THE COMPLETE BOOK OF THE BRITISH CHARTS

SINGLES & ALBUMS

BY TONY BROWN
JON KUTNER &
NEIL WARWICK

OMNIBUS PRESS

Cover designed by Chloë Alexander

ISBN: 0.7119.9075.1
Order No: OP 48598

Exclusive Distributors
Music Sales Limited,
8/9 Frith Street,
London W1D 3JB, UK.

Music Sales Corporation,
257 Park Avenue South,
New York, NY 10010, USA.

Macmillan Distribution Services,
53 Park West Drive,
Derrimut, Vic 3030,
Australia.

To the Music Trade only
Music Sales Limited,
8/9 Frith Street,
London W1D 3JB, UK.

Printed by Mackays of Chatham, Lordswood, Kent.

A catalogue record for this book is available from the British Library.

Visit Omnibus Press on the web at: www.omnibuspress.com

CONTENTS

INTRODUCTION

Well here we are with the second edition of *The Complete Book Of The British Charts.* It's quite a bit bigger this time around: we've added a further 1,680 singles to the 23,354 that appeared in our first edition, and the number of albums included has risen by 1,083 to a new total of 13,772. (Our publishers, alarmed at the frightening rate at which the size of this book is increasing, are glad the EP chart was just a Sixties phenomenon and that their numbers have been pegged at 481.) As well as the extra hits we've also put together a new facts and feats section at the back of the book for those interested in superlatives.

Being quiet, shy types we'd prefer the statistics within this book to speak for themselves, but we would like to take this opportunity to put at least one thing straight. On numerous occasions over the years we have been approached by a variety of media people to comment upon the awful state of the charts compared with some supposed halcyon era or else to talk about the imminent demise of the record industry. They all seem to be quite disappointed when we try to tell them anything different. The truth is there have always been records of questionable quality in the charts – singles we love and those we love to hate. And, good or bad, those records still sell in large quantities; Britons buy more singles – many more singles – per capita than any nation on earth. Granted, current singles sales are not at the same super-high levels of the late-Seventies or mid-Nineties, but they compare favourably with other periods of chart history. And sales of albums, despite competition from a range of other forms of entertainment, are higher than ever.

In November 2002 it will be fifty years since the likes of Al Martino, Nat 'King' Cole, Vera Lynn and Max Bygraves lined up alongside one another in the very first British Chart. All these years later there are still millions of us who are thrilled – and sometimes appalled – as we tune in to the Top 40 countdown, hearing our favourite artists do battle with each other week after week. Whether you are one of those listeners, one of those artists or just anybody who has ever bought a record, please join the three of us in wishing the British Charts a very happy birthday. At fifty she may be getting on a bit, but she is still in rude health.

The authors would like to thank Paul Barber, Tim Fuller, Robert Richland, Gene Robertson and Simon Ward for their help in the compilation of this edition. We would also welcome any comments or suggestions from our readers. Feel free to e-mail us at thechartbook@hotmail.com

Tony Brown, Jon Kutner & Neil Warwick, February, 2002

ABOUT THE AUTHORS

NEIL WARWICK

Neil's collection of more than 20,000 singles and 1,000 albums was kick-started on his fifth birthday by the acquisition of 'Day Tripper' by The Beatles. An avid music fan and pop quiz aficionado, it is his extensive database that forms the structure of this book.

NEIL'S TOP 10 SINGLES:

1 **Strawberry Fields Forever –** The Beatles
2 **The Wonder Of You –** Elvis Presley
3 **Don't Look Back In Anger –** Oasis
4 **Life On Mars –** David Bowie
5 **Rockin' All Over The World –** Status Quo
6 **Mr. Blue Sky –** Electric Light Orchestra
7 **Suburbia –** Pet Shop Boys
8 **The Legend Of Xanadu –** Dave Dee, Dozy, Beaky, Mick and Tich
9 **I Don't Wanna Dance –** Eddy Grant
10 **Goodbye Yellow Brick Road –** Elton John

NEIL'S TOP 10 ALBUMS:

1 **The Joshua Tree –** U2
2 **Sgt. Pepper's Lonely Hearts Club Band –** The Beatles
3 **Bat Out Of Hell –** Meat Loaf
4 **The Dark Side Of The Moon –** Pink Floyd
5 **Out Of The Blue –** Electric Light Orchestra
6 **Off The Wall –** Michael Jackson
7 **Hysteria –** Def Leppard
8 **The Invisible Band –** Travis
9 **Appetite For Destruction –** Guns N' Roses
10 **A Tonic For The Troops –** Boomtown Rats

JON KUTNER

After a stint in the Radio 1 production department, Jon became a full-time DJ and compere of music quizzes across London and the South East. He has been a contributor to *Record Collector* magazine and his own library of more than 70,000 discs includes nearly all of the singles listed in this book.

JON'S TOP 10 SINGLES:

1 **We've Got Tonite –** Bob Seger
2 **The Love Inside –** Barbra Streisand
3 **5.15 –** The Who
4 **Joanna –** Scott Walker
5 **Right Next Door (Because Of Me) –** Robert Cray Band
6 **What's Up? –** 4 Non Blondes
7 **Superstar –** Carpenters

8 **These Are The Days Of Our Lives –** Queen
9 **While You See A Chance –** Steve Winwood
10 **Nobody Knows –** Mike & The Mechanics

JON'S TOP 10 ALBUMS:

1 **Between The Lines –** Janis Ian
2 **So Close –** Dina Carroll
3 **Blood On The Tracks –** Bob Dylan
4 **The Vanishing Race –** Air Supply
5 **Hello I Must Be Going –** Phil Collins
6 **The Game –** Queen
7 **Sgt. Pepper's Lonely Hearts Club Band –** The Beatles
8 **Eat To The Beat –** Blondie
9 **Joseph & The Amazing Technicolor Dreamcoat (OST)**
10 **Tango In The Night –** Fleetwood Mac

TONY BROWN

Tony was the editorial associate for the *Guinness Book of British Hit Singles* from 1987 to 1997 and from 1990 he also worked in the chart department of *Music Week*. His other books include *The Complete Eurovision Song Contest Companion.*

TONY'S TOP 10 SINGLES:

1 **Standing Outside A Broken Phone Booth With Money In My Hand –** Primitive Radio Gods
2 **Coney Island –** Van Morrison
3 **Ceremony –** New Order
4 **How Can I Love You More? –** M People
5 **Frozen Orange Juice –** Peter Sarstedt
6 **Don't Walk –** The Big Supreme
7 **The Killing Jar –** Siouxsie and The Banshees
8 **Something For The Girl With Everything –** Sparks
9 **Goin' Back –** Dusty Springfield
10 **Lemon –** U2

TONY'S TOP 10 ALBUMS:

1 **If You're Feeling Sinister –** Belle and Sebastian
2 **A Different Kind Of Weather –** Dream Academy
3 **Bladerunner (OST) –** Vangelis
4 **The Wall –** Pink Floyd
5 **The Hounds Of Love –** Kate Bush
6 **Bookends –** Simon & Garfunkel
7 **The World Won't Listen –** Smiths
8 **Behaviour –** Pet Shop Boys
9 **Frequently Asked Questions –** Tram
10 **Judy At Carnegie Hall –** Judy Garland

15 Nov 52: First singles chart published in the *New Musical Express*. It comprised 15 records occupying 12 positions.

2 Oct 54: Chart increased to a Top 20.

31 Dec 55: Top 25 published for this week only.

14 Apr 56: Chart becomes a Top 30.

8 Nov 58: First album chart published in *Melody Maker*. It is a Top 10.

27 Jun 59: No album charts published until 8 Aug 59 due to newspaper strike. Chart of 20 Jun 59 repeated during this period.

5 Mar 60: Last *New Musical Express* chart used.

12 Mar 60: *Record Retailer* charts now utilised. Singles chart increased to a Top 50. EP chart commences with a Top 10.

19 Mar 60: EP chart increased to a Top 15.

26 Mar 60: Album chart increased to a Top 20; EP chart to a Top 20.

3 Jan 63: Charts now independently audited.

16 Apr 66: Album chart increased to a Top 30; EP chart reduced to a Top 10.

10 Dec 66: Album chart increased to a Top 40.

23 Sep 67: EP chart reduced to a Top 9.

2 Dec 67: Final EP chart published.

15 Feb 69: Chart now compiled for *Record Retailer* and the BBC by the British Market Research Bureau; album chart reduced to a Top 15.

8 Mar 69: Incorrect album chart including budget albums published. Correct chart found and used in this book.

29 Mar 69: Singles chart positions Nos. 33–50 incorrect. Correct chart researched and used.

12 Apr 69: Incorrect chart published. Correct chart researched and used.

19 Apr 69: Singles chart positions Nos. 42–50 incorrect. Correct chart researched and used.

14 Jun 69: Album chart increased to a Top 20.

28 Jun 69: Album chart increased to a Top 40.

9 Aug 69: Album chart a Top 32 for 1 week only.

11 Oct 69: Album chart decreases to a Top 25.

8 Nov 69: Until 24 Jan 70, album chart fluctuates between a Top 20 and a Top 24.

31 Jan 70: Until 9 Jan 71, album chart fluctuates between a Top 47 and a Top 77.

2 Jan 71: No *Record Retailer* published, though charts were compiled and used.

9 Jan 71: *Record Retailer* becomes *Record And Tape Retailer*.

16 Jan 71: Album chart increased to a Top 50.

6 Feb 71: Singles charts reduced to Top 40 for seven weeks due to postal strikes; no album charts published until 3 Apr 71 so the chart of 30 Jan 71 was repeated during this period.

7 Aug 71: Album chart has its full price and budget charts combined.

1 Jan 72: No *Record Retailer* published, though charts were compiled and used.

8 Jan 72: Album chart eliminates budget albums.

18 Mar 72: *Record And Tape Retailer* becomes *Music Week*.

May 72: *Music Week* did not publish singles chart though one was compiled and used.

3 Dec 72: *Music Week* did not publish singles chart though one was compiled and used.

Jan 73: Singles chart only reflected a Top 30, though a Top 50 has been calculated for this book.

3 Jan 73: Album chart only a Top 24.

7 Mar 73: Inaccurate singles Top 30 published in *Music Week* due to British Railways strike. Accurate Top 50 eventually compiled and used.

2 Dec 73: Singles chart only reflected a Top 30, though a Top 50 has been calculated for this book.

Jan 74: *Music Week* did not publish singles chart though one was compiled and used; album chart only a Top 42.

Jul 75: Album chart increases to a Top 60.

1 Feb 76: Incorrect chart published in *Music Week*. Correct chart issued and published the following week.

Jan 77: Singles chart restricted to a Top 30, though a Top 50 has been calculated for this book.

4 Dec 77: *Music Week* did not publish Singles chart though one was compiled and used.

Jan 78: Singles chart restricted to a Top 30, though a Top 50 has been calculated for this book.

4 Jan 78: Album chart only a Top 30.

3 May 78: Singles chart increased to a Top 75.

Dec 78: Album chart increased to a Top 75.

3 Oct 79: Two Album charts published as new system established allowing the calculation of the sales weeks to catch up.

0 Nov 79: Computer error gave incorrect singles at Number 1 and 2. Chart corrected.

Aug 81: Album chart increased to a Top 100.

Jan 83: Chart compilation taken over by Gallup.

4 Jan 89: Album charts split in two – a Top 75 artist chart and Top 20 compilation album chart.

2 Feb 94: Chart compilation taken over by Millward Brown. Charts are now © CIN (Chart Information Network).

0 Dec 94: Incorrect charts published due to incorrect data received. Correct chart compiled and used.

8 Jan 95: Incorrect Singles chart positions Nos. 50–75 published. Correct chart compiled and used.

Mar 95: Incorrect charts published due to incorrect data received. Correct chart compiled and published in following week's *Music Week*.

Oct 01: CIN changes name to The Official Charts Company.

Before 1983 charts were not published during the Christmas period and so the previous week's chart has been duplicated. The weeks in question are: 26 Dec 52, 25 Dec 53, 1 Jan 54, 24 Dec 54, 31 Dec 54, 31 Dec 64, 30 Dec 65, 29 Dec 66, 3 Jan 70, 26 Dec 70, 25 Dec 71, 30 Dec 72, 29 Dec 73, 28 Dec 74, 3 Jan 76, 1 Jan 77, 31 Dec 77, 30 Dec 78, 29 Dec 79, 3 Jan 81, 2 Jan 82, Jan 83, 31 Dec 83.

- The charts used to compile this book are taken from the following sources:

Singles:	*New Musical Express*	(15 November 1952 – 5 March 1960);
	Record Retailer/Music Week	(12 March 1960 – 31 December 2001).
EPs:	*Record Retailer*	(12 March 1960 – 2 December 1967).
Albums:	*Melody Maker*	(8 November 1958 – 5 March 1960);
	Record Retailer/Music Week	(12 March 1960 – 31 December 2001).
Compilation Albums:	*Music Week*	(14 January 1989 – 31 December 2001).

- All dates refer to the Saturday of the relevant week, not necessarily the date of the magazine's publication nor the date each chart was first announced.

- Artists are ordered alphabetically and under each artist is a list of their hit singles, followed by EPs, then albums.

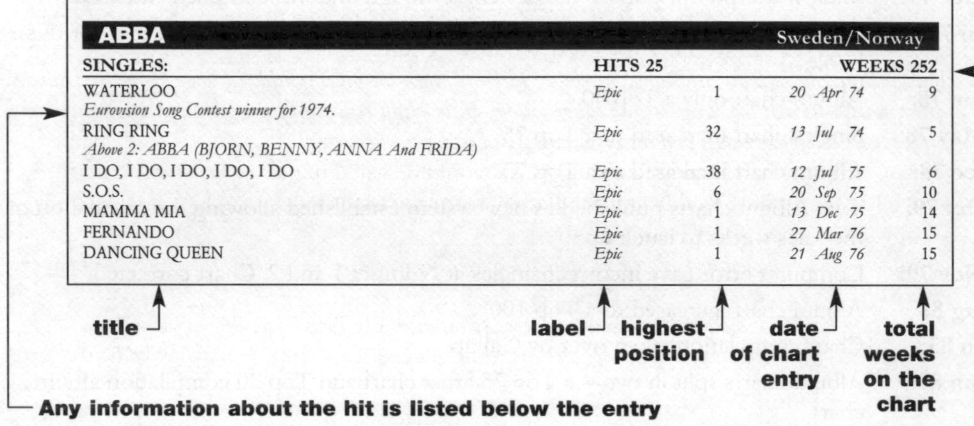

ABBA
Sweden/Norway
SINGLES:
HITS 25
WEEKS 252
WATERLOO Epic 1 20 Apr 74 9
Eurovision Song Contest winner for 1974.
RING RING Epic 32 13 Jul 74 5
Above 2: ABBA (BJORN, BENNY, ANNA And FRIDA)
I DO, I DO, I DO, I DO, I DO Epic 38 12 Jul 75 6
S.O.S. Epic 6 20 Sep 75 10
MAMMA MIA Epic 1 13 Dec 75 14
FERNANDO Epic 1 27 Mar 76 15
DANCING QUEEN Epic 1 21 Aug 76 15
title
label
highest position
date of chart entry
total weeks on the chart
Any information about the hit is listed below the entry
Each artist has hits and weeks totals at the top of the listing

- [RE] Re-entry
  [RI] Re-issue
  [RM] Re-mix
  [RR] Re-recording
  [M] Medley.

- Re-mixes and re-issues are classed as the same hit as the original while re-recordings are considered new hits.

- If the credit on the release is different to the main artist credit, then this is also highlighted below the hit.

- Any albums that appeared in the compilation chart, but where an artist had a major credit (i.e. featured on 50% or more of the tracks), are listed under the artist concerned, in chronological order and within the list of albums.

Each time a single enters the chart, it is given a separate listing, detailing date, highest position etc.

EPs, however, are accumulated totals and often include several re-entries.

Album totals are also accumulated, but re-entries are given a separate listing in the following circumstances:

If an album reaches its highest position six months or more after its original chart run.
If an album has a chart life of more than 10 years.
If an album is re-issued on a different label, or if on the same label, it has been given a new catalogue number.

In the case of duets and collaborations, the following criteria have been selected to define when a hit is attributed to the artists involved:

The words, 'and', 'versus', 'meets' between each artist defines an equal collaboration. Each artist has the hit listed under their name.

(e.g. Elton John and Kiki Dee; 808 State vs UB40; Man 2 Man meets Man Parrish.)

An equal collaboration of more than three artists warrants a separate entry in the book.

(e.g. All For Love is listed three times, under Bryan Adams, Rod Stewart and Sting; while Diana Ross, Marvin Gaye, Stevie Wonder and Smokey Robinson are considered a separate recording entity for Pops We Love You.)

If an artist credit includes 'featuring', 'with' or 'presents', then the hit is considered to be by the first named artist, and latter artist(s) are guests on the recording. If the credit reflects just one guest act, it is classed as a hit for both. More than one, and the hit is only listed under the first artist.

(e.g. A hit by Puff Daddy featuring Mase would be listed under each named artist; while a hit by Puff Daddy and the Family featuring the Notorious B.I.G. and Mase, is only listed under Puff Daddy's entry.)

Artists who have collaborated on four or more hit singles are considered a regular recording act and have their own separate entry.

(e.g. Ike and Tina Turner's hits are not combined with Tina Turner's solo output.)

Artists who record an album together are also considered a separate act, but only if all named have charted solo material too.

(e.g. McAlmont and Butler's hits are listed separately from their solo work, but Daniel O'Donnell and Mary Duff's album is to be found under the Daniel O'Donnell listing, because Mary Duff has not charted in her own right and the pair have charted fewer than four singles together.)

THE NUMBER ONE SINGLES

Figure in brackets indicates number of weeks spent at number one. Writers in italics.

*Denotes straight in at number one.

1952

15 Nov *Here In My Heart, Al Martino (9)
Best seller of the year including pre-chart: 'Auf Wiederseh'n Sweetheart', Vera Lynn with Soldiers & Airmen of her Majesty's Forces.
Bill Borrelli/Lou Levinson/Pat Genaro

1953

17 Jan You Belong To Me, Jo Stafford with Paul Weston & His Orchestra (1)
Chilton Price/Red Stewart/Pee Wee King

24 Jan Comes A-Long A-Love, Kay Starr (1)
Al Sherman

31 Jan Outside Of Heaven, Eddie Fisher with Hugo Winterhalter's Orchestra and Chorus (1)
Sammy Gallop/Chester Conn

7 Feb Don't Let The Stars Get In Your Eyes, Perry Como with The Ramblers (5)
Slim Willet

14 March She Wears Red Feathers, Guy Mitchell with Mitch Miller & His Orchestra and Chorus (4)
Bob Merrill

11 April Broken Wings, Stargazers (1)
John Jerome/Bernard Grun

18 April (How Much Is) That Doggie In The Window, Lita Roza (1)
Bob Merrill

25 April I Believe, Frankie Laine with Paul Weston & His Orchestra (9, *3 July* for 6, *22 Aug* for 3; best seller of the year)
Erwin Drake/Irvin Graham/Jimmy Shirl/Al Stillman

27 June I'm Walking Behind You, Eddie Fisher with Hugo Winterhalter and His Orchestra & Sally Sweetland (1)
Billy Reid

15 Aug The Song From The Moulin Rouge (Where Is Your Heart), Mantovani & His Orchestra (1)
Georges Auric

12 Sept Look At That Girl, Guy Mitchell (6)
Bob Merrill

24 Oct Hey Joe!, Frankie Laine with Paul Weston & His Orchestra and The Norman Luboff Choir (Carl Fischer: piano) (2)
Boudleaux Bryant

7 Nov Answer Me, David Whitfield with Stanley Black & His Orchestra (1, *12 Dec* for 1)
Bunny Sigman/Gerhard Winkler/Fred Rauch

14 Nov Answer Me, Frankie Laine with Paul Weston & His Orchestra and The Norman Luboff Choir (Carl Fischer: piano) (8)
Bunny Sigman/Gerhard Winkler/Fred Rauch

12 Dec Above two were joint No. 1s.

1954

9 Jan Oh, Mein Papa, Eddie Calvert (The Man With The Golden Trumpet) with Norrie Paramor & His Orchestra (9)
Paul Burkhart

13 March I See The Moon, Stargazers with Syd Dean & His Orchestra (5, *24 April* for 1)
Meredith Wilson

17 April Secret Love, Doris Day (1, *8 May* for 8; best seller of the year)
Paul Francis Webster/Sammy Fain

1 May Such A Night, Johnnie Ray (1)
Lincoln Chase

3 July Cara Mia, David Whitfield with Mantovani & His Orchestra and Chorus (10)
Tulio Trapani/Lee Lange

11 Sept Little Things Mean A Lot, Kitty Kallen (1)
Carl Stutz/Edith Lindeman

18 Sept Three Coins In The Fountain, Frank Sinatra (3)
Jule Styne/Sammy Cahn

9 Oct Hold My Hand, Don Cornell (4, *20 Nov* for 2)
Jack Lawrence/Richard Myers

6 Nov My Son My Son, Vera Lynn and Frank Weir & His Saxophone, His Chorus and Orchestra (2)
Eddie Calvert/Melville Farley/Bob Howard

27 Nov This Ole House, Rosemary Clooney with Buddy Cole & His Orchestra (1)
Stuart Hamblen

4 Dec Let's Have Another Party [M], Winifred Atwell & Her "Other" Piano (5)
Various

1955

8 Jan The Finger Of Suspicion, Dickie Valentine with The Stargazers (1, *22 Jan* for 2)
Paul Mann/Al Lewis

15 Jan Mambo Italiano, Rosemary Clooney & The Mellomen (1, *5 Feb* for 2)
Bob Merrill

19 Feb Softly Softly, Ruby Murray and Ray Martin & His Orchestra (3)
Mark Paul/Paddy Roberts/Pierre Dudan

12 March Give Me Your Word, "Tennessee" Ernie Ford (7)
George Wyler/Irving Taylor

30 April Cherry Pink And Apple Blossom White, Perez 'Prez' Prado & His Orchestra, (The King of the Mambo) (2)
Louis Louvigny/Mack David

14 May Stranger In Paradise, Tony Bennett with Percy Faith & His Orchestra and Chorus (2)
Robert Wright/George Forrest

28 May Cherry Pink (And Apple Blossom White), Eddie Calvert (The Man with the Golden Trumpet) (4)
Louis Louvigny/Mack David

25 June Unchained Melody, Jimmy Young with Bob Sharples & His Music (3)
Alex North/Hy Zaret

16 July Dreamboat, Alma Cogan (2)
Al Hoffman

30 July Rose Marie, Slim Whitman (11; best seller of the year)
Otto Harbach/Oscar Hammerstein II/Rudolf Friml/Stothart

15 Oct The Man From Laramie, Jimmy Young with Bob Sharples & His Music (4)
Lester Lee/Ned Washington

12 Nov Hernando's Hideaway, Johnston Brothers (2)
Richard Adler/Jerry Ross

26 Nov (We're Gonna) Rock Around The Clock, Bill Haley & His Comets (3)
Jimmy DeKnight/Max Freedman

17 Dec Christmas Alphabet, Dickie Valentine with Johnny Douglas & His Orchestra (3)
Buddy Kaye/Jules Loman

1956

7 Jan (We're Gonna) Rock Around The Clock, Bill Haley & His Comets (2)
Jimmy DeKnight/Max Freedman

21 Jan Sixteen Tons, "Tennessee" Ernie Ford (4)
Merle Travis

18 Feb Memories Are Made Of This, Dean Martin (4)
Terry Gilkyson/Richard Dehr/Frank Miller

17 March It's Almost Tomorrow, Dream Weavers (2, *7 April* for 1)
Wade Buff/Eugene Adkinson

31 March Rock And Roll Waltz, Kay Starr with Hugo Winterhalter's Orchestra & Chorus (1)
Dick Ware/Shorty Allen

14 April The Poor People Of Paris, Winifred Atwell & Her "Other" Piano (3)
Marguerite Monnot/Rene Rouzaud

5 May No Other Love, Ronnie Hilton (6)
Richard Rodgers/Oscar Hammerstein II

16 June I'll Be Home, Pat Boone (5; best seller of the year)
Ferdinand Washington/Stan Lewis

21 July Why Do Fools Fall In Love, Teenagers featuring Frankie Lymon (3)
Frankie Lymon/George Goldner

11 Aug Whatever Will Be Will Be (Que Sera Sera), Doris Day with Frank De Vol & His Orchestra (6)
Jay Livingstone/Ray Evans

22 Sept Lay Down Your Arms, Anne Shelton with Wally Stott & His Orchestra & Chorus (4)
Leon Land/Ake Gerhard/Paddy Roberts

20 Oct A Woman In Love, Frankie Laine with Percy Faith & His Orchestra (4)
Frank Loesser

17 Nov Just Walking In The Rain, Johnnie Ray with Ray Conniff & His Orchestra (7)
Johnny Bragg/Robert S.Riley

1957

5 Jan Singing The Blues, Guy Mitchell with Ray Conniff & His Orchestra (1, *18 Jan* for 1, *2 Feb* for 1)
Melvin Endsley

12 Jan Singing The Blues, Tommy Steele & The Steelmen (1)
Melvin Endsley

26 Jan The Garden Of Eden, Frankie Vaughan with Wally Stott & His Orchestra & Chorus (3)
Dennise Haas Norwood

2 Feb The Garden Of Eden and Singing The Blues (by Guy Mitchell) joint No. 1s.

23 Feb Young Love, Tab Hunter with Billy Vaughn's Orchestra & Chorus (7)
Carole Joyner/Ric Cartey

13 April Cumberland Gap, Lonnie Donegan & His Skiffle Group (5)
Trad arr Lonnie Donegan

18 May Rock-A-Billy, Guy Mitchell with Jimmy Carroll (1)
Woody Harris/Eddie Deane

25 May Butterfly, Andy Williams (2)
Bernie Lowe/Kal Mann

8 June Yes Tonight, Josephine, Johnnie Ray with Ray Conniff (3)
Winfield Scott/Dorothy Goodman

29 June Putting' On The Style/Gamblin' Man, Lonnie Donegan & His Skiffle Group (2)
Norman Cazden: Woody Guthrie/Lonnie Donegan

13 July All Shook Up, Elvis Presley with The Jordanaires (7)
Otis Blackwell/Elvis Presley

31 Aug Diana, Paul Anka (9; best seller of the year)
Paul Anka

2 Nov That'll Be The Day, Crickets (3)
Jerry Allison/Norman Petty/Buddy Holly

23 Nov Mary's Boy Child, Harry Belafonte (7)
Jester Hairston

1958

11 Jan Great Balls Of Fire, Jerry Lee Lewis (2)
Jack Hammer/Otis Blackwell

25 Jan *Jailhouse Rock, Elvis Presley (3; best seller of the year)
Jerry Leiber/Mike Stoller

15 Feb The Story Of My Life, Michael Holliday (2)
Burt Bacharach/Hal David

1 March Magic Moments, Perry Como with Mitchell Ayres' Orchestra & The Ray Charles Singers (8)
Burt Bacharach/Hal David

26 April Whole Lotta Woman, Marvin Rainwater (3)
Marvin Rainwater

17 May Who's Sorry Now, Connie Francis (6)
Ted Snyder/Bert Kalmer/Herman Ruby

28 June On The Street Where You Live, Vic Damone with Percy Faith & His Orchestra & Chorus (2)
Alan Jay Lerner/Frederick Lowe

5 July All I Have To Do Is Dream/Claudette, Everly Brothers (Joint No. 1 with above for first week) (7)
Felice & Boudleaux Bryant: Roy Orbison

23 Aug When, Kalin Twins (5)
Jack Reardon/Paul Evans

27 Sept Stupid Cupid/Carolina Moon, Connie Francis (6)
Neil Sedaka/Howard Greenfield: Benny Davis/Joe Burke

8 Nov It's All In The Game, Tommy Edwards (3)
Charlie Gates Dawes/Carl Sigman

29 Nov Hoots Mon, Jack Good presents Lord Rockingham's XI (3)
Harry Robinson

20 Dec It's Only Make Believe, Conway Twitty (5)
Conway Twitty/Jack Nance

1959

24 Jan The Day The Rains Came, Jane Morgan (1)
Gilbert Becaud/Carl Sigman

31 Jan One Night/I Got Stung, Elvis Presley (3)
Dave Bartholomew/Pearl King: Aaron Schroeder/David Hill

21 Feb As I Love You, Shirley Bassey with Wally Stott & His Orchestra (4)
Jay Livingstone/Ray Evans

21 March Smoke Gets In Your Eyes, Platters (1)
Otto Harbach/Jerome Kern

28 March Side Saddle, Russ Conway (4)
Trevor Stanford

25 April It Doesn't Matter Anymore, Buddy Holly (3)
Paul Anka

16 May A Fool Such As I/I Need Your Love Tonight, Elvis Presley with The Jordanaires (5)
William Trader: Sid Wayne/Bix Reichner

20 June Roulette, Russ Conway (2)
Trevor Stanford

4 July Dream Lover, Bobby Darin (4)
Bobby Darin

1 Aug Living Doll, Cliff Richard & The Drifters (6; best seller of the year)
Lionel Bart

12 Sept Only Sixteen, Craig Douglas (4)
Barbara Campbell (aka Lou Adler/Herb Alpert/Sam Cooke)

10 Oct Here Comes Summer, Jerry Keller (1)
Jerry Keller

17 Oct Mack The Knife, Bobby Darin (2)
Kurt Weil/Marc Blitzstein/Bertolt Brecht

31 Oct Travellin' Light, Cliff Richard & The Shadows (5)
Sid Tepper/Roy Bennett

5 Dec What Do You Want?, Adam Faith (3)
Les Vandyke

19 Dec What Do You Want To Make Those Eyes At Me For?, Emile Ford & The Checkmates (Joint No. 1 with above for first week) (6)
Jimmy Monaco/Joseph McCarthy/Howard Johnson

1960

30 Jan Starry Eyed, Michael Holliday with the Michael Sammes Singers (1)
Earl Shuman/Mort Garson

6 Feb Why, Anthony Newley (4)
Bob Marcucci/Peter De Angelis

6 March Poor Me, Adam Faith (2)
Les Vandyke

19 March Running Bear, Johnny Preston (2)
Jiles Perry Richardson

2 April My Old Man's A Dustman (Ballad Of A Refuse Disposal Officer), Lonnie Donegan & His Group (4)
Lonnie Donegan/Peter Buchanan

30 April Do You Mind, Anthony Newley (1; the 100th No. 1)
Lionel Bart

7 May Cathy's Clown, Everly Brothers (7)
Everly Brothers

5 June Three Steps To Heaven, Eddie Cochran (2)
Eddie Cochran

9 July Good Timin', Jimmy Jones (3)
Fred Tobias/Clint Ballard Jr

30 July Please Don't Tease, Cliff Richard & The Shadows (1, *13 Aug* for 1)
Bruce Welch/Pete Chester

6 Aug Shakin' All Over, Johnny Kidd & The Pirates (1)
Johnny Kidd/Gus Robinson

27 Aug Apache, Shadows (5)
Jerry Lordan

1 Oct Tell Laura I Love Her, Ricky Valance (3)
Jeff Barry/Ben Raleigh

22 Oct Only The Lonely (Know How I Feel), Roy Orbison (2)
Roy Orbison/Joe Melson

5 Nov *It's Now Or Never (O Sole Mio), Elvis Presley with The Jordanires (8; best seller of the year)
Eduardo Di Capua/Aaron Schroeder/Wally Gold

31 Dec I Love You, Cliff Richard & The Shadows (2)
Bruce Welch

1961

14 Jan Poetry In Motion, Johnny Tillotson (2)
Paul Kaufman/Mike Anthony

28 Jan Are You Lonesome Tonight?, Elvis Presley with The Jordanaires (4; best seller of the year)
Roy Turk/Lou Handman

25 Feb Sailor, Petula Clark, Peter Knight Orchestra & Chorus (1)
Werner Scharfenberger/Fini Busch/David West

4 March Walk Right Back/Ebony Eyes, Everly Brothers (3)
Sonny Curtis: John D.Loudermilk

25 March Wooden Heart, Elvis Presley (6)
Fred Wise/Ben Weisman/Kay Twomey/Bert Kaempfert

6 May Blue Moon, Marcels (2)
Richard Rodgers/Lorenz Hart

20 May On The Rebound, Floyd Cramer (1)
Floyd Cramer

27 May You're Driving Me Crazy, Temperance Seven, vocal refrain by Mr. Paul MacDowall (1)
Walter Donaldson

3 June Surrender (Torna A Surriento), Elvis Presley with the Jordanaires (4)
Ernesto DeCurtis/Doc Pomus/Mort Shuman

1 July Runaway, Del Shannon (3)
Del Shannon/Max Crook

22 July Temptation, Everly Brothers (2)
Nacio Herb Brown/Arthur Freed

5 Aug Well I Ask You, Eden Kane (1)
Les Vandyke

12 Aug You Don't Know, Helen Shapiro (3)
John Schroeder/Mike Hawker

2 Sept Johnny Remember Me, John Leyton (3, *30 Sept* for 1)
Geoff Goddard

23 Sept Reach For The Stars/Climb Ev'ry Mountain, Shirley Bassey with Geoff Love & His Orchestra (1)
Udo Jurgens/David West: Richard Rodgers/Oscar Hammerstein II

7 Oct Kon-Tiki, Shadows (1)
Michael Carr

14 Oct Michael, Highwaymen (1)
Trad arr Dave Fisher

21 Oct Walkin' Back To Happiness, Helen Shapiro (3)
John Schroeder/Mike Hawker

11 Nov (Marie's The Name) His Latest Flame, Elvis Presley (4)
Doc Pomus/Mort Shuman

9 Dec Tower Of Strength, Frankie Vaughan (3)
Burt Bacharach/Bob Hilliard

30 Dec Moon River, Danny Williams with Geoff Love & His Orchestra (2)
Henry Mancini/Johnny Mercer

1962

13 Jan *The Young Ones, Cliff Richard & The Shadows (6)
Sid Tepper/Roy Bennett

24 Feb Rock-A-Hula Baby ("Twist Special")/Can't Help Falling In Love, Elvis Presley with The Jordanaires (4)
Fred Wise/Ben Weisman/Delores Fuller: Hugo Peretti/Luigi Creatore/Fred Weiss

24 March Wonderful Land, Shadows (8)
Jerry Lordan

19 May Nut Rocker, B. Bumble & The Stingers (1)
Tchaikovsky/Kim Fowley

26 May Good Luck Charm, Elvis Presley with The Jordanaires (5)
Aaron Schroeder/Wally Gold

30 June Come Outside, Mike Sarne featuring Wendy Richard (2)
Charles Blackwell

14 July I Can't Stop Loving You, Ray Charles (2)
Don Gibson

28 July I Remember You, Frank Ifield (7; best seller of the year)
Johnny Mercer/Victor Schertzinger

15 Sept She's Not You, Elvis Presley with The Jordanaires (3)
Doc Pomus/Mort Shuman/Jerry Leiber

6 Oct Telstar, Tornados (5)
Joe Meek

10 Nov Lovesick Blues, Frank Ifield with Norrie Paramor & His Orchestra (5)
Cliff Friend/Irving Mills

15 Dec Return To Sender, Elvis Presley with The Jordanaires (3)
Otis Blackwell/Winfield Scott

1963

5 Jan The Next Time/Bachelor Boy, Cliff Richard, The Shadows & The Norrie Paramor Strings (3)
Buddy Kaye/Philip Springer: Cliff Richard/Bruce Welch

26 Jan Dance On!, Shadows (1)
Valerie & Eileen Murtagh/Ray Adams

2 Feb Diamonds, Jet Harris & Tony Meehan (3)
Jerry Lordon

23 Feb The Wayward Wind, Frank Ifield with Norrie Paramor & His Orchestra (3)
Herb Newman/Stan Lebowsky

16 March Summer Holiday, Cliff Richard, The Shadows & The Norrie Paramor Strings (2, *6 April* for 1)
Bruce Welch/Brian Bennett

30 March Foot Tapper, Shadows (1)
Hank Marvin/Bruce Welch

13 April How Do You Do It?, Gerry & The Pacemakers (3)
Mitch Murray

4 May From Me To You, Beatles (7)
John Lennon/Paul McCartney

22 June I Like It, Gerry & The Pacemakers (4)
Mitch Murray

20 July Confessin' (That I Love You), Frank Ifield (2)
Doc Daugherty/Ellis Reynolds/Al Neiburg

3 Aug (You're The) Devil In Disguise, Elvis Presley with The Jordanaires (1)
Bill Giant/Bernie Baum/Florence Kaye

10 Aug Sweets For My Sweet, Searchers (2)
Doc Pomus/Mort Shuman

24 Aug Bad To Me, Billy J. Kramer & The Dakotas (3)
John Lennon/Paul McCartney

14 Sept She Loves You, Beatles (4, *30 Nov* for 2; best seller of the year
John Lennon/Paul McCartney

12 Oct Do You Love Me, Brian Poole & The Tremeloes (3)
Berry Gordy Jnr

2 Nov You'll Never Walk Alone, Gerry & The Pacemakers (4)
Richard Rodgers/Oscar Hammerstein II

14 Dec I Want To Hold Your Hand, Beatles (5)
John Lennon/Paul McCartney

1964

18 Jan Glad All Over, Dave Clark Five (2)
Dave Clark/Mike Smith

1 Feb Needles And Pins, Searchers (3)
Sonny Bono/Jack Nitzche

22 Feb Diane, Bachelors (1)
Erno Rapee/Lew Pollack

29 Feb Anyone Who Had A Heart, Cilla Black (3)
Burt Bacharach/Hal David

21 March Little Children, Billy J. Kramer & The Dakotas (2)
Mort Shuman/John McFarland

4 April Can't Buy Me Love, Beatles (3; best seller of the year)
John Lennon/Paul McCartney

25 April A World Without Love, Peter & Gordon (2)
John Lennon/Paul McCartney

9 May Don't Throw Your Love Away, Searchers (2)
Billy Jackson/Jimmy Wisner

23 May Juliet, Four Pennies (1)
Mike Wilsh/Fritz Fryer/Lionel Morton

30 May You're My World (Il Mio Mondo), Cilla Black (4)
Umberto Bindi/Carl Sigman/Gino Paoli

27 June It's Over, Roy Orbison (2)
Roy Orbison/Bill Dees

11 July The House Of The Rising Sun, Animals (1)
Trad arr Alan Price

18 July It's All Over Now, Rolling Stones (1)
Bobby & Shirley Womack

25 July A Hard Day's Night, Beatles (3)
John Lennon/Paul McCartney

15 Aug Do Wah Diddy Diddy, Manfred Mann (2)
Jeff Barry/Ellie Greenwich

29 Aug Have I The Right?, Honeycombs (2)
Howard Blaikley

12 Sept You Really Got Me, Kinks (2)
Ray Davies

26 Sept I'm Into Something Good, Herman's Hermits (2)
Gerry Goffin/Carole King

10 Oct Oh, Pretty Woman, Roy Orbison (2, *14 Nov* for 1)
Roy Orbison/Bill Dees

24 Oct (There's) Always Something There To Remind Me, Sandie Shaw (3)
Burt Bacharach/Hal David

21 Nov Baby Love, Supremes (2)
Brian Holland/Lamont Dozier/Edward Holland

5 Dec Little Red Rooster, Rolling Stones (1)
Willie Dixon

12 Dec I Feel Fine, Beatles (5)
John Lennon/Paul McCartney

1965

16 Jan Yeh, Yeh, Georgie Fame & The Blue Flames (2)
Rodgers Grant/Pat Patrick/Jon Hendricks

30 Jan Go Now!, Moody Blues (1)
Larry Banks/Milton Bennett

6 Feb You've Lost That Lovin' Feelin', Righteous Brothers (2)
Phil Spector/Barry Mann/Cynthia Weil

20 Feb Tired Of Waiting For You, Kinks (1)
Ray Davies

27 Feb I'll Never Find Another You, Seekers (2)
Tom Springfield

13 March It's Not Unusual, Tom Jones (1)
Gordon Mills/Les Reed

20 March The Last Time, Rolling Stones (3)
Mick Jagger/Keith Richards

10 April Concrete And Clay, Unit Four Plus Two (1)
Tommy Moeller/Brian Parker

17 April The Minute You're Gone, Cliff Richard (1)
Jimmy Gateley

24 April Ticket To Ride, Beatles (3)
John Lennon/Paul McCartney

15 May King Of The Road, Roger Miller (1)
Roger Miller

22 May Where Are You Now, Jackie Trent (1)
Tony Hatch/Jackie Trent

29 May Long Live Love, Sandie Shaw (3)
Chris Andrews

19 June Crying In The Chapel, Elvis Presley with The Jordanaires (1, *3 July* for 1)
Artie Glenn

26 June I'm Alive, Hollies (1, *10 July* for 2)
Clint Ballard Jr

24 July Mr. Tambourine Man, Byrds (2)
Bob Dylan

7 Aug Help!, Beatles (3; the 200th No. 1)
John Lennon/Paul McCartney

28 Aug I Got You Babe, Sonny & Cher (2)
Sonny Bono

11 Sept (I Can't Get No) Satisfaction, Rolling Stones (2)
Mick Jagger/Keith Richards

25 Sept Make It Easy On Yourself, Walker Brothers (1)
Burt Bacharach/Hal David

2 Oct Tears, Ken Dodd with Geoff Love & His Orchestra (5; best seller of the year)
Billy Ubre/Frank Capano

6 Nov Get Off Of My Cloud, Rolling Stones (3)
Mick Jagger/Keith Richards

27 Nov The Carnival Is Over, Seekers (3)
Tom Springfield

18 Dec Day Tripper/We Can Work It Out, Beatles (5)
John Lennon/Paul McCartney

1966

22 Jan Keep On Running, Spencer Davis Group (1)
Jackie Edwards

29 Jan Michelle, Overlanders (3)
John Lennon/Paul McCartney

19 Feb These Boots Are Made For Walkin', Nancy Sinatra (4)
Lee Hazelwood

19 March The Sun Ain't Gonna Shine Anymore, Walker Brothers (4)
Bob Gaudio/Bob Crewe

16 April Somebody Help Me, Spencer Davis Group (2)
Jackie Edwards

30 April You Don't Have To Say You Love Me (Io Che No Vivo Senza Te), Dusty Springfield (1)
Pino Donnagio/Vito Pallavicini/Vicki Wickham/Simon Napier-Bell

7 May Pretty Flamingo, Manfred Mann (3)
Mark Barkan

28 May Paint It, Black, Rolling Stones (1)
Mick Jagger/Keith Richards

4 June Strangers In The Night, Frank Sinatra (3)
Charlie Singleton/Eddie Snyder/Bert Kaempfert

25 June Paperback Writer, Beatles (2)
John Lennon/Paul McCartney

9 July Sunny Afternoon, Kinks (2)
Ray Davies

23 July Get Away, Georgie Fame & The Blue Flames (1)
Clive Powell

30 July Out Of Time, Chris Farlowe (1)
Mick Jagger/Keith Richards

6 Aug With A Girl Like You, Troggs (2)
Reg Presley

20 Aug Yellow Submarine/Eleanor Rigby, Beatles (4)
John Lennon/Paul McCartney

17 Sept All Or Nothing, Small Faces (1)
Steve Marriott/Ronnie Lane

24 Sept Distant Drums, Jim Reeves (5)
Cindy Walker

29 Oct Reach Out I'll Be There, Four Tops (3)
Brian Holland/Lamont Dozier/Edward Holland

19 Nov Good Vibrations, Beach Boys (2)
Beach Boys

3 Dec Green, Green Grass Of Home, Tom Jones (7; best seller of the year)
Curly Putnam

1967

21 Jan I'm A Believer, Monkees (4)
Neil Diamond

18 Feb This Is My Song, Petula Clark (2)
Charles Chaplin

4 March Release Me, Engelbert Humperdinck (6; best seller of the year)
Eddie Miller/Robert Yount/Dub Williams/Robert Harris

15 April Somethin' Stupid, Nancy Sinatra & Frank Sinatra (2)
C.Carson Parks

29 April Puppet On A String, Sandie Shaw (3)
Bill Martin/Phil Coulter

20 May Silence Is Golden, Tremeloes (3)
Bob Gaudio/Bob Crewe

10 June A Whiter Shade Of Pale, Procol Harum (6)
Gary Brooker/Keith Reid

22 July All You Need Is Love, Beatles (3)
John Lennon/Paul McCartney

12 Aug San Francisco (Be Sure To Wear Flowers In Your Hair), Scott McKenzie (4)
John Phillips

9 Sept The Last Waltz, Engelbert Humperdinck (5)
Les Reed/Barry Mason

14 Oct Massachusetts (The Lights Went Out In), Bee Gees (4)
Barry Gibb/Maurice Gibb/Robin Gibb

11 Nov Baby, Now That I've Found You, Foundations (2)
John MacLeod/Tony Macauley

25 Nov Let The Heartaches Begin, Long John Baldry (2)
John MacLeod/Tony Macauley

9 Dec Hello Goodbye, Beatles (7)
John Lennon/Paul McCartney

1968

27 Jan The Ballad Of Bonnie And Clyde, Georgie Fame (1)
Mitch Murray/Peter Callander

3 Feb Everlasting Love, Love Affair (2)
Buzz Cason/Mac Gayden

17 Feb Mighty Quinn, Manfred Mann (2)
Bob Dylan

2 March Cinderella Rockafella, Esther & Abi Ofarim (3)
Mason Williams

23 March The Legend Of Xanadu, Dave Dee, Dozy, Beaky, Mick & Tich (1)
Howard Blaikley

30 March Lady Madonna, Beatles (2)
John Lennon/Paul McCartney

13 April Congratulations, Cliff Richard (2)
Bill Martin/Phil Coulter

27 April What A Wonderful World/Cabaret, Louis Armstrong Orchestra & Chorus/Louis Armstrong & His All Stars (4)
George Weiss/George Douglas: John Kander/Fred Ebb

25 May Young Girl, Union Gap featuring Gary Puckett (4)
Jerry Fuller

22 June Jumpin' Jack Flash, Rolling Stones (2)
Mick Jagger/Keith Richards

6 July Baby Come Back, Equals (3)
Eddy Grant

27 July I Pretend, Des O'Connor (1)
Les Reed/Barry Mason

3 Aug Mony, Mony, Tommy James & The Shondells (2, *24 Aug* for 1)
Bo Gentry/Ritchie Cordell/Tommy James/Bobby Bloom

17 Aug Fire!, Crazy World Of Arthur Brown (1)
Arthur Brown/Vince Crane

31 Aug Do It Again, Beach Boys (1)
Brian Wilson/Mike Love

7 Sept I've Gotta Get A Message To You, Bee Gees (1)
Barry Gibb/Maurice Gibb/Robin Gibb

14 Sept Hey Jude, Beatles (2; best seller of the year)
John Lennon/Paul McCartney

28 Sept Those Were The Days, Mary Hopkin (6)
Gene Raskin/Alexander Vertinski

9 Nov With A Little Help From My Friends, Joe Cocker (1)
John Lennon/Paul McCartney

16 Nov The Good, The Bad And The Ugly, Hugo Montenegro, His Orchestra & Chorus (4)
Ennio Morricone

14 Dec Lily The Pink, Scaffold (3)
Roger McGough/Mike McGear/John Gorman

1969

4 Jan Ob-La-Di Ob-La-Da, Marmalade (1, *18 Jan* for 1)
John Lennon/Paul McCartney

11 Jan Lily The Pink, Scaffold (1)
Roger McGough/Mike McGear/John Gorman

1 Feb Albatross, Fleetwood Mac (1)
Peter Green

8 Feb Blackberry Way, Move (1)
Roy Wood

15 Feb (If Paradise Is) Half As Nice, Amen Corner (2)
Lucio Battisti/Jack Fishman

1 March Where Do You Go To (My Lovely), Peter Sarstedt (4)
Peter Sarstedt

29 March I Heard It Through The Grapevine, Marvin Gaye (3)
Norman Whitfield/Barrett Strong

19 April Israelites, Desmond Dekker & The Aces (1)
Desmond Dacres/Leslie Kong

26 April *Get Back, Beatles with Billy Preston (6)
John Lennon/Paul McCartney

7 June Dizzy, Tommy Roe (1)
Tommy Roe/Freddie Weller

14 June The Ballad Of John And Yoko, Beatles (3)
John Lennon/Paul McCartney

5 July Something In The Air, Thunderclap Newman (3)
Speedy Keen

26 July Honky Tonk Women, Rolling Stones (5)
Mick Jagger/Keith Richards

30 Aug In The Year 2525 (Exordium And Terminus), Zager & Evans (3)
Rick Evans

20 Sept Bad Moon Rising, Creedence Clearwater Revival (3)
John Fogerty

11 Oct Je T'aime . . . Moi Non Plus, Jane Birkin & Serge Gainsbourg (1)
Serge Gainsbourg

18 Oct I'll Never Fall In Love Again, Bobbie Gentry (1)
Burt Bacharach/Hal David

25 Oct Sugar, Sugar, Archies (8; best seller of the year)
Jeff Barry/Andy Kim

20 Dec Two Little Boys, Rolf Harris (6)
Alan Braden/Edward Madden/Theodore Morse

1970

31 Jan Love Grows (Where My Rosemary Goes), Edison Lighthouse (5)
Barry Mason/Tony Macauley

7 March Wand'rin Star, Lee Marvin (3)
Alan Jay Lerner/Frederick Loewe

28 March Bridge Over Troubled Water, Simon & Garfunkel (3)
Paul Simon

18 April All Kinds Of Everything, Dana (2)
Derry Lindsay/Jackie Smith

2 May Spirit In The Sky, Norman Greenbaum (2)
Norman Greenbaum

16 May Back Home, England Football World Cup Squad "70" (3)
Bill Martin/Phil Coulter

6 June Yellow River, Christie (1)
Jeff Christie

13 June In The Summertime, Mungo Jerry (7)
Ray Dorset

1 Aug The Wonder Of You, Elvis Presley (6; best seller of the year)
Baker Knight

12 Sept The Tears Of A Clown, Smokey Robinson & The Miracles (1)
Henry Cosby/Smokey Robinson/Stevie Wonder

19 Sept Band Of Gold, Freda Payne (6)
Ron Dunbar/Edith Wayne

31 Oct Woodstock, Matthews Southern Comfort (3)
Joni Mitchell

21 Nov Voodoo Chile, Jimi Hendrix Experience (1)
Jimi Hendrix

28 Nov I Hear You Knocking, Dave Edmunds Rockpile (6)
Pearl King/Dave Bartholomew

1971

9 Jan Grandad, Clive Dunn (3)
Herbie Flowers/Kenny Pickett

30 Jan My Sweet Lord, George Harrison (5; best seller of the year)
George Harrison

6 March Baby Jump, Mungo Jerry (2)
Ray Dorset

20 March Hot Love, T. Rex (6)
Marc Bolan

1 May Double Barrel, Dave & Ansil Collins (2)
Winston Riley/Ansil Collins

15 May Knock Three Times, Dawn (5; the 300th No. 1)
Irwin Levine/Larry Russell-Brown

19 June Chirpy Chirpy Cheep Cheep, Middle Of The Road (5)
Lally Stott

24 July Get It On, T. Rex (4)
Marc Bolan

21 Aug I'm Still Waiting, Diana Ross (4)
Deke Richards

18 Sept Hey Girl Don't Bother Me, Tams (3)
Ray Whitley

9 Oct Maggie May, Rod Stewart (5)
Rod Stewart/Martin Quittenton

13 Nov Coz I Luv You, Slade (4)
Noddy Holder/Dave Lea

11 Dec Ernie (The Fastest Milkman In The West), Benny Hill (4)
Benny Hill

1972

8 Jan I'd Like To Teach The World To Sing (In Perfect Harmony), New Seekers (4; best seller of the year)
William Becker/Roquel Davis/Roger Cook/Roger Greenaway

5 Feb Telegram Sam, T. Rex (2)
Marc Bolan

19 Feb Son Of My Father, Chicory Tip (3)
Giorgio Moroder/Pete Bellotti/Michael Holm

11 March Without You, Nilsson (5)
Pete Ham/Tom Evans

15 April Amazing Grace, Pipes & Drums & Military Band of The Royal Scots Dragoon Guards (Carabiniers & Greys) Bandmaster W.O.I.C.I. Herbert, Pipe Major W.O.I.I.J. Pryde (5)
Judy Collins

20 May Metal Guru, T. Rex (4)
Marc Bolan

17 June Vincent, Don McLean (2)
Don McLean

1 July Take Me Bak 'Ome, Slade (1)
Noddy Holder/Jim Lea

8 July Puppy Love, Donny Osmond (5)
Paul Anka

12 Aug School's Out, Alice Cooper (3)
Alice Cooper/Michael Bruce

2 Sept You Wear It Well, Rod Stewart (1)
Rod Stewart/Martin Quittenton

9 Sept Mama Weer All Crazee Now, Slade (3)
Noddy Holder/Dave Lea

30 Sept How Can I Be Sure, David Cassidy (2)
Felix Cavaliere/Eddie Brigatti

14 Oct Mouldy Old Dough, Lieutenant Pigeon (4)
Rob Woodward/Nigel Fletcher

11 Nov Clair, Gilvert O'Sullivan (2)
Raymond O'Sullivan

25 Nov My Ding-A-Ling, Chuck Berry (4)
Chuck Berry

23 Dec Long Haired Lover From Liverpool, Little Jimmy Osmond with The Mike Curb Congregation (5)
Christopher Kingsley

1973

27 Jan Block Buster!, Sweet (5)
Nicky Chinn/Mike Chapman

3 March *Cum On Feel The Noize, Slade (4)
Noddy Holder/Dave Lea

31 March The Twelfth Of Never, Donny Osmond (1)
Paul Francis Webster/Jay Livingstone

7 April Get Down, Gilbert O'Sullivan (2)
Raymond O'Sullivan

21 April Tie A Yellow Ribbon Round The Ole Oak Tree, Dawn featuring Tony Orlando (4)
Irwin Levine/Larry Russell-Brown

19 May See My Baby Jive, Wizzard, vocal backing - The Suedettes (4)
Roy Wood

16 June Can The Can, Suzi Quatro (1)
Nicky Chinn/Mike Chapman

23 June Rubber Bullets, 10cc (1)
Kevin Godley/Lol Creme/Graham Gouldman

30 June *Skweeze Me, Pleeze Me, Slade (3)
Noddy Holder/Dave Lea

21 July Welcome Home, Peters & Lee (1)
Jean-Alphonse Dupre/Stanislas Beldone/Bryan Blackburn

28 July I'm The Leader Of The Gang (I Am), Gary Glitter (4)
Gary Glitter/Mike Leander

25 Aug Young Love, Donny Osmond (4)
Carole Joyner/Ric Cartey

22 Sept Angel Fingers (A Teen Ballad), Wizzard, vocal backing - The Suedettes & The Bleach Boys (1)
Roy Wood

29 Sept Eye Level (Theme From The Thames T.V. Series "Van Der Valk"), Simon Park Orchestra (4)
Simon Park/Jack Trombey

27 Oct Daydreamer/The Puppy Song, David Cassidy (3)
Terry Dempsey: Harry Nilsson

17 Nov *I Love You Love Me Love, Gary Glitter (4; best seller of the year)
Gary Glitter/Mike Leander

15 Dec *Merry Xmas Everybody, Slade (5)
Noddy Holder/Dave Lea

1974

19 Jan You Won't Find Another Fool Like Me, New Seekers featuring Lyn Paul (1; best seller of the year)
Tony Macauley/Geoff Stevens

26 Jan Tiger Feet, Mud (4)
Nicky Chinn/Mike Chapman

23 Feb Devil Gate Drive, Suzi Quatro (2)
Nicky Chinn/Mike Chapman

9 March Jealous Mind, Alvin Stardust (1)
Peter Shelley

16 March Billy - Don't Be A Hero, Paper Lace (3)
Mitch Murray/Peter Callander

6 April Seasons In The Sun, Terry Jacks (4)
Jaques Brel/Rod McKuen

4 May Waterloo, Abba (Bjorn, Benny, Anna & Frida) (2)
Benny Anderson/Bjorn Ulvaeus/Stig Anderson

18 May Sugar Baby Love, Rubettes (4)
Wayne Bickerton/Tony Waddington

15 June The Streak, Ray Stevens (1)
Ray Stevens

22 June Always Yours, Gary Glitter (1)
Gary Glitter/Mike Leander

29 June She, Charles Aznavour (4)
Charles Aznavour/Herbert Kretzmer

27 July Rock Your Baby, George McCrae (3)
Harry Casey/Richard Finch

17 Aug When Will I See You Again, Three Degrees (2)
Kenny Gamble/Leon Huff

31 Aug Love Me For A Reason, Osmonds (3)
Johnny Bristol

21 Sept Kung Fu Fighting, Carl Douglas (3)
Carl Douglas

12 Oct Annie's Song, John Denver (1)
John Denver

19 Oct Sad Sweet Dreamer, Sweet Sensation (1)
Des Parton

26 Oct Everything I Own, Ken Boothe (3)
David Gates

16 Nov Gonna Make You A Star, David Essex (3)
David Essex

7 Dec You're The First, The Last, My Everything, Barry White (2)
Barry White/Tony Sepe/Peter Radcliffe

21 Dec Lonely This Christmas, Mud (4)
Nicky Chinn/Mike Chapman

1975

18 Jan Down Down, Status Quo (1)
Francis Rossi/Robert Young

25 Jan M/s Grace, Tymes (1)
Joanna Hall/John Hall

1 Feb January, Pilot (3)
Dave Paton

22 Feb Make Me Smile (Come Up And See Me), Steve Harley & Cockney Rebel (2)
Steve Harley

8 March If, Telly Savalas (2)
David Gates

22 March Bye Bye Baby, Bay City Rollers (6)
Bob Gaudio/Bob Crewe

3 May Oh Boy, Mud (2)
Sonny West/Norman Petty/Bill Tilghman

17 May Stand By Your Man, Tammy Wynette (3)
Billy Sherrill/Tammy Wynette

7 June Whispering Grass, Windsor Davis as B.S.M. Williams & Don Estelle as Gunner Sugden (Lofty) (3)
Fred & Doris Fisher

28 June I'm Not In Love, 10cc (2)
Eric Stewart/Graham Gouldman

12 July Tears On My Pillow (I Can't Take It), Johnny Nash (1)
Ernie Smith

19 July Give A Little Love, Bay City Rollers (3)
Johnny Goodison/Phil Wainman

9 Aug Barbados, Typically Tropical (1)
Jeff Calvert/Max West

16 Aug Can't Give You Anything (But My Love), Stylistics (3)
Hugo Peretti/Luigi Creatore/David Weiss

6 Sept Sailing, Rod Stewart (4)
Gavin Sutherland

4 Oct Hold Me Close, David Essex (3)
David Essex

25 Oct I Only Have Eyes For You, Art Garfunkel (2)
Al Dubin/Harry Warren

8 Nov Space Oddity, David Bowie (2)
David Bowie

22 Nov D.I.V.O.R.C.E., Billy Connolly (1)
Bobby Braddock/Claude Putnam Jnr.

29 Nov Bohemian Rhapsody, Queen (9; best seller of the year)
Freddie Mercury

1976

31 Jan Mamma Mia, Abba (2)
Benny Anderson/Bjorn Ulvaeus/Stig Anderson

14 Feb Forever And Ever, Slik (1)
Bill Martin/Phil Coulter

21 Feb December, 1963 (Oh, What A Night), Four Seasons (2)
Bob Gaudio/Judy Parker

6 March I Love To Love (But My Baby Loves To Dance), Tina Charles (3)
Jack Robinson/James Bolden

27 March Save Your Kisses For Me, Brotherhood Of Man (6; best seller of the year)
Tony Hiller/Martin Lee/Lee Sheridan

8 May Fernando, Abba (4)
Benny Anderson/Bjorn Ulvaeus/Stig Anderson

5 June No Charge, J.J. Barrie (1)
Harland Howard

12 June The Combine Harvester (Brand New Key), Wurzels (2)
Melanie Safka

26 June You To Me Are Everything, Real Thing (3)
Ken Gold/Micky Denne

17 July Excerpts From The Roussos Phenomenon [EP], Demis Roussos (1). Lead track: Forever And Ever
Stylianos Vlaviano/Robert Costandinos

24 July Don't Go Breaking My Heart, Elton John & Kiki Dee (6)
Ann Orson And Carte Blanche

4 Sept Dancing Queen, Abba (6)
Benny Anderson/Bjorn Ulvaeus/Stig Anderson

16 Oct Mississippi, Pussycat (4)
Werner Theunissen

13 Nov If You Leave Me Now, Chicago (3)
Peter Cetera

4 Dec Under The Moon Of Love, Showaddywaddy (3)
Tommy Boyce/Curtis Lee

25 Dec When A Child Is Born (Soleado), Johnny Mathis (3)
Fred Jay/Di Damicco Ciro

1977

15 Jan Don't Give Up On Us, David Soul (4)
Tony Macauley

12 Feb Don't Cry For Me Argentina, Julie Covington (1; the 400th No. 1)
Andrew Lloyd Webber/Tim Rice

19 Feb When I Need You, Leo Sayer (3)
Albert Hammond/Carole Bayer Sager

12 March Chanson D'Amour, Manhattan Transfer (3)
Wayne Shanklin

2 April Knowing Me, Knowing You, Abba (5)
Benny Anderson/Bjorn Ulvaeus/Stig Anderson

7 May Free, Deniece Williams (2)
Deniece Williams/Hank Redd/Nathan Watts/Susaye Greene

21 May I Don't Want To Talk About It/First Cut Is The Deepest, Rod Stewart (4)
Danny Whitten: Cat Stevens

18 June Lucille, Kenny Rogers (1)
Roger Bowling/Hal Bynum

25 June Show You The Way To Go, Jacksons (1)
Kenny Gamble/Leon Huff

2 July So You Win Again, Hot Chocolate (3)
Russ Ballard

23 July I Feel Love, Donna Summer (4)
Donna Summer/Georgio Moroder/Pete Bellotte

20 Aug Angelo, Brotherhood Of Man (1)
Tony Hiller/Martin Lee/Lee Sheridan

27 Aug Float On, Floaters (1)
Marvin Willis/Arnold Ingram/James Mitchell

3 Sept Way Down, Elvis Presley (5)
Laine Martine Jr

8 Oct Silver Lady, David Soul (3)
Geoff Stephens/Tony Macauley

29 Oct Yes Sir, I Can Boogie, Baccara (1)
Rolf Soja/Frank Dostal

5 Nov The Name Of The Game, Abba (4)
Benny Anderson/Bjorn Ulvaeus/Stig Anderson

3 Dec Mull Of Kintyre/Girls' School, Wings (9; best seller of the year)
Paul McCartney: Paul McCartney/Denny Laine

1978

4 Feb Up Town Top Ranking, Althia & Donna (1)
Errol Thompson/Althia Forest/Donna Reid

11 Feb Figaro, Brotherhood Of Man (1)
Tony Hiller/Martin Lee/Lee Sheridan

18 Feb Take A Chance On Me, Abba (3)
Benny Anderson/Bjorn Ulvaeus

11 March Wuthering Heights, Kate Bush (4)
Kate Bush

8 April Matchstalk Men And Matchstalk Cats And Dogs (Lowry's Song), Brian & Michael (Burke & Jerk) (3)
Michael Coleman/Brian Burke

29 April Night Fever, Bee Gees (2)
Barry Gibb/Maurice Gibb/Robin Gibb

13 May Rivers Of Babylon, Boney M (5; best seller of the year)
Frank Farian/Georg Reyam/Brent Dowe/Trevor McNaughton: Frank Farian

17 June You're The One That I Want, John Travolta & Olivia Newton-John (9)
John Farrar

19 Aug Three Times A Lady, Commodores (5)
Lionel Richie

23 Sept Dreadlock Holiday, 10cc (1)
Eric Stewart/Graham Gouldman

30 Sept Summer Nights, John Travolta, Olivia Newton-John & Cast (7)
Jim Jacobs/Warren Casey

18 Nov Rat Trap, Boomtown Rats (2)
Bob Geldof

2 Dec Da 'Ya' Think I'm Sexy?, Rod Stewart (1)
Rod Stewart/Carmine Appice

9 Dec Mary's Boy Child/Oh My Lord [M], Boney M (4)
Jester Hairston/Frank Farian

1979

6 Jan Y.M.C.A., Village People (3; best seller of the year)
Jacques Morali/Henri Belolo/Victor Willis

27 Jan Hit Me With Your Rhythm Stick, Ian & The Blockheads (1)
Ian Dury/Chas Jankel

3 Feb Heart Of Glass, Blondie (4)
Chris Stein/Debbie Harry

3 March Tragedy, Bee Gees (2)
Barry Gibb/Maurice Gibb/Robin Gibb

17 March I Will Survive, Gloria Gaynor (4)
Freddie Perren/Dino Fekaris

14 April Bright Eyes, Art Garfunkel (6)
Mike Batt

26 May Sunday Girl, Blondie (3)
Chris Stein

16 June Ring My Bell, Anita Ward (2)
Frederick Knight

30 June Are 'Friends' Electric?, Tubeway Army (4)
Gary Numan

28 July I Don't Like Mondays, Boomtown Rats (4)
Bob Geldof

25 Aug We Don't Talk Anymore, Cliff Richard (4)
Alan Tarney

22 Sept Cars, Gary Numan (1)
Gary Numan

29 Sept Message In A Bottle, Police (3)
Sting

20 Oct Video Killed The Radio Star, Buggles (1)
Trevor Horn/Geoff Downes/Bruce Wooley

27 Oct One Day At A Time, Lena Martell (3)
MariJohn Wilkin/Kris Kristofferson

17 Nov When You're In Love With A Beautiful Woman, Dr. Hook (3)
Evan Stevens

8 Dec Walking On The Moon, Police (1)
Sting

15 Dec Another Brick In The Wall Part II, Pink Floyd (5)
Roger Waters

1980

19 Jan Brass In Pocket, Pretenders (2)
Chrissie Hynde/James Honeyman-Scott

2 Feb The Special A.K.A. Live! [EP], Specials featuring Rico (2). Lead track: Too Much Too Young
Jerry Dammers/Lloyd Chalmers

16 Feb Coward Of The County, Kenny Rogers (2)
Roger Bowling/Billy Wheeler

1 March Atomic, Blondie (2)
Debbie Harry/Jimmy Destri

15 March Together We Are Beautiful, Fern Kinney (1)
Ken Leray

22 March *Going Underground/The Dreams Of Children, Jam (3)
Paul Weller

12 April Working My Way Back To You, Detroit Spinners (2)
Sandy Linzer/Denny Randell

26 April Call Me, Blondie (1)
Giorgio Moroder/Deborah Harry

3 May Geno, Dexy's Midnight Runners (2)
Kevin Rowland/Al Archer

17 May What's Another Year, Johnny Logan (2)
Shay Healey

31 May Theme From M*A*S*H*(Suicide Is Painless), Mash (3)
Mike Altman/Johnny Mandel

21 June Crying, Don McLean (3)
Roy Orbison/Joe Melson

12 July Xanadu, Olivia Newton-John/Electric Light Orchestra (2)
Jeff Lynne

26 July Use It Up And Wear It Out, Odyssey (2)
Sandy Linzer/L.Russell Brown

9 Aug The Winner Takes It All, Abba (2)
Benny Anderson/Bjorn Ulvaeus

23 Aug Ashes To Ashes, David Bowie (2)
David Bowie

6 Sept Start, Jam (1)
Paul Weller

13 Sept Feels Like I'm In Love, Kelly Marie (2)
Ray Dorset

27 Sept *Don't Stand So Close To Me, Police (4; best seller of the year)
Sting

25 Oct Woman In Love, Barbra Streisand (3)
Barry Gibb/Robin Gibb

15 Nov The Tide Is High, Blondie (2)
John Holt

29 Nov Super Trouper, Abba (3)
Benny Anderson/Bjorn Ulvaeus

20 Dec (Just Like) Starting Over, John Lennon (1)
John Lennon

27 Dec There's No One Quite Like Grandma, St. Winifred's School Choir (2)
Gordon Lorenz

1981

10 Jan Imagine, John Lennon (4)
John Lennon

7 Feb Woman, John Lennon (2)
John Lennon

21 Feb Shaddap You Face, Joe Dolce Music Theatre (3)
Joe Dolce

14 March Jealous Guy, Roxy Music (2)
John Lennon

28 March This Ole House, Shakin' Stevens (3)
Stuart Hamblen

18 April Making Your Mind Up, Bucks Fizz (3)
Andy Hill/John Danter

9 May *Stand And Deliver, Adam & The Ants (5)
Adam Ant/Marco Pirroni

13 June Being With You, Smokey Robinson (2)
Smokey Robinson

27 June One Day In Your Life, Michael Jackson (2)
Sam Brown III/Renee Armand

11 July Ghost Town, Specials (3)
Jerry Dammers

1 Aug Green Door, Shakin' Stevens (4)
Bob Davie/Marvin Moore

29 Aug Japanese Boy, Aneka (1)
Bobby Heatlie

5 Sept Tainted Love, Soft Cell (2)
Ed Cobb

19 Sept Prince Charming, Adam & The Ants (4)
Adam Ant/Marco Pirroni

17 Oct It's My Party, Dave Stewart with Barbara Gaskin (4)
John Weiner/Wally Gold/John Gluck Jr

14 Nov Every Little Thing She Does Is Magic, Police (1)
Sting

21 Nov Under Pressure, Queen & David Bowie (2)
Queen/David Bowie

5 Dec Begin The Beguine (Volver A Empezar), Julio Iglesias (1)
Cole Porter

12 Dec Don't You Want Me, Human League (5; best seller of the year)
Jo Callis/Phil Oakey/Adrian Wright

1982

16 Jan The Land Of Make Believe, Bucks Fizz (2)
Andy Hill/Pete Sinfield

30 Jan Oh Julie, Shakin' Stevens (1)
Shakin' Stevens

6 Feb The Model/Computer Love, Kraftwerk (1)
Ralf Hutter/Karl Bartos/Emil Schmitt

13 Feb *Town Called Malice/Precious, Jam (3)
Paul Weller

6 March The Lion Sleeps Tonight, Tight Fit (3)
Hugo Peretti/Luigi Creatore/George David Weiss/Solomon Linda/Paul Campbell

27 March Seven Tears, Goombay Dance Band (3)
Wolff Eckehardt Stein/Wolfgang Jass

17 April My Camera Never Lies, Bucks Fizz (1)
Andy Hill/Nicola Martin

24 April Ebony And Ivory, Paul McCartney with additional vocals by Stevie Wonder (3)
Paul McCartney

15 May A Little Peace, Nicole (2; the 500th No. 1)
Ralph Siegel/Paul Greedus

29 May House Of Fun, Madness (2)
Mike Barson/LeeThompson

12 June Goody Two Shoes, Adam Ant (2)
Adam Ant/Marco Pirroni

26 June I've Never Been To Me, Charlene (1)
Ron Miller/Ken Hirsch

3 July Happy Talk, Captain Sensible (2)
Richard Rodgers/Oscar Hammerstein II

17 July Fame, Irene Cara (3)
Martin Gore/Dean Pitchford

7 Aug Come On Eileen, Dexys Midnight Runners & The Emerald Express (4; best seller of the year)
Kevin Rowland/Jimmy Patterson/Kevin Adams

4 Sept Eye Of The Tiger, Survivor (4)
Jim Peterik/Frankie Sullivan

2 Oct Pass The Dutchie, Musical Youth (3)
Jackie Mittoo/Fitzroy Simpson/Lloyd Ferguson

23 Oct Do You Really Want To Hurt Me, Culture Club (3)
Culture Club

13 Nov I Don't Wanna Dance, Eddy Grant (3)
Eddy Grant

4 Dec *Beat Surrender, Jam (2)
Paul Weller

18 Dec Save Your Love, Renee & Renato (4)
John Edward/Sue Edward

1983

15 Jan You Can't Hurry Love, Phil Collins (2)
Brian Holland/Lamont Dozier/Edward Holland

29 Jan Down Under, Men At Work (3)
Colin Hay/Ron Strykert

19 Feb Too Shy, Kajagoogoo (2)
Kajagoogoo

5 March Billie Jean, Michael Jackson (1)
Michael Jackson

12 March Total Eclipse Of The Heart, Bonnie Tyler (2)
Jim Steinman

26 March *Is There Something I Should Know?, Duran Duran (2)
Duran Duran

9 April Let's Dance, David Bowie (3)
David Bowie

30 April True, Spandau Ballet (4)
Gary Kemp

28 May Candy Girl, New Edition (1)
Maurice Starr/Michael Jonzun

4 June Every Breath You Take, Police (4)
Sting

2 July Baby Jane, Rod Stewart (3)
Rod Stewart/Jay Davis

23 July Wherever I Lay My Hat (That's My Home), Paul Young (3)
Marvin Gaye/Norman Whitfield/Barrett Strong

13 Aug Give It Up, KC & The Sunshine Band (3)
Harry Casey

3 Sept Red Red Wine, UB40 (3)
Neil Diamond

24 Sept Karma Chameleon, Culture Club (6; best seller of the year)
Culture Club

5 Nov Uptown Girl, Billy Joel (5)
Billy Joel

10 Dec Only You, Flying Pickets (5)
Vince Clarke

1984

14 Jan Pipes Of Peace, Paul McCartney (2)
Paul McCartney

28 Jan Relax, Frankie Goes To Hollywood (5)
Peter Gill/Holly Johnson/Mark O'Toole

3 March 99 Red Balloons, Nena (3)
Joern-Uwe Fahrenkrog-Petersen/Carlo Karges/Kevin McAlea

24 March Hello, Lionel Richie (6)
Lionel Richie

5 May The Reflex, Duran Duran (4)
Duran Duran

2 June Wake Me Up Before You Go Go, Wham! (2)
George Michael

16 June *Two Tribes, Frankie Goes To Hollywood (9)
Peter Gill/Holly Johnson/Mark O'Toole

18 Aug Careless Whisper, George Michael (3)
George Michael

8 Sept I Just Called To Say I Love You, Stevie Wonder (6)
Stevie Wonder

20 Oct Freedom, Wham! (3)
George Michael

10 Nov I Feel For You, Chaka Khan (3)
Prince

1 Dec I Should Have Known Better, Jim Diamond (1)
Jim Diamond/Graham Lyle

8 Dec The Power Of Love, Frankie Goes To Hollywood (1)
Peter Gill/Holly Johnson/Mark O'Toole

15 Dec *Do They Know It's Christmas?, Band Aid (5; best seller of the year)
Midge Ure/Bob Geldof

1985

19 Jan I Want To Know What Love Is, Foreigner (3)
Mick Jones

9 Feb I Know Him So Well, Elaine Paige & Barbara Dickson (4)
Benny Anderson/Bjorn Ulvaeus

9 March You Spin Me Round (Like A Record), Dead Or Alive (2)
Dead Or Alive

23 March Easy Lover, Philip Bailey (duet with Phil Collins) (4)
Philip Bailey/Phil Collins/Nathan East

20 April We Are The World, USA For Africa (2)
Michael Jackson/Lionel Richie

4 May Move Closer, Phyllis Nelson (1)
Phyllis Nelson

11 May 19, Paul Hardcastle (5)
Paul Hardcastle/William Coutourie/Jonas McCord

15 June You'll Never Walk Alone, Crowd (2)
Richard Rodgers/Oscar Hammerstein II

29 June Frankie, Sister Sledge (4)
Denise Rich

27 July There Must Be An Angel (Playing With My Heart), Eurythmics (1)
Annie Lennox/Dave Stewart

3 Aug Into The Groove, Madonna (4)
Madonna/Stephen Bray

31 Aug I Got You Babe, UB40 Guest vocals by Chrissie Hynde (1)
Sonny Bono

Sept *Dancing In The Street, David Bowie & Mick Jagger (4)
Ivy Hunter/William Stevenson/Marvin Gaye

Oct If I Was, Midge Ure (1)
Midge Ure/Danny Mitchell

2 Oct The Power Of Love, Jennifer Rush (5; best seller of the year)
Candy De Rouge/Gunther Mende/Jennifer Rush/Mary Susan Applegate

6 Nov A Good Heart, Feargal Sharkey (2)
Maria McKee

0 Nov I'm Your Man, Wham! (2)
George Michael

4 Dec Saving All My Love For You, Whitney Houston (2)
Michael Masser/Gerry Goffin

28 Dec Merry Christmas Everyone, Shakin' Stevens (2)
Bob Heatlie

1986

11 Jan West End Girls, Pet Shop Boys (2)
Neil Tennant/Chris Lowe

25 Jan The Sun Always Shines On T.V., A-Ha (2)
Pal Waaktaar

8 Feb When The Going Gets Tough, The Tough Get Going, Billy Ocean (4)
Wayne Briathwaite/Barry Eastmond/Billy Ocean/Robert Lange

8 March Chain Reaction, Diana Ross (3)
Barry Gibb/Maurice Gibb/Robin Gibb

29 March Living Doll, Comic Relief present Cliff Richard & The Young Ones featuring Hank Marvin (3)
Lionel Bart

19 April A Different Corner, George Michael (3)
George Michael

10 May Rock Me Amadeus, Falco (1)
Rob Bolland/Falco/Ferdi Bolland

17 May The Chicken Song, Spitting Image (3)
Rob Grant/Doug Naylor

7 June Spirit In The Sky, Doctor & The Medics (3)
Norman Greenbaum

28 June The Edge Of Heaven, Wham! (2)
George Michael

12 July Papa Don't Preach, Madonna (3)
Madonna/Brian Elliot

2 Aug The Lady In Red, Chris De Burgh (3)
Chris De Burgh

23 Aug I Wanna Wake Up With You, Boris Gardiner (3)
Mac Davis

13 Sept Don't Leave Me This Way, Communards with Sarah Jane Morris (4)
Kenny Gamble/Leon Huff

11 Oct True Blue, Madonna (1)
Madonna/Stephen Bray

18 Oct Every Loser Wins, Nick Berry (3; best seller of the year)
Simon May/Stewart & Bradley James

8 Nov Take My Breath Away (Love Theme From "Top Gun"), Berlin (4)
Giorgio Moroder/Tom Whitlock

6 Dec The Final Countdown, Europe (2)
Joey Tempest

20 Dec Caravan Of Love, Housemartins (1)
Ernie Isley/Chris Jasper/Marvin Isley

27 Dec Reet Petite (The Sweetest Girl In Town), Jackie Wilson (4)
Tyran Carlo/Berry Gordy Jnr

1987

24 Jan Jack Your Body, Steve 'Silk' Hurley (2)
Steve 'Silk' Hurley

7 Feb I Knew You Were Waiting (For Me), Aretha Franklin & George Michael (2)
Simon Climie/Denis Morgan

21 Feb Stand By Me, Ben E. King (3)
Ben E.King/Jerry Leiber/Mike Stoller

14 March Everything I Own, Boy George (2)
David Gates

28 March Respectable, Mel & Kim (1)
Mike Stock/Matt Aitken/Pete Waterman

4 April *Let It Be, Ferry Aid (3)
John Lennon/Paul McCartney

25 April La Isla Bonita, Madonna (2)
Madonna/Stephen Bray/Bruce Gaitsch

9 May Nothing's Gonna Stop Us Now, Starship (4)
Albert Hammond/Diane Warren

6 June I Wanna Dance With Somebody (Who Loves Me), Whitney Houston (2)
Shannon Rubicam/George Merrill

20 June Star Trekkin', Firm (2)
Grahame Lister/John O'Connor

4 July It's A Sin, Pet Shop Boys (3)
Neil Tennant/Chris Lowe

25 July Who's That Girl, Madonna (1)
Madonna/Patrick Leonard

1 Aug La Bamba, Los Lobos (2)
Richie Valens

15 Aug I Just Can't Stop Loving You, Michael Jackson with Siedah Garrett (2)
Michael Jackson

29 Aug Never Gonna Give You Up, Rick Astley (5; best seller of the year)
Mike Stock/Matt Aitken/Pete Waterman

3 Oct Pump Up The Volume/Anitina (The First Time I See She Dance), M/A/R/R/S (2)
Steve Young: A.R Kane/Colourbox

17 Oct You Win Again, Bee Gees (4)
Barry Gibb/Maurice Gibb/Robin Gibb

14 Nov China In Your Hand, T'Pau (5; the 600th No. 1)
Carol Decker/Ronnie Rogers

19 Dec Always On My Mind, Pet Shop Boys (4)
Wayne Thompson/Johnny Christopher/Mark James

1988

16 Jan Heaven Is A Place On Earth, Belinda Carlisle (2)
Rick Nowels/Ellen Shipley

30 Jan I Think We're Alone Now, Tiffany (3)
Richard Cordell

20 Feb I Should Be So Lucky, Kylie Minogue (5)
Mike Stock/Matt Aitken/Pete Waterman

26 March Don't Turn Around, Aswad (2)
Diane Warren/Albert Hammond

9 April Heart, Pet Shop Boys (3)
Neil Tennant/Chris Lowe

30 April Theme From S-Express, S-Express (2)
Mark Moore/Pascal Gabriel

14 May Perfect, Fairground Attraction (1)
Mark E. Nevin

21 May With A Little Help From My Friends/She's Leaving Home, Wet Wet Wet/Billy Bragg with Cara Tivey (4)
John Lennon/Paul McCartney

18 June Doctorin' The Tardis, Timelords (1)
Nicky Chinn/Mike Chapman/Ron Grainer/Gary Glitter/Mike Leander/Timelords

25 June I Owe You Nothing, Bros (2)
Luke Goss/Matt Goss

9 July Nothing's Gonna Change My Love For You, Glenn Medeiros (4)
Michael Masser/Gerry Goffin

6 Aug The Only Way Is Up, Yazz & The Plastic Population (5)
George Jackson/Johnny Henderson

10 Sept A Groovy Kind Of Love, Phil Collins (2)
Toni Wine/Carole Bayer Sager

24 Sept He Ain't Heavy, He's My Brother, Hollies (2)
Bert Russell/Bobby Scott

8 Oct Desire, U2 (1)
U2

15 Oct One Moment In Time, Whitney Houston (2)
Albert Hammond/John Bettis

29 Oct Orinoco Flow (Sail Away), Enya (3)
Enya/Rona Ryan

19 Nov The First Time, Robin Beck (3)
Gavin Spencer/Tom Anthony/Terry boyle

10 Dec Mistletoe And Wine, Cliff Richard (4; best seller of the year)
Leslie Stewart/Jeremy Paul/Keith Strachan

1989

7 Jan Especially For You, Kylie Minogue & Jason Donovan (3)
Mike Stock/Matt Aitken/Pete Waterman

28 Jan Something's Gotten Hold Of My Heart, Marc Almond featuring special guest star Gene Pitney (4)
Roger Cook/Roger Greenaway

25 Feb Belfast Child, Simple Minds (2)
Simple Minds

11 March Too Many Broken Hearts, Jason Donovan (2)
Mike Stock/Matt Aitken/Pete Waterman

25 March Like A Prayer, Madonna (3)
Madonna/Patrick Leonard

15 April Eternal Flame, Bangles (4)
Susanne Hoffs/Billy Steinberg/Thomas Kelly

13 May Hand On Your Heart, Kylie Minogue (1)
Mike Stock/Matt Aitken/Pete Waterman

20 May *Ferry 'Cross The Mersey, Christians, Holly Johnson, Paul McCartney, Gerry Marsden & Stock Atken Waterman (3)
Gerry Marsden

10 June *Sealed With A Kiss, Jason Donovan (2)
Gary Geld/Peter Udell

24 June Back To Life (However Do You Want Me), Soul II Soul featuring Caron Wheeler (4)
Beresford Romeo/Caron Wheeler/Simon Law/Nellee Hooper

22 July You'll Never Stop Me Loving You, Sonia (2)
Mike Stock/Matt Aitken/Pete Waterman

5 Aug Swing The Mood, Jive Bunny & The Mastermixers (5)
Various

9 Sept Ride On Time, Black Box (6; best seller of the year)
Mirko Limoni/Daniele Davoli/Valerio Semplici

21 Oct That's What I Like, Jive Bunny & The Mastermixers (3)
Various

11 Nov All Around The World, Lisa Stansfield (2)
Lisa Stansfield/Ian Devaney/Andy Morris

25 Nov You Got It (The Right Stuff), New Kids On The Block (3)
Maurice Starr

16 Dec *Let's Party, Jive Bunny & The Mastermixers (1)
Various

23 Dec *Do They Know It's Christmas?, Band Aid II (3)
Midge Ure/Bob Geldof

1990

13 Jan Hangin' Tough, New Kids On The Block (2)
Maurice Starr

27 Jan Tears On My Pillow, Kylie Minogue (1)
Sylvester Bradford/Al Lewis

3 Feb Nothing Compares 2 U, Sinead O'Connor (4)
Prince

3 March Dub Be Good To Me, Beats International featuring Lindy (4)
Norman Cook/James Harris III/Terry Lewis

31 March The Power, Snap! (2)
Benito Benites/John Garrett

14 April Vogue, Madonna (4)
Madonna/Shep Pettibone

12 May Killer, Adamski (4)
Adamski/Seal

9 June World In Motion . . ., Englandneworder (2)
New Order/Keith Allen

23 June Sacrifice/Healing Hands, Elton John (5)
Elton John/Bernie Taupin

28 July Turtle Power, Partners In Kryme (4)
James Alpern/Richard Usher

25 Aug Itsy Bitsy Teeny Weeny Yellow Polka Dot Bikini, Bombalurina (3)
Paul Vance/Lee Pockriss

15 Sept The Joker, Steve Miller Band (2)
Steve Miller

29 Sept Show Me Heaven, Maria McKee (4)
Joshua Rifkin/Eric Rackin/Maria McKee

27 Oct A Little Time, Beautiful South (1)
Paul Heaton/Dave Rotheray

3 Nov Unchained Melody, Righteous Brothers (4; best seller of the year)
Alex North/Hy Zaret

1 Dec Ice Ice Baby, Vanilla Ice (4)
Vanilla Ice/Earthquake/David Bowie/Freddie Mercury

29 Dec Saviours Day, Cliff Richard (1)
Chris Eaton

1991

5 Jan *Bring Your Daughter . . . To The Slaughter, Iron Maiden (2)
Bruce Dickinson

19 Jan Sadness Part 1, Enigma (1)
Curly M.C/David Fairstein

26 Jan *Innuendo, Queen (1)
Queen

2 Feb 3 A.M. Eternal (Live At The S.S.I.), KLF featuring the Children of the Revolution (2)
Jimmy Cauty/Bill Drummond/Ricardo Lyte

16 Feb Do The Bartman, Simpsons (3)
Bryan Loren

9 March Should I Stay Or Should I Go, Clash (2)
The Clash

23 March The Stonk, Hale and Pace & The Stonkers (1)
Joe Griffiths/Gareth Hale/Norman Pace

30 March The One And Only, Chesney Hawkes (5)
Nik Kershaw

4 May The Shoop Shoop Song (It's In His Kiss), Cher (5)
Rudy Clark

8 June I Wanna Sex You Up, Color Me Badd (3)
Dr Freeze

29 June Any Dream Will Do, Jason Donovan (2)
Andrew Lloyd Webber/Tim Rice

13 July (Everything I Do) I Do It For You, Bryan Adams (16; best seller of the year)
Bryan Adams/Robert Lange/Michael Kamen

2 Nov *The Fly, U2 (1)
U2

9 Nov Dizzy, Vic Reeves & The Wonder Stuff (2)
Freddy Weller/Tommy Roe

23 Nov *Black Or White, Michael Jackson (2)
Michael Jackson/Bill Bottrell

7 Dec *Don't Let The Sun Go Down On Me, George Michael with Elton John (2)
Elton John/Bernie Taupin

21 Dec *Bohemian Rhapsody/These Are The Days Of Our Lives, Queen (5)
Freddie Mercury: Queen

1992

25 Jan Goodnight Girl, Wet Wet Wet (4)
Graeme Clark/Tommy Cunningham/Marti Pellow/Neil Mitchell

22 Feb Stay, Shakespears Sister (8)
Siobhan Fahey/Marcella Detroit/Guiot (Dave Stewart)

18 April Deeply Dippy, Right Said Fred (3)
Fred Fairbrass/Rob Manzoli/Richard Fairbrass

9 May Please Don't Go/Game Boy, K.W.S. (5)
Harry Casey/Richard Finch: Chris King/Winston Williams

13 June *Abba-Esque [EP], Erasure (5). Lead track: Lay All Your Love On Me
Abba

18 July Ain't No Doubt, Jimmy Nail (3)
Guy Pratt/Danny Schogger/Jimmy Nail/Charlie Dore

8 Aug Rhythm Is A Dancer, Snap! (6)
Benito Benites/John Garrett/Thea Austin/Durron Butler

19 Sept Ebeneezer Goode, Shamen (4)
Colin Angus/Richard West

17 Oct Sleeping Satellite, Tasmin Archer (2)
Tasmin Archer/John Beck/John Hughes

31 Oct End Of The Road, Boyz II Men (3)
L.A.Reid/Babyface/Daryl Simmons

21 Nov Would I Lie To You, Charles & Eddie (2)
Mick Leeson/Peter Vale

5 Dec I Will Always Love You, Whitney Houston (10; best seller of the year)
Dolly Parton

1993

13 Feb No Limit, 2 Unlimited (5)
Anita Dells/Ray Slijngaard/Phil Wilde/Jean-Paul De Coster

20 March Oh Carolina, Shaggy (2)
Trad arr Shaggy

3 April Young At Heart, Bluebells (4)
Roger Hodgens/Siobhan Fahey

1 May *Five Live [EP], George Michael & Queen with Lisa Stansfield (3). Lead track: Somebody To Love
Freddie Mercury

22 May All That She Wants, Ace Of Base (3)
Joker/Buddah

12 June (I Can't Help) Falling In Love With You, UB40 (2)
George David Weiss/Hugo Perretti/Luigi Creatore

26 June Dreams, Gabrielle (3)
Gabrielle/Tim Laws

17 July *Pray, Take That (4)
Gary Barlow

14 Aug Living On My Own, Freddie Mercury (2)
Freddie Mercury

28 Aug Mr. Vain, Culture Beat (4)
Torsten Fenslau/Peter Zweier/Nosie Katzmann/Jay Supreme

25 Sept Boom! Shake The Room, Jazzy Jeff & The Fresh Prince (2)
Will Smith/Lee Haggard/Walter Williams/Ken Mayberry

9 Oct *Relight My Fire, Take That featuring Lulu (2)
Dan Hartman

23 Oct I'd Do Anything For Love (But I Won't Do That), Meat Loaf (7; best seller of the year)
Jim Steinman

11 Dec Mr Blobby, Mr Blobby (1, *25 Dec* for 2)
Paul Shaw/David Rogers

18 Dec *Babe, Take That (1)
Gary Barlow

1994

8 Jan Twist And Shout, Chaka Demus & Pliers with Jack Radics & Taxi Gang (2; the 700th No. 1)
Bert Burns/Phil Medley

22 Jan Things Can Only Get Better, D:Ream (4)
Peter Cunnah/Jamie Petrie

19 Feb *Without You, Mariah Carey (4)
Pete Ham/Tom Evans

19 March Doop, Doop (3)
Frederick Ridderhoff

9 April *Everything Changes, Take That (2)
Gary Barlow/Mike Ward/Elliot Kennedy/Cary Bayliss

23 April The Most Beautiful Girl In The World, Symbol (2)
Symbol

7 May The Real Thing, Tony Di Bart (1)
Tony Di Bart/Andy Blissett/Lucinda Drayton

14 May Inside, Stiltskin (1)
Peter Lawlor

21 May Come On You Reds, Manchester United Football Squad (2)
Francis Rossi/Andy Bown/John Edwards

4 June Love Is All Around, Wet Wet Wet (15; best seller of the year)
Reg Presley

17 Sept *Saturday Night, Whigfield (4)
Alfredo Pignagnoli/Davide Riva

15 Oct *Sure, Take That (2)
Gary Barlow/Mark Owen/Robbie Williams

29 Oct Baby Come Back, Pato Banton featuring Ali & Robin Campbell of UB40 (4)
Eddy Grant

26 Nov Let Me Be Your Fantasy, Baby D (2)
Floyd Dyce

10 Dec Stay Another Day, East 17 (5)
Tony Mortimer/Rob Kean/Dominic Hawken

1995

14 Jan Cotton Eye Joe, Rednex (3)
Jan Ericsson/Orjan Oberg/Pat Reiniz

4 Feb Think Twice, Celine Dion (7)
Andy Hill/Pete Sinfield

25 March Love Can Build A Bridge, Cher, Chrissie Hynde & Neneh Cherry with Eric Clapton (1)
Naomi Judd/John Jarvis/Paul Overstreet

1 April Don't Stop (Wiggle Wiggle), Outhere Brothers (1)
Hula Mahone/ Craig Simpkins/ Keith Mayberry/ Aladino

8 April *Back For Good, Take That (4)
Gary Barlow

6 May *Some Might Say, Oasis (1)
Noel Gallagher

13 May *Dreamer, Livin' Joy (1)
Gianni Visnadi/ Janice Robinson

20 May *Unchained Melody/(There'll Be Bluebirds Over) The White Cliffs Of Dover, Robson Green & Jerome Flynn (7; best seller of the year)
Alex North/ Hy Zaret: Walter Kent/ Nat Burton

8 July Boom Boom Boom, Outhere Brothers (4)
Hula/ Ken Mayberry

5 Aug *Never Forget, Take That (3)
Gary Barlow

26 Aug *Country House, Blur (2)
Damon Albarn/ Blur

9 Sept You Are Not Alone, Michael Jackson (2)
R.Kelly

23 Sept *Boombastic, Shaggy (1)
Orville Burrell/ Robert Livingston

30 Sept *Fairground, Simply Red (4)
Mick Hucknall

28 Oct *Gangsta's Paradise, Coolio featuring L.V. (2)
Artis Ivey Jr/ Larry Sanders/ Doug Rasheed/ Stevie Wonder

11 Nov *I Believe/Up On The Roof, Robson & Jerome (4)
Erwin Drake/ Irvin Graham/ Jimmy Shirl/ Al Stillman: Gerry Goffin/ Carole King

9 Dec *Earth Song, Michael Jackson (6)
Michael Jackson

1996

20 Jan *Jesus To A Child, George Michael (1)
George Michael

27 Jan *Spaceman, Babylon Zoo (5)
Jas Mann

2 March *Don't Look Back In Anger, Oasis (1)
Noel Gallagher

9 March *How Deep Is Your Love, Take That (3)
Barry Gibb/ Maurice Gibb/ Robin Gibb

30 March *Firestarter, Prodigy (2)
Liam Howlett

20 April Return Of The Mack, Mark Morrison (2)
Mark Morrison

4 May *Fastlove, George Michael (3)
George Michael/ Patrice Rushen/ Freddie Washington

25 May Ooh Aah . . . Just A Little Bit, Gina G (1)
Simon Tauber/ Steve Rodway

1 June *Three Lions (The Official Song Of The England Football Team), Baddiel & Skinner & Lightning Seeds (1, *6 July* for 1)
Ian Broudie

8 June *Killing Me Softly, Fugees (Refugee Camp) (4, *13 July* for 1; best seller of the year)
Norman Gimbel/ Charles Fox

20 July *Forever Love, Gary Barlow (1)
Gary Barlow

27 July Wannabe, Spice Girls (7)
Spice Girls/ Richard Stannard/ Matt Rowe

14 Sept *Flava, Peter Andre (1)
Peter Andre/ Andy Whitmore/ Wayne Hector/ Cee Lo

21 Sept Ready Or Not, Fugees (Refugee Camp) (2)
Wyclef Jean/ Pras Michel/ Lauryn Hill/ William Hart/ Thom Bell

5 Oct Breakfast At Tiffany's, Deep Blue Something (1)
Todd Pipes/ Deep Blue Something

12 Oct *Setting Sun, Chemical Brothers (1)
Tom Rowlands/ Ed Simons/ Noel Gallagher

19 Oct *Words, Boyzone (1)
Barry Gibb/ Maurice Gibb/ Robin Gibb

26 Oct *Say You'll Be There, Spice Girls (2)
Spice Girls/ Elliot Kennedy

9 Nov *What Becomes Of The Broken Hearted / Saturday Night At The Movies/ You'll Never Walk Alone, Robson & Jerome (2)
James Dean/ Paul Riser/ William Weatherspoon: Barry Mann/ Cynthia Weil: Richard Rodgers/ Oscar Hammerstein II

23 Nov *Breathe, Prodigy (2)
Liam Howlett/ Keith Flint/ Maxim Reality

7 Dec *I Feel You, Peter Andre (1)
Peter Andre/ Terry Jones/ Glen Goldsmith

14 Dec *A Different Beat, Boyzone (1)
Boyzone

21 Dec *Knockin' On Heaven's Door/Throw These Guns Away, Dunblane (1)
Bob Dylan: Ted Christopher

28 Dec *2 Become 1, Spice Girls (3)
Spice Girls/ Richard Stannard/ Matt Rowe

1997

18 Jan Professional Widow (It's Got To Be Big), Tori Amos (1)
Tori Amos

25 Jan *Your Woman, White Town (1)
Jyoti Mistra

1 Feb *Beetlebum, Blur (1)
Blur

8 Feb *Ain't Nobody, LL Cool J (1)
David Wolinski

15 Feb *Discotheque, U2 (1)
Bono/U2

22 Feb *Don't Speak, No Doubt (3)
Gwen Stefani

15 March *Mama / Who Do You Think You Are, Spice Girls (3)
Richard Stannard/Matt Rowe/Spice Girls: Spice Girls/ Adam Watkins/Paul Wilson

5 April *Block Rockin' Beats, Chemical Brothers (1)
Tom Rowlands/Ed Simons/Jesse B. Weaver

12 April I Believe I Can Fly, R. Kelly (3)
R.Kelly

3 May *Blood On The Dance Floor, Michael Jackson (1)
Michael Jackson/Teddy Riley

10 May *Love Won't Wait, Gary Barlow (1)
Shep Pettibone/Madonna

17 May *You're Not Alone, Olive (2)
Tim Kellett/Robin Taylor-Firth

31 May *I Wanna Be The Only One, Eternal featuring Bebe Winans (1)
Bebe Winans/Rhett Lawrence

7 June *Mmmbop, Hanson (3)
Isaac Hanson/Taylor Hanson/Zach Hanson

28 June *I'll Be Missing You, Puff Daddy & Faith Evans (featuring 112) (3, *26 July* for 3)
Sting

19 July *D'you Know What I Mean?, Oasis (1)
Noel Gallagher

16 Aug *Men In Black, Will Smith (4)
Will Smith/Patrice Rushen/Gene McFadden/ Freddie Washington

13 Sept *The Drugs Don't Work, Verve (1)
Richard Ashcroft

20 Sept *Something About The Way You Look Tonight/Candle In The Wind 1997, Elton John (5; best seller of the year)
Elton John/Bernie Taupin

25 Oct *Spice Up Your Life, Spice Girls (1)
Spice Girls/Richard Stannard/Matt Rowe

1 Nov Barbie Girl, Aqua (4)
Soren Rasted/Claus Noreen/Rene Dif/Lene Nystrom

29 Nov *Perfect Day, Various Artists (2)
Lou Reed

13 Dec *Teletubbies Say "Eh-Oh!", Teletubbies (2)
Andrew McCrorie-Shand/Andrew Davenport

27 Dec *Too Much, Spice Girls (2)
Spice Girls/Andy Watkins/Paul Wilson

1998

10 Jan Perfect Day, Various Artists (1)
Lou Reed

17 Jan Never Ever, All Saints (1)
Rickidy Raw/Shaznay Lewis

24 Jan *All Around The World, Oasis (1)
Noel Gallagher

31 Jan *You Make Me Wanna . . ., Usher (1)
Jermaine Dupri/Seal/Usher Raymond

7 Feb *Doctor Jones, Aqua (2)
Anders Oland/Soren Rashed/Claus Noreen/Rene Dif

21 Feb *My Heart Will Go On, Celine Dion (1, *14 March* for 1)
James Horner/Will Jennings

28 Feb *Brimful Of Asha, Cornershop (1)
Tjinder Singh

7 March *Frozen, Madonna (1)
Madonna/Patrick Leonard

21 March *It's Like That, Run-DMC vs Jason Nevins (6)
Christian Smith/Joseph Simmons/Daryl McDaniels

2 May *All That I Need, Boyzone (1)
Carl Sturken/Evan Rogers

9 May *Under The Bridge / Lady Marmalade, All Saints (1, *23 May* for 1)
Anthony Keldis/Michael Belzary/John Frusciante/Chad Smith: Bob Crewe/Kenny Nolan

16 May *Turn Back Time, Aqua (1)
Soren Rasted/Claus Noreen

30 May Feel It, Tamperer featuring Maya (1)
Michael Jackson/Jermaine Jackson

6 June *C'est La Vie, B*Witched (2)
*B*Witched/Ray Hedges/Tracy Ackerman/Martin Brannigan*

20 June *3 Lions '98, Baddiel, Skinner & The Lightning Seeds (3)
Ian Broudie/David Baddiel/Frank Skinner

11 July *Because We Want To, Billie (1)
Dion Rambo/Jacques Richmond/Wendy Page/Jim Marr

18 July *Freak Me, Another Level (1)
Roy Murray/Keith Sweat

25 July *Deeper Underground, Jamiriquai (1)
Jay Kay/Toby Smith

1 Aug *Viva Forever, Spice Girls (2)
Spice Girls/Richard Stannard/Matt Rowe

15 Aug *No Matter What, Boyzone (3)
Andrew Lloyd Webber/Jim Steinman

5 Sept *If You Tolerate This Your Children Will Be Next, Manic Street Preachers (1)
Nick Jones/James Dean Bradfield/Sean Moore

12 Sept *Bootie Call, All Saints (1; the 800th No. 1)
Shaznay Lewis/Karl Gordon

19 Sept *Millennium, Robbie Williams (1)
Robbie Williams/Guy Chambers/Les Bricusse/John Barry

26 Sept *I Want You Back, Melanie B featuring Missy "Misdemeanor" Elliott (1)
Missy Elliot/Gerald Thomas/Lenny Holmes

3 Oct *Rollercoaster, B*Witched (2)
*B*Witched/Ray Hedges/Tracy Ackerman/Martin Brannigan*

17 Oct *Girlfriend, Billie (1)
Dion Rambo/Jacques Richmond

24 Oct *Gym And Tonic, Spacedust (1)
Spacedust

31 Oct *Believe, Cher (7; best seller of the year)
Brian Higgins/Paul Barry/Steve Torch/Matt Gray/Stuart McLennen/Tim Powell

19 Dec *To You I Belong, B*Witched (1)
*B*Witched/Ray Hedges/Martin Brannigan*

26 Dec *Goodbye, Spice Girls (1)
Spice Girls/Richard Stannard/Matt Rowe

1999

2 Jan Chocolate Salty Balls (P.S. I Love), Chef (1)
Trey Parker

9 Jan Heartbeat/Tragedy, Steps (1)
Jackie James: Barry Gibb/Maurice Gibb/Robin Gibb

16 Jan *Praise You, Fatboy Slim (1)
Norman Cook/Camille Yarborough

23 Jan *A Little Bit More, 911 (1)
Bob Gosh

30 Jan *Pretty Fly (For A White Guy), Offspring (1)
Dexter Holland/Robert Lange/Joey Elliot/Steve Clarke

6 Feb *You Don't Know Me, Armand Van Helden featuring Duane Harden (1)
Armand Van Helden/Duane Harden

13 Feb *Maria, Blondie (1)
Jimmy Destri

20 Feb *Fly Away, Lenny Kravitz (1)
Lenny Kravitz

27 Feb *. . . Baby One More Time, Britney Spears (2; best seller of the year)
Max Martin

13 March *When The Going Gets Tough, Boyzone (2)
Wayne Braitwaite/Barry Eastmond/Robert Lange/Billy Ocean

27 March *Blame It On The Weatherman, B*Witched (1)
Ray Hedges/Martin Brannigan/Tracy Ackerman/Andy Caine

3 April *Flat Beat, Mr. Oizo (2)
Quentin Dupieux

17 April *Perfect Moment, Martine McCutcheon (2)
Wendy Page/Jim Marr

1 May *Swear It Again, Westlife (2)
Steve Mac/Wayne Hector

15 May *I Want It That Way, Backstreet Boys (1)
Max Martin/Andreas Carlsson

22 May *You Needed Me, Boyzone (1)
Randy Goodrum

29 May *Sweet Like Chocolate, Shanks & Bigfoot (2)
Stephen Meade/Daniel Langsman

12 June *Everybody's Free (To Wear Sunscreen) The Sunscreen Song (Class Of '99), Baz Luhrmann (1)
Tim Cox/Nigel Swanston/Mary Scmich

19 June *Bring It All Back, S Club 7 (1)
Elliot Kennedy/Mike Percy/Tim Lever

26 June *Boom, Boom, Boom, Boom!!, Vengaboys (1)
Danski/DJ Delmundo

3 July *9PM (Till I Come), ATB (2)
Anor Tenneberger

17 July *Livin' La Vida Loca, Ricky Martin (3)
Robi Rosa/Desmond Child

7 Aug *When You Say Nothing At All, Ronan Keating (2)
Paul Overstreet/Don Schlitz

21 Aug *If I Let You Go, Westlife (1)
Jorg Elofsson/Per Magnusson/David Kreuger

28 Aug *Mi Chico Latino, Geri Halliwell (1)
Geri Halliwell/Andy Watkins/Paul Wilson

4 Sept *Mambo No. 5 (A Little Bit Of . . .), Lou Bega (2)
Lou Bega/Zippy

18 Sept *We're Going To Ibiza! Vengaboys (1)
Jeff Calvert/Glen Hughes

25 Sept *Blue [Da Ba Dee], Eiffel 65 (3)
Massimo Gabutti/Maurizio Lobina/Gianfranco Randono

16 Oct *Genie In A Bottle, Christina Aguilera (2)
Stave Kipner/David Frank/Pam Sheyne

30 Oct *Flying Without Wings, Westlife (1)
Steve Mac/Wayne Hector

6 Nov *Keep On Movin', Five (1)
Richard Stannard/Julian Gallagher/Jay Brown/Abs Breen/Sean Conlon

13 Nov *Lift Me Up, Geri Halliwell (1)
Geri Halliwell/Andy Watkins/Paul Wilson/Tracy Ackerman

20 Nov *She's The One / It's Only Us, Robbie Williams (1)
Guy Chambers/Steve Power: Karl Wallinger

27 Nov *King Of My Castle, Wamdue Project (1)
Chris Brann

4 Dec The Millennium Prayer, Cliff Richard (3)
Trad arr Paul Fields/Stephen Deal/Cliff Richard/Nigel Wright

25 Dec *I Have A Dream/Seasons In The Sun, Westlife (4)
Benny Anderson/Bjorn Ulvaeus: Jacques Brel/Rod McKuen

2000

22 Jan *The Masses Against The Classes, Manic Street Preachers (1)
Nick Jones/James Dean Bradfield/Sean Moore

29 Jan *Born To Make You Happy, Britney Spears (1)
Kristian Lundin/Andreas Carlsson

5 Feb *Rise, Gabrielle (2)
Bob Dylan/Gabrielle/Under Hamilton/Ollie Dagois

19 Feb *Go Let It Out, Oasis (1)
Noel Gallagher

26 Feb *Pure Shores, All Saints (2)
William Orbit/Shaznay Lewis

11 March *American Pie, Madonna (1)
Don McLean

18 March *Don't Give Up, Chicane featuring Bryan Adams (1)
Nick Bracegirdle/Bryan Adams/Ray Hedges

25 March *Bag It Up, Geri Halliwell (1)
Geri Halliwell/Andy Watkins/Paul Wilson

1 April *Never Be The Same Again, Melanie C featuring Lisa 'Left-Eye' Lopes (1)
Melanie Chisholm/Rhett Lawrence/Paul F Cruz/Lisa Lopes/ Loranzo Martin

8 April *Fool Again, Westlife(1)
Jorgen Elofsson/Per Magnusson/David Kruger

15 April *Fill Me In, Craig David (1)
Craig David/Mark Hill

22 April *Toca's Miracle, Fragma (2)
Ramon Zenker/Dirk Duderstadt/Marco Duderstadt/Victor Imbress/Rob Davie

6 May *Bound 4 Da Reload (Casualty), Oxide And Neutrino (1)
Ken Freeman/Oxide/Neutrino

13 May *Oops! . . . I Did It Again, Britney Spears (1)
Max Martin/Rami

20 May *Don't Call Me Baby, Madison Avenue (1)
Cheyne Coates/Andy Van Dorsselaer/Duane Morrison

27 May *Day & Night, Billie Piper (1)
Billie Piper/Elliot Kennedy/Tim Lever/Mark Cawley/Mike Percy

3 June *It Feels So Good, Sonique (3)
Sonique/Sserious/Graeme Pleeth/Linus Burdick

24 June *You See The Trouble With Me, Black Legend (1)
Barry White/Ray Parker Jr

1 July *Spinning Around, Kylie Minogue (1)
Ira Shickman/Osborne Bingham/Kara Dio Guardi/Paula Abdul

8 July *The Real Slim Shady, Eminem (1)
Marshall Mathers/Andre Young/Mike Bradford

15 July *Breathless, Corrs (1)
Robert Lange/Corrs

22 July *Life Is A Rollercoaster, Ronan Keating (1)
Gregg Alexander/Rick Nowels

29 July *We Will Rock You, Five + Queen (1)
Brian May/Jay Brown/Abs Breen

5 Aug *7 Days, Craig David (1)
Craig David/Mark Hill/Darren Hill

12 Aug *Rock DJ, Robbie Williams (1)
Robbie Williams/Guy Chambers/Kelvin Andrews/Nelson Pigford/ Ekundayo Paris

19 Aug *I Turn To You, Melanie C (1)
Melanie Chisholm/Rick Nowels/Billy Steinberg

1 Sept *Groovejet (If This Ain't Love), Spiller. Lead vocal: Sophie Ellis-Bextor (1)
Cristiano Spiller/Sophie Ellis-Bextor/Rob Davis

8 Sept *Music, Madonna (1)
Madonna/Mirwais Ahmadzai

9 Sept *Take On Me, A1 (1)
Pal Waaktaar/Mags Furuholmen/Morten Harket

22 Sept *Lady (Hear Me Tonight), Modjo (2)
Yann Destagno/Romain Tranchart/Bernard Edwards/Nile Rodgers

30 Sept *Against All Odds (Take A Look At Me Now), Mariah Carey featuring Westlife (2)
Phil Collins

20 Oct Black Coffee, All Saints (1)
Tom Nichols/Alex Von Soos/Kirsty Elizabeth

21 Oct *Beautiful Day, U2 (1)
U2/Bono

3 Nov *Stomp, Steps (1)
Mark Topham/Karl Twigg/Pete Waterman/Ellie Campbell

4 Nov *Holler / Let Love Lead The Way, Spice Girls (1)
Rodney Jerkins/La Shawn Daniels/Fred Jerkins III: Spice Girls/Harvey Mason Jr

17 Nov *My Love, Westlife (1)
Jorgen Elofsson/Pelle Nylen/David Kreuger/Per Magnusson

24 Nov *Same Old Brand New You, A1 (1)
Eric Foster White/Ben Adams/Christian Ingebrigtsen/Mark Read

1 Dec *Can't Fight The Moonlight, Leann Rimes (1)
Diane Warren

8 Dec *Independent Women, (Part 1), Destiny's Child (1)
Samuel J Barnes/Jean Claude Olivier/Cory Rooney/Beyonce Knowles

15 Dec *Never Had A Dream Come True, S Club 7 (1)
Cathy Dennis/Simon Ellis

16 Dec *Stan, Eminem (1)
Marshall Matthers/Dido Armstrong/Paulie Herman

23 Dec Can We Fix It?, Bob The Builder (3; best seller of the year for 2000)
Paul K. Joyce

2001

13 Jan *Touch Me, Rui Da Silva featuring Cassandra (1)
Rui Da Silva/Cassandra Fox

20 Jan *Love Don't Cost A Thing, Jennifer Lopez (1)
Damon Sharpe/Greg Lawson/Georgette Franklin/Jeremy Monroe/Amii Harris

27 Jan *Rollin', Limp Bizkit (2)
Wes Borland/Sam Rivers/Jon Otto/Fred Durst

10 Feb *Whole Again, Atomic Kitten (4)
Stuart Kershaw/Andy McCluskey/Bill Padley/Jeremy Godfrey

10 March *It Wasn't Me, Shaggy featuring Ricardo 'Rikrok' Ducent (1; best seller of the year for 2001)
Orville Burrell/Ricardo Ducent/Shaun Pizzonia/Kevin Thompson

17 March *Uptown Girl, Westlife (1)
Billy Joel

24 March *Pure And Simple, Hear'Say (3)
Tim Hawes/Pete Kirtley/Alison Clarkson

14 April *What Took You So Long, Emma Bunton (2)
Richard Stannard/Emma Bunton/Julian Gallagher/John Themis/ Martin Harrington

28 April *Survivor, Destiny's Child (1)
Anthony Dent/Beyonce Knowles/Mathew Knowles

5 May *Don't Stop Movin', S Club 7 (2; *26 May* for 1 week)
Simon Ellis/Sheppard Solomon/S Club 7

12 May *It's Raining Men, Geri Halliwell (2)
Paul Jabara/Paul Schaffer

2 June *Do You Really Like It?, DJ Pied Piper And The Master Of Ceremonies (1)
Eugene Nwohia/Steve Wickham/Paul Newman/Ashley Livingstone

9 June *Angel, Shaggy featuring Rayvon (3)
Orville Burrell/Ricardo Ducent/Nigel Staff/Shaun Pizzonia/ Dave Kelly/Steve Miller/Chip Taylor

30 June *Lady Marmalade, Christina Aguilera, Lil' Kim, Mya And Pink (1; the 900th No. 1)
Bob Crewe/Ken Nolan

7 July *The Way To Your Love, Hear'Say (1)
Mikkel S.E./Hallgeir Rustan/Tor Erik Hermansen

14 July *Another Chance, Roger Sanchez (1)
Roger Sanchez/Steve Lukather

21 July *Eternity / The Road To Mandalay, Robbie Williams (1)
Robbie Williams/Guy Chambers

4 Aug *Eternal Flame, Atomic Kitten (2)
Billy Steinberg/Tom Kelly/Susanna Hoffs

18 Aug *21 Seconds, So Solid Crew (1)
Dwayne Vincent/Ashley Walters/Jermaine Williams/Shane Neil/Lisa Maffia/Michael Harvey/Marvin Dawkins/Jason Moore/Aminy Mahtari/Jason Phillips/Les Weir

25 Aug *Let's Dance, Five (2)
Richard Stannard/Julian Gallagher/Ash Howes/Martin Harrington/ Jay Brown/Sean Conlon

8 Sept *Too Close, Blue (2)
Kier Gist/Darren Lighty/Robert Huggar/Raphael Brown/ Robert Ford/Denyl Miller/James Moore/Kia Walker/Larry Smith

15 Sept *Mambo No. 5, Bob The Builder (1)
Perez Prado

22 Sept Hey Baby (Uuh Ahh), DJ Ötzi (1)
Bruce Channel/Ed Cobb

29 Sept *Can't Get You Out Of My Head, Kylie Minogue (4)
Cathy Dennis/Rob Davis

10 Nov *Because I Got High, Afroman (3)
Joseph Foreman

17 Nov *Queen Of My Heart, Westlife (1)
Steve Mac/Wayne Hector/John McLaughlin/Steve Robson

24 Nov *If You Come Back, Blue (1)
Ray Ruffin/Nicole Formescu/Ian Hope/Lee Brennan

1 Dec *Have You Ever, S Club 7 (1)
Cathy Dennis/Andrew Frampton/Chris Braide

8 Dec *Gotta Get Thru This, Daniel Bedingfield (2)
Daniel Bedingfield

22 Dec *Something Stupid, Robbie Williams & Nicole Kidman (3)
C.Carson Parks

THE NUMBER ONE EPS & ALBUMS

EPS and albums that reached the No. 1 position in the respective charts. Figure in brackets indicates number of weeks spent at number 1.

*Denotes straight in at No. 1.

1958

ALBUMS

8 Nov — *South Pacific, Original Soundtrack (70; best seller of the year)

1959

ALBUMS

No new No. 1's during the year. Best seller of the year: South Pacific, Original Soundtrack.

1960

EPS

12 March — *Expresso Bongo [OST], Cliff Richard & the Shadows (1, *23 April* for 1)

19 March — Strictly Elvis, Elvis Presley (5)

30 April — Strictly For Grown Ups, Paddy Roberts (1, *14 May* for 1, *4 June* for 12, *10 Sept* for 1, *24 Sept* for 3, *5 Nov* for 1)

7 May — Emile, Emile Ford & The Checkmates (1, *21 May* for 2)

27 Aug — Paddy Roberts Strikes Again, Paddy Roberts (2)

17 Sept — South Pacific No. 1, Original Soundtrack (1, *15 Oct* for 3, *12 Nov* for 5, *31 Dec* for 1)

17 Dec — Adam's Hit Parade, Adam Faith (1)

24 Dec — Cliff's Silver Discs, Cliff Richard & The Shadows (1)

ALBUMS

12 March — The Explosive Freddy Cannon, Freddy Cannon (1)

19 March — South Pacific, Original Soundtrack (19, *6 Aug* for 5, *15 Oct* for 13; best seller of the year)

30 July — Elvis Is Back, Elvis Presley (1)

10 Sept — Down Drury Lane To Memory Lane, One Hundred and One Strings (5)

1961

EPS

7 Jan — Cliff's Silver Discs, Cliff Richard & The Shadows (2)

21 Jan — Adam's Hit Parade, Adam Faith (1, *27 May* for 1)

28 Jan — The Shadows, Shadows (17, *3 June* for 3)

24 June — The Shadows To The Fore, Shadows (23)

2 Dec — Helen, Helen Shapiro (9)

ALBUMS

14 Jan — G.I. Blues [OST], Elvis Presley (7, *11 March* for 3, *8 April* for 12; best seller of the year)

4 March — South Pacific, Original Soundtrack (1, *1 April* for 1, *1 July* for 4, *26 Aug* for 1, *9 Sept* for 1)

29 July — The Black And White Minstrel Show, George Mitchell Minstrels (4, *2 Sept* for 1, *16 Sept* for 1, *21 Oct* for 1)

23 Sept — The Shadows, Shadows (4, *28 Oct* for 1)

4 Nov — I'm 21 Today, Cliff Richard & The Shadows (1)

11 Nov — Another Black And White Minstrel Show, George Mitchell Minstrels (8)

1962

EPS

3 Feb — The Shadows To The Fore, Shadows (4, *19 May* for 1)

3 March — Spotlight On The Shadows, Shadows (3, *14 April* for 5)

24 March — Helen's Hit Parade, Helen Shapiro (3, *26 May* for 1)

2 June — Hits From 'The Young Ones', Cliff Richard & The Shadows (2)

16 June — Follow That Dream [OST], Elvis Presley (20)

3 Nov — The Boys, Shadows (3)

24 Nov — Kid Galahad [OST], Elvis Presley (5)

29 Dec — The Black And White Minstrel Show, George Mitchell Minstrels (1)

ALBUMS

6 Jan — Blue Hawaii [OST], Elvis Presley (1, *24 Feb* for 17)

13 Jan — The Young Ones [OST], Cliff Richard & The Shadows (6)

23 June	West Side Story, Original Soundtracks (5, *1 Sept* for 1, *15 Sept* for 1, *29 Sept* for 3, *17 Nov* for 1, *15 Dec* for 1; best seller of the year)
28 July	Pot Luck, Elvis Presley (5, *8 Sept* for 1)
22 Sept	The Best Of Ball, Barber And Bilk, Kenny Ball, Chris Barber & Acker Bilk (1, *20 Oct* for 1)
27 Oct	Out Of The Shadows, Shadows (3, *24 Nov* for 1, *22 Dec* for 1)
1 Dec	On Stage With The George Mitchell Minstrels, George Mitchell Minstrels (2)
29 Dec	The Black And White Minstrel Show, George Mitchell Minstrels (2)

1963

EPS

5 Jan	Kid Galahad [OST], Elvis Presley (13)
6 April	Frank Ifield's Hits, Frank Ifield (8, *15 June* for 2, *6 July* for 2)
1 June	Just For Fun, Bobby Vee & The Crickets (1)
8 June	Holiday Carnival, Cliff Richard & The Shadows (1, *29 June* for 1, *20 July* for 1)
27 July	Twist And Shout, Beatles (10, *23 Nov* for 11)
5 Oct	Ain't Gonna Kiss You, Searchers (4)
2 Nov	The Beatles' Hits, Beatles (3)

ALBUMS

12 Jan	West Side Story, Original Soundtrack (1)
19 Jan	Out Of The Shadows, Shadows (2)
2 Feb	Summer Holiday [OST],Cliff Richard & The Shadows (14)
11 May	Please Please Me, Beatles (30)
7 Dec	With The Beatles, Beatles (21, best seller of the year)

1964

EPS

8 Feb	The Rolling Stones, Rolling Stones (3, *25 April* for 11)
29 Feb	All My Loving, Beatles (8)
11 July	Long Tall Sally, Beatles (7)
29 Aug	Five By Five, Rolling Stones (15)
12 Dec	A Hard Day's Night, Beatles (2)
26 Dec	Bachelors' Hits, Bachelors (2)

ALBUMS

2 May	Rolling Stones, Rolling Stones (12)
25 July	A Hard Day's Night, Beatles (21)
19 Dec	Beatles For Sale, Beatles (7; best seller of the year)

1965

EPS

9 Jan	A Hard Day's Night, Beatles (3, *6 Feb* for 1)
30 Jan	Five By Five, Rolling Stones (1, *13 Feb* for 1, *27 Feb* for 1, *27 March* for 3)
20 Feb	Kinksize Session, Kinks (1)
6 March	Green Shades Of Val Doonican, Val Doonican (3, *17 April* for 1)
24 April	Beatles For Sale, Beatles (5, *12 June* for 1)
29 May	Bumble Bee, Searchers (2)
19 June	The One In The Middle, Manfred Mann (1, *3 July* for 4, 7 Aug for 4)
26 June	Got Live If You Want It!, Rolling Stones (1, *31 July* for 1)
4 Sept	The Universal Soldier, DoNovan (8)
30 Oct	Kwyet Kinks, Kinks (7)
18 Dec	No Living Without Loving, Manfred Mann (7)

ALBUMS

6 Feb	Rolling Stones No. 2, Rolling Stones (3, *6 March* for 6, *24 April* for 1)
27 Feb	Beatles For Sale, Beatles (1, *1 May* for 3)
17 April	The Freewheelin' Bob Dylan, Bob Dylan (1, *22 May* for 1)
29 May	Bringing It All Back Home, Bob Dylan (1)
5 June	The Sound Of Music, Original Soundtrack (10, *16 Oct* for 10; best seller of the year)
14 Aug	*Help, Beatles (9)
25 Dec	Rubber Soul, Beatles (8)

1966

EPS

5 Feb	The Beatles' Million Sellers, Beatles (2, *12 March* for 2)
19 Feb	The Seekers, Seekers (3)
26 March	Yesterday, Beatles (8)
21 May	With God On Our Side, Joan Baez (1)
28 May	Machines, Manfred Mann (1)
4 June	The Beach Boy Hits, Beach Boys (4, *10 Sept* for 4, *29 Oct* for 7)
2 July	I Need You, Walker Brothers (10, *8 Oct* for 3)
17 Dec	Ready Steady Who, Who (5)

ALBUMS

19 Feb	The Sound Of Music, Original Soundtrack (10, *25 June* for 7, *1 Oct* for 18; best seller of the year)
30 April	Aftermath, Rolling Stones (8)
13 Aug	*Revolver, Beatles (7)

1967

EPS

21 Jan The Beach Boy Hits, Beach Boys (7, *12 Aug* for 6, *30 Sept* for 1, *14 Oct* for 1, *25 Nov* for 2)

11 March Morningtown Ride, Seekers (1)

18 March Four Tops Hits, Four Tops (10, *17 June* for 5, *23 Sept* for 1, *7 Oct* for 1, *21 Oct* for 5)

27 May Privilege, Paul Jones (3)

22 July Easy Come, Easy Go [OST], Elvis Presley (3)

The final EP chart was published on Dec 2, 1967.

ALBUMS

4 Feb The Monkees, Monkees (7)

25 March The Sound Of Music, Original Soundtrack (7, *20 May* for 1, *3 June* for 1, *18 Nov* for 1, *2 Dec* for 3)

13 May More Of The Monkees, Monkees (1, *27 May* for 1)

10 June Sergeant Pepper's Lonely Hearts Club Band, Beatles (23, *25 Nov* for 1, *23 Dec* for 2; best seller of the year)

1968

ALBUMS

6 Jan Val Doonican Rocks But Gently, Val Doonican (3)

27 Jan The Sound Of Music, Original Soundtrack (1, *23 Nov* for 1; best seller of the year)

3 Feb Sergeant Pepper's Lonely Hearts Club Band, Beatles (1)

10 Feb Four Tops Greatest Hits, Four Tops (1)

17 Feb Diana Ross & The Supremes Greatest Hits, Diana Ross & The Supremes (3)

9 March John Wesley Harding, Bob Dylan (10, *25 May* for 3)

18 May Scott 2, Scott Walker (1)

15 June Love Andy, Andy Williams (1)

22 June Dock Of The Bay, Otis Redding (1)

29 June Ogden's Nut Gone Flake, Small Faces (6)

10 Aug Delilah, Tom Jones (1, *21 Sept* for 1)

17 Aug Bookends, Simon & Garfunkel (5, *28 Sept* for 2)

12 Oct The Hollies' Greatest, Hollies (6, *30 Nov* for 1)

7 Dec *The Beatles (The White Album), Beatles (7)

1969

ALBUMS

25 Jan Best Of The Seekers, Seekers (1, *8 Feb* for 1, *29 March* for 2, *19 April* for 1, *3 May* for 1)

1 Feb The Beatles (The White Album), Beatles (1)

15 Feb Diana Ross & The Supremes Join The Temptations, Diana Ross & The Supremes with The Temptations (4)

15 March *Goodbye, Cream (2, *12 April* for 1, *26 April* for 1)

10 May On The Threshold Of A Dream, Moody Blues (2)

24 May Nashville Skyline, Bob Dylan (4)

21 June *His Orchestra, His Chorus, His Singers, His Sound, Ray Conniff (3)

12 July According To My Heart, Jim Reeves (4)

9 Aug *Stand Up, Jethro Tull (3, *6 Sept* for 2)

30 Aug From Elvis In Memphis, Elvis Presley (1)

20 Sept Blind Faith, Blind Faith (2)

4 Oct *Abbey Road, Beatles (11, *27 Dec* for 6; best seller of the year)

20 Dec *Let It Bleed, Rolling Stones (1)

1970

ALBUMS

7 Feb Led Zeppelin II, Led Zeppelin (1)

14 Feb Motown Chartbusters Volume 3, Tamla Motown Compilation (1)

21 Feb *Bridge Over Troubled Water, Simon & Garfunkel (13, *13 June* for 4, *18 July* for 5, *3 Oct* for 1, *17 Oct* for 1; best seller of the year)

23 May *Let It Be, Beatles (3)

11 July *Self Portrait, Bob Dylan (1)

22 Aug A Question Of Balance, Moody Blues (3)

12 Sept *Cosmo's Factory, Creedence Clearwater Revival (1)

19 Sept *Get Yer Ya-Ya's Out – The Rolling Stones In Concert, Rolling Stones (2)

10 Oct Paranoid, Black Sabbath (1)

24 Oct *Atom Heart Mother, Pink Floyd (1)

31 Oct Motown Chartbusters Volume 4, Tamla Motown Compilation (1)

7 Nov *Led Zeppelin 3, Led Zeppelin (3, *12 Dec* for 1)

28 Nov *New Morning, Bob Dylan (1)

5 Dec Andy Williams Greatest Hits, Andy Williams (1, *19 Dec* for 4)

1971

ALBUMS

16 Jan Bridge Over Troubled Water, Simon & Garfunkel (11, *3 July* for 5, 11 Sept for 1; best seller of the year)

3 April *Home Loving Man, Andy Williams (2)

17 April *Motown Chartbusters Volume 5, Tamla Motown Compilation (3)

8 May *Sticky Fingers, Rolling Stones (4, *19 June* for 1)

5 June *Ram, Paul & Linda McCartney (2)

26 June Tarkus, Emerson, Lake & Palmer (1)

7 Aug *Hot Hits 6, Anonymous (1)

14 Aug Every Good Boy Deserves Favour, Moody Blues (1)

21 Aug Top Of The Pops Volume 18, Anonymous (3)

18 Sept Who's Next, Who (1)

25 Sept Fireball, Deep Purple (1)

2 Oct Every Picture Tells A Story, Rod Stewart (4, *13 Nov* for 2)

30 Oct *Imagine, John Lennon & The Plastic Ono Band with The Flux Fiddlers (2)

27 Nov Top Of The Pops Volume 20, Anonymous (1)

4 Dec Four Symbols, Led Zeppelin (2)

18 Dec Electric Warrior, T. Rex (6)

1972

ALBUMS

29 Jan Concert For Bangladesh (Recorded Live), George Harrison & Friends (1)

5 Feb Electric Warrior, T. Rex (2)

19 Feb Neil Reid, Neil Reid (3)

11 March Harvest, Neil Young (1)

18 March Paul Simon, Paul Simon (1)

25 March Fog On The Tyne, Lindisfarne (4)

22 April Machine Head, Deep Purple (2, *13 May* for 1)

6 May Prophets, Seers And Sages The Angels Of The Ages / My People Were Fair And Had Sky In Their Hair But Now They're Content To Wear Stars On Their Brows, Tyrannosaurus Rex (1)

20 May *Bolan Boogie, T. Rex (3)

10 June *Exile On Main Street, Rolling Stones (1)

17 June 20 Dynamic Hits, K-Tel Compilation (8; best seller of the year)

12 Aug 20 Fantastic Hits, Arcade Compilation (5)

16 Sept Never A Dull Moment, Rod Stewart (2)

30 Sept 20 Fantastic Hits, Arcade Compilation (1)

7 Oct *20 All Time Hits Of The 50's, K-Tel Compilation (8, *23 Dec* for 3)

2 Dec *25 Rockin' And Rollin' Greats, K-Tel Compilation (3; the 100th No. 1 album)

1973

ALBUMS

13 Jan Slayed?, Slade (1, *27 Jan* for 2)

20 Jan Back To Front, Gilbert O'Sullivan (1)

10 Feb *Don't Shoot Me I'm Only The Piano Player, Elton John (6; best seller of the year)

24 March *Billion Dollar Babies, Alice Cooper (1)

31 March *20 Flashback Greats Of The Sixties, K-Tel Compilation (2)

14 April *Houses Of The Holy, Led Zeppelin (2)

28 April Ooh-La-La, Faces (1)

5 May *Aladdin Sane, David Bowie (5)

9 June Pure Gold, EMI Compilation (3)

30 June That'll Be The Day, Original Soundtrack (7)

18 Aug We Can Make It, Peters & Lee (2)

1 Sept Sing It Again Rod, Rod Stewart (3)

22 Sept *Goat's Head Soup, Rolling Stones (2)

6 Oct *Sladest, Slade (3)

27 Oct Hello, Status Quo (1)

3 Nov *Pin-Ups, David Bowie (5)

8 Dec Stranded, Roxy Music (1)

15 Dec Dreams Are Nuthin' More Than Wishes, David Cassidy (1)

22 Dec Goodbye Yellow Brick Road, Elton John (2)

1974

ALBUMS

5 Jan Tales From Topographic Oceans, Yes (2)

19 Jan Sladest, Slade (1)

26 Jan And I Love You So, Perry Como (1)

2 Feb The Singles 1969-1973, Carpenters (4, *9 March* for 11, *1 June* for 1, *6 July* for 1; best seller of the year)

2 March Old New Borrowed And Blue, Slade (1)

25 May Journey To The Centre Of The Earth, Rick Wakeman (1)

8 June *Diamond Dogs, David Bowie (4)

13 July *Caribou, Elton John (2)

27 July Band On The Run, Paul McCartney & Wings (7)

14 Sept *Hergest Ridge, Mike Oldfield (3)

5 Oct Tubular Bells, Mike Oldfield (1)

12 Oct *Rollin', Bay City Rollers (1, *26 Oct* for 1, *9 Nov* for 2)

19 Oct *Smiler, Rod Stewart (1, *2 Nov* for 1)

23 Nov *Elton John's Greatest Hits, Elton John (11)

1975

ALBUMS

8 Feb Engelbert Humperdinck – His Greatest Hits, Engelbert Humperdinck (3)

1 March *On The Level, Status Quo (2)

15 March *Physical Graffiti, Led Zeppelin (1)

22 March *20 Greatest Hits, Tom Jones (4)

19 April The Best Of The Stylistics, Stylistics (2, *24 May* for 5, *16 Aug* for 2; best seller of the year)

3 May *Once Upon A Star, Bay City Rollers (3)

28 June Venus And Mars, Wings (1, *19 July* for 1)

5 July Horizon, Carpenters (2, *26 July* for 3)

30 Aug *Atlantic Crossing, Rod Stewart (5, *11 Oct* for 2)

4 Oct Wish You Were Here, Pink Floyd (1)

25 Oct 40 Golden Greats, Jim Reeves (3)

15 Nov We All Had Doctors' Papers, Max Boyce (1)

22 Nov 40 Greatest Hits, Perry Como (5)

27 Dec A Night At The Opera, Queen (2)

1976

ALBUMS

10 Jan 40 Greatest Hits, Perry Como (1)

17 Jan A Night At The Opera, Queen (2)

31 Jan The Best Of Roy Orbison, Roy Orbison (1)

7 Feb The Very Best Of Slim Whitman, Slim Whitman (6)

20 March *Blue For You, Status Quo (3)

10 April *Rock Follies, TV Soundtrack (2, *1 May* for 1)

24 April *Presence, Led Zeppelin (1)

8 May Greatest Hits, Abba (9, *16 Oct* for 2; best seller of the year)

10 July A Night On The Town, Rod Stewart (2)

24 July *20 Golden Greats, Beach Boys (10)

2 Oct Best Of The Stylistics Volume 2, Stylistics (1)

9 Oct Stupidity, Dr. Feelgood (1)

30 Oct Soul Motion, K-Tel Compilation (2)

13 Nov The Song Remains The Same, Led Zeppelin (1)

20 Nov 22 Golden Guitar Greats, Bert Weedon (1)

27 Nov 20 Golden Greats, Glen Campbell (6)

1977

ALBUMS

8 Jan A Day At The Races, Queen (1)

15 Jan Arrival, Abba (1, *16 April* for 9; best seller of the year)

22 Jan Red River Valley, Slim Whitman (4)

19 Feb 20 Golden Greats, Shadows (6)

2 April Portrait Of Sinatra, Frank Sinatra (2)

18 June The Beatles Live At The Hollywood Bowl, Beatles (1)

25 June The Muppet Show, Muppets (1)

2 July A Star Is Born [OST], Barbra Streisand (2)

16 July The Johnny Mathis Collection, Johnny Mathis (4)

13 Aug Going For The One, Yes (2)

27 Aug 20 All Time Greats, Connie Francis (2)

10 Sept Elvis Presley's 40 Greatest Hits, Elvis Presley (1)

17 Sept *20 Golden Greats, Diana Ross & The Supremes (7)

5 Nov 40 Golden Greats, Cliff Richard & The Shadows (1)

12 Nov *Never Mind The Bollocks Here's The Sex Pistols, Sex Pistols (2)

26 Nov The Sound Of Bread, Bread (2)

10 Dec Disco Fever, K-Tel Compilation (6)

1978

ALBUMS

21 Jan The Sound Of Bread, Bread (1)

28 Jan Rumours, Fleetwood Mac (1)

4 Feb *The Album, Abba (7)

25 March 20 Golden Greats, Buddy Holly & The Crickets (3)

15 April 20 Golden Greats, Nat 'King' Cole (3)

6 May Saturday Night Fever, Original Soundtrack (18; best seller of the year)

9 Sept Night Flight To Venus, Boney M (4)

7 Oct Grease, Original Soundtrack (13)

1979

ALBUMS

6 Jan Greatest Hits, Showaddywaddy (2)

20 Jan Don't Walk – Boogie, EMI Compilation (3)

10 Feb Action Replay, K-Tel Compilation (1)

17 Feb Parallel Lines, Blondie (4; best seller of the year)

17 March Spirits Having Flown, Bee Gees (2)

31 March Barbra Streisand's Greatest Hits Volume 2, Barbra Streisand (4)

28 April The Very Best Of Leo Sayer, Leo Sayer (3)

19 May *Voulez-Vous, Abba (4)

16 June *Discovery, Electric Light Orchestra (5)

21 July Replicas, Tubeway Army (1)

28 July The Best Disco Album In The World, WEA Compilation (6)

8 Sept *In Through The Out Door, Led Zeppelin (2)

22 Sept *The Pleasure Principle, Gary Numan (1, *6 Oct* for 1)

29 Sept *Oceans Of Fantasy, Boney M (1)

13 Oct *Eat To The Beat, Blondie (1)

13 Oct *Reggatta De Blanc, Police, The (4; the 200th No. 1.)
[Two album charts were published for the week of 13 Oct.]

10 Nov Tusk, Fleetwood Mac (1)

17 Nov Greatest Hits Volume 2, Abba (3)

8 Dec Rod Stewart - Greatest Hits Vol. 1, Rod Stewart (5)

1980

ALBUMS

12 Jan Greatest Hits Volume 2, Abba (1)

19 Jan *Pretenders, Pretenders (4)

16 Feb The Last Dance, Motown Compilation (2)

1 March String Of Hits, Shadows (3)

22 March Tears And Laughter, Johnny Mathis (2)

5 April *Duke, Genesis (2)

19 April Greatest Hits, Rose Royce (2)

3 May Sky 2, Sky (2)

17 May The Magic Of Boney M, Boney M (2)

31 May *McCartney II, Paul McCartney (2)

14 June Peter Gabriel, Peter Gabriel (2)

28 June Flesh And Blood, Roxy Music (1, *23 Aug* for 3)

5 July *Emotional Rescue, Rolling Stones (2)

19 July The Game, Queen (2)

2 Aug Deepest Purple, Deep Purple (1)

9 Aug *Back In Black, AC/DC (2)

13 Sept *Telekon, Gary Numan (1)

20 Sept *Never For Ever, Kate Bush (1)

27 Sept *Scary Monsters And Super Creeps, David Bowie (2)

11 Oct *Zenyatta Mondatta, Police (4)

8 Nov Guilty, Barbra Streisand (2)

22 Nov *Super Trouper, Abba (9; best seller of the year)

1981

ALBUMS

24 Jan Kings Of The Wild Frontier, Adam & The Ants (2, *14 March* for 10; best seller of the year)

7 Feb Double Fantasy, John Lennon & Yoko Ono (2)

21 Feb *Face Value, Phil Collins (3)

23 May Stars On 45, Star Sound (5)

27 June *No Sleep Till Hammersmith, Motorhead (1)

4 July Disco Daze And Disco Nites, Ronco Compilation (1)

11 July Love Songs, Cliff Richard (5)

15 Aug The Official BBC Album Of The Royal Wedding, Royalty (2)

29 Aug Time, Electric Light Orchestra (2)

12 Sept *Dead Ringer, Meat Loaf (2)

26 Sept *Abacab, Genesis (2)

10 Oct *Ghost In The Machine, Police (3)

31 Oct Dare, Human League (1)

7 Nov Shaky, Shakin' Stevens (1)

14 Nov Qeen's Greatest Hits, Queen (4)

12 Dec Chart Hits '81, K-Tel Compilation (1)

19 Dec *The Visitors, Abba (3)

1982

ALBUMS

9 Jan Dare, Human League (3)

30 Jan Love Songs, Barbra Streisand (7, *27 March* for 2, best seller of the year)

20 March *The Gift, Jam (1)

10 April *The Number Of The Beast, Iron Maiden (2)

24 April *1982, Status Quo (1)

1 May *Barry Live In Britain, Barry Manilow (1)

8 May *Tug Of War, Paul McCartney (2)

22 May Complete Madness, Madness (2, *12 June* for 1)

5 June *Avalon, Roxy Music (1, *19 June* for 2)

3 July *The Lexicon Of Love, ABC (4)

24 July Fame, Original Soundtrack (2)
For 24 July, above two were joint at No. 1.

7 Aug The Kids From Fame, Kids From "Fame" (8, *30 Oct* for 4)

2 Oct *Love Over Gold, Dire Straits (4)

27 Nov The Singles - The First Ten Years, Abba (1)

4 Dec The John Lennon Collection, John Lennon (6)

1983

ALBUMS

15 Jan Raiders Of The Pop Charts, Ronco Compilation (2)

29 Jan Business As Usual, Men At Work (5)

5 March Thriller, Michael Jackson (1, *19 March* for 1, *21 May* for 5; best seller of the year)

12 March *War, U2 (1)

26 March The Hurting, Tears For Fears (1)

2 April *The Final Cut, Pink Floyd (2)

16 April *Faster Than The Speed Of Night, Bonnie Tyler (1)

23 April *Let's Dance, David Bowie (3)

14 May True, Spandau Ballet (1)

25 June *Synchronicity, Police (2)

9 July *Fantastic!, Wham! (2)

23 July You And Me Both, Yazoo (2)

6 Aug The Very Best Of The Beach Boys, Beach Boys (2, *10 Sept* for 1)

20 Aug 18 Greatest Hits, Michael Jackson plus the Jackson Five (3)

17 Sept No Parlez, Paul Young (1, *1 Oct* for 2, *10 Dec* for 1)

24 Sept *Labour Of Love, UB40 (1)

15 Oct *Genesis, Genesis (1)

22 Oct *Colour By Numbers, Culture Club (3, *19 Nov* for 2)

12 Nov Can't Slow Down, Lionel Richie (1)

3 Dec *Seven And The Ragged Tiger, Duran Duran (1)

17 Dec Now, That's What I Call Music, Compilation Series (4)

1984

ALBUMS

14 Jan No Parlez, Paul Young (1)

21 Jan Now, That's What I Call Music, Compilation Series (1)

28 Jan Thriller, Michael Jackson (1)

4 Feb Touch, Eurythmics (2)

18 Feb *Sparkle In The Rain, Simple Minds (1)

25 Feb *Into The Gap, Thompson Twins (3)

17 March *Human's Lib, Howard Jones (2)

31 March Can't Slow Down, Lionel Richie (2; best seller of the year)

14 April Now, That's What I Call Music II, Compilation Series (5)

19 May *Legend - The Best Of Bob Marley & The Wailers, Bob Marley & The Wailers (12)

11 Aug *Now, That's What I Call Music III, Compilations Series (8)

6 Oct *Tonight, David Bowie (1)

13 Oct *The Unforgettable Fire, U2 (2)

27 Oct *Steeltown, Big Country (1)

3 Nov *Give My Regards To Broad Street [OST], Paul McCartney (1)

10 Nov *Welcome To The Pleasuredome, Frankie Goes To Hollywood (1)

17 Nov *Make It Big, Wham! (2)

1 Dec *The Hits Album/The Hits Tape - 32 Original Hits, Compilation Series (7)

1985

ALBUMS

19 Jan Alf, Alison Moyet (1)

26 Jan Agent Provocateur, Foreigner (3)

16 Feb Born In The U.S.A., Bruce Springsteen (1, *6 July* for 4)

23 Feb *Meat Is Murder, Smiths (1)

2 March *No Jacket Required, Phil Collins (5)

6 April *The Secret Of Association, Paul Young (1)

13 April *The Hits Album 2/The Hits Tape 2, Compilation Series (6)

25 May *Brothers In Arms, Dire Straits (2, *3 Aug* for 2; best seller of the year)

8 June *Our Favourite Shop, Style Council (1)

15 June *Boys And Girls, Bryan Ferry (2; the 300th No. 1)

29 June *Misplaced Childhood, Marillion (1)

17 Aug *Now, That's What I Call Music 5, Compilation Series (5)

21 Sept Like A Virgin, Madonna (1, *12 Oct* for 1)

28 Sept *Hounds Of Love, Kate Bush (2, *19 Oct* for 1)

26 Oct The Love Songs, George Benson (1, *9 Nov* for 1)

2 Nov *Once Upon A Time, Simple Minds (1)

16 Nov *Promise, Sade (2)

30 Nov The Greatest Hits Of 1985, Compilation Series (1)

7 Dec *Now, That's What I Call Music 6, Compilation Series (2)

21 Dec Now - The Christmas Album, Compilation Series (2)

1986

ALBUMS

4 Jan Now, That's What I Call Music 6, Compilation Series (2)

18 Jan Brothers In Arms, Dire Straits (10)

29 March *Hits 4, Compilation Series (4)

26 April *Street Life - 20 Great Hits, Bryan Ferry & Roxy Music (5)

31 May *So, Peter Gabriel (2)

14 June *A Kind Of Magic, Queen (1)

21 June *Invisible Touch, Genesis (3)

12 July *True Blue, Madonna (6; best seller of the year)

23 Aug *Now, That's What I Call Music 7, Compilation Series (5)

27 Sept Silk And Steel, Five Star (1)

4 Oct Graceland, Paul Simon (5)

8 Nov *Every Breath You Take - The Singles, Police (2)

22 Nov *Hits 5, Compilation Series (2)

6 Dec *Now, That's What I Call Music 8, Compilation Series (6)

1987

ALBUMS

17 Jan The Whole Story, Kate Bush (2)

31 Jan Graceland, Paul Simon (3)

21 Feb *The Phantom Of The Opera, London Stage Cast (3)

14 March The Very Best Of Hot Chocolate, Hot Chocolate (1)

21 March *The Joshua Tree, U2 (2)

4 April *Now, That's What I Call Music 9, Compilation Series (5)

9 May *Keep Your Distance, Curiosity Killed The Cat (2)

23 May *It's Better To Travel, Swing Out Sister (2)

6 June *Live In The City Of Light, Simple Minds (1)

13 June *Whitney, Whiney Houston (6)

25 July *Introducing The Hardline According To Terence Trent D'Arby, Terence Trent D'Arby (1)

1 Aug Hits 6, Compilation Series (4, *5 Sept* for 1)

29 Aug *Hysteria, Def Leppard (1)

12 Sept *Bad, Michael Jackson (5; best seller of the year)

17 Oct *Tunnel Of Love, Bruce Springsteen (1)

24 Oct *Nothing Like The Sun, Sting (1)

31 Oct Tango In The Night, Fleetwood Mac (2)

14 Nov *Faith, George Michael (1)

21 Nov Bridge Of Spies, T'Pau (1)

28 Nov *Whenever You Need Somebody, Rick Astley (1)

5 Dec *Now That's What I Call Music 10, Compilation Series (6)

1988

ALBUMS

16 Jan Popped In Souled Out, Wet Wet Wet (1)

23 Jan *Turn Back The Clock, Johnny Hates Jazz (1)

30 Jan Introducing The Hardline According To Terence Trent D'Arby, Terence Trent D'Arby (8)

26 March *Viva Hate, Morrissey (1)

2 April *Now That's What I Call Music 11, Compilation Series (3)

23 April *Seventh Son Of A Seventh Son, Iron Maiden (1)

30 April *The Innocents, Erasure (1)

7 May Tango In The Night, Fleetwood Mac (2, *28 May* for 1)

21 May *Lovesexy, Princc (1)

4 June Nite Flite, CBS Compilation (4)

2 July Tracy Chapman, Tracy Chapman (3)

23 July *Now That's What I Call Music 12, Compilation Series (5)

27 Aug Kylie - The Album, Kylie Minogue (4, *19 Nov* for 2; best seller of the year)

24 Sept Hot City Nights, Vertigo Compilation (1)

1 Oct *New Jersey, Bon Jovi (2)

15 Oct *Flying Colours, Chris De Burgh (1)

22 Oct *Rattle And Hum, U2 (1)

29 Oct *Money For Nothing, Dire Straits (3)

3 Dec *Now That's What I Call Music 13, Compilation Series (3)

24 Dec Private Collection 1979-1988, Cliff Richard (2)

1989

ALBUMS

7 Jan Now That's What I Call Music 13, Compilation Series (1)
[From 14 Jan, 1989, the compilation chart was instituted, eliminating all various artist albums from the main chart.]

14 Jan The Innocents, Erasure (1)

21 Jan The Legendary Roy Orbison, Roy Orbison (3)

11 Feb *Technique, New Order (1)

18 Feb *The Raw And The Cooked, Fine Young Cannibals (1)

25 Feb *A New Flame, Simply Red (4, *29 April* for 1, *22 July* for 2)

25 March Anything For You, Gloria Estefan & Miami Sound Machine (1)

1 April *Like A Prayer, Madonna (2)

15 April *When The World Knows Your Name, Deacon Blue (2)

6 May *Blast!, Holly Johnson (1)

13 May *Street Fighting Years, Simple Minds (1)

20 May Ten Good Reasons, Jason Donovan (2, *10 June* for 2; best seller of the year)

3 June *The Miracle, Queen (1)

24 June Flowers In The Dirt, Paul McCartney (1)

1 July *Batman [OST], Prince (1)

8 July *Velveteen, Tranvision Vamp (1)

15 July Club Classics Volume One, Soul II Soul (1)

5 Aug *Cuts Both Ways, Gloria Estefan (6)

16 Sept *Aspects Of Love, London Stage Cast (1)

23 Sept *We Too Are One, Eurythmics (1)

30 Sept *Foreign Affair, Tina Turner (1)

7 Oct *The Seeds Of Love, Tears For Fears (1)

14 Oct *Crossroads, Tracy Chapman (1)

21 Oct *Enjoy Yourself, Kylie Minogue (1)

28 Oct *Wild!, Erasure (2)

11 Nov *The Road To Hell, Chris Rea (3)

2 Dec *. . . But Seriously, Phil Collins (8)

1990

ALBUMS

27 Jan *Colour, Christians (1)

3 Feb . . . But Seriously, Phil Collins (7; best seller of the year)

24 March *I Do Not Want What I Haven't Got, Sinead O'Connor (1)

31 March Changesbowie, David Bowie (1)

7 April Only Yesterday – Richard & Karen Carpenter's Greatest Hits, Carpenters (2; *28 April* for 5)

21 April *Behind The Mask, Fleetwood Mac (1)

2 June *Volume II (1990 A New Decade), Soul II Soul (3)

23 June The Essential Pavarotti, Luciano Pavarotti (1, *7 July* for 3)

30 June *Step By Step, New Kids On The Block (1)

28 July Sleeping With The Past, Elton John (5)

1 Sept *Grafitti Bridge, Prince (1)

8 Sept In Concert, Carreras Domingo Pavarotti Orchestra del Maggio Musical Fiorentino Orchestra del Teatro dell'opera di Roma Zubin Mehta (1, *22 Sept* for 4)

15 Sept *Listen Without Prejudice Volume 1, George Michael (1)

20 Oct *Some Friendly, Charlatans (1)

27 Oct *The Rhythm Of The Saints, Paul Simon (2)

10 Nov *The Very Best Of Elton John, Elton John (2; the 400th No. 1)

24 Nov *The Immaculate Collection, Madonna (9)

1991

ALBUMS

26 Jan MCMCX A.D., Enigma (1)

2 Feb *The Soul Cages, Sting (1)

9 Feb *Doubt, Jesus Jones (1)

16 Feb *Innuendo, Queen (2)

2 March Circle Of One Adems, Oleta (1)

9 March *Auberge, Chris Rea (1)

16 March *Spartacus, Farm (1)

23 March *Out Of Time, R.E.M. (1)

30 March *Greatest Hits, Eurythmics (9, *22 June* for 1)

1 June *Seal, Seal (3)

29 June *Love Hurts, Cher (6)

10 Aug Essential Pavarotti II, Luciano Pavarotti (2)

24 Aug *Metallica, Metallica (1)

31 Aug *Joseph And The Amazing Technicolor Dreamcoat, London Stage Cast (2)

14 Sept *From Time To Time – The Singles Collection, Paul Young (1)

21 Sept *On Every Street, Dire Straits (1)

28 Sept *Use Your Illusion II, Guns N' Roses (1)

5 Oct *Waking Up The Neighbours, Bryan Adams (1)

12 Oct *Stars, Simply Red (2, *2 Nov* for 1; best seller of the year)

26 Oct *Chorus, Erasure (1)

9 Nov *Greatest Hits II, Queen (1, *7 Dec* for 4)

16 Nov *Shepherd Moons, Enya (1)

23 Nov *We Can't Dance, Genesis (1)

30 Nov *Dangerous, Michael Jackson (1)

1992

ALBUMS

4 Jan Stars, Simply Red (5, *22 Feb* for 3, *9 May* for 1; best seller of the year)

8 Feb *High On The Happy Side, Wet Wet Wet (2)

14 March Divine Madness, Madness (3)

4 April *Human Touch, Bruce Springsteen (1)

11 April *Adrenalize, Def Leppard (1)

18 April *Diva, Annie Lennox (1)

25 April Up, Right Said Fred (1)

2 May *Wish, Cure (1)

16 May *1992 - The Love Album, Carter - The Unstoppable Sex Machine (1)

23 May *Fear Of The Dark, Iron Maiden (1)

30 May *Michael Ball, Michael Ball (1)

6 June *Back To Front, Lionel Richie (6)

18 July *U.F. Orb, Orb (1)

25 July The Greatest Hits 1966-1992, Neil Diamond (3)

15 Aug *Welcome To Wherever You Are, INXS (1)

22 Aug We Can't Dance, Genesis (1)

29 Aug *Best . . . I, Smiths (1)

5 Sept *Kylie Greatest Hits, Kylie Minogue (1)

12 Sept *Tubular Bells II, Mike Oldfield (2)

26 Sept The Best Of Belinda Volume 1, Belinda Carlisle (1)

3 Oct *Gold - Greatest Hits, Abba (1)

10 Oct *Automatic For The People, R.E.M. (1)

17 Oct *Symbol, Prince & The New Power Generation (1)

24 Oct *Glittering Prize 81/92, Simple Minds (3)

14 Nov *Keep The Faith, Bon Jovi (1)

21 Nov *Cher's Greatest Hits: 1965-1992, Cher (1, *12 Dec* for 6)

28 Nov *Pop! - The First 20 Hits, Erasure (2)

1993

ALBUMS

23 Jan *Live - The Way We Walk Volume 2: The Longs, Genesis (2)

6 Feb *Jam, Little Angels (1)

13 Feb *Pure Cult, Cult (1)

20 Feb *Words Of Love, Buddy Holly & The Crickets (1)

27 Feb *Walthamstow, East 17 (1)

6 March Diva, Annie Lennox (1)

13 March *Are You Gonna Go My Way, Lenny Kravitz (2)

27 March Their Greatest Hits, Hot Chocolate (1)

3 April *Songs Of Faith And Devotion, Depeche Mode (1)

10 April *Suede, Suede (1)

17 April *Black Tie White Noise, David Bowie (1)

24 April Automatic For The People, R.E.M. (1, *8 May* for 1, *22 May* for 1)

1 May *Cliff Richard - The Album, Cliff Richard (1)

15 May *Republic, New Order (1)

29 May *Janet, Janet Jackson (2)

12 June No Limits, Two Unlimited (1)

19 June *What's Love Got To Do With It [OST], Tina Turner (1)

26 June *Emergency On Planet Earth, Jamiroquai (3)

17 July *Zooropa, U2 (1)

24 July *Promises And Lies, UB40 (7)

11 Sept *Music Box, Mariah Carey (1)

18 Sept *Bat Out Of Hell II - Back Into Hell, Meat Loaf (1, *2 Oct* for 1, *16 Oct* for 1, *30 Oct* for 3, *27 Nov* for 5; best seller of the year)

25 Sept *In Utero, Nirvana (1)

9 Oct *Very, Pet Shop Boys (1)

23 Oct *Everything Changes, Take That (1)

20 Nov *Both Sides, Phil Collinsl (1)

1994

ALBUMS

1 Jan One Woman - The Ultimate Collection, Diana Ross (1, *22 Jan* for 1)

8 Jan Everything Changes, Take That (1)

15 Jan So Far So Good, Bryan Adams (1)

29 Jan Tease Me, Chaka Demus & Pliers (2)

12 Feb *Under The Pink, Tori Amos (1)

19 Feb *The Cross Of Changes, Enigma (1)

26 Feb Music Box, Mariah Carey (4, *2 April* for 1)

26 March *Vauxhall And I, Morrissey (1)

9 April *The Division Bell, Pink Floyd (4)

7 May *Parklife, Blur (1)

14 May Our Town - The Greatest Hits Of Deacon Blue, Deacon Blue (2)

28 May *I Say I Say I Say, Erasure (1)

4 June *Seal, Seal (2)

18 June *Real Things, Two Unlimited (1)

25 June Everybody Else Is Doing It, So Why Can't We?, Cranberries (1)

2 July *Happy Nation, Ace Of Base (2)

16 July *Music For The Jilted Generation, Prodigy (1)

23 July *Voodoo Lounge, Rolling Stones (1)

30 July End Of Part One (Their Greatest Hits), Wet Wet Wet (4, *3 Sept* for 1)

27 Aug *Come, Prince (1)

10 Sept *Definitely Maybe, Oasis (1)

17 Sept The Three Tenors In Concert 1994, Carreras Domingo Pavarotti with Orchestra conducted by Zubin Mehta (1)

24 Sept *From The Cradle, Eric Clapton (1)

1 Oct *Songs, Luther Vandross (1)

8 Oct *Monster, R.E.M. (2)

22 Oct *Cross Road - The Best Of Bon Jovi, Bon Jovi (3, *19 Nov* for 2; best seller of the year)

12 Nov *Unplugged In New York, Nirvana (1)

3 Dec Carry On Up The Charts - The Best Of The Beautiful South, Beautiful South (1, *17 Dec* for 6; the 500th No. 1)

10 Dec *Live At The BBC, Beatles (1)

1995

ALBUMS

28 Jan The Colour Of My Love, Celine Dion (6, *1 April* for 1)

11 March *Greatest Hits, Bruce Springsteen (1, *15 April* for 1)

18 March *Medusa, Annie Lennox (1)

25 March *Elastica, Elastica (1)

8 April *Wake Up!, Boo Radleys (1)

22 April *Picture This, Wet Wet Wet (3)

13 May *Nobody Else, Take That (2)

27 May *Stanley Road, Paul Weller (1)

3 June *Singles, Alison Moyet (1)

10 June *Pulse, Pink Floyd (2)

24 June *History - Past, Present And Future, Book 1, Michael Jackson (1)

1 July *These Days, Bon Jovi (4)

29 July I Should Coco, Supergrass (3)

19 Aug *It's Great When You're Straight . . . Yeah, Black Grape (2)

2 Sept *Said And Done, Boyzone (1)

9 Sept *The Charlatans, Charlatans (1)

16 Sept Zeitgeist, Levellers (1)

23 Sept *The Great Escape, Blur (2)

7 Oct *Daydream, Mariah Carey (1)

14 Oct *(What's The Story) Morning Glory?, Oasis (1)

21 Oct *Life, Simply Red (3)

11 Nov *Different Class, Pulp (1)

18 Nov *Made In Heaven, Queen (1)

25 Nov *Robson & Jerome, Robson & Jerome (7; best seller of the year)

1996

ALBUMS

13 Jan (What's The Story) Morning Glory?, Oasis (6, *2 March* for 3)

24 Feb *Expecting To Fly, Bluetones (1)

23 March *Falling Into You, Celine Dion (1)

30 March *Anthology 2, Beatles (1)

6 April *Greatest Hits, Take That (4)

4 May Jagged Little Pill, Alanis Morissette (2, *29 June* for 1, *20 July* for 8; best seller of the year)

18 May *1977, Ash (1)

25 May *Older, George Michael (3)

15 June *Load, Metallica (1)

22 June *18 Til I Die, Bryan Adams (1)

6 July *Recurring Dream - The Very Best Of Crowded House, Crowded House (2)

14 Sept *Coming Up, Suede (1)

21 Sept *New Adventures In Hi-Fi, R.E.M. (1)

28 Sept *K, Kula Shaker (2)

12 Oct *Natural, Peter Andre (1)

19 Oct *Greatest Hits, Simply Red (2)

2 Nov *Blue Is The Colour, Beautiful South (1)

9 Nov *A Different Beat, Boyzone (1)

16 Nov *Spice, Spice Girls (1, *7 Dec* for 8)

23 Nov *Take Two, Robson & Jerome (2)

1997

ALBUMS

1 Feb Evita [OST], Madonna & Various Artists (1)

8 Feb *Glow, Reef (1)

15 Feb *White On Blonde, Texas (1, *23 Aug* for 1)

22 Feb *Blur, Blur (1)

1 March *Attack Of The Grey Lantern, Mansun (1)

8 March Spice, Spice Girls (1, *22 March* for 4, *17 May* for 1)

15 March *Pop, U2 (1)

19 April *Dig Your Own Hole, Chemical Brothers (1)

26 April *Ultra, Depeche Mode (1)

3 May *Tellin' Stories, Charlatans (2)

24 May *Blood On The Dance Floor – History In The Mix, Michael Jackson (2)

7 June *Open Road, Gary Barlow (1)

14 June *Wu-Tang Forever, Wu-Tang Clan (1)

21 June *Middle Of Nowhere, Hanson (1)

28 June *OK Computer, Radiohead (2)

12 July *The Fat Of The Land, Prodigy (6)

30 Aug *Be Here Now, Oasis (4, *4 Oct* for (1; best seller of the year)

27 Sept *Marchin' Already, Ocean Colour Scene (1)

11 Oct *Urban Hymns, Verve (5)

15 Nov *Spiceworld, Spice Girls (2, *13 Dec* for 1)

29 Nov *Let's Talk About Love, Celine Dion (2, *20 Dec* for 2)

1998

ALBUMS

3 Jan Urban Hymns, Verve (6, *21 Feb* for 1)

14 Feb Titanic [OST], Music composed and conducted by James Horner (1, *28 Feb* for 2)

14 March *Ray Of Light, Madonna (2)

28 March Let's Talk About Love, Celine Dion (1)

4 April *The Best Of James, James (1)

11 April *This Is Hardcore, Pulp (1)

18 April Life Thru A Lens, Robbie Williams (2)

2 May *Mezzanine, Massive Attack (2)

16 May International Velvet, Catatonia (1)

23 May *Version 2.0, Garbage (1)

30 May *Blue, Simply Red (1, *13 June* for 1)

6 June *Where We Belong, Boyzone (1, *5 Sept* for 2)

20 June *The Good Will Out, Embrace (1)

27 June Talk On Corners, Corrs (1, *11 July* for 1, *15 Aug* for 3, *19 Sept* for 1; best seller of the year)

4 July Five, Five (1)

18 July *Hello Nasty, Beastie Boys (1)

25 July *Jane McDonald, Jane McDonald (3)

26 Sept *This Is My Truth Tell Me Yours, Manic Street Preachers (3)

17 Oct *Hits, Phil Collins (1)

24 Oct *Quench, Beautiful South (2)

7 Nov *I've Been Expecting You, Robbie Williams (1)

14 Nov *The Best Of 1980-1990 & B-Sides, U2 (1)

21 Nov *Ladies & Gentlemen – The Best Of George Michael, George Michael (8)

1999

ALBUMS

16 Jan I've Been Expecting You, Robbie Williams (1, *20 Feb* for 1)

23 Jan You've Come A Long Way, Baby, Fatboy Slim (4)

27 Feb Talk On Corners, Corrs (3, *10 April* for 1)

20 March *Peformance And Cocktails, Stereophonics (1)

27 March *13, Blur (2)

17 April Gold - Greatest Hits, Abba (1, *1 May* for 2, *29 May* for 2)

24 April *Equally Cursed And Blessed, Catatonia (1)

15 May *Head Music, Suede (1)

22 May *Hush, Texas (1)

12 June *By Request, Boyzone (2, *10 July* for 7)

26 June *Synkronized, Jamiroquai (1)

3 July *Surrender, Chemical Brothers (1)

28 Aug The Man Who, Travis (2)

11 Sept Come On Over, Shania Twain (3, *16 Oct* for 3, *11 Dec* for 5; best seller of the year)

2 Oct *Rhythm And Stealth, Leftfield (1)

9 Oct *Reload, Tom Jones (1)

6 Nov *Steptacular, Steps (3, *4 Dec* for 1)

27 Nov *All The Way . . . A Decade Of Song, Celine Dion (1; the 600th No. 1)

2000

ALBUMS

15 Jan The Man Who, Travis (5, *18 March* for 2)

19 Feb Rise, Gabrielle (3)

11 March *Standing On The Shoulder Of Giants, Oasis (1)

1 April Supernatural Santana (2)

15 April Play, Moby (5)

20 May Reload, Tom Jones (1, *17 June* for 1)

27 May *The Greatest Hits, Whitney Houston (2)

10 June *Crush, Bon Jovi (1)

24 June *7, S Club 7 (1)

1 July The Marshall Mathers LP, Eminem (1, *15 July* for 1)

8 July *Alone With Everybody, Richard Ashcroft (1)

22 July *Parachutes, Coldplay (1)

29 July *In Blue, Corrs (2)

12 Aug *Ronan, Ronan Keating (2)

25 Aug *Born To Do It, Craig David (2)

9 Sept *Sing When You're Winning, Robbie Williams (3)

30 Sept *Music, Madonna (2)

14 Oct *Kid A, Radiohead (2)

28 Oct *Saints & Sinners, All Saints (1)

4 Nov *The Greatest Hits, Texas (1)

11 Nov *All That You Can't Leave Behind, U2 (1)

18 Nov *Coast To Coast, Westlife (1)

25 Nov *1, Beatles (9; best seller of the year)

2001

ALBUMS

27 Jan The Greatest Hits, Texas (1)

3 Feb Chocolate Starfish And The Hot Dog Flavoured Water, Limp Bizkit (1)

10 Feb No Angel, Dido (6, *6 Oct* for 1; best seller of the year)

24 March Songbird, Eva Cassidy (2)

7 April *Popstars, Hear'Say (2)

21 April *Just Enough Education To Perform, Stereophonics (2)

5 May *Free All Angels, Ash (1)

12 May *Survivor, Destiny's Child (2, *28 July* for 2)

26 May *Reveal, R.E.M. (2)

9 June Hot Shot, Shaggy (1)

16 June *Amnesiac, Radiohead (1)

23 June *The Invisible Band, Travis (4)

21 July *8701, Usher (1)

11 Aug White Ladder, David Gray (1, *25 Aug* for 1)

18 Aug Right Now, Atomic Kitten (1)

1 Sept *Break The Cycle, Staind (1)

8 Sept *Iowa, Slipknot (1)

15 Sept *A Funk Odyssey, Jamiroquai (2)

29 Sept *The Id, Macy Gray (1)

13 Oct *Fever, Kylie Minogue (2)

27 Oct *Gold – The Greatest Hits, Steps (2, *17 Nov* for 1)

10 Nov *Invincible, Michael Jackson (1)

24 Nov *World Of Our Own, Westlife (1)

1 Dec *Swing When You're Winning, Robbie Williams (5)

A — UK

SINGLES:	HITS 6			WEEKS 6
FOGHORN	*Tycoon*	63	*7 Feb 98*	1
NUMBER ONE	*Tycoon*	47	*11 Apr 98*	1
SING-A-LONG	*Tycoon*	57	*27 Jun 98*	1
SUMMER ON THE UNDERGROUND	*Tycoon*	72	*24 Oct 98*	1
OLD FOLKS	*Tycoon*	54	*5 Jun 99*	1
I LOVE LAKE TAHOE	*Tycoon*	59	*21 Aug 99*	1
ALBUMS:	**HITS 1**			**WEEKS 1**
MONKEY KONG	*Tycoon*	62	*28 Aug 99*	1

A+ — US

SINGLES:	HITS 1			WEEKS 9
ENJOY YOURSELF	*Universal*	5	*13 Feb 99*	9

Samples Walter Murphy And The Big Apple Band's A Fifth Of Beethoven.

A vs B — UK/Greece

SINGLES:	HITS 1			WEEKS 1
RIPPED IN 2 MINUTES	*Positiva*	49	*9 May 98*	1

Amalgam of Jomanda's Make My Body Work and Bug Kann's Made In 2 Minutes.

A-HA — Norway

SINGLES:	HITS 19			WEEKS 133
TAKE ON ME	*Warner Brothers*	2	*28 Sep 85*	19
THE SUN ALWAYS SHINES ON TV	*Warner Brothers*	1	*28 Dec 85*	12
TRAIN OF THOUGHT	*Warner Brothers*	8	*5 Apr 86*	8
HUNTING HIGH AND LOW	*Warner Brothers*	5	*14 Jun 86*	10
I'VE BEEN LOSING YOU	*Warner Brothers*	8	*4 Oct 86*	7
CRY WOLF	*Warner Brothers*	5	*6 Dec 86*	9
MANHATTAN SKYLINE	*Warner Brothers*	13	*28 Feb 87*	6
THE LIVING DAYLIGHTS	*Warner Brothers*	5	*4 Jul 87*	9
From the James Bond film of the same name.				
STAY ON THESE ROADS	*Warner Brothers*	5	*26 Mar 88*	6
THE BLOOD THAT MOVES THE BODY	*Warner Brothers*	25	*18 Jun 88*	4
TOUCHY!	*Warner Brothers*	11	*27 Aug 88*	7
YOU ARE THE ONE	*Warner Brothers*	13	*3 Dec 88*	10
CRYING IN THE RAIN	*Warner Brothers*	13	*13 Oct 90*	7
I CALL YOUR NAME	*Warner Brothers*	44	*15 Dec 90*	5
MOVE TO MEMPHIS	*Warner Brothers*	47	*26 Oct 91*	2
DARK IS THE NIGHT	*Warner Brothers*	19	*5 Jun 93*	4
ANGEL	*Warner Brothers*	41	*18 Sep 93*	3
SHAPES THAT GO TOGETHER	*Warner Brothers*	27	*26 Mar 94*	3
SUMMER MOVED ON	*WEA*	33	*3 Jun 00*	2
ALBUMS:	**HITS 7**			**WEEKS 147**
HUNTING HIGH AND LOW	*Warner Brothers*	2	*9 Nov 85*	78
Includes re-entry in 1995.				
SCOUNDREL DAYS	*Warner Brothers*	2	*18 Oct 86*	29
STAY ON THESE ROADS	*Warner Brothers*	2	*14 May 88*	19
EAST OF THE SUN, WEST OF THE MOON	*Warner Brothers*	12	*3 Nov 90*	4
HEADLINES AND DEADLINES – THE HITS OF A-HA	*Warner Brothers*	12	*16 Nov 91*	12
Includes re-entry in 2000.				
MEMORIAL BEACH	*Warner Brothers*	17	*26 Jun 93*	3
MINOR EARTH MAJOR SKY	*WEA*	27	*17 Jun 00*	2

A.B.'S — Japan

ALBUMS:	HITS 1			WEEKS 2
DEJA VU	*Street Sounds*	80	*14 Apr 84*	2

12" single not eligible for the singles chart.

A.D.A.M. featuring AMY — France

SINGLES:	HITS 1			WEEKS 11
ZOMBIE	*Eternal*	16	*1 Jul 95*	11

A.K.A. — UK

SINGLES:	HITS 1			WEEKS 2
WARNING	*RCA*	43	*12 Oct 96*	2

Re-works the riff from an old reggae standard also titled Warning.

A.R.E. WEAPONS — UK

SINGLES:	HITS 1			WEEKS 1
STREET GANG	*Rough Trade*	72	*4 Aug 01*	1

A.S.A.P. — UK

SINGLES:	HITS 2			WEEKS 4
SILVER AND GOLD	*EMI*	60	*14 Oct 89*	2
DOWN THE WIRE	*EMI*	67	*3 Feb 90*	2
ALBUMS:	**HITS 1**			**WEEKS 1**
SILVER AND GOLD	*EMI*	70	*4 Nov 89*	1

A.T.F.C. presents ONEPHATDEEVA — UK/US

SINGLES:	HITS 2			WEEKS 8
IN AND OUT OF MY LIFE	*Defected*	11	*30 Oct 99*	5
Samples Adeva's In And Out Of My Life with Fatboy Slim's Right Here Right Now.				
BAD HABIT	*Defected*	17	*16 Sep 00*	3
Samples Bad Habits' Bad Habits and Chaka Khan's I Know You – I Love You.				
Above hit: ATFC presents ONEPHATDEEVA featuring Lisa MILLETT.				

A.T.G.O.C. — Italy

SINGLES:	HITS 1			WEEKS 2
REPEATED LOVE	*Wonderboy*	38	*21 Nov 98*	2

A*TEENS — Sweden

SINGLES:	HITS 4			WEEKS 19
MAMMA MIA	*Stockholm*	12	*4 Sep 99*	5
SUPER TROUPER	*Stockholm*	21	*11 Dec 99*	5
UPSIDE DOWN	*Stockholm*	10	*26 May 01*	7
HALFWAY AROUND THE WORLD	*Stockholm*	30	*27 Oct 01*	2

AALIYAH — US

SINGLES:	HITS 15			WEEKS 50
BACK AND FORTH	*Jive*	16	*2 Jul 94*	5
(AT YOUR BEST) YOU ARE LOVE	*Jive*	27	*15 Oct 94*	2
Originally recorded by the Isley Brothers on their 1976 album Harvest For The World.				
AGE AIN'T NOTHING BUT A NUMBER	*Jive*	32	*11 Mar 95*	2
DOWN WITH THE CLIQUE	*Jive*	33	*13 May 95*	2
Above 3: AALIYAH (AH-LEE-YAH).				
THE THING I LIKE	*Jive*	33	*9 Sep 95*	2
I NEED YOU TONIGHT	*Big Beat*	66	*3 Feb 96*	1
Above hit: JUNIOR M.A.F.I.A. featuring AALIYAH.				
IF YOUR GIRL ONLY KNEW	*Atlantic*	21	*24 Aug 96*	2
GOT TO GIVE IT UP	*Atlantic*	37	*23 Nov 96*	2
Features Slick Rick.				
IF YOUR GIRL ONLY KNEW [RI] / ONE IN A MILLION	*Atlantic*	15	*24 May 97*	3
4 PAGE LETTER	*Atlantic*	24	*30 Aug 97*	2
THE ONE I GAVE MY HEART TO / HOT LIKE FIRE	*Atlantic*	30	*22 Nov 97*	2
JOURNEY TO THE PAST	*Atlantic*	22	*18 Apr 98*	3
From the film 'Anastasia'.				
ARE YOU THAT SOMEBODY?	*Atlantic*	11	*12 Sep 98*	4
From the film 'Dr. Dolittle'.				
TRY AGAIN	*Virgin*	5	*22 Jul 00*	11
From the film 'Romeo Must Die'.				
TRY AGAIN [RE]	*Virgin*	75	*21 Oct 00*	1
WE NEED A RESOLUTION	*Virgin*	20	*21 Jul 01*	4
Above hit: AALIYAH featuring TIMBALAND.				
WE NEED A RESOLUTION [RE]	*Virgin*	65	*1 Sep 01*	2
ALBUMS:	**HITS 3**			**WEEKS 16**
AGE AIN'T NOTHING BUT A NUMBER	*Jive*	23	*23 Jul 94*	6
ONE IN A MILLION	*Atlantic*	33	*7 Sep 96*	3
AALIYAH	*Virgin*	25	*28 Jul 01*	7

ABBA — Sweden/Norway

SINGLES:	HITS 25			WEEKS 252
WATERLOO	*Epic*	1	*20 Apr 74*	9
Eurovision Song Contest winner in 1974.				
RING RING	*Epic*	32	*13 Jul 74*	5
Above 2: ABBA (BJORN, BENNY, ANNA and FRIDA).				
I DO, I DO, I DO, I DO, I DO	*Epic*	38	*12 Jul 75*	6
SOS	*Epic*	6	*20 Sep 75*	10
Only example of a palindromic artist and title.				
MAMMA MIA	*Epic*	1	*13 Dec 75*	14
FERNANDO	*Epic*	1	*27 Mar 76*	15
DANCING QUEEN	*Epic*	1	*21 Aug 76*	15
MONEY, MONEY, MONEY	*Epic*	3	*20 Nov 76*	12
KNOWING ME, KNOWING YOU	*Epic*	1	*26 Feb 77*	13
THE NAME OF THE GAME	*Epic*	1	*22 Oct 77*	12
TAKE A CHANCE ON ME	*Epic*	1	*4 Feb 78*	10

SUMMER NIGHT CITY	*Epic*	5	*16 Sep 78*	9
CHIQUITITA	*Epic*	2	*3 Feb 79*	9
DOES YOUR MOTHER KNOW	*Epic*	4	*5 May 79*	9
ANGELEYES / VOULEZ-VOUS	*Epic*	3	*14 Jul 79*	11
GIMME, GIMME, GIMME (A MAN AFTER MIDNIGHT)	*Epic*	3	*20 Oct 79*	12
I HAVE A DREAM	*Epic*	2	*15 Dec 79*	10
THE WINNER TAKES IT ALL	*Epic*	1	*2 Aug 80*	10
SUPER TROUPER	*Epic*	1	*15 Nov 80*	12
LAY ALL YOUR LOVE ON ME	*Epic*	7	*18 Jul 81*	7
ONE OF US	*Epic*	3	*12 Dec 81*	10
HEAD OVER HEELS	*Epic*	25	*20 Feb 82*	7
THE DAY BEFORE YOU CAME	*Epic*	32	*23 Oct 82*	6
UNDER ATTACK	*Epic*	26	*11 Dec 82*	8
THANK YOU FOR THE MUSIC	*Epic*	33	*12 Nov 83*	6
DANCING QUEEN [RI]	*Polydor*	16	*5 Sep 92*	5

ALBUMS:	**HITS 16**			**WEEKS 862**
WATERLOO	*Epic*	28	*8 Jun 74*	2

Above hit: ABBA (BJORN, BENNY, ANNA and FRIDA).

ABBA	*Epic*	13	*31 Jan 76*	10
GREATEST HITS	*Epic*	1	*10 Apr 76*	130
ARRIVAL	*Epic*	1	*27 Nov 76*	92
THE ALBUM	*Epic*	1	*4 Feb 78*	61
VOULEZ-VOUS	*Epic*	1	*19 May 79*	43
GREATEST HITS VOL 2	*Epic*	1	*10 Nov 79*	63
SUPER TROUPER	*Epic*	1	*22 Nov 80*	43
THE VISITORS	*Epic*	1	*19 Dec 81*	21
THE SINGLES - THE FIRST TEN YEARS	*Epic*	1	*20 Nov 82*	22
THANK YOU FOR THE MUSIC	*Epic*	17	*19 Nov 83*	12
ABSOLUTE ABBA	*Telstar*	70	*19 Nov 88*	7
GOLD - GREATEST HITS	*Polydor*	1	*3 Oct 92*	206
MORE ABBA GOLD - MORE ABBA HITS	*Polydor*	14	*5 Jun 93*	14
LOVE STORIES	*Polydor*	51	*7 Nov 98*	2
GOLD - GREATEST HITS [RE]	*Polydor*	1	*30 Jan 99*	117

Longest gap between separate runs at No.1.

MORE ABBA GOLD - MORE ABBA HITS [RE]	*Polydor*	13	*7 Aug 99*	9
THE DEFINITIVE COLLECTION	*Polydor*	17	*10 Nov 01*	8

ABBACADABRA — UK

SINGLES:	**HITS 1**			**WEEKS 1**
DANCING QUEEN	*PWL International*	57	*5 Sep 92*	1

Russ ABBOT — UK

SINGLES:	**HITS 3**			**WEEKS 22**
A DAY IN THE LIFE OF VINCE PRINCE [M]	*EMI*	61	*6 Feb 82*	1
A DAY IN THE LIFE OF VINCE PRINCE [M] [RE]	*EMI*	75	*20 Feb 82*	1
ATMOSPHERE	*Spirit*	7	*29 Dec 84*	13
ALL NIGHT HOLIDAY	*Spirit*	20	*13 Jul 85*	7

ALBUMS:	**HITS 2**			**WEEKS 16**
RUSS ABBOT'S MADHOUSE	*Ronco*	41	*5 Nov 83*	7
I LOVE A PARTY	*K-Tel*	12	*23 Nov 85*	9

Gregory ABBOTT — US

SINGLES:	**HITS 1**			**WEEKS 13**
SHAKE YOU DOWN	*CBS*	6	*22 Nov 86*	13

ALBUMS:	**HITS 1**			**WEEKS 5**
SHAKE YOU DOWN	*CBS*	53	*10 Jan 87*	5

ABC — UK

SINGLES:	**HITS 8**			**WEEKS 91**
TEARS ARE NOT ENOUGH	*Neutron*	19	*31 Oct 81*	8
POISON ARROW	*Neutron*	6	*20 Feb 82*	11
THE LOOK OF LOVE	*Neutron*	4	*15 May 82*	11
ALL OF MY HEART	*Neutron*	5	*4 Sep 82*	8
THE LOOK OF LOVE [RE]	*Neutron*	71	*15 Jan 83*	1
THAT WAS THEN BUT THIS IS NOW	*Neutron*	18	*5 Nov 83*	4
S.O.S.	*Neutron*	39	*21 Jan 84*	5

Backing vocals by Frankie Goes To Hollywood.

HOW TO BE A MILLIONAIRE	*Neutron*	49	*10 Nov 84*	4
BE NEAR ME	*Neutron*	26	*6 Apr 85*	4
VANITY KILLS	*Neutron*	70	*15 Jun 85*	1
OCEAN BLUE	*Neutron*	51	*18 Jan 86*	3
WHEN SMOKEY SINGS	*Neutron*	11	*6 Jun 87*	10

Tribute to Smokey Robinson.

THE NIGHT YOU MURDERED LOVE	*Neutron*	31	*5 Sep 87*	8
KING WITHOUT A CROWN	*Neutron*	44	*28 Nov 87*	3

ONE BETTER WORLD	*Neutron*	32	*27 May 89*	4
THE REAL THING	*Neutron*	68	*23 Sep 89*	1
THE LOOK OF LOVE (1990 MIX) [RM]	*Neutron*	68	*14 Apr 90*	1
LOVE CONQUERS ALL	*Parlophone*	47	*27 Jul 91*	2
SAY IT	*Parlophone*	42	*11 Jan 92*	3
STRANGER THINGS	*Blatant*	57	*22 Mar 97*	1
ALBUMS:	**HITS 8**			**WEEKS 91**
THE LEXICON OF LOVE	*Neutron*	1	*3 Jul 82*	50
BEAUTY STAB	*Neutron*	12	*26 Nov 83*	13
HOW TO BE A ZILLIONAIRE	*Neutron*	28	*26 Oct 85*	3
ALPHABET CITY	*Neutron*	7	*24 Oct 87*	10
UP	*Neutron*	58	*28 Oct 89*	1
ABSOLUTELY	*Neutron*	7	*21 Apr 90*	12
Compilation.				
ABRACADABRA	*Parlophone*	50	*24 Aug 91*	1
THE LOOK OF LOVE – THE VERY BEST OF ABC	*Mercury*	69	*4 Aug 01*	1

Paula ABDUL — US

SINGLES:	**HITS 11**			**WEEKS 67**
STRAIGHT UP	*Siren*	3	*4 Mar 89*	13
FOREVER YOUR GIRL	*Siren*	24	*3 Jun 89*	6
KNOCKED OUT	*Siren*	45	*19 Aug 89*	3
Original release reached No. 98 in 1988.				
(IT'S JUST) THE WAY THAT YOU LOVE ME	*Siren*	74	*2 Dec 89*	1
OPPOSITES ATTRACT	*Siren*	2	*7 Apr 90*	13
Above hit: Paula ABDUL (duet with the WILD PAIR).				
KNOCKED OUT [RM]	*Virgin America*	21	*21 Jul 90*	5
Remixed by Shep Pettibone.				
COLD HEARTED	*Virgin America*	46	*29 Sep 90*	3
RUSH RUSH	*Virgin America*	6	*22 Jun 91*	11
THE PROMISE OF A NEW DAY	*Virgin America*	52	*31 Aug 91*	2
VIBEOLOGY	*Virgin America*	19	*18 Jan 92*	6
WILL YOU MARRY ME?	*Virgin America*	73	*8 Aug 92*	1
MY LOVE IS FOR REAL	*Virgin*	28	*17 Jun 95*	3
Features vocals by Ofra Haza.				
ALBUMS:	**HITS 4**			**WEEKS 51**
FOREVER YOUR GIRL	*Siren*	5	*15 Apr 89*	21
FOREVER YOUR GIRL [RE]	*Siren*	3	*12 May 90*	18
SHUT UP AND DANCE (THE DANCE MIXES)	*Virgin America*	40	*10 Nov 90*	2
SPELLBOUND	*Virgin America*	4	*27 Jul 91*	9
HEAD OVER HEELS	*Virgin*	61	*1 Jul 95*	1

ABI — UK

SINGLES:	**HITS 1**			**WEEKS 2**
COUNTING THE DAYS	*Kuku*	44	*13 Jun 98*	2

ABIGAIL — UK

SINGLES:	**HITS 1**			**WEEKS 4**
SMELLS LIKE TEEN SPIRIT	*Klone*	29	*16 Jul 94*	4

ABNEA – See Johan GIELEN featuring ABNEA

Colonel ABRAMS — US

SINGLES:	**HITS 4**			**WEEKS 35**
TRAPPED	*MCA*	3	*17 Aug 85*	23
THE TRUTH	*MCA*	53	*7 Dec 85*	3
I'M NOT GONNA LET YOU	*MCA*	24	*8 Feb 86*	7
HOW SOON WE FORGET	*MCA*	75	*15 Aug 87*	2

ABSOLUTE — US

SINGLES:	**HITS 2**			**WEEKS 3**
I BELIEVE	*AM:PM*	38	*18 Jan 97*	2
Above hit: ABSOLUTE featuring Suzanne PALMER.				
CATCH ME	*AM:PM*	69	*14 Mar 98*	1

ABSOLUTELY FABULOUS – See PET SHOP BOYS

AC/DC — Australia/UK

SINGLES:	**HITS 27**			**WEEKS 126**
ROCK 'N' ROLL DAMNATION	*Atlantic*	24	*10 Jun 78*	9
HIGHWAY TO HELL	*Atlantic*	56	*1 Sep 79*	4
TOUCH TOO MUCH	*Atlantic*	29	*2 Feb 80*	9
WHOLE LOTTA ROSIE	*Atlantic*	36	*28 Jun 80*	8
DIRTY DEEDS DONE DIRT CHEAP	*Atlantic*	47	*28 Jun 80*	3
HIGH VOLTAGE (LIVE VERSION)	*Atlantic*	48	*28 Jun 80*	3

IT'S A LONG WAY TO THE TOP (IF YOU WANNA ROCK 'N' ROLL)	*Atlantic*	55	*28 Jun 80*	3
YOU SHOOK ME ALL NIGHT LONG	*Atlantic*	38	*13 Sep 80*	6
ROCK 'N' ROLL AIN'T NOISE POLLUTION	*Atlantic*	15	*29 Nov 80*	8
LET'S GET IT UP	*Atlantic*	13	*6 Feb 82*	6
FOR THOSE ABOUT TO ROCK (WE SALUTE YOU)	*Atlantic*	15	*3 Jul 82*	6
GUNS FOR HIRE	*Atlantic*	37	*29 Oct 83*	4
NERVOUS SHAKEDOWN	*Atlantic*	35	*4 Aug 84*	5
DANGER	*Atlantic*	48	*6 Jul 85*	4
SHAKE YOUR FOUNDATIONS	*Atlantic*	24	*18 Jan 86*	5
WHO MADE WHO	*Atlantic*	16	*24 May 86*	5
YOU SHOOK ME ALL NIGHT LONG [RI]	*Atlantic*	46	*30 Aug 86*	4
HEATSEEKER	*Atlantic*	12	*16 Jan 88*	6
THAT'S THE WAY I WANNA ROCK N ROLL	*Atlantic*	22	*2 Apr 88*	5
THUNDERSTRUCK	*Atco*	13	*22 Sep 90*	5
MONEYTALKS	*Atco*	36	*24 Nov 90*	3
ARE YOU READY	*Atco*	34	*27 Apr 91*	3
HIGHWAY TO HELL (LIVE) [RR]	*Atco*	14	*17 Oct 92*	4
DIRTY DEEDS DONE DIRT CHEAP (LIVE) [RR]	*Atco*	68	*6 Mar 93*	1
Above 2 are live recordings from their 1990-91 World Tour.				
BIG GUN	*Atco*	23	*10 Jul 93*	3
HARD AS A ROCK	*Atlantic*	33	*30 Sep 95*	2
HAIL CAESAR	*East West*	56	*11 May 96*	1
STIFF UPPER LIP	*EMI*	65	*15 Apr 00*	1

ALBUMS:	**HITS 14**			**WEEKS 255**
LET THERE BE ROCK	*Atlantic*	17	*5 Nov 77*	5
POWERAGE	*Atlantic*	26	*20 May 78*	9
IF YOU WANT BLOOD YOU'VE GOT IT	*Atlantic*	13	*28 Oct 78*	58
HIGHWAY TO HELL	*Atlantic*	8	*18 Aug 79*	32
BACK IN BLACK	*Atlantic*	1	*9 Aug 80*	40
FOR THOSE ABOUT TO ROCK WE SALUTE YOU	*Atlantic*	3	*5 Dec 81*	29
FLICK OF THE SWITCH	*Atlantic*	4	*3 Sep 83*	9
FLY ON THE WALL	*Atlantic*	7	*13 Jul 85*	10
WHO MADE WHO	*Atlantic*	11	*7 Jun 86*	12
Original soundtrack to the film 'Maximum Overdrive'.				
BLOW UP YOUR VIDEO	*Atlantic*	2	*13 Feb 88*	14
THE RAZOR'S EDGE	*Atco*	4	*6 Oct 90*	18
AC/DC LIVE	*Atco*	5	*7 Nov 92*	7
Live recordings from their 1990-91 World Tour.				
BALLBREAKER	*East West*	6	*7 Oct 95*	8
STIFF UPPER LIP	*EMI*	12	*11 Mar 00*	4

ACADEMY of ANCENT MUSIC conducted by Christopher HOGWOOD — UK

ALBUMS:	**HITS 1**			**WEEKS 2**
VIVALDI'S THE FOUR SEASONS	*L'Oiseau Lyre*	85	*16 Mar 85*	2

ACADEMY OF ST MARTIN IN THE FIELDS - See Neville MARRINER and the ACADEMY OF ST MARTIN IN THE FIELDS

ACCEPT — Germany

ALBUMS:	**HITS 4**			**WEEKS 5**
RESTLESS AND WILD	*Heavy Metal International*	98	*7 May 83*	2
METAL HEART	*Portrait*	50	*30 Mar 85*	1
KAIZOKU-BAN	*Portrait*	91	*15 Feb 86*	1
RUSSIAN ROULETTE	*Portrait*	80	*3 May 86*	1

ACE — UK

SINGLES:	**HITS 1**			**WEEKS 10**
HOW LONG	*Anchor*	20	*9 Nov 74*	10

ACE OF BASE — Sweden

SINGLES:	**HITS 12**			**WEEKS 100**
ALL THAT SHE WANTS	*London*	1	*8 May 93*	16
WHEEL OF FORTUNE	*London*	20	*28 Aug 93*	6
HAPPY NATION	*London*	42	*13 Nov 93*	3
THE SIGN	*London*	2	*26 Feb 94*	16
DON'T TURN AROUND	*London*	5	*11 Jun 94*	11
HAPPY NATION [RI]	*London*	40	*15 Oct 94*	3
LIVING IN DANGER	*London*	18	*14 Jan 95*	4
LUCKY LOVE	*London*	20	*11 Nov 95*	5
BEAUTIFUL LIFE	*London*	15	*27 Jan 96*	6
LIFE IS A FLOWER	*London*	5	*25 Jul 98*	11
CRUEL SUMMER	*London*	8	*10 Oct 98*	5
ALWAYS HAVE, ALWAYS WILL	*London*	12	*19 Dec 98*	10
EVERYTIME IT RAINS	*London*	22	*17 Apr 99*	4

ALBUMS:	**HITS 4**			**WEEKS 45**
HAPPY NATION	*London*	21	*19 Jun 93*	7

HAPPY NATION [RE]	*London*	1	*26 Mar 94*	31
Repackaged with additional track.				
THE BRIDGE	*London*	66	*2 Dec 95*	1
FLOWERS	*London*	15	*22 Aug 98*	5
SINGLES OF THE 90'S	*Polydor*	62	*27 Nov 99*	1
Compilation.				

Richard ACE — Jamaica

SINGLES:	HITS 1			WEEKS 2
STAYIN' ALIVE	*Blue Inc.*	66	*2 Dec 78*	2

ACEN — UK

SINGLES:	HITS 1			WEEKS 4
TRIP II THE MOON	*Production House*	38	*8 Aug 92*	3
TRIP II THE MOON (KALEIDOSCOPIKLIMAX) [RM]	*Production House*	71	*10 Oct 92*	1

Tracy ACKERMAN - See Q

ACT — UK/Germany

SINGLES:	HITS 1			WEEKS 2
SNOBBERY AND DECAY	*ZTT*	60	*23 May 87*	2

ACT ONE — US

SINGLES:	HITS 1			WEEKS 6
TOM THE PEEPER	*Mercury*	40	*18 May 74*	6

ACZESS — UK

SINGLES:	HITS 1			WEEKS 1
DO WHAT WE WOULD	*INCredible*	65	*27 Oct 01*	1

ADAM and the ANTS - See Adam ANT

Arthur ADAMS — US

SINGLES:	HITS 1			WEEKS 5
YOU GOT THE FLOOR	*RCA*	38	*24 Oct 81*	5

Bryan ADAMS — Canada

(See also Various Artists: Films – Original Soundtracks 'Robin Hood: Prince Of Thieves'.)

SINGLES:	HITS 33			WEEKS 235
RUN TO YOU	*A&M*	11	*12 Jan 85*	12
SOMEBODY	*A&M*	35	*16 Mar 85*	7
HEAVEN	*A&M*	38	*25 May 85*	5
SUMMER OF '69	*A&M*	42	*10 Aug 85*	7
IT'S ONLY LOVE	*A&M*	29	*2 Nov 85*	6
Above hit: Bryan ADAMS and Tina TURNER.				
CHRISTMAS TIME	*A&M*	55	*21 Dec 85*	2
THIS TIME	*A&M*	41	*22 Feb 86*	7
STRAIGHT FROM THE HEART	*A&M*	51	*12 Jul 86*	3
HEAT OF THE NIGHT	*A&M*	50	*28 Mar 87*	2
HEARTS ON FIRE	*A&M*	57	*20 Jun 87*	3
VICTIM OF LOVE	*A&M*	68	*17 Oct 87*	2
(EVERYTHING I DO) I DO IT FOR YOU	*A&M*	1	*29 Jun 91*	24
From the film 'Robin Hood (Prince Of Thieves)'.				
CAN'T STOP THIS THING WE STARTED	*A&M*	12	*14 Sep 91*	6
THERE WILL NEVER BE ANOTHER TONIGHT	*A&M*	32	*23 Nov 91*	3
(EVERYTHING I DO) I DO IT FOR YOU [RE]	*A&M*	73	*28 Dec 91*	1
THOUGHT I'D DIED AND GONE TO HEAVEN	*A&M*	8	*22 Feb 92*	7
ALL I WANT IS YOU	*A&M*	22	*18 Jul 92*	5
DO I HAVE TO SAY THE WORDS?	*A&M*	30	*26 Sep 92*	3
PLEASE FORGIVE ME	*A&M*	2	*30 Oct 93*	16
ALL FOR LOVE	*A&M*	2	*15 Jan 94*	13
From the film 'The Three Musketeers'.				
Above hit: Bryan ADAMS, Rod STEWART and STING.				
HAVE YOU EVER REALLY LOVE A WOMAN?	*A&M*	4	*22 Apr 95*	9
Featuring guitarist Paco De Lucia & taken from the film 'Juan De Marco'.				
ROCK STEADY	*Capitol*	50	*11 Nov 95*	2
Above hit: Bonnie RAITT and Bryan ADAMS.				
THE ONLY THING THAT LOOKS GOOD ON ME IS YOU	*A&M*	6	*1 Jun 96*	7
LET'S MAKE A NIGHT TO REMEMBER	*A&M*	10	*24 Aug 96*	8
STAR	*A&M*	13	*23 Nov 96*	4
I FINALLY FOUND SOMEONE	*A&M*	10	*8 Feb 97*	7
From the film 'The Mirror Has Two Faces'.				
Above hit: Barbra STREISAND and Bryan ADAMS.				
18 TILL I DIE	*A&M*	22	*19 Apr 97*	3
BACK TO YOU	*A&M*	18	*20 Dec 97*	7

I'M READY	*A&M*	20	*21 Mar 98*	4
Above 2 are live recordings for MTV from New York's Hammersmith Ballroom, 26 Sep 97.				
ON A DAY LIKE TODAY	*A&M*	13	*10 Oct 98*	5
WHEN YOU'RE GONE	*A&M*	3	*12 Dec 98*	19
Above hit: Bryan ADAMS featuring Melanie C.				
CLOUD #9	*A&M*	6	*15 May 99*	9
THE BEST OF ME	*A&M*	47	*18 Dec 99*	1
THE BEST OF ME [RE]	*A&M*	55	*22 Jan 00*	2
DON'T GIVE UP	*Xtravaganza*	1	*18 Mar 00*	14
Above hit: CHICANE featuring Bryan ADAMS.				
ALBUMS:	**HITS 11**			**WEEKS 393**
RECKLESS	*A&M*	7	*2 Mar 85*	115
Includes re-entries through to 1992.				
YOU WANT IT, YOU GOT IT	*A&M*	78	*24 Aug 85*	5
Originally released in 1981.				
CUTS LIKE A KNIFE	*A&M*	21	*15 Mar 86*	6
Originally released in 1983.				
INTO THE FIRE	*A&M*	10	*11 Apr 87*	21
WAKING UP THE NEIGHBOURS	*A&M*	1	*5 Oct 91*	54
SO FAR SO GOOD	*A&M*	1	*20 Nov 93*	55
Compilation. Includes re-entry in 2000.				
LIVE! LIVE! LIVE!	*A&M*	17	*6 Aug 94*	4
Live recordings from Wercher, Belgium during the summer of '88.				
18 TIL I DIE	*A&M*	1	*22 Jun 96*	40
UNPLUGGED	*A&M*	19	*13 Dec 97*	19
Live recordings from New York's Hammersmith Ballroom, 26 Sep 97.				
ON A DAY LIKE TODAY	*A&M*	11	*31 Oct 98*	35
Repackaged, May 99 to include Chicane remix (hit single version) of Cloud #9.				
THE BEST OF ME	*A&M*	12	*27 Nov 99*	39
Compilation.				

Ryan ADAMS — US

SINGLES:	**HITS 1**			**WEEKS 1**
NEW YORK NEW YORK	*Lost Highway*	53	*8 Dec 01*	1
ALBUMS:	**HITS 1**			**WEEKS 6**
GOLD	*Lost Highway*	20	*6 Oct 01*	6

Cliff ADAMS SINGERS — UK

SINGLES:	**HITS 1**			**WEEKS 2**
THE LONELY MAN THEME	*Pye International*	39	*30 Apr 60*	2
Used in the Strand cigarettes commercial.				
Above hit: CLIFF ADAMS ORCHESTRA.				
ALBUMS:	**HITS 4**			**WEEKS 20**
SING SOMETHING SIMPLE	*Pye*	18	*16 Apr 60*	1
SING SOMETHING SIMPLE [RE]	*Pye*	15	*18 Feb 61*	3
SING SOMETHING SIMPLE	*Pye Golden Guinea*	15	*24 Nov 62*	2
SING SOMETHING SIMPLE '76	*Warwick*	23	*20 Nov 76*	8
SING SOMETHING SIMPLE	*Ronco*	39	*25 Dec 82*	6
Title taken from the BBC Radio 2 show. All albums are different recordings.				

Gayle ADAMS — US

SINGLES:	**HITS 1**			**WEEKS 1**
STRETCH'IN OUT	*Epic*	64	*26 Jul 80*	1

Marie ADAMS - See Johnny OTIS with Marie ADAMS

Oleta ADAMS — US

SINGLES:	**HITS 9**			**WEEKS 36**
RHYTHM OF LIFE	*Fontana*	52	*24 Mar 90*	2
RHYTHM OF LIFE [RE]	*Fontana*	56	*3 Nov 90*	3
GET HERE	*Fontana*	4	*12 Jan 91*	12
Originally recorded by Brenda Russell.				
YOU'VE GOT TO GIVE ME ROOM / RHYTHM OF LIFE [RI]	*Fontana*	49	*13 Apr 91*	3
CIRCLE OF ONE	*Fontana*	73	*29 Jun 91*	1
Original release reached No. 95 in 1990.				
DON'T LET THE SUN GO DOWN ON ME	*Fontana*	33	*28 Sep 91*	5
WOMAN IN CHAINS	*Fontana*	57	*25 Apr 92*	1
Adams was not credited on the original release in 1989.				
Above hit: TEARS FOR FEARS featuring Oleta ADAMS.				
I JUST HAD TO HEAR YOUR VOICE	*Fontana*	42	*10 Jul 93*	3
NEVER KNEW LOVE	*Fontana*	22	*7 Oct 95*	3
RHYTHM OF LIFE - THE REMIXES [RM]	*Fontana*	38	*16 Dec 95*	2
Remixed by Reverend Jefferson.				
WE WILL MEET AGAIN	*Mercury*	51	*10 Feb 96*	1

ALBUMS:	HITS 3			WEEKS 34
CIRCLE OF ONE	*Fontana*	49	*26 May 90*	2
CIRCLE OF ONE [RE]	*Fontana*	1	*2 Mar 91*	24
EVOLUTION	*Fontana*	10	*7 Aug 93*	7
MOVING ON	*Fontana*	59	*4 Nov 95*	1

ADAMSKI — UK

SINGLES:	HITS 8			WEEKS 39
N-R-G	*MCA*	12	*20 Jan 90*	6
KILLER	*MCA*	1	*7 Apr 90*	18
Vocals by Seal.				
THE SPACE JUNGLE	*MCA*	7	*8 Sep 90*	8
FLASHBACK JACK	*MCA*	46	*17 Nov 90*	2
NEVER GOIN' DOWN (INCORPORATING FUTURE FREAK) / BORN TO BE ALIVE!	*MCA*	51	*9 Nov 91*	2
Above hit: ADAMSKI + Jimi POLO / ADAMSKI + SOHO.				
GET YOUR BODY!	*MCA*	68	*4 Apr 92*	1
Above hit: ADAMSKI featuring Nina HAGEN.				
BACK TO FRONT	*MCA*	63	*4 Jul 92*	1
ONE OF THE PEOPLE	*ZTT*	56	*11 Jul 98*	1
Vocals by Gerideau.				
Above hit: ADAMSKI'S THING.				

ALBUMS:	HITS 2			WEEKS 17
LIVEANDIRECT	*MCA*	65	*9 Dec 89*	1
LIVEANDIRECT [RE]	*MCA*	47	*17 Feb 90*	11
Re-released.				
DOCTOR ADAMSKI'S MUSICAL PHARMACY	*MCA*	8	*13 Oct 90*	5

Barry ADAMSON — UK

ALBUMS:	HITS 1			WEEKS 1
OEDIPUS SCHMOEDIPUS	*Mute*	51	*10 Aug 96*	1

ADDAMS and GEE — UK

SINGLES:	HITS 1			WEEKS 1
CHUNG KUO (REVISITED)	*Debut*	72	*20 Apr 91*	1
Original by Vangelis, from the album China.				

ADDIS BLACK WIDOW — US

SINGLES:	HITS 1			WEEKS 2
INNOCENT	*Mercury*	42	*3 Feb 96*	2
Samples Running For Your Love by Brothers Johnson.				

ADDRISI BROTHERS — US

SINGLES:	HITS 1			WEEKS 3
GHOST DANCER	*Scotti Brothers*	57	*6 Oct 79*	3

King Sunny ADE and his AFRICAN BEATS — Nigeria

ALBUMS:	HITS 1			WEEKS 1
SYNCHRO SYSTEM	*Island*	93	*9 Jul 83*	1

ADEVA — US

SINGLES:	HITS 15			WEEKS 66
RESPECT	*Cooltempo*	17	*14 Jan 89*	9
MUSICAL FREEDOM (MOVING ON UP)	*Cooltempo*	22	*25 Mar 89*	8
Above hit: Paul SIMPSON featuring ADEVA.				
WARNING!	*Cooltempo*	17	*12 Aug 89*	8
I THANK YOU	*Cooltempo*	17	*21 Oct 89*	7
Originally recorded by Sam and Dave in 1968.				
BEAUTIFUL LOVE	*Cooltempo*	57	*16 Dec 89*	5
TREAT ME RIGHT	*Cooltempo*	62	*28 Apr 90*	2
RING MY BELL	*Cooltempo*	20	*6 Apr 91*	5
Above hit: Monie LOVE Vs ADEVA.				
IT SHOULD'VE BEEN ME	*Cooltempo*	48	*19 Oct 91*	3
Original by Kim Weston in 1963.				
DON'T LET IT SHOW ON YOUR FACE	*Cooltempo*	34	*29 Feb 92*	4
UNTIL YOU COME BACK TO ME	*Cooltempo*	45	*6 Jun 92*	3
I'M THE ONE FOR YOU	*Cooltempo*	51	*17 Oct 92*	2
RESPECT '93 [RM]	*Network*	65	*11 Dec 93*	1
Remixed by Mental Instrum.				
TOO MANY FISH	*Virgin*	34	*27 May 95*	2
WHADDA U WANT (FROM ME)	*Virgin*	36	*18 Nov 95*	2
Above 2: Frankie KNUCKLES featuring ADEVA.				
DO WATCHA DO	*Avex UK*	54	*6 Apr 96*	1
Above hit: HYPER GO GO and ADEVA.				

'HANK YOU [RM]	*Cooltempo*	37	*4 May 96*	2
emixed by Love To Infinity and Dancing Divas.				
O WATCHA DO [RM]	*Distinct'ive*	60	*12 Apr 97*	1
emixed by K-Klass.				
bove hit: HYPER GO GO and ADEVA.				
'HERE IS THE LOVE? / THE WAY THAT YOU FEEL	*Distinct'ive*	54	*26 Jul 97*	1
acking vocals Incognito and Rachel Macfarlane.				
LBUMS:	**HITS 1**			**WEEKS 24**
DEVA	*Cooltempo*	6	*9 Sep 89*	24

ADICTS — UK

INGLES:	**HITS 1**			**WEEKS 1**
AD BOY	*Razor*	75	*14 May 83*	1
LBUMS:	**HITS 1**			**WEEKS 1**
OUND OF MUSIC	*Razor*	99	*4 Dec 82*	1

ADIEMUS — UK/South Africa

INGLES:	**HITS 1**			**WEEKS 2**
DIEMUS	*Venture*	48	*14 Oct 95*	2
rom the Delta Airlines TV commercial.				
LBUMS:	**HITS 3**			**WEEKS 22**
ONGS OF SANCTUARY	*Venture*	38	*1 Jul 95*	4
ONGS OF SANCTUARY [RE]	*Venture*	35	*3 Feb 96*	8
DIEMUS II - CANTATA MUNDI	*Venture*	15	*1 Mar 97*	9
Above hit: Miriam STOCKLEY/LONDON PHILHARMONIC ORCHESTRA conducted: Karl JENKINS.				
DIEMUS III - DANCES OF TIME	*Venture*	58	*24 Oct 98*	1

Larry ADLER — US

INGLES:	**HITS 1**			**WEEKS 2**
HE MAN I LOVE	*Mercury*	27	*30 Jul 94*	2
Above hit: Larry ADLER and Kate BUSH.				
LBUMS:	**HITS 1**			**WEEKS 18**
HE GLORY OF GERSHWIN	*Mercury*	2	*6 Aug 94*	18
eatures Peter Gabriel, Elton John, Kate Bush among others.				
Above hit: Larry ADLER and VARIOUS ARTISTS.				

ADONIS (featuring 2 PUERTO RICANS, a BLACKMAN and a DOMINICAN) — US

INGLES:	**HITS 1**			**WEEKS 4**
O WAY BACK / DO IT PROPERLY ("NO WAY BACK'")	*London*	47	*13 Jun 87*	4
eaturing 2 Puerto Ricans etc. not credited on the label for No Way Back.				

ADORABLE — UK

LBUMS:	**HITS 1**			**WEEKS 1**
GAINST PERFECTION	*Creation*	70	*13 Mar 93*	1

ADRENALIN M.O.D. — US

SINGLES:	**HITS 1**			**WEEKS 5**
)-O-O	*MCA*	49	*8 Oct 88*	5

ADULT NET — UK/US

SINGLES:	**HITS 1**			**WEEKS 2**
WHERE WERE YOU	*Fontana*	66	*10 Jun 89*	2
Original by the Grassroots reached No. 28 in the US in 1966.				

ADVENTURES — UK

SINGLES:	**HITS 6**			**WEEKS 24**
ANOTHER SILENT DAY	*Chrysalis*	71	*15 Sep 84*	2
SEND MY HEART	*Chrysalis*	62	*1 Dec 84*	4
FEEL THE RAINDROPS	*Chrysalis*	58	*13 Jul 85*	3
BROKEN LAND	*Elektra*	20	*9 Apr 88*	10
DROWNING IN THE SEA OF LOVE	*Elektra*	44	*2 Jul 88*	4
RAINING ALL OVER THE WORLD	*Polydor*	68	*13 Jun 92*	1
ALBUMS:	**HITS 2**			**WEEKS 11**
THE SEA OF LOVE	*Elektra*	30	*21 May 88*	10
TRADING SECRETS WITH THE MOON	*Elektra*	64	*17 Mar 90*	1

ADVENTURES OF STEVIE V — US

SINGLES:	**HITS 3**			**WEEKS 22**
DIRTY CASH	*Mercury*	2	*21 Apr 90*	13
BODY LANGUAGE (MONEY TALKS)	*Mercury*	29	*29 Sep 90*	5
JEALOUSY	*Mercury*	58	*2 Mar 91*	3

DIRTY CASH [RM]	*Avex Trax*	69	*27 Sep 97*
Remixed by Todd Terry.			
Above hit: ADVENTURES OF STEVIE V featuring NAZLYN.			

ADVERTS — UK

SINGLES:	HITS 2		WEEKS
GARY GILMORE'S EYES	*Anchor*	18	*27 Aug 77*
Refers to the death-row criminal who offered to donate his eyes to science.			
NO TIME TO BE 21	*Bright*	34	*4 Feb 78*
ALBUMS:	**HITS 1**		**WEEKS**
CROSSING THE RED SEA WITH THE ADVERTS	*Bright*	38	*11 Mar 78*

AEROSMITH — US

SINGLES:	HITS 17		WEEKS
DUDE (LOOKS LIKE A LADY)	*Geffen*	45	*17 Oct 87*
ANGEL	*Geffen*	69	*16 Apr 88*
LOVE IN AN ELEVATOR	*Geffen*	13	*9 Sep 89*
DUDE (LOOKS LIKE A LADY) [RI]	*Geffen*	20	*24 Feb 90*
Used in the film Mrs Doubtfire.			
RAG DOLL	*Geffen*	42	*14 Apr 90*
THE OTHER SIDE	*Geffen*	46	*1 Sep 90*
LIVIN' ON THE EDGE	*Geffen*	19	*10 Apr 93*
EAT THE RICH	*Geffen*	34	*3 Jul 93*
From the film of the same name.			
CRYIN'	*Geffen*	17	*30 Oct 93*
AMAZING	*Geffen*	57	*18 Dec 93*
SHUT UP AND DANCE	*Geffen*	24	*2 Jul 94*
SWEET EMOTION	*Columbia*	74	*20 Aug 94*
From the film 'Dazed And Confused'.			
CRAZY/BLIND MAN	*Geffen*	23	*5 Nov 94*
FALLING IN LOVE (IS HARD ON THE KNEES)	*Columbia*	22	*8 Mar 97*
HOLE IN MY SOUL	*Columbia*	29	*21 Jun 97*
PINK	*Columbia*	38	*27 Dec 97*
I DON'T WANT TO MISS A THING	*Columbia*	4	*12 Sep 98*
From the film 'Armageddon'.			
PINK [RI]	*Columbia*	13	*26 Jun 99*
Re-released to coincide with their Wembley gig with Lenny Kravitz, 26 Jun 99.			
JADED	*Columbia*	13	*17 Mar 01*
ALBUMS:	**HITS 8**		**WEEKS**
PERMANENT VACATION	*Geffen*	37	*5 Sep 87*
PUMP	*Geffen*	3	*23 Sep 89*
GET A GRIP	*Geffen*	2	*1 May 93*
BIG ONES	*Geffen*	7	*12 Nov 94*
Compilation.			
PUMP [RE]	*Geffen*	50	*4 Mar 95*
Re-released at mid-price.			
NINE LIVES	*Columbia*	4	*22 Mar 97*
A LITTLE SOUTH OF SANITY	*Geffen*	36	*31 Oct 98*
Live recordings from their 92/94 and 98/98 tours.			
JUST PUSH PLAY	*Columbia*	7	*24 Mar 01*
YOUNG LUST - THE AEROSMITH ANTHOLOGY	*Universal Music TV*	41	*8 Dec 01*

AFGHAN WHIGS — UK

ALBUMS:	HITS 2		WEEKS
GENTLEMEN	*Blast*	58	*16 Oct 93*
BLACK LOVE	*Mute*	41	*23 Mar 96*

AFRICAN BUSINESS — Italy

SINGLES:	HITS 1		WEEKS
IN ZAIRE	*Urban*	73	*17 Nov 90*

AFRO CELT SOUND SYSTEM — UK/Ireland/Africa

SINGLES:	HITS 1		WEEKS
RELEASE	*Realworld*	71	*29 Apr 00*
Vocals by Sinead O'Connor.			
ALBUMS:	**HITS 2**		**WEEKS**
VOLUME I - SOUND MAGIC	*Realworld*	59	*27 Jul 96*
VOLUME 2: RELEASE	*Realworld*	38	*8 May 99*

AFRO MEDUSA — UK/Spain

SINGLES:	HITS 1		WEEKS
PASILDA	*Rulin*	31	*28 Oct 00*

AFROMAN — US

NGLES:	HITS 1			WEEKS 13
CAUSE I GOT HIGH	*Universal*	45	*6 Oct 01*	3
port.				
CAUSE I GOT HIGH	*Universal*	1	*27 Oct 01*	10
m the film 'Jay and Silent Bob Strike Back'.				

AFTER DARK — UK

BUMS:	HITS 1			WEEKS 5
TE NIGHT SAX	*EMI TV*	18	*3 Feb 96*	5
interpretations of classic hits.				

AFTER 7 — US

NGLES:	HITS 1			WEEKS 3
N'T STOP	*Virgin America*	54	*3 Nov 90*	3

AFTER THE FIRE — UK

NGLES:	HITS 3			WEEKS 12
NE RULE FOR YOU	*CBS*	40	*9 Jun 79*	6
SER LOVE	*CBS*	62	*8 Sep 79*	2
R KOMMISSAR	*CBS*	47	*9 Apr 83*	4
iginally recorded by Falco.				
BUMS:	**HITS 3**			**WEEKS 4**
SER LOVE	*CBS*	57	*13 Oct 79*	1
F	*Epic*	69	*1 Nov 80*	1
TTERIES NOT INCLUDED	*CBS*	82	*3 Apr 82*	2

AFTERSHOCK — US

NGLES:	HITS 1			WEEKS 8
AVE TO THE VIBE	*Virgin America*	11	*21 Aug 93*	8

FX - See APHEX TWIN

AGE OF CHANCE — UK

NGLES:	HITS 3			WEEKS 13
SS	*FON*	50	*17 Jan 87*	6
HO'S AFRAID OF THE BIG BAD NOISE!	*Virgin*	65	*30 May 87*	2
IGHER THAN HEAVEN	*Virgin*	53	*20 Jan 90*	5

AGE OF LOVE — Italy/Belgium

NGLES:	HITS 1			WEEKS 6
HE AGE OF LOVE - THE REMIXES	*React*	17	*5 Jul 97*	4
iginally released in 1990 and 1992.				
HE AGE OF LOVE [RM]	*React*	38	*19 Sep 98*	2
emixed by Brainbug and Johnny Vicious.				

AGENT 00 — UK

NGLES:	HITS 1			WEEKS 1
HE MAGNIFICENT	*Inferno*	65	*7 Mar 98*	1
amples Dave & Ansil Collins' Double Barrel.				

AGENT PROVOCATEUR — UK

NGLES:	HITS 1			WEEKS 1
GENT DAN	*Epic*	49	*22 Mar 97*	1

AGENT SUMO — UK

NGLES:	HITS 1			WEEKS 2
4 HOURS	*Virgin*	44	*9 Jun 01*	2
amples Gladys Knight & the Pips' The Way We Were and Bell & James' Moses Theme.				

AGNELLI and NELSON — UK

NGLES:	HITS 5			WEEKS 13
L NINO	*Xtravaganza*	21	*15 Aug 98*	4
VERYDAY	*Xtravaganza*	17	*11 Sep 99*	4
MBRACE	*Xtravaganza*	35	*17 Jun 00*	2
UDSON STREET	*Xtravaganza*	29	*9 Sep 00*	2
EGAS	*Xtravaganza*	48	*7 Apr 01*	1

Christina AGUILERA — U

(See also Christina Aguilera, Lil' Kim, Mya and Pink.)

SINGLES:	HITS 5		WEEKS
GENIE IN A BOTTLE *Import.*	*RCA*	50	*11 Sep 99*
GENIE IN A BOTTLE	*RCA*	1	*16 Oct 99*
WHAT A GIRL WANTS *Originally recorded by Ophelie Winter in 1998 as Ce Que Je Suis.*	*RCA*	3	*26 Feb 00*
I TURN TO YOU *Originally recorded by All-4-One in 1997 for the Space Jam OST.*	*RCA*	19	*22 Jul 00*
COME ON OVER BABY (ALL I WANT IS YOU)	*RCA*	8	*11 Nov 00*
COME ON OVER BABY (ALL I WANT IS YOU) [RE]	*RCA*	65	*6 Jan 01*
NOBODY WANTS TO BE LONELY *Above hit: Ricky MARTIN with Christina AGUILERA.*	*Columbia*	4	*10 Mar 01*

ALBUMS:	HITS 1		WEEKS
CHRISTINA AGUILERA	*RCA*	14	*30 Oct 99*

Christina AGUILERA, LIL' KIM, MYA and PINK — U

(See also Christina Aguilera; Lil' Kim; Mya; Pink.)

SINGLES:	HITS 1		WEEKS
LADY MARMALADE *From the Baz Luhrmann film 'Moulin Rouge'. Originally recorded by Eleventh Hour.*	*Interscope*	1	*30 Jun 01*

AHEAD OF OUR TIME ORCHESTRA - See COLDCUT

AHMAD — U

SINGLES:	HITS 1		WEEK
BACK IN THE DAY	*Giant*	64	*9 Jul 94*

AIDA — Holland

SINGLES:	HITS 1		WEEK
FAR AND AWAY *Inspired by David's Song by Vladimir Cosma.*	*48K*	58	*19 Feb 00*

Alyn AINSWORTH and his Orchestra - See Des O'CONNOR; Frankie VAUGHAN

AIR — France

SINGLES:	HITS 5		WEEKS
SEXY BOY	*Virgin/Sam*	13	*21 Feb 98*
KELLY WATCH THE STARS *Single is tribute to Kelly from the 1970s TV series 'Charlie's Angels'.*	*Virgin*	18	*16 May 98*
ALL I NEED	*Virgin*	29	*21 Nov 98*
PLAYGROUND LOVE *From the film 'Virgin Suicides'.* *Above hit: AIR (sung by Gordon TRACKS).*	*Virgin*	25	*26 Feb 00*
RADIO #1	*Virgin*	31	*2 Jun 01*

ALBUMS:	HITS 4		WEEKS
MOON SAFARI	*Virgin*	6	*31 Jan 98*
PREMIERS SYMPTOMES *This was their first release in France.*	*Virgin*	12	*18 Sep 99*
THE VIRGIN SUICIDES [OST]	*Virgin*	14	*11 Mar 00*
10,000 HZ LEGEND	*Virgin*	7	*9 Jun 01*

AIR SUPPLY — UK/Australia

SINGLES:	HITS 3		WEEKS
ALL OUT OF LOVE	*Arista*	11	*27 Sep 80*
EVEN THE NIGHTS ARE BETTER	*Arista*	44	*2 Oct 82*
GOODBYE	*Giant*	66	*20 Nov 93*

AIRHEAD — UK

SINGLES:	HITS 3		WEEKS
FUNNY HOW	*Korova*	57	*5 Oct 91*
COUNTING SHEEP	*Korova*	35	*21 Dec 91*
RIGHT NOW	*Korova*	50	*7 Mar 92*

ALBUMS:	HITS 1		WEEKS
BOING!	*Korova*	29	*1 Feb 92*

AIRHEADZ — UK

SINGLES:	HITS 1		WEEKS
STANLEY (HERE I AM) *Originally a bootleg of Stan, but re-recorded as an answer record to the Eminem track.*	*AM:PM*	36	*28 Apr 01*

AIRSCAPE — Belgium/Holland

ee also Balearic Bill.)

INGLES:	HITS 3			WEEKS 5
ACIFIC MELODY	*Xtravaganza*	27	*9 Aug 97*	2
MAZON CHANT	*Xtravaganza*	46	*29 Aug 98*	1
eatured on BBC1 TV's 'Grandstand'.				
ESPERANZA	*Xtravaganza*	33	*4 Dec 99*	2

Laurel AITKEN and the UNITONE — Jamaica/Cuba

INGLES:	HITS 1			WEEKS 3
UDI GOT MARRIED	*I-Spy*	60	*17 May 80*	3

AKABU featuring Linda CLIFFORD — UK

INGLES:	HITS 1			WEEKS 1
IDE THE STORM	*NRK Sound Division*	69	*15 Sep 01*	1

KABU – See Gary CLAIL ON-U SOUND SYSTEM

Jewel AKENS — US

INGLES:	HITS 1			WEEKS 8
HE BIRDS AND THE BEES	*London*	29	*27 Mar 65*	8

AKIN — UK

INGLES:	HITS 1			WEEKS 1
TAY RIGHT HERE	*WEA*	60	*14 Jun 97*	1

ALABAMA – See Lionel RICHIE

ALABAMA 3 — UK

INGLES:	HITS 2			WEEKS 3
PEED AT THE SOUND OF LONELINESS	*El-e-mental*	72	*22 Nov 97*	1
AIN'T GOIN' TO GOA	*El-e-mental*	40	*11 Apr 98*	2
Original release reached No. 98 in 1996.				

Roberto ALAGNA/Angela GHEORGIU — Italy/Romania

ALBUMS:	HITS 1			WEEKS 5
DUETS & ARIAS	*EMI Classics*	42	*18 May 96*	5

ALANA – See MK

ALARM — UK

SINGLES:	HITS 16			WEEKS 64
68 GUNS	*I.R.S.*	17	*24 Sep 83*	7
WHERE WERE YOU HIDING WHEN THE STORM BROKE	*I.R.S.*	22	*21 Jan 84*	6
THE DECEIVER	*I.R.S.*	51	*31 Mar 84*	4
THE CHANT HAS JUST BEGUN	*I.R.S.*	48	*3 Nov 84*	4
ABSOLUTE REALITY	*I.R.S.*	35	*2 Mar 85*	6
STRENGTH	*I.R.S.*	40	*28 Sep 85*	4
SPIRIT OF 76	*I.R.S.*	22	*18 Jan 86*	5
KNIFE EDGE	*I.R.S.*	43	*26 Apr 86*	3
RAIN IN THE SUMMERTIME	*I.R.S.*	18	*17 Oct 87*	5
RESCUE ME	*I.R.S.*	48	*12 Dec 87*	2
PRESENCE OF LOVE (LAUGHARNE)	*I.R.S.*	44	*20 Feb 88*	3
SOLD ME DOWN THE RIVER / YN GYMREAG	*I.R.S.*	43	*16 Sep 89*	3
Yn Gymreag only listed for week of 16 Sep 89.				
A NEW SOUTH WALES / THE ROCK	*I.R.S.*	31	*4 Nov 89*	5
Above hit: ALARM featuring the MORRISTON ORPHEUS MALE VOICE CHOIR / ALARM.				
LOVE DON'T COME EASY	*I.R.S.*	48	*3 Feb 90*	3
UNSAFE BUILDING 1990	*I.R.S.*	54	*27 Oct 90*	2
RAW	*I.R.S.*	51	*13 Apr 91*	2

ALBUMS:	HITS 7			WEEKS 29
DECLARATION	*I.R.S.*	6	*25 Feb 84*	11
STRENGTH	*I.R.S.*	18	*26 Oct 85*	6
EYE OF THE HURRICANE	*I.R.S.*	23	*14 Nov 87*	4
ELECTRIC FOLKLORE LIVE	*I.R.S.*	62	*5 Nov 88*	2
CHANGE	*I.R.S.*	13	*30 Sep 89*	3
STANDARDS	*I.R.S.*	47	*24 Nov 90*	1
RAW	*I.R.S.*	33	*4 May 91*	2

Morris ALBERT — Brazil

SINGLES:	HITS 1			WEEKS 10
FEELINGS	*Decca*	4	*27 Sep 75*	10

ALBERTA — UK

SINGLES:	HITS 1		WEEKS
YOYO BOY	*RCA*	48	*26 Dec 98*

ALBERTO Y LOST TRIOS PARANOIAS — UK

SINGLES:	HITS 1		WEEKS
HEADS DOWN NO NONSENSE MINDLESS BOOGIE	*Logo*	47	*23 Sep 78*

Al ALBERTS – See FOUR ACES

ALBION — Holland

SINGLES:	HITS 1		WEEKS
AIR 2000	*Platipus*	59	*3 Jun 00*

Original release reached No. 106 in 1998.

ALCATRAZ — US

SINGLES:	HITS 1		WEEKS
GIVE ME LUV	*AM:PM*	12	*17 Feb 96*

ALCAZAR — Sweden

SINGLES:	HITS 1		WEEKS
CRYING AT THE DISCOTHEQUE	*Arista*	13	*8 Dec 01*

Samples Sheila B Devotion's 'Spacer'.

ALDA — Iceland

SINGLES:	HITS 2		WEEKS 1
REAL GOOD TIME	*Wildstar*	7	*29 Aug 98*
GIRLS NIGHT OUT	*Wildstar*	20	*26 Dec 98*

Robert ALDA – See Vivian BLAINE and Robert ALDA with the HOT BOX GIRLS

John ALDISS – See LONDON PHILHARMONIC CHOIR

Cali ALEMAN – See Tito PUENTE Jr. and the LATIN RHYTHM featuring Tito PUENTE, INDIA and Cali ALEMAN

ALENA — Jamaica

SINGLES:	HITS 1		WEEKS
TURN IT AROUND	*Wonderboy*	14	*13 Nov 99*

ALESSANDRA – See DJAIMIN featuring ALESSANDRA

ALESSI — US

SINGLES:	HITS 1		WEEKS 1
OH, LORI	*A&M*	8	*11 Jun 77* 1

ALEX PARTY — UK/Italy

SINGLES:	HITS 3		WEEKS 2
ALEX PARTY (SATURDAY NIGHT PARTY)	*Cleveland City Imports*	49	*18 Dec 93*
SATURDAY NIGHT PARTY (READ MY LIPS) [RE]	*Cleveland City Imports*	29	*28 May 94*
Although same catalogue number was used, it was issued with different title.			
DON'T GIVE ME YOUR LIFE	*Systematic*	2	*18 Feb 95*
WRAP ME UP	*Systematic*	17	*18 Nov 95*
READ MY LIPS [RM]	*Systematic*	28	*19 Oct 96*

A vocal remix of Saturday Night Party.

Jeff ALEXANDER CHOIR – See Mario LANZA

ALEXANDER BROTHERS — UK

EPS:	HITS 1		WEEKS
NOBDODY'S CHILD	*Pye*	20	*5 Mar 66*

ALBUMS:	HITS 1		WEEKS
THESE ARE MY MOUNTAINS	*Pye Golden Guinea*	29	*10 Dec 66*

ALEXIA — Italy

SINGLES:	HITS 3		WEEKS 1
UH LA LA LA	*Dance Pool*	10	*21 Mar 98*
GIMME LOVE	*Dance Pool*	17	*13 Jun 98*
THE MUSIC I LIKE	*Dance Pool*	31	*10 Oct 98*

ALFI and HARRY — US

(See also David Seville.)

SINGLES:	HITS 1		WEEKS 5
THE TROUBLE WITH HARRY	*London*	15	*24 Mar 56* 5

From the film of the same name.

ALFIE — UK

SINGLES:	HITS 1			WEEKS 1
YOU MAKE NO BONES	*Twisted Nerve*	61	*8 Sep 01*	1
ALBUMS:	**HITS 1**			**WEEKS 1**
IF YOU HAPPY WITH YOU NEED DO NOTHING	*Twisted Nerve*	62	*7 Apr 01*	1

John ALFORD — UK

SINGLES:	HITS 3			WEEKS 12
SMOKE GETS IN YOUR EYES *Originally recorded by Paul Whiteman.*	*Love This*	13	*17 Feb 96*	5
BLUE MOON / ONLY YOU *Originally recorded by the Glen Gray Orchestra in 1933.*	*Love This*	9	*25 May 96*	4
IF / KEEP ON RUNNING	*Love This*	24	*23 Nov 96*	3

ALI — UK

SINGLES:	HITS 2			WEEKS 2
LOVE LETTERS *Theme to the US sitcom 'Days Of Our Lives'.*	*Wild Card*	63	*23 May 98*	1
FEELIN' YOU	*Wild Card*	63	*24 Oct 98*	1

Tatyana ALI — US

SINGLES:	HITS 3			WEEKS 18
DAYDREAMIN' *Features rappers Lord Tariq and Peter Gunz.*	*MJJ*	6	*14 Nov 98*	5
BOY YOU KNOCK ME OUT *Samples Bobby Caldwell's What You Won't Do For Love.* *Above hit: Tatyana ALI featuring Will SMITH.*	*MJJ*	3	*13 Feb 99*	8
BOY YOU KNOCK ME OUT [RE]	*MJJ*	69	*15 May 99*	1
EVERYTIME	*MJJ*	20	*19 Jun 99*	4
ALBUMS:	**HITS 1**			**WEEKS 4**
KISS THE SKY	*MJJ*	41	*20 Feb 99*	4

ALI and FRAZIER — UK

SINGLES:	HITS 1			WEEKS 4
UPTOWN TOP RANKING	*Arista*	33	*7 Aug 93*	4

ALIBI — UK

SINGLES:	HITS 2			WEEKS 2
I'M NOT TO BLAME	*Urgent*	51	*15 Feb 97*	1
HOW MUCH I FEEL	*Urgent*	58	*7 Feb 98*	1

ALICE BAND — UK/US/Ireland

SINGLES:	HITS 1			WEEKS 1
ONE DAY AT A TIME	*Instant Karma*	52	*23 Jun 01*	1

ALICE COOPER - See Alice COOPER

ALICE DEEJAY — Holland

SINGLES:	HITS 5			WEEKS 50
BETTER OFF ALONE *Above hit: DJ JURGEN presents ALICE DEEJAY.*	*Positiva*	2	*31 Jul 99*	16
BACK IN MY LIFE	*Positiva*	4	*4 Dec 99*	15
WILL I EVER	*Positiva*	7	*15 Jul 00*	10
THE LONELY ONE	*Positiva*	16	*21 Oct 00*	5
CELEBRATE OUR LOVE	*Positiva*	17	*10 Feb 01*	4
ALBUMS:	**HITS 1**			**WEEKS 11**
WHO NEEDS GUITARS ANYWAY?	*Positiva*	8	*29 Jul 00*	11

ALICE IN CHAINS — US

SINGLES:	HITS 6			WEEKS 14
WOULD?	*Columbia*	19	*23 Jan 93*	3
THEM BONES	*Columbia*	26	*20 Mar 93*	3
ANGRY CHAIR	*Columbia*	33	*5 Jun 93*	2
DOWN IN A HOLE	*Columbia*	36	*23 Oct 93*	2
GRIND	*Columbia*	23	*11 Nov 95*	2
HEAVEN BESIDE YOU	*Columbia*	35	*10 Feb 96*	2
ALBUMS:	**HITS 4**			**WEEKS 22**
DIRT	*Columbia*	42	*24 Oct 92*	13
JAR OF FLIES/SAP *Jar Of Flies is a 7-track mini-LP. Sap is a 4-track EP.*	*Columbia*	4	*5 Feb 94*	5
ALICE IN CHAINS	*Columbia*	37	*18 Nov 95*	2

MTV UNPLUGGED *Live recordings from Brooklyn, 10 Apr 96.*	*Columbia*	20	*10 Aug 96*	[illegible]

ALIEN ANT FARM — US

SINGLES:	HITS 2			WEEKS 1[illegible]
MOVIES	*Dreamworks*	53	*30 Jun 01*	[illegible]
SMOOTH CRIMINAL *Import.*	*Dreamworks*	74	*8 Sep 01*	[illegible]
SMOOTH CRIMINAL	*Dreamworks*	3	*29 Sep 01*	1[illegible]
SMOOTH CRIMINAL [RE]	*Dreamworks*	73	*29 Dec 01*	[illegible]
ALBUMS:	**HITS 1**			**WEEKS 14**
ANTHOLOGY	*Dreamworks*	11	*18 Aug 01*	14

ALIEN SEX FIEND — UK

ALBUMS:	HITS 1			WEEKS 1
MAXIMUM SECURITY	*Anagram*	100	*12 Oct 85*	1

ALIEN VOICES featuring the THREE DEGREES — UK/US

See also Three Degrees.

SINGLES:	HITS 1			WEEKS 2
LAST CHRISTMAS	*Wildstar*	54	*26 Dec 98*	2

ALISHA — US

SINGLES:	HITS 1			WEEKS 2
BABY TALK	*Total Control*	67	*25 Jan 86*	2

ALISHA'S ATTIC — UK

SINGLES:	HITS 9			WEEKS 47
I AM, I FEEL	*Mercury*	14	*3 Aug 96*	10
ALISHA RULES THE WORLD	*Mercury*	12	*2 Nov 96*	6
INDESTRUCTIBLE	*Mercury*	12	*15 Mar 97*	6
AIR WE BREATHE	*Mercury*	12	*12 Jul 97*	6
THE INCIDENTALS	*Mercury*	13	*19 Sep 98*	7
WISH I WERE YOU	*Mercury*	29	*9 Jan 99*	5
BARBARELLA	*Mercury*	34	*17 Apr 99*	2
PUSH IT ALL ASIDE	*Mercury*	24	*24 Mar 01*	4
PRETENDER GOT MY HEART	*Mercury*	43	*28 Jul 01*	1
ALBUMS:	**HITS 3**			**WEEKS 47**
ALISHA RULES THE WORLD	*Mercury*	14	*23 Nov 96*	43
ILLUMINA	*Mercury*	15	*17 Oct 98*	3
THE HOUSE WE BUILT	*Mercury*	55	*4 Aug 01*	1

ALL ABOUT EVE — UK

SINGLES:	HITS 13			WEEKS 47
IN THE CLOUDS	*Mercury*	47	*31 Oct 87*	5
WILD HEARTED WOMAN	*Mercury*	33	*23 Jan 88*	4
EVERY ANGEL	*Mercury*	30	*9 Apr 88*	5
MARTHA'S HARBOUR	*Mercury*	10	*30 Jul 88*	8
WHAT KIND OF FOOL	*Mercury*	29	*12 Nov 88*	4
ROAD TO YOUR SOUL	*Mercury*	37	*30 Sep 89*	4
DECEMBER	*Mercury*	34	*16 Dec 89*	5
SCARLET	*Mercury*	34	*28 Apr 90*	2
FAREWELL MR. SORROW	*Mercury*	36	*15 Jun 91*	2
STRANGE WAY	*Vertigo*	50	*10 Aug 91*	3
THE DREAMER	*Vertigo*	41	*19 Oct 91*	2
PHASED [EP] *Lead track: Phased.*	*MCA*	38	*10 Oct 92*	2
SOME FINER DAY	*MCA*	57	*28 Nov 92*	1
ALBUMS:	**HITS 4**			**WEEKS 37**
ALL ABOUT EVE	*Mercury*	7	*27 Feb 88*	29
SCARLET AND OTHER STORIES	*Mercury*	9	*28 Oct 89*	4
TOUCHED BY JESUS	*Vertigo*	17	*7 Sep 91*	3
ULTRAVIOLET	*MCA*	46	*7 Nov 92*	1

ALL BLUE — UK

SINGLES:	HITS 1			WEEKS 1
PRISONER	*WEA*	73	*21 Aug 99*	1

ALL-4-ONE — US

SINGLES:	HITS 3			WEEKS 23
SO MUCH IN LOVE *Originally recorded by the Tymes.*	*Atlantic*	60	*2 Apr 94*	1

I SWEAR	*Atlantic*	2	*18 Jun 94*	18
Originally recorded by John Michael Montgomery.				
SO MUCH IN LOVE [RM]	*Atlantic*	49	*19 Nov 94*	2
Remixed by Tim O'Brien.				
I CAN LOVE YOU LIKE THAT	*Atlantic*	33	*15 Jul 95*	2
Originally recorded by John Michael Montgomery.				

ALBUMS:	HITS 1			WEEKS 5
ALL-4-ONE	*Atlantic*	25	*23 Jul 94*	5

ALL SAINTS — UK/Canada

SINGLES:	HITS 8			WEEKS 109
I KNOW WHERE IT'S AT	*London*	4	*6 Sep 97*	8
NEVER EVER	*London*	1	*22 Nov 97*	24
UNDER THE BRIDGE / LADY MARMALADE	*London*	1	*9 May 98*	14
Lady Marmalade originally recorded by Eleventh Hour.				
BOOTIE CALL	*London*	1	*12 Sep 98*	11
WAR OF NERVES	*London*	7	*5 Dec 98*	11
PURE SHORES	*London*	1	*26 Feb 00*	16
From the film 'The Beach'.				
BLACK COFFEE	*London*	1	*14 Oct 00*	16
ALL HOOKED UP	*London*	7	*27 Jan 01*	6
BLACK COFFEE [RE-1ST]	*London*	71	*24 Feb 01*	1
BLACK COFFEE [RE-2ND]	*London*	69	*10 Mar 01*	1
ALL HOOKED UP [RE]	*London*	59	*17 Mar 01*	1

ALBUMS:	HITS 3			WEEKS 96
ALL SAINTS	*London*	2	*6 Dec 97*	63
ALL SAINTS [RE]	*London*	27	*29 Apr 00*	8
Re-released with new catalogue number.				
SAINTS & SINNERS	*London*	1	*28 Oct 00*	21
ALL HITS	*London*	18	*17 Nov 01*	4

ALL SEEING I — UK

SINGLES:	HITS 3			WEEKS 17
BEAT GOES ON	*ffrr*	11	*28 Mar 98*	7
Sampled vocals from a version by Buddy Rich and his 12 year old daughter.				
WALK LIKE A PANTHER	*ffrr*	10	*23 Jan 99*	7
Above hit: ALL SEEING I featuring Tony CHRISTIE.				
1ST MAN IN SPACE	*ffrr*	28	*18 Sep 99*	3
Vocals by Phil Oakey (Human League).				

ALBUMS:	HITS 1			WEEKS 1
PICKLED EGGS & SHERBET	*ffrr*	45	*2 Oct 99*	1

ALL STAR CHOIR – See Donna SUMMER

ALL STAR HIT PARADE — UK

(See also entries for each artist.)

SINGLES:	HITS 2			WEEKS 16
ALL STAR HIT PARADE [M]	*Decca*	2	*30 Jun 56*	9
6 song medley over 2 sides. Artists credited: Dave King, Lita Roza, David Whitfield, Dickie Valentine, Joan Regan, Winifred Atwell.				
ALL STAR HIT PARADE NO. 2 [M]	*Decca*	15	*27 Jul 57*	7
6 song medley over 2 sides. Artists credited: Johnston Brothers, Billy Cotton, Jimmy Young, Max Bygraves, Beverly Sisters, Tommy Steele.				

ALL STARS – See Louis ARMSTRONG

ALL STARS – See PRINCE BUSTER and ALL STARS

ALLSTARS — UK

SINGLES:	HITS 2			WEEKS 11
BEST FRIENDS	*Island*	20	*23 Jun 01*	5
Theme to the TV show 'StarStreet'.				
BEST FRIENDS [RE]	*Island*	66	*1 Sep 01*	2
THINGS THAT GO BUMP IN THE NIGHT/ IS THERE SOMETHING I SHOULD KNOW?	*Island*	12	*22 Sep 01*	4

ALL SYSTEMS GO — UK

SINGLES:	HITS 1			WEEKS 2
POP MUZIK	*Unique*	63	*18 Jun 88*	2

Richard ALLAN — UK

SINGLES:	HITS 1			WEEKS 1
AS TIME GOES BY	*Parlophone*	43	*26 Mar 60*	1
Originally recorded by Jacques Renard in 1931.				

Steve ALLAN — UK

SINGLES:	HITS 1			WEEKS 2
TOGETHER WE ARE BEAUTIFUL	*Creole*	67	*27 Jan 79*	1
TOGETHER WE ARE BEAUTIFUL [RE]	*Creole*	70	*10 Feb 79*	1

Donna ALLEN — US

SINGLES:	HITS 4			WEEKS 27
SERIOUS	*Portrait*	8	*18 Apr 87*	12
JOY AND PAIN	*BCM*	10	*3 Jun 89*	10
REAL	*Epic*	34	*21 Jan 95*	2
From the film 'The Specialist'.				
SATURDAY	*AM:PM*	29	*11 Oct 97*	3
Original release was an instrumental reaching No. 110 in 1996.				
Above hit: EAST 57TH ST featuring Donna ALLEN.				

Keith ALLEN - See BLACK GRAPE; FAT LES

Patrick ALLEN - See Kevin PEEK and Rick WAKEMAN

Ed ALLEYNE-JOHNSON — UK

ALBUMS:	HITS 1			WEEKS 1
ULTRAVIOLET	*Equation*	68	*18 Jun 94*	1

Mose ALLISON — US

ALBUMS:	HITS 1			WEEKS 1
MOSE ALIVE	*Atlantic*	30	*4 Jun 66*	1

ALLISONS — UK

SINGLES:	HITS 3			WEEKS 27
ARE YOU SURE	*Fontana*	2	*25 Feb 61*	16
UK's Eurovision entry in 1961, it came 2nd.				
WORDS	*Fontana*	34	*20 May 61*	5
LESSONS IN LOVE	*Fontana*	30	*17 Feb 62*	6
Originally recorded by Cliff Richard.				

ALLMAN BROTHERS BAND — US

ALBUMS:	HITS 2			WEEKS 4
BROTHERS AND SISTERS	*Warner Brothers*	42	*6 Oct 73*	3
THE ROAD GOES ON FOREVER	*Capricorn*	54	*6 Mar 76*	1
Compilation.				

ALLNIGHT BAND — UK

SINGLES:	HITS 1			WEEKS 3
THE JOKER (THE WIGAN JOKER)	*Casino Classics*	50	*3 Feb 79*	3
Originally recorded by Butch Baker.				

ALLURE — US

SINGLES:	HITS 2			WEEKS 8
HEAD OVER HEELS	*Epic*	18	*14 Jun 97*	3
Samples MC Shan's The Bridge.				
Above hit: ALLURE featuring NAS.				
ALL CRIED OUT	*Epic*	12	*10 Jan 98*	5
Originally recorded by Lisa Lisa and Cult Jam.				
Above hit: ALLURE featuring 112.				

ALMIGHTY — UK/Canada

SINGLES:	HITS 11			WEEKS 22
WILD AND WONDERFUL	*Polydor*	50	*30 Jun 90*	2
FREE 'N' EASY	*Polydor*	35	*2 Mar 91*	2
DEVIL'S TOY	*Polydor*	36	*11 May 91*	2
LITTLE LOST SOMETIMES	*Polydor*	42	*29 Jun 91*	2
ADDICTION	*Polydor*	38	*3 Apr 93*	2
OUT OF SEASON	*Polydor*	41	*29 May 93*	2
OVER THE EDGE	*Polydor*	38	*30 Oct 93*	2
WRENCH	*Chrysalis*	26	*24 Sep 94*	2
JONESTOWN MIND	*Chrysalis*	26	*14 Jan 95*	3
ALL SUSSED OUT	*Chrysalis*	28	*16 Mar 96*	2
DO YOU UNDERSTAND	*Raw Power*	38	*25 May 96*	1

ALBUMS:	HITS 5			WEEKS 13
BLOOD, FIRE AND LIVE	*Polydor*	62	*20 Oct 90*	1
SOUL DESTRUCTION	*Polydor*	22	*30 Mar 91*	4
POWERTRIPPIN'	*Polydor*	5	*17 Apr 93*	4
CRANK	*Chrysalis*	15	*8 Oct 94*	2
JUST ADD LIFE	*Chrysalis*	34	*30 Mar 96*	2

Marc ALMOND — UK

(See also Soft Cell.)

SINGLES:	HITS 24			WEEKS 101
BLACK HEART	*Some Bizzare*	49	*2 Jul 83*	3
Above hit: MARC and the MAMBAS.				
THE BOY WHO CAME BACK	*Some Bizzare*	52	*2 Jun 84*	5
YOU HAVE	*Some Bizzare*	57	*1 Sep 84*	3
I FEEL LOVE [M]	*Forbidden Fruit*	3	*20 Apr 85*	12
Above hit: BRONSKI BEAT/Marc ALMOND.				
STORIES OF JOHNNY	*Some Bizzare*	23	*24 Aug 85*	5
LOVE LETTER	*Some Bizzare*	68	*26 Oct 85*	3
Features the Westminster City School Choir.				
THE HOUSE IS HAUNTED (BY THE ECHO OF YOUR LAST GOODBYE)	*Some Bizzare*	55	*4 Jan 86*	3
Vocals by Sally Timms.				
A WOMAN'S STORY	*Some Bizzare*	41	*7 Jun 86*	5
Originally recorded by Cher in 1976.				
Above hit: Marc ALMOND and the WILLING SINNERS.				
RUBY RED	*Some Bizzare*	47	*18 Oct 86*	3
MELANCHOLY ROSE	*Some Bizzare*	71	*14 Feb 87*	1
TEARS RUN RINGS	*Parlophone*	26	*3 Sep 88*	7
BITTER SWEET	*Parlophone*	40	*5 Nov 88*	3
SOMETHING'S GOTTEN HOLD OF MY HEART	*Parlophone*	1	*14 Jan 89*	12
Above hit: Marc ALMOND featuring special guest star Gene PITNEY.				
ONLY THE MOMENT	*Parlophone*	45	*8 Apr 89*	2
A LOVER SPURNED	*Parlophone*	29	*3 Mar 90*	4
THE DESPERATE HOURS	*Parlophone*	45	*19 May 90*	2
JACKY	*Some Bizzare*	17	*28 Sep 91*	6
MY HAND OVER MY HEART	*Some Bizzare*	33	*11 Jan 92*	5
THE DAYS OF PEARLY SPENCER	*Some Bizzare*	4	*25 Apr 92*	7
Originally recorded by David McWilliams.				
WHAT MAKES A MAN A MAN (LIVE)	*Some Bizzare*	60	*27 Mar 93*	2
Live recording from the Royal Albert Hall.				
ADORED AND EXPLORED	*Some Bizarre*	25	*13 May 95*	3
THE IDOL	*Some Bizarre*	44	*29 Jul 95*	2
CHILD STAR	*Some Bizarre*	41	*30 Dec 95*	1
YESTERDAY HAS GONE	*EMI Premier*	58	*28 Dec 96*	1
Original by Teddy Randazzo.				
YESTERDAY HAS GONE [RE]	*EMI Premier*	69	*11 Jan 97*	1
Above hit: P.J. PROBY; Marc ALMOND featuring the MY LIFE STORY ORCHESTRA.				

ALBUMS:	HITS 10			WEEKS 39
UNTITLED	*Some Bizzare*	12	*16 Oct 82*	4
TORMENT AND TOREROS	*Some Bizzare*	28	*20 Aug 83*	5
Above 2: MARC and the MAMBAS.				
VERMIN IN ERMINE	*Some Bizzare*	36	*10 Nov 84*	2
Above hit: Marc ALMOND and the WILLING SINNERS.				
STORIES OF JOHNNY	*Some Bizzare*	22	*5 Oct 85*	3
MOTHER FIST AND HER FIVE DAUGHTERS	*Some Bizzare*	41	*18 Apr 87*	2
Above hit: Marc ALMOND and the WILLING SINNERS.				
THE STARS WE ARE	*Parlophone*	41	*8 Oct 88*	4
THE STARS WE ARE [RE]	*Parlophone*	68	*4 Mar 89*	1
Repackaged with additional track.				
ENCHANTED	*Parlophone*	52	*16 Jun 90*	1
MEMORABILIA - THE SINGLES	*Mercury*	8	*1 Jun 91*	13
Includes both Almond's solo and group material.				
Above hit: SOFT CELL Marc ALMOND.				
TENEMENT SYMPHONY	*Some Bizzare*	48	*26 Oct 91*	1
TENEMENT SYMPHONY [RE]	*Some Bizzare*	39	*16 May 92*	2
FANTASTIC STAR	*Some Bizarre*	54	*9 Mar 96*	1

ALOOF — UK

SINGLES:	HITS 4			WEEKS 6
ON A MISSION	*Cowboy*	64	*19 Sep 92*	1
WISH YOU WERE HERE . . .	*East West*	61	*18 May 96*	1
ONE NIGHT STAND	*East West*	30	*30 Nov 96*	2
WISH YOU WERE HERE . . . [RI]	*East West*	43	*1 Mar 97*	1
WHAT I MISS THE MOST	*East West*	70	*29 Aug 98*	1

Herb ALPERT and the TIJUANA BRASS — US

SINGLES:	HITS 11			WEEKS 106
THE LONELY BULL (EL SOLO TORRO)	*Stateside*	22	*5 Jan 63*	9
SPANISH FLEA	*Pye International*	3	*11 Dec 65*	20
TIJUANA TAXI	*Pye International*	37	*26 Mar 66*	4
CASINO ROYALE	*A&M*	27	*29 Apr 67*	14
THIS GUY'S IN LOVE WITH YOU	*A&M*	3	*6 Jul 68*	16
THIS GUY'S IN LOVE WITH YOU [RE-1ST]	*A&M*	46	*29 Mar 69*	1
THIS GUY'S IN LOVE WITH YOU [RE-2ND]	*A&M*	49	*12 Apr 69*	1

THIS GUY'S IN LOVE WITH YOU [RE-3RD]	*A&M*	50	*10 May 69*	1
Above 4: Herb ALPERT.				
WITHOUT HER	*A&M*	36	*21 Jun 69*	5
Originally recorded by Harry Nilsson.				
JERUSALEM	*A&M*	47	*12 Dec 70*	1
JERUSALEM [RE]	*A&M*	42	*2 Jan 71*	2
RISE	*A&M*	13	*13 Oct 79*	13
ROTATION	*A&M*	46	*19 Jan 80*	3
KEEP YOUR EYE ON ME - SPECIAL MIX	*Breakout*	19	*21 Mar 87*	9
DIAMONDS	*Breakout*	27	*6 Jun 87*	7
Features vocals by Janet Jackson and Lisa Keith.				
Above 4: Herb ALPERT.				
ALBUMS:	**HITS 16**			**WEEKS 322**
GOING PLACES	*Pye*	5	*29 Jan 66*	22
WHIPPED CREAM AND OTHER DELIGHTS	*Pye*	2	*23 Apr 66*	42
WHAT NOW MY LOVE	*Pye*	18	*28 May 66*	12
GOING PLACES [RE]	*Pye*	4	*13 Aug 66*	116
Re-issued on the A&M label from 1 Jul 67.				
S.R.O.	*Pye*	5	*11 Feb 67*	26
Acronym of Standing Room Only.				
WHAT NOW MY LOVE [RI]	*A&M*	19	*15 Jul 67*	5
SOUNDS LIKE	*A&M*	21	*15 Jul 67*	10
NINTH	*A&M*	26	*3 Feb 68*	19
BEAT OF THE BRASS	*A&M*	4	*29 Jun 68*	21
WARM	*A&M*	30	*9 Aug 69*	4
THE BRASS ARE COMIN'	*A&M*	40	*14 Mar 70*	1
GREATEST HITS	*A&M*	8	*30 May 70*	27
DOWN MEXICO WAY	*A&M*	64	*27 Jun 70*	1
AMERICA	*A&M*	45	*13 Nov 71*	1
40 GREATEST	*K-Tel*	45	*12 Nov 77*	2
RISE	*A&M*	37	*17 Nov 79*	7
KEEP YOUR EYE ON ME	*Breakout*	79	*4 Apr 87*	3
THE VERY BEST OF HERB ALPERT	*A&M*	34	*28 Sep 91*	3
Above 3: Herb ALPERT.				

ALPHAVILLE — Germany

SINGLES:	**HITS 1**			**WEEKS 13**
BIG IN JAPAN	*WEA International*	8	*18 Aug 84*	13

ALSOU — Russia

SINGLES:	**HITS 1**			**WEEKS 3**
BEFORE YOU LOVE ME	*Mercury*	27	*12 May 01*	3

Gerald ALSTON — US

SINGLES:	**HITS 1**			**WEEKS 1**
ACTIVATED	*RCA*	73	*15 Apr 89*	1

ALT — UK/Ireland/New Zealand

ALBUMS:	**HITS 1**			**WEEKS 1**
ALTITUDE	*Parlophone*	67	*24 Jun 95*	1

ALTERED IMAGES — UK

SINGLES:	**HITS 8**			**WEEKS 60**
DEAD POP STARS	*Epic*	67	*28 Mar 81*	2
HAPPY BIRTHDAY	*Epic*	2	*26 Sep 81*	17
I COULD BE HAPPY	*Epic*	7	*12 Dec 81*	12
SEE THOSE EYES	*Epic*	11	*27 Mar 82*	7
PINKY BLUE	*Epic*	35	*22 May 82*	6
DON'T TALK TO ME ABOUT LOVE	*Epic*	7	*19 Mar 83*	7
BRING ME CLOSER	*Epic*	29	*28 May 83*	6
LOVE TO STAY	*Epic*	46	*16 Jul 83*	3
ALBUMS:	**HITS 3**			**WEEKS 40**
HAPPY BIRTHDAY	*Epic*	26	*19 Sep 81*	21
PINKY BLUE	*Epic*	12	*15 May 82*	10
BITE	*Epic*	16	*25 Jun 83*	9

ALTERN 8 — UK

SINGLES:	**HITS 8**			**WEEKS 34**
INFILTRATE 202	*Network*	28	*13 Jul 91*	7
ACTIV 8 (COME WITH ME)	*Network*	3	*16 Nov 91*	9
FREQUENCY	*Network*	41	*8 Feb 92*	1
EVAPOR 8	*Network*	6	*11 Apr 92*	6
Above hit: ALTERN 8 guest vocal P.P. ARNOLD.				
HYPNOTIC ST-8	*Network*	16	*4 Jul 92*	4

SHAME (HARDCORE MIX)	*Network*	74	*10 Oct 92*	1
Remix of Evelyn King's original.				
Above hit: ALTERN 8 vs Evelyn KING.				
BRUTAL-8-E	*Network*	43	*12 Dec 92*	5
EVERYBODY	*Network*	58	*3 Jul 93*	1
ALBUMS:	**HITS 1**			**WEEKS 4**
FULL ON..MASK HYSTERIA	*Network*	11	*25 Jul 92*	4

ALTHIA and DONNA — Jamaica

SINGLES:	**HITS 1**			**WEEKS 11**
UP TOWN TOP RANKING	*Lightning*	1	*24 Dec 77*	11
Originally recorded by Trinity as Three Piece Suite. Uptown Top Ranking is a Jamaican slang term for showing off in the city.				

ALVIN and the CHIPMUNKS – See CHIPMUNKS

ALY-US — US

SINGLES:	**HITS 1**			**WEEKS 2**
FOLLOW ME	*Cooltempo*	43	*21 Nov 92*	2

Shola AMA — UK

SINGLES:	**HITS 8**			**WEEKS 50**
YOU MIGHT NEED SOMEBODY	*WEA*	4	*19 Apr 97*	14
Original by Turley Richards in 1980.				
YOU'RE THE ONE I LOVE	*WEA*	3	*30 Aug 97*	8
WHO'S LOVING MY BABY	*WEA*	13	*29 Nov 97*	7
MUCH LOVE	*WEA*	17	*21 Feb 98*	3
SOMEDAY I'LL FIND YOU	*EMI*	28	*11 Apr 98*	3
[AA] listed with I've Been To A Marvellous Party by the Divine Comedy. From the Noel Coward commemorative album Twentieth Century Blues.				
Above hit: Shola AMA with Craig ARMSTRONG.				
TABOO	*WEA*	10	*17 Apr 99*	8
Above hit: GLAMMA KID featuring Shola AMA.				
STILL BELIEVE	*WEA*	26	*6 Nov 99*	3
IMAGINE	*WEA*	24	*29 Apr 00*	4
ALBUMS:	**HITS 1**			**WEEKS 32**
MUCH LOVE	*WEA*	6	*13 Sep 97*	32

Eddie AMADOR — US

SINGLES:	**HITS 2**			**WEEKS 5**
HOUSE MUSIC	*Pukka*	37	*24 Oct 98*	2
RISE	*Defected*	19	*22 Jan 00*	3
Vocals by David Gordan.				

AMAR — UK

SINGLES:	**HITS 1**			**WEEKS 1**
SOMETIMES IT SNOWS IN APRIL	*Blanco Y Negro*	48	*9 Sep 00*	1
Sleeve has additional title credit: Feel It Comin' In Comin' On.				

AMBASSADOR — Holland

SINGLES:	**HITS 1**			**WEEKS 1**
ONE OF THESE DAYS	*Platipus*	67	*12 Feb 00*	1

AMAZULU — UK

SINGLES:	**HITS 6**			**WEEKS 57**
EXCITABLE	*Island*	12	*6 Jul 85*	13
DON'T YOU JUST KNOW IT	*Island*	15	*23 Nov 85*	11
Original by Huey 'Piano' Smith reached No. 9 in the US in 1958.				
THE THINGS THE LONELY DO	*Island*	43	*15 Mar 86*	6
TOO GOOD TO BE FORGOTTEN	*Island*	5	*31 May 86*	13
MONTEGO BAY	*Island*	16	*13 Sep 86*	9
MONY MONY	*EMI*	38	*10 Oct 87*	5
ALBUMS:	**HITS 1**			**WEEKS 1**
AMAZULU	*Island*	97	*6 Dec 86*	1

AMBASSADORS OF FUNK featuring M.C. MARIO — UK

(See also Simon Harris.)

SINGLES:	**HITS 1**			**WEEKS 8**
SUPERMARIOLAND	*Living Beat*	8	*31 Oct 92*	8
Based upon the theme to the Nintendo game of the same name.				

AMBER — US

(See also Stars On 54: Ultra Nate, Amber, Jocelyn Enriquez.)

SINGLES:	HITS 1			WEEKS 2
SEXUAL	*Substance*	34	*24 Jun 00*	2

AMEN — US

SINGLES:	HITS 2			WEEKS 2
TOO HARD TO BE FREE	*Virgin*	72	*17 Feb 01*	1
THE WAITING 18	*Virgin*	61	*21 Jul 01*	1

AMEN CORNER — UK

SINGLES:	HITS 6			WEEKS 67
GIN HOUSE BLUES	*Deram*	12	*29 Jul 67*	10
THE WORLD OF BROKEN HEARTS	*Deram*	24	*14 Oct 67*	6
BEND ME SHAPE ME	*Deram*	3	*20 Jan 68*	12
Originally recorded by the Models.				
HIGH IN THE SKY	*Deram*	6	*3 Aug 68*	13
(IF PARADISE IS) HALF AS NICE	*Immediate*	1	*1 Feb 69*	11
HELLO SUZIE	*Immediate*	4	*28 Jun 69*	10
Originally recorded by Roy Wood.				
(IF PARADISE IS) HALF AS NICE [RI]	*Immediate*	34	*14 Feb 76*	5
ALBUMS:	**HITS 2**			**WEEKS 8**
ROUND AMEN CORNER	*Deram*	26	*30 Mar 68*	7
EXPLOSIVE COMPANY	*Immediate*	19	*1 Nov 69*	1

AMEN! UK — UK/Greece

SINGLES:	HITS 2			WEEKS 6
PASSION	*Feverpitch*	15	*8 Feb 97*	4
PEOPLE OF LOVE	*Feverpitch*	36	*28 Jun 97*	2

AMERICA — US/UK

SINGLES:	HITS 3			WEEKS 20
A HORSE WITH NO NAME	*Warner Brothers*	49	*18 Dec 71*	2
A HORSE WITH NO NAME [RE]	*Warner Brothers*	3	*8 Jan 72*	11
VENTURA HIGHWAY	*Warner Brothers*	43	*25 Nov 72*	4
YOU CAN DO MAGIC	*Capitol*	59	*6 Nov 82*	3
ALBUMS:	**HITS 4**			**WEEKS 22**
AMERICA	*Warner Brothers*	14	*22 Jan 72*	13
HOMECOMING	*Warner Brothers*	21	*9 Dec 72*	5
HAT TRICK	*Warner Brothers*	41	*10 Nov 73*	3
HISTORY - AMERICA'S GREATEST HITS	*Warner Brothers*	60	*7 Feb 76*	1

AMERICAN BREED — US

SINGLES:	HITS 1			WEEKS 6
BEND ME SHAPE ME	*Stateside*	24	*10 Feb 68*	6

AMERICAN HI-FI — US

SINGLES:	HITS 1			WEEKS 3
FLAVOR OF THE WEAK	*Mercury*	31	*8 Sep 01*	3

AMERICAN MUSIC CLUB — US

SINGLES:	HITS 2			WEEKS 4
JOHNNY MATHIS' FEET	*Virgin*	58	*24 Apr 93*	2
WISH THE WORLD AWAY	*Virgin*	46	*10 Sep 94*	2
ALBUMS:	**HITS 2**			**WEEKS 3**
MERCURY	*Virgin*	41	*27 Mar 93*	2
SAN FRANCISCO	*Virgin*	72	*24 Sep 94*	1

AMES BROTHERS with Hugo WINTERHALTER and his Orchestra — US

SINGLES:	HITS 1			WEEKS 6
THE NAUGHTY LADY OF SHADY LANE	*His Master's Voice*	6	*5 Feb 55*	6

AMIL Of MAJOR COINZ - See JAY-Z

AMIRA — US

SINGLES:	HITS 1			WEEKS 7
MY DESIRE	*VC Recordings*	51	*13 Dec 97*	1
MY DESIRE [RM-1ST]	*VC Recordings*	46	*8 Aug 98*	2
Remixed by Club Asylum.				
MY DESIRE [RM-2ND]	*VC Recordings*	20	*10 Feb 01*	4
Remixed by Dreemhouse.				

AMNESIA - See Frank O'MOIRAGHI featuring AMNESIA

Johnny AMOBI - See Jason DONOVAN

Cherie AMORE — France

SINGLES:	HITS 1			WEEKS 2
I DON'T WANT NOBODY (TELLIN' ME WHAT TO DO)	*Eternal*	33	*15 Apr 00*	2
Samples Inner Life.				

Vanessa AMOROSI — Australia

SINGLES:	HITS 1			WEEKS 10
ABSOLUTELY EVERYBODY	*Mercury*	7	*23 Sep 00*	10
Performed at the opening ceremony of the Olympic Games in Sydney, Australia, on 15 Sep 00.				

AMOS — UK

SINGLES:	HITS 5			WEEKS 12
ONLY SAW TODAY/INSTANT KARMA [M]	*Positiva*	48	*3 Sep 94*	2
LET LOVE SHINE	*Positiva*	31	*25 Mar 95*	2
CHURCH OF FREEDOM	*Positiva*	54	*7 Oct 95*	1
STAMP!	*Positiva*	11	*12 Oct 96*	5
ARGENTINA	*Positiva*	30	*31 May 97*	2
Above 2: Jeremy HEALY and AMOS.				

Tori AMOS — US

SINGLES:	HITS 14			WEEKS 64
SILENT ALL THESE YEARS	*East West*	51	*23 Nov 91*	3
CHINA	*East West*	51	*1 Feb 92*	2
WINTER	*East West*	25	*21 Mar 92*	4
CRUCIFY	*East West*	15	*20 Jun 92*	6
SILENT ALL THESE YEARS [RI]	*East West*	26	*22 Aug 92*	4
CORNFLAKE GIRL	*East West*	4	*22 Jan 94*	6
PRETTY GOOD YEAR	*East West*	7	*19 Mar 94*	4
PAST THE MISSION	*East West*	31	*28 May 94*	3
Vocals by Trent Reznor of Nine Inch Nails.				
GOD	*East West*	44	*15 Oct 94*	2
CAUGHT A LITE SNEEZE	*East West*	20	*13 Jan 96*	3
TALULA	*East West*	22	*23 Mar 96*	2
HEY JUPITER / PROFESSIONAL WIDOW	*East West*	20	*3 Aug 96*	9
Professional Widow mixed by Armand Van Holden.				
BLUE SKIES	*Perfecto*	26	*9 Nov 96*	2
Above hit: BT featuring Tori AMOS.				
PROFESSIONAL WIDOW (IT'S GOT TO BE BIG) [RI]	*East West*	1	*11 Jan 97*	10
SPARK	*Atlantic*	16	*2 May 98*	3
GLORY OF THE 80'S	*Atlantic*	46	*13 Nov 99*	1
ALBUMS:	**HITS 6**			**WEEKS 51**
LITTLE EARTHQUAKES	*East West*	14	*18 Jan 92*	23
UNDER THE PINK	*East West*	1	*12 Feb 94*	13
BOYS FOR PELE	*East West*	2	*3 Feb 96*	6
FROM THE CHOIRGIRL HOTEL	*Atlantic*	6	*16 May 98*	5
TO VENUS AND BACK	*Atlantic*	22	*2 Oct 99*	2
Comprises a studio set and live recordings from her 1998 'Plugged' tour.				
STRANGE LITTLE GIRLS	*Atlantic*	16	*29 Sep 01*	2

AMOURE - See WHO WANTS TO BE A MILLIONAIRE

AMPS — US

SINGLES:	HITS 1			WEEKS 1
TIPP CITY	*4AD*	61	*21 Oct 95*	1
ALBUMS:	**HITS 1**			**WEEKS 1**
PACER	*4AD*	60	*11 Nov 95*	1

AMY - See A.D.A.M. featuring AMY

ANADIN BROTHERS - See DOCTOR and the MEDICS

ANASTACIA — US

SINGLES:	HITS 5			WEEKS 38
I'M OUTTA LOVE	*Epic*	6	*30 Sep 00*	17
NOT THAT KIND	*Epic*	11	*3 Feb 01*	7
NOT THAT KIND [RE]	*Epic*	62	*31 Mar 01*	1
COWBOYS AND KISSES	*Epic*	28	*2 Jun 01*	5
MADE FOR LOVIN' YOU	*Epic*	27	*25 Aug 01*	3
PAID MY DUES	*Epic*	14	*1 Dec 01*	5
ALBUMS:	**HITS 2**			**WEEKS 54**
NOT THAT KIND	*Epic*	2	*14 Oct 00*	50
FREAK OF NATURE	*Epic*	14	*8 Dec 01*	4

. . . AND YOU WILL KNOW US BY THE TRAIL OF DEAD — US

SINGLES:	HITS 1			WEEKS 1
MISTAKES & REGRETS	*Domino Recordings*	69	*11 Nov 00*	1

AND WHY NOT? — UK

SINGLES:	HITS 3			WEEKS 18
RESTLESS DAYS (SHE SCREAMS OUT LOUD)	*Island*	38	*14 Oct 89*	7
THE FACE	*Island*	13	*13 Jan 90*	8
SOMETHING YOU GOT	*Island*	39	*21 Apr 90*	3
ALBUMS:	**HITS 1**			**WEEKS 3**
MOVE YOUR SKIN	*Island*	24	*10 Mar 90*	3

Angry ANDERSON — Australia

SINGLES:	HITS 1			WEEKS 13
SUDDENLY (THE WEDDING THEME FROM NEIGHBOURS)	*Food For Thought*	3	*19 Nov 88*	13

Played at the marriage of Scott (Jason Donovan) and Charlene (Kylie Minogue).

Carl ANDERSON — US

SINGLES:	HITS 1			WEEKS 4
BUTTERCUP	*Streetwave*	49	*8 Jun 85*	4

Carleen ANDERSON — US

SINGLES:	HITS 6			WEEKS 17
NERVOUS BREAKDOWN	*Circa*	27	*12 Feb 94*	4
MAMA SAID	*Circa*	26	*28 May 94*	4
TRUE SPIRIT	*Circa*	24	*13 Aug 94*	3
LET IT LAST	*Circa*	16	*14 Jan 95*	3
MAYBE I'M AMAZED	*Circa*	24	*7 Feb 98*	2
WOMAN IN ME	*Circa*	74	*25 Apr 98*	1
ALBUMS:	**HITS 3**			**WEEKS 7**
DUSKY SAPPHO [EP]	*Circa*	38	*13 Nov 93*	1
TRUE SPIRIT	*Circa*	12	*18 Jun 94*	4
BLESSED BURDEN	*Circa*	51	*2 May 98*	2

Gillian ANDERSON - See HAL featuring Gillian ANDERSON

Ian ANDERSON — UK

ALBUMS:	HITS 1			WEEKS 1
WALK INTO LIGHT	*Chrysalis*	78	*26 Nov 83*	1

John ANDERSON BIG BAND — UK

SINGLES:	HITS 1			WEEKS 5
GLENN MILLER MEDLEY [M]	*Modern*	63	*21 Dec 85*	2
GLENN MILLER MEDLEY [M] [RE]	*Modern*	61	*11 Jan 86*	3

John ANDERSON ORCHESTRA — Ireland

ALBUMS:	HITS 1			WEEKS 5
PAN PIPES - ROMANCE OF IRELAND	*MCA*	56	*25 Nov 95*	5

Jon ANDERSON — UK

(See also Anderson Bruford Wakeman Howe; Jon and Vangelis.)

ALBUMS:	HITS 3			WEEKS 19
OLIAS OF SUNHILLOW	*Atlantic*	8	*24 Jul 76*	10
SONG OF SEVEN	*Atlantic*	38	*15 Nov 80*	3
ANIMATION	*Polydor*	43	*5 Jun 82*	6

Laurie ANDERSON — US

SINGLES:	HITS 1			WEEKS 6
O SUPERMAN	*Warner Brothers*	2	*17 Oct 81*	6
ALBUMS:	**HITS 2**			**WEEKS 8**
BIG SCIENCE	*Warner Brothers*	29	*1 May 82*	6
MISTER HEARTBREAK	*Warner Brothers*	93	*10 Mar 84*	2

Leroy ANDERSON and his POPS CONCERT ORCHESTRA — US

SINGLES:	HITS 1			WEEKS 4
FORGOTTEN DREAMS	*Brunswick*	28	*29 Jun 57*	1
FORGOTTEN DREAMS [RE-1ST]	*Brunswick*	30	*13 Jul 57*	1
FORGOTTEN DREAMS [RE-2ND]	*Brunswick*	24	*7 Sep 57*	2

Lynn ANDERSON — US

INGLES:	HITS 1			WEEKS 20
OSE GARDEN	*CBS*	3	*20 Feb 71*	20
riginally recorded by Joe South.				
LBUMS:	**HITS 1**			**WEEKS 1**
OSE GARDEN	*CBS*	45	*17 Apr 71*	1

Moira ANDERSON — UK

ee also Harry Secombe and Moira Anderson.

INGLES:	HITS 1			WEEKS 2
OLY CITY	*Decca*	43	*27 Dec 69*	2
LBUMS:	**HITS 1**			**WEEKS 1**
HESE ARE MY SONGS	*Decca*	50	*20 Jun 70*	1

Sunshine ANDERSON — US

INGLES:	HITS 2			WEEKS 8
EARD IT ALL BEFORE	*Atlantic*	9	*2 Jun 01*	7
UNCH OR DINNER	*Atlantic*	57	*22 Sep 01*	1
LBUMS:	**HITS 1**			**WEEKS 6**
OUR WOMAN	*Atlantic*	39	*26 May 01*	6

ANDERSON BRUFORD WAKEMAN HOWE — UK

See also Jon Anderson; Steve Howe; Rick Wakeman.)

INGLES:	HITS 1			WEEKS 2
ROTHER OF MINE	*Arista*	63	*24 Jun 89*	2
LBUMS:	**HITS 1**			**WEEKS 6**
NDERSON BRUFORD WAKEMAN HOWE	*Arista*	14	*8 Jul 89*	6

Peter ANDRE — UK

INGLES:	HITS 10			WEEKS 83
URN IT UP	*Mushroom*	64	*10 Jun 95*	1
YSTERIOUS GIRL	*Mushroom*	53	*16 Sep 95*	2
hough Bubbler Ranx was credited on the re-issue, he was not credited on this release.				
NLY ONE	*Mushroom*	16	*16 Mar 96*	3
NLY ONE [RE]	*Mushroom*	69	*13 Apr 96*	1
YSTERIOUS GIRL [RI]	*Mushroom*	2	*1 Jun 96*	18
bove hit: Peter ANDRE featuring BUBBLER RANX.				
LAVA	*Mushroom*	1	*14 Sep 96*	9
FEEL YOU	*Mushroom*	1	*7 Dec 96*	9
FEEL YOU [RE-1ST]	*Mushroom*	65	*1 Mar 97*	1
ATURAL	*Mushroom*	6	*8 Mar 97*	8
FEEL YOU [RE-2ND]	*Mushroom*	74	*15 Mar 97*	1
ATURAL [RE-1ST]	*Mushroom*	58	*10 May 97*	1
ATURAL [RE-2ND]	*Mushroom*	68	*24 May 97*	2
LL ABOUT US	*Mushroom*	3	*9 Aug 97*	8
eatures rapper Little Bo Peep.				
LL ABOUT US [RE]	*Mushroom*	75	*1 Nov 97*	1
ONELY	*Mushroom*	6	*8 Nov 97*	5
ONELY [RE]	*Mushroom*	68	*3 Jan 98*	4
LL NIGHT ALL RIGHT	*Mushroom*	16	*24 Jan 98*	4
amples A Taste Of Honey's Boogie Oogie Oogie.				
Above hit: Peter ANDRE featuring Warren G.				
KISS THE GIRL	*Mushroom*	9	*25 Jul 98*	5
From the Walt Disney film 'The Little Mermaid'.				
ALBUMS:	**HITS 2**			**WEEKS 27**
NATURAL	*Mushroom*	1	*12 Oct 96*	23
TIME	*Mushroom*	28	*29 Nov 97*	4

Chris ANDREWS — UK

SINGLES:	HITS 5			WEEKS 36
YESTERDAY MAN	*Decca*	3	*9 Oct 65*	15
TO WHOM IT CONCERNS	*Decca*	13	*4 Dec 65*	10
SOMETHING ON MY MIND	*Decca*	45	*16 Apr 66*	1
SOMETHING ON MY MIND [RE]	*Decca*	41	*30 Apr 66*	2
WHAT'CHA GONNA DO NOW	*Decca*	40	*4 Jun 66*	4
STOP THAT GIRL	*Decca*	36	*27 Aug 66*	4

Eamonn ANDREWS with Ron GOODWIN and his Orchestra and Chorus — Ireland

SINGLES:	HITS 1			WEEKS 3
THE SHIFTING WHISPERING SANDS	*Parlophone*	18	*21 Jan 56*	3
Originally recorded by Billy Vaughn and his Orchestra.				

Julie ANDREWS — UK

(See also Various Artists: Films - Original Soundtracks 'Mary Poppins', 'The Sound Of Music', 'Thoroughly Modern Millie', 'Star! Stage Cast - Broadway 'My Fair Lady'; Studio Cast 'The King And I'.)

ALBUMS:	HITS 1			WEEKS
LOVE ME TENDER	*Peach River*	63	*16 Jul 83*	

ANEKA — UK

SINGLES:	HITS 2			WEEKS 1
JAPANESE BOY	*Hansa*	1	*8 Aug 81*	1
LITTLE LADY	*Hansa*	50	*7 Nov 81*	

Dave ANGEL — UK

SINGLES:	HITS 1			WEEKS
TOKYO STEALTH FIGHTER	*Fourth & Broadway*	58	*2 Aug 97*	

Simone ANGEL — Holland

SINGLES:	HITS 1			WEEKS
LET THIS FEELING	*A&M*	60	*13 Nov 93*	

ANGELETTES — UK

SINGLES:	HITS 1			WEEKS
DON'T LET HIM TOUCH YOU	*Decca*	35	*13 May 72*	

ANGELHEART — UK

SINGLES:	HITS 2			WEEKS
COME BACK TO ME	*Hi-Life*	68	*6 Apr 96*	
Above hit: ANGELHEART featuring Rochelle HARRIS.				
I'M STILL WAITING	*Hi-Life*	74	*22 Mar 97*	
Above hit: ANGELHEART featuring Aletia BOURNE.				

ANGELIC — UK

SINGLES:	HITS 3			WEEKS 1
IT'S MY TURN	*Serious*	11	*17 Jun 00*	1
From the film 'Brothers'.				
CAN'T KEEP ME SILENT	*Serious*	12	*24 Feb 01*	
STAY WITH ME	*Serious*	36	*10 Nov 01*	

ANGELIC UPSTARTS — UK

SINGLES:	HITS 7			WEEKS 30
I'M AN UPSTART	*Warner Brothers*	31	*21 Apr 79*	
TEENAGE WARNING	*Warner Brothers*	29	*11 Aug 79*	
NEVER 'AD NOTHIN'	*Warner Brothers*	52	*3 Nov 79*	4
OUT OF CONTROL	*Warner Brothers*	58	*9 Feb 80*	3
WE GOTTA GET OUT OF THIS PLACE	*Warner Brothers*	65	*22 Mar 80*	2
LAST NIGHT ANOTHER SOLDIER	*Zonophone*	51	*2 Aug 80*	4
KIDS ON THE STREET	*Zonophone*	57	*7 Feb 81*	3
ALBUMS:	**HITS 4**			**WEEKS 20**
TEENAGE WARNING	*Warner Brothers*	29	*18 Aug 79*	7
WE'VE GOTTA GET OUT OF THIS PLACE	*Warner Brothers*	54	*12 Apr 80*	3
2,000,000 VOICES	*Zonophone*	32	*27 Jun 81*	3
Title refers to UK unemployment figure.				
ANGELIC UPSTARTS	*Zonophone*	27	*26 Sep 81*	7

Bobby ANGELO and the TUXEDOS — UK

SINGLES:	HITS 1			WEEKS 6
BABY SITTIN'	*His Master's Voice*	30	*12 Aug 61*	6
Originally recorded by Myron Lee.				

ANGELS — US

SINGLES:	HITS 1			WEEKS 1
MY BOYFRIEND'S BACK	*Mercury*	50	*5 Oct 63*	1

ANGELS OF LIGHT - See PSYCHIC TV

ANGELWITCH — UK

SINGLES:	HITS 1			WEEKS 1
SWEET DANGER	*EMI*	75	*7 Jun 80*	1

ANIMAL — US

SINGLES:	HITS 1			WEEKS 3
WIPE OUT	*BMG Kidz*	38	*23 Jul 94*	3

ANIMALHOUSE — UK

SINGLES:	HITS 1			WEEKS 1
READY TO RECEIVE	*Boiler House!*	61	*15 Jul 00*	1

ANIMAL NIGHTLIFE — UK

SINGLES:	HITS 4			WEEKS 22
NATIVE BOY (UPTOWN)	*Inner Vision*	60	*13 Aug 83*	3
MR. SOLITARE	*Island*	25	*18 Aug 84*	12
LOVE IS JUST THE GREAT PRETENDER '85	*Island*	28	*6 Jul 85*	6
PREACHER, PREACHER	*Island*	67	*5 Oct 85*	1
ALBUMS:	**HITS 1**			**WEEKS 6**
SHANGRI-LA	*Island*	36	*24 Aug 85*	6

ANIMALS — UK

SINGLES:	HITS 15			WEEKS 147
BABY LET ME TAKE YOU HOME	*Columbia*	21	*18 Apr 64*	8
THE HOUSE OF THE RISING SUN	*Columbia*	1	*27 Jun 64*	12
Originally recorded by Josh White.				
I'M CRYING	*Columbia*	8	*19 Sep 64*	10
DON'T LET ME BE MISUNDERSTOOD	*Columbia*	3	*6 Feb 65*	9
Originally recorded by Nina Simone.				
BRING IT ON HOME TO ME	*Columbia*	7	*10 Apr 65*	11
Original by Sam Cooke reached No. 13 in the US in 1962.				
WE'VE GOTTA GET OUT OF THIS PLACE	*Columbia*	2	*17 Jul 65*	12
IT'S MY LIFE	*Columbia*	7	*30 Oct 65*	11
INSIDE-LOOKING OUT	*Decca*	12	*19 Feb 66*	8
DON'T BRING ME DOWN	*Decca*	6	*4 Jun 66*	8
HELP ME GIRL	*Decca*	14	*29 Oct 66*	10
WHEN I WAS YOUNG	*MGM*	45	*17 Jun 67*	3
GOOD TIMES	*MGM*	20	*9 Sep 67*	11
SAN FRANCISCAN NIGHTS	*MGM*	7	*21 Oct 67*	10
Above 4: Eric BURDON and the ANIMALS.				
SKY PILOT	*MGM*	40	*17 Feb 68*	3
Above hit: Eric BURDON.				
RING OF FIRE	*MGM*	35	*18 Jan 69*	5
Above hit: Eric BURDON and the ANIMALS.				
THE HOUSE OF THE RISING SUN [RI]	*RAK*	25	*7 Oct 72*	6
THE HOUSE OF THE RISING SUN [RI] [RE]	*RAK*	11	*18 Sep 82*	10
EPS:	**HITS 3**			**WEEKS 55**
THE ANIMALS IS HERE	*Columbia*	3	*9 Jan 65*	37
THE ANIMALS ARE BACK	*Columbia*	8	*23 Oct 65*	14
ANIMAL TRACKS	*Columbia*	7	*17 Sep 66*	4
ALBUMS:	**HITS 4**			**WEEKS 86**
THE ANIMALS	*Columbia*	6	*14 Nov 64*	20
ANIMAL TRACKS	*Columbia*	6	*22 May 65*	26
THE MOST OF THE ANIMALS	*Columbia*	4	*16 Apr 66*	20
ANIMALISMS	*Decca*	4	*28 May 66*	17
THE MOST OF THE ANIMALS [RI]	*Music For Pleasure*	18	*25 Sep 71*	3

ANIMOTION — US/UK

SINGLES:	HITS 1			WEEKS 12
OBSESSION	*Mercury*	5	*11 May 85*	12

Paul ANKA — Canada

SINGLES:	HITS 14			WEEKS 134
DIANA	*Columbia*	1	*10 Aug 57*	25
Written about his baby sitter Diana Ayoub.				
I LOVE YOU, BABY	*Columbia*	3	*9 Nov 57*	15
TELL ME THAT YOU LOVE ME	*Columbia*	25	*9 Nov 57*	2
Above 2 entries were separate sides of the same release, each had its own chart run.				
YOU ARE MY DESTINY	*Columbia*	6	*1 Feb 58*	13
CRAZY LOVE	*Columbia*	26	*31 May 58*	1
MIDNIGHT	*Columbia*	26	*27 Sep 58*	1
(ALL OF A SUDDEN) MY HEART SINGS	*Columbia*	10	*31 Jan 59*	13
Originally recorded by Kathryn Grayson in 1945.				
LONELY BOY	*Columbia*	3	*11 Jul 59*	17
From the film 'Girl's Town'.				

PUT YOUR HEAD ON MY SHOULDER	*Columbia*	7	*31 Oct 59*	12
IT'S TIME TO CRY	*Columbia*	28	*27 Feb 60*	1
From the film 'Girl's Town'.				
PUPPY LOVE	*Columbia*	33	*2 Apr 60*	4
IT'S TIME TO CRY [RI]	*Columbia*	47	*16 Apr 60*	1
PUPPY LOVE [RI]	*Columbia*	37	*7 May 60*	3
HELLO YOUNG LOVERS	*Columbia*	44	*17 Sep 60*	1
LOVE ME WARM AND TENDER	*RCA*	19	*17 Mar 62*	11
A STEEL GUITAR AND A GLASS OF WINE	*RCA*	41	*28 Jul 62*	4
Above hit: Paul ANKA with Ray ELLIS and his Orchestra.				
'YOU'RE' HAVING MY BABY	*United Artists*	6	*28 Sep 74*	10
Duet with Odia Coates.				

ANNETTE – See VARIOUS ARTISTS (EPs) 'The Further Adventures Of North – More Underground Dance EP'

ANNIHILATOR — UK

ALBUMS:	HITS 1			WEEKS 1
NEVER, NEVERLAND	*Roadrunner*	48	*11 Aug 90*	1

ANOTHER LEVEL — UK

SINGLES:	HITS 7			WEEKS 81
BE ALONE NO MORE	*Northwestside*	6	*28 Feb 98*	9
FREAK ME	*Northwestside*	1	*18 Jul 98*	12
GUESS I WAS A FOOL	*Northwestside*	5	*7 Nov 98*	13
I WANT YOU FOR MYSELF	*Northwestside*	2	*23 Jan 99*	8
Chart also credits Ghostface Killah.				
BE ALONE NO MORE [RM]	*Northwestside*	11	*10 Apr 99*	9
Remixed by Cutfather and Joe. CD2 has Holding Back The Years as the first track. Charity record in aid of Capital Radio's Help A London Child.				
Above hit: ANOTHER LEVEL featuring JAY Z.				
FROM THE HEART	*Northwestside*	6	*12 Jun 99*	10
From the film 'Notting Hill'.				
FROM THE HEART [RE]	*Northwestside*	74	*28 Aug 99*	1
SUMMERTIME	*Northwestside*	7	*4 Sep 99*	7
Above hit: ANOTHER LEVEL featuring TQ.				
BOMB DIGGY	*Northwestside*	6	*13 Nov 99*	12
Used as the theme music for Channel 4's 'North Hollywood High'.				
ALBUMS:	**HITS 2**			**WEEKS 40**
ANOTHER LEVEL	*Northwestside*	13	*21 Nov 98*	25
NEXUS . . .	*Northwestside*	7	*25 Sep 99*	15

Adam ANT — UK

SINGLES:	HITS 22			WEEKS 199
KINGS OF THE WILD FRONTIER	*CBS*	48	*2 Aug 80*	5
DOG EAT DOG	*CBS*	4	*11 Oct 80*	16
ANTMUSIC	*CBS*	2	*6 Dec 80*	18
YOUNG PARISIANS	*Decca*	9	*27 Dec 80*	13
Originally released in 1978.				
CARTROUBLE	*Do It*	33	*24 Jan 81*	9
Originally released in 1980.				
ZEROX	*Do It*	45	*24 Jan 81*	9
Originally released in 1979.				
KINGS OF THE WILD FRONTIER [RE]	*CBS*	2	*21 Feb 81*	13
STAND AND DELIVER	*CBS*	1	*9 May 81*	15
PRINCE CHARMING	*CBS*	1	*12 Sep 81*	12
ANT RAP	*CBS*	3	*12 Dec 81*	10
Above 10: ADAM and the ANTS.				
DEUTSCHER GIRLS	*E'G*	13	*27 Feb 82*	6
From the 1977 film 'Jubilee'.				
Above hit: Original ADAM and the ANTS.				
THE ANTMUSIC (EP) (THE B-SIDES) [EP]	*Do It*	46	*13 Mar 82*	4
Lead track: Friends.				
Above hit: ADAM and the ANTS.				
GOODY TWO SHOES	*CBS*	1	*22 May 82*	11
FRIEND OR FOE	*CBS*	9	*18 Sep 82*	8
DESPERATE BUT NOT SERIOUS	*CBS*	33	*27 Nov 82*	7
PUSS 'N BOOTS	*CBS*	5	*29 Oct 83*	11
STRIP	*CBS*	41	*10 Dec 83*	6
APOLLO 9	*CBS*	13	*22 Sep 84*	8
VIVE LE ROCK	*CBS*	50	*13 Jul 85*	4
ROOM AT THE TOP	*MCA*	13	*17 Feb 90*	7
CAN'T SET RULES ABOUT LOVE	*MCA*	47	*28 Apr 90*	2
WONDERFUL	*EMI*	32	*11 Feb 95*	3
GOTTA BE A SIN	*EMI*	48	*3 Jun 95*	2

ALBUMS:	HITS 10			WEEKS 157
KINGS OF THE WILD FRONTIER	*CBS*	1	*15 Nov 80*	66
DIRK WEARS WHITE SOX	*Do It*	16	*17 Jan 81*	29
PRINCE CHARMING	*CBS*	2	*14 Nov 81*	21
Above 3: ADAM and the ANTS.				
FRIEND OR FOE	*CBS*	5	*23 Oct 82*	12
STRIP	*CBS*	20	*19 Nov 83*	8
VIVE LE ROCK	*CBS*	42	*14 Sep 85*	3
MANNERS AND PHYSIQUE	*MCA*	19	*24 Mar 90*	3
ANTMUSIC - THE VERY BEST OF ADAM ANT	*Arcade*	6	*28 Aug 93*	11
Includes both solo and group material. From 26 Mar 94, album was repackaged with a live CD.				
WONDERFUL	*EMI*	24	*15 Apr 95*	2
THE VERY BEST OF ADAM AND THE ANTS	*Columbia*	56	*3 Apr 99*	2
Above hit: ADAM and the ANTS.				

ANT and DEC — UK

SINGLES:	HITS 14			WEEKS 81
TONIGHT I'M FREE	*XSRhythm*	62	*18 Dec 93*	3
Above hit: PJ and DUNCAN (BYKER GROVE).				
WHY ME?	*XSRhythm*	27	*23 Apr 94*	4
Above hit: PJ and DUNCAN (A.K.A. ANT and DECLAN).				
LET'S GET READY TO RHUMBLE	*XSRhythm*	9	*23 Jul 94*	11
IF I GIVE YOU MY NUMBER	*XSRhythm*	15	*8 Oct 94*	7
ETERNAL LOVE	*XSRhythm*	12	*3 Dec 94*	9
OUR RADIO ROCKS	*XSRhythm*	15	*25 Feb 95*	5
Above 4: PJ and DUNCAN A.K.A.				
STUCK ON U	*Telstar*	12	*29 Jul 95*	5
U KRAZY KATZ	*XSRhythm*	15	*14 Oct 95*	4
Features Jamiroquai's brass section.				
PERFECT	*Telstar*	16	*2 Dec 95*	7
STEPPING STONE	*Telstar*	11	*30 Mar 96*	5
Originally recorded by Paul Revere and the Raiders In 1966.				
Above 4: PJ and DUNCAN.				
BETTER WATCH OUT	*Telstar*	10	*24 Aug 96*	4
Above hit: The Cult Of . . . ANT and DEC.				
WHEN I FALL IN LOVE	*Telstar*	12	*23 Nov 96*	8
SHOUT	*Telstar*	10	*15 Mar 97*	5
Features Andy Bell of Erasure on backing vocals and samples Walk On The Wild Side by Lou Reed.				
FALLING	*Telstar*	14	*10 May 97*	4

ALBUMS:	HITS 3			WEEKS 31
PSYCHE - THE ALBUM	*XSRhythm*	5	*19 Nov 94*	20
Above hit: PJ and DUNCAN (AKA).				
TOP KATZ - THE ALBUM	*Telstar*	46	*18 Nov 95*	8
Above hit: PJ and DUNCAN.				
THE CULT OF ANT & DEC	*Telstar*	15	*24 May 97*	3

ANTARCTICA — Australia

SINGLES:	HITS 2			WEEKS 2
RETURN TO REALITY	*React*	53	*29 Jan 00*	1
ADRIFT (CAST YOUR MIND)	*React*	72	*8 Jul 00*	1

Mark ANTHONI - See FIRE ISLAND

Billie ANTHONY with Eric JUPP and his Orchestra — UK

SINGLES:	HITS 1			WEEKS 16
THIS OLE HOUSE	*Columbia*	4	*16 Oct 54*	16

Marc ANTHONY — US

SINGLES:	HITS 2			WEEKS 7
RIDE ON THE RHYTHM	*Atlantic*	71	*5 Oct 91*	1
Above hit: Little Louie VEGA and Marc ANTHONY.				
RIDE ON THE RHYTHM [RI]	*Atlantic*	70	*23 May 92*	1
Above hit: Louie VEGA and Marc ANTHONY.				
RIDE ON THE RHYTHM [RM]	*Perfecto Red*	36	*31 Jan 98*	2
Remixed by Mr. Roy.				
Above hit: "Little" LOUIE and Marc ANTHONY.				
I NEED TO KNOW	*Columbia*	28	*13 Nov 99*	3

Ray ANTHONY and his Orchestra — US

SINGLES:	HITS 1			WEEKS 2
DRAGNET	*Capitol*	7	*5 Dec 53*	1
DRAGNET [RE]	*Capitol*	11	*9 Jan 54*	1
Originally recorded by Henry Mancini.				

Richard ANTHONY — France

SINGLES:	HITS 2			WEEKS 15
WALKING ALONE	*Columbia*	37	*14 Dec 63*	5
IF I LOVED YOU	*Columbia*	48	*4 Apr 64*	1
From the film 'Carousel'.				
IF I LOVED YOU [RE]	*Columbia*	18	*25 Apr 64*	9
EPS:	**HITS 2**			**WEEKS 11**
RICHARD ANTHONY	*Columbia*	18	*2 May 64*	1
WALKIN' ALONE	*Columbia*	6	*11 Jul 64*	10

Truth ANTHONY - See Ronny JORDAN

ANTHRAX — US

SINGLES:	HITS 10			WEEKS 37
I AM THE LAW	*Island*	32	*28 Feb 87*	5
INDIANS	*Island*	44	*27 Jun 87*	4
I'M THE MAN (DEF UNCENSORED VERSION)	*Island*	20	*5 Dec 87*	6
MAKE ME LAUGH	*Island*	26	*10 Sep 88*	3
ANTI-SOCIAL	*Island*	44	*18 Mar 89*	3
IN MY WORLD	*Island*	29	*1 Sep 90*	2
GOT THE TIME	*Island*	16	*5 Jan 91*	4
Originally recorded by Joe Jackson.				
BRING THE NOISE	*Island*	14	*6 Jul 91*	5
Above hit: ANTHRAX featuring Chuck D from PUBLIC ENEMY.				
ONLY	*Elektra*	36	*8 May 93*	3
BLACK LODGE	*Elektra*	53	*11 Sep 93*	2
ALBUMS:	**HITS 6**			**WEEKS 23**
AMONG THE LIVING	*Island*	18	*18 Apr 87*	5
STATE OF EUPHORIA	*Island*	12	*24 Sep 88*	4
PERSISTENCE OF TIME	*Island*	13	*8 Sep 90*	5
ATTACK OF THE KILLER BS	*Island*	13	*20 Jul 91*	5
B-sides and remixes.				
SOUND OF WHITE NOISE	*Elektra*	14	*29 May 93*	3
VOLUME 8 - THE THREAT IS REAL!	*Ignition*	73	*1 Aug 98*	1

ANTI-NOWHERE LEAGUE

SINGLES:	HITS 3			WEEKS 10
STREETS OF LONDON	*WXYZ*	48	*23 Jan 82*	5
I HATE . . . PEOPLE	*WXYZ*	46	*20 Mar 82*	3
WOMAN	*WXYZ*	72	*3 Jul 82*	2
ALBUMS:	**HITS 2**			**WEEKS 12**
WE ARE . . . THE LEAGUE	*WXYZ*	24	*22 May 82*	11
LIVE IN YUGOSLAVIA	*Identity*	88	*5 Nov 83*	1

ANTI-PASTI — UK

SINGLES:	HITS 1			WEEKS 1
DON'T LET 'EM GRIND YOU DOWN EP (EXTRACTS FROM THE EDINBURGH LIVE NITE [EP]	*Superville*	70	*5 Dec 81*	1
Live recordings with one side for each group. there is no actual track listing.				
Above hit: EXPLOITED / ANTI-PASTI.				
ALBUMS:	**HITS 1**			**WEEKS 7**
THE LAST CALL	*Rondelet*	31	*15 Aug 81*	7

ANTICAPPELLA — Italy/UK

SINGLES:	HITS 4			WEEKS 12
$\sqrt[2]{231}$	*PWL Continental*	24	*16 Nov 91*	4
EVERYDAY	*PWL Continental*	45	*18 Apr 92*	2
MOVE YOUR BODY	*Media*	21	*25 Jun 94*	3
Above hit: ANTICAPPELLA (featuring MC FIXX IT).				
EXPRESS YOUR FREEDOM	*Media*	31	*1 Apr 95*	2
$\sqrt[2]{231}$ [RM] / MOVE YOUR BODY [RI]	*Media*	54	*25 May 96*	1
Remixed by Ben Keen and Paul Thompson.				

ANTONIA - See BOMB THE BASS

Miki ANTONY — UK

SINGLES:	HITS 1			WEEKS 7
IF IT WASN'T FOR THE REASON THAT I LOVE YOU	*Bell*	27	*3 Feb 73*	7

ANUNA and the RTE CONCERT ORCHESTRA - See Bill WHELAN

A1 — UK/Norway

SINGLES:	HITS 7			WEEKS 74
BE THE FIRST TO BELIEVE	*Columbia*	6	*3 Jul 99*	9

SUMMERTIME OF OUR LIVES	*Columbia*	5	*11 Sep 99*	6
SUMMERTIME OF OUR LIVES [RE]	*Columbia*	62	*13 Nov 99*	2
EVERYTIME / READY OR NOT	*Columbia*	3	*20 Nov 99*	11
LIKE A ROSE	*Columbia*	6	*4 Mar 00*	12
TAKE ON ME	*Columbia*	1	*9 Sep 00*	10
SAME OLD BRAND NEW YOU	*Columbia*	1	*18 Nov 00*	10
TAKE ON ME [RE]	*Columbia*	69	*2 Dec 00*	1
NO MORE	*Columbia*	6	*3 Mar 01*	8
NO MORE [RE]	*Columbia*	64	*12 May 01*	5

ALBUMS:	**HITS 2**			**WEEKS 17**
HERE WE COME	*Columbia*	20	*4 Dec 99*	8
THE A LIST	*Columbia*	14	*2 Dec 00*	9

APACHE INDIAN

UK

SINGLES:	**HITS 10**			**WEEKS 33**
FE REAL	*Ten Records*	33	*28 Nov 92*	3
[AA] listed with Just Wanna Know by Maxi Priest.				
Above hit: Maxi PRIEST and APACHE INDIAN.				
ARRANGED MARRIAGE	*Island*	16	*2 Jan 93*	6
CHOK THERE	*Island*	30	*27 Mar 93*	4
NUFF VIBES [EP]	*Island*	5	*14 Aug 93*	10
Lead track: Caste System, though Boom Shack A Lak received more airplay.				
MOVIN' ON	*Island*	48	*23 Oct 93*	2
A response to the election of a right wing candidate to Tower Hamlets council.				
WRECKX SHOP	*MCA*	26	*7 May 94*	2
Above hit: WRECKX 'N' EFFECT (featuring APACHE INDIAN).				
MAKE WAY FOR THE INDIAN	*Island*	29	*11 Feb 95*	2
Above hit: APACHE INDIAN and Tim DOG.				
RAGGAMUFFIN GIRL	*Island*	31	*22 Apr 95*	2
Above hit: APACHE INDIAN with Frankie PAUL.				
LOVIN' (LET ME LOVE YOU)	*Coalition*	53	*29 Mar 97*	1
Vocals by Sameera Singh.				
REAL PEOPLE	*Coalition*	66	*18 Oct 97*	1

ALBUMS:	**HITS 1**			**WEEKS 2**
NO RESERVATIONS	*Island*	36	*6 Feb 93*	2

APHEX TWIN

UK

(See also Polygon Window.)

SINGLES:	**HITS 7**			**WEEKS 13**
DIGERIDOO	*R&S*	55	*9 May 92*	2
ON	*Warp*	32	*27 Nov 93*	3
VENTOLIN	*Warp*	49	*8 Apr 95*	1
GIRL/BOY [EP]	*Warp*	64	*26 Oct 96*	1
Lead track: Girl Boy. With 6 tracks, it should have qualified as an entry to the album charts.				
COME TO DADDY	*Warp*	36	*18 Oct 97*	2
WINDOWLICKER	*Warp*	16	*3 Apr 99*	3
Above hit: APHEXTWIN.				
2 REMIXES BY AFX	*Men 1*	69	*11 Aug 01*	1
Above hit: AFX.				

ALBUMS:	**HITS 5**			**WEEKS 10**
SELECTED AMBIENT WORKS VOLUME II	*Warp*	11	*19 Mar 94*	3
CLASSICS	*R&S*	24	*11 Feb 95*	2
Compilation of early tracks.				
. . . I CARE BECAUSE YOU DO	*Warp*	24	*6 May 95*	2
RICHARD D. JAMES ALBUM	*Warp*	62	*16 Nov 96*	1
DRUKQS	*Warp*	22	*3 Nov 01*	2

APHRODITE'S CHILD

Greece

SINGLES:	**HITS 1**			**WEEKS 7**
RAIN AND TEARS	*Mercury*	29	*9 Nov 68*	7

APOLLO FOUR FORTY

UK

SINGLES:	**HITS 11**			**WEEKS 52**
ASTRAL AMERICA	*Stealth Sonic*	36	*22 Jan 94*	2
LIQUID COOL (THEME FROM CRYONIC SUSPENSION)	*Stealth Sonic*	35	*5 Nov 94*	2
(DON'T FEAR) THE REAPER	*Stealth Sonic*	35	*25 Mar 95*	2
Above 3: APOLLO 440.				
KRUPA	*Stealth Sonic*	23	*27 Jul 96*	4
Tribute to jazz drummer Gene Krupa.				
KRUPA [RE]	*Stealth Sonic*	24	*28 Sep 96*	4
AIN'T TALKIN' 'BOUT DUB	*Stealth Sonic*	7	*15 Feb 97*	7
Samples Van Halen's Ain't Talking About Love.				
RAW POWER	*Stealth Sonic*	32	*5 Jul 97*	3

RENDEZ-VOUS 98 *Theme to ITV's sports coverage of the World Cup 1998.* *Above hit: Jean Michel JARRE and APOLLO FOUR FORTY.*	*Epic*	12	*11 Jul 98*	6
LOST IN SPACE (THEME) *From the film of the same name.*	*Stealth Sonic*	4	*8 Aug 98*	9
STOP THE ROCK *Vocals by Mary Mary (former lead singer with Gaye Bykers On Acid). Based on Status Quo's Caroline.*	*Stealth Sonic*	10	*28 Aug 99*	6
HEART GO BOOM	*Stealth Sonic*	57	*27 Nov 99*	1
CHARLIE'S ANGELS 2000 – THEME FROM THE MOTION PICTURE *From the film 'Charlie's Angels'.*	*Stealth Sonic*	29	*9 Dec 00*	6
ALBUMS:	**HITS 2**			**WEEKS 4**
ELECTRO GLIDE IN BLUE	*Stealth Sonic*	62	*15 Mar 97*	1
GETTIN' HIGH ON YOUR OWN SUPPLY	*Stealth Sonic*	20	*18 Sep 99*	3

APOLLO presents – See HOUSE OF VIRGINISM

APOLLO 2000 — UK

ALBUMS:	**HITS 1**			**WEEKS 3**
OUT OF THIS WORLD *Instrumental music from science fiction films and TV.*	*Telstar*	43	*27 Apr 96*	3

Carmine APPICE – See Jeff BECK, Tim BOGERT and Carmine APPICE

Fiona APPLE — US

SINGLES:	**HITS 1**			**WEEKS 2**
FAST AS YOU CAN	*Columbia*	33	*26 Feb 00*	2
ALBUMS:	**HITS 1**			**WEEKS 1**
WHEN THE PAWN HITS THE CONFLICTS HE THINKS LIKE A KING WHAT HE KNOWS THROWS THE BLOWS WHEN HE GOES TO THE FIGHT AND HE'LL WIN THE WHOLE THING 'FORE HE ENTERS THE RING THERE'S NOBODY TO BATTER WHEN YOUR MIND IS YOUR MIGHT SO WHEN YOU GO SOLO YOU HOLD YOUR OWN HAND AND REMEMBER THAT DEPTH IS THE GREATEST OF HEIGHTS AND IF YOU KNOW WHERE YOU STAND THEN YOU KNOW WHERE TO LAND AND IF YOU FALL IT WON'T MATTER CUZ YOU'LL KNOW THAT YOU'RE RIGHT	*Columbia*	46	*11 Mar 00*	1

Stan APPLEBAUM and His ORCHESTRA – See Neil SEDAKA

Kim APPLEBY — UK

(See also Mel and Kim.)

SINGLES:	**HITS 7**			**WEEKS 31**
DON'T WORRY	*Parlophone*	2	*3 Nov 90*	10
G.L.A.D.	*Parlophone*	10	*9 Feb 91*	6
MAMA	*Parlophone*	19	*29 Jun 91*	8
IF YOU CARED	*Parlophone*	44	*19 Oct 91*	3
LIGHT OF THE WORLD	*Parlophone*	41	*31 Jul 93*	2
BREAKAWAY	*Parlophone*	56	*13 Nov 93*	1
FREE SPIRIT	*Parlophone*	51	*12 Nov 94*	1
ALBUMS:	**HITS 1**			**WEEKS 13**
KIM APPLEBY	*Parlophone*	23	*8 Dec 90*	13

APPLEJACKS — UK

SINGLES:	**HITS 3**			**WEEKS 29**
TELL ME WHEN	*Decca*	7	*7 Mar 64*	13
LIKE DREAMERS DO *Written by Lennon/McCartney.*	*Decca*	20	*13 Jun 64*	11
THREE LITTLE WORDS (I LOVE YOU)	*Decca*	23	*17 Oct 64*	5

APPLES — UK

SINGLES:	**HITS 1**			**WEEKS 1**
EYE WONDER	*Epic*	75	*23 Mar 91*	1

Charlie APPLEWHITE with Victor YOUNG and his Orchestra and Chorus — US

SINGLES:	**HITS 1**			**WEEKS 1**
BLUE STAR *Theme to the TV series 'The Medic'.*	*Brunswick*	20	*24 Sep 55*	1

Helen APRIL – See John DUMMER and Helen APRIL

APRIL WINE — Canada

SINGLES:	**HITS 2**			**WEEKS 9**
I LIKE TO ROCK	*Capitol*	41	*15 Mar 80*	5
JUST BETWEEN YOU AND ME	*Capitol*	52	*11 Apr 81*	4

ALBUMS:	HITS 2			WEEKS 8
HARDER . . . FASTER	*Capitol*	34	*15 Mar 80*	5
THE NATURE OF THE BEAST	*Capitol*	48	*24 Jan 81*	3

AQUA — Denmark/Norway

SINGLES:	HITS 7			WEEKS 85
BARBIE GIRL	*Universal*	1	*25 Oct 97*	24
DOCTOR JONES	*Universal*	1	*7 Feb 98*	14
BARBIE GIRL [RE]	*Universal*	66	*25 Apr 98*	2
TURN BACK TIME	*Universal*	1	*16 May 98*	10
From the film 'Sliding Doors'.				
MY OH MY	*Universal*	6	*1 Aug 98*	9
MY OH MY [RE]	*Universal*	66	*17 Oct 98*	2
GOOD MORNING SUNSHINE	*Universal*	18	*26 Dec 98*	7
CARTOON HEROES	*Universal*	7	*26 Feb 00*	9
CARTOON HEROES [RE]	*Universal*	73	*13 May 00*	2
AROUND THE WORLD	*Universal*	26	*10 Jun 00*	6

ALBUMS:	HITS 2			WEEKS 49
AQUARIUM	*Universal*	6	*15 Nov 97*	47
AQUARIUS	*Universal*	24	*11 Mar 00*	2

AQUA MARINA - See F.A.B.

AQUAGEN - See WARP BROTHERS

AQUARIAN DREAM — US

SINGLES:	HITS 1			WEEKS 1
YOU'RE A STAR	*Elektra*	67	*24 Feb 79*	1

ARAB STRAP — UK

SINGLES:	HITS 4			WEEKS 4
THE GIRLS OF SUMMER [EP]	*Chemikal Underground*	74	*13 Sep 97*	1
Lead track: Hey! Fever.				
HERE WE GO / TRIPPY	*Chemikal Underground*	48	*4 Apr 98*	1
Trippy credits Tremendon O'Hare.				
(AFTERNOON) SOAPS	*Chemikal Underground*	74	*10 Oct 98*	1
LOVE DETECTIVE - MOTION PICTURE SOUNDTRACK	*Chemikal Underground*	66	*10 Feb 01*	1
Sleeve has additional title credit: If You've Nothing To Hide . . . Why Hide It?				

ALBUMS:	HITS 1			WEEKS 2
PHILOPHOBIA	*Chemikal Underground*	37	*2 May 98*	2

ARCADIA — UK

SINGLES:	HITS 3			WEEKS 13
ELECTION DAY	*Parlophone Odean Series*	7	*26 Oct 85*	7
Includes narration by Grace Jones.				
THE PROMISE	*Parlophone Odean Series*	37	*25 Jan 86*	4
THE FLAME	*Parlophone Odean Series*	58	*26 Jul 86*	2

ALBUMS:	HITS 1			WEEKS 10
SO RED THE ROSE	*Parlophone Odean Series*	30	*7 Dec 85*	10

Tasmin ARCHER — UK

SINGLES:	HITS 6			WEEKS 37
SLEEPING SATELLITE	*EMI*	1	*12 Sep 92*	15
SLEEPING SATELLITE [RE]	*EMI*	67	*2 Jan 93*	2
IN YOUR CARE	*EMI*	16	*20 Feb 93*	6
LORDS OF THE NEW CHURCH	*EMI*	26	*29 May 93*	4
ARIENNE	*EMI*	30	*21 Aug 93*	4
SHIPBUILDING	*EMI*	40	*8 Jan 94*	4
Sleeve also gives title as an EP.				
ONE MORE GOOD NIGHT WITH THE BOYS	*EMI*	45	*23 Mar 96*	2

ALBUMS:	HITS 1			WEEKS 42
GREAT EXPECTATIONS	*EMI*	8	*31 Oct 92*	42

ARCHIES — US

SINGLES:	HITS 1			WEEKS 26
SUGAR, SUGAR	*RCA Victor*	1	*11 Oct 69*	26
Originally written for and rejected by the Monkees.				

ARCHITECHS — UK

SINGLES:	HITS 2			WEEKS 19
BODY GROOVE	*Go.Beat*	3	*7 Oct 00*	14
Above hit: ARCHITECHS featuring NANA.				
SHOW ME THE MONEY	*Go.Beat*	20	*7 Apr 01*	4
SHOW ME THE MONEY [RE]	*Go.Beat*	65	*18 Aug 01*	1

Jann ARDEN — Canada

SINGLES:	HITS 1			WEEKS 2
INSENSITIVE *From the film 'Bed Of Roses'.*	*A&M*	40	*13 Jul 96*	2

Tina ARENA — Australia

SINGLES:	HITS 8			WEEKS 32
CHAINS	*Columbia*	6	*15 Apr 95*	11
HEAVEN HELP MY HEART	*Columbia*	25	*12 Aug 95*	5
SHOW ME HEAVEN	*Columbia*	29	*2 Dec 95*	3
SORRENTO MOON (I REMEMBER)	*Columbia*	22	*3 Aug 96*	4
WHISTLE DOWN THE WIND *From the Andrew Lloyd Webber/Jim Steinman musical of the same name.*	*Really Useful*	24	*27 Jun 98*	5
IF I WAS A RIVER	*Columbia*	43	*24 Oct 98*	2
BURN	*Columbia*	47	*13 Mar 99*	1
LIVE FOR THE ONE I LOVE *From the English production of the French musical 'Notre Dame De Paris'.*	*Columbia*	63	*20 May 00*	1
ALBUMS:	**HITS 1**			**WEEKS 15**
DON'T ASK	*Columbia*	11	*20 May 95*	15

ARGENT — UK

(See also San Jose featuring Rodriguez Argentina; Silsoe.)

SINGLES:	HITS 3			WEEKS 27
HOLD YOUR HEAD UP	*Epic*	5	*4 Mar 72*	12
TRAGEDY	*Epic*	34	*10 Jun 72*	7
GOD GAVE ROCK AND ROLL TO YOU	*Epic*	18	*24 Mar 73*	8
ALBUMS:	**HITS 2**			**WEEKS 9**
ALL TOGETHER NOW	*Epic*	13	*29 Apr 72*	8
IN DEEP	*Epic*	49	*31 Mar 73*	1

India. ARIE — US

SINGLES:	HITS 2			WEEKS 5
VIDEO	*Motown*	32	*30 Jun 01*	3
BROWN SKIN	*Motown*	29	*20 Oct 01*	2
ALBUMS:	**HITS 1**			**WEEKS 3**
ACOUSTIC SOUL	*Motown*	55	*7 Jul 01*	3

ARIEL — UK

SINGLES:	HITS 1			WEEKS 2
LET IT SLIDE	*Deconstruction*	57	*27 Mar 93*	2

ARIEL — UK

SINGLES:	HITS 2			WEEKS 4
DEEP (I'M FALLING DEEPER) *Originally released in 1992 on the Pilot Music label.*	*Wonderboy*	47	*21 Jun 97*	1
A9	*Essential Recordings*	28	*17 Jun 00*	3

ARIZONA featuring ZEITIA — UK

SINGLES:	HITS 1			WEEKS 1
I SPECIALIZE IN LOVE	*Union*	74	*12 Mar 94*	1

Ship's Company and Royal Marine Band Of H.M.S. ARK ROYAL — UK

SINGLES:	HITS 1			WEEKS 6
THE LAST FAREWELL *Conductor: W.O. Keith Whittall.*	*BBC*	46	*23 Dec 78*	6

ARKARNA — UK

SINGLES:	HITS 2			WEEKS 3
HOUSE ON FIRE	*WEA*	33	*25 Jan 97*	2
SO LITTLE TIME	*WEA*	46	*2 Aug 97*	1

Joan ARMATRADING — UK

SINGLES:	HITS 10			WEEKS 53
LOVE AND AFFECTION	*A&M*	10	*16 Oct 76*	9
ROSIE	*A&M*	49	*23 Feb 80*	5
ME MYSELF I	*A&M*	21	*14 Jun 80*	11
ALL THE WAY FROM AMERICA	*A&M*	54	*6 Sep 80*	3
I'M LUCKY	*A&M*	46	*12 Sep 81*	5
NO LOVE	*A&M*	50	*16 Jan 82*	5
DROP THE PILOT	*A&M*	11	*19 Feb 83*	10
TEMPTATION	*A&M*	65	*16 Mar 85*	2

MORE THAN ONE KIND OF LOVE	*A&M*	75	*26 May 90*	1
WRAPPED AROUND HER	*A&M*	56	*23 May 92*	2
ALBUMS:	**HITS 14**			**WEEKS 193**
JOAN ARMATRADING	*A&M*	12	*4 Sep 76*	27
SHOW SOME EMOTION	*A&M*	6	*1 Oct 77*	11
TO THE LIMIT	*A&M*	13	*14 Oct 78*	10
ME MYSELF I	*A&M*	5	*24 May 80*	23
WALK UNDER LADDERS	*A&M*	6	*12 Sep 81*	29
THE KEY	*A&M*	10	*12 Mar 83*	14
TRACK RECORD	*A&M*	18	*26 Nov 83*	32
SECRET SECRETS	*A&M*	14	*16 Feb 85*	12
SLEIGHT OF HAND	*A&M*	34	*24 May 86*	6
THE SHOUTING STAGE	*A&M*	28	*16 Jul 88*	10
HEARTS AND FLOWERS	*A&M*	29	*16 Jun 90*	4
THE VERY BEST OF JOAN ARMATRADING	*A&M*	9	*16 Mar 91*	11
SQUARE THE CIRCLE	*A&M*	34	*20 Jun 92*	2
WHAT'S INSIDE	*RCA*	48	*10 Jun 95*	2

ARMIN

Holland

SINGLES:	**HITS 2**			**WEEKS 4**
BLUE FEAR	*Xtravaganza*	45	*14 Feb 98*	1
COMMUNICATON	*AM:PM*	18	*12 Feb 00*	3

ARMOURY SHOW

UK

SINGLES:	**HITS 3**			**WEEKS 6**
CASTLES IN SPAIN	*Parlophone*	69	*25 Aug 84*	2
WE CAN BE BRAVE AGAIN	*Parlophone*	66	*26 Jan 85*	1
LOVE IN ANGER	*Parlophone*	63	*17 Jan 87*	3
ALBUMS:	**HITS 1**			**WEEKS 1**
WAITING FOR THE FLOODS	*Parlophone*	57	*21 Sep 85*	1

Craig ARMSTRONG - See Shola AMA

Louis ARMSTRONG

US

(See also Various Artists: Films – Original Soundtracks 'The Five Pennies'.)

SINGLES:	**HITS 8**			**WEEKS 93**
TAKES TWO TO TANGO	*Brunswick*	6	*20 Dec 52*	10
A THEME FROM THE THREEPENNY OPERA (MACK THE KNIFE)	*Philips*	8	*14 Apr 56*	11
TAKE IT SATCH [EP] *Lead track: Tiger Rag. First hit single released in a picture sleeve.*	*Philips*	29	*16 Jun 56*	1
THE FAITHFUL HUSSAR	*Philips*	27	*14 Jul 56*	2
MACK THE KNIFE (THE THEME FROM THE THREEPENNY OPERA) [RI] *Above 4: Louis ARMSTRONG and his ALL STARS.*	*Philips*	24	*7 Nov 59*	1
HELLO, DOLLY! *From the musical of the same name.* *Above hit: Louis ARMSTRONG and the ALL STARS.*	*London*	4	*6 Jun 64*	14
WHAT A WONDERFUL WORLD / CABARET *Cabaret listed from 17 Feb 68.* *Above hit: Louis ARMSTRONG ORCHESTRA and CHORUS/Louis ARMSTRONG and his ALL STARS.*	*His Master's Voice*	1	*10 Feb 68*	29
THE SUNSHINE OF LOVE	*Stateside*	41	*29 Jun 68*	7
WHAT A WONDERFUL WORLD [RI] *From the film 'Good Morning Vietnam'.*	*A&M*	53	*16 Apr 88*	5
WE HAVE ALL THE TIME IN THE WORLD *Originally from the James Bond film 'On Her Majesty's Secret Service', re-issued after its inclusion in a Guinness TV commercial.*	*EMI*	3	*19 Nov 94*	11
WE HAVE ALL THE TIME IN THE WORLD [RE]	*EMI*	66	*18 Mar 95*	2
ALBUMS:	**HITS 7**			**WEEKS 29**
SATCHMO PLAYS KING OLIVER	*Audio Fidelity*	20	*22 Oct 60*	1
JAZZ CLASSICS	*Ace Of Hearts*	20	*28 Oct 61*	1
HELLO DOLLY	*London*	11	*27 Jun 64*	6
WHAT A WONDERFUL WORLD	*Stateside*	37	*16 Nov 68*	3
THE VERY BEST OF LOUIS ARMSTRONG	*Warwick*	30	*20 Feb 82*	3
THE ULTIMATE COLLECTION	*Bluebird*	48	*21 May 94*	3
WE HAVE ALL THE TIME IN THE WORLD - THE VERY BEST OF LOUIS ARMSTRONG	*EMI*	10	*17 Dec 94*	12

ARMY OF LOVERS

Sweden/France

SINGLES:	**HITS 3**			**WEEKS 12**
CRUCIFIED	*Ton Son Ton*	47	*17 Aug 91*	5
OBSESSION	*Ton Son Ton*	67	*28 Dec 91*	1
CRUCIFIED [RI]	*Ton Son Ton*	31	*15 Feb 92*	5
RIDE THE BULLET	*Ton Son Ton*	67	*18 Apr 92*	1

ARNEE and the TERMINATERS — UK

SINGLES:	HITS 1			WEEKS
I'LL BE BACK	*Epic*	5	*24 Aug 91*	[illegible]

ARNIE'S LOVE — US

SINGLES:	HITS 1			WEEKS
I'M OUT OF YOUR LIFE	*Streetwave*	67	*26 Nov 83*	[illegible]

David ARNOLD — UK

SINGLES:	HITS 4			WEEKS 1[illegible]
PLAY DEAD	*Island*	12	*23 Oct 93*	[illegible]
From the film 'The Young Americans'.				
Above hit: BJORK and David ARNOLD.				
ON HER MAJESTY'S SECRET SERVICE	*East West*	7	*18 Oct 97*	[illegible]
Above hit: PROPELLERHEADS/David ARNOLD.				
DIAMONDS ARE FOREVER	*East West*	39	*22 Nov 97*	[illegible]
Above hit: David McALMONT/David ARNOLD.				
THEME FROM RANDALL AND HOPKIRK (DECEASED)	*Island*	49	*29 Apr 00*	[illegible]
Theme from the BBC1 TV series starring Vic Reeves and Bob Mortimer.				
Above hit: Nina PERSSON and David ARNOLD.				
ALBUMS:	**HITS 2**			**WEEKS 1[illegible]**
INDEPENDENCE DAY [OST]	*RCA Victor*	71	*17 Aug 96*	[illegible]
SHAKEN AND STIRRED	*East West*	11	*1 Nov 97*	[illegible]
Reworked James Bond themes.				

Eddy ARNOLD — US

SINGLES:	HITS 3			WEEKS 2[illegible]
MAKE THE WORLD GO AWAY	*RCA Victor*	8	*19 Feb 66*	1[illegible]
Originally recorded by Ray Price.				
I WANT TO GO WITH YOU	*RCA Victor*	49	*28 May 66*	[illegible]
I WANT TO GO WITH YOU [RE]	*RCA Victor*	46	*11 Jun 66*	[illegible]
IF YOU WERE MINE MARY	*RCA Victor*	49	*30 Jul 66*	[illegible]

P.P. ARNOLD — US

SINGLES:	HITS 7			WEEKS 47
THE FIRST CUT IS THE DEEPEST	*Immediate*	18	*6 May 67*	10
THE TIME HAS COME	*Immediate*	47	*5 Aug 67*	2
(IF YOU THINK) YOU'RE GROOVY	*Immediate*	41	*27 Jan 68*	4
ANGEL OF THE MORNING	*Immediate*	29	*13 Jul 68*	11
BURN IT UP	*Rhythm King*	14	*24 Sep 88*	10
Above hit: BEATMASTERS with P.P. ARNOLD.				
EVAPOR 8	*Network*	6	*11 Apr 92*	6
Above hit: ALTERN 8 Guest Vocal P.P. ARNOLD.				
IT'S A BEAUTIFUL THING	*MCA*	12	*28 Feb 98*	4
Above hit: OCEAN COLOUR SCENE with PP ARNOLD.				

ARPEGGIO — US

SINGLES:	HITS 1			WEEKS 3
LOVE AND DESIRE	*Polydor*	63	*31 Mar 79*	3

ARRESTED DEVELOPMENT — US

SINGLES:	HITS 4			WEEKS 39
TENNESSEE	*Cooltempo*	46	*16 May 92*	4
TENNESSEE [RE]	*Cooltempo*	54	*11 Jul 92*	3
PEOPLE EVERYDAY	*Cooltempo*	2	*24 Oct 92*	14
Originally recorded by Sly & The Family Stone.				
MR. WENDAL / REVOLUTION	*Cooltempo*	4	*9 Jan 93*	9
TENNESSEE [RI]	*Cooltempo*	18	*3 Apr 93*	6
EASE MY MIND	*Cooltempo*	33	*28 May 94*	3
ALBUMS:	**HITS 3**			**WEEKS 40**
3 YEARS, 5 MONTHS AND 2 DAYS IN THE LIFE OF ARRESTED DEVELOPMENT	*Cooltempo*	3	*31 Oct 92*	34
Title refers to the time it took for the band to get a recording contract.				
UNPLUGGED	*Cooltempo*	40	*10 Apr 93*	3
ZINGALAMDUNI	*Cooltempo*	16	*18 Jun 94*	3

Steve ARRINGTON — US

SINGLES:	HITS 2			WEEKS 19
FEEL SO REAL	*Atlantic*	5	*27 Apr 85*	10
DANCIN' IN THE KEY OF LIFE	*Atlantic*	21	*6 Jul 85*	8
DANCIN' IN THE KEY OF LIFE [RE]	*Atlantic*	75	*7 Sep 85*	1
ALBUMS:	**HITS 1**			**WEEKS 11**
DANCIN' IN THE KEY OF LIFE	*Atlantic*	41	*13 Apr 85*	11

ARRIVAL — UK

SINGLES:	HITS 2			WEEKS 20
FRIENDS *Originally recorded by Terry Reid.*	*Decca*	8	*10 Jan 70*	9
I WILL SURVIVE	*Decca*	16	*6 Jun 70*	11

ARROLA – See RUFF DRIVERZ

ARROW — Montserrat

SINGLES:	HITS 2			WEEKS 15
HOT-HOT-HOT	*Cooltempo*	59	*28 Jul 84*	5
LONG TIME	*London*	30	*13 Jul 85*	7
HOT HOT HOT [RM] *Remixed by Les Adams.*	*The Hit Label*	38	*3 Sep 94*	3

ARROWS — US

SINGLES:	HITS 2			WEEKS 16
TOUCH TOO MUCH	*RAK*	8	*25 May 74*	9
MY LAST NIGHT WITH YOU	*RAK*	25	*1 Feb 75*	7

ARSENAL F.C. — UK

SINGLES:	HITS 4			WEEKS 16
GOOD OLD ARSENAL *Above hit: ARSENAL 1ST TEAM SQUAD.*	*Pye*	16	*8 May 71*	7
SHOUTING FOR THE GUNNERS *Above hit: ARSENAL F.A. CUP FINAL SQUAD '93 featuring Tippa IRIE and Peter HUNNINGDALE.*	*London*	34	*15 May 93*	3
HOT STUFF	*Grapevine*	9	*23 May 98*	5
ARSENAL NUMBER ONE (ADAPTED FROM MAMBO NO. 5)/OUR GOAL *Arsenal Number One is based on Lou Bega's Mambo No. 5, Our Goal has vocals by Irish tenor Finbar Wright and former Gunners striker Ian Wright. Released to coincide with their UEFA Cup Final appearance on 17 May 2000 (they lost on penalties to Galatasaray).*	*Grapevine*	46	*3 Jun 00*	1

ART COMPANY — Holland

SINGLES:	HITS 1			WEEKS 11
SUSANNA	*Epic*	12	*26 May 84*	11

ART OF NOISE — UK

SINGLES:	HITS 12			WEEKS 65
CLOSE (TO THE EDIT)	*ZTT*	8	*24 Nov 84*	19
MOMENTS IN LOVE / BEAT BOX *Beat Box originally reached No. 92 in 1984.*	*ZTT*	51	*13 Apr 85*	4
LEGS	*China*	69	*9 Nov 85*	1
PETER GUNN *Above hit: ART OF NOISE featuring Duane EDDY.*	*China*	8	*22 Mar 86*	9
PARANOIMIA *Above hit: ART OF NOISE with Max HEADROOM.*	*China*	12	*21 Jun 86*	9
DRAGNET	*China*	60	*18 Jul 87*	4
KISS *Above hit: ART OF NOISE featuring Tom JONES.*	*China*	5	*29 Oct 88*	7
YEBO! *Above hit: ART OF NOISE featuring MAHLATHINI and the MAHOTELLA QUEENS.*	*China*	63	*12 Aug 89*	3
ART OF LOVE	*China*	67	*16 Jun 90*	1
INSTRUMENTS OF DARKNESS (ALL OF US ARE ONE PEOPLE)	*China*	45	*11 Jan 92*	5
SHADES OF PARANOIMIA *Homage to the French poet Charles Baudelaire. Includes narration by John Hurt.* *Above hit: ART OF NOISE Your Forecaster: RAKIM.*	*China*	53	*29 Feb 92*	2

ALBUMS:	HITS 4			WEEKS 37
(WHO'S AFRAID OF?) THE ART OF NOISE	*ZTT*	27	*3 Nov 84*	17
IN VISIBLE SILENCE	*China*	18	*26 Apr 86*	15
IN NO SENSE/NONSENSE	*China*	55	*10 Oct 87*	2
THE BEST OF THE ART OF NOISE	*China*	55	*3 Dec 88*	3

ART OF TRANCE — UK

SINGLES:	HITS 1			WEEKS 3
MADAGASGA	*Platipus*	69	*31 Oct 98*	1
MADAGASCAR [RM] *Remixed by Ferry Corsten.*	*Platipus*	48	*7 Aug 99*	2

ARTEMESIA — Holland

(See also Ethics; Moving Melodies; Subliminal Cuts.)

SINGLES:	HITS 1			WEEKS 4
BITS + PIECES	*Hooj Choons*	46	*15 Apr 95*	2

BITS + PIECES [RE]	*Hooj Choons*	75	*23 Sep 95*	1
BITS + PIECES [RI]	*Tidy Trax*	51	*12 Aug 00*	1

Track 1 is the original edit, additional mixes by Hi-Jackers and Tidy Boys.
Above hit: MOVIN' MELODIES presents ARTEMESIA.

ARTFUL DODGER — UK

SINGLES:	HITS 7			WEEKS 69
RE-REWIND THE CROWD SAY BO SELECTA *Chart – though not the single – credited vocalist Craig David.*	*Relentless*	2	*11 Dec 99*	17
MOVIN TOO FAST *Above hit: ARTFUL DODGER and Romina JOHNSON.*	*Locked On*	2	*4 Mar 00*	11
MOVIN TOO FAST [RE]	*Locked On*	64	*10 Jun 00*	1
WOMAN TROUBLE *Above hit: ARTFUL DODGER and Robbie CRAIG featuring Craig DAVID.*	*ffrr*	6	*15 Jul 00*	10
PLEASE DON'T TURN ME ON *Above hit: ARTFUL DODGER featuring vocals by LIFFORD.*	*ffrr*	4	*25 Nov 00*	10
THINK ABOUT ME *Above hit: ARTFUL DODGER featuring Michelle ESCOFFERY.*	*ffrr*	11	*17 Mar 01*	8
TWENTYFOURSEVEN *Above hit: ARTFUL DODGER featuring Melanie BLATT.*	*ffrr*	6	*15 Sep 01*	9
IT AIN'T ENOUGH *Above hit: DREEM TEEM vs ARTFUL DODGER featuring MZ MAY & MC ALISTAIR.*	*ffrr*	20	*15 Dec 01*	3

ALBUMS:	HITS 1			WEEKS 27
IT'S ALL ABOUT THE STRAGGLERS	*ffrr*	24	*2 Dec 00*	22
IT'S ALL ABOUT THE STRAGGLERS [RE]	*ffrr*	18	*29 Sep 01*	5

Neil ARTHUR — UK

SINGLES:	HITS 1			WEEKS 2
I LOVE I HATE	*Chrysalis*	50	*5 Feb 94*	2

ARTIST - See PRINCE

ARTISTS AGAINST AIDS WORLDWIDE — US/Canada/Australia/Ireland

SINGLES:	HITS 1			WEEKS 7
WHAT'S GOING ON	*Columbia*	6	*17 Nov 01*	7

ARTISTS UNITED AGAINST APARTHEID — Multi-National

SINGLES:	HITS 1			WEEKS 8
SUN CITY *Charity assembly for the Africa Fund.*	*Manhattan*	21	*23 Nov 85*	8

ASCENSION — UK

SINGLES:	HITS 1			WEEKS 3
SOMEONE *Based around Barber's Adagio For Strings.*	*Perfecto*	55	*5 Jul 97*	1
SOMEONE [RM] *Remixed by Steve Helstrip. Vocals by Joanna Law.*	*Code Blue*	43	*15 Jul 00*	2

ASEND - See DEAD DRED featuring ASEND and ULTRAVIBE

ASH — UK

SINGLES:	HITS 12			WEEKS 53
KUNG FU	*Infectious*	57	*1 Apr 95*	1
GIRL FROM MARS	*Infectious*	11	*12 Aug 95*	5
ANGEL INTERCEPTOR	*Infectious*	14	*21 Oct 95*	4
GOLDFINGER	*Infectious*	5	*27 Apr 96*	5
OH YEAH	*Infectious*	6	*6 Jul 96*	7
OH YEAH [RE]	*Infectious*	69	*28 Sep 96*	1
A LIFE LESS ORDINARY *From the film of the same name.*	*Infectious*	10	*25 Oct 97*	5
JESUS SAYS	*Infectious*	15	*3 Oct 98*	4
WILD SURF	*Infectious*	31	*5 Dec 98*	2
SHINING LIGHT	*Infectious*	8	*10 Feb 01*	4
BURN BABY BURN	*Infectious*	13	*14 Apr 01*	6
SOMETIMES	*Infectious*	21	*21 Jul 01*	6
CANDY *Samples Make It Easy On Yourself by The Walker Brothers.*	*Infectious*	20	*13 Oct 01*	3

ALBUMS:	HITS 3			WEEKS 56
1977	*Infectious*	1	*18 May 96*	27
NU-CLEAR SOUNDS	*Infectious*	7	*17 Oct 98*	4
FREE ALL ANGELS	*Infectious*	1	*5 May 01*	25

Leslie ASH - See QUENTIN and ASH

ASHA — Italy

SINGLES:	HITS 1			WEEKS 2
J.J. TRIBUTE *Tribute to Janis Joplin.*	*Ffrreedom*	38	*8 Jul 95*	2

ASHAYE — UK

SINGLES:	HITS 1			WEEKS 3
DON'T STOP TIL YOU GET ENOUGH (MICHAEL JACKSON MEDLEY) [M]	*Record Shack*	45	*15 Oct 83*	3

Richard ASHCROFT — UK

SINGLES:	HITS 3			WEEKS 18
A SONG FOR THE LOVERS	*Hut*	3	*15 Apr 00*	10
MONEY TO BURN	*Hut*	17	*24 Jun 00*	4
A SONG FOR THE LOVERS [RE]	*Hut*	61	*1 Jul 00*	1
C'MON PEOPLE (WE'RE MAKING IT NOW)	*Hut*	21	*23 Sep 00*	3
ALBUMS:	**HITS 1**			**WEEKS 20**
ALONE WITH EVERYBODY	*Hut*	1	*8 Jul 00*	20

Harry ASHER D - See O.B.I. PROJECT featuring Harry ASHER D and DJ WHAT?

John ASHER — UK

SINGLES:	HITS 1			WEEKS 6
LET'S TWIST AGAIN	*Creole*	14	*15 Nov 75*	6

ASHFORD and SIMPSON — UK

SINGLES:	HITS 3			WEEKS 22
IT SEEMS TO HANG ON	*Warner Brothers*	48	*18 Nov 78*	4
SOLID	*Capitol*	3	*5 Jan 85*	15
BABIES	*Capitol*	56	*20 Apr 85*	3
ALBUMS:	**HITS 1**			**WEEKS 6**
SOLID	*Capitol*	42	*16 Feb 85*	6

ASHTON, GARDNER AND DYKE — UK

SINGLES:	HITS 1			WEEKS 14
THE RESURRECTION SHUFFLE	*Capitol*	3	*16 Jan 71*	14

ASIA — UK

SINGLES:	HITS 3			WEEKS 13
HEAT OF THE MOMENT	*Geffen*	46	*3 Jul 82*	5
ONLY TIME WILL TELL	*Geffen*	54	*18 Sep 82*	3
DON'T CRY	*Geffen*	33	*13 Aug 83*	5
ALBUMS:	**HITS 3**			**WEEKS 50**
ASIA	*Geffen*	11	*10 Apr 82*	38
ALPHA	*Geffen*	5	*20 Aug 83*	11
ASTRA	*Geffen*	68	*14 Dec 85*	1

ASIA BLUE — UK

SINGLES:	HITS 1			WEEKS 2
ESCAPING	*Atomic*	50	*27 Jun 92*	2

ASIAN DUB FOUNDATION — UK

SINGLES:	HITS 5			WEEKS 7
FREE SATPAL RAM *In 1986 Satpal Ram was attacked by six fascists, he fought back killing one and is serving a life sentence.*	*ffrr*	56	*21 Feb 98*	1
BUZZIN'	*ffrr*	31	*2 May 98*	2
BLACK WHITE	*ffrr*	52	*4 Jul 98*	1
REAL GREAT BRITAIN	*ffrr*	41	*18 Mar 00*	2
NEW WAY, NEW LIFE *Tribute to the 60s TV programme 'Naya Zindagi Naya Jeeva', the first UK show for British Asians.*	*ffrr*	49	*3 Jun 00*	1
ALBUMS:	**HITS 2**			**WEEKS 6**
RAFI'S REVENGE *Remix/repackage of their 1997 album R.A.F.I., dedicated to Bollywood singer Mohamed Rafi.*	*ffrr*	20	*23 May 98*	3
COMMUNITY MUSIC	*ffrr*	20	*1 Apr 00*	3

ASSEMBLY — UK

SINGLES:	HITS 1			WEEKS 10
NEVER NEVER	*Mute*	4	*12 Nov 83*	10

ASSOCIATES — UK

SINGLES:	HITS 7			WEEKS 47
PARTY FEARS TWO	*Associates*	9	*20 Feb 82*	10
CLUB COUNTRY	*Associates*	13	*8 May 82*	10
18 CARAT LOVE AFFAIR / LOVE HANGOVER	*Associates*	21	*7 Aug 82*	8
Love Hangover no longer listed from 28 Aug 82.				
THOSE FIRST IMPRESSIONS	*WEA*	43	*16 Jun 84*	6
WAITING FOR THE LOVEBOAT	*WEA*	53	*1 Sep 84*	4
BREAKFAST	*WEA*	49	*19 Jan 85*	6
HEART OF GLASS	*WEA*	56	*17 Sep 88*	3

ALBUMS:	HITS 3			WEEKS 28
SULK	*Associates*	10	*22 May 82*	20
PERHAPS	*WEA*	23	*16 Feb 85*	7
WILD AND LONELY	*Circa*	71	*31 Mar 90*	1

ASSOCIATION — US

SINGLES:	HITS 1			WEEKS 8
TIME FOR LIVIN'	*Warner Brothers*	23	*25 May 68*	8

Rick ASTLEY — UK

SINGLES:	HITS 12			WEEKS 91
NEVER GONNA GIVE YOU UP	*RCA*	1	*8 Aug 87*	18
WHENEVER YOU NEED SOMEBODY	*RCA*	3	*31 Oct 87*	12
Originally recorded by Ochi Brown in 1985.				
WHEN I FALL IN LOVE / MY ARMS KEEP MISSING YOU	*RCA*	2	*12 Dec 87*	10
When I Fall In Love listed only until 9 Jan 88 after which My Arms Keep Missing You was the side listed. When I Fall In Love originally recorded by Doris Day.				
TOGETHER FOREVER	*RCA*	2	*27 Feb 88*	9
SHE WANTS TO DANCE WITH ME	*RCA*	6	*24 Sep 88*	10
TAKE ME TO YOUR HEART	*RCA*	8	*26 Nov 88*	10
HOLD ME IN YOUR ARMS	*RCA*	10	*11 Feb 89*	8
CRY FOR HELP	*RCA*	7	*26 Jan 91*	7
MOVE RIGHT OUT	*RCA*	58	*30 Mar 91*	2
NEVER KNEW LOVE	*RCA*	70	*29 Jun 91*	1
THE ONES YOU LOVE	*RCA*	48	*4 Sep 93*	2
HOPELESSLY	*RCA*	33	*13 Nov 93*	2

ALBUMS:	HITS 3			WEEKS 62
WHENEVER YOU NEED SOMEBODY	*RCA*	1	*28 Nov 87*	34
HOLD ME IN YOUR ARMS	*RCA*	8	*10 Dec 88*	19
FREE	*RCA*	9	*2 Mar 91*	9

ASTRO TRAX TEAM featuring Shola PHILLIPS — UK

SINGLES:	HITS 1			WEEKS 1
THE ENERGY (FEEL THE VIBE)	*Satellite*	74	*24 Oct 98*	1

ASWAD — UK

SINGLES:	HITS 16			WEEKS 80
CHASING FOR THE BREEZE	*Island*	51	*3 Mar 84*	3
54-46 (WAS MY NUMBER)	*Island*	70	*6 Oct 84*	3
Originally recorded by the Maytals.				
DON'T TURN AROUND	*Island*	1	*27 Feb 88*	12
Original version by Tina Turner.				
GIVE A LITTLE LOVE	*Mango*	11	*21 May 88*	8
Original version by Albert Hammond.				
SET THEM FREE	*Mango*	70	*24 Sep 88*	2
BEAUTY'S ONLY SKIN DEEP	*Mango*	31	*1 Apr 89*	6
ON AND ON	*Mango*	25	*22 Jul 89*	8
Original by Stephen Bishop reached No. 11 in the US in 1977.				
NEXT TO YOU	*Mango*	24	*18 Aug 90*	6
SMILE	*Mango*	53	*17 Nov 90*	2
Above hit: ASWAD featuring Sweetie IRIE.				
TOO WICKED [EP]	*Mango*	61	*30 Mar 91*	2
Lead track: Best Of My Love.				
HOW LONG	*Polydor*	31	*31 Jul 93*	5
Above hit: YAZZ and ASWAD.				
DANCE HALL MOOD	*Bubblin'*	48	*9 Oct 93*	2
SHINE	*Bubblin'*	5	*18 Jun 94*	14
WARRIORS	*Bubblin'*	33	*17 Sep 94*	3
YOU'RE NO GOOD	*Bubblin'*	35	*18 Feb 95*	3
IF I WAS	*Bubblin'*	58	*5 Aug 95*	1

ALBUMS:	HITS 9			WEEKS 60
NOT SATISFIED	*CBS*	50	*24 Jul 82*	6
LIVE AND DIRECT	*Island*	57	*10 Dec 83*	16
REBEL SOULS	*Island*	48	*3 Nov 84*	2

TO THE TOP	*Simba*	71	*28 Jun 86*	3
DISTANT THUNDER	*Mango*	10	*9 Apr 88*	15
RENAISSANCE	*Stylus*	52	*3 Dec 88*	8
TOO WICKED	*Mango*	51	*29 Sep 90*	2
RISE AND SHINE	*Bubblin'*	38	*9 Jul 94*	5
GREATEST HITS	*Bubblin'*	20	*12 Aug 95*	3

AT THE DRIVE-IN — US

SINGLES:	HITS 3			WEEKS 3
ONE ARMED SCISSOR	*Grand Royal*	64	*19 Aug 00*	1
ROLODEX PROPAGANDA	*Grand Royal*	54	*16 Dec 00*	1
INVALID LETTER DEPT.	*Grand Royal*	50	*24 Mar 01*	1
ALBUMS:	**HITS 1**			**WEEKS 2**
RELATIONSHIP OF COMMAND	*Grand Royal*	33	*30 Sep 00*	2

Gali ATARI – See MILK and HONEY featuring Gali ATARI

ATB — Germany

SINGLES:	HITS 5			WEEKS 52
(9PM) 'TIL I COME *German import.*	*Data*	68	*13 Mar 99*	1
9PM (TILL I COME) *Austrian import.*	*Club Tools*	72	*22 May 99*	3
9PM (TILL I COME)	*DanceNet*	63	*19 Jun 99*	1
9PM (TILL I COME) [RE]	*Club Tools*	47	*19 Jun 99*	2
9PM (TILL I COME) [RM] *Remixed by Andre 'ATB' Tanneberger.*	*Sound Of Ministry*	1	*3 Jul 99*	15
DON'T STOP *Import. Vocals by Yolanda Rivera.*	*Club Tools*	61	*9 Oct 99*	2
DON'T STOP [RM]	*Sound Of Ministry*	3	*23 Oct 99*	9
DON'T STOP [RM][RE] *Different mix.*	*Sound Of Ministry*	48	*1 Jan 00*	4
KILLER	*Sound Of Ministry*	4	*25 Mar 00*	8
KILLER [RE]	*Sound Of Ministry*	74	*17 Jun 00*	1
THE FIELDS OF LOVE *Above hit: ATB featuring YORK.*	*Club Tools*	16	*27 Jan 01*	4
LET U GO *Vocals by Roberta Carter.*	*Kontor*	34	*30 Jun 01*	2
ALBUMS:	**HITS 1**			**WEEKS 3**
MOVIN MELODIES *Album was first released in November 1999 but was excluded from the chart because it contained a free CD-ROM.*	*Sound Of Ministry*	32	*8 Apr 00*	3

ATHENIANS – See Nana MOUSKOURI

ATHLETICO SPIZZ 80 — UK

ALBUMS:	HITS 1			WEEKS 5
DO A RUNNER	*A&M*	27	*26 Jul 80*	5

Chet ATKINS — US

(See also Chet Atkins and Mark Knopfler.)

SINGLES:	HITS 1			WEEKS 2
TEENSVILLE	*RCA*	46	*19 Mar 60*	1
TEENSVILLE [RE]	*RCA*	49	*7 May 60*	1
EPS:	**HITS 1**			**WEEKS 1**
GUITAR GENIUS	*RCA Victor*	19	*21 Dec 63*	1
ALBUMS:	**HITS 3**			**WEEKS 5**
THE OTHER CHET ATKINS	*RCA*	20	*18 Mar 61*	1
CHET ATKINS' WORKSHOP	*RCA*	19	*17 Jun 61*	1
CARIBBEAN GUITAR	*RCA Victor*	17	*25 Feb 63*	3

Chet ATKINS and Mark KNOPFLER — US

(See also Chet Atkins; Mark Knopfler.)

ALBUMS:	HITS 1			WEEKS 11
NECK AND NECK	*CBS*	41	*24 Nov 90*	11

Rowan ATKINSON — UK

ALBUMS:	HITS 1			WEEKS 9
LIVE IN BELFAST	*Arista*	44	*7 Feb 81*	9

ATLANTA RHYTHM SECTION — US

SINGLES:	HITS 1			WEEKS 4
SPOOKY	*Polydor*	48	*27 Oct 79*	4

Originally recorded by Mike Sharpe.

ATLANTIC OCEAN — Holland

SINGLES:	HITS 3			WEEKS 14
WATERFALL	*Eastern Bloc*	22	*19 Feb 94*	6
BODY IN MOTION	*Eastern Bloc*	15	*2 Jul 94*	4
MUSIC IS A PASSION	*Eastern Bloc*	59	*26 Nov 94*	1
Vocals by Farida and Rowetta.				
WATERFALL [RI]	*Eastern Bloc*	21	*30 Nov 96*	3

ATLANTIC STARR — US

SINGLES:	HITS 8			WEEKS 48
GIMME YOUR LUVIN'	*A&M*	66	*9 Sep 78*	3
SILVER SHADOW	*A&M*	41	*29 Jun 85*	6
ONE LOVE	*A&M*	58	*7 Sep 85*	4
SECRET LOVERS	*A&M*	10	*15 Mar 86*	12
IF YOUR HEART IS'NT IN IT	*A&M*	48	*24 May 86*	4
ALWAYS	*Warner Brothers*	3	*13 Jun 87*	14
ONE LOVER AT A TIME	*Warner Brothers*	57	*12 Sep 87*	3
EVERYBODY'S GOT SUMMER	*Arista*	36	*27 Aug 94*	2
ALBUMS:	**HITS 3**			**WEEKS 19**
AS THE BAND TURNS	*A&M*	64	*15 Jun 85*	3
THE ARTISTS VOLUME 2	*Street Sounds*	45	*13 Jul 85*	4
Compilation album with tracks by each artist.				
Above hit: Luther VANDROSS/Teddy PENDERGRASS/CHANGE/ATLANTIC STARR.				
ALL IN THE NAME OF LOVE	*Warner Brothers*	48	*11 Jul 87*	12

ATLANTIS vs AVATAR featuring Miriam STOCKLEY — UK/South Africa

SINGLES:	HITS 1			WEEKS 2
FIJI	*Inferno*	52	*28 Oct 00*	2

Samples Miriam Stockley's vocals from Praise's Only You.

Natacha ATLAS – See Jean Michel JARRE

ATMOSFEAR — UK

SINGLES:	HITS 1			WEEKS 7
DANCING IN OUTER SPACE	*MCA*	46	*17 Nov 79*	7

ATOMIC KITTEN — UK

SINGLES:	HITS 6			WEEKS 63
RIGHT NOW	*Innocent*	10	*11 Dec 99*	9
SEE YA	*Innocent*	6	*8 Apr 00*	6
SEE YA [RE]	*Innocent*	74	*1 Jul 00*	1
I WANT YOUR LOVE	*Innocent*	10	*15 Jul 00*	5
Samples the City Of Prague Philharmonic Orchestra's The Big Country and the KLF's Justified And Ancient.				
FOLLOW ME	*Innocent*	20	*21 Oct 00*	5
WHOLE AGAIN	*Innocent*	1	*10 Feb 01*	22
WHOLE AGAIN [RE]	*Innocent*	73	*21 Jul 01*	1
ETERNAL FLAME	*Innocent*	1	*4 Aug 01*	14
ALBUMS:	**HITS 1**			**WEEKS 24**
RIGHT NOW	*Innocent*	39	*4 Nov 00*	4
RIGHT NOW [RE]	*Innocent*	1	*18 Aug 01*	20

Repackaged with two extra tracks.

ATOMIC ROOSTER — UK

SINGLES:	HITS 2			WEEKS 25
TOMORROW NIGHT	*B&C*	11	*6 Feb 71*	12
DEVIL'S ANSWER	*B&C*	4	*10 Jul 71*	13
ALBUMS:	**HITS 3**			**WEEKS 13**
ATOMIC ROOSTER	*B&C*	49	*13 Jun 70*	1
DEATH WALKS BEHIND YOU	*Charisma*	12	*16 Jan 71*	8
IN HEARING OF ATOMIC ROOSTER	*Pegasus*	18	*21 Aug 71*	4

Winifred ATWELL and her 'Other Piano' — UK

(See also All Star Hit Parade.)

SINGLES:	HITS 15			WEEKS 117
BRITTANNIA RAG	*Decca*	11	*13 Dec 52*	1
BRITTANNIA RAG [RE]	*Decca*	5	*10 Jan 53*	5

ORONATION RAG	*Decca*	12	*16 May 53*	1
ORONATION RAG [RE]	*Decca*	5	*30 May 53*	5
LIRTATION WALTZ	*Decca*	12	*26 Sep 53*	1
LIRTATION WALTZ [RE-1ST]	*Decca*	10	*10 Oct 53*	1
LIRTATION WALTZ [RE-2ND]	*Decca*	12	*7 Nov 53*	1
ET'S HAVE A PARTY [M]	*Philips*	2	*5 Dec 53*	9
ACHMANINOFF'S 18TH VARIATION ON A THEME BY PAGANINI *rom the film 'The Story Of Three Loves'.* *bove hit: Winifred ATWELL with Wally STOTT and his Orchestra (and re-entry below).*	*Philips*	9	*24 Jul 54*	7
ACHMANINOFF'S 18TH VARIATION ON A THEME BY PAGANINI [RE]	*Philips*	19	*2 Oct 54*	2
ET'S HAVE A PARTY [M] [RE]	*Philips*	14	*27 Nov 54*	6
ET'S HAVE ANOTHER PARTY [M]	*Philips*	1	*27 Nov 54*	8
ET'S HAVE A DING DONG [M]	*Decca*	3	*5 Nov 55*	10
HE POOR PEOPLE OF PARIS	*Decca*	1	*17 Mar 56*	16
ORT-AU-PRINCE *bove hit: Winifred ATWELL and Frank CHACKSFIELD.*	*Decca*	18	*19 May 56*	6
HE LEFT BANK (C'EST A HAMBOURG)	*Decca*	14	*21 Jul 56*	7
AKE IT A PARTY [M]	*Decca*	7	*27 Oct 56*	12
ET'S ROCK 'N' ROLL [M]	*Decca*	28	*23 Feb 57*	2
ET'S ROCK 'N' ROLL [M] [RE]	*Decca*	24	*16 Mar 57*	2
ET'S HAVE A BALL [M]	*Decca*	4	*7 Dec 57*	6
HE SUMMER OF THE SEVENTEENTH DOLL	*Decca*	24	*8 Aug 59*	2
IANO PARTY [M]	*Decca*	10	*28 Nov 59*	7

AU PAIRS — UK

LBUMS:	HITS 2		WEEKS 10	
LAYING WITH A DIFFERENT SEX	*Human*	33	*6 Jun 81*	7
ENSE AND SENSUALITY	*Kamera*	79	*4 Sep 82*	3

AUDIOWEB — UK

INGLES:	HITS 8		WEEKS 12	
LEEPER	*Mother*	74	*14 Oct 95*	1
EAH?	*Mother*	73	*9 Mar 96*	1
NTO MY WORLD	*Mother*	42	*15 Jun 96*	1
LEEPER [RI]	*Mother*	50	*19 Oct 96*	2
ANKROBBER	*Mother*	19	*15 Feb 97*	2
AKER	*Mother*	70	*24 May 97*	1
OLICEMAN SKANK . . . (THE STORY OF MY LIFE)	*Mother*	21	*25 Apr 98*	2
ERSONAL FEELING	*Mother*	65	*4 Jul 98*	1
EST THE THEORY	*Mother*	56	*20 Feb 99*	1
LBUMS:	**HITS 1**		**WEEKS 1**	
UDIOWEB	*Mother*	70	*9 Nov 96*	1

Brian AUGER – See Julie DRISCOLL, Brian AUGER and the TRINITY

URA – See POPPERS present AURA

AURORA — UK

INGLES:	HITS 2		WEEKS 12	
HEAR YOU CALLING *Vocals by Sally Anne Marsh.*	*Additive*	71	*5 Jun 99*	1
HEAR YOU CALLING [RI] *Edited version of original.*	*Positiva*	17	*5 Feb 00*	4
ORDINARY WORLD *Above hit: AURORA featuring Naimee COLEMAN.*	*Positiva*	5	*23 Sep 00*	7

AURRA — US

SINGLES:	HITS 2		WEEKS 18	
LIKE I LIKE IT	*10 Records*	51	*4 May 85*	5
YOU AND ME TONIGHT	*10 Records*	12	*19 Apr 86*	8
LIKE I LIKE IT [RM] *Remixed by Timmy Reggisford and Boyd Jarvis.*	*10 Records*	43	*21 Jun 86*	5

Adam AUSTIN — UK

SINGLES:	HITS 1		WEEKS 1	
CENTERFOLD	*Power Station*	41	*13 Feb 99*	1

David AUSTIN — UK

SINGLES:	HITS 1		WEEKS 3	
TURN TO GOLD	*Parlophone*	68	*21 Jul 84*	3

Patti AUSTIN — US

(See also Quincy Jones.)

SINGLES:	HITS 2		WEEKS
BABY, COME TO ME *Above hit: Patti AUSTIN and James INGRAM.*	*Qwest*	11	*12 Feb 83*
I'LL KEEP YOUR DREAMS ALIVE *Above hit: George BENSON and Patti AUSTIN.*	*Ammi*	68	*5 Sep 92*
ALBUMS:	**HITS 1**		**WEEKS**
EVERY HOME SHOULD HAVE ONE	*Qwest*	99	*26 Sep 81*

AUTECHRE — UK

SINGLES:	HITS 1		WEEKS
BASSCAD [EP] *Various mixes of the track Basscadetmxs spread over 3 10"/1 CD formats.*	*Warp*	56	*7 May 94*

AUTEURS — UK

SINGLES:	HITS 5		WEEKS
LENNY VALENTINO	*Hut*	41	*27 Nov 93*
CHINESE BAKERY	*Hut*	42	*23 Apr 94*
BACK WITH THE KILLER [EP] *Lead track: Unsolved Child Murder.*	*Hut*	45	*6 Jan 96*
LIGHT AIRCRAFT ON FIRE	*Hut*	58	*24 Feb 96*
THE RUBETTES	*Hut*	66	*3 Jul 99*
ALBUMS:	**HITS 3**		**WEEKS**
NEW WAVE	*Hut*	35	*6 Mar 93*
NOW I'M A COWBOY	*Hut*	27	*21 May 94*
AFTER MURDER PARK	*Hut*	53	*16 Mar 96*

AUTUMN — UK

SINGLES:	HITS 1		WEEKS
MY LITTLE GIRL	*Pye*	37	*16 Oct 71*

Peter AUTY – See SNOWMAN

AVALANCHES — Australia

SINGLES:	HITS 2		WEEKS 1	
SINCE I LEFT YOU	*XL Recordings*	16	*7 Apr 01*	
FRONTIER PSYCHIATRIST	*XL Recordings*	18	*21 Jul 01*	
ALBUMS:	**HITS 1**		**WEEKS 2**	
SINCE I LEFT YOU	*XL Recordings*	8	*28 Apr 01*	2

Frankie AVALON — US

SINGLES:	HITS 4		WEEKS 1
GINGER BREAD	*His Master's Voice*	30	*11 Oct 58*
VENUS	*His Master's Voice*	16	*25 Apr 59*
WHY	*His Master's Voice*	20	*23 Jan 60*
DON'T THROW AWAY ALL THOSE TEARDROPS	*His Master's Voice*	37	*30 Apr 60*

AVALON BOYS – See LAUREL and HARDY

AVATAR – See ATLANTIS vs AVATAR featuring Miriam STOCKLEY

AVERAGE WHITE BAND — UK

SINGLES:	HITS 7		WEEKS 4	
PICK UP THE PIECES	*Atlantic*	6	*22 Feb 75*	
CUT THE CAKE	*Atlantic*	31	*26 Apr 75*	
QUEEN OF MY SOUL	*Atlantic*	23	*9 Oct 76*	
WALK ON BY	*RCA Victor*	46	*28 Apr 79*	
WHEN WILL YOU BE MINE	*RCA*	49	*25 Aug 79*	
LET'S GO ROUND AGAIN	*RCA*	12	*26 Apr 80*	11
FOR YOU FOR LOVE	*RCA*	46	*26 Jul 80*	4
LET'S GO ROUND AGAIN [RM] *Remixed by CCN.*	*The Hit Label*	56	*26 Mar 94*	2
ALBUMS:	**HITS 6**		**WEEKS 50**	
AVERAGE WHITE BAND	*Atlantic*	6	*1 Mar 75*	14
CUT THE CAKE	*Atlantic*	28	*5 Jul 75*	4
SOUL SEARCHING TIME	*Atlantic*	60	*31 Jul 76*	1
I FEEL NO FRET	*RCA Victor*	15	*10 Mar 79*	15
SHINE	*RCA*	14	*31 May 80*	13
LET'S GO ROUND AGAIN - THE BEST OF THE AVERAGE WHITE BAND	*The Hit Label*	38	*2 Apr 94*	3

Kevin AVIANCE — US

SINGLES:	HITS 1			WEEKS 1
DIN DA DA	*Distinct'ive*	65	*13 Jun 98*	1

Originally recorded by George Krantz.

AVONS — UK

SINGLES:	HITS 4			WEEKS 22
SEVEN LITTLE GIRLS SITTING IN THE BACK SEAT	*Columbia*	3	*14 Nov 59*	13
WE'RE ONLY YOUNG ONCE	*Columbia*	49	*9 Jul 60*	1
WE'RE ONLY YOUNG ONCE [RE]	*Columbia*	45	*23 Jul 60*	1
FOUR LITTLE HEELS	*Columbia*	45	*29 Oct 60*	2
FOUR LITTLE HEELS [RE]	*Columbia*	49	*3 Dec 60*	1
RUBBER BALL	*Columbia*	30	*28 Jan 61*	4

AWAKENING – See MISTA E featuring the AWAKENING

AWESOME — UK

SINGLES:	HITS 2			WEEKS 2
RUMOURS	*Universal*	58	*8 Nov 97*	1
CRAZY	*Universal*	63	*21 Mar 98*	1

AWESOME 3 — UK

SINGLES:	HITS 2			WEEKS 8
HARD UP	*A&M*	55	*8 Sep 90*	3
DON'T GO	*Citybeat*	75	*3 Oct 92*	1
DON'T GO '94 [RM-1ST]	*Citybeat*	45	*4 Jun 94*	2
Remixed by Mark and Adrian Luvdup.				
DON'T GO [RM-2ND]	*XL Recordings*	27	*26 Oct 96*	2
Remixed by Dancing Divas.				
Above hit: AWESOME 3 featuring Julie McDERMOTT.				

Hoyt AXTON — US

SINGLES:	HITS 1			WEEKS 4
DELLA AND THE DEALER	*Young Blood*	48	*7 Jun 80*	4

AXUS — UK

SINGLES:	HITS 1			WEEKS 1
ABACUS (WHEN I FALL IN LOVE)	*INCredible*	62	*26 Sep 98*	1

Roy AYERS — US

SINGLES:	HITS 4			WEEKS 13
GET ON UP, GET ON DOWN	*Polydor*	41	*21 Oct 78*	4
HEAT OF THE BEAT	*Polydor*	43	*13 Jan 79*	5
Above hit: Roy AYERS/Wayne HENDERSON.				
DON'T STOP THE FEELING	*Polydor*	56	*2 Feb 80*	3
EXPANSIONS	*Soma Recordings*	68	*16 May 98*	1
Above hit: Scott GROOVES featuring Roy AYERS.				

ALBUMS:	HITS 1			WEEKS 2
YOU MIGHT BE SURPRISED	*CBS*	91	*26 Oct 85*	2

AYLA — Germany

SINGLES:	HITS 1			WEEKS 3
AYLA	*Positiva*	22	*4 Sep 99*	3

Original release on the Additive label reached No. 198 in 1998.

Mitchell AYRES' ORCHESTRA – See Perry COMO

Pam AYRES — UK

ALBUMS:	HITS 2			WEEKS 29
SOME OF ME POEMS AND SONGS	*Galaxy*	13	*27 Mar 76*	23
SOME MORE OF ME POEMS AND SONGS	*Galaxy*	23	*11 Dec 76*	6

Live recordings from the Queen Elizabeth Hall, London, 22 Sep 76.

AZ — US

SINGLES:	HITS 1			WEEKS 1
SUGARHILL	*Cooltempo*	67	*30 Mar 96*	1

AZ YET — US

SINGLES:	HITS 2			WEEKS 10
LAST NIGHT	*LaFace*	21	*1 Mar 97*	3
From the film 'The Nutty Professor'.				
HARD TO SAY I'M SORRY	*LaFace*	7	*21 Jun 97*	7
Above hit: AZ YET featuring Peter CETERA.				

Charles AZNAVOUR — France

SINGLES:	HITS 2			WEEKS 29
THE OLD FASHIONED WAY (LES PLAISIRS DEMODES)	*Barclay*	50	*22 Sep 73*	1
THE OLD FASHIONED WAY (LES PLAISIRS DEMODES) [RE-1ST]	*Barclay*	38	*20 Oct 73*	12
SHE	*Barclay*	1	*22 Jun 74*	14
Theme from the ITV series 'Seven Faces Of Woman'.				
THE OLD FASHIONED WAY (LES PLAISIRS DEMODES) [RE-2ND]	*Barclay*	47	*27 Jul 74*	2
ALBUMS:	**HITS 3**			**WEEKS 21**
AZNAVOUR SINGS AZNAVOUR VOLUME 3	*Barclay*	23	*29 Jun 74*	7
A TAPESTRY OF DREAMS	*Barclay*	9	*7 Sep 74*	13
HIS GREATEST LOVE SONGS	*K-Tel*	73	*2 Aug 80*	1

AZTEC CAMERA — UK

SINGLES:	HITS 11			WEEKS 74
OBLIVIOUS	*Rough Trade*	47	*19 Feb 83*	6
WALK OUT TO THE WINTER	*Rough Trade*	64	*4 Jun 83*	4
OBLIVIOUS [RI]	*WEA*	18	*5 Nov 83*	11
ALL I NEED IS EVERYTHING / JUMP	*WEA*	34	*1 Sep 84*	6
Jump listed from 22 Sep 84.				
HOW MEN ARE	*WEA*	25	*13 Feb 88*	9
SOMEWHERE IN MY HEART	*WEA*	3	*23 Apr 88*	14
WORKING IN A GOLDMINE	*WEA*	31	*6 Aug 88*	5
DEEP & WIDE & TALL	*WEA*	55	*8 Oct 88*	3
Original release reached No. 79 in 1987.				
THE CRYING SCENE	*WEA*	70	*7 Jul 90*	3
GOOD MORNING BRITAIN	*WEA*	19	*6 Oct 90*	8
Above hit: AZTEC CAMERA and Mick JONES.				
SPANISH HORSES	*WEA*	52	*18 Jul 92*	3
DREAM SWEET DREAMS	*WEA*	67	*1 May 93*	2
ALBUMS:	**HITS 6**			**WEEKS 80**
HIGH LAND, HARD RAIN	*Rough Trade*	22	*23 Apr 83*	18
KNIFE	*WEA*	14	*29 Sep 84*	6
LOVE	*WEA*	49	*21 Nov 87*	12
LOVE [RE]	*WEA*	10	*23 Apr 88*	31
STRAY	*WEA*	22	*16 Jun 90*	7
DREAMLAND	*WEA*	21	*29 May 93*	2
THE BEST OF AZTEC CAMERA	*warner.esp*	36	*7 Aug 99*	4

AZTEC MYSTIC – See DJ ROLANDO AKA The AZTEC MYSTIC

AZURE — Italy

SINGLES:	HITS 1			WEEKS 2
MAMA USED TO SAY	*Inferno*	56	*25 Apr 98*	2

AZYMUTH — Brazil

SINGLES:	HITS 1			WEEKS 8
JAZZ CARNIVAL	*Milestone*	19	*12 Jan 80*	8

Bob AZZAM and his Orchestra — Egypt

SINGLES:	HITS 1			WEEKS 14
MUSTAPHA	*Decca*	23	*28 May 60*	14

AZZIDO DA BASS — Germany

SINGLES:	HITS 1			WEEKS 12
DOOMS NIGHT	*Club Tools*	58	*4 Mar 00*	1
Original release reached No. 149 in 1999.				
DOOMS NIGHT [RE]	*Club Tools*	46	*24 Jun 00*	2
DOOMS NIGHT [RI]	*Club Tools*	8	*21 Oct 00*	8
DOOOMS NIGHT [RI] [RE]	*Club Tools*	70	*13 Jan 01*	1

B

Derek B — UK

SINGLES:	HITS 3			WEEKS 15
GOODGROOVE	*Music Of Life*	16	*27 Feb 88*	6
BAD YOUNG BROTHER	*Tuff Audio*	16	*7 May 88*	6
WE'VE GOT THE JUICE	*Tuff Audio*	56	*2 Jul 88*	3
ALBUMS:	**HITS 1**			**WEEKS 9**
BULLET FROM A GUN	*Tuff Audio*	11	*28 May 88*	9

Eric B. and RAKIM — UK

(See also Rakim.)

SINGLES:	HITS 6			WEEKS 26
PAID IN FULL (THE COLD CUT REMIX)	*Fourth & Broadway*	15	*7 Nov 87*	6
MOVE THE CROWD	*Fourth & Broadway*	53	*20 Feb 88*	2
I KNOW YOU GOT SOUL (THE DOUBLE TROUBLE REMIX)	*Cooltempo*	13	*12 Mar 88*	6
Original release reached No. 76 in 1987.				
FOLLOW THE LEADER	*MCA*	21	*2 Jul 88*	5
MICROPHONE FIEND	*MCA*	74	*19 Nov 88*	1
FRIENDS	*MCA*	21	*12 Aug 89*	6
Above hit: Jody WATLEY with Eric B. and RAKIM.				
ALBUMS:	**HITS 4**			**WEEKS 10**
PAID IN FULL	*Fourth & Broadway*	85	*12 Sep 87*	4
FOLLOW THE LEADER	*MCA*	25	*6 Aug 88*	4
LET THE RHYTHM HIT 'EM	*MCA*	58	*7 Jul 90*	1
DON'T SWEAT THE TECHNIQUE	*MCA*	73	*11 Jul 92*	1

Howie B — UK

SINGLES:	HITS 3			WEEKS 4
ANGELS GO BALD: TOO	*Polydor*	36	*19 Jul 97*	2
SWITCH	*Polydor*	62	*18 Oct 97*	1
TAKE YOUR PARTNER BY THE HAND	*Polydor*	74	*11 Apr 98*	1
Above hit: Howie B featuring Robbie ROBERTSON.				
ALBUMS:	**HITS 1**			**WEEKS 1**
TURN THE DARK OFF	*Polydor*	58	*9 Aug 97*	1

Jazzie B – See Maxi PRIEST; SOUL II SOUL

Jon B — US

SINGLES:	HITS 2			WEEKS 5
THEY DON'T KNOW	*Epic*	32	*17 Oct 98*	2
DON'T TALK	*Epic*	29	*26 May 01*	3

Lisa B — US

SINGLES:	HITS 3			WEEKS 9
GLAM	*ffrr*	49	*12 Jun 93*	2
FASCINATED	*ffrr*	35	*25 Sep 93*	3
YOU AND ME	*ffrr*	39	*8 Jun 94*	4

Lorna B – See DJ SCOTT featuring Lorna B; ZERO VU featuring Lorna B

Mark B and BLADE — UK

SINGLES:	HITS 2			WEEKS 4
THE UNKNOWN	*Wordplay*	49	*10 Feb 01*	1
YA DON'T SEE THE SIGNS	*Wordplay*	23	*26 May 01*	3

Melanie B — UK

SINGLES:	HITS 5			WEEKS 36
I WANT YOU BACK	*Virgin*	1	*26 Sep 98*	9
From the film 'Why Do Fools Fall In Love'.				
Melanie B featuring Missy "Misdemeanor" ELLIOTT				
WORD UP	*Virgin*	14	*10 Jul 99*	7
From the film 'Austin Powers – The Spy Who Shagged Me'.				
Above hit: Melanie G.				
WORD UP [RE]	*Virgin*	71	*25 Sep 99*	1
TELL ME	*Virgin*	4	*7 Oct 00*	7
FEELS SO GOOD	*Virgin*	5	*3 Mar 01*	8
LULLABY	*Virgin*	13	*16 Jun 01*	4
ALBUMS:	**HITS 1**			**WEEKS 2**
HOT	*Virgin*	28	*21 Oct 00*	2

Sandy B — US

SINGLES:	HITS 3			WEEKS 8
FEEL LIKE SINGIN'	*Nervous*	60	*20 Feb 93*	1
Originally recorded by Tak Tix.				
MAKE THE WORLD GO ROUND	*Champion*	73	*18 May 96*	1
MAKE THE WORLD GO ROUND [RM]	*Champion*	35	*24 May 97*	2
Remixed by Deep Dish.				
AIN'T NO NEED TO HIDE	*Champion*	60	*8 Nov 97*	1
MAKE THE WORLD GO ROUND [RM] [RI]	*Champion*	20	*28 Feb 98*	3

Stevie B — US

SINGLES:	HITS 1			WEEKS 9
BECAUSE I LOVE YOU (THE POSTMAN SONG)	*Polydor*	6	*23 Feb 91*	9

Tairrie B — US

SINGLES:	HITS 1			WEEKS 2
MURDER SHE WROTE	*MCA*	71	*1 Dec 90*	2

B.A.D. – See BIG AUDIO DYNAMITE

B B and Q BAND — US

SINGLES:	HITS 4			WEEKS 15
ON THE BEAT	*Capitol*	41	*18 Jul 81*	5
GENIE	*Cooltempo*	40	*6 Jul 85*	4
Above hit: BROOKLYN BRONX and QUEENS (B.B.& Q.).				
DREAMER	*Cooltempo*	35	*20 Sep 86*	5
Above hit: BB + Q BROOKLYN BRONX and QUEENS.				
RICCOCHET	*Cooltempo*	71	*17 Oct 87*	1
Above hit: B B and Q.				

B.B.E. — France/Italy

SINGLES:	HITS 4			WEEKS 20
SEVEN DAYS AND ONE WEEK	*Positiva*	3	*28 Sep 96*	9
Title refers to how long track took to make.				
FLASH	*Positiva*	5	*29 Mar 97*	5
DESIRE	*Positiva*	19	*14 Feb 98*	3
DEEPER LOVE (SYMPHONIC PARADISE)	*Positiva*	19	*30 May 98*	3
ALBUMS:	**HITS 1**			**WEEKS 2**
GAMES	*Positiva*	60	*28 Feb 98*	2

B BOYS — US

ALBUMS:	HITS 1			WEEKS 1
CUTTIN' HERBIE	*Street Sounds*	90	*28 Jan 84*	1

B-CREW featuring Barbara TUCKER, Ultra NATE, DAJAE, MONE — US

SINGLES:	HITS 1			WEEKS 1
PARTAY FEELING	*Positiva*	45	*20 Sep 97*	1

B.E.F. — UK/US

SINGLES:	HITS 1			WEEKS 5
FAMILY AFFAIR	*Ten Records*	37	*27 Jul 91*	5
Originally recorded by Sly and the Family Stone.				
Above hit: B.E.F. featuring Lalah HATHAWAY.				

B-15 PROJECT featuring Crissy D and LADY G — UK/Jamaica

SINGLES:	HITS 1			WEEKS 10
GIRLS LIKE US	*Relentless*	7	*17 Jun 00*	8
GIRLS LIKE US [RE]	*Relentless*	55	*19 Aug 00*	2

B-52'S — US

SINGLES:	HITS 10			WEEKS 61
ROCK LOBSTER	*Island*	37	*11 Aug 79*	5
GIVE ME BACK MY MAN	*Island*	61	*9 Aug 80*	3
SONG FOR A FUTURE GENERATION	*Island*	63	*7 May 83*	2
ROCK LOBSTER [RI] / PLANET CLARE	*Island*	12	*10 May 86*	7
Planet Clare listed from 17 May 86.				
LOVE SHACK	*Reprise*	2	*3 Mar 90*	13
ROAM	*Reprise*	17	*19 May 90*	7
CHANNEL Z	*Reprise*	61	*18 Aug 90*	2
GOOD STUFF	*Reprise*	21	*20 Jun 92*	6
TELL IT LIKE IT T-I-IS	*Reprise*	61	*12 Sep 92*	3
(MEET) THE FLINTSTONES	*MCA*	3	*9 Jul 94*	12
From the film 'The Flintstones'.				
Above hit: BC-52'S.				
LOVE SHACK 99 [RM]	*Reprise*	66	*30 Jan 99*	1
Remixed by Mike Koglin and Vanessa Quinones (Espiritiu).				
ALBUMS:	**HITS 9**			**WEEKS 69**
THE B-52'S	*Island*	22	*4 Aug 79*	12
WILD PLANET	*Island*	18	*13 Sep 80*	4
THE PARTY MIX ALBUM	*Island*	36	*11 Jul 81*	5
MESOPOTAMIA	*EMI*	18	*27 Feb 82*	6
WHAMMY!	*Island*	33	*21 May 83*	4
BOUNCING OFF THE SATELLITES	*Island*	74	*8 Aug 87*	2

COSMIC THING	*Reprise*	75	*29 Jul 89*	1
COSMIC THING [RE]	*Reprise*	8	*31 Mar 90*	26
THE BEST OF THE B-52'S - DANCE THIS MESS AROUND	*Island*	36	*14 Jul 90*	3
GOOD STUFF	*Reprise*	8	*11 Jul 92*	6

B.G. THE PRINCE OF RAP — Germany

SINGLES:	HITS 1			WEEKS 2
TAKE CONTROL OF THE PARTY	*Columbia*	71	*18 Jan 92*	2

B M EX — UK

(See also Sasha.)

ALBUMS:	HITS 1			WEEKS 2
APPOLONIA / FEEL THE DROP	*Union City*	17	*30 Jan 93*	2

12" double-pack single. Four mixes of Appolonia, two of Feel The Drop.

B.M.R. Featuring FELICIA — Germany/UK

SINGLES:	HITS 1			WEEKS 2
CHECK IT OUT (EVERYBODY)	*Almo Sounds*	29	*1 May 99*	2

Samples MFSB's TSOP.

B.M.U. (BLACK MEN UNITED) — US/UK

SINGLES:	HITS 1			WEEKS 2
U WILL KNOW	*Mercury*	23	*18 Feb 95*	2

From the film 'Jason's Lyric'.

B-MOVIE — UK

SINGLES:	HITS 2			WEEKS 7
REMEMBRANCE DAY	*Deram*	61	*18 Apr 81*	3
NOWHERE GIRL	*Some Bizzare*	67	*27 Mar 82*	4

B REAL, Busta RHYMES, COOLIO, LL COOL J and METHOD MAN — US

SINGLES:	HITS 1			WEEKS 6
HIT 'EM HIGH (THE MONSTARS' ANTHEM)	*Atlantic*	8	*5 Apr 97*	6

From the film 'Space Jam'.

B.O.N.

SINGLES:	HITS 1			WEEKS 5
BOYS	*Epic*	15	*3 Feb 01*	5

B.T. EXPRESS — US

SINGLES:	HITS 2			WEEKS 11
EXPRESS	*Pye International*	34	*29 Mar 75*	6
DOES IT FEEL GOOD / GIVE UP THE FUNK (LET'S DANCE)	*Calibre*	52	*26 Jul 80*	4
EXPRESS [RM]	*PWL*	67	*23 Apr 94*	1

Remixed by Mother.

B-TRIBE — Spain

SINGLES:	HITS 1			WEEKS 4
¡FIESTA FATAL!	*East West*	64	*25 Sep 93*	4

B.V.S.M.P. — US

SINGLES:	HITS 1			WEEKS 12
I NEED YOU	*Debut*	3	*23 Jul 88*	12

B*WITCHED — UK

(See also Steps Tina Cousins Cleopatra B*Witched Billie.)

SINGLES:	HITS 7			WEEKS 85
C'EST LA VIE	*Glow Worm*	1	*6 Jun 98*	19
ROLLERCOASTER	*Glow Worm*	1	*3 Oct 98*	15
TO YOU I BELONG	*Glow Worm*	1	*19 Dec 98*	12
BLAME IT ON THE WEATHERMAN	*Glow Worm*	1	*27 Mar 99*	9
TO YOU I BELONG [RE]	*Glow Worm*	64	*27 Mar 99*	2
JESSE HOLD ON	*Glow Worm*	4	*16 Oct 99*	10
I SHALL BE THERE	*Glow Worm*	13	*18 Dec 99*	9
*Above hit: B*WITCHED featuring LADYSMITH BLACK MAMBAZO.*				
JESSE HOLD ON [RE]	*Glow Worm*	60	*8 Jan 00*	2
JUMP DOWN	*Glow Worm*	16	*8 Apr 00*	5
JUMP DOWN [RE]	*Glow Worm*	62	*27 May 00*	2
ALBUMS:	**HITS 2**			**WEEKS 48**
B*WITCHED	*Glow Worm*	3	*24 Oct 98*	36
AWAKE AND BREATHE	*Glow Worm*	5	*30 Oct 99*	12

BABE INSTINCT — UK

SINGLES:	HITS 1			WEEKS 2
DISCO BABES FROM OUTER SPACE	*Positiva*	21	*16 Jan 99*	2

BABES IN TOYLAND — US

ALBUMS:	HITS 2			WEEKS 3
FONTANELLE	*Southern*	24	*5 Sep 92*	2
PAINKILLERS	*Southern*	53	*3 Jul 93*	1

Alice BABS — Sweden

SINGLES:	HITS 1			WEEKS 1
AFTER YOU'VE GONE	*Fontana*	43	*17 Aug 63*	1
Originally recorded by Henry Burr and Albert Campbell in 1918.				

BABY ANIMALS — Australia

ALBUMS:	HITS 1			WEEKS 1
BABY ANIMALS	*Imago*	70	*14 Mar 92*	1

BABY BUMPS — UK

SINGLES:	HITS 2			WEEKS 6
BURNING	*Delirious*	17	*8 Aug 98*	4
Samples the Trammps' Disco Inferno.				
I GOT THIS FEELING	*Sound Of Ministry*	22	*26 Feb 00*	2
Samples Michael Jackson's Don't Stop 'Til You Get Enough.				

BABY D — UK

SINGLES:	HITS 6			WEEKS 45
DESTINY	*Production House*	69	*18 Dec 93*	1
CASANOVA	*Production House*	67	*23 Jul 94*	1
LET ME BE YOUR FANTASY	*Systematic*	1	*19 Nov 94*	14
Original release reached No. 87 in 1992.				
(EVERYBODY'S GOT TO LEARN SOMETIME) I NEED YOUR LOVING	*Systematic*	3	*3 Jun 95*	12
SO PURE	*Systematic*	3	*13 Jan 96*	7
TAKE ME TO HEAVEN	*Systematic*	15	*6 Apr 96*	5
LET ME BE YOUR FANTASY [RM]	*Systematic*	16	*2 Sep 00*	5
Remixed by Trick or Treat.				
ALBUMS:	**HITS 1**			**WEEKS 5**
DELIVERANCE	*Systematic*	5	*10 Feb 96*	5

BABY DC featuring IMAJIN — US

SINGLES:	HITS 1			WEEKS 1
BOUNCE, ROCK, SKATE, ROLL	*Jive*	45	*24 Apr 99*	1

BABY JUNE — UK

SINGLES:	HITS 1			WEEKS 1
HEY! WHAT'S YOUR NAME	*Arista*	75	*15 Aug 92*	1

BABY O — US

SINGLES:	HITS 1			WEEKS 5
IN THE FOREST	*Calibre*	46	*26 Jul 80*	5

BABY ROOTS — UK

SINGLES:	HITS 1			WEEKS 1
ROCK ME BABY	*ZYX*	71	*1 Aug 92*	1

BABYBIRD — UK

SINGLES:	HITS 9			WEEKS 35
GOODNIGHT	*Echo*	28	*10 Aug 96*	2
YOU'RE GORGEOUS	*Echo*	3	*12 Oct 96*	16
CANDY GIRL	*Echo*	14	*1 Feb 97*	3
CORNERSHOP	*Echo*	37	*17 May 97*	2
BAD OLD MAN	*Echo*	31	*9 May 98*	2
IF YOU'LL BE MINE	*Echo*	28	*22 Aug 98*	4
BACK TOGETHER	*Echo*	22	*27 Feb 99*	3
THE F-WORD	*Echo*	35	*25 Mar 00*	2
OUT OF SIGHT	*Echo*	58	*3 Jun 00*	1
ALBUMS:	**HITS 2**			**WEEKS 14**
UGLY BEAUTIFUL	*Echo*	9	*2 Nov 96*	12
Compilation from 5 earlier albums.				
THERE'S SOMETHING GOING ON	*Echo*	28	*5 Sep 98*	2

BABYFACE — US

(See also Jay-Z.)

SINGLES:	HITS 5			WEEKS 21
ROCK BOTTOM	*Epic*	50	*9 Jul 94*	4
WHEN CAN I SEE YOU	*Epic*	35	*1 Oct 94*	3
THIS IS FOR THE LOVER IN YOU	*Epic*	12	*9 Nov 96*	5
Above hit: BABYFACE featuring LL COOL J, Jody WATLEY, Howard HEWETT and Jeffrey DANIELS.				
EVERYTIME I CLOSE MY EYES	*Epic*	13	*8 Mar 97*	4
Features Mariah Carey on backing vocals and Kenny G on sax.				
HOW COME, HOW LONG	*Epic*	10	*19 Jul 97*	5
Above hit: BABYFACE featuring Stevie WONDER.				
ALBUMS:	**HITS 1**			**WEEKS 5**
THE DAY	*Epic*	34	*16 Nov 96*	5

BABYLON ZOO — UK

SINGLES:	HITS 4			WEEKS 20
SPACEMAN	*EMI*	1	*27 Jan 96*	14
Featured in the Levi's Jeans TV commercial.				
ANIMAL ARMY	*EMI*	17	*27 Apr 96*	3
THE BOY WITH THE X-RAY EYES	*EMI*	32	*5 Oct 96*	2
ALL THE MONEY'S GONE	*EMI*	46	*6 Feb 99*	1
ALBUMS:	**HITS 1**			**WEEKS 5**
THE BOY WITH THE X-RAY EYES	*EMI*	6	*17 Feb 96*	5

BABYS — US/UK

SINGLES:	HITS 1			WEEKS 3
ISN'T IT TIME	*Chrysalis*	45	*21 Jan 78*	3

BACCARA — Spain

SINGLES:	HITS 2			WEEKS 26
YES SIR, I CAN BOOGIE	*RCA Victor*	1	*17 Sep 77*	17
SORRY I'M A LADY	*RCA Victor*	8	*14 Jan 78*	9
ALBUMS:	**HITS 1**			**WEEKS 6**
BACCARA	*RCA Victor*	26	*4 Mar 78*	6

Burt BACHARACH his Orchestra and Chorus — US

SINGLES:	HITS 2			WEEKS 12
TRAINS AND BOATS AND PLANES	*London*	4	*22 May 65*	11
TOLEDO	*Mercury*	72	*1 May 99*	1
Above hit: Elvis COSTELLO with Burt BACHARACH.				
ALBUMS:	**HITS 5**			**WEEKS 46**
HIT MAKER-BURT BACHARACH	*London*	3	*22 May 65*	18
CASINO ROYALE [OST]	*RCA Victor*	35	*22 Jul 67*	1
Includes tracks by Herb Alpert and Dusty Springfield.				
REACH OUT	*A&M*	52	*28 Nov 70*	3
PORTRAIT IN MUSIC	*A&M*	5	*3 Apr 71*	22
PAINTED FROM MEMORY	*Mercury*	32	*10 Oct 98*	2
Above hit: Elvis COSTELLO with Burt BACHARACH.				

BACHELORS — Ireland

SINGLES:	HITS 17			WEEKS 187
CHARMAINE	*Decca*	6	*26 Jan 63*	19
Originally recorded by Rudy Valee.				
FARAWAY PLACES	*Decca*	36	*6 Jul 63*	3
WHISPERING	*Decca*	18	*31 Aug 63*	10
Originally recorded by Paul Whiteman in 1920.				
DIANE	*Decca*	1	*25 Jan 64*	19
Originally recorded by Nat Shilkret Orchestra in 1928.				
I BELIEVE	*Decca*	2	*21 Mar 64*	17
RAMONA	*Decca*	4	*6 Jun 64*	13
Originally recorded by Gene Austin.				
I WOULDN'T TRADE YOU FOR THE WORLD	*Decca*	4	*15 Aug 64*	16
NO ARMS CAN EVER HOLD YOU	*Decca*	7	*5 Dec 64*	12
TRUE LOVE FOR EVERMORE	*Decca*	34	*3 Apr 65*	6
MARIE	*Decca*	9	*22 May 65*	12
Originally recorded by Tommy Dorsey in 1940.				
IN THE CHAPEL IN THE MOONLIGHT	*Decca*	27	*30 Oct 65*	10
Originally recorded by Shep Fields in 1936.				
HELLO, DOLLY!	*Decca*	38	*8 Jan 66*	4
From the musical of the same name.				
THE SOUND OF SILENCE	*Decca*	3	*19 Mar 66*	13
CAN I TRUST YOU	*Decca*	26	*9 Jul 66*	7

WALK WITH FAITH IN YOUR HEART	*Decca*	22	*3 Dec 66*	9
OH HOW I MISS YOU	*Decca*	30	*8 Apr 67*	8
MARTA	*Decca*	20	*8 Jul 67*	9
EPS:	**HITS 4**			**WEEKS 98**
BACHELORS VOLUME 2	*Decca*	7	*14 Mar 64*	30
THE BACHELORS	*Decca*	5	*21 Mar 64*	22
THE BACHELORS' HITS	*Decca*	1	*5 Dec 64*	32
THE BACHELORS' HITS VOLUME 2	*Decca*	9	*8 Jan 66*	14
ALBUMS:	**HITS 8**			**WEEKS 103**
THE BACHELORS + 16 GREAT SONGS	*Decca*	2	*27 Jun 64*	44
MORE GREAT SONG HITS FROM THE BACHELORS	*Decca*	15	*9 Oct 65*	6
HITS OF THE SIXTIES	*Decca*	12	*9 Jul 66*	9
BACHELORS' GIRLS	*Decca*	24	*5 Nov 66*	8
GOLDEN ALL TIME HITS	*Decca*	19	*1 Jul 67*	7
WORLD OF THE BACHELORS	*Decca*	8	*14 Jun 69*	18
WORLD OF THE BACHELORS VOLUME 2	*Decca*	11	*23 Aug 69*	7
25 GOLDEN GREATS	*Warwick*	38	*22 Dec 79*	4

Randy BACHMAN – See BUS STOP

Tal BACHMAN — Canada

SINGLES:	**HITS 1**			**WEEKS 2**
SHE'S SO HIGH	*Columbia*	30	*30 Oct 99*	2

BACHMAN-TURNER OVERDRIVE — Canada

SINGLES:	**HITS 2**			**WEEKS 18**
YOU AIN'T SEEN NOTHING YET	*Mercury*	2	*16 Nov 74*	12
Written about Randy Bachman's brother Gary who stuttered.				
ROLL ON DOWN THE HIGHWAY	*Mercury*	22	*1 Feb 75*	6
ALBUMS:	**HITS 1**			**WEEKS 13**
NOT FRAGILE	*Mercury*	12	*14 Dec 74*	13

BACK TO THE PLANET — UK

SINGLES:	**HITS 2**			**WEEKS 2**
TEENAGE TURTLES	*Parallel*	52	*10 Apr 93*	1
DAYDREAM	*Parallel*	52	*4 Sep 93*	1
ALBUMS:	**HITS 1**			**WEEKS 2**
MIND AND SOUL COLLABORATORS	*Parallel*	32	*18 Sep 93*	2

BACKBEAT BAND — US

SINGLES:	**HITS 2**			**WEEKS 5**
MONEY	*Virgin*	48	*26 Mar 94*	3
Original by Barrett Strong reached No. 23 in the US in 1960.				
MONEY [RE]	*Virgin*	73	*23 Apr 94*	1
PLEASE MR. POSTMAN	*Virgin*	69	*14 May 94*	1
Original by the Marvelettes reached No. 1 in the US in 1961.				
ALBUMS:	**HITS 1**			**WEEKS 2**
BACKBEAT [OST]	*Virgin*	39	*16 Apr 94*	2
Film chronicles the early days of the Beatles.				

BACKROOM BOYS – See CHAS and DAVE

BACKSTREET BOYS — US

SINGLES:	**HITS 15**			**WEEKS 154**
WE'VE GOT IT GOIN' ON	*Jive*	54	*28 Oct 95*	1
I'LL NEVER BREAK YOUR HEART	*Jive*	42	*16 Dec 95*	3
GET DOWN (YOU'RE THE ONE FOR ME)	*Jive*	14	*1 Jun 96*	8
WE'VE GOT IT GOIN' ON [RI]	*Jive*	3	*24 Aug 96*	7
I'LL NEVER BREAK YOUR HEART [RI]	*Jive*	8	*16 Nov 96*	8
QUIT PLAYING GAMES (WITH MY HEART)	*Jive*	2	*18 Jan 97*	10
ANYWHERE FOR YOU	*Jive*	4	*29 Mar 97*	6
ANYWHERE FOR YOU [RE-1ST]	*Jive*	72	*31 May 97*	1
ANYWHERE FOR YOU [RE-2ND]	*Jive*	70	*14 Jun 97*	1
EVERYBODY (BACKSTREET'S BACK)	*Jive*	3	*2 Aug 97*	11
AS LONG AS YOU LOVE ME	*Jive*	3	*11 Oct 97*	19
ALL I HAVE TO GIVE	*Jive*	2	*14 Feb 98*	12
I WANT IT THAT WAY	*Jive*	1	*15 May 99*	14
LARGER THAN LIFE	*Jive*	5	*30 Oct 99*	14
SHOW ME THE MEANING OF BEING LONELY	*Jive*	66	*26 Feb 00*	1
Import				
SHOW ME THE MEANING OF BEING LONELY	*Jive*	3	*4 Mar 00*	9
SHOW ME THE MEANING OF BEING LONELY [RE]	*Jive*	51	*3 Jun 00*	2
THE ONE	*Jive*	8	*24 Jun 00*	7
THE ONE [RE]	*Jive*	75	*9 Sep 00*	1
SHAPE OF MY HEART	*Jive*	4	*18 Nov 00*	9

THE CALL	*Jive*	8	*24 Feb 01*	5
MORE THAN THAT	*Jive*	12	*7 Jul 01*	5
ALBUMS:	**HITS 5**			**WEEKS 136**
BACKSTREET BOYS	*Jive*	12	*21 Sep 96*	19
BACKSTREET'S BACK	*Jive*	2	*23 Aug 97*	44
MILLENNIUM	*Jive*	2	*29 May 99*	56
BLACK & BLUE	*Jive*	13	*2 Dec 00*	9
GREATEST HITS – CHAPTER ONE	*Jive*	5	*10 Nov 01*	8

BACKYARD DOG — UK

SINGLES:	**HITS 1**			**WEEKS 6**
BADDEST RUFFEST	*East West*	15	*7 Jul 01*	5
BADDEST RUFFEST [RE]	*East West*	69	*25 Aug 01*	1

BAD BOYS INC. — UK

SINGLES:	**HITS 6**			**WEEKS 31**
DON'T TALK ABOUT LOVE	*A&M*	19	*14 Aug 93*	5
WHENEVER YOU NEED SOMEONE	*A&M*	26	*2 Oct 93*	3
WALKING ON AIR	*A&M*	24	*11 Dec 93*	6
MORE TO THIS WORLD	*A&M*	8	*21 May 94*	7
TAKE ME AWAY (I'LL FOLLOW YOU)	*A&M*	15	*23 Jul 94*	6
LOVE HERE I COME	*A&M*	26	*17 Sep 94*	4
ALBUMS:	**HITS 1**			**WEEKS 6**
BAD BOYS INC	*A&M*	13	*18 Jun 94*	6

BAD COMPANY — UK

SINGLES:	**HITS 3**			**WEEKS 23**
CAN'T GET ENOUGH	*Island*	15	*1 Jun 74*	8
GOOD LOVIN' GONE BAD	*Island*	31	*22 Mar 75*	6
FEEL LIKE MAKIN' LOVE	*Island*	20	*30 Aug 75*	9
ALBUMS:	**HITS 6**			**WEEKS 87**
BAD COMPANY	*Island*	3	*15 Jun 74*	25
STRAIGHT SHOOTER	*Island*	3	*12 Apr 75*	27
RUN WITH THE PACK	*Island*	4	*21 Feb 76*	12
BURNIN' SKY	*Island*	17	*19 Mar 77*	8
DESOLATION ANGELS	*Swan Song*	10	*17 Mar 79*	9
ROUGH DIAMONDS	*Swan Song*	15	*28 Aug 82*	6

BAD ENGLISH — UK/US

SINGLES:	**HITS 1**			**WEEKS 3**
WHEN I SEE YOU SMILE	*Epic*	61	*25 Nov 89*	3
ALBUMS:	**HITS 2**			**WEEKS 2**
BAD ENGLISH	*Epic*	74	*16 Sep 89*	1
BACKLASH	*Epic*	64	*19 Oct 91*	1

BAD HABIT BOYS — Germany

SINGLES:	**HITS 1**			**WEEKS 1**
WEEKEND	*Inferno*	41	*1 Jul 00*	1

BAD MANNERS — UK

SINGLES:	**HITS 12**			**WEEKS 111**
NE-NE NA-NA NA-NA NU-NU *Originally recorded by Dicky Doo and the Dont's.*	*Magnet*	28	*1 Mar 80*	14
LIP UP FATTY	*Magnet*	15	*14 Jun 80*	14
SPECIAL BREW	*Magnet*	3	*27 Sep 80*	13
LORRAINE	*Magnet*	21	*6 Dec 80*	12
JUST A FEELING	*Magnet*	13	*28 Mar 81*	9
CAN CAN	*Magnet*	3	*27 Jun 81*	13
WALKING IN THE SUNSHINE	*Magnet*	10	*26 Sep 81*	9
BUONA SERA / DON'T BE ANGRY *Sleeve gives title as an EP: Special 'R'N'B' Party Four.*	*Magnet*	34	*21 Nov 81*	9
GOT NO BRAINS	*Magnet*	44	*1 May 82*	5
MY GIRL LOLLIPOP (MY BOY LOLLIPOP)	*Magnet*	9	*31 Jul 82*	7
SAMSON AND DELILAH	*Magnet*	58	*30 Oct 82*	3
THAT'LL DO NICELY	*Magnet*	49	*14 May 83*	3
ALBUMS:	**HITS 5**			**WEEKS 44**
SKA 'N' B	*Magnet*	34	*26 Apr 80*	13
LOONEE TUNES	*Magnet*	36	*29 Nov 80*	12
GOSH IT'S BAD MANNERS	*Magnet*	18	*24 Oct 81*	12
FORGING AHEAD	*Magnet*	78	*27 Nov 82*	1
THE HEIGHT OF BAD MANNERS *Compilation.*	*Telstar*	23	*7 May 83*	6

BAD MEETS EVIL featuring EMINEM and ROYCE DA 5′9″ — US

(See also Eminem.)

SINGLES:	HITS 1			WEEKS 1
SCARY MOVIES	*Mole UK*	63	*1 Sep 01*	1

BAD NEWS — UK

SINGLES:	HITS 1			WEEKS 5
BOHEMIAN RHAPSODY	*EMI*	44	*12 Sep 87*	5
ALBUMS:	**HITS 1**			**WEEKS 1**
BAD NEWS	*EMI*	69	*24 Oct 87*	1

BAD RELIGION — US

SINGLES:	HITS 1			WEEKS 2
21ST CENTURY (DIGITAL BOY)	*Columbia*	41	*11 Feb 95*	2

BAD SEEDS - See Nick CAVE and the BAD SEEDS

BAD YARD CLUB - See David MORALES

Angelo BADALAMENTI — US

(See also Booth and the Bad Angel.)

SINGLES:	HITS 1			WEEKS 3
BEACHED	*ffrr*	36	*11 Mar 00*	3
Samples Angelo Badalamenti's The Beach Theme. From the film 'The Beach'.				
Above hit: ORBITAL and Angelo BADALAMENTI.				
ALBUMS:	**HITS 1**			**WEEKS 25**
MUSIC FROM 'TWIN PEAKS' [OST-TV]	*Warner Brothers*	27	*17 Nov 90*	25
Includes re-entry in 2000.				
Above hit: Angelo BADALAMENTI with Julee CRUISE and VARIOUS ARTISTS.				

Wally BADAROU — France

SINGLES:	HITS 1			WEEKS 6
CHIEF INSPECTOR	*Fourth & Broadway*	46	*19 Oct 85*	6

BADDIEL and SKINNER and the LIGHTNING SEEDS — UK

SINGLES:	HITS 2			WEEKS 28
THREE LIONS (THE OFFICIAL SONG OF THE ENGLAND FOOTBALL TEAM)	*Epic*	1	*1 Jun 96*	15
Official anthem for England's football team in Euro 96				
3 LIONS '98 [RR]	*Epic*	1	*20 Jun 98*	13
Re-recorded for the 1998 World Cup in France.				

BADFINGER — UK

(See also Various Artists (EPs) 'The Apple EP'.)

SINGLES:	HITS 3			WEEKS 34
COME AND GET IT	*Apple*	4	*10 Jan 70*	11
From the film 'Magic Christian'. Originally recorded by the Beatles.				
NO MATTER WHAT	*Apple*	5	*9 Jan 71*	12
DAY AFTER DAY	*Apple*	10	*29 Jan 72*	11
Features George Harrison on guitar and Leon Russell on piano.				

BADLANDS — UK

ALBUMS:	HITS 2			WEEKS 3
BADLANDS	*WEA*	39	*24 Jun 89*	2
VOODOO HIGHWAY	*Atlantic*	74	*22 Jun 91*	1

BADLY DRAWN BOY — UK

SINGLES:	HITS 4			WEEKS 9
ONCE AROUND THE BLOCK	*Twisted Nerve*	46	*4 Sep 99*	2
ANOTHER PEARL	*Twisted Nerve*	41	*17 Jun 00*	1
DISILLUSION	*Twisted Nerve*	26	*16 Sep 00*	2
ONCE AROUND THE BLOCK [RI]	*Twisted Nerve*	27	*25 Nov 00*	2
SPITTING IN THE WIND	*Twisted Nerve*	22	*19 May 01*	2
Chart has title as Pissing In The Wind, the un-edited original version of the song which appears as track 2 on CD1.				
ALBUMS:	**HITS 1**			**WEEKS 47**
THE HOUR OF BEWILDERBEAST	*Twisted Nerve*	13	*8 Jul 00*	47
Winner of the 2000 Technics Mercury Music Prize.				

BADMAN — UK

SINGLES:	HITS 1			WEEKS 3
MAGIC STYLE	*Citybeat*	61	*2 Feb 91*	3

Erykah BADU — US

SINGLES:	HITS 6			WEEKS 17
ON & ON	*Universal*	12	*19 Apr 97*	4
NEXT LIFETIME	*Universal*	30	*14 Jun 97*	3
APPLE TREE	*Universal*	47	*29 Nov 97*	1
ONE	*Elektra*	23	*11 Jul 98*	3
Above hit: Busta RHYMES (featuring Erykah BADU).				
YOU GOT ME	*MCA*	31	*6 Mar 99*	2
Above hit: ROOTS featuring Erykah BADU.				
SWEET BABY	*Epic*	23	*15 Sep 01*	4
Above hit: Macy GRAY featuring Erykah BADU.				
ALBUMS:	**HITS 1**			**WEEKS 25**
BADUIZM	*MCA*	17	*1 Mar 97*	25

Joan BAEZ — US

SINGLES:	HITS 6			WEEKS 47
WE SHALL OVERCOME	*Fontana*	26	*8 May 65*	10
THERE BUT FOR FORTUNE	*Fontana*	8	*10 Jul 65*	12
Originally recorded by Phil Ochs.				
IT'S ALL OVER NOW, BABY BLUE	*Fontana*	22	*4 Sep 65*	8
FAREWELL ANGELINA	*Fontana*	35	*25 Dec 65*	3
FAREWELL ANGELINA [RE]	*Fontana*	49	*22 Jan 66*	1
PACK UP YOUR SORROWS	*Fontana*	50	*30 Jul 66*	1
THE NIGHT THEY DROVE OLD DIXIE DOWN	*Vanguard*	6	*9 Oct 71*	12
Originally recorded by the Band.				
EPS:	**HITS 4**			**WEEKS 97**
DON'T THINK TWICE, IT'S ALRIGHT	*Fontana*	10	*17 Apr 65*	23
SILVER DAGGER AND OTHER THINGS	*Philips*	3	*17 Apr 65*	33
WITH GOD ON OUR SIDE	*Fontana*	1	*26 Mar 66*	36
A HARD RAIN'S GONNA FALL	*Fontana*	7	*2 Jul 66*	5
ALBUMS:	**HITS 6**			**WEEKS 88**
JOAN BAEZ IN CONCERT VOLUME 2	*Fontana*	15	*18 Jul 64*	4
JOAN BAEZ NUMBER 5	*Fontana*	3	*15 May 65*	27
JOAN BAEZ	*Fontana*	9	*19 Jun 65*	13
JOAN BAEZ IN CONCERT VOLUME 2 [RE]	*Fontana*	8	*10 Jul 65*	15
FAREWELL ANGELINA	*Fontana*	5	*27 Nov 65*	23
JOAN BAEZ ON VANGUARD	*Vanguard*	15	*19 Jul 69*	5
FIRST TEN YEARS	*Vanguard*	41	*3 Apr 71*	1

BAHA MEN — Bahamas

SINGLES:	HITS 2			WEEKS 28
WHO LET THE DOGS OUT	*Edel*	2	*14 Oct 00*	23
Originally recorded by Anslem Douglas.				
YOU ALL DAT	*Edel*	14	*3 Feb 01*	5
Samples The Lion Sleeps Tonight by Tight Fit				
Above hit: BAHA MEN: Guest vocal Imani COPPOLA.				

Carol BAILEY — UK

SINGLES:	HITS 1			WEEKS 2
FEEL IT	*Multiply*	41	*25 Feb 95*	2

Philip BAILEY — US

SINGLES:	HITS 2			WEEKS 20
EASY LOVER	*CBS*	1	*9 Mar 85*	12
Above hit: Philip BAILEY (Duet with Phil COLLINS).				
WALKING ON THE CHINESE WALL	*CBS*	34	*18 May 85*	8
ALBUMS:	**HITS 1**			**WEEKS 17**
CHINESE WALL	*CBS*	29	*30 Mar 85*	17

Merril BAINBRIDGE — Australia

SINGLES:	HITS 1			WEEKS 1
MOUTH	*Gotham*	51	*7 Dec 96*	1

Adrian BAKER — UK

SINGLES:	HITS 1			WEEKS 8
SHERRY	*Magnet*	10	*19 Jul 75*	8

Anita BAKER — US

SINGLES:	HITS 5			WEEKS 22
SWEET LOVE	*Elektra*	13	*15 Nov 86*	10
CAUGHT UP IN THE RAPTURE	*Elektra*	51	*31 Jan 87*	5
GIVING YOU THE BEST THAT I GOT	*Elektra*	55	*8 Oct 88*	3

TALK TO ME	*Elektra*	68	*30 Jun 90*	2
BODY AND SOUL	*Elektra*	48	*17 Sep 94*	2
ALBUMS:	**HITS 4**			**WEEKS 81**
RAPTURE	*Elektra*	53	*3 May 86*	6
RAPTURE [RE]	*Elektra*	13	*9 Aug 86*	41
GIVING YOU THE BEST THAT I GOT	*Elektra*	9	*29 Oct 88*	20
COMPOSITIONS	*Elektra*	7	*14 Jul 90*	9
RHYTHM OF LOVE	*Elektra*	14	*24 Sep 94*	5

Arthur BAKER and the BACKBEAT DISCIPLES — US

SINGLES:	**HITS 2**			**WEEKS 7**
IT'S YOUR TIME	*Breakout*	64	*20 May 89*	2
Above hit: Arthur BAKER and the BACKBEAT DISCIPLES (featuring Shirley LEWIS).				
THE MESSAGE IS LOVE	*Breakout*	38	*21 Oct 89*	5
Above hit: Arthur BAKER and the BACKBEAT DISCIPLES featuring Al GREEN.				

George BAKER SELECTION — UK

SINGLES:	**HITS 1**			**WEEKS 10**
PALOMA BLANCA	*Warner Brothers*	10	*6 Sep 75*	10

Ginger BAKER'S AIR FORCE — UK

(See also Baker-Gurvitz Army.)

ALBUMS:	**HITS 1**			**WEEKS 1**
GINGER BAKER'S AIR FORCE	*Polydor*	37	*13 Jun 70*	1

Hylda BAKER and Arthur MULLARD — UK

SINGLES:	**HITS 1**			**WEEKS 6**
YOU'RE THE ONE THAT I WANT	*Pye*	22	*9 Sep 78*	6

Kenny BAKER - See Ted HEATH and his Music

BAKER-GURVITZ ARMY — UK

(See also Ginger Baker's Air Force; Adrian Gurvitz.)

ALBUMS:	**HITS 1**			**WEEKS 5**
BAKER-GURVITZ ARMY	*Vertigo*	22	*22 Feb 75*	5

BALAAM AND THE ANGEL — UK

SINGLES:	**HITS 1**			**WEEKS 2**
SHE KNOWS	*Virgin*	70	*29 Mar 86*	2
ALBUMS:	**HITS 1**			**WEEKS 2**
THE GREATEST STORY EVER TOLD	*Virgin*	67	*16 Aug 86*	2

Long John BALDRY — UK

SINGLES:	**HITS 4**			**WEEKS 36**
LET THE HEARTACHES BEGIN	*Pye*	1	*11 Nov 67*	13
WHEN THE SUN COMES SHINING THRU'	*Pye*	29	*31 Aug 68*	7
MEXICO	*Pye*	15	*26 Oct 68*	8
IT'S TOO LATE NOW	*Pye*	21	*1 Feb 69*	8

BALEARIC BILL — Belgium/Holland

(See also Airscape.)

SINGLES:	**HITS 1**			**WEEKS 2**
DESTINATION SUNSHINE	*Xtravaganza*	36	*2 Oct 99*	2

Edward BALL — UK

SINGLES:	**HITS 2**			**WEEKS 2**
THE MILL HILL SELF HATE CLUB	*Creation*	57	*20 Jul 96*	1
LOVE IS BLUE	*Creation*	59	*22 Feb 97*	1

Kenny BALL and his JAZZMEN — UK

SINGLES:	**HITS 14**			**WEEKS 136**
SAMANTHA	*Pye Jazz Today*	13	*25 Feb 61*	15
From the film 'High Society'.				
Above hit: Lonnie DONEGAN presents – Kenny BALL and his JAZZMEN.				
I STILL LOVE YOU ALL	*Pye Jazz Today*	24	*13 May 61*	6
SOMEDAY (YOU'LL BE SORRY)	*Pye Jazz Today*	28	*2 Sep 61*	6
Above 3 has sub credit: vocal: Kenny BALL.				
MIDNIGHT IN MOSCOW	*Pye Jazz Today*	2	*11 Nov 61*	21
Based on a Russian song Padmeskoveeye Vietchera.				
MARCH OF THE SIAMESE CHILDREN	*Pye Jazz Today*	4	*17 Feb 62*	13
From the film 'The King And I'.				

THE GREEN LEAVES OF SUMMER *From the film 'The Alamo'.*	*Pye*	7	*19 May 62*	14
SO DO I *Above hit: Kenny BALL and his JAZZMEN; vocal: Kenny BALL.*	*Pye Jazz Today*	14	*25 Aug 62*	8
THE PAY-OFF (A MOI DE PAYER) *Above hit: Kenny BALL and his JAZZMEN; clarinet-Dave JONES.*	*Pye Jazz Today*	23	*20 Oct 62*	6
SUKIYAKI	*Pye Jazz Today*	10	*19 Jan 63*	13
CASABLANCA	*Pye Jazz Today*	21	*27 Apr 63*	11
RONDO (BASED ON MOZART'S "RONDO A LA TURK") *From the film 'Live It Up'.*	*Pye Jazz Today*	24	*15 Jun 63*	8
ACAPULCO 1922	*Pye Jazz Today*	27	*24 Aug 63*	6
HELLO DOLLY *From the musical of the same name.* *Above hit: Kenny BALL and his JAZZMEN; vocal: Kenny BALL and the BOYS.*	*Pye Jazz Today*	30	*13 Jun 64*	7
WHEN I'M SIXTY-FOUR *Originally recorded by the Beatles.*	*Pye*	43	*22 Jul 67*	2
EPS:	**HITS 2**			**WEEKS 67**
KENNY'S BIG FOUR	*Pye Jazz*	3	*2 Dec 61*	24
KENNY BALL'S HIT PARADE	*Pye*	5	*3 Mar 62*	43
ALBUMS:	**HITS 2**			**WEEKS 50**
THE BEST OF BALL, BARBER AND BILK *Above hit: Mr. Acker BILK'S PARAMOUNT JAZZ BAND/Kenny BALL and his JAZZMEN/Chris BARBER'S JAZZ BAND.*	*Pye Golden Guinea*	1	*25 Aug 62*	24
KENNY BALL'S GOLDEN HITS *Above hit: Kenny BALL.*	*Pye Golden Guinea*	4	*7 Sep 63*	26

Michael BALL — UK

(See also Various Artists: Stage Cast - London 'Aspects Of Love'; Studio Cast 'Leonard Bernstein's West Side Story'.)

SINGLES:	**HITS 10**			**WEEKS 39**
LOVE CHANGES EVERYTHING *From the musical 'Aspects Of Love'.*	*Really Useful*	2	*28 Jan 89*	14
THE FIRST MAN YOU REMEMBER *Above hit: Michael BALL and Diana MORRISON.*	*Really Useful*	68	*28 Oct 89*	2
IT'S STILL YOU	*Polydor*	58	*10 Aug 91*	2
ONE STEP OUT OF TIME *UK's Eurovision entry in 1992, it came 2nd.*	*Polydor*	20	*25 Apr 92*	7
IF I CAN DREAM [EP] *Lead track: If I Can Dream.*	*Polydor*	51	*12 Dec 92*	1
IF I CAN DREAM [EP] [RE]	*Polydor*	68	*26 Dec 92*	1
SUNSET BOULEVARD	*Polydor*	72	*11 Sep 93*	1
FROM HERE TO ETERNITY	*Columbia*	36	*30 Jul 94*	3
THE LOVERS WE WERE	*Columbia*	63	*17 Sep 94*	2
THE ROSE *Theme from the TV series 'The Ladykillers'. Original by Bette Midler reached No. 3 in the US in 1980.*	*Columbia*	42	*9 Dec 95*	4
(SOMETHING INSIDE) SO STRONG	*Columbia*	40	*17 Feb 96*	2
ALBUMS:	**HITS 10**			**WEEKS 89**
MICHAEL BALL	*Polydor*	1	*30 May 92*	10
ALWAYS	*Polydor*	3	*17 Jul 93*	11
ONE CAREFUL OWNER	*Columbia*	7	*13 Aug 94*	6
THE BEST OF MICHAEL BALL	*PolyGram TV*	25	*19 Nov 94*	7
FIRST LOVE	*Columbia*	4	*27 Jan 96*	6
THE MUSICALS	*PolyGram TV*	20	*16 Nov 96*	10
THE MOVIES	*PolyGram TV*	13	*7 Nov 98*	17
THE VERY BEST OF MICHAEL BALL IN CONCERT AT THE ROYAL ALBERT HALL / CHRISTMAS *Double album package.*	*Universal Music TV*	18	*20 Nov 99*	7
THIS TIME . . . IT'S PERSONAL	*Universal Music TV*	20	*11 Nov 00*	8
CENTRE STAGE	*Universal Music TV*	11	*29 Sep 01*	7

BALTIMORA — Ireland

SINGLES:	**HITS 1**			**WEEKS 12**
TARZAN BOY	*Columbia*	3	*10 Aug 85*	12

Charli BALTIMORE — US

SINGLES:	**HITS 1**			**WEEKS 4**
MONEY *Remake of the O'Jays' 'For The Love Of Money'; from the film 'Woo'.*	*Epic*	12	*1 Aug 98*	4

BAM-BAM — US

SINGLES:	**HITS 1**			**WEEKS 2**
GIVE IT TO ME	*Serious*	65	*19 Mar 88*	2

Afrika BAMBAATAA — US

(See also Time Zone featuring John Lydon and Afrika Bambaataa.)

SINGLES:	HITS 6			WEEKS 33
PLANET ROCK *Samples Kraftwerk's 'Trans Euro Express'.*	*Polydor*	53	*28 Aug 82*	3
THE RENEGADES OF FUNK *Above 2: Afrika BAMBAATAA and the SOUL SONIC FORCE.*	*Tommy Boy*	30	*10 Mar 84*	4
UNITY (PART 1 - THE THIRD COMING) *Above hit: Afrika BAMBAATAA and the Godfather of Soul – James BROWN.*	*Tommy Boy*	49	*1 Sep 84*	5
RECKLESS *Above hit: Afrika BAMBAATAA and FAMILY featuring UB40.*	*EMI*	17	*27 Feb 88*	8
JUST GET UP AND DANCE	*EMI USA*	45	*12 Oct 91*	3
GOT TO GET UP [RM] *Remixes by Tall Paul and Loop Da Loop.* *Above hit: Afrika BAMBAATAA vs. CARPE DIEM.*	*Multiply*	22	*17 Oct 98*	4
AFRIKA SHOX *Above hit: LEFTFIELD. BAMBAATAA.*	*Hard Hands*	7	*18 Sep 99*	5
PLANET ROCK [RM] *Above hit: Paul OAKENFOLD presents Afrika BAMBAATAA and the SOULSONIC FORCE.*	*Tommy Boy*	47	*25 Aug 01*	1

BAMBOO — UK

SINGLES:	HITS 2			WEEKS 12
BAMBOOGIE *Featured in the Bud Ice TV commercial.*	*VC Recordings*	2	*17 Jan 98*	10
THE STRUTT	*VC Recordings*	36	*4 Jul 98*	2

BANANARAMA — UK

SINGLES:	HITS 26			WEEKS 202
IT AIN'T WHAT YOU DO IT'S THE WAY THAT YOU DO IT *Originally recorded by Jimmy Lunceford.* *Above hit: FUN BOY THREE with BANANARAMA.*	*Chrysalis*	4	*13 Feb 82*	10
REALLY SAYING SOMETHING (HE WAS REALLY SAYIN' SOMETHIN') *Originally recorded by the Velvelettes.* *Above hit: BANANARAMA and the FUN BOY THREE.*	*Deram*	5	*10 Apr 82*	10
SHY BOY	*London*	4	*3 Jul 82*	11
CHEERS THEN	*London*	45	*4 Dec 82*	7
NA NA HEY HEY KISS HIM GOODBYE	*London*	5	*26 Feb 83*	10
CRUEL SUMMER	*London*	8	*9 Jul 83*	10
ROBERT DE NIRO'S WAITING	*London*	3	*3 Mar 84*	11
ROUGH JUSTICE	*London*	23	*26 May 84*	7
HOT LINE TO HEAVEN	*London*	58	*24 Nov 84*	2
DO NOT DISTURB	*London*	31	*24 Aug 85*	6
VENUS	*London*	8	*31 May 86*	13
MORE THAN PHYSICAL	*London*	41	*16 Aug 86*	5
TRICK OF THE NIGHT	*London*	32	*14 Feb 87*	5
I HEARD A RUMOUR	*London*	14	*11 Jul 87*	9
LOVE IN THE FIRST DEGREE / MR. SLEAZE *Mr. Sleaze listed from 24 Oct 87.*	*London*	3	*10 Oct 87*	12
I CAN'T HELP IT	*London*	20	*9 Jan 88*	6
I WANT YOU BACK	*London*	5	*9 Apr 88*	10
LOVE, TRUTH AND HONESTLY	*London*	23	*24 Sep 88*	8
NATHAN JONES	*London*	15	*19 Nov 88*	9
HELP *In aid of Comic Relief.* *Above hit: BANANARAMA LA NA NEE NEE NOO NOO.*	*London*	3	*25 Feb 89*	9
CRUEL SUMMER (SWING BEAT VERSION) [RM] *Remixed by Atkins, Atkins and Trottman.*	*London*	19	*10 Jun 89*	6
ONLY YOUR LOVE	*London*	27	*28 Jul 90*	4
PREACHER MAN	*London*	20	*5 Jan 91*	6
LONG TRAIN RUNNING	*London*	30	*20 Apr 91*	5
MOVIN' ON	*London*	24	*29 Aug 92*	5
LAST THING ON MY MIND	*London*	71	*28 Nov 92*	2
MORE, MORE, MORE	*London*	24	*20 Mar 93*	4

ALBUMS:	HITS 8			WEEKS 99
DEEP SEA SKIVING	*London*	7	*19 Mar 83*	16
BANANARAMA	*London*	16	*28 Apr 84*	11
TRUE CONFESSIONS	*London*	46	*19 Jul 86*	5
WOW!	*London*	26	*19 Sep 87*	26
THE GREATEST HITS COLLECTION	*London*	3	*22 Oct 88*	37
POP LIFE	*London*	42	*25 May 91*	1
PLEASE YOURSELF	*London*	46	*10 Apr 93*	1
THE VERY BEST OF BANANARAMA	*London*	43	*10 Nov 01*	2

BANCO DE GAIA — UK

ALBUMS:	HITS 2			WEEKS 4
MAYA	*Ultimate*	34	*12 Mar 94*	2
LAST TRAIN TO LHASA	*Planet Dog*	31	*13 May 95*	2
Lhasa is the capital of Tibet.				

BAND — US/Canada

SINGLES:	HITS 2			WEEKS 18
THE WEIGHT	*Capitol*	21	*21 Sep 68*	9
Single shows full credit as Jamie Robbie Robertson-Rick Danko-Richard Manuel-Gartha Hudson-Leyon Helm-(The Band).				
RAG MAMA RAG	*Capitol*	16	*4 Apr 70*	9
ALBUMS:	**HITS 4**			**WEEKS 23**
THE BAND	*Capitol*	25	*31 Jan 70*	11
STAGE FRIGHT	*Capitol*	15	*3 Oct 70*	6
CAHOOTS	*Capitol*	41	*27 Nov 71*	1
THE LAST WALTZ [OST]	*Warner Brothers*	39	*6 May 78*	4
Live recordings from their final concert at the Winterland, San Francisco, 25 Nov 76. Features guests Eric Clapton, Bob Dylan, Neil Diamond, Joni Mitchell, Van Morrison, Ringo Starr, Muddy Waters and Neil Young.				
THE BAND [RE]	*Capitol*	41	*30 Aug 97*	1
Re-released. Charted after being featured on BBC1 TV's 'Classic Albums' series.				

BAND A.K.A. — US

SINGLES:	HITS 2			WEEKS 12
GRACE	*Epic*	41	*15 May 82*	5
JOY	*Epic*	24	*5 Mar 83*	7

BAND AID — International

SINGLES:	HITS 2			WEEKS 26
DO THEY KNOW IT'S CHRISTMAS?	*Mercury*	1	*15 Dec 84*	13
DO THEY KNOW IT'S CHRISTMAS? [RE]	*Mercury*	3	*7 Dec 85*	7
DO THEY KNOW IT'S CHRISTMAS? [RR]	*PWL/Polydor*	1	*23 Dec 89*	6
Above hit: BAND AID II.				

BAND OF GOLD — Holland

SINGLES:	HITS 1			WEEKS 11
LOVE SONGS ARE BACK AGAIN [M]	*RCA*	24	*14 Jul 84*	11
9 track medley of ballads.				

BANDA SONORA — UK

SINGLES:	HITS 1			WEEKS 2
GUITARRA G	*Defected*	50	*6 Oct 01*	2

BANDERAS — UK

SINGLES:	HITS 2			WEEKS 16
THIS IS YOUR LIFE	*London*	16	*23 Feb 91*	10
SHE SELLS	*London*	41	*15 Jun 91*	6
ALBUMS:	**HITS 1**			**WEEKS 3**
RIPE	*London*	40	*13 Apr 91*	3

BANDITS – See Billy COTTON and his BAND

BANDWAGON – See Johnny JOHNSON and the BANDWAGON

Honey BANE — UK

SINGLES:	HITS 2			WEEKS 8
TURN ME ON TURN ME OFF	*Zonophone*	37	*24 Jan 81*	5
BABY LOVE	*Zonophone*	58	*18 Apr 81*	3

BANG — UK

SINGLES:	HITS 1			WEEKS 2
YOU'RE THE ONE	*RCA*	74	*6 May 89*	2

BANGLES — US

SINGLES:	HITS 11			WEEKS 94
MANIC MONDAY	*CBS*	2	*15 Feb 86*	12 ●
Written by Prince under the pseudonym Christopher.				
IF SHE KNEW WHAT SHE WANTS	*CBS*	31	*26 Apr 86*	7
Originally recorded by Jules Shear.				
GOING DOWN TO LIVERPOOL	*CBS*	56	*5 Jul 86*	3
Original release reached No. 79 in 1985. Originally recorded by Katrina and the Waves.				
WALK LIKE AN EGYPTIAN	*CBS*	3	*13 Sep 86*	19

WALKING DOWN YOUR STREET	*CBS*	16	*10 Jan 87*	6
FOLLOWING	*CBS*	55	*18 Apr 87*	3
HAZY SHADE OF WINTER	*Def Jam*	11	*6 Feb 88*	10
From the film 'Less Than Zero'. Original by Simon and Garfunkel reached No. 13 in the US in 1966.				
IN YOUR ROOM	*CBS*	35	*5 Nov 88*	6
ETERNAL FLAME	*CBS*	1	*18 Feb 89*	18
BE WITH YOU	*CBS*	23	*10 Jun 89*	8
I'LL SET YOU FREE	*CBS*	74	*14 Oct 89*	1
WALK LIKE AN EGYPTIAN [RI]	*CBS*	73	*9 Jun 90*	1
ALBUMS:	**HITS 5**			**WEEKS 104**
ALL OVER THE PLACE	*CBS*	86	*16 Mar 85*	1
DIFFERENT LIGHT	*CBS*	30	*15 Mar 86*	14
DIFFERENT LIGHT [RE]	*CBS*	3	*4 Oct 86*	33
EVERYTHING	*CBS*	5	*10 Dec 88*	26
GREATEST HITS	*CBS*	4	*9 Jun 90*	19
GREATEST HITS [RI]	*Columbia*	37	*7 May 94*	4
Re-released at mid-price. Peak position reached in 1995 (1994 peak No. 64).				
ETERNAL FLAME - THE BEST OF THE BANGLES	*Columbia*	15	*4 Aug 01*	7

Tony BANKS — UK

SINGLES:	**HITS 1**			**WEEKS 1**
SHORTCUT TO SOMEWHERE	*Charisma*	75	*18 Oct 86*	1
Above hit: FISH and Tony BANKS.				
ALBUMS:	**HITS 2**			**WEEKS 7**
A CURIOUS FEELING	*Charisma*	21	*20 Oct 79*	5
THE FUGITIVE	*Charisma*	50	*25 Jun 83*	2

BANNED — UK

SINGLES:	**HITS 1**			**WEEKS 6**
LITTLE GIRL	*Harvest*	36	*17 Dec 77*	6
Original by Syndicate Of Sound reached No. 8 in the US in 1966.				

Buju BANTON — Jamaica

(See also Jamaica United.)

SINGLES:	**HITS 1**			**WEEKS 1**
MAKE MY DAY	*Mercury*	72	*7 Aug 93*	1

Pato BANTON — UK

SINGLES:	**HITS 5**			**WEEKS 37**
BABY COME BACK	*Virgin*	1	*1 Oct 94*	18
Above hit: Pato BANTON featuring Ali and Robin CAMPBELL of UB40.				
THIS COWBOY SONG	*A&M*	15	*11 Feb 95*	6
Above hit: STING (featuring Pato BANTON).				
BUBBLING HOT	*Virgin*	15	*8 Apr 95*	7
Above hit: Pato BANTON with RANKING ROGER.				
SPIRITS IN THE MATERIAL WORLD	*MCA*	36	*20 Jan 96*	2
From the film 'Ace Ventura When Nature Calls'. Above hit: Pato BANTON with STING.				
GROOVIN'	*I.R.S.*	14	*27 Jul 96*	4
Above hit: Pato BANTON and the REGGAE REVOLUTION.				

BAR-CODES featuring Alison BROWN — UK

SINGLES:	**HITS 1**			**WEEKS 1**
SUPERMARKET SWEEP (WILL YOU DANCE WITH ME)	*Blanca Casa*	72	*17 Dec 94*	1
With M.C. Dale (Winton), from ITV show of the same name. Later copies were credited as M.C. Dale and the Bar-Codes.				

BAR-KAYS — US

SINGLES:	**HITS 3**			**WEEKS 15**
SOUL FINGER	*Stax*	33	*26 Aug 67*	7
SHAKE YOUR RUMP TO THE FUNK	*Mercury*	41	*22 Jan 77*	4
SEXOMATIC	*Club*	51	*12 Jan 85*	4

Chris BARBER'S JAZZ BAND — UK

(See also Van Morrison/Lonnie Donegan/Chris Barber.)

SINGLES:	**HITS 3**			**WEEKS 30**
PETITE FLEUR	*Pye Nixa*	3	*14 Feb 59*	22
Originally recorded by Sidney Bechet. Above hit: Chris BARBER'S JAZZ BAND; Clarinet Solo – Monty SUNSHINE.				
PETITE FLEUR [RE]	*Pye Nixa*	22	*1 Aug 59*	2
LONESOME (SI TU VOIS MA MERE)	*Columbia*	27	*10 Oct 59*	2
Above hit: Chris BARBER'S JAZZ BAND featuring Monty SUNSHINE.				
REVIVAL	*Columbia*	50	*6 Jan 62*	2

REVIVAL [RE]	*Columbia*	43	*3 Feb 62*	2
EPS:	**HITS 1**			**WEEKS 1**
BARBERS BEST VOLUME 1	*Decca*	11	*25 Jun 60*	1
ALBUMS:	**HITS 6**			**WEEKS 88**
CHRIS BARBER BAND BOX NUMBER 2	*Columbia*	17	*24 Sep 60*	1
ELITE SYNCOPATIONS	*Columbia*	18	*5 Nov 60*	1
THE BEST OF CHRIS BARBER	*Ace Of Clubs*	17	*12 Nov 60*	1
Above hit: Chris BARBER'S JAZZ BAND with guest artist - Lonnie DONEGAN.				
THE BEST OF BARBER AND BILK VOLUME ONE	*Pye Golden Guinea*	4	*27 May 61*	43
THE BEST OF BARBER AND BILK VOLUME TWO	*Pye Golden Guinea*	8	*11 Nov 61*	18
Above 2 albums have one side by each artist.				
Above 2: Chris BARBER'S JAZZ BAND/MR. ACKER BILK and his PARAMOUNT JAZZ BAND.				
THE BEST OF BALL, BARBER AND BILK	*Pye Golden Guinea*	1	*25 Aug 62*	24
Compilation with 4 tracks by each band.				
Above hit: Mr. Acker BILK'S PARAMOUNT JAZZ BAND/Kenny Ball and his Jazzmen /Chris BARBER'S JAZZ BAND.				

BARBRA and NEIL - See Barbra STREISAND; Neil DIAMOND

BARCLAY JAMES HARVEST — UK

SINGLES:	**HITS 4**			**WEEKS 9**
LIVE [EP]	*Polydor*	49	*2 Apr 77*	1
Lead track: Rock 'N Roll Star.				
LIVE [EP] [RE]	*Polydor*	49	*16 Apr 77*	1
LOVE ON THE LINE	*Polydor*	63	*26 Jan 80*	2
LIFE IS FOR LIVING	*Polydor*	61	*22 Nov 80*	3
JUST A DAY AWAY	*Polydor*	68	*21 May 83*	2
ALBUMS:	**HITS 10**			**WEEKS 42**
BARCLAY JAMES HARVEST LIVE	*Polydor*	40	*14 Dec 74*	2
TIME HONOURED GHOST	*Polydor*	32	*18 Oct 75*	3
OCTOBERON	*Polydor*	19	*23 Oct 76*	4
GONE TO EARTH	*Polydor*	30	*1 Oct 77*	7
BARCLAY JAMES HARVEST XII	*Polydor*	31	*21 Oct 78*	2
TURN OF THE TIDE	*Polydor*	55	*23 May 81*	2
A CONCERT FOR THE PEOPLE (BERLIN)	*Polydor*	15	*24 Jul 82*	11
RING OF CHANGES	*Polydor*	36	*28 May 83*	4
VICTIMS OF CIRCUMSTANCE	*Polydor*	33	*14 Apr 84*	6
FACE TO FACE	*Polydor*	65	*14 Feb 87*	1

BARDO — UK

SINGLES:	**HITS 1**			**WEEKS 8**
ONE STEP FURTHER	*Epic*	2	*10 Apr 82*	8
UK's Eurovision entry in 1982, it came 7th.				

BARDOT — Australia

SINGLES:	**HITS 1**			**WEEKS 1**
POISON	*East West*	45	*14 Apr 01*	1
Featured in the Australian version of the 'Popstars' TV show				

Bobby BARE - See Bill PARSONS

BAREFOOT MAN — Germany

SINGLES:	**HITS 1**			**WEEKS 7**
BIG PANTY WOMAN	*Plaza*	21	*5 Dec 98*	7

BARENAKED LADIES — Canada

SINGLES:	**HITS 4**			**WEEKS 12**
ONE WEEK	*Reprise*	5	*20 Feb 99*	8
IT'S ALL BEEN DONE	*Reprise*	28	*15 May 99*	2
CALL AND ANSWER	*Reprise*	52	*24 Jul 99*	1
From the film 'EDtv'.				
BRIAN WILSON (2000)	*Reprise*	73	*11 Dec 99*	1
First appeared on the 1993 album Gordon.				
ALBUMS:	**HITS 3**			**WEEKS 18**
MAYBE YOU SHOULD DRIVE	*Reprise*	57	*27 Aug 94*	1
STUNT	*Reprise*	20	*6 Mar 99*	16
MAROON	*Reprise*	64	*30 Sep 00*	1

Daniel BARENBOIM - See John WILLIAMS

BARKIN BROTHERS featuring Johnnie FIORI — UK

SINGLES:	**HITS 1**			**WEEKS 2**
GONNA CATCH YOU	*Brothers Organisation*	51	*15 Apr 00*	2
Samples Lonnie Gordon's Gonna Catch You.				

Gary BARLOW — UK

SINGLES:	HITS 6			WEEKS 47
FOREVER LOVE *From the film 'The Leading Man'.*	*RCA*	1	*20 Jul 96*	16
LOVE WON'T WAIT *Co-written with Madonna.*	*RCA*	1	*10 May 97*	7
LOVE WON'T WAIT [RE-1ST]	*RCA*	64	*26 Jul 97*	1
SO HELP ME GIRL *Originally recorded by Joe Diffie.*	*RCA*	11	*26 Jul 97*	7
LOVE WON'T WAIT [RE-2ND]	*RCA*	67	*9 Aug 97*	1
SO HELP ME GIRL [RE]	*RCA*	64	*20 Sep 97*	4
OPEN ROAD	*RCA*	7	*15 Nov 97*	5
STRONGER	*RCA*	16	*17 Jul 99*	4
FOR ALL THAT YOU WANT	*RCA*	24	*9 Oct 99*	2
ALBUMS:	**HITS 2**			**WEEKS 27**
OPEN ROAD	*RCA*	1	*7 Jun 97*	26
TWELVE MONTHS, ELEVEN DAYS	*RCA*	35	*23 Oct 99*	1

BARNBRACK — UK

SINGLES:	HITS 1			WEEKS 7
BELFAST	Homespun	45	*16 Mar 85*	7

Jimmy BARNES and INXS — Australia

(See also INXS.)

SINGLES:	HITS 1			WEEKS 8
GOOD TIMES *From the film 'The Lost Boys'. Originally recorded by the Easybeats.*	*Atlantic*	18	*26 Jan 91*	8

Richard BARNES — UK

SINGLES:	HITS 2			WEEKS 10
TAKE TO THE MOUNTAINS	*Philips*	35	*23 May 70*	6
GO NORTH	*Philips*	49	*24 Oct 70*	1
GO NORTH [RE]	*Philips*	38	*7 Nov 70*	3

Kathy BARNET - See Claude FRANCOIS; girl vocal: Kathy BARNET

Gary BARNICLE - See BIG FUN; SONIA

BAROCK-AND-ROLL ENSEMBLE — Germany

EPS:	HITS 1			WEEKS 12
EINE KLEINE BEATLEMUSIK *Although not credited on the cover, the B-side of this EP is titled On The Bayreuth Beat and is by Val Kyrie and the Rhine Maidens.*	*HMV*	4	*29 May 65*	12

BARRACUDAS — UK/US

SINGLES:	HITS 1			WEEKS 6
SUMMER FUN	*EMI-Wipe Out*	37	*16 Aug 80*	6

Syd BARRETT — UK

ALBUMS:	HITS 1			WEEKS 1
THE MADCAP LAUGHS	*Harvest*	40	*7 Feb 70*	1

Amanda BARRIE and Johnny BRIGGS - See CORONATION STREET CAST

J.J. BARRIE — Canada

SINGLES:	HITS 1			WEEKS 11
NO CHARGE *Original by Melba Montgomery reached No. 39 in the US in 1974.*	*Power Exchange*	1	*24 Apr 76*	11

Ken BARRIE — UK

SINGLES:	HITS 1			WEEKS 15
POSTMAN PAT *Theme from the Children's BBC TV series.*	*Post Music*	44	*10 Jul 82*	8
POSTMAN PAT [RE-1ST]	*Post Music*	54	*25 Dec 82*	3
POSTMAN PAT [RE-2ND]	*Post Music*	59	*24 Dec 83*	4

BARRON KNIGHTS — UK

SINGLES:	HITS 13			WEEKS 95
CALL UP THE GROUPS [M]	*Columbia*	3	*11 Jul 64*	13
COME TO THE DANCE	*Columbia*	42	*24 Oct 64*	2
POP GO THE WORKERS [M]	*Columbia*	5	*27 Mar 65*	13
MERRY GENTLE POPS [M]	*Columbia*	9	*18 Dec 65*	7
UNDER NEW MANAGEMENT [M] *Above 5: BARRON KNIGHTS with Duke D'MOND.*	*Columbia*	15	*3 Dec 66*	9

AN OLYMPIC RECORD [M]	*Columbia*	35	*26 Oct 68*	4
LIVE IN TROUBLE [M]	*Epic*	7	*29 Oct 77*	11
A TASTE OF AGGRO [M]	*Epic*	3	*2 Dec 78*	10
FOOD FOR THOUGHT [M]	*Epic*	46	*8 Dec 79*	6
THE SIT SONG	*Epic*	44	*4 Oct 80*	4
Spoof of dog trainer Barbara Woodhouse.				
NEVER MIND THE PRESENTS [M]	*Epic*	17	*6 Dec 80*	8
BLACKBOARD JUMBLE [M]	*Epic*	52	*5 Dec 81*	5
All medleys listed above are parodies of contemporary hits.				
BUFFALO BILL'S LAST SCRATCH	*Epic*	49	*19 Mar 83*	3
ALBUMS:	**HITS 3**			**WEEKS 22**
NIGHT GALLERY	*Epic*	15	*2 Dec 78*	13
TEACH THE WORLD TO LAUGH	*Epic*	51	*1 Dec 79*	4
JUST A GIGGLE	*Epic*	45	*13 Dec 80*	5

Joe BARRY — US

SINGLES:	**HITS 1**			**WEEKS 1**
I'M A FOOL TO CARE	*Mercury*	49	*26 Aug 61*	1
Originally recorded by Les Paul and Mary Ford.				

John BARRY — UK

(See also Russ Conway; Adam Faith; Nina and Frederik.)

SINGLES:	**HITS 10**			**WEEKS 79**
HIT AND MISS	*Columbia*	10	*5 Mar 60*	13
Above hit: John BARRY SEVEN plus FOUR.				
BEAT FOR BEATNIKS	*Columbia*	40	*30 Apr 60*	2
Above hit: John BARRY and his Orchestra.				
HIT AND MISS [RE]	*Columbia*	45	*11 Jun 60*	1
NEVER LET GO	*Columbia*	49	*16 Jul 60*	1
BLUEBERRY HILL	*Columbia*	34	*20 Aug 60*	3
Above 2 entries were separate sides of the same release, each had its own chart run.				
Above 2: John BARRY ORCHESTRA.				
WALK DON'T RUN	*Columbia*	49	*10 Sep 60*	1
WALK DON'T RUN [RE]	*Columbia*	11	*24 Sep 60*	13
BLACK STOCKINGS	*Columbia*	27	*10 Dec 60*	9
THE MAGNIFICENT SEVEN	*Columbia*	48	*4 Mar 61*	1
From the film of the same name.				
THE MAGNIFICENT SEVEN [RE-1ST]	*Columbia*	45	*18 Mar 61*	2
THE MAGNIFICENT SEVEN [RE-2ND]	*Columbia*	50	*8 Apr 61*	1
THE MAGNIFICENT SEVEN [RE-3RD]	*Columbia*	47	*10 Jun 61*	1
Above 7: John BARRY SEVEN.				
CUTTY SARK	*Columbia*	35	*28 Apr 62*	2
THE JAMES BOND THEME	*Columbia*	13	*3 Nov 62*	11
From the film 'Doctor No'.				
FROM RUSSIA WITH LOVE	*Ember*	44	*23 Nov 63*	1
From the James Bond film of the same name.				
FROM RUSSIA WITH LOVE [RE]	*Ember*	39	*21 Dec 63*	2
Above 4: John BARRY SEVEN and ORCHESTRA.				
THEME FROM "THE PERSUADERS"	*CBS*	13	*11 Dec 71*	15
From the TV series.				
EPS:	**HITS 1**			**WEEKS 25**
THE JOHN BARRY SOUND	*Columbia*	4	*25 Feb 61*	25
Above hit: John BARRY 7 + 4.				
ALBUMS:	**HITS 8**			**WEEKS 35**
BEAT GIRL [OST]	*Columbia*	11	*11 Feb 61*	3
Above hit: Adam FAITH/John BARRY SEVEN /John BARRY ORCHESTRA.				
JAMES BOND 007 - GOLDFINGER [OST]	*United Artists*	14	*31 Oct 64*	5
Includes title track by Shirley Bassey.				
THE PERSUADERS [OST-TV]	*CBS*	18	*29 Jan 72*	9
JAMES BOND 007 - A VIEW TO A KILL [OST]	*Parlophone*	81	*22 Jun 85*	1
Includes title track by Duran Duran.				
OUT OF AFRICA [OST]	*MCA*	81	*26 Apr 86*	2
JAMES BOND 007 - THE LIVING DAYLIGHTS [OST]	*Warner Brothers*	57	*1 Aug 87*	6
Includes tracks by A-ha and Pretenders.				
DANCES WITH WOLVES [OST]	*Epic*	45	*20 Apr 91*	8
THE BEYONDNESS OF THINGS	*Decca*	67	*8 May 99*	1
Above hit: ENGLISH CHAMBER ORCHESTRA Conducted by John BARRY.				

Len BARRY — US

SINGLES:	**HITS 2**			**WEEKS 24**
1-2-3	*Brunswick*	3	*6 Nov 65*	14
LIKE A BABY	*Brunswick*	10	*15 Jan 66*	10

Michael BARRYMORE — UK

SINGLES:	HITS 1			WEEKS 4
TOO MUCH FOR ONE HEART	*EMI*	25	*16 Dec 95*	4

Lionel BART — UK

SINGLES:	HITS 1			WEEKS 3
HAPPY ENDINGS (GIVE YOURSELF A PINCH)	*EMI*	68	*25 Nov 89*	1
Featured in the Abbey National TV commercial.				
HAPPY ENDINGS (GIVE YOURSELF A PINCH) [RE]	*EMI*	71	*23 Dec 89*	2
EPS:	**HITS 1**			**WEEKS 1**
BART FOR BART'S SAKE	*Decca*	20	*26 Mar 60*	1

BART and HOMER – See SIMPSONS

BARTHEZZ — Holland

SINGLES:	HITS 1			WEEKS 4
ON THE MOVE	*Positiva*	18	*22 Sep 01*	4

BAS NOIR — US

SINGLES:	HITS 1			WEEKS 1
MY LOVE IS MAGIC	*10 Records*	73	*11 Feb 89*	1

Rob BASE and D.J. E-Z ROCK — US

SINGLES:	HITS 3			WEEKS 19
IT TAKES TWO	*Citybeat*	24	*16 Apr 88*	6
Samples Lyn Collins' Think.				
GET ON THE DANCE FLOOR	*Supreme*	14	*14 Jan 89*	7
IT TAKES TWO [RE]	*Citybeat*	49	*4 Mar 89*	3
JOY AND PAIN	*Supreme*	47	*22 Apr 89*	3
Features rap by Omar Chandler.				

BASEMENT BOYS – See Ultra NATE

BASEMENT JAXX — UK

SINGLES:	HITS 8			WEEKS 48
FLY LIFE	*Multiply*	19	*31 May 97*	3
RED ALERT	*XL Recordings*	5	*1 May 99*	10
Samples Locksmith's Far Beyond.				
RENDEZ-VU	*XL Recordings*	4	*14 Aug 99*	8
JUMP N' SHOUT	*XL Recordings*	12	*6 Nov 99*	5
Vocals by Slarta John and Madman Swyli.				
Above hit: BASEMENT JAXX Featuring SLARTA JOHN.				
BINGO BANGO	*XL Recordings*	13	*15 Apr 00*	4
Keyboard solo performed by Ugo Delmirani.				
Samples Merenque by Boliva.				
ROMEO	*XL Recordings*	6	*16 Jun 01*	10
Vocals by Kele Le Roc.				
JUS 1 KISS	*XL Recordings*	23	*6 Oct 01*	3
Vocals by Clix.				
JUS 1 KISS [RE]	*XL Recordings*	66	*3 Nov 01*	1
WHERE'S YOUR HEAD AT?	*XL Recordings*	9	*8 Dec 01*	4
Samples This Wreckage by Gary Numan.				
ALBUMS:	**HITS 2**			**WEEKS 64**
REMEDY	*XL Recordings*	4	*22 May 99*	45
ROOTY	*XL Recordings*	5	*7 Jul 01*	19

BASIA — Poland

SINGLES:	HITS 3			WEEKS 9
PROMISES (FRENCH MIX)	*Epic*	48	*23 Jan 88*	4
TIME AND TIDE	*Epic*	61	*28 May 88*	3
DRUNK ON LOVE	*Epic*	41	*14 Jan 95*	2
ALBUMS:	**HITS 2**			**WEEKS 4**
TIME AND TIDE	*Portrait*	61	*13 Feb 88*	3
LONDON WARSAW NEW YORK	*Epic*	68	*3 Mar 90*	1

Count BASIE and his Orchestra — US

(See also Frank Sinatra and Count Basie and his Orchestra.)

ALBUMS:	HITS 1			WEEKS 1
CHAIRMAN OF THE BOARD	*Columbia*	17	*16 Apr 60*	1

Toni BASIL — US

SINGLES:	HITS 2			WEEKS 16
MICKEY *Originally recorded by Racey (as Kitty).*	*Radialchoice*	2	*6 Feb 82*	12
NOBODY	*Radialchoice*	52	*1 May 82*	4
ALBUMS:	**HITS 1**			**WEEKS 16**
WORD OF MOUTH	*Radialchoice*	15	*6 Feb 82*	16

Olav BASOSKI — Holland

SINGLES:	HITS 1			WEEKS 1
OPIUM SCUMBAGZ	*Defected*	56	*26 Aug 00*	1

Fontella BASS — US

SINGLES:	HITS 2			WEEKS 15
RESCUE ME	*Chess*	11	*4 Dec 65*	10
RECOVERY	*Chess*	32	*22 Jan 66*	5

Norman BASS — Germany

SINGLES:	HITS 1			WEEKS 4
HOW U LIKE BASS?	*Substance*	17	*21 Apr 01*	4

Sid BASS' ORCHESTRA - See FOUR ESQUIRES - vocal with the Sid BASS' ORCHESTRA

BASS BOYZ — UK

(See also Pianoman.)

SINGLES:	HITS 1			WEEKS 1
GUNZ AND PIANOZ *Based around the guitar riff from Sweet Child Of Mine by Guns N'Roses.*	*Polydor*	74	*28 Sep 96*	1

BASS BUMPERS — Germany/UK

SINGLES:	HITS 2			WEEKS 4
RUNNIN'	*Vertigo*	68	*25 Sep 93*	1
THE MUSIC'S GOT ME	*Vertigo*	25	*5 Feb 94*	3

BASS JUMPERS — Holland

SINGLES:	HITS 1			WEEKS 1
MAKE UP YOUR MIND	*Pepper*	44	*13 Feb 99*	1

BASS-O-MATIC — UK

SINGLES:	HITS 4			WEEKS 19
IN THE REALM OF THE SENSES	*Virgin*	66	*12 May 90*	3
FASCINATING RHYTHM	*Virgin*	9	*1 Sep 90*	11
EASE ON BY	*Virgin*	61	*22 Dec 90*	4
FUNKY LOVE VIBRATIONS	*Virgin*	71	*3 Aug 91*	1
ALBUMS:	**HITS 1**			**WEEKS 2**
SET THE CONTROLS FOR THE HEART OF THE BASS	*Virgin*	57	*13 Oct 90*	2

Shirley BASSEY — UK

SINGLES:	HITS 30			WEEKS 326
THE BANANA BOAT SONG	*Philips*	8	*16 Feb 57*	10
FIRE DOWN BELOW *Inspired by the film 'Fire Down Below'.*	*Philips*	30	*24 Aug 57*	1
YOU, YOU ROMEO *Above 2 entries were separate sides of the same release, each had its own chart run.*	*Philips*	29	*7 Sep 57*	2
AS I LOVE YOU *From the film 'The Big Beat'. Originally recorded by Carmen McCrae.*	*Philips*	27	*20 Dec 58*	2
KISS ME, HONEY HONEY, KISS ME *Originally recorded by Gogi Grant.*	*Philips*	3	*27 Dec 58*	17
AS I LOVE YOU [RE] *Above 6: Shirley BASSEY with Wally STOTT and his Orchestra.*	*Philips*	1	*10 Jan 59*	17
WITH THESE HANDS	*Columbia*	38	*2 Apr 60*	2
WITH THESE HANDS [RE-1ST]	*Columbia*	31	*23 Apr 60*	2
WITH THESE HANDS [RE-2ND]	*Columbia*	41	*14 May 60*	2
AS LONG AS HE NEEDS ME *From the musical 'Oliver!'.*	*Columbia*	2	*6 Aug 60*	30
YOU'LL NEVER KNOW *Originally recorded by Dick Haymes in 1943.* *Above 5: Shirley BASSEY with the Rita WILLIAMS SINGERS and Geoff LOVE and his Orchestra.*	*Columbia*	6	*13 May 61*	17
REACH FOR THE STARS / CLIMB EV'RY MOUNTAIN *Climb Ev'ry Mountain from the musical 'The Sound Of Music'; it was not listed from 30 Sep 61.* *Above hit: Shirley BASSEY with Geoff LOVE and his Orchestra.*	*Columbia*	1	*29 Jul 61*	16

REACH FOR THE STARS [RE]	*Columbia*	40	*25 Nov 61*	2
I'LL GET BY (AS LONG AS I HAVE YOU)	*Columbia*	10	*25 Nov 61*	8
Originally recorded by Ruth Etting.				
Above hit: Shirley BASSEY with the WILLIAMS SINGERS and Geoff LOVE and his Orchestra.				
TONIGHT	*Columbia*	21	*17 Feb 62*	8
From the film/show 'West Side Story'.				
Above hit: Shirley BASSEY and the Rita WILLIAMS SINGERS with Geoff LOVE and his Orchestra.				
AVE MARIA	*Columbia*	31	*28 Apr 62*	4
Ave Maria is a Catholic form of address to the Virgin Mary.				
FAR AWAY	*Columbia*	24	*2 Jun 62*	13
From the musical 'Blitz'.				
Above hit: Shirley BASSEY with Geoff LOVE and his Orchestra.				
WHAT NOW MY LOVE?	*Columbia*	5	*1 Sep 62*	17
Above hit: Shirley BASSEY with Nelson RIDDLE and his Orchestra.				
WHAT KIND OF FOOL AM I?	*Columbia*	47	*2 Mar 63*	2
From the show 'Stop The World I Want To Get Off'.				
Above hit: Shirley BASSEY with Frank BARBER and his Orchestra.				
I (WHO HAVE NOTHING) (UNO DEI TANTI)	*Columbia*	6	*28 Sep 63*	20
Original by Ben E. King reached No. 29 in the US in 1963.				
MY SPECIAL DREAM (THEME FROM "THE VICTORS")	*Columbia*	32	*25 Jan 64*	7
GONE	*Columbia*	36	*11 Apr 64*	5
GOLDFINGER	*Columbia*	21	*17 Oct 64*	9
From the James Bond film of the same name.				
NO REGRETS (NON JE NE REGRETTE RIEN)	*Columbia*	39	*22 May 65*	4
Originally recorded by Edith Piaf.				
BIG SPENDER	*United Artists*	21	*14 Oct 67*	15
From 'Sweet Charity'.				
SOMETHING	*United Artists*	4	*20 Jun 70*	21
Written by George Harrison.				
THE FOOL ON THE HILL	*United Artists*	48	*2 Jan 71*	1
Originally written and recorded by the Beatles.				
SOMETHING [RE]	*United Artists*	50	*23 Jan 71*	1
(WHERE DO I BEGIN) LOVE STORY	*United Artists*	34	*27 Mar 71*	9
From the film 'Love Story'.				
FOR ALL WE KNOW	*United Artists*	46	*7 Aug 71*	1
From the film 'Lovers And Other Strangers'. Originally recorded by Larry Meredith.				
FOR ALL WE KNOW [RE]	*United Artists*	6	*21 Aug 71*	23
DIAMONDS ARE FOREVER	*United Artists*	38	*15 Jan 72*	6
From the James Bond film of the same name.				
NEVER, NEVER, NEVER (GRANDE, GRANDE, GRANDE)	*United Artists*	8	*3 Mar 73*	18
NEVER, NEVER, NEVER (GRANDE, GRANDE, GRANDE) [RE]	*United Artists*	48	*14 Jul 73*	1
THE RHYTHM DIVINE	*Mercury*	54	*22 Aug 87*	2
Backing vocals by Billy Mackenzie (The Associates).				
Above hit: YELLO featuring Shirley BASSEY.				
'DISCO' LA PASSIONE	*East West*	41	*16 Nov 96*	1
From the film 'La Passione'.				
Above hit: Chris REA/Shirley BASSEY.				
• HISTORY REPEATING	*Wall Of Sound*	19	*20 Dec 97*	7
Above hit: PROPELLERHEADS featuring Miss Shirley BASSEY.				
WORLD IN UNION	*Decca*	35	*23 Oct 99*	3
Official ITV theme of the 1999 Rugby World Cup. Features The Morriston Rugby Club Choir and the City of Prague Philharmonic Orchestra.				
Above hit: Shirley BASSEY, Bryn TERFEL and the BLACK MOUNTAIN MALE CHORUS.				

EPS:	**HITS 5**			**WEEKS 78**
THE FABULOUS MISS BASSEY	*Columbia*	5	*22 Oct 60*	15
AS LONG AS HE NEEDS ME	*Columbia*	3	*21 Jan 61*	57
THE FABULOUS SHIRLEY BASSEY (NO. 2)	*Columbia*	15	*18 Feb 61*	2
SHIRLEY (NO. 2)	*Columbia*	15	*2 Dec 61*	3
DYNAMIC SHIRLEY BASSEY	*Columbia*	15	*28 Nov 64*	1

ALBUMS:	**HITS 35**			**WEEKS 298**
FABULOUS SHIRLEY BASSEY	*Columbia*	12	*28 Jan 61*	2
Originally released in 1959.				
SHIRLEY	*Columbia*	9	*25 Feb 61*	10
SHIRLEY BASSEY	*Columbia*	14	*17 Feb 62*	11
LET'S FACE THE MUSIC	*Columbia*	12	*15 Dec 62*	7
Above hit: Shirley BASSEY with the NELSON RIDDLE ORCHESTRA.				
SHIRLEY BASSEY AT THE PIGALLE	*Columbia*	15	*4 Dec 65*	7
I'VE GOT A SONG FOR YOU	*United Artists*	26	*27 Aug 66*	1
TWELVE OF THOSE SONGS	*Columbia*	38	*17 Feb 68*	3
GOLDEN HITS OF SHIRLEY BASSEY	*Columbia*	28	*7 Dec 68*	40
LIVE AT THE TALK OF THE TOWN	*United Artists*	38	*11 Jul 70*	6
SOMETHING	*United Artists*	5	*29 Aug 70*	28
SOMETHING ELSE	*United Artists*	7	*15 May 71*	9
BIG SPENDER	*Sunset*	27	*2 Oct 71*	8

IT'S MAGIC	*Starline*	32	*30 Oct 71*	1
Above 2 were budget releases.				
THE FABULOUS SHIRLEY BASSEY	*Music For Pleasure*	48	*6 Nov 71*	1
WHAT NOW MY LOVE	*Music For Pleasure*	17	*4 Dec 71*	5
THE SHIRLEY BASSEY COLLECTION	*United Artists*	37	*8 Jan 72*	1
I CAPRICORN	*United Artists*	13	*19 Feb 72*	11
AND I LOVE YOU SO	*United Artists*	24	*25 Nov 72*	9
NEVER NEVER NEVER	*United Artists*	10	*2 Jun 73*	10
THE SHIRLEY BASSEY SINGLES ALBUM	*United Artists*	2	*15 Mar 75*	23
GOOD, BAD BUT BEAUTIFUL	*United Artists*	13	*1 Nov 75*	7
LOVE, LIFE AND FEELINGS	*United Artists*	13	*15 May 76*	5
THOUGHTS OF LOVE	*United Artists*	15	*4 Dec 76*	9
YOU TAKE MY HEART AWAY	*United Artists*	34	*25 Jun 77*	5
25TH ANNIVERSARY ALBUM	*United Artists*	3	*4 Nov 78*	12
THE MAGIC IS YOU	*United Artists*	40	*12 May 79*	5
LOVE SONGS	*Applause*	48	*17 Jul 82*	5
I AM WHAT I AM	*Towerbell*	25	*20 Oct 84*	18
Above hit: Shirley BASSEY with the LONDON SYMPHONY ORCHESTRA.				
KEEP THE MUSIC PLAYING	*Freestyle*	25	*18 May 91*	7
THE BEST OF SHIRLEY BASSEY	*Dino*	27	*5 Dec 92*	5
SHIRLEY BASSEY SINGS ANDREW LLOYD WEBBER	*Premier*	34	*4 Dec 93*	5
SHIRLEY BASSEY SINGS THE MOVIES	*PolyGram TV*	24	*11 Nov 95*	9
THE SHOW MUST GO ON	*PolyGram TV*	47	*9 Nov 96*	8
Compilation to coincide with her 60th birthday.				
THE REMIX ALBUM . . . DIAMONDS ARE FOREVER	*EMI*	62	*9 Sep 00*	1
THE GREATEST HITS – THIS IS MY LIFE	*Liberty*	54	*25 Nov 00*	4

BASSHEADS — UK

SINGLES:	HITS 4			WEEKS 19
IS THERE ANYBODY OUT THERE?	*Deconstruction*	5	*16 Nov 91*	8
BACK TO THE OLD SCHOOL	*Deconstruction*	12	*30 May 92*	4
WHO CAN MAKE ME FEEL GOOD?	*Deconstruction*	38	*28 Nov 92*	2
START A BRAND NEW LIFE (SAVE ME)	*Deconstruction*	49	*28 Aug 93*	2
IS THERE ANYBODY OUT THERE? [RI]	*Deconstruction*	24	*15 Jul 95*	3

BASSTOY — US

SINGLES:	HITS 1			WEEKS 1
RUNNIN	*Neo*	62	*27 May 00*	1
Vocals by Dana.				

BATES — Germany

SINGLES:	HITS 1			WEEKS 1
BILLIE JEAN	*Virgin*	67	*3 Feb 96*	1

Mike BATT (with the NEW EDITION) — UK

(See also Justin Hayward with Mike Batt and the London Philharmonic Orchestra.)

SINGLES:	HITS 1			WEEKS 8
SUMMERTIME CITY	*Epic*	4	*16 Aug 75*	8

BAUHAUS — UK

SINGLES:	HITS 8			WEEKS 35
KICK IN THE EYE	*Beggars Banquet*	59	*18 Apr 81*	3
THE PASSION OF LOVERS	*Beggars Banquet*	56	*4 Jul 81*	2
KICK IN THE EYE – SEARCHING FOR SATORI [EP]	*Beggars Banquet*	45	*6 Mar 82*	4
Lead track: Kick In The Eye (Searching For Satori).				
SPIRIT	*Beggars Banquet*	42	*19 Jun 82*	5
ZIGGY STARDUST	*Beggars Banquet*	15	*9 Oct 82*	7
LAGARTIJA NICK	*Beggars Banquet*	44	*22 Jan 83*	4
SHE'S IN PARTIES	*Beggars Banquet*	26	*9 Apr 83*	6
THE SINGLES 1981-1983 [EP]	*Beggars Banquet*	52	*29 Oct 83*	4
Lead track: The Passion Of Lovers. 6 track 12" only release featuring their first 6 hits.				
ALBUMS:	**HITS 5**			**WEEKS 24**
IN THE FLAT FIELD	*4AD*	72	*15 Nov 80*	1
MASK	*Beggars Banquet*	30	*24 Oct 81*	5
THE SKY'S GONE OUT	*Beggars Banquet*	4	*30 Oct 82*	6
BURNING FROM THE INSIDE	*Beggars Banquet*	13	*23 Jul 83*	10
1979-1983	*Beggars Banquet*	36	*30 Nov 85*	2

Les BAXTER his Chorus and Orchestra — US

SINGLES:	HITS 1			WEEKS 9
UNCHAINED MELODY	*Capitol*	10	*14 May 55*	9
From the film 'Unchained'.				

BAY CITY ROLLERS — UK

SINGLES:	HITS 12			WEEKS 113
KEEP ON DANCING	*Bell*	9	*18 Sep 71*	13
Jonathan King is actually the vocalist on this hit. Originally recorded by Avantis in 1963.				
REMEMBER (SHA-LA-LA)	*Bell*	6	*9 Feb 74*	12
Some copies only show title as 'Remember'.				
SHANG-A-LANG	*Bell*	2	*27 Apr 74*	10
SUMMERLOVE SENSATION	*Bell*	3	*27 Jul 74*	10
ALL OF ME LOVE ALL OF YOU	*Bell*	4	*12 Oct 74*	10
BYE BYE BABY	*Bell*	1	*8 Mar 75*	16
Original by the Four Seasons reached No. 12 in the US in 1965.				
GIVE A LITTLE LOVE	*Bell*	1	*12 Jul 75*	9
MONEY HONEY	*Bell*	3	*22 Nov 75*	9
LOVE ME LIKE I LOVE YOU	*Bell*	4	*10 Apr 76*	6
I ONLY WANNA BE WITH YOU	*Bell*	4	*11 Sep 76*	9
IT'S A GAME	*Arista*	16	*7 May 77*	6
Originally recorded by String Driven Thing.				
YOU MADE ME BELIEVE IN MAGIC	*Arista*	34	*30 Jul 77*	3

ALBUMS:	HITS 5			WEEKS 127
ROLLIN'	*Bell*	1	*12 Oct 74*	62
ONCE UPON A STAR	*Bell*	1	*3 May 75*	37
WOULDN'T YOU LIKE IT	*Bell*	3	*13 Dec 75*	12
DEDICATION	*Bell*	4	*25 Sep 76*	12
IT'S A GAME	*Arista*	18	*13 Aug 77*	4

Duke BAYSEE — UK

SINGLES:	HITS 2			WEEKS 6
SUGAR SUGAR	*Bell*	30	*3 Sep 94*	4
DO YOU LOVE ME?	*Double Dekker*	46	*21 Jan 95*	2

BAZ — UK

SINGLES:	HITS 1			WEEKS 2
BELIEVERS	*One Little Indian*	36	*15 Dec 01*	2

BBC CONCERT ORCHESTRA/BBC SYMPHONY CHORUS Conducted by Stephen JACKSON — UK

SINGLES:	HITS 1			WEEKS 3
ODE TO JOY (FROM BEETHOVEN SYMPHONY NO. 9)	*Virgin*	36	*22 Jun 96*	3
BBC-TV theme to the European Football Championships, 1996.				

BBC SYMPHONY ORCHESTRA, SINGERS and SYMPHONY CHORUS — UK

EPS:	HITS 1			WEEKS 1
PLANET SUITE – MARS AND JUPITER	*HMV*	14	*26 Mar 60*	1
Above hit: BBC SYMPHONY ORCHESTRA.				

ALBUMS:	HITS 3			WEEKS 7
LAST NIGHT OF THE PROMS	*Philips*	36	*4 Oct 69*	1
Above hit: Colin DAVIS conducting the BBC SYMPHONY ORCHESTRA, SINGERS and CHORUS.				
HIGHLIGHTS OF THE LAST NIGHT OF THE PROMS '82	*K-Tel*	69	*11 Dec 82*	5
Above hit: BBC SYMPHONY ORCHESTRA, SINGERS and SYMPHONY CHORUS conducted by James LOUGHRAN.				
ELGAR/PAYNE: SYMPHONY NO. 3	*NMC*	44	*28 Feb 98*	1
Above hit: BBC SYMPHONY ORCHESTRA conducted by Andrew DAVIS.				

BBC WELSH SYMPHONY ORCHESTRA and CHORUS – See Aled JONES

BBD – See BELL BIV DEVOE

BBG — UK

SINGLES:	HITS 4			WEEKS 10
SNAPPINESS	*Urban*	28	*28 Apr 90*	5
Samples Soul II Soul's Happiness.				
Above hit: BBG featuring Dina TAYLOR.				
SOME KIND OF HEAVEN	*Urban*	65	*11 Aug 90*	2
LET THE MUSIC PLAY	*MCA*	46	*23 Mar 96*	1
Above hit: BBG featuring ERIN.				
SNAPPINESS [RM]	*Hi-Life*	50	*18 May 96*	1
Remixed by Bob and Tony Newland.				
JUST BE TONIGHT	*Hi-Life*	45	*5 Jul 97*	1
Above hit: BBG featuring ERIN.				

BBM — UK

SINGLES:	HITS 1			WEEKS 2
WHERE IN THE WORLD	*Virgin*	57	*6 Aug 94*	2

ALBUMS:		HITS 1			WEEKS 4
AROUND THE NEXT DREAM		*Virgin*	9	*18 Jun 94*	4

BBMAK UK

SINGLES:	HITS 2			WEEKS 16
BACK HERE	*Telstar*	37	*28 Aug 99*	2
BACK HERE [RI]	*Telstar*	5	*24 Feb 01*	10
STILL ON YOUR SIDE	*Telstar*	8	*26 May 01*	4
ALBUMS:	**HITS 1**			**WEEKS 3**
SOONER OR LATER	*Telstar*	16	*9 Jun 01*	3

BC-52's – See B-52'S

BE-BOP DELUXE UK

SINGLES:	HITS 2			WEEKS 13
SHIPS IN THE NIGHT	*Harvest*	23	*21 Feb 76*	8
HOT VALVES [EP]	*Harvest*	36	*13 Nov 76*	5
Lead track: Maid In Heaven.				
ALBUMS:	**HITS 4**			**WEEKS 28**
SUNBURST FINISH	*Harvest*	17	*31 Jan 76*	12
MODERN MUSIC	*Harvest*	12	*25 Sep 76*	6
LIVE! IN THE AIR AGE	*Harvest*	10	*6 Aug 77*	5
DRASTIC PLASTIC	*Harvest*	22	*25 Feb 78*	5

BEACH BOYS US

SINGLES:	HITS 30			WEEKS 281
SURFIN' U.S.A.	*Capitol*	34	*3 Aug 63*	7
Adapted lyrics to Chuck Berry's Sweet Little Sixteen.				
I GET AROUND	*Capitol*	7	*11 Jul 64*	13
WHEN I GROW UP (TO BE A MAN)	*Capitol*	44	*31 Oct 64*	2
WHEN I GROW UP (TO BE A MAN) [RE]	*Capitol*	27	*21 Nov 64*	5
DANCE DANCE DANCE	*Capitol*	24	*23 Jan 65*	6
HELP ME RHONDA	*Capitol*	27	*5 Jun 65*	10
CALIFORNIA GIRLS	*Capitol*	26	*4 Sep 65*	8
BARBARA ANN	*Capitol*	3	*19 Feb 66*	10
Original by the Regents reached No. 13 in the US in 1961. Dean Torrence of Jan & Dean and Glen Campbell on backing vocals.				
SLOOP JOHN B	*Capitol*	2	*23 Apr 66*	15
GOD ONLY KNOWS	*Capitol*	2	*30 Jul 66*	14
GOOD VIBRATIONS	*Capitol*	1	*5 Nov 66*	13
Glen Campbell on lead guitar.				
THEN I KISSED HER	*Capitol*	4	*6 May 67*	11
HEROES AND VILLANS	*Capitol*	8	*26 Aug 67*	9
WILD HONEY	*Capitol*	29	*25 Nov 67*	6
DARLIN'	*Capitol*	11	*20 Jan 68*	14
FRIENDS	*Capitol*	25	*11 May 68*	7
DO IT AGAIN	*Capitol*	1	*27 Jul 68*	14
BLUEBIRDS OVER THE MOUNTAIN	*Capitol*	33	*28 Dec 68*	5
I CAN HEAR MUSIC	*Capitol*	10	*1 Mar 69*	13
Originally recorded by Ellie Greenwich.				
BREAK AWAY	*Capitol*	6	*14 Jun 69*	11
COTTONFIELDS	*Capitol*	5	*16 May 70*	17
CALIFORNIA SAGA/CALIFORNIA	*Reprise*	37	*3 Mar 73*	5
GOOD VIBRATIONS [RI]	*Capitol*	18	*3 Jul 76*	7
ROCK AND ROLL MUSIC	*Reprise*	36	*10 Jul 76*	4
HERE COMES THE NIGHT	*Caribou*	37	*31 Mar 79*	8
LADY LYNDA	*Caribou*	6	*16 Jun 79*	11
SUMAHAMA	*Caribou*	45	*29 Sep 79*	4
THE BEACH BOYS MEDLEY [M]	*Capitol*	47	*29 Aug 81*	4
WIPEOUT	*Urban*	2	*22 Aug 87*	12
Above hit: FAT BOYS and the BEACH BOYS.				
KOKOMO	*Elektra*	25	*19 Nov 88*	9
From the film 'Cocktail'.				
WOULDN'T IT BE NICE	*Capitol*	58	*2 Jun 90*	1
DO IT AGAIN [RI]	*Capitol*	61	*29 Jun 91*	2
FUN FUN FUN	*PolyGram TV*	24	*2 Mar 96*	4
Above hit: STATUS QUO with the BEACH BOYS.				
EPS:	**HITS 4**			**WEEKS 108**
FUN, FUN, FUN	*Capitol*	19	*29 Aug 64*	1
FOUR BY THE BEACH BOYS	*Capitol*	11	*14 Nov 64*	8
THE BEACH BOY HITS	*Capitol*	1	*14 May 66*	82
GOD ONLY KNOWS	*Capitol*	3	*12 Nov 66*	17
ALBUMS:	**HITS 30**			**WEEKS 569**
SURFIN' USA	*Capitol*	17	*25 Sep 65*	7
BEACH BOYS PARTY	*Capitol*	3	*19 Feb 66*	14

BEACH BOYS TODAY	*Capitol*	6	*16 Apr 66*	25
PET SOUNDS	*Capitol*	2	*9 Jul 66*	39
SUMMER DAYS (AND SUMMER NIGHTS!!)	*Capitol*	4	*16 Jul 66*	22
BEST OF THE BEACH BOYS	*Capitol*	2	*12 Nov 66*	142
SURFER GIRL	*Capitol*	13	*11 Mar 67*	14
BEST OF THE BEACH BOYS VOLUME 2	*Capitol*	3	*21 Oct 67*	39
SMILEY SMILE	*Capitol*	9	*18 Nov 67*	8
WILD HONEY	*Capitol*	7	*16 Mar 68*	15
FRIENDS	*Capitol*	13	*21 Sep 68*	8
BEST OF THE BEACH BOYS VOLUME 3	*Capitol*	8	*23 Nov 68*	12
20/20	*Capitol*	3	*29 Mar 69*	10
GREATEST HITS	*Capitol*	5	*19 Sep 70*	30
SUNFLOWER	*Stateside*	29	*5 Dec 70*	6
SURF'S UP	*Stateside*	15	*27 Nov 71*	7
CARL AND THE PASSIONS/SO TOUGH	*Reprise*	25	*24 Jun 72*	1
HOLLAND	*Reprise*	20	*17 Feb 73*	7
20 GOLDEN GREATS *Includes re-entries through to 1981.*	*Capitol*	1	*10 Jul 76*	86
15 BIG ONES	*Reprise*	31	*24 Jul 76*	3
THE BEACH BOYS LOVE YOU	*Reprise*	28	*7 May 77*	1
LA (LIGHT ALBUM)	*Caribou*	32	*21 Apr 79*	6
KEEPING THE SUMMER ALIVE	*Caribou*	54	*12 Apr 80*	3
THE VERY BEST OF THE BEACH BOYS	*Capitol*	1	*30 Jul 83*	17
THE BEACH BOYS	*Caribou*	60	*22 Jun 85*	2
SUMMER DREAMS - 28 CLASSIC TRACKS	*Capitol*	2	*23 Jun 90*	27
THE BEST OF THE BEACH BOYS *First compilation to feature all their Top 30 hits.*	*Capitol*	25	*1 Jul 95*	6
PET SOUNDS [RI]	*Fame*	70	*16 Sep 95*	2
GREATEST HITS	*EMI*	28	*11 Jul 98*	4
ENDLESS HARMONY SOUNDTRACK *Previously unreleased live tracks, demos, remixes and alternative recordings.*	*Capitol*	56	*19 Sep 98*	1
THE VERY BEST OF THE BEACH BOYS *Identically titled albums are different.*	*Capitol*	31	*21 Jul 01*	5

Walter BEASLEY — US

SINGLES:	HITS 1			WEEKS 3
I'M SO HAPPY	*Urban*	70	*23 Jan 88*	3

BEASTIE BOYS — US

SINGLES:	HITS 12			WEEKS 59
(YOU GOTTA) FIGHT FOR YOUR RIGHT (TO PARTY)	*Def Jam*	11	*28 Feb 87*	11
NO SLEEP TILL BROOKLYN	*Def Jam*	14	*30 May 87*	7
SHE'S ON IT	*Def Jam*	10	*18 Jul 87*	8
GIRLS / SHE'S CRAFTY	*Def Jam*	34	*3 Oct 87*	4
PASS THE MIC	*Grand Royal*	47	*11 Apr 92*	2
FROZEN METAL HEAD [EP] *Lead track: Jimmy James.*	*Grand Royal*	55	*4 Jul 92*	1
GET IT TOGETHER / SABOTAGE	*Grand Royal*	19	*9 Jul 94*	4
SURE SHOT	*Grand Royal*	27	*26 Nov 94*	3
..INTERGALACTIC..	*Grand Royal*	5	*4 Jul 98*	7
THE BODY MOVIN'	*Grand Royal*	15	*7 Nov 98*	4
THE BODY MOVIN' [RE]	*Grand Royal*	69	*16 Jan 99*	1
REMOTE CONTROL / 3 MCS & 1 DJ	*Grand Royal*	21	*29 May 99*	3
ALIVE *Samples Boogie Down Productions' I'm Still #1.*	*Grand Royal*	28	*18 Dec 99*	4

ALBUMS:	HITS 7			WEEKS 88
LICENSE TO ILL	*Def Jam*	7	*31 Jan 87*	40
PAUL'S BOUTIQUE	*Capitol*	44	*5 Aug 89*	2
ILL COMMUNICATION	*Grand Royal*	10	*4 Jun 94*	15
ROOT DOWN [EP] *3 mixes of Root Down and 7 tracks recorded live on their European tour.*	*Grand Royal*	23	*10 Jun 95*	2
THE IN SOUND FROM WAY OUT! *Includes B-sides, alternative versions and unreleased material.*	*Grand Royal*	45	*6 Apr 96*	1
HELLO NASTY	*Grand Royal*	1	*18 Jul 98*	21
ANTHOLOGY - THE SOUNDS OF SCIENCE *Rarities and unreleased tracks packaged with an 80 page booklet.*	*Grand Royal*	36	*4 Dec 99*	7

BEAT — UK

(See also Various Artists (EPs) 'The 2 Tone EP'.)

SINGLES:	HITS 13			WEEKS 92
TEARS OF A CLOWN / RANKING FULL STOP	*2-Tone*	6	*8 Dec 79*	11
HANDS OFF . . . SHE'S MINE	*Go-Feet*	9	*23 Feb 80*	9
MIRROR IN THE BATHROOM	*Go-Feet*	4	*3 May 80*	9
BEST FRIEND / STAND DOWN MARGARET (DUB)	*Go-Feet*	22	*16 Aug 80*	9
TOO NICE TO TALK TO	*Go-Feet*	7	*13 Dec 80*	11
DROWNING / ALL OUT TO GET YOU	*Go-Feet*	22	*18 Apr 81*	8

DOORS OF YOUR HEART	*Go-Feet*	33	*20 Jun 81*	6
HIT IT	*Go-Feet*	70	*5 Dec 81*	2
SAVE IT FOR LATER	*Go-Feet*	47	*17 Apr 82*	4
JEANETTE	*Go-Feet*	45	*18 Sep 82*	3
I CONFESS	*Go-Feet*	54	*4 Dec 82*	3
CAN'T GET USED TO LOSING YOU	*Go-Feet*	3	*30 Apr 83*	11
ACKEE 1-2-3	*Go-Feet*	54	*2 Jul 83*	4
MIRROR IN THE BATHROOM [RM]	*Go-Feet*	44	*27 Jan 96*	2
Remixed by Mark "Spike" Stent.				

ALBUMS:	**HITS 5**			**WEEKS 73**
JUST CAN'T STOP IT	*Go-Feet*	3	*31 May 80*	32
WHA'PPEN	*Go-Feet*	3	*16 May 81*	18
SPECIAL BEAT SERVICE	*Go-Feet*	21	*9 Oct 82*	6
WHAT IS BEAT? (THE BEST OF THE BEAT)	*Go-Feet*	10	*11 Jun 83*	13
BPM . . . THE VERY BEST OF THE BEAT	*Go-Feet*	13	*10 Feb 96*	4

BEAT BOYS - See Gene VINCENT

BEAT RENEGADES — UK

SINGLES:	**HITS 1**			**WEEKS 1**
AUTOMATIK	*Slinky Music*	73	*19 May 01*	1
Vocals by L'aura.				

BEAT SYSTEM — UK

SINGLES:	**HITS 2**			**WEEKS 3**
WALK ON THE WILD SIDE	*Fourth & Broadway*	63	*3 Mar 90*	2
TO A BRIGHTER DAY (O'HAPPY DAY)	*London*	70	*18 Sep 93*	1

BEATCHUGGERS featuring Eric CLAPTON — Denmark/UK

SINGLES:	**HITS 1**			**WEEKS 2**
FOREVER MAN (HOW MANY TIMES?)	*ffrr*	26	*18 Nov 00*	2
Samples Eric Clapton's Forever Man.				

BEATLES — UK

SINGLES:	**HITS 32**			**WEEKS 456**
LOVE ME DO	*Parlophone*	17	*13 Oct 62*	18
PLEASE PLEASE ME	*Parlophone*	2	*19 Jan 63*	18
FROM ME TO YOU	*Parlophone*	1	*20 Apr 63*	21
MY BONNIE	*Polydor*	48	*8 Jun 63*	1
First released in 1962.				
Above hit: Tony SHERIDAN and the BEATLES.				
SHE LOVES YOU	*Parlophone*	1	*31 Aug 63*	31
The best selling single of all-time in the UK until 1977.				
I WANT TO HOLD YOUR HAND	*Parlophone*	1	*7 Dec 63*	21
CAN'T BUY ME LOVE	*Parlophone*	1	*28 Mar 64*	14
SHE LOVES YOU [RE-1ST]	*Parlophone*	42	*11 Apr 64*	2
I WANT TO HOLD YOUR HAND [RE-1ST]	*Parlophone*	48	*16 May 64*	1
AIN'T SHE SWEET	*Polydor*	29	*13 Jun 64*	6
CAN'T BUY ME LOVE [RE-1ST]		47	*11 Jul 64*	1
A HARD DAY'S NIGHT	*Parlophone*	1	*18 Jul 64*	13
From the film of the same name.				
I FEEL FINE	*Parlophone*	1	*5 Dec 64*	13
TICKET TO RIDE	*Parlophone*	1	*17 Apr 65*	12
HELP!	*Parlophone*	1	*31 Jul 65*	14
From the film of the same name.				
DAY TRIPPER / WE CAN WORK IT OUT	*Parlophone*	1	*11 Dec 65*	12
PAPERBACK WRITER	*Parlophone*	1	*18 Jun 66*	11
YELLOW SUBMARINE / ELEANOR RIGBY	*Parlophone*	1	*13 Aug 66*	13
PENNY LANE / STRAWBERRY FIELDS FOREVER	*Parlophone*	2	*25 Feb 67*	11
ALL YOU NEED IS LOVE	*Parlophone*	1	*15 Jul 67*	13
Song featured on the BBC TV show 'Our World', 25 Jun 67 as part of a live global TV satelitte link-up.				
HELLO, GOODBYE	*Parlophone*	1	*2 Dec 67*	12
MAGICAL MYSTERY TOUR (DOUBLE EP) [EP]	*Parlophone*	2	*16 Dec 67*	12
6 tracks from the TV film. Lead track: Magical Mystery Tour.				
LADY MADONNA	*Parlophone*	1	*23 Mar 68*	8
HEY JUDE	*Apple*	1	*7 Sep 68*	16
GET BACK	*Apple*	1	*26 Apr 69*	17
Above hit: BEATLES with Billy PRESTON.				
THE BALLAD OF JOHN AND YOKO	*Apple*	1	*7 Jun 69*	14
SOMETHING / COME TOGETHER	*Apple*	4	*8 Nov 69*	12
LET IT BE	*Apple*	2	*14 Mar 70*	9
LET IT BE [RE]	*Apple*	43	*24 Oct 70*	1
YESTERDAY	*Apple*	8	*13 Mar 76*	7
Originally written for but turned down by Billy J.Kramer.				
PAPERBACK WRITER [RE]	*Parlophone*	23	*27 Mar 76*	5
HEY JUDE [RE]	*Apple*	12	*27 Mar 76*	7

STRAWBERRY FIELDS FOREVER [RE-1ST]	*Parlophone*	32	*3 Apr 76*	3
GET BACK [RE-1ST]	*Apple*	28	*3 Apr 76*	5
Above hit: BEATLES with Billy PRESTON.				
HELP! [RE]	*Parlophone*	37	*10 Apr 76*	3
Though the entries in 1976 had the same catalogue numbers, they were re-issued with green and black sleeves.				
BACK IN THE U.S.S.R.	*Parlophone*	19	*10 Jul 76*	6
SGT. PEPPER'S LONELY HEARTS CLUB BAND/WITH A LITTLE HELP FROM MY FRIENDS [M]	*Parlophone*	63	*7 Oct 78*	3
BEATLES MOVIE MEDLEY [M]	*Parlophone*	10	*5 Jun 82*	9
7 track medley from their films.				
LOVE ME DO [RE-1ST]	*Parlophone*	4	*16 Oct 82*	7
All re-entries from this date were released to mark the 20th anniversary of their original issue.				
PLEASE PLEASE ME [RE]	*Parlophone*	29	*22 Jan 83*	4
FROM ME TO YOU [RE]	*Parlophone*	40	*23 Apr 83*	4
SHE LOVES YOU [RE-2ND]	*Parlophone*	45	*3 Sep 83*	3
I WANT TO HOLD YOUR HAND [RE-2ND]	*Parlophone*	62	*26 Nov 83*	2
CAN'T BUY ME LOVE [RE-2ND]	*Parlophone*	53	*31 Mar 84*	2
A HARD DAY'S NIGHT [RE]	*Parlophone*	52	*21 Jul 84*	2
I FEEL FINE [RE]	*Parlophone*	65	*8 Dec 84*	1
TICKET TO RIDE [RE]	*Parlophone*	70	*20 Apr 85*	2
YELLOW SUBMARINE / ELEANOR RIGBY [RE]	*Parlophone*	63	*30 Aug 86*	1
STRAWBERRY FIELDS FOREVER / PENNY LANE [RE-2ND]	*Parlophone*	65	*28 Feb 87*	2
ALL YOU NEED IS LOVE [RE]	*Parlophone*	47	*18 Jul 87*	3
HELLO, GOODBYE [RE]	*Parlophone*	63	*5 Dec 87*	1
LADY MADONNA [RE]	*Parlophone*	67	*26 Mar 88*	1
HEY JUDE [RE-2ND]	*Apple*	52	*10 Sep 88*	2
GET BACK [RE-2ND]	*Apple*	74	*22 Apr 89*	1
Above hit: BEATLES with Billy PRESTON.				
LOVE ME DO [RE-2ND]	*Parlophone*	53	*17 Oct 92*	1
30th Anniversary re-issue.				
BABY IT'S YOU	*Apple*	7	*1 Apr 95*	6
Recorded at the BBC on 1 Jun 63 for 'Pop Go The Beatles'.				
BABY IT'S YOU [RE]	*Apple*	71	*8 Jul 95*	1
FREE AS A BIRD	*Apple*	2	*16 Dec 95*	8
First new recording in 25 years. Written by John Lennon in 1977.				
REAL LOVE	*Apple*	4	*16 Mar 96*	7
John Lennon's vocal from circa 1979.				
EPS:	**HITS 12**			**WEEKS 392**
TWIST AND SHOUT	*Parlophone*	1	*20 Jul 63*	64
THE BEATLES' HITS	*Parlophone*	1	*21 Sep 63*	43
THE BEATLES (NO. 1)	*Parlophone*	2	*9 Nov 63*	29
ALL MY LOVING	*Parlophone*	1	*8 Feb 64*	44
LONG TALL SALLY	*Parlophone*	1	*4 Jul 64*	37
Last song the Beatles ever performed at their final concert at Candlestick Park, San Francisco.				
EXTRACTS FROM THE FILM A HARD DAY'S NIGHT	*Parlophone*	1	*14 Nov 64*	30
A HARD DAY'S NIGHT VOLUME 2	*Parlophone*	8	*9 Jan 65*	17
BEATLES FOR SALE	*Parlophone*	1	*10 Apr 65*	47
BEATLES FOR SALE (NO. 2)	*Parlophone*	5	*12 Jun 65*	24
THE BEATLES' MILLION SELLERS	*Parlophone*	1	*11 Dec 65*	26
YESTERDAY	*Parlophone*	1	*12 Mar 66*	13
NOWHERE MAN	*Parlophone*	4	*16 Jul 66*	18
ALBUMS:	**HITS 31**			**WEEKS 1285**
PLEASE PLEASE ME	*Parlophone*	1	*6 Apr 63*	70
WITH THE BEATLES	*Parlophone*	1	*30 Nov 63*	51
A HARD DAY'S NIGHT [OST]	*Parlophone*	1	*18 Jul 64*	38
BEATLES FOR SALE	*Parlophone*	1	*12 Dec 64*	46
HELP! [OST]	*Parlophone*	1	*14 Aug 65*	37
RUBBER SOUL	*Parlophone*	1	*11 Dec 65*	42
REVOLVER	*Parlophone*	1	*13 Aug 66*	34
A COLLECTION OF BEATLES' OLDIES	*Parlophone*	7	*10 Dec 66*	34
SGT. PEPPER'S LONELY HEARTS CLUB BAND	*Parlophone*	1	*3 Jun 67*	148
The best selling album of all time in the UK.				
MAGICAL MYSTERY TOUR	*Capitol*	31	*13 Jan 68*	2
US import.				
THE BEATLES (THE WHITE ALBUM)	*Apple*	1	*7 Dec 68*	22
YELLOW SUBMARINE	*Apple*	3	*1 Feb 69*	10
Above hit: BEATLES featuring the George MARTIN ORCHESTRA.				
ABBEY ROAD	*Apple*	1	*4 Oct 69*	81
LET IT BE	*Apple*	1	*23 May 70*	59
A HARD DAY'S NIGHT [RE-1ST]	*Parlophone*	30	*16 Jan 71*	1
HELP! [RE-1ST]	*Parlophone*	33	*24 Jul 71*	2
Above 2 were re-released with new catalogue numbers.				
THE BEATLES 1962-1966	*Apple*	3	*5 May 73*	114
THE BEATLES 1967-1970	*Apple*	2	*5 May 73*	106
ROCK 'N' ROLL MUSIC	*Parlophone*	11	*26 Jun 76*	15
THE BEATLES TAPES	*Polydor*	45	*21 Aug 76*	1
THE BEATLES AT THE HOLLYWOOD BOWL	*Parlophone*	1	*21 May 77*	17

.OVE SONGS	*Parlophone*	7	*17 Dec 77*	17
₹ARITIES	*Parlophone*	71	*3 Nov 79*	1
3EATLES BALLADS	*Parlophone*	40	*15 Nov 80*	5
'HE BEATLES 1962-1966 [RE-1ST]	*Apple*	37	*20 Dec 80*	34
'HE BEATLES 1967-1970 [RE-1ST]	*Apple*	66	*20 Dec 80*	7
3EATLES BALLADS [RE]	*Parlophone*	17	*29 Aug 81*	11
20 GREATEST HITS	*Parlophone*	10	*30 Oct 82*	30
\ HARD DAY'S NIGHT [RE-2ND]	*Parlophone*	30	*7 Mar 87*	4
'LEASE PLEASE ME [RE]	*Parlophone*	32	*7 Mar 87*	4
VITH THE BEATLES [RE-1ST]	*Parlophone*	40	*7 Mar 87*	2
BEATLES FOR SALE [RE]	*Parlophone*	45	*7 Mar 87*	2
REVOLVER [RE-1ST] *'ncludes re-entry in 1997.*	*Parlophone*	55	*9 May 87*	6
RUBBER SOUL [RE-1ST] *'ncludes re-entry in 1997.*	*Parlophone*	60	*9 May 87*	4
HELP! [RE-2ND]	*Parlophone*	61	*9 May 87*	2
SGT. PEPPER'S LONELY HEARTS CLUB BAND [RE-1ST]	*Parlophone*	3	*6 Jun 87*	16
THE BEATLES (THE WHITE ALBUM) [RE-1ST]	*Apple*	18	*5 Sep 87*	2
YELLOW SUBMARINE [RE] *Above hit: BEATLES featuring the George MARTIN ORCHESTRA.*	*Apple*	60	*5 Sep 87*	1
MAGICAL MYSTERY TOUR [RI]	*Parlophone*	52	*3 Oct 87*	1
ABBEY ROAD [RE-1ST]	*Apple*	30	*31 Oct 87*	2
LET IT BE [RE] *All re-entries/re-issues listed above were available for the first time on CD.*	*Apple*	50	*31 Oct 87*	1
PAST MASTERS VOLUME 2	*Parlophone*	46	*19 Mar 88*	1
PAST MASTERS VOLUME 1	*Parlophone*	49	*19 Mar 88*	1
SGT. PEPPER'S LONELY HEARTS CLUB BAND[RE-2ND] *Re-promoted to celebrate the 25th anniversary of its release. Includes re-entries through to 1999.*	*Parlophone*	6	*20 Jun 92*	33
THE BEATLES 1962-1966 [RE-2ND]	*Apple*	3	*2 Oct 93*	24
THE BEATLES 1967-1970 [RE-2ND] *Above 2 were available for the first time on CD.*	*Apple*	4	*2 Oct 93*	24
LIVE AT THE BBC *Compilation of songs recorded by the BBC during 1963-65.*	*Apple*	1	*10 Dec 94*	20
ANTHOLOGY 1	*Apple*	2	*2 Dec 95*	10
ANTHOLOGY 2	*Apple*	1	*30 Mar 96*	12
ANTHOLOGY 3 *Above 3 are collections of out-takes, demos or previously unreleased songs.*	*Apple*	4	*9 Nov 96*	11
ABBEY ROAD [RE-2ND]	*Apple*	42	*8 Mar 97*	9
WITH THE BEATLES [RE-2ND]	*Parlophone*	72	*22 Mar 97*	1
REVOLVER [RE-2ND]	*Parlophone*	46	*11 Apr 98*	6
RUBBER SOUL [RE-2ND]	*Parlophone*	62	*25 Apr 98*	1
YELLOW SUBMARINE SONGTRACK [OST] *Now includes all Beatles songs from the film less tracks by the George Martin Orchestra.*	*Parlophone*	8	*25 Sep 99*	5
1 *All their UK and US No.1s plus Something*	*Apple*	1	*25 Nov 00*	45

BEATMASTERS — UK

SINGLES:	HITS 7			WEEKS 47
ROK DA HOUSE *Original release reached No. 79 in 1987.* *Above hit: BEATMASTERS featuring the COOKIE CREW.*	*Rhythm King*	5	*9 Jan 88*	11
BURN IT UP *Above hit: BEATMASTERS with P.P. ARNOLD.*	*Rhythm King*	14	*24 Sep 88*	10
WHO'S IN THE HOUSE (THE HIP HOUSE ANTHEM) *Above hit: BEATMASTERS with MERLIN.*	*Rhythm King*	8	*22 Apr 89*	9
HEY DJ/I CAN'T DANCE (TO THAT MUSIC YOUR PLAYING) /SKA TRAIN *Backing vocals: Claudia Fontaine. I Can't Dance originally recorded by Martha and the Vandellas.* *Above hit: BEATMASTERS featuring Betty BOO.*	*Rhythm King*	7	*12 Aug 89*	11
WARM LOVE *Above hit: BEATMASTERS featuring Claudia FONTAINE.*	*Rhythm King*	51	*2 Dec 89*	2
BOULEVARD OF BROKEN DREAMS *Vocals by JC001.*	*Rhythm King*	62	*21 Sep 91*	1
DUNNO WHAT IT IS (ABOUT YOU) *Original release reached No. 82 in 1991.* *Above hit: BEATMASTERS featuring Elaine VASSELL.*	*Rhythm King*	43	*16 May 92*	3

ALBUMS:	HITS 1			WEEKS 10
ANYWAYAWANNA	*Rhythm King*	30	*1 Jul 89*	10

BEATNUTS — US

SINGLES:	HITS 1			WEEKS 1
NO ESCAPIN' THIS	*Epic*	47	*14 Jul 01*	1

BEATRICE – See Mike KOGLIN

BEATS INTERNATIONAL — UK

(See also Norman Cook.)

SINGLES:	HITS 6			WEEKS 3
DUB BE GOOD TO ME *Above hit: BEATS INTERNATIONAL featuring LINDY.*	*Go.Beat*	1	*10 Feb 90*	1
WON'T TALK ABOUT IT	*Go.Beat*	9	*12 May 90*	[illegible]
BURUNDI BLUES *Features vocals by Janet Kay.*	*Go.Beat*	51	*15 Sep 90*	[illegible]
ECHO CHAMBER	*Go.Beat*	60	*2 Mar 91*	[illegible]
THE SUN DOESN'T SHINE	*Go.Beat*	66	*21 Sep 91*	[illegible]
IN THE GHETTO	*Go.Beat*	44	*23 Nov 91*	[illegible]
ALBUMS:	**HITS 1**			**WEEKS 1**
LET THEM EAT BINGO	*Go.Beat*	17	*14 Apr 90*	1

BEAUTIFUL PEOPLE — UK

SINGLES:	HITS 1			WEEKS
IF 60'S WERE 90'S *Features Jimi Hendrix samples.*	*Essential*	74	*28 May 94*	[illegible]

BEAUTIFUL SOUTH — UK

SINGLES:	HITS 26			WEEKS 15
SONG FOR WHOEVER	*Go! Discs*	2	*3 Jun 89*	1
YOU KEEP IT ALL IN	*Go! Discs*	8	*23 Sep 89*	[illegible]
I'LL SAIL THIS SHIP ALONE	*Go! Discs*	31	*2 Dec 89*	[illegible]
A LITTLE TIME	*Go! Discs*	1	*6 Oct 90*	1
MY BOOK	*Go! Discs*	43	*8 Dec 90*	[illegible]
LET LOVE SPEAK UP ITSELF	*Go! Discs*	51	*16 Mar 91*	[illegible]
OLD RED EYES IS BACK	*Go! Discs*	22	*11 Jan 92*	[illegible]
WE ARE EACH OTHER	*Go! Discs*	30	*14 Mar 92*	[illegible]
BELL BOTTOMED TEAR	*Go! Discs*	16	*13 Jun 92*	[illegible]
36D	*Go! Discs*	46	*26 Sep 92*	[illegible]
GOOD AS GOLD	*Go! Discs*	23	*12 Mar 94*	[illegible]
EVERYBODY'S TALKIN' *Originally recorded by Fred Neil.*	*Go! Discs*	12	*4 Jun 94*	8
PRETTIEST EYES	*Go! Discs*	37	*3 Sep 94*	[illegible]
ONE LAST LOVE SONG	*Go! Discs*	14	*12 Nov 94*	[illegible]
PRETENDERS TO THE THRONE	*Go! Discs*	18	*18 Nov 95*	[illegible]
ROTTERDAM	*Go! Discs*	5	*12 Oct 96*	9
DON'T MARRY HER	*Go! Discs*	8	*14 Dec 96*	10
BLACKBIRD ON THE WIRE	*Go! Discs*	23	*29 Mar 97*	[illegible]
LIARS' BAR *Featuring the Black Dyke Mills Band.*	*Go! Discs*	43	*5 Jul 97*	[illegible]
PERFECT 10	*Go! Discs*	2	*3 Oct 98*	14
DUMB	*Go! Discs*	16	*19 Dec 98*	7
DUMB [RE]	*Go! Discs*	72	*13 Mar 99*	1
HOW LONG'S A TEAR TAKE TO DRY?	*Go! Discs*	12	*20 Mar 99*	6
THE TABLE *Features the London Community Gospel Choir.*	*Go! Discs*	47	*10 Jul 99*	2
CLOSER THAN MOST	*Go! Discs*	22	*7 Oct 00*	4
THE RIVER/JUST CHECKIN'	*Go! Discs*	59	*23 Dec 00*	1
THE ROOT OF ALL EVIL	*Go! Discs*	50	*17 Nov 01*	1
ALBUMS:	**HITS 10**			**WEEKS 278**
WELCOME TO THE BEAUTIFUL SOUTH *Includes re-entry in 1998.*	*Go! Discs*	2	*4 Nov 89*	23
CHOKE	*Go! Discs*	2	*10 Nov 90*	22
0898: BEAUTIFUL SOUTH	*Go! Discs*	4	*11 Apr 92*	17
MIAOW	*Go! Discs*	6	*9 Apr 94*	24
CARRY ON UP THE CHARTS – THE BEST OF THE BEAUTIFUL SOUTH	*Go! Discs*	1	*19 Nov 94*	89
BLUE IS THE COLOUR	*Go! Discs*	1	*2 Nov 96*	46
QUENCH	*Go! Discs*	1	*24 Oct 98*	37
PAINTING IT RED	*Go! Discs*	2	*21 Oct 00*	11
SOLID BRONZE – GREAT HITS	*Go! Discs*	10	*24 Nov 01*	6

BEAVIS and BUTT-HEAD – See CHER

Gilbert BECAUD — France

SINGLES:	HITS 1			WEEKS 12
A LITTLE LOVE AND UNDERSTANDING	*Decca*	10	*29 Mar 75*	12

BECK — US

SINGLES:	HITS 9			WEEKS 27
LOSER *Samples Walking On Guilded Splinters by Dr John.*	*Geffen*	15	*5 Mar 94*	6
WHERE IT'S AT *Samples Get Up And Dance by Mantronix.*	*Geffen*	35	*29 Jun 96*	2

·VILS HAIRCUT	*Geffen*	22	*16 Nov 96*	2
·ples Them's Out Of Sight and Bernard Purdie's Soul Drums.				
·E NEW POLLUTION	*Geffen*	14	*8 Mar 97*	5
·SYNECK	*Geffen*	30	*24 May 97*	2
·n the film 'Feather In Your Cap'.				
·ADWEIGHT	*Geffen*	23	*8 Nov 97*	3
·n the film 'A Life Less Ordinary'.				
·OPICALIA	*Geffen*	39	*19 Dec 98*	2
·XX LAWS	*Geffen*	27	*20 Nov 99*	3
·XED BIZNESS	*Geffen*	34	*8 Apr 00*	2
·BUMS:	**HITS 4**			**WEEKS 75**
·LLOW GOLD	*Geffen*	41	*2 Apr 94*	4
·DE-LAY	*Geffen*	18	*6 Jul 96*	10
·DE-LAY [RE]	*Geffen*	17	*11 Jan 97*	41
·JTATIONS	*Geffen*	24	*14 Nov 98*	6
·DNITE VULTURES	*Geffen*	19	*4 Dec 99*	14

Jeff BECK — UK

·e also Jeff Beck, Tim Bogert and Carmine Appice.)

·NGLES:	**HITS 6**			**WEEKS 57**
·HO SILVER LINING	*Columbia*	14	*25 Mar 67*	14
·ginally recorded by The Attack in 1966.				
·LLYMAN	*Columbia*	30	*5 Aug 67*	3
·VE IS BLUE (L'AMOUR EST BLEU)	*Columbia*	23	*2 Mar 68*	7
·ginally Luxembourg's entry for the Eurovision Song Contest in 1967 by Vicky Leandros.				
·OO GOO BARABAJAGAL (LOVE IS HOT)	*Pye*	12	*12 Jul 69*	9
·ne issues only had title listed as 'Barabajagal'.				
·ove hit: DONOVAN and Jeff BECK GROUP.				
·HO SILVER LINING [RI]	*RAK*	17	*4 Nov 72*	11
·E BEEN DRINKING	*RAK*	27	*5 May 73*	6
·st released in 1968.				
·ove hit: Jeff BECK GROUP Vocal: Rod STEWART.				
·HO SILVER LINING [RI] [RE]	*RAK*	62	*9 Oct 82*	4
·OPLE GET READY	*Epic*	49	*7 Mar 92*	3
·ginally recorded by Curtis Mayfield.				
·ove hit: Jeff BECK and Rod STEWART.				
·BUMS:	**HITS 5**			**WEEKS 12**
·SA NOSTRA BECK - OLA	*Columbia*	39	*13 Sep 69*	1
·IRED	*CBS*	38	*24 Jul 76*	5
·IERE AND BACK	*Epic*	38	*19 Jul 80*	4
·ASH	*Epic*	83	*17 Aug 85*	1
·HO ELSE?	*Epic*	74	*27 Mar 99*	1

Jeff BECK, Tim BOGERT and Carmine APPICE — UK

·BUMS:	**HITS 1**			**WEEKS 3**
·F BECK, TIM BOGERT & CARMINE APPICE	*Epic*	28	*28 Apr 73*	3

Robin BECK — Canada

·NGLES:	**HITS 1**			**WEEKS 13**
·IE FIRST TIME	*Mercury*	1	*22 Oct 88*	13
Coca-Cola TV commercial theme.				

Victoria BECKHAM — UK

·ee also Dane; True Steppers.)

·NGLES:	**HITS 1**			**WEEKS 8**
·OT SUCH AN INNOCENT GIRL	*Virgin*	6	*29 Sep 01*	5
·OT SUCH AN INNOCENT GIRL [RE]	*Virgin*	46	*24 Nov 01*	3
·LBUMS:	**HITS 1**			**WEEKS 2**
·CTORIA BECKHAM	*Virgin*	10	*13 Oct 01*	2

·eter BECKETT – See Barry GRAY ORCHESTRA

·helton BECTON – See Frankie KNUCKLES

BEDAZZLED — UK

·NGLES:	**HITS 1**			**WEEKS 1**
·UMMER SONG	*Columbia*	73	*4 Jul 92*	1

Daniel BEDINGFIELD — UK

·NGLES:	**HITS 1**			**WEEKS 4**
·OTTA GET THRU THIS	*Relentless*	1	*8 Dec 01*	4

BEDLAM U

SINGLES:	HITS 1		WEEK
DA-FORCE	*Playola*	68	*6 Feb 99*
Samples the Real Thing's Can You Feel The Force.			

BEDLAM AGO GO U

SINGLES:	HITS 1		WEEK
SEASON NO. 5	*Sony S2*	57	*4 Apr 98*

BEDROCK U

SINGLES:	HITS 4		WEEK
FOR WHAT YOU DREAM OF	*Stress*	25	*1 Jun 96*
From the film 'Trainspotting'.			
Above hit: John DIGWEED and Nick MUIR present BEDROCK featuring KYO (aka Carole LEEMING).			
SET IN STONE / FORBIDDEN ZONE	*Stress*	71	*12 Jul 97*
Above hit: John DIGWEED and Nick MUIR present BEDROCK.			
HEAVEN SCENT	*Bedrock*	35	*6 Nov 99*
VOICES	*Bedrock*	44	*8 Jul 00*

BEDROCKS U

SINGLES:	HITS 1		WEEK
OB-LA-DI, OB-LA-DA	*Columbia*	20	*21 Dec 68*
Written and originally recorded by the Beatles.			

Celi BEE and the BUZZY BUNCH U

SINGLES:	HITS 1		WEEK
HOLD YOUR HORSES, BABE	*TK*	72	*17 Jun 78*

BEE GEES U

(See also Various Artists: Films – Original Soundtracks 'Saturday Night Fever'; 'Sgt. Pepper's Lonely Hearts Club Band'; 'Stayin' Aliv

SINGLES:	HITS 38		WEEKS 3
NEW YORK MINING DISASTER 1941	*Polydor*	12	*29 Apr 67*
TO LOVE SOMEBODY	*Polydor*	50	*15 Jul 67*
Originally written for, but turned down by, Otis Redding.			
TO LOVE SOMEBODY [RE]	*Polydor*	41	*29 Jul 67*
MASSACHUSETTS (THE LIGHTS WENT OUT IN)	*Polydor*	1	*23 Sep 67*
WORLD	*Polydor*	9	*25 Nov 67*
WORDS	*Polydor*	8	*3 Feb 68*
JUMBO / THE SINGER SANG HIS SONG	*Polydor*	25	*30 Mar 68*
I'VE GOTTA GET A MESSAGE TO YOU	*Polydor*	1	*10 Aug 68*
FIRST OF MAY	*Polydor*	6	*22 Feb 69*
TOMORROW, TOMORROW	*Polydor*	23	*7 Jun 69*
DON'T FORGET TO REMEMBER	*Polydor*	2	*16 Aug 69*
Above 2: BEE GEES featuring Barry GIBB, Maurice GIBB and Colin PETERSON.			
I.O.I.O.	*Polydor*	49	*28 Mar 70*
Above hit: BEE GEES featuring Barry and Maurice GIBB.			
LONELY DAYS	*Polydor*	33	*5 Dec 70*
MY WORLD	*Polydor*	16	*29 Jan 72*
RUN TO ME	*Polydor*	9	*22 Jul 72*
JIVE TALKIN'	*RSO*	5	*28 Jun 75*
YOU SHOULD BE DANCING	*RSO*	5	*31 Jul 76*
LOVE SO RIGHT	*RSO*	41	*13 Nov 76*
HOW DEEP IS YOUR LOVE	*RSO*	3	*29 Oct 77*
Originally written for Yvonne Elliman.			
STAYIN' ALIVE	*RSO*	4	*4 Feb 78*
NIGHT FEVER	*RSO*	1	*15 Apr 78*
Above 3 from the film 'Saturday Night Fever'.			
STAYIN' ALIVE [RE]	*RSO*	63	*13 May 78*
TOO MUCH HEAVEN	*RSO*	3	*25 Nov 78*
TRAGEDY	*RSO*	1	*17 Feb 79*
LOVE YOU INSIDE OUT	*RSO*	13	*14 Apr 79*
SPIRITS (HAVING FLOWN)	*RSO*	16	*5 Jan 80*
SOMEONE BELONGING TO SOMEONE	*RSO*	49	*17 Sep 83*
From the film 'Stayin' Alive'.			
YOU WIN AGAIN	*Warner Brothers*	1	*26 Sep 87*
E.S.P.	*Warner Brothers*	51	*12 Dec 87*
ORDINARY LIVES	*Warner Brothers*	54	*15 Apr 89*
ONE	*Warner Brothers*	71	*24 Jun 89*
SECRET LOVE	*Warner Brothers*	5	*2 Mar 91*
PAYING THE PRICE OF LOVE	*Polydor*	23	*21 Aug 93*
FOR WHOM THE BELLS TOLLS	*Polydor*	4	*27 Nov 93*
HOW TO FALL IN LOVE PART 1	*Polydor*	30	*16 Apr 94*
ALONE	*Polydor*	5	*1 Mar 97*
I COULD NOT LOVE YOU MORE	*Polydor*	14	*21 Jun 97*

ILL WATERS (RUN DEEP)	*Polydor*	18	*8 Nov 97*	3
MORTALITY	*Epic*	5	*18 Jul 98*	12
bove hit: Celine DION with special guests the BEE GEES.				
HIS IS WHERE I CAME IN	*Polydor*	18	*7 Apr 01*	5
LBUMS:	**HITS 18**			**WEEKS 378**
EE GEES FIRST	*Polydor*	8	*12 Aug 67*	26
ORIZONTAL	*Polydor*	16	*24 Feb 68*	15
DEA	*Polydor*	4	*28 Sep 68*	18
DESSA	*Polydor*	10	*5 Apr 69*	1
EST OF THE BEE GEES	*Polydor*	7	*8 Nov 69*	22
UCUMBER CASTLE	*Polydor*	57	*9 May 70*	2
PIRITS HAVING FLOWN	*RSO*	1	*17 Feb 79*	33
EE GEES GREATEST	*RSO*	6	*10 Nov 79*	25
IVING EYES	*RSO*	73	*7 Nov 81*	8
S.P.	*Warner Brothers*	5	*3 Oct 87*	24
NE	*Warner Brothers*	29	*29 Apr 89*	3
HE VERY BEST OF THE BEE GEES	*Polydor*	8	*17 Nov 90*	46
IGH CIVILZATION	*Warner Brothers*	24	*6 Apr 91*	5
ZE ISN'T EVERYTHING	*Polydor*	23	*25 Sep 93*	13
HE VERY BEST OF THE BEE GEES [RE]	*Polydor*	6	*22 Feb 97*	62
TILL WATERS	*Polydor*	2	*22 Mar 97*	19
IVE ONE NIGHT ONLY	*Polydor*	4	*19 Sep 98*	44
ive recordings from the MGM Grand, Las Vegas, November 97.				
HIS IS WHERE I CAME IN	*Polydor*	6	*14 Apr 01*	6
HEIR GREATEST HITS – THE RECORD	*Polydor*	5	*24 Nov 01*	6

ir Thomas BEECHAM – See ORCHESTRE NATIONALE DE LA RADIO DIFFUSION FRANCAISE conducted by ir Thomas BEECHAM

BEENIE MAN — Jamaica

INGLES:	**HITS 5**			**WEEKS 21**
DANCEHALL QUEEN	*Island Jamaica*	70	*20 Sep 97*	1
rom the film 'Dancehall Queen'.				
Above hit: Chevelle FRANKLYN featuring BEENIE MAN.				
WHO AM I (ZIM-ZIMMA)	*Greensleeves*	10	*7 Mar 98*	5
OUNDATION	*Jetstar*	69	*8 Aug 98*	1
hould not have charted as its track listing violated chart rules.				
Above hit: BEENIE MAN and the TAXI GANG.				
MONEY	*Parlophone Rhythm Series*	5	*4 Mar 00*	9
Above hit: JAMELLA featuring BEENIE MAN.				
GIRLS DEM SUGAR	*Virgin*	13	*24 Mar 01*	5
Above hit: BEENIE MAN featuring MYA.				

Lou BEGA — Germany

SINGLES:	**HITS 2**			**WEEKS 21**
MAMBO NO. 5 (A LITTLE BIT OF . . .)	*Lautstark*	31	*7 Aug 99*	4
German import.				
MAMBO NO. 5 (A LITTLE BIT OF . . .)	*RCA*	1	*4 Sep 99*	15
Theme to Channel 4's cricket coverage.				
GOT A GIRL	*RCA*	55	*18 Dec 99*	2
ALBUMS:	**HITS 1**			**WEEKS 2**
A LITTLE BIT OF MAMBO	*RCA*	50	*18 Sep 99*	2

BEGGAR and CO. — UK

SINGLES:	**HITS 2**			**WEEKS 15**
(SOMEBODY) HELP ME OUT	*Ensign*	15	*7 Feb 81*	10
MULE (CHANT NO. 2)	*RCA*	37	*12 Sep 81*	5
Backing by Spandau Ballet.				

BEGINNING OF THE END — Bahamas

SINGLES:	**HITS 1**			**WEEKS 6**
FUNKY NASSAU	*Atlantic*	31	*23 Feb 74*	6

BEIJING SPRING — UK

SINGLES:	**HITS 2**			**WEEKS 5**
I WANNA BE IN LOVE AGAIN	*MCA*	43	*23 Jan 93*	3
SUMMERLANDS	*MCA*	53	*8 May 93*	2

BEL AMOUR — France

SINGLES:	**HITS 1**			**WEEKS 3**
BEL AMOUR	*Credence*	23	*12 May 01*	3
Vocals by Sydney.				

BEL CANTO — UK

SINGLES:	HITS 1			WEEKS
WE'VE GOT TO WORK IT OUT	*Good Groove*	65	*14 Oct 95*	

Harry BELAFONTE — US

SINGLES:	HITS 7			WEEKS
BANANA BOAT SONG (DAY-O)	*His Master's Voice*	2	*2 Mar 57*	
Above hit: Harry BELAFONTE with Tony SCOTT'S ORCHESTRA and Chorus and Millard THOMAS, guitar.				
ISLAND IN THE SUN	*RCA*	3	*15 Jun 57*	
SCARLET RIBBONS	*His Master's Voice*	18	*7 Sep 57*	
Originally recorded by Jo Stafford.				
Above hit: Harry BELAFONTE and Millard THOMAS.				
MARY'S BOY CHILD	*RCA*	1	*2 Nov 57*	
LITTLE BERNADETTE	*RCA*	16	*23 Aug 58*	
Above hit: BELAFONTE.				
MARY'S BOY CHILD [RE-1ST]	*RCA*	10	*29 Nov 58*	
THE SON OF MARY	*RCA*	18	*13 Dec 58*	
MARY'S BOY CHILD [RE-2ND]	*RCA*	30	*12 Dec 59*	
THERE'S A HOLE IN THE BUCKET	*RCA*	32	*23 Sep 61*	
Harry BELAFONTE and ODETTA				
THERE'S A HOLE IN THE BUCKET [RE]	*RCA*	34	*14 Oct 61*	

EPS:	HITS 2			WEEKS
SCARLET RIBBONS	*RCA*	18	*16 Apr 60*	
BELAFONTE AT CHRISTMASTIDE	*RCA*	18	*9 Dec 61*	

Archie BELL and the DRELLS — US

SINGLES:	HITS 5			WEEKS 3
HERE I GO AGAIN	*Atlantic*	11	*7 Oct 72*	1
(THERE'S GONNA BE) A SHOWDOWN	*Atlantic*	36	*27 Jan 73*	
THE SOUL CITY WALK	*Philadelphia International*	13	*8 May 76*	1
EVERYBODY HAVE A GOOD TIME	*Philadelphia International*	43	*11 Jun 77*	
DON'T LET LOVE GET YOU DOWN	*Portrait*	49	*28 Jun 86*	

Freddie BELL and the BELL BOYS — US

SINGLES:	HITS 1			WEEKS 1
GIDDY-UP-A DING DONG	*Mercury*	4	*29 Sep 56*	1

Maggie BELL — UK

SINGLES:	HITS 2			WEEKS 1
HAZELL	*Swan Song*	37	*15 Apr 78*	
Theme from the Thames TV series of the same name.				
HAZELL [RE]	*Swan Song*	74	*13 May 78*	
HOLD ME	*Swan Song*	11	*17 Oct 81*	
Above hit: B.A. ROBERTSON and Maggie BELL.				

William BELL — US

SINGLES:	HITS 3			WEEKS 2
A TRIBUTE TO A KING	*Stax*	31	*1 Jun 68*	
A tribute to Otis Redding.				
PRIVATE NUMBER	*Stax*	8	*23 Nov 68*	1
Above hit: Judy CLAY and William BELL.				
HEADLINE NEWS	*Absolute*	70	*26 Apr 86*	

BELL and JAMES — US

SINGLES:	HITS 1			WEEKS
LIVIN' IT UP (FRIDAY NIGHT)	*A&M*	68	*31 Mar 79*	
LIVIN' IT UP (FRIDAY NIGHT)[RE]	*A&M*	59	*14 Apr 79*	

BELL & SPURLING — UK

SINGLES:	HITS 1			WEEKS
SVEN SVEN SVEN (COME ON ENGLAND)	*Eternal*	7	*13 Oct 01*	

BELL BIV DEVOE — US

(See also Janet Jackson; Luther Vandross.)

SINGLES:	HITS 3			WEEKS
POISON	*MCA*	19	*30 Jun 90*	
DO ME	*MCA*	56	*22 Sep 90*	
SOMETHING IN YOUR EYES	*MCA*	60	*9 Oct 93*	

ALBUMS:	HITS 1			WEEKS
POISON	*MCA*	35	*1 Sep 90*	

BELL BOOK AND CANDLE — Germany

SINGLES:	HITS 1			WEEKS 1
RESCUE ME	*Logic*	63	*17 Oct 98*	1

BELLAMY BROTHERS — US

SINGLES:	HITS 3			WEEKS 29
LET YOUR LOVE FLOW	*Warner Brothers*	7	*17 Apr 76*	12
SATIN SHEETS	*Warner Brothers*	43	*21 Aug 76*	3
IF I SAID YOU HAVE A BEAUTIFUL BODY WOULD YOU HOLD IT AGAINST ME	*Warner Brothers*	3	*11 Aug 79*	14
ALBUMS:	**HITS 1**			**WEEKS 6**
BELLAMY BROTHERS	*Warner Brothers*	21	*19 Jun 76*	6

BELLATRIX — Iceland

SINGLES:	HITS 1			WEEKS 1
JEDI WANNABE	*Fierce Panda*	65	*16 Sep 00*	1
Originally reached No. 141 in 1999.				

Regina BELLE — US

SINGLES:	HITS 2			WEEKS 13
GOOD LOVIN'	*CBS*	73	*21 Oct 89*	1
A WHOLE NEW WORLD (ALADDIN'S THEME)	*Columbia*	12	*11 Dec 93*	12
From the Walt Disney film 'Aladdin'.				
Above hit: Regina BELLE and Peabo BRYSON.				
ALBUMS:	**HITS 2**			**WEEKS 5**
ALL BY MYSELF	*CBS*	53	*1 Aug 87*	4
STAY WITH ME	*CBS*	62	*16 Sep 89*	1

BELLE and the DEVOTIONS — UK

SINGLES:	HITS 1			WEEKS 8
LOVE GAMES	*CBS*	11	*21 Apr 84*	8
UK's Eurovision entry in 1984, it came 7th.				

BELLE AND SEBASTIAN — UK

SINGLES:	HITS 6			WEEKS 12
DOG ON WHEELS	*Jeepster*	59	*24 May 97*	1
LAZY LINE PAINTER JANE	*Jeepster*	41	*9 Aug 97*	2
3.. 6.. 9 SECONDS OF LIGHT [EP]	*Jeepster*	32	*25 Oct 97*	2
Lead track: A Century Of Fakers.				
LEGAL MAN	*Jeepster*	15	*3 Jun 00*	3
Above hit: BELLE AND SEBASTIAN featuring the MAISONETTES.				
JONATHAN DAVID	*Jeepster*	31	*30 Jun 01*	2
I'M WAKING UP TO US	*Jeepster*	39	*8 Dec 01*	2
ALBUMS:	**HITS 3**			**WEEKS 13**
THE BOY WITH THE ARAB STRAP	*Jeepster*	12	*19 Sep 98*	6
TIGERMILK	*Jeepster*	13	*24 Jul 99*	4
Originally released in 1996 on the Electric Honey label.				
FOLD YOUR HANDS CHILD YOU WALK LIKE A PEASANT	*Jeepster*	10	*17 Jun 00*	3

La BELLE EPOQUE — France

SINGLES:	HITS 1			WEEKS 14
BLACK IS BLACK	*Harvest*	48	*27 Aug 77*	1
BLACK IS BLACK [RE]	*Harvest*	2	*10 Sep 77*	13

BELLE STARS — UK

SINGLES:	HITS 7			WEEKS 42
IKO IKO	*Stiff*	35	*5 Jun 82*	6
Originally recorded by James 'Sugarboy' Crawford as Jock-O-Mo.				
THE CLAPPING SONG	*Stiff*	11	*17 Jul 82*	9
MOCKINGBIRD	*Stiff*	51	*16 Oct 82*	3
SIGN OF THE TIMES	*Stiff*	3	*15 Jan 83*	11
SWEET MEMORY	*Stiff*	22	*16 Apr 83*	9
INDIAN SUMMER	*Stiff*	52	*13 Aug 83*	3
80'S ROMANCE	*Stiff*	71	*14 Jul 84*	1
ALBUMS:	**HITS 1**			**WEEKS 12**
THE BELLE STARS	*Stiff*	15	*5 Feb 83*	12

BELLEFIRE — Ireland

SINGLES:	HITS 1			WEEKS 4
PERFECT BLISS	*Virgin*	18	*14 Jul 01*	4

BELLINI — Brazil/Thailand/Indonesia/Germany

SINGLES:	HITS 1			WEEKS 7
SAMBA DE JANEIRO *Melody based on Airto Moreira's 'Celebration Suit'.*	*Virgin*	8	*27 Sep 97*	7

BELLY — US

SINGLES:	HITS 4			WEEKS 9
FEED THE TREE	*4AD*	32	*23 Jan 93*	3
GEPETTO	*4AD*	49	*10 Apr 93*	2
NOW THEY'LL SLEEP	*4AD*	28	*4 Feb 95*	2
SEAL MY FATE	*4AD*	35	*22 Jul 95*	2
ALBUMS:	**HITS 2**			**WEEKS 13**
STAR	*4AD*	2	*13 Feb 93*	10
KING	*4AD*	6	*25 Feb 95*	3

Pierre BELMONDE — France

ALBUMS:	HITS 1			WEEKS 10
THEMES FOR DREAMS	*K-Tel*	13	*7 Jun 80*	10

BELMONTS - See DION

BELOVED — UK

SINGLES:	HITS 10			WEEKS 47
THE SUN RISING	*WEA*	26	*21 Oct 89*	7
HELLO	*WEA*	19	*27 Jan 90*	7
YOUR LOVE TAKES ME HIGHER *Original release reached No. 91 in 1989.*	*East West*	39	*24 Mar 90*	3
TIME AFTER TIME	*East West*	46	*9 Jun 90*	4
IT'S ALRIGHT NOW	*East West*	48	*10 Nov 90*	3
SWEET HARMONY	*East West*	8	*23 Jan 93*	10
YOU'VE GOT ME THINKING	*East West*	23	*10 Apr 93*	4
OUTERSPACE GIRL	*East West*	38	*14 Aug 93*	2
SATELLITE	*East West*	19	*30 Mar 96*	3
EASE THE PRESSURE	*East West*	43	*10 Aug 96*	2
THE SUN RISING [RI]	*East West*	31	*30 Aug 97*	2
ALBUMS:	**HITS 4**			**WEEKS 31**
HAPPINESS	*East West*	14	*3 Mar 90*	14
BLISSED OUT	*East West*	38	*1 Dec 90*	2
CONSCIENCE	*East West*	2	*20 Feb 93*	12
X	*East West*	25	*20 Apr 96*	3

BELTRAM — US

SINGLES:	HITS 2			WEEKS 4
ENERGY FLASH [EP] *Lead track: Energy Flash.*	*R&S*	52	*28 Sep 91*	2
THE OMEN *Above hit: PROGRAM 2 BELTRAM.*	*R&S*	53	*7 Dec 91*	2

Pat BENATAR — US

SINGLES:	HITS 9			WEEKS 53
LOVE IS A BATTLEFIELD *Originally recorded by Holly Knight.*	*Chrysalis*	49	*21 Jan 84*	5
WE BELONG	*Chrysalis*	22	*12 Jan 85*	9
LOVE IS A BATTLEFIELD [RI]	*Chrysalis*	17	*23 Mar 85*	10
SHADOWS OF THE NIGHT *Original release reached No. 83 in 1983.*	*Chrysalis*	50	*15 Jun 85*	4
INVINCIBLE (THEME FROM 'THE LEGEND OF BILLIE JEAN')	*Chrysalis*	53	*19 Oct 85*	3
SEX AS A WEAPON	*Chrysalis*	67	*15 Feb 86*	3
ALL FIRED UP	*Chrysalis*	19	*2 Jul 88*	10
DON'T WALK AWAY	*Chrysalis*	42	*1 Oct 88*	5
ONE LOVE	*Chrysalis*	59	*14 Jan 89*	3
SOMEBODY'S BABY	*Chrysalis*	48	*30 Oct 93*	1
ALBUMS:	**HITS 9**			**WEEKS 84**
PRECIOUS TIME	*Chrysalis*	30	*25 Jul 81*	7
GET NERVOUS	*Chrysalis*	73	*13 Nov 82*	6
LIVE FROM EARTH *Live recordings (except for 2 studio tracks).*	*Chrysalis*	60	*15 Oct 83*	5
TROPICO	*Chrysalis*	31	*17 Nov 84*	25
IN THE HEAT OF THE NIGHT	*Chrysalis*	98	*24 Aug 85*	1
SEVEN THE HARD WAY	*Chrysalis*	69	*7 Dec 85*	4
BEST SHOTS	*Chrysalis*	6	*7 Nov 87*	19
WIDE AWAKE IN DREAMLAND	*Chrysalis*	11	*16 Jul 88*	14
TRUE LOVE	*Chrysalis*	40	*4 May 91*	3

David BENDETH — Canada

SINGLES:	HITS 1			WEEKS 5
FEEL THE REAL	*Sidewalk*	44	*8 Sep 79*	5

BENELUX and Nancy DEE — Belgium/Luxembourg/Holland

SINGLES:	HITS 1			WEEKS 4
SWITCH	*Scope*	52	*25 Aug 79*	4

Eric BENET — US

SINGLES:	HITS 3			WEEKS 5
SPIRITUAL THANG	*Warner Brothers*	62	*22 Mar 97*	1
GEORGY PORGY	*Warner Brothers*	28	*1 May 99*	3
Original by Toto reached No. 48 in the US in 1978.				
Above hit: Eric BENET featuring Faith EVANS.				
WHY YOU FOLLOW ME	*Warner Brothers*	48	*5 Feb 00*	1
ALBUMS:	**HITS 1**			**WEEKS 1**
A DAY IN THE LIFE	*Warner Brothers*	67	*15 May 99*	1

Addell BENJAMIN - See 2 FOR JOY

Nigel BENN - See PACK featuring Nigel BENN

Simone BENN - See VOLATILE AGENTS featuring Simone BENN

BENNET — UK

SINGLES:	HITS 2			WEEKS 3
MUM'S GONE TO ICELAND	*Roadrunner*	34	*22 Feb 97*	2
SOMEONE ALWAYS GETS THERE FIRST	*Roadrunner*	69	*3 May 97*	1
Original release reached No. 145 in 1996.				

Boyd BENNETT and his ROCKETS (Vocal by BIG MOE) — US

SINGLES:	HITS 1			WEEKS 2
SEVENTEEN	*Parlophone*	16	*24 Dec 55*	2

Chris BENNETT - See MUSIC MACHINE

Cliff BENNETT and the REBEL ROUSERS — UK

SINGLES:	HITS 3			WEEKS 23
ONE WAY LOVE	*Parlophone*	9	*3 Oct 64*	9
I'LL TAKE YOU HOME	*Parlophone*	42	*6 Feb 65*	3
Above 2 originally recorded by the Drifters.				
GOT TO GET YOU INTO MY LIFE	*Parlophone*	6	*13 Aug 66*	11
Originally written and recorded by the Beatles.				
ALBUMS:	**HITS 1**			**WEEKS 3**
DRIVIN' ME WILD	*Music For Pleasure*	25	*22 Oct 66*	3

Peter E. BENNETT with the CO-OPERATION CHOIR — UK

SINGLES:	HITS 1			WEEKS 1
THE SEAGULL'S NAME WAS NELSON	*RCA Victor*	45	*7 Nov 70*	1

Tony BENNETT — US

SINGLES:	HITS 8			WEEKS 61
STRANGER IN PARADISE	*Philips*	1	*16 Apr 55*	16
From the show 'Kismet'.				
Above hit: Tony BENNETT with Percy FAITH and his Orchestra and Chorus.				
CLOSE YOUR EYES	*Philips*	18	*17 Sep 55*	1
COME NEXT SPRING	*Philips*	29	*14 Apr 56*	1
TILL	*Philips*	35	*7 Jan 61*	2
Incorrectly listed on the chart as a double A-side with Serenata.				
THE GOOD LIFE	*CBS*	27	*20 Jul 63*	13
IF I RULED THE WORLD	*CBS*	40	*8 May 65*	5
Above hit: Tony BENNETT with the Will BRONSON CHORUS conducted by Don COSTA.				
(I LEFT MY HEART) IN SAN FRANCISCO	*CBS*	46	*29 May 65*	2
(I LEFT MY HEART) IN SAN FRANCISCO [RE-1ST]	*CBS*	40	*2 Oct 65*	5
(I LEFT MY HEART) IN SAN FRANCISCO [RE-2ND]	*CBS*	25	*11 Dec 65*	7
THE VERY THOUGHT OF YOU	*CBS*	21	*25 Dec 65*	9
Above hit: Tony BENNETT featuring Bobby HACKETT.				
EPS:	**HITS 3**			**WEEKS 72**
WHEN JOANNA LOVED ME	*CBS*	5	*4 Dec 65*	19
TILL	*CBS*	7	*21 May 66*	6
THE BEST OF BENNETT	*CBS*	2	*7 Jan 67*	47
ALBUMS:	**HITS 7**			**WEEKS 67**
I LEFT MY HEART IN SAN FRANCISCO	*CBS*	20	*29 May 65*	1
I LEFT MY HEART IN SAN FRANCISCO [RE]	*CBS*	13	*4 Dec 65*	13

A STRING OF TONY'S HITS	*CBS*	9	*19 Feb 66*	13
TONY'S GREATEST HITS	*CBS*	14	*10 Jun 67*	24
TONY MAKES IT HAPPEN	*CBS*	31	*23 Sep 67*	3
FOR ONCE IN MY LIFE	*CBS*	29	*23 Mar 68*	5
THE VERY BEST OF TONY BENNETT - 20 GREATEST HITS	*Warwick*	23	*26 Feb 77*	4
THE ESSENTIAL TONY BENNETT	*Columbia*	49	*28 Nov 98*	4

Gary BENSON — UK

SINGLES:	HITS 1			WEEKS 8
DON'T THROW IT ALL AWAY	*State*	20	*9 Aug 75*	8

George BENSON — US

(See also George Benson and Earl Klugh.)

SINGLES:	HITS 22			WEEKS 143
SUPERSHIP	*CTI*	30	*25 Oct 75*	6
Above hit: George 'Bad' BENSON.				
NATURE BOY	*Warner Brothers*	26	*4 Jun 77*	6
THE GREATEST LOVE OF ALL	*Arista*	27	*24 Sep 77*	7
From the film 'The Greatest'.				
LOVE BALLAD	*Warner Brothers*	29	*31 Mar 79*	9
Original by L.T.D. reached No. 20 in the US in 1976.				
GIVE ME THE NIGHT	*Warner Brothers*	7	*26 Jul 80*	10
LOVE X LOVE	*Warner Brothers*	10	*4 Oct 80*	8
WHAT'S ON YOUR MIND	*Warner Brothers*	45	*7 Feb 81*	5
LOVE ALL THE HURT AWAY	*Arista*	49	*19 Sep 81*	3
Above hit: Aretha FRANKLIN and George BENSON.				
TURN YOUR LOVE AROUND	*Warner Brothers*	29	*14 Nov 81*	11
NEVER GIVE UP ON A GOOD THING	*Warner Brothers*	14	*23 Jan 82*	10
LADY LOVE ME (ONE MORE TIME)	*Warner Brothers*	11	*21 May 83*	10
FEEL LIKE MAKIN' LOVE	*Warner Brothers*	28	*16 Jul 83*	7
IN YOUR EYES	*Warner Brothers*	7	*24 Sep 83*	10
Co-written and originally recorded by Dan Hill.				
INSIDE LOVE (SO PERSONAL)	*Warner Brothers*	57	*17 Dec 83*	5
20/20	*Warner Brothers*	29	*19 Jan 85*	9
BEYOND THE SEA (LA MER)	*Warner Brothers*	60	*20 Apr 85*	3
KISSES IN THE MOONLIGHT	*Warner Brothers*	60	*16 Aug 86*	4
SHIVER	*Warner Brothers*	19	*29 Nov 86*	9
TEASER	*Warner Brothers*	45	*14 Feb 87*	4
LET'S DO IT AGAIN	*Warner Brothers*	56	*27 Aug 88*	3
I'LL KEEP YOUR DREAMS ALIVE	*Ammi*	68	*5 Sep 92*	1
Above hit: George BENSON and Patti AUSTIN.				
SEVEN DAYS	*MCA*	22	*11 Jul 98*	3
Above hit: Mary J. BLIGE featuring George BENSON.				

ALBUMS:	HITS 14			WEEKS 274
IN FLIGHT	*Warner Brothers*	19	*19 Mar 77*	23
WEEKEND IN L.A.	*Warner Brothers*	47	*18 Feb 78*	1
LIVING INSIDE YOUR LOVE	*Warner Brothers*	24	*24 Mar 79*	14
GIVE ME THE NIGHT	*Warner Brothers*	3	*26 Jul 80*	40
THE GEORGE BENSON COLLECTION	*Warner Brothers*	19	*14 Nov 81*	35
IN YOUR EYES	*Warner Brothers*	3	*11 Jun 83*	53
20/20	*Warner Brothers*	9	*26 Jan 85*	19
THE LOVE SONGS	*K-Tel*	1	*19 Oct 85*	26
WHILE THE CITY SLEEPS . .	*Warner Brothers*	13	*6 Sep 86*	27
TWICE THE LOVE	*Warner Brothers*	16	*10 Sep 88*	10
TENDERLY	*Warner Brothers*	52	*8 Jul 89*	3
MIDNIGHT MOODS - THE LOVE COLLECTION	*Telstar*	25	*26 Oct 91*	12
THAT'S RIGHT	*GRP*	61	*29 Jun 96*	1
ESSENTIALS . . . THE VERY BEST OF GEORGE BENSON	*warner.esp/Jive*	8	*25 Apr 98*	10

George BENSON and Earl KLUGH — UK/US

(See also George Benson.)

ALBUMS:	HITS 1			WEEKS 6
COLLABORATION	*Warner Brothers*	47	*11 Jul 87*	6

BENTLEY RHYTHM ACE — UK

SINGLES:	HITS 3			WEEKS 7
BENTLEYS GONNA SORT YOU OUT!	*Parlophone*	17	*6 Sep 97*	4
THEME FROM GUTBUSTER	*Parlophone*	29	*27 May 00*	2
Samples Piero Umilani's Open Face, Kim Fowley's Whittier Boulevard and E-Man Groovin by the Jimmy Castor Bunch featuring the Everything Man.				
HOW'D I DO DAT???	*Parlophone*	57	*2 Sep 00*	1
Features Kernit (ex-Black Grape) on vocals.				

ALBUMS:	HITS 2			WEEKS 6
BENTLEY RHYTHM ACE	*Skint*	13	*24 May 97*	5
FOR YOUR EARS ONLY	*Parlophone*	48	*10 Jun 00*	1

Brook BENTON — US

SINGLES:	HITS 4			WEEKS 18
ENDLESSLY	*Mercury*	28	*11 Jul 59*	2
KIDDIO	*Mercury*	42	*8 Oct 60*	3
Originally recorded by Teddy Randazzo.				
KIDDIO [RE]	*Mercury*	41	*5 Nov 60*	3
FOOLS RUSH IN (WHERE ANGELS FEAR TO TREAD)	*Mercury*	50	*18 Feb 61*	1
THE BOLL WEEVIL SONG	*Mercury*	30	*15 Jul 61*	9
Originally recorded by Dave Bartholomew.				

BENZ — UK

SINGLES:	HITS 5			WEEKS 9
BOOM ROCK SOUL	*RCA*	62	*16 Dec 95*	2
URBAN CITY GIRL	*Hacktown*	31	*16 Mar 96*	3
MISS PARKER	*RCA*	35	*25 May 96*	2
IF I REMEMBER	*Hendricks*	59	*29 Mar 97*	1
ON A SUN-DAY	*Hendricks*	73	*9 Aug 97*	1

Spragga BENZ - See Foxy BROWN

Ingrid BERGMAN - See Dooley WILSON with the voices of Humphrey BOGART and Ingrid BERGMAN

BERLIN — US

SINGLES:	HITS 3			WEEKS 39
TAKE MY BREATH AWAY (LOVE THEME FROM "TOP GUN")	*CBS*	1	*25 Oct 86*	15
From the film 'Top Gun'.				
YOU DON'T KNOW	*Mercury*	39	*17 Jan 87*	6
LIKE FLAMES	*Mercury*	47	*14 Mar 87*	3
TAKE MY BREATH AWAY (LOVE THEME FROM "TOP GUN") [RE]	*CBS*	52	*20 Feb 88*	3
TAKE MY BREATH AWAY (LOVE THEME FROM "TOP GUN") [RI]	*CBS*	3	*13 Oct 90*	12
Re-Issued after the first showing of 'Top Gun' on British TV.				

ALBUMS:	HITS 1			WEEKS 11
COUNT THREE AND PRAY	*Mercury*	32	*17 Jan 87*	11

BERLIN PHILHARMONIC ORCHESTRA - See Herbert VON KARAJAN conducting the BERLIN PHILHARMONIC ORCHESTRA

Shelley BERMAN — US

ALBUMS:	HITS 1			WEEKS 4
INSIDE SHELLEY BERMAN	*Capitol*	12	*19 Nov 60*	4

Elmer BERNSTEIN — US

SINGLES:	HITS 1			WEEKS 11
STACCATO'S THEME	*Capitol*	4	*19 Dec 59*	10
STACCATO'S THEME [RE]	*Capitol*	40	*12 Mar 60*	1

EPS:	HITS 1			WEEKS 1
STACCATO	*Capitol*	6	*12 Mar 60*	1

Orchestra and Chorus conducted by Leonard BERNSTEIN — US

(See also Various Artists: Studio Cast 'West Side Story'.)

SINGLES:	HITS 1			WEEKS 4
AMERICA - THE OFFICIAL 1994 BBC WORLD CUP THEME	*Deutsche Grammophon*	44	*2 Jul 94*	4

ALBUMS:	HITS 1			WEEKS 2
BERNSTEIN IN BERLIN - BEETHOVEN SYMPHONY NO. 9	*Deutsche Grammophon*	54	*10 Feb 90*	2

BERRI — UK

SINGLES:	HITS 2			WEEKS 22
THE SUNSHINE AFTER THE RAIN	*Ffrreedom*	26	*26 Nov 94*	6
Above hit: NEW ATLANTIC/U4EA featuring BERRI.				
THE SUNSHINE AFTER THE RAIN [RI]	*Ffrreedom*	4	*2 Sep 95*	11
SHINE LIKE A STAR	*Ffrreedom*	20	*2 Dec 95*	5

LaKiesha BERRI — US

SINGLES:	HITS 1			WEEKS 1
LIKE THIS AND LIKE THAT	*Adept*	54	*5 Jul 97*	1

Chuck BERRY — US

SINGLES:	HITS 11			WEEKS 91
SCHOOL DAY (RING! RING! GOES THE BELL)	*Columbia*	24	*22 Jun 57*	2
SCHOOL DAY (RING! RING! GOES THE BELL) [RE]	*Columbia*	24	*13 Jul 57*	2
SWEET LITTLE SIXTEEN	*London*	16	*26 Apr 58*	5
GO, GO, GO	*Pye International*	38	*13 Jul 63*	6
LET IT ROCK / MEMPHIS TENNESSEE	*Pye International*	6	*12 Oct 63*	13

RUN RUDOLPH RUN	*Pye International*	36	*21 Dec 63*	6
NADINE (IS IT YOU)	*Pye International*	27	*15 Feb 64*	6
NADINE (IS IT YOU) [RE]	*Pye International*	43	*4 Apr 64*	1
NO PARTICULAR PLACE TO GO	*Pye International*	3	*9 May 64*	12
YOU NEVER CAN TELL	*Pye International*	23	*22 Aug 64*	8
THE PROMISED LAND	*Pye International*	26	*16 Jan 65*	6
MY DING-A-LING	*Chess*	1	*28 Oct 72*	17
Originally recorded by Dave Bartholomew in 1952. Backing musicians are the Average White Band.				
REELIN' AND ROCKIN'	*Chess*	18	*3 Feb 73*	7
Above 2: Live recordings from Lanchester Arts Festival, Coventry.				
EPS:	**HITS 5**			**WEEKS 68**
CHUCK BERRY	*Pye International*	7	*5 Oct 63*	14
CHUCK AND BO	*Pye International*	6	*5 Oct 63*	22
CHUCK AND BO, VOLUME 2	*Pye International*	15	*30 Nov 63*	2
Above 2: Chuck BERRY and Bo DIDDLEY.				
THE BEST OF CHUCK BERRY	*Pye International*	5	*8 Feb 64*	25
CHUCK AND BO, VOLUME 3	*Pye International*	12	*15 Feb 64*	5
Above hit: Chuck BERRY and Bo DIDDLEY.				
ALBUMS:	**HITS 6**			**WEEKS 53**
CHUCK BERRY	*Pye International*	12	*25 May 63*	16
CHUCK BERRY ON STAGE	*Pye International*	6	*5 Oct 63*	11
MORE CHUCK BERRY	*Pye International*	9	*7 Dec 63*	8
THE LATEST AND THE GREATEST	*Pye International*	8	*30 May 64*	7
YOU NEVER CAN TELL	*Pye International*	18	*3 Oct 64*	2
MOTORVATIN'	*Chess*	7	*12 Feb 77*	9

Dave BERRY — UK

SINGLES:	**HITS 8**			**WEEKS 76**
MEMPHIS TENNESSEE	*Decca*	19	*21 Sep 63*	13
Above hit: Dave BERRY and the CRUISERS.				
MY BABY LEFT ME	*Decca*	41	*11 Jan 64*	1
Originally recorded by Arthur 'Bigboy' Cruddup.				
MY BABY LEFT ME [RE]	*Decca*	37	*25 Jan 64*	8
BABY IT'S YOU	*Decca*	24	*2 May 64*	6
THE CRYING GAME	*Decca*	5	*8 Aug 64*	12
ONE HEART BETWEEN TWO	*Decca*	41	*28 Nov 64*	2
LITTLE THINGS	*Decca*	5	*27 Mar 65*	12
Original by Bobby Goldsboro reached No. 13 in the US in 1965.				
THIS STRANGE EFFECT	*Decca*	37	*24 Jul 65*	6
Written by Ray Davies of the Kinks.				
MAMA	*Decca*	5	*2 Jul 66*	16
Original by B.J.Thomas reached No. 22 in the US in 1966.				
EPS:	**HITS 1**			**WEEKS 6**
CAN I GET IT FROM YOU	*Decca*	12	*10 Jul 65*	6

Mike BERRY — UK

SINGLES:	**HITS 6**			**WEEKS 51**
TRIBUTE TO BUDDY HOLLY	*His Master's Voice*	24	*14 Oct 61*	6
DON'T YOU THINK IT'S TIME	*His Master's Voice*	6	*5 Jan 63*	12
MY LITTLE BABY	*His Master's Voice*	34	*13 Apr 63*	7
Above 3: Mike BERRY with the OUTLAWS.				
THE SUNSHINE OF YOUR SMILE	*Polydor*	9	*2 Aug 80*	12
Originally recorded by John McCormack in 1916. Produced by Chas Hodeges of Chas & Dave.				
IF I COULD ONLY MAKE YOU CARE	*Polydor*	37	*29 Nov 80*	9
MEMORIES	*Polydor*	55	*5 Sep 81*	5
EPS:	**HITS 1**			**WEEKS 4**
A TRIBUTE TO BUDDY HOLLY	*HMV*	17	*31 Aug 63*	4
Above hit: Mike BERRY with the OUTLAWS.				
ALBUMS:	**HITS 1**			**WEEKS 3**
THE SUNSHINE OF YOUR SMILE	*Polydor*	63	*24 Jan 81*	3

Nick BERRY — UK

SINGLES:	**HITS 3**			**WEEKS 24**
EVERY LOSER WINS	*BBC*	1	*4 Oct 86*	11
EVERY LOSER WINS [RE]	*BBC*	72	*27 Dec 86*	2
HEARTBEAT	*Columbia*	2	*13 Jun 92*	8
Theme from the Yorkshire TV series of the same name.				
LONG LIVE LOVE	*Columbia*	47	*31 Oct 92*	3
ALBUMS:	**HITS 2**			**WEEKS 8**
NICK BERRY	*BBC*	99	*20 Dec 86*	1
NICK BERRY	*Columbia*	28	*21 Nov 92*	7
Identically titled albums are different.				

Adele BERTEI - See JELLYBEAN

BEST COMPANY — UK

SINGLES:	HITS 1			WEEKS 1
DON'T YOU FORGET ABOUT ME	*ZYX*	65	*27 Mar 93*	1

BEST SHOT — UK

SINGLES:	HITS 1			WEEKS 2
UNITED COLOURS	*East West*	64	*5 Feb 94*	2

BETA BAND — UK

SINGLES:	HITS 2			WEEKS 3
BROKE/WON	*Regal Recordings*	30	*14 Jul 01*	2
HUMAN BEING	*Regal Recordings*	57	*27 Oct 01*	1
Samples Carole King's 'It's Too Late'.				
ALBUMS:	**HITS 3**			**WEEKS 6**
THE THREE E.P.S	*Regal Recordings*	35	*10 Oct 98*	1
12 track set bringing together tracks from their limited edition EPs.				
THE BETA BAND	*Regal Recordings*	18	*3 Jul 99*	2
HOT SHOTS II	*Regal Recordings*	13	*28 Jul 01*	3

Martin BETTINGHAUS - See Timo MAAS

BEVERLEY-PHILLIPS ORCHESTRA — UK

ALBUMS:	HITS 1			WEEKS 9
GOLD ON SILVER	*Warwick*	22	*9 Oct 76*	9

BEVERLEY SISTERS — UK

(See also All Star Hit Parade.)

SINGLES:	HITS 6			WEEKS 34
I SAW MOMMY KISSING SANTA CLAUS	*Philips*	11	*28 Nov 53*	1
I SAW MOMMY KISSING SANTA CLAUS [RE]	*Philips*	6	*12 Dec 53*	4
WILLIE CAN	*Decca*	23	*14 Apr 56*	4
I DREAMED	*Decca*	24	*2 Feb 57*	2
Above hit: BEVERLEY SISTERS with the Roland SHAW ORCHESTRA.				
THE LITTLE DRUMMER BOY	*Decca*	6	*14 Feb 59*	13
LITTLE DONKEY	*Decca*	14	*21 Nov 59*	7
GREEN FIELDS	*Columbia*	48	*25 Jun 60*	1
GREEN FIELDS [RE]	*Columbia*	29	*9 Jul 60*	2
EPS:	**HITS 1**			**WEEKS 2**
THE BEVS FOR CHRISTMAS	*Decca*	11	*24 Dec 60*	2

Frankie BEVERLY - See MAZE featuring Frankie BEVERLY

BEYOND — UK

SINGLES:	HITS 1			WEEKS 1
RAGING [EP]	*Harvest*	68	*21 Sep 91*	1
Lead track: Great Indifference.				

BIBLE — UK

SINGLES:	HITS 2			WEEKS 8
GRACELAND	*Ensign*	51	*20 May 89*	4
Released in 1986, reached No. 87; a year later it peaked at No. 86.				
HONEY BE GOOD	*Ensign*	54	*26 Aug 89*	4
ALBUMS:	**HITS 2**			**WEEKS 2**
EUREKA	*Chrysalis*	71	*4 Jun 88*	1
THE BIBLE	*Ensign*	67	*7 Oct 89*	1

BIDDU ORCHESTRA — UK

SINGLES:	HITS 3			WEEKS 13
SUMMER OF '42	*Epic*	14	*2 Aug 75*	8
RAIN FOREST	*Epic*	39	*17 Apr 76*	4
JOURNEY TO THE MOON	*Epic*	41	*11 Feb 78*	1

BIG APPLE BAND - See Walter MURPHY and the BIG APPLE BAND

BIG AUDIO DYNAMITE — UK/US

SINGLES:	HITS 6			WEEKS 27
E = MC^2	*CBS*	11	*22 Mar 86*	9
MEDICINE SHOW	*CBS*	29	*7 Jun 86*	5
C'MON EVERY BEATBOX	*CBS*	51	*18 Oct 86*	3
V. THIRTEEN	*CBS*	49	*21 Feb 87*	5
JUST PLAY MUSIC!	*CBS*	51	*28 May 88*	3

LOOKING FOR A SONG	*Columbia*	68	*12 Nov 94*	2
Above hit: BIG AUDIO.				
ALBUMS:	**HITS 6**			**WEEKS 43**
THIS IS BIG AUDIO DYNAMITE	*CBS*	27	*16 Nov 85*	27
NO. 10 UPPING STREET	*CBS*	11	*8 Nov 86*	8
TIGHTEN UP VOLUME 88	*CBS*	33	*9 Jul 88*	3
MEGATOP PHOENIX	*CBS*	26	*16 Sep 89*	3
KOOL-AID	*CBS*	55	*3 Nov 90*	1
THE GLOBE	*Columbia*	63	*17 Aug 91*	1
Above 2: BIG AUDIO DYNAMITE II.				

BIG BAD HORNS – See LITTLE ANGELS

BIG BAM BOO — UK/Canada

SINGLES:	**HITS 1**			**WEEKS 2**
SHOOTING FROM MY HEART	*MCA*	61	*28 Jan 89*	2

BIG BASS vs Michelle NARINE — Canada

SINGLES:	**HITS 1**			**WEEKS 1**
WHAT YOU DO	*Edel*	67	*2 Sep 00*	1
Recreates Bizarre Inc's Playing With Knives.				

BIG BEN — UK

SINGLES:	**HITS 1**			**WEEKS 2**
MILLENNIUM CHIMES	*London*	53	*1 Jan 00*	2
Donation from sales goes towards the Children's Promise – The Millennium Final Hour Appeal.				

BIG BEN BANJO BAND — UK

SINGLES:	**HITS 2**			**WEEKS 6**
LET'S GET TOGETHER NO. 1 [M]	*Columbia*	6	*11 Dec 54*	4
LET'S GET TOGETHER AGAIN - NO. 1 [M]	*Columbia*	19	*10 Dec 55*	1
LET'S GET TOGETHER AGAIN - NO. 1 [M] [RE]	*Columbia*	18	*31 Dec 55*	1
ALBUMS:	**HITS 1**			**WEEKS 1**
MORE MINSTREL MELODIES	*Columbia*	20	*17 Dec 60*	1

BIG BOPPER — US

SINGLES:	**HITS 1**			**WEEKS 8**
CHANTILLY LACE	*Mercury*	30	*27 Dec 58*	1
CHANTILLY LACE [RE]	*Mercury*	12	*10 Jan 59*	7

BIG BOSS STYLUS presents RED VENOM — UK

SINGLES:	**HITS 1**			**WEEKS 1**
LET'S GET IT ON	*All Around The World*	72	*31 Jul 99*	1

BIG C – See Alex WHITCOMBE and BIG C

BIG COUNTRY — UK

SINGLES:	**HITS 23**			**WEEKS 103**
FIELDS OF FIRE (400 MILES)	*Mercury*	10	*26 Feb 83*	12
IN A BIG COUNTRY	*Mercury*	17	*28 May 83*	7
CHANCE	*Mercury*	9	*3 Sep 83*	9
WONDERLAND	*Mercury*	8	*21 Jan 84*	8
EAST OF EDEN	*Mercury*	17	*29 Sep 84*	6
WHERE THE ROSE IS SOWN	*Mercury*	29	*1 Dec 84*	7
JUST A SHADOW	*Mercury*	26	*19 Jan 85*	4
LOOK AWAY	*Mercury*	7	*12 Apr 86*	8
THE TEACHER	*Mercury*	28	*21 Jun 86*	4
ONE GREAT THING	*Mercury*	19	*20 Sep 86*	6
HOLD THE HEART	*Mercury*	55	*29 Nov 86*	2
KING OF EMOTION	*Mercury*	16	*20 Aug 88*	5
KING OF EMOTION [RE]	*Mercury*	74	*1 Oct 88*	1
BROKEN HEART (THIRTEEN VALLEYS)	*Mercury*	47	*5 Nov 88*	4
PEACE IN OUR TIME	*Mercury*	39	*4 Feb 89*	3
SAVE ME	*Mercury*	41	*12 May 90*	3
HEART OF THE WORLD	*Mercury*	50	*21 Jul 90*	2
REPUBLICAN PARTY REPTILE [EP]	*Vertigo*	37	*31 Aug 91*	2
Lead track: Republican Party Reptile.				
BEAUTIFUL PEOPLE	*Vertigo*	72	*19 Oct 91*	1
ALONE	*Compulsion*	24	*13 Mar 93*	3
SHIPS (WHERE WERE YOU?)	*Compulsion*	29	*1 May 93*	3
I'M NOT ASHAMED	*Transatlantic*	69	*10 Jun 95*	1
YOU DREAMER	*Transatlantic*	68	*9 Sep 95*	1
FRAGILE THING	*Track Record*	69	*21 Aug 99*	1
Above hit: BIG COUNTRY (featuring Eddi READER).				

ALBUMS:	HITS 10			WEEKS 148
THE CROSSING	*Mercury*	3	*6 Aug 83*	80
STEELTOWN	*Mercury*	1	*27 Oct 84*	21
THE SEER	*Mercury*	2	*12 Jul 86*	16
PEACE IN OUR TIME	*Mercury*	9	*8 Oct 88*	6
THROUGH A BIG COUNTRY - GREATEST HITS	*Mercury*	2	*26 May 90*	17
NO PLACE LIKE HOME	*Vertigo*	28	*28 Sep 91*	2
THE BUFFALO SKINNERS	*Compulsion*	25	*3 Apr 93*	2
WITHOUT THE AID OF A SAFETY NET (LIVE)	*Compulsion*	35	*18 Jun 94*	1 •
Live recordings from 1993/94.				
WHY THE LONG FACE	*Transatlantic*	48	*24 Jun 95*	2
ECLECTIC	*Transatlantic*	41	*24 Aug 96*	1
Live recordings from Dingwall's, London, March 96.				

BIG DADDY — US

SINGLES:	HITS 1			WEEKS 8
DANCING IN THE DARK [EP]	*Making Waves*	21	*9 Mar 85*	8
Lead track: I Right The Songs, though Dancing In The Dark received more airplay.				

BIG DADDY KANE — US

SINGLES:	HITS 3			WEEKS 6
RAP SUMMARY / WRATH OF KANE	*Cold Chillin'*	52	*13 May 89*	2
SMOOTH OPERATOR	*Cold Chillin'*	65	*26 Aug 89*	1
AIN'T NO STOPPIN' US NOW	*Cold Chillin'*	44	*13 Jan 90*	3
ALBUMS:	**HITS 1**			**WEEKS 3**
IT'S A BIG DADDY THING	*Cold Chillin'*	37	*30 Sep 89*	3

BIG DISH — UK

SINGLES:	HITS 1			WEEKS 5
MISS AMERICA	*East West*	37	*12 Jan 91*	5
ALBUMS:	**HITS 2**			**WEEKS 3**
SWIMMER	*Virgin*	85	*11 Oct 86*	1
SATELLITES	*East West*	43	*23 Feb 91*	2

BIG FUN — UK

SINGLES:	HITS 5			WEEKS 33
BLAME IT ON THE BOOGIE	*Jive*	4	*12 Aug 89*	11
CAN'T SHAKE THE FEELING	*Jive*	8	*25 Nov 89*	9
HANDFUL OF PROMISES	*Jive*	21	*17 Mar 90*	6
YOU'VE GOT A FRIEND	*Jive*	14	*23 Jun 90*	6
Charity record in aid of Childline.				
Above hit: BIG FUN and SONIA featuring Gary BARNACLE on saxophone.				
HEY THERE LONELY GIRL	*Jive*	62	*4 Aug 90*	1
ALBUMS:	**HITS 1**			**WEEKS 11**
A POCKETFUL OF DREAMS	*Jive*	7	*12 May 90*	11

BIG MOE – See Boyd BENNETT and his ROCKETS (Vocal by BIG MOE)

BIG MOUNTAIN — US

SINGLES:	HITS 2			WEEKS 15
BABY, I LOVE YOUR WAY	*RCA*	2	*4 Jun 94*	14
From the film 'Reality Bites'.				
SWEET SENSUAL LOVE	*Giant*	51	*24 Sep 94*	1

BIG PUN – See Jennifer LOPEZ

BIG RON — UK

SINGLES:	HITS 1			WEEKS 1
LET THE FREAK	*48K*	57	*11 Mar 00*	1 •
Samples Dan Hartman's Relight My Fire and Sinnamon's I Need You Now.				

BIG ROOM GIRL featuring Darryl PANDY — UK/US

(See also Darryl Pandy.)

SINGLES:	HITS 1			WEEKS 2
RAISE YOUR HANDS	*VC Recordings*	40	*20 Feb 99*	2

BIG SOUND AUTHORITY — UK

SINGLES:	HITS 2			WEEKS 12
THIS HOUSE (IS WHERE YOUR LOVE STANDS)	*Source*	21	*19 Jan 85*	9
A BAD TOWN	*Source*	54	*8 Jun 85*	3

BIG SUPREME — UK

SINGLES:	HITS 2			WEEKS 5
DON'T WALK	*Polydor*	58	*20 Sep 86*	3
PLEASE YOURSELF	*Polydor*	64	*14 Mar 87*	2

BIG THREE — UK

SINGLES:	HITS 2			WEEKS 17
• SOME OTHER GUY	*Decca*	37	*13 Apr 63*	7
BY THE WAY	*Decca*	22	*13 Jul 63*	10
EPS:	**HITS 1**			**WEEKS 17**
AT THE CAVERN	*Decca*	6	*14 Dec 63*	17

BIG TIME CHARLIE — UK

SINGLES:	HITS 2			WEEKS 4
ON THE RUN *Samples Ecstasy's Touch And Go.*	*Inferno*	22	*23 Oct 99*	2
MR. DEVIL *Samples Chic's My Forbidden Lover.* *Above hit: BIG TIME CHARLIE featuring Soozy Q.*	*Inferno*	39	*18 Mar 00*	2

Barry BIGGS — Jamaica

SINGLES:	HITS 6			WEEKS 46
WORK ALL DAY	*Dynamic*	38	*28 Aug 76*	5
SIDE SHOW *Originally recorded by Blue Magic.*	*Dynamic*	3	*4 Dec 76*	16
YOU'RE MY LIFE	*Dynamic*	36	*23 Apr 77*	4
THREE RING CIRCUS *Originally recorded by Blue Magic.*	*Dynamic*	22	*9 Jul 77*	8
WHAT'S YOUR SIGN GIRL	*Dynamic*	55	*15 Dec 79*	7
WIDE AWAKE IN A DREAM	*Dynamic*	44	*20 Jun 81*	6

Ivor BIGGUN — UK

SINGLES:	HITS 2			WEEKS 15
THE WINKER'S SONG (MISPRINT) *Above hit: Ivor BIGGUN and the RED NOSED-BURGLARS.*	*Beggars Banquet*	22	*2 Sep 78*	12
BRAS ON 45 (FAMILY VERSION) *Spoof of the Stars On 45 hits.* *Above hit: Ivor BIGGUN and the D-KUPS.*	*Dead Badger*	50	*12 Sep 81*	3

BIKINI KILL/HUGGY BEAR — US/UK

COMPILATION ALBUMS:	HITS 1			WEEKS 2
YEAH YEAH YEAH YEAH / OUR TROUBLED YOUTH *Listed on the compilation chart, one side by Bikini Kill, the other by Huggy Bear.*	*Catcall*	12	*20 Mar 93*	2

BILBO — UK

SINGLES:	HITS 1			WEEKS 7
SHE'S GONNA WIN	*Lightning*	42	*26 Aug 78*	7

Mr. Acker BILK — UK

SINGLES:	HITS 12			WEEKS 172
• SUMMER SET *Above hit: Mr. Acker BILK and his PARAMOUNT JAZZ BAND.*	*Columbia*	5	*23 Jan 60*	20
GOODBYE SWEET PRINCE *Above hit: Mister Acker BILK.*	*Melodisc*	50	*11 Jun 60*	1
WHITE CLIFFS OF DOVER	*Columbia*	30	*20 Aug 60*	9
BUONA SERA	*Columbia*	7	*10 Dec 60*	18
THAT'S MY HOME *Sub credit: (Vocal Mr. Acker BILK)*	*Columbia*	7	*15 Jul 61*	17
STARS AND STRIPES FOREVER / CREOLE JAZZ *Above 4: Mr. Acker BILK and his PARAMOUNT JAZZ BAND.*	*Columbia*	22	*4 Nov 61*	10
• STRANGER ON THE SHORE *Theme from the BBC TV series of the same name. Originally called 'Jenny'.* *Above hit: Mr. Acker BILK with the Leon YOUNG STRING CHORALE.*	*Columbia*	2	*2 Dec 61*	55
FRANKIE AND JOHNNY *From the film 'It's Trad Dad'.*	*Columbia*	42	*17 Mar 62*	2
GOTTA SEE BABY TONIGHT *Above 2: Mr. Acker BILK and his PARAMOUNT JAZZ BAND (Vocal by Mr. Acker BILK).*	*Columbia*	24	*28 Jul 62*	9
LONELY *From the film 'Band Of Thieves'.*	*Columbia*	14	*29 Sep 62*	11
A TASTE OF HONEY *Above 2: Mr. Acker BILK with the Leon YOUNG STRING CHORALE.*	*Columbia*	16	*26 Jan 63*	9
ARIA *Above hit: Acker BILK, his clarinet and strings.*	*Pye*	5	*21 Aug 76*	11

PS:	HITS 11			WEEKS 134
CKER'S AWAY	*Columbia*	16	*26 Mar 60*	2
bove hit: Mr. Acker BILK and his PARAMOUNT JAZZ BAND.				
R. ACKER BILK REQUESTS, VOLUME 2	*Pye*	11	*2 Apr 60*	8
R. ACKER BILK MARCHES ON	*Pye*	12	*7 May 60*	2
R. ACKER BILK SINGS	*Pye Jazz*	15	*11 Jun 60*	1
bove 3: Mr. Acker BILK's PARAMOUNT JAZZ BAND.				
HE SEVEN AGES OF ACKER, VOLUME 1	*Columbia*	6	*5 Nov 60*	23
bove hit: Mr. Acker BILK and his PARAMOUNT JAZZ BAND.				
LARINET JAMBOREE	*Columbia*	19	*4 Mar 61*	1
bove hit: Mr. Acker BILK and Terry LIGHTFOOT.				
HE SEVEN AGES OF ACKER, VOLUME 2	*Columbia*	9	*18 Mar 61*	12
CKER, VOLUME 1	*Columbia*	6	*26 Aug 61*	5
CKER, VOLUME 2	*Columbia*	11	*13 Jan 62*	7
OUR HITS AND A MISTER	*Columbia*	2	*14 Apr 62*	56
AND OF THIEVES	*Columbia*	6	*29 Sep 62*	17
bove 5: Mr. Acker BILK and his PARAMOUNT JAZZ BAND.				

LBUMS:	HITS 12			WEEKS 161
EVEN AGES OF ACKER	*Columbia*	6	*19 Mar 60*	6
CKER BILK'S OMNIBUS	*Pye*	14	*9 Apr 60*	3
CKER	*Columbia*	17	*4 Mar 61*	1
OLDEN TREASURY OF BILK	*Columbia*	11	*1 Apr 61*	6
HE BEST OF BARBER AND BILK VOLUME ONE	*Pye Golden Guinea*	4	*27 May 61*	43
HE BEST OF BARBER AND BILK VOLUME TWO	*Pye Golden Guinea*	8	*11 Nov 61*	18
bove 2 albums have one side by each artist.				
bove 2: Chris BARBER'S JAZZ BAND/MR. ACKER BILK and his PARAMOUNT JAZZ BAND.				
TRANGER ON THE SHORE	*Columbia*	6	*26 May 62*	28
HE BEST OF BALL, BARBER AND BILK	*Pye Golden Guinea*	1	*25 Aug 62*	24
Compilation with 4 tracks by each band.				
bove hit: Mr. Acker BILK'S PARAMOUNT JAZZ BAND/Kenny BALL and his JAZZMEN / Chris BARBER'S JAZZ BAND				
TASTE OF HONEY	*Columbia*	17	*4 May 63*	4
HE ONE FOR ME	*Pye*	38	*9 Oct 76*	6
HEER MAGIC	*Warwick*	5	*4 Jun 77*	8
VERGREEN	*Warwick*	17	*11 Nov 78*	14

BILL — UK

SINGLES:	HITS 1			WEEKS 1
CAR BOOT SALE	*Mercury*	73	*23 Oct 93*	1
Character featured on Steve Wright's BBC Radio 1 afternoon show.				

BILLIE – See Billie PIPER

BIMBO JET — France

SINGLES:	HITS 1			WEEKS 10
EL BIMBO	*EMI*	12	*26 Jul 75*	10

BINARY FINARY — UK

SINGLES:	HITS 1			WEEKS 9
1998	*Positiva*	24	*10 Oct 98*	3
1999 [RM]	*Positiva*	11	*28 Aug 99*	6
Remix of 1998 by Kaycee.				

Umberto BINDI — Italy

SINGLES:	HITS 1			WEEKS 1
IL NOSTRO CONCERTO (OUR CONCERTO)	*Oriole*	47	*12 Nov 60*	1

BINI + MARTINI — Italy

(See also Goodfellas featuring Lisa Millett.)

SINGLES:	HITS 2			WEEKS 2
HAPPINESS	*Azuli*	53	*4 Mar 00*	1
BURNING UP	*Azuli*	65	*10 Mar 01*	1
Vocals by Lisa Millett.				
Above hit: BINI + MARTINI.				

BIOHAZARD — US

SINGLES:	HITS 2			WEEKS 4
TALES FROM THE HARD SIDE	*Warner Brothers*	47	*9 Jul 94*	2
HOW IT IS	*Warner Brothers*	62	*20 Aug 94*	2
Vocals by Sen Dog of Cypress Hill.				

ALBUMS:	HITS 2			WEEKS 2
STATE OF THE WORLD ADDRESS	*Warner Brothers*	72	*14 May 94*	1
MATA LEAO	*Warner Brothers*	72	*8 Jun 96*	1

La BIONDA — Italy

SINGLES:	HITS 1		WEEKS	
ONE FOR YOU ONE FOR ME	*Philips*	54	*7 Oct 78*	

BIOSPHERE — Norway

SINGLES:	HITS 1		WEEKS	
NOVELTY WAVES *Featured in a Levi's Jeans TV commerical.*	*Apollo*	51	*29 Apr 95*	

ALBUMS:	HITS 1		WEEKS	
PATASHNIK	*Apollo*	50	*5 Mar 94*	

BIRDLAND — UK

SINGLES:	HITS 5		WEEKS	
HOLLOW HEART	*Lazy*	70	*1 Apr 89*	
PARADISE	*Lazy*	70	*8 Jul 89*	
SLEEP WITH ME	*Lazy*	32	*3 Feb 90*	
ROCK AND ROLL NIGGER *Originally recorded by Patti Smith.*	*Lazy*	47	*22 Sep 90*	
EVERYBODY NEEDS SOMEBODY	*Lazy*	44	*2 Feb 91*	

ALBUMS:	HITS 1		WEEKS	
BIRDLAND	*Lazy*	44	*2 Mar 91*	

BIRDS — UK

SINGLES:	HITS 1		WEEKS	
LEAVING HERE *Originally recorded by Eddie Holland in 1964.*	*Decca*	45	*29 May 65*	

Jane BIRKIN and Serge GAINSBOURG — UK/France

SINGLES:	HITS 1		WEEKS 34	
JE T'AIME . . . MOI NON PLUS	*Fontana*	2	*2 Aug 69*	1
JE T'AIME . . . MOI NON PLUS [RI-1ST] *Major Minor picked up license after Fontana deleted the release.*	*Major Minor*	1	*4 Oct 69*	1
JE T'AIME . . . MOI NON PLUS [RI-2ND] *Above hit: Serge GAINSBOURG and Jane BIRKIN.*	*Antic*	31	*7 Dec 74*	9

BIRTHDAY PARTY — Australia

ALBUMS:	HITS 1		WEEKS 3	
JUNKYARD	*4AD*	73	*24 Jul 82*	3

BIS — UK

SINGLES:	HITS 7		WEEKS 9	
THE SECRET VAMPIRE SOUNDTRACK [EP] *Lead track: Kandy Pop.*	*Chemikal Underground*	25	*30 Mar 96*	2
BIS VS. THE D.I.Y. CORPS [EP] *Lead track: This Is Fake D.I.Y.*	*Teen-C*	45	*22 Jun 96*	1
ATOM POWERED ACTION! [EP] *Lead track: Starbright Boy.*	*Wiiija*	54	*9 Nov 96*	1
SWEET SHOP AVENGERZ	*Wiiija*	46	*15 Mar 97*	1
EVERYBODY THINKS THEY'RE GOING TO GET THEIRS	*Wiiija*	64	*10 May 97*	1
EURODISCO	*Wiiija*	37	*14 Nov 98*	2
ACTION AND DRAMA	*Wiiija*	50	*27 Feb 99*	1

ALBUMS:	HITS 1		WEEKS 1	
THE NEW TRANSISTOR HEROES	*Wiiija*	55	*19 Apr 97*	1

BISCUIT BOY AKA CRACKER MAN — UK

SINGLES:	HITS 1		WEEKS 1	
MITCH	*Mercury*	75	*15 Sep 01*	1

Elvin BISHOP — US

SINGLES:	HITS 1		WEEKS 4	
FOOLED AROUND AND FELL IN LOVE *Uncredited vocals by Mickey Thomas of Starship.*	*Capricorn*	34	*15 May 76*	4

Stephen BISHOP — US

ALBUMS:	HITS 1		WEEKS 3	
GREIG AND SCHUMANN PIANO CONCERTOS	*Philips*	34	*1 Apr 72*	3

BITI – See DEGREES OF MOTION featuring BITI

BIZARRE INC — UK

SINGLES:	HITS 7		WEEKS 49	
PLAYING WITH KNIVES	*Vinyl Solution*	43	*16 Mar 91*	5

SUCH A FEELING	*Vinyl Solution*	13	*14 Sep 91*	9
PLAYING WITH KNIVES [RM-1ST]	*Vinyl Solution*	4	*23 Nov 91*	8
I'M GONNA GET YOU	*Vinyl Solution*	3	*3 Oct 92*	12
I'M GONNA GET YOU [RE]	*Vinyl Solution*	72	*2 Jan 93*	1
TOOK MY LOVE	*Vinyl Solution*	19	*27 Feb 93*	5
Above 3: BIZARRE INC featuring Angie BROWN.				
KEEP THE MUSIC STRONG	*Mercury*	33	*23 Mar 96*	2
SURPRISE	*Mercury*	21	*6 Jul 96*	3
Guest vocals by Julie Driscoll.				
GET UP SUNSHINE STREET	*Mercury*	45	*14 Sep 96*	2
PLAYING WITH KNIVES [RM-2ND]	*Vinyl Solution*	30	*13 Mar 99*	2
Remixed by Tarrentella and Al Scott.				

ALBUMS:	**HITS 1**			**WEEKS 2**
ENERGIQUE	*Vinyl Solution*	41	*7 Nov 92*	2

BIZZ NIZZ — US/Belgium

SINGLES:	**HITS 1**			**WEEKS 11**
DON'T MISS THE PARTYLINE	*Cooltempo*	7	*31 Mar 90*	11

BIZZI — UK

SINGLES:	**HITS 1**			**WEEKS 1**
BIZZI'S PARTY	*Parlophone*	62	*6 Dec 97*	1

BJORK — Iceland

SINGLES:	**HITS 18**			**WEEKS 73**
OOOPS	*ZTT*	42	*27 Apr 91*	3
Above hit: 808 STATE featuring BJORK.				
HUMAN BEHAVIOUR	*One Little Indian*	36	*19 Jun 93*	2
VENUS AS A BOY	*One Little Indian*	29	*4 Sep 93*	4
PLAY DEAD	*Island*	12	*23 Oct 93*	6
From the film 'The Young Americans'.				
Above hit: BJORK and David ARNOLD.				
BIG TIME SENSUALITY	*One Little Indian*	17	*4 Dec 93*	8
VIOLENTLY HAPPY	*One Little Indian*	13	*19 Mar 94*	4
ARMY OF ME	*One Little Indian*	10	*6 May 95*	5
ISOBEL	*One Little Indian*	23	*26 Aug 95*	3
IT'S OH SO QUIET	*One Little Indian*	4	*25 Nov 95*	15
Originally recorded by Betty Hutton in 1948.				
HYPERBALLAD	*One Little Indian*	8	*24 Feb 96*	4
POSSIBLY MAYBE	*One Little Indian*	13	*9 Nov 96*	3
I MISS YOU	*One Little Indian*	36	*1 Mar 97*	2
BACHELORETTE	*One Little Indian*	21	*20 Dec 97*	5
HUNTER	*One Little Indian*	44	*17 Oct 98*	1
ALARM CALL	*One Little Indian*	33	*12 Dec 98*	2
ALL IS FULL OF LOVE	*One Little Indian*	24	*19 Jun 99*	2
HIDDEN PLACE	*One Little Indian*	21	*18 Aug 01*	2
PAGAN POETRY	*One Little Indian*	38	*17 Nov 01*	2

ALBUMS:	**HITS 5**			**WEEKS 125**
DEBUT	*One Little Indian*	3	*17 Jul 93*	69
Repackaged with additional track from 25 Dec 93. Includes re-entres through to 1999.				
POST	*One Little Indian*	2	*24 Jun 95*	37
Initital copies were withdrawn on first day of sale due to an uncleared sample of 'Mass Observation' by Scanner.				
POST / TELEGRAM [RE]	*One Little Indian*	59	*7 Dec 96*	1
Telegram was a remix album, sales were combined.				
HOMOGENIC	*One Little Indian*	4	*4 Oct 97*	13
SELMA SONGS [OST]	*One Little Indian*	34	*30 Sep 00*	1
Soundtrack to the film 'Dancer In The Dark' in which Bjork made her acting debut.				
VESPERTINE	*One Little Indian*	8	*8 Sep 01*	4

BJORN, BENNY, ANNA and FRIDA – See ABBA

BJORN AGAIN — Australia

SINGLES:	**HITS 3**			**WEEKS 8**
ERASURE-ISH - (A LITTLE RESPECT / STOP!)	*M&G*	25	*24 Oct 92*	3
SANTA CLAUS IS COMING TO TOWN	*M&G*	55	*12 Dec 92*	4
FLASHDANCE . . . WHAT A FEELING	*M&G*	65	*27 Nov 93*	1

BK — UK

(See also Various Artists (EPs) – Hard Beat EP 19.)

SINGLES:	**HITS 2**			**WEEKS 3**
HOOVERS AND HORNS	*Nukleuz*	57	*25 Nov 00*	2
Above hit: FERGIE and BK.				
FLASH	*Nukleuz*	67	*8 Dec 01*	1
Above hit: BK and Nick SENTIENCE.				

BLACK — UK

SINGLES:	HITS 8			WEEKS 35
WONDERFUL LIFE	*Ugly Man*	72	*27 Sep 86*	1
SWEETEST SMILE	*A&M*	8	*27 Jun 87*	10
WONDERFUL LIFE [RR]	*A&M*	8	*22 Aug 87*	9
PARADISE	*A&M*	38	*16 Jan 88*	3
THE BIG ONE	*A&M*	54	*24 Sep 88*	4
NOW YOU'RE GONE	*A&M*	66	*21 Jan 89*	2
FEEL LIKE CHANGE	*A&M*	56	*4 May 91*	2
HERE IT COMES AGAIN	*A&M*	70	*15 Jun 91*	1
WONDERFUL LIFE [RR] [RI]	*PolyGram TV*	42	*5 Mar 94*	3
Featured in TV commercials for Standard Life Assurance and Cadbury's.				
ALBUMS:	**HITS 3**			**WEEKS 29**
WONDERFUL LIFE	*A&M*	3	*26 Sep 87*	23
COMEDY	*A&M*	32	*29 Oct 88*	4
BLACK	*A&M*	42	*1 Jun 91*	2

Bill BLACK'S COMBO — US

SINGLES:	HITS 2			WEEKS 8
WHITE SILVER SANDS	*London*	50	*10 Sep 60*	1
Originally recorded by Dave Gardner.				
DON'T BE CRUEL	*London*	32	*5 Nov 60*	7

Cilla BLACK — UK

SINGLES:	HITS 21			WEEKS 194
LOVE OF THE LOVED	*Parlophone*	35	*19 Oct 63*	6
Written by Lennon/McCartney.				
ANYONE WHO HAD A HEART	*Parlophone*	1	*8 Feb 64*	17
Originally recorded by Dionne Warwick.				
YOU'RE MY WORLD (IL MIO MONDO)	*Parlophone*	1	*9 May 64*	17
Originally recorded by Umberto Bindi.				
IT'S FOR YOU	*Parlophone*	7	*8 Aug 64*	10
Written by Lennon/McCartney.				
YOU'VE LOST THAT LOVIN' FEELIN'	*Parlophone*	2	*16 Jan 65*	9
I'VE BEEN WRONG BEFORE	*Parlophone*	17	*24 Apr 65*	8
LOVE'S JUST A BROKEN HEART	*Parlophone*	5	*15 Jan 66*	11
ALFIE	*Parlophone*	9	*2 Apr 66*	12
From the film of the same name.				
DON'T ANSWER ME	*Parlophone*	6	*11 Jun 66*	10
A FOOL AM I (DIMMELO PARLAMI)	*Parlophone*	13	*22 Oct 66*	9
WHAT GOOD AM I?	*Parlophone*	24	*10 Jun 67*	7
I ONLY LIVE TO LOVE YOU	*Parlophone*	26	*2 Dec 67*	11
STEP INSIDE LOVE	*Parlophone*	8	*16 Mar 68*	9
Written by Lennon/McCartney.				
WHERE IS TOMORROW?	*Parlophone*	39	*15 Jun 68*	3
SURROUND YOURSELF WITH SORROW	*Parlophone*	3	*15 Feb 69*	12
CONVERSATIONS	*Parlophone*	7	*12 Jul 69*	12
IF I THOUGHT YOU'D EVER CHANGE YOUR MIND	*Parlophone*	20	*13 Dec 69*	9
SOMETHING TELLS ME (SOMETHING'S GONNA HAPPEN TONIGHT)	*Parlophone*	3	*20 Nov 71*	14
Theme from her BBC1 TV show.				
BABY WE CAN'T GO WRONG	*EMI*	36	*2 Feb 74*	6
THROUGH THE YEARS	*Columbia*	54	*18 Sep 93*	1
HEART AND SOUL	*Columbia*	75	*30 Oct 93*	1
Above hit: Cilla BLACK and Dusty SPRINGFIELD.				
EPS:	**HITS 3**			**WEEKS 29**
ANYONE WHO HAD A HEART	*Parlophone*	5	*25 Apr 64*	17
IT'S FOR YOU	*Parlophone*	12	*17 Oct 64*	8
CILLA'S HITS	*Parlophone*	6	*17 Sep 66*	4
ALBUMS:	**HITS 7**			**WEEKS 63**
CILLA	*Parlophone*	5	*13 Feb 65*	11
CILLA SINGS A RAINBOW	*Parlophone*	4	*14 May 66*	15
SHER-OO	*Parlophone*	7	*13 Apr 68*	11
THE BEST OF CILLA BLACK	*Parlophone*	21	*30 Nov 68*	11
SWEET INSPIRATION	*Parlophone*	42	*25 Jul 70*	4
THE VERY BEST OF CILLA BLACK	*Parlophone*	20	*29 Jan 83*	9
THROUGH THE YEARS	*Columbia*	41	*2 Oct 93*	2
Album released to mark her 30th year in showbusiness.				

Frank BLACK — US

SINGLES:	HITS 3			WEEKS 4
HEADACHE	*4AD*	53	*21 May 94*	1
MEN IN BLACK	*Dragnet*	37	*20 Jan 96*	2
I DON'T WANT TO HURT YOU (EVERY SINGLE TIME)	*Dragnet*	63	*27 Jul 96*	1
ALBUMS:	**HITS 4**			**WEEKS 8**
FRANK BLACK	*4AD*	9	*20 Mar 93*	3

TEENAGER OF THE YEAR	*4AD*	21	*4 Jun 94*	2
THE CULT OF RAY	*Dragnet*	39	*3 Feb 96*	2
FRANK BLACK AND THE CATHOLICS	*Play It*	61	*16 May 98*	1

Above hit: Frank BLACK and the CATHOLICS.

Jeanne BLACK — US

SINGLES:	HITS 1			WEEKS 4
HE'LL HAVE TO STAY	*Capitol*	41	*25 Jun 60*	4

Answer version to Jim Reeves' He'll Have To Go.

Mary BLACK — Ireland

ALBUMS:	HITS 4			WEEKS 10
THE HOLY GROUND	*Grapevine*	58	*3 Jul 93*	2
CIRCUS	*Grapevine*	16	*16 Sep 95*	4
SHINE	*Grapevine*	33	*29 Mar 97*	3
SPEAKING WITH THE ANGEL	*Grapevine*	63	*28 Aug 99*	1

Stanley BLACK and his Orchestra - See David WHITFIELD

BLACK AND WHITE ARMY — UK

SINGLES:	HITS 1			WEEKS 2
BLACK & WHITE ARMY (BRING THE PRIDE BACK HOME)	*Toon*	26	*23 May 98*	2

The official F.A. Cup song for Newcastle United.

BLACK BOX — Italy

SINGLES:	HITS 11			WEEKS 74
RIDE ON TIME	*Deconstruction*	1	*12 Aug 89*	22
I DON'T KNOW ANYBODY ELSE	*Deconstruction*	4	*17 Feb 90*	8
EVERYBODY EVERYBODY	*Deconstruction*	16	*2 Jun 90*	5
FANTASY (REMIXED)	*Deconstruction*	5	*3 Nov 90*	11
THE TOTAL MIX [M]	*Deconstruction*	12	*15 Dec 90*	8
Mix of their hits.				
STRIKE IT UP	*Deconstruction*	16	*6 Apr 91*	8
OPEN YOUR EYES	*Deconstruction*	48	*14 Dec 91*	4
ROCKIN' TO THE MUSIC	*Deconstruction*	39	*14 Aug 93*	2
NOT ANYONE	*Mercury*	31	*24 Jun 95*	2
I GOT THE VIBRATION / A POSITIVE VIBRATION	*Manifesto*	21	*20 Apr 96*	3
Samples Love Hangover by Diana Ross.				
NATIVE NEW YORKER	*Manifesto*	46	*22 Feb 97*	1
Above 2: BLACKBOX.				
ALBUMS:	**HITS 1**			**WEEKS 30**
DREAMLAND	*Deconstruction*	14	*5 May 90*	30

BLACK BOX RECORDER — UK

SINGLES:	HITS 2			WEEKS 4
THE FACTS OF LIFE	*Nude*	20	*22 Apr 00*	3
THE ART OF DRIVING	*Nude*	53	*15 Jul 00*	1
ALBUMS:	**HITS 1**			**WEEKS 1**
THE FACTS OF LIFE	*Nude*	37	*13 May 00*	1

BLACK CONNECTION — Italy

SINGLES:	HITS 2			WEEKS 3
GIVE ME RHYTHM	*Xtravaganza*	32	*14 Mar 98*	2
I'M GONNA GET YA BABY	*Xtravaganza*	62	*24 Oct 98*	1

BLACK CROWES — US

SINGLES:	HITS 11			WEEKS 28
HARD TO HANDLE	*Def American*	45	*1 Sep 90*	5
TWICE AS HARD	*Def American*	47	*12 Jan 91*	3
JEALOUS AGAIN / SHE TALKS TO ANGELS	*Def American*	70	*22 Jun 91*	1
HARD TO HANDLE [RI]	*Def American*	39	*24 Aug 91*	4
SEEING THINGS	*Def American*	72	*26 Oct 91*	1
REMEDY	*Def American*	24	*2 May 92*	3
STING ME	*Def American*	42	*26 Sep 92*	2
HOTEL ILLNESS	*Def American*	47	*28 Nov 92*	3
HIGH HEAD BLUES / A CONSPIRACY	*American Recordings*	25	*11 Feb 95*	2
WISER TIME	*American Recordings*	34	*22 Jul 95*	2
ONE MIRROR TOO MANY	*American Recordings*	51	*27 Jul 96*	1
KICKING MY HEART AROUND	*American Recordings*	55	*7 Nov 98*	1
ALBUMS:	**HITS 6**			**WEEKS 29**
SHAKE YOUR MONEY MAKER	*Def American*	36	*24 Aug 91*	11
THE SOUTHERN HARMONY AND MUSICAL COMPANION	*Def American*	2	*23 May 92*	7
AMORICA	*American Recordings*	8	*12 Nov 94*	4
THREE SNAKES AND ONE CHARM	*American Recordings*	17	*3 Aug 96*	3

BY YOUR SIDE	*Columbia*	34	*23 Jan 99*	2
LIONS	*V2*	37	*19 May 01*	2

BLACK DIAMOND — US

SINGLES:	HITS 1			WEEKS 1
LET ME BE	*Systematic*	56	*17 Sep 94*	1

BLACK DOG — UK

SINGLES:	HITS 1			WEEKS 1
BABYLON	*warner.esp*	65	*3 Apr 99*	1
Above hit: BLACK DOG featuring Ofra HAZA.				
ALBUMS:	**HITS 1**			**WEEKS 2**
SPANNERS	*Warp*	30	*28 Jan 95*	2

BLACK DUCK — UK

SINGLES:	HITS 1			WEEKS 5
WHIGGLE IN LINE	*Flying South*	33	*17 Dec 94*	5
Based around Whigfield's Saturday Night.				

BLACK EYED PEAS — US

SINGLES:	HITS 2			WEEKS 4
JOINTS AND JAM	*Interscope*	53	*10 Oct 98*	1
REQUEST + LINE	*Interscope*	31	*12 May 01*	3
Samples Paulinho Dacosta's Love Till The End Of Time.				
Above hit: BLACK EYED PEAS featuring Macy GRAY.				

BLACK GORILLA — UK

SINGLES:	HITS 1			WEEKS 6
GIMME DAT BANANA	*Response*	29	*27 Aug 77*	6

BLACK GRAPE — UK

SINGLES:	HITS 7			WEEKS 25
REVEREND BLACK GRAPE	*Radioactive*	9	*10 Jun 95*	5
IN THE NAME OF THE FATHER	*Radioactive*	8	*5 Aug 95*	4
KELLY'S HEROES	*Radioactive*	17	*2 Dec 95*	5
FAT NECK	*Radioactive*	10	*25 May 96*	3
ENGLAND'S IRIE	*Radioactive*	6	*29 Jun 96*	4
Above hit: BLACK GRAPE featuring Joe STRUMMER and Keith ALLEN.				
GET HIGHER	*Radioactive*	24	*1 Nov 97*	3
MARBLES	*Radioactive*	46	*7 Mar 98*	1
ALBUMS:	**HITS 2**			**WEEKS 46**
IT'S GREAT WHEN YOU'RE STRAIGHT . . . YEAH	*Radioactive*	1	*19 Aug 95*	39
STUPID STUPID STUPID	*Radioactive*	11	*22 Nov 97*	7

BLACK LACE — UK

SINGLES:	HITS 10			WEEKS 83
MARY ANN	*EMI*	42	*31 Mar 79*	4
UK's Eurovision entry in 1979, it came 7th.				
SUPERMAN (GIOCA JOUER)	*Flair*	9	*24 Sep 83*	18
Originally recorded by Phil Charles as 'The Joker'.				
AGADOO	*Flair*	2	*30 Jun 84*	30
Originally recorded by the Saragossa Band in 1981.				
DO THE CONGA	*Flair*	10	*24 Nov 84*	9
EL VINO COLLAPSO	*Flair*	42	*1 Jun 85*	5
I SPEAKA DA LINGO	*Flair*	49	*7 Sep 85*	4
THE HOKEY-COKEY	*Flair*	31	*7 Dec 85*	6
WIG WAM BAM	*Flair*	63	*20 Sep 86*	3
I AM THE MUSIC MAN	*Flair*	52	*26 Aug 89*	3
AGADOO [RR]	*N.O.W.*	64	*22 Aug 98*	1
ALBUMS:	**HITS 3**			**WEEKS 26**
PARTY PARTY - 16 GREAT PARTY ICEBREAKERS	*Telstar*	4	*8 Dec 84*	14
PARTY PARTY 2	*Telstar*	18	*7 Dec 85*	6
PARTY CRAZY	*Telstar*	58	*6 Dec 86*	6

BLACK LEGEND — Italy

SINGLES:	HITS 2			WEEKS 22
YOU SEE THE TROUBLE WITH ME	*Rise*	52	*20 May 00*	5
Import.				
YOU SEE THE TROUBLE WITH ME	*Eternal*	1	*24 Jun 00*	15
SOMEBODY	*WEA*	37	*4 Aug 01*	2
Above hit: SHORTIE vs BLACK LEGEND.				

BLACK MACHINE — France/Nigeria

SINGLES:	HITS 1			WEEKS 5
HOW GEE	*London*	17	*9 Apr 94*	5

BLACK MAGIC: A LIL' LOUIS PAINTING — US

(See also Lil' Louis.)

SINGLES:	HITS 1			WEEKS 2
FREEDOM (MAKE IT FUNKY)	*Positiva*	41	*1 Jun 96*	2

BLACK MOUNTAIN MALE CHORUS – See Shirley BASSEY; Bryn TERFEL

BLACK RIOT – See Todd TERRY

BLACK ROB — US

SINGLES:	HITS 2			WEEKS 8
WHOA!	*Puff Daddy*	44	*12 Aug 00*	2
Additional vocals: Harve 'Joe Hooker' Pierre.				
BAD BOY FOR LIFE	*Puff Daddy*	13	*6 Oct 01*	6
Above hit: P. DIDDY, BLACK ROB & Mark CURRY.				

BLACK, ROCK and RON — US

ALBUMS:	HITS 1			WEEKS 1
STOP THE WORLD	*Supreme*	72	*22 Apr 89*	1

BLACK SABBATH — UK

SINGLES:	HITS 9			WEEKS 70
PARANOID	*Vertigo*	4	*29 Aug 70*	18
NEVER SAY DIE	*Vertigo*	21	*3 Jun 78*	8
HARD ROAD	*Vertigo*	33	*14 Oct 78*	4
NEON KNIGHTS	*Vertigo*	22	*5 Jul 80*	9
PARANOID [RI]	*NEMS*	14	*16 Aug 80*	12
DIE YOUNG	*Vertigo*	41	*6 Dec 80*	7
MOB RULES	*Vertigo*	46	*7 Nov 81*	4
TURN UP THE NIGHT	*Vertigo*	37	*13 Feb 82*	5
HEADLESS CROSS	*I.R.S.*	62	*15 Apr 89*	1
TV CRIMES	*I.R.S.*	33	*13 Jun 92*	2
ALBUMS:	**HITS 23**			**WEEKS 217**
BLACK SABBATH	*Vertigo*	8	*7 Mar 70*	42
PARANOID	*Vertigo*	1	*26 Sep 70*	27
MASTER OF REALITY	*Vertigo*	5	*21 Aug 71*	13
BLACK SABBATH VOLUME 4	*Vertigo*	8	*30 Sep 72*	10
SABBATH BLOODY SABBATH	*WWA*	4	*8 Dec 73*	11
SABOTAGE	*NEMS*	7	*27 Sep 75*	7
WE SOLD OUR SOUL FOR ROCK 'N' ROLL	*NEMS*	35	*7 Feb 76*	5
TECHNICAL ECSTASY	*Vertigo*	13	*6 Nov 76*	6
NEVER SAY DIE	*Vertigo*	12	*14 Oct 78*	6
HEAVEN AND HELL	*Vertigo*	9	*26 Apr 80*	22
BLACK SABBATH LIVE AT LAST	*NEMS*	5	*5 Jul 80*	15
Live recordings from 1975.				
PARANOID [RI]	*NEMS*	54	*27 Sep 80*	2
MOB RULES	*Mercury*	12	*14 Nov 81*	14
LIVE EVIL	*Vertigo*	13	*22 Jan 83*	11
BORN AGAIN	*Vertigo*	4	*24 Sep 83*	7
SEVENTH STAR	*Vertigo*	27	*1 Mar 86*	5
Above hit: BLACK SABBATH featuring Tony IOMMI.				
THE ETERNAL IDOL	*Vertigo*	66	*28 Nov 87*	1
HEADLESS CROSS	*I.R.S.*	31	*29 Apr 89*	2
TYR	*I.R.S.*	24	*1 Sep 90*	3
DEHUMANIZER	*I.R.S.*	28	*4 Jul 92*	2
CROSS PURPOSES	*I.R.S.*	41	*12 Feb 94*	1
FORBIDDEN	*I.R.S.*	71	*17 Jun 95*	1
REUNION	*Epic*	41	*31 Oct 98*	1
Live recordings from the NEC, Birmingham, 5 Dec 97 plus 2 studio tracks.				
THE BEST OF BLACK SABBATH	*Metal Is*	24	*17 Jun 00*	3

BLACK SCIENCE ORCHESTRA — UK

ALBUMS:	HITS 1			WEEKS 1
WALTERS ROOM	*Junior Boy's Own*	68	*3 Aug 96*	1

BLACK SHEEP — US

SINGLES:	HITS 1			WEEKS 1
WITHOUT A DOUBT	*Mercury*	60	*19 Nov 94*	1

BLACK SLATE — UK/Jamaica

SINGLES:	HITS 2			WEEKS 15
AMIGO	*Ensign*	9	*20 Sep 80*	9
BOOM BOOM	*Ensign*	51	*6 Dec 80*	6

BLACK STAR LINER — UK

ALBUMS:	HITS 1			WEEKS 1
YEMEN CUTTA CONNECTION	*EXP*	66	*7 Sep 96*	1

BLACK UHURU — Jamaica

SINGLES:	HITS 2			WEEKS 9
WHAT IS LIFE?	*Island*	56	*8 Sep 84*	6
THE GREAT TRAIN ROBBERY	*Real Authentic Sound*	62	*31 May 86*	3
ALBUMS:	**HITS 4**			**WEEKS 22**
RED	*Island*	28	*13 Jun 81*	13
BLACK UHURU	*Virgin*	81	*22 Aug 81*	2
CHILL OUT	*Island*	38	*19 Jun 82*	6
ANTHEM	*Island*	90	*25 Aug 84*	1

Band of the BLACK WATCH — UK

SINGLES:	HITS 2			WEEKS 22
SCOTCH ON THE ROCKS	*Spark*	8	*30 Aug 75*	14
DANCE OF THE CUCKOOS (THE "LAUREL & HARDY" THEME)	*Spark*	37	*13 Dec 75*	8
ALBUMS:	**HITS 1**			**WEEKS 13**
SCOTCH ON THE ROCKS	*Spark*	11	*7 Feb 76*	13

BLACK WIDOW — UK

ALBUMS:	HITS 1			WEEKS 2
SACRIFICE	*CBS*	32	*4 Apr 70*	2

Tony BLACKBURN — UK

SINGLES:	HITS 2			WEEKS 7
SO MUCH LOVE	*MGM*	31	*27 Jan 68*	4
IT'S ONLY LOVE	*MGM*	41	*29 Mar 69*	3

Originally recorded by Tommy James and the Shondells.
Above hit: Tony BLACKBURN with the MAJORITY.

BLACKBYRDS — US

SINGLES:	HITS 1			WEEKS 6
WALKING IN RHYTHM	*Fantasy*	23	*31 May 75*	6

BLACKFOOT — US

SINGLES:	HITS 2			WEEKS 5
FOUR FROM BLACKFOOT [EP] *Lead track: Dry County.*	*Atco*	43	*6 Mar 82*	4
SEND ME AN ANGEL	*Atco*	66	*18 Jun 83*	1
ALBUMS:	**HITS 4**			**WEEKS 22**
MARAUDER	*Atco*	38	*18 Jul 81*	12
HIGHWAY SONG - BLACKFOOT LIVE	*Atco*	14	*11 Sep 82*	6
SIOGO	*Atlantic*	28	*21 May 83*	3
VERTICAL SMILES	*Atco*	82	*29 Sep 84*	1

J. BLACKFOOT — US

SINGLES:	HITS 1			WEEKS 4
TAXI	Allegiance	48	*17 Mar 84*	4

BLACKFOOT SUE — UK

SINGLES:	HITS 2			WEEKS 15
STANDING IN THE ROAD	*Jam*	4	*12 Aug 72*	10
SING DON'T SPEAK	*Jam*	36	*16 Dec 72*	5

BLACKGIRL — US

SINGLES:	HITS 1			WEEKS 3
90'S GIRL	*RCA*	23	*16 Jul 94*	3

Features rap from Menton 'Peanut' Smith.

Honor BLACKMAN - See Patrick MacNEE and Honor BLACKMAN

Ritchie BLACKMORE'S RAINBOW - See RAINBOW

BLACKNUSS featuring Stephen SIMMONDS-ADL-Richie PASTA-MULADOE — Sweden

SINGLES:	HITS 1			WEEKS 1
DINAH	*Arista*	56	*28 Jun 97*	1

BLACKOUT — UK

SINGLES:	HITS 3			WEEKS 9
GOTTA HAVE HOPE	*Multiply*	46	*27 Mar 99*	1
Original release reached No. 139 in 1997. Samples 2001: A Space Odyssey.				
MR DJ	*Independiente*	19	*31 Mar 01*	7
Vocals by Vanya Raeburn.				
GET UP	*Independiente*	67	*6 Oct 01*	1

BLACKSTREET — US

SINGLES:	HITS 14			WEEKS 70
BABY BE MINE	*MCA*	37	*19 Jun 93*	3
Above hit: BLACKSTREET featuring Teddy RILEY.				
BOOTI CALL	*Interscope*	56	*13 Aug 94*	1
Features rapper Antwone Dickey – T-Pirate.				
U BLOW MY MIND	*Interscope*	39	*11 Feb 95*	2
JOY	*Interscope*	56	*27 May 95*	2
NO DIGGITY	*Interscope*	9	*19 Oct 96*	7
Above hit: BLACKSTREET (featuring DR. DRE).				
GET ME HOME	*Def Jam*	11	*8 Mar 97*	5
Based on Eugene Wilde's Gotta Get You Home Tonight.				
Above hit: Foxy BROWN featuring BLACKSTREET.				
DON'T LEAVE ME	*Interscope*	6	*26 Apr 97*	10
Samples 2 Pac's I Ain't Mad At Cha.				
FIX	*Interscope*	7	*27 Sep 97*	5
Samples Grandmaster Flash's The Message. Features Slash (Guns N' Roses) and Ol' Dity Bastard (Wu-Tang Clan).				
(MONEY CAN'T) BUY ME LOVE	*Interscope*	18	*13 Dec 97*	6
I GET LONELY	*Virgin*	5	*4 Apr 98*	7
Above hit: JANET (featuring BLACKSTREET).				
THE CITY IS MINE	*Northwestside*	38	*27 Jun 98*	2
Above hit: JAY-Z featuring BLACKSTREET.				
TAKE ME THERE	*Interscope*	7	*12 Dec 98*	9
From the film 'The Rugrats Movie'.				
Above hit: BLACKSTREET and MYA featuring MASE and BLINKY BLINK.				
GIRLFRIEND / BOYFRIEND	*Interscope*	11	*17 Apr 99*	7
This is just one song title. Rap by Ja Rule and Eve.				
Above hit: BLACKSTREET featuring JANET.				
GET READY	*Puff Daddy*	32	*10 Jul 99*	4
Samples Shalamar's A Night To Remember.				
Above hit: MASE (featuring BLACKSTREET).				
ALBUMS:	**HITS 3**			**WEEKS 36**
BLACKSTREET	*Interscope*	35	*9 Jul 94*	6
ANOTHER LEVEL	*Interscope*	26	*21 Sep 96*	26
FINALLY	*Interscope*	27	*3 Apr 99*	4

Charles BLACKWELL - See Michael COX; Billie DAVIS; Rita PAVONE; Mike SARNE

Roger BLACKWELL and his Orchestra - See LITTLE RICHARD

BLACKWELLS — US

SINGLES:	HITS 1			WEEKS 2
LOVE OR MONEY	*London*	46	*20 May 61*	2

Richard BLACKWOOD — UK

SINGLES:	HITS 3			WEEKS 16
MAMA - WHO DA MAN?	*East West*	3	*17 Jun 00*	7
Samples Junior's Mama Used To Say.				
1 2 3 4 GET WITH THE WICKED	*East West*	10	*16 Sep 00*	6
Above hit: Richard BLACKWOOD featuring DEETAH.				
SOMEONE THERE FOR ME	*East West*	23	*25 Nov 00*	3
ALBUMS:	**HITS 1**			**WEEKS 2**
YOU'LL LOVE TO HATE THIS	*East West*	35	*30 Sep 00*	2

BLADE - See Mark B and BLADE

BLAGGERS I.T.A. — UK

SINGLES:	HITS 3			WEEKS 7
STRESS	*Parlophone*	56	*12 Jun 93*	2
OXYGEN	*Parlophone*	51	*9 Oct 93*	2
ABANDON SHIP	*Parlophone*	48	*8 Jan 94*	3

BLAHZAY BLAHZAY — US

SINGLES:	HITS 1			WEEKS 1
DANGER	*Mercury*	56	*2 Mar 96*	1

Vivian BLAINE and Robert ALDA with the HOT BOX GIRLS — US

SINGLES:	HITS 1			WEEKS 1
BUSHEL AND A PECK	*Brunswick*	12	*11 Jul 53*	1

BLAIR — UK

SINGLES:	HITS 2			WEEKS 5
HAVE FUN, GO MAD!	*Mercury*	37	*2 Sep 95*	3
LIFE?	*Mercury*	44	*6 Jan 96*	2

Theme to the BBC childrens TV show 'Dear Dilemma'.

BLAIR and ANOUCHKA – See Terry HALL

Howard BLAKE conducting the SINFONIA OF LONDON, Narration: Bernard CRIBBINS — UK

(See also Snowman.)

ALBUMS:	HITS 1			WEEKS 12
THE SNOWMAN	*CBS*	89	*22 Dec 84*	2
THE SNOWMAN [RE-1ST]	*CBS*	78	*14 Dec 85*	6
THE SNOWMAN [RE-2ND]	*CBS*	54	*12 Dec 87*	4

Peter BLAKE — UK

SINGLES:	HITS 1			WEEKS 4
LIPSMACKIN' ROCK 'N ROLLIN'	*Pepper/United Artists*	40	*8 Oct 77*	4

Featured in a TV commercial for Pepsi.

BLAME — UK

SINGLES:	HITS 1			WEEKS 2
MUSIC TAKES YOU	*Moving Shadow*	48	*11 Apr 92*	2

BLAMELESS — UK

SINGLES:	HITS 3			WEEKS 5
TOWN CLOWNS	*China*	56	*4 Nov 95*	1
BREATHE (A LITTLE DEEPER)	*China*	27	*23 Mar 96*	3
SIGNS . . .	*China*	49	*1 Jun 96*	1

BLANCMANGE — UK

SINGLES:	HITS 10			WEEKS 71
GOD'S KITCHEN / I'VE SEEN THE WORD	*London*	65	*17 Apr 82*	2
FEEL ME	*London*	46	*31 Jul 82*	5
LIVING ON THE CEILING	*London*	7	*30 Oct 82*	14
WAVES	*London*	19	*19 Feb 83*	9
BLIND VISION	*London*	10	*7 May 83*	8
THAT'S LOVE, THAT IT IS	*London*	33	*26 Nov 83*	8
DON'T TELL ME	*London*	8	*14 Apr 84*	10
THE DAY BEFORE YOU CAME	*London*	22	*21 Jul 84*	8
WHAT'S YOUR PROBLEM	*London*	40	*7 Sep 85*	5
I CAN SEE IT	*London*	71	*10 May 86*	2
ALBUMS:	**HITS 3**			**WEEKS 57**
HAPPY FAMILIES	*London*	30	*9 Oct 82*	38
MANGE TOUT	*London*	8	*26 May 84*	17
BELIEVE YOU ME	*London*	54	*26 Oct 85*	2

Billy BLAND — US

SINGLES:	HITS 1			WEEKS 10
LET THE LITTLE GIRL DANCE	*London*	15	*21 May 60*	10

BLANK and JONES — Germany

SINGLES:	HITS 4			WEEKS 7
CREAM	*Deviant*	24	*26 Jun 99*	3
AFTER LOVE	*Nebula*	57	*27 May 00*	1
THE NIGHTFLY	*Nebula*	55	*30 Sep 00*	1
BEYOND TIME	*Gang Go*	53	*3 Mar 01*	2

BLAQUE IVORY — US

SINGLES:	HITS 1			WEEKS 3
808	*Columbia*	31	*3 Jul 99*	3

BLAST featuring V.D.C. — Italy

SINGLES:	HITS 2			WEEKS 5
CRAYZY MAN	*MCA*	22	*18 Jun 94*	3
PRINCES OF THE NIGHT	*MCA*	40	*12 Nov 94*	2

Melanie BLATT - See ARTFUL DODGER

BLAZE featuring Palmer BROWN — US

SINGLES:	HITS 1			WEEKS 2
MY BEAT *Originally released in 1998.*	*Kickin*	53	*10 Mar 01*	2

BLEACH BOYS - See WIZZARD

BLEACHIN' — UK

(See also Jeremy Healey and Amos.)

SINGLES:	HITS 1			WEEKS 4
PEAKIN' *Recreates the vocals from Fleetwood Mac's Big Love.*	*Boiler House!*	32	*22 Jul 00*	3
PEAKIN' [RE]	*Boiler House!*	70	*2 Sep 00*	1

Memphis BLEEK featuring JAY-Z — US

(See also Jay-Z.)

SINGLES:	HITS 1			WEEKS 1
WHAT YOU THINK OF THAT *Samples Keith Mansfield's High Velocity.*	*Roc-A-Fella*	58	*4 Dec 99*	1

BLESSID UNION OF SOULS — US

SINGLES:	HITS 2			WEEKS 6
I BELIEVE	*EMI*	29	*27 May 95*	5
LET ME BE THE ONE	*EMI*	74	*23 Mar 96*	1

BLESSING — UK

SINGLES:	HITS 2			WEEKS 13
HIGHWAY 5	*MCA*	42	*11 May 91*	6
HIGHWAY 5 '92 [RM]	*MCA*	30	*18 Jan 92*	6
SOUL LOVE *Above hit: BLESSING featuring Cutty RANKS.*	*MCA*	73	*19 Feb 94*	1

Archie BLEYER and his Orchestra - See Bill HAYES

Mary J. BLIGE — US

SINGLES:	HITS 22			WEEKS 105
REAL LOVE	*MCA*	68	*28 Nov 92*	2
REMINISCE	*MCA*	31	*27 Feb 93*	4
YOU REMIND ME	*MCA*	48	*12 Jun 93*	3
REAL LOVE [RM] *Remixed by Blacksmith and the Funky Mob.*	*MCA*	26	*28 Aug 93*	4
YOU DON'T HAVE TO WORRY *From the film 'Who's The Man'. Samples Papa Don't Take No Mess by James Brown.*	*Uptown*	36	*4 Dec 93*	2
MY LOVE	*Uptown*	29	*14 May 94*	3
BE HAPPY *Samples You're Too Good To Me by Curtis Mayfield.*	*Uptown*	30	*10 Dec 94*	4
I'M GOIN' DOWN *Originally recorded by Rose Royce in 1978.*	*Uptown*	12	*15 Apr 95*	4
I'LL BE THERE FOR YOU/YOU'RE ALL I NEED TO GET BY [M] *Above hit: METHOD MAN featuring Mary J. BLIGE.*	*Def Jam*	10	*29 Jul 95*	5
MARY JANE (ALL NIGHT LONG)	*Uptown*	17	*30 Sep 95*	4
(YOU MAKE ME FEEL LIKE A) NATURAL WOMAN *Originally recorded by Carole King.*	*Uptown*	23	*16 Dec 95*	3
NOT GON' CRY *From the film 'Waiting To Exhale'.*	*Arista*	39	*30 Mar 96*	2
CAN'T KNOCK THE HUSTLE *Above hit: JAY-Z featuring Mary J. BLIGE.*	*Northwestside*	30	*1 Mar 97*	2
LOVE IS ALL WE NEED *Samples 'Moonchild' by Rick James.*	*MCA*	15	*17 May 97*	4
EVERYTHING *Based on Diana Ross and Marvin Gaye's 'You Are Everything'.*	*MCA*	6	*16 Aug 97*	9
MISSING YOU	*MCA*	19	*29 Nov 97*	3
MISSING YOU [RE-1ST]	*MCA*	72	*3 Jan 98*	1
MISSING YOU [RE-2ND]	*MCA*	74	*31 Jan 98*	1
SEVEN DAYS *Above hit: Mary J. BLIGE featuring George BENSON.*	*MCA*	22	*11 Jul 98*	3

AS	*Epic*	4	*13 Mar 99*	10
Originally recorded by Stevie Wonder's on his 1976 album Songs In The Key Of Life.				
Above hit: George MICHAEL – Mary J. BLIGE.				
ALL THAT I CAN SAY	*MCA*	29	*21 Aug 99*	3
DEEP INSIDE	*MCA*	42	*11 Dec 99*	2
Samples Elton John's Bennie And The Jets.				
GIVE ME YOU	*MCA*	19	*29 Apr 00*	4
Lead guitar: Eric Clapton.				
911	*Columbia*	9	*16 Dec 00*	10
Above hit: Wyclef JEAN featuring Mary J. BLIGE.				
FAMILY AFFAIR	*MCA*	8	*6 Oct 01*	13
ALBUMS:	**HITS 5**			**WEEKS 58**
WHAT'S THE 411?	*MCA*	53	*20 Mar 93*	1
MY LIFE	*Uptown*	59	*17 Dec 94*	3
SHARE MY WORLD	*MCA*	8	*26 Apr 97*	32
MARY	*MCA*	5	*28 Aug 99*	6
NO MORE DRAMA	*MCA*	20	*8 Sep 01*	16

BLIND FAITH — UK

ALBUMS:	**HITS 1**			**WEEKS 10**
BLIND FAITH	*Polydor*	1	*13 Sep 69*	10

BLIND MELON — US

SINGLES:	**HITS 4**			**WEEKS 13**
TONES OF HOME [EP]	*Capitol*	62	*12 Jun 93*	2
Lead track: Tones Of Home.				
NO RAIN	*Capitol*	17	*11 Dec 93*	6
CHANGE	*Capitol*	35	*9 Jul 94*	3
GALAXIE	*Capitol*	37	*5 Aug 95*	2
ALBUMS:	**HITS 2**			**WEEKS 4**
BLIND MELON	*Capitol*	53	*22 Jan 94*	3
SOUP	*Capitol*	48	*19 Aug 95*	1

BLINK — Ireland

SINGLES:	**HITS 1**			**WEEKS 1**
HAPPY DAY	*Parlophone*	57	*16 Jul 94*	1

BLINK-182- — US

SINGLES:	**HITS 4**			**WEEKS 29**
WHAT'S MY AGE AGAIN?	*MCA*	38	*2 Oct 99*	2
ALL THE SMALL THINGS	*MCA*	2	*25 Mar 00*	10
WHAT'S MY AGE AGAIN? [RI]	*MCA*	17	*8 Jul 00*	6
THE ROCK SHOW	*MCA*	14	*14 Jul 01*	7
FIRST DATE	*MCA*	31	*6 Oct 01*	3
FIRST DATE [RE]	*MCA*	74	*3 Nov 01*	1
ALBUMS:	**HITS 3**			**WEEKS 53**
ENEMA OF THE STATE	*MCA*	15	*11 Mar 00*	29
THE MARK, TOM AND TRAVIS SHOW (THE ENEMA STRIKES BACK)	*MCA*	69	*18 Nov 00*	1
TAKE OFF YOUR PANTS AND JACKET	*MCA*	4	*23 Jun 01*	23

BLINKY BLINK – See BLACKSTREET

BLITZ — UK

ALBUMS:	**HITS 1**			**WEEKS 3**
VOICE OF A GENERATION	*No Future*	27	*6 Nov 82*	3

Brandon BLOCK – See BLOCKSTER; GRIFTERS featuring TALL PAUL and Brandon BLOCK

BLOCKHEADS — UK

(See also Ian Dury and the Blockheads'.)

ALBUMS:	**HITS 1**			**WEEKS 3**
BRAND NEW BOOTS AND PANTIES	*East Central One*	44	*21 Apr 01*	3
Re-recording of Ian Dury's 1977 album New Boots And Panties with various artists.				

BLOCKSTER — UK

SINGLES:	**HITS 2**			**WEEKS 11**
YOU SHOULD BE . . .	*Sound Of Ministry*	3	*16 Jan 99*	9
GROOVELINE	*Sound Of Ministry*	18	*24 Jul 99*	2

BLODWYN PIG — UK

ALBUMS:	**HITS 2**			**WEEKS 11**
AHEAD RINGS OUT	*Island*	9	*16 Aug 69*	4
GETTING TO THIS	*Chrysalis*	8	*25 Apr 70*	7

Kristine BLOND — Denmark

SINGLES:	HITS 1			WEEKS 5
LOVE SHY	*Reverb*	22	*11 Apr 98*	3
LOVE SHY [RM]	*Relentless*	28	*11 Nov 00*	2
Remixed by Club Asylum.				

BLONDIE — US/UK

SINGLES:	HITS 16			WEEKS 169
DENIS (DENEE)	*Chrysalis*	2	*18 Feb 78*	14
Original by Randy and the Rainbows reached No. 10 in the US in 1963.				
(I'M ALWAYS TOUCHED BY YOUR) PRESENCE DEAR	*Chrysalis*	10	*6 May 78*	9
PICTURE THIS	*Chrysalis*	12	*26 Aug 78*	11
HANGING ON THE TELEPHONE	*Chrysalis*	5	*11 Nov 78*	12
Originally recorded by Jack Lee.				
HEART OF GLASS	*Chrysalis*	1	*27 Jan 79*	12
SUNDAY GIRL	*Chrysalis*	1	*19 May 79*	13
DREAMING	*Chrysalis*	2	*29 Sep 79*	8
UNION CITY BLUE	*Chrysalis*	13	*24 Nov 79*	10
ATOMIC	*Chrysalis*	1	*23 Feb 80*	9
CALL ME	*Chrysalis*	1	*12 Apr 80*	9
From the film 'An American Gigolo'.				
THE TIDE IS HIGH	*Chrysalis*	1	*8 Nov 80*	12
Originally recorded by the Paragons.				
RAPTURE	*Chrysalis*	5	*24 Jan 81*	8
ISLAND OF LOST SOULS	*Chrysalis*	11	*8 May 82*	9
WAR CHILD	*Chrysalis*	39	*24 Jul 82*	4
DENIS (THE '88 REMIX) [RM]	*Chrysalis*	50	*3 Dec 88*	3
Remixed by Danny D.				
CALL ME [RM]	*Chrysalis*	61	*11 Feb 89*	2
Remixed by Ben Liebrand.				
ATOMIC: REMIXES [RM]	*Chrysalis*	19	*10 Sep 94*	4
HEART OF GLASS [RM]	*Chrysalis*	15	*8 Jul 95*	3
UNION CITY BLUE [RM]	*Chrysalis*	31	*28 Oct 95*	2
Above 3 remixed by Diddy.				
MARIA	*Beyond*	1	*13 Feb 99*	12
NOTHING IS REAL BUT THE GIRL	*Beyond*	26	*12 Jun 99*	3

ALBUMS:	HITS 12			WEEKS 343
PLASTIC LETTERS	*Chrysalis*	10	*4 Mar 78*	54
PARALLEL LINES	*Chrysalis*	1	*23 Sep 78*	105
BLONDIE	*Chrysalis*	75	*10 Mar 79*	1
Originally released in 1977.				
EAT TO THE BEAT	*Chrysalis*	1	*13 Oct 79*	38
AUTOAMERICAN	*Chrysalis*	3	*29 Nov 80*	16
THE BEST OF BLONDIE	*Chrysalis*	4	*31 Oct 81*	40
THE HUNTER	*Chrysalis*	9	*5 Jun 82*	12
ONCE MORE INTO THE BLEACH	*Chrysalis*	50	*17 Dec 88*	1
Remix album of Debbie Harry's solo and group material.				
Above hit: Debbie HARRY and BLONDIE.				
THE COMPLETE PICTURE – THE VERY BEST OF DEBORAH HARRY AND BLONDIE	*Chrysalis*	3	*16 Mar 91*	22
Above hit: Deborah HARRY and BLONDIE.				
BEAUTIFUL – THE REMIX ALBUM	*Chrysalis*	25	*29 Jul 95*	2
ATOMIC – THE VERY BEST OF BLONDE	*EMI*	12	*25 Jul 98*	13
ATOMIC/ATOMIX – THE VERY BEST OF BLONDIE [RE]	*EMI*	12	*20 Feb 99*	21
Repackaged with remix album.				
NO EXIT	*Beyond*	3	*27 Feb 99*	15

BLOOD, SWEAT AND TEARS — UK/US/Canada

SINGLES:	HITS 1			WEEKS 6
YOU'VE MADE ME SO VERY HAPPY	*CBS*	35	*3 May 69*	6
Originally recorded by Brenda Holloway.				

ALBUMS:	HITS 3			WEEKS 21
CHILD IS THE FATHER TO THE MAN	*CBS*	40	*13 Jul 68*	1
BLOOD SWEAT AND TEARS	*CBS*	15	*12 Apr 69*	8
BLOOD SWEAT AND TEARS 3	*CBS*	14	*8 Aug 70*	12

BLOODHOUND GANG — US

SINGLES:	HITS 3			WEEKS 21
WHY'S EVERYBODY ALWAYS PICKIN' ON ME?	*Geffen*	56	*23 Aug 97*	1
THE BAD TOUCH	*Geffen*	4	*15 Apr 00*	14
THE BALLAD OF CHASEY LAIN	*Geffen*	15	*2 Sep 00*	6
Chasey Lain is a pornographic film actress.				

ALBUMS:	HITS 1			WEEKS 7
HOORAY FOR BOOBIES	*Geffen*	37	*6 May 00*	7

Major Denis BLOODNOK, 43RD DESERTERS (Rtd.) - See GOONS

BLOODSTONE — US

SINGLES:	HITS 1			WEEKS 4
NATURAL HIGH	*Decca*	40	*18 Aug 73*	4

Bobby BLOOM — US

SINGLES:	HITS 2			WEEKS 24
MONTEGO BAY	*Polydor*	3	*29 Aug 70*	14
MONTEGO BAY [RE-1ST]	*Polydor*	42	*12 Dec 70*	3
MONTEGO BAY [RE-2ND]	*Polydor*	47	*9 Jan 71*	2
HEAVY MAKES YOU HAPPY	*Polydor*	31	*9 Jan 71*	5

BLOOMSBURY SET — UK

SINGLES:	HITS 1			WEEKS 3
HANGING AROUND WITH THE BIG BOYS	*Stiletto*	56	*25 Jun 83*	3

Tanya BLOUNT — US

SINGLES:	HITS 1			WEEKS 1
I'M GONNA MAKE YOU MINE	*Polydor*	69	*11 Jun 94*	1

Kurtis BLOW — US

SINGLES:	HITS 6			WEEKS 23
CHRISTMAS RAPPIN'	*Mercury*	30	*15 Dec 79*	6
THE BREAKS	*Mercury*	47	*11 Oct 80*	4
PARTY TIME (THE GO-GO EDIT)	*Club*	67	*16 Mar 85*	1
SAVE YOUR LOVE (FOR # 1)	*Club*	66	*15 Jun 85*	2
Above hit: RENE and ANGELA with Kurtis BLOW.				
IF I RULED THE WORLD	*Club*	24	*18 Jan 86*	8
I'M CHILLIN'	*Club*	64	*8 Nov 86*	2

BLOW MONKEYS — UK

SINGLES:	HITS 10			WEEKS 46
DIGGING YOUR SCENE	*RCA*	12	*1 Mar 86*	10
WICKED WAYS	*RCA*	60	*17 May 86*	2
IT DOESN'T HAVE TO BE THIS WAY	*RCA*	5	*31 Jan 87*	8
OUT WITH HER	*RCA*	30	*28 Mar 87*	6
(CELEBRATE) THE DAY AFTER YOU	*RCA*	52	*30 May 87*	2
Above hit: BLOW MONKEYS with Curtis MAYFIELD.				
SOME KIND OF WONDERFUL	*RCA*	67	*15 Aug 87*	1
THIS IS YOUR LIFE	*RCA*	70	*6 Aug 88*	2
THIS IS YOUR LIFE [RM]	*RCA*	32	*8 Apr 89*	5
CHOICE?	*RCA*	22	*15 Jul 89*	6
SLAVES NO MORE	*RCA*	73	*14 Oct 89*	2
Above 2: BLOW MONKEYS featuring Sylvia TELLA.				
SPRINGTIME FOR THE WORLD	*RCA*	69	*26 May 90*	2
ALBUMS:	**HITS 4**			**WEEKS 27**
ANIMAL MAGIC	*RCA*	21	*19 Apr 86*	8
SHE WAS ONLY A GROCER'S DAUGHTER	*RCA*	20	*25 Apr 87*	8
WHOOPS! THERE GOES THE NEIGHBOURHOOD	*RCA*	46	*11 Feb 89*	2
CHOICES - THE SINGLES COLLECTION	*RCA*	5	*26 Aug 89*	9

BLOWING FREE — UK

(See also Harmonium; Hypnosis; In Tune; Raindance; School Of Excellence.)

ALBUMS:	HITS 2			WEEKS 14
SAX MOODS	*Dino*	6	*29 Jul 95*	13
SAX MOODS - VOLUME 2	*Dino*	70	*30 Nov 96*	1

BLU PETER — UK

SINGLES:	HITS 1			WEEKS 1
TELL ME WHAT YOU WANT / JAMES HAS KITTENS	*React*	70	*21 Mar 98*	1

BLUE — UK

SINGLES:	HITS 1			WEEKS 8
GONNA CAPTURE YOUR HEART	*Rocket*	18	*30 Apr 77*	8

BLUE — UK

SINGLES:	HITS 3			WEEKS 32
ALL RISE	*Innocent*	4	*2 Jun 01*	13
TOO CLOSE	*Innocent*	1	*8 Sep 01*	13
IF YOU COME BACK	*Innocent*	1	*24 Nov 01*	6

ALBUMS:	HITS 1			WEEKS 4
ALL RISE	*Innocent*	2	*8 Dec 01*	4

Babbity BLUE — UK

SINGLES:	HITS 1			WEEKS 2
DON'T MAKE ME (FALL IN LOVE WITH YOU)	*Decca*	48	*13 Feb 65*	2

Barry BLUE — UK

(See also Cry Sisco!)

SINGLES:	HITS 5			WEEKS 48
DANCIN' (ON A SATURDAY NIGHT) *Originally recorded by Lynsey De Paul.*	*Bell*	2	*28 Jul 73*	15
DO YOU WANNA DANCE?	*Bell*	7	*3 Nov 73*	12
SCHOOL LOVE	*Bell*	11	*2 Mar 74*	9
MISS HIT AND RUN	*Bell*	26	*3 Aug 74*	7
HOT SHOT	*Bell*	23	*26 Oct 74*	5

BLUE ADONIS featuring LIL' MISS MAX — Belgium

SINGLES:	HITS 1			WEEKS 3
DISCO COP	*Serious*	27	*17 Oct 98*	3

BLUE AEROPLANES — UK

SINGLES:	HITS 2			WEEKS 3
JACKET HANGS	*Ensign*	72	*17 Feb 90*	1
. . . AND STONES	*Ensign*	63	*26 May 90*	2
ALBUMS:	**HITS 3**			**WEEKS 5**
SWAGGER	*Ensign*	54	*24 Feb 90*	1
BEATSONGS	*Ensign*	33	*17 Aug 91*	3
LIFE MODEL	*Beggars Banquet*	59	*12 Mar 94*	1

BLUE AMAZON — UK

SINGLES:	HITS 2			WEEKS 2
AND THEN THE RAIN FALLS	*Sony*	53	*17 May 97*	1
BREATHE	*Subversive*	73	*1 Jul 00*	1

BLUE BAMBOO — Belgium

SINGLES:	HITS 1			WEEKS 4
ABC AND D . . .	*Escapade*	23	*3 Dec 94*	4

BLUE CAPS – See Gene VINCENT

BLUE FEATHER — Holland

SINGLES:	HITS 1			WEEKS 4
LET'S FUNK TONIGHT	*Mercury*	50	*3 Jul 82*	4

BLUE FLAMES – See Georgie FAME

BLUE HAZE — UK

SINGLES:	HITS 1			WEEKS 6
SMOKE GETS IN YOUR EYES *Originally recorded by Paul Whiteman in 1933.*	*A&M*	32	*18 Mar 72*	6

BLUE MELONS — UK

SINGLES:	HITS 1			WEEKS 1
DO WAH DIDDY DIDDY (THE WIGGLE MIX)	Fundamental	70	*8 Jun 96*	1

BLUE MERCEDES — UK

SINGLES:	HITS 3			WEEKS 18
I WANT TO BE YOUR PROPERTY	*MCA*	23	*10 Oct 87*	11
SEE WANT MUST HAVE	*MCA*	57	*13 Feb 88*	2
LOVE IS THE GUN	*MCA*	46	*23 Jul 88*	5

BLUE MINK — UK

SINGLES:	HITS 7			WEEKS 83
MELTING POT	*Philips*	3	*15 Nov 69*	15
GOOD MORNING FREEDOM	*Philips*	10	*28 Mar 70*	10
OUR WORLD	*Philips*	17	*19 Sep 70*	9
THE BANNER MAN	*Regal Zonophone*	3	*29 May 71*	14
STAY WITH ME	*Regal Zonophone*	11	*11 Nov 72*	13
STAY WITH ME [RE]	*Regal Zonophone*	43	*17 Feb 73*	2
BY THE DEVIL (I WAS TEMPTED)	*EMI*	26	*3 Mar 73*	9
RANDY	*EMI*	9	*23 Jun 73*	11

BLUE MURDER — US

ALBUMS:	HITS 1			WEEKS 3
BLUE MURDER	*Geffen*	45	*6 May 89*	3

BLUE NILE — UK

SINGLES:	HITS 3			WEEKS 4
THE DOWNTOWN LIGHTS	*Linn*	67	*30 Sep 89*	1
HEADLIGHTS ON THE PARADE	*Linn*	72	*29 Sep 90*	1
SATURDAY NIGHT	*Linn*	50	*19 Jan 91*	2
ALBUMS:	**HITS 3**			**WEEKS 10**
A WALK ACROSS THE ROOFTOPS	*Linn*	80	*19 May 84*	2
HATS	*Linn*	12	*21 Oct 89*	4
PEACE AT LAST	*Warner Brothers*	13	*22 Jun 96*	4

BLUE NOTES – See Neil YOUNG

BLUE OYSTER CULT — US

SINGLES:	HITS 1			WEEKS 14
(DON'T FEAR) THE REAPER	*CBS*	16	*20 May 78*	14
ALBUMS:	**HITS 8**			**WEEKS 40**
AGENTS OF FORTUNE	*CBS*	26	*3 Jul 76*	10
SPECTURES	*CBS*	60	*4 Feb 78*	1
SOME ENCHANTED EVENING	*CBS*	18	*28 Oct 78*	4
Live recordings.				
MIRRORS	*CBS*	46	*18 Aug 79*	5
CULTOSAURUS ERECTUS	*CBS*	12	*19 Jul 80*	7
FIRE OF UNKNOWN ORIGIN	*CBS*	29	*25 Jul 81*	7
EXTRATERRESTRIAL LIVE	*CBS*	39	*22 May 82*	5
THE REVOLUTION BY NIGHT	*CBS*	95	*19 Nov 83*	1

BLUE PEARL — UK/US

SINGLES:	HITS 6			WEEKS 29
NAKED IN THE RAIN	*Big Life*	4	*7 Jul 90*	13
LITTLE BROTHER	*Big Life*	31	*3 Nov 90*	5
(CAN YOU) FEEL THE PASSION	*Big Life*	14	*11 Jan 92*	6
MOTHER DAWN	*Big Life*	50	*25 Jul 92*	2
FIRE OF LOVE	*Logic*	71	*27 Nov 93*	1
Above hit: JUNGLE HIGH with BLUE PEARL.				
NAKED IN THE RAIN '98 [RR]	*Malarky*	22	*4 Jul 98*	2
ALBUMS:	**HITS 1**			**WEEKS 2**
NAKED	*Big Life*	58	*1 Dec 90*	2

BLUE RONDO A LA TURK — UK

SINGLES:	HITS 2			WEEKS 9
ME AND MR. SANCHEZ	*Diable Noir*	40	*14 Nov 81*	4
KLACTOVEESEDSTEIN	*Diable Noir*	50	*13 Mar 82*	5
ALBUMS:	**HITS 1**			**WEEKS 2**
CHEWING THE FAT	*Diable Noir*	80	*6 Nov 82*	2

BLUE ZOO — UK

SINGLES:	HITS 3			WEEKS 17
I'M YOUR MAN	*Magnet*	55	*12 Jun 82*	3
CRY BOY CRY	*Magnet*	13	*16 Oct 82*	10
(I JUST CAN'T) FORGIVE AND FORGET	*Magnet*	60	*28 May 83*	4

BLUEBELLS — UK

SINGLES:	HITS 6			WEEKS 49
CATH	*London*	62	*12 Mar 83*	2
SUGAR BRIDGE (IT WILL STAND)	*London*	72	*9 Jul 83*	1
I'M FALLING	*London*	11	*24 Mar 84*	12
YOUNG AT HEART	*London*	8	*23 Jun 84*	12
CATH [RI] / WILL SHE ALWAYS BE WAITING	*London*	38	*1 Sep 84*	7
ALL I AM (IS LOVING YOU)	*London*	58	*9 Feb 85*	3
YOUNG AT HEART [RI]	*London*	1	*27 Mar 93*	12
Featured in the Volkswagen TV commercial.				
ALBUMS:	**HITS 2**			**WEEKS 15**
SISTERS	*London*	22	*11 Aug 84*	10
THE BLUEBELLS - THE SINGLES COLLECTION	*London*	27	*17 Apr 93*	5

BLUEBOY — UK

SINGLES:	HITS 2			WEEKS 16
REMEMBER ME *Samples Marlena Shaw's Woman Of The Ghetto.*	*Pharm*	8	*1 Feb 97*	13
SANDMAN *Samples Undisputed Truth's You + Me = Love.*	*Sidewalk*	25	*23 Aug 97*	3

BLUES BAND — UK

SINGLES:	HITS 1			WEEKS 2
THE BLUES BAND [EP] *Lead tack: Maggie's Farm.*	*Arista*	68	*12 Jul 80*	2
ALBUMS:	**HITS 3**			**WEEKS 18**
OFFICIAL BOOTLEG ALBUM	*Arista*	40	*8 Mar 80*	9
READY	*Arista*	36	*18 Oct 80*	6
ITCHY FEET	*Arista*	60	*17 Oct 81*	3

BLUES BROTHERS — US

SINGLES:	HITS 1			WEEKS 8
EVERYBODY NEEDS SOMEBODY TO LOVE *[AA] listed with Think by Aretha Franklin. Originally recorded by Solomon Burke.*	*Atlantic*	12	*7 Apr 90*	8
ALBUMS:	**HITS 1**			**WEEKS 26**
THE BLUES BROTHERS [OST] *Features tracks by James Brown, Ray Charles and Aretha Franklin.*	*Atlantic*	64	*11 Apr 87*	18
THE BLUES BROTHERS [OST] [RE]	*Atlantic*	59	*3 Sep 88*	8
COMPILATION ALBUMS:	**HITS 1**			**WEEKS 80**
THE BLUES BROTHERS [OST] *Relegated to the Compilation chart as it included tracks by other artists.*	*Atlantic*	9	*21 Jan 89*	37
THE BLUES BROTHERS [OST] [RE]	*Atlantic*	4	*20 Jan 90*	43

BLUESBREAKERS – See John MAYALL

BLUETONES — UK

SINGLES:	HITS 10			WEEKS 41
ARE YOU BLUE OR ARE YOU BLIND?	*Superior Quality Recordings*	31	*17 Jun 95*	2
BLUETONIC	*Superior Quality Recordings*	19	*14 Oct 95*	3
SLIGHT RETURN *Originally released in 1994.*	*Superior Quality Recordings*	2	*3 Feb 96*	8
CUT SOME RUG / CASTLE ROCK	*Superior Quality Recordings*	7	*11 May 96*	5
CUT SOME RUG / CASTLE ROCK [RE]	*Superior Quality Recordings*	73	*20 Jul 96*	1
MARBLEHEAD JOHNSON	*Superior Quality Recordings*	7	*28 Sep 96*	6
SOLOMON BITES THE WORM	*Superior Quality Recordings*	10	*21 Feb 98*	3
IF...	*Superior Quality Recordings*	13	*9 May 98*	5
SLEAZY BED TRACK	*Superior Quality Recordings*	35	*8 Aug 98*	2
KEEP THE HOME FIRES BURNING	*Superior Quality Recordings*	13	*4 Mar 00*	3
AUTOPHILIA OR HOW I LEARNED TO STOP WORRYING AND LOVE MY CAR	*Superior Quality Recordings*	18	*20 May 00*	3
ALBUMS:	**HITS 3**			**WEEKS 45**
EXPECTING TO FLY	*Superior Quality Recordings*	1	*24 Feb 96*	25
RETURN TO THE LAST CHANCE SALOON	*Superior Quality Recordings*	10	*21 Mar 98*	16
SCIENCE & NATURE	*Superior Quality Recordings*	7	*27 May 00*	4

Colin BLUNSTONE — UK

(See also Neil MacArthur.)

SINGLES:	HITS 6			WEEKS 30
SAY YOU DON'T MIND *Originally recorded by Denny Laine.*	*Epic*	15	*12 Feb 72*	9
I DON'T BELIEVE IN MIRACLES	*Epic*	31	*11 Nov 72*	6
HOW COULD WE DARE TO BE WRONG	*Epic*	45	*17 Feb 73*	2
WHAT BECOMES OF THE BROKEN HEARTED? *Above hit: Dave STEWART guest vocals Colin BLUNSTONE.*	*Stiff*	13	*14 Mar 81*	10
TRACKS OF MY TEARS	PRT	60	*29 May 82*	2
OLD AND WISE *Above hit: Alan PARSONS PROJECT: lead vocals by Colin BLUNSTONE.*	*Arista*	74	*15 Jan 83*	1

BLUR — UK

SINGLES:	HITS 23			WEEKS 132
SHE'S SO HIGH	*Food*	48	*27 Oct 90*	3
THERE'S NO OTHER WAY	*Food*	8	*27 Apr 91*	8
BANG	*Food*	24	*10 Aug 91*	4
POPSCENE	*Food*	32	*11 Apr 92*	2
FOR TOMORROW	*Food*	28	*1 May 93*	4
CHEMICAL WORLD	*Food*	28	*10 Jul 93*	4
SUNDAY SUNDAY	*Food*	26	*16 Oct 93*	3
GIRLS AND BOYS	*Food*	5	*19 Mar 94*	7

TO THE END *Features Laetitia from Stereolab on backing vocals.*	*Food*	16	*11 Jun 94*	5
PARKLIFE *Above hit: BLUR starring Phil DANIELS.*	*Food*	10	*3 Sep 94*	7
END OF A CENTURY	*Food*	19	*19 Nov 94*	3
COUNTRY HOUSE	*Food*	1	*26 Aug 95*	11
COUNTRY HOUSE *Sales of 7" format which, due to chart eligibility rules, was listed separately.*	*Food*	57	*9 Sep 95*	1
THE UNIVERSAL	*Food*	5	*25 Nov 95*	9
STEREOTYPES	*Food*	7	*24 Feb 96*	5
CHARMLESS MAN	*Food*	5	*11 May 96*	6
BEETLEBUM	*Food*	1	*1 Feb 97*	5
SONG 2	*Food*	2	*19 Apr 97*	5
BEETLEBUM [RE]	*Food*	59	*26 Apr 97*	2
ON YOUR OWN	*Food*	5	*28 Jun 97*	5
M.O.R.	*Food*	15	*27 Sep 97*	3
TENDER	*Food*	2	*6 Mar 99*	10
COFFEE + TV	*Food*	11	*10 Jul 99*	7
NO DISTANCE LEFT TO RUN	*Food*	14	*27 Nov 99*	3
NO DISTANCE LEFT TO RUN [RE]	*Food*	65	*22 Jan 00*	1
MUSIC IS MY RADAR	*Food*	10	*28 Oct 00*	7
MUSIC IS MY RADAR [RE]	*Food*	66	*13 Jan 01*	2
ALBUMS:	**HITS 7**			**WEEKS 299**
LEISURE *Includes re-entries through to 1999.*	*Food*	7	*7 Sep 91*	12
MODERN LIFE IS RUBBISH	*Food*	15	*22 May 93*	14
PARKLIFE *Includes re-entries through to 1999.*	*Food*	1	*7 May 94*	106
THE GREAT ESCAPE	*Food*	1	*23 Sep 95*	47
BLUR	*Food*	1	*22 Feb 97*	65
13	*Food*	1	*27 Mar 99*	27
BLUR: BEST OF	*Food*	3	*11 Nov 00*	28

BM DUBS presents MR RUMBLE featuring BRASSTOOTH and KEE — UK

SINGLES:	**HITS 1**			**WEEKS 2**
WHOOMP! . . . THERE IT IS	*Incentive*	32	*17 Mar 01*	2

BOB and EARL — US

SINGLES:	**HITS 1**			**WEEKS 13**
HARLEM SHUFFLE	*Island*	7	*15 Mar 69*	13

BOB and MARCIA — Jamaica

SINGLES:	**HITS 2**			**WEEKS 25**
YOUNG, GIFTED AND BLACK *Originally recorded by Nina Simone and features Boris Gardiner on bass.*	*Harry J*	5	*14 Mar 70*	12
PIED PIPER	*Trojan*	11	*5 Jun 71*	13

BOB THE BUILDER — UK

SINGLES:	**HITS 2**			**WEEKS 38**
CAN WE FIX IT?	*BBC Music*	1	*16 Dec 00*	18
CAN WE FIX IT? [RE-1ST]	*BBC Music*	59	*28 Apr 01*	2
CAN WE FIX IT? [RE-2ND]	*BBC Music*	54	*2 Jun 01*	2
MAMBO NO. 5	*BBC Music*	1	*15 Sep 01*	16
ALBUMS:	**HITS 1**			**WEEKS 12**
THE ALBUM	*BBC Music*	4	*13 Oct 01*	12

BOBBYSOCKS — Sweden/Norway

SINGLES:	**HITS 1**			**WEEKS 4**
LET IT SWING *Eurovision Song Contest winner for Norway in 1985.*	*RCA*	44	*25 May 85*	4

Su Su BOBIEN – See MASS SYNDICATE featuring Su Su BOBIEN

Andrea BOCELLI — Italy

SINGLES:	**HITS 3**			**WEEKS 24**
TIME TO SAY GOODBYE (CON TE PARTIRO) *Above hit: Sarah BRIGHTMAN and Andrea BOCELLI.*	*Coalition*	2	*24 May 97*	14
CANTO DELLA TERRA	*Polydor*	25	*25 Sep 99*	4
AVE MARIA *With the Coro Di Voci Bianche Dell'Arcum (Chorus Master: Paulo Lucci). Ave Maria is a Catholic form of address to the Virgin Mary.* *Above hit: Andrea BOCELLI and the ORCHESTRA E CORO DELL'ACCADEMIA NAZIONALE DI SANTA CECILIA conducted by Myung-Whun CHUNG.*	*Philips*	65	*18 Dec 99*	1
CANTO DELLA TERRA [RE] *Theme to BBC-TV's coverage of the Euro 2000 football championships.*	*Polydor*	24	*1 Jul 00*	5

ALBUMS:	HITS 7			WEEKS 107
ROMANZA	*Philips*	6	*31 May 97*	25
ARIA - THE OPERA ALBUM	*Philips*	33	*9 May 98*	5
VIAGGIO ITALIANO	*Philips*	55	*13 Feb 99*	3
SOGNO	*Philips*	4	*10 Apr 99*	42
SACRED ARIAS	*Philips*	20	*20 Nov 99*	12
With the Orchestra dell'Accademia Nazionale di Santa Cecila conducted by Myung-Whun Chung.				
VERDI	*Philips*	17	*23 Sep 00*	10
With the Israeli Philharmonic Orchestra conducted by Zubin Mehta.				
CIELI DI TOSCANA	*Polydor*	3	*27 Oct 01*	10

Karen BODDINGTON and Mark WILLIAMS — Australia

SINGLES:	HITS 1			WEEKS 1
HOME AND AWAY	*First Night*	73	*2 Sep 89*	1

BODINES — UK

ALBUMS:	HITS 1			WEEKS 1
PLAYED	*Pop*	94	*29 Aug 87*	1

BODY COUNT — US

SINGLES:	HITS 2			WEEKS 4
BORN DEAD	*Virgin*	28	*8 Oct 94*	2
NECESSARY EVIL	*Virgin*	45	*17 Dec 94*	2
ALBUMS:	**HITS 1**			**WEEKS 2**
BORN DEAD	*Virgin*	15	*17 Sep 94*	2

BODYSNATCHERS — UK

SINGLES:	HITS 2			WEEKS 12
LETS DO ROCK STEADY	*2-Tone*	22	*15 Mar 80*	9
EASY LIFE	*2-Tone*	50	*19 Jul 80*	3

Humphrey BOGART - See Dooley WILSON with the Voices of Humphrey BOGART and Ingrid BERGMAN

Tim BOGERT - See Jeff BECK, Tim BOGERT and Carmine APPICE

Suzy BOGGUSS — US

ALBUMS:	HITS 1			WEEKS 1
SOMETHING UP MY SLEEVE	*Liberty*	69	*25 Sep 93*	1

Hamilton BOHANNON — US

SINGLES:	HITS 6			WEEKS 38
SOUTH AFRICAN MAN	*Brunswick*	22	*15 Feb 75*	8
DISCO STOMP	*Brunswick*	6	*24 May 75*	12
FOOT STOMPIN' MUSIC	*Brunswick*	23	*5 Jul 75*	6
HAPPY FEELING	*Brunswick*	49	*6 Sep 75*	3
LET'S START THE DANCE	*Mercury*	56	*26 Aug 78*	4
LET'S START TO DANCE AGAIN	*London*	49	*13 Feb 82*	5

BOILING POINT — US

SINGLES:	HITS 1			WEEKS 6
LET'S GET FUNKTIFIED	*Bang*	41	*27 May 78*	6

Marc BOLAN - See T. REX

C.J. BOLLAND — UK

(See also Ravesignal III.)

SINGLES:	HITS 3			WEEKS 10
SUGAR IS SWEETER	*Internal*	11	*5 Oct 96*	5
THE PROPHET	*ffrr*	19	*17 May 97*	3
IT AIN'T GONNA BE ME	*Essential Recordings*	35	*3 Jul 99*	2
Samples Samuel L. Jackson's vocal from the film 'Jackie Brown'. The track is from the film 'Human Traffic'.				
ALBUMS:	**HITS 1**			**WEEKS 2**
THE ANALOGUE THEATRE	*Internal*	43	*26 Oct 96*	2

BOLSHOI — UK

ALBUMS:	HITS 1			WEEKS 1
LINDY'S PARTY	*Beggars Banquet*	100	*3 Oct 87*	1

Michael BOLTON — US

SINGLES:	HITS 18			WEEKS 113
HOW AM I SUPPOSED TO LIVE WITHOUT YOU	*CBS*	3	*17 Feb 90*	10

HOW CAN WE BE LOVERS	*CBS*	10	*28 Apr 90*	1
WHEN I'M BACK ON MY FEET AGAIN	*CBS*	44	*21 Jul 90*	[illegible]
LOVE IS A WONDERFUL THING	*Columbia*	23	*20 Apr 91*	[illegible]
TIME, LOVE AND TENDERNESS	*Columbia*	28	*27 Jul 91*	[illegible]
WHEN A MAN LOVES A WOMAN	*Columbia*	8	*9 Nov 91*	[illegible]
STEEL BARS	*Columbia*	17	*8 Feb 92*	[illegible]
Co-written by Bob Dylan.				
MISSING YOU KNOW	*Columbia*	28	*9 May 92*	[illegible]
Above hit: Michael BOLTON featuring Kenny G.				
TO LOVE SOMEBODY	*Columbia*	16	*31 Oct 92*	6
DRIFT AWAY	*Columbia*	18	*26 Dec 92*	5
Originally recorded by Dobie Gray.				
REACH OUT I'LL BE THERE	*Columbia*	37	*13 Mar 93*	4
SAID I LOVED YOU, BUT I LIED	*Columbia*	15	*13 Nov 93*	8
SOUL OF MY SOUL	*Columbia*	32	*26 Feb 94*	3
LEAN ON ME	*Columbia*	14	*14 May 94*	7
CAN I TOUCH YOU . . . THERE?	*Columbia*	6	*9 Sep 95*	9
A LOVE SO BEAUTIFUL	*Columbia*	27	*2 Dec 95*	5
Originally recorded by Roy Orbison.				
SOUL PROVIDER	*Columbia*	35	*16 Mar 96*	3
THE BEST OF LOVE / GO THE DISTANCE	*Columbia*	14	*8 Nov 97*	4
Go The Distance from the Walt Disney film 'Hercules'.				

ALBUMS:	HITS 9			WEEKS 226
SOUL PROVIDER	*CBS*	4	*17 Mar 90*	72
THE HUNGER	*CBS*	44	*11 Aug 90*	5
TIME, LOVE AND TENDERNESS	*Columbia*	2	*18 May 91*	57
TIMELESS (THE CLASSICS)	*Columbia*	3	*10 Oct 92*	24
THE ONE THING	*Columbia*	4	*27 Nov 93*	24
GREATEST HITS 1985-1995	*Columbia*	2	*30 Sep 95*	30
ALL THAT MATTERS	*Columbia*	20	*22 Nov 97*	7
MY SECRET PASSION - THE ARIAS	*Sony Classical*	25	*2 May 98*	5
TIMELESS - THE CLASSICS VOLUME 2	*Columbia*	50	*4 Dec 99*	2

BOMB THE BASS — UK

SINGLES:	HITS 10			WEEKS 50
BEAT DIS	*Rhythm King*	2	*20 Feb 88*	9
MEGABLAST / DON'T MAKE ME WAIT	*Mister-ron*	6	*27 Aug 88*	9
Above hit: BOMB THE BASS featuring MERLIN and ANTONIA / BOMB THE BASS featuring LORRAINE.				
SAY A LITTLE PRAYER	*Rhythm King*	10	*26 Nov 88*	10
Above hit: BOMB THE BASS featuring MAUREEN.				
WINTER IN JULY	*Rhythm King*	7	*27 Jul 91*	9
THE AIR YOU BREATHE	*Rhythm King*	52	*9 Nov 91*	3
KEEP GIVING ME LOVE	*Rhythm King*	62	*2 May 92*	2
BUG POWDER DUST	*Stoned Heights*	24	*1 Oct 94*	3
Above hit: BOMB THE BASS featuring Justin WARFIELD.				
DARKHEART	*Stoned Heights*	35	*17 Dec 94*	3
Above hit: BOMB THE BASS featuring SPIKEY TEE.				
1 TO 1 RELIGION	*Stoned Heights*	53	*1 Apr 95*	1
Above hit: BOMB THE BASS featuring CARLTON.				
SANDCASTLES	*Fourth & Broadway*	54	*16 Sep 95*	1
Above hit: BOMB THE BASS featuring Bernard FOWLER.				

ALBUMS:	HITS 3			WEEKS 16
INTO THE DRAGON	*Rhythm King*	18	*22 Oct 88*	10
UNKNOWN TERRITORY	*Rhythm King*	19	*31 Aug 91*	4
CLEAR	*Fourth & Broadway*	22	*15 Apr 95*	2

BOMBALURINA — UK

SINGLES:	HITS 2			WEEKS 20
ITSY BITSY TEENY WEENY YELLOW POLKA DOT BIKINI	*Carpet*	1	*28 Jul 90*	13
SEVEN LITTLE GIRLS (SITTING IN THE BACKSEAT)	*Carpet*	18	*24 Nov 90*	7
Above hit: BOMBALURINA featuring Timmy MALLETT.				

ALBUMS:	HITS 1			WEEKS 5
HUGGIN' AN'A KISSIN'	*Polydor*	55	*15 Dec 90*	5
Above hit: BOMBALURINA featuring Timmy MALLETT.				

BOMBERS — Canada

SINGLES:	HITS 2			WEEKS 10
(EVERYBODY) GET DANCIN'	*Flamingo*	37	*5 May 79*	7
LET'S DANCE	*Flamingo*	58	*18 Aug 79*	3

BOMFUNK MCs — Finland/UK

SINGLES:	HITS 2			WEEKS 21
FREESTYLER	*Dance Pool*	2	*5 Aug 00*	12
UPROCKING BEATS	*INCredible*	11	*2 Dec 00*	9

ALBUMS:	HITS 1			WEEKS 2
IN STEREO	*Epidrome*	33	*26 Aug 00*	2

BON JOVI — US

(See also Jon Bon Jovi.)

SINGLES:	HITS 29			WEEKS 215
HARDEST PART IS THE NIGHT	*Vertigo*	68	*31 Aug 85*	1
YOU GIVE LOVE A BAD NAME	*Vertigo*	14	*9 Aug 86*	10
LIVIN' ON A PRAYER	*Vertigo*	4	*25 Oct 86*	15
WANTED DEAD OR ALIVE	*Vertigo*	13	*11 Apr 87*	7
NEVER SAY GOODBYE	*Vertigo*	21	*15 Aug 87*	5
BAD MEDICINE	*Vertigo*	17	*24 Sep 88*	7
BORN TO BE MY BABY	*Vertigo*	22	*10 Dec 88*	7
I'LL BE THERE FOR YOU	*Vertigo*	18	*29 Apr 89*	7
LAY YOUR HANDS ON ME	*Vertigo*	18	*26 Aug 89*	6
LIVING IN SIN	*Vertigo*	35	*9 Dec 89*	6
KEEP THE FAITH	*Jambco*	5	*24 Oct 92*	6
BED OF ROSES	*Jambco*	13	*23 Jan 93*	6
IN THESE ARMS	*Jambco*	9	*15 May 93*	7
I'LL SLEEP WHEN I'M DEAD	*Jambco*	17	*7 Aug 93*	5
I BELIEVE	*Jambco*	11	*2 Oct 93*	6
DRY COUNTY	*Jambco*	9	*26 Mar 94*	6
ALWAYS	*Jambco*	2	*24 Sep 94*	18
PLEASE COME HOME FOR CHRISTMAS	*Jambco*	7	*17 Dec 94*	6
SOMEDAY I'LL BE SATURDAY NIGHT	*Jambco*	7	*25 Feb 95*	7
PLEASE COME HOME FOR CHRISTMAS [RE]	*Jambco*	46	*4 Mar 95*	4
THIS AIN'T A LOVE SONG	*Mercury*	6	*10 Jun 95*	9
SOMETHING FOR THE PAIN	*Mercury*	8	*30 Sep 95*	7
LIE TO ME	*Mercury*	10	*25 Nov 95*	8
THESE DAYS	*Mercury*	7	*9 Mar 96*	6
HEY GOD	*Mercury*	13	*6 Jul 96*	5
REAL LIFE	*Reprise*	21	*10 Apr 99*	5
From the film 'EDtv'.				
IT'S MY LIFE	*Mercury*	3	*3 Jun 00*	13
SAY IT ISN'T SO	*Mercury*	10	*9 Sep 00*	6
SAY IT ISN'T SO [RE]	*Mercury*	73	*18 Nov 00*	1
THANK YOU FOR LOVING ME	*Mercury*	12	*9 Dec 00*	6
ONE WILD NIGHT	*Mercury*	10	*19 May 01*	7

ALBUMS:	HITS 9			WEEKS 411
BON JOVI	*Vertigo*	71	*28 Apr 84*	3
7800° FAHRENHEIT	*Vertigo*	28	*11 May 85*	12
SLIPPERY WHEN WET	*Vertigo*	6	*20 Sep 86*	123
NEW JERSEY	*Vertigo*	1	*1 Oct 88*	47
Album 2 includes re-entries through to 1996.				
KEEP THE FAITH	*Jambco*	1	*14 Nov 92*	70
CROSS ROAD - THE BEST OF BON JOVI	*Jambco*	1	*22 Oct 94*	68
Includes re-entries through to 2000.				
THESE DAYS	*Mercury*	1	*1 Jul 95*	50
CRUSH	*Mercury*	1	*10 Jun 00*	29
ONE WILD NIGHT - LIVE 1985-2001	*Mercury*	2	*26 May 01*	9

Jon BON JOVI — US

(See also Bon Jovi.)

SINGLES:	HITS 5			WEEKS 27
BLAZE OF GLORY	*Vertigo*	13	*4 Aug 90*	8
From the film 'Young Guns II', also features Jeff Beck on guitar and Randy Jackson on bass.				
MIRACLE	*Vertigo*	29	*10 Nov 90*	5
MIDNIGHT AT CHELSEA	*Mercury*	4	*14 Jun 97*	7
QUEEN OF NEW ORLEANS	*Mercury*	10	*30 Aug 97*	4
JANIE, DON'T TAKE YOUR LOVE TO TOWN	*Mercury*	13	*15 Nov 97*	3

ALBUMS:	HITS 2			WEEKS 41
BLAZE OF GLORY/YOUNG GUNS II [OST]	*Vertigo*	2	*25 Aug 90*	23
DESTINATION ANYWHERE	*Mercury*	2	*28 Jun 97*	18

BOND — UK//Australia

ALBUMS:	HITS 1			WEEKS 18
BORN	*Decca*	16	*14 Oct 00*	12
BORN [RE]	*Decca*	23	*9 Jun 01*	6
Repackaged.				

Graham BOND — UK

ALBUMS:	HITS 1			WEEKS 2
SOLID BOND	*Warner Brothers*	40	*20 Jun 70*	2

Ronnie BOND — UK

SINGLES:	HITS 1			WEEKS 5
IT'S WRITTEN ON YOUR BODY *Featured in a Levi's Jeans TV commercial.*	*Mercury*	52	*31 May 80*	5

Gary U.S. BONDS — US

SINGLES:	HITS 6			WEEKS 39
● NEW ORLEANS	*Top Rank*	16	*21 Jan 61*	11
QUARTER TO THREE *Above 2: U.S. BONDS.*	*Top Rank*	7	*22 Jul 61*	13
THIS LITTLE GIRL *Originally recorded by Bruce Springsteen.*	*EMI America*	43	*30 May 81*	6
JOLE BLON *Originally recorded by Moon Mullican in 1947.* *Above hit: Gary U.S. BONDS with Bruce SPRINGSTEEN.*	*EMI America*	51	*22 Aug 81*	3
IT'S ONLY LOVE	*EMI America*	43	*31 Oct 81*	3
SOUL DEEP	*EMI America*	59	*17 Jul 82*	3
ALBUMS:	**HITS 2**			**WEEKS 8**
DEDICATION	*EMI America*	43	*22 Aug 81*	3
ON THE LINE	*EMI America*	55	*10 Jul 82*	5

BONE — UK

SINGLES:	HITS 1			WEEKS 1
WINGS OF LOVE	*Deconstruction*	55	*2 Apr 94*	1

BONE THUGS-N-HARMONY — US

SINGLES:	HITS 4			WEEKS 22
1ST OF THA MONTH	*Epic*	32	*4 Nov 95*	2
THA CROSSROADS *Samples the Isley Brothers' Make Me Say It Again.*	*Epic*	8	*10 Aug 96*	11
1ST OF THA MONTH [RI]	*Epic*	15	*9 Nov 96*	4
DAYS OF OUR LIVEZ *From the film 'Set It Off'.*	*East West America*	37	*15 Feb 97*	2
LOOK INTO MY EYES *From the film 'Batman And Robin'.*	*Epic*	16	*26 Jul 97*	3
ALBUMS:	**HITS 2**			**WEEKS 4**
E.1999 ETERNAL	*Epic*	39	*31 Aug 96*	3
THE ART OF WAR	*Epic*	42	*9 Aug 97*	1

Elbow BONES and the RACKETEERS — US

SINGLES:	HITS 1			WEEKS 9
A NIGHT IN NEW YORK *Produced by Kid Creole (August Darnell).*	*EMI America*	33	*14 Jan 84*	9

BONEY M — Jamaica/Antilles/Montserrat

SINGLES:	HITS 17			WEEKS 170
DADDY COOL	*Atlantic*	6	*18 Dec 76*	13
SUNNY	*Atlantic*	3	*12 Mar 77*	10
MA BAKER	*Atlantic*	2	*25 Jun 77*	13
BELFAST	*Atlantic*	8	*29 Oct 77*	13
RIVERS OF BABYLON / BROWN GIRL IN THE RING *Brown Girl in The Ring listed from 5 Aug 78 and the song climbed back to No. 2. Rivers of Babylon originally recorded by the Melodians; Brown Girl In The Ring originally recorded by Exuma.*	*Atlantic*	1	*29 Apr 78*	40
RASPUTIN	*Atlantic*	2	*7 Oct 78*	10
MARY'S BOY CHILD/OH MY LORD [M]	*Atlantic*	1	*2 Dec 78*	8
PAINTER MAN	*Atlantic*	10	*3 Mar 79*	6
HOORAY HOORAY, IT'S A HOLI - HOLIDAY	*Atlantic*	3	*28 Apr 79*	9
GOTTA GO HOME/EL LUTE *El Lute listed from 29 Sep 79.*	*Atlantic*	12	*11 Aug 79*	11
I'M BORN AGAIN	*Atlantic*	35	*15 Dec 79*	7
MY FRIEND JACK *Originally recorded by the Smoke.*	*Atlantic*	57	*26 Apr 80*	5
CHILDREN OF PARADISE	*Atlantic*	66	*14 Feb 81*	2
WE KILL THE WORLD (DON'T KILL THE WORLD)	*Atlantic*	39	*21 Nov 81*	5
MEGAMIX [M] / MARY'S BOY CHILD [RM]	*Ariola*	52	*24 Dec 88*	3
BONEY M MEGAMIX [M] *Both Megamixes are different.*	*Arista*	7	*5 Dec 92*	9
BROWN GIRL IN THE RING (REMIX '93) [RM]	*Arista*	38	*17 Apr 93*	3
MA BAKER / SOMEBODY SCREAM [M] *Chorus of Ma Baker is sampled.* *Above hit: BONEY M vs HORNY UNITED.*	*Logic*	22	*8 May 99*	2
DADDY COOL 2001 [RM] *Remixed by Jewels & Stone.*	*BMG*	47	*29 Dec 01*	1

ALBUMS:	HITS 8			WEEKS 143
TAKE THE HEAT OFF ME	*Atlantic*	40	*23 Apr 77*	15
LOVE FOR SALE	*Atlantic*	60	*6 Aug 77*	1
NIGHT FLIGHT TO VENUS	*Atlantic*	1	*29 Jul 78*	65
OCEANS OF FANTASY	*Atlantic*	1	*29 Sep 79*	18
THE MAGIC OF BONEY M - 20 GOLDEN HITS	*Atlantic*	1	*12 Apr 80*	26
THE BEST OF 10 YEARS - 32 SUPERHITS	*Stylus*	35	*6 Sep 86*	5
THE GREATEST HITS	*Telstar*	14	*27 Mar 93*	10
THE GREATEST HITS	*BMG*	66	*15 Dec 01*	3
Above 2 albums are different.				

BONFIRE — Germany

ALBUMS:	HITS 1			WEEKS 1
POINT BLANK	*MSA*	74	*21 Oct 89*	1

Graham BONNET — UK

SINGLES:	HITS 2			WEEKS 15
NIGHT GAMES	*Vertigo*	6	*21 Mar 81*	11
LIAR	*Vertigo*	51	*13 Jun 81*	4
ALBUMS:	**HITS 1**			**WEEKS 3**
LINE UP	*Vertigo*	62	*7 Nov 81*	3

Graham BONNEY with Johnny SCOTT and his Orchestra — UK

SINGLES:	HITS 1			WEEKS 8
SUPER GIRL	*Columbia*	19	*26 Mar 66*	8

BONO — Ireland

SINGLES:	HITS 4			WEEKS 25
IN A LIFETIME *Above hit: CLANNAD/ additional vocals: BONO.*	*RCA*	20	*25 Jan 86*	5
IN A LIFETIME [RI] *Above hit: CLANNAD (guest vocal: BONO).*	*RCA*	17	*10 Jun 89*	7
I'VE GOT YOU UNDER MY SKIN *[AA] listed with Stay (Faraway, So Close) by U2. It was not available on the 2nd CD format.* *Above hit: Frank SINATRA with BONO.*	*Island*	4	*4 Dec 93*	9
IN THE NAME OF THE FATHER *From the film of the same name.* *Above hit: BONO and Gavin FRIDAY.*	*Island*	46	*9 Apr 94*	2
NEW DAY *Official Single of the Net Aid concert, 9 Oct 99 at London, New York, Geneva. Charity record in aid of Net Aid, Wyclef Jean Foundation and War Child.* *Above hit: Wyclef JEAN featuring BONO.*	*Columbia*	23	*23 Oct 99*	2

BONZO DOG DOO-DAH BAND — UK

SINGLES:	HITS 1			WEEKS 14
I'M THE URBAN SPACEMAN *Produced by Paul McCartney under the pseudonym Apollo C. Vermouth.*	*Liberty*	5	*9 Nov 68*	14
ALBUMS:	**HITS 3**			**WEEKS 4**
DOUGHNUT IN GRANNY'S GREENHOUSE	*Liberty*	40	*18 Jan 69*	1
TADPOLES	*Liberty*	36	*30 Aug 69*	1
THE HISTORY OF THE BONZOS	*United Artists*	41	*22 Jun 74*	2

BOO - See R. KELLY

Betty BOO — UK

SINGLES:	HITS 7			WEEKS 55
HEY DJ/I CAN'T DANCE (TO THAT MUSIC YOUR PLAYING) / SKA TRAIN *Backing vocals: Claudia Fontaine. I Can't Dance originally recorded by Martha and the Vandellas.* *Above hit: BEATMASTERS featuring Betty BOO.*	*Rhythm King*	7	*12 Aug 89*	11
DOIN' THE DO *Samples Reparata and the Delrons' Captain Of Your Ship.*	*Rhythm King*	7	*19 May 90*	12
WHERE ARE YOU BABY?	*Rhythm King*	3	*11 Aug 90*	10
24 HOURS	*Rhythm King*	25	*1 Dec 90*	8
LET ME TAKE YOU THERE *Samples the Four Tops' It's All In The Game.*	*WEA*	12	*8 Aug 92*	8
I'M ON MY WAY *Tune based around the Beatles Lady Madonna.*	*WEA*	44	*3 Oct 92*	3
HANGOVER	*WEA*	50	*10 Apr 93*	3
ALBUMS:	**HITS 2**			**WEEKS 25**
BOOMANIA	*Rhythm King*	4	*22 Sep 90*	24
GRRR! IT'S BETTY BOO	*WEA*	62	*24 Oct 92*	1

BOO RADLEYS — UK

SINGLES:	HITS 12			WEEKS 27
DOES THIS HURT? / BOO! FOREVER	*Creation*	67	*20 Jun 92*	1
WISH I WAS SKINNY	*Creation*	75	*23 Oct 93*	1
BARNEY (. . . AND ME)	*Creation*	48	*12 Feb 94*	2
LAZARUS	*Creation*	50	*11 Jun 94*	2
Original reached No. 76 in 1992.				
WAKE UP BOO!	*Creation*	9	*11 Mar 95*	8
FIND THE ANSWER WITHIN	*Creation*	37	*13 May 95*	3
IT'S LULU	*Creation*	25	*29 Jul 95*	2
FROM THE BENCH AT BELVIDERE	*Creation*	24	*7 Oct 95*	2
WHAT'S IN THE BOX? (SEE WHATCHA GOT)	*Creation*	25	*17 Aug 96*	2
C'MON KIDS	*Creation*	18	*19 Oct 96*	2
RIDE THE TIGER	*Creation*	38	*1 Feb 97*	1
FREE HUEY	*Creation*	54	*17 Oct 98*	1
The Huey in the song is Huey Newton, a prominent member of the Black Panther movement in the 1960s.				
ALBUMS:	**HITS 5**			**WEEKS 29**
EVERYTHING'S ALRIGHT FOREVER	*Creation*	55	*4 Apr 92*	1
GIANT STEPS	*Creation*	17	*28 Aug 93*	4
WAKE UP!	*Creation*	1	*8 Apr 95*	21
C'MON KIDS	*Creation*	20	*21 Sep 96*	2
KINGSIZE	*Creation*	62	*31 Oct 98*	1

BOO-YAA T.R.I.B.E. — US

SINGLES:	HITS 2			WEEKS 6
PSYKO FUNK	*Fourth & Broadway*	43	*30 Jun 90*	3
ANOTHER BODY MURDERED	*Epic*	26	*6 Nov 93*	3
From the film 'Judgment Night'.				
Above hit: FAITH NO MORE and BOO-YAA TRIBE.				
ALBUMS:	**HITS 1**			**WEEKS 1**
NEW FUNKY NATION	*Fourth & Broadway*	74	*14 Apr 90*	1

BOOGIE BOX HIGH — UK

SINGLES:	HITS 1			WEEKS 11
JIVE TALKIN'	*Hardback*	7	*4 Jul 87*	11
Vocals by George Michael.				

BOOGIE DOWN PRODUCTIONS — US

SINGLES:	HITS 1			WEEKS 2
MY PHILOSOPHY / STOP THE VIOLENCE	*Jive*	69	*4 Jun 88*	2
ALBUMS:	**HITS 3**			**WEEKS 9**
BY ALL MEANS NECESSARY	*Jive*	38	*18 Jun 88*	3
GHETTO MUSIC: THE BLUEPRINT OF HIP HOP	*Jive*	32	*22 Jul 89*	4
EDUTAINMENT	*Jive*	52	*25 Aug 90*	2

BOOKER T. and the M.G.s — US

SINGLES:	HITS 4			WEEKS 43
SOUL LIMBO	*Stax*	30	*14 Dec 68*	9
Theme to BBC TV's cricket coverage.				
TIME IS TIGHT	*Stax*	4	*10 May 69*	18
From the film 'Uptight'.				
SOUL CLAP '69	*Stax*	35	*30 Aug 69*	4
GREEN ONIONS	*Atlantic*	7	*15 Dec 79*	12
Originally released in 1962.				
EPS:	**HITS 1**			**WEEKS 1**
R&B WITH BOOKER T VOL. 2	*Atlantic*	19	*27 Feb 65*	1
ALBUMS:	**HITS 2**			**WEEKS 5**
GREEN ONIONS	*London*	11	*25 Jul 64*	4
MCLEMORE AVENUE	*Stax*	70	*11 Jul 70*	1

Taka BOOM – See EYE TO EYE featuring Taka BOOM; Joey NEGRO

BOOM! — UK

SINGLES:	HITS 1			WEEKS 5
FALLING	*London*	11	*27 Jan 01*	5

BOOM BOOM ROOM — UK

SINGLES:	HITS 1			WEEKS 1
HERE COMES THE MAN	*Fun After All*	74	*8 Mar 86*	1

BOOMTOWN RATS — Ireland

SINGLES:	HITS 14			WEEKS 123
LOOKING AFTER NO. 1	*Ensign*	11	*27 Aug 77*	9
MARY OF THE 4TH FORM	*Ensign*	15	*19 Nov 77*	9
SHE'S SO MODERN	*Ensign*	12	*15 Apr 78*	11
LIKE CLOCKWORK	*Ensign*	6	*17 Jun 78*	13
RAT TRAP	*Ensign*	1	*14 Oct 78*	15
I DON'T LIKE MONDAYS	*Ensign*	1	*21 Jul 79*	12
Written about San Diego schoolgirl Brenda Spencer who shot two people because she didn't like Mondays.				
DIAMOND SMILES	*Ensign*	13	*17 Nov 79*	10
SOMEONE'S LOOKING AT YOU	*Ensign*	4	*26 Jan 80*	9
BANANA REPUBLIC	*Ensign*	3	*22 Nov 80*	11
THE ELEPHANTS GRAVEYARD (GUILTY)	*Mercury*	26	*31 Jan 81*	6
NEVER IN A MILLION YEARS	*Mercury*	62	*12 Dec 81*	4
HOUSE ON FIRE	*Mercury*	24	*20 Mar 82*	8
TONIGHT	*Mercury*	73	*18 Feb 84*	1
DRAG ME DOWN	*Mercury*	50	*19 May 84*	3
I DON'T LIKE MONDAYS [RI]	*Vertigo*	38	*2 Jul 94*	2
ALBUMS:	**HITS 6**			**WEEKS 96**
BOOMTOWN RATS	*Ensign*	18	*17 Sep 77*	11
A TONIC FOR THE TROOPS	*Ensign*	8	*8 Jul 78*	44
THE FINE ART OF SURFACING	*Ensign*	7	*3 Nov 79*	26
MONDO BONGO	*Mercury*	6	*24 Jan 81*	7
V DEEP	*Mercury*	64	*3 Apr 82*	5
LOUDMOUTH – THE BEST OF THE BOOMTOWN RATS AND BOB GELDOF	*Vertigo*	10	*9 Jul 94*	3
Includes solo and group material.				
Above hit: BOOMTOWN RATS and Bob GELDOF.				

Clint BOON EXPERIENCE! — UK

SINGLES:	HITS 3			WEEKS 3
WHITE NO SUGAR	*Artful*	61	*6 Nov 99*	1
Original release on the Rabid Badger label reached No. 84 in 1998.				
THE BIGGEST HORIZON	*Artful*	70	*5 Feb 00*	1
DO WHAT YOU DO (EARWORM SONG)	*Artful*	63	*5 Aug 00*	1

Daniel BOONE — UK

SINGLES:	HITS 3			WEEKS 3
DADDY DON'T YOU WALK SO FAST	*Penny Farthing*	17	*14 Aug 71*	15
BEAUTIFUL SUNDAY	*Penny Farthing*	48	*1 Apr 72*	1
BEAUTIFUL SUNDAY [RE]	*Penny Farthing*	21	*15 Apr 72*	9
THE BIGGEST HORIZON	*Artful*	70	*5 Feb 00*	1
DO WHAT YOU DO (EARWORM SONG)	*Artful*	63	*5 Aug 00*	1

Debby BOONE — US

SINGLES:	HITS 1			WEEKS 3
YOU LIGHT UP MY LIFE	*Warner Brothers*	48	*24 Dec 77*	3
From the film of the same name. Originally recorded by Kacey Cisyk.				

Pat BOONE — US

SINGLES:	HITS 26			WEEKS 308
AIN'T THAT A SHAME	*London*	7	*19 Nov 55*	9
I'LL BE HOME	*London*	1	*28 Apr 56*	22
Originally recorded by the Flamingos.				
LONG TALL SALLY	*London*	27	*28 Jul 56*	3
I ALMOST LOST MY MIND	*London*	14	*18 Aug 56*	7
Originally recorded by Ivory Joe Hunter.				
LONG TALL SALLY [RE]	*London*	18	*25 Aug 56*	4
FRIENDLY PERSUASION (THEE I LOVE)	*London*	3	*8 Dec 56*	21
From the film 'Friendly Persuasion'.				
AIN'T THAT A SHAME [RE]	*London*	22	*12 Jan 57*	2
I'LL BE HOME [RE]	*London*	19	*12 Jan 57*	2
DON'T FORBID ME	*London*	2	*2 Feb 57*	16
WHY BABY WHY	*London*	17	*27 Apr 57*	7
LOVE LETTERS IN THE SAND	*London*	2	*6 Jul 57*	21
Whistling by Neil Sedaka. Originally recorded by Ted Black.				
REMEMBER YOU'RE MINE / THERE'S A GOLD MINE IN THE SKY	*London*	5	*28 Sep 57*	18
There's A Gold Mine In Sky only listed for its first chart week.				
Above 2: Pat BOONE with Billy VAUGHN'S ORCHESTRA.				
APRIL LOVE	*London*	7	*7 Dec 57*	23
From the film of the same name.				
WHITE CHRISTMAS	*London*	29	*14 Dec 57*	1
Above hit: Pat BOONE with Mort LINDSEY and his Orchestra and the Artie MALVERN SINGERS.				
A WONDERFUL TIME UP THERE	*London*	2	*5 Apr 58*	17
Originally recorded by Sister Rosetta Tharpe.				

IT'S TOO SOON TO KNOW	*London*	7	*12 Apr 58*	12
Above 2 entries were separate sides of the same release, each had its own chart run. Originally recorded by the Orioles.				
SUGAR MOON	*London*	6	*28 Jun 58*	12
Originally recorded by Collins and Harlan.				
IF DREAMS CAME TRUE	*London*	16	*30 Aug 58*	11
GEE, BUT IT'S LONELY	*London*	30	*6 Dec 58*	1
Written by Phil Everly.				
I'LL REMEMBER TONIGHT	*London*	28	*17 Jan 59*	1
From the film 'Mardi Gras'.				
I'LL REMEMBER TONIGHT [RE-1ST]	*London*	21	*7 Feb 59*	1
I'LL REMEMBER TONIGHT [RE-2ND]	*London*	18	*21 Feb 59*	7
WITH THE WIND AND THE RAIN IN YOUR HAIR	*London*	21	*11 Apr 59*	3
FOR A PENNY	*London*	28	*23 May 59*	3
FOR A PENNY [RE]	*London*	19	*27 Jun 59*	6
TWIXT TWELVE AND TWENTY	*London*	18	*1 Aug 59*	6
TWIXT TWELVE AND TWENTY [RE]	*London*	26	*19 Sep 59*	1
WALKING THE FLOOR OVER YOU	*London*	40	*25 Jun 60*	2
Originally recorded by Ernest Tubb in 1941.				
WALKING THE FLOOR OVER YOU [RE-1ST]	*London*	46	*16 Jul 60*	1
WALKING THE FLOOR OVER YOU [RE-2ND]	*London*	39	*6 Aug 60*	2
MOODY RIVER	*London*	18	*8 Jul 61*	10
JOHNNY WILL	*London*	4	*9 Dec 61*	13
Written by Paul Evans.				
I'LL SEE YOU IN MY DREAMS	*London*	27	*17 Feb 62*	9
QUANDO, QUANDO, QUANDO	*London*	41	*26 May 62*	4
Originally recorded by Tony Renis.				
SPEEDY GONZALES	*London*	2	*14 Jul 62*	19
Originally recorded by Dave Dante.				
THE MAIN ATTRACTION	*London*	12	*17 Nov 62*	11
From the film of the same name.				
EPS:	**HITS 1**			**WEEKS 5**
JOURNEY TO THE CENTRE OF THE EARTH [OST]	*London*	8	*12 Mar 60*	5
ALBUMS:	**HITS 4**			**WEEKS 12**
STARDUST	*London*	10	*22 Nov 58*	1
HYMNS WE HAVE LOVED	*London*	12	*28 May 60*	2
HYMNS WE LOVE	*London*	14	*25 Jun 60*	1
PAT BOONE ORIGINALS	*ABC*	16	*24 Apr 76*	8

BOOOM - See Boris DLUGOSCH

BOOT ROOM BOYZ - See LIVERPOOL FOOTBALL CLUB

Duke BOOTEE - See Melle MEL

BOOTH and the BAD ANGEL — US/UK

(See also Angelo Badalamenti.)

SINGLES:	**HITS 2**			**WEEKS 4**
I BELIEVE	*Fontana*	25	*22 Jun 96*	3
FALL IN LOVE WITH ME	*Mercury*	57	*11 Jul 98*	1
From the film 'Martha Meet Frank, Daniel & Laurence'.				
Above hit: BOOTH and the BAD ANGEL featuring Tim BOOTH of JAMES.				
ALBUMS:	**HITS 1**			**WEEKS 2**
BOOTH AND THE BAD ANGEL	*Fontana*	35	*13 Jul 96*	2

Ken BOOTHE — Jamaica

SINGLES:	**HITS 2**			**WEEKS 22**
EVERYTHING I OWN	*Trojan*	1	*21 Sep 74*	12
CRYING OVER YOU	*Trojan*	11	*14 Dec 74*	10

BOOTHILL FOOT-TAPPERS — UK

SINGLES:	**HITS 1**			**WEEKS 3**
GET YOUR FEET OUT OF MY SHOES	*Go! Discs*	64	*14 Jul 84*	3

BOOTSY'S RUBBER BAND — US

SINGLES:	**HITS 1**			**WEEKS 3**
BOOTZILLA	*Warner Brothers*	43	*8 Jul 78*	3

BOOTZILLA ORCHESTRA - See Malcolm McLAREN

Victor BORGE — Denmark

EPS:	**HITS 1**			**WEEKS 2**
PHONETIC PUNCTUATION	*Philips*	15	*7 Jan 61*	2

BOSS — US

(See also David Morales.)

SINGLES:	HITS 1			WEEKS 1
CONGO	*Cooltempo*	54	*27 Aug 94*	1

BOSTON — US

SINGLES:	HITS 2			WEEKS 13
MORE THAN A FEELING	*Epic*	22	*29 Jan 77*	8
DON'T LOOK BACK	*Epic*	43	*7 Oct 78*	5
ALBUMS:	**HITS 4**			**WEEKS 44**
BOSTON	*Epic*	11	*5 Feb 77*	20
DON'T LOOK BACK	*Epic*	9	*9 Sep 78*	10
BOSTON [RE]	*Epic*	58	*4 Apr 81*	2
Re-released with a different catalogue number.				
THIRD STAGE	*MCA*	37	*18 Oct 86*	11
WALK ON	*MCA*	56	*25 Jun 94*	1

Eve BOSWELL with Glenn SOMERS and his ORCHESTRA — Hungary

SINGLES:	HITS 1			WEEKS 13
PICKIN' A - CHICKEN	*Parlophone*	9	*31 Dec 55*	7
PICKIN' A - CHICKEN [RE-1ST]	*Parlophone*	16	*3 Mar 56*	3
PICKIN' A - CHICKEN [RE-2ND]	*Parlophone*	20	*7 Apr 56*	3

La BOUCHE — US

SINGLES:	HITS 3			WEEKS 12
SWEET DREAMS	*Bell*	63	*24 Sep 94*	1
BE MY LOVER	*Arista*	27	*15 Jul 95*	4
FALLING IN LOVE	*Arista*	43	*30 Sep 95*	2
BE MY LOVER [RI]	*Arista*	25	*2 Mar 96*	4
SWEET DREAMS [RI]	*Arista*	44	*7 Sep 96*	1

Judy BOUCHER — UK

SINGLES:	HITS 2			WEEKS 23
CAN'T BE WITH YOU TONIGHT	*Orbitone*	2	*4 Apr 87*	14
YOU CAUGHT MY EYE	*Orbitone*	18	*4 Jul 87*	9
ALBUMS:	**HITS 1**			**WEEKS 1**
CAN'T BE WITH YOU TONIGHT	*Orbitone*	95	*25 Apr 87*	1

Peter BOUNCER - See SHUT UP AND DANCE

BOUNCING CZECKS featuring Charlene DUCALL — UK

SINGLES:	HITS 1			WEEKS 1
I'M A LITTLE CHRISTMAS CRACKER	*RCA*	72	*29 Dec 84*	1

BOUNTY KILLER (featuring COCOA BROVAZ, Nona HENDRYX and FREE) — Jamaica

SINGLES:	HITS 1			WEEKS 1
IT'S A PARTY	*Edel*	65	*27 Feb 99*	1
Additional vocals by Mr. Gentleman and DaNaCeE.				

BOURGEOIS TAGG — US

SINGLES:	HITS 1			WEEKS 6
I DON'T MIND AT ALL	*Island*	35	*6 Feb 88*	6

BOURGIE BOURGIE — UK

SINGLES:	HITS 1			WEEKS 4
BREAKING POINT	*MCA*	48	*3 Mar 84*	4

Toby BOURKE with George MICHAEL — UK

(See also George Michael.)

SINGLES:	HITS 1			WEEKS 4
WALTZ AWAY DREAMING	*Aegean*	10	*7 Jun 97*	4
Dedicated to George Michael's late mother.				

Aletia BOURNE - See ANGELHEART

BOW WOW WOW — UK

SINGLES:	HITS 9			WEEKS 54
C'30, C'60, C'90, G0	*EMI*	34	*26 Jul 80*	7
The first cassette single released.				
YOUR CASSETTE PET [EP]	*EMI*	58	*6 Dec 80*	6
Cassette only release. Lead track: Louis Quatorze, which was listed on its own for the chart of 6 Dec 80.				

W.O.R.K. (N.O. NAH NO! NO! MY DADDY DON'T)	*EMI*	62	*28 Mar 81*	3
PRINCE OF DARKNESS	*RCA*	58	*15 Aug 81*	4
CHIHUAHUA	*RCA*	51	*7 Nov 81*	4
GO WILD IN THE COUNTRY	*RCA*	7	*30 Jan 82*	13
SEE JUNGLE! (JUNGLE BOY) / (I'M A) TV SAVAGE	*RCA*	45	*1 May 82*	3
I WANT CANDY	*RCA*	9	*5 Jun 82*	8
Originally recorded by the Strangeloves. Reached No. 12 in the US in 1965.				
LOUIS QUATORZE [RI]	*RCA*	66	*31 Jul 82*	2
The lead track from the Your Cassette Pet [EP].				
DO YOU WANNA HOLD ME?	*RCA*	47	*12 Mar 83*	4
ALBUMS:	**HITS 2**			**WEEKS 38**
SEE JUNGLE! SEE JUNGLE! GO JOIN YOUR GANG YEAH, CITY ALL OVER! GO APE CRAZY!	*RCA*	26	*24 Oct 81*	32
I WANT CANDY	*EMI*	26	*7 Aug 82*	6

BOWA featuring MALA — US

SINGLES:	**HITS 1**			**WEEKS 1**
DIFFERENT STORY	*Dead Dead Good*	64	*7 Dec 91*	1

Dane BOWERS - See DANE

David BOWIE — UK

SINGLES:	**HITS 63**			**WEEKS 447**
SPACE ODDITY	*Philips*	48	*6 Sep 69*	1
SPACE ODDITY [RE]	*Philips*	5	*20 Sep 69*	13
STARMAN	*RCA Victor*	10	*24 Jun 72*	11
JOHN, I'M ONLY DANCING	*RCA Victor*	12	*16 Sep 72*	10
THE JEAN GENIE	*RCA Victor*	2	*9 Dec 72*	13
DRIVE-IN SATURDAY (SEATTLE - PHOENIX)	*RCA Victor*	3	*14 Apr 73*	10
LIFE ON MARS?	*RCA Victor*	3	*30 Jun 73*	13
THE LAUGHING GNOME	*Deram*	6	*15 Sep 73*	12
Originally released in 1967.				
SORROW	*RCA Victor*	3	*20 Oct 73*	15
REBEL REBEL	*RCA Victor*	5	*23 Feb 74*	7
ROCK 'N' ROLL SUICIDE	*RCA Victor*	22	*20 Apr 74*	7
DIAMOND DOGS	*RCA Victor*	21	*22 Jun 74*	6
KNOCK ON WOOD	*RCA Victor*	10	*28 Sep 74*	6
Above 3: BOWIE.				
YOUNG AMERICANS	*RCA Victor*	18	*1 Mar 75*	7
Features backing vocals by Luther Vandross and David Sanborn on saxophone.				
FAME	*RCA Victor*	17	*2 Aug 75*	8
Co written and backing vocals by John Lennon.				
SPACE ODDITY [RI]	*RCA Victor Maximillion*	1	*11 Oct 75*	10
GOLDEN YEARS	*RCA Victor*	8	*29 Nov 75*	10
Above hit: BOWIE.				
TVC 15	*RCA Victor*	33	*22 May 76*	4
SOUND AND VISION	*RCA Victor*	3	*19 Feb 77*	11
Backing vocals by Mary Hopkin.				
HEROES	*RCA Victor*	24	*15 Oct 77*	8
BEAUTY AND THE BEAST	*RCA Victor*	39	*21 Jan 78*	3
BREAKING GLASS [EP]	*RCA Victor*	54	*2 Dec 78*	7
Lead track: Breaking Glass. Live recordings from Philadelphia (8 & 29 Apr 78).				
BOYS KEEP SWINGING	*RCA Victor*	7	*5 May 79*	10
D.J.	*RCA Victor*	29	*21 Jul 79*	5
JOHN, I'M ONLY DANCING (AGAIN)(1975)/JOHN, I'M ONLY DANCING (1972) [RR]	*RCA*	12	*15 Dec 79*	8
ALABAMA SONG	*RCA*	23	*1 Mar 80*	5
Originally recorded by Lotte Lenya.				
ASHES TO ASHES	*RCA*	1	*16 Aug 80*	10
FASHION	*RCA*	5	*1 Nov 80*	12
SCARY MONSTERS (AND SUPER CREEPS)	*RCA*	20	*10 Jan 81*	6
UP THE HILL BACKWARDS	*RCA*	32	*28 Mar 81*	6
UNDER PRESSURE	*EMI*	1	*14 Nov 81*	11
Above hit: QUEEN and David BOWIE.				
WILD IS THE WIND	*RCA*	24	*28 Nov 81*	10
BAAL'S HYMN [EP]	*RCA*	29	*6 Mar 82*	5
From the BBC TV production of Berthold Brecht's 'Baal' in which Bowie took title role. Lead track: Baal's Hymm.				
CAT PEOPLE (PUTTING OUT FIRE)	*MCA*	26	*10 Apr 82*	6
From the film of the same name.				
PEACE ON EARTH / LITTLE DRUMMER BOY [M]	*RCA*	3	*27 Nov 82*	8
Recorded in 1977 on Bing Crosby's Christmas TV show.				
Above hit: David BOWIE and Bing CROSBY.				
LET'S DANCE	*EMI America*	1	*26 Mar 83*	14
CHINA GIRL	*EMI America*	2	*11 Jun 83*	8
Originally recorded by Iggy Pop.				
MODERN LOVE	*EMI America*	2	*24 Sep 83*	8
Features Stevie Ray Vaughan on guitar.				
WHITE LIGHT/WHITE HEAT	*RCA*	46	*5 Nov 83*	3

BLUE JEAN	*EMI America*	6	*22 Sep 84*	8
TONIGHT	*EMI America*	53	*8 Dec 84*	4
Backing vocals by Tina Turner.				
THIS IS NOT AMERICA (THE THEME FROM "THE FALCON AND THE SNOWMAN")	*EMI America*	14	*9 Feb 85*	7
From the film 'The Falcon And The Snowman'.				
Above hit: David BOWIE/Pat METHENY GROUP.				
LOVING THE ALIEN	*EMI America*	19	*8 Jun 85*	6
LOVING THE ALIEN [RE]	*EMI America*	67	*27 Jul 85*	1
DANCING IN THE STREET	*EMI America*	1	*7 Sep 85*	12
Above hit: David BOWIE and Mick JAGGER.				
ABSOLUTE BEGINNERS	*Virgin*	2	*15 Mar 86*	9
From the film of the same name.				
UNDERGROUND	*EMI America*	21	*21 Jun 86*	6
From the film 'Labyrinth'.				
WHEN THE WIND BLOWS	*Virgin*	44	*8 Nov 86*	4
From the film of the same name.				
DAY-IN DAY-OUT	*EMI America*	17	*4 Apr 87*	6
TIME WILL CRAWL	*EMI America*	33	*27 Jun 87*	4
NEVER LET ME DOWN	*EMI America*	34	*29 Aug 87*	6
FAME 90 (GASS MIX) [RM]	*EMI USA*	28	*7 Apr 90*	4
Remixed by Jon Gass. From the film 'Pretty Woman'.				
REAL COOL WORLD	*Warner Brothers*	53	*22 Aug 92*	1
Theme from the film 'Cool World'.				
JUMP THEY SAY	*Arista*	9	*27 Mar 93*	6
BLACK TIE WHITE NOISE	*Arista*	36	*12 Jun 93*	2
Above hit: David BOWIE featuring Al B. SURE!				
MIRACLE GOODNIGHT	*Arista*	40	*23 Oct 93*	2
BUDDHA OF SUBURBIA	*Arista*	35	*4 Dec 93*	3
Theme from the BBC TV series of the same name.				
Above hit: David BOWIE (featuring Lenny KRAVITZ on guitar).				
THE HEARTS FILTHY LESSON	*RCA*	35	*23 Sep 95*	2
STRANGERS WHEN WE MEET / THE MAN WHO SOLD THE WORLD (LIVE)	*RCA*	39	*2 Dec 95*	2
HALLO SPACEBOY	*RCA*	12	*2 Mar 96*	4
Duet with the Pet Shop Boys.				
LITTLE WONDER	*RCA*	14	*8 Feb 97*	3
DEAD MAN WALKING	*RCA*	32	*26 Apr 97*	2
SEVEN YEARS IN TIBET	*RCA*	61	*30 Aug 97*	1
From the film of the same name.				
I CAN'T READ	*Velvet*	73	*21 Feb 98*	1
From the film 'The Ice Storm'.				
THURSDAY'S CHILD	*Virgin*	16	*2 Oct 99*	3
UNDER PRESSURE [RM]	*Parlophone*	14	*18 Dec 99*	7
Remixed by Queen, Joshua J. Macrae and Justin Shirley Smith.				
Above hit: QUEEN + David BOWIE.				
SURVIVE	*Virgin*	20	*5 Feb 00*	2
SEVEN	*Virgin*	32	*29 Jul 00*	2
ALBUMS:	**HITS 36**			**WEEKS 931**
THE RISE AND FALL OF ZIGGY STARDUST AND THE SPIDERS FROM MARS	*RCA Victor*	5	*1 Jul 72*	106
HUNKY DORY	*RCA Victor*	3	*23 Sep 72*	69
THE MAN WHO SOLD THE WORLD	*RCA Victor*	26	*25 Nov 72*	22
Originally released in April 71 with 'dress' cover sleeve.				
SPACE ODDITY	*RCA Victor*	17	*25 Nov 72*	37
Originally titled David Bowie when released on the Philips label in 1969.				
ALADDIN SANE	*RCA Victor*	1	*5 May 73*	47
PIN-UPS	*RCA Victor*	1	*3 Nov 73*	21
DIAMOND DOGS	*RCA Victor*	1	*8 Jun 74*	17
DAVID LIVE	*RCA Victor*	2	*16 Nov 74*	12
Live recordings from The Tower, Philadelphia, during his 1974 "Diamond Dogs" tour.				
YOUNG AMERICANS	*RCA Victor*	2	*5 Apr 75*	12
STATION TO STATION	*RCA Victor*	5	*7 Feb 76*	16
CHANGESONEBOWIE	*RCA Victor*	2	*12 Jun 76*	28
Compilation. Includes re-entries in 1983.				
LOW	*RCA Victor*	2	*29 Jan 77*	18
HEROES	*RCA Victor*	3	*29 Oct 77*	18
STAGE	*RCA Victor*	5	*14 Oct 78*	10
Live recordings from Philadelphia (8 & 29 Apr 78).				
LODGER	*RCA Victor*	4	*9 Jun 79*	17
SCARY MONSTERS AND SUPER CREEPS	*RCA*	1	*27 Sep 80*	32
THE VERY BEST OF DAVID BOWIE	*K-Tel*	3	*10 Jan 81*	20
HUNKY DORY [RI-1ST]	*RCA International*	32	*17 Jan 81*	51
Peak position reached in 1983 (1981 peak No. 68).				
THE RISE AND FALL OF ZIGGY STARDUST AND THE SPIDERS FROM MARS [RI-1ST]	*RCA International*	33	*31 Jan 81*	62
Peak position reached in 1983. (1981 peak No. 61).				
CHANGESTWOBOWIE	*RCA*	24	*28 Nov 81*	17
Compilation.				

ALADDIN SANE [RI-1ST]	*RCA International*	49	*6 Mar 82*	24
Peak position reached in 1983 (1982 peak No. 98).				
RARE	*RCA*	34	*15 Jan 83*	11
LET'S DANCE	*EMI America*	1	*23 Apr 83*	56
PIN-UPS [RI-1ST]	*RCA International*	57	*30 Apr 83*	15
THE MAN WHO SOLD THE WORLD [RI-1ST]	*RCA International*	64	*30 Apr 83*	8
DIAMOND DOGS [RI-1ST]	*RCA International*	60	*14 May 83*	14
HEROES [RI]	*RCA International*	75	*11 Jun 83*	8
LOW [RI-1ST]	*RCA International*	85	*11 Jun 83*	5
GOLDEN YEARS	*RCA*	33	*20 Aug 83*	5
ZIGGY STARDUST - THE MOTION PICTURE	*RCA*	17	*5 Nov 83*	6
FAME AND FASHION (BOWIE'S ALL TIME GREATEST HITS)	*RCA*	40	*28 Apr 84*	6
LOVE YOU TILL TUESDAY	*Deram*	53	*19 May 84*	4
TONIGHT	*EMI America*	1	*6 Oct 84*	19
NEVER LET ME DOWN	*EMI America*	6	*2 May 87*	16
CHANGESBOWIE	*EMI*	1	*24 Mar 90*	29
Compilation.				
HUNKY DORY [RI-2ND]	*EMI*	39	*14 Apr 90*	3
Includes re-entry in 1997.				
SPACE ODDITY [RI]	*EMI*	64	*14 Apr 90*	1
THE MAN WHO SOLD THE WORLD [RI-2ND]	*EMI*	66	*14 Apr 90*	1
THE RISE AND FALL OF ZIGGY STARDUST AND THE SPIDERS FROM MARS [RI-2ND]	*EMI*	25	*23 Jun 90*	4
ALADDIN SANE [RI-2ND]	*EMI*	43	*28 Jul 90*	1
PIN-UPS [RI-2ND]	*EMI*	52	*28 Jul 90*	1
DIAMOND DOGS [RI-2ND]	*EMI*	67	*27 Oct 90*	3
Includes re-entry in 1997.				
YOUNG AMERICANS [RI]	*EMI*	54	*4 May 91*	1
STATION TO STATION [RI]	*EMI*	57	*4 May 91*	1
LOW [RI-2ND]	*EMI*	64	*7 Sep 91*	1
All re-issues listed above were available for the first time on CD and included bonus tracks.				
BLACK TIE WHITE NOISE	*Arista*	1	*17 Apr 93*	11
THE SINGLES COLLECTION	*EMI*	9	*20 Nov 93*	15
SANTA MONICA '72	*Trident*	74	*7 May 94*	1
OUTSIDE	*RCA*	8	*7 Oct 95*	4
EARTHLING	*RCA*	6	*15 Feb 97*	4
THE BEST OF DAVID BOWIE 1969/1974	*EMI*	13	*8 Nov 97*	10
THE BEST OF DAVID BOWIE 1974/1979	*EMI*	39	*2 May 98*	2
HOURS . . .	*Virgin*	5	*16 Oct 99*	5
BOWIE AT THE BEEB - THE BEST OF THE BBC SESSIONS 68-72	*EMI*	7	*7 Oct 00*	4
Limited edition triple CD of BBC sessions.				

George BOWYER and William McCLINTOCK BUNBURY — UK

SINGLES:	HITS 1			WEEKS 2
GUARDIANS OF THE LAND	*BOYS*	33	*22 Aug 98*	2
Song is a defence of fox hunting. Backing fiddle and banjo playing by the Pedigrees.				

BOX TOPS — US

SINGLES:	HITS 3			WEEKS 33
THE LETTER	*Stateside*	5	*16 Sep 67*	12
CRY LIKE A BABY	*Bell*	15	*23 Mar 68*	12
SOUL DEEP	*Bell*	22	*23 Aug 69*	9

BOXCAR WILLIE — US

ALBUMS:	HITS 1			WEEKS 12
KING OF THE ROAD	*Warwick*	5	*31 May 80*	12

BOY GEORGE — UK

(See also Jesus Loves You; Culture Club.)

SINGLES:	HITS 13			WEEKS 46
EVERYTHING I OWN	*Virgin*	1	*7 Mar 87*	9
KEEP ME IN MIND	*Virgin*	29	*6 Jun 87*	4
SOLD	*Virgin*	24	*18 Jul 87*	5
TO BE REBORN	*Virgin*	13	*21 Nov 87*	7
LIVE MY LIFE	*Virgin*	62	*5 Mar 88*	2
NO CLAUSE 28	*Virgin*	57	*18 Jun 88*	3
DON'T CRY	*Virgin*	60	*8 Oct 88*	2
DON'T TAKE MY MIND ON A TRIP	*Virgin*	68	*4 Mar 89*	2
THE CRYING GAME	*Spaghetti*	22	*19 Sep 92*	4
From the film of the same name.				
MORE THAN LIKELY	*Gee Street*	40	*12 Jun 93*	3
Above hit: PM DAWN featuring BOY GEORGE.				
FUNTIME	*Virgin*	45	*1 Apr 95*	2
Originally recorded by Iggy Pop.				
IL ADORE	*Virgin*	50	*1 Jul 95*	2
SAME THING IN REVERSE	*Virgin*	56	*21 Oct 95*	1

ALBUMS:	HITS 4			WEEKS 14
SOLD	*Virgin*	29	*27 Jun 87*	6
AT WORST . . . THE BEST OF BOY GEORGE & CULTURE CLUB	*Virgin*	24	*2 Oct 93*	5
Also includes Jesus Loves You tracks.				
Above hit: BOY GEORGE/CULTURE CLUB.				
THE DEVIL IN SISTER GEORGE	*Virgin*	26	*12 Mar 94*	2
Remix album.				
Above hit: BOY GEORGE/JESUS LOVES YOU/CULTURE CLUB.				
CHEAPNESS AND BEAUTY	*Virgin*	44	*3 Jun 95*	1

BOY MEETS GIRL — US

SINGLES:	HITS 1			WEEKS 13
WAITING FOR A STAR TO FALL	*RCA*	9	*3 Dec 88*	13
ALBUMS:	**HITS 1**			**WEEKS 1**
REEL LIFE	*RCA*	74	*4 Feb 89*	1

BOY WUNDA – See PROGRESS presents The BOY WUNDA

Max BOYCE — UK

ALBUMS:	HITS 7			WEEKS 105
LIVE AT TREORCHY	*One Up*	21	*5 Jul 75*	32
Live recordings from the Treorchy Rugby Club, Rhondda Valley, 23 Nov 73.				
WE ALL HAD DOCTORS' PAPERS	*EMI*	1	*1 Nov 75*	17
Live recording from Pontardulais Rugby Football Club.				
THE INCREDIBLE PLAN	*EMI*	9	*20 Nov 76*	12
THE ROAD AND THE MILES	*EMI*	50	*7 Jan 78*	3
LIVE AT TREORCHY [RE]	*One Up*	42	*11 Mar 78*	6
Re-released with a different catalogue number.				
I KNOW COS I WAS THERE	*EMI*	6	*27 May 78*	14
NOT THAT I'M BIASED	*EMI*	27	*13 Oct 79*	13
ME AND BILLY WILLIAMS	*EMI*	37	*15 Nov 80*	8

Jimmy BOYD — US

SINGLES:	HITS 2			WEEKS 22
TELL ME A STORY	*Philips*	5	*9 May 53*	15
Features accompaniment by Norman Luboff and Carl Fischer on piano.				
Above hit: Jimmy BOYD-Frankie LAINE.				
TELL ME A STORY [RE]	*Philips*	12	*12 Sep 53*	1
I SAW MOMMY KISSING SANTA CLAUS	*Columbia*	3	*28 Nov 53*	6

Jacqueline BOYER — France

SINGLES:	HITS 1			WEEKS 2
TOM PILLIBI	*Columbia*	33	*30 Apr 60*	2
Eurovision Song Contest winner in 1960.				

BOYS — US

SINGLES:	HITS 2			WEEKS 5
DIAL MY HEART	*Motown*	61	*12 Nov 88*	2
CRAZY	*Motown*	57	*29 Sep 90*	3
ALBUMS:	**HITS 1**			**WEEKS 1**
THE BOYS	*NEMS*	50	*1 Oct 77*	1

BOYSTOWN GANG — US

SINGLES:	HITS 3			WEEKS 20
AIN'T NO MOUNTAIN HIGH ENOUGH/REMEMBER ME [M]	*WEA*	46	*22 Aug 81*	6
CAN'T TAKE MY EYES OFF YOU	*ERC*	4	*31 Jul 82*	11
Original by Frankie Valli reached No. 2 in the US in 1967.				
SIGNED, SEALED, DELIVERED (I'M YOURS)	*ERC*	50	*9 Oct 82*	3

BOYZ II MEN — US

SINGLES:	HITS 12			WEEKS 81
END OF THE ROAD	*Motown*	1	*5 Sep 92*	21
From the film 'Boomerang'.				
MOTOWNPHILLY	*Motown*	23	*19 Dec 92*	6
Rap is by Michael Bivins of Bell Biv Devoe.				
IN THE STILL OF THE NITE (I'LL REMEMBER)	*Motown*	27	*27 Feb 93*	4
From the film 'The Jacksons – An American Dream'.				
I'LL MAKE LOVE TO YOU	*Motown*	5	*3 Sep 94*	12
ON BENDED KNEE	*Motown*	20	*26 Nov 94*	3
I'LL MAKE LOVE TO YOU [RE]	*Motown*	57	*24 Dec 94*	3
THANK YOU	*Motown*	26	*22 Apr 95*	3
Samples La-Di-Da-Di by Doug E.Fresh.				
WATER RUNS DRY	*Motown*	24	*8 Jul 95*	3

ONE SWEET DAY	*Columbia*	6	*9 Dec 95*	11
Song spent 16 weeks at No. 1 in the US.				
Above hit: Mariah CAREY and BOYZ II MEN.				
HEY LOVER	*Def Jam*	17	*20 Jan 96*	4
Based on Michael Jackson's Lady In My Life.				
Above hit: LL COOL J featuring BOYZ II MEN.				
4 SEASONS OF LONELINESS	*Motown*	10	*20 Sep 97*	6
A SONG FOR MAMA	*Motown*	34	*6 Dec 97*	2
CAN'T LET HER GO	*Motown*	23	*25 Jul 98*	3
ALBUMS:	**HITS 4**			**WEEKS 29**
COOLEYHIGHHARMONY	*Motown*	7	*31 Oct 92*	18
II	*Motown*	17	*24 Sep 94*	5
EVOLUTION	*Motown*	12	*4 Oct 97*	5
NATHAN MICHAEL SHAWN WANYA	*Universal*	54	*23 Sep 00*	1

BOYZONE — Ireland

SINGLES:	**HITS 16**			**WEEKS 213**
LOVE ME FOR A REASON	*Polydor*	2	*10 Dec 94*	13
KEY TO MY LIFE	*Polydor*	3	*29 Apr 95*	8
SO GOOD	*Polydor*	3	*12 Aug 95*	6
FATHER AND SON	*Polydor*	2	*25 Nov 95*	16
Originally recorded by Cat Stevens.				
COMING HOME NOW	*Polydor*	4	*9 Mar 96*	9
WORDS	*Polydor*	1	*19 Oct 96*	14
A DIFFERENT BEAT	*Polydor*	1	*14 Dec 96*	10
A DIFFERENT BEAT [RE-1ST]	*Polydor*	74	*1 Mar 97*	1
A DIFFERENT BEAT [RE-2ND]	*Polydor*	62	*15 Mar 97*	4
ISN'T IT A WONDER	*Polydor*	2	*22 Mar 97*	7
ISN'T IT A WONDER [RE]	*Polydor*	44	*17 May 97*	7
PICTURE OF YOU	*Polydor*	2	*2 Aug 97*	18
From the film 'Bean: The Movie'.				
BABY CAN I HOLD YOU / SHOOTING STAR	*Polydor*	2	*6 Dec 97*	14
Baby Can I Hold You was originally recorded by Tracy Chapman in 1988. Shooting Star from the film 'Hercules'.				
ALL THAT I NEED	*Polydor*	1	*2 May 98*	10
ALL THAT I NEED [RE]	*Polydor*	49	*18 Jul 98*	4
NO MATTER WHAT	*Polydor*	1	*15 Aug 98*	15
From the musical 'Whistle Down The Wind'. At the request of Polydor, the single was removed from chart while at No. 34.				
I LOVE THE WAY YOU LOVE ME	*Polydor*	2	*5 Dec 98*	13
Originally recorded by John Michael Montgomery.				
WHEN THE GOING GETS TOUGH	*Polydor*	1	*13 Mar 99*	14
Charity record in aid of Comic Relief.				
YOU NEEDED ME	*Polydor*	1	*22 May 99*	12
WHEN THE GOING GETS TOUGH [RE]	*Polydor*	57	*17 Jul 99*	2
YOU NEEDED ME [RE]	*Polydor*	60	*28 Aug 99*	3
EVERY DAY I LOVE YOU	*Polydor*	3	*4 Dec 99*	13
ALBUMS:	**HITS 4**			**WEEKS 194**
SAID AND DONE	*Polydor*	1	*2 Sep 95*	58
A DIFFERENT BEAT	*Polydor*	1	*9 Nov 96*	24
WHERE WE BELONG	*Polydor*	1	*6 Jun 98*	55
... BY REQUEST	*Polydor*	1	*12 Jun 99*	57
Includes Ronan Keating's solo single When You Say Nothing At All.				

BRAD — US

SINGLES:	**HITS 1**			**WEEKS 1**
20TH CENTURY	*Epic*	64	*26 Jun 93*	1
ALBUMS:	**HITS 1**			**WEEKS 1**
SHAME	*Epic*	72	*15 May 93*	1

James Dean BRADFIELD - See 808 STATE; MANIC STREET PREACHERS

Scott BRADLEY — UK

SINGLES:	**HITS 1**			**WEEKS 1**
ZOOM	*Hidden Agenda*	61	*15 Oct 94*	1
Backing vocals by Motown session singer Pat Lewis.				

Paul BRADY — UK

SINGLES:	**HITS 1**			**WEEKS 1**
THE WORLD IS WHAT YOU MAKE IT	*Mercury*	67	*13 Jan 96*	1
Theme from the ITV series 'Faith In The Future'.				
ALBUMS:	**HITS 1**			**WEEKS 1**
TRICK OR TREAT	*Fontana*	62	*6 Apr 91*	1

Billy BRAGG — UK

(See also Billy Bragg and Wilco.)

SINGLES:	HITS 12			WEEKS 51
BETWEEN THE WARS [EP]	*Go! Discs*	15	*16 Mar 85*	6
Lead track: Between The Wars.				
DAYS LIKE THESE	*Go! Discs*	43	*28 Dec 85*	5
LEVI STUBBS TEARS [EP]	*Go! Discs*	29	*28 Jun 86*	6
Lead track; Levi Stubbs Tears.				
GREETINGS TO THE NEW BRUNETTE	*Go! Discs*	58	*15 Nov 86*	2
Above hit: Billy BRAGG with Johnny MARR and Kirsty MacCOLL.				
SHE'S LEAVING HOME	*Childline*	1	*14 May 88*	11
Charity record in aid of Childline. [AA] listed with With A Little Help From My Friends by Wet Wet Wet.				
Above hit: Billy BRAGG with Cara TIVEY.				
WAITING FOR THE GREAT LEAP FORWARDS	*Go! Discs*	52	*10 Sep 88*	3
WON'T TALK ABOUT IT	*Go.Beat*	29	*8 Jul 89*	6
Above hit: Norman COOK featuring Billy BRAGG.				
SEXUALITY	*Go! Discs*	27	*6 Jul 91*	5
YOU WOKE UP MY NEIGHBOURHOOD	*Go! Discs*	54	*7 Sep 91*	2
ACCIDENT WAITING TO HAPPEN [EP]	*Go! Discs*	33	*29 Feb 92*	3
Lead track: Accident Waiting To Happen.				
UPFIELD	*Cooking Vinyl*	46	*31 Aug 96*	1
THE BOY DONE GOOD	*Cooking Vinyl*	55	*17 May 97*	1

ALBUMS:	HITS 10			WEEKS 83
LIFE'S A RIOT WITH SPY VS SPY	*Go! Discs*	32	*21 Jan 84*	15
BREWING UP WITH BILLY BRAGG	*Go! Discs*	16	*20 Oct 84*	21
LIFE'S A RIOT WITH SPY VS SPY [RE]	*Go! Discs*	30	*2 Feb 85*	15
TALKING WITH THE TAXMAN ABOUT POETRY	*Go! Discs*	8	*4 Oct 86*	8
BACK TO BASICS	*Go! Discs*	37	*13 Jun 87*	4
WORKERS' PLAYTIME	*Go! Discs*	17	*1 Oct 88*	4
THE INTERNATIONALE	*Utility*	34	*12 May 90*	4
DON'T TRY THIS AT HOME	*Go! Discs*	8	*28 Sep 91*	6
WILLIAM BLOKE	*Cooking Vinyl*	16	*21 Sep 96*	3
BLOKE ON BLOKE	*Cooking Vinyl*	72	*28 Jun 97*	1
Album of rarities and previously unavailable tracks.				
REACHING TO THE CONVERTED	*Cooking Vinyl*	41	*11 Sep 99*	2
Compilation of rarities, B-sides and live recordings.				

Billy BRAGG and WILCO — UK/US

(See also Billy Bragg; Wilco.)

ALBUMS:	HITS 2			WEEKS 3
MERMAID AVENUE	*Elektra*	34	*11 Jul 98*	2
MERMAID AVENUE VOLUME 2	*Elektra*	61	*10 Jun 00*	1

BRAIDS — US

SINGLES:	HITS 1			WEEKS 3
BOHEMIAN RHAPSODY	*Atlantic*	21	*2 Nov 96*	3
From the film 'High School High'.				

BRAIN BASHERS — UK

SINGLES:	HITS 1			WEEKS 1
DO IT NOW	*Tidy Trax*	64	*1 Jul 00*	1

BRAINBUG — Italy

SINGLES:	HITS 2			WEEKS 7
NIGHTMARE	*Positiva*	11	*3 May 97*	5
BENEDICTUS / NIGHTMARE [RI]	*Positiva*	24	*22 Nov 97*	2

BRAINCHILD — Germany

SINGLES:	HITS 1			WEEKS 2
SYMMETRY C	*Multiply*	31	*30 Oct 99*	2
Originally released in 1992.				

Wilfred BRAMBELL and Harry H. CORBETT — UK

SINGLES:	HITS 1			WEEKS 12
STEPTOE & SON AT BUCKINGHAM PALACE	*Pye*	25	*30 Nov 63*	12
Live recording from the Royal Variety Performance of 1963.				

EPS:	HITS 2			WEEKS 36
THE FACTS OF LIFE FROM STEPTOE AND SON	*Pye*	4	*8 Jun 63*	28
WAGES OF SIN	*Pye*	10	*21 Dec 63*	8

ALBUMS:	HITS 3			WEEKS 34
STEPTOE AND SON	*Pye*	4	*23 Mar 63*	28

STEPTOE AND SON *Both albums are different.*	*Pye Golden Guinea*	14	*11 Jan 64*	5
MORE JUNK	*Pye*	19	*14 Mar 64*	1

Bekka BRAMLETT - See Joe COCKER

BRAN VAN 3000

Canada

SINGLES:	HITS 2			WEEKS 15
DRINKING IN L.A.	*Capitol*	34	*6 Jun 98*	2
DRINKING IN L.A. [RI] *Featured in the Rolling Rock beer TV commercial.*	*Capitol*	3	*21 Aug 99*	11
ASTOUNDED *Samples Curtis Mayfield's Move On Up.* *Above hit: BRAN VAN 3000 featuring Curtis MAYFIELD.*	*Grand Royal*	40	*16 Jun 01*	2

BRAND NEW HEAVIES

UK/US

SINGLES:	HITS 16			WEEKS 68
NEVER STOP	*ffrr*	43	*5 Oct 91*	3
DREAM COME TRUE	*ffrr*	24	*15 Feb 92*	4
ULTIMATE TRUNK FUNK - THE EP [EP] *Lead track: Never Stop, a remix by David Morales of their first hit.*	*ffrr*	19	*18 Apr 92*	6
DON'T LET IT GO TO YOUR HEAD *Originally recorded by Jean Carn.*	*ffrr*	24	*1 Aug 92*	4
STAY THIS WAY *Remix of a track from the Ultimate Trunk Funk EP.* *Above 5: BRAND NEW HEAVIES featuring N'Dea DAVENPORT.*	*ffrr*	40	*19 Dec 92*	5
DREAM ON DREAMER	*ffrr*	15	*26 Mar 94*	4
BACK TO LOVE	*ffrr*	23	*11 Jun 94*	4
MIDNIGHT AT THE OASIS	*ffrr*	13	*13 Aug 94*	6
SPEND SOME TIME	*ffrr*	26	*5 Nov 94*	4
CLOSE TO YOU *From the film 'Pret A Porter'.*	*ffrr*	38	*11 Mar 95*	3
SOMETIMES	*ffrr*	11	*12 Apr 97*	5
YOU ARE THE UNIVERSE	*ffrr*	21	*28 Jun 97*	4
YOU'VE GOT A FRIEND	*ffrr*	9	*18 Oct 97*	8
SHELTER	*ffrr*	31	*10 Jan 98*	4
SATURDAY NITE	*ffrr*	35	*11 Sep 99*	2
APPARENTLY NOTHING	*ffrr*	32	*29 Jan 00*	2

ALBUMS:	HITS 6			WEEKS 103
BRAND NEW HEAVIES *Repackaged from 29 Aug 92.*	*ffrr*	25	*14 Mar 92*	16
HEAVY RHYME EXPERIENCE VOLUME 1 *Features various rappers.*	*ffrr*	38	*5 Sep 92*	2
BROTHER SISTER	*ffrr*	4	*16 Apr 94*	48
ORIGINAL FLAVA *Album of early Brand New Heavies material.*	*Acid Jazz*	64	*12 Nov 94*	1
SHELTER	*ffrr*	5	*3 May 97*	33
TRUNK FUNK - THE BEST OF THE BRAND NEW HEAVIES	*ffrr*	13	*25 Sep 99*	3

BRAND X

UK

ALBUMS:	HITS 2			WEEKS 6
MOROCCAN ROLL	*Charisma*	37	*21 May 77*	5
IS THERE ANYTHING ABOUT?	*CBS*	93	*11 Sep 82*	1

Johnny BRANDON with the PHANTOMS

UK

SINGLES:	HITS 2			WEEKS 12
• TOMORROW	*Polygon*	8	*12 Mar 55*	6
TOMORROW [RE] *Above hit: Johnny BRANDON with the PHANTOMS and the Norman WARREN MUSIC.*	*Polygon*	16	*30 Apr 55*	2
DON'T WORRY	*Polygon*	18	*2 Jul 55*	4

BRANDY

US

SINGLES:	HITS 7			WEEKS 62
I WANNA BE DOWN	*Atlantic*	44	*10 Dec 94*	3
I WANNA BE DOWN [RI]	*Atlantic*	36	*3 Jun 95*	3
SITTIN' UP IN MY ROOM *From the film 'Waiting To Exhale'.*	*Arista*	30	*3 Feb 96*	4
THE BOY IS MINE *Above hit: BRANDY and MONICA.*	*Atlantic*	2	*6 Jun 98*	20
TOP OF THE WORLD *Above hit: BRANDY featuring MASE.*	*Atlantic*	2	*10 Oct 98*	8
HAVE YOU EVER?	*Atlantic*	13	*12 Dec 98*	8
TOP OF THE WORLD [RE] *Above hit: BRANDY featuring MASE.*	*Atlantic*	61	*9 Jan 99*	1
ALMOST DOESN'T COUNT	*Atlantic*	15	*19 Jun 99*	5

ANOTHER DAY IN PARADISE *Above hit: BRANDY and RAY-J*	*WEA*	5	*16 Jun 01*	10
ALBUMS:	**HITS 1**			**WEEKS 31**
NEVER S-A-Y NEVER	*Atlantic*	19	*20 Jun 98*	31

Laura BRANIGAN — US

SINGLES:	**HITS 3**			**WEEKS 33**
GLORIA *Originally recorded by Umberto Tozzi.*	*Atlantic*	6	*18 Dec 82*	13
SELF CONTROL *Originally recorded by RAF.*	*Atlantic*	5	*7 Jul 84*	17
THE LUCKY ONE	*Atlantic*	56	*6 Oct 84*	3
ALBUMS:	**HITS 2**			**WEEKS 18**
SELF CONTROL	*Atlantic*	16	*18 Aug 84*	14
HOLD ME	*Atlantic*	64	*24 Aug 85*	4

BRASS CONSTRUCTION — US

SINGLES:	**HITS 8**			**WEEKS 35**
MOVIN'	*United Artists*	23	*3 Apr 76*	6
HA CHA CHA (FUNKTION)	*United Artists*	37	*5 Feb 77*	5
MUSIC MAKES YOU FEEL LIKE DANCING	*United Artists*	39	*26 Jan 80*	6
WALKIN' THE LINE	*Capitol*	47	*28 May 83*	3
WE CAN WORK IT OUT	*Capitol*	70	*16 Jul 83*	2
PARTYLINE	*Capitol*	56	*7 Jul 84*	4
INTERNATIONAL	*Capitol*	70	*27 Oct 84*	2
GIVE AND TAKE	*Capitol*	62	*9 Nov 85*	3
MOVIN' - 1988 [RM] *Remixed by Phil Harding.*	*Syncopate*	24	*28 May 88*	4
ALBUMS:	**HITS 2**			**WEEKS 12**
BRASS CONSTRUCTION	*United Artists*	9	*20 Mar 76*	11
RENEGADES	*Capitol*	94	*30 Jun 84*	1

BRASSTOOTH - See BM DUBS presents MR RUMBLE featuring BRASSTOOTH and KEE

BRAT — UK

SINGLES:	**HITS 1**			**WEEKS 8**
CHALK DUST - THE UMPIRE STRIKES BACK	*Hansa*	19	*10 Jul 82*	8

BRAVADO — UK

SINGLES:	**HITS 1**			**WEEKS 3**
HARMONICA MAN *Harmonica playing is by world harmonica champion Paul Lamb.*	*Peach*	37	*18 Jun 94*	3

BRAVEHEARTS - See QB FINEST featuring NAS and BRAVEHEARTS

BRAVO ALL STARS — UK/US/Germany

SINGLES:	**HITS 1**			**WEEKS 2**
LET THE MUSIC HEAL YOUR SOUL *Profits to Nordoff Robbins Music Therapy.*	*Edel*	36	*29 Aug 98*	2

Los BRAVOS — Spain/Germany

SINGLES:	**HITS 2**			**WEEKS 24**
BLACK IS BLACK	*Decca*	2	*2 Jul 66*	13
I DON'T CARE	*Decca*	16	*10 Sep 66*	11
ALBUMS:	**HITS 1**			**WEEKS 1**
BLACK IS BLACK	*Decca*	29	*8 Oct 66*	1

Alan BRAXE & Fred FALKE presents . . . — France

SINGLES:	**HITS 1**			**WEEKS 3**
"INTRO" *Samples the Jets' Crush On You.*	*Credence*	35	*25 Nov 00*	3

Dhar BRAXTON — US

SINGLES:	**HITS 1**			**WEEKS 8**
JUMP BACK (SET ME FREE)	*Fourth & Broadway*	32	*31 May 86*	8

Toni BRAXTON — US

SINGLES:	**HITS 9**			**WEEKS 83**
ANOTHER SAD LOVE SONG	*LaFace*	51	*18 Sep 93*	2
BREATHE AGAIN	*LaFace*	2	*15 Jan 94*	12
ANOTHER SAD LOVE SONG [RI]	*LaFace*	15	*2 Apr 94*	8
YOU MEAN THE WORLD TO ME	*LaFace*	30	*9 Jul 94*	5
LOVE SHOULDA BROUGHT YOU HOME	*LaFace*	33	*3 Dec 94*	3

YOU'RE MAKIN ME HIGH	*LaFace*	7	*13 Jul 96*	11
UN-BREAK MY HEART	*LaFace*	2	*2 Nov 96*	19
Backing vocals by Shanice.				
I DON'T WANT TO	*LaFace*	9	*24 May 97*	8
HOW COULD AN ANGEL BREAK MY HEART	*LaFace*	22	*8 Nov 97*	4
Above hit: Toni BRAXTON with Kenny G.				
HE WASN'T MAN ENOUGH	*LaFace*	5	*29 Apr 00*	11

ALBUMS:	HITS 3			WEEKS 133
TONI BRAXTON	*LaFace*	4	*29 Jan 94*	33
SECRETS	*LaFace*	53	*29 Jun 96*	3
This chart run was from import sales.				
SECRETS [RE]	*LaFace*	10	*27 Jul 96*	78
Peak position reached on 25 Jan 97.				
THE HEAT	*LaFace*	3	*6 May 00*	19

BRAXTONS — US

SINGLES:	HITS 3			WEEKS 7
SO MANY WAYS	*Atlantic*	32	*1 Feb 97*	2
From the film 'High School High'.				
THE BOSS	*Atlantic*	31	*29 Mar 97*	3
SLOW FLOW	*Atlantic*	26	*19 Jul 97*	2

BREAD — US

SINGLES:	HITS 5			WEEKS 46
MAKE IT WITH YOU	*Elektra*	5	*1 Aug 70*	14
BABY I'M-A WANT YOU	*Elektra*	14	*15 Jan 72*	10
EVERYTHING I OWN	*Elektra*	32	*29 Apr 72*	6
THE GUITAR MAN	*Elektra*	16	*30 Sep 72*	9
LOST WITHOUT YOUR LOVE	*Elektra*	27	*25 Dec 76*	7

ALBUMS:	HITS 8			WEEKS 198
ON THE WATERS	*Elektra*	34	*26 Sep 70*	5
BABY I'M A-WANT YOU	*Elektra*	9	*18 Mar 72*	19
THE BEST OF BREAD	*Elektra*	7	*28 Oct 72*	100
THE BEST OF BREAD VOLUME 2	*Elektra*	48	*27 Jul 74*	1
LOST WITHOUT YOUR LOVE	*Elektra*	17	*29 Jan 77*	6
THE SOUND OF BREAD	*Elektra*	1	*5 Nov 77*	46
Includes re-entry in 1987.				
THE COLLECTION – THE VERY BEST OF BREAD AND DAVID GATES	*Telstar*	84	*28 Nov 87*	2
Above hit: BREAD and David GATES.				
DAVID GATES AND BREAD: ESSENTIALS	*warner.esp/Jive*	9	*5 Jul 97*	19
Above hit: David GATES and BREAD.				
Above 2 albums include Gates solo and group recordings.				

BREAK MACHINE — US

SINGLES:	HITS 3			WEEKS 32
STREET DANCE	*Record Shack*	3	*4 Feb 84*	14
BREAK DANCE PARTY	*Record Shack*	9	*12 May 84*	8
BREAK DANCE PARTY [RE]	*Record Shack*	65	*14 Jul 84*	2
ARE YOU READY	*Record Shack*	27	*11 Aug 84*	8

ALBUMS:	HITS 1			WEEKS 16
BREAK MACHINE	*Record Shack*	17	*9 Jun 84*	16

BREAKBEAT ERA — UK

SINGLES:	HITS 3			WEEKS 5
BREAKBEAT ERA	*XL Recordings*	38	*18 Jul 98*	2
ULTRA-OBSCENE	*XL Recordings*	48	*21 Aug 99*	2
BULLITPROOF	*XL Recordings*	65	*11 Mar 00*	1

ALBUMS:	HITS 1			WEEKS 2
ULTRA OBSCENE	*XL Recordings*	31	*11 Sep 99*	2

BREAKFAST CLUB — US

SINGLES:	HITS 1			WEEKS 3
RIGHT ON TRACK	*MCA*	54	*27 Jun 87*	3

Julian BREAM — UK

ALBUMS:	HITS 1			WEEKS 2
THE ULTIMATE GUITAR COLLECTION	*RCA Victor*	66	*27 Apr 96*	2
Compilation covering the period 1955–1983.				

BREATHE — UK

SINGLES:	HITS 4			WEEKS 27
HANDS TO HEAVEN	*Siren*	4	*30 Jul 88*	12
JONAH	*Siren*	60	*22 Oct 88*	3

HOW CAN I FALL?	*Siren*	48	*3 Dec 88*	7
DON'T TELL ME LIES	*Siren*	45	*11 Mar 89*	5
ALBUMS:	**HITS 1**			**WEEKS 5**
ALL THAT JAZZ	*Siren*	22	*8 Oct 88*	5

Freddy BRECK — Germany

SINGLES:	**HITS 1**			**WEEKS 4**
SO IN LOVE WITH YOU	*Decca*	44	*13 Apr 74*	4

BRECKER BROTHERS — US

SINGLES:	**HITS 1**			**WEEKS 5**
EAST RIVER	*Arista*	34	*4 Nov 78*	5

BREEDERS — US/UK

SINGLES:	**HITS 4**			**WEEKS 6**
SAFARI [EP]	*4AD*	69	*18 Apr 92*	1
Lead track: Do You Love Me Now.				
CANNONBALL [EP]	*4AD*	40	*21 Aug 93*	3
Lead track: Cannonball.				
DIVINE HAMMER	*4AD*	59	*6 Nov 93*	1
HEAD TO TOE [EP]	*4AD*	68	*23 Jul 94*	1
10" only release. Lead track: Head To Toe.				
ALBUMS:	**HITS 2**			**WEEKS 8**
POD	*4AD*	22	*9 Jun 90*	3
LAST SPLASH	*4AD*	5	*11 Sep 93*	5

BREEKOUT KREW — US

SINGLES:	**HITS 1**			**WEEKS 3**
MATT'S MOOD	*London*	51	*24 Nov 84*	3

Ann BREEN — Ireland

SINGLES:	**HITS 1**			**WEEKS 2**
PAL OF MY CRADLE DAYS	*Homespun*	69	*19 Mar 83*	1
PAL OF MY CRADLE DAYS [RE]	*Homespun*	74	*7 Jan 84*	1

Jo BREEZER — UK

SINGLES:	**HITS 1**			**WEEKS 2**
VENUS AND MARS	*Columbia*	27	*13 Oct 01*	2

BRENDON — UK

SINGLES:	**HITS 1**			**WEEKS 9**
GIMME SOME	*Magnet*	14	*19 Mar 77*	9
Originally recorded by Jimmy Bo Horne.				

Maire BRENNAN — Ireland

SINGLES:	**HITS 2**			**WEEKS 12**
AGAINST THE WIND	*RCA*	64	*16 May 92*	2
SALTWATER	*Xtravaganza*	6	*5 Jun 99*	10
Based aroud Clannad's Theme From Harry's Game.				
Above hit: CHICANE (featuring Maire BRENNAN of CLANNAD).				
ALBUMS:	**HITS 1**			**WEEKS 2**
MAIRE	*RCA*	53	*13 Jun 92*	2

Rose BRENNAN — Ireland

SINGLES:	**HITS 1**			**WEEKS 9**
TALL DARK STRANGER	*Philips*	31	*9 Dec 61*	9

Walter BRENNAN with the Johnny MANN SINGERS — US

SINGLES:	**HITS 1**			**WEEKS 3**
OLD RIVERS	*Liberty*	38	*30 Jun 62*	3

Tony BRENT — UK

SINGLES:	**HITS 8**			**WEEKS 52**
WALKIN' TO MISSOURI	*Columbia*	9	*20 Dec 52*	2
Above hit: Tony BRENT with Norrie PARAMOR, his Chorus and Orchestra.				
MAKE IT SOON	*Columbia*	9	*3 Jan 53*	4
WALKIN' TO MISSOURI [RE]	*Columbia*	7	*10 Jan 53*	5
GOT YOU ON MY MIND	*Columbia*	12	*24 Jan 53*	1
MAKE IT SOON [RE]	*Columbia*	9	*14 Mar 53*	3
CINDY OH CINDY	*Columbia*	16	*1 Dec 56*	6
CINDY OH CINDY [RE]	*Columbia*	30	*9 Feb 57*	1

DARK MOON *Originally recorded by Bonny Guitar.* *Above 3: Tony BRENT with Eric JUPP and his Orchestra.*	*Columbia*	17	*29 Jun 57*	14
THE CLOUDS WILL SOON ROLL BY	*Columbia*	24	*1 Mar 58*	3
THE CLOUDS WILL SOON ROLL BY [RE]	*Columbia*	20	*10 May 58*	2
GIRL OF MY DREAMS *Originally recorded by Gene Austin.* *Above hit: Tony BRENT with Eric JUPP and his Orchestra.*	*Columbia*	16	*6 Sep 58*	7
WHY SHOULD I BE LONELY ?	*Columbia*	24	*25 Jul 59*	4

Bernard BRESSLAW — UK

(See also Michael Medwin, Bernard Bresslaw, Alfie Bass and Leslie Fyson.)

SINGLES:	HITS 1			WEEKS 11
MAD PASSIONATE LOVE	*His Master's Voice*	6	*6 Sep 58*	11

Adrian BRETT — UK

ALBUMS:	HITS 1			WEEKS 11
ECHOES OF GOLD	*Warwick*	19	*10 Nov 79*	11

Paul BRETT — UK

ALBUMS:	HITS 1			WEEKS 7
ROMANTIC GUITAR	*K-Tel*	24	*19 Jul 80*	7

Teresa BREWER — US

SINGLES:	HITS 5			WEEKS 53
LET ME GO LOVER *Originally recorded by Georgia Shaw in 1953 as LET ME GO DEVIL.* *Above hit: Teresa BREWER with the LANCERS.*	*Vogue Coral*	9	*12 Feb 55*	10
A TEAR FELL	*Vogue Coral*	2	*14 Apr 56*	15
A SWEET OLD FASHIONED GIRL	*Vogue Coral*	3	*14 Jul 56*	15
NORA MALONE	*Vogue Coral*	26	*11 May 57*	2
HOW DO YOU KNOW IT'S LOVE	*Coral*	21	*25 Jun 60*	11

BRIAN and MICHAEL (BURKE and JERK) — UK

SINGLES:	HITS 1			WEEKS 19
MATCHSTALK MEN AND MATCHSTALK CATS AND DOGS (LOWRY'S SONG)	*Pye*	1	*25 Feb 78*	19

BRICK — US

SINGLES:	HITS 1			WEEKS 4
DAZZ	*Bang*	36	*5 Feb 77*	4

Edie BRICKELL and the NEW BOHEMIANS — US

SINGLES:	HITS 3			WEEKS 10
WHAT I AM	*Geffen*	31	*4 Feb 89*	7
CIRCLE	*Geffen*	74	*27 May 89*	1
GOOD TIMES *Features vocals by Barry White.* *Above hit: Edie BRICKELL.*	*Geffen*	40	*1 Oct 94*	2

ALBUMS:	HITS 3			WEEKS 19
SHOOTING RUBBERBANDS AT THE STARS	*Geffen*	25	*4 Feb 89*	17
GHOST OF A DOG	*Geffen*	63	*10 Nov 90*	1
PICTURE PERFECT MORNING *Above hit: Edie BRICKELL.*	*Geffen*	59	*3 Sep 94*	1

Alicia BRIDGES — US

SINGLES:	HITS 1			WEEKS 11
I LOVE THE NIGHT LIFE (DISCO 'ROUND)	*Polydor*	32	*11 Nov 78*	10
I LOVE THE NIGHTLIFE (DISCO 'ROUND) [RM] *From the film 'The Adventures Of Priscilla Queen Of The Desert'. Remixed by the Rapino Brothers.*	*Mother*	61	*8 Oct 94*	1

Johnny BRIGGS - See CORONATION STREET CAST

BRIGHOUSE and RASTRICK BRASS BAND — UK

SINGLES:	HITS 1			WEEKS 13
THE FLORAL DANCE	*Transatlantic*	2	*12 Nov 77*	13

ALBUMS:	HITS 1			WEEKS 11
FLORAL DANCE	*Logo*	10	*28 Jan 78*	11

Bette BRIGHT — UK

SINGLES:	HITS 1			WEEKS 5
HELLO, I AM YOUR HEART *Originally recorded by Dennis Linde.*	*Korova*	50	*8 Mar 80*	5

Sarah BRIGHTMAN — UK

(See also Andrew Lloyd Webber; Various Artists: Stage Cast – London 'The Phantom Of The Opera'; Television – Soundtracks 'Song And Dance'.)

SINGLES:	HITS 13			WEEKS 98
I LOST MY HEART TO A STARSHIP TROOPER	*Ariola Hansa*	6	*11 Nov 78*	14
Above hit: Sarah BRIGHTMAN and HOT GOSSIP.				
THE ADVENTURES OF THE LOVE CRUSADER	*Ariola Hansa*	53	*7 Apr 79*	5
Above hit: Sarah BRIGHTMAN and the STARSHIP TROOPERS.				
HIM	*Polydor*	55	*30 Jul 83*	4
Above hit: Sarah BRIGHTMAN and the ROYAL PHILHARMONIC ORCHESTRA.				
PIE JESU	*His Master's Voice*	3	*23 Mar 85*	8
Above hit: Sarah BRIGHTMAN and Paul MILES-KINGSTON; WINCHESTER CATHEDRAL CHOIR Director, Martin NEARY, James LANCELOT – Organ; ENGLISH CHAMBER ORCHESTRA conducted by Lorin MAAZEL.				
THE PHANTOM OF THE OPERA	*Polydor*	7	*11 Jan 86*	10
Above hit: Sarah BRIGHTMAN and Steve HARLEY.				
ALL I ASK OF YOU	*Polydor*	3	*4 Oct 86*	16
Above hit: Cliff RICHARD and Sarah BRIGHTMAN with the ROYAL PHILHARMONIC ORCHESTRA conducted by David CADDICK.				
WISHING YOU WERE SOMEHOW HERE AGAIN	*Polydor*	7	*10 Jan 87*	11
Above 3 from the musical 'The Phantom Of The Opera'. [AA] listed with The Music Of The Night by Michael Crawford.				
AMIGOS PARA SIEMPRE (FRIENDS FOR LIFE)	*Really Useful*	11	*11 Jul 92*	11
The theme to the Barcelona 1992 Olympic Games.				
Above hit: Jose CARRERAS and Sarah BRIGHTMAN.				
TIME TO SAY GOODBYE (CON TE PARTIRO)	*Coalition*	2	*24 May 97*	14
Above hit: Sarah BRIGHTMAN and Andrea BOCELLI.				
WHO WANTS TO LIVE FOREVER	*Coalition*	45	*23 Aug 97*	1
Above hit: Sarah BRIGHTMAN and the LONDON SYMPHONY ORCHESTRA.				
JUST SHOW ME HOW TO LOVE YOU	*Coalition*	54	*6 Dec 97*	2
Above hit: Sarah BRIGHTMAN and the LONDON SYMPHONY ORCHESTRA featuring Jose CURA.				
STARSHIP TROOPERS	*Coalition*	58	*14 Feb 98*	1
Featuring re-recorded vocals from Brightman's first hit.				
Above hit: UNITED CITIZEN FEDERATION featuring Sarah BRIGHTMAN.				
EDEN	*Coalition*	68	*13 Feb 99*	1

ALBUMS:	HITS 4			WEEKS 27
THE SONGS THAT GOT AWAY	*Really Useful*	48	*17 Jun 89*	2
THE UNEXPECTED SONGS – SURRENDER	*Really Useful*	45	*11 Nov 95*	2
Album of Andrew Lloyd Webber songs.				
TIMELESS	*Coalition*	2	*14 Jun 97*	21
Recorded with the London Philharmonic Orchestra.				
LA LUNA	*East West*	37	*20 Jan 00*	2

BRIGHTON AND HOVE ALBION F.C. – See SEAGULLS – BRIGHTON and HOVE ALBION FOOTBALL CLUB

BRILLIANT — UK

SINGLES:	HITS 3			WEEKS 13
IT'S A MAN'S MAN'S MAN'S WORLD	*Food*	58	*19 Oct 85*	5
LOVE IS WAR	*Food*	64	*22 Mar 86*	4
SOMEBODY	*Food*	67	*2 Aug 86*	4

ALBUMS:	HITS 1			WEEKS 1
KISS THE LIPS OF LIFE	*Food*	83	*20 Sep 86*	1

Danielle BRISEBOIS — US

SINGLES:	HITS 1			WEEKS 1
GIMME LITTLE SIGN	*Epic*	75	*9 Sep 95*	1

Johnny BRISTOL — US

SINGLES:	HITS 2			WEEKS 16
HANG ON IN THERE BABY	*MGM*	3	*24 Aug 74*	11
MY GUY – MY GIRL [M]	*Atlantic*	39	*19 Jul 80*	5
Above hit: Amii STEWART and Johnny BRISTOL.				

ALBUMS:	HITS 1			WEEKS 7
HANG ON IN THERE BABY	*MGM*	12	*5 Oct 74*	7

BRIT PACK — UK

SINGLES:	HITS 1			WEEKS 2
SET ME FREE	*When!*	41	*12 Feb 00*	2

BROCK LANDARS — UK

SINGLES:	HITS 1			WEEKS 2
S.M.D.U.	*Parlophone*	49	*11 Jul 98*	2
Samples Blur's Song 2 and Prodigy's Smack My Bitch Up. Acronym for Smack My Dick Up.				

BRODSKY QUARTET – See Elvis COSTELLO and the ATTRACTIONS

BROKEN ENGLISH — UK

SINGLES:	HITS 2			WEEKS 13
COMIN' ON STRONG	*EMI*	18	*30 May 87*	10
LOVE ON THE SIDE	*EMI*	69	*3 Oct 87*	3

June BRONHILL and Thomas ROUND — UK/Australia

ALBUMS:	HITS 1			WEEKS 1
LILAC TIME	*His Master's Voice*	17	*18 Jun 60*	1

BRONSKI BEAT — UK

(See also Jimmy Somerville.)

SINGLES:	HITS 7			WEEKS 78
SMALLTOWN BOY	*Forbidden Fruit*	3	*2 Jun 84*	13
WHY?	*Forbidden Fruit*	6	*22 Sep 84*	10
IT AIN'T NECESSARILY SO	*Forbidden Fruit*	16	*1 Dec 84*	11
I FEEL LOVE [M]	*Forbidden Fruit*	3	*20 Apr 85*	12
Above hit: BRONSKI BEAT/Marc ALMOND.				
HIT THAT PERFECT BEAT	*Forbidden Fruit*	3	*30 Nov 85*	14
COME ON, COME ON	*Forbidden Fruit*	20	*29 Mar 86*	7
Sleeve reads 'C'mon! C'mon!'.				
CHA CHA HEELS	*Arista*	32	*1 Jul 89*	7
Above hit: Eartha KITT and BRONSKI BEAT.				
SMALLTOWN BOY (1991 REMIX) [RM]	*London*	32	*2 Feb 91*	4
Above hit: Jimmy SOMERVILLE with BRONSKI BEAT.				

ALBUMS:	HITS 4			WEEKS 69
THE AGE OF CONSENT	*Forbidden Fruit*	4	*20 Oct 84*	53
HUNDREDS AND THOUSANDS	*Forbidden Fruit*	24	*21 Sep 85*	6
TRUTHDARE DOUBLEDARE	*Forbidden Fruit*	18	*10 May 86*	6
THE VERY BEST OF JIMMY SOMERVILLE - BRONSKI BEAT AND THE COMMUNARDS	*London*	29	*22 Sep 01*	4
17 track compilation. 5 solo tracks, 4 with Bronski Beat, 8 with Communards.				
Above hit: Jimmy SOMERVILLE – BRONSKI BEAT and the COMMUNARDS.				

Will BRONSON CHORUS – See Tony BENNETT

Jet BRONX and the FORBIDDEN — UK

SINGLES:	HITS 1			WEEKS 1
AIN'T DOIN' NOTHIN'	*Lightning*	49	*17 Dec 77*	1

Michael BROOK – See Nusrat Fateh Ali KHAN/Michael BROOK

BROOK BROTHERS — UK

SINGLES:	HITS 5			WEEKS 35
WARPAINT	*Pye*	5	*1 Apr 61*	14
Originally recorded by Barry Mann.				
Above hit: BROOK BROTHERS with the Tony HATCH GROUP.				
AIN'T GONNA WASH FOR A WEEK	*Pye*	13	*26 Aug 61*	10
Originally recorded by Eddie Hodges.				
HE'S OLD ENOUGH TO KNOW BETTER	*Pye*	37	*27 Jan 62*	1
WELCOME HOME, BABY	*Pye*	33	*18 Aug 62*	6
TROUBLE IS MY MIDDLE NAME	*Pye*	38	*23 Feb 63*	4

Bruno BROOKES – See Liz KERSHAW and Bruno BROOKES

BROOKLYN BOUNCE — Germany

SINGLES:	HITS 1			WEEKS 1
THE MUSIC'S GOT ME	*Club Tools*	67	*30 May 98*	1

BROOKLYN BRONX and QUEENS – See B B and Q BAND

Elkie BROOKS — UK

SINGLES:	HITS 13			WEEKS 91
PEARL'S A SINGER	*A&M*	8	*2 Apr 77*	9
Originally recorded by Dino and Sembello.				
SUNSHINE AFTER THE RAIN	*A&M*	10	*20 Aug 77*	9
Originally recorded by Carole King.				
LILAC WINE	*A&M*	16	*25 Feb 78*	7
Originally recorded by Eartha Kitt.				
ONLY LOVE CAN BREAK YOUR HEART	*A&M*	43	*3 Jun 78*	5
Original by Neil Young reached No. 33 in the US in 1970.				
DON'T CRY OUT LOUD	*A&M*	12	*11 Nov 78*	11
Originally recorded by Peter Allen.				
THE RUNAWAY	*A&M*	50	*5 May 79*	5
FOOL IF YOU THINK IT'S OVER	*A&M*	17	*16 Jan 82*	10

OUR LOVE	*A&M*	43	*1 May 82*	5
NIGHTS IN WHITE SATIN	*A&M*	33	*17 Jul 82*	5
GASOLINE ALLEY	*A&M*	52	*22 Jan 83*	5
NO MORE THE FOOL	*Legend*	5	*22 Nov 86*	16
Originally recorded by Russ Ballard.				
BREAK THE CHAIN	*Legend*	55	*4 Apr 87*	3
WE'VE GOT TONIGHT	*Legend*	69	*11 Jul 87*	1
ALBUMS:	**HITS 15**			**WEEKS 223**
TWO DAYS AWAY	*A&M*	16	*18 Jun 77*	20
SHOOTING STAR	*A&M*	20	*13 May 78*	13
LIVE AND LEARN	*A&M*	34	*13 Oct 79*	6
PEARLS	*A&M*	2	*14 Nov 81*	79
PEARLS II	*A&M*	5	*13 Nov 82*	25
MINUTES	*A&M*	35	*14 Jul 84*	7
SCREEN GEMS	*EMI*	35	*8 Dec 84*	11
NO MORE THE FOOL	*Legend*	5	*6 Dec 86*	23
THE VERY BEST OF ELKIE BROOKS	*Telstar*	10	*27 Dec 86*	18
BOOKBINDER'S KID	*Legend*	57	*11 Jun 88*	3
INSPIRATIONS	*Telstar*	58	*18 Nov 89*	3
ROUND MIDNIGHT	*Castle Communications*	27	*13 Mar 93*	4
NOTHIN' BUT THE BLUES	*Castle Communications*	58	*16 Apr 94*	2
AMAZING	*Carlton Premiere*	49	*13 Apr 96*	2
Re-recordings of her greatest hits.				
Above hit: Elkie BROOKS with the ROYAL PHILHARMONIC ORCHESTRA.				
THE VERY BEST OF ELKIE BROOKS	*PolyGram TV*	23	*15 Mar 97*	7
Both Best Of albums are different.				

Garth BROOKS — US

SINGLES:	**HITS 6**			**WEEKS 15**
SHAMELESS	*Capitol*	71	*1 Feb 92*	1
Originally recorded by Billy Joel.				
THE RED STROKES / AIN'T GOING DOWN (TILL THE SUN COMES UP)	*Liberty*	13	*22 Jan 94*	5
STANDING OUTSIDE THE FIRE	*Liberty*	28	*16 Apr 94*	4
THE DANCE / FRIENDS IN LOW PLACES	*Capitol*	36	*18 Feb 95*	3
SHE'S EVERY WOMAN	*Capitol*	55	*17 Feb 96*	1
LOST IN YOU	*Capitol*	70	*13 Nov 99*	1
Chris Gaines is a fictional character played by Brooks in the film 'The Lamb'.				
Above hit: Garth BROOKS as Chris GAINES.				
ALBUMS:	**HITS 6**			**WEEKS 48**
ROPIN' THE WIND	*Capitol*	41	*15 Feb 92*	2
IN PIECES	*Capitol*	2	*12 Feb 94*	11
Label changed to Liberty from 26 Feb 94.				
THE HITS	*Liberty*	11	*24 Dec 94*	21
FRESH HORSES	*Capitol*	22	*2 Dec 95*	6
SEVENS	*Capitol*	34	*13 Dec 97*	7
DOUBLE LIVE	*Capitol*	57	*28 Nov 98*	1
Live recordings made between 1991–98.				

Mel BROOKS — US

SINGLES:	**HITS 1**			**WEEKS 10**
TO BE OR NOT TO BE (THE HITLER RAP)	*Island*	12	*18 Feb 84*	10
From the film 'To Be Or Not To Be'.				

Meredith BROOKS — US

SINGLES:	**HITS 3**			**WEEKS 13**
BITCH	*Capitol*	6	*2 Aug 97*	10
I NEED	*Capitol*	28	*6 Dec 97*	2
WHAT WOULD HAPPEN	*Capitol*	49	*7 Mar 98*	1
ALBUMS:	**HITS 1**			**WEEKS 10**
BLURRING THE EDGES	*Capitol*	5	*23 Aug 97*	10

Nigel BROOKS SINGERS — UK

ALBUMS:	**HITS 2**			**WEEKS 17**
SONGS OF JOY	*K-Tel*	5	*29 Nov 75*	16
20 ALL TIME EUROVISION FAVOURITES	*K-Tel*	44	*5 Jun 76*	1

Norman BROOKS — Canada

SINGLES:	**HITS 1**			**WEEKS 1**
A SKY-BLUE SHIRT AND A RAINBOW TIE	*London*	17	*13 Nov 54*	1

BROS — UK

SINGLES:	**HITS 11**			**WEEKS 84**
WHEN WILL I BE FAMOUS?	*CBS*	62	*5 Dec 87*	2
WHEN WILL I BE FAMOUS? [RE]	*CBS*	2	*9 Jan 88*	13

DROP THE BOY	*CBS*	2	*19 Mar 88*	10
I OWE YOU NOTHING	*CBS*	1	*18 Jun 88*	11
Original release reached No. 80 in 1987.				
I QUIT	*CBS*	4	*17 Sep 88*	8
CAT AMONG THE PIGEONS / SILENT NIGHT	*CBS*	2	*3 Dec 88*	8
TOO MUCH	*CBS*	2	*29 Jul 89*	7
CHOCOLATE BOX	*CBS*	9	*7 Oct 89*	6
SISTER	*CBS*	10	*16 Dec 89*	6
Dedicated to their sister who died in a car crash.				
MADLY IN LOVE	*CBS*	14	*10 Mar 90*	4
ARE YOU MINE?	*Columbia*	12	*13 Jul 91*	5
TRY	*Columbia*	27	*21 Sep 91*	4
ALBUMS:	**HITS 3**			**WEEKS 69**
PUSH	*CBS*	2	*9 Apr 88*	54
THE TIME	*CBS*	4	*28 Oct 89*	13
CHANGING FACES	*Columbia*	18	*12 Oct 91*	2

BROTHER BEYOND — UK

SINGLES:	**HITS 10**			**WEEKS 58**
HOW MANY TIMES	*EMI*	62	*4 Apr 87*	3
CHAIN-GANG SMILE	*Parlophone*	57	*8 Aug 87*	3
CAN YOU KEEP A SECRET?	*Parlophone*	56	*23 Jan 88*	4
THE HARDER I TRY	*Parlophone*	2	*30 Jul 88*	14
HE AIN'T NO COMPETITION	*Parlophone*	6	*5 Nov 88*	10
BE MY TWIN	*Parlophone*	14	*21 Jan 89*	6
CAN YOU KEEP A SECRET? (89 MIX) [RM]	*Parlophone*	22	*1 Apr 89*	5
Remixed by Phil Harding.				
DRIVE ON	*Parlophone*	39	*28 Oct 89*	4
WHEN WILL I SEE YOU AGAIN	*Parlophone*	43	*9 Dec 89*	5
TRUST	*Parlophone*	53	*10 Mar 90*	2
THE GIRL I USED TO KNOW	*Parlophone*	48	*19 Jan 91*	2
ALBUMS:	**HITS 2**			**WEEKS 24**
GET EVEN	*Parlophone*	9	*26 Nov 88*	23
TRUST	*Parlophone*	60	*25 Nov 89*	1

BROTHER BROWN featuring FRANK'EE — Denmark

SINGLES:	**HITS 2**			**WEEKS 5**
UNDER THE WATER	*ffrr*	18	*2 Oct 99*	4
Vocals by Marie Frank.				
STAR CATCHING GIRL	*Rulin*	51	*24 Nov 01*	1

BROTHERHOOD — UK

SINGLES:	**HITS 1**			**WEEKS 1**
ONE SHOT / NOTHING IN PARTICULAR	*Bite It*	55	*27 Jan 96*	1
ALBUMS:	**HITS 1**			**WEEKS 1**
ELEMENTALZ	*Bite It*	50	*17 Feb 96*	1

BROTHERHOOD OF MAN — UK

SINGLES:	**HITS 10**			**WEEKS 97**
UNITED WE STAND	*Deram*	10	*14 Feb 70*	9
WHERE ARE YOU GOING TO MY LOVE	*Deram*	22	*4 Jul 70*	10
SAVE YOUR KISSES FOR ME	*Pye*	1	*13 Mar 76*	16
UK's Eurovision entry in 1976, it came 1st.				
MY SWEET ROSALIE	*Pye*	30	*19 Jun 76*	7
OH BOY (THE MOOD I'M IN)	*Pye*	8	*26 Feb 77*	12
Originally recorded by Diana Trask.				
ANGELO	*Pye*	1	*9 Jul 77*	12
FIGARO	*Pye*	1	*14 Jan 78*	11
BEAUTIFUL LOVER	*Pye*	15	*27 May 78*	12
MIDDLE OF THE NIGHT	*Pye*	41	*30 Sep 78*	6
LIGHTNING FLASH	*EMI*	67	*3 Jul 82*	2
ALBUMS:	**HITS 4**			**WEEKS 40**
LOVE AND KISSES FROM	*Pye*	20	*24 Apr 76*	8
B FOR BROTHERHOOD	*Pye*	18	*12 Aug 78*	9
BROTHERHOOD OF MAN	*K-Tel*	6	*7 Oct 78*	15
BROTHERHOOD OF MAN SING 20 NUMBER ONE HITS	*Warwick*	14	*29 Nov 80*	8

BROTHERLOVE - See PRATT and McLAIN with BROTHERLOVE

BROTHERS — UK

SINGLES:	**HITS 1**			**WEEKS 9**
SING ME	*Bus Stop*	8	*29 Jan 77*	9

BROTHERS FOUR — US

SINGLES:	HITS 1			WEEKS 2
GREENFIELDS	*Philips*	49	*25 Jun 60*	1
GREENFIELDS [RE]	*Philips*	40	*9 Jul 60*	1

BROTHERS IN RHYTHM — UK

SINGLES:	HITS 2			WEEKS 12
SUCH A GOOD FEELING	*Fourth & Broadway*	64	*16 Mar 91*	2
SUCH A GOOD FEELING [RI]	*Fourth & Broadway*	14	*14 Sep 91*	8
FOREVER AND A DAY	*Stress*	51	*30 Apr 94*	2

Above hit: BROTHERS IN RHYTHM present CHARVONI.

BROTHERS JOHNSON — US

SINGLES:	HITS 6			WEEKS 34
STRAWBERRY LETTER 23	*A&M*	35	*9 Jul 77*	5
Originally recorded by Shuggie Otis.				
AIN'T WE FUNKIN' NOW	*A&M*	43	*2 Sep 78*	6
RIDE-O-ROCKET	*A&M*	50	*4 Nov 78*	4
STOMP	*A&M*	6	*23 Feb 80*	12
LIGHT UP THE NIGHT	*A&M*	47	*31 May 80*	4
THE REAL THING	*A&M*	50	*25 Jul 81*	3
ALBUMS:	**HITS 3**			**WEEKS 22**
BLAM!!	*A&M*	48	*19 Aug 78*	8
LIGHT UP THE NIGHT	*A&M*	22	*23 Feb 80*	12
WINNERS	*A&M*	42	*18 Jul 81*	2

BROTHERS LIKE OUTLAW featuring Alison EVELYN — UK

SINGLES:	HITS 1			WEEKS 1
GOOD VIBRATIONS	*Gee Street*	74	*23 Jan 93*	1

Edgar BROUGHTON BAND — UK

SINGLES:	HITS 2			WEEKS 10
OUT DEMONS OUT	*Harvest*	39	*18 Apr 70*	5
APACHE DROPOUT [M]	*Harvest*	49	*23 Jan 71*	1
APACHE DROPOUT [M] [RE-1ST]	*Harvest*	35	*6 Feb 71*	2
APACHE DROPOUT [M] [RE-2ND]	*Harvest*	35	*13 Mar 71*	1
APACHE DROPOUT [M] [RE-3RD]	*Harvest*	33	*27 Mar 71*	1
ALBUMS:	**HITS 2**			**WEEKS 6**
SING BROTHER SING	*Harvest*	18	*20 Jun 70*	4
THE EDGAR BROUGHTON BAND	*Harvest*	28	*5 Jun 71*	2

Angie BROWN – See BIZARRE INC; MOTIV 8

Arthur BROWN – See CRAZY WORLD OF ARTHUR BROWN

Bobby BROWN — US

SINGLES:	HITS 14			WEEKS 123
DON'T BE CRUEL	*MCA*	42	*6 Aug 88*	7
MY PREROGATIVE	*MCA*	6	*17 Dec 88*	17
DON'T BE CRUEL [RM]	*MCA*	13	*25 Mar 89*	8
EVERY LITTLE STEP	*MCA*	6	*20 May 89*	9
ON OUR OWN	*MCA*	4	*15 Jul 89*	9
From the film 'Ghostbusters II'.				
ROCK WIT'CHA	*MCA*	33	*23 Sep 89*	6
RONI	*MCA*	21	*25 Nov 89*	7
THE FREE STYLE MEGA-MIX [M]	*MCA*	14	*9 Jun 90*	7
Mix of his earlier hits.				
SHE AIN'T WORTH IT	*London*	12	*30 Jun 90*	9
Above hit: Glenn MEDEIROS (featuring Bobby BROWN).				
HUMPIN' AROUND	*MCA*	19	*22 Aug 92*	6
GOOD ENOUGH	*MCA*	41	*17 Oct 92*	4
THAT'S THE WAY LOVE IS	*MCA*	56	*19 Jun 93*	2
SOMETHING IN COMMON	*MCA*	16	*22 Jan 94*	5
Above hit: Bobby BROWN (Duet with Whitney HOUSTON).				
TWO CAN PLAY THAT GAME	*MCA*	38	*25 Jun 94*	3
TWO CAN PLAY THAT GAME [RE]	*MCA*	3	*1 Apr 95*	12
HUMPIN' AROUND [RM]	*MCA*	8	*8 Jul 95*	6
Remixed by K Klass.				
MY PREROGATIVE [RM]	*MCA*	17	*14 Oct 95*	3
Remixed by Joe T. Vannelli.				
EVERY LITTLE STEP [RM]	*MCA*	25	*3 Feb 96*	2
Remixed by CJ Mackintosh.				
FEELIN' INSIDE	*MCA*	40	*22 Nov 97*	1
ALBUMS:	**HITS 5**			**WEEKS 65**
DON'T BE CRUEL	*MCA*	3	*28 Jan 89*	41

KING OF STAGE	*MCA*	40	*5 Aug 89*	6
DANCE! . . . YA KNOW IT!	*MCA*	26	*2 Dec 89*	10
BOBBY	*MCA*	11	*5 Sep 92*	5
TWO CAN PLAY THAT GAME	*MCA*	24	*5 Aug 95*	3
Compilation (mainly remixes of hit singles).				

Carl BROWN - See DOUBLE TROUBLE

Dennis BROWN — Jamaica

SINGLES:	HITS 3			WEEKS 18
MONEY IN MY POCKET	*Lightning*	14	*3 Mar 79*	9
LOVE HAS FOUND ITS WAY	*A&M*	47	*3 Jul 82*	6
HALFWAY UP, HALFWAY DOWN	*A&M*	56	*11 Sep 82*	3
ALBUMS:	**HITS 1**			**WEEKS 6**
LOVE HAS FOUND ITS WAY	*A&M*	72	*26 Jun 82*	6

Diana BROWN and Barrie K. SHARPE — UK

SINGLES:	HITS 4			WEEKS 11
THE MASTERPLAN	*ffrr*	39	*2 Jun 90*	6
SUN WORSHIPPERS (POSITIVE THINKING)	*ffrr*	61	*1 Sep 90*	2
LOVE OR NOTHING	*ffrr*	71	*23 Mar 91*	1
EATING ME ALIVE	*ffrr*	53	*27 Jun 92*	2

Errol BROWN — UK

SINGLES:	HITS 2			WEEKS 10
PERSONAL TOUCH	*WEA*	25	*4 Jul 87*	8
BODY ROCKIN'	*WEA*	51	*28 Nov 87*	2
ALBUMS:	**HITS 1**			**WEEKS 2**
STILL SEXY - THE ALBUM	*Universal Music TV*	44	*9 Jun 01*	2

Foxy BROWN — US

(See also Nas Escobar, Foxy Brown, AZ and Nature present the Firm featuring Dawn Robinson; Jay-Z.)

SINGLES:	HITS 7			WEEKS 23
TOUCH ME TEASE ME	*Def Jam*	26	*21 Sep 96*	3
From the film 'The Nutty Professor'.				
Above hit: CASE featuring Foxxy BROWN.				
GET ME HOME	*Def Jam*	11	*8 Mar 97*	5
Based on Eugene Wilde's Gotta Get You Home Tonight.				
Above hit: Foxy BROWN featuring BLACKSTREET.				
AIN'T NO PLAYA	*Northwestside*	31	*10 May 97*	2
Above hit: JAY-Z featuring Foxy BROWN.				
I'LL BE	*Def Jam*	9	*21 Jun 97*	5
Samples Rene And Angela's I'll Be Good and Blondie's Rapture.				
Above hit: Foxy BROWN featuring JAY Z.				
BIG BAD MAMMA	*Def Jam*	12	*11 Oct 97*	3
From the film 'How To Be A Player'.				
Above hit: Foxy BROWN featuring DRU HILL.				
HOT SPOT	*Def Jam*	31	*13 Mar 99*	2
OH YEAH	*Def Jam*	27	*8 Sep 01*	3
Samples Africa Unite and Lively Yourself Up by Bob Marley and Byron Lee's version of 54–46 (That's My Number).				
Above hit: Foxy BROWN featuring Spragga BENZ.				
ALBUMS:	**HITS 1**			**WEEKS 1**
CHYNA DOLL	*Def Jam*	51	*6 Feb 99*	1

Gloria D. BROWN — US

SINGLES:	HITS 1			WEEKS 3
THE MORE THEY KNOCK THE MORE I LOVE YOU	*10 Records*	57	*8 Jun 85*	3

Horace BROWN — US

SINGLES:	HITS 3			WEEKS 7
TASTE YOUR LOVE	*Uptown*	58	*25 Feb 95*	1
ONE FOR THE MONEY	*Motown*	12	*18 May 96*	4
THINGS WE DO FOR LOVE	*Motown*	27	*12 Oct 96*	2
ALBUMS:	**HITS 1**			**WEEKS 1**
HORACE BROWN	*Motown*	48	*6 Jul 96*	1

Ian BROWN — UK

SINGLES:	HITS 8			WEEKS 30
MY STAR	*Polydor*	5	*24 Jan 98*	4
CORPSES	*Polydor*	14	*4 Apr 98*	4
Backing vocals by Noel Gallagher.				
CAN'T SEE ME	*Polydor*	21	*20 Jun 98*	3

BE THERE	*Mo Wax*	8	*20 Feb 99*	6
Above hit: UNKLE featuring Ian BROWN.				
LOVE LIKE A FOUNTAIN	*Polydor*	23	*6 Nov 99*	3
DOLPHINS WERE MONKEYS	*Polydor*	5	*19 Feb 00*	4
GOLDEN GAZE	*Polydor*	29	*17 Jun 00*	2
F.E.A.R.	*Polydor*	13	*29 Sep 01*	4
ALBUMS:	**HITS 3**			**WEEKS 35**
UNFINISHED MONKEY BUSINESS	*Polydor*	4	*14 Feb 98*	24
GOLDEN GREATS	*Polydor*	14	*20 Nov 99*	6
MUSIC OF THE SPHERES	*Polydor*	3	*13 Oct 01*	5

Jackie BROWN – See Anthony STEEL with the RADIO REVELLERS and Jackie BROWN and his Music

James BROWN — US

SINGLES:	**HITS 18**			**WEEKS 104**
PAPA'S GOT A BRAND NEW BAG	*London*	25	*25 Sep 65*	7
I GOT YOU (I FEEL GOOD)	*Pye International*	29	*26 Feb 66*	6
IT'S A MAN'S MAN'S MAN'S WORLD	*Pye International*	13	*18 Jun 66*	9
Above 3: James BROWN and the FAMOUS FLAMES.				
GET UP I FEEL LIKE BEING A SEX MACHINE	*Polydor*	32	*10 Oct 70*	7
HEY AMERICA !	*Mojo*	47	*27 Nov 71*	3
GET UP OFFA THAT THING	*Polydor*	22	*18 Sep 76*	6
Sub credit: James Brown – Minister Of New New Super Heavy Funk.				
BODYHEAT	*Polydor*	36	*29 Jan 77*	4
Sub credit: James Brown – Brand New Sound.				
RAPP PAYBACK (WHERE IZ MOSES ?)	*RCA*	39	*10 Jan 81*	5
BRING IT ON . . . BRING IT ON	*Sonet*	45	*2 Jul 83*	4
UNITY (PART 1 - THE THIRD COMING)	*Tommy Boy*	49	*1 Sep 84*	5
Above hit: Afrika BAMBAATAA and the Godfather Of Soul – James BROWN.				
FROGGY MIX [M]	*Boiling Point*	50	*27 Apr 85*	3
Megamix of 12 songs.				
GET UP I FEEL LIKE BEING A SEX MACHINE [RI-1ST]	*Boiling Point*	47	*1 Jun 85*	5
LIVING IN AMERICA	*Scotti Brothers*	5	*25 Jan 86*	10
From the film 'Rocky IV'.				
GET UP I FEEL LIKE BEING A SEX MACHINE [RI-1ST] [RE]	*Boiling Point*	46	*1 Mar 86*	4
GRAVITY	*Scotti Brothers*	65	*18 Oct 86*	2
SHE'S THE ONE	*Urban*	45	*30 Jan 88*	3
THE PAYBACK MIX PART ONE [M]	*Urban*	12	*23 Apr 88*	6
Mixed by Coldcut.				
I'M REAL	*Scotti Brothers*	31	*4 Jun 88*	4
Above hit: James BROWN with FULL FORCE.				
I GOT YOU (I FEEL GOOD) [RI]	*A&M*	52	*23 Jul 88*	3
[AA] listed with Nowhere To Run by Martha Reeves and the Vandellas.				
GET UP (I FEEL LIKE BEING A) SEX MACHINE [RI-2ND]	*Polydor*	69	*16 Nov 91*	2
I GOT YOU (I FEEL GOOD) [RM]	*FBI*	72	*24 Oct 92*	1
Above hit: James BROWN v DAKEYNE.				
CAN'T GET ANY HARDER	*Polydor*	59	*17 Apr 93*	2
FUNK ON AH ROLL	*Eagle*	40	*17 Apr 99*	2
Samples his own track, Hot Pants.				
FUNK ON AH ROLL [RM]	*Eagle*	63	*22 Apr 00*	1
Samples his own Hot Pants. Remixed by Bump & Flex, their mix was track 3 on the original release.				
ALBUMS:	**HITS 4**			**WEEKS 51**
GRAVITY	*Scotti Brothers*	85	*18 Oct 86*	3
THE BEST OF JAMES BROWN - THE GODFATHER OF SOUL	*K-Tel*	17	*10 Oct 87*	21
I'M REAL	*Scotti Brothers*	27	*25 Jun 88*	5
SEX MACHINE - THE VERY BEST OF JAMES BROWN	*Polydor*	19	*16 Nov 91*	22

Jennifer BROWN — Sweden

SINGLES:	**HITS 1**			**WEEKS 1**
TUESDAY AFTERNOON	*RCA*	57	*1 May 99*	1

Joanne BROWN – See Tony OSBORNE SOUND featuring Joanne BROWN

Jocelyn BROWN — US

(See also Todd Terry.)

SINGLES:	**HITS 17**			**WEEKS 62**
SOMEBODY ELSE'S GUY	*Fourth & Broadway*	13	*21 Apr 84*	9
I WISH YOU WOULD	*Fourth & Broadway*	51	*22 Sep 84*	3
LOVE'S GONNA GET YOU	*Warner Brothers*	70	*15 Mar 86*	1
ALWAYS THERE	*Talkin Loud*	6	*29 Jun 91*	9
Above hit: INCOGNITO featuring Jocelyn BROWN.				
SHE GOT SOUL	*A&M*	57	*14 Sep 91*	3
Above hit: JAMESTOWN featuring Jocelyn BROWN.				
DON'T TALK JUST KISS	*Tug*	3	*7 Dec 91*	11
Above hit: RIGHT SAID FRED guest vocal Jocelyn BROWN.				

TAKE ME UP	*A&M*	61	*20 Mar 93*	1
Above hit: SONIC SURFERS featuring Jocelyn BROWN.				
NO MORE TEARS (ENOUGH IS ENOUGH)	*Bell*	13	*11 Jun 94*	7
Above hit: Kym MAZELLE and Jocelyn BROWN.				
GIMME ALL YOUR LOVIN'	*Bell*	22	*8 Oct 94*	3
Above hit: Jocelyn BROWN and Kym MAZELLE.				
IT'S ALRIGHT, I FEEL IT!	*Talkin Loud*	26	*10 May 97*	2
I AM THE BLACK GOLD OF THE SUN	*Talkin Loud*	31	*25 Oct 97*	2
Originally recorded by Minnie Riperton's band the Rotary Connection.				
Above 2: NUYORICAN SOUL featuring Jocelyn BROWN.				
HAPPINESS	S3	45	*22 Nov 97*	1
Above hit: KAMASULTRA featuring Jocelyn BROWN.				
FUN	*INCredible*	33	*2 May 98*	2
Above hit: DA MOB featuring Jocelyn BROWN.				
AIN'T NO MOUNTAIN HIGH ENOUGH	*INCredible*	35	*29 Aug 98*	2
I BELIEVE	*Playola*	62	*27 Mar 99*	1
Above hit: JAMESTOWN featuring Jocelyn BROWN.				
IT'S ALL GOOD	*INCredible*	54	*3 Jul 99*	1
Above hit: DA MOB featuring Jocelyn BROWN.				
BELIEVE	*Defected*	45	*11 Mar 00*	2
Above hit: MINISTERS DE-LA-FUNK featuring Jocelyn BROWN.				
BELIEVE [RM]	*Defected*	42	*27 Jan 01*	2
Remixed by Full Intention.				

Joe BROWN and the BRUVVERS — UK

SINGLES:	HITS 11			WEEKS 92
• THE DARKTOWN STRUTTERS BALL	*Decca*	34	*19 Mar 60*	6
Originally recorded by Original Dixieland Jazz Band.				
SHINE	*Pye*	33	*28 Jan 61*	6
Above hit: Joe BROWN.				
WHAT A CRAZY WORLD WE'RE LIVING IN	*Piccadilly*	37	*13 Jan 62*	2
Recorded during his act at the Granada, Woolwich.				
• A PICTURE OF YOU	*Piccadilly*	2	*19 May 62*	19
YOUR TENDER LOOK	*Piccadilly*	31	*15 Sep 62*	6
IT ONLY TOOK A MINUTE	*Piccadilly*	6	*17 Nov 62*	13
THAT'S WHAT LOVE WILL DO	*Piccadilly*	3	*9 Feb 63*	14
IT ONLY TOOK A MINUTE [RE]	*Piccadilly*	50	*23 Feb 63*	1
NATURE'S TIME FOR LOVE	*Piccadilly*	26	*29 Jun 63*	6
SALLY ANN	*Piccadilly*	28	*28 Sep 63*	9
WITH A LITTLE HELP FROM MY FRIENDS	*Pye*	32	*2 Jul 67*	4
HEY MAMA	*Ammo*	33	*14 Apr 73*	6
Above 2: Joe BROWN.				

EPS:	HITS 1			WEEKS 1
JOE BROWN HIT PARADE	*Piccadilly*	20	*28 Sep 63*	1
Above hit: Joe BROWN.				

ALBUMS:	HITS 2			WEEKS 47
A PICTURE OF YOU	*Pye Golden Guinea*	3	*1 Sep 62*	39
JOE BROWN - LIVE	*Piccadilly*	14	*25 May 63*	8
Above hit: Joe BROWN.				

Karen BROWN – See DJs RULE

Kathy BROWN — US

SINGLES:	HITS 4			WEEKS 9
TURN ME OUT	*Stress*	44	*25 Nov 95*	2
Original release reached No. 86 in 1994.				
TURN ME OUT (TURN TO SUGAR) [RM]	*ffrr*	35	*20 Sep 97*	3
Remixed by The Sol Brothers.				
Above 2: PRAXIS featuring Kathy BROWN.				
JOY	*Azuli*	63	*10 Apr 99*	1
LOVE IS NOT A GAME	*Defected*	34	*5 May 01*	2
Above hit: J. MAJIK featuring Kathy BROWN.				
OVER YOU	*Defected*	42	*2 Jun 01*	1
Above hit: Warren CLARKE featuring Kathy BROWN.				

Miquel BROWN — US

SINGLES:	HITS 2			WEEKS 7
HE'S A SAINT, HE'S A SINNER	*Record Shack*	68	*18 Feb 84*	4
CLOSE TO PERFECTION	*Record Shack*	63	*24 Aug 85*	3

Palmer BROWN – See BLAZE featuring Palmer BROWN

Peter BROWN — US

SINGLES:	HITS 2			WEEKS 9
DO YA WANNA GET FUNKY WITH ME	*TK*	43	*11 Feb 78*	4
DANCE WITH ME	*TK*	57	*17 Jun 78*	5
Above hit: Peter BROWN – Special background vocals: Betty WRIGHT.				

Polly BROWN — UK

SINGLES:	HITS 1			WEEKS 5
UP IN A PUFF OF SMOKE	*GTO*	43	*14 Sep 74*	5

Roy 'Chubby' BROWN — UK

SINGLES:	HITS 2			WEEKS 22
LIVING NEXT DOOR TO ALICE (WHO THE F**K IS ALICE?)	*N.O.W.*	64	*13 May 95*	2
Above hit: SMOKIE featuring Roy Chubby BROWN.				
LIVING NEXT DOOR TO ALICE (WHO THE F**K IS ALICE?) [RE]	*N.O.W.*	3	*26 Aug 95*	17
ROCKIN' GOOD CHRISTMAS	*PolyStar*	51	*21 Dec 96*	3
ALBUMS:	**HITS 2**			**WEEKS 8**
TAKE FAT AND PARTY	*PolyStar*	29	*25 Nov 95*	7
FAT OUT OF HELL	*PolyStar*	67	*7 Dec 96*	1

Sam BROWN — UK

SINGLES:	HITS 5			WEEKS 35
STOP	*A&M*	52	*11 Jun 88*	3
STOP [RE]	*A&M*	4	*4 Feb 89*	12
CAN I GET A WITNESS?	*A&M*	15	*13 May 89*	7
WITH A LITTLE LOVE	*A&M*	44	*3 Mar 90*	4
KISSING GATE	*A&M*	23	*5 May 90*	8
JUST GOOD FRIENDS	*The Dick Brothers*	63	*26 Aug 95*	1
Above hit: FISH featuring Sam BROWN.				
ALBUMS:	**HITS 2**			**WEEKS 30**
STOP!	*A&M*	4	*11 Mar 89*	18
APRIL MOON	*A&M*	38	*14 Apr 90*	12

Sharon BROWN — US

SINGLES:	HITS 1			WEEKS 11
I SPECIALIZE IN LOVE	*Virgin*	38	*17 Apr 82*	9
I SPECIALIZE IN LOVE [RM]	*Deep Distraxion*	62	*26 Feb 94*	2
Remixed by Tommy D & Paul Gotel.				

BROWN SAUCE — UK

SINGLES:	HITS 1			WEEKS 12
I WANNA BE A WINNER	*BBC*	15	*12 Dec 81*	12

Duncan BROWNE — UK

SINGLES:	HITS 2			WEEKS 8
JOURNEY	*RAK*	23	*19 Aug 72*	6
THEME FROM TRAVELLING MAN	*Towerbell*	68	*22 Dec 84*	2
From the Granada TV series.				

Jackson BROWNE — US

SINGLES:	HITS 3			WEEKS 14
STAY	*Asylum*	12	*1 Jul 78*	11
IN THE SHAPE OF A HEART	*Elektra*	66	*18 Oct 86*	2
EVERYWHERE I GO	*Elektra*	67	*25 Jun 94*	1
ALBUMS:	**HITS 8**			**WEEKS 37**
THE PRETENDER	*Asylum*	26	*4 Dec 76*	5
RUNNING ON EMPTY	*Asylum*	28	*21 Jan 78*	7
HOLD OUT	*Asylum*	44	*12 Jul 80*	5
LAWYERS IN LOVE	*Asylum*	37	*13 Aug 83*	7
LIVES IN THE BALANCE	*Asylum*	36	*8 Mar 86*	7
WORLD IN MOTION	*Elektra*	39	*17 Jun 89*	2
I'M ALIVE	*Elektra*	35	*6 Nov 93*	3
LOOKING EAST	*Elektra*	47	*9 Mar 96*	1

Ronnie BROWNE – See SCOTTISH RUGBY TEAM with Ronnie BROWNE

Tom BROWNE — US

SINGLES:	HITS 3			WEEKS 24
FUNKIN' FOR JAMAICA (N.Y.)	*Arista*	10	*19 Jul 80*	11
THIGHS HIGH (GRIP YOUR HIPS AND MOVE)	*Arista*	45	*25 Oct 80*	5
FUNGI MAMA (BEBOPAFUNKADISCOLYPSO)	*Arista*	58	*30 Jan 82*	4
FUNKIN' FOR JAMAICA (1991 REMIX) [RM]	*Arista*	45	*11 Jan 92*	4

BROWNS — US

SINGLES:	HITS 1			WEEKS 13
THE THREE BELLS (LES TROIS CLOCHES)	*RCA*	6	*19 Sep 59*	13

BROWNSTONE — US

SINGLES:	HITS 5			WEEKS 24
IF YOU LOVE ME	*MJJ Productions*	8	*1 Apr 95*	12
GRAPEVYNE	*MJJ Productions*	16	*15 Jul 95*	4
I CAN'T TELL YOU WHY	*MJJ Productions*	27	*23 Sep 95*	2
Originally recorded by the Eagles.				
5 MILES TO EMPTY	*Epic*	12	*17 May 97*	4
KISS AND TELL	*Epic*	21	*27 Sep 97*	2
ALBUMS:	**HITS 2**			**WEEKS 16**
FROM THE BOTTOM UP	*MJJ Productions*	18	*29 Apr 95*	13
STILL CLIMBING	*Epic*	19	*31 May 97*	3

BROWNSVILLE STATION — US

SINGLES:	HITS 1			WEEKS 6
SMOKIN' IN THE BOY'S ROOM	*Philips*	27	*2 Mar 74*	6

Dave BRUBECK QUARTET — US

SINGLES:	HITS 3			WEEKS 30
TAKE FIVE	*Fontana*	6	*28 Oct 61*	15
IT'S A RAGGY WALTZ	*Fontana*	36	*10 Feb 62*	3
UNSQUARE DANCE	*CBS*	14	*19 May 62*	12
EPS:	**HITS 2**			**WEEKS 41**
THE DAVE BRUBECK QUARTET IN EUROPE - NO. 1	*Fontana*	15	*26 Mar 60*	1
TAKE FIVE	*Fontana*	4	*30 Sep 61*	40
ALBUMS:	**HITS 2**			**WEEKS 17**
TIME OUT	*Fontana*	11	*25 Jun 60*	1
TIME FURTHER OUT	*Fontana*	12	*7 Apr 62*	16

Jack BRUCE — UK

ALBUMS:	HITS 1			WEEKS 9
SONGS FOR A TAILOR	*Polydor*	6	*27 Sep 69*	9

Tommy BRUCE and the BRUISERS — US

(See also Bruisers.)

SINGLES:	HITS 3			WEEKS 21
AIN'T MISBEHAVIN'	*Columbia*	3	*28 May 60*	16
Originally recorded by Fats Waller.				
BROKEN DOLL	*Columbia*	36	*10 Sep 60*	4
BABETTE	*Columbia*	50	*24 Feb 62*	1
Above hit: Tommy BRUCE.				

Claudia BRUCKEN — Germany

SINGLES:	HITS 2			WEEKS 2
ABSOLUT(E)	*Island*	71	*11 Aug 90*	1
KISS LIKE ETHER	*Island*	63	*16 Feb 91*	1

BRUISERS — UK

(See also Tommy Bruce and the Bruisers.)

SINGLES:	HITS 1			WEEKS 7
BLUE GIRL	*Parlophone*	31	*10 Aug 63*	6
BLUE GIRL [RE]	*Parlophone*	47	*28 Sep 63*	1

Frank BRUNO — UK

SINGLES:	HITS 1			WEEKS 4
EYE OF THE TIGER	*RCA*	28	*23 Dec 95*	4

BRUNO and LIZ and the RADIO 1 POSSE - See Liz KERSHAW and Bruno BROOKES

Tyrone BRUNSON — US

SINGLES:	HITS 1			WEEKS 5
THE SMURF	*Epic*	52	*25 Dec 82*	5

Dora BRYAN — UK

SINGLES:	HITS 1			WEEKS 6
ALL I WANT FOR CHRISTMAS IS A BEATLE	*Fontana*	20	*7 Dec 63*	6

Kelle BRYAN — UK

SINGLES:	HITS 1			WEEKS 4
HIGHER THAN HEAVEN	*Mercury*	14	*2 Oct 99*	4

Anita BRYANT — US

SINGLES:	HITS 2			WEEKS 6
PAPER ROSES •	*London*	49	*28 May 60*	1
PAPER ROSES [RE-1ST]	*London*	45	*2 Jul 60*	1
PAPER ROSES [RE-2ND]	*London*	24	*16 Jul 60*	2
MY LITTLE CORNER OF THE WORLD	*London*	48	*8 Oct 60*	2

Sharon BRYANT – See David MORALES

Peabo BRYSON — US

(See also Peabo Bryson and Roberta Flack.)

SINGLES:	HITS 3			WEEKS 22
BEAUTY AND THE BEAST *From the Walt Disney film of the same name.* *Above hit: Celine DION and Peabo BRYSON.*	*Epic*	9	*16 May 92*	7
BY THE TIME THIS NIGHT IS OVER *Above hit: Kenny G with Peabo BRYSON.*	*Arista*	56	*17 Jul 93*	3
A WHOLE NEW WORLD (ALADDIN'S THEME) *From the Walt Disney film 'Aladdin'.* *Above hit: Regina BELLE and Peabo BRYSON.*	*Columbia*	12	*11 Dec 93*	12

Peabo BRYSON and Roberta FLACK — US

(See also Peabo Bryson; Roberta Flack; Roberta Flack and Donny Hathaway.)

SINGLES:	HITS 1			WEEKS 13
TONIGHT I CELEBRATE MY LOVE	*Capitol*	2	*20 Aug 83*	13
ALBUMS:	**HITS 1**			**WEEKS 10**
BORN TO LOVE	*Capitol*	15	*17 Sep 83*	10

BT — US

SINGLES:	HITS 10			WEEKS 26
EMBRACING THE SUNSHINE	*East West*	34	*18 Mar 95*	2
LOVING YOU MORE	*Perfecto*	28	*16 Sep 95*	2
LOVING YOU MORE [RM] *Above 2: BT featuring Vincent COVELLO.*	*Perfecto*	14	*10 Feb 96*	3
BLUE SKIES *Above hit: BT featuring Tori AMOS.*	*Perfecto*	26	*9 Nov 96*	2
FLAMING JUNE	*Perfecto*	19	*19 Jul 97*	4
LOVE, PEACE AND GREASE	*Perfecto*	41	*29 Nov 97*	1
FLAMING JUNE [RI]	*Perfecto*	28	*10 Jan 98*	4
REMEMBER	*Perfecto*	27	*18 Apr 98*	2
GODSPEED	*Renaissance Music*	54	*21 Nov 98*	1
MERCURY AND SOLACE *Above hit: BT featuring vocals by Jan JOHNSTON.*	*Headspace*	38	*9 Oct 99*	2
DREAMING *Samples Judie Tzuke's We'll Go Dreaming.* *Above hit: BT featuring Kirsty HAWKSHAW.*	*Headspace*	38	*24 Jun 00*	2
NEVER GONNA COME BACK DOWN	*Ministry Of Sound*	51	*23 Jun 01*	1
ALBUMS:	**HITS 2**			**WEEKS 5**
IMA	*Perfecto*	45	*21 Oct 95*	4
ESCM	*Perfecto*	35	*4 Oct 97*	1

BUBBLER RANX – See Peter ANDRE

BUBBLEROCK – See Jonathan KING

BUCCANEER – See PHOEBE ONE featuring RED RAT, GOOFY and BUCCANEER

Catherine BUCHANAN – See JELLYBEAN

Roy BUCHANAN — US

SINGLES:	HITS 1			WEEKS 3
SWEET DREAMS *Originally recorded by Don Gibson.*	*Polydor*	40	*31 Mar 73*	3

Kenny "Dope" presents the BUCKETHEADS — US

SINGLES:	HITS 2			WEEKS 16
THE BOMB (THESE SOUNDS FALL INTO MY MIND) *Samples Chicago's Streetplayer.*	*Positiva*	5	*4 Mar 95*	13
GOT MYSELF TOGETHER *Samples Brass Construction's Movin'.*	*Positiva*	12	*20 Jan 96*	3
ALBUMS:	**HITS 1**			**WEEKS 1**
ALL IN THE MIND	*Positiva*	74	*27 Jan 96*	1

Lindsey BUCKINGHAM — US

SINGLES:	HITS 1		WEEKS
TROUBLE	*Mercury*	31	*▪16 Jan 82*	

ALBUMS:	HITS 1		WEEKS
OUT OF THE CRADLE	*Mercury*	51	*8 Aug 92*

Jeff BUCKLEY — US

SINGLES:	HITS 2		WEEKS
LAST GOODBYE	*Columbia*	54	*27 May 95*
EVERYBODY HERE WANTS YOU	*Columbia*	43	*6 Jun 98*

ALBUMS:	HITS 3		WEEKS 1
GRACE	*Columbia*	50	*27 Aug 94*
SKETCHES FOR MY SWEETHEART THE DRUNK *Compilation including his final session recordings.*	*Columbia*	7	*23 May 98*
MYSTERY WHITE BOY – LIVE 95-96	*Columbia*	8	*20 May 00*

BUCKS FIZZ — UK

SINGLES:	HITS 20			WEEKS 15
MAKING YOUR MIND UP *UK's Eurovision entry in 1981, it came 1st.*	*RCA*	1	*28 Mar 81*	1
PIECE OF THE ACTION	*RCA*	12	*6 Jun 81*	
ONE OF THOSE NIGHTS	*RCA*	20	*15 Aug 81*	1
THE LAND OF MAKE BELIEVE	*RCA*	1	*28 Nov 81*	1
MY CAMERA NEVER LIES	*RCA*	1	*27 Mar 82*	
NOW THOSE DAYS ARE GONE	*RCA*	8	*19 Jun 82*	
IF YOU CAN'T STAND THE HEAT	*RCA*	10	*27 Nov 82*	1
RUN FOR YOUR LIFE	*RCA*	14	*12 Mar 83*	
WHEN WE WERE YOUNG	*RCA*	10	*18 Jun 83*	
LONDON TOWN	*RCA*	34	*1 Oct 83*	
RULES OF THE GAME	*RCA*	57	*17 Dec 83*	
TALKING IN YOUR SLEEP	*RCA*	15	*25 Aug 84*	
GOLDEN DAYS	*RCA*	42	*27 Oct 84*	
I HEAR TALK	*RCA*	34	*29 Dec 84*	
YOU AND YOUR HEART SO BLUE	*RCA*	43	*22 Jun 85*	
MAGICAL	*RCA*	57	*14 Sep 85*	
NEW BEGINNING (MAMBA SEYRA)	*Polydor*	8	*7 Jun 86*	1
LOVE THE ONE YOU'RE WITH	*Polydor*	47	*30 Aug 86*	
KEEP EACH OTHER WARM	*Polydor*	45	*15 Nov 86*	
HEART OF STONE	*RCA*	50	*5 Nov 88*	

ALBUMS:	HITS 6			WEEKS 8
BUCKS FIZZ	*RCA*	14	*8 Aug 81*	2
ARE YOU READY?	*RCA*	10	*8 May 82*	2
HAND CUT	*RCA*	17	*19 Mar 83*	1
GREATEST HITS	*RCA*	25	*3 Dec 83*	1
I HEAR TALK	*RCA*	66	*24 Nov 84*	2
THE WRITING ON THE WALL	*Polydor*	89	*13 Dec 86*	1

BUCKSHOT LEFONQUE — US

SINGLES:	HITS 1			WEEKS 1
ANOTHER DAY	*Columbia*	65	*6 Dec 97*	1

Harold BUDD, Elizabeth FRASER, Robin GUTHRIE and Simon RAYMONDE — UK

ALBUMS:	HITS 1			WEEKS 2
THE MOON AND THE MELODIES	*4AD*	46	*22 Nov 86*	2

Roy BUDD — UK

SINGLES:	HITS 1			WEEKS 1
THE THEME FROM GET CARTER	*Cinephile*	68	*10 Jul 99*	1

ALBUMS:	HITS 1			WEEKS 1
GET CARTER [OST] *First UK release of the original 1970 film soundtrack.*	*Cinephile*	68	*19 Sep 98*	1

BUDGIE — UK

SINGLES:	HITS 1			WEEKS 2
KEEPING A RENDEZVOUS	*RCA*	71	*3 Oct 81*	2

ALBUMS:	HITS 4			WEEKS 10
IN FOR THE KILL	*MCA*	29	*8 Jun 74*	3
BANDOLIER	*MCA*	36	*27 Sep 75*	4
NIGHT FLIGHT	*RCA*	68	*31 Oct 81*	2
DELIVER US FROM EVIL	*RCA*	62	*23 Oct 82*	1

BUFFALO G — Ireland

INGLES:	HITS 1			WEEKS 4
'E'RE REALLY SAYING SOMETHING	*Epic*	17	*10 Jun 00*	3
'E'RE REALLY SAYING SOMETHING [RE]	*Epic*	74	*8 Jul 00*	1

BUFFALO TOM — US

INGLES:	HITS 1			WEEKS 5
OING UNDERGROUND	*Ignition*	6	*23 Oct 99*	5
A] listed with Carnation by Liam Gallagher and Steve Cradock. From the Jam tribute album Fire & Skill.				
LBUMS:	**HITS 3**			**WEEKS 5**
ET ME COME OVER	*Situation Two*	49	*14 Mar 92*	1
IG RED LETTER DAY)	*Beggars Banquet*	17	*9 Oct 93*	3
EEPY EYED	*Beggars Banquet*	31	*22 Jul 95*	1

BUG KANN and the PLASTIC JAM — UK

INGLES:	HITS 1			WEEKS 2
IADE IN TWO MINUTES	*Optimum Dance*	70	*31 Aug 91*	1
bove hit: BUG KANN and the PLASTIC JAM featuring Patti LOW and DOOGIE.				
IADE IN TWO MINUTES [RM]	*PWL*	64	*26 Feb 94*	1

BUGGLES — UK

INGLES:	HITS 4			WEEKS 28
IDEO KILLED THE RADIO STAR	*Island*	1	*22 Sep 79*	11
he first video shown on MTV in America. Originally recorded by Bruce Wooley and the Camera Club.				
HE PLASTIC AGE	*Island*	16	*26 Jan 80*	8
LEAN, CLEAN	*Island*	38	*5 Apr 80*	5
riginally recorded by Bruce Wooley and the Camera Club.				
LSTREE	*Island*	55	*8 Nov 80*	4
LBUMS:	**HITS 1**			**WEEKS 6**
HE AGE OF PLASTIC	*Island*	27	*16 Feb 80*	6

LTJ BUKEM — UK

LBUMS:	HITS 1			WEEKS 3
OURNEY INWARDS	*Good Looking*	40	*8 Apr 00*	3

James BULLER — UK

INGLES:	HITS 1			WEEKS 1
AN'T SMILE WITHOUT YOU	*BBC Music*	51	*6 Mar 99*	1
rom the BBC TV series 'Sunburn'. Originally recorded by David Martin.				

BULLETPROOF — UK

SINGLES:	HITS 1			WEEKS 1
SAY YEAH/DANCE TO THE RHYTHM	*Tidy Trax*	62	*10 Mar 01*	1

B. BUMBLE and the STINGERS — US

SINGLES:	HITS 1			WEEKS 26
NUT ROCKER	*Top Rank*	1	*21 Apr 62*	15
Based upon Tchaikovsky's Nutcracker Suite. Originally recorded by Jack B. Nimble and the Quicks.				
NUT ROCKER [RI]	*Stateside*	19	*3 Jun 72*	11

BUMP — UK

SINGLES:	HITS 1			WEEKS 5
I'M RUSHING	*Good Boy*	40	*4 Jul 92*	4
I'M RUSHIN' 95 [RM]	*Deconstruction*	45	*11 Nov 95*	1
Remixed by David Valentine.				

BUMP and FLEX — UK

SINGLES:	HITS 1			WEEKS 1
LONG TIME COMING	*Heat Recordings*	73	*23 May 98*	1
Originally released in 1997.				

BUNKER KRU/HARLEQUIN 4'S — US

SINGLES:	HITS 1			WEEKS 4
SET IT OFF (BUNKER '88 MIX)	*Champion*	55	*19 Mar 88*	4
Original release reached No. 78 in 1986.				

Emma BUNTON — UK

SINGLES:	HITS 4			WEEKS 35
WHAT I AM	*VC Recordings*	2	*13 Nov 99*	24
Above hit: TIN TIN OUT featuring Emma BUNTON.				

WHAT TOOK YOU SO LONG?	*Virgin*	1	*14 Apr 01*
TAKE MY BREATH AWAY	*Virgin*	5	*8 Sep 01*
WE'RE NOT GONNA SLEEP TONIGHT	*Virgin*	20	*22 Dec 01*
ALBUMS:	**HITS 1**		**WEEKS**
A GIRL LIKE ME	*Virgin*	4	*28 Apr 01*

Eric BURDON and WAR — UK

(See also Animals; War.)

ALBUMS:	**HITS 1**		**WEEKS**
ERIC BURDON DECLARES WAR	*Polydor*	50	*3 Oct 70*

Geoffrey BURGON — UK

SINGLES:	**HITS 1**		**WEEKS**
BRIDESHEAD THEME *From the Granada ITV series.*	*Chrysalis*	48	*26 Dec 81*
ALBUMS:	**HITS 1**		**WEEKS**
BRIDESHEAD REVISITED [OST-TV]	*Chrysalis*	50	*21 Nov 81*

Keni BURKE — US

SINGLES:	**HITS 2**		**WEEKS**
LET SOMEBODY LOVE YOU	*RCA*	59	*27 Jun 81*
RISIN' TO THE TOP *Original release reached No. 96 in 1987.*	*RCA*	70	*18 Apr 92*

Jean-Jacques BURNEL — UK

(See also Dave Greenfield and Jean-Jacques Burnel.)

ALBUMS:	**HITS 1**		**WEEKS**
EUROMAN COMETH	*United Artists*	40	*21 Apr 79*

Hank C. BURNETTE — Sweden

SINGLES:	**HITS 1**		**WEEKS**
SPINNING ROCK BOOGIE	*Sonet*	21	*30 Oct 76*

Johnny BURNETTE — US

SINGLES:	**HITS 5**		**WEEKS 4**
DREAMIN'	*London*	5	*1 Oct 60*
• YOU'RE SIXTEEN *Originally called You're 13.*	*London*	3	*14 Jan 61*
LITTLE BOY SAD	*London*	12	*15 Apr 61*
GIRLS	*London*	37	*12 Aug 61*
CLOWN SHOES	*Liberty*	35	*19 May 62*

Rocky BURNETTE — US

SINGLES:	**HITS 1**		**WEEKS**
TIRED OF TOEIN' THE LINE *Features Dave Edmunds on guitar.*	*EMI*	58	*17 Nov 79*

Jerry BURNS — UK

SINGLES:	**HITS 1**		**WEEKS**
PALE RED	*Columbia*	64	*25 Apr 92*

Ray BURNS — UK

SINGLES:	**HITS 2**		**WEEKS 1**
• MOBILE *Above hit: Ray BURNS with Eric JUPP and his Orchestra.*	*Columbia*	4	*12 Feb 55*
• THAT'S HOW A LOVE SONG WAS BORN *Above hit: Ray BURNS with the CORONETS.*	*Columbia*	14	*27 Aug 55*

BURRELLS – See RESONANCE featuring the BURRELLS

Malandra BURROWS — UK

SINGLES:	**HITS 3**		**WEEKS 1**
JUST THIS SIDE OF LOVE *From the Yorkshire TV series 'Emmerdale'.*	*Yorkshire Television Entertainment*	11	*1 Dec 90*
CARNIVAL IN HEAVEN	*warner.esp*	49	*18 Oct 97*
DON'T LEAVE ME	*warner.esp*	54	*29 Aug 98*

Jenny BURTON — US

SINGLES:	**HITS 1**		**WEEKS 2**
BAD HABITS	*Atlantic*	68	*30 Mar 85*

BURUNDI STEIPHENSON BLACK — Burundi/France

SINGLES:	HITS 1			WEEKS 14
URUNDI BLACK	*Barclay*	31	*13 Nov 71*	14

BUS STOP — UK/Jamaica

SINGLES:	HITS 4			WEEKS 19
UNG FU FIGHTING	*All Around The World*	8	*23 May 98*	11
amples Douglas' original vocal.				
Above hit: BUS STOP featuring Carl DOUGLAS.				
OU AIN'T SEEN NOTHING YET	*All Around The World*	22	*24 Oct 98*	4
eatured in the ITV series 'Gladiators', accompanying a game called Vertigo.				
Above hit: BUS STOP featuring Randy BACHMAN.				
UMP	*All Around The World*	23	*10 Apr 99*	3
ET IT ON	*All Around The World*	59	*7 Oct 00*	1
amples T-Rex's Get It On.				
Above hit: BUS STOP featuring T-REX				

BUS75 - See WHALE

Lou BUSCH and his Orchestra — US

(See also Joe 'Fingers' Carr.)

SINGLES:	HITS 1			WEEKS 17
ZAMBESI	*Capitol*	2	*28 Jan 56*	17

BUSH — UK

SINGLES:	HITS 7			WEEKS 13
MACHINEHEAD	*Interscope*	48	*8 Jun 96*	2
SWALLOWED	*Interscope*	7	*1 Mar 97*	5
GREEDY FLY	*Interscope*	22	*7 Jun 97*	2
BONEDRIVEN	*Interscope*	49	*1 Nov 97*	1
THE CHEMICALS BETWEEN US	*Trauma*	46	*4 Dec 99*	1
WARM MACHINE	*Trauma*	45	*18 Mar 00*	1
LETTING THE CABLES SLEEP	*Trauma*	51	*3 Jun 00*	1
ALBUMS:	**HITS 4**			**WEEKS 18**
SIXTEEN STONE	*Atlantic*	42	*15 Jun 96*	3
RAZORBLADE SUITCASE	*Interscope*	4	*1 Feb 97*	12
THE SCIENCE OF THINGS	*Polydor*	28	*6 Nov 99*	2
GOLDEN STATE	*Atlantic*	53	*10 Nov 01*	1

Kate BUSH — UK

SINGLES:	HITS 26			WEEKS 168
WUTHERING HEIGHTS	*EMI*	1	*11 Feb 78*	12
WUTHERING HEIGHTS [RE]	*EMI*	75	*13 May 78*	1
THE MAN WITH THE CHILD IN HIS EYES	*EMI*	6	*10 Jun 78*	11
HAMMER HORROR	*EMI*	44	*11 Nov 78*	6
WOW	*EMI*	14	*17 Mar 79*	10
KATE BUSH ON STAGE [EP]	*EMI*	10	*15 Sep 79*	9
Lead track: Them Heavy People. Live recordings from a benefit concert at Hammersmith Odeon, London, 12 May 79.				
BREATHING	*EMI*	16	*26 Apr 80*	7
BABOOSHKA	*EMI*	5	*5 Jul 80*	10
ARMY DREAMERS	*EMI*	16	*4 Oct 80*	9
DECEMBER WILL BE MAGIC AGAIN	*EMI*	29	*6 Dec 80*	7
SAT IN YOUR LAP	*EMI*	11	*11 Jul 81*	7
THE DREAMING	*EMI*	48	*7 Aug 82*	3
RUNNING UP THAT HILL	*EMI*	3	*17 Aug 85*	11
CLOUDBUSTING	*EMI*	20	*26 Oct 85*	6
HOUNDS OF LOVE	*EMI*	18	*1 Mar 86*	5
THE BIG SKY	*EMI*	37	*10 May 86*	3
DON'T GIVE UP	*Virgin*	9	*1 Nov 86*	11
Above hit: Peter GABRIEL and Kate BUSH.				
EXPERIMENT IV	*EMI*	23	*8 Nov 86*	4
THE SENSUAL WORLD	*EMI*	12	*30 Sep 89*	5
THIS WOMAN'S WORK	*EMI*	25	*2 Dec 89*	5
LOVE AND ANGER	*EMI*	38	*10 Mar 90*	3
ROCKET MAN (I THINK IT'S GOING TO BE A LONG, LONG TIME)	*Mercury*	12	*7 Dec 91*	8
RUBBERBAND GIRL	*EMI*	12	*18 Sep 93*	5
MOMENTS OF PLEASURE	*EMI*	26	*27 Nov 93*	3
THE RED SHOES	*EMI*	21	*16 Apr 94*	3
THE MAN I LOVE	*Mercury*	27	*30 Jul 94*	2
Above hit: Larry ADLER and Kate BUSH.				
AND SO IS LOVE	*EMI*	26	*19 Nov 94*	2
ALBUMS:	**HITS 8**			**WEEKS 281**
THE KICK INSIDE	*EMI*	3	*11 Mar 78*	70
LIONHEART	*EMI*	6	*25 Nov 78*	36

NEVER FOR EVER	*EMI*	1	*20 Sep 80*	
THE DREAMING	*EMI*	3	*25 Sep 82*	
HOUNDS OF LOVE	*EMI*	1	*28 Sep 85*	
The second side is titled The Ninth Wave.				
THE WHOLE STORY	*EMI*	1	*22 Nov 86*	
Compilation. Includes re-entries through to 1995.				
THE SENSUAL WORLD	*EMI*	2	*28 Oct 89*	
THE RED SHOES	*EMI*	2	*13 Nov 93*	
THE WHOLE STORY [RE]	*EMI*	45	*13 Oct 01*	

BUSTER — UK

SINGLES:	HITS 1			WEEKS
SUNDAY	*RCA Victor*	49	*19 Jun 76*	

Sam BUTERA and the WITNESSES – See Louis PRIMA

Bernard BUTLER — UK

(See also McAlmont and Butler.)

SINGLES:	HITS 4			WEEKS
STAY	*Creation*	12	*17 Jan 98*	
NOT ALONE	*Creation*	27	*28 Mar 98*	
A CHANGE OF HEART	*Creation*	45	*27 Jun 98*	
YOU MUST GO ON	*Creation*	44	*23 Oct 99*	
ALBUMS:	**HITS 2**			**WEEKS**
PEOPLE MOVE ON	*Creation*	11	*18 Apr 98*	
FRIENDS AND LOVERS	*Creation*	43	*6 Nov 99*	

Gerry BUTLER STRINGS – See WHITE PLAINS

Jonathan BUTLER — US

SINGLES:	HITS 2			WEEKS 1
IF YOU'RE READY (COME GO WITH ME)	*Jive*	30	*25 Jan 86*	
Above hit: Ruby TURNER featuring Jonathan BUTLER.				
LIES	*Jive*	18	*8 Aug 87*	1
ALBUMS:	**HITS 2**			**WEEKS 1**
JONATHAN BUTLER	*Jive*	12	*12 Sep 87*	1
MORE THAN FRIENDS	*Jive*	29	*4 Feb 89*	

BUTTERSCOTCH — UK

SINGLES:	HITS 1			WEEKS 1
DON'T YOU KNOW (SHE SAID HELLO)	*RCA Victor*	17	*2 May 70*	1

BUTTHOLE SURFERS — US

SINGLES:	HITS 1			WEEKS
PEPPER	*Capitol*	59	*5 Oct 96*	
ALBUMS:	**HITS 2**			**WEEKS 2**
PIOUHGD	*Rough Trade*	68	*16 Mar 91*	
INDEPENDENT WORM SALOON	*Capitol*	73	*3 Apr 93*	

BUZZCOCKS — UK

SINGLES:	HITS 9			WEEKS 53
WHAT DO I GET?	*United Artists*	37	*18 Feb 78*	3
I DON'T MIND	*United Artists*	55	*13 May 78*	2
LOVE YOU MORE	*United Artists*	34	*15 Jul 78*	6
EVER FALLEN IN LOVE (WITH SOMEONE YOU SHOULDN'T'VE)	*United Artists*	12	*23 Sep 78*	11
PROMISES	*United Artists*	20	*25 Nov 78*	10
EVERYBODY'S HAPPY NOWADAYS	*United Artists*	29	*10 Mar 79*	6
HARMONY IN MY HEAD	*United Artists*	32	*21 Jul 79*	6
SPIRAL SCRATCH [EP]	*New Hormones*	31	*25 Aug 79*	6
Lead track: Breakdown. Originally released in 1977.				
Above hit: BUZZCOCKS with Howard DEVOTO.				
ARE EVERYTHING / WHY SHE'S A GIRL FROM THE CHAINSTORE	*United Artists*	61	*6 Sep 80*	3
Why She's A Girl From The Chainstore listed from 13 Sep 80.				
ALBUMS:	**HITS 3**			**WEEKS 23**
ANOTHER MUSIC IN A DIFFERENT KITCHEN	*United Artists*	15	*25 Mar 78*	11
LOVE BITES	*United Artists*	13	*7 Oct 78*	9
A DIFFERENT KIND OF TENSION	*United Artists*	26	*6 Oct 79*	3

BY ALL MEANS — US

SINGLES:	HITS 1			WEEKS 2
I SURRENDER TO YOUR LOVE	*Fourth & Broadway*	65	*18 Jun 88*	2
ALBUMS:	**HITS 1**			**WEEKS 1**
BY ALL MEANS	*Fourth & Broadway*	80	*16 Jul 88*	1

Max BYGRAVES — UK

(See also All Star Hit Parade.)

SINGLES:	HITS 18			WEEKS 131
COWPUNCHER'S CANTATA [M]	*His Master's Voice*	11	*15 Nov 52*	1
COWPUNCHER'S CANTATA [M] [RE-1ST]	*His Master's Voice*	8	*3 Jan 53*	1
COWPUNCHER'S CANTATA [M] [RE-2ND]	*His Master's Voice*	6	*24 Jan 53*	5
COWPUNCHER'S CANTATA [M] [RE-3RD]	*His Master's Voice*	10	*7 Mar 53*	1
THE GANG THAT SANG HEART OF MY HEART	*His Master's Voice*	7	*15 May 54*	8
Above hit: Max BYGRAVES and vocal quartet.				
GILLY GILLY OSSENFEFFER KATZENELLENBOGEN BY THE SEA	*His Master's Voice*	7	*11 Sep 54*	7
Above hit: Max BYGRAVES with CHILDREN'S CHORUS.				
GILLY GILLY OSSENFEFFER KATZENELLENBOGEN BY THE SEA [RE]	*His Master's Voice*	20	*6 Nov 54*	1
MISTER SANDMAN	*His Master's Voice*	16	*22 Jan 55*	1
Originally recorded by Vaughan Monroe.				
MEET ME ON THE CORNER	*His Master's Voice*	2	*19 Nov 55*	11
THE BALLAD OF DAVY CROCKETT	*His Master's Voice*	20	*18 Feb 56*	1
Above hit: Max BYGRAVES with CHILDREN'S CHORUS.				
OUT OF TOWN	*His Master's Voice*	18	*26 May 56*	7
HEART	*Decca*	14	*6 Apr 57*	8
Above hit: Max BYGRAVES with Malcolm LOCKYER and his Orchestra.				
TULIPS FROM AMSTERDAM / YOU NEED HANDS	*Decca*	3	*3 May 58*	25
Tulips From Amsterdam listed from 10.May 58.				
Above hit: Max BYGRAVES with Eric RODGERS and his Orchestra / Max BYGRAVES with the CLARKE BROTHERS and Eric RODGERS and his Orchestra.				
LITTLE TRAIN / GOTTA HAVE RAIN	*Decca*	28	*23 Aug 58*	2
Little Train from the film 'A Cry From The Streets'.				
(I LOVE TO PLAY) MY UKELELE	*Decca*	19	*3 Jan 59*	4
JINGLE BELL ROCK	*Decca*	7	*19 Dec 59*	4
Original by Bobby Helms reached No. 6 in the US in 1957.				
FINGS AIN'T WOT THEY USED T'BE	*Decca*	5	*12 Mar 60*	15
Originally recorded by Lionel Bart.				
CONSIDER YOURSELF	*Decca*	50	*30 Jul 60*	1
THE BELLS OF AVIGNON	*Decca*	36	*3 Jun 61*	5
Above hit: Max BYGRAVES with the CORONA CHILDREN.				
YOU'RE MY EVERYTHING	*Pye*	50	*22 Feb 69*	1
From the film 'The Laugh Parade'.				
YOU'RE MY EVERYTHING [RE]	*Pye*	34	*8 Mar 69*	3
DECK OF CARDS	*Pye*	13	*6 Oct 73*	15
WHITE CHRISTMAS	*Parkfield*	71	*9 Dec 89*	4

ALBUMS:	HITS 12			WEEKS 176
SING ALONG WITH MAX	*Pye*	4	*23 Sep 72*	44
SING ALONG WITH MAX VOLUME 2	*Pye*	11	*2 Dec 72*	23
SINGALONGAMAX VOLUME 3	*Pye*	5	*5 May 73*	30
SINGALONGAMAX VOLUME 4	*Pye*	7	*29 Sep 73*	12
SINGALONGPARTY SONG	*Pye*	15	*15 Dec 73*	6
YOU MAKE ME FEEL LIKE SINGING A SONG	*Pye*	39	*12 Oct 74*	3
SINGALONGAXMAS	*Pye*	21	*7 Dec 74*	6
100 GOLDEN GREATS	*Ronco*	3	*13 Nov 76*	21
LINGALONGAMAX	*Ronco*	39	*28 Oct 78*	5
THE SONG AND DANCE MEN	*Pye*	67	*16 Dec 78*	1
SINGALONGAWARYEARS	*Parkfield Music*	5	*19 Aug 89*	19
SINGALONGAWARYEARS VOLUME 2	*Parkfield*	33	*25 Nov 89*	6

BYKER GROOOVE! — UK

SINGLES:	HITS 1			WEEKS 3
LOVE YOUR SEXY . . . !!	*Groove*	48	*24 Dec 94*	3

Charlie BYRD – See Stan GETZ and Charlie BYRD

Debra BYRD – See Barry MANILOW

Donald BYRD — US

SINGLES:	HITS 1			WEEKS 6
LOVE HAS COME AROUND / LOVING YOU	*Elektra*	41	*26 Sep 81*	6

ALBUMS:	HITS 1			WEEKS 3
LOVE BYRD	*Elektra*	70	*10 Oct 81*	3

Gary BYRD and the GB EXPERIENCE — US

SINGLES:	HITS 1			WEEKS 9
THE CROWN	*Motown*	6	*23 Jul 83*	9
Features vocals by and co written with Stevie Wonder.				

BYRDS — US

SINGLES:	HITS 6			WEEKS 52
MR. TAMBOURINE MAN	*CBS*	1	*19 Jun 65*	14
Originally recorded by Bob Dylan.				
ALL I REALLY WANT TO DO	*CBS*	4	*14 Aug 65*	10
TURN! TURN! TURN! (TO EVERYTHING THERE IS A SEASON)	*CBS*	26	*13 Nov 65*	8
Lyrics adapted from the Book Of Ecclesiastes by Pete Seeger.				
EIGHT MILES HIGH	*CBS*	24	*7 May 66*	9
YOU AIN'T GOING NOWHERE	*CBS*	45	*8 Jun 68*	3
Written by Bob Dylan.				
CHESTNUT MARE	*CBS*	19	*13 Feb 71*	8

EPS:	HITS 2			WEEKS 5
THE TIMES THEY ARE A' CHANGIN'	*CBS*	15	*19 Feb 66*	4
EIGHT MILES HIGH	*CBS*	8	*15 Oct 66*	1

ALBUMS:	HITS 10			WEEKS 42
MR. TAMBOURINE MAN	*CBS*	7	*28 Aug 65*	12
TURN, TURN, TURN	*CBS*	11	*9 Apr 66*	5
5TH DIMENSION	*CBS*	27	*1 Oct 66*	2
YOUNGER THAN YESTERDAY	*CBS*	37	*22 Apr 67*	4
THE NOTORIOUS BYRD BROTHERS	*CBS*	12	*4 May 68*	11
DR. BYRDS AND MR HYDE	*CBS*	15	*24 May 69*	1
BALLAD OF EASY RIDER	*CBS*	41	*14 Feb 70*	1
UNTITLED	*CBS*	11	*28 Nov 70*	4
BYRDS	*Asylum*	31	*14 Apr 73*	1
HISTORY OF THE BYRDS	*CBS*	47	*19 May 73*	1

David BYRNE — UK

(See also Brian Eno and David Byrne.)

ALBUMS:	HITS 4			WEEKS 10
REI MOMO	*Sire*	52	*21 Oct 89*	2
UH-OH	*Luaka Bop*	26	*14 Mar 92*	5
DAVID BYRNE	*Luaka Bop*	44	*4 Jun 94*	2
LOOK INTO THE EYEBALL	*Luaka Bop*	58	*19 May 01*	1

Ed BYRNES — US

SINGLES:	HITS 1			WEEKS 8
KOOKIE, KOOKIE (LEND ME YOUR COMB)	*Warner Brothers*	27	*7 May 60*	8
From '77 Sunset Strip'.				
Above hit: Ed BYRNES and Connie STEVENS with the Big Sound of Don RALKE.				

EPS:	HITS 1			WEEKS 1
KOOKIE	*Warner Brothers*	20	*25 Mar 61*	1

BYSTANDERS — UK

SINGLES:	HITS 1			WEEKS 1
98.6	*Piccadilly*	45	*11 Feb 67*	1

C

Andy C – See SHIMON and Andy C

Melanie C — UK

SINGLES:	HITS 6			WEEKS 74
WHEN YOU'RE GONE	*Mercury*	3	*12 Dec 98*	19
Above hit: Bryan ADAMS featuring Melanie C.				
GOIN' DOWN	*Virgin*	4	*9 Oct 99*	4
GOIN' DOWN [RE]	*Virgin*	64	*13 Nov 99*	2
NORTHERN STAR	*Virgin*	4	*4 Dec 99*	11
NEVER BE THE SAME AGAIN	*Virgin*	1	*1 Apr 00*	14
Above hit: Melanie C featuring Lisa 'Left Eye' LOPES.				
NEVER BE THE SAME AGAIN [RE]	*Virgin*	70	*22 Jul 00*	2
I TURN TO YOU	*Virgin*	1	*19 Aug 00*	12
IF THAT WERE ME	*Virgin*	18	*9 Dec 00*	8
Proceeds to Kandu Arts For Sustainable Development, a charity to support the young homeless.				
IF THAT WERE ME [RE]	*Virgin*	72	*3 Mar 01*	2

ALBUMS:	HITS 1			WEEKS 64
NORTHERN STAR	*Virgin*	10	*30 Oct 99*	13
NORTHERN STAR [RE]	*Virgin*	4	*26 Feb 00*	51

Roy C — US

SINGLES:	HITS 1			WEEKS 24
SHOTGUN WEDDING	*Island*	6	*23 Apr 66*	11
SHOTGUN WEDDING [RI]	*UK*	8	*25 Nov 72*	13

C&C MUSIC FACTORY — US

SINGLES:	HITS 10			WEEKS 53
GONNA MAKE YOU SWEAT (EVERYBODY DANCE NOW)	*CBS*	3	*15 Dec 90*	12
HERE WE GO	*Columbia*	20	*30 Mar 91*	7
THINGS THAT MAKE YOU GO HMMM . . .	*Columbia*	4	*6 Jul 91*	11
Above 3: C&C MUSIC FACTORY (featuring Freedom WILLIAMS).				
JUST A TOUCH OF LOVE (EVERYDAY)	*Columbia*	31	*23 Nov 91*	3
Above hit: C&C MUSIC FACTORY featuring Zelma DAVIS.				
PRIDE (IN THE NAME OF LOVE)	*Columbia*	15	*18 Jan 92*	5
A DEEPER LOVE	*Columbia*	15	*14 Mar 92*	5
Above 2: CLIVILLES and COLE.				
KEEP IT COMIN' (DANCE TIL YOU CAN'T DANCE NO MORE)	*Columbia*	34	*3 Oct 92*	3
From the film 'Buffy The Vampire Slayer'.				
Above hit: C&C MUSIC FACTORY featuring Q UNIQUE and Deborah COOPER.				
DO YOU WANNA GET FUNKY	*Columbia*	27	*27 Aug 94*	3
I FOUND LOVE / TAKE A TOKE	*Columbia*	26	*18 Feb 95*	2
The 12" format of Take A Toke featured Martha Wash.				
Above hit: C & C MUSIC FACTORY featuring Zelma DAVIS / C & C MUSIC FACTORY featuring TRILOGY.				
I'LL ALWAYS BE AROUND	*MCA*	42	*11 Nov 95*	2
Above hit: C+C MUSIC FACTORY.				

ALBUMS:	HITS 2			WEEKS 14
GONNA MAKE YOU SWEAT	*Columbia*	8	*9 Feb 91*	13
GREATEST REMIXES VOLUME 1	*Columbia*	45	*28 Mar 92*	1
Above hit: CLIVILLES and COLE.				

C.C.S. — UK

SINGLES:	HITS 5			WEEKS 55
WHOLE LOTTA LOVE	*RAK*	13	*31 Oct 70*	13
The theme to the BBC 1's 'Top Of The Pops' in the 1970s.				
WALKING	*RAK*	7	*27 Feb 71*	16
TAP TURNS ON THE WATER	*RAK*	5	*4 Sep 71*	13
BROTHER	*RAK*	25	*4 Mar 72*	8
THE BAND PLAYED THE BOOGIE	*RAK*	36	*4 Aug 73*	5

ALBUMS:	HITS 1			WEEKS 5
C.C.S.	*RAK*	23	*8 Apr 72*	5

C.J. and CO. — US

SINGLES:	HITS 1			WEEKS 2
DEVIL'S GUN	*Atlantic*	43	*30 Jul 77*	2

C.L.S. — US

SINGLES:	HITS 1			WEEKS 1
CAN YOU FEEL IT?	*Satellite*	46	*30 May 98*	1

C.O.D. — US

SINGLES:	HITS 1			WEEKS 2
IN THE BOTTLE	*Streetwave*	54	*14 May 83*	2

ÇA VA ÇA VA — UK

SINGLES:	HITS 2			WEEKS 8
WHERE'S ROMEO?	*Regard*	49	*18 Sep 82*	5
BROTHER BRIGHT	*Regard*	65	*19 Feb 83*	3

Montserrat CABALLE – See Placido DOMINGO, Jose CARRERAS and Montserrat CABALLE; Freddie MERCURY and Montserrat CABALLE

CABANA — Brazil

SINGLES:	HITS 1			WEEKS 1
BAILANDO CON LOBOS	*Hi-Life*	65	*15 Jul 95*	1

CABARET VOLTAIRE — UK

SINGLES:	HITS 4			WEEKS 8
DON'T ARGUE	*Parlophone*	69	*18 Jul 87*	2
HYPNOTISED	*Parlophone*	66	*4 Nov 89*	2
KEEP ON	*Parlophone*	55	*12 May 90*	2
EASY LIFE	*Parlophone*	61	*18 Aug 90*	2

ALBUMS:	HITS 5			WEEKS 11
2 X 45	*Rough Trade*	98	*26 Jun 82*	1
THE CRACKDOWN	*Some Bizzare*	31	*13 Aug 83*	5
MICRO-PHONIES	*Some Bizzare*	69	*10 Nov 84*	1
DRINKING GASOLINE	*Some Bizzare*	71	*3 Aug 85*	2
THE COVENANT, THE SWORD AND THE ARM OF THE LAW	*Some Bizzare*	57	*26 Oct 85*	2

CABLE — UK

SINGLES:	HITS 1			WEEKS 2
FREEZE THE ATLANTIC	*Infectious*	44	*14 Jun 97*	2

Albert CABRERA – See David MORALES and Albert CABRERA present MOCA featuring DEANNA

CACIQUE — UK

SINGLES:	HITS 1			WEEKS 1
DEVOTED TO YOU	*Diamond Duel*	69	*1 Jun 85*	1

CACTUS WORLD NEWS — Ireland

SINGLES:	HITS 3			WEEKS 7
YEARS LATER	*MCA*	59	*8 Feb 86*	3
WORLDS APART	*MCA*	58	*26 Apr 86*	3
THE BRIDGE	*MCA*	74	*20 Sep 86*	1
ALBUMS:	**HITS 1**			**WEEKS 2**
URBAN BEACHES	*MCA*	56	*24 May 86*	2

David CADDICK – See Michael CRAWFORD

CADETS with Eileen REED Lead vocal — Ireland

SINGLES:	HITS 1			WEEKS 1
JEALOUS HEART	*Pye*	42	*5 Jun 65*	1

Susan CADOGAN — UK

SINGLES:	HITS 2			WEEKS 19
HURT SO GOOD *Originally recorded by Katie Love and The Four Shades of Black.*	*Magnet*	4	*5 Apr 75*	12
LOVE ME BABY	*Magnet*	22	*19 Jul 75*	7

Athena CAGE – See Keith SWEAT

Al CAIOLA and his Orchestra — US

SINGLES:	HITS 1			WEEKS 6
THEME FROM 'THE MAGNIFICENT SEVEN' *From 24 Jun 61 sales were combined for issues on both the HMV and London labels.*	*His Master's Voice / London*	34	*17 Jun 61*	6

CAKE — US

SINGLES:	HITS 4			WEEKS 7
THE DISTANCE	*Capricorn*	22	*22 Mar 97*	3
I WILL SURVIVE	*Capricorn*	29	*31 May 97*	2
NEVER THERE	*Capricorn*	66	*1 May 99*	1
SHORT SKIRT/LONG JACKET *One song.*	*Columbia*	63	*3 Nov 01*	1
ALBUMS:	**HITS 1**			**WEEKS 2**
FASHION NUGGET	*Capricorn*	53	*5 Apr 97*	2

J.J. CALE — US

ALBUMS:	HITS 6			WEEKS 24
TROUBADOUR	*Island*	53	*2 Oct 76*	1
5	*Shelter*	40	*25 Aug 79*	6
SHADES	*Shelter*	44	*21 Feb 81*	7
GRASSHOPPER	*Shelter*	36	*20 Mar 82*	5
NUMBER 8	*Mercury*	47	*24 Sep 83*	3
NUMBER 10	*Silvertone*	58	*26 Sep 92*	2

John CALE – See Lou REED

CALEXICO — US

ALBUMS:	HITS 1			WEEKS 1
HOT RAIL	*Columbia*	60	*20 May 00*	1

CALIBRE CUTS — Multi National

SINGLES:	HITS 1			WEEKS 2
CALIBRE CUTS [M] *16 track montage of 13 singles plus 3 re-makes of hit titles.*	*Calibre*	75	*17 May 80*	2

CALIFORNIA SUNSHINE — Israel/Italy

SINGLES:	HITS 1			WEEKS 1
SUMMER '89	*Perfecto Fluoro*	56	*16 Aug 97*	1

CALL — US

SINGLES:	HITS 1			WEEKS 6
LET THE DAY BEGIN	*MCA*	42	*30 Sep 89*	6

Maria CALLAS — Greece

ALBUMS:	HITS 4			WEEKS 19
THE MARIA CALLAS COLLECTION	*Stylus*	50	*20 Jun 87*	7
DIVA - THE ULTIMATE COLLECTION	*EMI*	61	*24 Feb 96*	1
POPULAR MUSIC FROM TV, FILM AND OPERA	*EMI Classics*	45	*11 Nov 00*	8
THE BEST OF . . . ROMANTIC CALLAS	*EMI Classics*	32	*27 Oct 01*	3

Terry CALLIER — US

(See also Beth Orton.)

SINGLES:	HITS 1			WEEKS 1
LOVE THEME FROM SPARTACUS	*Talkin Loud*	57	*23 May 98*	1

Constantine CALLINICOS - See Mario LANZA

Eddie CALVERT (The Man with the Golden Trumpet) with Norrie PARAMOR and his Orchestra — UK

SINGLES:	HITS 7			WEEKS 80
OH, MEIN PAPA	*Columbia*	1	*19 Dec 53*	21
Originally recorded by Lys Assia.				
CHERRY PINK (AND APPLE BLOSSOM WHITE)	*Columbia*	1	*9 Apr 55*	21
STRANGER IN PARADISE	*Columbia*	14	*14 May 55*	4
From the musical 'Kismet'.				
JOHN AND JULIE	*Columbia*	6	*30 Jul 55*	11
From the film of the same name.				
ZAMBESI	*Columbia*	18	*10 Mar 56*	1
ZAMBESI [RE]	*Columbia*	13	*24 Mar 56*	6
MANDY (THE PANSY)	*Columbia*	9	*8 Feb 58*	14
LITTLE SERENADE (PICCOLISSIMA SERENATA)	*Columbia*	28	*21 Jun 58*	2

Donnie CALVIN - See ROCKERS REVENGE featuring Donnie CALVIN

CAMEL — UK

ALBUMS:	HITS 8			WEEKS 47
THE SNOW GOOSE	*Decca*	22	*24 May 75*	13
MOON MADNESS	*Decca*	15	*17 Apr 76*	6
RAIN DANCES	*Decca*	20	*17 Sep 77*	8
BREATHLESS	*Decca*	26	*14 Oct 78*	1
I CAN SEE YOUR HOUSE FROM HERE	*Decca*	45	*27 Oct 79*	3
NUDE	*Decca*	34	*31 Jan 81*	7
THE SINGLE FACTOR	*Decca*	57	*15 May 82*	5
STATIONARY TRAVELLER	*Decca*	57	*21 Apr 84*	4

CAMEO — US

SINGLES:	HITS 10			WEEKS 71
SHE'S STRANGE	*Club*	37	*31 Mar 84*	8
ATTACK ME WITH YOUR LOVE	*Club*	65	*13 Jul 85*	2
SINGLE LIFE	*Club*	15	*14 Sep 85*	10
SHE'S STRANGE [RI]	*Club*	22	*7 Dec 85*	8
A GOODBYE	*Club*	65	*22 Mar 86*	2
WORD UP	*Club*	3	*30 Aug 86*	13
CANDY	*Club*	27	*29 Nov 86*	9
BACK AND FORTH	*Club*	11	*25 Apr 87*	9
SHE'S MINE	*Club*	35	*17 Oct 87*	4
YOU MAKE ME WORK	*Club*	74	*29 Oct 88*	1
LOVERBOY	*Columbia*	12	*28 Jul 01*	4
Mariah CAREY featuring CAMEO				
LOVERBOY [RE]	*Columbia*	53	*15 Sep 01*	1

ALBUMS:	HITS 3			WEEKS 47
SINGLE LIFE	*Club*	66	*10 Aug 85*	12
WORD UP	*Club*	7	*18 Oct 86*	34
MACHISMO	*Club*	86	*26 Nov 88*	1

Andy CAMERON — UK

SINGLES:	HITS 1			WEEKS 8
ALLY'S TARTAN ARMY	*Klub*	6	*4 Mar 78*	8
A tribute to the Scottish World Cup football squad.				

CAMILLA - See MOJOLATORS featuring CAMILLA

Tony CAMILLO'S BAZUKA — US

SINGLES:	HITS 1			WEEKS 5
DYNOMITE	*A&M*	28	*31 May 75*	5

CAMISRA — UK

SINGLES:	HITS 3			WEEKS 12
LET ME SHOW YOU	*VC Recordings*	5	*21 Feb 98*	8
FEEL THE BEAT	*VC Recordings*	32	*11 Jul 98*	2
CLAP YOUR HANDS	*VC Recordings*	34	*22 May 99*	2

CAMOUFLAGE featuring 'MYSTI' — UK

SINGLES:	HITS 1			WEEKS 3
BEE STING	*State*	48	*24 Sep 77*	3

A CAMP — Sweden

SINGLES:	HITS 1			WEEKS 1
I CAN BUY YOU	*Stockholm*	46	*1 Sep 01*	1

CAMP LO — US

SINGLES:	HITS 1			WEEKS 1
LUCHINI AKA (THIS IS IT)	*ffrr*	74	*16 Aug 97*	1

CAMPAG VELOCET — UK

SINGLES:	HITS 1			WEEKS 1
VITO SATAN	*PIAS Recordings*	75	*19 Feb 00*	1

Ali CAMPBELL — UK

(See also Pato Banton.)

SINGLES:	HITS 3			WEEKS 18
THAT LOOK IN YOUR EYE	*Kuff*	5	*20 May 95*	10
Features vocals by Pamela Starks.				
LET YOUR YEAH BE YEAH	*Kuff*	25	*26 Aug 95*	4
SOMETHIN' STUPID	*Kuff*	30	*9 Dec 95*	4
Above hit: Ali and Kibibi CAMPBELL.				
ALBUMS:	**HITS 1**			**WEEKS 11**
BIG LOVE	*Kuff*	6	*17 Jun 95*	11

Ali and Robin CAMPBELL of UB40 - See Pato BANTON

Danny CAMPBELL and SASHA — UK

SINGLES:	HITS 1			WEEKS 1
TOGETHER	*ffrr*	57	*31 Jul 93*	1

Don CAMPBELL - See GENERAL SAINT

Ellie CAMPBELL — UK

SINGLES:	HITS 3			WEEKS 5
SWEET LIES	*Jive*	42	*3 Apr 99*	1
SO MANY WAYS	*Jive*	26	*14 Aug 99*	3
DON'T WANT YOU BACK	*Jive*	50	*9 Jun 01*	1

Ethna CAMPBELL — UK

SINGLES:	HITS 1			WEEKS 11
THE OLD RUGGED CROSS	*Philips*	33	*27 Dec 75*	11

Glen CAMPBELL — US

(See also Bobbie Gentry and Glen Campbell.)

SINGLES:	HITS 9			WEEKS 84
WICHITA LINEMAN	*Ember*	7	*1 Feb 69*	13
GALVESTON	*Ember*	14	*10 May 69*	10
Originally recorded by Don Ho.				
TRY A LITTLE KINDNESS	*Capitol*	45	*7 Feb 70*	2
HONEY COME BACK	*Capitol*	4	*9 May 70*	19
EVERYTHING A MAN COULD EVER NEED	*Capitol*	32	*26 Sep 70*	5
IT'S ONLY MAKE BELIEVE	*Capitol*	4	*21 Nov 70*	14
DREAM BABY (HOW LONG MUST I DREAM)	*Capitol*	39	*27 Mar 71*	3
RHINESTONE COWBOY	*Capitol*	4	*4 Oct 75*	12
Originally recorded by Larry Weiss.				
SOUTHERN NIGHTS	*Capitol*	28	*26 Mar 77*	6
Originally recorded by Allan Toussaint.				
ALBUMS:	**HITS 9**			**WEEKS 184**
GLEN CAMPBELL LIVE	*Capitol*	16	*31 Jan 70*	14

TRY A LITTLE KINDNESS	*Capitol*	37	*30 May 70*	10
THE GLEN CAMPBELL ALBUM	*Capitol*	16	*12 Dec 70*	5
GLEN CAMPBELL'S GREATEST HITS	*Capitol*	8	*27 Nov 71*	113
RHINESTONE COWBOY	*Capitol*	38	*25 Oct 75*	9
GLEN CAMPBELL'S TWENTY GOLDEN GREATS	*Capitol*	1	*20 Nov 76*	27
SOUTHERN NIGHTS	*Capitol*	51	*23 Apr 77*	1
THE COMPLETE GLEN CAMPBELL	*Stylus*	47	*22 Jul 89*	4
MY HITS AND LOVE SONGS	*Capitol*	50	*2 Oct 99*	1

Ian CAMPBELL FOLK GROUP — UK

SINGLES:	HITS 1			WEEKS 5
• THE TIMES THEY ARE A CHANGIN'	*Transatlantic*	42	*13 Mar 65*	2
THE TIMES THEY ARE A CHANGIN' [RE-1ST]	*Transatlantic*	47	*3 Apr 65*	1
THE TIMES THEY ARE A CHANGIN' [RE-2ND]	*Transatlantic*	46	*17 Apr 65*	2

Jo Ann CAMPBELL — US

SINGLES:	HITS 1			WEEKS 3
• MOTORCYCLE MICHAEL	*His Master's Voice*	41	*10 Jun 61*	3

Junior CAMPBELL — UK

SINGLES:	HITS 2			WEEKS 18
HALLELUJAH FREEDOM	*Deram*	10	*14 Oct 72*	9
SWEET ILLUSION	*Deram*	15	*2 Jun 73*	9

Kibibi CAMPBELL - See Ali CAMPBELL

Naomi CAMPBELL — UK

SINGLES:	HITS 1			WEEKS 3
LOVE AND TEARS	*Epic*	40	*24 Sep 94*	3

Backing vocals by Chrissie Hynde.

Pat CAMPBELL — Ireland

SINGLES:	HITS 1			WEEKS 5
THE DEAL	*Major Minor*	31	*15 Nov 69*	5

Stan CAMPBELL — UK

SINGLES:	HITS 1			WEEKS 3
YEARS GO BY	*WEA*	65	*6 Jun 87*	3

Tevin CAMPBELL — US

SINGLES:	HITS 1			WEEKS 2
TELL ME WHAT YOU WANT ME TO DO	*Qwest*	63	*18 Apr 92*	2

CAM'RON featuring MASE — US

SINGLES:	HITS 1			WEEKS 4
HORSE & CARRIAGE	*Epic*	12	*19 Sep 98*	4

CAN — Germany

SINGLES:	HITS 1			WEEKS 10
I WANT MORE	*Virgin*	26	*28 Aug 76*	10

CANDIDO — US

SINGLES:	HITS 1			WEEKS 3
JINGO	*Excaliber*	55	*18 Jul 81*	3

Originally recorded by Michael Olatunji.

CANDLEWICK GREEN — UK

SINGLES:	HITS 1			WEEKS 8
WHO DO YOU THINK YOU ARE?	*Decca*	21	*23 Feb 74*	8

CANDY FLIP — UK

SINGLES:	HITS 2			WEEKS 14
STRAWBERRY FIELDS FOREVER	*Debut*	3	*17 Mar 90*	10
THIS CAN BE REAL (SMALLER)	*Debut*	60	*14 Jul 90*	4

CANDY GIRLS — UK

SINGLES:	HITS 3			WEEKS 10
FEE FI FO FUM	*VC Recordings*	23	*30 Sep 95*	4
WHAM BAM	*VC Recordings*	20	*24 Feb 96*	4

Above 2: CANDY GIRLS featuring SWEET PUSSY PAULINE.

I WANT CANDY	*Feverpitch*	30	*7 Dec 96*	2
Original by the Strangeloves reached No. 11 in the US in 1965.				
Above hit: CANDY GIRLS featuring Valerie MALCOLM.				

CANDYLAND — UK

SINGLES:	HITS 1			WEEKS 1
FOUNTAIN O' YOUTH	*Non Fiction*	72	*9 Mar 91*	1

CANDYSKINS — UK

SINGLES:	HITS 3			WEEKS 4
MRS HOOVER	*Ultimate*	65	*19 Oct 96*	1
MONDAY MORNING	*Ultimate*	34	*8 Feb 97*	2
HANG MYSELF ON YOU	*Ultimate*	65	*3 May 97*	1

CANIBUS — US

SINGLES:	HITS 2			WEEKS 3
SECOND ROUND K.O.	*Universal*	35	*27 Jun 98*	2
Features boxer Mike Tyson on backing vocals.				
HOW COME	*Interscope*	52	*10 Oct 98*	1
From the film 'Bulworth'.				
Above hit: Youssou N'DOUR and CANIBUS.				
ALBUMS:	**HITS 1**			**WEEKS 1**
CAN-I-BUS	*Universal*	43	*19 Sep 98*	1

CANNED HEAT — US

SINGLES:	HITS 4			WEEKS 41
• ON THE ROAD AGAIN	*Liberty*	8	*27 Jul 68*	15
GOING UP THE COUNTRY	*Liberty*	19	*4 Jan 69*	10
Based around Bull Doze Blues by Henry Thomas.				
LET'S WORK TOGETHER	*Liberty*	2	*17 Jan 70*	15
Original by Wilbert Harrison reached No. 32 in the US in 1970.				
SUGAR BEE	*Liberty*	49	*11 Jul 70*	1
ALBUMS:	**HITS 4**			**WEEKS 40**
BOOGIE WITH CANNED HEAT	*Liberty*	5	*29 Jun 68*	21
CANNED HEAT COOKBOOK	*Liberty*	8	*14 Feb 70*	12
Compilation.				
CANNED HEAT '70 CONCERT	*Liberty*	15	*4 Jul 70*	3
Live recordings from European shows.				
FUTURE BLUES	*Liberty*	27	*10 Oct 70*	4

Freddie CANNON — US

SINGLES:	HITS 6			WEEKS 54
TALLAHASSEE LASSIE	*Top Rank*	17	*15 Aug 59*	8
Co-written by Freddie's mother.				
Above hit: Freddy CANNON.				
• WAY DOWN YONDER IN NEW ORLEANS	*Top Rank*	3	*2 Jan 60*	18
Originally recorded by Layton & Johnson.				
CALIFORNIA HERE I COME	*Top Rank*	25	*5 Mar 60*	2
Originally recorded by Al Jolson.				
INDIANA	*Top Rank*	42	*19 Mar 60*	1
Above 2 entries were separate sides of the same release, each had its own chart run.				
CALIFORNIA HERE I COME [RE]	*Top Rank*	46	*26 Mar 60*	1
THE URGE	*Top Rank*	18	*21 May 60*	10
MUSKRAT RAMBLE	*Top Rank*	32	*22 Apr 61*	5
PALISADES PARK	*Stateside*	20	*30 Jun 62*	9
Above 3: Freddy CANNON with Frank SLAY and his Orchestra.				
ALBUMS:	**HITS 1**			**WEEKS 11**
THE EXPLOSIVE FREDDY CANNON	*Top Rank*	1	*27 Feb 60*	11
Above hit: Freddy CANNON.				

Blu CANTRELL — US

SINGLES:	HITS 1			WEEKS 6
HIT 'EM UP STYLE (OOPS!)	*Arista*	12	*24 Nov 01*	6

Jim CAPALDI — UK

SINGLES:	HITS 2			WEEKS 17
IT'S ALL UP TO YOU	*Island*	27	*27 Jul 74*	6
LOVE HURTS	*Island*	4	*25 Oct 75*	11
Originally recorded by Roy Orbison.				

CAPERCAILLIE — UK

SINGLES:	HITS 2			WEEKS 3
A PRINCE AMONG ISLANDS [EP]	*Survival*	39	*23 May 92*	2
Music from the TV programme 'A Prince Among Islands'. Lead track: Coisich A Ruin (Walk My Beloved).				
DARK ALAN (AILEIN DUINN)	*Survival*	65	*17 Jun 95*	1
From the film 'Rob Roy'.				
ALBUMS:	**HITS 4**			**WEEKS 8**
SECRET PEOPLE	*Arista*	40	*25 Sep 93*	3
CAPERCAILLIE	*Survival*	61	*17 Sep 94*	1
TO THE MOON	*Survival*	41	*4 Nov 95*	2
BEAUTIFUL WASTELAND	*Survival*	55	*20 Sep 97*	2

CAPPADONNA — US

SINGLES:	HITS 1			WEEKS 1
TRIUMPH	*Loud*	46	*16 Aug 97*	1
Above hit: WU-TANG CLAN (featuring CAPPADONNA).				
ALBUMS:	**HITS 1**			**WEEKS 1**
THE PILLAGE	*Epic*	43	*4 Apr 98*	1

CAPPELLA — UK/Italy

SINGLES:	HITS 12			WEEKS 68
PUSH THE BEAT/BAUHAUS	*Fast Globe*	60	*9 Apr 88*	2
One song title, not a double 'A' side.				
HELYOM HALIB	*Music Man*	11	*6 May 89*	9
HOUSE ENERGY REVENGE	*Music Man*	73	*23 Sep 89*	1
EVERYBODY	*ffrr*	66	*27 Apr 91*	1
TAKE ME AWAY	*PWL Continental*	25	*18 Jan 92*	5
Above hit: CAPPELLA featuring Loleatta HOLLOWAY.				
U GOT 2 KNOW	*Internal Dance*	6	*3 Apr 93*	11
U GOT 2 KNOW REVISITED [RM]	*Internal Dance*	43	*14 Aug 93*	3
Remixed by Paul Newman & Craig Daniel Michael Yefet.				
U GOT 2 LET THE MUSIC	*Internal Dance*	2	*23 Oct 93*	12
MOVE ON BABY	*Internal Dance*	7	*19 Feb 94*	7
U & ME	*Internal Dance*	10	*18 Jun 94*	7
MOVE IT UP / BIG BEAT	*Internal Dance*	16	*15 Oct 94*	6
TELL ME THE WAY	*Systematic*	17	*16 Sep 95*	3
BE MY BABY	*Nukleuz*	53	*6 Sep 97*	1
ALBUMS:	**HITS 1**			**WEEKS 9**
U GOT 2 KNOW	*Internal Dance*	10	*26 Mar 94*	9

CAPRICCIO — UK

SINGLES:	HITS 1			WEEKS 2
EVERYBODY GET UP	*Defected*	44	*27 Mar 99*	2
Samples Jazzy Dee's Get On Up.				

CAPRICE — US

SINGLES:	HITS 2			WEEKS 5
OH YEAH	*Virgin*	24	*4 Sep 99*	3
ONCE AROUND THE SUN	*Virgin*	24	*10 Mar 01*	2

CAPRICORN — Belgium

SINGLES:	HITS 1			WEEKS 1
20HZ (NEW FREQUENCIES)	*R&S*	73	*29 Nov 97*	1

Tony CAPSTICK-CARLTON MAIN/FRICKLEY COLLIERY BAND — UK

SINGLES:	HITS 1			WEEKS 8
CAPSTICK COMES HOME / THE SHEFFIELD GRINDER	*Dingle's*	3	*21 Mar 81*	8

CAPTAIN and TENNILLE — US

SINGLES:	HITS 4			WEEKS 24
LOVE WILL KEEP US TOGETHER	*A&M*	32	*2 Aug 75*	5
Originally recorded by Neil Sedaka.				
THE WAY I WANT TO TOUCH YOU	*A&M*	28	*24 Jan 76*	6
YOU NEVER DONE IT LIKE THAT	*A&M*	63	*4 Nov 78*	3
DO THAT TO ME ONE MORE TIME	*Casablanca*	7	*16 Feb 80*	10
ALBUMS:	**HITS 1**			**WEEKS 6**
MAKE YOUR MOVE	*Casablanca*	33	*22 Mar 80*	6

CAPTAIN BEAKY and His BAND – See Keith MICHELL

CAPTAIN BEEFHEART and his MAGIC BAND — US

ALBUMS:	HITS 5			WEEKS 16
TROUT MASK REPLICA	*Straight*	21	*6 Dec 69*	1
LICK MY DECALS OFF BABY	*Straight*	20	*23 Jan 71*	10
MIRROR MAN	*Buddah*	49	*29 May 71*	1
THE SPOTLIGHT KID	*Reprise*	44	*19 Feb 72*	2
ICE CREAM FOR CROW	*Virgin*	90	*18 Sep 82*	2

CAPTAIN HOLLYWOOD PROJECT — US/Germany

(See also Twenty 4 Seven featuring Captain Hollywood.)

SINGLES:	HITS 4			WEEKS 12
ONLY WITH YOU	*Pulse 8*	67	*27 Mar 93*	1
MORE AND MORE	*Pulse 8*	23	*6 Nov 93*	6
Originally reached No. 113 in 1992.				
IMPOSSIBLE	*Pulse 8*	29	*5 Feb 94*	3
ONLY WITH YOU [RI]	*Pulse 8*	61	*11 Jun 94*	1
FLYING HIGH	*Pulse 8*	58	*1 Apr 95*	1

CAPTAIN SENSIBLE — UK

SINGLES:	HITS 5			WEEKS 31
HAPPY TALK	*A&M*	1	*26 Jun 82*	8
Backing vocals by the Dolly Mixtures. Originally recorded by Juanita Hall.				
WOT!	*A&M*	26	*14 Aug 82*	7
GLAD IT'S ALL OVER/ DAMNED ON 45 [M]	*A&M*	6	*24 Mar 84*	10
THERE ARE MORE SNAKES THAN LADDERS	*A&M*	57	*28 Jul 84*	5
THE HOKEY COKEY	*Have A Nice Day*	71	*10 Dec 94*	1
Charity record in aid of Great Ormond Street Children's Hospital.				

ALBUMS:	HITS 1			WEEKS 3
WOMEN AND CAPTAIN FIRST	*A&M*	64	*11 Sep 82*	3

Irene CARA — US

SINGLES:	HITS 3			WEEKS 33
FAME	*RSO*	1	*3 Jul 82*	16
OUT HERE ON MY OWN	*RSO*	58	*4 Sep 82*	3
Above 2 from the film 'Fame'.				
FLASHDANCE . . . WHAT A FEELING	*Casablanca*	2	*4 Jun 83*	14
From the film 'Flashdance'.				

CARAMBA — Sweden

SINGLES:	HITS 1			WEEKS 6
FEDORA (I'LL BE YOUR DAWG)	*Billco*	56	*12 Nov 83*	6

CARAVAN — UK

ALBUMS:	HITS 2			WEEKS 2
CUNNING STUNTS	*Decca*	50	*30 Aug 75*	1
BLIND DOG AT ST. DUNSTAN'S	*BTM*	53	*15 May 76*	1

CARAVELLES — UK

SINGLES:	HITS 1			WEEKS 13
YOU DON'T HAVE TO BE A BABY TO CRY	*Decca*	6	*10 Aug 63*	13

CARCASS — UK

ALBUMS:	HITS 2			WEEKS 2
HEARTWORK	*Earache*	67	*6 Nov 93*	1
SWANSONG	*Earache*	68	*6 Jul 96*	1

CARDIGANS — Sweden

SINGLES:	HITS 10			WEEKS 66
CARNIVAL	*Stockholm*	72	*17 Jun 95*	1
SICK & TIRED	*Stockholm*	34	*30 Sep 95*	3
CARNIVAL [RE]	*Stockholm*	35	*2 Dec 95*	2
RISE & SHINE	*Stockholm*	29	*17 Feb 96*	2
Their debut release in Sweden.				
LOVEFOOL	*Stockholm*	21	*21 Sep 96*	4
BEEN IT	*Stockholm*	56	*7 Dec 96*	1
LOVEFOOL [RI]	*Stockholm*	2	*3 May 97*	13
From the film 'Romeo & Juliet'.				
YOUR NEW CUCKOO	*Stockholm*	35	*6 Sep 97*	2
MY FAVOURITE GAME	*Stockholm*	14	*17 Oct 98*	18
ERASE/REWIND	*Stockholm*	7	*6 Mar 99*	9
One song.				
HANGING AROUND	*Stockholm*	17	*24 Jul 99*	4

URNING DOWN THE HOUSE	*Gut*	7	*25 Sep 99*	7
riginally recorded by Talking Heads on their 1983 album Speaking In Tongues.				
bove hit: Tom JONES and the CARDIGANS.				

LBUMS:	HITS 3			WEEKS 68
IFE	*Stockholm*	51	*8 Jul 95*	9
IRST BAND ON THE MOON	*Stockholm*	18	*12 Oct 96*	10
RAN TURISMO	*Stockholm*	27	*31 Oct 98*	4
RAN TURISMO [RE]	*Stockholm*	8	*9 Jan 99*	45

CARE — UK

INGLES:	HITS 1			WEEKS 4
LAMING SWORD	*Arista*	48	*12 Nov 83*	4

Mariah CAREY — US

INGLES:	HITS 28			WEEKS 252
ISION OF LOVE	*CBS*	9	*4 Aug 90*	12
OVE TAKES TIME	*CBS*	37	*10 Nov 90*	8
OMEDAY	*Columbia*	38	*26 Jan 91*	5
HERE'S GOT TO BE A WAY	*Columbia*	54	*1 Jun 91*	3
MOTIONS	*Columbia*	17	*5 Oct 91*	9
AN'T LET GO	*Columbia*	20	*11 Jan 92*	7
AKE IT HAPPEN	*Columbia*	17	*18 Apr 92*	5
LL BE THERE	*Columbia*	2	*27 Jun 92*	9
ncredited duet with Trey Lorenz.				
REAMLOVER	*Columbia*	9	*21 Aug 93*	10
ERO	*Columbia*	7	*6 Nov 93*	15
ITHOUT YOU	*Columbia*	1	*19 Feb 94*	14
riginally recorded by Badfinger.				
NYTIME YOU NEED A FRIEND	*Columbia*	8	*18 Jun 94*	10
NDLESS LOVE	*Epic*	3	*17 Sep 94*	10
bove hit: Luther VANDROSS and Mariah CAREY.				
LL I WANT FOR CHRISTMAS IS YOU	*Columbia*	2	*10 Dec 94*	7
NDLESS LOVE [RE-1ST]	*Epic*	70	*7 Jan 95*	2
NDLESS LOVE [RE-2ND]	*Epic*	55	*4 Feb 95*	4
LL I WANT FOR CHRISTMAS IS YOU [RE]	*Columbia*	59	*11 Mar 95*	1
ANTASY	*Columbia*	4	*23 Sep 95*	11
amples Tom Tom Club's Genius Of Love.				
NE SWEET DAY	*Columbia*	6	*9 Dec 95*	11
ong spent 16 weeks at No.1 in the US.				
bove hit: Mariah CAREY and BOYZ II MEN.				
PEN ARMS	*Columbia*	4	*17 Feb 96*	6
riginal by Journey reached No. 2 in the US in 1982.				
LWAYS BE MY BABY	*Columbia*	3	*22 Jun 96*	10
ONEY	*Columbia*	3	*6 Sep 97*	8
amples The Body Rock by Treacherous.				
UTTERFLY	*Columbia*	22	*13 Dec 97*	6
Y ALL	*Columbia*	4	*13 Jun 98*	8
HEN YOU BELIEVE (FROM THE PRINCE OF EGYPT)	*Columbia*	4	*19 Dec 98*	11
rom the film 'The Prince Of Egypt'.				
bove hit: Mariah CAREY and Whitney HOUSTON.				
HEN YOU BELIEVE (FROM THE PRINCE OF EGYPT) [RE]	*Columbia*	68	*27 Mar 99*	2
STILL BELIEVE	*Columbia*	16	*10 Apr 99*	7
riginal by Brenda K. Starr reached No. 13 in the US in 1988.				
EARTBREAKER	*Columbia*	5	*6 Nov 99*	13
amples Stacy Lattisaw's Attack Of The Name Game.				
bove hit: Mariah CAREY featuring JAY-Z.				
HANK GOD I FOUND YOU	*Columbia*	10	*11 Mar 00*	9
e and 98 Degrees only listed on a sticky label on the sleeve.				
bove hit: MARIAH featuring JOE and 98 DEGREES.				
HANK GOD I FOUND YOU [RE]	*Columbia*	71	*20 May 00*	1
GAINST ALL ODDS (TAKE A LOOK AT ME NOW)	*Columbia*	1	*30 Sep 00*	11
bove hit: Mariah CAREY featuring WESTLIFE.				
GAINST ALL ODDS (TAKE A LOOK AT ME NOW) [RE]	*Columbia*	68	*13 Jan 01*	1
OVERBOY	*Columbia*	12	*28 Jul 01*	4
ariah CAREY featuring CAMEO.				
amples Candy by Cameo.				
OVERBOY [RE]	*Columbia*	53	*15 Sep 01*	1
EVER TOO FAR/DON'T STOP (FUNKIN' 4 JAMAICA)	*Virgin*	32	*29 Dec 01*	1
bove hit: Mariah CAREY/Mariah CAREY featuring MYSTIKAL.				

LBUMS:	HITS 11			WEEKS 300
ARIAH CAREY	*CBS*	6	*15 Sep 90*	40
MOTIONS	*Columbia*	4	*26 Oct 91*	40
TV UNPLUGGED [EP]	*Columbia*	3	*18 Jul 92*	10
ive recordings for the TV station, 16 Mar 92.				
USIC BOX	*Columbia*	1	*11 Sep 93*	77
ERRY CHRISTMAS	*Columbia*	32	*19 Nov 94*	7
AYDREAM	*Columbia*	1	*7 Oct 95*	46

BUTTERFLY	*Columbia*	2	*20 Sep 97*	27
#1S	*Columbia*	10	*28 Nov 98*	32
Compilation.				
RAINBOW	*Columbia*	8	*13 Nov 99*	15
GLITTER	*Virgin*	10	*22 Sep 01*	3
GREATEST HITS	*Columbia*	46	*15 Dec 01*	3

CARL - See CLUBHOUSE

Belinda CARLISLE — US

SINGLES:	HITS 23			WEEKS 145
HEAVEN IS A PLACE ON EARTH	*Virgin*	1	*12 Dec 87*	14
I GET WEAK	*Virgin*	10	*27 Feb 88*	9
CIRCLE IN THE SAND	*Virgin*	4	*7 May 88*	11
MAD ABOUT YOU	*I.R.S.*	67	*6 Aug 88*	3
WORLD WITHOUT YOU	*Virgin*	34	*10 Sep 88*	6
LOVE NEVER DIES . . .	*Virgin*	54	*10 Dec 88*	5
LEAVE A LIGHT ON	*Virgin*	4	*7 Oct 89*	10
Features slide guitar by George Harrison.				
LA LUNA	*Virgin*	38	*9 Dec 89*	6
RUNAWAY HORSES	*Virgin*	40	*24 Feb 90*	5
VISION OF YOU	*Virgin*	41	*26 May 90*	4
(WE WANT) THE SAME THING	*Virgin*	6	*13 Oct 90*	10
SUMMER RAIN	*Virgin*	23	*22 Dec 90*	10
VISION OF YOU [RE]	*Virgin*	71	*20 Apr 91*	1
LIVE YOUR LIFE BE FREE	*Virgin*	12	*28 Sep 91*	7
DO YOU FEEL LIKE I FEEL?	*Virgin*	29	*16 Nov 91*	4
HALF THE WORLD	*Virgin*	35	*11 Jan 92*	4
LITTLE BLACK BOOK	*Virgin*	28	*29 Aug 92*	5
BIG SCARY ANIMAL	*Virgin*	12	*25 Sep 93*	6
LAY DOWN YOUR ARMS	*Virgin*	27	*27 Nov 93*	6
IN TOO DEEP	*Chrysalis*	6	*13 Jul 96*	7
Originally recorded by Jenny Morris in May 1996				
ALWAYS BREAKING MY HEART	*Chrysalis*	8	*21 Sep 96*	6
LOVE IN THE KEY OF C	*Chrysalis*	20	*30 Nov 96*	3
CALIFORNIA	*Chrysalis*	31	*1 Mar 97*	2
Beach Boy Brian Wilson is on backing vocals.				
ALL GOD'S CHILDREN	*Virgin*	66	*27 Nov 99*	1
ALBUMS:	**HITS 7**			**WEEKS 160**
HEAVEN ON EARTH	*Virgin*	4	*2 Jan 88*	53
RUNAWAY HORSES	*Virgin*	4	*4 Nov 89*	39
HEAVEN ON EARTH [RE]	*Virgin*	46	*15 Jun 91*	1
Re-released at mid-price.				
LIVE YOUR LIFE BE FREE	*Virgin*	7	*26 Oct 91*	16
THE BEST OF BELINDA VOLUME 1	*Virgin*	1	*19 Sep 92*	35
REAL	*Virgin*	9	*23 Oct 93*	5
A WOMAN AND A MAN	*Chrysalis*	12	*5 Oct 96*	5
A PLACE ON EARTH - THE GREATEST HITS	*Virgin*	15	*13 Nov 99*	6

Bob CARLISLE — US

SINGLES:	HITS 1			WEEKS 2
BUTTERFLY KISSES	*Jive*	56	*30 Aug 97*	2

Sara CARLSON - See MANIC MC'S featuring Sara CARLSON

CARLTON — UK

SINGLES:	HITS 2			WEEKS 3
LOVE AND PAIN	*3 Stripe*	56	*16 Feb 91*	2
1 TO 1 RELIGION	*Stoned Heights*	53	*1 Apr 95*	1
Above hit: BOMB THE BASS featuring CARLTON.				

Carl CARLTON — US

SINGLES:	HITS 1			WEEKS 8
SHE'S A BAD MAMA JAMA (SHE'S BUILT, SHE'S STACKED)	*20th Century*	34	*18 Jul 81*	8
Originally recorded by Leon Haywood.				

Larry CARLTON - See Mike POST

CARLTON MAIN/FRICKLEY COLLIERY BAND - See Tony CAPSTICK-CARLTON MAIN/FRICKLEY COLLIERY BAND

CARMEL — UK

SINGLES:	HITS 3			WEEKS 19
BAD DAY	*London*	15	*6 Aug 83*	9
MORE, MORE, MORE	*London*	23	*11 Feb 84*	7
SALLY	*London*	60	*14 Jun 86*	3
ALBUMS:	**HITS 3**			**WEEKS 11**
CARMEL 6-TRACK [EP]	*Red Flame*	94	*1 Oct 83*	2

THE DRUM IS EVERYTHING	*London*	19	*24 Mar 84*	8
THE FALLING	*London*	88	*27 Sep 86*	1

Eric CARMEN — US

SINGLES:	HITS 1			WEEKS 7
ALL BY MYSELF	*Arista*	12	*10 Apr 76*	7
ALBUMS:	**HITS 1**			**WEEKS 1**
ERIC CARMEN	*Arista*	58	*15 May 76*	1

Tracey CARMEN - See RUTHLESS RAP ASSASSINS

Ian CARMICHAEL — UK

EPS:	HITS 1			WEEKS 3
THE HOUSE AT POOH CORNER	*HMV*	10	*23 Dec 61*	3

Jean CARN - See Bobby M featuring Jean CARN

Kim CARNEGIE — UK

SINGLES:	HITS 1			WEEKS 1
JAZZ RAP	*Best*	73	*19 Jan 91*	1

Kim CARNES — US

SINGLES:	HITS 3			WEEKS 15
BETTE DAVIES EYES *Originally recorded by Jackie De Shannon.*	*EMI America*	10	*9 May 81*	9
DRAW OF THE CARDS	*EMI America*	49	*8 Aug 81*	4
VOYEUR	*EMI America*	68	*9 Oct 82*	2
ALBUMS:	**HITS 1**			**WEEKS 16**
MISTAKEN IDENTITY	*EMI America*	26	*20 Jun 81*	16

CARNIVAL featuring. R.I.P. vs. RED RAT - See R.I.P. PRODUCTIONS; RED RAT

Renato CAROSONE and His SEXTET — Italy

SINGLES:	HITS 1			WEEKS 1
TORERO - CHA CHA CHA	*Parlophone*	25	*5 Jul 58*	1

CAROUSEL - ORIGINAL SOUNDTRACK - See VARIOUS ARTISTS: FILMS - ORIGINAL SOUNDTRACKS

CARPE DIEM - See Afrika BAMBAATAA

Mary Chapin CARPENTER — US

SINGLES:	HITS 3			WEEKS 6
HE THINKS HE'LL KEEP HER	*Columbia*	71	*20 Nov 93*	1
ONE COOL REMOVE *Above hit: Shawn COLVIN with Mary Chapin CARPENTER.*	*Columbia*	40	*7 Jan 95*	3
SHUT UP AND KISS ME	*Columbia*	35	*3 Jun 95*	2
ALBUMS:	**HITS 4**			**WEEKS 9**
STONES IN THE ROAD	*Columbia*	26	*29 Oct 94*	5
A PLACE IN THE WORLD	*Columbia*	36	*2 Nov 96*	2
PARTY DOLL AND OTHER FAVORITES *Compilation includes live recordings.*	*Columbia*	65	*5 Jun 99*	1
TIME*SEX*LOVE	*Columbia*	57	*26 May 01*	1

CARPENTERS — US

SINGLES:	HITS 19			WEEKS 173
THEY LONG TO BE CLOSE TO YOU *Originally recorded by Richard Chamberlain.*	*A&M*	6	*5 Sep 70*	18
WE'VE ONLY JUST BEGUN	*A&M*	28	*9 Jan 71*	7
SUPERSTAR / FOR ALL WE KNOW *Superstar originally recorded by Delaney & Bonnie & Friends and Eric Clapton as Groupie (Superstar). For All We Know from the film 'Lovers And Other Strangers'.*	*A&M*	18	*18 Sep 71*	13
MERRY CHRISTMAS DARLING	*A&M*	45	*1 Jan 72*	1
GOODBYE TO LOVE / I WON'T LAST A DAY WITHOUT YOU *I Won't Last A Day Without You listed on 23 Sep 72 (at No. 49). From 30 Sep 72 only Goodbye To Love was listed.*	*A&M*	9	*23 Sep 72*	16
YESTERDAY ONCE MORE	*A&M*	2	*7 Jul 73*	17
TOP OF THE WORLD	*A&M*	5	*20 Oct 73*	18
JAMBALAYA (ON THE BAYOU) / MR. GUDER *Mr. Guder listed from 16 Mar 74.*	*A&M*	12	*2 Mar 74*	11
I WON'T LAST A DAY WITHOUT YOU [RI]	*A&M*	32	*8 Jun 74*	5
PLEASE MR POSTMAN *Original by the Marvelettes reached No. 1 in the US in 1961.*	*A&M*	2	*18 Jan 75*	12
ONLY YESTERDAY	*A&M*	7	*19 Apr 75*	10
SOLITAIRE	*A&M*	32	*30 Aug 75*	5
SANTA CLAUS IS COMIN' TO TOWN *Originally recorded by George Hall in 1934.*	*A&M*	37	*20 Dec 75*	4

THERE'S A KIND OF HUSH (ALL OVER THE WORLD)	A&M	22	27 Mar 76	6
Originally recorded by New Vaudeville Band.				
I NEED TO BE IN LOVE	A&M	36	3 Jul 76	5
CALLING OCCUPANTS OF INTERPLANETARY CRAFT (THE RECOGNIZED ANTHEM OF WORLD CONTACT DAY)	A&M	9	8 Oct 77	9
Originally recorded by Klaatu.				
SWEET, SWEET SMILE	A&M	40	11 Feb 78	4
MAKE BELIEVE IT'S YOUR FIRST TIME	A&M	60	22 Oct 83	3
MERRY CHRISTMAS DARLING [RI] / (THEY LONG TO BE) CLOSE TO YOU [RI]	A&M	25	8 Dec 90	5
RAINY DAYS AND MONDAYS	A&M	63	13 Feb 93	2
Released to commemorate 10th anniversary of Karen's death.				
TRYIN' TO GET THE FEELING AGAIN	A&M	44	24 Dec 94	2
First recorded in 1975 and re-discovered in 1991.				
ALBUMS:	**HITS 19**			**WEEKS 606**
CLOSE TO YOU	A&M	23	23 Jan 71	82
CARPENTERS	A&M	12	30 Oct 71	36
TICKET TO RIDE	A&M	20	15 Apr 72	3
A SONG FOR YOU	A&M	13	23 Sep 72	37
NOW & THEN	A&M	2	7 Jul 73	65
THE SINGLES 1969-1973	A&M	1	26 Jan 74	116
Includes re-entry in 1983.				
HORIZON	A&M	1	28 Jun 75	27
TICKET TO RIDE [RI]	Hamlet	35	23 Aug 75	2
Re-released at mid-price.				
A KIND OF HUSH	A&M	3	3 Jul 76	15
LIVE AT THE PALLADIUM	A&M	28	8 Jan 77	3
PASSAGE	A&M	12	8 Oct 77	12
THE SINGLES 1974-1978	A&M	2	2 Dec 78	20
MADE IN AMERICA	A&M	12	27 Jun 81	10
VOICE OF THE HEART	A&M	6	15 Oct 83	19
YESTERDAY ONCE MORE	EMI	10	20 Oct 84	26
THE SINGLES 1969-1973 [RE]	A&M	24	13 Jan 90	9
THE SINGLES 1974-1978 [RE]	A&M	42	13 Jan 90	7
LOVELINES	A&M	73	13 Jan 90	1
ONLY YESTERDAY - RICHARD & KAREN CARPENTER'S GREATEST HITS	A&M	1	31 Mar 90	82
Includes re-entries through to 1996.				
INTERPRETATIONS	A&M	29	15 Oct 94	10
Album of cover versions.				
LOVE SONGS	A&M	47	22 Nov 97	8
GOLD - GREATEST HITS	A&M	21	9 Dec 00	16

Dick CARR And His BUSHLANDERS - See Slim DUSTY with Dick CARR and his BUSHLANDERS

Joe 'Fingers' CARR — US

SINGLES:	**HITS 1**			**WEEKS 5**
• PORTUGUESE WASHERWOMAN	Capitol	20	30 Jun 56	5

Linda CARR — US

SINGLES:	**HITS 2**			**WEEKS 12**
HIGHWIRE	Chelsea	15	12 Jul 75	8
Above hit: Linda CARR and the LOVE SQUAD.				
SOLD MY ROCK 'N' ROLL (GAVE IT FOR FUNKY SOUL)	Spark	36	5 Jun 76	4
Above hit: LINDA and the FUNKY BOYS.				

Pearl CARR - See Teddy JOHNSON and Pearl CARR

Suzi CARR — US

SINGLES:	**HITS 1**			**WEEKS 1**
ALL OVER ME	Cowboy	45	8 Oct 94	1

Valerie CARR with Hugo PERETTI and his Orchestra — US

SINGLES:	**HITS 1**			**WEEKS 2**
WHEN THE BOYS TALK ABOUT THE GIRLS	Columbia	29	5 Jul 58	1
WHEN THE BOYS TALK ABOUT THE GIRLS [RE]	Columbia	30	19 Jul 58	1

Vikki CARR — US

SINGLES:	**HITS 3**			**WEEKS 26**
• IT MUST BE HIM (SEUL SUR SON E TOILE)	Liberty	2	3 Jun 67	20
THERE I GO (SE PER TE C'E SOLTANTO QUELL'UOMO)	Liberty	50	2 Sep 67	1
WITH PEN IN HAND	Liberty	43	15 Mar 69	1
Originally recorded by Bobby Goldsboro.				
WITH PEN IN HAND [RE-1ST]	Liberty	39	29 Mar 69	2
WITH PEN IN HAND [RE-2ND]	Liberty	40	3 May 69	2
ALBUMS:	**HITS 2**			**WEEKS 12**
WAY OF TODAY	Liberty	31	22 Jul 67	2
IT MUST BE HIM	Liberty	12	12 Aug 67	10

Raffaella CARRA — Italy

SINGLES:	HITS 1			WEEKS 12
DO IT, DO IT AGAIN	*Epic*	9	*15 Apr 78*	12

Paul CARRACK — UK

SINGLES:	HITS 4			WEEKS 18
WHEN YOU WALK IN THE ROOM	*Chrysalis*	48	*16 May 87*	5
DON'T SHED A TEAR	*Chrysalis*	60	*18 Mar 89*	3
EYES OF BLUE	*I.R.S.*	40	*6 Jan 96*	4
HOW LONG?	*I.R.S.*	32	*6 Apr 96*	5
EYES OF BLUE [RI]	*I.R.S.*	45	*24 Aug 96*	1
ALBUMS:	**HITS 2**			**WEEKS 8**
BLUE VIEWS	*I.R.S.*	55	*3 Feb 96*	7
SATISFY MY SOUL	*Carrack-UK*	63	*24 Jun 00*	1

José CARRERAS — Spain

(See also Placido Domingo, Diana Ross and José Carreras; Placido Domingo, José Carreras and Montserrat Caballe; 3 Tenors: José Carreras, Placido Domingo, Luciano Pavarotti; Various Artists: Studio Cast 'West Side Story, South Pacific'.)

SINGLES:	HITS 1			WEEKS 11
AMIGOS PARA SIEMPRE (FRIENDS FOR LIFE) *The official theme to the Barcelona 1992 Olympic Games.* *Above hit: Jose CARRERAS and Sarah BRIGHTMAN.*	*Really Useful*	11	*11 Jul 92*	11
ALBUMS:	**HITS 7**			**WEEKS 35**
JOSÉ CARRERAS COLLECTION	*Stylus*	90	*1 Oct 88*	4
JOSÉ CARRERAS SINGS ANDREW LLOYD WEBBER	*WEA*	42	*23 Dec 89*	6
THE ESSENTIAL JOSÉ CARRERAS	*Philips*	24	*23 Feb 91*	9
HOLLYWOOD GOLDEN CLASSICS	*East West*	47	*6 Apr 91*	3
AMIGOS PARA SIEMPRE (FRIENDS FOR LIFE)	*East West*	53	*8 Aug 92*	4
WITH A SONG IN MY HEART	*Teldec*	73	*16 Oct 93*	1
PASSION	*Erato*	21	*3 Feb 96*	8

Tia CARRERE — US

SINGLES:	HITS 1			WEEKS 6
BALLROOM BLITZ *From the film 'Wayne's World'.*	*Reprise*	26	*30 May 92*	6

Jim CARREY — US

SINGLES:	HITS 1			WEEKS 3
CUBAN PETE *From the film 'The Mask'.*	*Columbia*	31	*21 Jan 95*	3

CARRIE — UK/US/Australia,

SINGLES:	HITS 2			WEEKS 2
MOLLY	*Island*	56	*14 Mar 98*	1
CALIFORNIA SCREAMIN'	*Island*	55	*9 May 98*	1

Dina CARROLL — UK

SINGLES:	HITS 14			WEEKS 99
IT'S TOO LATE *Above hit: QUARTZ introducing Dina CARROLL.*	*Mercury*	8	*2 Feb 91*	14
NAKED LOVE (JUST SAY YOU WANT ME) *Above hit: QUARTZ and Dina CARROLL.*	*Mercury*	39	*15 Jun 91*	3
AIN'T NO MAN	*A&M*	16	*11 Jul 92*	8
SPECIAL KIND OF LOVE	*A&M*	16	*10 Oct 92*	5
SO CLOSE	*A&M*	20	*5 Dec 92*	8
THIS TIME	*A&M*	23	*27 Feb 93*	6
EXPRESS	*A&M*	12	*15 May 93*	6
DON'T BE A STRANGER	*A&M*	3	*16 Oct 93*	13
THE PERFECT YEAR *From the musical 'Sunset Boulevard'.*	*A&M*	5	*11 Dec 93*	11
ESCAPING	*Mercury*	3	*28 Sep 96*	8
ONLY HUMAN	*Mercury*	33	*21 Dec 96*	4
ONE, TWO, THREE	*Mercury*	16	*24 Oct 98*	4
WITHOUT LOVE	*Manifesto*	13	*24 Jul 99*	7
SOMEONE LIKE YOU *From the film 'Bridget Jones's Diary'.*	*Mercury*	38	*16 Jun 01*	2
ALBUMS:	**HITS 3**			**WEEKS 80**
SO CLOSE	*A&M*	2	*30 Jan 93*	63
ONLY HUMAN	*Mercury*	2	*26 Oct 96*	13
THE VERY BEST OF DINA CARROLL	*Mercury*	15	*23 Jun 01*	4

Jimmy CARROLL and his Orchestra - See Frankie LAINE; Guy MITCHELL

Ron CARROLL - See KLUSTER featuring Ron CARROLL; SUPRFUNK

Ronnie CARROLL — UK

SINGLES:	HITS 7			WEEKS 50
WALK HAND IN HAND	*Philips*	13	*28 Jul 56*	8
Above hit: Ronnie CARROLL with Wally STOTT and his Orchestra.				
THE WISDOM OF A FOOL	*Philips*	20	*30 Mar 57*	2
Originally recorded by Annette Klooger with the Ted Heath Band.				
FOOTSTEPS	*Philips*	36	*2 Apr 60*	3
RING-A-DING GIRL	*Philips*	46	*24 Feb 62*	3
ROSES ARE RED (MY LOVE)	*Philips*	3	*4 Aug 62*	16
IF ONLY TOMORROW (COULD BE LIKE TODAY)	*Philips*	33	*17 Nov 62*	4
UK's Eurovision entry in 1962, it came 4th.				
SAY WONDERFUL THINGS	*Philips*	6	*9 Mar 63*	14
UK's Eurovision entry in 1963, it came 4th.				
All 6 above: Ronnie CARROLL with Wally STOTT and his Orchestra and Chorus.				

Jasper CARROTT — UK

SINGLES:	HITS 1			WEEKS 15
FUNKY MOPED / MAGIC ROUNDABOUT	*DJM*	5	*16 Aug 75*	15
ALBUMS:	**HITS 8**			**WEEKS 66**
RABBITS ON AND ON	*DJM*	10	*18 Oct 75*	7
CARROTT IN NOTTS	*DJM*	56	*6 Nov 76*	1
THE BEST OF JASPER CARROTT	*DJM*	38	*25 Nov 78*	13
THE UNRECORDED JASPER CARROTT	*DJM*	19	*20 Oct 79*	15
BEAT THE CARROTT	*DJM*	13	*19 Sep 81*	16
CARROTT'S LIB	*DJM*	80	*25 Dec 82*	3
THE STUN (CARROTT TELLS ALL)	*DJM*	57	*19 Nov 83*	8
COSMIC CARROTT	*Portrait*	66	*7 Feb 87*	3

CARS — US

SINGLES:	HITS 5			WEEKS 51
MY BEST FRIEND'S GIRL	*Elektra*	3	*11 Nov 78*	10
The first single released on picture disc.				
JUST WHAT I NEEDED	*Elektra*	17	*17 Feb 79*	10
LET'S GO	*Elektra*	51	*28 Jul 79*	4
SINCE YOU'RE GONE	*Elektra*	37	*5 Jun 82*	4
DRIVE	*Elektra*	5	*29 Sep 84*	11
DRIVE [RE]	*Elektra*	4	*3 Aug 85*	12
Re-entered after its airing at Live Aid.				
ALBUMS:	**HITS 5**			**WEEKS 72**
CARS	*Elektra*	29	*2 Dec 78*	15
CANDY-O	*Elektra*	30	*7 Jul 79*	6
HEARTBEAT CITY	*Elektra*	27	*6 Oct 84*	15
HEARTBEAT CITY [RE]	*Elektra*	25	*27 Jul 85*	15
THE CARS GREATEST HITS	*Elektra*	27	*9 Nov 85*	19
DOOR TO DOOR	*Elektra*	72	*5 Sep 87*	2

Aaron CARTER — US

SINGLES:	HITS 6			WEEKS 29
CRUSH ON YOU	*Ultra Pop*	9	*29 Nov 97*	8
CRAZY LITTLE PARTY GIRL	*Ultra Pop*	7	*7 Feb 98*	6
I'M GONNA MISS YOU FOREVER	*Ultra Pop*	24	*28 Mar 98*	5
SURFIN' USA	*Ultra Pop*	18	*4 Jul 98*	5
I WANT CANDY	*Jive*	31	*16 Sep 00*	3
Original version by the Strangeloves reached No. 11 in the US in 1965.				
AARON'S PARTY (COME GET IT)	*Jive*	51	*28 Oct 00*	2
ALBUMS:	**HITS 1**			**WEEKS 8**
AARON CARTER	*Ultra Pop*	12	*28 Feb 98*	8

Clarence CARTER — US

SINGLES:	HITS 1			WEEKS 13
PATCHES	*Atlantic*	2	*10 Oct 70*	13
Originally recorded by Chairmen Of The Board.				

CARTER FAMILY - See Johnny CASH

CARTER - THE UNSTOPPABLE SEX MACHINE — UK

SINGLES:	HITS 13			WEEKS 46
BLOODSPORTS FOR ALL	*Rough Trade*	48	*26 Jan 91*	2
SHERIFF FATMAN	*Big Cat*	23	*22 Jun 91*	7
Originally released in 1989.				
AFTER THE WATERSHED (EARLY LEARNING THE HARD WAY)	*Chrysalis*	11	*26 Oct 91*	5
RUBBISH	*Big Cat*	14	*11 Jan 92*	5
Originally released in 1990.				
THE ONLY LIVING BOY IN NEW CROSS	*Big Cat*	7	*25 Apr 92*	5

DO RE ME, SO FAR SO GOOD	*Chrysalis*	22	*4 Jul 92*	3
THE IMPOSSIBLE DREAM	*Chrysalis*	21	*28 Nov 92*	3
LEAN ON ME I WON'T FALL OVER	*Chrysalis*	16	*4 Sep 93*	3
LENNY AND TERENCE	*Chrysalis*	40	*16 Oct 93*	2
GLAM ROCK COPS	*Chrysalis*	24	*12 Mar 94*	3
LET'S GET TATTOOS	*Chrysalis*	30	*19 Nov 94*	3
THE YOUNG OFFENDER'S MUM	*Chrysalis*	34	*4 Feb 95*	3
BORN ON THE 5TH OF NOVEMBER	*Chrysalis*	35	*30 Sep 95*	2

ALBUMS:	**HITS 8**			**WEEKS 40**
30 SOMETHING	*Rough Trade*	8	*2 Mar 91*	9
101 DAMNATIONS	*Big Cat*	29	*21 Sep 91*	6
30 SOMETHING [RI]	*Chrysalis*	21	*1 Feb 92*	4
1992 - THE LOVE ALBUM	*Chrysalis*	1	*16 May 92*	9
POST HISTORIC MONSTERS	*Chrysalis*	5	*18 Sep 93*	4
STARRY EYED AND BOLLOCK NAKED	*Chrysalis*	22	*26 Mar 94*	2
WORRY BOMB	*Chrysalis*	9	*18 Feb 95*	3
STRAW DONKEY . . . THE SINGLES	*Chrysalis*	37	*14 Oct 95*	2
A WORLD WITHOUT DAVE	*Cooking Vinyl*	73	*5 Apr 97*	1

6 track mini-LP.

CARTER TWINS — Ireland

SINGLES:	**HITS 1**			**WEEKS 1**
THE TWELFTH OF NEVER / TOO RIGHT TO BE WRONG	*RCA*	61	*8 Mar 97*	1

Junior CARTIER — UK

(See also Money Mafia.)

SINGLES:	**HITS 1**			**WEEKS 1**
WOMEN BEAT THEIR MEN	*Nucamp*	70	*6 Nov 99*	1

Samples Dominatrix's The Dominatrix Sleeps Tonight.

CARTOONS — Denmark

SINGLES:	**HITS 3**			**WEEKS 30**
WITCH DOCTOR	*Flex*	2	*3 Apr 99*	13
DOODAH!	*Flex*	7	*19 Jun 99*	11
AISY WAISY	*Island*	16	*4 Sep 99*	5
DOODAH! [RE]	*Flex*	73	*16 Oct 99*	1

ALBUMS:	**HITS 1**			**WEEKS 14**
TOONAGE	*Flex*	17	*17 Apr 99*	14

Sam CARTWRIGHT - See VOLCANO

CARVELLS — UK

SINGLES:	**HITS 1**			**WEEKS 4**
THE L.A. RUN	*Creole*	31	*26 Nov 77*	4

CASCADES — US

SINGLES:	**HITS 1**			**WEEKS 16**
RHYTHM OF THE RAIN	*Warner Brothers*	5	*2 Mar 63*	16

CASE — US

SINGLES:	**HITS 2**			**WEEKS 7**
TOUCH ME TEASE ME *From the film 'The Nutty Professor'.* *Above hit: CASE featuring Foxy BROWN.*	*Def Jam*	26	*21 Sep 96*	3
LIVIN' IT UP *Above hit: JA RULE featuring CASE.*	*Def Jam*	27	*10 Nov 01*	4

Ed CASE — UK

SINGLES:	**HITS 2**			**WEEKS 4**
SOMETHING IN YOUR EYES	*Red Rose*	38	*21 Oct 00*	2
WHO?	*Columbia*	29	*15 Sep 01*	2

Above hit: Ed CASE and Sweetie IRIE.

Natalie CASEY — UK

SINGLES:	**HITS 1**			**WEEKS 1**
CHICK CHICK CHICKEN	*Polydor*	72	*7 Jan 84*	1

Plays Carol Groves in Channel 4 Soap 'Hollyoaks'. Youngest artist to have a chart hit at the age of 3.

Johnny CASH — US

SINGLES:	**HITS 5**			**WEEKS 59**
IT AIN'T ME BABE	*CBS*	28	*5 Jun 65*	8

Originally recorded by Bob Dylan.

A BOY NAMED SUE	*CBS*	4	*6 Sep 69*	19
Originally recorded by Shel Silverstein.				
WHAT IS TRUTH	*CBS*	21	*23 May 70*	11
A THING CALLED LOVE	*CBS*	4	*15 Apr 72*	13
Originally recorded by Jerry Reed.				
Above hit: Johnny CASH and the EVANGEL TEMPLE CHOIR.				
A THING CALLED LOVE [RE]	*CBS*	48	*22 Jul 72*	1
ONE PIECE AT A TIME	*CBS*	32	*3 Jul 76*	7
Above hit: Johnny CASH and the TENNESSEE THREE.				
EPS:	**HITS 1**			**WEEKS 2**
MEAN AS HELL!	*CBS*	8	*4 Jun 66*	2
Above hit: Johnny CASH with the STATLER BROTHERS and the CARTER FAMILY.				
ALBUMS:	**HITS 17**			**WEEKS 290**
EVERYBODY LOVES A NUT	*CBS*	28	*23 Jul 66*	1
FROM SEA TO SHINING SEA	*CBS*	40	*4 May 68*	1
OLD GOLDEN THROAT	*CBS*	37	*6 Jul 68*	2
JOHNNY CASH AT FOLSOM PRISON	*CBS*	8	*24 Aug 68*	53
JOHNNY CASH AT SAN QUENTIN	*CBS*	2	*23 Aug 69*	114
Above 2 are live recordings at the respective prisons. Johnny Cash at San Quentin was also a TV soundtrack for a Granada ITV documentary.				
GREATEST HITS VOLUME 1	*CBS*	23	*4 Oct 69*	25
HELLO I'M JOHNNY CASH	*CBS*	6	*7 Mar 70*	16
THE WORLD OF JOHNNY CASH	*CBS*	5	*15 Aug 70*	31
THE JOHNNY CASH SHOW	*CBS*	18	*12 Dec 70*	6
MAN IN BLACK	*CBS*	18	*18 Sep 71*	7
JOHNNY CASH	*Hallmark*	43	*13 Nov 71*	2
A THING CALLED LOVE	*CBS*	8	*20 May 72*	11
STAR PORTRAIT	*CBS*	16	*14 Oct 72*	7
ONE PIECE AT A TIME	*CBS*	49	*10 Jul 76*	3
THE BEST OF JOHNNY CASH	*CBS*	48	*9 Oct 76*	2
ITCHY FEET	*CBS*	36	*2 Sep 78*	4
THE MAN IN BLACK - DEFINITIVE COLLECTION	*Columbia*	15	*27 Aug 94*	5

Pat CASH - See John McENROE and Pat CASH with the FULL METAL RACKETS

CASHFLOW — US

SINGLES:	**HITS 1**			**WEEKS 8**
MINE ALL MINE / PARTY FREAK	*Club*	15	*24 May 86*	8
ALBUMS:	**HITS 1**			**WEEKS 3**
CASHFLOW	*Club*	33	*28 Jun 86*	3

CASHMERE — US

SINGLES:	**HITS 2**			**WEEKS 11**
CAN I	*Fourth & Broadway*	29	*19 Jan 85*	8
WE NEED LOVE	*Fourth & Broadway*	52	*23 Mar 85*	3
ALBUMS:	**HITS 1**			**WEEKS 5**
CASHMERE	*Fourth & Broadway*	63	*2 Mar 85*	5

CASINO — UK

SINGLES:	**HITS 2**			**WEEKS 2**
SOUND OF EDEN	*Worx*	52	*17 May 97*	1
ONLY YOU	*POW!*	72	*10 Jul 99*	1

CASINOS — US

SINGLES:	**HITS 1**			**WEEKS 7**
THEN YOU CAN TELL ME GOODBYE	*President*	28	*25 Feb 67*	7
Originally recorded by John D. Loudermilk.				

Nove CASPER - See MJ COLE

CASSANDRA - See Rui DA SILVA featuring CASSANDRA

David CASSIDY — US

(See also Partridge Family.)

SINGLES:	**HITS 11**			**WEEKS 109**
COULD IT BE FOREVER / CHERISH	*Bell*	2	*8 Apr 72*	17
Cherish was originally recorded by the Association and reached No. 1 in the US in 1966.				
HOW CAN I BE SURE	*Bell*	1	*16 Sep 72*	11
Original by the Young Rascals reached No. 4 in the US in 1967.				
ROCK ME BABY	*Bell*	11	*25 Nov 72*	9
I AM A CLOWN / SOME KIND OF A SUMMER	*Bell*	3	*24 Mar 73*	12
DAYDREAMER / THE PUPPY SONG	*Bell*	1	*13 Oct 73*	15
IF I DIDN'T CARE	*Bell*	9	*11 May 74*	8
Originally recorded by Inkspots.				

PLEASE PLEASE ME *Live recording.*	*Bell*	16	*27 Jul 74*	6
I WRITE THE SONGS / GET IT UP FOR LOVE *I Write The Songs originally recorded by Bruce Johnston.*	*RCA Victor*	11	*5 Jul 75*	8
DARLIN'	*RCA Victor*	16	*25 Oct 75*	8
THE LAST KISS *Backing vocals by George Michael.*	*Arista*	6	*23 Feb 85*	9
ROMANCE (LET YOUR HEART GO)	*Arista*	54	*11 May 85*	6
ALBUMS:	**HITS 7**			**WEEKS 106**
CHERISH	*Bell*	2	*20 May 72*	43
ROCK ME BABY	*Bell*	2	*24 Feb 73*	20
DREAMS ARE NUTHIN' MORE THAN WISHES	*Bell*	1	*24 Nov 73*	13
CASSIDY LIVE	*Bell*	9	*3 Aug 74*	7
THE HIGHER THEY CLIMB	*RCA Victor*	22	*9 Aug 75*	5
ROMANCE	*Arista*	20	*8 Jun 85*	6
THEN AND NOW *Re-recordings of his solo and Partridge Family material.*	*Universal Music TV*	5	*13 Oct 01*	12

Eva CASSIDY — US

SINGLES:	**HITS 1**			**WEEKS 9**
OVER THE RAINBOW *Originally recorded by Judy Garland in 1939.*	*Blix Street*	61	*21 Apr 01*	1
OVER THE RAINBOW [RE-1ST]	*Blix Street*	42	*12 May 01*	6
OVER THE RAINBOW [RE-2ND]	*Blix Street*	74	*30 Jun 01*	1
OVER THE RAINBOW [RE-3RD]	*Blix Street*	73	*25 Aug 01*	1
ALBUMS:	**HITS 2**			**WEEKS 61**
TIME AFTER TIME	*Blix Street*	52	*3 Jun 00*	3
SONGBIRD *Compilation.*	*Blix Street*	1	*10 Feb 01*	47
TIME AFTER TIME [RE]	*Blix Street*	25	*24 Mar 01*	11

CASSIUS — France

SINGLES:	**HITS 3**			**WEEKS 12**
CASSIUS 99 *Samples Donna Summer's Love Is Just A Breath Away.*	*Virgin*	7	*23 Jan 99*	7
FEELING FOR YOU *Samples Gwen McCrae's All The Love That I'm Giving.*	*Virgin*	16	*15 May 99*	4
LA MOUCHE *Title is French for the fly. Single is based around the Scientist's hit The Bee.*	*Virgin*	53	*20 Nov 99*	1
ALBUMS:	**HITS 1**			**WEEKS 2**
1999	*Virgin*	28	*6 Feb 99*	2

CAST — UK

SINGLES:	**HITS 12**			**WEEKS 55**
FINETIME	*Polydor*	17	*15 Jul 95*	4
ALRIGHT	*Polydor*	13	*30 Sep 95*	4
SANDSTORM	*Polydor*	8	*20 Jan 96*	5
WALKAWAY	*Polydor*	9	*30 Mar 96*	7
FLYING	*Polydor*	4	*26 Oct 96*	5
FREE ME	*Polydor*	7	*5 Apr 97*	6
FREE ME [RE]	*Polydor*	61	*21 Jun 97*	1
GUIDING STAR	*Polydor*	9	*28 Jun 97*	6
LIVE THE DREAM	*Polydor*	7	*13 Sep 97*	5
I'M SO LONELY	*Polydor*	14	*15 Nov 97*	3
BEAT MAMA	*Polydor*	9	*8 May 99*	5
MAGIC HOUR	*Polydor*	28	*7 Aug 99*	3
DESERT DROUGHT	*Polydor*	45	*28 Jul 01*	1
ALBUMS:	**HITS 3**			**WEEKS 116**
ALL CHANGE	*Polydor*	7	*28 Oct 95*	67
MOTHER NATURE CALLS	*Polydor*	3	*26 Apr 97*	42
MAGIC HOUR	*Polydor*	6	*29 May 99*	7

CAST FROM CASUALTY — UK

SINGLES:	**HITS 1**			**WEEKS 6**
EVERLASTING LOVE	*warner.esp*	5	*14 Mar 98*	6

CAST OF THE NEW ROCKY HORROR SHOW — UK

SINGLES:	**HITS 1**			**WEEKS 1**
THE TIMEWARP	*Damm It Janet*	57	*12 Dec 98*	1

Roy CASTLE with Wally STOTT and his ORCHESTRA — UK

SINGLES:	**HITS 1**			**WEEKS 3**
LITTLE WHITE BERRY	*Philips*	40	*24 Dec 60*	3

CASUALS — UK

SINGLES:	HITS 2			WEEKS 26
JESAMINE	*Decca*	2	*17 Aug 68*	18
Originally recorded by the Bystanders. •				
TOY	*Decca*	30	*7 Dec 68*	8

Elaine CASWELL - See Joe JACKSON

CAT — UK

SINGLES:	HITS 1			WEEKS 4
TONGUE TIED	*EMI*	17	*23 Oct 93*	4

CATATONIA — UK

(See also Space.)

SINGLES:	HITS 13			WEEKS 50
SWEET CATATONIA	*Blanco Y Negro*	61	*3 Feb 96*	1
LOST CAT	*Blanco Y Negro*	41	*4 May 96*	1
YOU'VE GOT A LOT TO ANSWER FOR	*Blanco Y Negro*	35	*7 Sep 96*	2
BLEED	*Blanco Y Negro*	46	*30 Nov 96*	1
Original release on the Nursery label in 1995 reached No. 158.				
I AM THE MOB	*Blanco Y Negro*	40	*18 Oct 97*	2
MULDER AND SCULLY	*Blanco Y Negro*	3	*31 Jan 98*	10
ROAD RAGE	*Blanco Y Negro*	5	*2 May 98*	8
STRANGE GLUE	*Blanco Y Negro*	11	*1 Aug 98*	6
GAME ON	*Blanco Y Negro*	33	*7 Nov 98*	2
DEAD FROM THE WAIST DOWN	*Blanco Y Negro*	7	*10 Apr 99*	8
LONDINIUM	*Blanco Y Negro*	20	*24 Jul 99*	3
KARAOKE QUEEN	*Blanco Y Negro*	36	*13 Nov 99*	2
STONE BY STONE	*Blanco Y Negro*	19	*4 Aug 01*	3
STONE BY STONE [RE]	*Blanco Y Negro*	68	*8 Sep 01*	4
ALBUMS:	**HITS 4**			**WEEKS 123**
WAY BEYOND BLUE	*Blanco Y Negro*	40	*12 Oct 96*	1
INTERNATIONAL VELVET	*Blanco Y Negro*	1	*14 Feb 98*	93
EQUALLY CURSED AND BLESSED	*Blanco Y Negro*	1	*24 Apr 99*	23
WAY BEYOND BLUE [RE]	*Blanco Y Negro*	32	*24 Apr 99*	2
PAPER SCISSORS STONE	*Blanco Y Negro*	6	*18 Aug 01*	4

CATCH — UK

SINGLES:	HITS 1			WEEKS 1
FREE (C'MON)	*ffrr*	70	*17 Nov 90*	1

CATCH — UK

SINGLES:	HITS 2			WEEKS 6
BINGO	*Virgin*	23	*11 Oct 97*	4
DIVE IN	*Virgin*	44	*21 Feb 98*	2

CATHERINE WHEEL — UK

SINGLES:	HITS 10			WEEKS 12
BLACK METALLIC [EP]	*Fontana*	68	*23 Nov 91*	1
Lead track: Black Metallic.				
BALLOON	*Fontana*	59	*8 Feb 92*	1
I WANT TO TOUCH YOU	*Fontana*	35	*18 Apr 92*	2
30 CENTURY MAN	*Fontana*	47	*9 Jan 93*	2
Cover of a Scott Walker song from his 1969 album Scott 3.				
CRANK	*Fontana*	66	*10 Jul 93*	1
SHOW ME MARY	*Fontana*	62	*16 Oct 93*	1
WAYDOWN	*Fontana*	67	*5 Aug 95*	1
DELICIOUS	*Chrysalis*	53	*13 Dec 97*	1
MA SOLITUDA	*Chrysalis*	53	*28 Feb 98*	1
BROKEN NOSE	*Chrysalis*	48	*2 May 98*	1
ALBUMS:	**HITS 3**			**WEEKS 3**
FERMENT	*Fontana*	36	*29 Feb 92*	1
CHROME	*Fontana*	58	*31 Jul 93*	1
ADAM AND EVE	*Chrysalis*	53	*16 May 98*	1

CATHOLICS - See Frank BLACK

Lorraine CATO — UK

SINGLES:	HITS 2			WEEKS 3
HOW CAN YOU TELL ME IT'S OVER?	*Columbia*	46	*6 Feb 93*	2
I WAS MADE TO LOVE YOU	*MCA*	41	*3 Aug 96*	1

CATS — UK

SINGLES:	HITS 1			WEEKS 2
SWAN LAKE	*BAF*	48	*12 Apr 69*	1
SWAN LAKE [RE]	*BAF*	50	*24 May 69*	1

CATS U.K. — UK

SINGLES:	HITS 1			WEEKS 8
LUTON AIRPORT *The catch phrase from the Lorraine Chase Campari TV commercial.*	*WEA*	22	*6 Oct 79*	8

Nick CAVE and the BAD SEEDS — Australia/Germany

SINGLES:	HITS 9			WEEKS 12
STRAIGHT TO YOU / JACK THE RIPPER	*Mute*	68	*11 Apr 92*	1
WHAT A WONDERFUL WORLD *Above hit: Nick CAVE and Shane MacGOWAN.*	*Mute*	72	*12 Dec 92*	1
DO YOU LOVE ME?	*Mute*	68	*9 Apr 94*	1
WHERE THE WILD ROSES GROW *Above hit: Nick CAVE and the BAD SEEDS + Kylie MINOGUE.*	*Mute*	11	*14 Oct 95*	4
HENRY LEE *Above hit: Nick CAVE and PJ HARVEY and the BAD SEEDS.*	*Mute*	36	*9 Mar 96*	1
INTO MY ARMS	*Mute*	53	*22 Feb 97*	1
(ARE YOU) THE ONE THAT I'VE BEEN WAITING FOR?	*Mute*	67	*31 May 97*	1
AS I SAT SADLY BY HER SIDE	*Mute*	42	*31 Mar 01*	1
FIFTEEN FEET OF PURE WHITE SNOW	*Mute*	52	*2 Jun 01*	1
ALBUMS:	**HITS 12**			**WEEKS 27**
FROM HER TO ETERNITY *Above hit: Nick CAVE featuring the BAD SEEDS.*	*Mute*	40	*2 Jun 84*	3
THE FIRST BORN IS DEAD	*Mute*	53	*15 Jun 85*	1
KICKING AGAINST THE PRICKS	*Mute*	89	*30 Aug 86*	1
TENDER PREY	*Mute*	67	*1 Oct 88*	1
THE GOOD SON	*Mute*	47	*28 Apr 90*	1
HENRY'S DREAM	*Mute*	29	*9 May 92*	2
LIVE SEEDS	*Mute*	67	*18 Sep 93*	1
LET LOVE IN	*Mute*	12	*30 Apr 94*	2
MURDER BALLADS	*Mute*	8	*17 Feb 96*	5
THE BOATMAN'S CALL	*Mute*	22	*15 Mar 97*	3
THE BEST OF NICK CAVE AND THE BAD SEEDS	*Mute*	11	*23 May 98*	4
NO MORE SHALL WE PART	*Mute*	15	*14 Apr 01*	3

CAVEMAN — UK

SINGLES:	HITS 1			WEEKS 2
I'M READY	*Profile*	65	*9 Mar 91*	2
ALBUMS:	**HITS 1**			**WEEKS 2**
POSITIVE REACTION	*Profile*	43	*13 Apr 91*	2

CECIL — UK

SINGLES:	HITS 2			WEEKS 2
HOSTAGE IN A FROCK	*Parlophone*	68	*25 Oct 97*	1
THE MOST TIRING DAY	*Parlophone*	69	*28 Mar 98*	1

CELEDA — UK

SINGLES:	HITS 2			WEEKS 5
MUSIC IS THE ANSWER (DANCIN' AND PRANCIN') *Above hit: Danny TENAGLIA + CELEDA.*	*Twisted UK*	36	*5 Sep 98*	3
BE YOURSELF	*Twisted UK*	61	*12 Jun 99*	1
MUSIC IS THE ANSWER '99 (DANCIN' AND PRANCIN') [RM] *Remixed by Future Shock.* *Above hit: Danny TENAGLIA + CELEDA.*	*Twisted UK*	50	*23 Oct 99*	1

CELETIA — UK

SINGLES:	HITS 2			WEEKS 3
REWIND	*Big Life*	29	*11 Apr 98*	2
RUNAWAY SKIES	*Big Life*	66	*8 Aug 98*	1

CELTIC SPIRIT — UK

ALBUMS:	HITS 1			WEEKS 1
CELTIC DREAMS	*PolyGram TV*	62	*31 Jan 98*	1

CENTORY — US

SINGLES:	HITS 1			WEEKS 1
POINT OF NO RETURN	*EMI*	67	*17 Dec 94*	1

CENTRAL LINE — UK

SINGLES:	HITS 6			WEEKS 30
(YOU KNOW) YOU CAN DO IT	*Mercury*	67	*31 Jan 81*	3
WALKING INTO SUNSHINE	*Mercury*	42	*15 Aug 81*	10
DON'T TELL ME	*Mercury*	55	*30 Jan 82*	3
YOU'VE SAID ENOUGH	*Mercury*	58	*20 Nov 82*	3
NATURE BOY	*Mercury*	21	*22 Jan 83*	8
SURPRISE SURPRISE	*Mercury*	48	*11 Jun 83*	3
ALBUMS:	**HITS 1**			**WEEKS 5**
BREAKING POINT	*Mercury*	64	*13 Feb 82*	5

CERRONE — France

SINGLES:	HITS 3			WEEKS 21
LOVE IS 'C' MINOR	*Atlantic*	31	*5 Mar 77*	4
SUPERNATURE	*Atlantic*	8	*29 Jul 78*	12
Features Stephanie De Sykes and Madeline Bell (Blue Mink) on vocals.				
JE SUIS MUSIC	*CBS*	39	*13 Jan 79*	4
SUPERNATURE [RM]	*Encore*	66	*10 Aug 96*	1
Remixed by the Candy Girls.				
ALBUMS:	**HITS 1**			**WEEKS 1**
SUPERNATURE	*Atlantic*	60	*30 Sep 78*	1

A CERTAIN RATIO — UK

SINGLES:	HITS 1			WEEKS 3
WON'T STOP LOVING YOU	*A&M*	55	*16 Jun 90*	3
Original release reached No. 96 in 1989.				
ALBUMS:	**HITS 1**			**WEEKS 3**
SEXTET	*Factory*	53	*30 Jan 82*	3

CERYS of CATATONIA - See Tom JONES; SPACE

Peter CETERA — US

SINGLES:	HITS 2			WEEKS 20
GLORY OF LOVE (THEME FROM KARATE KID PT. II)	*Full Moon*	3	*2 Aug 86*	13
From the film 'The Karate Kid Part II'.				
HARD TO SAY I'M SORRY	*LaFace*	7	*21 Jun 97*	7
Above hit: AZ YET featuring Peter CETERA.				
ALBUMS:	**HITS 1**			**WEEKS 4**
SOLITUDE/SOLITAIRE	*Full Moon*	56	*13 Sep 86*	4

Frank CHACKSFIELD and His Orchestra — UK

SINGLES:	HITS 6			WEEKS 41
LITTLE RED MONKEY	*Parlophone*	10	*4 Apr 53*	3
Above hit: Frank CHACKSFIELD'S TUNESMITHS with Jack JORDAN (clavioline).				
TERRY'S THEME FROM "LIMELIGHT"	*Decca*	2	*23 May 53*	24
From the film 'Limelight'.				
EBB TIDE	*Decca*	9	*13 Feb 54*	2
Originally recorded by Robert Maxwell.				
IN OLD LISBON	*Decca*	15	*25 Feb 56*	4
PORT-AU-PRINCE	*Decca*	18	*19 May 56*	6
Above hit: Winifred ATWELL and Frank CHACKSFIELD.				
THE DONKEY CART	*Decca*	26	*1 Sep 56*	2

CHAIRMEN OF THE BOARD — US

SINGLES:	HITS 10			WEEKS 78
GIVE ME JUST A LITTLE MORE TIME	*Invictus*	3	*22 Aug 70*	13
YOU'VE GOT ME DANGLING ON A STRING	*Invictus*	5	*14 Nov 70*	13
EVERYTHING'S TUESDAY	*Invictus*	12	*20 Feb 71*	9
PAY TO THE PIPER	*Invictus*	34	*15 May 71*	7
CHAIRMAN OF THE BOARD	*Invictus*	48	*4 Sep 71*	2
WORKING ON A BUILDING OF LOVE	*Invictus*	20	*15 Jul 72*	8
ELMO JAMES	*Invictus*	21	*7 Oct 72*	7
I'M ON MY WAY TO A BETTER PLACE	*Invictus*	38	*16 Dec 72*	1
I'M ON MY WAY TO A BETTER PLACE [RE]	*Invictus*	30	*6 Jan 73*	6
FINDERS KEEPERS	*Invictus*	21	*23 Jun 73*	9
LOVER BOY	*EMI*	56	*13 Sep 86*	3
Above hit: CHAIRMEN OF THE BOARD featuring GENERAL JOHNSON.				

CHAKACHAS — Belgium

SINGLES:	HITS 2			WEEKS 8
TWIST TWIST	*RCA*	48	*13 Jan 62*	1
JUNGLE FEVER	*Polydor*	29	*27 May 72*	7

George CHAKIRIS — US

SINGLES:	HITS 1			WEEKS 1
HEART OF A TEENAGE GIRL	*Triumph*	49	*4 Jun 60*	1

CHAKKA BOOM BANG — Holland

SINGLES:	HITS 1			WEEKS 1
TOSSING AND TURNING	*Hooj Choons*	57	*20 Jan 96*	1

CHAKRA — UK

SINGLES:	HITS 3			WEEKS 5
I AM *Originally released in 1996.*	*WEA*	24	*18 Jan 97*	2
HOME	*WEA*	46	*23 Aug 97*	1
LOVE SHINES THROUGH *Vocals by Kate Cameron.*	*WEA*	67	*23 Oct 99*	1
HOME [RM] *Remixed by Above and Beyond.*	*WEA*	47	*26 Aug 00*	1

Sue CHALONER — UK

SINGLES:	HITS 1			WEEKS 1
MOVE ON UP	*Pulse 8*	64	*22 May 93*	1

Richard CHAMBERLAIN — US

SINGLES:	HITS 4			WEEKS 36
THEME FROM DR. KILDARE (THREE STARS WILL SHINE TONIGHT)	*MGM*	12	*9 Jun 62*	10
LOVE ME TENDER	*MGM*	15	*3 Nov 62*	11
HI-LILI, HI-LO *Originally recorded by Leslie Caron.*	*MGM*	20	*23 Feb 63*	9
TRUE LOVE	*MGM*	30	*20 Jul 63*	6
ALBUMS:	**HITS 1**			**WEEKS 8**
RICHARD CHAMBERLAIN SINGS	*MGM*	8	*16 Mar 63*	8

Bryan CHAMBERS - See CLEPTOMANIACS featuring Bryan CHAMBERS

CHAMELEON — UK

SINGLES:	HITS 1			WEEKS 2
THE WAY IT IS *First released through DMC in 1995.*	*Stress*	34	*18 May 96*	2

CHAMELEONS — UK

ALBUMS:	HITS 2			WEEKS 4
WHAT DOES ANYTHING MEAN? BASICALLY	*Statik*	60	*25 May 85*	2
STRANGE TIMES	*Geffen*	44	*20 Sep 86*	2

CHAMPAIGN — US

SINGLES:	HITS 1			WEEKS 13
HOW 'BOUT US	*CBS*	5	*9 May 81*	13
ALBUMS:	**HITS 1**			**WEEKS 4**
HOW 'BOUT US	*CBS*	38	*27 Jun 81*	4

CHAMPIONS - See MANCHESTER UNITED FOOTBALL SQUAD

CHAMPS — US

SINGLES:	HITS 2			WEEKS 10
TEQUILA	*London*	5	*5 Apr 58*	9
TOO MUCH TEQUILA	*London*	49	*19 Mar 60*	1

CHAMPS BOYS — France

SINGLES:	HITS 1			WEEKS 6
TUBULAR BELLS	*Philips*	41	*19 Jun 76*	6

CHANCE - See SUNKIDS featuring CHANCE

Gene CHANDLER — US

SINGLES:	HITS 4			WEEKS 29
NOTHING CAN STOP ME	*Soul City*	41	*8 Jun 68*	4
GET DOWN	*20th Century*	11	*3 Feb 79*	11
WHEN YOU'RE NUMBER 1	*20th Century*	43	*1 Sep 79*	5
DOES SHE HAVE A FRIEND?	*20th Century*	28	*28 Jun 80*	9

George CHANDLER - See OLYMPIC RUNNERS

CHANELLE — US

SINGLES:	HITS 1			WEEKS 9
ONE MAN	*Cooltempo*	16	*11 Mar 89*	8
ONE MAN [RM]	*Deep Distraxion*	50	*10 Dec 94*	1
Remixed by Joey Musaphia.				

CHANGE — US

SINGLES:	HITS 7			WEEKS 43
A LOVER'S HOLIDAY / THE GLOW OF LOVE	*WEA*	14	*28 Jun 80*	8
SEARCHING	*WEA*	11	*6 Sep 80*	10
CHANGE OF HEART	*WEA*	17	*2 Jun 84*	10
YOU ARE MY MELODY	*WEA*	48	*11 Aug 84*	4
LET'S GO TOGETHER	*Cooltempo*	37	*16 Mar 85*	7
OH WHAT A FEELING	*Cooltempo*	56	*25 May 85*	2
MUTUAL ATTRACTION	*Cooltempo*	60	*13 Jul 85*	2
ALBUMS:	**HITS 3**			**WEEKS 27**
CHANGE OF HEART	*WEA*	34	*19 May 84*	17
TURN ON THE RADIO	*Cooltempo*	39	*27 Apr 85*	6
THE ARTISTS VOLUME 2	*Street Sounds*	45	*13 Jul 85*	4
Compilation album with tracks by each artist.				
Above hit: Luther VANDROSS/Teddy PENDERGRASS/CHANGE/ATLANTIC STARR.				

CHANGING FACES — US

SINGLES:	HITS 5			WEEKS 12
STROKE YOU UP	*Atlantic*	43	*24 Sep 94*	3
G.H.E.T.T.O.U.T.	*Atlantic*	10	*26 Jul 97*	5
I GOT SOMEBODY ELSE	*Atlantic*	42	*1 Nov 97*	1
TIME AFTER TIME	*Atlantic*	35	*4 Apr 98*	2
Above hit: CHANGING FACES (featuring JAY-Z).				
SAME TEMPO	*A&M*	53	*1 Aug 98*	1
From the film 'The Players Club'.				

CHANNEL X — Belgium

SINGLES:	HITS 1			WEEKS 1
GROOVE TO MOVE	*PWL Continental*	67	*14 Dec 91*	1

Bruce CHANNEL — US

SINGLES:	HITS 2			WEEKS 28
• HEY! BABY	*Mercury*	2	*24 Mar 62*	12
Features Delbert McClinton on harmonica.				
KEEP ON	*Bell*	12	*29 Jun 68*	16

CHANSON — US

SINGLES:	HITS 1			WEEKS 7
DON'T HOLD BACK	*Ariola*	33	*13 Jan 79*	7

CHANTAL – See MOONMAN

CHANTAYS — US

SINGLES:	HITS 1			WEEKS 14
• PIPELINE	*London*	16	*20 Apr 63*	14

CHANTER SISTERS — UK

SINGLES:	HITS 1			WEEKS 5
SIDESHOW	*Polydor*	43	*17 Jul 76*	5

CHAOS — UK

SINGLES:	HITS 1			WEEKS 2
FAREWELL MY SUMMER LOVE	*Arista*	55	*3 Oct 92*	2

Harry CHAPIN — US

SINGLES:	HITS 1			WEEKS 5
W.O.L.D.	*Elektra*	34	*11 May 74*	5

Michael CHAPMAN — UK

ALBUMS:	HITS 1			WEEKS 1
FULLY QUALIFIED SURVIVOR	*Harvest*	45	*21 Mar 70*	1

Simone CHAPMAN – See ILLEGAL MOTION featuring Simone CHAPMAN

Tracy CHAPMAN — US

SINGLES:	HITS 2			WEEKS 15
FAST CAR	*Elektra*	5	*11 Jun 88*	12
CROSSROADS	*Elektra*	61	*30 Sep 89*	3

ALBUMS:	HITS 4			WEEKS 217
TRACY CHAPMAN	*Elektra*	1	*21 May 88*	75
CROSSROADS	*Elektra*	1	*14 Oct 89*	16
MATTERS OF THE HEART	*Elektra*	19	*9 May 92*	3
TRACY CHAPMAN [RE-1ST]	*Elektra*	12	*2 Apr 94*	110
Re-released at mid-price. 1994 peak No. 34, 1999 peak No. 19, 2000 peak No. 12.				
COLLECTION	*Elektra*	3	*6 Oct 01*	13

CHAPTERHOUSE — UK

SINGLES:	HITS 2			WEEKS 3
PEARL	*Dedicated*	67	*30 Mar 91*	1
MESMERISE	*Dedicated*	60	*12 Oct 91*	2

ALBUMS:	HITS 1			WEEKS 3
WHIRLPOOL	*Dedicated*	23	*11 May 91*	3

CHAQUITO ORCHESTRA — UK

SINGLES:	HITS 1			WEEKS 1
NEVER ON SUNDAY (JAMIAS LE DIMANCHE)	*Fontana*	50	*29 Oct 60*	1

ALBUMS:	HITS 2			WEEKS 2
THIS IS CHAQUITO	*Fontana*	36	*24 Feb 68*	1
Above hit: CHAQUITO and QUEDO BRASS.				
THRILLER THEMES	*Philips*	48	*4 Mar 72*	1

CHARGED GBH — UK

SINGLES:	HITS 2			WEEKS 5
NO SURVIVORS	*Clay*	63	*6 Feb 82*	2
GIVE ME FIRE	*Clay*	69	*20 Nov 82*	3

ALBUMS:	HITS 1			WEEKS 6
CITY BABY ATTACKED BY RATS	*Clay*	17	*14 Aug 82*	6

CHARLATANS — UK

SINGLES:	HITS 22			WEEKS 77
THE ONLY ONE I KNOW	*Situation Two*	9	*2 Jun 90*	9
THEN	*Situation Two*	12	*22 Sep 90*	5
OVER RISING	*Situation Two*	15	*9 Mar 91*	5
INDIAN ROPE	*Dead Dead Good*	57	*17 Aug 91*	1
ME. IN TIME	*Situation Two*	28	*9 Nov 91*	3
WEIRDO	*Situation Two*	19	*7 Mar 92*	4
TREMELO SONG [EP]	*Situation Two*	44	*18 Jul 92*	2
Lead track: Tremelo Song.				
CAN'T GET OUT OF BED	*Beggars Banquet*	24	*5 Feb 94*	3
I NEVER WANT AN EASY LIFE IF ME AND HE WERE EVER TO GET THERE	*Beggars Banquet*	38	*19 Mar 94*	1
Limited edition boxed CD.				
JESUS HAIRDO	*Beggars Banquet*	48	*2 Jul 94*	2
Title taken from quote in Douglas Couplan's Novel 'Shampoo Planet'.				
CRASHIN' IN	*Beggars Banquet*	31	*7 Jan 95*	2
JUST LOOKIN / BULLET COMES	*Beggars Banquet*	32	*27 May 95*	3
JUST WHEN YOU'RE THINKIN' THINGS OVER	*Beggars Banquet*	12	*26 Aug 95*	3
ONE TO ANOTHER	*Beggars Banquet*	3	*7 Sep 96*	6
NORTH COUNTRY BOY	*Beggars Banquet*	4	*5 Apr 97*	5
Recorded before the death of keyboardist Rob Collins the previous year.				
HOW HIGH	*Beggars Banquet*	6	*21 Jun 97*	5
NORTH COUNTRY BOY [RE]	*Beggars Banquet*	74	*21 Jun 97*	1
TELLIN' STORIES	*Beggars Banquet*	16	*1 Nov 97*	3
FOREVER	*Universal*	12	*16 Oct 99*	3
MY BEAUTIFUL FRIEND	*Universal*	31	*18 Dec 99*	3
IMPOSSIBLE	*Universal*	15	*27 May 00*	3
LOVE IS THE KEY	*Universal*	16	*8 Sep 01*	3
A MAN NEEDS TO BE TOLD	*Universal*	31	*1 Dec 01*	2

ALBUMS:	HITS 8			WEEKS 105
SOME FRIENDLY	*Situation Two*	1	*20 Oct 90*	17
BETWEEN 10TH AND 11TH	*Situation Two*	21	*4 Apr 92*	4
UP TO OUR HIPS	*Beggars Banquet*	8	*2 Apr 94*	3
THE CHARLATANS	*Beggars Banquet*	1	*9 Sep 95*	13
TELLIN' STORIES	*Beggars Banquet*	1	*3 May 97*	28
MELTING POT	*Beggars Banquet*	4	*7 Mar 98*	25
Compilation made up of live favourites and rare alternative mixes.				
US AND US ONLY	*Universal*	2	*30 Oct 99*	10
WONDERLAND	*Universal*	2	*22 Sep 01*	5

CHARLENE — US

SINGLES:	HITS 1			WEEKS 12
I'VE NEVER BEEN TO ME *Originally recorded by Nancy Wilson.*	*Motown*	1	*15 May 82*	12

ALBUMS:	HITS 1			WEEKS 4
I'VE NEVER BEEN TO ME	*Motown*	43	*17 Jul 82*	4

Don CHARLES — UK

SINGLES:	HITS 1			WEEKS 5
WALK WITH ME MY ANGEL *Originally recorded by John Leyton.*	*Decca*	39	*24 Feb 62*	5

Don CHARLES presents the SINGING DOGS — Denmark

SINGLES:	HITS 1			WEEKS 4
PAT-A-CAKE, PAT-A-CAKE/THREE BLIND MICE/JINGLE BELLS [M] / OH SUSANNA *Chart reflects the entry only as 'The Singing Dogs'.* *The above entry only lists both sides.*	*Pye Nixa*	13	*26 Nov 55*	4

Ray CHARLES — US

(See also Quincy Jones.)

SINGLES:	HITS 16			WEEKS 123
GEORGIA ON MY MIND *Originally recorded by Hoagy Carmichael.*	*His Master's Voice*	47	*3 Dec 60*	1
GEORGIA ON MY MIND [RE]	*His Master's Voice*	24	*17 Dec 60*	7
HIT THE ROAD JACK *Originally recorded by Percy Mayfield.* *Above hit: Ray CHARLES and his Orchestra. Vocal by Ray CHARLES with the RAELETS.*	*His Master's Voice*	6	*21 Oct 61*	12
I CAN'T STOP LOVING YOU *Originally recorded by Don Gibson.*	*His Master's Voice*	1	*16 Jun 62*	17
YOU DON'T KNOW ME *Originally recorded by Eddy Arnold.*	*His Master's Voice*	9	*15 Sep 62*	13
YOUR CHEATING HEART *Originally recorded by Hank Williams.* *Above hit: Ray CHARLES with the Jack HALLORAN SINGERS.*	*His Master's Voice*	13	*15 Dec 62*	8
DON'T SET ME FREE *Above hit: Ray CHARLES and his Orchestra with the RAELETTES featuring Margie HENDRIX.*	*His Master's Voice*	37	*30 Mar 63*	3
TAKE THESE CHAINS FROM MY HEART *Originally recorded by Hank Williams.* *Above hit: Ray CHARLES with the Jack HALLORAN SINGERS.*	*His Master's Voice*	5	*18 May 63*	20
NO ONE *Above hit: Ray CHARLES and the RAELETS.*	*His Master's Voice*	35	*14 Sep 63*	7
BUSTED *Originally recorded by Johnny Cash.* *Above hit: Ray CHARLES and his Orchestra.*	*His Master's Voice*	21	*2 Nov 63*	10
NO-ONE TO CRY TO	*His Master's Voice*	38	*26 Sep 64*	3
MAKIN' WHOOPEE	*His Master's Voice*	42	*23 Jan 65*	4
CRYIN' TIME *Above hit: Ray CHARLES with the Jack HALLORAN SINGERS and the Ray CHARLES ORCHESTRA with the RAELETS.*	*His Master's Voice*	50	*12 Feb 66*	1
TOGETHER AGAIN *Above 2 originally recorded by Buck Owens.*	*His Master's Voice*	48	*23 Apr 66*	1
HERE WE GO AGAIN	*His Master's Voice*	38	*8 Jul 67*	1
HERE WE GO AGAIN [RE]	*His Master's Voice*	45	*22 Jul 67*	2
YESTERDAY	*Stateside*	44	*23 Dec 67*	4
ELEANOR RIGBY	*Stateside*	36	*3 Aug 68*	9

EPS:	HITS 2			WEEKS 41
I CAN'T STOP LOVING YOU	*HMV*	10	*12 Jan 63*	36
TAKE THESE CHAINS FROM MY HEART	*HMV*	16	*21 Sep 63*	5

ALBUMS:	HITS 8			WEEKS 50
MODERN SOUNDS IN COUNTRY AND WESTERN MUSIC	*His Master's Voice*	6	*28 Jul 62*	16
MODERN SOUNDS IN COUNTRY AND WESTERN MUSIC VOLUME 2	*His Master's Voice*	15	*23 Feb 63*	5
GREATEST HITS	*His Master's Voice*	16	*20 Jul 63*	5
GREATEST HITS VOLUME 2	*Stateside*	24	*5 Oct 68*	8
HEART TO HEART - 20 HOT HITS	*London*	29	*19 Jul 80*	5
COLLECTION	*Westmoor*	36	*24 Mar 90*	3
RAY CHARLES - THE LIVING LEGEND	*Arcade*	48	*13 Mar 93*	3
THE DEFINITIVE RAY CHARLES	*warner.esp*	13	*25 Aug 01*	5

Ray CHARLES SINGERS - See Perry COMO

Suzette CHARLES — US

SINGLES:	HITS 1			WEEKS 2
FREE TO LOVE AGAIN	*RCA*	58	*21 Aug 93*	2

Tina CHARLES — UK

SINGLES:	HITS 7			WEEKS 63
I LOVE TO LOVE (BUT MY BABY LOVES TO DANCE)	*CBS*	1	*7 Feb 76*	12
LOVE ME LIKE A LOVER	*CBS*	28	*1 May 76*	7
DANCE LITTLE LADY DANCE	*CBS*	6	*21 Aug 76*	13
DR. LOVE	*CBS*	4	*4 Dec 76*	10
Originally recorded by the Electric Dolls.				
RENDEZVOUS	*CBS*	27	*14 May 77*	6
LOVE BUG - SWEETS FOR MY SWEET [M]	*CBS*	26	*29 Oct 77*	4
I'LL GO WHERE YOUR MUSIC TAKES ME	*CBS*	27	*11 Mar 78*	8
I LOVE TO LOVE (TEENAGE MIX) [RM]	*Disco Mix Club*	67	*30 Aug 86*	3
ALBUMS:	**HITS 1**			**WEEKS 7**
HEART 'N' SOUL	*CBS*	35	*3 Dec 77*	7

CHARLES and EDDIE — US

SINGLES:	HITS 4			WEEKS 30
WOULD I LIE TO YOU?	*Capitol*	1	*31 Oct 92*	17
N.Y.C. (CAN YOU BELIEVE THIS CITY?)	*Capitol*	33	*20 Feb 93*	5
HOUSE IS NOT A HOME	*Capitol*	29	*22 May 93*	4
24-7-365	*Capitol*	38	*13 May 95*	4
ALBUMS:	**HITS 1**			**WEEKS 15**
DUOPHONIC	*Capitol*	19	*12 Dec 92*	15

Dick CHARLESWORTH and his CITY GENTS — UK

SINGLES:	HITS 1			WEEKS 1
BILLY BOY	*Top Rank*	43	*6 May 61*	1

CHARLOTTE — UK

SINGLES:	HITS 4			WEEKS 4
QUEEN OF HEARTS	*Big Life*	54	*12 Mar 94*	1
BE MINE	*Parlophone*	59	*2 May 98*	1
SKIN	*Parlophone Rhythm Series*	56	*29 May 99*	1
SOMEDAY	*Parlophone Rhythm Series*	74	*4 Sep 99*	1

CHARME — US

SINGLES:	HITS 1			WEEKS 2
GEORGY PORGY	*RCA*	68	*17 Nov 84*	2
Originally recorded by Toto				

CHARO and the SALSOUL ORCHESTRA — US

SINGLES:	HITS 1			WEEKS 4
DANCE A LITTLE BIT CLOSER	*Salsoul*	44	*29 Apr 78*	4

CHARVONI - See BROTHERS IN RHYTHM

CHAS and DAVE — UK

(See also Tottenham Hotspur FA Cup Final Squad.)

SINGLES:	HITS 10			WEEKS 66
STRUMMIN' / I'M IN TROUBLE	*EMI*	52	*11 Nov 78*	3
I'm In Trouble listed from 18 Nov 78.				
Above hit: CHAS and DAVE with ROCKNEY.				
GERTCHA	*EMI*	20	*26 May 79*	8
THE SIDEBOARD SONG (GOT MY BEER IN THE SIDEBOARD HERE)	*EMI*	55	*1 Sep 79*	3
RABBIT	*Rockney*	8	*29 Nov 80*	11
Above 3 and Margate used in the Courage Best Bitter TV commercials.				
STARS OVER 45 [M]	*Rockney*	21	*12 Dec 81*	8
Medley of sing-a-long songs from the early 20th century.				
AIN'T NO PLEASING YOU	*Rockney*	2	*13 Mar 82*	11
MARGATE	*Rockney*	46	*17 Jul 82*	4
LONDON GIRLS	*Rockney*	63	*19 Mar 83*	3
MY MELANCHOLY BABY	*Rockney*	51	*3 Dec 83*	6
SNOOKER LOOPY	*Rockney*	6	*3 May 86*	9
Vocals by snooker stars Steve Davis, Terry Griffiths, Tony Meo, Dennis Taylor and Willie Thorne.				
Above hit: MATCHROOM MOB with CHAS and DAVE.				
ALBUMS:	**HITS 9**			**WEEKS 101**
CHAS AND DAVE'S CHRISTMAS JAMBOREE BAG	*Warwick*	25	*5 Dec 81*	15
Title per sleeve, though label reads title as Stars Over 45 - The Christmas Jamboree Bag.				
MUSTN'T GRUMBLE	*Rockney*	35	*17 Apr 82*	11
JOB LOT	*Rockney*	59	*8 Jan 83*	15
CHAS AND DAVE'S KNEES-UP - JAMBOREE BAG NO. 2	*Rockney*	7	*15 Oct 83*	17
WELL PLEASED	*Rockney*	27	*11 Aug 84*	10
CHAS AND DAVE'S GREATEST HITS	*Rockney*	16	*17 Nov 84*	10
CHAS AND DAVE'S CHRISTMAS JAMBOREE BAG [RI]	*Rockney*	87	*15 Dec 84*	1

JAMBOREE BAG NUMBER 3	*Rockney*	15	*9 Nov 85*	13
CHAS AND DAVE'S CHRISTMAS CAROL ALBUM	*Telstar*	37	*13 Dec 86*	4
STREET PARTY	*Telstar*	3	*29 Apr 95*	5
50-track medley of war songs, released in time for the 50th anniversary of VE day.				
Above hit: CHAS 'N' DAVE.				

Tara CHASE – See Sonny JONES featuring Tara CHASE

Ingrid CHAVEZ – See Riuichi SAKAMOTO; David SYLVIAN

CHEAP TRICK — US

SINGLES:	HITS 3			WEEKS 14
I WANT YOU TO WANT ME	*Epic*	29	*5 May 79*	9
WAY OF THE WORLD	*Epic*	73	*2 Feb 80*	2
IF YOU WANT MY LOVE	*Epic*	57	*31 Jul 82*	3
ALBUMS:	**HITS 3**			**WEEKS 15**
CHEAP TRICK AT BUDOKAN	*Epic*	29	*24 Feb 79*	9
DREAM POLICE	*Epic*	41	*6 Oct 79*	5
ONE ON ONE	*Epic*	95	*5 Jun 82*	1

Oliver CHEATHAM — US

SINGLES:	HITS 1			WEEKS 5
GET DOWN SATURDAY NIGHT	*MCA*	38	*2 Jul 83*	5

CHEB MAMI – See STING

CHECK 1-2 – See Craig McLACHLAN

Chubby CHECKER — US

SINGLES:	HITS 10			WEEKS 112
THE TWIST	*Columbia*	49	*24 Sep 60*	1
Originally recorded by Hank Ballard and the Midnighters.				
THE TWIST [RE-1ST]	*Columbia*	44	*8 Oct 60*	1
PONY TIME	*Columbia*	27	*1 Apr 61*	6
Originally recorded by Don Covay and the Goodtimers.				
LET'S TWIST AGAIN	*Columbia*	37	*19 Aug 61*	3
LET'S TWIST AGAIN [RE-1ST]	*Columbia*	2	*30 Dec 61*	27
THE TWIST [RE-2ND]	*Columbia*	14	*13 Jan 62*	10
SLOW TWISTIN'	*Columbia*	23	*7 Apr 62*	8
TEACH ME TO TWIST	*Columbia*	45	*21 Apr 62*	1
Above hit: Chubby CHECKER; Bobby RYDELL.				
DANCIN' PARTY	*Columbia*	19	*11 Aug 62*	13
LET'S TWIST AGAIN [RE-2ND]	*Columbia*	46	*25 Aug 62*	1
LET'S TWIST AGAIN [RE-3RD]	*Columbia*	49	*15 Sep 62*	3
LIMBO ROCK	*Cameo-Parkway*	32	*3 Nov 62*	10
JINGLE BELL ROCK	*Cameo-Parkway*	40	*22 Dec 62*	3
Above hit: Bobby RYDELL and Chubby CHECKER.				
WHAT DO YA SAY	*Cameo-Parkway*	37	*2 Nov 63*	4
LET'S TWIST AGAIN [RI] / THE TWIST [RI]	*London*	5	*29 Nov 75*	10
THE TWIST (YO, TWIST)	*Urban*	2	*18 Jun 88*	11
Above hit: FAT BOYS (lead vocal: Chubby CHECKER).				
EPS:	**HITS 2**			**WEEKS 46**
KING OF THE TWIST	*Columbia*	3	*17 Mar 62*	43
DANCING PARTY	*Cameo Parkway*	17	*2 Feb 63*	3
ALBUMS:	**HITS 2**			**WEEKS 7**
TWIST WITH CHUBBY CHECKER	*Columbia*	13	*27 Jan 62*	4
FOR TWISTERS ONLY	*Columbia*	17	*3 Mar 62*	3

CHECKMATES LTD. featuring Sonny CHARLES — US

SINGLES:	HITS 1			WEEKS 8
PROUD MARY	*A&M*	30	*15 Nov 69*	8

CHEEKAH – See VENGABOYS

Judy CHEEKS — US

SINGLES:	HITS 4			WEEKS 15
SO IN LOVE (THE REAL DEAL)	*Positiva*	27	*13 Nov 93*	3
REACH	*Positiva*	17	*7 May 94*	4
THIS TIME/RESPECT	*Positiva*	23	*4 Mar 95*	2
YOU'RE THE STORY OF MY LIFE / AS LONG AS YOU'RE GOOD TO ME	*Positiva*	30	*17 Jun 95*	3
REACH [RM]	*Positiva*	22	*13 Jan 96*	3
Remixed by Dancing Divaz.				

CHEETAHS — UK

SINGLES:	HITS 2			WEEKS 6
MECCA	*Philips*	36	*3 Oct 64*	3
Originally recorded by Gene Pitney.				
SOLDIER BOY	*Philips*	39	*23 Jan 65*	3

CHEF — US

(See also Isaac Hayes.)

SINGLES:	HITS 1			WEEKS 13
CHOCOLATE SALTY BALLS (P.S. I LOVE YOU)	*Columbia*	1	*26 Dec 98*	13

CHELSEA FOOTBALL TEAM — UK

SINGLES:	HITS 4			WEEKS 22
BLUE IS THE COLOUR	*Penny Farthing*	5	*26 Feb 72*	12
NO ONE CAN STOP US NOW	*RCA*	23	*14 May 94*	3
BLUE DAY	*WEA*	22	*17 May 97*	5
Above hit: SUGGS and CO. featuring the CHELSEA TEAM.				
BLUE TOMORROW	*Telstar TV*	22	*27 May 00*	2
The commemorative single of the 2000 FA Cup Final, in which Chelsea beat Aston Villa 1–0.				
Above hit: CHELSEA and CO.				

CHEMICAL BROTHERS — UK

SINGLES:	HITS 10			WEEKS 53
LEAVE HOME	*Junior Boy's Own*	17	*17 Jun 95*	4
LIFE IS SWEET	*Junior Boy's Own*	25	*9 Sep 95*	3
Features vocals by Tim Burgess of the Charlatans.				
LOOPS OF FURY [EP]	*Junior Boy's Own*	13	*27 Jan 96*	1
Lead track: Loops Of Fury.				
SETTING SUN	*Virgin*	1	*12 Oct 96*	7
Features vocals by Noel Gallagher of Oasis.				
BLOCK ROCKIN' BEATS	*Virgin*	1	*5 Apr 97*	6
Vocals by Schooly D.				
BLOCK ROCKIN' BEATS [RE]	*Virgin*	69	*28 Jun 97*	1
ELEKTROBANK	*Virgin*	17	*20 Sep 97*	4
HEY BOY HEY GIRL	*Virgin*	3	*12 Jun 99*	10
LET FOREVER BE	*Virgin*	9	*14 Aug 99*	7
Vocals by Noel Gallagher.				
OUT OF CONTROL	*Virgin*	21	*23 Oct 99*	4
Vocal and guitar by Bernard Summer (New Order) and additional vocals by Bobby Gillespie (Primal Scream).				
IT BEGAN IN AFRIKA	*Virgin*	8	*22 Sep 01*	4
IT BEGAN IN AFRIKA [RE]	*Virgin*	53	*3 Nov 01*	2
ALBUMS:	**HITS 3**			**WEEKS 115**
EXIT PLANET DUST	*Junior Boy's Own*	9	*8 Jul 95*	41
DIG YOUR OWN HOLE	*Virgin*	1	*19 Apr 97*	27
SURRENDER	*Virgin*	1	*3 Jul 99*	47

CHEQUERS — UK

SINGLES:	HITS 2			WEEKS 10
ROCK ON BROTHER	*Creole*	21	*18 Oct 75*	5
HEY MISS PAYNE	*Creole*	32	*28 Feb 76*	5

CHER — US

(See also Cher, Chrissie Hynde and Neneh Cherry with Eric Clapton; Sonny and Cher; Various Artists: Films - Original Soundtracks 'Mermaids'.)

SINGLES:	HITS 30			WEEKS 218
ALL I REALLY WANT TO DO	*Liberty*	9	*21 Aug 65*	10
BANG BANG (MY BABY SHOT ME DOWN)	*Liberty*	3	*2 Apr 66*	12
I FEEL SOMETHING IN THE AIR	*Liberty*	43	*6 Aug 66*	2
SUNNY	*Liberty*	32	*24 Sep 66*	5
GYPSYS, TRAMPS AND THIEVES	*MCA*	4	*6 Nov 71*	13
Originally called Gypsies and White Trash.				
DARK LADY	*MCA*	36	*16 Feb 74*	3
DARK LADY [RE]	*MCA*	45	*16 Mar 74*	1
I FOUND SOMEONE	*Geffen*	5	*19 Dec 87*	10
Written and produced by Michael Bolton.				
WE ALL SLEEP ALONE	*Geffen*	47	*2 Apr 88*	5
IF I COULD TURN BACK TIME	*Geffen*	6	*2 Sep 89*	14
JUST LIKE JESSE JAMES	*Geffen*	11	*13 Jan 90*	11
HEART OF STONE	*Geffen*	43	*7 Apr 90*	5
YOU WOULDN'T KNOW LOVE	*Geffen*	55	*11 Aug 90*	3
THE SHOOP SHOOP SONG (IT'S IN HIS KISS)	*Epic*	1	*13 Apr 91*	15
From the film 'Mermaids'. Originally recorded by Merry Clayton in 1963.				

LOVE AND UNDERSTANDING	*Geffen*	10	*13 Jul 91*	8
SAVE UP ALL YOUR TEARS	*Geffen*	37	*12 Oct 91*	5
Robin Beck's original reached No. 84 in 1989.				
LOVE HURTS	*Geffen*	43	*7 Dec 91*	5
COULD'VE BEEN YOU	*Geffen*	31	*18 Apr 92*	4
OH NO NOT MY BABY	*Geffen*	33	*14 Nov 92*	4
Originally recorded by The Shirelles				
MANY RIVERS TO CROSS (LIVE FROM THE MIRAGE)	*Geffen*	37	*16 Jan 93*	3
WHENEVER YOU'RE NEAR	*Geffen*	72	*6 Mar 93*	1
I GOT YOU BABE	*Geffen*	35	*15 Jan 94*	3
Beavis and Butt-Head are cartoon characters from MTV.				
Above hit: CHER with BEAVIS and BUTT-HEAD.				
WALKING IN MEMPHIS	*WEA*	11	*28 Oct 95*	7
ONE BY ONE	*WEA*	7	*20 Jan 96*	9
Originally recorded by Jo Jo and the Real People in 1987.				
NOT ENOUGH LOVE IN THE WORLD	*WEA*	31	*27 Apr 96*	2
Originally recorded by Don Henley from his album Building The Perfect Beast.				
THE SUN AIN'T GONNA SHINE ANYMORE	*WEA*	26	*17 Aug 96*	3
BELIEVE	*WEA*	1	*31 Oct 98*	26
STRONG ENOUGH	*WEA*	5	*6 Mar 99*	10
BELIEVE [RE]	*WEA*	59	*8 May 99*	2
ALL OR NOTHING	*WEA*	12	*19 Jun 99*	7
DOV'E L'AMOURE	*WEA*	21	*6 Nov 99*	3
THE MUSIC'S NO GOOD WITHOUT YOU	*WEA*	8	*17 Nov 01*	7
EPS:	**HITS 1**			**WEEKS 1**
THE HITS OF CHER	*Liberty*	10	*22 Oct 66*	1
ALBUMS:	**HITS 10**			**WEEKS 296**
ALL I REALLY WANT TO DO	*Liberty*	7	*2 Oct 65*	9
SONNY SIDE OF CHER	*Liberty*	11	*7 May 66*	11
CHER	*Geffen*	26	*16 Jan 88*	22
HEART OF STONE	*Geffen*	15	*22 Jul 89*	13
HEART OF STONE [RE-1ST]	*Geffen*	7	*30 Dec 89*	47
HEART OF STONE [RE-2ND]	*Geffen*	43	*27 Apr 91*	22
Re-released at mid-price. Chart position reached in 1992 (1991 peak No. 49).				
LOVE HURTS	*Geffen*	1	*29 Jun 91*	51
CHER'S GREATEST HITS: 1965-1992	*Geffen*	1	*21 Nov 92*	33
IT'S A MAN'S WORLD	*WEA*	10	*18 Nov 95*	18
Tracks on the album were all originally written and performed by men.				
BELIEVE	*WEA*	7	*7 Nov 98*	44
THE GREATEST HITS	*WEA/Universal Music TV*	7	*20 Nov 99*	24
LIVING PROOF	*WEA*	46	*1 Dec 01*	2

CHER, Chrissie HYNDE and Neneh CHERRY with Eric CLAPTON — UK/US/Sweden

(See also Cher; Neneh Cherry; Eric Clapton.)

SINGLES:	**HITS 1**			**WEEKS 8**
LOVE CAN BUILD A BRIDGE	*London*	1	*18 Mar 95*	8
In aid of Comic Relief. Originally recorded by the Judds in 1990.				

CHERI — US

SINGLES:	**HITS 1**			**WEEKS 9**
MURPHY'S LAW	*Polydor*	13	*19 Jun 82*	9

CHEROKEES — UK

SINGLES:	**HITS 1**			**WEEKS 5**
SEVEN DAFFODILS	*Columbia*	33	*5 Sep 64*	5

CHERRELLE — US

SINGLES:	**HITS 5**			**WEEKS 26**
SATURDAY LOVE	*Tabu*	6	*28 Dec 85*	11
Above hit: CHERRELLE with Alexander O'NEAL.				
WILL YOU SATISFY?	*Tabu*	57	*1 Mar 86*	3
NEVER KNEW LOVE LIKE THIS	*Tabu*	26	*6 Feb 88*	7
Above hit: Alexander O'NEAL featuring CHERRELLE.				
AFFAIR	*Tabu*	67	*6 May 89*	2
SATURDAY LOVE (FEELIN' LUV MIX) [RM]	*Tabu*	55	*24 Mar 90*	2
Remixed by Olimar and D.J. Shapps.				
Above hit: CHERRELLE with Alexander O'NEAL.				
BABY COME TO ME	*One World Entertainment*	56	*2 Aug 97*	1
Above hit: Alexander O'NEAL and CHERRELLE.				
ALBUMS:	**HITS 1**			**WEEKS 9**
HIGH PRIORITY	*Tabu*	17	*25 Jan 86*	9

Don CHERRY — US

SINGLES:	HITS 1			WEEKS 11
BAND OF GOLD	*Philips*	6	*11 Feb 56*	11
Above hit: Don CHERRY with Ray CONNIFF and his Orchestra. Originally recorded by Kit Carson.				

Eagle-Eye CHERRY — Sweden

SINGLES:	HITS 5			WEEKS 28
SAVE TONIGHT	*Polydor*	6	*4 Jul 98*	13
FALLING IN LOVE AGAIN	*Polydor*	8	*14 Nov 98*	8
PERMANENT TEARS	*Polydor*	43	*20 Mar 99*	1
ARE YOU STILL HAVING FUN?	*Polydor*	21	*29 Apr 00*	4
LONG WAY AROUND	*Polydor*	48	*11 Nov 00*	2
Above hit: EAGLE-EYE featuring Neneh CHERRY.				
ALBUMS:	**HITS 2**			**WEEKS 32**
DESIRELESS	*Polydor*	3	*1 Aug 98*	29
LIVING IN THE PRESENT FUTURE	*Polydor*	12	*20 May 00*	3

Neneh CHERRY — Sweden

(See also Cher, Chrissie Hynde and Neneh Cherry with Eric Clapton.)

SINGLES:	HITS 12			WEEKS 90
BUFFALO STANCE	*Circa*	3	*10 Dec 88*	13
MANCHILD	*Circa*	5	*20 May 89*	10
KISSES ON THE WIND	*Circa*	20	*12 Aug 89*	6
INNA CITY MAMMA	*Circa*	31	*23 Dec 89*	7
I'VE GOT YOU UNDER MY SKIN	*Circa*	25	*29 Sep 90*	5
From the Red, Hot and Blue album to benefit AIDS research.				
MONEY LOVE	*Circa*	23	*3 Oct 92*	4
BUDDY X	*Circa*	35	*19 Jun 93*	3
Samples Juicy's Sugar Free. Features rap by the Notorious B.I.G.				
7 SECONDS	*Columbia*	3	*25 Jun 94*	21
Above hit: Youssou N'DOUR (featuring Neneh CHERRY).				
7 SECONDS [RE]	*Columbia*	54	*24 Dec 94*	4
WOMAN	*Hut*	9	*3 Aug 96*	7
Based on James Brown's It's A Man's World.				
KOOTCHI	*Hut*	38	*14 Dec 96*	2
FEEL IT	*Hut*	68	*22 Feb 97*	1
A tribute to her father.				
BUDDY X 99 [RM]	*4 Liberty*	15	*6 Nov 99*	5
Remixed produced by B. Simms. Additional vocals by PSG.				
Above hit: DREEM TEEM 'v' Neneh CHERRY.				
LONG WAY AROUND	*Polydor*	48	*11 Nov 00*	2
Above hit: EAGLE EYE featuring Neneh CHERRY.				
ALBUMS:	**HITS 3**			**WEEKS 49**
RAW LIKE SUSHI	*Circa*	2	*17 Jun 89*	43
HOMEBREW	*Circa*	27	*7 Nov 92*	2
MAN	*Hut*	16	*14 Sep 96*	4

Maurice CHEVALIER and Hayley MILLS — France/UK

(See also Hayley Mills; Various Artists: Films - Original Soundtracks 'Can-Can'.)

EPS:	HITS 1			WEEKS 1
IN SEARCH OF THE CASTAWAYS [OST]	*Decca*	18	*9 Feb 63*	1

CHI-LITES — US

SINGLES:	HITS 9			WEEKS 89
(FOR GOD'S SAKE) GIVE MORE POWER TO THE PEOPLE	*MCA*	32	*28 Aug 71*	6
HAVE YOU SEEN HER	*MCA*	3	*15 Jan 72*	12
OH GIRL	*MCA*	14	*27 May 72*	9
HOMELY GIRL	*Brunswick*	5	*23 Mar 74*	13
I FOUND SUNSHINE	*Brunswick*	35	*20 Jul 74*	5
TOO GOOD TO BE FORGOTTEN	*Brunswick*	10	*2 Nov 74*	11
HAVE YOU SEEN HER? [RI]/OH GIRL [RI]	*Brunswick*	5	*21 Jun 75*	9
IT'S TIME FOR LOVE	*Brunswick*	5	*13 Sep 75*	10
YOU DON'T HAVE TO GO	*Brunswick*	3	*31 Jul 76*	11
CHANGING FOR YOU	*R&B*	61	*13 Aug 83*	3

CHIC — US

(See also Romina Johnson.)

SINGLES:	HITS 10			WEEKS 90
DANCE, DANCE, DANCE (YOWSAH, YOWSAH, YOWSAH)	*Atlantic*	6	*26 Nov 77*	12
EVERYBODY DANCE	*Atlantic*	9	*1 Apr 78*	11
LE FREAK	*Atlantic*	7	*18 Nov 78*	16
Backing vocals by Luther Vandross.				

I WANT YOUR LOVE	*Atlantic*	4	*24 Feb 79*	11
GOOD TIMES	*Atlantic*	5	*30 Jun 79*	11
MY FORBIDDEN LOVER	*Atlantic*	15	*13 Oct 79*	8
MY FEET KEEP DANCING	*Atlantic*	21	*8 Dec 79*	9
HANGIN'	*Atlantic*	64	*12 Mar 83*	1
JACK LE FREAK [RM]	*Atlantic*	19	*19 Sep 87*	6
CHIC MEDLEY [M]	*Atlantic*	58	*14 Jul 90*	2
Above hit: MEGACHIC.				
CHIC MYSTIQUE	*Warner Brothers*	48	*15 Feb 92*	3
ALBUMS:	**HITS 4**			**WEEKS 47**
COMPILATION ALBUMS:	**HITS 1**			**WEEKS 6**
C'EST CHIC	*Atlantic*	2	*3 Feb 79*	24
RISQUE	*Atlantic*	29	*18 Aug 79*	12
THE BEST OF CHIC	*Atlantic*	30	*15 Dec 79*	8
FREAK OUT	*Telstar*	72	*5 Dec 87*	3
Compilation of hits from the two groups.				
Above hit: CHIC and SISTER SLEDGE.				
CHIC AND ROSE ROYCE - THEIR GREATEST HITS - SIDE BY SIDE	*Dino*	8	*27 Jul 91*	6
LP contained two different recording acts and was thus ineligible for the main album chart.				
Above hit: ROSE ROYCE and CHIC.				

CHICAGO — US

SINGLES:	**HITS 7**			**WEEKS 81**
I'M A MAN	*CBS*	8	*10 Jan 70*	11
25 OR 6 TO 4	*CBS*	7	*18 Jul 70*	13
IF YOU LEAVE ME NOW	*CBS*	1	*9 Oct 76*	16
BABY, WHAT A BIG SURPRISE	*CBS*	41	*5 Nov 77*	3
HARD TO SAY I'M SORRY	*Full Moon*	4	*21 Aug 82*	15
HARD HABIT TO BREAK	*Full Moon*	8	*27 Oct 84*	13
YOU'RE THE INSPIRATION	*Full Moon*	14	*26 Jan 85*	10
ALBUMS:	**HITS 10**			**WEEKS 121**
CHICAGO TRANSIT AUTHORITY	*CBS*	9	*27 Sep 69*	14
Above hit: CHICAGO TRANSIT AUTHORITY.				
CHICAGO	*CBS*	6	*4 Apr 70*	27
CHICAGO 3	*CBS*	31	*3 Apr 71*	1
CHICAGO 5	*CBS*	24	*30 Sep 72*	2
CHICAGO X	*CBS*	21	*23 Oct 76*	11
CHICAGO 16	*Full Moon*	44	*2 Oct 82*	9
LOVE SONGS	*TV Records*	42	*4 Dec 82*	8
CHICAGO 17	*Full Moon*	24	*1 Dec 84*	20
THE HEART OF CHICAGO	*Reprise*	15	*25 Nov 89*	14
THE HEART OF CHICAGO [RE]	*Reprise*	6	*19 Feb 94*	11
Re-released at mid-price.				
THE HEART OF CHICAGO - 1967-1997	*Reprise*	21	*13 Feb 99*	4
Updated version of their 1989 compilation.				

CHICANE — UK

(See also Disco Citizens.)

SINGLES:	**HITS 8**			**WEEKS 48**
OFFSHORE	*Xtravaganza*	14	*21 Dec 96*	7
SUNSTROKE	*Xtravaganza*	21	*14 Jun 97*	3
OFFSHORE '97 [RM]	*Xtravaganza*	17	*13 Sep 97*	4
Remixed by Anthony Pappa.				
Above hit: CHICANE with POWER CIRCLE.				
LOST YOU SOMEWHERE	*Xtravaganza*	35	*20 Dec 97*	3
STRONG IN LOVE	*Xtravaganza*	32	*10 Oct 98*	2
Above hit: CHICANE featuring MASON.				
SALTWATER	*Xtravaganza*	6	*5 Jun 99*	10
Based on Clannad's Theme From Harry's Game.				
Above hit: CHICANE (featuring Maire BRENNAN of CLANNAD).				
DON'T GIVE UP	*Xtravaganza*	1	*18 Mar 00*	14
Above hit: CHICANE featuring Bryan ADAMS.				
NO ORDINARY MORNING/HALCYON	*Xtravaganza*	28	*22 Jul 00*	3
AUTUMN TACTICS	*Xtravaganza*	44	*28 Oct 00*	2
ALBUMS:	**HITS 2**			**WEEKS 9**
FAR FROM THE MADDENING CROWDS	*Xtravaganza*	49	*1 Nov 97*	1
BEHIND THE SUN	*Xtravaganza*	10	*8 Apr 00*	8

CHICKEN SHACK — UK

SINGLES:	**HITS 2**			**WEEKS 19**
• I'D RATHER GO BLIND	*Blue Horizon*	14	*10 May 69*	13
Originally recorded by Etta James.				
TEARS IN THE WIND	*Blue Horizon*	29	*6 Sep 69*	6

ALBUMS:	HITS 2			WEEKS 9
FORTY BLUE FINGERS FRESHLY PACKED	*Blue Horizon*	12	*22 Jun 68*	8
OK KEN?	*Blue Horizon*	9	*15 Feb 69*	1

CHICKEN SHED — UK

SINGLES:	HITS 1			WEEKS 6
I AM IN LOVE WITH THE WORLD *Charity record with proceeds to Diana, Princess Of Wales Memorial Fund.*	*Columbia*	15	*27 Dec 97*	6

CHICORY TIP — UK

SINGLES:	HITS 3			WEEKS 34
SON OF MY FATHER *Originally recorded by Georgio.*	*CBS*	1	*29 Jan 72*	13
WHAT'S YOUR NAME	*CBS*	13	*20 May 72*	8
GOOD GRIEF CHRISTINA	*CBS*	17	*31 Mar 73*	13

CHIEFTAINS — Ireland

(See also James Galway and the Chieftains; Van Morrison and the Chieftains.)

SINGLES:	HITS 1			WEEKS 3
I KNOW MY LOVE *Above hit: CHIEFTAINS featuring the CORRS.*	*RCA Victor*	37	*12 Jun 99*	3
ALBUMS:	**HITS 2**			**WEEKS 13**
THE LONG BLACK VEIL	*RCA*	17	*4 Feb 95*	9
TEARS OF STONE	*RCA Victor*	36	*6 Mar 99*	4

CHIFFONS — US

SINGLES:	HITS 3			WEEKS 40
• HE'S SO FINE	*Stateside*	16	*13 Apr 63*	12
ONE FINE DAY	*Stateside*	29	*20 Jul 63*	6
• SWEET TALKIN' GUY	*Stateside*	31	*28 May 66*	8
SWEET TALKIN' GUY [RI]	*London*	4	*18 Mar 72*	14

CHILD — UK

SINGLES:	HITS 3			WEEKS 22
WHEN YOU WALK IN THE ROOM	*Ariola Hansa*	38	*29 Apr 78*	5
IT'S ONLY MAKE BELIEVE	*Ariola Hansa*	10	*22 Jul 78*	12
ONLY YOU (AND YOU ALONE)	*Ariola Hansa*	33	*28 Apr 79*	5

Jane CHILD — Canada

SINGLES:	HITS 1			WEEKS 8
DON'T WANNA FALL IN LOVE	*Warner Brothers*	22	*12 May 90*	8

CHILDLINERS — UK/US/Australia

SINGLES:	HITS 1			WEEKS 6
THE GIFT OF CHRISTMAS *In aid of the charity Childline.*	*London*	9	*16 Dec 95*	6

CHILDREN FOR RWANDA — UK

SINGLES:	HITS 1			WEEKS 2
LOVE CAN BUILD A BRIDGE *Proceeds to Rwandan aid charities. Originally recorded by the Judds in 1990.*	*East West*	57	*10 Sep 94*	2

CHILDREN OF THE NIGHT — UK

SINGLES:	HITS 1			WEEKS 2
IT'S A TRIP (TUNE IN, TURN ON, DROP OUT)	*Jive*	52	*26 Nov 88*	2

CHILDREN OF THE REVOLUTION – See KLF

CHILDREN'S CHORUS – See Max BYGRAVES; Guy MITCHELL

Toni CHILDS — US

SINGLES:	HITS 1			WEEKS 4
DON'T WALK AWAY	*A&M*	53	*25 Mar 89*	4
ALBUMS:	**HITS 1**			**WEEKS 1**
UNION	*A&M*	73	*22 Apr 89*	1

CHILI HI FLY — Australia

SINGLES:	HITS 1			WEEKS 2
IS IT LOVE? *Samples Kool & The Gang's Be My Lady.*	*Sound Of Ministry*	37	*18 Mar 00*	2

CHILL FAC-TORR — US

SINGLES:	HITS 1			WEEKS 8
TWIST (ROUND 'N' ROUND)	*Phillyworld*	37	*2 Apr 83*	8

CHILLI featuring CARRAPICHO — US/Ghana/Brazil

SINGLES:	HITS 1			WEEKS 1
TIC, TIC TAC	*Arista*	59	*20 Sep 97*	1

Song has its own dance, the Boi Bumba.

CHIMES — UK

SINGLES:	HITS 5			WEEKS 28
1-2-3	*CBS*	60	*19 Aug 89*	3
HEAVEN	*CBS*	66	*2 Dec 89*	2
HEAVEN [RE]	*CBS*	69	*6 Jan 90*	3
I STILL HAVEN'T FOUND WHAT I'M LOOKING FOR	*CBS*	6	*19 May 90*	9
TRUE LOVE	*CBS*	48	*28 Jul 90*	3
HEAVEN [RI]	*CBS*	24	*29 Sep 90*	6
LOVE COMES TO MIND	*CBS*	49	*1 Dec 90*	2
ALBUMS:	**HITS 1**			**WEEKS 19**
THE CHIMES	*CBS*	17	*23 Jun 90*	19

CHIMIRA — South Africa

SINGLES:	HITS 1			WEEKS 1
SHOW ME HEAVEN	*Neoteric*	70	*6 Dec 97*	1

CHINA BLACK — UK

SINGLES:	HITS 4			WEEKS 35
SEARCHING	*Wild Card*	4	*16 Jul 94*	16
Originally released in 1992.				
STARS	*Wild Card*	19	*29 Oct 94*	7
SEARCHING [RE]	*Wild Card*	54	*17 Dec 94*	4
ALMOST SEE YOU (SOMEWHERE)	*Wild Card*	31	*11 Feb 95*	2
SWING LOW SWEET CHARIOT	*PolyGram TV*	15	*3 Jun 95*	6
The England Rugby World Cup Squad's theme tune.				
Above hit: LADYSMITH BLACK MAMBAZO featuring CHINA BLACK.				
ALBUMS:	**HITS 1**			**WEEKS 4**
BORN	*Wild Card*	27	*11 Mar 95*	4

CHINA CRISIS — UK

SINGLES:	HITS 11			WEEKS 66
AFRICAN AND WHITE	*Inevitable*	45	*7 Aug 82*	5
CHRISTIAN	*Virgin*	12	*22 Jan 83*	9
TRAGEDY AND MYSTERY	*Virgin*	46	*21 May 83*	6
WORKING WITH FIRE AND STEEL	*Virgin*	48	*15 Oct 83*	5
WISHFUL THINKING	*Virgin*	9	*14 Jan 84*	8
HANNA HANNA	*Virgin*	44	*10 Mar 84*	3
BLACK MAN RAY	*Virgin*	14	*30 Mar 85*	9
KING IN A CATHOLIC STYLE (WAKE UP)	*Virgin*	19	*1 Jun 85*	9
YOU DID CUT ME	*Virgin*	54	*7 Sep 85*	3
ARIZONA SKY	*Virgin*	47	*8 Nov 86*	4
BEST KEPT SECRET	*Virgin*	36	*24 Jan 87*	5
ALBUMS:	**HITS 6**			**WEEKS 68**
DIFFICULT SHAPES AND PASSIVE RHYTHMS SOME PEOPLE THINK IT'S FUN TO ENTERTAIN	*Virgin*	21	*20 Nov 82*	18
WORKING WITH FIRE AND STEEL – POSSIBLE POP SONGS VOLUME 2	*Virgin*	20	*12 Nov 83*	16
FLAUNT THE IMPERFECTION	*Virgin*	9	*11 May 85*	22
WHAT PRICE PARADISE?	*Virgin*	63	*6 Dec 86*	6
DIARY OF A HOLLOW HORSE	*Virgin*	58	*13 May 89*	2
CHINA CRISIS COLLECTION – THE VERY BEST OF CHINA CRISIS	*Virgin*	32	*15 Sep 90*	4

CHINA DRUM — UK

SINGLES:	HITS 4			WEEKS 4
CAN'T STOP THESE THINGS	*Mantra*	65	*2 Mar 96*	1
LAST CHANCE	*Mantra*	60	*20 Apr 96*	1
FICTION OF LIFE	*Mantra*	65	*9 Aug 97*	1
SOMEWHERE ELSE	*Mantra*	74	*27 Sep 97*	1
ALBUMS:	**HITS 1**			**WEEKS 1**
GOOSEFAIR	*Mantra*	53	*11 May 96*	1

Jonny CHINGAS — US

SINGLES:	HITS 1			WEEKS 6
PHONE HOME	*CBS*	43	*19 Feb 83*	6

CHIPMUNKS — US

(See also David Seville.)

SINGLES:	HITS 3			WEEKS 12
RAGTIME COWBOY JOE	*London*	11	*25 Jul 59*	8
Above hit: David SEVILLE and the CHIPMUNKS.				
ACHY BREAKY HEART	*Epic*	53	*19 Dec 92*	3
Above hit: ALVIN and the CHIPMUNKS (with special guest Billy Ray CYRUS).				
MACARENA	*Sony Wonder*	65	*14 Dec 96*	1
Above hit: LOS DEL CHIPMUNKS.				

CHIPPENDALES — UK/US

SINGLES:	HITS 1			WEEKS 4
GIVE ME YOUR BODY	*XSRhythm*	28	*31 Oct 92*	4

George CHISHOLM - See Clinton FORD; JOHNSTON BROTHERS

CHOCOLATE PUMA — Holland

SINGLES:	HITS 1			WEEKS 9
I WANNA BE U	*Cream*	6	*24 Mar 01*	8
Vocals by Evo.				
I WANNA BE U [RE]	*Cream*	68	*2 Jun 01*	1

CHOIR OF NEW COLLEGE OXFORD/Edward HIGGINBOTTOM — UK

ALBUMS:	HITS 2			WEEKS 7
AGNUS DEI	*Erato*	49	*12 Oct 96*	5
AGNUS DEI II	*Erato*	57	*18 Apr 98*	2

CHOO CHOO PROJECT - See Harry 'Choo Choo' ROMERO

CHOPS-EMC and EXTENSIVE — UK

SINGLES:	HITS 1			WEEKS 1
ME' ISRAELITES	*Faze 2*	60	*8 Aug 92*	1

CHORDETTES — US

SINGLES:	HITS 3			WEEKS 25
MR. SANDMAN	*Columbia*	11	*18 Dec 54*	8
Originally recorded by Vaughan Monroe.				
BORN TO BE WITH YOU	*London*	8	*1 Sep 56*	9
LOLLIPOP	*London*	6	*19 Apr 58*	8
Original by Ronald and Ruby reached No. 20 in the US in the same year.				

CHORDS — UK

SINGLES:	HITS 5			WEEKS 17
NOW IT'S GONE	*Polydor*	63	*6 Oct 79*	2
MAYBE TOMORROW	*Polydor*	40	*2 Feb 80*	5
SOMETHING'S MISSING	*Polydor*	55	*26 Apr 80*	3
THE BRITISH WAY OF LIFE	*Polydor*	54	*12 Jul 80*	3
IN MY STREET	*Polydor*	50	*18 Oct 80*	4
ALBUMS:	**HITS 1**			**WEEKS 3**
SO FAR AWAY	*Polydor*	30	*24 May 80*	3

CHORUS GIRLS with the PLAYBOYS - See Dorothy PROVINE

CHRIS and JAMES — UK

SINGLES:	HITS 3			WEEKS 3
CALM DOWN (BASS KEEPS PUMPIN')	*Stress*	74	*17 Sep 94*	1
FOX FORCE FIVE	*Stress*	71	*4 Nov 95*	1
CLUB FOR LIFE '98	*Stress*	66	*7 Nov 98*	1

Neil CHRISTIAN — UK

SINGLES:	HITS 1			WEEKS 10
THAT'S NICE	*Strike*	14	*9 Apr 66*	10

Roger CHRISTIAN — UK

SINGLES:	HITS 1			WEEKS 3
TAKE IT FROM ME	*Island*	63	*30 Sep 89*	3

CHRISTIANS — UK

(See also Christians, Holly Johnson, Paul McCartney, Gerry Marsden, Stock Aitken Waterman.)

SINGLES:	HITS 12			WEEKS 77
FORGOTTEN TOWN	*Island*	22	*31 Jan 87*	11
HOOVERVILLE (AND THEY PROMISED US THE WORLD)	*Island*	21	*13 Jun 87*	10
WHEN THE FINGERS POINT	*Island*	34	*26 Sep 87*	7

IDEAL WORLD	*Island*	14	*5 Dec 87*	13
BORN AGAIN	*Island*	25	*23 Apr 88*	7
HARVEST FOR THE WORLD	*Island*	8	*15 Oct 88*	7
WORDS	*Island*	18	*23 Dec 89*	8
I FOUND OUT	*Island*	56	*7 Apr 90*	2
GREENBACK DRIVE	*Island*	63	*15 Sep 90*	2
WHAT'S IN A WORD	*Island*	33	*5 Sep 92*	5
FATHER	*Island*	55	*14 Nov 92*	2
THE BOTTLE	*Island*	39	*6 Mar 93*	3
ALBUMS:	**HITS 4**			**WEEKS 96**
THE CHRISTIANS	*Island*	2	*31 Oct 87*	68
COLOUR	*Island*	1	*27 Jan 90*	17
HAPPY IN HELL	*Island*	18	*10 Oct 92*	3
THE BEST OF THE CHRISTIANS	*Island*	22	*20 Nov 93*	8

CHRISTIANS, Holly JOHNSON, Paul McCARTNEY, Gerry MARSDEN and STOCK AITKEN WATERMAN — UK

(See also Christians; Gerry and the Pacemakers; Holly Johnson; Paul McCartney; Stock Aitken Waterman.)

SINGLES:	**HITS 1**			**WEEKS 7**
FERRY 'CROSS THE MERSEY	*PWL*	1	*20 May 89*	7

CHRISTIE — UK

SINGLES:	**HITS 3**			**WEEKS 37**
YELLOW RIVER	*CBS*	1	*2 May 70*	22
Originally recorded by the Tremeloes.				
SAN BERNADINO	*CBS*	49	*10 Oct 70*	1
SAN BERNADINO [RE]	*CBS*	7	*24 Oct 70*	13
IRON HORSE	*CBS*	47	*25 Mar 72*	1

David CHRISTIE — France

SINGLES:	**HITS 1**			**WEEKS 12**
SADDLE UP	*KR*	9	*14 Aug 82*	12

John CHRISTIE — Australia

SINGLES:	**HITS 1**			**WEEKS 6**
HERE'S TO LOVE (AULD LANG SYNE)	*EMI*	24	*25 Dec 76*	6

Lou CHRISTIE — US

SINGLES:	**HITS 4**			**WEEKS 35**
• LIGHTNIN' STRIKES	*MGM*	11	*26 Feb 66*	8
RHAPSODY IN THE RAIN	*MGM*	37	*30 Apr 66*	2
I'M GONNA MAKE YOU MINE	*Buddah*	2	*13 Sep 69*	17
SHE SOLD ME MAGIC	*Buddah*	25	*27 Dec 69*	8

Tony CHRISTIE — UK

(See also Various Artists: Studio Cast 'Evita'.)

SINGLES:	**HITS 6**			**WEEKS 54**
LAS VEGAS	*MCA*	21	*9 Jan 71*	9
I DID WHAT I DID FOR MARIA	*MCA*	2	*8 May 71*	17
(IS THIS THE WAY TO) AMARILLO	*MCA*	18	*20 Nov 71*	13
Originally recorded by Neil Sedaka.				
AVENUES AND ALLEYWAYS	*MCA*	37	*10 Feb 73*	4
DRIVE SAFELY DARLIN'	*MCA*	35	*17 Jan 76*	4
From the TV series 'The Protectors'.				
WALK LIKE A PANTHER	*ffrr*	10	*23 Jan 99*	7
Above hit: ALL SEEING I featuring Tony CHRISTIE.				
ALBUMS:	**HITS 4**			**WEEKS 10**
I DID WHAT I DID FOR MARIA	*MCA*	37	*24 Jul 71*	1
WITH LOVING FEELING	*MCA*	19	*17 Feb 73*	2
TONY CHRISTIE - LIVE	*MCA*	33	*31 May 75*	3
BEST OF TONY CHRISTIE	*MCA*	28	*6 Nov 76*	4

Shawn CHRISTOPHER — US

SINGLES:	**HITS 3**			**WEEKS 11**
ANOTHER SLEEPLESS NIGHT	*Arista*	74	*22 Sep 90*	1
Above hit: Mike 'Hitman' WILSON featuring Shawn CHRISTOPHER.				
ANOTHER SLEEPLESS NIGHT [RI]	*Arista*	50	*4 May 91*	4
DON'T LOSE THE MAGIC	*Arista*	30	*21 Mar 92*	5
MAKE MY LOVE	*BTB*	57	*2 Jul 94*	1

CHRON GEN — UK

ALBUMS:	**HITS 1**			**WEEKS 3**
CHRONIC GENERATION	*Secret*	53	*3 Apr 82*	3

CHUBBY CHUNKS — UK

SINGLES:	HITS 2			WEEKS 2
TESTAMENT 4	*Cleveland City*	52	*4 Jun 94*	1
Above hit: CHUBBY CHUNKS VOLUME II.				
I'M TELLIN YOU	*Cleveland City*	61	*29 May 99*	1
Re-recording of Testament 1 from 1993, with added vocals.				
Above hit: KENTISH MAN presents CHUBBY CHUNKS featuring Kim RUFFIN.				

CHUCKLE STAR - See Sid OWEN

CHUCKS — UK

SINGLES:	HITS 1			WEEKS 7
LOO-BE-LOO	*Decca*	22	*26 Jan 63*	7

CHUMBAWAMBA — UK

SINGLES:	HITS 5			WEEKS 31
ENOUGH IS ENOUGH	*One Little Indian*	56	*18 Sep 93*	2
Above hit: CHUMBAWAMBA and CREDIT TO THE NATION.				
TIMEBOMB	*One Little Indian*	59	*4 Dec 93*	1
TUBTHUMPING	*EMI*	2	*23 Aug 97*	20
AMNESIA	*EMI*	10	*31 Jan 98*	5
TOP OF THE WORLD (OLE, OLE, OLE)	*EMI*	21	*13 Jun 98*	3
ALBUMS:	**HITS 3**			**WEEKS 10**
ANARCHY	*One Little Indian*	29	*7 May 94*	2
SWINGIN' WITH RAYMOND	*One Little Indian*	70	*4 Nov 95*	1
TUBTHUMPER	*EMI*	19	*13 Sep 97*	7

Myung- Whun CHUNG - See Andrea BOCELLI

CHUPITO — Spain

SINGLES:	HITS 1			WEEKS 2
AMERICAN PIE	*Eternal*	54	*23 Sep 95*	2

Charlotte CHURCH — UK

SINGLES:	HITS 1			WEEKS 4
JUST WAVE HELLO	*Sony Classical*	31	*25 Dec 99*	4
With the London Symphony Orchestra. Featured in the Ford Global TV commercial.				
ALBUMS:	**HITS 4**			**WEEKS 45**
VOICE OF AN ANGEL	*Sony Classical*	4	*21 Nov 98*	20
CHARLOTTE CHURCH	*Sony Classical*	8	*27 Nov 99*	10
DREAM A DREAM	*Sony Classical*	30	*2 Dec 00*	6
ENCHANTMENT	*Sony Classical*	24	*3 Nov 01*	9

Sir Winston CHURCHILL — UK

ALBUMS:	HITS 1			WEEKS 8
THE VOICE OF CHURCHILL	*Decca*	6	*13 Feb 65*	8

CHYNA - See INCOGNITO

CICA - See PQM featuring CICA

CICCONE YOUTH - See SONIC YOUTH

CICERO — UK

SINGLES:	HITS 3			WEEKS 12
LOVE IS EVERYWHERE	*Spaghetti*	19	*18 Jan 92*	8
THAT LOVING FEELING	*Spagetti*	46	*18 Apr 92*	3
HEAVEN MUST HAVE SENT YOU BACK TO ME	*Spagetti*	70	*1 Aug 92*	1

CINDERELLA — US

SINGLES:	HITS 4			WEEKS 7
GYPSY ROAD	*Vertigo*	54	*6 Aug 88*	2
DON'T KNOW WHAT YOU GOT (TIL IT'S GONE)	*Vertigo*	54	*4 Mar 89*	2
SHELTER ME	*Vertigo*	55	*17 Nov 90*	2
HEARTBREAK STATION	*Vertigo*	63	*27 Apr 91*	1
ALBUMS:	**HITS 2**			**WEEKS 8**
LONG COLD WINTER	*Vertigo*	30	*23 Jul 88*	6
HEARTBREAK STATION	*Vertigo*	36	*1 Dec 90*	2

CINDY and the SAFFRONS — UK

SINGLES:	HITS 1			WEEKS 3
PAST, PRESENT AND FUTURE	*Stilletto*	56	*15 Jan 83*	3
Originally recorded by The Shangrila's.				

CINERAMA — UK

SINGLES:	HITS 1			WEEKS 1
KERRY KERRY	*Cooking Vinyl*	71	*18 Jul 98*	1

Gigliola CINQUETTI — Italy

SINGLES:	HITS 2			WEEKS 27
NON HO L'ETA' PER AMARTI *Eurovision Song Contest winner for 1964.*	*Decca*	17	*25 Apr 64*	17
GO (BEFORE YOU BREAK MY HEART) *Italian Eurovision entry in 1974, it came 2nd.*	*CBS*	8	*4 May 74*	10

CIRCA featuring DESTRY — UK/US

SINGLES:	HITS 1			WEEKS 1
SUN SHINING DOWN *Vocals by Destry Spigner. Samples the O'Jays Backstabbers.*	*Inferno*	70	*27 Nov 99*	1

CIRCUIT — UK

SINGLES:	HITS 1			WEEKS 3
SHELTER ME *Original release reached No. 82 in 1990.*	*Cooltempo*	44	*20 Jul 91*	2
SHELTER ME [RI]	*Pukka*	50	*1 Apr 95*	1

CIRCULATION — UK

SINGLES:	HITS 1			WEEKS 1
TURQUOISE	*Hooj Choons*	64	*1 Sep 01*	1

CIRRUS — UK

SINGLES:	HITS 1			WEEKS 1
ROLLIN' ON	*Jet*	62	*30 Sep 78*	1

CITIZEN CANED — UK

SINGLES:	HITS 1			WEEKS 2
THE JOURNEY	*Serious*	41	*7 Apr 01*	2

CITY BOY — UK

SINGLES:	HITS 3			WEEKS 20
5.7.0.5.	*Vertigo*	8	*8 Jul 78*	12
WHAT A NIGHT	*Vertigo*	39	*28 Oct 78*	5
THE DAY THE EARTH CAUGHT FIRE	*Vertigo*	67	*15 Sep 79*	3

CITY HIGH — US

SINGLES:	HITS 1			WEEKS 13
WHAT WOULD YOU DO? *Samples Things Done Changed by Notorious B.I.G.*	*Interscope*	3	*6 Oct 01*	13

CITY SPUD - See NELLY

Gary CLAIL ON-U SOUND SYSTEM — UK

SINGLES:	HITS 5			WEEKS 19
BEEF *Above hit: Gary CLAIL ON-U SOUND SYSTEM featuring Bim SHERMAN.*	*RCA*	64	*14 Jul 90*	2
HUMAN NATURE	*Perfecto*	10	*30 Mar 91*	9
ESCAPE *Above hit: Gary CLAIL ON-U SOUND SYSTEM (additional vocals By AKABU).*	*Perfecto*	44	*8 Jun 91*	3
WHO PAYS THE PIPER?	*Perfecto*	31	*14 Nov 92*	3
THESE THINGS ARE WORTH FIGHTING FOR	*Perfecto*	45	*22 May 93*	2
ALBUMS:	**HITS 1**			**WEEKS 2**
THE EMOTIONAL HOOLIGAN	*Perfecto*	35	*4 May 91*	2

CLAIRE and FRIENDS — UK

SINGLES:	HITS 1			WEEKS 11
IT'S 'ORRIBLE BEING IN LOVE (WHEN YOU'RE 8½) *From BBC1 TV's 'Saturday Superstore'.*	*BBC*	13	*7 Jun 86*	11

CLANCY BROTHERS and Tommy MAKEM — Ireland

ALBUMS:	HITS 1			WEEKS 5
ISN'T IT GRAND BOYS?	*CBS*	22	*16 Apr 66*	5

CLANNAD — Ireland

SINGLES:	HITS 5			WEEKS 29
THEME FROM HARRY'S GAME *Theme from the ITV series 'Harry's Game'.*	*RCA*	5	*6 Nov 82*	10

NEW GRANGE	RCA	65	2 Jul 83	1
ROBIN (THE HOODED MAN)	RCA	42	12 May 84	5
Theme from the TV series 'Robin Of Sherwood'.				
IN A LIFETIME	RCA	20	25 Jan 86	5
Above hit: CLANNAD/ additional vocals: BONO				
IN A LIFETIME [RI]	RCA	17	10 Jun 89	7
Above hit: CLANNAD (guest vocal: BONO).				
BOTH SIDES NOW	MCA	74	10 Aug 91	1
Above hit: CLANNAD and Paul YOUNG.				
ALBUMS:	**HITS 11**			**WEEKS 150**
MAGICAL RING	RCA	26	2 Apr 83	21
LEGEND (MUSIC FROM ROBIN OF SHERWOOD)	RCA	16	12 May 84	14
MAGICAL RING [RE]	RCA	91	2 Jun 84	1
Re-released.				
LEGEND (MUSIC FROM ROBIN OF SHERWOOD) [RE]	RCA	15	16 Mar 85	26
MACALLA	RCA	33	26 Oct 85	24
SIRIUS	RCA	34	7 Nov 87	4
ATLANTIC REALM [OST-TV]	BBC	41	4 Feb 89	3
PAST PRESENT	RCA	5	6 May 89	23
Re-released.				
ANAM	RCA	14	20 Oct 90	7
BANBA	RCA	5	15 May 93	11
PAST PRESENT [RE]	RCA	55	16 Sep 95	3
Re-released.				
LORE	RCA	14	6 Apr 96	7
THE ULTIMATE COLLECTION	RCA	46	31 May 97	4
LANDMARKS	RCA	34	11 Apr 98	2

Jimmy CLANTON — US

SINGLES:	**HITS 1**			**WEEKS 1**
ANOTHER SLEEPLESS NIGHT	Top Rank	50	23 Jul 60	1
Written and originally recorded by Neil Sedaka.				

Eric CLAPTON — UK

(See also Cher, Chrissie Hynde and Neneh Cherry with Eric Clapton; Derek and the Dominos; B. B. King and Eric Clapton.)

SINGLES:	**HITS 23**			**WEEKS 121**
COMIN' HOME	Atlantic	16	20 Dec 69	9
Above hit: DELANEY and BONNIE and FRIENDS featuring Eric CLAPTON.				
I SHOT THE SHERIFF	RSO	9	27 Jul 74	9
Originally recorded by Bob Marley & the Wailers.				
SWING LOW SWEET CHARIOT	RSO	19	10 May 75	9
KNOCKIN' ON HEAVEN'S DOOR	RSO	38	16 Aug 75	4
LAY DOWN SALLY	RSO	39	21 Dec 77	6
PROMISES	RSO	37	21 Oct 78	7
I SHOT THE SHERIFF [RI]	RSO	64	5 Jun 82	2
THE SHAPE YOU'RE IN	Duck	75	23 Apr 83	1
FOREVER MAN	Warner Brothers	51	16 Mar 85	4
EDGE OF DARKNESS	BBC	65	4 Jan 86	3
Theme from the BBC TV series of the same name.				
Above hit: Eric CLAPTON with Michael KAMEN.				
BEHIND THE MASK	Duck	15	17 Jan 87	11
Originally recorded by the Yellow Magic Orchestra.				
TEARING US APART	Duck	56	20 Jun 87	3
Above hit: Eric CLAPTON and Tina TURNER.				
BAD LOVE	Duck	25	27 Jan 90	7
Backing vocals by Phil Collins.				
NO ALIBIS	Duck	53	14 Apr 90	3
WONDERFUL TONIGHT	Duck	30	16 Nov 91	7
Live recording from the Royal Albert Hall, London.				
TEARS IN HEAVEN	Reprise	50	8 Feb 92	3
From the film 'Rush'. Written about his dead son Connor.				
TEARS IN HEAVEN [RE]	Reprise	5	7 Mar 92	9
RUNAWAY TRAIN	Rocket	31	1 Aug 92	4
Above hit: Elton JOHN and Eric CLAPTON.				
IT'S PROBABLY ME	A&M	30	29 Aug 92	5
From the film 'Lethal Weapon 3'.				
Above hit: STING with Eric CLAPTON.				
LAYLA (ACOUSTIC)	Duck	45	3 Oct 92	3
MOTHERLESS CHILD	Duck	63	15 Oct 94	1
CHANGE THE WORLD	Reprise	18	20 Jul 96	5
From the film 'Phenomenon'.				
MY FATHER'S EYES	Duck	33	4 Apr 98	2
CIRCUS	Duck	39	4 Jul 98	2
First performed at Clapton's MTV Unplugged concert.				
FOREVER MAN (HOW MANY TIMES?) [RM]	ffrr	26	18 Nov 00	2
Samples Eric Clapton's Forever Man.				
Above hit: BEATCHUGGERS featuring Eric CLAPTON.				

ALBUMS:	HITS 25			WEEKS 527
BLUES BREAKERS	*Decca*	6	*30 Jul 66*	17
Above hit: John MAYALL with Eric CLAPTON.				
ERIC CLAPTON	*Polydor*	17	*5 Sep 70*	8
HISTORY OF ERIC CLAPTON	*Polydor*	20	*26 Aug 72*	6
461 OCEAN BOULEVARD	*RSO*	3	*24 Aug 74*	19
THERE'S ONE IN EVERY CROWD	*RSO*	15	*12 Apr 75*	8
E.C. WAS HERE	*RSO*	14	*13 Sep 75*	6
NO REASON TO CRY	*RSO*	8	*11 Sep 76*	7
SLOWHAND	*RSO*	23	*26 Nov 77*	13
BACKLESS	*RSO*	18	*9 Dec 78*	12
JUST ONE NIGHT	*RSO*	3	*10 May 80*	12
ANOTHER TICKET	*RSO*	18	*7 Mar 81*	8
TIME PIECES - THE BEST OF ERIC CLAPTON	*RSO*	20	*24 Apr 82*	13
MONEY & CIGARETTES	*Duck*	13	*19 Feb 83*	17
BACKTRACKIN'	*Starblend*	29	*9 Jun 84*	16
BEHIND THE SUN	*Duck*	8	*23 Mar 85*	14
AUGUST	*Duck*	3	*6 Dec 86*	42
THE CREAM OF ERIC CLAPTON	*Polydor*	3	*26 Sep 87*	98
Above hit: Eric CLAPTON and CREAM.				
JOURNEYMAN	*Duck*	2	*18 Nov 89*	34
24 NIGHTS	*Duck*	17	*26 Oct 91*	7
Live recordings from the Royal Albert Hall, London, 1990.				
UNPLUGGED	*Duck*	2	*12 Sep 92*	90
Peak position reached on 20 Mar 93.				
TIME PIECES - THE BEST OF ERIC CLAPTON [RE]	*RSO*	58	*6 Mar 93*	1
Re-released at mid-price.				
THE CREAM OF ERIC CLAPTON [RE-1ST] / THE BEST OF ERIC CLAPTON	*Polydor*	25	*10 Jul 93*	6
The re-package The Best Of Eric Clapton listed from 17 Jul 93.				
Above hit: Eric CLAPTON and CREAM.				
FROM THE CRADLE	*Duck*	1	*24 Sep 94*	18
A collection of old Blues numbers.				
AUGUST [RE]	*Duck*	38	*4 Mar 95*	4
Re-released at mid-price.				
PILGRIM	*Duck*	6	*21 Mar 98*	15
THE CREAM OF ERIC CLAPTON [RE-2ND]	*Polydor*	52	*18 Apr 98*	5
Re-released.				
Above hit: Eric CLAPTON and CREAM.				
BLUES	*Polydor*	52	*26 Jun 99*	2
Includes studio and live recordings from 1970-80.				
CLAPTON CHRONICLES - THE BEST OF ERIC CLAPTON	*Duck*	6	*30 Oct 99*	20
TIME PIECES - THE BEST OF ERIC CLAPTON [RI]	*Polydor*	73	*15 Jul 00*	2
REPTILE	*Reprise*	7	*17 Mar 01*	7

CLARISSA - See DJ VISAGE featuring CLARISSA

Dave CLARK FIVE — UK

SINGLES:	HITS 22			WEEKS 174
DO YOU LOVE ME	*Columbia*	30	*5 Oct 63*	6
Originally recorded by the Contours.				
GLAD ALL OVER	*Columbia*	1	*23 Nov 63*	19
BITS AND PIECES	*Columbia*	2	*22 Feb 64*	11
CAN'T YOU SEE THAT SHE'S MINE	*Columbia*	10	*30 May 64*	11
THINKING OF YOU BABY	*Columbia*	26	*15 Aug 64*	4
ANY WAY YOU WANT IT	*Columbia*	25	*24 Oct 64*	5
EVERYBODY KNOWS	*Columbia*	37	*16 Jan 65*	4
REELIN' AND ROCKIN'	*Columbia*	24	*13 Mar 65*	8
COME HOME	*Columbia*	16	*29 May 65*	8
CATCH US IF YOU CAN	*Columbia*	5	*17 Jul 65*	11
OVER AND OVER	*Columbia*	45	*13 Nov 65*	4
Originally recorded by Bobby Day.				
LOOK BEFORE YOU LEAP	*Columbia*	50	*21 May 66*	1
YOU GOT WHAT IT TAKES	*Columbia*	28	*18 Mar 67*	8
EVERYBODY KNOWS	*Columbia*	2	*4 Nov 67*	14
Song is different from their 1965 hit.				
NO ONE CAN BREAK A HEART LIKE YOU	*Columbia*	28	*2 Mar 68*	7
THE RED BALLOON	*Columbia*	7	*21 Sep 68*	11
Originally recorded by Raymond Froggatt.				
LIVE IN THE SKY	*Columbia*	39	*30 Nov 68*	6
PUT A LITTLE LOVE IN YOUR HEART	*Columbia*	31	*25 Oct 69*	4
Originally recorded by Jackie De Shannon.				
GOOD OLD ROCK 'N' ROLL [M]	*Columbia*	7	*6 Dec 69*	12
Originally recorded by Cat Mother and the All Night News Boys.				
EVERYBODY GET TOGETHER	*Columbia*	8	*7 Mar 70*	8
Originally recorded by Dino Valente in 1963.				
HERE COMES SUMMER	*Columbia*	44	*4 Jul 70*	3
MORE GOOD OLD ROCK 'N ROLL [M]	*Columbia*	34	*7 Nov 70*	6
GLAD ALL OVER [RI]	*EMI*	37	*1 May 93*	3

EPS:	HITS 3			WEEKS 35
THE DAVE CLARK FIVE	*Columbia*	3	*18 Jan 64*	24
THE HITS OF THE DAVE CLARK FIVE	*Columbia*	20	*23 Jan 65*	1
WILD WEEKEND	*Columbia*	10	*25 Sep 65*	10
ALBUMS:	**HITS 4**			**WEEKS 31**
A SESSION WITH THE DAVE CLARK FIVE	*Columbia*	3	*18 Apr 64*	8
CATCH US IF YOU CAN	*Columbia*	8	*14 Aug 65*	8
25 THUMPING GREAT HITS	*Polydor*	7	*4 Mar 78*	10
GLAD ALL OVER AGAIN	*EMI*	28	*17 Apr 93*	5

Dee CLARK — US

SINGLES:	HITS 2			WEEKS 9
JUST KEEP IT UP (AND SEE WHAT HAPPENS)	*London*	26	*3 Oct 59*	1
RIDE A WILD HORSE	*Chelsea*	16	*11 Oct 75*	8

Gary CLARK — UK

SINGLES:	HITS 3			WEEKS 8
WE SAIL ON THE STORMY WATERS	*Circa*	34	*30 Jan 93*	4
FREEFLOATING	*Circa*	50	*3 Apr 93*	3
MAKE A FAMILY	*Circa*	70	*19 Jun 93*	1
ALBUMS:	**HITS 1**			**WEEKS 2**
TEN SHORT SONGS ABOUT LOVE	*Circa*	25	*8 May 93*	2

Loni CLARK — US

SINGLES:	HITS 3			WEEKS 6
RUSHING	*A&M*	37	*5 Jun 93*	2
U	*A&M*	28	*22 Jan 94*	3
Shortest title for a hit single.				
LOVE'S GOT ME ON A TRIP SO HIGH	*A&M*	59	*17 Dec 94*	1

Louis CLARK – See ROYAL PHILHARMONIC ORCHESTRA

Petula CLARK — UK

SINGLES:	HITS 27			WEEKS 247
THE LITTLE SHOEMAKER (LES PETIT CORDONNIER)	*Polygon*	12	*12 Jun 54*	1
Above hit: Petula CLARK with Malcolm LOCKYER and his Orchestra.				
THE LITTLE SHOEMAKER (LES PETIT CORDONNIER) [RE]	*Polygon*	7	*26 Jun 54*	9
MAJORCA	*Polygon*	12	*19 Feb 55*	4
Above hit: Petula CLARK with Laurie JOHNSON and his Orchestra.				
MAJORCA [RE]	*Polygon*	18	*26 Mar 55*	1
Above hit: Petula CLARK with Laurie JOHNSON and his Orchestra.				
SUDDENLY THERE'S A VALLEY	*Pye Nixa*	7	*26 Nov 55*	10
Originally recorded by Gogi Grant.				
WITH ALL MY HEART	*Pye Nixa*	4	*27 Jul 57*	18
Originally recorded by Jodie Sands.				
Above 2: Petula CLARK with Tony OSBORNE and his Orchestra.				
ALONE	*Pye Nixa*	8	*16 Nov 57*	12
Above hit: Petula CLARK with the Kim DRAKE ORCHESTRA and the Beryl STOTT GROUP.				
BABY LOVER	*Pye Nixa*	12	*1 Mar 58*	7
Above hit: Petula CLARK with the Peter KNIGHT ORCHESTRA with the Beryl STOTT GROUP.				
SAILOR	*Pye*	1	*28 Jan 61*	15
Original by Lolita reached No. 5 in the US in 1960.				
SOMETHING MISSING (L'ABSENT)	*Pye*	44	*15 Apr 61*	1
From the film 'Top Hat'.				
Above 2: Petula CLARK; Peter KNIGHT ORCHESTRA.				
ROMEO	*Pye*	3	*15 Jul 61*	15
MY FRIEND THE SEA	*Pye*	7	*18 Nov 61*	13
I'M COUNTING ON YOU	*Pye*	41	*10 Feb 62*	2
YA YA TWIST	*Pye*	14	*30 Jun 62*	11
YA YA TWIST [RE]	*Pye*	45	*22 Sep 62*	2
CASANOVA / CHARIOT	*Pye*	39	*4 May 63*	7
Above hit: Petula CLARK with the Henry MAYER ORCHESTRA (on Casanova only).				
DOWNTOWN	*Pye*	2	*14 Nov 64*	15
I KNOW A PLACE	*Pye*	17	*13 Mar 65*	8
YOU'D BETTER COME HOME	*Pye*	44	*14 Aug 65*	3
ROUND EVERY CORNER	*Pye*	43	*16 Oct 65*	3
YOU'RE THE ONE	*Pye*	23	*6 Nov 65*	9
MY LOVE	*Pye*	4	*12 Feb 66*	9
A SIGN OF THE TIMES	*Pye*	49	*23 Apr 66*	1
I COULDN'T LIVE WITHOUT YOUR LOVE	*Pye*	6	*2 Jul 66*	11
THIS IS MY SONG	*Pye*	1	*4 Feb 67*	14
From the film 'A Countess From Hong Kong'. Written by Charlie Chaplin.				
DON'T SLEEP IN THE SUBWAY	*Pye*	12	*27 May 67*	11
THE OTHER MAN'S GRASS (IS ALWAYS GREENER)	*Pye*	20	*16 Dec 67*	9

KISS ME GOODBYE	*Pye*	50	*9 Mar 68*	1
THE SONG OF MY LIFE	*Pye*	41	*30 Jan 71*	1
THE SONG OF MY LIFE [RE]	*Pye*	32	*13 Feb 71*	11
I DON'T KNOW HOW TO LOVE HIM	*Pye*	47	*15 Jan 72*	1
I DON'T KNOW HOW TO LOVE HIM [RE]	*Pye*	49	*29 Jan 72*	1
DOWNTOWN '88 [RM]	*PRT*	10	*19 Nov 88*	11
Remixed by Peter Slaghuis.				
EPS:	**HITS 2**			**WEEKS 12**
DOWNTOWN	*Pye*	12	*20 Feb 65*	6
THIS IS MY SONG	*Pye*	6	*29 Apr 67*	6
ALBUMS:	**HITS 6**			**WEEKS 43**
I COULDN'T LIVE WITHOUT YOUR LOVE	*Pye*	11	*30 Jul 66*	10
HIT PARADE	*Pye*	18	*4 Feb 67*	13
COLOUR MY WORLD	*Pye*	16	*18 Feb 67*	9
THESE ARE MY SONGS	*Pye*	38	*7 Oct 67*	3
THE OTHER MAN'S GRASS IS ALWAYS GREENER	*Pye*	37	*6 Apr 68*	1
20 ALL TIME GREATEST	*K-Tel*	18	*5 Feb 77*	7

Roland CLARK - See Armand VAN HELDEN

Dave CLARKE — UK

SINGLES:	**HITS 4**			**WEEKS 7**
RED THREE [EP]	*Bush*	45	*30 Sep 95*	2
Lead Track: Thunder.				
SOUTHSIDE	*Bush*	34	*3 Feb 96*	2
NO ONE'S DRIVING	*Bush*	37	*15 Jun 96*	2
THE COMPASS	*Skint*	46	*8 Dec 01*	1
ALBUMS:	**HITS 1**			**WEEKS 2**
ARCHIVE ONE	*Bush*	36	*17 Feb 96*	2

Gilby CLARKE — US

ALBUMS:	**HITS 1**			**WEEKS 1**
PAWNSHOP GUITARS	*Virgin*	39	*6 Aug 94*	1

John Cooper CLARKE — UK

SINGLES:	**HITS 1**			**WEEKS 3**
¡ GIMMIX ! PLAY LOUD	*Epic*	39	*10 Mar 79*	3
ALBUMS:	**HITS 2**			**WEEKS 9**
SNAP CRACKLE AND BOP	*Epic*	26	*19 Apr 80*	7
ZIP STYLE METHOD	*Epic*	97	*5 Jun 82*	2

Rick CLARKE — UK

SINGLES:	**HITS 1**			**WEEKS 2**
I'LL SEE YOU ALONG THE WAY	*WA*	63	*30 Apr 88*	2

Sharon Dee CLARKE - See F.P.I. PROJECT; SERIOUS ROPE

Warren CLARKE featuring Kathy BROWN — UK

SINGLES:	**HITS 1**			**WEEKS 1**
OVER YOU	*Defected*	42	*2 Jun 01*	1

Stanley CLARKE — US

ALBUMS:	**HITS 1**			**WEEKS 2**
ROCKS PEBBLES AND SAND	*Epic*	42	*12 Jul 80*	2

CLARKE BROTHERS - See Max BYGRAVES

CLASH — UK

SINGLES:	**HITS 18**			**WEEKS 135**
WHITE RIOT	*CBS*	38	*2 Apr 77*	3
COMPLETE CONTROL	*CBS*	28	*8 Oct 77*	2
CLASH CITY ROCKERS	*CBS*	35	*4 Mar 78*	4
(WHITE MAN) IN HAMMERSMITH PALAIS	*CBS*	32	*24 Jun 78*	7
TOMMY GUN	*CBS*	19	*2 Dec 78*	10
ENGLISH CIVIL WAR (JOHNNY COMES MARCHING HOME)	*CBS*	25	*3 Mar 79*	6
THE COST OF LIVING [EP]	*CBS*	22	*19 May 79*	8
Lead track: I Fought The Law.				
LONDON CALLING	*CBS*	11	*15 Dec 79*	10
BANKROBBER	*CBS*	12	*9 Aug 80*	10
THE CALL UP	*CBS*	40	*6 Dec 80*	6
HITSVILLE UK	*CBS*	56	*24 Jan 81*	4
THE MAGNIFICENT SEVEN	*CBS*	34	*25 Apr 81*	5
THIS IS RADIO CLASH	*CBS*	47	*28 Nov 81*	6
KNOW YOUR RIGHTS	*CBS*	43	*1 May 82*	3

ROCK THE CASBAH	*CBS*	30	*26 Jun 82*	10
SHOULD I STAY OR SHOULD I GO / STRAIGHT TO HELL	*CBS*	17	*25 Sep 82*	9
THIS IS ENGLAND	*CBS*	24	*12 Oct 85*	5
I FOUGHT THE LAW	*CBS*	29	*12 Mar 88*	5
LONDON CALLING [RI-1ST]	*CBS*	46	*7 May 88*	3
RETURN TO BRIXTON	*CBS*	57	*21 Jul 90*	2
SHOULD I STAY OR SHOULD I GO [RI]	*Columbia*	1	*2 Mar 91*	9
Featured in a Levi's jeans TV commercial.				
ROCK THE CASBAH [RI]	*Columbia*	15	*13 Apr 91*	6
LONDON CALLING [RI-2ND]	*Columbia*	64	*8 Jun 91*	2
ALBUMS:	**HITS 9**			**WEEKS 112**
CLASH	*CBS*	12	*30 Apr 77*	16
GIVE 'EM ENOUGH ROPE	*CBS*	2	*25 Nov 78*	14
LONDON CALLING	*CBS*	9	*22 Dec 79*	20
SANDINISTA	*CBS*	19	*20 Dec 80*	9
COMBAT ROCK	*CBS*	2	*22 May 82*	23
CUT THE CRAP	*CBS*	16	*16 Nov 85*	3
THE STORY OF THE CLASH - VOLUME 1	*CBS*	7	*2 Apr 88*	10
THE STORY OF THE CLASH - VOLUME 1 [RI]	*Columbia*	13	*30 Mar 91*	10
THE SINGLES COLLECTION	*Columbia*	68	*16 Nov 91*	2
FROM HERE TO ETERNITY	*Columbia*	13	*16 Oct 99*	3
Live recordings from 1977–1982. Released to coincide with the airing of a BBC TV documentary about the band, 'Westway To The World' on 2 Oct 99.				
LONDON CALLING [RE]	*Columbia*	63	*16 Oct 99*	1
THE STORY OF THE CLASH - VOLUME 1 [RE]	*Columbia*	70	*16 Oct 99*	1

CLASS ACTION featuring Chris WILTSHIRE — US

SINGLES:	**HITS 1**			**WEEKS 3**
WEEKEND	*Jive*	49	*7 May 83*	3
Originally recorded by Patrick Adams presents Phreak.				

CLASSICS IV — US

SINGLES:	**HITS 1**			**WEEKS 1**
SPOOKY	*Liberty*	46	*2 Mar 68*	1
Originally recorded by Mike Sharpe.				

CLASSIX NOUVEAUX — UK

SINGLES:	**HITS 7**			**WEEKS 34**
GUILTY	*Liberty*	43	*28 Feb 81*	7
TOKYO	*Liberty*	67	*16 May 81*	3
INSIDE OUTSIDE	*Liberty*	45	*8 Aug 81*	5
NEVER AGAIN (THE DAYS TIME ERASED)	*Liberty*	44	*7 Nov 81*	4
IS IT A DREAM	*Liberty*	11	*13 Mar 82*	9
BECAUSE YOU'RE YOUNG	*Liberty*	43	*29 May 82*	4
THE END . . . OR THE BEGINNING?	*Liberty*	60	*30 Oct 82*	2
ALBUMS:	**HITS 2**			**WEEKS 6**
NIGHT PEOPLE	*Liberty*	66	*30 May 81*	2
LA VERITE	*Liberty*	44	*24 Apr 82*	4

CLAWFINGER — Norway/Sweden

SINGLES:	**HITS 1**			**WEEKS 1**
WARFAIR	*East West*	54	*19 Mar 94*	1

Judy CLAY and William BELL — US

(See also William Bell.)

SINGLES:	**HITS 1**			**WEEKS 14**
PRIVATE NUMBER	*Stax*	8	*23 Nov 68*	14

Richard CLAYDERMAN — France

(See also Richard Clayderman and James Last.)

ALBUMS:	**HITS 14**			**WEEKS 189**
RICHARD CLAYDERMAN	*Decca*	2	*13 Nov 82*	64
THE MUSIC OF RICHARD CLAYDERMAN	*Decca*	21	*8 Oct 83*	28
THE MUSIC OF LOVE	*Decca*	28	*24 Nov 84*	21
RICHARD CLAYDERMAN - CHRISTMAS	*Decca*	53	*1 Dec 84*	5
THE CLASSIC TOUCH	*Decca*	17	*23 Nov 85*	18
Above hit: Richard CLAYDERMAN with the ROYAL PHILHARMONIC ORCHESTRA.				
HOLLYWOOD AND BROADWAY	*Decca*	28	*22 Nov 86*	9
SONGS OF LOVE	*Decca*	19	*28 Nov 87*	13
A LITTLE NIGHT MUSIC	*Decca Delphine*	52	*3 Dec 88*	5
THE LOVE SONGS OF ANDREW LLOYD WEBBER	*Decca Delphine*	18	*25 Nov 89*	10
MY CLASSIC COLLECTION	*Decca*	29	*24 Nov 90*	7

THE VERY BEST OF RICHARD CLAYDERMAN *Above 2: Richard CLAYDERMAN with the ROYAL PHILHARMONIC ORCHESTRA.*	*Decca Delphine*	47	*14 Nov 92*	5
THE CARPENTERS COLLECTION	*PolyGram TV*	65	*25 Nov 95*	2
THE BEST OF RICHARD CLAYDERMAN	*Decca Delphine*	73	*20 Dec 97*	1
. . . WITH LOVE	*Music Collection*	62	*18 Sep 99*	1

Richard CLAYDERMAN and James LAST — France/Germany

(See also Richard Clayderman; James Last.)

ALBUMS:	HITS 2			WEEKS 22
TOGETHER AT LAST	*Decca Delphine*	14	*9 Nov 91*	15
IN HARMONY	*Polydor*	28	*19 Nov 94*	7

Adam CLAYTON and Larry MULLEN — Ireland

SINGLES:	HITS 1			WEEKS 12
THEME FROM MISSION: IMPOSSIBLE	*Mother*	7	*15 Jun 96*	12

Merry CLAYTON — US

SINGLES:	HITS 1			WEEKS 1
YES *From the film 'Dirty Dancing'.*	*RCA*	70	*21 May 88*	1

CLAYTOWN TROUPE — UK

SINGLES:	HITS 2			WEEKS 3
WAYS OF LOVE	*Island*	57	*16 Jun 90*	2
WANTED IT ALL	*EMI USA*	74	*14 Mar 92*	1
ALBUMS:	**HITS 1**			**WEEKS 1**
THROUGH THE VEIL	*Island*	72	*21 Oct 89*	1

Johnny CLEGG and SAVUKA — UK/South Africa

SINGLES:	HITS 1			WEEKS 1
SCATTERLINGS OF AFRICA	*EMI*	75	*16 May 87*	1

CLEOPATRA — UK

(See also Steps Tina Cousins Cleopatra B*Witched Billie.)

SINGLES:	HITS 5			WEEKS 31
CLEOPATRA'S THEME	*WEA*	3	*14 Feb 98*	10
LIFE AIN'T EASY	*WEA*	4	*16 May 98*	7
I WANT YOU BACK	*WEA*	4	*22 Aug 98*	7
A TOUCH OF LOVE	*WEA*	24	*6 Mar 99*	4
COME AND GET ME	*WEA*	29	*29 Jul 00*	3
ALBUMS:	**HITS 1**			**WEEKS 4**
COMIN' ATCHA!	*WEA*	20	*6 Jun 98*	4

CLEPTOMANIACS featuring Bryan CHAMBERS — UK

SINGLES:	HITS 1			WEEKS 3
ALL I DO *Originally recorded by Stevie Wonder on the Hotter Than July LP.*	*Defected*	23	*3 Feb 01*	3

CLICK — US

SINGLES:	HITS 1			WEEKS 1
SCANDALOUS	*Jive*	54	*29 Jun 96*	1

Jimmy CLIFF — Jamaica

SINGLES:	HITS 4			WEEKS 33
• WONDERFUL WORLD, BEAUTIFUL PEOPLE	*Trojan*	6	*25 Oct 69*	13
VIETNAM	*Trojan*	47	*14 Feb 70*	1
VIETNAM [RE]	*Trojan*	46	*28 Feb 70*	2
WILD WORLD *Originally recorded by Cat Stevens.*	*Island*	8	*8 Aug 70*	12
I CAN SEE CLEARLY NOW *From the film 'Cool Runnings'.*	*Columbia*	23	*19 Mar 94*	5

Buzz CLIFFORD — US

SINGLES:	HITS 1			WEEKS 13
• BABY SITTIN' BOOGIE	*Fontana*	17	*4 Mar 61*	13

Linda CLIFFORD — US

SINGLES:	HITS 3			WEEKS 13
IF MY FRIENDS COULD SEE ME NOW	*Curtom*	50	*10 Jun 78*	5
BRIDGE OVER TROUBLED WATER	*RSO*	28	*5 May 79*	7
RIDE THE STORM	*NRK Sound Division*	69	*15 Sep 01*	1

Above hit: AKABU featuring Linda CLIFFORD.

CLIMAX BLUES BAND — UK

SINGLES:	HITS 1			WEEKS 9
COULDN'T GET IT RIGHT	*BTM*	10	*9 Oct 76*	9
ALBUMS:	**HITS 1**			**WEEKS 1**
GOLD PLATED	*BTM*	56	*13 Nov 76*	1

Simon CLIMIE — UK

SINGLES:	HITS 1			WEEKS 2
SOUL INSPIRATION	*Epic*	60	*19 Sep 92*	2

CLIMIE FISHER — UK

SINGLES:	HITS 6			WEEKS 44
LOVE CHANGES (EVERYTHING)	*EMI*	67	*5 Sep 87*	2
Originally intended for Rod Stewart.				
RISE TO THE OCCASION	*EMI*	10	*12 Dec 87*	11
LOVE CHANGES (EVERYTHING) [RM]	*EMI*	2	*12 Mar 88*	12
THIS IS ME	*EMI*	22	*21 May 88*	5
I WON'T BLEED FOR YOU	*EMI*	35	*20 Aug 88*	4
LOVE LIKE A RIVER	*EMI*	22	*24 Dec 88*	7
FACTS OF LOVE	*EMI*	50	*23 Sep 89*	3
ALBUMS:	**HITS 2**			**WEEKS 38**
EVERYTHING	*EMI*	14	*13 Feb 88*	36
COMING IN FOR THE KILL	*EMI*	35	*21 Oct 89*	2

Patsy CLINE — US

SINGLES:	HITS 3			WEEKS 17
SHE'S GOT YOU	*Brunswick*	43	*28 Apr 62*	1
HEARTACHES	*Brunswick*	31	*1 Dec 62*	5
CRAZY	*MCA*	14	*8 Dec 90*	11
First released 1961. A previous re issue reached No. 79 in 1987. Originally recorded by Willie Nelson.				
ALBUMS:	**HITS 4**			**WEEKS 28**
SWEET DREAMS	*MCA*	18	*19 Jan 91*	10
DREAMING . . .	*Platinum Music*	55	*19 Jan 91*	4
THE DEFINITIVE PATSY CLINE 1932–1963	*Arcade*	11	*5 Sep 92*	8
THE VERY BEST OF PATSY CLINE	*MCA*	21	*6 Jul 96*	6

Above 4 are all compilations.

CLINIC — UK

SINGLES:	HITS 2			WEEKS 2
THE RETURN OF EVIL BILL	*Domino Recordings*	70	*22 Apr 00*	1
THE SECOND LINE	*Domino Recordings*	56	*4 Nov 00*	1

Featured in the Levi's 'engineered' TV commercial.

George CLINTON — US

(See also Ice Cube; Xavier featuring George Clinton and Bootsy Collins.)

SINGLES:	HITS 2			WEEKS 7
LOOPZILLA	*Capitol*	57	*4 Dec 82*	5
DO FRIES GO WITH THAT SHAKE	*Capitol*	57	*26 Apr 86*	2

CLIVILLES and COLE – See C&C MUSIC FACTORY

CLOCK — UK

SINGLES:	HITS 15			WEEKS 70
HOLDING ON	*Media*	66	*30 Oct 93*	1
Vocals by Ann-Marie Smith. Samples the 49ers' Move Your Feet.				
THE RHYTHM	*Media*	28	*21 May 94*	2
KEEP THE FIRES BURNING	*Media*	36	*10 Sep 94*	3
AXEL F / KEEP PUSHIN'	*Media*	7	*4 Mar 95*	9
WHOOMPH! (THERE IT IS)	*Media*	4	*1 Jul 95*	9
EVERYBODY	*Media*	6	*26 Aug 95*	5
IN THE HOUSE	*Media*	23	*18 Nov 95*	3
HOLDING ON 4 U [RR]	*Media*	27	*24 Feb 96*	2
Vocals by O.D.C. MC and Tinka.				
OH WHAT A NIGHT	*Media*	13	*7 Sep 96*	10
IT'S OVER	*Media*	10	*22 Mar 97*	5

U SEXY THING	*Media*	11	*18 Oct 97*	9
THAT'S THE WAY (I LIKE IT)	*Media*	11	*17 Jan 98*	4
ROCK YOUR BODY	*Media*	30	*11 Jul 98*	3
BLAME IT ON THE BOOGIE	*Media*	16	*28 Nov 98*	4
SUNSHINE DAY	*Power Station*	58	*31 Jul 99*	1

ALBUMS:	**HITS 2**			**WEEKS 4**
IT'S TIME . . .	*Media*	27	*23 Sep 95*	2
ABOUT TIME 2	*Media*	56	*5 Apr 97*	2

Rosemary CLOONEY — US

SINGLES:	**HITS 7**			**WEEKS 81**
• HALF AS MUCH *Originally recorded by Hank Williams.* *Above hit: Rosemary CLOONEY with Percy FAITH and his Orchestra.*	*Columbia*	3	*15 Nov 52*	9
MAN (UH - HUH) *[AA] listed with Woman (Uh – Huh) by Jose Ferrer.*	*Philips*	7	*6 Feb 54*	5
• THIS OLE HOUSE *Originally recorded by Stuart Hamblen.* *Above hit: Rosemary CLOONEY with Buddy COLE and his Orchestra.*	*Philips*	1	*9 Oct 54*	18
• MAMBO ITALIANO *Above hit: Rosemary CLOONEY and the MELLOMEN.*	*Philips*	1	*18 Dec 54*	16
WHERE WILL THE DIMPLE BE? *Above hit: Rosemary CLOONEY and the MELLOMEN with the Buddy COLE QUARTET Bass solo: Thurl RAVENSCROFT.*	*Philips*	6	*21 May 55*	13
HEY THERE *From the film 'The Pajama Game'. Originally recorded by John Raitt. (Bonnie Raitt's father).* *Above hit: Rosemary CLOONEY with Buddy COLE and his Orchestra.*	*Philips*	4	*1 Oct 55*	11
MANGOS *Above hit: Rosemary CLOONEY with Frank COMSTOCK.*	*Philips*	25	*30 Mar 57*	2
MANGOS [RE]	*Philips*	17	*27 Apr 57*	7

CLOUD — UK

SINGLES:	**HITS 1**			**WEEKS 1**
ALL NIGHT LONG / TAKE IT TO THE TOP	*UK Champagne*	72	*31 Jan 81*	1

CLOUDBURST – SS DISCO TEX presents CLOUDBURST

CLOUT — South Africa

SINGLES:	**HITS 1**			**WEEKS 15**
SUBSTITUTE *Originally recorded by the Righteous Brothers.*	*Carrere*	2	*17 Jun 78*	15

CLUB NOUVEAU — US

SINGLES:	**HITS 1**			**WEEKS 12**
LEAN ON ME	*Warner Brothers*	3	*21 Mar 87*	12

CLUB 69 — Austria/US

SINGLES:	**HITS 2**			**WEEKS 6**
LET ME BE YOUR UNDERWEAR	*ffrr*	33	*5 Dec 92*	5
ALRIGHT *Above hit: CLUB 69 featuring Suzanne PALMER.*	*Twisted UK*	70	*14 Nov 98*	1

CLUBHOUSE — Italy

SINGLES:	**HITS 7**			**WEEKS 40**
DO IT AGAIN / BILLIE JEAN [M]	*Island*	11	*23 Jul 83*	6
SUPERSTITION / GOOD TIMES [M] *Above 2: CLUB HOUSE.*	*Island*	59	*3 Dec 83*	3
I'M A MAN/YE KE YE KE [M]	*Music Man*	69	*1 Jul 89*	3
DEEP IN MY HEART	*ffrr*	59	*20 Apr 91*	2
DEEP IN MY HEART [RE]	*ffrr*	55	*22 Jun 91*	2
LIGHT MY FIRE *Above hit: CLUB HOUSE featuring CARL.*	*PWL International*	59	*4 Sep 93*	1
LIGHT MY FIRE [RE-1ST]	*PWL International*	45	*13 Nov 93*	5
LIGHT MY FIRE [RE-2ND]	*PWL International*	53	*25 Dec 93*	6
LIGHT MY FIRE [RM] *Remixed by Cappella.*	*PWL*	7	*30 Apr 94*	8
LIVING IN THE SUNSHINE	*PWL Continental*	21	*23 Jul 94*	3
NOWHERE LAND *Above 3: CLUBHOUSE featuring CARL.*	*PWL International*	56	*11 Mar 95*	1

CLUBZONE — UK/Germany

SINGLES:	**HITS 1**			**WEEKS 1**
HANDS UP	*Logic*	50	*19 Nov 94*	1

CLUELESS — US

SINGLES:	HITS 1			WEEKS 1
DON'T SPEAK	*ZYX*	61	*5 Apr 97*	1

Jeremy CLYDE - See Chad STUART and Jeremy CLYDE

CLYDE VALLEY STOMPERS — UK

SINGLES:	HITS 1			WEEKS 8
PETER AND THE WOLF	*Parlophone*	25	*11 Aug 62*	8

CO-CO — UK

SINGLES:	HITS 1			WEEKS 7
BAD OLD DAYS *UK's Eurovision entry in 1978, it came 11th.*	*Ariola Hansa*	13	*22 Apr 78*	7

CO-OPERATION CHOIR - See Peter BENNETT with the CO-OPERATION CHOIR

CO.RO featuring TARLISA — Germany

SINGLES:	HITS 1			WEEKS 1
BECAUSE THE NIGHT	*ZYX*	61	*12 Dec 92*	1

COAL CHAMBER — US

ALBUMS:	HITS 1			WEEKS 2
CHAMBER MUSIC	*Roadrunner*	21	*18 Sep 99*	2

COAST TO COAST — UK

SINGLES:	HITS 2			WEEKS 22
(DO) THE HUCKLEBUCK *Originally recorded by Paul Williams.*	*Polydor*	5	*31 Jan 81*	15
LET'S JUMP THE BROOMSTICK	*Polydor*	28	*23 May 81*	7

COAST 2 COAST featuring DISCOVERY — Ireland

SINGLES:	HITS 1			WEEKS 1
HOME	*Religion Music*	44	*16 Jun 01*	1

COASTERS — US

SINGLES:	HITS 5			WEEKS 32
SEARCHIN'	*London*	30	*28 Sep 57*	1
YAKETY YAK	*London*	12	*16 Aug 58*	8
CHARLIE BROWN	*London*	6	*28 Mar 59*	12
POISON IVY	*London*	15	*31 Oct 59*	7
SORRY BUT I'M GONNA HAVE TO PASS *Featured in the Volkswagen TV commercial. Originally released in 1958.*	*Atlantic*	41	*9 Apr 94*	4

Odia COATES - See Paul ANKA

Luis COBOS — Spain

SINGLES:	HITS 1			WEEKS 2
TURANDOT 'NESSUM DORMA' *Above hit: Luis COBOS featuring Placido DOMINGO.*	*Epic*	59	*16 Jun 90*	2

ALBUMS:	HITS 1			WEEKS 1
OPERA EXTRAVAGANZA *Sleeve credits The Royal Philharmonic Orchestra, Chorus Royal Opera House, the London Symphony Orchestra, conductor Luis Cobos.*	*Epic*	72	*21 Apr 90*	1

Eddie COCHRAN — US

SINGLES:	HITS 9			WEEKS 90
SUMMERTIME BLUES	*London*	18	*8 Nov 58*	6
C'MON EVERYBODY *Originally titled Lets Get Together.*	*London*	6	*14 Mar 59*	13
SOMETHIN' ELSE	*London*	22	*17 Oct 59*	3
HALLELUJAH, I LOVE HER SO *Originally recorded by Ray Charles.*	*London*	28	*23 Jan 60*	1
HALLELUJAH, I LOVE HER SO [RE]	*London*	22	*6 Feb 60*	3
THREE STEPS TO HEAVEN	*London*	1	*14 May 60*	15
SWEETIE PIE	*London*	38	*8 Oct 60*	3
LONELY *A-side was Sweetie Pie but not listed on this entry.*	*London*	41	*5 Nov 60*	1
WEEKEND	*London*	15	*17 Jun 61*	16
JEANNIE, JEANNIE, JEANNIE *Originally recorded by Jimmie Madden.*	*London*	31	*2 Dec 61*	4
MY WAY	*Liberty*	23	*27 Apr 63*	10
SUMMERTIME BLUES [RI]	*Liberty*	34	*27 Apr 68*	8

C'MON EVERYBODY [RI] *Featured in the Levi's Jeans TV commercial.*	*Liberty*	14	*13 Feb 88*	7
EPS:	**HITS 3**			**WEEKS 51**
SOMETHIN' ELSE	*London*	6	*7 May 60*	11
C'MON EVERYBODY	*London*	2	*18 Jun 60*	38
NEVER TO BE FORGOTTEN	*Liberty*	18	*16 Feb 63*	2
ALBUMS:	**HITS 6**			**WEEKS 47**
SINGING TO MY BABY	*London*	19	*30 Jul 60*	1
EDDIE COCHRAN MEMORIAL ALBUM	*London*	9	*1 Oct 60*	12
CHERISHED MEMORIES	*Liberty*	15	*12 Jan 63*	3
EDDIE COCHRAN MEMORIAL ALBUM [RI]	*Liberty*	11	*20 Apr 63*	18
SINGING TO MY BABY [RI]	*Liberty*	20	*19 Oct 63*	1
VERY BEST OF EDDIE COCHRAN	*Liberty*	34	*9 May 70*	3
THE EDDIE COCHRAN SINGLES ALBUM	*United Artists*	39	*18 Aug 79*	6
C'MON EVERYBODY	*Liberty*	53	*16 Apr 88*	3

Brenda COCHRANE — UK

ALBUMS:	**HITS 2**			**WEEKS 14**
THE VOICE	*Polydor*	14	*14 Apr 90*	11
IN DREAMS	*Polydor*	55	*6 Apr 91*	3

Tom COCHRANE — Canada

SINGLES:	**HITS 1**			**WEEKS 2**
LIFE IS A HIGHWAY	*Capitol*	62	*27 Jun 92*	2

COCK ROBIN — US

SINGLES:	**HITS 1**			**WEEKS 12**
THE PROMISE YOU MADE	*CBS*	28	*31 May 86*	12

Joe COCKER — UK

SINGLES:	**HITS 15**			**WEEKS 89**
MARJORINE	*Regal Zonophone*	48	*25 May 68*	1
WITH A LITTLE HELP FROM MY FRIENDS *Originally recorded by the Beatles.*	*Regal Zonophone*	1	*5 Oct 68*	13
DELTA LADY *Written and originally recorded by Leon Russell about Rita Coolidge.*	*Regal Zonophone*	10	*27 Sep 69*	11
THE LETTER	*Regal Zonophone*	39	*4 Jul 70*	6
I'M SO GLAD I'M STANDING HERE TODAY *Above hit: CRUSADERS, featured vocalist Joe COCKER.*	*MCA*	61	*26 Sep 81*	3
UP WHERE WE BELONG *From the film 'An Officer And A Gentleman'. Originally recorded by Buffy Saint-Marie.* *Above hit: JOE COCKER and Jennifer WARNES.*	*Island*	7	*15 Jan 83*	13
UNCHAIN MY HEART	*Capitol*	46	*14 Nov 87*	4
WHEN THE NIGHT COMES	*Capitol*	65	*13 Jan 90*	2
FEELS LIKE FOREVER	*Capitol*	25	*7 Mar 92*	5
NOW THAT THE MAGIC HAS GONE	*Capitol*	28	*9 May 92*	6
UNCHAIN MY HEART [RM] *Remixed by Chris Lord-Alge.*	*Capitol*	17	*4 Jul 92*	6
WHEN THE NIGHT COMES [RI]	*Capitol*	61	*21 Nov 92*	3
THE SIMPLE THINGS	*Capitol*	17	*13 Aug 94*	5
TAKE ME HOME *Above hit: Joe COCKER featuring Bekka BRAMLETT.*	*Capitol*	41	*22 Oct 94*	3
LET THE HEALING BEGIN	*Capitol*	32	*17 Dec 94*	5
HAVE A LITTLE FAITH	*Capitol*	67	*23 Sep 95*	2
DON'T LET ME BE MISUNDERSTOOD	*Parlophone*	53	*12 Oct 96*	1
ALBUMS:	**HITS 9**			**WEEKS 66**
MAD DOGS AND ENGLISHMEN	*A&M*	16	*26 Sep 70*	8
JOE COCKER / WITH A LITTLE HELP FROM MY FRIENDS *Re-issue of albums originally released in 1969.*	*Double Back*	29	*6 May 72*	4
A CIVILISED MAN	*Capitol*	100	*30 Jun 84*	1
NIGHT CALLS	*Capitol*	25	*11 Apr 92*	14
THE LEGEND – THE ESSENTIAL COLLECTION	*PolyGram TV*	4	*27 Jun 92*	20
HAVE A LITTLE FAITH	*Capitol*	9	*17 Sep 94*	15
ORGANIC *Re-recorded versions of Cocker's songs.*	*Parlophone*	49	*26 Oct 96*	1
GREATEST HITS	*EMI*	24	*20 Feb 99*	2
NO ORDINARY WORLD	*Parlophone*	63	*23 Oct 99*	1

COCKEREL CHORUS — UK

SINGLES:	**HITS 1**			**WEEKS 12**
NICE ONE CYRIL	*Young Blood*	14	*24 Feb 73*	12

COCKNEY REBEL – See Steve HARLEY and COCKNEY REBEL

COCKNEY REJECTS — UK

SINGLES:	HITS 6			WEEKS 22
I'M NOT A FOOL	*EMI*	65	*1 Dec 79*	2
BADMAN	*EMI*	65	*16 Feb 80*	3
THE GREATEST COCKNEY RIP-OFF	*Zonophone*	21	*26 Apr 80*	7
I'M FOREVER BLOWING BUBBLES	*Zonophone*	35	*17 May 80*	5
WE CAN DO ANYTHING	*Zonophone*	65	*12 Jul 80*	2
WE ARE THE FIRM	*Zonophone*	54	*25 Oct 80*	3
ALBUMS:	**HITS 3**			**WEEKS 17**
GREATEST HITS VOLUME 1	*Zonophone*	22	*15 Mar 80*	11
GREATEST HITS VOLUME 2	*Zonophone*	23	*25 Oct 80*	3
GREATEST HITS VOLUME 3 (LIVE AND LOUD)	*Zonophone*	27	*18 Apr 81*	3

COCO — UK

SINGLES:	HITS 1			WEEKS 2
I NEED A MIRACLE	*Positiva*	39	*8 Nov 97*	2

EI COCO — US

SINGLES:	HITS 1			WEEKS 4
COCOMOTION	*Pye International*	31	*14 Jan 78*	4

COCOA BROVAZ - See BOUNTY KILLER (featuring COCOA BROVAZ, Nona HENDRYX and FREE)

COCONUTS — US

SINGLES:	HITS 1			WEEKS 3
DID YOU HAVE TO LOVE ME LIKE YOU DID	*EMI America*	60	*11 Jun 83*	3

COCTEAU TWINS — UK

SINGLES:	HITS 13			WEEKS 25
PEARLY-DEWDROPS DROPS	*4AD*	29	*28 Apr 84*	5
AIKEA-GUINEA	*4AD*	41	*30 Mar 85*	3
TINY DYNAMINE [EP]	*4AD*	52	*23 Nov 85*	2
Lead track: Pink Orange Red.				
ECHOES IN A SHALLOW BAY [EP]	*4AD*	65	*7 Dec 85*	1
Lead track: Great Spangled Fritillary.				
LOVE'S EASY TEARS	*4AD*	53	*25 Oct 86*	1
ICEBLINK LUCK	*4AD*	38	*8 Sep 90*	3
EVANGELINE	*Fontana*	34	*2 Oct 93*	2
WINTER WONDERLAND / FROSTY THE SNOWMAN	*Fontana*	58	*18 Dec 93*	1
BLUEBEARD	*Fontana*	33	*26 Feb 94*	2
TWINLIGHTS [EP]	*Fontana*	59	*7 Oct 95*	1
Lead track: Rilkean Heart.				
OTHERNESS [EP]	*Fontana*	59	*4 Nov 95*	1
Lead track: Feet Like Fins.				
TISHBITE	*Fontana*	34	*30 Mar 96*	2
VIOLAINE	*Fontana*	56	*20 Jul 96*	1
ALBUMS:	**HITS 8**			**WEEKS 46**
HEAD OVER HEELS	*4AD*	51	*29 Oct 83*	15
TREASURE	*4AD*	29	*24 Nov 84*	8
VICTORIALAND	*4AD*	10	*26 Apr 86*	7
BLUE BELL KNOLL	*4AD*	15	*1 Oct 88*	4
HEAVEN OR LAS VEGAS	*4AD*	7	*29 Sep 90*	5
FOUR-CALENDAR CAFE	*Fontana*	13	*30 Oct 93*	3
MILK & KISSES	*Fontana*	17	*27 Apr 96*	3
STARS AND TOPSOIL - A COLLECTION 1982-1990	*4AD*	63	*28 Oct 00*	1

CODE RED — UK

SINGLES:	HITS 5			WEEKS 7
I GAVE YOU EVERYTHING	*Polydor*	50	*6 Jul 96*	1
THIS IS OUR SONG	*Polydor*	59	*16 Nov 96*	1
CAN WE TALK . . .	*Polydor*	29	*14 Jun 97*	2
Original by Tevin Campbell reached No. 92 in 1993.				
IS THERE SOMEONE OUT THERE?	*Polydor*	34	*9 Aug 97*	2
WHAT WOULD YOU DO IF . . . ?	*Polydor*	55	*4 Jul 98*	1

COFFEE — US

SINGLES:	HITS 2			WEEKS 13
CASANOVA	*De-Lite*	13	*27 Sep 80*	10
Originally recorded by Ruby Andrews.				
SLIP AND DIP / I WANNA BE WITH YOU	*De-Lite*	57	*6 Dec 80*	3

Alma COGAN — UK

SINGLES:	HITS 18			WEEKS 110
BELL BOTTOM BLUES	*His Master's Voice*	4	*20 Mar 54*	9
Originally recorded by Teresa Brewer.				
LITTLE THINGS MEAN A LOT	*His Master's Voice*	11	*28 Aug 54*	2
LITTLE THINGS MEAN A LOT [RE-1ST]	*His Master's Voice*	19	*9 Oct 54*	1
LITTLE THINGS MEAN A LOT [RE-2ND]	*His Master's Voice*	18	*23 Oct 54*	2
I CAN'T TELL A WALTZ FROM A TANGO	*His Master's Voice*	6	*4 Dec 54*	11
Originally recorded by Patti Page.				
DREAMBOAT	*His Master's Voice*	1	*28 May 55*	16
THE BANJO'S BACK IN TOWN	*His Master's Voice*	17	*24 Sep 55*	1
GO ON BY	*His Master's Voice*	16	*15 Oct 55*	4
Above 2 entries were separate sides of the same release, each had its own chart run.				
TWENTY TINY FINGERS	*His Master's Voice*	17	*17 Dec 55*	1
Majority of singles listed above featured an Orchestra conducted by Frank Cordell.				
NEVER DO A TANGO WITH AN ESKIMO	*His Master's Voice*	6	*24 Dec 55*	5
Above 2 entries were separate sides of the same release, each had its own chart run.				
WILLIE CAN	*His Master's Voice*	13	*31 Mar 56*	8
Above hit: Alma COGAN with Desmond LANE – penny whistle.				
(THE SAME THINGS HAPPEN WITH) THE BIRDS AND THE BEES	*His Master's Voice*	25	*14 Jul 56*	4
WHY DO FOOLS FALL IN LOVE	*His Master's Voice*	22	*11 Aug 56*	3
Above 2 entries were separate sides of the same release, each had its own chart run.				
Above 2: Alma COGAN with vocal group and Orchestra.				
IN THE MIDDLE OF THE HOUSE	*His Master's Voice*	26	*3 Nov 56*	1
IN THE MIDDLE OF THE HOUSE [RE]	*His Master's Voice*	20	*24 Nov 56*	3
YOU, ME AND US	*His Master's Voice*	18	*19 Jan 57*	6
WHATEVER LOLA WANTS (LOLA GETS)	*His Master's Voice*	26	*30 Mar 57*	2
THE STORY OF MY LIFE	*His Master's Voice*	25	*1 Feb 58*	2
SUGARTIME	*His Master's Voice*	16	*15 Feb 58*	10
SUGARTIME [RE]	*His Master's Voice*	30	*3 May 58*	1
LAST NIGHT ON THE BACK PORCH	*His Master's Voice*	27	*24 Jan 59*	2
Above 3: Alma COGAN with the Michael SAMMES SINGERS.				
WE GOT LOVE	*His Master's Voice*	26	*19 Dec 59*	4
Above hit: Alma COGAN with the Don RIDDELLE SINGERS.				
DREAM TALK	*His Master's Voice*	48	*14 May 60*	1
THE TRAIN OF LOVE	*His Master's Voice*	27	*13 Aug 60*	5
Above 2: Alma COGAN with the Michael SAMMES SINGERS.				
COWBOY JIMMY JOE	*Columbia*	37	*22 Apr 61*	6
Above hit: Alma COGAN with Geoff LOVE and his Orchestra and the Rita WILLIAMS SINGERS.				

Shaye COGAN — US

SINGLES:	HITS 1			WEEKS 1
MEAN TO ME	*MGM*	40	*26 Mar 60*	1
Originally recorded by Ruth Etting.				

Izhar COHEN and the 'ALPHA-BETA' — Israel

SINGLES:	HITS 1			WEEKS 7
A-BA-NI-BI	*Polydor*	20	*13 May 78*	7
Eurovision Song Contest winner in 1978.				

Leonard COHEN — Canada

ALBUMS:	HITS 11			WEEKS 153
SONGS OF LEONARD COHEN	*CBS*	18	*31 Aug 68*	12
SONGS OF LEONARD COHEN [RE]	*CBS*	13	*26 Apr 69*	59
SONGS FROM A ROOM	*CBS*	2	*3 May 69*	26
SONGS OF LOVE AND HATE	*CBS*	4	*24 Apr 71*	18
NEW SKIN FOR THE OLD CEREMONY	*CBS*	24	*28 Sep 74*	3
DEATH OF A LADIES' MAN	*CBS*	35	*10 Dec 77*	5
VARIOUS POSITIONS	*CBS*	52	*16 Feb 85*	6
I'M YOUR MAN	*CBS*	48	*27 Feb 88*	13
GREATEST HITS	*CBS*	99	*6 Aug 88*	1
THE FUTURE	*Columbia*	36	*5 Dec 92*	3
COHEN LIVE	*Columbia*	35	*6 Aug 94*	4
Live recordings dating from 1988–93.				
TEN NEW SONGS	*Columbia*	26	*20 Oct 01*	3

Marc COHN — US

SINGLES:	HITS 3			WEEKS 15
WALKING IN MEMPHIS	*Atlantic*	66	*25 May 91*	4
SILVER THUNDERBIRD	*Atlantic*	54	*10 Aug 91*	3
WALKING IN MEMPHIS [RI]	*Atlantic*	22	*12 Oct 91*	5
WALK THROUGH THE WORLD	*Atlantic*	37	*29 May 93*	3

ALBUMS:	HITS 2			WEEKS 23
MARC COHN	*Atlantic*	27	*29 Jun 91*	20
THE RAINY SEASON	*Atlantic*	24	*12 Jun 93*	3

COLA BOY — UK

SINGLES:	HITS 1			WEEKS 7
7 WAYS TO LOVE	*Arista*	8	*6 Jul 91*	7

COLDCUT — UK

SINGLES:	HITS 10			WEEKS 39
DOCTORIN' THE HOUSE	*Ahead Our Our Time*	6	*20 Feb 88*	9
Above hit: COLDCUT featuring YAZZ and the PLASTIC POPULATION.				
STOP THIS CRAZY THING	*Ahead Our Our Time*	21	*10 Sep 88*	7
Above hit: COLDCUT featuring Junior REID and the AHEAD OF OUR TIME ORCHESTRA.				
PEOPLE HOLD ON	*Ahead Our Our Time*	11	*25 Mar 89*	9
Above hit: COLDCUT featuring Lisa STANSFIELD.				
MY TELPHONE	*Ahead Our Our Time*	52	*3 Jun 89*	2
COLDCUT'S CHRISTMAS BREAK	*Ahead Our Our Time*	67	*16 Dec 89*	3
FIND A WAY	*Ahead Our Our Time*	52	*26 May 90*	2
Above hit: COLDCUT featuring QUEEN LATIFAH.				
DREAMER	*Arista*	54	*4 Sep 93*	2
AUTUMN LEAVES	*Arista*	50	*22 Jan 94*	2
MORE BEATS + PIECES	*Ninja Tune*	37	*16 Aug 97*	2
RE:VOLUTION	*Ninja Tune*	67	*16 Jun 01*	1
Above hit: COLDCUT and the GUILTY PARTY.				

ALBUMS:	HITS 2			WEEKS 5
WHAT'S THAT NOISE	*Ahead Our Our Time*	20	*29 Apr 89*	4
LET US PLAY!	*Ninja Tune*	33	*20 Sep 97*	1

COLDJAM featuring GRACE — US

SINGLES:	HITS 1			WEEKS 2
LAST NIGHT A DJ SAVED MY LIFE	*Big Wave*	64	*28 Jul 90*	2

COLDPLAY — UK

SINGLES:	HITS 3			WEEKS 23
SHIVER	*Parlophone*	35	*18 Mar 00*	3
YELLOW	*Parlophone*	4	*8 Jul 00*	11
TROUBLE	*Parlophone*	10	*4 Nov 00*	9

ALBUMS:	HITS 1			WEEKS 70
PARACHUTES	*Parlophone*	1	*22 Jul 00*	70

Andy COLE — UK

SINGLES:	HITS 1			WEEKS 1
OUTSTANDING	*WEA*	68	*18 Sep 99*	1

Buddy COLE QUARTET/TRIO - See Bing CROSBY; Rosemary CLOONEY; Johnnie RAY

Cozy COLE — US

SINGLES:	HITS 1			WEEKS 1
TOPSY	*London*	29	*6 Dec 58*	1

George COLE - See Dennis WATERMAN

Lloyd COLE — UK

SINGLES:	HITS 15			WEEKS 62
PERFECT SKIN	*Polydor*	71	*26 May 84*	1
PERFECT SKIN [RE]	*Polydor*	26	*9 Jun 84*	8
FOREST FIRE	*Polydor*	41	*25 Aug 84*	6
RATTLESNAKES	*Polydor*	65	*17 Nov 84*	2
BRAND NEW FRIEND	*Polydor*	19	*14 Sep 85*	8
LOST WEEKEND	*Polydor*	17	*9 Nov 85*	7
CUT ME DOWN	*Polydor*	38	*18 Jan 86*	4
MY BAG	*Polydor*	46	*3 Oct 87*	4
JENNIFER SHE SAID	*Polydor*	31	*9 Jan 88*	5
FROM THE HIP [EP]	*Polydor*	59	*23 Apr 88*	2
Lead track: From The Hip.				
Above 10: Lloyd COLE and the COMMOTIONS.				
NO BLUE SKIES	*Polydor*	42	*3 Feb 90*	4
DON'T LOOK BACK	*Polydor*	59	*7 Apr 90*	3
SHE'S A GIRL AND I'M A MAN	*Polydor*	55	*31 Aug 91*	2
SO YOU'D LIKE TO SAVE THE WORLD	*Fontana*	72	*25 Sep 93*	2
LIKE LOVERS DO	*Fontana*	24	*16 Sep 95*	3
A collaboration with former Commotion guitarist Neil Clark.				
SENTIMENTAL FOOL	*Fontana*	73	*2 Dec 95*	1

ALBUMS:	HITS 9			WEEKS 92
RATTLESNAKES	*Polydor*	13	*20 Oct 84*	30
EASY PIECES	*Polydor*	5	*30 Nov 85*	18
MAINSTREAM	*Polydor*	9	*7 Nov 87*	20
1984–1989	*Polydor*	14	*8 Apr 89*	7
Above 4: Lloyd COLE and the COMMOTIONS.				
LLOYD COLE	*Polydor*	11	*3 Mar 90*	6
DON'T GET WEIRD ON ME BABE	*Polydor*	21	*28 Sep 91*	3
BAD VIBES	*Fontana*	38	*23 Oct 93*	2
LOVE STORY	*Fontana*	27	*7 Oct 95*	2
THE COLLECTION	*Mercury*	24	*23 Jan 99*	4

MJ COLE — UK

SINGLES:	HITS 3			WEEKS 16
SINCERE	*AM:PM*	38	*23 May 98*	2
CRAZY LOVE	*Talkin Loud*	10	*6 May 00*	7
Vocals by Elisabeth Troy.				
SINCERE [RM]	*Talkin Loud*	13	*12 Aug 00*	5
Remixed by MJ Cole.				
Above hit: MJ COLE; featuring Nove CASPER and Jay DEE.				
HOLD ON TO ME	*Talkin Loud*	35	*2 Dec 00*	2
Above hit: MJ COLE featuring Elisabeth TROY.				

ALBUMS:	HITS 1			WEEKS 4
SINCERE	*Talkin Loud*	14	*19 Aug 00*	4

Nat 'King' COLE — US

(See also Nat King Cole/The George Shearing Quintet.)

SINGLES:	HITS 30			WEEKS 235
SOMEWHERE ALONG THE WAY	*Capitol*	3	*15 Nov 52*	7
BECAUSE YOU'RE MINE	*Capitol*	6	*20 Dec 52*	2
FAITH CAN MOVE MOUNTAINS	*Capitol*	11	*3 Jan 53*	1
Above 2 entries were separate sides of the same release, each had its own chart run.				
FAITH CAN MOVE MOUNTAINS [RE-1ST]	*Capitol*	12	*17 Jan 53*	2
BECAUSE YOU'RE MINE [RE-1ST]	*Capitol*	10	*24 Jan 53*	1
FAITH CAN MOVE MOUNTAINS [RE-2ND]	*Capitol*	10	*7 Feb 53*	1
BECAUSE YOU'RE MINE [RE-2ND]	*Capitol*	11	*14 Feb 53*	1
PRETEND	*Capitol*	2	*25 Apr 53*	18
CAN'T I	*Capitol*	9	*15 Aug 53*	3
Above hit: Nat "King" COLE and Billy MAY and His Orchestra.				
MOTHER NATURE AND FATHER TIME	*Capitol*	7	*19 Sep 53*	7
CAN'T I [RE-1ST]	*Capitol*	6	*19 Sep 53*	4
CAN'T I [RE-2ND]	*Capitol*	10	*31 Oct 53*	1
TENDERLY	*Capitol*	10	*17 Apr 54*	1
SMILE	*Capitol*	2	*11 Sep 54*	14
MAKE HER MINE	*Capitol*	11	*9 Oct 54*	2
Above 2 entries were separate sides of the same release, each had its own chart run.				
A BLOSSOM FELL	*Capitol*	3	*26 Feb 55*	10
MY ONE SIN (IN LIFE)	*Capitol*	18	*27 Aug 55*	1
MY ONE SIN (IN LIFE) [RE]	*Capitol*	17	*17 Sep 55*	1
DREAMS CAN TELL A LIE	*Capitol*	10	*28 Jan 56*	9
TOO YOUNG TO GO STEADY	*Capitol*	8	*12 May 56*	14
From the film 'Strip For Action'.				
Nat "King" COLE with the Music of Nelson RIDDLE.				
LOVE ME AS IF THERE WERE NO TOMORROW	*Capitol*	24	*15 Sep 56*	2
LOVE ME AS IF THERE WERE NO TOMORROW [RE]	*Capitol*	11	*6 Oct 56*	13
WHEN I FALL IN LOVE	*Capitol*	2	*20 Apr 57*	20
Originally recorded by Doris Day.				
WHEN ROCK AND ROLL COME TO TRINIDAD	*Capitol*	28	*6 Jul 57*	1
MY PERSONAL POSSESSION	*Capitol*	21	*19 Oct 57*	2
The majority of hits above also had the credit 'Orchestra conducted by Nelson Riddle'.				
Above hit: Nat "King" COLE and the FOUR KNIGHTS with Nelson RIDDLE's Music.				
STARDUST	*Capitol*	24	*26 Oct 57*	2
Originally recorded by Irving Mills.				
YOU MADE ME LOVE YOU	*Capitol*	22	*30 May 59*	3
Originally recorded by Al Jolson in 1913.				
MIDNIGHT FLYER	*Capitol*	27	*5 Sep 59*	1
MIDNIGHT FLYER [RE]	*Capitol*	23	*19 Sep 59*	3
TIME AND THE RIVER	*Capitol*	29	*13 Feb 60*	1
TIME AND THE RIVER [RE-1ST]	*Capitol*	23	*27 Feb 60*	3
TIME AND THE RIVER [RE-2ND]	*Capitol*	47	*2 Apr 60*	1
THAT'S YOU	*Capitol*	10	*28 May 60*	8
Nat King COLE with the music of Nelson RIDDLE.				
JUST AS MUCH AS EVER	*Capitol*	18	*12 Nov 60*	10
THE WORLD IN MY ARMS	*Capitol*	36	*4 Feb 61*	10
LET TRUE LOVE BEGIN	*Capitol*	29	*18 Nov 61*	10
BRAZILIAN LOVE SONG (ANDORHINA PRETA)	*Capitol*	34	*24 Mar 62*	4

THE RIGHT THING TO SAY	*Capitol*	42	*2 Jun 62*	4
RAMBLIN' ROSE	*Capitol*	5	*29 Sep 62*	14
DEAR LONELY HEARTS	*Capitol*	37	*22 Dec 62*	3
WHEN I FALL IN LOVE [RI]	*Capitol*	4	*12 Dec 87*	7
UNFORGETTABLE	*Elektra*	19	*22 Jun 91*	8
Above hit: Natalie COLE with Nat 'King' COLE.				
THE CHRISTMAS SONG (CHESTNUTS ROASTING ON AN OPEN FIRE)	*Capitol*	69	*14 Dec 91*	2
Originally recorded by Mel Torme.				
LET'S FACE THE MUSIC AND DANCE	*EMI*	30	*19 Mar 94*	3
Featured in an Allied Dunbar TV Commercial.				
EPS:	**HITS 3**			**WEEKS 94**
LOVE IS THE THING, PART 1	*Capitol*	2	*28 May 60*	23
UNFORGETTABLE	*Capitol*	2	*15 Oct 60*	62
TENDERLY	*Capitol*	9	*22 Apr 61*	9
ALBUMS:	**HITS 10**			**WEEKS 126**
STRING ALONG WITH NAT 'KING' COLE	*Encore*	12	*19 Aug 61*	9
UNFORGETTABLE NAT 'KING' COLE	*Capitol*	11	*27 Mar 65*	8
THE BEST OF NAT 'KING' COLE	*Capitol*	5	*7 Dec 68*	18
THE BEST OF NAT 'KING' COLE VOLUME 2	*Capitol*	39	*5 Dec 70*	2
WHITE CHRISTMAS	*Music for Pleasure*	45	*27 Nov 71*	1
Budget compilation.				
Above hit: Nat 'King' COLE and Dean MARTIN.				
20 GOLDEN GREATS	*Capitol*	1	*8 Apr 78*	30
20 GREATEST LOVE SONGS	*Capitol*	7	*20 Nov 82*	26
20 GOLDEN GREATS [RI]	*EMI*	66	*19 Dec 87*	7
CHRISTMAS WITH NAT 'KING' COLE	*Stylus*	25	*26 Nov 88*	9
THE UNFORGETTABLE NAT 'KING' COLE	*EMI*	23	*23 Nov 91*	9
THE ULTIMATE COLLECTION	*EMI*	26	*20 Nov 99*	7

Nat King COLE/The George SHEARING QUINTET — US

(See also Nat 'King' Cole; George Shearing Quintet with Strings.)

SINGLES:	**HITS 1**			**WEEKS 14**
LET THERE BE LOVE	*Capitol*	11	*21 Jul 62*	14
ALBUMS:	**HITS 1**			**WEEKS 7**
NAT KING COLE SINGS AND THE GEORGE SHEARING QUINTET PLAYS	*Capitol*	8	*20 Oct 62*	7

Natalie COLE — US

(See also Johnny Mathis and Natalie Cole.)

SINGLES:	**HITS 11**			**WEEKS 87**
THIS WILL BE	*Capitol*	32	*11 Oct 75*	5
JUMP START	*Manhattan*	44	*8 Aug 87*	8
PINK CADILLAC	*Manhattan*	5	*26 Mar 88*	12
Originally recorded by Bruce Springsteen.				
EVERLASTING	*Manhattan*	28	*25 Jun 88*	6
JUMP START [RI]	*Manhattan*	36	*20 Aug 88*	5
I LIVE FOR YOUR LOVE	*Manhattan*	23	*26 Nov 88*	14
Original release reached No. 86 in 1987.				
MISS YOU LIKE CRAZY	*EMI USA*	2	*15 Apr 89*	15
REST OF THE NIGHT	*EMI USA*	56	*22 Jul 89*	2
STARTING OVER AGAIN	*EMI USA*	56	*16 Dec 89*	4
WILD WOMEN DO	*EMI USA*	16	*21 Apr 90*	7
From the film 'Pretty Woman'.				
UNFORGETTABLE	*Elektra*	19	*22 Jun 91*	8
Originally recorded by her father Nat 'King' Cole.				
Above hit: Natalie COLE with Nat 'King' COLE.				
THE VERY THOUGHT OF YOU	*Elektra*	71	*16 May 92*	1
ALBUMS:	**HITS 4**			**WEEKS 49**
EVERLASTING	*Manhattan*	62	*7 May 88*	4
GOOD TO BE BACK	*EMI-USA*	10	*20 May 89*	12
UNFORGETTABLE - WITH LOVE	*Elektra*	11	*27 Jul 91*	29
TAKE A LOOK	*Elektra*	16	*26 Jun 93*	4

Paula COLE — US

SINGLES:	**HITS 2**			**WEEKS 9**
WHERE HAVE ALL THE COWBOYS GONE?	*Warner Brothers*	15	*28 Jun 97*	8
I DON'T WANT TO WAIT	*Warner Brothers*	43	*1 Aug 98*	1
From the film 'City Of Angels'.				
ALBUMS:	**HITS 1**			**WEEKS 1**
THIS FIRE	*Warner Brothers*	60	*26 Jul 97*	1

Naimee COLEMAN - See AURORA featuring Naimee COLEMAN

COLETTE - See SISTER BLISS

John Ford COLEY - See ENGLAND DAN and John Ford COLEY

COLLAGE — US/Canada/Philippines

SINGLES:	HITS 1			WEEKS 5
ROMEO WHERE'S JULIET?	*MCA*	46	*21 Sep 85*	5

COLLAPSED LUNG — UK

SINGLES:	HITS 1			WEEKS 8
LONDON TONIGHT / EAT MY GOAL *Eat My Goal was used in the TV commercial for Coca Cola during the Euro '96 football championships.*	*Deceptive*	31	*22 Jun 96*	3
EAT MY GOAL [RI]	*Deceptive*	18	*30 May 98*	5

Albert COLLINS - See Gary MOORE

Bootsy COLLINS - See XAVIER featuring George CLINTON and Bootsy COLLINS

Dave and Ansil COLLINS — Jamaica

SINGLES:	HITS 2			WEEKS 27
DOUBLE BARREL	*Technique*	1	*27 Mar 71*	15
MONKEY SPANNER	*Technique*	7	*26 Jun 71*	12
ALBUMS:	**HITS 1**			**WEEKS 2**
DOUBLE BARREL	*Trojan*	41	*7 Aug 71*	2

Edwyn COLLINS — UK

SINGLES:	HITS 5			WEEKS 25
PALE BLUE EYES *Above hit: Paul QUINN and Edwyn COLLINS.*	*Swamplands*	72	*11 Aug 84*	2
EXPRESSLY [EP] *Lead track: A Girl Like You.*	*Setanta*	42	*12 Nov 94*	3
A GIRL LIKE YOU [RI]	*Setanta*	4	*17 Jun 95*	14
KEEP ON BURNING	*Setanta*	45	*2 Mar 96*	2
THE MAGIC PIPER (OF LOVE) *From the film 'Austin Powers'.*	*Setanta*	32	*2 Aug 97*	3
ADIDAS WORLD	*Setanta*	71	*18 Oct 97*	1
ALBUMS:	**HITS 2**			**WEEKS 9**
GORGEOUS GEORGE	*Setanta*	8	*22 Jul 95*	8
I'M NOT FOLLOWING YOU	*Setanta*	55	*13 Sep 97*	1

Felicia COLLINS - See LUKK featuring Felicia COLLINS

Jeff COLLINS — UK

SINGLES:	HITS 1			WEEKS 8
ONLY YOU	*Polydor*	40	*18 Nov 72*	8

Joan COLLINS - See Anthony NEWLEY, Peter SELLERS, Joan COLLINS

Judy COLLINS — US

SINGLES:	HITS 3			WEEKS 86
BOTH SIDES NOW *Originally recorded by Joni Mitchell.*	*Elektra*	14	*17 Jan 70*	11
AMAZING GRACE	*Elektra*	5	*5 Dec 70*	32
AMAZING GRACE [RE-1ST]	*Elektra*	48	*24 Jul 71*	1
AMAZING GRACE [RE-2ND]	*Elektra*	40	*4 Sep 71*	7
AMAZING GRACE [RE-3RD]	*Elektra*	50	*20 Nov 71*	1
AMAZING GRACE [RE-4TH]	*Elektra*	48	*18 Dec 71*	2
AMAZING GRACE [RE-5TH]	*Elektra*	20	*22 Apr 72*	19
AMAZING GRACE [RE-6TH]	*Elektra*	46	*9 Sep 72*	2
AMAZING GRACE [RE-7TH]	*Elektra*	49	*23 Dec 72*	3
SEND IN THE CLOWNS *Originally recorded by Glynis Johns.*	*Elektra*	6	*17 May 75*	8
ALBUMS:	**HITS 3**			**WEEKS 18**
WHALES AND NIGHTINGALES	*Elektra*	37	*10 Apr 71*	2
JUDITH	*Elektra*	7	*31 May 75*	12
AMAZING GRACE	*Telstar*	34	*14 Dec 85*	4

Michael COLLINS and his Concert Orchestra - See Russ CONWAY

Michelle COLLINS — UK

SINGLES:	HITS 1			WEEKS 3
SUNBURN *Theme from the BBC TV series of the same name.*	*BBC Music*	28	*27 Feb 99*	3

Phil COLLINS — UK

(See also Various Artists: Films - Original Soundtracks 'Buster'.)

SINGLES:	HITS 30			WEEKS 228
IN THE AIR TONIGHT	*Virgin*	2	*17 Jan 81*	10

I MISSED AGAIN	*Virgin*	14	*7 Mar 81*	8
IF LEAVING ME IS EASY	*Virgin*	17	*30 May 81*	8
THRU' THESE WALLS	*Virgin*	56	*23 Oct 82*	2
YOU CAN'T HURRY LOVE	*Virgin*	1	*4 Dec 82*	16
DON'T LET HIM STEAL YOUR HEART AWAY	*Virgin*	45	*19 Mar 83*	5
Above hit: Phil COLLINS with the Martyn FORD ORCHESTRA.				
AGAINST ALL ODDS (TAKE A LOOK AT ME NOW)	*Virgin*	2	*7 Apr 84*	14
From the film 'Against All Odds'.				
SUSSUDIO	*Virgin*	12	*26 Jan 85*	9
EASY LOVER	*CBS*	1	*9 Mar 85*	12
Above hit: Philip BAILEY (duet with Phil COLLINS).				
ONE MORE NIGHT	*Virgin*	4	*13 Apr 85*	9
TAKE ME HOME	*Virgin*	19	*27 Jul 85*	9
SEPARATE LIVES	*Virgin*	4	*23 Nov 85*	13
From the film 'White Nights'.				
Above hit: Phil COLLINS and Marilyn MARTIN. Originally recorded by Steven Bishop in 1982.				
IN THE AIR TONIGHT ('88 REMIX) [RM]	*Virgin*	4	*18 Jun 88*	9
This remix had an identical catalogue number to the original. Remixed by Phil Collins and Hugh Padgham.				
A GROOVY KIND OF LOVE	*Virgin*	1	*3 Sep 88*	13
Originally recorded by Diane and Annita in 1963.				
TWO HEARTS	*Virgin*	6	*26 Nov 88*	11
Above 2 from the film 'Buster'.				
ANOTHER DAY IN PARADISE	*Virgin*	2	*4 Nov 89*	11
I WISH IT WOULD RAIN DOWN	*Virgin*	7	*27 Jan 90*	9
SOMETHING HAPPENED ON THE WAY TO HEAVEN	*Virgin*	15	*28 Apr 90*	7
THAT'S JUST THE WAY IT IS	*Virgin*	26	*28 Jul 90*	5
HANG IN LONG ENOUGH	*Virgin*	34	*6 Oct 90*	3
DO YOU REMEMBER (LIVE)	*Virgin*	57	*8 Dec 90*	5
HERO	*Atlantic*	56	*15 May 93*	3
Above hit: David CROSBY featuring Phil COLLINS.				
BOTH SIDES OF THE STORY	*Virgin*	7	*30 Oct 93*	5
BOTH SIDES OF THE STORY [RE]	*Virgin*	61	*1 Jan 94*	1
EVERYDAY	*Virgin*	15	*15 Jan 94*	5
WE WAIT AND WE WONDER	*Virgin*	45	*7 May 94*	2
DANCE INTO THE LIGHT	*Face Value*	9	*5 Oct 96*	6
IT'S IN YOUR EYES	*Face Value*	30	*14 Dec 96*	4
WEAR MY HAT	*Face Value*	43	*12 Jul 97*	2
TRUE COLORS	*Virgin*	26	*7 Nov 98*	4
YOU'LL BE IN MY HEART	*Walt Disney*	17	*6 Nov 99*	6
From the Walt Disney film 'Tarzan'.				
IN THE AIR TONITE [RR]	*WEA*	26	*22 Sep 01*	2
Above hit: LIL' KIM featuring Phil COLLINS.				
ALBUMS:	**HITS 8**			**WEEKS 796**
FACE VALUE	*Virgin*	1	*21 Feb 81*	274
Includes re-entries through to 1990.				
HELLO, I MUST BE GOING!	*Virgin*	2	*13 Nov 82*	135
NO JACKET REQUIRED	*Virgin*	1	*2 Mar 85*	176
Includes re-entries through to 1990.				
HELLO, I MUST BE GOING! [RE]	*Virgin*	48	*16 Jul 88*	28
Re-released at mid-price. Chart position reached in 1990 (1988 peak No. 83, 1989 peak No. 59)				
BUT SERIOUSLY	*Virgin*	1	*2 Dec 89*	72
SERIOUS HITS . . . LIVE!	*Virgin*	2	*17 Nov 90*	50
Live recordings from the 1990 Serious Tour.				
BOTH SIDES	*Virgin*	1	*20 Nov 93*	21
DANCE INTO THE LIGHT	*Face Value*	4	*2 Nov 96*	13
. . . HITS	*Virgin*	1	*17 Oct 98*	27

Rodger COLLINS — US

SINGLES:	**HITS 1**			**WEEKS 6**
YOU SEXY SUGAR PLUM (BUT I LIKE IT)	*Fantasy*	22	*3 Apr 76*	6

Willie COLLINS — US

SINGLES:	**HITS 1**			**WEEKS 4**
WHERE YOU GONNA BE TONIGHT?	*Capitol*	46	*28 Jun 86*	4
ALBUMS:	**HITS 1**			**WEEKS 1**
WHERE YOU GONNA BE TONIGHT?	*Capitol*	97	*14 Jun 86*	1

Michel COLOMBIER – See Pierre HENRY/Michel COLOMBIER

Willie COLON — US

SINGLES:	**HITS 1**			**WEEKS 7**
SET FIRE TO ME	*A&M*	41	*28 Jun 86*	7

COLOR ME BADD — US

SINGLES:	HITS 6			WEEKS 31
I WANNA SEX YOU UP *From the film 'New Jack City'.*	*Giant*	1	*18 May 91*	14
ALL 4 LOVE	*Giant*	5	*3 Aug 91*	10
I ADORE MI AMOR	*Giant*	44	*12 Oct 91*	2
I ADORE MI AMOR [RI]	*Giant*	59	*9 Nov 91*	2
HEARTBREAKER	*Giant*	58	*22 Feb 92*	1
TIME AND CHANCE	*Giant*	62	*20 Nov 93*	1
CHOOSE	*Giant*	65	*16 Apr 94*	1
ALBUMS:	**HITS 1**			**WEEKS 22**
C.M.B.	*Giant*	3	*24 Aug 91*	22

COLORADO — UK

SINGLES:	HITS 1			WEEKS 3
CALIFORNIA DREAMING	*Pinnacle*	45	*21 Oct 78*	3

COLOSSEUM — UK

ALBUMS:	HITS 4			WEEKS 14
COLOSSEUM	*Fontana*	15	*17 May 69*	1
VALENTYNE SUITE	*Vertigo*	15	*22 Nov 69*	2
DAUGHTER OF TIME	*Vertigo*	23	*5 Dec 70*	5
COLOSSEUM LIVE	*Bronze*	17	*26 Jun 71*	6

COLOUR GIRL — UK

SINGLES:	HITS 3			WEEKS 5
CAN'T GET USED TO LOSING YOU	*4 Liberty*	31	*11 Mar 00*	3
JOYRIDER (YOU'RE PLAYING WITH FIRE)	*4 Liberty*	51	*9 Sep 00*	1
MAS QUE NADA *Originally recorded by Jorge Ben in 1963.* *Above hit: COLOUR GIRL featuring PSG.*	*4 Liberty*	57	*3 Feb 01*	1

COLOURBOX — UK

ALBUMS:	HITS 1			WEEKS 2
COLOURBOX	*4AD*	67	*24 Aug 85*	2

COLOURFIELD — UK

SINGLES:	HITS 4			WEEKS 18
THE COLOUR FIELD *Above hit: COLOUR FIELD.*	*Chrysalis*	43	*21 Jan 84*	4
TAKE	*Chrysalis*	70	*28 Jul 84*	1
THINKING OF YOU	*Chrysalis*	12	*26 Jan 85*	10
CASTLES IN THE AIR	*Chrysalis*	51	*13 Apr 85*	3
ALBUMS:	**HITS 2**			**WEEKS 8**
VIRGINS AND PHILISTINES	*Chrysalis*	12	*4 May 85*	7
DECEPTION	*Chrysalis*	95	*4 Apr 87*	1

COLOURS featuring Stephen EMMANUEL and ESKA — UK

SINGLES:	HITS 1			WEEKS 1
WHAT U DO	*Inferno*	51	*27 Feb 99*	1

Alice COLTRANE - See Carlos SANTANA and Alice COLTRANE

COLUMBIA PICTURES ORCHESTRA - See Morris STOLOFF conducting the Columbia PICTURES ORCHESTRA

COLUMBO presents IN FULL ROCK-A-PHONIC SOUND featuring OOE — UK

SINGLES:	HITS 1			WEEKS 1
ROCKABILLY BOB	V2	59	*15 May 99*	1

Shawn COLVIN — US

SINGLES:	HITS 6			WEEKS 12
I DON'T KNOW WHY	*Columbia*	62	*27 Nov 93*	1
ROUND OF BLUES	*Columbia*	73	*12 Feb 94*	1
EVERY LITTLE THING HE DOES IS MAGIC	*Columbia*	65	*3 Sep 94*	2
ONE COOL REMOVE *Above hit: Shawn COLVIN with Mary Chapin CARPENTER.*	*Columbia*	40	*7 Jan 95*	3
I DON'T KNOW WHY [RI] *From the film 'Clockwork Mice'.*	*Columbia*	52	*12 Aug 95*	1
GET OUT OF THIS HOUSE	*Columbia*	70	*15 Mar 97*	1
SUNNY CAME HOME	*Columbia*	29	*30 May 98*	3
ALBUMS:	**HITS 1**			**WEEKS 1**
COVER GIRL	*Columbia*	67	*17 Sep 94*	1

COMETS - See Bill HALEY and his COMETS

COMIC RELIEF — UK

ALBUMS:	HITS 1			WEEKS 8
COMIC RELIEF PRESENTS UTTERLY UTTERLY LIVE!	*WEA*	10	*10 May 86*	8

COMING OUT CREW — US

SINGLES:	HITS 1			WEEKS 1
FREE GAY AND HAPPY	*Out On Vinyl*	50	*18 Mar 95*	1
Vocals by Sabrina Johnston.				

COMMADER TOM — Germany

SINGLES:	HITS 1			WEEKS 1
EYE BEE M	*Tripoli Trax*	75	*23 Dec 00*	1

COMME CI COMME CA – See LONYO

COMMENTATORS — UK

SINGLES:	HITS 1			WEEKS 7
N-N-NINETEEN NOT OUT	*Oval*	13	*22 Jun 85*	7
A pastiche of Paul Hardcastle's 19.				

COMMITMENTS — Ireland

SINGLES:	HITS 1			WEEKS 1
MUSTANG SALLY	*MCA*	63	*30 Nov 91*	1
ALBUMS:	**HITS 2**			**WEEKS 141**
THE COMMITMENTS [OST]	*MCA*	4	*26 Oct 91*	130
Includes re-entries through to 1997.				
THE COMMITMENTS VOLUME 2	*MCA*	13	*25 Apr 92*	11

COMMODORES — US

SINGLES:	HITS 16			WEEKS 121
MACHINE GUN	*Tamla Motown*	20	*24 Aug 74*	11
THE ZOO (THE HUMAN ZOO)	*Tamla Motown*	44	*23 Nov 74*	2
EASY	*Motown*	9	*2 Jul 77*	10
BRICK HOUSE / SWEET LOVE	*Motown*	32	*8 Oct 77*	6
TOO HOT TA TROT / ZOOM	*Motown*	38	*11 Mar 78*	4
FLYING HIGH	*Motown*	37	*24 Jun 78*	7
THREE TIMES A LADY	*Motown*	1	*5 Aug 78*	14
JUST TO BE CLOSE TO YOU	*Motown*	62	*25 Nov 78*	4
SAIL ON	*Motown*	8	*25 Aug 79*	10
STILL	*Motown*	4	*3 Nov 79*	11
WONDERLAND	*Motown*	40	*19 Jan 80*	4
LADY (YOU BRING ME UP)	*Motown*	56	*1 Aug 81*	5
OH NO	*Motown*	44	*21 Nov 81*	3
NIGHTSHIFT	*Motown*	3	*26 Jan 85*	14
ANIMAL INSTINCT	*Motown*	74	*11 May 85*	1
GOIN' TO THE BANK	*Polydor*	43	*25 Oct 86*	4
EASY [RI]	*Motown*	15	*13 Aug 88*	11
ALBUMS:	**HITS 10**			**WEEKS 129**
COMMODORES LIVE!	*Motown*	60	*13 May 78*	1
NATURAL HIGH	*Motown*	8	*10 Jun 78*	23
GREATEST HITS	*Motown*	19	*2 Dec 78*	16
MIDNIGHT MAGIC	*Motown*	15	*18 Aug 79*	25
HEROES	*Motown*	50	*28 Jun 80*	5
IN THE POCKET	*Motown*	69	*18 Jul 81*	5
LOVE SONGS	*K Tel*	5	*14 Aug 82*	28
NIGHTSHIFT	*Motown*	13	*23 Feb 85*	10
THE VERY BEST OF COMMODORES - 16 CLASSIC TRACKS	*Telstar*	25	*9 Nov 85*	13
THE VERY BEST OF THE COMMODORES	*Motown*	26	*6 May 95*	3

COMMON — US

SINGLES:	HITS 3			WEEKS 3
REMINDING ME (OF SEF)	*Epic*	59	*8 Nov 97*	1
Above hit: COMMON featuring Chantay SAVAGE.				
THE LIGHT/THE 6TH SENSE (SOMETHING U FEEL)	*MCA*	56	*14 Oct 00*	1
The Light samples Bobby Caldwell's Open Your Eyes.				
GETO HEAVEN (THE SOUND OF ILLADELPH)	*MCA*	48	*28 Apr 01*	1
Based around the Family Stand's Ghetto Heaven.				
Above hit: COMMON featuring Macy GRAY.				

COMMUNARDS — UK

(See also Jimmy Somerville.)

SINGLES:	HITS 8			WEEKS 76
YOU ARE MY WORLD	*London*	30	*12 Oct 85*	8
Above hit: COMMUNARDS/Jimmy SOMERVILLE – Richard COLES.				

DISENCHANTED	*London*	29	*24 May 86*	5
DON'T LEAVE ME THIS WAY	*London*	1	*23 Aug 86*	14
Above hit: COMMUNARDS with Sarah Jane MORRIS.				
SO COLD THE NIGHT	*London*	8	*29 Nov 86*	10
YOU ARE MY WORLD ('87) [RM]	*London*	21	*21 Feb 87*	6
TOMORROW	*London*	23	*12 Sep 87*	7
NEVER CAN SAY GOODBYE	*London*	4	*7 Nov 87*	11
Originally recorded by the Jackson 5.				
FOR A FRIEND	*London*	28	*20 Feb 88*	7
THERE'S MORE TO LOVE	*London*	20	*11 Jun 88*	8
ALBUMS:	**HITS 3**			**WEEKS 78**
COMMUNARDS	*London*	7	*2 Aug 86*	45
RED	*London*	4	*17 Oct 87*	29
THE VERY BEST OF JIMMY SOMERVILLE - BRONSKI BEAT AND THE COMMUNARDS	*London*	29	*22 Sep 01*	4
17 track compilation. 5 solo tracks, 4 with Bronski Beat, 8 with Communards.				
Above hit: Jimmy SOMERVILLE – BRONSKI BEAT and the COMMUNARDS.				

Perry COMO — US

SINGLES:	**HITS 23**			**WEEKS 323**
• DON'T LET THE STARS GET IN YOUR EYES	*His Master's Voice*	1	*17 Jan 53*	15
Originally recorded by Slim Willet.				
Above hit: Perry COMO with the RAMBLERS.				
WANTED	*His Master's Voice*	4	*5 Jun 54*	14
Above hit: Perry COMO with Hugo WINTERHALTER'S ORCHESTRA and CHORUS.				
IDLE GOSSIP	*His Master's Voice*	3	*26 Jun 54*	15
Above hit: Perry COMO with Hugo WINTERHALTER and his Orchestra.				
WANTED [RE]	*His Master's Voice*	18	*2 Oct 54*	1
PAPA LOVES MAMBO	*His Master's Voice*	16	*11 Dec 54*	1
Above hit: Perry COMO and the Ray CHARLES SINGERS.				
TINA MARIE	*His Master's Voice*	24	*31 Dec 55*	1
Above hit: Perry COMO and the Ray CHARLES SINGERS with Mitchell AYRES and his Orchestra.				
• JUKE BOX BABY	*His Master's Voice*	22	*28 Apr 56*	6
HOT DIGGITY (DOG ZIGGITY BOOM)	*His Master's Voice*	4	*26 May 56*	13
Above hit: Perry COMO with Mitchell AYRES and his Orchestra and the Ray CHARLES SINGERS.				
MORE	*His Master's Voice*	10	*22 Sep 56*	11
GLENDORA	*His Master's Voice*	18	*29 Sep 56*	6
Above 2 entries were separate sides of the same release, each had its own chart run.				
MORE [RE]	*His Master's Voice*	29	*15 Dec 56*	1
Above 3: Perry COMO and the Ray CHARLES SINGERS with Mitchell AYRES and his Orchestra.				
• MAGIC MOMENTS	*RCA*	1	*8 Feb 58*	17
CATCH A FALLING STAR	*RCA*	9	*8 Mar 58*	10
Above 2 entries were separate sides of the same release, each had its own chart run.				
KEWPIE DOLL	*RCA*	9	*10 May 58*	7
I MAY NEVER PASS THIS WAY AGAIN	*RCA*	15	*31 May 58*	8
MOON TALK	*RCA*	17	*6 Sep 58*	11
LOVE MAKES THE WORLD GO 'ROUND (YEAH, YEAH)	*RCA*	6	*8 Nov 58*	14
MANDOLINS IN THE MOONLIGHT	*RCA*	13	*22 Nov 58*	12
Above 2 entries were separate sides of the same release, each had its own chart run.				
TOMBOY	*RCA*	10	*28 Feb 59*	12
I KNOW	*RCA*	13	*11 Jul 59*	16
DELAWARE	*RCA*	3	*27 Feb 60*	14
Above 10: Perry COMO with Mitchell AYRES ORCHESTRA and the Ray CHARLES SINGERS.				
CATERINA	*RCA*	37	*12 May 62*	4
Above hit: Perry COMO with the Ray CHARLES SINGERS; Mitchell AYRES and his Orchestra.				
CATERINA [RE]	*RCA*	45	*16 Jun 62*	2
IT'S IMPOSSIBLE	*RCA Victor*	4	*30 Jan 71*	23
Originally recorded by Armando Manzanero.				
I THINK OF YOU	*RCA Victor*	14	*15 May 71*	11
• AND I LOVE YOU SO	*RCA Victor*	3	*21 Apr 73*	31
Originally recorded by Don McLean.				
FOR THE GOOD TIMES	*RCA Victor*	7	*25 Aug 73*	27
Originally recorded by Kris Kristofferson.				
WALK RIGHT BACK	*RCA Victor*	33	*8 Dec 73*	10
AND I LOVE YOU SO [RE]	*RCA Victor*	40	*12 Jan 74*	4
I WANT TO GIVE (AHORA QUE SOY LIBRE)	*RCA Victor*	31	*25 May 74*	6
EPS:	**HITS 1**			**WEEKS 1**
YOU'LL NEVER WALK ALONE	*RCA*	20	*18 Jun 60*	1
ALBUMS:	**HITS 9**			**WEEKS 193**
DEAR PERRY	*RCA*	6	*8 Nov 58*	5
Above hit: Perry COMO with Mitchell AYRES and his ORCHESTRA and the Ray CHARLES SINGERS				

COMO'S GOLDEN RECORDS	*RCA*	4	*31 Jan 59*	5
IT'S IMPOSSIBLE	*RCA Victor*	13	*10 Apr 71*	13
AND I LOVE YOU SO	*RCA Victor*	1	*7 Jul 73*	109
Peak position reached on 26 Jan 74.				
PERRY	*RCA Victor*	26	*24 Aug 74*	3
MEMORIES ARE MADE OF HITS	*RCA Victor*	14	*19 Apr 75*	16
40 GREATEST HITS	*K-Tel*	1	*25 Oct 75*	34
FOR THE GOOD TIMES	*Telstar*	41	*3 Dec 83*	6
GOLD – GREATEST HITS	*RCA*	55	*17 Nov 01*	2

COMPAGNONS DE LA CHANSON — France

SINGLES:	HITS 1			WEEKS 3
THE THREE BELLS (THE JIMMY BROWN SONG) •	*Columbia*	27	*10 Oct 59*	1
THE THREE BELLS (THE JIMMY BROWN SONG) [RE]	*Columbia*	21	*24 Oct 59*	2

COMPULSION — Ireland/Holland

ALBUMS:	HITS 1			WEEKS 1
COMFORTER	*One Little Indian*	59	*9 Apr 94*	1

COMSAT ANGELS — UK

SINGLES:	HITS 1			WEEKS 2
INDEPENDENCE DAY	*Jive*	75	*21 Jan 84*	1
INDEPENDENCE DAY [RE]	*Jive*	71	*4 Feb 84*	1
ALBUMS:	**HITS 3**			**WEEKS 9**
SLEEP NO MORE	*Polydor*	51	*5 Sep 81*	5
FICTION	*Polydor*	94	*18 Sep 82*	2
LAND	*Jive*	91	*8 Oct 83*	2

Frank COMSTOCK – See Rosemary CLOONEY

CON FUNK SHUN — US

SINGLES:	HITS 1			WEEKS 2
BURNIN' LOVE	*Club*	68	*19 Jul 86*	2

CONCEPT — US

SINGLES:	HITS 1			WEEKS 6
MR. D.J.	*Fourth & Broadway*	27	*14 Dec 85*	6

CONDUCTOR and the COWBOY — UK

SINGLES:	HITS 1			WEEKS 2
FEELING THIS WAY	*Serious*	35	*20 May 00*	2
Vocals by Laura Hallett.				

CONFEDERATES – See Elvis COSTELLO and the ATTRACTIONS

CONGREGATION — UK

SINGLES:	HITS 1			WEEKS 14
SOFTLY WHISPERING I LOVE YOU	*Columbia*	4	*27 Nov 71*	14
Originally recorded by David and Jonathan.				

CONGRESS — UK

SINGLES:	HITS 1			WEEKS 4
40 MILES	*Inner Rhythm*	26	*26 Oct 91*	4

Arthur CONLEY — US

SINGLES:	HITS 2			WEEKS 15
SWEET SOUL MUSIC •	*Atlantic*	7	*29 Apr 67*	14
Based on a Sam Cooke track called 'Yeah Man'.				
FUNKY STREET	*Atlantic*	46	*13 Apr 68*	1

Jud CONLON'S RHYTHMAIRES and ORCHESTRA – See Bing CROSBY

CONNELLS — US

SINGLES:	HITS 1			WEEKS 11
'74–'75	*TNT*	14	*12 Aug 95*	8
'74–'75 [RE]	*TNT*	21	*16 Mar 96*	3
ALBUMS:	**HITS 1**			**WEEKS 2**
RING	*London*	36	*9 Sep 95*	2

Harry CONNICK Jr. — US

SINGLES:	HITS 3			WEEKS 11
RECIPE FOR LOVE / IT HAD TO BE YOU	*Columbia*	32	*25 May 91*	6
Recipe For Love originally reached No. 86 in 1990. It Had To Be You from the film 'When Harry Met Sally' and originally recorded by Isham Jones.				

WE ARE IN LOVE	*Columbia*	62	*3 Aug 91*	2
BLUE LIGHT, RED LIGHT (SOMEONE'S THERE)	*Columbia*	54	*23 Nov 91*	3
ALBUMS:	**HITS 5**			**WEEKS 67**
WE ARE IN LOVE *Re-issued on the Columbia label from 12 Jan 91.*	*CBS*	17	*22 Sep 90*	27
WE ARE IN LOVE [RI]	*Columbia*	7	*25 May 91*	19
BLUE LIGHT, RED LIGHT	*Columbia*	16	*26 Oct 91*	11
25	*Columbia*	35	*30 Jan 93*	2
FOREVER FOR NOW	*Columbia*	32	*12 Jun 93*	5
SHE	*Columbia*	21	*27 Aug 94*	3

Ray CONNIFF — US

(See also Don Cherry; Frankie Laine; Guy Mitchell; Johnnie Ray.)

ALBUMS:	**HITS 11**			**WEEKS 96**
IT'S THE TALK OF THE TOWN *Above hit: Ray CONNIFF SINGERS.*	*Philips*	15	*28 May 60*	1
'S AWFUL NICE *Above hit: Ray CONNIFF ORCHESTRA.*	*Philips*	13	*25 Jun 60*	1
THE RAY CONNIFF HI-FI COMPANION ALBUM *Above hit: Ray CONNIFF and his Orchestra and Chorus.*	*Philips*	3	*26 Nov 60*	44
MEMORIES ARE MADE OF THIS	*Philips*	14	*20 May 61*	4
'S WONDERFUL 'S MARVELLOUS	*CBS*	18	*29 Dec 62*	3
WE WISH YOU A MERRY CHRISTMAS	*CBS*	12	*29 Dec 62*	1
THE RAY CONNIFF HI-FI COMPANION ALBUM [RI] *Above hit: Ray CONNIFF and his Orchestra and Chorus.*	*CBS*	24	*16 Apr 66*	4
SOMEWHERE MY LOVE	*CBS*	34	*9 Sep 67*	3
HIS ORCHESTRA, HIS CHORUS, HIS SINGERS, HIS SOUND	*CBS*	1	*21 Jun 69*	16
BRIDGE OVER TROUBLED WATER	*CBS*	30	*23 May 70*	14
LOVE STORY	*CBS*	34	*12 Jun 71*	1
I'D LIKE TO TEACH THE WORLD TO SING	*CBS*	17	*19 Feb 72*	4

Billy CONNOLLY — UK

SINGLES:	**HITS 4**			**WEEKS 31**
D.I.V.O.R.C.E. *Live recording from the Apollo, Glasgow. A parody of the Tammy Wynette hit.*	*Polydor*	1	*1 Nov 75*	10
NO CHANCE (NO CHARGE) *Parody of the J.J. Barrie hit.*	*Polydor*	24	*17 Jul 76*	5
IN THE BROWNIES *Parody of the Village People hit In The Navy.*	*Polydor*	38	*25 Aug 79*	7
SUPER GRAN (THEME) *Theme from the Tyne Tees TV series 'Super Gran'.*	*Stiff*	32	*9 Mar 85*	9
ALBUMS:	**HITS 8**			**WEEKS 108**
SOLO CONCERT	*Transatlantic*	8	*20 Jul 74*	33
COP YER WHACK FOR THIS	*Polydor*	10	*18 Jan 75*	29
WORDS AND MUSIC	*Transatlantic*	34	*20 Sep 75*	10
GET RIGHT INTAE HIM	*Polydor*	6	*6 Dec 75*	14
ATLANTIC BRIDGE	*Polydor*	20	*11 Dec 76*	9
RAW MEAT FOR THE BALCONY	*Polydor*	57	*28 Jan 78*	3
THE PICK OF BILLY CONNOLLY	*Polydor*	23	*5 Dec 81*	8
BILLY AND ALBERT	*10 Records*	81	*5 Dec 87*	2

Sarah CONNOR featuring TQ — Germany/US

(See also TQ.)

SINGLES:	**HITS 1**			**WEEKS 5**
LET'S GET BACK TO BED - BOY	*Epic*	16	*13 Oct 01*	5

CONQUERING LION — UK

SINGLES:	**HITS 1**			**WEEKS 1**
CODE RED ('94 REMIX) *Includes samples from Supercat and Reggie Stepper.*	*Mango*	53	*8 Oct 94*	1

Leena CONQUEST and HIP HOP FINGER — US

SINGLES:	**HITS 1**			**WEEKS 1**
BOUNDARIES	*Naturalresponse*	67	*18 Jun 94*	1

Jess CONRAD — UK

SINGLES:	**HITS 3**			**WEEKS 13**
CHERRY PIE	*Decca*	39	*2 Jul 60*	1
MYSTERY GIRL	*Decca*	44	*28 Jan 61*	1
MYSTERY GIRL [RE]	*Decca*	18	*11 Feb 61*	9
PRETTY JENNY	*Decca*	50	*13 Oct 62*	2

CONSOLIDATED — US

ALBUMS:	HITS 1			WEEKS 1
BUSINESS OF PUNISHMENT	*London*	53	*30 Jul 94*	1

CONSORTIUM — UK

SINGLES:	HITS 1			WEEKS 9
ALL THE LOVE IN THE WORLD •	*Pye*	22	*15 Feb 69*	9

Ann CONSUELO - See SUBTERRANIA featuring Ann CONSUELO

CONTOURS — US

SINGLES:	HITS 1			WEEKS 6
JUST A LITTLE MISUNDERSTANDING	*Tamla Motown*	31	*24 Jan 70*	6

CONTRABAND — Germany/US

SINGLES:	HITS 1			WEEKS 2
ALL THE WAY FROM MEMPHIS	*Impact American*	65	*20 Jul 91*	2

CONTROL — UK

SINGLES:	HITS 1			WEEKS 5
DANCE WITH ME (I'M YOUR ECSTASY)	*All Around The World*	17	*2 Nov 91*	5

CONVERT — Belgium

SINGLES:	HITS 2			WEEKS 7
NIGHTBIRD	*A&M*	39	*11 Jan 92*	4
ROCKIN' TO THE RHYTHM	*A&M*	42	*29 May 93*	2
NIGHTBIRD [RM]	*Wonderboy*	45	*31 Jan 98*	1
Remixed by Tin Tin Out.				

Russ CONWAY — UK

SINGLES:	HITS 20			WEEKS 179
PARTY POPS [M]	*Columbia*	24	*30 Nov 57*	5
GOT A MATCH	*Columbia*	30	*30 Aug 58*	1
The week Got A Match charted, Yakety Yak by the Coasters was inadvertently omitted. The mistake allowed Russ Conway to sneak in at No.30.				
MORE PARTY POPS [M]	*Columbia*	10	*29 Nov 58*	7
THE WORLD OUTSIDE (THEME FROM THE WARSAW CONCERTO)	*Columbia*	24	*24 Jan 59*	1
Above hit: Russ CONWAY with Geoff LOVE and his Orchestra and the Rita WILLIAMS SINGERS.				
SIDE SADDLE •	*Columbia*	1	*21 Feb 59*	30
THE WORLD OUTSIDE (THEME FROM THE WARSAW CONCERTO) [RE]	*Columbia*	24	*07 Mar 59*	3
Above hit: Russ CONWAY with Geoff LOVE and his Orchestra and the Rita WILLIAMS SINGERS.				
ROULETTE	*Columbia*	1	*16 May 59*	19
CHINA TEA	*Columbia*	5	*22 Aug 59*	13
SNOW COACH	*Columbia*	7	*14 Nov 59*	9
MORE AND MORE PARTY POPS [M]	*Columbia*	5	*21 Nov 59*	8
ROYAL EVENT	*Columbia*	15	*5 Mar 60*	8
FINGS AIN'T WOT THEY USED T'BE	*Columbia*	47	*23 Apr 60*	1
LUCKY FIVE	*Columbia*	14	*21 May 60*	9
PASSING BREEZE	*Columbia*	16	*1 Oct 60*	10
Above hit: Russ CONWAY with Tony OSBORNE and his Orchestra.				
EVEN MORE PARTY POPS [M]	*Columbia*	27	*26 Nov 60*	9
PEPE	*Columbia*	19	*21 Jan 61*	9
Above hit: Russ CONWAY with John BARRY and his Orchestra.				
PABLO	*Columbia*	45	*27 May 61*	2
Above hit: Russ CONWAY with Tony OSBORNE and his Orchestra.				
SAY IT WITH FLOWERS	*Columbia*	23	*26 Aug 61*	10
Above hit: Dorothy SQUIRES/Russ CONWAY with Tony OSBORNE and his Orchestra.				
TOY BALLOONS	*Columbia*	7	*2 Dec 61*	11
LESSON ONE	*Columbia*	21	*24 Feb 62*	7
ALWAYS YOU AND ME	*Columbia*	33	*1 Dec 62*	4
Majority of the above hits had the credit 'accompaniment directed by Geoff Love'.				
Above hit: Russ CONWAY with Geoff LOVE and his Orchestra.				
ALWAYS YOU AND ME [RE]	*Columbia*	35	*5 Jan 63*	3

EPS:	HITS 5			WEEKS 25
TIME TO CELEBRATE	*Columbia*	17	*9 Apr 60*	3
ANOTHER SIX	*Columbia*	12	*13 Aug 60*	5
ROCKING HORSE COWBOY	*Columbia*	12	*29 Oct 60*	3
MORE PARTY POPS	*Columbia*	7	*24 Dec 60*	8
MY CONCERTO FOR YOU NO. 2	*Columbia*	11	*29 Apr 61*	6

ALBUMS:	HITS 7			WEEKS 69
PACK UP YOUR TROUBLES	*Columbia*	9	*22 Nov 58*	5
SONGS TO SING IN YOUR BATH	*Columbia*	8	*2 May 59*	10

FAMILY FAVOURITES	*Columbia*	3	*19 Sep 59*	16
TIME TO CELEBRATE	*Columbia*	3	*19 Dec 59*	7
MY CONCERTO FOR YOU	*Columbia*	5	*26 Mar 60*	17
Above hit: Russ CONWAY with Michael COLLINS and his Concert Orchestra and the WILLIAMS SINGERS.				
PARTY TIME	*Columbia*	7	*17 Dec 60*	11
RUSS CONWAY PRESENTS 24 PIANO GREATS	*Ronco*	25	*23 Apr 77*	3

CONWAY BROTHERS — US

SINGLES:	HITS 1			WEEKS 10
TURN IT UP	*10 Records*	11	*22 Jun 85*	10

Ry COODER — US

(See also Ali Farka Toure and Ry Cooder.)

ALBUMS:	HITS 5			WEEKS 45
BOP TILL YOU DROP	*Warner Brothers*	36	*11 Aug 79*	9
BORDER LINE	*Warner Brothers*	35	*18 Oct 80*	6
THE SLIDE AREA	*Warner Brothers*	18	*24 Apr 82*	12
GET RHYTHM	*Warner Brothers*	75	*14 Nov 87*	3
BUENA VISTA SOCIAL CLUB	*World Circuit*	44	*5 Jul 97*	15
Collaboration with various Cuban musicians.				

Martin COOK - See Richard DENTON and Martin COOK

Norman COOK — UK

(See also Fatboy Slim; Mighty Dub Katz.)

SINGLES:	HITS 2			WEEKS 10
WON'T TALK ABOUT IT / BLAME IT ON THE BASSLINE	*Go.Beat*	29	*8 Jul 89*	6
Above hit: Norman COOK featuring Billy BRAGG / Norman COOK featuring M.C. WILDSKI.				
FOR SPACIOUS LIES	*Go.Beat*	48	*21 Oct 89*	4
Above hit: Norman COOK featuring LESTER.				

Peter COOK and Dudley MOORE — UK

SINGLES:	HITS 2			WEEKS 15
GOODBYEEE	*Decca*	18	*19 Jun 65*	10
Above hit: Peter COOK and Dudley MOORE with the Dudley MOORE TRIO.				
THE BALLAD OF SPOTTY MULDOON	*Decca*	34	*17 Jul 65*	5
Above hit: Peter COOK with the Dudley MOORE TRIO.				
EPS:	**HITS 1**			**WEEKS 3**
BY APPOINTMENT	*Decca*	18	*29 Jan 66*	3
ALBUMS:	**HITS 3**			**WEEKS 34**
ONCE MOORE WITH COOK	*Decca*	25	*21 May 66*	1
DEREK AND CLIVE LIVE	*Island*	12	*18 Sep 76*	25
COME AGAIN	*Virgin*	18	*24 Dec 77*	8

Brandon COOKE featuring Roxanne SHANTE — US

(See also Roxanne Shante.)

SINGLES:	HITS 1			WEEKS 3
SHARP AS A KNIFE	*Club*	45	*29 Oct 88*	3

Sam COOKE — US

SINGLES:	HITS 8			WEEKS 82
YOU SEND ME	*London*	29	*18 Jan 58*	1
ONLY SIXTEEN	*His Master's Voice*	23	*15 Aug 59*	4
WONDERFUL WORLD	*His Master's Voice*	27	*9 Jul 60*	8
CHAIN GANG	*RCA*	9	*1 Oct 60*	11
CUPID	*RCA*	7	*29 Jul 61*	14
TWISTIN' THE NIGHT AWAY	*RCA Victor*	6	*10 Mar 62*	14
ANOTHER SATURDAY NIGHT	*RCA Victor*	23	*18 May 63*	12
FRANKIE AND JOHNNY	*RCA Victor*	30	*7 Sep 63*	6
WONDERFUL WORLD [RI]	*RCA*	2	*22 Mar 86*	11
Featured in the Levi's Jeans TV commercial.				
ANOTHER SATURDAY NIGHT [RI]	*RCA Victor*	75	*10 May 86*	1
ALBUMS:	**HITS 1**			**WEEKS 27**
THE MAN AND HIS MUSIC	*RCA*	8	*26 Apr 86*	27

COOKIE CREW — UK

SINGLES:	HITS 5			WEEKS 31
ROK DA HOUSE	*Rhythm King*	5	*9 Jan 88*	11
Original release reached No. 79 in 1987.				
Above hit: BEATMASTERS featuring the COOKIE CREW.				
BORN THIS WAY (LET'S DANCE)	*ffrr*	23	*7 Jan 89*	5

GOT TO KEEP ON	*ffrr*	17	*1 Apr 89*	9
COME ON AND GET SOME	*ffrr*	42	*15 Jul 89*	3
SECRETS (OF SUCCESS)	*ffrr*	53	*27 Jul 91*	3
Above hit: COOKIE CREW featuring Danny D.				
ALBUMS:	**HITS 1**			**WEEKS 4**
BORN THIS WAY!	*London*	24	*6 May 89*	4

COOKIES — US

SINGLES:	**HITS 1**			**WEEKS 1**
CHAINS	*London*	50	*12 Jan 63*	1

COOL, the FAB and the GROOVY present Quincy JONES — UK

(See also Quincy Jones.)

SINGLES:	**HITS 1**			**WEEKS 1**
SOUL BOSSA NOVA	*Manifesto*	47	*1 Aug 98*	1
Originally released by Quincy Jones in 1962. Featured in the Nike TV commercial.				

COOL DOWN ZONE — UK

SINGLES:	**HITS 1**			**WEEKS 4**
HEAVEN KNOWS	*10 Records*	52	*30 Jun 90*	4

COOL JACK — Italy

SINGLES:	**HITS 1**			**WEEKS 1**
JUS' COME	*AM:PM*	44	*9 Nov 96*	1

COOL NOTES — UK

SINGLES:	**HITS 6**			**WEEKS 28**
YOU'RE NEVER TOO YOUNG	*Abstract Dance*	42	*18 Aug 84*	5
I FORGOT	*Abstract Dance*	63	*17 Nov 84*	2
SPEND THE NIGHT	*Abstract Dance*	11	*23 Mar 85*	9
IN YOUR CAR	*Abstract Dance*	13	*13 Jul 85*	9
HAVE A GOOD FOREVER . . .	*Abstract Dance*	73	*19 Oct 85*	1
INTO THE MOTION	*Abstract Dance*	66	*17 May 86*	2
ALBUMS:	**HITS 1**			**WEEKS 2**
HAVE A GOOD FOREVER . . .	*Abstract Dance*	66	*9 Nov 85*	2

Rita COOLIDGE — US

(See also Kris Kristofferson and Rita Coolidge.)

SINGLES:	**HITS 4**			**WEEKS 24**
WE'RE ALL ALONE	*A&M*	6	*25 Jun 77*	13
Originally recorded by Boz Scaggs				
(YOUR LOVE HAS LIFTED ME) HIGHER AND HIGHER	*A&M*	49	*15 Oct 77*	1
(YOUR LOVE HAS LIFTED ME) HIGHER AND HIGHER [RE]	*A&M*	48	*29 Oct 77*	1
WORDS	*A&M*	25	*4 Feb 78*	8
ALL TIME HIGH	*A&M*	75	*25 Jun 83*	1
Theme song from the James Bond film 'Octopussy'.				
ALBUMS:	**HITS 3**			**WEEKS 40**
ANYTIME ANYWHERE	*A&M*	6	*6 Aug 77*	28
LOVE ME AGAIN	*A&M*	51	*8 Jul 78*	1
THE VERY BEST OF RITA COOLIDGE	*A&M*	6	*14 Mar 81*	11

COOLIO — US

(See also B Real, Busta Rhymes, Coolio, LL Cool J and Method Man; Quincy Jones.)

SINGLES:	**HITS 9**			**WEEKS 56**
FANTASTIC VOYAGE	*Tommy Boy*	41	*23 Jul 94*	2
Originally recorded by Lakeside.				
I REMEMBER	*Tommy Boy*	73	*15 Oct 94*	1
Samples Float On by the Floaters.				
GANGSTA'S PARADISE	*Tommy Boy*	1	*28 Oct 95*	20
From the film 'Dangerous Minds'. Samples Stevie Wonder's Pastime Paradise.				
Above hit: COOLIO featuring L.V.				
TOO HOT	*Tommy Boy*	9	*20 Jan 96*	6
Kool And The Gang's JT Taylor re-recorded his vocal sample for this hit.				
1, 2, 3, 4 (SUMPIN' NEW)	*Tommy Boy*	13	*6 Apr 96*	7
Samples Wikka Wrap by the Evasions.				
IT'S ALL THE WAY LIVE (NOW)	*Tommy Boy*	34	*17 Aug 96*	2
From the film 'Eddie'. Originally recorded by Lakeside.				
THE WINNER	*Atlantic*	53	*7 Jun 97*	1
From the film 'Space Jam'.				
C U WHEN U GET THERE	*Tommy Boy*	3	*19 Jul 97*	12
From the film 'Nothing To Lose'. Song based on Pacelbel's 'Canon'.				
Above hit: COOLIO featuring 40 THEVZ.				

OOH LA LA *Samples Grace Jones' Pull Up To The Bumper.*	*Tommy Boy*	14	*11 Oct 97*	5
ALBUMS:	**HITS 3**			**WEEKS 27**
IT TAKES A THIEF	*Tommy Boy*	67	*29 Oct 94*	1
GANGSTA'S PARADISE	*Tommy Boy*	18	*18 Nov 95*	24
MY SOUL	*Tommy Boy*	28	*13 Sep 97*	2

COOLY'S HOT BOX - See Roger SANCHEZ

Alice COOPER — US

SINGLES:	**HITS 19**			**WEEKS 104**
SCHOOL'S OUT	*Warner Brothers*	1	*15 Jul 72*	12
ELECTED	*Warner Brothers*	4	*7 Oct 72*	10
HELLO HURRAY	*Warner Brothers*	6	*10 Feb 73*	12
NO MORE MR. NICE GUY	*Warner Brothers*	10	*21 Apr 73*	10
TEENAGE LAMENT '74	*Warner Brothers*	12	*19 Jan 74*	7
(NO MORE) LOVE AT YOUR CONVENIENCE	*Warner Brothers*	44	*21 May 77*	2
HOW YOU GONNA SEE ME NOW	*Warner Brothers*	61	*23 Dec 78*	6
SEVEN AND SEVEN IS (LIVE VERSION)	*Warner Brothers*	62	*6 Mar 82*	3
FOR BRITAIN ONLY / UNDER MY WHEELS (LIVE)	*Warner Brothers*	66	*8 May 82*	2
HE'S BACK (THE MAN BEHIND THE MASK)	*MCA*	61	*18 Oct 86*	2
FREEDOM	*MCA*	50	*9 Apr 88*	3
POISON	*Epic*	2	*29 Jul 89*	11
BED OF NAILS	*Epic*	38	*7 Oct 89*	5
HOUSE OF FIRE	*Epic*	65	*2 Dec 89*	2
HEY STOOPID	*Epic*	21	*22 Jun 91*	6
LOVE'S A LOADED GUN	*Epic*	38	*5 Oct 91*	3
FEED MY FRANKENSTEIN *From the film 'Wayne's World'.*	*Epic*	27	*6 Jun 92*	3
LOST IN AMERICA	*Epic*	22	*28 May 94*	3
IT'S ME	*Epic*	34	*23 Jul 94*	2
ALBUMS:	**HITS 19**			**WEEKS 133**
KILLER	*Warner Brothers*	27	*5 Feb 72*	18
SCHOOL'S OUT	*Warner Brothers*	4	*22 Jul 72*	20
LOVE IT TO DEATH	*Warner Brothers*	28	*9 Sep 72*	7
BILLION DOLLAR BABIES	*Warner Brothers*	1	*24 Mar 73*	23
MUSCLE OF LOVE	*Warner Brothers*	34	*12 Jan 74*	4
WELCOME TO MY NIGHTMARE	*Anchor*	19	*15 Mar 75*	8
ALICE COOPER GOES TO HELL	*Warner Brothers*	23	*24 Jul 76*	7
LACE AND WHISKY	*Warner Brothers*	33	*28 May 77*	3
FROM THE INSIDE	*Warner Brothers*	68	*23 Dec 78*	3
FLUSH THE FASHION	*Warner Brothers*	56	*17 May 80*	3
SPECIAL FORCES	*Warner Brothers*	96	*12 Sep 81*	1
DADA	*Warner Brothers*	93	*12 Nov 83*	1
CONSTRICTOR	*MCA*	41	*1 Nov 86*	2
RAISE YOUR FIST AND YELL	*MCA*	48	*7 Nov 87*	3
TRASH	*Epic*	2	*26 Aug 89*	12
HEY STOOPID	*Epic*	4	*13 Jul 91*	7
THE LAST TEMPTATION	*Epic*	6	*18 Jun 94*	5
BRUTAL PLANET	*Eagle*	38	*24 Jun 00*	1
THE DEFINITIVE ALICE COOPER	*Rhino*	33	*10 Mar 01*	5

Deborah COOPER - See C&C MUSIC FACTORY

Tommy COOPER — UK

SINGLES:	**HITS 1**			**WEEKS 3**
DON'T JUMP OFF THE ROOF DAD	*Palette*	40	*1 Jul 61*	2
DON'T JUMP OFF THE ROOF DAD [RE]	*Palette*	50	*22 Jul 61*	1

COOPER TEMPLE CLAUSE — UK

SINGLES:	**HITS 1**			**WEEKS 1**
LET'S KILL MUSIC	*Morning*	41	*29 Sep 01*	1

Julian COPE — UK

SINGLES:	**HITS 15**			**WEEKS 59**
SUNSHINE PLAYROOM	*Mercury*	64	*19 Nov 83*	1
THE GREATNESS AND PERFECTION OF LOVE	*Mercury*	52	*31 Mar 84*	5
WORLD SHUT YOUR MOUTH	*Island*	19	*27 Sep 86*	8
TRAMPOLENE	*Island*	31	*17 Jan 87*	6
EVE'S VOLCANO (COVERED IN SIN)	*Island*	41	*11 Apr 87*	5
CHARLOTTE ANNE	*Island*	35	*24 Sep 88*	6
5 O'CLOCK WORLD *Originally recorded by the Vogues.*	*Island*	42	*21 Jan 89*	4
CHINA DOLL	*Island*	53	*24 Jun 89*	2
BEAUTIFUL LOVE	*Island*	32	*9 Feb 91*	6
EAST EASY RIDER	*Island*	51	*20 Apr 91*	3

HEAD	*Island*	57	*3 Aug 91*	2
WORLD SHUT YOUR MOUTH [RI]	*Island*	44	*8 Aug 92*	3
FEAR LOVES THIS PLACE	*Island*	42	*17 Oct 92*	2
TRY TRY TRY	*Echo*	24	*12 Aug 95*	3
I COME FROM ANOTHER PLANET, BABY	*Echo*	34	*27 Jul 96*	2
PLANETARY SIT-IN (EVERY GIRL HAS YOUR NAME)	*Echo*	34	*5 Oct 96*	1
ALBUMS:	**HITS 10**			**WEEKS 35**
WORLD SHUT YOUR MOUTH	*Mercury*	40	*3 Mar 84*	4
"FRIED"	*Mercury*	87	*24 Nov 84*	1
SAINT JULIAN	*Island*	11	*14 Mar 87*	10
MY NATION UNDERGROUND	*Island*	42	*29 Oct 88*	2
PEGGY SUICIDE	*Island*	23	*16 Mar 91*	7
FLOORED GENIUS – THE BEST OF JULIAN COPE AND THE TEARDROP EXPLODES	*Island*	22	*15 Aug 92*	3
Includes his solo and group material.				
Above hit: Julian COPE and the TEARDROP EXPLODES.				
JEHOVAHKILL	*Island*	20	*31 Oct 92*	2
AUTOGEDDON	*Echo*	16	*16 Jul 94*	3
JULIAN COPE PRESENTS 20 MOTHERS	*Echo*	20	*9 Sep 95*	2
INTERPRETER	*Echo*	39	*26 Oct 96*	1

Imani COPPOLA — US

SINGLES:	**HITS 1**			**WEEKS 3**
LEGEND OF A COWGIRL	*Columbia*	32	*28 Feb 98*	3
YOU ALL DAT	*Edel*	14	*3 Feb 01*	5
Samples The Lion Sleeps Tonight.				
Above hit: BAHA MEN: Guest vocal Imani COPPOLA.				

Frank CORDELL and his Orchestra — UK

SINGLES:	**HITS 1**			**WEEKS 4**
SADIE'S SHAWL (SANTIE SE KOPDOEK)	*His Master's Voice*	29	*25 Aug 56*	2
THE BLACK BEAR (THE THEME FROM "TUNES OF GLORY")	*His Master's Voice*	44	*18 Feb 61*	2

Louise CORDET — UK

SINGLES:	**HITS 1**			**WEEKS 13**
I'M JUST A BABY	*Decca*	13	*7 Jul 62*	13

CORDUROY — UK

ALBUMS:	**HITS 1**			**WEEKS 1**
OUT OF HERE	*Acid Jazz*	73	*8 Oct 94*	1

Chris CORNELL — US

SINGLES:	**HITS 1**			**WEEKS 1**
CAN'T CHANGE ME	*A&M*	62	*23 Oct 99*	1
ALBUMS:	**HITS 1**			**WEEKS 1**
EUPHORIA MORNING	*A&M*	31	*2 Oct 99*	1

Don CORNELL — US

SINGLES:	**HITS 2**			**WEEKS 23**
HOLD MY HAND	*Vogue*	1	*4 Sep 54*	21
From the film 'Susan Slept Here'.				
STRANGER IN PARADISE	*Vogue Coral*	19	*23 Apr 55*	2
Above hit: Don CORNELL with the Roland SHAW ORCHESTRA.				

Lyn CORNELL — UK

SINGLES:	**HITS 1**			**WEEKS 9**
NEVER ON SUNDAY	*Decca*	30	*22 Oct 60*	9

CORNERSHOP — UK

SINGLES:	**HITS 2**			**WEEKS 16**
BRIMFUL OF ASHA	*Wiiija*	60	*30 Aug 97*	1
BRIMFUL OF ASHA [RI]	*Wiiija*	1	*28 Feb 98*	12
Though the main track is a re-issue, it was the B-side Norman Cook remix that was more popular.				
SLEEP ON THE LEFT SIDE	*Wiiija*	23	*16 May 98*	3
ALBUMS:	**HITS 1**			**WEEKS 15**
WHEN I WAS BORN FOR THE 7TH TIME	*Wiiija*	17	*20 Sep 97*	15

Charlotte CORNWELL – See Julie COVINGTON, Charlotte CORNWELL, Rula LENSKA, Sue JONES-DAVIES

Hugh CORNWELL — UK

SINGLES:	HITS 2			WEEKS 3
FACTS + FIGURES	*Virgin*	61	*24 Jan 87*	2
ANOTHER KIND OF LOVE	*Virgin*	71	*7 May 88*	1
ALBUMS:	**HITS 1**			**WEEKS 1**
WOLF	*Virgin*	98	*18 Jun 88*	1

CORO DE MUNJES DEL MONASTERIO BENEDICTINO DE SANTO DOMINGO DE SILOS — Spain

(Popularly known as the Monks Chorus Silos.)

ALBUMS:	HITS 2			WEEKS 28
CANTO GREGORIANO	*EMI Classics*	7	*5 Mar 94*	25
CANTO NOEL	*EMI Classics*	53	*17 Dec 94*	3

CORONA — Brazil/Italy

SINGLES:	HITS 5			WEEKS 44
THE RHYTHM OF THE NIGHT	*WEA*	2	*10 Sep 94*	14
THE RHYTHM OF THE NIGHT [RE]	*WEA*	55	*31 Dec 94*	4
BABY BABY	*Eternal*	5	*8 Apr 95*	8
TRY ME OUT	*Eternal*	6	*22 Jul 95*	10
I DON'T WANNA BE A STAR	*Eternal*	22	*23 Dec 95*	6
MEGAMIX [M]	*Eternal*	36	*22 Feb 97*	2
Megamix of previous 4 hits.				
ALBUMS:	**HITS 1**			**WEEKS 7**
THE RHYTHM OF THE NIGHT	*Eternal*	18	*20 May 95*	7

CORONA SCHOOL CHILDREN – See Max BYGRAVES; Norman VAUGHAN

CORONATION STREET CAST featuring Bill WADDINGTON (Percy Sugden) / Amanda BARRIE and Johnny BRIGGS (Alma & Mike Baldwin) — UK

SINGLES:	HITS 1			WEEKS 3
THE CORONATION STREET SINGLE: – ALWAYS LOOK ON THE BRIGHT SIDE OF LIFE / SOMETHING STUPID	*EMI Premier*	35	*16 Dec 95*	3

CORONETS — UK

SINGLES:	HITS 2			WEEKS 7
THAT'S HOW A LOVE SONG WAS BORN	*Columbia*	14	*27 Aug 55*	6
Above hit: Ray BURNS with the CORONETS.				
TWENTY TINY FINGERS	*Columbia*	20	*26 Nov 55*	1
Above hit: CORONETS with Eric JUPP and his Orchestra.				

CORRIES — UK

ALBUMS:	HITS 2			WEEKS 5
SCOTTISH LOVE SONGS	*Fontana*	46	*9 May 70*	4
SOUND OF PIBROCH	*Columbia*	39	*16 Sep 72*	1

Briana CORRIGAN — UK

SINGLES:	HITS 1			WEEKS 2
LOVE ME NOW	*East West*	48	*11 May 96*	2

CORROSION OF CONFORMITY — US

ALBUMS:	HITS 1			WEEKS 1
WISEBLOOD	*Columbia*	43	*14 Sep 96*	1

CORRS — Ireland

SINGLES:	HITS 13			WEEKS 92
RUNAWAY	*Atlantic*	49	*17 Feb 96*	2
RUNAWAY [RE]	*Atlantic*	60	*7 Dec 96*	1
LOVE TO LOVE YOU / RUNAWAY [RI]	*Atlantic*	62	*1 Feb 97*	1
Re-issue of Runaway is a slightly longer version than the original chart entry.				
ONLY WHEN I SLEEP	*Atlantic*	58	*25 Oct 97*	1
I NEVER LOVED YOU ANYWAY	*Atlantic*	43	*20 Dec 97*	2
WHAT CAN I DO	*Atlantic*	53	*28 Mar 98*	1
DREAMS	*Atlantic*	6	*16 May 98*	10
WHAT CAN I DO [RM]	*Atlantic*	3	*29 Aug 98*	11
Remixed by Tin Tin Out.				
SO YOUNG	*Atlantic*	6	*28 Nov 98*	13
RUNAWAY [RM]	*Atlantic*	2	*27 Feb 99*	11
Remixed by Tin Tin Out.				
I KNOW MY LOVE	*RCA Victor*	37	*12 Jun 99*	3
Above hit: CHIEFTAINS featuring the CORRS.				
RADIO	*Atlantic*	18	*11 Dec 99*	9

BREATHLESS	*Atlantic*	1	*15 Jul 00*	13
IRRESISTIBLE	*Atlantic*	20	*11 Nov 00*	5
IRRESISTIBLE [RE]	*Atlantic*	60	*13 Jan 01*	2
GIVE ME A REASON	*Atlantic*	27	*28 Apr 01*	2
WOULD YOU BE HAPPIER?	*Atlantic*	14	*10 Nov 01*	5
ALBUMS:	**HITS 5**			**WEEKS 333**
FORGIVEN, NOT FORGOTTEN	*Atlantic*	36	*2 Mar 96*	47
TALK ON CORNERS	*Atlantic*	7	*1 Nov 97*	15
TALK ON CORNERS [RE] *Peak position reached on 27 Jun 98.*	*Atlantic*	1	*21 Mar 98*	127
FORGIVEN, NOT FORGOTTEN [RE]	*Atlantic*	2	*16 Jan 99*	66
UNPLUGGED *Recorded for MTV at Ardmore Studios, Co. Wicklow, Ireland, 5 Oct 99.*	*Atlantic*	7	*27 Nov 99*	26
IN BLUE	*Atlantic*	1	*29 Jul 00*	45
THE BEST OF THE CORRS	*Atlantic*	6	*17 Nov 01*	7

CORTINA — UK

SINGLES:	**HITS 1**			**WEEKS 2**
MUSIC IS MOVING *Original release reached No. 153 in 2000.*	*Nukleuz*	42	*24 Mar 01*	2

Vladimir COSMA — Hungary

SINGLES:	**HITS 1**			**WEEKS 1**
DAVID'S SONG (MAIN THEME FROM "KIDNAPPED") *Theme from the ITV series 'Kidnapped'.* *Above hit: Arranged and conducted by Vladimir COSMA.*	*Decca*	64	*14 Jul 79*	1
ALBUMS:	**HITS 1**			**WEEKS 3**
MISTRAL'S DAUGHTER [OST-TV] *Above hit: Conducted by Vladimir COSMA featuring Nana MOUSKOURI.*	*Carrere*	53	*1 Feb 86*	3

COSMIC BABY — Germany

SINGLES:	**HITS 1**			**WEEKS 1**
LOOPS OF INFINITY	*Logic*	70	*26 Feb 94*	1
ALBUMS:	**HITS 1**			**WEEKS 1**
THINKING ABOUT MYSELF	*Logic*	60	*23 Apr 94*	1

COSMIC GATE — Germany

SINGLES:	**HITS 1**			**WEEKS 7**
FIRE WIRE	*Data*	9	*4 Aug 01*	7

COSMIC ROUGH RIDERS — UK

SINGLES:	**HITS 2**			**WEEKS 2**
REVOLUTION (IN THE SUMMERTIME)	*Poptones*	35	*4 Aug 01*	1
THE PAIN INSIDE	*Poptones*	36	*29 Sep 01*	1

COSMOS — UK

SINGLES:	**HITS 1**			**WEEKS 1**
SUMMER IN SPACE *Vocals by David Laudat.*	*Island Blue*	49	*18 Sep 99*	1

Don COSTA and his Orchestra and Chorus — US

(See also Paul Anka; Tony Bennett; Lloyd Price.)

SINGLES:	**HITS 1**			**WEEKS 10**
NEVER ON SUNDAY *From the film of the same name.*	*London*	27	*15 Oct 60*	9
NEVER ON SUNDAY [RE]	*London*	41	*24 Dec 60*	1

Nikka COSTA — US

SINGLES:	**HITS 1**			**WEEKS 1**
LIKE A FEATHER	*Virgin*	53	*11 Aug 01*	1

Elvis COSTELLO and the ATTRACTIONS — UK

SINGLES:	**HITS 35**			**WEEKS 179**
WATCHING THE DETECTIVES *Above hit: Elvis COSTELLO.*	*Stiff*	15	*5 Nov 77*	11
(I DON'T WANT TO GO TO) CHELSEA	*Radar*	16	*11 Mar 78*	10
PUMP IT UP	*Radar*	24	*13 May 78*	10
RADIO RADIO	*Radar*	29	*28 Oct 78*	7
OLIVER'S ARMY	*Radar*	2	*10 Feb 79*	12
ACCIDENTS WILL HAPPEN	*Radar*	28	*12 May 79*	8

I CAN'T STAND UP FOR FALLING DOWN *Originally recorded by Sam & Dave.*	*F-Beat*	4	*16 Feb 80*	8
HIGH FIDELITY	*F-Beat*	30	*12 Apr 80*	5
NEW AMSTERDAM *Above hit: Elvis COSTELLO.*	*F-Beat*	36	*7 Jun 80*	6
CLUBLAND	*F-Beat*	60	*20 Dec 80*	4
A GOOD YEAR FOR THE ROSES *Originally recorded by George Jones.*	*F-Beat*	6	*3 Oct 81*	11
SWEET DREAMS *Originally recorded by Don Gibson.*	*F-Beat*	42	*12 Dec 81*	8
I'M YOUR TOY *Originally recorded by the Flying Burrito Brothers as Hot Burrito #1.* *Above hit: Elvis COSTELLO and the ATTRACTIONS with the ROYAL PHILHARMONIC ORCHESTRA.*	*F-Beat*	51	*10 Apr 82*	3
YOU LITTLE FOOL	*F-Beat*	52	*19 Jun 82*	3
MAN OUT OF TIME	*F-Beat*	58	*31 Jul 82*	2
FROM HEAD TO TOE	*F-Beat*	43	*25 Sep 82*	4
PARTY PARTY *From the film of the same name. Features Gary Barnacle on tenor and baritone sax & Annie Whitehead on Trombone.* *Above hit: Elvis COSTELLO and the ATTRACTIONS with the ROYAL GUARD HORNS.*	*A&M*	48	*11 Dec 82*	6
PILLS AND SOAP *Above hit: IMPOSTER.*	*IMP*	16	*11 Jun 83*	4
EVERYDAY I WRITE THE BOOK	*F-Beat*	28	*9 Jul 83*	8
LET THEM ALL TALK *Above hit: Elvis COSTELLO and the ATTRACTIONS with the TKO HORNS.*	*F-Beat*	59	*17 Sep 83*	2
PEACE IN OUR TIME *Above hit: IMPOSTER.*	*Imposter*	48	*28 Apr 84*	3
I WANNA BE LOVED / TURNING THE TOWN RED *Turning The Town Red from the Granda TV series 'Scully'.*	*F-Beat*	25	*16 Jun 84*	6
THE ONLY FLAME IN TOWN	*F-Beat*	71	*25 Aug 84*	2
GREEN SHIRT	*F-Beat*	71	*4 May 85*	1
GREEN SHIRT [RE]	*F-Beat*	68	*18 May 85*	1
DON'T LET ME BE MISUNDERSTOOD *Above hit: COSTELLO SHOW featuring the CONFEDERATES.*	*F-Beat*	33	*1 Feb 86*	4
TOKYO STORM WARNING	*IMP*	73	*30 Aug 86*	1
VERONICA *Co-written by Paul McCartney.*	*Warner Brothers*	31	*4 Mar 89*	6
BABY PLAYS AROUND [EP] *Lead track: Baby Plays Around.*	*Warner Brothers*	65	*20 May 89*	1
THE OTHER SIDE OF SUMMER	*Warner Brothers*	43	*4 May 91*	4
SULKY GIRL	*Warner Brothers*	22	*5 Mar 94*	3
13 STEPS LEAD DOWN *Above 5: Elvis COSTELLO.*	*Warner Brothers*	59	*30 Apr 94*	1
LONDON'S BRILLIANT PARADE [EP] *Lead track: London's Brilliant Parade.*	*Warner Brothers*	48	*26 Nov 94*	2
IT'S TIME	*Warner Brothers*	58	*11 May 96*	1
TOLEDO *Above hit: Elvis COSTELLO with Burt BACHARACH.*	*Mercury*	72	*1 May 99*	1
SHE *From the film 'Notting Hill'. Features the London Symphony Orchestra.* *Above hit: Elvis COSTELLO.*	*Mercury*	19	*31 Jul 99*	8
SHE [RE]	*Mercury*	57	*9 Oct 99*	2
ALBUMS:	**HITS 23**			**WEEKS 219**
MY AIM IS TRUE	*Stiff*	14	*6 Aug 77*	12
THIS YEAR'S MODEL *Above 2: Elvis COSTELLO.*	*Radar*	4	*1 Apr 78*	14
ARMED FORCES	*Radar*	2	*20 Jan 79*	28
GET HAPPY!	*F-Beat*	2	*23 Feb 80*	14
TRUST	*F-Beat*	9	*31 Jan 81*	7
ALMOST BLUE	*F-Beat*	7	*31 Oct 81*	18
IMPERIAL BEDROOM	*F-Beat*	6	*10 Jul 82*	12
PUNCH THE CLOCK	*F-Beat*	3	*6 Aug 83*	13
GOODBYE CRUEL WORLD	*F-Beat*	10	*7 Jul 84*	10
THE BEST OF ELVIS COSTELLO - THE MAN	*Telstar*	8	*20 Apr 85*	17
KING OF AMERICA *Above hit: COSTELLO SHOW.*	*F-Beat*	11	*1 Mar 86*	9
BLOOD AND CHOCOLATE	*Imp*	16	*27 Sep 86*	5
SPIKE	*Warner Brothers*	5	*18 Feb 89*	16
GIRLS GIRLS GIRLS *Compilation. Other formats not available on vinyl have different track listing.*	*Demon*	67	*28 Oct 89*	1
MIGHTY LIKE A ROSE *Above 3: Elvis COSTELLO.*	*Warner Brothers*	5	*25 May 91*	6
THE JULIET LETTERS *Above hit: Elvis COSTELLO and the BRODSKY QUARTET.*	*Warner Brothers*	18	*30 Jan 93*	3
BRUTAL YOUTH	*Warner Brothers*	2	*19 Mar 94*	5
THE BEST OF ELVIS COSTELLO - THE MAN [RI]	*Demon*	50	*19 Mar 94*	8
THE VERY BEST OF ELVIS COSTELLO AND THE ATTRACTIONS	*Demon*	57	*12 Nov 94*	2

KOJAK VARIETY	*Warner Brothers*	21	*27 May 95*	2
Title refers to a brand of lager sold in Barbados.				
Above hit: Elvis COSTELLO.				
KING OF AMERICA [RI]	*Demon*	71	*12 Aug 95*	1
Re-issued with additional tracks				
Above hit: COSTELLO SHOW.				
ALL THIS USELESS BEAUTY	*Warner Brothers*	28	*25 May 96*	3
PAINTED FROM MEMORY	*Mercury*	32	*10 Oct 98*	2
Above hit: Elvis COSTELLO with Burt BACHARACH.				
THE VERY BEST OF ELVIS COSTELLO	*Universal Music TV*	4	*14 Aug 99*	10
Above hit: Elvis COSTELLO.				
FOR THE STARS	*Deutsche Grammophon*	67	*31 Mar 01*	1
Above hit: Anne VON OTTER meets Elvis COSTELLO.				

Billy COTTON and His BAND — UK

(See also All Star Hit Parade.)

SINGLES:	HITS 3			WEEKS 25
IN A GOLDEN COACH (THERE'S A HEART OF GOLD) •	*Decca*	3	*2 May 53*	10
Above hit: Billy COTTON and his BAND with Doreen STEPHENS and CHORUS.				
I SAW MOMMY KISSING SANTA CLAUS	*Decca*	11	*19 Dec 53*	3
Above hit: Billy COTTON and his BAND featuring the MILL GIRLS and the BANDITS.				
FRIENDS AND NEIGHBOURS	*Decca*	12	*1 May 54*	1
Above hit: Billy COTTON and his BAND featuring the BANDITS (and re-entry below).				
FRIENDS AND NEIGHBOURS [RE]	*Decca*	3	*15 May 54*	11

Mike COTTON JAZZMEN — UK

SINGLES:	HITS 1			WEEKS 4
SWING THAT HAMMER •	*Columbia*	36	*22 Jun 63*	4

John COUGAR - See John Cougar MELLENCAMP

COUGARS — UK

SINGLES:	HITS 1			WEEKS 8
SATURDAY NIGHT AT THE DUCK POND •	*Parlophone*	33	*2 Mar 63*	8

Phil COULTER — Ireland

ALBUMS:	HITS 2			WEEKS 15
SEA OF TRANQUILITY	*K-Tel Ireland*	46	*13 Oct 84*	14
From 27 Oct 84 it got an official release in the UK.				
PHIL COULTER'S IRELAND	*K-Tel*	86	*18 May 85*	1

COUNCIL COLLECTIVE — UK/US

SINGLES:	HITS 1			WEEKS 6
SOUL DEEP (PART 1)	*Polydor*	24	*22 Dec 84*	6
Charity record with proceeds to striking miners and the widow of taxi driver David Wilkie (killed when a concrete block was dropped on his car).				

COUNTING CROWS — US

SINGLES:	HITS 7			WEEKS 11
MR. JONES	*Geffen*	28	*30 Apr 94*	2
ROUND HERE	*Geffen*	70	*9 Jul 94*	1
RAIN KING	*Geffen*	49	*15 Oct 94*	3
ANGELS OF THE SILENCES	*Geffen*	41	*19 Oct 96*	1
A LONG DECEMBER	*Geffen*	62	*14 Dec 96*	1
DAYLIGHT FADING	*Geffen*	54	*31 May 97*	1
A LONG DECEMBER [RE]	*Geffen*	68	*20 Dec 97*	1
HANGINAROUND	*Geffen*	46	*30 Oct 99*	1
ALBUMS:	**HITS 4**			**WEEKS 49**
AUGUST AND EVERYTHING AFTER	*Geffen*	16	*12 Mar 94*	38
RECOVERING THE SATELLITES	*Geffen*	4	*26 Oct 96*	4
ACROSS A WIRE - LIVE IN NEW YORK	*Geffen*	27	*25 Jul 98*	4
Consists of 2 discs divided between live recordings for MTV and the other of acoustic versions.				
THIS DESERT LIFE	*Geffen*	19	*13 Nov 99*	3

COUNTRYMEN — UK

SINGLES:	HITS 1			WEEKS 2
I KNOW WHERE I'M GOING •	*Piccadilly*	45	*5 May 62*	2

COURSE — Holland

SINGLES:	HITS 3			WEEKS 15
READY OR NOT	*The Brothers*	5	*19 Apr 97*	7
AIN'T NOBODY	*The Brothers*	8	*5 Jul 97*	6
BEST LOVE	*The Brothers*	51	*20 Dec 97*	2

Tina COUSINS — UK

(See also Steps Tina Cousins Cleopatra B*Witched Billie.)

SINGLES:	HITS 5			WEEKS 22
MYSTERIOUS TIMES	*Multiply*	2	*15 Aug 98*	12
Above hit: SASH! featuring Tina COUSINS.				
PRAY	*Jive*	20	*21 Nov 98*	3
KILLIN' TIME	*Jive*	15	*27 Mar 99*	4
FOREVER	*Jive*	45	*10 Jul 99*	2
ANGEL	*Jive*	46	*9 Oct 99*	1
ALBUMS:	**HITS 1**			**WEEKS 1**
KILLING TIME	*Jive*	50	*24 Jul 99*	1

Don COVAY — US

SINGLES:	HITS 1			WEEKS 6
IT'S BETTER TO HAVE (AND DON'T NEED)	*Mercury*	29	*7 Sep 74*	6

Vincent COVELLO - See BT

COVENTRY CITY F.A. CUP SQUAD — UK

SINGLES:	HITS 1			WEEKS 2
GO FOR IT!	*Sky Blue*	61	*23 May 87*	2

COVER GIRLS — US

SINGLES:	HITS 1			WEEKS 4
WISHING ON A STAR	*Epic*	38	*1 Aug 92*	4

David COVERDALE — UK

(See also Coverdale Page; Whitesnake.)

ALBUMS:	HITS 2			WEEKS 2
NORTHWINDS	*Purple*	78	*27 Feb 82*	1
Originally released in 1978.				
INTO THE LIGHT	*EMI*	75	*7 Oct 00*	1

COVERDALE PAGE — UK

(See also David Coverdale; Jimmy Page and Robert Plant; Jimmy Page.)

SINGLES:	HITS 2			WEEKS 3
TAKE ME FOR A LITTLE WHILE	*EMI*	29	*3 Jul 93*	2
TAKE A LOOK AT YOURSELF	*EMI*	43	*23 Oct 93*	1
ALBUMS:	**HITS 1**			**WEEKS 8**
COVERDALE PAGE	*EMI*	4	*27 Mar 93*	8

Julie COVINGTON — UK

(See also Julie Covington, Charlotte Cornwell, Rula Lenska, SueJones-Davies; Various Artists: Studio Cast 'Evita'.)

SINGLES:	HITS 2			WEEKS 29
DON'T CRY FOR ME ARGENTINA	*MCA*	1	*25 Dec 76*	15
From the musical 'Evita'.				
ONLY WOMEN BLEED	*Virgin*	12	*3 Dec 77*	11
Original by Alice Cooper reached No. 12 in the US in 1975.				
DON'T CRY FOR ME ARGENTINA [RE]	*MCA*	63	*15 Jul 78*	3

Julie COVINGTON, Charlotte CORNWELL, Rula LENSKA, Sue JONES-DAVIES — UK

(See also Julie Covington; Various Artists: Television - Soundtracks 'Rock Follies'.)

SINGLES:	HITS 1			WEEKS 6
O.K?	*Polydor*	10	*21 May 77*	6
From the ITV series 'Rock Follies II'.				

COWBOY JUNKIES — US

ALBUMS:	HITS 2			WEEKS 7
THE CAUTION HORSES	*RCA*	33	*24 Mar 90*	4
BLACK EYED MAN	*RCA*	21	*15 Feb 92*	3

COWBOY TIMMY - See MR. HANKY POO

Patrick COWLEY - See SYLVESTER

Carl COX — UK

SINGLES:	HITS 7			WEEKS 19
I WANT YOU (FOREVER)	*Perfecto*	23	*28 Sep 91*	7
DOES IT FEEL GOOD TO YOU	*Perfecto*	35	*8 Aug 92*	3
Above hit: DJ Carl COX.				
THE PLANET OF LOVE	*Perfecto*	44	*6 Nov 93*	2
Above hit: Carl COX CONCEPT.				

TWO PAINTINGS AND A DRUM [EP]	*Edel*	24	*9 Mar 96*	2
Lead track: Phoebus Apollo.				
SENSUAL SOPHIS-TI-CAT / THE PLAYER	*Edel*	25	*8 Jun 96*	2
THE LATIN THEME	*Edel*	52	*12 Dec 98*	1
PHUTURE 2000	*Worldwide Ultimation*	40	*22 May 99*	2
ALBUMS:	**HITS 1**			**WEEKS 4**
AT THE END OF THE CLICHE	*Edel:*	23	*15 Jun 96*	4

Deborah COX — US

SINGLES:	**HITS 4**			**WEEKS 8**
SENTIMENTAL	*Arista*	34	*11 Nov 95*	3
WHO DO U LOVE	*Arista*	31	*24 Feb 96*	3
Backing vocals by Danny Madden.				
IT'S OVER NOW	*Arista*	49	*31 Jul 99*	1
Samples Harold Melvin and the Blue Notes' Bad Luck.				
NOBODY'S SUPPOSED TO BE HERE	*Arista*	55	*9 Oct 99*	1

Michael COX — UK

SINGLES:	**HITS 2**			**WEEKS 15**
ANGELA JONES	*Triumph*	7	*11 Jun 60*	13
Originally recorded by John D.Loudermilk.				
ALONG CAME CAROLINE	*His Master's Voice*	41	*22 Oct 60*	2
Above 2: Michael COX; Charles BLACKWELL'S ORCHESTRA.				

Peter COX — UK

SINGLES:	**HITS 3**			**WEEKS 6**
AIN'T GONNA CRY AGAIN	*Chrysalis*	37	*2 Aug 97*	2
IF YOU WALK AWAY	*Chrysalis*	24	*15 Nov 97*	2
WHAT A FOOL BELIEVES	*Chrysalis*	39	*20 Jun 98*	2
ALBUMS:	**HITS 1**			**WEEKS 1**
PETER COX	*Chrysalis*	64	*29 Nov 97*	1

Graham COXON — UK

ALBUMS:	**HITS 1**			**WEEKS 2**
THE SKY IS TOO HIGH	*Transcopic*	31	*22 Aug 98*	2

CRACKER — US

SINGLES:	**HITS 2**			**WEEKS 9**
LOW	*Virgin*	43	*28 May 94*	4
GET OFF THIS	*Virgin*	41	*23 Jul 94*	3
LOW [RE]	*Virgin*	54	*3 Dec 94*	2
ALBUMS:	**HITS 1**			**WEEKS 2**
KEROSENE HAT	*Virgin*	44	*25 Jun 94*	2

Sarah CRACKNELL — UK

SINGLES:	**HITS 1**			**WEEKS 1**
ANYMORE	*Gut*	39	*14 Sep 96*	1

CRADLE OF FILTH — UK

ALBUMS:	**HITS 3**			**WEEKS 3**
CRUELTY AND THE BEAST	*Music For Nations*	48	*16 May 98*	1
MIDIAN	*Music For Nations*	63	*11 Nov 00*	1
Named after the underworld city in Clive Barker's novel 'Nightbreed'.				
BITTER SUITES TO SUCCUBI	*Snapper Music*	63	*30 Jun 01*	1

Steve CRADOCK – See Liam GALLAGHER and Steve CRADOCK

CRAIG — UK

SINGLES:	**HITS 1**			**WEEKS 6**
AT THIS TIME OF YEAR	*Eternal*	14	*23 Dec 00*	5
Charity record in support of the Downs Syndrome Association.				
AT THIS TIME OF YEAR [RE]	*Eternal*	56	*10 Feb 01*	1

Robbie CRAIG – See ARTFUL DODGER

Floyd CRAMER — US

SINGLES:	**HITS 3**			**WEEKS 24**
ON THE REBOUND	*RCA*	1	*15 Apr 61*	14
SAN ANTONIO ROSE	*RCA*	36	*22 Jul 61*	8
Originally recorded by Bob Wills and the Texas Playboys.				
HOT PEPPER	*RCA*	46	*25 Aug 62*	2

CRAMPS — US

SINGLES:	HITS 2			WEEKS 4
CAN YOUR PUSSY DO THE DOG?	*Big Beat*	68	*9 Nov 85*	1
BIKINI GIRLS WITH MACHINE GUNS	*Enigma*	35	*10 Feb 90*	3
ALBUMS:	**HITS 4**			**WEEKS 13**
OFF THE BONE	*Illegal*	44	*25 Jun 83*	4
SMELL OF FEMALE	*Ace*	74	*26 Nov 83*	2
A DATE WITH ELVIS	*Big Beat*	34	*1 Mar 86*	6
STAY STICK!	*Ensign*	62	*24 Feb 90*	1

CRANBERRIES — Ireland

(See also Jah Wobble's Invaders Of The Heart.)

SINGLES:	HITS 10			WEEKS 50
LINGER	*Island*	74	*27 Feb 93*	1
LINGER [RI]	*Island*	14	*12 Feb 94*	11
DREAMS	*Island*	27	*7 May 94*	5
ZOMBIE	*Island*	14	*1 Oct 94*	6
ODE TO MY FAMILY	*Island*	26	*3 Dec 94*	6
I CAN'T BE WITH YOU	*Island*	23	*11 Mar 95*	5
RIDICULOUS THOUGHTS	*Island*	20	*12 Aug 95*	3
From the film 'Butterfly Kiss'.				
SALVATION	*Island*	13	*20 Apr 96*	5
FREE TO DECIDE	*Island*	33	*13 Jul 96*	3
PROMISES	*Island US*	13	*17 Apr 99*	4
ANIMAL INSTINCT	*Island US*	54	*17 Jul 99*	1
ALBUMS:	**HITS 5**			**WEEKS 189**
EVERYBODY ELSE IS DOING IT, SO WHY CAN'T WE?	*Island*	64	*13 Mar 93*	1
EVERYBODY ELSE IS DOING IT, SO WHY CAN'T WE? [RE]	*Island*	1	*12 Mar 94*	85
NO NEED TO ARGUE	*Island*	2	*15 Oct 94*	78
TO THE FAITHFUL DEPARTED	*Island*	2	*11 May 96*	19
BURY THE HATCHET	*Island US*	7	*1 May 99*	5
WAKE UP AND SMELL THE COFFEE	*Island US*	61	*3 Nov 01*	1

Les CRANE — US

SINGLES:	HITS 1			WEEKS 14
DESIDERATA	*Warner Brothers*	7	*19 Feb 72*	14

Whitfield CRANE – See MOTORHEAD

CRANES — UK

SINGLES:	HITS 2			WEEKS 2
JEWEL	*Dedicated*	29	*25 Sep 93*	1
SHINING ROAD	*Dedicated*	57	*3 Sep 94*	1
ALBUMS:	**HITS 2**			**WEEKS 2**
WINGS OF JOY	*Dedicated*	52	*28 Sep 91*	1
FOREVER	*Dedicated*	40	*8 May 93*	1

CRASH TEST DUMMIES — Canada

SINGLES:	HITS 3			WEEKS 20
MMM MMM MMM MMM	*RCA*	2	*23 Apr 94*	11
AFTERNOONS AND COFFEESPOONS	*RCA*	23	*16 Jul 94*	5
THE BALLAD OF PETER PUMPKINHEAD	*RCA*	30	*15 Apr 95*	4
From the film 'Dumb And Dumber'.				
Above hit: CRASH TEST DUMMIES featuring Ellen REID.				
ALBUMS:	**HITS 1**			**WEEKS 23**
GOD SHUFFLED HIS FEET	*RCA*	2	*14 May 94*	23

CRASS — UK

ALBUMS:	HITS 1			WEEKS 2
CHRIST THE ALBUM	*Crass*	26	*28 Aug 82*	2

Beverley CRAVEN — UK

SINGLES:	HITS 6			WEEKS 33
PROMISE ME	*Epic*	3	*20 Apr 91*	13
HOLDING ON	*Epic*	32	*20 Jul 91*	7
WOMAN TO WOMAN	*Epic*	40	*5 Oct 91*	5
MEMORIES	*Epic*	68	*7 Dec 91*	2
LOVE SCENES	*Epic*	34	*25 Sep 93*	4
MOLLIE'S SONG	*Epic*	61	*20 Nov 93*	2
ALBUMS:	**HITS 3**			**WEEKS 67**
BEVERLEY CRAVEN	*Epic*	3	*2 Mar 91*	52
LOVE SCENES	*Epic*	4	*9 Oct 93*	13
MIXED EMOTIONS	*Epic*	46	*12 Jun 99*	2

Billy CRAWFORD — Philippines

SINGLES:	HITS 1			WEEKS 2
URGENTLY IN LOVE	*V2*	48	*10 Oct 98*	2

Jimmy CRAWFORD — UK

SINGLES:	HITS 2			WEEKS 11
LOVE OR MONEY	*Columbia*	49	*10 Jun 61*	1
I LOVE HOW YOU LOVE ME	*Columbia*	18	*18 Nov 61*	10
Original by the Paris Sisters reached No. 5 in the US in 1961.				

Michael CRAWFORD — UK

(See also Various Artists: Stage Cast - London 'The Phantom Of The Opera'.)

SINGLES:	HITS 2			WEEKS 14
THE MUSIC OF THE NIGHT	*Polydor*	7	*10 Jan 87*	11
[AA] listed with Wishing You Were Somehow Here Again by Sarah Brightman.				
Above hit: Michael CRAWFORD with the ROYAL PHILHARMONIC ORCHESTRA conducted by David CADDICK.				
THE MUSIC OF THE NIGHT [RR]	*Columbia*	54	*15 Jan 94*	3
Above 2 from the musical 'The Phantom Of The Opera'.				
Above hit: Barbra STREISAND (duet with Michael CRAWFORD).				
ALBUMS:	**HITS 7**			**WEEKS 73**
SONGS FROM STAGE AND SCREEN	*Telstar*	12	*28 Nov 87*	13
Above hit: Michael CRAWFORD and the LONDON SYMPHONY ORCHESTRA.				
WITH LOVE	*Telstar*	31	*2 Dec 89*	7
MICHAEL CRAWFORD PERFORMS ANDREW LLOYD WEBBER	*Telstar*	3	*9 Nov 91*	36
Above hit: Michael CRAWFORD and the ROYAL PHILHARMONIC ORCHESTRA.				
A TOUCH OF MUSIC IN THE NIGHT	*Telstar*	12	*13 Nov 93*	11
THE LOVE SONGS ALBUM	*Telstar*	64	*19 Nov 94*	3
ON EAGLE'S WINGS	*Atlantic*	65	*21 Nov 98*	2
THE MOST WONDERFUL TIME OF THE YEAR	*Telstar TV*	69	*25 Dec 99*	1

Randy CRAWFORD — US

(See also Crusaders.)

SINGLES:	HITS 12			WEEKS 75
LAST NIGHT AT DANCELAND	*Warner Brothers*	61	*21 Jun 80*	2
ONE DAY I'LL FLY AWAY	*Warner Brothers*	2	*30 Aug 80*	11
YOU MIGHT NEED SOMEBODY	*Warner Brothers*	11	*30 May 81*	13
Originally recorded by Turley Richards.				
RAINY NIGHT IN GEORGIA	*Warner Brothers*	18	*8 Aug 81*	9
Written by Tony Joe White and originally recorded by Brook Benton.				
SECRET COMBINATION	*Warner Brothers*	48	*31 Oct 81*	3
IMAGINE	*Warner Brothers*	60	*30 Jan 82*	1
Live recording.				
Above hit: Randy CRAWFORD accompanied by YELLOW JACKETS.				
IMAGINE [RE]	*Warner Brothers*	75	*13 Feb 82*	1
ONE HELLO	*Warner Brothers*	48	*5 Jun 82*	4
HE REMINDS ME	*Warner Brothers*	65	*19 Feb 83*	2
NIGHTLINE	*Warner Brothers*	51	*8 Oct 83*	4
ALMAZ	*Warner Brothers*	4	*29 Nov 86*	17
DIAMANTE	*London*	44	*18 Jan 92*	7
Above hit: ZUCCHERO with Randy CRAWFORD.				
GIVE ME THE NIGHT	*WEA*	60	*15 Nov 97*	1
ALBUMS:	**HITS 10**			**WEEKS 155**
NOW WE MAY BEGIN	*Warner Brothers*	10	*28 Jun 80*	16
SECRET COMBINATION	*Warner Brothers*	2	*16 May 81*	60
WINDSONG	*Warner Brothers*	7	*12 Jun 82*	17
NIGHTLINE	*Warner Brothers*	37	*22 Oct 83*	4
MISS RANDY CRAWFORD - THE GREATEST HITS	*K-Tel*	10	*13 Oct 84*	17
ABSTRACT EMOTIONS	*Warner Brothers*	78	*28 Jun 86*	1
ABSTRACT EMOTIONS [RE]	*Warner Brothers*	14	*31 Jan 87*	9
THE LOVE SONGS	*Telstar*	27	*10 Oct 87*	13
RICH AND POOR	*Warner Brothers*	63	*21 Oct 89*	1
THE VERY BEST OF RANDY CRAWFORD	*Dino*	8	*27 Mar 93*	13
LOVE SONGS - THE VERY BEST OF RANDY CRAWFORD	*warner.esp*	22	*12 Feb 00*	4

Robert CRAY BAND — US

SINGLES:	HITS 2			WEEKS 5
RIGHT NEXT DOOR (BECAUSE OF ME)	*Mercury*	50	*20 Jun 87*	4
BABY LEE	*Silvertone*	65	*20 Apr 96*	1
Featured in a TV commercial for Lee Jeans.				
Above hit: John Lee HOOKER with Robert CRAY.				
ALBUMS:	**HITS 7**			**WEEKS 53**
FALSE ACCUSATIONS	*Demon*	68	*12 Oct 85*	1
STRONG PERSUADER	*Mercury*	41	*15 Nov 86*	11

STRONG PERSUADER [RE]	*Mercury*	34	*13 Jun 87*	17
DON'T BE AFRAID OF THE DARK	*Mercury*	13	*3 Sep 88*	12
MIDNIGHT STROLL	*Mercury*	19	*29 Sep 90*	7
Above hit: Robert CRAY BAND with the MEMPHIS HORNS.				
I WAS WARNED	*Mercury*	29	*12 Sep 92*	3
Above hit: Robert CRAY.				
SHAME AND SIN	*Mercury*	48	*16 Oct 93*	1
SOME RAINY MORNING	*Mercury*	63	*20 May 95*	1
Above hit: Robert CRAY.				

CRAZY ELEPHANT — US

SINGLES:	HITS 1			WEEKS 13
GIMME GIMME GOOD LOVIN'	*Major Minor*	12	*24 May 69*	13

CRAZY HORSE – See Ian McNABB; Neil YOUNG

CRAZY TOWN — US

SINGLES:	HITS 2			WEEKS 18
BUTTERFLY	*Columbia*	3	*7 Apr 01*	13
Samples Red Hot Chili Peppers' Pretty Little Ditty.				
REVOLVING DOOR	*Columbia*	23	*11 Aug 01*	5
ALBUMS:	**HITS 1**			**WEEKS 9**
THE GIFT OF GAME	*Columbia*	15	*21 Apr 01*	9

CRAZY WORLD OF ARTHUR BROWN — UK

SINGLES:	HITS 1			WEEKS 14
FIRE!	*Track*	1	*29 Jun 68*	14
ALBUMS:	**HITS 1**			**WEEKS 16**
THE CRAZY WORLD OF ARTHUR BROWN	*Track*	2	*6 Jul 68*	16

CRAZYHEAD — UK

(See also Various Artists (EPs) 'The Food Christmas EP 1989'.)

SINGLES:	HITS 2			WEEKS 4
TIME HAS TAKEN IT'S TOLL ON YOU	*Food*	65	*16 Jul 88*	2
HAVE LOVE, WILL TRAVEL [EP]	*Food*	68	*25 Feb 89*	2
Lead track: Have Love, Will Travel.				

CREAM — UK

SINGLES:	HITS 7			WEEKS 59
WRAPPING PAPER	*Reaction*	34	*22 Oct 66*	6
I FEEL FREE	*Reaction*	11	*17 Dec 66*	12
STRANGE BREW	*Reaction*	17	*10 Jun 67*	9
ANYONE FOR TENNIS (THE SAVAGE SEVEN THEME)	*Polydor*	40	*8 Jun 68*	3
SUNSHINE OF YOUR LOVE	*Polydor*	25	*12 Oct 68*	7
WHITE ROOM	*Polydor*	28	*18 Jan 69*	8
BADGE	*Polydor*	18	*12 Apr 69*	10
BADGE [RI]	*Polydor*	42	*28 Oct 72*	4
ALBUMS:	**HITS 9**			**WEEKS 291**
FRESH CREAM	*Reaction*	6	*24 Dec 66*	19
DISRAELI GEARS	*Reaction*	5	*18 Nov 67*	42
WHEELS OF FIRE (SINGLE: IN THE STUDIO)	*Polydor*	7	*17 Aug 68*	13
WHEELS OF FIRE (DOUBLE: LIVE AND STUDIO)	*Polydor*	3	*17 Aug 68*	26
Live recordings from the Fillmore West in San Francisco.				
GOODBYE	*Polydor*	1	*15 Mar 69*	28
THE BEST OF CREAM	*Polydor*	6	*8 Nov 69*	34
LIVE CREAM	*Polydor*	4	*4 Jul 70*	15
LIVE CREAM VOLUME 2	*Polydor*	15	*24 Jun 72*	5
THE CREAM OF ERIC CLAPTON	*Polydor*	3	*26 Sep 87*	98
THE CREAM OF ERIC CLAPTON [RE-1ST] / THE BEST OF ERIC CLAPTON	*Polydor*	25	*10 Jul 93*	6
The re-package The Best Of Eric Clapton listed from 17 Jul 93.				
THE CREAM OF ERIC CLAPTON [RE-2ND]	*Polydor*	52	*18 Apr 98*	5
Re-released.				
Above hit: Eric CLAPTON and CREAM.				

CREATION — UK

SINGLES:	HITS 2			WEEKS 3
MAKING TIME	*Planet*	49	*9 Jul 66*	1
PAINTER MAN	*Planet*	36	*5 Nov 66*	2

CREATURES — UK

SINGLES:	HITS 5			WEEKS 27
MAD EYED SCREAMER	*Polydor*	24	*3 Oct 81*	7
Sleeve gives title as an EP: Wild Things.				
MISS THE GIRL	*Wonderland*	21	*23 Apr 83*	7

IGHT NOW	*Wonderland*	14	*16 Jul 83*	10
)riginally recorded by Mel Torme.				
TANDING THERE	*Wonderland*	53	*14 Oct 89*	2
AY	*Siouxs*	72	*27 Mar 99*	1
LBUMS:	**HITS 1**			**WEEKS 9**
EAST	*Wonderland*	17	*28 May 83*	9

CREDIT TO THE NATION — UK

INGLES:	**HITS 6**			**WEEKS 11**
ALL IT WHAT YOU WANT	*One Little Indian*	57	*22 May 93*	3
NOUGH IS ENOUGH	*One Little Indian*	56	*18 Sep 93*	2
Above hit: CHUMBAWAMBA and CREDIT TO THE NATION.				
TEENAGE SENSATION	*One Little Indian*	24	*12 Mar 94*	3
OWING THE SEEDS OF HATRED	*One Little Indian*	72	*14 May 94*	1
IAR LIAR	*One Little Indian*	60	*22 Jul 95*	1
ACKY LOVE SONG	*Chrysalis*	60	*12 Sep 98*	1
amples Radiohead's High And Dry.				
LBUMS:	**HITS 1**			**WEEKS 3**
AKE DIS	*One Little Indian*	20	*9 Apr 94*	3

CREED — US

SINGLES:	**HITS 2**			**WEEKS 7**
HIGHER	*Epic*	47	*15 Jan 00*	1
WITH ARMS WIDE OPEN	*Epic*	13	*20 Jan 01*	5
HIGHER [RI]	*Epic*	64	*29 Sep 01*	1
ALBUMS:	**HITS 2**			**WEEKS 6**
HUMAN CLAY	*Epic*	29	*3 Feb 00*	4
WEATHERED	*Epic*	48	*1 Dec 01*	2

CREEDENCE CLEARWATER REVIVAL — UK

SINGLES:	**HITS 9**			**WEEKS 94**
PROUD MARY •	*Liberty*	8	*31 May 69*	13
BAD MOON RISING •	*Liberty*	1	*16 Aug 69*	15
GREEN RIVER	*Liberty*	19	*15 Nov 69*	11
DOWN ON THE CORNER •	*Liberty*	31	*14 Feb 70*	6
TRAVELIN' BAND	*Liberty*	8	*4 Apr 70*	12
UP AROUND THE BEND	*Liberty*	3	*20 Jun 70*	12
TRAVELIN' BAND [RE]	*Liberty*	46	*4 Jul 70*	1
LONG AS I CAN SEE THE LIGHT	*Liberty*	20	*5 Sep 70*	9
HAVE YOU EVER SEEN THE RAIN •	*Liberty*	36	*20 Mar 71*	6
SWEET HITCH-HIKER	*United Artists*	36	*24 Jul 71*	8
BAD MOON RISING [RI]	*Epic*	71	*2 May 92*	1
ALBUMS:	**HITS 7**			**WEEKS 65**
GREEN RIVER	*Liberty*	20	*24 Jan 70*	6
WILLY AND THE POOR BOYS	*Liberty*	10	*28 Mar 70*	24
BAYOU COUNTRY	*Liberty*	62	*2 May 70*	1
COSMO'S FACTORY	*Liberty*	1	*12 Sep 70*	15
PENDULUM	*Liberty*	23	*23 Jan 71*	12
GREATEST HITS	*Fantasy*	35	*30 Jun 79*	5
THE CREEDENCE COLLECTION	*Impression*	68	*19 Oct 85*	2

Kid CREOLE and the COCONUTS — US

(See also Coconuts.)

SINGLES:	**HITS 8**			**WEEKS 58**
ME NO POP I	*Ze*	32	*13 Jun 81*	7
Above hit: Kid CREOLE and the COCONUTS present Coati MUNDI.				
I'M A WONDERFUL THING, BABY	*Ze*	4	*15 May 82*	11
STOOL PIGEON	*Ze*	7	*24 Jul 82*	9
ANNIE, I'M NOT YOUR DADDY	*Ze*	2	*9 Oct 82*	8
DEAR ADDY	*Ze*	29	*11 Dec 82*	7
Sleeve gives title as an EP: Christmas In B'Dilli Bay.				
THERE'S SOMETHING WRONG IN PARADISE	*Island*	35	*10 Sep 83*	5
THE LIFEBOAT PARTY	*Ze*	49	*19 Nov 83*	4
THE SEX OF IT	*CBS*	29	*14 Apr 90*	5
I'M A WONDERFUL THING, BABY [RM]	*Island*	60	*10 Apr 93*	2
Remixed by Brothers In Rhythm.				
ALBUMS:	**HITS 4**			**WEEKS 54**
TROPICAL GANGSTERS	*Ze*	3	*22 May 82*	40
FRESH FRUIT IN FOREIGN PLACES	*Ze*	99	*26 Jun 82*	1
DOPPELGANGER	*Island*	21	*17 Sep 83*	6
CRE-OLE (BEST OF KID CREOLE AND COCONUTS)	*Island*	21	*15 Sep 84*	7

CRESCENDO — UK/US

SINGLES:	HITS 1			WEEKS
ARE YOU OUT THERE	*ffrr*	20	*23 Dec 95*	

CRESTERS – See Mike SAGAR and CRESTERS

CREW-CUTS — Canada

SINGLES:	HITS 2			WEEKS 2
SH-BOOM (LIFE COULD BE A DREAM)	*Mercury*	12	*2 Oct 54*	
EARTH ANGEL	*Mercury*	4	*16 Apr 55*	2

Originally recorded by the Penguins.
Above hit: CREW-CUTS with David CARROLL and his Orchestra.

Bernard CRIBBINS — UK

(See also Howard Blake conducting the Sinfonia of London, Narration: Bernard Cribbins.)

SINGLES:	HITS 3			WEEKS 29
THE HOLE IN THE GROUND	*Parlophone*	9	*17 Feb 62*	13
RIGHT, SAID FRED	*Parlophone*	10	*7 Jul 62*	10
GOSSIP CALYPSO	*Parlophone*	25	*15 Dec 62*	6

CRICKETS — US

(See also Buddy Holly; Bobby Vee and the Crickets.)

SINGLES:	HITS 12			WEEKS 97
THAT'LL BE THE DAY	*Vogue Coral*	1	*28 Sep 57*	14
OH, BOY	*Coral*	3	*28 Dec 57*	15
THAT'LL BE THE DAY [RE]	*Vogue Coral*	29	*11 Jan 58*	1
MAYBE BABY	*Coral*	4	*15 Mar 58*	10
THINK IT OVER	*Coral*	11	*26 Jul 58*	7
LOVE'S MADE A FOOL OF YOU	*Coral*	26	*25 Apr 59*	1
LOVE'S MADE A FOOL OF YOU [RE]	*Coral*	30	*9 May 59*	1
WHEN YOU ASK ABOUT LOVE	*Coral*	27	*16 Jan 60*	1
MORE THAN I CAN SAY	*Coral*	42	*14 May 60*	1
BABY MY HEART	*Coral*	33	*28 May 60*	4
Above 2 entries were separate sides of the same release, each had its own chart run.				
DON'T EVER CHANGE	*Liberty*	5	*23 Jun 62*	13
MY LITTLE GIRL	*Liberty*	17	*26 Jan 63*	9
DON'T TRY TO CHANGE ME	*Liberty*	37	*8 Jun 63*	4
YOU'VE GOT LOVE	*Coral*	40	*16 May 64*	6
Above hit: Buddy HOLLY and the CRICKETS.				
(THEY CALL HER) LA BAMBA	*Liberty*	21	*4 Jul 64*	10

EPS:	HITS 2			WEEKS 6
FOUR MORE	*Coral*	7	*18 Jun 60*	5
IT'S SO EASY	*Coral*	18	*20 Jan 62*	1

ALBUMS:	HITS 1			WEEKS 7
IN STYLE WITH THE CRICKETS	*Coral*	13	*25 Mar 61*	7

CRIMINAL ELEMENT ORCHESTRA – See Wally JUMP JR. and the CRIMINAL ELEMENT

CRISPY and COMPANY — US

SINGLES:	HITS 2			WEEKS 11
BRAZIL	*Creole*	26	*16 Aug 75*	5
Originally recorded by Eddy Duchin in 1942.				
GET IT TOGETHER	*Creole*	21	*27 Dec 75*	6
Above hit: CRISPY and CO.				

CRITTERS — US

SINGLES:	HITS 1			WEEKS 5
YOUNGER GIRL	*London*	38	*2 Jul 66*	5

Originally recorded by Lovin' Spoonful.

Tony CROMBIE and his ROCKETS — UK

(See also Ray Ellington with Tony Crombie, his Orchestra and Chorus.)

SINGLES:	HITS 1			WEEKS 2
TEACH YOU TO ROCK / SHORT'NIN' BREAD ROCK	*Columbia*	25	*20 Oct 56*	2

Bing CROSBY — US

(See also Various Artists: Films – Original Soundtracks 'High Society'.)

SINGLES:	HITS 12			WEEKS 97
THE ISLE OF INNISFREE	*Brunswick*	3	*15 Nov 52*	12
Above hit: Bing CROSBY with John Scott TROTTER and his Orchestra.				
ZING A LITTLE ZONG	*Brunswick*	10	*6 Dec 52*	2
From the film 'Just For You'.				
Above hit: Bing CROSBY and Jane WYMAN with Jud CONLON'S RHYTHMAIRES and ORCHESTRA.				

SILENT NIGHT, HOLY NIGHT	*Brunswick*	8	*20 Dec 52*	2
Above hit: Bing CROSBY; vocal with the Max TERR CHOIR and John Scott TROTTER and his Orchestra.				
CHANGING PARTNERS	*Brunswick*	10	*20 Mar 54*	1
Above hit: Bing CROSBY with Jud CONLON'S RHYTHMAIRES.				
CHANGING PARTNERS [RE-1ST]	*Brunswick*	9	*3 Apr 54*	1
CHANGING PARTNERS [RE-2ND]	*Brunswick*	11	*24 Apr 54*	1
COUNT YOUR BLESSINGS INSTEAD OF SHEEP	*Brunswick*	18	*8 Jan 55*	1
COUNT YOUR BLESSINGS INSTEAD OF SHEEP [RE]	*Brunswick*	11	*22 Jan 55*	2
STRANGER IN PARADISE	*Brunswick*	17	*30 Apr 55*	2
IN A LITTLE SPANISH TOWN ('TWAS ON A NIGHT LIKE THIS)	*Brunswick*	22	*28 Apr 56*	3
Originally recorded by Paul Whiteman in 1927.				
Above hit: Bing CROSBY with the Buddy COLE TRIO.				
TRUE LOVE	*Capitol*	4	*24 Nov 56*	27
From the film 'High Society'.				
Above hit: Bing CROSBY and Grace KELLY.				
AROUND THE WORLD	*Brunswick*	5	*25 May 57*	15
From the film 'Around The World In Eighty Days'.				
THAT'S WHAT LIFE IS ALL ABOUT	*United Artists*	41	*9 Aug 75*	4
Above hit: Bing CROSBY with the Peter MOORE ORCHESTRA.				
WHITE CHRISTMAS	*MCA*	5	*3 Dec 77*	7
Originally released in 1942. It was the best selling single in the world until the release of Elton John's 'Candle In The Wind' in 1997.				
PEACE ON EARTH / LITTLE DRUMMER BOY [M]	*RCA*	3	*27 Nov 82*	8
Recorded in 1977 on Bing Crosby's Christmas TV show.				
Above hit: David BOWIE and Bing CROSBY.				
TRUE LOVE [RI]	*Capitol*	70	*17 Dec 83*	3
Above hit: Bing CROSBY and Grace KELLY.				
WHITE CHRISTMAS [RI-1ST]	*MCA*	69	*21 Dec 85*	2
WHITE CHRISTMAS [RE-2ND]	*MCA*	29	*19 Dec 98*	4
EPS:	**HITS 1**			**WEEKS 6**
MERRY CHRISTMAS, PART 1	*Columbia*	9	*3 Dec 60*	6
ALBUMS:	**HITS 9**			**WEEKS 45**
JOIN BING AND SING ALONG	*Warner Brothers*	7	*8 Oct 60*	11
WHITE CHRISTMAS	*MCA*	45	*21 Dec 74*	3
THAT'S WHAT LIFE IS ALL ABOUT	*United Artists*	28	*20 Sep 75*	6
LIVE AT THE LONDON PALLADIUM	*K-Tel*	9	*5 Nov 77*	2
Live recordings from the theatre in London.				
THE BEST OF BING	*MCA*	41	*5 Nov 77*	7
SEASONS	*Polydor*	25	*17 Dec 77*	7
SONGS OF A LIFETIME	*Philips*	29	*5 May 79*	3
CHRISTMAS WITH BING CROSBY	*Telstar*	66	*14 Dec 91*	3
THE BEST OF BING CROSBY	*MCA*	59	*23 Nov 96*	3

David CROSBY — US

(See also Crosby, Stills, Nash and Young.)

SINGLES:	**HITS 1**			**WEEKS 3**
HERO	*Atlantic*	56	*15 May 93*	3
Above hit: David CROSBY featuring Phil COLLINS.				
ALBUMS:	**HITS 1**			**WEEKS 7**
IF ONLY I COULD REMEMBER MY NAME	*Atlantic*	12	*24 Apr 71*	7

CROSBY, STILLS, NASH and YOUNG — US/UK

(See also David Crosby; Graham Nash and David Crosby; Graham Nash; Steven Stills; Stephen Stills' Manassas; Stills-Young Band, Neil Young.)

SINGLES:	**HITS 2**			**WEEKS 12**
MARRAKESH EXPRESS	*Atlantic*	17	*16 Aug 69*	9
Above hit: CROSBY, STILLS and NASH.				
AMERICAN DREAM	*Atlantic*	55	*21 Jan 89*	3
ALBUMS:	**HITS 6**			**WEEKS 94**
CROSBY, STILLS AND NASH	*Atlantic*	25	*23 Aug 69*	5
Above hit: CROSBY, STILLS and NASH.				
DEJA VU	*Atlantic*	5	*30 May 70*	61
FOUR-WAY STREET	*Atlantic*	5	*22 May 71*	12
SO FAR	*Atlantic*	25	*21 Sep 74*	6
CSN	*Atlantic*	23	*9 Jul 77*	9
Above hit: CROSBY, STILLS and NASH.				
LOOKING FORWARD	*Reprise*	54	*6 Nov 99*	1

CROSS — UK/US

SINGLES:	**HITS 1**			**WEEKS 1**
COWBOYS AND INDIANS	*Virgin*	74	*17 Oct 87*	1
ALBUMS:	**HITS 1**			**WEEKS 2**
SHOVE IT	*Virgin*	58	*6 Feb 88*	2

Christopher CROSS — US

SINGLES:	HITS 4			WEEKS 27
RIDE LIKE THE WIND	*Warner Brothers*	69	*19 Apr 80*	1
SAILING	*Warner Brothers*	48	*14 Feb 81*	6
ARTHUR'S THEME (BEST THAT YOU CAN DO) *From the film 'Arthur'.*	*Warner Brothers*	56	*17 Oct 81*	4
ARTHUR'S THEME (BEST THAT YOU CAN DO) [RE]	*Warner Brothers*	7	*9 Jan 82*	11
ALL RIGHT	*Warner Brothers*	51	*5 Feb 83*	5
ALBUMS:	**HITS 2**			**WEEKS 93**
CHRISTOPHER CROSS	*Warner Brothers*	14	*21 Feb 81*	77
ANOTHER PAGE	*Warner Brothers*	4	*19 Feb 83*	16

Lynn CROUCH - See QWILO and FELIX DA HOUSECAT featuring Lynn CROUCH

CROW — Germany

SINGLES:	HITS 1			WEEKS 1
WHAT YA LOOKIN' AT?	*Tidy Trax*	60	*19 May 01*	1

Sheryl CROW — US

SINGLES:	HITS 16			WEEKS 77
LEAVING LAS VEGAS	*A&M*	66	*18 Jun 94*	1
ALL I WANNA DO	*A&M*	4	*5 Nov 94*	13
STRONG ENOUGH *From the film 'Kalifornia'.*	*A&M*	33	*11 Feb 95*	4
CAN'T CRY ANYMORE	*A&M*	33	*27 May 95*	3
RUN, BABY, RUN *Originally reached No. 92 in 1994.*	*A&M*	24	*29 Jul 95*	4
WHAT I CAN DO FOR YOU	*A&M*	43	*11 Nov 95*	1
IF IT MAKES YOU HAPPY	*A&M*	9	*21 Sep 96*	6
EVERYDAY IS A WINDING ROAD	*A&M*	12	*30 Nov 96*	6
HARD TO MAKE A STAND	*A&M*	22	*29 Mar 97*	3
A CHANGE WOULD DO YOU GOOD	*A&M*	8	*12 Jul 97*	5
HOME	*A&M*	25	*18 Oct 97*	2
TOMORROW NEVER DIES *From the James Bond film of the same name.*	*A&M*	12	*13 Dec 97*	9
MY FAVORITE MISTAKE	*A&M*	9	*12 Sep 98*	6
THERE GOES THE NEIGHBORHOOD	*A&M*	19	*5 Dec 98*	7
ANYTHING BUT DOWN	*A&M*	19	*6 Mar 99*	4
SWEET CHILD O' MINE *From the film 'Big Daddy'.*	*Columbia*	30	*11 Sep 99*	3
ALBUMS:	**HITS 3**			**WEEKS 157**
TUESDAY NIGHT MUSIC CLUB	*A&M*	68	*12 Feb 94*	1
TUESDAY NIGHT MUSIC CLUB [RE] *Peak position reached on 3 June 95.*	*A&M*	8	*26 Nov 94*	54
SHERYL CROW	*A&M*	5	*12 Oct 96*	70
THE GLOBE SESSIONS	*A&M*	2	*3 Oct 98*	32

CROWD — Multi-National

SINGLES:	HITS 1			WEEKS 11
YOU'LL NEVER WALK ALONE	*Spartan*	1	*1 Jun 85*	11

CROWDED HOUSE — Australia/New Zealand/US

SINGLES:	HITS 13			WEEKS 64
DON'T DREAM IT'S OVER	*Capitol*	27	*6 Jun 87*	8
CHOCOLATE CAKE	*Capitol*	69	*22 Jun 91*	2
FALL AT YOUR FEET	*Capitol*	17	*2 Nov 91*	7
WEATHER WITH YOU	*Capitol*	7	*29 Feb 92*	9
FOUR SEASONS IN ONE DAY	*Capitol*	26	*20 Jun 92*	5
IT'S ONLY NATURAL	*Capitol*	24	*26 Sep 92*	4
DISTANT SUN	*Capitol*	19	*2 Oct 93*	6
NAILS IN MY FEET	*Capitol*	22	*20 Nov 93*	4
LOCKED OUT	*Capitol*	12	*19 Feb 94*	4
FINGERS OF LOVE	*Capitol*	25	*11 Jun 94*	3
PINEAPPLE HEAD	*Capitol*	27	*24 Sep 94*	3
INSTINCT	*Capitol*	12	*22 Jun 96*	4
NOT THE GIRL YOU THINK YOU ARE	*Capitol*	20	*17 Aug 96*	3
DON'T DREAM IT'S OVER [RI]	*Capitol*	25	*9 Nov 96*	2
ALBUMS:	**HITS 4**			**WEEKS 186**
WOODFACE	*Capitol*	34	*13 Jul 91*	4
WOODFACE [RE]	*Capitol*	6	*29 Feb 92*	82
TOGETHER ALONE	*Capitol*	4	*23 Oct 93*	32
RECURRING DREAM - THE VERY BEST OF CROWDED HOUSE *Includes re-entries through to 2001.*	*Capitol*	1	*6 Jul 96*	66
AFTERGLOW *Compilation of B-sides and rarities.*	*Capitol*	18	*19 Feb 00*	2

CROWN HEIGHTS AFFAIR — US

SINGLES:	HITS 5			WEEKS 34
GALAXY OF LOVE	*Mercury*	24	*19 Aug 78*	10
I'M GONNA LOVE YOU FOREVER	*Mercury*	47	*11 Nov 78*	4
DANCE LADY DANCE	*Mercury*	44	*14 Apr 79*	4
YOU GAVE ME LOVE	*De-Lite*	10	*3 May 80*	12
YOU'VE BEEN GONE	*De-Lite*	44	*9 Aug 80*	4
ALBUMS:	**HITS 1**			**WEEKS 3**
DREAM WORLD	*Philips*	40	*23 Sep 78*	3

Julee CRUISE — US

(See also Angelo Badalamenti with Julee Cruise and Various Artists.)

SINGLES:	HITS 3			WEEKS 14
FALLING	*Warner Brothers*	7	*10 Nov 90*	11
From the TV series 'Twin Peaks'.				
ROCKIN' BACK INSIDE MY HEART	*Warner Brothers*	66	*2 Mar 91*	2
IF I SURVIVE	*Distinct'ive*	52	*11 Sep 99*	1
Above hit: HYBRID featuring Julee CRUISE.				

CRUISERS – See Dave BERRY.

CRUSADERS — US

SINGLES:	HITS 3			WEEKS 16
STREET LIFE	*MCA*	5	*18 Aug 79*	11
Vocals by Randy Crawford.				
I'M SO GLAD I'M STANDING HERE TODAY	*MCA*	61	*26 Sep 81*	3
Above hit: CRUSADERS, featured vocalist Joe COCKER.				
NIGHT LADIES	*MCA*	55	*7 Apr 84*	2
ALBUMS:	**HITS 4**			**WEEKS 30**
STREET LIFE	*MCA*	10	*21 Jul 79*	16
RHAPSODY AND BLUE	*MCA*	40	*19 Jul 80*	5
STANDING TALL	*MCA*	47	*12 Sep 81*	5
GHETTO BLASTER	*MCA*	46	*7 Apr 84*	4

CRUSH — UK

SINGLES:	HITS 2			WEEKS 3
JELLYHEAD	*Telstar*	50	*24 Feb 96*	2
LUV'D UP	*Telstar*	45	*3 Aug 96*	1

Bobby CRUSH — UK

SINGLES:	HITS 1			WEEKS 4
BORSALINO	*Philips*	37	*4 Nov 72*	4
ALBUMS:	**HITS 2**			**WEEKS 12**
BOBBY CRUSH	*Philips*	15	*25 Nov 72*	7
THE BOBBY CRUSH INCREDIBLE DOUBLE DECKER PARTY 101 GREAT SONGS	*Warwick*	53	*18 Dec 82*	5

CRW — Italy

SINGLES:	HITS 2			WEEKS 6
I FEEL LOVE	*VC Recordings*	15	*26 Feb 00*	4
Original release reached No. 88 in 1999. Featured in the film 'Keven & Perry Go Large'.				
LOVIN'	*VC Recordings*	49	*25 Nov 00*	2

CRY BEFORE DAWN — Ireland

SINGLES:	HITS 1			WEEKS 2
WITNESS FOR THE WORLD	*Epic*	67	*17 Jun 89*	2

CRY FREEDOM (solo voice: Thuli DUMAKUDE) / CRY FREEDOM (solo voices: George FENTON, Jonas GWANGWA) — UK/South Africa

SINGLES:	HITS 1			WEEKS 1
THE FUNERAL (SEPTEMBER 25, 1977) / CRY FREEDOM	*MCA*	75	*2 Jan 88*	1
From the film 'Cry Freedom'.				

CRY OF LOVE — US

SINGLES:	HITS 1			WEEKS 1
BAD THING	*Columbia*	60	*15 Jan 94*	1

CRY SISCO! — UK

SINGLES:	HITS 1			WEEKS 9
AFRO DIZZI ACT	*Escape*	42	*2 Sep 89*	8
AFRO DIZZI ACT [RE]	*Escape*	70	*20 Jan 90*	1

CRYIN' SHAMES — UK

SINGLES:	HITS 1			WEEKS 7
PLEASE STAY *Originally recorded by Drifters.*	*Decca*	26	*2 Apr 66*	7

CRYSTAL METHOD — US

SINGLES:	HITS 3			WEEKS 4
(CAN'T YOU) TRIP LIKE I DO *From the film 'Spawn'.* *Above hit: FILTER and the CRYSTAL METHOD.*	*Epic*	39	*11 Oct 97*	2
KEEP HOPE ALIVE *Title inspired by Jesse Jackson's speech at the 1992 Democratic party convention.*	*Sony S2*	71	*7 Mar 98*	1
COMIN' BACK	*Sony S2*	73	*8 Aug 98*	1

CRYSTAL PALACE FC 1990 FA CUP FINAL SQUAD featuring the "FAB FOUR" — UK

SINGLES:	HITS 1			WEEKS 2
GLAD ALL OVER / WHERE EAGLES FLY	*Parkfield*	50	*12 May 90*	2

CRYSTALS — US

SINGLES:	HITS 4			WEEKS 54
HE'S A REBEL *Originally recorded by Vicki Carr.*	*London*	19	*24 Nov 62*	13
DA DOO RON RON	*London*	5	*22 Jun 63*	16
THEN HE KISSED ME	*London*	2	*21 Sep 63*	14
I WONDER	*London*	36	*7 Mar 64*	3
DA DOO RON RON [RI]	*Warner Spector*	15	*19 Oct 74*	8
EPS:	**HITS 1**			**WEEKS 1**
DA DOO RON RON	*London*	18	*1 Feb 64*	1

CSILLA — Hungary

SINGLES:	HITS 1			WEEKS 1
MAN IN THE MOON	*Worx*	69	*13 Jul 96*	1

CUBAN BOYS — UK

SINGLES:	HITS 1			WEEKS 9
COGNOSCENTI VS INTELLIGENTSIA *Samples the Hamsterdance website and Roger Miller's Whistle Stop.*	*EMI*	4	*25 Dec 99*	7
COGNOSCENTI VS INTELLIGENTSIA [RE]	*EMI*	58	*19 Feb 00*	2

CUBIC 22 — Belgium

SINGLES:	HITS 1			WEEKS 7
NIGHT IN MOTION	*XL Recordings*	15	*22 Jun 91*	7

CUD — UK

SINGLES:	HITS 8			WEEKS 16
OH NO WON'T DO [EP] *Lead track: Oh No Won't Do.*	*A&M*	49	*19 Oct 91*	2
THROUGH THE ROOF	*A&M*	44	*28 Mar 92*	2
RICH AND STRANGE	*A&M*	24	*30 May 92*	3
PURPLE LOVE BALLOON	*A&M*	27	*15 Aug 92*	3
ONCE AGAIN	*A&M*	45	*10 Oct 92*	1
NEUROTICA	*A&M*	37	*12 Feb 94*	2
STICKS AND STONES	*A&M*	68	*2 Apr 94*	1
ONE GIANT LOVE	*A&M*	52	*3 Sep 94*	2
ALBUMS:	**HITS 2**			**WEEKS 2**
ASQUARIUS	*A&M*	30	*11 Jul 92*	1
SHOWBIZ	*A&M*	46	*23 Apr 94*	1

CUDDLES – See Keith HARRIS and ORVILLE

CUFF-LINKS — US

SINGLES:	HITS 2			WEEKS 30
TRACY	*MCA*	4	*29 Nov 69*	16
WHEN JULIE COMES AROUND *Lead vocals by Rupert Holmes.*	*MCA*	10	*14 Mar 70*	14

CULPRITS – See Craig McLACHLAN

CULT — UK

SINGLES:	HITS 15			WEEKS 80
RESURRECTION JOE	*Beggars Banquet*	74	*22 Dec 84*	2
SHE SELLS SANCTUARY	*Beggars Banquet*	15	*25 May 85*	17
SHE SELLS SANCTUARY [RE]	*Beggars Banquet*	61	*28 Sep 85*	2
RAIN	*Beggars Banquet*	17	*5 Oct 85*	8

REVOLUTION	*Beggars Banquet*	30	*30 Nov 85*	7
LOVE REMOVAL MACHINE	*Beggars Banquet*	18	*28 Feb 87*	7
LIL' DEVIL	*Beggars Banquet*	11	*2 May 87*	7
WILD FLOWER	*Beggars Banquet*	24	*22 Aug 87*	2
This entry was based on sales of a 7" doublepack.				
WILD FLOWER	*Beggars Banquet*	30	*29 Aug 87*	1
FIRE WOMAN	*Beggars Banquet*	15	*1 Apr 89*	4
EDIE (CIAO BABY)	*Beggars Banquet*	32	*8 Jul 89*	5
SUN KING / EDIE (CIAO BABY) [RI]	*Beggars Banquet*	39	*18 Nov 89*	2
SWEET SOUL SISTER	*Beggars Banquet*	42	*10 Mar 90*	4
WILD HEARTED SON	*Beggars Banquet*	40	*14 Sep 91*	2
HEART OF SOUL	*Beggars Banquet*	51	*29 Feb 92*	1
SHE SELLS SANCTUARY (MCMXCIII) [RM]	*Beggars Banquet*	15	*30 Jan 93*	4
Remixes by Youth/Butch Vig/J.G. Thilwell.				
COMING DOWN	*Beggars Banquet*	50	*8 Oct 94*	1
STAR	*Beggars Banquet*	65	*7 Jan 95*	1
ALBUMS:	**HITS 9**			**WEEKS 86**
THE SOUTHERN DEATH CULT	*Beggars Banquet*	43	*18 Jun 83*	3
Above hit: SOUTHERN DEATH CULT.				
DREAMTIME	*Beggars Banquet*	21	*8 Sep 84*	8
LOVE	*Beggars Banquet*	4	*26 Oct 85*	22
ELECTRIC	*Beggars Banquet*	4	*18 Apr 87*	27
SONIC TEMPLE	*Beggars Banquet*	3	*22 Apr 89*	11
CEREMONY	*Beggars Banquet*	9	*5 Oct 91*	4
PURE CULT	*Beggars Banquet*	1	*13 Feb 93*	8
Compilation.				
THE CULT	*Beggars Banquet*	21	*22 Oct 94*	2
BEYOND GOOD AND EVIL	*Atlantic*	69	*23 Jun 01*	1

CULTURE

Jamaica

ALBUMS:	**HITS 1**			**WEEKS 1**
TWO SEVENS CLASH	*Lightning*	60	*1 Apr 78*	1

CULTURE BEAT

UK/US/Germany

SINGLES:	**HITS 8**			**WEEKS 46**
(CHERRY LIPS) DER ERDBEERMUND	*Epic*	55	*3 Feb 90*	3
MR. VAIN	*Epic*	1	*7 Aug 93*	15
GOT TO GET IT	*Epic*	4	*6 Nov 93*	11
ANYTHING	*Epic*	5	*15 Jan 94*	8
WORLD IN YOUR HANDS	*Epic*	20	*2 Apr 94*	4
INSIDE OUT	*Epic*	32	*27 Jan 96*	2
CRYING IN THE RAIN	*Epic*	29	*15 Jun 96*	2
TAKE ME AWAY	*Epic*	52	*28 Sep 96*	1
ALBUMS:	**HITS 1**			**WEEKS 10**
SERENITY	*Dance Pool*	13	*25 Sep 93*	10

CULTURE CLUB

UK

(See also Boy George.)

SINGLES:	**HITS 13**			**WEEKS 119**
DO YOU REALLY WANT TO HURT ME	*Virgin*	1	*18 Sep 82*	18
TIME (CLOCK OF THE HEART)	*Virgin*	3	*27 Nov 82*	12
CHURCH OF THE POISON MIND	*Virgin*	2	*9 Apr 83*	9
KARMA CHAMELEON	*Virgin*	1	*17 Sep 83*	20
VICTIMS	*Virgin*	3	*10 Dec 83*	10
IT'S A MIRACLE	*Virgin*	4	*24 Mar 84*	9
Above 4 feature backing vocals from Helen Terry.				
THE WAR SONG	*Virgin*	2	*6 Oct 84*	8
THE MEDAL SONG	*Virgin*	32	*1 Dec 84*	4
THE MEDAL SONG [RE]	*Virgin*	74	*5 Jan 85*	1
MOVE AWAY	*Virgin*	7	*15 Mar 86*	7
GOD THANK YOU WOMAN	*Virgin*	31	*31 May 86*	5
I JUST WANNA BE LOVED	*Virgin*	4	*31 Oct 98*	10
YOUR KISSES ARE CHARITY	*Virgin*	25	*7 Aug 99*	4
COLD SHOULDER / STARMAN	*Virgin*	43	*27 Nov 99*	2
ALBUMS:	**HITS 8**			**WEEKS 163**
KISSING TO BE CLEVER	*Virgin*	5	*16 Oct 82*	59
COLOUR BY NUMBERS	*Virgin*	1	*22 Oct 83*	56
WAKING UP WITH THE HOUSE ON FIRE	*Virgin*	2	*3 Nov 84*	13
FROM LUXURY TO HEARTACHE	*Virgin*	10	*12 Apr 86*	6
THIS TIME: THE FIRST FOUR YEARS	*Virgin*	8	*18 Apr 87*	10
AT WORST. . .THE BEST OF BOY GEORGE & CULTURE CLUB	*Virgin*	24	*2 Oct 93*	5
Also includes Jesus Loves You tracks.				
Above hit: BOY GEORGE/CULTURE CLUB.				
GREATEST MOMENTS	*Virgin*	15	*21 Nov 98*	13
DON'T MIND IF I DO	*Virgin*	64	*4 Dec 99*	1

Smiley CULTURE — UK

SINGLES:	HITS 3			WEEKS 13
POLICE OFFICER	*Fashion*	12	*15 Dec 84*	10
COCKNEY TRANSLATION	*Fashion*	71	*6 Apr 85*	1
SCHOOLTIME CHRONICLE	*Polydor*	59	*13 Sep 86*	2

Larry CUNNINGHAM and the MIGHTY AVONS — Ireland

SINGLES:	HITS 1			WEEKS 11
TRIBUTE TO JIM REEVES	*King*	40	*12 Dec 64*	8
Includes words and music from 4 songs (3 hits) recorded by Jim Reeves.				
TRIBUTE TO JIM REEVES [RE]	*King*	46	*27 Feb 65*	3

CUPID'S INSPIRATION — UK

SINGLES:	HITS 2			WEEKS 19
YESTERDAY HAS GONE	*Nems*	4	*22 Jun 68*	11
Originally recorded by Teddy Randazzo.				
MY WORLD	*Nems*	33	*5 Oct 68*	8

Jose CURA - See Sarah BRIGHTMAN

Mike CURB CONGREGATION - See Little Jimmy OSMOND

CURE — UK

SINGLES:	HITS 27			WEEKS 145
A FOREST	*Fiction*	31	*12 Apr 80*	8
PRIMARY	*Fiction*	43	*4 Apr 81*	6
CHARLOTTE SOMETIMES	*Fiction*	44	*17 Oct 81*	4
THE HANGING GARDEN	*Fiction*	34	*24 Jul 82*	4
LET'S GO TO BED	*Fiction*	44	*27 Nov 82*	4
LET'S GO TO BED [RE]	*Fiction*	75	*8 Jan 83*	1
THE WALK	*Fiction*	12	*9 Jul 83*	8
THE LOVE CATS	*Fiction*	7	*29 Oct 83*	11
THE CATERPILLAR	*Fiction*	14	*7 Apr 84*	7
IN BETWEEN DAYS	*Fiction*	15	*27 Jul 85*	10
CLOSE TO ME	*Fiction*	24	*21 Sep 85*	8
BOYS DON'T CRY	*Fiction*	22	*3 May 86*	6
WHY CAN'T I BE YOU?	*Fiction*	21	*18 Apr 87*	5
CATCH	*Fiction*	27	*4 Jul 87*	6
JUST LIKE HEAVEN	*Fiction*	29	*17 Oct 87*	5
HOT HOT HOT!!!	*Fiction*	45	*20 Feb 88*	3
LULLABY	*Fiction*	5	*22 Apr 89*	6
LOVESONG	*Fiction*	18	*2 Sep 89*	7
PICTURES OF YOU	*Fiction*	24	*31 Mar 90*	6
NEVER ENOUGH	*Fiction*	13	*29 Sep 90*	5
CLOSE TO ME [RM]	*Fiction*	13	*3 Nov 90*	5
HIGH	*Fiction*	8	*28 Mar 92*	3
HIGH [RM]	*Fiction*	44	*11 Apr 92*	1
FRIDAY I'M IN LOVE	*Fiction*	6	*23 May 92*	7
A LETTER TO ELISE	*Fiction*	28	*17 Oct 92*	2
THE 13TH	*Fiction*	15	*4 May 96*	2
MINT CAR	*Fiction*	31	*29 Jun 96*	2
GONE!	*Fiction*	60	*14 Dec 96*	1
WRONG NUMBER	*Fiction*	62	*29 Nov 97*	1
CUT HERE	*Fiction*	54	*10 Nov 01*	1

ALBUMS:	HITS 21			WEEKS 205
THREE IMAGINARY BOYS	*Fiction*	44	*2 Jun 79*	3
17 SECONDS	*Fiction*	20	*3 May 80*	10
FAITH	*Fiction*	14	*25 Apr 81*	8
PORNOGRAPHY	*Fiction*	8	*15 May 82*	9
BOYS DON'T CRY	*Fiction*	77	*3 Sep 83*	5
Chart position reached in 1994 (1983 peak No. 93).				
JAPANESE WHISPERS: SINGLES NOV 82 - NOV 83	*Fiction*	26	*24 Dec 83*	14
THE TOP	*Fiction*	10	*12 May 84*	10
CONCERT - THE CURE LIVE	*Fiction*	26	*3 Nov 84*	4
THE HEAD ON THE DOOR	*Fiction*	7	*7 Sep 85*	13
BOYS DON'T CRY [RE]	*Fiction*	71	*10 May 86*	2
STANDING ON A BEACH - THE SINGLES	*Fiction*	4	*31 May 86*	35
CD format was titled Staring At The Sea.				
KISS ME KISS ME KISS ME	*Fiction*	6	*6 Jun 87*	15
DISINTEGRATION	*Fiction*	3	*13 May 89*	26
MIXED UP	*Fiction*	8	*17 Nov 90*	17
ENTREAT	*Fiction*	10	*6 Apr 91*	5
WISH	*Fiction*	1	*2 May 92*	13
SHOW	*Fiction*	29	*25 Sep 93*	2
PARIS	*Fiction*	56	*6 Nov 93*	1
WILD MOOD SWINGS	*Fiction*	9	*18 May 96*	6
GALORE - THE SINGLES 1987-1997	*Fiction*	37	*15 Nov 97*	2

BLOODFLOWERS	*Fiction*	14	*26 Feb 00*	2
GREATEST HITS	*Fiction*	33	*24 Nov 01*	3

CURIOSITY KILLED THE CAT — UK

SINGLES:	HITS 8			WEEKS 58
DOWN TO EARTH	*Mercury*	3	*13 Dec 86*	18
ORDINARY DAY	*Mercury*	11	*4 Apr 87*	7
MISFIT	*Mercury*	7	*20 Jun 87*	9
Original release reached No. 76 in 1986.				
FREE	*Mercury*	56	*19 Sep 87*	2
NAME AND NUMBER	*Mercury*	14	*16 Sep 89*	9
HANG ON IN THERE BABY	*RCA*	3	*25 Apr 92*	10
I NEED YOUR LOVIN'	*RCA*	47	*29 Aug 92*	2
GIMME THE SUNSHINE	*RCA*	73	*30 Oct 93*	1
Above 3: CURIOSITY.				
ALBUMS:	**HITS 2**			**WEEKS 27**
KEEP YOUR DISTANCE	*Mercury*	1	*9 May 87*	24
GETAHEAD	*Mercury*	29	*4 Nov 89*	3

CURLS – See Paul EVANS

Mark CURRY – See BLACK ROB; PUFF DADDY

Chantal CURTIS — France

SINGLES:	HITS 1			WEEKS 3
GET ANOTHER LOVE	*Pye International*	51	*14 Jul 79*	3

T.C. CURTIS backing vocals by GALAXY — Jamaica

SINGLES:	HITS 1			WEEKS 4
YOU SHOULD HAVE KNOWN BETTER	*Hot Melt*	50	*23 Feb 85*	4

CURVE — UK

SINGLES:	HITS 7			WEEKS 14
THE BLINDFOLD [EP]	*AnXious*	68	*16 Mar 91*	1
Lead track: Ten Little Girls.				
COAST IS CLEAR	*AnXious*	34	*25 May 91*	3
CLIPPED	*AnXious*	36	*9 Nov 91*	2
FAIT ACCOMPLI	*AnXious*	22	*7 Mar 92*	3
HORROR HEAD	*AnXious*	31	*18 Jul 92*	2
BLACKERTHREETRACKER [EP]	*AnXious*	39	*4 Sep 93*	2
Lead track: Missing Link.				
COMING UP ROSES	*Universal*	51	*16 May 98*	1
ALBUMS:	**HITS 3**			**WEEKS 6**
DOPPELGANGER	*Anxious*	11	*21 Mar 92*	3
RADIO SESSIONS	*Anxious*	72	*19 Jun 93*	1
CUCKOO	*Anxious*	23	*25 Sep 93*	2

CURVED AIR — UK

SINGLES:	HITS 1			WEEKS 12
BACK STREET LUV	*Warner Brothers*	4	*7 Aug 71*	12
ALBUMS:	**HITS 3**			**WEEKS 32**
AIR CONDITIONING	*Warner Brothers*	8	*5 Dec 70*	21
CURVED AIR	*Warner Brothers*	11	*9 Oct 71*	6
PHANTASMAGORIA	*Reprise*	20	*13 May 72*	5

CUT 'N' MOVE — Denmark

SINGLES:	HITS 2			WEEKS 4
GIVE IT UP	*EMI*	61	*2 Oct 93*	2
I'M ALIVE	*EMI*	49	*9 Sep 95*	2

Frankie CUTLASS — US

SINGLES:	HITS 1			WEEKS 1
THE CYPHER: PART 3	*Epic*	59	*5 Apr 97*	1

Adge CUTLER and the WURZELS – See WURZELS

CUTTING CREW — UK/Canada

SINGLES:	HITS 4			WEEKS 37
(I JUST) DIED IN YOUR ARMS	*Siren*	4	*16 Aug 86*	12
I'VE BEEN IN LOVE BEFORE	*Siren*	31	*25 Oct 86*	9
I'VE BEEN IN LOVE BEFORE [RE]	*Siren*	70	*10 Jan 87*	1
ONE FOR THE MOCKINGBIRD	*Siren*	52	*7 Mar 87*	5
I'VE BEEN IN LOVE BEFORE [RM]	*Siren*	24	*21 Nov 87*	8
Mixed by Steve Thompson and Michael Barbiero.				

(BETWEEN A) ROCK AND A HARD PLACE	*Siren*	66	*22 Jul 89*	2
ALBUMS:	**HITS 1**			**WEEKS 6**
BROADCAST	*Siren*	41	*29 Nov 86*	6

CYBERSONIK — US

SINGLES:	**HITS 1**			**WEEKS 1**
TECHNARCHY	*Champion*	73	*10 Nov 90*	1

CYGNUS X — Germany

SINGLES:	**HITS 2**			**WEEKS 5**
THE ORANGE THEME *Original release reached No. 127 in 1995.*	*Hooj Choons*	43	*11 Mar 00*	2
SUPERSTRING	*Xtravaganza*	33	*18 Aug 01*	3

Johnny CYMBAL — UK

SINGLES:	**HITS 1**			**WEEKS 10**
MR. BASS MAN	*London*	24	*16 Mar 63*	10

CYPRESS HILL — US

SINGLES:	**HITS 11**			**WEEKS 43**
INSANE IN THE BRAIN	*Columbia*	32	*31 Jul 93*	4
WHEN THE SH** GOES DOWN	*Columbia*	19	*2 Oct 93*	4
I AIN'T GOIN' OUT LIKE THAT	*Columbia*	15	*11 Dec 93*	7
INSANE IN THE BRAIN [RI]	*Columbia*	21	*26 Feb 94*	4
LICK A SHOT	*Columbia*	20	*7 May 94*	3
THROW YOUR SET IN THE AIR	*Columbia*	15	*7 Oct 95*	3
ILLUSIONS	*Columbia*	23	*17 Feb 96*	2
TEQULA SUNRISE	*Columbia*	23	*10 Oct 98*	2
DR. GREENTHUMB	*Columbia*	34	*10 Apr 99*	2
INSANE IN THE BRAIN [RM] *Remixed by Jason Nevins.* *Above hit: Jason NEVINS vs. CYPRESS HILL.*	*INCredible*	19	*26 Jun 99*	3
(RAP) SUPERSTAR/(ROCK) SUPERSTAR *(Rap) Superstar is track 1 of CD1; (Rock) Superstar is track 1 on CD2. (Rock) Superstar features China from the Deftones and Everlast.*	*Columbia*	13	*29 Apr 00*	5
CAN'T GET THE BEST OF ME/HIGHLIFE	*Columbia*	35	*16 Sep 00*	2
TROUBLE/LOWRIDER	*Columbia*	33	*8 Dec 01*	2
ALBUMS:	**HITS 6**			**WEEKS 67**
BLACK SUNDAY	*Columbia*	13	*7 Aug 93*	49
CYPRESS HILL III (TEMPLES OF BOOM)	*Columbia*	11	*11 Nov 95*	5
UNRELEASED & REVAMPED [EP] *Consists of tracks previously unreleased.*	*Columbia*	29	*24 Aug 96*	4
IV	*Columbia*	25	*17 Oct 98*	3
SKULL & BONES	*Columbia*	6	*6 May 00*	5
STONED RAIDERS	*Columbia*	71	*15 Dec 01*	1

Billy Ray CYRUS — US

SINGLES:	**HITS 4**			**WEEKS 18**
ACHY BREAKY HEART *Originally recorded by the Marci Brothers as Don't Tell My Heart.*	*Mercury*	3	*25 Jul 92*	10
COULD'VE BEEN ME	*Mercury*	24	*10 Oct 92*	4
THESE BOOTS ARE MADE FOR WALKIN'	*Mercury*	63	*28 Nov 92*	1
ACHY BREAKY HEART [RR] *Above hit: ALVIN and the CHIPMUNKS (with Special Guest Billy Ray CYRUS).*	*Epic*	53	*19 Dec 92*	3
ALBUMS:	**HITS 1**			**WEEKS 10**
SOME GAVE ALL	*Mercury*	9	*29 Aug 92*	10

CZR featuring DELANO — US

SINGLES:	**HITS 1**			**WEEKS 1**
I WANT YOU	*Credence*	57	*30 Sep 00*	1

Holgar CZUKAY – See David SYLVIAN

D

Chuck D — US

SINGLES:	**HITS 3**			**WEEKS 9**
BRING THE NOISE *Above hit: ANTHRAX featuring Chuck D from PUBLIC ENEMY.*	*Island*	14	*6 Jul 91*	5
NO	*Mercury*	55	*26 Oct 96*	1
ROCK DA FUNKY BEATS *Above hit: PUBLIC DOMAIN featuring Chuck D.*	*Xtrahard*	19	*23 Jun 01*	3

Crissy D - See B-15 PROJECT featuring Crissy D and LADY G

Danny D - See COOKIE CREW; D-MOB

Maxwell D — UK

SINGLES:	HITS 1			WEEKS 2
SERIOUS	*4 Liberty*	38	*15 Sep 01*	2

Dimples D — US

SINGLES:	HITS 1			WEEKS 10
SUCKER DJ	*FBI*	17	*17 Nov 90*	10
Recorded in 1983 and samples the TV theme 'I Dream Of Jeannie'.				

Longsy D's HOUSE SOUND — UK

SINGLES:	HITS 1			WEEKS 7
THIS IS SKA	*Big One*	56	*4 Mar 89*	7

Nikki D — US

SINGLES:	HITS 2			WEEKS 6
MY LOVE IS SO RAW	*Def Jam*	34	*6 May 89*	5
Above hit: Alyson WILLIAMS featuring NIKKI-D.				
DADDY'S LITTLE GIRL	*Def Jam*	75	*30 Mar 91*	1

Vicky "D" — US

SINGLES:	HITS 1			WEEKS 6
THIS BEAT IS MINE	*Virgin/Sam*	42	*13 Mar 82*	6

D.B.M. — Germany

SINGLES:	HITS 1			WEEKS 3
DISCOBEATLEMANIA [M]	*Atlantic*	45	*12 Nov 77*	3

D. B. M. and T. — UK

SINGLES:	HITS 1			WEEKS 8
MR. PRESIDENT	*Fontana*	33	*1 Aug 70*	8

D.BO GENERAL - See URBAN SHAKEDOWN featuring Micky FINN

D-INFLUENCE — UK

SINGLES:	HITS 5			WEEKS 10
GOOD LOVER	*East West America*	46	*20 Jun 92*	2
GOOD LOVER [RI]	*East West America*	61	*27 Mar 93*	1
Samples Eleanore Mills' Mr. Right.				
MIDNITE	*East West America*	58	*24 Jun 95*	1
HYPNOTIZE	*Echo*	33	*16 Aug 97*	2
MAGIC	*Echo*	45	*11 Oct 97*	1
ROCK WITH YOU	*Echo*	30	*5 Sep 98*	3
ALBUMS:	**HITS 1**			**WEEKS 1**
LONDON	*Echo*	56	*25 Oct 97*	1

D.J.H. featuring STEFY — Italy

SINGLES:	HITS 3			WEEKS 14
THINK ABOUT . . .	*RCA*	22	*16 Feb 91*	6
Samples Aretha Franklin's Rock-A-Lott.				
I LIKE IT	*RCA*	16	*13 Jul 91*	7
MOVE YOUR LOVE	*RCA*	73	*19 Oct 91*	1
Also samples Aretha Franklin's Rock-A-Lott.				

D-KUPS - See Ivor BIGGUN

D'LUX — UK

SINGLES:	HITS 1			WEEKS 1
LOVE RESURRECTION	*Logic*	58	*22 Jun 96*	1

D'MENACE — UK

SINGLES:	HITS 1			WEEKS 3
DEEP MENACE (SPANK)	*Inferno*	20	*8 Aug 98*	3

D-MOB — UK

SINGLES:	HITS 7			WEEKS 48
WE CALL IT ACIEED	*ffrr*	3	*15 Oct 88*	12
Above hit: D. MOB (featuring Gary HAISMAN).				
IT IS TIME TO GET FUNKY	*ffrr*	9	*3 Jun 89*	10
Above hit: D. MOB featuring L.R.S. and D.C. SAROME.				

C'MON AND GET MY LOVE *Above hit: D MOB introducing Cathy DENNIS.*	*ffrr*	15	*21 Oct 89*	10
PUT YOUR HANDS TOGETHER *Above hit: D. MOB featuring NUFF JUICE.*	*ffrr*	7	*6 Jan 90*	8
THAT'S THE WAY OF THE WORLD *Above hit: D MOB featuring Cathy DENNIS.*	*ffrr*	48	*7 Apr 90*	3
WHY *Above hit: D-MOB with Cathy DENNIS.*	*ffrr*	23	*12 Feb 94*	3
ONE DAY *Vocals by Steven Dante.* *Above hit: Danny D presents D:MOB*	*ffrr*	41	*3 Sep 94*	2
ALBUMS:	**HITS 1**			**WEEKS 11**
A LITTLE BIT OF THIS, A LITTLE BIT OF THAT	*ffrr*	46	*11 Nov 89*	11

D*NOTE — UK

SINGLES:	**HITS 2**			**WEEKS 2**
WAITING HOPEFULLY	*VC Recordings*	46	*12 Jul 97*	1
LOST AND FOUND	*VC Recordings*	59	*15 Nov 97*	1

D.O.P. — UK

SINGLES:	**HITS 2**			**WEEKS 2**
STOP STARTING TO START STOPPING [EP] *Lead track: Gusta.*	*Hi-Life*	58	*3 Feb 96*	1
GROOVY BEAT *Originally released in 1992.*	*Hi-Life*	54	*13 Jul 96*	1

D.O.S.E. featuring Mark E. SMITH — UK

SINGLES:	**HITS 1**			**WEEKS 1**
PLUG MYSELF IN	*Coliseum*	50	*23 Mar 96*	1

D:REAM — UK

SINGLES:	**HITS 8**			**WEEKS 74**
U R THE BEST THING	*FXU*	72	*4 Jul 92*	1
THINGS CAN ONLY GET BETTER	*Magnet*	24	*30 Jan 93*	5
U R THE BEST THING [RM-1ST]	*Magnet*	19	*24 Apr 93*	8
UNFORGIVEN	*Magnet*	29	*31 Jul 93*	3
STAR / I LIKE IT	*Magnet*	26	*2 Oct 93*	4
THINGS CAN ONLY GET BETTER [RM]	*Magnet*	1	*8 Jan 94*	16
U R THE BEST THING [RM-2ND] *Remixed by Paul Oakenfold and Steve Osborne.*	*Magnet*	4	*26 Mar 94*	10
TAKE ME AWAY	*Magnet*	18	*18 Jun 94*	5
BLAME IT ON ME	*Magnet*	25	*10 Sep 94*	5
SHOOT ME WITH YOUR LOVE	*Magnet*	7	*8 Jul 95*	7
PARTY UP THE WORLD	*Magnet*	20	*9 Sep 95*	6
THE POWER (OF ALL THE LOVE IN THE WORLD)	*Magnet*	40	*11 Nov 95*	1
THINGS CAN ONLY GET BETTER [RM] [RI] *Used as a Labour party anthem in the 1997 general election.*	*Magnet*	19	*3 May 97*	3
ALBUMS:	**HITS 2**			**WEEKS 41**
D:REAM ON VOLUME 1	*Magnet*	44	*30 Oct 93*	3
D:REAM ON VOLUME 1 [RE] *Re-packaged.*	*Magnet*	5	*5 Feb 94*	34
WORLD	*Magnet*	5	*30 Sep 95*	4

D.S.M. — US

SINGLES:	**HITS 1**			**WEEKS 4**
WARRIOR GROOVE	*10 Records*	68	*7 Dec 85*	4

D-SHAKE — Holland

SINGLES:	**HITS 2**			**WEEKS 8**
YAAAH / TECHNO TRANCE	*Cooltempo*	20	*2 Jun 90*	6
MY HEART, THE BEAT	*Cooltempo*	42	*2 Feb 91*	2

D-TEK — UK

SINGLES:	**HITS 1**			**WEEKS 1**
DROP THE ROCK [EP] *Lead track: Drop The Rock.*	*Positiva*	70	*6 Nov 93*	1

D-TRAIN — US

(See also David Morales.)

SINGLES:	**HITS 4**			**WEEKS 36**
YOU'RE THE ONE FOR ME	*Epic*	30	*6 Feb 82*	8
WALK ON BY	*Epic*	44	*8 May 82*	6
MUSIC	*Prelude*	23	*7 May 83*	7

KEEP GIVING ME LOVE	*Prelude*	65	*16 Jul 83*	2
YOU'RE THE ONE FOR ME (LABOUR OF LOVE MIX) [RM]	*Prelude*	15	*27 Jul 85*	11
MUSIC [RM]	*Prelude*	62	*12 Oct 85*	2
Above 2 remixed by Paul Hardcastle.				
ALBUMS:	**HITS 1**			**WEEKS 4**
D-TRAIN	*Epic*	72	*8 May 82*	4

DA BRAT — US

(See also Lil' Kim.)

SINGLES:	**HITS 2**			**WEEKS 3**
FUNKDAFIED	*Columbia*	65	*22 Oct 94*	1
SOCKIT2ME	*East West*	33	*29 Nov 97*	2
Above hit: Missy Misdemeanor ELLIOTT featuring DA BRAT.				

DA CLICK — UK

SINGLES:	**HITS 2**			**WEEKS 8**
GOOD RHYMES	*ffrr*	14	*16 Jan 99*	6
Based around Chic's Good Times.				
WE ARE DA CLICK	*ffrr*	38	*29 May 99*	2
Samples Tom Browne's Funkin' For Jamaica.				

DA FOOL — UK

SINGLES:	**HITS 1**			**WEEKS 2**
NO GOOD (FORMERLY KNOWN AS "MEET HIM AT THE BLUE OYSTER BAR")	*ffrr*	38	*16 Jan 99*	2
Samples SIL's Blue Oyster.				

Ricardo DA FORCE — UK

SINGLES:	**HITS 3**			**WEEKS 14**
PUMP UP THE VOLUME	*Stress*	51	*18 Mar 95*	2
Above hit: GREED featuring Ricardo DA FORCE.				
STAYIN' ALIVE	*All Around the World*	2	*16 Sep 95*	11
Above hit: N-TRANCE featuring Ricardo DA FORCE.				
WHY?	*ffrr*	58	*31 Aug 96*	1

DA HOOL — Germany

SINGLES:	**HITS 2**			**WEEKS 13**
MEET HER AT THE LOVE PARADE	*Manifesto*	15	*14 Feb 98*	4
BORA BORA	*Manifesto*	35	*22 Aug 98*	3
Bora Bora is an island 150 miles northwest at Tahiti.				
MEET HER AT THE LOVE PARADE 2001 [RM]	*Manifesto*	11	*28 Jul 01*	6
Remixed by Fergie.				

DA LENCH MOB — US

SINGLES:	**HITS 1**			**WEEKS 2**
FREEDOM GOT AN A.K.	*East West America*	51	*20 Mar 93*	2

DA MOB featuring Jocelyn BROWN — US

(See also Jocelyn Brown.)

SINGLES:	**HITS 2**			**WEEKS 3**
FUN	*INCredible*	33	*2 May 98*	2
IT'S ALL GOOD	*INCredible*	54	*3 Jul 99*	1

DA MUTTZ — UK

SINGLES:	**HITS 1**			**WEEKS 10**
WASSUUP!	*Eternal*	11	*9 Dec 00*	10
Inspired by the Budweiser TV commercial.				

Rui DA SILVA featuring CASSANDRA — Portugal/UK

SINGLES:	**HITS 1**			**WEEKS 14**
TOUCH ME	*Arista*	1	*13 Jan 01*	14

DA SLAMMIN PHROGZ — France

SINGLES:	**HITS 1**			**WEEKS 1**
SOMETHIN' ABOUT THE MUSIC	*WEA*	53	*29 Apr 00*	1
Samples Bratt Packs' Can You Feel It and Love Committee's Just As Long As I Have You.				

DA TECHNO BOHEMIAN — Holland

SINGLES:	**HITS 1**			**WEEKS 1**
BANGIN' BASS	*Hi-Life*	63	*25 Jan 97*	1

Paul DA VINCI — UK

SINGLES:	HITS 1			WEEKS 8
YOUR BABY AIN'T YOUR BABY ANYMORE	*Penny Farthing*	20	*20 Jul 74*	8

Terry DACTYL and the DINOSAURS — UK

(See also Jona Lewie.)

SINGLES:	HITS 2			WEEKS 16
SEASIDE SHUFFLE	*UK*	2	*15 Jul 72*	12
ON A SATURDAY NIGHT	*UK*	45	*13 Jan 73*	4
Label has minor credit 'featuring John G. Lewis'.				

DADA — US

SINGLES:	HITS 1			WEEKS 1
DOG	*I.R.S.*	71	*4 Dec 93*	1

DADDY FREDDY – See Simon HARRIS

DADDY'S FAVOURITE — UK

SINGLES:	HITS 1			WEEKS 3
I FEEL GOOD THINGS FOR YOU	*Go.Beat*	44	*21 Nov 98*	2
Samples Patrice Rushen's Haven't You Heard.				
I FEEL GOOD THINGS FOR YOU [RI]	*Go.Beat*	50	*9 Oct 99*	1

DAFFY DUCK featuring the GROOVE GANG — Germany

SINGLES:	HITS 1			WEEKS 3
PARTY ZONE	*WEA*	58	*6 Jul 91*	3

DAFT PUNK — France

SINGLES:	HITS 7			WEEKS 35
DA FUNK / MUSIQUE	*Virgin*	7	*22 Feb 97*	5
AROUND THE WORLD	*Virgin*	5	*26 Apr 97*	5
BURNIN'	*Virgin*	30	*4 Oct 97*	2
REVOLUTION 909	*Virgin*	47	*28 Feb 98*	1
ONE MORE TIME	*Virgin*	2	*25 Nov 00*	12
Above hit: DAFT PUNK vocals performed by ROMANTHONY.				
DIGITAL LOVE	*Virgin*	14	*23 Jun 01*	7
Samples George Duke's Love You More.				
HARDER BETTER FASTER STRONGER	*Virgin*	25	*17 Nov 01*	3
Samples Cola Bottle Baby by Edwin Birdsong.				
ALBUMS:	**HITS 2**			**WEEKS 50**
HOMEWORK	*Virgin*	8	*1 Feb 97*	15
DISCOVERY	*Virgin*	2	*24 Mar 01*	35

Gigi D'AGOSTINO – See R.A.F.

Etienne DAHO – See SAINT ETIENNE

DAINTEES – See Martin STEPHENSON and the DAINTEES

DAISY CHAINSAW — UK/Canada

SINGLES:	HITS 2			WEEKS 6
LOVE YOUR MONEY	*Deva*	26	*18 Jan 92*	5
Chart for 18 Jan 92 listed the EP title: Lovesick Pleasure.				
PINK FLOWER / ROOM ELEVEN	*Deva*	65	*28 Mar 92*	1
ALBUMS:	**HITS 1**			**WEEKS 1**
ELEVENTEEN	*Deva*	62	*10 Oct 92*	1

DAJAE – See B-CREW featuring Barbara TUCKER, Ultra NATE, DAJAE, MONE; Junior SANCHEZ featuring DAJAE

DAKEYNE – See James BROWN; TINMAN

DAKOTAS — UK

(See also Billy J. Kramer with the Dakotas.)

SINGLES:	HITS 1			WEEKS 13
THE CRUEL SEA	*Parlophone*	18	*13 Jul 63*	13
EPS:	**HITS 1**			**WEEKS 1**
MEET THE DAKOTAS	*Parlophone*	19	*14 Dec 63*	1

Jim DALE — UK

SINGLES:	HITS 3			WEEKS 22
BE MY GIRL	*Parlophone*	2	*12 Oct 57*	16
Originally recorded by Johnny Madara.				
JUST BORN (TO BE YOUR BABY)	*Parlophone*	27	*11 Jan 58*	1

CRAZY DREAM	*Parlophone*	24	*18 Jan 58*	2
Above 2 entries were separate sides of the same release, each had its own chart run.				
SUGARTIME	*Parlophone*	25	*8 Mar 58*	3

DALE and GRACE — US

SINGLES:	HITS 1			WEEKS 2
I'M LEAVING IT UP TO YOU	*London*	42	*11 Jan 64*	2

DALE SISTERS — US

SINGLES:	HITS 1			WEEKS 6
MY SUNDAY BABY (UN TELEGRAMA)	*Ember*	36	*25 Nov 61*	6

DALEK I — UK

ALBUMS:	HITS 1			WEEKS 2
COMPASS KUMPAS	*Backdoor*	54	*9 Aug 80*	2

DALI'S CAR — UK

SINGLES:	HITS 1			WEEKS 2
THE JUDGEMENT IS THE MIRROR	*Paradox*	66	*3 Nov 84*	2
ALBUMS:	**HITS 1**			**WEEKS 1**
THE WAKING HOUR	*Paradox*	84	*1 Dec 84*	1

Roger DALTREY — UK

SINGLES:	HITS 8			WEEKS 46
GIVING IT ALL AWAY	*Track*	5	*14 Apr 73*	11
I'M FREE	*Ode*	13	*4 Aug 73*	10
Above hit: Roger DALTREY with LONDON SYMPHONY ORCHESTRA and ENGLISH CHAMBER CHOIR conducted by David MEASHAM.				
WRITTEN ON THE WIND	*Polydor*	46	*14 May 77*	2
FREE ME	*Polydor*	39	*2 Aug 80*	6
WITHOUT YOUR LOVE	*Polydor*	55	*11 Oct 80*	4
Above 2 from the film 'McVicar'.				
WALKING IN MY SLEEP	*WEA International*	56	*3 Mar 84*	3
AFTER THE FIRE	*10 Records*	50	*5 Oct 85*	5
UNDER A RAGING MOON	*10 Records*	43	*8 Mar 86*	5
Features 7 different drummers including Roger Taylor, Cozy Powell, Stewart Copeland and Zak Starkley.				
ALBUMS:	**HITS 4**			**WEEKS 24**
RIDE A ROCK HORSE	*Polydor*	14	*26 Jul 75*	10
ONE OF THE BOYS	*Polydor*	45	*4 Jun 77*	1
MCVICAR [OST]	*Polydor*	39	*23 Aug 80*	11
UNDER A RAGING MOON	*10 Records*	52	*2 Nov 85*	2

Glen DALY — UK

ALBUMS:	HITS 1			WEEKS 2
GLASGOW NIGHT OUT	*Golden Guinea*	28	*20 Nov 71*	2

DAMAGE — UK

SINGLES:	HITS 11			WEEKS 59
ANYTHING	*Big Life*	68	*20 Jul 96*	1
Features US rapper Little Caesar from the Junior M.A.F.I.A. collective.				
LOVE II LOVE	*Big Life*	12	*12 Oct 96*	6
FOREVER	*Big Life*	6	*14 Dec 96*	9
LOVE GUARANTEED	*Big Life*	7	*22 Mar 97*	6
WONDERFUL TONIGHT	*Big Life*	3	*17 May 97*	8
Originally recorded by Eric Clapton in 1977.				
LOVE GUARANTEED [RE]	*Big Life*	73	*14 Jun 97*	1
LOVE LADY	*Big Life*	33	*9 Aug 97*	2
GHETTO ROMANCE	*Cooltempo*	7	*1 Jul 00*	7
RUMOURS	*Cooltempo*	22	*28 Oct 00*	4
STILL BE LOVIN' YOU	*Cooltempo*	11	*31 Mar 01*	6
Features Emma Bunton on backing vocals.				
STILL BE LOVIN' YOU [RE]	*Cooltempo*	74	*19 May 01*	1
SO WHAT IF I	*Cooltempo*	12	*14 Jul 01*	5
SO WHAT IF I [RE]	*Cooltempo*	70	*25 Aug 01*	1
AFTER THE LOVE HAS GONE	*Cooltempo*	42	*15 Dec 01*	2
ALBUMS:	**HITS 2**			**WEEKS 22**
FOREVER	*Big Life*	13	*19 Apr 97*	12
SINCE YOU'VE BEEN GONE	*Cooltempo*	16	*14 Apr 01*	5
SINCE YOU'VE BEEN GONE [RE]	*Cooltempo*	28	*21 Jul 01*	5
Repackaged.				

Carolina DAMAS – See SUENO LATINO featuring Carolina DAMAS

Bobby D'AMBROSIO featuring Michelle WEEKS — US

SINGLES:	HITS 1			WEEKS 3
MOMENT OF MY LIFE	*Ministry Of Sound*	23	*2 Aug 97*	3

Originally recorded by Inner Life in 1982.

DAMIAN — UK

SINGLES:	HITS 2			WEEKS 26
THE TIME WARP II (BRAND NEW VERSION)	*Jive*	51	*26 Dec 87*	6
The dance routine from 'the Rocky Horror Show'. Original release reached No. 94 in 1986.				
THE TIME WARP 2 (BRAND NEW VERSION) [RI]	*Jive*	64	*27 Aug 88*	3
THE TIME WARP (PWL REMIX) [RM]	*Jive*	7	*19 Aug 89*	13
Remixed by Peter Hammond.				
WIG WAM BAM	*Jive*	49	*16 Dec 89*	4

DAMNED — UK

SINGLES:	HITS 15			WEEKS 77
LOVE SONG	*Chiswick*	20	*5 May 79*	8
SMASH IT UP	*Chiswick*	35	*20 Oct 79*	5
I JUST CAN'T BE HAPPY TODAY	*Chiswick*	46	*1 Dec 79*	5
THE HISTORY OF THE WORLD	*Chiswick*	51	*4 Oct 80*	4
FRIDAY THE THIRTEENTH [EP]	*Stale One*	50	*28 Nov 81*	4
Lead track: Disco Man.				
LOVELY MONEY	*Bronze*	42	*10 Jul 82*	4
THANKS FOR THE NIGHT	*Plus One*	43	*9 Jun 84*	4
GRIMLY FIENDISH	*MCA*	21	*30 Mar 85*	7
THE SHADOW OF LOVE (EDITION PREMIERE)	*MCA*	25	*22 Jun 85*	8
IS IT A DREAM "WILD WEST END MIX"	*MCA*	34	*21 Sep 85*	4
ELOISE	*MCA*	3	*8 Feb 86*	9
ELOISE [RE]	*MCA*	72	*19 Apr 86*	1
ANYTHING	*MCA*	32	*22 Nov 86*	4
GIGOLO	*MCA*	29	*7 Feb 87*	3
ALONE AGAIN OR	*MCA*	27	*25 Apr 87*	6
IN DULCE DECORUM	*MCA*	72	*28 Nov 87*	1

ALBUMS:	HITS 8			WEEKS 54
DAMNED DAMNED DAMNED	*Stiff*	36	*12 Mar 77*	10
MACHINE GUN ETIQUETTE	*Chiswick*	31	*17 Nov 79*	5
THE BLACK ALBUM	*Chiswick*	29	*29 Nov 80*	3
THE BEST OF THE DAMNED	*Big Beat*	43	*28 Nov 81*	12
STRAWBERRIES	*Bronze*	15	*23 Oct 82*	4
PHANTASMAGORIA	*MCA*	11	*27 Jul 85*	17
ANYTHING	*MCA*	40	*13 Dec 86*	2
LIGHT AT THE END OF THE TUNNEL	*MCA*	87	*12 Dec 87*	1

Kenny DAMON — US

SINGLES:	HITS 1			WEEKS 1
WHILE I LIVE	*Mercury*	45	*21 May 66*	1

Vic DAMONE — US

SINGLES:	HITS 3			WEEKS 22
AN AFFAIR TO REMEMBER (OUR LOVE AFFAIR)	*Philips*	29	*7 Dec 57*	1
Originally recorded by Carmen Cavallaro & his Orchestra.				
AN AFFAIR TO REMEMBER (OUR LOVE AFFAIR) [RE]	*Philips*	30	*1 Feb 58*	1
ON THE STREET WHERE YOU LIVE	*Philips*	1	*10 May 58*	17
From the musical 'My Fair Lady'.				
Above hit: Vic DAMONE with Percy FAITH and his Orchestra and Chorus.				
THE ONLY MAN ON THE ISLAND	*Philips*	24	*2 Aug 58*	3
Above hit: Vic DAMONE with Frank DE VOL and his Orchestra.				

ALBUMS:	HITS 2			WEEKS 8
NOW!	*RCA International*	28	*25 Apr 81*	7
VIC DAMONE SINGS THE GREAT SONGS	*Cameo*	87	*2 Apr 83*	1

Richie DAN — UK

SINGLES:	HITS 1			WEEKS 3
CALL IT FATE	*Pure Silk*	34	*12 Aug 00*	3

DAN-I — UK

SINGLES:	HITS 1			WEEKS 9
MONKEY CHOP	*Island*	30	*10 Nov 79*	9

DANA — UK

SINGLES:	HITS 8			WEEKS 75
ALL KINDS OF EVERYTHING	*Rex*	1	*4 Apr 70*	15

Eurovision Song Contest winner for Ireland in 1970.

ALL KINDS OF EVERYTHING [RE]	*Rex*	47	*25 Jul 70*	1
WHO PUT THE LIGHTS OUT	*Rex*	14	*13 Feb 71*	11
PLEASE TELL HIM THAT I SAID HELLO	*GTO*	8	*25 Jan 75*	14
IT'S GONNA BE A COLD COLD CHRISTMAS	*GTO*	4	*13 Dec 75*	6
NEVER GONNA FALL IN LOVE AGAIN	*GTO*	31	*6 Mar 76*	4
Originally recorded by Eric Carmen.				
FAIRYTALE	*GTO*	13	*16 Oct 76*	16
SOMETHING'S COOKING IN THE KITCHEN	*GTO*	44	*31 Mar 79*	5
I FEEL LOVE COMIN' ON	*Creole*	66	*15 May 82*	3
ALBUMS:	**HITS 1**			**WEEKS 3**
EVERYTHING IS BEAUTIFUL	*Warwick*	43	*27 Dec 80*	3

DANA INTERNATIONAL — Israel

SINGLES:	**HITS 1**			**WEEKS 4**
DIVA	*Dance Pool*	11	*27 Jun 98*	4
Eurovision Song Contest winner in 1998.				

DANCE CONSPIRACY — UK

SINGLES:	**HITS 1**			**WEEKS 1**
DUB WAR	*XL Recordings*	72	*3 Oct 92*	1

DANCE FLOOR VIRUS — Italy

SINGLES:	**HITS 1**			**WEEKS 2**
MESSAGE IN A BOTTLE	*Epic*	49	*21 Oct 95*	2

DANCE 2 TRANCE — Germany

SINGLES:	**HITS 3**			**WEEKS 8**
P.OWER OF A.MERICAN N.ATIVES	*Logic*	25	*24 Apr 93*	4
TAKE A FREE FALL	*Logic*	36	*24 Jul 93*	3
WARRIOR	*Logic*	56	*4 Feb 95*	1

Evan DANDO – See Kirsty MacCOLL

Suzanne DANDO — UK

ALBUMS:	**HITS 1**			**WEEKS 1**
SHAPE UP AND DANCE WITH SUZANNE DANDO	*Lifestyle*	87	*17 Mar 84*	1

DANDY WARHOLS — US

SINGLES:	**HITS 6**			**WEEKS 20**
EVERY DAY SHOULD BE A HOLIDAY	*Capitol*	29	*28 Feb 98*	2
NOT IF YOU WERE THE LAST JUNKIE ON EARTH	*Capitol*	13	*2 May 98*	4
BOYS BETTER	*Capitol*	36	*8 Aug 98*	2
GET OFF	*Capitol*	38	*10 Jun 00*	2
BOHEMIAN LIKE YOU	*Capitol*	42	*9 Sep 00*	1
GODLESS	*Capitol*	66	*7 Jul 01*	1
BOHEMIAN LIKE YOU [RI]	*Capitol*	5	*10 Nov 01*	8
Featured in the Vodafone TV commercial.				
ALBUMS:	**HITS 2**			**WEEKS 11**
COME DOWN	*Capitol*	16	*16 May 98*	8
THIRTEEN TALES FROM URBAN BOHEMIA	*Capitol*	51	*24 Jun 00*	1
THIRTEEN TALES FROM URBAN BOHEMIA [RE]	*Capitol*	32	*17 Nov 01*	2

DANDYS — UK

SINGLES:	**HITS 2**			**WEEKS 2**
YOU MAKE ME WANT TO SCREAM	*Artificial*	71	*14 Mar 98*	1
ENGLISH COUNTRY GARDEN	*Artificial*	57	*30 May 98*	1

DANE

SINGLES:	**HITS 4**			**WEEKS 38**
BUGGIN	*NuLife*	6	*29 Apr 00*	8
Above hit: TRUE STEPPERS and Dane BOWERS from ANOTHER LEVEL.				
OUT OF YOUR MIND	*NuLife*	2	*26 Aug 00*	16
Above hit: TRUE STEPPERS and Dane BOWERS featuring Victoria BECKHAM.				
OUT OF YOUR MIND [RE]	*NuLife*	58	*6 Jan 01*	4
SHUT UP . . . AND FORGET ABOUT IT	*Arista*	9	*3 Mar 01*	5
ANOTHER LOVER	*Arista*	9	*7 Jul 01*	5

D'ANGELO — US

(See also Genius/GZA.)

SINGLES:	**HITS 4**			**WEEKS 9**
BROWN SUGAR	*Cooltempo*	24	*28 Oct 95*	3
CRUISIN'	*Cooltempo*	31	*2 Mar 96*	2
Original by Smokey Robinson reached No. 4 in the US in 1979.				

LADY	*Cooltempo*	21	*15 Jun 96*	2
BREAK UPS 2 MAKE UPS	*Def Jam*	33	*22 May 99*	2
Above hit: METHOD MAN featuring D'ANGELO.				
ALBUMS:	**HITS 2**			**WEEKS 5**
BROWN SUGAR	*Cooltempo*	57	*28 Oct 95*	2
VOODOO	*Cooltempo*	21	*26 Feb 00*	3

DANGER DANGER — US

SINGLES:	**HITS 3**			**WEEKS 5**
MONKEY BUSINESS	*Epic*	42	*8 Feb 92*	2
I STILL THINK ABOUT YOU	*Epic*	46	*28 Mar 92*	2
COMIN' HOME	*Epic*	75	*13 Jun 92*	1

Charlie DANIELS BAND — US

SINGLES:	**HITS 1**			**WEEKS 10**
THE DEVIL WENT DOWN TO GEORGIA	*Epic*	14	*22 Sep 79*	10
ALBUMS:	**HITS 1**			**WEEKS 1**
MILLION MILE REFLECTIONS	*Epic*	74	*10 Nov 79*	1

Jeffrey DANIELS – See BABYFACE

Phil DANIELS – See BLUR

Johnny DANKWORTH and his Orchestra — UK

SINGLES:	**HITS 2**			**WEEKS 33**
EXPERIMENTS WITH MICE	*Parlophone*	7	*23 Jun 56*	12
AFRICAN WALTZ	*Columbia*	9	*25 Feb 61*	21

DANNII – See Dannii MINOGUE

DANNY and the JUNIORS — US

SINGLES:	**HITS 1**			**WEEKS 19**
• AT THE HOP	*His Master's Voice*	3	*18 Jan 58*	14
Originally written as Do The Bop.				
AT THE HOP [RI]	*ABC*	39	*10 Jul 76*	5

DANNY WILSON — UK

SINGLES:	**HITS 3**			**WEEKS 28**
MARY'S PRAYER	*Virgin*	42	*22 Aug 87*	7
MARY'S PRAYER [RM]	*Virgin*	3	*2 Apr 88*	11
Remixed by Paul Staveley and issued with the same catalogue number as the previous entry.				
THE SECOND SUMMER OF LOVE	*Virgin*	23	*17 Jun 89*	9
NEVER GONNA BE THE SAME	*Virgin*	69	*16 Sep 89*	1
ALBUMS:	**HITS 3**			**WEEKS 11**
MEET DANNY WILSON	*Virgin*	65	*30 Apr 88*	5
BEEBOP MOPTOP	*Virgin*	24	*29 Jul 89*	5
SWEET DANNY WILSON	*Virgin*	54	*31 Aug 91*	1

DANSE SOCIETY — UK

SINGLES:	**HITS 2**			**WEEKS 5**
WAKE UP	*Society*	61	*27 Aug 83*	3
HEAVEN IS WAITING	*Society*	60	*5 Nov 83*	2
ALBUMS:	**HITS 1**			**WEEKS 4**
HEAVEN IS WAITING	*Society*	39	*11 Feb 84*	4

DANSKI and DJ DELMUNDO present VENGABOYS – See VENGABOYS

Steven DANTE — UK

(See also D-Mob.)

SINGLES:	**HITS 2**			**WEEKS 16**
THE REAL THING	*Chrysalis*	13	*26 Sep 87*	10
Above hit: JELLYBEAN featuring Steven DANTE.				
I'M TOO SCARED	*Cooltempo*	34	*9 Jul 88*	6
ALBUMS:	**HITS 1**			**WEEKS 1**
FIND OUT	*Cooltempo*	87	*3 Sep 88*	1

Tonja DANTZLER — US

SINGLES:	**HITS 1**			**WEEKS 1**
IN AND OUT OF MY LIFE	*ffrr*	66	*17 Dec 94*	1

DANY – See DOUBLE DEE (featuring DANY)

DANZIG — US

SINGLES:	HITS 1			WEEKS 1
MOTHER	*American*	62	*14 May 94*	1

DAPHNE — US

SINGLES:	HITS 1			WEEKS 1
CHANGE	*Stress*	71	*9 Dec 95*	1

DAPHNE and CELESTE — US

SINGLES:	HITS 3			WEEKS 28
OOH STICK YOU!	*Universal*	8	*5 Feb 00*	12
U.G.L.Y.	*Universal*	18	*17 Jun 00*	12
Originally recorded by Fishbone.				
SCHOOL'S OUT!	*Universal*	12	*2 Sep 00*	4

Terence Trent D'ARBY — US

SINGLES:	HITS 11			WEEKS 77
IF YOU LET ME STAY	*CBS*	7	*14 Mar 87*	13
WISHING WELL	*CBS*	4	*20 Jun 87*	11
DANCE LITTLE SISTER (PART ONE)	*CBS*	20	*10 Oct 87*	7
SIGN YOUR NAME	*CBS*	2	*9 Jan 88*	10
TO KNOW SOMEONE DEEPLY IS TO KNOW SOMEONE SOFTLY	*CBS*	55	*20 Jan 90*	3
DO YOU LOVE ME LIKE YOU SAY?	*Columbia*	14	*17 Apr 93*	6
DELICATE	*Columbia*	14	*19 Jun 93*	6
Above hit: Terence Trent D'ARBY featuring DES'REE.				
SHE KISSED ME	*Columbia*	16	*28 Aug 93*	7
LET HER DOWN EASY	*Columbia*	18	*20 Nov 93*	7
HOLDING ON TO YOU	*Columbia*	20	*8 Apr 95*	6
VIBRATOR	*Columbia*	57	*5 Aug 95*	1
ALBUMS:	**HITS 4**			**WEEKS 96**
INTRODUCING THE HARDLINE ACCORDING TO TERENCE TRENT D'ARBY	*CBS*	1	*25 Jul 87*	65
NEITHER FISH NOR FLESH	*CBS*	12	*4 Nov 89*	5
SYMPHONY OR DAMN	*Columbia*	4	*15 May 93*	19
TERENCE TRENT D'ARBY'S VIBRATOR	*Columbia*	11	*29 Apr 95*	5
INTRODUCING THE HARDLINE ACCORDING TO TERENCE TRENT D'ARBY [RI]	*Columbia*	53	*16 Sep 95*	2

Richard DARBYSHIRE — UK

SINGLES:	HITS 3			WEEKS 7
COMING BACK FOR MORE	*Chrysalis*	41	*20 Aug 88*	3
Above hit: JELLYBEAN featuring Richard DARBYSHIRE.				
THIS I SWEAR	*Dome*	50	*24 Jul 93*	3
WHEN ONLY LOVE WILL DO	*Dome*	54	*12 Feb 94*	1

DARE — UK

SINGLES:	HITS 4			WEEKS 7
THE RAINDANCE	*A&M*	62	*29 Apr 89*	2
ABANDON	*A&M*	71	*29 Jul 89*	2
Original release reached No. 99 in 1988.				
WE DON'T NEED A REASON	*A&M*	52	*10 Aug 91*	2
REAL LOVE	*A&M*	67	*5 Oct 91*	1
ALBUMS:	**HITS 1**			**WEEKS 1**
BLOOD FROM STONE	*A&M*	48	*14 Sep 91*	1

Matt DAREY — UK

SINGLES:	HITS 4			WEEKS 10
LIBERATION (TEMPTATION - FLY LIKE AN ANGEL)	*Incentive*	19	*9 Oct 99*	3
Above hit: Matt DAREY presents MASH UP.				
FROM RUSSIA WITH LOVE	*Liquid Asset*	40	*22 Apr 00*	2
Track is based around an earlier Darey release (Li Kwan's Point Zero) and the orchestration of the 1963 James Bond film 'From Russia With Love'.				
Above hit: Matt DAREY presents DSP.				
BEAUTIFUL	*Incentive*	21	*15 Jul 00*	4
Above hit: Matt DAREY'S MASH UP featuring Marcella WOODS.				
MASH IT UP	*NuLife*	66	*27 Oct 01*	1
Above hit: MDM.				

Bobby DARIN — US

SINGLES:	HITS 17			WEEKS 162
SPLISH SPLASH •	*London*	28	*2 Aug 58*	1
SPLISH SPLASH [RE]	*London*	18	*16 Aug 58*	6
QUEEN OF THE HOP	*London*	24	*10 Jan 59*	2
DREAM LOVER •	*London*	1	*30 May 59*	19
MACK THE KNIFE •	*London*	1	*26 Sep 59*	16

MACK THE KNIFE [RE-1ST]	*London*	30	*23 Jan 60*	1
LA MER (BEYOND THE SEA)	*London*	8	*30 Jan 60*	11
Originally recorded by Charles Trenet.				
MACK THE KNIFE [RE-2ND]	*London*	50	*12 Mar 60*	1
CLEMENTINE	*London*	8	*2 Apr 60*	12
LA MER (BEYOND THE SEA) [RE]	*London*	40	*23 Apr 60*	2
BILL BAILEY WON'T YOU PLEASE COME HOME	*London*	36	*2 Jul 60*	1
Originally recorded by Arthur Collins in 1902.				
BILL BAILEY WON'T YOU PLEASE COME HOME [RE]	*London*	34	*16 Jul 60*	1
• LAZY RIVER	*London*	2	*18 Mar 61*	13
Originally recorded by Hoagy Carmichael.				
NATURE BOY	*London*	24	*8 Jul 61*	7
Originally recorded by Dick Haymes and the Song Spinners.				
YOU MUST HAVE BEEN A BEAUTIFUL BABY	*London*	10	*14 Oct 61*	11
Originally recorded by Bing Crosby.				
THEME FROM "COME SEPTEMBER"	*London*	50	*28 Oct 61*	1
Above hit: Bobby DARIN and his Orchestra.				
MULTIPLICATION	*London*	5	*23 Dec 61*	13
Above 2 from the film 'Come September'.				
THINGS	*London*	2	*21 Jul 62*	17
IF A MAN ANSWERS	*Capitol*	24	*6 Oct 62*	6
From the film 'If A Man Answers'.				
BABY FACE	*London*	40	*1 Dec 62*	4
Originally recorded by Al Jolson in 1949.				
EIGHTEEN YELLOW ROSES	*Capitol*	37	*27 Jul 63*	4
IF I WERE A CARPENTER	*Atlantic*	9	*15 Oct 66*	12
DREAM LOVER [RI] / MACK THE KNIFE [RI]	*Lightning*	64	*14 Apr 79*	1
EPS:	**HITS 1**			**WEEKS 9**
THAT'S ALL	*London*	6	*19 Mar 60*	9
ALBUMS:	**HITS 3**			**WEEKS 15**
THIS IS DARIN	*London*	4	*19 Mar 60*	8
THAT'S ALL	*London*	15	*9 Apr 60*	1
THE LEGEND OF BOBBY DARIN - HIS GREATEST HITS	*Stylus*	39	*5 Oct 85*	6

DARIO G — UK

SINGLES:	**HITS 5**			**WEEKS 39**
SUNCHYME	*Eternal*	2	*27 Sep 97*	18
Samples Dream Academy's Life In A Northern Town.				
CARNAVAL DE PARIS	*Eternal*	5	*20 Jun 98*	9
SUNMACHINE	*Eternal*	17	*12 Sep 98*	4
Based around David Bowie's Memory Of A Free Festival, from the Space Oddity album.				
VOICES	*Eternal*	37	*25 Mar 00*	2
From the film 'The Beach'.				
Above hit: DARIO G featuring Vanessa QUINONES.				
DREAM TO ME	*Manifesto*	9	*3 Feb 01*	6
Based around a line from the Cranberries' Dreams.				
ALBUMS:	**HITS 1**			**WEEKS 4**
SUNMACHINE	*Eternal*	26	*11 Jul 98*	4

DARK STAR — UK

SINGLES:	**HITS 3**			**WEEKS 6**
ABOUT 3AM	*Harvest*	50	*26 Jun 99*	1
GRACEADELICA	*Harvest*	25	*15 Jan 00*	3
Originally released in October 1998.				
I AM THE SUN	*Harvest*	31	*13 May 00*	2

DARKMAN — UK

SINGLES:	**HITS 4**			**WEEKS 8**
YABBA DABBA DOO	*Wild Card*	49	*14 May 94*	2
WHO'S THE DARKMAN?	*Wild Card*	46	*20 Aug 94*	2
YABBA DABBA DOO [RM]	*Wild Card*	37	*3 Dec 94*	2
Remixed by Paul Waller and Seamus Haji.				
BRAND NEW DAY	*Wild Card*	74	*21 Oct 95*	1
REPUTATIONS (JUST BE GOOD TO ME)	*WEA*	75	*14 Nov 98*	1
Above hit: Andrea GRANT featuring DARKMAN.				

DARLING BUDS — UK

SINGLES:	**HITS 6**			**WEEKS 20**
BURST	*Epic*	50	*8 Oct 88*	5
HIT THE GROUND	*Epic*	27	*7 Jan 89*	5
LET'S GO ROUND THERE	*Epic*	49	*25 Mar 89*	4
YOU'VE GOT TO CHOOSE	*Epic*	45	*22 Jul 89*	3
TINY MACHINE	*Epic*	60	*2 Jun 90*	2
SURE THING	*Epic*	71	*12 Sep 92*	1

ALBUMS:	HITS 1			WEEKS 3
POP SAID	*Epic*	23	*18 Feb 89*	3

Guy DARRELL — UK

SINGLES:	HITS 1			WEEKS 13
I'VE BEEN HURT *Originally recorded in 1966.*	*Santa Ponsa*	12	*18 Aug 73*	13

James DARREN — US

SINGLES:	HITS 4			WEEKS 25
BECAUSE THEY'RE YOUNG	*Pye International*	29	*13 Aug 60*	7
GOODBYE CRUEL WORLD *Originally recorded by Gloria Shayne.*	*Pye International*	28	*16 Dec 61*	9
HER ROYAL MAJESTY	*Pye International*	36	*31 Mar 62*	3
CONSCIENCE	*Pye International*	30	*23 Jun 62*	6

DARTS — UK

SINGLES:	HITS 12			WEEKS 117
DADDY COOL/THE GIRL CAN'T HELP IT [M] *Originally recorded by the Rays/Little Richard.*	*Magnet*	6	*5 Nov 77*	13
COME BACK MY LOVE *Originally recorded by the Wrens.*	*Magnet*	2	*28 Jan 78*	12
THE BOY FROM NEW YORK CITY *Original by the Ad-Libs reached No. 8 in the US in 1965.*	*Magnet*	2	*6 May 78*	13
IT'S RAINING	*Magnet*	2	*5 Aug 78*	11
DON'T LET IT FADE AWAY	*Magnet*	18	*11 Nov 78*	11
GET IT	*Magnet*	10	*10 Feb 79*	9
DUKE OF EARL *Originally recorded by Gene Chandler.*	*Magnet*	6	*21 Jul 79*	11
CAN'T GET ENOUGH OF YOUR LOVE	*Magnet*	43	*20 Oct 79*	6
REET PETITE	*Magnet*	51	*1 Dec 79*	7
LET'S HANG ON	*Magnet*	11	*31 May 80*	14
PEACHES *Originally recorded by Ikettes as Peaches and Cream in 1966.*	*Magnet*	66	*6 Sep 80*	3
WHITE CHRISTMAS / SH-BOOM (LIFE COULD BE A DREAM)	*Magnet*	48	*29 Nov 80*	7

ALBUMS:	HITS 4			WEEKS 57
DARTS	*Magnet*	9	*3 Dec 77*	22
EVERYONE PLAYS DARTS	*Magnet*	12	*3 Jun 78*	18
AMAZING DARTS	*Magnet*	8	*18 Nov 78*	13
DART ATTACK	*Magnet*	38	*6 Oct 79*	4

DARUDE — Finland

SINGLES:	HITS 3			WEEKS 29
SANDSTORM	*Neo*	3	*24 Jun 00*	15
FEEL THE BEAT	*Neo*	5	*25 Nov 00*	10
OUT OF CONTROL (BACK FOR MORE) *Vocals by Tammy Marie.*	*Neo*	13	*15 Sep 01*	4

DAS EFX — US

SINGLES:	HITS 2			WEEKS 5
CHECK YO SELF *Samples Grand Master Flash The Message.* *Above hit: ICE CUBE (featuring DAS EFX).*	*Fourth & Broadway*	36	*7 Aug 93*	4
RAP SCHOLAR *Above hit: DAS EFX featuring REDMAN.*	*East West America*	42	*25 Apr 98*	1

N'Dea DAVENPORT — US

(See also Brand New Heavies.)

SINGLES:	HITS 2			WEEKS 3
TRUST ME *Above hit: GURU featuring N'Dea DAVENPORT.*	*Cooltempo*	34	*11 Sep 93*	2
BRING IT ON	*V2*	52	*20 Jun 98*	1

Anne-Marie DAVID — France

SINGLES:	HITS 1			WEEKS 9
WONDERFUL DREAM *Eurovision Song Contest winner for Luxembourg in 1973.*	*Epic*	13	*28 Apr 73*	9

Craig DAVID — UK

(See also Artful Dodger.)

SINGLES:	HITS 4			WEEKS 52
FILL ME IN	*Wildstar*	1	*15 Apr 00*	14
7 DAYS	*Wildstar*	1	*5 Aug 00*	14

7 DAYS [RE]	*Wildstar*	74	*18 Nov 00*	1
WALKING AWAY	*Wildstar*	3	*2 Dec 00*	13
RENDEZVOUS	*Wildstar*	8	*31 Mar 01*	10
ALBUMS:	**HITS 1**			**WEEKS 48**
BORN TO DO IT	*Wildstar*	1	*26 Aug 00*	48

F.R. DAVID — France

SINGLES:	**HITS 2**			**WEEKS 13**
WORDS	*Carrere*	2	*2 Apr 83*	12
MUSIC	*Carrere*	71	*18 Jun 83*	1
ALBUMS:	**HITS 1**			**WEEKS 6**
WORDS	*Carrere*	46	*7 May 83*	6

DAVID and JONATHAN — UK

SINGLES:	**HITS 2**			**WEEKS 22**
MICHELLE	*Columbia*	11	*15 Jan 66*	6
Originally recorded by the Beatles.				
LOVERS OF THE WORLD UNITE	*Columbia*	7	*9 Jul 66*	16

DAVID DEVANT AND HIS SPIRIT WIFE — UK

SINGLES:	**HITS 2**			**WEEKS 2**
GINGER	*Kindness*	54	*5 Apr 97*	1
THIS IS FOR REAL	*Kindness*	61	*21 Jun 97*	1
ALBUMS:	**HITS 1**			**WEEKS 1**
WORK, LOVELIFE, MISCELLANEOUS	*Kindness*	70	*5 Jul 97*	1

Jim DAVIDSON — UK

SINGLES:	**HITS 1**			**WEEKS 4**
WHITE CHRISTMAS / TOO RISKY	*Scratch*	52	*27 Dec 80*	4

Paul DAVIDSON — Jamaica

SINGLES:	**HITS 1**			**WEEKS 10**
MIDNIGHT RIDER	*Tropical*	10	*27 Dec 75*	10
Originally recorded by the Allman Brothers.				

Hutch DAVIE ORCHESTRA - See Linda SCOTT

Dave DAVIES — UK

SINGLES:	**HITS 2**			**WEEKS 17**
DEATH OF A CLOWN	*Pye*	3	*22 Jul 67*	10
SUZANAH'S STILL ALIVE	*Pye*	20	*9 Dec 67*	7

Ray DAVIES - See Ken THORNE and his Orchestra

Windsor DAVIES as B.S.M. WILLIAMS and Don ESTELLE as GUNNER SUGDEN (LOFTY) — UK

SINGLES:	**HITS 2**			**WEEKS 16**
WHISPERING GRASS	*EMI*	1	*17 May 75*	12
Originally recorded by Inkspots.				
PAPER DOLL	*EMI*	41	*25 Oct 75*	4
Above hit: Don ESTELLE and Windsor DAVIES.				
ALBUMS:	**HITS 1**			**WEEKS 8**
SING LOFTY	*EMI*	10	*10 Jan 76*	8
Above hit: Don ESTELLE and Windsor DAVIES.				

Andrew DAVIS - See BBC SYMPHONY ORCHESTRA, SINGERS and SYMPHONY CHORUS

Billie DAVIS — UK

SINGLES:	**HITS 4**			**WEEKS 33**
WILL I WHAT	*Parlophone*	18	*1 Sep 62*	10
Above hit: Mike SARNE featuring Billie DAVIS with the Charles BLACKWELL ORCHESTRA.				
TELL HIM	*Decca*	10	*9 Feb 63*	12
HE'S THE ONE	*Decca*	40	*1 Jun 63*	3
I WANT YOU TO BE MY BABY	*Decca*	33	*12 Oct 68*	8
Backing vocals by Madeline Bell, Doris Troy and Kiki Dee.				

Billy DAVIS, JR. - See Marilyn McCOO and Billy DAVIS, JR.

Carl DAVIS and the ROYAL LIVERPOOL PHILHARMONIC ORCHESTRA and CHOIR — UK

ALBUMS:	**HITS 1**			**WEEKS 4**
PAUL McCARTNEY'S LIVERPOOL ORATORIO	*EMI Classics*	36	*19 Oct 91*	4

Colin DAVIS - See BBC SYMPHONY ORCHESTRA, SINGERS and SYMPHONY CHORUS

Darlene DAVIS — US

SINGLES:	HITS 1			WEEKS 5
I FOUND LOVE	*Serious*	55	*7 Feb 87*	5

John DAVIS and the MONSTER ORCHESTRA — US

SINGLES:	HITS 1			WEEKS 2
AIN'T THAT ENOUGH FOR YOU	*Miracle*	70	*10 Feb 79*	2

Mac DAVIS — US

SINGLES:	HITS 2			WEEKS 22
BABY DON'T GET HOOKED ON ME	*CBS*	29	*4 Nov 72*	6
IT'S HARD TO BE HUMBLE	*Casablanca*	27	*15 Nov 80*	16

Miles DAVIS — US

ALBUMS:	HITS 6			WEEKS 9
BITCHES BREW	*CBS*	71	*11 Jul 70*	1
YOU'RE UNDER ARREST	*CBS*	88	*15 Jun 85*	1
TUTU	*Warner Brothers*	74	*18 Oct 86*	2
AMANDLA	*Warner Brothers*	49	*3 Jun 89*	2
THE VERY BEST OF MILES DAVIS	*Columbia*	64	*5 Oct 96*	1
Released to commemorate the 5th anniversary of his death.				
KIND OF BLUE	*Columbia*	63	*28 Apr 01*	2
Originally released in April 1959.				

Richie DAVIS – See SHUT UP AND DANCE

Roy DAVIS JR. featuring Peven EVERETT — US

SINGLES:	HITS 1			WEEKS 4
GABRIEL	*XL Recordings*	22	*1 Nov 97*	4

Ruth DAVIS – See Bo KIRKLAND and Ruth DAVIS

Sammy DAVIS JR. — US

SINGLES:	HITS 8			WEEKS 37
SOMETHING'S GOTTA GIVE •	*Brunswick*	19	*30 Jul 55*	2
SOMETHING'S GOTTA GIVE [RE]	*Brunswick*	11	*20 Aug 55*	5
LOVE ME OR LEAVE ME	*Brunswick*	8	*10 Sep 55*	6
Originally recorded by Ruth Etting. Above 2 entries were separate sides of the same release, each had its own chart run.				
THAT OLD BLACK MAGIC	*Brunswick*	16	*1 Oct 55*	1
Originally recorded by Glenn Miller. •				
HEY THERE	*Brunswick*	19	*8 Oct 55*	1
From the film 'The Pajama Game'. Originally recorded by John Raitt (Bonnie Raitt's father).				
LOVE ME OR LEAVE ME [RE]	*Brunswick*	18	*5 Nov 55*	2
IN A PERSIAN MARKET	*Brunswick*	28	*21 Apr 56*	1
ALL OF YOU	*Brunswick*	28	*29 Dec 56*	1
Above 8: Sammy DAVIS.				
HAPPY TO MAKE YOUR ACQUAINTANCE	*Brunswick*	46	*18 Jun 60*	1
Above hit: Sammy DAVIS JR. and Carmen McRAE.				
WHAT KIND OF FOOL AM I / GONNA BUILD A MOUNTAIN	*Reprise*	26	*24 Mar 62*	8
ME AND MY SHADOW	*Reprise*	20	*15 Dec 62*	7
Above hit: Frank SINATRA and Sammy DAVIS Jnr.				
ME AND MY SHADOW [RE]	*Reprise*	47	*9 Feb 63*	2
EPS:	**HITS 2**			**WEEKS 3**
STARRING SAMMY DAVIS, VOLUME 1	*Brunswick*	20	*30 Jul 60*	1
SAMMY DAVIS JR. IMPERSONATING	*Reprise*	18	*31 Aug 63*	2
ALBUMS:	**HITS 1**			**WEEKS 1**
SAMMY DAVIS JR. AT THE COCONUT GROVE	*Reprise*	19	*13 Apr 63*	1
COMPILATION ALBUMS:	**HITS 1**			**WEEKS 4**
EEE- O 11 - THE BEST OF THE RAT PACK	*Capitol*	2	*8 Dec 01*	4
Solo recordings and 2 duets. Above entry listed in the compilation chart.				
Above hit: Frank SINATRA Dean MARTIN Sammy DAVIS Jr.				

Skeeter DAVIS — US

SINGLES:	HITS 1			WEEKS 13
THE END OF THE WORLD	*RCA Victor*	18	*16 Mar 63*	13

Spencer DAVIS GROUP — UK

SINGLES:	HITS 10			WEEKS 71
I CAN'T STAND IT	*Fontana*	47	*5 Nov 64*	3
Original by the Soul Sisters.				
EVERY LITTLE BIT HURTS	*Fontana*	43	*27 Feb 65*	2
EVERY LITTLE BIT HURTS [RE]	*Fontana*	41	*20 Mar 65*	1
STRONG LOVE	*Fontana*	50	*12 Jun 65*	1

STRONG LOVE [RE]	*Fontana*	44	*26 Jun 65*	3
KEEP ON RUNNING	*Fontana*	1	*4 Dec 65*	14
SOMEBODY HELP ME	*Fontana*	1	*26 Mar 66*	10
Above 2 originally recorded by Jackie Edwards.				
WHEN I COME HOME	*Fontana*	12	*3 Sep 66*	9
GIMME SOME LOVING	*Fontana*	2	*5 Nov 66*	12
I'M A MAN	*Fontana*	9	*28 Jan 67*	7
TIME SELLER	*Fontana*	30	*12 Aug 67*	5
MR. SECOND CLASS	*United Artists*	35	*13 Jan 68*	4
EPS:	**HITS 2**			**WEEKS 34**
YOU PUT THE HURT ON ME	*Fontana*	4	*23 Oct 65*	27
SITTIN' AND THINKIN'	*Fontana*	3	*21 May 66*	7
ALBUMS:	**HITS 3**			**WEEKS 47**
THEIR FIRST LP	*Fontana*	6	*8 Jan 66*	9
THE SECOND ALBUM	*Fontana*	3	*22 Jan 66*	18
AUTUMN '66	*Fontana*	4	*10 Sep 66*	20

T.J. DAVIS — UK

SINGLES:	**HITS 1**			**WEEKS 1**
BRILLIANT FEELING	*Arista*	72	*27 Jul 96*	1
Above hit: FULL MONTY ALLSTARS featuring T.J. DAVIS.				
WONDERFUL LIFE	*Melting Pot*	42	*29 Dec 01*	1

Zelma DAVIS - See C&C MUSIC FACTORY

DAVIS PINCKNEY PROJECT - See GO GO LORENZO and the DAVIS PINCKNEY PROJECT

DAWN — US

SINGLES:	**HITS 6**			**WEEKS 109**
CANDIDA	*Bell*	9	*16 Jan 71*	11
KNOCK THREE TIMES	*Bell*	1	*10 Apr 71*	27
WHAT ARE YOU DOING SUNDAY	*Bell*	3	*31 Jul 71*	12
TIE A YELLOW RIBBON ROUND THE OLE OAK TREE	*Bell*	1	*10 Mar 73*	39
SAY, HAS ANYBODY SEEN MY SWEET GYPSY ROSE	*Bell*	12	*4 Aug 73*	15
TIE A YELLOW RIBBON ROUND THE OLE OAK TREE [RE]	*Bell*	41	*5 Jan 74*	1
WHO'S IN THE STRAWBERRY PATCH WITH SALLY	*Bell*	37	*9 Mar 74*	4
Above 4: DAWN featuring Tony ORLANDO.				
ALBUMS:	**HITS 1**			**WEEKS 2**
GOLDEN RIBBONS	*Bell*	46	*4 May 74*	2

DAWN OF THE REPLICANTS — UK

SINGLES:	**HITS 2**			**WEEKS 2**
CANDLEFIRE	*East West*	52	*7 Feb 98*	1
HOGWASH FARM (THE DIESEL HANDS E.P.) [EP]	*East West*	65	*4 Apr 98*	1
Lead track: Hogwash Farm (Re-Built).				
ALBUMS:	**HITS 1**			**WEEKS 1**
ONE HEAD, TWO ARMS, TWO LEGS	*East West*	62	*28 Feb 98*	1

Julie DAWN - See Cyril STAPLETON and his Orchestra

Liz DAWN - See Joe LONGTHORNE

Dana DAWSON — US

SINGLES:	**HITS 4**			**WEEKS 14**
3 IS FAMILY	*EMI*	9	*15 Jul 95*	8
GOT TO GIVE ME LOVE	*EMI*	27	*28 Oct 95*	2
SHOW ME	*EMI*	28	*4 May 96*	3
HOW I WANNA BE LOVED	*EMI*	42	*20 Jul 96*	1

Bobby DAY — US

SINGLES:	**HITS 1**			**WEEKS 2**
● ROCKIN' ROBIN	*London*	29	*8 Nov 58*	2

Darren DAY — UK

SINGLES:	**HITS 3**			**WEEKS 7**
YOUNG GIRL	*Bell*	42	*8 Oct 94*	2
SUMMER HOLIDAY MEDLEY [M]	*RCA*	17	*8 Jun 96*	4
Backing vocals by Cliff Richard. From the musical 'Summer Holiday'.				
HOW CAN I BE SURE?	*EastCoast*	71	*9 May 98*	1
ALBUMS:	**HITS 1**			**WEEKS 1**
DARREN DAY	*EastCoast*	62	*18 Apr 98*	1

Doris DAY — US

SINGLES:	HITS 14			WEEKS 146
SUGAR BUSH	*Columbia*	8	*15 Nov 52*	2
Above hit: Doris DAY and Frankie LAINE with Carl FISCHER'S ORCHESTRA and the Norman LUBOFF CHOIR.				
MY LOVE AND DEVOTION	*Columbia*	10	*22 Nov 52*	2
Above hit: Doris DAY with Percy FAITH and his Orchestra.				
SUGAR BUSH [RE]	*Columbia*	8	*6 Dec 52*	6
MA SAYS, PA SAYS	*Columbia*	12	*4 Apr 53*	1
A FULL TIME JOB	*Columbia*	11	*18 Apr 53*	1
Above 2 entries were separate sides of the same release, each had its own chart run.				
LET'S WALK THAT-A-WAY	*Philips*	4	*25 Jul 53*	14
Above 3: Doris DAY-Johnnie RAY with Paul WESTON and his Orchestra.				
SECRET LOVE	*Philips*	1	*3 Apr 54*	29
THE BLACK HILLS OF DAKOTA	*Philips*	7	*28 Aug 54*	8
Above 2 from the film 'Calamity Jane'.				
IF I GIVE MY HEART TO YOU	*Philips*	4	*2 Oct 54*	11
Above hit: Doris DAY with the MELLOMEN.				
READY, WILLING AND ABLE	*Philips*	7	*9 Apr 55*	9
From the film 'Young At Heart'.				
Above hit: Doris DAY with Buddy COLE and his Orchestra.				
LOVE ME OR LEAVE ME	*Philips*	20	*10 Sep 55*	1
Originally recorded by Ruth Etting.				
I'LL NEVER STOP LOVING YOU	*Philips*	17	*22 Oct 55*	2
I'LL NEVER STOP LOVING YOU [RE]	*Philips*	19	*26 Nov 55*	1
Above hit: Doris DAY with Percy FAITH and his Orchestra.				
WHATEVER WILL BE, WILL BE (QUE SERA, SERA)	*Philips*	1	*30 Jun 56*	22
From the film 'The Man Who Knew Too Much'.				
A VERY PRECIOUS LOVE	*Philips*	16	*14 Jun 58*	11
From the film 'Marjorie Morningstar'.				
EVERYBODY LOVES A LOVER	*Philips*	25	*16 Aug 58*	3
EVERYBODY LOVES A LOVER [RE]	*Philips*	27	*27 Sep 58*	1
Above 4: Doris DAY with Frank DE VOL and his Orchestra.				
MOVE OVER DARLING	*CBS*	8	*14 Mar 64*	16
From the film of the same name.				
MOVE OVER DARLING [RI]	*CBS*	45	*18 Apr 87*	6
Featured in the Pretty Polly tights TV commercial.				
EPS:	**HITS 1**			**WEEKS 6**
PILLOW TALK	*Philips*	11	*19 Mar 60*	6
ALBUMS:	**HITS 5**			**WEEKS 36**
20 GOLDEN GREATS	*Warwick*	12	*6 Jan 79*	11
A PORTRAIT OF DORIS DAY	*Stylus*	32	*11 Nov 89*	9
GREATEST HITS	*Telstar*	14	*6 Nov 93*	12
THE LOVE ALBUM	*Vision*	64	*10 Dec 94*	3
THE MAGIC OF THE MOVIES	*Columbia*	63	*20 Nov 99*	1

Inaya DAY — US

SINGLES:	HITS 2			WEEKS 3
JUST CAN'T GET ENOUGH	*Almo Sounds*	39	*22 May 99*	2
Above hit: Harry 'Choo Choo' ROMERO presents Inaya DAY				
FEEL IT	*Positiva*	51	*7 Oct 00*	1

Patti DAY — US

SINGLES:	HITS 1			WEEKS 1
RIGHT BEFORE MY EYES	*Debut*	69	*9 Dec 89*	1

DAY ONE — UK

SINGLES:	HITS 1			WEEKS 1
I'M DOIN' FINE	*Melankolic*	68	*13 Nov 99*	1
ALBUMS:	**HITS 1**			**WEEKS 1**
ORDINARY MAN	*Melankolic*	70	*25 Mar 00*	1

DAYEENE — Sweden

SINGLES:	HITS 1			WEEKS 1
AND IT HURTS	*Pukka*	63	*17 Jul 99*	1

Taylor DAYNE — US

SINGLES:	HITS 10			WEEKS 54
TELL IT TO MY HEART	*Arista*	3	*23 Jan 88*	13
PROVE YOUR LOVE	*Arista*	8	*19 Mar 88*	10
I'LL ALWAYS LOVE YOU	*Arista*	41	*11 Jun 88*	7
WITH EVERY BEAT OF MY HEART	*Arista*	53	*18 Nov 89*	2
I'LL BE YOUR SHELTER	*Arista*	43	*14 Apr 90*	5
LOVE WILL LEAD YOU BACK	*Arista*	69	*4 Aug 90*	1

CAN'T GET ENOUGH OF YOUR LOVE	*Arista*	14	*3 Jul 93*	8
I'LL WAIT	*Arista*	29	*16 Apr 94*	3
ORIGINAL SIN (THEME FROM THE SHADOW) *From the film 'The Shadow'.*	*Arista*	63	*4 Feb 95*	1
SAY A PRAYER	*Arista*	58	*18 Nov 95*	1
TELL IT TO MY HEART [RM] *Remixed by T-Empo.*	*Arista*	23	*13 Jan 96*	3
ALBUMS:	**HITS 1**			**WEEKS 17**
TELL IT TO MY HEART	*Arista*	24	*5 Mar 88*	17

DAYTON — US

SINGLES:	**HITS 1**			**WEEKS 1**
THE SOUND OF MUSIC	*Capitol*	75	*10 Dec 83*	1

DAZZ BAND — US

SINGLES:	**HITS 1**			**WEEKS 12**
LET IT ALL BLOW	*Motown*	12	*3 Nov 84*	12

Darryl D'BONNEAU – See Lenny FONTANA; Barbara TUCKER

D'BORA — US

SINGLES:	**HITS 3**			**WEEKS 4**
DREAM ABOUT YOU	*Polydor*	75	*14 Sep 91*	1
GOING ROUND	*Vibe*	40	*1 Jul 95*	2
GOOD LOVE REAL LOVE	*MCA/Music Plant*	58	*30 Mar 96*	1

Nino DE ANGELO — Germany

SINGLES:	**HITS 1**			**WEEKS 5**
GUARDIAN ANGEL	*Carrere*	57	*21 Jul 84*	5

DE BOS — Holland

SINGLES:	**HITS 1**			**WEEKS 1**
ON THE RUN	*Jive*	51	*25 Oct 97*	1

Chris DE BURGH — Ireland

SINGLES:	**HITS 14**			**WEEKS 71**
DON'T PAY THE FERRYMAN	*A&M*	48	*23 Oct 82*	5
HIGH ON EMOTION	*A&M*	44	*12 May 84*	5
THE LADY IN RED	*A&M*	1	*12 Jul 86*	14
FATAL HESITATION	*A&M*	44	*20 Sep 86*	4
A SPACEMAN CAME TRAVELLING / THE BALLROOM OF ROMANCE	*A&M*	40	*13 Dec 86*	5
THE LADY IN RED [RE]	*A&M*	74	*21 Feb 87*	1
THE SIMPLE TRUTH (A CHILD IS BORN)	*A&M*	69	*12 Dec 87*	2
THE SIMPLE TRUTH (A CHILD IS BORN) [RE]	*A&M*	55	*2 Jan 88*	1
MISSING YOU	*A&M*	3	*29 Oct 88*	12
TENDER HANDS	*A&M*	43	*7 Jan 89*	6
THIS WAITING HEART	*A&M*	59	*14 Oct 89*	3
THE SIMPLE TRUTH: CAMPAIGN FOR KURDISH REFUGEES [RI] *Charity record for the Red Cross campaign for the protection of war victims.*	*A&M*	36	*25 May 91*	2
SEPARATE TABLES	*A&M*	30	*11 Apr 92*	4
BLONDE HAIR, BLUE JEANS	*A&M*	51	*21 May 94*	1
THE SNOWS OF NEW YORK	*A&M*	60	*9 Dec 95*	1
SO BEAUTIFUL	*A&M*	29	*27 Sep 97*	4
WHEN I THINK OF YOU	*A&M*	59	*18 Sep 99*	1
ALBUMS:	**HITS 16**			**WEEKS 280**
BEST MOVES	*A&M*	65	*12 Sep 81*	4
THE GETAWAY	*A&M*	30	*9 Oct 82*	16
MAN ON THE LINE	*A&M*	11	*19 May 84*	24
THE VERY BEST OF CHRIS DE BURGH	*Telstar*	6	*29 Dec 84*	70
SPANISH TRAIN AND OTHER STORIES	*A&M*	78	*24 Aug 85*	3
INTO THE LIGHT	*A&M*	2	*7 Jun 86*	59
CRUSADER	*A&M*	72	*4 Oct 86*	1
FLYING COLOURS	*A&M*	1	*15 Oct 88*	30
FROM A SPARK TO A FLAME – THE VERY BEST OF CHRIS DE BURGH	*A&M*	4	*4 Nov 89*	29
HIGH ON EMOTION – LIVE FROM DUBLIN	*A&M*	15	*22 Sep 90*	6
POWER OF TEN	*A&M*	3	*9 May 92*	10
THIS WAY UP	*A&M*	5	*28 May 94*	6
BEAUTIFUL DREAMS	*A&M*	33	*18 Nov 95*	8
THE LOVE SONGS	*A&M*	8	*11 Oct 97*	7
QUIET REVOLUTION	*A&M*	23	*2 Oct 99*	3
THE ULTIMATE COLLECTION – NOTES FROM PLANET EARTH	*A&M*	19	*31 Mar 01*	4

DE CASTRO SISTERS vocal with the Skip MARTIN Orchestra — Cuba

SINGLES:	HITS 1			WEEKS 1
TEACH ME TONIGHT	*London*	20	*12 Feb 55*	1
Originally recorded by Janet Brace.				

DE-CODE featuring Beverli SKEETE — UK

SINGLES:	HITS 1			WEEKS 1
WONDERWALL / SOME MIGHT SAY	*Neoteric*	69	*18 May 96*	1

Etienne DE CRECY — France

SINGLES:	HITS 2			WEEKS 3
PRIX CHOC	*Different*	60	*28 Mar 98*	1
AM I WRONG	*XL Recordings*	44	*20 Jan 01*	2
Samples Millie Jackson's If Loving You Is Wrong (I Don't Want To Be Right).				

DE FUNK featuring F45 — UK

SINGLES:	HITS 1			WEEKS 1
PLEASURE LOVE	*INCredible*	49	*25 Sep 99*	1
Features guitar sample from Earth, Wind And Fire's September.				

Lennie DE ICE — UK

SINGLES:	HITS 1			WEEKS 1
WE ARE I.E.	*Distinct'ive*	61	*17 Apr 99*	1

DE LA SOUL — US

(See also Jungle Brothers.)

SINGLES:	HITS 14			WEEKS 62
ME MYSELF AND I	*Big Life*	22	*8 Apr 89*	8
SAY NO GO	*Big Life*	18	*8 Jul 89*	7
EYE KNOW	*Big Life*	14	*21 Oct 89*	7
Samples Otis Redding's (Sittin' On) The Dock Of The Bay.				
THE MAGIC NUMBER / BUDDY	*Big Life*	7	*23 Dec 89*	8
Buddy no longer listed from 14 Jan 90, hit peaked at No. 8.				
Above hit: DE LA SOUL / DE LA SOUL featuring the JUNGLE BROTHERS, Monie LOVE, QUEEN LATIFAH and Q-TIP.				
MAMMA GAVE BIRTH TO THE SOUL CHILDREN	*Gee Street*	14	*24 Mar 90*	7
Above hit: QUEEN LATIFAH + DE LA SOUL.				
RING RING RING (HA HA HEY)	*Big Life*	10	*27 Apr 91*	7
A ROLLER SKATING JAM NAMED "SATURDAYS"	*Big Life*	22	*3 Aug 91*	5
Samples Frankie Valli's Grease.				
KEEPIN' THE FAITH	*Big Life*	50	*23 Nov 91*	2
BREAKADAWN	*Big Life*	39	*18 Sep 93*	3
Samples Michael Jackson's I Can't Help It, Smokey Robinson's Quiet Storm, Bar Kays Song And Dance, Grand Funk's Nothing Is The Same and Kleer's Intimate Collection.				
FALLIN'	*Epic*	59	*2 Apr 94*	1
From the film 'Judgement Night'. Samples Tom Petty's Free Fallin'.				
Above hit: TEENAGE FANCLUB and DE LA SOUL.				
STAKES IS HIGH	*Tommy Boy*	55	*29 Jun 96*	1
4 MORE	*Tommy Boy*	52	*8 Mar 97*	1
Recreates Sharon Redd's Never Give You Up.				
Above hit: DE LA SOUL featuring ZHANE.				
OOOH.	*Tommy Boy*	29	*22 Jul 00*	2
Samples Lalo Schifrin's Enter The Dragon Theme.				
Above hit: DE LA SOUL featuring REDMAN.				
ALL GOOD? IT AIN'T - AND THAT'S THE TRUTH	*Tommy Boy*	33	*11 Nov 00*	3
Above hit: DE LA SOUL featuring Chaka KHAN.				

ALBUMS:	HITS 5			WEEKS 76
3 FEET HIGH AND RISING	*Big Life*	27	*25 Mar 89*	12
3 FEET HIGH AND RISING [RE]	*Big Life*	13	*15 Jul 89*	44
Peak position reached on 27 Jan 90.				
DE LA SOUL IS DEAD	*Big Life*	7	*25 May 91*	11
BUHLOONE MINDSTATE	*Big Life*	37	*9 Oct 93*	2
STAKES IS HIGH	*Tommy Boy*	42	*13 Jul 96*	1
3 FEET HIGH AND RISING [RI]	*Tommy Boy*	17	*9 Oct 99*	2
ART OFFICIAL INTELLIGENCE: MOSAIC THUMP	*Tommy Boy*	22	*19 Aug 00*	4

DE LEON – See DUMONDE

Donna DE LORY — US

SINGLES:	HITS 1			WEEKS 1
JUST A DREAM	*MCA*	71	*24 Jul 93*	1

Waldo DE LOS RIOS — Argentina

SINGLES:	HITS 1			WEEKS 16
MOZART SYMPHONY NO. 40 IN G MINOR K550 1ST MOVEMENT (ALLEGRO MOLTO)	*A&M*	5	*10 Apr 71*	16

ALBUMS:	HITS 1			WEEKS 26
SYMPHONIES FOR THE SEVENTIES	*A&M*	6	*1 May 71*	26

Vincent DE MOOR — Holland

SINGLES:	HITS 2			WEEKS 4
FLOWTATION	*XL Recordings*	54	*16 Aug 97*	1
FLY AWAY	*VC Recordings*	30	*7 Apr 01*	3

DE NADA — UK

SINGLES:	HITS 1			WEEKS 4
LOVE YOU ANYWAY	*Wildstar*	15	*25 Aug 01*	4

Lynsey DE PAUL — UK

SINGLES:	HITS 7			WEEKS 54
SUGAR ME	*MAM*	5	*19 Aug 72*	11
GETTING A DRAG	*MAM*	18	*2 Dec 72*	8
WON'T SOMBODY DANCE WITH ME	*MAM*	14	*27 Oct 73*	7
OOH I DO	*Warner Brothers*	25	*8 Jun 74*	6
NO HONESTLY	*Jet*	7	*2 Nov 74*	11
From the ITV series of the same name.				
MY MAN AND ME	*Jet*	40	*22 Mar 75*	4
ROCK BOTTOM	*Polydor*	19	*26 Mar 77*	7
UK's Eurovision entry in 1977, it came 2nd.				
Above hit: Lynsey DE PAUL and Mike MORAN.				

Tullio DE PISCOPO — Italy

SINGLES:	HITS 1			WEEKS 4
STOP BAJON . . . PRIMAVERA	*Greyhound*	58	*28 Feb 87*	4

Manitas DE PLATA — Spain

ALBUMS:	HITS 1			WEEKS 1
FLAMENCO GUITAR	*Philips*	40	*29 Jul 67*	1

Rebecca DE RUVO — Sweden

SINGLES:	HITS 1			WEEKS 1
I CAUGHT YOU OUT	*Arista*	72	*1 Oct 94*	1

Teri DE SARIO — US

SINGLES:	HITS 1			WEEKS 5
AIN'T NOTHING GONNA KEEP ME FROM YOU	*Casablanca*	52	*2 Sep 78*	5

Stephanie DE SYKES — UK

SINGLES:	HITS 2			WEEKS 17
BORN WITH A SMILE ON MY FACE	*Bradley's*	2	*20 Jul 74*	10
Above hit: Stephanie DE SYKES (with RAIN).				
WE'LL FIND OUR DAY	*Bradley's*	17	*19 Apr 75*	7

DE VANTE - See VARIOUS ARTISTS (EPs) 'Dangerous Minds EP'

Tony DE VIT — UK

(See also Various Artists (EPs) 'Trade EP 2'.)

SINGLES:	HITS 5			WEEKS 11
BURNING UP	*Icon*	25	*4 Mar 95*	3
HOOKED	*Labello Dance*	28	*12 Aug 95*	2
Above hit: 99TH FLOOR ELEVATORS featuring Tony DE VIT.				
TO THE LIMIT	*Xplode*	44	*9 Sep 95*	2
I'LL BE THERE	*Labello Dance*	37	*30 Mar 96*	2
Vocals by Lorraine.				
Above hit: 99TH FLOOR ELEVATORS featuring Tony DE VIT.				
THE DAWN	*Tidy Trax*	56	*28 Oct 00*	2
Originally released in November 1998.				

Frank DE VOL and his Orchestra - See Vic DAMONE; Doris DAY

DEACON BLUE — UK

SINGLES:	HITS 20			WEEKS 112
DIGNITY	*CBS*	31	*23 Jan 88*	8
WHEN WILL YOU MAKE MY TELEPHONE RING	*CBS*	34	*9 Apr 88*	7
Original release reached No. 86 in 1987.				

CHOCOLATE GIRL	*CBS*	43	*16 Jul 88*	7
REAL GONE KID	*CBS*	8	*15 Oct 88*	13
WAGES DAY	*CBS*	18	*4 Mar 89*	6
FERGUS SINGS THE BLUES	*CBS*	14	*20 May 89*	6
LOVE AND REGRET	*CBS*	28	*16 Sep 89*	5
QUEEN OF THE NEW YEAR	*CBS*	21	*6 Jan 90*	5
FOUR BACHARACH AND DAVID SONGS [EP]	*CBS*	2	*25 Aug 90*	9
Lead track: I'll Never Fall In Love Again.				
YOUR SWAYING ARMS	*Columbia*	23	*25 May 91*	4
TWIST AND SHOUT	*Columbia*	10	*27 Jul 91*	9
CLOSING TIME	*Columbia*	42	*12 Oct 91*	3
COVER FROM THE SKY	*Columbia*	31	*14 Dec 91*	4
YOUR TOWN	*Columbia*	14	*28 Nov 92*	8
WILL WE BE LOVERS	*Columbia*	31	*13 Feb 93*	4
ONLY TENDER LOVE	*Columbia*	22	*24 Apr 93*	4
HANG YOUR HEAD [EP]	*Columbia*	21	*17 Jul 93*	3
Lead track: Hang Your Head.				
I WAS RIGHT AND YOU WERE WRONG	*Columbia*	32	*2 Apr 94*	3
DIGNITY [RR]	*Columbia*	20	*28 May 94*	3
The original version first issued in 1987.				
EVERYTIME YOU SLEEP	*Papillon*	64	*28 Apr 01*	1
ALBUMS:	**HITS 8**			**WEEKS 217**
RAINTOWN	*CBS*	82	*6 Jun 87*	2
RAINTOWN [RE-1ST]	*CBS*	33	*5 Mar 88*	16
RAINTOWN [RE-2ND]	*CBS*	14	*16 Jul 88*	59
WHEN THE WORLD KNOWS YOUR NAME	*CBS*	1	*15 Apr 89*	54
OOH LAS VEGAS	*CBS*	3	*22 Sep 90*	8
FELLOW HOODLUMS	*Columbia*	2	*15 Jun 91*	27
WHATEVER YOU SAY, SAY NOTHING	*Columbia*	4	*13 Mar 93*	10
OUR TOWN - THE GREATEST HITS	*Columbia*	1	*16 Apr 94*	38
WALKING BACK HOME	*Columbia*	39	*23 Oct 99*	2
HOMESICK	*Papillon*	59	*12 May 01*	1

DEAD CAN DANCE — Australia

ALBUMS:	**HITS 2**			**WEEKS 3**
INTO THE LABYRINTH	*4AD*	47	*25 Sep 93*	1
SPIRITCHASER	*4AD*	43	*29 Jun 96*	2

DEAD DRED featuring ASEND and ULTRAVIBE — UK

SINGLES:	**HITS 1**			**WEEKS 2**
DRED BASS	*Moving Shadow*	60	*5 Nov 94*	2

DEAD END KIDS — UK

SINGLES:	**HITS 1**			**WEEKS 10**
HAVE I THE RIGHT	*CBS*	6	*26 Mar 77*	10

DEAD KENNEDYS — US

SINGLES:	**HITS 2**			**WEEKS 9**
KILL THE POOR	*Cherry Red*	49	*1 Nov 80*	3
TOO DRUNK TO FUCK	*Cherry Red*	36	*30 May 81*	6
ALBUMS:	**HITS 2**			**WEEKS 8**
FRESH FRUIT FOR ROTTING VEGETABLES	*Cherry Red*	33	*13 Sep 80*	6
GIVE ME CONVENIENCE	*Alternative Tentacles*	84	*4 Jul 87*	2

DEAD OR ALIVE — UK

SINGLES:	**HITS 10**			**WEEKS 70**
THAT'S THE WAY (I LIKE IT)	*Epic*	22	*24 Mar 84*	9
YOU SPIN ME ROUND (LIKE A RECORD)	*Epic*	1	*1 Dec 84*	23
LOVER COME BACK TO ME	*Epic*	11	*20 Apr 85*	8
IN TOO DEEP	*Epic*	14	*29 Jun 85*	8
MY HEART GOES BANG (GET ME TO THE DOCTOR)	*Epic*	23	*21 Sep 85*	6
BRAND NEW LOVER	*Epic*	31	*20 Sep 86*	4
SOMETHING IN MY HOUSE	*Epic*	12	*10 Jan 87*	7
HOOKED ON LOVE	*Epic*	69	*4 Apr 87*	2
TURN AROUND AND COUNT 2 TEN	*Epic*	70	*3 Sep 88*	1
COME HOME WITH ME BABY	*Epic*	62	*22 Jul 89*	2
ALBUMS:	**HITS 3**			**WEEKS 22**
SOPHISTICATED BOOM BOOM	*Epic*	29	*28 Apr 84*	3
YOUTHQUAKE	*Epic*	9	*25 May 85*	15
MAD, BAD AND DANGEROUS TO KNOW	*Epic*	27	*14 Feb 87*	4

DEAD PREZ — US

SINGLES:	**HITS 1**			**WEEKS 2**
HIP HOP	*Epic*	41	*11 Mar 00*	2

DEADLY SINS

UK/Italy

SINGLES:	HITS 1			WEEKS 2
WE ARE GOING ON DOWN	*Ffreedom*	45	*30 Apr 94*	2

Hazell DEAN

UK

SINGLES:	HITS 11			WEEKS 71
EVERGREEN / JEALOUS LOVE	*Proto*	63	*18 Feb 84*	3
SEARCHIN'	*Proto*	6	*21 Apr 84*	15
Original release reached No. 76 in 1983.				
WHATEVER I DO (WHEREVER I GO)	*Proto*	4	*28 Jul 84*	11
BACK IN MY ARMS (ONCE AGAIN)	*Proto*	41	*3 Nov 84*	4
NO FOOL (FOR LOVE)	*Proto*	41	*2 Mar 85*	5
THEY SAY IT'S GONNA RAIN	*Parlophone*	58	*12 Oct 85*	4
WHO'S LEAVING WHO	*EMI*	4	*2 Apr 88*	11
Originally recorded by Anne Murray.				
MAYBE (WE SHOULD CALL IT A DAY)	*EMI*	15	*25 Jun 88*	6
TURN IT INTO LOVE	*EMI*	21	*24 Sep 88*	7
LOVE PAINS	*Lisson*	48	*26 Aug 89*	4
BETTER OFF WITHOUT YOU	*Lisson*	72	*23 Mar 91*	1
ALBUMS:	**HITS 1**			**WEEKS 3**
ALWAYS	*EMI*	38	*22 Oct 88*	3

Jimmy DEAN

US

SINGLES:	HITS 2			WEEKS 17
BIG BAD JOHN	*Philips*	2	*28 Oct 61*	13
LITTLE BLACK BOOK	*CBS*	33	*10 Nov 62*	4

Letitia DEAN and Paul MEDFORD

UK

SINGLES:	HITS 1			WEEKS 7
SOMETHING OUTA NOTHING	*BBC*	12	*25 Oct 86*	7
Sung as The Banned in the BBC TV soap 'EastEnders'.				

Syd DEAN and his Band – See STARGAZERS

Sheryl DEANE – See THRILLSEEKERS featuring Sheryl DEANE

DEANNA – See David MORALES and Albert CABRERA present MOCA featuring DEANNA

DEAR JON

UK

SINGLES:	HITS 1			WEEKS 1
ONE GIFT OF LOVE	*MDMC*	68	*22 Apr 95*	1
Beaten into second place by Gina G in the contest to represent the UK at Eurovision.				

DEATH IN VEGAS

UK

SINGLES:	HITS 4			WEEKS 8
DIRT	*Concrete*	61	*2 Aug 97*	1
Original release reached No. 88 in 1996.				
ROCCO	*Concrete*	51	*1 Nov 97*	1
AISHA	*Concrete*	9	*12 Feb 00*	4
Vocals by Iggy Pop.				
DIRGE	*Concrete*	24	*6 May 00*	2
Vocals by Dot Allison.				
ALBUMS:	**HITS 2**			**WEEKS 13**
DEAD ELVIS	*Concrete*	52	*29 Mar 97*	1
THE CONTINO SESSIONS	*Concrete*	19	*25 Sep 99*	12
Named after the band's studio.				

DEBARGE

US

SINGLES:	HITS 2			WEEKS 17
RHYTHM OF THE NIGHT	*Gordy*	4	*6 Apr 85*	14
From the film 'The Last Dragon'.				
YOU WEAR IT WELL	*Gordy*	54	*21 Sep 85*	3
Above hit: El DEBARGE with DEBARGE.				
ALBUMS:	**HITS 1**			**WEEKS 2**
RHYTHM OF THE NIGHT	*Gordy*	94	*25 May 85*	2

Chico DEBARGE

US

SINGLES:	HITS 1			WEEKS 1
IGGIN' ME	*Universal*	50	*14 Mar 98*	1

El DEBARGE — US

(See also DeBarge; Quincy Jones.)

SINGLES:	HITS 1			WEEKS 2
WHO'S JOHNNY ("SHORT CIRCUIT" THEME)	*Gordy*	60	*28 Jun 86*	2
From the film 'Short Circuit'.				

Diana DECKER — US

SINGLES:	HITS 1			WEEKS 10
POPPA PICCOLINO	*Columbia*	2	*24 Oct 53*	8
POPPA PICCOLINO [RE]	*Columbia*	5	*9 Jan 54*	2

Dave DEE — UK

(See also Dave Dee, Dozy, Beaky, Mick and Tich.)

SINGLES:	HITS 1			WEEKS 4
MY WOMAN'S MAN	*Fontana*	42	*14 Mar 70*	4

Dave DEE, DOZY, BEAKY, MICK and TICH — UK

(See also D. B. M. and T.; Dave Dee.)

SINGLES:	HITS 13			WEEKS 141
YOU MAKE IT MOVE	*Fontana*	26	*25 Dec 65*	8
HOLD TIGHT!	*Fontana*	4	*5 Mar 66*	17
HIDEAWAY	*Fontana*	10	*11 Jun 66*	11
BEND IT!	*Fontana*	2	*17 Sep 66*	12
SAVE ME	*Fontana*	4	*10 Dec 66*	10
TOUCH ME, TOUCH ME	*Fontana*	13	*11 Mar 67*	9
OKAY!	*Fontana*	4	*20 May 67*	11
ZABADAK!	*Fontana*	3	*14 Oct 67*	14
THE LEGEND OF XANADU	*Fontana*	1	*17 Feb 68*	12
LAST NIGHT IN SOHO	*Fontana*	8	*6 Jul 68*	11
THE WRECK OF THE 'ANTOINETTE'	*Fontana*	14	*5 Oct 68*	9
DON JUAN	*Fontana*	23	*8 Mar 69*	9
SNAKE IN THE GRASS	*Fontana*	23	*17 May 69*	8
EPS:	**HITS 1**			**WEEKS 3**
LOOS OF ENGLAND	*Fontana*	8	*4 Mar 67*	3
ALBUMS:	**HITS 2**			**WEEKS 15**
DAVE DEE, DOZY, BEAKY, MICK AND TICH	*Fontana*	11	*2 Jul 66*	10
IF MUSIC BE THE FOOD OF LOVE ... PREPARE FOR INDIGESTION	*Fontana*	27	*7 Jan 67*	5

Jay DEE - See MJ COLE

Jazzy DEE — US

SINGLES:	HITS 1			WEEKS 5
GET ON UP	*Laurie*	53	*5 Mar 83*	5

Joey DEE and the STARLITERS — US

SINGLES:	HITS 1			WEEKS 8
PEPPERMINT TWIST	*Columbia*	33	*10 Feb 62*	8

Kiki DEE — UK

SINGLES:	HITS 10			WEEKS 79
AMOUREUSE	*Rocket*	13	*10 Nov 73*	13
Originally recorded by Veronique Sanson.				
I GOT THE MUSIC IN ME	*Rocket*	19	*7 Sep 74*	8
Originally recorded by Sabrina Lory.				
(YOU DON'T KNOW) HOW GLAD I AM	*Rocket*	33	*12 Apr 75*	4
Originally recorded by Nancy Wilson. Some labels only show title as How Glad I Am.				
Above 2: Kiki DEE BAND.				
DON'T GO BREAKING MY HEART	*Rocket*	1	*3 Jul 76*	14
Above hit: Elton JOHN and Kiki DEE.				
LOVING AND FREE / AMOUREUSE [RI]	*Rocket*	13	*11 Sep 76*	8
Amoureuse listed from 11 Sep 76 for 2 weeks and 9 Oct 76 for 4 weeks.				
FIRST THING IN THE MORNING	*Rocket*	32	*19 Feb 77*	5
CHICAGO	*Rocket*	28	*11 Jun 77*	4
[AA] listed with Bite Your Lip (Get Up and Dance) by Elton John.				
STAR	*Ariola*	13	*21 Feb 81*	10
PERFECT TIMING	*Ariola*	66	*23 May 81*	3
TRUE LOVE	*Rocket*	2	*20 Nov 93*	10
Above hit: Elton JOHN – duet with Kiki DEE.				
ALBUMS:	**HITS 3**			**WEEKS 11**
KIKI DEE	*Rocket*	24	*26 Mar 77*	5
PERFECT TIMING	*Ariola*	47	*18 Jul 81*	4
THE VERY BEST OF KIKI DEE	*Rocket*	62	*9 Apr 94*	2

Nancy DEE – See BENELUX and Nancy DEE

DEE – TAH — Chile

SINGLES:	HITS 3			WEEKS 16
RELAX *Samples Dire Straits' Why Worry.*	*ffrr*	11	*26 Sep 98*	8
EL PARAISCO RICO *Based around Madonna's La Isla Bonita.*	*ffrr*	39	*1 May 99*	2
1 2 3 4 GET WITH THE WICKED *Above hit: Richard BLACKWOOD featuring DEETAH.*	*East West*	10	*16 Sep 00*	6

DEEE-LITE — US/Russia/Japan

SINGLES:	HITS 6			WEEKS 30
GROOVE IS IN THE HEART / WHAT IS LOVE? *Bootsy Collins on backing vocals on Groove Is In The Heart. Samples Vernon Burch's Get Up. What Is Love? listed from 25 Aug 90.*	*Elektra*	2	*18 Aug 90*	13
POWER OF LOVE / DEEE-LITE THEME	*Elektra*	25	*24 Nov 90*	7
HOW DO YOU SAY . . . LOVE / GROOVE IS IN THE HEART (BOOTSIFIED TO THE NTH MIX) [RM]	*Elektra*	52	*23 Feb 91*	2
GOOD BEAT / RIDING ON THROUGH	*Elektra*	53	*27 Apr 91*	3
RUNAWAY	*Elektra*	45	*13 Jun 92*	3
PICNIC IN THE SUMMERTIME	*Elektra*	43	*30 Jul 94*	2
ALBUMS:	**HITS 2**			**WEEKS 19**
WORLD CLIQUE	*Elektra*	14	*8 Sep 90*	18
INFINITY WITHIN	*Elektra*	37	*4 Jul 92*	1

DEEJAY DAVY T – See PORN KINGS

DEEJAY PUNK-ROC — US

SINGLES:	HITS 4			WEEKS 5
DEAD HUSBAND	*Independiente*	71	*21 Mar 98*	1
MY BEATBOX	*Independiente*	43	*9 May 98*	1
FAR OUT	*Independiente*	43	*8 Aug 98*	2
ROC-IN-IT *Above hit: DEEJAY PUNK-ROC vs ONYX.*	*Independiente*	59	*20 Feb 99*	1
ALBUMS:	**HITS 1**			**WEEKS 1**
CHICKENEYE	*Independiente*	47	*30 May 98*	1

DEEJAY SVEN – See M.C. MIKER 'G' and DEEJAY SVEN

Carol DEENE — UK

SINGLES:	HITS 4			WEEKS 25
• SAD MOVIES	*His Master's Voice*	44	*28 Oct 61*	3
NORMAN *Above two originally recorded by John D.Loudermilk.*	*His Master's Voice*	24	*27 Jan 62*	8
• JOHNNY GET ANGRY *Above hit: Carol DEENE with the Michael SAMMES SINGERS.*	*His Master's Voice*	32	*7 Jul 62*	4
SOME PEOPLE *From the film of the same name.*	*His Master's Voice*	25	*25 Aug 62*	10

Scotti DEEP — US

SINGLES:	HITS 1			WEEKS 1
BROOKLYN BEATS	*Extravaganza*	67	*15 Mar 97*	1

DEEP BLUE — UK

SINGLES:	HITS 1			WEEKS 2
THE HELICOPTER TUNE	*Moving Shadow*	68	*16 Apr 94*	2

DEEP BLUE SOMETHING — US

SINGLES:	HITS 2			WEEKS 17
BREAKFAST AT TIFFANY'S	*Interscope*	55	*6 Jul 96*	2
BREAKFAST AT TIFFANY'S [RE]	*Interscope*	1	*21 Sep 96*	12
JOSEY	*Interscope*	27	*7 Dec 96*	3
ALBUMS:	**HITS 1**			**WEEKS 5**
HOME	*Interscope*	24	*5 Oct 96*	5

DEEP C — UK

SINGLES:	HITS 2			WEEKS 3
AFRICAN REIGN	*M&G*	75	*19 Jan 91*	1
CHILL TO THE PANIC *Above hit: DEEP C featuring DEZZ the DEZZ and SHOLA.*	*M&G*	73	*8 Jun 91*	2

DEEP CREED 94

US

(See also Armand Van Helden.)

SINGLES:	HITS 1			WEEKS 1
CAN U FEEL IT	*Eastern Bloc*	59	*7 May 94*	1

DEEP DISH

US

SINGLES:	HITS 2			WEEKS 4
STAY GOLD	*Deconstruction*	41	*26 Oct 96*	1
STRANDED	*Deconstruction*	60	*1 Nov 97*	1
THE FUTURE OF THE FUTURE (STAY GOLD) [RM]	*Deconstruction*	31	*3 Oct 98*	2
Remixed by Ben Watt/David Morales and includes vocals by Tracy Thorn.				
Above hit: DEEP DISH with EVERYTHING BUT THE GIRL.				

ALBUMS:	HITS 1			WEEKS 2
JUNK SCIENCE	*Deconstruction*	37	*18 Jul 98*	2

DEEP FEELING

UK

SINGLES:	HITS 1			WEEKS 5
DO YOU LOVE ME	*Page One*	45	*25 Apr 70*	1
DO YOU LOVE ME [RE]	*Page One*	34	*9 May 70*	4

DEEP FOREST

France

SINGLES:	HITS 4			WEEKS 14
SWEET LULLABY	*Columbia*	10	*5 Feb 94*	6
DEEP FOREST	*Columbia*	20	*21 May 94*	4
SAVANNA DANCE	*Columbia*	28	*23 Jul 94*	2
MARTA'S SONG	*Columbia*	26	*24 Jun 95*	2
Vocals by Marta Sebestyen. From the film 'Pret-A-Porter'.				

ALBUMS:	HITS 3			WEEKS 17
DEEP FOREST	*Columbia*	15	*26 Feb 94*	11
BOHEME	*Columbia*	12	*3 Jun 95*	5
COMPARSA	*Columbia*	60	*31 Jan 98*	1

DEEP PURPLE

UK

SINGLES:	HITS 13			WEEKS 85
BLACK NIGHT	*Harvest*	2	*15 Aug 70*	21
STRANGE KIND OF WOMAN	*Harvest*	8	*27 Feb 71*	12
FIREBALL	*Harvest*	15	*13 Nov 71*	13
NEVER BEFORE	*Purple*	35	*1 Apr 72*	6
SMOKE ON THE WATER	*Purple*	21	*16 Apr 77*	7
Song is about the fire at the Montreux Casino, Swizerland, 3 Dec 71.				
NEW LIVE AND RARE [EP]	*Purple*	31	*15 Oct 77*	4
Lead track: Black Night (Live Version).				
NEW LIVE AND RARE VOL. II [EP]	*Purple*	45	*7 Oct 78*	3
Lead track: Burn (Edited Version).				
BLACK NIGHT [RI]	*Harvest*	43	*2 Aug 80*	6
NEW LIVE AND RARE VOLUME 3 [EP]	*Harvest*	48	*1 Nov 80*	3
Lead track: Smoke On The Water (Live).				
PERFECT STRANGERS	*Polydor*	48	*26 Jan 85*	3
KNOCKING AT YOUR BACK DOOR / PERFECT STRANGERS [RI]	*Polydor*	68	*15 Jun 85*	1
HUSH	*Polydor*	62	*18 Jun 88*	2
Re-recording of their first single which was originally released in 1968 on the Parlophone label.				
KING OF DREAMS	*RCA*	70	*20 Oct 90*	1
LOVE CONQUERS ALL	*RCA*	57	*2 Mar 91*	2
BLACK NIGHT [RM]	*EMI*	66	*24 Jun 95*	1
Released to coincide with 25th anniversary of the Deep Purple In Rock album. Remixed by Roger Glover.				

ALBUMS:	HITS 23			WEEKS 278

COMPILATION ALBUMS:	HITS 1			WEEKS 13
CONCERTO FOR GROUP AND ORCHESTRA	*Harvest*	26	*24 Jan 70*	4
Live recordings from the Royal Albert Hall on 15 Sep 70 with the Royal Philharmonic Orchestra conducted by Malcolm Arnold.				
DEEP PURPLE IN ROCK	*Harvest*	4	*20 Jun 70*	68
FIREBALL	*Harvest*	1	*18 Sep 71*	25
MACHINE HEAD	*Purple*	1	*15 Apr 72*	24
MADE IN JAPAN	*Purple*	16	*6 Jan 73*	14
Live recordings from Tokyo and Osako on 16 & 17 Aug 72.				
WHO DO WE THINK WE ARE	*Purple*	4	*17 Feb 73*	11
BURN	*Purple*	3	*2 Mar 74*	21
STORM BRINGER	*Purple*	6	*23 Nov 74*	12
24 CARAT PURPLE	*Purple*	14	*5 Jul 75*	17
COME TASTE THE BAND	*Purple*	19	*22 Nov 75*	4
DEEP PURPLE LIVE	*Purple*	12	*27 Nov 76*	6
Live recordings from their 1975 European tour.				
THE MARK II PURPLE SINGLES	*Purple*	24	*21 Apr 79*	6

DEEPEST PURPLE	*Harvest*	1	*19 Jul 80*	15
IN CONCERT	*Harvest*	30	*13 Dec 80*	8
Live recordings from 1970–72.				
DEEP PURPLE LIVE IN LONDON	*Harvest*	23	*4 Sep 82*	5
Recorded in 1974 for the BBC.				
PERFECT STRANGERS	*Polydor*	5	*10 Nov 84*	15
THE ANTHOLOGY	*Harvest*	50	*29 Jun 85*	3
THE HOUSE OF BLUE LIGHT	*Polydor*	10	*24 Jan 87*	9
NOBODY'S PERFECT	*Polydor*	38	*16 Jul 88*	2
SLAVES AND MASTERS	*RCA*	45	*3 Nov 90*	2
PURPLE RAINBOWS	*PolyGram TV/EMI*	1	*13 Jul 91*	13
Majority of tracks are by Deep Purple but as it included tracks by Rainbow, Whitesnake, Graham Bonnet and Dio it was relegated to the Compilation Chart.				
THE BATTLE RAGES ON . . .	*RCA*	21	*7 Aug 93*	3
PURPENDICULAR	*RCA*	58	*17 Feb 96*	1
MADE IN JAPAN [RI]	*EMI*	73	*31 Jan 98*	1
Re-issued with bonus CD of 3 encores.				
30: VERY BEST OF DEEP PURPLE	*EMI*	39	*24 Oct 98*	2

DEEP RIVER BOYS with Sid PHILLIPS and his Orchestra — US

SINGLES:	HITS 1			WEEKS 1
THAT'S RIGHT	*His Master's Voice*	29	*8 Dec 56*	1

Rick DEES and his CAST OF IDIOTS — US

SINGLES:	HITS 1			WEEKS 9
DISCO DUCK	*RSO*	6	*18 Sep 76*	9
Features duck noises by Ken Pruitt.				

DEF LEPPARD — UK

SINGLES:	HITS 24			WEEKS 112
WASTED	*Vertigo*	61	*17 Nov 79*	3
HELLO AMERICA	*Vertigo*	45	*23 Feb 80*	4
PHOTOGRAPH	*Vertigo*	66	*5 Feb 83*	3
ROCK OF AGES	*Vertigo*	41	*27 Aug 83*	4
ANIMAL	*Bludgeon Riffola*	6	*1 Aug 87*	9
POUR SOME SUGAR ON ME	*Bludgeon Riffola*	18	*19 Sep 87*	6
HYSTERIA	*Bludgeon Riffola*	26	*28 Nov 87*	5
HYSTERIA [RE]	*Bludgeon Riffola*	74	*9 Jan 88*	1
ARMAGEDDON IT (THE ATOMIC MIX)	*Bludgeon Riffola*	20	*9 Apr 88*	5
LOVE BITES	*Bludgeon Riffola*	11	*16 Jul 88*	8
ROCKET	*Bludgeon Riffola*	15	*11 Feb 89*	7
LET'S GET ROCKED	*Bludgeon Riffola*	2	*28 Mar 92*	7
MAKE LOVE LIKE A MAN	*Bludgeon Riffola*	12	*27 Jun 92*	5
HAVE YOU EVER NEEDED SOMEONE SO BAD	*Bludgeon Riffola*	16	*12 Sep 92*	5
HEAVEN IS	*Bludgeon Riffola*	13	*30 Jan 93*	5
TONIGHT	*Bludgeon Riffola*	34	*1 May 93*	3
TWO STEPS BEHIND	*Bludgeon Riffola*	32	*18 Sep 93*	4
From the film 'Last Action Hero'.				
ACTION	*Bludgeon Riffola*	14	*15 Jan 94*	5
WHEN LOVE & HATE COLLIDE	*Bludgeon Riffola*	2	*14 Oct 95*	10
SLANG	*Bludgeon Riffola*	17	*4 May 96*	5
WORK IT OUT	*Bludgeon Riffola*	22	*13 Jul 96*	3
ALL I WANT IS EVERYTHING	*Bludgeon Riffola*	38	*28 Sep 96*	2
BREATHE A SIGH	*Bludgeon Riffola*	43	*30 Nov 96*	1
PROMISES	*Bludgeon Riffola*	41	*24 Jul 99*	1
GOODBYE	*Bludgeon Riffola*	54	*9 Oct 99*	1
ALBUMS:	**HITS 9**			**WEEKS 187**
ON THROUGH THE NIGHT	*Vertigo*	15	*22 Mar 80*	8
HIGH 'N' DRY	*Vertigo*	26	*25 Jul 81*	8
PYROMANIA	*Vertigo*	18	*12 Mar 83*	8
HYSTERIA	*Bludgeon Riffola*	1	*29 Aug 87*	101
Includes re-entries through to 1992.				
ADRENALIZE	*Bludgeon Riffola*	1	*11 Apr 92*	30
RETRO ACTIVE	*Bludgeon Riffola*	6	*16 Oct 93*	5
VAULT - THE GREATEST HITS 1980-1995	*Bludgeon Riffola*	3	*4 Nov 95*	14
SLANG	*Bludgeon Riffola*	5	*25 May 96*	8
EUPHORIA	*Bludgeon Riffola*	11	*26 Jun 99*	5

DEFINITION OF SOUND — UK

SINGLES:	HITS 9			WEEKS 26
WEAR YOUR LOVE LIKE HEAVEN	*Circa*	17	*9 Mar 91*	9
NOW IS TOMORROW	*Circa*	46	*1 Jun 91*	4
Above hit: DEFINITION OF SOUND (vocals by Elaine VASSELL).				
MOIRA JANE'S CAFE	*Circa*	34	*8 Feb 92*	4
WHAT ARE YOU UNDER	*Circa*	68	*19 Sep 92*	1
CAN I GET OVER	*Circa*	61	*14 Nov 92*	2

BOOM BOOM	*Fontana*	59	*20 May 95*	1
Track based around a piano sample of the Moody Blues' Go Now.				
PASS THE VIBES	*Fontana*	23	*2 Dec 95*	3
CHILD	*Fontana*	48	*24 Feb 96*	1
HERE WE GO	*Freskanova*	45	*24 Jul 99*	1
Above hit: FREESTYLERS featuring DEFINITION OF SOUND.				
ALBUMS:	**HITS 1**			**WEEKS 3**
LOVE AND LIFE	*Circa*	38	*29 Jun 91*	3

DEFTONES — US

SINGLES:	**HITS 3**			**WEEKS 4**
MY OWN SUMMER (SHOVE IT)	*Maverick*	29	*21 Mar 98*	2
BE QUITE AND DRIVE (FAR AWAY)	*Maverick*	50	*11 Jul 98*	1
CHANGE (IN THE HOUSE OF FLIES)	*Maverick*	53	*26 Aug 00*	1
ALBUMS:	**HITS 3**			**WEEKS 5**
AROUND THE FUR	*Maverick*	56	*8 Nov 97*	1
WHITE PONY	*Maverick*	13	*1 Jul 00*	2
BACK TO SCHOOL (MINI MAGGIT)	*Maverick*	35	*24 Mar 01*	2
8 track mini album.				

DEGREES OF MOTION featuring BITI — US

SINGLES:	**HITS 3**			**WEEKS 21**
DO YOU WANT IT RIGHT NOW	*ffrr*	31	*25 Apr 92*	5
Originally recorded by Taylor Dayne.				
SHINE ON	*ffrr*	43	*18 Jul 92*	3
Above hit: DEGREES OF MOTION featuring BITI with Kit WEST.				
SOUL FREEDOM - FREE YOUR SOUL	*ffrr*	64	*7 Nov 92*	1
SHINE ON [RM]	*ffrr*	8	*19 Mar 94*	8
DO YOU WANT IT RIGHT NOW [RM]	*ffrr*	26	*25 Jun 94*	4
Above 2 remixed by Richie Jones.				
Above hit: DEGREES OF MOTION.				

DEICIDE — US

ALBUMS:	**HITS 1**			**WEEKS 1**
ONCE UPON THE CROSS	*Roadrunner*	66	*13 May 95*	1

DEJA — US

SINGLES:	**HITS 1**			**WEEKS 1**
SERIOUS	*10 Records*	75	*29 Aug 87*	1

DEJA VU — UK

SINGLES:	**HITS 1**			**WEEKS 1**
WHY? WHY? WHY?	*Cowboy*	57	*5 Feb 94*	1

Desmond DEKKER and the ACES — Jamaica

SINGLES:	**HITS 6**			**WEEKS 71**
007 (SHANTY TOWN)	*Pyramid*	14	*15 Jul 67*	11
Some labels credit simply 007.				
ISRAELITES	*Pyramid*	1	*22 Mar 69*	14
First reggae song to top the UK chart.				
IT MIEK	*Pyramid*	7	*28 Jun 69*	11
ISRAELITES [RE]	*Pyramid*	45	*5 Jul 69*	1
PICKNEY GAL	*Pyramid*	42	*10 Jan 70*	3
YOU CAN GET IT IF YOU REALLY WANT	*Trojan*	2	*22 Aug 70*	15
ISRAELITES [RI]	*Cactus*	10	*10 May 75*	9
SING A LITTLE SONG	*Cactus*	16	*30 Aug 75*	7
Above 4: Desmond DEKKER.				
ALBUMS:	**HITS 1**			**WEEKS 4**
THIS IS DESMOND DEKKER	*Trojan*	27	*5 Jul 69*	4
Above hit: Desmond DEKKER.				

DEL AMITRI — UK

SINGLES:	**HITS 16**			**WEEKS 69**
KISS THIS THING GOODBYE	*A&M*	59	*19 Aug 89*	2
NOTHING EVER HAPPENS	*A&M*	11	*13 Jan 90*	9
KISS THIS THING GOODBYE [RI]	*A&M*	43	*24 Mar 90*	4
MOVE AWAY JIMMY BLUE	*A&M*	36	*16 Jun 90*	6
SPIT IN THE RAIN	*A&M*	21	*3 Nov 90*	6
ALWAYS THE LAST TO KNOW	*A&M*	13	*9 May 92*	7
BE MY DOWNFALL	*A&M*	30	*11 Jul 92*	4
JUST LIKE A MAN	*A&M*	25	*12 Sep 92*	4
WHEN YOU WERE YOUNG	*A&M*	20	*23 Jan 93*	3
HERE AND NOW	*A&M*	21	*18 Feb 95*	4
DRIVING WITH THE BRAKES ON	*A&M*	18	*29 Apr 95*	4

ROLL TO ME	*A&M*	22	*8 Jul 95*	4
TELL HER THIS	*A&M*	32	*28 Oct 95*	2
NOT WHERE IT'S AT	*A&M*	21	*21 Jun 97*	3
SOME OTHER SUCKER'S PARADE	*A&M*	46	*6 Dec 97*	1
DON'T COME HOME TOO SOON (OFFICIAL TEAM SCOTLAND SONG WORLD CUP '98)	*A&M*	15	*13 Jun 98*	4
CRY TO BE FOUND	*Mercury*	40	*5 Sep 98*	2
ALBUMS:	**HITS 5**			**WEEKS 105**
WAKING HOURS	*A&M*	6	*24 Feb 90*	44
CHANGE EVERYTHING	*A&M*	2	*13 Jun 92*	20
TWISTED	*A&M*	3	*11 Mar 95*	25
SOME OTHER SUCKER'S PARADE	*A&M*	6	*12 Jul 97*	5
THE BEST OF DEL AMITRI - HATFUL OF RAIN	*Mercury*	5	*19 Sep 98*	11

Also released at same time was an album of B-sides, ineligible for the chart because of its low price.

DE'LACY — US

SINGLES:	**HITS 2**			**WEEKS 16**
HIDEAWAY	*Deconstruction*	9	*2 Sep 95*	10
THAT LOOK	*Deconstruction*	19	*31 Aug 96*	4
HIDEAWAY 1998 [RM]	*Deconstruction*	21	*14 Feb 98*	2

Remixed by Nu Birth.

ALBUMS:	**HITS 1**			**WEEKS 1**
HIDEAWAY	*Slip'n'Slide*	53	*1 Jul 95*	1

Doublepack 12" single featuring 4 mixes.

DELAGE — UK

SINGLES:	**HITS 1**			**WEEKS 2**
ROCK THE BOAT	*PWL/Polydor*	63	*15 Dec 90*	2

DELAKOTA — UK

SINGLES:	**HITS 3**			**WEEKS 3**
THE ROCK	*Go.Beat*	60	*18 Jul 98*	1
C'MON CINCINNATI	*Go.Beat*	55	*19 Sep 98*	1
Above hit: DELAKOTA featuring Rose SMITH.				
555	*Go.Beat*	42	*13 Feb 99*	1
ALBUMS:	**HITS 1**			**WEEKS 1**
ONE LOVE	*Go.Beat*	58	*3 Oct 98*	1

DELANEY and BONNIE and FRIENDS — US

SINGLES:	**HITS 1**			**WEEKS 9**
COMIN' HOME	*Atlantic*	16	*20 Dec 69*	9
Above hit: DELANEY and BONNIE and FRIENDS featuring Eric CLAPTON.				
ALBUMS:	**HITS 1**			**WEEKS 3**
ON TOUR	*Atlantic*	39	*6 Jun 70*	3

DELANO - See CZR featuring DELANO

DELEGATION — UK

SINGLES:	**HITS 2**			**WEEKS 7**
WHERE IS THE LOVE (WE USED TO KNOW)	*State*	22	*23 Apr 77*	6
YOU'RE BEEN DOING ME WRONG	*State*	49	*20 Aug 77*	1

DELERIUM — Canada

SINGLES:	**HITS 4**			**WEEKS 23**
SILENCE	*Nettwerk*	73	*12 Jun 99*	1
Vocals by Sarah McLachlan.				
HEAVEN'S EARTH	*Nettwerk*	44	*5 Feb 00*	1
SILENCE [RM]	*Nettwerk*	3	*14 Oct 00*	16
Remixed by Airscape.				
Above hit: DELERIUM featuring Sarah McLACHLAN.				
INNOCENTE (FALLING IN LOVE)	*Nettwerk*	32	*7 Jul 01*	3
Above hit: DELERIUM featuring Leigh NASH (Of SIXPENCE NONE THE RICHER)				
UNDERWATER	*Nettwerk*	33	*24 Nov 01*	2
Above hit: DELERIUM featuring RANI.				

DELFONICS — US

SINGLES:	**HITS 3**			**WEEKS 23**
DIDN'T I (BLOW YOUR MIND THIS TIME)	*Bell*	43	*10 Apr 71*	1
DIDN'T I (BLOW YOUR MIND THIS TIME) [RE]	*Bell*	22	*24 Apr 71*	8
LA-LA MEANS I LOVE YOU	*Bell*	19	*10 Jul 71*	10
READY OR NOT HERE I COME (CAN'T HIDE THE LOVE)	*Bell*	41	*16 Oct 71*	4

DELGADOS — UK

SINGLES:	HITS 2			WEEKS 2
PULL THE WIRES FROM THE WALL	*Chemikal Underground*	69	*23 May 98*	1
AMERICAN TRILOGY	*Chemikal Underground*	61	*3 Jun 00*	1
ALBUMS:	**HITS 2**			**WEEKS 2**
PELOTON	*Chemikal Underground*	56	*20 Jun 98*	1
THE GREAT EASTERN	*Chemikal Underground*	72	*29 Apr 00*	1

Named after the Great Eastern Hotel for the homeless in Glasgow.

DELIRIOUS? — UK

SINGLES:	HITS 7			WEEKS 17
WHITE RIBBON DAY	*Furious?*	41	*1 Mar 97*	2
DEEPER	*Furious?*	20	*17 May 97*	3
PROMISE	*Furious?*	20	*26 Jul 97*	2
DEEPER [RI]	*Furious?*	36	*15 Nov 97*	2
SEE THE STAR	*Furious?*	16	*27 Mar 99*	2
IT'S OK	*Furious?*	18	*4 Mar 00*	2
WAITING FOR THE SUMMER	*Furious?*	26	*16 Jun 01*	2
I COULD SING OF YOUR LOVE FOREVER	*Furious?*	40	*22 Dec 01*	2
ALBUMS:	**HITS 3**			**WEEKS 6**
KING OF FOOLS	*Furious?*	13	*28 Jun 97*	3
MEZZAMORPHIS	*Furious?*	25	*24 Apr 99*	2
AUDIO LESSONOVER?	*Furious?*	58	*18 Aug 01*	1

'DELIVERANCE' SOUNDTRACK — US

SINGLES:	HITS 1			WEEKS 7
DUELLING BANJOS	*Warner Brothers*	17	*31 Mar 73*	7

From the film 'Deliverance'. Originally recorded by Arthur 'Guitar Boogie' Smith in 1955 as the Feuding Banjos.

DELLS — US

SINGLES:	HITS 1			WEEKS 9
MEDLEY: (a) SING A RAINBOW (b) LOVE IS BLUE [M]	*Chess*	15	*19 Jul 69*	9

DELORES – See MONOBOY featuring DELORES

DELTA – See David MORALES

DELUXE — US

SINGLES:	HITS 1			WEEKS 1
JUST A LITTLE MORE	*Unyque*	74	*18 Mar 89*	1

DEM 2 — UK

SINGLES:	HITS 1			WEEKS 2
DESTINY	*Locked On*	58	*24 Oct 98*	2

DEMETREUS – See Christian FALK featuring DEMETREUS

DEMOLITION MAN – See PRIZNA featuring the DEMOLITION MAN

DEMON — UK

ALBUMS:	HITS 2			WEEKS 5
THE UNEXPECTED GUEST	*Carrere*	47	*14 Aug 82*	3
THE PLAGUE	*Clay*	73	*2 Jul 83*	2

DEMON vs HEARTBREAKER — France

SINGLES:	HITS 1			WEEKS 1
YOU ARE MY HIGH	*Source*	70	*19 May 01*	1

Samples the Gap Band's You Are My High.

D'EMPRESS – See 187 LOCKDOWN

Chaka DEMUS and PLIERS — Jamaica

SINGLES:	HITS 8			WEEKS 55
TEASE ME	*Mango*	3	*12 Jun 93*	15
SHE DON'T LET NOBODY	*Mango*	4	*18 Sep 93*	10
Originally recorded by Curtis Mayfield.				
TWIST AND SHOUT	*Mango*	1	*18 Dec 93*	13
Above hit: Chaka DEMUS and PLIERS with JACK RADICS and TAXI GANG.				
MURDER SHE WROTE	*Mango*	27	*12 Mar 94*	4
I WANNA BE YOUR MAN	*Mango*	19	*18 Jun 94*	6
GAL WINE	*Mango*	20	*27 Aug 94*	4
This was their first release as a duo in 1992.				
TWIST AND SHOUT [RE]	*Mango*	67	*1 Apr 95*	1
EVERY KINDA PEOPLE	*Island Jamaica*	47	*31 Aug 96*	1

EVERY LITTLE THING SHE DOES IS MAGIC	*Virgin*	51	*30 Aug 97*	1
ALBUMS:	**HITS 1**			**WEEKS 30**
TEASE ME	*Mango*	26	*10 Jul 93*	10
TEASE ME [RE]	*Mango*	1	*29 Jan 94*	20
Repackaged with additional track.				

Terry DENE with the Malcolm LOCKYER GROUP — UK

SINGLES:	**HITS 3**			**WEEKS 20**
A WHITE SPORT'S COAT (AND A PINK CARNATION)	*Decca*	18	*8 Jun 57*	6
START MOVIN' (IN MY DIRECTION)	*Decca*	15	*20 Jul 57*	8
A WHITE SPORT'S COAT (AND A PINK CARNATION) [RE]	*Decca*	30	*27 Jul 57*	1
STAIRWAY OF LOVE	*Decca*	16	*17 May 58*	5

DENISE and JOHNNY — UK

SINGLES:	**HITS 1**			**WEEKS 12**
ESPECIALLY FOR YOU	*RCA*	3	*26 Dec 98*	10
Backing vocals by Steps. Charity record in aid of BBC's Children In Need.				
ESPECIALLY FOR YOU [RE]	*RCA*	53	*10 Apr 99*	2

Cathy DENNIS — UK

SINGLES:	**HITS 13**			**WEEKS 68**
C'MON AND GET MY LOVE	*ffrr*	15	*21 Oct 89*	10
Above hit: D MOB introducing Cathy DENNIS.				
THAT'S THE WAY OF THE WORLD	*ffrr*	48	*7 Apr 90*	3
Above hit: D MOB featuring Cathy DENNIS.				
TOUCH ME (ALL NIGHT LONG)	*Polydor*	5	*4 May 91*	10
JUST ANOTHER DREAM	*Polydor*	13	*20 Jul 91*	7
First release reached No. 93 in 1989 then No. 95 in 1990.				
TOO MANY WALLS	*Polydor*	17	*5 Oct 91*	7
EVERYBODY MOVE	*Polydor*	25	*7 Dec 91*	8
YOU LIED TO ME	*Polydor*	34	*29 Aug 92*	4
IRRESISTIBLE	*Polydor*	24	*21 Nov 92*	6
FALLING (THE PM DAWN VERSION)	*Polydor*	32	*6 Feb 93*	2
WHY	*ffrr*	23	*12 Feb 94*	3
Above hit: D-MOB with Cathy DENNIS.				
WEST END PAD	*Polydor*	25	*10 Aug 96*	2
WATERLOO SUNSET	*Polydor*	11	*1 Mar 97*	5
WHEN DREAMS TURN TO DUST	*Polydor*	43	*21 Jun 97*	1
ALBUMS:	**HITS 2**			**WEEKS 35**
MOVE TO THIS	*Polydor*	3	*10 Aug 91*	31
INTO THE SKYLINE	*Polydor*	8	*23 Jan 93*	4

Jackie DENNIS — UK

SINGLES:	**HITS 2**			**WEEKS 10**
LA DEE DAH	*Decca*	4	*15 Mar 58*	9
Originally recorded by Billie and Lillie.				
THE PURPLE PEOPLE EATER	*Decca*	29	*28 Jun 58*	1

Stefan DENNIS — Australia

SINGLES:	**HITS 2**			**WEEKS 8**
DON'T IT MAKE YOU FEEL GOOD	*Sublime*	16	*6 May 89*	7
THIS LOVE AFFAIR	*Sublime*	67	*7 Oct 89*	1

DENNISONS — UK

SINGLES:	**HITS 2**			**WEEKS 13**
(COME ON) BE MY GIRL	*Decca*	46	*17 Aug 63*	6
WALKING THE DOG	*Decca*	36	*9 May 64*	7

Sandy DENNY — UK

ALBUMS:	**HITS 1**			**WEEKS 2**
THE NORTH STAR GRASSMAN AND THE RAVENS	*Island*	31	*2 Oct 71*	2

Richard DENTON and Martin COOK — UK

SINGLES:	**HITS 1**			**WEEKS 7**
THEME FROM 'HONG KONG BEAT'	*BBC*	25	*15 Apr 78*	7
From the BBC1 TV series.				

John DENVER — US

(See also Placido Domingo and John Denver.)

SINGLES:	**HITS 1**			**WEEKS 13**
ANNIE'S SONG	*RCA Victor*	1	*17 Aug 74*	13

ALBUMS:	HITS 16			WEEKS 228
ROCKY MOUNTAIN HIGH	*RCA Victor*	11	*17 Mar 73*	15
POEMS, PRAYERS AND PROMISES	*RCA Victor*	19	*2 Jun 73*	5
RHYMES AND REASONS	*RCA Victor*	21	*23 Jun 73*	5
THE BEST OF JOHN DENVER	*RCA Victor*	7	*30 Mar 74*	69
BACK HOME AGAIN	*RCA Victor*	3	*7 Sep 74*	29
AN EVENING WITH JOHN DENVER	*RCA Victor*	31	*22 Mar 75*	4
Live recordings from the Universal City Amphitheater, California.				
WIND SONG	*RCA Victor*	14	*11 Oct 75*	21
LIVE IN LONDON	*RCA Victor*	2	*15 May 76*	29
Live recordings from the London Palladium during the week of 29 Mar 76.				
SPIRIT	*RCA Victor*	9	*4 Sep 76*	11
BEST OF JOHN DENVER VOLUME 2	*RCA Victor*	9	*19 Mar 77*	9
I WANT TO LIVE	*RCA Victor*	25	*11 Feb 78*	5
JOHN DENVER	*RCA Victor*	68	*21 Apr 79*	1
IT'S ABOUT TIME	*RCA*	90	*22 Oct 83*	2
JOHN DENVER - COLLECTION	*Telstar*	20	*1 Dec 84*	11
ONE WORLD	*RCA*	91	*23 Aug 86*	3
THE ROCKY MOUNTAIN COLLECTION	*RCA*	19	*22 Mar 97*	9

Karl DENVER — UK

SINGLES:	HITS 12			WEEKS 127
MARCHETA	*Decca*	8	*24 Jun 61*	20
MEXICALI ROSE	*Decca*	8	*21 Oct 61*	11
Originally recorded by Bing Crosby.				
WIMOWEH	*Decca*	4	*27 Jan 62*	17
NEVER GOODBYE	*Decca*	9	*24 Feb 62*	18
A LITTLE LOVE, A LITTLE KISS	*Decca*	19	*9 Jun 62*	10
BLUE WEEK-END	*Decca*	33	*22 Sep 62*	5
CAN YOU FORGIVE ME	*Decca*	32	*23 Mar 63*	8
INDIAN LOVE CALL	*Decca*	32	*15 Jun 63*	8
STILL	*Decca*	13	*24 Aug 63*	15
MY WORLD OF BLUE	*Decca*	29	*7 Mar 64*	6
LOVE ME WITH ALL YOUR HEART	*Decca*	37	*6 Jun 64*	6
Originally recorded by Los Hermanos Riguel as Cuando Caliente El Sol.				
LAZYITIS - ONE ARMED BOXER	*Factory*	46	*9 Jun 90*	3
Above hit: HAPPY MONDAYS and Karl DENVER.				

EPS:	HITS 2			WEEKS 29
BY A SLEEPY LAGOON	*Decca*	2	*15 Sep 62*	20
KARL DENVER HITS	*Decca*	7	*24 Nov 62*	9

ALBUMS:	HITS 1			WEEKS 27
WIMOWEH	*Ace Of Clubs*	7	*23 Dec 61*	27

DENZIE - See MONSTA BOY featuring DENZIE

DEODATO arranged and conducted by Eumir DEODATO — US

SINGLES:	HITS 1			WEEKS 9
ALSO SPRACH ZARATHUSTRA (2001)	*CTI*	7	*5 May 73*	9

DEPARTMENT S — UK

SINGLES:	HITS 2			WEEKS 13
IS VIC THERE?	*RCA*	22	*4 Apr 81*	10
Chart incorrectly lists Demon label.				
GOING LEFT RIGHT	*Stiff*	55	*11 Jul 81*	3

DEPECHE MODE — UK

SINGLES:	HITS 38			WEEKS 240
DREAMING OF ME	*Mute*	57	*4 Apr 81*	4
NEW LIFE	*Mute*	11	*13 Jun 81*	15
JUST CAN'T GET ENOUGH	*Mute*	8	*19 Sep 81*	10
SEE YOU	*Mute*	6	*13 Feb 82*	10
THE MEANING OF LOVE	*Mute*	12	*8 May 82*	8
LEAVE IN SILENCE	*Mute*	18	*28 Aug 82*	10
GET THE BALANCE RIGHT!	*Mute*	13	*12 Feb 83*	8
EVERYTHING COUNTS	*Mute*	6	*23 Jul 83*	11
LOVE IN ITSELF . 2	*Mute*	21	*1 Oct 83*	7
PEOPLE ARE PEOPLE	*Mute*	4	*24 Mar 84*	10
MASTER AND SERVANT	*Mute*	9	*1 Sep 84*	9
SOMEBODY / BLASPHEMOUS RUMOURS	*Mute*	16	*10 Nov 84*	6
From 17 Nov 84 titles were listed in reverse. Somebody was not available on a second 7" format.				
SHAKE THE DISEASE	*Mute*	18	*11 May 85*	9
IT'S CALLED A HEART	*Mute*	18	*28 Sep 85*	4
STRIPPED	*Mute*	15	*22 Feb 86*	5
A QUESTION OF LUST	*Mute*	28	*26 Apr 86*	5
A QUESTION OF TIME	*Mute*	17	*23 Aug 86*	6
STRANGELOVE	*Mute*	16	*9 May 87*	5

NEVER LET ME DOWN AGAIN	*Mute*	22	*5 Sep 87*	4
BEHIND THE WHEEL	*Mute*	21	*9 Jan 88*	5
LITTLE 15 *Import.*	*Mute*	60	*28 May 88*	2
EVERYTHING COUNTS [RR] *Live recording.*	*Mute*	22	*25 Feb 89*	7
PERSONAL JESUS *Above hit: DM*	*Mute*	13	*9 Sep 89*	8
ENJOY THE SILENCE	*Mute*	6	*17 Feb 90*	9
POLICY OF TRUTH	*Mute*	16	*19 May 90*	6
WORLD IN MY EYES	*Mute*	17	*29 Sep 90*	6
I FEEL YOU	*Mute*	8	*27 Feb 93*	7
WALKING IN MY SHOES	*Mute*	14	*8 May 93*	4
CONDEMNATION [EP] *Lead track: Condemnation.*	*Mute*	9	*25 Sep 93*	4
IN YOUR ROOM	*Mute*	8	*22 Jan 94*	4
BARREL OF A GUN	*Mute*	4	*15 Feb 97*	4
IT'S NO GOOD	*Mute*	5	*12 Apr 97*	5
HOME	*Mute*	23	*28 Jun 97*	4
USELESS	*Mute*	28	*1 Nov 97*	2
ONLY WHEN I LOSE MYSELF	*Mute*	17	*19 Sep 98*	3
DREAM ON	*Mute*	6	*5 May 01*	4
DREAM ON [RE]	*Mute*	75	*23 Jun 01*	1
I FEEL LOVED	*Mute*	12	*11 Aug 01*	6
FREELOVE	*Mute*	19	*17 Nov 01*	3
ALBUMS:	**HITS 13**			**WEEKS 181**
SPEAK AND SPELL	*Mute*	10	*14 Nov 81*	33
A BROKEN FRAME	*Mute*	8	*9 Oct 82*	11
CONSTRUCTION TIME AGAIN	*Mute*	6	*3 Sep 83*	12
SOME GREAT REWARD	*Mute*	5	*6 Oct 84*	12
THE SINGLES 81-85	*Mute*	6	*26 Oct 85*	22
BLACK CELEBRATION	*Mute*	4	*29 Mar 86*	11
MUSIC FOR THE MASSES	*Mute*	10	*10 Oct 87*	4
101	*Mute*	5	*25 Mar 89*	8
VIOLATOR	*Mute*	2	*31 Mar 90*	30
SONGS OF FAITH AND DEVOTION	*Mute*	1	*3 Apr 93*	16
ULTRA	*Mute*	1	*26 Apr 97*	11
THE SINGLES 86>98	*Mute*	5	*10 Oct 98*	6
THE SINGLES 81-85 [RE] *Re-released with a new catalogue number.*	*Mute*	57	*7 Nov 98*	1
EXCITER	*Mute*	9	*26 May 01*	4

DEPTH CHARGE

UK

SINGLES:	**HITS 1**			**WEEKS 1**
LEGEND OF THE GOLDEN SNAKE	*DC Recordings*	75	*29 Jul 95*	1

DER DRITTE RAUM

Germany

SINGLES:	**HITS 1**			**WEEKS 1**
HALE BOPP	*Additive*	75	*4 Sep 99*	1

Van DER TOORN - See PAPPA BEAR featuring Van DER TOORN

DEREK and the DOMINOS

UK

SINGLES:	**HITS 1**			**WEEKS 21**
LAYLA	*Polydor*	7	*12 Aug 72*	11
LAYLA [RI]	*RSO*	4	*6 Mar 82*	10
ALBUMS:	**HITS 1**			**WEEKS 1**
DEREK AND THE DOMINOS IN CONCERT	*RSO*	36	*24 Mar 73*	1

Yves DERUYTER

Belgium

SINGLES:	**HITS 1**			**WEEKS 1**
BACK TO EARTH	*UK Bonzai*	63	*14 Apr 01*	1

DESERT

UK

SINGLES:	**HITS 1**			**WEEKS 1**
LETTIN' YA MIND GO	*Future Groove*	74	*20 Oct 01*	1

DESIDERIO

UK/Holland

SINGLES:	**HITS 1**			**WEEKS 1**
STARLIGHT	*Code Blue*	57	*3 Jun 00*	1

Kevin DESIMONE - See Barry MANILOW

DESIRELESS — France

SINGLES:	HITS 1			WEEKS 19
VOYAGE VOYAGE	*CBS*	53	*31 Oct 87*	6
VOYAGE VOYAGE [RM]	*CBS*	5	*14 May 88*	13
Remixed by Pete Hammond and Peter Waterman.				

DESIYA featuring Melissa YIANNAKOU — UK

SINGLES:	HITS 1			WEEKS 1
COMIN' ON STRONG	*Black Market*	74	*1 Feb 92*	1

DESKEE — UK

SINGLES:	HITS 2			WEEKS 3
LET THERE BE HOUSE	*Big One*	52	*3 Feb 90*	2
DANCE, DANCE	*Big One*	74	*8 Sep 90*	1

DES'REE — UK

SINGLES:	HITS 10			WEEKS 72
FEEL SO HIGH	*Dusted Sound*	51	*31 Aug 91*	5
FEEL SO HIGH [RI]	*Dusted Sound*	13	*11 Jan 92*	7
MIND ADVENTURES	*Dusted Sound*	43	*21 Mar 92*	3
WHY SHOULD I LOVE YOU?	*Dusted Sound*	44	*27 Jun 92*	3
DELICATE	*Columbia*	14	*19 Jun 93*	6
Above hit: Terence Trent D'ARBY featuring DES'REE.				
YOU GOTTA BE	*Dusted Sound*	20	*9 Apr 94*	7
I AIN'T MOVIN'	*Dusted Sound*	44	*18 Jun 94*	3
LITTLE CHILD	*Dusted Sound*	69	*3 Sep 94*	1
YOU GOTTA BE [RI]	*Dusted Sound*	14	*11 Mar 95*	8
LIFE	*Dusted Sound*	8	*20 Jun 98*	15
WHAT'S YOUR SIGN?	*Dusted Sound*	19	*7 Nov 98*	4
YOU GOTTA BE 1999 MIX [RM]	*Dusted Sound*	10	*3 Apr 99*	8
Featured in the Ford Focus TV commercial. Remixed by Brian Tench.				
AIN'T NO SUNSHINE	*Universal*	42	*16 Oct 99*	2
Original by Bill Withers reached No. 3 in the US in 1971.				
Above hit: LADYSMITH BLACK MAMBAZO featuring DES'REE.				
ALBUMS:	**HITS 3**			**WEEKS 27**
MIND ADVENTURES	*Dusted Sound*	26	*29 Feb 92*	5
I AIN'T MOVIN'	*Dusted Sound*	13	*21 May 94*	6
SUPERNATURAL	*Dusted Sound*	16	*11 Jul 98*	16

DESTINY'S CHILD — UK

SINGLES:	HITS 12			WEEKS 102
NO NO NO	*Columbia*	5	*28 Mar 98*	8
Above hit: DESTINY'S CHILD (featuring Wyclef JEAN).				
WITH ME	*Columbia*	19	*11 Jul 98*	3
Above hit: DESTINY'S CHILD (featuring JD).				
SHE'S GONE	*Columbia*	24	*7 Nov 98*	3
Above hit: Matthew MARSDEN (featuring DESTINY'S CHILD).				
GET ON THE BUS	*East West*	15	*23 Jan 99*	5
From the film 'Why Do Fools Fall In Love'.				
Above hit: DESTINY'S CHILD (featuring TIMBALAND).				
BILLS, BILLS, BILLS	*Columbia*	6	*24 Jul 99*	9
BUG A BOO	*Columbia*	9	*30 Oct 99*	7
SAY MY NAME	*Columbia*	3	*8 Apr 00*	11
JUMPIN' JUMPIN'	*Columbia*	5	*29 Jul 00*	11
INDEPENDENT WOMEN PART 1	*Columbia*	1	*2 Dec 00*	15
From the film 'Charlie's Angels'.				
SURVIVOR	*Columbia*	1	*28 Apr 01*	13
BOOTYLICIOUS	*Columbia*	2	*4 Aug 01*	11
Samples Edge of Seventeen by Stevie Nicks.				
EMOTION	*Columbia*	3	*24 Nov 01*	6
ALBUMS:	**HITS 3**			**WEEKS 125**
DESTINY'S CHILD	*Columbia*	45	*14 Mar 98*	4
THE WRITING'S ON THE WALL	*Columbia*	12	*7 Aug 99*	26
THE WRITING'S ON THE WALL [RE]	*Columbia*	10	*18 Mar 00*	61
Peak position reached on 6 Jan 01.				
SURVIVOR	*Columbia*	1	*12 May 01*	34

DESTROYERS - See George THOROGOOD and the DESTROYERS

DESTRY - See CIRCA featuring DESTRY; ZOO EXPERIENCE - featuring DESTRY

Marcella DETROIT — US

SINGLES:	HITS 3			WEEKS 16
I BELIEVE	*London*	11	*12 Mar 94*	8

AIN'T NOTHING LIKE THE REAL THING	*London*	24	*14 May 94*	4
Above hit: Marcella DETROIT and Elton JOHN.				
I'M NO ANGEL	*London*	33	*16 Jul 94*	4
ALBUMS:	**HITS 1**			**WEEKS 5**
JEWEL	*London*	15	*9 Apr 94*	5

DETROIT EMERALDS — US

SINGLES:	HITS 4			WEEKS 44
FEEL THE NEED IN ME	*Janus*	4	*10 Feb 73*	15
YOU WANT IT, YOU GOT IT	*Westbound*	12	*5 May 73*	9
I THINK OF YOU	*Westbound*	27	*11 Aug 73*	9
FEEL THE NEED [RR]	*Atlantic*	12	*18 Jun 77*	11

DETROIT GRAND PU BAHS — US

SINGLES:	HITS 1			WEEKS 3
SANDWICHES	*Jive Electro*	29	*8 Jul 00*	3

DETROIT SPINNERS — US

(See also Rappin-4-Tay.)

SINGLES:	HITS 10			WEEKS 89
IT'S A SHAME	*Tamla Motown*	20	*14 Nov 70*	11
Above hit: MOTOWN SPINNERS.				
COULD IT BE I'M FALLING IN LOVE	*Atlantic*	11	*21 Apr 73*	11
GHETTO CHILD	*Atlantic*	7	*29 Sep 73*	10
THEN CAME YOU	*Atlantic*	29	*19 Oct 74*	6
Above hit: Dionne WARWICKE and the DETROIT SPINNERS.				
THE RUBBERBAND MAN	*Atlantic*	16	*11 Sep 76*	11
WAKE UP SUSAN	*Atlantic*	29	*29 Jan 77*	6
COULD IT BE I'M FALLING IN LOVE [EP]	*Atlantic*	32	*7 May 77*	3
Lead track: Could It Be I'm Falling In Love. (This is a re-issue.)				
WORKING MY WAY BACK TO YOU	*Atlantic*	1	*23 Feb 80*	14
Although not credited on the label, it is also known and was listed on the chart as a medley with Forgive Me Girl.				
BODY LANGUAGE	*Atlantic*	40	*10 May 80*	7
MEDLEY: a. CUPID; b. I'VE LOVED YOU FOR A LONG TIME [M]	*Atlantic*	4	*28 Jun 80*	10
ALBUMS:	**HITS 1**			**WEEKS 3**
DETROIT SPINNERS' SMASH HITS	*Atlantic*	37	*14 May 77*	3

DEUCE — UK

SINGLES:	HITS 4			WEEKS 23
CALL IT LOVE	*London*	11	*21 Jan 95*	10
I NEED YOU	*London*	10	*22 Apr 95*	5
Beaten into third place by Gina G and Dear Jon in the contest to represent the UK at Eurovision.				
ON THE BIBLE	*London*	13	*19 Aug 95*	6
NO SURRENDER	*Love This*	29	*29 Jun 96*	2
ALBUMS:	**HITS 1**			**WEEKS 2**
ON THE LOOSE!	*London*	18	*9 Sep 95*	2

dEUS — Belgium

SINGLES:	HITS 6			WEEKS 7
HOTELLOUNGE (BE THE DEATH OF ME)	*Island*	55	*11 Feb 95*	1
THEME FROM TURNPIKE [EP]	*Island*	68	*13 Jul 96*	1
Lead track: Theme From Turnpike.				
LITTLE ARITHMETICS	*Island*	44	*19 Oct 96*	2
ROSES	*Island*	56	*15 Mar 97*	1
INSTANT STREET	*Island*	49	*24 Apr 99*	1
SISTER DEW	*Island*	62	*3 Jul 99*	1
ALBUMS:	**HITS 1**			**WEEKS 1**
THE IDEAL CRASH	*Island*	64	*3 Apr 99*	1

William DEVAUGHN — US

SINGLES:	HITS 2			WEEKS 10
BE THANKFUL FOR WHAT YOU GOT	*Chelsea*	31	*6 Jul 74*	5
BE THANKFUL FOR WHAT YOU GOT [RR]	*EMI*	44	*20 Sep 80*	5

Sidney DEVINE — UK

SINGLES:	HITS 1			WEEKS 1
SCOTLAND FOR EVER	*Philips*	48	*1 Apr 78*	1
ALBUMS:	**HITS 2**			**WEEKS 11**
DOUBLE DEVINE	*Philips*	14	*10 Apr 76*	10
DEVINE TIME	*Philips*	49	*11 Dec 76*	1

DEVO — UK

SINGLES:	HITS 5			WEEKS 23
(I CAN'T GET ME NO) SATISFACTION	*Stiff*	41	*22 Apr 78*	8
JOCKO HOMO	*Stiff*	62	*13 May 78*	3
BE STIFF	*Stiff*	71	*12 Aug 78*	1
COME BACK JONEE	*Virgin*	60	*2 Sep 78*	4
WHIP IT	*Virgin*	51	*22 Nov 80*	7
ALBUMS:	**HITS 4**			**WEEKS 22**
Q: ARE WE NOT MEN? A: NO WE ARE DEVO	*Virgin*	12	*16 Sep 78*	7
DUTY NOW FOR THE FUTURE	*Virgin*	49	*23 Jun 79*	6
FREEDOM OF CHOICE	*Virgin*	47	*24 May 80*	5
NEW TRADITIONALISTS	*Virgin*	50	*5 Sep 81*	4

Howard DEVOTO — UK

(See also Buzzcocks.)

ALBUMS:	HITS 1			WEEKS 2
JERKY VERSIONS OF THE DREAM	*Virgin*	57	*6 Aug 83*	2

DEXY'S MIDNIGHT RUNNERS — UK

SINGLES:	HITS 11			WEEKS 93
DANCE STANCE	*Oddball Productions*	40	*19 Jan 80*	6
GENO	*Late Night Feelings*	1	*22 Mar 80*	14
THERE THERE MY DEAR	*Late Night Feelings*	7	*12 Jul 80*	9
PLAN B	*Parlophone*	58	*21 Mar 81*	2
SHOW ME	*Mercury*	16	*11 Jul 81*	9
Above hit: DEXYS MIDNIGHT RUNNERS.				
THE CELTIC SOUL BROTHERS	*Mercury*	45	*20 Mar 82*	4
COME ON EILEEN	*Mercury*	1	*3 Jul 82*	17
Above 2: DEXYS MIDNIGHT RUNNERS and the EMERALD EXPRESS.				
JACKIE WILSON SAID (I'M IN HEAVEN WHEN YOU SMILE	*Mercury*	5	*2 Oct 82*	7
Originally recorded by Van Morrison.				
LET'S GET THIS STRAIGHT (FROM THE START) / OLD	*Mercury*	17	*4 Dec 82*	9
THE CELTIC SOUL BROTHERS (MORE, PLEASE, THANK YOU) [RR]	*Mercury*	20	*2 Apr 83*	6
Above 3: Kevin ROWLAND and DEXYS MIDNIGHT RUNNERS.				
BECAUSE OF YOU	*Mercury*	13	*22 Nov 86*	10
Theme from the BBC1 TV comedy series 'Brush Strokes'.				
Above hit: Kevin ROWLAND featuring DEXY'S MIDNIGHT RUNNERS.				
ALBUMS:	**HITS 5**			**WEEKS 79**
SEARCHING FOR THE YOUNG SOUL REBELS	*Parlophone*	6	*26 Jul 80*	10
TOO-RYE-AY	*Mercury*	2	*7 Aug 82*	46
Above hit: Kevin ROWLAND and DEXYS MIDNIGHT RUNNERS.				
GENO	*EMI*	79	*26 Mar 83*	2
Originally released in 1980.				
DON'T STAND ME DOWN	*Mercury*	22	*21 Sep 85*	6
THE VERY BEST OF DEXY'S MIDNIGHT RUNNERS	*Mercury*	12	*8 Jun 91*	15

DEZZ the DEZZ and SHOLA - See DEEP C

Tony DI BART — UK

SINGLES:	HITS 4			WEEKS 19
THE REAL THING	*Cleveland City Blues*	1	*9 Apr 94*	12
Original release reached No. 83 in 1993.				
DO IT	*Cleveland City Blues*	21	*20 Aug 94*	4
WHY DID YA	*Cleveland City Blues*	46	*20 May 95*	1
TURN YOUR LOVE AROUND	*Cleveland City Blues*	66	*2 Mar 96*	1
THE REAL THING [RM]	*Cleveland City*	51	*17 Oct 98*	1
Remixed by Mellonheads.				

Gregg DIAMOND BIONIC BOOGIE — US

SINGLES:	HITS 1			WEEKS 3
CREAM (ALWAYS RISES TO THE TOP)	*Polydor*	61	*20 Jan 79*	3

Jim DIAMOND — UK

SINGLES:	HITS 4			WEEKS 30
I SHOULD HAVE KNOWN BETTER	*A&M*	1	*3 Nov 84*	13
I SLEEP ALONE AT NIGHT	*A&M*	72	*2 Feb 85*	1
REMEMBER I LOVE YOU	*A&M*	42	*18 May 85*	5
HI HO SILVER	*A&M*	5	*22 Feb 86*	11
Theme from the ITV series 'Boon'.				
ALBUMS:	**HITS 1**			**WEEKS 5**
JIM DIAMOND	*PolyGram TV*	16	*22 May 93*	5

Neil DIAMOND — US

SINGLES:	HITS 13			WEEKS 121
CRACKLIN' ROSIE	*Uni*	3	*7 Nov 70*	17
SWEET CAROLINE	*Uni*	8	*20 Feb 71*	11
I AM . . . I SAID	*Uni*	4	*8 May 71*	12
SONG SUNG BLUE	*Uni*	14	*13 May 72*	13
IF YOU KNOW WHAT I MEAN	*CBS*	35	*14 Aug 76*	4
BEAUTIFUL NOISE	*CBS*	13	*23 Oct 76*	9
DESIREE	*CBS*	39	*24 Dec 77*	6
YOU DON'T BRING ME FLOWERS	*CBS*	5	*25 Nov 78*	12
Originally by Neil Diamond on his 1977 album I'm Glad You're Here With Me Tonight.				
Above hit: BARBRA and NEIL.				
FOREVER IN BLUE JEANS	*CBS*	16	*3 Mar 79*	12
LOVE ON THE ROCKS	*Capitol*	17	*15 Nov 80*	12
HELLO AGAIN	*Capitol*	51	*14 Feb 81*	4
Above 2 from the film 'The Jazz Singer'.				
HEARTLIGHT	*CBS*	47	*20 Nov 82*	7
MORNING HAS BROKEN	*Columbia*	36	*21 Nov 92*	2

ALBUMS:	HITS 34			WEEKS 572
TAP ROOT MANUSCRIPT	*Uni*	19	*3 Apr 71*	12
GOLD	*Uni*	23	*3 Apr 71*	11
STONES	*Uni*	18	*11 Dec 71*	14
MOODS	*Uni*	7	*5 Aug 72*	19
HOT AUGUST NIGHT	*Uni*	32	*12 Jan 74*	2
Live recordings from the Greek Theatre, Los Angeles, 24 Aug 72.				
JONATHAN LIVINGSTON SEAGULL [OST]	*CBS*	35	*16 Feb 74*	1
RAINBOW	*MCA*	39	*9 Mar 74*	5
HIS 12 GREATEST HITS	*MCA*	13	*29 Jun 74*	78
SERENADE	*CBS*	11	*9 Nov 74*	14
BEAUTIFUL NOISE	*CBS*	10	*10 Jul 76*	26
LOVE AT THE GREEK GREEK - RECORDED LIVE AT THE GREEK THEATRE, LOS ANGELES	*CBS*	3	*12 Mar 77*	32
Live recordings from the Greek Theatre, Los Angeles, Aug 76.				
HOT AUGUST NIGHT [RI]	*MCA*	60	*6 Aug 77*	1
I'M GLAD YOU'RE HERE WITH ME TONIGHT	*CBS*	16	*17 Dec 77*	12
20 GOLDEN GREATS	*MCA*	2	*25 Nov 78*	26
YOU DON'T BRING ME FLOWERS	*CBS*	15	*6 Jan 79*	23
SEPTEMBER MORN	*CBS*	14	*19 Jan 80*	11
THE JAZZ SINGER [OST]	*Capitol*	3	*22 Nov 80*	110
LOVE SONGS	*MCA*	43	*28 Feb 81*	6
THE WAY TO THE SKY	*CBS*	39	*5 Dec 81*	13
12 GREATEST HITS VOLUME 2	*CBS*	32	*19 Jun 82*	8
HEARTLIGHT	*CBS*	43	*13 Nov 82*	10
THE VERY BEST OF NEIL DIAMOND	*K-Tel*	33	*10 Dec 83*	11
PRIMITIVE	*CBS*	7	*28 Jul 84*	10
HEADED FOR THE FUTURE	*CBS*	36	*24 May 86*	8
HOT AUGUST NIGHT II	*CBS*	74	*28 Nov 87*	4
Live recordings from the Greek Theatre, Los Angeles.				
THE BEST YEARS OF OUR LIVES	*CBS*	55	*25 Feb 89*	3
THE BEST YEARS OF OUR LIVES [RE]	*CBS*	42	*18 Nov 89*	3
LOVESCAPE	*Columbia*	36	*9 Nov 91*	13
THE GREATEST HITS 1966-1992	*Columbia*	1	*4 Jul 92*	30
20 GOLDEN GREATS [RE]	*MCA*	48	*25 Jul 92*	3
Re-released with a new catalogue number.				
THE CHRISTMAS ALBUM	*Columbia*	50	*28 Nov 92*	6
UP ON THE ROOF - SONGS FROM THE BRILL BUILDING	*Columbia*	28	*9 Oct 93*	10
TENNESSEE MOON (THE NASHVILLE COLLECTION)	*Columbia*	12	*17 Feb 96*	13
A collaboration with Nashville country stars.				
THE BEST OF NEIL DIAMOND	*MCA*	68	*25 May 96*	1
THE ULTIMATE COLLECTION	*Sony TV/MCA*	5	*31 Aug 96*	20
THE MOVIE ALBUM - AS TIME GOES BY	*Columbia*	68	*14 Nov 98*	2
Live recordings, conducted by Elmer Bernstein.				
THREE CHORD OPERA	*Columbia*	49	*15 Sep 01*	1

DIAMOND HEAD — UK

SINGLES:	HITS 1			WEEKS 2
IN THE HEAT OF THE NIGHT	*MCA*	67	*11 Sep 82*	2

ALBUMS:	HITS 2			WEEKS 9
BORROWED TIME	*MCA*	24	*23 Oct 82*	5
CANTERBURY	*MCA*	32	*24 Sep 83*	4

DIAMONDS — Canada

SINGLES:	HITS 1			WEEKS 17
● LITTLE DARLIN'	*Mercury*	3	*1 Jun 57*	17
Originally by the Gladiolas reached No. 51 in the US in 1957.				

DIANA - See Diana ROSS

DICK and DEEDEE — US

SINGLES:	HITS 1			WEEKS 3
THE MOUNTAIN'S HIGH	*London*	37	*28 Oct 61*	3

Charles DICKENS — UK

SINGLES:	HITS 1			WEEKS 8
THAT'S THE WAY LOVE GOES	*Pye*	37	*3 Jul 65*	8

Gwen DICKEY — US

(See also Rose Royce.)

SINGLES:	HITS 3			WEEKS 10
CAR WASH	*Swanyard*	72	*27 Jan 90*	2
AIN'T NOBODY (LOVES ME BETTER)	*X-Clusive*	21	*2 Jul 94*	4
Sleeve reflects artist credits in reverse.				
Above hit: Gwen DICKEY and K.W.S.				
WISHING ON A STAR	*Northwestside*	13	*14 Feb 98*	4
Above hit: JAY-Z featuring Gwen DICKEY.				

Neville DICKIE — UK

SINGLES:	HITS 1			WEEKS 10
THE ROBIN'S RETURN	*Major Minor*	33	*25 Oct 69*	7
THE ROBIN'S RETURN [RE]	*Major Minor*	43	*20 Dec 69*	3

DICKIES — US

SINGLES:	HITS 6			WEEKS 28
SILENT NIGHT	*A&M*	47	*16 Dec 78*	4
BANANA SPLITS (THE TRA LA LA SONG)	*A&M*	7	*21 Apr 79*	8
PARANOID	*A&M*	45	*21 Jul 79*	6
NIGHTS IN WHITE SATIN	*A&M*	39	*15 Sep 79*	5
FAN MAIL	*A&M*	57	*16 Feb 80*	3
GIGANTOR	*A&M*	72	*19 Jul 80*	2
ALBUMS:	**HITS 2**			**WEEKS 19**
THE INCREDIBLE SHRINKING DICKIES	*A&M*	18	*17 Feb 79*	17
DAWN OF THE DICKIES	*A&M*	60	*24 Nov 79*	2

Bruce DICKINSON — UK

SINGLES:	HITS 8			WEEKS 23
TATTOOED MILLIONAIRE	*EMI*	18	*28 Apr 90*	5
ALL THE YOUNG DUDES	*EMI*	23	*23 Jun 90*	5
DIVE! DIVE! DIVE!	*EMI*	45	*25 Aug 90*	2
(I WANT TO BE) ELECTED	*London*	9	*4 Apr 92*	5
Mr. Bean is a character played by comedian Rowan Atkinson.				
Above hit: MR. BEAN and SMEAR CAMPAIGN (featuring Bruce DICKINSON).				
TEARS OF THE DRAGON	*EMI*	28	*28 May 94*	2
SHOOT ALL THE CLOWNS	*EMI*	37	*8 Oct 94*	2
BACK FROM THE EDGE	*Raw Power*	68	*13 Apr 96*	1
ACCIDENT OF BIRTH	*Raw Power*	54	*3 May 97*	1
ALBUMS:	**HITS 5**			**WEEKS 15**
TATTOOED MILLIONAIRE	*EMI*	14	*19 May 90*	9
BALLS TO PICASSO	*EMI*	21	*18 Jun 94*	3
SKUNKWORKS	*Raw Power*	41	*9 Mar 96*	1
ACCIDENT OF BIRTH	*Raw Power*	53	*24 May 97*	1
THE CHEMICAL WEDDING	*Air Raid*	55	*26 Sep 98*	1

Barbara DICKSON — UK

(See also Various Artists: Studio Cast 'Evita'.)

SINGLES:	HITS 6			WEEKS 49
ANSWER ME	*RSO*	9	*17 Jan 76*	7
ANOTHER SUITCASE IN ANOTHER HALL	*MCA*	18	*26 Feb 77*	7
From the musical 'Evita'.				
CARAVAN SONG	*Epic*	41	*19 Jan 80*	7
Above hit: Song from the film "CARAVANS" featuring Barbara DICKSON.				
JANUARY FEBRUARY	*Epic*	11	*15 Mar 80*	10
IN THE NIGHT	*Epic*	48	*14 Jun 80*	2
I KNOW HIM SO WELL	*RCA*	1	*5 Jan 85*	16
From the musical 'Chess'.				
Above hit: Elaine PAIGE and Barbara DICKSON.				
ALBUMS:	**HITS 14**			**WEEKS 143**
MORNING COMES QUICKLY	*RSO*	58	*18 Jun 77*	1
THE BARBARA DICKSON ALBUM	*Epic*	7	*12 Apr 80*	12
YOU KNOW IT'S ME	*Epic*	39	*16 May 81*	6

ALL FOR A SONG	*Epic*	3	*6 Feb 82*	38
TELL ME IT'S NOT TRUE 'FROM THE MUSICAL BLOOD BROTHERS'	*Legacy*	100	*24 Sep 83*	1
HEARTBEATS	*Epic*	21	*23 Jun 84*	8
THE BARBARA DICKSON SONGBOOK	*K-Tel*	5	*12 Jan 85*	19
GOLD	*K-Tel*	11	*23 Nov 85*	18
THE VERY BEST OF BARBARA DICKSON	*Telstar*	78	*15 Nov 86*	8
THE RIGHT MOMENT	*K-Tel*	39	*29 Nov 86*	8
COMING ALIVE AGAIN	*Telstar*	30	*6 May 89*	7
DON'T THINK TWICE IT'S ALL RIGHT	*Columbia*	32	*15 Aug 92*	5
THE BEST OF ELAINE PAIGE AND BARBARA DICKSON	*Telstar*	22	*28 Nov 92*	9
Above hit: Elaine PAIGE and Barbara DICKSON.				
PARCEL OF ROGUES	*Castle Communication*	30	*5 Mar 94*	3

DICTATORS

US

SINGLES:	HITS 1			WEEKS 2
SEARCH AND DESTROY	*Asylum*	49	*17 Sep 77*	1
Originally recorded by Iggy Pop.				
SEARCH AND DESTROY [RE]	*Asylum*	50	*1 Oct 77*	1

Bo DIDDLEY

US

SINGLES:	HITS 2			WEEKS 10
PRETTY THING	*Pye International*	34	*12 Oct 63*	6
HEY GOOD LOOKIN'	*Chess*	39	*20 Mar 65*	4
EPS:	**HITS 3**			**WEEKS 29**
CHUCK AND BO	*Pye International*	6	*5 Oct 63*	22
CHUCK AND BO, VOLUME 2	*Pye International*	15	*30 Nov 63*	2
CHUCK AND BO, VOLUME 3	*Pye International*	12	*15 Feb 64*	5
Above 3: Chuck BERRY and Bo DIDDLEY.				
ALBUMS:	**HITS 4**			**WEEKS 16**
BO DIDDLEY	*Pye International*	11	*5 Oct 63*	8
BO DIDDLEY IS A GUNSLINGER	*Pye*	20	*9 Nov 63*	1
BO DIDDLEY RIDES AGAIN	*Pye International*	19	*30 Nov 63*	1
BO DIDDLEY'S BEACH PARTY	*Pye*	13	*15 Feb 64*	6

DIDDY

UK

SINGLES:	HITS 1			WEEKS 3
GIVE ME LOVE	*Positiva*	52	*19 Feb 94*	1
GIVE ME LOVE [RM]	*Feverpitch*	23	*12 Jul 97*	2
Remixed by Diddy.				

DIDO

UK

SINGLES:	HITS 3			WEEKS 30
HERE WITH ME	*Arista*	4	*24 Feb 01*	12
THANK YOU	*Arista*	3	*2 Jun 01*	10
HUNTER	*Arista*	17	*22 Sep 01*	8
ALBUMS:	**HITS 1**			**WEEKS 62**
NO ANGEL	*Arista*	1	*28 Oct 00*	62
Peak position reached on 10 Feb 01.				

DIESEL PARK WEST

UK

(See also Various Artists (EPs) 'The Food Christmas EP 1989'.)

SINGLES:	HITS 6			WEEKS 15
ALL THE MYTHS ON SUNDAY	*Food*	66	*4 Feb 89*	2
LIKE PRINCES DO	*Food*	58	*1 Apr 89*	3
WHEN THE HOODOO COMES	*Food*	62	*5 Aug 89*	2
FALL TO LOVE	*Food*	48	*18 Jan 92*	3
BOY ON TOP OF THE NEWS	*Food*	58	*21 Mar 92*	2
GOD ONLY KNOWS	*Food*	57	*5 Sep 92*	3
ALBUMS:	**HITS 2**			**WEEKS 3**
SHAKESPEARE ALABAMA	*Food*	55	*11 Feb 89*	2
DECENCY	*Food*	57	*15 Feb 92*	1

DIFFERENT GEAR vs the POLICE

UK/Italy

SINGLES:	HITS 1			WEEKS 3
WHEN THE WORLD IS RUNNING DOWN (YOU CAN'T GO WRONG)	*Pagan*	28	*5 Aug 00*	3
Remix of a track from the Police's 1980 album Zenyatta Mondatta.				

DIFFORD and TILBROOK

UK

SINGLES:	HITS 1			WEEKS 2
LOVE'S CRASHING WAVES	*A&M*	57	*30 Jun 84*	2
ALBUMS:	**HITS 1**			**WEEKS 3**
DIFFORD AND TILBROOK	*A&M*	47	*14 Jul 84*	3

DIGABLE PLANETS — US

SINGLES:	HITS 1			WEEKS 2
REBIRTH OF SLICK (COOL LIKE DAT)	*Elektra*	67	*13 Feb 93*	2

DIGITAL DREAM BABY — UK

SINGLES:	HITS 1			WEEKS 4
WALKING IN THE AIR (FROM THE SNOWMAN) *Dance remix of Walking In the Air by the Snowman.*	*Columbia*	49	*14 Dec 91*	4

DIGITAL EXCITATION — Belgium

SINGLES:	HITS 1			WEEKS 2
PURE PLEASURE	*R&S*	37	*29 Feb 92*	2

DIGITAL ORGASM — Belgium

SINGLES:	HITS 3			WEEKS 14
RUNNING OUT OF TIME	*Dead Dead Good*	16	*7 Dec 91*	9
STARTOUCHERS	*DDG International*	31	*18 Apr 92*	3
MOOG ERUPTION	*DDG International*	62	*25 Jul 92*	2

DIGITAL UNDERGROUND — US

SINGLES:	HITS 1			WEEKS 4
SAME SONG	*Big Life*	52	*16 Mar 91*	4
ALBUMS:	**HITS 2**			**WEEKS 2**
SEX PACKETS	*BCM*	59	*7 Apr 90*	1
DOOWUTCHYALIKE / PACKET MAN *12"/CD single too long to be eligible for the singles charts.*	*BCM*	59	*30 Jun 90*	1

John DIGWEED – See BEDROCK

DILEMMA — Italy

SINGLES:	HITS 1			WEEKS 1
IN SPIRIT *First released in 1991.*	*ffrr*	42	*6 Apr 96*	1

Ricky DILLARD – See Farley "Jackmaster" FUNK

Richard DIMBLEBY — UK

ALBUMS:	HITS 1			WEEKS 5
THE VOICE OF RICHARD DIMBLEBY	*Music For Pleasure*	14	*4 Jun 66*	5

DIMESTARS — UK

SINGLES:	HITS 1			WEEKS 1
MY SUPERSTAR	*Polydor*	72	*16 Jun 01*	1

Paolo DINI – See F.P.I. PROJECT

Mark DINNING — US

SINGLES:	HITS 1			WEEKS 4
TEEN ANGEL *Written by Mark's sister Jeannie.*	*MGM*	37	*12 Mar 60*	3
TEEN ANGEL [RE]	*MGM*	42	*9 Apr 60*	1

DINOSAUR JR — US

SINGLES:	HITS 7			WEEKS 13
THE WAGON	*Blanco Y Negro*	49	*2 Feb 91*	2
GET ME	*Blanco Y Negro*	44	*14 Nov 92*	1
START CHOPPIN	*Blanco Y Negro*	20	*30 Jan 93*	3
OUT THERE	*Blanco Y Negro*	44	*12 Jun 93*	2
FEEL THE PAIN	*Blanco Y Negro*	25	*27 Aug 94*	3
I DON'T THINK SO	*Blanco Y Negro*	67	*11 Feb 95*	1
TAKE A RUN AT THE SUN	*Blanco Y Negro*	53	*5 Apr 97*	1
ALBUMS:	**HITS 3**			**WEEKS 7**
GREEN MIND	*Blanco Y Negro*	36	*2 Mar 91*	2
WHERE YOU BEEN	*Blanco Y Negro*	10	*20 Feb 93*	3
WITHOUT A SOUND	*Blanco Y Negro*	24	*10 Sep 94*	2

DIO — UK/US

SINGLES:	HITS 7			WEEKS 22
HOLY DIVER	*Vertigo*	72	*20 Aug 83*	2
RAINBOW IN THE DARK	*Vertigo*	46	*29 Oct 83*	3
WE ROCK	*Vertigo*	42	*11 Aug 84*	3
MYSTERY	*Vertigo*	34	*29 Sep 84*	4
ROCK 'N' ROLL CHILDREN	*Vertigo*	26	*10 Aug 85*	6

HUNGRY FOR HEAVEN	*Vertigo*	72	*2 Nov 85*	1
HUNGRY FOR HEAVEN [RI]	*Vertigo*	56	*17 May 86*	2
I COULD HAVE BEEN A DREAMER	*Vertigo*	69	*1 Aug 87*	1
ALBUMS:	**HITS 6**			**WEEKS 48**
HOLY DIVER	*Vertigo*	13	*11 Jun 83*	15
THE LAST IN LINE	*Vertigo*	4	*21 Jul 84*	14
SACRED HEART	*Vertigo*	4	*7 Sep 85*	6
INTERMISSION	*Vertigo*	22	*5 Jul 86*	5
DREAM EVIL	*Vertigo*	8	*22 Aug 87*	5
LOCK UP THE WOLVES	*Vertigo*	28	*26 May 90*	3

DION — US

SINGLES:	**HITS 4**			**WEEKS 35**
A TEENAGER IN LOVE *Above hit: DION and the BELMONTS.*	*London*	28	*27 Jun 59*	2
LONELY TEENAGER	*Top Rank*	47	*21 Jan 61*	1
RUNAROUND SUE	*Top Rank*	11	*4 Nov 61*	9
THE WANDERER	*His Master's Voice*	10	*17 Feb 62*	12
THE WANDERER [RI]	*Philips*	16	*22 May 76*	9
KING OF THE NEW YORK STREETS	*Arista*	74	*19 Aug 89*	2
ALBUMS:	**HITS 1**			**WEEKS 5**
20 GOLDEN GREATS *Above hit: DION and the BELMONTS.*	*K-Tel*	31	*12 Apr 80*	5

Celine DION — Canada

SINGLES:	**HITS 22**			**WEEKS 230**
BEAUTY AND THE BEAST *From the Walt Disney film of the same name.* *Above hit: Celine DION and Peabo BRYSON.*	*Epic*	9	*16 May 92*	7
IF YOU ASKED ME TO *Originally recorded by Patti Labelle in 1989.*	*Epic*	60	*4 Jul 92*	2
LOVE CAN MOVE MOUNTAINS	*Epic*	46	*14 Nov 92*	2
IF YOU ASKED ME TO [RE]	*Epic*	57	*26 Dec 92*	3
WHERE DOES MY HEART BEAT NOW *Originally released in 1991.*	*Epic*	72	*3 Apr 93*	1
THE POWER OF LOVE	*Epic*	4	*29 Jan 94*	10
MISLED	*Epic*	40	*23 Apr 94*	3
THINK TWICE	*Epic*	1	*22 Oct 94*	31
ONLY ONE ROAD	*Epic*	8	*20 May 95*	8
TU M'AIMES ENCORE (TO LOVE ME AGAIN)	*Epic*	7	*9 Sep 95*	9
MISLED [RI]	*Epic*	15	*2 Dec 95*	6
FALLING INTO YOU	*Epic*	10	*2 Mar 96*	10
BECAUSE YOU LOVED ME (THEME FROM "UP CLOSE & PERSONAL") *From the film 'Up Close And Personal'.*	*Epic*	5	*1 Jun 96*	16
IT'S ALL COMING BACK TO ME NOW	*Epic*	3	*5 Oct 96*	14
ALL BY MYSELF *Based on Rachmaninoff's Piano Concerto composed around 1892.*	*Epic*	6	*21 Dec 96*	10
ALL BY MYSELF [RE]	*Epic*	58	*15 Mar 97*	3
CALL THE MAN	*Epic*	11	*28 Jun 97*	6
TELL HIM *Above hit: Barbra STREISAND/Celine DION.*	*Columbia*	3	*15 Nov 97*	15
THE REASON	*Epic*	11	*20 Dec 97*	8
MY HEART WILL GO ON (LOVE THEME FROM TITANIC) *From the film 'Titanic'.*	*Epic*	1	*21 Feb 98*	20
IMMORTALITY *Above hit: Celine DION with special guests the BEE GEES.*	*Epic*	5	*18 Jul 98*	12
I'M YOUR ANGEL *Above hit: Celine DION and R. KELLY.*	*Epic*	3	*28 Nov 98*	13
TREAT HER LIKE A LADY	*Epic*	29	*10 Jul 99*	3
THAT'S THE WAY IT IS	*Epic*	12	*11 Dec 99*	11
THE FIRST TIME EVER I SAW YOUR FACE *Originally recorded by Peggy Seeger.*	*Epic*	19	*8 Apr 00*	6
THE FIRST TIME EVER I SAW YOUR FACE [RE]	*Epic*	74	*10 Jun 00*	1
ALBUMS:	**HITS 12**			**WEEKS 368**
THE COLOUR OF MY LOVE	*Epic*	10	*5 Mar 94*	4
THE COLOUR OF MY LOVE [RE]	*Epic*	1	*24 Dec 94*	105
UNISON *Originally released in 1991.*	*Epic*	56	*16 Sep 95*	2
D'EUX - THE FRENCH ALBUM	*Epic*	7	*7 Oct 95*	9
FALLING INTO YOU	*Epic*	1	*23 Mar 96*	113
UNISON [RE]	*Epic*	55	*19 Oct 96*	1
LIVE A PARIS *Live recordings from the Zenith Theatre, Paris, Autumn 1995.*	*Epic*	53	*9 Nov 96*	1
C'EST POUR VIVRE *French recordings from 1983-87.*	*Nectar Masters*	49	*15 Mar 97*	3
LET'S TALK ABOUT LOVE	*Epic*	1	*29 Nov 97*	73

S'IL SUFFISAIT D'AIMER	*Epic*	17	*19 Sep 98*	4
CELINE DION	*Epic*	70	*26 Sep 98*	2
First released 1992.				
THESE ARE SPECIAL TIMES	*Epic*	20	*14 Nov 98*	10
ALL THE WAY . . . A DECADE OF SONG	*Epic*	1	*27 Nov 99*	38
Compilation plus 7 new tracks.				
THE COLLECTORS SERIES VOLUME 1	*Epic*	30	*11 Nov 00*	3

Kathryn DION – See 2 FUNKY 2 featuring Kathryn DION

DIONNE — Canada

SINGLES:	HITS 1			WEEKS 2
COME GET MY LOVIN'	*Citybeat*	69	*23 Sep 89*	2

Wasis DIOP featuring Lena FIAGBE — Senegal/UK

SINGLES:	HITS 1			WEEKS 2
AFRICAN DREAM	*Mercury*	44	*10 Feb 96*	2

DIPPY – See Keith HARRIS and ORVILLE

DIRE STRAITS — UK

SINGLES:	HITS 18			WEEKS 119
SULTANS OF SWING	*Vertigo*	8	*10 Mar 79*	11
LADY WRITER	*Vertigo*	51	*28 Jul 79*	6
ROMEO AND JULIET	*Vertigo*	8	*17 Jan 81*	11
SKATEAWAY	*Vertigo*	37	*4 Apr 81*	5
TUNNEL OF LOVE	*Vertigo*	54	*10 Oct 81*	3
PRIVATE INVESTIGATIONS	*Vertigo*	2	*4 Sep 82*	8
TWISTING BY THE POOL	*Vertigo*	14	*22 Jan 83*	7
Sleeve gives title as an EP: Dance Play.				
LOVE OVER GOLD (LIVE) / SOLID ROCK (LIVE)	*Vertigo*	50	*18 Feb 84*	3
SO FAR AWAY	*Vertigo*	20	*20 Apr 85*	6
MONEY FOR NOTHING	*Vertigo*	4	*6 Jul 85*	16
Features vocals by Sting.				
BROTHERS IN ARMS	*Vertigo*	16	*26 Oct 85*	13
WALK OF LIFE	*Vertigo*	2	*11 Jan 86*	11
YOUR LATEST TRICK	*Vertigo*	26	*3 May 86*	6
Royalties from this single donated to Great Ormond Street Hospital.				
SULTANS OF SWING [RI]	*Vertigo*	62	*5 Nov 88*	1
CALLING ELVIS	*Vertigo*	21	*31 Aug 91*	4
HEAVY FUEL	*Vertigo*	55	*2 Nov 91*	2
ON EVERY STREET	*Vertigo*	42	*29 Feb 92*	2
THE BUG	*Vertigo*	67	*27 Jun 92*	1
ENCORES [EP]	*Vertigo*	31	*22 May 93*	3
Live recordings, lead track: Your Latest Trick.				

ALBUMS:	HITS 11			WEEKS 1133
DIRE STRAITS	*Vertigo*	5	*22 Jul 78*	130
Includes re-entries through to 1988.				
COMMUNIQUE	*Vertigo*	5	*23 Jun 79*	32
MAKING MOVIES	*Vertigo*	4	*25 Oct 80*	249
LOVE OVER GOLD	*Vertigo*	1	*2 Oct 82*	198
Above 2 include re-entries through to 1988.				
ALCHEMY - DIRE STRAITS LIVE	*Vertigo*	3	*24 Mar 84*	163
BROTHERS IN ARMS	*Vertigo*	1	*25 May 85*	203
Includes re-entries through to 1994.				
MONEY FOR NOTHING	*Vertigo*	1	*29 Oct 88*	64
Compilation. Includes re-entries through to 1994.				
ON EVERY STREET	*Vertigo*	1	*21 Sep 91*	35
ON THE NIGHT	*Vertigo*	4	*22 May 93*	7
LIVE AT THE BBC	*Windsong*	71	*8 Jul 95*	1
Various sessions recorded for Radio 1 in 1978.				
BROTHERS IN ARMS [RE]	*Vertigo*	19	*15 Jun 96*	25
Includes re-entries through to 2000.				
LOVE OVER GOLD [RE]	*Vertigo*	66	*15 Jun 96*	2
DIRE STRAITS [RE]	*Vertigo*	69	*15 Jun 96*	2
MAKING MOVIES [RE]	*Vertigo*	70	*15 Jun 96*	2
Above 4 were digitally remastered.				
SULTANS OF SWING - THE VERY BEST OF DIRE STRAITS	*Vertigo*	6	*31 Oct 98*	20

DIRECKT — UK

(See also E-Lustrious.)

SINGLES:	HITS 1			WEEKS 2
TWO FATT GUITARS (REVISITED)	*UFG*	36	*13 Aug 94*	2

DIRECT DRIVE
UK

SINGLES:	HITS 2			WEEKS
ANYTHING?	*Polydor*	67	*26 Jan 85*	
A.B.C. (FALLING IN LOVE'S NOT EASY)	*Boiling Point*	75	*4 May 85*	

DIRTY ROTTEN SCOUNDRELS – See Lisa STANSFIELD

DIRTY VEGAS
UK

SINGLES:	HITS 1			WEEKS
DAYS GO BY	*Credence*	27	*19 May 01*	

DISCHARGE
UK

SINGLES:	HITS 1			WEEKS
NEVER AGAIN	*Clay*	64	*24 Oct 81*	
ALBUMS:	**HITS 1**			**WEEKS**
HEAR NOTHING, SEE NOTHING, SAY NOTHING	*Clay*	40	*15 May 82*	

DISCIPLES OF SOUL – See LITTLE STEPHEN

DISCO ANTHEM
Holland

SINGLES:	HITS 1			WEEKS 2
SCREAM *Samples Daryl Pandy's vocals from Love Can't Turn Around by Farley Jackmaster Funk.*	*Sweat*	47	*18 Jun 94*	2

DISCO CITIZENS
UK

SINGLES:	HITS 3			WEEKS 5
RIGHT HERE RIGHT NOW	*Deconstruction*	40	*22 Jul 95*	2
FOOTPRINT	*Xtravaganza*	34	*12 Apr 97*	2
NAGASAKI BADGER	*Xtravaganza*	56	*4 Jul 98*	1

DISCO EVANGELISTS
UK

SINGLES:	HITS 1			WEEKS 2
DE NIRO	*Positiva*	59	*8 May 93*	2

DISCO TEX presents CLOUDBURST
UK

SINGLES:	HITS 1			WEEKS 2
I CAN CAST A SPELL *Vocals by Shena.* *Based around a line from Chaka Khan's I'm Every Woman.*	*Absolution*	35	*24 Mar 01*	2

DISCO TEX and the SEX-O-LETTES
US

SINGLES:	HITS 2			WEEKS 22
GET DANCIN'	*Chelsea*	8	*23 Nov 74*	12
I WANNA DANCE WIT' CHOO (DOO DAT DANEE) *Features backing vocals by Jocelyn Brown.*	*Chelsea*	6	*26 Apr 75*	10

DISCOVERY – See COAST 2 COAST featuring DISCOVERY

DISPOSABLE HEROES OF HIPHOPRISY
US

SINGLES:	HITS 2			WEEKS 7
TELEVISION, THE DRUG OF THE NATION	*Fourth & Broadway*	57	*4 Apr 92*	2
LANGUAGE OF VIOLENCE	*Fourth & Broadway*	68	*30 May 92*	1
TELEVISION, THE DRUG OF THE NATION [RE]	*Fourth & Broadway*	44	*19 Dec 92*	4
ALBUMS:	**HITS 1**			**WEEKS 3**
HYPOCRISY IS THE GREATEST LUXURY	*Fourth & Broadway*	40	*16 May 92*	3

Sacha DISTEL
France

SINGLES:	HITS 1			WEEKS 27
RAIN DROPS KEEP FALLING ON MY HEAD *From the film 'Butch Cassidy and the Sundance Kid'. Originally recorded by B.J.Thomas.*	*Warner Brothers*	50	*10 Jan 70*	1
RAIN DROPS KEEP FALLING ON MY HEAD [RE-1ST]	*Warner Brothers*	10	*24 Jan 70*	20
RAIN DROPS KEEP FALLING ON MY HEAD [RE-2ND]	*Warner Brothers*	43	*27 Jun 70*	4
RAIN DROPS KEEP FALLING ON MY HEAD [RE-3RD]	*Warner Brothers*	47	*1 Aug 70*	1
RAIN DROPS KEEP FALLING ON MY HEAD [RE-4TH]	*Warner Brothers*	44	*15 Aug 70*	1
ALBUMS:	**HITS 1**			**WEEKS 14**
SACHA DISTEL	*Warner Brothers*	21	*2 May 70*	14

DISTURBED
US

SINGLES:	HITS 1			WEEKS 1
VOICES	*Giant*	52	*7 Apr 01*	1

DIVA — Norway

SINGLES:	HITS 2			WEEKS 2
THE SUN ALWAYS SHINES ON TV	*East West*	53	*7 Oct 95*	1
EVERYBODY (MOVE YOUR BODY)	*East West*	44	*20 Jul 96*	1

DIVA SURPRISE featuring Georgia JONES — US/Spain

SINGLES:	HITS 1			WEEKS 2
ON THE TOP OF THE WORLD	*Positiva*	29	*14 Nov 98*	2

DIVE — UK

SINGLES:	HITS 1			WEEKS 1
BOOGIE	*WEA*	35	*21 Feb 98*	1

DIVERSIONS — UK

SINGLES:	HITS 1			WEEKS 3
FATTIE BUM-BUM	*Gull*	34	*20 Sep 75*	3
Features sax solo by Lene Lovich.				

DIVINE — US

SINGLES:	HITS 5			WEEKS 24
LOVE REACTION	*Design Communications*	65	*15 Oct 83*	2
YOU THINK YOU'RE A MAN	*Proto*	16	*14 Jul 84*	10
I'M SO BEAUTIFUL	*Proto*	52	*20 Oct 84*	2
WALK LIKE A MAN	*Proto*	23	*27 Apr 85*	7
TWISTIN' THE NIGHT AWAY	*Proto*	47	*20 Jul 85*	3

DIVINE — US

SINGLES:	HITS 1			WEEKS 1
LATELY	*Red Ant*	52	*16 Oct 99*	1

DIVINE COMEDY — UK

SINGLES:	HITS 13			WEEKS 38
SOMETHING FOR THE WEEKEND	*Setanta*	14	*29 Jun 96*	5
BECOMING MORE LIKE ALFIE	*Setanta*	27	*24 Aug 96*	2
THE FROG PRINCESS	*Setanta*	15	*16 Nov 96*	2
EVERYBODY KNOWS (EXCEPT YOU)	*Setanta*	14	*22 Mar 97*	4
Features 30 piece orchestra conducted by Christopher Austin.				
I'VE BEEN TO A MARVELLOUS PARTY	*EMI*	28	*11 Apr 98*	3
[AA] listed with Someday I'll Find You by Shola Ama. From the Noel Coward commemorative album Twentieth Century Blues.				
GENERATION SEX	*Setanta*	19	*26 Sep 98*	3
THE CERTAINTY OF CHANCE	*Setanta*	49	*28 Nov 98*	1
NATIONAL EXPRESS	*Setanta*	8	*6 Feb 99*	7
THE POP SINGER'S FEAR OF THE POLLEN COUNT	*Setanta*	17	*21 Aug 99*	4
Originally appeared on their 1993 album Liberation.				
GIN SOAKED BOY	*Setanta*	38	*13 Nov 99*	2
LOVE WHAT YOU DO	*Parlophone*	26	*10 Mar 01*	2
BAD AMBASSADOR	*Parlophone*	34	*26 May 01*	2
PERFECT LOVESONG	*Parlophone*	42	*10 Nov 01*	1
ALBUMS:	**HITS 5**			**WEEKS 43**
CASANOVA	*Setanta*	48	*11 May 96*	9
A SHORT ALBUM ABOUT LOVE	*Setanta*	13	*22 Feb 97*	6
Orchestral love songs recorded on 19 Oct 96 at the Shepherd's Bush Empire with the Brunel Ensemble.				
FIN DE SIECLE	*Setanta*	9	*12 Sep 98*	14
A SECRET HISTORY - THE BEST OF THE DIVINE COMEDY	*Setanta*	3	*11 Sep 99*	11
REGENERATION	*Parlophone*	14	*24 Mar 01*	3

DIVINE WORKS — Europe

(See also Sacred Spirit.)

ALBUMS:	HITS 1			WEEKS 2
DIVINE WORKS	*Virgin*	43	*16 Aug 97*	2

DIVINYLS — Australia

SINGLES:	HITS 1			WEEKS 12
I TOUCH MYSELF	*Virgin America*	10	*18 May 91*	12
ALBUMS:	**HITS 1**			**WEEKS 1**
DIVINYLS	*Virgin America*	59	*20 Jul 91*	1

DIXIE CHICKS — US

SINGLES:	HITS 2			WEEKS 6
THERE'S YOUR TROUBLE	*Epic*	26	*3 Jul 99*	5

READY TO RUN	*Epic*	53	*6 Nov 99*	1

ALBUMS:	HITS 2			WEEKS 8
WIDE OPEN SPACE	*Epic*	29	*3 Jul 99*	6
Originally released in 1998.				
FLY	*Epic*	38	*11 Sep 99*	2

DIXIE CUPS — US

SINGLES:	HITS 2			WEEKS 16
CHAPEL OF LOVE	*Pye International*	22	*20 Jun 64*	8
IKO IKO	*Red Bird*	23	*15 May 65*	8
Originally recorded by James 'Sugarboy' Crawford as Jock-O-Mo.				

DIXIE HUMMINGBIRDS - See Paul SIMON

DIZZY HEIGHTS — UK

SINGLES:	HITS 1			WEEKS 4
CHRISTMAS RAPPING	*Polydor*	49	*18 Dec 82*	4

DJ ALIGATOR PROJECT — Denmark

SINGLES:	HITS 1			WEEKS 1
THE WHISTLE SONG	*Liberty*	57	*7 Oct 00*	1

DJ ARABESQUE - See Mario PIU

DJ BADMARSH & SHRI featuring UK APACHE — UK/India

(See also UK APACHI with SHY FX)

SINGLES:	HITS 1			WEEKS 1
SIGNS	*Outcaste*	63	*28 Jul 01*	1

D.J. BOBO — Switzerland

SINGLES:	HITS 2			WEEKS 4
EVERYBODY	*PWL*	47	*24 Sep 94*	2
LOVE IS ALL AROUND	*Avex UK*	49	*17 Jun 95*	2

DJ Carl COX - See Carl COX

DJ DADO — Italy

SINGLES:	HITS 4			WEEKS 9
X-FILES	*ZYX*	8	*6 Apr 96*	6
Dance version of theme to the TV series.				
COMING BACK	*Ffrreedom*	63	*14 Mar 98*	1
GIVE ME LOVE	*VC Recordings*	59	*11 Jul 98*	1
Above hit: DJ DADO vs Michelle WEEKS.				
READY OR NOT	*Chemistry*	51	*8 May 99*	1
Above hit: DJ DADO and Simone JAY.				

DJ DAN presents NEEDLE DAMAGE — US

SINGLES:	HITS 1			WEEKS 1
THAT ZIPPER TRACK	*Duty Free*	53	*5 May 01*	1
Original release reached No. 77 in 1999.				

DJ DEE KLINE — UK

SINGLES:	HITS 1			WEEKS 6
I DON'T SMOKE	*East West*	11	*3 Jun 00*	6
Features samples from the Channel 4 TV show 'Barking'.				

DJ DISCIPLE — US

SINGLES:	HITS 1			WEEKS 1
ON THE DANCEFLOOR	*Mother*	67	*12 Nov 94*	1

DJ DUKE — US

SINGLES:	HITS 2			WEEKS 7
BLOW YOUR WHISTLE	*ffrr*	15	*8 Jan 94*	5
TURN IT UP (SAY YEAH)	*ffrr*	31	*16 Jul 94*	2

D.J. E-Z ROCK - See Rob BASE and D.J. E-Z ROCK

DJ EMPIRE presents Giorgio MORODER — Italy

SINGLES:	HITS 1			WEEKS 1
THE CHASE	*Logic*	46	*12 Feb 00*	1

DJ ERIC presents — UK

SINGLES:	HITS 2			WEEKS 3
WE ARE LOVE	*Distinct'ive*	37	*13 Feb 99*	2
Samples Daryl Hall and John Oates' I Can't Go For That (No Can Do) and Alexander Hope's Brothers & Sisters.				
DESIRE	*Distinct'ive*	67	*10 Jun 00*	1
Samples Ian Dury and the Blockheads' Hit Me With Your Rhythm Stick.				

DJ FAST EDDIE — US

SINGLES:	HITS 4			WEEKS 15
CAN U DANCE	*Champion*	71	*11 Apr 87*	2
Above hit: Kenny "Jammin" JASON and "Fast" Eddie SMITH.				
CAN U DANCE [RE]	*Champion*	67	*14 Nov 87*	2
HIP HOUSE / I CAN DANCE	*DJ International*	47	*21 Jan 89*	4
YO YO GET FUNKY	*DJ International*	54	*11 Mar 89*	3
Label credit: Fast Eddie.				
GIT ON UP	*DJ International*	49	*28 Oct 89*	4
Above hit: FAST EDDIE featuring SUNDANCE.				

DJ FLAVOURS — UK

SINGLES:	HITS 1			WEEKS 4
YOUR CARESS (ALL I NEED)	*All Around the World*	19	*11 Oct 97*	4
Samples Pacha's One Kiss.				

DJ GERT — Holland

SINGLES:	HITS 1			WEEKS 1
GIVE ME SOME MORE	*Mostika*	50	*26 May 01*	1
Samples Together Forever by Exodus.				

DJ HYPE — UK

(See also Various Artists (EPs) 'Subplates Volume 1 EP'.)

SINGLES:	HITS 2			WEEKS 2
SHOT IN THE DARK	*Suburban Base*	63	*20 Mar 93*	1
DEAD A'S	*True Playaz*	58	*2 Jun 01*	1
Double A side with Casino Royale by DJ Zinc.				
Above hit: TRUE PLAYAZ present DJ HYPE.				
ALBUMS:	**HITS 1**			**WEEKS 1**
NEW FRONTIERS [EP]	*Parousia*	56	*30 Aug 97*	1
Above hit: DJ HYPE presents GANJA KRU.				

DJ JAZZY JEFF and the FRESH PRINCE – See JAZZY JEFF and the FRESH PRINCE

DJ JEAN — Holland

SINGLES:	HITS 1			WEEKS 11
THE LAUNCH	*AM:PM*	2	*11 Sep 99*	11

DJ JURGEN presents ALICE DEEJAY – See ALICE DEEJAY

DJ KOOL — US

SINGLES:	HITS 1			WEEKS 7
LET ME CLEAR MY THROAT	*American Recordings*	8	*22 Feb 97*	7
Guest rapper is Doug E Fresh. Samples Kool and the Gang's Hollywood Swingin'.				

DJ KRUSH — Japan

SINGLES:	HITS 2			WEEKS 2
MEISO	*Mo Wax*	52	*16 Mar 96*	1
ONLY THE STRONG SURVIVE	*Mo Wax*	71	*12 Oct 96*	1
ALBUMS:	**HITS 2**			**WEEKS 2**
BAD BROTHERS	*Island*	58	*3 Sep 94*	1
Mixes of Ronny Jordan material by DJ Krush.				
Above hit: Ronny JORDAN meets DJ KRUSH.				
MEISO	*Mo Wax*	64	*11 Nov 95*	1

DJ LUCK and MC NEAT — UK

SINGLES:	HITS 5			WEEKS 42
A LITTLE BIT OF LUCK	*Red Rose*	9	*25 Dec 99*	15
MASTERBLASTER 2000	*Red Rose*	5	*27 May 00*	8
AIN'T NO STOPPIN' US	*Red Rose*	8	*7 Oct 00*	6
Above 2: DJ LUCK and MC NEAT featuring JJ.				
PIANO LOCO	*Island*	12	*17 Mar 01*	8
I'M ALL ABOUT YOU	*Island*	18	*8 Sep 01*	4
Above hit: DJ LUCK and MC NEAT featuring Ari GOLD.				
I'M ALL ABOUT YOU [RE]	*Island*	71	*20 Oct 01*	1

DJ MANTA — Holland

SINGLES:	HITS 1			WEEKS 1
HOLDING ON	*A&M*	47	*9 Oct 99*	1

Samples Orchestral Manoeuvres In The Dark's Maid Of Orleans (The Waltz Joan Of Arc).

DJ MIKO — Italy

SINGLES:	HITS 1			WEEKS 10
WHAT'S UP	*Systematic*	6	*13 Aug 94*	10

Features female vocalist Louise Gard.

DJ MILANO featuring Samantha FOX — Italy

(See also Samantha Fox.)

SINGLES:	HITS 1			WEEKS 2
SANTA MARIA	*All Around the World*	31	*28 Mar 98*	2

Rap by Eagle E.

DJ MISJAH and DJ TIM — Holland

SINGLES:	HITS 1			WEEKS 4
ACCESS	*Ffreedom*	16	*23 Mar 96*	3
ACCESS [RM]	*Tripoli Trax*	45	*27 May 00*	1

Remixed by Mick Shiner and Steve Hill.

DJ MUGGS – See TRICKY

DJ ÖTZI — Ausria

SINGLES:	HITS 3			WEEKS 26
HEY BABY (UUH, AAH)	*EMI*	1	*18 Aug 01*	20
Single charted on import for the first five weeks; the UK release had the same catalogue number as the import and was thus not listed as a new entry.				
DO WAH DIDDY	*EMI*	9	*1 Dec 01*	5
Originally recorded by The Exciters in 1961 as 'Do Wah Diddy Diddy'.				
X-MAS TIME	*EMI*	51	*29 Dec 01*	1

DJ PIED PIPER and the MASTER OF CEREMONIES — UK

SINGLES:	HITS 1			WEEKS 14
DO YOU REALLY LIKE IT?	*Relentless*	1	*2 Jun 01*	14

DJ POWER — Italy

SINGLES:	HITS 1			WEEKS 2
EVERYBODY PUMP	*Cooltempo*	46	*7 Mar 92*	2

DJ PROFESSOR — Italy

SINGLES:	HITS 4			WEEKS 6
WE GOTTA DO IT	*Fourth & Broadway*	57	*10 Aug 91*	2
Above hit: DJ PROFESSOR and Francesco ZAPPALA.				
ROCK ME STEADY	*PWL Continental*	49	*28 Mar 92*	2
ROCKIN' ME	*Citra*	56	*8 Oct 94*	1
Above hit: PROFESSOR.				
WALKIN' ON UP	*Nukleuz*	64	*1 Mar 97*	1
Above hit: DJ PROF-X-OR.				

DJ QUICKSILVER — Turkey

SINGLES:	HITS 3			WEEKS 29
BELLISSIMA	*Positiva*	4	*5 Apr 97*	17
FREE	*Positiva*	7	*6 Sep 97*	7
PLANET LOVE	*Positiva*	12	*21 Feb 98*	5
ALBUMS:	**HITS 1**			**WEEKS 3**
QUICKSILVER	*Positiva*	26	*7 Mar 98*	3

DJ QUIK – See TONY! TONI! TONE!

DJ RAP — UK

SINGLES:	HITS 3			WEEKS 5
BAD GIRL	*Higher Ground*	32	*4 Jul 98*	2
GOOD TO BE ALIVE	*Higher Ground*	36	*17 Oct 98*	2
EVERYDAY GIRL	*Higher Ground*	47	*3 Apr 99*	1

DJ ROLANDO AKA the AZTEC MYSTIC — US

SINGLES:	HITS 1			WEEKS 2
JAGUAR	*430 West*	43	*21 Oct 00*	2

First appeared on Aztec Mystic's Knight Of The Jaguar EP on the Underground Resistance label in 1999.

DJ SAKIN and FRIENDS — Germany

SINGLES:	HITS 2			WEEKS 18
PROTECT YOUR MIND (FOR THE LOVE OF A PRINCESS) *Samples James Horner's For The Love Of A Princess (from the film 'Braveheart').*	*Positiva*	4	*20 Feb 99*	10
PROTECT YOUR MIND (FOR THE LOVE OF A PRINCESS) [RE]	*Positiva*	71	*8 May 99*	1
NOMANSLAND (DAVID'S SONG) *Samples the theme from the 1970s TV show 'The Adventures Of David Belfour'.*	*Positiva*	14	*5 Jun 99*	7

DJ SANDY vs HOUSETRAP — Germany

SINGLES:	HITS 1			WEEKS 2
OVERDRIVE	*Positiva*	32	*1 Jul 00*	2

DJ SCOT PROJECT — Germany

SINGLES:	HITS 1			WEEKS 1
Y (HOW DEEP IS YOUR LOVE)	*Perfecto Mainline*	57	*14 Feb 98*	1

DJ Doc SCOTT — UK

SINGLES:	HITS 1			WEEKS 2
N.H.S. [EP] *Lead track: Surgery.*	*Absolute*	64	*1 Feb 92*	2

DJ SCOTT featuring Lorna B — UK

SINGLES:	HITS 2			WEEKS 5
DO YOU WANNA PARTY *Originally released in 1994.*	*Steppin' Out*	36	*28 Jan 95*	3
SWEET DREAMS	*Steppin' Out*	37	*1 Apr 95*	2

DJ SEDUCTION — UK

SINGLES:	HITS 2			WEEKS 8
HARDCORE HEAVEN/YOU AND ME	*Ffreedom*	26	*22 Feb 92*	5
COME ON	*Ffreedom*	37	*11 Jul 92*	3

DJ SHADOW — US

SINGLES:	HITS 5			WEEKS 7
WHAT DOES YOUR SOUL LOOK LIKE	*Mo Wax*	59	*25 Mar 95*	1
MIDNIGHT IN A PERFECT WORLD	*Mo Wax*	54	*14 Sep 96*	1
STEM	*Mo Wax*	74	*9 Nov 96*	1
HIGH NOON	*Mo Wax*	22	*11 Oct 97*	2
CAMEL BOBSLED RACE *24 minute megamix of 7 DJ Shadow tracks mixed by DJ Q-Bert.*	*Mo Wax*	62	*20 Dec 97*	1
WHAT DOES YOUR SOUL LOOK LIKE (PART 1) [RM] *Remixed by Peshay and DJ Die.*	*Mo Wax*	54	*24 Jan 98*	1
ALBUMS:	**HITS 1**			**WEEKS 3**
ENDTRODUCING	*Mo Wax*	17	*28 Sep 96*	3

DJ SHORTY - See Lenny FORTUNA

DJ SUPREME — UK

SINGLES:	HITS 4			WEEKS 11
THA WILDSTYLE *Samples The Badman Is Robbin' by Hijack.*	*Distinct'ive*	39	*5 Oct 96*	2
THA WILDSTYLE [RM] *Remixed by Klubbheads.*	*Distinct'ive*	24	*3 May 97*	2
ENTER THE SCENE *Above hit: DJ SUPREME vs the RHYTHM MASTERS.*	*Distinct'ive*	49	*6 Dec 97*	1
THA HORNS OF JERICHO	*All Around the World*	29	*21 Feb 98*	2
UP TO THE WILDSTYLE [RR] *Above hit: PORN KINGS vs DJ SUPREME.*	*All Around The World*	10	*16 Jan 99*	4

DJ TAUCHER — Germany

SINGLES:	HITS 1			WEEKS 1
CHILD OF THE UNIVERSE (SANVEAN)	*Additive*	74	*8 May 99*	1

DJ TIESTO — Holland

SINGLES:	HITS 2			WEEKS 4
FLIGHT 643	*Nebula*	56	*12 May 01*	1
URBAN TRAIN	*VC Recordings*	22	*29 Sep 01*	3

DJ TIM - See DJ MISJAH and DJ TIM

DJAIMIN featuring ALESSANDRA — Switzerland

SINGLES:	HITS 1			WEEKS 2
GIVE YOU	*Cooltempo*	45	*19 Sep 92*	2

DJPC — Belgium

SINGLES:	HITS 1			WEEKS 5
INSSOMNIAK	*Hype*	62	*26 Oct 91*	4
INSSOMNIAK [RM]	*Hype*	64	*29 Feb 92*	1

DJ'S RULE — Canada

SINGLES:	HITS 1			WEEKS 2
GET INTO THE MUSIC	*Distinct'ive*	72	*2 Mar 96*	1
GET INTO THE MUSIC [RI]	*Distinct'ive*	65	*5 Apr 97*	1
Above hit: DJ'S RULE featuring Karen BROWN.				

DJ'S UNITE – See VARIOUS ARTISTS (EPs) 'Fourplay Volume 1 EP'

DJ VISAGE featuring CLARISSA — Denmark/Germany

SINGLES:	HITS 1			WEEKS 1
THE RETURN (TIME TO SAY GOODBYE)	*One Step Music*	58	*10 Jun 00*	1
Featured in the Red Square TV commercial.				

DJUM DJUM – See LEFTFIELD

DJ WHAT? – See O.B.I. PROJECT featuring Harry ASHER D and DJ WHAT?

DJ ZINC — UK

SINGLES:	HITS 2			WEEKS 4
138 TREK	*Phaze One*	27	*18 Nov 00*	3
CASINO ROYALE	*True Playaz*	58	*2 Jun 01*	1
Double A side with Dead A's by DJ Hype.				
Above hit: TRUE PLAYAZ present DJ ZINC.				

Boris DLUGOSCH — US/Germany

SINGLES:	HITS 3			WEEKS 8
KEEP PUSHIN'	*Manifesto*	41	*7 Dec 96*	2
HOLD YOUR HEAD UP HIGH	*Positiva*	23	*13 Sep 97*	2
Above 2: Boris DLUGOSCH presents BOOOM.				
NEVER ENOUGH	*Positiva*	16	*16 Jun 01*	4
Above hit: Boris DLUGOSCH featuring Rosin MURPHY.				

Duke D'MOND – See BARRON KNIGHTS

DMX — US

SINGLES:	HITS 2			WEEKS 5
SLIPPIN'	*Def Jam*	30	*15 May 99*	2
Samples Grover Washington Jr.'s Moonstream.				
WHO WE BE	*Def Jam*	34	*15 Dec 01*	3
ALBUMS:	**HITS 1**			**WEEKS 3**
THE GREAT DEPRESSION	*Def Jam*	20	*3 Nov 01*	3

DNA — UK

SINGLES:	HITS 5			WEEKS 29
TOM'S DINER	*A&M*	2	*28 Jul 90*	10
DNA remix of a 1987 Suzanne Vega hit.				
Above hit: DNA featuring Suzanne VEGA.				
LA SERENISSIMA	*Raw Bass*	34	*18 Aug 90*	8
REBEL WOMAN	*DNA*	42	*3 Aug 91*	4
Samples David Bowie's Rebel Rebel.				
Above hit: DNA rap performed by Jazzi P.				
CAN YOU HANDLE IT	*EMI*	17	*1 Feb 92*	5
Above hit: DNA featuring Sharon REDD.				
BLUE LOVE (CALL MY NAME)	*EMI*	66	*9 May 92*	2
Above hit: DNA featuring Joe NYE.				

Carl DOBKINS — US

SINGLES:	HITS 1			WEEKS 1
LUCKY DEVIL	*Brunswick*	44	*2 Apr 60*	1

Anita DOBSON — UK

SINGLES:	HITS 2			WEEKS 13
ANYONE CAN FALL IN LOVE	*BBC*	4	*9 Aug 86*	9
Above hit: Anita DOBSON and the Simon MAY ORCHESTRA.				
TALKING OF LOVE	*Parlophone*	43	*18 Jul 87*	4

DOCTOR and the MEDICS — UK

SINGLES:	HITS 3			WEEKS 25
SPIRIT IN THE SKY	*I.R.S.*	1	*10 May 86*	15

BURN	*I.R.S.*	29	*9 Aug 86*	6
WATERLOO	*I.R.S.*	45	*22 Nov 86*	4
Above hit: DOCTOR and the MEDICS with Roy WOOD starring the ANADIN BROTHERS.				
ALBUMS:	**HITS 1**			**WEEKS 3**
LAUGHING AT THE PIECES	*I.R.S.*	25	*21 Jun 86*	3

DR. ALBAN — Nigeria

SINGLES:	**HITS 6**			**WEEKS 28**
IT'S MY LIFE	*Logic*	2	*5 Sep 92*	12
ONE LOVE	*Logic*	45	*14 Nov 92*	2
SING HALLELUJAH!	*Logic*	16	*10 Apr 93*	8
LOOK WHO'S TALKING	*Logic*	55	*26 Mar 94*	3
AWAY FROM HOME	*Logic*	42	*13 Aug 94*	2
SWEET DREAMS	*Logic*	59	*29 Apr 95*	1
Above hit: SWING featuring DR. ALBAN.				

DR. BARNARDO'S CHILDREN – See Joan REGAN

DR. DRE — US

(See also Scarface.)

SINGLES:	**HITS 11**			**WEEKS 66**
NUTHIN' BUT A 'G' THANG / LET ME RIDE	*Death Row*	31	*22 Jan 94*	3
Original release reached No. 81 in 1993. Nuthin' But A 'G' Thang features vocals by Snoop Doggy Dog.				
DRE DAY	*Death Row*	59	*3 Sep 94*	2
NATURAL BORN KILLAZ	*Death Row*	45	*15 Apr 95*	2
From the film 'Murder Was The Case'.				
Above hit: DR. DRE and ICE CUBE.				
KEEP THEIR HEADS RINGIN'	*Priority*	25	*10 Jun 95*	4
From the film 'Friday'.				
CALIFORNIA LOVE	*Death Row*	6	*13 Apr 96*	8
Samples Zapp's So Ruff So Tuff and Joe Cocker's Woman To Woman.				
Above hit: 2PAC featuring DR DRE.				
NO DIGGITY	*Interscope*	9	*19 Oct 96*	7
Above hit: BLACKSTREET (featuring DR. DRE).				
ZOOM	*Interscope*	15	*11 Jul 98*	3
From the film 'Bulworth'.				
Above hit: DR. DRE LL COOL J.				
GUILTY CONSCIENCE	*Interscope*	5	*14 Aug 99*	8
Samples the track Go Home Pigs. From the film 'Getting Straight'.				
Above hit: EMINEM featuring DR. DRE.				
STILL D.R.E.	*Interscope*	6	*25 Mar 00*	10
Above hit: DR. DRE featuring SNOOP DOGG.				
FORGET ABOUT DRE	*Interscope*	7	*10 Jun 00*	9
Above hit: DR. DRE featuring EMINEM.				
THE NEXT EPISODE	*Interscope*	3	*3 Feb 01*	10
Above hit: DR. DRE featuring SNOOP DOGG.				
ALBUMS:	**HITS 2**			**WEEKS 75**
2001	*Interscope*	48	*27 Nov 99*	2
2001 [RE]	*Interscope*	4	*8 Jan 00*	71
THE CHRONIC	*Interscope*	52	*9 Sep 00*	2
Originally released in 1993.				

DR. FEELGOOD — UK

SINGLES:	**HITS 6**			**WEEKS 29**
SNEAKIN' SUSPICION	*United Artists*	47	*11 Jun 77*	3
SHE'S A WIND UP	*United Artists*	34	*24 Sep 77*	5
DOWN AT THE DOCTORS	*United Artists*	48	*30 Sep 78*	5
Originally recorded by Mickey Jupp.				
MILK AND ALCOHOL	*United Artists*	9	*20 Jan 79*	9
Co-written by Nick Lowe.				
AS LONG AS THE PRICE IS RIGHT	*United Artists*	40	*5 May 79*	6
PUT HIM OUT OF YOUR MIND	*United Artists*	73	*8 Dec 79*	1
ALBUMS:	**HITS 6**			**WEEKS 33**
MALPRACTICE	*United Artists*	17	*18 Oct 75*	6
STUPIDITY	*United Artists*	1	*2 Oct 76*	9
Live recordings. Side 1 from Sheffield City Hall 23 May 76, side 2 from Southend Kursaal 8 Nov 75.				
SNEAKIN' SUSPICION	*United Artists*	10	*4 Jun 77*	6
BE SEEING YOU	*United Artists*	55	*8 Oct 77*	3
PRIVATE PRACTICE	*United Artists*	41	*7 Oct 78*	5
AS IT HAPPENS	*United Artists*	42	*2 Jun 79*	4

DR. HOOK — US

SINGLES:	HITS 10			WEEKS 105
SYLVIA'S MOTHER	*CBS*	2	*24 Jun 72*	13
Originally recorded by Shel Silverstein.				
Above hit: DR HOOK and the MEDICINE SHOW.				
A LITTLE BIT MORE	*Capitol*	2	*26 Jun 76*	14
IF NOT YOU	*Capitol*	5	*30 Oct 76*	11
MORE LIKE THE MOVIES	*Capitol*	14	*25 Mar 78*	10
Originally recorded by Shel Silverstein.				
WHEN YOU'RE IN LOVE WITH A BEAUTIFUL WOMAN	*Capitol*	1	*22 Sep 79*	17
BETTER LOVE NEXT TIME	*Capitol*	8	*5 Jan 80*	8
SEXY EYES	*Capitol*	4	*29 Mar 80*	9
YEARS FROM NOW	*Capitol*	47	*23 Aug 80*	6
SHARING THE NIGHT TOGETHER	*Capitol*	43	*8 Nov 80*	4
Originally recorded by Dobie Gray.				
GIRLS CAN GET IT	*Mercury*	40	*22 Nov 80*	5
WHEN YOU'RE IN LOVE WITH A BEAUTIFUL WOMAN [RI]	*Capitol*	44	*1 Feb 92*	4
A LITTLE BIT MORE [RI]	*EMI*	47	*6 Jun 92*	4

ALBUMS:	HITS 9			WEEKS 157
A LITTLE BIT MORE	*Capitol*	5	*26 Jun 76*	42
MAKING LOVE AND MUSIC	*Capitol*	39	*29 Oct 77*	4
PLEASURE AND PAIN	*Capitol*	47	*27 Oct 79*	6
SOMETIMES YOU WIN	*Capitol*	14	*17 Nov 79*	44
Peak position reached on 10 May 80.				
RISING	*Mercury*	44	*29 Nov 80*	5
DR. HOOK GREATEST HITS	*Capitol*	2	*6 Dec 80*	28
DR. HOOK LIVE IN THE UK	*Capitol*	90	*14 Nov 81*	1
COMPLETELY HOOKED - THE BEST OF DR. HOOK	*Capitol*	3	*13 Jun 92*	19
LOVE SONGS	*EMI*	8	*13 Feb 99*	8

DR. JOHN — US

ALBUMS:	HITS 1			WEEKS 3
ANUTHA ZONE	*Parlophone*	33	*27 Jun 98*	3

DR. MOUTHQUAKE - See E-ZEE POSSEE

DR. OCTAGON — US

SINGLES:	HITS 1			WEEKS 1
BLUE FLOWERS	*Mo Wax*	66	*7 Sep 96*	1

DOCTOR SPIN — UK

SINGLES:	HITS 1			WEEKS 8
TETRIS	*Carpet*	6	*3 Oct 92*	8
Theme to the Nintendo computer game.				

Ken DODD — UK

SINGLES:	HITS 19			WEEKS 233
LOVE IS LIKE A VIOLIN	*Decca*	8	*9 Jul 60*	18
ONCE IN EVERY LIFETIME	*Decca*	28	*17 Jun 61*	7
ONCE IN EVERY LIFETIME [RE-1ST]	*Decca*	47	*12 Aug 61*	1
ONCE IN EVERY LIFETIME [RE-2ND]	*Decca*	31	*26 Aug 61*	10
PIANISSIMO	*Decca*	21	*3 Feb 62*	15
STILL	*Columbia*	35	*31 Aug 63*	10
Above hit: Ken DODD with Geoff LOVE and his Orchestra.				
EIGHT BY TEN	*Columbia*	22	*8 Feb 64*	11
HAPPINESS	*Columbia*	31	*25 Jul 64*	13
Above 3: originally recorded by Bill Anderson.				
SO DEEP IS THE NIGHT	*Columbia*	31	*28 Nov 64*	7
TEARS	*Columbia*	1	*4 Sep 65*	24
THE RIVER (LE COLLINE SONO IN FIORE)	*Columbia*	3	*20 Nov 65*	14
PROMISES	*Columbia*	6	*14 May 66*	14
Above 3: Ken DODD with Geoff LOVE and his Orchestra.				
MORE THAN LOVE	*Columbia*	14	*6 Aug 66*	11
Above hit: Ken DODD with Johnny PEARSON and his Orchestra.				
IT'S LOVE (IN UN FIORE)	*Columbia*	36	*29 Oct 66*	7
Above hit: Ken DODD with Brian FAHEY and his Orchestra.				
LET ME CRY ON YOUR SHOULDER	*Columbia*	11	*21 Jan 67*	10
Above hit: Ken DODD with Geoff LOVE and his Orchestra.				
TEARS WON'T WASH AWAY THESE HEARTACHES	*Columbia*	22	*2 Aug 69*	11
BROKENHEARTED	*Columbia*	15	*5 Dec 70*	9
BROKENHEARTED [RE]	*Columbia*	38	*13 Feb 71*	1
WHEN LOVE COMES ROUND AGAIN (L'ARCA DI NOE)	*Columbia*	19	*10 Jul 71*	16
JUST OUT OF REACH (OF MY TWO EMPTY ARMS)	*Columbia*	29	*18 Nov 72*	11
THINK OF ME (WHEREVER YOU ARE)	*EMI*	21	*29 Nov 75*	8
HOLD MY HAND	*Images*	44	*26 Dec 81*	5

EPS:	HITS 3			WEEKS 19
STILL	*Columbia*	18	*22 Feb 64*	1
DODDY AND THE DIDDY MEN	*Columbia*	4	*25 Dec 65*	17
Above hit: Ken DODD with the DIDDYMEN.				
DIDDYNESS	*Columbia*	8	*7 Jan 67*	1
Above hit: Ken DODD with the DIDDYMEN and DODDY'S DIDDY BAND.				

ALBUMS:	HITS 4			WEEKS 36
TEARS OF HAPPINESS	*Columbia*	6	*25 Dec 65*	12*
HITS FOR NOW AND ALWAYS	*Columbia*	14	*23 Jul 66*	11
FOR SOMEONE SPECIAL	*Columbia*	40	*14 Jan 67*	1
20 GOLDEN GREATS OF KEN DODD	*Warwick*	8	*29 Nov 80*	12

DODGY UK

SINGLES:	HITS 11			WEEKS 41
LOVEBIRDS	*A&M*	65	*8 May 93*	2
I NEED ANOTHER [EP]	*A&M*	67	*3 Jul 93*	2
Lead track: I Need Another.				
THE MELOD-E.P. [EP]	*A&M*	53	*6 Aug 94*	1
Lead track: Melodies Haunt You.				
STAYING OUT FOR THE SUMMER	*A&M*	38	*1 Oct 94*	2
SO LET ME GO FAR	*A&M*	30	*7 Jan 95*	3
MAKING THE MOST OF	*A&M*	22	*11 Mar 95*	3
Above hit: DODGY with the KICK HORNS.				
STAYING OUT FOR THE SUMMER (SUMMER '95) [RM]	*A&M*	19	*10 Jun 95*	5
IN A ROOM	*A&M*	12	*8 Jun 96*	6
GOOD ENOUGH	*A&M*	4	*10 Aug 96*	8
IF YOU'RE THINKING OF ME	*A&M*	11	*16 Nov 96*	4
FOUND YOU	*A&M*	19	*15 Mar 97*	3
EVERY SINGLE DAY	*A&M*	32	*26 Sep 98*	2

ALBUMS:	HITS 4			WEEKS 54
THE DODGY ALBUM	*A&M*	75	*5 Jun 93*	1
HOMEGROWN	*A&M*	43	*5 Nov 94*	1
HOMEGROWN [RE]	*A&M*	28	*24 Jun 95*	13
FREE PEACE SWEET	*A&M*	7	*29 Jun 96*	38
ACE A'S + KILLER B'S	*A&M*	55	*17 Oct 98*	1

DOG EAT DOG US

SINGLES:	HITS 2			WEEKS 7
NO FRONTS - THE REMIXES	*Roadrunner*	64	*19 Aug 95*	1
NO FRONTS - THE REMIXES [RE]	*Roadrunner*	9	*3 Feb 96*	5
ISMS	*Roadrunner*	43	*13 Jul 96*	1

ALBUMS:	HITS 1			WEEKS 2
PLAY GAMES	*Roadrunner*	40	*27 Jul 96*	2

Tim DOG US

SINGLES:	HITS 2			WEEKS 3
BITCH WITH A PERM	*Dis-stress*	49	*29 Oct 94*	1
MAKE WAY FOR THE INDIAN	*Island*	29	*11 Feb 95*	2
Above hit: APACHE INDIAN and Tim DOG.				

Nate DOGG – See Warren G; LUDACRIS; Pharoahe MONCH; MOS DEF; SHADE SHEIST featuring Nate DOGG & KURUPT

DOGS D'AMOUR UK

SINGLES:	HITS 6			WEEKS 15
HOW COME IT NEVER RAINS	*China*	44	*4 Feb 89*	3
SATELLITE KID	*China*	26	*5 Aug 89*	3
TRAIL OF TEARS	*China*	47	*14 Oct 89*	3
VICTIMS OF SUCCESS	*China*	36	*23 Jun 90*	3
EMPTY WORLD	*China*	61	*15 Sep 90*	2
ALL OR NOTHING	*China*	53	*19 Jun 93*	1

ALBUMS:	HITS 6			WEEKS 12
IN THE DYNAMITE JET SALOON	*China*	97	*22 Oct 88*	1
A GRAVEYARD OF EMPTY BOTTLES	*China*	16	*25 Mar 89*	4
ERROL FLYNN	*China*	22	*30 Sep 89*	3
STRAIGHT	*China*	32	*6 Oct 90*	2
DOG'S HITS AND THE BOOTLEG ALBUM	*China*	58	*7 Sep 91*	1
. . . MORE UNCHARTERED HEIGHTS OF DISGRACE	*China*	30	*15 May 93*	1

Ken DOH UK

SINGLES:	HITS 1			WEEKS 7
NAKASAKI EP (I NEED A LOVER TONIGHT) [EP]	*ffrr*	7	*30 Mar 96*	7
Various mixes of the track I Need A Lover Tonight.				

DOKKEN — UK

ALBUMS:	HITS 1			WEEKS 1
BACK FOR THE ATTACK	*Elektra*	96	*21 Nov 87*	1

Joe DOLAN — Ireland

SINGLES:	HITS 4			WEEKS 40
• MAKE ME AN ISLAND	*Pye*	3	*28 Jun 69*	18
TERESA	*Pye*	20	*1 Nov 69*	7
MAKE ME AN ISLAND [RE]	*Pye*	48	*8 Nov 69*	1
YOU'RE SUCH A GOOD LOOKING WOMAN	*Pye*	17	*28 Feb 70*	13
I NEED YOU	*Pye*	43	*17 Sep 77*	1

Thomas DOLBY — UK

SINGLES:	HITS 9			WEEKS 51
EUROPA AND THE PIRATE TWINS	*Parlophone*	48	*3 Oct 81*	3
WINDPOWER	*Venice In Peril*	31	*14 Aug 82*	8
SHE BLINDED ME WITH SCIENCE	*Venice In Peril*	49	*6 Nov 82*	4
Features vocals from Dr. Magnus Pike.				
SHE BLINDED ME WITH SCIENCE [RI]	*Venice In Peril*	56	*16 Jul 83*	4
HYPERACTIVE!	*Parlophone Odean Series*	17	*21 Jan 84*	9
I SCARE MYSELF	*Parlophone Odean Series*	46	*31 Mar 84*	5
Originally recorded by Dan Hicks and his Hot Licks.				
AIRHEAD	*Manhattan*	53	*16 Apr 88*	3
CLOSE BUT NO CIGAR	*Virgin*	22	*9 May 92*	5
I LOVE YOU GOODBYE	*Virgin*	36	*11 Jul 92*	4
SILK PYJAMAS	*Virgin*	62	*26 Sep 92*	2
HYPERACTIVE! [RI]	*Parlophone*	23	*22 Jan 94*	4
ALBUMS:	**HITS 4**			**WEEKS 29**
THE GOLDEN AGE OF WIRELESS	*Venice In Peril*	65	*22 May 82*	10
THE FLAT EARTH	*Parlophone*	14	*18 Feb 84*	14
ALIENS ATE MY BUICK	*Manhattan*	30	*7 May 88*	3
ASTRONAUTS AND HERETICS	*Virgin*	35	*8 Aug 92*	2

Joe DOLCE MUSIC THEATRE — US

SINGLES:	HITS 1			WEEKS 10
SHADDAP YOU FACE	*Epic*	1	*7 Feb 81*	10

DOLL — UK

SINGLES:	HITS 1			WEEKS 8
DESIRE ME	*Beggars Banquet*	28	*13 Jan 79*	8

DOLLAR — UK

SINGLES:	HITS 14			WEEKS 128
SHOOTING STAR	*Carrere*	14	*11 Nov 78*	12
WHO WERE YOU WITH IN THE MOONLIGHT	*Carrere*	14	*19 May 79*	12
LOVE'S GOTTA HOLD ON ME	*Carrere*	4	*18 Aug 79*	13
I WANNA HOLD YOUR HAND	*Carrere*	9	*24 Nov 79*	14
TAKIN' A CHANCE ON YOU	*WEA*	62	*25 Oct 80*	3
HAND HELD IN BLACK AND WHITE	*WEA*	19	*15 Aug 81*	12
MIRROR MIRROR (MON AMOUR)	*WEA*	4	*14 Nov 81*	17
RING RING	*Carrere*	61	*20 Mar 82*	2
Originally recorded by Christopher Rainbow in 1979.				
GIVE ME BACK MY HEART	*WEA*	4	*27 Mar 82*	9
VIDEOTHEQUE	*WEA*	17	*19 Jun 82*	10
GIVE ME SOME KINDA MAGIC	*WEA*	34	*18 Sep 82*	6
WE WALKED IN LOVE	*Arista*	61	*16 Aug 86*	4
O L'AMOUR	*London*	7	*26 Dec 87*	11
Originally recorded by Erasure.				
IT'S NATURE'S WAY (NO PROBLEM)	*London*	58	*16 Jul 88*	3
ALBUMS:	**HITS 3**			**WEEKS 28**
SHOOTING STARS	*Carrere*	36	*15 Sep 79*	8
THE VERY BEST OF DOLLAR	*Carrere*	31	*24 Apr 82*	9
THE DOLLAR ALBUM	*WEA*	18	*30 Oct 82*	11

DOLORES – See CRANBERRIES; Jah WOBBLE'S INVADERS OF THE HEART

Placido DOMINGO — Spain

(See also Placido Domingo and John Denver; Placido Domingo, Diana Ross and José Carreras; Placido Domingo, José Carreras and Montserrat Caballe; Andrew Lloyd Webber; 3 Tenors: Jose Carreras, Placido Domingo, Luciano Pavarotti; Dionne Warwick Placido Domingo.)

SINGLES:	HITS 2			WEEKS 11
TILL I LOVED YOU	*CBS*	24	*27 May 89*	9
Above hit: Placido DOMINGO and Jennifer RUSH.				

TURANDOT 'NESSUM DORMA'	*Epic*	59	*16 Jun 90*	2
Above hit: Luis COBOS featuring Placido DOMINGO.				
ALBUMS:	**HITS 9**			**WEEKS 59**
MY LIFE FOR A SONG	*CBS*	31	*21 May 83*	8
PLACIDO DOMINGO COLLECTION	*Stylus*	30	*27 Dec 86*	14
GREATEST LOVE SONGS	*CBS*	63	*23 Apr 88*	2
THE ESSENTIAL DOMINGO	*Deutsche Grammophon*	20	*17 Jun 89*	8
GOYA . . . A LIFE IN A SONG	*CBS*	36	*17 Jun 89*	4
BE MY LOVE . . . AN ALBUM OF LOVE	*EMI*	14	*24 Nov 90*	12
THE BROADWAY I LOVE	*East West*	45	*7 Dec 91*	6
Above hit: Placido DOMINGO with the LONDON SYMPHONY ORCHESTRA conducted by Eugene KOHN.				
DOMINGO: ARIAS AND SPANISH SONGS	*Deutsche Grammophon*	47	*13 Jun 92*	3
SONGS OF LOVE	*EMI*	53	*28 Oct 00*	2

Placido DOMINGO, José CARRERAS and Montserrat CABALLE — Spain/Italy

(See also José Carreras; Placido Domingo; Freddie Mercury and Montserrat Caballe.)

ALBUMS:	**HITS 1**			**WEEKS 3**
FROM THE OFFICAL BARCELONA GAMES CEREMONY	*RCA Red Seal*	41	*8 Aug 92*	3

Placido DOMINGO and John DENVER — Spain/US

(See also John Denver; Placido Domingo.)

SINGLES:	**HITS 1**			**WEEKS 9**
PERHAPS LOVE	*CBS*	46	*12 Dec 81*	9
Above hit: Placido DOMINGO and John DENVER, vocal duet – John DENVER, guitar.				
ALBUMS:	**HITS 1**			**WEEKS 21**
PERHAPS LOVE	*CBS*	17	*28 Nov 81*	21

Placido DOMINGO, Diana ROSS and José CARRERAS — Spain/US

(See also José Carreras; Placido Domingo; Diana Ross.)

ALBUMS:	**HITS 1**			**WEEKS 2**
CHRISTMAS IN VIENNA	*Sony Classical*	71	*25 Dec 93*	2
Live recordings from the Rathaus, Vienna, 21 Dec 92.				

DOMINO — US

SINGLES:	**HITS 2**			**WEEKS 6**
GETTO JAM	*Outburst*	33	*22 Jan 94*	4
SWEET POTATOE PIE	*Outburst*	42	*14 May 94*	2

Fats DOMINO — UK

SINGLES:	**HITS 20**			**WEEKS 110**
I'M IN LOVE AGAIN	*London*	28	*28 Jul 56*	1
I'M IN LOVE AGAIN [RE]	*London*	12	*18 Aug 56*	13
BLUEBERRY HILL	*London*	26	*1 Dec 56*	1
Originally recorded by Glenn Miller.				
BLUEBERRY HILL [RE]	*London*	6	*22 Dec 56*	14
AIN'T THAT A SHAME	*London*	23	*26 Jan 57*	2
HONEY CHILE	*London*	29	*2 Feb 57*	1
BLUE MONDAY	*London*	23	*30 Mar 57*	1
I'M WALKIN'	*London*	19	*20 Apr 57*	7
BLUE MONDAY [RE]	*London*	30	*20 Apr 57*	1
VALLEY OF TEARS	*London*	25	*20 Jul 57*	1
THE BIG BEAT	*London*	20	*29 Mar 58*	4
SICK AND TIRED	*London*	26	*5 Jul 58*	1
Originally recorded by Guy Lombardo.				
MARGIE	*London*	18	*23 May 59*	5
Originally recorded by Eddie Cantor.				
I WANT TO WALK YOU HOME	*London*	14	*17 Oct 59*	5
BE MY GUEST	*London*	11	*19 Dec 59*	8
BE MY GUEST [RE]	*London*	19	*20 Feb 60*	4
COUNTRY BOY	*London*	19	*19 Mar 60*	11
WALKING TO NEW ORLEANS	*London*	19	*23 Jul 60*	10
THREE NIGHTS A WEEK	*London*	45	*12 Nov 60*	2
MY GIRL JOSEPHINE	*London*	32	*7 Jan 61*	4
IT KEEPS RAININ'	*London*	49	*29 Jul 61*	1
WHAT A PARTY	*London*	43	*2 Dec 61*	1
JAMBALAYA	*London*	41	*31 Mar 62*	1
RED SAILS IN THE SUNSET	*His Master's Voice*	34	*2 Nov 63*	6
BLUEBERRY HILL [RI]	*United Artists*	41	*24 Apr 76*	5
ALBUMS:	**HITS 1**			**WEEKS 1**
VERY BEST OF FATS DOMINO	*Liberty*	56	*16 May 70*	1

DOMINOS – See Billy WARD and the DOMINOES

DON-E UK

SINGLES:	HITS 3			WEEKS 8
LOVE MAKES THE WORLD GO ROUND	*Fourth & Broadway*	18	*9 May 92*	6
PEACE IN THE WORLD *Single was removed from the chart when evidence of hyping was uncovered.*	*Fourth & Broadway*	41	*25 Jul 92*	1
DELICIOUS *Above hit: Deni HINES featuring DON-E*	*Mushroom*	52	*28 Feb 98*	1

DON PABLO'S ANIMALS Italy

SINGLES:	HITS 1			WEEKS 10
VENUS	*Rumour*	4	*19 May 90*	10

Lonnie DONEGAN UK

(See also Chris Barber's Jazz Band; Miki and Griff; Van Morrison, Lonnie Donegan and Chris Barber.)

SINGLES:	HITS 30			WEEKS 321
ROCK ISLAND LINE *Sub credit: (Lonnie Donegan-guitar and vocal; Chris Barber-bass; Beryl Bryden-washboard). Originally recorded by Leadbelly.*	*Decca*	8	*7 Jan 56*	13
ROCK ISLAND LINE [RE-1ST]	*Decca*	16	*14 Apr 56*	3
STEWBALL	*Pye Nixa*	27	*21 Apr 56*	1
LOST JOHN / STEWBALL *Stewball was only listed from 12 May 56 for 3 weeks, peaking at No. 7.*	*Pye Nixa*	2	*28 Apr 56*	17
ROCK ISLAND LINE [RE-2ND]	*Decca*	19	*12 May 56*	6
LONNIE DONEGAN SKIFFLE SESSION [EP] *Lead track: Railroad Bill.* *Above 6: Lonnie DONEGAN SKIFFLE GROUP.*	*Pye Nixa*	20	*7 Jul 56*	2
BRING A LITTLE WATER, SYLVIE / DEAD OR ALIVE *Dead Or Alive listed from 15 Sep 56. Bring A Litle Water Sylvie originally recorded by Leadbelly.*	*Pye Nixa*	7	*8 Sep 56*	12
LONNIE DONEGAN SHOWCASE [LP] *8 track LP, first track: Wabash Cannonball.*	*Pye Nixa*	26	*22 Dec 56*	3
BRING A LITTLE WATER, SYLVIE / DEAD OR ALIVE [RE]	*Pye Nixa*	30	*12 Jan 57*	1
DON'T YOU ROCK ME DADDY-O	*Pye Nixa*	4	*19 Jan 57*	17
CUMBERLAND GAP	*Pye Nixa*	1	*6 Apr 57*	12
PUTTIN' ON THE STYLE / GAMBLIN' MAN *Gamblin' Man listed from 22 Jun 57 and had first credit. Both sides are live recordings from the London Palladium, 9 May 57. Some copies have Putting rather than Puttin'.*	*Pye Nixa*	1	*8 Jun 57*	19
MY DIXIE DARLING *Originally recorded by the Carter Family.*	*Pye Nixa*	10	*12 Oct 57*	15
JACK O' DIAMONDS	*Pye Nixa*	14	*21 Dec 57*	7
THE GRAND COOLIE DAM *From the film 'Six Five Special'. Title on some copies is Grand Coulee Dam. Originally recorded by Woody Guthrie.*	*Pye Nixa*	6	*12 Apr 58*	15
SALLY DON'T YOU GRIEVE / BETTY, BETTY, BETTY *Sally Don't You Grieve originally recorded by Woody Guthrie.*	*Pye Nixa*	11	*12 Jul 58*	7
LONESOME TRAVELLER	*Pye Nixa*	28	*27 Sep 58*	1
LONNIE'S SKIFFLE PARTY [M]	*Pye Nixa*	23	*15 Nov 58*	5
TOM DOOLEY	*Pye Nixa*	3	*22 Nov 58*	14
DOES YOUR CHEWING GUM LOSE ITS FLAVOUR (ON THE BEDPOST OVERNIGHT) *Live recording from the New Theatre, Oxford, 13 Dec 58. Originally recorded by Ernest Hare & Billy Jones in 1924.*	*Pye Nixa*	3	*7 Feb 59*	12
FORT WORTH JAIL	*Pye Nixa*	14	*9 May 59*	5
BATTLE OF NEW ORLEANS *Recorded at the Bristol Hippodrome. Originally recorded by Jimmie Driftwood.*	*Pye*	2	*27 Jun 59*	16
SAL'S GOT A SUGAR LIP *Recorded at the Royal Aquarium, Great Yarmouth.*	*Pye*	13	*12 Sep 59*	4
SAN MIGUEL *Above 18: Lonnie DONEGAN and his SKIFFLE GROUP.*	*Pye*	19	*5 Dec 59*	4
MY OLD MAN'S A DUSTMAN (BALLAD OF A REFUSE DISPOSAL OFFICER) *Live recording from the Gaumont Cinema, Doncaster.* *Above hit: Lonnie DONEGAN and his Group.*	*Pye*	1	*26 Mar 60*	13
I WANNA GO HOME (THE WRECK OF THE JOHN "B") *Above hit: Lonnie DONEGAN; Wally STOTT ORCHESTRA.*	*Pye*	5	*28 May 60*	17
LORELEI	*Pye*	10	*27 Aug 60*	8
LIVELY *Above hit: Lonnie DONEGAN and his Group.*	*Pye*	13	*26 Nov 60*	9
VIRGIN MARY	*Pye*	27	*10 Dec 60*	5
HAVE A DRINK ON ME	*Pye*	8	*13 May 61*	15
MICHAEL, ROW THE BOAT / LUMBERED *From 14 Oct 61, Lumbered no longer listed on the chart. Recorded at the Winter Gardens Pavilion Theatre, Blackpool. Lumered from the show 'Stop The World – I Want To Get Off'.* *Above 2: Lonnie DONEGAN and his Group.*	*Pye*	6	*2 Sep 61*	11
THE COMANCHEROS	*Pye*	14	*20 Jan 62*	10
THE PARTY'S OVER *From the musical 'Bells Are Ringing'.*	*Pye*	9	*7 Apr 62*	12

PICK A BALE OF COTTON *Originally recorded by Leadbelly.* *Above hit: Lonnie DONEGAN and his Group.*	*Pye*	11	*18 Aug 62*	10
EPS:	**HITS 1**			**WEEKS 8**
YANKEE DOODLE DONEGAN	*Pye Nixa*	8	*1 Oct 60*	8
ALBUMS:	**HITS 3**			**WEEKS 29**
GOLDEN AGE OF DONEGAN	*Pye Golden Guinea*	3	*1 Sep 62*	23
GOLDEN AGE OF DONEGAN VOLUME 2	*Pye Golden Guinea*	15	*9 Feb 63*	3
PUTTIN' ON THE STYLE	*Chrysalis*	51	*25 Feb 78*	3

Tanya DONELLY — US

SINGLES:	**HITS 2**			**WEEKS 2**
PRETTY DEEP	*4AD*	55	*30 Aug 97*	1
THE BRIGHT LIGHT	*4AD*	64	*6 Dec 97*	1
ALBUMS:	**HITS 1**			**WEEKS 1**
LOVESONGS FOR UNDERDOGS	*4AD*	36	*20 Sep 97*	1

Ral DONNER — US

SINGLES:	**HITS 1**			**WEEKS 10**
YOU DON'T KNOW WHAT YOU'VE GOT (UNTIL YOU LOSE IT)	*Parlophone*	25	*23 Sep 61*	10

DONOVAN — UK

SINGLES:	**HITS 11**			**WEEKS 100**
CATCH THE WIND	*Pye*	4	*27 Mar 65*	13
COLOURS	*Pye*	4	*5 Jun 65*	12
TURQUOISE	*Pye*	30	*13 Nov 65*	6
SUNSHINE SUPERMAN *Features Jimmy Page on guitar.*	*Pye*	2	*10 Dec 66*	11
MELLOW YELLOW *Backing vocals by Paul McCartney.*	*Pye*	8	*11 Feb 67*	8
THERE IS A MOUNTAIN	*Pye*	8	*28 Oct 67*	11
JENNIFER JUNIPER	*Pye*	5	*24 Feb 68*	11
HURDY GURDY MAN	*Pye*	4	*1 Jun 68*	10
ATLANTIS	*Pye*	23	*7 Dec 68*	8
GOO GOO BARABAJAGAL (LOVE IS HOT) *Some issues only had title listed as Barabajagal.* *Above hit: DONOVAN and Jeff BECK GROUP.*	*Pye*	12	*12 Jul 69*	9
JENNIFER JUNIPER *Above hit: SINGING CORNER meets DONOVAN.*	*Fontana*	68	*1 Dec 90*	1
EPS:	**HITS 2**			**WEEKS 36**
THE UNIVERSAL SOLDIER	*Pye*	1	*21 Aug 65*	30
DONOVAN, VOLUME ONE	*Pye*	12	*5 Mar 66*	6
ALBUMS:	**HITS 7**			**WEEKS 73**
WHAT'S BIN DID AND WHAT'D BIN HID	*Pye*	3	*5 Jun 65*	16
FAIRY TALE	*Pye*	20	*6 Nov 65*	2
SUNSHINE SUPERMAN	*Pye*	25	*8 Jul 67*	7
UNIVERSAL SOLDIER	*Marble Arch*	5	*14 Oct 67*	18
A GIFT FROM A FLOWER TO A GARDEN	*Pye*	13	*11 May 68*	14
OPEN ROAD	*Dawn*	30	*12 Sep 70*	4
COSMIC WHEELS	*Epic*	15	*24 Mar 73*	12

Jason DONOVAN — Australia

(See also Various Artists: Stage Cast – London 'Joseph and the Amazing Technicolor Dreamcoat'.)

SINGLES:	**HITS 17**			**WEEKS 137**
NOTHING CAN DIVIDE US	*PWL*	5	*10 Sep 88*	12
ESPECIALLY FOR YOU *Above hit: Kylie MINOGUE and Jason DONOVAN.*	*PWL*	1	*10 Dec 88*	14
TOO MANY BROKEN HEARTS	*PWL*	1	*4 Mar 89*	13
SEALED WITH A KISS	*PWL*	1	*10 Jun 89*	10
EVERY DAY (I LOVE YOU MORE)	*PWL*	2	*9 Sep 89*	9
WHEN YOU COME BACK TO ME	*PWL*	2	*9 Dec 89*	11
HANG ON TO YOUR LOVE	*PWL*	8	*7 Apr 90*	7
ANOTHER NIGHT	*PWL*	18	*30 Jun 90*	5
RHYTHM OF THE RAIN	*PWL*	9	*1 Sep 90*	6
I'M DOING FINE	*PWL*	22	*27 Oct 90*	6
R.S.V.P.	*PWL*	17	*18 May 91*	5
ANY DREAM WILL DO *From the musical 'Joseph and the Amazing Technicolor Dreamcoat'.*	*Really Useful*	1	*22 Jun 91*	12
HAPPY TOGETHER	*PWL*	10	*24 Aug 91*	6
JOSEPH MEGA-REMIX [M] *From the musical 'Joseph and the Amazing Technicolor Dreamcoat'.* *Above hit: Jason DONOVAN with the ORIGNAL LONDON CAST featuring Linzi HATELEY, David EASTER and Johnny AMOBI.*	*Really Useful*	13	*7 Dec 91*	8
MISSION OF LOVE	*Polydor*	26	*18 Jul 92*	4

AS TIME GOES BY	*Polydor*	26	*28 Nov 92*	6
Originally recorded by Jacques Renard in 1931.				
ALL AROUND THE WORLD	*Polydor*	41	*7 Aug 93*	3
ALBUMS:	**HITS 4**			**WEEKS 99**
TEN GOOD REASONS	*PWL*	1	*13 May 89*	54
BETWEEN THE LINES	*PWL*	2	*9 Jun 90*	26
GREATEST HITS	*PWL*	9	*28 Sep 91*	17
ALL AROUND THE WORLD	*Polydor*	27	*11 Sep 93*	2

DOOBIE BROTHERS — US

SINGLES:	**HITS 6**			**WEEKS 45**
LISTEN TO THE MUSIC	*Warner Brothers*	29	*9 Mar 74*	7
TAKE ME IN YOUR ARMS (ROCK ME A LITTLE WHILE)	*Warner Brothers*	29	*7 Jun 75*	5
WHAT A FOOL BELIEVES	*Warner Brothers*	31	*17 Feb 79*	10
WHAT A FOOL BELIEVES [RE]	*Warner Brothers*	72	*5 May 79*	1
MINUTE BY MINUTE	*Warner Brothers*	47	*14 Jul 79*	4
WHAT A FOOL BELIEVES [RI]	*Warner Brothers*	57	*24 Jan 87*	3
Above hit: DOOBIE BROTHERS featuring Michael McDONALD.				
THE DOCTOR	*Capitol*	73	*29 Jul 89*	2
LONG TRAIN RUNNIN'	*Warner Brothers*	7	*27 Nov 93*	10
First released 1974, but never charted. Remixed twice, No.125 in 1990 and No. 76 in 1993. This entry was remixed by Sure Is Pure.				
LISTEN TO THE MUSIC [RM]	*Warner Brothers*	37	*14 May 94*	3
Remixed by Motiv8.				
ALBUMS:	**HITS 5**			**WEEKS 30**
WHAT WERE ONCE VICES ARE NOW HABITS	*Warner Brothers*	19	*30 Mar 74*	10
STAMPEDE	*Warner Brothers*	14	*17 May 75*	11
TAKIN' IT TO THE STREETS	*Warner Brothers*	42	*10 Apr 76*	2
LIVING ON THE FAULT LINE	*Warner Brothers*	25	*17 Sep 77*	5
ONE STEP CLOSER	*Warner Brothers*	53	*11 Oct 80*	2

DOOLALLY — UK

(See also Shanks & Bigfoot.)

SINGLES:	**HITS 1**			**WEEKS 16**
STRAIGHT FROM THE HEART	*Locked On*	20	*14 Nov 98*	6
Vocals by Sharon Woolf.				
STRAIGHT FROM THE HEART [RE]	*Locked On*	63	*2 Jan 99*	4
STRAIGHT FROM THE HEART [RI]	*Locked On*	9	*7 Aug 99*	6

DOOLEYS — UK

SINGLES:	**HITS 10**			**WEEKS 83**
THINK I'M GONNA FALL IN LOVE WITH YOU	*GTO*	13	*13 Aug 77*	10
LOVE OF MY LIFE	*GTO*	9	*12 Nov 77*	11
DON'T TAKE IT LYIN' DOWN	*GTO*	60	*13 May 78*	3
A ROSE HAS TO DIE	*GTO*	11	*2 Sep 78*	11
Originally recorded by the Ryders.				
HONEY I'M LOST	*GTO*	24	*10 Feb 79*	9
WANTED	*GTO*	3	*16 Jun 79*	14
THE CHOSEN FEW	*GTO*	7	*22 Sep 79*	11
LOVE PATROL	*GTO*	29	*8 Mar 80*	7
BODY LANGUAGE	*GTO*	46	*6 Sep 80*	4
Originally recorded by Hendy.				
AND I WISH	*GTO*	52	*10 Oct 81*	3
ALBUMS:	**HITS 3**			**WEEKS 27**
THE BEST OF THE DOOLEYS	*GTO*	6	*30 Jun 79*	21
THE CHOSEN FEW	*GTO*	56	*3 Nov 79*	4
FULL HOUSE	*GTO*	54	*25 Oct 80*	2

Val DOONICAN — Ireland

SINGLES:	**HITS 14**			**WEEKS 143**
WALK TALL	*Decca*	3	*17 Oct 64*	21
THE SPECIAL YEARS	*Decca*	7	*23 Jan 65*	12
I'M GONNA GET THERE SOMEHOW	*Decca*	25	*10 Apr 65*	5
THE SPECIAL YEARS [RE]	*Decca*	49	*24 Apr 65*	1
ELUSIVE BUTTERFLY	*Decca*	5	*19 Mar 66*	12
WHAT WOULD I BE	*Decca*	2	*5 Nov 66*	17
MEMORIES ARE MADE OF THIS	*Decca*	11	*25 Feb 67*	12
TWO STREETS	*Decca*	39	*27 May 67*	4
IF THE WHOLE WORLD STOPPED LOVIN'	*Pye*	3	*21 Oct 67*	19
YOU'RE THE ONLY ONE	*Pye*	37	*24 Feb 68*	4
NOW	*Pye*	43	*15 Jun 68*	2
IF I KNEW THEN WHAT I KNOW NOW	*Pye*	14	*26 Oct 68*	13
RING OF BRIGHT WATER	*Pye*	48	*26 Apr 69*	1
MORNING	*Philips*	12	*4 Dec 71*	13
HEAVEN IS MY WOMAN'S LOVE	*Philips*	34	*10 Mar 73*	6

HEAVEN IS MY WOMAN'S LOVE [RE]	*Philips*	47	*28 Apr 73*	1
EPS:	**HITS 2**			**WEEKS 44**
THE GREEN SHADES OF VAL DOONICAN	*Decca*	1	*20 Feb 65*	39
DOONICAN'S IRISH STEW	*Decca*	4	*28 May 66*	5
ALBUMS:	**HITS 11**			**WEEKS 170**
THE LUCKY 13 SHADES OF VAL DOONICAN	*Decca*	2	*12 Dec 64*	27
GENTLE SHADES OF VAL DOONICAN	*Decca*	5	*3 Dec 66*	52
VAL DOONICAN ROCKS, BUT GENTLY	*Pye*	1	*2 Dec 67*	23
VAL	*Pye*	6	*30 Nov 68*	11
THE WORLD OF VAL DOONICAN	*Decca*	2	*14 Jun 69*	31
SOUNDS GENTLE	*Pye*	22	*13 Dec 69*	9
THE MAGIC OF VAL DOONICAN	*Philips*	34	*19 Dec 70*	3
THIS IS VAL DOONICAN	*Philips*	40	*27 Nov 71*	1
I LOVE COUNTRY MUSIC	*Philips*	37	*22 Feb 75*	2
SOME OF MY BEST FRIENDS ARE SONGS	*Philips*	29	*21 May 77*	5
SONGS FROM MY SKETCH BOOK	*Parkfield*	33	*24 Mar 90*	6

DOOP — Holland

SINGLES:	**HITS 1**			**WEEKS 12**
DOOP *Based on the Charleston.*	*Citybeat*	1	*12 Mar 94*	12

DOORS — US

SINGLES:	**HITS 4**			**WEEKS 42**
LIGHT MY FIRE	*Elektra*	49	*19 Aug 67*	1
HELLO I LOVE YOU, WON'T YOU TELL ME YOUR NAME?	*Elektra*	15	*31 Aug 68*	12
RIDERS ON THE STORM	*Elektra*	50	*16 Oct 71*	1
RIDERS ON THE STORM [RE]	*Elektra*	22	*30 Oct 71*	10
RIDERS ON THE STORM [RI-1ST]	*Elektra*	33	*20 Mar 76*	5
HELLO I LOVE YOU [RI]	*Elektra*	71	*3 Feb 79*	2
BREAK ON THROUGH	*Elektra*	64	*27 Apr 91*	2
LIGHT MY FIRE [RI]	*Elektra*	7	*1 Jun 91*	8
RIDERS ON THE STORM [RI-2ND]	*Elektra*	68	*10 Aug 91*	1
ALBUMS:	**HITS 11**			**WEEKS 99**
WAITING FOR THE SUN	*Elektra*	16	*28 Sep 68*	10
MORRISON HOTEL	*Elektra*	12	*11 Apr 70*	8
ABSOLUTELY LIVE *Live recordings from New York's Felt Forum, January 70.*	*Elektra*	69	*26 Sep 70*	1
L.A. WOMAN	*Elektra*	28	*31 Jul 71*	3
WEIRD SCENES INSIDE THE GOLD MINE	*Elektra*	50	*1 Apr 72*	1
ALIVE, SHE CRIED *From lost tapes discovered in an LA warehouse.*	*Elektra*	36	*29 Oct 83*	5
LIVE AT THE HOLLYWOOD BOWL *Live recordings from the Hollywood Bowl, Los Angeles, 5 Jul 68.*	*Elektra*	51	*4 Jul 87*	3
THE DOORS [OST] *Only the CD format contains material by other artists.* *Above hit: DOORS and Jim MORRISON and VARIOUS ARTISTS.*	*Elektra*	11	*6 Apr 91*	17
THE BEST OF THE DOORS	*Elektra*	17	*20 Apr 91*	18
THE DOORS	*Elektra*	43	*20 Apr 91*	12
L.A. WOMAN [RE]	*Elektra*	73	*20 Apr 91*	1
IN CONCERT	*Elektra*	24	*1 Jun 91*	5
THE DOORS [RE]	*Elektra*	70	*9 Apr 94*	1
THE BEST OF THE DOORS [RE-1ST] *Above 2 re-released at mid-price.*	*Elektra*	37	*21 Mar 98*	8
THE BEST OF THE DOORS [RE-2ND] *Digitally remastered version of the 1991 album with bonus CD.*	*Elektra*	9	*23 Sep 00*	6

DOPE SMUGGLAZ — UK

SINGLES:	**HITS 2**			**WEEKS 5**
THE WORD *Based around Frankie Valli's Grease.*	*Perfecto*	62	*5 Dec 98*	1
DOUBLE DOUBLE DUTCH	*Perfecto*	15	*7 Aug 99*	4

Charlie DORE — UK

SINGLES:	**HITS 1**			**WEEKS 2**
PILOT OF THE AIRWAVES	*Island*	66	*17 Nov 79*	2

DO'REEN – See SOUL II SOUL

DOROTHY — UK

SINGLES:	**HITS 1**			**WEEKS 5**
WHAT'S THAT TUNE? (DOO DOO, DOO DOO, DOO-DOO-DOO-DOO-DOO-DOO . . .) *Dance version of the theme tune from LWT's 'Blind Date'.*	*RCA*	31	*9 Dec 95*	5

Lee DORSEY — US

SINGLES:	HITS 4			WEEKS 36
GET OUT OF MY LIFE, WOMAN	*Stateside*	22	*5 Feb 66*	7
CONFUSION	*Stateside*	38	*7 May 66*	6
WORKING IN THE COAL MINE	*Stateside*	8	*13 Aug 66*	11
HOLY COW	*Stateside*	6	*29 Oct 66*	12
EPS:	**HITS 1**			**WEEKS 4**
YOU'RE BREAKIN' ME UP	*Stateside*	7	*3 Sep 66*	4
ALBUMS:	**HITS 1**			**WEEKS 4**
NEW LEE DORSEY	*Stateside*	34	*17 Dec 66*	4

Marc DORSEY — US

SINGLES:	HITS 1			WEEKS 1
IF YOU REALLY WANNA KNOW	*Jive*	58	*19 Jun 99*	1

Tommy DORSEY ORCHESTRA starring Warren COVINGTON — US

SINGLES:	HITS 1			WEEKS 19
TEA FOR TWO CHA CHA	*Brunswick*	3	*18 Oct 58*	19

DOUBLE — Switzerland

SINGLES:	HITS 2			WEEKS 10
THE CAPTAIN OF HER HEART	*Polydor*	8	*25 Jan 86*	9
DEVIL'S BALL	*Polydor*	71	*5 Dec 87*	1
ALBUMS:	**HITS 1**			**WEEKS 4**
BLUE	*Polydor*	69	*8 Mar 86*	4

DOUBLE DEE (featuring DANY) — Italy

SINGLES:	HITS 1			WEEKS 4
FOUND LOVE	*Epic*	63	*1 Dec 90*	2
FOUND LOVE [RM]	*Sony*	33	*25 Nov 95*	2
Remixed by Strike.				

DOUBLE 99 — UK

(See also R.I.P. Productions.)

SINGLES:	HITS 1			WEEKS 9
RIPGROOVE	*Satellite*	31	*31 May 97*	3
RIP GROOVE [RM]	*Satellite*	14	*1 Nov 97*	6
Remixes by Karl 'Tuff Enough' Brown & Matt 'Jam' Lamont.				
Above hit: DOUBLE 99 featuring TOP CAT.				

007 – See also RED RAW featuring 007

DOUBLE SIX — UK

SINGLES:	HITS 2			WEEKS 2
REAL GOOD	*Multiply*	66	*19 Sep 98*	1
BREAKDOWN	*Multiply*	59	*12 Jun 99*	1
Vocals by Steve Eusebe.				

DOUBLE TROUBLE — UK

SINGLES:	HITS 5			WEEKS 35
JUST KEEP ROCKIN'	*Desire*	11	*27 May 89*	12
Above hit: DOUBLE TROUBLE and the REBEL MC.				
STREET TUFF	*Desire*	3	*7 Oct 89*	14
Above hit: REBEL MC DOUBLE TROUBLE.				
TALK BACK	*Desire*	71	*12 May 90*	1
Above hit: DOUBLE TROUBLE vocals by Janette SEWELL.				
LOVE DON'T LIVE HERE ANYMORE	*Desire*	21	*30 Jun 90*	6
Above hit: DOUBLE TROUBLE vocals – Janette SEWELL voice-overs – Carl BROWN.				
RUB-A-DUB	*Desire*	66	*15 Jun 91*	2
ALBUMS:	**HITS 1**			**WEEKS 1**
AS ONE	*Desire*	73	*4 Aug 90*	1

DOUBLE YOU? — Italy

SINGLES:	HITS 1			WEEKS 3
PLEASE DON'T GO	*ZYX*	41	*2 May 92*	3

Rob DOUGAN — UK

SINGLES:	HITS 1			WEEKS 1
FURIOUS ANGELS	*Cheeky*	62	*4 Apr 98*	1

Carl DOUGLAS — Jamaica

(See also Bus Stop.)

SINGLES:	HITS 3			WEEKS 28
KUNG FU FIGHTING	*Pye*	1	*17 Aug 74*	13
DANCE THE KUNG FU	*Pye*	35	*30 Nov 74*	5
RUN BACK	*Pye*	25	*3 Dec 77*	10

Carol DOUGLAS — US

SINGLES:	HITS 1			WEEKS 4
NIGHT FEVER *From the film 'Saturday Night Fever'.*	*Gull*	66	*22 Jul 78*	4

Craig DOUGLAS — UK

SINGLES:	HITS 11			WEEKS 113
A TEENAGER IN LOVE	*Top Rank*	13	*13 Jun 59*	11
ONLY SIXTEEN	*Top Rank*	1	*8 Aug 59*	15
PRETTY BLUE EYES *Originally recorded by Steve Lawrence.*	*Top Rank*	4	*23 Jan 60*	15
HEART OF A TEENAGE GIRL	*Top Rank*	10	*30 Apr 60*	9
OH! WHAT A DAY	*Top Rank*	43	*13 Aug 60*	1
A HUNDRED POUNDS OF CLAY *Originally recorded by Gene McDaniels.*	*Top Rank*	9	*22 Apr 61*	9
TIME *Originally recorded by Jerry Jackson.*	*Top Rank*	9	*1 Jul 61*	14
WHEN MY LITTLE GIRL IS SMILING	*Top Rank*	9	*24 Mar 62*	13
OUR FAVOURITE MELODIES *Originally recorded by Gary Criss.* *Above 4: Craig DOUGLAS with Harry ROBINSON and his Orchestra.*	*Columbia*	9	*30 Jun 62*	10
OH, LONESOME ME	*Decca*	15	*20 Oct 62*	12
TOWN CRIER *Originally recorded by Linda Scott.*	*Decca*	36	*2 Mar 63*	4
ALBUMS:	**HITS 1**			**WEEKS 2**
CRAIG DOUGLAS	*Top Rank*	17	*6 Aug 60*	2

Johnny DOUGLAS and his Orchestra - See JOHNSTON BROTHERS; Joan REGAN; Dickie VALENTINE

DOVE — Ireland

SINGLES:	HITS 1			WEEKS 2
DON'T DREAM	*ZTT*	37	*11 Sep 99*	2

DOVES — UK

SINGLES:	HITS 4			WEEKS 7
HERE IT COMES	*Casino*	73	*14 Aug 99*	1
THE CEDAR ROOM *Originally released on their own Casino label in November 1999*	*Heavenly*	30	*1 Apr 00*	2
CATCH THE SUN	*Heavenly*	32	*10 Jun 00*	2
THE MAN WHO TOLD EVERYTHING	*Heavenly*	32	*11 Nov 00*	2
ALBUMS:	**HITS 1**			**WEEKS 10**
LOST SOULS	*Heavenly*	16	*15 Apr 00*	10

DOWLANDS — UK

SINGLES:	HITS 1			WEEKS 7
ALL MY LOVING *Originally recorded by the Beatles.*	*Oriole*	33	*11 Jan 64*	7

DOWN — US

ALBUMS:	HITS 1			WEEKS 1
NOLA	*Atlantic*	68	*30 Sep 95*	1

Jason DOWNS — US

SINGLES:	HITS 2			WEEKS 6
WHITE BOY WITH A FEATHER	*Pepper*	19	*12 May 01*	5
CAT'S IN THE CRADLE *Originally recorded by Harry Chapin.* *Above 2: Jason DOWNS featuring MILK.*	*Pepper*	65	*14 Jul 01*	1
ALBUMS:	**HITS 1**			**WEEKS 1**
WHITE BOY WITH A FEATHER	*Pepper*	64	*28 Jul 01*	1

Robert DOWNEY Jr. — US

SINGLES:	HITS 1			WEEKS 1
SMILE *From the film 'Chaplin'.*	*Epic*	68	*30 Jan 93*	1

Don DOWNING — US

SINGLES:	HITS 1			WEEKS 10
LONELY DAYS LONELY NIGHTS	*People*	32	*10 Nov 73*	10

Will DOWNING — US

SINGLES:	HITS 7			WEEKS 35
A LOVE SUPREME *Originally recorded by John Coltrane.*	*Fourth & Broadway*	14	*2 Apr 88*	10
IN MY DREAMS	*Fourth & Broadway*	34	*25 Jun 88*	6
FREE	*Fourth & Broadway*	58	*1 Oct 88*	5
WHERE IS THE LOVE *Above hit: Mica PARIS and Will DOWNING.*	*Fourth & Broadway*	19	*21 Jan 89*	7
TEST OF TIME	*Fourth & Broadway*	67	*28 Oct 89*	2
COME TOGETHER AS ONE	*Fourth & Broadway*	48	*24 Feb 90*	4
THERE'S NO LIVING WITHOUT YOU	*Fourth & Broadway*	67	*18 Sep 93*	1
ALBUMS:	**HITS 3**			**WEEKS 28**
WILL DOWNING	*Fourth & Broadway*	20	*26 Mar 88*	23
COME TOGETHER AS ONE	*Fourth & Broadway*	36	*18 Nov 89*	2
A DREAM FULFILLED	*Fourth & Broadway*	43	*6 Apr 91*	3

DOWNSIDE ABBEY MONKS and CHOIRBOYS — UK

ALBUMS:	HITS 2			WEEKS 6
THE ABBEY	*Virgin*	54	*2 Nov 96*	5
GREGORIAN MOODS	*Virgin*	59	*3 Jan 98*	1

Lamont DOZIER - See HOLLAND-DOZIER featuring Lamont DOZIER

Charlie DRAKE — UK

SINGLES:	HITS 5			WEEKS 37
SPLISH SPLASH	*Parlophone*	7	*9 Aug 58*	11
VOLARE	*Parlophone*	28	*25 Oct 58*	2
MR. CUSTER *Originally recorded by Larry Verne.*	*Parlophone*	12	*29 Oct 60*	12
MY BOOMERANG WON'T COME BACK	*Parlophone*	14	*7 Oct 61*	11
PUCKWUDGIE	*Columbia*	47	*1 Jan 72*	1

Kim DRAKE - See Petula CLARK; Lance FORTUNE; David MacBETH - Kim DRAKE MUSIC - Beryl STOTT GROUP; Gary MILLER

DRAMATIS — UK

SINGLES:	HITS 2			WEEKS 8
LOVE NEEDS NO DISGUISE *Above hit: Gary NUMAN and DRAMATIS.*	*Beggars Banquet*	33	*5 Dec 81*	7
I CAN SEE HER NOW	*Rocket*	57	*13 Nov 82*	1

Rusty DRAPER — US

SINGLES:	HITS 1			WEEKS 4
MULE SKINNER BLUES *Originally recorded by Jimmie Rodgers.*	*Mercury*	39	*13 Aug 60*	4

DREAD ZEPPELIN — US

SINGLES:	HITS 2			WEEKS 3
YOUR TIME IS GONNA COME	*I.R.S.*	59	*1 Dec 90*	1
STAIRWAY TO HEAVEN	*I.R.S.*	62	*13 Jul 91*	2
ALBUMS:	**HITS 1**			**WEEKS 2**
UN-LED-ED	*I.R.S.*	71	*11 Aug 90*	2

DREADZONE — UK

SINGLES:	HITS 7			WEEKS 15
ZION YOUTH	*Virgin*	49	*6 May 95*	2
CAPTAIN DREAD	*Virgin*	49	*29 Jul 95*	2
MAXIMUM [EP] *Lead track: Fight the Power 95.*	*Virgin*	56	*23 Sep 95*	2
LITTLE BRITAIN	*Virgin*	20	*6 Jan 96*	6
LIFE LOVE & UNITY	*Virgin*	56	*30 Mar 96*	1
EARTH ANGEL	*Virgin*	51	*10 May 97*	1
MOVING ON	*Virgin*	58	*26 Jul 97*	1
ALBUMS:	**HITS 2**			**WEEKS 5**
SECOND LIGHT	*Virgin*	37	*10 Jun 95*	4
BIOLOGICAL RADIO	*Virgin*	45	*9 Aug 97*	1

DREAM — US

SINGLES:	HITS 1			WEEKS 7
HE LOVES U NOT	*Puff Daddy*	17	*17 Mar 01*	7

DREAM ACADEMY — UK

SINGLES:	HITS 2			WEEKS 10
LIFE IN A NORTHERN TOWN	*Blanco Y Negro*	15	*30 Mar 85*	8
THE LOVE PARADE	*Blanco Y Negro*	68	*14 Sep 85*	2
ALBUMS:	**HITS 1**			**WEEKS 2**
THE DREAM ACADEMY	*Blanco Y Negro*	58	*12 Oct 85*	2

DREAM FREQUENCY — UK

SINGLES:	HITS 5			WEEKS 12
LOVE, PEACE AND HARMONY	*Citybeat*	71	*12 Jan 91*	2
FEEL SO REAL	*Citybeat*	23	*25 Jan 92*	5
TAKE ME	*Citybeat*	39	*25 Apr 92*	3
Above 2: DREAM FREQUENCY featuring Debbie SHARP.				
GOOD TIMES / THE DREAM	*Citybeat*	67	*21 May 94*	1
YOU MAKE ME FEEL MIGHTY REAL	*Citybeat*	65	*10 Sep 94*	1

DREAM THEATER — US

ALBUMS:	HITS 1			WEEKS 1
AWAKE	*East West*	65	*15 Oct 94*	1

DREAM WARRIORS — Canada

SINGLES:	HITS 3			WEEKS 19
WASH YOUR FACE IN MY SINK	*Fourth & Broadway*	16	*14 Jul 90*	8
MY DEFINITION OF A BOOMBASTIC JAZZ STYLE	*Fourth & Broadway*	13	*24 Nov 90*	8
LUDI	*Fourth & Broadway*	39	*2 Mar 91*	3
ALBUMS:	**HITS 1**			**WEEKS 7**
AND NOW THE LEGACY BEGINS	*Fourth & Broadway*	18	*16 Feb 91*	7

DREAM WEAVERS — US

SINGLES:	HITS 1			WEEKS 18
IT'S ALMOST TOMORROW	*Brunswick*	1	*11 Feb 56*	18

DREAMHOUSE — UK

SINGLES:	HITS 1			WEEKS 2
STAY	*Chase*	62	*3 Jun 95*	2

DREAMKEEPER — UK

ALBUMS:	HITS 1			WEEKS 1
SPIRIT OF RELAXATION	*Flute*	71	*9 Aug 97*	1

DREEM TEEM — UK

SINGLES:	HITS 3			WEEKS 12
THE THEME	*Deconstruction*	34	*13 Dec 97*	4
BUDDY X 99	*4 Liberty*	15	*6 Nov 99*	5
Remixed by B. Simms. Additional vocals by PSG.				
Above hit: DREEM TEEM 'n' Neneh CHERRY.				
IT AIN'T ENOUGH	*ffrr*	20	*15 Dec 01*	3
Above hit: DREEM TEEM vs ARTFUL DODGER featuring MZ MAY & MC ALISTAIR.				

Eddie DRENNON and B.B.S. UNLIMITED — US

SINGLES:	HITS 1			WEEKS 6
LET'S DO THE LATIN HUSTLE	*Pye International*	20	*28 Feb 76*	6

Alan DREW — UK

SINGLES:	HITS 1			WEEKS 2
ALWAYS THE LONELY ONE	*Columbia*	48	*28 Sep 63*	2

DRIFTERS – See Cliff RICHARD

DRIFTERS — US

SINGLES:	HITS 19			WEEKS 176
DANCE WITH ME	*London*	17	*9 Jan 60*	4
DANCE WITH ME [RE]	*London*	35	*12 Mar 60*	1
SAVE THE LAST DANCE FOR ME	*London*	2	*5 Nov 60*	18
I COUNT THE TEARS	*London*	28	*18 Mar 61*	6
WHEN MY LITTLE GIRL IS SMILING	*London*	31	*7 Apr 62*	3
I'LL TAKE YOU HOME	*London*	37	*12 Oct 63*	5
UNDER THE BOARDWALK	*Atlantic*	45	*26 Sep 64*	4
AT THE CLUB	*Atlantic*	35	*10 Apr 65*	7
COME ON OVER TO MY PLACE	*Atlantic*	40	*1 May 65*	5
BABY WHAT I MEAN	*Atlantic*	49	*4 Feb 67*	1

AT THE CLUB [RI]	*Atlantic*	39	*25 Mar 72*	1
AT THE CLUB [RI] / SATURDAY NIGHT AT THE MOVIES [RE]	*Atlantic*	3	*8 Apr 72*	19
COME ON OVER TO MY PLACE [RI]	*Atlantic*	9	*26 Aug 72*	11
LIKE SISTER AND BROTHER	*Bell*	7	*4 Aug 73*	12
KISSIN' IN THE BACK ROW OF THE MOVIES	*Bell*	2	*15 Jun 74*	13
DOWN ON THE BEACH TONIGHT	*Bell*	7	*12 Oct 74*	9
LOVE GAMES	*Bell*	33	*8 Feb 75*	6
THERE GOES MY FIRST LOVE	*Bell*	3	*6 Sep 75*	12
CAN I TAKE YOU HOME LITTLE GIRL	*Bell*	10	*29 Nov 75*	10
HELLO HAPPINESS	*Bell*	12	*13 Mar 76*	8
Originally recorded by Claude Francois.				
EVERY NITE'S A SATURDAY NIGHT WITH YOU	*Bell*	29	*11 Sep 76*	7
YOU'RE MORE THAN A NUMBER IN MY LITTLE RED BOOK	*Arista*	5	18 Dec 76	12
SAVE THE LAST DANCE FOR ME [RI] /WHEN MY LITTLE GIRL IS SMILING [RI]	*Lightning*	69	*14 Apr 79*	2

ALBUMS:	**HITS 7**			**WEEKS 92**
GOLDEN HITS	*Atlantic*	27	*18 May 68*	7
GOLDEN HITS [RE]	*Atlantic*	26	*10 Jun 72*	8
Re-released with a new catalogue number.				
24 ORIGINAL HITS	*Atlantic*	2	*8 Nov 75*	34
LOVE GAMES	*Bell*	51	*13 Dec 75*	1
THE VERY BEST OF THE DRIFTERS	*Telstar*	24	*18 Oct 86*	15
STAND BY ME (THE ULTIMATE COLLECTION)	*Atlantic*	14	*14 Mar 87*	8
The Drifters are only on 3 tracks.				
THE VERY BEST OF BEN E. KING AND THE DRIFTERS	*Telstar*	15	*20 Oct 90*	16
THE VERY BEST OF BEN E. KING AND THE DRIFTERS	*Warner.esp/Global TV*	41	*7 Nov 98*	3

Above 2 albums are different.
Above 3: Ben E. KING and the DRIFTERS.

Julie DRISCOLL, Brian AUGER and the TRINITY — UK

SINGLES:	**HITS 1**			**WEEKS 16**
THIS WHEEL'S ON FIRE	*Marmalade*	5	*20 Apr 68*	16
Originally recorded by Bob Dylan.				

ALBUMS:	**HITS 1**			**WEEKS 13**
OPEN	*Marmalade*	12	*8 Jun 68*	13

Above hit: Julie DRISCOLL and the Brian AUGER TRINITY.

DRIVER 67 — UK

SINGLES:	**HITS 1**			**WEEKS 12**
CAR 67	*Logo*	7	*23 Dec 78*	12

DRIZA-BONE — US

SINGLES:	**HITS 5**			**WEEKS 18**
REAL LOVE	*Fourth & Broadway*	16	*22 Jun 91*	8
CATCH THE FIRE	*Fourth & Broadway*	54	*26 Oct 91*	2
PRESSURE	*Fourth & Broadway*	33	*23 Apr 94*	2
BRIGHTEST STAR	*Fourth & Broadway*	45	*15 Oct 94*	2
REAL LOVE [RR]	*Fourth & Broadway*	24	*4 Mar 95*	4

ALBUMS:	**HITS 1**			**WEEKS 1**
CONSPIRACY	*Fourth & Broadway*	72	*19 Nov 94*	1

Frank D'RONE — US

SINGLES:	**HITS 1**			**WEEKS 6**
STRAWBERRY BLONDE (THE BAND ROCKED ON)	*Mercury*	24	*24 Dec 60*	6

DRU HILL — US

SINGLES:	**HITS 7**			**WEEKS 42**
TELL ME	*Fourth & Broadway*	30	*15 Feb 97*	3
From the film 'Eddie'.				
IN MY BED	*Fourth & Broadway*	16	*10 May 97*	3
BIG BAD MAMMA	*Def Jam*	12	*11 Oct 97*	3
From the film 'How To Be A Player'.				
Above hit: Foxy BROWN featuring DRU HILL.				
5 STEPS	*Island Black Music*	22	*6 Dec 97*	3
Above hit: DRU HILL.				
HOW DEEP IS YOUR LOVE	*Island Black Music*	9	*24 Oct 98*	7
Above hit: DRU HILL (featuring REDMAN).				
HOW DEEP IS YOUR LOVE [RE]	*Island Black Music*	75	*16 Jan 99*	1
Above hit: DRU HILL (featuring REDMAN).				
THESE ARE THE TIMES	*Island Black Music*	4	*6 Feb 99*	6
WILD WILD WEST	*Columbia*	2	*10 Jul 99*	16
Samples Stevie Wonder' I Wish. From the film of the same name.				
Above hit: Will SMITH (featuring DRU HILL).				

ALBUMS:	**HITS 1**			**WEEKS 7**
ENTER THE DRU	*Island Black Music*	42	*7 Nov 98*	7

DRUGSTORE — UK/US/Brazil

SINGLES:	HITS 3			WEEKS 5
FADER	*Honey*	72	*10 Jun 95*	1
EL PRESIDENT	*Roadrunner*	20	*2 May 98*	3
Features vocals from Thom Yorke of Radiohead.				
SOBER	*Roadrunner*	68	*4 Jul 98*	1

ALBUMS:	HITS 2			WEEKS 3
DRUGSTORE	*Honey*	31	*8 Apr 95*	2
WHITE MAGIC FOR LOVERS	*Roadrunner*	45	*16 May 98*	1

DRUM CLUB — UK

SINGLES:	HITS 1			WEEKS 1
SOUND SYSTEM	*Butterfly*	62	*6 Nov 93*	1

ALBUMS:	HITS 1			WEEKS 1
DRUMS ARE DANGEROUS	*Butterfly*	53	*20 Aug 94*	1

DRUM THEATRE — UK

SINGLES:	HITS 2			WEEKS 8
LIVING IN THE PAST	*Epic*	67	*15 Feb 86*	2
ELDORADO	*Epic*	44	*17 Jan 87*	6

DRUPI — Italy

SINGLES:	HITS 1			WEEKS 12
VADO VIA	*A&M*	17	*1 Dec 73*	12

DSK — UK

SINGLES:	HITS 1			WEEKS 4
WHAT WOULD WE DO / READ MY LIPS	*Boys Own Productions*	46	*31 Aug 91*	3
Read My Lips listed from 7 Sep 91, once single had dropped to No. 51.				
WHAT WOULD WE DO? [RM]	*Fresh*	55	*22 Nov 97*	1
Remixed by Industry Standard.				

DSP – See Matt DAREY

DTI — US

SINGLES:	HITS 1			WEEKS 1
KEEP THIS FREQUENCY CLEAR	*Premiere UK*	73	*16 Apr 88*	1

DTOX — UK

SINGLES:	HITS 1			WEEKS 1
SHATTERED GLASS	*Vitality*	75	*21 Nov 92*	1
Originally recorded by Ellie Warren in 1980.				

D12 — US

SINGLES:	HITS 3			WEEKS 24
SH!T ON YOU	*Interscope*	10	*17 Mar 01*	7
PURPLE PILLS	*Interscope*	2	*21 Jul 01*	12
Samples Curtis Mayfield's If There Is A Hell Down Below, We're All Going To Go.				
FIGHT MUSIC	*Interscope*	11	*17 Nov 01*	5

ALBUMS:	HITS 1			WEEKS 17
DEVIL'S NIGHT	*Interscope*	2	*30 Jun 01*	17

John DU CANN — UK

SINGLES:	HITS 1			WEEKS 6
DON'T BE A DUMMY	*Vertigo*	33	*22 Sep 79*	6
Featured in the Levi's Jeans TV commercial.				

John DU PREZ – See MODERN ROMANCE

DUB CONSPIRACY – See TRU FAITH and DUB CONSPIRACY

DUB PISTOLS — UK

SINGLES:	HITS 1			WEEKS 1
CYCLONE	*Concrete*	63	*10 Oct 98*	1
Vocals by rapper: T.K. Lawrence.				

DUB WAR — UK

SINGLES:	HITS 4			WEEKS 5
STRIKE IT	*Earache*	70	*3 Jun 95*	1
ENEMY MAKER	*Earache*	41	*27 Jan 96*	2
CRY DIGNITY	*Earache*	59	*24 Aug 96*	1
MILLION DOLLAR LOVE	*Earache*	73	*29 Mar 97*	1

DUBLINERS — Ireland

SINGLES:	HITS 5			WEEKS 45
SEVEN DRUNKEN NIGHTS	*Major Minor*	7	*1 Apr 67*	17
BLACK VELVET BAND •	*Major Minor*	15	*2 Sep 67*	15
Originally recorded by the Kinsfolk Folk Group.				
MAIDS. WHEN YOU'RE YOUNG. NEVER WED AN OLD MAN	*Major Minor*	43	*23 Dec 67*	3
THE IRISH ROVER	*Stiff*	8	*28 Mar 87*	8
JACK'S HEROES / WHISKEY IN THE JAR	*Pogue Mahone*	63	*16 Jun 90*	2
Above 2: POGUES and the DUBLINERS.				
ALBUMS:	**HITS 5**			**WEEKS 88**
A DROP OF THE HARD STUFF	*Major Minor*	5	*13 May 67*	41
BEST OF THE DUBLINERS	*Transatlantic*	25	*9 Sep 67*	11
MORE OF THE HARD STUFF	*Major Minor*	8	*7 Oct 67*	23
DRINKIN' AND COURTIN'	*Major Minor*	31	*2 Mar 68*	3
THE DUBLINERS 25 YEARS CELEBRATION	*Stylus*	43	*25 Apr 87*	10

DUBSTAR — UK

SINGLES:	HITS 8			WEEKS 26
STARS	*Food*	40	*8 Jul 95*	3
ANYWHERE	*Food*	37	*30 Sep 95*	3
NOT SO MANIC NOW	*Food*	18	*6 Jan 96*	5
STARS [RI]	*Food*	15	*30 Mar 96*	6
ELEVATOR SONG – THE MIXES	*Food*	25	*3 Aug 96*	2
NO MORE TALK	*Food*	20	*19 Jul 97*	3
CATHEDRAL PARK	*Food*	41	*20 Sep 97*	1
I WILL BE YOUR GIRLFRIEND	*Food*	28	*7 Feb 98*	2
I (FRIDAY NIGHT)	*Food*	37	*27 May 00*	1
ALBUMS:	**HITS 2**			**WEEKS 20**
DISGRACEFUL	*Food*	33	*21 Oct 95*	5
DISGRACEFUL [RE]	*Food*	30	*6 Apr 96*	13
GOODBYE	*Food*	18	*4 Oct 97*	2

Ricardo "Rikrok" DUCENT – See SHAGGY

Anne DUDLEY – See TRAVIS

Mary DUFF – See Daniel O'DONNELL

DUFFO — Australia

SINGLES:	HITS 1			WEEKS 2
GIVE ME BACK ME BRAIN	*Beggars Banquet*	60	*24 Mar 79*	2

Stephen 'Tin Tin' DUFFY — UK

SINGLES:	HITS 3			WEEKS 24
HOLD IT	*Curve*	55	*9 Jul 83*	4
Above hit: TINTIN.				
KISS ME	*10 Records*	4	*2 Mar 85*	11
Original release reached No. 78 in 1984.				
ICING ON THE CAKE	*10 Records*	14	*18 May 85*	9
ALBUMS:	**HITS 1**			**WEEKS 7**
THE UPS AND DOWNS	*10 Records*	35	*20 Apr 85*	7

DUKE — UK

SINGLES:	HITS 1			WEEKS 6
SO IN LOVE WITH YOU	*Encore*	66	*25 May 96*	1
SO IN LOVE WITH YOU [RI]	*Pukka*	22	*26 Oct 96*	4
SO IN LOVE WITH YOU [RM]	*48K*	65	*11 Nov 00*	1
Remixed by Full Intention; it originally appeared as track 2 on the 1996 re-issue.				

George DUKE — US

SINGLES:	HITS 1			WEEKS 6
BRAZILIAN LOVE AFFAIR	*Epic*	36	*12 Jul 80*	6
ALBUMS:	**HITS 1**			**WEEKS 4**
BRAZILIAN LOVE AFFAIR	*Epic*	33	*26 Jul 80*	4

DUKES – See Steve EARL

DUKES — UK

SINGLES:	HITS 2			WEEKS 13
MYSTERY GIRL	*WEA*	47	*17 Oct 81*	7
THANK YOU FOR THE PARTY	*WEA*	53	*1 May 82*	6
Above hit: DUKES (BUGATTI and MUSKER).				

Candy DULFER — Holland

(See also David A. Stewart.)

ALBUMS:	HITS 2			WEEKS 11
LILY WAS HERE	*AnXious*	6	*24 Feb 90*	12
Above hit: David A. STEWART featuring Candy DULFER.				
SAXUALITY	*RCA*	60	*4 Aug 90*	2
SINGLES:	**HITS 2**			**WEEKS 14**
SAXUALITY	*RCA*	27	*18 Aug 90*	9
SAX-A-GO-GO	*Ariola*	56	*13 Mar 93*	2

DUM DUMS — UK

SINGLES:	HITS 4			WEEKS 15
EVERYTHING	*Good Behaviour*	21	*11 Mar 00*	5
CAN'T GET YOU OUT OF MY THOUGHTS	*Good Behaviour*	18	*8 Jul 00*	5
YOU DO SOMETHING TO ME	*Good Behaviour*	27	*23 Sep 00*	3
ARMY OF TWO	*Good Behaviour*	27	*17 Feb 01*	2
ALBUMS:	**HITS 1**			**WEEKS 2**
IT GOES WITHOUT SAYING	*Good Behaviour*	27	*30 Sep 00*	2

Thuli DUMAKUDE – See CRY FREEDOM

John DUMMER and Helen APRIL — UK

SINGLES:	HITS 1			WEEKS 3
BLUE SKIES	*Speed*	54	*28 Aug 82*	3

DUMONDE — Germany

SINGLES:	HITS 2			WEEKS 3
TOMORROW	*Variation*	60	*27 Jan 01*	1
NEVER LOOK BACK	*Manifesto*	36	*19 May 01*	2
Above hit: JAMX + DELEON present DUMONDE.				

Sly DUNBAR and Robert SHAKESPEARE – See SLY and ROBBIE

DUNBLANE — UK

SINGLES:	HITS 1			WEEKS 15
KNOCKIN' ON HEAVEN'S DOOR / THROW THESE GUNS AWAY	*BMG*	1	*21 Dec 96*	15
Recorded in memory of the children murdered in the Dunblaine shooting in March '96.				

Johnny DUNCAN and the BLUE GRASS BOYS — US

SINGLES:	HITS 3			WEEKS 20
LAST TRAIN TO SAN FERNANDO •	*Columbia*	2	*27 Jul 57*	17
BLUE, BLUE HEARTACHE	*Columbia*	27	*26 Oct 57*	1
FOOTPRINTS IN THE SNOW •	*Columbia*	27	*30 Nov 57*	1
FOOTPRINTS IN THE SNOW [RE]	*Columbia*	28	*4 Jan 58*	1

David DUNDAS — UK

SINGLES:	HITS 2			WEEKS 14
JEANS ON	*Air*	3	*24 Jul 76*	9
Featured in the Brutus Jeans TV commercial.				
ANOTHER FUNNY HONEYMOON	*Air*	29	*9 Apr 77*	5

DUNE – See Quincy JONES

Errol DUNKLEY — Jamaica

SINGLES:	HITS 2			WEEKS 14
O.K. FRED	*Scope*	11	*22 Sep 79*	11
Originally recorded by John Holt.				
SIT DOWN AND CRY	*Scope*	52	*2 Feb 80*	3
Originally recorded by Willie Dixon.				

Clive DUNN — UK

SINGLES:	HITS 1			WEEKS 28
GRANDAD	*Columbia*	1	*28 Nov 70*	27
GRANDAD [RE]	*Columbia*	50	*26 Jun 71*	1

Simon DUPREE and the BIG SOUND — UK

SINGLES:	HITS 2			WEEKS 16
KITES •	*Parlophone*	9	*25 Nov 67*	13
FOR WHOM THE BELL TOLLS	*Parlophone*	43	*6 Apr 68*	3
ALBUMS:	**HITS 1**			**WEEKS 1**
WITHOUT RESERVATIONS	*Parlophone*	39	*19 Aug 67*	1

DURAN DURAN — UK

SINGLES:	HITS 30			WEEKS 222
PLANET EARTH	*EMI*	12	*21 Feb 81*	11
CARELESS MEMORIES	*EMI*	37	*9 May 81*	7
GIRLS ON FILM	*EMI*	5	*25 Jul 81*	11
MY OWN WAY	*EMI*	14	*28 Nov 81*	11
HUNGRY LIKE THE WOLF	*EMI*	5	*15 May 82*	12
SAVE A PRAYER	*EMI*	2	*21 Aug 82*	9
RIO	*EMI*	9	*13 Nov 82*	11
IS THERE SOMETHING I SHOULD KNOW?	*EMI*	1	*26 Mar 83*	9
UNION OF THE SNAKE	*EMI*	3	*29 Oct 83*	7
UNION OF THE SNAKE [RE]	*EMI*	66	*24 Dec 83*	4
NEW MOON ON MONDAY	*EMI*	9	*4 Feb 84*	7
THE REFLEX	*EMI*	1	*28 Apr 84*	14
THE WILD BOYS	*Parlophone*	2	*3 Nov 84*	14
A VIEW TO A KILL	*Parlophone*	2	*18 May 85*	16
Theme from the James Bond film of the same name.				
NOTORIOUS	*EMI*	7	*1 Nov 86*	6
NOTORIOUS [RE]	*EMI*	73	*3 Jan 87*	1
SKIN TRADE	*EMI*	22	*21 Feb 87*	6
MEET EL PRESIDENTE	*EMI*	24	*25 Apr 87*	5
I DON'T WANT YOUR LOVE	*EMI*	14	*1 Oct 88*	5
ALL SHE WANTS IS	*EMI*	9	*7 Jan 89*	5
DO YOU BELIEVE IN SHAME?	*EMI*	30	*22 Apr 89*	4
Above 3: DURANDURAN.				
BURNING THE GROUND [M]	*EMI*	31	*16 Dec 89*	5
Medley of earlier hits.				
VIOLENCE OF SUMMER (LOVE'S TAKING OVER)	*Parlophone*	20	*4 Aug 90*	4
SERIOUS	*Parlophone*	48	*17 Nov 90*	3
ORDINARY WORLD	*Parlophone*	6	*30 Jan 93*	9
COME UNDONE	*Parlophone*	13	*10 Apr 93*	8
TOO MUCH INFORMATION	*Parlophone*	35	*4 Sep 93*	3
PERFECT DAY	*Parlophone*	28	*25 Mar 95*	4
Cover of a Lou Reed track from his 1973 album Transformer.				
WHITE LINES (DON'T DO IT)	*Parlophone*	17	*17 Jun 95*	5
Above hit: DURAN DURAN featuring Mele MEL and GRANDMASTER FLASH and the FURIOUS FIVE.				
OUT OF MY MIND	*Virgin*	21	*24 May 97*	2
From the film 'The Saint'.				
ELECTRIC BARBARELLA	*EMI*	23	*30 Jan 99*	3
SOMEONE ELSE NOT ME	*Hollywood*	53	*10 Jun 00*	1

ALBUMS:	HITS 13			WEEKS 398
DURAN DURAN	*EMI*	3	*27 Jun 81*	118
RIO	*EMI*	2	*22 May 82*	109
SEVEN AND THE RAGGED TIGER	*EMI*	1	*3 Dec 83*	47
ARENA	*Parlophone*	6	*24 Nov 84*	31
Live recordings from their 1984 world tour.				
NOTORIOUS	*EMI*	16	*6 Dec 86*	16
BIG THING	*EMI*	15	*29 Oct 88*	5
Above hit: DURANDURAN.				
DECADE	*EMI*	5	*25 Nov 89*	15
LIBERTY	*Parlophone*	8	*1 Sep 90*	4
DURAN DURAN (THE WEDDING ALBUM)	*Parlophone*	4	*27 Feb 93*	23
DECADE [RI]	*Parlophone*	66	*24 Sep 94*	1
THANK YOU	*Parlophone*	12	*8 Apr 95*	3
Album of cover versions.				
GREATEST	*EMI*	15	*21 Nov 98*	24
STRANGE BEHAVIOUR	*EMI*	70	*27 Mar 99*	1
12" versions and remixes.				
POP TRASH	*Hollywood*	53	*1 Jul 00*	1

Jimmy DURANTE — US

SINGLES:	HITS 1			WEEKS 1
MAKE SOMEONE HAPPY	*Warner Brothers*	69	*14 Dec 96*	1

Deanna DURBIN — Canada

ALBUMS:	HITS 1			WEEKS 4
THE BEST OF DEANNA DURBIN	*MCA*	84	*30 Jan 82*	4

Tyler DURDEN – See DUST BROTHERS (Michael SIMPSON and John KING) featuring Tyler DURDEN

Judith DURHAM — Australia

(See also Seekers.)

SINGLES:	HITS 1			WEEKS 5
THE OLIVE TREE	*Columbia*	33	*17 Jun 67*	5

ALBUMS:	HITS 2			WEEKS 16
CARNIVAL OF HITS	*EMI*	7	*23 Apr 94*	14
Features both solo and group material. Includes re-entries through to 2000.				
Above hit: Judith DURHAM and the SEEKERS.				
MONA LISAS	*EMI Premier*	46	*30 Mar 96*	2

Ian DURY and the BLOCKHEADS — UK

(See also Blockheads.)

SINGLES:	HITS 7			WEEKS 56
WHAT A WASTE	*Stiff*	9	*29 Apr 78*	12
Above hit: Ian DURY and the BLOCKHEADS and JANKEL and JENNER and LATHAM.				
HIT ME WITH YOUR RHYTHM STICK	*Stiff*	1	*9 Dec 78*	15
Above hit: IAN and the BLOCKHEADS.				
REASONS TO BE CHEERFUL, PART 3	*Stiff*	3	*4 Aug 79*	8
I WANT TO BE STRAIGHT	*Stiff*	22	*30 Aug 80*	7
SUEPERMAN'S BIG SISTER	*Stiff*	51	*15 Nov 80*	3
HIT ME WITH YOUR RHYTHM STICK [RM-1ST]	*Stiff*	55	*25 May 85*	4
Remixed by Paul Hardcastle.				
PROFOUNDLY IN LOVE WITH PANDORA	*EMI*	45	*26 Oct 85*	5
Theme from the ITV series 'The Secret Diary Of Adrian Mole'.				
Above hit: Ian DURY.				
HIT ME WITH YOUR RHYTHM STICK '91 [RM-2ND]	*Flying*	73	*27 Jul 91*	1
DRIP FED FRED	*Virgin*	55	*11 Mar 00*	1
The campaign theme for London Mayoral candidate Fredrick C. Threwe.				
Above hit: MADNESS featuring Ian DURY.				

ALBUMS:	HITS 7			WEEKS 122
NEW BOOTS AND PANTIES!!	*Stiff*	5	*22 Oct 77*	90
Above hit: Ian DURY.				
DO IT YOURSELF	*Stiff*	2	*2 Jun 79*	18
LAUGHTER	*Stiff*	48	*6 Dec 80*	4
LORD UPMINSTER	*Polydor*	53	*10 Oct 81*	4
4,000 WEEKS HOLIDAY	*Polydor*	54	*4 Feb 84*	2
Above hit: Ian DURY and the MUSIC STUDENTS.				
MR. LOVE PANTS	*Ronnie Harris*	57	*11 Jul 98*	2
REASONS TO BE CHEERFUL - THE VERY BEST OF IAN DURY AND THE BLOCKHEADS	*EMI*	40	*9 Oct 99*	2

DUST BROTHERS (Michael SIMPSON and John KING) featuring Tyler DURDEN — US

SINGLES:	HITS 1			WEEKS 1
THIS IS YOUR LIFE - MUSIC FROM FIGHT CLUB	*Restless*	60	*11 Dec 99*	1
From the film 'The Fight Club'. Features vocals by Brad Pitt.				

DUST JUNKYS — UK

SINGLES:	HITS 3			WEEKS 5
(NONSTOPOPERATION)	*Polydor*	47	*15 Nov 97*	2
WHAT TIME IS IT?	*Polydor*	39	*28 Feb 98*	2
NOTHIN' PERSONAL	*Polydor*	62	*16 May 98*	1
Samples Oh Well by Fleetwood Mac.				

ALBUMS:	HITS 1			WEEKS 2
DONE AND DUSTED	*Polydor*	35	*21 Mar 98*	2

DUSTED — UK

SINGLES:	HITS 1			WEEKS 2
ALWAYS REMEMBER TO RESPECT AND HONOUR YOUR MOTHER (PART 1)	*Go.Beat*	31	*20 Jan 01*	2
Features vocals by 12-year-old choirboy Alan Young.				

Slim DUSTY with Dick CARR and his BUSHLANDERS — Australia

SINGLES:	HITS 1			WEEKS 15
A PUB WITH NO BEER	*Columbia*	3	*31 Jan 59*	15

DUTCH FORCE — Holland

SINGLES:	HITS 1			WEEKS 2
DEADLINE	*Inferno*	35	*6 May 00*	2

Ondrea DUVERNEY – See HUSTLERS CONVENTION featuring Dave LAUDAT and Ondrea DUVERNEY

DWEEB — UK

SINGLES:	HITS 2			WEEKS 2
SCOOBY DOO	*Blanco Y Negro*	63	*22 Feb 97*	1
OH YEAH, BABY	*Blanco Y Negro*	70	*7 Jun 97*	1

Bob DYLAN US

(See also Bob Dylan and the Grateful Dead.)

SINGLES:	HITS 19			WEEKS 137
TIMES THEY ARE A-CHANGIN'	*CBS*	9	*27 Mar 65*	11
SUBTERRANEAN HOMESICK BLUES	*CBS*	9	*1 May 65*	9
MAGGIE'S FARM	*CBS*	22	*19 Jun 65*	8
LIKE A ROLLING STONE	*CBS*	4	*21 Aug 65*	12
Features Al Kooper (from Blood Sweat & Tears) on organ.				
POSITIVELY 4TH STREET	*CBS*	8	*30 Oct 65*	12
CAN YOU PLEASE CRAWL OUT YOUR WINDOW	*CBS*	17	*29 Jan 66*	5
ONE OF US MUST KNOW (SOONER OR LATER)	*CBS*	33	*16 Apr 66*	5
RAINY DAY WOMEN NOS. 12 & 35	*CBS*	7	*14 May 66*	8
I WANT YOU	*CBS*	16	*23 Jul 66*	9
I THREW IT ALL AWAY	*CBS*	30	*17 May 69*	6
LAY LADY LAY	*CBS*	5	*13 Sep 69*	12
Written for his wife at the time Sarah Lowndres.				
WATCHING THE RIVER FLOW	*CBS*	24	*10 Jul 71*	9
KNOCKIN' ON HEAVEN'S DOOR	*CBS*	14	*6 Oct 73*	9
From the film 'Pat Garrett And Billy The Kid'.				
HURRICANE	*CBS*	43	*7 Feb 76*	4
BABY STOP CRYING	*CBS*	13	*29 Jul 78*	11
IS YOUR LOVE IN VAIN?	*CBS*	56	*28 Oct 78*	3
DIGNITY	*Columbia*	33	*20 May 95*	2
LOVE SICK	*Columbia*	64	*11 Jul 98*	1
THINGS HAVE CHANGED	*Columbia*	58	*14 Oct 00*	1
From the film 'The Wonder Boys'.				

EPS:	HITS 3			WEEKS 57
BOB DYLAN	*CBS*	3	*3 Jul 65*	41
ONE TOO MANY MORNINGS	*CBS*	8	*19 Feb 66*	8
MR. TAMBOURINE MAN	*CBS*	4	*15 Oct 66*	8

ALBUMS:	HITS 42			WEEKS 617
THE FREEWHEELIN' BOB DYLAN	*CBS*	11	*23 May 64*	17
THE TIMES THEY ARE A-CHANGIN'	*CBS*	15	*11 Jul 64*	6
ANOTHER SIDE OF BOB DYLAN	*CBS*	8	*21 Nov 64*	19
THE FREEWHEELIN' BOB DYLAN [RE]	*CBS*	1	*13 Mar 65*	32
THE TIMES THEY ARE A-CHANGIN' [RE]	*CBS*	4	*20 Mar 65*	14
BOB DYLAN	*CBS*	13	*8 May 65*	6
BRINGING IT ALL BACK HOME	*CBS*	1	*15 May 65*	29
HIGHWAY 61 REVISITED	*CBS*	4	*9 Oct 65*	15
BLONDE ON BLONDE	*CBS*	3	*20 Aug 66*	15
GREATEST HITS	*CBS*	6	*14 Jan 67*	82
JOHN WESLEY HARDING	*CBS*	1	*2 Mar 68*	29
NASHVILLE SKYLINE	*CBS*	1	*17 May 69*	42
SELF PORTRAIT	*CBS*	1	*11 Jul 70*	15
NEW MORNING	*CBS*	1	*28 Nov 70*	18
MORE BOB DYLAN GREATEST HITS	*CBS*	12	*25 Dec 71*	15
PAT GARRETT & BILLY THE KID [OST]	*CBS*	29	*29 Sep 73*	11
Only 3 tracks are included with his vocals, though he wrote the soundtrack and appeared in the film as outlaw Alias.				
PLANET WAVES	*Island*	7	*23 Feb 74*	8
BEFORE THE FLOOD	*Asylum*	8	*13 Jul 74*	7
Live recordings from the January & February 74 US tour. Supported by the Band.				
BLOOD ON THE TRACKS	*CBS*	4	*15 Feb 75*	16
THE BASEMENT TAPES	*CBS*	8	*26 Jul 75*	10
DESIRE	*CBS*	3	*31 Jan 76*	35
HARD RAIN	*CBS*	3	*9 Oct 76*	7
Live recordings from Forth Worth, Texas and Fort Collins, Colarado.				
STREET LEGAL	*CBS*	2	*1 Jul 78*	20
BOB DYLAN AT BUDOKAN	*CBS*	4	*26 May 79*	19
Live recordings from Japan 1 March 78.				
SLOW TRAIN COMING	*CBS*	2	*8 Sep 79*	13
SAVED	*CBS*	3	*28 Jun 80*	8
SHOT OF LOVE	*CBS*	6	*29 Aug 81*	8
INFIDELS	*CBS*	9	*12 Nov 83*	12
REAL LIVE	*CBS*	54	*15 Dec 84*	2
Live recordings from his Summer 1984 European tour.				
EMPIRE BURLESQUE	*CBS*	11	*22 Jun 85*	6
KNOCKED OUT LOADED	*CBS*	35	*2 Aug 86*	5
GREATEST HITS [RE]	*CBS*	99	*23 Apr 88*	1
Re-released at mid-price.				
DOWN IN THE GROOVE	*CBS*	32	*25 Jun 88*	3
OH MERCY	*CBS*	6	*14 Oct 89*	7
UNDER THE SKY	*CBS*	13	*29 Sep 90*	3
THE BOOTLEG SERIES VOLUMES 1-3	*Columbia*	32	*13 Apr 91*	5
GOOD AS I BEEN TO YOU	*Columbia*	18	*14 Nov 92*	3
WORLD GONE WRONG	*Columbia*	35	*20 Nov 93*	2

UNPLUGGED	*Columbia*	10	*29 Apr 95*	5
Recorded for MTV on 17 Nov 94.				
GREATEST HITS [RI]	*Columbia*	47	*23 Sep 95*	2
THE BEST OF BOB DYLAN	*Columbia*	6	*14 Jun 97*	18
TIME OUT OF MIND	*Columbia*	10	*11 Oct 97*	6
LIVE AT THE ROYAL ALBERT HALL	*Legacy*	19	*24 Oct 98*	2
Live recordings actually from Manchester's Free Trade Hall in the mid 1960s.				
THE BEST OF BOB DYLAN VOLUME 2	*Columbia*	22	*20 May 00*	2
THE ESSENTIAL BOB DYLAN	*Columbia*	9	*2 Jun 01*	12
LOVE AND THEFT	*Columbia*	3	*22 Sep 01*	5

Bob DYLAN and the GRATEFUL DEAD — US

(See also Bob Dylan; Grateful Dead.)

ALBUMS:	HITS 1			WEEKS 3
DYLAN AND THE DEAD	*CBS*	38	*18 Feb 89*	3
Live recordings recorded Summer 1987.				

DYNAMIX II featuring: TOO TOUGH TEE — US

SINGLES:	HITS 1			WEEKS 4
JUST GIVE THE DJ A BREAK	*Cooltempo*	50	*8 Aug 87*	4

DYNASTY — US

SINGLES:	HITS 3			WEEKS 20
I DON'T WANT TO BE A FREAK (BUT I CAN'T HELP MYSELF)	*Solar*	20	*13 Oct 79*	13
I'VE JUST BEGUN TO LOVE YOU	*Solar*	51	*9 Aug 80*	4
DOES THAT RING A BELL	*Solar*	53	*21 May 83*	3

DYNASTY OF TWO featuring ROWETTA – See VARIOUS ARTISTS (EPs) 'The Further Adventures Of North – More Underground Dance EP'

Ronnie DYSON — US

SINGLES:	HITS 1			WEEKS 6
WHEN YOU GET RIGHT DOWN TO IT	*CBS*	34	*4 Dec 71*	6
Originally recorded by Barry Mann.				

E

Katherine E — US

SINGLES:	HITS 2			WEEKS 7
I'M ALRIGHT	*Dead Dead Good*	41	*6 Apr 91*	5
THEN I FEEL GOOD	*PWL Continental*	56	*18 Jan 92*	2

Lizz E – See FRESH 4 (CHILDREN OF THE GHETTO) featuring Lizz E

Sheila E — US

SINGLES:	HITS 1			WEEKS 9
THE BELLE OF ST. MARK	*Warner Brothers*	18	*23 Feb 85*	9

E-LUSTRIOUS — UK

(See also Direkt.)

SINGLES:	HITS 2			WEEKS 2
DANCE NO MORE	*MOS*	58	*15 Feb 92*	1
Above hit: E-LUSTRIOUS featuring Deborah FRENCH.				
IN YOUR DANCE	*UFG*	69	*2 Jul 94*	1

E-MALE — UK

SINGLES:	HITS 1			WEEKS 1
WE ARE E-MALE	*East West*	44	*31 Jan 98*	1

E-MOTION — UK

SINGLES:	HITS 2			WEEKS 7
THE NAUGHTY NORTH & THE SEXY SOUTH	*Sound Proof*	20	*3 Feb 96*	3
I STAND ALONE	*Sound Proof*	60	*17 Aug 96*	1
THE NAUGHTY NORTH & THE SEXY SOUTH [RI]	*Sound Proof*	17	*26 Oct 96*	3

E – ROTIC — US/Germany

SINGLES:	HITS 1			WEEKS 2
MAX DON'T HAVE SEX WITH YOUR EX	*Stip*	45	*3 Jun 95*	2

E-17 – See EAST 17

E-SMOOVE featuring Latanza WATERS — UK/US

SINGLES:	HITS 1			WEEKS 1
DEJA VU	*AM:PM*	63	*15 Aug 98*	1

E STREET BAND – See Bruce SPRINGSTEEN

E-TRAX — Holland

SINGLES:	HITS 1			WEEKS 1
LET'S ROCK	*Tidy Trax*	60	*9 Jun 01*	1

E-TYPE — Sweden

SINGLES:	HITS 2			WEEKS 2
THIS IS THE WAY	*Ffrreedom*	53	*23 Sep 95*	1
CAMPIONE 2000	*Polydor*	58	*24 Jun 00*	1
The official anthem to the Euro 2000 football championships in Holland and Belgium.				

E.U. – See SALT-N-PEPA

E.V.E. — UK/US

SINGLES:	HITS 2			WEEKS 5
GROOVE OF LOVE	*MCA*	30	*1 Oct 94*	3
GOOD LIFE	*MCA*	39	*28 Jan 95*	2

E'VOKE — UK

SINGLES:	HITS 2			WEEKS 6
RUNAWAY	*Ffrreedom*	30	*25 Nov 95*	3
ARMS OF LOREN	*Manifesto*	25	*24 Aug 96*	3

E.Y.C. — US

SINGLES:	HITS 7			WEEKS 36
FEELIN' ALRIGHT	*MCA*	16	*11 Dec 93*	8
THE WAY YOU WORK IT	*MCA*	14	*5 Mar 94*	7
NUMBER ONE	*MCA*	27	*14 May 94*	5
BLACK BOOK	*MCA*	13	*30 Jul 94*	6
ONE MORE CHANCE	*MCA*	25	*10 Dec 94*	6
OOH-AH-AA (I FEEL IT)	*MCA*	33	*23 Sep 95*	2
IN THE BEGINNING	*MCA*	41	*2 Dec 95*	2
ALBUMS:	**HITS 1**			**WEEKS 5**
EXPRESS YOURSELF CLEARLY	*MCA*	14	*16 Apr 94*	5

E-Z ROLLERS — UK

SINGLES:	HITS 1			WEEKS 3
WALK THIS LAND	*Moving Shadow*	18	*24 Apr 99*	3
From the film 'Lock, Stock And Two Smoking Barrels'.				

E-ZEE POSSEE — UK

SINGLES:	HITS 4			WEEKS 16
EVERYTHING STARTS WITH AN 'E'	*More Protein*	69	*26 Aug 89*	1
Sleeve shows title as Everything Begins With An 'E'.				
LOVE ON LOVE	*More Protein*	59	*20 Jan 90*	3
Above hit: E-ZEE POSSEE featuring DR. MOUTHQUAKE.				
EVERYTHING STARTS WITH AN 'E' [RE]	*More Protein*	15	*17 Mar 90*	8
THE SUN MACHINE	*More Protein*	62	*30 Jun 90*	3
BREATHING IS E-ZEE	*More Protein*	72	*21 Sep 91*	1
Above hit: E-ZEE POSSEE featuring Tara NEWLEY.				

EAGLES — US

SINGLES:	HITS 9			WEEKS 51
ONE OF THESE NIGHTS	*Asylum*	23	*9 Aug 75*	7
LYIN' EYES	*Asylum*	23	*1 Nov 75*	7
TAKE IT TO THE LIMIT	*Asylum*	12	*6 Mar 76*	7
NEW KID IN TOWN	*Asylum*	20	*15 Jan 77*	7
HOTEL CALIFORNIA	*Asylum*	8	*16 Apr 77*	10
PLEASE COME HOME FOR CHRISTMAS	*Asylum*	30	*16 Dec 78*	5
Originally recorded by Charles Brown.				
HEARTACHE TONIGHT	*Asylum*	40	*13 Oct 79*	5
Co-written by Bob Seger.				
THE LONG RUN	*Elektra*	66	*1 Dec 79*	2
LOVE WILL KEEP US ALIVE	*Geffen*	52	*13 Jul 96*	1
ALBUMS:	**HITS 11**			**WEEKS 409**
ON THE BORDER	*Asylum*	28	*27 Apr 74*	9
DESPERADO	*Asylum*	39	*12 Jul 75*	9
ONE OF THESE NIGHTS	*Asylum*	8	*12 Jul 75*	40

THEIR GREATEST HITS 1971-1975	*Asylum*	2	*6 Mar 76*	77
Includes re-entries through to 1982.				
HOTEL CALIFORNIA	*Asylum*	2	*25 Dec 76*	61
THE LONG RUN	*Asylum*	4	*13 Oct 79*	16
LIVE	*Asylum*	24	*22 Nov 80*	13
Compiled from onstage recordings during the 1970s.				
THE BEST OF EAGLES	*Asylum*	10	*18 May 85*	24
HOTEL CALIFORNIA [RE-1ST]	*Asylum*	56	*28 Feb 87*	8
Includes re-entries through to 1996. Peak position reached in 1994 (1987 peak No. 87, 1991 peak No. 59).				
THE BEST OF EAGLES [RE-1ST]	*Asylum*	8	*13 Aug 88*	41
Includes re-entries through to 1993.				
THE BEST OF EAGLES [RE-2ND]	*Asylum*	15	*30 Apr 94*	8
Re-released at mid-price.				
THE VERY BEST OF THE EAGLES	*Elektra*	4	*23 Jul 94*	54
Includes re-entries through to 2000.				
HELL FREEZES OVER	*Geffen*	28	*19 Nov 94*	11
ONE OF THESE NIGHTS [RE]	*Asylum*	57	*11 Mar 95*	1
Re-released at mid-price.				
HELL FREEZES OVER [RE]	*Geffen*	18	*13 Jul 96*	10
HOTEL CALIFORNIA [RE-2ND]	*Asylum*	72	*8 Jan 00*	1
THE VERY BEST OF THE EAGLES	*Elektra*	3	*9 Jun 01*	26
Expanded and repacked version of their 1994 album.				

Robert EARL — UK

SINGLES:	HITS 3			WEEKS 27
I MAY NEVER PASS THIS WAY AGAIN	*Philips*	14	*26 Apr 58*	13
MORE THAN EVER (COME PRIMA)	*Philips*	26	*25 Oct 58*	2
MORE THAN EVER (COME PRIMA) [RE]	*Philips*	28	*22 Nov 58*	2
THE WONDERFUL SECRET OF LOVE	*Philips*	17	*14 Feb 59*	10
Above 3: Robert EARL with Wally STOTT and his Orchestra and Chorus.				

Charles EARLAND — US

SINGLES:	HITS 1			WEEKS 5
LET THE MUSIC PLAY	*Mercury*	46	*19 Aug 78*	5

Steve EARLE — US

SINGLES:	HITS 2			WEEKS 7
COPPERHEAD ROAD	*MCA*	45	*15 Oct 88*	6
JOHNNY COME LATELY	*MCA*	75	*31 Dec 88*	1
ALBUMS:	**HITS 8**			**WEEKS 21**
EXIT O	*MCA*	77	*4 Jul 87*	2
COPPERHEAD ROAD	*MCA*	42	*19 Nov 88*	8
THE HARD WAY	*MCA*	22	*7 Jul 90*	4
SHUT UP AND DIE LIKE AN AVIATOR	*MCA*	62	*19 Oct 91*	1
Above 2: Steve EARLE and the DUKES.				
I FEEL ALRIGHT	*Transatlantic*	44	*23 Mar 96*	3
EL COROZON	*Warner Brothers*	59	*18 Oct 97*	1
THE MOUNTAIN	*Grapevine*	51	*6 Mar 99*	1
Above hit: Steve EARLE and the Del McCOURY BAND.				
TRANSCENDENTAL BLUES	*Epic*	32	*17 Jun 00*	1

EARLY MUSIC CONSORT, directed by David MUNROW — UK

SINGLES:	HITS 1			WEEKS 1
HENRY VIII SUITE: THE SIX WIVES OF HENRY VIII [OST-TV] [EP]	*BBC*	49	*3 Apr 71*	1
Lead track: Fanfare, Passomezo Du Roy, Gaillard De Escosse. This was the theme and incidental music from the six plays written for BBC-TV.				

EARTH, WIND AND FIRE — US

(See also Various Artists: Films – Original Soundtracks 'Sgt. Pepper's Lonely Hearts Club Band'.)

SINGLES:	HITS 17			WEEKS 128
SATURDAY NITE	*CBS*	17	*12 Feb 77*	9
FANTASY	*CBS*	14	*11 Feb 78*	10
JUPITER	*CBS*	41	*13 May 78*	5
MAGIC MIND	*CBS*	75	*29 Jul 78*	1
MAGIC MIND [RE]	*CBS*	54	*12 Aug 78*	4
GOT TO GET YOU INTO MY LIFE	*CBS*	33	*7 Oct 78*	7
Originally recorded by the Beatles.				
SEPTEMBER	*CBS*	3	*9 Dec 78*	13
BOOGIE WONDERLAND	*CBS*	4	*12 May 79*	13
Above hit: EARTH, WIND AND FIRE with the EMOTIONS.				
AFTER THE LOVE HAS GONE	*CBS*	4	*28 Jul 79*	10
STAR	*CBS*	16	*6 Oct 79*	8
CAN'T LET GO	*CBS*	46	*15 Dec 79*	7
IN THE STONE	*CBS*	53	*8 Mar 80*	3
LET ME TALK	*CBS*	29	*11 Oct 80*	5

BACK ON THE ROAD	*CBS*	63	*20 Dec 80*	4
LET'S GROOVE	*CBS*	3	*7 Nov 81*	13
I'VE HAD ENOUGH	*CBS*	29	*6 Feb 82*	6
FALL IN LOVE WITH ME	*CBS*	47	*5 Feb 83*	4
SYSTEM OF SURVIVAL	*CBS*	54	*7 Nov 87*	3
SEPTEMBER 99 [RM]	*INCredible*	*25*	*31 Jul 99*	*3*
Remixed by Phats and Small.				
ALBUMS:	**HITS 10**			**WEEKS 171**
ALL 'N' ALL	*CBS*	13	*21 Jan 78*	23
THE BEST OF EARTH WIND AND FIRE VOLUME 1	*CBS*	6	*16 Dec 78*	42
I AM	*CBS*	5	*23 Jun 79*	41
FACES	*CBS*	10	*1 Nov 80*	6
RAISE!	*CBS*	14	*14 Nov 81*	22
POWERLIGHT	*CBS*	22	*19 Feb 83*	7
THE ARTISTS VOLUME 1	*Street Sounds*	65	*9 Mar 85*	4
Compilation album with tracks by each artist.				
Above hit: EARTH WIND AND FIRE/Jean CARN/ROSE ROYCE.				
THE COLLECTION - 24 ESSENTIAL HITS	*K-Tel*	5	*10 May 86*	13
THE VERY BEST OF EARTH, WIND AND FIRE	*Telstar*	40	*28 Nov 92*	6
BOOGIE WONDERLAND - THE VERY BEST OF EARTH, WIND AND FIRE [RE]	*Telstar*	29	*28 Sep 96*	4
Repackage of The Very Best Of Earth, Wind And Fire.				
THE ULTIMATE COLLECTION	*Columbia*	34	*7 Aug 99*	3

EARTHLING — UK

SINGLES:	**HITS 2**			**WEEKS 2**
ECHO ON MY MIND PART II	*Cooltempo*	61	*14 Oct 95*	1
BLOOD MUSIC [EP]	*Cooltempo*	69	*1 Jun 96*	1
Lead track: 1st Transmission.				
ALBUMS:	**HITS 1**			**WEEKS 1**
RADAR	*Cooltempo*	66	*3 Jun 95*	1
Features guest female vocalist Segun.				

EAST 57TH ST featuring Donna ALLEN — UK

SINGLES:	**HITS 1**			**WEEKS 3**
SATURDAY	*AM:PM*	29	*11 Oct 97*	3
Originally recorded by Norma Jean. Original release in instrumental form reached No. 110 in 1996.				

EAST OF EDEN — UK

SINGLES:	**HITS 1**			**WEEKS 12**
JIG-A-JIG	*Deram*	7	*17 Apr 71*	12
ALBUMS:	**HITS 1**			**WEEKS 2**
SNAFU	*Deram*	29	*14 Mar 70*	2

EAST 17 — UK

SINGLES:	**HITS 18**			**WEEKS 170**
HOUSE OF LOVE	*London*	10	*29 Aug 92*	9
GOLD	*London*	28	*14 Nov 92*	4
GOLD [RE]	*London*	64	*19 Dec 92*	4
DEEP	*London*	5	*30 Jan 93*	10
SLOW IT DOWN	*London*	13	*10 Apr 93*	7
WEST END GIRLS	*London*	11	*26 Jun 93*	7
IT'S ALRIGHT	*London*	3	*4 Dec 93*	14
AROUND THE WORLD	*London*	3	*14 May 94*	13
STEAM	*London*	7	*1 Oct 94*	8
STAY ANOTHER DAY	*London*	1	*3 Dec 94*	15
LET IT RAIN	*London*	10	*25 Mar 95*	7
STAY ANOTHER DAY [RE]	*London*	64	*6 May 95*	1
HOLD MY BODY TIGHT	*London*	12	*17 Jun 95*	7
THUNDER	*London*	4	*4 Nov 95*	14
Above hit: E.17.				
DO U STILL?	*London*	7	*10 Feb 96*	7
SOMEONE TO LOVE	*London*	16	*10 Aug 96*	8
Above hit: EAST 7EVENTEEN.				
IF YOU EVER	*London*	2	*2 Nov 96*	15
Original by Shai reached No.2 in the US in 1992.				
Above hit: EAST SEVENTEEN featuring GABRIELLE.				
HEY CHILD	*London*	3	*18 Jan 97*	5
Written for Mortimer's daughters Atlanta and Ocean.				
Above hit: EAST SEVENTEEN.				
EACH TIME	*Telstar*	2	*14 Nov 98*	10
BETCHA CAN'T WAIT	*Telstar*	12	*13 Mar 99*	5
Above 2: E-17.				
ALBUMS:	**HITS 5**			**WEEKS 102**
WALTHAMSTOW	*London*	1	*27 Feb 93*	14
WALTHAMSTOW [RE]	*London*	16	*17 Jul 93*	19
Repackaged with additional track.				

STEAM	*London*	3	*29 Oct 94*	36
UP ALL NIGHT	*London*	7	*25 Nov 95*	15
AROUND THE WORLD – THE JOURNEY SO FAR *Compilation.*	*London*	3	*16 Nov 96*	16
RESURRECTION *Above hit: E-17.*	*Telstar*	43	*28 Nov 98*	2

EAST SIDE BEAT — Italy

SINGLES:	HITS 3			WEEKS 18
RIDE LIKE THE WIND	*ffrr*	3	*30 Nov 91*	11
ALIVE AND KICKING	*ffrr*	26	*19 Dec 92*	6
YOU'RE MY EVERYTHING	*ffrr*	65	*29 May 93*	1

David EASTER – See Jason DONOVAN

EASTERHOUSE — UK

ALBUMS:	HITS 1			WEEKS 1
CONTENDERS	*Rough Trade*	91	*28 Jun 86*	1

Sheena EASTON — UK

SINGLES:	HITS 15			WEEKS 104
MODERN GIRL	*EMI*	56	*5 Apr 80*	3
9 TO 5	*EMI*	3	*19 Jul 80*	15
MODERN GIRL [RE]	*EMI*	8	*9 Aug 80*	12
ONE MAN WOMAN	*EMI*	14	*25 Oct 80*	6
TAKE MY TIME	*EMI*	44	*14 Feb 81*	5
WHEN HE SHINES	*EMI*	12	*2 May 81*	8
FOR YOUR EYES ONLY *From the James Bond film of the same name.*	*EMI*	8	*27 Jun 81*	13
JUST ANOTHER BROKEN HEART	*EMI*	33	*12 Sep 81*	8
YOU COULD HAVE BEEN WITH ME	*EMI*	54	*5 Dec 81*	3
MACHINERY	*EMI*	38	*31 Jul 82*	5
WE'VE GOT TONIGHT *Above hit: Kenny ROGERS and Sheena EASTON.*	*Liberty*	28	*12 Feb 83*	7
THE LOVER IN ME	*MCA*	15	*21 Jan 89*	8
DAYS LIKE THIS	*MCA*	43	*18 Mar 89*	3
101	*MCA*	54	*15 Jul 89*	2
THE ARMS OF ORION *Above hit: PRINCE with Sheena EASTON.*	*Warner Brothers*	27	*18 Nov 89*	5
GIVING UP, GIVING IN	*Universal*	54	*9 Dec 00*	1

ALBUMS:	HITS 5			WEEKS 27
TAKE MY TIME	*EMI*	17	*31 Jan 81*	9
YOU COULD HAVE BEEN WITH ME	*EMI*	33	*3 Oct 81*	6
MADNESS, MONEY AND MUSIC	*EMI*	44	*25 Sep 82*	4
BEST KEPT SECRET	*EMI*	99	*15 Oct 83*	1
THE LOVER IN ME	*MCA*	30	*4 Mar 89*	7

EASTSIDE CONNECTION — US

SINGLES:	HITS 1			WEEKS 3
YOU'RE SO RIGHT FOR ME	*Creole*	44	*8 Apr 78*	3

Clint EASTWOOD — US

(See also Various Artists: Films – Original Soundtracks 'Paint Your Wagon'.)

SINGLES:	HITS 1			WEEKS 2
I TALK TO THE TREES *From the film 'Paint Your Wagon'. [AA] listed with Wand'rin' Star by Lee Marvin.*	*Paramount*	18	*7 Feb 70*	2

Clint EASTWOOD and GENERAL SAINT — UK

SINGLES:	HITS 1			WEEKS 3
LAST PLANE (ONE WAY TICKET)	*MCA*	51	*29 Sep 84*	3

ALBUMS:	HITS 2			WEEKS 3
TWO BAD DJ	*Greensleeves*	99	*6 Feb 82*	2
STOP THAT TRAIN	*Greensleeves*	98	*28 May 83*	1

EASY RIDERS – See Frankie LAINE

EASYBEATS — Australia

SINGLES:	HITS 2			WEEKS 24
FRIDAY ON MY MIND •	*United Artists*	6	*29 Oct 66*	15
HELLO, HOW ARE YOU	*United Artists*	20	*13 Apr 68*	9

EAT — UK

SINGLES:	HITS 1			WEEKS 1
BLEED ME WHITE	*Fiction*	73	*12 Jun 93*	1

EAT STATIC — UK

SINGLES:	HITS 3			WEEKS 3
HYBRID	*Planet Dog*	41	*22 Feb 97*	1
INTERCEPTOR	*Planet Dog*	44	*27 Sep 97*	1
CONTACT . . .	*Planet Dog*	67	*27 Jun 98*	1
ALBUMS:	**HITS 3**			**WEEKS 5**
ABDUCTION	*Ultimate*	62	*15 May 93*	1
IMPLANT	*Planet Dog*	13	*25 Jun 94*	3
SCIENCE OF THE GODS	*Planet Dog*	60	*25 Oct 97*	1

Dedicated to Jon Pertwee and Timothy Leary.

Cleveland EATON — US

SINGLES:	HITS 1			WEEKS 6
BAMA BOOGIE WOOGIE	*Gull*	35	*23 Sep 78*	6

EAV (ERSTE ALLGEMEINE VERUNSICHERUNG) — Austria

SINGLES:	HITS 1			WEEKS 4
BA-BA-BANKROBBERY (ENGLISH VERSION??)	*Columbia*	63	*27 Sep 86*	4

EAZY-E — US

SINGLES:	HITS 1			WEEKS 3
JUST TAH LET U KNOW	*Epic*	30	*6 Jan 96*	3
ALBUMS:	**HITS 1**			**WEEKS 1**
STR8 OFF THA STREETZ OF MUTHAPHUKKIN COMPTON	*Epic*	66	*10 Feb 96*	1

Bernard EBBINGHOUSE and his Orchestra - See Cliff RICHARD

EBTG - See EVERYTHING BUT THE GIRL

ECHO and the BUNNYMEN — UK

(See also England United.)

SINGLES:	HITS 18			WEEKS 86
RESCUE	*Korova*	62	*17 May 80*	1
CROCODILES	*Korova*	37	*18 Apr 81*	4
A PROMISE	*Korova*	49	*18 Jul 81*	4
THE BACK OF LOVE	*Korova*	19	*29 May 82*	7
THE CUTTER	*Korova*	8	*22 Jan 83*	8
NEVER STOP	*Korova*	15	*16 Jul 83*	7
THE KILLING MOON	*Korova*	9	*28 Jan 84*	6
SILVER	*Korova*	30	*21 Apr 84*	5
SEVEN SEAS	*Korova*	16	*14 Jul 84*	7
BRING ON THE DANCING HORSES	*Korova*	21	*19 Oct 85*	7
THE GAME	*WEA*	28	*13 Jun 87*	4
LIPS LIKE SUGAR	*WEA*	36	*1 Aug 87*	4
PEOPLE ARE STRANGE	*WEA*	29	*20 Feb 88*	5
PEOPLE ARE STRANGE [RI]	*East West*	34	*2 Mar 91*	4
From the film 'The Lost Boys'.				
NOTHING LASTS FOREVER	*London*	8	*28 Jun 97*	6
I WANT TO BE THERE WHEN YOU COME	*London*	30	*13 Sep 97*	2
DON'T LET IT GET YOU DOWN	*London*	50	*8 Nov 97*	1
RUST	*London*	22	*27 Mar 99*	3
IT'S ALRIGHT	*Cooking Vinyl*	41	*5 May 01*	1
ALBUMS:	**HITS 10**			**WEEKS 100**
CROCODILES	*Korova*	17	*26 Jul 80*	6
HEAVEN UP HERE	*Korova*	10	*6 Jun 81*	16
PORCUPINE	*Korova*	2	*12 Feb 83*	17
OCEAN RAIN	*Korova*	4	*12 May 84*	26
SONGS TO LEARN AND SING	*Korova*	6	*23 Nov 85*	15
ECHO AND THE BUNNYMEN	*WEA*	4	*18 Jul 87*	9
BALLYHOO - THE BEST OF ECHO AND THE BUNNYMEN	*Korova*	59	*21 Jun 97*	1
EVERGREEN	*London*	8	*26 Jul 97*	7
WHAT ARE YOU GOING TO DO WITH YOUR LIFE?	*London*	21	*17 Apr 99*	2
FLOWERS	*Cooking Vinyl*	56	*26 May 01*	1

ECHOBASS — UK

SINGLES:	HITS 1			WEEKS 1
YOU ARE THE WEAKEST LINK	*House Of Bush*	53	*14 Jul 01*	1

Samples Anne Robinson's catchphrase from BBC TV's The Weakest Link.

ECHOBEATZ — UK

SINGLES:	HITS 1			WEEKS 5
MAS QUE NADA	*Eternal*	10	*25 Jul 98*	5

Dance version of the track featured in the Nike TV commercial.

ECHOBELLY — UK

SINGLES:	HITS 8			WEEKS 16
INSOMNIAC	*Fauve*	47	*2 Apr 94*	1
I CAN'T IMAGINE THE WORLD WITHOUT ME	*Fauve*	39	*2 Jul 94*	2
CLOSE . . . BUT	*Fauve*	59	*5 Nov 94*	1
GREAT THINGS	*Fauve*	13	*2 Sep 95*	3
KING OF THE KERB	*Fauve*	25	*4 Nov 95*	3
DARK THERAPY	*Fauve*	20	*2 Mar 96*	3
THE WORLD IS FLAT	*Epic*	31	*23 Aug 97*	2
HERE COMES THE BIG RUSH	*Epic*	56	*8 Nov 97*	1
ALBUMS:	**HITS 3**			**WEEKS 28**
EVERYONE'S GOT ONE	*Fauve*	8	*3 Sep 94*	3
ON	*Fauve*	4	*30 Sep 95*	24
LUSTRA	*Epic*	47	*22 Nov 97*	1

Billy ECKSTINE — US

SINGLES:	HITS 3			WEEKS 48
NO ONE BUT YOU *From the film 'Flame And The Flesh'.*	*MGM*	3	*13 Nov 54*	17
PASSING STRANGERS • *Above hit: Blly VAUGHAN and Billy ECKSTINE.*	*Mercury*	22	*28 Sep 57*	2
GIGI *From the film of the same name.*	*Mercury*	8	*14 Feb 59*	14
PASSING STRANGERS [RI] *Above hit: Blly VAUGHAN and Billy ECKSTINE.*	*Mercury*	20	*15 Mar 69*	15

ECLIPSE — Italy

SINGLES:	HITS 1			WEEKS 4
MAKES ME LOVE YOU *Samples Sister Sledge's Thinking Of You.*	*Azuli*	25	*14 Aug 99*	4

Silvio ECOMO — Holland

SINGLES:	HITS 1			WEEKS 1
STANDING	*Hooj Choons*	70	*15 Jul 00*	1

EDDIE and the HOT RODS — UK

SINGLES:	HITS 5			WEEKS 26
LIVE AT THE MARQUEE [EP] *Lead Track: 96 Tears.*	*Island*	43	*11 Sep 76*	5
TEENAGE DEPRESSION	*Island*	35	*13 Nov 76*	4
I MIGHT BE LYING	*Island*	44	*23 Apr 77*	3
DO ANYTHING YOU WANNA DO *Above hit: RODS.*	*Island*	9	*13 Aug 77*	10
QUIT THIS TOWN	*Island*	36	*21 Jan 78*	4
ALBUMS:	**HITS 3**			**WEEKS 5**
TEENAGE DEPRESSION	*Island*	43	*18 Dec 76*	1
LIFE ON THE LINE	*Island*	27	*3 Dec 77*	3
THRILLER	*Island*	50	*24 Mar 79*	1

EDDY — UK

SINGLES:	HITS 1			WEEKS 2
SOMEDAY	*Positiva*	49	*9 Jul 94*	2

Duane EDDY — US

SINGLES:	HITS 22			WEEKS 202
REBEL-ROUSER • *Above hit: Duane EDDY and his twangy guitar.*	*London*	19	*6 Sep 58*	10
CANNONBALL *Above hit: Duane EDDY, his "twangy" guitar and the REBELS.*	*London*	22	*3 Jan 59*	4
PETER GUNN • *Originally recorded by Henry Mancini.*	*London*	6	*20 Jun 59*	10
YEP! *Above 2 entries were separate sides of the same release, each had its own chart run.*	*London*	17	*25 Jul 59*	5
FORTY MILES OF BAD ROAD	*London*	11	*5 Sep 59*	9
PETER GUNN [RE]	*London*	27	*12 Sep 59*	1
SOME KIND-A EARTHQUAKE	*London*	12	*19 Dec 59*	5
BONNIE CAME BACK	*London*	12	*20 Feb 60*	11
SHAZAM!	*London*	4	*30 Apr 60*	13
BECAUSE THEY'RE YOUNG *Above 2 from the film 'Because They're Young'.*	*London*	2	*23 Jul 60*	18
KOMMOTION	*London*	13	*12 Nov 60*	10
PEPE *From the film of the same name.*	*London*	2	*14 Jan 61*	14
THEME FROM DIXIE	*London*	7	*22 Apr 61*	10

RING OF FIRE	*London*	17	*24 Jun 61*	10
DRIVIN' HOME	*London*	30	*16 Sep 61*	4
CARAVAN *Originally recorded by Duke Ellington.*	*Parlophone*	42	*7 Oct 61*	3
DEEP IN THE HEART OF TEXAS *Originally recorded by Alvino Rey & his Orchestra.*	*RCA*	19	*26 May 62*	8
BALLAD OF PALADIN *Originally recorded by Johnny Western.*	*RCA*	10	*25 Aug 62*	10
(DANCE WITH THE) GUITAR MAN	*RCA*	4	*10 Nov 62*	16
BOSS GUITAR *Above 2: Duane EDDY and the REBELETTES.*	*RCA Victor*	27	*16 Feb 63*	8
LONELY BOY LONELY GUITAR	*RCA Victor*	35	*1 Jun 63*	4
YOUR BABY'S GONE SURFIN'	*RCA Victor*	49	*31 Aug 63*	1
PLAY ME LIKE YOU PLAY YOUR GUITAR *Above hit: Duane EDDY and the REBELETTES.*	*GTO*	9	*8 Mar 75*	9
PETER GUNN *Above hit: ART OF NOISE featuring Duane EDDY.*	*China*	8	*22 Mar 86*	9
EPS:	**HITS 5**			**WEEKS 37**
YEP!	*London*	16	*30 Jul 60*	2
TWANGY	*London*	4	*10 Dec 60*	30
BECAUSE THEY'RE YOUNG	*London*	17	*18 Feb 61*	1
THE LONELY ONE	*London*	16	*20 May 61*	1
PEPE	*London*	10	*1 Jul 61*	3
ALBUMS:	**HITS 9**			**WEEKS 88**
HAVE "TWANGY" GUITAR WILL TRAVEL	*London*	6	*6 Jun 59*	3
ESPECIALLY FOR YOU	*London*	6	*31 Oct 59*	8
THE "TWANG'S" THE THANG *Above hit: Duane EDDY, his "twangy" guitar and the REBELS.*	*London*	2	*19 Mar 60*	25
SONGS OF OUR HERITAGE	*London*	13	*26 Nov 60*	5
A MILLION DOLLARS' WORTH OF TWANG	*London*	5	*1 Apr 61*	19
A MILLION DOLLARS' WORTH OF TWANG VOLUME 2	*London*	18	*9 Jun 62*	1
TWISTIN' AND TWANGIN'	*RCA*	8	*21 Jul 62*	12
TWANGY GUITAR - SILKY STRINGS	*RCA Victor*	13	*8 Dec 62*	11
DANCE WITH THE GUITAR MAN	*RCA Victor*	14	*16 Mar 63*	4

Nelson EDDY
US

EPS:	**HITS 1**			**WEEKS 1**
INDIAN LOVE CALL	*RCA*	12	*23 Apr 60*	1

EDDY and the SOULBAND
US

SINGLES:	**HITS 1**			**WEEKS 7**
THEME FROM SHAFT	*Club*	13	*23 Feb 85*	7

Randy EDELMAN
US

SINGLES:	**HITS 4**			**WEEKS 18**
CONCRETE AND CLAY	*20th Century*	11	*6 Mar 76*	7
THE UPTOWN, UPTEMPO WOMAN	*20th Century*	25	*18 Sep 76*	7
YOU	*20th Century*	49	*15 Jan 77*	2
NOBODY MADE ME	*Rocket*	60	*17 Jul 82*	2

EDELWEISS
Austria

SINGLES:	**HITS 1**			**WEEKS 10**
BRING ME EDELWEISS *Tune based on Abba's S.O.S.*	*WEA*	5	*29 Apr 89*	10

EDEN
UK/Australia

SINGLES:	**HITS 1**			**WEEKS 2**
DO U FEEL 4 ME	*Logic*	51	*6 Mar 93*	2

Lyn EDEN – See SMOKIN BEATS featuring Lyn EDEN

EDISON LIGHTHOUSE
UK

SINGLES:	**HITS 2**			**WEEKS 13**
LOVE GROWS (WHERE MY ROSEMARY GOES) *Originally recorded by Jeff Barry.*	*Bell*	1	*24 Jan 70*	12
IT'S UP TO YOU PETULA	*Bell*	49	*30 Jan 71*	1

EDMONTON SYMPHONY ORCHESTRA – See PROCOL HARUM

Dave EDMUNDS
UK

(See also Rockpile.)

SINGLES:	**HITS 12**			**WEEKS 93**
I HEAR YOU KNOCKING *Originally recorded by Smiley Lewis.* *Above hit: Dave EDMUND'S ROCKPILE.*	*MAM*	1	*21 Nov 70*	14

BABY I LOVE YOU	*Rockfield*	8	*20 Jan 73*	13
BORN TO BE WITH YOU	*Rockfield*	5	*9 Jun 73*	12
I KNEW THE BRIDE	*Swan Song*	26	*2 Jul 77*	8
GIRLS TALK	*Swan Song*	4	*30 Jun 79*	11
Originally recorded by Elvis Costello and the Attractions.				
QUEEN OF HEARTS	*Swan Song*	11	*22 Sep 79*	9
CRAWLING FROM THE WRECKAGE	*Swan Song*	59	*24 Nov 79*	4
SINGING THE BLUES	*Swan Song*	28	*9 Feb 80*	8
ALMOST SATURDAY NIGHT	*Swan Song*	58	*28 Mar 81*	3
Originally recorded by John Fogerty.				
THE RACE IS ON	*Swan Song*	34	*20 Jun 81*	6
Originally recorded by George Jones.				
Above hit: Dave EDMUNDS and the STRAY CATS.				
SLIPPING AWAY	*Arista*	60	*26 Mar 83*	4
Written and produced by Jeff Lynne.				
KING OF LOVE	*Capitol*	68	*7 Apr 90*	1
Features Brian Setzer on backing vocals and Lee Rocker (both of the Stray Cats) on bass.				
ALBUMS:	**HITS 4**			**WEEKS 21**
REPEAT WHEN NECESSARY	*Swan Song*	39	*23 Jun 79*	12
TWANGIN'	*Swan Song*	37	*18 Apr 81*	4
DE 7	*Arista*	60	*3 Apr 82*	3
INFORMATION	*Arista*	92	*30 Apr 83*	2

Alton EDWARDS — Zimbabwe

SINGLES:	**HITS 1**			**WEEKS 9**
I JUST WANNA (SPEND SOME TIME WITH YOU)	*Streetwave*	20	*9 Jan 82*	9

Dennis EDWARDS — US

SINGLES:	**HITS 1**			**WEEKS 10**
DON'T LOOK ANY FURTHER	*Gordy*	45	*24 Mar 84*	5
Above hit: Dennis EDWARDS featuring Siedah GARRETT.				
DON'T LOOK ANY FURTHER [RE]	*Gordy*	55	*20 Jun 87*	5
ALBUMS:	**HITS 1**			**WEEKS 1**
DON'T LOOK ANY FURTHER	*Gordy*	91	*14 Apr 84*	1

Doreen EDWARDS - See T-EMPO

Rupie EDWARDS — Jamaica

SINGLES:	**HITS 2**			**WEEKS 16**
IRE FEELINGS (SKANGA)	*Cactus*	9	*23 Nov 74*	10
LEGO SKANGA	*Cactus*	32	*8 Feb 75*	6

Todd EDWARDS — US

ALBUMS:	**HITS 1**			**WEEKS 1**
SAVED MY LIFE	*ffrr*	69	*24 Aug 96*	1
12" single, too long to be eligible for the singles chart.				

Tommy EDWARDS — US

SINGLES:	**HITS 2**			**WEEKS 18**
IT'S ALL IN THE GAME •	*MGM*	1	*4 Oct 58*	17
Co-writer Carl Sigman was Vice President of the United States from 1925–1929. Originally recorded in 1951.				
MY MELANCHOLY BABY	*MGM*	29	*8 Aug 59*	1
Originally recorded by Walter Van Brunt in 1915.				
EPS:	**HITS 1**			**WEEKS 1**
THE WAYS OF LOVE	*MGM*	15	*16 Apr 60*	1

EEK-A-MOUSE — Jamaica

ALBUMS:	**HITS 1**			**WEEKS 3**
SKIDIP	*Greensleeves*	61	*14 Aug 82*	3

EELS — US

SINGLES:	**HITS 8**			**WEEKS 23**
NOVOCAINE FOR THE SOUL	*Dreamworks*	10	*15 Feb 97*	5
SUSAN'S HOUSE	*Dreamworks*	9	*17 May 97*	5
YOUR LUCKY DAY IN HELL	*Dreamworks*	35	*13 Sep 97*	2
LAST STOP: THIS TOWN	*Dreamworks*	23	*26 Sep 98*	3
CANCER FOR THE CURE	*Dreamworks*	60	*12 Dec 98*	1
MR E'S BEAUTIFUL BLUES	*Dreamworks*	11	*26 Feb 00*	4
FLYSWATTER	*Dreamworks*	55	*24 Jun 00*	1
SOULJACKER PART 1	*Dreamworks*	30	*22 Sep 01*	2
ALBUMS:	**HITS 4**			**WEEKS 38**
BEAUTIFUL FREAK	*Dreamworks*	5	*8 Feb 97*	27
ELECTRO-SHOCK BLUES	*Dreamworks*	12	*3 Oct 98*	4

DAISIES OF THE GALAXY	*Dreamworks*	8	*11 Mar 00*	5
SOULJACKER	*Dreamworks*	12	*6 Oct 01*	2

EFUA — UK

SINGLES:	HITS 1			WEEKS 5
SOMEWHERE	*Virgin*	42	*3 Jul 93*	5

EGG — UK

SINGLES:	HITS 1			WEEKS 1
GETTING AWAY WITH IT	*Indochina*	58	*30 Jan 99*	1

EGGS ON LEGS — UK

SINGLES:	HITS 1			WEEKS 1
COCK A DOODLE DO IT	*Avex UK*	42	*23 Sep 95*	1
Theme from Channel 4's 'The Big Breakfast "Eggs On Legs"' tour.				

EGYPTIAN EMPIRE — UK

SINGLES:	HITS 1			WEEKS 2
THE HORN TRACK	*Ffreedom*	61	*24 Oct 92*	2

EIFFEL 65 — Italy

SINGLES:	HITS 2			WEEKS 36
BLUE [DA BA DEE]	*Logic*	39	*21 Aug 99*	5
Import.				
BLUE [DA BA DEE]	*Eternal*	1	*25 Sep 99*	21
MOVE YOUR BODY	*Eternal*	3	*19 Feb 00*	10
ALBUMS:	**HITS 1**			**WEEKS 4**
EUROPOP	*Eternal*	12	*4 Mar 00*	4

18 WHEELER — UK

SINGLES:	HITS 1			WEEKS 1
STAY	*Creation*	59	*15 Mar 97*	1

EIGHTH WONDER — UK

SINGLES:	HITS 4			WEEKS 25
STAY WITH ME	*CBS*	65	*2 Nov 85*	2
I'M NOT SCARED	*CBS*	7	*20 Feb 88*	13
CROSS MY HEART	*CBS*	13	*25 Jun 88*	8
BABY BABY	*CBS*	65	*1 Oct 88*	2
ALBUMS:	**HITS 1**			**WEEKS 4**
FEARLESS	*CBS*	47	*23 Jul 88*	4

801 — UK

ALBUMS:	HITS 1			WEEKS 2
801 LIVE	*Island*	52	*20 Nov 76*	2

808 STATE — UK

SINGLES:	HITS 15			WEEKS 70
PACIFIC	*ZTT*	10	*18 Nov 89*	9
THE EXTENDED PLEASURE OF DANCE [EP]	*ZTT*	56	*31 Mar 90*	1
12" vinyl release only. Lead track: Ancodia.				
THE ONLY RHYME THAT BITES	*ZTT*	10	*2 Jun 90*	10
TUNES SPLITS THE ATOM	*ZTT*	18	*15 Sep 90*	7
Above 2: MC TUNES versus 808 STATE.				
CUBIK / OLYMPIC	*ZTT*	10	*10 Nov 90*	10
Cubik first appeared on the Extended Pleasure Of Dance EP.				
IN YER FACE	*ZTT*	9	*16 Feb 91*	6
OOOPS	*ZTT*	42	*27 Apr 91*	3
Above hit: 808 STATE featuring BJORK.				
LIFT / OPEN YOUR MIND	*ZTT*	38	*17 Aug 91*	4
TIME BOMB / NIMBUS	*ZTT*	59	*29 Aug 92*	1
ONE IN TEN	*ZTT*	17	*12 Dec 92*	8
Above hit: 808 STATE UB40.				
PLAN 9	*ZTT*	50	*30 Jan 93*	2
10 X 10	*ZTT*	67	*26 Jun 93*	1
BOMBADIN	*ZTT*	67	*13 Aug 94*	1
BOND	*ZTT*	57	*29 Jun 96*	1
LOPEZ (METAPHORICALLY)	*ZTT*	20	*8 Feb 97*	2
Above hit: 808 STATE via the PROPELLERHEADS, Brian ENO and themselves; viva! the guest vocals of James Dean BRADFIELD.				
PACIFIC 808:98 [RM] / CUBIK [RI]	*ZTT*	21	*16 May 98*	3
Remixed by Grooverider.				

THE ONLY RHYME THAT BITES 99 [RI]	*ZTT*	53	*6 Mar 99*	1

Though billed as a remix, the lead track is just a longer version of the original.
Above hit: MC TUNES vs 808 STATE.

ALBUMS:	HITS 4			WEEKS 20
NINETY	*ZTT*	57	*16 Dec 89*	5
EX:EL	*ZTT*	4	*16 Mar 91*	10
GORGEOUS	*ZTT*	17	*13 Feb 93*	3
808:88:98	*ZTT*	40	*30 May 98*	2

88.3 featuring Lisa MAY — UK

SINGLES:	HITS 1			WEEKS 1
WISHING ON A STAR	*Urban Gorilla*	61	*15 Jul 95*	1

EINSTEIN - See AMBASSADORS OF FUNK featuring M.C. MARIO; Simon HARRIS; TECHNOTRONIC; SNAP!

EL MARIACHI — US

SINGLES:	HITS 1			WEEKS 2
CUBA	*ffrr*	38	*9 Nov 96*	2

ELASTICA — UK

SINGLES:	HITS 4			WEEKS 12
LINE UP	*Deceptive*	20	*12 Feb 94*	3
CONNECTION	*Deceptive*	17	*22 Oct 94*	4
WAKING UP	*Deceptive*	13	*25 Feb 95*	4
Based on the Stranglers' No More Heroes.				
MAD DOG	*Deceptive*	44	*24 Jun 00*	1

ALBUMS:	HITS 2			WEEKS 27
ELASTICA	*Deceptive*	1	*25 Mar 95*	25
THE MENACE	*Deceptive*	24	*15 Apr 00*	2

ELATE — UK

SINGLES:	HITS 1			WEEKS 2
SOMEBODY LIKE YOU	*VC Recordings*	38	*26 Jul 97*	2

Samples Clannad's Theme From Harry's Game.

Donnie ELBERT — US

SINGLES:	HITS 3			WEEKS 29
WHERE DID OUR LOVE GO	*London*	8	*8 Jan 72*	10
I CAN'T HELP MYSELF	*Avco*	11	*26 Feb 72*	10
A LITTLE PIECE OF LEATHER	*London*	27	*29 Apr 72*	9

ELBOW — UK

SINGLES:	HITS 3			WEEKS 3
RED	*V2*	36	*5 May 01*	1
POWDER BLUE	*V2*	41	*21 Jul 01*	1
Originally released on The Noisebox EP in 1998.				
NEWBORN	*V2*	42	*20 Oct 01*	1

ALBUMS:	HITS 1			WEEKS 3
ASLEEP IN THE BACK	*V2*	14	*19 May 01*	3

ELECTRA — UK

SINGLES:	HITS 2			WEEKS 7
JIBARO	*ffrr*	54	*6 Aug 88*	3
IT'S YOUR DESTINY / AUTUMN LOVE	*ffrr*	51	*30 Dec 89*	4

Autumn Love listed from 13 Jan 90.

ELECTRAFIXION — UK

SINGLES:	HITS 4			WEEKS 6
ZEPHYR	*Spacejunk*	47	*19 Nov 94*	2
LOWDOWN	*Spacejunk*	54	*9 Sep 95*	2
NEVER	*Spacejunk*	58	*4 Nov 95*	1
SISTER PAIN	*Spacejunk*	27	*16 Mar 96*	1

ALBUMS:	HITS 1			WEEKS 2
BURNED	*Spacejunk*	38	*7 Oct 95*	2

ELECTRASY — UK

SINGLES:	HITS 3			WEEKS 7
LOST IN SPACE	*MCA*	60	*13 Jun 98*	1
MORNING AFTERGLOW	*MCA*	19	*5 Sep 98*	4
BEST FRIEND'S GIRL	*MCA*	41	*28 Nov 98*	2

ALBUMS:	HITS 1			WEEKS 1
BEAUTIFUL INSANE	*MCA*	48	*26 Sep 98*	1

ELECTRIBE 101 — UK/Germany

SINGLES:	HITS 3			WEEKS 15
TELL ME WHEN THE FEVER ENDED	*Mercury*	32	*28 Oct 89*	5
TALKING WITH MYSELF	*Mercury*	23	*24 Feb 90*	5
YOU'RE WALKING	*Mercury*	50	*22 Sep 90*	3
TALKING WITH MYSELF '98 [RM]	*Manifesto*	39	*10 Oct 98*	2
Remixed by Canny.				

ALBUMS:	HITS 1			WEEKS 3
ELECTRIBAL MEMORIES	*Mercury*	26	*20 Oct 90*	3

ELECTRIC BOYS — Sweden

ALBUMS:	HITS 1			WEEKS 1
GROOVUS MAXIMUS	*Vertigo*	61	*6 Jun 92*	1

ELECTRIC LIGHT ORCHESTRA — UK

SINGLES:	HITS 29			WEEKS 255
10538 OVERTURE	*Harvest*	9	*29 Jul 72*	8
ROLL OVER BEETHOVEN	*Harvest*	6	*27 Jan 73*	10
SHOWDOWN	*Harvest*	12	*6 Oct 73*	10
MA-MA-MA-BELLE	*Warner Brothers*	22	*9 Mar 74*	8
EVIL WOMAN	*Jet*	10	*10 Jan 76*	8
STRANGE MAGIC	*Jet*	38	*3 Jul 76*	3
LIVIN' THING	*Jet*	4	*13 Nov 76*	12
ROCKARIA!	*Jet*	9	*19 Feb 77*	9
TELEPHONE LINE	*Jet*	8	*21 May 77*	10
TURN TO STONE	*Jet*	18	*29 Oct 77*	12
MR. BLUE SKY	*Jet*	6	*28 Jan 78*	11
WILD WEST HERO	*Jet*	6	*10 Jun 78*	14
SWEET TALKIN' WOMAN	*Jet*	6	*7 Oct 78*	9
THE ELO EP [EP]	*Jet*	34	*9 Dec 78*	8
EP of old releases. Lead track: Can't Get It Out Of My Head.				
SHINE A LITTLE LOVE	*Jet*	6	*19 May 79*	10
THE DIARY OF HORACE WIMP	*Jet*	8	*21 Jul 79*	9
DON'T BRING ME DOWN	*Jet*	3	*1 Sep 79*	9
CONFUSION / LAST TRAIN TO LONDON	*Jet*	8	*17 Nov 79*	10
I'M ALIVE	*Jet*	20	*24 May 80*	9
XANADU	*Jet*	1	*21 Jun 80*	11
Above hit: Olivia NEWTON-JOHN/ELECTRIC LIGHT ORCHESTRA.				
ALL OVER THE WORLD	*Jet*	11	*2 Aug 80*	8
DON'T WALK AWAY	*Jet*	21	*22 Nov 80*	10
Above 4 from the film 'Xanadu'.				
HOLD ON TIGHT	*Jet*	4	*1 Aug 81*	12
Above hit: ELO.				
TWILIGHT	*Jet*	30	*24 Oct 81*	7
HERE IS THE NEWS / TICKET TO THE MOON	*Jet*	24	*9 Jan 82*	8
Here Is the News listed from 16 Jan 82.				
Above hit: ELO.				
ROCK 'N' ROLL IS KING	*Jet*	13	*18 Jun 83*	9
SECRET MESSAGES	*Jet*	48	*3 Sep 83*	3
CALLING AMERICA	*Epic*	28	*1 Mar 86*	7
HONEST MEN	*Telstar*	60	*11 May 91*	1
Above hit: ELECTRIC LIGHT ORCHESTRA PART TWO.				

ALBUMS:	HITS 17			WEEKS 410
ELECTRIC LIGHT ORCHESTRA	*Harvest*	32	*12 Aug 72*	4
ELECTRIC LIGHT ORCHESTRA II	*Harvest*	35	*31 Mar 73*	1
A NEW WORLD RECORD	*Jet*	6	*11 Dec 76*	100
OUT OF THE BLUE	*Jet*	4	*12 Nov 77*	108
Above 2 albums were on the Jet label when first released but had United Artists catalogue numbers. From 1978 they were re-issued with Jet catalogue numbers.				
THREE LIGHT YEARS	*Jet*	38	*6 Jan 79*	9
Boxed set of On the Third Day/Eldorado/Face the Music, 3 uncharted early ELO albums.				
DISCOVERY	*Jet*	1	*16 Jun 79*	46
ELO'S GREATEST HITS	*Jet*	7	*1 Dec 79*	18
XANADU [OST]	*Jet*	2	*19 Jul 80*	17
Album divided with one side by each artist.				
Above hit: Olivia NEWTON-JOHN/ELECTRIC LIGHT ORCHESTRA.				
TIME	*Jet*	1	*8 Aug 81*	32
Above hit: ELO.				
SECRET MESSAGES	*Jet*	4	*2 Jul 83*	15
BALANCE OF POWER	*Epic*	9	*15 Mar 86*	12
THE GREATEST HITS	*Telstar*	23	*16 Dec 89*	12
THE VERY BEST OF THE ELECTRIC LIGHT ORCHESTRA [RE]	*Telstar*	28	*20 Oct 90*	9
Repackage of The Greatest Hits.				
ELECTRIC LIGHT ORCHESTRA PART TWO	*Telstar*	34	*1 Jun 91*	4
Above hit: ELECTRIC LIGHT ORCHESTRA PART TWO.				
THE VERY BEST OF THE ELECTRIC LIGHT ORCHESTRA	*Dino*	4	*2 Jul 94*	11

LIGHT YEARS - THE VERY BEST OF ELECTRIC LIGHT ORCHESTRA	*Epic*	60	*8 Nov 97*	4
ZOOM	*Epic*	34	*23 Jun 01*	2
THE ULTIMATE COLLECTION	*Columbia*	18	*3 Nov 01*	6

ELECTRIC PRUNES — US

SINGLES:	HITS 2			WEEKS 5
I HAD TOO MUCH TO DREAM (LAST NIGHT)	*Reprise*	49	*11 Feb 67*	1
GET ME TO THE WORLD ON TIME	*Reprise*	42	*13 May 67*	4

ELECTRIC SOFT PARADE — UK

SINGLES:	HITS 1			WEEKS 1
EMPTY AT THE END/SUMATRAN *Above hit: SOFT PARADE.*	*DB*	65	*4 Aug 01*	1
THERE'S A SILENCE	*DB*	52	*10 Nov 01*	1

ELECTRIC WIND ENSEMBLE — UK

ALBUMS:	HITS 1			WEEKS 9
HAUNTING MELODIES	*Nouveau Music*	28	*18 Feb 84*	9

ELECTRIQUE BOUTIQUE — UK/France

SINGLES:	HITS 1			WEEKS 2
REVELATION *Originally released on the Continental label in 1999, first re-release on Data reached No. 109 in October 1999.*	*Data*	37	*26 Aug 00*	2

ELECTRONIC — UK

SINGLES:	HITS 8			WEEKS 36
GETTING AWAY WITH IT *Vocals by Neil Tennant (Pet Shop Boys).*	*Factory*	12	*16 Dec 89*	9
GET THE MESSAGE	*Factory*	8	*27 Apr 91*	7
FEEL EVERY BEAT	*Factory*	39	*21 Sep 91*	4
DISAPPOINTED	*Parlophone*	6	*4 Jul 92*	5
FORBIDDEN CITY	*Parlophone*	14	*6 Jul 96*	4
FOR YOU	*Parlophone*	16	*28 Sep 96*	2
SECOND NATURE *Keyboardist is Karl Bartos from Kraftwerk. Denise Johnson provides backing vocals.*	*Parlophone*	35	*15 Feb 97*	2
VIVID	*Parlophone*	17	*24 Apr 99*	3
ALBUMS:	**HITS 3**			**WEEKS 24**
ELECTRONIC	*Factory*	2	*8 Jun 91*	16
RAISE THE PRESSURE	*Parlophone*	8	*20 Jul 96*	5
TWISTED TENDERNESS	*Parlophone*	9	*8 May 99*	3

ELECTRONICA'S — Holland

SINGLES:	HITS 1			WEEKS 8
THE ORIGINAL BIRD DANCE	*Polydor*	22	*19 Sep 81*	8

ELECTROSET — UK

SINGLES:	HITS 2			WEEKS 4
HOW DOES IT FEEL? (THEME FROM TECHNO BLUES) *Based on Blue Monday by New Order.*	*ffrr*	27	*21 Nov 92*	3
SENSATION *Based on New Sensation by INXS.*	*Ffrreedom*	69	*15 Jul 95*	1

ELEGANTS — US

SINGLES:	HITS 1			WEEKS 2
LITTLE STAR	*His Master's Voice*	25	*27 Sep 58*	2

ELEMENTFOUR — UK

SINGLES:	HITS 1			WEEKS 11
BIG BROTHER UK TV THEME *Theme to the Channel 4 TV programme 'Big Brother'.*	*Channel 4 Music*	4	*9 Sep 00*	9
BIG BROTHER UK TV THEME [RE] *Re-entered during the run of 'Big Brother 2'.*	*Channel 4 Music*	63	*4 Aug 01*	2

ELEPHANT'S MEMORY - See John LENNON

ELEVATION — UK

SINGLES:	HITS 1			WEEKS 1
CAN U FEEL IT	*Nova*	62	*23 May 92*	1

ELEVATOR SUITE — UK

SINGLES:	HITS 1			WEEKS 1
EVERYTHING THAT GOES AROUND COMES BACKAROUND	*Infectious*	71	*12 Aug 00*	1

ELEVATORMAN — UK

SINGLES:	HITS 2			WEEKS 4
FUNK AND DRIVE	*Wired*	37	*14 Jan 95*	3
FIRED UP	*Wired*	44	*1 Jul 95*	1

Danny ELFMAN — US

ALBUMS:	HITS 1			WEEKS 6
BATMAN [OST]	*Warner Brothers*	45	*19 Aug 89*	6

ELGINS — US

SINGLES:	HITS 2			WEEKS 20
HEAVEN MUST HAVE SENT YOU	*Tamla Motown*	3	*1 May 71*	13
PUT YOURSELF IN MY PLACE	*Tamla Motown*	28	*9 Oct 71*	7

ELIAS and his ZIG-ZAG JIVE FLUTES — South Africa

SINGLES:	HITS 1			WEEKS 14
TOM HARK	*Columbia*	2	*26 Apr 58*	14
Theme to the TV series 'The Killing Stone'. Tom Hark is South African slang for a police van.				

Yvonne ELLIMAN — US

SINGLES:	HITS 5			WEEKS 44
I DON'T KNOW HOW TO LOVE HIM	*MCA*	47	*29 Jan 72*	1
From the musical 'Jesus Christ Superstar'. This was a maxi-single of which only 2 tracks were listed, this, and Superstar by Murray Head with the Trinidad Singers.				
Above hit: Yvonne ELLIMAN/VARIOUS ARTISTS.				
LOVE ME	*RSO*	6	*6 Nov 76*	13
Originally recorded by the Bee Gees.				
HELLO STRANGER	*RSO*	26	*7 May 77*	5
I CAN'T GET YOU OUTA MY MIND	*RSO*	17	*13 Aug 77*	13
IF I CAN'T HAVE YOU	*RSO*	4	*6 May 78*	12
From the film 'Saturday Night Fever'.				

Duke ELLINGTON — US

SINGLES:	HITS 1			WEEKS 4
SKIN DEEP	*Philips*	7	*6 Mar 54*	4
Above hit: Duke ELLINGTON and his Orchestra (featuring Louis BELLSON, drums).				
ALBUMS:	**HITS 1**			**WEEKS 2**
NUT CRACKER SUITE	*Philips*	11	*8 Apr 61*	2

Lance ELLINGTON — UK

SINGLES:	HITS 1			WEEKS 1
LONELY (HAVE WE LOST OUR LOVE)	*RCA*	57	*21 Aug 93*	1

Ray ELLINGTON with Tony CROMBIE, his Orchestra and Chorus — UK

SINGLES:	HITS 1			WEEKS 4
THE MADISON	*Ember*	41	*17 Nov 62*	2
Originally recorded by Al Brown.				
THE MADISON [RE]	*Ember*	36	*22 Dec 62*	2

Bern ELLIOTT and the FENMEN — UK

SINGLES:	HITS 2			WEEKS 22
MONEY	*Decca*	14	*23 Nov 63*	13
Original by Barrett Strong reached No. 23 in the US in 1960.				
NEW ORLEANS	*Decca*	24	*21 Mar 64*	9
EPS:	**HITS 1**			**WEEKS 5**
BERN ELLIOTT AND THE FENMEN	*Decca*	10	*18 Jan 64*	5

Joe ELLIOTT – See Mick RONSON

Missy "Misdemeanor" ELLIOTT — US

(See also Lil' Kim; Nicole; Timbaland.)

SINGLES:	HITS 10			WEEKS 48
THE RAIN (SUPA DUPA FLY)	*East West*	16	*30 Aug 97*	3
Based around Ann Peebles' I Can't Stand the Rain.				
SOCKIT2ME	*East West*	33	*29 Nov 97*	2
Above hit: Missy Misdemeanor ELLIOTT featuring DA BRAT.				
BEEP ME 911	*East West America*	14	*25 Apr 98*	3
Above hit: Missy Misdemeanor ELLIOTT (featuring 702 and MAGOO).				
HIT 'EM WITH DA HEE	*East West America*	25	*22 Aug 98*	3
Above hit: Missy Misdemeanor ELLIOTT featuring LIL' KIM and MOCHA.				
I WANT YOU BACK	*Virgin*	1	*26 Sep 98*	9
Above hit: Melanie B featuring Missy "Misdemeanor" ELLIOTT.				

5 MINUTES	*East West America*	72	*21 Nov 98*	1
Above 2 from the film 'Why Do Fools Fall In Love'.				
Above hit: LIL 'LIL' MO featuring Missy "Misdemeanor" ELLIOTT.				
ALL N MY GRILL	*Elektra*	20	*25 Sep 99*	4
Above hit: Missy Misdemeanor ELLIOTT featuring MC SOLAAR.				
HOT BOYZ	*Elektra*	18	*22 Jan 00*	3
GET UR FREAK ON	*Elektra*	4	*28 Apr 01*	11
ONE MINUTE MAN	*Elektra*	10	*18 Aug 01*	8
Above hit: "Missy Misdemeanor" ELLIOTT featuring LUDACRIS.				
GET UR FREAK ON [RM]	*Elektra*	72	*13 Oct 01*	1
Remixed by Superchumbo.				
ALBUMS:	**HITS 2**			**WEEKS 16**
DA REAL WORLD	*Elektra*	40	*10 Jul 99*	2
MISS E . . . SO ADDICTIVE	*Elektra*	10	*26 May 01*	14

Greg ELLIS – See Reva RICE and Greg ELLIS

Sophie ELLIS-BEXTOR

SINGLES:	**HITS 3**			**WEEKS 39**
GROOVEJET (IF THIS AIN'T LOVE)	*Positiva*	1	*26 Aug 00*	24
Samples Love Is You by Carol Williams.				
Above hit: SPILLER; Lead vocals by Sophie ELLIS-BEXTOR.				
TAKE ME HOME (A GIRL LIKE ME)	*Polydor*	2	*25 Aug 01*	12
MURDER ON THE DANCEFLOOR	*Polydor*	2	*15 Dec 01*	3
ALBUMS:	**HITS 1**			**WEEKS 8**
READ MY LIPS	*Polydor*	4	*15 Sep 01*	8

Joey B. ELLIS — US

SINGLES:	**HITS 2**			**WEEKS 10**
GO FOR IT! (HEART AND FIRE)	*Capitol*	20	*16 Feb 91*	8
From the film 'Rocky V'.				
Above hit: "ROCKY V" featuring Joey B. ELLIS and Tynetta HARE.				
THOUGHT U WERE THE ONE FOR ME	*Capitol*	58	*18 May 91*	2

Ray ELLIS and his Orchestra – See Johnny MATHIS; Frankie VAUGHAN

Shirley ELLIS — US

SINGLES:	**HITS 2**			**WEEKS 17**
THE CLAPPING SONG	*London*	6	*8 May 65*	13
THE CLAPPING SONG [EP]	*MCA*	59	*8 Jul 78*	4
Lead track: The Clapping Song.				

ELLIS, BEGGS and HOWARD — UK

SINGLES:	**HITS 1**			**WEEKS 8**
BIG BUBBLES, NO TROUBLES	*RCA*	59	*2 Jul 88*	3
BIG BUBBLES, NO TROUBLES [RE]	*RCA*	41	*11 Mar 89*	5
Though listed as a re-entry with same catalogue number, there was also a re-mixed version available.				

Ben ELTON — UK

ALBUMS:	**HITS 1**			**WEEKS 2**
MOTORMOUTH	*Mercury*	86	*14 Nov 87*	2

ELWOOD — US

SINGLES:	**HITS 1**			**WEEKS 1**
SUNDOWN	*Palm Pictures*	72	*26 Aug 00*	1

EMBRACE — UK

SINGLES:	**HITS 11**			**WEEKS 38**
FIREWORKS [EP]	*Hut*	34	*17 May 97*	2
Lead track: The Last Gas.				
ONE BIG FAMILY [EP]	*Hut*	21	*19 Jul 97*	3
Lead track: One Big Family.				
ALL YOU GOOD GOOD PEOPLE [EP]	*Hut*	8	*8 Nov 97*	4
Lead track: All You Good Good People.				
COME BACK TO WHAT YOU KNOW	*Hut*	6	*6 Jun 98*	8
MY WEAKNESS IS NONE OF YOUR BUSINESS	*Hut*	9	*29 Aug 98*	4
HOOLIGAN	*Hut*	18	*13 Nov 99*	3
YOU'RE NOT ALONE	*Hut*	14	*25 Mar 00*	3
SAVE ME	*Hut*	29	*10 Jun 00*	2
SAVE ME [RE]	*Hut*	67	*15 Jul 00*	1
I WOULDN'T WANNA HAPPEN TO YOU	*Hut*	23	*19 Aug 00*	2
WONDER	*Hut*	14	*1 Sep 01*	3
WONDER [RE]	*Hut*	59	*13 Oct 01*	1
MAKE IT LAST	*Hut*	35	*17 Nov 01*	2

ALBUMS:	HITS 3			WEEKS 37
THE GOOD WILL OUT	*Hut*	1	*20 Jun 98*	21
DRAWN FROM MEMORY	*Hut*	8	*8 Apr 00*	13
IF YOU'VE NEVER BEEN	*Hut*	9	*15 Sep 01*	3

EMERALD EXPRESS – See DEXY'S MIDNIGHT RUNNERS

Keith EMERSON — UK

(See also Emerson, Lake and Palmer; Emerson, Lake and Powell.)

SINGLES:	HITS 1			WEEKS 5
HONKY TONK TRAIN BLUES *Originally recorded by Meade Lux Lewis.*	*Manticore*	21	*10 Apr 76*	5

EMERSON, LAKE and PALMER — UK

(See also Keith Emerson; Emerson, Lake and Powell; Greg Lake.)

SINGLES:	HITS 1			WEEKS 13
FANFARE FOR THE COMMON MAN	*Atlantic*	2	*4 Jun 77*	13

ALBUMS:	HITS 9			WEEKS 135
EMERSON, LAKE AND PALMER	*Island*	4	*5 Dec 70*	28
TARKUS	*Island*	1	*19 Jun 71*	17
PICTURES AT AN EXHIBITION *Live recordings from the City Hall, Newcastle, 26 Mar 71*	*Island*	3	*4 Dec 71*	5
TRILOGY	*Island*	2	*8 Jul 72*	29
BRAIN SALAD SURGERY	*Manticore*	2	*22 Dec 73*	17
WELCOME BACK MY FRIENDS TO THE SHOW THAT NEVER ENDS – LADIES AND GENTLEMEN: EMERSON, LAKE AND PALMER *Live recordings.*	*Manticore*	5	*24 Aug 74*	5
WORKS	*Atlantic*	9	*9 Apr 77*	25
WORKS VOLUME 2 *Above 2 were essentially solo recordings.*	*Atlantic*	20	*10 Dec 77*	5
LOVE BEACH	*Atlantic*	48	*9 Dec 78*	4

EMERSON, LAKE and POWELL — UK

(See also Keith Emerson; Emerson, Lake and Powell; Cozy Powell.)

ALBUMS:	HITS 1			WEEKS 5
EMERSON, LAKE AND POWELL	*Polydor*	35	*14 Jun 86*	5

Dick EMERY — UK

SINGLES:	HITS 2			WEEKS 8
IF YOU LOVE HER	*Pye*	32	*1 Mar 69*	4
YOU ARE AWFUL (BUT I LIKE YOU)	*Pye*	43	*13 Jan 73*	4

EMF — UK

SINGLES:	HITS 10			WEEKS 50
UNBELIEVABLE	*Parlophone*	3	*3 Nov 90*	13
I BELIEVE	*Parlophone*	6	*2 Feb 91*	7
CHILDREN	*Parlophone*	19	*27 Apr 91*	5
LIES	*Parlophone*	28	*31 Aug 91*	3
UNEXPLAINED [EP] *Lead track: Getting Through.*	*Parlophone*	18	*2 May 92*	4
THEY'RE HERE	*Parlophone*	29	*19 Sep 92*	3
IT'S YOU	*Parlophone*	23	*21 Nov 92*	3
PERFECT DAY	*Parlophone*	27	*25 Feb 95*	3
I'M A BELIEVER *Above hit: EMF and REEVES and MORTIMER.*	*Parlophone*	3	*8 Jul 95*	8
AFRO KING	*Parlophone*	51	*28 Oct 95*	1

ALBUMS:	HITS 3			WEEKS 22
SCHUBERT DIP	*Parlophone*	3	*18 May 91*	19
STIGMA	*Parlophone*	19	*10 Oct 92*	2
CHA CHA CHA	*Parlophone*	30	*18 Mar 95*	1

EMILIA — Sweden

SINGLES:	HITS 2			WEEKS 14
BIG BIG WORLD	*Universal*	5	*12 Dec 98*	13
GOOD SIGN	*Universal*	54	*1 May 99*	1

EMINEM — US

(See also Bad Meets Evil featuring Eminem and Royce Da 5'9".)

SINGLES:	HITS 6			WEEKS 70
MY NAME IS *Samples Labi Siffre's I Got The.*	*Interscope*	2	*10 Apr 99*	11
MY NAME IS [RE]	*Interscope*	68	*24 Jul 99*	1

GUILTY CONSCIENCE *Samples the track Go Home Pigs. From the film 'Getting Straight'.* *Above hit: EMINEM featuring DR. DRE.*	*Interscope*	5	*14 Aug 99*	8
FORGET ABOUT DRE *Above hit: DR. DRE featuring EMINEM.*	*Interscope*	7	*10 Jun 00*	9
THE REAL SLIM SHADY	*Interscope*	1	*8 Jul 00*	15
THE WAY I AM	*Interscope*	8	*14 Oct 00*	9
STAN *Samples Dido's Thank You.*	*Interscope*	1	*16 Dec 00*	16
STAN [RE]	*Interscope*	74	*21 Apr 01*	1
ALBUMS:	**HITS 2**			**WEEKS 172**
THE SLIM SHADY LP *Available as an explicit vocal or clean version.*	*Interscope*	12	*24 Apr 99*	35
THE SLIM SHADY LP [RE]	*Interscope*	10	*4 Mar 00*	73
THE MARSHALL MATHERS LP	*Interscope*	1	*3 Jun 00*	64

EMMA — UK

SINGLES:	**HITS 1**			**WEEKS 6**
GIVE A LITTLE LOVE BACK TO THE WORLD *UK's Eurovision entry in 1990, it came 6th.*	*Big Wave*	33	*28 Apr 90*	6

Ivor EMMANUEL — UK

EPS:	**HITS 1**			**WEEKS 5**
LAND OF SONG	*Delyse*	13	*21 Jan 61*	5

Stephen EMMANUEL – See COLOURS featuring Stephen EMMANUEL and ESKA; EN-CORE featuring ESKA and Stephen EMMANUEL

EMMIE — UK

SINGLES:	**HITS 1**			**WEEKS 8**
MORE THAN THIS	*Manifesto*	5	*23 Jan 99*	8

An EMOTIONAL FISH — Ireland

SINGLES:	**HITS 1**			**WEEKS 5**
CELEBRATE	*East West*	46	*23 Jun 90*	5
ALBUMS:	**HITS 1**			**WEEKS 3**
AN EMOTIONAL FISH	*East West*	40	*25 Aug 90*	3

EMOTIONS — US

SINGLES:	**HITS 3**			**WEEKS 28**
BEST OF MY LOVE	*CBS*	4	*10 Sep 77*	10
I DON'T WANNA LOSE YOUR LOVE	*CBS*	40	*24 Dec 77*	5
BOOGIE WONDERLAND *Above hit: EARTH, WIND AND FIRE with the EMOTIONS.*	*CBS*	4	*12 May 79*	13

EMPIRION — UK

SINGLES:	**HITS 2**			**WEEKS 2**
NARCOTIC INFLUENCE	*XL Recordings*	64	*6 Jul 96*	1
BETA	*XL Recordings*	75	*21 Jun 97*	1

EN-CORE featuring ESKA and Stephen EMMANUEL — UK

SINGLES:	**HITS 1**			**WEEKS 2**
COOCHY-COO	*VC Recordings*	32	*9 Sep 00*	2

EN VOGUE — US

SINGLES:	**HITS 13**			**WEEKS 83**
HOLD ON *Samples James Brown' The Payback.*	*Atlantic*	5	*5 May 90*	11
LIES	*Atlantic*	44	*21 Jul 90*	4
MY LOVIN'	*East West America*	69	*4 Apr 92*	3
MY LOVIN' [RE]	*East West America*	4	*9 May 92*	9
GIVING HIM SOMETHING HE CAN FEEL *Originally recorded by Aretha Franklin as Something He Can Feel.*	*East West America*	44	*15 Aug 92*	3
FREE YOUR MIND / GIVING HIM SOMETHING HE CAN FEEL [RI]	*East West America*	16	*7 Nov 92*	8
GIVE IT UP, TURN IT LOOSE	*East West America*	22	*16 Jan 93*	4
LOVE DON'T LOVE YOU	*East West America*	64	*10 Apr 93*	1
RUNAWAY LOVE	*East West America*	36	*9 Oct 93*	3
WHATTA MAN *Originally recorded by Linda Lyndell.* *Above hit: SALT 'N' PEPA with EN VOGUE.*	*ffrr*	7	*19 Mar 94*	10
DON'T LET GO (LOVE) *From the film 'Set It Off'. Backing vocals by Mariah Carey, saxophone by Kenny G.*	*East West America*	5	*11 Jan 97*	16
WHATEVER	*East West America*	14	*14 Jun 97*	5
TOO GONE, TOO LONG	*East West America*	20	*6 Sep 97*	3

Title	Label	Pos	Date	Wks
HOLD ON [RM]	*East West America*	53	*28 Nov 98*	1
Remixed by Tuff Jam.				
RIDDLE	*Elektra*	33	*1 Jul 00*	2
ALBUMS:	**HITS 4**			**WEEKS 52**
BORN TO SING	*Atlantic*	23	*2 Jun 90*	13
FUNKY DIVAS	*East West America*	26	*23 May 92*	10
FUNKY DIVAS [RE]	*East West America*	4	*16 Jan 93*	19
EV3	*East West America*	9	*28 Jun 97*	8
BEST OF EN VOGUE	*East West America*	39	*31 Oct 98*	2

ENCORE — France

SINGLES:	**HITS 1**			**WEEKS 4**
LE DISC JOCKEY	*Sum*	12	*14 Feb 98*	4

ENERGISE — UK

SINGLES:	**HITS 1**			**WEEKS 1**
REPORT TO THE DANCEFLOOR	*Network*	69	*16 Feb 91*	1

ENERGY 52 — Germany

SINGLES:	**HITS 1**			**WEEKS 7**
CAFE DEL MAR	*Hooj Choons*	51	*8 Mar 97*	1
CAFE DEL MAR '98 [RI]	*Hooj Choons*	12	*25 Jul 98*	6
Though listed as a remix, the lead track of the CD format is a straight re-issue.				

ENERGY ORCHARD — Ireland

SINGLES:	**HITS 2**			**WEEKS 6**
BELFAST	*MCA*	52	*27 Jan 90*	4
SAILORTOWN	*MCA*	73	*7 Apr 90*	2
ALBUMS:	**HITS 1**			**WEEKS 2**
ENERGY ORCHARD	*MCA*	53	*12 May 90*	2

Harry ENFIELD — UK

SINGLES:	**HITS 1**			**WEEKS 7**
LOADSAMONEY (DOIN' UP THE HOUSE)	*Mercury*	4	*7 May 88*	7

ENGLAND DAN and John Ford COLEY — US

SINGLES:	**HITS 2**			**WEEKS 12**
I'D REALLY LOVE TO SEE YOU TONIGHT	*Atlantic*	26	*25 Sep 76*	7
LOVE IS THE ANSWER	*Big Tree*	45	*23 Jun 79*	5
Originally recorded by Utopia.				

ENGLAND RUGBY WORLD CUP SQUAD – See UNION

ENGLAND SISTERS — UK

SINGLES:	**HITS 1**			**WEEKS 1**
HEARTBEAT	*His Master's Voice*	33	*19 Mar 60*	1

ENGLAND SUPPORTERS BAND — UK

SINGLES:	**HITS 2**			**WEEKS 4**
THE GREAT ESCAPE	*V2*	46	*27 Jun 98*	2
THE GREAT ESCAPE 2000 [RR]	*V2*	26	*24 Jun 00*	2

ENGLAND UNITED — UK

SINGLES:	**HITS 1**			**WEEKS 11**
(HOW DOES IT FEEL TO BE) ON TOP OF THE WORLD	*London*	9	*13 Jun 98*	9
The official song of the 1998 England World Cup Team.				
Above hit: ENGLAND UNITED : ECHO & THE BUNNYMEN, OCEAN COLOUR SCENE, SPACE, SPICE GIRLS.				
(HOW DOES IT FEEL TO BE) ON TOP OF THE WORLD [RE]	*London*	61	*22 Aug 98*	2

ENGLAND WORLD CUP SQUAD — UK

SINGLES:	**HITS 5**			**WEEKS 46**
BACK HOME	*Pye*	1	*18 Apr 70*	16
Above hit: ENGLAND WORLD CUP SQUAD "70".				
BACK HOME [RE]	*Pye*	46	*15 Aug 70*	1
THIS TIME (WE'LL GET IT RIGHT) / ENGLAND, WE'LL FLY THE FLAG	*England*	2	*10 Apr 82*	13
WE'VE GOT THE WHOLE WORLD AT OUR FEET / WHEN WE ARE FAR FROM HOME	*Columbia*	66	*19 Apr 86*	2
Above hit: ENGLAND WORLD CUP SQUAD 1986.				
ALL THE WAY	*MCA*	64	*21 May 88*	2
Above hit: ENGLAND FOOTBALL TEAM with the 'Sound' Of STOCK, AITKEN and WATERMAN				

WORLD IN MOTION . . . *New Order and the England World Cup Squad for Italia 1990.* *Above hit: ENGLANDNEWORDER.*	*Factory*	1	*2 Jun 90*	12
ALBUMS:	**HITS 2**			**WEEKS 18**
THE WORLD BEATERS SING THE WORLD BEATERS *Above hit: ENGLAND FOOTBALL WORLD CUP SQUAD 1970.*	*Pye*	4	*16 May 70*	8
THIS TIME	*K-Tel*	37	*15 May 82*	10

ENGLAND'S BARMY ARMY — UK

SINGLES:	**HITS 1**			**WEEKS 1**
COME ON ENGLAND! *A reworking of Booker T. & the MGs' Soul Limbo by supporters of the England World Cup cricket squad.*	*Wildstar*	45	*12 Jun 99*	1

Kim ENGLISH — US

SINGLES:	**HITS 4**			**WEEKS 7**
NITE LIFE	*Hi-Life*	35	*23 Jul 94*	2
TIME FOR LOVE	*Hi-Life*	48	*4 Mar 95*	1
I KNOW A PLACE	*Hi-Life*	52	*9 Sep 95*	1
NITE LIFE [RM] *Remixed by J.T. Vannelli.*	*Hi-Life*	35	*30 Nov 96*	2
SUPERNATURAL	*Hi-Life*	50	*26 Apr 97*	1

Scott ENGLISH — US

SINGLES:	**HITS 1**			**WEEKS 10**
BRANDY	*Horse*	12	*9 Oct 71*	10

ENGLISH CHAMBER CHOIR - See Roger DALTREY; Rick WAKEMAN

ENGLISH CHAMBER ORCHESTRA — UK

(See also Nigel Kennedy; Andrew Lloyd Webber; Kiri Te Kanawa; John Williams.)

ALBUMS:	**HITS 1**			**WEEKS 1**
THE BEYONDNESS OF THINGS *Above hit: ENGLISH CHAMBER ORCHESTRA conducted by John BARRY.*	*Decca*	67	*8 May 99*	1

ENIAC - See Tom NOVY

ENIGMA — UK

SINGLES:	**HITS 2**			**WEEKS 15**
AIN'T NO STOPPING - DISCO MIX '81 [M]	*Creole*	11	*23 May 81*	8
I LOVE MUSIC [M] *Above 2 are segued tracks of disco hits.*	*Creole*	25	*8 Aug 81*	7
ALBUMS:	**HITS 1**			**WEEKS 3**
AIN'T NO STOPPIN'	*Creole*	80	*5 Sep 81*	3

ENIGMA — Romania/Germany

SINGLES:	**HITS 9**			**WEEKS 45**
SADNESS PART 1	*Virgin International*	1	*15 Dec 90*	12
MEA CULPA PART II	*Virgin International*	55	*30 Mar 91*	3
PRINCIPLES OF LUST	*Virgin International*	59	*10 Aug 91*	2
THE RIVERS OF BELIEF	*Virgin International*	68	*11 Jan 92*	2
RETURN TO INNOCENCE	*Virgin*	3	*29 Jan 94*	14
THE EYES OF TRUTH	*Virgin*	21	*14 May 94*	4
AGE OF LONELINESS *From the film 'Sliver'.*	*Virgin*	21	*20 Aug 94*	5
BEYOND THE INVISIBLE	*Virgin*	26	*25 Jan 97*	2
T.N.T. FOR THE BRAIN	*Virgin*	60	*19 Apr 97*	1
ALBUMS:	**HITS 5**			**WEEKS 140**
MCMXC A.D.	*Virgin International*	1	*22 Dec 90*	57
MCMXC A.D. [RI]	*Virgin*	38	*22 Jan 94*	26
THE CROSS OF CHANGES *Above hit: ENIGMA 2.*	*Virgin*	1	*19 Feb 94*	35
LE ROI EST MORT, VIVE LE ROI!	*Virgin*	12	*7 Dec 96*	12
THE SCREEN BEHIND THE MIRROR	*Virgin*	7	*29 Jan 00*	6
LOVE SENSUALITY DEVOTION - GREATEST HITS	*Virgin*	29	*17 Nov 01*	4

Brian ENO — UK

(See also 808 State; Brian Eno and David Byrne; Brian Eno and Jah Wobble.)

ALBUMS:	**HITS 5**			**WEEKS 7**
HERE COME THE WARM JETS	*Island*	26	*9 Mar 74*	2
MUSIC FOR FILMS	*Polydor*	55	*21 Oct 78*	1
AMBIENT 4 ON LAND	*E'G*	93	*8 May 82*	1
NERVE NET	*Opal*	70	*12 Sep 92*	1

WAH WAH	*Fontana*	11	*24 Sep 94*	2
Though credited, Eno is more the producer/ remixer on the album. Consists of re-workings/ alternate versions/ studio jams recorded by James at the same time as their Laid album.				
Above hit: JAMES and Brian ENO.				

Brian ENO and David BYRNE — UK

(See also David Byrne; Brian Eno.)

ALBUMS:	HITS 1			WEEKS 8
MY LIFE IN THE BUSH OF GHOSTS	*E'G*	29	*21 Feb 81*	8

Brian ENO and Jah WOBBLE — UK

(See also Brian Eno; Jah Wobble's Invaders Of The Heart.)

ALBUMS:	HITS 1			WEEKS 1
SPINNER	*All Saints*	71	*14 Oct 95*	1
Music composed by Eno and remixed by Wobble. Several tracks are from the film 'Glitterbug'.				

ENRICO - See Marc VAN DALE with ENRICO

Jocelyn ENRIQUEZ - See STARS ON 54: Ultra NATE, AMBER, Jocelyn ENRIQUEZ

ENTOMBED — Sweden

ALBUMS:	HITS 1			WEEKS 1
TO RIDE, SHOOT STRAIGHT AND SPEAK THE TRUTH	*Threeman Recordings*	75	*15 Mar 97*	1

ENUFF Z'NUFF — US

ALBUMS:	HITS 1			WEEKS 1
STRENGTH	*Atco*	56	*13 Apr 91*	1

ENYA — Ireland

SINGLES:	HITS 12			WEEKS 63
ORINOCO FLOW (SAIL AWAY)	*WEA*	1	*15 Oct 88*	13
EVENING FALLS . . .	*WEA*	20	*24 Dec 88*	4
STORMS IN AFRICA (PART II)	*WEA*	41	*10 Jun 89*	4
CARIBBEAN BLUE	*WEA*	13	*19 Oct 91*	7
HOW CAN I KEEP FROM SINGING?	*WEA*	32	*7 Dec 91*	5
BOOK OF DAYS	*WEA*	10	*1 Aug 92*	6
From the film 'Far and Away'.				
THE CELTS	*WEA*	29	*14 Nov 92*	4
ANYWHERE IS	*WEA*	7	*18 Nov 95*	12
ON MY WAY HOME	*WEA*	26	*7 Dec 96*	2
ONLY IF . . .	*WEA*	43	*13 Dec 97*	2
ONLY TIME	*WEA*	32	*25 Nov 00*	3
From the film 'Sweet November'.				
WILD CHILD	*WEA*	72	*31 Mar 01*	1
ALBUMS:	**HITS 6**			**WEEKS 274**
ENYA [OST-TV]	*BBC*	69	*6 Jun 87*	4
Music from the TV series 'The Celts'.				
WATERMARK	*WEA*	5	*15 Oct 88*	92
Includes re-entries through to 1994.				
SHEPHERD MOONS	*WEA*	1	*16 Nov 91*	90
THE CELTS [RI]	*WEA*	10	*28 Nov 92*	19
Repackaged version of her debut album. Includes re-entry in 1998.				
THE MEMORY OF TREES	*WEA*	5	*2 Dec 95*	24
PAINT THE SKY WITH STARS - THE BEST OF ENYA	*WEA*	4	*15 Nov 97*	28
A DAY WITHOUT RAIN	*WEA*	6	*2 Dec 00*	17

EON — UK

SINGLES:	HITS 1			WEEKS 1
FEAR: THE MINDKILLER [EP]	*Vinyl Solution*	63	*17 Aug 91*	1
Lead track: Fear (Prologue).				

EPMD — US

SINGLES:	HITS 1			WEEKS 1
STRICTLY BUSINESS	*Parlophone*	43	*15 Aug 98*	1
Samples Eric Clapton's I Shot the Sheriff.				
Above hit: MANTRONIK vs EPMD.				
ALBUMS:	**HITS 1**			**WEEKS 1**
BUSINESS AS USUAL	*Def Jam*	69	*16 Feb 91*	1
Above hit: E.P.M.D.				

EQ - See VARIOUS ARTISTS (EPs) 'Fourplay Volume 1 EP'

EQUALS
UK/Guyana

SINGLES:	HITS 8			WEEKS 69
I GET SO EXCITED •	*President*	44	*24 Feb 68*	4
BABY COME BACK •	*President*	50	*4 May 68*	1
BABY COME BACK [RE]	*President*	1	*18 May 68*	17
LAUREL AND HARDY	*President*	35	*24 Aug 68*	5
SOFTLY SOFTLY	*President*	48	*30 Nov 68*	3
MICHAEL AND THE SLIPPER TREE	*President*	24	*5 Apr 69*	7
VIVA BOBBY JOE	*President*	6	*2 Aug 69*	14
RUB A DUB DUB	*President*	34	*27 Dec 69*	7
BLACK SKIN BLUE EYED BOYS •	*President*	9	*19 Dec 70*	11

ALBUMS:	HITS 2			WEEKS 10
UNEQUALLED EQUALS	*President*	10	*18 Nov 67*	9
EQUALS EXPLOSION	*President*	32	*9 Mar 68*	1

ERASURE
UK

SINGLES:	HITS 26			WEEKS 203
WHO NEEDS LOVE LIKE THAT	*Mute*	55	*5 Oct 85*	2
SOMETIMES	*Mute*	2	*25 Oct 86*	17
IT DOESN'T HAVE TO BE	*Mute*	12	*28 Feb 87*	9
VICTIM OF LOVE	*Mute*	7	*30 May 87*	9
THE CIRCUS	*Mute*	6	*3 Oct 87*	10
SHIP OF FOOLS	*Mute*	6	*5 Mar 88*	8
CHAINS OF LOVE	*Mute*	11	*11 Jun 88*	7
A LITTLE RESPECT	*Mute*	4	*1 Oct 88*	10
CRACKERS INTERNATIONAL [EP]	*Mute*	2	*10 Dec 88*	13
Lead track: Stop!				
DRAMA!	*Mute*	4	*30 Sep 89*	8
YOU SURROUND ME	*Mute*	15	*9 Dec 89*	9
BLUE SAVANNAH	*Mute*	3	*10 Mar 90*	10
STAR	*Mute*	11	*2 Jun 90*	7
CHORUS	*Mute*	3	*29 Jun 91*	9
LOVE TO HATE YOU	*Mute*	4	*21 Sep 91*	9
AM I RIGHT?	*Mute*	15	*7 Dec 91*	6
AM I RIGHT? [RM]	*Mute*	22	*11 Jan 92*	3
The remix entry was a 2nd 12"/CD format. As chart rules allowed only 4 formats, it was listed separately.				
BREATH OF LIFE	*Mute*	8	*28 Mar 92*	6
ABBA-ESQUE [EP]	*Mute*	1	*13 Jun 92*	12
Lead track: Lay All Your Love On Me, though all 4 tracks received airplay. Take A Chance On Me featured a rap by MC Kinky.				
WHO NEEDS LOVE (LIKE THAT) [RM]	*Mute*	10	*7 Nov 92*	4
Remixed by Dave Bascombe and Erasure.				
ALWAYS	*Mute*	4	*23 Apr 94*	9
RUN TO THE SUN	*Mute*	6	*30 Jul 94*	5
I LOVE SATURDAY	*Mute*	20	*3 Dec 94*	6
STAY WITH ME	*Mute*	15	*23 Sep 95*	4
FINGERS & THUMBS (COLD SUMMER'S DAY)	*Mute*	20	*9 Dec 95*	3
IN MY ARMS	*Mute*	13	*18 Jan 97*	4
DON'T SAY YOUR LOVE IS KILLING ME	*Mute*	23	*8 Mar 97*	2
FREEDOM	*Mute*	27	*21 Oct 00*	2

ALBUMS:	HITS 10			WEEKS 316
WONDERLAND	*Mute*	71	*14 Jun 86*	7
THE CIRCUS	*Mute*	6	*11 Apr 87*	107
THE INNOCENTS	*Mute*	1	*30 Apr 88*	78
WILD!	*Mute*	1	*28 Oct 89*	48
CHORUS	*Mute*	1	*26 Oct 91*	25
POP! - THE FIRST 20 HITS	*Mute*	1	*28 Nov 92*	26
I SAY I SAY I SAY	*Mute*	1	*28 May 94*	15
ERASURE	*Mute*	14	*4 Nov 95*	5
COWBOY	*Mute*	10	*12 Apr 97*	4
LOVEBOAT	*Mute*	45	*4 Nov 00*	1

ERIC and BILLY - See S-EXPRESS

ERIC and the GOOD GOOD FEELING
UK

(See also S-Express.)

SINGLES:	HITS 1			WEEKS 1
GOOD GOOD FEELING	*Equinox*	73	*3 Jun 89*	1

ERIK
UK

SINGLES:	HITS 3			WEEKS 5
LOOKS LIKE I'M IN LOVE AGAIN	*PWL Sanctuary*	46	*10 Apr 93*	2
Above hit: KEY WEST featuring ERIK.				
GOT TO BE REAL	*PWL International*	42	*29 Jan 94*	2
WE GOT THE LOVE	*PWL International*	55	*1 Oct 94*	1

ERIN - See BBG; SHUT UP AND DANCE

ERIRE - See SCIENCE DEPT. featuring ERIRE

EROTIC DRUM BAND — Canada

SINGLES:	HITS 1		WEEKS 3	
LOVE DISCO STYLE	*Scope*	47	*9 Jun 79*	3

ERUPTION — UK

SINGLES:	HITS 2		WEEKS 21	
I CAN'T STAND THE RAIN	*Atlantic*	5	*18 Feb 78*	11
Originally recorded by Ann Peebles. Some copies do not credit Precious Wilson.				
Above hit: ERUPTION featuring Precious WILSON.				
ONE WAY TICKET	*Atlantic*	9	*21 Apr 79*	10
Originally recorded by Neil Sedaka in 1959 (B-side to Oh! Carol).				

Nas ESCOBAR - See Nas ESCOBAR, Foxy BROWN, AZ and NATURE present the FIRM featuring Dawn ROBINSON

Shaun ESCOFFERY — UK

SINGLES:	HITS 1		WEEKS 1	
SPACE RIDER	*Oyster Music*	52	*10 Mar 01*	1

ESCORTS — UK

SINGLES:	HITS 1		WEEKS 2	
THE ONE TO CRY	*Fontana*	49	*4 Jul 64*	2

ESCRIMA — UK

SINGLES:	HITS 2		WEEKS 4	
TRAIN OF THOUGHT	*Ffrreedom*	36	*11 Feb 95*	2
Features a sample from King Bee's Back By Dope Demand.				
DEEPER	*Hooj Choons*	27	*7 Oct 95*	2

ESKA - See COLOURS featuring Stephen EMMANUEL and ESKA; EN-CORE featuring ESKA and Stephen EMMANUEL; Nitin SAWHNEY

ESKIMOS AND EGYPT — UK

SINGLES:	HITS 2		WEEKS 4	
FALL FROM GRACE	*One Little Indian*	51	*13 Feb 93*	2
UK - USA	*One Little Indian*	52	*29 May 93*	2

ESPIRITU — UK/France

SINGLES:	HITS 4		WEEKS 10	
CONQUISTADOR	*Heavenly*	47	*6 Mar 93*	2
LOS AMERICANOS	*Heavenly*	45	*7 Aug 93*	2
BONITA MANANA	*Columbia*	50	*20 Aug 94*	1
ALWAYS SOMETHING THERE TO REMIND ME	*WEA*	14	*25 Mar 95*	5
Above hit: TIN TIN OUT featuring ESPIRITU.				

ESSENCE — UK

SINGLES:	HITS 1		WEEKS 2	
THE PROMISE	*Innocent*	27	*21 Mar 98*	2

ESSEX — US

SINGLES:	HITS 1		WEEKS 5	
EASIER SAID THAN DONE	*Columbia*	41	*10 Aug 63*	5

David ESSEX — UK

SINGLES:	HITS 25		WEEKS 199	
ROCK ON	*CBS*	3	*18 Aug 73*	11
LAMPLIGHT	*CBS*	7	*10 Nov 73*	15
AMERICA	*CBS*	32	*11 May 74*	5
GONNA MAKE YOU A STAR	*CBS*	1	*12 Oct 74*	17
STARDUST	*CBS*	7	*14 Dec 74*	10
From the film of the same name.				
ROLLING STONE	*CBS*	5	*5 Jul 75*	7
HOLD ME CLOSE	*CBS*	1	*13 Sep 75*	10
IF I COULD	*CBS*	13	*6 Dec 75*	8
CITY LIGHTS	*CBS*	24	*20 Mar 76*	4
COMING HOME	*CBS*	24	*16 Oct 76*	6
COOL OUT TONIGHT	*CBS*	23	*17 Sep 77*	6
STAY WITH ME BABY	*CBS*	45	*11 Mar 78*	5
OH WHAT A CIRCUS	*Mercury*	3	*19 Aug 78*	11
BRAVE NEW WORLD	*CBS*	55	*21 Oct 78*	3
Above hit: featuring the vocal performance of David ESSEX from Jeff WAYNE'S "THE WAR OF THE WORLDS".				

IMPERIAL WIZARD	*Mercury*	32	*3 Mar 79*	8
SILVER DREAM MACHINE	*Mercury*	4	*5 Apr 80*	11
From the film 'Silver Dream Racer'.				
HOT LOVE	*Mercury*	57	*14 Jun 80*	4
ME AND MY GIRL (NIGHT-CLUBBING)	*Mercury*	13	*26 Jun 82*	10
A WINTER'S TALE	*Mercury*	2	*11 Dec 82*	10
THE SMILE	*Mercury*	52	*4 Jun 83*	4
TAHITI	*Mercury*	8	*27 Aug 83*	11
From the musical 'Mutiny On The Bounty'.				
YOU'RE IN MY HEART	*Mercury*	67	*26 Nov 83*	2
YOU'RE IN MY HEART [RE]	*Mercury*	59	*17 Dec 83*	4
FALLING ANGELS RIDING	*Mercury*	29	*23 Feb 85*	7
MYFANWY	*Arista*	41	*18 Apr 87*	7
From the musical 'Betjeman'.				
TRUE LOVE WAYS	*PolyGram TV*	38	*26 Nov 94*	3
Above hit: David ESSEX and Catherine Zeta JONES.				

ALBUMS:	**HITS 20**			**WEEKS 178**
ROCK ON	*CBS*	7	*24 Nov 73*	22
DAVID ESSEX	*CBS*	2	*19 Oct 74*	24
ALL THE FUN OF THE FAIR	*CBS*	3	*27 Sep 75*	20
ON TOUR	*CBS*	51	*5 Jun 76*	1
OUT ON THE STREET	*CBS*	31	*30 Oct 76*	9
GOLD AND IVORY	*CBS*	29	*8 Oct 77*	4
THE DAVID ESSEX ALBUM	*CBS*	29	*6 Jan 79*	7
IMPERIAL WIZARD	*Mercury*	12	*31 Mar 79*	9
HOT LOVE	*Mercury*	75	*12 Jul 80*	1
STAGE-STRUCK	*Mercury*	31	*19 Jun 82*	15
THE VERY BEST OF DAVID ESSEX	*TV Records*	37	*27 Nov 82*	11
MUTINY (STUDIO CAST RECORDING)	*Mercury*	39	*15 Oct 83*	4
This show was not staged until 1985.				
Above hit: David ESSEX, Frank FINLAY and VARIOUS ARTISTS.				
THE WHISPER	*Mercury*	67	*17 Dec 83*	6
CENTRE STAGE	*K-Tel*	82	*6 Dec 86*	4
HIS GREATEST HITS	*Mercury*	13	*19 Oct 91*	13
COVER SHOT	*PolyGram TV*	3	*10 Apr 93*	8
BACK TO BACK	*PolyGram TV*	33	*22 Oct 94*	2
MISSING YOU	*PolyGram TV*	26	*9 Dec 95*	9
A NIGHT AT THE MOVIES	*PolyGram TV*	14	*17 May 97*	5
Features the Royal Philharmonic Orchestra.				
GREATEST HITS	*PolyGram TV*	31	*13 Jun 98*	4

Gloria ESTEFAN US

SINGLES:	**HITS 32**			**WEEKS 207**
DR. BEAT	*Epic*	6	*11 Aug 84*	14
BAD BOY	*Epic*	16	*17 May 86*	11
Above 2: MIAMI SOUND MACHINE.				
ANYTHING FOR YOU	*Epic*	10	*16 Jul 88*	16
1-2-3	*Epic*	9	*22 Oct 88*	9
RHYTHM IS GONNA GET YOU	*Epic*	16	*17 Dec 88*	9
1-2-3 [RE]	*Epic*	72	*31 Dec 88*	1
CAN'T STAY AWAY FROM YOU	*Epic*	7	*11 Feb 89*	12
Originally reached No. 88 in 1988.				
Above 5: Gloria ESTEFAN and MIAMI SOUND MACHINE.				
DON'T WANNA LOSE YOU	*Epic*	6	*15 Jul 89*	10
OYE MI CANTO (HEAR MY VOICE)	*Epic*	16	*16 Sep 89*	8
GET ON YOUR FEET	*Epic*	23	*25 Nov 89*	7
HERE WE ARE	*Epic*	23	*3 Mar 90*	6
CUTS BOTH WAYS	*Epic*	49	*26 May 90*	5
COMING OUT OF THE DARK	*Epic*	25	*26 Jan 91*	5
Backing vocals by Jon Secada and Betty Wright.				
SEAL OUR FATE	*Epic*	24	*6 Apr 91*	7
REMEMBER ME WITH LOVE	*Epic*	22	*8 Jun 91*	6
LIVE FOR LOVING YOU	*Epic*	33	*21 Sep 91*	5
ALWAYS TOMORROW	*Epic*	24	*24 Oct 92*	4
MIAMI HIT MIX [M] / CHRISTMAS THROUGH YOUR EYES	*Epic*	8	*12 Dec 92*	9
Medley of 5 earlier hits. Christmas Through Your Eyes listed from 19 Dec 92.				
I SEE YOUR SMILE	*Epic*	48	*13 Feb 93*	2
GO AWAY	*Epic*	13	*3 Apr 93*	6
MI TIERRA	*Epic*	36	*3 Jul 93*	3
IF WE WERE LOVERS / CON LOS ANOS QUE ME QUEDAN	*Epic*	40	*14 Aug 93*	3
MONTUNO	*Epic*	55	*18 Dec 93*	2
TURN THE BEAT AROUND	*Epic*	21	*15 Oct 94*	6
From the film 'The Specialist'. Original by Vicki Sue Robinson reached No. 10 in the US in 1976.				
HOLD ME, THRILL ME, KISS ME	*Epic*	11	*3 Dec 94*	10
Originally recorded by Harry Noble and his Orchestra.				
EVERLASTING LOVE	*Epic*	19	*18 Feb 95*	5
HOLD ME, THRILL ME, KISS ME [RE]	*Epic*	68	*18 Mar 95*	1

REACH *The official anthem of the Atlanta 1996 Olympic Games.*	*Epic*	15	*25 May 96*	6
REACH [RE-1ST]	*Epic*	68	*3 Aug 96*	1
REACH [RE-2ND]	*Epic*	55	*17 Aug 96*	1
YOU'LL BE MINE (PARTY TIME) *Performed at the closing ceremony of the 1996 Olympic Games.*	*Epic*	18	*24 Aug 96*	3
I'M NOT GIVING YOU UP	*Epic*	28	*14 Dec 96*	3
HEAVEN'S WHAT I FEEL	*Epic*	17	*6 Jun 98*	4
OYE	*Epic*	33	*10 Oct 98*	2
DON'T LET THIS MOMENT END *Above 2: GLORIA!*	*Epic*	28	*16 Jan 99*	2
MUSIC OF MY HEART *Above hit: 'NSYNC Gloria ESTEFAN.*	*Epic*	34	*8 Jan 00*	3
ALBUMS:	**HITS 11**			**WEEKS 247**
ANYTHING FOR YOU *Originally released in 1987 with title 'Let It Loose'.* *Above hit: Gloria ESTEFAN and MIAMI SOUND MACHINE.*	*Epic*	1	*19 Nov 88*	54
CUTS BOTH WAYS	*Epic*	1	*5 Aug 89*	64
INTO THE LIGHT	*Epic*	2	*16 Feb 91*	36
GREATEST HITS	*Epic*	2	*14 Nov 92*	47
MI TIERRA	*Epic*	11	*10 Jul 93*	11
HOLD ME, THRILL ME, KISS ME *Album of cover versions.*	*Epic*	5	*29 Oct 94*	19
ABRIENDO PUERTAS	*Epic*	70	*21 Oct 95*	1
DESTINY	*Epic*	12	*15 Jun 96*	9
GLORIA!	*Epic*	16	*13 Jun 98*	4
ALMA CARIBENA - CARIBBEAN SOUL	*Epic*	44	*27 May 00*	1
GREATEST HITS VOLUME 2	*Epic*	60	*24 Feb 01*	1

Don ESTELLE and Windsor DAVIES - See Windsor DAVIES as B.S.M. WILLIAMS and Don ESTELLE as GUNNER SUGDEN

Deon ESTUS — US

SINGLES:	**HITS 2**			**WEEKS 7**
MY GUY, MY GIRL [M] *Above hit: Amii STEWART and Dion ESTUS.*	*Sedition*	63	*25 Jan 86*	3
HEAVEN HELP ME *Features backing vocals by George Michael.*	*Mika*	41	*29 Apr 89*	4

ESTHERO - See Ian POOLEY

ETA — Denmark

SINGLES:	**HITS 1**			**WEEKS 5**
CASUAL SUB (BURNING SPEAR)	*East West*	28	*28 Jun 97*	3
CASUAL SUB (BURNING SPEAR) [RI]	*East West Dance*	28	*31 Jan 98*	2

ETERNAL — UK

SINGLES:	**HITS 15**			**WEEKS 134**
STAY *Originally recorded by Glenn Jones in 1990.*	*EMI*	4	*2 Oct 93*	9
SAVE OUR LOVE	*EMI*	8	*15 Jan 94*	7
JUST A STEP FROM HEAVEN	*EMI*	8	*30 Apr 94*	10
SO GOOD	*EMI*	13	*20 Aug 94*	7
OH BABY I . . .	*EMI*	4	*5 Nov 94*	13
CRAZY	*EMI*	15	*24 Dec 94*	7
POWER OF A WOMAN	*EMI*	5	*21 Oct 95*	8
I AM BLESSED	*EMI*	7	*9 Dec 95*	12
GOOD THING	*EMI*	8	*9 Mar 96*	6
SOMEDAY *From the film 'The Hunchback of Notre Dame'.*	*EMI*	4	*17 Aug 96*	9
SECRETS	*EMI*	9	*7 Dec 96*	7
DON'T YOU LOVE ME	*EMI*	3	*8 Mar 97*	7
I WANNA BE THE ONLY ONE *Above hit: ETERNAL featuring BeBe WINANS.*	*EMI*	1	*31 May 97*	15
ANGEL OF MINE	*EMI*	4	*11 Oct 97*	13
WHAT'CHA GONNA DO	*EMI*	16	*30 Oct 99*	4
ALBUMS:	**HITS 4**			**WEEKS 163**
ALWAYS & FOREVER	*EMI*	9	*11 Dec 93*	16
ALWAYS & FOREVER [RE] *Peak position reached on 7 Jan 95.*	*EMI*	2	*7 May 94*	60
POWER OF A WOMAN	*EMI*	6	*11 Nov 95*	31
BEFORE THE RAIN	*EMI*	3	*29 Mar 97*	29
GREATEST HITS	*EMI*	2	*1 Nov 97*	27

ETHER — UK

SINGLES:	HITS 1			WEEKS 1
WATCHING YOU	*Parlophone*	74	*28 Mar 98*	1

Melissa ETHERIDGE — US

ALBUMS:	HITS 2			WEEKS 2
BRAVE AND CRAZY	*Island*	63	*30 Sep 89*	1
NEVER ENOUGH	*Island*	56	*9 May 92*	1

ETHICS — Holland

(See also Artemesia; Movin' Melodies; Subliminal Cuts.)

SINGLES:	HITS 1			WEEKS 5
TO THE BEAT OF THE DRUM (LA LUNA)	*VC Recordings*	13	*25 Nov 95*	5
Song was originally released by Movin' Melodies.				

ETHIOPIANS — Jamaica

SINGLES:	HITS 1			WEEKS 6
TRAIN TO SKAVILLE	*Rio*	40	*16 Sep 67*	6

Tony ETORIA — UK

SINGLES:	HITS 1			WEEKS 8
I CAN PROVE IT	*GTO*	21	*4 Jun 77*	8

EUROGROOVE — UK

SINGLES:	HITS 3			WEEKS 7
MOVE YOUR BODY	*Avex UK*	29	*20 May 95*	2
DIVE TO PARADISE	*Avex UK*	31	*5 Aug 95*	2
IT'S ON YOU (SCAN ME)	*Avex UK*	25	*21 Oct 95*	2
MOVE YOUR BODY [RM]	*Avex UK*	44	*3 Feb 96*	1
Remixed by Boyz With Pride.				

EUROPE — Sweden

SINGLES:	HITS 7			WEEKS 50
THE FINAL COUNTDOWN	*Epic*	1	*1 Nov 86*	15
ROCK THE NIGHT	*Epic*	12	*31 Jan 87*	9
CARRIE	*Epic*	22	*18 Apr 87*	8
SUPERSTITIOUS	*Epic*	34	*20 Aug 88*	5
I'LL CRY FOR YOU	*Epic*	28	*1 Feb 92*	5
HALFWAY TO HEAVEN	*Epic*	42	*21 Mar 92*	4
THE FINAL COUNTDOWN 2000 [RR]	*Epic*	36	*25 Dec 99*	4
Initial copies of the single contained a printing error on the sleeve whereby the 'o' in countdown was omitted.				

ALBUMS:	HITS 3			WEEKS 43
THE FINAL COUNTDOWN	*Epic*	9	*22 Nov 86*	37
OUT OF THIS WORLD	*Epic*	12	*17 Sep 88*	5
PRISONERS IN PARADISE	*Epic*	61	*19 Oct 91*	1

EUROPEANS — UK

ALBUMS:	HITS 1			WEEKS 1
LIVE	*A&M*	100	*11 Feb 84*	1

EURYTHMICS — UK

SINGLES:	HITS 26			WEEKS 208
NEVER GONNA CRY AGAIN	*RCA*	63	*4 Jul 81*	3
LOVE IS A STRANGER	*RCA*	54	*20 Nov 82*	5
SWEET DREAMS (ARE MADE OF THIS)	*RCA*	2	*12 Feb 83*	14
LOVE IS A STRANGER [RE]	*RCA*	6	*9 Apr 83*	8
WHO'S THAT GIRL?	*RCA*	3	*9 Jul 83*	10
RIGHT BY YOUR SIDE	*RCA*	10	*5 Nov 83*	11
HERE COMES THE RAIN AGAIN	*RCA*	8	*21 Jan 84*	8
SEX CRIME (NINETEEN EIGHTY-FOUR)	*Virgin*	4	*3 Nov 84*	13
From the film 'Nineteen-Eighty Four'.				
JULIA	*Virgin*	44	*19 Jan 85*	4
WOULD I LIE TO YOU?	*RCA*	17	*20 Apr 85*	8
THERE MUST BE AN ANGEL (PLAYING WITH MY HEART)	*RCA*	1	*6 Jul 85*	13
Features harmonica playing by Stevie Wonder.				
SISTERS ARE DOIN' IT FOR THEMSELVES	*RCA*	9	*2 Nov 85*	11
Above hit: EURYTHMICS and Aretha FRANKLIN.				
IT'S ALRIGHT (BABY'S COMING BACK)	*RCA*	12	*11 Jan 86*	8
WHEN TOMORROW COMES	*RCA*	30	*14 Jun 86*	6
THORN IN MY SIDE	*RCA*	5	*6 Sep 86*	11
THE MIRACLE OF LOVE	*RCA*	23	*29 Nov 86*	9
MISSIONARY MAN	*RCA*	31	*28 Feb 87*	4

BEETHOVEN (I LOVE TO LISTEN TO)	*RCA*	25	*24 Oct 87*	5
SHAME	*RCA*	41	*26 Dec 87*	6
I NEED A MAN	*RCA*	26	*9 Apr 88*	5
YOU HAVE PLACED A CHILL IN MY HEART	*RCA*	16	*11 Jun 88*	8
REVIVAL	*RCA*	26	*26 Aug 89*	6
DON'T ASK ME WHY	*RCA*	25	*4 Nov 89*	6
THE KING AND QUEEN OF AMERICA	*RCA*	29	*3 Feb 90*	5
ANGEL	*RCA*	23	*12 May 90*	6
LOVE IS A STRANGER [RI]	*RCA*	46	*9 Mar 91*	3
SWEET DREAMS (ARE MADE OF THIS) '91 [RM]	*RCA*	48	*16 Nov 91*	2
I SAVED THE WORLD TODAY	*RCA*	11	*16 Oct 99*	6
17 AGAIN	*RCA*	27	*5 Feb 00*	4
ALBUMS:	**HITS 11**			**WEEKS 476**
SWEET DREAMS (ARE MADE OF THIS)	*RCA*	3	*12 Feb 83*	59
TOUCH	*RCA*	1	*26 Nov 83*	48
TOUCH DANCE	*RCA*	31	*9 Jun 84*	5
Remixes of four tracks from Touch.				
1984 (FOR THE LOVE OF BIG BROTHER) [OST]	*Virgin*	23	*24 Nov 84*	17
BE YOURSELF TONIGHT	*RCA*	3	*11 May 85*	80
REVENGE	*RCA*	3	*12 Jul 86*	52
SAVAGE	*RCA*	7	*21 Nov 87*	33
WE TOO ARE ONE	*RCA*	1	*23 Sep 89*	32
GREATEST HITS	*RCA*	1	*30 Mar 91*	122
Includes re-entries through to 2001.				
SWEET DREAMS (ARE MADE OF THIS) [RE]	*RCA*	64	*15 Jun 91*	1
Re-released at mid-price.				
EURYTHMICS LIVE 1983-1989	*RCA*	22	*27 Nov 93*	7
PEACE	*RCA*	4	*30 Oct 99*	20

EUSEBE — UK

SINGLES:	**HITS 1**			**WEEKS 3**
SUMMERTIME HEALING	*Mama's Yard*	32	*26 Aug 95*	3

EVANGEL TEMPLE CHOIR – See Johnny CASH

Faith EVANS — US

(See also Whitney Houston; A Tribe Called Quest.)

SINGLES:	**HITS 5**			**WEEKS 33**
YOU USED TO LOVE ME	*Puff Daddy*	42	*14 Oct 95*	2
I'LL BE MISSING YOU	*Puff Daddy*	1	*28 Jun 97*	21
Sleeve gives title as an EP:Tribute To the Notorious B.I.G. Based on the Police's Every Breath You Take.				
Above hit: PUFF DADDY and Faith EVANS (featuring 112).				
LOVE LIKE THIS	*Puff Daddy*	24	*14 Nov 98*	4
Samples Chic's Chic Cheer.				
GEORGY PORGY	*Warner Brothers*	28	*1 May 99*	3
Original by Toto reached No.48 in the US in 1978.				
Above hit: Eric BENET featuring Faith EVANS.				
ALL NIGHT LONG	*Puff Daddy*	23	*1 May 99*	3
Samples Unlimited Touch's I Hear Music In The Street.				
Above hit: Faith EVANS (featuring PUFF DADDY).				
ALBUMS:	**HITS 1**			**WEEKS 1**
KEEP THE FAITH	*Puff Daddy*	69	*7 Nov 98*	1

Maureen EVANS — UK

SINGLES:	**HITS 5**			**WEEKS 37**
THE BIG HURT •	*Oriole*	26	*23 Jan 60*	2
Above hit: Maureen EVANS with Norman PERCIVAL and his Orchestra.				
LOVE KISSES AND HEARTACHES	*Oriole*	44	*19 Mar 60*	1
PAPER ROSES	*Oriole*	40	*4 Jun 60*	5
LIKE I DO	*Oriole*	3	*1 Dec 62*	18
I LOVE HOW YOU LOVE ME	*Oriole*	34	*29 Feb 64*	10
I LOVE HOW YOU LOVE ME [RE]	*Oriole*	50	*16 May 64*	1

Paul EVANS — US

SINGLES:	**HITS 3**			**WEEKS 14**
SEVEN LITTLE GIRLS SITTING IN THE BACK SEAT •	*London*	25	*28 Nov 59*	1
Above hit: Paul EVANS and the CURLS.				
MIDNITE SPECIAL	*London*	41	*2 Apr 60*	1
HELLO, THIS IS JOANNIE (THE TELEPHONE ANSWERING MACHINE SONG) •	*Spring*	6	*16 Dec 78*	12

EVASIONS — UK

SINGLES:	**HITS 1**			**WEEKS 8**
WIKKA WRAP	*Groove*	20	*13 Jun 81*	8
Spoof take-off of Alan Whicker against the tune of Tom Browne's Funkin' For Jamaica.				

EVE — US

SINGLES:	HITS 2			WEEKS 20
WHO'S THAT GIRL	*Interscope*	6	*19 May 01*	8
LET ME BLOW YA MIND	*Interscope*	4	*25 Aug 01*	12
Above hit: EVE featuring Gwen STEFANI.				
ALBUMS:	**HITS 1**			**WEEKS 8**
SCORPION	*Interscope*	22	*11 Aug 01*	8

Alison EVELYN – See BROTHERS LIKE OUTLAW featuring Alison EVELYN

EVERCLEAR — US

SINGLES:	HITS 4			WEEKS 7
HEARTSPARK DOLLARSIGN	*Capitol*	48	*1 Jun 96*	2
SANTA MONICA (WATCH THE WORLD DIE)	*Capitol*	40	*31 Aug 96*	2
EVERYTHING TO EVERYONE	*Capitol*	41	*9 May 98*	1
WONDERFUL	*Capitol*	36	*14 Oct 00*	2
ALBUMS:	**HITS 3**			**WEEKS 3**
SO MUCH FOR THE AFTERGLOW	*Capitol*	63	*14 Mar 98*	1
SONGS FROM AN AMERICAN MOVIE – VOLUME ONE: LEARNING HOW TO SMILE	*Capitol*	51	*19 Aug 00*	1
SONGS FROM AN AMERICAN MOVIE – VOLUME TWO: GOOD TIME FOR A BAD ATTITUDE	*Capitol*	69	*28 Apr 01*	1

Betty EVERETT — US

SINGLES:	HITS 2			WEEKS 14
GETTING MIGHTY CROWDED	*Fontana*	29	*16 Jan 65*	7
IT'S IN HIS KISS (THE SHOOP SHOOP SONG)	*President*	34	*2 Nov 68*	7

Kenny EVERETT — UK

SINGLES:	HITS 2			WEEKS 12
CAPTAIN KREMMEN (RETRIBUTION)	*DJM*	32	*12 Nov 77*	4
Captain Kremmen was a fictional character in Everett's Capital Radio show.				
Above hit: Kenny EVERETT and Mike VICKERS.				
SNOT RAP	*RCA*	9	*26 Mar 83*	8
Sid Snot and Cupid Stunt were 2 characters from his BBC TV show.				
Above hit: Kenny EVERETT featuring Sid SNOT and Cupid STUNT.				

Peven EVERETT – See Roy DAVIS JR. featuring Peven EVERETT

EVERLAST — US

SINGLES:	HITS 3			WEEKS 5
WHAT IT'S LIKE	*Tommy Boy*	34	*27 Feb 99*	2
ENDS	*Tommy Boy*	47	*3 Jul 99*	1
Samples Wu Tang Clan's C.R.E.A.M.				
BLACK JESUS	*Tommy Boy*	37	*20 Jan 01*	2
ALBUMS:	**HITS 1**			**WEEKS 1**
WHITEY FORD SINGS THE BLUES	*Tommy Boy*	65	*13 Mar 99*	1

Phil EVERLY — US

SINGLES:	HITS 3			WEEKS 24
LOUISE	*Capitol*	47	*6 Nov 82*	6
SHE MEANS NOTHING TO ME	*Capitol*	9	*19 Feb 83*	9
Above hit: Phil EVERLY / Cliff RICHARD.				
ALL I HAVE TO DO IS DREAM	*EMI*	14	*10 Dec 94*	6
[AA] listed with the re-issue of Miss You Nights by Cliff Richard.				
Above hit: Cliff RICHARD (with Phil EVERLY).				
ALL I HAVE TO DO IS DREAM [RE]	*EMI*	58	*25 Feb 95*	3
ALBUMS:	**HITS 1**			**WEEKS 1**
PHIL EVERLY	*Capitol*	61	*7 May 83*	1

EVERLY BROTHERS — US

SINGLES:	HITS 29			WEEKS 345
BYE BYE, LOVE •	*London*	6	*13 Jul 57*	16
WAKE UP LITTLE SUSIE •	*London*	2	*9 Nov 57*	13
ALL I HAVE TO DO IS DREAM / CLAUDETTE	*London*	1	*24 May 58*	21
Claudette listed from 31 May 58. Originally written and recorded by Roy Orbison.				
BIRD DOG •	*London*	2	*13 Sep 58*	16
PROBLEMS	*London*	6	*24 Jan 59*	12
TAKE A MESSAGE TO MARY	*London*	29	*23 May 59*	1
POOR JENNY	*London*	14	*30 May 59*	11
Above 2 entries were separate sides of the same release, each had its own chart run.				
TAKE A MESSAGE TO MARY [RE-1ST]	*London*	27	*20 Jun 59*	1

TAKE A MESSAGE TO MARY [RE-2ND]	*London*	20	*4 Jul 59*	8
('TIL) I KISSED YOU *The Crickets on backing vocals.*	*London*	2	*12 Sep 59*	15
LET IT BE ME *French version by Gilbert Becaud in 1955 and first recorded in English by Jill Corey in 1957.*	*London*	13	*13 Feb 60*	6
LET IT BE ME [RE]	*London*	26	*2 Apr 60*	4
CATHY'S CLOWN *The first release on the Warner Brothers label.*	*Warner Brothers*	1	*16 Apr 60*	18
WHEN WILL I BE LOVED	*London*	4	*16 Jul 60*	16
LUCILLE / SO SAD (TO WATCH GOOD LOVE GO BAD)	*Warner Brothers*	4	*24 Sep 60*	15
LIKE STRANGERS	*London*	11	*17 Dec 60*	10
EBONY EYES / WALK RIGHT BACK *Ebony Eyes only listed on 11 Feb 61. Both sides listed for the next 3 weeks. From 11 Mar 61 Walk Right Back had first credit and from 1 Apr 61 it was the only side listed.*	*Warner Brothers*	1	*11 Feb 61*	16
TEMPTATION *Originally recorded by Bing Crosby.*	*Warner Brothers*	1	*17 Jun 61*	15
MUSKRAT / DON'T BLAME ME *Don't Blame Me only listed from 14 Oct 61 for 4 weeks. Originally recorded by Ethel Waters in 1933.*	*Warner Brothers*	20	*7 Oct 61*	6
CRYING IN THE RAIN	*Warner Brothers*	6	*20 Jan 62*	15
HOW CAN I MEET HER	*Warner Brothers*	12	*19 May 62*	10
NO ONE CAN MAKE MY SUNSHINE SMILE	*Warner Brothers*	11	*27 Oct 62*	11
(SO IT WAS . . . SO IT IS) SO IT WILL ALWAYS BE	*Warner Brothers*	23	*23 Mar 63*	11
IT'S BEEN NICE (GOODNIGHT) *From the film 'Just For Fun'.*	*Warner Brothers*	26	*15 Jun 63*	5
THE GIRL SANG THE BLUES	*Warner Brothers*	25	*19 Oct 63*	9
THE FERRIS WHEEL	*Warner Brothers*	22	*18 Jul 64*	10
GONE GONE GONE	*Warner Brothers*	36	*5 Dec 64*	7
THAT'LL BE THE DAY	*Warner Brothers*	30	*8 May 65*	4
THE PRICE OF LOVE	*Warner Brothers*	2	*22 May 65*	14
I'LL NEVER GET OVER YOU	*Warner Brothers*	35	*28 Aug 65*	5
LOVE IS STRANGE *Originally recorded by Micky and Sylvia.*	*Warner Brothers*	11	*23 Oct 65*	9
IT'S MY TIME	*Warner Brothers*	39	*11 May 68*	6
ON THE WINGS OF A NIGHTINGALE	*Mercury*	41	*22 Sep 84*	9
EPS:	**HITS 4**			**WEEKS 13**
THE EVERLY BROTHERS - NO. 5	*London*	7	*7 May 60*	6
THE EVERLY BROTHERS	*London*	15	*23 Jul 60*	1
THE EVERLY BROTHERS - NO. 4	*London*	8	*23 Jul 60*	5
THE EVERLY BROTHERS - NO. 6	*London*	20	*9 Jun 62*	1
ALBUMS:	**HITS 12**			**WEEKS 123**
IT'S EVERLY TIME	*Warner Brothers*	2	*2 Jul 60*	23
FABULOUS STYLE OF THE EVERLY BROTHERS	*London*	4	*15 Oct 60*	11
A DATE WITH THE EVERLY BROTHERS	*Warner Brothers*	3	*4 Mar 61*	14
INSTANT PARTY	*Warner Brothers*	20	*21 Jul 62*	1
ORIGINAL GREATEST HITS	*CBS*	7	*12 Sep 70*	16
THE VERY BEST OF THE EVERLY BROTHERS	*Warner Brothers*	43	*8 Jun 74*	1
WALK RIGHT BACK WITH THE EVERLYS	*Warner Brothers*	10	*29 Nov 75*	10
LIVING LEGENDS	*Warwick*	12	*9 Apr 77*	10
LOVE HURTS	*K-Tel*	31	*18 Dec 82*	10
EVERLY BROTHERS REUNION CONCERT - LIVE AT THE ROYAL ALBERT HALL *Live recordings from 23 Sep 83.*	*Impression*	47	*7 Jan 84*	6
THE EVERLY BROTHERS	*Mercury*	36	*3 Nov 84*	4
LOVE HURTS [RE]	*K-Tel*	22	*29 Dec 84*	12
THE GOLDEN YEARS OF THE EVERLY BROTHERS - THEIR 24 GREATEST HITS	*Warner Brothers*	26	*29 May 93*	5

EVERTON FOOTBALL CLUB

UK

SINGLES:	**HITS 2**			**WEEKS 8**
HERE WE GO *Above hit: EVERTON 1985 (the OFFICIAL TEAM RECORD).*	*Columbia*	14	*11 May 85*	5
ALL TOGETHER NOW *Features vocals by Keith Mullen of the Farm.*	*MDMC*	24	*20 May 95*	3

EVERYTHING BUT THE GIRL

UK

SINGLES:	**HITS 21**			**WEEKS 96**
EACH AND EVERYONE	*Blanco Y Negro*	28	*12 May 84*	7
MINE	*Blanco Y Negro*	58	*21 Jul 84*	2
NATIVE LAND	*Blanco Y Negro*	73	*6 Oct 84*	2
COME ON HOME	*Blanco Y Negro*	44	*2 Aug 86*	7
DON'T LEAVE ME BEHIND	*Blanco Y Negro*	72	*11 Oct 86*	2
THESE EARLY DAYS	*Blanco Y Negro*	75	*13 Feb 88*	1
I DON'T WANT TO TALK ABOUT IT	*Blanco Y Negro*	3	*9 Jul 88*	9
DRIVING	*Blanco Y Negro*	54	*27 Jan 90*	2
COVERS [EP] *Lead track: Love Is Strange.*	*Blanco Y Negro*	13	*22 Feb 92*	6
THE ONLY LIVING BOY IN NEW YORK [EP] *Lead track: The Only Living Boy In New York. Originally recorded by Simon and Garfunkel.*	*Blanco Y Negro*	42	*24 Apr 93*	5

I DIDN'T KNOW I WAS LOOKING FOR LOVE [EP]	*Blanco Y Negro*	72	*19 Jun 93*	1
Lead track: I Didn't Know I Was Looking For Love.				
ROLLERCOASTER [EP]	*Blanco Y Negro*	65	*4 Jun 94*	1
Lead track: Rollercoaster.				
MISSING	*Blanco Y Negro*	69	*20 Aug 94*	1
MISSING [RM]	*Blanco Y Negro*	3	*28 Oct 95*	22
Remixed by Todd Terry.				
WALKING WOUNDED	*Virgin*	6	*20 Apr 96*	6
WRONG	*Virgin*	8	*29 Jun 96*	7
SINGLE	*Virgin*	20	*5 Oct 96*	3
DRIVING [RM]	*Blanco Y Negro*	36	*7 Dec 96*	2
Remixed by Todd Terry.				
BEFORE TODAY	*Virgin*	25	*1 Mar 97*	2
THE FUTURE OF THE FUTURE (STAY GOLD) [RM]	*Deconstruction*	31	*3 Oct 98*	2
Remixed by Ben Watt and David Morales, it features Thorn's vocals.				
Above hit: DEEP DISH with EVERYTHING BUT THE GIRL.				
FIVE FATHOMS	*Virgin*	27	*25 Sep 99*	3
TEMPERAMENTAL	*Virgin*	72	*4 Mar 00*	1
TRACEY IN MY ROOM	*VC Recordings*	34	*27 Jan 01*	2
Ben Watt mix of Everything But The Girl's Wrong and Soul Vision's 1999 remix of Sandy Rivera's Come Into My Room.				
Above hit: EBTG vs SOUL VISION.				

ALBUMS:	HITS 11			WEEKS 131
EDEN	*Blanco Y Negro*	14	*16 Jun 84*	22
LOVE NOT MONEY	*Blanco Y Negro*	10	*27 Apr 85*	9
BABY THE STARS SHINE BRIGHT	*Blanco Y Negro*	22	*6 Sep 86*	9
IDLEWILD	*Blanco Y Negro*	13	*12 Mar 88*	9
IDLEWILD [RE]	*Blanco Y Negro*	21	*6 Aug 88*	6
Repackaged with additional track.				
THE LANGUAGE OF LIFE	*Blanco Y Negro*	10	*17 Feb 90*	6
WORLDWIDE	*Blanco Y Negro*	29	*5 Oct 91*	5
HOME MOVIES - THE BEST OF EVERYTHING BUT THE GIRL	*Blanco Y Negro*	5	*22 May 93*	8
AMPLIFIED HEART	*Blanco Y Negro*	20	*25 Jun 94*	15
WALKING WOUNDED	*Virgin*	4	*18 May 96*	27
THE BEST OF EVERYTHING BUT THE GIRL	*Blanco Y Negro*	23	*9 Nov 96*	12
TEMPERAMENTAL	*Virgin*	16	*9 Oct 99*	3

EVOLUTION

UK

SINGLES:	HITS 5			WEEKS 12
LOVE THING	*Deconstruction*	32	*20 Mar 93*	2
EVERYBODY DANCE	*Deconstruction*	19	*3 Jul 93*	5
EVOLUTIONDANCE PART ONE [EP]	*Deconstruction*	52	*8 Jan 94*	3
Lead track: Escape To Alcatraz.				
LOOK UP TO THE LIGHT	*Deconstruction*	55	*4 Nov 95*	1
YOUR LOVE IS CALLING	*Deconstruction*	60	*19 Oct 96*	1

EX PISTOLS

UK

(See also Sex Pistols.)

SINGLES:	HITS 1			WEEKS 2
LAND OF HOPE AND GLORY	*Virgin*	69	*2 Feb 85*	2

EXCITERS

US

SINGLES:	HITS 2			WEEKS 7
TELL HIM •	*United Artists*	46	*23 Feb 63*	1
REACHING FOR THE BEST	*20th Century*	31	*4 Oct 75*	6

EXETER BRAMDEAN BOYS' CHOIR

UK

SINGLES:	HITS 1			WEEKS 3
REMEMBERING CHRISTMAS [EP]	*Golden Sounds*	46	*18 Dec 93*	3
Lead track: No Room At The Inn. Charity record in aid of the Bosnian Children Appeal and the Bramdean Chapel Foundation Trust.				

EXILE

US

SINGLES:	HITS 3			WEEKS 18
KISS YOU ALL OVER	*RAK*	6	*19 Aug 78*	12
HOW CAN THIS GO WRONG	*RAK*	67	*12 May 79*	2
HEART AND SOUL	*RAK*	54	*12 Sep 81*	4

EXODUS

US

ALBUMS:	HITS 1			WEEKS 1
FABULOUS DISASTER	*Music For Nations*	67	*11 Feb 89*	1

EXOTERIX — UK

SINGLES:	HITS 2			WEEKS 2
VOID	*Positiva*	58	*24 Apr 93*	1
SATISFY MY LOVE	*Union*	62	*5 Feb 94*	1

EXOTICA featuring Itsy FOSTER — UK/Italy

SINGLES:	HITS 1			WEEKS 1
THE SUMMER IS MAGIC '95	*Polydor*	68	*16 Sep 95*	1

EXPLOITED — UK

SINGLES:	HITS 4			WEEKS 13
DOGS OF WAR	*Secret*	63	*18 Apr 81*	4
DEAD CITIES	*Secret*	31	*17 Oct 81*	5
DON'T LET 'EM GRIND YOU DOWN EP (EXTRACTS FROM THE EDINBURGH LIVE NITE [EP]	*Superville*	70	*5 Dec 81*	1
One side of single for each group. There is no actual track listing. Above hit: EXPLOITED / ANTI-PASTI.				
ATTACK	*Secret*	50	*8 May 82*	3
ALBUMS:	**HITS 3**			**WEEKS 26**
PUNK'S NOT DEAD	*Secret*	20	*16 May 81*	11
EXPLOITED LIVE	*Superville*	52	*14 Nov 81*	3
TROOPS OF TOMORROW	*Secret*	17	*19 Jun 82*	12

EXPOSE — US

SINGLES:	HITS 1			WEEKS 1
I'LL NEVER GET OVER YOU (GETTING OVER ME)	*Arista*	75	*28 Aug 93*	1

EXPRESS OF SOUND — Italy

SINGLES:	HITS 1			WEEKS 1
REAL VIBRATION (WANT LOVE)	*Positiva*	45	*2 Nov 96*	1
Originally released in 1995.				

EXPRESSOS — UK

SINGLES:	HITS 2			WEEKS 5
HEY GIRL	*WEA*	60	*21 Jun 80*	3
TANGO IN MONO	*WEA*	70	*14 Mar 81*	2

EXTREME — US

SINGLES:	HITS 9			WEEKS 46
GET THE FUNK OUT	*A&M*	19	*8 Jun 91*	7
MORE THAN WORDS	*A&M*	2	*27 Jul 91*	11
DECADENCE DANCE	*A&M*	36	*12 Oct 91*	3
HOLE HEARTED	*A&M*	12	*23 Nov 91*	7
SONG FOR LOVE	*A&M*	12	*2 May 92*	6
REST IN PEACE	*A&M*	13	*5 Sep 92*	5
STOP THE WORLD	*A&M*	22	*14 Nov 92*	2
TRAGIC COMIC	*A&M*	15	*6 Feb 93*	4
HIP TODAY	*A&M*	44	*11 Mar 95*	1
ALBUMS:	**HITS 3**			**WEEKS 75**
EXTREME II PORNOGRAFFITTI	*A&M*	12	*1 Jun 91*	61
III SIDES TO EVERY STORY	*A&M*	2	*26 Sep 92*	11
WAITING FOR THE PUNCHLINE	*A&M*	10	*11 Feb 95*	3

EYE TO EYE featuring Taka BOOM — UK/US

SINGLES:	HITS 1			WEEKS 2
JUST CAN'T GET ENOUGH (NO NO NO NO)	*Xtravaganza*	36	*9 Jun 01*	2
Samples the bassline of Apollo 440's Stop The Rock and the vocals from Soulsearchers' Can't Get Enough.				

EYES CREAM — Italy

SINGLES:	HITS 1			WEEKS 1
FLY AWAY (BYE BYE)	*Accolade*	53	*16 Oct 99*	1
Samples Sylvester's You Make Me Fell Mighty Real.				

F

Adam F — UK

SINGLES:	HITS 4			WEEKS 14
CIRCLES	*Positiva*	20	*27 Sep 97*	3

MUSIC IN MY MIND	*Positiva*	27	*7 Mar 98*	3
SMASH SUMTHIN'	*Def Jam*	11	*15 Sep 01*	7
Above hit: REDMAN featuring Adam F.				
STAND CLEAR	*Chrysalis*	43	*1 Dec 01*	1
Above hit: Adam F featuring M.O.P.				
ALBUMS:	**HITS 2**			**WEEKS 3**
COLOURS	*Positiva*	47	*15 Nov 97*	1
KAOS - THE ANTI ACOUSTIC WARFARE	*Chrysalis*	44	*22 Sep 01*	2

F.A.B. — UK

SINGLES:	**HITS 3**			**WEEKS 11**
THUNDERBIRDS ARE GO	*Brothers Organisation*	5	*7 Jul 90*	8
Above hit: F.A.B. featuring M.C. PARKER.				
THE PRISONER	*Brothers Organisation*	56	*20 Oct 90*	2
Above hit: F.A.B. featuring MC NUMBER 6.				
THE STINGRAY MEGAMIX	*Brothers Organisation*	66	*1 Dec 90*	1
Above hit: F.A.B. featuring AQUA MARINA.				
ALBUMS:	**HITS 1**			**WEEKS 3**
POWER THEMES 90	*Telstar*	53	*10 Nov 90*	3

F.P.I. PROJECT — Italy

SINGLES:	**HITS 3**			**WEEKS 17**
GOING BACK TO MY ROOTS / RICH IN PARADISE	*Rumour*	9	*9 Dec 89*	12
Re-issued from 27 Jan 90 with new vocals by Sharon Dee Clarke on Going Back To My Roots.				
Above hit: F.P.I. PROJECT present RICH IN PARADISE featuring vocals of Paolo DINI.				
EVERYBODY (ALL OVER THE WORLD)	*Rumour*	65	*9 Mar 91*	3
COME ON (AND DO IT)	*Synthetic*	59	*7 Aug 93*	1
EVERYBODY ALL OVER THE WORLD [RM]	*99 North*	67	*13 Mar 99*	1
Remixed by Dillon and Dickins.				
Above hit: FPI PROJECT.				

FAB! — Ireland

SINGLES:	**HITS 1**			**WEEKS 1**
TURN AROUND	*Break Records 2000*	59	*1 Aug 98*	1

Shelley FABARES — US

SINGLES:	**HITS 1**			**WEEKS 4**
JOHNNY ANGEL	*Pye International*	41	*28 Apr 62*	4
Backing vocals by the Blossoms.				

FABIAN — US

SINGLES:	**HITS 1**			**WEEKS 1**
HOUND DOG MAN	*His Master's Voice*	46	*12 Mar 60*	1

Lara FABIAN — Belgium

SINGLES:	**HITS 1**			**WEEKS 1**
I WILL LOVE AGAIN	*Columbia*	63	*28 Oct 00*	1

FABULOUS BAKER BOYS — UK

SINGLES:	**HITS 1**			**WEEKS 2**
OH BOY	*Multiply*	34	*15 Nov 97*	2
Originally released in 1992.				

FABULOUS FLEE-RAKKERS — UK

SINGLES:	**HITS 1**			**WEEKS 13**
GREEN JEANS	*Triumph*	23	*21 May 60*	13

FACE – See David MORALES

FACES — UK

SINGLES:	**HITS 5**			**WEEKS 46**
STAY WITH ME	*Warner Brothers*	6	*18 Dec 71*	14
CINDY INCIDENTALLY	*Warner Brothers*	2	*17 Feb 73*	9
POOL HALL RICHARD / I WISH IT WOULD RAIN (WITH A TRUMPET)	*Warner Brothers*	8	*8 Dec 73*	11
YOU CAN MAKE ME DANCE, SING OR ANYTHING (EVEN TAKE THE DOG FOR A WALK, MEND A FUSE, FOLD AWAY THE IRONING BOARD, OR ANY OTHER DOMESTIC SHORT COMINGS)	*Warner Brothers*	12	*7 Dec 74*	9
Above hit: FACES/Rod STEWART.				
THE FACES [EP]	*Riva*	41	*4 Jun 77*	3
Lead track: Memphis.				
ALBUMS:	**HITS 7**			**WEEKS 57**
FIRST STEP	*Warner Brothers*	45	*4 Apr 70*	1
LONG PLAYER	*Warner Brothers*	31	*8 May 71*	7

A NOD'S AS GOOD AS A WINK . . . TO A BLIND HORSE	*Warner Brothers*	2	*25 Dec 71*	22
OOH-LA-LA	*Warner Brothers*	1	*21 Apr 73*	13
OVERTURE AND BEGINNERS	*Mercury*	3	*26 Jan 74*	7
Above hit: Rod STEWART and the FACES.				
THE BEST OF THE FACES	*Riva*	24	*21 May 77*	6
THE BEST OF ROD STEWART AND THE FACES 1971-1975	*Mercury*	58	*7 Nov 92*	1
Features both Rod Stewart's solo and group material.				
Above hit: Rod STEWART and the FACES.				

FACTORY OF UNLIMITED RHYTHM — Jamaica

SINGLES:	HITS 1			WEEKS 1
THE SWEETEST SURRENDER	*Kuff*	59	*1 Jun 96*	1

Donald FAGEN — US

SINGLES:	HITS 1			WEEKS 2
TOMORROW'S GIRLS	*Reprise*	46	*3 Jul 93*	2
ALBUMS:	**HITS 2**			**WEEKS 25**
THE NIGHTFLY	*Warner Brothers*	44	*30 Oct 82*	16
KAMAKIRIAD	*Reprise*	3	*5 Jun 93*	9

Joe FAGIN — UK

SINGLES:	HITS 2			WEEKS 20
THAT'S LIVING ALRIGHT	*Towerbell*	3	*7 Jan 84*	11
The original A-side was Breakin' Away though this was not listed on the charts.				
BACK WITH THE BOYS AGAIN / GET IT RIGHT	*Towerbell*	53	*5 Apr 86*	9
Above 2: From the Central ITV series 'Auf Wiedersehen, Pet'.				

Brian FAHEY and his Orchestra – See Ken DODD

Yvonne FAIR — US

SINGLES:	HITS 1			WEEKS 11
IT SHOULD HAVE BEEN ME	*Tamla Motown*	5	*24 Jan 76*	11
Originally recorded by Kim Weston in 1963.				

FAIR WEATHER — UK

SINGLES:	HITS 1			WEEKS 12
NATURAL SINNER	*RCA Victor*	6	*18 Jul 70*	12

FAIRGROUND ATTRACTION — UK

SINGLES:	HITS 4			WEEKS 27
PERFECT	*RCA*	1	*16 Apr 88*	13
FIND MY LOVE	*RCA*	7	*30 Jul 88*	10
A SMILE IN A WHISPER	*RCA*	75	*19 Nov 88*	1
CLARE	*RCA*	49	*28 Jan 89*	3
ALBUMS:	**HITS 2**			**WEEKS 54**
THE FIRST OF A MILLION KISSES	*RCA*	2	*28 May 88*	52
AY FOND KISS	*RCA*	55	*30 Jun 90*	2

FAIRPORT CONVENTION — UK

SINGLES:	HITS 1			WEEKS 9
SI TU DOIS PARTIR (IF YOU GOTTA GO, GO NOW)	*Island*	21	*26 Jul 69*	8
SI TU DOIS PARTIR (IF YOU GOTTA GO, GO NOW) [RE]	*Island*	49	*27 Sep 69*	1
ALBUMS:	**HITS 6**			**WEEKS 41**
UNHALFBRICKING	*Island*	12	*2 Aug 69*	8
LIEGE AND LIEF	*Island*	17	*17 Jan 70*	15
FULL HOUSE	*Island*	13	*18 Jul 70*	11
ANGEL DELIGHT	*Island*	8	*3 Jul 71*	5
RISING FOR THE MOON	*Island*	52	*12 Jul 75*	1
RED AND GOLD	*New Routes*	74	*28 Jan 89*	1

Andy FAIRWEATHER LOW — UK

SINGLES:	HITS 2			WEEKS 18
REGGAE TUNE	*A&M*	10	*21 Sep 74*	8
WIDE EYED AND LEGLESS	*A&M*	6	*6 Dec 75*	10

Adam FAITH — UK

SINGLES:	HITS 24			WEEKS 252
WHAT DO YOU WANT?	*Parlophone*	1	*21 Nov 59*	19
POOR ME	*Parlophone*	1	*23 Jan 60*	18
SOMEONE ELSE'S BABY	*Parlophone*	2	*16 Apr 60*	13
JOHNNY COMES MARCHING HOME / MADE YOU	*Parlophone*	5	*2 Jul 60*	13
Johnny Comes Marching Home from the film 'Never Let Go'; Made You from the film 'Beat Girl'.				

HOW ABOUT THAT!	*Parlophone*	4	*17 Sep 60*	14
Above 2: Adam FAITH with John BARRY and his Orchestra.				
LONELY PUP (IN A CHRISTMAS SHOP)	*Parlophone*	4	*19 Nov 60*	11
Above hit: Adam FAITH with the Children.				
WHO AM I? / THIS IS IT	*Parlophone*	5	*11 Feb 61*	14
This Is It had first billing for the first 2 weeks, and from 11 Mar 61 it was no longer listed.				
EASY GOING ME	*Parlophone*	12	*29 Apr 61*	10
DON'T YOU KNOW IT?	*Parlophone*	12	*22 Jul 61*	10
THE TIME HAS COME	*Parlophone*	4	*28 Oct 61*	14
From the film 'What A Whopper!'.				
LONESOME	*Parlophone*	12	*20 Jan 62*	9
AS YOU LIKE IT	*Parlophone*	5	*5 May 62*	15
Above 2: Adam FAITH with John BARRY and his Orchestra.				
DON'T THAT BEAT ALL	*Parlophone*	8	*1 Sep 62*	11
Above hit: Adam FAITH with Johnny KEATING and his Orchestra.				
BABY TAKE A BOW	*Parlophone*	22	*15 Dec 62*	6
Though not billed, single had accompaniment directed by Johnny Keating.				
WHAT NOW	*Parlophone*	31	*2 Feb 63*	5
WALKIN' TALL	*Parlophone*	23	*13 Jul 63*	6
Above 2: Adam FAITH with Johnny KEATING and his Orchestra.				
THE FIRST TIME	*Parlophone*	5	*21 Sep 63*	13
Written by Chris Andrews.				
WE ARE IN LOVE	*Parlophone*	11	*14 Dec 63*	12
IF HE TELLS YOU	*Parlophone*	25	*14 Mar 64*	9
I LOVE BEING IN LOVE WITH YOU	*Parlophone*	33	*30 May 64*	6
Above 4: Adam FAITH with the ROULETTES.				
A MESSAGE TO MARTHA (KENTUCKY BLUEBIRD)	*Parlophone*	12	*28 Nov 64*	11
STOP FEELING SORRY FOR YOURSELF	*Parlophone*	23	*13 Feb 65*	6
SOMEONE'S TAKEN MARIA AWAY	*Parlophone*	34	*19 Jun 65*	5
Above 2: Adam FAITH with the ROULETTES.				
CHERYL'S GOIN' HOME	*Parlophone*	46	*22 Oct 66*	2
Originally recorded by Bob Lind.				
EPS:	**HITS 4**			**WEEKS 95**
ADAM'S HIT PARADE	*Parlophone*	1	*17 Sep 60*	77
ADAM NO. 1	*Parlophone*	4	*11 Mar 61*	13
ADAM FAITH NO. 1	*Parlophone*	12	*17 Mar 62*	4
A MESSAGE TO MARTHA - FROM ADAM	*Parlophone*	17	*13 Mar 65*	1
ALBUMS:	**HITS 5**			**WEEKS 46**
ADAM	*Parlophone*	6	*19 Nov 60*	36
BEAT GIRL [OST]	*Columbia*	11	*11 Feb 61*	3
Includes tracks featuring the John Barry Seven and the John Barry Orchestra.				
Above hit: Adam FAITH/John BARRY SEVEN /John BARRY ORCHESTRA.				
ADAM FAITH	*Parlophone*	20	*24 Mar 62*	1
FAITH ALIVE	*Parlophone*	19	*25 Sep 65*	1
20 GOLDEN GREATS	*Warwick*	61	*19 Dec 81*	3
MIDNIGHT POSTCARDS	*PolyGram TV*	43	*27 Nov 93*	2

Horace FAITH — Jamaica

SINGLES:	**HITS 1**			**WEEKS 10**
BLACK PEARL	*Trojan*	13	*12 Sep 70*	10
Originally recorded by Sonny Charles.				

Percy FAITH and his Orchestra — Canada

(See also Tony Bennett; Rosemary Clooney; Vic Damone; Doris Day; Johnny Mathis; Frankie Laine; Johnnie Ray.)

SINGLES:	**HITS 1**			**WEEKS 31**
THE THEME FROM "A SUMMER PLACE"	*Philips*	2	*5 Mar 60*	31
Originally recorded by Hugo Winterhalter and his Orchestra. From the film of the same name.				

FAITH BROTHERS — UK

SINGLES:	**HITS 2**			**WEEKS 6**
THE COUNTRY OF THE BLIND	*Siren*	63	*13 Apr 85*	3
A STRANGER ON HOME GROUND	*Siren*	69	*6 Jul 85*	3
ALBUMS:	**HITS 1**			**WEEKS 1**
EVENTIDE	*Siren*	66	*9 Nov 85*	1

FAITH HOPE and CHARITY — US

SINGLES:	**HITS 1**			**WEEKS 4**
JUST ONE LOOK	*RCA Victor*	38	*31 Jan 76*	4

FAITH HOPE and CHARITY — UK

SINGLES:	**HITS 1**			**WEEKS 3**
BATTLE OF THE SEXES	*WEA*	53	*23 Jun 90*	3

FAITH NO MORE — US

SINGLES:	HITS 16			WEEKS 65
WE CARE A LOT	*Slash*	53	*6 Feb 88*	3
EPIC	*Slash*	37	*10 Feb 90*	4
FROM OUT OF NOWHERE	*Slash*	23	*14 Apr 90*	6
FALLING TO PIECES	*Slash*	41	*14 Jul 90*	3
EPIC [RI]	*Slash*	25	*8 Sep 90*	5
MIDLIFE CRISIS	*Slash*	10	*6 Jun 92*	5
A SMALL VICTORY	*Slash*	29	*15 Aug 92*	5
A SMALL VICTORY [RM]	*Slash*	55	*12 Sep 92*	1
Remixed by Youth.				
EVERYTHING'S RUINED	*Slash*	28	*21 Nov 92*	3
I'M EASY / BE AGGRESSIVE	*Slash*	3	*16 Jan 93*	7
I'M EASY / BE AGGRESSIVE [RE]	*Slash*	75	*13 Mar 93*	1
ANOTHER BODY MURDERED	*Epic*	26	*6 Nov 93*	3
From the film 'Judgement Night'.				
Above hit: FAITH NO MORE and BOO-YAA TRIBE.				
DIGGING THE GRAVE	*Slash*	16	*11 Mar 95*	4
RICOCHET	*Slash*	27	*27 May 95*	2
EVIDENCE	*Slash*	32	*29 Jul 95*	3
ASHES TO ASHES	*Slash*	15	*31 May 97*	3
LAST CUP OF SORROW	*Slash*	51	*16 Aug 97*	1
THIS TOWN AIN'T BIG ENOUGH FOR BOTH OF US	*Roadrunner*	40	*13 Dec 97*	2
Above hit: SPARKS vs. FAITH NO MORE.				
ASHES TO ASHES [RI]	*Slash*	29	*17 Jan 98*	3
I STARTED A JOKE	*Slash*	49	*7 Nov 98*	1
Originally recorded by the Bee Gees.				

ALBUMS:	HITS 6			WEEKS 74
THE REAL THING	*Slash*	30	*17 Feb 90*	35
LIVE AT THE BRIXTON ACADEMY	*Slash*	20	*16 Feb 91*	4
ANGEL DUST	*Slash*	2	*20 Jun 92*	25
KING FOR A DAY, FOOL FOR A LIFETIME	*Slash*	5	*25 Mar 95*	6
ALBUM OF THE YEAR	*Slash*	7	*21 Jun 97*	3
WHO CARES A LOT? – THE GREATEST HITS	*Slash*	37	*21 Nov 98*	1
Sales of CD doublepack only due to chart rules. The standard release only reached No. 93.				

Marianne FAITHFULL — UK

SINGLES:	HITS 7			WEEKS 59
AS TEARS GO BY	*Decca*	9	*15 Aug 64*	13
Originally recorded by Rolling Stones.				
COME AND STAY WITH ME	*Decca*	4	*20 Feb 65*	13
Written by Jackie De Shannon.				
THIS LITTLE BIRD	*Decca*	6	*8 May 65*	11
Originally recorded by John D. Loudermilk.				
SUMMER NIGHTS	*Decca*	10	*24 Jul 65*	10
YESTERDAY	*Decca*	36	*6 Nov 65*	4
IS THIS WHAT I GET FROM LOVING YOU?	*Decca*	43	*11 Mar 67*	2
THE BALLAD OF LUCY JORDAN	*Island*	48	*24 Nov 79*	6
Originally recorded by Shel Silverstein.				

EPS:	HITS 1			WEEKS 19
GO AWAY FROM MY WORLD	*Decca*	4	*19 Jun 65*	19

ALBUMS:	HITS 6			WEEKS 19
COME MY WAY	*Decca*	12	*5 Jun 65*	7
MARIANNE FAITHFULL	*Decca*	15	*5 Jun 65*	2
BROKEN ENGLISH	*Island*	57	*24 Nov 79*	3
DANGEROUS ACQUAINTANCES	*Island*	45	*17 Oct 81*	4
A CHILD'S ADVENTURE	*Island*	99	*26 Mar 83*	1
STRANGE WEATHER	*Island*	78	*8 Aug 87*	2

FAITHLESS — UK

SINGLES:	HITS 10			WEEKS 65
SALVA MEA (SAVE ME)	*Cheeky*	30	*5 Aug 95*	2
INSOMNIA	*Cheeky*	27	*9 Dec 95*	2
DON'T LEAVE	*Cheeky*	34	*23 Mar 96*	2
INSOMNIA [RI]	*Cheeky*	3	*26 Oct 96*	13
SALVA MEA [RM]	*Cheeky*	9	*21 Dec 96*	7
Additional vocals by Collette.				
REVERENCE	*Cheeky*	10	*26 Apr 97*	3
DON'T LEAVE [RI]	*Cheeky*	21	*15 Nov 97*	2
From the film 'A Life Less Ordinary'.				
GOD IS A DJ	*Cheeky*	6	*5 Sep 98*	8
TAKE THE LONG WAY HOME	*Cheeky*	15	*5 Dec 98*	6
BRING MY FAMILY BACK	*Cheeky*	14	*1 May 99*	5
From the film 'Forces Of Nature'.				
WE COME 1	*Cheeky*	3	*16 Jun 01*	10
MUHAMMAD ALI	*Cheeky*	29	*29 Sep 01*	2

MUHAMMAD ALI [RE]	*Cheeky*	52	*27 Oct 01*	2
TARANTULA	*Cheeky*	29	*29 Dec 01*	1
ALBUMS:	**HITS 3**			**WEEKS 36**
REVERENCE	*Cheeky*	26	*23 Nov 96*	14
Sales were combined with Irreverence, a remix CD.				
SUNDAY 8PM	*Cheeky*	10	*3 Oct 98*	7
OUTROSPECTIVE	*Cheeky*	4	*30 Jun 01*	15

FALCO — Austria

SINGLES:	**HITS 4**			**WEEKS 26**
ROCK ME AMADEUS	*A&M*	1	*22 Mar 86*	15
Tribute to composer Wolfgang Amadeus Mozart.				
VIENNA CALLING	*A&M*	10	*31 May 86*	8
JEANNY	*A&M*	68	*2 Aug 86*	1
THE SOUND OF MUSIK	*WEA*	61	*27 Sep 86*	2
ALBUMS:	**HITS 1**			**WEEKS 15**
FALCO 3	*A&M*	32	*26 Apr 86*	15

Christian FALK featuring DEMETREUS — Sweden

SINGLES:	**HITS 1**			**WEEKS 3**
MAKE IT RIGHT	*London*	22	*26 Aug 00*	3

Fred FALKE – See Alan BRAXE & Fred FALKE presents . . .

FALL — UK

SINGLES:	**HITS 14**			**WEEKS 25**
MR. PHARMACIST	*Beggars Banquet*	75	*13 Sep 86*	1
Originally recorded by The Other Half.				
HEY! LUCIANI	*Beggars Banquet*	59	*20 Dec 86*	1
THERE'S A GHOST IN MY HOUSE	*Beggars Banquet*	30	*9 May 87*	4
HIT THE NORTH	*Beggars Banquet*	57	*31 Oct 87*	5
VICTORIA	*Beggars Banquet*	35	*30 Jan 88*	3
BIG NEW PRINZ / JERUSALEM	*Beggars Banquet*	59	*26 Nov 88*	2
Jerusalem based on the 1804 poem by Milton: And Did Those Feet In Ancient Time by William Blake.				
TELEPHONE THING	*Cog Sinister*	58	*27 Jan 90*	1
WHITE LIGHTNING	*Cog Sinister*	56	*8 Sep 90*	2
FREE RANGE	*Cog Sinister*	40	*14 Mar 92*	1
WHY ARE PEOPLE GRUDGEFUL?	*Permanent*	43	*17 Apr 93*	1
BEHIND THE COUNTER [EP]	*Permanent*	75	*25 Dec 93*	1
Lead track: Behind The Counter.				
15 WAYS	*Permanent*	65	*30 Apr 94*	1
THE CHISELLERS	*Jet*	60	*17 Feb 96*	1
MASQUERADE	*Artful*	69	*21 Feb 98*	1
ALBUMS:	**HITS 15**			**WEEKS 30**
HEX EDUCATION HOUR	*Kamera*	71	*20 Mar 82*	3
THE WONDERFUL AND FRIGHTENING WORLD OF . . .	*Beggars Banquet*	62	*20 Oct 84*	2
THIS NATION'S SAVING GRACE	*Beggars Banquet*	54	*5 Oct 85*	2
BEND SINISTER	*Beggars Banquet*	36	*11 Oct 86*	3
THE FRENZ EXPERIMENT	*Beggars Banquet*	19	*12 Mar 88*	4
I AM KURIOUS, ORANJ	*Beggars Banquet*	54	*12 Nov 88*	2
SEMINAL LIVE	*Beggars Banquet*	40	*8 Jul 89*	2
EXTRICATE	*Cog Sinister*	31	*3 Mar 90*	3
458489 A SIDES	*Beggars Banquet*	44	*15 Sep 90*	2
Compilation.				
SHIFT-WORK	*Cog Sinister*	17	*4 May 91*	2
CODE: SELFISH	*Cog Sinister*	21	*28 Mar 92*	1
INFOTAINMENT SCAN	*Permanent*	9	*8 May 93*	3
MIDDLE CLASS REVOLT	*Permanent*	48	*14 May 94*	1
CEREBRAL CAUSTIC	*Permanent*	67	*11 Mar 95*	1
THE LIGHT USER SYNDROME	*Jet*	54	*22 Jun 96*	1

Harold FALTERMEYER — Germany

SINGLES:	**HITS 2**			**WEEKS 23**
AXEL F	*MCA*	62	*23 Mar 85*	4
AXEL F [RE]	*MCA*	2	*1 Jun 85*	18
"FLETCH" THEME	*MCA*	74	*24 Aug 85*	1
All singles from the film' Beverly Hills Cop'.				

Agnetha FALTSKOG — Sweden

SINGLES:	**HITS 3**			**WEEKS 12**
THE HEAT IS ON	*Epic*	35	*28 May 83*	6
WRAP YOUR ARMS AROUND ME	*Epic*	44	*13 Aug 83*	5
Originally recorded by Holly Knight.				
CAN'T SHAKE LOOSE	*Epic*	63	*22 Oct 83*	1

ALBUMS:	HITS 3			WEEKS 17
WRAP YOUR ARMS AROUND ME	*Epic*	18	*11 Jun 83*	13
EYES OF A WOMAN	*Epic*	38	*4 May 85*	3
I STAND ALONE	*WEA*	72	*12 Mar 88*	1

Georgie FAME — UK

(See also Mondo Kane featuring Dee Lewis and Coral Gordon Guest star Georgie Fame.)

SINGLES:	HITS 13			WEEKS 115
YEH, YEH	*Columbia*	1	*19 Dec 64*	12
Originally recorded by Jon Hendricks.				
IN THE MEANTIME	*Columbia*	22	*6 Mar 65*	8
LIKE WE USED TO BE	*Columbia*	33	*31 Jul 65*	7
SOMETHING	*Columbia*	23	*30 Oct 65*	7
GETAWAY	*Columbia*	1	*25 Jun 66*	11
Above 5: Georgie FAME and the BLUE FLAMES.				
SUNNY	*Columbia*	13	*24 Sep 66*	8
SITTING IN THE PARK	*Columbia*	12	*24 Dec 66*	10
BECAUSE I LOVE YOU	*CBS*	15	*25 Mar 67*	8
TRY MY WORLD	*CBS*	37	*16 Sep 67*	5
THE BALLAD OF BONNIE AND CLYDE	*CBS*	1	*16 Dec 67*	13
PEACEFUL	*CBS*	16	*12 Jul 69*	9
SEVENTH SON	*CBS*	25	*13 Dec 69*	7
ROSETTA	*CBS*	11	*10 Apr 71*	10
Above hit: FAME and PRICE, PRICE and FAME TOGETHER.				

EPS:	HITS 4			WEEKS 48
RHYTHM AND BLUES AT THE FLAMINGO	*Columbia*	8	*16 Jan 65*	13
Live recordings from the Flamingo club in Soho, London.				
FATS FOR FAME	*Columbia*	15	*5 Jun 65*	2
GETAWAY	*Columbia*	7	*10 Dec 66*	7
GEORGIE FAME	*CBS*	2	*10 Jun 67*	26

ALBUMS:	HITS 5			WEEKS 72
FAME AT LAST	*Columbia*	15	*17 Oct 64*	8
SWEET THINGS	*Columbia*	6	*14 May 66*	22
SOUND VENTURE	*Columbia*	9	*15 Oct 66*	9
HALL OF FAME	*Columbia*	12	*11 Mar 67*	18
TWO FACES OF FAME	*CBS*	22	*1 Jul 67*	15

FAMILY — UK

SINGLES:	HITS 4			WEEKS 44
NO MULE'S FOOL	*Reprise*	29	*1 Nov 69*	7
STRANGE BAND: THE WEAVERS ANSWER	*Reprise*	11	*22 Aug 70*	12
IN MY OWN TIME	*Reprise*	4	*17 Jul 71*	13
BURLESQUE	*Reprise*	13	*23 Sep 72*	12

ALBUMS:	HITS 7			WEEKS 41
MUSIC IN THE DOLLS HOUSE	*Reprise*	35	*10 Aug 68*	3
FAMILY ENTERTAINMENT	*Reprise*	6	*22 Mar 69*	3
A SONG FOR ME	*Reprise*	4	*7 Feb 70*	13
ANYWAY	*Reprise*	7	*28 Nov 70*	7
FEARLESS	*Reprise*	14	*20 Nov 71*	2
BANDSTAND	*Reprise*	15	*30 Sep 72*	10
IT'S ONLY A MOVIE	*Raft*	30	*29 Sep 73*	3

FAMILY – See Afrika BAMBAATAA

FAMILY – See PUFF DADDY

FAMILY CAT — UK

SINGLES:	HITS 3			WEEKS 5
AIRPLANE GARDENS / ATMOSPHERIC ROAD	*Dedicated*	69	*28 Aug 93*	1
WONDERFUL EXCUSE	*Dedicated*	48	*21 May 94*	2
GOLDENBOOK	*Dedicated*	42	*30 Jul 94*	2

ALBUMS:	HITS 1			WEEKS 1
FURTHEST FROM THE SUN	*Dedicated*	55	*4 Jul 92*	1

FAMILY DOGG — UK

SINGLES:	HITS 1			WEEKS 14
A WAY OF LIFE	*Bell*	6	*31 May 69*	14

FAMILY FOUNDATION — UK

SINGLES:	HITS 1			WEEKS 4
XPRESS YOURSELF	*380 PEW*	42	*13 Jun 92*	4

FAMILY STAND — US

SINGLES:	HITS 1			WEEKS 13
GHETTO HEAVEN	*Atlantic*	10	*31 Mar 90*	11
GHETTO HEAVEN [RM]	*Perfecto Red*	30	*17 Jan 98*	2
Remixed by Jeff Ishmael.				
ALBUMS:	**HITS 1**			**WEEKS 3**
CHAIN	*Atlantic*	52	*19 May 90*	3

FAMOUS FLAMES – See James BROWN

FANTASTIC FOUR — US

SINGLES:	HITS 1			WEEKS 4
B.Y.O.F. (BRING YOUR OWN FUNK)	*Atlantic*	62	*24 Feb 79*	4

FANTASTICS — US

SINGLES:	HITS 1			WEEKS 12
SOMETHING OLD, SOMETHING NEW	*Bell*	9	*27 Mar 71*	12

FANTASY U.F.O. — UK

SINGLES:	HITS 2			WEEKS 6
FANTASY	*XL Recordings*	56	*29 Sep 90*	3
MIND, BODY, SOUL	*East West*	50	*10 Aug 91*	3
Above hit: FANTASY U.F.O. featuring Jay GROOVE.				

FAR CORPORATION — UK/US/Germany

SINGLES:	HITS 1			WEEKS 11
STAIRWAY TO HEAVEN	*Arista*	8	*26 Oct 85*	11
Originally recorded by Led Zeppelin.				

Sonny FARAR and his Banjo Band – See STARGAZERS

Don FARDON — UK

SINGLES:	HITS 2			WEEKS 22
BELFAST BOY	*Young Blood*	32	*18 Apr 70*	5
INDIAN RESERVATION	*Young Blood*	3	*10 Oct 70*	17
Originally recorded by John D. Loudermilk.				

FARGETTA — UK/Italy

SINGLES:	HITS 2			WEEKS 3
MUSIC	*Synthetic*	34	*23 Jan 93*	2
Above hit: FARGETTA and Anne-Marie SMITH.				
THE MUSIC IS MOVING	*Arista*	74	*10 Aug 96*	1

Chris FARLOWE — UK

SINGLES:	HITS 6			WEEKS 36
THINK	*Immediate*	49	*29 Jan 66*	1
THINK [RE]	*Immediate*	37	*12 Feb 66*	2
OUT OF TIME	*Immediate*	1	*25 Jun 66*	13
RIDE ON BABY	*Immediate*	31	*29 Oct 66*	7
Above 3 originally recorded by Rolling Stones.				
MY WAY OF GIVING IN	*Immediate*	48	*18 Feb 67*	1
Originally recorded by Small Faces.				
MOANIN'	*Immediate*	46	*2 Jul 67*	2
Originally recorded by Art Blakey and the Jazz Messengers.				
HANDBAGS AND GLADRAGS	*Immediate*	33	*16 Dec 67*	6
Originally recorded by Mike D'Abo.				
OUT OF TIME [RI]	*Immediate*	44	*27 Sep 75*	4
EPS:	**HITS 1**			**WEEKS 13**
FARLOWE IN THE MIDNIGHT HOUR	*Immediate*	6	*15 Jan 66*	13
ALBUMS:	**HITS 2**			**WEEKS 3**
14 THINGS TO THINK ABOUT	*Immediate*	19	*2 Apr 66*	1
THE ART OF CHRIS FARLOWE	*Immediate*	37	*10 Dec 66*	2

FARM — UK

SINGLES:	HITS 9			WEEKS 54
STEPPING STONE / FAMILY OF MAN	*Produce*	58	*5 May 90*	4
GROOVY TRAIN	*Produce*	6	*1 Sep 90*	10
ALL TOGETHER NOW	*Produce*	4	*8 Dec 90*	12
SINFUL! (SCARY JIGGIN' WITH DOCTOR LOVE)	*Siren*	28	*13 Apr 91*	5
Above hit: Pete WYLIE (and the FARM).				
DON'T LET ME DOWN	*Produce*	36	*4 May 91*	3
MIND	*Produce*	31	*24 Aug 91*	4
LOVE SEE NO COLOUR	*Produce*	58	*14 Dec 91*	4

RISING SUN	*End Product*	48	*4 Jul 92*	3
DON'T YOU WANT ME	*End Product*	18	*17 Oct 92*	5
Track from the NME 40th Anniversary album 'Ruby Trax'.				
LOVE SEE NO COLOUR [RI]	*End Product*	35	*2 Jan 93*	4
ALBUMS:	**HITS 1**			**WEEKS 17**
SPARTACUS	*Produce*	1	*16 Mar 91*	17

FARMER'S BOYS — UK

SINGLES:	**HITS 4**			**WEEKS 17**
MUCK IT OUT!	*EMI*	48	*9 Apr 83*	6
FOR YOU	*EMI*	66	*30 Jul 83*	3
IN THE COUNTRY	*EMI*	44	*4 Aug 84*	5
PHEW WOW	*EMI*	59	*3 Nov 84*	3
ALBUMS:	**HITS 1**			**WEEKS 1**
GET OUT AND WALK	*EMI*	49	*29 Oct 83*	1

John FARNHAM — Australia

SINGLES:	**HITS 1**			**WEEKS 17**
YOU'RE THE VOICE	*Wheatley*	6	*25 Apr 87*	17
ALBUMS:	**HITS 1**			**WEEKS 9**
WHISPERING JACK	*RCA*	35	*11 Jul 87*	9

FARRAR - See MARVIN, WELCH and FARRAR

Sonny FARRAR and his Banjo Band - See STARGAZERS

Joanne FARRELL — US

SINGLES:	**HITS 1**			**WEEKS 2**
ALL I WANNA DO	*Big Beat*	40	*24 Jun 95*	2

Joe FARRELL — US

SINGLES:	**HITS 1**			**WEEKS 4**
NIGHT DANCING	*Warner Brothers*	57	*16 Dec 78*	4

Dionne FARRIS — US

SINGLES:	**HITS 2**			**WEEKS 6**
I KNOW	*Columbia*	47	*18 Mar 95*	2
I KNOW [RE]	*Columbia*	41	*27 May 95*	3
HOPELESS	*Columbia*	42	*7 Jun 97*	1
From the film 'Love Jones'.				

Gene FARROW with the G. F. BAND — UK

SINGLES:	**HITS 2**			**WEEKS 8**
MOVE YOUR BODY	*Magnet*	33	*1 Apr 78*	5
MOVE YOUR BODY [RE]	*Magnet*	67	*13 May 78*	1
DON'T STOP NOW	*Magnet*	71	*5 Aug 78*	1
DON'T STOP NOW [RE]	*Magnet*	74	*19 Aug 78*	1

FASCINATIONS — US

SINGLES:	**HITS 1**			**WEEKS 6**
GIRLS ARE OUT TO GET YOU	*Mojo*	32	*3 Jul 71*	6

FASHION — UK

SINGLES:	**HITS 3**			**WEEKS 12**
STREETPLAYER (MECHANIK)	*Arista*	46	*3 Apr 82*	5
LOVE SHADOW	*Arista*	51	*21 Aug 82*	5
EYE TALK	*Epic*	69	*18 Feb 84*	2
ALBUMS:	**HITS 2**			**WEEKS 17**
FABRIQUE	*Arista*	10	*3 Jul 82*	16
TWILIGHT OF IDOLS	*De Stijl*	69	*16 Jun 84*	1

Susan FASSBENDER — UK

SINGLES:	**HITS 1**			**WEEKS 8**
TWILIGHT CAFE	*CBS*	21	*17 Jan 81*	8

FAST EDDIE - See DJ FAST EDDIE

FASTBALL — US

SINGLES:	**HITS 1**			**WEEKS 5**
THE WAY	*Hollywood*	21	*3 Oct 98*	5

FASTER PUSSYCAT
US

ALBUMS:	HITS 2			WEEKS 3
WAKE ME WHEN IT'S OVER	*Elektra*	35	*16 Sep 89*	2
WHIPPED!	*Elektra*	58	*22 Aug 92*	1

FASTWAY
UK

SINGLES:	HITS 1			WEEKS 1
EASY LIVIN'	*CBS*	74	*2 Apr 83*	1
ALBUMS:	**HITS 1**			**WEEKS 2**
FASTWAY	*CBS*	43	*30 Apr 83*	2

FAT BOYS
US

SINGLES:	HITS 4			WEEKS 29
JAIL HOUSE RAP	*Sultra*	63	*4 May 85*	2
WIPEOUT	*Urban*	2	*22 Aug 87*	12
Above hit: FAT BOYS and the BEACH BOYS.				
THE TWIST (YO, TWIST)	*Urban*	2	*18 Jun 88*	11
Original by Hank Ballard and the Midniters reached No. 28 in the US in 1960.				
Above hit: FAT BOYS (Lead Vocal: Chubby CHECKER).				
LOUIE LOUIE	*Urban*	46	*5 Nov 88*	4
Originally recorded by Richard Berry and the Pharoahs in 1957.				
ALBUMS:	**HITS 2**			**WEEKS 5**
CRUSHIN'	*Urban*	49	*3 Oct 87*	4
COMING BACK HARD AGAIN	*Urban*	98	*30 Jul 88*	1

FAT JOE - See Jennifer LOPEZ

FAT LADY SINGS
Ireland

SINGLES:	HITS 1			WEEKS 2
DRUNKARD LOGIC	*East West*	56	*17 Jul 93*	2
ALBUMS:	**HITS 1**			**WEEKS 1**
TWIST	*East West*	50	*18 May 91*	1

FAT LARRY'S BAND
US

SINGLES:	HITS 4			WEEKS 26
CENTER CITY	*WMOT*	31	*2 Jul 77*	5
BOOGIE TOWN	*Fantasy*	46	*10 Mar 79*	4
Above hit: FLB.				
LOOKIN' FOR LOVE TONIGHT	*Fantasy*	46	*18 Aug 79*	6
Above hit: FAT LARRY'S BAND (FLB).				
ZOOM	*WMOT*	2	*18 Sep 82*	11
ALBUMS:	**HITS 1**			**WEEKS 4**
BREAKIN' OUT	*WMOT*	58	*9 Oct 82*	4

FAT LES
UK

SINGLES:	HITS 3			WEEKS 22
VINDALOO	*Telstar*	2	*20 Jun 98*	12
NAUGHTY CHRISTMAS (GOBLIN IN THE OFFICE)	*Turtleneck*	21	*19 Dec 98*	5
JERUSALEM	*Parlophone*	10	*17 Jun 00*	3
The official England song for the Euro 2000 football championships. Based on Milton: And Did Those Feet In Ancient Time, an 1804 poem by William Blake.				
Above hit: FAT LES 2000				
JERUSALEM [RE]	*Parlophone*	55	*5 Aug 00*	2

FATBACK BAND
US

SINGLES:	HITS 9			WEEKS 67
YUM, YUM (GIMME SOME)	*Polydor*	40	*6 Sep 75*	6
(ARE YOU READY) DO THE BUS STOP	*Polydor*	18	*6 Dec 75*	10
(DO THE) SPANISH HUSTLE	*Polydor*	10	*21 Feb 76*	7
PARTY TIME	*Polydor*	41	*29 May 76*	4
NIGHT FEVER	*Spring*	38	*14 Aug 76*	4
DOUBLE DUTCH	*Spring*	31	*12 Mar 77*	4
BACKSTROKIN'	*Spring*	41	*9 Aug 80*	9
Above hit: FATBACK.				
I FOUND LOVIN'	*Master Mix*	49	*23 Jun 84*	4
GIRLS ON MY MIND	*Atlantic*	69	*4 May 85*	2
Above hit: FATBACK.				
I FOUND LOVIN' [RM] + [RE-1ST]	*Important & Master Mix*	55	*6 Sep 86*	5
Sales were combined for the original and the remix.				
I FOUND LOVIN' [RE-2ND]	*Master Mix*	7	*5 Sep 87*	12
ALBUMS:	**HITS 2**			**WEEKS 7**
RAISING HELL	*Polydor*	19	*6 Mar 76*	6

FATBACK LIVE	*Start*	80	*4 Jul 87*	1
Above hit: FATBACK.				

FATBOY SLIM — UK

(See also Norman Cook; Mighty Dub Katz.)

SINGLES:	HITS 11			WEEKS 72
GOING OUT OF MY HEAD / MICHAEL JACKSON	*Skint*	57	*3 May 97*	1
EVERYBODY NEEDS A 303	*Skint*	34	*1 Nov 97*	2
THE ROCKAFELLER SKANK	*Skint*	6	*20 Jun 98*	10
Samples the Just Brothers' Sliced Tomatoes and the John Barry Seven's Beat Girl.				
GANGSTA TRIPPIN	*Skint*	3	*17 Oct 98*	8
Samples DJ Shadow's Entropy and Dust Junkys Beatbox Wash.				
PRAISE YOU	*Skint*	1	*16 Jan 99*	12
Samples Camille Yarborough's Take Yo Praise.				
RIGHT HERE RIGHT NOW	*Skint*	2	*1 May 99*	10
Samples the James Gang's Ashes, The Rain And I.				
BADDER BADDER SCHWING	*Eye Q*	34	*1 May 99*	2
Above hit: Freddy FRESH (featuring FATBOY SLIM).				
SUNSET (BIRD OF PREY)	*Skint*	9	*28 Oct 00*	7
Samples Jim Morrison's Bird Of Prey from his posthumously released (1978) American Prayer album.				
SUNSET (BIRD OF PREY) [RE]	*Skint*	54	*30 Dec 00*	6
DEMONS	*Skint*	16	*20 Jan 01*	5
Samples Bill Withers' I Can't Write Left Handed.				
Above hit: FATBOY SLIM featuring Macy GRAY.				
STAR 69 WHAT THE F**K	*Skint*	10	*5 May 01*	7
Samples Roland Clarke's I Get Deep.				
YA MAMA/SONG FOR SHELTER	*Skint*	30	*15 Sep 01*	2
ALBUMS:	**HITS 3**			**WEEKS 104**
BETTER LIVING THROUGH CHEMISTRY	*Skint*	69	*28 Sep 96*	3
YOU'VE COME A LONG WAY, BABY	*Skint*	1	*31 Oct 98*	86
HALFWAY BETWEEN THE GUTTER AND THE STARS	*Skint*	8	*18 Nov 00*	15

FATHER ABRAHAM and the SMURFS – See SMURFS

FATHER ABRAPHART and the SMURPS – See Jonathan KING

FATHER Colm KILCOYNE – See POPE JOHN PAUL II

FATIMA MANSIONS — Ireland

SINGLES:	HITS 4			WEEKS 11
EVIL MAN	*Radioactive*	59	*23 May 92*	1
1000%	*Radioactive*	61	*1 Aug 92*	3
EVERYTHING I DO (I DO IT FOR YOU)	*Columbia*	7	*19 Sep 92*	6
[AA] listed with Theme From M.A.S.H. (Suicide Is Painless) by Manic Street Preachers. Both were tracks from the NME 40th Anniversary album 'Ruby Trax'.				
THE LOYALISER	*Kitchenware*	58	*6 Aug 94*	1
ALBUMS:	**HITS 1**			**WEEKS 1**
VALHALLA AVENUE	*Radioactive*	52	*6 Jun 92*	1

FE-M@IL — UK

SINGLES:	HITS 1			WEEKS 2
FLEE FLY FLO	*Jive*	46	*5 Aug 00*	2

FEAR FACTORY — US

SINGLES:	HITS 1			WEEKS 1
CARS	*Roadrunner*	57	*9 Oct 99*	1
Includes vocals by Gary Numan.				
ALBUMS:	**HITS 4**			**WEEKS 6**
DEMANUFACTURE	*Roadrunner*	27	*1 Jul 95*	1
REMANUFACTURE - CLONING TECHNOLOGY	*Roadrunner*	22	*14 Jun 97*	1
Tracks from Demanufacture, remixed by Rhys Fulber, DJ Dano, Kingsize and Junkie XL.				
OBSOLETE	*Roadrunner*	20	*8 Aug 98*	2
DIGIMORTAL	*Roadrunner*	24	*5 May 01*	2

Phil FEARON — UK

(See also T.C. Curtis.)

SINGLES:	HITS 9			WEEKS 63
DANCING TIGHT	*Ensign*	4	*23 Apr 83*	11
WAIT UNTIL TONIGHT (MY LOVE)	*Ensign*	20	*30 Jul 83*	8
Above 2: GALAXY featuring Phil FEARON.				
FANTASY REAL	*Ensign*	41	*22 Oct 83*	6
WHAT DO I DO?	*Ensign*	5	*10 Mar 84*	10
EVERYBODY'S LAUGHING	*Ensign*	10	*14 Jul 84*	10
YOU DON'T NEED A REASON	*Ensign*	42	*15 Jun 85*	4
Above 4: Phil FEARON and GALAXY.				

THIS KIND OF LOVE	*Ensign*	70	*27 Jul 85*	3
Above hit: Phil FEARON and GALAXY featuring Dee GALDES.				
I CAN PROVE IT	*Ensign*	8	*2 Aug 86*	9
Originally recorded by Tony Etoria.				
AIN'T NOTHING BUT A HOUSE PARTY	*Ensign*	60	*15 Nov 86*	2
ALBUMS:	**HITS 2**			**WEEKS 9**
PHIL FEARON AND GALAXY	*Ensign*	8	*25 Aug 84*	8
THIS KIND OF LOVE	*Ensign*	98	*14 Sep 85*	1
Above 2: Phil FEARON and GALAXY.				

FEEBI – See T-EMPO

FEEDER — UK

SINGLES:	**HITS 13**			**WEEKS 32**
TANGERINE	*Echo*	60	*8 Mar 97*	1
CEMENT	*Echo*	53	*10 May 97*	1
CRASH	*Echo*	48	*23 Aug 97*	1
HIGH	*Echo*	24	*18 Oct 97*	2
SUFFOCATE	*Echo*	37	*28 Feb 98*	1
DAY IN DAY OUT	*Echo*	31	*3 Apr 99*	2
INSOMNIA	*Echo*	22	*12 Jun 99*	3
YESTERDAY WENT TOO SOON	*Echo*	20	*21 Aug 99*	3
PAPERFACES	*Echo*	41	*20 Nov 99*	2
BUCK ROGERS	*Echo*	5	*20 Jan 01*	6
SEVEN DAYS IN THE SUN	*Echo*	14	*14 Apr 01*	4
SEVEN DAYS IN THE SUN [RE]	*Echo*	57	*19 May 01*	2
TURN	*Echo*	27	*14 Jul 01*	2
JUST A DAY [EP]	*Echo*	12	*22 Dec 01*	2
Lead track: Just A Day.				
ALBUMS:	**HITS 3**			**WEEKS 12**
POLYTHENE	*Echo*	65	*31 May 97*	1
YESTERDAY WENT TOO SOON	*Echo*	8	*11 Sep 99*	3
ECHO PARK	*Echo*	5	*5 May 01*	8

Wilton FELDER — US

SINGLES:	**HITS 2**			**WEEKS 7**
INHERIT THE WIND	*MCA*	39	*1 Nov 80*	5
Lead vocals by Bobby Womack.				
(NO MATTER HOW HIGH I GET) I'LL STILL BE LOOKIN' UP TO YOU	*MCA*	63	*16 Feb 85*	2
Above hit: Wilton FELDER featuring Bobby WOMACK and introducing Alltrinna GRAYSON.				
ALBUMS:	**HITS 1**			**WEEKS 3**
SECRETS	*MCA*	77	*23 Feb 85*	3
Above hit: Wilton FELDER featuring Bobby WOMACK and introducing Alltrina GRAYSON.				

FELICIA – See B.M.R. featuring FELICIA

Jose FELICIANO — US

SINGLES:	**HITS 2**			**WEEKS 23**
LIGHT MY FIRE	*RCA Victor*	6	*21 Sep 68*	16
AND THE SUN WILL SHINE	*RCA Victor*	25	*18 Oct 69*	7
Originally recorded by The Bee Gees.				
ALBUMS:	**HITS 4**			**WEEKS 40**
FELICIANO	*RCA Victor*	6	*2 Nov 68*	36
JOSE FELICIANO	*RCA Victor*	29	*29 Nov 69*	2
10 TO 23	*RCA Victor*	38	*14 Feb 70*	1
FIREWORKS	*RCA Victor*	65	*22 Aug 70*	1

FELIX — UK

SINGLES:	**HITS 3**			**WEEKS 29**
DON'T YOU WANT ME	*Deconstruction*	6	*8 Aug 92*	11
IT WILL MAKE ME CRAZY	*Deconstruction*	11	*24 Oct 92*	6
Vocals by Steele.				
STARS	*Deconstruction*	29	*22 May 93*	3
DON'T YOU WANT ME [RM-1ST]	*Deconstruction*	10	*12 Aug 95*	5
Remixed by Patrick Prins.				
DON'T YOU WANT ME ('96 PUGILIST MIX) [RM-2ND]	*Deconstruction*	17	*19 Oct 96*	4
Featured in the Tango Blackcurrant TV commercial. Remixed by Tom Hayes.				
ALBUMS:	**HITS 1**			**WEEKS 4**
FELIX #1	*Deconstruction*	26	*10 Apr 93*	4

Julie FELIX — US

SINGLES:	HITS 2			WEEKS 19
(EL CONDOR PASA) IF I COULD *Originally recorded by Simon And Garfunkel.*	*RAK*	19	*18 Apr 70*	11
HEAVEN IS HERE	*RAK*	22	*17 Oct 70*	8
EPS:	**HITS 1**			**WEEKS 6**
SONGS FROM 'THE FROST REPORT'	*Fontana*	5	*13 Aug 66*	6
ALBUMS:	**HITS 1**			**WEEKS 4**
CHANGES	*Fontana*	27	*10 Sep 66*	4

FELIX DA HOUSECAT — US

SINGLES:	HITS 2			WEEKS 2
DIRTY MOTHA *Above hit: QWILO and FELIX DA HOUSECAT featuring Lynn CROUCH.*	*Manifesto*	66	*6 Sep 97*	1
SILVER SCREEN SHOWER SCENE *Above hit: FELIX DA HOUSECAT featuring MS. KITTIN*	*City Rockers*	55	*14 Jul 01*	1

FELLY - See TECHNOTRONIC

FEMME FATALE — US

SINGLES:	HITS 1			WEEKS 2
FALLING IN AND OUT OF LOVE	*MCA*	69	*11 Feb 89*	2

FEN - See RAMSEY and FEN featuring Lynsey MOORE

FENDERMEN — US

SINGLES:	HITS 1			WEEKS 9
MULE SKINNER BLUES *Originally recorded by Jimmie Rodgers in 1931.*	*Top Rank*	50	*20 Aug 60*	1
MULE SKINNER BLUES [RE-1ST]	*Top Rank*	37	*3 Sep 60*	2
MULE SKINNER BLUES [RE-2ND]	*Top Rank*	32	*1 Oct 60*	6

George FENTON - See Cry Freedom

Peter FENTON — UK

SINGLES:	HITS 1			WEEKS 3
MARBLE BREAKS IRON BENDS *Originally recorded by Drafi.*	*Fontana*	46	*12 Nov 66*	3

Shane FENTON and the FENTONES — UK

(See also Fentones; Alvin Stardust.)

SINGLES:	HITS 4			WEEKS 28
I'M A MOODY GUY	*Parlophone*	22	*28 Oct 61*	8
WALK AWAY	*Parlophone*	38	*3 Feb 62*	5
IT'S ALL OVER NOW	*Parlophone*	29	*7 Apr 62*	7
CINDY'S BIRTHDAY *Originally recorded by Johnny Crawford.*	*Parlophone*	19	*14 Jul 62*	8

FENTONES — UK

(See also Shane Fenton and the Fentones.)

SINGLES:	HITS 2			WEEKS 4
THE MEXICAN	*Parlophone*	41	*21 Apr 62*	3
THE BREEZE AND I	*Parlophone*	48	*29 Sep 62*	1

FERGIE — Ireland

SINGLES:	HITS 2			WEEKS 3
DECEPTION	*Duty Free*	47	*9 Sep 00*	1
HOOVERS AND HORNS *Above hit: FERGIE and BK.*	*Nukleuz*	57	*25 Nov 00*	2

Sheila FERGUSON — US

SINGLES:	HITS 1			WEEKS 1
WHEN WILL I SEE YOU AGAIN	*XSRhythm*	60	*5 Feb 94*	1

FERKO STRING BAND — US

SINGLES:	HITS 1			WEEKS 2
ALABAMA JUBILEE *Originally recorded by Arthur Collins and Byron Harlan in 1915.*	*London*	20	*13 Aug 55*	2

Luisa FERNANDEZ — Spain

SINGLES:	HITS 1			WEEKS 8
LAY LOVE ON YOU	*Warner Brothers*	31	*11 Nov 78*	8

Pamela FERNANDEZ — US

SINGLES:	HITS 2			WEEKS 3
KICKIN' IN THE BEAT	*Ore*	43	*17 Sep 94*	2
LET'S START OVER / KICKIN' IN THE BEAT [RM]	*Ore*	59	*3 Jun 95*	1
Kickin' In the Beat remixed by Todd Terry.				

FERRANTE and TEICHER — US

SINGLES:	HITS 2			WEEKS 18
THEME FROM 'THE APARTMENT'	*London*	44	*20 Aug 60*	1
Title originally called Jealous Lover in 1949.				
THEME FROM "EXODUS"	*London*	6	*11 Mar 61*	17
Issued on HMV during chart run when United Artists changed UK outlets. Both labels listed on the chart from 10 Jun 61. The HMV label reads title as Exodus (Theme From "Exodus").				

Ibrahim FERRER — Cuba

ALBUMS:	HITS 1			WEEKS 3
BUENA VISTA SOCIAL CLUB PRESENTS . . .	*World Circuit*	42	*5 Jun 99*	3

Jose FERRER — US

SINGLES:	HITS 1			WEEKS 3
WOMAN (UH - HUH)	*Philips*	7	*20 Feb 54*	3
[AA] listed with Man (Uh - Huh) by Rosemary Clooney.				

Tony FERRINO — UK

SINGLES:	HITS 1			WEEKS 2
HELP YOURSELF / BIGAMY AT CHRISTMAS	*RCA*	42	*23 Nov 96*	2

Bryan FERRY — UK

SINGLES:	HITS 22			WEEKS 133
A HARD RAIN'S A-GONNA FALL	*Island*	10	*29 Sep 73*	9
Originally recorded by Bob Dylan.				
THE 'IN' CROWD	*Island*	13	*25 May 74*	6
SMOKE GETS IN YOUR EYES	*Island*	17	*31 Aug 74*	8
Originally recorded by Paul Whiteman in 1933.				
YOU GO TO MY HEAD	*Island*	33	*5 Jul 75*	3
LET'S STICK TOGETHER (LET'S WORK TOGETHER)	*Island*	4	*12 Jun 76*	10
Originally recorded by Wilbert Harrison.				
EXTENDED PLAY [EP]	*Island*	7	*7 Aug 76*	9
Lead track: Price Of Love.				
THIS IS TOMORROW	*Polydor*	9	*5 Feb 77*	9
TOKYO JOE	*Polydor*	15	*14 May 77*	7
WHAT GOES ON	*Polydor*	67	*13 May 78*	2
SIGN OF THE TIMES	*Polydor*	37	*5 Aug 78*	8
SLAVE TO LOVE	*E'G*	10	*11 May 85*	9
DON'T STOP THE DANCE	*E'G*	21	*31 Aug 85*	7
WINDSWEPT	*E'G*	46	*7 Dec 85*	3
IS YOUR LOVE STRONG ENOUGH	*E'G*	22	*29 Mar 86*	7
THE RIGHT STUFF	*Virgin*	37	*10 Oct 87*	6
KISS AND TELL	*Virgin*	41	*13 Feb 88*	5
From the film 'Bright Lights Big City'.				
LET'S STICK TOGETHER WESTSIDE '88 REMIX [RM]	*E'G*	12	*29 Oct 88*	7
THE PRICE OF LOVE: THE R&B '89 REMIX [RM]	*E'G*	49	*11 Feb 89*	3
Above 2 remixed by Bruce Lampcov and Rhett Davies.				
HE'LL HAVE TO GO	*E'G*	63	*22 Apr 89*	1
I PUT A SPELL ON YOU	*Virgin*	18	*6 Mar 93*	5
WILL YOU LOVE ME TOMORROW	*Virgin*	23	*29 May 93*	5
GIRL OF MY BEST FRIEND	*Virgin*	57	*4 Sep 93*	2
YOUR PAINTED SMILE	*Virgin*	52	*29 Oct 94*	1
MAMOUNA	*Virgin*	57	*11 Feb 95*	1

ALBUMS:	HITS 14			WEEKS 320
THESE FOOLISH THINGS	*Island*	5	*3 Nov 73*	42
ANOTHER TIME, ANOTHER PLACE	*Island*	4	*20 Jul 74*	25
LET'S STICK TOGETHER	*Island*	19	*2 Oct 76*	5
IN YOUR MIND	*Polydor*	5	*5 Mar 77*	17
THE BRIDE STRIPPED BARE	*Polydor*	13	*30 Sep 78*	5
BOYS AND GIRLS	*E'G*	1	*15 Jun 85*	44
STREET LIFE - 20 GREAT HITS	*E'G*	1	*26 Apr 86*	77
Above hit: Bryan FERRY ROXY MUSIC.				
BETE NOIRE	*Virgin*	9	*14 Nov 87*	16
THE ULTIMATE COLLECTION	*E'G*	6	*19 Nov 88*	27
Above hit: Bryan FERRY and ROXY MUSIC.				
TAXI	*Virgin*	2	*3 Apr 93*	14
MAMOUNA	*Virgin*	11	*17 Sep 94*	4
THE ULTIMATE COLLECTION [RI]	*Virgin*	26	*17 Sep 94*	8
Above hit: Bryan FERRY and ROXY MUSIC.				

MORE THAN THIS - THE BEST OF BRYAN FERRY AND ROXY MUSIC *Above hit: Bryan FERRY and ROXY MUSIC.*	*Virgin*	15	*4 Nov 95*	15
AS TIME GOES BY *Compilation of songs from the 1930s.*	*Virgin*	16	*6 Nov 99*	10
SLAVE TO LOVE	*Virgin*	11	*22 Jul 00*	11

FERRY AID — International

SINGLES:	HITS 1			WEEKS 7
LET IT BE *Proceeds to the Sun's Zeebrugge Disaster Fund.*	*The Sun*	1	*4 Apr 87*	7

FEVER featuring Tippa IRIE — UK

SINGLES:	HITS 1			WEEKS 1
STAYING ALIVE 95	*Telstar*	48	*8 Jul 95*	1

F45 - See DE FUNK featuring F45

FFWD — UK/Germany

ALBUMS:	HITS 1			WEEKS 1
FFWD	*Inter*	48	*13 Aug 94*	1

Lena FIAGBE — UK

SINGLES:	HITS 5			WEEKS 13
YOU COME FROM EARTH *Above hit: LENA.*	*Mother*	69	*24 Jul 93*	1
GOTTA GET IT RIGHT	*Mother*	20	*23 Oct 93*	5
WHAT'S IT LIKE TO BE BEAUTIFUL	*Mother*	52	*16 Apr 94*	3
VISIONS	*Mother*	48	*25 Jun 94*	2
AFRICAN DREAM *Above hit: Wasis DIOP featuring Lena FIAGBE.*	*Mercury*	44	*10 Feb 96*	2

Karel FIALKA — UK

SINGLES:	HITS 2			WEEKS 12
THE EYES HAVE IT	*Blueprint*	52	*17 May 80*	4
HEY MATTHEW *Features Karel's step-son Matthew.*	*I.R.S.*	9	*5 Sep 87*	8

FIAT LUX — UK

SINGLES:	HITS 2			WEEKS 4
SECRETS	*Polydor*	65	*28 Jan 84*	3
BLUE EMOTION	*Polydor*	59	*17 Mar 84*	1

FICTION FACTORY — UK

SINGLES:	HITS 2			WEEKS 11
(FEELS LIKE) HEAVEN	*CBS*	6	*14 Jan 84*	9
GHOST OF LOVE	*CBS*	64	*17 Mar 84*	2

FIDDLER'S DRAM — UK

SINGLES:	HITS 1			WEEKS 9
DAYTRIP TO BANGOR (DIDN'T WE HAVE A LOVELY TIME)	*Dingle's*	3	*15 Dec 79*	9

FIDELFATTI featuring RONNETTE — Italy

SINGLES:	HITS 1			WEEKS 1
JUST WANNA TOUCH ME *Original release reached No. 88 in 1989.*	*Urban*	65	*27 Jan 90*	1

Brad FIEDEL — Germany

ALBUMS:	HITS 1			WEEKS 7
TERMINATOR 2 [OST]	*Varese Sarabande*	26	*31 Aug 91*	7

Billy FIELD — Australia

SINGLES:	HITS 1			WEEKS 3
YOU WEREN'T IN LOVE WITH ME	*CBS*	67	*12 Jun 82*	3

Ernie FIELD'S ORCHESTRA — US

SINGLES:	HITS 1			WEEKS 8
IN THE MOOD *Originally recorded by Glenn Miller in 1939.*	*London*	13	*26 Dec 59*	8

Gracie FIELDS — UK

SINGLES:	HITS 2			WEEKS 15
AROUND THE WORLD	*Columbia*	8	*1 Jun 57*	8
From the film 'Around the World In 80 Days'.				
Above hit: Gracie FIELDS with Tony OSBORNE and his Orchestra and Chorus.				
AROUND THE WORLD [RE]	*Columbia*	24	*3 Aug 57*	1
LITTLE DONKEY	*Columbia*	30	*7 Nov 59*	1
Above hit: Gracie FIELDS with the Rita WILLIAMS SINGERS.				
LITTLE DONKEY [RE]	*Columbia*	21	*21 Nov 59*	5
EPS:	**HITS 1**			**WEEKS 1**
OUR GRACIE SINGS COMEDY SONGS	*HMV*	16	*26 Nov 60*	1
ALBUMS:	**HITS 1**			**WEEKS 3**
THE GOLDEN YEARS	*Warwick*	48	*20 Dec 75*	3

Richard 'Dimples' FIELDS — US

SINGLES:	HITS 1			WEEKS 4
I'VE GOT TO LEARN TO SAY NO!	*Epic*	56	*20 Feb 82*	4

FIELDS OF THE NEPHILIM — UK

SINGLES:	HITS 5			WEEKS 9
BLUE WATER	*Situation Two*	75	*24 Oct 87*	1
MOONCHILD	*Situation Two*	28	*4 Jun 88*	3
PSYCHONAUT	*Situation Two*	35	*27 May 89*	3
FOR HER LIGHT	*Beggars Banquet*	54	*4 Aug 90*	1
SUMERLAND (DREAMED)	*Beggars Banquet*	37	*24 Nov 90*	1
ALBUMS:	**HITS 4**			**WEEKS 9**
DAWNRAZOR	*Situation Two*	62	*30 May 87*	2
THE NEPHILIM	*Situation Two*	14	*17 Sep 88*	3
ELIZIUM	*Beggars Banquet*	22	*6 Oct 90*	2
EARTH INFERNO	*Beggars Banquet*	39	*6 Apr 91*	2

FIERCE — UK

SINGLES:	HITS 4			WEEKS 23
RIGHT HERE RIGHT NOW	*Wildstar*	25	*9 Jan 99*	5
DAYS LIKE THAT	*Wildstar*	11	*15 May 99*	5
SO LONG	*Wildstar*	15	*14 Aug 99*	5
SWEET LOVE 2K	*Wildstar*	3	*12 Feb 00*	8
ALBUMS:	**HITS 1**			**WEEKS 2**
RIGHT HERE RIGHT NOW	*Wildstar*	27	*28 Aug 99*	2

5TH DIMENSION — US

SINGLES:	HITS 2			WEEKS 21
MEDLEY: AQUARIUS/LET THE SUNSHINE IN (THE FLESH FAILURES) [M]	*Liberty*	11	*19 Apr 69*	12
From the musical 'Hair'.				
WEDDING BELL BLUES	*Liberty*	16	*17 Jan 70*	9
Originally recorded by Laura Nyro.				

50.GRIND featuring POKEMON ALLSTARS — UK

SINGLES:	HITS 1			WEEKS 1
GOTTA CATCH 'EM ALL	*Recognition*	57	*22 Dec 01*	1

5050

SINGLES:	HITS 1			WEEKS 1
WHO'S COMING AROUND	*Obsessive*	54	*13 Oct 01*	1

52ND STREET — UK

SINGLES:	HITS 3			WEEKS 13
TELL ME (HOW IT FEELS)	*10 Records*	54	*2 Nov 85*	5
YOU'RE MY LAST CHANCE	*10 Records*	49	*11 Jan 86*	4
I CAN'T LET YOU GO	*10 Records*	57	*8 Mar 86*	4
ALBUMS:	**HITS 1**			**WEEKS 1**
CHILDREN OF THE NIGHT	*10 Records*	71	*19 Apr 86*	1

53RD & 3RD featuring the SOUND OF SHAG - See Jonathan KING

FILTER — US

SINGLES:	HITS 2			WEEKS 5
(CAN'T YOU) TRIP LIKE I DO	*Epic*	39	*11 Oct 97*	2
From the film 'Spawn'.				
Above hit: FILTER and the CRYSTAL METHOD.				
TAKE A PICTURE	*Reprise*	25	*18 Mar 00*	3

ALBUMS:	HITS 1			WEEKS 1
TITLE OF RECORD	*Reprise*	75	*4 Sep 99*	1

FINAL CUT – See TRUE FAITH and Bridgette GRACE with FINAL CUT

FINE YOUNG CANNIBALS — UK

SINGLES:	HITS 11			WEEKS 81
JOHNNY COME HOME	*London*	8	*8 Jun 85*	13
BLUE	*London*	41	*9 Nov 85*	6
SUSPICIOUS MINDS	*London*	8	*11 Jan 86*	9
FUNNY HOW LOVE IS	*London*	58	*12 Apr 86*	4
EVER FALLEN IN LOVE	*London*	9	*21 Mar 87*	10
SHE DRIVES ME CRAZY	*London*	5	*7 Jan 89*	11
GOOD THING	*London*	7	*15 Apr 89*	8
From the film 'Tin Men'.				
DON'T LOOK BACK	*London*	34	*19 Aug 89*	4
I'M NOT THE MAN I USED TO BE	*London*	20	*18 Nov 89*	8
I'M NOT SATISFIED	*London*	46	*24 Feb 90*	3
THE FLAME	*ffrr*	17	*16 Nov 96*	3
SHE DRIVES ME CRAZY [RI]	*ffrr*	36	*11 Jan 97*	2
ALBUMS:	**HITS 4**			**WEEKS 107**
FINE YOUNG CANNIBALS	*London*	11	*21 Dec 85*	27
THE RAW & THE COOKED	*London*	1	*18 Feb 89*	66
THE RAW AND THE REMIX	*London*	61	*15 Dec 90*	1
Remixed tracks from The Raw And The Cooked.				
Above hit: FYC.				
THE FINEST	*ffrr*	10	*23 Nov 96*	13

FINITRIBE — UK

SINGLES:	HITS 2			WEEKS 2
FOREVERGREEN	*One Little Indian*	51	*11 Jul 92*	1
BRAND NEW	*ffrr*	69	*19 Nov 94*	1

FINK BROTHERS — UK

SINGLES:	HITS 1			WEEKS 4
MUTANTS IN MEGA CITY ONE	*Zarjazz*	50	*9 Feb 85*	4

Frank FINLAY – See David ESSEX

FINN — New Zealand

SINGLES:	HITS 2			WEEKS 5
SUFFER NEVER	*Parlophone*	29	*14 Oct 95*	3
ANGEL'S HEAP	*Parlophone*	41	*9 Dec 95*	2
ALBUMS:	**HITS 1**			**WEEKS 3**
FINN	*Parlophone*	15	*28 Oct 95*	3

Micky FINN – See URBAN SHAKEDOWN featuring Micky FINN

Neil FINN — New Zealand

SINGLES:	HITS 4			WEEKS 6
SHE WILL HAVE HER WAY	*Parlophone*	26	*13 Jun 98*	2
SINNER	*Parlophone*	39	*17 Oct 98*	1
WHEREVER YOU ARE	*Parlophone*	32	*7 Apr 01*	2
HOLE IN THE ICE	*Parlophone*	43	*22 Sep 01*	1
ALBUMS:	**HITS 2**			**WEEKS 15**
TRY WHISTLING THIS	*Parlophone*	5	*27 Jun 98*	11
ONE NIL	*Parlophone*	14	*21 Apr 01*	4

Tim FINN — New Zealand

SINGLES:	HITS 2			WEEKS 6
PERSUASION	*Capitol*	43	*26 Jun 93*	3
HIT THE GROUND RUNNING	*Capitol*	50	*18 Sep 93*	3
ALBUMS:	**HITS 1**			**WEEKS 2**
BEFORE AND AFTER	*Capitol*	29	*10 Jul 93*	2

Johnnie FIORI – See BARKIN BROTHERS featuring Johnnie FIORI

Elisa FIORILLO — US

SINGLES:	HITS 2			WEEKS 14
WHO FOUND WHO	*Chrysalis*	10	*28 Nov 87*	10
Above hit: JELLYBEAN featuring Elisa FIORILLO.				
HOW CAN I FORGET YOU	*Chrysalis*	50	*13 Feb 88*	4

FIRE INC. – See Jim STEINMAN

FIRE ISLAND — UK

(See also Heller and Farley Project.)

SINGLES:	HITS 4			WEEKS 7
IN YOUR BONES / FIRE ISLAND	*Boy's Own Productions*	66	*8 Aug 92*	1
THERE BUT FOR THE GRACE OF GOD *Originally recorded by Kid Creole and the Coconuts.* *Above hit: FIRE ISLAND featuring: LOVE NELSON.*	*Junior Boy's Own*	32	*12 Mar 94*	3
IF YOU SHOULD NEED A FRIEND *Originally recorded by Blaze in 1987.* *Above hit: FIRE ISLAND featuring Mark ANTHONI.*	*Junior Boy's Own*	51	*4 Mar 95*	1
SHOUT TO THE TOP *Above hit: FIRE ISLAND featuring Loleatta HOLLOWAY.*	*JBO*	23	*11 Apr 98*	2

FIREBALLS — US

SINGLES:	HITS 2			WEEKS 17
QUITE A PARTY	*Pye International*	29	*29 Jul 61*	9
SUGAR SHACK *Above hit: Jimmy GILMER and the FIREBALLS.*	*London*	45	*16 Nov 63*	4
SUGAR SHACK [RE]	*London*	46	*21 Dec 63*	4

FIREHOUSE — US

SINGLES:	HITS 2			WEEKS 2
DON'T TREAT ME BAD	*Epic*	71	*13 Jul 91*	1
WHEN I LOOK INTO YOUR EYES	*Epic*	65	*19 Dec 92*	1

FIRM — UK

SINGLES:	HITS 2			WEEKS 21
ARTHUR DALEY ('E'S ALRIGHT) *Arthur Daley is character from the Thames ITV series 'Minder'.*	*Bark*	14	*17 Jul 82*	9
STAR TREKKIN' *Novelty single based around characters from 'Star Trek'.*	*Bark*	1	*6 Jun 87*	12

FIRM — UK

ALBUMS:	HITS 2			WEEKS 8
THE FIRM	*Atlantic*	15	*2 Mar 85*	5
MEAN BUSINESS	*Atlantic*	46	*5 Apr 86*	3

Nas ESCOBAR, Foxy BROWN, AZ and NATURE present the FIRM featuring Dawn ROBINSON — US

(See also AZ; Foxy Brown; Nas.)

SINGLES:	HITS 1			WEEKS 3
FIRM BIZ	*Columbia*	18	*29 Nov 97*	3

FIRST CHOICE — UK

SINGLES:	HITS 2			WEEKS 21
ARMED AND EXTREMELY DANGEROUS	*Bell*	16	*19 May 73*	10
SMARTY PANTS	*Bell*	9	*4 Aug 73*	11

FIRST CIRCLE — US

ALBUMS:	HITS 1			WEEKS 2
BOY'S NIGHT OUT	*EMI America*	70	*2 May 87*	2

FIRST CLASS — UK

SINGLES:	HITS 1			WEEKS 10
BEACH BABY	UK	13	*15 Jun 74*	10

FIRST EDITION – See Kenny ROGERS

FIRST LIGHT — UK

SINGLES:	HITS 2			WEEKS 5
EXPLAIN THE REASONS	*London*	65	*21 May 83*	3
WISH YOU WERE HERE	*London*	71	*28 Jan 84*	2

FIRSTBORN — Ireland

SINGLES:	HITS 1			WEEKS 1
THE MOOD CLUB *From the film 'Human Traffic'.*	*Independiente*	69	*19 Jun 99*	1

Carl FISCHER – See Doris DAY; Frankie LAINE.

FISCHER-Z — UK

SINGLES:	HITS 2			WEEKS 7
THE WORKER	*United Artists*	53	*26 May 79*	5
SO LONG	*United Artists*	72	*3 May 80*	2
ALBUMS:	**HITS 1**			**WEEKS 1**
WORD SALAD	*United Artists*	66	*23 Jun 79*	1

FISH — UK

SINGLES:	HITS 10			WEEKS 20
SHORTCUT TO SOMEWHERE	*Charisma*	75	*18 Oct 86*	1
Above hit: FISH and Tony BANKS.				
STATE OF MIND	*EMI*	32	*28 Oct 89*	3
BIG WEDGE	*EMI*	25	*6 Jan 90*	4
A GENTLEMAN'S EXCUSE ME	*EMI*	30	*17 Mar 90*	3
INTERNAL EXILE	*Polydor*	37	*28 Sep 91*	2
CREDO	*Polydor*	38	*11 Jan 92*	2
SOMETHING IN THE AIR	*Polydor*	51	*4 Jul 92*	2
LADY LET IT LIE	*The Dick Brothers*	46	*16 Apr 94*	1
FORTUNES OF WAR	*The Dick Brothers*	67	*1 Oct 94*	1
JUST GOOD FRIENDS	*The Dick Brothers*	63	*26 Aug 95*	1
Above hit: FISH featuring Sam BROWN.				
ALBUMS:	**HITS 8**			**WEEKS 17**
VIGIL IN A WILDERNESS OF MIRRORS	*EMI*	5	*10 Feb 90*	6
INTERNAL EXILE	*Polydor*	21	*9 Nov 91*	3
SONGS FROM THE MIRROR	*Polydor*	46	*30 Jan 93*	2
SUITS	*The Dick Brothers*	18	*11 Jun 94*	2
YANG	*The Dick Brothers*	52	*16 Sep 95*	1
YIN	*The Dick Brothers*	58	*16 Sep 95*	1
Above 2 feature remixes/re-recordings of Marillion and solo material.				
SUNSETS ON EMPIRE	*The Dick Brothers*	42	*31 May 97*	1
RAINGODS WITH ZIPPOS	*Roadrunner*	57	*1 May 99*	1

FISHBONE — US

SINGLES:	HITS 2			WEEKS 3
EVERYDAY SUNSHINE / FIGHT THE YOUTH	*Columbia*	60	*1 Aug 92*	2
SWIM	*Columbia*	54	*28 Aug 93*	1
ALBUMS:	**HITS 1**			**WEEKS 1**
THE REALITY OF MY SURROUNDINGS	*Columbia*	75	*13 Jul 91*	1

Cevin FISHER — US

SINGLES:	HITS 5			WEEKS 9
THE FREAKS COME OUT	*Sound Of Ministry*	34	*3 Oct 98*	2
Above hit: Cevin FISHER'S BIG BREAK.				
(YOU GOT ME) BURNING UP	*Wonderboy*	14	*20 Feb 99*	4
Samples Loleatta Holloway's Love Sensation.				
Above hit: Cevin FISHER featuring Loleatta HOLLOWAY.				
MUSIC SAVED MY LIFE	*Sm:)e Communications*	67	*7 Aug 99*	1
IT'S A GOOD LIFE	*Wonderboy*	54	*20 Jan 01*	1
Above hit: Cevin FISHER featuring Ramona KELLER.				
LOVE YOU SOME MORE	*Subversive*	60	*24 Feb 01*	1
Above hit: Cevin FISHER featuring Sheila SMITH.				

Eddie FISHER — US

SINGLES:	HITS 9			WEEKS 105
OUTSIDE OF HEAVEN	*His Master's Voice*	1	*3 Jan 53*	16
EVERYTHING I HAVE IS YOURS	*His Master's Voice*	12	*24 Jan 53*	1
EVERYTHING I HAVE IS YOURS [RE]	*His Master's Voice*	8	*7 Feb 53*	4
Above 3: Eddie FISHER with Hugo WINTERHALTER's ORCHESTRA and CHORUS.				
DOWNHEARTED	*His Master's Voice*	3	*2 May 53*	1
Above hit : Eddie FISHER with Hugo WINTERHALTER and his Orchestra.				
OUTSIDE OF HEAVEN [RE]	*His Master's Voice*	12	*2 May 53*	1
Above hit: Eddie FISHER with Hugo WINTERHALTER's ORCHESTRA and CHORUS.				
I'M WALKING BEHIND YOU	*His Master's Voice*	1	*23 May 53*	18
Above hit: Eddie FISHER with Hugo WINTERHALTER and his Orchestra and Sally SWEETLAND.				
WISH YOU WERE HERE	*His Master's Voice*	8	*7 Nov 53*	9
From the musical of the same name.				
Above hit : Eddie FISHER with Hugo WINTERHALTER and his Orchestra.				
OH MY PAPA (O MEIN PAPA)	*His Master's Voice*	9	*23 Jan 54*	1
Above hit: Eddie FISHER with Hugo WINTERHALTER's ORCHESTRA and CHORUS.				
OH MY PAPA (O MEIN PAPA) [RE-1ST]	*His Master's Voice*	11	*6 Feb 54*	1
OH MY PAPA (O MEIN PAPA) [RE-2ND]	*His Master's Voice*	10	*27 Feb 54*	1

OH MY PAPA (O MEIN PAPA) [RE-3RD]	*His Master's Voice*	11	*13 Mar 54*	1
I NEED YOU NOW	*His Master's Voice*	16	*30 Oct 54*	2
Above hit : Eddie FISHER with Hugo WINTERHALTER and his Orchestra.				
I NEED YOU NOW [RE-1ST]	*His Master's Voice*	13	*20 Nov 54*	7
I NEED YOU NOW [RE-2ND]	*His Master's Voice*	19	*22 Jan 55*	1
(I'M ALWAYS HEARING) WEDDING BELLS	*His Master's Voice*	5	*19 Mar 55*	11
CINDY, OH CINDY	*His Master's Voice*	5	*24 Nov 56*	16
Above 2: Eddie FISHER with Hugo WINTERHALTER's ORCHESTRA and CHORUS.				

Mark FISHER (featuring Dotty GREEN) — UK

SINGLES:	HITS 1			WEEKS 2
LOVE SITUATION	*Total Control*	59	*29 Jun 85*	2

Toni FISHER — US

SINGLES:	HITS 1			WEEKS 1
THE BIG HURT	*Top Rank*	30	*13 Feb 60*	1
First hit to use a phasing gimmick.				

Martin FISHLEY – See PRESSURE DROP

FITS OF GLOOM — UK/Italy

SINGLES:	HITS 2			WEEKS 4
HEAVEN	*MCA*	47	*4 Jun 94*	2
THE POWER OF LOVE	*Media*	49	*5 Nov 94*	2
Above hit: FITS OF GLOOM featuring Lizzy MACK.				

Ella FITZGERALD — US

SINGLES:	HITS 6			WEEKS 29
THE SWINGIN' SHEPHERD BLUES	*His Master's Voice*	15	*24 May 58*	5
Above hit: Ella FITZGERALD and her SHEPHERDS.				
BUT NOT FOR ME	*His Master's Voice*	25	*17 Oct 59*	2
From the film of the same name.				
BUT NOT FOR ME [RE]	*His Master's Voice*	29	*26 Dec 59*	1
MACK THE KNIFE	*His Master's Voice*	19	*23 Apr 60*	9
HOW HIGH THE MOON	*His Master's Voice*	46	*8 Oct 60*	1
From the film 'Two For The Show'. Originally recorded by Benny Goodman in 1940.				
Above 2: Ella FITZGERALD with the Paul SMITH QUARTET.				
DESAFINADO (SLIGHTLY OUT OF TUNE)	*Verve*	38	*24 Nov 62*	4
DESAFINADO (SLIGHTLY OUT OF TUNE) [RE]	*Verve*	41	*29 Dec 62*	2
CAN'T BUY ME LOVE	*Verve*	34	*2 May 64*	5
EPS:	**HITS 3**			**WEEKS 7**
WITH A SONG IN MY HEART	*HMV*	10	*11 Jun 60*	3
MOODS OF ELLA	*HMV*	17	*13 Aug 60*	1
ELLA SINGS IRVING BERLIN	*HMV*	17	*27 Aug 60*	3
ALBUMS:	**HITS 7**			**WEEKS 43**
ELLA SINGS GERSHWIN	*Brunswick*	13	*11 Jun 60*	3
ELLA AT THE OPERA HOUSE	*Columbia*	16	*18 Jun 60*	1
ELLA SINGS GERSHWIN VOLUME 5	*His Master's Voice*	18	*23 Jul 60*	2
THE INCOMPARABLE ELLA	*Polydor*	40	*10 May 80*	7
A PORTRAIT OF ELLA FITZGERALD	*Stylus*	42	*27 Feb 88*	10
ESSENTIAL ELLA	*PolyGram TV*	35	*19 Nov 94*	14
Recordings from 1956 and 1960.				
FOREVER ELLA	*Verve/PolyGram TV*	19	*23 Mar 96*	6

Scott FITZGERALD — UK

SINGLES:	HITS 2			WEEKS 12
IF I HAD WORDS	*Pepper/United Artists*	3	*14 Jan 78*	10
Above hit: Scott FITZGERALD and Yvonne KEELY (with the ST. THOMAS MORE SCHOOL CHOIR).				
GO	*PRT*	52	*7 May 88*	2
UK's Eurovision entry in 1988, it came 2nd.				

FIVE — UK

SINGLES:	HITS 11			WEEKS 130
SLAM DUNK (DA FUNK)	*RCA*	10	*13 Dec 97*	9
WHEN THE LIGHTS GO OUT	*RCA*	4	*14 Mar 98*	9
GOT THE FEELIN'	*RCA*	3	*20 Jun 98*	13
Above 3: 5.				
EVERYBODY GET UP	*RCA*	2	*12 Sep 98*	12
Samples Joan Jett and the Blackhearts' I Love Rock and Roll.				
UNTIL THE TIME IS THROUGH	*RCA*	2	*28 Nov 98*	12
IF YA GETTIN' DOWN	*RCA*	2	*31 Jul 99*	12
Samples Indeep's Last Night A DJ Saved My Life.				
KEEP ON MOVIN'	*RCA*	1	*6 Nov 99*	17

DON'T WANNA LET YOU GO	*RCA*	9	*18 Mar 00*	12
WE WILL ROCK YOU	*RCA*	1	*29 Jul 00*	12
Above hit: FIVE + QUEEN.				
Originally recorded by Queen, B-side of We Are The Champions.				
WE WILL ROCK YOU [RE]	*RCA*	72	*4 Nov 00*	1
LET'S DANCE	*RCA*	1	*25 Aug 01*	12
CLOSER TO ME	*RCA*	4	*3 Nov 01*	9
ALBUMS:	**HITS 4**			**WEEKS 91**
FIVE	*RCA*	1	*4 Jul 98*	36
INVINCIBLE	*RCA*	4	*20 Nov 99*	39
KINGSIZE	*RCA*	3	*8 Sep 01*	11
GREATEST HITS	*RCA*	9	*1 Dec 01*	5

FIVE PENNY PIECE — UK

ALBUMS:	**HITS 2**			**WEEKS 6**
MAKING TRACKS	*Columbia*	37	*24 Mar 73*	1
KING COTTON	*EMI*	9	*3 Jul 76*	5

FIVE SMITH BROTHERS — UK

SINGLES:	**HITS 1**			**WEEKS 1**
I'M IN FAVOUR OF FRIENDSHIP	*Decca*	20	*23 Jul 55*	1

FIVE STAR — UK

SINGLES:	**HITS 21**			**WEEKS 140**
ALL FALL DOWN	*Tent*	15	*4 May 85*	12
LET ME BE THE ONE	*Tent*	18	*20 Jul 85*	9
LOVE TAKE OVER	*Tent*	25	*14 Sep 85*	9
R.S.V.P.	*Tent*	45	*16 Nov 85*	5
SYSTEM ADDICT	*Tent*	3	*11 Jan 86*	11
CAN'T WAIT ANOTHER MINUTE	*Tent*	7	*12 Apr 86*	10
Originally recorded by Lewis.				
FIND THE TIME	*Tent*	7	*26 Jul 86*	10
RAIN OR SHINE	*Tent*	2	*13 Sep 86*	11
IF I SAY YES	*Tent*	15	*22 Nov 86*	9
STAY OUT OF MY LIFE	*Tent*	9	*7 Feb 87*	8
THE SLIGHTEST TOUCH	*Tent*	4	*18 Apr 87*	9
WHENEVER YOU'RE READY	*Tent*	11	*22 Aug 87*	6
STRONG AS STEEL	*Tent*	16	*10 Oct 87*	7
SOMEWHERE SOMEBODY	*Tent*	23	*5 Dec 87*	6
ANOTHER WEEKEND	*Tent*	18	*4 Jun 88*	4
ROCK MY WORLD	*Tent*	28	*6 Aug 88*	4
THERE'S A BRAND NEW WORLD	*Tent*	61	*17 Sep 88*	2
LET ME BE YOURS	*Tent*	51	*19 Nov 88*	3
WITH EVERY HEARTBEAT	*Tent*	49	*8 Apr 89*	2
TREAT ME LIKE A LADY	*Tent*	54	*10 Mar 90*	2
HOT LOVE	*Tent*	68	*7 Jul 90*	1
ALBUMS:	**HITS 5**			**WEEKS 153**
LUXURY OF LIFE	*Tent*	24	*3 Aug 85*	21
LUXURY OF LIFE [RE]	*Tent*	12	*4 Jan 86*	49
SILK AND STEEL	*Tent*	1	*30 Aug 86*	58
BETWEEN THE LINES	*Tent*	7	*26 Sep 87*	17
ROCK THE WORLD	*Tent*	17	*27 Aug 88*	5
GREATEST HITS	*Tent*	53	*21 Oct 89*	3

FIVE THIRTY — UK

SINGLES:	**HITS 4**			**WEEKS 4**
ABSTAIN	*East West*	75	*4 Aug 90*	1
13TH DISCIPLE	*East West*	67	*25 May 91*	1
SUPERNOVA	*East West*	75	*3 Aug 91*	1
YOU [EP]	*East West*	72	*2 Nov 91*	1
Lead track: You.				
ALBUMS:	**HITS 1**			**WEEKS 1**
BED	*East West*	57	*31 Aug 91*	1

5000 VOLTS — UK

SINGLES:	**HITS 2**			**WEEKS 18**
I'M ON FIRE	*Philips*	4	*6 Sep 75*	9
DOCTOR KISS - KISS	*Philips*	8	*24 Jul 76*	9
Vocals by Linda Kelly.				

FIXATE — UK

SINGLES:	**HITS 1**			**WEEKS 1**
24/7	*ePARK*	42	*14 Jul 01*	1

FIXX — UK

SINGLES:	HITS 2			WEEKS 8
STAND OR FALL	*MCA*	54	*24 Apr 82*	4
RED SKIES	*MCA*	57	*17 Jul 82*	4
ALBUMS:	**HITS 2**			**WEEKS 7**
SHUTTERED ROOM	*MCA*	54	*22 May 82*	6
REACH THE BEACH	*MCA*	91	*21 May 83*	1

FKW — UK

SINGLES:	HITS 4			WEEKS 8
NEVER GONNA GIVE YOU UP	*PWL International*	48	*2 Oct 93*	2
SEIZE THE DAY	*PWL International*	45	*11 Dec 93*	2
JINGO	*PWL International*	30	*5 Mar 94*	3
THIS IS THE WAY	*PWL International*	63	*4 Jun 94*	1

Roberta FLACK — US

(See also Peabo Bryson and Roberta Flack; Roberta Flack and Donny Hathaway.)

SINGLES:	HITS 5			WEEKS 44
THE FIRST TIME EVER I SAW YOUR FACE	*Atlantic*	14	*27 May 72*	14
Originally recorded by Peggy Seeger. Featured in the Clint Eastwood film 'Play Misty For Me'.				
KILLING ME SOFTLY WITH HIS SONG	*Atlantic*	6	*17 Feb 73*	14
Originally recorded by Lori Leiberman in 1972. Inspired by a Don McLean concert.				
FEEL LIKE MAKIN' LOVE	*Atlantic*	34	*24 Aug 74*	7
DON'T MAKE ME WAIT TOO LONG	*Atlantic*	44	*30 Aug 80*	7
UH-UH OOH OOH LOOK OUT (HERE IT COMES)	*Atlantic*	72	*29 Jul 89*	2
ALBUMS:	**HITS 4**			**WEEKS 28**
FIRST TAKE	*Atlantic*	47	*15 Jul 72*	2
KILLING ME SOFTLY	*Atlantic*	40	*13 Oct 73*	2
ROBERTA FLACK'S GREATEST HITS	*K-Tel*	35	*31 Mar 84*	14
SOFTLY WITH THESE SONGS - THE BEST OF ROBERTA FLACK	*Atlantic*	7	*19 Feb 94*	10

Roberta FLACK and Donny HATHAWAY — US

(See also Peabo Bryson and Roberta Flack; Roberta Flack.)

SINGLES:	HITS 3			WEEKS 22
WHERE IS THE LOVE	*Atlantic*	29	*5 Aug 72*	7
THE CLOSER I GET TO YOU	*Atlantic*	42	*6 May 78*	4
Above hit: Roberta FLACK with Donny HATHAWAY.				
BACK TOGETHER AGAIN	*Atlantic*	3	*17 May 80*	11
ALBUMS:	**HITS 1**			**WEEKS 7**
ROBERTA FLACK AND DONNY HATHAWAY	*Atlantic*	31	*7 Jun 80*	7

FLAJ - See GETO BOYS featuring FLAJ

FLAMING LIPS — US

SINGLES:	HITS 3			WEEKS 4
THIS HERE GIRAFFE	*Warner Brothers*	72	*9 Mar 96*	1
RACE FOR THE PRIZE	*Warner Brothers*	39	*26 Jun 99*	2
WAITIN' FOR A SUPERMAN	*Warner Brothers*	73	*20 Nov 99*	1
ALBUMS:	**HITS 1**			**WEEKS 2**
THE SOFT BULLETIN	*Warner Brothers*	39	*29 May 99*	2

FLAMINGOS — US

SINGLES:	HITS 1			WEEKS 5
THE BOOGALOO PARTY	*Philips*	26	*7 Jun 69*	5
Originally released in 1966.				

Michael FLANDERS and Donald SWANN — UK

ALBUMS:	HITS 2			WEEKS 12
AT THE DROP OF A HAT	*Parlophone*	9	*26 Mar 60*	1
Recorded during a performance at the Fortune Theatre, London				
AT THE DROP OF ANOTHER HAT	*Parlophone*	12	*22 Feb 64*	11

Michael FLANDERS with the Michael SAMMES SINGERS — UK

SINGLES:	HITS 1			WEEKS 3
THE LITTLE DRUMMER BOY	*Parlophone*	20	*28 Feb 59*	2
THE LITTLE DRUMMER BOY [RE]	*Parlophone*	24	*18 Apr 59*	1

FLASH AND THE PAN — Australia

SINGLES:	HITS 2			WEEKS 15
AND THE BAND PLAYED ON (DOWN AMONG THE DEAD MEN)	*Ensign*	54	*23 Sep 78*	4
WAITING FOR A TRAIN	*Easybeat*	7	*21 May 83*	11

ALBUMS:	HITS 1			WEEKS 2
PAN-ORAMA	*Easybeat*	69	*16 Jul 83*	2

Lester FLATT and Earl SCRUGGS — US

SINGLES:	HITS 1			WEEKS 6
FOGGY MOUNTAIN BREAKDOWN *Sales of two different recordings (CBS from 1965, Mercury from 1949) were combined. Theme from the film 'Bonnie and Clyde'.*	*CBS & Mercury*	39	*18 Nov 67*	6

Fogwell FLAX and the ANKLE BITERS from FREEHOLD JUNIOR SCHOOL — UK

SINGLES:	HITS 1			WEEKS 2
ONE-NINE FOR SANTA	*EMI*	68	*26 Dec 81*	2

FLB – See FAT LARRY'S BAND

FLEETWOOD MAC — UK/US

SINGLES:	HITS 25			WEEKS 223
BLACK MAGIC WOMAN	*Blue Horizon*	37	*13 Apr 68*	7
NEED YOUR LOVE SO BAD *Originally recorded by Little Willie John.*	*Blue Horizon*	31	*20 Jul 68*	13
ALBATROSS	*Blue Horizon*	1	*7 Dec 68*	20
MAN OF THE WORLD	*Immediate*	2	*19 Apr 69*	14
NEED YOUR LOVE SO BAD [RI]	*Blue Horizon*	32	*26 Jul 69*	6
NEED YOUR LOVE SO BAD [RI] [RE]	*Blue Horizon*	42	*13 Sep 69*	3
OH WELL	*Reprise*	2	*4 Oct 69*	16
THE GREEN MANALISHI (WITH THE TWO PRONG CROWN)	*Reprise*	10	*23 May 70*	12
ALBATROSS [RI]	*CBS*	2	*12 May 73*	15
SAY YOU LOVE ME	*Reprise*	40	*13 Nov 76*	4
GO YOUR OWN WAY	*Warner Brothers*	38	*19 Feb 77*	4
DON'T STOP	*Warner Brothers*	32	*30 Apr 77*	5
DREAMS	*Warner Brothers*	24	*9 Jul 77*	9
YOU MAKE LOVING FUN	*Warner Brothers*	45	*22 Oct 77*	2
RHIANNON *Originally released in 1976.*	*Reprise*	46	*11 Mar 78*	3
TUSK	*Warner Brothers*	6	*6 Oct 79*	10
SARA	*Warner Brothers*	37	*22 Dec 79*	8
GYPSY	*Warner Brothers*	46	*25 Sep 82*	3
OH DIANE	*Warner Brothers*	9	*18 Dec 82*	15
BIG LOVE	*Warner Brothers*	9	*4 Apr 87*	12
SEVEN WONDERS	*Warner Brothers*	56	*11 Jul 87*	4
LITTLE LIES	*Warner Brothers*	5	*26 Sep 87*	12
FAMILY MAN	*Warner Brothers*	54	*26 Dec 87*	5
EVERYWHERE	*Warner Brothers*	4	*2 Apr 88*	10
ISN'T IT MIDNIGHT	*Warner Brothers*	60	*18 Jun 88*	2
AS LONG AS YOU FOLLOW	*Warner Brothers*	66	*17 Dec 88*	3
SAVE ME	*Warner Brothers*	53	*5 May 90*	3
IN THE BACK OF MY MIND	*Warner Brothers*	58	*25 Aug 90*	3

ALBUMS:	HITS 17			WEEKS 850
PETER GREEN'S FLEETWOOD MAC *Above hit: Peter GREEN'S FLEETWOOD MAC.*	*Blue Horizon*	4	*2 Mar 68*	37
MR. WONDERFUL	*Blue Horizon*	10	*7 Sep 68*	11
THE PIOUS BIRD OF GOOD OMEN *Compilation.*	*Blue Horizon*	18	*30 Aug 69*	4
THEN PLAY ON	*Reprise*	6	*4 Oct 69*	11
KILN HOUSE	*Reprise*	39	*10 Oct 70*	2
GREATEST HITS	*CBS*	36	*19 Feb 72*	11
FLEETWOOD MAC	*Reprise*	23	*6 Nov 76*	19
RUMOURS *Peak position reached on 28 Jan.78. Includes re-entries through to 1987.*	*Warner Brothers*	1	*26 Feb 77*	402
TUSK *Includes re-entries in 1988.*	*Warner Brothers*	1	*27 Oct 79*	26
FLEETWOOD MAC LIVE	*Warner Brothers*	31	*13 Dec 80*	9
MIRAGE	*Warner Brothers*	5	*10 Jul 82*	39
TANGO IN THE NIGHT *Peak position reached on 31 Oct 87.*	*Warner Brothers*	1	*25 Apr 87*	100
RUMOURS [RE-1ST]	*Warner Brothers*	28	*9 Jan 88*	41
GREATEST HITS [RE] *Repackaged.*	*CBS*	81	*14 May 88*	2
GREATEST HITS *The 2 Greatest Hits albums are different.*	*Warner Brothers*	3	*3 Dec 88*	31
BEHIND THE MASK	*Warner Brothers*	1	*21 Apr 90*	21
TANGO IN THE NIGHT [RE-] *Re-released at mid-price. Peak position reached in 1995, (1994 peak No. 45). Includes re-entries through to 2000.*	*Warner Brothers*	28	*2 Apr 94*	15
GREATEST HITS [RE] *Repackaged at mid-price.*	*Warner Brothers*	38	*30 Apr 94*	21

LIVE AT THE BBC *Recorded for the BBC between 1967–69.*	*Essential*	48	*23 Sep 95*	2
GREATEST HITS [RI]	*Columbia*	73	*23 Sep 95*	1
TIME	*Warner Brothers*	47	*21 Oct 95*	1
THE DANCE *Compilation with 4 new tracks.*	*Reprise*	15	*6 Sep 97*	10
RUMOURS [RE-2ND] *Initially re-charted after featuring on BBC-TV's 'Classic Albums' series. Includes re-entries through to 2000.*	*Warner Brothers*	18	*6 Sep 97*	34

FLEETWOODS — US

SINGLES:	HITS 1			WEEKS 8
COME SOFTLY TO ME	*London*	6	*25 Apr 59*	8

John '00' FLEMING — UK

SINGLES:	HITS 2			WEEKS 2
LOST IN EMOTION	*React*	74	*25 Dec 99*	1
FREE	*React*	61	*12 Aug 00*	1

La FLEUR — Holland

SINGLES:	HITS 1			WEEKS 4
BOOGIE NIGHTS	*Proto*	51	*30 Jul 83*	4

FLICKMAN — Italy

SINGLES:	HITS 2			WEEKS 6
THE SOUND OF BAMBOO *Samples Eddy Grant's 1983 recording of The House Of Bamboo.*	*Inferno*	11	*4 Mar 00*	5
HEY! PARADISE	*Inferno*	69	*28 Apr 01*	1

KC FLIGHTT — US

SINGLES:	HITS 2			WEEKS 5
PLANET E	*RCA*	48	*1 Apr 89*	4
VOICES *Samples the Police's Voices In My Head from their Zenyatta Mondatta album.* *Above hit: KC FLIGHTT vs FUNKY JUNCTION.*	*Hooj Choons*	59	*12 May 01*	1

Dread FLIMSTONE and the MODERN TONE AGE FAMILY — US

SINGLES:	HITS 1			WEEKS 1
FROM THE GHETTO	*Urban*	66	*30 Nov 91*	1

Berni FLINT — UK

SINGLES:	HITS 2			WEEKS 11
I DON'T WANT TO PUT A HOLD ON YOU	*EMI*	3	*19 Mar 77*	10
SOUTHERN COMFORT	*EMI*	48	*23 Jul 77*	1
ALBUMS:	**HITS 1**			**WEEKS 6**
I DON'T WANT TO PUT A HOLD ON YOU	*EMI*	37	*2 Jul 77*	6

FLINTLOCK — UK

SINGLES:	HITS 1			WEEKS 5
DAWN	*Pinnacle*	30	*29 May 76*	5

FLIP&FILL featuring Kelly LLOENNA — UK

SINGLES:	HITS 1			WEEKS 3
TRUE LOVE NEVER DIES	*All Around The World*	34	*24 Mar 01*	3

FLIPMODE SQUAD (Starring Busta RHYMES, BABY SHAM, RAH DIGGA and SPLIFF STAR) — US

(See also Busta Rhymes.)

SINGLES:	HITS 1			WEEKS 1
CHA CHA CHA	*Elektra*	54	*31 Oct 98*	1

FLOATERS — US

SINGLES:	HITS 1			WEEKS 11
FLOAT ON	*ABC*	1	*23 Jul 77*	11
ALBUMS:	**HITS 1**			**WEEKS 8**
FLOATERS	*ABC*	17	*20 Aug 77*	8

FLOCK — UK

ALBUMS:	HITS 1			WEEKS 2
FLOCK	*CBS*	59	*2 May 70*	2

A FLOCK OF SEAGULLS — UK

SINGLES:	HITS 7			WEEKS 46
I RAN	*Jive*	43	*27 Mar 82*	6
SPACE AGE LOVE SONG	*Jive*	34	*12 Jun 82*	6
WISHING (IF I HAD A PHOTOGRAPH OF YOU)	*Jive*	10	*6 Nov 82*	12
NIGHTMARES	*Jive*	53	*23 Apr 83*	3
TRANSFER AFFECTION	*Jive*	38	*25 Jun 83*	5
THE MORE YOU LIVE, THE MORE YOU LOVE	*Jive*	26	*14 Jul 84*	11
WHO'S THAT GIRL? SHE'S GOT IT	*Jive*	66	*19 Oct 85*	3
ALBUMS:	**HITS 3**			**WEEKS 59**
A FLOCK OF SEAGULLS	*Jive*	32	*17 Apr 82*	44
LISTEN	*Arista*	16	*7 May 83*	10
THE STORY OF A YOUNG HEART	*Jive*	30	*1 Sep 84*	5

FLOORPLAY — UK

SINGLES:	HITS 1			WEEKS 1
AUTOMATIC	*Perfecto*	50	*27 Jan 96*	1

FLOWER POT MEN — UK

SINGLES:	HITS 1			WEEKS 12
LET'S GO TO SAN FRANCISCO	*Deram*	4	*26 Aug 67*	12

FLOWERED UP — UK

(See also Various Artists (EPs) 'The Fred EP'.)

SINGLES:	HITS 5			WEEKS 17
IT'S ON	*Heavenly*	54	*28 Jul 90*	4
PHOBIA	*Heavenly*	75	*24 Nov 90*	1
TAKE IT	*London*	34	*11 May 91*	4
IT'S ON [RI] / EGG RUSH	*London*	38	*17 Aug 91*	3
WEEKENDER	*Heavenly*	20	*2 May 92*	5
ALBUMS:	**HITS 1**			**WEEKS 3**
A LIFE WITH BRIAN	*London*	23	*7 Sep 91*	3

Mike FLOWERS POPS — UK

SINGLES:	HITS 3			WEEKS 14
WONDERWALL	*London*	2	*30 Dec 95*	7
WONDERWALL [RE]	*London*	52	*13 Apr 96*	2
LIGHT MY FIRE / PLEASE RELEASE ME	*London*	39	*8 Jun 96*	2
DON'T CRY FOR ME ARGENTINA	*Love This*	30	*28 Dec 96*	3

Eddie FLOYD — US

SINGLES:	HITS 3			WEEKS 29
KNOCK ON WOOD	*Atlantic*	50	*4 Feb 67*	1
KNOCK ON WOOD [RE]	*Atlantic*	19	*4 Mar 67*	17
RAISE YOUR HAND	*Stax*	42	*18 Mar 67*	3
THINGS GET BETTER	*Stax*	31	*12 Aug 67*	8
ALBUMS:	**HITS 1**			**WEEKS 5**
KNOCK ON WOOD	*Stax*	36	*29 Apr 67*	5

FLUFFY — UK

SINGLES:	HITS 2			WEEKS 2
HUSBAND	*Parkway*	58	*17 Feb 96*	1
NOTHING	*Virgin*	52	*5 Oct 96*	1

FLUKE — UK

SINGLES:	HITS 9			WEEKS 20
SLID	*Circa*	59	*20 Mar 93*	1
ELECTRIC GUITAR	*Circa*	58	*19 Jun 93*	2
Samples Jimi Hendrix's Crossstown Traffic.				
GROOVY FEELING	*Circa*	45	*11 Sep 93*	3
BUBBLE	*Circa*	37	*23 Apr 94*	2
BULLET	*Circa*	23	*29 Jul 95*	3
TOSH	*Circa*	32	*16 Dec 95*	3
ATOM BOMB	*Circa*	20	*16 Nov 96*	3
Song is featured on the WipeOut2 2097 Game for Playstation.				
ABSURD	*Circa*	25	*31 May 97*	2
SQUIRT	*Circa*	46	*27 Sep 97*	1
ALBUMS:	**HITS 3**			**WEEKS 3**
SIX WHEELS ON MY WAGON	*Circa*	41	*23 Oct 93*	1
Live recordings.				
OTO	*Circa*	44	*19 Aug 95*	1
RISOTTO	*Circa*	45	*11 Oct 97*	1

FLUSH – See SLADE

FLUX FIDDLERS – See John LENNON

A FLUX OF PINK INDIANS — UK

ALBUMS:	HITS 1			WEEKS 2
STRIVE TO SURVIVE CAUSING LEAST SUFFERING POSSIBLE	*Spiderleg*	79	*5 Feb 83*	2

FLYING LIZARDS — UK

SINGLES:	HITS 2			WEEKS 16
MONEY	*Virgin*	5	*4 Aug 79*	10
Original by Barrett Strong reached No. 23 in the US in 1960.				
TV	*Virgin*	43	*9 Feb 80*	6
ALBUMS:	**HITS 1**			**WEEKS 3**
FLYING LIZARDS	*Virgin*	60	*16 Feb 80*	3

FLYING PICKETS — UK

SINGLES:	HITS 3			WEEKS 20
ONLY YOU	*10 Records*	1	*26 Nov 83*	11
First a cappella song to top the chart.				
(WHEN YOU'RE) YOUNG AND IN LOVE	*10 Records*	7	*21 Apr 84*	8
Originally recorded by the Marvelettes.				
WHO'S THAT GIRL	*10 Records*	71	*8 Dec 84*	1
ALBUMS:	**HITS 2**			**WEEKS 22**
LIVE AT THE ALBANY EMPIRE	*VAM*	48	*17 Dec 83*	11
LOST BOYS	*10 Records*	11	*9 Jun 84*	11

Jerome FLYNN – See ROBSON and JEROME

FM — UK

SINGLES:	HITS 5			WEEKS 11
FROZEN HEART	*Portrait*	64	*31 Jan 87*	2
Original release reached No. 92 in 1985.				
LET LOVE BE THE LEADER	*Portrait*	71	*20 Jun 87*	2
BAD LUCK	*Epic*	54	*5 Aug 89*	4
SOMEDAY (YOU'LL COME RUNNING)	*CBS*	64	*7 Oct 89*	2
EVERYTIME I THINK OF YOU	*Epic*	73	*10 Feb 90*	1
ALBUMS:	**HITS 2**			**WEEKS 3**
INDISCREET	*Portrait*	76	*20 Sep 86*	1
TOUGH IT OUT	*Epic*	34	*14 Oct 89*	2

FOCUS — Holland

SINGLES:	HITS 2			WEEKS 21
HOCUS POCUS	*Polydor*	20	*20 Jan 73*	10
SYLVIA	*Polydor*	4	*27 Jan 73*	11
ALBUMS:	**HITS 5**			**WEEKS 65**
MOVING WAVES	*Polydor*	2	*11 Nov 72*	34
FOCUS 3	*Polydor*	6	*2 Dec 72*	15
FOCUS AT THE RAINBOW	*Polydor*	23	*20 Oct 73*	5
HAMBURGER CONCERTO	*Polydor*	20	*25 May 74*	5
FOCUS	*Polydor*	23	*9 Aug 75*	6

FOG — US

SINGLES:	HITS 1			WEEKS 4
BEEN A LONG TIME	*Columbia*	44	*19 Feb 94*	2
BEEN A LONG TIME [RM]	*Pukka*	27	*6 Jun 98*	2
Remixed by Full Intention.				

Dan FOGELBERG — US

SINGLES:	HITS 1			WEEKS 4
LONGER	*Full Moon*	59	*15 Mar 80*	4
ALBUMS:	**HITS 1**			**WEEKS 3**
PHOENIX	*Full Moon*	42	*29 Mar 80*	3

John FOGERTY — US

ALBUMS:	HITS 1			WEEKS 11
CENTERFIELD	*Warner Brothers*	48	*16 Feb 85*	11

Ben FOLDS FIVE — US

SINGLES:	HITS 6			WEEKS 13
UNDERGROUND	*Caroline*	37	*14 Sep 96*	2
BATTLE OF WHO COULD CARE LESS	*Epic*	26	*1 Mar 97*	3
KATE	*Epic*	39	*7 Jun 97*	2

BRICK	*Epic*	26	*18 Apr 98*	3
ARMY	*Epic*	28	*24 Apr 99*	2
ROCKIN' THE SUBURBS	*Epic*	53	*29 Sep 01*	1
Above hit: Ben FOLDS.				
ALBUMS:	**HITS 4**			**WEEKS 7**
WHATEVER AND EVER AMEN	*Epic*	30	*15 Mar 97*	3
NAKED BABY PHOTOS	*Virgin*	65	*24 Jan 98*	1
Compilation of live versions/out-takes from 1994-98.				
THE UNAUTHORIZED BIOGRAPHY OF REINHOLD MESSNER	*Epic*	22	*8 May 99*	2
Messner was the first mountaineer to scale Everest without oxygen.				
ROCKIN' THE SUBURBS	*Epic*	73	*6 Oct 01*	1
Above hit: Ben FOLDS.				

Ellen FOLEY — US

ALBUMS:	**HITS 2**			**WEEKS 3**
NIGHT OUT	*Epic*	68	*17 Nov 79*	1
SPIRIT OF ST. LOUIS	*Epic*	57	*4 Apr 81*	2

FOLK IMPLOSION — US

SINGLES:	**HITS 1**			**WEEKS 1**
NATURAL ONE	*London*	45	*15 Jun 96*	1
From the film 'Kids'.				

Jane FONDA — US

ALBUMS:	**HITS 2**			**WEEKS 51**
JANE FONDA'S WORKOUT RECORD	*CBS*	7	*29 Jan 83*	47
Instructions by Jane Fonda with backing music by the Jacksons, REO Speedwagon, Brothers Johnson, Linda Clifford, Billy Ocean and William Ackerman. Disc 1 titled: Workout - Beginners; Disc 2 titled: Workout - Advanced.				
JANE FONDA'S WORKOUT RECORD: NEW AND IMPROVED	*CBS*	60	*22 Sep 84*	4

Claudia FONTAINE - See BEATMASTERS

Lenny FONTANA — US

SINGLES:	**HITS 2**			**WEEKS 3**
CHOCOLATE SENSATION	*ffrr*	39	*4 Mar 00*	2
Samples Johnny Hammond's Los Conquistadores Chocolates and Loleatta Holloway's vocal from Salsoul Orchestra's Love Sensation.				
Above hit: Lenny FONTANA and DJ SHORTY.				
POW POW POW	*Strictly Rhythm UK*	62	*24 Mar 01*	1
Above hit: FONTANA featuring Darryl D'BONNEAU.				

Wayne FONTANA — UK

(See also Wayne Fontana and the Mindbenders.)

SINGLES:	**HITS 4**			**WEEKS 31**
IT WAS EASIER TO HURT HER	*Fontana*	36	*11 Dec 65*	6
COME ON HOME	*Fontana*	16	*23 Apr 66*	12
GOODBYE BLUEBIRD	*Fontana*	49	*27 Aug 66*	1
PAMELA, PAMELA	*Fontana*	11	*10 Dec 66*	12

Wayne FONTANA and the MINDBENDERS — UK

(See also Wayne Fontana; Mindbenders.)

SINGLES:	**HITS 6**			**WEEKS 45**
HELLO JOSEPHINE	*Fontana*	46	*13 Jul 63*	2
STOP LOOK AND LISTEN	*Fontana*	37	*30 May 64*	4
UM, UM, UM, UM, UM, UM	*Fontana*	5	*10 Oct 64*	15
THE GAME OF LOVE	*Fontana*	2	*6 Feb 65*	11
IT'S JUST A LITTLE BIT TOO LATE	*Fontana*	20	*19 Jun 65*	7
SHE NEEDS LOVE	*Fontana*	32	*2 Oct 65*	6
EPS:	**HITS 2**			**WEEKS 20**
UM, UM, UM, UM, UM, UM	*Fontana*	7	*12 Dec 64*	19
THE GAME OF LOVE	*Fontana*	19	*15 May 65*	1
ALBUMS:	**HITS 1**			**WEEKS 1**
WAYNE FONTANA AND THE MINDBENDERS	*Fontana*	18	*20 Feb 65*	1

FOO FIGHTERS — US

SINGLES:	**HITS 11**			**WEEKS 32**
THIS IS A CALL	*Roswell*	5	*1 Jul 95*	4
I'LL STICK AROUND	*Roswell*	18	*16 Sep 95*	3
FOR ALL THE COWS	*Roswell*	28	*2 Dec 95*	2
BIG ME	*Roswell*	19	*6 Apr 96*	3
MONKEY WRENCH	*Roswell*	12	*10 May 97*	4
EVERLONG	*Roswell*	18	*30 Aug 97*	3
MY HERO	*Roswell*	21	*31 Jan 98*	2

WALKING AFTER YOU	*Elektra*	20	*29 Aug 98*	3
[AA] listed with Beacon Light by Ween. From the film 'The X Files'.				
LEARN TO FLY	*RCA*	21	*30 Oct 99*	3
BREAKOUT	*RCA*	29	*30 Sep 00*	3
NEXT YEAR	*RCA*	42	*16 Dec 00*	2
ALBUMS:	**HITS 3**			**WEEKS 45**
FOO FIGHTERS	*Roswell*	3	*8 Jul 95*	17
THE COLOUR AND THE SHAPE	*Roswell*	3	*24 May 97*	12
THERE IS NOTHING LEFT TO LOSE	*RCA*	10	*13 Nov 99*	16

FOOL BOONA — UK

SINGLES:	**HITS 1**			**WEEKS 1**
POPPED!!	*VC Recordings*	52	*10 Apr 99*	1
Contains re-recorded samples from Iggy Pop's The Passenger.				

FOOL'S GARDEN — Germany

SINGLES:	**HITS 1**			**WEEKS 4**
LEMON TREE	*Encore*	61	*25 May 96*	1
LEMON TREE [RI]	*Encore*	26	*3 Aug 96*	3

FOR REAL — US

SINGLES:	**HITS 2**			**WEEKS 2**
YOU DON'T KNOW NOTHIN'	*A&M*	54	*1 Jul 95*	1
LIKE I DO	*Arista*	45	*12 Jul 97*	1

Steve FORBERT — US

ALBUMS:	**HITS 2**			**WEEKS 3**
ALIVE ON ARRIVAL	*Epic*	56	*9 Jun 79*	1
JACK RABBIT SLIM	*Epic*	54	*24 Nov 79*	2

Bill FORBES — UK

SINGLES:	**HITS 1**			**WEEKS 1**
TOO YOUNG	*Columbia*	29	*16 Jan 60*	1

David FORBES — UK

SINGLES:	**HITS 1**			**WEEKS 1**
QUESTIONS (MUST BE ASKED)	*Serious*	57	*25 Aug 01*	1

FORCE M.D.'S — US

SINGLES:	**HITS 1**			**WEEKS 9**
TENDER LOVE	*Tommy Boy*	23	*12 Apr 86*	9
From the film 'Krush Groove'.				

FORCE and STYLES featuring Kelly LLORENNA — UK

(See also Kelly Llorenna.)

SINGLES:	**HITS 1**			**WEEKS 1**
HEART OF GOLD	*Diverse*	55	*25 Jul 98*	1

Baby FORD — UK

SINGLES:	**HITS 4**			**WEEKS 16**
OOCHY KOOCHY (F.U. BABY YEAH YEAH)	*Rhythm King*	58	*10 Sep 88*	6
CHIKKI CHIKKI AHH AHH	*Rhythm King*	75	*24 Dec 88*	1
CHIKKI CHIKKI AHH AHH [RE]	*Rhythm King*	54	*7 Jan 89*	3
CHILDREN OF THE REVOLUTION	*Rhythm King*	53	*17 Jun 89*	4
BEACH BUMP	*Rhythm King*	68	*17 Feb 90*	2

Clinton FORD — UK

SINGLES:	**HITS 4**			**WEEKS 25**
OLD SHEP	*Oriole*	27	*24 Oct 59*	1
TOO MANY BEAUTIFUL GIRLS (AND NOT ENOUGH TIME)	*Oriole*	48	*19 Aug 61*	1
FANLIGHT FANNY	*Oriole*	22	*10 Mar 62*	10
Above hit: Clinton FORD with the George CHISHOLM ALL-STARS.				
RUN TO THE DOOR	*Piccadilly*	25	*7 Jan 67*	13
ALBUMS:	**HITS 1**			**WEEKS 4**
CLINTON FORD	*Oriole*	16	*26 May 62*	4

Emile FORD and the CHECKMATES — US

SINGLES:	**HITS 8**			**WEEKS 89**
WHAT DO YOU WANT TO MAKE THOSE EYES AT ME FOR?	*Pye Nixa*	1	*31 Oct 59*	26
Originally recorded by Ada Jones and Billy Murray in 1917.				
ON A SLOW BOAT TO CHINA	*Pye*	3	*6 Feb 60*	15
Originally recorded by Kay Kyser in 1948.				

YOU'LL NEVER KNOW WHAT YOU'RE MISSIN' 'TIL YOU TRY	*Pye*	12	*28 May 60*	9
THEM THERE EYES	*Pye*	18	*3 Sep 60*	16
Above hit: Emile FORD; Johnny KEATING MUSIC; Babs KNIGHT GROUP.				
COUNTING TEARDROPS	*Pye*	4	*10 Dec 60*	12
Originally recorded by Barry Mann.				
WHAT AM I GONNA DO	*Pye*	33	*4 Mar 61*	6
HALF OF MY HEART	*Piccadilly*	50	*20 May 61*	1
HALF OF MY HEART [RE]	*Piccadilly*	42	*24 Jun 61*	3
I WONDER WHO'S KISSING HER NOW	*Piccadilly*	43	*10 Mar 62*	1
Originally recorded by Ada Reeve and Harry Woodruff in 1909.				
EPS:	**HITS 1**			**WEEKS 23**
EMILE	*Pye*	1	*9 Apr 60*	23

Tennessee Ernie FORD — US

SINGLES:	**HITS 3**			**WEEKS 42**
GIVE ME YOUR WORD	*Capitol*	1	*22 Jan 55*	24
SIXTEEN TONS	*Capitol*	1	*7 Jan 56*	11
Originally recorded by Merle Travis.				
THE BALLAD OF DAVY CROCKETT	*Capitol*	3	*14 Jan 56*	7
From the film 'Davy Crockett, King Of The Wild Frontier'.				

Lita FORD — UK

SINGLES:	**HITS 3**			**WEEKS 7**
KISS ME DEADLY	*RCA*	75	*17 Dec 88*	1
CLOSE MY EYES FOREVER	*Dreamland*	47	*20 May 89*	3
Above hit: Lita FORD (Duet with Ozzy OSBOURNE).				
SHOT OF POISON	*RCA*	63	*11 Jan 92*	3
ALBUMS:	**HITS 3**			**WEEKS 4**
DANCIN' ON THE EDGE	*Vertigo*	96	*26 May 84*	1
STILETTO	*RCA*	66	*23 Jun 90*	1
DANGEROUS CURVES	*RCA*	51	*25 Jan 92*	2

Martyn FORD ORCHESTRA — UK

(See also Phil Collins.)

SINGLES:	**HITS 1**			**WEEKS 3**
LET YOUR BODY GO DOWNTOWN	*Mountain*	38	*14 May 77*	3

Mary FORD – See Les PAUL and Mary FORD

Penny FORD — US

SINGLES:	**HITS 2**			**WEEKS 7**
DANGEROUS	*Total Experience*	43	*4 May 85*	5
Above hit: Pennye FORD.				
DAYDREAMING	*Columbia*	43	*29 May 93*	2

Julia FORDHAM — UK

SINGLES:	**HITS 5**			**WEEKS 32**
HAPPY EVER AFTER	*Circa*	27	*2 Jul 88*	9
WHERE DOES THE TIME GO?	*Circa*	41	*25 Feb 89*	5
I THOUGHT IT WAS YOU	*Circa*	64	*31 Aug 91*	2
LOVE MOVES (IN MYSTERIOUS WAYS)	*Circa*	19	*18 Jan 92*	9
From the film 'The Butcher's Wife'.				
I THOUGHT IT WAS YOU [RM]	*Circa*	45	*30 May 92*	3
DIFFERENT TIME DIFFERENT PLACE	*Circa*	41	*30 Apr 94*	3
I CAN'T HELP MYSELF	*Circa*	62	*23 Jul 94*	1
ALBUMS:	**HITS 4**			**WEEKS 36**
JULIA FORDHAM	*Circa*	41	*18 Jun 88*	16
JULIA FORDHAM [RE]	*Circa*	20	*18 Mar 89*	6
PORCELAIN	*Circa*	13	*21 Oct 89*	5
SWEPT	*Circa*	33	*2 Nov 91*	3
SWEPT [RE]	*Circa*	46	*7 Mar 92*	3
Repackaged.				
FALLING FORWARD	*Circa*	21	*21 May 94*	3

FOREIGNER — US

SINGLES:	**HITS 11**			**WEEKS 78**
FEELS LIKE THE FIRST TIME	*Atlantic*	39	*6 May 78*	6
COLD AS ICE	*Atlantic*	24	*15 Jul 78*	10
Above 2 originally released in 1977.				
HOT BLOODED	*Atlantic*	42	*28 Oct 78*	3
BLUE MORNING, BLUE DAY	*Atlantic*	45	*24 Feb 79*	4
URGENT	*Atlantic*	54	*29 Aug 81*	4
Features Junior Walker on saxophone.				
JUKE BOX HERO	*Atlantic*	48	*10 Oct 81*	4

WAITING FOR A GIRL LIKE YOU	*Atlantic*	8	*12 Dec 81*	13
URGENT [RI]	*Atlantic*	45	*8 May 82*	5
I WANT TO KNOW WHAT LOVE IS	*Atlantic*	1	*8 Dec 84*	16
Features Tom Bailey of the Thompson Twins on keyboards and Jennifer Holliday on backing vocals.				
THAT WAS YESTERDAY	*Atlantic*	28	*6 Apr 85*	6
COLD AS ICE [RM]	*Atlantic*	64	*22 Jun 85*	2
SAY YOU WILL	*Atlantic*	71	*19 Dec 87*	4
WHITE LIE	*Arista*	58	*22 Oct 94*	1

ALBUMS:	**HITS 8**			**WEEKS 126**
DOUBLE VISION	*Atlantic*	32	*26 Aug 78*	5
4	*Atlantic*	5	*25 Jul 81*	62
Peak position reached on 6 Feb 82.				
RECORDS: THE BEST OF FOREIGNER	*Atlantic*	58	*18 Dec 82*	11
AGENT PROVOCATEUR	*Atlantic*	1	*22 Dec 84*	32
INSIDE INFORMATION	*Atlantic*	64	*19 Dec 87*	7
UNUSUAL HEAT	*Atlantic*	56	*6 Jul 91*	1
THE VERY BEST OF FOREIGNER	*Atlantic*	19	*2 May 92*	7
MR. MOONLIGHT	*Arista*	59	*12 Nov 94*	1

FORMATIONS — US

SINGLES:	**HITS 1**			**WEEKS 11**
AT THE TOP OF THE STAIRS	*Mojo*	50	*31 Jul 71*	1
AT THE TOP OF THE STAIRS [RE]	*Mojo*	28	*14 Aug 71*	10

George FORMBY with the Beryl STOTT CHORUS — UK

SINGLES:	**HITS 1**			**WEEKS 3**
HAPPY GO LUCKY ME / BANJO BOY	*Pye*	40	*23 Jul 60*	3

FORREST — US

SINGLES:	**HITS 3**			**WEEKS 20**
ROCK THE BOAT	*CBS*	4	*26 Feb 83*	10
FEEL THE NEED IN ME	*CBS*	17	*14 May 83*	8
ONE LOVER (DON'T STOP THE SHOW)	*CBS*	67	*17 Sep 83*	2

Sharon FORRESTER — Jamaica

SINGLES:	**HITS 1**			**WEEKS 1**
LOVE INSIDE	*ffrr*	50	*11 Feb 95*	1

FORTE – See FUGEES

Lance FORTUNE — UK

SINGLES:	**HITS 2**			**WEEKS 18**
BE MINE (ALLE MADCHEN WOLLEN KUSSEN)	*Pye*	4	*20 Feb 60*	13
THIS LOVE I HAVE FOR YOU	*Pye*	26	*7 May 60*	5
Above hit: Lance FORTUNE, Kim DRAKE MUSIC.				

FORTUNES — UK

SINGLES:	**HITS 5**			**WEEKS 65**
YOU'VE GOT YOUR TROUBLES	*Decca*	2	*10 Jul 65*	14
Originally recorded by David and Jonathan.				
HERE IT COMES AGAIN	*Decca*	4	*9 Oct 65*	14
THIS GOLDEN RING	*Decca*	15	*5 Feb 66*	9
Originally recorded by Cook & Greenaway.				
FREEDOM COME, FREEDOM GO	*Capitol*	6	*11 Sep 71*	17
STORM IN A TEACUP	*Capitol*	7	*29 Jan 72*	11
Originally recorded by Lynsey De Paul.				

40 THEVZ – See COOLIO

45 KING — US

SINGLES:	**HITS 1**			**WEEKS 6**
THE KING IS HERE / THE 900 NUMBER	*Trax*	60	*28 Oct 89*	5
THE 900 NUMBER [RE]	*Trax*	73	*11 Aug 90*	1

49ERS — Italy

SINGLES:	**HITS 6**			**WEEKS 27**
TOUCH ME	*Fourth & Broadway*	3	*16 Dec 89*	13
Samples Alisha Warren's recording of the same song title.				
DON'T YOU LOVE ME	*Fourth & Broadway*	12	*17 Mar 90*	6
GIRL TO GIRL	*Fourth & Broadway*	31	*9 Jun 90*	3
GOT TO BE FREE	*Fourth & Broadway*	46	*6 Jun 92*	2
THE MESSAGE	*Fourth & Broadway*	68	*29 Aug 92*	1

ROCKIN' MY BODY	*Media*	31	*18 Mar 95*	2
Above hit: 49ERS featuring Ann-Marie SMITH.				
ALBUMS:	**HITS 1**			**WEEKS 5**
THE 49ERS	*Fourth & Broadway*	51	*10 Mar 90*	5

Itsy FOSTER – See EXOTICA featuring Itsy FOSTER

Lawrence FOSTER – See LONDON SYMPHONY ORCHESTRA

FOSTER and ALLEN — Ireland

SINGLES:	**HITS 6**			**WEEKS 47**
A BUNCH OF THYME	*Ritz*	18	*27 Feb 82*	11
OLD FLAMES	*Ritz*	51	*30 Oct 82*	8
MAGGIE	*Ritz*	27	*19 Feb 83*	9
I WILL LOVE YOU ALL OF MY LIFE	*Ritz*	49	*29 Oct 83*	6
Title on label: I Will Love You All My Life.				
JUST FOR OLD TIME'S SAKE	*Ritz*	47	*30 Jun 84*	6
AFTER ALL THESE YEARS	*Ritz*	43	*29 Mar 86*	7
ALBUMS:	**HITS 23**			**WEEKS 205**
COMPILATION ALBUMS:	**HITS 1**			**WEEKS 3**
MAGGIE	*Ritz*	72	*14 May 83*	6
I WILL LOVE YOU ALL OF MY LIFE	*Ritz*	71	*5 Nov 83*	6
THE VERY BEST OF FOSTER AND ALLEN	*Ritz*	18	*17 Nov 84*	18
AFTER ALL THESE YEARS	*Ritz*	82	*29 Mar 86*	2
REMINISCING	*Stylus*	11	*25 Oct 86*	15
LOVE SONGS - THE VERY BEST OF FOSTER AND ALLEN VOLUME 2	*Ritz*	92	*27 Jun 87*	1
REFLECTIONS	*Stylus*	16	*10 Oct 87*	16
REMEMBER YOU'RE MINE	*Stylus*	16	*30 Apr 88*	15
THE WORLDS OF FOSTER AND ALLEN	*Stylus*	21	*1 Oct 88*	15
Album consisted only of solo recordings, thus it was eligible for the compilation chart from 1989.				
THE WORLDS OF FOSTER AND ALLEN	*Stylus*	16	*14 Jan 89*	3
This is an entry in the compilation chart.				
THE MAGIC OF FOSTER AND ALLEN (THEIR GREATEST HITS)	*Stylus*	29	*28 Oct 89*	12
FOSTER AND ALLEN'S CHRISTMAS COLLECTION	*Stylus*	40	*9 Dec 89*	4
Chart shows title as 'The Foster And Allen Christmas Album'.				
SOUVENIRS	*Telstar*	15	*10 Nov 90*	12
THE CHRISTMAS COLLECTION	*Telstar*	44	*8 Dec 90*	4
MEMORIES	*Telstar*	18	*2 Nov 91*	11
HEART STRINGS	*Telstar*	37	*31 Oct 92*	10
BY REQUEST	*Telstar*	14	*23 Oct 93*	12
SONGS WE LOVE TO SING	*Telstar*	41	*5 Nov 94*	9
100 GOLDEN GREATS	*Telstar*	30	*4 Nov 95*	12
SOMETHING SPECIAL - 100 GOLDEN LOVE SONGS	*Telstar*	46	*2 Nov 96*	10
SHADES OF GREEN	*Telstar*	55	*26 Apr 97*	2
BEST FRIENDS	*Telstar TV*	36	*15 Nov 97*	8
GREATEST HITS	*Telstar TV*	52	*12 Dec 98*	4
ONE DAY AT A TIME	*Telstar TV*	61	*25 Dec 99*	1

FOTHERINGAY — UK

ALBUMS:	**HITS 1**			**WEEKS 6**
FOTHERINGAY	*Island*	18	*11 Jul 70*	6

FOUNDATIONS — UK

SINGLES:	**HITS 6**			**WEEKS 57**
BABY, NOW THAT I'VE FOUND YOU	*Pye*	1	*30 Sep 67*	16
BACK ON MY FEET AGAIN	*Pye*	18	*27 Jan 68*	10
ANY OLD TIME YOU'RE SAD AND LONELY	*Pye*	48	*4 May 68*	1
ANY OLD TIME YOU'RE SAD AND LONELY [RE]	*Pye*	50	*18 May 68*	1
BUILD ME UP BUTTERCUP	*Pye*	2	*23 Nov 68*	15
Co-written by Mike D'Abo from Manfred Mann.				
IN THE BAD, BAD OLD DAYS (BEFORE YOU LOVED ME)	*Pye*	8	*15 Mar 69*	10
BORN TO LIVE, BORN TO DIE	*Pye*	46	*13 Sep 69*	3
BUILD ME UP BUTTERCUP [RI]	*Sequal*	71	*12 Dec 98*	1
From the film 'There's Something About Mary'.				

FOUNTAINS OF WAYNE — US

SINGLES:	**HITS 5**			**WEEKS 7**
RADIATION VIBE	*Atlantic*	32	*22 Mar 97*	2
SINK TO THE BOTTOM	*Atlantic*	42	*10 May 97*	1
SURVIVAL CAR	*Atlantic*	53	*26 Jul 97*	1
I WANT AN ALIEN FOR CHRISTMAS	*Atlantic*	36	*27 Dec 97*	2
DENISE	*Atlantic*	57	*20 Mar 99*	1
ALBUMS:	**HITS 1**			**WEEKS 1**
FOUNTAINS OF WAYNE	*Atlantic*	67	*7 Jun 97*	1

FOUR ACES — US

SINGLES:	HITS 7			WEEKS 40
THREE COINS IN THE FOUNTAIN *From the film of the same name.*	*Brunswick*	5	*31 Jul 54*	5
THREE COINS IN THE FOUNTAIN [RE]	*Brunswick*	17	*23 Oct 54*	1
MISTER SANDMAN *Originally recorded by Vaughan Monroe.*	*Brunswick*	9	*8 Jan 55*	5
STRANGER IN PARADISE	*Brunswick*	6	*21 May 55*	6
LOVE IS A MANY SPLENDOURED THING *From the film of the same name.*	*Brunswick*	2	*19 Nov 55*	13
A WOMAN IN LOVE *Above 6: FOUR ACES featuring Al ALBERTS.*	*Brunswick*	19	*20 Oct 56*	3
FRIENDLY PERSUASION (THEE I LOVE) *From the film of the same name.*	*Brunswick*	29	*5 Jan 57*	1
THE WORLD OUTSIDE (THEME FROM WARSAW CONCERTO)	*Brunswick*	18	*24 Jan 59*	6

FOUR BUCKETEERS — UK

SINGLES:	HITS 1			WEEKS 6
THE BUCKET OF WATER SONG *From the ITV children's show 'Tiswas'.*	*CBS*	26	*3 May 80*	6

FOUR ESQUIRES – vocal with the Sid BASS' ORCHESTRA — US

SINGLES:	HITS 1			WEEKS 2
LOVE ME FOREVER	*London*	23	*1 Feb 58*	2

4 HERO — UK

SINGLES:	HITS 4			WEEKS 6
COMBAT DANCING [EP] *Only the lead track Mr. Kirk's Nightmare was listed on 1 Dec 90.*	*Reinforced*	73	*24 Nov 90*	2
COOKIN' UP YAH BRAIN	*Reinforced*	59	*9 May 92*	2
STAR CHASERS	*Talkin Loud*	41	*15 Aug 98*	1
LES FLEUR *Originally recorded by Minnie Riperton in 1969.*	*Talkin Loud*	53	*3 Nov 01*	1
ALBUMS:	**HITS 2**			**WEEKS 7**
TWO PAGES	*Talkin Loud*	38	*25 Jul 98*	6
CREATING PATTERNS	*Talkin Loud*	65	*10 Nov 01*	1

400 BLOWS — UK

SINGLES:	HITS 1			WEEKS 4
MOVIN'	*Illuminated*	54	*29 Jun 85*	4

FOUR JAYS – See Billy FURY

FOUR KESTRELS – See Billy FURY

FOUR KNIGHTS — US

SINGLES:	HITS 2			WEEKS 13
I GET SO LONELY (WHEN I DREAM ABOUT YOU)	*Capitol*	5	*5 Jun 54*	7
I GET SO LONELY (WHEN I DREAM ABOUT YOU) [RE]	*Capitol*	10	*31 Jul 54*	4
MY PERSONAL POSSESSION *Above hit: Nat "King" COLE and the FOUR KNIGHTS with Nelson RIDDLE's MUSIC.*	*Capitol*	21	*19 Oct 57*	2

FOUR LADS — Canada

SINGLES:	HITS 3			WEEKS 23
FAITH CAN MOVE MOUNTAINS *Above hit: Johnnie RAY with the FOUR LADS.*	*Columbia*	7	*20 Dec 52*	2
FAITH CAN MOVE MOUNTAINS [RE]	*Columbia*	9	*10 Jan 53*	1
RAIN, RAIN, RAIN *Above hit: Frankie LAINE and the FOUR LADS with the Buddy COLE QUARTET.*	*Philips*	8	*23 Oct 54*	16
STANDING ON THE CORNER *From the musical 'The Most Happy Fella'.*	*Philips*	34	*30 Apr 60*	4

4 NON BLONDES — US

SINGLES:	HITS 2			WEEKS 19
WHAT'S UP?	*Interscope*	2	*19 Jun 93*	17
SPACEMAN	*Interscope*	53	*16 Oct 93*	2
ALBUMS:	**HITS 1**			**WEEKS 18**
BIGGER, BETTER, FASTER, MORE!	*Interscope*	4	*17 Jul 93*	18

4 OF US — Ireland

SINGLES:	HITS 2			WEEKS 6
SHE HITS ME	*Columbia*	35	*27 Feb 93*	4
I MISS YOU	*Columbia*	62	*1 May 93*	2

ALBUMS:	HITS 1			WEEKS 1
MAN ALIVE	*Columbia*	64	*20 Mar 93*	1

FOUR PENNIES — UK

SINGLES:	HITS 6			WEEKS 56
DO YOU WANT ME TO	*Philips*	47	*18 Jan 64*	1
DO YOU WANT ME TO [RE]	*Philips*	49	*8 Feb 64*	1
JULIET	*Philips*	1	*4 Apr 64*	15
The flip side, Tell Me Girl (What Are You Gonna Do), was initially promoted as the A-side.				
I FOUND OUT THE HARD WAY	*Philips*	14	*18 Jul 64*	11
BLACK GIRL	*Philips*	20	*31 Oct 64*	12
Originally recorded by Leadbelly.				
UNTIL IT'S TIME FOR YOU TO GO	*Philips*	19	*9 Oct 65*	11
Originally recorded by Buffy St Marie.				
TROUBLE IS MY MIDDLE NAME	*Philips*	32	*19 Feb 66*	5
EPS:	**HITS 1**			**WEEKS 15**
SPIN WITH THE PENNIES	*Philips*	6	*1 Aug 64*	15
ALBUMS:	**HITS 1**			**WEEKS 5**
TWO SIDES OF FOUR PENNIES	*Philips*	13	*7 Nov 64*	5

FOUR PREPS — US

SINGLES:	HITS 3			WEEKS 23
BIG MAN	*Capitol*	2	*14 Jun 58*	13
BIG MAN [RE]	*Capitol*	22	*20 Sep 58*	1
GOT A GIRL	*Capitol*	28	*28 May 60*	6
GOT A GIRL [RE]	*Capitol*	47	*16 Jul 60*	1
MORE MONEY FOR YOU AND ME [M]	*Capitol*	39	*4 Nov 61*	2

FOUR SEASONS — US

SINGLES:	HITS 17			WEEKS 151
SHERRY	*Stateside*	8	*6 Oct 62*	16
BIG GIRLS DON'T CRY	*Stateside*	13	*19 Jan 63*	10
WALK LIKE A MAN	*Stateside*	12	*30 Mar 63*	12
AIN'T THAT A SHAME	*Stateside*	38	*29 Jun 63*	3
Above 4: 4 SEASONS.				
RAG DOLL	*Philips*	2	*29 Aug 64*	13
LET'S HANG ON!	*Philips*	4	*20 Nov 65*	16
WORKING MY WAY BACK TO YOU	*Philips*	50	*2 Apr 66*	3
OPUS 17 (DON'T YOU WORRY 'BOUT ME)	*Philips*	20	*4 Jun 66*	9
I'VE GOT YOU UNDER MY SKIN	*Philips*	12	*1 Oct 66*	11
Originally recorded by Ray Noble and his Orchestra in 1936.				
TELL IT TO THE RAIN	*Philips*	37	*14 Jan 67*	5
Above 6: 4 SEASONS featuring the "Sound" Of Frankie VALLI.				
THE NIGHT	*Mowest*	7	*19 Apr 75*	9
Originally released in 1972.				
Above hit: Frankie VALLI and the FOUR SEASONS.				
WHO LOVES YOU	*Warner Brothers*	6	*20 Sep 75*	9
DECEMBER, 1963 (OH, WHAT A NIGHT)	*Warner Brothers*	1	*31 Jan 76*	10
The song's original year was 1933, and it was about the repeal of prohibition in the US.				
SILVER STAR	*Warner Brothers*	3	*24 Apr 76*	9
WE CAN WORK IT OUT	*Warner Brothers*	34	*27 Nov 76*	4
RHAPSODY	*Warner Brothers*	37	*18 Jun 77*	3
DOWN THE HALL	*Warner Brothers*	34	*20 Aug 77*	5
DECEMBER, 1963 (OH, WHAT A NIGHT) [RM]	*BR*	49	*29 Oct 88*	4
Remixed by Ben Liebrand.				
Above hit: Frankie VALLI and the FOUR SEASONS.				
ALBUMS:	**HITS 9**			**WEEKS 68**
SHERRY	*Stateside*	20	*6 Jul 63*	1
EDIZIOBE D'ORO	*Philips*	11	*10 Apr 71*	7
THE BIG ONES	*Philips*	37	*20 Nov 71*	1
THE FOUR SEASONS STORY	*Private Stock*	20	*6 Mar 76*	8
WHO LOVES YOU	*Warner Brothers*	12	*6 Mar 76*	17
GREATEST HITS	*K-Tel*	4	*20 Nov 76*	6
THE COLLECTION - THE 20 GREATEST HITS	*Telstar*	38	*21 May 88*	9
CD format is titled The 22 Greatest Hits.				
THE VERY BEST OF FRANKIE VALLI AND THE FOUR SEASONS	*PolyGram TV*	7	*7 Mar 92*	15
THE DEFINITIVE FRANKIE VALLI AND THE FOUR SEASONS	*WSM*	26	*13 Oct 01*	4
Above 3 contain Frankie Valli's solo and group material.				
Above 3: Frankie VALLI and the FOUR SEASONS.				

FOUR SHEPHERD BOYS – See Michael HOLLIDAY

4 STRINGS — Holland

SINGLES:	HITS 1			WEEKS 3
DAY TIME	*AM:PM*	48	*23 Dec 00*	3

4 THE CAUSE — US

SINGLES:	HITS 1			WEEKS 9
STAND BY ME	*RCA*	12	*10 Oct 98*	9

FOUR TOPS — US

(See also Supremes and the Four Tops.)

SINGLES:	HITS 27			WEEKS 298
I CAN'T HELP MYSELF	*Tamla Motown*	23	*3 Jul 65*	9
IT'S THE SAME OLD SONG	*Tamla Motown*	34	*4 Sep 65*	8
LOVING YOU IS SWEETER THAN EVER	*Tamla Motown*	21	*23 Jul 66*	12
Co-written by Stevie Wonder.				
REACH OUT I'LL BE THERE	*Tamla Motown*	1	*15 Oct 66*	16
STANDING IN THE SHADOWS OF LOVE	*Tamla Motown*	6	*14 Jan 67*	8
BERNADETTE	*Tamla Motown*	8	*1 Apr 67*	10
7-ROOMS OF GLOOM	*Tamla Motown*	12	*17 Jun 67*	9
YOU KEEP RUNNING AWAY	*Tamla Motown*	26	*14 Oct 67*	7
WALK AWAY RENEE	*Tamla Motown*	3	*16 Dec 67*	11
Original by Left Banke reached No. 5 in the US in 1966.				
IF I WERE A CARPENTER	*Tamla Motown*	7	*16 Mar 68*	11
YESTERDAY'S DREAMS	*Tamla Motown*	23	*24 Aug 68*	15
I'M IN A DIFFERENT WORLD	*Tamla Motown*	27	*16 Nov 68*	13
WHAT IS A MAN	*Tamla Motown*	16	*31 May 69*	11
DO WHAT YOU GOTTA DO	*Tamla Motown*	11	*27 Sep 69*	11
I CAN'T HELP MYSELF [RI]	*Tamla Motown*	10	*21 Mar 70*	11
IT'S ALL IN THE GAME	*Tamla Motown*	5	*30 May 70*	14
IT'S ALL IN THE GAME [RE]	*Tamla Motown*	48	*12 Sep 70*	2
STILL WATER (LOVE)	*Tamla Motown*	10	*3 Oct 70*	10
STILL WATER (LOVE) [RE]	*Tamla Motown*	44	*19 Dec 70*	2
JUST SEVEN NUMBERS (CAN STRAIGHTEN OUT MY LIFE)	*Tamla Motown*	36	*1 May 71*	5
SIMPLE GAME	*Tamla Motown*	3	*25 Sep 71*	11
Originally recorded by Moody Blues.				
BERNADETTE [RI]	*Tamla Motown*	23	*11 Mar 72*	7
WALK WITH ME TALK WITH ME DARLING	*Tamla Motown*	32	*5 Aug 72*	6
KEEPER OF THE CASTLE	*Probe*	18	*18 Nov 72*	9
SWEET UNDERSTANDING LOVE	*Probe*	29	*10 Nov 73*	10
WHEN SHE WAS MY GIRL	*Casablanca*	3	*17 Oct 81*	10
DON'T WALK AWAY	*Casablanca*	16	*19 Dec 81*	11
TONIGHT I'M GONNA LOVE YOU ALL OVER	*Casablanca*	43	*6 Mar 82*	4
BACK TO SCHOOL AGAIN	*RSO*	62	*26 Jun 82*	2
From the film 'Grease 2'.				
REACH OUT, I'LL BE THERE [RM]	*Motown*	11	*23 Jul 88*	9
INDESTRUCTIBLE [RM]	*Arista*	55	*17 Sep 88*	4
Above 2: remixed by Phil Harding and Ian Curnow.				
Above hit: FOUR TOPS featuring Smokey ROBINSON.				
LOCO IN ACAPULCO	*Arista*	7	*3 Dec 88*	13
From the film 'Buster'.				
INDESTRUCTIBLE	*Arista*	30	*25 Feb 89*	7
This was actually the original US recording, it charted after the UK mix. Smokey Robinson was only credited on the back of the sleeves of both releases.				
Above hit: FOUR TOPS featuring Smokey ROBINSON.				

EPS:	HITS 2			WEEKS 97
THE FOUR TOPS	*Tamla Motown*	2	*29 Oct 66*	58
FOUR TOPS HITS	*Tamla Motown*	1	*11 Mar 67*	39

ALBUMS:	HITS 11			WEEKS 244
FOUR TOPS ON TOP	*Tamla Motown*	9	*19 Nov 66*	23
FOUR TOPS LIVE!	*Tamla Motown*	4	*11 Feb 67*	72
Live recordings from the Roostertail in Detroit.				
REACH OUT	*Tamla Motown*	4	*25 Nov 67*	34
FOUR TOPS GREATEST HITS	*Tamla Motown*	1	*20 Jan 68*	67
YESTERDAY'S DREAMS	*Tamla Motown*	37	*8 Feb 69*	1
STILL WATERS RUN DEEP	*Tamla Motown*	29	*27 Jun 70*	8
FOUR TOPS' GREATEST HITS VOLUME 2	*Tamla Motown*	25	*27 Nov 71*	10
THE FOUR TOPS STORY 1964-72	*Tamla Motown*	35	*10 Nov 73*	5
THE BEST OF THE FOUR TOPS	*K-Tel*	13	*13 Feb 82*	13
THEIR GREATEST HITS	*Telstar*	47	*8 Dec 90*	6
THE SINGLES COLLECTION	*PolyGram TV*	11	*19 Sep 92*	5

4MANDU — UK

SINGLES:	HITS 3			WEEKS 6
THIS IS IT	*Arista*	45	*29 Jul 95*	3
DO IT FOR LOVE	*Arista*	45	*17 Feb 96*	2
BABY DON'T GO	*Arista*	47	*15 Jun 96*	1

FOURMOST — UK

SINGLES:	HITS 6			WEEKS 64
HELLO LITTLE GIRL	*Parlophone*	9	*14 Sep 63*	17
I'M IN LOVE	*Parlophone*	17	*28 Dec 63*	12
Above 2 written by Lennon & McCartney.				
A LITTLE LOVING	*Parlophone*	6	*25 Apr 64*	13
HOW CAN I TELL HER	*Parlophone*	33	*15 Aug 64*	4
BABY I NEED YOUR LOVING	*Parlophone*	24	*28 Nov 64*	12
GIRLS GIRLS GIRLS	*Parlophone*	33	*11 Dec 65*	6
Originally recorded by the Coasters.				
EPS:	**HITS 1**			**WEEKS 5**
FOURMOST SOUND	*Parlophone*	15	*29 Feb 64*	5

4-SKINS — UK

ALBUMS:	HITS 1			WEEKS 4
THE GOOD, THE BAD AND THE 4-SKINS	*Secret*	80	*17 Apr 82*	4

14–18 — UK

SINGLES:	HITS 1			WEEKS 4
GOOD-BYE-EE	*Magnet*	33	*1 Nov 75*	4

Bernard FOWLER – See BOMB THE BASS

FOX — UK

SINGLES:	HITS 3			WEEKS 29
ONLY YOU CAN	*GTO*	3	*15 Feb 75*	11
IMAGINE ME IMAGINE YOU	*GTO*	15	*10 May 75*	8
S-S-S-SINGLE BED	*GTO*	4	*10 Apr 76*	10
ALBUMS:	**HITS 1**			**WEEKS 8**
FOX	*GTO*	7	*17 May 75*	8

Noosha FOX — UK

SINGLES:	HITS 1			WEEKS 6
GEORGINA BAILEY	*GTO*	31	*12 Nov 77*	6

Samantha FOX — UK

SINGLES:	HITS 13			WEEKS 73
TOUCH ME (I WANT YOUR BODY)	*Jive*	3	*22 Mar 86*	10
DO YA DO YA (WANNA PLEASE ME)	*Jive*	10	*28 Jun 86*	7
HOLD ON TIGHT	*Jive*	26	*6 Sep 86*	5
I'M ALL YOU NEED	*Jive*	41	*13 Dec 86*	6
NOTHING'S GONNA STOP ME NOW	*Jive*	8	*30 May 87*	9
I SURRENDER (TO THE SPIRIT OF THE NIGHT)	*Jive*	25	*25 Jul 87*	7
I PROMISE YOU (GET READY)	*Jive*	58	*17 Oct 87*	3
TRUE DEVOTION	*Jive*	62	*19 Dec 87*	3
NAUGHTY GIRLS (NEED LOVE TOO)	*Jive*	31	*21 May 88*	5
LOVE HOUSE	*Jive*	32	*19 Nov 88*	6
I ONLY WANNA BE WITH YOU	*Jive*	16	*28 Jan 89*	8
I WANNA HAVE SOME FUN	*Jive*	63	*17 Jun 89*	2
SANTA MARIA	*All Around the World*	31	*28 Mar 98*	2
Rap by Eagle E.				
Above hit: DJ MILANO featuring Samantha FOX.				
ALBUMS:	**HITS 3**			**WEEKS 18**
TOUCH ME	*Jive*	17	*26 Jul 86*	10
SAMANTHA FOX	*Jive*	22	*1 Aug 87*	6
I WANNA HAVE SOME FUN	*Jive*	46	*18 Feb 89*	2

Bruce FOXTON — UK

SINGLES:	HITS 3			WEEKS 9
FREAK	*Arista*	23	*30 Jul 83*	5
THIS IS THE WAY	*Arista*	56	*29 Oct 83*	3
IT MAKES ME WONDER	*Arista*	74	*21 Apr 84*	1
ALBUMS:	**HITS 1**			**WEEKS 4**
TOUCH SENSITIVE	*Arista*	68	*12 May 84*	4

Charlie FOXX – See Inez FOXX

Inez FOXX — US

SINGLES:	HITS 2			WEEKS 8
HURT BY LOVE	*Sue*	40	*25 Jul 64*	3
MOCKINGBIRD	*United Artists*	36	*22 Feb 69*	2
Above hit: Inez and Charlie FOXX.				
MOCKINGBIRD [RE]	*United Artists*	33	*22 Mar 69*	3

John FOXX — UK

SINGLES:	HITS 7			WEEKS 31
UNDERPASS	*Metal Beat*	31	*26 Jan 80*	8
NO-ONE DRIVING	*Metal Beat*	32	*29 Mar 80*	4
Also available as a double single with the same catalogue number as the standard 7".				
BURNING CAR	*Metal Beat*	35	*19 Jul 80*	7
MILES AWAY	*Metal Beat*	51	*8 Nov 80*	3
EUROPE AFTER THE RAIN	*Metal Beat*	40	*29 Aug 81*	5
ENDLESSLY	*Virgin*	66	*2 Jul 83*	3
YOUR DRESS	*Virgin*	61	*17 Sep 83*	1
ALBUMS:	**HITS 4**			**WEEKS 17**
METAMATIC	*Metal Beat*	18	*2 Feb 80*	7
THE GARDEN	*Metal Beat*	24	*3 Oct 81*	6
THE GOLDEN SECTION	*Virgin*	27	*8 Oct 83*	3
IN MYSTERIOUS WAYS	*Virgin*	85	*5 Oct 85*	1

FRAGGLES — UK/US

SINGLES:	HITS 1			WEEKS 8
FRAGGLE ROCK THEME	*RCA*	33	*18 Feb 84*	8
Theme from the Children's ITV series of the same name.				
ALBUMS:	**HITS 1**			**WEEKS 4**
FRAGGLE ROCK	*RCA*	38	*21 Apr 84*	4

FRAGMA — Germany/Spain

SINGLES:	HITS 5			WEEKS 45
TOCA ME	*Positiva*	11	*25 Sep 99*	6
TOCA'S MIRACLE	*Positiva*	1	*22 Apr 00*	15
Mix of Fragma's Toca Me and the vocals from Coco's I Need A Miracle.				
TOCA'S MIRACLE [RE]	*Positiva*	52	*12 Aug 00*	2
EVERYTIME YOU NEED ME	*Positiva*	3	*13 Jan 01*	11
Above hit: FRAGMA featuring Maria RUBIA.				
YOU ARE ALIVE	*Positiva*	4	*19 May 01*	9
SAY THAT YOU'RE HERE	*Illustrious*	25	*8 Dec 01*	2
ALBUMS:	**HITS 1**			**WEEKS 12**
TOCA	*Positiva*	19	*27 Jan 00*	12

Grazina FRAME - See Cliff RICHARD

Roddy FRAME — UK

SINGLES:	HITS 1			WEEKS 2
REASON FOR LIVING	*Independiente*	45	*19 Sep 98*	2
ALBUMS:	**HITS 1**			**WEEKS 1**
THE NORTH STAR	*Independiente*	55	*3 Oct 98*	1

Peter FRAMPTON — UK

(See also Various Artists: Films - Original Soundtracks 'Sgt.Pepper's Lonely Hearts Club Band'.)

SINGLES:	HITS 4			WEEKS 24
SHOW ME THE WAY	*A&M*	10	*1 May 76*	12
BABY I LOVE YOUR WAY	*A&M*	43	*11 Sep 76*	5
DO YOU FEEL LIKE WE DO	*A&M*	39	*6 Nov 76*	4
Above 3 are live recordings.				
I'M IN YOU	*A&M*	41	*23 Jul 77*	3
ALBUMS:	**HITS 2**			**WEEKS 49**
FRAMPTON COMES ALIVE	*A&M*	6	*22 May 76*	39
Live recordings from the Winterland, San Francisco. Biggest selling live album of all time.				
I'M IN YOU	*A&M*	19	*18 Jun 77*	10

Connie FRANCIS — US

SINGLES:	HITS 23			WEEKS 244
WHO'S SORRY NOW	*MGM*	1	*5 Apr 58*	25
Originally recorded by Isham Jones in 1923.				
I'M SORRY I MADE YOU CRY	*MGM*	11	*28 Jun 58*	10
Originally recorded by Henry Burr in 1918.				
STUPID CUPID / CAROLINA MOON	*MGM*	1	*23 Aug 58*	19
Carolina Moon had first credit on the charts of 22 Aug 58 and 29 Aug 58. Stupid Cupid originally recorded by Neil Sedaka, Carolina Moon originally recorded by Gene Austin in 1929.				
I'LL GET BY	*MGM*	19	*1 Nov 58*	6
Originally recorded by Ruth Etting in 1929.				
FALLIN'	*MGM*	20	*22 Nov 58*	5
Above 2 entries were separate sides of the same release, each had its own chart run.				
YOU ALWAYS HURT THE ONE YOU LOVE	*MGM*	13	*27 Dec 58*	7

MY HAPPINESS	*MGM*	4	*14 Feb 59*	14
Originally recorded by Jon and Sondra Steele in 1948.				
Above hit: Connie FRANCIS: David ROSE and his Orchestra.				
MY HAPPINESS [RE]	*MGM*	30	*30 May 59*	1
LIPSTICK ON YOUR COLLAR	*MGM*	3	*4 Jul 59*	16
PLENTY GOOD LOVIN'	*MGM*	18	*12 Sep 59*	6
AMONG MY SOUVENIRS	*MGM*	11	*5 Dec 59*	10
Originally recorded by Paul Whiteman in 1928.				
VALENTINO	*MGM*	27	*19 Mar 60*	8
MAMA / ROBOT MAN	*MGM*	2	*21 May 60*	19
Robot Man listed from 4 Jun 60.				
EVERYBODY'S SOMEBODY'S FOOL	*MGM*	5	*20 Aug 60*	13
MY HEART HAS A MIND OF ITS OWN	*MGM*	3	*5 Nov 60*	15
MANY TEARS AGO	*MGM*	12	*14 Jan 61*	9
WHERE THE BOYS ARE / BABY ROO	*MGM*	5	*18 Mar 61*	14
Baby Roo had first billing on 18 Mar 61, and from 13 May 61 was no longer listed. Where the Boys Are written by Neil Sedaka and from the film of same name.				
BREAKIN' IN A BRAND NEW BROKEN HEART	*MGM*	12	*17 Jun 61*	11
TOGETHER	*MGM*	6	*16 Sep 61*	11
Originally recorded by Paul Whiteman in 1928.				
BABY'S FIRST CHRISTMAS	*MGM*	30	*16 Dec 61*	4
DON'T BREAK THE HEART THAT LOVES YOU	*MGM*	39	*28 Apr 62*	3
VACATION	*MGM*	10	*4 Aug 62*	9
I'M GONNA BE WARM THIS WINTER	*MGM*	48	*22 Dec 62*	1
MY CHILD	*MGM*	26	*12 Jun 65*	6
JEALOUS HEART	*MGM*	44	*22 Jan 66*	2
Originally recorded by Al Morgan in 1949.				
EPS:	**HITS 2**			**WEEKS 17**
HEARTACHES	*MGM*	14	*7 Jan 61*	2
FIRST LADY OF RECORD	*MGM*	7	*21 Jan 61*	15
ALBUMS:	**HITS 4**			**WEEKS 31**
ROCK 'N' ROLL MILLION SELLERS	*MGM*	12	*26 Mar 60*	1
CONNIE'S GREATEST HITS	*MGM*	16	*11 Feb 61*	3
20 ALL TIME GREATS	*Polydor*	1	*18 Jun 77*	22
First solo female to top the album chart.				
THE SINGLES COLLECTION	*PolyGram TV*	12	*24 Apr 93*	5

Jill FRANCIS — UK

SINGLES:	**HITS 1**			**WEEKS 1**
MAKE LOVE TO ME	*Glady Wax*	70	*3 Jul 93*	1

Claude FRANCOIS; Girl vocal: Kathy BARNET — France

SINGLES:	**HITS 1**			**WEEKS 4**
TEARS ON THE TELEPHONE	*Bradley's*	35	*10 Jan 76*	4

Joe FRANK - See HAMILTON, Joe FRANK and REYNOLDS

FRANK AND WALTERS — Ireland

SINGLES:	**HITS 4**			**WEEKS 13**
HAPPY BUSMAN	*Setanta*	49	*21 Mar 92*	2
THIS IS NOT A SONG	*Setanta*	46	*12 Sep 92*	3
AFTER ALL	*Setanta*	11	*9 Jan 93*	5
FASHION CRISIS HITS NEW YORK	*Setanta*	42	*17 Apr 93*	3
ALBUMS:	**HITS 1**			**WEEKS 1**
TRAINS, BOATS AND PLANES	*Setanta*	36	*7 Nov 92*	1

FRANKE — UK

(See also Our Tribe/One Tribe/O.T. Quartet.)

SINGLES:	**HITS 1**			**WEEKS 2**
UNDERSTAND THIS GROOVE	*China*	60	*7 Nov 92*	2

FRANK'EE - See BROTHER BROWN featuring FRANK'EE

FRANKIE GOES TO HOLLYWOOD — UK

SINGLES:	**HITS 7**			**WEEKS 147**
RELAX	*ZTT*	1	*26 Nov 83*	48
Reached No. 1 on 28 Jan 84, it dropped down the chart and climbed back to No. 2 on 7 Jul 84.				
TWO TRIBES	*ZTT*	1	*16 Jun 84*	20
Features the voice of actor Patrick Allen.				
TWO TRIBES [RE]	*ZTT*	73	*10 Nov 84*	1
THE POWER OF LOVE	*ZTT*	1	*1 Dec 84*	11
RELAX [RE]	*ZTT*	58	*16 Feb 85*	4
THE POWER OF LOVE [RE]	*ZTT*	64	*23 Feb 85*	1
WELCOME TO THE PLEASURE DOME	*ZTT*	2	*30 Mar 85*	11

RAGE HARD	*ZTT*	4	*6 Sep 86*	7
WARRIORS (OF THE WASTELAND)	*ZTT*	19	*22 Nov 86*	8
WATCHING THE WILDLIFE	*ZTT*	28	*7 Mar 87*	6
RELAX [RI]	*ZTT*	5	*2 Oct 93*	7
WELCOME TO THE PLEASUREDOME [RM-1ST] *This is the original 7" mix before the 1985 single release was remixed.*	*ZTT*	18	*20 Nov 93*	3
THE POWER OF LOVE [RI]	*ZTT*	10	*18 Dec 93*	7
TWO TRIBES [RM] *Remixed by Fluke.*	*ZTT*	16	*26 Feb 94*	3
THE POWER OF LOVE [RM] *Remixed by Rob Searle.*	*ZTT*	6	*1 Jul 00*	6
TWO TRIBES [RM-2ND] *Remixed by Rob Searle.*	*ZTT*	17	*9 Sep 00*	3
WELCOME TO THE PLEASUREDOME [RM-2ND] *Remixed by Sleazesisters.*	*ZTT*	45	*18 Nov 00*	1

ALBUMS:	**HITS 4**			**WEEKS 95**
WELCOME TO THE PLEASUREDOME	*ZTT*	1	*10 Nov 84*	58
LIVERPOOL	*ZTT*	5	*1 Nov 86*	13
BANG! - GREATEST HITS OF FRANKIE GOES TO HOLLYWOOD	*ZTT*	4	*30 Oct 93*	15
WELCOME TO THE PLEASUREDOME [RE-1ST] *Re-released at mid-price.*	*ZTT*	24	*18 Feb 95*	5
WELCOME TO THE PLEASUREDOME [RE-2ND] *Repackaged.*	*ZTT*	16	*10 Jul 99*	3
MAXIMUM JOY	*ZTT*	54	*7 Oct 00*	1

Aretha FRANKLIN — US

SINGLES:	**HITS 29**			**WEEKS 182**
RESPECT *Written by Otis Redding and features King Curtis on saxophone.*	*Atlantic*	10	*10 Jun 67*	14
BABY I LOVE YOU	*Atlantic*	39	*26 Aug 67*	4
CHAIN OF FOOLS / SATISFACTION *Chain Of Fools features Joe South on guitar. Originally recorded by Don Covay.*	*Atlantic*	43	*23 Dec 67*	2
SATISFACTION [RE]	*Atlantic*	37	*13 Jan 68*	5
(SWEET SWEET BABY) SINCE YOU'VE BEEN GONE	*Atlantic*	47	*16 Mar 68*	1
THINK	*Atlantic*	26	*25 May 68*	9
I SAY A LITTLE PRAYER *Originally recorded by Dionne Warwick.*	*Atlantic*	4	*10 Aug 68*	14
DON'T PLAY THAT SONG *Originally recorded by Ben E. King in 1962.*	*Atlantic*	13	*22 Aug 70*	11
SPANISH HARLEM	*Atlantic*	14	*2 Oct 71*	9
ANGEL *Originally recorded by Jimi Hendrix.*	*Atlantic*	37	*8 Sep 73*	5
UNTIL YOU COME BACK TO ME (THAT'S WHAT I'M GONNA DO) *Co-written by Stevie Wonder.*	*Atlantic*	26	*16 Feb 74*	8
WHAT A FOOL BELIEVES	*Arista*	46	*6 Dec 80*	7
LOVE ALL THE HURT AWAY *Above hit: Aretha FRANKLIN and George BENSON.*	*Arista*	49	*19 Sep 81*	3
JUMP TO IT	*Arista*	42	*4 Sep 82*	5
GET IT RIGHT	*Arista*	74	*23 Jul 83*	2
FREEWAY OF LOVE	*Arista*	68	*13 Jul 85*	3
SISTERS ARE DOIN' IT FOR THEMSELVES *Above hit: EURYTHMICS and Aretha FRANKLIN.*	*RCA*	9	*2 Nov 85*	11
WHO'S ZOOMIN' WHO	*Arista*	11	*23 Nov 85*	14
ANOTHER NIGHT	*Arista*	54	*22 Feb 86*	6
FREEWAY OF LOVE [RE]	*Arista*	51	*10 May 86*	3
JUMPIN' JACK FLASH *From the film of the same name and produced by Keith Richards.*	*Arista*	58	*25 Oct 86*	3
I KNEW YOU WERE WAITING (FOR ME) *Co-written by Simon Climie of Climie Fisher.* *Above hit: Aretha FRANKLIN and George MICHAEL.*	*Epic*	1	*31 Jan 87*	9
JIMMY LEE	*Arista*	46	*14 Mar 87*	4
THROUGH THE STORM *Above hit: Aretha FRANKLIN and Elton JOHN.*	*Arista*	41	*6 May 89*	3
IT ISN'T, IT WASN'T, IT AIN'T NEVER GONNA BE *Label only credits Aretha Franklin.* *Above hit: ARETHA and WHITNEY.*	*Arista*	29	*9 Sep 89*	5
THINK [RR] *[AA] listed with Everybody Needs Somebody To Love by the Blues Brothers. From the film 'The Blues Brothers'.*	*Atlantic*	31	*7 Apr 90*	2
EVERYDAY PEOPLE	*Arista*	69	*27 Jul 91*	1
A DEEPER LOVE *From the film 'Sister Act 2: Back In The Habit'.*	*Arista*	5	*12 Feb 94*	7
WILLING TO FORGIVE	*Arista*	17	*25 Jun 94*	7
A ROSE IS STILL A ROSE	*Arista*	22	*9 May 98*	4
HERE WE GO AGAIN	*Arista*	68	*26 Sep 98*	1

ALBUMS:	**HITS 10**			**WEEKS 76**
I NEVER LOVED A MAN	*Atlantic*	36	*12 Aug 67*	2

LADY SOUL	*Atlantic*	25	*13 Apr 68*	18
ARETHA NOW	*Atlantic*	6	*14 Sep 68*	11
WHO'S ZOOMIN' WHO?	*Arista*	49	*18 Jan 86*	12
THE FIRST LADY OF SOUL	*Stylus*	89	*24 May 86*	1
ARETHA	*Arista*	51	*8 Nov 86*	13
THROUGH THE STORM	*Arista*	46	*3 Jun 89*	1
GREATEST HITS 1980-1994	*Arista*	27	*19 Mar 94*	3
QUEEN OF SOUL - THE VERY BEST OF ARETHA FRANKLIN	*Atlantic*	20	*29 Oct 94*	5
GREATEST HITS	*Global Television*	38	*21 Nov 98*	10

Erma FRANKLIN — US

SINGLES:	HITS 1			WEEKS 10
(TAKE A LITTLE) PIECE OF MY HEART	*Epic*	9	*10 Oct 92*	10
Featured in the Levi's Jeans TV commercial.				

Kirk FRANKLIN – See GOD'S PROPERTY from Kirk FRANKLIN'S NU NATION featuring Kirk FRANKLIN and "SALT"

Rodney FRANKLIN — US

SINGLES:	HITS 1			WEEKS 9
THE GROOVE	*CBS*	7	*19 Apr 80*	9
ALBUMS:	**HITS 1**			**WEEKS 2**
YOU'LL NEVER KNOW	*CBS*	64	*24 May 80*	2

Chevelle FRANKLYN featuring BEENIE MAN — Jamaica

SINGLES:	HITS 1			WEEKS 1
DANCEHALL QUEEN	*Island Jamaica*	70	*20 Sep 97*	1
From the film of the same name.				

FRANTIC FIVE – See Don LANG

FRANTIQUE — US

SINGLES:	HITS 1			WEEKS 12
STRUT YOUR FUNKY STUFF	*Philadelphia International*	10	*11 Aug 79*	12

Elizabeth FRASER – See Harold BUDD, Elizabeth FRASER, Robin GUTHRIE and Simon RAYMONDE; FUTURE SOUND OF LONDON; Ian McCULLOCH.

Wendy FRASER – See Patrick SWAYZE featuring Wendy FRASER

FRASH — UK

SINGLES:	HITS 1			WEEKS 1
HERE I GO AGAIN	*PWL International*	69	*18 Feb 95*	1

FRAZIER CHORUS — UK

SINGLES:	HITS 6			WEEKS 14
DREAM KITCHEN	*Virgin*	57	*4 Feb 89*	3
TYPICAL!	*Virgin*	53	*15 Apr 89*	2
SLOPPY HEART	*Virgin*	73	*15 Jul 89*	1
CLOUD 8	*Virgin*	52	*9 Jun 90*	3
NOTHING	*Virgin*	51	*25 Aug 90*	3
WALKING ON AIR	*Virgin*	60	*16 Feb 91*	2
ALBUMS:	**HITS 2**			**WEEKS 2**
SUE	*Virgin*	56	*20 May 89*	1
RAY	*Virgin*	66	*16 Mar 91*	1

FREAK OF NATURE — US/Denmark

ALBUMS:	HITS 1			WEEKS 1
GATHERING OF FREAKS	*Music For Nations*	66	*1 Oct 94*	1

FREAK POWER — UK/Canada

SINGLES:	HITS 4			WEEKS 20
TURN ON, TUNE IN, COP OUT	*Fourth & Broadway*	29	*16 Oct 93*	5
RUSH	*Fourth & Broadway*	62	*26 Feb 94*	2
TURN ON, TUNE IN, COP OUT [RI]	*Fourth & Broadway*	3	*18 Mar 95*	9
Featured in the Levi's Jeans 'Taxi' TV commercial.				
NEW DIRECTION	*Fourth & Broadway*	60	*8 Jun 96*	1
NO WAY	*Deconstruction*	29	*9 May 98*	3
ALBUMS:	**HITS 1**			**WEEKS 5**
DRIVE-THRU BOOTY	*Fourth & Broadway*	11	*15 Apr 95*	5

FREAKY REALISTIC — UK/Japan

SINGLES:	HITS 2			WEEKS 3
KOOCHIE RYDER	*Frealism*	52	*3 Apr 93*	2
LEONARD NIMOY	*Polydor*	71	*3 Jul 93*	1

FREAKYMAN — Holland

SINGLES:	HITS 1			WEEKS 1
DISCOBUG '97	*Xtravaganza*	68	*27 Sep 97*	1
Originally released in 1996.				

Stan FREBERG — US

SINGLES:	HITS 3			WEEKS 5
SH-BOOM (LIFE COULD BE A DREAM)	*Capitol*	15	*20 Nov 54*	2
Above hit: Stan FREBERG with the TOADS featuring Jessie WHITE Music by Billy MAY with the TOADS.				
ROCK ISLAND LINE / HEARTBREAK HOTEL	*Capitol*	24	*28 Jul 56*	1
Above hit: Stan FREBERG and his SNIFFLE GROUP Interruptions by Peter LEEDS / Stan FREBERG Echo by MAMMOTH CAVE.				
ROCK ISLAND LINE / HEARTBREAK HOTEL [RE]	*Capitol*	29	*11 Aug 56*	1
THE OLD PAYOLA ROLL BLUES	*Capitol*	40	*14 May 60*	1
Above hit: Stan FREBERG with the TOADS featuring Jessie WHITE Music by Billy MAY with the TOADS.				

John FRED and his PLAYBOY BAND — US

SINGLES:	HITS 1			WEEKS 12
JUDY IN DISGUISE (WITH GLASSES)	*Pye International*	3	*6 Jan 68*	12
Title based on Lucy In The Sky With Diamonds.				

FRED and ROXY — UK

SINGLES:	HITS 1			WEEKS 2
SOMETHING FOR THE WEEKEND	*Echo*	36	*5 Feb 00*	2

FREDDIE and the DREAMERS — UK

SINGLES:	HITS 9			WEEKS 85
IF YOU GOTTA MAKE A FOOL OF SOMEBODY	*Columbia*	3	*11 May 63*	14
Original by James Ray reached No. 22 in the US in 1962.				
I'M TELLIN' YOU NOW	*Columbia*	2	*10 Aug 63*	11
YOU WERE MADE FOR ME	*Columbia*	3	*9 Nov 63*	15
OVER YOU	*Columbia*	13	*22 Feb 64*	11
I LOVE YOU BABY	*Columbia*	16	*16 May 64*	8
Guitar solo by Big Jim Sullivan.				
JUST FOR YOU	*Columbia*	41	*18 Jul 64*	3
I UNDERSTAND	*Columbia*	5	*7 Nov 64*	15
A LITTLE YOU	*Columbia*	26	*24 Apr 65*	5
THOU SHALT NOT STEAL	*Columbia*	44	*6 Nov 65*	3
Originally recorded by Dick & Deedee in 1964.				
EPS:	**HITS 3**			**WEEKS 14**
IF YOU GOTTA MAKE A FOOL OF SOMEBODY	*Columbia*	8	*19 Oct 63*	11
SONGS FROM THE FILM "WHAT A CRAZY WORLD"	*Columbia*	15	*8 Feb 64*	2
OVER YOU	*Columbia*	17	*4 Jul 64*	1
ALBUMS:	**HITS 1**			**WEEKS 26**
FREDDIE AND THE DREAMERS	*Columbia*	5	*9 Nov 63*	26

FREDERIK – See NINA and FREDERIK

Dee FREDRIX — UK

SINGLES:	HITS 2			WEEKS 5
AND SO I WILL WAIT FOR YOU	*East West*	56	*27 Feb 93*	4
DIRTY MONEY	*East West*	74	*3 Jul 93*	1

FREE — UK

SINGLES:	HITS 5			WEEKS 75
ALL RIGHT NOW	*Island*	2	*6 Jun 70*	16
MY BROTHER JAKE	*Island*	4	*1 May 71*	11
LITTLE BIT OF LOVE	*Island*	13	*27 May 72*	10
WISHING WELL	*Island*	7	*13 Jan 73*	10
ALL RIGHT NOW [RE]	*Island*	15	*21 Jul 73*	9
FREE [EP]	*Island*	11	*18 Feb 78*	7
Lead track: All Right Now (re-issue).				
FREE [EP] [RE]	*Island*	57	*23 Oct 82*	3
ALL RIGHT NOW [RM]	*Island*	8	*9 Feb 91*	9
Featured in the Wrigley's Chewing Gum TV commercial. Remixed by Bob Clearmountain.				
ALBUMS:	**HITS 7**			**WEEKS 71**
FIRE AND WATER	*Island*	2	*11 Jul 70*	18
HIGHWAY	*Island*	41	*23 Jan 71*	10
FREE LIVE!	*Island*	4	*26 Jun 71*	12
FREE AT LAST	*Island*	9	*17 Jun 72*	9
HEARTBREAKER	*Island*	9	*3 Feb 73*	7

THE FREE STORY	*Island*	2	*16 Mar 74*	6
THE BEST OF FREE - ALL RIGHT NOW	*Island*	9	*2 Mar 91*	9

FREE - See BOUNTY KILLER (featuring COCOA BROVAZ, Nona HENDRYX and FREE) Wyclef JEAN; QUEEN; QUEEN LATIFAH

FREE SPIRIT — UK

SINGLES:	HITS 1			WEEKS 1
NO MORE RAINY DAYS *Vocals by Elaine Vassel.*	*Columbia*	68	*13 May 95*	1

FREE THE SPIRIT — UK

ALBUMS:	HITS 3			WEEKS 42
PAN PIPE MOODS	*PolyGram TV*	2	*4 Feb 95*	26
PAN PIPES MOODS TWO	*PolyGram TV*	18	*4 Nov 95*	11
PAN PIPE MOODS IN PARADISE	*PolyGram TV*	26	*25 May 96*	5

FREEEZ — UK

SINGLES:	HITS 5			WEEKS 48
KEEP IN TOUCH	*Calibre*	49	*7 Jun 80*	3
SOUTHERN FREEEZ	*Beggars Banquet*	8	*7 Feb 81*	11
FLYING HIGH	*Beggars Banquet*	35	*18 Apr 81*	5
I.O.U.	*Beggars Banquet*	2	*18 Jun 83*	15
POP GOES MY LOVE	*Beggars Banquet*	26	*1 Oct 83*	6
I.O.U. (THE ULTIMATE MIXES - '87) [RM] *Above hit: FREEEZ featuring John ROCCA.*	*Citybeat*	23	*17 Jan 87*	6
SOUTHERN FREEEZ [RM]	*Total Control*	63	*30 May 87*	2
ALBUMS:	**HITS 2**			**WEEKS 18**
SOUTHERN FREEEZ	*Beggars Banquet*	17	*7 Feb 81*	15
GONNA GET YOU	*Beggars Banquet*	46	*22 Oct 83*	3

FREEFALL featuring Jan JOHNSTON — UK/US

SINGLES:	HITS 1			WEEKS 5
SKYDIVE	*Stress*	75	*28 Nov 98*	1
SKYDIVE [RI]	*Renaissance*	43	*22 Jul 00*	2
SKYDIVE (I FEEL WONDERFUL) [RI-2ND]	*Incentive*	35	*8 Sep 01*	2

FREEFALL featuring PSYCHOTROPIC — UK/Australia

SINGLES:	HITS 1			WEEKS 1
FEEL SURREAL	*ffrr*	63	*27 Jul 91*	1

Claire FREELAND — UK

SINGLES:	HITS 1			WEEKS 1
FREE *From the ITV series 'Popstars'.*	*Statuesque*	44	*21 Jul 01*	1

FREESTYLERS — UK

SINGLES:	HITS 3			WEEKS 5
B-BOY STANCE *Above hit: FREESTYLERS featuring TENOR FLY.*	*Freskanova*	23	*7 Feb 98*	3
WARNING *Above hit: FREESTYLERS featuring NAVIGATOR.*	*Freskanova*	68	*14 Nov 98*	1
HERE WE GO *Additional vocals by Navigator.* *Above hit: FREESTYLERS featuring DEFINITION OF SOUND.*	*Freskanova*	45	*24 Jul 99*	1
ALBUMS:	**HITS 1**			**WEEKS 3**
WE ROCK HARD	*Freskanova*	33	*15 Aug 98*	3

FREHLEY'S COMET — US

ALBUMS:	HITS 1			WEEKS 1
SECOND SIGHTING	*Atlantic*	79	*18 Jun 88*	1

FREIHEIT — Germany

SINGLES:	HITS 1			WEEKS 9
KEEPING THE DREAM ALIVE	*CBS*	14	*17 Dec 88*	9

Debbie FRENCH - See Joey NEGRO

Deborah FRENCH - See E-LUSTRIOUS

Nicki FRENCH — UK

SINGLES:	HITS 4			WEEKS 18
TOTAL ECLIPSE OF THE HEART	*Bags Of Fun*	54	*15 Oct 94*	1
TOTAL ECLIPSE OF THE HEART [RE]	*Bags Of Fun*	5	*14 Jan 95*	12

FOR ALL WE KNOW	*Bags Of Fun*	42	*22 Apr 95*	2
DID YOU EVER REALLY LOVE ME?	*Love This*	55	*15 Jul 95*	1
DON'T PLAY THAT SONG AGAIN	*RCA*	34	*27 May 00*	2

UK's Eurovision entry in 2000, it came 16th.

FRENCH AFFAIR — France

SINGLES:	HITS 1			WEEKS 3
MY HEART GOES BOOM	*Arista*	44	*16 Sep 00*	3

FREQUENCY 9 - See VARIOUS ARTISTS (EPs) 'The Further Adventures Of North - More Underground Dance EP'

Doug E. FRESH and the GET FRESH CREW — US

SINGLES:	HITS 1			WEEKS 11
THE SHOW	*Cooltempo*	7	*9 Nov 85*	11

Freddy FRESH — US

SINGLES:	HITS 2			WEEKS 3
BADDER BADDER SCHWING	*Eye Q*	34	*1 May 99*	2
Above hit: Freddy FRESH (featuring FATBOY SLIM).				
WHAT IT IS	*Eye Q*	63	*31 Jul 99*	1

FRESH 4 (CHILDREN OF THE GHETTO) featuring Lizz E — UK

SINGLES:	HITS 1			WEEKS 9
WISHING ON A STAR	*10 Records*	10	*7 Oct 89*	9

FRESH PRINCE - See JAZZY JEFF and the FRESH PRINCE

FRESHIES — UK

SINGLES:	HITS 1			WEEKS 3
I'M IN LOVE WITH THE GIRL ON A CERTAIN VIRGIN MANCHESTER MEGASTORE CHECKOUT DESK	*MCA*	54	*14 Feb 81*	3

Originally released on the Razz record label in 1980. Later copies on MCA removed the word Virgin from the title.

Matt FRETTON — UK

SINGLES:	HITS 1			WEEKS 5
IT'S SO HIGH	*Chrysalis*	50	*11 Jun 83*	5

FREUR — UK

SINGLES:	HITS 1			WEEKS 4
DOOT DOOT	*CBS*	59	*23 Apr 83*	4

Glenn FREY — US

SINGLES:	HITS 2			WEEKS 20
THE HEAT IS ON	*MCA*	12	*2 Mar 85*	12
From the film 'Beverly Hills Cop'.				
SMUGGLER'S BLUES	*BBC*	22	*22 Jun 85*	8
From the BBC TV series 'Miami Vice'.				
ALBUMS:	**HITS 1**			**WEEKS 9**
THE ALLNIGHTER	*MCA*	31	*6 Jul 85*	9

FRIDA — Norway

SINGLES:	HITS 2			WEEKS 12
I KNOW THERE'S SOMETHING GOING ON	*Epic*	43	*21 Aug 82*	7
Production and drums by Phil Collins.				
TIME	*Epic*	45	*17 Dec 83*	5
Above hit: FRIDA and B.A. ROBERTSON.				
ALBUMS:	**HITS 2**			**WEEKS 8**
SOMETHING'S GOING ON	*Epic*	18	*18 Sep 82*	7
SHINE	*Epic*	67	*20 Oct 84*	1

Gavin FRIDAY - See BONO

Ralph FRIDGE — Germany

SINGLES:	HITS 2			WEEKS 4
PARADISE	*Additive*	68	*24 Apr 99*	1
ANGEL	*Incentive*	20	*8 Apr 00*	3

Samples the vocal from Spectrasonics' Symphony Of Voices.

Dean FRIEDMAN — US

SINGLES:	HITS 3			WEEKS 22
WOMAN OF MINE	*Lifesong*	52	*3 Jun 78*	5

LUCKY STARS *This is a duet with female vocalist Denise Marser.*	*Lifesong*	3	*23 Sep 78*	10
LYDIA	*Lifesong*	31	*18 Nov 78*	7
ALBUMS:	**HITS 1**			**WEEKS 14**
WELL, WELL, SAID THE ROCKING CHAIR	*Lifesong*	21	*21 Oct 78*	14

FRIENDS AGAIN — UK

SINGLES:	**HITS 1**			**WEEKS 3**
THE FRIENDS AGAIN [EP] *Lead track: Lullaby No. 2 Love On Board.*	*Mercury*	59	*4 Aug 84*	3

FRIENDS OF MATTHEW — UK

SINGLES:	**HITS 1**			**WEEKS 1**
OUT THERE *Originally released on Pulse-8 Records in 1991. Vocals by Sally Kemp.*	*Serious*	61	*10 Jul 99*	1

FRIGID VINEGAR — UK

SINGLES:	**HITS 1**			**WEEKS 1**
DOGMONAUT 2000 (IS THERE ANYBODY OUT THERE?) *Samples Les Reed's brass arrangement of It's Not Unusual.*	*Gut*	53	*21 Aug 99*	1

FRIJID PINK — US

SINGLES:	**HITS 1**			**WEEKS 16**
THE HOUSE OF THE RISING SUN	*Deram*	4	*28 Mar 70*	16

Robert FRIPP — UK

(See also David Sylvian and Robert Fripp.)

ALBUMS:	**HITS 1**			**WEEKS 1**
EXPOSURE	*Polydor*	71	*12 May 79*	1

FROG CHORUS – See Paul McCARTNEY

Jane FROMAN — US

SINGLES:	**HITS 1**			**WEEKS 4**
I WONDER	*Capitol*	14	*18 Jun 55*	4

FRONT 242 — US/Belgium

SINGLES:	**HITS 1**			**WEEKS 1**
RELIGION	*RRE*	46	*1 May 93*	1
ALBUMS:	**HITS 3**			**WEEKS 3**
TYRANNY FOR YOU	*RRE*	49	*2 Feb 91*	1
06:21:03:11 UP EVIL	*RRE*	44	*22 May 93*	1
05:22:09:12 OFF	*RRE*	46	*4 Sep 93*	1

Bernard FROST – See Francis ROSSI

Christian FRY — UK

SINGLES:	**HITS 2**			**WEEKS 3**
YOU GOT ME	*Mushroom*	45	*14 Nov 98*	2
WON'T YOU STAY	*Mushroom*	48	*3 Apr 99*	1

FSOL – See FUTURE SOUND OF LONDON

FUGAZI — US

SINGLES:	**HITS 1**			**WEEKS 1**
FURNITURE	*Dischord*	61	*20 Oct 01*	1
ALBUMS:	**HITS 5**			**WEEKS 7**
STEADY DIET OF NOTHING	*Dischord*	63	*21 Sep 91*	1
IN ON THE KILLTAKER	*Dischord*	24	*19 Jun 93*	2
RED MEDICINE	*Dischord*	18	*13 May 95*	2
END HITS	*Dischord*	47	*25 Apr 98*	1
THE ARGUMENT	*Dischord*	63	*20 Oct 01*	1

FUGEES (REFUGEE CAMP) — US

(See also Brian Harvey.)

SINGLES:	**HITS 7**			**WEEKS 61**
FU-GEE-LA *Samples Ooh La La La by Teena Marie.*	*Columbia*	21	*6 Apr 96*	5
KILLING ME SOFTLY	*Columbia*	1	*8 Jun 96*	20
READY OR NOT *Samples Enya's Song For Bodecia.* *Samples Enya's Song For Bodecia , Rotary Connections' Memory Band, The Headhunters' God Made Me Funky.*	*Columbia*	1	*14 Sep 96*	12

NO WOMAN, NO CRY *Features Bob Marley's son Steve.*	*Columbia*	2	*30 Nov 96*	9
RUMBLE IN THE JUNGLE *Samples Abba's The Name Of The Game. From the film 'When We Were Kings'.* *Above hit: FUGEES featuring A TRIBE CALLED QUEST, Busta RHYMES and FORTE.*	*Mercury*	3	*15 Mar 97*	8
THE SWEETEST THING *Rap by John Forte. From the film 'Love Jones'.* *Above hit: REFUGEE CAMP ALLSTARS featuring Lauryn HILL.*	*Columbia*	18	*6 Sep 97*	4

ALBUMS:	HITS 2			WEEKS 72
THE SCORE *Peak position reached on 5 Oct 96.*	*Columbia*	2	*30 Mar 96*	70
THE BOOTLEG VERSIONS *Mini album features mixes from their first album 'Blunted On Reality'.*	*Columbia*	55	*7 Dec 96*	2

FULL CIRCLE — US

SINGLES:	HITS 1			WEEKS 5
WORKIN' UP A SWEAT	*EMI America*	41	*7 Mar 87*	5

FULL FORCE — US

SINGLES:	HITS 3			WEEKS 32
I WONDER IF I TAKE YOU HOME *Above hit: LISA LISA and CULT JAM with FULL FORCE.*	*CBS*	53	*4 May 85*	6
I WONDER IF I TAKE YOU HOME [RE]	*CBS*	12	*3 Aug 85*	11
ALICE, I WANT YOU JUST FOR ME!	*CBS*	9	*21 Dec 85*	11
I'M REAL *Above hit: James BROWN with FULL FORCE.*	*Scotti Brothers*	31	*4 Jun 88*	4

ALBUMS:	HITS 1			WEEKS 1
LISA LISA AND CULT JAM WITH FULL FORCE *Above hit: LISA LISA and CULT JAM with FULL FORCE.*	*CBS*	96	*21 Sep 85*	1

FULL INTENTION — UK

SINGLES:	HITS 5			WEEKS 8
AMERICA (I LOVE AMERICA)	*Stress*	32	*6 Apr 96*	2
UPTOWN DOWNTOWN	*Stress*	61	*10 Aug 96*	1
SHAKE YOUR BODY (DOWN TO THE GROUND)	*Sugar Daddy*	34	*26 Jul 97*	2
AMERICA (I LOVE AMERICA) [RE]	*Stress*	56	*22 Nov 97*	1
YOU ARE SOMEBODY	*Sugar Daddy*	75	*6 Jun 98*	1
I'LL BE WAITING *Above hit: FULL INTENTION presents SHENA.*	*Rulin*	44	*1 Sep 01*	1

FULL MONTY — UK

SINGLES:	HITS 1			WEEKS 1
THE FULL MONTY MONSTER MIX [M] *Medley of 3 tracks from the film.*	*RCA Victor*	62	*12 Sep 98*	1

FULL MONTY ALLSTARS featuring T.J. DAVIS — UK

SINGLES:	HITS 1			WEEKS 1
BRILLIANT FEELING	*Arista*	72	*27 Jul 96*	1

Bobby FULLER FOUR — US

SINGLES:	HITS 1			WEEKS 4
I FOUGHT THE LAW *Originally recorded by Sonny Curtis.*	*London*	33	*16 Apr 66*	4

FUN BOY THREE — UK

SINGLES:	HITS 8			WEEKS 70
THE LUNATICS (HAVE TAKEN OVER THE ASYLUM)	*Chrysalis*	20	*7 Nov 81*	12
IT AIN'T WHAT YOU DO IT'S THE WAY THAT YOU DO IT *Originally recorded by Jimmy Lunceford.* *Above hit: FUN BOY THREE with BANANARAMA.*	*Chrysalis*	4	*13 Feb 82*	10
REALLY SAYING SOMETHING (HE WAS REALLY SAYIN' SOMETHIN') *Originally recorded by the Velvetlettes.* *Above hit: BANANARAMA and the FUN BOY THREE.*	*Deram*	5	*10 Apr 82*	10
THE TELEPHONE ALWAYS RINGS	*Chrysalis*	17	*8 May 82*	9
SUMMERTIME	*Chrysalis*	18	*31 Jul 82*	8
THE MORE I SEE (THE LESS I BELIEVE)	*Chrysalis*	68	*15 Jan 83*	1
TUNNEL OF LOVE	*Chrysalis*	10	*5 Feb 83*	10
OUR LIPS ARE SEALED	*Chrysalis*	7	*30 Apr 83*	10

ALBUMS:	HITS 2			WEEKS 40
THE FUN BOY THREE	*Chrysalis*	7	*20 Mar 82*	20
WAITING	*Chrysalis*	14	*19 Feb 83*	20

FUN DA MENTAL — UK

ALBUMS:	HITS 1			WEEKS 1
SIEZE THE TIME	*Nation*	74	*25 Jun 94*	1

FUN LOVIN' CRIMINALS — US

SINGLES:	HITS 10			WEEKS 31
THE GRAVE AND THE CONSTANT	*Chrysalis*	72	*8 Jun 96*	1
SCOOBY SNACKS	*Chrysalis*	22	*17 Aug 96*	3
THE FUN LOVIN' CRIMINAL	*Chrysalis*	26	*16 Nov 96*	3
KING OF NEW YORK	*Chrysalis*	28	*29 Mar 97*	3
I'M NOT IN LOVE / SCOOBY SNACKS [RI]	*Chrysalis*	12	*5 Jul 97*	5
LOVE UNLIMITED	*Chrysalis*	18	*15 Aug 98*	4
Tribute to Barry White.				
BIG NIGHT OUT	*Chrysalis*	29	*17 Oct 98*	2
Samples Tom Petty's American Girl and Marshall Tucker Band's Can't You See.				
KOREAN BODEGA	*Chrysalis*	15	*8 May 99*	3
LOCO	*Chrysalis*	5	*17 Feb 01*	6
Samples Little River Band's Happy Anniversary.				
BUMP/RUN DADDY RUN	*Chrysalis*	50	*1 Sep 01*	1
ALBUMS:	**HITS 4**			**WEEKS 113**
COME FIND YOURSELF	*Chrysalis*	10	*13 Jul 96*	28
Chart position reached in 1997, (1996 peak No. 52).				
COME FIND YOURSELF [RE]	*Chrysalis*	7	*28 Jun 97*	44
100% COLOMBIAN	*Chrysalis*	3	*5 Sep 98*	26
MIMOSA	*Chrysalis*	37	*11 Dec 99*	9
LOCO	*Chrysalis*	5	*10 Mar 01*	6

Farley "Jackmaster" FUNK — US

SINGLES:	HITS 2			WEEKS 16
LOVE CAN'T TURN AROUND	*DJ International*	10	*23 Aug 86*	12
Above hit: Farley "Jackmaster" FUNK and Jessie SAUNDERS.				
AS ALWAYS	*Champion*	49	*11 Feb 89*	2
Above hit: Farley 'Jackmaster' FUNK Presents Ricky DILLARD.				
LOVE CAN'T TURN AROUND [RM]	*4 Liberty*	40	*14 Dec 96*	2
Above hit: Farley 'Jackmaster' FUNK featuring Darryl PANDY.				

FUNK D'VOID — UK

SINGLES:	HITS 1			WEEKS 1
DIABLA	*Soma Recordings*	70	*20 Oct 01*	1

FUNK JUNKEEZ — US

SINGLES:	HITS 1			WEEKS 1
GOT FUNK	*Evocative*	57	*21 Feb 98*	1

FUNK MASTER — UK

SINGLES:	HITS 1			WEEKS 12
IT'S OVER	*Master-Funk*	8	*18 Jun 83*	12

FUNKADELIC — US

(See also Scott Grooves.)

SINGLES:	HITS 1			WEEKS 12
ONE NATION UNDER A GROOVE	*Warner Brothers*	9	*9 Dec 78*	12
ALBUMS:	**HITS 1**			**WEEKS 5**
ONE NATION UNDER A GROOVE	*Warner Brothers*	56	*23 Dec 78*	5

FUNKAPOLITAN — UK

SINGLES:	HITS 1			WEEKS 7
AS THE TIME GOES BY	*London*	41	*22 Aug 81*	7

FUNKDOOBIEST — US

SINGLES:	HITS 2			WEEKS 6
WOPBABALUBOP	*Epic*	37	*11 Dec 93*	4
BOW WOW WOW	*Epic*	34	*5 Mar 94*	2
ALBUMS:	**HITS 1**			**WEEKS 1**
BROTHAS DOOBIE	*Epic*	62	*15 Jul 95*	1

FUNKSTAR DE LUXE — Denmark

SINGLES:	HITS 4			WEEKS 18
THE SUN IS SHINING	*Club Tools*	3	*25 Sep 99*	10
Marley first recorded the track for the Trojan label in the late 1960s and re-recorded it in 1978 for the Kaya album. This is the Trojan version remixed by Funkstar De Luxe.				
Above hit: Bob MARLEY vs FUNKSTAR DE LUXE REMIX.				

RAINBOW COUNTRY	*Club Tools*	11	*22 Jan 00*	6
Above hit: Bob MARLEY vs FUNKSTAR DE LUXE.				
WALKIN' IN THE NAME	*Club Tools*	42	*13 May 00*	1
Above hit: FUNKSTAR DE LUXE vs Terry MAXX.				
PULL UP TO THE BUMPER	*Club Tools*	60	*25 Nov 00*	1
Above hit: Grace JONES vs FUNKSTAR DE LUXE.				
ALBUMS:	**HITS 1**			**WEEKS 3**
THE SUN IS SHINING	*Club Tools*	40	*4 Sep 99*	3
Import single. It was too long and expensive to be eligible for the singles chart. See also entry in the singles section above.				
Above hit: Bob MARLEY vs FUNKSTAR DE LUXE.				

FUNKY CHOAD featuring Nick SKITZ — Australia/Italy

SINGLES:	**HITS 1**			**WEEKS 1**
THE ULTIMATE	*ffrr*	51	*29 Aug 98*	1

FUNKY GREEN DOGS — US

SINGLES:	**HITS 4**			**WEEKS 6**
FIRED UP!	*Twisted UK*	17	*12 Apr 97*	3
THE WAY	*Twisted UK*	43	*28 Jun 97*	1
UNTIL THE DAY	*Twisted UK*	75	*20 Jun 98*	1
BODY	*Twisted UK*	46	*27 Feb 99*	1

FUNKY JUNCTION – See KC FLIGHTT

FUNKY POETS — US

SINGLES:	**HITS 1**			**WEEKS 1**
BORN IN THE GHETTO	*Epic*	72	*7 May 94*	1

FUNKY WORM — UK

SINGLES:	**HITS 3**			**WEEKS 14**
HUSTLE! (TO THE MUSIC . . .)	*FON*	13	*30 Jul 88*	8
THE SPELL!	*FON*	61	*26 Nov 88*	3
U + ME = LOVE	*FON*	46	*20 May 89*	3

FUREYS and Davey ARTHUR — Ireland

SINGLES:	**HITS 2**			**WEEKS 14**
WHEN YOU WERE SWEET SIXTEEN	*Ritz*	14	*10 Oct 81*	11
Originally recorded by George C. Gaskin in 1900.				
I WILL LOVE YOU (EVERYTIME WHEN WE ARE GONE)	*Ritz*	54	*3 Apr 82*	3
Above hit: FUREYS.				
ALBUMS:	**HITS 4**			**WEEKS 38**
WHEN YOU WERE SWEET SIXTEEN	*Ritz*	99	*8 May 82*	1
GOLDEN DAYS	*K-Tel*	17	*10 Nov 84*	19
AT THE END OF THE DAY	*K-Tel*	35	*26 Oct 85*	11
FUREYS FINEST	*Telstar*	65	*21 Nov 87*	7

FURIOUS FIVE – See DURAN DURAN; GRANDMASTER FLASH and the FURIOUS FIVE; Melle MEL

FURNITURE — UK

SINGLES:	**HITS 1**			**WEEKS 10**
BRILLIANT MIND	*Stiff*	21	*14 Jun 86*	10

Nelly FURTADO — Canada

SINGLES:	**HITS 2**			**WEEKS 26**
I'M LIKE A BIRD	*Dreamworks*	5	*10 Mar 01*	16
TURN OFF THE LIGHT	*Dreamworks*	4	*1 Sep 01*	10
ALBUMS:	**HITS 1**			**WEEKS 35**
WHOA NELLY!	*Dreamworks*	2	*24 Mar 01*	35

Billy FURY — UK

SINGLES:	**HITS 29**			**WEEKS 281**
MAYBE TOMORROW	*Decca*	22	*28 Feb 59*	3
MAYBE TOMORROW [RE]	*Decca*	18	*28 Mar 59*	6
MARGO	*Decca*	28	*27 Jun 59*	1
COLLETTE	*Decca*	9	*12 Mar 60*	10
THAT'S LOVE	*Decca*	19	*28 May 60*	11
Above hit: Billy FURY with the FOUR JAYS.				
WONDEROUS PLACE	*Decca*	25	*24 Sep 60*	9
A THOUSAND STARS	*Decca*	14	*21 Jan 61*	10
Originally recorded by The Rivileers.				
DON'T WORRY	*Decca*	40	*29 Apr 61*	2
Originally recorded by Marty Robbins.				
Above hit: Billy FURY and the FOUR KESTRELS.				

HALFWAY TO PARADISE	*Decca*	3	*13 May 61*	23
Original by Tony Orlando reached No. 39 in the US in 1961.				
JEALOUSY	*Decca*	2	*9 Sep 61*	12
I'D NEVER FIND ANOTHER YOU	*Decca*	5	*16 Dec 61*	15
LETTER FULL OF TEARS	*Decca*	32	*17 Mar 62*	6
LAST NIGHT WAS MADE FOR LOVE	*Decca*	4	*5 May 62*	16
ONCE UPON A DREAM	*Decca*	7	*21 Jul 62*	13
From the film 'Play It Cool'.				
BECAUSE OF LOVE	*Decca*	18	*27 Oct 62*	14
Originally recorded by Elvis Presley.				
LIKE I'VE NEVER BEEN GONE	*Decca*	3	*16 Feb 63*	15
WHEN WILL YOU SAY I LOVE YOU	*Decca*	3	*18 May 63*	12
IN SUMMER	*Decca*	5	*27 Jul 63*	11
SOMEBODY ELSE'S GIRL	*Decca*	18	*5 Oct 63*	7
DO YOU REALLY LOVE ME TOO (FOOLS ERRAND)	*Decca*	13	*4 Jan 64*	10
I WILL	*Decca*	14	*2 May 64*	12
Originally recorded by Vic Dana.				
IT'S ONLY MAKE BELIEVE	*Decca*	10	*25 Jul 64*	10
I'M LOST WITHOUT YOU	*Decca*	16	*16 Jan 65*	10
Originally recorded by Teddy Randazzo.				
IN THOUGHTS OF YOU	*Decca*	9	*24 Jul 65*	11
RUN TO MY LOVIN' ARMS	*Decca*	25	*18 Sep 65*	7
Originally recorded by Jay and the Americans.				
I'LL NEVER QUITE GET OVER YOU	*Decca*	35	*12 Feb 66*	5
GIVE ME YOUR WORD	*Decca*	27	*6 Aug 66*	7
LOVE OR MONEY	*Polydor*	57	*4 Sep 82*	5
DEVIL OR ANGEL	*Polydor*	58	*13 Nov 82*	4
FORGET HIM	*Polydor*	59	*4 Jun 83*	4

EPS:	**HITS 3**			**WEEKS 91**
PLAY IT COOL	*Decca*	2	*9 Jun 62*	45
BILLY FURY HITS	*Decca*	8	*10 Nov 62*	30
BILLY FURY AND THE TORNADOS	*Decca*	2	*25 May 63*	16
Above hit: Billy FURY and the TORNADOS.				

ALBUMS:	**HITS 6**			**WEEKS 51**
THE SOUND OF FURY	*Decca*	18	*4 Jun 60*	2
HALFWAY TO PARADISE	*Ace Of Clubs*	5	*23 Sep 61*	9
BILLY	*Decca*	6	*11 May 63*	21
WE WANT BILLY	*Decca*	14	*26 Oct 63*	2
Live recordings, also features the Tornados.				
THE BILLY FURY HIT PARADE	*Decca*	44	*19 Feb 83*	15
THE ONE AND ONLY BILLY FURY	*Polydor*	56	*26 Mar 83*	2

FUSE — Canada

(See also Plastik Man.)

ALBUMS:	**HITS 1**			**WEEKS 1**
DIMENSION INTRUSION	*Warp*	63	*19 Jun 93*	1

FUSED — Sweden

SINGLES:	**HITS 1**			**WEEKS 1**
THIS PARTY SUCKS!	*Columbia*	64	*20 Mar 99*	1

FUTURE BREEZE — Germany

SINGLES:	**HITS 2**			**WEEKS 2**
WHY DON'T YOU DANCE WITH ME	*AM:PM*	50	*6 Sep 97*	1
SMILE	*Nebula*	67	*20 Jan 01*	1

FUTURE FORCE — UK/US

SINGLES:	**HITS 1**			**WEEKS 1**
WHAT YOU WANT	*AM:PM*	47	*17 Aug 96*	1

FUTURE SOUND OF LONDON — UK

SINGLES:	**HITS 7**			**WEEKS 25**
PAPUA NEW GUINEA	*Jumpin' & Pumpin'*	22	*23 May 92*	6
CASCADE	*Virgin*	27	*6 Nov 93*	3
EXPANDER	*Jumpin' & Pumpin'*	72	*30 Jul 94*	1
LIFEFORMS	*Virgin*	14	*13 Aug 94*	3
Above hit: FSOL with vocals by Elizabeth FRASER.				
FAR-OUT SON OF LUNG AND THE RAMBLINGS OF A MADMAN	*Virgin*	22	*27 May 95*	3
MY KINGDOM	*Virgin*	13	*26 Oct 96*	3
Samples Mary Hopkin's vocals from Vangelis' Rachel's Song.				
WE HAVE EXPLOSIVE	*Virgin*	12	*12 Apr 97*	3
Soundtrack to the Playstation's Wipeout 2097 computer game.				
PAPUA NEW GUINES 2001 [RI]	*Jumpin' Pumpin'*	28	*29 Sep 01*	3

ALBUMS:	HITS 5			WEEKS 10
ACCELERATOR	*Jumpin' & Pumpin'*	75	*18 Jul 92*	1
LIFEFORMS	*Virgin*	6	*4 Jun 94*	5
ISDN	*Virgin*	62	*17 Dec 94*	1
Recorded from live radio broadcasts transmitted down from ISDN phonelines from their studio.				
ISDN (REMIX)	*Virgin*	44	*17 Jun 95*	1
DEAD CITIES	*Virgin*	26	*9 Nov 96*	2

FUZZBOX – See WE'VE GOT A FUZZBOX AND WE'RE GONNA USE IT

FUZZBUBBLE – See PUFF DADDY

FYC – See FINE YOUNG CANNIBALS

Leslie FYSON – See Michael MEDWIN, Bernard BRESSLAW, Alfie BASS and Leslie FYSON

G

Andy G'S STARSKY and HUTCH ALLSTARS featuring HUGGY BEAR — UK

SINGLES:	HITS 1			WEEKS 1
STARSKY & HUTCH - THE THEME	*Virgin*	51	*3 Oct 98*	1
Song is dance reworking of the 1970s TV theme.				

Bobby G — UK

SINGLES:	HITS 1			WEEKS 12
BIG DEAL (THEME FROM THE BBC TV SERIES)	*BBC*	75	*1 Dec 84*	1
BIG DEAL (THEME FROM THE BBC TV SERIES) [RE-1ST]	*BBC*	65	*15 Dec 84*	5
BIG DEAL (THEME FROM THE BBC TV SERIES) [RE-2ND]	*BBC*	46	*19 Oct 85*	6

Dennis G – See WIDEBOYS featuring Dennis G

Gina G — Australia

SINGLES:	HITS 6			WEEKS 51
OOH AAH . . . JUST A LITTLE BIT	*Eternal*	1	*6 Apr 96*	23
UK's Eurovision entry in 1996, it came 7th.				
OOH AAH . . . JUST A LITTLE BIT [RE-1ST]	*Eternal*	62	*21 Sep 96*	1
OOH AAH . . . JUST A LITTLE BIT [RE-2ND]	*Eternal*	64	*5 Oct 96*	1
I BELONG TO YOU	*Eternal*	6	*9 Nov 96*	11
FRESH!	*Eternal*	6	*22 Mar 97*	7
TI AMO	*Eternal*	11	*7 Jun 97*	5
GIMME SOME LOVE	*Eternal*	25	*6 Sep 97*	2
EVERY TIME I FALL	*Eternal*	52	*15 Nov 97*	1

ALBUMS:	HITS 1			WEEKS 4
FRESH!	*Eternal*	12	*5 Apr 97*	4

Kenny G — US

SINGLES:	HITS 7			WEEKS 26
HI! HOW YA DOIN'?	*Arista*	70	*21 Apr 84*	3
WHAT DOES IT TAKE (TO WIN YOUR LOVE)	*Arista*	64	*30 Aug 86*	2
SONGBIRD	*Arista*	22	*4 Jul 87*	7
MISSING YOU KNOW	*Columbia*	28	*9 May 92*	4
Above hit: Michael BOLTON featuring Kenny G.				
FOREVER IN LOVE	*Arista*	47	*24 Apr 93*	3
BY THE TIME THIS NIGHT IS OVER	*Arista*	56	*17 Jul 93*	3
Above hit: Kenny G with Peabo BRYSON.				
HOW COULD AN ANGEL BREAK MY HEART	*LaFace*	22	*8 Nov 97*	4
Above hit: Toni BRAXTON with Kenny G.				

ALBUMS:	HITS 6			WEEKS 58
G FORCE	*Arista*	56	*17 Mar 84*	5
DUOTONES	*Arista*	28	*8 Aug 87*	5
MONTAGE	*Arista*	32	*14 Apr 90*	7
BREATHLESS	*Arista*	4	*15 May 93*	27
THE MOMENT	*Arista*	19	*19 Oct 96*	9
GREATEST HITS	*Arista*	38	*13 Dec 97*	5

Warren G — US

SINGLES:	HITS 8			WEEKS 59
REGULATE	*Death Row*	5	*23 Jul 94*	14
From the film 'Above The Rim'. Samples Michael McDonald's I Keep Forgettin'.				
Above hit: Warren G and Nate DOGG.				
THIS DJ	*RAL*	12	*12 Nov 94*	5
THIS DJ [RE]	*RAL*	68	*31 Dec 94*	2
DO YOU SEE	*RAL*	29	*25 Mar 95*	2
Samples Junior's Mama Used To Say.				

WHAT'S LOVE GOT TO DO WITH IT	*Interscope*	2	*23 Nov 96*	12
Above hit: Warren G featuring Adina HOWARD.				
I SHOT THE SHERIFF	*Def Jam*	2	*22 Feb 97*	8
SMOKIN' ME OUT	*Def Jam*	14	*31 May 97*	5
Cover of the Isley Brothers' Coolin' Me Out from their 1978 album Shakedown.				
Above hit: Warren G featuring Ron ISLEY.				
PRINCE IGOR	*Def Jam*	15	*10 Jan 98*	7
Based on music composed by Borodin.				
Above hit: RAPSODY: Warren G and SISSEL.				
ALL NIGHT ALL RIGHT	*Mushroom*	16	*24 Jan 98*	4
Samples A Taste Of Honey's Boogie Oogie Oogie.				
Above hit: Peter ANDRE featuring Warren G.				
ALBUMS:	**HITS 2**			**WEEKS 10**
REGULATE ... G FUNK ERA	*RAL*	25	*6 Aug 94*	6
TAKE A LOOK OVER YOUR SHOULDER (REALITY)	*Def Jam*	20	*8 Mar 97*	4

G.B.H. – See CHARGED G.B.H.

G-CLEFS — US

SINGLES:	**HITS 1**			**WEEKS 12**
I UNDERSTAND (JUST HOW YOU FEEL)	*London*	17	*2 Dec 61*	12
Originally recorded by the Four Tunes in 1954.				

G NATION featuring ROSIE — UK

SINGLES:	**HITS 1**			**WEEKS 1**
FEEL THE NEED	*Cooltempo*	58	*9 Aug 97*	1

G.O.S.H. — UK

SINGLES:	**HITS 1**			**WEEKS 11**
THE WISHING WELL	*MSS*	22	*28 Nov 87*	11
G.O.S.H. stands for 'Great Ormond Street Help'. Charity record for the hospital's Wishing Well appeal.				

G.Q. — US

SINGLES:	**HITS 1**			**WEEKS 6**
DISCO NIGHTS-(ROCK FREAK)	*Arista*	42	*10 Mar 79*	6

G.S.P. — UK

SINGLES:	**HITS 1**			**WEEKS 3**
THE BANANA SONG	*Yoyo*	37	*3 Oct 92*	3

G.T.O. — UK

(See also Technohead; Tricky Disco.)

SINGLES:	**HITS 3**			**WEEKS 7**
PURE	*Cooltempo*	57	*4 Aug 90*	3
LISTEN TO THE RHYTHM FLOW / BULLFROG	*React*	72	*7 Sep 91*	2
ELEVATION	*React*	59	*2 May 92*	2

G.T.R. — UK

ALBUMS:	**HITS 1**			**WEEKS 4**
GTR	*Arista*	41	*19 Jul 86*	4

G.U.N. – See GUN

G.U.S. (FOOTWEAR) BAND and the MORRISTOWN ORPHEUS CHOIR — UK

ALBUMS:	**HITS 1**			**WEEKS 1**
LAND OF HOPE AND GLORY	*Columbia*	54	*3 Oct 70*	1

Eric GABLE — US

SINGLES:	**HITS 1**			**WEEKS 1**
PROCESS OF ELIMINATION	*Epic*	63	*19 Mar 94*	1

Peter GABRIEL — UK

SINGLES:	**HITS 19**			**WEEKS 112**
SOLSBURY HILL	*Charisma*	13	*9 Apr 77*	9
GAMES WITHOUT FRONTIERS	*Charisma*	4	*9 Feb 80*	11
Features uncredited vocals by Kate Bush. Whistling by producers Steve Lillywhite & Hugh Progham.				
NO SELF CONTROL	*Charisma*	33	*10 May 80*	6
BIKO	*Charisma*	38	*23 Aug 80*	3
Written about black activist Steven Biko.				

SHOCK THE MONKEY	*Charisma*	58	*25 Sep 82*	5
I DON'T REMEMBER	*Charisma*	62	*9 Jul 83*	3
WALK THROUGH THE FIRE	*Virgin*	69	*2 Jun 84*	3
From the film 'Against All Odds'.				
SLEDGEHAMMER	*Virgin*	4	*26 Apr 86*	16
DON'T GIVE UP	*Virgin*	9	*1 Nov 86*	11
Above hit: Peter GABRIEL and Kate BUSH.				
BIG TIME	*Virgin*	13	*28 Mar 87*	7
Features the Police's Stewart Copeland on drums.				
RED RAIN	*Virgin*	46	*11 Jul 87*	3
BIKO [RR]	*Virgin*	49	*21 Nov 87*	6
Live recording from the Blossom Music Centre, Cleveland, 27 Jul 87.				
SHAKIN' THE TREE	*Virgin*	61	*3 Jun 89*	3
Above hit: Youssou N'DOUR and Peter GABRIEL.				
SOLSBURY HILL [RI] / SHAKING THE TREE [RI]	*Virgin*	57	*22 Dec 90*	4
Above hit: Peter GABRIEL / Peter GABRIEL and Youssou N'DOUR.				
DIGGING IN THE DIRT	*Virgin*	24	*19 Sep 92*	4
STEAM	*Realworld*	10	*16 Jan 93*	7
BLOOD OF EDEN	*Realworld*	43	*3 Apr 93*	4
KISS THAT FROG	*Realworld*	46	*25 Sep 93*	3
LOVETOWN	*Epic*	49	*25 Jun 94*	2
From the film 'Philadelphia'.				
SW LIVE [EP]	*Realworld*	39	*3 Sep 94*	2
Lead track: Red Rain. Live recording from Palasport Nouvo, Modena, Italy, 16+17 Nov 93.				

ALBUMS:	HITS 12			WEEKS 204
PETER GABRIEL	*Charisma*	7	*12 Mar 77*	19
PETER GABRIEL	*Charisma*	10	*17 Jun 78*	8
PETER GABRIEL	*Charisma*	1	*7 Jun 80*	18
PETER GABRIEL	*Charisma*	6	*18 Sep 82*	16
All 4 self-titled albums above are different.				
PETER GABRIEL PLAYS LIVE	*Charisma*	8	*18 Jun 83*	9
BIRDY [OST]	*Charisma*	51	*30 Mar 85*	3
SO	*Virgin*	1	*31 May 86*	76
PASSION	*Virgin*	29	*17 Jun 89*	5
SHAKING THE TREE	*Virgin*	11	*1 Dec 90*	15
Compilation. CD format also has the credit '16 Golden Greats', while the vinyl format has '12 Golden Greats'.				
US	*Realworld*	2	*10 Oct 92*	29
SECRET WORLD LIVE	*Realworld*	10	*10 Sep 94*	4
Live recordings from Modena, Italy, Nov 93.				
OVO - THE MILLENNIUM SHOW	*Realworld*	24	*24 Jun 00*	2
Music from the main show at the Millennium Dome.				

GABRIELLE — UK

SINGLES:	HITS 15			WEEKS 144
DREAMS	*Go.Beat*	1	*19 Jun 93*	15
GOING NOWHERE	*Go.Beat*	9	*2 Oct 93*	7
I WISH	*Go.Beat*	26	*11 Dec 93*	5
BECAUSE OF YOU	*Go.Beat*	24	*26 Feb 94*	5
GIVE ME A LITTLE MORE TIME	*Go.Beat*	5	*24 Feb 96*	18
FORGET ABOUT THE WORLD	*Go.Beat*	23	*22 Jun 96*	5
IF YOU REALLY CARED	*Go.Beat*	15	*5 Oct 96*	5
IF YOU EVER	*London*	2	*2 Nov 96*	15
Original by Shai reached No. 2 in the US in 1992.				
Above hit: EAST SEVENTEEN featuring GABRIELLE.				
WALK ON BY	*Go.Beat*	7	*1 Feb 97*	8
SUNSHINE	*Go.Beat*	9	*9 Oct 99*	8
RISE	*Go.Beat*	1	*5 Feb 00*	15
Samples Bob Dylan's Knocking On Heaven's Door.				
WHEN A WOMAN	*Go.Beat*	6	*17 Jun 00*	8
SHOULD I STAY	*Go.Beat*	13	*4 Nov 00*	7
OUT OF REACH	*Go.Beat*	4	*21 Apr 01*	16
DON'T NEED THE SUN TO SHINE (TO MAKE ME SMILE)	*Go.Beat*	9	*3 Nov 01*	7

ALBUMS:	HITS 4			WEEKS 145
FIND YOUR WAY	*Go.Beat*	9	*30 Oct 93*	22
GABRIELLE	*Go.Beat*	11	*8 Jun 96*	30
RISE	*Go.Beat*	1	30 Oct 99	59
RISE [RE]	*Go.Beat*	5	*12 May 01*	28
Re-issued with extra track.				
DREAMS CAN COME TRUE - GREATEST HITS VOLUME 1	*Go.Beat*	2	*24 Nov 01*	6

Yvonne GAGE — US

SINGLES:	HITS 1			WEEKS 4
DOIN' IT IN A HAUNTED HOUSE	*Epic*	45	*16 Jun 84*	4

Danni'elle GAHA — Australia

SINGLES:	HITS 3			WEEKS 7
STUCK IN THE MIDDLE	*Epic*	68	*1 Aug 92*	2
DO IT FOR LOVE	*Epic*	52	*27 Feb 93*	2
SECRET LOVE	*Epic*	41	*12 Jun 93*	3

Billy and Sarah GAINES — US

SINGLES:	HITS 1			WEEKS 1
I FOUND SOMEONE	*Expansion*	48	*14 Jun 97*	1

Originally released in 1991.

Chris GAINES - See Garth BROOKS.

Rosie GAINES — US

SINGLES:	HITS 3			WEEKS 15
I WANT U	*Motown*	70	*11 Nov 95*	1
CLOSER THAN CLOSE	*Big Bang*	4	*31 May 97*	12
I SURRENDER	*Big Bang*	39	*29 Nov 97*	2

Serge GAINSBOURG and Jane BIRKIN - See Jane BIRKIN and Serge GAINSBOURG

GALA — Italy

SINGLES:	HITS 3			WEEKS 24
FREED FROM DESIRE	*Big Life*	2	*19 Jul 97*	14
LET A BOY CRY	*Big Life*	11	*6 Dec 97*	8
COME INTO MY LIFE	*Big Life*	38	*22 Aug 98*	2

GALAXY featuring Phil FEARON - See Phil FEARON

Dee GALDES - See Phil FEARON

Eve GALLAGHER — UK

SINGLES:	HITS 4			WEEKS 8
LOVE COME DOWN	*More Protein*	61	*1 Dec 90*	3
LOVE COME DOWN [RE]	*More Protein*	68	*29 Dec 90*	1
YOU CAN HAVE IT ALL	*Cleveland City*	43	*15 Apr 95*	2
LOVE COME DOWN [RR]	*Cleveland City*	57	*28 Oct 95*	1
HEARTBREAK	*React*	44	*6 Jul 96*	1

Above hit: MRS WOOD featuring Eve GALLAGHER.

Liam GALLAGHER and Steve CRADOCK — UK

SINGLES:	HITS 1			WEEKS 5
CARNATION	*Ignition*	6	*23 Oct 99*	5

[AA] listed with Going Underground by Buffalo Tom. From the Jam tribute album Fire & Skill.

Rory GALLAGHER — UK

ALBUMS:	HITS 10			WEEKS 43
RORY GALLAGHER	*Polydor*	32	*29 May 71*	2
DEUCE	*Polydor*	39	*4 Dec 71*	1
LIVE! IN EUROPE	*Polydor*	9	*20 May 72*	15
BLUE PRINT	*Polydor*	12	*24 Feb 73*	7
TATTOO	*Polydor*	32	*17 Nov 73*	3
IRISH TOUR '74	*Polydor*	36	*27 Jul 74*	2
CALLING CARD	*Chrysalis*	32	*30 Oct 76*	1
TOP PRIORITY	*Chrysalis*	56	*22 Sep 79*	4
STAGE STRUCK	*Chrysalis*	40	*8 Nov 80*	3
JINX	*Chrysalis*	68	*8 May 82*	5

GALLAGHER and LYLE — UK

SINGLES:	HITS 4			WEEKS 27
I WANNA STAY WITH YOU	*A&M*	6	*28 Feb 76*	9
HEART ON MY SLEEVE	*A&M*	6	*22 May 76*	10
BREAKAWAY	*A&M*	35	*11 Sep 76*	4
EVERY LITTLE TEARDROP	*A&M*	32	*29 Jan 77*	4
ALBUMS:	**HITS 2**			**WEEKS 44**
BREAKAWAY	*A&M*	6	*28 Feb 76*	35
LOVE ON THE AIRWAYS	*A&M*	19	*29 Jan 77*	9

Patsy GALLANT — Canada

SINGLES:	HITS 1			WEEKS 9
FROM NEW YORK TO L.A.	*EMI*	6	*10 Sep 77*	9

Luke GALLIANA — UK

SINGLES:	HITS 1			WEEKS 1
TO DIE FOR	*Jive*	42	*12 May 01*	1
Unsuccessful contender in the UK's Song For Europe competition.				

GALLIANO — UK

SINGLES:	HITS 6			WEEKS 14
SKUNK FUNK	*Talkin Loud*	41	*30 May 92*	2
PRINCE OF PEACE	*Talkin Loud*	47	*1 Aug 92*	3
JUS' REACH (RECYCLED)	*Epic*	66	*10 Oct 92*	2
LONG TIME GONE	*Talkin Loud*	15	*28 May 94*	3
Originally recorded by Crosby, Stills, Nash and Young in 1971.				
TWYFORD DOWN	*Talkin Loud*	37	*30 Jul 94*	2
EASE YOUR MIND	*Talkin Loud*	45	*27 Jul 96*	2
ALBUMS:	**HITS 2**			**WEEKS 15**
A JOYFUL NOISE UNTO THE CREATOR	*Talkin Loud*	28	*20 Jun 92*	3
THE PLOT THICKENS	*Talkin Loud*	7	*11 Jun 94*	12

GALLON DRUNK — UK

ALBUMS:	HITS 1			WEEKS 1
FROM THE HEART OF TOWN	*Clawfist*	67	*13 Mar 93*	1

James GALWAY — Ireland

(See also Cleo Laine and James Galway; James Galway and Henry Mancini with the National Philharmonic Orchestra; James Galway and the Chieftains.)

SINGLES:	HITS 1			WEEKS 13
ANNIE'S SONG	*RCA Red Seal*	3	*27 May 78*	13
Above hit: James GALWAY, flute: NATIONAL PHILHARMONIC ORCHESTRA; Charles GERHART, conductor.				
ALBUMS:	**HITS 8**			**WEEKS 75**
THE MAGIC FLUTE OF JAMES GALWAY	*RCA Red Seal*	43	*27 May 78*	6
THE MAN WITH THE GOLDEN FLUTE	*RCA Red Seal*	52	*1 Jul 78*	3
JAMES GALWAY PLAYS SONGS FOR ANNIE	*RCA Red Seal*	7	*9 Sep 78*	40
Above hit: James GALWAY, flute; NATIONAL PHILHARMONIC ORCHESTRA; Charles GERHARDT, conductor.				
SONGS OF THE SEASHORE	*Solar*	39	*15 Dec 79*	6
THE JAMES GALWAY COLLECTION	*Telstar*	41	*18 Dec 82*	8
MASTERPIECES - THE ESSENTIAL FLUTE OF JAMES GALWAY	*RCA Victor*	30	*17 Apr 93*	5
I WILL ALWAYS LOVE YOU	*RCA Victor*	59	*18 Feb 95*	2
CLASSICAL MEDITATIONS	*RCA Victor*	45	*20 Jul 96*	5
1 of 2 albums released on the same day. The other, The Celtic Minstrel, entered at No.168.				

James GALWAY and the CHIEFTAINS — UK/Ireland

(See also Chieftains; James Galway.)

ALBUMS:	HITS 1			WEEKS 5
JAMES GALWAY AND THE CHIEFTAINS IN IRELAND	*RCA Red Seal*	32	*28 Mar 87*	5

James GALWAY and Henry MANCINI with the NATIONAL PHILHARMONIC ORCHESTRA — UK/US

(See also James Galway; Henry Mancini and his Orchestra.)

ALBUMS:	HITS 1			WEEKS 6
IN THE PINK	*RCA Red Seal*	62	*8 Dec 84*	6

GAMBAFREAKS — Italy

SINGLES:	HITS 2			WEEKS 2
INSTANT REPLAY	*Evocative*	57	*12 Sep 98*	1
Above hit: GAMBAFREAKS featuring Paco RIVAZ.				
DOWN DOWN DOWN	*Azuli*	57	*13 May 00*	1

GAMBLE – See PHILADELPHIA INTERNATIONAL ALL STARS: Lou RAWLS, Billy PAUL, Archie BELL, Teddy PENDERGRASS, O'JAYS, Dee Dee SHARP, GAMBLE

GANG OF FOUR — UK

SINGLES:	HITS 2			WEEKS 5
AT HOME HE'S A TOURIST	*EMI*	58	*16 Jun 79*	3
I LOVE A MAN IN UNIFORM	*EMI*	65	*22 May 82*	2
ALBUMS:	**HITS 3**			**WEEKS 9**
ENTERTAINMENT	*EMI*	45	*13 Oct 79*	3
SOLID GOLD	*EMI*	52	*21 Mar 81*	2
SONGS OF THE FREE	*EMI*	61	*29 May 82*	4

GANG STARR — US

SINGLES:	HITS 4			WEEKS 8
JAZZ THING	*CBS*	66	*13 Oct 90*	2
TAKE A REST	*Cooltempo*	63	*23 Feb 91*	1
LOVESICK	*Cooltempo*	50	*25 May 91*	3
2 DEEP	*Cooltempo*	67	*13 Jun 92*	2
ALBUMS:	**HITS 4**			**WEEKS 9**
STEP IN THE ARENA	*Cooltempo*	36	*26 Jan 91*	3
HARD TO EARN	*Cooltempo*	29	*12 Mar 94*	3
MOMENT OF TRUTH	*Cooltempo*	43	*11 Apr 98*	1
FULL CLIP: A DECADE OF GANG STARR	*Cooltempo*	47	*7 Aug 99*	2

GANJA KRU – See DJ HYPE

GANT — UK

SINGLES:	HITS 1			WEEKS 1
SOUND BWOY BURIAL / ALL NIGHT LONG	*Positiva*	67	*27 Dec 97*	1

GAP BAND — US

SINGLES:	HITS 12			WEEKS 82
OOPS UP SIDE YOUR HEAD	*Mercury*	6	*12 Jul 80*	14
PARTY LIGHTS	*Mercury*	30	*27 Sep 80*	8
BURN RUBBER ON ME (WHY YOU WANNA HURT ME)	*Mercury*	22	*27 Dec 80*	11
HUMPIN'	*Mercury*	36	*11 Apr 81*	6
YEARNING FOR YOUR LOVE	*Mercury*	47	*27 Jun 81*	4
EARLY IN THE MORNING	*Mercury*	55	*5 Jun 82*	3
OUTSTANDING	*Total Experience*	68	*19 Feb 83*	2
SOMEDAY	*Total Experience*	17	*31 Mar 84*	8
JAMMIN' IN AMERICA	*Total Experience*	64	*23 Jun 84*	2
BIG FUN	*Total Experience*	4	*13 Dec 86*	12
HOW MUSIC CAME ABOUT (BOP B DA B DA DA)	*Total Experience*	61	*14 Mar 87*	2
OOPS UPSIDE YOUR HEAD ('87 MIX) [RM]	*Club*	20	*11 Jul 87*	8
Remixed by Lonnie Simmons and Rudy Taylor.				
I'M GONNA GIT YOU SUCKA	*Arista*	63	*18 Feb 89*	2
ALBUMS:	**HITS 1**			**WEEKS 3**
GAP BAND 8	*Total Experience*	47	*7 Feb 87*	3

GARBAGE — UK/US

SINGLES:	HITS 12			WEEKS 59
SUBHUMAN	*Mushroom*	50	*19 Aug 95*	1
Originally released on the Discordant label.				
ONLY HAPPY WHEN IT RAINS	*Mushroom*	29	*30 Sep 95*	3
QUEER	*Mushroom*	13	*2 Dec 95*	4
STUPID GIRL	*Mushroom*	4	*23 Mar 96*	7
Samples Train In Vain by the Clash.				
MILK	*Mushroom*	10	*23 Nov 96*	7
Though credited on the chart, Tricky's contribution was only as a remixer of a secondary track of the CD.				
Above hit: GARBAGE featuring TRICKY.				
MILK [RE]	*Mushroom*	74	*18 Jan 97*	1
PUSH IT	*Mushroom*	9	*9 May 98*	5
I THINK I'M PARANOID	*Mushroom*	9	*18 Jul 98*	5
SPECIAL	*Mushroom*	15	*17 Oct 98*	4
Samples The Pretenders' The Talk Of The Town.				
WHEN I GROW UP	*Mushroom*	9	*6 Feb 99*	7
YOU LOOK SO FINE	*Mushroom*	19	*5 Jun 99*	4
THE WORLD IS NOT ENOUGH	*Radioactivell*	11	*27 Nov 99*	9
Theme from the James Bond film of the same name.				
ANDROGYNY	*Mushroom*	24	*6 Oct 01*	2
ALBUMS:	**HITS 3**			**WEEKS 169**
GARBAGE	*Mushroom*	23	*14 Oct 95*	4
GARBAGE [RE]	*Mushroom*	6	*9 Dec 95*	95
Peak position reached on 27 Apr 96.				
VERSION 2.0	*Mushroom*	1	*23 May 98*	65
BEAUTIFULGARBAGE	*Mushroom*	6	*13 Oct 01*	4

Jan GARBAREK — Norway

ALBUMS:	HITS 1			WEEKS 1
VISIBLE WORLD	*ECM*	69	*4 May 96*	1

Adam GARCIA — Australia

SINGLES:	HITS 1			WEEKS 5
NIGHT FEVER	*Polydor*	15	*16 May 98*	5
From the musical 'Saturday Night Fever'.				

Scott GARCIA featuring MC STYLES — UK

SINGLES:	HITS 1			WEEKS 3
A LONDON THING	*Connected*	29	*1 Nov 97*	3
Originally released in 1996.				

Boris GARDINER — Jamaica

SINGLES:	HITS 4			WEEKS 38
ELIZABETHAN REGGAE	*Duke*	48	*17 Jan 70*	1
Original copies credited Byron Lee as the artist (he recorded the B-side). This entry and for the first 4 weeks of the re-entry, the charts credited him instead of Boris Gardner.				
Above hit: Boris GARDNER.				
ELIZABETHAN REGGAE [RE]	*Duke*	14	*31 Jan 70*	13
I WANNA WAKE UP WITH YOU	*Revue*	1	*26 Jul 86*	15
Originally recorded by Mac Davis in 1980.				
YOU'RE EVERYTHING TO ME	*Revue*	11	*4 Oct 86*	8
Some copies of the above 2 hits have his surname as Gardner.				
THE MEANING OF CHRISTMAS	*Revue*	69	*27 Dec 86*	1

Paul GARDINER — UK

SINGLES:	HITS 1			WEEKS 4
STORMTROOPER IN DRAG	*Beggars Banquet*	49	*25 Jul 81*	4
Features vocals by Gary Numan.				

Art GARFUNKEL — US

(See also Simon and Garfunkel.)

SINGLES:	HITS 3			WEEKS 37
I ONLY HAVE EYES FOR YOU	*CBS*	1	*13 Sep 75*	11
Originally recorded by Ben Selvin in 1934.				
BRIGHT EYES	*CBS*	1	*3 Mar 79*	19
From the film 'Watership Down'.				
SINCE I DON'T HAVE YOU	*CBS*	38	*7 Jul 79*	7
Originally recorded by the Skyliners.				
ALBUMS:	**HITS 7**			**WEEKS 64**
ANGEL CLARE	*CBS*	14	*13 Oct 73*	7
BREAKAWAY	*CBS*	7	*1 Nov 75*	10
WATER MARK	*CBS*	25	*18 Mar 78*	5
FATE FOR BREAKFAST	*CBS*	2	*21 Apr 79*	20
SCISSORS CUT	*CBS*	51	*19 Sep 81*	3
THE ART GARFUNKEL ALBUM	*CBS*	12	*17 Nov 84*	13
THE VERY BEST OF ART GARFUNKEL - ACROSS AMERICA	*Virgin*	35	*14 Dec 96*	6

Judy GARLAND — US

SINGLES:	HITS 1			WEEKS 2
THE MAN THAT GOT AWAY	*Philips*	18	*11 Jun 55*	2
EPS:	**HITS 1**			**WEEKS 3**
MAGGIE MAY	*Capitol*	18	*5 Dec 64*	3
ALBUMS:	**HITS 1**			**WEEKS 3**
JUDY AT CARNEGIE HALL	*Capitol*	13	*3 Mar 62*	3

Errol GARNER — US

ALBUMS:	HITS 1			WEEKS 1
CLOSE UP IN SWING	*Philips*	20	*14 Jul 62*	1

Laurent GARNIER — France

SINGLES:	HITS 3			WEEKS 4
CRISPY BACON	*F Communications*	60	*15 Feb 97*	1
THE MAN WITH THE RED FACE	*F Communications*	65	*22 Apr 00*	1
GREED/THE MAN WITH THE RED FACE [RI]	*F Communications*	36	*11 Nov 00*	2
The Man With The Red Face is an edited version of the original.				

Lee GARRETT — US

SINGLES:	HITS 1			WEEKS 7
YOU'RE MY EVERYTHING	*Chrysalis*	15	*29 May 76*	7

Leif GARRETT — US

SINGLES:	HITS 2			WEEKS 14
I WAS MADE FOR DANCIN'	*Scotti Brothers*	4	*20 Jan 79*	10
FEEL THE NEED	*Scotti Brothers*	38	*21 Apr 79*	4

Lesley GARRETT — UK

SINGLES:	HITS 1			WEEKS 10
AVE MARIA	*Internal Affairs*	16	*6 Nov 93*	10

Duet with leukaemia sufferer Thompson was broadcast on BBC TV's 'Hearts Of Gold' on 26 Sep 93. Ave Maria is a Catholic form of address to the Virgin Mary.
Above hit: Lesley GARRETT with Amanda THOMPSON.

ALBUMS:	HITS 8			WEEKS 44
AVE MARIA - THE ALBUM	*Telstar*	25	*12 Feb 94*	7
SOPRANO IN RED	*Silva Classics*	59	*18 Nov 95*	8
SOPRANO IN HOLLYWOOD	*Silva Classics*	53	*19 Oct 96*	4
Features the BBC Concert Orchestra and includes songs from the 1930s/40s.				
THE SOPRANO'S GREATEST HITS	*Silva Classics*	53	*18 Oct 97*	2
Recorded with the Royal Philharmonic Orchestra.				
A SOPRANO INSPIRED	*Conifer Classics*	48	*22 Nov 97*	7
LESLEY GARRETT	*BBC*	34	*14 Nov 98*	8
I WILL WAIT FOR YOU	*Conifer*	28	*27 May 00*	7
TRAVELLING LIGHT	*EMI Classics*	75	*24 Nov 01*	1

Siedah GARRETT - See Dennis EDWARDS; Michael JACKSON

David GARRICK — UK

SINGLES:	HITS 2			WEEKS 16
LADY JANE	*Piccadilly*	28	*11 Jun 66*	7
Originally recorded by the Rolling Stones.				
DEAR MRS. APPLEBEE	*Piccadilly*	22	*24 Sep 66*	9
Originally recorded by Flip Cartridge.				

GARY'S GANG — US

SINGLES:	HITS 3			WEEKS 18
KEEP ON DANCIN'	*CBS*	8	*24 Feb 79*	10
LET'S LOVEDANCE TONIGHT	*CBS*	49	*2 Jun 79*	4
KNOCK ME OUT	*Arista*	45	*6 Nov 82*	4

Barbara GASKIN - See Dave STEWART

GAT DECOR — UK

SINGLES:	HITS 1			WEEKS 10
PASSION	*Effective*	29	*16 May 92*	4
PASSION [RM]	*Way Of Life*	6	*9 Mar 96*	6

The theme to BBC1 TV's 'Ski Sunday'. Remixed by Northern Scum and new vocals by Beverli Skeete.

Stephen GATELEY — Ireland

SINGLES:	HITS 3			WEEKS 19
NEW BEGINNING/BRIGHT EYES	*A&M*	3	*10 Jun 00*	11
Bright Eyes was the theme to the new TV version of 'Watership Down'.				
I BELIEVE	*A&M*	11	*14 Oct 00*	4
From the film 'Billy Elliot'.				
STAY	*A&M*	13	*12 May 01*	4

ALBUMS:	HITS 1			WEEKS 4
NEW BEGINNING	*A&M*	9	*1 Jul 00*	4

David GATES — US

SINGLES:	HITS 1			WEEKS 2
TOOK THE LAST TRAIN	*Elektra*	50	*22 Jul 78*	2

ALBUMS:	HITS 4			WEEKS 25
NEVER LET HER GO	*Elektra*	32	*31 May 75*	1
GOODBYE GIRL	*Elektra*	28	*29 Jul 78*	3
THE COLLECTION - THE VERY BEST OF BREAD AND DAVID GATES	*Telstar*	84	*28 Nov 87*	2
Above hit: BREAD and David GATES.				
DAVID GATES AND BREAD: ESSENTIALS	*Warner.esp/Jive*	9	*5 Jul 97*	19

Above 2 albums include Gates' solo and group recordings.
Above hit: David GATES and BREAD.

GAY DAD — UK

SINGLES:	HITS 5			WEEKS 10
TO EARTH WITH LOVE	*London*	10	*30 Jan 99*	4
JOY!	*London*	22	*5 Jun 99*	3
OH JIM	*London*	47	*14 Aug 99*	1
NOW ALWAYS AND FOREVER	*B-Unique*	41	*31 Mar 01*	1
TRANSMISSION	*B-Unique*	58	*22 Sep 01*	1

ALBUMS:	HITS 1			WEEKS 3
LEISURE NOISE	*London*	14	*19 Jun 99*	3

GAY GORDON and the MINCE PIES — UK

SINGLES:	HITS 1			WEEKS 5
THE ESSENTIAL WALLY PARTY MEDLEY [M]	*Lifestyle*	60	*6 Dec 86*	5

Marvin GAYE — US

(See also Marvin Gaye and Tammi Terrell; Diana Ross and Marvin Gaye; Diana Ross, Marvin Gaye, Smokey Robinson and Stevie Wonder.)

SINGLES:	HITS 15			WEEKS 116
ONCE UPON A TIME	*Stateside*	50	*1 Aug 64*	1
Above hit: Marvin GAYE and Mary WELLS.				
HOW SWEET IT IS	*Stateside*	49	*12 Dec 64*	1
LITTLE DARLIN' (I NEED YOU)	*Tamla Motown*	50	*1 Oct 66*	1
IT TAKES TWO	*Tamla Motown*	16	*28 Jan 67*	11
Above hit: Marvin GAYE and Kim WESTON.				
I HEARD IT THROUGH THE GRAPEVINE	*Tamla Motown*	1	*15 Feb 69*	15
Originally recorded by Smokey Robinson & the Miracles.				
TOO BUSY THINKING ABOUT MY BABY	*Tamla Motown*	5	*26 Jul 69*	16
ABRAHAM, MARTIN AND JOHN	*Tamla Motown*	9	*9 May 70*	14
Originally recorded by Dion.				
SAVE THE CHILDREN	*Tamla Motown*	41	*11 Dec 71*	6
LET'S GET IT ON	*Tamla Motown*	31	*22 Sep 73*	7
GOT TO GIVE IT UP	*Motown*	7	*7 May 77*	10
Live Recording from the London Palladium.				
SEXUAL HEALING	*CBS*	4	*30 Oct 82*	14
MY LOVE IS WAITING	*CBS*	34	*8 Jan 83*	5
SANCTIFIED LADY	*CBS*	51	*18 May 85*	4
I HEARD IT THROUGH THE GRAPEVINE [RI]	*Motown*	8	*26 Apr 86*	8
Featured in the Levi's 501 jeans TV commercial.				
LUCKY LUCKY ME	*Motown*	67	*14 May 94*	1
MUSIC	*Polydor*	36	*6 Oct 01*	2
Above hit: Erick SERMON featuring Marvin GAYE.				

EPS:	HITS 1			WEEKS 8
ORIGINALS FROM MARVIN GAYE	*Tamla Motown*	3	*15 Apr 67*	8

ALBUMS:	HITS 14			WEEKS 141
GREATEST HITS	*Tamla Motown*	40	*16 Mar 68*	1
LET'S GET IT ON	*Tamla Motown*	39	*10 Nov 73*	1
I WANT YOU	*Tamla Motown*	22	*15 May 76*	5
THE BEST OF MARVIN GAYE	*Tamla Motown*	56	*30 Oct 76*	1
IN OUR LIFETIME	*Motown*	48	*28 Feb 81*	4
MIDNIGHT LOVE	*CBS*	10	*20 Nov 82*	16
GREATEST HITS	*Telstar*	13	*12 Nov 83*	61
The two Greatest Hits albums are different.				
DREAM OF A LIFETIME	*CBS*	46	*15 Jun 85*	4
LOVE SONGS	*Telstar*	69	*12 Nov 88*	9
Compilation, one side for each artist.				
Above hit: Marvin GAYE and Smokey ROBINSON.				
LOVE SONGS	*Telstar*	39	*3 Nov 90*	5
THE VERY BEST OF MARVIN GAYE	*Motown*	3	*9 Apr 94*	19
Includes re-entry in 1999.				
WHAT'S GOING ON?	*Motown*	69	*24 Jul 99*	1
Originally released in 1971.				
THE LOVE SONGS	*Motown*	8	*19 Feb 00*	7
WHAT'S GOING ON? [RE]	*Motown*	56	*1 Apr 00*	3
THE VERY BEST OF MARVIN GAYE	*Motown*	15	*1 Sep 01*	4

Marvin GAYE and Tammi TERRELL — US

(See also Marvin Gaye.)

SINGLES:	HITS 6			WEEKS 61
IF I COULD BUILD MY WHOLE WORLD AROUND YOU	*Tamla Motown*	41	*20 Jan 68*	7
AIN'T NOTHIN' LIKE THE REAL THING	*Tamla Motown*	34	*15 Jun 68*	7
YOU'RE ALL I NEED TO GET BY	*Tamla Motown*	19	*5 Oct 68*	19
YOU AIN'T LIVIN' TILL YOU'RE LOVIN'	*Tamla Motown*	21	*25 Jan 69*	8
GOOD LOVIN' AIN'T EASY TO COME BY	*Tamla Motown*	26	*7 Jun 69*	7
GOOD LOVIN' AIN'T EASY TO COME BY [RE]	*Tamla Motown*	48	*2 Aug 69*	1
THE ONION SONG	*Tamla Motown*	9	*15 Nov 69*	12
Female vocal on the above two was actually Valerie Simpson, due to Terrell's ill health.				

ALBUMS:	HITS 1			WEEKS 4
GREATEST HITS	*Tamla Motown*	60	*22 Aug 70*	4

GAYE BYKERS ON ACID — UK

SINGLES:	HITS 1			WEEKS 2
GIT DOWN (SHAKE YOUR THANG)	*Virgin*	54	*31 Oct 87*	2

ALBUMS:	HITS 1			WEEKS 1
DRILL YOUR OWN HOLE	*Virgin*	95	*14 Nov 87*	1

Crystal GAYLE — US

SINGLES:	HITS 2			WEEKS 28
DON'T IT MAKE MY BROWN EYES BLUE *Originally recorded by Richard Leigh.*	*United Artists*	5	*12 Nov 77*	14
TALKING IN YOUR SLEEP *Originally recorded by Marmalade.*	*United Artists*	11	*26 Aug 78*	14
ALBUMS:	**HITS 3**			**WEEKS 25**
WE MUST BELIEVE IN MAGIC	*United Artists*	15	*21 Jan 78*	7
WHEN I DREAM	*United Artists*	25	*23 Sep 78*	8
THE CRYSTAL GAYLE SINGLES ALBUM	*United Artists*	7	*22 Mar 80*	10

Michelle GAYLE — UK

SINGLES:	HITS 7			WEEKS 52
LOOKING UP	*RCA*	11	*7 Aug 93*	6
SWEETNESS	*RCA*	4	*24 Sep 94*	16
I'LL FIND YOU	*RCA*	26	*17 Dec 94*	7
FREEDOM	*RCA*	16	*27 May 95*	6
HAPPY JUST TO BE WITH YOU *Samples Chic's Good Times.*	*RCA*	11	*26 Aug 95*	7
DO YOU KNOW	*RCA*	6	*8 Feb 97*	6
SENSATIONAL *Based on For The Love Of You by the Isley Brothers.*	*RCA*	14	*26 Apr 97*	4
ALBUMS:	**HITS 2**			**WEEKS 13**
MICHELLE GAYLE	*RCA*	30	*22 Oct 94*	10
SENSATIONAL	*RCA*	17	*10 May 97*	3

Roy GAYLE – See MIRAGE

GAYLE and GILLIAN — Australia

SINGLES:	HITS 2			WEEKS 2
MAD IF YA DON'T!	*Mushroom*	75	*3 Jul 93*	1
WANNA BE YOUR LOVER	*Mushroom*	62	*19 Mar 94*	1

Gloria GAYNOR — US

SINGLES:	HITS 8			WEEKS 73
NEVER CAN SAY GOODBYE	*MGM*	2	*7 Dec 74*	13
REACH OUT, I'LL BE THERE	*MGM*	14	*8 Mar 75*	8
ALL I NEED IS YOUR SWEET LOVIN'	*MGM*	44	*9 Aug 75*	3
HOW HIGH THE MOON *Originally recorded by Benny Goodman in 1940.*	*MGM*	33	*17 Jan 76*	4
I WILL SURVIVE	*Polydor*	1	*3 Feb 79*	15
LET ME KNOW (I HAVE A RIGHT)	*Polydor*	32	*6 Oct 79*	7
I AM WHAT I AM (FROM 'LA CAGE AUX FOLLES') *From the stage show.*	*Chrysalis*	13	*24 Dec 83*	12
I WILL SURVIVE [RM] *Remixed by Phil Kelsey.*	*Polydor*	5	*26 Jun 93*	10
LAST NIGHT	*Logic*	67	*3 Jun 00*	1
ALBUMS:	**HITS 3**			**WEEKS 17**
NEVER CAN SAY GOODBYE	*MGM*	32	*8 Mar 75*	8
LOVE TRACKS	*Polydor*	31	*24 Mar 79*	7
THE POWER OF GLORIA GAYNOR	*Stylus*	81	*16 Aug 86*	2

GAZ — US

SINGLES:	HITS 1			WEEKS 4
SING SING	*Salsoul*	60	*24 Feb 79*	4

GAZZA — UK

SINGLES:	HITS 2			WEEKS 14
FOG ON THE TYNE (REVISITED) *Above hit: GAZZA and LINDISFARNE.*	*Best*	2	*10 Nov 90*	9
GEORDIE BOYS (GAZZA RAP)	*Best*	31	*22 Dec 90*	5

Nigel GEE — UK

SINGLES:	HITS 1			WEEKS 1
HOOTIN'	*Neo*	57	*27 Jan 01*	1

J. GEILS BAND — US

SINGLES:	HITS 4			WEEKS 20
ONE LAST KISS	*EMI America*	74	*9 Jun 79*	1
CENTERFOLD	*EMI America*	3	*13 Feb 82*	9
FREEZE-FRAME	*EMI America*	27	*10 Apr 82*	7
ANGEL IN BLUE	*EMI America*	55	*26 Jun 82*	3

ALBUMS:	HITS 1			WEEKS 15
FREEZE-FRAME	*EMI America*	12	*27 Feb 82*	15

Bob GELDOF — Ireland

SINGLES:	HITS 4			WEEKS 15
THIS IS THE WORLD CALLING	*Mercury*	25	*1 Nov 86*	5
LOVE LIKE A ROCKET	*Mercury*	61	*21 Feb 87*	3
THE GREAT SONG OF INDIFFERENCE	*Mercury*	15	*23 Jun 90*	6
CRAZY	*Vertigo*	65	*7 May 94*	1
Backing vocals by Sting.				

ALBUMS:	HITS 3			WEEKS 10
DEEP IN THE HEART OF NOWHERE	*Mercury*	79	*6 Dec 86*	1
THE VEGETARIANS OF LOVE	*Mercury*	21	*4 Aug 90*	6
LOUDMOUTH - THE BEST OF THE BOOMTOWN RATS AND BOB GELDOF	*Vertigo*	10	*9 Jul 94*	3
Includes both solo and group material.				
Above hit: BOOMTOWN RATS and Bob GELDOF.				

GEM - See OUR TRIBE/ONE TRIBE/O.T. QUARTET

GEMINI — UK

SINGLES:	HITS 3			WEEKS 7
EVEN THOUGH YOU BROKE MY HEART	*EMI*	40	*30 Sep 95*	3
STEAL YOUR LOVE AWAY	*EMI*	37	*10 Feb 96*	2
COULD IT BE FOREVER	*EMI*	38	*29 Jun 96*	2

GEMS FOR JEM — UK

SINGLES:	HITS 1			WEEKS 2
LIFTING ME HIGHER	*Box 21*	28	*6 May 95*	2
Samples Evelyn Thomas' High Energy.				

GEN X - See GENERATION X

GENE — UK

SINGLES:	HITS 11			WEEKS 22
BE MY LIGHT, BE MY GUIDE	*Costermonger*	54	*13 Aug 94*	1
SLEEP WELL TONIGHT	*Costermonger*	36	*12 Nov 94*	2
HAUNTED BY YOU	*Costermonger*	32	*4 Mar 95*	2
OLYMPIAN	*Costermonger*	18	*22 Jul 95*	2
FOR THE DEAD	*Costermonger*	14	*13 Jan 96*	3
FIGHTING FIT	*Polydor*	22	*2 Nov 96*	2
WE COULD BE KINGS	*Polydor*	17	*1 Feb 97*	2
WHERE ARE THEY NOW?	*Polydor*	22	*10 May 97*	2
SPEAK TO ME SOMEONE	*Polydor*	30	*9 Aug 97*	2
AS GOOD AS IT GETS	*Polydor*	23	*27 Feb 99*	2
FILL HER UP	*Polydor*	36	*24 Apr 99*	2

ALBUMS:	HITS 4			WEEKS 14
OLYMPIAN	*Costermonger*	8	*1 Apr 95*	6
TO SEE THE LIGHTS	*Costermonger*	11	*3 Feb 96*	3
DRAWN TO THE DEEP END	*Polydor*	8	*1 Mar 97*	3
REVELATIONS	*Polydor*	25	*13 Mar 99*	2

GENE AND JIM ARE INTO SHAKES — UK

SINGLES:	HITS 1			WEEKS 2
SHAKE! (HOW ABOUT A SAMPLING, GENE?)	*Rough Trade*	68	*19 Mar 88*	2

GENE LOVES JEZEBEL — UK

SINGLES:	HITS 4			WEEKS 7
SWEETEST THING	*Beggars Banquet*	75	*29 Mar 86*	1
HEARTACHE	*Beggars Banquet*	71	*14 Jun 86*	2
THE MOTION OF LOVE	*Beggars Banquet*	56	*5 Sep 87*	3
GORGEOUS	*Beggars Banquet*	68	*5 Dec 87*	1

ALBUMS:	HITS 2			WEEKS 5
DISCOVER	*Beggars Banquet*	32	*19 Jul 86*	4
HOUSE OF DOLLS	*Beggars Banquet*	81	*24 Oct 87*	1

GENERAL DEGREE - See Richie STEPHENS featuring GENERAL DEGREE

GENERAL LEVY — UK

SINGLES:	HITS 2			WEEKS 13
MONKEY MAN	*London*	75	*4 Sep 93*	1
INCREDIBLE	*Renk*	39	*18 Jun 94*	3
Above hit: M-BEAT featuring GENERAL LEVY.				
INCREDIBLE [RM]	*Renk*	8	*10 Sep 94*	9

GENERAL PUBLIC
UK

SINGLES:	HITS 2			WEEKS 4
GENERAL PUBLIC	*Virgin*	60	*10 Mar 84*	3
I'LL TAKE YOU THERE *From the film 'Threesome'.*	*Epic*	73	*2 Jul 94*	1

GENERAL SAINT
UK

(See also Clint Eastwood and General Saint.)

SINGLES:	HITS 2			WEEKS 6
OH CAROL! *Above hit: GENERAL SAINT featuring Don CAMPBELL.*	*Copasetic*	54	*2 Apr 94*	5
SAVE THE LAST DANCE FOR ME *Above hit: SAINT and CAMPBELL.*	*Copasetic*	75	*6 Aug 94*	1

GENERATION X
UK

SINGLES:	HITS 7			WEEKS 31
YOUR GENERATION	*Chrysalis*	36	*17 Sep 77*	4
READY STEADY GO	*Chrysalis*	47	*11 Mar 78*	3
KING ROCKER	*Chrysalis*	11	*20 Jan 79*	9
VALLEY OF THE DOLLS	*Chrysalis*	23	*7 Apr 79*	7
FRIDAYS ANGELS	*Chrysalis*	62	*30 Jun 79*	2
DANCING WITH MYSELF	*Chrysalis*	62	*18 Oct 80*	2
DANCING WITH MYSELF [EP] *Lead track: Dancing With Myself.* *Above 2: GEN X.*	*Chrysalis*	60	*24 Jan 81*	4

ALBUMS:	HITS 2			WEEKS 9
GENERATION X	*Chrysalis*	29	*8 Apr 78*	4
VALLEY OF THE DOLLS	*Chrysalis*	51	*17 Feb 79*	5

GENERATOR
Holland

SINGLES:	HITS 1			WEEKS 1
WHERE ARE YOU NOW? *Originally released on the Polar State label in 1998.*	*Tidy Trax*	60	*23 Oct 99*	1

GENESIS
UK

SINGLES:	HITS 29			WEEKS 187
I KNOW WHAT I LIKE (IN YOUR WARDROBE)	*Charisma*	21	*6 Apr 74*	7
YOUR OWN SPECIAL WAY	*Charisma*	43	*26 Feb 77*	3
SPOT THE PIGEON [EP] *Lead track: Match Of The Day.*	*Charisma*	14	*28 May 77*	7
FOLLOW YOU FOLLOW ME *First hit to feature Phil Collins on vocals.*	*Charisma*	7	*11 Mar 78*	13
MANY TOO MANY	*Charisma*	43	*8 Jul 78*	5
TURN IT ON AGAIN	*Charisma*	8	*15 Mar 80*	10
DUCHESS	*Charisma*	46	*17 May 80*	5
MISUNDERSTANDING	*Charisma*	42	*13 Sep 80*	5
ABACAB *Title is the chord sequence of the song.*	*Charisma*	9	*22 Aug 81*	8
KEEP IT DARK	*Charisma*	33	*31 Oct 81*	4
MAN ON THE CORNER	*Charisma*	41	*13 Mar 82*	5
3 X 3 [EP] *Lead track: Paperlate.*	*Charisma*	10	*22 May 82*	8
MAMA	*Charisma*	4	*3 Sep 83*	10
THAT'S ALL	*Charisma*	16	*12 Nov 83*	11
ILLEGAL ALIEN	*Charisma*	46	*11 Feb 84*	3
ILLEGAL ALIEN [RE]	*Charisma*	70	*10 Mar 84*	1
INVISIBLE TOUCH	*Virgin*	15	*31 May 86*	8
IN TOO DEEP (FROM THE FILM 'MONA LISA')	*Virgin*	19	*30 Aug 86*	9
LAND OF CONFUSION	*Virgin*	14	*22 Nov 86*	12
TONIGHT, TONIGHT, TONIGHT	*Virgin*	18	*14 Mar 87*	6
THROWING IT ALL AWAY	*Virgin*	22	*20 Jun 87*	8
NO SON OF MINE	*Virgin*	6	*2 Nov 91*	6
NO SON OF MINE [RE]	*Virgin*	70	*4 Jan 92*	1
I CAN'T DANCE	*Virgin*	7	*11 Jan 92*	9
HOLD ON MY HEART	*Virgin*	16	*18 Apr 92*	5
JESUS HE KNOWS ME	*Virgin*	20	*25 Jul 92*	7
INVISIBLE TOUCH (LIVE) [RR]	*Virgin*	7	*21 Nov 92*	4
TELL ME WHY	*Virgin*	40	*20 Feb 93*	3
CONGO	*Virgin*	29	*27 Sep 97*	2
SHIPWRECKED	*Virgin*	54	*13 Dec 97*	1
NOT ABOUT US	*Virgin*	66	*7 Mar 98*	1

ALBUMS:	HITS 21			WEEKS 488
FOXTROT	*Charisma*	12	*14 Oct 72*	7
GENESIS LIVE	*Charisma*	9	*11 Aug 73*	10
SELLING ENGLAND BY THE POUND	*Charisma*	3	*20 Oct 73*	21

NURSERY CRYME	*Charisma*	39	*11 May 74*	1
THE LAMB LIES DOWN ON BROADWAY	*Charisma*	10	*7 Dec 74*	6
A TRICK OF THE TRAIL	*Charisma*	3	*28 Feb 76*	39
WIND AND WUTHERING	*Charisma*	7	*15 Jan 77*	22
SECONDS OUT	*Charisma*	4	*29 Oct 77*	17
. . . AND THEN THERE WERE THREE . . .	*Charisma*	3	*15 Apr 78*	32
DUKE	*Charisma*	1	*5 Apr 80*	30
ABACAB	*Charisma*	1	*26 Sep 81*	27
THREE SIDES LIVE	*Charisma*	2	*12 Jun 82*	19
Live recordings apart from the fourth side, which contains studio cuts from 1979–81.				
GENESIS	*Charisma*	1	*15 Oct 83*	51
NURSERY CRYME [RE]	*Charisma*	68	*31 Mar 84*	1
Repackaged.				
TRESPASS	*Charisma*	98	*21 Apr 84*	1
Originally released in 1970.				
INVISIBLE TOUCH	*Charisma*	1	*21 Jun 86*	96
Includes re-entries through to 1992.				
WE CAN'T DANCE	*Virgin*	1	*23 Nov 91*	61
LIVE – THE WAY WE WALK VOLUME 1: THE SHORTS	*Virgin*	3	*28 Nov 92*	18
LIVE / THE WAY WE WALK – VOLUME TWO: THE LONGS	*Virgin*	1	*23 Jan 93*	9
CALLING ALL STATIONS	*Virgin*	2	*13 Sep 97*	7
ARCHIVE 1967–75	*Virgin*	35	*4 Jul 98*	1
4 CD box set containing a live version of The Lamb Lies Down On Broadway and live tracks/B-sides and demos.				
TURN IT ON AGAIN – THE HITS	*Virgin*	4	*6 Nov 99*	12

Lee A. GENESIS – See Bob SINCLAR

GENEVA — UK

SINGLES:	HITS 6			WEEKS 9
NO ONE SPEAKS	*Nude*	32	*26 Oct 96*	2
INTO THE BLUE	*Nude*	26	*8 Feb 97*	2
TRANQUILLIZER	*Nude*	24	*31 May 97*	2
BEST REGRETS	*Nude*	38	*16 Aug 97*	1
DOLLARS IN THE HEAVENS	*Nude*	59	*27 Nov 99*	1
IF YOU HAVE TO GO	*Nude*	69	*11 Mar 00*	1
ALBUMS:	**HITS 1**			**WEEKS 2**
FURTHER	*Nude*	20	*21 Jun 97*	2

GENEVEVE — UK

SINGLES:	HITS 1			WEEKS 1
ONCE	*CBS*	43	*7 May 66*	1

GENIUS CRU — UK

SINGLES:	HITS 2			WEEKS 7
BOOM SELECTION	*Incentive*	12	*3 Feb 01*	5
COURSE BRUV . . .	*Incentive*	39	*27 Oct 01*	2

GENIUS/GZA — US

SINGLES:	HITS 1			WEEKS 2
COLD WORLD	*Geffen*	40	*2 Mar 96*	2
Above hit: GENIUS/GZA featuring D'ANGELO and INSPEKTAH DECK A.K.A. ROLLIE FINGERS.				
ALBUMS:	**HITS 2**			**WEEKS 2**
LIQUID SWORDS	*Geffen*	73	*2 Dec 95*	1
BENEATH THE SURFACE	*MCA*	56	*10 Jul 99*	1

Jackie GENOVA — UK

ALBUMS:	HITS 1			WEEKS 2
WORK THAT BODY	*Island*	74	*21 May 83*	2

Bobbie GENTRY — US

(See also Bobbie Gentry and Glen Campbell.)

SINGLES:	HITS 3			WEEKS 34
ODE TO BILLY JOE	*Capitol*	13	*16 Sep 67*	11
I'LL NEVER FALL IN LOVE AGAIN	*Capitol*	1	*30 Aug 69*	19
Originally recorded by Dionne Warwick.				
RAINDROPS KEEP FALLING ON MY HEAD	*Capitol*	40	*21 Feb 70*	4
ALBUMS:	**HITS 1**			**WEEKS 1**
TOUCH 'EM WITH LOVE	*Capitol*	21	*25 Oct 69*	1

Bobbie GENTRY and Glen CAMPBELL — US

(See also Glen Campbell; Bobbie Gentry.)

SINGLES:	HITS 1			WEEKS 14
ALL I HAVE TO DO IS DREAM	*Capitol*	3	*6 Dec 69*	14
ALBUMS:	**HITS 1**			**WEEKS 1**
BOBBIE GENTRY AND GLEN CAMPBELL	*Capitol*	50	*28 Feb 70*	1

GEORDIE — UK

SINGLES:	HITS 4			WEEKS 35
DON'T DO THAT	*Regal Zonophone*	32	*2 Dec 72*	7
ALL BECAUSE OF YOU	*EMI*	6	*17 Mar 73*	13
CAN YOU DO IT	*EMI*	13	*16 Jun 73*	9
ELECTRIC LADY	*EMI*	32	*25 Aug 73*	6

Lowell GEORGE — US

ALBUMS:	HITS 1			WEEKS 1
THANKS BUT I'LL EAT IT HERE	*Warner Brothers*	71	*21 Apr 79*	1

Robin GEORGE — UK

SINGLES:	HITS 1			WEEKS 2
HEARTLINE	*Bronze*	68	*27 Apr 85*	2
ALBUMS:	**HITS 1**			**WEEKS 3**
DANGEROUS MUSIC	*Bronze*	65	*2 Mar 85*	3

Sophia GEORGE — Jamaica

SINGLES:	HITS 1			WEEKS 11
GIRLIE GIRLIE	*Winner*	7	*7 Dec 85*	11

GEORGIA SATELLITES — US

SINGLES:	HITS 3			WEEKS 8
KEEP YOUR HANDS TO YOURSELF	*Elektra*	69	*7 Feb 87*	1
BATTLESHIP CHAINS (KICK 'N' LICK REMIX)	*Elektra*	44	*16 May 87*	4
HIPPY HIPPY SHAKE	*Elektra*	63	*21 Jan 89*	3
ALBUMS:	**HITS 2**			**WEEKS 9**
GEORGIA SATELLITES	*Elektra*	52	*7 Feb 87*	7
OPEN ALL NIGHT	*Elektra*	39	*2 Jul 88*	2

GEORGIE PORGIE — US

SINGLES:	HITS 3			WEEKS 3
EVERYBODY MUST PARTY	*Vibe*	61	*12 Aug 95*	1
TAKE ME HIGHER	*MCA/Music Plant*	61	*4 May 96*	1
LIFE GOES ON	*Neo*	54	*26 Aug 00*	1

GEORGIO — US

SINGLES:	HITS 1			WEEKS 3
LOVER'S LANE	*Motown*	54	*20 Feb 88*	3

Danyel GERARD — France

SINGLES:	HITS 1			WEEKS 12
BUTTERFLY	*CBS*	11	*18 Sep 71*	12

Charles GERHARDT – See James GALWAY.

GERIDEAU — US

SINGLES:	HITS 2			WEEKS 2
BRING IT BACK 2 LUV *Above hit: PROJECT featuring GERIDEAU.*	*Fruittree*	65	*27 Aug 94*	1
MASQUERADE	*Inferno*	63	*4 Jul 98*	1

Lisa GERRARD – See Hans ZIMMER

GERRY and the PACEMAKERS — UK

SINGLES:	HITS 9			WEEKS 114
HOW DO YOU DO IT? *Originally written for Adam Faith.*	*Columbia*	1	*16 Mar 63*	18
I LIKE IT	*Columbia*	1	*1 Jun 63*	15
YOU'LL NEVER WALK ALONE *Originally recorded by Frank Sinatra. From the film 'Carousel'. Also the terrace chant for Liverpool FC.*	*Columbia*	1	*12 Oct 63*	19
I'M THE ONE	*Columbia*	2	*18 Jan 64*	15
DON'T LET THE SUN CATCH YOU CRYING *Originally recorded by Louise Cordet.*	*Columbia*	6	*18 Apr 64*	11

IT'S GONNA BE ALL RIGHT	*Columbia*	24	*5 Sep 64*	7
FERRY CROSS THE MERSEY	*Columbia*	8	*19 Dec 64*	13
Above 2: From the film 'Ferry 'Cross The Mersey'.				
I'LL BE THERE	*Columbia*	15	*27 Mar 65*	9
Originally recorded by Bobby Darin.				
WALK HAND IN HAND	*Columbia*	29	*20 Nov 65*	7
EPS:	**HITS 4**			**WEEKS 49**
HOW DO YOU DO IT?	*Columbia*	2	*13 Jul 63*	35
YOU'LL NEVER WALK ALONE	*Columbia*	8	*22 Feb 64*	8
I'M THE ONE	*Columbia*	11	*18 Apr 64*	5
DON'T LET THE SUN CATCH YOU CRYING	*Columbia*	15	*10 Oct 64*	1
ALBUMS:	**HITS 2**			**WEEKS 29**
HOW DO YOU LIKE IT?	*Columbia*	2	*26 Oct 63*	28
FERRY ACROSS THE MERSEY	*Columbia*	19	*6 Feb 65*	1

GET READY — UK

SINGLES:	**HITS 1**			**WEEKS 1**
WILD, WILD WEST	*Mega*	65	*3 Jun 95*	1

GETO BOYS featuring FLAJ — US

SINGLES:	**HITS 1**			**WEEKS 1**
THE WORLD IS A GHETTO	*Virgin*	49	*11 May 96*	1

Stan GETZ — US

(See also Stan Getz and Charlie Byrd.)

SINGLES:	**HITS 1**			**WEEKS 16**
THE GIRL FROM IPANEMA (GAROTA DE IPANEMA)	*Verve*	29	*25 Jul 64*	10
Above hit: Stan GETZ Joao GILBERTO vocal by Astrud GILBERTO.				
THE GIRL FROM IPANEMA [RI]	*Verve*	55	*25 Aug 84*	6
Above hit: Astrud GILBERTO.				

Stan GETZ and Charlie BYRD — US

(See also Stan Getz.)

SINGLES:	**HITS 1**			**WEEKS 13**
DESAFINADO	*His Master's Voice*	11	*10 Nov 62*	13
ALBUMS:	**HITS 1**			**WEEKS 7**
JAZZ SAMBA	*Verve*	15	*23 Feb 63*	7

Angela GHEORGIU – See Roberto ALAGNA/Angela GHEORGIU

Amanda GHOST — UK

SINGLES:	**HITS 1**			**WEEKS 1**
IDOL	*Warner Brothers*	63	*8 Apr 00*	1

GHOST DANCE — UK

SINGLES:	**HITS 1**			**WEEKS 2**
DOWN TO THE WIRE	*Chrysalis*	66	*17 Jun 89*	2

GHOSTFACE KILLAH — US

SINGLES:	**HITS 1**			**WEEKS 4**
ALL THAT I GOT IS YOU	*Epic Street*	11	*12 Jul 97*	4
Samples the Jackson 5's Maybe Tomorrow.				
ALBUMS:	**HITS 1**			**WEEKS 2**
IRONMAN	*Epic*	38	*9 Nov 96*	2

Andy GIBB — UK

SINGLES:	**HITS 4**			**WEEKS 30**
I JUST WANNA BE YOUR EVERYTHING	*RSO*	26	*25 Jun 77*	7
SHADOW DANCING	*RSO*	42	*13 May 78*	6
AN EVERLASTING LOVE	*RSO*	10	*12 Aug 78*	10
(OUR LOVE) DON'T THROW IT ALL AWAY	*RSO*	32	*27 Jan 79*	7
ALBUMS:	**HITS 1**			**WEEKS 9**
SHADOW DANCING	*RSO*	15	*19 Aug 78*	9

Barry GIBB — UK

SINGLES:	**HITS 1**			**WEEKS 10**
GUILTY	*CBS*	34	*6 Dec 80*	10
Above hit: Barbra STREISAND and Barry GIBB.				
ALBUMS:	**HITS 1**			**WEEKS 2**
NOW VOYAGER	*Polydor*	85	*20 Oct 84*	2

Robin GIBB — UK

SINGLES:	HITS 3			WEEKS 21
SAVED BY THE BELL	*Polydor*	2	*12 Jul 69*	16
SAVED BY THE BELL [RE]	*Polydor*	49	*15 Nov 69*	1
AUGUST OCTOBER	*Polydor*	45	*7 Feb 70*	3
ANOTHER LONELY NIGHT IN NEW YORK	*Polydor*	71	*11 Feb 84*	1

Steve GIBBONS BAND — UK

SINGLES:	HITS 2			WEEKS 14
TULANE *Originally recorded by Chuck Berry.*	*Polydor*	12	*6 Aug 77*	10
EDDY VORTEX	*Polydor*	56	*13 May 78*	4
ALBUMS:	**HITS 1**			**WEEKS 3**
CAUGHT IN THE ACT	*Polydor*	22	*22 Oct 77*	3

Georgia GIBBS — US

SINGLES:	HITS 2			WEEKS 2
TWEEDLEE DEE *Above hit: Georgia GIBBS with Glenn OSSER and his Orchestra.*	*Mercury*	20	*23 Apr 55*	1
KISS ME ANOTHER	*Mercury*	24	*14 Jul 56*	1

Debbie GIBSON — US

(See also Various Artists: Stage Cast – London 'Grease'.)

SINGLES:	HITS 11			WEEKS 70
ONLY IN MY DREAMS	*Atlantic*	54	*26 Sep 87*	5
SHAKE YOUR LOVE	*Atlantic*	7	*23 Jan 88*	8
ONLY IN MY DREAMS [RE]	*Atlantic*	11	*19 Mar 88*	7
OUT OF THE BLUE	*Atlantic*	19	*7 May 88*	7
FOOLISH BEAT	*Atlantic*	9	*9 Jul 88*	9
STAYING TOGETHER	*Atlantic*	53	*15 Oct 88*	2
LOST IN YOUR EYES	*Atlantic*	34	*28 Jan 89*	7
ELECTRIC YOUTH	*Atlantic*	14	*29 Apr 89*	8
WE COULD BE TOGETHER	*Atlantic*	22	*19 Aug 89*	8
ANYTHING IS POSSIBLE	*Atlantic*	51	*9 Mar 91*	2
SHOCK YOUR MAMA	*Atlantic*	74	*3 Apr 93*	1
YOU'RE THE ONE THAT I WANT *From the musical 'Grease'.* *Above hit: Craig McLACHLAN and Debbie GIBSON.*	*Epic*	13	*24 Jul 93*	6
ALBUMS:	**HITS 3**			**WEEKS 52**
OUT OF THE BLUE	*Atlantic*	26	*30 Jan 88*	35
ELECTRIC YOUTH	*Atlantic*	8	*11 Feb 89*	16
ANYTHING IS POSSIBLE	*Atlantic*	69	*30 Mar 91*	1

Don GIBSON — US

SINGLES:	HITS 2			WEEKS 16
SEA OF HEARTBREAK	*RCA*	14	*2 Sep 61*	13
LONESOME NUMBER ONE	*RCA*	47	*3 Feb 62*	3
ALBUMS:	**HITS 1**			**WEEKS 10**
COUNTRY NUMBER ONE	*Warwick*	13	*22 Mar 80*	10

Wayne GIBSON — UK

SINGLES:	HITS 2			WEEKS 13
KELLY *Originally recorded by Del Shannon.*	*Pye*	48	*5 Sep 64*	2
UNDER MY THUMB *Originally recorded by the Rolling Stones.*	*Pye Disco Demand*	17	*23 Nov 74*	11

GIBSON BROTHERS — Martinique

SINGLES:	HITS 6			WEEKS 54
CUBA	*Island*	41	*10 Mar 79*	9
OOH! WHAT A LIFE	*Island*	10	*21 Jul 79*	12
QUE SERA MI VIDA (IF YOU SHOULD GO)	*Island*	5	*17 Nov 79*	11
CUBA [RI] / BETTER DO IT SALSA	*Island*	12	*23 Feb 80*	9
MARIANA	*Island*	11	*12 Jul 80*	10
MY HEART'S BEATING WILD (TIC TAC TIC TAC)	*Stiff*	56	*9 Jul 83*	3
ALBUMS:	**HITS 1**			**WEEKS 3**
ON THE RIVIERA	*Island*	50	*30 Aug 80*	3

GIDEA PARK — UK

SINGLES:	HITS 2			WEEKS 19
BEACH BOY GOLD [M]	*Stone*	11	*4 Jul 81*	13

SEASONS OF GOLD [M]	*Polo*	28	*12 Sep 81*	6

Above 2 medleys are of Beach Boys and Four Seasons songs.

Johan GIELEN presents ABNEA — Belgium

(See also Svenson & Gielen.)

SINGLES:	HITS 1			WEEKS 1
VELVET MOODS	*Data*	74	*18 Aug 01*	1

GIFTED — UK

SINGLES:	HITS 1			WEEKS 1
DO I	*Perfecto*	60	*23 Aug 97*	1

GIGOLO AUNTS — US

SINGLES:	HITS 2			WEEKS 4
MRS. WASHINGTON	*Fire*	74	*23 Apr 94*	1
WHERE I FIND MY HEAVEN	*Fire*	29	*13 May 95*	3

From the film 'Dumb And Dummer'. Originally released in 1994.

Astrud GILBERTO – See Stan GETZ

Joao GILBERTO – See Stan GETZ

Donna GILES — US

SINGLES:	HITS 1			WEEKS 4
AND I'M TELLING YOU I'M NOT GOING	*Ore*	43	*13 Aug 94*	2
AND I'M TELLING YOU I'M NOT GOING [RM]	*Ore*	27	*10 Feb 96*	2

From the film 'Dreamgirls'. Remixed by Stonebridge and Nick Nice.

Johnny GILL — US

SINGLES:	HITS 4			WEEKS 12
WRAP MY BODY TIGHT	*Motown*	57	*23 Feb 91*	2
SLOW AND SEXY	*Epic*	17	*28 Nov 92*	7
Above hit: Shabba RANKS (featuring Johnny GILL).				
THE FLOOR	*Motown*	53	*17 Jul 93*	1
A CUTE, SWEET, LOVE ADDICTION	*Motown*	46	*29 Jan 94*	2
ALBUMS:	**HITS 1**			**WEEKS 3**
PROVOCATIVE	*Motown*	41	*19 Jun 93*	3

Vince GILL – See Amy GRANT; Barbra STREISAND

GILLAN — UK

(See also Ian Gillan.)

SINGLES:	HITS 8			WEEKS 46
SLEEPING ON THE JOB	*Virgin*	55	*14 Jun 80*	3
TROUBLE	*Virgin*	14	*4 Oct 80*	6
MUTUALLY ASSURED DESTRUCTION	*Virgin*	32	*14 Feb 81*	5
NEW ORLEANS	*Virgin*	17	*21 Mar 81*	10
NO LAUGHING IN HEAVEN	*Virgin*	31	*20 Jun 81*	6
NIGHTMARE	*Virgin*	36	*10 Oct 81*	6
RESTLESS	*Virgin*	25	*23 Jan 82*	7
LIVING FOR THE CITY	*Virgin*	50	*4 Sep 82*	3
ALBUMS:	**HITS 6**			**WEEKS 53**
CHILD IN TIME	*Polydor*	55	*17 Jul 76*	1
Above hit: Ian GILLAN BAND.				
MR. UNIVERSE	*Acrobat*	11	*20 Oct 79*	6
GLORY ROAD	*Virgin*	3	*16 Aug 80*	12
FUTURE SHOCK	*Virgin*	2	*25 Apr 81*	13
DOUBLE TROUBLE	*Virgin*	12	*7 Nov 81*	15
MAGIC	*Virgin*	17	*2 Oct 82*	6

Ian GILLAN — UK

(See also Gillan.)

ALBUMS:	HITS 1			WEEKS 1
NAKED THUNDER	*Teldec*	63	*28 Jul 90*	1

GILLETTE – See 20 FINGERS

Stuart GILLIES — UK

SINGLES:	HITS 1			WEEKS 10
AMANDA	*Philips*	13	*31 Mar 73*	10

Jimmy GILMER and the FIREBALLS – See FIREBALLS

David GILMOUR — UK

ALBUMS:	HITS 2			WEEKS 18
DAVID GILMOUR	*Harvest*	17	*10 Jun 78*	9
ABOUT FACE	*Harvest*	21	*17 Mar 84*	9

James GILREATH — US

SINGLES:	HITS 1			WEEKS 10
LITTLE BAND OF GOLD	*Pye International*	29	*4 May 63*	10

Jim GILSTRAP — US

SINGLES:	HITS 1			WEEKS 11
SWING YOUR DADDY	*Chelsea*	4	*15 Mar 75*	11

Gordon GILTRAP — UK

SINGLES:	HITS 2			WEEKS 10
HEARTSONG *Occasionally used as the BBC's Holiday programme theme.*	*Electric*	21	*14 Jan 78*	7
FEAR OF THE DARK *Above hit: Gordon GILTRAP BAND.*	*Electric*	58	*28 Apr 79*	3
ALBUMS:	**HITS 1**			**WEEKS 7**
PERILOUS JOURNEY	*Electric*	29	*18 Feb 78*	7

GIN BLOSSOMS — US

SINGLES:	HITS 4			WEEKS 12
HEY JEALOUSY	*Fontana*	24	*5 Feb 94*	5
FOUND OUT ABOUT YOU	*Fontana*	40	*16 Apr 94*	3
TIL I HEAR IT FROM YOU *From the film 'Empire'.*	*A&M*	39	*10 Feb 96*	2
FOLLOW YOU DOWN	*A&M*	30	*27 Apr 96*	2
ALBUMS:	**HITS 2**			**WEEKS 6**
NEW MISERABLE EXPERIENCE	*Fontana*	53	*26 Feb 94*	4
CONGRATULATIONS, I'M SORRY	*A&M*	42	*24 Feb 96*	2

GINUWINE — US

SINGLES:	HITS 5			WEEKS 22
PONY	*Epic*	16	*25 Jan 97*	6
TELL ME DO U WANNA	*Epic*	16	*24 May 97*	3
WHEN DOVES CRY	*Epic*	10	*6 Sep 97*	5
HOLLER *Additional vocals by Maria Wallace.*	*Epic*	13	*14 Mar 98*	4
WHAT'S SO DIFFERENT? *Samples the Monkees' Valleri.*	*Epic*	10	*13 Mar 99*	4
ALBUMS:	**HITS 2**			**WEEKS 2**
GINUWINE . . . THE BACHELOR	*Epic*	74	*28 Mar 98*	1
100% GINUWINE	*Epic*	42	*27 Mar 99*	1

GIORGIO – See Giorgio MORODER

GIPSY KINGS — France

SINGLES:	HITS 1			WEEKS 2
HITS MEDLEY [M] *Medley of 5 previous uncharted single releases.*	*Columbia*	53	*3 Sep 94*	2
ALBUMS:	**HITS 5**			**WEEKS 65**
GIPSY KINGS	*Telstar*	16	*15 Apr 89*	29
MOSAIQUE	*Telstar*	27	*25 Nov 89*	13
ESTE MUNDO	*Columbia*	19	*13 Jul 91*	7
GREATEST HITS	*Columbia*	11	*6 Aug 94*	11
VOLARE - THE VERY BEST OF THE GIPSY KINGS	*Columbia*	20	*24 Jul 99*	5

Martine GIRAULT — UK

SINGLES:	HITS 2			WEEKS 7
REVIVAL	*ffrr*	53	*29 Aug 92*	2
REVIVAL [RI-1ST]	*ffrr*	37	*30 Jan 93*	3
BEEN THINKING ABOUT YOU	*RCA*	63	*28 Oct 95*	1
REVIVAL [RI-2ND]	*RCA*	61	*1 Feb 97*	1

GIRESSE — UK

SINGLES:	HITS 1			WEEKS 1
MON AMI *Features a recreated sample of Tubeway Army's 1997 remix of Are Friends Electric?*	*Inferno*	61	*14 Apr 01*	1

GIRL — UK

SINGLES:	HITS 1			WEEKS 3
HOLLYWOOD TEASE	*Jet*	50	*12 Apr 80*	3
ALBUMS:	**HITS 2**			**WEEKS 6**
SHEER GREED	*Jet*	33	*9 Feb 80*	5
WASTED YOUTH	*Jet*	92	*23 Jan 82*	1

GIRL NEXT DOOR - See M&S presents The GIRL NEXT DOOR

GIRL THING — UK/Holland

SINGLES:	HITS 2			WEEKS 13
LAST ONE STANDING	*RCA*	8	*1 Jul 00*	8
LAST ONE STANDING [RE]	*RCA*	65	*9 Sep 00*	2
GIRLS ON TOP	*RCA*	25	*18 Nov 00*	3

GIRLFRIEND — UK

SINGLES:	HITS 2			WEEKS 5
TAKE IT FROM ME	*Arista*	47	*30 Jan 93*	4
GIRL'S LIFE	*Arista*	68	*15 May 93*	1

GIRLS AT OUR BEST — UK

ALBUMS:	HITS 1			WEEKS 3
PLEASURE	*Happy Birthday*	60	*7 Nov 81*	3

GIRLS@PLAY — UK

SINGLES:	HITS 2			WEEKS 7
AIRHEAD	*GSM*	18	*24 Feb 01*	5
RESPECTABLE	*Redbus Music*	29	*13 Oct 01*	2

GIRLSCHOOL — UK

SINGLES:	HITS 5			WEEKS 25
RACE WITH THE DEVIL	*Bronze*	49	*2 Aug 80*	6
ST. VALENTINE'S DAY MASSACRE [EP]	*Bronze*	5	*21 Feb 81*	8
Lead track: Please Don't Touch.				
Above hit: HEADGIRL (MOTORHEAD and GIRLSCHOOL).				
HIT AND RUN	*Bronze*	32	*11 Apr 81*	6
C'MON LET'S GO	*Bronze*	42	*11 Jul 81*	3
WILDLIFE [EP]	*Bronze*	58	*3 Apr 82*	2
Lead track: Don't Call It Love.				
ALBUMS:	**HITS 4**			**WEEKS 23**
DEMOLITION	*Bronze*	28	*5 Jul 80*	10
HIT 'N' RUN	*Bronze*	5	*25 Apr 81*	6
SCREAMING BLUE MURDER	*Bronze*	27	*12 Jun 82*	6
PLAY DIRTY	*Bronze*	66	*12 Nov 83*	1

Junior GISCOMBE - See JUNIOR

GITTA — Denmark/Italy

SINGLES:	HITS 1			WEEKS 1
NO MORE TURNING BACK	*Pepper*	54	*19 Aug 00*	1

GLADEZZ - See SOUND OF ONE featuring GLADEZZ

GLADIATORS — UK

SINGLES:	HITS 1			WEEKS 1
THE BOYS ARE BACK IN TOWN	*RCA*	70	*30 Nov 96*	1
Title music to ITV's 5th series of 'Gladiators'.				
COMPILATION ALBUMS:	**HITS 1**			**WEEKS 10**
GLADIATORS - THE ALBUM	*PolyGram TV*	11	*28 Nov 92*	10
Above entry was in the compilation chart.				

GLAM — Italy

SINGLES:	HITS 1			WEEKS 2
HELL'S PARTY	*Six6*	42	*1 May 93*	2

GLAM METAL DETECTIVES — UK

SINGLES:	HITS 1			WEEKS 2
EVERYBODY UP!	*ZTT*	29	*11 Mar 95*	2
Theme from the BBC2 TV series 'Glam Metal Detectives'.				

GLAMMA KID — UK

SINGLES:	HITS 4			WEEKS 25
FASHION 98	*WEA*	49	*21 Nov 98*	1

TABOO	*WEA*	10	*17 Apr 99*	8
Above hit: GLAMMA KID featuring Shola AMA.				
WHY	*WEA*	10	*27 Nov 99*	10
Includes vocals by Marcelle Duprey.				
BILLS 2 PAY	*WEA*	17	*2 Sep 00*	5
Samples Blondie's Rapture and Visage's Fade To Grey.				
BILLS 2 PAY [RE]	*WEA*	69	*14 Oct 00*	1
ALBUMS:	**HITS 1**			**WEEKS 1**
KIDOLOGY	*WEA*	66	*16 Sep 00*	1

GLASGOW RANGERS FOOTBALL CLUB — UK

SINGLES:	**HITS 1**			**WEEKS 2**
GLASGOW RANGERS (NINE IN A ROW)	*Gers*	54	*4 Oct 97*	2

GLASS TIGER — Canada

SINGLES:	**HITS 3**			**WEEKS 18**
DON'T FORGET ME (WHEN I'M GONE)	*Manhattan*	29	*18 Oct 86*	9
Backing vocals by Bryan Adams.				
SOMEDAY	*Manhattan*	66	*31 Jan 87*	2
MY TOWN	*EMI*	33	*26 Oct 91*	7
Vocals by Rod Stewart.				

Mayson GLEN ORCHESTRA – See Paul HENRY and the Mayson GLEN ORCHESTRA

GLENN and CHRIS — UK

SINGLES:	**HITS 1**			**WEEKS 8**
DIAMOND LIGHTS	*Record Shack*	12	*18 Apr 87*	8

GLIDE – See VARIOUS ARTISTS (EPs) 'Fourplay Volume 1 EP'

Gary GLITTER — UK

SINGLES:	**HITS 23**			**WEEKS 170**
ROCK AND ROLL PART 1 / ROCK AND ROLL PART 2	*Bell*	2	*10 Jun 72*	15
Part 2 was listed on the chart from 24 Jun 72.				
I DIDN'T KNOW I LOVED YOU (TILL I SAW YOU ROCK AND ROLL)	*Bell*	4	*23 Sep 72*	11
DO YOU WANNA TOUCH ME? (OH YEAH!)	*Bell*	2	*20 Jan 73*	11
HELLO! HELLO! I'M BACK AGAIN	*Bell*	2	*7 Apr 73*	14
I'M THE LEADER OF THE GANG (I AM!)	*Bell*	1	*21 Jul 73*	12
I LOVE YOU LOVE ME LOVE	*Bell*	1	*17 Nov 73*	14
REMEMBER ME THIS WAY	*Bell*	3	*30 Mar 74*	8
ALWAYS YOURS	*Bell*	1	*15 Jun 74*	9
OH YES! YOU'RE BEAUTIFUL	*Bell*	2	*23 Nov 74*	10
LOVE LIKE YOU AND ME	*Bell*	10	*3 May 75*	6
DOING ALL RIGHT WITH THE BOYS	*Bell*	6	*21 Jun 75*	7
PAPA OOM MOW MOW	*Bell*	38	*8 Nov 75*	5
Original by the Rivingtons reached No. 48 in the US in 1962.				
YOU BELONG TO ME	*Bell*	40	*13 Mar 76*	5
IT TAKES ALL NIGHT LONG	*Arista*	25	*22 Jan 77*	6
A LITTLE BOOGIE WOOGIE IN THE BACK OF MY MIND	*Arista*	31	*16 Jul 77*	5
GARY GLITTER [EP]	*GTO*	57	*20 Sep 80*	3
Lead track: I'm The Leader Of The Gang (I Am). This and the other tracks are all re-issues.				
AND THEN SHE KISSED ME	*Bell*	39	*10 Oct 81*	5
ALL THAT GLITTERS [M]	*Bell*	48	*5 Dec 81*	5
DANCE ME UP	*Arista*	25	*23 Jun 84*	5
ANOTHER ROCK AND ROLL CHRISTMAS	*Arista*	7	*1 Dec 84*	7
AND THE LEADER ROCKS ON [M]	*EMI*	58	*10 Oct 92*	2
THROUGH THE YEARS	*EMI*	49	*21 Nov 92*	3
HELLO, HELLO, I'M BACK AGAIN (AGAIN!) [RR]	*Carlton Sounds*	50	*16 Dec 95*	2
Sleeve gives title as an EP: By Public Demand.				
ALBUMS:	**HITS 5**			**WEEKS 100**
GLITTER	*Bell*	8	*21 Oct 72*	40
TOUCH ME	*Bell*	2	*16 Jun 73*	33
REMEMBER ME THIS WAY	*Bell*	5	*29 Jun 74*	14
GARY GLITTER'S GREATEST HITS	*Bell*	33	*27 Mar 76*	5
MANY HAPPY RETURNS - THE HITS	*EMI*	35	*14 Nov 92*	8

GLITTER BAND — UK

SINGLES:	**HITS 7**			**WEEKS 60**
ANGEL FACE	*Bell*	4	*23 Mar 74*	10
JUST FOR YOU	*Bell*	10	*3 Aug 74*	8
LET'S GET TOGETHER AGAIN	*Bell*	8	*19 Oct 74*	8
GOODBYE MY LOVE	*Bell*	2	*18 Jan 75*	9
THE TEARS I CRIED	*Bell*	8	*12 Apr 75*	8
LOVE IN THE SUN	*Bell*	15	*9 Aug 75*	8
PEOPLE LIKE YOU AND PEOPLE LIKE ME	*Bell*	5	*28 Feb 76*	9

ALBUMS:	HITS 3			WEEKS 17
HEY	*Bell*	13	*14 Sep 74*	12
ROCK 'N' ROLL DUDES	*Bell*	17	*3 May 75*	4
GREATEST HITS	*Bell*	52	*19 Jun 76*	1

GLOBAL COMMUNICATION — UK

SINGLES:	HITS 1			WEEKS 1
THE WAY / THE DEEP	*Dedicated*	51	*11 Jan 97*	1

GLORIA! - See Gloria ESTEFAN

GLOVE — UK

SINGLES:	HITS 1			WEEKS 3
LIKE A ANIMAL	*Wonderland*	52	*20 Aug 83*	3
ALBUMS:	**HITS 1**			**WEEKS 3**
BLUE SUNSHINE	*Wonderland*	35	*17 Sep 83*	3

GLOWORM — UK/US

SINGLES:	HITS 2			WEEKS 17
I LIFT MY CUP	*Pulse 8*	20	*6 Feb 93*	4
CARRY ME HOME	*Go! Discs*	9	*14 May 94*	11
I LIFT MY CUP [RI]	*Pulse 8*	46	*6 Aug 94*	2

GO-BETWEENS — Australia

ALBUMS:	HITS 2			WEEKS 2
TALLULAH	*Beggars Banquet*	91	*13 May 87*	1
16 LOVER'S LANE	*Beggars Banquet*	81	*10 Sep 88*	1

GO GO LORENZO and the DAVIS PINCKNEY PROJECT — US

SINGLES:	HITS 1			WEEKS 8
YOU CAN DANCE IF YOU WANT TO	*Boiling Point*	46	*6 Dec 86*	8

GO-GO'S — US

SINGLES:	HITS 3			WEEKS 10
OUR LIPS ARE SEALED	*I.R.S.*	47	*15 Jun 82*	6
COOL JERK	*I.R.S.*	60	*26 Jan 91*	1
THE WHOLE WORLD LOST IT'S HEAD	*I.R.S.*	29	*18 Feb 95*	3
Single was issued as a double-A side with Our Lips Are Sealed, though not listed on the chart as such.				
ALBUMS:	**HITS 2**			**WEEKS 4**
VACATION	*I.R.S.*	75	*21 Aug 82*	3
RETURN TO THE VALLEY OF THE GO-GO'S	*I.R.S.*	52	*18 Mar 95*	1
Compilation of singles, live tracks and B-sides with 3 new tracks.				

GO WEST — UK

SINGLES:	HITS 12			WEEKS 85
WE CLOSE OUR EYES	*Chrysalis*	5	*23 Feb 85*	14
CALL ME	*Chrysalis*	12	*11 May 85*	10
GOODBYE GIRL	*Chrysalis*	25	*3 Aug 85*	7
DON'T LOOK DOWN - THE SEQUEL	*Chrysalis*	13	*23 Nov 85*	10
TRUE COLOURS	*Chrysalis*	48	*29 Nov 86*	7
I WANT TO HEAR IT FROM YOU	*Chrysalis*	43	*9 May 87*	3
THE KING IS DEAD	*Chrysalis*	67	*12 Sep 87*	2
THE KING OF WISHFUL THINKING	*Chrysalis*	18	*28 Jul 90*	10
FAITHFUL	*Chrysalis*	13	*17 Oct 92*	6
WHAT YOU WON'T DO FOR LOVE	*Chrysalis*	15	*16 Jan 93*	5
Original by Bobby Caldwell reached No. 8 in the US in 1979.				
STILL IN LOVE	*Chrysalis*	43	*27 Mar 93*	3
TRACKS OF MY TEARS	*Chrysalis*	16	*2 Oct 93*	5
WE CLOSE OUR EYES '93 [RM]	*Chrysalis*	40	*4 Dec 93*	3
Remixed by Tom Lord Alge.				
ALBUMS:	**HITS 4**			**WEEKS 119**
GO WEST / BANGS AND CRASHES	*Chrysalis*	8	*13 Apr 85*	83
Peak position reached on 8 Mar 86. Bangs and Crashes was a remix album listed from 31 May 86, sales were combined.				
DANCING ON THE COUCH	*Chrysalis*	19	*6 Jun 87*	5
INDIAN SUMMER	*Chrysalis*	13	*14 Nov 92*	16
ACES AND KINGS - THE BEST OF GO WEST	*Chrysalis*	5	*16 Oct 93*	15

GOATS — US

SINGLES:	HITS 1			WEEKS 2
AAAH D YAAA / TYPICAL AMERICAN	*Columbia*	53	*29 May 93*	2
Typical American only listed on 5 Jun 93 once it had dropped to No. 65.				

ALBUMS:	HITS 1			WEEKS 1
NO GOATS, NO GLORY	*Columbia*	58	*27 Aug 94*	1

GOD MACHINE — US

SINGLES:	HITS 1			WEEKS 2
HOME	*Fiction*	65	*30 Jan 93*	2
ALBUMS:	**HITS 1**			**WEEKS 1**
SCENES FROM THE SECOND STOREY	*Fiction*	55	*20 Feb 93*	1

GODFATHERS — UK

ALBUMS:	HITS 2			WEEKS 3
BIRTH, SCHOOL, WORK, DEATH	*Epic*	80	*13 Feb 88*	2
MORE SONGS ABOUT LOVE AND HATE	*Epic*	49	*20 May 89*	1

GODIEGO — US/Japan

SINGLES:	HITS 2			WEEKS 11
THE WATER MARGIN *Theme sung in English from the BBC1 TV series of the same name. [AA] listed with Pete Mac Junior's Japanese version.*	*BBC*	37	*15 Oct 77*	4
GANDHARA *Theme from the BBC TV series 'Monkey'.*	*BBC*	56	*16 Feb 80*	7

GODLEY and CREME — UK

SINGLES:	HITS 3			WEEKS 36
UNDER YOUR THUMB	*Polydor*	3	*12 Sep 81*	11
WEDDING BELLS	*Polydor*	7	*21 Nov 81*	11
CRY	*Polydor*	19	*30 Mar 85*	11
CRY [RE]	*Polydor*	66	*16 Aug 86*	3
ALBUMS:	**HITS 4**			**WEEKS 34**
CONSEQUENCES *Above hit: Kevin GODLEY and Lol CRÈME.*	*Mercury*	52	*19 Nov 77*	1
L	*Mercury*	47	*9 Sep 78*	2
ISMISM	*Polydor*	29	*17 Oct 81*	13
CHANGING FACES - THE VERY BEST OF 10CC AND GODLEY AND CREME *Above hit: 10CC and GODLEY and CRÈME.*	*ProTV*	4	*29 Aug 87*	18

GOD'S PROPERTY from Kirk FRANKLIN'S NU NATION featuring Kirk FRANKLIN and "SALT" — US

SINGLES:	HITS 1			WEEKS 1
STOMP *Based around Funkadelic's One Nation Under A Groove.*	*B-rite Music*	60	*22 Nov 97*	1

GODSPEED YOU BLACK EMPEROR! — Canada

ALBUMS:	HITS 1			WEEKS 1
LIFT YOUR SKINNY FISTS LIKE ANTENNAS TO HEAVEN	*Kranky*	66	*21 Oct 00*	1

Andrew GOLD — US

SINGLES:	HITS 4			WEEKS 36
LONELY BOY *Backing vocals by Linda Ronstadt.*	*Asylum*	11	*2 Apr 77*	9
NEVER LET HER SLIP AWAY	*Asylum*	5	*25 Mar 78*	13
HOW CAN THIS BE LOVE	*Asylum*	19	*24 Jun 78*	10
THANK YOU FOR BEING A FRIEND	*Asylum*	42	*14 Oct 78*	4
ALBUMS:	**HITS 1**			**WEEKS 7**
ALL THIS AND HEAVEN TOO	*Asylum*	31	*15 Apr 78*	7

Ari GOLD - See DJ LUCK and MC NEAT

Brian and Tony GOLD - See RED DRAGON with Brian and Tony GOLD

GOLD BLADE — UK

SINGLES:	HITS 1			WEEKS 1
STRICTLY HARDCORE	*Ultimate*	64	*22 Mar 97*	1

GOLDBUG — UK

SINGLES:	HITS 1			WEEKS 5
WHOLE LOTTA LOVE *Samples the Pearl & Dean cinema tune called Asteroid.*	*Acid Jazz*	3	*27 Jan 96*	5

GOLDEN EARRING — Holland

SINGLES:	HITS 2			WEEKS 16
RADAR LOVE	*Track*	7	*8 Dec 73*	13

RADAR LOVE [RR] *Live recording.* *Above hit: GOLDEN EARRING 'LIVE'.*	*Polydor*	44	*8 Oct 77*	3
ALBUMS:	**HITS 1**			**WEEKS 4**
MOONTAN	*Track*	24	*2 Feb 74*	4

GOLDEN GIRLS — UK

SINGLES:	**HITS 1**			**WEEKS 3**
KINETIC *Original release reached No. 86 in 1993.*	*Distinct'ive*	38	*3 Oct 98*	2
KINETIC '99 [RM] *Remixed by Commie.*	*Distinct'ive*	56	*4 Dec 99*	1

GOLDENSCAN — UK

SINGLES:	**HITS 1**			**WEEKS 1**
SUNRISE	*VC Recordings*	52	*11 Nov 00*	1

GOLDFRAPP — UK

SINGLES:	**HITS 2**			**WEEKS 2**
UTOPIA	*Mute*	62	*23 Jun 01*	1
PILOTS (ON A STAR)/LOVELY HEAD	*Mute*	68	*17 Nov 01*	1
ALBUMS:	**HITS 1**			**WEEKS 5**
FELT MOUNTAIN	*Mute*	57	*25 Aug 01*	5

GOLDIE — UK

SINGLES:	**HITS 1**			**WEEKS 11**
MAKING UP AGAIN	*Bronze*	7	*27 May 78*	11

GOLDIE — UK

SINGLES:	**HITS 5**			**WEEKS 16**
INNER CITY LIFE *Above hit: GOLDIE Presents METALHEADS.*	*ffrr*	49	*3 Dec 94*	2
ANGEL	*ffrr*	41	*9 Sep 95*	3
INNER CITY LIFE [RI] *All three entries above feature vocals by Diane Charlamagne (of Urban Cookie Collective).*	*ffrr*	39	*11 Nov 95*	2
DIGITAL *Above hit: GOLDIE featuring KRS ONE.*	*ffrr*	13	*1 Nov 97*	3
TEMPER TEMPER *Features Noel Gallagher on vocal and guitar.*	*ffrr*	13	*24 Jan 98*	4
BELIEVE *Samples Loose Ends' Hanging On A String.*	*ffrr*	36	*18 Apr 98*	2
ALBUMS:	**HITS 2**			**WEEKS 16**
TIMELESS	*ffrr*	7	*19 Aug 95*	12
SATURNZ RETURN	*ffrr*	15	*14 Feb 98*	4

GOLDIE and the GINGERBREADS — US

SINGLES:	**HITS 1**			**WEEKS 5**
CAN'T YOU HEAR MY HEARTBEAT? *Originally recorded by John Leyton.*	*Decca*	25	*27 Feb 65*	5

Bobby GOLDSBORO — US

SINGLES:	**HITS 3**			**WEEKS 47**
HONEY *Originally recorded by Bob Shane.*	*United Artists*	2	*20 Apr 68*	15
SUMMER (THE FIRST TIME)	*United Artists*	9	*4 Aug 73*	10
HELLO, SUMMERTIME *Featured in the Coca-Cola TV commercial.*	*United Artists*	14	*3 Aug 74*	10
HONEY [RI]	*United Artists*	2	*29 Mar 75*	12

Glen GOLDSMITH — UK

SINGLES:	**HITS 4**			**WEEKS 24**
I WON'T CRY	*Reproduction*	34	*7 Nov 87*	7
DREAMING	*Reproduction*	12	*12 Mar 88*	11
WHAT YOU SEE IS WHAT YOU GET	*Reproduction*	33	*11 Jun 88*	5
SAVE A LITTLE BIT	*Reproduction*	73	*3 Sep 88*	1
ALBUMS:	**HITS 1**			**WEEKS 9**
WHAT YOU SEE IS WHAT YOU GET	*RCA*	14	*23 Jul 88*	9

GOMEZ — UK

SINGLES:	**HITS 6**			**WEEKS 13**
78 STONE WOBBLE	*Hut*	44	*11 Apr 98*	1
GET MYSELF ARRESTED	*Hut*	45	*13 Jun 98*	1

WHIPPIN' PICCADILLY	*Hut*	35	*12 Sep 98*	3
BRING IT ON	*Hut*	21	*10 Jul 99*	3
RHYTHM & BLUES ALIBI	*Hut*	18	*11 Sep 99*	3
WE HAVEN'T TURNED AROUND	*Hut*	38	*27 Nov 99*	2
ALBUMS:	**HITS 3**			**WEEKS 92**
BRING IT ON	*Hut*	11	*25 Apr 98*	60
Peak position reached on 3 Oct 98. Mercury Music Price winner of 1998.				
LIQUID SKIN	*Hut*	2	*25 Sep 99*	28
ABANDONED SHOPPING TROLLEY HOTLINE	*Hut*	10	*7 Oct 00*	4

Leroy GOMEZ - See SANTA ESMERALDA and Leroy GOMEZ

GOMPIE — Holland

SINGLES:	**HITS 1**			**WEEKS 12**
ALICE (WHO THE X IS ALICE?) (LIVING NEXT DOOR TO ALICE)	*Habana*	34	*20 May 95*	5
ALICE (WHO THE X IS ALICE?) (LIVING NEXT DOOR TO ALICE) [RE]	*Habana*	17	*02 Sep 95*	7

GONZALEZ — UK/US

SINGLES:	**HITS 1**			**WEEKS 11**
HAVEN'T STOPPED DANCING YET	*Sidewalk*	15	*31 Mar 79*	11
Written by Marc Bolan's girlfriend Gloria Jones.				

GOO GOO DOLLS — US

SINGLES:	**HITS 2**			**WEEKS 4**
IRIS	*Reprise*	50	*1 Aug 98*	1
From the film 'City Of Angels'.				
SLIDE	*Hollywood*	43	*27 Mar 99*	1
IRIS [RI]	*Hollywood*	26	*17 Jul 99*	2
ALBUMS:	**HITS 1**			**WEEKS 1**
DIZZY UP THE GIRL	*Hollywood*	47	*31 Jul 99*	1

GOOD GIRLS — US

SINGLES:	**HITS 1**			**WEEKS 1**
JUST CALL ME	*Motown*	75	*24 Jul 93*	1

Jack GOOD - See LORD ROCKINGHAM'S XI

GOODBYE MR. MACKENZIE — UK

SINGLES:	**HITS 5**			**WEEKS 13**
GOODBYE MR. MACKENZIE	*Capitol*	62	*20 Aug 88*	2
THE RATTLER	*Capitol*	37	*11 Mar 89*	6
GOODWILL CITY / I'M SICK OF YOU	*Capitol*	49	*29 Jul 89*	2
LOVE CHILD	*Parlophone*	52	*21 Apr 90*	2
BLACKER THAN BLACK	*Parlophone*	61	*23 Jun 90*	1
ALBUMS:	**HITS 2**			**WEEKS 4**
GOOD DEEDS AND DIRTY RAGS	*Capitol*	26	*22 Apr 89*	3
HAMMER AND TONGS	*Radioactive*	61	*16 Mar 91*	1
Original release was due in 1990 on the Parlophone label, but was not issued.				

GOODFELLAS featuring Lisa MILLETT — Italy/UK

(See also Bini + Martini.)

SINGLES:	**HITS 1**			**WEEKS 2**
SOUL HEAVEN	*Direction*	27	*21 Jul 01*	2

GOODFELLAZ — US

SINGLES:	**HITS 1**			**WEEKS 2**
SUGAR HONEY ICE TEA	*Wild Card*	25	*10 May 97*	2

GOODIES — UK

SINGLES:	**HITS 5**			**WEEKS 38**
THE INBETWEENIES / FATHER CHRISTMAS DO NOT TOUCH ME	*Bradley's*	7	*7 Dec 74*	9
THE FUNKY GIBBON / SICK-MAN BLUES	*Bradley's*	4	*15 Mar 75*	10
BLACK PUDDING BERTHA (THE QUEEN OF NORTHERN SOUL)	*Bradley's*	19	*21 Jun 75*	7
NAPPY LOVE / WILD THING	*Bradley's*	21	*27 Sep 75*	6
MAKA A DAFT NOISE FOR CHRISTMAS	*Bradley's*	20	*13 Dec 75*	6
ALBUMS:	**HITS 1**			**WEEKS 11**
THE NEW GOODIES LP	*Bradley's*	25	*8 Nov 75*	11

Cuba GOODING — US

SINGLES:	**HITS 1**			**WEEKS 2**
HAPPINESS IS JUST AROUND THE BEND	*London*	72	*19 Nov 83*	2
Originally recorded by Brian Auger.				

Benny GOODMAN — US

ALBUMS:	HITS 1			WEEKS 1
BENNY GOODMAN TODAY	*Decca*	49	*3 Apr 71*	1

GOODMEN — Holland

SINGLES:	HITS 1			WEEKS 19
GIVE IT UP	*Ffrreedom*	23	*7 Aug 93*	5
GIVE IT UP [RE]	*Ffrreedom*	5	*9 Oct 93*	14

Ron GOODWIN and his Orchestra — UK

(See also Eammon Andrews; Dick James; Glen Mason.)

SINGLES:	HITS 2			WEEKS 24
THE THEME FROM THE FILM "LIMELIGHT"	*Parlophone*	3	*16 May 53*	23
BLUE STAR (THE MEDIC THEME)	*Parlophone*	20	*29 Oct 55*	1
ALBUMS:	**HITS 1**			**WEEKS 1**
LEGEND OF THE GLASS MOUNTAIN	*Studio Two*	49	*2 May 70*	1

GOODY GOODY — US

SINGLES:	HITS 1			WEEKS 5
#1 DEE JAY	*Atlantic*	55	*2 Dec 78*	5

GOOFY – See Phoebe ONE featuring RED RAT, GOOFY and BUCCANEER (MAIN STREET CREW)

GOOMBAY DANCE BAND — Germany/Montserrat

SINGLES:	HITS 2			WEEKS 16
SEVEN TEARS	*Epic*	1	*27 Feb 82*	12
SUN OF JAMAICA	*Epic*	50	*15 May 82*	4
ALBUMS:	**HITS 1**			**WEEKS 9**
SEVEN TEARS	*Epic*	16	*10 Apr 82*	9

GOONS — UK

(See also Harry Secombe, Peter Sellers and Spike Milligan.)

SINGLES:	HITS 2			WEEKS 30
I'M WALKING BACKWARDS FOR CHRISTMAS / THE BLUEBOTTLE BLUES *The Bluebottle Blues listed from 14 Jul 56.* *Above hit: GOONS with Nick RAUCHEN conducting the BALL'S POND ROAD Near "The ONE-IN-HARMONY" / GOONS with Maurice PONKE and his Orchestre Fromage.*	*Decca*	4	*30 Jun 56*	10
THE YING TONG SONG / BLOODNOK'S ROCK'N'ROLL CALL *Bloodnok's Rock'n'Roll Call had first credit for the week 15 Sep 56.* *Above hit: GOONS with Maurice PONKE and his Orchestre Fromage / GOONS featuring Major Dennis BLOODNOK, 43rd Deserters (Rtd.), with Roland ROCKCAKE and his WHOLLY ROLLERS directed by Maestro PONKE.*	*Decca*	3	*15 Sep 56*	10
YING TONG SONG [RI]	*Decca*	9	*21 Jul 73*	10
ALBUMS:	**HITS 3**			**WEEKS 31**
BEST OF THE GOONS SHOWS	*Parlophone*	8	*28 Nov 59*	14
BEST OF THE GOONS SHOWS VOLUME 2	*Parlophone*	11	*17 Dec 60*	6
LAST GOON SHOW OF ALL	*BBC*	8	*4 Nov 72*	11

Coral GORDON – See MONDO KANE featuring Dee LEWIS and Coral GORDON Guest star Georgie FAME

Lonnie GORDON — US

SINGLES:	HITS 6			WEEKS 23
(I'VE GOT YOUR) PLEASURE CONTROL *Above hit: Simon HARRIS featuring Lonnie GORDON.*	*ffrr*	60	*24 Jun 89*	3
HAPPENIN' ALL OVER AGAIN	*Supreme*	4	*27 Jan 90*	10
BEYOND YOUR WILDEST DREAMS	*Supreme*	48	*11 Aug 90*	2
IF I HAVE TO STAND ALONE	*Supreme*	68	*17 Nov 90*	1
GONNA CATCH YOU	*Supreme*	32	*4 May 91*	5
LOVE EVICTION *Above hit: QUARTZ LOCK featuring Lonnie GORDON.*	*Xplode*	32	*7 Oct 95*	2

Lesley GORE — US

SINGLES:	HITS 2			WEEKS 20
IT'S MY PARTY *Originally recorded by Helen Shapiro.*	*Mercury*	9	*22 Jun 63*	12
MAYBE I KNOW	*Mercury*	20	*26 Sep 64*	8

Martin L. GORE — UK

ALBUMS:	HITS 1			WEEKS 1
COUNTERFEIT [EP]	*Mute*	51	*24 Jun 89*	1

GORILLAZ — UK

SINGLES:	HITS 3			WEEKS 35
CLINT EASTWOOD	*Parlophone*	4	*17 Mar 01*	17
19/2000	*Parlophone*	6	*7 Jul 01*	10
ROCK THE HOUSE	*Parlophone*	18	*3 Nov 01*	8
ALBUMS:	**HITS 1**			**WEEKS 39**
GORILLAZ	*Parlophone*	3	*7 Apr 00*	39

GORKY'S ZYGOTIC MYNCI — UK

SINGLES:	HITS 8			WEEKS 8
PATIO SONG	*Fontana*	41	*9 Nov 96*	1
DIAMOND DEW	*Fontana*	42	*29 Mar 97*	1
YOUNG GIRLS & HAPPY ENDINGS / DARK NIGHT	*Fontana*	49	*21 Jun 97*	1
SWEET JOHNNY	*Fontana*	60	*6 Jun 98*	1
LET'S GET TOGETHER (IN OUR MINDS)	*Fontana*	43	*29 Aug 98*	1
SPANISH DANCE TROUPE	*Mantra*	47	*2 Oct 99*	1
POODLE ROCKIN'	*Mantra*	52	*4 Mar 00*	1
STOOD ON GOLD	*Mantra*	65	*15 Sep 01*	1
ALBUMS:	**HITS 2**			**WEEKS 2**
BARAFUNDLE	*Fontana*	46	*19 Apr 97*	1
GORKY 5	*Fontana*	67	*12 Sep 98*	1

Eydie GORME — US

SINGLES:	HITS 4			WEEKS 33
LOVE ME FOREVER	*His Master's Voice*	21	*25 Jan 58*	5
YES MY DARLING DAUGHTER	*CBS*	10	*23 Jun 62*	9
BLAME IT ON THE BOSSA NOVA	*CBS*	32	*2 Feb 63*	6
I WANT TO STAY HERE	*CBS*	3	*24 Aug 63*	13

Above hit: STEVE and EYDIE.

Luke GOSS and the BAND OF THIEVES — UK

SINGLES:	HITS 2			WEEKS 3
SWEETER THAN THE MIDNIGHT TRAIN	*Sabre*	52	*12 Jun 93*	2
GIVE ME ONE MORE CHANCE	*Sabre*	68	*21 Aug 93*	1

Matt GOSS — UK

SINGLES:	HITS 2			WEEKS 5
THE KEY	*Atlas*	40	*26 Aug 95*	2
IF YOU WERE HERE TONIGHT	*Atlas*	23	*27 Apr 96*	3

GOTTI - See R. KELLY

Donald GOULD - See UNITED KINGDOM SYMPHONY ORCHESTRA conducted by Donald GOULD

Nigel GOULDING - See Abigail MEAD and Nigel GOULDING

Graham GOULDMAN — UK

SINGLES:	HITS 1			WEEKS 4
SUNBURN	*Mercury*	52	*23 Jun 79*	4

From the film of the same name.

GOURYELLA — Holland

SINGLES:	HITS 3			WEEKS 11
GOURYELLA	*Code Blue*	15	*10 Jul 99*	7
WALHALLA *Vocals by Rachiel Spier.*	*Code Blue*	27	*4 Dec 99*	2
TENSHI *Tenshi means Angel in Japanese.*	*Code Blue*	45	*23 Dec 00*	2

GRACE — UK

SINGLES:	HITS 6			WEEKS 24
NOT OVER YET *Originally released in 1993.*	*Perfecto*	6	*8 Apr 95*	8
I WANT TO LIVE *Written by Gavin Friday and originally intended for Bono.*	*Perfecto*	30	*23 Sep 95*	2
SKIN ON SKIN *Vocal re-working of Orange (a remix of U2's Lemon).*	*Perfecto*	21	*24 Feb 96*	3
DOWN TO EARTH	*Perfecto*	20	*1 Jun 96*	2
IF I COULD FLY	*Perfecto*	29	*28 Sep 96*	2
HAND IN HAND	*Perfecto*	38	*3 May 97*	1
DOWN TO EARTH [RM]	*Perfecto*	29	*26 Jul 97*	2

Remixed by Stephen Jones. The first track on the CD format was You're Not Mine, but this was not common to all formats.

NOT OVER YET 99 [RI]	*Code Blue*	16	*14 Aug 99*	4
Edited version of the original release.				
Above hit: PLANET PERFECTO featuring GRACE.				

GRACE BROTHERS — UK

SINGLES:	HITS 1			WEEKS 1
ARE YOU BEING SERVED?	*EMI Premier*	51	*20 Apr 96*	1

Bridgette GRACE – See TRUE FAITH and Bridgette GRACE with FINAL CUT

Janey Lee GRACE – See HYPERSTATE featuring Janey Lee GRACE

Charlie GRACIE — US

SINGLES:	HITS 4			WEEKS 41
BUTTERFLY	*Parlophone*	12	*20 Apr 57*	8
FABULOUS	*Parlophone*	8	*15 Jun 57*	16
I LOVE YOU SO MUCH IT HURTS / WANDERING EYES	*London*	14	*24 Aug 57*	2
From 7 Sep 57, both sides started separate chart runs.				
I LOVE YOU SO MUCH IT HURTS	*London*	20	*7 Sep 57*	2
Originally recorded by Jimmy Wakely in 1948.				
WANDERING EYES	*London*	6	*7 Sep 57*	12
COOL BABY	*London*	26	*11 Jan 58*	1

Eve GRAHAM – See NEW SEEKERS

Jaki GRAHAM — UK

SINGLES:	HITS 12			WEEKS 75
COULD IT BE I'M FALLING IN LOVE	*Chrysalis*	5	*23 Mar 85*	11
Originally recorded by Detroit Spinners.				
Above hit: David GRANT and Jaki GRAHAM.				
ROUND AND AROUND	*EMI*	9	*29 Jun 85*	11
HEAVEN KNOWS	*EMI*	59	*31 Aug 85*	3
Original release reached No. 80 in 1984.				
MATED	*EMI*	20	*16 Nov 85*	10
Originally recorded by Utopia.				
Above hit: David GRANT and Jaki GRAHAM.				
SET ME FREE	*EMI*	7	*3 May 86*	12
BREAKING AWAY	*EMI*	16	*9 Aug 86*	8
STEP RIGHT UP	*EMI*	15	*15 Nov 86*	12
NO MORE TEARS	*EMI*	60	*9 Jul 88*	2
FROM NOW ON	*EMI*	73	*24 Jun 89*	2
AIN'T NOBODY	*Pulse 8*	44	*16 Jul 94*	3
YOU CAN COUNT ON ME	*Avex UK*	62	*4 Feb 95*	1
ABSOLUTE E-SENSUAL	*Avex UK*	69	*8 Jul 95*	1
ALBUMS:	**HITS 2**			**WEEKS 10**
HEAVEN KNOWS	*EMI*	48	*14 Sep 85*	5
BREAKING AWAY	*EMI*	25	*20 Sep 86*	5

Larry GRAHAM — US

SINGLES:	HITS 1			WEEKS 4
SOONER OR LATER	*Warner Brothers*	54	*3 Jul 82*	4

Mikey GRAHAM — Ireland

SINGLES:	HITS 2			WEEKS 6
YOU'RE MY ANGEL	*Public*	13	*10 Jun 00*	5
YOU COULD BE MY EVERYTHING	*Public*	62	*14 Apr 01*	1

Ron GRAINER ORCHESTRA — UK

SINGLES:	HITS 1			WEEKS 7
A TOUCH OF VELVET - A STING OF BRASS	*Casino Classics*	60	*9 Dec 78*	7
EPS:	**HITS 1**			**WEEKS 1**
THEME MUSIC FROM "INSPECTOR MAIGRET"	*Warner Brothers*	13	*20 Jan 62*	1

GRAM'MA FUNK – See GROOVE ARMADA; ILLICIT featuring GRAM'MA FUNK

GRAND FUNK RAILROAD — US

SINGLES:	HITS 1			WEEKS 1
INSIDE LOOKING OUT	*Capitol*	40	*6 Feb 71*	1

GRAND PLAZ — UK

SINGLES:	HITS 1			WEEKS 4
WOW WOW - NA NA	*Urban*	41	*8 Sep 90*	4
Based around Steam's Na Na Hey Hey Kiss Him Goodbye.				

GRAND PRIX

UK

SINGLES:	HITS 1			WEEKS 1
KEEP ON BELIEVING	*RCA*	75	*27 Feb 82*	1
ALBUMS:	**HITS 1**			**WEEKS 2**
SAMURAI	*Chrysalis*	65	*18 Jun 83*	2

GRAND PUBA – See INFINITI featuring GRAND PUBA; SHAGGY

GRAND THEFT AUDIO

UK

SINGLES:	HITS 0			WEEKS 0
WE LUV U *From the film 'Dude Where's My Car?'.*	*Sci-Fi*	70	*24 Mar 01*	1

GRANDAD ROBERTS and his son ELVIS

UK

SINGLES:	HITS 1			WEEKS 1
MEAT PIE SAUSAGE ROLL (COME ON ENGLAND GI'S A GOAL) *Originally a terrace chant at Oldham Athletic FC.*	*WEA*	67	*20 Jun 98*	1

GRANDADDY

US

SINGLES:	HITS 2			WEEKS 3
HEWLETT'S DAUGHTER	*V2*	71	*2 Sep 00*	1
THE CRYSTAL LAKE *Original release reached No. 80 in June 2000.*	*V2*	38	*10 Feb 01*	2
ALBUMS:	**HITS 1**			**WEEKS 4**
SOPHTWARE SLUMP	*V2*	36	*20 May 00*	4

GRANDMASTER FLASH and the FURIOUS FIVE

US

(See also Duran Duran.)

SINGLES:	HITS 3			WEEKS 56
THE MESSAGE	*Sugar Hill*	8	*28 Aug 82*	9
WHITE LINES (DON'T DON'T DO IT) *Above hit: GRAND MASTER and Melle MEL.*	*Sugar Hill*	60	*19 Nov 83*	3
WHITE LINES (DON'T DON'T DO IT) [RE-1ST] *Peak position reached on 28 Jul 84.*	*Sugar Hill*	7	*11 Feb 84*	38
WHITE LINES (DON'T DON'T DO IT) [RE-2ND]	*Sugar Hill*	75	*24 Nov 84*	1
WHITE LINES (DON'T DON'T DO IT) [RE-3RD]	*Sugar Hill*	73	*5 Jan 85*	1
SIGN OF THE TIMES *Above hit: GRANDMASTER FLASH.*	*Elektra*	72	*16 Feb 85*	1
WHITE LINES (DON'T DO IT) [RM] *Remixed by D & S.* *Above hit: GRANDMASTER FLASH and Melle MEL.*	*WGAF*	59	*8 Jan 94*	3
ALBUMS:	**HITS 3**			**WEEKS 20**
THE MESSAGE	*Sugar Hill*	77	*23 Oct 82*	3
GREATEST MESSAGES	*Sugar Hill*	41	*23 Jun 84*	16
THEY SAID IT COULDN'T BE DONE *Above hit: GRANDMASTER FLASH.*	*Elektra*	95	*23 Feb 85*	1

GRANDMASTER Melle MEL and the FURIOUS FIVE – See Melle MEL

GRANDMIXER D.ST

US

SINGLES:	HITS 1			WEEKS 3
CRAZY CUTS	*Island*	73	*24 Dec 83*	2
CRAZY CUTS [RE]	*Island*	71	*14 Jan 84*	1

GRANGE HILL CAST (Rap: Mmoloki CHRYSTIE)

UK

SINGLES:	HITS 1			WEEKS 6
JUST SAY NO	*BBC*	5	*19 Apr 86*	6

Gerri GRANGER

US

SINGLES:	HITS 1			WEEKS 3
I GO TO PIECES (EVERYTIME)	*Casino Classics*	50	*30 Sep 78*	3

Amy GRANT

US

SINGLES:	HITS 8			WEEKS 39
BABY BABY *Written about Grant's six-year-old daughter, Millie.*	*A&M*	2	*11 May 91*	13
EVERY HEARTBEAT	*A&M*	25	*3 Aug 91*	7
THAT'S WHAT LOVE IS FOR	*A&M*	60	*2 Nov 91*	3
GOOD FOR ME	*A&M*	60	*15 Feb 92*	1
LUCKY ONE	*A&M*	60	*13 Aug 94*	1
SAY YOU'LL BE MINE	*A&M*	41	*22 Oct 94*	2
BIG YELLOW TAXI	*A&M*	20	*24 Jun 95*	10

HOUSE OF LOVE	*A&M*	46	*14 Oct 95*	2
Above hit: Amy GRANT with Vince GILL.				

ALBUMS:	HITS 1			WEEKS 15
HEART IN MOTION	*A&M*	25	*22 Jun 91*	15

Andrea GRANT featuring DARKMAN — UK

SINGLES:	HITS 1			WEEKS 1
REPUTATIONS (JUST BE GOOD TO ME)	*WEA*	75	*14 Nov 98*	1

Boysie GRANT - See Ezz RECO and the LAUNCHERS with Boysie GRANT

David GRANT — UK

SINGLES:	HITS 8			WEEKS 59
STOP AND GO	*Chrysalis*	19	*30 Apr 83*	9
WATCHING YOU, WATCHING ME	*Chrysalis*	10	*16 Jul 83*	13
LOVE WILL FIND A WAY	*Chrysalis*	24	*8 Oct 83*	6
ROCK THE MIDNIGHT	*Chrysalis*	46	*26 Nov 83*	4
COULD IT BE I'M FALLING IN LOVE	*Chrysalis*	5	*23 Mar 85*	11
Originally recorded by Detroit Spinners.				
MATED	*EMI*	20	*16 Nov 85*	10
Originally recorded by Utopia.				
Above 2: David GRANT and Jaki GRAHAM.				
CHANGE	*Polydor*	55	*1 Aug 87*	4
KEEP IT TOGETHER	*Fourth & Broadway*	56	*12 May 90*	2

ALBUMS:	HITS 2			WEEKS 7
DAVID GRANT	*Chrysalis*	32	*5 Nov 83*	6
HOPES AND DREAMS	*Chrysalis*	96	*18 May 85*	1

Eddy GRANT — Guyana

SINGLES:	HITS 11			WEEKS 107
LIVING ON THE FRONT LINE	*Ensign*	11	*2 Jun 79*	11
DO YOU FEEL MY LOVE?	*Ensign*	8	*15 Nov 80*	11
CAN'T GET ENOUGH OF YOU	*Ensign*	13	*4 Apr 81*	10
I LOVE YOU, YES I LOVE YOU	*Ensign*	37	*25 Jul 81*	6
I DON'T WANNA DANCE	*Ice*	1	*16 Oct 82*	15
ELECTRIC AVENUE	*Ice*	2	*15 Jan 83*	9
LIVING ON THE FRONT LINE [RI] / DO YOU FEEL MY LOVE [RI]	*Mercury*	47	*19 Mar 83*	4
WAR PARTY	*Ice*	42	*23 Apr 83*	4
TILL I CAN'T TAKE LOVE NO MORE	*Ice*	42	*29 Oct 83*	7
ROMANCING THE STONE	*Ice*	52	*19 May 84*	3
GIMME HOPE JO'ANNA	*Ice*	7	*23 Jan 88*	12
WALKING ON SUNSHINE	*Blue Wave*	63	*27 May 89*	2
ELECTRIC AVENUE [RM]	*East West*	5	*9 Jun 01*	10
Remixed by Peter Black.				
ELECTRIC AVENUE [RM] [RE]	*East West*	71	*25 Aug 01*	2
WALKING ON SUNSHINE [RM]	*East West*	57	*24 Nov 01*	1
Remixed by Stargate.				

ALBUMS:	HITS 5			WEEKS 62
CAN'T GET ENOUGH	*Ice*	39	*30 May 81*	6
KILLER ON THE RAMPAGE	*Ice*	7	*27 Nov 82*	23
ALL THE HITS	*K-Tel*	23	*17 Nov 84*	10
WALKING ON SUNSHINE (THE VERY BEST OF EDDY GRANT)	*Parlophone*	20	*1 Jul 89*	8
THE GREATEST HITS	*East West*	3	*19 May 01*	15

Gogi GRANT — US

SINGLES:	HITS 1			WEEKS 11
WAYWARD WIND	*London*	9	*30 Jun 56*	11

Julie GRANT — UK

SINGLES:	HITS 3			WEEKS 17
UP ON THE ROOF	*Pye*	33	*5 Jan 63*	3
COUNT ON ME	*Pye*	24	*30 Mar 63*	9
COME TO ME	*Pye*	31	*26 Sep 64*	5

Rudy GRANT — Guyana

SINGLES:	HITS 1			WEEKS 3
LATELY	*Ensign*	58	*14 Feb 81*	3

GRANT LEE BUFFALO — US

ALBUMS:	HITS 3			WEEKS 5
FUZZY	*Slash*	74	*10 Jul 93*	1
MIGHTY JOE MOON	*Slash*	24	*1 Oct 94*	2
COPPEROPOLIS	*Slash*	34	*15 Jun 96*	2

GRAPEFRUIT — UK

SINGLES:	HITS 2			WEEKS 19
DEAR DELILAH	*RCA Victor*	21	*17 Feb 68*	9
C'MON MARIANNE	*RCA Victor*	31	*17 Aug 68*	10

GRASS-SHOW — Sweden

SINGLES:	HITS 2			WEEKS 2
1962	*Food*	53	*22 Mar 97*	1
OUT OF THE VOID	*Food*	75	*23 Aug 97*	1
Original release reached No. 128 in 1996.				

GRATEFUL DEAD — US

(See also Bob Dylan and the Grateful Dead.)

ALBUMS:	HITS 6			WEEKS 9
WORKINGMAN'S DEAD	*Warner Brothers*	69	*19 Sep 70*	2
GRATEFUL DEAD FROM THE MARS HOTEL	*Warner Brothers*	47	*3 Aug 74*	1
BLUES FOR ALLAH	*United Artists*	45	*1 Nov 75*	1
STEAL YOUR FACE	*United Artists*	42	*4 Sep 76*	1
Early releases were issued with bonus album titled For Dead Heads Only.				
TERRAPIN STATION	*Arista*	30	*20 Aug 77*	1
IN THE DARK	*Arista*	57	*19 Sep 87*	3

Jorn GRAUENGAARD and his Orchestra – See NINA and FREDERIK

GRAVEDIGGAZ — US

SINGLES:	HITS 4			WEEKS 6
SIX FEET DEEP [EP]	*Gee Street*	64	*11 Mar 95*	1
Lead track: Bang Your Head.				
THE HELL [EP]	*Fourth & Broadway*	12	*5 Aug 95*	3
Lead track: Hell Is Around The Corner.				
Above hit: TRICKY vs. the GRAVEDIGGAZ.				
THE NIGHT THE EARTH CRIED	*Gee Street*	44	*24 Jan 98*	1
UNEXPLAINED	*Gee Street*	48	*25 Apr 98*	1
ALBUMS:	**HITS 1**			**WEEKS 1**
THE PICK, THE SICKLE AND THE SHOVEL	*Gee Street*	24	*4 Oct 97*	1

Barry GRAY ORCHESTRA — UK

SINGLES:	HITS 2			WEEKS 8
THUNDERBIRDS	*PRT*	61	*11 Jul 81*	2
JOE 90 (THEME)('86 DANCE MIX) / CAPTAIN SCARLET THEME	*PRT*	53	*14 Jun 86*	6
Above hit: Barry GRAY ORCHESTRA featuring keyboards by Peter BECKETT.				

David GRAY — UK

SINGLES:	HITS 5			WEEKS 31
PLEASE FORGIVE ME	*IHT*	72	*4 Dec 99*	1
BABYLON	*East West*	5	*1 Jul 00*	12
PLEASE FORGIVE ME [RI]	*East West*	18	*28 Oct 00*	6
THIS YEAR'S LOVE	*East West*	20	*17 Mar 01*	5
From the film of the same name.				
SAIL AWAY	*East West*	26	*28 Jul 01*	6
SAY HELLO WAVE GOODBYE	*East West*	26	*29 Dec 01*	1
ALBUMS:	**HITS 3**			**WEEKS 98**
WHITE LADDER	*East West*	1	*13 May 00*	86
Originally released on the 1HT label in 1998. Peak position reached on 11 Aug 01, the longest uninterrupted climb to No.1.				
LOST SONGS 95-98	*1HT*	55	*12 Aug 00*	1
LOST SONGS 95-98 [RE]	*East West*	7	*24 Feb 01*	10
THE EPs 92-94	*Hut*	68	*14 Jul 01*	1

David GRAY and Tommy TYCHO — UK

ALBUMS:	HITS 1			WEEKS 6
ARMCHAIR MELODIES	*K-Tel*	21	*16 Oct 76*	6

Dobie GRAY — UK

SINGLES:	HITS 2			WEEKS 11
THE IN CROWD	*London*	25	*27 Feb 65*	7
OUT ON THE FLOOR	*Black Magic*	42	*27 Sep 75*	4

Dorian GRAY — UK

SINGLES:	HITS 1			WEEKS 7
I'VE GOT YOU ON MY MIND	*Parlophone*	36	*30 Mar 68*	7

Johnnie GRAY and the BAND OF THE DAY – See STARGAZERS

Les GRAY — UK

SINGLES:	HITS 1			WEEKS 5
A GROOVY KIND OF LOVE	*Warner Brothers*	32	*26 Feb 77*	5

Macy GRAY — US

SINGLES:	HITS 9			WEEKS 49
DO SOMETHING	*Epic*	51	*3 Jul 99*	1
I TRY	*Epic*	6	*9 Oct 99*	22
STILL	*Epic*	18	*25 Mar 00*	7
STILL [RE]	*Epic*	65	*20 May 00*	2
WHY DIDN'T YOU CALL ME	*Epic*	38	*5 Aug 00*	2
WHY DIDN'T YOU CALL ME [RE]	*Epic*	74	*26 Aug 00*	1
DEMONS	*Skint*	16	*20 Jan 01*	5
Samples Bill Withers' I Can't Write Left Handed.				
Above hit: FATBOY SLIM featuring Macy GRAY.				
GETO HEAVEN (THE SOUND OF ILLADELPH)	*MCA*	48	*28 Apr 01*	1
Above hit: COMMON featuring Macy GRAY.				
REQUEST + LINE	*Interscope*	31	*12 May 01*	3
Samples Paulinho Dacosta's Love Till The End Of Time.				
Above hit: BLACK EYED PEAS featuring Macy GRAY.				
SWEET BABY	*Epic*	23	*15 Sep 01*	4
Above hit: Macy GRAY featuring Erykah BADU.				
SEXUAL REVOLUTION	*Epic*	45	*8 Dec 01*	1
ALBUMS:	**HITS 2**			**WEEKS 75**
ON HOW LIFE IS	*Epic*	3	*17 Jul 99*	67
THE ID	*Epic*	1	*29 Sep 01*	8

Alltrinna GRAYSON – See Wilton FELDER

GREASE – See TRICKY

GREAT WHITE — US

SINGLES:	HITS 3			WEEKS 5
HOUSE OF BROKEN LOVE	*Capitol*	44	*24 Feb 90*	2
CONGO SQUARE	*Capitol*	62	*16 Feb 91*	1
CALL IT ROCK N' ROLL	*Capitol*	67	*7 Sep 91*	2
ALBUMS:	**HITS 1**			**WEEKS 1**
HOOKED	*Capitol*	43	*9 Mar 91*	1

Buddy GRECO — US

SINGLES:	HITS 1			WEEKS 8
THE LADY IS A TRAMP	*Fontana*	26	*9 Jul 60*	8

GREED featuring Ricardo DA FORCE — UK

SINGLES:	HITS 1			WEEKS 2
PUMP UP THE VOLUME	*Stress*	51	*18 Mar 95*	2

GREEDIES — UK/Ireland/US

SINGLES:	HITS 1			WEEKS 5
A MERRY JINGLE	*Vertigo*	28	*15 Dec 79*	5

Al GREEN — US

SINGLES:	HITS 9			WEEKS 67
TIRED OF BEING ALONE	*London*	4	*9 Oct 71*	13
LET'S STAY TOGETHER	*London*	7	*8 Jan 72*	12
LOOK WHAT YOU DONE FOR ME	*London*	44	*20 May 72*	4
I'M STILL IN LOVE WITH YOU	*London*	35	*19 Aug 72*	5
SHA-LA-LA (MAKE ME HAPPY)	*London*	20	*16 Nov 74*	10
L.O.V.E. (LOVE)	*London*	24	*15 Mar 75*	8
PUT A LITTLE LOVE IN YOUR HEART	*A&M*	28	*3 Dec 88*	8
Originally recorded by Jackie de Shannon.				
Above hit: Annie LENNOX and Al GREEN.				
THE MESSAGE IS LOVE	*Breakout*	38	*21 Oct 89*	5
Above hit: Arthur BAKER and the BACKBEAT DISCIPLES featuring Al GREEN.				
LOVE IS A BEAUTIFUL THING	*Arista*	56	*2 Oct 93*	2
ALBUMS:	**HITS 3**			**WEEKS 25**
AL GREEN'S GREATEST HITS	*London*	18	*26 Apr 75*	16
HI LIFE - THE BEST OF AL GREEN	*K-Tel*	34	*1 Oct 88*	7
AL	*Beechwood*	41	*24 Oct 92*	2

Dotty GREEN – See Mark FISHER (featuring Dotty GREEN)

Jesse GREEN — US

SINGLES:	HITS 3			WEEKS 26
NICE AND SLOW	*EMI*	17	*7 Aug 76*	12
FLIP	*EMI*	26	*18 Dec 76*	8
COME WITH ME	*EMI*	29	*11 Jun 77*	6

Peter GREEN — UK

ALBUMS:	HITS 4			WEEKS 19
IN THE SKIES	*Creole*	32	*9 Jun 79*	13
LITTLE DREAMER	*PUK*	34	*24 May 80*	4
SPLINTER GROUP *Includes live tracks recorded in late 1996.*	*Artisan*	71	*24 May 97*	1
THE ROBERT JOHNSON SONGBOOK *Above hit: Peter GREEN with Nigel WATSON and the SPLINTER GROUP.*	*Artisan*	57	*30 May 98*	1

Robson GREEN and Jerome FLYNN - See ROBSON and JEROME

GREEN DAY — US

SINGLES:	HITS 13			WEEKS 43
BASKET CASE	*Reprise*	55	*20 Aug 94*	2
WELCOME TO PARADISE	*Reprise*	20	*29 Oct 94*	3
BASKET CASE [RI]	*Reprise*	7	*28 Jan 95*	6
LONGVIEW	*Reprise*	30	*18 Mar 95*	3
WHEN I COME AROUND	*Reprise*	27	*20 May 95*	3
GEEK STINK BREATH	*Reprise*	16	*7 Oct 95*	3
STUCK WITH ME	*Reprise*	24	*6 Jan 96*	3
BRAIN STEW / JADED [M]	*Reprise*	28	*6 Jul 96*	2
HITCHIN' A RIDE	*Reprise*	25	*11 Oct 97*	2
TIME OF YOUR LIFE (GOOD RIDDANCE)	*Reprise*	11	*31 Jan 98*	5
REDUNDANT	*Reprise*	27	*9 May 98*	2
MINORITY	*Reprise*	18	*30 Sep 00*	3
WARNING	*Reprise*	27	*23 Dec 00*	4
WAITING	*Reprise*	34	*10 Nov 01*	2

ALBUMS:	HITS 5			WEEKS 91
DOOKIE *Includes re-entries through to 2000.*	*Reprise*	13	*5 Nov 94*	55
INSOMNIAC	*Reprise*	8	*21 Oct 95*	5
NIMROD	*Reprise*	11	*25 Oct 97*	11
WARNING	*Reprise*	4	*14 Oct 00*	14
INTERNATIONAL SUPERHITS! *Compilation.*	*Reprise*	15	*24 Nov 01*	6

GREEN JELLY — US

SINGLES:	HITS 3			WEEKS 15
THREE LITTLE PIGS	*Zoo*	5	*5 Jun 93*	8
ANARCHY IN THE UK	*Zoo*	27	*14 Aug 93*	3
I'M THE LEADER OF THE GANG *Above hit: Hulk HOGAN with GREEN JELLY and the WRESTLING BOOT TRASH CAN BAND.*	*Arista*	25	*25 Dec 93*	4

ALBUMS:	HITS 1			WEEKS 10
CEREAL KILLER SOUNDTRACK	*Zoo*	18	*3 Jul 93*	10

GREEN ON RED — US

ALBUMS:	HITS 1			WEEKS 1
NO FREE LUNCH	*Mercury*	99	*26 Oct 85*	1

Gavin GREENAWAY - See Hans ZIMMER

Norman GREENBAUM — US

SINGLES:	HITS 1			WEEKS 20
SPIRIT IN THE SKY	*Reprise*	1	*21 Mar 70*	20

Lorne GREENE — US

SINGLES:	HITS 1			WEEKS 8
RINGO	*RCA Victor*	22	*19 Dec 64*	8

Dave GREENFIELD and Jean-Jacques BURNEL — UK

(See also Jean-Jacques Burnel.)

ALBUMS:	HITS 1			WEEKS 1
BURNEL FIRE AND WATER	*Epic*	94	*3 Dec 83*	1

GREENSLADE — UK

ALBUMS:	HITS 1			WEEKS 3
SPYGLASS GUEST	*Warner Brothers*	34	*14 Sep 74*	3

Lee GREENWOOD — US

SINGLES:	HITS 1			WEEKS 6
THE WIND BENEATH MY WINGS	*MCA*	49	*19 May 84*	6

Christina GREGG — UK

ALBUMS:	HITS 1			WEEKS 1
MUSIC 'N' MOTION	*Warwick*	51	*27 May 78*	1

Iain GREGORY — UK

SINGLES:	HITS 1			WEEKS 2
CAN'T YOU HEAR THE BEAT OF A BROKEN HEART	*Pye*	39	*6 Jan 62*	2

Johnny GREGORY and his Orchestra - See Russ HAMILTON

GREYHOUND — Jamaica

SINGLES:	HITS 3			WEEKS 33
BLACK AND WHITE *Originally recorded by (UK) Spinners.*	*Trojan*	6	*26 Jun 71*	13
MOON RIVER	*Trojan*	12	*8 Jan 72*	11
I AM WHAT I AM	*Trojan*	20	*25 Mar 72*	9

GRID — UK

SINGLES:	HITS 9			WEEKS 47
FLOATATION	*East West*	60	*7 Jul 90*	2
A BEAT CALLED LOVE	*East West*	64	*29 Sep 90*	4
FIGURE OF EIGHT	*Virgin*	50	*25 Jul 92*	3
HEARTBEAT	*Virgin*	72	*3 Oct 92*	2
CRYSTAL CLEAR	*Virgin*	27	*13 Mar 93*	4
TEXAS COWBOYS	*Deconstruction*	21	*30 Oct 93*	3
SWAMP THING	*Deconstruction*	3	*4 Jun 94*	17
ROLLERCOASTER	*Deconstruction*	19	*17 Sep 94*	4
TEXAS COWBOYS [RI]	*Deconstruction*	17	*3 Dec 94*	6
DIABLO	*Deconstruction*	32	*23 Sep 95*	2
ALBUMS:	**HITS 2**			**WEEKS 4**
EVOLVER	*Deconstruction*	14	*1 Oct 94*	3
MUSIC FOR DANCING	*Deconstruction*	67	*14 Oct 95*	1

Zaine GRIFF — New Zealand

SINGLES:	HITS 2			WEEKS 6
TONIGHT	*Automatic*	54	*16 Feb 80*	3
ASHES AND DIAMONDS	*Automatic*	68	*31 May 80*	3

Billy GRIFFIN — US

SINGLES:	HITS 2			WEEKS 12
HOLD ME TIGHTER IN THE RAIN	*CBS*	17	*8 Jan 83*	9
SERIOUS	*CBS*	64	*14 Jan 84*	3

Clive GRIFFIN — UK

SINGLES:	HITS 2			WEEKS 5
HEAD ABOVE WATER	*Mercury*	60	*24 Jun 89*	2
I'LL BE WAITING	*Mercury*	56	*11 May 91*	3

Nanci GRIFFITH — US

ALBUMS:	HITS 8			WEEKS 27
LITTLE LOVE AFFAIRS	*MCA*	78	*26 Mar 88*	1
STORMS	*MCA*	38	*23 Sep 89*	3
LATE NIGHT GRANDE HOTEL	*MCA*	40	*28 Sep 91*	5
OTHER VOICES/OTHER ROOMS	*MCA*	18	*20 Mar 93*	6
THE BEST OF NANCI GRIFFITH	*MCA*	27	*13 Nov 93*	4
FLYER	*MCA*	20	*1 Oct 94*	4
BLUE ROSES FROM THE MOONS *Features the Crickets.*	*Elektra*	64	*5 Apr 97*	3
CLOCK WITHOUT HANDS	*Elektra*	61	*11 Aug 01*	1

Roni GRIFFITH — US

SINGLES:	HITS 1			WEEKS 4
(THE BEST PART OF) BREAKIN' UP *Original release reached No. 85 in 1983.*	*Making Waves*	63	*30 Jun 84*	4

GRIFTERS featuring TALL PAUL and Brandon BLOCK — UK

(See also Blockster; Tall Paul.)

SINGLES:	HITS 1			WEEKS 1
FLASH *Samples Liason D's Future FJP.*	*Duty Free*	63	*20 Feb 99*	1

GRIMETHORPE COLLIERY BAND — UK

(See also Peter Skellern.)

ALBUMS:	HITS 1			WEEKS 4
BRASSED OFF [OST] *First released 1996. Charted after the film was aired on Channel 4.*	*RCA Victor*	36	*6 Jun 98*	4

Dave GROHL – See PUFF DADDY

GROOVE ARMADA — UK

SINGLES:	HITS 5			WEEKS 22
IF EVERYBODY LOOKED THE SAME *Samples the Chi-Lites' We Are Neighbors and A Tribe Called Quest's Ince Again (The Twister Mix).*	*Pepper*	25	*8 May 99*	2
AT THE RIVER *Samples Patti Page's Old Cape Cod. Originally released in 1997.*	*Pepper*	19	*7 Aug 99*	5
I SEE YOU BABY *Above hit: GROOVE ARMADA featuring GRAM'MA FUNK.*	*Pepper*	17	*27 Nov 99*	4
I SEE YOU BABY [RE]	*Pepper*	70	*15 Jan 00*	2
SUPERSTYLIN'	*Pepper*	12	*25 Aug 01*	6
SUPERSTYLIN' [RE]	*Pepper*	67	*13 Oct 01*	1
MY FRIEND	*Pepper*	36	*17 Nov 01*	2
ALBUMS:	**HITS 3**			**WEEKS 23**
VERTIGO	*Pepper*	23	*5 Jun 99*	14
THE REMIXES	*Pepper*	68	*6 May 00*	1
GOODBYE COUNTRY (HELLO NIGHTCLUB)	*Pepper*	5	*22 Sep 01*	8

GROOVE CONNEKTION 2 — UK

SINGLES:	HITS 1			WEEKS 1
CLUB LONELY	*XL Recordings*	54	*11 Apr 98*	1

GROOVE CORPORATION featuring ROMILLIE — UK/Italy

SINGLES:	HITS 1			WEEKS 1
RAIN	*Six6*	71	*16 Apr 94*	1

GROOVE GENERATION featuring Leo SAYER — UK

SINGLES:	HITS 1			WEEKS 3
YOU MAKE ME FEEL LIKE DANCING *Re-recorded vocals by Leo Sayer.*	*Brothers Organisation*	32	*8 Aug 98*	3

GROOVE THEORY — UK

(See also Sweetback featuring Amel Larrieux from Groove Theory.)

SINGLES:	HITS 1			WEEKS 3
TELL ME	*Epic*	31	*18 Nov 95*	3

Jay GROOVE – See FANTASY U.F.O.

GROOVERIDER — UK

SINGLES:	HITS 2			WEEKS 3
RAINBOWS OF COLOUR *Above hit: GROOVERIDER with Guest Vocalist ROYA ARAB.*	*Higher Ground*	40	*26 Sep 98*	2
WHERE'S JACK THE RIPPER?	*Higher Ground*	61	*19 Jun 99*	1
ALBUMS:	**HITS 1**			**WEEKS 1**
MYSTERIES OF FUNK	*Higher Ground*	50	*10 Oct 98*	1

Scott GROOVES — US

SINGLES:	HITS 2			WEEKS 3
EXPANSIONS *Above hit: Scott GROOVES featuring Roy AYERS.*	*Soma Recordings*	68	*16 May 98*	1
MOTHERSHIP RECONNECTION *Samples Parliament-Funkadelic's Mothership Connection Live.* *Above hit: Scott GROOVES featuring PARLIAMENT / FUNKADELIC.*	*Soma Recordings*	55	*28 Nov 98*	1
MOTHERSHIP RECONNECTION [RM] *Remixed by Daft Punk.* *Above hit: Scott GROOVES featuring PARLIAMENT-FUNKADELIC.*	*Virgin*	55	*21 Aug 99*	1

Henry GROSS — US

SINGLES:	HITS 1			WEEKS 4
SHANNON	*Lifesong*	32	*28 Aug 76*	4

Written about his dog that died.

GROUND LEVEL — Australia

SINGLES:	HITS 1			WEEKS 2
DREAMS OF HEAVEN	*Faze 2*	54	*30 Jan 93*	2

GROUNDHOGS — UK

ALBUMS:	HITS 4			WEEKS 50
THANK CHRIST FOR THE BOMB	*Liberty*	9	*6 Jun 70*	13
SPLIT	*Liberty*	5	*3 Apr 71*	27
WHO WILL SAVE THE WORLD	*United Artists*	8	*18 Mar 72*	9
SOLID	*WWA*	31	*13 Jul 74*	1

GROUP THERAPY — US

SINGLES:	HITS 1			WEEKS 1
EAST COAST/WEST COAST KILLAS	*Interscope*	51	*30 Nov 96*	1

Boring Bob GROVER – See PIRANHAS

Sir Charles GROVES – See ROYAL PHILHARMONIC ORCHESTRA

GUESS WHO — Canada

SINGLES:	HITS 2			WEEKS 14
HIS GIRL	*King*	45	*18 Feb 67*	1
AMERICAN WOMAN	*RCA Victor*	45	*9 May 70*	2
AMERICAN WOMAN [RE]	*RCA Victor*	19	*30 May 70*	11

GUILDFORD CATHEDRAL CHOIR conductor: Barry ROSE — UK

ALBUMS:	HITS 1			WEEKS 4
CHRISTMAS CAROLS FROM GUILDFORD CATHEDRAL	*Music For Pleasure*	24	*10 Dec 66*	4

GUILTY PARTY – See COLDCUT

GUITAR CORPORATION — UK

ALBUMS:	HITS 1			WEEKS 5
IMAGES	*Quality Television*	41	*15 Feb 92*	5

GUN — UK

SINGLES:	HITS 1			WEEKS 11
RACE WITH THE DEVIL	*CBS*	8	*23 Nov 68*	11

GUN — UK

SINGLES:	HITS 14			WEEKS 46
BETTER DAYS	*A&M*	33	*1 Jul 89*	9
MONEY (EVERYBODY LOVES HER)	*A&M*	73	*16 Sep 89*	2
INSIDE OUT	*A&M*	57	*11 Nov 89*	2
TAKING ON THE WORLD	*A&M*	50	*10 Feb 90*	3
SHAME ON YOU	*A&M*	33	*14 Jul 90*	4
STEAL YOUR FIRE	*A&M*	24	*14 Mar 92*	4
HIGHER GROUND	*A&M*	48	*2 May 92*	2
WELCOME TO THE REAL WORLD	*A&M*	43	*4 Jul 92*	2
WORD UP	*A&M*	8	*9 Jul 94*	7
DON'T SAY IT'S OVER	*A&M*	19	*24 Sep 94*	3
THE ONLY ONE	*A&M*	29	*25 Feb 95*	3
SOMETHING WORTHWHILE	*A&M*	39	*15 Apr 95*	2
CRAZY YOU	*A&M*	21	*26 Apr 97*	2
MY SWEET JANE	*A&M*	51	*12 Jul 97*	1

Above 2: G.U.N.

ALBUMS:	HITS 4			WEEKS 23
TAKING ON THE WORLD	*A&M*	44	*22 Jul 89*	10
GALLUS	*A&M*	14	*18 Apr 92*	4
SWAGGER	*A&M*	5	*13 Aug 94*	7
0141 632 6326	*A&M*	32	*24 May 97*	2

Title is phone number set up for fans to leave messages.
Above hit: G.U.N.

GUNS N' ROSES — US

SINGLES:	HITS 15			WEEKS 107
WELCOME TO THE JUNGLE	*Geffen*	67	*3 Oct 87*	2
SWEET CHILD O' MINE	*Geffen*	24	*20 Aug 88*	8

Written about his then girlfriend Erin Everly.

WELCOME TO THE JUNGLE [RI] / NIGHTRAIN	*Geffen*	24	*29 Oct 88*	5
PARADISE CITY	*Geffen*	6	*18 Mar 89*	9
SWEET CHILD O' MINE [RM]	*Geffen*	6	*3 Jun 89*	9
Remixed by Steve Thomson and Michael Barbiero.				
PATIENCE	*Geffen*	10	*1 Jul 89*	7
NIGHTRAIN [RI]	*Geffen*	17	*2 Sep 89*	5
YOU COULD BE MINE	*Geffen*	3	*13 Jul 91*	10
From the film 'Terminator 2 Judgement Day'.				
DON'T CRY	*Geffen*	8	*21 Sep 91*	4
LIVE AND LET DIE	*Geffen*	5	*21 Dec 91*	7
NOVEMBER RAIN	*Geffen*	4	*7 Mar 92*	5
KNOCKIN' ON HEAVEN'S DOOR	*Geffen*	2	*23 May 92*	9
Live recording from Wembley Stadium at the Freddie Mercury Tribute Concert on 20 Apr 92.				
YESTERDAYS / NOVEMBER RAIN [RI]	*Geffen*	8	*21 Nov 92*	9
November Rain listed from 28 Nov 92.				
THE "CIVIL WAR" [EP]	*Geffen*	11	*29 May 93*	3
Lead track: Civil War (LP Version).				
AIN'T IT FUN	*Geffen*	9	*20 Nov 93*	3
SINCE I DON'T HAVE YOU	*Geffen*	10	*4 Jun 94*	6
Original by the Skyliners reached No. 12 in the US in 1959.				
SYMPATHY FOR THE DEVIL	*Geffen*	9	*14 Jan 95*	6
Originally recorded by The Rolling Stones. From the film 'Interview With The Vampire'.				

ALBUMS:	HITS 6			WEEKS 374
APPETITE FOR DESTRUCTION	*Geffen*	15	*1 Aug 87*	20
Peak position reached in 1988, (1987 peak No. 68).				
G N' R THE LIES, THE SEX, THE DRUGS, THE VIOLENCE, THE SHOCKING TRUTH	*Geffen*	32	*17 Dec 89*	9
APPETITE FOR DESTRUCTION [RE-1ST]	*Geffen*	5	*7 Jan 89*	65
Peak position reached on 22 Jul 89.				
G N' R THE LIES, THE SEX, THE DRUGS, THE VIOLENCE, THE SHOCKING TRUTH [RE-1ST]	*Geffen*	22	*18 Mar 89*	30
APPETITE FOR DESTRUCTION [RE-2ND]	*Geffen*	31	*24 Aug 91*	68
Re-released. Peak position reached in 1992, (1991 peak No. 53). Includes re-entries through to 2000.				
USE YOUR ILLUSION I	*Geffen*	2	*28 Sep 91*	84
USE YOUR ILLUSION II	*Geffen*	1	*28 Sep 91*	84
Above 2 includes re-entries through to 1997.				
G N' R THE LIES, THE SEX, THE DRUGS, THE VIOLENCE, THE SHOCKING TRUTH [RE-2ND]	*Geffen*	69	*23 May 92*	2
Re-released.				
THE SPAGHETTI INCIDENT?	*Geffen*	2	*4 Dec 93*	10
LIVE - ERA '87-'93	*Geffen*	45	*11 Dec 99*	2

GUNSHOT — UK

ALBUMS:	HITS 1			WEEKS 1
PATRIOT GAMES	*Vinyl Solution*	60	*19 Jun 93*	1

David GUNSON — UK

ALBUMS:	HITS 1			WEEKS 2
WHAT GOES UP MIGHT COME DOWN	*Big Ben*	92	*25 Dec 82*	2

Peter GUNZ – See LORD TARIQ and Peter GUNZ; Shaquille O'NEAL

GURU — US

(See also Various Artists (EPs) 'Help EP'.)

SINGLES:	HITS 7			WEEKS 13
TRUST ME	*Cooltempo*	34	*11 Sep 93*	2
Above hit: GURU featuring N'Dea DAVENPORT.				
NO TIME TO PLAY	*Cooltempo*	25	*13 Nov 93*	3
Above hit: GURU featuring vocals by D.C. LEE.				
WATCH WHAT YOU SAY	*Cooltempo*	28	*19 Aug 95*	3
Sleeve gives title as an EP: Jazzmatazz Vol.2, The New Reality. Above hit: GURU featuring Chaka KHAN.				
FEEL THE MUSIC	*Cooltempo*	34	*18 Nov 95*	2
Above hit: GURU: JAZZAMATAZZ VOL. II THE NEW REALITY.				
LIVIN' IN THE WORLD / LIFESAVER	*Cooltempo*	61	*13 Jul 96*	1
Features Donald Byrd on trumpet and vocals by N'Dea Davenport.				
FED UP	*Tommy Boy*	68	*05 Oct 96*	1
Featured in the Lucozade TV commercial. Samples Mitch Ryder's Blessing In Disguise. Above hit: HOUSE OF PAIN (featuring GURU).				
KEEP YOUR WORRIES	*Virgin*	57	*16 Dec 00*	1
Above hit: GURU'S JAZZMATAZZ featuring Angie STONE.				

ALBUMS:	HITS 3			WEEKS 12
JAZZAMATAZZ	*Cooltempo*	58	*29 May 93*	2
Above hit: GURU featuring VARIOUS ARTISTS.				
JAZZMATAZZ VOLUME II - THE NEW REALITY	*Cooltempo*	12	*15 Jul 95*	9

STREETSOUL	*Virgin*	74	*14 Oct 00*	1

Above hit: GURU'S JAZZMATAZZ.

GURU JOSH — UK

SINGLES:	HITS 2			WEEKS 14
INFINITY (1990'S: TIME FOR THE GURU)	*Deconstruction*	5	*24 Feb 90*	10
WHOSE LAW (IS IT ANYWAY?)	*Deconstruction*	26	*16 Jun 90*	4
ALBUMS:	**HITS 1**			**WEEKS 2**
INFINITY	*Deconstruction*	41	*14 Jul 90*	2

Adrian GURVITZ — UK

SINGLES:	HITS 2			WEEKS 16
CLASSIC	*RAK*	8	*30 Jan 82*	13
YOUR DREAM	*RAK*	61	*12 Jun 82*	3

GUSGUS — Iceland

SINGLES:	HITS 3			WEEKS 3
POLYESTERDAY	*4AD*	55	*21 Feb 98*	1
LADYSHAVE	*4AD*	64	*13 Mar 99*	1
STARLOVERS	*4AD*	62	*24 Apr 99*	1

GUSTO — US

SINGLES:	HITS 2			WEEKS 8
DISCO'S REVENGE	*Manifesto*	9	*2 Mar 96*	5
Samples Harvey Mason's 70s disco hit Groovin You.				
LET'S ALL CHANT	*Manifesto*	21	*7 Sep 96*	3

Arlo GUTHRIE — US

ALBUMS:	HITS 1			WEEKS 1
ALICE'S RESTAURANT	*Reprise*	44	*7 Mar 70*	1

Gwen GUTHRIE — US

SINGLES:	HITS 3			WEEKS 25
AIN'T NOTHIN' GOIN' ON BUT THE RENT	*Boiling Point*	5	*19 Jul 86*	12
(THEY LONG TO BE) CLOSE TO YOU	*Boiling Point*	25	*11 Oct 86*	7
GOOD TO GO LOVER / OUTSIDE IN THE RAIN	*Boiling Point*	37	*14 Feb 87*	4
AIN'T NOTHIN' GOIN' ON BUT THE RENT [RM]	*Polydor*	42	*4 Sep 93*	2
Remixed by Nigel Wright.				
ALBUMS:	**HITS 1**			**WEEKS 14**
GOOD TO GO LOVER	*Boiling Point*	42	*23 Aug 86*	14

GUY — US

(See also Various Artists (EPs) 'New York Undercover 4-Track EP'.)

SINGLES:	HITS 1			WEEKS 4
HER	*MCA*	58	*4 May 91*	4
ALBUMS:	**HITS 1**			**WEEKS 1**
III	*MCA*	55	*5 Feb 00*	1

Buddy GUY — US

ALBUMS:	HITS 2			WEEKS 9
DAMM RIGHT, I'VE GOT THE BLUES	*Silvertone*	43	*22 Jun 91*	5
FEELS LIKE RAIN	*Silvertone*	36	*13 Mar 93*	4

A GUY CALLED GERALD — UK

SINGLES:	HITS 2			WEEKS 23
VOODOO RAY [EP]	*Rham!*	55	*8 Apr 89*	8
Lead track: Voodoo Ray.				
VOODOO RAY [EP] [RE]	*Rham!*	12	*24 Jun 89*	10
FX / EYES OF SORROW	*Subscape*	52	*16 Dec 89*	5
ALBUMS:	**HITS 2**			**WEEKS 2**
AUTOMANIKK	*Subscape*	68	*14 Apr 90*	1
BLACK SECRET TECHNOLOGY	*Juice Box*	64	*1 Apr 95*	1

GUYS 'N' DOLLS — UK

SINGLES:	HITS 5			WEEKS 33
THERE'S A WHOLE LOT OF LOVING	*Magnet*	2	*1 Mar 75*	11
HERE I GO AGAIN	*Magnet*	33	*17 May 75*	5
YOU DON'T HAVE TO SAY YOU LOVE ME	*Magnet*	5	*21 Feb 76*	8
STONEY GROUND	*Magnet*	38	*6 Nov 76*	4

ONLY LOVING DOES IT *Song used in the Oxo TV commercial.*	*Magnet*	42	*13 May 78*	5
ALBUMS:	**HITS 1**			**WEEKS 1**
GUYS 'N' DOLLS	*Magnet*	43	*31 May 75*	1

Jonas GWANGWA – See CRY FREEDOM

GWENT CHORALE – See Bryn YEMM

GYPSYMEN — US

(See also Todd Terry.)

SINGLES:	**HITS 1**			**WEEKS 2**
BABARABATIRI *Samples Babarabatiri by Beny Moore & Perez Prado.*	*Sound Design*	32	*11 Aug 01*	2

GYRES — UK

SINGLES:	**HITS 2**			**WEEKS 2**
POP COP	*Sugar*	71	*13 Apr 96*	1
ARE YOU READY?	*Sugar*	71	*6 Jul 96*	1

H

H.H.C. — UK

SINGLES:	**HITS 1**			**WEEKS 1**
WE'RE NOT ALONE	*Perfecto*	44	*19 Apr 97*	1

H.W.A. featuring SONIC The HEDGEHOG — UK

SINGLES:	**HITS 1**			**WEEKS 6**
SUPERSONIC	*Internal Affairs*	33	*5 Dec 92*	6

HABIT — UK

SINGLES:	**HITS 1**			**WEEKS 2**
LUCY	*Virgin*	56	*30 Apr 88*	2

Bobby HACKETT – See Tony BENNETT

Steve HACKETT — UK

SINGLES:	**HITS 1**			**WEEKS 2**
CELL 151	*Charisma*	66	*2 Apr 83*	2
ALBUMS:	**HITS 8**			**WEEKS 38**
VOYAGE OF THE ACOLYTE	*Charisma*	26	*1 Nov 75*	4
PLEASE DON'T TOUCH	*Charisma*	38	*6 May 78*	5
SPECTRAL MORNINGS	*Charisma*	22	*26 May 79*	11
DEFECTOR	*Charisma*	9	*21 Jun 80*	7
CURED	*Charisma*	15	*29 Aug 81*	5
HIGHLY STRUNG	*Charisma*	16	*30 Apr 83*	3
BAY OF KINGS	*Lamborghini*	70	*19 Nov 83*	1
TILL WE HAVE FACES	*Lamborghini*	54	*22 Sep 84*	2

HADDAWAY — Trinidad & Tobago

SINGLES:	**HITS 6**			**WEEKS 52**
WHAT IS LOVE	*Logic*	2	*5 Jun 93*	15
LIFE	*Logic*	6	*25 Sep 93*	9
I MISS YOU	*Logic*	9	*18 Dec 93*	14
ROCK MY HEART	*Logic*	9	*2 Apr 94*	9
FLY AWAY	*Logic*	20	*24 Jun 95*	3
CATCH A FIRE	*Logic*	39	*23 Sep 95*	2
ALBUMS:	**HITS 1**			**WEEKS 16**
HADDAWAY - THE ALBUM	*Logic*	19	*23 Oct 93*	5
HADDAWAY - THE ALBUM [RE] *Repackaged.*	*Logic*	9	*29 Jan 94*	11

Tony HADLEY — UK

SINGLES:	**HITS 4**			**WEEKS 9**
LOST IN YOUR LOVE	*EMI*	42	*7 Mar 92*	4
FOR YOUR BLUE EYES ONLY	*EMI*	67	*29 Aug 92*	2
THE GAME OF LOVE	*EMI*	72	*16 Jan 93*	1
DANCE WITH ME *Above hit: TIN TIN OUT featuring Tony HADLEY.*	*VC Recordings*	35	*10 May 97*	2
ALBUMS:	**HITS 1**			**WEEKS 3**
TONY HADLEY	*PolyGram TV*	45	*20 Sep 97*	3

Sammy HAGAR — US

(See also Hagar, Schon, Aaronson, Shrieve.)

SINGLES:	HITS 4			WEEKS 15
THIS PLANET'S ON FIRE (BURN IN HELL) / SPACE STATION NO. 5	*Capitol*	52	*15 Dec 79*	5
I'VE DONE EVERYTHING FOR YOU	*Capitol*	36	*16 Feb 80*	5
HEARTBEAT / LOVE OR MONEY	*Capitol*	67	*24 May 80*	2
PIECE OF MY HEART	*Geffen*	67	*16 Jan 82*	1
PIECE OF MY HEART [RE]	*Geffen*	67	*30 Jan 82*	2
ALBUMS:	**HITS 5**			**WEEKS 19**
STREET MACHINE	*Capitol*	38	*29 Sep 79*	4
LOUD AND CLEAR	*Capitol*	12	*22 Mar 80*	8
DANGER ZONE	*Capitol*	25	*7 Jun 80*	3
STANDING HAMPTON	*Geffen*	84	*13 Feb 82*	2
SAMMY HAGAR	*Geffen*	86	*4 Jul 87*	2

HAGAR, SCHON, AARONSON, SHRIEVE — US

(See also Sammy Hagar.)

ALBUMS:	HITS 1			WEEKS 1
THROUGH THE FIRE	*Geffen*	92	*19 May 84*	1

Nina HAGEN – See ADAMSKI

Paul HAIG — UK

SINGLES:	HITS 1			WEEKS 3
HEAVEN SENT	*Island*	74	*28 May 83*	3
ALBUMS:	**HITS 1**			**WEEKS 2**
RHYTHM OF LIFE	*Island*	82	*22 Oct 83*	2

HAIRCUT ONE HUNDRED — UK

SINGLES:	HITS 5			WEEKS 47
FAVOURITE SHIRTS (BOY MEETS GIRL)	*Arista*	4	*24 Oct 81*	14
LOVE PLUS ONE	*Arista*	3	*30 Jan 82*	12
FANTASTIC DAY	*Arista*	9	*10 Apr 82*	9
NOBODY'S FOOL	*Arista*	9	*21 Aug 82*	7
PRIME TIME	*Polydor*	46	*6 Aug 83*	5
ALBUMS:	**HITS 1**			**WEEKS 34**
PELICAN WEST	*Arista*	2	*6 Mar 82*	34

Curtis HAIRSTON — US

SINGLES:	HITS 3			WEEKS 16
I WANT YOU (ALL TONIGHT)	*RCA*	44	*15 Oct 83*	5
I WANT YOUR LOVIN' (JUST A LITTLE BIT)	*London*	13	*27 Apr 85*	7
CHILLIN' OUT	*Atlantic*	57	*6 Dec 86*	4

Gary HAISMAN – See D-MOB

HAL featuring Gillian ANDERSON — UK

SINGLES:	HITS 1			WEEKS 3
EXTREMIS	*Virgin*	23	*24 May 97*	3

HALE and PACE and the STONKERS — UK

SINGLES:	HITS 1			WEEKS 7
THE STONK *Charity record in aid of Comic Relief's Red Nose Day.*	*London*	1	*9 Mar 91*	7

Bill HALEY and his COMETS — US

SINGLES:	HITS 14			WEEKS 199
SHAKE, RATTLE AND ROLL *Originally recorded by Joe Turner. Additional credit reads: featuring Bill Haley and Ensemble.*	*Brunswick*	4	*18 Dec 54*	14
(WE'RE GONNA) ROCK AROUND THE CLOCK *From the film 'The Blackboard Jungle'. Originally recorded by Sonny Dae and the Knights in 1952.*	*Brunswick*	17	*8 Jan 55*	2
MAMBO ROCK	*Brunswick*	14	*16 Apr 55*	2
(WE'RE GONNA) ROCK AROUND THE CLOCK [RE-1ST]	*Brunswick*	1	*15 Oct 55*	17
ROCK-A-BEATIN' BOOGIE *Originally recorded by Esquire Boys in 1953.*	*Brunswick*	4	*31 Dec 55*	9
SEE YOU LATER, ALLIGATOR *Originally recorded by Bobby Charles.*	*Brunswick*	7	*10 Mar 56*	13
THE SAINTS ROCK 'N ROLL	*Brunswick*	5	*26 May 56*	24
ROCKIN' THROUGH THE RYE	*Brunswick*	3	*18 Aug 56*	18
RAZZLE DAZZLE	*Brunswick*	13	*15 Sep 56*	8
SEE YOU LATER, ALLIGATOR [RE]	*Brunswick*	12	*22 Sep 56*	8
(WE'RE GONNA) ROCK AROUND THE CLOCK [RE-2ND]	*Brunswick*	5	*22 Sep 56*	11

ROCK 'N' ROLL STAGE SHOW [LP]	*Brunswick*	30	*10 Nov 56*	1
12-track album, first track: Calling All Comets.				
RIP IT UP	*Brunswick*	4	*10 Nov 56*	18
RUDY'S ROCK	*Brunswick*	30	*24 Nov 56*	1
RUDY'S ROCK [RE]	*Brunswick*	26	*15 Dec 56*	4
(WE'RE GONNA) ROCK AROUND THE CLOCK [RE-3RD]	*MCA*	24	*15 Dec 56*	2
ROCKIN' THROUGH THE RYE [RE]	*Brunswick*	19	*5 Jan 57*	5
(WE'RE GONNA) ROCK AROUND THE CLOCK [RE-4TH]	*MCA*	25	*5 Jan 57*	2
(WE'RE GONNA) ROCK AROUND THE CLOCK [RE-5TH]	*Brunswick*	22	*26 Jan 57*	2
ROCK THE JOINT	*London*	20	*2 Feb 57*	4
Originally recorded by the Treniers.				
DON'T KNOCK THE ROCK	*Brunswick*	7	*9 Feb 57*	8
(WE'RE GONNA) ROCK AROUND THE CLOCK [RI-1ST]	*MCA*	20	*6 Apr 68*	11
(WE'RE GONNA) ROCK AROUND THE CLOCK [R1-2ND]	*MCA*	12	*16 Mar 74*	10
HALEY'S GOLDEN MEDLEY [M]	*MCA*	50	*25 Apr 81*	5

ALBUMS:	HITS 1			WEEKS 5
ROCK AROUND THE CLOCK	*Ace Of Hearts*	34	*18 May 68*	5

HALF MAN HALF BISCUIT — UK

ALBUMS:	HITS 2			WEEKS 14
BACK IN THE D.H.S.S.	*Probe*	60	*8 Feb 86*	9
BACK AGAIN IN THE D.H.S.S.	*Probe*	59	*21 Feb 87*	5

Aaron HALL — US

(See also Various Artists (EPs) 'Dangerous Minds EP'.)

SINGLES:	HITS 2			WEEKS 3
DON'T BE AFRAID	*MCA*	56	*13 Jun 92*	2
GET A LITTLE FREAKY WITH ME	*MCA*	66	*23 Oct 93*	1

Audrey HALL — Jamaica

SINGLES:	HITS 2			WEEKS 20
ONE DANCE WON'T DO	*Germain*	20	*25 Jan 86*	11
SMILE	*Germain*	14	*5 Jul 86*	9
Above hit: Audrey HALL featuring Sly DUNBAR and Robert SHAKESPEARE.				

Daryl HALL — US

(See also Daryl Hall and John Oates.)

SINGLES:	HITS 6			WEEKS 26
DREAMTIME	*RCA*	28	*2 Aug 86*	8
I'M IN A PHILLY MOOD	*Epic*	59	*25 Sep 93*	2
STOP LOVING ME, STOP LOVING YOU	*Epic*	30	*8 Jan 94*	6
Originally recorded by Marvin Gaye.				
I'M IN A PHILLY MOOD [RE]	*Epic*	52	*26 Mar 94*	2
HELP ME FIND A WAY TO YOUR HEART	*Epic*	70	*14 May 94*	1
GLORYLAND	*Mercury*	36	*2 Jul 94*	4
The official theme song of the USA 1994 World Cup.				
Above hit: Daryl HALL and SOUNDS OF BLACKNESS.				
WHEREVER WOULD I BE	*Columbia*	44	*10 Jun 95*	3
Above hit: Dusty SPRINGFIELD and Daryl HALL.				

ALBUMS:	HITS 2			WEEKS 9
THREE HEARTS IN THE HAPPY ENDING MACHINE	*RCA*	26	*23 Aug 86*	5
SOUL ALONE	*Epic*	57	*23 Oct 93*	1
SOUL ALONE [RI]	*Columbia*	55	*12 Feb 94*	3

Daryl HALL and John OATES — US

(See also Daryl Hall.)

SINGLES:	HITS 16			WEEKS 84
SHE'S GONE	*Atlantic*	42	*16 Oct 76*	4
Originally recorded by Tavares in 1974.				
RUNNING FROM PARADISE	*RCA*	41	*14 Jun 80*	6
YOU'VE LOST THAT LOVIN' FEELIN'	*RCA*	55	*20 Sep 80*	3
KISS ON MY LIST	*RCA*	33	*15 Nov 80*	8
I CAN'T GO FOR THAT (NO CAN DO)	*RCA*	8	*23 Jan 82*	10
PRIVATE EYES	*RCA*	32	*10 Apr 82*	7
MANEATER	*RCA*	6	*30 Oct 82*	11
ONE ON ONE	*RCA*	63	*22 Jan 83*	3
FAMILY MAN	*RCA*	15	*30 Apr 83*	7
SAY IT ISN'T SO	*RCA*	69	*12 Nov 83*	3
ADULT EDUCATION	*RCA*	63	*10 Mar 84*	2
OUT OF TOUCH	*RCA*	48	*20 Oct 84*	5
METHOD OF MODERN LOVE	*RCA*	21	*9 Feb 85*	8
OUT OF TOUCH [RM]	*RCA*	62	*22 Jun 85*	3

A NITE AT THE APOLLO LIVE! [M]	*RCA*	58	*21 Sep 85*	2
Medley of The Way You Do The Things You Do and My Girl.				
Above hit: Daryl HALL and John OATES featuring David RUFFIN and Eddie KENDRICK.				
SO CLOSE	*Arista*	69	*29 Sep 90*	1
EVERYWHERE I LOOK	*Arista*	74	*26 Jan 91*	1
ALBUMS:	**HITS 12**			**WEEKS 152**
HALL AND OATES	*RCA Victor*	56	*3 Jul 76*	1
BIGGER THAN BOTH OF US	*RCA Victor*	25	*18 Sep 76*	7
BEAUTY ON A BACK STREET	*RCA Victor*	40	*15 Oct 77*	2
PRIVATE EYES	*RCA*	8	*6 Feb 82*	21
H2O	*RCA*	24	*23 Oct 82*	35
ROCK 'N' SOUL PART ONE	*RCA*	16	*29 Oct 83*	45
Compilation.				
BIG BAM BOOM	*RCA*	28	*27 Oct 84*	13
HALL AND OATES LIVE AT THE APOLLO WITH DAVID RUFFIN AND EDDIE KENDRICK	*RCA*	32	*28 Sep 85*	5
Live recordings from the Apollo Theater, Harlem, May 85 to benefit the United Negro College Fund.				
OOH YEAH!	*RCA*	52	*18 Jun 88*	3
CHANGE OF SEASON	*Arista*	44	*27 Oct 90*	2
THE BEST OF DARYL HALL AND JOHN OATES – LOOKING BACK	*Arista*	9	*19 Oct 91*	16
THE ESSENTIAL COLLECTION	*RCA*	26	*6 Oct 01*	2

Lynden David HALL — UK

SINGLES:	**HITS 6**			**WEEKS 12**
SEXY CINDERELLA	*Cooltempo*	45	*25 Oct 97*	2
Features Me'shell Ndegeocello on bass guitar.				
DO I QUALIFY?	*Cooltempo*	26	*14 Mar 98*	2
CRESCENT MOON	*Cooltempo*	45	*4 Jul 98*	1
SEXY CINDERELLA [RI]	*Cooltempo*	17	*31 Oct 98*	3
FORGIVE ME	*Cooltempo*	30	*11 Mar 00*	2
SLEEPING WITH VICTOR	*Cooltempo*	49	*27 May 00*	1
Features Me'Shell Ndegeocello on bass.				
LET'S DO IT AGAIN	*Cooltempo*	69	*23 Sep 00*	1
Features Hinda Hicks on vocals and also samples the original version by the Staple Singers, a US No. 1 in 1975.				
ALBUMS:	**HITS 2**			**WEEKS 4**
MEDICINE 4 MY PAIN	*Cooltempo*	43	*14 Nov 98*	2
Originally released in 1997, charted after being repackaged with additional tracks.				
THE OTHER SIDE	*Cooltempo*	36	*10 Jun 00*	2

Pam HALL — Jamaica

SINGLES:	**HITS 1**			**WEEKS 4**
DEAR BOOPSIE	*Bluemountain*	54	*16 Aug 86*	4

Terry HALL — UK

SINGLES:	**HITS 5**			**WEEKS 6**
MISSING	*Chrysalis*	75	*11 Nov 89*	1
Credit is as per sleeve. Label only lists Terry Hall.				
Above hit: TERRY, BLAIR and ANOUCHKA.				
FOREVER J	*AnXious*	67	*27 Aug 94*	1
SENSE	*AnXious*	54	*12 Nov 94*	2
RAINBOWS [EP]	*AnXious*	62	*28 Oct 95*	1
Lead track: Chasing A Rainbow (with Damon Albarn).				
BALLAD OF A LANDLORD	*Southsea Bubble Co*	50	*14 Jun 97*	1
ALBUMS:	**HITS 1**			**WEEKS 1**
LAUGH	*Southsea Bubble Co*	50	*18 Oct 97*	1

Toni HALLIDAY – See LEFTFIELD

Geri HALLIWELL — UK

SINGLES:	**HITS 7**			**WEEKS 87**
LOOK AT ME	*EMI*	2	*22 May 99*	12
LOOK AT ME [RE]	*EMI*	60	*28 Aug 99*	2
MI CHICO LATINO	*EMI*	1	*28 Aug 99*	13
LIFT ME UP	*EMI*	1	*13 Nov 99*	15
LIFT ME UP [RE]	*EMI*	61	*4 Mar 00*	2
BAG IT UP	*EMI*	1	*25 Mar 00*	11
Features Pepsi and Shirlie on backing vocals.				
BAG IT UP [RE]	*EMI*	55	*24 Jun 00*	2
IT'S RAINING MEN	*EMI*	1	*12 May 01*	15
From the film 'Bridget Jones's Diary'.				
SCREAM IF YOU WANNA GO FASTER	*EMI*	8	*11 Aug 01*	9
SCREAM IF YOU WANNA GO FASTER [RE]	*EMI*	64	*27 Oct 01*	2
CALLING	*EMI*	7	*8 Dec 01*	4

ALBUMS:	HITS 2			WEEKS 58
SCHIZOPHONIC	*EMI*	4	*19 Jun 99*	43
SCREAM IF YOU WANNA GO FASTER	*EMI*	5	*26 May 01*	15

Jack HALLORAN SINGERS - See Ray CHARLES

HALO JAMES — UK

SINGLES:	HITS 4			WEEKS 24
WANTED	*Epic*	45	*7 Oct 89*	5
COULD HAVE TOLD YOU SO	*Epic*	6	*23 Dec 89*	12
BABY	*Epic*	43	*17 Mar 90*	4
MAGIC HOUR	*Epic*	59	*19 May 90*	3
ALBUMS:	**HITS 1**			**WEEKS 4**
WITNESS	*Epic*	18	*14 Apr 90*	4

HAMBURG STUDENTS CHOIR — Germany

ALBUMS:	HITS 1			WEEKS 6
HARK THE HERALD ANGELS SING	*Pye Golden Guinea*	11	*17 Dec 60*	6

HAMILTON, Joe FRANK and REYNOLDS — US

SINGLES:	HITS 1			WEEKS 6
FALLIN' IN LOVE	*Pye International*	33	*13 Sep 75*	6

George HAMILTON IV — US

SINGLES:	HITS 2			WEEKS 13
WHY DON'T THEY UNDERSTAND	*His Master's Voice*	22	*8 Mar 58*	9
I KNOW WHERE I'M GOIN'	*His Master's Voice*	29	*19 Jul 58*	1
I KNOW WHERE I'M GOIN' [RE]	*His Master's Voice*	23	*9 Aug 58*	3
ALBUMS:	**HITS 3**			**WEEKS 11**
CANADIAN PACIFIC	*RCA Victor*	45	*10 Apr 71*	1
REFLECTIONS	*Lotus*	25	*10 Feb 79*	9
SONGS FOR A WINTER'S NIGHT	*Ronco*	94	*13 Nov 82*	1

Lynne HAMILTON — UK

SINGLES:	HITS 1			WEEKS 11
ON THE INSIDE (THEME FROM 'PRISONER CELL BLOCK H') *Theme from the TV soap.*	*A.1*	3	*29 Apr 89*	11

Mike 'Tone' HAMILTON - See Ian McNABB

Russ HAMILTON — UK

SINGLES:	HITS 2			WEEKS 26
WE WILL MAKE LOVE	*Oriole*	2	*25 May 57*	20
WEDDING RING	*Oriole*	20	*28 Sep 57*	6

Above hit: Russ HAMILTON Johnny GREGORY and his Orchestra with the TONETTES.

Marvin HAMLISCH — US

SINGLES:	HITS 1			WEEKS 13
THE ENTERTAINER - MUSIC FROM "THE STING" *From the film 'The Sting'. Composed by Scott Joplin in 1901.* *Above hit: featuring Marvin HAMLISCH on Piano.*	*MCA*	25	*30 Mar 74*	13
ALBUMS:	**HITS 1**			**WEEKS 35**
THE STING [OST]	*MCA*	7	*23 Mar 74*	35

HAMMER — US

SINGLES:	HITS 12			WEEKS 68
U CAN'T TOUCH THIS *Based around Super Freak by Rick James.*	*Capitol*	3	*9 Jun 90*	16
HAVE YOU SEEN HER	*Capitol*	8	*6 Oct 90*	7
PRAY *Based around Prince's When Doves Cry.*	*Capitol*	8	*8 Dec 90*	10
HERE COMES THE HAMMER	*Capitol*	15	*23 Feb 91*	5
YO!! SWEETNESS	*Capitol*	16	*1 Jun 91*	5
(HAMMER HAMMER) THEY PUT ME IN THE MIX *Above 6: M.C. HAMMER.*	*Capitol*	20	*20 Jul 91*	4
2 LEGIT 2 QUIT *Above hit: HAMMER (Introducing SAJA).*	*Capitol*	60	*26 Oct 91*	2
ADDAMS GROOVE *From the film 'The Addams Family'.*	*Capitol*	4	*21 Dec 91*	9
DO NOT PASS ME BY *Above hit: HAMMER (featuring Tremaine HAWKINS introducing Trina JOHNSON & VOICES).*	*Capitol*	14	*21 Mar 92*	6
IT'S ALL GOOD	*RCA*	52	*12 Mar 94*	2
DON'T STOP	*RCA*	72	*13 Aug 94*	1

STRAIGHT TO MY FEET	*Priority*	57	*3 Jun 95*	1
From the film 'Street Fighter II'.				
Above hit: HAMMER/Deion SANDERS.				
ALBUMS:	**HITS 3**			**WEEKS 67**
PLEASE HAMMER DON'T HURT 'EM	*Capitol*	8	*28 Jul 90*	59
LET'S GET IT STARTED	*Capitol*	46	*6 Apr 91*	2
Above 2: M.C. HAMMER.				
TOO LEGIT TO QUIT	*Capitol*	41	*2 Nov 91*	6

Jan HAMMER — Czechoslovakia

SINGLES:	HITS 3			WEEKS 26
MIAMI VICE THEME	*MCA*	5	*12 Oct 85*	8
CROCKETT'S THEME	*MCA*	2	*19 Sep 87*	12
Above 2 from the TV series 'Miami Vice'.				
CROCKETT'S THEME [RI] / CHANCER	*MCA*	47	*1 Jun 91*	6
ALBUMS:	**HITS 1**			**WEEKS 12**
ESCAPE FROM TV	*MCA*	34	*14 Nov 87*	12

Albert HAMMOND — UK

THE SINGLES:	HITS 1			WEEKS 11
FREE ELECTRIC BAND	*Mums*	19	*30 Jun 73*	11

Beres HAMMOND – See Maxi PRIEST

Herbie HANCOCK — US

SINGLES:	HITS 6			WEEKS 41
I THOUGHT IT WAS YOU	*CBS*	15	*26 Aug 78*	9
YOU BET YOUR LOVE	*CBS*	18	*3 Feb 79*	10
ROCKIT	*Epic*	8	*30 Jul 83*	12
AUTODRIVE	*CBS*	33	*8 Oct 83*	4
FUTURE SHOCK	*CBS*	54	*21 Jan 84*	3
HARDROCK	*CBS*	65	*4 Aug 84*	3
ALBUMS:	**HITS 3**			**WEEKS 24**
SUNLIGHT	*CBS*	27	*9 Sep 78*	6
FEETS DON'T FAIL ME NOW	*CBS*	28	*24 Feb 79*	8
FUTURE SHOCK	*CBS*	27	*27 Aug 83*	10

Tony HANCOCK — UK

EPS:	HITS 1			WEEKS 39
LITTLE PIECES OF HANCOCK	*Pye*	6	*12 May 62*	39
ALBUMS:	**HITS 3**			**WEEKS 51**
THIS IS HANCOCK	*Pye*	2	*9 Apr 60*	22
PIECES OF HANCOCK	*Pye*	17	*12 Nov 60*	3
HANCOCK	*Pye*	12	*3 Mar 62*	23
THIS IS HANCOCK [RI]	*Pye Golden Guinea*	16	*14 Sep 63*	4

HANDBAGGERS — UK

SINGLES:	HITS 1			WEEKS 1
U FOUND OUT	*Tidy Trax*	55	*15 Jun 96*	1
Samples Depeche Modes' Just Can't Get Enough.				

Vernon HANDLEY – See Nigel KENNEDY

HANDLEY FAMILY — UK

SINGLES:	HITS 1			WEEKS 7
WAM BAM	*GL*	30	*7 Apr 73*	7

HANDS OF DR. TELENY – See Peter STRAKER and the HANDS OF DR. TELENY

HANI — US

SINGLES:	HITS 1			WEEKS 1
BABY WANTS TO RIDE	*Neo*	70	*11 Mar 00*	1

Jayn HANNA — UK

SINGLES:	HITS 2			WEEKS 2
LOVELIGHT (RIDE ON A LOVE TRAIN)	*VC Recordings*	42	*13 Apr 96*	1
LOST WITHOUT YOU	*VC Recordings*	44	*1 Feb 97*	1

HANNAH – See MAN WITH NO NAME

HANNAH — UK

SINGLES:	HITS 1			WEEKS 2
OUR KIND OF LOVE	*Telstar*	41	*21 Oct 00*	2
From the Ben Elton/Andrew Lloyd Webber musical 'The Beautiful Game'.				

HANNAH and Her SISTERS - See Hannah JONES; PJB Featuring HANNAH and Her SISTERS

Bo HANNSON — Sweden

ALBUMS:	HITS 1			WEEKS 2
LORD OF THE RINGS	*Charisma*	34	*18 Nov 72*	2

HANOI ROCKS — UK/Finland

SINGLES:	HITS 1			WEEKS 2
UP AROUND THE BEND	*CBS*	61	*7 Jul 84*	2
ALBUMS:	**HITS 2**			**WEEKS 4**
BACK TO MYSTERY CITY	Lick	87	*11 Jun 83*	1
TWO STEPS FROM THE MOVE	*CBS*	28	*20 Oct 84*	3

HANSON — US

SINGLES:	HITS 6			WEEKS 47
MMMBOP *First debut single to simultaneously top the UK & US single chart.*	*Mercury*	1	*7 Jun 97*	13
WHERE'S THE LOVE	*Mercury*	4	*13 Sep 97*	9
I WILL COME TO YOU	*Mercury*	5	*22 Nov 97*	9
WEIRD *From the film 'The Borrowers'.*	*Mercury*	19	*28 Mar 98*	5
THINKING OF YOU	*Mercury*	23	*4 Jul 98*	6
THINKING OF YOU [RE]	*Mercury*	69	*5 Sep 98*	1
IF ONLY *Features John Popper of Blues Traveler on harmonica.*	*Mercury*	15	*29 Apr 00*	4
ALBUMS:	**HITS 3**			**WEEKS 31**
MIDDLE OF NOWHERE	*Mercury*	1	*21 Jun 97*	29
3 CAR GARAGE - INDIE RECORDINGS 95-96 *Tracks culled from two earlier US-only releases.*	*Mercury*	39	*13 Jun 98*	1
THIS TIME AROUND	*Mercury*	33	*13 May 00*	1

John HANSON — UK

ALBUMS:	HITS 3			WEEKS 12
THE STUDENT PRINCE	*Pye*	17	*23 Apr 60*	1
THE STUDENT PRINCE / THE VAGABOND KING *'The Student Prince' was a 1954 film musical featuring the voice of Mario Lanza. 'The Vagabond King' was a musical from 1956.*	*Pye Golden Guinea*	9	*2 Sep 61*	7
JOHN HANSON SINGS 20 SHOWTIME GREATS	*K-Tel*	16	*10 Dec 77*	4

HAPPENINGS — US

SINGLES:	HITS 2			WEEKS 14
I GOT RHYTHM *Originally recorded by Red Nichols in 1931.*	*Stateside*	28	*20 May 67*	9
MY MAMMY *Originally recorded by Paul Whiteman in 1921. From 26 Aug 68 the US B.T Puppy label was credited on the chart.*	*Pye International*	34	*19 Aug 67*	5

HAPPY CLAPPERS — UK

SINGLES:	HITS 4			WEEKS 19
I BELIEVE	*Shindig*	21	*3 Jun 95*	3
HOLD ON	*Shindig*	27	*26 Aug 95*	2
I BELIEVE [RI]	*Shindig*	7	*18 Nov 95*	8
CAN'T HELP IT	*Coliseum*	18	*15 Jun 96*	3
NEVER AGAIN	*Coliseum*	49	*21 Dec 96*	1
I BELIEVE 97 [RM] *Remixed by Sash.*	*Coalition*	28	*22 Nov 97*	2

HAPPY MONDAYS — UK

SINGLES:	HITS 10			WEEKS 53
W.F.L. (WROTE FOR LUCK)	*Factory*	68	*30 Sep 89*	2
MADCHESTER RAVE ON [EP] *Lead track: Hallelujah. From 13 Jan 90 repackaged as a remixed version climbing back up to No. 22.*	*Factory*	19	*25 Nov 89*	14
STEP ON *Above hit: HAPPY MONDAYS Guest Vocal: ROWETTA.*	*Factory*	5	*7 Apr 90*	11
LAZYITIS - ONE ARMED BOXER *Above hit: HAPPY MONDAYS and Karl DENVER.*	*Factory*	46	*9 Jun 90*	3
KINKY AFRO	*Factory*	5	*20 Oct 90*	7
LOOSE FIT	*Factory*	17	*9 Mar 91*	7
JUDGE FUDGE	*Factory*	24	*30 Nov 91*	3
STINKIN' THINKIN'	*Factory*	31	*19 Sep 92*	3
SUNSHINE AND LOVE	*Factory*	62	*21 Nov 92*	1
THE BOYS ARE BACK IN TOWN	*London*	24	*22 May 99*	2

ALBUMS:	HITS 6			WEEKS 55
BUMMED	*Factory*	59	*27 Jan 90*	14
PILLS 'N' THRILLS AND BELLYACHES	*Factory*	4	*17 Nov 90*	29
HAPPY MONDAYS – LIVE	*Factory*	21	*12 Oct 91*	3
. . . YES PLEASE!	*Factory*	14	*10 Oct 92*	3
LOADS – THE BEST OF THE HAPPY MONDAYS	*Factory*	41	*18 Nov 95*	2
GREATEST HITS	*London*	11	*5 Jun 99*	4

Paul HARDCASTLE — UK

(See also Direct Drive; First Light; Silent Underdog.)

SINGLES:	HITS 11			WEEKS 66
YOU'RE THE ONE FOR ME – DAYBREAK – A.M.	*Total Control*	41	*7 Apr 84*	4
Above hit: Paul HARDCASTLE vocals by Kevin HENRY.				
GUILTY	*Total Control*	55	*28 Jul 84*	3
RAIN FOREST	*BlueBird*	41	*22 Sep 84*	5
EAT YOUR HEART OUT	*Cooltempo*	59	*17 Nov 84*	4
Above hit: Paul HARDCASTLE vocals by Kevin HENRY.				
19	*Chrysalis*	1	*4 May 85*	16
19 was the average age of an American soldier in the Vietnam war.				
RAIN FOREST [RI]	*BlueBird*	53	*15 Jun 85*	4
JUST FOR MONEY	*Chrysalis*	19	*9 Nov 85*	5
Features the voices of Laurence Olivier, Bob Hoskins, Ed O'Ross and AlanTalbot.				
DON'T WASTE MY TIME	*Chrysalis*	8	*1 Feb 86*	11
Above hit: Paul HARDCASTLE Lead vocals – Carol KENYON				
FOOLIN' YOURSELF	*Chrysalis*	51	*21 Jun 86*	3
Above hit: Paul HARDCASTLE introducing Kevin HENRY.				
THE WIZARD	*Chrysalis*	15	*11 Oct 86*	6
Theme to BBC TV's 'Top Of The Pops'.				
WALK IN THE NIGHT	*Chrysalis*	54	*9 Apr 88*	3
40 YEARS	*Chrysalis*	53	*4 Jun 88*	2

ALBUMS:	HITS 1			WEEKS 5
PAUL HARDCASTLE	*Chrysalis*	53	*30 Nov 85*	5

HARDCORE RHYTHM TEAM — UK

SINGLES:	HITS 1			WEEKS 1
HARDCORE – THE FINAL CONFLICT	*Furious*	69	*14 Mar 92*	1

Duane HARDEN – See POWERHOUSE featuring Duane HARDEN; Armand VAN HELDEN

HARDFLOOR — Germany

SINGLES:	HITS 2			WEEKS 6
HARDTRANCE ACPERIENCE [EP]	*Harthouse UK*	56	*26 Dec 92*	4
Various mixes of the track Acperience.				
TRANCESCRIPT	*Harthouse UK*	72	*10 Apr 93*	1
ACPERIENCE [RM]	*Eye-Q*	60	*25 Oct 97*	1
Remixed by Dex and Jonsey.				

ALBUMS:	HITS 1			WEEKS 1
HOME RUN	*Harthouse*	68	*29 Jun 96*	1

Ronan HARDIMAN — Ireland

ALBUMS:	HITS 1			WEEKS 8
MICHAEL FLATLEY'S LORD OF THE DANCE	*PolyGram TV*	37	*2 Nov 96*	8

Tim HARDIN — US

SINGLES:	HITS 1			WEEKS 1
HANG ON A DREAM	*Verve*	50	*7 Jan 67*	1

Carolyn HARDING – See PROSPECT PARK Featuring Carolyn HARDING

Mike HARDING — UK

SINGLES:	HITS 1			WEEKS 8
ROCHDALE COWBOY	*Rubber*	22	*2 Aug 75*	8

ALBUMS:	HITS 4			WEEKS 24
MRS 'ARDIN'S KID	*Rubber*	24	*30 Aug 75*	6
ONE MAN SHOW	*Philips*	19	*10 Jul 76*	10
OLD FOUR EYES IS BACK	*Philips*	31	*11 Jun 77*	6
CAPTAIN PARALYTIC AND THE BROWN ALE COWBOY	*Philips*	60	*24 Jun 78*	2

Francoise HARDY — France

SINGLES:	HITS 3			WEEKS 26
TOUS LES GARCONS ET LES FILLES	*Pye*	36	*27 Jun 64*	7
HOWEVER MUCH (ET MEME)	*Pye*	31	*9 Jan 65*	4
ALL OVER THE WORLD	*Pye*	16	*27 Mar 65*	15

EPS:	HITS 2			WEEKS 23
C'EST FAB!	*Pye*	5	*4 Jul 64*	21
C'EST FRANCOISE	*Pye*	18	*10 Oct 64*	2

Tynetta HARE - See Joey B. ELLIS

Niki HARE - See SNAP!

Morten HARKET — Norway

SINGLES:	HITS 1			WEEKS 1
A KIND OF CHRISTMAS CARD	*Warner Brothers*	53	*19 Aug 95*	1

HARLEM COMMUNITY CHOIR - See John LENNON

HARLEQUIN 4'S - See BUNKER KRU/HARLEQUIN 4'S

Steve HARLEY and COCKNEY REBEL — UK

SINGLES:	HITS 9			WEEKS 69
JUDY TEEN	*EMI*	5	*11 May 74*	11
MR. SOFT	*EMI*	8	*10 Aug 74*	9
Above 2: COCKNEY REBEL.				
MAKE ME SMILE (COME UP AND SEE ME)	*EMI*	1	*8 Feb 75*	9
MR. RAFFLES (MAN, IT WAS MEAN)	*EMI*	13	*7 Jun 75*	6
HERE COMES THE SUN	*EMI*	10	*31 Jul 76*	7
Originally recorded by the Beatles.				
(I BELIEVE) LOVE'S A PRIMA DONNA	*EMI*	41	*6 Nov 76*	4
FREEDOM'S PRISONER	*EMI*	58	*20 Oct 79*	3
Above hit: Steve HARLEY.				
BALLERINA (PRIMA DONNA)	*Stiletto*	51	*13 Aug 83*	5
THE PHANTOM OF THE OPERA	*Polydor*	7	*11 Jan 86*	10
From the musical 'The Phantom Of The Opera'.				
Above hit: Sarah BRIGHTMAN and Steve HARLEY.				
MAKE ME SMILE (COME UP AND SEE ME) [RI-1ST]	*EMI*	46	*25 Apr 92*	2
MAKE ME SMILE (COME UP AND SEE ME) [R1-2ND]	*EMI*	33	*30 Dec 95*	3
Featured in the Carlsberg lager TV commercial.				

ALBUMS:	HITS 5			WEEKS 52
THE PSYCHOMODO	*EMI*	8	*22 Jun 74*	20
Above hit: COCKNEY REBEL.				
THE BEST YEARS OF OUR LIVES	*EMI*	4	*22 Mar 75*	19
TIMELESS FLIGHT	*EMI*	18	*14 Feb 76*	6
LOVE'S A PRIMA DONNA	*EMI*	28	*27 Nov 76*	3
FACE TO FACE - A LIVE RECORDING	*EMI*	40	*30 Jul 77*	4
Live recordings dating from 1974/75.				

HARLEY QUINNE — UK

SINGLES:	HITS 1			WEEKS 8
NEW ORLEANS	*Bell*	19	*14 Oct 72*	8

HARMONIUM — UK

(See also Blowing Free; Hypnosis; In Tune; Raindance; School Of Excellence.)

ALBUMS:	HITS 1			WEEKS 4
SPIRIT OF TRANQUILITY	*Global Television*	25	*21 Mar 98*	4

HARMONIX — UK

SINGLES:	HITS 1			WEEKS 2
LANDSLIDE	*Deconstruction*	28	*30 Mar 96*	2
Samples U2's Where The Streets Have No Name.				

HARMONY GRASS — UK

SINGLES:	HITS 1			WEEKS 7
MOVE IN A LITTLE CLOSER BABY	*RCA Victor*	24	*1 Feb 69*	7

Ben HARPER — US

SINGLES:	HITS 1			WEEKS 1
FADED	*Virgin*	54	*4 Apr 98*	1

Charlie HARPER — UK

SINGLES:	HITS 1			WEEKS 1
BARMY LONDON ARMY	*Gems*	68	*19 Jul 80*	1

Roy HARPER — UK

ALBUMS:	HITS 4			WEEKS 9
VALENTINE	*Harvest*	27	*9 Mar 74*	1
H.Q.	*Harvest*	31	*21 Jun 75*	2

BULLINAMINGVASE	*Harvest*	25	*12 Mar 77*	2
WHATEVER HAPPENED TO JUGULA?	*Beggars Banquet*	44	*16 Mar 85*	4

Above hit: Roy HARPER with Jimmy PAGE.

HARPERS BIZARRE — US

SINGLES:	HITS 2			WEEKS 13
59TH STREET BRIDGE SONG (FEELIN' GROOVY) *Originally recorded by Simon and Garfunkel.*	*Warner Brothers*	34	*1 Apr 67*	7
ANYTHING GOES *Written by Cole Porter in 1934.*	*Warner Brothers*	33	*7 Oct 67*	6

HARPO — Sweden

SINGLES:	HITS 1			WEEKS 6
MOVIE STAR *Features Agnetha and Frida from Abba on backing vocals.*	*DJM*	24	*17 Apr 76*	6

Anita HARRIS — UK

SINGLES:	HITS 4			WEEKS 50
JUST LOVING YOU	*CBS*	6	*2 Jul 67*	30
THE PLAYGROUND	*CBS*	46	*14 Oct 67*	3
ANNIVERSARY WALTZ	*CBS*	21	*27 Jan 68*	9
DREAM A LITTLE DREAM OF ME	*CBS*	33	*17 Aug 68*	8
ALBUMS:	**HITS 1**			**WEEKS 5**
JUST LOVING YOU	*CBS*	29	*27 Jan 68*	5

Emmylou HARRIS — US

(See also Dolly Parton, Linda Ronstadt and Emmylou Harris.)

SINGLES:	HITS 1			WEEKS 6
HERE, THERE & EVERYWHERE *Originally recorded by the Beatles.*	*Reprise*	30	*6 Mar 76*	6
ALBUMS:	**HITS 8**			**WEEKS 32**
ELITE HOTEL	*Reprise*	17	*14 Feb 76*	11
LUXURY LINER	*Warner Brothers*	17	*29 Jan 77*	6
QUARTER MOON IN A TEN CENT TOWN	*Warner Brothers*	40	*4 Feb 78*	5
HER BEST SONGS	*K-Tel*	36	*29 Mar 80*	3
EVANGELINE	*Warner Brothers*	53	*14 Feb 81*	4
WRECKING BALL	*Grapevine*	46	*7 Oct 95*	1
SPYBOY *Live recordings from the end of her 1997 tour.*	*Grapevine*	57	*29 Aug 98*	1
RED DIRT GIRL	*Grapevine*	45	*30 Sep 00*	1

Jet HARRIS — UK

(See also Jet Harris and Tony Meehan.)

SINGLES:	HITS 2			WEEKS 18
BESAME MUCHO	*Decca*	22	*26 May 62*	7
MAIN TITLE THEME (FROM "THE MAN WITH THE GOLDEN ARM") *Theme from the film.*	*Decca*	12	*18 Aug 62*	11

Jet HARRIS and Tony MEEHAN — UK

(See also Jet Harris; Tony Meehan.)

SINGLES:	HITS 3			WEEKS 39
DIAMONDS	*Decca*	1	*12 Jan 63*	13
SCARLET O'HARA	*Decca*	2	*27 Apr 63*	13
APPLEJACK	*Decca*	4	*7 Sep 63*	13
EPS:	**HITS 1**			**WEEKS 21**
JET AND TONY	*Decca*	3	*29 Jun 63*	21

Keith HARRIS and ORVILLE — UK

SINGLES:	HITS 3			WEEKS 20
ORVILLE'S SONG	*BBC*	4	*18 Dec 82*	11
COME TO MY PARTY *Above hit: Keith HARRIS and ORVILLE with DIPPY.*	*BBC*	44	*24 Dec 83*	4
WHITE CHRISTMAS	*Columbia*	40	*14 Dec 85*	5
ALBUMS:	**HITS 1**			**WEEKS 1**
AT THE END OF THE RAINBOW *Above hit: Keith HARRIS, ORVILLE and CUDDLES.*	*BBC*	92	*4 Jun 83*	1

Major HARRIS — US

SINGLES:	HITS 2			WEEKS 9
LOVE WON'T LET ME WAIT	*Atlantic*	37	*9 Aug 75*	7
ALL MY LIFE	*London*	61	*5 Nov 83*	2

Max HARRIS with his Group — UK

SINGLES:	HITS 1			WEEKS 10
GURNEY SLADE *From the TV series 'The Strange World Of Gurney Slade'.*	*Fontana*	11	*3 Dec 60*	10

Rahni HARRIS and F.L.O. vocals by T. HARRINGTON and O. RASBURY — US

SINGLES:	HITS 1			WEEKS 7
SIX MILLION STEPS (WEST RUNS SOUTH)	*Mercury*	43	*16 Dec 78*	7

Richard HARRIS — Ireland

SINGLES:	HITS 1			WEEKS 18
MACARTHUR PARK	*RCA Victor*	4	*29 Jun 68*	12
MACARTHUR PARK [RI]	*Probe*	38	*8 Jul 72*	6

Rochelle HARRIS - See ANGELHEART

Rolf HARRIS — Australia

SINGLES:	HITS 9			WEEKS 77
TIE ME KANGAROO DOWN SPORT *Above hit: Rolf HARRIS with his Wobble Board and the RHYTHM SPINNERS.*	*Columbia*	9	*23 Jul 60*	13
SUN ARISE	*Columbia*	3	*27 Oct 62*	16
JOHNNY DAY	*Columbia*	44	*2 Mar 63*	2
BLUER THAN BLUE	*Columbia*	30	*19 Apr 69*	8
TWO LITTLE BOYS *Originally recorded in 1903 by Harry Lauder about the American Civil War.*	*Columbia*	1	*22 Nov 69*	24
TWO LITTLE BOYS [RE]	*Columbia*	50	*20 Jun 70*	1
STAIRWAY TO HEAVEN	*Vertigo*	7	*13 Feb 93*	6
BOHEMIAN RHAPSODY	*Living Beat*	50	*1 Jun 96*	1
SUN ARISE [RR]	*EMI*	26	*25 Oct 97*	3
FINE DAY	*Tommy Boy Silver Label*	24	*14 Oct 00*	3
EPS:	**HITS 1**			**WEEKS 2**
ROLF HARRIS AND SHAMUS O'SEAN THE LEPRECHAUN	*Columbia*	9	*22 Oct 66*	2
ALBUMS:	**HITS 1**			**WEEKS 1**
CAN YOU TELL WHAT IT IS YET?	*EMI*	70	*1 Nov 97*	1

Ronnie HARRIS — UK

SINGLES:	HITS 1			WEEKS 3
THE STORY OF TINA	*Columbia*	12	*25 Sep 54*	3

Sam HARRIS — US

SINGLES:	HITS 1			WEEKS 2
HEARTS ON FIRE / OVER THE RAINBOW *The second white male solo to hit on Motown after R. Dean Taylor.*	*Motown*	67	*9 Feb 85*	2

Simon HARRIS — UK

(See also Ambassadors Of Funk featuring MC Mario; World Warrior.)

SINGLES:	HITS 5			WEEKS 17
BASS (HOW LOW CAN YOU GO)	*ffrr*	12	*19 Mar 88*	6
HERE COMES THAT SOUND	*ffrr*	38	*29 Oct 88*	4
(I'VE GOT YOUR) PLEASURE CONTROL *Above hit: Simon HARRIS featuring Lonnie GORDON.*	*ffrr*	60	*24 Jun 89*	3
ANOTHER MONSTERJAM *Above hit: Simon HARRIS featuring EINSTEIN.*	*ffrr*	65	*18 Nov 89*	1
RAGGA HOUSE (ALL NIGHT LONG) *Above hit: Simon HARRIS Starring DADDY FREDDY.*	*Living Beat*	56	*10 Mar 90*	3

George HARRISON — UK

SINGLES:	HITS 10			WEEKS 82
MY SWEET LORD *Originally recorded by Billy Preston and backing vocals from Phil Spector.*	*Apple*	1	*23 Jan 71*	17
BANGLA-DESH	*Apple*	10	*14 Aug 71*	9
GIVE ME LOVE (GIVE ME PEACE ON EARTH)	*Apple*	8	*2 Jun 73*	10
DING DONG	*Apple*	38	*21 Dec 74*	5
YOU	*Apple*	38	*11 Oct 75*	5
BLOW AWAY	*Dark Horse*	51	*10 Mar 79*	5
ALL THOSE YEARS AGO *A tribute to John Lennon.*	*Dark Horse*	13	*23 May 81*	7
GOT MY MIND SET ON YOU *Originally recorded by James Ray.*	*Dark Horse*	2	*24 Oct 87*	14
WHEN WE WAS FAB	*Dark Horse*	25	*6 Feb 88*	7
THIS IS LOVE	*Dark Horse*	55	*25 Jun 88*	3
ALBUMS:	**HITS 7**			**WEEKS 78**
ALL THINGS MUST PASS	*Apple*	4	*26 Dec 70*	24

LIVING IN THE MATERIAL WORLD	*Apple*	2	*7 Jul 73*	12
EXTRA TEXTURE (READ ALL ABOUT IT)	*Apple*	16	*18 Oct 75*	4
THIRTY THREE AND A THIRD	*Dark Horse*	35	*18 Dec 76*	4
GEORGE HARRISON	*Dark Horse*	39	*17 Mar 79*	5
SOMEWHERE IN ENGLAND	*Dark Horse*	13	*13 Jun 81*	4
CLOUD NINE	*Dark Horse*	10	*14 Nov 87*	23
ALL THINGS MUST PASS [RI]	*Parlophone*	68	*3 Feb 00*	2
30th anniversary re-issue with extra tracks.				

Jane HARRISON — UK

ALBUMS:	HITS 1			WEEKS 1
NEW DAY	*Stylus*	70	*4 Feb 89*	1

Noel HARRISON — UK

SINGLES:	HITS 1			WEEKS 14
THE WINDMILLS OF YOUR MIND	*Reprise*	8	*1 Mar 69*	14
From the film 'The Thomas Crown Affair'.				

Deborah HARRY — US

SINGLES:	HITS 10			WEEKS 52
BACKFIRED	*Chrysalis*	32	*1 Aug 81*	6
FRENCH KISSIN' IN THE USA	*Chrysalis*	8	*15 Nov 86*	10
FREE TO FALL	*Chrysalis*	46	*28 Feb 87*	4
IN LOVE WITH LOVE	*Chrysalis*	45	*9 May 87*	5
Above 4: Debbie HARRY.				
I WANT THAT MAN	*Chrysalis*	13	*7 Oct 89*	10
BRITE SIDE	*Chrysalis*	59	*2 Dec 89*	4
SWEET AND LOW	*Chrysalis*	57	*31 Mar 90*	3
WELL, DID YOU EVAH!	*Chrysalis*	42	*5 Jan 91*	4
Above hit: Deborah HARRY and Iggy POP.				
I CAN SEE CLEARLY	*Chrysalis*	23	*3 Jul 93*	4
STRIKE ME PINK	*Chrysalis*	46	*18 Sep 93*	2

ALBUMS:	HITS 6			WEEKS 53
KOO KOO	*Chrysalis*	6	*8 Aug 81*	7
ROCKBIRD	*Chrysalis*	31	*29 Nov 86*	11
Above 2 Debbie HARRY.				
ONCE MORE INTO THE BLEACH	*Chrysalis*	50	*17 Dec 88*	4
Remix album of Debbie Harry's solo and group material.				
Above hit: Debbie HARRY and BLONDIE.				
DEF DUMB AND BLONDE	*Chrysalis*	12	*28 Oct 89*	7
THE COMPLETE PICTURE - THE VERY BEST OF DEBORAH HARRY AND BLONDIE	*Chrysalis*	3	*16 Mar 91*	22
Above hit: Deborah HARRY and BLONDIE.				
DEBRAVATION	*Chrysalis*	24	*31 Jul 93*	2

HARRY J. ALL STARS — Jamaica

SINGLES:	HITS 1			WEEKS 25
LIQUIDATOR	*Harry J*	9	*25 Oct 69*	20
LIQUIDATOR [RI]	*Trojan*	42	*29 Mar 80*	5
[AA] listed with Long Shot Kick De Bucket by the Pioneers.				

Keef HARTLEY BAND — UK

ALBUMS:	HITS 1			WEEKS 3
THE TIME IS NEAR	*Deram*	41	*5 Sep 70*	3

Richard HARTLEY - See Michael REED ORCHESTRA

Dan HARTMAN — US

SINGLES:	HITS 5			WEEKS 34
INSTANT REPLAY	*Blue Sky*	8	*21 Oct 78*	15
THIS IS IT	*Blue Sky*	17	*13 Jan 79*	8
SECOND NATURE	*MCA*	66	*18 May 85*	2
I CAN DREAM ABOUT YOU	*MCA*	12	*24 Aug 85*	8
Original release reached No. 78 in 1984.				
KEEP THE FIRE BURNIN'	*Columbia*	49	*1 Apr 95*	1
Above hit: Dan HARTMAN Starring Loleatta HOLLOWAY.				

Alex HARVEY - See SENSATIONAL ALEX HARVEY BAND

Brian HARVEY — UK

(See also True Steppers.)

SINGLES:	HITS 2			WEEKS 5
STRAIGHT UP (NO BENDS)	*Edel*	26	*28 Apr 01*	2
LOVING YOU (OLE OLE OLE)	*Edel*	20	*27 Oct 01*	3
Above hit: Brian HARVEY and the REFUGEE CREW.				

HARVEY – See OXIDE and NEUTRINO

Lee HARVEY – See N*E*R*D featuring Lee HARVEY and VITA

PJ HARVEY — UK

(See also John Parish + Polly Jean Harvey; Various Artists (EPs) 'The Help EP'.)

SINGLES:	HITS 13			WEEKS 23
SHEELA-NA-GIG	*Too Pure*	69	*29 Feb 92*	1
50 FT QUEENIE	*Island*	27	*1 May 93*	2
MAN-SIZE	*Island*	42	*17 Jul 93*	2
DOWN BY THE WATER	*Island*	38	*18 Feb 95*	2
C'MON BILLY	*Island*	29	*22 Jul 95*	2
SEND HIS LOVE TO ME	*Island*	34	*28 Oct 95*	2
HENRY LEE	*Mute*	36	*9 Mar 96*	1
Based on a traditional folk tale.				
Above hit: Nick CAVE and PJ HARVEY and the BAD SEEDS.				
BROKEN HOMES	*Island*	25	*30 May 98*	2
[AA] listed with Money Greedy by Tricky.				
Above hit: TRICKY featuring Polly Jean HARVEY.				
A PERFECT DAY ELISE	*Island*	25	*26 Sep 98*	2
THE WIND	*Island*	29	*23 Jan 99*	2
GOOD FORTUNE	*Island*	41	*25 Nov 00*	2
A PLACE CALLED HOME	*Island*	43	*10 Mar 01*	2
THIS IS LOVE	*Island*	41	*20 Oct 01*	1

ALBUMS:	HITS 6			WEEKS 30
DRY	*Too Pure*	11	*11 Apr 92*	5
RID OF ME	*Island*	3	*8 May 93*	4
4-TRACK DEMOS	*Island*	19	*30 Oct 93*	2
Budget album of demos from the time of Rid Of Me.				
TO BRING YOU MY LOVE	*Island*	12	*11 Mar 95*	6
IS THIS DESIRE?	*Island*	17	*10 Oct 98*	2
STORIES FROM THE CITY STORIES FROM THE SEA	*Island*	23	*4 Nov 00*	11

Richard HARVEY and FRIENDS — UK

ALBUMS:	HITS 1			WEEKS 1
EVENING FALLS	*Telstar*	72	*6 May 89*	1

Steve HARVEY — UK

SINGLES:	HITS 2			WEEKS 6
SOMETHING SPECIAL	*London*	46	*28 May 83*	4
TONIGHT	*London*	63	*29 Oct 83*	2

HARVEY DANGER — US

SINGLES:	HITS 1			WEEKS 1
FLAGPOLE SITTA	*Slash*	57	*1 Aug 98*	1

Gordon HASKELL — UK

SINGLES:	HITS 1			WEEKS 1
HOW WONDERFUL YOU ARE	*Flying Sparks*	2	*29 Dec 01*	1

David HASSELHOFF — US

SINGLES:	HITS 1			WEEKS 2
IF I COULD ONLY SAY GOODBYE	*Arista*	35	*13 Nov 93*	2

Tony HATCH — UK

(See also Brook Brothers.)

SINGLES:	HITS 1			WEEKS 1
OUT OF THIS WORLD	*Pye*	50	*6 Oct 62*	1

Linzi HATELEY, David EASTER and Johnny AMOBI – See Jason DONOVAN

Juliana HATFIELD — US

SINGLES:	HITS 2			WEEKS 2
MY SISTER	*East West*	71	*11 Sep 93*	1
Above hit: Juliana HATFIELD THREE.				
UNIVERSAL HEART-BEAT	*East West*	65	*18 Mar 95*	1

ALBUMS:	HITS 2			WEEKS 3
BECOME WHAT YOU ARE	*East West*	44	*14 Aug 93*	2
Above hit: Juliana HATFIELD THREE.				
ONLY EVERYTHING	*East West*	59	*8 Apr 95*	1

HATFIELD AND THE NORTH — UK

ALBUMS:	HITS 1			WEEKS 1
ROTTERS CLUB	*Virgin*	43	*29 Mar 75*	1

Donny HATHAWAY – See Roberta FLACK and Donny HATHAWAY

Lalah HATHAWAY — US

SINGLES:	HITS 3			WEEKS 10
HEAVEN KNOWS	*Virgin America*	66	*1 Sep 90*	2
BABY DON'T CRY	*Virgin America*	54	*2 Feb 91*	3
FAMILY AFFAIR	*Ten Records*	37	*27 Jul 91*	5
Above hit: B.E.F. featuring Lalah HATHAWAY.				

HATIRAS featuring SLARTA JOHN — UK/Canada

SINGLES:	HITS 1			WEEKS 5
SPACED INVADER	*Defected*	14	*27 Jan 01*	5

HAVANA — UK

SINGLES:	HITS 1			WEEKS 1
ETHNIC PRAYER	*Limbo*	71	*6 Mar 93*	1

HAVEN — UK

SINGLES:	HITS 1			WEEKS 1
LET IT LIVE	*Radiate*	72	*22 Sep 01*	1

Nic HAVERSON — UK

SINGLES:	HITS 1			WEEKS 3
HEAD OVER HEELS	*Telstar*	48	*30 Jan 93*	3
From the Carlton ITV series of the same name.				

Chesney HAWKES — UK

SINGLES:	HITS 4			WEEKS 25
THE ONE AND ONLY	*Chrysalis*	1	*23 Feb 91*	16
Written by Nik Kershaw.				
I'M A MAN NOT A BOY	*Chrysalis*	27	*22 Jun 91*	5
SECRETS OF THE HEART	*Chrysalis*	57	*28 Sep 91*	3
Above 3 from the film 'Buddy's Song'.				
WHAT'S WRONG WITH THIS PICTURE?	*Chrysalis*	63	*29 May 93*	1
ALBUMS:	**HITS 1**			**WEEKS 8**
BUDDY'S SONG [OST]	*Chrysalis*	18	*13 Apr 91*	8

Edwin HAWKINS SINGERS. Soloist: Dorothy Combs MORRISON — US

SINGLES:	HITS 1			WEEKS 13
OH HAPPY DAY	*Buddah*	2	*24 May 69*	12
Produced by Paul Anka.				
OH HAPPY DAY [RE]	*Buddah*	43	*23 Aug 69*	1

Screamin' Jay HAWKINS — US

SINGLES:	HITS 1			WEEKS 3
HEART ATTACK AND VINE	*Columbia*	42	*3 Apr 93*	3
Featured in the Levi's Jeans TV commercial. Originally recorded by Tom Waits from his 1980 album of the same name.				

Sophie B. HAWKINS — US

SINGLES:	HITS 6			WEEKS 37
DAMN I WISH I WAS YOUR LOVER	*Columbia*	14	*4 Jul 92*	9
CALIFORNIA HERE I COME	*Columbia*	53	*12 Sep 92*	3
I WANT YOU	*Columbia*	49	*6 Feb 93*	2
RIGHT BESIDE YOU	*Columbia*	13	*13 Aug 94*	12
DON'T DON'T TELL ME NO	*Columbia*	36	*26 Nov 94*	5
AS I LAY ME DOWN	*Columbia*	24	*11 Mar 95*	6
ALBUMS:	**HITS 2**			**WEEKS 6**
TONGUES AND TAILS	*Columbia*	46	*1 Aug 92*	2
WHALER	*Columbia*	46	*3 Sep 94*	4

Ted HAWKINS — US

ALBUMS:	HITS 1			WEEKS 1
HAPPY HOUR	*Windows*	82	*18 Apr 87*	1

Tremaine HAWKINS – See HAMMER

HAWKLORDS – See HAWKWIND

Kirsty HAWKSHAW - See BT

HAWKWIND — UK

SINGLES:	HITS 3			WEEKS 28
SILVER MACHINE	*United Artists*	3	*1 Jul 72*	15
Live recording from the Roundtree, 13 Feb 72.				
URBAN GUERRILLA	*United Artists*	39	*11 Aug 73*	3
SILVER MACHINE [RE-1ST]	*United Artists*	34	*21 Oct 78*	5
SHOT DOWN IN THE NIGHT	*Bronze*	59	*19 Jul 80*	3
SILVER MACHINE [RE-2ND]	*United Artists*	67	*15 Jan 83*	2
ALBUMS:	**HITS 22**			**WEEKS 101**
IN SEARCH OF SPACE	*United Artists*	18	*6 Nov 71*	19
DOREMI FASOL LATIDO	*United Artists*	14	*23 Dec 72*	5
SPACE RITUAL ALIVE	*United Artists*	9	*2 Jun 73*	5
From their tour in Dec 73.				
HALL OF THE MOUNTAIN GRILL	*United Artists*	16	*21 Sep 74*	5
WARRIOR ON THE EDGE OF TIME	*United Artists*	13	*31 May 75*	7
ROAD HAWKS	*United Artists*	34	*24 Apr 76*	4
Compilation.				
ASTONISHING SOUNDS, AMAZING MUSIC	*Charisma*	33	*18 Sep 76*	5
QUARK STRANGENESS AND CHARM	*Charisma*	30	*9 Jul 77*	6
25 YEARS ON	*Charisma*	48	*21 Oct 78*	3
Above hit: HAWKLORDS.				
PXR 5	*Charisma*	59	*30 Jun 79*	5
LIVE 1979	*Bronze*	15	*9 Aug 80*	7
Live recordings from St. Albans, Nov 79.				
LEVITATION	*Bronze*	21	*8 Nov 80*	4
SONIC ATTACK	*RCA*	19	*24 Oct 81*	5
THE CHURCH OF HAWKWIND	*RCA*	26	*22 May 82*	6
CHOOSE YOUR MASQUES	*RCA*	29	*23 Oct 82*	5
ZONES	*Flicknife*	57	*5 Nov 83*	2
HAWKWIND	*Liberty*	75	*25 Feb 84*	1
Re-issue of their debut album from 1970.				
CHRONICLE OF THE BLACK SWORD	*Flicknife*	65	*16 Nov 85*	2
THE XENON CODEX	*GWR*	79	*14 May 88*	2
SPACE BANDITS	*GWR*	70	*6 Oct 90*	1
ELECTRIC TEPEE	*Essential*	53	*23 May 92*	1
IT IS THE BUSINESS OF THE FUTURE TO BE DANGEROUS	*Essential*	75	*6 Nov 93*	1

Bill HAYES — US

SINGLES:	HITS 1			WEEKS 9
BALLAD OF DAVY CROCKETT	*London*	2	*7 Jan 56*	9
From the Walt Disney film 'Davy Crockett'.				
Above hit: Bill HAYES with Archie BLEYER'S ORCHESTRA.				

Isaac HAYES — US

(See also Chef.)

SINGLES:	HITS 2			WEEKS 22
THEME FROM "SHAFT"	*Stax*	4	*4 Dec 71*	12
Theme from the film.				
DISCO CONNECTION	*ABC*	10	*3 Apr 76*	9
Above hit: Isaac HAYES MOVEMENT.				
THEME FROM SHAFT [RI]	*LaFace*	53	*30 Sep 00*	1
From the film of the same name (remade in 2000 with Samuel L. Jackson in the lead role).				
ALBUMS:	**HITS 2**			**WEEKS 14**
SHAFT [OST]	*Polydor*	17	*18 Dec 71*	13
BLACK MOSES	*Stax*	38	*12 Feb 72*	1

HAYSI FANTAYZEE — UK

SINGLES:	HITS 4			WEEKS 25
JOHN WAYNE IS BIG LEGGY	*Regard*	11	*24 Jul 82*	10
HOLY JOE	*Regard*	51	*13 Nov 82*	3
SHINY SHINY	*Regard*	16	*22 Jan 83*	10
SISTER FRICTION	*Regard*	62	*25 Jun 83*	2
ALBUMS:	**HITS 1**			**WEEKS 5**
BATTLE HYMNS FOR CHILDREN SINGING	*Regard*	53	*26 Feb 83*	5

Justin HAYWARD — UK

(See also Justin Hayward and John Lodge; Justin Hayward with Mike Batt and the London Philharmonic Orchestra.)

SINGLES:	HITS 1			WEEKS 13
FOREVER AUTUMN	*CBS*	5	*8 Jul 78*	13
Originally recorded by Vigrass and Osbourne.				
Above hit: From Jeff WAYNE'S "WAR OF THE WORLDS" featuring Justin HAYWARD.				

ALBUMS:	HITS 3			WEEKS 10
SONGWRITER	*Deram*	28	*5 Mar 77*	5
NIGHT FLIGHT	*Decca*	41	*19 Jul 80*	4
MOVING MOUNTAINS	*Towerbell*	78	*19 Oct 85*	1

Justin HAYWARD with Mike BATT and the LONDON PHILHARMONIC ORCHESTRA — UK

(See also Mike Batt; Justin Hayward; London Philharmonic Orchestra.)

ALBUMS:	HITS 1			WEEKS 7
CLASSIC BLUE	*Trax*	47	*28 Oct 89*	7

Justin HAYWARD and John LODGE — UK

(See also Justin Hayward; John Lodge.)

SINGLES:	HITS 1			WEEKS 7
BLUE GUITAR	*Threshold*	8	*25 Oct 75*	7
ALBUMS:	**HITS 1**			**WEEKS 18**
BLUE JAYS	*Threshold*	4	*29 Mar 75*	18

Leon HAYWOOD — US

SINGLES:	HITS 1			WEEKS 11
DON'T PUSH IT DON'T FORCE IT	*20th Century*	12	*15 Mar 80*	11

HAYWOODE — UK

SINGLES:	HITS 4			WEEKS 31
A TIME LIKE THIS	*CBS*	48	*17 Sep 83*	7
I CAN'T LET YOU GO	*CBS*	63	*29 Sep 84*	4
ROSES	*CBS*	65	*13 Apr 85*	3
GETTING CLOSER	*CBS*	67	*5 Oct 85*	2
ROSES [RI]	*CBS*	11	*21 Jun 86*	11
I CAN'T LET YOU GO [RI]	*CBS*	50	*13 Sep 86*	4

Ofra HAZA — Israel

SINGLES:	HITS 2			WEEKS 9
IM NIN'ALU	*WEA*	15	*30 Apr 88*	8
BABYLON	*warner.esp*	65	*3 Apr 99*	1
Above hit: BLACK DOG featuring Ofra HAZA.				

HAZIZA — Sweden

SINGLES:	HITS 1			WEEKS 1
ONE MORE	*Tidy Trax*	75	*28 Apr 01*	1

Lee HAZLEWOOD – See Nancy SINATRA and Lee HAZLEWOOD

Murray HEAD — UK

SINGLES:	HITS 2			WEEKS 15
SUPERSTAR	*MCA*	47	*29 Jan 72*	1
From the musical 'Jesus Christ Superstar'. This was a 4 -track maxi single, but only Superstar and I Don't Know How To Love Him by Yvonne Elliman/ Various Artists were credited.				
Above hit: Murray HEAD with the TRINIDAD SINGERS.				
ONE NIGHT IN BANGKOK	*RCA*	12	*10 Nov 84*	13
From the musical 'Chess'.				
ONE NIGHT IN BANGKOK [RE]	*RCA*	74	*16 Feb 85*	1

Roy HEAD — US

SINGLES:	HITS 1			WEEKS 5
TREAT HER RIGHT	*Vocalion*	30	*6 Nov 65*	5

HEADBANGERS — UK

SINGLES:	HITS 1			WEEKS 3
STATUS ROCK [M]	*Magnet*	60	*10 Oct 81*	3
Medley of Status Quo hits.				

HEADBOYS — UK

SINGLES:	HITS 1			WEEKS 8
THE SHAPE OF THINGS TO COME	*RSO*	45	*22 Sep 79*	8

HEADGIRL – See GIRLSCHOOOL; MOTORHEAD

Max HEADROOM – See ART OF NOISE

HEADS — UK

SINGLES:	HITS 1			WEEKS 4
AZTEC LIGHTNING - THEME FROM BBC WORLD CUP GRANDSTAND	*BBC*	45	*21 Jun 86*	4

HEADS with Shaun RYDER — UK/US

(See also Talking Heads.)

SINGLES:	HITS 1			WEEKS 1
DON'T TAKE MY KINDNESS FOR WEAKNESS	*Radioactive*	60	*9 Nov 96*	1

HEADSWIM — UK

SINGLES:	HITS 3			WEEKS 5
CRAWL	*Epic*	64	*25 Feb 95*	1
TOURNIQUET	*Epic*	30	*14 Feb 98*	3
BETTER MADE	*Epic*	42	*16 May 98*	1
ALBUMS:	**HITS 1**			**WEEKS 2**
DESPITE YOURSELF	*Epic*	24	*30 May 98*	2

Jeff HEALEY BAND — Canada

ALBUMS:	HITS 4			WEEKS 16
SEE THE LIGHT	*Arista*	58	*14 Jan 89*	7
HELL TO PAY	*Arista*	18	*9 Jun 90*	6
FEEL THIS	*Arista*	72	*28 Nov 92*	1
COVER TO COVER	*Arista*	50	*18 Mar 95*	2

Jeremy HEALY and AMOS — UK

(See also Amos.)

SINGLES:	HITS 2			WEEKS 7
STAMP!	*Positiva*	11	*12 Oct 96*	5
ARGENTINA	*Positiva*	30	*31 May 97*	2

Both songs were recorded to accompany John Galliano's fashion shows.

Imogen HEAP – See URBAN SPECIES

HEAR 'N AID — UK/US

SINGLES:	HITS 1			WEEKS 6
STARS	*Vertigo*	26	*19 Apr 86*	6

Charity record for famine relief in Africa.

HEAR'SAY — UK

SINGLES:	HITS 3			WEEKS 46
PURE AND SIMPLE	*Polydor*	1	*24 Mar 01*	25
From the ITV series 'Popstars'. Originally recorded by Girl Thing.				
THE WAY TO YOUR LOVE	*Polydor*	1	*7 Jul 01*	13
THE WAY TO YOUR LOVE [RE]	*Polydor*	60	*13 Oct 01*	4
EVERYBODY	*Polydor*	4	*8 Dec 01*	4
ALBUMS:	**HITS 2**			**WEEKS 27**
POPSTARS	*Polydor*	1	*7 Apr 01*	24
EVERYBODY	*Polydor*	24	*15 Dec 01*	3

HEART — US

SINGLES:	HITS 12			WEEKS 76
THESE DREAMS	*Capitol*	62	*29 Mar 86*	4
ALONE	*Capitol*	3	*13 Jun 87*	16
Originally recorded by I-Ten.				
WHO WILL YOU RUN TO	*Capitol*	30	*19 Sep 87*	7
THERE'S THE GIRL	*Capitol*	34	*12 Dec 87*	7
NEVER / THESE DREAMS [RI]	*Capitol*	8	*5 Mar 88*	9
WHAT ABOUT LOVE	*Capitol*	14	*14 May 88*	6
NOTHIN' AT ALL	*Capitol*	38	*22 Oct 88*	3
Original release reached No. 76 in 1986.				
ALL I WANNA DO IS MAKE LOVE TO YOU	*Capitol*	8	*24 Mar 90*	13
I DIDN'T WANT TO NEED YOU	*Capitol*	47	*28 Jul 90*	3
STRANDED	*Capitol*	60	*17 Nov 90*	2
YOU'RE THE VOICE	*Capitol*	56	*14 Sep 91*	2
Live recording.				
WILL YOU BE THERE (IN THE MORNING)	*Capitol*	19	*20 Nov 93*	4
ALBUMS:	**HITS 9**			**WEEKS 143**
DREAMBOAT ANNIE	*Arista*	36	*22 Jan 77*	8
LITTLE QUEEN	*Portrait*	34	*23 Jul 77*	4
PRIVATE AUDITION	*Epic*	77	*19 Jun 82*	2
HEART	*Capitol*	46	*26 Oct 85*	17
BAD ANIMALS	*Capitol*	7	*6 Jun 87*	56
HEART [RE]	*Capitol*	19	*5 Mar 88*	26
BRIGADE	*Capitol*	3	*14 Apr 90*	20
ROCK THE HOUSE 'LIVE'	*Capitol*	45	*28 Sep 91*	2
DESIRE WALKS ON	*Capitol*	32	*11 Dec 93*	2
THESE DREAMS - GREATEST HITS	*Capitol*	33	*19 Apr 97*	6

HEARTBEAT — UK

SINGLES:	HITS 2			WEEKS 5
TEARS FROM HEAVEN	*Priority*	32	*24 Oct 87*	4
THE WINNER	*Priority*	70	*23 Apr 88*	1

HEARTBEAT COUNTRY — UK

SINGLES:	HITS 1			WEEKS 1
HEARTBEAT	*Mmmm*	75	*31 Dec 94*	1

HEARTBREAKER – See DEMON vs HEARTBREAKER

HEARTBREAKERS — US

ALBUMS:	HITS 1			WEEKS 1
L.A.M.F.	*Track*	55	*5 Nov 77*	1

HEARTISTS — Italy

SINGLES:	HITS 1			WEEKS 5
BELO HORIZONTI	*VC Recordings*	42	*9 Aug 97*	3
Samples Celebration Suite by Airto Moreira.				
BELO HORIZONTI [RI]	*VC Recordings*	40	*31 Jan 98*	2

Ted HEATH and his Music — UK

SINGLES:	HITS 9			WEEKS 56
VANESSA	*Decca*	11	*17 Jan 53*	1
HOT TODDY	*Decca*	6	*4 Jul 53*	11
DRAGNET	*Decca*	12	*24 Oct 53*	1
DRAGNET [RE-1ST]	*Decca*	9	*28 Nov 53*	1
DRAGNET [RE-2ND]	*Decca*	11	*12 Dec 53*	1
DRAGNET [RE-3RD]	*Decca*	11	*16 Jan 54*	1
DRAGNET [RE-4TH]	*Decca*	12	*6 Feb 54*	1
SKIN DEEP	*Decca*	9	*13 Feb 54*	3
Above hit: Ted HEATH and his Music featuring Runnig VERRELL – drums and Bobby PRATT and Kenny BAKER – trumpets.				
THE FAITHFUL HUSSAR	*Decca*	18	*7 Jul 56*	9
SWINGIN' SHEPHERD BLUES	*Decca*	3	*15 Mar 58*	14
TEQUILA	*Decca*	21	*12 Apr 58*	6
TOM HARK	*Decca*	24	*5 Jul 58*	2
SUCU SUCU (THEME FROM "TOP SECRET")	*Decca*	36	*7 Oct 61*	4
SUCU SUCU (THEME FROM "TOP SECRET") [RE]	*Decca*	47	*11 Nov 61*	1

ALBUMS:	HITS 1			WEEKS 5
BIG BAND PERCUSSION	*Decca*	17	*21 Apr 62*	5

HEATWAVE — US/UK

SINGLES:	HITS 9			WEEKS 80
BOOGIE NIGHTS	*GTO*	2	*22 Jan 77*	14
TOO HOT TO HANDLE / SLIP YOUR DISC TO THIS	*GTO*	15	*7 May 77*	11
THE GROOVE LINE	*GTO*	12	*14 Jan 78*	8
MIND BLOWING DECISIONS	*GTO*	12	*3 Jun 78*	11
ALWAYS AND FOREVER / MIND BLOWING DECISIONS [RM]	*GTO*	9	*4 Nov 78*	14
Mind Blowing Decisions is a remixed version of the original.				
RAZZLE DAZZLE	*GTO*	43	*26 May 79*	5
GANSTERS OF THE GROOVE	*GTO*	19	*17 Jan 81*	8
JITTERBUGGIN'	*GTO*	34	*21 Mar 81*	7
MIND BLOWING DECISIONS [RR]	*Brothers Organisation*	65	*1 Sep 90*	2
Rap by Johnny Daviz.				

ALBUMS:	HITS 4			WEEKS 27
TOO HOT TO HANDLE	*GTO*	46	*11 Jun 77*	2
CENTRAL HEATING	*GTO*	26	*6 May 78*	15
CANDLES	*GTO*	29	*14 Feb 81*	9
GANGSTERS OF THE GROOVE - THE 90'S MIX	*Telstar*	56	*23 Feb 91*	1

HEAVEN 17 — UK

SINGLES:	HITS 12			WEEKS 87
(WE DON'T NEED THIS) FASCIST GROOVE THANG	*Virgin*	45	*21 Mar 81*	5
PLAY TO WIN	*Virgin*	46	*5 Sep 81*	7
PENTHOUSE AND PAVEMENT	*Virgin*	57	*14 Nov 81*	3
LET ME GO	*Virgin*	41	*30 Oct 82*	6
TEMPTATION	*Virgin*	2	*16 Apr 83*	13
Female vocal by Carol Kenyon.				
COME LIVE WITH ME	*Virgin*	5	*25 Jun 83*	11
CRUSHED BY THE WHEELS OF INDUSTRY	*Virgin*	17	*10 Sep 83*	7
SUNSET NOW	*Virgin*	24	*1 Sep 84*	6
THIS IS MINE	*Virgin*	23	*27 Oct 84*	7
. . . (AND THAT'S NO LIE)	*Virgin*	52	*19 Jan 85*	5

TROUBLE	*Virgin*	51	*17 Jan 87*	3
TEMPTATION [RM]	*Virgin*	4	*21 Nov 92*	11
Female vocal by Carol Kenyon, remixed by Brothers In Rhythm.				
(WE DON'T NEED THIS) FASCIST GROOVE THANG [RR]	*Virgin*	40	*27 Feb 93*	2
PENTHOUSE AND PAVEMENT [RM]	*Virgin*	54	*10 Apr 93*	1
Remixed by Tommy D.				
ALBUMS:	**HITS 6**			**WEEKS 128**
PENTHOUSE AND PAVEMENT	*Virgin*	14	*26 Sep 81*	76
THE LUXURY GAP	*Virgin*	4	*7 May 83*	36
HOW MEN ARE	*Virgin*	12	*6 Oct 84*	11
ENDLESS	*Virgin*	70	*12 Jul 86*	2
First album to chart on Cassette and CD formats only.				
PLEASURE ONE	*Virgin*	78	*29 Nov 86*	1
HIGHER AND HIGHER - THE BEST OF HEAVEN 17	*Virgin*	31	*20 Mar 93*	2

HEAVEN'S CRY — Holland

SINGLES:	**HITS 1**			**WEEKS 1**
TIL TEARS DO US PART	*Tidy Trax*	68	*6 Oct 01*	1

HEAVY D and the BOYZ — US

SINGLES:	**HITS 5**			**WEEKS 28**
MR. BIG STUFF	*MCA*	61	*6 Dec 86*	8
Originally recorded by Jean Knight.				
WE GOT OUR OWN THANG	*MCA*	69	*15 Jul 89*	2
Chart for 15 Jul 89 lists an import catalogue number.				
NOW THAT WE'VE FOUND LOVE	*MCA*	2	*6 Jul 91*	12
Originally recorded by the O'Jays.				
IS IT GOOD TO YOU	*MCA*	46	*28 Sep 91*	3
Samples Junior's Mama Used To Say.				
THIS IS YOUR NIGHT	*MCA*	30	*8 Oct 94*	3
Samples Kool and The Gang's Ladies Night and George Benson's Give Me The Night.				
ALBUMS:	**HITS 1**			**WEEKS 3**
PEACEFUL JOURNEY	*MCA*	40	*10 Aug 91*	3

HEAVY PETTIN' — UK

SINGLES:	**HITS 1**			**WEEKS 2**
LOVE TIMES LOVE	*Polydor*	69	*17 Mar 84*	2
ALBUMS:	**HITS 2**			**WEEKS 4**
LETTIN' LOOSE	*Polydor*	55	*29 Oct 83*	2
ROCK AIN'T DEAD	*Polydor*	81	*13 Jul 85*	2

HEAVY STEREO — UK

SINGLES:	**HITS 4**			**WEEKS 4**
SLEEP FREAK	*Creation*	46	*22 Jul 95*	1
SMILER	*Creation*	46	*28 Oct 95*	1
CHINESE BURN	*Creation*	45	*10 Feb 96*	1
MOUSE IN A HOLE	*Creation*	53	*24 Aug 96*	1

HEAVY WEATHER — US

SINGLES:	**HITS 1**			**WEEKS 1**
LOVE CAN'T TURN AROUND	*Pukka*	56	*29 Jun 96*	1

Bobby HEBB — US

SINGLES:	**HITS 2**			**WEEKS 15**
SUNNY	*Philips*	12	*10 Sep 66*	9
Written about Hebb's brother, Hal, who was killed in a mugging.				
LOVE LOVE LOVE	*Philips*	32	*19 Aug 72*	6
Originally recorded by William Bonney.				

HED BOYS — UK

SINGLES:	**HITS 1**			**WEEKS 6**
GIRLS + BOYS	*Deconstruction*	21	*6 Aug 94*	4
Samples Girls Out On The Floor by Jessie Veles.				
GIRLS & BOYS [RI]	*Deconstruction*	36	*4 Nov 95*	2

HED PLANET EARTH — US

ALBUMS:	**HITS 1**			**WEEKS 1**
BROKE	*Music For Nations*	73	*2 Sep 00*	1

HEDGEHOPPERS ANONYMOUS — UK

SINGLES:	**HITS 1**			**WEEKS 12**
IT'S GOOD NEWS WEEK	*Decca*	5	*2 Oct 65*	12
Written & produced by Jonathan King.				

HEFNER — UK

SINGLES:	HITS 3			WEEKS 3
GOOD FRUIT	*Too Pure*	50	*26 Aug 00*	1
THE GREEDY UGLY PEOPLE	*Too Pure*	64	*14 Oct 00*	1
ALAN BEAN	*Too Pure*	58	*8 Sep 01*	1

Neal HEFTI — US

SINGLES:	HITS 1			WEEKS 4
BATMAN THEME	*RCA*	55	*9 Apr 88*	4

Original 1966 TV version.

Den HEGARTY — UK

SINGLES:	HITS 1			WEEKS 2
VOODOO VOODOO	*Magnet*	73	*31 Mar 79*	2

Anita HEGERLAND and Barry PALMER – See Mike OLDFIELD

HEIDI – See Mark 'Ruff' RYDER; Vocals by SPECIAL MC and HEIDI

HEINZ — UK

SINGLES:	HITS 5			WEEKS 35
JUST LIKE EDDIE	*Decca*	5	*10 Aug 63*	15
COUNTRY BOY	*Decca*	26	*30 Nov 63*	9
YOU WERE THERE	*Decca*	26	*29 Feb 64*	8
QUESTIONS I CAN'T ANSWER	*Columbia*	39	*17 Oct 64*	2
DIGGIN' MY POTATOES	*Columbia*	49	*20 Mar 65*	1

Above hit: HEINZ and the WILD BOYS.

EPS:	HITS 1			WEEKS 9
LIVE IT UP	*Decca*	12	*1 Feb 64*	9

HELEN LOVE — UK

SINGLES:	HITS 2			WEEKS 2
DOES YOUR HEART GO BOOM	*Che*	71	*20 Sep 97*	1
LONG LIVE THE UK MUSIC SCENE	*Che*	65	*19 Sep 98*	1

HELICOPTER — UK

SINGLES:	HITS 1			WEEKS 4
ON YA WAY	*Helicopter*	32	*27 Aug 94*	2
Originally released in 1992.				
ON YA WAY [RM]	*Systematic*	37	*22 Jun 96*	2

HELIOCENTRIC WORLD — UK

SINGLES:	HITS 1			WEEKS 2
WHERE'S YOUR LOVE BEEN	*Talkin Loud*	71	*14 Jan 95*	2

HELIOTROPIC featuring Verna V. — UK

SINGLES:	HITS 1			WEEKS 2
ALIVE	*Multiply*	33	*16 Oct 99*	2

Pete HELLER — UK

(See also Fire Island.)

SINGLES:	HITS 2			WEEKS 14
ULTRA FLAVA	*AM:PM*	22	*24 Feb 96*	3
ULTRA FLAVA [RM]	*AM:PM*	32	*28 Dec 96*	4
Remixed by Rhythm Masters.				
Above 2: HELLER and FARLEY PROJECT.				
BIG LOVE	*Essential Recordings*	12	*15 May 99*	7
Samples Stargard's Wear It Out.				

HELLO — UK

SINGLES:	HITS 2			WEEKS 21
TELL HIM	*Bell*	6	*9 Nov 74*	12
Originally recorded by the Exciters.				
NEW YORK GROOVE	*Bell*	9	*18 Oct 75*	9
Originally recorded by Russ Ballard.				

HELLOWEEN — US

SINGLES:	HITS 3			WEEKS 7
DR STEIN	*Noise International*	57	*27 Aug 88*	3
I WANT OUT	*Noise International*	69	*12 Nov 88*	2
KIDS OF THE CENTURY	*EMI*	56	*2 Mar 91*	2

ALBUMS:	HITS 3			WEEKS 9
KEEPER OF THE SEVEN KEYS PART 2	*Noise International*	24	*17 Sep 88*	5
LIVE IN THE UK	*EMI*	26	*15 Apr 89*	2
PINK BUBBLES GO APE	*EMI*	41	*23 Mar 91*	2

HELMET — US

ALBUMS:	HITS 1			WEEKS 1
BETTY	*Interscope*	38	*2 Jul 94*	1

Bobby HELMS — US

SINGLES:	HITS 3			WEEKS 7
MY SPECIAL ANGEL	*Brunswick*	22	*30 Nov 57*	3
Above hit: Bobby HELMS and Anita KERR SINGERS.				
NO OTHER BABY	*Brunswick*	30	*22 Feb 58*	1
Originally recorded by Dickie Bishop and the Sidekicks.				
JACQUELINE	*Brunswick*	20	*2 Aug 58*	3
From the film 'The Case Against Brooklyn'.				
Above hit: Bobby HELMS and Anita KERR SINGERS.				

Jimmy HELMS — UK

SINGLES:	HITS 1			WEEKS 10
GONNA MAKE YOU AN OFFER YOU CAN'T REFUSE	*Cube*	8	*24 Feb 73*	10

HELTAH SKELTER and ORIGINOO GUNN CLAPPAZ as the FABULOUS FIVE — US

SINGLES:	HITS 1			WEEKS 1
BLAH	*Priority*	60	*1 Jun 96*	1

Eddie HENDERSON — US

SINGLES:	HITS 1			WEEKS 6
PRANCE ON	*Capitol*	44	*28 Oct 78*	6

Joe "Mr. Piano" HENDERSON — UK

SINGLES:	HITS 5			WEEKS 23
SING IT WITH JOE [M]	*Polygon*	14	*4 Jun 55*	4
SING IT AGAIN WITH JOE [M]	*Polygon*	18	*3 Sep 55*	3
Above 2: Joe 'Mr. Piano' HENDERSON and his Friends.				
TRUDIE	*Pye Nixa*	14	*26 Jul 58*	12
Above hit: Joe "Mr. Piano" HENDERSON with the Beryl STOTT CHORUS.				
TRUDIE [RE]	*Pye Nixa*	23	*25 Oct 58*	2
TREBLE CHANCE	*Pye*	28	*24 Oct 59*	1
OOH LA LA	*Pye*	44	*26 Mar 60*	1

Wayne HENDERSON – See Roy AYERS

Billy HENDRIX — Germany

SINGLES:	HITS 1			WEEKS 2
THE BODY SHINE [EP]	*Hooj Choons*	55	*12 Sep 98*	2
Various mixes of track The Body Shine.				

Jimi HENDRIX — US

SINGLES:	HITS 10			WEEKS 87
HEY JOE	*Polydor*	6	*7 Jan 67*	10
Originally recorded by the Leaves.				
PURPLE HAZE	*Track*	3	*25 Mar 67*	14
THE WIND CRIES MARY	*Track*	6	*13 May 67*	11
BURNING OF THE MIDNIGHT LAMP	*Track*	18	*2 Sep 67*	9
ALL ALONG THE WATCHTOWER	*Track*	5	*26 Oct 68*	11
Originally recorded by Bob Dylan.				
CROSSTOWN TRAFFIC	*Track*	37	*19 Apr 69*	3
VOODOO CHILE	*Track*	1	*7 Nov 70*	13
GYPSY EYES/REMEMBER	*Track*	35	*30 Oct 71*	5
Above 8: Jimi HENDRIX EXPERIENCE.				
JOHNNY B. GOODE	*Polydor*	35	*12 Feb 72*	5
Originally recorded by Chuck Berry.				
CROSSTOWN TRAFFIC [RI]	*Polydor*	61	*21 Apr 90*	3
ALL ALONG THE WATCHTOWER [EP]	*Polydor*	52	*20 Oct 90*	3
Lead track: Alll Along The Watchtower. (This and the other tracks are re-issues).				

ALBUMS:	HITS 27			WEEKS 270
ARE YOU EXPERIENCED	*Track*	2	*27 May 67*	33
AXIS: BOLD AS LOVE	*Track*	5	*16 Dec 67*	16
SMASH HITS	*Track*	4	*27 Apr 68*	25
Above 3: Jimi HENDRIX EXPERIENCE.				
GET THAT FEELING	*London*	39	*18 May 68*	2
Above hit: Jimi HENDRIX and Curtis KNIGHT.				

ELECTRIC LADYLAND *Above hit: Jimi HENDRIX EXPERIENCE.*	*Track*	6	*16 Nov 68*	12
BAND OF GYPSIES *Live recordings from Fillmore East, New York, 31 Dec 69.*	*Track*	6	*4 Jul 70*	30
CRY OF LOVE	*Track*	2	*3 Apr 71*	14
EXPERIENCE	*Ember*	9	*28 Aug 71*	6
JIMI HENDRIX AT THE ISLE OF WIGHT *Live recordings from the festival, 30 Aug 70.*	*Track*	17	*20 Nov 71*	2
RAINBOW BRIDGE [OST] *Recordings from 1968-70.*	*Reprise*	16	*4 Dec 71*	8
HENDRIX IN THE WEST	*Polydor*	7	*5 Feb 72*	14
WAR HEROES	*Polydor*	23	*11 Nov 72*	3
SOUNDTRACK RECORDINGS FROM THE FILM 'JIMI HENDRIX' [OST]	*Warner Brothers*	37	*21 Jul 73*	1
JIMI HENDRIX	*Polydor*	35	*29 Mar 75*	4
CRASH LANDING	*Polydor*	35	*30 Aug 75*	3
MIDNIGHT LIGHTNING	*Polydor*	46	*29 Nov 75*	1
THE JIMI HENDRIX CONCERTS *Live recordings from 1968-70.*	*CBS*	16	*14 Aug 82*	11
THE SINGLES ALBUM	*Polydor*	77	*19 Feb 83*	4
RADIO ONE *Recordings made for BBC Radio 1.*	*Castle Collectors*	30	*11 Mar 89*	6
CORNERSTONES - JIMI HENDRIX 1967-1970	*Polydor*	5	*3 Nov 90*	16
JIMI HENDRIX - THE ULTIMATE EXPERIENCE	*PolyGram TV*	25	*14 Nov 92*	26
BLUES	*Polydor*	10	*30 Apr 94*	3
WOODSTOCK *Live recordings from Woodstock, Aug 69.*	*Polydor*	32	*13 Aug 94*	3
FIRST RAYS OF THE NEW RISING SUN *Recreation of the album Hendrix was working on at the time of his death.*	*MCA*	37	*10 May 97*	2
ELECTRIC LADYLAND [RI] *Charted after being featured on BBC1 TV's 'Classic Albums' series.* *Above hit: Jimi HENDRIX EXPERIENCE.*	*MCA*	47	*2 Aug 97*	1
EXPERIENCE HENDRIX - THE BEST OF JIMI HENDRIX	*Telstar TV*	18	*13 Sep 97*	15
BBC SESSIONS *Collection of BBC Radio and TV performances.* *Above hit: Jimi HENDRIX EXPERIENCE.*	*MCA*	42	*13 Jun 98*	2
EXPERIENCE HENDRIX - THE BEST OF JIMI HENDRIX [RE] *Repackaged version of the 1997 album with bonus CD.*	*Universal Music TV*	10	*23 Sep 00*	7

Nona HENDRYX — US

(See also Bounty Killer (featuring Cocoa Brovaz, Nona Hendryx and Free).)

SINGLES:	HITS 1			WEEKS 2
WHY SHOULD I CRY?	*EMI America*	60	*16 May 87*	2

Don HENLEY — US

SINGLES:	HITS 4			WEEKS 30
DIRTY LAUNDRY *Features guitar solo by Joe Walsh.*	*Asylum*	59	*12 Feb 83*	3
THE BOYS OF SUMMER	*Geffen*	12	*9 Feb 85*	10
THE END OF THE INNOCENCE *Features Bruce Hornsby on piano.*	*Geffen*	48	*29 Jul 89*	5
SOMETIMES LOVE JUST AIN'T ENOUGH *Above hit: Patty SMYTH with Don HENLEY.*	*MCA*	22	*3 Oct 92*	6
THE BOYS OF SUMMER [RI] *This re-issue has longer intro than original chart entry.*	*Geffen*	12	*18 Jul 98*	6

ALBUMS:	HITS 3			WEEKS 30
BUILDING THE PERFECT BEAST	*Geffen*	14	*9 Mar 85*	11
THE END OF THE INNOCENCE	*Geffen*	17	*8 Jul 89*	16
INSIDE JOB	*Warner Brothers*	25	*3 Jun 00*	3

Clarence "Frogman" HENRY — US

SINGLES:	HITS 3			WEEKS 35
BUT I DO	*Pye International*	3	*6 May 61*	19
YOU ALWAYS HURT THE ONE YOU LOVE *Originally recorded by the Mills Brothers in 1944.*	*Pye International*	6	*15 Jul 61*	12
LONELY STREET / WHY CAN'T YOU	*Pye International*	42	*23 Sep 61*	2
(I DON'T KNOW WHY) BUT I DO [RI] *Featured in the Fiat Cinquecento TV commercial.*	*MCA*	65	*17 Jul 93*	2

Kevin HENRY - See Paul HARDCASTLE; L.A. MIX

Paul HENRY and the Mayson GLEN ORCHESTRA — UK

SINGLES:	HITS 1			WEEKS 2
BENNY'S THEME *From the ATV soap 'Crossroads'.*	*Pye*	39	*14 Jan 78*	2

Pauline HENRY — UK

SINGLES:	HITS 8			WEEKS 21
TOO MANY PEOPLE	*Sony S2*	38	*18 Sep 93*	2
FEEL LIKE MAKING LOVE	*Sony S2*	12	*6 Nov 93*	7
CAN'T TAKE YOUR LOVE	*Sony S2*	30	*29 Jan 94*	3
WATCH THE MIRACLE START	*Sony S2*	54	*21 May 94*	1
SUGAR FREE	*Sony S2*	57	*30 Sep 95*	2
LOVE HANGOVER	*Sony S2*	37	*23 Dec 95*	3
NEVER KNEW LOVE LIKE THIS	*Sony S2*	40	*24 Feb 96*	2
Above hit: Pauline HENRY featuring Wayne MARSHALL.				
HAPPY	*Sony S2*	46	*1 Jun 96*	1
ALBUMS:	**HITS 1**			**WEEKS 1**
PAULINE	*Sony S2*	45	*19 Feb 94*	1

Pierre HENRY/Michel COLOMBIER — France

SINGLES:	HITS 1			WEEKS 1
PSYCHE ROCK	*Hi-Life*	58	*4 Oct 97*	1

HEPBURN — UK

SINGLES:	HITS 3			WEEKS 15
I QUIT	*Columbia*	8	*29 May 99*	7
BUGS	*Columbia*	14	*28 Aug 99*	5
DEEP DEEP DOWN	*Columbia*	16	*19 Feb 00*	3
ALBUMS:	**HITS 1**			**WEEKS 2**
HEPBURN	*Columbia*	28	*11 Sep 99*	2

Band and Chorus Of HER MAJESTY'S GUARDS DIVISION — UK

ALBUMS:	HITS 1			WEEKS 4
30 SMASH HITS OF THE WAR YEARS	*Warwick*	38	*22 Nov 75*	4

HERBIE - See 3T

HERD — UK

SINGLES:	HITS 3			WEEKS 35
FROM THE UNDERWORLD	*Fontana*	6	*16 Sep 67*	13
PARADISE LOST	*Fontana*	15	*23 Dec 67*	9
I DON'T WANT OUR LOVING TO DIE	*Fontana*	5	*13 Apr 68*	13
ALBUMS:	**HITS 1**			**WEEKS 1**
PARADISE LOST	*Fontana*	38	*24 Feb 68*	1

HERMAN'S HERMITS — UK

SINGLES:	HITS 20			WEEKS 211
I'M INTO SOMETHING GOOD	*Columbia*	1	*22 Aug 64*	15
Originally recorded by Earl Jean.				
SHOW ME GIRL	*Columbia*	19	*21 Nov 64*	9
SILHOUETTES	*Columbia*	3	*20 Feb 65*	12
Original by the Rays reached No. 3 in the US in 1957.				
WONDERFUL WORLD	*Columbia*	7	*1 May 65*	9
JUST A LITTLE BIT BETTER	*Columbia*	15	*4 Sep 65*	9
A MUST TO AVOID	*Columbia*	6	*25 Dec 65*	11
YOU WON'T BE LEAVING	*Columbia*	20	*26 Mar 66*	7
THIS DOOR SWINGS BOTH WAYS	*Columbia*	18	*25 Jun 66*	7
NO MILK TODAY	*Columbia*	7	*8 Oct 66*	11
EAST WEST	*Columbia*	37	*3 Dec 66*	7
THERE'S A KIND OF HUSH	*Columbia*	7	*11 Feb 67*	11
Originally recorded by New Vaudeville Band.				
I CAN TAKE OR LEAVE YOUR LOVING	*Columbia*	11	*20 Jan 68*	9
SLEEPY JOE	*Columbia*	12	*4 May 68*	10
SUNSHINE GIRL	*Columbia*	8	*20 Jul 68*	14
SOMETHING'S HAPPENING	*Columbia*	6	*21 Dec 68*	15
Originally recorded by Ricardo del Turco as Luglio.				
MY SENTIMENTAL FRIEND	*Columbia*	2	*26 Apr 69*	12
HERE COMES THE STAR	*Columbia*	33	*8 Nov 69*	9
YEARS MAY COME, YEARS MAY GO	*Columbia*	7	*7 Feb 70*	11
YEARS MAY COME, YEARS MAY GO [RE]	*Columbia*	45	*2 May 70*	1
BET YER LIFE I DO	*RAK*	22	*23 May 70*	10
LADY BARBARA	*RAK*	13	*14 Nov 70*	12
Above two co-written by Errol Brown from Hot Chocolate.				
Above hit: Peter NOONE and HERMAN'S HERMITS.				
EPS:	**HITS 4**			**WEEKS 42**
HERMANIA	*Columbia*	19	*30 Jan 65*	1
MRS BROWN YOU'VE GOT A LOVELY DAUGHTER	*Columbia*	3	*12 Jun 65*	21
HERMAN'S HERMITS HITS	*Columbia*	10	*25 Sep 65*	10
MUSIC FROM THE SOUNDTRACK "HOLD ON"	*Columbia*	4	*27 Aug 66*	10

ALBUMS:	HITS 3			WEEKS 11
HERMAN'S HERMITS	*Columbia*	16	*18 Sep 65*	2
THE MOST OF HERMAN'S HERMITS	*Music For Pleasure*	14	*25 Sep 71*	5
GREATEST HITS	*Columbia*	37	*8 Oct 77*	4

HERMES HOUSE BAND — Holland

SINGLES:	HITS 1			WEEKS 3
COUNTRY ROADS	*Liberty*	7	*15 Dec 01*	3
Originally recorded by John Denver in 1971.				

HERNANDEZ — UK

SINGLES:	HITS 1			WEEKS 3
ALL MY LOVE	*Epic*	58	*15 Apr 89*	3

Patrick HERNANDEZ — France

SINGLES:	HITS 1			WEEKS 14
BORN TO BE ALIVE	*GEM*	10	*16 Jun 79*	14

HERREY'S — Sweden

SINGLES:	HITS 1			WEEKS 3
DIGGI LOO - DIGGI LEY	*Panther*	46	*26 May 84*	3
Eurovision Song Contest winners in 1984.				

Kristin HERSH — US

SINGLES:	HITS 2			WEEKS 3
YOUR GHOST	*4AD*	45	*22 Jan 94*	2
Features vocals by Michael Stipe (R.E.M.).				
STRINGS [EP]	*4AD*	60	*16 Apr 94*	1
Lead track: A Loon.				
ALBUMS:	**HITS 2**			**WEEKS 5**
HIPS AND MAKERS	*4AD*	7	*5 Feb 94*	4
STRANGE ANGELS	*4AD*	64	*14 Feb 98*	1

Howard HEWETT - See BABYFACE

Nick HEYWARD — UK

SINGLES:	HITS 13			WEEKS 65
WHISTLE DOWN THE WIND	*Arista*	13	*19 Mar 83*	8
TAKE THAT SITUATION	*Arista*	11	*4 Jun 83*	10
BLUE HAT FOR A BLUE DAY	*Arista*	14	*24 Sep 83*	8
ON A SUNDAY	*Arista*	52	*3 Dec 83*	5
LOVE ALL DAY	*Arista*	31	*2 Jun 84*	6
WARNING SIGN	*Arista*	25	*3 Nov 84*	8
WARNING SIGN [RE]	*Arista*	72	*5 Jan 85*	1
LAURA	*Arista*	45	*8 Jun 85*	4
OVER THE WEEKEND	*Arista*	43	*10 May 86*	5
YOU'RE MY WORLD	*Warner Brothers*	67	*10 Sep 88*	2
KITE	*Epic*	44	*21 Aug 93*	2
HE DOESN'T LOVE YOU LIKE I DO	*Epic*	58	*16 Oct 93*	2
THE WORLD	*Epic*	47	*30 Sep 95*	2
ROLLERBLADE	*Epic*	37	*13 Jan 96*	2
ALBUMS:	**HITS 1**			**WEEKS 13**
NORTH OF A MIRACLE	*Arista*	10	*29 Oct 83*	13

HI-FIVE — US

SINGLES:	HITS 2			WEEKS 8
I LIKE THE WAY (THE KISSING GAME)	*Jive*	43	*1 Jun 91*	6
SHE'S PLAYING HARD TO GET	*Jive*	55	*24 Oct 92*	2

HI-GATE — UK

SINGLES:	HITS 3			WEEKS 14
PITCHIN' (IN EVERY DIRECTION)	*Incentive*	6	*29 Jan 00*	6
I CAN HEAR VOICES/CANED AND UNABLE	*Incentive*	12	*26 Aug 00*	5
GONNA WORK IT OUT	*Incentive*	25	*7 Apr 01*	3

HI-GLOSS — US

SINGLES:	HITS 1			WEEKS 13
YOU'LL NEVER KNOW	*Epic*	12	*8 Aug 81*	13

HI-JACK — US

ALBUMS:	HITS 1			WEEKS 1
THE HORNS OF JERICO	*Warner Brothers*	54	*19 Oct 91*	1

HI-LUX — UK

SINGLES:	HITS 2			WEEKS 3
FEEL IT	*Cheeky*	41	*18 Feb 95*	2
NEVER FELT THIS WAY / FEEL IT	*Champion*	58	*2 Sep 95*	1

HI POWER — Germany

SINGLES:	HITS 1			WEEKS 1
CULT OF SNAP / SIMBA GROOVE	*Rumour*	73	*1 Sep 90*	1

HI TEK featuring JONELL — US

SINGLES:	HITS 1			WEEKS 1
ROUND AND ROUND	*Rawkus*	73	*20 Oct 01*	1

HI TEK 3 featuring YA KID K — Belgium

(See also Technotronic.)

SINGLES:	HITS 1			WEEKS 10
SPIN THAT WHEEL	*Brothers Organisation*	69	*3 Feb 90*	3
SPIN THAT WHEEL (TURTLES GET REAL) [RI]	*Brothers Organisation*	15	*29 Sep 90*	7
From the film 'Teenage Mutant Ninja Turtles'.				

HI TENSION — US

SINGLES:	HITS 2			WEEKS 23
HI-TENSION	*Island*	13	*6 May 78*	12
BRITISH HUSTLE / PEACE ON EARTH	*Island*	8	*12 Aug 78*	11
Peace On Earth listed from 2 Sep 78.				
ALBUMS:	**HITS 1**			**WEEKS 4**
HI TENSION	*Island*	74	*6 Jan 79*	4

John HIATT — US

ALBUMS:	HITS 3			WEEKS 3
STOLEN MOMENTS	*A&M*	72	*7 Jul 90*	1
PERFECTLY GOOD GUITAR	*A&M*	67	*11 Sep 93*	1
WALK ON	*Capitol*	74	*11 Nov 95*	1

Toots HIBBERT - See JAMAICA UNITED

Al HIBBLER — US

SINGLES:	HITS 1			WEEKS 17
UNCHAINED MELODY	*Brunswick*	2	*14 May 55*	17
From the film 'Unchained'.				

Hinda HICKS — UK

SINGLES:	HITS 5			WEEKS 15
IF YOU WANT ME	*Island*	25	*7 Mar 98*	3
Samples Kool And The Gang's Too Hot.				
YOU THINK YOU OWN ME	*Island*	19	*16 May 98*	4
I WANNA BE YOUR LADY	*Island*	14	*15 Aug 98*	5
Original release reached No. 109 in 1997. Features backing vocals by Shaznay Lewis of All Saints.				
TRULY	*Island*	31	*24 Oct 98*	2
MY REMEDY	*Island*	61	*14 Oct 00*	1
ALBUMS:	**HITS 1**			**WEEKS 4**
HINDA	*Island*	20	*29 Aug 98*	4

Bertie HIGGINS — US

SINGLES:	HITS 1			WEEKS 4
KEY LARGO	*Epic*	60	*5 Jun 82*	4

HIGH — UK

SINGLES:	HITS 4			WEEKS 11
UP AND DOWN	*London*	53	*25 Aug 90*	4
TAKE YOUR TIME	*London*	56	*27 Oct 90*	2
BOX SET GO	*London*	28	*12 Jan 91*	3
Original release reached No. 76 in 1990.				
MORE . . .	*London*	67	*6 Apr 91*	2
ALBUMS:	**HITS 1**			**WEEKS 2**
SOMEWHERE SOON	*London*	59	*17 Nov 90*	2

HIGH FIDELITY — UK

SINGLES:	HITS 1			WEEKS 1
LUV DUP	*Plastique*	70	*25 Jul 98*	1

HIGH LLAMAS — UK/Ireland

ALBUMS:	HITS 1			WEEKS 1
HAWAII	*Alpaca Park*	62	*6 Apr 96*	1

HIGH NUMBERS — UK

(See also Who.)

SINGLES:	HITS 1			WEEKS 4
I'M THE FACE	*Back Door*	49	*5 Apr 80*	4
Originally released in 1964 on the Fontana label.				

HIGH SOCIETY — UK

SINGLES:	HITS 1			WEEKS 4
I NEVER GO OUT IN THE RAIN	*Eagle*	53	*15 Nov 80*	4

HIGHLY LIKELY — UK

SINGLES:	HITS 1			WEEKS 4
WHATEVER HAPPENED TO YOU (LIKELY LADS THEME)	*BBC*	35	*21 Apr 73*	4
Theme from the BBC1 TV comedy 'Whatever Happened To The Likely Lads'.				

HIGHWAYMEN — US

SINGLES:	HITS 2			WEEKS 18
MICHAEL	*His Master's Voice*	1	*9 Sep 61*	14
GYPSY ROVER (THE WHISTLING GYPSY)	*His Master's Voice*	41	*9 Dec 61*	3
GYPSY ROVER (THE WHISTLING GYPSY) [RE]	*His Master's Voice*	43	*13 Jan 62*	1

HIJACK — UK

SINGLES:	HITS 1			WEEKS 3
THE BADMAN IS ROBBIN'	*Rhyme Syndicate*	56	*6 Jan 90*	3

Benny HILL — UK

SINGLES:	HITS 4			WEEKS 43
GATHER IN THE MUSHROOMS	*Pye*	12	*18 Feb 61*	8
TRANSISTOR RADIO	*Pye*	24	*3 Jun 61*	6
THE HARVEST OF LOVE	*Pye*	20	*18 May 63*	8
Above hit: Benny HILL with the KESTRELS.				
ERNIE (THE FASTEST MILKMAN IN THE WEST)	*Columbia*	1	*13 Nov 71*	17
ERNIE (THE FASTEST MILKMAN IN THE WEST) [RI]	*EMI*	29	*30 May 92*	4
ALBUMS:	**HITS 1**			**WEEKS 8**
WORDS AND MUSIC	*Columbia*	9	*11 Dec 71*	8

Chris HILL — UK

SINGLES:	HITS 2			WEEKS 14
RENTA SANTA	*Philips*	10	*6 Dec 75*	7
BIONIC SANTA	*Philips*	10	*4 Dec 76*	7
Above 2 weave comic storylines around copious samples from other hits.				

Dan HILL — Canada

SINGLES:	HITS 1			WEEKS 13
SOMETIMES WHEN WE TOUCH	*20th Century*	46	*18 Feb 78*	1
SOMETIMES WHEN WE TOUCH [RE]	*20th Century*	13	*4 Mar 78*	12

Faith HILL — US

SINGLES:	HITS 5			WEEKS 35
THIS KISS	*Warner Brothers*	13	*14 Nov 98*	11
LET ME LET GO	*Warner Brothers*	72	*17 Apr 99*	1
From the film 'Message In A Bottle'.				
BREATHE	*Warner Brothers*	33	*20 May 00*	2
THE WAY YOU LOVE ME	*Warner Brothers*	15	*21 Apr 01*	5
THERE YOU'LL BE	*Hollywood/Warner Brothers*	3	*30 Jun 01*	14
From the film 'Pearl Harbor'.				
BREATHE [RM]	*Warner Brothers*	36	*13 Oct 01*	2
Remixed by Tin Tin Out.				
ALBUMS:	**HITS 2**			**WEEKS 26**
BREATHE	*Warner Brothers*	21	*3 Jun 00*	4
BREATHE [RE]	*Warner Brothers*	19	*28 Apr 01*	12
THERE YOU'LL BE	*Warner Brothers*	6	*27 Oct 01*	10

Lauryn HILL — US

SINGLES:	HITS 6			WEEKS 35
THE SWEETEST THING	*Columbia*	18	*6 Sep 97*	4
From the film 'Love Jones'. Male rap by John Forte.				
Above hit: REFUGEE CAMP ALLSTARS featuring Lauryn HILL.				

ALL MY TIME	*One World Entertainment*	57	*27 Dec 97*	1
Above hit: PAID and LIVE featuring Lauryn HILL.				
DOO WOP (THAT THING)	*Ruffhouse*	3	*3 Oct 98*	7
EX-FACTOR	*Ruffhouse*	4	*27 Feb 99*	9
Samples Wu Tang Clan's Can It All Be So Simple (which was itself an interpretation of Gladys Knight's The Way We Were).				
EX-FACTOR [RE]	*Ruffhouse*	67	*22 May 99*	1
EVERYTHING IS EVERYTHING	*Ruffhouse*	19	*10 Jul 99*	6
TURN YOUR LIGHTS DOWN LOW	*Columbia*	15	*11 Dec 99*	7
From the film 'The Best Man'.				
Above hit: Bob MARLEY featuring Lauryn HILL.				
ALBUMS:	**HITS 1**			**WEEKS 70**
THE MISEDUCATION OF LAURYN HILL	*Ruffhouse*	2	*10 Oct 98*	70

Lonnie HILL — US

SINGLES:	**HITS 1**			**WEEKS 4**
GALVESTON BAY	*10 Records*	51	*22 Mar 86*	4

Roni HILL — US

SINGLES:	**HITS 1**			**WEEKS 4**
YOU KEEP ME HANGING ON / STOP! IN THE NAME OF LOVE [M]	*Creole*	36	*7 May 77*	4

Vince HILL — UK

SINGLES:	**HITS 11**			**WEEKS 91**
THE RIVER'S RUN DRY	*Piccadilly*	49	*9 Jun 62*	1
THE RIVER'S RUN DRY [RE]	*Piccadilly*	41	*30 Jun 62*	1
TAKE ME TO YOUR HEART AGAIN (LA VIE EN ROSE)	*Columbia*	13	*8 Jan 66*	11
HEARTACHES	*Columbia*	28	*19 Mar 66*	5
Above hit: Vince HILL with the Eddie LESTER SINGERS.				
MERCI CHERI	*Columbia*	36	*4 Jun 66*	6
EDELWEISS	*Columbia*	2	*11 Feb 67*	17
From the film 'The Sound Of Music'.				
ROSES OF PICARDY	*Columbia*	13	*13 May 67*	11
LOVE LETTERS IN THE SAND	*Columbia*	23	*30 Sep 67*	9
THE IMPORTANCE OF YOUR LOVE (L'IMPORTANT, C'EST LA ROSE)	*Columbia*	32	*29 Jun 68*	12
Originally recorded by Gilbert Becaud.				
Above 4: Vince HILL with the Eddie LESTER SINGERS.				
DOESN'T ANYBODY KNOW MY NAME?	*Columbia*	50	*15 Feb 69*	1
LITTLE BLUEBIRD	*Columbia*	42	*25 Oct 69*	1
LOOK AROUND (AND YOU'LL FIND ME THERE)	*Columbia*	12	*25 Sep 71*	16
From the film 'Love Story'.				
ALBUMS:	**HITS 2**			**WEEKS 10**
EDELWEISS	*Columbia*	23	*20 May 67*	9
THAT LOVING FEELING	*K-Tel*	51	*29 Apr 78*	1

Steve HILLAGE — UK

ALBUMS:	**HITS 8**			**WEEKS 41**
FISH RISING	*Virgin*	33	*3 May 75*	3
L	*Virgin*	10	*16 Oct 76*	12
MOTIVATION RADIO	*Virgin*	28	*22 Oct 77*	5
GREEN VIRGIN	*Virgin*	30	*29 Apr 78*	8
LIVE HERALD	*Virgin*	54	*17 Feb 79*	5
RAINBOW DOME MUSIC	*Virgin*	52	*5 May 79*	5
OPEN	*Virgin*	71	*27 Oct 79*	1
FOR TO NEXT	*Virgin*	48	*5 Mar 83*	2

HILLMAN MINX — UK/France

SINGLES:	**HITS 1**			**WEEKS 1**
I'VE HAD ENOUGH	*Mercury*	72	*5 Sep 98*	1

HILLTOPPERS — US

SINGLES:	**HITS 3**			**WEEKS 30**
ONLY YOU (AND YOU ALONE)	*London*	3	*28 Jan 56*	22
ONLY YOU (AND YOU ALONE) [RE]	*London*	24	*11 Aug 56*	1
TRYING	*London*	30	*15 Sep 56*	1
MARIANNE	*London*	20	*6 Apr 57*	2
Originally recorded by Terry Gilkyson and the Easyriders.				
Above hit: HILLTOPPERS with Billy VAUGHN'S ORCHESTRA.				
MARIANNE [RE]	*London*	23	*27 Apr 57*	4

Ronnie HILTON — UK

SINGLES:	**HITS 17**			**WEEKS 136**
I STILL BELIEVE	*His Master's Voice*	3	*27 Nov 54*	14

VENI VIDI VICI	*His Master's Voice*	12	*11 Dec 54*	8
Above 2 entries were separate sides of the same release, each had its own chart run.				
A BLOSSOM FELL	*His Master's Voice*	10	*12 Mar 55*	5
STARS SHINE IN YOUR EYES	*His Master's Voice*	13	*27 Aug 55*	7
From the film 'La Strada'.				
THE YELLOW ROSE OF TEXAS	*His Master's Voice*	15	*12 Nov 55*	2
YOUNG AND FOOLISH	*His Master's Voice*	17	*11 Feb 56*	1
YOUNG AND FOOLISH [RE-1ST]	*His Master's Voice*	20	*25 Feb 56*	1
YOUNG AND FOOLISH [RE-2ND]	*His Master's Voice*	19	*10 Mar 56*	1
NO OTHER LOVE	*His Master's Voice*	1	*21 Apr 56*	14
From the film 'Me And Juliet'.				
WHO ARE WE	*His Master's Voice*	6	*30 Jun 56*	12
A WOMAN IN LOVE	*His Master's Voice*	30	*22 Sep 56*	1
From the film 'Guys And Dolls'.				
TWO DIFFERENT WORLDS	*His Master's Voice*	13	*10 Nov 56*	13
AROUND THE WORLD	*His Master's Voice*	4	*25 May 57*	18
From the film 'Around The World In Eighty Days'.				
WONDERFUL, WONDERFUL	*His Master's Voice*	27	*3 Aug 57*	2
MAGIC MOMENTS	*His Master's Voice*	22	*22 Feb 58*	2
I MAY NEVER PASS THIS WAY AGAIN	*His Master's Voice*	30	*19 Apr 58*	1
I MAY NEVER PASS THIS WAY AGAIN [RE-1ST]	*His Master's Voice*	30	*3 May 58*	1
I MAY NEVER PASS THIS WAY AGAIN [RE-2ND]	*His Master's Voice*	27	*7 Jun 58*	1
THE WORLD OUTSIDE	*His Master's Voice*	18	*10 Jan 59*	6
Above 4: Ronnie HILTON with the Michael SAMMES SINGERS.				
THE WONDER OF YOU	*His Master's Voice*	22	*22 Aug 59*	3
Above hit: Ronnie HILTON with the RIDDELLE SINGERS.				
DON'T LET THE RAIN COME DOWN (CROOKED LITTLE MAN)	*His Master's Voice*	21	*23 May 64*	10
Above hit: Ronnie HILTON with the Michael SAMMES SINGERS.				
A WINDMILL IN OLD AMSTERDAM	*His Master's Voice*	23	*13 Feb 65*	13
Above hit: Ronnie HILTON with the Michael SAMMES SINGERS and ORCHESTRA.				

HINDSIGHT — UK

SINGLES:	HITS 1			WEEKS 3
LOWDOWN	*Circa*	62	*5 Sep 87*	3

Deni HINES — Australia

SINGLES:	HITS 4			WEEKS 6
IT'S ALRIGHT	*Mushroom*	35	*14 Jun 97*	2
I LIKE THE WAY	*Mushroom*	37	*20 Sep 97*	2
DELICIOUS	*Mushroom*	52	*28 Feb 98*	1
Above hit: Deni HINES featuring DON-E.				
JOY	*Mushroom*	47	*23 May 98*	1

Gregory HINES – See Luther VANDROSS

HIPSWAY — UK

SINGLES:	HITS 6			WEEKS 21
THE BROKEN YEARS	*Mercury*	72	*13 Jul 85*	3
ASK THE LORD	*Mercury*	72	*14 Sep 85*	1
THE HONEYTHIEF	*Mercury*	17	*22 Feb 86*	9
ASK THE LORD [RR]	*Mercury*	50	*10 May 86*	5
LONG WHITE CAR	*Mercury*	55	*20 Sep 86*	2
YOUR LOVE	*Mercury*	66	*1 Apr 89*	1
ALBUMS:	**HITS 1**			**WEEKS 23**
HIPSWAY	*Mercury*	42	*19 Apr 86*	23

David HIRSCHFELDER — Australia

ALBUMS:	HITS 1			WEEKS 9
SHINE [OST]	*Philips*	46	*2 Aug 97*	9

HISTORY featuring Q-TEE — UK

SINGLES:	HITS 1			WEEKS 5
AFRIKA	*SBK One*	42	*21 Apr 90*	5

Carol HITCHCOCK — Australia

SINGLES:	HITS 1			WEEKS 5
GET READY	*A&M*	56	*30 May 87*	5

HITHOUSE — Holland

SINGLES:	HITS 2			WEEKS 13
JACK TO THE SOUND OF THE UNDERGROUND	*Supreme*	14	*5 Nov 88*	12
MOVE YOUR FEET TO THE RHYTHM OF THE BEAT	*Supreme*	69	*19 Aug 89*	1

HITMAN HOWIE TEE – See REAL ROXANNE

Chorus of Members of HM FORCES – See Vera LYNN

Helen HOBSON – See Cliff RICHARD

Edmund HOCKRIDGE — Canada

SINGLES:	HITS 3			WEEKS 18
YOUNG AND FOOLISH	*Pye Nixa*	10	*18 Feb 56*	7
From the musical 'Plain And Fancy'.				
Above hit: Edmund HOCKRIDGE with Tony OSBORNE and his Orchestra.				
YOUNG AND FOOLISH [RE-1ST]	*Pye Nixa*	28	*14 Apr 56*	1
YOUNG AND FOOLISH [RE-2ND]	*Pye Nixa*	26	*5 May 56*	1
NO OTHER LOVE	*Pye Nixa*	24	*12 May 56*	2
NO OTHER LOVE [RE-1ST]	*Pye Nixa*	29	*2 Jun 56*	1
NO OTHER LOVE [RE-2ND]	*Pye Nixa*	30	*16 Jun 56*	1
BY THE FOUNTAINS OF ROME	*Pye Nixa*	17	*1 Sep 56*	5
Above hit: Edmund HOCKRIDGE with Beryl STOTT CHORUS and Tony OSBORNE ORCHESTRA.				

EPS:	HITS 2			WEEKS 6
MOST HAPPY FELLA	*Pye*	8	*21 May 60*	4
THE MUSIC MAN	*Pye*	20	*8 Apr 61*	2

Eddie HODGES — US

SINGLES:	HITS 2			WEEKS 10
I'M GONNA KNOCK ON YOUR DOOR	*London*	37	*30 Sep 61*	6
Originally recorded by the Isley Brothers.				
(GIRLS GIRLS GIRLS) MADE TO LOVE	*London*	37	*11 Aug 62*	4
Written by Phil Everly.				

Roger HODGSON — UK

(See also Supertramp.)

ALBUMS:	HITS 1			WEEKS 4
IN THE EYE OF THE STORM	*A&M*	70	*20 Oct 84*	4

Gerard HOFFNUNG — Germany

ALBUMS:	HITS 1			WEEKS 20
AT THE OXFORD UNION	*Decca*	4	*3 Sep 60*	20

Susanna HOFFS — US

SINGLES:	HITS 3			WEEKS 8
MY SIDE OF THE BED	*Columbia*	44	*2 Mar 91*	4
UNCONDITIONAL LOVE	*Columbia*	65	*11 May 91*	2
ALL I WANT	*London*	32	*19 Oct 96*	2

ALBUMS:	HITS 1			WEEKS 2
WHEN YOU'RE A BOY	*Columbia*	56	*6 Apr 91*	2

Hulk HOGAN with GREEN JELLY and the WRESTLING BOOT TRASH CAN BAND — US

SINGLES:	HITS 1			WEEKS 4
I'M THE LEADER OF THE GANG	*Arista*	25	*25 Dec 93*	4

Christopher HOGWOOD – See ACADEMY Of ANCENT MUSIC conducted by Christopher HOGWOOD

HOLE — US

SINGLES:	HITS 7			WEEKS 15
BEAUTIFUL SON	*City Slang*	54	*17 Apr 93*	1
MISS WORLD	*City Slang*	64	*9 Apr 94*	1
DOLL PARTS	*Geffen*	16	*15 Apr 95*	3
VIOLET	*Geffen*	17	*29 Jul 95*	2
CELEBRITY SKIN	*Geffen*	19	*12 Sep 98*	4
MALIBU	*Geffen*	22	*30 Jan 99*	2
AWFUL	*Geffen*	42	*10 Jul 99*	2

ALBUMS:	HITS 3			WEEKS 10
PRETTY ON THE INSIDE	*City Slang*	59	*12 Oct 91*	1
LIVE THROUGH THIS	*City Slang*	13	*23 Apr 94*	5
CELEBRITY SKIN	*Geffen*	11	*19 Sep 98*	4

HOLE IN ONE — Holland

SINGLES:	HITS 1			WEEKS 2
LIFE'S TOO SHORT	*Manifesto*	36	*15 Feb 97*	2

Billie HOLIDAY — US

ALBUMS:	HITS 2			WEEKS 11
THE LEGEND OF BILLIE HOLIDAY	*MCA*	60	*16 Nov 85*	10
LADY DAY – THE VERY BEST OF BILLIE HOLIDAY	*Columbia*	63	*6 Sep 97*	1

Jools HOLLAND and his R&B ORCHESTRA — UK

SINGLES:	HITS 1			WEEKS 3
I'M IN THE MOOD FOR LOVE	*WSM*	29	*24 Feb 01*	3
Originally recorded by Little Jack Little & Orchestra in 1935.				
Above hit: Jools HOLLAND and JAMIROQUAI with the RHYTHM AND BLUES ORCHESTRA.				

ALBUMS:	HITS 4			WEEKS 9
WORLD OF HIS OWN	*I.R.S.*	71	*5 May 90*	1
Above hit: Jools HOLLAND.				
SEX & JAZZ & ROCK & ROLL	*Coliseum*	38	*26 Oct 96*	2
LIFT THE LID	*Coalition*	50	*25 Oct 97*	1
SMALL WORLD BIG BAND	*WSM*	14	*1 Dec 01*	5

HOLLAND-DOZIER featuring Lamont DOZIER — US

SINGLES:	HITS 1			WEEKS 5
WHY CAN'T WE BE LOVERS	*Invictus*	29	*28 Oct 72*	5

Jennifer HOLLIDAY — US

SINGLES:	HITS 1			WEEKS 6
AND I'M TELLING YOU I'M NOT GOING	*Geffen*	32	*4 Sep 82*	6
From the musical 'Dream Girls'.				

Michael HOLLIDAY — UK

SINGLES:	HITS 10			WEEKS 66
NOTHIN' TO DO	*Columbia*	20	*31 Mar 56*	1
Above hit: Michael HOLLIDAY with Norrie PARAMOR and his Orchestra and Chorus.				
NOTHIN' TO DO [RE]	*Columbia*	23	*28 Apr 56*	2
THE GAL WITH THE YALLER SHOES	*Columbia*	13	*16 Jun 56*	3
From the film 'Viva Las Vegas'.				
HOT DIGGITY (DOG ZIGGITY BOOM)	*Columbia*	14	*23 Jun 56*	5
Above 2 entries were separate sides of the same release, each had its own chart run.				
HOT DIGGITY (DOG ZIGGITY BOOM) / THE GAL WITH THE YALLER SHOES [RE]	*Columbia*	17	*4 Aug 56*	3
The Gal With The Yaller Shoes only listed on 18 Aug 56 once single had dropped to No. 25.				
Above 3: Michael HOLLIDAY with Norrie PARAMOR and his Orchestra and the FOUR SHEPHERD BOYS.				
TEN THOUSAND MILES	*Columbia*	24	*6 Oct 56*	3
Above hit: Michael HOLLIDAY with Norrie PARAMOR and his Orchestra with the Michael SAMMES SINGERS.				
THE STORY OF MY LIFE	*Columbia*	1	*18 Jan 58*	15
Original by Marty Robbins reached No. 15 in the US in 1957.				
IN LOVE	*Columbia*	26	*15 Mar 58*	3
STAIRWAY OF LOVE	*Columbia*	3	*17 May 58*	13
Originally recorded by Marty Robbins.				
I'LL ALWAYS BE IN LOVE WITH YOU	*Columbia*	27	*12 Jul 58*	1
Above 2: Michael HOLLIDAY with Norrie PARAMOR and his Orchestra.				
STARRY EYED	*Columbia*	1	*2 Jan 60*	13
Originally recorded by Gary Stites in 1959.				
Above hit: Michael HOLLIDAY with the Michael SAMMES SINGERS.				
SKYLARK	*Columbia*	39	*16 Apr 60*	3
LITTLE BOY LOST	*Columbia*	50	*3 Sep 60*	1
Above hit: Michael HOLLIDAY with Norrie PARAMOR and his Orchestra.				

HOLLIES — UK

SINGLES:	HITS 29			WEEKS 318
(AIN'T THAT) JUST LIKE ME	*Parlophone*	25	*1 Jun 63*	10
SEARCHIN'	*Parlophone*	12	*31 Aug 63*	14
Originally recorded by the Coasters.				
STAY	*Parlophone*	8	*23 Nov 63*	16
JUST ONE LOOK	*Parlophone*	2	*29 Feb 64*	13
Original by Doris Troy reached No. 10 in the US in 1963.				
HERE I GO AGAIN	*Parlophone*	4	*23 May 64*	12
WE'RE THROUGH	*Parlophone*	7	*19 Sep 64*	11
YES I WILL	*Parlophone*	9	*30 Jan 65*	13
I'M ALIVE	*Parlophone*	1	*29 May 65*	14
LOOK THROUGH ANY WINDOW	*Parlophone*	4	*4 Sep 65*	11
IF I NEEDED SOMEONE	*Parlophone*	20	*11 Dec 65*	9
I CAN'T LET GO	*Parlophone*	2	*26 Feb 66*	10
Originally recorded by Evie Sands.				
BUS STOP	*Parlophone*	5	*25 Jun 66*	9
STOP STOP STOP	*Parlophone*	2	*15 Oct 66*	12
ON A CAROUSEL	*Parlophone*	4	*18 Feb 67*	11
CARRIE ANNE	*Parlophone*	3	*3 Jun 67*	11
Written for Marianne Faithfull.				
KING MIDAS IN REVERSE	*Parlophone*	18	*30 Sep 67*	8

JENNIFER ECCLES *Jennifer was Allan Clarke's wife's name, and Eccles was Graham Nash's wife's maiden name.*	*Parlophone*	7	*30 Mar 68*	11
LISTEN TO ME	*Parlophone*	11	*5 Oct 68*	11
SORRY SUZANNE	*Parlophone*	3	*8 Mar 69*	12
HE AIN'T HEAVY . . . HE'S MY BROTHER *Originally recorded by Kelly Gordon.*	*Parlophone*	3	*4 Oct 69*	15
I CAN'T TELL THE BOTTOM FROM THE TOP *Above two feature Elton John on Piano.*	*Parlophone*	7	*18 Apr 70*	10
GASOLINE ALLEY BRED	*Parlophone*	14	*3 Oct 70*	7
HEY WILLY	*Parlophone*	22	*22 May 71*	7
THE BABY *Originally recorded by Chip Taylor.*	*Polydor*	26	*26 Feb 72*	6
LONG COOL WOMAN IN A BLACK DRESS	*Parlophone*	32	*2 Sep 72*	8
THE DAY THAT CURLY BILLY SHOT CRAZY SAM MCGEE	*Polydor*	24	*13 Oct 73*	6
THE AIR THAT I BREATHE *Originally recorded by Albert Hammond.*	*Polydor*	2	*9 Feb 74*	13
SOLDIER'S SONG	*Polydor*	58	*14 Jun 80*	3
HOLLIEDAZE (A MEDLEY) [M] *Medley of old hits.*	*EMI*	28	*29 Aug 81*	7
HE AIN'T HEAVY, HE'S MY BROTHER [RI] *Featured in the Miller Lite lager TV commercial.*	*EMI*	1	*3 Sep 88*	11
THE AIR THAT I BREATHE [RI]	*EMI*	60	*3 Dec 88*	5
THE WOMAN I LOVE *Released to celebrate their 30th Anniversary.*	*EMI*	42	*20 Mar 93*	2
EPS:	**HITS 4**			**WEEKS 33**
THE HOLLIES	*Parlophone*	6	*6 Jun 64*	8
JUST ONE LOOK	*Parlophone*	10	*27 Jun 64*	8
I'M ALIVE	*Parlophone*	5	*25 Sep 65*	15
I CAN'T LET GO	*Parlophone*	9	*9 Jul 66*	2
ALBUMS:	**HITS 13**			**WEEKS 150**
STAY WITH THE HOLLIES	*Parlophone*	2	*15 Feb 64*	25
HOLLIES	*Parlophone*	8	*2 Oct 65*	14
WOULD YOU BELIEVE?	*Parlophone*	16	*16 Jul 66*	8
FOR CERTAIN BECAUSE	*Parlophone*	23	*17 Dec 66*	7
EVOLUTION	*Parlophone*	13	*17 Jun 67*	10
THE HOLLIES' GREATEST	*Parlophone*	1	*17 Aug 68*	27
HOLLIES SING DYLAN	*Parlophone*	3	*17 May 69*	7
CONFESSIONS OF THE MIND	*Parlophone*	30	*28 Nov 70*	5
HOLLIES *Both self titled albums are different.*	*Polydor*	38	*16 Mar 74*	3
HOLLIES LIVE HITS *Live recordings from Christchurch, New Zealand, Feb 76.*	*Polydor*	4	*19 Mar 77*	12
20 GOLDEN GREATS	*EMI*	2	*22 Jul 78*	15
20 GOLDEN GREATS [RE]	*EMI*	64	*10 Sep 88*	5
ALL THE HITS AND MORE	*EMI*	51	*1 Oct 88*	5
THE AIR THAT I BREATHE – THE BEST OF THE HOLLIES	*EMI*	15	*3 Apr 93*	7

Mark HOLLIS UK

ALBUMS:	**HITS 1**			**WEEKS 1**
MARK HOLLIS	*Polydor*	53	*14 Feb 98*	1

Laurie HOLLOWAY – See SOUTH BANK ORCHESTRA conducted by Joseph MOROVITZ and Laurie HOLLOWAY

Loleatta HOLLOWAY US

SINGLES:	**HITS 7**			**WEEKS 21**
GOOD VIBRATIONS *Samples Loleatta Holloway's Love Sensation.* *Above hit: MARKY MARK and the FUNKY BUNCH (featuring Loleatta HOLLOWAY).*	*Interscope*	14	*31 Aug 91*	7
TAKE ME AWAY *Above hit: CAPPELLA featuring Loleatta HOLLOWAY.*	*PWL Continental*	25	*18 Jan 92*	5
STAND UP	*Six6*	68	*26 Mar 94*	1
KEEP THE FIRE BURNIN' *Above hit: Dan HARTMAN Starring Loleatta HOLLOWAY.*	*Columbia*	49	*1 Apr 95*	1
SHOUT TO THE TOP *Above hit: FIRE ISLAND featuring Loleatta HOLLOWAY.*	*JBO*	23	*11 Apr 98*	2
(YOU GOT ME) BURNING UP *Samples Loleatta Holloway's Love Sensation.* *Above Hit: Cevin FISHER featuring Loleatta HOLLOWAY.*	*Wonderboy*	14	*20 Feb 99*	4
DREAMIN' *Remixed by Satoshi Tomiie. Holloway's original reached No. 72 in the US in 1977.*	*Defected*	59	*25 Nov 00*	1

HOLLOWAY and CO. UK

SINGLES:	**HITS 1**			**WEEKS 1**
I'LL DO ANYTHING – TO MAKE YOU MINE	*INCredible*	58	*21 Aug 99*	1

Buddy HOLLY — US

(See also Crickets.)

SINGLES:	HITS 19			WEEKS 190
PEGGY SUE	*Vogue Coral*	6	*7 Dec 57*	17
Title originally called Cindy-Lou.				
LISTEN TO ME	*Coral*	16	*15 Mar 58*	2
RAVE ON	*Coral*	5	*21 Jun 58*	14
Originally recorded by Sonny West.				
EARLY IN THE MORNING	*Coral*	17	*30 Aug 58*	4
Originally recorded by Bobby Darin and the Rinky Dinks.				
HEARTBEAT	*Coral*	30	*17 Jan 59*	1
IT DOESN'T MATTER ANYMORE	*Coral*	1	*28 Feb 59*	21
Originally recorded by Paul Anka.				
MIDNIGHT SHIFT	*Brunswick*	26	*1 Aug 59*	3
PEGGY SUE GOT MARRIED	*Coral*	13	*12 Sep 59*	10
HEARTBEAT [RI]	*Coral*	30	*30 Apr 60*	3
TRUE LOVE WAYS	*Coral*	25	*28 May 60*	7
LEARNING THE GAME	*Coral*	36	*22 Oct 60*	3
WHAT TO DO	*Coral*	34	*28 Jan 61*	6
BABY I DON'T CARE / VALLEY OF TEARS	*Coral*	12	*8 Jul 61*	14
Valley of Tears listed from 22 Jul 61. Baby I Don't Care originally recorded by Elvis Presley.				
LISTEN TO ME [RI]	*Coral*	48	*17 Mar 62*	1
REMINISCING	*Coral*	17	*15 Sep 62*	11
BROWN EYED HANDSOME MAN	*Coral*	3	*16 Mar 63*	17
Originally recorded by Chuck Berry in 1956.				
BO DIDDLEY	*Coral*	4	*8 Jun 63*	12
Originally recorded by Bo Diddley.				
WISHING	*Coral*	10	*7 Sep 63*	11
WHAT TO DO [RR]	*Coral*	27	*21 Dec 63*	8
YOU'VE GOT LOVE	*Coral*	40	*16 May 64*	6
Above hit: Buddy HOLLY and the CRICKETS.				
LOVE'S MADE A FOOL OF YOU	*Coral*	39	*12 Sep 64*	6
PEGGY SUE [RI] / RAVE ON [RI]	*MCA*	32	*6 Apr 68*	9
TRUE LOVE WAYS [RI]	*MCA*	65	*10 Dec 88*	4
EPS:	**HITS 5**			**WEEKS 90**
THE LATE GREAT BUDDY HOLLY	*Coral*	4	*19 Mar 60*	43
RAVE ON	*Coral*	9	*22 Jul 61*	22
BUDDY HOLLY NO. 1	*Brunswick*	18	*26 Aug 61*	2
HEARTBEAT	*Coral*	13	*2 Sep 61*	6
LISTEN TO ME	*Coral*	12	*17 Mar 62*	17
ALBUMS:	**HITS 13**			**WEEKS 339**
THE BUDDY HOLLY STORY	*Coral*	2	*2 May 59*	156
Includes re-entries through to 1964.				
THE BUDDY HOLLY STORY VOLUME 2	*Coral*	7	*15 Oct 60*	14
THAT'LL BE THE DAY	*Ace Of Hearts*	5	*21 Oct 61*	14
REMINISCING	*Coral*	2	*6 Apr 63*	31
BUDDY HOLLY SHOWCASE	*Coral*	3	*13 Jun 64*	16
HOLLY IN THE HILLS	*Coral*	13	*26 Jun 65*	6
Above 6: Buddy HOLLY and the CRICKETS.				
BUDDY HOLLY'S GREATEST HITS	*Ace Of Hearts*	10	*15 Jul 67*	21
BUDDY HOLLY'S GREATEST HITS [RE]	*Ace Of Hearts*	9	*11 May 68*	19
GIANT	*MCA*	13	*12 Apr 69*	1
Above hit: Buddy HOLLY and the CRICKETS.				
BUDDY HOLLY'S GREATEST HITS [RI-1ST]	*Coral*	32	*21 Aug 71*	6
BUDDY HOLLY'S GREATEST HITS [RI-1ST] [RE]	*Coral*	42	*12 Jul 75*	3
Repackaged with additional tracks.				
20 GOLDEN GREATS	*MCA*	1	*11 Mar 78*	20
Above hit: Buddy HOLLY and the CRICKETS.				
BUDDY HOLLY'S GREATEST HITS [RI-2ND]	*MCA*	100	*8 Sep 84*	1
TRUE LOVE WAYS	*Telstar*	8	*18 Feb 89*	11
WORDS OF LOVE	*PolyGram TV/MCA*	1	*20 Feb 93*	9
Above hit: Buddy HOLLY and the CRICKETS.				
THE VERY BEST OF BUDDY HOLLY	*Dino*	24	*7 Dec 96*	8
THE VERY BEST OF BUDDY HOLLY AND THE CRICKETS	*Universal Music TV*	25	*28 Aug 99*	3
Above hit: Buddy HOLLY and the CRICKETS.				

HOLLY and the IVYS — UK

SINGLES:	HITS 1			WEEKS 4
CHRISTMAS ON 45 [M]	*Decca*	40	*19 Dec 81*	4

HOLLYWOOD ARGYLES — US

SINGLES:	HITS 1			WEEKS 10
ALLEY-OOP	*London*	24	*23 Jul 60*	10

HOLLYWOOD BEYOND — UK

SINGLES:	HITS 2			WEEKS 14
WHAT'S THE COLOUR OF MONEY? *Features Mica Paris on backing vocals.*	*WEA*	7	*12 Jul 86*	10
NO MORE TEARS	*WEA*	47	*20 Sep 86*	4

Eddie HOLMAN — US

SINGLES:	HITS 1			WEEKS 13
(HEY THERE) LONELY GIRL	*ABC*	4	*19 Oct 74*	13

Dave HOLMES — UK

SINGLES:	HITS 1			WEEKS 1
DEVOTION	*Tidy Trax*	66	*26 May 01*	1

David HOLMES — UK

SINGLES:	HITS 5			WEEKS 8
GONE *Vocals by Sarah Cracknell of Saint Etienne.*	*Go! Discs*	75	*6 Apr 96*	1
GRITTY SHAKER	*Go.Beat*	53	*23 Aug 97*	1
DON'T DIE JUST YET	*Go.Beat*	33	*10 Jan 98*	3
MY MATE PAUL	*Go.Beat*	39	*4 Apr 98*	2
69 POLICE	*Go.Beat*	53	*19 Aug 00*	1
ALBUMS:	**HITS 3**			**WEEKS 5**
THIS FILM'S CRAP, LET'S SLASH THE SEATS	*Go! Discs*	51	*22 Jul 95*	1
LET'S GET KILLED	*Go.Beat*	34	*13 Sep 97*	2
BOW DOWN TO THE EXIT SIGN	*Go.Beat*	22	*24 Jun 00*	2

Rupert HOLMES — US

SINGLES:	HITS 2			WEEKS 14
ESCAPE (THE PINA COLADA SONG)	*Infinity*	23	*12 Jan 80*	7
HIM	*MCA*	31	*22 Mar 80*	7

Adele HOLNESS – See Ben SHAW featuring Adele HOLNESS

John HOLT — Jamaica

SINGLES:	HITS 1			WEEKS 14
HELP ME MAKE IT THROUGH THE NIGHT *Originally recorded by Kris Kristofferson.*	*Trojan*	6	*14 Dec 74*	14
ALBUMS:	**HITS 1**			**WEEKS 2**
A THOUSAND VOLTS OF HOLT	*Trojan*	42	*1 Feb 75*	2

Nichola HOLT — UK

SINGLES:	HITS 1			WEEKS 1
THE GAME	*RCA*	72	*21 Oct 00*	1

HOME — UK

ALBUMS:	HITS 1			WEEKS 1
DREAMER	*CBS*	41	*11 Nov 72*	1

A HOMEBOY, A HIPPIE and A FUNKI DREDD — UK

SINGLES:	HITS 3			WEEKS 9
TOTAL CONFUSION	*Tam Tam*	56	*13 Oct 90*	3
FREEDOM	*Tam Tam*	68	*29 Dec 90*	4
HERE WE GO AGAIN	*Polydor*	57	*8 Jan 94*	2

HOMER – See SIMPSONS

HONDY — Italy

SINGLES:	HITS 1			WEEKS 2
HONDY (NO ACCESS)	*Manifesto*	26	*12 Apr 97*	2

HONEYBUS — UK

SINGLES:	HITS 1			WEEKS 12
I CAN'T LET MAGGIE GO	*Deram*	8	*23 Mar 68*	12

HONEYCOMBS — UK

SINGLES:	HITS 4			WEEKS 39
HAVE I THE RIGHT?	*Pye*	1	*25 Jul 64*	15
IS IT BECAUSE?	*Pye*	38	*24 Oct 64*	6
SOMETHING BETTER BEGINNING *Originally recorded by the Kinks.*	*Pye*	39	*1 May 65*	4
THAT'S THE WAY	*Pye*	12	*7 Aug 65*	14

HONEYCRACK — UK

SINGLES:	HITS 4			WEEKS 9
SITTING AT HOME	*Epic*	42	*4 Nov 95*	2
GO AWAY	*Epic*	41	*24 Feb 96*	2
KING OF MISERY	*Epic*	32	*11 May 96*	2
SITTING AT HOME [RI]	*Epic*	32	*20 Jul 96*	2
ANYWAY	*E'G*	67	*16 Nov 96*	1
ALBUMS:	**HITS 1**			**WEEKS 1**
PROZAIC	*Epic*	34	*1 Jun 96*	1

HONEYDRIPPERS — UK/US

SINGLES:	HITS 1			WEEKS 3
SEA OF LOVE	*Es Paranza*	56	*2 Feb 85*	3
ALBUMS:	**HITS 1**			**WEEKS 10**
THE HONEYDRIPPERS VOLUME ONE	*Es Paranza*	56	*1 Dec 84*	10

HONEYZ — UK/France

SINGLES:	HITS 7			WEEKS 57
FINALLY FOUND	*Mercury*	4	*5 Sep 98*	12
END OF THE LINE	*Mercury*	5	*19 Dec 98*	12
END OF THE LINE [RE]	*Mercury*	64	*24 Apr 99*	2
LOVE OF A LIFETIME	*Mercury*	9	*24 Apr 99*	9
NEVER LET YOU DOWN	*Mercury*	7	*23 Oct 99*	6
WON'T TAKE IT LYING DOWN	*Mercury*	7	*11 Mar 00*	7
WON'T TAKE IT LYING DOWN [RE]	*Mercury*	72	*13 May 00*	1
NOT EVEN GONNA TRIP	*Mercury*	24	*28 Oct 00*	3
From the film 'The Nutty Professor II: The Klumps'.				
NOT EVEN GONNA TRIP [RE-1ST]	*Mercury*	68	*25 Nov 00*	1
NOT EVEN GONNA TRIP [RE-2ND]	*Mercury*	71	*13 Jan 01*	1
I DON'T KNOW	*Mercury*	28	*18 Aug 01*	3
ALBUMS:	**HITS 1**			**WEEKS 22**
WONDER NO.8	*Mercury*	33	*5 Dec 98*	19
WONDER NO.8 [RE]	*Mercury*	46	*13 Nov 99*	3
Re-released with additional track.				

HONKY — UK

SINGLES:	HITS 1			WEEKS 5
JOIN THE PARTY	*Creole*	28	*28 May 77*	5

HONKY — UK

SINGLES:	HITS 4			WEEKS 5
THE HONKY DOODLE DAY [EP]	*ZTT*	61	*30 Oct 93*	1
Lead track: K.K.K. (Boom Boom Tra La La La).				
THE WHISTLER	*ZTT*	41	*19 Feb 94*	2
HIP HOP DON'T YA DROP	*Higher Ground*	70	*20 Apr 96*	1
WHAT'S GOIN DOWN	*Higher Ground*	49	*10 Aug 96*	1
Samples Ian Dury's Sex & Drugs & Rock & Roll.				

Frank HOOKER and POSITIVE PEOPLE — US

SINGLES:	HITS 1			WEEKS 4
THIS FEELIN'	*DJM*	48	*5 Jul 80*	4

John Lee HOOKER — US

SINGLES:	HITS 6			WEEKS 23
DIMPLES	*Stateside*	23	*13 Jun 64*	10
BOOM BOOM	*Pointblank*	16	*24 Oct 92*	5
Featured in the Lee Jeans TV commercial. Originally released in 1963.				
BOOGIE AT RUSSIAN HILL	*Pointblank*	53	*16 Jan 93*	2
GLORIA	*Exile*	31	*15 May 93*	3
Original by Them was the B-side to Baby Please Don't Go in 1964.				
Above hit: Van MORRISON and John Lee HOOKER.				
CHILL OUT (THINGS GONNA CHANGE)	*Pointblank*	45	*11 Feb 95*	2
Features Carlos Santana.				
BABY LEE	*Silvertone*	65	*20 Apr 96*	1
Featured in the Lee Jeans TV commercial.				
Above hit: John Lee HOOKER with Robert CRAY.				
ALBUMS:	**HITS 6**			**WEEKS 31**
HOUSE OF THE BLUES	*Marble Arch*	34	*4 Feb 67*	2
THE HEALER	*Silvertone*	63	*11 Nov 89*	8
Above hit: John Lee HOOKER and FRIENDS.				
MR. LUCKY	*Silvertone*	3	*21 Sep 91*	10
BOOM BOOM	*Pointblank*	15	*7 Nov 92*	4

CHILL OUT	*Pointblank*	23	*4 Mar 95*	5
DON'T LOOK BACK	*Pointblank*	63	*22 Mar 97*	2

HOOTERS — US

SINGLES:	HITS 1			WEEKS 9
SATELLITE	*CBS*	22	*21 Nov 87*	9

HOOTIE AND THE BLOWFISH — US

SINGLES:	HITS 4			WEEKS 6
HOLD MY HAND	*Atlantic*	50	*25 Feb 95*	3
LET HER CRY	*Atlantic*	75	*27 May 95*	1
OLD MAN & ME (WHEN I GET TO HEAVEN)	*Atlantic*	57	*4 May 96*	1
I WILL WAIT	*Atlantic*	57	*7 Nov 98*	1
ALBUMS:	**HITS 3**			**WEEKS 30**
CRACKED REAR VIEW	*Atlantic*	12	*18 Mar 95*	11
FAIRWEATHER JOHNSON	*Atlantic*	9	*4 May 96*	16
MUSICAL CHAIRS	*Atlantic*	15	*26 Sep 98*	3

HOPE A.D. — UK

(See also Mind Of Kane.)

SINGLES:	HITS 1			WEEKS 1
TREE FROG *Originally released in 1993.*	*Sun-Up*	73	*4 Jun 94*	1

Mary HOPKIN — UK

(See also Various Artists (EPs) 'The Apple EP'.)

SINGLES:	HITS 7			WEEKS 74
THOSE WERE THE DAYS *Originally recorded in English by the Limeliters.*	*Apple*	1	*7 Sep 68*	21
GOODBYE *Written by Lennon/McCartney.*	*Apple*	2	*5 Apr 69*	14
TEMMA HARBOUR	*Apple*	6	*31 Jan 70*	11
KNOCK, KNOCK WHO'S THERE? *UK's Eurovision entry in 1970, it came 2nd.*	*Apple*	2	*28 Mar 70*	14
THINK ABOUT YOUR CHILDREN *Written by Errol Brown and Tony Wilson of Hot Chocolate.*	*Apple*	19	*31 Oct 70*	7
THINK ABOUT YOUR CHILDREN [RE]	*Apple*	46	*2 Jan 71*	2
LET MY NAME BE SORROW	*Apple*	46	*31 Jul 71*	1
IF YOU LOVE ME (I WON'T CARE) *Originally recorded by Edith Piaf.*	*Good Earth*	32	*20 Mar 76*	4
ALBUMS:	**HITS 1**			**WEEKS 9**
POSTCARD	*Apple*	3	*1 Mar 69*	9

Anthony HOPKINS — UK

SINGLES:	HITS 1			WEEKS 1
DISTANT STAR	*Juice*	75	*27 Dec 86*	1

Nick HORNBY – See VARIOUS ARTISTS (EPs) 'Fever Pitch The EP'

James HORNER — US

ALBUMS:	HITS 3			WEEKS 82
BRAVEHEART [OST] *Above hit: LONDON SYMPHONY ORCHESTRA, conductor James HORNER.*	*Decca*	27	*23 Sep 95*	9
TITANIC [OST] *Above hit: Music composed and conducted by James HORNER.*	*Sony Classical*	1	*31 Jan 98*	55
BACK TO TITANIC	*Sony Classical*	10	*12 Sep 98*	18

Bruce HORNSBY and the RANGE — US

SINGLES:	HITS 3			WEEKS 15
THE WAY IT IS	*RCA*	15	*2 Aug 86*	10
MANDOLIN RAIN	*RCA*	70	*25 Apr 87*	1
THE VALLEY ROAD	*RCA*	44	*28 May 88*	4
ALBUMS:	**HITS 4**			**WEEKS 54**
THE WAY IT IS	*RCA*	16	*13 Sep 86*	26
SCENES FROM THE SOUTHSIDE	*RCA*	18	*14 May 88*	18
A NIGHT ON THE TOWN	*RCA*	23	*30 Jun 90*	7
HARBOR LIGHTS *Above hit: Bruce HORNSBY.*	*RCA*	32	*8 May 93*	3

HORNY UNITED – See BONEY M

Jane HORROCKS — UK

ALBUMS:	HITS 1			WEEKS 1
THE FURTHER ADVENTURES OF LITTLE VOICE	*Liberty*	63	*21 Oct 00*	1

HORSE — UK

SINGLES:	HITS 4			WEEKS 10
CAREFUL	*Capitol*	52	*24 Nov 90*	3
SHAKE THIS MOUNTAIN	*Oxygen*	52	*21 Aug 93*	2
GOD'S HOME MOVIE	*Oxygen*	56	*23 Oct 93*	1
CELEBRATE	*Oxygen*	49	*15 Jan 94*	2
CAREFUL [RM]	*Stress*	44	*5 Apr 97*	2
Remixed by Brothers In Rhythm.				

ALBUMS:	HITS 2			WEEKS 4
THE SAME SKY	*Echo Chamber*	44	*23 Jun 90*	2
GOD'S HOME MOVIE	*Oxygen*	42	*13 Nov 93*	2

HORSLIPS — Ireland

ALBUMS:	HITS 1			WEEKS 3
THE BOOK OF INVASIONS - A CELTIC SYMPHONY	*DJM*	39	*30 Apr 77*	3

Johnny HORTON — US

SINGLES:	HITS 2			WEEKS 15
THE BATTLE OF NEW ORLEANS	*Philips*	16	*27 Jun 59*	4
NORTH TO ALASKA	*Philips*	23	*21 Jan 61*	11
From the film of the same name.				

Robert HORTON — US

EPS:	HITS 1			WEEKS 8
ROBERT HORTON IN SUNDAY NIGHT AT THE LONDON PALLADIUM	*Pye*	7	*12 Mar 60*	8

HOT BLOOD — France

SINGLES:	HITS 1			WEEKS 5
SOUL DRACULA	*Creole*	32	*9 Oct 76*	5

HOT BOX GIRLS - See Vivian BLAINE and Robert ALDA with the HOT BOX GIRLS

HOT BUTTER — US

SINGLES:	HITS 1			WEEKS 19
POPCORN	*Pye International*	5	*22 Jul 72*	16
Originally recorded by Phantom Surfers.				
POPCORN [RE]	*Pye International*	50	*23 Dec 72*	3

HOT CHOCOLATE — UK

SINGLES:	HITS 30			WEEKS 283
LOVE IS LIFE	*RAK*	6	*15 Aug 70*	12
Accompanied by the Trinidad Singers.				
YOU COULD'VE BEEN A LADY	*RAK*	22	*6 Mar 71*	9
I BELIEVE (IN LOVE)	*RAK*	8	*28 Aug 71*	11
YOU'LL ALWAYS BE A FRIEND	*RAK*	23	*28 Oct 72*	8
BROTHER LOUIE	*RAK*	7	*14 Apr 73*	10
RUMOURS	*RAK*	44	*18 Aug 73*	3
EMMA	*RAK*	3	*16 Mar 74*	10
CHERI BABY	*RAK*	31	*30 Nov 74*	9
DISCO QUEEN	*RAK*	11	*24 May 75*	7
A CHILD'S PRAYER	*RAK*	7	*9 Aug 75*	10
YOU SEXY THING	*RAK*	2	*8 Nov 75*	12
DON'T STOP IT NOW	*RAK*	11	*20 Mar 76*	8
MAN TO MAN	*RAK*	14	*26 Jun 76*	8
HEAVEN IS IN THE BACK SEAT OF MY CADILLAC	*RAK*	25	*21 Aug 76*	8
SO YOU WIN AGAIN	*RAK*	1	*18 Jun 77*	11
PUT YOUR LOVE IN ME	*RAK*	10	*26 Nov 77*	9
EVERY 1'S A WINNER	*RAK*	12	*4 Mar 78*	11
I'LL PUT YOU TOGETHER AGAIN (FROM DEAR ANYONE)	*RAK*	13	*2 Dec 78*	11
Originally recorded by Pandora and the Correspondants.				
MINDLESS BOOGIE	*RAK*	46	*19 May 79*	5
GOING THROUGH THE MOTIONS	*RAK*	53	*28 Jul 79*	4
NO DOUBT ABOUT IT	*RAK*	2	*3 May 80*	11
ARE YOU GETTING ENOUGH OF WHAT MAKES YOU HAPPY	*RAK*	17	*19 Jul 80*	7
LOVE ME TO SLEEP	*RAK*	50	*13 Dec 80*	5
YOU'LL NEVER BE SO WRONG	*RAK*	52	*30 May 81*	4
GIRL CRAZY	*RAK*	7	*17 Apr 82*	11
IT STARTED WITH A KISS	*RAK*	5	*10 Jul 82*	12
CHANCES	*RAK*	32	*25 Sep 82*	5
WHAT KINDA BOY YOU'RE LOOKIN' FOR (GIRL)	*RAK*	10	*7 May 83*	9

TEARS ON THE TELEPHONE	*RAK*	37	*17 Sep 83*	5
I GAVE YOU MY HEART (DIDN'T I)	*RAK*	13	*4 Feb 84*	10
YOU SEXY THING [RM]	*EMI*	10	*17 Jan 87*	10
Remixed by Ben Liebrand.				
EVERY 1'S A WINNER (GROOVE MIX) [RM]	*EMI*	69	*4 Apr 87*	2
IT STARTED WITH A KISS [RI-1ST]	*EMI*	31	*6 Mar 93*	5
YOU SEXY THING [RI]	*EMI*	6	*22 Nov 97*	8
From the film 'The Full Monty'.				
IT STARTED WITH A KISS [RI-2ND]	*EMI*	18	*14 Feb 98*	3
Above hit: HOT CHOCOLATE featuring Errol BROWN.				
ALBUMS:	**HITS 8**			**WEEKS 153**
HOT CHOCOLATE	*RAK*	34	*15 Nov 75*	7
MAN TO MAN	*RAK*	32	*7 Aug 76*	7
GREATEST HITS	*RAK*	6	*20 Nov 76*	35
EVERY 1'S A WINNER	*RAK*	30	*8 Apr 78*	8
20 HOTTEST HITS	*RAK*	3	*15 Dec 79*	19
MYSTERY	*RAK*	24	*25 Sep 82*	7
THE VERY BEST OF HOT CHOCOLATE	*RAK*	1	*21 Feb 87*	28
THEIR GREATEST HITS	*EMI*	1	*20 Mar 93*	42
Includes re-entries through to 2001.				

HOT GOSSIP - See Sarah BRIGHTMAN

HOT HOUSE — UK

SINGLES:	**HITS 1**			**WEEKS 3**
DON'T COME TO STAY	*Deconstruction*	74	*14 Feb 87*	1
DON'T COME TO STAY [RI]	*Deconstruction*	70	*24 Sep 88*	2

HOT 'N' JUICY - See MOUSSE T.

HOT STREAK — US

SINGLES:	**HITS 1**			**WEEKS 8**
BODY WORK	*Polydor*	19	*10 Sep 83*	8

HOTHOUSE FLOWERS — Ireland

SINGLES:	**HITS 10**			**WEEKS 36**
DON'T GO	*London*	11	*14 May 88*	8
I'M SORRY	*London*	53	*23 Jul 88*	3
GIVE IT UP	*London*	30	*12 May 90*	5
I CAN SEE CLEARLY NOW	*London*	23	*28 Jul 90*	7
MOVIES	*London*	68	*20 Oct 90*	2
AN EMOTIONAL TIME	*London*	38	*13 Feb 93*	4
ONE TONGUE	*London*	45	*8 May 93*	3
ISN'T IT AMAZING	*London*	46	*19 Jun 93*	2
THIS IS IT (YOUR SOUL)	*London*	67	*27 Nov 93*	1
YOU CAN LOVE ME NOW	*London*	65	*16 May 98*	1
ALBUMS:	**HITS 3**			**WEEKS 51**
PEOPLE	*London*	2	*18 Jun 88*	19
HOME	*London*	5	*16 Jun 90*	21
SONGS FROM THE RAIN	*London*	7	*20 Mar 93*	11

HOTLEGS — UK

SINGLES:	**HITS 1**			**WEEKS 14**
NEANDERTHAL MAN	*Fontana*	2	*4 Jul 70*	14

HOTSHOTS — UK

SINGLES:	**HITS 1**			**WEEKS 15**
SNOOPY VERSUS THE RED BARON	*Mooncrest*	4	*2 Jun 73*	15

Steven HOUGHTON — UK

SINGLES:	**HITS 2**			**WEEKS 22**
WIND BENEATH MY WINGS	*RCA*	3	*29 Nov 97*	15
Originally recorded by Sheena Easton.				
TRULY	*RCA*	23	*7 Mar 98*	5
Both songs were featured in the ITV series 'London's Burning'.				
TRULY [RE]	*RCA*	72	*2 May 98*	2
ALBUMS:	**HITS 1**			**WEEKS 7**
STEVEN HOUGHTON	*RCA*	21	*29 Nov 97*	7

HOUND DOG and the MEGAMIXERS — UK

ALBUMS:	**HITS 1**			**WEEKS 9**
THE GREATEST EVER JUNIOR PARTY MEGAMIX	*Pop & Arts*	34	*1 Dec 90*	9

A HOUSE — Ireland

SINGLES:	HITS 4			WEEKS 8
ENDLESS ART	*Setanta*	46	*13 Jun 92*	3
TAKE IT EASY ON ME	*Setanta*	55	*8 Aug 92*	2
WHY ME?	*Setanta*	52	*25 Jun 94*	1
HERE COME THE GOOD TIMES	*Setanta*	37	*1 Oct 94*	2

HOUSE ENGINEERS — UK

SINGLES:	HITS 1			WEEKS 2
GHOST HOUSE	*Syncopate*	69	*5 Dec 87*	2

HOUSE MASTER BOYZ and the RUDE BOY OF HOUSE — US

SINGLES:	HITS 1			WEEKS 14
HOUSE NATION	*Magnetic Dance*	48	*9 May 87*	6
HOUSE NATION [RE]	*Magnetic Dance*	8	*12 Sep 87*	8

HOUSE OF GLASS — Italy

SINGLES:	HITS 1			WEEKS 1
DISCO DOWN	*Azuli*	72	*14 Apr 01*	1

HOUSE OF LOVE — UK/Germany/New Zealand

SINGLES:	HITS 8			WEEKS 21
NEVER	*Fontana*	41	*22 Apr 89*	2
I DON'T KNOW WHY I LOVE YOU	*Fontana*	41	*18 Nov 89*	3
SHINE ON	*Fontana*	20	*3 Feb 90*	4
BEATLES AND THE STONES	*Fontana*	36	*7 Apr 90*	4
THE GIRL WITH THE LONELIEST EYES	*Fontana*	58	*26 Oct 91*	1
FEEL	*Fontana*	45	*2 May 92*	3
YOU DON'T UNDERSTAND	*Fontana*	46	*27 Jun 92*	3
CRUSH ME	*Fontana*	67	*5 Dec 92*	1
ALBUMS:	**HITS 4**			**WEEKS 14**
HOUSE OF LOVE	*Fontana*	8	*10 Mar 90*	10
THE HOUSE OF LOVE	*Fontana*	49	*10 Nov 90*	1
BABE RAINBOW	*Fontana*	34	*18 Jul 92*	2
AUDIENCE WITH THE MIND	*Fontana*	38	*3 Jul 93*	1

HOUSE OF PAIN — US

SINGLES:	HITS 7			WEEKS 24
JUMP AROUND	*XL Recordings*	32	*10 Oct 92*	4
JUMP AROUND [RI] / TOP O' THE MORNING TO YA	*XL Recordings*	8	*22 May 93*	7
SHAMROCKS AND SHENANIGANS / WHO'S THE MAN	*XL Recordings*	23	*23 Oct 93*	4
Shamrocks And Shenanigans originally reached No. 97 in Jan 93. Shamrocks And Shenanigans samples David Bowie's Fame. Who'sThe Man samples the Kay Gees The Masterplan.				
ON POINT	*XL Recordings*	19	*16 Jul 94*	3
Samples Cannonball Adderley's Inside Straight				
IT AIN'T A CRIME	*XL Recordings*	37	*12 Nov 94*	2
Samples Red Hot Chili Pepper's Under The Bridge.				
OVER THERE (I DON'T CARE)	*XL Recordings*	20	*1 Jul 95*	3
FED UP	*Tommy Boy*	68	*5 Oct 96*	1
Featured in the Lucozade TV commercial. Samples Mitch Ryder's Blessing In Disguise.				
Above hit: HOUSE OF PAIN (featuring GURU).				
ALBUMS:	**HITS 2**			**WEEKS 7**
HOUSE OF PAIN	*XL Recordings*	73	*21 Nov 92*	1
SAME AS IT EVER WAS	*XL Recordings*	8	*30 Jul 94*	6

HOUSE OF VIRGINISM — Sweden

SINGLES:	HITS 3			WEEKS 6
I'LL BE THERE FOR YOU (DOYA DODODO DOYA)	*ffrr*	29	*20 Nov 93*	3
REACHIN	*ffrr*	35	*30 Jul 94*	2
EXCLUSIVE	*Logic*	67	*17 Feb 96*	1
Above hit: APOLLO Presents HOUSE OF VIRGINISM.				

HOUSE OF ZEKKARIYAS – See WOMACK and WOMACK

HOUSE TRAFFIC — UK/Italy

SINGLES:	HITS 1			WEEKS 3
EVERYDAY OF MY LIFE	*Logic*	24	*4 Oct 97*	3
Originally reached No. 101 in 1994.				

HOUSEMARTINS — UK

SINGLES:	HITS 8			WEEKS 59
SHEEP	*Go! Discs*	54	*8 Mar 86*	3
SHEEP [RE]	*Go! Discs*	71	*5 Apr 86*	1

HAPPY HOUR	*Go! Discs*	3	*7 Jun 86*	13
THINK FOR A MINUTE (NEW VERSION)	*Go! Discs*	18	*4 Oct 86*	8
CARAVAN OF LOVE	*Go! Discs*	1	*6 Dec 86*	11
Originally recorded by Isley Jasper Isley.				
FIVE GET OVEREXCITED	*Go! Discs*	11	*23 May 87*	6
ME AND THE FARMER	*Go! Discs*	15	*5 Sep 87*	5
BUILD	*Go! Discs*	15	*21 Nov 87*	8
THERE IS ALWAYS SOMETHING THERE TO REMIND ME	*Go! Discs*	35	*23 Apr 88*	4
ALBUMS:	**HITS 4**			**WEEKS 71**
LONDON 0 HULL 4	*Go! Discs*	3	*5 Jul 86*	41
THE HOUSEMARTINS' CHRISTMAS SINGLES BOX	*Go! Discs*	84	*27 Dec 86*	1
4 singles in foldout sleeve.				
THE PEOPLE WHO GRINNED THEMSELVES TO DEATH	*Go! Discs*	9	*3 Oct 87*	18
NOW THAT'S WHAT I CALL QUITE GOOD!	*Go! Discs*	8	*21 May 88*	11

HOUSETRAP – See DJ SANDY vs HOUSETRAP

Thelma HOUSTON — US

SINGLES:	**HITS 4**			**WEEKS 22**
DON'T LEAVE ME THIS WAY	*Motown*	13	*5 Feb 77*	8
IF YOU FEEL IT	*RCA*	48	*27 Jun 81*	4
YOU USED TO HOLD ME SO TIGHT	*MCA*	49	*1 Dec 84*	8
DON'T LEAVE ME THIS WAY [RR]	*Dynamo*	35	*21 Jan 95*	2

Whitney HOUSTON — US

(See also Various Artists: Films – Original Soundtracks 'The Bodyguard'; 'Waiting To Exhale'.)

SINGLES:	**HITS 32**			**WEEKS 312**
SAVING ALL MY LOVE FOR YOU	*Arista*	1	*16 Nov 85*	16
Originally recorded by Billy Davis Jr & Marilyn McCoo.				
HOLD ME	*Asylum*	44	*25 Jan 86*	5
Above hit: Teddy PENDERGRASS with Whitney HOUSTON.				
HOW WILL I KNOW	*Arista*	5	*25 Jan 86*	12
Originally written for Janet Jackson, backing vocals by Whitney's mother Cissy.				
GREATEST LOVE OF ALL	*Arista*	8	*12 Apr 86*	11
I WANNA DANCE WITH SOMEBODY (WHO LOVES ME)	*Arista*	1	*23 May 87*	16
Written by Boy Meets Girl.				
DIDN'T WE ALMOST HAVE IT ALL	*Arista*	14	*22 Aug 87*	8
SO EMOTIONAL	*Arista*	5	*14 Nov 87*	11
WHERE DO BROKEN HEARTS GO	*Arista*	14	*12 Mar 88*	8
LOVE WILL SAVE THE DAY	*Arista*	10	*28 May 88*	7
ONE MOMENT IN TIME	*Arista*	1	*24 Sep 88*	12
The official theme for the Olympic Games in Seoul, South Korea.				
IT ISN'T, IT WASN'T, IT AIN'T NEVER GONNA BE	*Arista*	29	*9 Sep 89*	5
Label only credits Aretha Franklin.				
Above hit: ARETHA and WHITNEY.				
I'M YOUR BABY TONIGHT	*Arista*	5	*20 Oct 90*	9
ALL THE MAN THAT I NEED	*Arista*	13	*22 Dec 90*	10
Originally recorded by Linda Clifford in 1978, features Kenny G on saxophone.				
I'M YOUR BABY TONIGHT [RE]	*Arista*	69	*29 Dec 90*	1
MY NAME IS NOT SUSAN	*Arista*	29	*6 Jul 91*	5
I BELONG TO YOU	*Arista*	54	*28 Sep 91*	2
I WILL ALWAYS LOVE YOU	*Arista*	1	*14 Nov 92*	23
Originally recorded by Dolly Parton in 1974.				
I'M EVERY WOMAN	*Arista*	4	*20 Feb 93*	11
Backing vocals by Jeanie Tracy.				
I HAVE NOTHING	*Arista*	3	*24 Apr 93*	10
RUN TO YOU	*Arista*	15	*31 Jul 93*	6
QUEEN OF THE NIGHT	*Arista*	14	*6 Nov 93*	5
Above 5 from the film 'The Bodyguard'.				
I WILL ALWAYS LOVE YOU [RE]	*Arista*	25	*18 Dec 93*	6
SOMETHING IN COMMON	*MCA*	16	*22 Jan 94*	5
Above hit: Bobby BROWN (Duet with Whitney HOUSTON).				
EXHALE (SHOOP SHOOP)	*Arista*	11	*18 Nov 95*	9
COUNT ON ME	*Arista*	12	*24 Feb 96*	6
Above 2 from the film 'Waiting To Exhale'.				
Above hit: Whitney HOUSTON and CeCe WINANS.				
STEP BY STEP	*Arista*	13	*21 Dec 96*	13
Backing vocals by Annie Lennox.				
I BELIEVE IN YOU AND ME	*Arista*	16	*29 Mar 97*	5
Above 2 from the film 'The Preacher's Wife'.				
WHEN YOU BELIEVE (FROM THE PRINCE OF EGYPT)	*Columbia*	4	*19 Dec 98*	11
From the film 'The Prince Of Egypt'.				
Above hit: Mariah CAREY and Whitney HOUSTON.				
IT'S NOT RIGHT BUT IT'S OKAY	*Arista*	3	*6 Mar 99*	15
WHEN YOU BELIEVE (FROM THE PRINCE OF EGYPT) [RE]	*Columbia*	68	*27 Mar 99*	2
MY LOVE IS YOUR LOVE	*Arista*	2	*3 Jul 99*	12
Including backing vocals from the Family Friends Community Choir.				

I LEARNED FROM THE BEST	*Arista*	19	*11 Dec 99*	11
IF I TOLD YOU THAT	*Arista*	9	*17 Jun 00*	9
Above hit: Whitney HOUSTON and George MICHAEL.				
IF I TOLD YOU THAT [RE]	*Arista*	51	*26 Aug 00*	2
COULD I HAVE THIS KISS FOREVER	*Arista*	7	*14 Oct 00*	8
Above hit: Whitney HOUSTON and Enrique IGLESIAS.				
HEARTBREAK HOTEL	*Arista*	25	*30 Dec 00*	5
Above hit: Whitney HOUSTON (featuring Faith EVANS and Kelly PRICE).				
ALBUMS:	**HITS 6**			**WEEKS 374**
WHITNEY HOUSTON	*Arista*	2	*14 Dec 85*	119
WHITNEY	*Arista*	1	*13 Jun 87*	101
I'M YOUR BABY TONIGHT	*Arista*	4	*17 Nov 90*	29
THE PREACHER'S WIFE [OST]	*Arista*	35	*4 Jan 97*	7
MY LOVE IS YOUR LOVE	*Arista*	4	*28 Nov 98*	68
Peak position reached on 24 Jul 99.				
THE GREATEST HITS	*Arista*	1	*27 May 00*	50

Adina HOWARD — US

SINGLES:	**HITS 2**			**WEEKS 16**
FREAK LIKE ME	*East West America*	67	*4 Mar 95*	1
FREAK LIKE ME [RE]	*East West America*	33	*6 May 95*	3
WHAT'S LOVE GOT TO DO WITH IT	*Interscope*	2	*23 Nov 96*	12
Above hit: Warren G featuring Adina HOWARD.				

Billy HOWARD — UK

SINGLES:	**HITS 1**			**WEEKS 12**
KING OF THE COPS	*Penny Farthing*	6	*13 Dec 75*	12
Impersonations of TV cops to the music of King Of The Road.				

Miki HOWARD — US

SINGLES:	**HITS 1**			**WEEKS 2**
UNTIL YOU COME BACK TO ME (THAT'S WHAT I'M GONNA DO)	*Atlantic*	67	*26 May 90*	2

Nick HOWARD — Australia

SINGLES:	**HITS 1**			**WEEKS 1**
EVERYBODY NEEDS SOMEBODY	*Bell*	64	*21 Jan 95*	1

Robert HOWARD and Kym MAZELLE — UK/US

(See also Kym Mazelle.)

SINGLES:	**HITS 1**			**WEEKS 10**
WAIT	*RCA*	7	*14 Jan 89*	10

Steve HOWE — UK

ALBUMS:	**HITS 2**			**WEEKS 6**
BEGINNINGS	*Atlantic*	22	*15 Nov 75*	4
THE STEVE HOWE ALBUM	*Atlantic*	68	*24 Nov 79*	2

HOWLIN' WOLF — US

SINGLES:	**HITS 1**			**WEEKS 5**
SMOKESTACK LIGHTNIN'	*Pye International*	42	*6 Jun 64*	5
EPS:	**HITS 1**			**WEEKS 4**
TELL ME	*Pye International*	16	*10 Oct 64*	4

H2O — UK

SINGLES:	**HITS 2**			**WEEKS 16**
I DREAM TO SLEEP	*RCA*	17	*21 May 83*	10
Title as per sleeve. Label just shows Dream To Sleep.				
JUST OUTSIDE OF HEAVEN	*RCA*	38	*13 Aug 83*	6

H2O featuring BILLIE — US/Switzerland

SINGLES:	**HITS 2**			**WEEKS 4**
NOBODY'S BUSINESS	*AM:PM*	19	*14 Sep 96*	3
SATISFIED (TAKE ME HIGHER)	*AM:PM*	66	*30 Aug 97*	1
Above hit: H2O.				

HUDDERSFIELD CHORAL SOCIETY — UK

ALBUMS:	**HITS 2**			**WEEKS 14**
THE HYMNS ALBUM	*His Master's Voice*	8	*15 Mar 86*	10
Above hit: HUDDERSFIELD CHORAL SOCIETY conductor Owain Arwel HUGHES.				
THE CAROLS ALBUM	*EMI*	29	*13 Dec 86*	4

Al HUDSON — US

SINGLES:	HITS 4			WEEKS 22
DANCE, GET DOWN (FEEL THE GROOVE) / HOW DO YOU DO	*ABC*	57	*9 Sep 78*	4
YOU CAN DO IT	*MCA*	15	*15 Sep 79*	10
Above hit: Al HUDSON and the PARTNERS.				
MUSIC	*MCA*	56	*8 Dec 79*	6
Above hit: ONE WAY featuring Al HUDSON.				
LET'S TALK ABOUT SHHHH	*MCA*	64	*29 Jun 85*	2
Sleeve reads as Let's Talk (Parts 1 & 2).				
Above hit: ONE WAY.				

Lavine HUDSON — UK

SINGLES:	HITS 1			WEEKS 3
INTERVENTION	*Virgin*	57	*21 May 88*	3

HUDSON-FORD — UK

(See also Monks.)

SINGLES:	HITS 3			WEEKS 20
PICK UP THE PIECES	*A&M*	8	*18 Aug 73*	9
BURN BABY BURN	*A&M*	15	*16 Feb 74*	9
FLOATING IN THE WIND	*A&M*	35	*29 Jun 74*	2

HUE AND CRY — UK

SINGLES:	HITS 10			WEEKS 59
LABOUR OF LOVE	*Circa*	6	*13 Jun 87*	16
STRENGTH TO STRENGTH	*Circa*	46	*19 Sep 87*	5
I REFUSE	*Circa*	47	*30 Jan 88*	3
Original release reached No. 85 in 1987.				
ORDINARY ANGEL	*Circa*	42	*22 Oct 88*	6
LOOKING FOR LINDA	*Circa*	15	*28 Jan 89*	9
VIOLENTLY [EP]	*Circa*	21	*6 May 89*	6
Lead track: Violently.				
SWEET INVISIBILITY	*Circa*	55	*30 Sep 89*	3
MY SALT HEART	*Circa*	47	*25 May 91*	3
LONG TERM LOVERS OF PAIN [EP]	*Circa*	48	*3 Aug 91*	3
Lead track: Long Term Lovers Of Pain.				
PROFOUNDLY YOURS	*Fidelity*	74	*11 Jul 92*	1
LABOUR OF LOVE [RM]	*Circa*	25	*13 Mar 93*	4
Remixed by Dave Lee and Doc Livingstone.				
ALBUMS:	**HITS 5**			**WEEKS 74**
SEDUCED AND ABANDONED	*Circa*	22	*7 Nov 87*	11
REMOTE	*Circa*	10	*10 Dec 88*	40
REMOTE / THE BITTER SUITE [RE]	*Circa*	47	*16 Dec 89*	8
The Bitter Suite was a remix album listed from 10 Jan 90, sales were combined.				
STARS CRASH DOWN	*Circa*	10	*29 Jun 91*	9
TRUTH AND LOVE	*Fidelity*	33	*29 Aug 92*	2
LABOURS OF LOVE - THE BEST OF HUE AND CRY	*Circa*	27	*10 Apr 93*	4

HUES CORPORATION — US

SINGLES:	HITS 2			WEEKS 16
ROCK THE BOAT	*RCA Victor*	6	*27 Jul 74*	10
ROCKIN' SOUL	*RCA Victor*	24	*19 Oct 74*	6

HUFF — UK

SINGLES:	HITS 2			WEEKS 8
HELP ME MAKE IT	*Skyway*	31	*2 Nov 96*	2
Samples Gladys Knight's live version of Help Me Make It Through The Night.				
HELP ME MAKE IT THROUGH THE NIGHT [RM]	*Skyway*	37	*21 Jun 97*	2
Remixed by Rollo and Sister Bliss.				
Above 2: HUFF and PUFF.				
FEELING GOOD	*Planet 3*	31	*6 Dec 97*	3
FEELING GOOD 98 [RM]	*Planet 3*	69	*7 Nov 98*	1
Remixed by Curtis & Moore.				
Above 2: HUFF and HERB.				

HUGGY BEAR – See Andy G'S STARSKY and HUTCH ALLSTARS

David HUGHES with the Wally STOTT ORCHESTRA — UK

SINGLES:	HITS 1			WEEKS 1
BY THE FOUNTAINS OF ROME	*Philips*	27	*22 Sep 56*	1

Owain Arwel HUGHES – See HUDDERSFIELD CHORAL SOCIETY

HUGO and LUIGI their Orchestra and Children's Chorus — US

SINGLES:	HITS 1			WEEKS 2
LA PLUME DE MA TANTE	*RCA*	29	*23 Jul 59*	2

Alan HULL — UK

ALBUMS:	HITS 1			WEEKS 3
PIPEDREAM	*Charisma*	29	*28 Jul 73*	3

HUMAN LEAGUE — UK

SINGLES:	HITS 22			WEEKS 156
HOLIDAY 80 [EP]	*Virgin*	56	*3 May 80*	5
Double-pack single, lead track: Being Boiled.				
EMPIRE STATE HUMAN	*Virgin*	62	*21 Jun 80*	2
BOYS AND GIRLS	*Virgin*	48	*28 Feb 81*	4
THE SOUND OF THE CROWD	*Virgin*	12	*2 May 81*	10
LOVE ACTION (I BELIEVE IN LOVE)	*Virgin*	3	*8 Aug 81*	13
Above 2: HUMAN LEAGUE RED.				
OPEN YOUR HEART	*Virgin*	6	*10 Oct 81*	9
Above hit: HUMAN LEAGUE BLUE.				
DON'T YOU WANT ME	*Virgin*	1	*5 Dec 81*	13
First No.1 hit on the Virgin label.				
Above hit: HUMAN LEAGUE 100.				
BEING BOILED	*Fast Product*	6	*9 Jan 82*	9
Originally released in 1978.				
HOLIDAY 80 [EP] [RE]	*Virgin*	46	*6 Feb 82*	5
MIRROR MAN	*Virgin*	2	*20 Nov 82*	10
(KEEP FEELING) FASCINATION	*Virgin*	2	*23 Apr 83*	9
THE LEBANON	*Virgin*	11	*5 May 84*	6
THE LEBANON [RE]	*Virgin*	75	*23 Jun 84*	1
LIFE ON YOUR OWN	*Virgin*	16	*30 Jun 84*	6
LOUISE	*Virgin*	13	*17 Nov 84*	10
HUMAN	*Virgin*	8	*23 Aug 86*	8
I NEED YOUR LOVING	*Virgin*	72	*22 Nov 86*	1
Above hit: HUMAN LEAGUE RED.				
LOVE IS ALL THAT MATTERS	*Virgin*	41	*15 Oct 88*	5
HEART LIKE A WHEEL	*Virgin*	29	*18 Aug 90*	5
TELL ME WHEN	*East West*	6	*7 Jan 95*	9
ONE MAN IN MY HEART	*East West*	13	*18 Mar 95*	8
FILLING UP WITH HEAVEN	*East West*	36	*17 Jun 95*	2
DON'T YOU WANT ME [RM]	*Virgin*	16	*28 Oct 95*	3
Remixed by Red Jerry.				
STAY WITH ME TONIGHT	*East West*	40	*20 Jan 96*	2
ALL I EVER WANTED	*Papillon*	47	*11 Aug 01*	1

ALBUMS:	HITS 10			WEEKS 260
TRAVELOGUE	*Virgin*	16	*31 May 80*	42
REPRODUCTION	*Virgin*	34	*22 Aug 81*	23
First released 1979. This is a mid-price re-issue.				
DARE	*Virgin*	1	*24 Oct 81*	71
LOVE AND DANCING	*Virgin*	3	*17 Jul 82*	52
Mini-album containing dance remixes from Dare.				
Above hit: LEAGUE UNLIMITED ORCHESTRA.				
HYSTERIA	*Virgin*	3	*19 May 84*	18
CRASH	*Virgin*	7	*20 Sep 86*	6
GREATEST HITS	*Virgin*	3	*12 Nov 88*	24
Includes re-entries during 1994/1995.				
ROMANTIC?	*Virgin*	24	*29 Sep 90*	2
OCTOPUS	*East West*	6	*4 Feb 95*	12
GREATEST HITS [RE]	*Virgin*	28	*11 Nov 95*	8
Repackaged with additional tracks.				
SECRETS	*Papillon*	44	*18 Aug 01*	1
DARE [RE]	*Virgin*	75	*20 Oct 01*	1

HUMAN MOVEMENT featuring Sophie MOLETA — UK/Australia

SINGLES:	HITS 1			WEEKS 1
LOVE HAS COME AGAIN	*Renaissance Recordings*	53	*3 Feb 01*	1

HUMAN NATURE — Australia

SINGLES:	HITS 4			WEEKS 7
WISHES	*Epic*	44	*10 May 97*	1
WHISPER YOUR NAME	*Epic*	53	*30 Aug 97*	1
HE DON'T LOVE YOU	*Epic*	18	*10 Mar 01*	4
WHEN WE WERE YOUNG	*Epic*	43	*30 Jun 01*	1

HUMAN RESOURCE
Holland

SINGLES:	HITS 2			WEEKS 14
DOMINATOR	*R&S*	36	*14 Sep 91*	7
THE COMPLETE DOMINATOR [RM]	*R&S*	18	*21 Dec 91*	7
Remixed by Beltram.				

HUMANOID
UK

SINGLES:	HITS 2			WEEKS 14
STAKKER HUMANOID	*Westside*	17	*26 Nov 88*	8
SLAM	*Westside*	54	*22 Apr 89*	2
STAKKER HUMANOID [RI]	*Jumpin' & Pumpin'*	40	*8 Aug 92*	3
STAKKER HUMANOID 2001 [RM]	*Jumpin' & Pumpin'*	65	*3 Mar 01*	1
Remixed by Krafty Kuts.				

HUMATE
Germany

SINGLES:	HITS 1			WEEKS 4
LOVE SIMULATION	*Deviant*	18	*30 Jan 99*	4
Originally released in 1992.				

HUMBLE PIE
UK

SINGLES:	HITS 1			WEEKS 10
NATURAL BORN BUGIE	*Immediate*	4	*23 Aug 69*	10
ALBUMS:	**HITS 4**			**WEEKS 10**
AS SAFE AS YESTERDAY IS	*Immediate*	32	*6 Sep 69*	1
ROCKING AT THE FILLMORE	*A&M*	32	*22 Jan 72*	2
SMOKIN'	*A&M*	28	*15 Apr 72*	5
EAT IT	*A&M*	34	*7 Apr 73*	2

Engelbert HUMPERDINCK
UK

SINGLES:	HITS 16			WEEKS 239
RELEASE ME	*Decca*	1	*28 Jan 67*	56
Originally recorded by Eddie Miller.				
THERE GOES MY EVERYTHING	*Decca*	2	*27 May 67*	29
Originally recorded by Jack Greene.				
THE LAST WALTZ	*Decca*	1	*26 Aug 67*	27
AM I THAT EASY TO FORGET	*Decca*	3	*13 Jan 68*	13
Originally recorded by Carl Belew.				
A MAN WITHOUT LOVE	*Decca*	2	*27 Apr 68*	15
LES BICYCLETTES DE BELSIZE	*Decca*	5	*28 Sep 68*	15
THE WAY IT USED TO BE	*Decca*	3	*8 Feb 69*	14
I'M A BETTER MAN (FOR HAVING LOVED YOU)	*Decca*	15	*9 Aug 69*	13
WINTER WORLD OF LOVE	*Decca*	7	*15 Nov 69*	13
MY MARIE	*Decca*	31	*30 May 70*	7
SWEETHEART	*Decca*	22	*12 Sep 70*	6
Originally recorded by the Bee Gees.				
SWEETHEART [RE]	*Decca*	50	*31 Oct 70*	1
ANOTHER TIME, ANOTHER PLACE	*Decca*	13	*11 Sep 71*	12
TOO BEAUTIFUL TO LAST	*Decca*	14	*4 Mar 72*	10
From the film 'Nicholas And Alexandra'.				
LOVE IS ALL	*Decca*	44	*20 Oct 73*	3
LOVE IS ALL [RE]	*Decca*	45	*17 Nov 73*	1
QUANDO QUANDO QUANDO	*The Hit Label*	40	*30 Jan 99*	3
HOW TO WIN YOUR LOVE	*Universal Music TV*	59	*6 May 00*	1
ALBUMS:	**HITS 14**			**WEEKS 255**
RELEASE ME	*Decca*	6	*20 May 67*	58
THE LAST WALTZ	*Decca*	3	*25 Nov 67*	33
A MAN WITHOUT LOVE	*Decca*	3	*3 Aug 68*	45
ENGELBERT	*Decca*	3	*1 Mar 69*	8
ENGELBERT HUMPERDINCK	*Decca*	5	*6 Dec 69*	23
WE MADE IT HAPPEN	*Decca*	17	*11 Jul 70*	11
ANOTHER TIME, ANOTHER PLACE	*Decca*	48	*18 Sep 71*	1
LIVE AT THE RIVIERA LAS VEGAS	*Decca*	45	*26 Feb 72*	1
ENGELBERT HUMPERDINCK – HIS GREATEST HITS	*Decca*	1	*21 Dec 74*	34
GETTING SENTIMENTAL	*Telstar*	35	*4 May 85*	10
THE ENGELBERT HUMPERDINCK COLLECTION	*Telstar*	35	*4 Apr 87*	9
LOVE UNCHAINED	*EMI*	16	*10 Jun 95*	6
AT HIS VERY BEST	*Universal Music TV*	5	*8 Apr 00*	14
I WANT TO WAKE UP WITH YOU	*Universal Music TV*	42	*20 Oct 01*	2

HUNDRED REASONS
UK

SINGLES:	HITS 2			WEEKS 3
EP TWO	*Columbia*	47	*18 Aug 01*	1
Lead track: Remmus.				
EP THREE	*Columbia*	37	*15 Dec 01*	2
Lead track: I'll Find You.				

Peter HUNNINGDALE – See ARSENAL F.C.

Geraldine HUNT — Canada

SINGLES:	HITS 1			WEEKS 5
CAN'T FAKE THE FEELING	*Champagne*	44	*25 Oct 80*	5

Lisa HUNT – See LOVESTATION

Marsha HUNT — US

SINGLES:	HITS 2			WEEKS 3
WALK ON GILDED SPLINTERS	*Track*	46	*24 May 69*	2
Originally recorded by Dr John.				
KEEP THE CUSTOMER SATISFIED	*Track*	41	*2 May 70*	1
Originally recorded by Simon and Garfunkel.				

Tommy HUNT — US

SINGLES:	HITS 3			WEEKS 17
CRACKIN' UP	*Spark*	39	*11 Oct 75*	5
Originally recorded by Roy Hamilton as Crackin' Up Over You.				
LOVING ON THE LOSING SIDE	*Spark*	28	*21 Aug 76*	9
ONE FINE MORNING	*Spark*	44	*4 Dec 76*	3

HUNTER featuring Ruby TURNER — UK

(See also Ruby Turner.)

SINGLES:	HITS 1			WEEKS 1
SHAKABOOM!	*Telstar*	64	*9 Dec 95*	1
Featured on 'Junior Gladiators' on TV's 'Scratchy And Co.'.				

Alfonzo HUNTER — US

SINGLES:	HITS 1			WEEKS 2
JUST THE WAY	*Cooltempo*	38	*22 Feb 97*	2

Ian HUNTER — UK

SINGLES:	HITS 1			WEEKS 10
ONCE BITTEN TWICE SHY	*CBS*	14	*3 May 75*	10
ALBUMS:	**HITS 5**			**WEEKS 26**
IAN HUNTER	*CBS*	21	*12 Apr 75*	15
ALL AMERICAN ALIEN BOY	*CBS*	29	*29 May 76*	4
YOU'RE NEVER ALONE WITH A SCHIZOPHRENIC	*Chrysalis*	49	*5 May 79*	3
WELCOME TO THE CLUB	*Chrysalis*	61	*26 Apr 80*	2
SHORT BACK 'N' SIDES	*Chrysalis*	79	*29 Aug 81*	2

Tab HUNTER — US

SINGLES:	HITS 2			WEEKS 30
YOUNG LOVE	*London*	1	*9 Feb 57*	18
Originally recorded by Ric Cartey.				
Above hit: Tab HUNTER with Billy VAUGHN's ORCHESTRA and Chorus.				
NINETY-NINE WAYS	*London*	5	*13 Apr 57*	11
Originally recorded by Charlie Gracie.				
Above hit: Tab HUNTER with Billy VAUGHN's ORCHESTRA.				
NINETY-NINE WAYS [RE]	*London*	29	*6 Jul 57*	1

Terry HUNTER — US

SINGLES:	HITS 1			WEEKS 1
HARVEST FOR THE WORLD	*Delirious*	48	*26 Jul 97*	1
Lead vocals: Curtis Harmon Additional vocals: Paul Johnson.				

HUNTERS – See Dave SAMPSON and the HUNTERS

HURLEY and TODD — UK/South Africa

SINGLES	HITS 1			WEEKS 2
SUNSTORM (FEATURING 'SONG FOR GUY')	*Multiply*	38	*29 Apr 00*	2
Samples Elton John's Song For Guy. Originally released on Liquid Asset Records in 1999.				

Steve 'Silk' HURLEY — US

SINGLES:	HITS 1			WEEKS 9
JACK YOUR BODY	*London*	1	*10 Jan 87*	9

HURRAH! — UK

ALBUMS:	HITS 1			WEEKS 1
TELL GOD I'M HERE	*Kitchenware*	71	*28 Feb 87*	1

HURRICANE G – See PUFF DADDY

HURRICANE #1 — UK

SINGLES:	HITS 6			WEEKS 17
STEP INTO MY WORLD	*Creation*	29	*10 May 97*	2
JUST ANOTHER ILLUSION	*Creation*	35	*5 Jul 97*	2
CHAIN REACTION	*Creation*	30	*6 Sep 97*	2
STEP INTO MY WORLD [RM] *Remixed by Paul Oakenfold and Steve Osbourne.*	*Creation*	19	*1 Nov 97*	3
ONLY THE STRONGEST SURVIVE	*Creation*	19	*21 Feb 98*	6
RISING SIGN	*Creation*	47	*24 Oct 98*	1
THE GREATEST HIGH	*Creation*	43	*3 Apr 99*	1
ALBUMS:	**HITS 2**			**WEEKS 3**
HURRICANE #1	*Creation*	11	*27 Sep 97*	2
ONLY THE STRONG SURVIVE	*Creation*	55	*1 May 99*	1

Phil HURTT — US

SINGLES:	HITS 1			WEEKS 5
GIVING IT BACK	*Fantasy*	36	*11 Nov 78*	5

HUSKER DU — US

ALBUMS:	HITS 1			WEEKS 1
WAREHOUSE: SONGS AND STORIES	*Warner Brothers*	72	*14 Feb 87*	1

HUSTLERS CONVENTION featuring Dave LAUDAT and Ondrea DUVERNEY — UK

SINGLES:	HITS 1			WEEKS 1
THE 'DANCE' TO THE MUSIC [EP] *Lead track: Dance To The Music.*	*Stress*	71	*20 May 95*	1

Willie HUTCH — US

SINGLES:	HITS 2			WEEKS 8
IN AND OUT	*Motown*	51	*4 Dec 82*	7
KEEP ON JAMMIN'	*Motown*	73	*6 Jul 85*	1

June HUTTON and Axel STORDAHL with the BOYS NEXT DOOR and the STORDAHL ORCHESTRA — US

SINGLES:	HITS 1			WEEKS 7
SAY YOU'RE MINE AGAIN	*Capitol*	10	*8 Aug 53*	3
SAY YOU'RE MINE AGAIN [RE]	*Capitol*	6	*5 Sep 53*	4

HYBRID — UK

SINGLES:	HITS 3			WEEKS 4
FINISHED SYMPHONY *All orchestral parts performed by the Russian Federal Orchestra.*	*Distinct'ive*	58	*10 Jul 99*	1
IF I SURVIVE *Above hit: HYBRID featuring Julee CRUISE.*	*Distinct'ive*	52	*11 Sep 99*	1
KID 2000 *Above hit: HYBRID featuring Chrissie HYNDE.*	*Distinct'ive*	32	*3 Jun 00*	2
ALBUMS:	**HITS 1**			**WEEKS 1**
WIDE ANGLE	*Distinct'ive*	45	*25 Sep 99*	1

Brian HYLAND — US

SINGLES:	HITS 6			WEEKS 72
ITSY BITSY TEENIE WEENIE YELLOW POLKADOT BIKINI *Spoken female voice is Trudy Packer.*	*London*	8	*9 Jul 60*	13
FOUR LITTLE HEELS	*London*	29	*22 Oct 60*	6
GINNY COME LATELY	*His Master's Voice*	5	*12 May 62*	15
SEALED WITH A KISS	*His Master's Voice*	3	*4 Aug 62*	15
WARMED OVER KISSES (LEFT OVER LOVE)	*His Master's Voice*	28	*10 Nov 62*	6
GYPSY WOMAN	*Uni*	45	*27 Mar 71*	1
GYPSY WOMAN [RE]	*Uni*	42	*10 Apr 71*	5
SEALED WITH A KISS [RI]	*ABC*	7	*28 Jun 75*	11

Sheila HYLTON — Jamaica

SINGLES:	HITS 2			WEEKS 12
BREAKFAST IN BED *Originally recorded by Dusty Springfield.*	*Ballistic*	57	*15 Sep 79*	5
THE BED'S TOO BIG WITHOUT YOU	*Island*	35	*17 Jan 81*	7

Unforgettable Sound of the Dick HYMAN TRIO — US

SINGLES:	HITS 1			WEEKS 10
THEME FROM "THE THREEPENNY OPERA"	*MGM*	9	*17 Mar 56*	10

Phyllis HYMAN — US

SINGLES:	HITS 2			WEEKS 9
YOU KNOW HOW TO LOVE ME	*Arista*	47	*16 Feb 80*	6
YOU SURE LOOK GOOD TO ME	*Arista*	56	*12 Sep 81*	3
ALBUMS:	**HITS 1**			**WEEKS 1**
LIVING ALL ALONE	*Philadelphia International*	97	*20 Sep 86*	1

Chrissie HYNDE – See CHER, Chrissie HYNDE and Neneh CHERRY with Eric CLAPTON; HYBRID; MOODSWINGS features the voice of Chrissie HYNDE; UB40

HYPER GO-GO — UK

SINGLES:	HITS 5			WEEKS 15
HIGH	*Deconstruction*	30	*22 Aug 92*	5
NEVER LET GO	*Positiva*	45	*31 Jul 93*	3
RAISE	*Positiva*	36	*5 Feb 94*	2
IT'S ALRIGHT	*Positiva*	49	*26 Nov 94*	1
DO WATCHA DO	*Avex UK*	54	*6 Apr 96*	1
Above hit: HYPER GO GO and ADEVA.				
HIGH [RM]	*Distinct'ive*	32	*12 Oct 96*	2
Remixed by Rhythm Masters.				
DO WATCHA DO [RM]	*Distinct'ive*	60	*12 Apr 97*	1
Remixed by K-Klass.				
Above hit: HYPER GO GO and ADEVA.				

HYPERLOGIC — UK

SINGLES:	HITS 1			WEEKS 3
ONLY ME	*Systematic*	35	*29 Jul 95*	2
Samples New Year's Day by U2 and Sleep Talk by Alyson Williams.				
ONLY ME [RM]	*Tidy Trax*	48	*9 May 98*	1
Remixed by Red Vinyl.				

HYPERSTATE featuring Janey Lee GRACE — UK

SINGLES:	HITS 1			WEEKS 1
TIME AFTER TIME	*M&G*	71	*6 Feb 93*	1
Janey Lee Grace was only credited on the back of the sleeve and not on the chart.				

HYPNOSIS — UK

(See also Blowing Free; Harmonium; In Tune; Raindance; School Of Excellence.)

ALBUMS:	HITS 2			WEEKS 16
VOICES OF TRANQUILITY	*Dino*	16	*17 Aug 96*	12
VOICES OF TRANQUILITY VOLUME 2	*Dino*	32	*15 Mar 97*	4

HYPNOTIST — UK

SINGLES:	HITS 2			WEEKS 5
THE HOUSE IS MINE	*Rising High*	65	*28 Sep 91*	2
THE HARDCORE [EP]	*Rising High*	68	*21 Dec 91*	3
Lead track: Hardcore U Know The Score.				

HYSTERIC EGO — UK

SINGLES:	HITS 3			WEEKS 8
WANT LOVE	*WEA*	28	*31 Aug 96*	4
MINISTRY OF LOVE	*WEA*	39	*21 Jun 97*	2
WANT LOVE - THE REMIXES [RM]	*WEA*	46	*28 Feb 98*	1
Remixed by the Timewriter.				
TIME TO GET BACK	*WEA*	50	*13 Feb 99*	1
Samples N-Joi's Adrenalin.				

HYSTERICS — UK

SINGLES:	HITS 1			WEEKS 5
JINGLE BELLS LAUGHING ALL THE WAY (OVER THE RAINBOW MUSIC)	*Recorded Delivery*	44	*12 Dec 81*	5

HYSTERIX — UK

SINGLES:	HITS 2			WEEKS 4
MUST BE THE MUSIC	*Deconstruction*	40	*7 May 94*	3
EVERYTHING	*Deconstruction*	65	*18 Feb 95*	1

I

I-LEVEL — UK

SINGLES:	HITS 2			WEEKS 9
MINEFIELD	*Virgin*	52	*16 Apr 83*	6
TEACHER	*Virgin*	56	*18 Jun 83*	3
ALBUMS:	**HITS 1**			**WEEKS 4**
I-LEVEL	*Virgin*	50	*9 Jul 83*	4

I MONSTER — UK

SINGLES:	HITS 1			WEEKS 6
DAYDREAM IN BLUE	*Instant Karma*	20	*16 Jun 01*	6
Originally recorded by Wallace Collection in 1969 as Daydream.				

IAN and the BLOCKHEADS - See Ian DURY and the BLOCKHEADS

Janis IAN — US

SINGLES:	HITS 2			WEEKS 10
FLY TOO HIGH	*CBS*	44	*17 Nov 79*	7
THE OTHER SIDE OF THE SUN	*CBS*	44	*28 Jun 80*	3

ICE CUBE — US

(See also Scarface.)

SINGLES:	HITS 9			WEEKS 23
IT WAS A GOOD DAY	*Fourth & Broadway*	27	*27 Mar 93*	4
Samples the Isley Brothers' Footsteps In The Dark and the Moments Sexy Mama.				
CHECK YO SELF	*Fourth & Broadway*	36	*7 Aug 93*	4
Samples Grand Master Flash The Message.				
Above hit: ICE CUBE (featuring DAS EFX).				
WICKED	*Fourth & Broadway*	62	*11 Sep 93*	1
Samples Ohio Players Funky Worm, Public Enemy's Welcome To The Terrodome and Can't Truss It, Das EFX's Looseys.				
Above hit: ICE CUBE featuring Don JAGUAR.				
REALLY DOE	*Fourth & Broadway*	66	*18 Dec 93*	1
YOU KNOW HOW WE DO IT	*Fourth & Broadway*	41	*26 Mar 94*	3
BOP GUN (ONE NATION)	*Fourth & Broadway*	22	*27 Aug 94*	3
Samples Funkadelic's One Nation Under A Groove.				
Above hit: ICE CUBE featuring George CLINTON.				
YOU KNOW HOW WE DO IT [RE]	*Fourth & Broadway*	46	*24 Dec 94*	2
HAND OF THE DEAD BODY	*Virgin*	41	*11 Mar 95*	2
Above hit: SCARFACE (featuring ICE CUBE).				
NATURAL BORN KILLAZ	*Death Row*	45	*15 Apr 95*	2
From the film 'Murder Was The Case'.				
Above hit: DR. DRE and ICE CUBE.				
THE WORLD IS MINE	*Jive*	60	*22 Mar 97*	1
From the film 'Dangerous Ground'.				
ALBUMS:	**HITS 5**			**WEEKS 11**
AMERIKKKA'S MOST WANTED	*Fourth & Broadway*	48	*28 Jul 90*	5
KILL AT WILL	*Fourth & Broadway*	66	*9 Mar 91*	3
THE PREDATOR	*Fourth & Broadway*	73	*5 Dec 92*	1
LETHAL INJECTION	*Fourth & Broadway*	52	*18 Dec 93*	1
WAR & PEACE - VOLUME II (THE PEACE DISC)	*Priority*	56	*1 Apr 00*	1
Volume One was released in 1998 and reached No. 141.				

ICE MC — UK

SINGLES:	HITS 2			WEEKS 5
THINK ABOUT THE WAY (BOM DIGI DIGI BOM . . .)	*WEA*	42	*6 Aug 94*	2
Features German vocalist Jasmine.				
IT'S A RAINY DAY	*Eternal*	73	*8 Apr 95*	1
BOM DIGI BOM (THINK ABOUT THE WAY) [RI]	*Eternal*	38	*14 Sep 96*	2
From the film 'Trainspotting'.				

ICE-T — US

SINGLES:	HITS 9			WEEKS 29
HIGH ROLLERS	*Sire*	63	*18 Mar 89*	2
YOU PLAYED YOURSELF	*Sire*	64	*17 Feb 90*	2
SUPERFLY 1990	*Capitol*	48	*29 Sep 90*	3
Above hit: Curtis MAYFIELD and ICE-T.				
I AIN'T NEW TA THIS	*Rhyme Syndicate*	62	*8 May 93*	2
THAT'S HOW I'M LIVIN'	*Rhyme Syndicate*	21	*18 Dec 93*	6
GOTTA LOTTA LOVE	*Rhyme Syndicate*	24	*9 Apr 94*	4
Samples Mike Oldfield's Tubular Bells.				

BORN TO RAISE HELL	*Fox*	47	*10 Dec 94*	2
From the film 'Airheads'.				
Above hit: MOTORHEAD with ICE-T and Whitfield CRANE.				
I MUST STAND	*Rhyme Syndicate*	23	*1 Jun 96*	3
Samples Portishead's Numb.				
THE LANE	*Rhyme Syndicate*	18	*7 Dec 96*	5
Samples Jean Jaques Perry's Eva.				

ALBUMS:	**HITS 4**			**WEEKS 15**
THE ICEBERG/FREEDOM OF SPEECH	*Sire*	42	*21 Oct 89*	2
O.G. ORIGINAL GANGSTER	*Sire*	38	*25 May 91*	4
HOME INVASION	*Rhyme Syndicate*	15	*3 Apr 93*	7
VI: RETURN OF THE REAL	*Rhyme Syndicate*	26	*8 Jun 96*	2

ICEBERG SLIMM — US

SINGLES:	**HITS 1**			**WEEKS 2**
NURSERY RHYMES	*Polydor*	37	*7 Oct 00*	2

ICEHOUSE — New Zealand/Australia/UK

SINGLES:	**HITS 5**			**WEEKS 28**
HEY LITTLE GIRL	*Chrysalis*	17	*5 Feb 83*	10
STREET CAFE	*Chrysalis*	62	*23 Apr 83*	4
NO PROMISES	*Chrysalis*	72	*3 May 86*	1
CRAZY	*Chrysalis*	74	*29 Aug 87*	1
CRAZY [RE]	*Chrysalis*	38	*13 Feb 88*	8
ELECTRIC BLUE	*Chrysalis*	53	*14 May 88*	4

ALBUMS:	**HITS 2**			**WEEKS 7**
LOVE IN MOTION	*Chrysalis*	64	*5 Mar 83*	6
Originally released in 1982 with the title Primitive Man.				
MAN OF COLOURS	*Chrysalis*	93	*2 Apr 88*	1

ICICLE WORKS — UK

SINGLES:	**HITS 7**			**WEEKS 28**
LOVE IS SUCH A WONDERFUL COLOUR	*Beggars Banquet*	15	*24 Dec 83*	8
BIRDS FLY (WHISPER TO A SCREAM) / IN THE CAULDRON OF LOVE	*Beggars Banquet*	53	*10 Mar 84*	4
Original release reached No. 90 in 1983.				
UNDERSTANDING JANE	*Beggars Banquet*	52	*26 Jul 86*	3
WHO DO YOU WANT FOR YOUR LOVE?	*Beggars Banquet*	54	*4 Oct 86*	4
EVANGELINE	*Beggars Banquet*	53	*14 Feb 87*	4
LITTLE GIRL LOST	*Beggars Banquet*	59	*30 Apr 88*	4
MOTORCYCLE RIDER	*Epic*	73	*17 Mar 90*	1

ALBUMS:	**HITS 6**			**WEEKS 19**
THE ICICLE WORKS	*Beggars Banquet*	24	*31 Mar 84*	6
THE SMALL PRICE OF A BICYCLE	*Beggars Banquet*	55	*28 Sep 85*	3
SEVEN SINGLES DEEP	*Beggars Banquet*	52	*1 Mar 86*	2
IF YOU WANT TO DEFEAT YOUR ENEMY SING HIS SONG	*Beggars Banquet*	28	*21 Mar 87*	4
BLIND	*Beggars Banquet*	40	*14 May 88*	3
THE BEST OF THE ICICLE WORKS	*Beggars Banquet*	60	*5 Sep 92*	1

ICON — UK

SINGLES:	**HITS 1**			**WEEKS 1**
TAINTED LOVE	*Eternal*	51	*15 Jun 96*	1

IDEAL — UK

SINGLES:	**HITS 1**			**WEEKS 2**
HOT	*Cleveland City*	49	*6 Aug 94*	2

IDEAL U.S. featuring LIL' MO — US

SINGLES:	**HITS 1**			**WEEKS 3**
WHATEVER	*Virgin*	31	*23 Sep 00*	3

IDES OF MARCH — US

SINGLES:	**HITS 1**			**WEEKS 9**
VEHICLE	*Warner Brothers*	31	*6 Jun 70*	9

Eric IDLE featuring Richard WILSON — UK

SINGLES:	**HITS 1**			**WEEKS 3**
ONE FOOT IN THE GRAVE	*Victa*	50	*17 Dec 94*	3
Dance mix of the theme from the BBC1 TV sitcom of the same name. Originally released in 1990.				

IDLEWILD — UK

SINGLES:	**HITS 8**			**WEEKS 15**
A FILM FOR THE FUTURE	*Food*	53	*9 May 98*	1

EVERYONE SAYS YOU'RE SO FRAGILE	*Food*	47	*25 Jul 98*	1
I'M A MESSAGE	*Food*	41	*24 Oct 98*	1
WHEN I ARGUE I SEE SHAPES	*Food*	19	*13 Feb 99*	2
LITTLE DISCOURAGE	*Food*	24	*2 Oct 99*	2
ACTUALLY IT'S DARKNESS	*Food*	23	*8 Apr 00*	3
THESE WOODEN IDEAS	*Food*	32	*24 Jun 00*	3
ROSEABILITY	*Food*	38	*28 Oct 00*	2
ALBUMS:	**HITS 2**			**WEEKS 5**
HOPE IS IMPORTANT	*Food*	53	*7 Nov 98*	1
100 BROKEN WINDOWS	*Food*	15	*22 Apr 00*	4

Billy IDOL — UK

SINGLES:	**HITS 15**			**WEEKS 106**
HOT IN THE CITY	*Chrysalis*	58	*11 Sep 82*	4
REBEL YELL	*Chrysalis*	62	*24 Mar 84*	2
EYES WITHOUT A FACE	*Chrysalis*	18	*30 Jun 84*	11
FLESH FOR FANTASY	*Chrysalis*	54	*29 Sep 84*	3
WHITE WEDDING	*Chrysalis*	6	*13 Jul 85*	15
REBEL YELL [RI]	*Chrysalis*	6	*14 Sep 85*	12
TO BE A LOVER	*Chrysalis*	22	*4 Oct 86*	8
Originally recorded by William Bell as I Forgot To Be Your Lover.				
DON'T NEED A GUN	*Chrysalis*	26	*7 Mar 87*	5
SWEET SIXTEEN	*Chrysalis*	17	*13 Jun 87*	9
MONY MONY (LIVE)	*Chrysalis*	7	*3 Oct 87*	10
HOT IN THE CITY (EXTERMINATOR FIX) [RM]	*Chrysalis*	13	*16 Jan 88*	9
Remixed by Billy Idol and Steve Stevens.				
CATCH MY FALL	*Chrysalis*	63	*13 Aug 88*	3
CRADLE OF LOVE	*Chrysalis*	34	*28 Apr 90*	4
L.A. WOMAN	*Chrysalis*	70	*11 Aug 90*	2
PRODIGAL BLUES	*Chrysalis*	47	*22 Dec 90*	4
SHOCK TO THE SYSTEM	*Chrysalis*	30	*26 Jun 93*	3
SPEED	*Fox*	47	*10 Sep 94*	2
From the film of the same name.				
ALBUMS:	**HITS 6**			**WEEKS 100**
VITAL IDOL	*Chrysalis*	7	*8 Jun 85*	34
Compilation.				
REBEL YELL	*Chrysalis*	36	*28 Sep 85*	11
WHIPLASH SMILE	*Chrysalis*	8	*1 Nov 86*	20
IDOL SONGS: 11 OF THE BEST	*Chrysalis*	2	*2 Jul 88*	25
CHARMED LIFE	*Chrysalis*	15	*12 May 90*	8
CYBERPUNK	*Chrysalis*	20	*10 Jul 93*	2

Frank IFIELD — UK

SINGLES:	**HITS 16**			**WEEKS 163**
LUCKY DEVIL	*Columbia*	22	*20 Feb 60*	6
LUCKY DEVIL [RE]	*Columbia*	33	*9 Apr 60*	2
GOTTA GET A DATE	*Columbia*	49	*1 Oct 60*	1
I REMEMBER YOU	*Columbia*	1	*7 Jul 62*	28
Song was originally from the 1942 film 'The Fleet's In'. Originally recorded by Jimmy Dorsey in 1942. Harmonica playing by Harry Pitch (of Mr. Bloe).				
LOVESICK BLUES	*Columbia*	1	*27 Oct 62*	17
Originally recorded by Elsie Clark in 1922.				
THE WAYWARD WIND	*Columbia*	1	*26 Jan 63*	13
Above 2: Frank IFIELD with Norrie PARAMOR and his Orchestra.				
NOBODY'S DARLIN' BUT MINE	*Columbia*	4	*13 Apr 63*	16
Originally recorded by Jimmy Davis.				
CONFESSIN' (THAT I LOVE YOU)	*Columbia*	1	*29 Jun 63*	16
MULE TRAIN	*Columbia*	22	*19 Oct 63*	6
DON'T BLAME ME	*Columbia*	8	*11 Jan 64*	13
Originally recorded by Ethel Waters in 1933.				
Above hit: Frank IFIELD with Norrie PARAMOR and his Orchestra.				
ANGRY AT THE BIG OAK TREE	*Columbia*	25	*25 Apr 64*	8
I SHOULD CARE	*Columbia*	33	*25 Jul 64*	3
SUMMER IS OVER	*Columbia*	25	*3 Oct 64*	6
PARADISE	*Columbia*	26	*21 Aug 65*	9
NO ONE WILL EVER KNOW	*Columbia*	25	*25 Jun 66*	4
CALL HER YOUR SWEETHEART	*Columbia*	24	*10 Dec 66*	11
THE YODELING SONG	*EMI*	40	*7 Dec 91*	4
Originally the B-side of Lovesick Blues.				
Above hit: Frank IFIELD featuring the BACKROOM BOYS.				
EPS:	**HITS 6**			**WEEKS 103**
FRANK IFIELD'S HITS	*Columbia*	1	*8 Dec 62*	59
MORE OF FRANK IFIELD'S HITS	*Columbia*	4	*22 Jun 63*	15
JUST ONE MORE CHANCE	*Columbia*	5	*21 Sep 63*	13
VIVA IFIELD	*Columbia*	11	*12 Oct 63*	11

PLEASE	*Columbia*	18	*25 Jan 64*	3
DON'T BLAME ME	*Columbia*	19	*18 Apr 64*	2
ALBUMS:	**HITS 4**			**WEEKS 83**
I'LL REMEMBER YOU	*Columbia*	3	*16 Feb 63*	36
BORN FREE	*Columbia*	3	*21 Sep 63*	32
Above hit: Frank IFIELD; Norrie PARAMOR and his Orchestra.				
BLUE SKIES	*Columbia*	10	*28 Mar 64*	12
GREATEST HITS	*Columbia*	9	*19 Dec 64*	3

IGGY and the STOOGES – See Iggy POP

Enrique IGLESIAS — Spain

SINGLES:	**HITS 3**			**WEEKS 19**
BAILAMOS	*Interscope*	4	*11 Sep 99*	9
From the film 'Wild Wild West'.				
RHYTHM DIVINE	*Interscope*	45	*18 Dec 99*	2
COULD I HAVE THIS KISS FOREVER	*Arista*	7	*14 Oct 00*	8
Above hit: Whitney HOUSTON and Enrique IGLESIAS.				

Julio IGLESIAS — Spain

SINGLES:	**HITS 9**			**WEEKS 75**
BEGIN THE BEGUINE (VOLVER A EMPEZAR)	*CBS*	1	*24 Oct 81*	14
Written by Cole Porter.				
QUIEREME MUCHO (YOURS)	*CBS*	3	*6 Mar 82*	9
AMOR	*CBS*	32	*9 Oct 82*	7
Originally recorded by Ginny Simms in 1943.				
HEY!	*CBS*	31	*9 Apr 83*	7
TO ALL THE GIRLS I'VE LOVED BEFORE	*CBS*	17	*7 Apr 84*	10
Originally recorded by Albert Hammond.				
Above hit: Julio IGLESIAS and Willie NELSON.				
ALL OF YOU	*CBS*	43	*7 Jul 84*	8
Above hit: Julio IGLESIAS and Diana ROSS.				
MY LOVE	*CBS*	5	*6 Aug 88*	11
Above hit: Julio IGLESIAS featuring Stevie WONDER.				
CRAZY	*Columbia*	43	*4 Jun 94*	3
CRAZY [RE]	*Columbia*	50	*27 Aug 94*	2
FRAGILE	*Columbia*	53	*26 Nov 94*	2
Backing vocals by Sting.				
FRAGILE [RE]	*Columbia*	66	*31 Dec 94*	2
ALBUMS:	**HITS 13**			**WEEKS 174**
DE NINA A MUJER	*CBS*	43	*7 Nov 81*	5
BEGIN THE BEGUINE	*CBS*	5	*28 Nov 81*	28
AMOR	*CBS*	14	*16 Oct 82*	14
JULIO	*CBS*	5	*2 Jul 83*	17
1100 BEL AIR PLACE	*CBS*	14	*1 Sep 84*	14
LIBRA	*CBS*	61	*19 Oct 85*	4
NON STOP	*CBS*	33	*3 Sep 88*	14
STARRY NIGHT	*CBS*	27	*1 Dec 90*	20
CRAZY	*Columbia*	6	*28 May 94*	37
LA CARRETERA	*Columbia*	6	*12 Aug 95*	6
TANGO	*Columbia*	56	*30 Nov 96*	3
MY LIFE: THE GREATEST HITS	*Columbia*	18	*7 Nov 98*	9
NOCHE DE CUATRO LUNAS	*Columbia*	32	*22 Jul 00*	3

IGNORANTS — UK

SINGLES:	**HITS 1**			**WEEKS 3**
PHAT GIRLS	*Spaghetti*	59	*25 Dec 93*	3

IIO — US

SINGLES:	**HITS 1**			**WEEKS 8**
RAPTURE	*Data*	2	*10 Nov 01*	8

ILLEGAL MOTION featuring Simone CHAPMAN — UK

SINGLES:	**HITS 1**			**WEEKS 1**
SATURDAY LOVE	*Arista*	67	*9 Oct 93*	1

ILLICIT featuring GRAM'MA FUNK — UK

SINGLES:	**HITS 1**			**WEEKS 1**
CHEEKY ARMADA	*Yola*	72	*2 Sep 00*	1
Samples You Can't Hide From Yourself by Teddy Pendergrass.				

IMAANI — UK

SINGLES:	**HITS 1**			**WEEKS 7**
WHERE ARE YOU	*EMI*	15	*9 May 98*	7
UK's Eurovision entry in 1998, it came 2nd.				

IMAGINATION — UK

SINGLES:	HITS 12			WEEKS 105
BODY TALK	*R&B*	4	*16 May 81*	18
IN AND OUT OF LOVE	*R&B*	16	*5 Sep 81*	9
FLASHBACK	*R&B*	16	*14 Nov 81*	13
JUST AN ILLUSION	*R&B*	2	*6 Mar 82*	11
MUSIC AND LIGHTS	*R&B*	5	*26 Jun 82*	9
IN THE HEAT OF THE NIGHT	*R&B*	22	*25 Sep 82*	8
CHANGES	*R&S*	31	*11 Dec 82*	8
LOOKING AT MIDNIGHT	*R&B*	29	*4 Jun 83*	7
NEW DIMENSION	*R&B*	56	*5 Nov 83*	3
STATE OF LOVE	*R&B*	67	*26 May 84*	2
THANK YOU MY LOVE	*R&B*	22	*24 Nov 84*	15
INSTINCTUAL	*RCA*	62	*16 Jan 88*	2
ALBUMS:	**HITS 5**			**WEEKS 122**
BODY TALK *Peak position reached on 10 Apr 82.*	*R&B*	20	*24 Oct 81*	53
IN THE HEAT OF THE NIGHT	*R&B*	7	*11 Sep 82*	29
NIGHT DUBBING	*R&M*	9	*14 May 83*	20
SCANDALOUS	*R&B*	25	*12 Nov 83*	8
IMAGINATION – ALL THE HITS	*Stylus*	4	*12 Aug 89*	12

IMAGINATIONS – See Mari WILSON

IMAJIN — US

SINGLES:	HITS 4			WEEKS 7
SHORTY (YOU KEEP PLAYIN' WITH MY MIND) *Above hit: IMAJIN featuring Keith MURRAY.*	*Jive*	22	*27 Jun 98*	3
NO DOUBT *Samples the Spinners It's A Natural Affair.*	*Jive*	42	*20 Feb 99*	2
BOUNCE, ROCK, SKATE, ROLL *Above hit: BABY DC featuring IMAJIN.*	*Jive*	45	*24 Apr 99*	1
FLAVA	*Jive*	64	*12 Feb 00*	1

Natalie IMBRUGLIA — Australia

SINGLES:	HITS 5			WEEKS 44
TORN *Originally recorded by Ednaswap in 1995.*	*RCA*	2	*8 Nov 97*	17
BIG MISTAKE	*RCA*	2	*14 Mar 98*	10
WISHING I WAS HERE	*RCA*	19	*6 Jun 98*	5
SMOKE	*RCA*	5	*17 Oct 98*	7
THAT DAY	*RCA*	11	*10 Nov 01*	4
THAT DAY [RE]	*RCA*	66	*29 Dec 01*	1
ALBUMS:	**HITS 2**			**WEEKS 90**
LEFT OF THE MIDDLE	*RCA*	5	*6 Dec 97*	87
WHITE LILIES ISLAND	*RCA*	15	*17 Nov 01*	3

IMMACULATE FOOLS — UK

SINGLES:	HITS 1			WEEKS 4
IMMACULATE FOOLS	*A&M*	51	*26 Jan 85*	4
ALBUMS:	**HITS 1**			**WEEKS 2**
HEARTS OF FORTUNE	*A&M*	65	*11 May 85*	2

IMMATURE (featuring SMOOTH) — US

SINGLES:	HITS 1			WEEKS 2
WE GOT IT	*MCA*	26	*16 Mar 96*	2

IMPALAS — US

SINGLES:	HITS 1			WEEKS 1
SORRY (I RAN ALL THE WAY HOME)	*MGM*	28	*22 Aug 59*	1

IMPEDANCE — UK

SINGLES:	HITS 1			WEEKS 4
TAINTED LOVE	*Jumpin' & Pumpin'*	54	*11 Nov 89*	4

Carlo IMPERATO and "the WATERS" – See KIDS FROM "FAME"

IMPERIAL DRAG — UK

SINGLES:	HITS 1			WEEKS 1
BOY OR A GIRL	*Columbia*	54	*12 Oct 96*	1

IMPERIAL TEEN — US

SINGLES:	HITS 1			WEEKS 1
YOU'RE ONE	*Slash*	69	*7 Sep 96*	1

IMPERIALS – See LITTLE ANTHONY and the IMPERIALS

IMPERIALS QUARTET – See Elvis PRESLEY

IMPOSTER – See Elvis COSTELLO and the ATTRACTIONS

IMPRESSIONS — US

SINGLES:	HITS 1			WEEKS 10
FIRST IMPRESSIONS	*Curtom*	16	*22 Nov 75*	10

IN CROWD — UK

SINGLES:	HITS 1			WEEKS 1
THAT'S HOW STRONG MY LOVE IS	*Parlophone*	48	*22 May 65*	1

IN FULL ROCK-A-PHONIC SOUND – See COLUMBO presents IN FULL ROCK-A-PHONIC SOUND featuring OOE

IN TUA NUA — Ireland

SINGLES:	HITS 1			WEEKS 2
ALL I WANTED	*Virgin*	69	*14 May 88*	2

IN TUNE — UK

(See also Blowing Free; Harmonium; Hypnosis; Raindance; School Of Excellence.)

ALBUMS:	HITS 1			WEEKS 3
ACOUSTIC MOODS	*Global Television*	21	*17 Jun 95*	3

INAURA — UK

SINGLES:	HITS 1			WEEKS 1
COMA AROMA	*EMI*	57	*18 May 96*	1

INCANTATION — UK

SINGLES:	HITS 1			WEEKS 12
CACHARPAYA (ANDES PUMPSA DESI)	*Beggars Banquet*	12	*4 Dec 82*	12
ALBUMS:	**HITS 3**			**WEEKS 52**
CACHARPAYA (PANPIPES OF THE ANDES)	*Beggars Banquet*	9	*11 Dec 82*	26
DANCE OF THE FLAMES	*Beggars Banquet*	61	*17 Dec 83*	7
THE BEST OF INCANTATION: MUSIC FROM THE ANDES	*West Five*	28	*28 Dec 85*	19

INCOGNITO — UK

SINGLES:	HITS 13			WEEKS 38
PARISIENNE GIRL	*Ensign*	73	*15 Nov 80*	2
ALWAYS THERE	*Talkin Loud*	6	*29 Jun 91*	9
Originally recorded by Ronnie Laws.				
Above hit: INCOGNITO featuring Jocelyn BROWN.				
CRAZY FOR YOU	*Talkin Loud*	59	*14 Sep 91*	2
Above hit: INCOGNITO featuring CHYNA.				
DON'T YOU WORRY 'BOUT A THING	*Talkin Loud*	19	*6 Jun 92*	6
Originally recorded by Stevie Wonder.				
CHANGE	*Talkin Loud*	52	*15 Aug 92*	2
STILL A FRIEND OF MINE	*Talkin Loud*	47	*21 Aug 93*	2
GIVIN' IT UP	*Talkin Loud*	43	*20 Nov 93*	2
PIECES OF A DREAM	*Talkin Loud*	35	*12 Mar 94*	2
EVERYDAY	*Talkin Loud*	23	*27 May 95*	3
Vocals by Pamela Anderson (cousin of Carleen Anderson).				
I HEAR YOUR NAME	*Talkin Loud*	42	*5 Aug 95*	3
JUMP TO MY LOVE / ALWAYS THERE [RR]	*Talkin Loud*	29	*11 May 96*	3
OUT OF THE STORM	*Talkin Loud*	57	*26 Oct 96*	1
NIGHTS OVER EGYPT	*Talkin Loud*	56	*10 Apr 99*	1
Originally recorded by the Jones Girls in 1981.				
ALBUMS:	**HITS 6**			**WEEKS 19**
JAZZ FUNK	*Ensign*	28	*18 Apr 81*	8
INSIDE LIFE	*Talkin Loud*	44	*27 Jul 91*	2
TRIBES, VIBES AND SCRIBES	*Talkin Loud*	41	*4 Jul 92*	2
POSITIVITY	*Talkin Loud*	55	*6 Nov 93*	2
100 DEGREES AND RISING	*Talkin Loud*	11	*17 Jun 95*	4
REMIXED	*Talkin Loud*	56	*1 Jun 96*	1

INCREDIBLE STRING BAND — UK

ALBUMS:	HITS 7			WEEKS 37
5,000 SPIRITS OR THE LAYERS OF THE ONION	*Elektra*	25	*21 Oct 67*	5
THE HANGMAN'S BEAUTIFUL DAUGHTER	*Elektra*	5	*6 Apr 68*	21

THE INCREDIBLE STRING BAND *Originally issued in 1966.*	*Elektra*	34	*20 Jul 68*	3
CHANGING HORSES	*Elektra*	30	*24 Jan 70*	1
I LOOKED UP	*Elektra*	30	*9 May 70*	4
U	*Elektra*	34	*31 Oct 70*	2
LIQUID ACROBAT AS REGARDS THE AIR	*Island*	46	*30 Oct 71*	1

INCUBUS — US

SINGLES:	HITS 2			WEEKS 3
PARDON ME	*Epic*	61	*20 May 00*	1
DRIVE	*Epic*	40	*23 Jun 01*	2
ALBUMS:	**HITS 1**			**WEEKS 3**
MORNING VIEW	*Epic*	15	*3 Nov 01*	3

INDEEP — US

SINGLES:	HITS 2			WEEKS 11
LAST NIGHT A D.J. SAVED MY LIFE	*Sound Of New York*	13	*22 Jan 83*	9
WHEN BOYS TALK	*Sound Of New York*	67	*14 May 83*	2

INDIA – See MASTERS AT WORK present INDIA; NUYORICAN SOUL; Tito PUENTO Jr. and the LATIN RHYTHM featuring Tito PUENTE, INDIA and Cali ALEMAN; RIVER OCEAN featuring INDIA

INDIAN VIBES — UK

SINGLES:	HITS 1			WEEKS 2
MATHAR *Original version by the Dave Pike Set.*	*Virgin*	68	*24 Sep 94*	1
MATHAR [RI]	*VC Recordings*	52	*2 May 98*	1

INDIGO GIRLS — US

ALBUMS:	HITS 2			WEEKS 3
SWAMP OPHELIA	*Epic*	66	*11 Jun 94*	1
4.5 THE BEST OF THE INDIGO GIRLS	*Epic*	43	*15 Jul 95*	2

Count INDIGO — UK

SINGLES:	HITS 1			WEEKS 1
MY UNKNOWN LOVE	*Cowboy*	59	*9 Mar 96*	1

Los INDIOS TABAJARAS — Brazil

SINGLES:	HITS 1			WEEKS 17
MARIA ELENA	*RCA Victor*	5	*2 Nov 63*	17

INDO — US

SINGLES:	HITS 1			WEEKS 3
R U SLEEPING *Original release reached No. 130 in 1996.*	*Satellite*	31	*18 Apr 98*	3

INDUSTRY STANDARD — UK

SINGLES:	HITS 1			WEEKS 3
INDUSTRY STANDARD VOL. 1 (WHAT YOU WANT)	*Satellite*	34	*10 Jan 98*	3

INFA RIOT — UK

ALBUMS:	HITS 1			WEEKS 4
STILL OUT OF ORDER	*Secret*	42	*7 Aug 82*	4

INFINITI featuring GRAND PUBA — US

SINGLES:	HITS 1			WEEKS 1
WILL YOU BE MY BABY?	*GHQ*	53	*30 Mar 96*	1

INGRAM — US

SINGLES:	HITS 1			WEEKS 2
SMOOTHIN' GROOVIN'	*Streetwave*	56	*11 Jun 83*	2

James INGRAM — US

(See also Quincy Jones.)

SINGLES:	HITS 4			WEEKS 41
BABY, COME TO ME *Above hit: Patti AUSTIN and James INGRAM.*	*Qwest*	11	*12 Feb 83*	10
YAH MO B THERE	*Qwest*	44	*18 Feb 84*	5
YAH MO B THERE [RE]	*Qwest*	69	*7 Apr 84*	3
YAH MO B THERE [RM]	*Qwest*	12	*12 Jan 85*	8

Remixed by John 'Jellybean' Benitez. This remix had the same catalogue number as the original.
Above 3: James INGRAM (with Michael McDONALD).

SOMEWHERE OUT THERE *From the film 'An American Tail'.* *Above hit: Linda RONSTADT and James INGRAM.*	*MCA*	8	*11 Jul 87*	13
THE DAY I FALL IN LOVE (LOVE THEME FROM BEETHOVEN'S 2ND) *From the film 'Beethoven's 2nd'.* *Above hit: Dolly PARTON and James INGRAM.*	*Columbia*	64	*16 Apr 94*	2
ALBUMS:	**HITS 2**			**WEEKS 19**
IT'S YOUR NIGHT	*Warner Brothers*	25	*31 Mar 84*	17
NEVER FELT SO GOOD	*Qwest*	72	*30 Aug 86*	2

INK SPOTS — US

SINGLES:	**HITS 1**			**WEEKS 4**
MELODY OF LOVE	*Parlophone*	10	*30 Apr 55*	4

John INMAN — UK

SINGLES:	**HITS 1**			**WEEKS 6**
ARE YOU BEING SERVED SIR?	*DJM*	39	*25 Oct 75*	6

INMATES — UK

SINGLES:	**HITS 1**			**WEEKS 9**
THE WALK *Originally recorded by Jimmy McCracklin.*	*Radar*	36	*8 Dec 79*	9

INNER CIRCLE — Jamaica

SINGLES:	**HITS 5**			**WEEKS 35**
EVERYTHING IS GREAT	*Island*	37	*24 Feb 79*	8
STOP BREAKING MY HEART	*Island*	50	*12 May 79*	3
SWEAT (A LA LA LA LA LONG)	*Magnet*	43	*31 Oct 92*	5
SWEAT (A LA LA LA LA LONG) [RE]	*Magnet*	3	*1 May 93*	14
BAD BOYS	*Magnet*	52	*31 Jul 93*	3
GAMES PEOPLE PLAY	*Magnet*	67	*10 Sep 94*	2
ALBUMS:	**HITS 1**			**WEEKS 2**
BAD TO THE BONE	*Magnet*	44	*29 May 93*	2

INNER CITY — US

SINGLES:	**HITS 17**			**WEEKS 81**
BIG FUN (RADIO FUN) *Above hit: INNER CITY (featuring Kevin SAUNDERSON) Vocals by PARIS.*	*10 Records*	8	*3 Sep 88*	14
GOOD LIFE	*10 Records*	4	*10 Dec 88*	12
AIN'T NOBODY BETTER	*10 Records*	10	*22 Apr 89*	7
DO YOU LOVE WHAT YOU FEEL	*10 Records*	16	*29 Jul 89*	7
WHATCHA GONNA DO WITH MY LOVIN'	*10 Records*	12	*18 Nov 89*	9
THAT MAN (HE'S ALL MINE)	*Ten Records*	42	*13 Oct 90*	4
TILL WE MEET AGAIN	*Ten Records*	47	*23 Feb 91*	2
LET IT REIGN	*Ten Records*	51	*7 Dec 91*	2
HALLELUJAH '92	*Ten Records*	22	*4 Apr 92*	4
PENNIES FROM HEAVEN *Background vocals from Members Of The House, Rachel Choate and Ann Saunderson.*	*Ten Records*	24	*13 Jun 92*	4
PRAISE	*Ten Records*	59	*12 Sep 92*	2
TILL WE MEET AGAIN [RM] *Remixed by Brothers In Rhythm.*	*Ten Records*	55	*27 Feb 93*	1
BACK TOGETHER AGAIN	*Six6*	49	*14 Aug 93*	1
DO YA	*Six6*	44	*5 Feb 94*	2
SHARE MY LIFE	*Six6*	62	*9 Jul 94*	1
YOUR LOVE	*Six6*	28	*10 Feb 96*	2
DO ME RIGHT	*Six6*	47	*5 Oct 96*	1
GOOD LIFE (BUENA VIDA) [RR]	*PIAS Recordings*	10	*6 Feb 99*	6
ALBUMS:	**HITS 4**			**WEEKS 39**
PARADISE	*10 Records*	3	*20 May 89*	30
PARADISE REMIXED	*10 Records*	17	*10 Feb 90*	6
PRAISE	*Ten Records*	52	*11 Jul 92*	1
TESTAMENT '93	*Ten Records*	33	*15 May 93*	2

INNER SANCTUM — Canada

SINGLES:	**HITS 1**			**WEEKS 1**
HOW SOON IS NOW	*Malarky*	75	*23 May 98*	1

INNERZONE ORCHESTRA — US

SINGLES:	**HITS 1**			**WEEKS 1**
BUG IN THE BASSBIN *First released in the US in 1992.*	*Mo Wax*	68	*28 Sep 96*	1

INNOCENCE — UK

SINGLES:	HITS 8			WEEKS 33
NATURAL THING	*Cooltempo*	16	*3 Mar 90*	7
SILENT VOICE	*Cooltempo*	37	*21 Jul 90*	5
LET'S PUSH IT	*Cooltempo*	25	*13 Oct 90*	6
A MATTER OF FACT	*Cooltempo*	37	*8 Dec 90*	7
REMEMBER THE DAY	*Cooltempo*	56	*30 Mar 91*	2
I'LL BE THERE	*Cooltempo*	26	*20 Jun 92*	3
ONE LOVE IN MY LIFETIME	*Cooltempo*	40	*3 Oct 92*	2
BUILD	*Cooltempo*	72	*21 Nov 92*	1
ALBUMS:	**HITS 2**			**WEEKS 20**
BELIEF	*Cooltempo*	24	*10 Nov 90*	19
BUILD	*Cooltempo*	66	*31 Oct 92*	1

INSANE CLOWN POSSE — US

SINGLES:	HITS 2			WEEKS 2
HALLS OF ILLUSIONS	*Island*	56	*17 Jan 98*	1
HOKUS POKUS	*Island*	53	*6 Jun 98*	1

INSPEKTAH DECK A.K.A. ROLLIE FINGERS - See GENIUS/GZA

INSPIRAL CARPETS — UK

SINGLES:	HITS 15			WEEKS 50
MOVE	*Cow*	49	*18 Nov 89*	2
THIS IS HOW IT FEELS	*Cow*	14	*17 Mar 90*	8
SHE COMES IN THE FALL	*Cow*	27	*30 Jun 90*	6
ISLAND HEAD [EP]	*Cow*	21	*17 Nov 90*	4
Lead track: Biggest Mountain.				
CARAVAN	*Cow*	30	*30 Mar 91*	5
PLEASE BE CRUEL	*Cow*	50	*22 Jun 91*	2
DRAGGING ME DOWN	*Cow*	12	*29 Feb 92*	5
TWO WORLDS COLLIDE	*Cow*	32	*30 May 92*	2
GENERATIONS	*Cow*	28	*19 Sep 92*	3
BITCHES BREW	*Cow*	36	*14 Nov 92*	2
HOW IT SHOULD BE	*Cow*	49	*5 Jun 93*	1
SATURN 5	*Cow*	20	*22 Jan 94*	4
I WANT YOU	*Cow*	18	*5 Mar 94*	3
Above hit: INSPIRAL CARPETS featuring Mark E. SMITH.				
UNIFORM	*Cow*	51	*7 May 94*	1
JOE	*Cow*	37	*16 Sep 95*	2
Originally released in 1989.				
ALBUMS:	**HITS 5**			**WEEKS 36**
LIFE	*Cow*	2	*5 May 90*	21
THE BEAST INSIDE	*Cow*	5	*4 May 91*	6
REVENGE OF THE GOLDFISH	*Cow*	17	*17 Oct 92*	3
DEVIL HOPPING	*Cow*	10	*19 Mar 94*	3
THE SINGLES	*Cow*	17	*30 Sep 95*	3

INSPIRATIONAL CHOIR — US

SINGLES:	HITS 1			WEEKS 11
ABIDE WITH ME	*Epic*	44	*22 Dec 84*	5
ABIDE WITH ME [RI]	*Portrait*	36	*14 Dec 85*	6
The Royal Choral Society not credited on the original issue.				
Above hit: INSPIRATIONAL CHOIR with the ROYAL CHORAL SOCIETY.				
ALBUMS:	**HITS 1**			**WEEKS 4**
SWEET INSPIRATION	*Portrait*	59	*18 Jan 86*	4

INSPIRATIONS — UK

ALBUMS:	HITS 5			WEEKS 35
PAN PIPE INSPIRATIONS	*Pure Music*	10	*29 Apr 95*	10
PAN PIPE DREAMS	*Pure Music*	10	*23 Sep 95*	8
PURE EMOTIONS	*Pure Music*	37	*11 Nov 95*	4
PAN PIPE IMAGES	*Telstar*	23	*6 Apr 96*	6
THE VERY BEST OF THE PAN PIPES	*Telstar*	37	*12 Oct 96*	7

INSTANT FUNK — US

SINGLES:	HITS 1			WEEKS 5
GOT MY MIND MADE UP	*Salsoul*	46	*20 Jan 79*	5

INTASTELLA — UK

SINGLES:	HITS 4			WEEKS 6
DREAM SOME PARADISE	*MCA*	69	*25 May 91*	1
PEOPLE	*MCA*	74	*24 Aug 91*	2

CENTURY	*MCA*	70	*16 Nov 91*	2
THE NIGHT	*Planet 3*	60	*23 Sep 95*	1

INTELLIGENT HOODLUM — US

SINGLES:	HITS 1			WEEKS 3
BACK TO REALITY	*A&M*	55	*6 Oct 90*	3

INTERACTIVE — Germany

SINGLES:	HITS 1			WEEKS 4
FOREVER YOUNG	*Ffrreedom*	28	*13 Apr 96*	4
Original recording by Alphaville in 1984.				

INTI ILLIMANI-GUAMARY — Chile

ALBUMS:	HITS 1			WEEKS 7
THE FLIGHT OF THE CONDOR [OST-TV]	*BBC*	62	*17 Dec 83*	7

INTRUDERS — US

SINGLES:	HITS 3			WEEKS 21
I'LL ALWAYS LOVE MY MAMA	*Philadelphia International*	32	*13 Apr 74*	7
WIN, PLACE OR SHOW (SHE'S A WINNER)	*Philadelphia International*	14	*06 Jul 74*	9
Features backing vocals by Daryl Hall.				
WHO DO YOU LOVE	*Streetwave*	65	*22 Dec 84*	5

INVISIBLE GIRLS – See Pauline MURRAY and the INVISIBLE GIRLS

INVISIBLE MAN — UK

SINGLES:	HITS 1			WEEKS 1
GIVE A LITTLE LOVE	*Serious*	48	*17 Apr 99*	1

INXS — Australia

SINGLES:	HITS 25			WEEKS 132
WHAT YOU NEED	*Mercury*	51	*19 Apr 86*	6
LISTEN LIKE THIEVES	*Mercury*	46	*28 Jun 86*	7
KISS THE DIRT (FALLING DOWN THE MOUNTAIN)	*Mercury*	54	*30 Aug 86*	3
NEED YOU TONIGHT	*Mercury*	58	*24 Oct 87*	3
NEW SENSATION	*Mercury*	25	*9 Jan 88*	6
DEVIL INSIDE	*Mercury*	47	*12 Mar 88*	5
NEVER TEAR US APART	*Mercury*	24	*25 Jun 88*	7
NEED YOU TONIGHT [RI]	*Mercury*	2	*12 Nov 88*	11
MYSTIFY	*Mercury*	14	*8 Apr 89*	7
SUICIDE BLONDE	*Mercury*	11	*15 Sep 90*	6
DISAPPEAR	*Mercury*	21	*8 Dec 90*	8
GOOD TIMES	*Atlantic*	18	*26 Jan 91*	8
From the film 'The Lost Boys'.				
Above hit: Jimmy BARNES and INXS.				
BY MY SIDE	*Mercury*	42	*30 Mar 91*	4
BITTER TEARS	*Mercury*	30	*13 Jul 91*	3
SHINING STAR [EP]	*Mercury*	27	*2 Nov 91*	3
Lead track: Shining Star.				
HEAVEN SENT	*Mercury*	31	*18 Jul 92*	3
BABY DON'T CRY	*Mercury*	20	*5 Sep 92*	5
TASTE IT	*Mercury*	21	*14 Nov 92*	4
BEAUTIFUL GIRL	*Mercury*	23	*13 Feb 93*	5
THE GIFT	*Mercury*	11	*23 Oct 93*	4
PLEASE (YOU GOT THAT . . .)	*Mercury*	50	*11 Dec 93*	3
Features vocals by Ray Charles.				
THE STRANGEST PARTY (THESE ARE THE TIMES)	*Mercury*	15	*22 Oct 94*	5
ELEGANTLY WASTED	*Mercury*	20	*22 Mar 97*	4
EVERYTHING	*Mercury*	71	*7 Jun 97*	1
PRECIOUS HEART	*Duty Free*	14	*18 Aug 01*	4
Above hit: TALL PAUL vs INXS.				
PRECIOUS HEART [RE]	*Duty Free*	57	*29 Sep 01*	1
I'M SO CRAZY	*Credence*	19	*3 Nov 01*	5
Samples Just Keep Walking by INXS.				
Above hit: PAR-T-ONE vs INXS.				
I'M SO CRAZY [RE]	*Credence*	71	*15 Dec 01*	1

ALBUMS:	HITS 8			WEEKS 237
LISTEN LIKE THIEVES	*Mercury*	48	*8 Feb 86*	15
KICK	*Mercury*	9	*28 Nov 87*	103
Includes re-entries through to 1993.				
X	*Mercury*	2	*6 Oct 90*	50
Includes re-entries through to 1998.				
LIVE BABY LIVE	*Mercury*	8	*16 Nov 91*	9
WELCOME TO WHEREVER YOU ARE	*Mercury*	1	*15 Aug 92*	33
FULL MOON, DIRTY HEARTS	*Mercury*	3	*13 Nov 93*	8

INXS - THE GREATEST HITS	*Mercury*	3	*12 Nov 94*	16
ELEGANTLY WASTED	*Mercury*	16	*19 Apr 97*	3

Tommy IOMMI - See BLACK SABBATH

IQ — UK

ALBUMS:	HITS 1			WEEKS 1
THE WAKE	*Sahara*	72	*22 Jun 85*	1

Sweetie IRIE - See ASWAD; Ed CASE; SCRITTI POLITTI

Tippa IRIE — UK

(See also Arsenal FC.)

SINGLES:	HITS 3			WEEKS 11
HELLO DARLING	*UK Bubblers*	22	*22 Mar 86*	7
HEARTBEAT	*UK Bubblers*	59	*19 Jul 86*	3
STAYING ALIVE 95	*Telstar*	48	*8 Jul 95*	1
Above hit: FEVER featuring Tippa IRIE.				

IRON MAIDEN — UK

SINGLES:	HITS 31			WEEKS 154
RUNNING FREE	*EMI*	34	*23 Feb 80*	5
SANCTUARY	*EMI*	29	*7 Jun 80*	5
WOMEN IN UNIFORM	*EMI*	35	*8 Nov 80*	4
TWILIGHT ZONE/WRATH CHILD	*EMI*	31	*14 Mar 81*	5
PURGATORY	*EMI*	52	*27 Jun 81*	3
MAIDEN JAPAN [EP]	*EMI*	43	*26 Sep 81*	4
Lead track: Running Free. Live recordings from their shows in Japan.				
RUN TO THE HILLS	*EMI*	7	*20 Feb 82*	10
THE NUMBER OF THE BEAST	*EMI*	18	*15 May 82*	8
FLIGHT OF ICARUS	*EMI*	11	*23 Apr 83*	6
THE TROOPER	*EMI*	12	*2 Jul 83*	7
2 MINUTES TO MIDNIGHT	*EMI*	11	*18 Aug 84*	6
ACES HIGH	*EMI*	20	*3 Nov 84*	5
RUNNING FREE [RR]	*EMI*	19	*5 Oct 85*	5
Live recording.				
RUN TO THE HILLS [RR]	*EMI*	26	*14 Dec 85*	6
Live recording from the Long Beach Arena, Mar 85.				
WASTED YEARS	*EMI*	18	*6 Sep 86*	4
STRANGER IN A STRANGE LAND	*EMI*	22	*22 Nov 86*	4
STRANGER IN A STRANGE LAND [RE]	*EMI*	71	*27 Dec 86*	2
CAN I PLAY WITH MADNESS	*EMI*	3	*26 Mar 88*	6
THE EVIL THAT MEN DO	*EMI*	5	*13 Aug 88*	6
THE CLAIRVOYANT	*EMI*	6	*19 Nov 88*	8
INFINITE DREAMS (LIVE)	*EMI*	6	*18 Nov 89*	5
Live recording from Birmingham NEC 27/28 Nov 88.				
INFINITE DREAMS (LIVE) [RE]	*EMI*	74	*30 Dec 89*	1
HOLY SMOKE	*EMI*	3	*22 Sep 90*	4
BRING YOUR DAUGHTER . . . TO THE SLAUGHTER	*EMI*	1	*5 Jan 91*	5
BE QUICK OR BE DEAD	*EMI*	2	*25 Apr 92*	4
FROM HERE TO ETERNITY	*EMI*	21	*11 Jul 92*	4
FEAR OF THE DARK (LIVE)	*EMI*	8	*13 Mar 93*	3
Live recording from the Ishallen, Helsinki, Finland 5 Jun 92.				
HALLOWED BE THY NAME (LIVE)	*EMI*	9	*16 Oct 93*	3
Live recording from the Olympic Arena, Moscow 4 Jun 93.				
MAN ON THE EDGE	*EMI*	10	*7 Oct 95*	3
VIRUS	*EMI*	16	*21 Sep 96*	3
THE ANGEL AND THE GAMBLER	*EMI*	18	*21 Mar 98*	3
THE WICKER MAN	*EMI*	9	*20 May 00*	4
OUT OF THE SILENT PLANET	*EMI*	20	*4 Nov 00*	3

ALBUMS:	HITS 27			WEEKS 198
IRON MAIDEN	*EMI*	4	*26 Apr 80*	15
KILLERS	*EMI*	12	*28 Feb 81*	8
THE NUMBER OF THE BEAST	*EMI*	1	*10 Apr 82*	31
PIECE OF MIND	*EMI*	3	*28 May 83*	18
POWERSLAVE	*EMI*	2	*15 Sep 84*	13
IRON MAIDEN [RI]	*Fame*	71	*15 Jun 85*	2
Mid-price re-issue.				
LIVE AFTER DEATH	*EMI*	2	*26 Oct 85*	14
Live recordings from their World Slavery tour between Apr 84 and Jul 85.				
SOMEWHERE IN TIME	*EMI*	3	*11 Oct 86*	11
THE NUMBER OF THE BEAST [RI]	*Fame*	98	*20 Jun 87*	1
Mid-price re-issue.				
SEVENTH SON OF A SEVENTH SON	*EMI*	1	*23 Apr 88*	18
RUNNING FREE/SANCTUARY	*EMI*	10	*24 Feb 90*	4
WOMEN IN UNIFORM/TWILIGHT ZONE	*EMI*	10	*3 Mar 90*	3
PURGATORY/MAIDEN JAPAN	*EMI*	5	*10 Mar 90*	3

RUN TO THE HILLS/THE NUMBER OF THE BEAST	EMI	3	17 Mar 90	2
FLIGHT OF ICARUS/THE TROOPER	EMI	7	24 Mar 90	2
2 MINUTES TO MIDNIGHT/ACES HIGH	EMI	11	31 Mar 90	2
RUNNING FREE (LIVE)/RUN TO THE HILLS (LIVE)	EMI	9	7 Apr 90	2
WASTED YEARS/STRANGER IN A STRANGE LAND	EMI	9	14 Apr 90	2
CAN I PLAY WITH MADNESS/THE EVIL THAT MEN DO	EMI	10	21 Apr 90	3
THE CLAIRVOYANT/INFINITE DREAMS (LIVE)	EMI	11	28 Apr 90	2
Above 10 are double 12"/CD singles, too long and expensive to be eligible for the singles chart.				
NO PRAYER FOR THE DYING	EMI	2	13 Oct 90	14
FEAR OF THE DARK	EMI	1	23 May 92	5
A REAL LIVE ONE	EMI	3	3 Apr 93	4
A REAL DEAD ONE	EMI	12	30 Oct 93	3
Above 2 are live recordings from their 1992/1993 European tour.				
LIVE AT DONNINGTON	EMI	23	20 Nov 93	1
Limited edition (5,000 copies) bootleg of their appearance at Donnington, issued as a farewell to Bruce Dickinson.				
THE X FACTOR	EMI	8	14 Oct 95	4
THE BEST OF THE BEAST	EMI	16	5 Oct 96	5
VIRTUAL XI	EMI	16	4 Apr 98	2
BRAVE NEW WORLD	EMI	7	10 Jun 00	4

IRONHORSE — Canada

SINGLES:	HITS 1			WEEKS 3
SWEET LUI-LOUISE	Scotti Brothers	60	5 May 79	3

Big Dee IRWIN — US

SINGLES:	HITS 1			WEEKS 17
SWINGING ON A STAR	Colpix	7	23 Nov 63	17
Although she is not credited, single is a duet with Little Eva. Originally recorded by Bing Crosby in 1944.				

Gregory ISAACS — Jamaica

ALBUMS:	HITS 2			WEEKS 6
MORE GREGORY	Pre	93	12 Sep 81	1
NIGHT NURSE	Island	32	4 Sep 82	5

Chris ISAAK — US

SINGLES:	HITS 5			WEEKS 22
WICKED GAME	London	10	24 Nov 90	10
From the film 'Wild At Heart'.				
BLUE HOTEL	Reprise	17	2 Feb 91	7
Original release reached No. 100 in 1987.				
CAN'T DO A THING (TO STOP ME)	Reprise	36	3 Apr 93	3
SAN FRANCISCO DAYS	Reprise	62	10 Jul 93	1
BABY DID A BAD BAD THING	Reprise	44	2 Oct 99	1
From the film 'Eyes Wide Shut'.				
ALBUMS:	**HITS 3**			**WEEKS 38**
WICKED GAME	Reprise	3	26 Jan 91	30
SAN FRANCISCO DAYS	Reprise	12	24 Apr 93	5
FOREVER BLUE	Reprise	27	3 Jun 95	3

ISHA-D — UK

SINGLES:	HITS 1			WEEKS 4
STAY (TONIGHT)	Cleveland City Blues	28	22 Jul 95	3
STAY [RM]	Satellite	58	5 Jul 97	1
Remixed by Andy Ling.				

Ronald ISLEY – See Warren G; R. KELLY; Rod STEWART

ISLEY BROTHERS — US

SINGLES:	HITS 13			WEEKS 108
TWIST AND SHOUT	Stateside	42	27 Jul 63	1
Originally recorded by the Top Notes in 1961.				
THIS OLD HEART OF MINE (IS WEAK FOR YOU)	Tamla Motown	47	30 Apr 66	1
I GUESS I'LL ALWAYS LOVE YOU	Tamla Motown	45	3 Sep 66	2
THIS OLD HEART OF MINE (IS WEAK FOR YOU) [RE]	Tamla Motown	3	26 Oct 68	16
I GUESS I'LL ALWAYS LOVE YOU [RI]	Tamla Motown	11	18 Jan 69	9
BEHIND A PAINTED SMILE	Tamla Motown	5	19 Apr 69	12
IT'S YOUR THING	Major Minor	30	28 Jun 69	5
PUT YOURSELF IN MY PLACE	Tamla Motown	13	30 Aug 69	11
THAT LADY	Epic	14	22 Sep 73	9
HIGHWAY OF MY LIFE	Epic	25	19 Jan 74	8
SUMMER BREEZE	Epic	16	25 May 74	8
Originally recorded by Seals and Croft.				
HARVEST FOR THE WORLD	Epic	10	10 Jul 76	8

TAKE ME TO THE NEXT PHASE (PARTS 1 & 2)	*Epic*	50	*13 May 78*	4
IT'S A DISCO NIGHT (ROCK DON'T STOP)	*Epic*	14	*3 Nov 79*	11
BETWEEN THE SHEETS	*Epic*	52	*16 Jul 83*	3
ALBUMS:	**HITS 5**			**WEEKS 24**
THIS OLD HEART OF MINE	*Tamla Motown*	23	*14 Dec 68*	6
HARVEST FOR THE WORLD	*Epic*	50	*14 Aug 76*	5
GO FOR YOUR GUNS	*Epic*	46	*14 May 77*	2
SHOWDOWN	*Epic*	50	*24 Jun 78*	1
GREATEST HITS	*Telstar*	41	*5 Mar 88*	10

ISLEY JASPER ISLEY — US

SINGLES:	**HITS 1**			**WEEKS 5**
CARAVAN OF LOVE	*Epic*	52	*23 Nov 85*	5

ISOTONIK — UK

SINGLES:	**HITS 2**			**WEEKS 9**
DIFFERENT STROKES	*Ffreedom*	12	*11 Jan 92*	5
EVERYWHERE I GO / LET'S GET DOWN	*Ffreedom*	25	*2 May 92*	4

Let's Get Down listed from 9 May 92. Sleeve gives title as an EP:The Isotronik E.P.

IT BITES — UK

SINGLES:	**HITS 4**			**WEEKS 21**
CALLING ALL THE HEROS	*Virgin*	6	*12 Jul 86*	12
WHOLE NEW WORLD	*Virgin*	54	*18 Oct 86*	3
THE OLD MAN AND THE ANGEL	*Virgin*	72	*23 May 87*	1
STILL TOO YOUNG TO REMEMBER	*Virgin*	66	*13 May 89*	3
STILL TOO YOUNG TO REMEMBER [RM]	*Virgin*	60	*24 Feb 90*	2

Remixed by Nick Davies.

ALBUMS:	**HITS 4**			**WEEKS 12**
THE BIG LAD IN THE WINDMILL	*Virgin*	35	*6 Sep 86*	5
ONCE AROUND THE WORLD	*Virgin*	43	*2 Apr 88*	3
EAT ME IN ST. LOUIS	*Virgin*	40	*24 Jun 89*	3
THANK YOU AND GOODNIGHT	*Virgin*	59	*31 Aug 91*	1

IT'S A BEAUTIFUL DAY — US

ALBUMS:	**HITS 2**			**WEEKS 3**
IT'S A BEAUTIFUL DAY	*CBS*	58	*23 May 70*	1
MARRYING MAIDEN	*CBS*	45	*18 Jul 70*	2

IT'S IMMATERIAL — UK

SINGLES:	**HITS 2**			**WEEKS 10**
DRIVING AWAY FROM HOME (JIM'S TUNE)	*Siren*	18	*12 Apr 86*	7
ED'S FUNKY DINER (FRIDAY NIGHT, SATURDAY MORNING)	*Siren*	65	*2 Aug 86*	3
ALBUMS:	**HITS 1**			**WEEKS 3**
LIFE'S HARD AND THEN YOU DIE	*Siren*	62	*27 Sep 86*	3

ITTY BITTY BOOZY WOOZY — Holland

(See also Klubbheads.)

SINGLES:	**HITS 1**			**WEEKS 2**
TEMPO FIESTA (PARTY TIME)	*Systematic*	34	*25 Nov 95*	2

Burl IVES — US

SINGLES:	**HITS 2**			**WEEKS 25**
A LITTLE BITTY TEAR	*Brunswick*	9	*27 Jan 62*	15
FUNNY WAY OF LAUGHIN'	*Brunswick*	29	*19 May 62*	10

IVY LEAGUE — UK

SINGLES:	**HITS 4**			**WEEKS 31**
FUNNY HOW LOVE CAN BE	*Piccadilly*	8	*6 Feb 65*	9
THAT'S WHY I'M CRYING	*Piccadilly*	22	*8 May 65*	8
TOSSING AND TURNING	*Piccadilly*	3	*26 Jun 65*	13
WILLOW TREE	*Piccadilly*	50	*16 Jul 66*	1

IZIT — UK

SINGLES:	**HITS 1**			**WEEKS 3**
STORIES	*ffrr*	52	*2 Dec 89*	3

J

J.A.L.N. BAND — UK/Jamaica

SINGLES:	HITS 3			WEEKS 17
DISCO MUSIC/I LIKE IT [M]	*Magnet*	21	*11 Sep 76*	9
I GOT TO SING	*Magnet*	40	*27 Aug 77*	4
GET UP (AND LET YOURSELF GO)	*Magnet*	53	*1 Jul 78*	4

J.B.'S ALL STARS — UK

SINGLES:	HITS 1			WEEKS 4
BACKFIELD IN MOTION	*RCA Victor*	48	*11 Feb 84*	4

Original by Mel and Tim reached No. 10 in the US in 1969.

J.C. — UK

SINGLES:	HITS 1			WEEKS 1
SO HOT	*East West Dance*	74	*7 Feb 98*	1

J.J. — UK

SINGLES:	HITS 1			WEEKS 3
IF THIS IS LOVE	*Columbia*	55	*9 Feb 91*	3

J.K.D. BAND featuring the voice of Bruce LEE — UK

SINGLES:	HITS 1			WEEKS 4
DRAGON POWER (A TRIBUTE TO BRUCE LEE)	*Satril*	58	*1 Jul 78*	4

J.M. SILK — US

SINGLES:	HITS 2			WEEKS 6
I CAN'T TURN AROUND	*RCA*	62	*25 Oct 86*	3
LET THE MUSIC TAKE CONTROL	*RCA*	47	*7 Mar 87*	3

J.M.D. – See TYREE

J.PAC — UK

SINGLES:	HITS 1			WEEKS 2
ROCK 'N' ROLL (DOLE)	*East West*	51	*22 Jul 95*	2

J.T. and the BIG FAMILY — Italy

SINGLES:	HITS 1			WEEKS 8
MOMENTS IN SOUL	*Champion*	7	*3 Mar 90*	8

JA RULE

(See also Jay-Z.)

SINGLES:	HITS 2			WEEKS 7
BETWEEN ME AND YOU	*Def Jam*	26	*3 Mar 01*	3
Above hit: JA RULE (featuring Christina MILLAN).				
LIVIN' IT UP	*Def Jam*	27	*10 Nov 01*	4
Above hit: JA RULE featuring CASE.				
ALBUMS:	**HITS 1**			**WEEKS 6**
PAIN IS LOVE	*Def Jam*	17	*27 Oct 01*	6

JACK 'N' CHILL — UK

SINGLES:	HITS 2			WEEKS 21
THE JACK THAT HOUSE BUILT	*10 Records*	48	*6 Jun 87*	5
THE JACK THAT HOUSE BUILT [RE]	*10 Records*	6	*9 Jan 88*	11
BEATIN' THE HEAT	*10 Records*	42	*9 Jul 88*	5

JACK RADICS – See Chaka DEMUS and PLIERS; SUPERCAT

Susan JACKS – See POPPY FAMILY (featuring Susan JACKS)

Terry JACKS — Canada

SINGLES:	HITS 2			WEEKS 21
SEASONS IN THE SUN	*Bell*	1	*23 Mar 74*	12
IF YOU GO AWAY	*Bell*	8	*29 Jun 74*	9

Above 2 originally recorded by Jacques Brel.

Chad JACKSON — UK

SINGLES:	HITS 1			WEEKS 10
HEAR THE DRUMMER (GET WICKED)	*Big Wave*	3	*2 Jun 90*	10

Dee D. JACKSON

UK

SINGLES:	HITS 2			WEEKS 14
AUTOMATIC LOVER	*Mercury*	4	*22 Apr 78*	9
METEOR MAN	*Mercury*	48	*2 Sep 78*	5

Freddie JACKSON

US

SINGLES:	HITS 8			WEEKS 31
YOU ARE MY LADY	*Capitol*	49	*23 Nov 85*	4
ROCK ME TONIGHT (FOR OLD TIME'S SAKE)	*Capitol*	18	*22 Feb 86*	9
TASTY LOVE	*Capitol*	73	*11 Oct 86*	1
HAVE YOU EVER LOVED SOMEBODY	*Capitol*	33	*7 Feb 87*	6
NICE AND SLOW	*Capitol*	56	*9 Jul 88*	2
CRAZY (FOR ME)	*Capitol*	41	*15 Oct 88*	3
ME AND MRS. JONES	*Capitol*	32	*5 Sep 92*	5
MAKE LOVE EASY	*RCA*	70	*15 Jan 94*	1
ALBUMS:	**HITS 4**			**WEEKS 48**
ROCK ME TONIGHT	*Capitol*	73	*18 May 85*	6
ROCK ME TONIGHT [RE]	*Capitol*	27	*25 Jan 86*	16
JUST LIKE THE FIRST TIME	*Capitol*	30	*8 Nov 86*	15
DON'T LET LOVE SLIP AWAY	*Capitol*	24	*30 Jul 88*	9
DO ME AGAIN	*Capitol*	48	*17 Nov 90*	2

Gisele JACKSON

US

SINGLES:	HITS 1			WEEKS 1
LOVE COMMANDMENTS	*Manifesto*	54	*30 Aug 97*	1

Janet JACKSON

US

SINGLES:	HITS 36			WEEKS 274
WHAT HAVE YOU DONE FOR ME LATELY	*A&M*	3	*22 Mar 86*	14
NASTY	*A&M*	19	*31 May 86*	9
WHEN I THINK OF YOU	*A&M*	10	*9 Aug 86*	10
CONTROL	*A&M*	42	*1 Nov 86*	5
LET'S WAIT AWHILE	*Breakout*	3	*21 Mar 87*	10
THE PLEASURE PRINCIPLE	*Breakout*	24	*13 Jun 87*	5
Label on 7" format reads Pleasure Principle Remix (The Shep Pettibone Mix).				
FUNNY HOW TIME FLIES (WHEN YOU'RE HAVING FUN)	*Breakout*	59	*14 Nov 87*	2
MISS YOU MUCH	*Breakout*	22	*2 Sep 89*	7
RHYTHM NATION	*Breakout*	23	*4 Nov 89*	5
COME BACK TO ME	*Breakout*	20	*27 Jan 90*	7
ESCAPADE	*Breakout*	17	*31 Mar 90*	7
ALRIGHT	*Breakout*	20	*7 Jul 90*	5
BLACK CAT	*A&M*	15	*8 Sep 90*	6
Lead guitar by Vernon Reid of Living Colour.				
LOVE WILL NEVER DO (WITHOUT YOU)	*A&M*	34	*27 Oct 90*	4
THE BEST THINGS IN LIFE ARE FREE	*Perspective*	2	*15 Aug 92*	13
From the film 'Mo' Money'.				
Above hit: Luther VANDROSS and Janet JACKSON with special guests BBD and Ralph TRESVANT.				
THAT'S THE WAY LOVE GOES	*Virgin*	2	*8 May 93*	10
IF	*Virgin*	14	*31 Jul 93*	7
AGAIN	*Virgin*	6	*20 Nov 93*	11
BECAUSE OF LOVE	*Virgin*	19	*12 Mar 94*	4
ANY TIME, ANY PLACE	*Virgin*	13	*18 Jun 94*	5
YOU WANT THIS	*Virgin*	14	*26 Nov 94*	3
Samples Love Child by Diana Ross and the Supremes.				
WHOOPS NOW / WHAT'LL I DO	*Virgin*	9	*18 Mar 95*	8
SCREAM	*Epic*	3	*10 Jun 95*	12
Above hit: Michael JACKSON (Duet with Michael JACKSON and Janet JACKSON).				
SCREAM [RM]	*Epic*	43	*24 Jun 95*	2
Remixed by David Morales.				
RUNAWAY	*A&M*	6	*23 Sep 95*	7
SCREAM [RE]	*Epic*	72	*2 Dec 95*	1
THE BEST THINGS IN LIFE ARE FREE [RM]	*A&M*	7	*16 Dec 95*	7
Remixed by K-Klass.				
Above hit: Luther VANDROSS and Janet JACKSON.				
TWENTY FOREPLAY	*A&M*	22	*6 Apr 96*	4
GOT 'TIL IT'S GONE	*Virgin*	6	*4 Oct 97*	9
Samples Joni Mitchell's Big Yellow Taxi.				
Above hit: JANET (featuring Q-TIP and Joni MITCHELL).				
TOGETHER AGAIN	*Virgin*	4	*13 Dec 97*	19
Above hit: JANET.				
I GET LONELY	*Virgin*	5	*4 Apr 98*	7
Above hit: JANET (featuring BLACKSTREET).				
GO DEEP	*Virgin*	13	*27 Jun 98*	5

EVERY TIME	*Virgin*	46	*19 Dec 98*	1
Above 2: JANET.				
GIRLFRIEND / BOYFRIEND	*Interscope*	11	*17 Apr 99*	7
One song. Rap by Ja Rule and Eve.				
Above hit: BLACKSTREET featuring JANET.				
WHAT'S IT GONNA BE?!	*Elektra*	6	*1 May 99*	7
Above hit: Busta RHYMES featuring JANET.				
DOESN'T REALLY MATTER	*Def Soul*	5	*19 Aug 00*	11
From the film 'The Nutty Professor II: The Klumps'.				
ALL FOR YOU	*Virgin*	3	*21 Apr 01*	11
Samples A Glow Of Love by Change.				
SOMEONE TO CALL MY LOVER	*Virgin*	11	*11 Aug 01*	5
Above 2: JANET.				
SON OF A GUN (I BETCHA THINK THIS SONG IS ABOUT YOU)	*Virgin*	13	*22 Dec 01*	2
Above hit: JANET featuring Carly SIMON.				

ALBUMS:	HITS 7			WEEKS 268
CONTROL	*A&M*	15	*5 Apr 86*	43
CONTROL [RE]	*A&M*	8	*21 Mar 87*	29
CONTROL - THE REMIXES	*Breakout*	20	*14 Nov 87*	14
JANET JACKSON'S RHYTHM NATION 1814	*A&M*	4	*30 Sep 89*	43
JANET	*Virgin*	1	*29 May 93*	49
Repackaged from 12 Feb 94.				
JANET / JANET - REMIXED [RE]	*Virgin*	15	*25 Mar 95*	8
Janet - Remixed was a remix album, sales were combined.				
DESIGN OF A DECADE - 1986/1996	*A&M*	2	*14 Oct 95*	21
Compilation.				
THE VELVET ROPE	*Virgin*	6	*18 Oct 97*	43
ALL FOR YOU	*Virgin*	2	*5 May 01*	18

Jermaine JACKSON — US

SINGLES:	HITS 7			WEEKS 43
LET'S GET SERIOUS	*Motown*	8	*10 May 80*	11
Written, produced and backing vocals by Stevie Wonder.				
BURNIN' HOT	*Motown*	32	*26 Jul 80*	6
YOU LIKE ME DON'T YOU	*Motown*	41	*30 May 81*	5
SWEETEST SWEETEST	*Arista*	52	*12 May 84*	4
WHEN THE RAIN BEGINS TO FALL	*Arista*	68	*27 Oct 84*	2
From the film 'Voyage Of The Rock Aliens'.				
Above hit: Jermaine JACKSON and Pia ZADORA.				
DO WHAT YOU DO	*Arista*	6	*16 Feb 85*	13
DON'T TAKE IT PERSONAL	*Arista*	69	*21 Oct 89*	2

ALBUMS:	HITS 2			WEEKS 12
LET'S GET SERIOUS	*Motown*	22	*31 May 80*	6
DYNAMITE	*Arista*	57	*12 May 84*	6

Joe JACKSON — UK

SINGLES:	HITS 8			WEEKS 49
IS SHE REALLY GOING OUT WITH HIM?	*A&M*	13	*4 Aug 79*	9
IT'S DIFFERENT FOR GIRLS	*A&M*	5	*12 Jan 80*	9
JUMPIN' JIVE	*A&M*	43	*4 Jul 81*	5
Originally recorded by Cab Calloway in 1939.				
Above hit: Joe JACKSON'S JUMPIN' JIVE.				
STEPPIN' OUT	*A&M*	6	*8 Jan 83*	8
BREAKING US IN TWO	*A&M*	59	*12 Mar 83*	4
HAPPY ENDING	*A&M*	58	*28 Apr 84*	3
Elaine Caswell was only credited on the back of the sleeve.				
Above hit: Joe JACKSON featuring Elaine CASWELL.				
BE MY NUMBER TWO	*A&M*	70	*7 Jul 84*	2
LEFT OF CENTRE	*A&M*	32	*7 Jun 86*	9
Sleeve has British spelling; the sleeve the US variant 'Center'.				
Above hit: Suzanne VEGA featuring Joe JACKSON on piano.				

ALBUMS:	HITS 11			WEEKS 106
LOOK SHARP	*A&M*	40	*17 Mar 79*	11
I'M THE MAN	*A&M*	12	*13 Oct 79*	16
BEAT CRAZY	*A&M*	42	*18 Oct 80*	3
JUMPIN' JIVE	*A&M*	14	*4 Jul 81*	14
Above hit: Joe JACKSON'S JUMPIN' JIVE.				
NIGHT AND DAY	*A&M*	44	*3 Jul 82*	11
NIGHT AND DAY [RE]	*A&M*	3	*22 Jan 83*	16
BODY AND SOUL	*A&M*	14	*7 Apr 84*	14
BIG WORLD	*A&M*	41	*5 Apr 86*	5
LIVE 1980-86	*A&M*	66	*7 May 88*	2
BLAZE OF GLORY	*A&M*	36	*29 Apr 89*	3
STEPPING OUT - THE VERY BEST OF JOE JACKSON	*A&M*	7	*15 Sep 90*	9
LAUGHTER AND LUST	*Virgin America*	41	*11 May 91*	2

Michael JACKSON — US

SINGLES:	HITS 51			WEEKS 493
GOT TO BE THERE	*Tamla Motown*	5	*12 Feb 72*	11
ROCKIN' ROBIN	*Tamla Motown*	3	*20 May 72*	14
AIN'T NO SUNSHINE	*Tamla Motown*	8	*19 Aug 72*	11
Originally recorded by Bill Withers in 1972.				
BEN	*Tamla Motown*	7	*25 Nov 72*	14
EASE ON DOWN THE ROAD	*MCA*	45	*18 Nov 78*	4
Originally recorded by the Consumer Rapport. From the film 'The Wiz'.				
Above hit: Diana ROSS / Michael JACKSON.				
DON'T STOP 'TILL YOU GET ENOUGH	*Epic*	3	*15 Sep 79*	12
OFF THE WALL	*Epic*	7	*24 Nov 79*	10
ROCK WITH YOU	*Epic*	7	*9 Feb 80*	9
SHE'S OUT OF MY LIFE	*Epic*	3	*3 May 80*	9
GIRLFRIEND	*Epic*	41	*26 Jul 80*	5
ONE DAY IN YOUR LIFE	*Tamla Motown*	1	*23 May 81*	14
Originally released in 1975.				
WE'RE ALMOST THERE	*Motown*	46	*1 Aug 81*	4
THE GIRL IS MINE	*Epic*	8	*6 Nov 82*	9
Above hit: Michael JACKSON and Paul McCARTNEY.				
THE GIRL IS MINE [RE]	*Epic*	75	*15 Jan 83*	1
BILLIE JEAN	*Epic*	1	*29 Jan 83*	15
BEAT IT	*Epic*	3	*9 Apr 83*	12
Features Eddie Van Halen on guitar.				
WANNA BE STARTIN' SOMETHIN'	*Epic*	8	*11 Jun 83*	9
HAPPY (LOVE THEME FROM 'LADY SINGS THE BLUES')	*Tamla Motown*	52	*23 Jul 83*	3
From the film 'Lady Sings The Blues'.				
SAY SAY SAY	*Parlophone*	2	*15 Oct 83*	15
Above hit: Paul McCARTNEY and Michael JACKSON.				
THRILLER	*Epic*	10	*19 Nov 83*	18
P.Y.T. (PRETTY YOUNG THING)	*Epic*	11	*31 Mar 84*	8
FAREWELL MY SUMMER LOVE	*Motown*	7	*2 Jun 84*	12
GIRL YOU'RE SO TOGETHER	*Motown*	33	*11 Aug 84*	8
I JUST CAN'T STOP LOVING YOU	*Epic*	1	*8 Aug 87*	9
Above hit: Michael JACKSON with Siedah GARRETT.				
BAD	*Epic*	3	*26 Sep 87*	11
THE WAY YOU MAKE ME FEEL	*Epic*	3	*5 Dec 87*	10
MAN IN THE MIRROR	*Epic*	21	*20 Feb 88*	5
Siedah Garrett and the Winans on backing vocals.				
GET IT	*Motown*	37	*28 May 88*	4
Above hit: Stevie WONDER and Michael JACKSON.				
DIRTY DIANA	*Epic*	4	*16 Jul 88*	8
ANOTHER PART OF ME	*Epic*	15	*10 Sep 88*	6
SMOOTH CRIMINAL	*Epic*	8	*26 Nov 88*	10
LEAVE ME ALONE	*Epic*	2	*25 Feb 89*	9
LIBERIAN GIRL	*Epic*	13	*15 Jul 89*	6
BLACK OR WHITE	*Epic*	1	*23 Nov 91*	10
Slash from Guns N' Roses on guitar, rap is by Bill Bottrell.				
BLACK OR WHITE [RM]	*Epic*	14	*18 Jan 92*	4
Remixed by Clivilles and Cole.				
REMEMBER THE TIME / COME TOGETHER	*Epic*	3	*15 Feb 92*	8
Come Together listed from 7 Mar 92 once single had dropped down to No.10.				
IN THE CLOSET	*Epic*	8	*2 May 92*	6
Above hit: Michael JACKSON and MYSTERY GIRL: Duet.				
WHO IS IT	*Epic*	10	*25 Jul 92*	7
JAM	*Epic*	13	*12 Sep 92*	5
Rap by Heavy D.				
PRELUDE/HEAL THE WORLD	*Epic*	2	*5 Dec 92*	15
GIVE IN TO ME	*Epic*	2	*27 Feb 93*	9
Above hit: Michael JACKSON featuring special guitar performance by SLASH.				
WILL YOU BE THERE	*Epic*	9	*10 Jul 93*	8
GONE TOO SOON	*Epic*	33	*18 Dec 93*	5
SCREAM	*Epic*	3	*10 Jun 95*	12
Above hit: Michael JACKSON (Duet with Michael JACKSON and Janet JACKSON).				
SCREAM [RM]	*Epic*	43	*24 Jun 95*	2
Remixed by David Morales.				
YOU ARE NOT ALONE	*Epic*	1	*2 Sep 95*	15
Written and produced by R.Kelly				
SCREAM [RE]	*Epic*	72	*2 Dec 95*	1
EARTH SONG	*Epic*	1	*9 Dec 95*	17
THEY DON'T CARE ABOUT US	*Epic*	4	*20 Apr 96*	12
THEY DON'T CARE ABOUT US [RE-1ST]	*Epic*	66	*3 Aug 96*	1
THEY DON'T CARE ABOUT US [RE-2ND]	*Epic*	66	*17 Aug 96*	1
WHY	*Epic*	2	*24 Aug 96*	9
Above hit: 3T featuring Michael JACKSON.				
STRANGER IN MOSCOW	*Epic*	4	*16 Nov 96*	10
STRANGER IN MOSCOW [RE]	*Epic*	69	*1 Mar 97*	1

BLOOD ON THE DANCE FLOOR	*Epic*	1	*3 May 97*	9
HISTORY / GHOSTS	*Epic*	5	*19 Jul 97*	8
Though listed as a double A-side, Ghosts did not appear on the second CD format.				
YOU ROCK MY WORLD	*Epic*	2	*20 Oct 01*	11
CRY	*Epic*	25	*22 Dec 01*	2
ALBUMS:	**HITS 23**			**WEEKS 861**

COMPILATION ALBUMS:	**HITS 1**			**WEEKS 2**
GOT TO BE THERE	*Tamla Motown*	37	*3 Jun 72*	5
BEN	*Tamla Motown*	17	*13 Jan 73*	7
OFF THE WALL	*Epic*	5	*29 Sep 79*	160
Includes re-entries through to 1987.				
THE BEST OF MICHAEL JACKSON	*Motown*	11	*4 Jul 81*	18
ONE DAY IN YOUR LIFE	*Motown*	29	*18 Jul 81*	8
THRILLER	*Epic*	1	*11 Dec 82*	173
Includes re-entries through to 1992.				
E.T. - THE EXTRA TERRESTRIAL STORYBOOK	*MCA*	82	*12 Feb 83*	2
18 GREATEST HITS	*Telstar*	1	*9 Jul 83*	55
Above hit: Michael JACKSON plus the JACKSON FIVE.				
MICHAEL JACKSON 9 SINGLE PACK	*Epic*	66	*3 Dec 83*	3
This is a package of 9 x 7" singles on red vinyl.				
FAREWELL MY SUMMER LOVE	*Motown*	9	*9 Jun 84*	14
DIANA, MICHAEL, GLADYS. STEVIE - THEIR VERY BEST - BACK TO BACK	*PriorityV*	21	*15 Nov 86*	10
Compilation featuring tracks by each act.				
Above hit: Diana ROSS/Michael JACKSON/Gladys KNIGHT/Stevie WONDER.				
BAD	*Epic*	1	*12 Sep 87*	115
LOVE SONGS	*Telstar*	12	*31 Oct 87*	24
Compilation of each artist's solo recordings. When the compilation chart commenced on 14 Jan 89 it was listed there. See separate entry below.				
Above hit: Michael JACKSON and Diana ROSS.				
THE MICHAEL JACKSON MIX	*Stylus*	27	*26 Dec 87*	25
THE MICHAEL JACKSON BAD SOUVENIR SINGLES PACK	*Epic*	91	*30 Jul 88*	1
5 x 7" square-shaped picture discs.				
OFF THE WALL [RE-1ST]	*Epic*	36	*16 Jul 88*	16
Re-released at mid-price. Includes re-entries in 1992.				
18 GREATEST HITS [RI]	*Motown*	85	*30 Jul 88*	3
Above hit: Michael JACKSON Plus the JACKSON FIVE.				
LOVE SONGS	*Telstar*	18	*14 Jan 89*	2
Above entry was in the compilation chart.				
Above hit: Michael JACKSON and Diana ROSS.				
DANGEROUS	*Epic*	1	*30 Nov 91*	96
MOTOWN'S GREATEST HITS: MICHAEL JACKSON	*Motown*	53	*29 Feb 92*	2
TOUR SOUVENIR PACK	*Epic*	32	*15 Aug 92*	3
4-picture CD box set.				
HISTORY - PAST, PRESENT AND FUTURE, BOOK 1	*Epic*	1	*24 Jun 95*	77
Double CD, one of which is a greatest hits compilation.				
OFF THE WALL [RE-2ND]	*Epic*	60	*23 Sep 95*	2
BLOOD ON THE DANCE FLOOR - HISTORY IN THE MIX	*Epic*	1	*24 May 97*	16
Features 5 new songs and mixes from last album.				
THE BEST OF MICHAEL JACKSON & THE JACKSON FIVE - THE MOTOWN YEARS	*PolyGram TV*	5	*19 Jul 97*	9
Contains both Jackson's solo and group material.				
Above hit: Michael JACKSON and the JACKSON FIVE.				
THE BEST OF MICHAEL JACKSON AND THE JACKSON FIVE - THE MOTOWN YEARS [RI]	*Universal Music TV*	33	*20 Oct 01*	3
THRILLER [RE]	*Epic*	52	*27 Oct 01*	3
BAD [RE]	*Epic*	53	*27 Oct 01*	2
INVINCIBLE	*Epic*	1	*10 Nov 01*	8
GREATEST HITS - HISTORY VOLUME 1	*Epic*	68	*24 Nov 01*	1
Single CD version of his 1995 entry.				

Mick JACKSON — UK

SINGLES:	**HITS 2**			**WEEKS 16**
BLAME IT ON THE BOOGIE	*Atlantic*	15	*30 Sep 78*	8
WEEKEND	*Atlantic*	38	*3 Feb 79*	8

Millie JACKSON — US

SINGLES:	**HITS 3**			**WEEKS 8**
MY MAN A SWEET MAN	*Mojo*	50	*18 Nov 72*	1
I FEEL LIKE WALKING IN THE RAIN	*Sire*	55	*10 Mar 84*	2
ACT OF WAR	*Rocket*	32	*15 Jun 85*	5
Above hit: Elton JOHN and Millie JACKSON.				
ALBUMS:	**HITS 2**			**WEEKS 7**
E.S.P.	*Sire*	59	*18 Feb 84*	5
LIVE AND UNCENSORED	*Important*	81	*6 Apr 85*	2
Originally released in 1980.				

Stonewall JACKSON — US

SINGLES:	HITS 1			WEEKS 2
WATERLOO	*Philips*	24	*18 Jul 59*	2

Tony JACKSON and the VIBRATIONS — UK

SINGLES:	HITS 1			WEEKS 3
BYE BYE BABY *Originally recorded by Mary Wells.*	*Pye*	38	*10 Oct 64*	3

Tony JACKSON - See Q

Wanda JACKSON — US

SINGLES:	HITS 2			WEEKS 11
LET'S HAVE A PARTY *Backing vocals by Gene Vincent's Blue Caps.*	*Capitol*	32	*3 Sep 60*	8
MEAN MEAN MAN	*Capitol*	46	*28 Jan 61*	1
MEAN MEAN MAN [RE]	*Capitol*	40	*11 Feb 61*	2

JACKSON FIVE - See JACKSONS

JACKSON SISTERS — US

SINGLES:	HITS 1			WEEKS 2
I BELIEVE IN MIRACLES	*Urban*	72	*20 Jun 87*	2

JACKSONS — US

(See also Stevie Wonder.)

SINGLES:	HITS 26			WEEKS 235
I WANT YOU BACK	*Tamla Motown*	2	*31 Jan 70*	13
A B C	*Tamla Motown*	8	*16 May 70*	11
THE LOVE YOU SAVE	*Tamla Motown*	7	*1 Aug 70*	9
I'LL BE THERE	*Tamla Motown*	4	*21 Nov 70*	16
MAMA'S PEARL	*Tamla Motown*	25	*10 Apr 71*	7
NEVER CAN SAY GOODBYE	*Tamla Motown*	33	*17 Jul 71*	7
LOOKIN' THROUGH THE WINDOWS	*Tamla Motown*	9	*11 Nov 72*	11
SANTA CLAUS IS COMIN' TO TOWN	*Tamla Motown*	43	*23 Dec 72*	3
DOCTOR MY EYES *Originally recorded by Jackson Browne.*	*Tamla Motown*	9	*17 Feb 73*	10
HALLELUJAH DAY *Above 10: JACKSON 5.*	*Tamla Motown*	20	*9 Jun 73*	9
SKYWRITER *Above hit: JACKSON FIVE.*	*Tamla Motown*	25	*8 Sep 73*	8
ENJOY YOURSELF *Originally released in 1976.*	*Epic*	42	*9 Apr 77*	4
SHOW YOU THE WAY TO GO	*Epic*	1	*4 Jun 77*	10
DREAMER	*Epic*	22	*13 Aug 77*	9
GOIN' PLACES	*Epic*	26	*5 Nov 77*	7
EVEN THOUGH YOU'VE GONE	*Epic*	31	*11 Feb 78*	4
BLAME IT ON THE BOOGIE	*Epic*	8	*23 Sep 78*	12
DESTINY	*Epic*	39	*3 Feb 79*	6
SHAKE YOUR BODY (DOWN TO THE GROUND)	*Epic*	4	*24 Mar 79*	12
LOVELY ONE	*Epic*	29	*25 Oct 80*	6
HEARTBREAK HOTEL	*Epic*	44	*13 Dec 80*	6
CAN YOU FEEL IT	*Epic*	6	*28 Feb 81*	15
WALK RIGHT NOW	*Epic*	7	*4 Jul 81*	11
STATE OF SHOCK *Above hit: JACKSONS lead vocals by Michael JACKSON and Mick JAGGER.*	*Epic*	14	*7 Jul 84*	8
TORTURE	*Epic*	26	*8 Sep 84*	6
I WANT YOU BACK ('88 REMIX) [RM] *Remixed by Phil Harding.* *Above hit: Michael JACKSON with the JACKSON FIVE.*	*Motown*	8	*16 Apr 88*	9
NOTHIN (THAT COMPARES 2 U)	*Epic*	33	*13 May 89*	6

ALBUMS:	HITS 13			WEEKS 152
DIANA ROSS PRESENTS THE JACKSON FIVE	*Tamla Motown*	16	*21 Mar 70*	4
ABC	*Tamla Motown*	22	*15 Aug 70*	6
GREATEST HITS	*Tamla Motown*	26	*7 Oct 72*	14
LOOKIN' THROUGH THE WINDOWS *Above 4: JACKSON 5.*	*Tamla Motown*	16	*18 Nov 72*	8
THE JACKSONS	*Epic*	54	*16 Jul 77*	1
GOIN' PLACES	*Epic*	45	*3 Dec 77*	1
DESTINY	*Epic*	33	*5 May 79*	7
TRIUMPH	*Epic*	13	*11 Oct 80*	16
THE JACKSONS - LIVE	*Epic*	53	*12 Dec 81*	9
18 GREATEST HITS *Above hit: Michael JACKSON plus the JACKSON FIVE.*	*Telstar*	1	*9 Jul 83*	55
VICTORY	*Epic*	3	*21 Jul 84*	13

18 GREATEST HITS [RI]	*Motown*	85	*30 Jul 88*	3
Above hit: Michael JACKSON plus the JACKSON FIVE.				
2300 JACKSON ST	*Epic*	39	*1 Jul 89*	3
THE BEST OF MICHAEL JACKSON AND THE JACKSON FIVE – THE MOTOWN YEARS	*PolyGram TV*	5	*19 Jul 97*	9
Contains both Jackson's solo and group material.				
Above hit: Michael JACKSON and the JACKSON FIVE.				
THE BEST OF MICHAEL JACKSON AND THE JACKSON FIVE – THE MOTOWN YEARS [RI]	*Universal Music TV*	33	*20 Oct 01*	3

JACKY – See Jackie LEE

JACQUELINE – MACK VIBE featuring JACQUELINE

JADA – See SKIP RAIDERS featuring JADA

JADE — US

SINGLES:	HITS 5			WEEKS 28
DON'T WALK AWAY	*Giant*	7	*20 Mar 93*	8
I WANNA LOVE YOU	*Giant*	13	*3 Jul 93*	7
ONE WOMAN	*Giant*	22	*18 Sep 93*	5
ALL THRU THE NITE	*Giant*	32	*5 Feb 94*	3
Above hit: P.O.V. duet with JADE.				
EVERY DAY OF THE WEEK	*Giant*	19	*11 Feb 95*	5
ALBUMS:	**HITS 1**			**WEEKS 3**
JADE TO THE MAX	*Giant*	43	*29 May 93*	3

JADE 4 U – See PRAGA KHAN

JAGGED EDGE — UK

SINGLES:	HITS 1			WEEKS 2
YOU DON'T LOVE ME	*Polydor*	66	*15 Sep 90*	2

JAGGED EDGE featuring NELLY — US

SINGLES:	HITS 1			WEEKS 3
WHERE THE PARTY AT?	*Columbia*	25	*27 Oct 01*	3

Mick JAGGER — UK

(See also Jacksons.)

SINGLES:	HITS 5			WEEKS 34
MEMO FROM TURNER	*Decca*	32	*14 Nov 70*	5
From the film 'Performance'.				
JUST ANOTHER NIGHT	*CBS*	32	*16 Feb 85*	6
DANCING IN THE STREET	*EMI America*	1	*7 Sep 85*	12
Charity record with proceeds to Live Aid.				
Above hit: David BOWIE and Mick JAGGER.				
LET'S WORK	*CBS*	31	*12 Sep 87*	7
SWEET THING	*Atlantic*	24	*6 Feb 93*	4
ALBUMS:	**HITS 4**			**WEEKS 24**
SHE'S THE BOSS	*CBS*	6	*16 Mar 85*	11
PRIMITIVE COOL	*CBS*	26	*26 Sep 87*	5
WANDERING SPIRIT	*Atlantic*	12	*20 Feb 93*	4
GODDESS IN THE DOORWAY	*Virgin*	44	*1 Dec 01*	4

JAGS — UK

SINGLES:	HITS 2			WEEKS 11
BACK OF MY HAND	*Island*	17	*8 Sep 79*	10
WOMAN'S WORLD	*Island*	75	*2 Feb 80*	1

JAHEIM — US

SINGLES:	HITS 2			WEEKS 5
COULD IT BE	*Warner Brothers*	33	*24 Mar 01*	3
JUST IN CASE	*Warner Brothers*	34	*11 Aug 01*	2
ALBUMS:	**HITS 1**			**WEEKS 1**
GHETTO LOVE	*Warner Brothers*	50	*7 Apr 01*	1

JAKATTA — UK

SINGLES:	HITS 1			WEEKS 15
AMERICAN DREAM	*Rulin*	3	*24 Feb 01*	13
Samples the soundtrack to the Sam Mendes film 'American Beauty'.				
AMERICAN DREAM [RE]	*Rulin*	73	*2 Jun 01*	1
AMERICAN DREAM – THE REMIXES [RM]	*Rulin*	63	*11 Aug 01*	1
Remixed by Lucid.				

Don JAGUAR – See ICE CUBE

JAM

UK

SINGLES:	HITS 18			WEEKS 205
IN THE CITY	*Polydor*	40	*7 May 77*	6
ALL AROUND THE WORLD	*Polydor*	13	*23 Jul 77*	8
THE MODERN WORLD	*Polydor*	36	*5 Nov 77*	4
NEWS OF THE WORLD	*Polydor*	27	*11 Mar 78*	5
DAVID WATTS / "A" BOMB IN WARDOUR STREET	*Polydor*	25	*26 Aug 78*	8
David Watts originally recorded by The Kinks.				
DOWN IN THE TUBE STATION AT MIDNIGHT	*Polydor*	15	*21 Oct 78*	7
STRANGE TOWN	*Polydor*	15	*17 Mar 79*	9
WHEN YOU'RE YOUNG	*Polydor*	17	*25 Aug 79*	7
THE ETON RIFLES	*Polydor*	3	*3 Nov 79*	12
GOING UNDERGROUND / THE DREAMS OF CHILDREN	*Polydor*	1	*22 Mar 80*	9
ALL AROUND THE WORLD [RE-1ST]	*Polydor*	43	*26 Apr 80*	3
DAVID WATTS / "A" BOMB IN WARDOUR STREET [RE]	*Polydor*	54	*26 Apr 80*	3
IN THE CITY [RE-1ST]	*Polydor*	40	*26 Apr 80*	4
NEWS OF THE WORLD [RE-1ST]	*Polydor*	53	*26 Apr 80*	3
STRANGE TOWN [RE-1ST]	*Polydor*	44	*26 Apr 80*	4
THE MODERN WORLD [RE-1ST]	*Polydor*	52	*26 Apr 80*	3
START	*Polydor*	1	*23 Aug 80*	8
THAT'S ENTERTAINMENT	*Metronome*	21	*7 Feb 81*	7
Import.				
FUNERAL PYRE	*Polydor*	4	*6 Jun 81*	6
ABSOLUTE BEGINNERS	*Polydor*	4	*24 Oct 81*	6
TOWN CALLED MALICE / PRECIOUS	*Polydor*	1	*13 Feb 82*	8
JUST WHO IS THE 5 O'CLOCK HERO	*Polydor*	8	*3 Jul 82*	5
Import.				
THE BITTEREST PILL (I EVER HAD TO SWALLOW)	*Polydor*	2	*18 Sep 82*	7
Vocals by Jenny McKeowen of the Belle Stars.				
BEAT SURRENDER	*Polydor*	1	*4 Dec 82*	9
ALL AROUND THE WORLD [RE-2ND]	*Polydor*	38	*22 Jan 83*	4
DAVID WATTS/"A" BOMB IN WARDOUR STREET [RE-2ND]	*Polydor*	50	*22 Jan 83*	4
DOWN IN THE TUBE STATION AT MIDNIGHT [RE]	*Polydor*	30	*22 Jan 83*	6
GOING UNDERGROUND / THE DREAMS OF CHILDREN [RE]	*Polydor*	21	*22 Jan 83*	6
IN THE CITY [RE-2ND]	*Polydor*	47	*22 Jan 83*	4
NEWS OF THE WORLD [RE-2ND]	*Polydor*	39	*22 Jan 83*	4
STRANGE TOWN [RE-2ND]	*Polydor*	42	*22 Jan 83*	5
THE MODERN WORLD [RE-2ND]	*Polydor*	51	*22 Jan 83*	4
WHEN YOU'RE YOUNG [RE]	*Polydor*	53	*22 Jan 83*	4
THAT'S ENTERTAINMENT [RI-1ST]	*Polydor*	60	*29 Jan 83*	3
START [RE]	*Polydor*	62	*5 Feb 83*	2
THE ETON RIFLES [RE]	*Polydor*	54	*5 Feb 83*	3
TOWN CALLED MALICE / PRECIOUS [RE]	*Polydor*	73	*5 Feb 83*	1
THAT'S ENTERTAINMENT [RE-2ND]	*Polydor*	57	*29 Jun 91*	2
THE BITTEREST PILL (I EVER HAD TO SWALLOW) [RI]	*Polydor*	30	*11 Oct 97*	2

ALBUMS:	HITS 14			WEEKS 190
IN THE CITY	*Polydor*	20	*28 May 77*	18
THIS IS THE MODERN WORLD	*Polydor*	22	*26 Nov 77*	5
ALL MOD CONS	*Polydor*	6	*11 Nov 78*	17
SETTING SONS	*Polydor*	4	*24 Nov 79*	19
SOUND AFFECTS	*Polydor*	2	*6 Dec 80*	19
THE GIFT	*Polydor*	1	*20 Mar 82*	24
DIG THE NEW BREED	*Polydor*	2	*18 Dec 82*	15
IN THE CITY [RE]	*Polydor*	100	*27 Aug 83*	1
Re-released.				
SNAP!	*Polydor*	2	*22 Oct 83*	30
GREATEST HITS	*Polydor*	2	*13 Jul 91*	21
EXTRAS	*Polydor*	15	*18 Apr 92*	4
LIVE JAM	*Polydor*	28	*6 Nov 93*	2
THE JAM COLLECTION	*Polydor*	58	*27 Jul 96*	1
Collection of B-sides and lesser-known album tracks.				
DIRECTION REACTION CREATION	*Polydor*	8	*7 Jun 97*	4
5 CD box set of their 6 studio albums and 22 unreleased tracks.				
THE VERY BEST OF THE JAM	*Polydor*	9	*25 Oct 97*	10

JAM MACHINE

US/Italy

SINGLES:	HITS 1			WEEKS 1
EVERYDAY	*Deconstruction*	68	*23 Dec 89*	1

JAM ON THE MUTHA

UK

SINGLES:	HITS 1			WEEKS 2
HOTEL CALIFORNIA	*M&G*	62	*11 Aug 90*	2

JAM and SPOON featuring PLAVKA — Germany

(See also Storm; Tokyo Ghetto Pussy.)

SINGLES:	HITS 5			WEEKS 24
TALES FROM A DANCEOGRAPHIC OCEAN [EP]	*R&S*	49	*2 May 92*	1
Lead track: Stella.				
THE COMPLETE STELLA [RM]	*Outer Rhythm*	66	*6 Jun 92*	2
Remix of the track Stella from the EP listed above.				
Above 2: JAM and SPOON.				
RIGHT IN THE NIGHT (FALL IN LOVE WITH MUSIC)	*Epic*	31	*26 Feb 94*	4
FIND ME (ODYSSEY TO ANYOONA)	*Epic*	37	*24 Sep 94*	3
RIGHT IN THE NIGHT (FALL IN LOVE WITH MUSIC) [RI]	*Epic*	10	*10 Jun 95*	8
FIND ME (ODYSSEY TO ANYOONA) [RI]	*Epic*	22	*16 Sep 95*	3
ANGEL (LADADI O-HEYO)	*Epic*	26	*25 Nov 95*	2
KALEIDOSCOPE SKIES	*Epic*	48	*30 Aug 97*	1
ALBUMS:	**HITS 1**			**WEEKS 1**
TRIPOMATIC FAIRYTALES 2001	*Epic*	71	*19 Feb 94*	1
Act released two albums simultaneously; the other, Tripomatic Fairytales 2002, charted at No. 119.				

JAM TRONIK — US/Germany

SINGLES:	HITS 1			WEEKS 7
ANOTHER DAY IN PARADISE	*Debut*	19	*24 Mar 90*	7

JAMAICA UNITED starring Ziggy MARLEY, Buju BANTON, Diana KING, SHAGGY, Maxi PRIEST, Ini KAMOZE, Toots HIBBER — Jamaica

SINGLES:	HITS 1			WEEKS 1
RISE UP	*Columbia*	54	*4 Jul 98*	1

JAMELIA — UK

SINGLES:	HITS 4			WEEKS 18
I DO	*Parlophone Rhythm Series*	36	*31 Jul 99*	2
MONEY	*Parlophone Rhythm Series*	5	*4 Mar 00*	9
Above hit: JAMELIA featuring BEENIE MAN.				
CALL ME	*Parlophone Rhythm Series*	11	*24 Jun 00*	5
BOY NEXT DOOR	*Parlophone Rhythm Series*	42	*21 Oct 00*	2
ALBUMS:	**HITS 1**			**WEEKS 2**
DRAMA	*Parlophone Rhythm Series*	39	*8 Jul 00*	2

JAMES — UK

SINGLES:	HITS 20			WEEKS 89
HOW WAS IT FOR YOU?	*Fontana*	32	*12 May 90*	3
COME HOME	*Fontana*	32	*7 Jul 90*	4
Original release reached No. 84 in 1989.				
LOSE CONTROL	*Fontana*	38	*8 Dec 90*	5
SIT DOWN	*Fontana*	2	*30 Mar 91*	10
Original release reached No. 77 in 1989.				
SOUND	*Fontana*	9	*30 Nov 91*	7
BORN OF FRUSTRATION	*Fontana*	13	*1 Feb 92*	6
RING THE BELLS	*Fontana*	37	*4 Apr 92*	2
SEVEN [EP]	*Fontana*	46	*18 Jul 92*	2
Lead track: Seven.				
SOMETIMES	*Fontana*	18	*11 Sep 93*	4
LAID	*Fontana*	25	*13 Nov 93*	4
JAM J / SAY SOMETHING	*Fontana*	24	*2 Apr 94*	4
Say Something only listed for first two weeks, it was not available on all formats.				
SHE'S A STAR	*Fontana*	9	*22 Feb 97*	5
TOMORROW	*Fontana*	12	*3 May 97*	3
WALTZING ALONE	*Fontana*	23	*5 Jul 97*	4
DESTINY CALLING	*Fontana*	17	*21 Mar 98*	4
RUNAGROUND	*Fontana*	29	*6 Jun 98*	2
SIT DOWN [RM]	*Fontana*	7	*21 Nov 98*	7
Remixed by Apollo 440 for the Manchester 2002 Commonwealth Games launch in Oct 98.				
I KNOW WHAT I'M HERE FOR	*Mercury*	22	*31 Jul 99*	5
JUST LIKE FRED ASTAIRE	*Mercury*	17	*16 Oct 99*	3
WE'RE GOING TO MISS YOU	*Mercury*	48	*25 Dec 99*	2
GETTING AWAY WITH IT (ALL MESSED UP)	*Mercury*	22	*7 Jul 01*	3
ALBUMS:	**HITS 10**			**WEEKS 155**
STUTTER	*Blanco Y Negro*	68	*2 Aug 86*	2
STRIP MINE	*Sire*	90	*8 Oct 88*	1
GOLD MOTHER	*Fontana*	16	*16 Jun 90*	12
GOLD MOTHER [RE]	*Fontana*	2	*4 May 91*	22
Repackaged with additional track.				
SEVEN	*Fontana*	2	*29 Feb 92*	14
LAID	*Fontana*	3	*9 Oct 93*	16

WAH WAH *Out-takes and alternate versions from the Laid sessions.* *Above hit: JAMES and Brian ENO.*	*Fontana*	11	*24 Sep 94*	2
WHIPLASH	*Fontana*	9	*8 Mar 97*	19
THE BEST OF JAMES	*Fontana*	1	*4 Apr 98*	53
MILLIONAIRES	*Mercury*	2	*23 Oct 99*	11
PLEASED TO MEET YOU	*Mercury*	11	*14 Jul 01*	3

David JAMES — UK

SINGLES:	HITS 1			WEEKS 1
(ALWAYS) A PERMANENT STATE	*Hooj Choons*	60	*11 Aug 01*	1

Dick JAMES — UK

SINGLES:	HITS 2			WEEKS 13
ROBIN HOOD *Above hit: Dick JAMES with Stephen JAMES and his CHUMS.*	*Parlophone*	14	*21 Jan 56*	8
ROBIN HOOD [RE] / THE BALLAD OF DAVY CROCKETT *The Ballad Of Davy Crockett is only credited to Dick James.*	*Parlophone*	29	*19 May 56*	1
THE GARDEN OF EDEN *Above hit: Dick JAMES with Ron GOODWIN and his Orchestra.*	*Parlophone*	18	*12 Jan 57*	4

Doris JAMES – See SLICK

Etta JAMES — UK

SINGLES:	HITS 1			WEEKS 7
I JUST WANT TO MAKE LOVE TO YOU *Featured in the Diet Coke TV commercial.*	*MCA*	5	*10 Feb 96*	7

Freddie JAMES — Canada

SINGLES:	HITS 1			WEEKS 3
GET UP AND BOOGIE	*Warner Brothers*	54	*24 Nov 79*	3

Jimmy JAMES and the VAGABONDS — UK

SINGLES:	HITS 3			WEEKS 25
RED RED WINE	*Pye*	36	*14 Sep 68*	8
I'LL GO WHERE YOUR MUSIC TAKES ME	*Pye*	23	*24 Apr 76*	8
NOW IS THE TIME	*Pye*	5	*17 Jul 76*	9

Joni JAMES — US

SINGLES:	HITS 2			WEEKS 2
WHY DON'T YOU BELIEVE ME? *Above hit: Joni JAMES with Lew DOUGLAS and his Orchestra.*	*MGM*	11	*7 Mar 53*	1
THERE MUST BE A WAY *Originally recorded by Johnnie Johnson in 1945.*	*MGM*	24	*31 Jan 59*	1

Rick JAMES — US

SINGLES:	HITS 6			WEEKS 30
YOU AND I	*Motown*	46	*8 Jul 78*	7
I'M A SUCKER FOR YOUR LOVE *Above hit: Teena MARIE Co-lead vocals: Rick JAMES.*	*Motown*	43	*7 Jul 79*	8
BIG TIME	*Motown*	41	*6 Sep 80*	6
GIVE IT TO ME BABY	*Motown*	47	*4 Jul 81*	3
STANDING ON THE TOP (PART 1) *Above hit: TEMPTATIONS featuring Rick JAMES.*	*Motown*	53	*12 Jun 82*	3
DANCE WIT' ME	*Motown*	53	*3 Jul 82*	3
ALBUMS:	**HITS 1**			**WEEKS 2**
THROWIN' DOWN	*Motown*	93	*24 Jul 82*	2

Sonny JAMES — US

SINGLES:	HITS 2			WEEKS 8
THE CAT CAME BACK	*Capitol*	30	*1 Dec 56*	1
YOUNG LOVE *Originally recorded by Ric Cartey.*	*Capitol*	11	*9 Feb 57*	7

Stephen JAMES and his CHUMS – See Dick JAMES

Tommy JAMES and the SHONDELLS — US

SINGLES:	HITS 2			WEEKS 25
HANKY PANKY *Originally recorded by The Raindrops in 1963.*	*Roulette*	38	*23 Jul 66*	7
MONY MONY	*Major Minor*	1	*8 Jun 68*	18

Wendy JAMES — UK

SINGLES:	HITS 2			WEEKS 4
THE NAMELESS ONE	*MCA*	34	*20 Feb 93*	3
LONDON'S BRILLIANT	*MCA*	62	*17 Apr 93*	1
ALBUMS:	**HITS 1**			**WEEKS 1**
NOW AIN'T THE TIME FOR YOUR TEARS	*MCA*	43	*20 Mar 93*	1

JAMES BOYS — UK

SINGLES:	HITS 1			WEEKS 6
OVER AND OVER	*Penny Farthing*	39	*19 May 73*	6

JAMESTOWN featuring Jocelyn BROWN — US

(See also Jocelyn Brown.)

SINGLES:	HITS 2			WEEKS 4
SHE GOT SOUL	*A&M*	57	*14 Sep 91*	3
I BELIEVE	*Playola*	62	*27 Mar 99*	1

JAMIROQUAI — UK

SINGLES:	HITS 19			WEEKS 128
WHEN YOU GONNA LEARN?	*Acid Jazz*	52	*31 Oct 92*	2
WHEN YOU GONNA LEARN? [RE]	*Acid Jazz*	69	*20 Feb 93*	1
TOO YOUNG TO DIE	*Sony S2*	10	*13 Mar 93*	7
BLOW YOUR MIND	*Sony S2*	12	*5 Jun 93*	6
EMERGENCY ON PLANET EARTH	*Sony S2*	32	*14 Aug 93*	3
WHEN YOU GONNA LEARN? [RI]	*Sony S2*	28	*25 Sep 93*	3
SPACE COWBOY	*Sony S2*	17	*8 Oct 94*	5
HALF THE MAN	*Sony S2*	15	*19 Nov 94*	8
STILLNESS IN TIME	*Sony S2*	9	*1 Jul 95*	5
DO U KNOW WHERE YOU'RE COMING FROM	*Renk*	12	*1 Jun 96*	5
Above hit: M-BEAT featuring JAMIROQUAI.				
VIRTUAL INSANITY	*Sony S2*	3	*31 Aug 96*	11
COSMIC GIRL	*Sony S2*	6	*7 Dec 96*	10
ALRIGHT	*Sony S2*	6	*10 May 97*	5
HIGH TIMES	*Sony S2*	20	*13 Dec 97*	6
DEEPER UNDERGROUND	*Sony S2*	1	*25 Jul 98*	11
From the film 'Godzilla'.				
CANNED HEAT	*Sony S2*	4	*5 Jun 99*	10
SUPERSONIC	*Sony S2*	22	*25 Sep 99*	4
KING FOR A DAY	*Sony S2*	20	*11 Dec 99*	7
I'M IN THE MOOD FOR LOVE	*WSM*	29	*24 Feb 01*	3
Originally recorded by Little Jack Little and his Orchestra in 1935.				
Above hit: Jools HOLLAND and JAMIROQUAI with the RHYTHM AND BLUES ORCHESTRA.				
LITTLE L	*Sony S2*	5	*25 Aug 01*	11
YOU GIVE ME SOMETHING	*Sony S2*	16	*1 Dec 01*	5
ALBUMS:	**HITS 5**			**WEEKS 180**
EMERGENCY ON PLANET EARTH	*Sony S2*	1	*26 Jun 93*	32
THE RETURN OF THE SPACE COWBOY	*Sony S2*	2	*29 Oct 94*	29
TRAVELLING WITHOUT MOVING	*Sony S2*	2	*21 Sep 96*	74
Includes re-entries through to 2001.				
SYNKRONIZED	*Sony S2*	1	*26 Jun 99*	29
A FUNK ODYSSEY	*Sony S2*	1	*15 Sep 01*	16

JAMMERS — US

SINGLES:	HITS 1			WEEKS 2
BE MINE TONIGHT	*Salsoul*	65	*29 Jan 83*	2

JAMX – See DUMONDE

JAN and DEAN — US

SINGLES:	HITS 2			WEEKS 18
HEART AND SOUL	*London*	24	*26 Aug 61*	8
Written by Hoagy Carmichael and originally recorded by Larry Clinton in 1938.				
SURF CITY	*Liberty*	26	*17 Aug 63*	10
Backing vocals by Brian Wilson of the Beach Boys.				
ALBUMS:	**HITS 1**			**WEEKS 2**
THE JAN AND DEAN STORY	*K-Tel*	67	*12 Jul 80*	2

JAN and KJELD — Denmark

SINGLES:	HITS 1			WEEKS 4
BANJO BOY	*Ember*	36	*23 Jul 60*	4
From the film 'Kein Mann Zua Heiraten'.				
Above hit: JAN and KJELD with Gert WILDEN'S ORCHESTRA.				

JANE'S ADDICTION — US

SINGLES:	HITS 2			WEEKS 4
BEEN CAUGHT STEALING	*Warner Brothers*	34	*23 Mar 91*	3
CLASSIC GIRL	*Warner Brothers*	60	*1 Jun 91*	1
ALBUMS:	**HITS 1**			**WEEKS 2**
RITUAL DE LO HABITUAL	*Warner Brothers*	37	*8 Sep 90*	2

JANET – See Janet JACKSON

Horst JANKOWSKI his Orchestra and Chorus — Germany

SINGLES:	HITS 1			WEEKS 18
A WALK IN THE BLACK FOREST (EINE SCHWARZWALDFAHRT)	*Mercury*	3	*31 Jul 65*	18

Samantha JANUS — UK

SINGLES:	HITS 1			WEEKS 3
A MESSAGE TO YOUR HEART	*Hollywood*	30	*11 May 91*	3
UK's Eurovision entry in 1991, it came 10th.				

Philip JAP — UK

SINGLES:	HITS 2			WEEKS 8
SAVE US	*A&M*	53	*31 Jul 82*	4
TOTAL ERASURE	*A&M*	41	*25 Sep 82*	4

JAPAN — UK

(See also Rain Tree Crow.)

SINGLES:	HITS 12			WEEKS 81
GENTLEMEN TAKE POLAROIDS	*Virgin*	60	*18 Oct 80*	2
THE ART OF PARTIES	*Virgin*	48	*9 May 81*	5
QUIET LIFE	*Hansa*	19	*19 Sep 81*	9
VISIONS OF CHINA	*Virgin*	32	*7 Nov 81*	12
EUROPEAN SON	*Hansa*	31	*23 Jan 82*	6
GHOSTS	*Virgin*	5	*20 Mar 82*	8
CANTONESE BOY	*Virgin*	24	*22 May 82*	6
I SECOND THAT EMOTION	*Hansa*	9	*3 Jul 82*	11
LIFE IN TOKYO	*Hansa*	28	*9 Oct 82*	6
NIGHTPORTER	*Virgin*	29	*20 Nov 82*	9
ALL TOMORROW'S PARTIES	*Hansa*	38	*12 Mar 83*	4
Originally recorded by Velvet Underground.				
CANTON (LIVE)	*Virgin*	42	*21 May 83*	3
ALBUMS:	**HITS 6**			**WEEKS 135**
QUIET LIFE	*Ariola Hansa*	72	*9 Feb 80*	2
GENTLEMEN TAKE POLAROIDS	*Virgin*	45	*15 Nov 80*	10
ASSEMBLAGE	*Hansa*	30	*26 Sep 81*	26
TIN DRUM	*Virgin*	12	*28 Nov 81*	50
QUIET LIFE [RE]	*Ariola Hansa*	53	*30 Jan 82*	6
ASSEMBLAGE [RE]	*Hansa*	26	*24 Jul 82*	20
OIL ON CANVAS	*Virgin*	5	*18 Jun 83*	14
Live recordings from their 1982 tour.				
EXORCISING GHOSTS	*Virgin*	45	*8 Dec 84*	7
Compilation.				

JARK PRONGO — Holland

SINGLES:	HITS 1			WEEKS 1
MOVIN' THRU YOUR SYSTEM	*Hooj Choons*	58	*3 Apr 99*	1

Jeff JARRATT and Don REEDMAN — UK

ALBUMS:	HITS 1			WEEKS 8
MASTERWORKS	*K-Tel*	39	*22 Nov 80*	8

Jean Michel JARRE — France

SINGLES:	HITS 10			WEEKS 40
OXYGENE (PART 4)	*Polydor*	4	*27 Aug 77*	9
EQUINOXE PART 5	*Polydor*	45	*20 Jan 79*	5
FOURTH RENDEZ-VOUS	*Polydor*	65	*23 Aug 86*	4
REVOLUTIONS	*Polydor*	52	*5 Nov 88*	2
LONDON KID	*Polydor*	52	*7 Jan 89*	3
Above hit: Jean Michel JARRE featuring Hank MARVIN.				
OXYGENE IV (NEW VERSION) [RM]	*Polydor*	65	*7 Oct 89*	2
CHRONOLOGIE PART 4	*Polydor*	55	*26 Jun 93*	2
CHRONOLOGIE PART IV [RM]	*Polydor*	56	*30 Oct 93*	1
OXYGENE 8	*Epic*	17	*22 Mar 97*	3
OXYGENE 10	*Epic*	21	*5 Jul 97*	2

RENDEZ-VOUS 98 [RR]	*Epic*	12	*11 Jul 98*	6
Theme to ITV's sports coverage of the 1988 World Cup.				
Above hit: Jean Michel JARRE and APOLLO FOUR FORTY.				
C'EST LA VIE	*Epic*	40	*26 Feb 00*	1
Above hit: Jean Michel JARRE featuring Natacha ATLAS.				
ALBUMS:	**HITS 17**			**WEEKS 236**
OXYGENE	*Polydor*	2	*20 Aug 77*	24
Includes re-entries through to 1986.				
EQUINOXE	*Polydor*	11	*16 Dec 78*	26
MAGNETIC FIELDS	*Polydor*	6	*6 Jun 81*	17
THE CONCERTS IN CHINA	*Polydor*	6	*15 May 82*	17
Live recordings from Oct 81.				
THE ESSENTIAL JEAN-MICHEL JARRE	*Polystar*	14	*12 Nov 83*	29
ZOOLOOK	*Polydor*	47	*24 Nov 84*	14
RENDEZ-VOUS	*Polydor*	9	*12 Apr 86*	38
JEAN-MICHEL JARRE IN CONCERT LYON/HOUSTON	*Polydor*	18	*18 Jul 87*	15
Lyon recording from 1985, Houston from Apr 86.				
REVOLUTIONS	*Polydor*	2	*8 Oct 88*	13
JARRE LIVE	*Polydor*	16	*14 Oct 89*	4
WAITING FOR COUSTEAU	*Polydor*	14	*23 Jun 90*	10
IMAGES - THE BEST OF JEAN MICHEL JARRE	*Polydor*	14	*26 Oct 91*	12
CHRONOLOGIE	*Polydor*	11	*5 Jun 93*	8
CHRONOLOGIE PART 6	*Polydor*	60	*28 May 94*	1
6 track CD single.				
OXYGENE 7-13	*Epic*	11	*1 Mar 97*	5
ODYSSEY THROUGH O2	*Epic*	50	*23 May 98*	2
Remixes of Oxygene 7-13.				
METAMORPHOSES	*Epic*	37	*12 Feb 00*	1

Maurice JARRE — France

EPS:	**HITS 1**			**WEEKS 15**
LAWRENCE OF ARABIA [OST]	*Colpix*	13	*9 May 64*	15
Above hit: Composed and conducted by Maurice JARRE; Performed by the LONDON PHILHARMONIC ORCHESTRA.				
ALBUMS:	**HITS 1**			**WEEKS 106**
DOCTOR ZHIVAGO [OST]	*MGM*	3	*10 Sep 66*	106
Above hit: M.G.M. STUDIO ORCHESTRA Composed and conducted by Maurice Jarre.				

Al JARREAU — US

SINGLES:	**HITS 7**			**WEEKS 30**
WE'RE IN THIS LOVE TOGETHER / EASY	*Warner Brothers*	55	*26 Sep 81*	4
Easy only listed on 26 Sep 81 at its chart entry position of No. 67.				
MORNIN'	*WEA*	28	*14 May 83*	6
TROUBLE IN PARADISE	*WEA International*	36	*16 Jul 83*	5
BOOGIE DOWN	*WEA*	63	*24 Sep 83*	3
DAY BY DAY	*Polydor*	53	*16 Nov 85*	3
Above hit: SHAKATAK with Al JARREAU.				
THE MUSIC OF GOODBYE (LOVE THEME FROM OUT OF AFRICA)	*MCA*	75	*5 Apr 86*	1
From the film.				
Above hit: MELISSA MANCHESTER and Al JARREAU.				
MOONLIGHTING "THEME"	*WEA*	8	*7 Mar 87*	8
Theme from the TV series.				
ALBUMS:	**HITS 4**			**WEEKS 37**
BREAKING AWAY	*Warner Brothers*	60	*5 Sep 81*	8
JARREAU	*WEA International*	39	*30 Apr 83*	18
HIGH CRIME	*WEA*	81	*17 Nov 84*	1
L IS FOR LOVER	*WEA*	50	*13 Sep 86*	4
L IS FOR LOVER [RE]	*WEA*	45	*4 Apr 87*	6
Repackaged.				

Kenny "Jammin" JASON and "Fast" Eddie SMITH — US

(See also DJ Fast Eddie.)

SINGLES:	**HITS 1**			**WEEKS 4**
CAN U DANCE	*Champion*	71	*11 Apr 87*	2
CAN U DANCE [RE]	*Champion*	67	*14 Nov 87*	2

JAVELLS featuring Nosmo KING — UK

SINGLES:	**HITS 1**			**WEEKS 8**
GOODBYE NOTHIN' TO SAY	*Pye Disco Demand*	26	*9 Nov 74*	8

Peter JAY and the JAYWALKERS — UK

SINGLES:	**HITS 1**			**WEEKS 11**
CAN-CAN '62	*Decca*	31	*10 Nov 62*	11

Simone JAY - See DJ DADO

JAY and the AMERICANS — US

EPS:	HITS 1			WEEKS 1
LIVING WITH JAY AND THE AMERICANS	*United Artists*	10	*1 Oct 66*	1

JAY-Z — US

(See also R. Kelly.)

SINGLES:	HITS 18			WEEKS 77
CAN'T KNOCK THE HUSTLE *Samples Much Too Much by Marcus Miller.* *Above hit: JAY-Z featuring Mary J. BLIGE.*	*Northwestside*	30	*1 Mar 97*	2
AIN'T NO PLAYA *Above hit: JAY-Z featuring Foxy BROWN.*	*Northwestside*	31	*10 May 97*	2
I'LL BE *Samples Rene and Angela's I'll Be Good and Blondie's Rapture.* *Above hit: Foxy BROWN featuring JAY Z.*	*Def Jam*	9	*21 Jun 97*	5
WHO YOU WIT *From the film 'Sprung'.*	*Qwest*	65	*23 Aug 97*	1
SUNSHINE *Above hit: JAY-Z featuring BABYFACE and Foxy BROWN.*	*Northwestside*	25	*25 Oct 97*	2
WISHING ON A STAR *Above hit: JAY-Z featuring Gwen DICKEY.*	*Northwestside*	13	*14 Feb 98*	4
TIME AFTER TIME *Above hit: CHANGING FACES (featuring JAY-Z).*	*Atlantic*	35	*4 Apr 98*	2
THE CITY IS MINE *Above hit: JAY-Z featuring BLACKSTREET.*	*Northwestside*	38	*27 Jun 98*	2
HARD KNOCK LIFE (GHETTO ANTHEM) *Samples It's A Hard Knock Life by the Original Broadway Cast of the show 'Annie'.*	*Northwestside*	2	*12 Dec 98*	11
CAN I GET A . . . *Sleeve gives title as an EP: Def Jam's Rush Hour. From the film 'Rush Hour'.* *Above hit: JAY-Z featuring (AMIL of MAJOR COINZ) and JA RULE.*	*Def Jam*	24	*13 Mar 99*	3
BE ALONE NO MORE *Jay-Z was not credited on the original release. Remix by Cutfather & Joe. Charity record in aid of Capital Radio's Help A London Child.* *Above hit: ANOTHER LEVEL featuring JAY Z.*	*Northwestside*	11	*10 Apr 99*	9
LOBSTER & SCRIMP *Above hit: TIMBALAND featuring JAY-Z.*	*Virgin*	48	*19 Jun 99*	1
HEARTBREAKER *Samples Stacy Lattisaw's Attack Of The Name Game.* *Above hit: Mariah CAREY featuring JAY-Z.*	*Columbia*	5	*6 Nov 99*	13
WHAT YOU THINK OF THAT *Samples Keith Mansfield's High Velocity.* *Above hit: Memphis BLEEK featuring JAY-Z.*	*Roc-A-Fella*	58	*4 Dec 99*	1
ANYTHING *Samples Jack Wild's vocals on I'll Do Anything from the Oliver! soundtrack.*	*Roc-A-Fella*	18	*26 Feb 00*	4
BIG PIMPIN' *Above hit: JAY-Z (featuring UGK).*	*Roc-A-Fella*	29	*24 Jun 00*	3
I JUST WANNA LOVE U (GIVE IT 2 ME) *Samples Give It To Me by Rick James.*	*Roc-A-Fella*	17	*16 Dec 00*	8
IZZO (H.O.V.A.)	*Roc-A-Fella*	21	*27 Oct 01*	4

ALBUMS:	HITS 1			WEEKS 4
THE BLUEPRINT	*Roc-A-Fella*	30	*29 Sep 01*	4

JAYDEE — Holland

SINGLES:	HITS 1			WEEKS 3
PLASTIC DREAMS *Original release reached No. 93 in 1993.*	*R&S*	18	*20 Sep 97*	3

Ollie JAYE - See JON THE DENTIST vs OLLIE JAYE

JAYHAWKS — US

SINGLES:	HITS 1			WEEKS 1
BAD TIME *Originally recorded by Grand Funk.*	*American Recordings*	70	*15 Jul 95*	1

ALBUMS:	HITS 3			WEEKS 3
TOMORROW THE GREEN GRASS	*American Recordings*	41	*25 Feb 95*	1
SOUND OF LIES	*American Recordings*	61	*3 May 97*	1
SMILE	*Columbia*	60	*20 May 00*	1

JAZZ and the BROTHERS GRIMM — UK

SINGLES:	HITS 1			WEEKS 2
(LET'S ALL GO BACK) DISCO NIGHTS	*Ensign*	57	*9 Jul 88*	2

JAZZY JEFF and the FRESH PRINCE — US

SINGLES:	HITS 8			WEEKS 49
GIRLS AIN'T NOTHIN BUT TROUBLE	*Champion*	21	*4 Oct 86*	8
SUMMERTIME	*Jive*	8	*3 Aug 91*	8
RING MY BELL	*Jive*	53	*9 Nov 91*	2
Above 3: D.J. JAZZY JEFF and the FRESH PRINCE.				
BOOM! SHAKE THE ROOM	*Jive*	1	*11 Sep 93*	13
Samples the Bar-Kays' 'Funky Worm'.				
I'M LOOKING FOR THE ONE (TO BE WITH ME)	*Jive*	24	*20 Nov 93*	4
CAN'T WAIT TO BE WITH YOU	*Jive*	29	*19 Feb 94*	4
Samples Never Too Much by Luther Vandross.				
TWINKLE TWINKLE (I'M NOT A STAR)	*Jive*	62	*4 Jun 94*	2
SUMMERTIME [RE]	*Jive*	29	*6 Aug 94*	4
Above hit: DJ JAZZY JEFF and the FRESH PRINCE.				
BOOM! SHAKE THE ROOM [RM]	*Jive*	40	*2 Dec 95*	2
Remixed by Hula of the Outhere Brothers.				
LOVELY DAZE	*Jive*	37	*11 Jul 98*	2
Samples Lovely Day by Bill Withers.				
Above hit: DJ JAZZY JEFF and FRESH PRINCE.				

ALBUMS:	HITS 5			WEEKS 15
ROCK THE HOUSE	*Champion*	97	*28 Feb 87*	1
HE'S THE DJ, I'M THE RAPPER	*Jive*	68	*21 May 88*	2
HOMEBASE	*Jive*	69	*14 Sep 91*	1
Above 3: D.J. JAZZY JEFF and the FRESH PRINCE.				
CODE RED	*Jive*	50	*11 Dec 93*	6
GREATEST HITS	*Jive*	20	*16 May 98*	5
Includes Will Smith's Men In Black.				
Above hit: DJ JAZZY JEFF and FRESH PRINCE.				

JAZZY JOYCE – See REGGAE PHILHARMONIC ORCHESTRA

JAZZY M — UK

SINGLES:	HITS 1			WEEKS 2
JAZZIN' THE WAY YOU KNOW	*Perfecto*	47	*21 Oct 00*	2

JC-001 — UK

SINGLES:	HITS 2			WEEKS 4
NEVER AGAIN	*AnXious*	67	*24 Apr 93*	2
CUPID	*AnXious*	56	*26 Jun 93*	2

JD – See DESTINY'S CHILD; SNOOP DOGGY DOG

JDS — UK/Italy

SINGLES:	HITS 2			WEEKS 3
NINE WAYS	*ffrr*	61	*27 Sep 97*	1
LONDON TOWN	*Pepper*	49	*23 May 98*	1
NINE WAYS [RM]	*ffrr*	47	*3 Mar 01*	1
Remixed by the Plum DJs.				

Norma JEAN – See Romina JOHNSON

Wyclef JEAN — US

SINGLES:	HITS 10			WEEKS 67
WE TRYING TO STAY ALIVE	*Columbia*	13	*28 Jun 97*	5
Samples the Bee Gees' Staying Alive.				
GUANTANAMERA	*Columbia*	25	*27 Sep 97*	2
Above 2: Wyclef JEAN featuring REFUGEE ALLSTARS.				
NO NO NO	*Columbia*	5	*28 Mar 98*	8
Above hit: DESTINY'S CHILD (featuring Wyclef JEAN).				
GONE TILL NOVEMBER	*Columbia*	3	*16 May 98*	9
ANOTHER ONE BITES THE DUST	*Dreamworks*	5	*14 Nov 98*	6
From the film 'Small Soldiers'.				
Above hit: QUEEN/Wyclef JEAN featuring PRAS and FREE.				
NEW DAY	*Columbia*	23	*23 Oct 99*	2
Official Single of the Net Aid concert, 9 Oct 99 at London, New York, Geneva. Charity record in aid of NetAid, Wyclef Jean Foundation and War Child.				
Above hit: Wyclef JEAN featuring BONO.				
IT DOESN'T MATTER	*Columbia*	3	*16 Sep 00*	8
Samples Longsy D's This Is Ska, John Denver's Take Me Home Country Roads and Slick Rick's Mona Lisa.				
Above hit: Wyclef JEAN featuring the ROCK and MELKY SEDECK.				
911	*Columbia*	9	*16 Dec 00*	10
Above hi: Wyclef JEAN featuring Mary J. BLIGE.				
PERFECT GENTLEMEN	*Columbia*	4	*21 Jul 01*	14
Features rapper Xzibit and reggae toaster Yelloe Man.				
WISH YOU WERE HERE	*Columbia*	28	*8 Dec 01*	3
Originally recorded by Pink Floyd.				

ALBUMS:	HITS 2			WEEKS 21
THE CARNIVAL	*Columbia*	40	*5 Jul 97*	6
Above hit: Wyclef JEAN and the REFUGEE ALLSTARS.				
THE ECLEFTIC - 2 SIDES II A BOOK	*Columbia*	34	*2 Sep 00*	4
THE ECLEFTIC - 2 SIDES II A BOOK [RE]	*Columbia*	5	*28 Jul 01*	11
Repackaged with 5 additional tracks and 3 videos.				

JEFFERSON — UK

SINGLES:	HITS 1			WEEKS 8
THE COLOUR OF MY LOVE	*Pye*	22	*12 Apr 69*	8
Originally recorded by Barry Ryan.				

JEFFERSON AIRPLANE - See STARSHIP

JEFFERSON STARSHIP - See STARSHIP

Garland JEFFREYS — US

SINGLES:	HITS 1			WEEKS 1
HAIL HAIL ROCK 'N' ROLL	*RCA*	72	*8 Feb 92*	1

JELLYBEAN — US

SINGLES:	HITS 6			WEEKS 47
SIDEWALK TALK	*EMI America*	47	*1 Feb 86*	4
Written by Madonna.				
Above hit: JELLYBEAN featuring Catherine BUCHANAN.				
THE REAL THING	*Chrysalis*	13	*26 Sep 87*	10
Above hit: JELLYBEAN featuring Steven DANTE.				
WHO FOUND WHO	*Chrysalis*	10	*28 Nov 87*	10
Above hit: JELLYBEAN featuring Elisa FIORILLO.				
JINGO	*Chrysalis*	12	*12 Dec 87*	10
Originally recorded by Michael Oluntunji.				
JUST A MIRAGE	*Chrysalis*	13	*12 Mar 88*	10
Above hit: JELLYBEAN featuring Adele BERTEI.				
COMING BACK FOR MORE	*Chrysalis*	41	*20 Aug 88*	3
Above hit: JELLYBEAN featuring Richard DARBYSHIRE.				
ALBUMS:	**HITS 2**			**WEEKS 35**
JUST VISITING THIS PLANET	*Chrysalis*	15	*31 Oct 87*	28
ROCKS THE HOUSE!	*Chrysalis*	16	*3 Sep 88*	7

JELLYFISH — US

SINGLES:	HITS 6			WEEKS 20
THE KING IS HALF UNDRESSED	*Charisma*	39	*26 Jan 91*	6
BABY'S COMING BACK	*Charisma*	51	*27 Apr 91*	4
THE SCARY-GO-ROUND [EP]	*Charisma*	49	*3 Aug 91*	3
Lead track: Now She Knows She's Wrong.				
I WANNA STAY HOME	*Charisma*	59	*26 Oct 91*	2
THE GHOST AT NUMBER ONE	*Charisma*	43	*1 May 93*	3
NEW MISTAKE	*Virgin*	55	*17 Jul 93*	2
ALBUMS:	**HITS 1**			**WEEKS 2**
SPILT MILK	*Charisma*	21	*22 May 93*	2

Gordon JENKINS and his Chorus and Orchestra - See Danny KAYE with Gordon JENKINS and his Chorus and Orchestra

Karl JENKINS - See ADIEMUS

JERU THE DAMAJA — US

SINGLES:	HITS 1			WEEKS 1
YA PLAYIN' YASELF	*ffrr*	67	*7 Dec 96*	1

JESSICA — Sweden

SINGLES:	HITS 1			WEEKS 1
HOW WILL I KNOW (WHO YOU ARE)	*Jive*	47	*20 Mar 99*	1

JESUS JONES — UK

(See also Various Artists (EPs) 'The Food Christmas EP 1989'.)

SINGLES:	HITS 12			WEEKS 52
INFO-FREAKO	*Food*	42	*25 Feb 89*	3
NEVER ENOUGH	*Food*	42	*8 Jul 89*	3
BRING IT ON DOWN	*Food*	46	*23 Sep 89*	3
REAL REAL REAL	*Food*	19	*7 Apr 90*	8
RIGHT HERE, RIGHT NOW	*Food*	31	*6 Oct 90*	4
INTERNATIONAL BRIGHT YOUNG THING	*Food*	7	*12 Jan 91*	7
WHO? WHERE? WHY?	*Food*	21	*2 Mar 91*	7
RIGHT HERE, RIGHT NOW [RI]	*Food*	31	*20 Jul 91*	4

THE DEVIL YOU KNOW	*Food*	10	*9 Jan 93*	5
THE RIGHT DECISION	*Food*	36	*10 Apr 93*	3
ZEROES AND ONES	*Food*	30	*10 Jul 93*	3
THE NEXT BIG THING	*Food*	49	*14 Jun 97*	1
CHEMICAL #1	*Food*	71	*16 Aug 97*	1
ALBUMS:	**HITS 3**			**WEEKS 31**
LIQUIDIZER	*Food*	32	*14 Oct 89*	3
DOUBT	*Food*	1	*9 Feb 91*	24
PERVERSE	*Food*	6	*6 Feb 93*	4

JESUS LIZARD — US

SINGLES:	**HITS 1**			**WEEKS 2**
PUSS	*Touch And Go*	12	*6 Mar 93*	2
[AA] listed with Oh, The Guilt by Nirvana.				
ALBUMS:	**HITS 1**			**WEEKS 1**
DOWN	*Touch And Go*	64	*10 Sep 94*	1

JESUS LOVES YOU — UK

(See also Boy George.)

SINGLES:	**HITS 4**			**WEEKS 18**
AFTER THE LOVE	*More Protein*	68	*11 Nov 89*	1
BOW DOWN MISTER	*More Protein*	27	*23 Feb 91*	8
GENERATIONS OF LOVE	*More Protein*	35	*8 Jun 91*	8
Original release reached No. 80 in 1990.				
SWEET TOXIC LOVE	*Virgin*	65	*12 Dec 92*	1
ALBUMS:	**HITS 1**			**WEEKS 1**
THE MARTYR MANTRAS	*More Protein*	60	*13 Apr 91*	1

JESUS AND MARY CHAIN — UK

SINGLES:	**HITS 20**			**WEEKS 59**
NEVER UNDERSTAND	*Blanco Y Negro*	47	*2 Mar 85*	4
YOU TRIP ME UP	*Blanco Y Negro*	55	*8 Jun 85*	3
JUST LIKE HONEY	*Blanco Y Negro*	45	*12 Oct 85*	3
SOME CANDY TALKING	*Blanco Y Negro*	13	*26 Jul 86*	5
APRIL SKIES	*Blanco Y Negro*	8	*2 May 87*	6
HAPPY WHEN IT RAINS	*Blanco Y Negro*	25	*15 Aug 87*	5
DARKLANDS	*Blanco Y Negro*	33	*7 Nov 87*	4
SIDEWALKING	*Blanco Y Negro*	30	*9 Apr 88*	3
BLUES FROM A GUN	*Blanco Y Negro*	32	*23 Sep 89*	2
HEAD ON	*Blanco Y Negro*	57	*18 Nov 89*	2
ROLLERCOASTER [EP]	*Blanco Y Negro*	46	*8 Sep 90*	2
Lead track: Rollercoaster.				
REVERENCE	*Blanco Y Negro*	10	*15 Feb 92*	4
FAR GONE AND OUT	*Blanco Y Negro*	23	*14 Mar 92*	3
ALMOST GOLD	*Blanco Y Negro*	41	*4 Jul 92*	2
SOUND OF SPEED [EP]	*Blanco Y Negro*	30	*10 Jul 93*	2
Lead track: Snakedriver.				
SOMETIMES ALWAYS	*Blanco Y Negro*	22	*30 Jul 94*	3
Vocals by Hope Sandoval of Mazzy Star.				
COME ON	*Blanco Y Negro*	52	*22 Oct 94*	2
I HATE ROCK 'N' ROLL	*Blanco Y Negro*	61	*17 Jun 95*	1
CRACKING UP	*Creation*	35	*18 Apr 98*	2
ILOVEROCKNROLL	*Creation*	38	*30 May 98*	1
ALBUMS:	**HITS 8**			**WEEKS 40**
PSYCHOCANDY	*Blanco Y Negro*	31	*30 Nov 85*	10
DARKLANDS	*Blanco Y Negro*	5	*12 Sep 87*	7
BARBED WIRE KISSES	*Blanco Y Negro*	9	*30 Apr 88*	7
AUTOMATIC	*Blanco Y Negro*	11	*21 Oct 89*	4
HONEY'S DEAD	*Blanco Y Negro*	14	*4 Apr 92*	5
THE SOUND OF SPEED	*Blanco Y Negro*	15	*24 Jul 93*	3
STONED AND DETHRONED	*Blanco Y Negro*	13	*27 Aug 94*	3
MUNKI	*Creation*	47	*13 Jun 98*	1

JETHRO TULL — UK

SINGLES:	**HITS 9**			**WEEKS 68**
LOVE STORY	*Island*	29	*4 Jan 69*	8
LIVING IN THE PAST	*Island*	3	*17 May 69*	14
SWEET DREAM	*Chrysalis*	7	*1 Nov 69*	11
THE WITCH'S PROMISE / TEACHER	*Chrysalis*	4	*24 Jan 70*	9
Some copies may only reflect title as Witch's Promise.				
LIFE IS A LONG SONG / UP THE POOL	*Chrysalis*	11	*18 Sep 71*	8
RING OUT SOLSTICE BELLS [EP]	*Chrysalis*	28	*11 Dec 76*	6
Lead track: Ring Out Solstice Bells.				
LAP OF LUXURY	*Chrysalis*	70	*15 Sep 84*	2
SAID SHE WAS A DANCER	*Chrysalis*	55	*16 Jan 88*	4

ROCKS ON THE ROAD	*Chrysalis*	47	*21 Mar 92*	3
LIVING IN THE (SLIGHTLY MORE RECENT) PAST [RI]	*Chrysalis*	32	*22 May 93*	3
Live recording from Montreal, Canada in 1992. CD2 track 1 was a re-issue of the original 1969 version.				
ALBUMS:	**HITS 26**			**WEEKS 236**
THIS WAS	*Island*	10	*2 Nov 68*	22
STAND UP	*Island*	1	*9 Aug 69*	29
BENEFIT	*Island*	3	*9 May 70*	13
AQUALUNG	*Island*	4	*3 Apr 71*	21
THICK AS A BRICK	*Chrysalis*	5	*18 Mar 72*	14
LIVING IN THE PAST	*Chrysalis*	8	*15 Jul 72*	11
Compilation of unreleased material plus one side recorded live at Carnegie Hall, New York.				
A PASSION PLAY	*Chrysalis*	13	*28 Jul 73*	8
Originally premiered as a live show.				
WAR CHILD	*Chrysalis*	14	*2 Nov 74*	4
MINSTREL IN THE GALLERY	*Chrysalis*	20	*27 Sep 75*	6
M.U. THE BEST OF JETHRO TULL	*Chrysalis*	44	*31 Jan 76*	5
TOO OLD TO ROCK 'N' ROLL: TOO YOUNG TO DIE	*Chrysalis*	25	*15 May 76*	10
SONGS FROM THE WOOD	*Chrysalis*	13	*19 Feb 77*	12
HEAVY HORSES	*Chrysalis*	20	*29 Apr 78*	10
LIVE BURSTING OUT	*Chrysalis*	17	*14 Oct 78*	8
STORM WATCH	*Chrysalis*	27	*6 Oct 79*	4
A	*Chrysalis*	25	*6 Sep 80*	5
BROADSWORD AND THE BEAST	*Chrysalis*	27	*17 Apr 82*	19
UNDER WRAPS	*Chrysalis*	18	*15 Sep 84*	5
ORIGINAL MASTERS	*Chrysalis*	63	*2 Nov 85*	3
Compilation of material up to 1977.				
CREST OF A KNAVE	*Chrysalis*	19	*19 Sep 87*	10
20 YEARS OF JETHRO TULL	*Chrysalis*	78	*9 Jul 88*	1
5-LP box set or 3-CD box set.				
ROCK ISLAND	*Chrysalis*	18	*2 Sep 89*	6
CATFISH RISING	*Chrysalis*	27	*14 Sep 91*	3
A LITTLE LIGHT MUSIC	*Chrysalis*	34	*26 Sep 92*	2
ROOTS TO BRANCHES	*Chrysalis*	20	*16 Sep 95*	3
AQUALUNG [RI]	*Chrysalis*	53	*29 Jun 96*	1
Digitally remastered, featuring 5 extra tracks recorded in the 1960s.				
J-TULL DOT COM	*Papillon*	44	*4 Sep 99*	1

JETS — UK

SINGLES:	**HITS 8**			**WEEKS 38**
SUGAR DOLL	*EMI*	55	*22 Aug 81*	3
Originally recorded by Johnny Jay.				
YES TONIGHT JOSEPHINE	*EMI*	25	*31 Oct 81*	11
LOVE MAKES THE WORLD GO ROUND	*EMI*	21	*6 Feb 82*	9
THE HONEYDRIPPER	*EMI*	58	*24 Apr 82*	3
SOMEBODY TO LOVE	*EMI*	56	*9 Oct 82*	3
Originally recorded by Bobby Darin.				
BLUE SKIES	*EMI*	53	*6 Aug 83*	3
ROCKIN' AROUND THE CHRISTMAS TREE	*PRT*	62	*17 Dec 83*	4
PARTY DOLL	*PRT*	72	*13 Oct 84*	2
ALBUMS:	**HITS 1**			**WEEKS 6**
100 PERCENT COTTON	*EMI*	30	*10 Apr 82*	6

JETS — US

SINGLES:	**HITS 3**			**WEEKS 19**
CRUSH ON YOU	*MCA*	5	*31 Jan 87*	13
CURIOSITY	*MCA*	41	*25 Apr 87*	4
ROCKET 2 U	*MCA*	69	*28 May 88*	2
ALBUMS:	**HITS 1**			**WEEKS 4**
CRUSH ON YOU	*MCA*	57	*11 Apr 87*	4

Joan JETT and the BLACKHEARTS — US

SINGLES:	**HITS 4**			**WEEKS 21**
I LOVE ROCK 'N ROLL	*Epic*	4	*24 Apr 82*	10
Originally recorded by the Arrows.				
CRIMSON AND CLOVER	*Epic*	60	*10 Jul 82*	3
Originally recorded by Tommy James & The Shondells.				
I HATE MYSELF FOR LOVING YOU	*London*	46	*20 Aug 88*	6
DIRTY DEEDS	*Chrysalis*	69	*31 Mar 90*	1
Above hit: Joan JETT.				
I LOVE ROCK AND ROLL [RI]	*Reprise*	75	*19 Feb 94*	1
ALBUMS:	**HITS 1**			**WEEKS 7**
I LOVE ROCK 'N' ROLL	*Epic*	25	*8 May 82*	7

JEWEL — US

SINGLES:	HITS 4			WEEKS 8
WHO WILL SAVE YOUR SOUL	*Atlantic*	52	*14 Jun 97*	1
YOU WERE MEANT FOR ME	*Atlantic*	53	*9 Aug 97*	1
YOU WERE MEANT FOR ME [RE]	*Atlantic*	32	*22 Nov 97*	2
HANDS	*Atlantic*	41	*21 Nov 98*	2
DOWN SO LONG	*Atlantic*	38	*26 Jun 99*	2

ALBUMS:	HITS 1			WEEKS 1
SPIRIT	*Atlantic*	54	*28 Nov 98*	1

JEZ and CHOOPIE — UK/Israel

SINGLES:	HITS 1			WEEKS 2
YIM	*Multiply*	36	*21 Mar 98*	2

JFK — UK

SINGLES:	HITS 1			WEEKS 1
GOOD GOD	*Y2K*	71	*15 Sep 01*	1

JHELISA — US

SINGLES:	HITS 1			WEEKS 1
FRIENDLY PRESSURE	*Dorado*	75	*1 Jul 95*	1

JIGSAW — UK

SINGLES:	HITS 2			WEEKS 16
SKY HIGH *From the film 'The Man From Hong Kong'.*	*Splash*	9	*1 Nov 75*	11
IF I HAVE TO GO AWAY	*Splash*	36	*6 Aug 77*	5

JILTED JOHN — UK

SINGLES:	HITS 1			WEEKS 12
JILTED JOHN *Originally released on the Rabd label.*	*EMI International*	4	*12 Aug 78*	12

JIMMY EAT WORLD — US

SINGLES:	HITS 1			WEEKS 1
SALT SWEAT SUGAR	*Dreamworks*	60	*17 Nov 01*	1

JIMMY THE HOOVER — UK

SINGLES:	HITS 1			WEEKS 8
TANTALISE (WO WO EE YEH YEH)	*Inner Vision*	18	*25 Jun 83*	8

JINGLE BELLES — UK/US

SINGLES:	HITS 1			WEEKS 4
CHRISTMAS SPECTRE	*Passion*	37	*17 Dec 83*	4

JINNY — US

SINGLES:	HITS 3			WEEKS 16
KEEP WARM	*Virgin*	68	*29 Jun 91*	3
FEEL THE RHYTHM	*Logic*	74	*22 May 93*	1
KEEP WARM [RI]	*Multiply*	11	*15 Jul 95*	8
WANNA BE WITH YOU	*Multiply*	30	*16 Dec 95*	4

JIVE BUNNY and the MASTERMIXERS — UK

(See also Liz Kershaw and Bruno Brookes.)

SINGLES:	HITS 10			WEEKS 68
SWING THE MOOD [M]	*Music Factory Dance*	1	*15 Jul 89*	19
THAT'S WHAT I LIKE [M]	*Music Factory Dance*	1	*14 Oct 89*	12
LET'S PARTY [M]	*Music Factory Dance*	1	*16 Dec 89*	6
THAT SOUNDS GOOD TO ME [M]	*Music Factory Dance*	4	*17 Mar 90*	6
CAN CAN YOU PARTY [M]	*Music Factory Dance*	8	*25 Aug 90*	6
LET'S SWING AGAIN [M]	*Music Factory Dance*	19	*17 Nov 90*	5
THE CRAZY PARTY MIXES [M] *This is title on the sleeve. The tracks on the 7" format were The Crazy Conga Mix on the A-side and Crazy Party Mix on the B-side.*	*Music Factory Dance*	13	*22 Dec 90*	5
OVER TO YOU JOHN (HERE WE GO AGAIN) [M] *Charity record with proceeds to St. John's Ambulance.*	*Music Factory Dance*	28	*23 Mar 91*	5
HOT SUMMER SALSA [M]	*Music Factory Dance*	43	*20 Jul 91*	2
ROCK 'N' ROLL DANCE PARTY [M]	*Music Factory Dance*	48	*23 Nov 91*	2

ALBUMS:	HITS 2			WEEKS 29
JIVE BUNNY - THE ALBUM	*Telstar*	2	*9 Dec 89*	22
IT'S PARTY TIME	*Telstar*	23	*8 Dec 90*	7

JJ – See DJ LUCK and MC NEAT

JJ72 — Ireland

SINGLES:	HITS 4			WEEKS 10
LONG WAY SOUTH	*Lakota*	68	*3 Jun 00*	1
OXYGEN	*Lakota*	23	*26 Aug 00*	3
OCTOBER SWIMMER	*Lakota*	29	*4 Nov 00*	3
Originally released in November 1999.				
SNOW	*Lakota*	21	*10 Feb 01*	3
Original release reached No. 80 in March 2000.				
ALBUMS:	**HITS 1**			**WEEKS 20**
JJ72	*Lakota*	16	*9 Sep 00*	20

JO JO GUNNE — US

SINGLES:	HITS 1			WEEKS 12
RUN RUN RUN	*Asylum*	6	*25 Mar 72*	12

JOAN COLLINS' FAN CLUB — UK

SINGLES:	HITS 1			WEEKS 3
LEADER OF THE PACK	*10 Records*	60	*18 Jun 88*	3

John Paul JOANS — UK

SINGLES:	HITS 1			WEEKS 7
THE MAN FROM NAZARETH	*RAK*	41	*19 Dec 70*	3
THE MAN FROM NAZARETH [RE]	*RAK*	25	*16 Jan 71*	4

JOBOXERS — UK

SINGLES:	HITS 4			WEEKS 33
BOXERBEAT	*RCA*	3	*19 Feb 83*	15
JUST GOT LUCKY	*RCA*	7	*21 May 83*	9
JOHNNY FRIENDLY	*RCA*	31	*13 Aug 83*	8
JEALOUS LOVE	*RCA*	72	*12 Nov 83*	1
ALBUMS:	**HITS 1**			**WEEKS 5**
LIKE GANGBUSTERS	*RCA*	18	*24 Sep 83*	5

JOCASTA — UK

SINGLES:	HITS 2			WEEKS 2
GO	*Epic*	50	*15 Feb 97*	1
Originally released in 1996.				
CHANGE ME	*Epic*	60	*3 May 97*	1

JOCKMASTER B.A. – See MAD JOCKS featuring JOCKMASTER B.A.

JOCKO — US

SINGLES:	HITS 1			WEEKS 3
RHYTHM TALK	*Philadelphia International*	56	*23 Feb 80*	3
Backing music is McFadden and Whitehead's 'Ain't No Stoppin' Us Now.				

JODE featuring YO-HANS — UK

SINGLES:	HITS 1			WEEKS 2
WALK . . . (THE DOG) LIKE AN EGYPTIAN	*Logic*	48	*19 Dec 98*	2

JODECI — US

SINGLES:	HITS 6			WEEKS 19
CHERISH	*MCA*	56	*16 Jan 93*	2
CRY FOR YOU	*MCA*	56	*11 Dec 93*	1
FEENIN'	*MCA*	18	*16 Jul 94*	3
CRY FOR YOU [RI]	*Uptown*	20	*28 Jan 95*	3
FREEK 'N YOU	*Uptown*	17	*24 Jun 95*	5
LOVE U 4 LIFE	*Uptown*	23	*9 Dec 95*	3
GET ON UP	*MCA*	20	*25 May 96*	2
Samples Velas by Quincy Jones.				
ALBUMS:	**HITS 1**			**WEEKS 8**
THE SHOW, THE AFTER-PARTY, THE HOTEL	*Uptown*	4	*29 Jul 95*	8

JODIE — Australia

SINGLES:	HITS 1			WEEKS 1
ANYTHING YOU WANT	*Mercury*	47	*25 Feb 95*	1

JOE — US

(See also Mariah Carey.)

SINGLES:	HITS 12			WEEKS 32
I'M IN LUV	*Mercury*	22	*22 Jan 94*	4
THE ONE FOR ME	*Mercury*	34	*25 Jun 94*	2
ALL OR NOTHING	*Mercury*	56	*22 Oct 94*	1
ALL THE THINGS (YOUR MAN WON'T DO)	*Island*	34	*27 Apr 96*	3
From the film 'Don't Be A Menace'.				
DON'T WANNA BE A PLAYER	*Jive*	16	*14 Jun 97*	3
From the film 'Booty Call'.				
THE LOVE SCENE	*Jive*	22	*27 Sep 97*	2
GOOD GIRLS	*Jive*	29	*10 Jan 98*	3
NO ONE ELSE COMES CLOSE	*Jive*	41	*22 Aug 98*	2
ALL THAT I AM	*Jive*	52	*31 Oct 98*	1
TREAT HER LIKE A LADY	*Jive*	60	*15 Jul 00*	1
STUTTER	*Jive*	7	*17 Feb 01*	8
Samples the Pharcyde's Passing Me By. From the film 'Double Take'.				
Above hit: JOE featuring MYSTIKAL.				
I WANNA KNOW	*Jive*	37	*5 May 01*	2

ALBUMS:	HITS 3			WEEKS 9
EVERYTHING	*Vertigo*	53	*12 Feb 94*	1
ALL THAT I AM	*Jive*	26	*9 Aug 97*	4
MY NAME IS JOE	*Jive*	55	*29 Apr 00*	2
MY NAME IS JOE [RE]	*Jive*	46	*3 Mar 01*	2

JOE PUBLIC — US

SINGLES:	HITS 2			WEEKS 5
LIVE AND LEARN	*Columbia*	43	*11 Jul 92*	4
I'VE BEEN WATCHIN'	*Columbia*	75	*28 Nov 92*	1

Billy JOEL — US

SINGLES:	HITS 20			WEEKS 146
JUST THE WAY YOU ARE	*CBS*	19	*11 Feb 78*	9
Written about his first wife & manager Elizabeth.				
MOVIN' OUT (ANTHONY'S SONG)	*CBS*	35	*24 Jun 78*	6
MY LIFE	*CBS*	12	*2 Dec 78*	15
Backing vocals by Peter Cetera.				
UNTIL THE NIGHT	*CBS*	50	*28 Apr 79*	3
ALL FOR LEYNA	*CBS*	40	*12 Apr 80*	4
IT'S STILL ROCK AND ROLL TO ME	*CBS*	14	*9 Aug 80*	11
UPTOWN GIRL	*CBS*	1	*15 Oct 83*	17
Written about his then girlfriend Christie Brinkley.				
TELL HER ABOUT IT	*CBS*	4	*10 Dec 83*	10
AN INNOCENT MAN	*CBS*	8	*18 Feb 84*	10
THE LONGEST TIME	*CBS*	25	*28 Apr 84*	8
GOODNIGHT SAIGON / LEAVE A TENDER MOMENT ALONE	*CBS*	29	*23 Jun 84*	7
Goodnight Saigon listed from 30 Jun 84 and took first credit.				
SHE'S ALWAYS A WOMAN / JUST THE WAY YOU ARE [RI]	*CBS*	53	*22 Feb 86*	1
A MATTER OF TRUST	*CBS*	52	*20 Sep 86*	4
WE DIDN'T START THE FIRE	*CBS*	7	*30 Sep 89*	10
LENINGRAD	*CBS*	53	*16 Dec 89*	4
I GO TO EXTREMES	*CBS*	70	*10 Mar 90*	2
ALL SHOOK UP	*Epic*	27	*29 Aug 92*	4
From the film 'Honeymoon In Vegas'.				
THE RIVER OF DREAMS	*Columbia*	3	*31 Jul 93*	14
ALL ABOUT SOUL	*Columbia*	32	*23 Oct 93*	4
Backing vocals by Color Me Badd.				
NO MAN'S LAND	*Columbia*	50	*26 Feb 94*	3

ALBUMS:	HITS 16			WEEKS 347
THE STRANGER	*CBS*	25	*25 Mar 78*	40
52ND STREET	*CBS*	10	*25 Nov 78*	43
Includes re-entry in 1984.				
GLASS HOUSES	*CBS*	9	*22 Mar 80*	24
SONGS IN THE ATTIC	*CBS*	57	*10 Oct 81*	3
THE NYLON CURTAIN	*CBS*	27	*2 Oct 82*	8
AN INNOCENT MAN	*CBS*	2	*10 Sep 83*	94
Peak position reached on 23 Jun 84.				
COLD SPRING HARBOUR	*CBS*	95	*4 Feb 84*	1
Originally released in 1972.				
PIANO MAN	*CBS*	98	*23 Jun 84*	1
Originally released in 1973.				
GREATEST HITS VOLUME I & VOLUME II	*CBS*	7	*20 Jul 85*	39
First disc titled Greatest Hits Vol. I 1973–1980; Second disc titled Greatest Hits Vol. II 1980–1985.				
THE BRIDGE	*CBS*	38	*16 Aug 86*	10

KOHYEPT - LIVE IN LENINGRAD	*CBS*	92	*28 Nov 87*	1
Live recordings from Apr 87.				
STORM FRONT	*CBS*	5	*4 Nov 89*	25
RIVER OF DREAMS	*Columbia*	3	*14 Aug 93*	26
AN INNOCENT MAN [RI]	*Columbia*	66	*23 Sep 95*	1
GREATEST HITS - VOLUME III	*Columbia*	23	*1 Nov 97*	4
GREATEST HITS - VOLUMES I, II & III [RI]	*Columbia*	33	*13 Jun 98*	4
Double re-issue of the 2 previous hits packages.				
2000 YEARS - THE MILLENNIUM CONCERT	*Columbia*	68	*27 May 00*	1
Recorded at his millennium eve concert in New York's Madison Square Gardens.				
THE ULTIMATE COLLECTION	*Columbia*	4	*31 Mar 01*	22

JOHANN — Germany

SINGLES:	HITS 1			WEEKS 1
NEW KICKS	*Perfecto*	54	*16 Mar 96*	1

Angela JOHN - See Jose PADILLA featuring Angela JOHN

Elton JOHN — UK

(See also Dionne Warwick; Various Artists: Films - Original Soundtracks 'The Lion King'.)

SINGLES:	HITS 74			WEEKS 567
YOUR SONG	*DJM*	7	*23 Jan 71*	12
ROCKET MAN (I THINK IT'S GOING TO BE A LONG LONG TIME)	*DJM*	2	*22 Apr 72*	13
HONKY CAT	*DJM*	31	*9 Sep 72*	6
CROCODILE ROCK	*DJM*	5	*4 Nov 72*	14
DANIEL	*DJM*	4	*20 Jan 73*	10
SATURDAY NIGHT'S ALRIGHT FOR FIGHTING	*DJM*	7	*7 Jul 73*	9
GOODBYE YELLOW BRICK ROAD	*DJM*	6	*29 Sep 73*	16
STEP INTO CHRISTMAS	*DJM*	24	*8 Dec 73*	7
CANDLE IN THE WIND	*DJM*	11	*2 Mar 74*	9
DON'T LET THE SUN GO DOWN ON ME	*DJM*	16	*1 Jun 74*	8
Backing vocals by Captain and Tennille and Carl Wilson and Bruce Johnston of the Beach Boys.				
THE BITCH IS BACK	*DJM*	15	*14 Sep 74*	7
Backing vocals by Dusty Springfield.				
LUCY IN THE SKY WITH DIAMONDS	*DJM*	10	*23 Nov 74*	10
Written by Lennon/McCartney.				
PHILADELPHIA FREEDOM	*DJM*	12	*8 Mar 75*	9
Tribute to tennis star Billie Jean King.				
Above hit: Elton JOHN BAND.				
SOMEONE SAVED MY LIFE TONIGHT	*DJM*	22	*28 Jun 75*	5
ISLAND GIRL	*DJM*	14	*4 Oct 75*	8
PINBALL WIZARD	*DJM*	7	*20 Mar 76*	7
From the film 'Tommy'.				
DON'T GO BREAKING MY HEART	*Rocket*	1	*3 Jul 76*	14
Above hit: Elton JOHN and Kiki DEE.				
BENNY AND THE JETS	*DJM*	37	*25 Sep 76*	5
SORRY SEEMS TO BE THE HARDEST WORD	*Rocket*	11	*13 Nov 76*	10
CRAZY WATER	*Rocket*	27	*26 Feb 77*	6
BITE YOUR LIP (GET UP AND DANCE)	*Rocket*	28	*11 Jun 77*	4
[AA] listed with Chicago by Kiki Dee.				
EGO	*Rocket*	34	*15 Apr 78*	6
PART TIME LOVE	*Rocket*	15	*21 Oct 78*	13
SONG FOR GUY	*Rocket*	4	*16 Dec 78*	10
Written about Rocket Records' messenger Guy Burchett who was killed in a motorcycle accident.				
ARE YOU READY FOR LOVE	*Rocket*	42	*12 May 79*	6
LITTLE JEANIE	*Rocket*	33	*24 May 80*	7
Sleeve reflects title as Little Jeannie.				
SARTORIAL ELOQUENCE	*Rocket*	44	*23 Aug 80*	5
I SAW HER STANDING THERE	*DJM*	40	*21 Mar 81*	4
Above hit: Elton JOHN BAND featuring John LENNON and the MUSCLE SHOALS HORNS.				
NOBODY WINS	*Rocket*	42	*23 May 81*	5
BLUE EYES	*Rocket*	8	*27 Mar 82*	10
EMPTY GARDEN	*Rocket*	51	*12 Jun 82*	4
Tribute to John Lennon.				
I GUESS THAT'S WHY THEY CALL IT THE BLUES	*Rocket*	5	*30 Apr 83*	15
Features Stevie Wonder on Harmonica.				
I'M STILL STANDING	*Rocket*	4	*30 Jul 83*	11
KISS THE BRIDE	*Rocket*	20	*15 Oct 83*	7
COLD AS CHRISTMAS (IN THE MIDDLE OF THE YEAR)	*Rocket*	33	*10 Dec 83*	6
Even though not listed, this was released as a double A-side with 'Crystal'.				
SAD SONGS (SAY SO MUCH)	*Rocket*	7	*26 May 84*	12
PASSENGERS	*Rocket*	5	*11 Aug 84*	11
WHO WEARS THESE SHOES?	*Rocket*	50	*20 Oct 84*	3
BREAKING HEARTS (AIN'T WHAT IT USED TO BE)	*Rocket*	59	*2 Mar 85*	3
ACT OF WAR	*Rocket*	32	*15 Jun 85*	5
Above hit: Elton JOHN and Millie JACKSON.				

NIKITA	*Rocket*	3	*12 Oct 85*	13
WRAP HER UP	*Rocket*	12	*7 Dec 85*	10
Above 2 features backing vocals by George Michael.				
CRY TO HEAVEN	*Rocket*	47	*1 Mar 86*	4
HEARTACHE ALL OVER THE WORLD	*Rocket*	45	*4 Oct 86*	4
SLOW RIVERS	*Rocket*	44	*29 Nov 86*	8
Backing vocals by Kiki Dee.				
Above hit: Elton JOHN and Cliff RICHARD.				
FLAMES OF PARADISE	*CBS*	59	*20 Jun 87*	3
Above hit: Jennifer RUSH (duet with Elton JOHN).				
CANDLE IN THE WIND [RR-1ST]	*Rocket*	5	*16 Jan 88*	11
With the Melbourne Symphony Orchestra, recorded live in Australia, 1986.				
I DON'T WANNA GO ON WITH YOU LIKE THAT	*Rocket*	30	*4 Jun 88*	8
TOWN OF PLENTY	*Rocket*	74	*3 Sep 88*	1
THROUGH THE STORM	*Arista*	41	*6 May 89*	3
Above hit: Aretha FRANKLIN and Elton JOHN.				
HEALING HANDS	*Rocket*	45	*26 Aug 89*	5
SACRIFICE	*Rocket*	55	*4 Nov 89*	3
SACRIFICE [RI] / HEALING HANDS [RI]	*Rocket*	1	*9 Jun 90*	15
CLUB AT THE END OF THE STREET / WHISPERS	*Rocket*	47	*18 Aug 90*	3
YOU GOTTA LOVE SOMEONE	*Rocket*	33	*20 Oct 90*	4
EASIER TO WALK AWAY	*Rocket*	67	*15 Dec 90*	1
EASIER TO WALK AWAY [RE]	*Rocket*	63	*29 Dec 90*	1
DON'T LET THE SUN GO DOWN ON ME	*Epic*	1	*7 Dec 91*	10
Live recording in London, Mar 91.				
Above hit: George MICHAEL with Elton JOHN.				
THE ONE	*Rocket*	10	*6 Jun 92*	8
RUNAWAY TRAIN	*Rocket*	31	*1 Aug 92*	4
Above hit: Elton JOHN and Eric CLAPTON.				
THE LAST SONG	*Rocket*	21	*7 Nov 92*	4
SIMPLE LIFE	*Rocket*	44	*22 May 93*	2
TRUE LOVE	*Rocket*	2	*20 Nov 93*	10
Above hit: Elton JOHN - duet with Kiki DEE.				
DON'T GO BREAKING MY HEART	*Rocket*	7	*26 Feb 94*	7
Above hit: Elton JOHN and RUPAUL.				
AIN'T NOTHING LIKE THE REAL THING	*London*	24	*14 May 94*	4
Above hit: Marcella DETROIT and Elton JOHN.				
CAN YOU FEEL THE LOVE TONIGHT	*Mercury*	14	*9 Jul 94*	9
Backing vocals by Gary Barlow, Kiki Dee and Rick Astley.				
CIRCLE OF LIFE	*Rocket*	11	*8 Oct 94*	12
Above 2 from the film 'The Lion King'.				
BELIEVE	*Rocket*	15	*4 Mar 95*	7
MADE IN ENGLAND	*Rocket*	18	*20 May 95*	5
PLEASE	*Rocket*	33	*3 Feb 96*	3
LIVE LIKE HORSES	*Rocket*	9	*14 Dec 96*	6
Above hit: Elton JOHN and Luciano PAVAROTTI.				
SOMETHING ABOUT THE WAY YOU LOOK TONIGHT / CANDLE IN THE WIND 1997 [RR 2ND]	*Rocket*	1	*20 Sep 97*	24
Biggest selling single of all time. Lyrics were changed for the funeral of Diana, Princess Of Wales on 6 Sep 97.				
RECOVER YOUR SOUL	*Rocket*	16	*14 Feb 98*	3
IF THE RIVER CAN BEND	*Rocket*	32	*13 Jun 98*	2
Proceeds from the majority of John's later singles were donated to charity.				
WRITTEN IN THE STARS	*Rocket*	10	*6 Mar 99*	7
From the Walt Disney film 'Aida'.				
Above hit: Elton JOHN and LeAnn RIMES.				
WRITTEN IN THE STARS [RE]	*Rocket*	63	*22 May 99*	1
I WANT LOVE	*Rocket*	9	*6 Oct 01*	10
ALBUMS:	**HITS 38**		**WEEKS 897**	
ELTON JOHN	*DJM*	11	*23 May 70*	14
TUMBLEWEED CONNECTION	*DJM*	6	*16 Jan 71*	20
THE ELTON JOHN LIVE ALBUM 17-11-70	*DJM*	20	*1 May 71*	2
Live recording of a concert in New York by the W-PLJ FM radio station.				
MADMAN ACROSS THE WATER	*DJM*	41	*20 May 72*	2
HONKY CHATEAU	*DJM*	2	*3 Jun 72*	23
DON'T SHOOT ME I'M ONLY THE PIANO PLAYER	*DJM*	1	*10 Feb 73*	42
GOODBYE YELLOW BRICK ROAD	*DJM*	1	*3 Nov 73*	84
CARIBOU	*DJM*	1	*13 Jul 74*	18
ELTON JOHN'S GREATEST HITS	*DJM*	1	*23 Nov 74*	84
CAPTAIN FANTASTIC AND THE BROWN DIRT COWBOY	*DJM*	2	*7 Jun 75*	24
ROCK OF THE WESTIES	*DJM*	5	*8 Nov 75*	12
HERE AND THERE	*DJM*	6	*15 May 76*	9
Live recordings from the Royal Festival Hall and Madison Square Garden, 1974.				
BLUE MOVES	*Rocket*	3	*6 Nov 76*	15
ELTON JOHN'S GREATEST HITS - VOLUME II	*DJM*	6	*15 Oct 77*	24
A SINGLE MAN	*Rocket*	8	*4 Nov 78*	26
VICTIM OF LOVE	*Rocket*	41	*20 Oct 79*	3
LADY SAMANTHA	*DJM*	56	*8 Mar 80*	2

21 AT 33	*Rocket*	12	*31 May 80*	13
THE VERY BEST OF ELTON JOHN	*K-Tel*	24	*25 Oct 80*	13
THE FOX	*Rocket*	12	*30 May 81*	12
JUMP UP	*Rocket*	13	*17 Apr 82*	12
LOVE SONGS	*TV Records*	39	*6 Nov 82*	13
TOO LOW FOR ZERO	*Rocket*	7	*11 Jun 83*	73
BREAKING HEARTS	*Rocket*	2	*30 Jun 84*	23
ICE ON FIRE	*Rocket*	3	*16 Nov 85*	23
LEATHER JACKETS	*Rocket*	24	*15 Nov 86*	9
LIVE IN AUSTRALIA	*Rocket*	70	*12 Sep 87*	2
Live recordings from his 1986 Australian tour. Melbourne Symphony Orchestra conducted by James Newton Howard. This was based on sales of a box set.				
Above hit: Elton JOHN and the MELBOURNE SYMPHONY ORCHESTRA.				
LIVE IN AUSTRALIA [RE]	*Rocket*	43	*5 Mar 88*	5
Standard package re-release.				
REG STRIKES BACK	*Rocket*	18	*16 Jul 88*	6
SLEEPING WITH THE PAST	*Rocket*	6	*23 Sep 89*	9
SLEEPING WITH THE PAST [RE]	*Rocket*	1	*16 Jun 90*	33
THE VERY BEST OF ELTON JOHN	*Rocket*	1	*10 Nov 90*	96
Includes re-entries through to 1997.				
THE ONE	*Rocket*	2	*27 Jun 92*	18
DUETS	*Rocket*	5	*4 Dec 93*	18
Above hit: Elton JOHN and VARIOUS ARTISTS.				
MADE IN ENGLAND	*Rocket*	3	*1 Apr 95*	14
LOVE SONGS	*Rocket*	4	*18 Nov 95*	48
THE BIG PICTURE	*Rocket*	3	*11 Oct 97*	23
ELTON JOHN AND TIM RICE'S AIDA	*Rocket*	29	*3 Apr 99*	2
Above hit: Elton JOHN and FRIENDS.				
ONE NIGHT ONLY - THE GREATEST HITS	*Rocket*	7	*25 Nov 00*	13
Recorded live at New York's Madison Square Garden on 22 Oct 00.				
SONGS FROM THE WEST COAST	*Rocket*	2	*13 Oct 01*	12
GOODBYE YELLOW BRICK ROAD [RI]	*Mercury*	41	*20 Oct 01*	3

Robert JOHN — US

SINGLES:	HITS 2			WEEKS 13
IF YOU DON'T WANT MY LOVE	*CBS*	42	*20 Jul 68*	5
SAD EYES	*EMI America*	31	*20 Oct 79*	8

JOHN and YOKO – See John LENNON

JOHNNA — US

SINGLES:	HITS 2			WEEKS 3
DO WHAT YOU FEEL	*PWL International*	43	*10 Feb 96*	2
IN MY DREAMS	*PWL*	66	*11 May 96*	1

JOHNNY CORPORATE — US

SINGLES:	HITS 1			WEEKS 2
SUNDAY SHOUTIN'	*Defected*	45	*28 Oct 00*	2

JOHNNY and CHARLEY — Spain

SINGLES:	HITS 1			WEEKS 1
LA YENKA	*Pye International*	49	*16 Oct 65*	1

JOHNNY HATES JAZZ — UK

SINGLES:	HITS 5			WEEKS 45
SHATTERED DREAMS	*Virgin*	5	*11 Apr 87*	14
I DON'T WANT TO BE A HERO	*Virgin*	11	*29 Aug 87*	10
TURN BACK THE CLOCK	*Virgin*	12	*21 Nov 87*	11
HEART OF GOLD	*Virgin*	19	*27 Feb 88*	7
DON'T SAY IT'S LOVE	*Virgin*	48	*9 Jul 88*	3
ALBUMS:	**HITS 1**			**WEEKS 39**
TURN BACK THE CLOCK	*Virgin*	1	*23 Jan 88*	39

JOHNNY and the HURRICANES — US

SINGLES:	HITS 7			WEEKS 88
RED RIVER ROCK	*London*	3	*10 Oct 59*	16
REVEILLE ROCK	*London*	14	*26 Dec 59*	5
BEATNIK FLY	*London*	8	*19 Mar 60*	19
DOWN YONDER	*London*	8	*18 Jun 60*	11
Originally recorded by Hare and Jones in 1921.				
ROCKING GOOSE	*London*	3	*1 Oct 60*	20
JA-DA	*London*	14	*4 Mar 61*	9
Originally recorded by Arthur Fields in 1919.				
OLD SMOKIE / HIGH VOLTAGE	*London*	24	*8 Jul 61*	8

ALBUMS:	HITS 2			WEEKS 5
STORMSVILLE	*London*	18	*3 Dec 60*	1
BIG SOUND OF JOHNNY AND THE HURRICANES	*London*	13	*1 Apr 61*	4

JOHNSON — UK

SINGLES:	HITS 1			WEEKS 1
SAY YOU LOVE ME	*Higher Ground*	56	*27 Mar 99*	1

Andreas JOHNSON — Sweden

SINGLES:	HITS 2			WEEKS 12
GLORIOUS	*WEA*	4	*5 Feb 00*	11
THE GAMES WE PLAY	*WEA*	41	*27 May 00*	1
ALBUMS:	**HITS 1**			**WEEKS 2**
LIEBLING	*WEA*	46	*19 Feb 00*	2

Bryan JOHNSON — UK

SINGLES:	HITS 1			WEEKS 11
LOOKING HIGH, HIGH, HIGH	*Decca*	20	*12 Mar 60*	11
UK's Eurovision entry in 1960, it came 2nd.				

Carey JOHNSON — Australia

SINGLES:	HITS 1			WEEKS 8
REAL FASHION REGGAE STYLE	*10 Records*	19	*25 Apr 87*	8

Denise JOHNSON — UK

SINGLES:	HITS 2			WEEKS 4
DON'T FIGHT IT, FEEL IT	*Creation*	41	*24 Aug 91*	2
Above hit: PRIMAL SCREAM featuring Denise JOHNSON.				
RAYS OF THE RISING SUN	*Magnet*	45	*14 May 94*	2

Don JOHNSON — US

SINGLES:	HITS 2			WEEKS 12
HEARTBEAT	*Epic*	46	*18 Oct 86*	5
TILL I LOVED YOU (THE LOVE THEME FROM GOYA)	*CBS*	16	*5 Nov 88*	7
Above hit: Barbra STREISAND and Don JOHNSON.				

General JOHNSON - See CHAIRMEN OF THE BOARD

Holly JOHNSON — UK

(See also Christians, Holly Johnson, Paul McCartney, Gerry Marsden, Stock Aitken Waterman.)

SINGLES:	HITS 6			WEEKS 31
LOVE TRAIN	*MCA*	4	*14 Jan 89*	11
Features Brian May on guitar.				
AMERICANOS	*MCA*	4	*1 Apr 89*	11
ATOMIC CITY	*MCA*	18	*24 Jun 89*	4
HEAVEN'S HERE	*MCA*	62	*30 Sep 89*	2
WHERE HAS LOVE GONE?	*MCA*	73	*1 Dec 90*	1
THE POWER OF LOVE	*Pleasuredome*	56	*25 Dec 99*	2
ALBUMS:	**HITS 1**			**WEEKS 17**
BLAST	*MCA*	1	*6 May 89*	17

Howard JOHNSON — US

SINGLES:	HITS 1			WEEKS 6
KEEPIN' LOVE NEW / SO FINE	*A&M*	45	*4 Sep 82*	6
Keepin' Love New listed only on 4 Sep 82 at its chart entry position of No. 64.				

Johnny JOHNSON and the BANDWAGON — US

SINGLES:	HITS 5			WEEKS 50
BREAKIN' DOWN THE WALLS OF HEARTACHE	*Direction*	4	*19 Oct 68*	15
Above hit: BANDWAGON.				
Some later copies credit Johnny Johnson and the Bandwagon.				
YOU	*Direction*	34	*8 Feb 69*	4
LET'S HANG ON	*Direction*	36	*31 May 69*	6
SWEET INSPIRATION	*Bell*	10	*25 Jul 70*	12
SWEET INSPIRATION [RE]	*Bell*	46	*24 Oct 70*	1
(BLAME IT) ON THE PONY EXPRESS	*Bell*	7	*28 Nov 70*	12

Kevin JOHNSON — Australia

SINGLES:	HITS 1			WEEKS 6
ROCK AND ROLL (I GAVE YOU THE BEST YEARS OF MY LIFE)	*UK*	23	*11 Jan 75*	6

L J JOHNSON — US

SINGLES:	HITS 1			WEEKS 6
YOUR MAGIC PUT A SPELL ON ME	*Philips*	27	*7 Feb 76*	6

Laurie JOHNSON ORCHESTRA — UK

SINGLES:	HITS 2			WEEKS 14
SUCU SUCU *Theme from the TV series 'Top Secret'.*	*Pye*	9	*30 Sep 61*	12
THEME FROM THE PROFESSIONALS *Theme from the 1970s ITV series.* *Above hit: Laurie JOHNSON'S LONDON BIG BAND.*	*Virgin*	36	*17 May 97*	2

Linton Kwesi JOHNSON — Jamaica

ALBUMS:	HITS 3			WEEKS 8
FORCE OF VICTORY	*Island*	66	*30 Jun 79*	1
BASS CULTURE	*Island*	46	*31 May 80*	5
MAKING HISTORY	*Island*	73	*10 Mar 84*	2

Lou JOHNSON — US

SINGLES:	HITS 1			WEEKS 2
MESSAGE TO MARTHA (KENTUCKY BLUEBIRD)	*London*	36	*28 Nov 64*	2

Marv JOHNSON — US

SINGLES:	HITS 5			WEEKS 40
YOU GOT WHAT IT TAKES	*London*	7	*13 Feb 60*	17
I LOVE THE WAY YOU LOVE	*London*	35	*7 May 60*	3
AIN'T GONNA BE THAT WAY	*London*	50	*13 Aug 60*	1
I'LL PICK A ROSE FOR MY ROSE	*Tamla Motown*	10	*25 Jan 69*	11
I MISS YOU BABY (HOW I MISS YOU)	*Tamla Motown*	25	*25 Oct 69*	8

Orlando JOHNSON – See SECCHI featuring Orlando JOHNSON

Paul JOHNSON — UK

SINGLES:	HITS 2			WEEKS 7
WHEN LOVE COMES CALLING	*CBS*	52	*21 Feb 87*	5
NO MORE TOMORROWS	*CBS*	67	*25 Feb 89*	2
ALBUMS:	**HITS 2**			**WEEKS 3**
PAUL JOHNSON	*CBS*	63	*4 Jul 87*	2
PERSONAL	*CBS*	70	*16 Sep 89*	1

Paul JOHNSON — US

SINGLES:	HITS 1			WEEKS 8
GET GET DOWN	*Defected*	5	*25 Sep 99*	8

Puff JOHNSON — US

SINGLES:	HITS 2			WEEKS 6
OVER AND OVER *From the film 'The First Wives Club'.*	*Columbia*	20	*18 Jan 97*	4
FOREVER MORE	*Columbia*	29	*12 Apr 97*	2

Romina JOHNSON — UK

SINGLES:	HITS 1			WEEKS 13
MOVIN TOO FAST *Above hit: ARTFUL DODGER and Romina JOHNSON.*	*Locked On*	2	*4 Mar 00*	11
MOVIN TOO FAST [RE]	*Locked On*	64	*10 Jun 00*	1
MY FORBIDDEN LOVER *Above hit: Romina JOHNSON featuring Lucie MARTIN and Norma JEAN from CHIC.*	*51 Lexington*	59	*17 Jun 00*	1

Teddy JOHNSON and Pearl CARR — UK

SINGLES:	HITS 2			WEEKS 19
SING LITTLE BIRDIE *UK's Eurovision entry in 1959, it came 2nd.*	*Columbia*	12	*21 Mar 59*	8
HOW WONDERFUL TO KNOW *Above hit: Teddy JOHNSON and Pearl CARR with Geoff LOVE and his Orchestra.*	*Columbia*	23	*8 Apr 61*	11

Trina JOHNSON and VOICES – See HAMMER

Bruce JOHNSTON — US

SINGLES:	HITS 1			WEEKS 4
PIPELINE	*CBS*	33	*27 Aug 77*	4

James A. JOHNSTON — US

ALBUMS:	HITS 2			WEEKS 17
WORLD WRESTLING FEDERATION - THE MUSIC - VOLUME 4	*Koch International*	44	*13 Nov 99*	9
Volume 4 is the first UK retail release, includes track by German rock group H-Blockx.				
WORLD WRESTLING FEDERATION - THE MUSIC - VOLUME 5	*Koch International*	11	*10 Mar 01*	8
Would have charted at No. 3 on 3 Mar 01, but was excluded from the chart because the album contained a weblink to a site where it could be purchased.				

Jan JOHNSTON — UK

SINGLES:	HITS 6			WEEKS 14
TAKE ME BY THE HAND	*AM:PM*	28	*8 Feb 97*	2
Above hit: SUB.MERGE featuring Jan JOHNSTON.				
SKYDIVE	*Stress*	75	*28 Nov 98*	1
Above hit: FREEFALL featuring Jan JOHNSTON.				
MERCURY AND SOLACE	*Headspace*	38	*9 Oct 99*	2
Above hit: BT featuring vocals by Jan JOHNSTON.				
LOVE WILL COME	*Xtravaganza*	31	*12 Feb 00*	2
Above hit: TOMSKI featuring Jan JOHNSTON.				
SKYDIVE [RI]	*Renaissance Recordings*	43	*22 Jul 00*	2
Above hit: FREEFALL featuring Jan JOHNSTON.				
FLESH	*Perfecto*	36	*21 Apr 01*	2
SILENT WORDS	*Perfecto*	57	*28 Jul 01*	1
SKYDIVE (I FEEL WONDERFUL) [RI-2ND]	*Incentive*	35	*8 Sep 01*	2
Above hit: FREEFALL featuring Jan JOHNSTON.				

Sabrina JOHNSTON — US

SINGLES:	HITS 4			WEEKS 19
PEACE	*East West*	8	*7 Sep 91*	10
FRIENDSHIP	*East West*	58	*7 Dec 91*	4
I WANNA SING	*East West*	46	*11 Jul 92*	2
PEACE [RM]	*Epic*	35	*3 Oct 92*	2
[AA] listed with a remix of Gypsy Woman by Crystal Waters. Remixed by David Morales. From the 'Red Hot + Dance' album (to benefit Aids research).				
SATISFY MY LOVE	*Champion*	62	*13 Aug 94*	1

JOHNSTON BROTHERS — UK

(See also All Star Hit Parade.)

SINGLES:	HITS 10			WEEKS 33
OH HAPPY DAY	*Decca*	4	*4 Apr 53*	8
WAIT FOR ME DARLING	*Decca*	18	*6 Nov 54*	1
Above hit: Joan REGAN and the JOHNSTON BROTHERS.				
HAPPY DAYS AND LONELY NIGHTS	*Decca*	14	*22 Jan 55*	2
Above hit: Suzi MILLER and the JOHNSTON BROTHERS.				
HERNANDO'S HIDEAWAY	*Decca*	1	*8 Oct 55*	13
Originally recorded by Carol Haney.				
Above hit: JOHNSTON BROTHERS with Johnny DOUGLAS and his Orchestra (Elsa BRUNELLESCHI-castanets).				
JOIN IN AND SING AGAIN [M]	*Decca*	9	*31 Dec 55*	1
Above hit: JOHNSTON BROTHERS and the George CHISHOLM SOUR-NOTE SIX.				
NO OTHER LOVE	*Decca*	22	*14 Apr 56*	1
Above hit: JOHNSTON BROTHERS with Bob SHARPLES and his Music.				
IN THE MIDDLE OF THE HOUSE	*Decca*	27	*1 Dec 56*	1
Above hit: JOHNSTON BROTHERS and the KEYNOTES.				
JOIN IN AND SING NO. 3 [M]	*Decca*	30	*8 Dec 56*	1
Above hit: JOHNSTON BROTHERS and the George CHISHOLM SOUR-NOTE SIX.				
JOIN IN AND SING NO. 3 [M] [RE]	*Decca*	24	*29 Dec 56*	1
GIVE HER MY LOVE	*Decca*	27	*9 Feb 57*	1
HEART	*Decca*	23	*20 Apr 57*	3
Above hit: JOHNSTON BROTHERS with Roland SHAW and his Orchestra.				

Brian JOHNSTONE — UK

ALBUMS:	HITS 1			WEEKS 3
AN EVENING WITH JOHNNERS	*Listen For Pleasure*	46	*5 Mar 94*	3

James JOLIS – See Barry MANILOW

JOLLY BROTHERS — Jamaica

SINGLES:	HITS 1			WEEKS 7
CONSCIOUS MAN	*United Artists*	46	*28 Jul 79*	7

JOLLY ROGER — UK

SINGLES:	HITS 1			WEEKS 12
ACID MAN	*10 Records*	23	*10 Sep 88*	12

Al JOLSON — US

ALBUMS:	HITS 2			WEEKS 11
20 GOLDEN GREATS	*MCA*	18	*14 Mar 81*	7
THE AL JOLSON COLLECTION	*Ronco*	67	*17 Dec 83*	4

JOMALSKI - See WILDCHILD

JOMANDA — US

SINGLES:	HITS 4			WEEKS 10
MAKE MY BODY ROCK (FEEL IT)	*RCA*	44	*22 Apr 89*	3
GOT A LOVE FOR YOU	*Giant*	43	*29 Jun 91*	4
I LIKE IT	*Atlantic*	67	*11 Sep 93*	1
NEVER	*Big Beat*	40	*13 Nov 93*	2

JON and VANGELIS — UK/Greece

(See also Jon Anderson; Anderson Bruford Wakeman Howe; Vangelis.)

SINGLES:	HITS 4			WEEKS 28
I HEAR YOU NOW	*Polydor*	8	*5 Jan 80*	11
I'LL FIND MY WAY HOME	*Polydor*	6	*12 Dec 81*	13
HE IS SAILING	*Polydor*	61	*30 Jul 83*	2
STATE OF INDEPENDENCE	*Polydor*	67	*18 Aug 84*	2
ALBUMS:	**HITS 4**			**WEEKS 53**
SHORT STORIES	*Polydor*	4	*26 Jan 80*	11
THE FRIENDS OF MR. CAIRO	*Polydor*	17	*11 Jul 81*	8
THE FRIENDS OF MR. CAIRO [RE] *Re-released with additional track.*	*Polydor*	6	*23 Jan 82*	15
PRIVATE COLLECTION	*Polydor*	22	*2 Jul 83*	10
THE BEST OF JON AND VANGELIS	*Polydor*	42	*11 Aug 84*	9

JON OF THE PLEASED WIMMIN — UK

SINGLES:	HITS 2			WEEKS 5
PASSION	*Perfecto*	27	*18 Feb 95*	3
GIVE ME STRENGTH	*Perfecto*	30	*6 Apr 96*	2

JON THE DENTIST vs Ollie JAYE — UK

SINGLES:	HITS 2			WEEKS 2
IMAGINATION	*Tidy Trax*	72	*24 Jul 99*	1
FEEL SO GOOD	*Tidy Trax*	72	*10 Jun 00*	1

JONAH — Holland

SINGLES:	HITS 1			WEEKS 4
SSSST... (LISTEN)	*VC Recordings*	25	*22 Jul 00*	4

JONES - See BLANK and JONES

Aled JONES — UK

(See also Mike Oldfield.)

SINGLES:	HITS 3			WEEKS 18
MEMORY: THEME FROM THE MUSICAL 'CATS' *Above hit: Aled JONES with the LONDON SYMPHONY ORCHESTRA.*	*BBC*	42	*20 Jul 85*	4
WALKING IN THE AIR *From 'The Snowman'.*	*EMI*	5	*30 Nov 85*	11
A WINTER STORY *From the S4C/Channel 4 TV film of the same name.*	*His Master's Voice*	51	*20 Dec 86*	3
ALBUMS:	**HITS 8**			**WEEKS 141**
VOICES FROM THE HOLY LAND *Above hit: BBC WELSH CHORUS/Aled JONES (treble) conducted By John Hugh THOMAS.*	*BBC*	6	*27 Apr 85*	43
ALL THROUGH THE NIGHT *Above hit: Aled JONES with the BBC WELSH SYMPHONY ORCHESTRA and BBC WELSH CHORUS (Chorus Master-John Hugh THOMAS) Conducted by Robin STAPLETON*	*BBC*	2	*29 Jun 85*	44
ALED JONES WITH THE BBC WELSH CHORUS *Above hit: Aled JONES with the BBC WELSH CHORUS conducted by John Hugh THOMAS.*	*10 Records*	11	*23 Nov 85*	10
WHERE E'ER YOU WALK	*10 Records*	36	*22 Feb 86*	6
PIE JESU	*10 Records*	25	*12 Jul 86*	16
AN ALBUM OF HYMNS	*Telstar*	18	*29 Nov 86*	11
ALED (MUSIC FROM THE TV SERIES) [OST-TV] *Above hit: Aled JONES with the BBC WELSH CHORUS.*	*10 Records*	52	*14 Mar 87*	6
THE BEST OF ALED JONES	*10 Records*	59	*5 Dec 87*	5

Barbara JONES — Jamaica

SINGLES:	HITS 1			WEEKS 7
JUST WHEN I NEEDED YOU MOST	*A Side*	31	*31 Jan 81*	7

Catherine Zeta JONES — UK

SINGLES:	HITS 3			WEEKS 9
FOR ALL TIME	*Columbia*	36	*19 Sep 92*	5
From the album Jeff Wayne's Musical Version Of 'Spartacus'.				
TRUE LOVE WAYS	*PolyGram TV*	38	*26 Nov 94*	3
Above hit: David ESSEX and Catherine Zeta JONES.				
IN THE ARMS OF LOVE	*Wow!*	72	*1 Apr 95*	1

Donell JONES — US

(See also True Steppers.)

SINGLES:	HITS 3			WEEKS 15
KNOCKS ME OFF MY FEET	*LaFace*	58	*15 Feb 97*	1
Originally recorded by Stevie Wonder.				
U KNOW WHAT'S UP	*LaFace*	2	*22 Jan 00*	11
SHORTY (GOT HER EYES ON ME)	*LaFace*	19	*20 May 00*	3
ALBUMS:	**HITS 1**			**WEEKS 3**
WHERE I WANNA BE	*LaFace*	47	*29 Jan 00*	3

Georgia JONES – See DIVA SURPRISE featuring Georgia JONES; PLUX featuring Georgia JONES.

Glenn JONES — US

ALBUMS:	HITS 1			WEEKS 1
GLENN JONES	*Jive*	62	*31 Oct 87*	1

Grace JONES — US

SINGLES:	HITS 8			WEEKS 46
PRIVATE LIFE	*Island*	17	*26 Jul 80*	8
Originally recorded by the Pretenders in 1980.				
PULL UP TO THE BUMPER	*Island*	53	*20 Jun 81*	4
THE APPLE STRETCHING / NIPPLE TO THE BOTTLE	*Island*	50	*30 Oct 82*	4
MY JAMAICAN GUY	*Island*	56	*9 Apr 83*	3
SLAVE TO THE RHYTHM	*ZTT*	12	*12 Oct 85*	8
PULL UP TO THE BUMPER [RI] / LA VIE EN ROSE	*Island*	12	*18 Jan 86*	9
La Vie En Rose listed from 1 Feb 86 and originally recorded by Edith Piaf. Titles listed in reverse from 8 Feb 86.				
LOVE IS THE DRUG	*Island*	35	*1 Mar 86*	4
I'M NOT PERFECT (BUT I'M PERFECT FOR YOU)	*Manhattan*	56	*15 Nov 86*	3
SLAVE TO THE RHYTHM [RI]	*ZTT*	28	*7 May 94*	2
Re-released to coincide with the ZTT label's 10th anniversary				
PULL UP TO THE BUMPER [RM]	*Club Tools*	60	*25 Nov 00*	1
Remixed by Martin Ottesen.				
Above hit: Grace JONES vs FUNKSTAR DE LUXE.				
ALBUMS:	**HITS 6**			**WEEKS 80**
WARM LEATHERETTE	*Island*	45	*30 Aug 80*	2
NIGHTCLUBBING	*Island*	35	*23 May 81*	16
LIVING MY LIFE	*Island*	15	*20 Nov 82*	22
SLAVE TO THE RHYTHM	*Island*	12	*9 Nov 85*	8
ISLAND LIFE	*Island*	4	*14 Dec 85*	30
Compilation.				
INSIDE STORY	*Manhattan*	61	*29 Nov 86*	2

Hannah JONES — US

SINGLES:	HITS 2			WEEKS 9
BRIDGE OVER TROUBLED WATER	*Dance Pool*	21	*14 Sep 91*	8
Above hit: PJB featuring HANNAH and her SISTERS.				
KEEP IT ON	*TMRC*	67	*30 Jan 93*	1

Howard JONES — UK

SINGLES:	HITS 14			WEEKS 103
NEW SONG	*WEA*	3	*17 Sep 83*	12
WHAT IS LOVE?	*WEA*	2	*26 Nov 83*	15
NEW SONG [RE]	*WEA*	60	*14 Jan 84*	3
HIDE AND SEEK	*WEA*	12	*18 Feb 84*	9
PEARL IN THE SHELL	*WEA*	7	*26 May 84*	10
LIKE TO GET TO KNOW YOU WELL	*WEA*	4	*11 Aug 84*	12
THINGS CAN ONLY GET BETTER	*WEA*	6	*9 Feb 85*	8
LOOK MAMA	*WEA*	10	*20 Apr 85*	6
LIFE IN ONE DAY	*WEA*	14	*29 Jun 85*	7
NO ONE IS TO BLAME	*WEA*	16	*15 Mar 86*	7
Drums and production by Phil Collins.				

ALL I WANT	*WEA*	35	*4 Oct 86*	4
YOU KNOW I LOVE YOU . . . DON'T YOU?	*WEA*	43	*29 Nov 86*	3
LITTLE BIT OF SNOW	*WEA*	70	*21 Mar 87*	1
EVERLASTING LOVE	*WEA*	62	*4 Mar 89*	3
LIFT ME UP	*East West*	52	*11 Apr 92*	3
ALBUMS:	**HITS 6**			**WEEKS 122**
HUMAN'S LIB	*WEA*	1	*17 Mar 84*	57
THE 12" ALBUM	*WEA*	15	*8 Dec 84*	33
Mini-album of remixes/extended version of previous singles.				
DREAM INTO ACTION	*WEA*	2	*23 Mar 85*	25
ONE TO ONE	*WEA*	10	*25 Oct 86*	4
CROSS THAT LINE	*WEA*	64	*1 Apr 89*	1
THE BEST OF HOWARD JONES	*East West*	36	*5 Jun 93*	2

Jack JONES — US

ALBUMS:	**HITS 6**			**WEEKS 70**
A SONG FOR YOU	*RCA Victor*	9	*29 Apr 72*	6
BREAD WINNERS	*RCA Victor*	7	*3 Jun 72*	36
Cover of songs originally recorded by Bread.				
TOGETHER	*RCA Victor*	8	*7 Apr 73*	10
HARBOUR	*RCA Victor*	10	*23 Feb 74*	5
THE FULL LIFE	*RCA Victor*	41	*19 Feb 77*	5
ALL TO YOURSELF	*RCA Victor*	10	*21 May 77*	8

Janie JONES — UK

SINGLES:	**HITS 1**			**WEEKS 3**
WITCHES BREW	*His Master's Voice*	46	*29 Jan 66*	3

Jimmy JONES — US

SINGLES:	**HITS 5**			**WEEKS 47**
HANDY MAN	*MGM*	3	*19 Mar 60*	21
GOOD TIMIN'	*MGM*	1	*18 Jun 60*	15
HANDY MAN [RE]	*MGM*	32	*20 Aug 60*	3
I JUST GO FOR YOU	*MGM*	35	*10 Sep 60*	4
READY FOR LOVE	*MGM*	46	*19 Nov 60*	1
I TOLD YOU SO	*MGM*	33	*1 Apr 61*	3

Fabulous Josie JONES – See Pete WYLIE

Juggy JONES — US

SINGLES:	**HITS 1**			**WEEKS 4**
INSIDE AMERICA	*Contempo*	39	*7 Feb 76*	4

Kelly JONES – See MANCHILD; TECHNATION

Lavina JONES — South Africa

SINGLES:	**HITS 1**			**WEEKS 2**
SING IT TO YOU (DEE - DOOB -DEE -DOO)	*Virgin*	45	*18 Feb 95*	2

Mick JONES – See AZTEC CAMERA

Oran "Juice" JONES — US

SINGLES:	**HITS 1**			**WEEKS 14**
THE RAIN	*Def Jam*	4	*15 Nov 86*	14

Paul JONES — UK

(See also Various Artists: Studio Cast 'Evita'.)

SINGLES:	**HITS 4**			**WEEKS 34**
HIGH TIME	*His Master's Voice*	4	*8 Oct 66*	15
I'VE BEEN A BAD, BAD BOY	*His Master's Voice*	5	*21 Jan 67*	9
From the film 'Privilege'.				
Above hit: Paul JONES with Mike LEANDER and his Orchestra.				
THINKIN' AIN'T FOR ME	*His Master's Voice*	47	*26 Aug 67*	1
THINKIN' AIN'T FOR ME [RE]	*His Master's Voice*	32	*16 Sep 67*	7
AQUARIUS	*Columbia*	45	*8 Feb 69*	2
EPS:	**HITS 1**			**WEEKS 31**
PRIVILEGE	*His Master's Voice*	1	*6 May 67*	31

Quincy JONES — US

(See also Frank Sinatra.)

SINGLES:	**HITS 8**			**WEEKS 42**
STUFF LIKE THAT	*A&M*	34	*29 Jul 78*	9
Vocals by Ashford and Simpson and Chaka Khan.				

AI NO CORRIDA (I-NO-KO-REE-DA)	*A&M*	14	*11 Apr 81*	10
Originally recorded by Chas Jankel.				
Above hit: Quincy JONES featuring the vocals of DUNE.				
RAZZAMATAZZ	*A&M*	11	*20 Jun 81*	9
Vocals by Patti Austin.				
BETCHA' WOULDN'T HURT ME	*A&M*	52	*5 Sep 81*	3
I'LL BE GOOD TO YOU	*Qwest*	21	*13 Jan 90*	7
Above hit: Quincy JONES featuring Ray CHARLES and Chaka KHAN.				
THE SECRET GARDEN (SWEET SEDUCTION SUITE)	*Qwest*	67	*31 Mar 90*	1
Above hit: Quincy JONES featuring Al B SURE!, James INGRAM, El DEBARGE and Barry WHITE.				
STOMP - THE REMIXES	*Qwest*	28	*14 Sep 96*	2
First track on CD remixed by Mousse-T.				
Above hit: Quincy JONES featuring: Melle MEL/COOLIO/YO-YO/Shaquille O'NEAL/LUNIZ.				
SOUL BOSSA NOVA	*Manifesto*	47	*1 Aug 98*	1
Original recorded by Jones in 1962, this mix was featured in a Nike TV commercial and the opening scene to the film 'Austin Powers'.				
Above hit: COOL, The FAB and the GROOVY present Quincy JONES.				

ALBUMS:	HITS 3			WEEKS 41
THE DUDE	*A&M*	19	*18 Apr 81*	25
THE BEST OF QUINCY JONES	*A&M*	41	*20 Mar 82*	4
BACK ON THE BLOCK	*Qwest*	26	*20 Jan 90*	12

Rickie Lee JONES — US

SINGLES:	HITS 1			WEEKS 9
CHUCK E.'S IN LOVE	*Warner Brothers*	18	*23 Jun 79*	9
Written about singer/songwriter Chuck E. Weiss.				

ALBUMS:	HITS 5			WEEKS 39
RICKIE LEE JONES	*Warner Brothers*	18	*16 Jun 79*	19
PIRATES	*Warner Brothers*	37	*8 Aug 81*	11
GIRL AT HER VOLCANO	*Warner Brothers*	51	*2 Jul 83*	3
10" format mini-album.				
THE MAGAZINE	*Warner Brothers*	40	*13 Oct 84*	4
FLYING COWBOYS	*Geffen*	50	*7 Oct 89*	2

Shirley JONES – See PARTRIDGE FAMILY

Sonny JONES featuring Tara CHASE — Germany/Canada

SINGLES:	HITS 1			WEEKS 2
FOLLOW YOU FOLLOW ME	*Logic*	42	*7 Oct 00*	2

Steve JONES – See SEX PISTOLS

Tammy JONES — UK

SINGLES:	HITS 1			WEEKS 10
LET ME TRY AGAIN	*Epic*	5	*26 Apr 75*	10

ALBUMS:	HITS 1			WEEKS 5
LET ME TRY AGAIN	*Epic*	38	*12 Jul 75*	5

Tom JONES — UK

(See also Various Artists: Studio Cast 'Matador'.)

SINGLES:	HITS 39			WEEKS 390
IT'S NOT UNUSUAL	*Decca*	1	*13 Feb 65*	14
Originally written for Sandie Shaw. Lead guitar by Big Jim Sullivan.				
ONCE UPON A TIME	*Decca*	32	*8 May 65*	4
WITH THESE HANDS	*Decca*	13	*10 Jul 65*	11
Originally recorded by Eddie Fisher in 1953.				
WHAT'S NEW PUSSYCAT?	*Decca*	11	*14 Aug 65*	10
From the film of the same name.				
THUNDERBALL	*Decca*	35	*15 Jan 66*	4
Theme from the James Bond film of the same name.				
ONCE THERE WAS A TIME / NOT RESPONSIBILE	*Decca*	18	*21 May 66*	9
THIS AND THAT	*Decca*	44	*20 Aug 66*	3
GREEN, GREEN GRASS OF HOME	*Decca*	1	*12 Nov 66*	22
Originally recorded by Johnny Darrell in 1964.				
DETROIT CITY	*Decca*	8	*18 Feb 67*	10
Original by Bobby Bare reached No. 16 in the US in 1963.				
FUNNY FAMILIAR FORGOTTEN FEELINGS	*Decca*	7	*15 Apr 67*	15
Originally recorded by Mickey Newbury.				
I'LL NEVER FALL IN LOVE AGAIN	*Decca*	2	*29 Jul 67*	25
Originally recorded by Lonnie Donegan.				
I'M COMING HOME	*Decca*	2	*25 Nov 67*	16
DELILAH	*Decca*	2	*2 Mar 68*	17
HELP YOURSELF	*Decca*	5	*20 Jul 68*	26
A MINUTE OF YOUR TIME	*Decca*	14	*30 Nov 68*	15

LOVE ME TONIGHT	*Decca*	9	*17 May 69*	12
WITHOUT LOVE	*Decca*	10	*13 Dec 69*	11
Originally recorded by Clyde McPhatter.				
WITHOUT LOVE [RE]	*Decca*	49	*14 Mar 70*	1
DAUGHTER OF DARKNESS	*Decca*	5	*18 Apr 70*	15
I (WHO HAVE NOTHING)	*Decca*	16	*15 Aug 70*	8
I (WHO HAVE NOTHING) [RE]	*Decca*	47	*17 Oct 70*	3
SHE'S A LADY	*Decca*	13	*16 Jan 71*	9
Written by Paul Anka.				
SHE'S A LADY [RE]	*Decca*	47	*27 Mar 71*	1
PUPPET MAN	*Decca*	49	*5 Jun 71*	1
Written by Neil Sedaka and Howard Greenfield and originally recorded by The Fifth Dimension..				
PUPPET MAN [RE]	*Decca*	50	*19 Jun 71*	1
TILL	*Decca*	2	*23 Oct 71*	15
Original by Roger Williams reached No. 22 in the US in 1957.				
THE YOUNG NEW MEXICAN PUPPETEER	*Decca*	6	*1 Apr 72*	12
LETTER TO LUCILLE	*Decca*	31	*14 Apr 73*	8
SOMETHIN' 'BOUT YOU BABY I LIKE	*Decca*	36	*7 Sep 74*	5
SAY YOU'LL STAY UNTIL TOMORROW	*EMI*	40	*16 Apr 77*	3
A BOY FROM NOWHERE	*Epic*	2	*18 Apr 87*	12
From the musical 'Matador'.				
IT'S NOT UNUSUAL [RI]	*Decca*	17	*30 May 87*	8
I WAS BORN TO BE ME	*Epic*	61	*2 Jan 88*	1
From the musical 'Matador'.				
KISS	*China*	5	*29 Oct 88*	7
Above hit: ART OF NOISE featuring Tom JONES.				
MOVE CLOSER	*Jive*	49	*29 Apr 89*	3
COULDN'T SAY GOODBYE	*Dover*	51	*26 Jan 91*	2
CARRYING A TORCH	*Dover*	57	*16 Mar 91*	2
Originally recorded by and features backing vocals by Van Morrison.				
DELILAH [RI]	*The Hit Label*	68	*4 Jul 92*	2
ALL YOU NEED IS LOVE	*Childline*	19	*6 Feb 93*	4
Charity record for the Childline Appeal. Backing vocals by Kiki Dee.				
Above hit: Tom JONES and Dave STEWART.				
IF I ONLY KNEW	*ZTT*	11	*5 Nov 94*	9
BURNING DOWN THE HOUSE	*Gut*	7	*25 Sep 99*	7
Originally recorded by Talking Heads on their 1983 album Speaking In Tongues.				
Above hit: Tom JONES and the CARDIGANS.				
BABY, IT'S COLD OUTSIDE	*Gut*	17	*18 Dec 99*	7
Originally recorded by Esther Williams and Ricardo Montalban.				
Above hit: Tom JONES and CERYS of CATATONIA.				
MAMA TOLD ME NOT TO COME	*Gut*	4	*18 Mar 00*	7
Originally recorded by the Animals.				
Above hit: Tom JONES and STEREOPHONICS				
SEX BOMB	*Gut*	3	*20 May 00*	10
Above hit: Tom JONES and MOUSSE T.				
YOU NEED LOVE LIKE I DO	*Gut*	24	*18 Nov 00*	3
Original by Gladys Knight and the Pips reached No. 25 in the US in 1970.				
Above hit: Tom JONES and Heather SMALL.				

EPS:	**HITS 1**			**WEEKS 28**
ON STAGE	*Decca*	3	*10 Apr 65*	28

ALBUMS:	**HITS 26**			**WEEKS 493**
ALONG CAME JONES	*Decca*	11	*5 Jun 65*	5
FROM THE HEART	*Decca*	23	*8 Oct 66*	8
GREEN GREEN GRASS OF HOME	*Decca*	3	*8 Apr 67*	49
TOM JONES LIVE! AT THE TALK OF THE TOWN	*Decca*	6	*24 Jun 67*	90
13 SMASH HITS	*Decca*	5	*30 Dec 67*	49
DELILAH	*Decca*	1	*27 Jul 68*	29
HELP YOURSELF	*Decca*	4	*21 Dec 68*	9
THIS IS TOM JONES	*Decca*	2	*28 Jun 69*	20
TOM JONES LIVE IN LAS VEGAS	*Decca*	2	*15 Nov 69*	45
TOM	*Decca*	4	*25 Apr 70*	18
I WHO HAVE NOTHING	*Decca*	10	*14 Nov 70*	10
SHE'S A LADY	*Decca*	9	*29 May 71*	7
LIVE AT CAESAR'S PALACE	*Decca*	27	*27 Nov 71*	5
CLOSE UP	*Decca*	17	*24 Jun 72*	4
THE BODY AND SOUL OF TOM JONES	*Decca*	31	*23 Jun 73*	1
GREATEST HITS	*Decca*	15	*5 Jan 74*	13
THE TENTH ANNIVERSARY ALBUM OF TOM JONES - 20 GREATEST HITS	*Decca*	1	*22 Mar 75*	21
I'M COMING HOME	*Lotus*	12	*7 Oct 78*	9
THE GREATEST HITS	*Telstar*	16	*16 May 87*	12
AT THIS MOMENT	*Jive*	34	*13 May 89*	3
TOM JONES AFTER DARK	*Stylus*	46	*8 Jul 89*	4
CARRYING A TORCH	*Dover*	44	*6 Apr 91*	4
THE COMPLETE TOM JONES	*Fontana*	8	*27 Jun 92*	6
THE LEAD AND HOW TO SWING IT	*ZTT*	55	*26 Nov 94*	1
THE ULTIMATE HITS COLLECTION	*PolyGram TV*	75	*14 Nov 98*	1

RELOAD *Duets album.*	*Gut*	1	*9 Oct 99*	65
THE ULTIMATE HITS COLLECTION [RI]	*Universal Music TV*	26	*9 Oct 99*	5

Trevor JONES — UK

ALBUMS:	HITS 1			WEEKS 2
LABYRINTH [OST] *Original score is by Trevor Jones and features David Bowie (who starred in the film) on certain tracks.*	*EMI America*	38	*5 Jul 86*	2

JONESTOWN — US

SINGLES:	HITS 1			WEEKS 1
SWEET THANG *Samples Sister Sledge's He's The Greatest Dancer.*	*Universal*	49	*13 Jun 98*	1

Janis JOPLIN — US

ALBUMS:	HITS 3			WEEKS 11
PEARL	*CBS*	50	*17 Apr 71*	1
JANIS JOPLIN IN CONCERT *First side is with Big Brother and the Holding Co., the second with the Full Tilt Boogie Band.*	*CBS*	30	*22 Jul 72*	6
THE ULTIMATE COLLECTION	*Columbia*	26	*29 Aug 98*	4

Alison JORDAN — UK

SINGLES:	HITS 1			WEEKS 4
BOY FROM NEW YORK CITY	*Arista*	23	*9 May 92*	4

Dick JORDAN — UK

SINGLES:	HITS 2			WEEKS 4
HALLELUJAH I LOVE HER SO	*Oriole*	47	*19 Mar 60*	1
LITTLE CHRISTINE	*Oriole*	39	*11 Jun 60*	3

Jack JORDAN – Clavioline - See Frank CHACKSFIELD and his Orchestra

Montell JORDAN — US

SINGLES:	HITS 5			WEEKS 21
THIS IS HOW WE DO IT	*Def Jam*	11	*13 May 95*	8
SOMETHIN' 4 DA HONEYZ *Samples Summer Madness by Kool and the Gang.*	*Def Jam*	15	*2 Sep 95*	4
I LIKE *From the film 'The Nutty Professor'. Samples I Get Lifted by KC & the Sunshine Band.* *Above hit: Montell JORDAN featuring SLICK RICK.*	*Def Jam*	24	*19 Oct 96*	3
LET'S RIDE *Above hit: Montell JORDAN featuring MASTER P and SILKK "THE SHOCKER".*	*Def Jam*	25	*23 May 98*	2
GET IT ON TONITE *Originally recorded by Derrick Demitri. Samples Claudia Berry's Love For The Sake Of Love.*	*Def Soul*	15	*8 Apr 00*	4
ALBUMS:	**HITS 2**			**WEEKS 3**
THIS IS HOW WE DO IT	*RAL*	53	*24 Jun 95*	2
MORE TO TELL	*Def Jam*	66	*14 Sep 96*	1

Ronny JORDAN — UK

SINGLES:	HITS 4			WEEKS 7
SO WHAT! *Originally recorded by Miles Davis.*	*Antilles*	32	*1 Feb 92*	4
UNDER YOUR SPELL *Above hit: Ronny JORDAN with Special Guests Fay SIMPSON and Truth ANTHONY.*	*Island*	72	*25 Sep 93*	1
TINSEL TOWN	*Island*	64	*15 Jan 94*	1
COME WITH ME *Originally recorded by Tania Marie in 1993.* *Above hit: Ronny JORDAN (Guest vocalist Fay SIMPSON).*	*Island*	63	*28 May 94*	1
ALBUMS:	**HITS 3**			**WEEKS 7**
THE ANTIDOTE	*Island*	52	*7 Mar 92*	4
THE QUIET REVOLUTION	*Island*	49	*9 Oct 93*	2
BAD BROTHERS *Mixes of Jordan's material by DJ Krush.* *Above hit: Ronny JORDAN Meets DJ KRUSH.*	*Island*	58	*3 Sep 94*	1

JORDANAIRES - See Elvis PRESLEY

JORIO — US

SINGLES:	HITS 1			WEEKS 1
REMEMBER ME	*Wonderboy*	54	*24 Feb 01*	1

David JOSEPH — UK

SINGLES:	HITS 4			WEEKS 21
YOU CAN'T HIDE (YOUR LOVE FROM ME)	*Island*	13	*26 Feb 83*	9
LET'S LIVE IT UP (NITE PEOPLE)	*Island*	26	*28 May 83*	5
JOYS OF LIFE	*Island*	61	*18 Feb 84*	2
EXPANSIONS '86 (EXPAND YOUR MIND)	*Fourth & Broadway*	58	*31 May 86*	5
Above hit: Chris PAUL featuring the voice of David JOSEPH.				

Dawn JOSEPH – See LOGO featuring Dawn JOSEPH

Martyn JOSEPH — UK

SINGLES:	HITS 4			WEEKS 10
DOLPHINS MAKE ME CRY	*Epic*	34	*20 Jun 92*	4
WORKING MOTHER	*Epic*	65	*12 Sep 92*	1
PLEASE SIR	*Epic*	45	*9 Jan 93*	3
TALK ABOUT IT IN THE MORNING	*Epic*	43	*3 Jun 95*	2

JOURNEY — US

SINGLES:	HITS 2			WEEKS 9
DON'T STOP BELIEVIN'	*CBS*	62	*27 Feb 82*	4
WHO'S CRYING NOW	*CBS*	46	*11 Sep 82*	5
ALBUMS:	**HITS 4**			**WEEKS 30**
ESCAPE	*CBS*	79	*20 Mar 82*	4
ESCAPE [RE]	*CBS*	32	*21 Aug 82*	12
FRONTIERS	*CBS*	6	*19 Feb 83*	8
EVOLUTION	*CBS*	100	*6 Aug 83*	1
Originally released in 1979.				
RAISED ON RADIO	*CBS*	22	*24 May 86*	5

JOY – See A VERY GOOD FRIEND OF MINE featuring JOY

Ruth JOY — UK

SINGLES:	HITS 3			WEEKS 4
DON'T PUSH IT	*MCA*	66	*26 Aug 89*	2
FEEL	*MCA*	67	*22 Feb 92*	1
WALKING ON SUNSHINE	*Network*	71	*14 Nov 92*	1
Above hit: KRUSH featuring Ruth JOY.				

JOY DIVISION — UK

SINGLES:	HITS 2			WEEKS 24
LOVE WILL TEAR US APART	*Factory*	13	*28 Jun 80*	9
LOVE WILL TEAR US APART [RE]	*Factory*	19	*29 Oct 83*	7
ATMOSPHERE	*Factory*	34	*18 Jun 88*	5
LOVE WILL TEAR US APART [RM]	*London*	19	*17 Jun 95*	3
Mixed by Don German.				
Above hit: JOY DIVISION 1995.				
ALBUMS:	**HITS 6**			**WEEKS 33**
CLOSER	*Factory*	6	*26 Jul 80*	8
UNKNOWN PLEASURES	*Factory*	71	*30 Aug 80*	1
First released in 1979.				
STILL	*Factory*	5	*17 Oct 81*	12
1977-1980 SUBSTANCE	*Factory*	7	*23 Jul 88*	8
PERMANENT: JOY DIVISION 1995	*London*	16	*1 Jul 95*	3
Released to coincide with Ian Curtis's biography, written by his widow.				
HEART AND SOUL	*London*	70	*7 Feb 98*	1
Re-issued 4CD box set, first released on 8 Dec 97.				

JOY STRINGS — UK

SINGLES:	HITS 2			WEEKS 11
IT'S AN OPEN SECRET	*Regal Zonophone*	32	*29 Feb 64*	7
A STARRY NIGHT	*Regal Zonophone*	35	*19 Dec 64*	4

Dale JOYNER – See XPANSIONS

JOYRIDER — UK

SINGLES:	HITS 2			WEEKS 4
RUSH HOUR	*Paradox*	22	*27 Jul 96*	3
ALL GONE AWAY	*A&M*	54	*28 Sep 96*	1

JT PLAYAZ — UK

SINGLES:	HITS 2			WEEKS 4
JUST PLAYIN'	*Pukka*	30	*5 Apr 97*	3
LET'S GET DOWN	*MCA*	64	*2 May 98*	1
Based around Kool And The Gang's Celebration.				

JTQ with Noel McKOY – See James TAYLOR QUARTET

JU JU HOUNDS – See Izzy STRADLIN'

JUDAS PRIEST — UK

SINGLES:	HITS 13			WEEKS 51
TAKE ON THE WORLD	*CBS*	14	*20 Jan 79*	10
EVENING STAR	*CBS*	53	*12 May 79*	4
LIVING AFTER MIDNIGHT	*CBS*	12	*29 Mar 80*	7
BREAKING THE LAW	*CBS*	12	*7 Jun 80*	6
UNITED	*CBS*	26	*23 Aug 80*	8
DON'T GO	*CBS*	51	*21 Feb 81*	3
HOT ROCKIN'	*CBS*	60	*25 Apr 81*	3
YOU'VE GOT ANOTHER THING COMIN'	*CBS*	66	*21 Aug 82*	2
FREEWHEEL BURNIN'	*CBS*	42	*21 Jan 84*	3
JOHNNY B. GOODE	*Atlantic*	64	*23 Apr 88*	2
PAIN KILLER	*CBS*	74	*15 Sep 90*	1
A TOUCH OF EVIL	*Columbia*	58	*23 Mar 91*	1
NIGHT CRAWLER	*Columbia*	63	*24 Apr 93*	1

ALBUMS:	HITS 13			WEEKS 78
SIN AFTER SIN	*CBS*	23	*14 May 77*	6
STAINED GLASS	*CBS*	27	*25 Feb 78*	5
KILLING MACHINE	*CBS*	32	*11 Nov 78*	9
UNLEASHED IN THE EAST	*CBS*	10	*6 Oct 79*	8
BRITISH STEEL	*CBS*	4	*19 Apr 80*	17
POINT OF ENTRY	*CBS*	14	*7 Mar 81*	5
SCREAMING FOR VENGEANCE	*CBS*	11	*17 Jul 82*	9
DEFENDERS OF THE FAITH	*CBS*	19	*28 Jan 84*	5
TURBO	*CBS*	33	*19 Apr 86*	4
PRIEST LIVE	*CBS*	47	*13 Jun 87*	2
Live recordings from their 1986 World tour.				
RAM IT DOWN	*CBS*	24	*28 May 88*	5
PAINKILLER	*CBS*	26	*29 Sep 90*	2
METAL WORKS 73 - 93	*Columbia*	37	*8 May 93*	1
Retrospective issued to commemorate their 20th anniversary.				

JUDGE DREAD — UK

SINGLES:	HITS 11			WEEKS 95
BIG SIX	*Big Shot*	11	*26 Aug 72*	27
BIG SEVEN	*Big Shot*	8	*9 Dec 72*	18
BIG EIGHT	*Big Shot*	14	*21 Apr 73*	10
JE T'AIME (MOI NON PLUS)	*Cactus*	9	*5 Jul 75*	9
BIG 10	*Cactus*	14	*27 Sep 75*	7
CHRISTMAS IN DREADLAND / COME OUTSIDE	*Cactus*	14	*6 Dec 75*	7
THE WINKLE MAN	*Cactus*	35	*8 May 76*	4
Y VIVA SUSPENDERS	*Cactus*	27	*28 Aug 76*	4
5TH ANNIVERSARY [EP]	*Cactus*	31	*2 Apr 77*	4
Lead track: Jamaica Jerk (Off).				
UP WITH THE COCK / BIG PUNK	*Cactus*	49	*14 Jan 78*	1
HOKEY COKEY / JINGLE BELLS	*EMI*	59	*16 Dec 78*	4

ALBUMS:	HITS 2			WEEKS 14
BEDTIME STORIES	*Cactus*	26	*6 Dec 75*	12
40 BIG ONES	*Creole*	51	*7 Mar 81*	2

JUICE — Denmark

SINGLES:	HITS 2			WEEKS 3
BEST DAYS	*Chrysalis*	28	*18 Apr 98*	2
I'LL COME RUNNIN'	*Chrysalis*	48	*22 Aug 98*	1

JUICY — US

SINGLES:	HITS 1			WEEKS 5
SUGAR FREE	*Epic*	45	*22 Feb 86*	5

JUICY LUCY — UK

SINGLES:	HITS 2			WEEKS 17
WHO DO YOU LOVE	*Vertigo*	14	*7 Mar 70*	12
PRETTY WOMAN	*Vertigo*	45	*10 Oct 70*	2
PRETTY WOMAN [RE]	*Vertigo*	44	*31 Oct 70*	3

ALBUMS:	HITS 2			WEEKS 5
JUICY LUCY	*Vertigo*	41	*18 Apr 70*	4
LIE BACK AND ENJOY IT	*Vertigo*	53	*21 Nov 70*	1

Thomas JULES-STOCK — UK

SINGLES:	HITS 1			WEEKS 1
DIDN'T I TELL YOU TRUE	*Mercury*	59	*15 Aug 98*	1

JULIA and COMPANY — US

SINGLES:	HITS 2			WEEKS 10
BREAKIN' DOWN (SUGAR SAMBA)	*London*	15	*3 Mar 84*	8
I'M SO HAPPY	*London*	56	*23 Feb 85*	2
Above hit: JULIA and CO.				

JULUKA — UK/South Africa

SINGLES:	HITS 1			WEEKS 4
SCATTERLINGS OF AFRICA	*Safari*	44	*12 Feb 83*	4
ALBUMS:	**HITS 1**			**WEEKS 3**
SCATTERLINGS	*Safari*	50	*23 Jul 83*	3

JUMP — UK

SINGLES:	HITS 1			WEEKS 1
FUNKATARIUM	*Heat Recordings*	56	*1 Mar 97*	1
Original release reached No. 156 in 1996.				

Wally JUMP JR. and the CRIMINAL ELEMENT — US

SINGLES:	HITS 5			WEEKS 19
TURN ME LOOSE	*London*	60	*28 Feb 87*	2
PUT THE NEEDLE TO THE RECORD	*Cooltempo*	63	*5 Sep 87*	3
Above hit: CRIMINAL ELEMENT ORCHESTRA.				
TIGHTEN UP/I JUST CAN'T STOP DANCIN'	*Breakout*	24	*12 Dec 87*	7
Above hit is one track.				
PRIVATE PARTY	*Breakout*	57	*19 Mar 88*	3
EVERYBODY (RAP)	*Deconstruction*	30	*6 Oct 90*	4
Based around Black Box's Everybody Everybody.				
Above hit: CRIMINAL ELEMENT ORCHESTRA featuring Wendell WILLIAMS.				

Rosemary JUNE — US

SINGLES:	HITS 1			WEEKS 9
"I'LL BE WITH YOU" IN APPLE BLOSSOM TIME	*Pye International*	14	*24 Jan 59*	9

JUNGLE BOOK DISNEY CAST — US

SINGLES:	HITS 1			WEEKS 8
THE JUNGLE BOOK GROOVE [M]	*Hollywood*	14	*8 May 93*	8

JUNGLE BROTHERS — US

(See also De La Soul.)

SINGLES:	HITS 10			WEEKS 35
I'LL HOUSE YOU	*Gee Street*	22	*22 Oct 88*	5
Above hit: Richie RICH Meets JUNGLE BROTHERS.				
BLACK IS BLACK / STRAIGHT OUT OF THE JUNGLE	*Gee Street*	72	*18 Mar 89*	1
WHAT "U" WAITIN' "4"?	*Eternal*	35	*31 Mar 90*	5
DOIN' OUR OWN DANG	*Eternal*	33	*21 Jul 90*	6
Above hit: JUNGLE BROTHERS featuring DE LA SOUL, Monie LOVE, TRIBE CALLED QUEST and QUEEN LATIFAH.				
BRAIN	*Gee Street*	52	*19 Jul 97*	1
JUNGLE BROTHER	*Gee Street*	56	*29 Nov 97*	1
JUNGLE BROTHER [RE]	*Gee Street*	18	*9 May 98*	4
I'LL HOUSE YOU '98 [RM]	*ffrr*	26	*11 Jul 98*	5
Remixed by The Hitmen.				
BECAUSE I GOT IT LIKE THAT	*Gee Street*	32	*28 Nov 98*	2
V.I.P.	*Gee Street*	33	*10 Jul 99*	3
Samples 'I Dream Of Jeanie'.				
GET DOWN	*Gee Street*	52	*6 Nov 99*	1
Vocal harmonies by Carol Gardenas. Samples Kool And The Gang's Get Down On It.				
FREAKIN' YOU	*Gee Street*	70	*25 Mar 00*	1
ALBUMS:	**HITS 1**			**WEEKS 3**
DONE BY THE FORCES OF NATURE	*Eternal*	41	*3 Feb 90*	3

JUNGLE HIGH with BLUE PEARL — UK/US

(See also Blue Pearl.)

SINGLES:	HITS 1			WEEKS 1
FIRE OF LOVE	*Logic*	71	*27 Nov 93*	1

JUNIOR — UK

SINGLES:	HITS 11			WEEKS 57
MAMA USED TO SAY	*Mercury*	7	*24 Apr 82*	13
Originally released in 1981.				
TOO LATE	*Mercury*	20	*10 Jul 82*	9
LET ME KNOW / I CAN'T HELP IT	*Mercury*	53	*25 Sep 82*	3

COMMUNICATION BREAKDOWN	*Mercury*	57	*23 Apr 83*	3
SOMEBODY	*London*	64	*8 Sep 84*	2
DO YOU REALLY (WANT MY LOVE)	*London*	47	*9 Feb 85*	4
OH LOUISE	*London*	74	*30 Nov 85*	3
ANOTHER STEP (CLOSER TO YOU)	*MCA*	6	*4 Apr 87*	11
Above hit: Kim WILDE and JUNIOR.				
STEP OFF	*MCA*	63	*25 Aug 90*	3
THEN CAME YOU	*MCA*	32	*15 Aug 92*	5
ALL OVER THE WORLD	*MCA*	74	*31 Oct 92*	1
Above 3: Junior GISCOMBE.				

ALBUMS:	**HITS 1**			**WEEKS 14**
JI	*Mercury*	28	*5 Jun 82*	14

JUNIOR JACK — Italy

SINGLES:	**HITS 1**			**WEEKS 4**
MY FEELING	*Defected*	31	*16 Dec 00*	4

Original release reached No. 79 in December 1999.

JUNIOR M.A.F.I.A. — US

SINGLES:	**HITS 2**			**WEEKS 2**
I NEED YOU TONIGHT	*Big Beat*	66	*3 Feb 96*	1
Above hit: JUNIOR M.A.F.I.A. featuring AALIYAH.				
GETTIN' MONEY (THE GET MONEY REMIX)	*Big Beat*	63	*19 Oct 96*	1

Rap by Notorious B.I.G. Sleeve shows title as Get Money (The Gettin' Money Remix).

JUNKIE XL — Holland

SINGLES:	**HITS 1**			**WEEKS 1**
ZEROTONINE	*Manifesto*	63	*22 Jul 00*	1

JUNO REACTOR — UK/Germany

SINGLES:	**HITS 1**			**WEEKS 1**
JUNGLE HIGH	*Perfecto*	45	*8 Feb 97*	1

Eric JUPP and his Orchestra - See Bille ANTHONY; Tony BRENT; Ray BURNS; CORONETS: Barbara LYON; Norman WISDOM

JURASSIC 5 — US

SINGLES:	**HITS 2**			**WEEKS 4**
JAYOU	*Pan*	56	*25 Jul 98*	1
CONCRETE SCHOOLYARD	*Pan*	35	*24 Oct 98*	3

ALBUMS:	**HITS 2**			**WEEKS 4**
JURASSIC 5	*Pan*	70	*13 Jun 98*	1
QUALITY CONTROL	*Interscope*	23	*1 Jul 00*	3

Christopher JUST — Austria

SINGLES:	**HITS 1**			**WEEKS 2**
I'M A DISCO DANCER (AND A SWEET ROMANCER)	*Slut Trax*	72	*13 Dec 97*	1
I'M A DISCO DANCER (AND A SWEET ROMANCER) [RM]	*XL Recordings*	69	*6 Feb 99*	1

This is the original Olav Basoski remix, recorded before the Fat Boy Slim remix charted in 1997.

JUST LUIS — Australia

SINGLES:	**HITS 1**			**WEEKS 3**
AMERICAN PIE	*Pro-activ*	31	*14 Oct 95*	2
AMERICAN PIE [RM]	*Pro-activ*	70	*17 Feb 96*	1

Remixed by Almighty Associates.

Jimmy JUSTICE — UK

SINGLES:	**HITS 3**			**WEEKS 35**
WHEN MY LITTLE GIRL IS SMILING	*Pye*	9	*31 Mar 62*	13
AIN'T THAT FUNNY	*Pye*	8	*16 Jun 62*	11
SPANISH HARLEM	*Pye*	20	*25 Aug 62*	11

JUSTIFIED ANCIENTS OF MU MU — UK

(See also KLF, Timelords, 2K.)

SINGLES:	**HITS 1**			**WEEKS 6**
IT'S GRIM UP NORTH	*KLF Commuications*	10	*9 Nov 91*	5
IT'S GRIM UP NORTH [RE]	*KLF Commuications*	67	*4 Jan 92*	1

JUSTIN — UK

SINGLES:	**HITS 4**			**WEEKS 13**
THIS BOY	*Streamline*	34	*22 Aug 98*	2
OVER YOU	*Streamline*	11	*16 Jan 99*	4
IT'S ALL ABOUT YOU	*Streamline*	34	*17 Jul 99*	3

LET IT BE ME *French version by Gilbert Becaud in 1955 & first recorded in English by Jill Corey in 1957.*	*Innocent*	15	*22 Jan 00*	4

Bill JUSTIS — US

SINGLES:	HITS 1			WEEKS 8
RAUNCHY	*London*	24	*11 Jan 58*	2
RAUNCHY [RE]	*London*	11	*1 Feb 58*	6

Patrick JUVET — France

SINGLES:	HITS 2			WEEKS 19
GOT A FEELING	*Casablanca*	34	*2 Sep 78*	7
I LOVE AMERICA	*Casablanca*	12	*4 Nov 78*	12

JX — UK

SINGLES:	HITS 4			WEEKS 33
SON OF A GUN	*Internal Dance*	13	*2 Apr 94*	6
YOU BELONG TO ME	*Ffrreedom*	17	*1 Apr 95*	5
SON OF A GUN [RI]	*Ffrreedom*	6	*19 Aug 95*	6
THERE'S NOTHING I WON'T DO *Vocals by Karlina.*	*Ffrreedom*	4	*18 May 96*	13
CLOSE TO YOUR HEART	*Ffrreedom*	18	*8 Mar 97*	3

K

Frank 'K' (featuring Wiston OFFICE) — US/Italy

SINGLES:	HITS 1			WEEKS 1
EVERYBODY LET'S SOMEBODY LOVE	*Urban*	61	*26 Jan 91*	1

Leila K — Sweden

SINGLES:	HITS 4			WEEKS 22
GOT TO GET *Above hit: ROB 'N' RAZ featuring Leila K.*	*Arista*	8	*25 Nov 89*	14
ROK THE NATION *Above hit: ROB 'N' RAZ with Leila K.*	*Arista*	41	*17 Mar 90*	3
OPEN SESAME	*Polydor*	23	*23 Jan 93*	4
CA PLANE POUR MOI	*Polydor*	69	*3 Jul 93*	1

K-CI – See Will SMITH

K-CI and JOJO — US

SINGLES:	HITS 6			WEEKS 29
HOW DO YOU WANT IT *Above hit: 2PAC (featuring KC and JOJO).*	*Death Row*	17	*27 Jul 96*	4
YOU BRING ME UP	*MCA*	21	*23 Aug 97*	2
ALL MY LIFE	*MCA*	8	*18 Apr 98*	11
DON'T RUSH (TAKE LOVE SLOWLY)	*MCA*	16	*19 Sep 98*	3
TELL ME IT'S REAL	*MCA*	40	*2 Oct 99*	2
TELL ME IT'S REAL [RM] *Remixed by Club Asylum.*	*AM:PM*	16	*23 Sep 00*	5
CRAZY	*MCA*	35	*12 May 01*	2
ALBUMS:	**HITS 2**			**WEEKS 3**
LOVE ALWAYS *This entry was based on import sales.*	*MCA*	64	*28 Jun 97*	1
LOVE ALWAYS [RE]	*MCA*	51	*9 May 98*	1
IT'S REAL	*MCA*	56	*3 Jul 99*	1

K-CREATIVE — UK

SINGLES:	HITS 1			WEEKS 2
THREE TIMES A MAYBE *[AA] listed with Feed The Feeling by Perception.*	*Talkin Loud*	58	*7 Mar 92*	2

Ernie K-DOE — US

SINGLES:	HITS 1			WEEKS 7
MOTHER-IN-LAW *Guest bass vocal by Benny Spellman.*	*London*	29	*13 May 61*	7

K-GEE — US

SINGLES:	HITS 1			WEEKS 3
I DON'T REALLY CARE	*Instant Karma*	22	*4 Nov 00*	3

K.I.D. — Antilles

SINGLES:	HITS 1			WEEKS 4
DON'T STOP	*EMI*	49	*28 Feb 81*	4

K-KLASS — UK

SINGLES:	HITS 6			WEEKS 31
RHYTHM IS A MYSTERY	*Creed*	61	*4 May 91*	2
Vocals by Bobby Depasois.				
RHYTHM IS A MYSTERY [RI]	*Deconstruction*	3	*9 Nov 91*	10
SO RIGHT	*Deconstruction*	20	*25 Apr 92*	5
DON'T STOP	*Deconstruction*	32	*7 Nov 92*	3
LET ME SHOW YOU	*Deconstruction*	13	*27 Nov 93*	7
WHAT YOU'RE MISSING	*Deconstruction*	24	*28 May 94*	3
BURNIN'	*Parlophone*	45	*1 Aug 98*	1
Vocals by Rachel McFarlane.				
ALBUMS:	**HITS 1**			**WEEKS 1**
UNIVERSAL	*Deconstruction*	73	*4 Jun 94*	1

K.P. and ENVYI — US

SINGLES:	HITS 1			WEEKS 4
SWING MY WAY	*East West America*	14	*13 Jun 98*	4

K.W.S. — UK

SINGLES:	HITS 7			WEEKS 37
PLEASE DON'T GO / GAME BOY	*Network*	1	*25 Apr 92*	16
Game Boy listed from 9 May 92.				
ROCK YOUR BABY / TOTAL STATE OF KONFUSION	*Network*	8	*22 Aug 92*	7
Total State Of Konfusion only listed for the week of 29 Aug 92.				
HOLD BACK THE NIGHT	*Network*	30	*12 Dec 92*	6
Above hit: KWS features guest vocals from the TRAMMPS.				
CAN'T GET ENOUGH OF YOUR LOVE	*Network*	71	*5 Jun 93*	1
IT SEEMS TO HANG ON	*X-Clusive*	58	*9 Apr 94*	1
Above 2: KWS.				
AIN'T NOBODY (LOVES ME BETTER)	*X-Clusive*	21	*2 Jul 94*	4
Sleeve reflects artist credits in reverse.				
Above hit: Gwen DICKEY and K.W.S.				
THE MORE I GET, THE MORE I WANT	*X-Clusive*	35	*19 Nov 94*	2
Originally recorded by Teddy Pendergrass when he was with Harold Melvin and the Blluenotes.				
Above hit: KWS featuring Teddy PENDERGRASS.				

KACI — US

SINGLES:	HITS 2			WEEKS 12
PARADISE	*Curb*	11	*10 Mar 01*	9
TU AMOR	*Curb*	24	*28 Jul 01*	3
Originally recorded by Nadine Renee.				

Joshua KADISON — US

SINGLES:	HITS 3			WEEKS 19
JESSIE	*SBK*	69	*26 Feb 94*	2
JESSIE [RE]	*SBK*	48	*1 Oct 94*	3
BEAUTIFUL IN MY EYES	*SBK*	65	*12 Nov 94*	1
JESSIE [RI]	*SBK*	15	*29 Apr 95*	10
Edited version to the original release.				
BEAUTIFUL IN MY EYES [RI]	*SBK*	37	*12 Aug 95*	3
ALBUMS:	**HITS 1**			**WEEKS 4**
PAINTED DESERT SERENADE	*SBK*	45	*27 May 95*	4

KADOC — Spain

SINGLES:	HITS 3			WEEKS 11
THE NIGHTRAIN	*Positiva*	14	*6 Apr 96*	8
Import reached No. 186 before its UK release. Originally recorded by Jimmy Forest.				
YOU GOT TO BE THERE	*Positiva*	45	*17 Aug 96*	1
ROCK THE BELLS	*Manifesto*	34	*23 Aug 97*	2

Bert KAEMPFERT and his Orchestra — Germany

SINGLES:	HITS 1			WEEKS 10
BYE BYE BLUES	*Polydor*	24	*25 Dec 65*	10
Originally recorded by Bert Lown's Orchestra in 1930.				
ALBUMS:	**HITS 10**			**WEEKS 104**
BYE BYE BLUES	*Polydor*	4	*5 Mar 66*	22
BEST OF BERT KAEMPFERT	*Polydor*	27	*16 Apr 66*	1
SWINGING SAFARI	*Polydor*	20	*28 May 66*	15
STRANGERS IN THE NIGHT	*Polydor*	13	*30 Jul 66*	26

RELAXING SOUND OF BERT KAEMPFERT	*Polydor*	33	*4 Feb 67*	3
BERT KAEMPFERT - BEST SELLER	*Polydor*	25	*18 Feb 67*	18
HOLD ME	*Polydor*	36	*29 Apr 67*	5
KAEMPFERT SPECIAL	*Polydor*	24	*26 Aug 67*	5
ORANGE COLOURED SKY	*Polydor*	49	*19 Jun 71*	1
SOUNDS SENSATIONAL	*Polydor*	17	*5 Jul 80*	8

KAISH - See OXIDE and NEUTRINO

KAJAGOOGOO — UK

SINGLES:	HITS 7			WEEKS 50
TOO SHY *Co-produced by Nick Rhodes of Duran Duran.*	*EMI*	1	*22 Jan 83*	13
OOH TO BE AH	*EMI*	7	*2 Apr 83*	8
HANG ON NOW	*EMI*	13	*4 Jun 83*	7
BIG APPLE	*EMI*	8	*17 Sep 83*	8
THE LION'S MOUTH	*EMI*	25	*3 Mar 84*	7
TURN YOUR BACK ON ME	*EMI*	47	*5 May 84*	4
SHOULDN'T DO THAT *Above hit: KAJA.*	*Parlophone*	63	*21 Sep 85*	3
ALBUMS:	**HITS 2**			**WEEKS 23**
WHITE FEATHERS	*EMI*	5	*30 Apr 83*	20
ISLANDS	*EMI*	35	*2 Jun 84*	3

KALEEF — UK

SINGLES:	HITS 5			WEEKS 12
WALK LIKE A CHAMPION *Above hit: KALIPHZ featuring PRINCE NASEEM.*	*Payday*	23	*30 Mar 96*	3
GOLDEN BROWN	*Unity*	22	*7 Dec 96*	4
TRIALS OF LIFE *Samples Brass In Pocket by the Pretenders. Charity record with proceeds donated to Manchester Drug Agency.*	*Unity*	75	*14 Jun 97*	1
I LIKE THE WAY (THE KISSING GAME)	*Unity*	58	*11 Oct 97*	1
SANDS OF TIME *Samples Clannad's Theme From Harry's Game.*	*Unity*	26	*24 Jan 98*	3

KALIN TWINS — US

SINGLES:	HITS 1			WEEKS 18
WHEN *Co-written by Paul Evans.*	*Brunswick*	1	*19 Jul 58*	18

KALIPHZ featuring PRINCE NASEEM - See KALEEF

KALLAGHAN - See N 'N' G featuring KALLAGHAN

Kitty KALLEN — US

SINGLES:	HITS 1			WEEKS 23
LITTLE THINGS MEAN A LOT	*Brunswick*	1	*3 Jul 54*	23

Gunter KALLMAN CHOIR — Germany

SINGLES:	HITS 1			WEEKS 3
ELISABETH SERENADE	*Polydor*	45	*26 Dec 64*	3

KAMASULTRA featuring Jocelyn BROWN — Italy

(See also Jocelyn Brown.)

SINGLES:	HITS 1			WEEKS 1
HAPPINESS	*S3*	45	*22 Nov 97*	1

Michael KAMEN - See Eric CLAPTON; VARIOUS ARTISTS: FILMS - ORIGINAL SOUNDTRACKS 'Robin Hood: Prince Of Thieves'

Nick KAMEN — UK

SINGLES:	HITS 5			WEEKS 33
EACH TIME YOU BREAK MY HEART *Co-written and produced by Madonna.*	*WEA*	5	*8 Nov 86*	12
LOVING YOU IS SWEETER THAN EVER	*WEA*	16	*28 Feb 87*	9
NOBODY ELSE	*WEA*	47	*16 May 87*	3
TELL ME	*WEA*	40	*28 May 88*	5
I PROMISED MYSELF	*WEA*	50	*28 Apr 90*	4
ALBUMS:	**HITS 1**			**WEEKS 7**
NICK KAMEN	*WEA*	34	*18 Apr 87*	7

Ini KAMOZE — Jamaica

(See also Jamaica United.)

SINGLES:	HITS 1			WEEKS 15
HERE COMES THE HOTSTEPPER *From the film 'Pret-A-Porter'.*	*Columbia*	4	*7 Jun 95*	15

KANDI — US

SINGLES:	HITS 1			WEEKS 10
DON'T THINK I'M NOT	*Columbia*	9	*11 Nov 00*	10

KANDIDATE — UK

SINGLES:	HITS 4			WEEKS 28
DON'T WANNA SAY GOODNIGHT	*RAK*	47	*19 Aug 78*	6
I DON'T WANNA LOSE YOU	*RAK*	11	*17 Mar 79*	12
GIRLS GIRLS GIRLS	*RAK*	34	*4 Aug 79*	7
LET ME ROCK YOU	*RAK*	58	*22 Mar 80*	3

KANE – See NALIN and KANE

Eden KANE — UK

SINGLES:	HITS 5			WEEKS 73
WELL I ASK YOU	*Decca*	1	*3 Jun 61*	21
GET LOST	*Decca*	10	*16 Sep 61*	11
FORGET ME NOT	*Decca*	3	*20 Jan 62*	14
I DON'T KNOW WHY	*Decca*	7	*12 May 62*	13
BOYS CRY	*Fontana*	8	*1 Feb 64*	14
EPS:	**HITS 1**			**WEEKS 8**
HITS	*Decca*	12	*29 Sep 62*	8

KANE GANG — UK

SINGLES:	HITS 6			WEEKS 37
SMALL TOWN CREED	*Kitchenware*	60	*19 May 84*	2
CLOSEST THING TO HEAVEN	*Kitchenware*	12	*7 Jul 84*	11
RESPECT YOURSELF	*Kitchenware*	21	*10 Nov 84*	10
RESPECT YOURSELF [RE]	*Kitchenware*	75	*26 Jan 85*	1
GUN LAW	*Kitchenware*	53	*9 Mar 85*	4
MOTORTOWN	*Kitchenware*	45	*27 Jun 87*	5
DON'T LOOK ANY FURTHER	*Kitchenware*	52	*16 Apr 88*	4
ALBUMS:	**HITS 2**			**WEEKS 12**
THE BAD AND LOWDOWN WORLD OF THE KANE GANG	*Kitchenware*	21	*23 Feb 85*	8
MIRACLE	*Kitchenware*	41	*8 Aug 87*	1

KANSAS — US

SINGLES:	HITS 1			WEEKS 7
CARRY ON WAYWARD SON	*Kirshner*	51	*1 Jul 78*	7

Mory KANTE — Guinea

SINGLES:	HITS 1			WEEKS 14
YE KE YE KE	*London*	29	*23 Jul 88*	9
YEKE YEKE [RM-1ST] *Remixed by Martin Young.*	*Ffrreedom*	25	*11 Mar 95*	3
YEKE YEKE - 96 REMIXES [RM-2ND] *Remixed by Hardfloor.*	*ffrr*	28	*30 Nov 96*	2

KAOMA — France

SINGLES:	HITS 2			WEEKS 20
LAMBADA	*CBS*	4	*21 Oct 89*	18
DANCANDO LAMBADA	*CBS*	62	*27 Jan 90*	2

KAOTIC CHEMISTRY — UK

SINGLES:	HITS 1			WEEKS 1
L.S.D. [EP] *Lead track: Space Cakes.*	*Moving Shadow*	68	*31 Oct 92*	1

KARIN – See UNIQUE 3

KARIYA — US

SINGLES:	HITS 1			WEEKS 9
LET ME LOVE YOU FOR TONIGHT	*Sleeping Bag*	44	*8 Jul 89*	6
LET ME LOVE YOU FOR TONIGHT [RE]	*Sleeping Bag*	57	*21 Oct 89*	3

Mick KARN — UK

SINGLES:	HITS 2			WEEKS 6
AFTER A FASHION *Above hit: Midge URE and Mick KARN.*	*Musicfest*	39	*9 Jul 83*	4
BUOY *Above hit: Mick KARN featuring David SYLVIAN.*	*Virgin*	63	*17 Jan 87*	2
ALBUMS:	**HITS 2**			**WEEKS 4**
TITLES	*Virgin*	74	*20 Nov 82*	3
DREAMS OF REASON PRODUCE MONSTERS	*Virgin*	89	*28 Feb 87*	1

KARTOON KREW — US

SINGLES:	HITS 1			WEEKS 6
INSPECTOR GADGET	*Champion*	58	*7 Dec 85*	6

KASENETZ-KATZ SINGING ORCHESTRAL CIRCUS — US

SINGLES:	HITS 1			WEEKS 15
QUICK JOEY SMALL (RUN JOEY RUN) *Lead vocals by Joey Levine.*	*Buddah*	19	*23 Nov 68*	15

KATCHA — UK

SINGLES:	HITS 1			WEEKS 1
TOUCHED BY GOD	*Hooj Choons*	57	*21 Aug 99*	1

KATRINA and the WAVES — US/UK

SINGLES:	HITS 3			WEEKS 34
WALKING ON SUNSHINE	*Capitol*	8	*4 May 85*	12
SUN STREET	*Capitol*	22	*5 Jul 86*	9
WALKING ON SUNSHINE [RI] *Used by GMTV for their Get Up And Give appeal.*	*EMI Premier*	53	*8 Jun 96*	1
LOVE SHINE A LIGHT *UK's Eurovision entry in 1997. It came 1st.*	*Eternal*	3	*10 May 97*	12
ALBUMS:	**HITS 2**			**WEEKS 7**
KATRINA AND THE WAVES	*Capitol*	28	*8 Jun 85*	6
WAVES	*Capitol*	70	*10 May 86*	1

KAVANA — UK

SINGLES:	HITS 8			WEEKS 26
CRAZY CHANCE *Co-written by Howard Donald of Take That.*	*Nemesis*	35	*11 May 96*	3
WHERE ARE YOU	*Nemesis*	26	*24 Aug 96*	2
I CAN MAKE YOU FEEL GOOD	*Nemesis*	8	*11 Jan 97*	5
MFEO *Acronym of Made For Each Other.*	*Nemesis*	8	*19 Apr 97*	4
CRAZY CHANCE 97 [RR]	*Nemesis*	16	*13 Sep 97*	3
SPECIAL KIND OF SOMETHING	*Virgin*	13	*29 Aug 98*	4
FUNKY LOVE	*Virgin/Sam*	32	*12 Dec 98*	2
FUNKY LOVE [RE]	*Virgin*	73	*9 Jan 99*	1
WILL YOU WAIT FOR ME	*Virgin*	29	*20 Mar 99*	2
ALBUMS:	**HITS 1**			**WEEKS 2**
KAVANA	*Nemesis*	29	*10 May 97*	2

Niamh KAVANAGH — Ireland

SINGLES:	HITS 1			WEEKS 5
IN YOUR EYES *Eurovision Song Contest winner in 1993.*	*Arista*	24	*12 Jun 93*	5

KAWALA — UK

SINGLES:	HITS 1			WEEKS 1
HUMANISTIC *Samples Simple Minds' New Gold Dream.*	*Pepper*	68	*26 Feb 00*	1

Janet KAY — UK

SINGLES:	HITS 2			WEEKS 24
SILLY GAMES	*Scope*	2	*9 Jun 79*	14
SILLY GAMES [RR] *Above hit: Lindy LAYTON featuring Janet KAY.*	*Arista*	22	*11 Aug 90*	7
SILLY GAMES (THE MUSIC FACTORY REMIX) [RM]	*Music Factory Dance*	62	*11 Aug 90*	3

Danny KAYE with Gordon JENKINS and his Chorus and Orchestra — US

(See also Various Artists: Films – Original Soundtracks 'The Five Pennies'.)

SINGLES:	HITS 1			WEEKS 10
WONDERFUL COPENHAGEN *From the film 'Hans Christian Andersen'.*	*Brunswick*	5	*28 Feb 53*	10

Gordon KAYE – See RENE and YVETTE featuring Gordon KAYE and Vicki MICHELLE

KAYE SISTERS — UK

SINGLES:	HITS 5			WEEKS 45
IVORY TOWER *Originally recorded by Cathy Carr.* *Above hit: THREE KAYES.*	*His Master's Voice*	20	*26 May 56*	5
GOT-TA HAVE SOMETHING IN THE BANK, FRANK *Originally recorded by Bob Jaxon.* *Above hit: Frankie VAUGHAN and the KAYE SISTERS with Wally STOTT and his Orchestra.*	*Philips*	8	*2 Nov 57*	11
SHAKE ME I RATTLE / ALONE *Above hit: KAYE SISTERS with Wally STOTT and his Orchestra.*	*Philips*	27	*4 Jan 58*	1
COME SOFTLY TO ME *Above hit: Frankie VAUGHAN and the KAYE SISTERS with Wally STOTT and his Orchestra.*	*Philips*	9	*2 May 59*	9
PAPER ROSES *Originally recorded by Lola Dee.*	*Philips*	7	*9 Jul 60*	19

KAYESTONE — UK

SINGLES:	HITS 1			WEEKS 1
ATMOSPHERE *Original release reached No. 200 on 13 Mar 99.*	*Distinct'ive*	55	*29 Jul 00*	1

KC and the SUNSHINE BAND — US

SINGLES:	HITS 13			WEEKS 104
QUEEN OF CLUBS	*Jay Boy*	7	*17 Aug 74*	12
SOUND YOUR FUNKY HORN	*Jay Boy*	17	*23 Nov 74*	9
GET DOWN TONIGHT	*Jay Boy*	21	*29 Mar 75*	9
THAT'S THE WAY (I LIKE IT)	*Jay Boy*	4	*2 Aug 75*	10
I'M SO CRAZY (BOUT YOU)	*Jay Boy*	34	*22 Nov 75*	3
(SHAKE, SHAKE, SHAKE) SHAKE YOUR BOOTY	*Jay Boy*	22	*17 Jul 76*	8
KEEP IT COMIN' LOVE	*Jay Boy*	31	*11 Dec 76*	8
I'M YOUR BOOGIE MAN	*TK*	41	*30 Apr 77*	4
BOOGIE SHOES *From the film 'Saturday Night Fever'. Originally was the B-side of I'm So Crazy (Bout You).*	*TK*	34	*6 May 78*	5
IT'S THE SAME OLD SONG	*TK*	47	*22 Jul 78*	5
PLEASE DON'T GO	*TK*	3	*8 Dec 79*	12
GIVE IT UP	*Epic*	1	*16 Jul 83*	14
(YOU SAID) YOU'D GIMME SOME MORE	*Epic*	41	*24 Sep 83*	3
THAT'S THE WAY (I LIKE IT) [RM]	*Music Factory Dance*	59	*11 May 91*	2
ALBUMS:	**HITS 3**			**WEEKS 17**
K.C. AND THE SUNSHINE BAND	*Jay Boy*	26	*30 Aug 75*	7
GREATEST HITS	*TK*	10	*1 Mar 80*	6
ALL IN A NIGHT'S WORK	*Epic*	46	*27 Aug 83*	4

KE — US

SINGLES:	HITS 1			WEEKS 1
STRANGE WORLD	*Venture*	73	*13 Apr 96*	1

Johnny KEATING — UK

(See also Adam Faith; Emile Ford and the Checkmates.)

SINGLES:	HITS 1			WEEKS 14
THEME FROM Z-CARS (JOHNNY TODD) *Theme from the BBC TV series.*	*Piccadilly*	8	*3 Mar 62*	14

Ronan KEATING — Ireland

SINGLES:	HITS 4			WEEKS 57
WHEN YOU SAY NOTHING AT ALL *From the film 'Notting Hill'. Originally recorded by Keith Whitley in 1987.*	*Polydor*	1	*7 Aug 99*	15
WHEN YOU SAY NOTHING AT ALL [RE-1ST]	*Polydor*	75	*27 Nov 99*	1
WHEN YOU SAY NOTHING AT ALL [RE-2ND]	*Polydor*	66	*1 Jan 00*	1
LIFE IS A ROLLERCOASTER	*Polydor*	1	*22 Jul 00*	14
THE WAY YOU MAKE ME FEEL *Written by Bryan Adams, who also provides backing vocals and guitar.*	*Polydor*	6	*2 Dec 00*	11
THE WAY YOU MAKE ME FEEL [RE]	*Polydor*	71	*10 Mar 01*	1
LOVIN' EACH DAY	*Polydor*	2	*28 Apr 01*	14

ALBUMS:	HITS 1			WEEKS 48
RONAN	*Polydor*	1	*12 Aug 00*	33
RONAN [RE]	*Polydor*	6	*21 Aug 01*	15
Repackaged with additional track.				

KEE – See BM DUBS presents MR RUMBLE featuring BRASSTOOTH and KEE

Kevin KEEGAN — UK

SINGLES:	HITS 1			WEEKS 6
HEAD OVER HEELS IN LOVE	*EMI*	31	*9 Jun 79*	6

KEEL — US

ALBUMS:	HITS 1			WEEKS 2
THE FINAL FRONTIER	*Vertigo*	83	*17 May 86*	2

Howard KEEL — US

ALBUMS:	HITS 3			WEEKS 36
AND I LOVE YOU SO	*Warwick*	6	*14 Apr 84*	19
REMINISCING - THE HOWARD KEEL COLLECTION	*Telstar*	20	*9 Nov 85*	12
JUST FOR YOU	*Telstar*	51	*26 Mar 88*	5

Yvonne KEELY – See Scott FITZGERALD

Nelson KEENE — UK

SINGLES:	HITS 1			WEEKS 5
IMAGE OF A GIRL	*His Master's Voice*	37	*27 Aug 60*	4
IMAGE OF A GIRL [RE]	*His Master's Voice*	45	*1 Oct 60*	1

KEITH — US

SINGLES:	HITS 2			WEEKS 8
98.6	*Mercury*	24	*28 Jan 67*	7
Backing vocals by the Tokens.				
TELL ME TO MY FACE	*Mercury*	50	*18 Mar 67*	1
Originally recorded by the Hollies.				

KEITH 'N' SHANE — Ireland

SINGLES:	HITS 1			WEEKS 3
GIRL YOU KNOW IT'S TRUE	*Polydor*	36	*23 Dec 00*	3
Originally recorded by Numarx. Samples Belouis Some's Imagination.				

KELIS — US

SINGLES:	HITS 6			WEEKS 34
CAUGHT OUT THERE	*Virgin*	52	*26 Feb 00*	1
Import.				
CAUGHT OUT THERE	*Virgin*	4	*4 Mar 00*	10
CAUGHT OUT THERE [RE]	*Virgin*	64	*20 May 00*	2
GOOD STUFF	*Virgin*	19	*17 Jun 00*	5
Terrar only credited on inlay.				
Above hit: KELIS featuring TERRAR.				
GOT YOUR MONEY	*Elektra*	11	*8 Jul 00*	8
Above hit: OL' DIRTY BASTARD featuring KELIS.				
GET ALONG WITH YOU	*Virgin*	51	*21 Oct 00*	1
HONEY	*Mute*	17	*28 Oct 00*	5
Remixed by Fafue with new vocals by Kelis. Listed with its flip side Why Does My Heart Feel So Bad by Moby.				
Above hit: MOBY (featuring KELIS).				
YOUNG FRESH N' NEW	*Virgin*	32	*3 Nov 01*	2

ALBUMS:	HITS 1			WEEKS 13
KALEIDOSCOPE	*Virgin*	43	*11 Mar 00*	13

Jerry KELLER — US

SINGLES:	HITS 1			WEEKS 14
HERE COMES SUMMER	*London*	1	*29 Aug 59*	14

Ramona KELLER – See Cevin FISHER

Frank KELLY — Ireland

SINGLES:	HITS 1			WEEKS 5
CHRISTMAS COUNTDOWN	*Ritz*	26	*24 Dec 83*	4
CHRISTMAS COUNTDOWN [RE]	*Ritz*	54	*29 Dec 84*	1

Frankie KELLY — US

SINGLES:	HITS 1			WEEKS 2
AIN'T THAT THE TRUTH	*10 Records*	65	*2 Nov 85*	2

Grace KELLY – See Bing CROSBY; VARIOUS ARTISTS: FILMS – ORIGINAL SOUNDTRACKS 'High Society'.

Janis KELLY – See Barrington PHELOUNG

Keith KELLY — UK

SINGLES:	HITS 2			WEEKS 5
(MUST YOU ALWAYS) TEASE ME	*Parlophone*	46	*7 May 60*	1
(MUST YOU ALWAYS) TEASE ME [RE]	*Parlophone*	27	*21 May 60*	3
LISTEN LITTLE GIRL	*Parlophone*	47	*20 Aug 60*	1

R. KELLY — US

SINGLES:	HITS 22			WEEKS 153
SHE'S GOT THAT VIBE	*Jive*	57	*9 May 92*	2
SEX ME	*Jive*	75	*20 Nov 93*	1
Above 2: R. KELLY and PUBLIC ANNOUNCEMENT.				
YOUR BODY'S CALLIN'	*Jive*	19	*14 May 94*	4
SUMMER BUNNIES	*Jive*	23	*3 Sep 94*	3
Samples Outstanding by the Gap Band.				
SHE'S GOT THAT VIBE [RI]	*Jive*	3	*22 Oct 94*	13
BUMP N' GRIND	*Jive*	8	*21 Jan 95*	9
Originally reached No. 79 in 1994.				
THE 4 PLAY [EP]	*Jive*	23	*6 May 95*	3
Lead track: Your Body's Callin'. This is a re-issue.				
YOU REMIND ME OF SOMETHING	*Jive*	24	*11 Nov 95*	3
DOWN LOW (NOBODY HAS TO KNOW) THE MOVIE	*Jive*	23	*2 Mar 96*	3
From the film 'Down Low'.				
Above hit: R. KELLY featuring Ronald ISLEY.				
THANK GOD IT'S FRIDAY	*Jive*	14	*22 Jun 96*	4
I BELIEVE I CAN FLY	*Jive*	1	*29 Mar 97*	17
GOTHAM CITY	*Jive*	9	*19 Jul 97*	8
From the film 'Batman And Robin'.				
BE CAREFUL	*Jive*	7	*18 Jul 98*	6
Above hit: SPARKLE featuring R. KELLY.				
BE CAREFUL [RE]	*Jive*	75	*5 Sep 98*	1
HALF ON A BABY	*Jive*	16	*26 Sep 98*	4
HOME ALONE	*Jive*	17	*14 Nov 98*	5
Above hit: R. KELLY featuring Keith MURRAY.				
I'M YOUR ANGEL	*Epic*	3	*28 Nov 98*	13
Above hit: Celine DION and R. KELLY.				
DID YOU EVER THINK	*Jive*	20	*31 Jul 99*	5
Samples Curtis Mayfield's Right On For The Darkness.				
Above hit: R. KELLY featuring NAS.				
IF I COULD TURN BACK THE HANDS OF TIME	*Jive*	57	*16 Oct 99*	2
Import. Background vocals Sparkle and Bruce Kelly (R. Kelly's brother). Tribute to Kelly's mother.				
IF I COULD TURN BACK THE HANDS OF TIME	*Jive*	2	*30 Oct 99*	19
SATISFY YOU	*Bad Boy*	13	*19 Feb 00*	1
Import.				
Above hit: PUFF DADDY featuring R. KELLY.				
SATISFY YOU [RE]	*Bad Boy*	73	*4 Mar 00*	1
SATISFY YOU	*Puff Daddy*	8	*11 Mar 00*	8
Samples I Got 5 On It by Luniz and Club Nouveau's Why You Treat Me So Bad.				
Above hit: PUFF DADDY (featuring R. KELLY).				
ONLY THE LOOT CAN MAKE ME HAPPY/ WHEN A WOMAN'S FED UP/I CAN'T SLEEP BABY (IF I)	*Jive*	24	*22 Apr 00*	3
I WISH	*Jive*	12	*21 Oct 00*	6
THE STORM IS OVER NOW	*Jive*	18	*31 Mar 01*	6
FIESTA	*Jive*	23	*23 Jun 01*	3
Above hit: R. KELLY featuring JAY-Z and BOO and GOTI.				

ALBUMS:	HITS 5			WEEKS 84
BORN INTO THE 90'S	*Jive*	67	*29 Feb 92*	1
Above hit: R. KELLY and PUBLIC ANNOUNCEMENT.				
12 PLAY	*Jive*	39	*27 Nov 93*	26
Peak position reached in 1994, (1993 peak No. 69).				
12 PLAY [RE]	*Jive*	20	*14 Jan 95*	18
R. KELLY	*Jive*	18	*25 Nov 95*	10
R.	*Jive*	27	*21 Nov 98*	26
TP-2.COM	*Jive*	21	*18 Nov 00*	3

Roberta KELLY — US

SINGLES:	HITS 1			WEEKS 3
ZODIACS	*Oasis*	48	*21 Jan 78*	1
ZODIACS [RE]	*Oasis*	44	*4 Feb 78*	2

KELLY FAMILY — Ireland

SINGLES:	HITS 1			WEEKS 1
AN ANGEL	*EMI*	69	*21 Oct 95*	1

Johnny KEMP — Barbados

SINGLES:	HITS 1			WEEKS 1
JUST GOT PAID	*CBS*	68	*27 Aug 88*	1

Tara KEMP — US

SINGLES:	HITS 1			WEEKS 2
HOLD YOU TIGHT	*Giant*	69	*20 Apr 91*	2

Felicity KENDAL — UK

ALBUMS:	HITS 1			WEEKS 47
SHAPE UP AND DANCE WITH FELICITY KENDAL (VOLUME ONE)	*Lifestyle*	53	*19 Jun 82*	14
SHAPE UP AND DANCE WITH FELICITY KENDAL (VOLUME ONE) [RE]	*Lifestyle*	29	*22 Jan 83*	33

Graham KENDRICK — UK

SINGLES:	HITS 1			WEEKS 4
LET THE FLAME BURN BRIGHTER	*Power*	55	*9 Sep 89*	4

Eddie KENDRICKS — US

SINGLES:	HITS 2			WEEKS 18
KEEP ON TRUCKIN'	*Tamla Motown*	18	*3 Nov 73*	14
BOOGIE DOWN	*Tamla Motown*	39	*16 Mar 74*	4

KENICKIE — UK

SINGLES:	HITS 6			WEEKS 13
PUNKA	*Emidisc*	43	*14 Sep 96*	2
MILLIONAIRE SWEEPER	*Emidisc*	60	*16 Nov 96*	1
IN YOUR CAR	*Emidisc*	24	*11 Jan 97*	3
NIGHTLIFE	*Emidisc*	27	*3 May 97*	2
PUNKA [RI]	*Emidisc*	38	*5 Jul 97*	2
I WOULD FIX YOU	*EMI*	36	*6 Jun 98*	2
STAY IN THE SUN	*EMI*	43	*22 Aug 98*	1
ALBUMS:	**HITS 2**			**WEEKS 5**
AT THE CLUB	*Emidisc*	9	*24 May 97*	3
GET IN	*EMI*	32	*12 Sep 98*	2

Jane KENNAWAY and STRANGE BEHAVIOUR — UK

SINGLES:	HITS 1			WEEKS 3
I.O.U.	*Deram*	65	*24 Jan 81*	3

Brian KENNEDY — UK

SINGLES:	HITS 3			WEEKS 8
A BETTER MAN	*RCA*	28	*22 Jun 96*	3
LIFE, LOVE & HAPPINESS	*RCA*	27	*21 Sep 96*	3
PUT THE MESSAGE IN THE BOX	*RCA*	37	*5 Apr 97*	2
ALBUMS:	**HITS 2**			**WEEKS 4**
THE GREAT WAR OF WORDS	*RCA*	64	*31 Mar 90*	1
A BETTER MAN	*RCA*	19	*19 Oct 96*	3

Kevin KENNEDY — UK

SINGLES:	HITS 1			WEEKS 1
BULLDOG NATION	*D2M*	70	*24 Jun 00*	1

Nigel KENNEDY — UK

ALBUMS:	HITS 8			WEEKS 123
ELGAR: VIOLIN CONCERTO *Above hit: Nigel KENNEDY with the LONDON PHILHARMONIC ORCHESTRA , conducted by Vernon HANDLEY.*	*EMI*	97	*1 Mar 86*	1
VIVALDI: THE FOUR SEASONS *Above hit: Nigel KENNEDY (violin and director); ENGLISH CHAMBER ORCHESTRA.*	*EMI*	3	*7 Oct 89*	81
MENDELSSOHN/BRUCH/SCHUBERT *Above hit: Nigel KENNEDY with Jeffrey TATE conducting the ENGLISH CHAMBER ORCHESTRA.*	*His Master's Voice*	28	*5 May 90*	15
BRAHMS: VIOLIN CONCERTO *Above hit: Nigel KENNEDY with the LONDON PHILHARMONIC ORCHESTRA conducted by Klaus TENNSTEDT.*	*EMI*	16	*6 Apr 91*	12
JUST LISTEN . . . *Above hit: Nigel KENNEDY with the LONDON PHILHARMONIC ORCHESTRA, conducted by Simon RATTLE.*	*EMI Classics*	56	*22 Feb 92*	1
BEETHOVEN VIOLIN CONCERTO, CORIOLAN OVERTURE *Above hit: Nigel KENNEDY with Klaus TENNSTEDT conducting the NORTH GERMAN RADIO SYMPHONY ORCHESTRA.*	*EMI Classics*	40	*21 Nov 92*	6
KAFKA	*EMI*	67	*29 Jun 96*	1

CLASSIC KENNEDY *Above hit: KENNEDY with the ENGLISH CHAMBER ORCHESTRA.*	*EMI Classics*	51	*6 Nov 99*	6

KENNY — Ireland

SINGLES:	HITS 2			WEEKS 16
HEART OF STONE	*RAK*	11	*3 Mar 73*	13
GIVE IT TO ME NOW	*RAK*	38	*30 Jun 73*	3

KENNY — UK

SINGLES:	HITS 4			WEEKS 39
THE BUMP *Originally recorded by the Bay City Rollers.*	*RAK*	3	*7 Dec 74*	15
FANCY PANTS	*RAK*	4	*8 Mar 75*	9
BABY I LOVE YOU, OK!	*RAK*	12	*7 Jun 75*	7
JULIE ANNE	*RAK*	10	*16 Aug 75*	8
ALBUMS:	**HITS 1**			**WEEKS 1**
THE SOUND OF SUPER K	*RAK*	56	*17 Jan 76*	1

Gerard KENNY — US

SINGLES:	HITS 4			WEEKS 21
NEW YORK, NEW YORK	*RCA Victor*	43	*9 Dec 78*	8
FANTASY	*RCA*	65	*21 Jun 80*	1
FANTASY [RE]	*RCA*	34	*5 Jul 80*	5
THE OTHER WOMAN, THE OTHER MAN	*Impression*	69	*18 Feb 84*	4
NO MAN'S LAND *Theme from the Thames ITV series 'Widows'.*	*WEA*	56	*4 May 85*	3
ALBUMS:	**HITS 1**			**WEEKS 4**
MADE IT THROUGH THE RAIN	*RCA Victor*	19	*21 Jul 79*	4

KENT — Sweden

SINGLES:	HITS 1			WEEKS 1
747	*RCA Victor*	61	*13 Mar 99*	1

Klark KENT — UK

SINGLES:	HITS 1			WEEKS 4
DON'T CARE *Stewart Copeland (from the Police) under a pseudonym.*	*A&M*	48	*26 Aug 78*	4

KENTISH MAN – See CHUBBY CHUNKS

Carol KENYON – See Paul HARDCASTLE; HEAVEN 17; RAPINATION

KERBDOG — Ireland

SINGLES:	HITS 4			WEEKS 5
DRY RISER	*Vertigo*	60	*12 Mar 94*	1
DUMMY CRUSHER	*Vertigo*	37	*6 Aug 94*	2
SALLY	*Fontana*	69	*12 Oct 96*	1
MEXICAN WAVE	*Fontana*	49	*29 Mar 97*	1
ALBUMS:	**HITS 1**			**WEEKS 1**
ON THE TURN	*Fontana*	64	*12 Apr 97*	1

Anita KERR SINGERS – See Bobby HELMS

KERRI-ANN — Ireland

SINGLES:	HITS 1			WEEKS 1
DO YOU LOVE ME BOY?	*Raglan Road*	58	*8 Aug 98*	1

KERRI and MICK — Australia

SINGLES:	HITS 1			WEEKS 3
"SONS AND DAUGHTERS" THEME *Theme from the Australian TV soap.*	*A.1*	68	*28 Apr 84*	3

Liz KERSHAW and Bruno BROOKES — UK

SINGLES:	HITS 2			WEEKS 3
IT TAKES TWO, BABY *Above hit: Liz KERSHAW, Bruno BROOKES, JIVE BUNNY and LONDONBEAT.*	*Spartan*	53	*2 Dec 89*	2
LET'S DANCE *Above 2 were charity records with proceeds to BBC's Children In Need.* *Above hit: BRUNO and LIZ and the RADIO 1 DJ POSSE.*	*Jive*	54	*1 Dec 90*	1

Nik KERSHAW — UK

SINGLES:	HITS 13			WEEKS 89
I WON'T LET THE SUN GO DOWN ON ME	*MCA*	47	*19 Nov 83*	5
WOULDN'T IT BE GOOD	*MCA*	4	*28 Jan 84*	14

DANCING GIRLS	*MCA*	13	*14 Apr 84*	9
I WON'T LET THE SUN GO DOWN ON ME [RI]	*MCA*	2	*16 Jun 84*	13
HUMAN RACING	*MCA*	19	*15 Sep 84*	7
THE RIDDLE	*MCA*	3	*17 Nov 84*	11
WIDE BOY	*MCA*	9	*16 Mar 85*	8
DON QUIXOTE	*MCA*	10	*3 Aug 85*	7
WHEN A HEART BEATS	*MCA*	27	*30 Nov 85*	7
NOBODY KNOWS	*MCA*	44	*11 Oct 86*	3
RADIO MUSICOLA	*MCA*	43	*13 Dec 86*	2
ONE STEP AHEAD	*MCA*	55	*4 Feb 89*	1
SOMEBODY LOVES YOU	*Eagle*	70	*27 Feb 99*	1
SOMETIMES	*Wall Of Sound*	56	*7 Aug 99*	1
Above hit: LES RYTHMES DIGITALES featuring Nik KERSHAW.				
ALBUMS:	**HITS 3**			**WEEKS 100**
HUMAN RACING	*MCA*	5	*10 Mar 84*	61
THE RIDDLE	*MCA*	8	*1 Dec 84*	36
RADIO MUSICOLA	*MCA*	47	*8 Nov 86*	3

KEVIN and PERRY – See PRECOCIOUS BRATS featuring KEVIN and PERRY

KEVIN THE GERBIL — UK

SINGLES:	**HITS 1**			**WEEKS 6**
SUMMER HOLIDAY	*Rodent*	50	*4 Aug 84*	6
Above hit: Roland RAT SUPERSTAR presents KEVIN THE GERBIL.				

KEY WEST featuring ERIK — UK

SINGLES:	**HITS 1**			**WEEKS 2**
LOOKS LIKE I'M IN LOVE AGAIN	*PWL Sanctuary*	46	*10 Apr 93*	2

KEYNOTES – See JOHNSTON BROTHERS, Dave KING

Alicia KEYS — US

SINGLES:	**HITS 1**			**WEEKS 8**
FALLIN'	*J*	3	*10 Nov 01*	8
ALBUMS:	**HITS 1**			**WEEKS 15**
SONGS IN A MINOR	*J*	7	*22 Sep 01*	15

Nusrat Fateh Ali KHAN/Michael BROOK — Pakistan/UK

ALBUMS:	**HITS 1**			**WEEKS 1**
NIGHT SONG	*Realworld*	65	*6 Apr 96*	1

Chaka KHAN — US

(See also Quincy Jones; Rufus.)

SINGLES:	**HITS 11**			**WEEKS 69**
I'M EVERY WOMAN	*Warner Brothers*	11	*2 Dec 78*	13
I FEEL FOR YOU	*Warner Brothers*	1	*20 Oct 84*	16
Features rap by Grandmaster Melle Mel and harmonica by Stevie Wonder. Written and originally recorded by Prince.				
THIS IS MY NIGHT	*Warner Brothers*	14	*19 Jan 85*	6
EYE TO EYE	*Warner Brothers*	16	*20 Apr 85*	7
LOVE OF A LIFETIME	*Warner Brothers*	52	*12 Jul 86*	4
IT'S MY PARTY	*Warner Brothers*	71	*21 Jan 89*	2
I'M EVERY WOMAN [RM]	*Warner Brothers*	8	*6 May 89*	8
Remixed by Dancin' Danny Dee.				
I FEEL FOR YOU [RM]	*Warner Brothers*	45	*7 Oct 89*	2
LOVE YOU ALL MY LIFETIME	*Warner Brothers*	49	*28 Mar 92*	3
DON'T LOOK AT ME THAT WAY	*Warner Brothers*	73	*17 Jul 93*	1
WATCH WHAT YOU SAY	*Cooltempo*	28	*19 Aug 95*	3
Sleeve gives title as an EP: Jazzmatazz Vol.2, The New Reality.				
Above hit: GURU featuring Chaka KHAN.				
NEVER MISS THE WATER	*Reprise*	59	*1 Mar 97*	1
Above hit: Chaka KHAN featuring Me'shell NDEGEOCELLO.				
ALL GOOD? IT AIN'T – AND THAT'S THE TRUTH	*Tommy Boy*	33	*11 Nov 00*	3
Above hit: DE LA SOUL featuring Chaka KHAN.				
ALBUMS:	**HITS 4**			**WEEKS 40**
I FEEL FOR YOU	*Warner Brothers*	15	*20 Oct 84*	22
DESTINY	*Warner Brothers*	77	*9 Aug 86*	2
LIFE IS A DANCE – THE REMIX PROJECT	*Warner Brothers*	14	*3 Jun 89*	15
Compilation.				
BEST OF CHAKA KHAN – I'M EVERY WOMAN	*warner.esp*	62	*4 Sep 99*	1

Aram KHATCHATURIAN – See VIENNA PHILHARMONIC ORCHESTRA conducted by Aram KHACHATURIAN

Mary KIANI — UK

SINGLES:	HITS 5			WEEKS 15
WHEN I CALL YOUR NAME	*Mercury*	18	*12 Aug 95*	4
I GIVE IT ALL TO YOU / I IMAGINE	*Mercury*	35	*23 Dec 95*	4
LET THE MUSIC PLAY	*Mercury*	19	*27 Apr 96*	3
100%	*Mercury*	23	*18 Jan 97*	3
WITH OR WITHOUT YOU	*Mercury*	46	*21 Jun 97*	1

KICK HORNS – See DODGY

KICK SQUAD — UK/Germany

SINGLES:	HITS 1			WEEKS 2
SOUND CLASH (CHAMPION SOUND)	*Kickin*	59	*10 Nov 90*	2

KICKING BACK with TAXMAN — UK

SINGLES:	HITS 2			WEEKS 8
DEVOTION	*10 Records*	47	*17 Mar 90*	4
EVERYTHING	*10 Records*	54	*7 Jul 90*	4

Sleeve has artist credit Kicking Back featuring Taxman.

KICKS LIKE A MULE — UK

SINGLES:	HITS 1			WEEKS 6
THE BOUNCER	*Tribal Bass*	7	*1 Feb 92*	6

KID 'N' PLAY — US

SINGLES:	HITS 3			WEEKS 7
LAST NIGHT	*Cooltempo*	71	*18 Jul 87*	1
DO THIS MY WAY	*Cooltempo*	48	*26 Mar 88*	3
GITTIN' FUNKY	*Cooltempo*	55	*17 Sep 88*	3

KID ROCK — US

SINGLES:	HITS 3			WEEKS 8
COWBOY	*Atlantic*	36	*23 Oct 99*	2
AMERICAN BAD ASS	*Atlantic*	25	*9 Sep 00*	4
BAWITDABA (BAH-WIT-DA-BAH)	*Atlantic*	41	*12 May 01*	2
ALBUMS:	**HITS 1**			**WEEKS 1**
THE HISTORY OF ROCK	*Atlantic*	73	*10 Jun 00*	1

Compilation.

KID UNKNOWN — UK

SINGLES:	HITS 1			WEEKS 1
NIGHTMARE	*Warp*	64	*2 May 92*	1

Carol KIDD featuring Terry WAITE — UK

SINGLES:	HITS 1			WEEKS 3
WHEN I DREAM	*The Hit Label*	58	*17 Oct 92*	3

Johnny KIDD and the PIRATES — UK

SINGLES:	HITS 9			WEEKS 62
PLEASE DON'T TOUCH	*His Master's Voice*	26	*13 Jun 59*	3
PLEASE DON'T TOUCH [RE]	*His Master's Voice*	25	*18 Jul 59*	2
YOU GOT WHAT IT TAKES	*His Master's Voice*	25	*13 Feb 60*	3
SHAKIN' ALL OVER	*His Master's Voice*	1	*18 Jun 60*	19
RESTLESS	*His Master's Voice*	22	*8 Oct 60*	7
LINDA LU	*His Master's Voice*	47	*15 Apr 61*	1
Originally recorded by Ray Sharpe in 1959.				
A SHOT OF RHYTHM AND BLUES	*His Master's Voice*	48	*12 Jan 63*	1
Originally recorded by Arthur Alexander.				
I'LL NEVER GET OVER YOU	*His Master's Voice*	4	*27 Jul 63*	15
HUNGRY FOR LOVE	*His Master's Voice*	20	*30 Nov 63*	10
ALWAYS AND EVER	*His Master's Voice*	46	*2 May 64*	1
EPS:	**HITS 1**			**WEEKS 7**
SHAKIN' ALL OVER	*His Master's Voice*	11	*14 Jan 61*	7

Nicole KIDMAN — Australia

SINGLES:	HITS 2			WEEKS 7
COME WHAT MAY	*Interscope*	27	*6 Oct 01*	5
From the film 'Moulin Rouge'.				
Above hit: Nicole KIDMAN and Ewan McGREGOR.				
SOMETHIN' STUPID	*Chrysalis*	1	*22 Dec 01*	2
Above hit: Robbie WILLIAMS and Nicole KIDMAN.				

KIDS FROM "FAME" — US

SINGLES:	HITS 4			WEEKS 36
HI-FIDELITY	RCA	5	14 Aug 82	10
Above hit: KIDS FROM "FAME" featuring Valerie LANDSBURG.				
STARMAKER	RCA	3	2 Oct 82	10
Originally recorded by Bruce Roberts.				
Above hit: KIDS FROM "FAME" featuring the KIDS FROM "FAME".				
MANNEQUIN	RCA	50	11 Dec 82	6
Above hit: KIDS FROM "FAME" featuring Gene Anthony RAY.				
FRIDAY NIGHT (LIVE VERSION)	RCA	13	9 Apr 83	10
Above hit: KIDS FROM FAME featuring Carlo IMPERATO and "The WATERS".				
ALBUMS:	**HITS 5**			**WEEKS 117**
THE KIDS FROM FAME	BBC	1	24 Jul 82	45
THE KIDS FROM FAME AGAIN	RCA	2	16 Oct 82	21
THE KIDS FROM FAME LIVE	RCA	8	26 Feb 83	28
THE KIDS FROM FAME SONGS	BBC	14	14 May 83	16
THE KIDS FROM FAME SING FOR YOU	BBC	28	20 Aug 83	7

Greg KIHN BAND — US

SINGLES:	HITS 1			WEEKS 2
JEOPARDY	Beserkley	63	23 Apr 83	2

KILLAH PRIEST — US

SINGLES:	HITS 1			WEEKS 1
ONE STEP	Geffen	45	7 Feb 98	1
Vocals by Tekitha.				

KILLING JOKE — UK

SINGLES:	HITS 15			WEEKS 48
FOLLOW THE LEADERS	E'G	55	23 May 81	5
EMPIRE SONG	E'G	43	20 Mar 82	4
BIRDS OF A FEATHER	E'G	64	30 Oct 82	2
LET'S ALL GO (TO THE FIRE DANCES)	E'G	51	25 Jun 83	3
ME OR YOU?	E'G	57	15 Oct 83	1
EIGHTIES	E'G	60	7 Apr 84	5
A NEW DAY	E'G	56	21 Jul 84	2
LOVE LIKE BLOOD	E'G	16	2 Feb 85	9
KINGS AND QUEENS	E'G	58	30 Mar 85	3
ADORATIONS	E'G	42	16 Aug 86	6
SANITY	E'G	70	18 Oct 86	1
MILLENIUM	Butterfly	34	7 May 94	2
THE PANDEMONIUM SINGLE [EP]	Butterfly	28	16 Jul 94	3
EP features Pandemonium and various mixes of the track.				
JANA	Butterfly	54	4 Feb 95	1
DEMOCRACY	Butterfly	39	23 Mar 96	1
ALBUMS:	**HITS 10**			**WEEKS 34**
KILLING JOKE	Polydor	39	25 Oct 80	4
WHAT'S THIS FOR	E'G	42	20 Jun 81	4
REVELATIONS	E'G	12	8 May 82	6
"HA" - KILLING JOKE LIVE	E'G	66	27 Nov 82	2
FIRE DANCES	E'G	29	23 Jul 83	3
NIGHT TIME	E'G	11	9 Mar 85	9
BRIGHTER THAN A THOUSAND SUNS	E'G	54	22 Nov 86	1
OUTSIDE THE GATE	E'G	92	9 Jul 88	1
PANDEMONIUM	Butterfly	16	6 Aug 94	3
DEMOCRACY	Butterfly	71	13 Apr 96	1

Andy KIM — Canada

SINGLES:	HITS 1			WEEKS 12
ROCK ME GENTLY	Capitol	2	24 Aug 74	12

KIMERA with the LONDON SYMPHONY ORCHESTRA — Korea

(See also London Symphony Orchestra.)

ALBUMS:	HITS 1			WEEKS 4
HITS ON OPERA	Stylus	38	26 Oct 85	4

KINANE — Ireland

SINGLES:	HITS 4			WEEKS 4
ALL THE LOVER I NEED	Coliseum	59	18 May 96	1
THE WOMAN IN ME	Coliseum	73	21 Sep 96	1
Above 2: Bianca KINANE.				
HEAVEN	Coalition	49	16 May 98	1
SO FINE	Coalition	63	22 Aug 98	1

KING — UK/Ireland

SINGLES:	HITS 5			WEEKS 44
LOVE AND PRIDE	*CBS*	2	*12 Jan 85*	14
Original release reached No. 84 in 1984.				
WON'T YOU HOLD MY HAND NOW	*CBS*	24	*23 Mar 85*	8
ALONE WITHOUT YOU	*CBS*	8	*17 Aug 85*	9
THE TASTE OF YOUR TEARS	*CBS*	11	*19 Oct 85*	9
TORTURE	*CBS*	23	*11 Jan 86*	4
ALBUMS:	**HITS 2**			**WEEKS 32**
STEPS IN TIME	*CBS*	6	*9 Feb 85*	21
BITTER SWEET	*CBS*	16	*23 Nov 85*	11

Albert KING – See Gary MOORE

B.B. KING — US

(See also B.B. King and Eric Clapton.)

SINGLES:	HITS 2			WEEKS 10
WHEN LOVE COMES TO TOWN	*Island*	6	*15 Apr 89*	7
Above hit: U2 with B.B. KING.				
SINCE I MET YOU BABY	*Virgin*	59	*18 Jul 92*	3
Above hit: Gary MOORE and B.B. KING.				
ALBUMS:	**HITS 2**			**WEEKS 9**
TAKE IT HOME	*MCA*	60	*25 Aug 79*	5
HIS DEFINITIVE GREATEST HITS	*Universal Music TV*	24	*1 May 99*	4
Compilation covering the years 1964–1993.				

B.B. KING and Eric CLAPTON — US/UK

(See also Eric Clapton; B.B. King.)

ALBUMS:	HITS 1			WEEKS 15
RIDING WITH THE KING	*Reprise*	15	*24 Jun 00*	15

Ben E. KING — US

SINGLES:	HITS 4			WEEKS 35
FIRST TASTE OF LOVE	*London*	27	*4 Feb 61*	11
STAND BY ME	*London*	50	*24 Jun 61*	1
STAND BY ME [RE]	*London*	27	*8 Jul 61*	6
AMOR, AMOR	*London*	38	*7 Oct 61*	4
Originally recorded by Ginny Simms in 1943.				
STAND BY ME [RI]	*Arista*	1	*14 Feb 87*	11
Featured in the Levi's 501 TV commercial.				
SAVE THE LAST DANCE FOR ME	*Manhattan*	69	*4 Jul 87*	2
ALBUMS:	**HITS 4**			**WEEKS 30**
SPANISH HARLEM	*Atlantic*	30	*1 Jul 67*	3
STAND BY ME (THE ULTIMATE COLLECTION)	*Atlantic*	14	*14 Mar 87*	8
THE VERY BEST OF BEN E. KING AND THE DRIFTERS	*Telstar*	15	*20 Oct 90*	16
THE VERY BEST OF BEN E. KING AND THE DRIFTERS	Warner.esp/Global TV	41	*7 Nov 98*	3
Above 2 albums are different and include both Ben E. King's solo and group material.				
Above 3: KING and the DRIFTERS				

Carole KING — UK

SINGLES:	HITS 2			WEEKS 29
IT MIGHT AS WELL RAIN UNTIL SEPTEMBER	*London*	3	*22 Sep 62*	13
She wrote it for Bobby Vee.				
IT'S TOO LATE	*A&M*	6	*7 Aug 71*	12
IT MIGHT AS WELL RAIN UNTIL SEPTEMBER [RI]	*London*	43	*28 Oct 72*	4
ALBUMS:	**HITS 4**			**WEEKS 108**
TAPESTRY	*A&M*	4	*24 Jul 71*	90
MUSIC	*A&M*	18	*15 Jan 72*	10
RHYMES AND REASONS	Ode	40	*2 Dec 72*	2
TAPESTRY [RI]	*Epic*	64	*7 Feb 98*	1
NATURAL WOMAN - THE VERY BEST OF CAROLE KING	*Columbia*	31	*30 Sep 00*	3
TAPESTRY [RI][RE]	*Epic*	24	*7 Jul 01*	2
Digitally remastered.				

Dave KING — UK

(See also All Star Hit Parade.)

SINGLES:	HITS 4			WEEKS 29
MEMORIES ARE MADE OF THIS	*Decca*	5	*18 Feb 56*	15
YOU CAN'T BE TRUE TO TWO	*Decca*	11	*14 Apr 56*	9
Above 2: Dave KING with the Roland SHAW ORCHESTRA and the KEYNOTES.				
CHRISTMAS AND YOU	*Decca*	23	*22 Dec 56*	2
THE STORY OF MY LIFE	*Decca*	20	*25 Jan 58*	3
Above hit: Dave KING and the Roland SHAW ORCHESTRA.				

Denis KING and his Orchestra — UK

SINGLES:	HITS 1			WEEKS 6
THE THEME FROM "WE'LL MEET AGAIN"	*Multi-Media Tapes*	36	*24 Apr 82*	6
Theme to the LWT ITV series. [AA] listed with The Song That I Sing by Stutz Bear Cats.				

Diana KING — Jamaica

(See also Jamaica United.)

SINGLES:	HITS 3			WEEKS 22
SHY GUY	*Columbia*	2	*8 Jul 95*	13
From the film 'Bad Boys'.				
AIN'T NOBODY	*Columbia*	13	*28 Oct 95*	5
I SAY A LITTLE PRAYER	*Columbia*	17	*1 Nov 97*	4
ALBUMS:	**HITS 1**			**WEEKS 2**
TOUGHER THAN LOVE	*Columbia*	50	*12 Aug 95*	2

Evelyn 'Champagne' KING — US

SINGLES:	HITS 11			WEEKS 76
SHAME	*RCA Victor*	39	*13 May 78*	23
I DON'T KNOW IF IT'S RIGHT	*RCA Victor*	67	*3 Feb 79*	2
I'M IN LOVE	*RCA*	27	*27 Jun 81*	11
IF YOU WANT MY LOVIN'	*RCA*	43	*26 Sep 81*	6
LOVE COME DOWN	*RCA*	7	*28 Aug 82*	13
BACK TO LOVE	*RCA*	40	*20 Nov 82*	4
GET LOOSE	*RCA*	45	*19 Feb 83*	5
Above 5: Evelyn KING.				
YOUR PERSONAL TOUCH	*RCA*	37	*9 Nov 85*	5
HIGH HORSE	*RCA*	55	*29 Mar 86*	3
HOLD ON TO WHAT YOU'VE GOT	*Manhattan*	47	*23 Jul 88*	3
SHAME (HARDCORE MIX) [RM]	*Network*	74	*10 Oct 92*	1
Above hit: ALTERN 8 vs Evelyn KING.				
ALBUMS:	**HITS 1**			**WEEKS 9**
GET LOOSE	*RCA*	35	*11 Sep 82*	9

John KING – See DUST BROTHERS (Michael SIMPSON and John KING) featuring Tyler DURDEN

Jonathan KING — UK

SINGLES:	HITS 17			WEEKS 128
EVERYONE'S GONE TO THE MOON	*Decca*	4	*31 Jul 65*	11
Above hit: Johnathan KING.				
LET IT ALL HANG OUT	*Decca*	26	*10 Jan 70*	7
IT'S THE SAME OLD SONG	*B&C*	19	*16 Jan 71*	9
Above hit: WEATHERMEN.				
SUGAR SUGAR	*RCA Victor*	12	*3 Apr 71*	14
Above hit: SAKKARIN.				
LAZYBONES	*Decca*	23	*29 May 71*	8
Originally recorded by the Hombres (as Let It Out).				
HOOKED ON A FEELING	*Decca*	23	*20 Nov 71*	10
Originally recorded by Mark James.				
FLIRT!	*Decca*	22	*5 Feb 72*	9
LOOP DI LOVE	*UK*	4	14 Oct 72	13
Originally recorded by J. Bastos.				
Above hit: SHAG.				
(I CAN'T GET NO) SATISFACTION	*UK*	29	*26 Jan 74*	5
Above hit: BUBBLEROCK.				
UNA PALOMA BLANCA (WHITE DOVE)	*UK*	5	*6 Sep 75*	11
CHICK-A-BOOM (DON'T YA JES LOVE IT)	*UK*	36	*20 Sep 75*	4
Originally recorded by Daddy Dewdrop.				
Above hit: 53RD & 3RD featuring the SOUND OF SHAG.				
IN THE MOOD	*UK*	46	*7 Feb 76*	3
Above hit: SOUND 9418.				
IT ONLY TAKES A MINUTE	*UK*	9	*26 Jun 76*	9
Above hit: ONE HUNDRED TON AND A FEATHER.				
ONE FOR YOU, ONE FOR ME	*GTO*	29	*7 Oct 78*	6
LICK A SMURP FOR CHRISTMAS (ALL FALL DOWN)	*Petrol/Magnet*	58	*16 Dec 78*	4
Initially issued as a single sided flexi disc on the Petrol label, it was then available on Magnet from 23 Dec 78.				
Above hit: FATHER ABRAPHART and the SMURPS.				
YOU'RE THE GREATEST LOVER	*UK International*	67	*16 Jun 79*	2
GLORIA	*Ariola*	65	*3 Nov 79*	3

Mark KING — UK

ALBUMS:	HITS 1			WEEKS 2
INFLUENCES	*Polydor*	77	*21 Jul 84*	2

Nosmo KING – See JAVELLS featuring Nosmo KING

Paul KING — UK

SINGLES:	HITS 1			WEEKS 3
I KNOW	*CBS*	59	*2 May 87*	3

Solomon KING — US

SINGLES:	HITS 2			WEEKS 28
SHE WEARS MY RING *Originally recorded by Roy Orbison.*	*Columbia*	3	*6 Jan 68*	18
WHEN WE WERE YOUNG	*Columbia*	21	*4 May 68*	10
ALBUMS:	**HITS 1**			**WEEKS 1**
SHE WEARS MY RING	*Columbia*	40	*22 Jun 68*	1

Tony KING – See VISION MASTERS and Tony KING featuring Kylie MINOGUE

KING ADORA — UK

SINGLES:	HITS 3			WEEKS 5
SMOULDER	*Superior Quality Recordings*	62	*4 Nov 00*	1
SUFFOCATE	*Superior Quality Recordings*	39	*3 Mar 01*	2
BIONIC *Original release reached No. 128 on 20 May 2000.*	*Superior Quality Recordings*	30	*26 May 01*	2
ALBUMS:	**HITS 1**			**WEEKS 1**
VIBRATE YOU	*Superior Quality Recordings*	30	*2 Jun 01*	1

KING BEE — UK

SINGLES:	HITS 2			WEEKS 6
MUST BEE THE MUSIC *Above hit: KING BEE featuring MICHELE.*	*Torso Dance*	44	*26 Jan 91*	4
BACK BY DOPE DEMAND	*1st Bass*	61	*23 Mar 91*	2

KING BROTHERS — UK

SINGLES:	HITS 8			WEEKS 74
A WHITE SPORT COAT (AND A PINK CARNATION) *Originally recorded by Marty Robbins.* *Above hit: KING BROTHERS with the KING BROTHERS and Geoff LOVE and his Orchestra.*	*Parlophone*	6	*1 Jun 57*	14
IN THE MIDDLE OF AN ISLAND *Above hit: KING BROTHERS with Geoff LOVE and his Orchestra and the Rita WILLIAMS SINGERS.*	*Parlophone*	19	*10 Aug 57*	13
WAKE UP LITTLE SUSIE	*Parlophone*	22	*7 Dec 57*	3
PUT A LIGHT IN THE WINDOW	*Parlophone*	29	*1 Feb 58*	1
PUT A LIGHT IN THE WINDOW [RE-1ST]	*Parlophone*	28	*15 Feb 58*	1
PUT A LIGHT IN THE WINDOW [RE-2ND] *Above 4: KING BROTHERS with Geoff LOVE and his Orchestra.*	*Parlophone*	25	*1 Mar 58*	2
STANDING ON THE CORNER *From the musical 'The Most Happy Fella'.*	*Parlophone*	4	*16 Apr 60*	11
MAIS OUI *Above 2: KING BROTHERS and the Rita WILLIAMS SINGERS with Geoff LOVE and his Orchestra.*	*Parlophone*	16	*30 Jul 60*	10
DOLL HOUSE *Above hit: KING BROTHERS and the Rita WILLIAMS SINGERS.*	*Parlophone*	21	*14 Jan 61*	8
SEVENTY-SIX TROMBONES *Originally recorded by Robert Preston.* *Above hit: KING BROTHERS and the Rita WILLIAMS SINGERS with Geoff LOVE and his Orchestra.*	*Parlophone*	19	*4 Mar 61*	11

KING CRIMSON — UK

ALBUMS:	HITS 11			WEEKS 54
IN THE COURT OF THE CRIMSON KING	*Island*	5	*1 Nov 69*	18
IN THE WAKE OF POSEIDON	*Island*	4	*30 May 70*	13
LIZARD	*Island*	30	*16 Jan 71*	1
ISLANDS	*Island*	30	*8 Jan 72*	1
LARKS' TONGUES IN ASPIC	*Island*	20	*7 Apr 73*	4
STARLESS AND BIBLE BLACK	*Island*	28	*13 Apr 74*	2
RED	*Island*	45	*26 Oct 74*	1
DISCIPLINE	*E'G*	41	*10 Oct 81*	4
BEAT *Songs based on work by US beat poet Jack Kerouac.*	*E'G*	39	*26 Jun 82*	5
THREE OF A PERFECT PAIR	*E'G*	30	*31 Mar 84*	4
THRAK	*Virgin*	58	*15 Apr 95*	1

KING KURT — UK

SINGLES:	HITS 5			WEEKS 16
DESTINATION ZULU LAND	*Stiff*	36	*15 Oct 83*	6
MACK THE KNIFE	*Stiff*	55	*28 Apr 84*	4

BANANA BANANA	*Stiff*	54	*4 Aug 84*	4
AMERICA	*Polydor*	73	*15 Nov 86*	1
THE LAND OF RING DANG DO	*Polydor*	67	*2 May 87*	1
ALBUMS:	**HITS 2**			**WEEKS 5**
OOH WALLAH WALLAH	*Stiff*	99	*10 Dec 83*	1
BIG COCK	*Stiff*	50	*8 Mar 86*	4

KING SUN-D MOET — US

SINGLES:	**HITS 1**			**WEEKS 3**
HEY LOVE	*Flame*	66	*11 Jul 87*	3

KING TRIGGER — UK

SINGLES:	**HITS 1**			**WEEKS 4**
RIVER	*Chrysalis*	57	*14 Aug 82*	4

KINGDOM COME — US

SINGLES:	**HITS 2**			**WEEKS 2**
GET IT ON	*Polydor*	75	*16 Apr 88*	1
DO YOU LIKE IT	*Polydor*	73	*6 May 89*	1
ALBUMS:	**HITS 2**			**WEEKS 10**
KINGDOM COME	*Polydor*	43	*26 Mar 88*	6
IN YOUR FACE	*Polydor*	25	*13 May 89*	4

KINGMAKER — UK

SINGLES:	**HITS 8**			**WEEKS 22**
IDIOTS AT THE WHEEL [EP] *Lead track: Really Scrape The Sky.*	*Scorch*	30	*18 Jan 92*	3
EAT YOURSELF WHOLE *Single also gives title as an EP: The Killjoy Was Here.*	*Scorch*	15	*23 May 92*	3
ARMCHAIR ANARCHIST	*Scorch*	47	*31 Oct 92*	2
10 YEARS ASLEEP	*Scorch*	15	*8 May 93*	4
QUEEN JANE	*Scorch*	29	*19 Jun 93*	4
SATURDAY'S NOT WHAT IT USED TO BE	*Scorch*	63	*30 Oct 93*	1
YOU AND I WILL NEVER SEE THINGS EYE TO EYE	*Chrysalis*	33	*15 Apr 95*	3
IN THE BEST POSSIBLE TASTE (PART 2)	*Chrysalis*	41	*3 Jun 95*	2
ALBUMS:	**HITS 2**			**WEEKS 10**
EAT YOURSELF WHOLE	*Scorch*	29	*19 Oct 91*	3
SLEEPWALKING	*Scorch*	15	*29 May 93*	7

Choir Of KING'S COLLEGE, CAMBRIDGE — UK

ALBUMS:	**HITS 1**			**WEEKS 3**
THE WORLD OF CHRISTMAS	*Argo*	38	*11 Dec 71*	3

KINGS OF CONVENIENCE — Norway

SINGLES:	**HITS 2**			**WEEKS 2**
TOXIC GIRL	*Source*	44	*21 Apr 01*	1
FAILURE	*Source*	63	*14 Jul 01*	1
ALBUMS:	**HITS 1**			**WEEKS 1**
QUIET IS THE NEW LOUD	*Source*	72	*10 Feb 01*	1

KINGS OF TOMORROW featuring Julie McKNIGHT — US

SINGLES:	**HITS 1**			**WEEKS 4**
FINALLY	*Distance*	54	*14 Apr 01*	1
FINALLY [RM] *Remixed by Danny Tenaglia..*	*Defected*	24	*29 Sep 01*	3

KINGS OF SWING ORCHESTRA — Australia

SINGLES:	**HITS 1**			**WEEKS 5**
SWITCHED ON SWING [M]	*Philips*	48	*1 May 82*	5
ALBUMS:	**HITS 1**			**WEEKS 11**
SWITCHED ON SWING	*K-Tel*	28	*29 May 82*	11

KINGS OF TOMORROW featuring Julie McKNIGHT — US

SINGLES:	**HITS 2**			**WEEKS 2**
TOXIC GIRL	*Source*	44	*21 Apr 01*	1
FAILURE	*Source*	63	*14 Jul 01*	1
ALBUMS:	**HITS 1**			**WEEKS 1**
QUIET IS THE NEW LOUD	*Source*	72	*10 Feb 01*	1

KING'S X — US

ALBUMS:	HITS 4			WEEKS 4
GRETCHEN GOES TO NEBRASKA	*Megaforce*	52	*1 Jul 89*	1
FAITH HOPE LOVE	*Megaforce*	70	*10 Nov 90*	1
KING'S X	*Atlantic*	46	*28 Mar 92*	1
DOGMAN	*Atlantic*	49	*12 Feb 94*	1

KINGSMEN — US

SINGLES:	HITS 1			WEEKS 7
LOUIE LOUIE	*Pye International*	26	*1 Feb 64*	7

Originally recorded by Richard Berry and the Pharoahs in 1957.

KINGSTON TRIO — US

SINGLES:	HITS 2			WEEKS 15
TOM DOOLEY	*Capitol*	5	*22 Nov 58*	14
Written as Tom Dula in 1958.				
SAN MIGUEL	*Capitol*	29	*5 Dec 59*	1

KINKS — UK

SINGLES:	HITS 23			WEEKS 215
YOU REALLY GOT ME	*Pye*	1	*15 Aug 64*	12
ALL DAY AND ALL OF THE NIGHT	*Pye*	2	*31 Oct 64*	14
TIRED OF WAITING FOR YOU	*Pye*	1	*23 Jan 65*	10
EVERYBODY'S GONNA BE HAPPY	*Pye*	17	*27 Mar 65*	8
SET ME FREE	*Pye*	9	*29 May 65*	11
SEE MY FRIEND	*Pye*	10	*7 Aug 65*	9
TILL THE END OF THE DAY	*Pye*	8	*4 Dec 65*	12
DEDICATED FOLLOWER OF FASHION	*Pye*	4	*5 Mar 66*	11
SUNNY AFTERNOON	*Pye*	1	*11 Jun 66*	13
DEAD END STREET	*Pye*	5	*26 Nov 66*	11
WATERLOO SUNSET	*Pye*	2	*13 May 67*	11
AUTUMN ALMANAC	*Pye*	3	*21 Oct 67*	11
WONDERBOY	*Pye*	36	*20 Apr 68*	5
DAY'S	*Pye*	12	*20 Jul 68*	10
PLASTIC MAN	*Pye*	31	*19 Apr 69*	4
VICTORIA	*Pye*	33	*10 Jan 70*	4
LOLA	*Pye*	2	*4 Jul 70*	14
APEMAN	*Pye*	5	*12 Dec 70*	14
SUPERSONIC ROCKET SHIP	*RCA Victor*	16	*27 May 72*	8
BETTER THINGS	*Arista*	46	*27 Jun 81*	5
COME DANCING	*Arista*	12	*6 Aug 83*	9
DON'T FORGET TO DANCE	*Arista*	58	*15 Oct 83*	3
YOU REALLY GOT ME [RI]	*PRT*	47	*15 Oct 83*	4
THE DAYS [EP]	*When!*	35	*18 Jan 97*	2

Lead track: Days. Featured in the Yellow Pages TV commercial. This and the other tracks are all re-issues.

EPS:	HITS 4			WEEKS 79
KINKSIZE SESSION	*Pye*	1	*12 Dec 64*	22
KINKSIZE HITS	*Pye*	3	*30 Jan 65*	21
KWYET KINKS	*Pye*	1	*25 Sep 65*	32
DEDICATED KINKS	*Pye*	7	*23 Jul 66*	4

ALBUMS:	HITS 13			WEEKS 135
KINKS	*Pye*	3	*17 Oct 64*	25
KINDA KINKS	*Pye*	3	*13 Mar 65*	15
KINDA KONTROVERSY	*Pye*	9	*4 Dec 65*	12
WELL RESPECTED KINKS	*Marble Arch*	5	*10 Sep 66*	31
FACE TO FACE	*Pye*	12	*5 Nov 66*	11
SOMETHING ELSE	*Pye*	35	*14 Oct 67*	2
SUNNY AFTERNOON	*Marble Arch*	9	*2 Dec 67*	11
GOLDEN HOUR OF THE KINKS	*Golden Hour*	21	*23 Oct 71*	4
20 GOLDEN GREATS	*Ronco*	19	*14 Oct 78*	6
KINKS GREATEST HITS - DEAD END STREET	*PRT*	96	*5 Nov 83*	1
THE ULTIMATE COLLECTION	*Castle Communications*	35	*16 Sep 89*	7
THE DEFINITIVE COLLECTION	*PolyGram TV*	18	*18 Sep 93*	7
THE VERY BEST OF THE KINKS	*PolyGram TV*	42	*12 Apr 97*	3

Includes Dave Davies' solo hits.

KINKY — UK

(See also Erasure; E-Z Posse.)

SINGLES:	HITS 1			WEEKS 1
EVERYBODY	*Feverpitch*	71	*24 Aug 96*	1

KINKY MACHINE — UK

SINGLES:	HITS 4			WEEKS 4
SUPERNATURAL GIVER	*Lemon*	70	*6 Mar 93*	1
SHOCKAHOLIC	*Oxygen*	70	*29 May 93*	1
GOING OUT WITH GOD	*Oxygen*	74	*14 Aug 93*	1
10 SECOND BIONIC MAN	*Oxygen*	66	*2 Jul 94*	1

Fern KINNEY — US

SINGLES:	HITS 1			WEEKS 11
TOGETHER WE ARE BEAUTIFUL	*WEA*	1	*16 Feb 80*	11

Originally recorded by Ken Leray.

KINSHASA BAND – See Johnny WAKELIN

Kathy KIRBY — UK

SINGLES:	HITS 5			WEEKS 54
DANCE ON	*Decca*	11	*17 Aug 63*	13
SECRET LOVE	*Decca*	4	*9 Nov 63*	18
LET ME GO, LOVER	*Decca*	10	*22 Feb 64*	11
YOU'RE THE ONE	*Decca*	17	*9 May 64*	9
I BELONG	*Decca*	36	*6 Mar 65*	3
UK's Eurovision entry in 1965, it came 2nd.				
EPS:	**HITS 2**			**WEEKS 10**
KATHY KIRBY VOLUME 2	*Decca*	20	*28 Nov 64*	1
BBC TV'S SONG FOR EUROPE	*Decca*	9	*6 Mar 65*	9
ALBUMS:	**HITS 1**			**WEEKS 8**
16 HITS FROM 'STARS AND GARTERS'	*Decca*	11	*4 Jan 64*	8
From the TV series.				

Bo KIRKLAND and Ruth DAVIS — US

SINGLES:	HITS 1			WEEKS 9
YOU'RE GONNA GET NEXT TO ME	*EMI International*	12	*4 Jun 77*	9

Dominic KIRWAN — Ireland

ALBUMS:	HITS 1			WEEKS 1
THE MUSIC'S BACK	*Ritz*	54	*1 Nov 97*	1

KISS — US

SINGLES:	HITS 13			WEEKS 57
I WAS MADE FOR LOVIN' YOU	*Casablanca*	50	*30 Jun 79*	7
A WORLD WITHOUT HEROES	*Casablanca*	55	*20 Feb 82*	3
CREATURES OF THE NIGHT	*Casablanca*	34	*30 Apr 83*	4
LICK IT UP	*Vertigo*	31	*29 Oct 83*	5
HEAVEN'S ON FIRE	*Vertigo*	43	*8 Sep 84*	3
TEARS ARE FALLING	*Vertigo*	57	*9 Nov 85*	2
CRAZY CRAZY NIGHTS	*Vertigo*	4	*3 Oct 87*	9
REASON TO LIVE	*Vertigo*	33	*5 Dec 87*	7
TURN ON THE NIGHT	*Vertigo*	41	*10 Sep 88*	3
HIDE YOUR HEART	*Vertigo*	59	*18 Nov 89*	2
FOREVER	*Vertigo*	65	*31 Mar 90*	2
Co-written by Michael Bolton.				
GOD GAVE ROCK AND ROLL TO YOU II	*Interscope*	4	*11 Jan 92*	8
From the film 'Bill And Ted's Bogus Journey'.				
UNHOLY	*Vertigo*	26	*9 May 92*	2
ALBUMS:	**HITS 19**			**WEEKS 71**
DESTROYER	*Casablanca*	22	*29 May 76*	5
ALIVE!	*Casablanca*	49	*26 Jun 76*	2
Live recordings from their 1975 tour.				
ALIVE	*Casablanca*	60	*17 Dec 77*	1
Titled 'Alive II' in the US. Live recordings from the LA Forum between 25 & 27 Aug 77.				
DYNASTY	*Casablanca*	50	*7 Jul 79*	6
UNMASKED	*Mercury*	48	*28 Jun 80*	3
THE ELDER	*Casablanca*	51	*5 Dec 81*	3
KILLERS	*Casablanca*	42	*26 Jun 82*	6
CREATURES OF THE NIGHT	*Casablanca*	22	*6 Nov 82*	4
LICK IT UP	*Casablanca*	7	*8 Oct 83*	7
ANIMALIZE	*Vertigo*	11	*6 Oct 84*	4
ASYLUM	*Vertigo*	12	*5 Oct 85*	3
CRAZY NIGHTS	*Vertigo*	4	*7 Nov 87*	14
SMASHES, THRASHES AND HITS	*Vertigo*	62	*10 Dec 88*	2
HOT IN THE SHADE	*Fontana*	35	*4 Nov 89*	2
REVENGE	*Mercury*	10	*23 May 92*	3
ALIVE III	*Mercury*	24	*29 May 93*	2
Live recordings from their 1992 concerts in Detroit, Cleveland and Indianapolis.				

ITV UNPLUGGED	*Mercury*	74	*23 Mar 96*	1
ive recordings for the TV station.				
REATEST HITS	*PolyGram TV*	58	*12 Jul 97*	2
SYCHO-CIRCUS	*Mercury*	47	*3 Oct 98*	1

KISS AMC — UK

SINGLES:	HITS 2			WEEKS 5
BIT OF . . .	*Syncopate*	58	*1 Jul 89*	2
amples U2's Pride (In The Name Of Love). A copyright dispute prevented the U2 credit.				
Above hit: <Kiss AMC.>				
BIT OF U2 [RE]	*Syncopate*	58	*19 Aug 89*	2
MY DOCS	*Syncopate*	66	*3 Feb 90*	1

KISSING THE PINK — UK

SINGLES:	HITS 1			WEEKS 14
LAST FILM	*Magnet*	19	*5 Mar 83*	14
Sleeve shows title as 'The Last Film'.				
ALBUMS:	**HITS 1**			**WEEKS 5**
NAKED	*Magnet*	54	*4 Jun 83*	5

Mac and Katie KISSOON — UK

SINGLES:	HITS 5			WEEKS 33
CHIRPY CHIRPY CHEEP CHEEP	*Young Blood*	41	*19 Jun 71*	1
Originally recorded by Lally Stott.				
SUGAR CANDY KISSES	*Polydor*	3	*18 Jan 75*	10
DON'T DO IT BABY	*State*	9	*3 May 75*	8
LIKE A BUTTERFLY	*State*	18	*30 Aug 75*	9
THE TWO OF US	*State*	46	*15 May 76*	5

Kevin KITCHEN — UK

SINGLES:	HITS 1			WEEKS 3
PUT MY ARMS AROUND YOU	*China*	64	*20 Apr 85*	3

KITCHENS OF DISTINCTION — UK

ALBUMS:	HITS 2			WEEKS 2
STRANGE FREE WORLD	*One Little Indian*	45	*30 Mar 91*	1
THE DEATH OF COOL	*One Little Indian*	72	*15 Aug 92*	1

Joy KITIKONTI — Italy

SINGLES:	HITS 1			WEEKS 2
JOYENERGIZER	*BXR*	57	*17 Nov 01*	2

Eartha KITT — US

SINGLES:	HITS 6			WEEKS 34
UNDER THE BRIDGES OF PARIS	*His Master's Voice*	7	*2 Apr 55*	9
Above hit: Eartha KITT with Henri RENE and his Orchestra.				
UNDER THE BRIDGES OF PARIS [RE]	*His Master's Voice*	20	*11 Jun 55*	1
WHERE IS MY MAN	*Record Shack*	36	*3 Dec 83*	11
I LOVE MEN	*Record Shack*	50	*7 Jul 84*	3
THIS IS MY LIFE	*Record Shack*	73	*12 Apr 86*	1
CHA CHA HEELS	*Arista*	32	*1 Jul 89*	7
Above hit: Eartha KITT and BRONSKI BEAT.				
IF I LOVE YA, THEN I NEED YA, IF I NEED YA, I WANT'CHA AROUND	*RCA*	43	*5 Mar 94*	2
Featured in the Flora margarine TV commercial.				
EPS:	**HITS 1**			**WEEKS 1**
EARTHA KITT REVISITED	*London*	18	*1 Dec 62*	1
ALBUMS:	**HITS 1**			**WEEKS 1**
REVISITED	*London*	17	*11 Feb 61*	1

KITTIE — Canada

SINGLES:	HITS 2			WEEKS 2
BRACKISH	*Epic*	46	*25 Mar 00*	1
CHARLOTTE	*Epic*	60	*22 Jul 00*	1

KLAXONS — Belgium

SINGLES:	HITS 1			WEEKS 6
CLAP CLAP SOUND	*PRT*	45	*10 Dec 83*	6
Originally recorded by the Pepe's.				

KLEEER — US

SINGLES:	HITS 2			WEEKS 10
KEEP YOUR BODY WORKING	*Atlantic*	51	*17 Mar 79*	6

GET TOUGH	*Atlantic*	49	*14 Mar 81*	
ALBUMS:	**HITS 2**			**WEEKS**
SEEKRET	*Atlantic*	96	*6 Jul 85*	
THE ARTISTS VOLUME III	*Street Sounds*	87	*12 Oct 85*	
Compilation featuring tracks by each artist.				
Above hit: WOMACK and WOMACK/The O'JAYS/KLEEER/The S.O.S. BAND.				

KLESHAY — UK

SINGLES:	**HITS 2**			**WEEKS**
REASONS	*Jerv*	33	*19 Sep 98*	
RUSH	*Jerv*	19	*20 Feb 99*	

KLF — UK

(See also Justified Ancients Of Mu Mu; Timelords, 2K.)

SINGLES:	**HITS 5**			**WEEKS 5**
WHAT TIME IS LOVE? (LIVE AT TRANCENTRAL)	*KLF Communications*	5	*11 Aug 90*	1
Samples Kick Out The Jams by MC5. Rap by MC Bello.				
3 A.M. ETERNAL (LIVE AT THE S.S.L.)	*KLF Communications*	1	*19 Jan 91*	1
Vocals by Maxine Harvey.				
Above 2: KLF featuring the CHILDREN OF THE REVOLUTION.				
LAST TRAIN TO TRANCENTRAL (LIVE FROM THE LOST CONTINENT)	*KLF Commuications*	2	*4 May 91*	
JUSTIFIED AND ANCIENT	*KLF Commuications*	2	*7 Dec 91*	1
Above hit: KLF (Lead Vocals: "the First Lady of Country" Miss Tammy WYNETTE).				
AMERICA: WHAT TIME IS LOVE? [RR]	*KLF Commuications*	4	*7 Mar 92*	
ALBUMS:	**HITS 1**			**WEEKS 4**
THE WHITE ROOM	*KLF Communications*	3	*16 Mar 91*	4

KLUBBHEADS — Holland

(See also Itty Bitty Boozy Woozy.)

SINGLES:	**HITS 3**			**WEEKS 1**
KLUBBHOPPING	*AM:PM*	10	*11 May 96*	
DISCOHOPPING	*AM:PM*	35	*16 Aug 97*	
Samples Born To Be Alive by Patrick Hernandez.				
KICKIN' HARD	*Wonderboy*	36	*15 Aug 98*	

Earl KLUGH – See George BENSON and Earl KLUGH

KLUSTER featuring Ron CARROLL — France/US

(See also Superfunk featuring Ron Carroll.)

SINGLES:	**HITS 1**			**WEEKS**
MY LOVE	*Scorpio Music*	73	*28 Apr 01*	

KNACK — US

SINGLES:	**HITS 2**			**WEEKS 12**
MY SHARONA	*Capitol*	6	*30 Jun 79*	10
GOOD GIRLS DON'T	*Capitol*	66	*13 Oct 79*	2
ALBUMS:	**HITS 1**			**WEEKS 2**
GET THE KNACK	*Capitol*	65	*4 Aug 79*	2

KNACK – See MOUNT RUSHMORE presents the KNACK

Beverley KNIGHT — UK

SINGLES:	**HITS 8**			**WEEKS 27**
FLAVOUR OF THE OLD SCHOOL	*Dome*	50	*8 Apr 95*	2
DOWN FOR THE ONE	*Dome*	55	*2 Sep 95*	1
FLAVOUR OF THE OLD SCHOOL [RI]	*Dome*	33	*21 Oct 95*	2
MOVING ON UP (ON THE RIGHT SIDE)	*Dome*	42	*23 Mar 96*	1
MADE IT BACK	*Parlophone*	21	*30 May 98*	3
Above hit: Beverley KNIGHT featuring REDMAN.				
REWIND (FIND A WAY)	*Parlophone Rhythm Series*	40	*22 Aug 98*	2
MADE IT BACK 99 [RM]	*Parlophone Rhythm Series*	19	*10 Apr 99*	5
Samples Chic's Good Times.				
Above hit: Beverley KNIGHT featuring REDMAN.				
GREATEST DAY	*Parlophone Rhythm Series*	14	*17 Jul 99*	5
SISTA SISTA	*Parlophone Rhythm Series*	31	*4 Dec 99*	2
GET UP	*Parlophone*	17	*17 Nov 01*	4
ALBUMS:	**HITS 1**			**WEEKS 14**
PRODIGAL SISTA	*Parlophone Rhythm Series*	54	*5 Sep 98*	2
PRODIGAL SISTA [RE]	*Parlophone Rhythm Series*	42	*1 May 99*	12
Re-release includes 3 new mixes by Mike Spencer, TNT and Jus Bounce.				

Curtis KNIGHT – See Jimmy HENDRIX

Frederick KNIGHT — US

SINGLES:	HITS 1			WEEKS 10
I'VE BEEN LONELY FOR SO LONG	*Stax*	22	*10 Jun 72*	10

Gladys KNIGHT and the PIPS — US

(See also Dionne Warwick.)

SINGLES:	HITS 23			WEEKS 179
TAKE ME IN YOUR ARMS AND LOVE ME	*Tamla Motown*	13	*10 Jun 67*	15
I HEARD IT THROUGH THE GRAPEVINE	*Tamla Motown*	47	*30 Dec 67*	1
JUST WALK IN MY SHOES	*Tamla Motown*	35	*17 Jun 72*	8
Originally released in 1966.				
HELP ME MAKE IT THROUGH THE NIGHT	*Tamla Motown*	11	*25 Nov 72*	17
THE LOOK OF LOVE	*Tamla Motown*	21	*3 Mar 73*	9
NEITHER ONE OF US (WANTS TO BE THE FIRST TO SAY GOODNIGHT)	*Tamla Motown*	31	*26 May 73*	7
THE WAY WE WERE/TRY TO REMEMBER [M]	*Buddah*	4	*5 Apr 75*	15
Live recording from Detroit. Song from the Broadway show 'The Fantasticks'.				
BEST THING THAT EVER HAPPENED TO ME	*Buddah*	7	*2 Aug 75*	10
PART TIME LOVE	*Buddah*	30	*15 Nov 75*	5
Certain copies were released with the title shown as 'Part Time Lover'. Originally recorded by David Gates.				
MIDNIGHT TRAIN TO GEORGIA	*Buddah*	10	*8 May 76*	9
Originally recorded by Cissy Houston.				
MAKE YOURS A HAPPY HOME	*Buddah*	35	*21 Aug 76*	4
SO SAD THE SONG	*Buddah*	20	*6 Nov 76*	10
NOBODY BUT YOU	*Buddah*	34	*15 Jan 77*	2
BABY DON'T CHANGE YOUR MIND	*Buddah*	4	*28 May 77*	12
HOME IS WHERE THE HEART IS	*Buddah*	35	*24 Sep 77*	4
THE ONE AND ONLY	*Buddah*	32	*8 Apr 78*	4
From the film of the same name.				
THE ONE AND ONLY [RE]	*Buddah*	66	*13 May 78*	1
COME BACK AND FINISH WHAT YOU STARTED	*Buddah*	15	*24 Jun 78*	13
IT'S A BETTER THAN GOOD TIME	*Buddah*	59	*30 Sep 78*	4
TASTE OF BITTER LOVE	*CBS*	35	*30 Aug 80*	6
BOURGIE, BOURGIE	*CBS*	32	*8 Nov 80*	6
Originally recorded by Ashford and Simpson.				
WHEN A CHILD IS BORN	*CBS*	74	*26 Dec 81*	2
Above hit: Johnny MATHIS and Gladys KNIGHT and the PIPS.				
LOVE OVERBOARD	*MCA*	42	*16 Jan 88*	4
LICENCE TO KILL	*MCA*	6	*10 Jun 89*	11
Theme from the James Bond film of the same name.				
Above hit: Gladys KNIGHT.				

ALBUMS:	HITS 9			WEEKS 117
I FEEL A SONG	*Buddah*	20	*31 May 75*	15
THE BEST OF GLADYS KNIGHT & THE PIPS	*Buddah*	6	*28 Feb 76*	43
STILL TOGETHER	*Buddah*	42	*16 Jul 77*	3
30 GREATEST	*K-Tel*	3	*12 Nov 77*	22
A TOUCH OF LOVE	*K-Tel*	16	*4 Oct 80*	6
THE COLLECTION - 20 GREATEST HITS	*Starblend*	43	*4 Feb 84*	5
DIANA . MICHAEL . GLADYS . STEVIE - THEIR VERY BEST - BACK TO BACK	*PrioriTyV*	21	*15 Nov 86*	10
Compilation featuring tracks by each artist.				
Above hit: Diana ROSS/Michael JACKSON/Gladys KNIGHT/Stevie WONDER.				
ALL OUR LOVE	*MCA*	80	*27 Feb 88*	1
THE SINGLES ALBUM	*PolyGram*	12	*28 Oct 89*	10
THE SINGLES ALBUM [RI]	*PolyGram TV*	69	*29 Mar 97*	2
Repackaged.				

Jordan KNIGHT — US

SINGLES:	HITS 1			WEEKS 9
GIVE IT TO YOU	*Interscope*	5	*16 Oct 99*	8
GIVE IT TO YOU [RE]	*Interscope*	61	*15 Jan 00*	1

Peter KNIGHT ORCHESTRA/SINGERS – See Petula CLARK; Nat 'King' COLE; Emile FORD and the CHECKMATES; Joan REGAN; Marion RYAN with the Peter KNIGHT Orchestra and the Beryl STOTT CHORUS; Frankie VAUGHAN; Malcolm VAUGHN.

Robert KNIGHT — US

SINGLES:	HITS 2			WEEKS 26
EVERLASTING LOVE	*Monument*	40	*20 Jan 68*	2
LOVE ON A MOUNTAIN TOP	*Monument*	10	*24 Nov 73*	16
EVERLASTING LOVE [RI]	*Monument*	19	*9 Mar 74*	8

KNIGHTSBRIDGE STRINGS — UK

ALBUMS:	HITS 1			WEEKS 1
STRING SWAY	*Top Rank*	20	*25 Jun 60*	1

David KNOPFLER — UK

ALBUMS:	HITS 1			WEEKS 1
RELEASE	*Peach River*	82	*19 Nov 83*	1

Mark KNOPFLER — UK

(See also Chet Atkins and Mark Knopfler.)

SINGLES:	HITS 3			WEEKS 7
GOING HOME: THEME OF THE LOCAL HERO *Theme from the film.*	*Vertigo*	56	*12 Mar 83*	3
DARLING PRETTY	*Vertigo*	33	*16 Mar 96*	2
CANNIBALS	*Vertigo*	42	*25 May 96*	2
ALBUMS:	**HITS 4**			**WEEKS 44**
LOCAL HERO [OST]	*Vertigo*	14	*16 Apr 83*	11
CAL [OST]	*Vertigo*	65	*20 Oct 84*	3
GOLDEN HEART	*Vertigo*	9	*6 Apr 96*	17
SAILING TO PHILADELPHIA	*Mercury*	4	*7 Oct 00*	13

KNOWLEDGE — Italy

SINGLES:	HITS 1			WEEKS 1
AS (UNTIL THE DAY) *Originally recorded by Stevie Wonder for his 1976 album 'Songs In The Key Of Life'.*	*ffrr*	70	*8 Nov 97*	1

Buddy KNOX — US

SINGLES:	HITS 2			WEEKS 5
PARTY DOLL *Above hit: Buddy KNOX with the RHYTHM ORCHIDS.*	*Columbia*	29	*11 May 57*	3
SHE'S GONE *Above hit: Buddy KNOX with the Johnny MANN SINGERS.*	*Liberty*	45	*18 Aug 62*	2

Frankie KNUCKLES — US

SINGLES:	HITS 7			WEEKS 19
TEARS *Above hit: Frankie KNUCKLES presents Satoshi TOMIIE featuring Robert OWENS.*	*ffrr*	50	*17 Jun 89*	3
YOUR LOVE	*Trax*	59	*21 Oct 89*	4
THE WHISTLE SONG	*Virgin America*	17	*27 Jul 91*	5
IT'S HARD SOMETIME *Above hit: Frankie KNUCKLES featuring Shelton BECTON.*	*Virgin America*	67	*23 Nov 91*	1
RAIN FALLS *Above hit: Frankie KNUCKLES featuring Lisa MICHAELIS.*	*Virgin America*	48	*6 Jun 92*	2
TOO MANY FISH	*Virgin*	34	*27 May 95*	2
WHADDA U WANT (FROM ME) *Above 2: Frankie KNUCKLES featuring ADEVA.*	*Virgin*	36	*18 Nov 95*	2
ALBUMS:	**HITS 1**			**WEEKS 2**
BEYOND THE MIX	*Virgin America*	59	*17 Aug 91*	2

Moe KOFFMAN QUARTETTE — Canada

SINGLES:	HITS 1			WEEKS 2
SWINGIN' SHEPHERD BLUES	*London*	23	*29 Mar 58*	2

KOFI – See SOUL II SOUL

Mike KOGLIN — Germany

SINGLES:	HITS 2			WEEKS 4
THE SILENCE	*Multiply*	20	*28 Nov 98*	2
ON MY WAY *Above hit: Mike KOGLIN featuring BEATRICE.*	*Multiply*	28	*29 May 99*	2

Eugene KOHN – See Placido DOMINGO

KOKOMO, his Piano and Orchestra — US

SINGLES:	HITS 1			WEEKS 7
ASIA MINOR *Adapted from Grieg's Piano Concerto.*	*London*	35	*15 Apr 61*	7

KOKOMO — UK

SINGLES:	HITS 1			WEEKS 3
A LITTLE BIT FURTHER AWAY	*CBS*	45	*29 May 82*	3

KON KAN — Canada

SINGLES:	HITS 1			WEEKS 13
I BEG YOUR PARDON *Samples Lynn Anderson's Rose Garden and Disco Nights (Rock Freak) by GQ.*	*Atlantic*	5	*4 Mar 89*	13

John KONGOS UK

SINGLES:	HITS 2			WEEKS 25
HE'S GONNA STEP ON YOU AGAIN	*Fly*	4	*22 May 71*	14
TOKOLOSHE MAN	*Fly*	4	*20 Nov 71*	11
ALBUMS:	**HITS 1**			**WEEKS 2**
KONGOS	*Fly*	29	*15 Jan 72*	2

KONKRETE UK

SINGLES:	HITS 1			WEEKS 1
LAW UNTO MYSELF	*Perfecto*	60	*22 Sep 01*	1

KOOL AND THE GANG US

SINGLES:	HITS 21			WEEKS 207
LADIES NIGHT	*Mercury*	9	*27 Oct 79*	12
TOO HOT	*Mercury*	23	*19 Jan 80*	8
HANGIN' OUT	*De-Lite*	52	*12 Jul 80*	4
CELEBRATION	*De-Lite*	7	*1 Nov 80*	13
JONES VS JONES / SUMMER MADNESS / FUNKY STUFF / HOLLYWOOD SWINGING	*De-Lite*	17	*21 Feb 81*	11
Though all 4 tracks were listed on the chart, the last 2 were only available on the 12" and 7" doublepack formats.				
TAKE IT TO THE TOP (CLIMBING)	*De-Lite*	15	*30 May 81*	9
STEPPIN' OUT	*De-Lite*	12	*31 Oct 81*	13
GET DOWN ON IT	*De-Lite*	3	*19 Dec 81*	12
TAKE MY HEART (YOU CAN HAVE IT IF YOU WANT IT)	*De-Lite*	29	*6 Mar 82*	7
BIG FUN	*De-Lite*	14	*7 Aug 82*	8
OOH LA LA LA (LET'S GO DANCIN')	*De-Lite*	6	*16 Oct 82*	9
HI DE HI, HI DE HO	*De-Lite*	29	*4 Dec 82*	8
STRAIGHT AHEAD	*De-Lite*	15	*10 Dec 83*	10
JOANNA / TONIGHT	*De-Lite*	2	*11 Feb 84*	11
(WHEN YOU SAY YOU LOVE SOMEBODY) IN THE HEART	*De-Lite*	7	*14 Apr 84*	8
FRESH	*De-Lite*	11	*24 Nov 84*	12
MISLED	*De-Lite*	28	*9 Feb 85*	5
CHERISH	*De-Lite*	4	*11 May 85*	22
EMERGENCY	*De-Lite*	50	*2 Nov 85*	3
VICTORY	*Club*	67	*22 Nov 86*	2
VICTORY [RE]	*Club*	30	*20 Dec 86*	10
STONE LOVE	*Club*	45	*21 Mar 87*	4
CELEBRATION [RM]	*Club*	56	*31 Dec 88*	5
Remixed by Stock Aitken Waterman.				
GET DOWN ON IT [RM]	*Mercury*	69	*6 Jul 91*	1
Remixed by Oliver Momm.				
ALBUMS:	**HITS 7**			**WEEKS 115**
SOMETHING SPECIAL	*De-Lite*	10	*21 Nov 81*	20
AS ONE	*De-Lite*	49	*2 Oct 82*	10
TWICE AS KOOL - THE HITS OF KOOL & THE GANG	*De-Lite*	4	*7 May 83*	23
IN THE HEART	*De-Lite*	18	*14 Jan 84*	23
EMERGENCY	*De-Lite*	47	*15 Dec 84*	25
THE SINGLES COLLECTION	*De-Lite*	28	*12 Nov 88*	13
KOOL LOVE	*Telstar*	50	*27 Oct 90*	1

KOOL ROCK STEADY - See TYREE

KOON + STEPHENSON - See WESTBAM

KORGIS UK

SINGLES:	HITS 3			WEEKS 27
IF I HAD YOU	*Rialto*	13	*23 Jun 79*	12
EVERYBODY'S GOT TO LEARN SOMETIME	*Rialto*	5	*24 May 80*	12
IF IT'S ALRIGHT WITH YOU BABY	*Rialto*	56	*30 Aug 80*	3
ALBUMS:	**HITS 1**			**WEEKS 4**
DUMB WAITERS	*Rialto*	40	*26 Jul 80*	4

KORN US

SINGLES:	HITS 7			WEEKS 14
NO PLACE TO HIDE	*Epic*	26	*19 Oct 96*	2
A.D.I.D.A.S.	*Epic*	22	*15 Feb 97*	2
Acronym for All Day I Dream About Sex.				
GOOD GOD	*Epic*	25	*7 Jun 97*	2
GOT THE LIFE	*Epic*	23	*22 Aug 98*	2
FREAK ON A LEASH	*Epic*	24	*8 May 99*	2
FALLING AWAY FROM ME	*Epic*	24	*12 Feb 00*	2
MAKE ME BAD	*Epic*	25	*3 Jun 00*	2
ALBUMS:	**HITS 3**			**WEEKS 7**
LIFE IS PEACHY	*Epic*	32	*26 Oct 96*	2

FOLLOW THE LEADER	*Epic*	5	*29 Aug 98*	4
ISSUES	*Epic*	37	*27 Nov 99*	1

KOSHEEN — UK

SINGLES:	HITS 3			WEEKS 12
EMPTY SKIES/HIDE U	*Moksha Recordings*	73	*17 Jun 00*	1
(SLIP & SLIDE) SUICIDE	*Moksha Recordings*	50	*14 Apr 01*	2
HIDE U [RM]	*Moksha Recordings*	6	*1 Sep 00*	6
Remixed by John Creamer and Stephan K.				
HIDE U [RM] [RE]	*Moksha Recordings*	55	*27 Oct 01*	1
CATCH	*Moksha Recordings*	15	*22 Dec 01*	2
ALBUMS:	**HITS 1**			**WEEKS 1**
RESIST	*Moksha Recordings*	56	*29 Sep 01*	1

KRAFTWERK — Germany

SINGLES:	HITS 9			WEEKS 72
AUTOBAHN	*Vertigo*	11	*10 May 75*	9
NEON LIGHTS	*Capitol*	53	*28 Oct 78*	3
POCKET CALCULATOR	*EMI*	39	*9 May 81*	6
COMPUTER LOVE / THE MODEL	*EMI*	36	*11 Jul 81*	8
THE MODEL / COMPUTER LOVE [RE]	*EMI*	1	*26 Dec 81*	13
SHOWROOM DUMMIES	*EMI*	25	*20 Feb 82*	5
TOUR DE FRANCE	*EMI*	22	*6 Aug 83*	8
TOUR DE FRANCE ('BREAKDANCE' REMIX) [RE]	*EMI*	24	*25 Aug 84*	11
Though this had the same catalogue number, it was actually a remix for the film 'Breakdance'.				
THE ROBOTS	*EMI*	20	*1 Jun 91*	4
RADIOACTIVITY	*EMI*	43	*2 Nov 91*	2
TOUR DE FRANCE [RI]	*EMI*	61	*23 Oct 99*	1
EXPO2000	*EMI*	27	*18 Mar 00*	2
Written to publicise the World Fair in Hanover.				
ALBUMS:	**HITS 6**			**WEEKS 71**
AUTOBAHN	*Vertigo*	4	*17 May 75*	18
THE MAN-MACHINE	*Capitol*	53	*20 May 78*	3
COMPUTER WORLD	*EMI*	15	*23 May 81*	22
THE MAN-MACHINE [RE]	*Capitol*	9	*23 Jan 82*	10
TRANS-EUROPE EXPRESS	*Capitol*	49	*6 Feb 82*	7
Originally released in 1977.				
AUTOBAHN [RI]	*Parlophone*	61	*22 Jun 85*	3
ELECTRIC CAFE	*EMI*	58	*15 Nov 86*	2
THE MIX	*EMI*	15	*22 Jun 91*	6

Diana KRALL — Canada

ALBUMS:	HITS 2			WEEKS 8
WHEN I LOOK IN YOUR EYES	*Verve*	72	*12 Jun 99*	1
THE LOOK OF LOVE	*Verve*	23	*29 Sep 01*	7

Billy J. KRAMER with the DAKOTAS — UK

SINGLES:	HITS 6			WEEKS 71
DO YOU WANT TO KNOW A SECRET	*Parlophone*	2	*4 May 63*	15
BAD TO ME	*Parlophone*	1	*3 Aug 63*	14
I'LL KEEP YOU SATISFIED	*Parlophone*	4	*9 Nov 63*	13
Above 3 written by Lennon/McCartney.				
LITTLE CHILDREN	*Parlophone*	1	*29 Feb 64*	13
FROM A WINDOW	*Parlophone*	10	*25 Jul 64*	8
Written by Lennon/ McCartney.				
TRAINS AND BOATS AND PLANES	*Parlophone*	12	*22 May 65*	8
EPS:	**HITS 1**			**WEEKS 13**
THE BILLY J. KRAMER HITS	*Parlophone*	8	*26 Oct 63*	13
ALBUMS:	**HITS 1**			**WEEKS 17**
LISTEN TO BILLY J. KRAMER	*Parlophone*	11	*16 Nov 63*	17

KRANKIES — UK

SINGLES:	HITS 1			WEEKS 6
FAN' DABI' DOZI	*Monarch*	71	*7 Feb 81*	1
FAN' DABI' DOZI [RE]	*Monarch*	46	*7 Mar 81*	5

Alison KRAUSS and UNION STATION — US

ALBUMS:	HITS 1			WEEKS 1
NEW FAVORITE	*Rounder*	72	*25 Aug 01*	1

Lenny KRAVITZ — US

SINGLES:	HITS 16			WEEKS 68
MR. CABDRIVER	*Virgin America*	58	*2 Jun 90*	2

LET LOVE RULE	*Virgin America*	39	*4 Aug 90*	4
ALWAYS ON THE RUN	*Virgin America*	41	*30 Mar 91*	3
IT AIN'T OVER 'TIL IT'S OVER	*Virgin America*	11	*15 Jun 91*	8
STAND BY MY WOMAN	*Virgin America*	55	*14 Sep 91*	3
ARE YOU GONNA GO MY WAY	*Virgin America*	4	*20 Feb 93*	11
BELIEVE	*Virgin America*	30	*22 May 93*	5
HEAVEN HELP	*Virgin*	20	*28 Aug 93*	7
IS THERE ANY LOVE IN YOUR HEART	*Virgin*	52	*4 Dec 93*	2
BUDDHA OF SUBURBIA	*Arista*	35	*4 Dec 93*	3
Theme from the BBC TV series of the same name.				
Above hit: David BOWIE (featuring Lenny KRAVITZ on Guitar).				
ROCK AND ROLL IS DEAD	*Virgin*	22	*9 Sep 95*	3
CIRCUS	*Virgin*	54	*23 Dec 95*	2
CAN'T GET YOU OFF MY MIND	*Virgin*	54	*2 Mar 96*	2
IF YOU CAN'T SAY NO	*Virgin*	48	*16 May 98*	2
I BELONG TO YOU	*Virgin*	75	*10 Oct 98*	1
FLY AWAY	*Virgin*	1	*20 Feb 99*	10
Featured in the Peugeot 206 TV commercial. Original release reached No. 162 in 1998.				

ALBUMS:	HITS 7			WEEKS 109
LET LOVE RULE	*Virgin America*	56	*26 May 90*	4
MAMA SAID	*Virgin America*	8	*13 Apr 91*	27
ARE YOU GONNA GO MY WAY	*Virgin*	1	*13 Mar 93*	47
CIRCUS	*Virgin*	5	*23 Sep 95*	4
5	*Virgin*	18	*23 May 98*	13
GREATEST HITS	*Virgin*	12	*4 Nov 00*	13
LENNY	*Virgin*	55	*10 Nov 01*	1

KRAZE — US

SINGLES:	HITS 2			WEEKS 6
THE PARTY	*MCA*	29	*22 Oct 88*	5
LET'S PLAY HOUSE	*MCA*	71	*17 Jun 89*	1

KREUZ — UK

SINGLES:	HITS 1			WEEKS 1
PARTY ALL NIGHT	*Diesel*	75	*8 Jul 95*	1
ALBUMS:	**HITS 1**			**WEEKS 2**
KREUZ KONTROL	*Diesel*	48	*18 Mar 95*	2

Chantal KREVIAZUK — Canada

SINGLES:	HITS 1			WEEKS 1
LEAVING ON A JET PLANE	*Epic*	59	*6 Mar 99*	1
From the film 'Armageddon'.				

KREW-KATS — UK

SINGLES:	HITS 1			WEEKS 10
TRAMBONE	*His Master's Voice*	33	*11 Mar 61*	9
Originally recorded by Chet Atkins.				
TRAMBONE [RE]	*His Master's Voice*	49	*20 May 61*	1

KRIS KROSS — US

SINGLES:	HITS 5			WEEKS 22
JUMP	*Columbia*	2	*30 May 92*	8
WARM IT UP	*Columbia*	16	*25 Jul 92*	6
I MISSED THE BUS	*Columbia*	57	*17 Oct 92*	1
IT'S A SHAME	*Columbia*	31	*19 Dec 92*	5
ALRIGHT	*Columbia*	47	*11 Sep 93*	2
Samples Slave's Just A Touch Of Love.				
Above hit: KRISS KROSS featuring SUPERCAT				
ALBUMS:	**HITS 1**			**WEEKS 8**
TOTALLY KROSSED OUT	*Columbia*	31	*27 Jun 92*	8

Kris KRISTOFFERSON and Rita COOLIDGE — US

(See also Rita Coolidge; Barbra Streisand.)

ALBUMS:	HITS 1			WEEKS 4
NATURAL ACT	*A&M*	35	*6 May 78*	4

KROKUS — Switzerland/Argentina

SINGLES:	HITS 1			WEEKS 2
INDUSTRIAL STRENGTH [EP]	*Ariola*	62	*16 May 81*	2
Lead track: Bedside Radio.				
ALBUMS:	**HITS 3**			**WEEKS 11**
HARDWARE	*Ariola*	44	*21 Feb 81*	4
ONE VICE AT A TIME	*Arista*	28	*20 Feb 82*	5

HEADHUNTERS	*Arista*	74	*16 Apr 83*	2

KRS ONE — US

SINGLES:	HITS 5			WEEKS 8
RAPPAZ R.N. DAINJA	*Jive*	47	*18 May 96*	1
WORD PERFECT	*Jive*	70	*8 Feb 97*	1
STEP INTO A WORLD (RAPTURE'S DELIGHT) *Track based on Blondie's 1981 hit Rapture.*	*Jive*	24	*26 Apr 97*	2
HEARTBEAT / A FRIEND *Above hit: KRS-ONE featuring REDMAN and Angie MARTINEZ.*	*Jive*	66	*20 Sep 97*	1
DIGITAL *Above hit: GOLDIE featuring KRS ONE.*	*ffrr*	13	*1 Nov 97*	3
ALBUMS:	**HITS 1**			**WEEKS 1**
I GOT NEXT	*Jive*	58	*31 May 97*	1

KRUSH — UK

SINGLES:	HITS 2			WEEKS 16
HOUSE ARREST	*Club*	3	*5 Dec 87*	15
WALKING ON SUNSHINE *Above hit: KRUSH featuring Ruth JOY.*	*Network*	71	*14 Nov 92*	1

KRUSH PERSPECTIVE — US

SINGLES:	HITS 1			WEEKS 2
LET'S GET TOGETHER (SO GROOVY NOW)	*Perspective*	61	*16 Jan 93*	2

KRUST featuring Saul WILLIAMS — UK

SINGLES:	HITS 1			WEEKS 1
CODED LANGUAGE	*Talkin Loud*	66	*23 Oct 99*	1

K7 — US

SINGLES:	HITS 3			WEEKS 22
COME BABY COME	*Big Life*	3	*11 Dec 93*	16
HI DE HO	*Big Life*	17	*2 Apr 94*	5
ZUNGA ZENG *Above 2: K7 and the SWING KIDS.*	*Big Life*	63	*25 Jun 94*	1
ALBUMS:	**HITS 1**			**WEEKS 3**
SWING BATTA SWING	*Big Life*	27	*5 Feb 94*	3

K3M — Italy

SINGLES:	HITS 1			WEEKS 1
LISTEN TO THE RHYTHM	*PWL Continental*	71	*21 Mar 92*	1

K2 FAMILY — UK

SINGLES:	HITS 1			WEEKS 3
BOUNCING FLOW	*Relentless*	27	*27 Oct 01*	3

KULA SHAKER — UK

SINGLES:	HITS 8			WEEKS 48
GRATEFUL WHEN YOU'RE DEAD/JERRY WAS THERE [M]	*Columbia*	35	*4 May 96*	3
TATTVA	*Columbia*	4	*6 Jul 96*	8
HEY DUDE	*Columbia*	2	*7 Sep 96*	7
GOVINDA *Originally recorded by Radha Krishna Temple.*	*Columbia*	7	*23 Nov 96*	8
HUSH *Originally recorded by Joe South in 1968, though the arrangement for this version was adapted from Deep Purple's version.*	*Columbia*	2	*8 Mar 97*	8
HUSH [RE]	*Columbia*	70	*9 Aug 97*	1
SOUND OF DRUMS	*Columbia*	3	*2 May 98*	6
MYSTICAL MACHINE GUN	*Columbia*	14	*6 Mar 99*	3
SHOWER YOUR LOVE	*Columbia*	14	*15 May 99*	4
ALBUMS:	**HITS 2**			**WEEKS 54**
K	*Columbia*	1	*28 Sep 96*	44
PEASANTS, PIGS & ASTRONAUTS	*Columbia*	9	*20 Mar 99*	10

KULAY — Philippines

SINGLES:	HITS 1			WEEKS 1
DELICIOUS	*INCredible*	73	*12 Sep 98*	1

KUMARA — Holland

SINGLES:	HITS 1			WEEKS 1
SNAP YOUR FINGAZ	*Y2K*	70	*7 Oct 00*	1

Charlie KUNZ — UK

SINGLES:	HITS 1			WEEKS 4
CHARLIE KUNZ PIANO MEDLEY NO. 114 [M]	*Decca*	20	*18 Dec 54*	3
Medley of songs from 1954.				
CHARLIE KUNZ PIANO MEDLEY NO. 114 [M] [RE]	*Decca*	16	*15 Jan 55*	1
ALBUMS:	**HITS 1**			**WEEKS 11**
THE WORLD OF CHARLIE KUNZ	*Decca*	9	*14 Jun 69*	11

KURSAAL FLYERS — UK

SINGLES:	HITS 1			WEEKS 10
LITTLE DOES SHE KNOW	*CBS*	14	*20 Nov 76*	10

KURUPT featuring Natina REED — US

(See also Shade Sheist featuring Nate Dogg & Kurupt.)

SINGLES:	HITS 1			WEEKS 3
IT'S OVER	*PIAS Recordings*	21	*13 Oct 01*	3

KUT KLOSE — US

SINGLES:	HITS 1			WEEKS 1
I LIKE	*Elektra*	72	*29 Apr 95*	1

Li KWAN — UK

(See also Joey Negro.)

SINGLES:	HITS 1			WEEKS 2
I NEED A MAN	*Deconstruction*	51	*17 Dec 94*	2

KY-MANI - See PM DAWN

KYO (aka Carole LEEMING) - See John DIGWEED and Nick MUIR Present BEDROCK

Val KYRIE and the RHINE MAIDENS - See BAROCK-AND-ROLL ENSEMBLE

L

Jonny L — UK

SINGLES:	HITS 2			WEEKS 2
OOH I LIKE IT	*XL Recordings*	73	*28 Aug 93*	1
20 DEGREES	*XL Recordings*	66	*31 Oct 98*	1
Above hit: Jonny L featuring SILVAH BULLET.				

L.A. GUNS — US

SINGLES:	HITS 2			WEEKS 4
SOME LIE 4 LOVE	*Mercury*	61	*30 Nov 91*	1
THE BALLAD OF JAYNE	*Mercury*	53	*21 Dec 91*	3
ALBUMS:	**HITS 3**			**WEEKS 4**
L.A. GUNS	*Vertigo*	73	*5 Mar 88*	1
COCKED AND LOADED	*Vertigo*	45	*30 Sep 89*	2
HOLLYWOOD VAMPIRES	*Mercury*	44	*13 Jul 91*	1

L.A. MIX — UK

SINGLES:	HITS 7			WEEKS 25
DON'T STOP (JAMMIN')	*Breakout*	47	*10 Oct 87*	4
CHECK THIS OUT	*Breakout*	6	*21 May 88*	7
GET LOOSE	*Breakout*	25	*8 Jul 89*	6
Above hit: L.A. MIX featuring Jazzi P.				
LOVE TOGETHER	*Breakout*	66	*16 Sep 89*	2
Above hit: L.A. MIX featuring Kevin HENRY.				
COMING BACK FOR MORE	*A&M*	50	*15 Sep 90*	3
MYSTERIES OF LOVE	*A&M*	46	*19 Jan 91*	2
WE SHOULDN'T HOLD HANDS IN THE DARK	*A&M*	69	*23 Mar 91*	1

L.R.S. - See D-MOB

L.T.D. — US

SINGLES:	HITS 1			WEEKS 3
HOLDING ON (WHEN LOVE IS GONE)	*A&M*	70	*9 Sep 78*	3

L.V. — US

SINGLES:	HITS 3			WEEKS 25
GANGSTA'S PARADISE *From the film 'Dangerous Minds'. Samples Stevie Wonder's Pastime Paradise.* *Above hit: COOLIO featuring L.V.*	*Tommy Boy*	1	*28 Oct 95*	20
THROW YOUR HANDS UP / GANGSTA'S PARADISE [RR]	*Tommy Boy*	24	*23 Dec 95*	4
I AM L.V.	*Tommy Boy*	64	*4 May 96*	1

L.W.S. — Italy

SINGLES:	HITS 1			WEEKS 1
GOSP	*Transworld*	65	*29 Oct 94*	1

LA GANZ (EL - E - GANZ) — US

SINGLES:	HITS 1			WEEKS 1
LIKE A PLAYA	*Jive*	75	*9 Nov 96*	1

LA NA NEE NEE NOO NOO – See BANANARAMA

Julius LA ROSA with Nick PERITO and his Orchestra — US

SINGLES:	HITS 1			WEEKS 9
TORERO	*RCA*	15	*5 Jul 58*	9

Danny LA RUE — UK

SINGLES:	HITS 1			WEEKS 9
ON MOTHER KELLY'S DOORSTEP	*Page One*	33	*21 Dec 68*	9

LA'S — UK

(See also Various Artists (EPs) 'Fever Pitch The EP'.)

SINGLES:	HITS 3			WEEKS 19
THERE SHE GOES	*Go! Discs*	59	*14 Jan 89*	4
TIMELESS MELODY	*Go! Discs*	57	*15 Sep 90*	2
THERE SHE GOES [RI]	*Go! Discs*	13	*3 Nov 90*	9
FEELIN'	*Go! Discs*	43	*16 Feb 91*	3
THERE SHE GOES [RI-2ND] *Released after the success of the cover by Sixpence None The Richer.*	*Polydor*	65	*2 Oct 99*	1

ALBUMS:	HITS 1			WEEKS 20
THE LA'S	*Go! Discs*	30	*13 Oct 90*	20

LA TREC – See SASH!

LABELLE — US

SINGLES:	HITS 1			WEEKS 9
LADY MARMALADE (VOULEZ-VOUS COUCHER AVEC MOI CE SOIR?) *Originally recorded by the Eleventh Hour.*	*Epic*	17	*22 Mar 75*	9

Patti LABELLE — US

SINGLES:	HITS 3			WEEKS 21
ON MY OWN *Above hit: Patti LABELLE and Michael McDONALD.*	*MCA*	2	*3 May 86*	13
OH, PEOPLE	*MCA*	26	*2 Aug 86*	6
THE RIGHT KINDA LOVER *From the film 'Beverly Hill Cop II'.*	*MCA*	50	*3 Sep 94*	2

ALBUMS:	HITS 1			WEEKS 17
WINNER IN YOU	*MCA*	30	*24 May 86*	17

LADIES CHOICE — UK

SINGLES:	HITS 1			WEEKS 4
FUNKY SENSATION	*Sure Delight*	41	*25 Jan 86*	4

LADIES FIRST — UK

SINGLES:	HITS 1			WEEKS 2
MESSIN'	*Polydor*	30	*24 Nov 01*	2

LADY G – See B-15 PROJECT featuring Crissy D and LADY G

LADY J and the SECRETARY OF ENT. – See RAZE

LADY JOJO, Queen of the GoGo – See TWA featuring LADY JOJO, Queen of the GoGo

LADY OF RAGE — US

SINGLES:	HITS 1			WEEKS 1
AFRO PUFFS *Features vocals by Dr. Dre and Snoop Doggy Dogg. From the film 'Above The Rim'.*	*Interscope*	72	*8 Oct 94*	1

LADY SAW - See M-DUBS featuring LADY SAW; UB40

LADYSMITH BLACK MAMBAZO — South Africa

SINGLES:	HITS 5			WEEKS 26
SWING LOW SWEET CHARIOT *The England theme for the Rugby World Cup.* *Above hit: LADYSMITH BLACK MAMBAZO featuring CHINA BLACK.*	*PolyGram TV*	15	*3 Jun 95*	6
WORLD IN UNION '95 The ITV Rugby World Cup theme. *Above hit: LADYSMITH BLACK MAMBAZO featuring P.J. POWERS.*	*PolyGram TV*	47	*3 Jun 95*	5
INKANYEZI NEZAZI (THE STAR AND THE WISEMAN) *Featured in the Heinz Beans TV commerical.*	*A&M*	33	*15 Nov 97*	3
INKANYEZI NEZAZI (THE STAR AND THE WISEMAN) [RI]	*AM:PM*	63	*11 Jul 98*	1
AIN'T NO SUNSHINE *Originally recorded by Bill Withers reaching No. 3 in the US in 1971.* *Above hit: LADYSMITH BLACK MAMBAZO featuring DES'REE.*	*Universal*	42	*16 Oct 99*	2
I SHALL BE THERE *Above hit: B*WITCHED featuring LADYSMITH BLACK MAMBAZO.*	*Glow Worm*	13	*18 Dec 99*	9

ALBUMS:	HITS 5			WEEKS 69
SHAKA ZULU	*Warner Brothers*	34	*11 Apr 87*	11
HEAVENLY	*A&M*	53	*22 Nov 97*	16
THE BEST OF LADYSMITH BLACK MAMBAZO - THE STAR AND THE WISEMAN *Label changed to Universal Music TV from 13 Mar 99.*	*PolyGram TV*	2	*3 Oct 98*	34
IN HARMONY	*Universal Music TV*	15	*16 Oct 99*	5
THE ULTIMATE COLLECTION	*Universal Music TV*	37	*12 May 01*	3

LAGUNA — Italy

SINGLES:	HITS 1			WEEKS 2
SPILLER FROM RIO (DO IT EASY)	*Positiva*	40	*1 Nov 97*	2

LAID BACK — Norway

SINGLES:	HITS 1			WEEKS 4
BAKERMAN	*Arista*	44	*5 May 90*	4

LAIN - See WOOKIE

Cleo LAINE — UK

(See also Cleo Laine and James Galway; Cleo Laine and John Williams.)

SINGLES:	HITS 2			WEEKS 14
LET'S SLIP AWAY	*Fontana*	42	*31 Dec 60*	1
YOU'LL ANSWER TO ME *Originally recorded by Patti Page*	*Fontana*	5	*16 Sep 61*	13

ALBUMS:	HITS 1			WEEKS 1
CLEO	*Arcade*	68	*2 Dec 78*	1

Cleo LAINE and James GALWAY — UK

(See also James Galway; Cleo Laine.)

ALBUMS:	HITS 1			WEEKS 14
SOMETIMES WHEN WE TOUCH	*RCA*	15	*31 May 80*	14

Cleo LAINE and John WILLIAMS — UK

(See also Cleo Laine; John Williams.)

ALBUMS:	HITS 1			WEEKS 22
BEST OF FRIENDS	*RCA Victor*	18	*7 Jan 78*	22

Frankie LAINE — US

SINGLES:	HITS 27			WEEKS 282
HIGH NOON (DO NOT FORSAKE ME) *From the film 'High Noon'.*	*Columbia*	7	*15 Nov 52*	7
SUGAR BUSH *Above hit: Doris DAY and Frankie LAINE with Carl FISCHER'S ORCHESTRA and the Norman LUBOFF CHOIR.*	*Columbia*	8	*15 Nov 52*	2
SUGAR BUSH [RE]	*Columbia*	8	*6 Dec 52*	6
THE GIRL IN THE WOOD *Above hit: Frankie LAINE with Paul WESTON and his Orchestra and the Norman LUBOFF CHOIR (Carl FISCHER at the piano).*	*Columbia*	11	*21 Mar 53*	1
I BELIEVE *The single to have spent the longest time at No. 1 (18 weeks).* *Above hit: Frankie LAINE with Paul WESTON and his Orchestra.*	*Philips*	1	*4 Apr 53*	36
TELL ME A STORY *Features accompaniment by Norman Luboff and Carl Fischer on piano.* *Above hit: Jimmy BOYD-Frankie LAINE.*	*Philips*	5	*9 May 53*	15
WHERE THE WINDS BLOW *Above hit: Frankie LAINE; Carl FISCHER-piano.*	*Philips*	2	*5 Sep 53*	12

Title	Label	Pos	Date	Wks
TELL ME A STORY [RE]	*Philips*	12	*12 Sep 53*	1
HEY JOE!	*Philips*	1	*17 Oct 53*	8
ANSWER ME	*Philips*	1	*31 Oct 53*	17
Above 2: Frankie LAINE with Paul WESTON and his Orchestra and the Norman LUBOFF CHOIR (Carl FISCHER-piano).				
BLOWING WILD (THE BALLAD OF BLACK GOLD)	*Philips*	2	*9 Jan 54*	12
From the film 'Blowing Wild'.				
Above hit: Frankie LAINE (Carl FISCHER: piano).				
GRANADA	*Philips*	10	*27 Mar 54*	1
Above hit: Frankie LAINE with Paul WESTON and his Orchestra (Carl FISCHER: piano).				
GRANADA [RE]	*Philips*	9	*10 Apr 54*	1
THE KID'S LAST FIGHT	*Philips*	3	*17 Apr 54*	10
Above hit: Frankie LAINE with Carl FISCHER At the Upright and the Norman LUBOFF CHOIR.				
MY FRIEND	*Philips*	3	*14 Aug 54*	15
Above hit: Frankie LAINE with Paul WESTON and his Orchestra and the Norman LUBOFF CHOIR.				
THERE MUST BE A REASON	*Philips*	9	*9 Oct 54*	9
Above hit: Frankie LAINE with Paul WESTON and his Orchestra (Carl FISCHER: piano).				
RAIN, RAIN, RAIN	*Philips*	8	*23 Oct 54*	16
Above hit: Frankie LAINE and the FOUR LADS with the Buddy COLE QUARTET				
IN THE BEGINNING	*Philips*	20	*12 Mar 55*	1
Above hit: Frankie LAINE with Paul WESTON his Orchestra and the Norman LUBOFF CHOIR.				
COOL WATER	*Philips*	2	*25 Jun 55*	22
Originally recorded by Sons Of The Pioneers in 1941.				
Above hit: Frankie LAINE with Paul WESTON and his Orchestra and the MELLOMEN.				
STRANGE LADY IN TOWN	*Philips*	6	*16 Jul 55*	13
From the film of the same name.				
Above hit: Frankie LAINE with Mitch MILLER and his Orchestra and Chorus.				
HUMMINGBIRD	*Philips*	16	*12 Nov 55*	1
HAWK-EYE	*Philips*	7	*26 Nov 55*	8
Above hit: Frankie LAINE with Ray CONNIFF and his Orchestra.				
SIXTEEN TONS	*Philips*	10	*21 Jan 56*	3
Above hit: Frankie LAINE with the MELLOMEN.				
HELL HATH NO FURY	*Philips*	28	*5 May 56*	1
From the film 'Meet Me In Las Vegas'.				
A WOMAN IN LOVE	*Philips*	1	*8 Sep 56*	21
Some copies only reflect title as 'Woman In Love'. From the film 'Guys And Dolls'. Originally recorded by Marlon Brando.				
Above hit: Frankie LAINE with Percy FAITH and his Orchestra.				
MOONLIGHT GAMBLER	*Philips*	13	*29 Dec 56*	12
Above hit: Frankie LAINE with Ray CONNIFF and his Orchestra.				
MOONLIGHT GAMBLER [RE]	*Philips*	28	*30 Mar 57*	1
LOVE IS A GOLDEN RING	*Philips*	19	*27 Apr 57*	5
Above hit: Frankie LAINE with the EASY RIDERS.				
UP ABOVE MY HEAD, I HEAR MUSIC IN THE AIR / GOOD EVENING FRIENDS	*Philips*	25	*5 Oct 57*	4
Up Above My Head originally recorded by Sister Rosetta Tharpe.				
Above hit: Johnnie RAY – Frankie LAINE with Ray CONNIFF and his Orchestra / Frankie LAINE – Johnnie RAY with Ray CONNIFF and his Orchestra.				
RAWHIDE	*Philips*	6	*14 Nov 59*	18
From the TV series of the same name.				
Above hit: Frankie LAINE with Jimmy CARROLL and his Orchestra.				
RAWHIDE [RE]	*Philips*	41	*2 Apr 60*	2
GUNSLINGER	*Philips*	50	*13 May 61*	1
Main title theme from the CBS-TV Network show of the same name.				
EPS:	**HITS 1**			**WEEKS 12**
WESTERN FAVOURITES	*Philips*	7	*22 Jul 61*	12
ALBUMS:	**HITS 2**			**WEEKS 29**
HELL BENT FOR LEATHER	*Philips*	7	*24 Jun 61*	23
THE VERY BEST OF FRANKIE LAINE	*Warwick*	7	*24 Sep 77*	6

Greg LAKE — UK

(See also Emerson, Lake and Palmer; Emerson, Lake and Powell.)

Title	Label	Pos	Date	Wks
SINGLES:	**HITS 1**			**WEEKS 12**
I BELIEVE IN FATHER CHRISTMAS	*Manticore*	2	*6 Dec 75*	7
I BELIEVE IN FATHER CHRISTMAS [RE-1ST]	*Manticore*	72	*25 Dec 82*	3
I BELIEVE IN FATHER CHRISTMAS [RE-2ND]	*Manticore*	65	*24 Dec 83*	2
ALBUMS:	**HITS 1**			**WEEKS 3**
GREG LAKE	*Chrysalis*	62	*17 Oct 81*	3

LAMB — UK

Title	Label	Pos	Date	Wks
SINGLES:	**HITS 3**			**WEEKS 4**
GORECKI	*Fontana*	30	*29 Mar 97*	2
Inspired by Polish composer Henri Gorecki's Symphony Of Sorrow Songs.				

B LINE	*Fontana*	52	*3 Apr 99*	1
ALL IN YOUR HANDS	*Fontana*	71	*22 May 99*	1
ALBUMS:	**HITS 2**			**WEEKS 2**
FEAR OF FOURS	*Fontana*	37	*29 May 99*	1
WHAT SOUND	*Mercury*	54	*20 Oct 01*	1

Annabel LAMB — UK

SINGLES:	**HITS 1**			**WEEKS 7**
RIDERS ON THE STORM	*A&M*	27	*27 Aug 83*	7
ALBUMS:	**HITS 1**			**WEEKS 1**
THE FLAME	*A&M*	84	*28 Apr 84*	1

LAMBCHOP — US

SINGLES:	**HITS 1**			**WEEKS 1**
THE "SPEAK UP" MUSICAL - UP WITH PEOPLE!	*City Slang*	66	*20 May 00*	1
ALBUMS:	**HITS 1**			**WEEKS 1**
NIXON	*City Slang*	60	*19 Feb 00*	1

LAMPIES — UK

SINGLES:	**HITS 1**			**WEEKS 2**
LIGHT UP THE WORLD FOR CHRISTMAS	*Bluecrest*	48	*22 Dec 01*	2

LAMBRETTAS — UK

SINGLES:	**HITS 3**			**WEEKS 24**
POISON IVY	*Rocket*	7	*1 Mar 80*	12
D-A-A-ANCE	*Rocket*	12	*24 May 80*	8
ANOTHER DAY (ANOTHER GIRL)	*Rocket*	49	*23 Aug 80*	4
ALBUMS:	**HITS 1**			**WEEKS 8**
BEAT BOYS IN THE JET AGE	*Rocket*	28	*5 Jul 80*	8

LANCASTRIANS — UK

SINGLES:	**HITS 1**			**WEEKS 2**
WE'LL SING IN THE SUNSHINE *Originally recorded by Gale Garnett.*	*Pye*	47	*26 Dec 64*	2

Major LANCE — US

SINGLES:	**HITS 1**			**WEEKS 2**
UM UM UM UM UM UM	*Columbia*	40	*15 Feb 64*	2

James LANCELOT - See Sarah BRIGHTMAN

LANCERS - See Teresa BREWER

Charlie LANDSBOROUGH — UK

ALBUMS:	**HITS 4**			**WEEKS 13**
WITH YOU IN MIND	*Ritz*	49	*12 Oct 96*	6
FURTHER DOWN THE ROAD	*Ritz*	42	*8 Nov 97*	3
THE VERY BEST OF CHARLIE LANDSBOROUGH	*Ritz*	41	*10 Oct 98*	2
STILL CAN'T SAY GOODBYE	*Ritz*	39	*2 Oct 99*	2

Valerie LANDSBURG - See KIDS FROM "FAME"

LANDSCAPE — UK

SINGLES:	**HITS 2**			**WEEKS 20**
EINSTEIN A GO-GO	*RCA*	5	*28 Feb 81*	13
NORMAN BATES	*RCA*	40	*23 May 81*	7
ALBUMS:	**HITS 1**			**WEEKS 13**
FROM THE TEAROOMS OF MARS TO THE HELLHOLES OF URANUS	*RCA*	16	*21 Mar 81*	13

Desmond LANE - See Alma COGAN; Cyril STAPLETON and his Orchestra

Ronnie LANE and the band SLIM CHANCE — UK

(See also Pete Townshend and Ronnie Lane.)

SINGLES:	**HITS 2**			**WEEKS 12**
HOW COME? *Above hit: Ronnie LANE Accompanied by the Band "SLIM CHANCE".*	*GM*	11	*12 Jan 74*	8
THE POACHER	*GM*	36	*15 Jun 74*	4
ALBUMS:	**HITS 1**			**WEEKS 1**
ANYMORE FOR ANYMORE	*GM*	48	*17 Aug 74*	1

Don LANG — UK

SINGLES:	HITS 4			WEEKS 18
CLOUDBURST	His Master's Voice	16	5 Nov 55	2
Originally recorded by Sam The Man Taylor				
Above hit: Don LANG with the MAIRANTS-LANGHORN BIG SIX.				
CLOUDBURST [RE-1ST]	His Master's Voice	18	3 Dec 55	1
CLOUDBURST [RE-2ND]	His Master's Voice	20	14 Jan 56	1
SCHOOL DAY (RING RING GOES THE BELL)	His Master's Voice	26	6 Jul 57	2
WITCH DOCTOR	His Master's Voice	5	24 May 58	11
Above 2: Don LANG and his "FRANTIC FIVE".				
SINK THE BISMARCK	His Master's Voice	43	12 Mar 60	1

k.d. lang — Canada

SINGLES:	HITS 7			WEEKS 25
CONSTANT CRAVING	Sire	52	16 May 92	4
CRYING	Virgin America	13	22 Aug 92	6
Above hit: Roy ORBISON (duet with k.d. lang).				
CONSTANT CRAVING [RI]	Sire	15	27 Feb 93	8
THE MIND OF LOVE (WHERE IS YOUR HEAD KATHRYN?)	Sire	72	1 May 93	1
MISS CHATELAINE	Sire	68	26 Jun 93	2
Original release reached No. 84 in 1992.				
JUST KEEP ME MOVING	Sire	59	11 Dec 93	1
From the film 'Even Cowgirls Get The Blues'.				
IF I WERE YOU	Sire	53	30 Sep 95	1
YOU'RE OK	Warner Brothers	44	18 May 96	2
ALBUMS:	**HITS 5**			**WEEKS 68**
INGENUE	Sire	28	28 Mar 92	13
INGENUE [RE]	Sire	3	27 Feb 93	39
EVEN COW GIRLS GET THE BLUES [OST]	Sire	36	13 Nov 93	2
ALL YOU CAN EAT	Warner Brothers	7	14 Oct 95	5
DRAG	Warner Brothers	19	12 Jul 97	3
All songs on the album have a reference to smoking.				
INVINCIBLE SUMMER	Warner Brothers	17	15 Jul 00	6

Thomas LANG — UK

SINGLES:	HITS 1			WEEKS 3
THE HAPPY MAN	Epic	67	30 Jan 88	3
ALBUMS:	**HITS 1**			**WEEKS 1**
SCALLYWAG JAZ	Epic	92	20 Feb 88	1

LANGE — UK

SINGLES:	HITS 1			WEEKS 1
I BELIEVE	Additive	68	19 Jun 99	1
Chart also credits Sarah Dyer.				

LANTERNS — UK

SINGLES:	HITS 1			WEEKS 1
HIGHRISE TOWN	Columbia	50	6 Feb 99	1

Mario LANZA — US

SINGLES:	HITS 4			WEEKS 32
BECAUSE YOU'RE MINE	His Master's Voice	3	15 Nov 52	24
From the film of the same name.				
Above hit: Mario LANZA-Tenor with RCA VICTOR ORCHESTRA and the Jeff ALEXANDER CHOIR Cond. by Constantine CALLINICOS.				
DRINKING SONG	His Master's Voice	13	5 Feb 55	1
From the film 'The Student Prince'.				
I'LL WALK WITH GOD	His Master's Voice	18	19 Feb 55	1
SERENADE	His Master's Voice	19	23 Apr 55	1
Above entry and Drinking Song were separate sides of the same release, each had its own chart run.				
I'LL WALK WITH GOD [RE]	His Master's Voice	20	7 May 55	1
SERENADE [RE]	His Master's Voice	15	7 May 55	2
Above 5 also had Orchestra and Chorus conducted by Constantine Callinicos.				
SERENADE	His Master's Voice	25	15 Sep 56	1
Both hits titled Serenade are different songs.				
SERENADE [RE]	His Master's Voice	29	13 Oct 56	1
EPS:	**HITS 3**			**WEEKS 30**
THE GREAT CARUSO	RCA	16	16 Apr 60	1
THE STUDENT PRINCE	RCA	8	23 Apr 60	27
SINGS CHRISTMAS CAROLS	RCA	10	3 Dec 60	2
ALBUMS:	**HITS 6**			**WEEKS 63**
THE STUDENT PRINCE / THE GREAT CARUSO [OST]	RCA	4	6 Dec 58	21
THE GREAT CARUSO	RCA	3	23 Jul 60	15
HIS GREATEST HITS VOLUME 1	RCA Victor	39	9 Jan 71	1

THE LEGEND OF MARIO LANZA	*K-Tel*	29	*5 Sep 81*	11
A PORTRAIT OF MARIO LANZA	*Stylus*	49	*14 Nov 87*	8
MARIO LANZA - THE ULTIMATE COLLECTION	*RCA Victor*	13	*12 Mar 94*	7

LAPTOP — US

SINGLES:	HITS 1			WEEKS 1
NOTHING TO DECLARE	*Island*	74	*12 Jun 99*	1

LARD — UK

ALBUMS:	HITS 1			WEEKS 1
THE LAST TEMPTATION OF REID	*Alternative Tentacles*	69	*6 Oct 90*	1

Amel LARRIEUX - See SWEETBACK featuring Amel LARRIEUX from GROOVE THEORY

Denise LASALLE — US

SINGLES:	HITS 1			WEEKS 13
MY TOOT TOOT	*Epic*	6	*15 Jun 85*	13
Originally recorded by Rockin' Sydney.				

Lisa LASHES - See TIDY GIRLS presents Lisa LASHES

James LAST — Germany

(See also Richard Clayderman and James Last.)

SINGLES:	HITS 1			WEEKS 4
THE SEDUCTION (LOVE THEME)	*Polydor*	48	*3 May 80*	4
Written by Giorgio Moroder and from the film 'American Gigolo'.				
Above hit: James LAST BAND.				

ALBUMS:	HITS 61			WEEKS 421
THIS IS JAMES LAST	*Polydor*	6	*15 Apr 67*	48
Above hit: James LAST BAND.				
HAMMOND A-GO-GO	*Polydor*	27	*22 Jul 67*	10
LOVE THIS IS MY SONG	*Polydor*	32	*26 Aug 67*	2
NON-STOP DANCING	*Polydor*	35	*26 Aug 67*	1
JAMES LAST GOES POP	*Polydor*	32	*22 Jun 68*	3
DANCING '68 VOLUME 1	*Polydor*	40	*8 Feb 69*	1
TRUMPET A-GO-GO	*Polydor*	13	*31 May 69*	1
NON-STOP DANCING '69	*Polydor*	26	*9 Aug 69*	1
NON-STOP DANCING '69/2	*Polydor*	27	*24 Jan 70*	3
NON-STOP EVERGREENS	*Polydor*	26	*23 May 70*	1
CLASSICS UP TO DATE	*Polydor*	44	*11 Jul 70*	1
NON-STOP DANCING '70	*Polydor*	67	*11 Jul 70*	1
VERY BEST OF JAMES LAST	*Polydor*	45	*24 Oct 70*	4
NON STOP DANCING '71	*Polydor*	21	*8 May 71*	4
SUMMER HAPPENING	*Polydor*	38	*26 Jun 71*	1
BEACH PARTY 2	*Polydor*	47	*18 Sep 71*	1
YESTERDAY'S MEMORIES	*Contour*	17	*2 Oct 71*	14
NON-STOP DANCING 12	*Polydor*	30	*16 Oct 71*	3
NON-STOP DANCING 13	*Polydor*	32	*19 Feb 72*	2
POLKA PARTY	*Polydor*	22	*4 Mar 72*	3
JAMES LAST IN CONCERT	*Polydor*	13	*29 Apr 72*	6
VOODOO PARTY	*Polydor*	45	*24 Jun 72*	1
CLASSICS UP TO DATE VOLUME 2	*Polydor*	49	*16 Sep 72*	1
LOVE MUST BE THE REASON	*Polydor*	32	*30 Sep 72*	2
THE MUSIC OF JAMES LAST	*Polydor*	19	*27 Jan 73*	12
JAMES LAST IN RUSSIA	*Polydor*	12	*24 Feb 73*	9
NON STOP DANCING VOLUME 14	*Polydor*	27	*24 Feb 73*	3
OLE	*Polydor*	24	*28 Jul 73*	5
NON-STOP DANCING VOLUME 15	*Polydor*	34	*1 Sep 73*	2
NON-STOP DANCING VOLUME 16	*Polydor*	43	*20 Apr 74*	2
IN CONCERT VOLUME 2	*Polydor*	49	*29 Jun 74*	1
GOLDEN MEMORIES	*Polydor*	39	*23 Nov 74*	2
TEN YEARS NON-STOP JUBILEE	*Polydor*	5	*26 Jul 75*	16
VIOLINS IN LOVE	*K-Tel*	60	*2 Aug 75*	1
MAKE THE PARTY LAST	*Polydor*	3	*22 Nov 75*	19
CLASSICS UP TO DATE VOLUME 3	*Polydor*	54	*8 May 76*	1
EAST TO WEST	*Polydor*	49	*6 May 78*	4
LAST THE WHOLE NIGHT LONG	*Polydor*	2	*14 Apr 79*	45
THE BEST FROM 150 GOLD RECORDS	*Polydor*	56	*23 Aug 80*	3
CLASSICS FOR DREAMING	*Polydor*	12	*1 Nov 80*	18
ROSES FROM THE SOUTH	*Polydor*	41	*14 Feb 81*	5
HANSIMANIA	*Polydor*	18	*21 Nov 81*	13
LAST FOREVER	*Polydor*	88	*28 Nov 81*	2
BLUEBIRD	*Polydor*	57	*5 Mar 83*	3
NON-STOP DANCING '83 - PARTY POWER	*Polydor*	56	*30 Apr 83*	2
THE BEST OF MY GOLD RECORDS	*Polydor*	42	*30 Apr 83*	5
THE GREATEST SONGS OF THE BEATLES	*Polydor*	52	*3 Dec 83*	8
THE ROSE OF TRALEE AND OTHER IRISH FAVOURITES	*Polydor*	21	*24 Mar 84*	11

PARADISE	*Polydor*	74	*13 Oct 84*	2
JAMES LAST IN SCOTLAND	*Polydor*	68	*8 Dec 84*	9
LEAVE THE BEST TO LAST	*Polydor*	11	*14 Sep 85*	27
BY REQUEST	*Polydor*	22	*18 Apr 87*	11
DANCE DANCE DANCE	*Polydor*	38	*26 Nov 88*	8
CLASSICS BY MOONLIGHT	*Polydor*	12	*14 Apr 90*	12
POP SYMPHONIES	*Polydor*	10	*15 Jun 91*	11
VIVA ESPANA	*PolyGram TV*	23	*12 Sep 92*	5
JAMES LAST PLAYS ANDREW LLOYD WEBBER	*Polydor*	12	*20 Nov 93*	10
THE VERY BEST OF JAMES LAST AND HIS ORCHESTRA	*Polydor*	36	*18 Nov 95*	7
POP SYMPHONIES 2	*Polydor*	32	*28 Mar 98*	3
COUNTRY ROADS	*Polydor*	18	*24 Apr 99*	5
JAMES LAST AND HIS ORCHESTRA PLAYS ABBA	*Polydor*	29	*3 Nov 01*	4

LAST RHYTHM — Italy

SINGLES:	HITS 1			WEEKS 1
LAST RHYTHM *Originally recorded in 1991.*	*Stress*	62	*14 Sep 96*	1

LATE SHOW — UK

SINGLES:	HITS 1			WEEKS 6
BRISTOL STOMP *Originally recorded by the Dovels.*	*Decca*	40	*3 Mar 79*	6

LATIN QUARTER — UK

SINGLES:	HITS 2			WEEKS 10
RADIO AFRICA *Original release reached No. 76 in 1985.*	*Rockin' Horse*	19	*18 Jan 86*	9
NOMZAMO (ONE PEOPLE ONE CAUSE)	*Rockin' Horse*	73	*18 Apr 87*	1
ALBUMS:	**HITS 2**			**WEEKS 3**
MODERN TIMES	*Rockin' Horse*	91	*1 Mar 86*	2
MICK AND CAROLINE	*Rockin' Horse*	96	*6 Jun 87*	1

LATIN RHYTHM - See Tito PUENTE Jr. and the LATIN RHYTHM featuring Tito PUENTE, INDIA and Cali ALEMAN

LATIN THING — Canada/Spain

SINGLES:	HITS 1			WEEKS 1
LATIN THING	*Faze 2*	41	*13 Jul 96*	1

Gino LATINO — Italy

SINGLES:	HITS 1			WEEKS 7
WELCOME	*ffrr*	17	*20 Jan 90*	7

LATINO RAVE — Italy

SINGLES:	HITS 2			WEEKS 13
DEEP HEAT '89 [M]	*Deep Heat*	12	*25 Nov 89*	11
THE SIXTH SENSE [M]	*Deep Heat*	49	*28 Apr 90*	2

LATOUR — US

SINGLES:	HITS 1			WEEKS 7
PEOPLE ARE STILL HAVING SEX	*Polydor*	15	*8 Jun 91*	7

Stacy LATTISAW — US

SINGLES:	HITS 2			WEEKS 14
JUMP TO THE BEAT	*Atlantic*	3	*14 Jun 80*	11
DYNAMITE	*Atlantic*	51	*30 Aug 80*	3

Dave LAUDAT - See HUSTLERS CONVENTION featuring Dave LAUDAT and Ondrea DUVERNEY

LAUNCHERS - See Ezz RECO and the LAUNCHERS with Boysie GRANT

Cyndi LAUPER — US

SINGLES:	HITS 17			WEEKS 103
GIRLS JUST WANT TO HAVE FUN	*Portrait*	2	*14 Jan 84*	12
TIME AFTER TIME	*Portrait*	54	*24 Mar 84*	4
TIME AFTER TIME [RE]	*Portrait*	3	*16 Jun 84*	13
SHE BOP	*Portrait*	46	*1 Sep 84*	5
ALL THROUGH THE NIGHT *Originally recorded by Jules Shear.*	*Portrait*	64	*17 Nov 84*	2
TRUE COLORS	*Portrait*	12	*20 Sep 86*	11
CHANGE OF HEART *Features the Bangles on backing vocals.*	*Portrait*	74	*27 Dec 86*	1
CHANGE OF HEART [RE]	*Portrait*	67	*10 Jan 87*	1
WHAT'S GOING ON	*Portrait*	57	*28 Mar 87*	3
I DROVE ALL NIGHT	*Epic*	7	*20 May 89*	12

MY FIRST NIGHT WITH YOU	*Epic*	53	*5 Aug 89*	4
HEADING WEST	*Epic*	68	*30 Dec 89*	1
THE WORLD IS STONE	*Epic*	15	*6 Jun 92*	7
THAT'S WHAT I THINK	*Epic*	31	*13 Nov 93*	4
WHO LET IN THE RAIN	*Epic*	32	*8 Jan 94*	4
HEY NOW (GIRLS JUST WANT TO HAVE FUN) [RR]	*Epic*	4	*17 Sep 94*	13
I'M GONNA BE STRONG	*Epic*	37	*11 Feb 95*	2
Originally recorded by Frankie Laine.				
COME ON HOME	*Epic*	39	*26 Aug 95*	2
YOU DON'T KNOW	*Epic*	27	*1 Feb 97*	2
ALBUMS:	**HITS 6**			**WEEKS 92**
SHE'S SO UNUSUAL	*Portrait*	16	*18 Feb 84*	31
TRUE COLORS	*Portrait*	25	*11 Oct 86*	12
A NIGHT TO REMEMBER	*Epic*	9	*1 Jul 89*	12
SHE'S SO UNUSUAL [RE]	*Portrait*	71	*5 Aug 89*	1
Repackaged.				
HAT FULL OF STARS	*Epic*	56	*27 Nov 93*	1
TWELVE DEADLY CYNS . . . AND THEN SOME	*Epic*	2	*3 Sep 94*	34
Compilation.				
SISTERS OF AVALON	*Epic*	59	*22 Feb 97*	1

LAUREL and HARDY — UK/US

SINGLES:	**HITS 1**			**WEEKS 10**
THE TRAIL OF THE LONESOME PINE	*United Artists*	2	*22 Nov 75*	10
Originally recorded by Henry Burr and Albert Campbell in 1913. From the 1937 film 'Way Out West'.				
Above hit: LAUREL and HARDY with the AVALON BOYS featuring Chill WILLS.				
ALBUMS:	**HITS 1**			**WEEKS 4**
THE GOLDEN AGE OF HOLLYWOOD COMEDY	*United Artists*	55	*6 Dec 75*	4

LAUREL and HARDY — UK

SINGLES:	**HITS 1**			**WEEKS 2**
CLUNK CLICK	*CBS*	65	*2 Apr 83*	2

LAURNEA — US

SINGLES:	**HITS 1**			**WEEKS 2**
DAYS OF YOUTH	*Epic*	36	*12 Jul 97*	2

Lauren LAVERNE - See MINT ROYALE

LAW — UK/US

ALBUMS:	**HITS 1**			**WEEKS 1**
THE LAW	*Atlantic*	61	*6 Apr 91*	1

Joanna LAW — UK

SINGLES:	**HITS 2**			**WEEKS 8**
FIRST TIME EVER	*Citybeat*	67	*7 Jul 90*	3
Originally recorded by Peggy Seeger.				
THE GIFT	*Deconstruction*	15	*14 Sep 96*	5
Samples Joanna Law's First Time Ever.				
Above hit: WAY OUT WEST featuring Miss Joanna LAW.				

Steve LAWLER; Vocal from PRINCE QUICK 'MELLOW' — UK

SINGLES:	**HITS 1**			**WEEKS 1**
RISE 'IN	*Bedrock*	50	*11 Nov 00*	1

Billy LAWRENCE – See RAMPAGE featuring Billy LAWRENCE

Joey LAWRENCE — US

SINGLES:	**HITS 4**			**WEEKS 15**
NOTHIN' MY LOVE CAN'T FIX	*EMI*	13	*26 Jun 93*	7
I CAN'T HELP MYSELF	*EMI*	27	*28 Aug 93*	4
STAY FOREVER	*EMI*	41	*30 Oct 93*	3
NEVER GONNA CHANGE MY MIND	*Curb*	49	*19 Sep 98*	1
ALBUMS:	**HITS 1**			**WEEKS 3**
JOEY LAWRENCE	*EMI*	39	*31 Jul 93*	3

Lee LAWRENCE — UK

SINGLES:	**HITS 2**			**WEEKS 10**
CRYING IN THE CHAPEL	*Decca*	11	*21 Nov 53*	1
CRYING IN THE CHAPEL [RE]	*Decca*	7	*12 Dec 53*	5

SUDDENLY THERE'S A VALLEY	Columbia	19	3 Dec 55	1
Above hit: Lee LAWRENCE with Ray MARTIN and his Orchestra.				
SUDDENLY THERE'S A VALLEY [RE]	Columbia	14	17 Dec 55	3

Sophie LAWRENCE — UK

SINGLES:	HITS 1			WEEKS 7
LOVE'S UNKIND	IQ	21	3 Aug 91	7

Steve LAWRENCE — US

SINGLES:	HITS 3			WEEKS 27
FOOTSTEPS	His Master's Voice	4	23 Apr 60	13
GIRLS GIRLS GIRLS	London	49	20 Aug 60	1
I WANT TO STAY HERE	CBS	3	24 Aug 63	13
Above hit: STEVE and EYDIE.				

Syd LAWRENCE — UK

ALBUMS:	HITS 4			WEEKS 9
MORE MILLER AND OTHER BIG BAND MAGIC	Philips	14	8 Aug 70	4
MUSIC OF GLENN MILLER IN SUPER STEREO	Philips	43	25 Dec 71	2
SYD LAWRENCE WITH THE GLENN MILLER SOUND	Fontana	31	25 Dec 71	2
Above hit: Syd LAWRENCE ORCHESTRA.				
SOMETHING OLD, SOMETHING NEW	Philips	34	26 Feb 72	1

Ronnie LAWS — US

ALBUMS:	HITS 1			WEEKS 1
SOLID GROUND	Liberty	100	17 Oct 81	1

Lindy LAYTON — UK

SINGLES:	HITS 6			WEEKS 28
DUB BE GOOD TO ME	Go.Beat	1	10 Feb 90	13
Above hit: BEATS INTERNATIONAL featuring LINDY.				
SILLY GAMES	Arista	22	11 Aug 90	7
Above hit: Lindy LAYTON featuring Janet KAY.				
ECHO MY HEART	Arista	42	26 Jan 91	2
WITHOUT YOU (ONE AND ONE)	Arista	71	31 Aug 91	2
WE GOT THE LOVE ('93 REMIX)	PWL International	38	24 Apr 93	3
SHOW ME	PWL International	47	30 Oct 93	1

Peter LAZONBY — UK

SINGLES:	HITS 1			WEEKS 1
SACRED CYCLES	Hooj Choons	49	10 Jun 00	1
Originally released on the Brainiac label in 1993.				

Doug LAZY — US

SINGLES:	HITS 2			WEEKS 9
LET IT ROLL	Atlantic	27	15 Jul 89	5
Chart has the credit as Raze Presents Doug Lazy, though this is not reflected on the single itself.				
LET THE RHYTHM PUMP	Atlantic	45	4 Nov 89	3
LET THE RHYTHM PUMP [RM]	Atlantic	63	26 May 90	1
Remixed by Dakeyne and Anderson of DMC UK.				
ALBUMS:	**HITS 1**			**WEEKS 1**
DOUG LAZY GETTIN' CRAZY	Atlantic	65	10 Mar 90	1

LCD — UK

SINGLES:	HITS 1			WEEKS 9
ZORBA'S DANCE	Virgin	20	27 Jun 98	5
ZORBA'S DANCE [RI]	Virgin	22	9 Oct 99	4

LE CLICK — US/Sweden

SINGLES:	HITS 1			WEEKS 2
CALL ME	Logic	38	30 Aug 97	2

Kele LE ROC — UK

(See also Curtis Lynch Jnr featuring Kele Le Roc and Red Rat.)

SINGLES:	HITS 2			WEEKS 14
LITTLE BIT OF LOVIN'	Wild Card	8	31 Oct 98	7
MY LOVE	Wild Card	8	27 Mar 99	7
ALBUMS:	**HITS 1**			**WEEKS 2**
EVERYBODY'S SOMEBODY	Wild Card	44	10 Apr 99	2

LEAGUE UNLIMITED ORCHESTRA - See HUMAN LEAGUE

Vicky LEANDROS — Greece

SINGLES:	HITS 3			WEEKS 29
COME WHAT May (APRES - TOI)	*Philips*	2	*8 Apr 72*	16
Eurovision Song Contest winner for Luxembourg in 1972.				
THE LOVE IN YOUR EYES	*Philips*	48	*23 Dec 72*	3
THE LOVE IN YOUR EYES [RE-1ST]	*Philips*	40	*20 Jan 73*	4
THE LOVE IN YOUR EYES [RE-2ND]	*Philips*	46	*7 Apr 73*	1
WHEN BOUZOUKIS PLAYED	*Philips*	44	*7 Jul 73*	2
WHEN BOUZOUKIS PLAYED [RE]	*Philips*	45	*28 Jul 73*	3

Denis LEARY — US

SINGLES:	HITS 1			WEEKS 2
ASSHOLE	*A&M*	58	*13 Jan 96*	2

Keith LeBLANC - See Malcolm X, music by Keith LeBLANC

LED ZEPPELIN — UK

SINGLES:	HITS 1			WEEKS 2
WHOLE LOTTA LOVE	*Atlantic*	21	*13 Sep 97*	2
This is their first official single release in the UK.				
ALBUMS:	**HITS 16**			**WEEKS 475**
LED ZEPPELIN	*Atlantic*	6	*12 Apr 69*	79
LED ZEPPELIN II	*Atlantic*	1	*8 Nov 69*	138
Repackaged from March 72.				
LED ZEPPELIN 3	*Atlantic*	1	*7 Nov 70*	40
FOUR SYMBOLS (LED ZEPPELIN 4)	*Atlantic*	1	*27 Nov 71*	57
Repackaged from March 72. Album was untitled, but was commonly referred to as per the two titles above. Includes re-entries through to 1981.				
HOUSES OF THE HOLY	*Atlantic*	1	*14 Apr 73*	13
PHYSICAL GRAFFITI	*Swan Song*	1	*15 Mar 75*	27
PRESENCE	*Swan Song*	1	*24 Apr 76*	14
THE SONG REMAINS THE SAME [OST]	*Swan Song*	1	*6 Nov 76*	15
Includes the Madison Square Garden concert from March 73.				
IN THROUGH THE OUT DOOR	*Swan Song*	1	*8 Sep 79*	16
FOUR SYMBOLS (LED ZEPPELIN 4) [RE-1ST]	*Atlantic*	69	*14 Aug 82*	6
Includes re-entries in 1983 & 1991. Chart position reached in 1991 (1982 peak No. 81).				
CODA	*Swan Song*	4	*4 Dec 82*	7
REMASTERS	*Atlantic*	10	*27 Oct 90*	45
Includes re-entries through to 1998.				
LED ZEPPELIN (BOX SET)	*Atlantic*	48	*10 Nov 90*	2
LED ZEPPELIN BOXED SET II	*Atlantic*	56	*9 Oct 93*	1
Above 2 are compilations.				
FOUR SYMBOLS (LED ZEPPELIN 4) [RE-2ND]	*Atlantic*	48	*2 Apr 94*	6
Includes re-entry in 1999.				
BBC SESSIONS	*Atlantic*	23	*29 Nov 97*	7
EARLY DAYS - THE BEST OF LED ZEPPELIN VOLUME ONE	*Atlantic*	55	*1 Apr 00*	1
LATTER DAYS - THE BEST OF LED ZEPPELIN VOLUME 2	*Atlantic*	40	*1 Apr 00*	1

Angel LEE — UK

SINGLES:	HITS 1			WEEKS 1
WHAT'S YOUR NAME?	*WEA*	39	*3 Jun 00*	1

Ann LEE — UK

SINGLES:	HITS 2			WEEKS 21
2 TIMES	*ZYX*	57	*11 Sep 99*	2
German import. Removed from chart when it was discovered the running time broke eligibility rules.				
2 TIMES	*Systematic*	2	*16 Oct 99*	16
VOICES	*Systematic*	27	*4 Mar 00*	3

Brenda LEE — US

SINGLES:	HITS 22			WEEKS 210
SWEET NUTHIN'S	*Brunswick*	45	*19 Mar 60*	1
SWEET NUTHIN'S [RE]	*Brunswick*	4	*9 Apr 60*	18
I'M SORRY	*Brunswick*	12	*2 Jul 60*	16
Features Floyd Cramer on piano.				
I WANT TO BE WANTED	*Brunswick*	31	*22 Oct 60*	6
LET'S JUMP THE BROOMSTICK	*Brunswick*	12	*21 Jan 61*	15
EMOTIONS	*Brunswick*	45	*8 Apr 61*	1
DUM DUM	*Brunswick*	22	*22 Jul 61*	8
Written by Jackie De Shannon.				
FOOL NUMBER ONE	*Brunswick*	38	*18 Nov 61*	3
Originally recorded by Loretta Lynn.				
BREAK IT TO ME GENTLY	*Brunswick*	46	*10 Feb 62*	2
SPEAK TO ME PRETTY	*Brunswick*	3	*7 Apr 62*	12
From the film 'Two Little Bears'.				

HERE COMES THAT FEELING	*Brunswick*	5	*23 Jun 62*	12
IT STARTED ALL OVER AGAIN	*Brunswick*	15	*15 Sep 62*	11
• ROCKIN' AROUND THE CHRISTMAS TREE	*Brunswick*	6	*1 Dec 62*	7
ALL ALONE AM I	*Brunswick*	7	*19 Jan 63*	17
LOSING YOU	*Brunswick*	10	*30 Mar 63*	16
I WONDER *Originally recorded by Cecil Gant and Roosevelt Sykes.*	*Brunswick*	14	*20 Jul 63*	9
SWEET IMPOSSIBLE YOU	*Brunswick*	28	*2 Nov 63*	6
AS USUAL	*Brunswick*	5	*11 Jan 64*	15
THINK	*Brunswick*	26	*11 Apr 64*	8
IS IT TRUE	*Brunswick*	17	*12 Sep 64*	8
CHRISTMAS WILL BE JUST ANOTHER LONELY DAY	*Brunswick*	29	*12 Dec 64*	5
THANKS A LOT *Originally recorded by Ernest Tubb in 1963.*	*Brunswick*	41	*6 Feb 65*	2
TOO MANY RIVERS	*Brunswick*	22	*31 Jul 65*	12
EPS:	**HITS 2**			**WEEKS 11**
SPEAK TO ME PRETTY	*Brunswick*	18	*10 Nov 62*	3
ALL ALONE AM I	*Brunswick*	8	*3 Aug 63*	8
ALBUMS:	**HITS 8**			**WEEKS 64**
ALL THE WAY	*Brunswick*	20	*24 Nov 62*	2
BRENDA - THAT'S ALL	*Brunswick*	13	*16 Feb 63*	9
ALL ALONE AM I	*Brunswick*	8	*13 Apr 63*	20
BYE BYE BLUES	*Brunswick*	21	*16 Jul 66*	2
LITTLE MISS DYNAMITE - BRENDA LEE	*Warwick*	15	*1 Nov 80*	11
25TH ANNIVERSARY	*MCA*	65	*7 Jan 84*	4
THE VERY BEST OF BRENDA LEE	*MCA*	16	*30 Mar 85*	9
THE VERY BEST OF BRENDA LEE . . . WITH LOVE	*Telstar*	20	*15 Oct 94*	7

Byron LEE - See Boris GARDINER

Curtis LEE — US

SINGLES:	**HITS 1**			**WEEKS 2**
PRETTY LITTLE ANGEL EYES *Backing vocals by the Halos.*	*London*	47	*2 Sep 61*	1
PRETTY LITTLE ANGEL EYES [RE]	*London*	48	*16 Sep 61*	1

Dee C. LEE — UK

(See also Style Council.)

SINGLES:	**HITS 3**			**WEEKS 20**
SEE THE DAY	*CBS*	3	*9 Nov 85*	12
COME HELL OR WATERS HIGH *Originally recorded by Judie Tzuke.*	*CBS*	46	*8 Mar 86*	5
NO TIME TO PLAY *Above hit: GURU featuring vocals by D.C. LEE.*	*Cooltempo*	25	*13 Nov 93*	3

Garry LEE and SHOWDOWN — Canada

SINGLES:	**HITS 1**			**WEEKS 3**
THE RODEO SONG	*Party Dish*	44	*31 Jul 93*	3

Jackie LEE — Ireland

SINGLES:	**HITS 2**			**WEEKS 31**
WHITE HORSES *Theme from the BBC1 TV children's series of the same name.* *Above hit: JACKY.*	*Philips*	10	*13 Apr 68*	14
RUPERT *Theme from the ITV children's series 'Rupert The Bear'.*	*Pye*	14	*2 Jan 71*	17

Leapy LEE — UK

SINGLES:	**HITS 2**			**WEEKS 28**
LITTLE ARROWS	*MCA*	2	*24 Aug 68*	21
GOOD MORNING	*MCA*	47	*20 Dec 69*	1
GOOD MORNING [RE]	*MCA*	29	*10 Jan 70*	6

Peggy LEE — US

SINGLES:	**HITS 3**			**WEEKS 29**
MR. WONDERFUL *From the musical of the same name.*	*Brunswick*	5	*25 May 57*	13
FEVER	*Capitol*	5	*16 Aug 58*	11
TILL THERE WAS YOU *From the film 'The Music Man'. Originally recorded by Robert Preston and Barbara Cook.* *Above 3: Peggy LEE with Jack MARSHALL'S MUSIC.*	*Capitol*	40	*25 Mar 61*	1
TILL THERE WAS YOU [RE]	*Capitol*	30	*8 Apr 61*	3
FEVER [RI]	*Capitol*	75	*22 Aug 92*	1

ALBUMS:	HITS 3			WEEKS 17
LATIN A LA LEE	*Capitol*	8	*4 Jun 60*	15
BEST OF PEGGY LEE VOLUME 2	*Brunswick*	18	*20 May 61*	1
BLACK COFFEE	*Ace Of Hearts*	20	*21 Oct 61*	1

Peggy LEE and George SHEARING — US

(See also Peggy Lee; George Shearing Quartet.)

ALBUMS:	HITS 1			WEEKS 6
BEAUTY AND THE BEAT	*Capitol*	16	*11 Jun 60*	6

Toney LEE — US

SINGLES:	HITS 1			WEEKS 4
REACH UP	*TMT Productions*	64	*29 Jan 83*	4

Tracey LEE — US

SINGLES:	HITS 1			WEEKS 1
THE THEME: IT'S PARTY TIME	*Universal*	51	*19 Jul 97*	1

Bruce LEE – See J.K.D. BAND featuring the voice of Bruce LEE

LEE-O – See K-WARREN featuring LEE-O

LEEDS UNITED FOOTBALL TEAM — UK

SINGLES:	HITS 2			WEEKS 13
LEEDS UNITED	*Chapter 1*	10	*29 Apr 72*	10
LEEDS, LEEDS, LEEDS, (MARCHING ON TOGETHER)	*Q Music*	61	*25 Apr 92*	1
Above hit: LEEDS UNITED A.F.C. (1970'S).				
LEEDS, LEEDS, LEEDS, (MARCHING ON TOGETHER) [RE]	*Q Music*	54	*9 May 92*	2

Carol LEEMING – BEDROCK; STAXX

Raymond LEFEVRE — France

SINGLES:	HITS 1			WEEKS 2
SOUL COAXING	*Major Minor*	46	*18 May 68*	2
Originally recorded by Michael Polnareff.				
ALBUMS:	**HITS 2**			**WEEKS 9**
RAYMOND LEFEVRE	*Major Minor*	10	*7 Oct 67*	7
RAYMOND LEFEVRE VOLUME 2	*Major Minor*	37	*17 Feb 68*	2

LEFT EYE – See LIL' KIM

LEFTFIELD — UK

SINGLES:	HITS 7			WEEKS 23
SONG OF LIFE	*Hard Hands*	59	*12 Dec 92*	1
OPEN UP	*Hard Hands*	13	*13 Nov 93*	5
Above hit: LEFTFIELD LYDON.				
ORIGINAL	*Hard Hands*	18	*25 Mar 95*	3
Above hit: LEFTFIELD HALLIDAY.				
THE AFRO-LEFT [EP]	*Hard Hands*	22	*5 Aug 95*	3
Lead track: Afro Left.				
Above hit: LEFTFIELD featuring DJUM DJUM.				
RELEASE THE PRESSURE	*Hard Hands*	13	*20 Jan 96*	3
AFRIKA SHOX	*Hard Hands*	7	*18 Sep 99*	5
Above hit: LEFTFIELD. BAMBAATAA.				
DUSTED	*Hard Hands*	28	*11 Dec 99*	2
Above hit: LEFTFIELD. ROOTS MANUVA.				
DUSTED [RE]	*Hard Hands*	75	*22 Jan 00*	1
ALBUMS:	**HITS 2**			**WEEKS 114**
LEFTISM	*Hard Hands*	3	*11 Feb 95*	94
Includes re-entries through to 2000.				
RHYTHM AND STEALTH	*Hard Hands*	1	*2 Oct 99*	20

LEGEND — US

(See also Razc.)

SINGLES:	HITS 1			WEEKS 1
CAN YOU FEEL IT (CHAMPION MEGAMIX) (M) / CAN YOU FEEL IT (RAZE MEGAMIX) (M)	*Champion*	62	*10 Feb 90*	1
Montage of tracks by Raze.				

LEGEND B — Germany

SINGLES:	HITS 1			WEEKS 1
LOST IN LOVE	*Perfecto*	45	*22 Feb 97*	1

Tom LEHRER — US

ALBUMS:	HITS 2			WEEKS 26
SONGS BY TOM LEHRER	*Decca*	7	*8 Nov 58*	19
AN EVENING WASTED WITH TOM LEHRER	*Decca*	7	*25 Jun 60*	7

Oliver LEIB presents SMOKED — Germany

SINGLES:	HITS 1			WEEKS 1
METROPOLIS	*Duty Free*	72	*30 Sep 00*	1

LEILANI — UK

SINGLES:	HITS 3			WEEKS 7
MADNESS THING	*ZTT*	19	*6 Feb 99*	4
DO YOU WANT ME?	*ZTT*	40	*12 Jun 99*	2
FLYING ELVIS	*ZTT*	73	*3 Jun 00*	1

Paul LEKAKIS — US

SINGLES:	HITS 1			WEEKS 4
BOOM BOOM (LET'S GO BACK TO MY ROOM)	*Champion*	60	*30 May 87*	4

LEMON PIPERS — US

SINGLES:	HITS 2			WEEKS 16
GREEN TAMBOURINE	*Pye International*	7	*10 Feb 68*	11
RICE IS NICE	*Pye International*	41	*4 May 68*	5

LEMON TREES — UK

SINGLES:	HITS 5			WEEKS 9
LOVE IS IN YOUR EYES	*Oxygen*	75	*26 Sep 92*	1
THE WAY I FEEL	*Oxygen*	62	*7 Nov 92*	2
LET IT LOOSE	*Oxygen*	55	*13 Feb 93*	2
CHILD OF LOVE	*Oxygen*	55	*17 Apr 93*	3
I CAN'T FACE THE WORLD	*Oxygen*	52	*3 Jul 93*	1

LEMONHEADS — US/Australia

SINGLES:	HITS 8			WEEKS 26
IT'S A SHAME ABOUT RAY	*Atlantic*	70	*17 Oct 92*	1
MRS. ROBINSON / BEING AROUND	*Atlantic*	19	*5 Dec 92*	9
CONFETTI / MY DRUG BUDDY	*Atlantic*	44	*6 Feb 93*	2
IT'S A SHAME ABOUT RAY [RI]	*Atlantic*	31	*10 Apr 93*	3
INTO YOUR ARMS	*Atlantic*	14	*16 Oct 93*	4
IT'S ABOUT TIME	*Atlantic*	57	*27 Nov 93*	2
BIG GAY HEART	*Atlantic*	55	*14 May 94*	2
IF I COULD TALK I'D TELL YOU	*Atlantic*	39	*28 Sep 96*	2
IT'S ALL TRUE	*Atlantic*	61	*14 Dec 96*	1
ALBUMS:	**HITS 3**			**WEEKS 32**
IT'S A SHAME ABOUT RAY	*Atlantic*	69	*1 Aug 92*	1
IT'S A SHAME ABOUT RAY [RE]	*Atlantic*	33	*26 Dec 92*	15
Repackaged.				
COME ON FEEL THE LEMONHEADS	*Atlantic*	5	*23 Oct 93*	14
CAR BUTTON CLOTH	*Atlantic*	28	*12 Oct 96*	2

LEN — Canada

SINGLES:	HITS 2			WEEKS 15
STEAL MY SUNSHINE	*Columbia*	8	*18 Dec 99*	13
Samples Andrea True Connection's More More More.				
CRYPTIK SOULS CREW	*Columbia*	28	*10 Jun 00*	2

LENA - See Lena FIAGBE

John LENNON — UK

SINGLES:	HITS 18			WEEKS 197
GIVE PEACE A CHANCE	*Apple*	2	*12 Jul 69*	13
Recorded in room 1742 Hotel La Reine Elizabeth, Montreal and features his son Sean.				
COLD TURKEY	*Apple*	14	*1 Nov 69*	8
Features Eric Clapton on guitar.				
Above 2: PLASTIC ONO BAND.				
INSTANT KARMA	*Apple*	5	*21 Feb 70*	9
Features George Harrison on guitar and Billy Preston on piano.				
Above hit: LENNON/ONO with the PLASTIC ONO BAND.				
POWER TO THE PEOPLE	*Apple*	7	*20 Mar 71*	9
Above hit: John LENNON/PLASTIC ONO BAND.				
HAPPY XMAS (WAR IS OVER)	*Apple*	4	*9 Dec 72*	8
Above hit: JOHN and YOKO/the PLASTIC ONO BAND with the HARLEM COMMUNITY CHOIR.				
MIND GAMES	*Apple*	26	*24 Nov 73*	9

WHATEVER GETS YOU THRU' THE NIGHT	*Apple*	36	*19 Oct 74*	4
Features Elton John on backing vocals.				
Above hit: John LENNON with the PLASTIC ONO NUCLEAR BAND.				
HAPPY XMAS (WAR IS OVER) [RE-1ST]	*Apple*	48	*4 Jan 75*	1
Above hit: JOHN and YOKO/the PLASTIC ONO BAND with the HARLEM COMMUNITY CHOIR.				
#9 DREAM	*Apple*	23	*8 Feb 75*	8
STAND BY ME	*Apple*	30	*3 May 75*	7
IMAGINE	*Apple*	6	*1 Nov 75*	11
(JUST LIKE) STARTING OVER	*Geffen*	1	*8 Nov 80*	15
HAPPY XMAS (WAR IS OVER) [RE-2ND]	*Apple*	2	*20 Dec 80*	9
Above hit: JOHN and YOKO and the PLASTIC ONO BAND with the HARLEM COMMUNITY CHOIR.				
IMAGINE [RE]	*Apple*	1	*27 Dec 80*	13
WOMAN	*Geffen*	1	*24 Jan 81*	11
GIVE PEACE A CHANCE [RE]	*Apple*	33	*24 Jan 81*	5
Above hit: PLASTIC ONO BAND.				
I SAW HER STANDING THERE	*DJM*	40	*21 Mar 81*	4
Above hit: Elton JOHN BAND featuring John LENNON and the MUSCLE SHOALS HORNS.				
WATCHING THE WHEELS	*Geffen*	30	*4 Apr 81*	6
Above hit: John LENNON and Yoko ONO.				
HAPPY XMAS (WAR IS OVER) [RE-3RD]	*Apple*	28	*19 Dec 81*	5
Above hit: JOHN and YOKO/the PLASTIC ONO BAND with the HARLEM COMMUNITY CHOIR.				
LOVE	*Parlophone*	41	*20 Nov 82*	7
HAPPY XMAS (WAR IS OVER) [RE-4TH]	*Apple*	56	*25 Dec 82*	3
Above hit: JOHN and YOKO/the PLASTIC ONO BAND with the HARLEM COMMUNITY CHOIR.				
NOBODY TOLD ME	*Polydor*	6	*21 Jan 84*	6
BORROWED TIME	*Polydor*	32	*17 Mar 84*	6
JEALOUS GUY	*Parlophone*	65	*30 Nov 85*	2
IMAGINE [RI-1ST] / JEALOUS GUY [RI] / HAPPY XMAS (WAR IS OVER) [RI-1ST]	*Parlophone*	45	*10 Dec 88*	5
IMAGINE [RI-2ND]	*Parlophone*	3	*25 Dec 99*	11
Above hit: John LENNON and the PLASTIC ONO BAND (with the FLUX FIDDLERS).				
IMAGINE [RI-2ND] [RE]	*Parlophone*	42	*18 Mar 00*	2

ALBUMS:	**HITS 14**			**WEEKS 335**
JOHN LENNON/PLASTIC ONO BAND	*Apple*	11	*16 Jan 71*	11
Above hit: John LENNON/PLASTIC ONO BAND.				
IMAGINE	*Apple*	1	*30 Oct 71*	85
Above hit: John LENNON; PLASTIC ONO BAND (with the FLUX FIDDLERS).				
SOMETIME IN NEW YORK CITY	*Apple*	11	*14 Oct 72*	6
Above hit: John and Yoko LENNON with the PLASTIC ONO BAND and ELEPHANT'S MEMORY.				
MIND GAMES	*Apple*	13	*8 Dec 73*	12
Above hit: John LENNON and PLASTIC U.F.ONO BAND.				
WALLS AND BRIDGES	*Apple*	6	*19 Oct 74*	10
ROCK'N'ROLL	*Apple*	6	*8 Mar 75*	25
Collection of Lennon's favourite rock'n'roll songs.				
SHAVED FISH (COLLECTABLE LENNON)	*Apple*	8	*8 Nov 75*	17
Compilation.				
DOUBLE FANTASY	*Geffen*	1	*22 Nov 80*	36
Tracks divided equally between each artist.				
Above hit: John LENNON and Yoko ONO.				
IMAGINE [RI]	*Parlophone*	5	*20 Dec 80*	16
Above hit: John LENNON and the PLASTIC ONO BAND (with the FLUX FIDDLERS).				
SHAVED FISH [RI]	*Parlophone*	11	*17 Jan 81*	12
ROCK AND ROLL [RI]	*Parlophone*	64	*17 Jan 81*	3
THE JOHN LENNON COLLECTION	*Parlophone*	1	*20 Nov 82*	42
MILK AND HONEY - A HEART PLAY	*Polydor*	3	*4 Feb 84*	13
Recordings from 1980. Tracks divided equally between each artist.				
Above hit: John LENNON and Yoko ONO.				
JOHN LENNON LIVE IN NEW YORK CITY	*Parlophone*	55	*8 Mar 86*	3
Live recordings from Madison Square Gardens, 30 Aug 72.				
IMAGINE: JOHN LENNON [OST]	*Parlophone*	64	*22 Oct 88*	6
Includes Beatles material.				
THE JOHN LENNON COLLECTION [RE]	*Parlophone*	73	*20 Apr 96*	1
LENNON LEGEND - THE VERY BEST OF JOHN LENNON	*Parlophone*	4	*8 Nov 97*	35
THE JOHN LENNON ANTHOLOGY	*Capitol*	62	*14 Nov 98*	1
4 CD box set titled 'Ascot', 'New York'. 'Lost Weekend' and 'Dakota'. A separate condensed version, Wonsaponatime, reached No. 76 the same week.				
IMAGINE [RI] [RE]	*Parlophone*	51	*26 Feb 00*	1
Remixed and remastered to mark the 20th anniversary of his death.				

Julian LENNON — UK

SINGLES:	**HITS 9**			**WEEKS 47**
TOO LATE FOR GOODBYES	*Charisma*	6	*6 Oct 84*	11

VALOTTE	*Charisma*	55	*15 Dec 84*	6
SAY YOU'RE WRONG	*Charisma*	75	*9 Mar 85*	1
BECAUSE	*EMI*	40	*7 Dec 85*	7
From the musical 'Time'.				
NOW YOU'RE IN HEAVEN	*Virgin*	59	*11 Mar 89*	3
SALTWATER	*Virgin*	6	*24 Aug 91*	13
HELP YOURSELF	*Virgin*	53	*30 Nov 91*	2
GET A LIFE	*Virgin*	56	*25 Apr 92*	3
DAY AFTER DAY	*Music From Another*	66	*23 May 98*	1
ALBUMS:	**HITS 3**			**WEEKS 20**
VALOTTE	*Charisma*	20	*3 Nov 84*	15
THE SECRET VALUE OF DAYDREAMING	*Charisma*	93	*5 Apr 86*	1
HELP YOURSELF	*Virgin*	42	*5 Oct 91*	4

Annie LENNOX — UK

SINGLES:	**HITS 10**			**WEEKS 68**
PUT A LITTLE LOVE IN YOUR HEART	*A&M*	28	*3 Dec 88*	8
Above hit: Annie LENNOX and Al GREEN.				
WHY	*RCA*	5	*28 Mar 92*	8
PRECIOUS	*RCA*	23	*6 Jun 92*	5
WALKING ON BROKEN GLASS	*RCA*	8	*22 Aug 92*	8
COLD	*RCA*	26	*31 Oct 92*	4
LITTLE BIRD / LOVE SONG FOR A VAMPIRE	*RCA*	3	*13 Feb 93*	12
Love Song For A Vampire from the film 'Bram Stoker's Dracula'.				
NO MORE "I LOVE YOU'S"	*RCA*	2	*18 Feb 95*	12
A WHITER SHADE OF PALE	*RCA*	16	*10 Jun 95*	6
WAITING IN VAIN	*RCA*	31	*30 Sep 95*	3
SOMETHING SO RIGHT	*RCA*	44	*9 Dec 95*	2
Originally recorded by Paul Simon, from his 1973 album There Goes Rhymin' Simon.				
Above hit: Annie LENNOX featuring Paul SIMON on guitar and vocals.				
ALBUMS:	**HITS 2**			**WEEKS 129**
DIVA	*RCA*	1	*18 Apr 92*	80
MEDUSA	*RCA*	1	*18 Mar 95*	49
Album of cover versions.				

Rula LENSKA - See Julie COVINGTON, Charlotte CORNWELL, Rula LENSKA, Sue JONES-DAVIES

Phillip LEO — UK

SINGLES:	**HITS 2**			**WEEKS 3**
SECOND CHANCE	*EMI*	57	*23 Jul 94*	2
THINKING ABOUT YOUR LOVE	*EMI*	64	*25 Mar 95*	1

LEON - See SCOTT and LEON

Deke LEONARD — UK

ALBUMS:	**HITS 1**			**WEEKS 1**
KAMIKAZE	*United Artists*	50	*13 Apr 74*	1

Paul LEONI — UK

ALBUMS:	**HITS 1**			**WEEKS 19**
FLIGHTS OF FANCY	*Nouveau Music*	17	*24 Sep 83*	19
Covers of popular hits.				

LeROYS - See Simon SCOTT and the LeROYS

LES RYTHMES DIGITALES — France

SINGLES:	**HITS 3**			**WEEKS 3**
MUSIC MAKES YOU LOSE CONTROL	*Wall Of Sound*	69	*25 Apr 98*	1
SOMETIMES	*Wall Of Sound*	56	*7 Aug 99*	1
Above hit: LES RYTHMES DIGITALES featuring Nik KERSHAW.				
JAQUES YOUR BODY [MAKE ME SWEAT] '99 MIX	*Wall Of Sound*	60	*30 Oct 99*	1
Featured in the Sunny Delight TV commercial.				
ALBUMS:	**HITS 1**			**WEEKS 1**
DARKDANCER	*Wall Of Sound*	53	*5 Jun 99*	1

LeSHAUN - See LL COOL J

LESS THAN JAKE — US

SINGLES:	**HITS 2**			**WEEKS 2**
ALL MY BEST FRIENDS ARE METALHEADS	*Golf*	51	*5 Aug 00*	1
GAINESVILLE ROCK CITY	*Golf*	57	*8 Sep 01*	1

LESTER - See Norman COOK

Eddie LESTER SINGERS - See Vince HILL

Ketty LESTER — US

SINGLES:	HITS 2			WEEKS 16
LOVE LETTERS	*London*	4	*21 Apr 62*	12
Originally recorded by Dick Haymes in 1945.				
BUT NOT FOR ME	*London*	45	*21 Jul 62*	4

LET LOOSE — UK

SINGLES:	HITS 8			WEEKS 62
CRAZY FOR YOU	*Vertigo*	44	*24 Apr 93*	3
SEVENTEEN	*Mercury*	44	*9 Apr 94*	2
CRAZY FOR YOU [RI]	*Mercury*	2	*25 Jun 94*	20
SEVENTEEN [RM]	*Mercury*	11	*22 Oct 94*	6
Remixed by Let Loose and Nick Kershaw.				
CRAZY FOR YOU [RI] [RE]	*Mercury*	46	*24 Dec 94*	4
SEVENTEEN [RM] [RE]	*Mercury*	47	*7 Jan 95*	3
ONE NIGHT STAND	*Mercury*	12	*28 Jan 95*	6
BEST IN ME	*Mercury*	8	*29 Apr 95*	5
EVERYBODY SAY EVERYBODY DO	*Mercury*	29	*4 Nov 95*	3
EVERYBODY SAY EVERYBODY DO [RE]	*Mercury*	71	*13 Jan 96*	1
MAKE IT WITH YOU	*Mercury*	7	*22 Jun 96*	6
TAKE IT EASY	*Mercury*	25	*7 Sep 96*	2
DARLING BE HOME SOON	*Mercury*	65	*16 Nov 96*	1
ALBUMS:	**HITS 2**			**WEEKS 15**
LET LOOSE	*Mercury*	20	*19 Nov 94*	14
ROLLERCOASTER	*Mercury*	42	*5 Oct 96*	1

Gerald LETHAN - See WALL OF SOUND featuring Gerald LETHAN

LETTERMEN — US

SINGLES:	HITS 1			WEEKS 3
THE WAY YOU LOOK TONIGHT	*Capitol*	36	*25 Nov 61*	3
Originally recorded by Fred Astaire in 1936.				

LEVEL 42 — UK

SINGLES:	HITS 29			WEEKS 177
LOVE MEETING LOVE	*Polydor*	61	*30 Aug 80*	4
LOVE GAMES	*Polydor*	38	*18 Apr 81*	6
TURN IT ON	*Polydor*	57	*8 Aug 81*	6
STARCHILD	*Polydor*	47	*14 Nov 81*	4
ARE YOU HEARING (WHAT I HEAR)?	*Polydor*	49	*8 May 82*	5
WEAVE YOUR SPELL	*Polydor*	43	*2 Oct 82*	4
THE CHINESE WAY	*Polydor*	24	*15 Jan 83*	8
OUT OF SIGHT OUT OF MIND	*Polydor*	41	*16 Apr 83*	4
THE SUN GOES DOWN (LIVING IT UP)	*Polydor*	10	*30 Jul 83*	12
MICRO-KID	*Polydor*	37	*22 Oct 83*	5
HOT WATER	*Polydor*	18	*1 Sep 84*	9
THE CHANT HAS BEGUN	*Polydor*	41	*3 Nov 84*	5
SOMETHING ABOUT YOU	*Polydor*	6	*21 Sep 85*	17
LEAVING ME NOW	*Polydor*	15	*7 Dec 85*	11
LESSONS IN LOVE	*Polydor*	3	*26 Apr 86*	13
RUNNING IN THE FAMILY	*Polydor*	6	*14 Feb 87*	10
TO BE WITH YOU AGAIN	*Polydor*	10	*25 Apr 87*	7
IT'S OVER	*Polydor*	10	*12 Sep 87*	8
CHILDREN SAY	*Polydor*	22	*12 Dec 87*	6
HEAVEN IN MY HANDS	*Polydor*	12	*3 Sep 88*	5
TAKE A LOOK	*Polydor*	32	*29 Oct 88*	4
TRACIE	*Polydor*	25	*21 Jan 89*	5
TAKE CARE OF YOURSELF	*Polydor*	39	*28 Oct 89*	3
GUARANTEED	*RCA*	17	*17 Aug 91*	4
OVERTIME	*RCA*	62	*19 Oct 91*	2
MY FATHER'S SHOES	*RCA*	55	*18 Apr 92*	1
FOREVER NOW	*RCA*	19	*26 Feb 94*	4
ALL OVER YOU	*RCA*	26	*30 Apr 94*	2
LOVE IN A PEACEFUL WORLD	*RCA*	31	*6 Aug 94*	3
ALBUMS:	**HITS 13**			**WEEKS 228**
LEVEL 42	*Polydor*	20	*29 Aug 81*	18
THE EARLY TAPES JULY-AUGUST 1980	*Polydor*	46	*10 Apr 82*	6
THE PURSUIT OF ACCIDENTS	*Polydor*	17	*18 Sep 82*	16
STANDING IN THE LIGHT	*Polydor*	9	*3 Sep 83*	13
TRUE COLOURS	*Polydor*	14	*13 Oct 84*	8
A PHYSICAL PRESENCE	*Polydor*	28	*6 Jul 85*	5
Live recordings, mainly from small club tours in the UK.				
WORLD MACHINE	*Polydor*	3	*26 Oct 85*	72
RUNNING IN THE FAMILY	*Polydor*	2	*28 Mar 87*	54
STARING AT THE SUN	*Polydor*	2	*1 Oct 88*	11

LEVEL BEST	*Polydor*	5	*18 Nov 89*	15
Compilation.				
GUARANTEED	*RCA*	3	*14 Sep 91*	5
FOREVER NOW	*RCA*	8	*26 Mar 94*	3
THE VERY BEST OF LEVEL 42	*Polydor*	41	*7 Nov 98*	2

LEVELLERS — UK

SINGLES:	HITS 17			WEEKS 56
ONE WAY	*China*	51	*21 Sep 91*	2
FAR FROM HOME	*China*	71	*7 Dec 91*	1
15 YEARS [EP]	*China*	11	*23 May 92*	5
Lead track: 15 years.				
BELARUSE	*China*	12	*10 Jul 93*	5
THIS GARDEN	*China*	12	*30 Oct 93*	4
THE JULIE [EP]	*China*	17	*14 May 94*	3
Lead track: Julie (New Version).				
HOPE ST.	*China*	12	*12 Aug 95*	5
FANTASY	*China*	16	*14 Oct 95*	3
JUST THE ONE	*China*	12	*23 Dec 95*	8
Above hit: LEVELLERS Special guest Joe STRUMMER on piano.				
EXODUS - LIVE	*China*	24	*20 Jul 96*	2
WHAT A BEAUTIFUL DAY	*China*	13	*9 Aug 97*	5
CELEBRATE	*China*	28	*18 Oct 97*	2
Vocals by Eddi Reader.				
DOG TRAIN	*China*	24	*20 Dec 97*	5
TOO REAL	*China*	46	*14 Mar 98*	1
BOZOS	*China*	44	*24 Oct 98*	2
ONE WAY [RR]	*China*	33	*6 Feb 99*	2
HAPPY BIRTHDAY REVOLUTION	*China*	57	*9 Sep 00*	1

ALBUMS:	HITS 7			WEEKS 81
LEVELLING THE LAND	*China*	14	*19 Oct 91*	22
LEVELLING THE LAND [RE]	*China*	40	*24 Jul 93*	8
Re-released.				
LEVELLERS	*China*	2	*4 Sep 93*	14
ZEITGEIST	*China*	1	*9 Sep 95*	14
BEST LIVE - HEADLIGHTS WHITE LINES BLACK TAR RIVERS: BEST LIVE	*China*	13	*31 Aug 96*	4
Live recordings from their European tour from Sep to Dec 95.				
MOUTH TO MOUTH	*China*	5	*6 Sep 97*	6
ONE WAY OF LIFE - THE BEST OF THE LEVELLERS	*China*	15	*7 Nov 98*	11
HELLO PIG	*China*	28	*16 Sep 00*	2

LEVERT — US

SINGLES:	HITS 1			WEEKS 10
CASANOVA	*Atlantic*	9	*22 Aug 87*	10

ALBUMS:	HITS 1			WEEKS 1
THE BIG THROWDOWN	*Atlantic*	86	*29 Aug 87*	1

LEVERT SWEAT GILL — US

SINGLES:	HITS 3			WEEKS 7
MY BODY	*East West America*	21	*14 Mar 98*	3
CURIOUS	*East West America*	23	*6 Jun 98*	2
Above hit: LEVERT SWEAT GILL featuring L.L. COOL J., Busta RHYMES and MC LYTE.				
DOOR #1	*East West America*	45	*12 Sep 98*	2

Hank LEVINE — US

SINGLES:	HITS 1			WEEKS 4
IMAGE	*His Master's Voice*	45	*23 Dec 61*	4

James LEVINE - See 3 TENORS: Jose CARRERAS, Placido DOMINGO, Luciano PAVAROTTI

LEVITATION — UK

ALBUMS:	HITS 1			WEEKS 1
NEED FOR NOT	*Rough Trade*	45	*16 May 92*	1

LEVITICUS — UK

SINGLES:	HITS 1			WEEKS 1
BURIAL	*ffrr*	66	*25 Mar 95*	1
Song based on Madamoiselle by Foxy.				

Barrington LEVY — Jamaica

(See also Rebel MC.)

SINGLES:	HITS 3			WEEKS 7
HERE I COME	*London*	41	*2 Feb 85*	4

WORK	*MCA*	65	*24 Sep 94*	1
HERE I COME (SING DJ)	*NuLife*	37	*13 Oct 01*	2
Above hit: TALISMAN P meets Barrington LEVY.				

Jona LEWIE — UK

(See also Terry Dactyl and the Dinosaurs.)

SINGLES:	HITS 2			WEEKS 20
YOU'LL ALWAYS FIND ME IN THE KITCHEN AT PARTIES	*Stiff*	16	*10 May 80*	9
Some copies have title as Kitchen At Parties.				
STOP THE CAVALRY	*Stiff*	3	*29 Nov 80*	11

C.J. LEWIS — UK

SINGLES:	HITS 5			WEEKS 32
SWEETS FOR MY SWEET	*Black Market*	3	*23 Apr 94*	13
EVERYTHING IS ALRIGHT (UPTIGHT)	*Black Market*	10	*23 Jul 94*	7
BEST OF MY LOVE	*Black Market*	13	*8 Oct 94*	6
DOLLARS	*Black Market*	34	*17 Dec 94*	4
R TO THE A	*Black Market*	34	*9 Sep 95*	2
ALBUMS:	**HITS 1**			**WEEKS 2**
DOLLARS	*Black Market*	44	*3 Sep 94*	2

Danny J LEWIS — UK

SINGLES:	HITS 1			WEEKS 2
SPEND THE NIGHT	*Locked On*	29	*20 Jun 98*	2

Darlene LEWIS - See LOVELAND featuring the voice of Rachel McFARLANE

Dee LEWIS — UK

(See also Mondo Kane featuring Dee Lewis and Coral Gordon, guest star Georgie Fame.)

SINGLES:	HITS 1			WEEKS 5
THE BEST OF MY LOVE	*Mercury*	47	*18 Jun 88*	5

Donna LEWIS — UK

SINGLES:	HITS 2			WEEKS 16
I LOVE YOU ALWAYS FOREVER	*Atlantic*	5	*7 Sep 96*	14
Inspired by the H.E. Bates novel 'Love For Lydia'.				
WITHOUT LOVE	*Atlantic*	39	*8 Feb 97*	2
ALBUMS:	**HITS 1**			**WEEKS 1**
NOW IN A MINUTE	*Atlantic*	52	*12 Oct 96*	1

Gary LEWIS and the PLAYBOYS — US

SINGLES:	HITS 1			WEEKS 7
MY HEART'S SYMPHONY	*United Artists*	36	*8 Feb 75*	7
Originally released in 1966, reaching No. 13 in the US.				

Georgia LEWIS - See TECHNICIAN 2 featuring Georgia LEWIS

Huey LEWIS and the NEWS — US

SINGLES:	HITS 8			WEEKS 66
IF THIS IS IT	*Chrysalis*	39	*27 Oct 84*	6
POWER OF LOVE	*Chrysalis*	11	*31 Aug 85*	10
From the film 'Back To The Future'.				
THE HEART AND SOUL [EP]	*Chrysalis*	61	*23 Nov 85*	4
Lead track: Heart And Soul.				
THE POWER OF LOVE [RE] + [RI] / DO YOU BELIEVE IN LOVE	*Chrysalis*	9	*8 Feb 86*	12
Do You Believe In Love listed from 15 Feb 86 on the re-issued release.				
THE HEART OF ROCK AND ROLL	*Chrysalis*	49	*10 May 86*	3
Original release reached No. 78 in 1984, it was also a track on The Heart And Soul EP.				
STUCK WITH YOU	*Chrysalis*	12	*23 Aug 86*	12
HIP TO BE SQUARE	*Chrysalis*	41	*6 Dec 86*	8
SIMPLE AS THAT	*Chrysalis*	47	*21 Mar 87*	5
PERFECT WORLD	*Chrysalis*	48	*16 Jul 88*	6
ALBUMS:	**HITS 5**			**WEEKS 94**
SPORTS	*Chrysalis*	23	*14 Sep 85*	24
FORE!	*Chrysalis*	8	*20 Sep 86*	52
SMALL WORLD	*Chrysalis*	12	*6 Aug 88*	8
HARD AT PLAY	*Chrysalis*	39	*18 May 91*	2
THE HEART OF ROCK AND ROLL - BEST OF HUEY LEWIS AND THE NEWS	*Chrysalis*	23	*21 Nov 92*	8

Jerry LEWIS — US

SINGLES:	HITS 1			WEEKS 8
ROCK-A-BYE YOUR BABY WITH A DIXIE MELODY *Originally recorded by Al Jolson in 1918.*	*Brunswick*	12	*9 Feb 57*	7
ROCK-A-BYE YOUR BABY WITH A DIXIE MELODY [RE]	*Brunswick*	22	*6 Apr 57*	1

Jerry Lee LEWIS — US

SINGLES:	HITS 10			WEEKS 68
WHOLE LOTTA SHAKIN' GOIN' ON *Originally recorded by Big Maybelle in 1955.*	*London*	8	*28 Sep 57*	10
GREAT BALLS OF FIRE *From the film 'Jamboree'.*	*London*	1	*21 Dec 57*	12
WHOLE LOTTA SHAKIN' GOIN' ON [RE]	*London*	26	*28 Dec 57*	1
BREATHLESS	*London*	8	*12 Apr 58*	7
HIGH SCHOOL CONFIDENTIAL *From the film of the same name.*	*London*	12	*24 Jan 59*	6
LOVIN' UP A STORM	*London*	28	*2 May 59*	1
BABY BABY BYE BYE	*London*	47	*11 Jun 60*	1
WHAT'D I SAY *Featuring the Anita Kerr Singers. Original by Ray Charles reached No. 6 in the US in 1959.*	*London*	10	*6 May 61*	12
WHAT'D I SAY [RE]	*London*	49	*5 Aug 61*	2
SWEET LITTLE SIXTEEN	*London*	38	*8 Sep 62*	5
GOOD GOLLY MISS MOLLY	*London*	31	*16 Mar 63*	6
CHANTILLY LACE	*Mercury*	33	*6 May 72*	5
EPS:	**HITS 2**			**WEEKS 11**
JERRY LEE LEWIS - NO. 4	*London*	13	*6 Oct 62*	5
JERRY LEE LEWIS - NO. 5	*London*	14	*27 Oct 62*	6
ALBUMS:	**HITS 1**			**WEEKS 6**
JERRY LEE LEWIS VOLUME 2	*London*	14	*2 Jun 62*	6

Linda LEWIS — UK

SINGLES:	HITS 5			WEEKS 31
ROCK A DOODLE DOO	*Raft*	15	*2 Jun 73*	11
IT'S IN HIS KISS	*Arista*	6	*12 Jul 75*	8
BABY I'M YOURS	*Arista*	33	*17 Apr 76*	6
I'D BE SURPRISINGLY GOOD FOR YOU	*Ariola*	40	*2 Jun 79*	5
REACH OUT *Above hit: MIDFIELD GENERAL featuring Linda LEWIS.*	*Skint*	61	*19 Aug 00*	1
ALBUMS:	**HITS 1**			**WEEKS 4**
NOT A LITTLE GIRL ANYMORE	*Arista*	40	*9 Aug 75*	4

Linda Gail LEWIS - See Van MORRISON

Ramsey LEWIS TRIO — US

SINGLES:	HITS 1			WEEKS 8
WADE IN THE WATER *Above hit: Ramsey LEWIS.*	*Chess*	31	*15 Apr 72*	8
ALBUMS:	**HITS 1**			**WEEKS 4**
HANG ON RAMSEY	*Chess*	20	*21 May 66*	4

Shirley LEWIS - See Arthur BAKER and the BACKBEAT DISCIPLES

John LEYTON — UK

SINGLES:	HITS 9			WEEKS 70
JOHNNY REMEMBER ME *Female backing vocals by Lissa Gray.*	*Top Rank*	1	*5 Aug 61*	15
WILD WIND	*Top Rank*	2	*7 Oct 61*	10
SON THIS IS SHE	*His Master's Voice*	15	*30 Dec 61*	10
LONE RIDER *Originally recorded by the Flee-Rekkers.*	*His Master's Voice*	40	*17 Mar 62*	5
LONELY CITY	*His Master's Voice*	14	*5 May 62*	11
DOWN THE RIVER NILE	*His Master's Voice*	42	*25 Aug 62*	3
CUPBOARD LOVE	*His Master's Voice*	22	*23 Feb 63*	12
I'LL CUT YOUR TAIL OFF	*His Master's Voice*	50	*20 Jul 63*	1
I'LL CUT YOUR TAIL OFF [RE]	*His Master's Voice*	36	*10 Aug 63*	2
MAKE LOVE TO ME	*His Master's Voice*	49	*22 Feb 64*	1
EPS:	**HITS 1**			**WEEKS 13**
JOHN LEYTON	*Top Rank*	11	*10 Mar 62*	13

LEYTON BUZZARDS — UK

SINGLES:	HITS 1			WEEKS 5
SATURDAY NIGHT (BENEATH THE PLASTIC PALM TREES)	*Chrysalis*	53	*3 Mar 79*	5

LFO — UK

SINGLES:	HITS 3			WEEKS 15
LFO	*Warp*	12	*14 Jul 90*	10
WE ARE BACK / NURTURE	*Warp*	47	*6 Jul 91*	3
WHAT IS HOUSE [EP] *Lead track: Tan Ta Ra.*	*Warp*	62	*1 Feb 92*	2
ALBUMS:	**HITS 2**			**WEEKS 3**
FREQUENCIES	*Warp*	42	*3 Aug 91*	2
ADVANCE	*Warp*	44	*10 Feb 96*	1

LIBERACE — US

SINGLES:	HITS 2			WEEKS 2
UNCHAINED MELODY *From the film 'Unchained'.*	*Philips*	20	*18 Jun 55*	1
I DON'T CARE (AS LONG AS YOU CARE FOR ME)	*Columbia*	28	*20 Oct 56*	1

LIBERATION — UK

SINGLES:	HITS 1			WEEKS 3
LIBERATION	*ZYX*	28	*24 Oct 92*	3

LIBERTY — UK

SINGLES:	HITS 2			WEEKS 11
THINKING IT OVER	*V2*	5	*6 Oct 01*	8
DOIN' IT	*V2*	14	*15 Dec 01*	3

LIBIDO — Norway

SINGLES:	HITS 1			WEEKS 1
OVERTHROWN	*Fire*	53	*31 Jan 98*	1

LIBRA presents TAYLOR — UK

SINGLES:	HITS 1			WEEKS 3
ANOMALY - CALLING YOUR NAME *Originally released in 1995.*	*Platipus*	71	*26 Oct 96*	1
ANOMALY - CALLING YOUR NAME [RM] *Remixed by Ferry Corsten.*	*Platipus*	43	*18 Mar 00*	2

LICK THE TINS — UK

SINGLES:	HITS 1			WEEKS 8
CAN'T HELP FALLING IN LOVE	*Sedition*	42	*29 Mar 86*	8

Ben LIEBRAND — Holland

SINGLES:	HITS 1			WEEKS 2
PULS(T)AR	*Epic*	68	*9 Jun 90*	2

LIEUTENANT PIGEON — UK

SINGLES:	HITS 2			WEEKS 29
MOULDY OLD DOUGH	*Decca*	1	*16 Sep 72*	19
DESPERATE DAN	*Decca*	17	*16 Dec 72*	10

LIFEHOUSE — US

SINGLES:	HITS 1			WEEKS 4
HANGING BY A MOMENT	*Dreamworks*	25	*8 Sep 01*	4

LIGHTFORCE — Germany

SINGLES:	HITS 1			WEEKS 1
JOIN ME	*Slinky Music*	53	*28 Oct 00*	1

LIGHT OF THE WORLD — UK

SINGLES:	HITS 6			WEEKS 25
SWINGIN'	*Ensign*	45	*14 Apr 79*	5
MIDNIGHT GROOVIN'	*Ensign*	72	*14 Jul 79*	1
LONDON TOWN	*Ensign*	41	*18 Oct 80*	5
I SHOT THE SHERIFF	*Ensign*	40	*17 Jan 81*	5
I'M SO HAPPY / TIME	*Mercury*	35	*28 Mar 81*	6
RIDE THE LOVE TRAIN	*EMI*	49	*21 Nov 81*	3
ALBUMS:	**HITS 1**			**WEEKS 1**
ROUND TRIP	*Ensign*	73	*24 Jan 81*	1

LIGHTER SHADE OF BROWN — US

SINGLES:	HITS 1			WEEKS 3
HEY D.J. *Samples the World Famous Supreme Team's Hey DJ.*	*Mercury*	33	*9 Jul 94*	3

Gordon LIGHTFOOT — Canada

SINGLES:	HITS 4			WEEKS 26
IF YOU COULD READ MY MIND	*Reprise*	30	*19 Jun 71*	9
SUNDOWN	*Reprise*	33	*3 Aug 74*	7
THE WRECK OF THE EDMUND FITZGERALD	*Reprise*	40	*15 Jan 77*	4
DAYLIGHT KATY	*Warner Brothers*	41	*16 Sep 78*	6
ALBUMS:	**HITS 2**			**WEEKS 2**
DON QUIXOTE	*Reprise*	44	*20 May 72*	1
SUNDOWN	*Reprise*	45	*17 Aug 74*	1

Terry LIGHTFOOT'S NEW ORLEANS JAZZMEN — UK

SINGLES:	HITS 3			WEEKS 17
TRUE LOVE	*Columbia*	33	*9 Sep 61*	4
KING KONG	*Columbia*	29	*25 Nov 61*	12
TAVERN IN THE TOWN	*Columbia*	49	*5 May 62*	1
EPS:	**HITS 1**			**WEEKS 1**
CLARINET JAMBOREE *Above hit: Mr. Acker BILK and Terry LIGHTFOOT.*	*Columbia*	19	*4 Mar 61*	1

LIGHTHOUSE FAMILY — UK

SINGLES:	HITS 10			WEEKS 82
LIFTED	*Wild Card*	61	*27 May 95*	2
OCEAN DRIVE *From the film 'Jack And Sarah'.*	*Wild Card*	34	*14 Oct 95*	3
LIFTED [RI]	*Wild Card*	4	*10 Feb 96*	10
OCEAN DRIVE [RI]	*Wild Card*	11	*1 Jun 96*	8
GOODBYE HEARTBREAK *Backing vocals by Nu Colours.*	*Wild Card*	14	*21 Sep 96*	6
LOVING EVERY MINUTE	*Wild Card*	20	*21 Dec 96*	7
RAINCLOUD	*Wild Card*	6	*11 Oct 97*	7
HIGH	*Wild Card*	4	*10 Jan 98*	14
LOST IN SPACE	*Wild Card*	6	*27 Jun 98*	8
QUESTION OF FAITH	*Wild Card*	21	*10 Oct 98*	5
POSTCARDS FROM HEAVEN	*Wild Card*	24	*9 Jan 99*	6
(I WISH I KNEW HOW IT WOULD FEEL TO BE) FREE/ONE [M]	*Wild Card*	6	*24 Nov 01*	6
ALBUMS:	**HITS 3**			**WEEKS 230**
OCEAN DRIVE	*Wild Card*	74	*18 Nov 95*	1
OCEAN DRIVE [RE] *Peak position reached on 8 Mar 97.*	*Wild Card*	3	*16 Mar 96*	153
POSTCARDS FROM HEAVEN	*Wild Card*	2	*1 Nov 97*	71
WHATEVER GETS YOU THROUGH THE DAY	*Wild Card*	7	*1 Dec 01*	5

LIGHTNING SEEDS — UK

SINGLES:	HITS 16			WEEKS 98
PURE	*Ghetto*	16	*22 Jul 89*	8
THE LIFE OF RILEY	*Virgin*	28	*14 Mar 92*	6
SENSE	*Virgin*	31	*30 May 92*	5
LUCKY YOU	*Epic*	43	*20 Aug 94*	2
CHANGE	*Epic*	13	*14 Jan 95*	6
MARVELLOUS	*Epic*	24	*15 Apr 95*	5
PERFECT	*Epic*	18	*22 Jul 95*	5
LUCKY YOU [RI]	*Epic*	15	*21 Oct 95*	6
READY OR NOT	*Epic*	20	*9 Mar 96*	4
THREE LIONS (THE OFFICIAL SONG OF THE ENGLAND FOOTBALL TEAM) *Official anthem for England's football team in Euro 1996.* *Above hit: BADDIEL and SKINNER and LIGHTNING SEEDS.*	*Epic*	1	*1 Jun 96*	15
WHAT IF . . .	*Epic*	14	*2 Nov 96*	3
WHAT IF . . . [RE]	*Epic*	64	*11 Jan 97*	1
SUGAR COATED ICEBERG *Co written by Stephen Jones (Babybird).*	*Epic*	12	*18 Jan 97*	4
YOU SHOWED ME *Originally recorded by the Byrds in 1964. The Turtles' version reached No. 6 in the US in 1969.*	*Epic*	8	*26 Apr 97*	5
WHAT YOU SAY	*Epic*	41	*13 Dec 97*	5
3 LIONS '98 [RR] *Re-recorded for the 1998 World Cup in France.* *Above hit: BADDIEL, SKINNER and the LIGHTNING SEEDS.*	*Epic*	1	*20 Jun 98*	13
LIFE'S TOO SHORT	*Epic*	27	*27 Nov 99*	3
LIFE'S TOO SHORT [RE]	*Epic*	73	*22 Jan 00*	1
SWEETEST SOUL SENSATIONS *Samples Al Green's Simply Beautiful.*	*Epic*	67	*18 Mar 00*	1

ALBUMS:	HITS 7			WEEKS 139
CLOUDCUCKOOLAND	*Ghetto*	50	*10 Feb 90*	2
SENSE	*Virgin*	53	*18 Apr 92*	1
JOLLIFICATION	*Epic*	30	*17 Sep 94*	7
Peak position reached in 1995 (1994 peak No 60).				
JOLLIFICATION [RE]	*Epic*	12	*15 Jul 95*	51
Peak position reached on 13 Jan 96.				
PURE LIGHTNING SEEDS	*Virgin*	27	*18 May 96*	9
DIZZY HEIGHTS	*Epic*	11	*23 Nov 96*	26
LIKE YOU DO . . . BEST OF THE LIGHTNING SEEDS	*Epic*	5	*22 Nov 97*	41
TILT	*Epic*	46	*4 Dec 99*	2

LIL BOW WOW — US

SINGLES:	HITS 1			WEEKS 9
BOW WOW (THAT'S MY NAME)	*So So Def*	6	*14 Apr 01*	9
Samples Andy Gibb's Shadow Dancing.				

LIL' DEVIOUS — UK

SINGLES:	HITS 1			WEEKS 1
COME HOME	*Rulin*	55	*15 Sep 01*	1

LIL' KIM — US

(See also Christina Aguilera, Lil' Kim, Mya and Pink; Missy "Misdemeanor" Elliott; Notorious B.I.G.; Puff Daddy.)

SINGLES:	HITS 6			WEEKS 16
NO TIME	*Atlantic*	45	*26 Apr 97*	1
Samples Just Take Me As I Am by Lyn Collins.				
Above hit: LIL' KIM featuring PUFF DADDY.				
CRUSH ON YOU	*Atlantic*	36	*5 Jul 97*	2
Samples Jeff Lorber's Rain Dance.				
NOT TONIGHT	*Atlantic*	11	*16 Aug 97*	5
From the film 'Nothing To Lose'; samples Kool And The Gang's Ladies Night.				
Above hit: LIL' KIM featuring DA BRAT, LEFT EYE, Missy "Misdemeanor" ELLIOTT and Angie MARTINEZ.				
CRUSH ON YOU [RE]	*Atlantic*	23	*25 Oct 97*	3
NO MATTER WHAT THEY SAY	*Atlantic*	35	*2 Sep 00*	2
Samples Jose "Cheo" Feliciano's Esto Es El Guaguango.				
WAIT A MINUTE	*Atlantic*	54	*11 Aug 01*	1
Above hit: RAY-J featuring LIL' KIM.				
IN THE AIR TONITE	*WEA*	26	*22 Sep 01*	2
Above hit: LIL' KIM featuring Phil COLLINS.				

ALBUMS:	HITS 1			WEEKS 1
THE NOTORIOUS K.I.M.	*Atlantic*	67	*8 Jul 00*	1

LIL' LOUIS — US

(See also Black Magic.)

SINGLES:	HITS 4			WEEKS 21
FRENCH KISS	*ffrr*	2	*29 Jul 89*	11
I CALLED U	*ffrr*	16	*13 Jan 90*	6
SAVED MY LIFE	*ffrr*	74	*26 Sep 92*	1
Above 2: LIL' LOUIS and the WORLD.				
HOW'S YOUR EVENING SO FAR? [RR]	*ffrr*	23	*12 Aug 00*	3
A re-recorded version of French Kiss.				
Above hit: Josh WINK and LIL' LOUIS.				

ALBUMS:	HITS 1			WEEKS 5
FRENCH KISSES	*ffrr*	35	*26 Aug 89*	5

LIL' MISS MAX – See BLUE ADONIS featuring LIL' MISS MAX

LIL' MO — US

SINGLES:	HITS 2			WEEKS 4
5 MINUTES	*East West America*	72	*21 Nov 98*	1
From the film 'Why Do Fools Fall In Love'.				
Above hit: LIL' MO featuring Missy Misdemeanor ELLIOTT.				
WHATEVER	*Virgin*	31	*23 Sep 00*	3
Above hit: IDEAL U.S. featuring LIL' MO.				

LIL MO' YIN YANG — US

SINGLES:	HITS 1			WEEKS 2
REACH	*Multiply*	28	*9 Mar 96*	2

LIL' ROMEO — US

SINGLES:	HITS 1			WEEKS 1
MY BABY	*Priority*	67	*22 Sep 01*	1

LILY – See MAXIMA featuring LILY

LILYS
US

SINGLES:	HITS 1			WEEKS 4
A NANNY IN MANHATTAN	*Che*	16	*21 Feb 98*	4
Featured in the Levi's Jeans TV commercial.				

LIMA – See Tom NOVY

LIMAHL
UK

SINGLES:	HITS 3			WEEKS 25
ONLY FOR LOVE	*EMI*	16	*5 Nov 83*	7
ONLY FOR LOVE [RE]	*EMI*	75	*7 Jan 84*	1
TOO MUCH TROUBLE	*EMI*	64	*2 Jun 84*	3
THE NEVER ENDING STORY	*EMI*	4	*13 Oct 84*	14
From the film of the same name. Duet with Beth Anderson.				
ALBUMS:	**HITS 1**			**WEEKS 3**
DON'T SUPPOSE	*EMI*	63	*1 Dec 84*	3

Alison LIMERICK
UK

SINGLES:	HITS 9			WEEKS 39
WHERE LOVE LIVES (COME ON IN)	*Arista*	27	*30 Mar 91*	8
Original release reached No. 87 in 1990.				
COME BACK (FOR REAL LOVE)	*Arista*	53	*12 Oct 91*	2
MAGIC'S BACK (THEME FROM 'THE GHOSTS OF OXFORD STREET')	*RCA*	42	*21 Dec 91*	4
Theme from the Channel 4 TV programme.				
Above hit: Malcolm McLAREN featuring Alison LIMERICK.				
MAKE IT ON MY OWN	*Arista*	16	*29 Feb 92*	6
GETTIN' IT RIGHT	*Arista*	57	*18 Jul 92*	2
HEAR MY CALL	*Arista*	73	*28 Nov 92*	1
TIME OF OUR LIVES	*Arista*	36	*8 Jan 94*	4
LOVE COME DOWN	*Arista*	36	*19 Mar 94*	2
LOVE WILL KEEP US TOGETHER	*Acid Jazz*	63	*25 Feb 95*	1
Above hit: James TAYLOR QUARTET featuring Alison LIMERICK.				
WHERE LOVE LIVES [RM]	*Arista*	9	*6 Jul 96*	6
MAKE IT ON MY OWN [RM]	*Arista*	30	*14 Sep 96*	2
Above 2 remixed by Dancing Divaz.				
PUT YOUR FAITH IN ME	*X-ES*	42	*23 Aug 97*	1
ALBUMS:	**HITS 1**			**WEEKS 2**
AND STILL I RISE	*Arista*	53	*4 Apr 92*	2

LIMIT
Holland

SINGLES:	HITS 1			WEEKS 8
SAY YEAH	*Portrait*	17	*5 Jan 85*	8

LIMMIE and FAMILY COOKIN'
US

SINGLES:	HITS 3			WEEKS 28
YOU CAN DO MAGIC	*Avco*	3	*21 Jul 73*	13
DREAMBOAT	*Avco*	31	*20 Oct 73*	5
A WALKIN' MIRACLE	*Avco*	6	*6 Apr 74*	10
Original by the Essex reached No. 12 in the US in 1963.				

LIMP BIZKIT
US

SINGLES:	HITS 5			WEEKS 49
TAKE A LOOK AROUND (THEME FROM MI: 2)	*Interscope*	3	*15 Jul 00*	13
From the film 'Mission Impossible 2'.				
MY GENERATION	*Interscope*	15	*11 Nov 00*	6
MY GENERATION [RE]	*Interscope*	65	*6 Jan 01*	2
ROLLIN'	*Interscope*	1	*27 Jan 01*	13
MY WAY	*Interscope*	6	*23 Jun 01*	10
BOILER/FAITH	*Interscope*	18	*10 Nov 01*	5
ALBUMS:	**HITS 3**			**WEEKS 90**
SIGNIFICANT OTHER	*Interscope*	26	*3 Jul 99*	13
THREE DOLLAR BILL Y'ALL$	*Interscope*	68	*9 Sep 00*	2
Reached No. 90 when first released in 1997.				
CHOCOLATE STARFISH AND THE HOTDOG FLAVOURED WATER	*Interscope*	1	*28 Oct 00*	48
Peak position reached on 3 Feb 01.				
SIGNIFICANT OTHER [RE]	*Interscope*	10	*3 Feb 01*	24
THREE DOLLAR BILL Y'ALL$ [RE]	*Interscope*	50	*17 Mar 01*	3

LINA
US

SINGLES:	HITS 1			WEEKS 1
PLAYA NO MO'	*Atlantic*	46	*3 Mar 01*	1

Bob LIND — US

SINGLES:	HITS 2			WEEKS 10
ELUSIVE BUTTERFLY	*Fontana*	5	*12 Mar 66*	9
REMEMBER THE RAIN	*Fontana*	46	*28 May 66*	1

LINDA and the FUNKY BOYS - See Linda CARR

LINDISFARNE — UK

SINGLES:	HITS 6			WEEKS 55
MEET ME ON THE CORNER	*Charisma*	5	*26 Feb 72*	11
LADY ELEANOR	*Charisma*	3	*13 May 72*	11
ALL FALL DOWN	*Charisma*	34	*23 Sep 72*	5
RUN FOR HOME	*Mercury*	10	*3 Jun 78*	15
JUKE BOX GYPSY	*Mercury*	56	*7 Oct 78*	4
FOG ON THE TYNE (REVISITED)	*Best*	2	*10 Nov 90*	9
Above hit: GAZZA and LINDISFARNE.				

ALBUMS:	HITS 8			WEEKS 118
FOG ON THE TYNE	*Charisma*	1	*30 Oct 71*	56
NICELY OUT OF TUNE	*Charisma*	8	*15 Jan 72*	30
DINGLY DELL	*Charisma*	95	*30 Sep 72*	10
LINDISFARNE LIVE	*Charisma*	25	*11 Aug 73*	6
FINEST HOUR	*Charisma*	55	*18 Oct 75*	1
Compilation.				
BACK AND FOURTH	*Mercury*	22	*24 Jun 78*	11
MAGIC IN THE AIR	*Mercury*	71	*9 Dec 78*	1
SLEEPLESS NIGHTS	*LMP*	59	*23 Oct 82*	3

LINDSAY — UK

SINGLES:	HITS 1			WEEKS 4
NO DREAM IMPOSSIBLE	*Universal Music TV*	32	*12 May 01*	4
The UK's Eurovision entry in 2001, it came 15th.				

Mort LINDSEY and his Orchestra - See Pat BOONE

LINER — UK

SINGLES:	HITS 2			WEEKS 6
KEEP REACHING OUT FOR LOVE	*Atlantic*	49	*10 Mar 79*	3
YOU AND ME	*Atlantic*	44	*26 May 79*	3

Max LINEN — UK

SINGLES:	HITS 1			WEEKS 1
THE SOULSHAKER	*Global Cuts*	55	*17 Nov 01*	1

Andy LING — UK

SINGLES:	HITS 1			WEEKS 1
FIXATION	*Hooj Choons*	55	*23 May 00*	1
Originally released on the Fluid Recordings label in 1999.				

Laurie LINGO and the DIPSTICKS — UK

SINGLES:	HITS 1			WEEKS 7
CONVOY G.B.	*State*	4	*17 Apr 76*	7
Parody of C.W. McCall's Convoy.				

LINK — US

SINGLES:	HITS 1			WEEKS 1
WHATCHA GONNA DO?	*Epic*	48	*7 Nov 98*	1

LINKIN PARK — US

SINGLES:	HITS 4			WEEKS 27
ONE STEP CLOSER	*Warner Brothers*	24	*27 Jan 01*	4
CRAWLING	*Warner Brothers*	16	*21 Apr 01*	8
PAPERCUT	*Warner Brothers*	14	*30 Jun 01*	6
IN THE END	*Warner Brothers*	8	*20 Oct 01*	9

ALBUMS:	HITS 1			WEEKS 50
HYBRID THEORY	*Warner Brothers*	4	*20 Jan 01*	50
Peak position reached on 3 Nov 01.				

LINOLEUM — UK

SINGLES:	HITS 1			WEEKS 1
MARQUIS	*Lino Vinyl*	73	*12 Jul 97*	1

LINX — UK

SINGLES:	HITS 6			WEEKS 45
YOU'RE LYING	*Chrysalis*	15	*20 Sep 80*	10
INTUITION	*Chrysalis*	7	*7 Mar 81*	11
THROW AWAY THE KEY	*Chrysalis*	21	*13 Jun 81*	9
SO THIS IS ROMANCE	*Chrysalis*	15	*5 Sep 81*	9
CAN'T HELP MYSELF	*Chrysalis*	55	*21 Nov 81*	3
PLAYTHING	*Chrysalis*	48	*10 Jul 82*	3

ALBUMS:	HITS 2			WEEKS 23
INTUITION	*Chrysalis*	8	*28 Mar 81*	19
GO AHEAD	*Chrysalis*	35	*31 Oct 81*	4

LIONROCK — UK

SINGLES:	HITS 8			WEEKS 14
LIONROCK	*Deconstruction*	63	*5 Dec 92*	1
PACKET OF PEACE	*Deconstruction*	32	*8 May 93*	3
CARNIVAL [EP]	*Arista*	34	*23 Oct 93*	2
Lead track: Are You Willing To Testify?				
TRIPWIRE	*Deconstruction*	44	*27 Aug 94*	1
STRAIGHT AT YER HEAD	*Deconstruction*	33	*6 Apr 96*	2
FIRE UP THE SHOESAW	*Deconstruction*	43	*27 Jul 96*	1
RUDE BOY ROCK	*Concrete*	20	*14 Mar 98*	3
SCATTER & SWING	*Concrete*	54	*30 May 98*	1

ALBUMS:	HITS 2			WEEKS 3
AN INSTINCT FOR DETECTION	*Deconstruction*	30	*20 Apr 96*	2
CITY DELIRIOUS	*Concrete*	73	*28 Mar 98*	1

LIPPS INC. — US

SINGLES:	HITS 1			WEEKS 13
FUNKYTOWN	*Casablanca*	2	*17 May 80*	13

LIQUID — UK

SINGLES:	HITS 7			WEEKS 20
SWEET HARMONY [EP]	*XL Recordings*	15	*21 Mar 92*	6
Lead track: Sweet Harmony.				
THE FUTURE MUSIC [EP]	*XL Recordings*	59	*5 Sep 92*	2
Lead track: Liquid Is Liquid.				
TIME TO GET UP	*XL Recordings*	46	*20 Mar 93*	2
SWEET HARMONY [RM] / ONE LOVE FAMILY	*XL Recordings*	14	*8 Jul 95*	6
Remixed by Liquid.				
CLOSER	*XL Recordings*	47	*21 Oct 95*	2
STRONG	*Higher Ground*	59	*25 Jul 98*	1
ORLANDO DAWN	*Xtravaganza*	53	*21 Oct 00*	1

LIQUID CHILD — Germany

SINGLES:	HITS 1			WEEKS 2
DIVING FACES	*Essential Recordings*	25	*23 Oct 99*	2
Original release on the Reef label reached No. 95 in 1998.				

LIQUID GOLD — UK

SINGLES:	HITS 6			WEEKS 46
ANYWAY YOU DO IT	*Creole*	41	*2 Dec 78*	7
DANCE YOURSELF DIZZY	*Polo*	2	*23 Feb 80*	14
SUBSTITUTE	*Polo*	8	*31 May 80*	9
THE NIGHT, THE WINE AND THE ROSES	*Polo*	32	*1 Nov 80*	7
DON'T PANIC	*Polo*	42	*28 Mar 81*	5
Was a contender for 'A Song For Europe'.				
WHERE DID WE GO WRONG	*Polo*	56	*21 Aug 82*	4

ALBUMS:	HITS 1			WEEKS 3
LIQUID GOLD	*Polo*	34	*16 Aug 80*	3

LIQUID OXYGEN — UK

SINGLES:	HITS 1			WEEKS 2
THE PLANET DANCE (MOVE YA BODY)	*Champion*	56	*28 Apr 90*	2

LISA LISA and CULT JAM — US

SINGLES:	HITS 4			WEEKS 32
I WONDER IF I TAKE YOU HOME	*CBS*	53	*4 May 85*	6
Above hit: LISA LISA and CULT JAM with FULL FORCE.				
I WONDER IF I TAKE YOU HOME [RE]	*CBS*	12	*3 Aug 85*	11
LOST IN EMOTION	*CBS*	58	*31 Oct 87*	4
LET THE BEAT HIT 'EM	*Columbia*	17	*13 Jul 91*	6
LET THE BEAT HIT 'EM PART 2 [RM]	*Columbia*	49	*24 Aug 91*	2

SKIP TO MY LU	*Chrysalis*	34	*26 Mar 94*	3
Above hit: LISA LISA.				
ALBUMS:	**HITS 1**			**WEEKS 1**
LISA LISA AND CULT JAM WITH FULL FORCE	*CBS*	96	*21 Sep 85*	1
Above hit: LISA LISA and CULT JAM with FULL FORCE.				

LISA MARIE EXPERIENCE — UK

SINGLES:	**HITS 2**			**WEEKS 15**
KEEP ON JUMPIN'	*ffrr*	7	*27 Apr 96*	10
Originally recorded by Musique in 1978.				
KEEP ON JUMPIN' [RE]	*ffrr*	61	*20 Jul 96*	3
DO THAT TO ME	*Positiva*	33	*10 Aug 96*	2
Originally released in 1995.				

LIT — US

SINGLES:	**HITS 3**			**WEEKS 7**
MY OWN WORST ENEMY	*RCA*	16	*26 Jun 99*	4
ZIP-LOCK	*RCA*	60	*25 Sep 99*	1
OVER MY HEAD - MUSIC FROM THE MOTION PICTURE TITAN A.E.	*Capitol*	37	*19 Aug 00*	2
ALBUMS:	**HITS 1**			**WEEKS 1**
A PLACE IN THE SUN	*RCA*	55	*10 Jul 99*	1

LITHIUM and Sonya MADAN — US

SINGLES:	**HITS 1**			**WEEKS 2**
RIDE A ROCKET	*ffrr*	40	*1 Mar 97*	2

De Etta LITTLE and Nelson PIGFORD — US

SINGLES:	**HITS 1**			**WEEKS 5**
YOU TAKE MY HEART AWAY	*United Artists*	35	*13 Aug 77*	5
From the film 'Rocky'.				

LITTLE ANGELS — UK

SINGLES:	**HITS 13**			**WEEKS 41**
BIG BAD [EP]	*Polydor*	74	*4 Mar 89*	1
Lead Track: She's A Little Angel.				
KICKING UP DUST	*Polydor*	46	*24 Feb 90*	4
RADICAL YOUR LOVER	*Polydor*	34	*12 May 90*	4
Above hit: LITTLE ANGELS (featuring the BIG BAD HORNS).				
SHE'S A LITTLE ANGEL	*Polydor*	21	*4 Aug 90*	3
BONEYARD	*Polydor*	33	*2 Feb 91*	4
Above has title as We're All Going Down To The Boneyard.				
PRODUCT OF THE WORKING CLASS	*Polydor*	40	*30 Mar 91*	2
YOUNG GODS	*Polydor*	34	*1 Jun 91*	2
I AIN'T GONNA CRY	*Polydor*	26	*20 Jul 91*	3
TOO MUCH TOO YOUNG	*Polydor*	22	*7 Nov 92*	3
WOMANKIND	*Polydor*	12	*9 Jan 93*	5
SOAPBOX	*Polydor*	33	*24 Apr 93*	4
SAIL AWAY	*Polydor*	45	*25 Sep 93*	3
TEN MILES HIGH	*Polydor*	18	*9 Apr 94*	3
ALBUMS:	**HITS 4**			**WEEKS 15**
YOUNG GODS	*Polydor*	17	*2 Mar 91*	6
JAM	*Polydor*	1	*6 Feb 93*	5
LITTLE OF THE PAST	*Polydor*	20	*23 Apr 94*	2
TOO POSH TO MOSH, TOO GOOD TO LAST!	*Essential*	18	*2 Jul 94*	2
Remixed/remastered version of their debut album from 1987.				

LITTLE ANTHONY and the IMPERIALS — US

SINGLES:	**HITS 2**			**WEEKS 13**
BETTER USE YOUR HEAD	*United Artists*	42	*31 Jul 76*	4
WHO'S GONNA LOVE ME	*Power Exchange*	17	*24 Dec 77*	9
Above hit: IMPERIALS.				

LITTLE BENNY and the MASTERS — US

SINGLES:	**HITS 1**			**WEEKS 7**
WHO COMES TO BOOGIE	*BlueBird*	33	*2 Feb 85*	7

LITTLE CAESAR — UK

SINGLES:	**HITS 1**			**WEEKS 3**
THE WHOLE OF THE MOON	*A.1.*	68	*9 Jun 90*	3

LITTLE EVA — US

(See also Big Dee Irwin.)

SINGLES:	HITS 3			WEEKS 45
THE LOCO-MOTION *Carole King on vocals and the Cookies on backing vocals.*	*London*	2	*8 Sep 62*	17
KEEP YOUR HANDS OFF MY BABY	*London*	30	*5 Jan 63*	5
LET'S TURKEY TROT	*London*	13	*9 Mar 63*	12
THE LOCO-MOTION [RE]	*London*	11	*29 Jul 72*	11

LITTLE FEAT — US

ALBUMS:	HITS 5			WEEKS 19
THE LAST RECORD ALBUM	*Warner Brothers*	36	*6 Dec 75*	3
TIME LOVES A HERO	*Warner Brothers*	8	*21 May 77*	11
WAITING FOR COLUMBUS *Live recordings.*	*Warner Brothers*	43	*11 Mar 78*	1
DOWN ON THE FARM	*Warner Brothers*	46	*1 Dec 79*	3
HOY=HOY! *Compilation.*	*Warner Brothers*	76	*8 Aug 81*	1

LITTLE LOUIE - See "Little" Louie VEGA and Marc ANTHONY

LITTLE MS MARCIE - See MELT featuring LITTLE MS MARCIE

LITTLE RICHARD — US

SINGLES:	HITS 16			WEEKS 116
RIP IT UP	*London*	30	*15 Dec 56*	1
LONG TALL SALLY	*London*	3	*9 Feb 57*	16
TUTTI FRUTTI *Above 2 entries were separate sides of the same release, each had its own chart run.*	*London*	29	*23 Feb 57*	1
SHE'S GOT IT	*London*	15	*9 Mar 57*	7
THE GIRL CAN'T HELP IT *Above 2 entries were separate sides of the same release, each had its own chart run.*	*London*	9	*16 Mar 57*	11
SHE'S GOT IT [RE]	*London*	28	*25 May 57*	2
LUCILLE	*London*	10	*29 Jun 57*	9
JENNY JENNY *Above 7: LITTLE RICHARD and his Band.*	*London*	11	*14 Sep 57*	5
KEEP A KNOCKIN'	*London*	21	*30 Nov 57*	7
GOOD GOLLY MISS MOLLY	*London*	8	*1 Mar 58*	9
OOH! MY SOUL	*London*	30	*12 Jul 58*	1
OOH! MY SOUL [RE]	*London*	22	*26 Jul 58*	3
BABY FACE	*London*	2	*3 Jan 59*	15
BY THE LIGHT OF THE SILVERY MOON	*London*	17	*4 Apr 59*	5
KANSAS CITY *Originally recorded by Little Willie Littlefield as KC Lovin'.*	*London*	26	*6 Jun 59*	5
HE GOT WHAT HE WANTED (BUT HE LOST WHAT HE HAD) *Above hit: LITTLE RICHARD with Roger BLACKWELL and his Orchestra.*	*Mercury*	38	*13 Oct 62*	4
BAMA LAMA BAMA LOO	*London*	20	*6 Jun 64*	7
GOOD GOLLY MISS MOLLY! [RR] / RIP IT UP! [RR]	*Creole*	37	*2 Jul 77*	4
GREAT GOSH A'MIGHTY (IT'S A MATTER OF TIME) *From the film 'Down And Out In Beverly Hills'.*	*MCA*	62	*14 Jun 86*	2
OPERATOR	*WEA*	67	*25 Oct 86*	2

LITTLE SHAWN - See VARIOUS ARTISTS (EPs) 'New York Undercover 4-Track EP'

LITTLE STEVEN — US

SINGLES:	HITS 1			WEEKS 3
BITTER FRUIT	*Manhattan*	66	*23 May 87*	3
ALBUMS:	**HITS 2**			**WEEKS 4**
MEN WITHOUT WOMEN *Above hit: LITTLE STEVEN and the DISCIPLES Of SOUL.*	*EMI America*	73	*6 Nov 82*	2
FREEDOM NO COMPROMISE	*Manhattan*	52	*6 Jun 87*	2

LITTLE T - See REBEL MC

LITTLE TONY and his BROTHERS — Italy

SINGLES:	HITS 1			WEEKS 3
TOO GOOD	*Decca*	19	*16 Jan 60*	3

LITTLE TREES — Denmark

SINGLES:	HITS 1			WEEKS 7
HELP! I'M A FISH (I'M A LITTLE YELLOW FISH) *Originally recorded by Creamy in 2000.*	*RCA*	11	*1 Sep 01*	7

LITTLE VILLAGE — UK/US

ALBUMS:	HITS 1			WEEKS 4
LITTLE VILLAGE	*Reprise*	23	*29 Feb 92*	4

LIVE — US

SINGLES:	HITS 7			WEEKS 13
I ALONE	*Radioactive*	48	*18 Feb 95*	4
SELLING THE DRAMA	*Radioactive*	30	*1 Jul 95*	2
ALL OVER YOU	*Radioactive*	48	*7 Oct 95*	1
LIGHTNING CRASHES	*Radioactive*	33	*13 Jan 96*	2
LAKINI'S JUICE	*Radioactive*	29	*15 Mar 97*	2
FREAKS	*Radioactive*	60	*12 Jul 97*	1
THE DOLPHIN'S CRY	*Radioactive*	62	*5 Feb 00*	1
ALBUMS:	**HITS 3**			**WEEKS 9**
THROWING COPPER	*Radioactive*	37	*15 Jul 95*	6
SECRET SAMADHI	*Radioactive*	31	*29 Mar 97*	2
THE DISTANCE TO HERE	*Radioactive*	56	*16 Oct 99*	1

LIVE REPORT — UK

SINGLES:	HITS 1			WEEKS 1
WHY DO I ALWAYS GET IT WRONG	*Brouhaha*	73	*20 May 89*	1
UK's Eurovision entry in 1989, it came 2nd.				

LIVERPOOL CATHEDRALS' CHOIRS - See Ian TRACEY with the LIVERPOOL CATHEDRALS' CHOIRS

LIVERPOOL EXPRESS — UK

SINGLES:	HITS 4			WEEKS 26
YOU ARE MY LOVE	*Warner Brothers*	11	*26 Jun 76*	9
HOLD TIGHT	*Warner Brothers*	46	*16 Oct 76*	2
EVERY MAN MUST HAVE A DREAM	*Warner Brothers*	17	*18 Dec 76*	11
DREAMIN'	*Warner Brothers*	40	*4 Jun 77*	4

LIVERPOOL FOOTBALL CLUB — UK

SINGLES:	HITS 5			WEEKS 21
WE CAN DO IT [EP]	*State*	15	*28 May 77*	4
Lead track: We Can Do It.				
Above hit: LIVERPOOL FOOTBALL TEAM 76/77.				
LIVERPOOL (WE'RE NEVER GONNA STOP) / LIVERPOOL (ANTHEM)	*Mean*	54	*23 Apr 83*	4
SITTING ON THE TOP OF THE WORLD	*Columbia*	50	*17 May 86*	2
Above hit: LIVERPOOL FOOTBALL TEAM 1986.				
ANFIELD RAP (RED MACHINE IN FULL EFFECT)	*Virgin*	3	*14 May 88*	6
Above hit: LIVERPOOL F.C.				
PASS & MOVE (IT'S THE LIVERPOOL GROOVE)	*Telstar*	4	*18 May 96*	5
Above hit: LIVERPOOL FC and the BOOT ROOM BOYZ.				

LIVIN' JOY — US/Italy

SINGLES:	HITS 5			WEEKS 41
DREAMER	*Undiscovered*	18	*3 Sep 94*	6
DREAMER [RI]	*Undiscovered*	1	*13 May 95*	11
DON'T STOP MOVIN'	*Undiscovered*	5	*15 Jun 96*	14
FOLLOW THE RULES	*Undiscovered*	9	*2 Nov 96*	5
WHERE CAN I FIND LOVE	*Undiscovered*	12	*5 Apr 97*	4
DEEP IN YOU	*Undiscovered*	17	*23 Aug 97*	4
ALBUMS:	**HITS 1**			**WEEKS 2**
DON'T STOP MOVIN	*Undiscovered*	41	*16 Nov 96*	2

LIVING BASS - See Jay MONDI and the LIVING BASS.

LIVING COLOUR — US

SINGLES:	HITS 6			WEEKS 22
TYPE	*Epic*	75	*27 Oct 90*	1
LOVE REARS ITS UGLY HEAD	*Epic*	12	*2 Feb 91*	11
SOLACE OF YOU	*Epic*	33	*1 Jun 91*	5
CULT OF PERSONALITY	*Epic*	67	*26 Oct 91*	2
LEAVE IT ALONE	*Epic*	34	*20 Feb 93*	2
AUSLANDER	*Epic*	53	*17 Apr 93*	1
ALBUMS:	**HITS 2**			**WEEKS 22**
TIME'S UP	*Epic*	20	*15 Sep 90*	19
STAIN	*Epic*	19	*6 Mar 93*	3

LIVING IN A BOX — UK

SINGLES:	HITS 8			WEEKS 62
LIVING IN A BOX	*Chrysalis*	5	*4 Apr 87*	13
SCALES OF JUSTICE	*Chrysalis*	30	*13 Jun 87*	6
SO THE STORY GOES	*Chrysalis*	34	*26 Sep 87*	8
Uncredited vocals by Bobby Womack.				
LOVE IS THE ART	*Chrysalis*	45	*30 Jan 88*	4

BLOW THE HOUSE DOWN *Features Brian May on guitar.*	*Chrysalis*	10	*18 Feb 89*	9
GATECRASHING	*Chrysalis*	36	*10 Jun 89*	6
ROOM IN YOUR HEART	*Chrysalis*	5	*23 Sep 89*	13
DIFFERENT AIR	*Chrysalis*	64	*30 Dec 89*	1
DIFFERENT AIR [RE]	*Chrysalis*	57	*13 Jan 90*	2
ALBUMS:	**HITS 2**			**WEEKS 35**
LIVING IN A BOX	*Chrysalis*	25	*9 May 87*	19
GATECRASHING	*Chrysalis*	21	*8 Jul 89*	13
GATECRASHING [RE] *Re-released.*	*Chrysalis*	59	*13 Jan 90*	3

Dandy LIVINGSTONE — Jamaica

SINGLES:	**HITS 2**			**WEEKS 19**
SUZANNE BEWARE OF THE DEVIL	*Horse*	14	*2 Sep 72*	11
BIG CITY / THINK ABOUT THAT	*Horse*	26	*13 Jan 73*	8

LL COOL J — US

(See also B Real, Busta Rhymes, Coolio, LL Cool J and Method Man; Babyface; Levert Sweat Gill.)

SINGLES:	**HITS 15**			**WEEKS 70**
I'M BAD	*Def Jam*	71	*4 Jul 87*	1
I NEED LOVE	*Def Jam*	8	*12 Sep 87*	10
GO CUT CREATOR GO	*Def Jam*	66	*21 Nov 87*	2
GOING BACK TO CALI / JACK THE RIPPER *Jack The Ripper listed from 20 Feb 88.*	*Def Jam*	37	*13 Feb 88*	4
I'M THAT TYPE OF GUY	*Def Jam*	43	*10 Jun 89*	5
AROUND THE WAY GIRL / MAMA SAID KNOCK YOU OUT	*Def Jam*	41	*1 Dec 90*	4
AROUND THE WAY GIRL [RE]	*Def Jam*	36	*9 Mar 91*	4
HOW I'M COMIN' *Samples Bobby Byrd's Hot Pants - I'm Coming - I'm Coming - I'm Coming.*	*Def Jam*	37	*10 Apr 93*	2
HEY LOVER *Song based on Michael Jackson's 'Lady In My Life' and features Boyz II Men on backing vocals.* *Above hit: LL COOL J featuring BOYZ II MEN.*	*Def Jam*	17	*20 Jan 96*	4
DOIN IT *Guest vocalist is Leshaun and samples My Jamaican Guy by Grace Jones.* *Above hit: LL COOL J (Guest Vocalist LeSHAUN).*	*Def Jam*	15	*1 Jun 96*	3
LOUNGIN *Features Total and samples Al B. Sures' Night And Day.*	*Def Jam*	7	*5 Oct 96*	8
AIN'T NOBODY *From the film 'Beavis And Butthead Do America'.*	*Geffen*	1	*8 Feb 97*	9
PHENOMENON *Samples Bill Withers' Who Is He And What Is He To You.*	*Def Jam*	9	*1 Nov 97*	5
FATHER *Featuring the Kirk Franklin Gospel Choir. Samples George Michael's Father Figure.*	*Def Jam*	10	*28 Mar 98*	5
ZOOM *From the film 'Bulworth'.* *Above hit: DR. DRE LL COOL J.*	*Interscope*	15	*11 Jul 98*	3
INCREDIBLE *Samples James Brown's Sportin' Life.* *Above hit: Keith MURRAY featuring LL COOL J.*	*Jive*	52	*5 Dec 98*	1
ALBUMS:	**HITS 8**			**WEEKS 40**
RADIO	*Def Jam*	71	*15 Feb 86*	1
BIGGER AND DEFFER	*Def Jam*	54	*13 Jun 87*	19
WALKING WITH A PANTHER	*Def Jam*	43	*8 Jul 89*	3
MAMA SAID KNOCK YOU OUT	*Def Jam*	49	*13 Oct 90*	2
14 SHOTS TO THE DOME	*Def Jam*	74	*17 Apr 93*	1
ALL WORLD *Compilation.*	*Def Jam*	23	*16 Nov 96*	8
PHENOMENON	*Def Jam*	37	*25 Oct 97*	4
G.O.A.T. FEATURING JAMES T. SMITH - THE GREATEST OF ALL TIME	*Def Jam*	29	*23 Sep 00*	2

LLAMA FARMERS — UK

SINGLES:	**HITS 2**			**WEEKS 2**
BIG WHEELS	*Beggars Banquet*	67	*6 Feb 99*	1
GET THE KEYS AND GO	*Beggars Banquet*	74	*15 May 99*	1

Kelly LLORENNA — UK

SINGLES:	**HITS 4**			**WEEKS 10**
SET YOU FREE *Original release reached No.81 in 1993.* *Above hit: N-TRANCE featuring Kelly LLORENNA.*	*All Around The World*	39	*7 May 94*	4
BRIGHTER DAY	*Pukka*	43	*24 Feb 96*	2
HEART OF GOLD *Above hit: FORCE and STYLES featuring Kelly LLORENNA.*	*Diverse*	55	*25 Jul 98*	1

TRUE LOVE NEVER DIES	*All Around The World*	34	*24 Mar 01*	3
Above hit: FLIP&FILL featuring Kelly LLORENNA.				

Andrew LLOYD WEBBER — UK

ALBUMS:	HITS 2			WEEKS 37
VARIATIONS	*MCA*	2	*11 Feb 78*	19
Above hit: Andrew LLOYD WEBBER featuring cellist Julian LLOYD WEBBER.				
ANDREW LLOYD WEBBER: REQUIEM	*His Master's Voice*	4	*23 Mar 85*	18
Above hit: Placido DOMINGO, Sarah BRIGHTMAN, Paul MILES-KINGSTON, WINCHESTER CATHEDRAL CHOIR and the ENGLISH CHAMBER ORCHESTRA conducted by Lorin MAAZEL.				

Julian LLOYD WEBBER — UK

(See also Andrew Lloyd Webber.)

ALBUMS:	HITS 3			WEEKS 19
PIECES	*Polydor*	59	*14 Sep 85*	5
Above hit: Julian LLOYD WEBBER and the LONDON SYMPHONY ORCHESTRA.				
ELGAR CELLO CONCERTO	*Philips*	94	*21 Feb 87*	1
Above hit: Julian LLOYD WEBBER with the ROYAL PHILHARMONIC ORCHESTRA conducted by Sir Yehudi MENUHIN.				
LLOYD WEBBER PLAYS LLOYD WEBBER	*Philips*	15	*27 Oct 90*	13
Above hit: Julian LLOYD WEBBER with the ROYAL PHILHARMONIC ORCHESTRA.				

Don LLOYDIE - See SOUNDMAN and Don LLOYDIE with Elisabeth TROY

LNR — US

SINGLES:	HITS 1			WEEKS 2
WORK IT TO THE BONE	*Kool Kat*	64	*3 Jun 89*	2

LO FIDELITY ALLSTARS — UK

SINGLES:	HITS 3			WEEKS 5
DISCO MACHINE GUN	*Skint*	50	*11 Oct 97*	1
VISION INCISION	*Skint*	30	*2 May 98*	2
BATTLEFLAG	*Skint*	36	*28 Nov 98*	2
Track started out as a remix of a single by Sub Pop act Pigeonhed.				
Above hit: LO FIDELITY ALLSTARS featuring PIGEONHED.				

ALBUMS:	HITS 1			WEEKS 4
HOW TO OPERATE WITH A BLOWN MIND	*Skint*	15	*6 Jun 98*	4

LO-PRO - See X-PRESS 2

LOBO — US

SINGLES:	HITS 2			WEEKS 25
ME AND YOU AND A DOG NAMED BOO	*Philips*	4	*19 Jun 71*	14
I'D LOVE YOU TO WANT ME	*UK*	5	*8 Jun 74*	11

LOBO — Holland

SINGLES:	HITS 1			WEEKS 11
THE CARIBBEAN DISCO SHOW [M]	*Polydor*	8	*25 Jul 81*	11
Medley of Calypso songs.				

Tone LOC — US

SINGLES:	HITS 3			WEEKS 19
WILD THING / LOC'ED AFTER DARK	*Fourth & Broadway*	21	*11 Feb 89*	8
FUNKY COLD MEDINA / ON FIRE	*Fourth & Broadway*	13	*20 May 89*	9
I GOT IT GOIN' ON	*Fourth & Broadway*	55	*5 Aug 89*	2
Samples Tom Browne's Funkin' For Jamaica.				

ALBUMS:	HITS 1			WEEKS 16
LOC'ED AFTER DARK	*Fourth & Broadway*	22	*25 Mar 89*	16

LOCK'N'LOAD — Holland

SINGLES:	HITS 2			WEEKS 13
BLOW YA MIND	*Pepper*	6	*15 Apr 00*	10
BLOW YA MIND [RE]	*Pepper*	69	*1 Jul 00*	1
HOUSE SOME MORE	*Pepper*	45	*3 Mar 01*	2

Josef LOCKE — Ireland

ALBUMS:	HITS 3			WEEKS 20
THE WORLD OF JOSEF LOCKE TODAY	*Decca*	29	*28 Jun 69*	1
HEAR MY SONG (THE BEST OF JOSEF LOCKE)	*EMI*	7	*21 Mar 92*	17
TAKE A PAIR OF SPARKLING EYES	*EMI*	41	*27 Jun 92*	2

Hank LOCKLIN — US

SINGLES:	HITS 4			WEEKS 41
PLEASE HELP ME, I'M FALLING	*RCA*	9	*13 Aug 60*	19
FROM HERE TO THERE TO YOU	*RCA*	44	*17 Feb 62*	3
WE'RE GONNA GO FISHIN'	*RCA*	18	*17 Nov 62*	11
I FEEL A CRY COMING ON	*RCA Victor*	29	*7 May 66*	8

LOCKSMITH — US

SINGLES:	HITS 1			WEEKS 6
UNLOCK THE FUNK	*Arista*	42	*23 Aug 80*	6

Malcolm LOCKYER - See Max BYGRAVES; Petula CLARK; Terry DENE with the Malcolm LOCKYER GROUP

LOCOMOTIVE — UK

SINGLES:	HITS 1			WEEKS 8
RUDI'S IN LOVE	*Parlophone*	25	*19 Oct 68*	8

John LODGE — UK

(See also Justin Hayward and John Lodge.)

ALBUMS:	HITS 1			WEEKS 2
NATURAL AVENUE	*Decca*	38	*19 Feb 77*	2

LODGER — UK

SINGLES:	HITS 1			WEEKS 2
I'M LEAVING *Features Supergrass drummer Danny Goffey.*	*Island*	40	*2 May 98*	2

Lisa LOEB and NINE STORIES — US

SINGLES:	HITS 2			WEEKS 17
STAY (I MISSED YOU) *From the film 'Reality Bites'.*	*RCA*	6	*3 Sep 94*	15
DO YOU SLEEP?	*Geffen*	45	*16 Sep 95*	2
ALBUMS:	**HITS 1**			**WEEKS 2**
TAILS	*Geffen*	39	*7 Oct 95*	2

Nils LOFGREN — US

SINGLES:	HITS 1			WEEKS 3
SECRETS IN THE STREET	*Towerbell*	53	*8 Jun 85*	3
ALBUMS:	**HITS 8**			**WEEKS 30**
CRY TOUGH	*A&M*	8	*17 Apr 76*	11
I CAME TO DANCE	*A&M*	30	*26 Mar 77*	4
NIGHT AFTER NIGHT	*A&M*	38	*5 Nov 77*	2
NIGHT FADES AWAY	*Backstreet/MCA*	50	*26 Sep 81*	3
A RHYTHM ROMANCE *Compilation.*	*A&M*	100	*1 May 82*	1
FLIP	*Towerbell*	36	*6 Jul 85*	7
CODE OF THE ROAD	*Towerbell*	86	*5 Apr 86*	1
SILVER LINING	*Essential*	61	*27 Apr 91*	1

Johnny LOGAN — Ireland

SINGLES:	HITS 3			WEEKS 24
WHAT'S ANOTHER YEAR *Eurovision Song Contest winner in 1980.*	*Epic*	1	*3 May 80*	8
HOLD ME NOW *Eurovision Song Contest winner in 1987.*	*Epic*	2	*23 May 87*	11
I'M NOT IN LOVE	*Epic*	51	*22 Aug 87*	5
ALBUMS:	**HITS 1**			**WEEKS 1**
HOLD ME NOW	*CBS*	83	*22 Aug 87*	1

Kenny LOGGINS — US

SINGLES:	HITS 2			WEEKS 21
FOOTLOOSE *From the film of the same name.*	*CBS*	6	*28 Apr 84*	10
DANGER ZONE *From the film 'Top Gun'.*	*CBS*	45	*1 Nov 86*	11

LOGO featuring Dawn JOSEPH — UK

SINGLES:	HITS 1			WEEKS 1
DON'T PANIC *Originally recorded by Coldplay as Beautiful World.*	*Manifesto*	42	*8 Dec 01*	1

LOLA — US

SINGLES:	HITS 1			WEEKS 1
WAX THE VAN *Originally recorded by Arthur Russell.*	*Syncopate*	65	*28 Mar 87*	1

LOLLY — UK

SINGLES:	HITS 5			WEEKS 44
VIVA LA RADIO	*Polydor*	6	*10 Jul 99*	9
MICKEY	*Polydor*	4	*18 Sep 99*	10
BIG BOYS DON'T CRY / ROCKIN' ROBIN	*Polydor*	10	*4 Dec 99*	9
PER SEMPRE AMORE (FOREVER IN LOVE)	*Polydor*	11	*6 May 00*	8
PER SEMPRE AMORE (FOREVER IN LOVE) [RE]	*Polydor*	63	*8 Jul 00*	2
GIRLS JUST WANNA HAVE FUN	*Polydor*	14	*9 Sep 00*	6
ALBUMS:	**HITS 1**			**WEEKS 12**
MY FIRST ALBUM	*Polydor*	21	*2 Oct 99*	12

Jackie LOMAX – See VARIOUS ARTISTS (EPs) 'The Apple EP'

Alain LOMBARD – See Mady MESPLE and Danielle MILLET, PARIS OPERA – COMIQUE ORCHESTRA conducted by Alain LOMBARD.

Julie LONDON — US

SINGLES:	HITS 1			WEEKS 3
CRY ME A RIVER *From the film 'The Girl Can't Help It'.*	*London*	22	*6 Apr 57*	3

Laurie LONDON with Geoff LOVE his Orchestra and Chorus — UK

SINGLES:	HITS 1			WEEKS 12
HE'S GOT THE WHOLE WORLD IN HIS HANDS	*Parlophone*	12	*9 Nov 57*	12

LONDON BOYS — UK

SINGLES:	HITS 6			WEEKS 46
REQUIEM	*WEA*	59	*10 Dec 88*	6
REQUIEM [RE]	*WEA*	4	*1 Apr 89*	15
LONDON NIGHTS	*WEA*	2	*1 Jul 89*	9
HARLEM DESIRE	*WEA*	17	*16 Sep 89*	7
MY LOVE	*WEA*	46	*2 Dec 89*	6
CHAPEL OF LOVE	*East West*	75	*16 Jun 90*	1
FREEDOM	*East West*	54	*19 Jan 91*	2
ALBUMS:	**HITS 1**			**WEEKS 29**
THE TWELVE COMMANDMENTS OF DANCE	*WEA*	2	*29 Jul 89*	29

LONDON COMMUNITY GOSPEL CHOIR – See Sal SOLO

LONDON PHILHARMONIC CHOIR — UK

ALBUMS:	HITS 3			WEEKS 20
THE MESSIAH *Above hit: LONDON PHILHARMONIC CHOIR with the LONDON ORCHESTRA conducted by Walter SUSSKIND.*	*Pye Golden Guinea*	10	*3 Dec 60*	7
SOUND OF GLORY	*Arcade*	10	*13 Nov 76*	10
PRAISE – 18 CHORAL MASTERPIECES *Above 2: LONDON PHILHARMONIC CHOIR with the NATIONAL PHILHARMONIC ORCHESTRA conducted by John ALDISS.*	*Pop & Arts*	54	*13 Apr 91*	3

LONDON PHILHARMONIC ORCHESTRA — UK

(See also Adiemus; Justin Hayward with Mike Batt and the London Philharmonic Orchestra; Maurice Jarre; Nigel Kennedy; Ennio Morricone; Cliff Richard; Various Artists: Studio Cast 'Evita')

ALBUMS:	HITS 2			WEEKS 5
RAVEL'S BOLERO	*London*	15	*23 Apr 60*	4
VICTORY AT SEA	*Pye Golden Guinea*	12	*8 Apr 61*	1

LONDON SINFONIETTA – See Dawn UPSHAW (Soprano)/The LONDON SINFONIETTA/David ZINMAN (conductor)

LONDON STRING CHORALE — UK

SINGLES:	HITS 1			WEEKS 13
GALLOPING HOME *Theme from the ITV children's series 'The Adventures Of Black Beauty'.*	*Polydor*	49	*15 Dec 73*	3
GALLOPING HOME [RE]	*Polydor*	31	*19 Jan 74*	10

LONDON SYMPHONY ORCHESTRA — UK

(See also Shirley Bassey; Sarah Brightman; Michael Crawford; Placido Domingo; Roger Daltrey; James Horner; Aled Jones; Julian Lloyd Webber; Kimera with the London Symphony Orchestra; Spike Milligan: Rick Wakeman; John Williams.)

SINGLES:	HITS 1			WEEKS 5
THEME FROM SUPERMAN (MAIN TITLE)	*Warner Brothers*	32	*6 Jan 79*	5
Theme from the film.				
Above hit: Composed and conducted by John WILLIAMS Performed by the LONDON SYMPHONY ORCHESTRA.				

ALBUMS:	HITS 15			WEEKS 173
TOP TV THEMES	*Studio Two*	13	*18 Mar 72*	7
THE STRAUSS FAMILY [OST-TV]	*Polydor*	2	*16 Dec 72*	21
Above hit: LONDON SYMPHONY ORCHESTRA conducted by Cyril ORNADEL.				
MUSIC FROM 'EDWARD VII' [OST-TV]	*Polydor*	52	*5 Jul 75*	1
Above 2 from the ITV drama series.				
CLASSIC ROCK	*K-Tel*	3	*8 Jul 78*	39
CLASSIC ROCK - THE SECOND MOVEMENT	*K-Tel*	26	*10 Feb 79*	8
RHAPSODY IN BLACK	*K-Tel*	34	*5 Jan 80*	5
CLASSIC ROCK - ROCK CLASSICS	*K-Tel*	5	*1 Aug 81*	23
Above hit: LONDON SYMPHONY ORCHESTRA with the ROYAL CHORAL SOCIETY.				
THE BEST OF CLASSIC ROCK	*K-Tel*	35	*27 Nov 82*	11
CLASSIC ROCK - ROCK SYMPHONIES	*K-Tel*	40	*27 Aug 83*	9
THE POWER OF CLASSIC ROCK	*Portrait*	13	*16 Nov 85*	15
Above 3: LONDON SYMPHONY ORCHESTRA with the ROYAL CHORAL SOCIETY and the Roger SMITH CHORALE.				
CLASSIC ROCK COUNTDOWN	*CBS*	32	*14 Nov 87*	16
CLASSIC ROCK - THE LIVING YEARS	*CBS*	51	*18 Nov 89*	6
WIND OF CHANGE - CLASSIC ROCK	*Columbia*	24	*18 Jan 92*	8
Above hit: LONDON SYMPHONY ORCHESTRA and the ROYAL CHORAL SOCIETY.				
THE WORKS OF RICE AND LLOYD WEBBER	*Vision*	55	*19 Nov 94*	2
PAUL MCCARTNEY'S STANDING STONE	*EMI Classics*	34	*25 Oct 97*	2
A 'symphonic poem' commissioned by EMI to mark their centenary.				
Above hit: LONDON SYMPHONY ORCHESTRA conducted by Lawrence FOSTER.				

LONDON WELSH MALE VOICE CHOIR — UK

ALBUMS:	HITS 1			WEEKS 10
SONGS OF THE VALLEYS	*K-Tel*	61	*5 Sep 81*	10

LONDONBEAT — UK/US

(See also Liz Kershaw and Bruno Brookes.)

SINGLES:	HITS 9			WEEKS 45
9 A.M. (THE COMFORT ZONE)	*AnXious*	19	*26 Nov 88*	10
FALLING IN LOVE AGAIN	*AnXious*	60	*18 Feb 89*	2
I'VE BEEN THINKING ABOUT YOU	*AnXious*	2	*1 Sep 90*	13
A BETTER LOVE	*AnXious*	52	*24 Nov 90*	5
NO WOMAN NO CRY	*AnXious*	64	*2 Mar 91*	2
A BETTER LOVE [RI]	*AnXious*	23	*20 Jul 91*	6
YOU BRING ON THE SUN	*AnXious*	32	*27 Jun 92*	4
THAT'S HOW I FEEL ABOUT YOU	*AnXious*	69	*24 Oct 92*	1
I'M JUST YOUR PUPPET ON A . . . (STRING!)	*AnXious*	55	*8 Apr 95*	1
One of the contenders for Eurovision's A Song For Europe, it came 6th (out of 8).				
COME BACK	*AnXious*	69	*20 May 95*	1

ALBUMS:	HITS 1			WEEKS 6
IN THE BLOOD	*Anxious*	34	*13 Oct 90*	6

LONE JUSTICE — US

SINGLES:	HITS 1			WEEKS 4
I FOUND LOVE	*Geffen*	45	*7 Mar 87*	4

ALBUMS:	HITS 2			WEEKS 5
LONE JUSTICE	*Geffen*	49	*6 Jul 85*	2
SHELTER	*Geffen*	84	*8 Nov 86*	3

LONE STAR — UK

ALBUMS:	HITS 2			WEEKS 7
LONE STAR	*Epic*	47	*2 Oct 76*	1
FIRING ON ALL SIX	*CBS*	36	*17 Sep 77*	6

LONESTAR — US

SINGLES:	HITS 2			WEEKS 24
AMAZED	*Grapevine*	21	*15 Apr 00*	22
SMILE	*Grapevine*	55	*7 Oct 00*	2

Shorty LONG — US

SINGLES:	HITS 1			WEEKS 7
HERE COMES THE JUDGE	*Tamla Motown*	30	*20 Jul 68*	7

LONG RYDERS — US

SINGLES:	HITS 1			WEEKS 4
LOOKING FOR LEWIS AND CLARKE	*Island*	59	*5 Oct 85*	4
ALBUMS:	**HITS 1**			**WEEKS 1**
STATE OF OUR UNION	*Island*	66	*16 Nov 85*	1

LONG AND THE SHORT — UK

SINGLES:	HITS 2			WEEKS 8
THE LETTER	*Decca*	35	*12 Sep 64*	5
CHOC ICE	*Decca*	49	*26 Dec 64*	3

LONGPIGS — UK

SINGLES:	HITS 7			WEEKS 17
SHE SAID	*Mother*	67	*22 Jul 95*	1
JESUS CHRIST	*Mother*	61	*28 Oct 95*	1
FAR	*Mother*	37	*17 Feb 96*	2
ON AND ON	*Mother*	16	*13 Apr 96*	3
SHE SAID [RI]	*Mother*	16	*22 Jun 96*	4
LOST MYSELF	*Mother*	22	*5 Oct 96*	3
BLUE SKIES	*Mother*	21	*9 Oct 99*	2
THE FRANK SONATA	*Mother*	57	*18 Dec 99*	1
ALBUMS:	**HITS 2**			**WEEKS 10**
THE SUN IS OFTEN OUT	*Mother*	26	*11 May 96*	9
MOBILE HOME	*Mother*	33	*23 Oct 99*	1

Joe LONGTHORNE — UK

SINGLES:	HITS 2			WEEKS 6
YOUNG GIRL	*EMI*	61	*30 Apr 94*	2
PASSING STRANGERS	*EMI*	34	*10 Dec 94*	4
Above hit: Joe LONGTHORNE and Liz DAWN.				
ALBUMS:	**HITS 5**			**WEEKS 32**
THE JOE LONGTHORNE SONGBOOK	*Telstar*	16	*3 Dec 88*	12
ESPECIALLY FOR YOU	*Telstar*	22	*29 Jul 89*	10
THE JOE LONGTHORNE CHRISTMAS ALBUM	*Telstar*	44	*9 Dec 89*	4
I WISH YOU LOVE	*EMI*	47	*13 Nov 93*	4
LIVE AT THE ROYAL ALBERT HALL	*Premier*	57	*8 Oct 94*	2

LONYO — UK

SINGLES:	HITS 2			WEEKS 9
SUMMER OF LOVE	*Riverhorse*	8	*8 Jul 00*	7
Samples Oscar D'Leon's Madre.				
Above hit: LONYO – COMME ÇI COMME ÇA.				
GARAGE GIRLS	*Riverhorse*	39	*7 Apr 01*	2
Above hit: LONYO – featuring MC ONYX STONE.				

LOOK — UK

SINGLES:	HITS 2			WEEKS 15
I AM THE BEAT	*MCA*	6	*20 Dec 80*	12
FEEDING TIME	*MCA*	50	*29 Aug 81*	3

LOOP — UK

ALBUMS:	HITS 2			WEEKS 2
FADE OUT	*Chapter 22*	51	*4 Feb 89*	1
A GILDED ETERNITY	*Situation Two*	39	*3 Feb 90*	1

LOOP DA LOOP — UK

SINGLES:	HITS 2			WEEKS 4
GO WITH THE FLOW	*Manifesto*	47	*7 Jun 97*	1
Features rap from MC Duke.				
HAZEL	*Manifesto*	20	*20 Feb 99*	3
Samples Stetasonic's Sally.				

LOOSE ENDS — UK

SINGLES:	HITS 12			WEEKS 76
TELL ME WHAT YOU WANT	*Virgin*	74	*25 Feb 84*	1
EMERGENCY (DIAL 999)	*Virgin*	41	*28 Apr 84*	6
CHOOSE ME (RESCUE ME)	*Virgin*	59	*21 Jul 84*	3
HANGIN' ON A STRING (CONTEMPLATING)	*Virgin*	13	*23 Feb 85*	13

MAGIC TOUCH	*Virgin*	16	*11 May 85*	7
GOLDEN YEARS	*Virgin*	59	*27 Jul 85*	4
STAY A LITTLE WHILE, CHILD	*Virgin*	52	*14 Jun 86*	5
SLOW DOWN	*Virgin*	27	*20 Sep 86*	7
NIGHTS OF PLEASURE	*Virgin*	42	*29 Nov 86*	7
MR. BACHELOR	*Virgin*	50	*4 Jun 88*	4
DON'T BE A FOOL	*10 Records*	13	*25 Aug 90*	9
LOVE'S GOT ME	*Ten Records*	40	*17 Nov 90*	4
HANGIN' ON A STRING [RM]	*Ten Records*	25	*20 Jun 92*	5
Remixed by Frankie Knuckles.				
MAGIC TOUCH [RM]	*Ten Records*	75	*5 Sep 92*	1
ALBUMS:	**HITS 6**			**WEEKS 41**
A LITTLE SPICE	*Virgin*	46	*21 Apr 84*	9
SO WHERE ARE YOU?	*Virgin*	13	*20 Apr 85*	13
ZAGORA	*Virgin*	15	*18 Oct 86*	8
THE REAL CHUCKEEBOO	*Virgin*	52	*2 Jul 88*	4
LOOK HOW LONG	*Ten Records*	19	*29 Sep 90*	5
TIGHTEN UP VOLUME 1	*Ten Records*	40	*19 Sep 92*	2

Lisa 'Left Eye' LOPES — US

SINGLES:	**HITS 2**			**WEEKS 20**
NEVER BE THE SAME AGAIN	*Virgin*	1	*1 Apr 00*	14
Above hit: Melanie C featuring Lisa 'Left Eye' LOPES.				
NEVER BE THE SAME AGAIN [RE]	*Virgin*	70	*22 Jul 00*	2
THE BLOCK PARTY	*LaFace*	16	*27 Oct 01*	4

Jennifer LOPEZ — US

SINGLES:	**HITS 7**			**WEEKS 71**
IF YOU HAD MY LOVE	*Columbia*	4	*3 Jul 99*	13
WAITING FOR TONIGHT	*Columbia*	5	*13 Nov 99*	12
FEELIN' SO GOOD	*Columbia*	15	*1 Apr 00*	6
Samples Strafe's Set It Off.				
Above hit: Jennifer LOPEZ (featuring BIG PUN and FAT JOE).				
LOVE DON'T COST A THING	*Epic*	1	*20 Jan 01*	10
LOVE DON'T COST A THING [RE]	*Epic*	67	*21 Apr 01*	1
PLAY	*Epic*	3	*12 May 01*	10
PLAY [RE]	*Epic*	70	*28 Jul 01*	2
AIN'T IT FUNNY	*Epic*	3	*18 Aug 01*	8
AIN'T IT FUNNY [RE]	*Epic*	59	*27 Oct 01*	1
I'M REAL	*Epic*	4	*10 Nov 01*	8
ALBUMS:	**HITS 2**			**WEEKS 67**
ON THE 6	*Columbia*	14	*17 Jul 99*	30
J.LO	*Epic*	2	*3 Feb 01*	30
J.LO [RE]	*Epic*	26	*17 Nov 01*	7
Repackaged with 3 extra tracks.				

Trini LOPEZ — US

SINGLES:	**HITS 5**			**WEEKS 37**
IF I HAD A HAMMER	*Reprise*	4	*14 Sep 63*	17
Originally recorded by the Weavers. Live recording from the Hollywood club P.J.'s.				
KANSAS CITY	*Reprise*	35	*14 Dec 63*	5
Live recording.				
I'M COMING HOME CINDY	*Reprise*	28	*14 May 66*	5
GONNA GET ALONG WITHOUT YA NOW	*Reprise*	41	*8 Apr 67*	5
TRINI-TRAX [M]	*RCA*	59	*19 Dec 81*	5
EPS:	**HITS 2**			**WEEKS 11**
TRINI LOPEZ AT P.J.'S	*Reprise*	11	*7 Dec 63*	7
AMERICA	*Reprise*	16	*19 Sep 64*	4
ALBUMS:	**HITS 2**			**WEEKS 42**
TRINI LOPEZ AT P.J.'S	*Reprise*	7	*26 Oct 63*	25
TRINI LOPEZ IN LONDON	*Reprise*	6	*25 Mar 67*	17
Above 2 are live recordings.				

Jeff LORBER — US

ALBUMS:	**HITS 1**			**WEEKS 2**
STEP BY STEP	*Club*	97	*18 May 85*	2

LORD ROCKINGHAM'S XI — UK/South Africa

SINGLES:	**HITS 2**			**WEEKS 21**
HOOTS MON	*Decca*	1	*25 Oct 58*	17
WEE TOM	*Decca*	16	*7 Feb 59*	3
Above 2 from the ITV series 'Oh! Boy'.				
Above 2: Jack GOOD presents LORD ROCKINGHAM'S XI.				
HOOTS MON [RI]	*Decca*	60	*25 Sep 93*	1
Featured in the Maynard's Wine Gums TV commercial.				

LORD TANAMO — Trinidad & Tobago

SINGLES:	HITS 1			WEEKS 2
I'M IN THE MOOD FOR LOVE	*Mooncrest*	58	*1 Dec 90*	2

Featured in the Paxo TV commercial. First released in 1965. Originally recorded by Little Jack Little.

LORD TARIQ and Peter GUNZ — US

SINGLES:	HITS 1			WEEKS 3
DEJA VU (UPTOWN BABY)	*Columbia*	21	*2 May 98*	3

Based around Steely Dan's Deja Vu.

Jerry LORDAN — UK

SINGLES:	HITS 3			WEEKS 16
I'LL STAY SINGLE	*Parlophone*	26	*9 Jan 60*	2
WHO COULD BE BLUER?	*Parlophone*	16	*27 Feb 60*	10
I'LL STAY SINGLE [RE]	*Parlophone*	41	*12 Mar 60*	1
WHO COULD BE BLUER? [RE]	*Parlophone*	45	*21 May 60*	1
SING LIKE AN ANGEL	*Parlophone*	36	*4 Jun 60*	2

Traci LORDS — US

SINGLES:	HITS 1			WEEKS 1
FALLEN ANGEL	*Radioactive*	72	*7 Oct 95*	1

LORDS OF THE UNDERGROUND — US

ALBUMS:	HITS 1			WEEKS 1
KEEPERS OF THE FUNK	*Pendulum*	68	*12 Nov 94*	1

Sophia LOREN – See Peter SELLERS and Sophia LOREN

Trey LORENZ — US

(See also Mariah Carey.)

SINGLES:	HITS 2			WEEKS 5
SOMEONE TO HOLD	*Epic*	65	*21 Nov 92*	2
PHOTOGRAPH OF MARY	*Epic*	38	*30 Jun 93*	3

LORI and the CHAMELEONS — UK

SINGLES:	HITS 1			WEEKS 1
TOUCH	*Sire*	70	*8 Dec 79*	1

LORRAINE – See BOMB THE BASS

LOS DEL CHIPMUNKS – See CHIPMUNKS

LOS DEL MAR featuring Wil. VELOZ — Canada/Cuba

SINGLES:	HITS 1			WEEKS 7
MACARENA	*Pulse 8*	66	*8 Jun 96*	2
MACARENA [RE]	*Pulse 8*	43	*6 Jul 96*	5

LOS DEL RIO — Spain

SINGLES:	HITS 1			WEEKS 19
MACARENA	*RCA*	64	*1 Jun 96*	1
MACARENA [RE]	*RCA*	2	*13 Jul 96*	18

LOS LOBOS — US

SINGLES:	HITS 3			WEEKS 24
DON'T WORRY BABY / WILL THE WOLF SURVIVE	*Slash*	57	*6 Apr 85*	4
LA BAMBA	*Slash*	1	*18 Jul 87*	11
COME ON, LET'S GO	*Slash*	18	*26 Sep 87*	9

Above 2 from the film 'La Bamba'.

ALBUMS:	HITS 3			WEEKS 24
HOW WILL THE WOLF SURVIVE?	*Slash*	77	*6 Apr 85*	6
BY THE LIGHT OF THE MOON	*Slash*	77	*7 Feb 87*	3
LA BAMBA [OST]	*London*	24	*22 Aug 87*	15

Majority of the tracks are by Los Lobos.
Above hit: LOS LOBOS/VARIOUS.

LOS UMBRELLOS — Denmark

SINGLES:	HITS 1			WEEKS 2
NO TENGO DINERO	*Virgin*	33	*3 Oct 98*	2

Melody is based on the theme from the film 'Never On Sunday'.

Joe LOSS and his Orchestra — UK

(See also George Mitchell Minstrels.)

SINGLES:	HITS 5			WEEKS 53
WHEELS - CHA CHA	*His Master's Voice*	21	*1 Jul 61*	21
SUCU SUCU	*His Master's Voice*	48	*21 Oct 61*	1
THE MAIGRET THEME	*His Master's Voice*	20	*31 Mar 62*	10
MUST BE MADISON	*His Master's Voice*	20	*3 Nov 62*	13
MARCH OF THE MODS (FINNJENKA DANCE)	*His Master's Voice*	35	*7 Nov 64*	4
MARCH OF THE MODS (FINNJENKA DANCE) [RE]	*His Master's Voice*	31	*26 Dec 64*	4
EPS:	**HITS 2**			**WEEKS 4**
DANCING TIME FOR LATINS	*HMV*	17	*16 Dec 61*	3
LATIN STYLE	*HMV*	19	*27 Jan 62*	1
ALBUMS:	**HITS 1**			**WEEKS 10**
ALL-TIME PARTY HITS	*Music For Pleasure*	24	*30 Oct 71*	10

LOST — UK

SINGLES:	HITS 1			WEEKS 1
TECHNOFUNK	*Perfecto*	75	*22 Jun 91*	1

LOST BOYZ — US

(See also Various Artists (EPs) 'New York Undercover 4-Track EP'.)

SINGLES:	HITS 2			WEEKS 2
MUSIC MAKES ME HIGH	*Universal*	42	*2 Nov 96*	1
LOVE, PEACE & NAPPINESS	*Universal*	57	*12 Jul 97*	1
ALBUMS:	**HITS 1**			**WEEKS 1**
LEGAL DRUG MONEY	*MCA*	64	*6 Jul 96*	1

LOST IT.COM — UK

SINGLES:	HITS 1			WEEKS 1
ANIMAL	*Perfecto*	70	*7 Apr 01*	1

Originally released on the Finiflex label in 1995.

LOST TRIBE — UK

SINGLES:	HITS 1			WEEKS 3
GAMEMASTER	*Hooj Choons*	24	*11 Sep 99*	3

Originally appeared on their Distant Voice EP, which reached No. 79 in 1997.

LOST WITNESS — UK

SINGLES:	HITS 3			WEEKS 10
HAPPINESS HAPPENING	*Sound Of Ministry*	18	*29 May 99*	4
RED SUN RISING	*Sound Of Ministry*	22	*18 Sep 99*	3
7 COLOURS	*Data*	28	*16 Dec 00*	3

Samples Nina James' After The Rain.

LOSTPROPHETS — UK

SINGLES:	HITS 1			WEEKS 2
SHINOBI VS DRAGON NINJA	*Visible Noise*	41	*8 Dec 01*	2

LOTUS EATERS — UK

SINGLES:	HITS 2			WEEKS 16
THE FIRST PICTURE OF YOU	*Sylvan*	15	*2 Jul 83*	12
YOU DON'T NEED SOMEONE NEW	*Sylvan*	53	*8 Oct 83*	4
ALBUMS:	**HITS 1**			**WEEKS 1**
NO SENSE OF SIN	*Sylvan*	96	*16 Jun 84*	1

Bonnie LOU — US

SINGLES:	HITS 1			WEEKS 10
TENNESSEE WIG WALK	*Parlophone*	4	*6 Feb 54*	10

Lippy LOU — UK

SINGLES:	HITS 1			WEEKS 2
LIBERATION	*More Protein*	57	*22 Apr 95*	2

Louchie LOU and Michie ONE — UK

SINGLES:	HITS 6			WEEKS 36
SHOUT	*ffrr*	7	*29 May 93*	8
SOMEBODY ELSE'S GUY (ME DID LOVE YOU)	*ffrr*	54	*14 Aug 93*	2
GET DOWN ON IT	*China*	58	*26 Aug 95*	1
CECILIA	*WEA*	4	*13 Apr 96*	17

Above hit: SUGGS featuring Louchie LOU and Michie ONE.

GOOD SWEET LOVIN'	*Indochina*	34	*15 Jun 96*	2
CECILIA [RE-1ST]	*WEA*	65	*24 Aug 96*	1
CECILIA [RE-2ND]	*WEA*	59	*7 Sep 96*	1
NO MORE ALCOHOL	*WEA*	24	*21 Sep 96*	4

Samples the Champs' Tequila.
Above hit: SUGGS featuring Louchie LOU and Michie ONE.

LOUD — UK

SINGLES:	HITS 1			WEEKS 2
EASY	*China*	67	*28 Mar 92*	2

John D. LOUDERMILK — US

SINGLES:	HITS 1			WEEKS 10
LANGUAGE OF LOVE	*RCA*	13	*6 Jan 62*	10

Louie LOUIE — US

SINGLES:	HITS 1			WEEKS 5
THE THOUGHT OF IT	*Hardback*	34	*19 Dec 92*	5

LOUISE — UK

SINGLES:	HITS 11			WEEKS 78
LIGHT OF MY LIFE	*EMI*	8	*7 Oct 95*	8
IN WALKED LOVE	*EMI*	17	*16 Mar 96*	6
Originally recorded by Expose.				
NAKED	*EMI*	5	*8 Jun 96*	8
UNDIVIDED LOVE	*EMI*	5	*31 Aug 96*	6
ONE KISS FROM HEAVEN	*EMI*	9	*30 Nov 96*	7
ARMS AROUND THE WORLD	*EMI*	4	*4 Oct 97*	7
LET'S GO ROUND AGAIN	*EMI*	10	*29 Nov 97*	9
ALL THAT MATTERS	*EMI*	11	*4 Apr 98*	5
Backing vocals by Miriam Stockley and Lance Ellington.				
ALL THAT MATTERS [RE]	*EMI*	73	*20 Jun 98*	1
2 FACED	*EMI*	3	*29 Jul 00*	8
BEAUTIFUL INSIDE	*EMI*	13	*11 Nov 00*	4
STUCK IN THE MIDDLE WITH YOU	*EMI*	4	*8 Sep 01*	9
ALBUMS:	**HITS 4**			**WEEKS 59**
NAKED	*EMI*	7	*6 Jul 96*	31
WOMAN IN ME	*EMI*	5	*18 Oct 97*	19
ELBOW BEACH	*EMI*	12	*12 Aug 00*	4
CHANGING FACES - THE BEST OF LOUISE	*EMI*	9	*22 Sep 01*	5

Jacques LOUSSIER — France

ALBUMS:	HITS 1			WEEKS 3
JACQUES LOUSSIER - THE BEST OF PLAY BACH	*Start*	58	*30 Mar 85*	3

LOVE — US

ALBUMS:	HITS 2			WEEKS 9
FOREVER CHANGES	*Elektra*	24	*24 Feb 68*	6
OUT HERE	*Harvest*	29	*16 May 70*	2
FOREVER CHANGES [RE]	*Elektra*	63	*3 Mar 01*	1

Darlene LOVE — US

SINGLES:	HITS 1			WEEKS 5
ALL ALONE ON CHRISTMAS	*Arista*	31	*19 Dec 92*	4
Features Little Steven and the Jersey Allstars. From the film 'Home Alone 2: Lost In New York'.				
ALL ALONE ON CHRISTMAS [RE]	*Arista*	72	*1 Jan 94*	1

Geoff LOVE and his Orchestra — UK

(See also Shirley Bassey; Alma Cogan; Russ Conway; Ken Dodd; Teddy Johnson and Pearl Carr; King Brothers; Laurie London with Geoff Love his Orchestra and Chorus; Manuel and the Music Of The Mountains; Rita Pavone; Peter and Gordon; Ann Shelton; Ricky Stevens with the Rita Williams Singers and Geoff Love and his Orchestra ; Frankie Vaughan; Danny Williams.)

ALBUMS:	HITS 3			WEEKS 28
BIG WAR MOVIE THEMES	*Music For Pleasure*	11	*7 Aug 71*	20
BIG WESTERN MOVIE THEMES	*Music For Pleasure*	38	*21 Aug 71*	3
BIG LOVE MOVIE THEMES	*Music For Pleasure*	28	*30 Oct 71*	5

Monie LOVE — UK

(See also De La Soul; Jungle Brothers.)

SINGLES:	HITS 11			WEEKS 51
I CAN DO THIS	*Cooltempo*	37	*4 Feb 89*	4
Samples the Whispers' And The Beat Goes On.				
GRANDPA'S PARTY	*Cooltempo*	16	*24 Jun 89*	9
MONIE IN THE MIDDLE	*Cooltempo*	46	*14 Jul 90*	3

IT'S A SHAME (MY SISTER)	*Cooltempo*	12	*22 Sep 90*	8
Above hit: Monie LOVE (featuring TRUE IMAGE).				
DOWN TO EARTH	*Cooltempo*	31	*1 Dec 90*	6
RING MY BELL	*Cooltempo*	20	*6 Apr 91*	5
Above hit: Monie LOVE vs ADEVA.				
FULL TERM LOVE	*Cooltempo*	34	*25 Jul 92*	4
From the film 'Class Act'.				
BORN 2 B.R.E.E.D.	*Cooltempo*	18	*13 Mar 93*	5
B.R.E.E.D is an acronym for Build Relationships where Education and Enlightenment Dominate.				
IN A WORD OR 2 / THE POWER	*Cooltempo*	33	*12 Jun 93*	3
NEVER GIVE UP	*Cooltempo*	41	*21 Aug 93*	2
SLICE OF DA PIE	*Relentless*	29	*22 Apr 00*	2
ALBUMS:	**HITS 1**			**WEEKS 3**
DOWN TO EARTH	*Cooltempo*	30	*20 Oct 90*	3

Vikki LOVE - See NUANCE featuring Vikki LOVE

LOVE AFFAIR — UK

SINGLES:	**HITS 5**			**WEEKS 56**
EVERLASTING LOVE	*CBS*	1	*6 Jan 68*	12
RAINBOW VALLEY	*CBS*	5	*20 Apr 68*	13
Above 2 originally recorded by Robert Knight.				
Above hit: LOVE AFFAIR with the Keith MANSFIELD ORCHESTRA.				
A DAY WITHOUT LOVE	*CBS*	6	*14 Sep 68*	12
ONE ROAD	*CBS*	16	*22 Feb 69*	9
BRINGING ON BACK THE GOOD TIMES	*CBS*	9	*19 Jul 69*	10

LOVE AND MONEY — UK

SINGLES:	**HITS 6**			**WEEKS 23**
CANDYBAR EXPRESS	*Mercury*	56	*24 May 86*	4
LOVE AND MONEY	*Mercury*	68	*25 Apr 87*	4
HALLELUIAH MAN	*Fontana*	63	*17 Sep 88*	4
STRANGE KIND OF LOVE	*Fontana*	45	*14 Jan 89*	5
JOCELYN SQUARE	*Fontana*	51	*25 Mar 89*	4
WINTER	*Fontana*	52	*16 Nov 91*	2
ALBUMS:	**HITS 2**			**WEEKS 2**
STRANGE KIND OF LOVE	*Fontana*	71	*29 Oct 88*	1
DOGS IN THE TRAFFIC	*Fontana*	41	*3 Aug 91*	1

LOVE BITE — Italy

SINGLES:	**HITS 1**			**WEEKS 1**
TAKE YOUR TIME	*AM:PM*	56	*7 Oct 00*	1

LOVE CITY GROOVE — UK

SINGLES:	**HITS 1**			**WEEKS 11**
LOVE CITY GROOVE	*Planet 3*	7	*8 Apr 95*	11
UK's Eurovision entry in 1995, it came 10th.				

LOVE CONNECTION — Italy/Germany

SINGLES:	**HITS 1**			**WEEKS 1**
THE BOMB	*Multiply*	53	*2 Dec 00*	1

LOVE DECADE — UK

SINGLES:	**HITS 5**			**WEEKS 14**
DREAM ON (IS THIS A DREAM)	*All Around The World*	52	*6 Jul 91*	2
SO REAL	*All Around The World*	14	*23 Nov 91*	7
I FEEL YOU	*All Around The World*	34	*11 Apr 92*	3
WHEN THE MORNING COMES	*All Around The World*	69	*6 Feb 93*	1
IS THIS A DREAM? [RR]	*All Around The World*	39	*17 Feb 96*	1

LOVE DECREE — UK

SINGLES:	**HITS 1**			**WEEKS 4**
SOMETHING SO REAL (THE CHINHEADS THEME)	*Ariola*	61	*16 Sep 89*	4

LOVE/HATE — US

SINGLES:	**HITS 2**			**WEEKS 4**
EVIL TWIN	*Columbia*	59	*30 Nov 91*	1
WASTED IN AMERICA	*Columbia*	38	*4 Apr 92*	3
ALBUMS:	**HITS 2**			**WEEKS 5**
WASTED IN AMERICA	*Columbia*	20	*7 Mar 92*	4
LET'S RUMBLE	*RCA*	24	*24 Jul 93*	1

LOVE INC featuring M.C. NOISE — UK

SINGLES:	HITS 1			WEEKS 3
LOVE IS THE MESSAGE	*Love*	59	*9 Feb 91*	3

LOVE NELSON - See FIRE ISLAND

LOVE SCULPTURE — UK

SINGLES:	HITS 1			WEEKS 14
SABRE DANCE *Composed by Khatchaturian.*	*Parlophone*	5	*30 Nov 68*	14

LOVE SQUAD - See Linda CARR

A LOVE SUPREME — UK

SINGLES:	HITS 1			WEEKS 2
NIALL QUINN'S DISCO PANTS *Based on a terrace chant of Sunderland FC supporters.*	*Cherry Red*	59	*17 Apr 99*	2

LOVE TATTOO — Australia

SINGLES:	HITS 1			WEEKS 1
DROP SOME DRUMS	*Positiva*	58	*6 Oct 01*	1

LOVE TO INFINITY — UK

SINGLES:	HITS 3			WEEKS 4
KEEP LOVE TOGETHER	*Mushroom*	38	*24 Jun 95*	2
SOMEDAY	*Mushroom*	75	*18 Nov 95*	1
PRAY FOR LOVE	*Mushroom*	69	*3 Aug 96*	1

LOVE TRIBE — US

SINGLES:	HITS 1			WEEKS 3
STAND UP *Song is based around Fire Island's There But For The Grace Of God.*	*AM:PM*	23	*29 Jun 96*	3

LOVE UNLIMITED — US

SINGLES:	HITS 2			WEEKS 19
WALKIN' IN THE RAIN WITH THE ONE I LOVE *Vocals midway through song at the 'telephone break' are by Barry White.*	*Uni*	14	*17 Jun 72*	10
IT MAY BE WINTER OUTSIDE (BUT IN MY HEART IT'S SPRING) *Originally recorded by Felice Taylor.*	*20th Century*	11	*25 Jan 75*	9

LOVE UNLIMITED ORCHESTRA — US

SINGLES:	HITS 1			WEEKS 10
LOVE'S THEME	*Pye International*	10	*2 Feb 74*	10
ALBUMS:	**HITS 1**			**WEEKS 1**
RHAPSODY IN WHITE	*Pye International*	50	*6 Apr 74*	1

LOVEBUG STARSKI — US

SINGLES:	HITS 1			WEEKS 9
AMITYVILLE (THE HOUSE ON THE HILL)	*Epic*	12	*31 May 86*	9

LOVEDEEJAY AKEMI - See YOSH presents LOVEDEEJAY AKEMI

LOVEHAPPY — UK/US

SINGLES:	HITS 1			WEEKS 3
MESSAGE OF LOVE *Vocals by Ellie Lawson. Backgound vocals by Lance Ellington and Miriam Stockley.*	*MCA*	37	*18 Feb 95*	2
MESSAGE OF LOVE [RM] *Remixed by K-Klass.*	*MCA*	70	*20 Jul 96*	1

Bill LOVELADY — UK

SINGLES:	HITS 1			WEEKS 10
REGGAE FOR IT NOW	*Charisma*	12	*18 Aug 79*	10

LOVELAND featuring the voice of Rachel McFARLANE — UK

SINGLES:	HITS 5			WEEKS 15
LET THE MUSIC (LIFT YOU UP) *Darlene Lewis' vocals did not appear on the lead track of this release.* *Above hit: LOVELAND featuring Rachel McFARLANE vs. Darlene LEWIS.*	*KMS*	16	*16 Apr 94*	4
(KEEP ON) SHINING / HOPE (NEVER GIVE UP) *Above hit: LOVELAND featuring Rachel McFARLANE.*	*Eastern Bloc*	37	*5 Nov 94*	2
I NEED SOMEBODY *Cover of a Keicha Jenkins track from 1989. Backing vocals by Yvonne Shelton.*	*Eastern Bloc*	21	*14 Jan 95*	3
DON'T MAKE ME WAIT	*Eastern Bloc*	22	*10 Jun 95*	3

THE WONDER OF LOVE	*Eastern Bloc*	53	*2 Sep 95*	1
I NEED SOMEBODY [RM]	*Eastern Bloc*	38	*11 Nov 95*	2

Remixed by Topham/Twigg/Waterman.

LOVER SPEAKS — UK

SINGLES:	HITS 1			WEEKS 5
NO MORE "I LOVE YOU'S"	*A&M*	58	*16 Aug 86*	5

Michael LOVESMITH — US

SINGLES:	HITS 1			WEEKS 1
AIN'T NOTHIN' LIKE IT	*Motown*	75	*5 Oct 85*	1

LOVESTATION — UK/US

SINGLES:	HITS 5			WEEKS 21
SHINE ON ME	*RCA*	71	*13 Mar 93*	1
Above hit: LOVESTATION featuring Lisa HUNT.				
BEST OF MY LOVE	*Fresh*	73	*13 Nov 93*	1
LOVE COME RESCUE ME	*Fresh*	42	*18 Mar 95*	2
Originally released in 1992.				
TEARDROPS	*Fresh*	14	*1 Aug 98*	6
SENSUALITY	*Fresh*	16	*5 Dec 98*	7
TEARDROPS (FOOTSTEPS ON THE DANCEFLOOR . . .) [RM]	*Fresh*	24	*5 Feb 00*	4
Remixed by Joey Negro. Featured in the Martini TV commercial.				

Lyle LOVETT — US

ALBUMS:	HITS 2			WEEKS 2
I LOVE EVERYBODY	*MCA*	54	*8 Oct 94*	1
THE ROAD TO ENSENADA	*MCA*	62	*29 Jun 96*	1

Lene LOVICH — US

SINGLES:	HITS 6			WEEKS 38
LUCKY NUMBER	*Stiff*	3	*17 Feb 79*	11
SAY WHEN	*Stiff*	19	*12 May 79*	10
BIRD SONG	*Stiff*	39	*20 Oct 79*	7
WHAT WILL I DO WITHOUT YOU	*Stiff*	58	*29 Mar 80*	3
NEW TOY	*Stiff*	53	*14 Mar 81*	5
IT'S YOU, ONLY YOU (MEIN SCHMERZ)	*Stiff*	68	*27 Nov 82*	2
ALBUMS:	**HITS 2**			**WEEKS 17**
STATELESS	*Stiff*	35	*17 Mar 79*	11
FLEX	*Stiff*	19	*2 Feb 80*	6

LOVIN' SPOONFUL — US/Canada

SINGLES:	HITS 4			WEEKS 33
DAYDREAM	*Pye International*	2	*16 Apr 66*	13
SUMMER IN THE CITY	*Kama Sultra*	8	*16 Jul 66*	11
NASHVILLE CATS	*Kama Sultra*	26	*7 Jan 67*	7
DARLING BE HOME SOON	*Kama Sultra*	44	*11 Mar 67*	2
From the film 'You're A Big Boy Now'.				
EPS:	**HITS 2**			**WEEKS 13**
DID YOU EVER HAVE TO MAKE UP YOUR MIND	*Kama Sutra*	3	*25 Jun 66*	11
JUG BAND MUSIC	*Kama Sutra*	8	*27 Aug 66*	2
ALBUMS:	**HITS 1**			**WEEKS 11**
DAYDREAM	*Pye International*	8	*7 May 66*	11

LOVINDEER — Jamaica

SINGLES:	HITS 1			WEEKS 3
MAN SHORTAGE	*TSOJ*	69	*27 Sep 86*	3

Gary LOW — Italy

SINGLES:	HITS 1			WEEKS 3
I WANT YOU	*Savoir*	52	*8 Oct 83*	3

Patti LOW and DOOGIE – See BUG KANN and the PLASTIC JAM

Jim LOWE with the HIGH FIVES — US

SINGLES:	HITS 1			WEEKS 9
THE GREEN DOOR	*London*	8	*27 Oct 56*	9

Nick LOWE — UK

SINGLES:	HITS 4			WEEKS 27
I LOVE THE SOUND OF BREAKING GLASS	*Radar*	7	*11 Mar 78*	8
CRACKING UP	*Radar*	34	*9 Jun 79*	5

CRUEL TO BE KIND	*Radar*	12	*25 Aug 79*	11
HALF A BOY AND HALF A MAN	*F-Beat*	53	*26 May 84*	3
ALBUMS:	**HITS 3**			**WEEKS 17**
THE JESUS OF COOL	*Radar*	72	*11 Mar 78*	9
LABOUR OF LUST	*Radar*	43	*23 Jun 79*	6
NICK THE KNIFE	*F-Beat*	99	*20 Feb 82*	2

LOWGOLD — UK

SINGLES:	**HITS 3**			**WEEKS 4**
BEAUTY DIES YOUNG	*Nude*	67	*30 Sep 00*	1
MERCURY	*Nude*	48	*10 Feb 01*	1
COUNTERFEIT	*Nude*	52	*12 May 01*	1
BEAUTY DIES YOUNG [RI]	*Nude*	40	*8 Sep 01*	1
ALBUMS:	**HITS 1**			**WEEKS 2**
JUST BACKWARD OF SQUARE	*Nude*	33	*24 Feb 01*	2

LOWRELL — US

SINGLES:	**HITS 1**			**WEEKS 9**
MELLOW MELLOW RIGHT ON	*AVI*	37	*24 Nov 79*	9

LOX - See PUFF DADDY

L7 — US

SINGLES:	**HITS 4**			**WEEKS 18**
PRETEND WE'RE DEAD	*Slash*	21	*4 Apr 92*	7
EVERGLADE	*Slash*	27	*30 May 92*	3
MONSTER	*Slash*	33	*12 Sep 92*	3
PRETEND WE'RE DEAD [RI]	*Slash*	50	*28 Nov 92*	3
ANDRES	*Slash*	34	*9 Jul 94*	2
ALBUMS:	**HITS 2**			**WEEKS 8**
BRICKS ARE HEAVY	*Slash*	24	*2 May 92*	6
HUNGRY FOR STINK	*Slash*	26	*23 Jul 94*	2

LSG — Germany

SINGLES:	**HITS 1**			**WEEKS 1**
NETHERWORLD	*Hooj Choons*	63	*10 May 97*	1

Norman LUBOFF CHOIR - See Doris DAY; Frankie LAINE; Jo STAFFORD

LUCAS — US

SINGLES:	**HITS 1**			**WEEKS 4**
LUCAS WITH THE LID OFF	*WEA*	37	*6 Aug 94*	4

Carrie LUCAS — US

SINGLES:	**HITS 1**			**WEEKS 6**
DANCE WITH YOU	*Solar*	40	*16 Jun 79*	6

Tammy LUCAS - See Teddy RILEY featuring Tammy LUCAS

LUCIANA — UK

SINGLES:	**HITS 3**			**WEEKS 5**
GET IT UP FOR LOVE	*Chrysalis*	55	*23 Apr 94*	2
IF YOU WANT	*Chrysalis*	47	*6 Aug 94*	2
WHAT GOES AROUND / ONE MORE RIVER	*Chrysalis*	67	*5 Nov 94*	1

One More River was featured in the TV detective series 'Anna Lee'.

LUCID — UK

SINGLES:	**HITS 3**			**WEEKS 15**
I CAN'T HELP MYSELF	*ffrr*	7	*8 Aug 98*	8
CRAZY	*ffrr*	14	*27 Feb 99*	5
STAY WITH ME TILL DAWN	*ffrr*	25	*16 Oct 99*	2

LUCKY MONKEYS — UK

SINGLES:	**HITS 1**			**WEEKS 1**
BJANGO	*Hi-Life*	50	*9 Nov 96*	1

LUCY PEARL — US

SINGLES:	**HITS 3**			**WEEKS 7**
DANCE TONIGHT	*Virgin*	36	*29 Jul 00*	2
DON'T MESS WITH MY MAN	*Virgin*	20	*25 Nov 00*	4
WITHOUT YOU	*Virgin*	51	*28 Jul 01*	1

LUDACRIS — US

SINGLES:	HITS 3			WEEKS 16
WHAT'S YOUR FANTASY *Above hit: LUDACRIS (featuring SHAWNA).*	*Def Jam South*	19	*9 Jun 01*	5
ONE MINUTE MAN *Above hit: Missy "Misdemeanor" ELLIOTT featuring LUDACRIS.*	*Elektra*	10	*18 Aug 01*	8
AREA CODES *Above hit: LUDACRIS featuring Nate DOGG.*	*Def Jam*	25	*29 Sep 01*	3

Baz LUHRMANN presents — Australia

SINGLES:	HITS 1			WEEKS 16
EVERYBODY'S FREE (TO WEAR SUNSCREEN) THE SUNSCREEN SONG (CLASS OF '99) *Vocals by Lee Perry. Samples the instrumental from Quindon Tarver's version of Everybody's Free (To Feel Good) from the film 'Romeo And Juliet'. Lyrics are from an article in the Chicago Tribune by Mary Schmich.*	*EMI*	1	*12 Jun 99*	16

Robin LUKE — US

SINGLES:	HITS 1			WEEKS 6
SUSIE DARLIN'	*London*	24	*18 Oct 58*	3
SUSIE DARLIN' [RE-1ST]	*London*	23	*22 Nov 58*	1
SUSIE DARLIN' [RE-2ND]	*London*	23	*6 Dec 58*	2

LUKK featuring Felicia COLLINS — US

SINGLES:	HITS 1			WEEKS 1
ON THE ONE	*Important/Towerbell*	72	*28 Sep 85*	1

LULU — UK

SINGLES:	HITS 26			WEEKS 175
SHOUT *Originally recorded by the Isley Brothers.* *Above hit: LULU and the LUVVERS.*	*Decca*	7	*16 May 64*	13
HERE COMES THE NIGHT	*Decca*	50	*14 Nov 64*	1
LEAVE A LITTLE LOVE	*Decca*	8	*19 Jun 65*	11
TRY TO UNDERSTAND	*Decca*	25	*4 Sep 65*	8
THE BOAT THAT I ROW *Originally recorded by Neil Diamond.*	*Columbia*	6	*15 Apr 67*	11
LET'S PRETEND	*Columbia*	11	*2 Jul 67*	11
LOVE LOVES TO LOVE, LOVE	*Columbia*	32	*11 Nov 67*	6
ME, THE PEACEFUL HEART	*Columbia*	9	*2 Mar 68*	9
BOY	*Columbia*	15	*8 Jun 68*	7
I'M A TIGER *Written by Marty Wilde.*	*Columbia*	9	*9 Nov 68*	13
BOOM BANG-A-BANG *UK's Eurovision entry in 1969, it came joint 1st.*	*Columbia*	2	*15 Mar 69*	13
OH ME OH MY (I'M A FOOL FOR YOU BABY)	*Atco*	47	*22 Nov 69*	2
THE MAN WHO SOLD THE WORLD *Originally recorded by David Bowie who plays saxophone on the track, John Bonham plays drums.*	*Polydor*	3	*26 Jan 74*	9
TAKE YOUR MAMA FOR A RIDE	*Chelsea*	37	*19 Apr 75*	4
I COULD NEVER MISS YOU (MORE THAN I DO)	*Alfa*	62	*12 Dec 81*	4
I COULD NEVER MISS YOU (MORE THAN I DO) [RE]	*Alfa*	63	*16 Jan 82*	1
SHOUT [RR]	*Jive*	8	*19 Jul 86*	10
SHOUT [RI] *Both versions were listed separately until 2 Aug 86 when sales for each were combined.* *Above hit: LULU and the LUVVERS.*	*Decca*	8	*26 Jul 86*	9
INDEPENDENCE	*Dome*	11	*30 Jan 93*	5
I'M BACK FOR MORE *Originally recorded by Al Johnson and Jean Carn.* *Above hit: LULU and Bobby WOMACK.*	*Dome*	27	*3 Apr 93*	5
LET ME WAKE UP IN YOUR ARMS	*Dome*	51	*4 Sep 93*	2
RELIGHT MY FIRE *Above hit: TAKE THAT featuring LULU.*	*RCA*	1	*9 Oct 93*	14
HOW 'BOUT US	*Dome*	46	*27 Nov 93*	3
GOODBYE BABY AND AMEN	*Dome*	40	*27 Aug 94*	2
EVERY WOMAN KNOWS	*Dome*	44	*26 Nov 94*	2
HURT ME SO BAD	*Rocket*	42	*29 May 99*	2
BETTER GET READY *Theme to the BBC 1 TV lottery show 'Red Alert', hosted by Lulu.*	*Mercury*	59	*8 Jan 00*	1
WHERE THE POOR BOYS DANCE	*Mercury*	24	*18 Mar 00*	5
ALBUMS:	**HITS 2**			**WEEKS 7**
THE MOST OF LULU	*Music For Pleasure*	15	*25 Sep 71*	6
INDEPENDENCE	*Dome*	67	*6 Mar 93*	1

Bob LUMAN — US

SINGLES:	HITS 3			WEEKS 21
LET'S THINK ABOUT LIVING	*Warner Brothers*	6	*10 Sep 60*	18
WHY WHY BYE BYE	*Warner Brothers*	46	*17 Dec 60*	1
THE GREAT SNOW MAN	*Warner Brothers*	49	*6 May 61*	2
Originally recorded by John D. Loudermilk.				
ALBUMS:	**HITS 1**			**WEEKS 1**
LET'S THINK ABOUT LIVING	*Warner Brothers*	18	*14 Jan 61*	1

LUMINAIRE - See Jonathan PETERS presents LUMINAIRE

LUNIZ — US

(See also Quincy Jones.)

SINGLES:	HITS 2			WEEKS 18
I GOT 5 ON IT	*Virgin*	3	*17 Feb 96*	13
Samples Timex Social Club's Rumours.				
PLAYA HATA	*Virgin*	20	*11 May 96*	3
Samples Bobby Caldwell's What You Won't Do For Love.				
I GOT 5 ON IT - URBAN TAKEOVER REMIX [RM]	*VC Recordings*	28	*31 Oct 98*	2
Remixed by Mickey Finn and Aphofite. Featured in Channel 5's advertising campaign.				
ALBUMS:	**HITS 1**			**WEEKS 3**
OPERATION STACKOLA	*Virgin*	41	*16 Mar 96*	3

LUPINE HOWL — UK

SINGLES:	HITS 1			WEEKS 1
VAPORIZER	*Vinyl Hiss*	68	*22 Jan 00*	1

LURKERS — UK

SINGLES:	HITS 5			WEEKS 11
AIN'T GOT A CLUE	*Beggars Banquet*	45	*3 Jun 78*	3
I DON'T NEED TO TELL HER	*Beggars Banquet*	49	*5 Aug 78*	4
JUST THIRTEEN	*Beggars Banquet*	66	*3 Feb 79*	2
OUT IN THE DARK / CYANIDE	*Beggars Banquet*	72	*9 Jun 79*	1
NEW GUITAR IN TOWN	*Beggars Banquet*	72	*17 Nov 79*	1
ALBUMS:	**HITS 1**			**WEEKS 1**
FULHAM FALLOUT	*Beggars Banquet*	57	*1 Jul 78*	1

LUSCIOUS JACKSON — US

SINGLES:	HITS 4			WEEKS 5
DEEP SHAG / CITYSONG	*Grand Royal*	69	*18 Mar 95*	1
HERE	*Grand Royal*	59	*21 Oct 95*	1
From the film 'Clueless'.				
NAKED EYE	*Grand Royal*	25	*12 Apr 97*	2
LADYFINGERS	*Grand Royal*	43	*3 Jul 99*	1
ALBUMS:	**HITS 1**			**WEEKS 1**
FEVER IN FEVER OUT	*Grand Royal*	55	*26 Apr 97*	1

LUSH — UK

SINGLES:	HITS 9			WEEKS 19
MAD LOVE [EP]	*4AD*	55	*10 Mar 90*	1
Lead track: De-Luxe.				
SWEETNESS AND LIGHT	*4AD*	47	*27 Oct 90*	2
NOTHING NATURAL	*4AD*	43	*19 Oct 91*	2
FOR LOVE [EP]	*4AD*	35	*11 Jan 92*	2
Lead track: For Love.				
DESIRE LINES	*4AD*	60	*11 Jun 94*	1
HYPOCRITE	*4AD*	52	*11 Jun 94*	2
SINGLE GIRL	*4AD*	21	*20 Jan 96*	3
LADYKILLERS	*4AD*	22	*9 Mar 96*	3
500 (SHAKE BABY SHAKE)	*4AD*	21	*27 Jul 96*	3
ALBUMS:	**HITS 3**			**WEEKS 10**
SPOOKY	*4AD*	7	*8 Feb 92*	3
SPLIT	*4AD*	19	*25 Jun 94*	2
LOVELIFE	*4AD*	8	*30 Mar 96*	5

LUSTRAL — UK

SINGLES:	HITS 1			WEEKS 3
EVERYTIME	*Hooj Choons*	60	*18 Oct 97*	1
Vocals by Tracey Ackerman. Samples Robert Flack's First Time Ever I Saw Your Face.				
EVERYTIME [RM]	*Hooj Choons*	30	*4 Dec 99*	2
Remixed by Way Out West.				

LUVVERS - See LULU

LUZON — US

SINGLES:	HITS 1			WEEKS 1
THE BAGUIO TRACK	*Renaissance Recordings*	67	*14 Jul 01*	1

Annabella LWIN — Burma

SINGLES:	HITS 1			WEEKS 1
DO WHAT YOU DO	*Sony S2*	61	*28 Jan 95*	1

John LYDON — UK

(See also Time Zone featuring John Lydon and Afrika Bambaataa.)

SINGLES:	HITS 2			WEEKS 6
OPEN UP	*Hard Hands*	13	*13 Nov 93*	5
Above hit: LEFTFIELD LYDON.				
SUN	*Virgin*	42	*2 Aug 97*	1

Frankie LYMON and the TEENAGERS — US

SINGLES:	HITS 3			WEEKS 38
WHY DO FOOLS FALL IN LOVE	*Columbia*	1	*30 Jun 56*	16
Above hit: TEENAGERS featuring Frankie LYMON.				
I'M NOT A JUVENILE DELINQUENT	*Columbia*	12	*30 Mar 57*	7
BABY, BABY	*Columbia*	4	*13 Apr 57*	12
Above 2 entries were separate sides of the same release, each had its own chart run. Both sides from the film 'Rock, Rock, Rock'.				
GOODY GOODY	*Columbia*	24	*21 Sep 57*	3
Originally recorded by Benny Goodman in 1936.				

Read by Des LYNAM performed by the WIMBLEDON CHORAL SOCIETY — UK

(See also Wimbledon Choral Society.)

SINGLES:	HITS 1			WEEKS 3
IF: KIPLING'S POEM WITH THE BBC WORLD CUP '98 THEME - PAVANE	*BBC Worldwide Music*	45	*12 Dec 98*	3
Read by Lynam at the end of the BBC's coverage of the 1998 World Cup.				

Curtis LYNCH Jnr featuring Kele LE ROC and RED RAT — UK/Jamaica

(See also Kele Le Roc.)

SINGLES:	HITS 1			WEEKS 1
THINKING OF YOU	*Telstar*	70	*30 Sep 00*	1

Kenny LYNCH — UK

SINGLES:	HITS 8			WEEKS 59
MOUNTAIN OF LOVE	*His Master's Voice*	33	*2 Jul 60*	3
Originally recorded by Harold Dorman.				
Above hit: Kenny LYNCH with the Michael SAMMES SINGERS.				
PUFF (UP IN SMOKE)	*His Master's Voice*	33	*15 Sep 62*	5
PUFF (UP IN SMOKE) [RE]	*His Master's Voice*	46	*27 Oct 62*	1
UP ON THE ROOF	*His Master's Voice*	10	*8 Dec 62*	12
Originally recorded by Little Eva.				
YOU CAN NEVER STOP ME LOVING YOU	*His Master's Voice*	10	*22 Jun 63*	14
STAND BY ME	*His Master's Voice*	39	*18 Apr 64*	7
WHAT AM I TO YOU	*His Master's Voice*	37	*29 Aug 64*	4
WHAT AM I TO YOU [RE]	*His Master's Voice*	44	*3 Oct 64*	2
I'LL STAY BY YOU	*His Master's Voice*	29	*19 Jun 65*	7
HALF THE DAY'S GONE AND WE HAVEN'T EARNE'D A PENNY	*Satril*	50	*20 Aug 83*	4

Cheryl LYNN — US

SINGLES:	HITS 1			WEEKS 2
ENCORE	*Streetwave*	68	*8 Sep 84*	2

Patti LYNN — UK

SINGLES:	HITS 1			WEEKS 5
JOHNNY ANGEL	*Fontana*	37	*12 May 62*	5

Tami LYNN — US

SINGLES:	HITS 1			WEEKS 20
I'M GONNA RUN AWAY FROM YOU	*Mojo*	4	*22 May 71*	14
I'M GONNA RUN AWAY FROM YOU [RI]	*Contempo Raries*	36	*3 May 75*	6

Vera LYNN — UK

SINGLES:	HITS 9			WEEKS 46
FORGET-ME-NOT	*Decca*	7	*15 Nov 52*	1
THE HOMING WALTZ	*Decca*	9	*15 Nov 52*	3
Above hit: Vera LYNN with SAILORS, SOLDIERS and AIRMEN Of HER MAJESTY'S FORCES.				

AUF WIEDERSEH'N SWEETHEART	*Decca*	10	*15 Nov 52*	1
Above hit: Vera LYNN with SOLDIERS and AIRMEN Of HER MAJESTY'S FORCES.				
FORGET-ME-NOT [RE]	*Decca*	5	*29 Nov 52*	5
THE WINDSOR WALTZ	*Decca*	11	*6 Jun 53*	1
Above hit: Vera LYNN with Chorus of Members of HM FORCES.				
MY SON, MY SON	*Decca*	1	*16 Oct 54*	14
Originally recorded by Eddie Calvert.				
Above hit: Vera LYNN and Frank WEIR and his Saxophone, his Chorus and Orchestra.				
WHO ARE WE	*Decca*	30	*9 Jun 56*	1
A HOUSE WITH LOVE IN IT	*Decca*	17	*27 Oct 56*	13
THE FAITHFUL HUSSAR (DON'T CRY MY LOVE)	*Decca*	29	*16 Mar 57*	2
TRAVELLIN' HOME	*Decca*	20	*22 Jun 57*	5
ALBUMS:	**HITS 2**			**WEEKS 15**
20 FAMILY FAVOURITES	*EMI*	25	*21 Nov 81*	12
WE'LL MEET AGAIN	*Telstar*	44	*9 Sep 89*	3

Jeff LYNNE — UK

(See also Various Artists: Films – Original Soundtracks 'Robin Hood: Prince Of Thieves'.)

SINGLES:	**HITS 1**			**WEEKS 4**
EVERY LITTLE THING	*Reprise*	59	*30 Jun 90*	4
ALBUMS:	**HITS 1**			**WEEKS 4**
ARMCHAIR THEATRE	*Reprise*	24	*4 Aug 90*	4

Shelby LYNNE — US

SINGLES:	**HITS 1**			**WEEKS 1**
LEAVIN'	*Mercury*	73	*29 Apr 00*	1

Philip LYNOTT — Ireland

SINGLES:	**HITS 4**			**WEEKS 36**
DEAR MISS LONELY HEARTS	*Vertigo*	32	*5 Apr 80*	6
KING'S CALL	*Vertigo*	35	*21 Jun 80*	6
Tribute to Elvis Presley. Features Mark Knopfler.				
YELLOW PEARL	*Vertigo*	56	*21 Mar 81*	3
YELLOW PEARL [RE]	*Vertigo*	14	*26 Dec 81*	9
Re-released after being used as the theme to BBC1 TV's Top Of The Pops.				
OUT IN THE FIELDS	*10 Records*	5	*18 May 85*	10
Above hit: Gary MOORE and Phil LYNOTT.				
KING'S CALL [RM]	*Vertigo*	68	*24 Jan 87*	2
ALBUMS:	**HITS 2**			**WEEKS 16**
SOLO IN SOHO	*Vertigo*	28	*26 Apr 80*	6
SOLDIER OF FORTUNE – THE BEST OF PHIL LYNOTT AND THIN LIZZY	*Telstar*	55	*14 Nov 87*	10
Features Lynott's solo and group material.				
Above hit: Phil LYNOTT and THIN LIZZY.				

LYNYRD SKYNYRD — US

SINGLES:	**HITS 1**			**WEEKS 21**
SWEET HOME ALABAMA / DOUBLE TROUBLE	*MCA*	31	*11 Sep 76*	4
Initial chart entry was listed as AA side, though later listed as an EP. Free Bird was the track on the flip side.				
FREE BIRD [EP] [RE-1ST]	*MCA*	43	*22 Dec 79*	8
A tribute to Duane Allman from the Allman Brothers.				
FREE BIRD [EP] [RE-2ND]	*MCA*	21	*19 Jun 82*	9
ALBUMS:	**HITS 6**			**WEEKS 19**
NUTHIN' FANCY	*MCA*	43	*3 May 75*	1
GIMME BACK MY BULLETS	*MCA*	34	*28 Feb 76*	5
ONE MORE FOR THE ROAD	*MCA*	17	*6 Nov 76*	4
Live recordings from Atlanta.				
STREET SURVIVORS	*MCA*	13	*12 Nov 77*	4
SKYNYRD'S FIRST AND LAST	*MCA*	50	*4 Nov 78*	1
Unreleased recordings from 1970–72.				
GOLD AND PLATINUM	*MCA*	49	*9 Feb 80*	4
Compilation.				

Barbara LYON — US

SINGLES:	**HITS 2**			**WEEKS 12**
STOWAWAY	*Columbia*	12	*25 Jun 55*	8
Above hit: Barbara LYON with Ray MARTIN and his Orchestra.				
LETTER TO A SOLDIER	*Columbia*	27	*22 Dec 56*	4
Above hit: Barbara LYON with Eric JUPP and his Orchestra.				

LYTE FUNKIE ONES — US

SINGLES:	**HITS 3**			**WEEKS 17**
CAN'T HAVE YOU	*Logic*	54	*22 May 99*	1

SUMMERGIRLS	*Logic*	16	*18 Sep 99*	7
Based around the melody of Extreme's More Than Words.				
GIRL ON TV	*Logic*	6	*5 Feb 00*	9
ALBUMS:	**HITS 1**			**WEEKS 1**
LYTE FUNKIE ONES	*Logic*	62	*26 Feb 00*	1

Humphrey LYTTELTON and his Band — UK

SINGLES:	**HITS 1**			**WEEKS 6**
BAD PENNY BLUES	*Parlophone*	19	*14 Jul 56*	6

M

M — UK

SINGLES:	**HITS 4**			**WEEKS 39**
POP MUZIK	*MCA*	2	*7 Apr 79*	14
MOONLIGHT AND MUZAK	*MCA*	33	*8 Dec 79*	9
THAT'S THE WAY THE MONEY GOES	*MCA*	45	*15 Mar 80*	5
OFFICIAL SECRETS	*MCA*	64	*22 Nov 80*	2
POP MUZIK (THE 1989 RE-MIX) [RM]	*Freestyle*	15	*10 Jun 89*	9
Remixed by Robin Scott and Simon Rogers.				

M&S presents The GIRL NEXT DOOR — UK

SINGLES:	**HITS 1**			**WEEKS 13**
SALSOUL NUGGET (IF U WANNA)	*ffrr*	6	*7 Apr 01*	13
Samples Double Exposure's Everyman and Loleatta Holloway's Hit And Run.				

Bobby M featuring Jean CARN — US

SINGLES:	**HITS 1**			**WEEKS 3**
LET'S STAY TOGETHER	*Gordy*	53	*29 Jan 83*	3

M.A.N.I.C. — UK

SINGLES:	**HITS 1**			**WEEKS 1**
I'M COMIN' HARDCORE	*Union City*	60	*18 Apr 92*	1

M/A/R/R/S — UK

SINGLES:	**HITS 1**			**WEEKS 14**
PUMP UP THE VOLUME / ANITINA (THE FIRST TIME I SEE SHE DANCE)	*4AD*	1	*5 Sep 87*	14

M-BEAT — UK

SINGLES:	**HITS 3**			**WEEKS 24**
INCREDIBLE	*Renk*	39	*18 Jun 94*	3
INCREDIBLE [RM]	*Renk*	8	*10 Sep 94*	9
Above 2: M-BEAT featuring GENERAL LEVY.				
SWEET LOVE	*Renk*	18	*17 Dec 94*	7
Above hit: M-BEAT featuring NAZLYN.				
DO U KNOW WHERE YOU'RE COMING FROM	*Renk*	12	*1 Jun 96*	5
Above hit: M-BEAT featuring JAMIROQUAI.				

M.C.R.B - See SUNSHIP featuring M.C.R.B

M-D-EMM — UK

SINGLES:	**HITS 2**			**WEEKS 3**
GET DOWN	*Strictly Underground*	55	*22 Feb 92*	2
MOVE YOUR FEET	*Strictly Underground*	67	*30 May 92*	1

M-DUBS featuring LADY SAW — UK/Jamaica

SINGLES:	**HITS 1**			**WEEKS 1**
BUMP 'N' GRIND (. . . I AM FEELING HOT TONIGHT)	*Telstar*	59	*16 Dec 00*	1
Samples Lady Saw's No Long Talking.				

M + M — Canada

(See also Martha and the Muffins.)

SINGLES:	**HITS 1**			**WEEKS 4**
BLACK STATIONS/WHITE STATIONS	*RCA*	46	*28 Jul 84*	4
One track (not AA).				

M. and O. BAND — UK

SINGLES:	HITS 1			WEEKS 6
LET'S DO THE LATIN HUSTLE	*Creole*	16	*28 Feb 76*	6

M.O.P. — US

SINGLES:	HITS 3			WEEKS 19
COLD AS ICE	*Epic*	4	*12 May 01*	10
Samples Foreigner's Cold As Ice.				
ANTE UP	*Epic*	7	*18 Aug 01*	7
Above hit: M.O.P. featuring Busta RHYMES, TEPHLON and Remy MARTIN.				
ANTE UP [RE]	*Epic*	65	*13 Oct 01*	1
STAND CLEAR	*EMI*	43	*1 Dec 01*	1
Above hit: Adam F featuring M.O.P.				
ALBUMS:	**HITS 1**			**WEEKS 3**
WARRIORZ	*Epic*	40	*25 Aug 01*	3

M PEOPLE — UK

SINGLES:	HITS 19			WEEKS 137
HOW CAN I LOVE YOU MORE?	*Deconstruction*	29	*26 Oct 91*	9
COLOUR MY LIFE	*Deconstruction*	35	*7 Mar 92*	4
SOMEDAY	*Deconstruction*	38	*18 Apr 92*	3
Above hit: M-PEOPLE with Heather SMALL.				
EXCITED	*Deconstruction*	29	*10 Oct 92*	5
HOW CAN I LOVE YOU MORE? [RM]	*Deconstruction*	8	*6 Feb 93*	8
Remixed by Sasha and Tom Frederikse.				
ONE NIGHT IN HEAVEN	*Deconstruction*	6	*26 Jun 93*	11
MOVING ON UP	*Deconstruction*	2	*25 Sep 93*	11
DON'T LOOK ANY FURTHER	*Deconstruction*	9	*4 Dec 93*	10
RENAISSANCE	*Deconstruction*	5	*12 Mar 94*	7
Theme from BBC2's 'The Living Soap'.				
ELEGANTLY AMERICAN [EP]	*Deconstruction*	31	*17 Sep 94*	2
3 remixes of One Night In Heaven by David Morales and 1 of Moving On Up by MK (Mark Kinchen).				
SIGHT FOR SORE EYES	*Deconstruction*	6	*19 Nov 94*	9
OPEN YOUR HEART	*Deconstruction*	9	*4 Feb 95*	7
SEARCH FOR THE HERO	*Deconstruction*	9	*24 Jun 95*	7
LOVE RENDEZVOUS	*Deconstruction*	32	*14 Oct 95*	4
ITCHYCOO PARK	*Deconstruction*	11	*25 Nov 95*	8
JUST FOR YOU	*M People*	8	*4 Oct 97*	7
FANTASY ISLAND	*M People*	33	*6 Dec 97*	8
Backing vocals by Will Downing.				
FANTASY ISLAND [RE]	*M People*	69	*28 Feb 98*	1
ANGEL ST	*M People*	8	*28 Mar 98*	6
TESTIFY	*M People*	12	*7 Nov 98*	6
DREAMING	*M People*	13	*13 Feb 99*	4
ALBUMS:	**HITS 5**			**WEEKS 278**
NORTHERN SOUL	*Deconstruction*	53	*6 Mar 93*	2
ELEGANT SLUMMING	*Deconstruction*	2	*16 Oct 93*	87
BIZARRE FRUIT	*Deconstruction*	4	*26 Nov 94*	52
NORTHERN SOUL [RE]	*Deconstruction*	26	*16 Sep 95*	3
BIZARRE FRUIT / BIZARRE FRUIT II [RE]	*Deconstruction*	3	*9 Dec 95*	63
Bizzarre Fruit II was a remix album, sales were combined.				
FRESCO	*M People*	2	*25 Oct 97*	40
THE BEST OF M PEOPLE	*M People*	2	*14 Nov 98*	31

Timo MAAS — Germany

SINGLES:	HITS 2			WEEKS 3
DER SCHIEBER	*48K*	50	*1 Apr 00*	1
UBIK (THE BREAKZ)	*Perfecto*	33	*30 Sep 00*	2
Above hit: Timo MAAS featuring Martin BETTINGHAUS.				

Lorin MAAZEL – See Andrew LLOYD WEBBER; PHILHARMONIA ORCHESTRA conducted by Lorin MAAZEL

Keith MAC PROJECT — UK

SINGLES:	HITS 1			WEEKS 1
DE DAH DAH (SPICE OF LIFE)	*Public Demand*	66	*25 Jun 94*	1

Pete MAC Junior — US

SINGLES:	HITS 1			WEEKS 4
THE WATER MARGIN	*BBC*	37	*15 Oct 77*	4
Japanese theme from the BBC1 TV series of the same name. [AA] listed with Godiego's English version.				

Scott MAC – See SIGNUM

MAC BAND featuring the McCAMPBELL BROTHERS — US

SINGLES:	HITS 2			WEEKS 17
ROSES ARE RED	*MCA*	8	*18 Jun 88*	13
Chart for 18 Jun 88 reflects 12" only import catalogue number. Originally written for the Whispers who rejected it.				
STALEMATE	*MCA*	40	*10 Sep 88*	4
ALBUMS:	**HITS 1**			**WEEKS 3**
THE MAC BAND	*MCA*	61	*20 Aug 88*	3

David McALMONT — UK

(See also McAlmont and Butler.)

SINGLES:	HITS 3			WEEKS 5
HYMN	*Blanco Y Negro*	65	*27 Apr 96*	1
Above hit: ULTRAMARINE (featuring David McALMONT).				
LOOK AT YOURSELF	*Hut*	40	*9 Aug 97*	2
DIAMONDS ARE FOREVER	*East West*	39	*22 Nov 97*	2
Above hit: David McALMONT/David ARNOLD.				

McALMONT and BUTLER — UK

(See also Bernard Butler; David McAlmont.)

SINGLES:	HITS 2			WEEKS 12
YES	*Hut*	8	*27 May 95*	8
YOU DO	*Hut*	17	*4 Nov 95*	4
ALBUMS:	**HITS 1**			**WEEKS 8**
THE SOUND OF MCALMONT AND BUTLER	*Hut*	33	*9 Dec 95*	8

Neil MacARTHUR — UK

(See also Colin Blunstone.)

SINGLES:	HITS 1			WEEKS 5
SHE'S NOT THERE	*Deram*	34	*8 Feb 69*	5

David MacBETH - Kim DRAKE MUSIC - Beryl STOTT GROUP — UK

SINGLES:	HITS 1			WEEKS 4
MR. BLUE	*Pye*	18	*31 Oct 59*	4

Nicko McBRAIN — UK

SINGLES:	HITS 1			WEEKS 1
RHYTHM OF THE BEAST	*EMI*	72	*13 Jul 91*	1

Frankie McBRIDE — Ireland

SINGLES:	HITS 1			WEEKS 15
FIVE LITTLE FINGERS	*Emerald*	19	*12 Aug 67*	15
Originally recorded by Bill Anderson.				
ALBUMS:	**HITS 1**			**WEEKS 3**
FRANKIE MCBRIDE	*Emerald*	29	*17 Feb 68*	3

MACC LADS — UK

ALBUMS:	HITS 1			WEEKS 1
FROM BEER TO ETERNITY	*Hectic House*	72	*7 Oct 89*	1

Dan McCAFFERTY — UK

SINGLES:	HITS 1			WEEKS 3
OUT OF TIME	*Mountain*	41	*13 Sep 75*	3

C.W. McCALL — US

SINGLES:	HITS 1			WEEKS 10
CONVOY	*MGM*	2	*14 Feb 76*	10
The song that brought the CB (Citizen Broadcast) Radio craze and slang to the public's attention in the UK.				

David McCALLUM — UK

SINGLES:	HITS 1			WEEKS 4
COMMUNICATION	*Capitol*	32	*16 Apr 66*	4

McCAMPBELL BROTHERS - See MAC BAND featuring the McCAMPBELL BROTHERS

Linda McCARTNEY — UK

(See also Paul and Linda McCartney.)

SINGLES:	HITS 2			WEEKS 2
WIDE PRAIRIE	*Parlophone*	74	*21 Nov 98*	1
THE LIGHT COMES FROM WITHIN	*Parlophone*	56	*6 Feb 99*	1

Paul McCARTNEY — UK

(See also Christians, Holly Johnson Paul McCartney, Gerry Marsden and Stock Aitken Waterman; Paul and Linda McCartney.)

SINGLES:	HITS 50			WEEKS 398
ANOTHER DAY	*Apple*	2	*27 Feb 71*	12
GIVE IRELAND BACK TO THE IRISH	*Apple*	16	*26 Feb 72*	8
MARY HAD A LITTLE LAMB	*Apple*	9	*27 May 72*	11
HI, HI, HI/C MOON	*Apple*	5	*9 Dec 72*	13
Above 3 WINGS.				
MY LOVE	*Apple*	9	*7 Apr 73*	11
Above hit: Paul McCARTNEY and WINGS.				
LIVE AND LET DIE	*Apple*	9	*9 Jun 73*	13
From the James Bond film of the same name.				
Above hit: WINGS.				
LIVE AND LET DIE [RE]	*Apple*	49	*15 Sep 73*	1
HELEN WHEELS	*Apple*	12	*3 Nov 73*	12
JET	*Apple*	7	*2 Mar 74*	9
BAND ON THE RUN	*Apple*	3	*6 Jul 74*	11
JUNIOR'S FARM	*Apple*	16	*9 Nov 74*	10
Above 4: Paul McCARTNEY and WINGS.				
LISTEN TO WHAT THE MAN SAID	*Capitol*	6	*31 May 75*	8
LETTING GO	*Capitol*	41	*18 Oct 75*	3
SILLY LOVE SONGS	*Parlophone*	2	*15 May 76*	11
LET 'EM IN	*Parlophone*	2	*7 Aug 76*	10
MAYBE I'M AMAZED	*Parlophone*	28	*19 Feb 77*	5
MULL OF KINTYRE / GIRLS' SCHOOL	*Capitol*	1	*19 Nov 77*	17
WITH A LITTLE LUCK	*Parlophone*	5	*1 Apr 78*	9
I'VE HAD ENOUGH	*Parlophone*	42	*1 Jul 78*	7
LONDON TOWN	*Parlophone*	60	*9 Sep 78*	4
GOODNIGHT TONIGHT	*Parlophone*	5	*7 Apr 79*	10
OLD SIAM, SIR	*Parlophone*	35	*16 Jun 79*	6
GETTING CLOSER / BABY'S REQUEST	*Parlophone*	60	*1 Sep 79*	3
Above 12: WINGS.				
WONDERFUL CHRISTMASTIME	*Parlophone*	6	*1 Dec 79*	8
COMING UP	*Parlophone*	2	*19 Apr 80*	9
WATERFALLS	*Parlophone*	9	*21 Jun 80*	8
EBONY AND IVORY	*Parlophone*	1	*10 Apr 82*	10
Above hit: Paul McCARTNEY with additional vocals by Stevie WONDER.				
TAKE IT AWAY	*Parlophone*	15	*3 Jul 82*	10
TUG OF WAR	*Parlophone*	53	*9 Oct 82*	3
THE GIRL IS MINE	*Epic*	8	*6 Nov 82*	9
Above hit: Michael JACKSON and Paul McCARTNEY.				
THE GIRL IS MINE [RE]	*Epic*	75	*15 Jan 83*	1
SAY SAY SAY	*Parlophone*	2	*15 Oct 83*	15
Above hit: Paul McCARTNEY and Michael JACKSON.				
PIPES OF PEACE	*Parlophone*	1	*17 Dec 83*	12
NO MORE LONELY NIGHTS (BALLAD)	*Parlophone*	2	*6 Oct 84*	15
From the film 'Give My Regards To Broad Street'.				
WE ALL STAND TOGETHER	*Parlophone*	3	*24 Nov 84*	13
From the animated film 'Rupert And The Frog Song'.				
Above hit: Paul McCARTNEY and the FROG CHORUS.				
SPIES LIKE US	*Parlophone*	13	*30 Nov 85*	10
From the film of the same name.				
WE ALL STAND TOGETHER [RE]	*Parlophone*	32	*21 Dec 85*	5
PRESS	*Parlophone*	25	*26 Jul 86*	8
ONLY LOVE REMAINS	*Parlophone*	34	*13 Dec 86*	5
ONCE UPON A LONG AGO	*Parlophone*	10	*28 Nov 87*	7
MY BRAVE FACE	*Parlophone*	18	*20 May 89*	5
Co-written by Elvis Costello.				
THIS ONE	*Parlophone*	18	*29 Jul 89*	6
FIGURE OF EIGHT	*Parlophone*	42	*25 Nov 89*	3
PUT IT THERE	*Parlophone*	32	*17 Feb 90*	2
BIRTHDAY	*Parlophone*	29	*20 Oct 90*	3
ALL MY TRIALS	*Parlophone*	35	*8 Dec 90*	5
HOPE OF DELIVERANCE	*Parlophone*	18	*9 Jan 93*	6
C'MON PEOPLE	*Parlophone*	41	*6 Mar 93*	3
YOUNG BOY	*Parlophone*	19	*10 May 97*	3
THE WORLD TONIGHT	*Parlophone*	23	*19 Jul 97*	2
BEAUTIFUL NIGHT	*Parlophone*	25	*27 Dec 97*	4

Features Ringo Starr on drums, George Martin on backing vocals and Jeff Lynne on guitar.

NO OTHER BABY / BROWN EYED HANDSOME MAN	*Parlophone*	42	*6 Nov 99*	2
No Other Baby originally recorded by Dickie Bishop and the Sidekicks but based on the Vipers' version from 1958. Brown Eyed Handsome Man originally recorded by Chuck Berry in 1956.				
FROM A LOVER TO A FRIEND	*Parlophone*	45	*10 Nov 01*	2
ALBUMS:	**HITS 27**			**WEEKS 533**
MCCARTNEY	*Apple*	2	*2 May 70*	32
WINGS WILDLIFE	*Apple*	11	*18 Dec 71*	9
Above hit: WINGS.				
RED ROSE SPEEDWAY	*Apple*	5	*19 May 73*	16
BAND ON THE RUN	*Apple*	1	*15 Dec 73*	124
Peak position reached on 27 Jul 74.				
Above 2: Paul McCARTNEY and WINGS.				
VENUS AND MARS	*Capitol*	1	*21 Jun 75*	29
WINGS AT THE SPEED OF SOUND	*Apple*	2	*17 Apr 76*	35
WINGS OVER AMERICA	*Parlophone*	8	*15 Jan 77*	22
Live recordings from their 1976 US tour.				
LONDON TOWN	*Parlophone*	4	*15 Apr 78*	23
WINGS GREATEST	*Parlophone*	5	*16 Dec 78*	32
BACK TO THE EGG	*Parlophone*	6	*23 Jun 79*	15
Above 6: WINGS.				
MCCARTNEY II	*Parlophone*	1	*31 May 80*	18
THE MCCARTNEY INTERVIEW	*EMI*	34	*7 Mar 81*	4
Originally a promotional record for US radio stations.				
TUG OF WAR	*Parlophone*	1	*8 May 82*	27
PIPES OF PEACE	*Parlophone*	4	*12 Nov 83*	23
GIVE MY REGARDS TO BROAD STREET [OST]	*Parlophone*	1	*3 Nov 84*	21
PRESS TO PLAY	*Parlophone*	8	*13 Sep 86*	6
ALL THE BEST!	*Parlophone*	2	*14 Nov 87*	21
FLOWERS IN THE DIRT	*Parlophone*	1	*17 Jun 89*	20
TRIPPING THE LIVE FANTASTIC	*Parlophone*	17	*17 Nov 90*	11
UNPLUGGED - THE OFFICIAL BOOTLEG	*Parlophone*	7	*1 Jun 91*	3
CHOBA B CCCP (THE RUSSIAN ALBUM)	*Parlophone*	63	*12 Oct 91*	1
Originally released in Russia,1988.				
OFF THE GROUND	*Parlophone*	5	*13 Feb 93*	4
PAUL IS LIVE	*Parlophone*	34	*20 Nov 93*	2
Live recordings from his 1993 tour.				
FLAMING PIE	*Parlophone*	2	*17 May 97*	15
BAND ON THE RUN [RI]	*Parlophone*	69	*27 Mar 99*	1
25th anniversary edition.				
Above hit: Paul McCARTNEY and WINGS.				
RUN DEVIL RUN	*Parlophone*	12	*16 Oct 99*	11
Collection of rock'n'roll covers.				
WINGSPAN - HITS AND HISTORY	*Parlophone*	5	*19 May 01*	7
DRIVING RAIN	*Parlophone*	46	*24 Nov 01*	1

Paul and Linda McCARTNEY — UK

(See also Linda McCartney; Paul McCartney.)

SINGLES:	**HITS 1**			**WEEKS 5**
THE BACK SEAT OF MY CAR	*Apple*	39	*28 Aug 71*	5
ALBUMS:	**HITS 1**			**WEEKS 24**
RAM	*Apple*	1	*5 Jun 71*	24

William McCLINTOCK BUNBURY - See George BOWYER and William McCLINTOCK BUNBURY

Kirsty MacCOLL — UK

(See also Billy Bragg.)

SINGLES:	**HITS 9**			**WEEKS 63**
THERE'S A GUY WORKS DOWN THE CHIP SHOP, SWEARS HE'S ELVIS	*Polydor*	14	*13 Jun 81*	9
A NEW ENGLAND	*Stiff*	7	*19 Jan 85*	10
Originally recorded by Billy Bragg.				
FAIRYTALE OF NEW YORK	*Pogue Mahone*	2	*5 Dec 87*	9
Above hit: POGUES featuring Kirsty MacCOLL.				
FREE WORLD	*Virgin*	43	*8 Apr 89*	6
DAYS	*Virgin*	12	*1 Jul 89*	9
WALKING DOWN MADISON	*Virgin*	23	*25 May 91*	7
MY AFFAIR	*Virgin*	56	*17 Aug 91*	2
FAIRYTALE OF NEW YORK [RI]	*PM*	36	*14 Dec 91*	5
Above hit: POGUES featuring Kirsty MacCOLL.				
CAROLINE	*Virgin*	58	*4 Mar 95*	2
PERFECT DAY	*Virgin*	75	*24 Jun 95*	1
Above hit: Kirsty MacCOLL andEvan DANDO.				
DAYS [RI]	*Virgin*	42	*29 Jul 95*	3
Featured in the Sony Handcam Camcorder TV commerical.				
ALBUMS:	**HITS 5**			**WEEKS 58**
KITE	*Virgin*	34	*20 May 89*	12
ELECTRIC LANDLADY	*Virgin*	17	*6 Jul 91*	8

TITANIC DAYS	*ZTT*	46	*12 Mar 94*	2
GALORE - THE BEST OF KIRSTY MACCOLL	*Virgin*	6	*18 Mar 95*	27
TROPICAL BRAINSTORM	*V2*	39	*1 Apr 00*	9

Marilyn McCOO and Billy DAVIS, JR. — US

SINGLES:	HITS 1			WEEKS 9
YOU DON'T HAVE TO BE A STAR (TO BE IN MY SHOW)	*ABC*	7	*19 Mar 77*	9

Del McCOURY BAND - See Steve EARLE

Van McCOY — US

SINGLES:	HITS 4			WEEKS 36
THE HUSTLE	*Avco*	3	*31 May 75*	12
Above hit: Van McCOY and the SOUL CITY SYMPHONY.				
CHANGE WITH THE TIMES	*Avco*	36	*1 Nov 75*	4
SOUL CHA CHA	*H&L*	34	*12 Feb 77*	6
THE SHUFFLE	*H&L*	4	*9 Apr 77*	14
ALBUMS:	**HITS 1**			**WEEKS 11**
DISCO BABY	*Avco*	32	*5 Jul 75*	11
Above hit: Van McCOY and the SOUL CITY SYMPHONY.				

McCOYS — US

SINGLES:	HITS 2			WEEKS 18
HANG ON SLOOPY	*Immediate*	5	*4 Sep 65*	14
Originally recorded by the Vibrations as My Girl Sloopy.				
FEVER	*Immediate*	44	*18 Dec 65*	4
Originally recorded by Little Willie John.				

George McCRAE — US

SINGLES:	HITS 8			WEEKS 62
ROCK YOUR BABY	*Jay Boy*	1	*29 Jun 74*	14
I CAN'T LEAVE YOU ALONE	*Jay Boy*	9	*5 Oct 74*	9
YOU CAN HAVE IT ALL	*Jay Boy*	23	*14 Dec 74*	9
SING A HAPPY SONG	*Jay Boy*	38	*22 Mar 75*	4
IT'S BEEN SO LONG	*Jay Boy*	4	*19 Jul 75*	11
I AIN'T LYIN'	*Jay Boy*	12	*18 Oct 75*	7
HONEY I	*Jay Boy*	33	*24 Jan 76*	4
ONE STEP CLOSER (TO LOVE)	*President*	57	*25 Feb 84*	4
ALBUMS:	**HITS 2**			**WEEKS 29**
ROCK YOUR BABY	*Jay Boy*	13	*3 Aug 74*	28
GEORGE MCCRAE	*Jay Boy*	54	*13 Sep 75*	1

Gwen McCRAE — US

SINGLES:	HITS 2			WEEKS 5
ALL THIS LOVE THAT I'M GIVING	*Flame*	63	*30 Apr 88*	2
ALL THIS LOVE I'M GIVING [RR]	*KTDA*	36	*13 Feb 93*	3
Above hit: MUSIC and MYSTERY featuring Gwen McCRAE.				

McCRARYS — US

SINGLES:	HITS 1			WEEKS 4
LOVE ON A SUMMER NIGHT	*Capitol*	52	*31 Jul 82*	4

Mindy McCREADY — US

SINGLES:	HITS 1			WEEKS 3
OH ROMEO	*BNA*	41	*1 Aug 98*	3

Ian McCULLOCH — UK

SINGLES:	HITS 4			WEEKS 14
SEPTEMBER SONG	*Korova*	51	*15 Dec 84*	5
Originally recorded by Walter Huston.				
PROUD TO FALL	*WEA*	51	*2 Sep 89*	4
CANDLELAND (THE SECOND COMING)	*East West*	75	*12 May 90*	1
Above hit: Ian McCULLOCH featuring Elizabeth FRASER.				
LOVER LOVER LOVER	*East West*	47	*22 Feb 92*	4
ALBUMS:	**HITS 2**			**WEEKS 4**
CANDLELAND	*WEA*	18	*7 Oct 89*	3
MYSTERIO	*East West*	46	*21 Mar 92*	1

Martine McCUTCHEON — UK

SINGLES:	HITS 6			WEEKS 65
ARE YOU MAN ENOUGH	*Avex UK*	62	*18 Nov 95*	1
Above hit: UNO CLIO featuring Martine McCUTCHEON.				

PERFECT MOMENT *Originally recorded by Edyta Gorniak in 1997.*	*Innocent*	1	*17 Apr 99*	15
PERFECT MOMENT [RE]	*Innocent*	59	*14 Aug 99*	5
I'VE GOT YOU	*Innocent*	6	*11 Sep 99*	10
TALKING IN YOUR SLEEP / LOVE ME *Charity record in aid of the BBC's Children In Need Appeal.*	*Innocent*	6	*4 Dec 99*	16
I'M OVER YOU	*Innocent*	2	*4 Nov 00*	10
ON THE RADIO	*Innocent*	7	*3 Feb 01*	8
ALBUMS:	**HITS 2**			**WEEKS 34**
YOU, ME & US	*Innocent*	2	*18 Sep 99*	20
WISHING	*Innocent*	25	*25 Nov 00*	14

Gene McDANIELS — US

SINGLES:	**HITS 1**			**WEEKS 2**
TOWER OF STRENGTH *Backing vocals by the Johnny Mann Singers.*	*London*	49	*18 Nov 61*	1
TOWER OF STRENGTH [RE]	*London*	49	*2 Dec 61*	1

Julie McDERMOTT – See AWESOME 3; THIRD DIMENSION featuring Julie McDERMOTT

Chas McDEVITT SKIFFLE GROUP (featuring Nancy WHISKEY) — UK

SINGLES:	**HITS 2**			**WEEKS 20**
FREIGHT TRAIN	*Oriole*	5	*13 Apr 57*	17
GREENBACK DOLLAR	*Oriole*	28	*15 Jun 57*	1
GREENBACK DOLLAR [RE]	*Oriole*	30	*6 Jul 57*	1
FREIGHT TRAIN [RE]	*Oriole*	27	*21 Sep 57*	1

Jane McDONALD — UK

SINGLES:	**HITS 1**			**WEEKS 7**
CRUISE INTO CHRISTMAS [M]	*Focus Music International*	10	*26 Dec 98*	7
ALBUMS:	**HITS 3**			**WEEKS 39**
JANE MCDONALD *First new act to debut at No. 1 without a hit single.*	*Focus Music International*	1	*25 Jul 98*	27
INSPIRATION	*Universal Music TV*	6	*17 Jun 00*	9
LOVE AT THE MOVIES	*Universal Music TV*	24	*27 Oct 01*	3

Michael McDONALD — US

(See also Doobie Brothers.)

SINGLES:	**HITS 4**			**WEEKS 45**
YAH MO B THERE	*Qwest*	44	*18 Feb 84*	5
YAH MO B THERE [RE]	*Qwest*	69	*7 Apr 84*	3
YAH MO B THERE [RM] *Remixed by John 'Jellybean' Benitez. The remix had the same catalogue number as the original.* *Above 3: James INGRAM (with Michael McDONALD).*	*Qwest*	12	*12 Jan 85*	8
ON MY OWN *Above hit: Patti LABELLE and Michael McDONALD.*	*MCA*	2	*3 May 86*	13
I KEEP FORGETTIN' *Originally released 1982, reaching No. 4 in the US. Originally recorded by Chuck Jackson.*	*Warner Brothers*	43	*26 Jul 86*	6
SWEET FREEDOM *From the film 'Running Scared'.*	*MCA*	12	*6 Sep 86*	10
ALBUMS:	**HITS 3**			**WEEKS 45**
SWEET FREEDOM: BEST OF MICHAEL McDONALD	*Warner Brothers*	6	*22 Nov 86*	35
TAKE IT TO HEART	*Reprise*	35	*26 May 90*	4
THE VERY BEST OF MICHAEL McDONALD *Includes 4 tracks by the Doobie Brothers.*	*Rhino*	21	*17 Mar 01*	6

Carrie McDOWELL — US

SINGLES:	**HITS 1**			**WEEKS 3**
UH UH, NO NO CASUAL SEX	*Motown*	68	*26 Sep 87*	3

John McENROE and Pat CASH with the FULL METAL RACKET — US/Australia

SINGLES:	**HITS 1**			**WEEKS 1**
ROCK AND ROLL	*Music For Nations*	66	*13 Jul 91*	1

Reba McENTIRE — US

SINGLES:	**HITS 1**			**WEEKS 1**
DOES HE LOVE YOU	*MCA Nashville*	62	*19 Jun 99*	1

MACEO and the MACKS — US

SINGLES:	**HITS 1**			**WEEKS 5**
CROSS THE TRACK (WE BETTER GO BACK)	*Urban*	54	*16 May 87*	5

McFADDEN and WHITEHEAD — US

SINGLES:	HITS 1			WEEKS 10
AIN'T NO STOPPIN' US NOW	*Philadelphia International*	5	*19 May 79*	10

Rachel McFARLANE — UK

(See also Loveland featuring the Voice Of Rachel McFarlane.)

SINGLES:	HITS 1			WEEKS 2
LOVER	*Multiply*	38	*1 Aug 98*	2

Bobby McFERRIN — US

SINGLES:	HITS 2			WEEKS 15
DON'T WORRY BE HAPPY	*Manhattan*	2	*24 Sep 88*	11
THINKIN' ABOUT YOUR BODY	*Manhattan*	46	*17 Dec 88*	4
Featured in the Cadbury's chocolate TV commercial with ammended words.				
ALBUMS:	**HITS 1**			**WEEKS 1**
SIMPLE PLEASURES	*Manhattan*	92	*29 Oct 88*	1

McGANNS — UK

SINGLES:	HITS 2			WEEKS 4
JUST MY IMAGINATION	*Coalition*	59	*14 Nov 98*	1
A HEARTBEAT AWAY	*Coalition*	42	*6 Feb 99*	3

Kate and Anna McGARRIGLE — Canada

ALBUMS:	HITS 1			WEEKS 4
DANCER WITH BRUISED KNEES	*Warner Brothers*	35	*26 Feb 77*	4

Mike McGEAR — UK

SINGLES:	HITS 1			WEEKS 4
LEAVE IT	*Warner Brothers*	36	*5 Oct 74*	4

Maureen McGOVERN — US

SINGLES:	HITS 1			WEEKS 8
THE CONTINENTAL	*20th Century*	16	*5 Jun 76*	8

Shane MacGOWAN — UK

SINGLES:	HITS 5			WEEKS 9
WHAT A WONDERFUL WORLD	*Mute*	72	*12 Dec 92*	1
Above hit: Nick CAVE and Shane MacGOWAN.				
THE CHURCH OF THE HOLY SPOOK	*ZTT*	74	*3 Sep 94*	1
THAT WOMAN'S GOT ME DRINKING	*ZTT*	34	*15 Oct 94*	3
Features actor Johnny Depp on guitar.				
Above 2: Shane MacGOWAN and the POPES.				
HAUNTED	*ZTT*	30	*29 Apr 95*	2
Above hit: Shane MacGOWAN and Sinead O'CONNOR.				
MY WAY	*ZTT*	29	*20 Apr 96*	2
Featured in the Nike Swoosh trainers TV commercial.				
ALBUMS:	**HITS 2**			**WEEKS 3**
THE SNAKE	*ZTT*	37	*29 Oct 94*	2
THE CROCK OF GOLD	*ZTT*	59	*8 Nov 97*	1
Above 2: Shane MacGOWAN and the POPES.				

Ewan McGREGOR — UK

SINGLES:	HITS 2			WEEKS 16
CHOOSE LIFE	*Positiva*	6	*15 Nov 97*	11
From the film 'Trainspotting'. Samples McGregor's opening monologue.				
Above hit: PF PROJECT featuring Ewan McGREGOR.				
COME WHAT MAY	*Interscope*	27	*6 Oct 01*	5
From the film 'Moulin Rouge'.				
Above hit: Nicole KIDMAN and Ewan McGREGOR.				

Freddie McGREGOR — Jamaica

SINGLES:	HITS 2			WEEKS 16
JUST DON'T WANT TO BE LONELY	*Germain*	9	*27 Jun 87*	11
Originally recorded by Ronnie Dyson.				
THAT GIRL (GROOVY SITUATION)	*Polydor*	47	*19 Sep 87*	5

Mary MacGREGOR — US

SINGLES:	HITS 1			WEEKS 10
TORN BETWEEN TWO LOVERS	*Ariola America*	4	*19 Feb 77*	10
ALBUMS:	**HITS 1**			**WEEKS 1**
TORN BETWEEN TWO LOVERS	*Ariola America*	59	*23 Apr 77*	1

McGUINNESS FLINT — UK

SINGLES:	HITS 2			WEEKS 26
WHEN I'M DEAD AND GONE	*Capitol*	2	*21 Nov 70*	14
MALT AND BARLEY BLUES	*Capitol*	5	*1 May 71*	12
ALBUMS:	**HITS 1**			**WEEKS 10**
MCGUINNESS FLINT	*Capitol*	9	*23 Jan 71*	10

Barry McGUIRE — US

SINGLES:	HITS 1			WEEKS 13
EVE OF DESTRUCTION	*RCA Victor*	3	*11 Sep 65*	13

Originally recorded by P.F.Sloan.

McGUIRE SISTERS — US

SINGLES:	HITS 4			WEEKS 24
NO MORE	*Vogue Coral*	20	*2 Apr 55*	1
SINCERELY	*Vogue Coral*	14	*16 Jul 55*	4
Above 2 entries were separate sides of the same release, each had its own chart run.				
DELILAH JONES	*Vogue Coral*	24	*2 Jun 56*	2
SUGARTIME	*Coral*	14	*15 Feb 58*	6
MAY YOU ALWAYS	*Coral*	15	*2 May 59*	10
MAY YOU ALWAYS [RE]	*Coral*	28	*18 Jul 59*	1

MACHEL — Trinidad

SINGLES:	HITS 1			WEEKS 1
COME DIG IT	*London*	56	*14 Sep 96*	1

Featured in the Lilt TV commercial.

MACHINE HEAD — US

SINGLES:	HITS 3			WEEKS 4
OLD	*Roadrunner*	43	*27 May 95*	2
TAKE MY SCARS	*Roadrunner*	73	*6 Dec 97*	1
FROM THIS DAY	*Roadrunner*	74	*18 Dec 99*	1
ALBUMS:	**HITS 4**			**WEEKS 9**
BURN MY EYES	*Roadrunner*	25	*20 Aug 94*	3
THE MORE THINGS CHANGE . . .	*Roadrunner*	16	*5 Apr 97*	3
THE BURNING RED	*Roadrunner*	13	*21 Aug 99*	2
SUPERCHARGER	*Roadrunner*	34	*13 Oct 01*	1

Hal McINTRYE and his Orchestra – See MILLS BROTHERS with Hal McINTRYE and his Orchestra

Craig MACK — US

(See also Various Artists (EPs) 'Dangerous Minds EP'.)

SINGLES:	HITS 3			WEEKS 5
FLAVA IN YA EAR	*Bad Boy*	57	*12 Nov 94*	2
Features rapping by Busta Rhymes.				
GET DOWN	*Puff Daddy*	54	*1 Apr 95*	1
SPIRIT	*A&M*	35	*7 Jun 97*	2

Above hit: SOUNDS OF BLACKNESS featuring Craig MACK.

Lizzy MACK — UK

SINGLES:	HITS 2			WEEKS 3
THE POWER OF LOVE	*Media*	49	*5 Nov 94*	2
Above hit: FITS OF GLOOM featuring Lizzy MACK.				
DON'T GO	*Media*	52	*4 Nov 95*	1

Lonnie MACK — US

SINGLES:	HITS 1			WEEKS 3
MEMPHIS	*Lightning*	47	*14 Apr 79*	3

[AA] listed with Let's Dance by Chris Montez. It was originally recorded by Chuck Berry in 1959; Mack's version reached No.5 in the US in 1963.

MACK VIBE featuring JACQUELINE — US

SINGLES:	HITS 1			WEEKS 1
I CAN'T LET YOU GO	*MCA*	53	*4 Feb 95*	1

Duff McKAGAN — US

ALBUMS:	HITS 1			WEEKS 2
BELIEVE IN ME	*Geffen*	27	*9 Oct 93*	2

Maria McKEE — US

SINGLES:	HITS 5			WEEKS 23
SHOW ME HEAVEN	*Epic*	1	*15 Sep 90*	14
From the film 'Days Of Thunder'.				
BREATHE	*Geffen*	59	*26 Jan 91*	1
SWEETEST CHILD	*Geffen*	45	*1 Aug 92*	4
I'M GONNA SOOTHE YOU	*Geffen*	35	*22 May 93*	3
I CAN'T MAKE IT ALONE	*Geffen*	74	*18 Sep 93*	1
ALBUMS:	**HITS 2**			**WEEKS 6**
MARIA MCKEE	*Geffen*	49	*24 Jun 89*	3
YOU GOTTA SIN TO GET SAVED	*Geffen*	26	*12 Jun 93*	3

Kenneth McKELLAR — UK

SINGLES:	HITS 1			WEEKS 4
A MAN WITHOUT LOVE	*Decca*	30	*12 Mar 66*	4
UK's Eurovision entry in 1966, it came 9th.				
EPS:	**HITS 4**			**WEEKS 7**
KENNETH McKELLAR SINGS HANDEL	*Decca*	12	*26 Mar 60*	3
HANDEL'S ARIAS	*Decca*	9	*3 Sep 60*	1
KENNETH McKELLAR NO. 2	*Decca*	13	*24 Sep 60*	1
ROAD TO THE ISLES	*Decca*	8	*24 Dec 60*	2
ALBUMS:	**HITS 2**			**WEEKS 10**
THE WORLD OF KENNETH MCKELLAR	*Decca*	27	*28 Jun 69*	7
ECCO DI NAPOLI	*Decca*	45	*31 Jan 70*	3

Terence McKENNA – See SHAMEN

Billy MacKENZIE — UK

ALBUMS:	HITS 1			WEEKS 1
BEYOND THE SUN	*Nude*	64	*18 Oct 97*	1
Charity record with proceeds to the Samaritans/Macmillan Cancer Relief Fund.				

Gisele MacKENZIE — Canada

SINGLES:	HITS 1			WEEKS 6
SEVEN LONELY DAYS	*Capitol*	12	*18 Jul 53*	1
SEVEN LONELY DAYS [RE-1ST]	*Capitol*	11	*1 Aug 53*	1
SEVEN LONELY DAYS [RE-2ND]	*Capitol*	6	*22 Aug 53*	4

Scott McKENZIE — US

SINGLES:	HITS 2			WEEKS 18
SAN FRANCISCO (BE SURE TO WEAR SOME FLOWERS IN YOUR HAIR)	*CBS*	1	*15 Jul 67*	17
LIKE AN OLD TIME MOVIE	*CBS*	50	*4 Nov 67*	1
Above hit: Voice Of Scott McKENZIE.				

Ken MacKINTOSH, his Saxophone and his Orchestra — UK

SINGLES:	HITS 3			WEEKS 9
THE CREEP	*His Master's Voice*	12	*16 Jan 54*	1
THE CREEP [RE]	*His Master's Voice*	10	*30 Jan 54*	1
RAUNCHY	*His Master's Voice*	19	*8 Feb 58*	6
NO HIDING PLACE	*His Master's Voice*	45	*12 Mar 60*	1
Above hit: Ken MACKINTOSH.				

Brian McKNIGHT — US

SINGLES:	HITS 2			WEEKS 4
ANYTIME	*Motown*	48	*6 Jun 98*	2
YOU SHOULD BE MINE (DON'T WASTE YOUR TIME)	*Motown*	36	*3 Oct 98*	2
Above hit: Brian McKNIGHT featuring MASE.				

Julie McKNIGHT – See KINGS OF TOMORROW featuring Julie McKNIGHT

Vivienne McKONE — UK

SINGLES:	HITS 2			WEEKS 5
SING	*ffrr*	47	*25 Jul 92*	4
BEWARE	*ffrr*	69	*31 Oct 92*	1

McKOY — UK

SINGLES:	HITS 1			WEEKS 2
FIGHT	*Rightrack*	54	*6 Mar 93*	2

Noel McKOY – See McKoy; James Taylor Quartet

Craig McLACHLAN — Australia

(See also Various Artists: Stage Cast – London 'Grease'.)

SINGLES:	HITS 8			WEEKS 40
MONA *Originally recorded by Bo Diddley.*	*Epic*	2	*16 Jun 90*	11
AMANDA	*Epic*	19	*4 Aug 90*	6
I ALMOST FELT LIKE CRYING *Above 3: Craig McLACHLAN and CHECK 1-2.*	*Epic*	50	*10 Nov 90*	3
ONE REASON WHY	*Epic*	29	*23 May 92*	6
ON MY OWN	*Columbia*	59	*14 Nov 92*	2
YOU'RE THE ONE THAT I WANT *Above hit: Craig McLACHLAN and Debbie GIBSON.*	*Epic*	13	*24 Jul 93*	6
GREASE *Above 2 from the show 'Grease'.*	*Epic*	44	*25 Dec 93*	4
EVERYDAY *Above hit: Craig McLACHLAN and the CULPRITS.*	*MDMC*	65	*8 Jul 95*	2

ALBUMS:	HITS 1			WEEKS 11
CRAIG MCLACHLAN AND CHECK 1-2 *Above hit: Craig McLACHLAN and CHECK 1-2.*	*Epic*	10	*21 Jul 90*	11

Sarah McLACHLAN — Canada

SINGLES:	HITS 2			WEEKS 21
ADIA	*Arista*	18	*3 Oct 98*	5
SILENCE [RM] *Original hit did not credit McLachlan.* *Above hit: DELERIUM featuring Sarah McLACHLAN.*	*Nettwerk*	3	*14 Oct 00*	16

ALBUMS:	HITS 1			WEEKS 2
SURFACING	*Arista*	47	*17 Oct 98*	2

Tommy McLAIN — US

SINGLES:	HITS 1			WEEKS 1
SWEET DREAMS *Originally recorded by Don Gibson.*	*London*	49	*10 Sep 66*	1

Malcolm McLAREN — UK

SINGLES:	HITS 11			WEEKS 66
BUFFALO GALS *Above hit: Malcolm McLAREN and the WORLD'S FAMOUS SUPREME TEAM.*	*Charisma*	9	*4 Dec 82*	12
SOWETO *Above hit: Malcolm McLAREN with the McLARENETTES.*	*Charisma*	32	*26 Feb 83*	5
DOUBLE DUTCH	*Charisma*	3	*2 Jul 83*	13
DUCK FOR THE OYSTER	*Charisma*	54	*17 Dec 83*	5
MADAM BUTTERFLY (UN BEL DI VEDREMO)	*Charisma*	13	*1 Sep 84*	9
WALTZ DARLING *Above hit: Malcolm McLAREN and the BOOTZILLA ORCHESTRA.*	*Epic*	31	*27 May 89*	8
SOMETHING'S JUMPIN' IN YOUR SHIRT *Sleeve credits Lisa Marie with Malcolm McLaren and the Bootzilla Orchestra.* *Above hit: Malcolm McLAREN and the BOOTZILLA ORCHESTRA.*	*Epic*	29	*19 Aug 89*	7
HOUSE OF THE BLUE DANUBE *Above hit: Malcolm McLAREN and the BOOTZILLA ORCHESTRA.*	*Epic*	73	*25 Nov 89*	1
OPERAA HOUSE *Above hit: Malcolm McLAREN presents the WORLD FAMOUS SUPREME TEAM SHOW.*	*Virgin*	75	*8 Dec 90*	1
MAGIC'S BACK (THEME FROM 'THE GHOSTS OF OXFORD STREET') *Theme from the Channel 4 TV programme.* *Above hit: Malcolm McLAREN featuring Alison LIMERICK.*	*RCA*	42	*21 Dec 91*	4
BUFFALO GALS STAMPEDE [RR] *Roger Sanchez remixed track 1 (as per CD order). Rakim appeared on track 2: Buffalo Gals (Back To Skool).* *Above hit: Malcolm McLAREN and the WORLD FAMOUS SUPREME TEAM versus RAKIM and Roger SANCHEZ.*	*Virgin*	65	*3 Oct 98*	1

ALBUMS:	HITS 5			WEEKS 41
DUCK ROCK	*Charisma*	18	*4 Jun 83*	17
WOULD YA LIKE MORE SCRATCHIN' *Above hit: Malcolm McLAREN and the WORLD'S FAMOUS SUPREME TEAM SHOW.*	*Charisma*	44	*26 May 84*	4
FANS	*Charisma*	47	*29 Dec 84*	8
WALTZ DARLING *Above hit: Malcolm McLAREN and the BOOTZILLA ORCHESTRA.*	*Epic*	30	*15 Jul 89*	11
PARIS	*No!*	44	*20 Aug 94*	1

McLARENETTES - See Malcolm McLAREN

Mahavishnu John McLAUGHLIN - See MAHAVISHNU ORCHESTRA; Carlos SANTANA and Mahavishnu John McLAUGHLIN

Bitty McLEAN — UK

SINGLES:	HITS 10			WEEKS 50
IT KEEPS RAININ' (TEARS FROM MY EYES)	*Brilliant*	2	*31 Jul 93*	15
PASS IT ON	*Brilliant*	35	*30 Oct 93*	3
Originally recorded by Bob Marley & The Wailers.				
HERE I STAND	*Brilliant*	10	*15 Jan 94*	6
Originally recorded by Wade Flemons.				
DEDICATED TO THE ONE I LOVE	*Brilliant*	6	*9 Apr 94*	10
Originally recorded by the Five Royales.				
WHAT GOES AROUND	*Brilliant*	36	*6 Aug 94*	3
OVER THE RIVER	*Brilliant*	27	*8 Apr 95*	4
Originally recorded by Justin Hinds.				
WE'VE ONLY JUST BEGUN	*Brilliant*	23	*17 Jun 95*	5
NOTHING CAN CHANGE THIS LOVE	*Brilliant*	55	*30 Sep 95*	2
Originally recorded by Sam Cooke reached No. 12 in the US in 1962.				
NATURAL HIGH	*Brilliant*	63	*27 Jan 96*	1
SHE'S ALRIGHT	*Kuff*	53	*5 Oct 96*	1
Originally recorded by Otis Redding in 1968.				

ALBUMS:	HITS 1			WEEKS 11
JUST TO LET YOU KNOW	*Brilliant*	19	*19 Feb 94*	11

Don McLEAN — US

SINGLES:	HITS 5			WEEKS 68
AMERICAN PIE	*United Artists*	2	*22 Jan 72*	16
Dedicated to Buddy Holly.				
VINCENT	*United Artists*	1	*13 May 72*	15
Dedicated to Vincent Van Gogh.				
EVERY DAY	*United Artists*	38	*14 Apr 73*	5
Originally recorded by Buddy Holly.				
CRYING	*EMI*	1	*10 May 80*	14
CASTLES IN THE AIR	*EMI*	47	*17 Apr 82*	8
New recording of a song first issued in 1972 as the B-side to Vincent.				
AMERICAN PIE [RI]	*Liberty*	12	*5 Oct 91*	10

ALBUMS:	HITS 6			WEEKS 92
AMERICAN PIE	*United Artists*	3	*11 Mar 72*	54
TAPESTRY	*United Artists*	16	*17 Jun 72*	12
PLAYIN' FAVORITES	*United Artists*	42	*24 Nov 73*	2
CHAIN LIGHTNING	*EMI International*	19	*14 Jun 80*	9
THE VERY BEST OF DON MCLEAN	*United Artists*	4	*27 Sep 80*	12
AMERICAN PIE - THE GREATEST HITS	*Capitol*	30	*15 Apr 00*	3

Jackie McLEAN — US

SINGLES:	HITS 1			WEEKS 4
DOCTOR JACKYLL AND MISTER FUNK	*RCA Victor*	53	*7 Jul 79*	4

Phil McLEAN — US

SINGLES:	HITS 1			WEEKS 4
SMALL SAD SAM	*Top Rank*	34	*20 Jan 62*	4
A parody of Big Bad John.				

Andy McNAB — UK

ALBUMS:	HITS 1			WEEKS 2
BRAVO TWO ZERO	*PolyGram TV*	45	*21 May 94*	2

Ian McNABB — UK

SINGLES:	HITS 5			WEEKS 6
IF LOVE WAS LIKE GUITARS	*This Way Up*	67	*23 Jan 93*	1
YOU MUST BE PREPARED TO DREAM	*This Way Up*	54	*2 Jul 94*	1
Above hit: Ian McNABB featuring Ralph MOLINA and Billy TALBOT of CRAZY HORSE with Mike 'Tone' HAMILTON - Rhythm guitar.				
GO INTO THE LIGHT	*This Way Up*	66	*17 Sep 94*	2
DON'T PUT YOUR SPELL ON ME	*This Way Up*	72	*27 Apr 96*	1
MERSEYBEAST	*This Way Up*	74	*6 Jul 96*	1

ALBUMS:	HITS 3			WEEKS 5
TRUTH AND BEAUTY	*This Way Up*	51	*30 Jan 93*	1
HEAD LIKE A ROCK	*This Way Up*	29	*16 Jul 94*	2
MERSEYBEAST	*This Way Up*	30	*18 May 96*	2

Lutricia McNEAL — US

SINGLES:	HITS 4			WEEKS 43
AIN'T THAT JUST THE WAY	*Wildstar*	6	*29 Nov 97*	18
Originally recorded by 1970s porn star Barbie Benton.				
STRANDED	*Wildstar*	3	*23 May 98*	12

SOMEONE LOVES YOU HONEY *Originally recorded by Brenda Lee.*	*Wildstar*	9	*26 Sep 98*	7
THE GREATEST LOVE YOU'LL NEVER KNOW	*Wildstar*	17	*19 Dec 98*	6
ALBUMS:	**HITS 1**			**WEEKS 16**
LUTRICIA MCNEAL	*Wildstar*	16	*25 Jul 98*	16

Patrick MacNEE and Honor BLACKMAN — UK

SINGLES:	**HITS 1**			**WEEKS 7**
KINKY BOOTS *Originally recorded in 1964; it charted after being championed by Simon Mayo's Radio 1 breakfast show.*	*Deram*	5	*1 Dec 90*	7

Rita MacNEIL — Canada

SINGLES:	**HITS 1**			**WEEKS 10**
WORKING MAN	*Polydor*	11	*6 Oct 90*	10
ALBUMS:	**HITS 1**			**WEEKS 4**
REASON TO BELIEVE	*Polydor*	32	*24 Nov 90*	4

Clyde McPHATTER — US

SINGLES:	**HITS 1**			**WEEKS 1**
TREASURE OF LOVE	*London*	27	*25 Aug 56*	1

Carmen McRAE - See Sammy DAVIS JR

Ian McSHANE — UK

ALBUMS:	**HITS 1**			**WEEKS 7**
FROM BOTH SIDES NOW	*PolyGram TV*	40	*21 Nov 92*	7

Ralph McTELL — UK

SINGLES:	**HITS 2**			**WEEKS 18**
STREETS OF LONDON	*Reprise*	2	*7 Dec 74*	12
DREAMS OF YOU	*Warner Brothers*	36	*20 Dec 75*	6
ALBUMS:	**HITS 3**			**WEEKS 17**
NOT TILL TOMORROW	*Reprise*	36	*18 Nov 72*	1
EASY	*Reprise*	31	*2 Mar 74*	4
STREETS	*Warner Brothers*	13	*15 Feb 75*	12

Christine McVIE — US

ALBUMS:	**HITS 1**			**WEEKS 4**
CHRISTINE MCVIE	*Warner Brothers*	58	*11 Feb 84*	4

David McWILLIAMS — UK

ALBUMS:	**HITS 3**			**WEEKS 9**
DAVID MCWILLIAMS SINGS	*Major Minor*	38	*10 Jun 67*	2
DAVID MCWILLIAMS VOLUME 2	*Major Minor*	23	*4 Nov 67*	6
DAVID MCWILLIAMS VOLUME 3	*Major Minor*	39	*9 Mar 68*	1

MAD COBRA featuring Richie STEPHENS — UK/Jamaica

SINGLES:	**HITS 1**			**WEEKS 1**
LEGACY	*Columbia*	64	*15 May 93*	1

MAD JOCKS featuring JOCKMASTER B.A. — UK

SINGLES:	**HITS 2**			**WEEKS 9**
JOCK MIX 1 [M]	*Debut*	46	*19 Dec 87*	5
PARTY FOUR [EP] *Lead track: No Lager, which was listed on the charts for 18 & 25 Dec 93.*	*SMP*	57	*18 Dec 93*	4

MAD MOSES — US

SINGLES:	**HITS 1**			**WEEKS 1**
PANTHER PARTY *Vocals by Bobby McFerrin.*	*Hi-Life*	50	*16 Aug 97*	1

MAD SEASON — UK

ALBUMS:	**HITS 1**			**WEEKS 1**
ABOVE	*Columbia*	41	*25 Mar 95*	1

MAD STUNTMAN - See REEL 2 REAL featuring the MAD STUNTMAN

Sonya MADAN - See LITHIUM and Sonya MADAN

MADASUN — UK

SINGLES:	HITS 3			WEEKS 13
DON'T YOU WORRY	V2	14	11 Mar 00	6
WALKING ON WATER	V2	14	27 May 00	4
FEEL GOOD	V2	29	2 Sep 00	3

Danny MADDEN — US

SINGLES:	HITS 1			WEEKS 2
THE FACTS OF LIFE	Eternal	72	14 Jul 90	2

MADDER ROSE — US

SINGLES:	HITS 2			WEEKS 2
PANIC ON	Atlantic	65	26 Mar 94	1
CAR SONG	Atlantic	68	16 Jul 94	1
ALBUMS:	**HITS 1**			**WEEKS 2**
PANIC ON	Atlantic	52	9 Apr 94	2

MADDOG – See STRETCH and VERN Present "MADDOG"

MADE IN LONDON — UK/Norway

SINGLES:	HITS 2			WEEKS 6
DIRTY WATER	RCA	15	13 May 00	5
SHUT YOUR MOUTH	RCA	74	9 Sep 00	1

MADEMOISELLE — France

SINGLES:	HITS 1			WEEKS 1
DO YOU LOVE ME?	RCA	56	8 Sep 01	1

MADISON AVENUE — Australia

SINGLES:	HITS 3			WEEKS 25
DON'T CALL ME BABY	VC Recordings	30	13 Nov 99	4
Samples Pino D'Anglo's version of the song.				
DON'T CALL ME BABY [RE-1ST]	VC Recordings	74	29 Jan 00	1
DON'T CALL ME BABY [RE-2ND]	VC Recordings	70	19 Feb 00	1
DON'T CALL ME BABY [RI]	VC Recordings	1	20 May 00	12
WHO THE HELL ARE YOU	VC Recordings	10	21 Oct 00	5
EVERYTHING YOU NEED	VC Recordings	33	27 Jan 01	2
ALBUMS:	**HITS 1**			**WEEKS 1**
THE POLYESTER EMBASSY	VC Recordings	74	4 Nov 00	1

MADNESS — UK

(See also Various Artists (EPs) 'The 2 Tone EP'.)

SINGLES:	HITS 28			WEEKS 268
THE PRINCE	2-Tone	16	1 Sep 79	11
ONE STEP BEYOND . . .	Stiff	7	10 Nov 79	14
Originally recorded by Prince Buster and the All-stars				
MY GIRL	Stiff	3	5 Jan 80	10
WORK REST AND PLAY [EP]	Stiff	6	5 Apr 80	8
Lead track: Night Boat To Cairo.				
BAGGY TROUSERS	Stiff	3	13 Sep 80	20
EMBARRASSMENT	Stiff	4	22 Nov 80	12
THE RETURN OF THE LOS PALMAS 7	Stiff	7	24 Jan 81	11
GREY DAY	Stiff	4	25 Apr 81	10
SHUT UP	Stiff	7	26 Sep 81	9
IT MUST BE LOVE	Stiff	4	5 Dec 81	12
CARDIAC ARREST	Stiff	14	20 Feb 82	10
HOUSE OF FUN	Stiff	1	22 May 82	9
DRIVING IN MY CAR	Stiff	4	24 Jul 82	8
OUR HOUSE	Stiff	5	27 Nov 82	13
TOMORROW'S (JUST ANOTHER DAY) / MADNESS IS ALL IN THE MIND	Stiff	8	19 Feb 83	9
WINGS OF A DOVE	Stiff	2	20 Aug 83	10
THE SUN AND THE RAIN	Stiff	5	5 Nov 83	10
MICHAEL CAINE	Stiff	11	11 Feb 84	8
ONE BETTER DAY	Stiff	17	2 Jun 84	7
YESTERDAY'S MEN	Zarjazz	18	31 Aug 85	7
UNCLE SAM	Zarjazz	21	26 Oct 85	11
SWEETEST GIRL	Zarjazz	35	1 Feb 86	6
(WAITING FOR) THE GHOST TRAIN	Zarjazz	18	8 Nov 86	7
(WAITING FOR) THE GHOST TRAIN [RE]	Zarjazz	74	3 Jan 87	1
I PRONOUNCE YOU	Virgin	44	19 Mar 88	4
Above hit: The MADNESS.				
IT MUST BE LOVE [RI]	Virgin	6	15 Feb 92	9
HOUSE OF FUN [RI]	Virgin	40	25 Apr 92	3
MY GIRL [RI]	Virgin	27	8 Aug 92	4

THE HARDER THEY COME	*Go! Discs*	44	*28 Nov 92*	3
NIGHT BOAT TO CAIRO [RI]	*Virgin*	56	*27 Feb 93*	2
Re-issue of track from the Work Rest And Play EP.				
LOVESTRUCK	*Virgin*	10	*31 Jul 99*	7
JOHNNY THE HORSE	*Virgin*	44	*6 Nov 99*	2
DRIP FED FRED	*Virgin*	55	*11 Mar 00*	1
The campaign theme for London Mayoral candidate Fredrick C. Threwe.				
Above hit: MADNESS featuring Ian DURY.				
ALBUMS:	**HITS 13**			**WEEKS 412**
ONE STEP BEYOND . . .	*Stiff*	2	*3 Nov 79*	78
ABSOLUTELY	*Stiff*	2	*4 Oct 80*	46
MADNESS 7	*Stiff*	5	*10 Oct 81*	29
COMPLETE MADNESS	*Stiff*	1	*1 May 82*	88
Compilation.				
MADNESS PRESENTS THE RISE AND FALL	*Stiff*	10	*13 Nov 82*	22
KEEP MOVING	*Stiff*	6	*3 Mar 84*	19
MAD NOT MAD	*Zarjazz*	16	*12 Oct 85*	9
UTTER MADNESS	*Zarjazz*	29	*6 Dec 86*	8
Compilation.				
THE MADNESS	*Virgin*	65	*7 May 88*	1
Above hit: The MADNESS.				
DIVINE MADNESS	*Virgin*	1	*7 Mar 92*	96
Compilation.				
MADSTOCK!	*Go! Discs*	22	*14 Nov 92*	9
Live recordings.				
THE HEAVY HEAVY HITS	*Virgin*	19	*13 Jun 98*	5
Repackage of Divine Madness with additional track The Harder They Come.				
WONDERFUL	*Virgin*	17	*13 Nov 99*	2
DIVINE MADNESS [RE]	*Virgin*	59	*17 Jun 00*	3
Digitally remastered with 2 additional tracks.				

MADONNA US

(See also Various Artists: Films – Original Soundtracks 'Who's That Girl'.)

SINGLES:	**HITS 53**			**WEEKS 568**
HOLIDAY	*Sire*	6	*14 Jan 84*	11
LUCKY STAR	*Sire*	14	*17 Mar 84*	9
BORDERLINE	*Sire*	56	*2 Jun 84*	4
LIKE A VIRGIN	*Sire*	3	*17 Nov 84*	18
MATERIAL GIRL	*Sire*	3	*2 Mar 85*	10
CRAZY FOR YOU	*Geffen*	2	*8 Jun 85*	15
From the film 'Vision Quest'.				
INTO THE GROOVE	*Sire*	1	*27 Jul 85*	14
From the film 'Desperately Seeking Susan'.				
HOLIDAY [RE]	*Sire*	2	*3 Aug 85*	10
ANGEL	*Sire*	5	*21 Sep 85*	9
GAMBLER	*Geffen*	4	*12 Oct 85*	11
From the film 'Vision Quest'.				
DRESS YOU UP	*Sire*	5	*7 Dec 85*	11
GAMBLER [RE]	*Geffen*	61	*4 Jan 86*	1
BORDERLINE [RE]	*Sire*	2	*25 Jan 86*	9
LIVE TO TELL	*Sire*	2	*26 Apr 86*	12
From the film 'Shanghai Surprise'.				
PAPA DON'T PREACH	*Sire*	1	*28 Jun 86*	14
TRUE BLUE	*Sire*	1	*4 Oct 86*	15
OPEN YOUR HEART	*Sire*	4	*13 Dec 86*	9
LA ISLA BONITA	*Sire*	1	*4 Apr 87*	11
WHO'S THAT GIRL	*Sire*	1	*18 Jul 87*	10
CAUSING A COMMOTION	*Sire*	4	*19 Sep 87*	9
THE LOOK OF LOVE	*Sire*	9	*12 Dec 87*	7
Above 3 from the film 'Who's That Girl'.				
LIKE A PRAYER	*Sire*	1	*18 Mar 89*	12
EXPRESS YOURSELF	*Sire*	5	*3 Jun 89*	10
CHERISH	*Sire*	3	*16 Sep 89*	8
DEAR JESSIE	*Sire*	5	*16 Dec 89*	9
VOGUE	*Sire*	1	*7 Apr 90*	14
HANKY PANKY	*Sire*	2	*21 Jul 90*	9
JUSTIFY MY LOVE	*Sire*	2	*8 Dec 90*	10
Co-written by Lenny Kravitz.				
CRAZY FOR YOU [RM]	*Sire*	2	*2 Mar 91*	8
Mixed by Shep Pettibone and Michael Hutchinson.				
RESCUE ME	*Sire*	3	*13 Apr 91*	8
HOLIDAY [RI]	*Sire*	5	*8 Jun 91*	7
THIS USED TO BE MY PLAYGROUND	*Sire*	3	*25 Jul 92*	9
EROTICA	*Maverick*	3	*17 Oct 92*	8
Samples Jungle Boogie by Kool and the Gang.				
DEEPER AND DEEPER	*Maverick*	6	*12 Dec 92*	9
EROTICA [RE]	*Maverick*	65	*9 Jan 93*	1

BAD GIRL	*Maverick*	10	*6 Mar 93*	7
FEVER	*Maverick*	6	*3 Apr 93*	6
RAIN	*Maverick*	7	*31 Jul 93*	8
I'LL REMEMBER (THEME FROM 'WITH HONOURS')	*Maverick*	7	*2 Apr 94*	8
From the film 'With Honors'.				
SECRET	*Maverick*	5	*8 Oct 94*	9
TAKE A BOW	*Maverick*	16	*17 Dec 94*	9
Backing vocals by Babyface.				
BEDTIME STORY	*Maverick*	4	*25 Feb 95*	8
Samples What You Need by Main Source.				
BEDTIME STORY [RE]	*Maverick*	66	*6 May 95*	1
HUMAN NATURE	*Maverick*	8	*26 Aug 95*	5
YOU'LL SEE	*Maverick*	5	*4 Nov 95*	13
OH FATHER	*Maverick*	16	*6 Jan 96*	6
From the 1989 album Like A Prayer.				
ONE MORE CHANCE	*Maverick*	11	*23 Mar 96*	4
YOU MUST LOVE ME	*Warner Brothers*	10	*2 Nov 96*	4
DON'T CRY FOR ME ARGENTINA	*Warner Brothers*	3	*28 Dec 96*	12
YOU MUST LOVE ME [RE-1ST]	*Warner Brothers*	75	*4 Jan 97*	1
YOU MUST LOVE ME [RE-2ND]	*Warner Brothers*	71	*18 Jan 97*	1
ANOTHER SUITCASE IN ANOTHER HALL	*Warner Brothers*	7	*29 Mar 97*	5
Above 3 hits from the film 'Evita'.				
FROZEN	*Maverick*	1	*7 Mar 98*	13
RAY OF LIGHT	*Maverick*	2	*9 May 98*	9
RAY OF LIGHT [RE]	*Maverick*	75	*18 Jul 98*	1
DROWNDED WORLD / SUBSTITUTE FOR LOVE	*Maverick*	10	*5 Sep 98*	5
THE POWER OF GOOD-BYE / LITTLE STAR	*Maverick*	6	*5 Dec 98*	9
NOTHING REALLY MATTERS	*Maverick*	7	*13 Mar 99*	8
NOTHING REALLY MATTERS [RE]	*Maverick*	75	*5 Jun 99*	1
BEAUTIFUL STRANGER	*Maverick*	2	*19 Jun 99*	16
From the film 'Austin Powers – The Spy Who Shagged Me'.				
AMERICAN PIE	*Maverick*	1	*11 Mar 00*	12
From the film 'The Next Best Thing'.				
AMERICAN PIE [RE]	*Maverick*	68	*17 Jun 00*	2
MUSIC	*Maverick*	1	*2 Sep 00*	23
DON'T TELL ME	*Maverick*	4	*9 Dec 00*	10
WHAT IT FEELS LIKE FOR A GIRL	*Maverick*	7	*28 Apr 01*	9
WHAT IT FEELS LIKE FOR A GIRL [RE]	*Maverick*	66	*14 Jul 01*	2

ALBUMS:	**HITS 14**			**WEEKS 947**
MADONNA	*Sire*	37	*11 Feb 84*	22
LIKE A VIRGIN	*Sire*	1	*24 Nov 84*	152
Repackaged from 10 Aug 95 with additional track. Peak position reached on 21 Sep 85. Includes re-entries through to 1990.				
MADONNA / THE FIRST ALBUM [RE]	*Sire*	6	*27 Jul 85*	101
Repackaged as The First Album from 14 Sep 85.				
TRUE BLUE	*Sire*	1	*12 Jul 86*	81
YOU CAN DANCE	*Sire*	5	*28 Nov 87*	16
Album of dance remixes.				
LIKE A PRAYER	*Sire*	1	*1 Apr 89*	65
I'M BREATHLESS	*Sire*	2	*2 Jun 90*	20
THE IMMACULATE COLLECTION	*Sire*	1	*24 Nov 90*	166
Includes re-entries through to 2000.				
EROTICA	*Maverick*	2	*24 Oct 92*	38
LIKE A PRAYER [RE]	*Sire*	32	*2 Apr 94*	5
Re-released at mid-price. Peak position reached in 1995 (1994 peak No. 58).				
TRUE BLUE [RE]	*Sire*	39	*9 Apr 94*	4
Re-released at mid-price. Peak position reached in 1995 (1994 peak No. 65).				
BEDTIME STORIES	*Maverick*	2	*5 Nov 94*	27
SOMETHING TO REMEMBER	*Maverick*	3	*18 Nov 95*	29
Compilation of ballads plus 3 new songs.				
EVITA [OST]	*Warner Brothers*	1	*9 Nov 96*	36
Madonna sings on 15 of the album's 19 tracks.				
Above hit: MADONNA and VARIOUS ARTISTS.				
RAY OF LIGHT	*Maverick*	1	*14 Mar 98*	110
MUSIC	*Maverick*	1	*30 Sep 00*	49
THE IMMACULATE COLLECTION [RE]	*Sire*	21	*6 Jan 01*	20
GHV2: GREATEST HITS VOLUME 2 – THE BEST SONGS OF A DECADE	*Maverick*	2	*24 Nov 01*	6

Lisa MAFFIA – See OXIDE and NEUTRINO

MAGAZINE — UK

SINGLES:	**HITS 2**			**WEEKS 7**
SHOT BY BOTH SIDES	*Virgin*	41	*11 Feb 78*	4
SWEET HEART CONTRACT	*Virgin*	54	*26 Jul 80*	3

ALBUMS:	**HITS 5**			**WEEKS 24**
REAL LIFE	*Virgin*	29	*24 Jun 78*	8
SECONDHAND DAYLIGHT	*Virgin*	38	*14 Apr 79*	8
CORRECT USE OF SOAP	*Virgin*	28	*10 May 80*	4

PLAY	*Virgin*	69	*13 Dec 80*	1
MAGIC, MURDER AND THE WEATHER	*Virgin*	39	*27 Jun 81*	3

MAGIC AFFAIR — US/Germany

SINGLES:	HITS 3			WEEKS 8
OMEN III	*EMI*	17	*4 Jun 94*	4
Vocal by Franco Morgano.				
GIVE ME ALL YOUR LOVE	*EMI*	30	*27 Aug 94*	2
IN THE MIDDLE OF THE NIGHT	*EMI*	38	*5 Nov 94*	2

MAGIC BAND – See CAPTAIN BEEFHEART and his MAGIC BAND

MAGIC LADY — US

SINGLES:	HITS 1			WEEKS 3
BETCHA CAN'T LOSE (WITH MY LOVE)	*Motown*	58	*14 May 88*	3

MAGIC LANTERNS — UK

SINGLES:	HITS 1			WEEKS 3
EXCUSE ME BABY	*CBS*	46	*9 Jul 66*	1
EXCUSE ME BABY [RE-1ST]	*CBS*	44	*30 Jul 66*	1
EXCUSE ME BABY [RE-2ND]	*CBS*	46	*13 Aug 66*	1

MAGNA CARTA — UK

ALBUMS:	HITS 1			WEEKS 2
SEASONS	*Vertigo*	55	*8 Aug 70*	2

MAGNUM — UK

SINGLES:	HITS 7			WEEKS 26
MAGNUM LIVE [EP]	*Jet*	47	*22 Mar 80*	6
Double single, lead track: Invasion (Live).				
LONELY NIGHT	*Polydor*	70	*12 Jul 86*	2
DAYS OF NO TRUST	*Polydor*	32	*19 Mar 88*	4
START TALKING LOVE	*Polydor*	22	*7 May 88*	4
IT MUST HAVE BEEN LOVE	*Polydor*	33	*2 Jul 88*	4
ROCKIN' CHAIR	*Polydor*	27	*23 Jun 90*	4
HEARTBROKE AND BUSTED	*Polydor*	49	*25 Aug 90*	2
ALBUMS:	**HITS 11**			**WEEKS 47**
KINGDOM OF MADNESS	*Jet*	58	*16 Sep 78*	1
MARAUDER	*Jet*	34	*19 Apr 80*	5
CHASE THE DRAGON	*Jet*	17	*6 Mar 82*	7
THE ELEVENTH HOUR	*Jet*	38	*21 May 83*	4
ON A STORYTELLER'S NIGHT	*FM*	24	*25 May 85*	7
VIGILANTE	*Polydor*	24	*4 Oct 86*	5
WINGS OF HEAVEN	*Polydor*	5	*9 Apr 88*	9
GOODNIGHT L.A.	*Polydor*	9	*21 Jul 90*	5
THE SPIRIT	*Polydor*	50	*14 Sep 91*	1
SLEEPWALKING	*Music For Nations*	27	*24 Oct 92*	2
ROCK ART	*EMI*	57	*18 Jun 94*	1

MAGOO — UK

SINGLES:	HITS 1			WEEKS 1
BLACK SABBATH	*Fierce Panda*	60	*4 Apr 98*	1
[AA] listed with Sweet Leaf by Mogwai.				

MAGOO – See Missy "Misdemeanor" ELLIOTT; TIMBALAND

Sean MAGUIRE — UK

SINGLES:	HITS 8			WEEKS 34
SOMEONE TO LOVE	*Parlophone*	14	*20 Aug 94*	7
TAKE THIS TIME	*Parlophone*	27	*5 Nov 94*	4
TAKE THIS TIME [RE]	*Parlophone*	74	*31 Dec 94*	1
SUDDENLY	*Parlophone*	18	*25 Mar 95*	5
NOW I'VE FOUND YOU	*Parlophone*	22	*24 Jun 95*	3
YOU TO ME ARE EVERYTHING	*Parlophone*	16	*18 Nov 95*	3
GOOD DAY	*Parlophone*	12	*25 May 96*	4
DON'T PULL YOUR LOVE	*Parlophone*	14	*3 Aug 96*	4
Originally recorded by Hamilton, Joe Frank and Reynolds reached No. 4 in the US in 1971.				
TODAY'S THE DAY	*Parlophone*	27	*29 Mar 97*	3
ALBUMS:	**HITS 2**			**WEEKS 3**
SEAN MAGUIRE	*Parlophone*	75	*26 Nov 94*	1
SPIRIT	*Parlophone*	43	*15 Jun 96*	2

MAHAVISHNU ORCHESTRA — UK

(See also Carlos Santana and Mahavishnu John McLaughlin.)

ALBUMS:	HITS 1			WEEKS 5
BIRDS OF FIRE	*CBS*	20	*31 Mar 73*	5

Siobhan MAHER – See OCEANIC

MAHLATHINI and the MAHOTELLA QUEENS – See ART OF NOISE

MAI TAI — Holland

SINGLES:	HITS 3			WEEKS 30
HISTORY	*Hot Melt*	8	*25 May 85*	13
BODY AND SOUL	*Hot Melt*	9	*3 Aug 85*	13
FEMALE INTUITION	*Hot Melt*	54	*15 Feb 86*	4
ALBUMS:	**HITS 1**			**WEEKS 1**
HISTORY	*Hot Melt*	91	*6 Jul 85*	1

MAIN INGREDIENT — US

SINGLES:	HITS 1			WEEKS 7
JUST DON'T WANT TO BE LONELY *Originally recorded by Ronnie Dyson.*	*RCA Victor*	27	*29 Jun 74*	7

MAIRANTS-LANGHORN BIG SIX – See Don LANG

MAISONETTES – See BELLE AND SEBASTIAN

MAISONETTES — UK

SINGLES:	HITS 1			WEEKS 12
HEARTACHE AVENUE	*Ready Steady Go!*	7	*11 Dec 82*	12

Raven MAIZE — UK

SINGLES:	HITS 2			WEEKS 7
FOREVER TOGETHER	*Republic*	67	*5 Aug 89*	1
THE REAL LIFE *Originally recorded by Corporation of One in 1989.*	*Rulin*	12	*18 Aug 01*	5
THE REAL LIFE [RE]	*Rulin*	60	*29 Sep 01*	1

MAJESTICS — UK

ALBUMS:	HITS 1			WEEKS 4
TUTTI FRUTTI	*BBC*	64	*4 Apr 87*	4

J. MAJIK featuring Kathy BROWN — UK/US

(See also Kathy Brown.)

SINGLES:	HITS 1			WEEKS 2
LOVE IS NOT A GAME	*Defected*	34	*5 May 01*	2

MAJORITY – See Barry RYAN

MAKADOPOULOS and his GREEK SERENADERS — Greece

SINGLES:	HITS 1			WEEKS 14
NEVER ON SUNDAY (JAMAIS LE DIMANCHE) *From the film of the same name.*	*Palette*	36	*22 Oct 60*	14

MAKAVELI – See 2PAC

Tommy MAKEM – See CLANCY BROTHERS and Tommy MAKEM

Jack E. MAKOSSA — Kenya

SINGLES:	HITS 1			WEEKS 5
THE OPERA HOUSE	*Champion*	48	*12 Sep 87*	5

MALA – See BOWA featuring MALA

MALAIKA — US

SINGLES:	HITS 1			WEEKS 1
GOTTA KNOW (YOUR NAME)	*A&M*	68	*31 Jul 93*	1

Carl MALCOLM — Jamaica

SINGLES:	HITS 1			WEEKS 8
FATTIE BUM BUM	*UK*	8	*13 Sep 75*	8

Valerie MALCOLM – See CANDY GIRLS

Stephen MALKMUS — US

SINGLES:	HITS 1			WEEKS 1
DISCRETION GROVE	*Domino Recordings*	60	*28 Apr 01*	1

ALBUMS:	HITS 1			WEEKS 1
STEPHEN MALKMUS	*Domino Recordings*	49	*24 Feb 01*	1

Timmy MALLETT - See BOMBALURINA

Yngwie J. MALMSTEEN — Sweden

ALBUMS:	HITS 4			WEEKS 11
ODYSSEY	*Polydor*	27	*21 May 88*	7
TRIAL BY FIRE - LIVE IN LENINGRAD	*Polydor*	65	*4 Nov 89*	1
ECLIPSE	*Polydor*	43	*28 Apr 90*	2
FIRE AND ICE	*Elektra*	57	*29 Feb 92*	1

Artie MALVERN SINGERS - See Pat BOONE

MAMA CASS — US

(See also Mamas and the Papas.)

SINGLES:	HITS 2			WEEKS 27
DREAM A LITTLE DREAM OF ME	*RCA Victor*	11	*17 Aug 68*	12
Originally recorded by Wayne King in 1931.				
Above hit: MAMA CASS with the MAMAS and PAPAS.				
IT'S GETTING BETTER	*Stateside*	8	*16 Aug 69*	15
Originally recorded by Paul Jones in 1967.				

MAMA'S BOYS — Ireland

ALBUMS:	HITS 1			WEEKS 4
POWER AND PASSION	*Jive*	55	*6 Apr 85*	4

MAMAS and the PAPAS — US/Canada

(See also Mama Cass.)

SINGLES:	HITS 6			WEEKS 71
CALIFORNIA DREAMIN'	*RCA Victor*	23	*30 Apr 66*	9
Originally recorded by Barry McGuire.				
MONDAY MONDAY	*RCA Victor*	3	*14 May 66*	13
I SAW HERE AGAIN	*RCA Victor*	11	*30 Jul 66*	11
WORDS OF LOVE	*RCA Victor*	47	*11 Feb 67*	3
DEDICATED TO THE ONE I LOVE	*RCA Victor*	2	*8 Apr 67*	17
Originally recorded by the Five Royales.				
CREEQUE ALLEY	*RCA Victor*	9	*29 Jul 67*	11
CALIFORNIA DREAMIN [RI]	*MCA*	9	*2 Aug 97*	7
Featured in the Carling Premier TV commercial.				

ALBUMS:	HITS 7			WEEKS 71
IF YOU CAN BELIEVE YOUR EYES AND EARS	*RCA Victor*	3	*25 Jun 66*	18
CASS, JOHN, MICHELLE, DENNY	*RCA Victor*	24	*28 Jan 67*	6
MAMAS AND PAPAS DELIVER	*RCA Victor*	4	*24 Jun 67*	22
HITS OF GOLD	*Stateside*	7	*26 Apr 69*	2
THE BEST OF THE MAMAS AND PAPAS	*Arcade*	6	*18 Jun 77*	13
CALIFORNIA DREAMIN' - THE VERY BEST OF THE MAMAS AND THE PAPAS	*PolyGram TV*	14	*28 Jan 95*	6
CALIFORNIA DREAMIN' - GREATEST HITS OF THE MAMAS AND THE PAPAS	*Telstar TV*	30	*6 Sep 97*	4
Repackaged version of the previous hits collection.				

MAMMOTH CAVE - See Stan FREBERG

MAN — UK

ALBUMS:	HITS 4			WEEKS 11
BACK INTO THE FUTURE	*United Artists*	23	*20 Oct 73*	3
RHINOS WINOS AND LUNATICS	*United Artists*	24	*25 May 74*	4
MAXIMUM DARKNESS	*United Artists*	25	*11 Oct 75*	2
WELSH CONNECTION	*MCA*	40	*17 Apr 76*	2

A MAN CALLED ADAM — UK

SINGLES:	HITS 1			WEEKS 4
BAREFOOT IN THE HEAD	*Big Life*	70	*29 Sep 90*	2
BAREFOOT IN THE HEAD [RE]	*Big Life*	60	*20 Oct 90*	2

MANCHILD — UK

SINGLES:	HITS 2			WEEKS 2
THE CLICHES ARE TRUE	*One Little Indian*	60	*16 Sep 00*	1
Above hit: MANCHILD featuring Kelly JONES.				
NOTHING WITHOUT ME	*One Little Indian*	40	*25 Aug 01*	1

MAN TO MAN — US

SINGLES:	HITS 2			WEEKS 19
MALE STRIPPER	*Bolts*	64	*13 Sep 86*	3
Above hit: MAN 2 MAN Meet Man PARRISH.				

MALE STRIPPER [RE-1ST]	*Bolts*	63	*3 Jan 87*	1
MALE STRIPPER [RE-2ND]	*Bolts*	4	*7 Feb 87*	12
I NEED A MAN / ENERGY IS EUROBEAT	*Bolts*	43	*4 Jul 87*	3

MAN WITH NO NAME — UK

SINGLES:	HITS 5			WEEKS 6
FLOOR-ESSENCE	*Perfecto*	68	*30 Sep 95*	1
PAINT A PICTURE	*Perfecto*	42	*20 Jan 96*	2
Above hit: MAN WITH NO NAME featuring HANNAH.				
TELEPORT / SUGAR RUSH	*Perfecto*	55	*12 Oct 96*	1
VAVOOM!	*Perfecto*	43	*2 May 98*	1
THE FIRST DAY (HORIZON)	*Perfecto Fluoro*	72	*18 Jul 98*	1

Melissa MANCHESTER and Al JARREAU — US

(See also Al Jarreau.)

SINGLES:	HITS 1			WEEKS 1
THE MUSIC OF GOODBYE (LOVE THEME FROM OUT OF AFRICA)	*MCA*	75	*5 Apr 86*	1
From the film.				

MANCHESTER BOYS CHOIR — UK

ALBUMS:	HITS 1			WEEKS 2
THE NEW SOUND OF CHRISTMAS	*K-Tel*	80	*21 Dec 85*	2

MANCHESTER UNITED FOOTBALL SQUAD — UK

SINGLES:	HITS 8			WEEKS 56
MANCHESTER UNITED	*Decca*	50	*8 May 76*	1
GLORY GLORY MAN. UNITED	*EMI*	13	*21 May 83*	5
Above 2: MANCHESTER UNITED FOOTBALL CLUB.				
WE ALL FOLLOW MAN. UNITED	*Columbia*	10	*18 May 85*	5
Above hit: MANCHESTER UNITED FOOTBALL TEAM.				
UNITED (WE LOVE YOU)	*Living Beat*	37	*19 Jun 93*	2
Above hit: MANCHESTER UNITED and the CHAMPIONS.				
COME ON YOU REDS	*PolyGram TV*	1	*30 Apr 94*	15
Based on Status Quo's Burning Bridges.				
WE'RE GONNA DO IT AGAIN	*PolyGram TV*	6	*13 May 95*	6
Based on Status Quo's Again And Again.				
Above hit: MANCHESTER UNITED 1995 FOOTBALL SQUAD featuring STRYKER.				
MOVE MOVE MOVE (THE RED TRIBE)	*Music Collection*	6	*4 May 96*	11
Above hit: 1996 MANCHESTER UNITED F.A. CUP SQUAD.				
MOVE MOVE MOVE (THE RED TRIBE) [RE]	*Music Collection*	30	*3 Aug 96*	4
LIFT IT HIGH (ALL ABOUT BELIEF)	*Music Collection*	11	*29 May 99*	6
Above hit: 1999 MANCHESTER UNITED SQUAD.				
LIFT IT HIGH (ALL ABOUT BELIEF) [RE]	*Music Collection*	75	*21 Aug 99*	1

Henry MANCINI and his Orchestra — US

(See also James Galway and Henry Mancini with the National Philharmonic Orchestra; Johnny Mathis and Henry Mancini; Luciano Pavarotti.)

SINGLES:	HITS 4			WEEKS 23
MOON RIVER	*RCA*	46	*9 Dec 61*	2
MOON RIVER [RE]	*RCA*	44	*30 Dec 61*	1
HOW SOON	*RCA Victor*	10	*26 Sep 64*	12
Theme from 'The Richard Boone Show'.				
THEME FROM 'CADE'S COUNTY'	*RCA Victor*	42	*25 Mar 72*	1
THE THORN BIRDS THEME	*Warner Brothers*	23	*11 Feb 84*	7
Theme from the BBC1 TV series.				

EPS:	HITS 1			WEEKS 10
THE PINK PANTHER	*RCA Victor*	14	*18 Apr 64*	10

ALBUMS:	HITS 1			WEEKS 8
HENRY MANCINI	*Arcade*	26	*16 Oct 76*	8

Steve MANDELL – See 'DELIVERANCE' SOUNDTRACK

MANFRED MANN — UK/South Africa

SINGLES:	HITS 22			WEEKS 217
5-4-3-2-1	*His Master's Voice*	5	*25 Jan 64*	13
HUBBLE BUBBLE (TOIL AND TROUBLE)	*His Master's Voice*	11	*18 Apr 64*	8
DO WAH DIDDY DIDDY	*His Master's Voice*	1	*18 Jul 64*	14
Originally recorded by the Exciters in 1961.				
SHA LA LA	*His Master's Voice*	3	*17 Oct 64*	12
Originally recorded by the Shirelles.				
COME TOMORROW	*His Master's Voice*	4	*16 Jan 65*	9
Originally recorded by Marie Knight.				
Above hit: MANFRED MANN; Vocal: Paul JONES.				

OH NO NOT MY BABY *Originally recorded by The Shirelles.*	*His Master's Voice*	11	*17 Apr 65*	10
IF YOU GOTTA GO, GO NOW *Originally recorded by Bob Dylan.*	*His Master's Voice*	2	*18 Sep 65*	12
PRETTY FLAMINGO	*His Master's Voice*	1	*23 Apr 66*	12
YOU GAVE ME SOMEBODY TO LOVE	*His Master's Voice*	36	*9 Jul 66*	4
JUST LIKE A WOMAN *Originally recorded by Bob Dylan.*	*Fontana*	10	*6 Aug 66*	10
SEMI-DETACHED, SUBURBAN MR. JAMES	*Fontana*	2	*29 Oct 66*	12
HA! HA! SAID THE CLOWN *Originally recorded by Tony Hazzard.*	*Fontana*	4	*1 Apr 67*	11
SWEET PEA *Originally recorded by Tommy Roe.*	*Fontana*	36	*27 May 67*	4
MIGHTY QUINN *Originally recorded by Bob Dylan.*	*Fontana*	1	*27 Jan 68*	11
MY NAME IS JACK *Originally recorded by John Simon.*	*Fontana*	8	*15 Jun 68*	11
FOX ON THE RUN *Originally recorded by Tony Hazzard.*	*Fontana*	5	*21 Dec 68*	12
RAGAMUFFIN MAN	*Fontana*	8	*3 May 69*	11
JOYBRINGER *Based on Jupiter from Holst's Plant Suite.*	*Vertigo*	9	*8 Sep 73*	10
BLINDED BY THE LIGHT *Originally recorded by Bruce Springsteen.*	*Bronze*	6	*28 Aug 76*	10
DAVY'S ON THE ROAD AGAIN *Originally recorded by John Simon.*	*Bronze*	6	*20 May 78*	12
YOU ANGEL YOU *Originally recorded by Bob Dylan.*	*Bronze*	54	*17 Mar 79*	5
DON'T KILL IT CAROL *Originally recorded by Heron.* *Above 5: MANFRED MANN'S EARTH BAND.*	*Bronze*	45	*7 Jul 79*	4

EPS:	**HITS 6**			**WEEKS 111**
GROOVIN' WITH MANFRED MANN	*HMV*	3	*21 Nov 64*	18
THE ONE IN THE MIDDLE	*HMV*	1	*12 Jun 65*	38
NO LIVING WITHOUT LOVING	*HMV*	1	*27 Nov 65*	24
MACHINES	*HMV*	1	*16 Apr 66*	13
INSTRUMENTAL ASYLUM	*HMV*	3	*11 Jun 66*	9
AS WAS	*HMV*	4	*15 Oct 66*	9

ALBUMS:	**HITS 12**			**WEEKS 101**
FIVE FACES OF MANFRED MANN	*His Master's Voice*	3	*19 Sep 64*	24
MANN MADE	*His Master's Voice*	7	*23 Oct 65*	11
MANN MADE HITS	*His Master's Voice*	11	*17 Sep 66*	18
AS IS	*Fontana*	22	*29 Oct 66*	4
SOUL OF MANN *Compilation of instrumental tracks.*	*His Master's Voice*	40	*21 Jan 67*	1
THE ROARING SILENCE *Above hit: MANFRED MANN'S EARTH BAND.*	*Bronze*	10	*18 Sep 76*	9
WATCH *Above hit: MANFRED MANN'S EARTH BAND.*	*Bronze*	33	*17 Jun 78*	6
ANGEL STATION *Above 3: MANFRED MANN'S EARTH BAND.*	*Bronze*	30	*24 Mar 79*	8
SEMI-DETACHED SUBURBAN	*EMI*	9	*15 Sep 79*	14
SOMEWHERE IN AFRIKA *Above hit: MANFRED MANN'S EARTH BAND.*	*Bronze*	87	*26 Feb 83*	1
AGES OF MANN - 22 CLASSIC HITS OF THE 60'S	*PolyGram TV*	23	*23 Jan 93*	4
THE VERY BEST OF MANFRED MANN'S EARTH BAND *Above hit: MANFRED MANN'S EARTH BAND.*	*Arcade*	69	*10 Sep 94*	1

MANHATTAN TRANSFER US

SINGLES:	**HITS 9**			**WEEKS 72**
TUXEDO JUNCTION *Originally recorded by Erskine Hawkins.*	*Atlantic*	24	*7 Feb 76*	6
CHANSON D'AMOUR *Originally recorded by Art and Dotty Todd.*	*Atlantic*	1	*5 Feb 77*	13
DON'T LET GO	*Atlantic*	32	*28 May 77*	6
WALK IN LOVE *Originally recorded by David Batteau.*	*Atlantic*	48	*18 Feb 78*	1
WALK IN LOVE [RE]	*Atlantic*	12	*4 Mar 78*	11
ON A LITTLE STREET IN SINGAPORE *Originally recorded by Jimmy Dorsey in 1940.*	*Atlantic*	20	*20 May 78*	9
WHERE DID OUR LOVE GO/JE VOULAIS (TE DIRE QUE JE T'ATTENDS)	*Atlantic*	40	*16 Sep 78*	4
WHO, WHAT, WHEN, WHERE, WHY	*Atlantic*	49	*23 Dec 78*	6
a. TWILIGHT ZONE b. TWILIGHT TONE [M]	*Atlantic*	25	*17 May 80*	8
SPICE OF LIFE	*Atlantic*	19	*21 Jan 84*	8

ALBUMS:	**HITS 6**			**WEEKS 85**
COMING OUT	*Atlantic*	12	*12 Mar 77*	20
MANHATTAN TRANSFER	*Atlantic*	49	*19 Mar 77*	7

PASTICHE	*Atlantic*	10	*25 Feb 78*	34
LIVE	*Atlantic*	4	*11 Nov 78*	17
EXTENSIONS	*Atlantic*	63	*17 Nov 79*	3
BODIES AND SOULS	*Atlantic*	53	*18 Feb 84*	4

MANHATTANS US

SINGLES:	HITS 5			WEEKS 31
KISS AND SAY GOODBYE	*CBS*	4	*19 Jun 76*	11
HURT	*CBS*	4	*2 Oct 76*	11
Originally recorded by Roy Hamiltion in 1954; Timi Yuro's version reached No. 4 in the US in 1961.				
IT'S YOU	*CBS*	43	*23 Apr 77*	3
SHINING STAR	*CBS*	45	*26 Jul 80*	4
CRAZY	*CBS*	63	*6 Aug 83*	2
ALBUMS:	**HITS 1**			**WEEKS 3**
MANHATTANS	*CBS*	37	*14 Aug 76*	3

MANIC MC'S featuring Sara CARLSON UK

SINGLES:	HITS 1			WEEKS 5
MENTAL	*RCA*	30	*12 Aug 89*	5

MANIC STREET PREACHERS UK

SINGLES:	HITS 27			WEEKS 145
YOU LOVE US	*Heavenly*	62	*25 May 91*	2
STAY BEAUTIFUL	*Columbia*	40	*10 Aug 91*	3
LOVE'S SWEET EXILE / REPEAT	*Columbia*	26	*9 Nov 91*	3
YOU LOVE US [RI-1ST]	*Columbia*	16	*1 Feb 92*	4
SLASH 'N' BURN	*Columbia*	20	*28 Mar 92*	4
MOTORCYCLE EMPTINESS	*Columbia*	17	*13 Jun 92*	6
THEME FROM M.A.S.H. (SUICIDE IS PAINLESS)	*Columbia*	7	*19 Sep 92*	6
[AA] listed with Everything I Do (I Do It For You) by the Fatima Mansions. Track from the NME 40th Anniversary album Ruby Trax.				
LITTLE BABY NOTHING	*Columbia*	29	*21 Nov 92*	3
Features porn star Traci Lords on vocals.				
FROM DESPAIR TO WHERE	*Columbia*	25	*12 Jun 93*	4
LA TRISTESSE DURERA (SCREAM TO A SIGH)	*Columbia*	22	*31 Jul 93*	5
ROSES IN THE HOSPITAL	*Columbia*	15	*2 Oct 93*	3
LIFE BECOMING A LANDSLIDE	*Columbia*	36	*12 Feb 94*	2
FASTER / P.C.P.	*Epic*	16	*11 Jun 94*	3
REVOL	*Epic*	22	*13 Aug 94*	3
SHE IS SUFFERING	*Epic*	25	*15 Oct 94*	3
A DESIGN FOR LIFE	*Epic*	2	*27 Apr 96*	10
A DESIGN FOR LIFE [RE]	*Epic*	71	*27 Jul 96*	1
EVERYTHING MUST GO	*Epic*	5	*3 Aug 96*	6
KEVIN CARTER	*Epic*	9	*12 Oct 96*	4
Kevin Carter was photographer friend of the band who had committed suicide.				
AUSTRALIA	*Epic*	7	*14 Dec 96*	7
LITTLE BABY NOTHING [RI]	*Epic*	50	*13 Sep 97*	1
LOVE'S SWEET EXILE [RI]	*Epic*	55	*13 Sep 97*	1
MOTORCYCLE EMPTINESS [RI]	*Epic*	41	*13 Sep 97*	2
SLASH 'N' BURN [RI]	*Epic*	54	*13 Sep 97*	1
STAY BEAUTIFUL [RI]	*Epic*	52	*13 Sep 97*	1
YOU LOVE US [RI-2ND]	*Epic*	49	*13 Sep 97*	1
IF YOU TOLERATE THIS YOUR CHILDREN WILL BE NEXT	*Epic*	1	*5 Sep 98*	10
IF YOU TOLERATE THIS YOUR CHILDREN WILL BE NEXT [RE]	*Epic*	69	*5 Dec 98*	1
THE EVERLASTING	*Epic*	11	*12 Dec 98*	8
YOU STOLE THE SUN FROM MY HEART	*Epic*	5	*20 Mar 99*	8
TSUNAMI	*Epic*	11	*17 Jul 99*	5
THE MASSES AGAINST THE CLASSES	*Epic*	1	*22 Jan 00*	6
THE MASSES AGAINST THE CLASSES [RE]	*Epic*	70	*1 Apr 00*	1
SO WHY SO SAD	*Epic*	8	*10 Mar 01*	7
FOUND THAT SOUL	*Epic*	9	*10 Mar 01*	3
FOUND THAT SOUL [RE]	*Epic*	68	*21 Apr 01*	1
OCEAN SPRAY	*Epic*	15	*16 Jun 01*	4
LET ROBESON SING	*Epic*	19	*22 Sep 01*	2
ALBUMS:	**HITS 6**			**WEEKS 188**
GENERATION TERRORISTS	*Columbia*	13	*22 Feb 92*	10
GOLD AGAINST THE SOUL	*Columbia*	8	*3 Jul 93*	11
THE HOLY BIBLE	*Epic*	6	*10 Sep 94*	4
EVERYTHING MUST GO	*Epic*	2	*1 Jun 96*	82
THIS IS MY TRUTH TELL ME YOURS	*Epic*	1	*26 Sep 98*	60
GENERATION TERRORISTS [RE]	*Columbia*	47	*23 Jan 99*	7
Re-released at mid-price.				
KNOW YOUR ENEMY	*Epic*	2	*31 Mar 01*	14

Barry MANILOW — UK

SINGLES:	HITS 19			WEEKS 136
MANDY	*Arista*	11	*22 Feb 75*	9
Based on Scott English's Brandy.				
CAN'T SMILE WITHOUT YOU	*Arista*	43	*6 May 78*	7
Originally recorded by David Martin.				
SOMEWHERE IN THE NIGHT / COPACABANA (AT THE COPA)	*Arista*	42	*29 Jul 78*	10
Copacabana (At The Copa) from the film 'Foul Play'. Somewhere In The Night originally recorded by Richard Kerr.				
COULD IT BE MAGIC	*Arista*	25	*23 Dec 78*	10
Originally released in 1975. Inspired by F. Chopin's Prelude in C Minor.				
LONELY TOGETHER	*Arista*	21	*8 Nov 80*	13
I MADE IT THROUGH THE RAIN	*Arista*	37	*7 Feb 81*	6
Originally recorded by Gerard Kenny.				
BERMUDA TRIANGLE	*Arista*	15	*11 Apr 81*	9
LET'S HANG ON	*Arista*	12	*26 Sep 81*	11
THE OLD SONGS	*Arista*	48	*12 Dec 81*	8
IF I SHOULD LOVE AGAIN	*Arista*	66	*20 Feb 82*	2
STAY	*Arista*	23	*17 Apr 82*	8
Sales of the live and studio recordings were combined.				
Above hit: Barry MANILOW featuring Kevin DESIMONE and James JOLIS.				
I WANNA DO IT WITH YOU	*Arista*	8	*16 Oct 82*	8
I'M GONNA SIT RIGHT DOWN AND WRITE MYSELF A LETTER	*Arista*	36	*4 Dec 82*	7
Originally recorded by Fats Waller.				
SOME KIND OF FRIEND	*Arista*	48	*25 Jun 83*	2
YOU'RE LOOKIN' HOT TONIGHT	*Arista*	47	*27 Aug 83*	6
READ 'EM AND WEEP	*Arista*	17	*10 Dec 83*	7
Originally recorded by Meatloaf.				
PLEASE DON'T BE SCARED	*Arista*	35	*8 Apr 89*	5
COPACABANA (AT THE COPA) - THE 1993 REMIX [RM]	*Arista*	22	*10 Apr 93*	4
Remixed by Dave Ford..				
COULD IT BE MAGIC 1993 [RR]	*Arista*	36	*20 Nov 93*	3
LET ME BE YOUR WINGS	*EMI*	73	*6 Aug 94*	1
From the film 'Thumbelina'. Features the Irish Film Orchestra.				
Above hit: Barry MANILOW and Debra BYRD.				

ALBUMS:	HITS 21			WEEKS 340
EVEN NOW	*Arista*	12	*23 Sep 78*	28
MANILOW MAGIC - THE BEST OF BARRY MANILOW	*Arista*	3	*3 Mar 79*	151
ONE VOICE	*Arista*	18	*20 Oct 79*	7
BARRY	*Arista*	5	*29 Nov 80*	34
GIFT SET	*Arista*	62	*25 Apr 81*	1
IF I SHOULD LOVE AGAIN	*Arista*	5	*3 Oct 81*	26
BARRY LIVE IN BRITAIN	*Arista*	1	*1 May 82*	23
I WANNA DO IT WITH YOU	*Arista*	7	*27 Nov 82*	9
A TOUCH MORE MAGIC	*Arista*	10	*8 Oct 83*	12
2.00 A.M. PARADISE CAFE	*Arista*	28	*1 Dec 84*	6
MANILOW	*RCA*	40	*16 Nov 85*	6
SWING STREET	*Arista*	81	*20 Feb 88*	1
SONGS TO MAKE THE WHOLE WORLD SING	*Arista*	20	*20 May 89*	4
LIVE ON BROADWAY	*Arista*	19	*17 Mar 90*	3
THE SONGS 1975-1990	*Arista*	13	*30 Jun 90*	7
SHOWSTOPPERS	*Arista*	53	*2 Nov 91*	3
HIDDEN TREASURES	*Arista*	36	*3 Apr 93*	7
Album of remixes, unreleased demos and 3 new tracks.				
THE PLATINUM COLLECTION - GREATEST HITS	*Arista*	37	*27 Nov 93*	6
BARRY MANILOW SINGIN' WITH THE BIG BANDS	*Arista*	54	*5 Nov 94*	2
Features the music of Glenn Miller, Benny Goodman and Jimmy Dorsey.				
SUMMER OF '78	*Arista*	66	*30 Nov 96*	2
BARRY SINGS SINATRA	*Arista*	72	*21 Nov 98*	2

MANIX — UK

SINGLES:	HITS 3			WEEKS 6
MANIC MINDS	*Reinforced*	63	*23 Nov 91*	2
OBLIVION (HEAD IN THE CLOUDS) [EP]	*Reinforced*	43	*7 Mar 92*	3
Lead track: I Can't Stand It. (The title of the EP is the 4th track).				
RAINBOW PEOPLE	*Reinforced*	57	*8 Aug 92*	1

MANKEY — UK

SINGLES:	HITS 1			WEEKS 1
BELIEVE IN ME	*Frisky*	74	*16 Nov 96*	1
Samples Yazoo's Situation.				

MANKIND — UK

SINGLES:	HITS 1			WEEKS 12
DR. WHO	*Pinnacle*	25	*25 Nov 78*	12

Aimee MANN — US

SINGLES:	HITS 2			WEEKS 6
I SHOULD'VE KNOWN	*Imago*	55	*28 Aug 93*	2
STUPID THING	*Imago*	47	*20 Nov 93*	2
I SHOULD'VE KNOWN [RI]	*Imago*	45	*5 Mar 94*	2
ALBUMS:	**HITS 2**			**WEEKS 2**
WHATEVER	*Imago*	39	*18 Sep 93*	1
I'M WITH STUPID	*Geffen*	51	*11 Nov 95*	1

Johnny MANN SINGERS — US

(See also Walter Brennan; Buddy Knox; Bobby Vee.)

SINGLES:	HITS 1			WEEKS 13
UP-UP AND AWAY	*Liberty*	6	*15 Jul 67*	13
Written by Jimmy Webb. Originally recorded by Fifth Dimension.				

Roberto MANN — UK

ALBUMS:	HITS 1			WEEKS 9
GREAT WALTZES	*Deram*	19	*9 Dec 67*	9

Shelley MANNE — US

ALBUMS:	HITS 1			WEEKS 1
MY FAIR LADY	Vogue	20	*18 Jun 60*	1

MANOWAR — US

ALBUMS:	HITS 2			WEEKS 3
HAIL TO ENGLAND	*Music For Nations*	83	*18 Feb 84*	2
SIGN OF THE HAMMER	*10 Records*	73	*6 Oct 84*	1

Keith MANSFIELD STRINGS - See LOVE AFFAIR; TREMELOES

MANSUN — UK

SINGLES:	HITS 14			WEEKS 44
ONE [EP]	*Parlophone*	37	*6 Apr 96*	2
Lead track: Egg Shaped Fred.				
TWO [EP]	*Parlophone*	32	*15 Jun 96*	2
Lead track: Take It Easy Chicken.				
THREE [EP]	*Parlophone*	19	*21 Sep 96*	3
Lead track: Stripper Vicar.				
FOUR [EP]	*Parlophone*	15	*7 Dec 96*	4
Lead track: Wide Open Space.				
FIVE [EP]	*Parlophone*	9	*15 Feb 97*	5
Lead track: She Makes My Noise Bleed.				
SIX [EP]	*Parlophone*	15	*10 May 97*	3
Lead track: Taxloss.				
SEVEN [EP]	*Parlophone*	10	*18 Oct 97*	3
Lead track: Closed For Business.				
EIGHT [EP]	*Parlophone*	7	*11 Jul 98*	4
Lead track: Legacy.				
NINE [EP]	*Parlophone*	13	*5 Sep 98*	3
Lead track: Being A Girl (Part One).				
TEN [EP]	*Parlophone*	27	*7 Nov 98*	2
Lead track: Negative.				
ELEVEN [EP]	*Parlophone*	16	*13 Feb 99*	3
Lead track: Six.				
Charts only reflected the lead tracks of the EPs Four through to Seven, Ten and Eleven.				
TWELVE [EP]	*Parlophone*	8	*12 Aug 00*	6
Lead track: I Can Only Disappoint U.				
THIRTEEN [EP]	*Parlophone*	23	*18 Nov 00*	2
Lead track: Electric Man.				
FOURTEEN [EP]	*Parlophone*	28	*10 Feb 01*	2
Lead track: Fool.				
ALBUMS:	**HITS 3**			**WEEKS 27**
ATTACK OF THE GREY LANTERN	*Parlophone*	1	*1 Mar 97*	19
SIX	*Parlophone*	6	*19 Sep 98*	4
LITTLE KIX	*Parlophone*	12	*26 Aug 00*	4

MANTOVANI and his Orchestra — UK

(See also David Whitfield.)

SINGLES:	HITS 5			WEEKS 52
WHITE CHRISTMAS	*Decca*	6	*20 Dec 52*	3
THE SONG FROM THE MOULIN ROUGE (WHERE IS YOUR HEART)	*Decca*	1	*30 May 53*	21
From the film 'Moulin Rouge'.				

SWEDISH RHAPSODY	*Decca*	2	*24 Oct 53*	17
From the film 'The Stranger Left No Card'.				
THE SONG FROM THE MOULIN ROUGE (WHERE IS YOUR HEART) [RE-1ST]	*Decca*	10	*14 Nov 53*	1
THE SONG FROM THE MOULIN ROUGE (WHERE IS YOUR HEART) [RE-2ND]	*Decca*	12	*5 Dec 53*	1
SWEDISH RHAPSODY [RE]	*Decca*	12	*27 Feb 54*	1
LONELY BALLERINA	*Decca*	16	*12 Feb 55*	3
LONELY BALLERINA [RE]	*Decca*	18	*19 Mar 55*	1
AROUND THE WORLD	*Decca*	20	*1 Jun 57*	4
From the film 'Around The World In Eighty Days'.				
EPS:	**HITS 3**			**WEEKS 70**
MANTOVANI'S BIG FOUR	*Decca*	6	*12 Mar 60*	31
DREAMS OF OLWEN	*Decca*	17	*2 Apr 60*	4
EXODUS AND OTHER THEMES	*Decca*	3	*1 Apr 61*	35
ALBUMS:	**HITS 12**			**WEEKS 151**
CONTINENTAL ENCORES	*Decca*	4	*21 Feb 59*	12
CONCERT SPECTACULAR	*Decca*	16	*18 Feb 61*	2
MANTOVANI MAGIC	*Decca*	3	*16 Apr 66*	15
MR. MUSIC . . . MANTOVANI	*Decca*	24	*15 Oct 66*	3
MANTOVANI'S GOLDEN HITS	*Decca*	10	*14 Jan 67*	43
MANTOVANI/HOLLYWOOD	*Decca*	37	*30 Sep 67*	1
THE WORLD OF MANTOVANI	*Decca*	6	*14 Jun 69*	31
THE WORLD OF MANTOVANI VOL 2	*Decca*	4	*4 Oct 69*	19
MANTOVANI TODAY	*Decca*	16	*16 May 70*	8
TO LOVERS EVERYWHERE	*Decca*	44	*26 Feb 72*	1
20 GOLDEN GREATS	*Warwick*	9	*3 Nov 79*	13
MANTOVANI MAGIC	*Telstar*	52	*16 Mar 85*	3
Above hit: MANTOVANI ORCHESTRA conducted by Roland SHAW.				

MANTRONIK vs EPMD — US

(See also EPMD; Mantronix.)

SINGLES:	**HITS 1**			**WEEKS 1**
STRICTLY BUSINESS	*Parlophone*	43	*15 Aug 98*	1
Samples Eric Clapton's I Shot The Sheriff.				

MANTRONIX — US/Jamaica

(See also Mantronik vs EPMD.)

SINGLES:	**HITS 10**			**WEEKS 48**
LADIES	*10 Records*	55	*22 Feb 86*	4
BASSLINE	*10 Records*	34	*17 May 86*	6
WHO IS IT?	*10 Records*	40	*7 Feb 87*	6
SCREAM	*10 Records*	46	*4 Jul 87*	4
SING A SONG (BREAK IT DOWN)	*10 Records*	61	*30 Jan 88*	2
SIMPLE SIMON (YOU GOTTA REGARD)	*10 Records*	72	*12 Mar 88*	2
GOT TO HAVE YOUR LOVE	*Capitol*	4	*6 Jan 90*	11
TAKE YOUR TIME	*Capitol*	10	*12 May 90*	7
Above 2: MANTRONIX featuring WONDRESS.				
DON'T GO MESSIN' WITH MY HEART	*Capitol*	22	*2 Mar 91*	5
STEP TO ME (DO ME)	*Capitol*	59	*22 Jun 91*	1
ALBUMS:	**HITS 5**			**WEEKS 17**
THE ALBUM	*10 Records*	45	*29 Mar 86*	3
MUSICAL MADNESS	*10 Records*	97	*13 Dec 86*	1
MUSICAL MADNESS [RE]	*10 Records*	66	*8 Aug 87*	2
IN FULL EFFECT	*10 Records*	39	*2 Apr 88*	3
THIS SHOULD MOVE YA	*Capitol*	18	*17 Feb 90*	6
THE INCREDIBLE SOUND MACHINE	*Capitol*	36	*30 Mar 91*	2

MANUEL and the MUSIC OF THE MOUNTAINS — UK

(See also Geoff Love and his Orchestra.)

SINGLES:	**HITS 4**			**WEEKS 31**
THE HONEYMOON SONG	*Columbia*	29	*29 Aug 59*	2
From the film 'Honeymoon'.				
THE HONEYMOON SONG [RE-1ST]	*Columbia*	22	*26 Sep 59*	5
THE HONEYMOON SONG [RE-2ND]	*Columbia*	27	*7 Nov 59*	2
NEVER ON SUNDAY (JAMAIS LE DIMANCHE)	*Columbia*	29	*15 Oct 60*	10
From the film of the same name.				
SOMEWHERE MY LOVE	*Columbia*	42	*15 Oct 66*	2
RODRIGO'S GUITAR CONCERTO DE ARANJUEZ (THEME FROM 2ND MOVEMENT)	*EMI*	3	*31 Jan 76*	10
ALBUMS:	**HITS 3**			**WEEKS 38**
MUSIC OF THE MOUNTAINS	*Columbia*	17	*10 Sep 60*	1
THIS IS MANUEL	*Studio Two*	18	*7 Aug 71*	19
CARNIVAL	*Studio Two*	3	*31 Jan 76*	18

Roots MANUVA — UK

SINGLES:	HITS 4			WEEKS 6
DUSTED	Hard Hands	28	11 Dec 99	2
Above hit: LEFTFIELD/Roots MANUVA.				
DUSTED [RE]	Hard Hands	75	22 Jan 00	1
WITNESS (1 HOPE)	Big Dada	45	4 Aug 01	2
DREAMY DAYS	Big Dada	53	20 Oct 01	1
ALBUMS:	**HITS 1**			**WEEKS 3**
RUN COME SAVE ME	Big Dada	33	25 Aug 01	3

Phil MANZANERA — UK

ALBUMS:	HITS 1			WEEKS 1
DIAMOND HEAD	Island	40	24 May 75	1

MARATHON — UK/Germany

SINGLES:	HITS 1			WEEKS 3
MOVIN'	Ten Records	36	25 Jan 92	3

MARAUDERS — UK

SINGLES:	HITS 1			WEEKS 4
THAT'S WHAT I WANT	Decca	48	10 Aug 63	1
THAT'S WHAT I WANT [RE]	Decca	43	24 Aug 63	3

MARBLES — UK

SINGLES:	HITS 2			WEEKS 18
ONLY ONE WOMAN	Polydor	5	28 Sep 68	12
Written by the Bee Gees.				
THE WALLS FELL DOWN	Polydor	28	29 Mar 69	6

MARC ET CLAUDE — Germany

SINGLES:	HITS 2			WEEKS 10
LA	Positiva	28	21 Nov 98	3
I NEED YOUR LOVIN' (LIKE THE SUNSHINE)	Positiva	12	22 Jul 00	7

MARC and the MAMBAS - See Marc ALMOND

MARCELS — US

SINGLES:	HITS 2			WEEKS 17
BLUE MOON	Pye International	1	15 Apr 61	13
Originally recorded by Glen Gray Orchestra in 1935.				
SUMMERTIME	Pye International	46	10 Jun 61	4

Little Peggy MARCH — US

SINGLES:	HITS 1			WEEKS 7
HELLO HEARTACHE GOODBYE LOVE	RCA Victor	29	14 Sep 63	7

MARCY PLAYGROUND — US

SINGLES:	HITS 1			WEEKS 3
SEX AND CANDY	EMI	29	18 Apr 98	3
ALBUMS:	**HITS 1**			**WEEKS 1**
MARCY PLAYGROUND	EMI	61	9 May 98	1

MARDI GRAS — US

SINGLES:	HITS 1			WEEKS 9
TOO BUSY THINKING ABOUT MY BABY	Bell	19	5 Aug 72	9

MARIA - See Maria NAYLER

Kelly MARIE — UK

SINGLES:	HITS 4			WEEKS 36
FEELS LIKE I'M IN LOVE	Calibre	1	2 Aug 80	16
Originally intended for Elvis Presley and originally recorded by Ray Dorset.				
LOVING JUST FOR FUN	Calibre	21	18 Oct 80	7
HOT LOVE	Calibre	22	7 Feb 81	10
LOVE TRIAL	Calibre	51	30 May 81	3

Lisa MARIE - See Malcolm McLAREN

Rose MARIE — UK

SINGLES:	HITS 1			WEEKS 5
WHEN I LEAVE THE WORLD BEHIND	*A.1*	75	*19 Nov 83*	1
Written by Irving Berlin and originally recorded by Henry Burr.				
WHEN I LEAVE THE WORLD BEHIND [RE-1ST]	*A.1*	63	*3 Dec 83*	2
WHEN I LEAVE THE WORLD BEHIND [RE-2ND]	*A.1*	66	*24 Dec 83*	2
ALBUMS:	**HITS 5**			**WEEKS 35**
ROSE MARIE SINGS JUST FOR YOU	*A.1*	30	*13 Apr 85*	13
SO LUCKY	*A.1*	62	*24 May 86*	3
SENTIMENTALLY YOURS	*Telstar*	22	*14 Nov 87*	11
TOGETHER AGAIN	*Telstar*	52	*19 Nov 88*	7
MEMORIES OF HOME	*Telstar*	51	*23 Mar 96*	1
Collection of traditional Irish songs.				

Teena MARIE — US

(See also Snoop Doggy Dogg.)

SINGLES:	HITS 5			WEEKS 28
I'M A SUCKER FOR YOUR LOVE	*Motown*	43	*7 Jul 79*	8
Above hit: Teena MARIE Co-lead vocals: Rick JAMES.				
BEHIND THE GROOVE	*Motown*	6	*31 May 80*	10
I NEED YOUR LOVIN'	*Motown*	28	*11 Oct 80*	6
OOO LA LA LA	*Epic*	74	*26 Mar 88*	2
SINCE DAY ONE	*Epic*	69	*10 Nov 90*	2

MARILLION — UK

SINGLES:	HITS 22			WEEKS 103
MARKET SQUARE HEROES	*EMI*	60	*20 Nov 82*	2
HE KNOWS YOU KNOW	*EMI*	35	*12 Feb 83*	4
MARKET SQUARE HEROES [RE]	*EMI*	53	*16 Apr 83*	6
GARDEN PARTY - THE GREAT CUCUMBER MASSACRE	*EMI*	16	*18 Jun 83*	5
PUNCH AND JUDY	*EMI*	29	*11 Feb 84*	4
ASSASSING	*EMI*	22	*12 May 84*	5
KAYLEIGH	*EMI*	2	*18 May 85*	14
LAVENDER	*EMI*	5	*7 Sep 85*	9
HEART OF LOTHIAN	*EMI*	29	*30 Nov 85*	6
INCOMMUNICADO	*EMI*	6	*23 May 87*	5
SUGAR MICE	*EMI*	22	*25 Jul 87*	5
WARM WET CIRCLES	*EMI*	22	*7 Nov 87*	4
FREAKS (LIVE)	*EMI*	24	*26 Nov 88*	3
HOOKS IN YOU	*EMI*	30	*9 Sep 89*	3
UNINVITED GUEST	*EMI*	53	*9 Dec 89*	2
EASTER	*EMI*	34	*14 Apr 90*	2
COVER MY EYES (PAIN AND HEAVEN)	*EMI*	34	*8 Jun 91*	4
NO ONE CAN	*EMI*	33	*3 Aug 91*	4
DRY LAND	*EMI*	34	*5 Oct 91*	2
SYMPATHY	*EMI*	17	*23 May 92*	3
NO ONE CAN [RI]	*EMI*	26	*1 Aug 92*	4
THE HOLLOW MAN	*EMI*	30	*26 Mar 94*	2
ALONE AGAIN IN THE LAP OF LUXURY	*EMI*	53	*7 May 94*	3
BEAUTIFUL	*EMI*	29	*10 Jun 95*	2
ALBUMS:	**HITS 16**			**WEEKS 165**
SCRIPT FOR A JESTER'S TEAR	*EMI*	7	*26 Mar 83*	31
FUGAZI	*EMI*	5	*24 Mar 84*	20
REAL TO REEL	*EMI*	8	*17 Nov 84*	22
Budget price album featuring live recordings from Leicester, UK and Montreal, Canada.				
MISPLACED CHILDHOOD	*EMI*	1	*29 Jun 85*	41
CLUTCHING AT STRAWS	*EMI*	2	*4 Jul 87*	15
B SIDES THEMSELVES	*EMI*	64	*23 Jul 88*	6
THE THIEVING MAGPIE	*EMI*	25	*10 Dec 88*	6
SEASON'S END	*EMI*	7	*7 Oct 89*	4
HOLIDAYS IN EDEN	*EMI*	7	*6 Jul 91*	7
A SINGLES COLLECTION 1982-1992	*EMI*	27	*20 Jun 92*	2
BRAVE	*EMI*	10	*19 Feb 94*	4
AFRAID OF SUNLIGHT	*EMI*	16	*8 Jul 95*	2
MADE AGAIN	*EMI*	37	*6 Apr 96*	1
Live recordings.				
THIS STRANGE ENGINE	*Raw Power*	27	*3 May 97*	2
RADIATION	*Raw Power*	35	*3 Oct 98*	1
MARILLION.COM	*Raw Power*	53	*30 Oct 99*	1

MARILYN — UK

SINGLES:	HITS 4			WEEKS 26
CALLING YOUR NAME	*Mercury*	4	*5 Nov 83*	12
CRY AND BE FREE	*Love*	31	*11 Feb 84*	6
YOU DON'T LOVE ME	*Love*	40	*21 Apr 84*	7
BABY U LEFT ME (IN THE COLD)	*Mercury*	70	*13 Apr 85*	1

MARILYN MANSON — US

SINGLES:	HITS 7			WEEKS 18
THE BEAUTIFUL PEOPLE	*Interscope*	18	*7 Jun 97*	3
10" format was titled 'The Horrible People'.				
TOURNIQUET	*Interscope*	28	*20 Sep 97*	2
THE DOPE SHOW	*Interscope*	12	*21 Nov 98*	3
ROCK IS DEAD	*Maverick*	23	*26 Jun 99*	2
From the film 'The Matrix'.				
DISPOSABLE TEENS	*Nothing*	12	*18 Nov 00*	3
THE FIGHT SONG	*Nothing*	24	*3 Mar 01*	3
THE NOBODIES	*Nothing*	34	*15 Sep 01*	2

ALBUMS:	HITS 4			WEEKS 8
ANTICHRIST SUPERSTAR	*Interscope*	73	*26 Oct 96*	1
MECHANICAL ANIMAL	*Interscope*	8	*26 Sep 98*	4
THE LAST TOUR ON EARTH	*Interscope*	61	*27 Nov 99*	1
Live recordings from their US Rock Is Dead tour, early 1999.				
HOLY WOOD	*Nothing*	23	*25 Nov 00*	2

Marino MARINI and his QUARTET — Italy

SINGLES:	HITS 2			WEEKS 23
VOLARE (NEL BLU DIPINTO DI BLU)	*Durium*	13	*4 Oct 58*	7
COME PRIMA	*Durium*	2	*11 Oct 58*	14
Above 2 entries were separate sides of the same release, each had its own chart run.				
CIAO CIAO BAMBINA	*Durium*	25	*21 Mar 59*	1
CIAO CIAO BAMBINA [RE]	*Durium*	24	*4 Apr 59*	1

MARION — UK

SINGLES:	HITS 5			WEEKS 9
SLEEP	*London*	53	*25 Feb 95*	1
TOYS FOR BOYS	*London*	57	*13 May 95*	1
LET'S ALL GO TOGETHER	*London*	37	*21 Oct 95*	2
TIME	*London*	29	*3 Feb 96*	2
SLEEP [RM]	*London*	17	*30 Mar 96*	2
CD1 is titled The Sleep EP; CD2 is titled The Acoustic EP. Featured in the Peugeot car TV commercial.				
MIYAKO HIDEAWAY	*London*	45	*7 Mar 98*	1
Named after a hotel in Japan.				

ALBUMS:	HITS 1			WEEKS 2
THIS WORLD AND BODY	*London*	10	*17 Feb 96*	2

MARK' OH — Germany

SINGLES:	HITS 1			WEEKS 3
TEARS DON'T LIE	*Systematic*	24	*6 May 95*	3
Based on an Italian folk song and Johnny Mathis' When A Child Is Born.				

Pigmeat MARKHAM — US

SINGLES:	HITS 1			WEEKS 8
HERE COMES THE JUDGE	*Chess*	19	*20 Jul 68*	8

Biz MARKIE — US

SINGLES:	HITS 1			WEEKS 2
JUST A FRIEND	*Cold Chillin'*	55	*26 May 90*	2

Yannis MARKOPOULOS — Greece

SINGLES:	HITS 1			WEEKS 8
WHO PAYS THE FERRYMAN?	*BBC*	11	*17 Dec 77*	8
Theme from the BBC TV series of the same name.				

ALBUMS:	HITS 1			WEEKS 8
WHO PAYS THE FERRYMAN	*BBC*	22	*26 Aug 78*	8

Guy MARKS — US

SINGLES:	HITS 1			WEEKS 8
LOVING YOU HAS MADE ME BANANAS	*ABC*	25	*13 May 78*	8

MARKSMEN – See Houston WELLS and the MARKSMEN

MARKY MARK and the FUNKY BUNCH — US

SINGLES:	HITS 3			WEEKS 14
GOOD VIBRATIONS	*Interscope*	14	*31 Aug 91*	7
Loletta Holoway's vocals are sampled from Love Sensation.				
Above hit: MARKY MARK and the FUNKY BUNCH (featuring Loletta HOLLOWAY).				
WILDSIDE	*Interscope*	42	*2 Nov 91*	3
YOU GOTTA BELIEVE	*Atlantic*	54	*12 Dec 92*	4

ALBUMS:	HITS 1			WEEKS 1
MUSIC FOR THE PEOPLE	*Interscope*	61	*5 Oct 91*	1

Bob MARLEY and the WAILERS

Jamaica

SINGLES:	HITS 19			WEEKS 167
NO WOMAN NO CRY	*Island*	22	*27 Sep 75*	7
EXODUS	*Island*	14	*25 Jun 77*	9
WAITING IN VAIN	*Island*	27	*10 Sep 77*	6
JAMMING / PUNKY REGGAE PARTY	*Island*	9	*10 Dec 77*	12
IS THIS LOVE	*Island*	9	*25 Feb 78*	9
SATISFY MY SOUL	*Island*	21	*10 Jun 78*	10
SO MUCH TROUBLE IN THE WORLD	*Island*	56	*20 Oct 79*	4
COULD YOU BE LOVED	*Island*	5	*21 Jun 80*	12
THREE LITTLE BIRDS	*Island*	17	*13 Sep 80*	9
NO WOMAN NO CRY [RE]	*Island*	8	*13 Jun 81*	11
BUFFALO SOLDIER	*Island*	4	*7 May 83*	12
ONE LOVE/PEOPLE GET READY [M]	*Island*	5	*21 Apr 84*	11
WAITING IN VAIN [RI]	*Island*	31	*23 Jun 84*	7
COULD YOU BE LOVED [RI]	*Island*	71	*8 Dec 84*	2
ONE LOVE - PEOPLE GET READY [M] [RI]	*Tuff Gong*	42	*18 May 91*	3
IRON LION ZION	*Tuff Gong*	5	*19 Sep 92*	9
WHY SHOULD I / EXODUS [RR]	*Tuff Gong*	42	*28 Nov 92*	3
Exodus was listed from 5 Dec 92, once single had dropped to No. 53.				
WHY SHOULD I / EXODUS [RR] [RE]	*Tuff Gong*	75	*2 Jan 93*	1
KEEP ON MOVING	*Tuff Gong*	17	*20 May 95*	4
'Re-modelled' from original 1977 recording by Trevor Wyatt and Ingmar Kianh.				
WHAT GOES AROUND COMES AROUND	*Anansi*	42	*8 Jun 96*	1
Above hit: Bob MARLEY.				
SUN IS SHINING	*Club Tools*	3	*25 Sep 99*	10
Marley first recorded the track for the Trojan label in the late 1960s and re-recorded it in 1978 for the Kaya album. This is the Trojan version remixed by Funkstar de Luxe.				
Above hit: Bob MARLEY vs. FUNKSTAR DE LUXE.				
TURN YOUR LIGHTS DOWN LOW	*Columbia*	15	*11 Dec 99*	7
From the film 'The Best Man'.				
Above hit: Bob MARLEY featuring Lauryn HILL.				
RAINBOW COUNTRY	*Club Tools*	11	*22 Jan 00*	6
Above hit: Bob MARLEY vs FUNKSTAR DELUXE.				
JAMMIN'	*Tuff Gong*	42	*24 Jun 00*	2
Above hit: Bob MARLEY with MC LYTE				

ALBUMS:	HITS 17			WEEKS 527
NATTY DREAD	*Island*	43	*4 Oct 75*	5
LIVE!	*Island*	38	*20 Dec 75*	5
Live recordings from the Lyceum Ballroom, London, summer 1975.				
RASTAMAN VIBRATION	*Island*	15	*8 May 76*	13
EXODUS	*Island*	8	*11 Jun 77*	56
KAYA	*Island*	4	*1 Apr 78*	24
BABYLON BY BUS	*Island*	40	*16 Dec 78*	11
Live recordings.				
SURVIVAL	*Island*	20	*13 Oct 79*	6
UPRISING	*Island*	6	*28 Jun 80*	17
LIVE AT THE LYCEUM [RE]	*Island*	68	*25 Jul 81*	6
CONFRONTATION	*Island*	5	*28 May 83*	19
LEGEND - THE BEST OF BOB MARLEY AND THE WAILERS	*Island*	1	*19 May 84*	106
REBEL MUSIC	*Island*	54	*28 Jun 86*	3
LEGEND - THE BEST OF BOB MARLEY AND THE WAILERS [RI]	*Tuff Gong*	11	*18 May 91*	216
Digitally remastered version. Includes re-entries through to 2000.				
SONGS OF FREEDOM	*Tuff Gong*	10	*3 Oct 92*	5
Above hit: Bob MARLEY.				
NATURAL MYSTIC	*Tuff Gong*	5	*3 Jun 95*	8
Released to celebate 50th anniversary of Marley's birth.				
THE SUN IS SHINING	*Club Tool*	40	*4 Sep 99*	3
Import single. It was too long and expensive to be eligible for the singles chart. See also entry in the singles section above.				
Above hit: Bob MARLEY vs FUNKSTAR DE LUXE.				
ONE LOVE - THE VERY BEST OF BOB MARLEY & THE WAILERS	*Tuff Gong*	5	*2 Jun 01*	15
LIVELY UP YOURSELF	*Music Collection*	75	*7 Jul 01*	1
Above hit: Bob MARLEY.				
ONE LOVE - THE VERY BEST OF BOB MARLEY & THE WAILERS	*Tuff Gong*	24	*10 Nov 01*	8
Repackaged with bonus CD of rarities.				

Ziggy MARLEY and the MELODY MAKERS

Jamaica

(See also Jamaica United.)

SINGLES:	HITS 2			WEEKS 11
TOMORROW PEOPLE	*Virgin*	22	*11 Jun 88*	10
Features Jerry Harrison (of Talking Heads) on organ.				
LOOK WHO'S DANCING	*Virgin America*	65	*23 Sep 89*	1

Lene MARLIN — Norway

SINGLES:	HITS 3			WEEKS 19
SITTING DOWN HERE	*Virgin*	5	*11 Mar 00*	11
UNFORGIVABLE SINNER	*Virgin*	13	*16 Sep 00*	6
Original release reached No. 170 on 6 Nov 99				
WHERE I'M HEADED	*Virgin*	31	*13 Jan 01*	2
ALBUMS:	**HITS 1**			**WEEKS 34**
PLAYING MY GAME	*Virgin*	18	*25 Mar 00*	34

MARLO — UK

SINGLES:	HITS 1			WEEKS 1
HOW DO I KNOW?	*Polydor*	56	*24 Jul 99*	1

MARMALADE — UK

SINGLES:	HITS 11			WEEKS 130
LOVIN' THINGS	*CBS*	6	*25 May 68*	13
Originally recorded by the Pathfinders.				
WAIT FOR ME MARY-ANNE	*CBS*	30	*26 Oct 68*	5
OB-LA-DI OB-LA-DA	*CBS*	1	*7 Dec 68*	20
Originally recorded by the Beatles.				
BABY MAKE IT SOON	*CBS*	9	*14 Jun 69*	13
REFLECTIONS OF MY LIFE	*Decca*	3	*20 Dec 69*	12
RAINBOW	*Decca*	3	*18 Jul 70*	14
MY LITTLE ONE	*Decca*	15	*27 Mar 71*	11
COUSIN NORMAN	*Decca*	6	*4 Sep 71*	11
BACK ON THE ROAD	*Decca*	35	*27 Nov 71*	7
BACK ON THE ROAD [RE]	*Decca*	50	*22 Jan 72*	1
RADANCER	*Decca*	6	*1 Apr 72*	12
FALLING APART AT THE SEAMS	*Target*	9	*21 Feb 76*	11

MARMION — Holland/Spain

SINGLES:	HITS 1			WEEKS 2
SCHONEBERG	*Hooj Choons*	53	*18 May 96*	1
First released in Germany, 1993.				
SCHONEBERG [RI]	*ffrr*	56	*14 Feb 98*	1

Johnny MARR – See Billy BRAGG

MARRADONA — UK

SINGLES:	HITS 1			WEEKS 5
OUT OF MY HEAD	*Peach*	38	*26 Feb 94*	3
OUT OF MY HEAD 97 [RM]	*Soopa*	39	*26 Jul 97*	2
Remixed by Twink.				

Neville MARRINER and the ACADEMY OF ST. MARTIN IN THE FIELDS — UK

ALBUMS:	HITS 1			WEEKS 6
AMADEUS [OST]	*London*	64	*6 Apr 85*	6

Bernie MARSDEN — UK

ALBUMS:	HITS 1			WEEKS 2
LOOK AT ME NOW	*Parlophone*	71	*5 Sep 81*	2

Gerry MARSDEN – See CHRISTIANS, Holly JOHNSON, Paul McCARTNEY, Gerry MARSDEN and STOCK AITKEN WATERMAN; GERRY and the PACEMAKERS

Matthew MARSDEN — UK

SINGLES:	HITS 2			WEEKS 10
THE HEART'S LONE DESIRE	*Columbia*	13	*11 Jul 98*	7
SHE'S GONE	*Columbia*	24	*7 Nov 98*	3
Above hit: Matthew MARSDEN (featuring DESTINY'S CHILD).				

Stevie MARSH — UK

SINGLES:	HITS 1			WEEKS 4
IF YOU WERE THE ONLY BOY IN THE WORLD	*Decca*	29	*5 Dec 59*	2
Originally recorded by comic George Robey in 1916.				
IF YOU WERE THE ONLY BOY IN THE WORLD [RE]	*Decca*	24	*26 Dec 59*	2

MARSHA – See SHAGGY

Amanda MARSHALL — Canada

ALBUMS:	HITS 1			WEEKS 2
AMANDA MARSHALL	*Epic*	47	*3 Aug 96*	2

Jack MARSHALL'S MUSIC – See Peggy LEE

Joy MARSHALL — UK

SINGLES:	HITS 1			WEEKS 2
THE MORE I SEE YOU	*Decca*	34	*25 Jun 66*	2

Keith MARSHALL — UK

SINGLES:	HITS 1			WEEKS 10
ONLY CRYING	*Arrival*	12	*4 Apr 81*	10

Louise Clare MARSHALL – See SILICONE SOUL featuring Louise Clare MARSHALL

Wayne MARSHALL — UK

SINGLES:	HITS 3			WEEKS 7
OOH AAH (G-SPOT)	*Soultown*	29	*1 Oct 94*	3
SPIRIT	*Soultown*	58	*3 Jun 95*	1
From the film 'Spirit Of The Pharoah'.				
NEVER KNEW LOVE LIKE THIS	*Sony S2*	40	*24 Feb 96*	2
Above hit: Pauline HENRY featuring Wayne MARSHALL.				
G SPOT [RM]	*MBA*	50	*7 Dec 96*	1
Remixed by Roger Benov.				

MARSHALL, HAIN — UK

SINGLES:	HITS 2			WEEKS 19
DANCING IN THE CITY	*Harvest*	3	*3 Jun 78*	15
COMING HOME	*Harvest*	39	*14 Oct 78*	4

MARTAY featuring ZZ TOP — UK/US

(See also ZZ Top.)

SINGLES:	HITS 1			WEEKS 2
GIMME ALL YOUR LOVIN' 2000	*Riverhorse*	28	*16 Oct 99*	2
Samples ZZ Top's Gimme All Your Lovin.				

Lena MARTELL — UK

SINGLES:	HITS 1			WEEKS 18
ONE DAY AT A TIME	*Pye*	1	*29 Sep 79*	18
Written by Kris Kristofferson and originally recorded by Marilyn Sellars reached No.37 in the US in 1974.				
ALBUMS:	**HITS 6**			**WEEKS 71**
THAT WONDERFUL SOUND OF LENA MARTELL	*Pye*	35	*25 May 74*	2
THE BEST OF LENA MARTELL	*Pye*	13	*8 Jan 77*	16
THE LENA MARTELL COLLECTION	*Ronco*	12	*27 May 78*	19
LENA'S MUSIC ALBUM	*Pye*	5	*20 Oct 79*	18
BY REQUEST	*Ronco*	9	*19 Apr 80*	9
BEAUTIFUL SUNDAY	*Ronco*	23	*29 Nov 80*	7

MARTHA and the MUFFINS — Canada

(See also M + M.)

SINGLES:	HITS 1			WEEKS 10
ECHO BEACH	*Dindisc*	10	*1 Mar 80*	10
ALBUMS:	**HITS 1**			**WEEKS 6**
METRO MUSIC	*DinDisc*	34	*15 Mar 80*	6

MARTHA and the VANDELLAS – See Martha REEVES and the VANDELLAS

MARTIKA — US

SINGLES:	HITS 7			WEEKS 57
TOY SOLDIERS	*CBS*	5	*29 Jul 89*	11
I FEEL THE EARTH MOVE	*CBS*	7	*14 Oct 89*	14
Originally recorded by Carole King.				
MORE THAN YOU KNOW	*CBS*	15	*13 Jan 90*	7
WATER	*CBS*	59	*17 Mar 90*	3
LOVE . . . THY WILL BE DONE	*Columbia*	9	*17 Aug 91*	9
MARTIKA'S KITCHEN	*Columbia*	17	*30 Nov 91*	10
Above 2 written by Prince.				
COLOURED KISSES	*Columbia*	41	*22 Feb 92*	3
ALBUMS:	**HITS 2**			**WEEKS 52**
MARTIKA	*CBS*	11	*16 Sep 89*	37
MARTIKA'S KITCHEN	*Columbia*	15	*7 Sep 91*	15

Billie Ray MARTIN — Germany

SINGLES:	HITS 5			WEEKS 20
YOUR LOVING ARMS	*Magnet*	38	*19 Nov 94*	3
YOUR LOVING ARMS [RI]	*Magnet*	6	*20 May 95*	10
RUNNING AROUND TOWN	*Magnet*	29	*2 Sep 95*	2

IMITATION OF LIFE	*Magnet*	29	*6 Jan 96*	3
SPACE OASIS	*Magnet*	66	*6 Apr 96*	1
HONEY	*React*	54	*21 Aug 99*	1

ALBUMS:	**HITS 1**			**WEEKS 2**
DEADLINE FOR MY MEMORIES	*Magnet*	47	*3 Feb 96*	2

Dean MARTIN — US

SINGLES:	**HITS 16**			**WEEKS 163**
KISS	*Capitol*	9	*19 Sep 53*	1
KISS [RE]	*Capitol*	5	*3 Oct 53*	7
THAT'S AMORE	*Capitol*	2	*23 Jan 54*	11
From the film 'The Caddy'.				
Above hit: Dean MARTIN with Dick STABILE and his Orchestra.				
SWAY	*Capitol*	6	*2 Oct 54*	7
HOW DO YOU SPEAK TO AN ANGEL?	*Capitol*	15	*23 Oct 54*	2
HOW DO YOU SPEAK TO AN ANGEL? [RE]	*Capitol*	17	*20 Nov 54*	4
THE NAUGHTY LADY OF SHADY LANE	*Capitol*	5	*29 Jan 55*	10
MAMBO ITALIANO	*Capitol*	14	*5 Feb 55*	2
LET ME GO LOVER	*Capitol*	3	*26 Feb 55*	9
Above entry and Naughty Lady Of Shady Lane were separate sides of the same release, each had its own chart run.				
UNDER THE BRIDGES OF PARIS	*Capitol*	6	*2 Apr 55*	8
MEMORIES ARE MADE OF THIS	*Capitol*	1	*11 Feb 56*	16
YOUNG AND FOOLISH	*Capitol*	20	*3 Mar 56*	1
INNAMORATA	*Capitol*	21	*28 Apr 56*	3
From the film 'Artists And Models'.				
THE MAN WHO PLAYS THE MANDOLINO (GUAGLIONE)	*Capitol*	21	*23 Mar 57*	2
From the film 'Ten Thousand Bedrooms'. Certain copies did not reflect (Guaglione) in the title.				
RETURN TO ME	*Capitol*	2	*14 Jun 58*	22
Originally recorded by Guy Lombardo.				
VOLARE (NEL BLU DIPINTO DI BLU)	*Capitol*	2	*30 Aug 58*	14
EVERYBODY LOVES SOMEBODY	*Reprise*	11	*29 Aug 64*	13
Originally recorded by Frank Sinatra in 1948.				
THE DOOR IS STILL OPEN TO MY HEART	*Reprise*	42	*14 Nov 64*	4
Originally recorded by the Cardinals in 1955.				
GENTLE ON MY MIND	*Reprise*	2	*8 Feb 69*	23
Originally recorded by Glen Campbell in 1967.				
GENTLE ON MY MIND [RE]	*Reprise*	49	*30 Aug 69*	1
THAT'S AMORE [RI]	*EMI Premier*	43	*22 Jun 96*	2
Featured in the Loyal Supporters TV commercial for the Euro '96 football championships.				
SWAY [RI]	*Capitol*	66	*21 Aug 99*	1
Featured in the Eurostar TV commercial.				

COMPILATION ALBUMS:	**HITS 1**			**WEEKS 4**

ALBUMS:	**HITS 10**			**WEEKS 56**
THIS TIME I'M SWINGIN'!	*Capitol*	18	*13 May 61*	1
AT EASE WITH DEAN	*Reprise*	35	*25 Feb 67*	1
WELCOME TO MY WORLD	*Reprise*	39	*4 Nov 67*	1
DEAN MARTIN'S GREATEST HITS VOLUME 1	*Reprise*	40	*12 Oct 68*	1
GENTLE ON MY MIND	*Reprise*	9	*22 Feb 69*	8
THE BEST OF DEAN MARTIN	*Capitol*	9	*22 Feb 69*	1
WHITE CHRISTMAS	*Music For Pleasure*	45	*27 Nov 71*	1
Budget compilation.				
Above hit: Nat 'King' COLE and Dean MARTIN.				
20 ORIGINAL DEAN MARTIN HITS	*Reprise*	7	*13 Nov 76*	11
THE VERY BEST OF DEAN MARTIN – THE CAPITOL & REPRISE YEARS	*EMI*	5	*5 Jun 99*	29
Originally released in 1998, it charted after a BBC TV 'Omnibus' programme on the artist.				
THE VERY BEST OF DEAN MARTIN VOLUME 2 – THE CAPITOL & REPRISE YEARS	*Capitol*	40	*26 Aug 00*	2
EEE- O 11 – THE BEST OF THE RAT PACK	*Capitol*	2	*8 Dec 01*	4
Solo recordings and 2 duets. Above entry listed in the compilation chart.				
Above hit: Frank SINATRA Dean MARTIN Sammy DAVIS Jr.				

George MARTIN — UK

(See also Beatles.)

ALBUMS:	**HITS 1**			**WEEKS 13**
IN MY LIFE	*Echo*	5	*4 Apr 98*	13
Features Celine Dion, Phil Collins, Jim Carrey, Robin Williams.				
Above hit: George MARTIN and VARIOUS ARTISTS.				

Juan MARTIN with the ROYAL PHILHARMONIC ORCHESTRA conducted by Louis CLARK — Spain

(See also Royal Philharmonic Orchestra.)

SINGLES:	**HITS 1**			**WEEKS 7**
LOVE THEME FROM THE THORN BIRDS	*WEA*	10	*28 Jan 84*	7
From the BBC1 TV series.				

ALBUMS:	HITS 1			WEEKS 9
SERENADE	*K-Tel*	21	*11 Feb 84*	9

Linda MARTIN — Ireland

SINGLES:	HITS 1			WEEKS 2
WHY ME?	*Columbia*	59	*30 May 92*	2
Eurovision Song Contest winner in 1992.				

Lucie MARTIN - See Romina JOHNSON

Marilyn MARTIN - See Phil COLLINS

Mary MARTIN — US

EPS:	HITS 1			WEEKS 2
SOUTH PACIFIC	*Philips*	20	*9 Apr 60*	2

Ray MARTIN and his Concert Orchestra — UK

(See also Lee Lawrence; Barbara Lyon; Jimmy Parkinson; Ruby Murray.)

SINGLES:	HITS 3			WEEKS 11
BLUE TANGO	*Columbia*	8	*15 Nov 52*	1
Originally recorded by Leroy Anderson.				
BLUE TANGO [RE]	*Columbia*	10	*29 Nov 52*	3
SWEDISH RHAPSODY	*Columbia*	10	*5 Dec 53*	1
SWEDISH RHAPSODY [RE]	*Columbia*	4	*19 Dec 53*	3
THE CAROUSEL WALTZ	*Columbia*	28	*16 Jun 56*	1
THE CAROUSEL WALTZ [RE]	*Columbia*	24	*4 Aug 56*	2

Remy MARTIN - See M.O.P.

Ricky MARTIN — US

SINGLES:	HITS 8			WEEKS 75
UN, DOS, TRES) MARIA	*Columbia*	6	*20 Sep 97*	6
THE CUP OF LIFE	*Columbia*	29	*11 Jul 98*	3
Official Song of the World Cup 1998, and performed at the opening ceremony.				
LIVIN' LA VIDA LOCA	*Columbia*	1	*17 Jul 99*	17
SHAKE YOUR BON-BON	*Columbia*	12	*20 Nov 99*	9
PRIVATE EMOTION	*Columbia*	9	*29 Apr 00*	9
Above hit: Ricky MARTIN featuring MEJA.				
SHE BANGS	*Columbia*	3	*4 Nov 00*	15
NOBODY WANTS TO BE LONELY	*Columbia*	4	*10 Mar 01*	12
Above hit: Ricky MARTIN with Christina AGUILERA.				
LOADED	*Columbia*	19	*28 Jul 01*	4
ALBUMS:	**HITS 3**			**WEEKS 74**
RICKY MARTIN	*Columbia*	2	*12 Jun 99*	48
SOUND LOADED	*Columbia*	14	*18 Nov 00*	21
THE BEST OF RICKY MARTIN	*Columbia*	42	*1 Dec 01*	5

Skip MARTIN and his Orchestra - See DE CASTRO SISTERS with Skip MARTIN and his Orchestra

Tony MARTIN with Hugo WINTERHALTER's Orchestra and Chorus — US

SINGLES:	HITS 2			WEEKS 28
STRANGER IN PARADISE	*His Master's Voice*	6	*23 Apr 55*	13
From the musical 'Kismet'.				
WALK HAND IN HAND	*His Master's Voice*	2	*14 Jul 56*	15

Vince MARTIN and the TARRIERS — UK

(See also Tarriers.)

SINGLES:	HITS 1			WEEKS 1
CINDY OH CINDY	*London*	26	*15 Dec 56*	1

Wink MARTINDALE — US

SINGLES:	HITS 1			WEEKS 41
DECK OF CARDS	*London*	18	*5 Dec 59*	5
Originally recorded by Texas T. Tyler.				
DECK OF CARDS [RE-1ST]	*London*	28	*16 Jan 60*	2
DECK OF CARDS [RE-2ND]	*London*	45	*2 Apr 60*	1
DECK OF CARDS [RE-3RD]	*London*	5	*20 Apr 63*	21
DECK OF CARDS [RI]	*Dot*	22	*20 Oct 73*	12
EPS:	**HITS 1**			**WEEKS 12**
DECK OF CARDS	*London*	11	*13 Jul 63*	12

Angie MARTINEZ - See KRS ONE; LIL' KIM

Al MARTINO — US

SINGLES:	HITS 10			WEEKS 87
HERE IN MY HEART	*Capitol*	1	*15 Nov 52*	18
The first No. 1 single.				
TAKE MY HEART	*Capitol*	9	*22 Nov 52*	1
NOW	*Capitol*	3	*31 Jan 53*	12
RACHEL	*Capitol*	10	*11 Jul 53*	4
RACHEL [RE]	*Capitol*	12	*12 Sep 53*	1
WANTED	*Capitol*	12	*5 Jun 54*	1
WANTED [RE-1ST]	*Capitol*	4	*19 Jun 54*	14
THE STORY OF TINA	*Capitol*	10	*2 Oct 54*	8
WANTED [RE-2ND]	*Capitol*	17	*2 Oct 54*	1
THE MAN FROM LARAMIE	*Capitol*	19	*24 Sep 55*	2
THE MAN FROM LARAMIE [RE]	*Capitol*	20	*29 Oct 55*	1
SUMMERTIME	*Top Rank*	49	*2 Apr 60*	1
I LOVE YOU BECAUSE	*Capitol*	48	*31 Aug 63*	1
SPANISH EYES	*Capitol*	49	*22 Aug 70*	1
SPANISH EYES [RE]	*Capitol*	5	*14 Jul 73*	21

MARTY - See NEW SEEKERS

John MARTYN — UK

SINGLES:	HITS 1			WEEKS 2
DELIVER ME	*Multiply*	31	*24 Mar 01*	2
Originally recorded by the Beloved for their 1996 album X.				
Above hit: SISTER BLISS featuring John MARTYN.				

ALBUMS:	HITS 10			WEEKS 30
ONE WORLD	*Island*	54	*4 Feb 78*	1
GRACE AND DANGER	*Island*	54	*1 Nov 80*	2
GLORIOUS FOOL	*Geffen*	25	*26 Sep 81*	7
WELL KEPT SECRET	*WEA*	20	*4 Sep 82*	7
SAPPHIRE	*Island*	57	*17 Nov 84*	2
PIECE BY PIECE	*Island*	28	*8 Mar 86*	4
COULDN'T LOVE YOU MORE	*Permanent*	65	*10 Oct 92*	2
AND	*Go! Discs*	32	*10 Aug 96*	3
THE CHURCH WITH ONE BELL	*Independiente*	51	*4 Apr 98*	1
Album of cover versions.				
GLASGOW WALKER	*Independiente*	66	*3 Jun 00*	1

MARVELETTES — US

SINGLES:	HITS 1			WEEKS 10
WHEN YOU'RE YOUNG AND IN LOVE	*Tamla Motown*	13	*17 Jun 67*	10

Hank MARVIN — UK

(See also Marvin, Welch and Farrar; Cliff Richard.)

SINGLES:	HITS 5			WEEKS 25
THROW DOWN A LINE	*Columbia*	7	*13 Sep 69*	9
THE JOY OF LIVING	*Columbia*	25	*21 Feb 70*	8
Above 2: CLIFF and HANK.				
DON'T TALK	*Polydor*	49	*6 Mar 82*	4
LONDON KID	*Polydor*	52	*7 Jan 89*	3
Above hit: Jean-Michel JARRE featuring Hank MARVIN.				
WE ARE THE CHAMPIONS	*PolyGram TV*	66	*17 Oct 92*	1
Above hit: Hank MARVIN featuring Brian MAY.				

ALBUMS:	HITS 11			WEEKS 66
HANK MARVIN	*Columbia*	14	*22 Nov 69*	2
WORDS AND MUSIC	*Polydor*	66	*20 Mar 82*	3
INTO THE LIGHT	*Polydor*	18	*31 Oct 92*	10
HEARTBEAT	*PolyGram TV*	17	*20 Nov 93*	9
THE BEST OF HANK MARVIN AND THE SHADOWS	*PolyGram TV*	19	*22 Oct 94*	11
Includes both solo and group material.				
Above hit: Hank MARVIN and the SHADOWS.				
HANK PLAYS CLIFF	*PolyGram TV*	33	*18 Nov 95*	7
Includes guest appearance from Cliff Richard.				
HANK PLAYS HOLLY	*PolyGram TV*	34	*23 Nov 96*	7
Album of Buddy Holly/Crickets covers.				
HANK PLAYS LIVE	*PolyGram TV*	71	*5 Apr 97*	1
Live recordings from Birmingham Symphony Hall, late 1996.				
PLAY ANDREW LLOYD WEBBER AND TIM RICE	*PolyGram TV*	41	*22 Nov 97*	6
Songs from their musicals.				
VERY BEST OF HANK MARVIN AND THE SHADOWS - THE FIRST 40 YEARS	*PolyGram TV*	56	*14 Nov 98*	5
Above 2 includes both solo and group material.				
Above 2: Hank MARVIN and the SHADOWS.				
MARVIN AT THE MOVIES	*Universal Music TV*	17	*15 Apr 00*	5

Lee MARVIN — US

(See also Various Artists: Films – Original Soundtracks 'Paint Your Wagon'.)

SINGLES:	HITS 1			WEEKS 23
WAND'RIN' STAR	*Paramount*	1	*7 Feb 70*	18
[AA] listed with I Talk To The Trees by Clint Eastwood, which was only listed for the first 2 weeks. From the film 'Paint Your Wagon'.				
WAND'RIN' STAR [RE-1ST]	*Paramount*	42	*20 Jun 70*	3
WAND'RIN' STAR [RE-2ND]	*Paramount*	47	*15 Aug 70*	2

MARVIN and TAMARA — UK

SINGLES:	HITS 2			WEEKS 9
GROOVE MACHINE	*Epic*	11	*7 Aug 99*	5
NORTH, SOUTH, EAST, WEST	*Epic*	38	*25 Dec 99*	4

MARVIN, WELCH and FARRAR — UK

(See also Hank Marvin.)

ALBUMS:	HITS 1			WEEKS 4
MARVIN, WELCH AND FARRAR	*Regal Zonophone*	30	*3 Apr 71*	4

MARVIN, THE PARANOID ANDROID — UK

SINGLES:	HITS 1			WEEKS 4
MARVIN	*Polydor*	53	*16 May 81*	4

Richard MARX — US

SINGLES:	HITS 15			WEEKS 75
SHOULD'VE KNOWN BETTER	*Manhattan*	50	*27 Feb 88*	5
ENDLESS SUMMER NIGHTS	*Manhattan*	50	*14 May 88*	3
SATISFIED	*EMI USA*	52	*17 Jun 89*	4
RIGHT HERE WAITING	*EMI USA*	2	*2 Sep 89*	10
ANGELIA	*EMI USA*	45	*11 Nov 89*	4
TOO LATE TO SAY GOODBYE	*EMI USA*	38	*24 Mar 90*	3
CHILDREN OF THE NIGHT	*EMI USA*	54	*7 Jul 90*	2
ENDLESS SUMMER NIGHTS [RI] / HOLD ON TO THE NIGHTS	*EMI USA*	60	*1 Sep 90*	2
KEEP COMING BACK	*Capitol*	55	*19 Oct 91*	2
HAZARD	*Capitol*	3	*9 May 92*	15
TAKE THIS HEART	*Capitol*	13	*29 Aug 92*	6
CHAINS AROUND MY HEART	*Capitol*	29	*28 Nov 92*	6
NOW AND FOREVER	*Capitol*	13	*29 Jan 94*	6
SILENT SCREAM	*Capitol*	32	*30 Apr 94*	4
THE WAY SHE LOVES ME	*Capitol*	38	*13 Aug 94*	3
ALBUMS:	**HITS 5**			**WEEKS 42**
RICHARD MARX	*Manhattan*	68	*9 Apr 88*	2
REPEAT OFFENDER	*EMI-USA*	8	*20 May 89*	12
RUSH STREET	*Capitol*	60	*16 Nov 91*	1
RUSH STREET [RE]	*Capitol*	7	*13 Jun 92*	19
PAID VACATION	*Capitol*	11	*19 Feb 94*	5
GREATEST HITS	*Capitol*	34	*21 Feb 98*	3

MARXMAN — UK/Ireland

SINGLES:	HITS 2			WEEKS 5
ALL ABOUT EVE	*Talkin Loud*	28	*6 Mar 93*	4
SHIP AHOY	*Talkin Loud*	64	*1 May 93*	1
Vocals by Sinead O'Connor.				
ALBUMS:	**HITS 1**			**WEEKS 1**
33 REVOLUTIONS PER MINUTE	*Talkin Loud*	69	*3 Apr 93*	1

MARY JANE GIRLS — US

SINGLES:	HITS 3			WEEKS 15
CANDY MAN	*Gordy*	60	*21 May 83*	4
ALL NIGHT LONG	*Gordy*	13	*25 Jun 83*	9
BOYS	*Gordy*	74	*8 Oct 83*	1
ALL NIGHT LONG [RM]	*Motown*	51	*18 Feb 95*	1
Remixed by Mike Gray and Jon Pearn.				
ALBUMS:	**HITS 1**			**WEEKS 9**
MARY JANE GIRLS	*Gordy*	51	*28 May 83*	9

MARY MARY — US

SINGLES:	HITS 2			WEEKS 14
SHACKLES (PRAISE YOU)	*Columbia*	5	*10 Jun 00*	12
I SINGS	*Columbia*	32	*18 Nov 00*	2

Carolyne MAS — US

SINGLES:	HITS 1			WEEKS 2
QUOTE GOODBYE QUOTE	*Mercury*	71	*2 Feb 80*	2

MA$E — US

(See also Blackstreet; Notorious B.I.G.; Puff Daddy.)

SINGLES:	HITS 7			WEEKS 36
CAN'T NOBODY HOLD ME DOWN *Samples Grandmaster Flash and the Furious Five's The Message.* *Above hit: PUFF DADDY (featuring MA$E).*	*Puff Daddy*	19	*29 Mar 97*	4
FEEL SO GOOD *Samples Kool And The Gang's Hollywood Swinging.*	*Puff Daddy*	10	*27 Dec 97*	8
WHAT YOU WANT *Above hit: MA$E featuring TOTAL.*	*Puff Daddy*	15	*18 Apr 98*	5
HORSE & CARRIAGE *Above hit: CAM'RON featuring MA$E.*	*Epic*	12	*19 Sep 98*	4
YOU SHOULD BE MINE (DON'T WASTE YOUR TIME) *Above hit: Brian McKNIGHT featuring MA$E.*	*Motown*	36	*3 Oct 98*	2
TOP OF THE WORLD *Above hit: BRANDY featuring MA$E.*	*Atlantic*	2	*10 Oct 98*	8
TOP OF THE WORLD [RE]	*Atlantic*	61	*9 Jan 99*	1
GET READY *Samples Shalamar's A Night To Remember.* *Above hit: MA$E (featuring BLACKSTREET).*	*Puff Daddy*	32	*10 Jul 99*	4
ALBUMS:	**HITS 2**			**WEEKS 9**
HARLEM WORLD	*Puff Daddy*	53	*24 Jan 98*	7
DOUBLE UP	*Puff Daddy*	47	*24 Jul 99*	2

M.A.S.H. — US

SINGLES:	HITS 1			WEEKS 12
THEME FROM M*A*S*H* (SUICIDE IS PAINLESS) *Theme from the TV series. Originally recorded in 1970.*	*CBS*	1	*10 May 80*	12

MASH! — UK/US

SINGLES:	HITS 2			WEEKS 3
U DON'T HAVE TO SAY U LOVE ME *Features vocals by Taffy.*	*React*	37	*21 May 94*	2
LET'S SPEND THE NIGHT TOGETHER	*Playa*	66	*4 Feb 95*	1

MASH UP - See Matt DAREY

MASON - See CHICANE

Barbara MASON — US

SINGLES:	HITS 1			WEEKS 5
ANOTHER MAN	*Streetwave*	45	*21 Jan 84*	5

Glen MASON — UK

SINGLES:	HITS 2			WEEKS 7
GLENDORA *Above hit: Glen MASON with Ron GOODWIN'S CHORUS and ORCHESTRA.*	*Parlophone*	28	*29 Sep 56*	2
THE GREEN DOOR	*Parlophone*	24	*17 Nov 56*	5

Mary MASON — UK

SINGLES:	HITS 1			WEEKS 6
ANGEL OF THE MORNING/ANY WAY THAT YOU WANT ME [M]	*Epic*	27	*8 Oct 77*	6

Sylvia MASON-JAMES - See SCOTT and LEON

MASQUERADE — UK

SINGLES:	HITS 2			WEEKS 10
ONE NATION	*Streetwave*	54	*11 Jan 86*	6
(SOLUTION TO) THE PROBLEM	*Streetwave*	65	*5 Jul 86*	2
(SOLUTION TO) THE PROBLEM [RE]	*Streetwave*	64	*26 Jul 86*	2

MASS ORDER — US

SINGLES:	HITS 2			WEEKS 5
LIFT EVERY VOICE (TAKE ME AWAY)	*Columbia*	35	*14 Mar 92*	3
LET'S GET HAPPY	*Columbia*	45	*23 May 92*	2

MASS PRODUCTION — US

SINGLES:	HITS 2			WEEKS 7
WELCOME TO OUR WORLD (OF MERRY MUSIC)	*Cotillion*	44	*12 Mar 77*	3
SHANTE	*Atlantic*	59	*17 May 80*	4

MASS SYNDICATE featuring Su Su BOBIEN — US

SINGLES:	HITS 1			WEEKS 1
YOU DON'T KNOW	*ffrr*	71	*24 Oct 98*	1

MASSED WELSH CHOIRS — UK

ALBUMS:	HITS 1			WEEKS 7
CYMANSA GANN	*BBC*	5	*9 Aug 69*	7

Zeitia MASSIAH — UK

SINGLES:	HITS 2			WEEKS 2
I SPECIALIZE IN LOVE	*Union*	74	*12 Mar 94*	1
Above hit: ARIZONA featuring ZEITIA.				
THIS IS THE PLACE	*Virgin*	62	*24 Sep 94*	1

MASSIEL — Spain

SINGLES:	HITS 1			WEEKS 4
LA LA LA	*Philips*	35	*27 Apr 68*	4
Eurovision Song Contest winner in 1968.				

MASSIVE ATTACK — UK

SINGLES:	HITS 9			WEEKS 42
UNFINISHED SYMPATHY	*Wild Bunch*	13	*23 Feb 91*	9
Group name cut from Massive Attack because of the Gulf War.				
Above hit: MASSIVE.				
SAFE FROM HARM	*Wild Bunch*	25	*8 Jun 91*	6
Above 2 feature vocals by Shara Nelson.				
MASSIVE ATTACK [EP]	*Wild Bunch*	27	*22 Feb 92*	4
Lead track: Hymn Of The Big Wheel.				
SLY	*Wild Bunch*	24	*29 Oct 94*	4
PROTECTION	*Wild Bunch*	14	*21 Jan 95*	4
Above hit: MASSIVE ATTACK with Tracey THORN.				
THE KARMACOMA [EP]	*Wild Bunch*	28	*1 Apr 95*	4
Various mixes of Karmacoma.				
RISINGSON	*Circa*	11	*19 Jul 97*	3
Samples the Velvet Underground's I Found A Reason.				
TEAR DROP	*Circa*	10	*9 May 98*	6
Features vocals by Elizabeth Fraser.				
ANGEL	*Circa*	30	*25 Jul 98*	2
Features vocals by Horace Andy.				
ALBUMS:	**HITS 3**			**WEEKS 205**
BLUE LINES	*Wild Bunch*	13	*20 Apr 91*	76
Includes re-entries through to 2000.				
Above hit: MASSIVE.				
PROTECTION	*Wild Bunch*	4	*8 Oct 94*	8
PROTECTION / NO PROTECTION [RE]	*Wild Bunch*	10	*7 Jan 95*	69
From 4 Mar 95 Protection was made available with an extra CD of remixes by Mad Professor. Includes re-entries through to 2000.				
MEZZANINE	*Wild Bunch*	1	*2 May 98*	52

MASSIVO featuring TRACY — UK

SINGLES:	HITS 1			WEEKS 11
LOVING YOU	*Debut*	25	*26 May 90*	11

MASTER OF CEREMONIES - See DJ PIED PIPER and the MASTER OF CEREMONIES

MASTER P and SILKK "THE SHOCKER" - See Montel JORDAN

MASTER SINGERS — UK

SINGLES:	HITS 2			WEEKS 7
THE HIGHWAY CODE	*Parlophone*	25	*16 Apr 66*	6
WEATHER FORECAST	*Parlophone*	50	*19 Nov 66*	1

Sammy MASTERS — US

SINGLES:	HITS 1			WEEKS 5
ROCKIN' RED WING	*Warner Brothers*	36	*11 Jun 60*	5

MASTERS AT WORK presents INDIA — US

(See also Nuyorican Soul; River Ocean featuring India.)

SINGLES:	HITS 2			WEEKS 5
I CAN'T GET NO SLEEP '95	*AM:PM*	44	*5 Aug 95*	2
TO BE IN LOVE	*Defected*	23	*31 Jul 99*	3
Above hit: MAW presents INDIA.				

MATCH — UK

SINGLES:	HITS 1			WEEKS 3
BOOGIE MAN	*Flamingo*	48	*16 Jun 79*	3

MATCHBOX — UK

SINGLES:	HITS 8			WEEKS 66
ROCKABILLY REBEL	*Magnet*	18	*3 Nov 79*	12
BUZZ BUZZ A DIDDLE IT	*Magnet*	22	*19 Jan 80*	8
Originally recorded by Freddie Cannon.				
MIDNITE DYNAMOS	*Magnet*	14	*10 May 80*	12
WHEN YOU ASK ABOUT LOVE	*Magnet*	4	*27 Sep 80*	12
OVER THE RAINBOW/YOU BELONG TO ME [M]	*Magnet*	15	*29 Nov 80*	11
BABES IN THE WOOD	*Magnet*	46	*4 Apr 81*	6
LOVE'S MADE A FOOL OF YOU	*Magnet*	63	*1 Aug 81*	3
ONE MORE SATURDAY NIGHT	*Magnet*	63	*29 May 82*	2
ALBUMS:	**HITS 2**			**WEEKS 14**
MATCHBOX	*Magnet*	44	*2 Feb 80*	5
MIDNITE DYNAMOS	*Magnet*	23	*11 Oct 80*	9

MATCHBOX 20 — US

SINGLES:	HITS 3			WEEKS 4
PUSH	*Atlantic*	38	*11 Apr 98*	2
3AM	*Atlantic*	64	*4 Jul 98*	1
IF YOU'RE GONE	*Atlantic*	50	*17 Feb 01*	1
Above hit: MATCHBOX TWENTY.				
ALBUMS:	**HITS 2**			**WEEKS 3**
YOURSELF OR SOMEONE LIKE YOU	*Atlantic*	50	*25 Apr 98*	1
MAD SEASON BY MATCHBOX TWENTY	*Atlantic*	31	*3 Jun 00*	2

MATCHROOM MOB with CHAS and DAVE - See CHAS and DAVE

Mireille MATHIEU — France

SINGLES:	HITS 1			WEEKS 7
LA DERNIERE VALSE (THE LAST WALTZ)	*Columbia*	26	*16 Dec 67*	7
EPS:	**HITS 1**			**WEEKS 6**
MIRIELLE MATHIEU	*Fontana*	9	*12 Aug 67*	6
ALBUMS:	**HITS 1**			**WEEKS 1**
MIREILLE MATHIEU	*Columbia*	39	*2 Mar 68*	1

Johnny MATHIS — US

(See also Johnny Mathis and Deniece Williams; Johnny Mathis and Henry Mancini; Johnny Mathis and Natalie Cole.)

SINGLES:	HITS 14			WEEKS 118
TEACHER, TEACHER	*Fontana*	27	*24 May 58*	5
A CERTAIN SMILE	*Fontana*	4	*27 Sep 58*	16
From the film of the same name.				
Above hit: Johnny MATHIS with Ray ELLIS and his Orchestra.				
WINTER WONDERLAND	*Fontana*	17	*20 Dec 58*	3
Above hit: Johnny MATHIS with Percy FAITH and his Orchestra				
SOMEONE	*Fontana*	6	*8 Aug 59*	15
Originally recorded by Jesse Belvin.				
Above hit: Johnny MATHIS with Ray ELLIS and his Orchestra.				
THE BEST OF EVERYTHING	*Fontana*	30	*28 Nov 59*	1
MISTY	*Fontana*	12	*30 Jan 60*	10
Originally recorded by Errol Garner.				
YOU ARE BEAUTIFUL	*Fontana*	38	*26 Mar 60*	8
Above hit: Johnny MATHIS with Ray ELLIS and his Orchestra.				
MISTY [RE]	*Fontana*	46	*16 Apr 60*	2
YOU ARE BEAUTIFUL [RE]	*Fontana*	46	*28 May 60*	1
STARBRIGHT	*Fontana*	47	*30 Jul 60*	2
MY LOVE FOR YOU	*Fontana*	9	*8 Oct 60*	18
WHAT WILL MARY SAY	*CBS*	49	*6 Apr 63*	1
I'M STONE IN LOVE WITH YOU	*CBS*	10	*25 Jan 75*	12
Originally recorded by Stylistics.				
WHEN A CHILD IS BORN (SOLEADO)	*CBS*	1	*13 Nov 76*	12
Originally recorded by the Daniel SentaCruz Ensemble As Soleado.				
Above hit: Johnny MATHIS and Gladys KNIGHT and the PIPS.				

GONE, GONE, GONE *Co-written by Leon Haywood.*	*CBS*	15	*11 Aug 79*	10
WHEN A CHILD IS BORN	*CBS*	74	*26 Dec 81*	2
EPS:	**HITS 4**			**WEEKS 4**
MEET MISTER MATHIS	*Fontana*	18	*7 May 60*	1
IT'S LOVE	*Fontana*	20	*15 Apr 61*	1
FOUR HITS	*Fontana*	17	*26 Aug 61*	1
FOUR SHOW HITS	*Fontana*	17	*7 Oct 61*	1
ALBUMS:	**HITS 24**			**WEEKS 193**
WARM	*Fontana*	6	*8 Nov 58*	2
SWING SOFTLY	*Fontana*	10	*24 Jan 59*	1
RIDE ON A RAINBOW	*Fontana*	10	*13 Feb 60*	2
RHYTHMS AND BALLADS OF BROADWAY	*Fontana*	6	*10 Dec 60*	10
I'LL BUY YOU A STAR	*Fontana*	18	*17 Jun 61*	1
RAINDROPS KEEP FALLING ON MY HEAD	*CBS*	23	*16 May 70*	10
LOVE STORY	*CBS*	27	*3 Apr 71*	5
FIRST TIME EVER I SAW YOUR FACE	*CBS*	40	*9 Sep 72*	3
MAKE IT EASY ON YOURSELF	*CBS*	49	*16 Dec 72*	1
I'M COMING HOME	*CBS*	18	*8 Mar 75*	11
THE HEART OF A WOMAN	*CBS*	39	*5 Apr 75*	2
WHEN WILL I SEE YOU AGAIN	*CBS*	13	*26 Jul 75*	10
I ONLY HAVE EYES FOR YOU	*CBS*	14	*3 Jul 76*	12
GREATEST HITS VOLUME IV	*CBS*	31	*19 Feb 77*	5
THE JOHNNY MATHIS COLLECTION	*CBS*	1	*18 Jun 77*	40
SWEET SURRENDER	*CBS*	55	*17 Dec 77*	1
YOU LIGHT UP MY LIFE	*CBS*	3	*29 Apr 78*	19
THE BEST DAYS OF MY LIFE	*CBS*	38	*7 Apr 79*	5
MATHIS MAGIC	*CBS*	59	*3 Nov 79*	4
TEARS AND LAUGHTER	*CBS*	1	*8 Mar 80*	15
ALL FOR YOU	*CBS*	20	*12 Jul 80*	8
CELEBRATION	*CBS*	9	*19 Sep 81*	16
FRIENDS IN LOVE	*CBS*	34	*15 May 82*	7
A SPECIAL PART OF ME	*CBS*	45	*15 Sep 84*	3

Johnny MATHIS and Natalie COLE — US

(See also Natalie Cole; Johnny Mathis.)

ALBUMS:	**HITS 1**			**WEEKS 16**
UNFORGETTABLE: A MUSICAL TRIBUTE TO NAT KING COLE	*CBS*	5	*17 Sep 83*	16

Johnny MATHIS and Henry MANCINI — US

(See also Henry Mancini and his Orchestra; Johnny Mathis.)

ALBUMS:	**HITS 1**			**WEEKS 8**
THE HOLLYWOOD MUSICALS	*CBS*	46	*13 Dec 86*	8

Johnny MATHIS and Deniece WILLIAMS — US

(See also Johnny Mathis; Deniece Williams.)

SINGLES:	**HITS 2**			**WEEKS 20**
TOO MUCH, TOO LITTLE, TOO LATE *Above hit: Johnny MATHIS/Deniece WILLIAMS.*	*CBS*	3	*25 Mar 78*	14
YOU'RE ALL I NEED TO GET BY	*CBS*	45	*29 Jul 78*	6
ALBUMS:	**HITS 1**			**WEEKS 11**
THAT'S WHAT FRIENDS ARE FOR	*CBS*	16	*26 Aug 78*	11

Ivan MATIAS — US

SINGLES:	**HITS 1**			**WEEKS 1**
SO GOOD (TO COME HOME TO) / I'VE HAD ENOUGH	*Arista*	69	*6 Apr 96*	1

MATT BIANCO — UK

SINGLES:	**HITS 10**			**WEEKS 65**
GET OUT OF YOUR LAZY BED	*WEA*	15	*11 Feb 84*	8
SNEAKING OUT THE BACK DOOR / MATT'S MOOD *Matt's Mood listed from 5 May 84. Titles were listed on the chart in reverse from 19 May 84.*	*WEA*	44	*14 Apr 84*	7
HALF A MINUTE	*WEA*	23	*10 Nov 84*	10
MORE THAN I CAN BEAR	*WEA*	50	*2 Mar 85*	7
YEH YEH	*WEA*	13	*5 Oct 85*	10
JUST CAN'T STAND IT	*WEA*	66	*1 Mar 86*	2
DANCING IN THE STREET	*WEA*	64	*14 Jun 86*	3
DON'T BLAME IT ON THAT GIRL / WAP-BAM-BOOGIE *Re-packaged from 2 July 88 with Wap-Bam-Boogie as first side.*	*WEA*	11	*4 Jun 88*	13
GOOD TIMES	*WEA*	55	*27 Aug 88*	3
NERVOUS (RE-RECORDED VERSION) / WAP BAM BOOGIE (LATIN REMIX) [RM] *Wap Bam Boogie remixed by Mixmaster Phil Harding.*	*WEA*	59	*4 Feb 89*	2

ALBUMS:	HITS 4			WEEKS 67
WHOSE SIDE ARE YOU ON	*WEA*	44	*8 Sep 84*	6
WHOSE SIDE ARE YOU ON [RE]	*WEA*	35	*10 Nov 84*	33
Peak position reached on 6 Apr 85.				
MATT BIANCO	*WEA*	26	*22 Mar 86*	13
INDIGO	*WEA*	23	*9 Jul 88*	13
THE BEST OF MATT BIANCO	*East West*	49	*3 Nov 90*	2

Kathy MATTEA — US

ALBUMS:	HITS 2			WEEKS 2
READY FOR THE STORM (FAVOURITE CUTS)	*Mercury*	61	*15 Apr 95*	1
Compilation of tracks from her 8 Mercury albums since 1984.				
LOVE TRAVELS	*Mercury*	65	*8 Feb 97*	1

Al MATTHEWS — US

SINGLES:	HITS 1			WEEKS 8
FOOL	*CBS*	16	*23 Aug 75*	8

Dave MATTHEWS BAND — US

SINGLES:	HITS 1			WEEKS 2
THE SPACE BETWEEN	*RCA*	35	*1 Dec 01*	2

John MATTHEWS – See UNDERCOVER

MATTHEWS' SOUTHERN COMFORT — UK

SINGLES:	HITS 1			WEEKS 18
WOODSTOCK	*Uni*	1	*26 Sep 70*	18
Originally recorded by Joni Mitchell.				
ALBUMS:	**HITS 1**			**WEEKS 4**
SECOND SPRING	*Uni*	52	*25 Jul 70*	4

MATUMBI — UK

SINGLES:	HITS 1			WEEKS 7
POINT OF VIEW (SQUEEZE A LITTLE LOVIN)	*Matumbi*	35	*29 Sep 79*	7

Susan MAUGHAN — UK

SINGLES:	HITS 3			WEEKS 25
BOBBY'S GIRL	*Philips*	3	*13 Oct 62*	19
Originally recorded by Marcie Blaine.				
Above hit: Susan MAUGHAN with Wally STOTT and his Orchestra and Chorus.				
HAND A HANDKERCHIEF TO HELEN	*Philips*	41	*16 Feb 63*	3
SHE'S NEW TO YOU	*Philips*	45	*11 May 63*	3
Above hit: Susan MAUGHAN with Wally STOTT and his Orchestra and Chorus.				

MAUREEN — UK

SINGLES:	HITS 3			WEEKS 22
SAY A LITTLE PRAYER	*Rhythm King*	10	*26 Nov 88*	10
Above hit: BOMB THE BASS featuring MAUREEN.				
THINKING OF YOU	*Urban*	11	*16 Jun 90*	9
Rap by Kev Won.				
Above hit: Maureen WALSH.				
WHERE HAS ALL THE LOVE GONE	*Urban*	51	*12 Jan 91*	3

Paul MAURIAT and his Orchestra — France

SINGLES:	HITS 1			WEEKS 14
LOVE IS BLUE (L'AMOUR EST BLEU)	*Philips*	12	*24 Feb 68*	14
Originally Luxembourg's entry for the Eurovision Song Contest in 1967 by Vicky, coming 4th.				

MAVERICKS — US

SINGLES:	HITS 3			WEEKS 23
DANCE THE NIGHT AWAY	*MCA*	4	*2 May 98*	18
I'VE GOT THIS FEELING	*MCA*	27	*26 Sep 98*	4
SOMEONE SHOULD TELL HER	*MCA Nashville*	45	*5 Jun 99*	1
ALBUMS:	**HITS 3**			**WEEKS 58**
MUSIC FOR ALL OCCASIONS	*MCA*	56	*11 May 96*	1
Originally released in 1995.				
TRAMPOLINE	*MCA Nashville*	10	*14 Mar 98*	48
THE BEST OF THE MAVERICKS	*Mercury*	40	*4 Dec 99*	9

MAW presents INDIA – See MASTERS AT WORK presents INDIA

MAX Q — Australia

SINGLES:	HITS 1			WEEKS 3
SOMETIMES	*Mercury*	53	*17 Feb 90*	3
ALBUMS:	**HITS 1**			**WEEKS 1**
MAX Q	*Mercury*	69	*4 Nov 89*	1

MAX WEBSTER — Canada

SINGLES:	HITS 1			WEEKS 3
PARADISE SKIES	*Capitol*	43	*19 May 79*	3

MAXEE — US

SINGLES:	HITS 1			WEEKS 1
WHEN I LOOK INTO YOUR EYES	*Mercury*	55	*17 Mar 01*	1

MAXIM — UK

SINGLES:	HITS 2			WEEKS 3
CARMEN QUEASY	*XL Recordings*	33	*10 Jun 00*	2
Vocals by Skin of Skunk Anansie.				
SCHEMING	*XL Recordings*	53	*23 Sep 00*	1
Vocals by Trina Allen.				

MAXIMA featuring LILY — UK/Spain

SINGLES:	HITS 1			WEEKS 2
IBIZA	*Yo! Yo!*	55	*14 Aug 93*	2

MAXWELL — US

SINGLES:	HITS 3			WEEKS 10
. . . TIL THE COPS COME KNOCKIN' THE OPUS	*Columbia*	63	*11 May 96*	1
ASCENSION NO ONE'S GONNA LOVE YOU, SO DON'T EVER WONDER	*Columbia*	39	*24 Aug 96*	3
SUMTHIN' SUMTHIN' THE MANTRA	*Columbia*	27	*1 Mar 97*	3
ASCENSION DON'T EVER WONDER THE ENCORE [RI]	*Columbia*	28	*24 May 97*	3
ALBUMS:	**HITS 4**			**WEEKS 20**
URBAN HANG SUITE	*Columbia*	57	*13 Apr 96*	1
URBAN HANG SUITE [RE]	*Columbia*	39	*1 Mar 97*	9
MTV UNPLUGGED [EP]	*Columbia*	45	*26 Jul 97*	2
Mini album of live recordings from New York, May 97.				
EMBRYA	*Columbia*	11	*4 Jul 98*	6
NOW	*Columbia*	46	*22 Sep 01*	2

MAXX — UK/Sweden/Germany

SINGLES:	HITS 4			WEEKS 24
GET-A-WAY	*Pulse 8*	4	*21 May 94*	12
NO MORE (I CAN'T STAND IT)	*Pulse 8*	8	*6 Aug 94*	8
YOU CAN GET IT	*Pulse 8*	21	*29 Oct 94*	3
I CAN MAKE YOU FEEL LIKE	*Pulse 8*	56	*22 Jul 95*	1
ALBUMS:	**HITS 1**			**WEEKS 1**
TO THE MAXXIMUM	*Pulse 8*	66	*23 Jul 94*	1

Terry MAXX - See FUNKSTAR DE LUXE

Billy MAY and his Orchestra — US

(See also Nat 'King' Cole; Frank Sinatra.)

SINGLES:	HITS 1			WEEKS 10
MAIN TITLE (FROM THE FILM "THE MAN WITH THE GOLDEN ARM")	*Capitol*	9	*28 Apr 56*	10

Brian MAY — UK

SINGLES:	HITS 9			WEEKS 33
STAR FLEET	*EMI*	65	*5 Nov 83*	3
Based on the theme of a Japanese children's puppet sci-fi series.				
Above hit: Brian May and FRIENDS.				
DRIVEN BY YOU	*Parlophone*	6	*7 Dec 91*	9
TOO MUCH LOVE WILL KILL YOU	*Parlophone*	5	*5 Sep 92*	9
WE ARE THE CHAMPIONS	*PolyGram TV*	66	*17 Oct 92*	1
Above hit: Hank MARVIN featuring Brian MAY.				
BACK TO THE LIGHT	*Parlophone*	19	*21 Nov 92*	4
RESURRECTION	*Parlophone*	23	*19 Jun 93*	3
Above hit: Brian May with Cozy POWELL.				
LAST HORIZON	*Parlophone*	51	*18 Dec 93*	2
THE BUSINESS (ROCK ON COZY MIX)	*Parlophone*	51	*6 Jun 98*	1
A tribute to Cozy Powell, who died in April that year.				
WHY DON'T WE TRY AGAIN	*Parlophone*	44	*12 Sep 98*	1

ALBUMS:	HITS 4			WEEKS 23
STAR FLEET PROJECT	*EMI*	35	*12 Nov 83*	4
Above hit: Brian May and FRIENDS.				
BACK TO THE LIGHT	*Parlophone*	6	*10 Oct 92*	14
LIVE AT BRIXTON ACADEMY	*Parlophone*	20	*19 Feb 94*	3
Live recordings from June 93.				
Above hit: Brian May BAND.				
ANOTHER WORLD	*Parlophone*	23	*13 Jun 98*	2

Lisa MAY — UK

SINGLES:	HITS 2			WEEKS 2
WISHING ON A STAR	*Urban Gorilla*	61	*15 Jul 95*	1
Above hit: 88.3 featuring Lisa MAY.				
THE CURSE OF VOODOO RAY	*Fontana*	64	*14 Sep 96*	1

Mary MAY — UK

SINGLES:	HITS 1			WEEKS 1
ANYONE WHO HAD A HEART	*Fontana*	49	*29 Feb 64*	1

Shernette MAY — UK

SINGLES:	HITS 1			WEEKS 1
ALL THE MAN THAT I NEED	*Virgin*	50	*6 Jun 98*	1

Simon MAY — UK

(See also Anita Dobson; Marti Webb.)

SINGLES:	HITS 3			WEEKS 21
THE SUMMER OF MY LIFE	*Pye*	7	*9 Oct 76*	8
WE'LL GATHER LILACS/ALL MY LOVING [M]	*Pye*	49	*21 May 77*	1
WE'LL GATHER LILACS/ALL MY LOVING [M] [RE]	*Pye*	50	*4 Jun 77*	1
HOWARDS' WAY (THEME FROM THE BBC TV SERIES)	*BBC*	21	*26 Oct 85*	11
Above hit: Simon May ORCHESTRA.				

ALBUMS:	HITS 1			WEEKS 7
SIMON'S WAY	*BBC*	59	*27 Sep 86*	7
Above hit: Simon May ORCHESTRA.				

MAYA – See TAMPERER featuring MAYA

John MAYALL — UK

ALBUMS:	HITS 14			WEEKS 115
BLUES BREAKERS	*Decca*	6	*30 Jul 66*	17
Above hit: John MAYALL with Eric CLAPTON.				
A HARD ROAD	*Decca*	10	*4 Mar 67*	19
CRUSADE	*Decca*	8	*23 Sep 67*	14
Above 2: John MAYALL and his BLUESBREAKERS.				
THE BLUES ALONE	*Ace Of Clubs*	24	*25 Nov 67*	5
THE DIARY OF A BAND VOLUME 1	*Decca*	27	*16 Mar 68*	9
THE DIARY OF A BAND VOLUME 2	*Decca*	28	*16 Mar 68*	5
Above 2 are live recordings from 1967.				
BARE WIRES	*Decca*	3	*20 Jul 68*	17
Above 3: John MAYALL'S BLUESBREAKERS.				
BLUES FROM LAUREL CANYON	*Decca*	33	*18 Jun 69*	3
LOOKING BACK	*Decca*	14	*23 Aug 69*	7
Compilation of tracks recorded during 1964–67.				
THE TURNING POINT	*Polydor*	11	*15 Nov 69*	7
EMPTY ROOMS	*Polydor*	9	*11 Apr 70*	8
U.S.A. UNION	*Polydor*	50	*12 Dec 70*	1
BACK TO THE ROOTS	*Polydor*	31	*26 Jun 71*	2
WAKE UP CALL	*Silvertone*	61	*17 Apr 93*	1

Henry MAYER ORCHESTRA – See Petula CLARK

Curtis MAYFIELD — US

SINGLES:	HITS 5			WEEKS 20
MOVE ON UP	*Buddah*	12	*31 Jul 71*	10
NO GOODBYES	*Curtom*	65	*2 Dec 78*	3
(CELEBRATE) THE DAY AFTER YOU	*RCA*	52	*30 May 87*	2
Above hit: BLOW MONKEYS with Curtis MAYFIELD.				
SUPERFLY 1990	*Capitol*	48	*29 Sep 90*	3
Above hit: Curtis MAYFIELD and ICE-T.				
ASTOUNDED	*Grand Royal*	40	*16 Jun 01*	2
Samples Curtis Mayfield's Move On Up.				
Above hit: BRAN VAN 3000 featuring Curtis MAYFIELD.				

ALBUMS:	HITS 2			WEEKS 4
SUPERFLY [OST]	*Buddah*	26	*31 Mar 73*	2
NEW WORLD ORDER	*Warner Brothers*	44	*15 Feb 97*	2

MAYTALS — Jamaica

SINGLES:	HITS 1			WEEKS 4
MONKEY MAN	*Trojan*	50	*25 Apr 70*	1
MONKEY MAN [RE]	*Trojan*	47	*9 May 70*	3

MAYTE — US

SINGLES:	HITS 1			WEEKS 1
IF EYE LOVE U 2 NIGHT	*NPG*	67	*18 Nov 95*	1
Written by Prince.				

MAZE featuring Frankie BEVERLY — US

SINGLES:	HITS 3			WEEKS 14
TOO MANY GAMES	*Capitol*	36	*20 Jul 85*	7
I WANNA BE WITH YOU	*Capitol*	55	*23 Aug 86*	3
JOY AND PAIN	*Capitol*	57	*27 May 89*	4
Above hit: MAZE.				
ALBUMS:	**HITS 4**			**WEEKS 25**
WE ARE ONE	*Capitol*	38	*7 May 83*	6
CAN'T STOP THE LOVE	*Capitol*	41	*9 Mar 85*	12
LIVE IN LOS ANGELES	*Capitol*	70	*27 Sep 86*	2
SILKY SOUL	*Warner Brothers*	43	*16 Sep 89*	5

Kym MAZELLE — UK

SINGLES:	HITS 13			WEEKS 66
USELESS (I DON'T NEED YOU NOW)	*Syncopate*	53	*12 Nov 88*	3
WAIT	*RCA*	7	*14 Jan 89*	10
Above hit: Robert HOWARD and Kym MAZELLE.				
GOT TO GET YOU BACK	*Syncopate*	29	*25 Mar 89*	4
LOVE STRAIN	*Syncopate*	52	*7 Oct 89*	3
WAS THAT ALL IT WAS	*Syncopate*	33	*20 Jan 90*	6
USELESS (I DON'T NEED YOU NOW) [RM]	*Syncopate*	48	*26 May 90*	2
Remixed by Norman Cook.				
MISSING YOU	*Ten Records*	22	*24 Nov 90*	7
Above hit: SOUL II SOUL (Vocals: Kym MAZELLE).				
NO ONE CAN LOVE YOU MORE THAN ME	*Parlophone*	62	*25 May 91*	2
LOVE ME THE RIGHT WAY	*Logic*	22	*26 Dec 92*	10
Above hit: RAPINATION and Kym MAZELLE.				
NO MORE TEARS (ENOUGH IS ENOUGH)	*Bell*	13	*11 Jun 94*	7
Above hit: Kym MAZELLE and Jocelyn BROWN.				
GIMME ALL YOUR LOVIN'	*Bell*	22	*8 Oct 94*	3
Above hit: Jocelyn BROWN and Kym MAZELLE.				
SEARCHING FOR THE GOLDEN EYE	*Eternal*	40	*23 Dec 95*	3
Above hit: MOTIV 8 and Kym MAZELLE.				
LOVE ME THE RIGHT WAY '96 [RM]	*Logic*	55	*28 Sep 96*	1
Remixed by the Rapino Brothers.				
Above hit: RAPINATION and Kym MAZELLE.				
YOUNG HEARTS RUN FREE	*EMI*	20	*16 Aug 97*	4
From the film 'Romeo + Juliet'.				
TRULY	*Island Blue*	55	*19 Feb 00*	1
Above hit: PESHAY featuring Kym MAZELLE.				

MAZZY STAR — US

SINGLES:	HITS 2			WEEKS 3
FADE INTO YOU	*Capitol*	48	*27 Aug 94*	1
FLOWERS IN DECEMBER	*Capitol*	40	*2 Nov 96*	2
ALBUMS:	**HITS 2**			**WEEKS 2**
SO TONIGHT THAT I MIGHT SEE	*Capitol*	68	*9 Oct 93*	1
AMONG MY SWAN	*Capitol*	57	*16 Nov 96*	1

MC ALISTAIR - See ARTFUL DODGER; DREAM TEEM

M.C. DUKE — UK

SINGLES:	HITS 1			WEEKS 1
I'M RIFFIN (ENGLISH RASTA)	*Music Of Life*	75	*11 Mar 89*	1

MC ERIC - See TECHNOTRONIC

MC FIXX IT - See ANTICAPPELLA

MC Mikee FREEDOM - See NOMAD

M.C. HAMMER - See HAMMER

MC KIE - See TEEBONE featuring MC KIE and MC SPARKS

MC LETHAL — UK

SINGLES:	HITS 1			WEEKS 1
THE RAVE DIGGER	*Network*	66	*14 Nov 92*	1

MC LYTE — US

(See also Levert Sweat Gill.)

SINGLES:	HITS 6			WEEKS 16
RUFFNECK	*Atlantic*	67	*15 Jan 94*	1
KEEP ON, KEEPIN' ON	*East West America*	39	*29 Jun 96*	2
From the film 'Sunset Park'. Samples Liberian Girl by Michael Jackson.				
Above hit: MC LYTE featuring XSCAPE.				
COLD ROCK A PARTY (BAD BOY REMIX)	*East West America*	15	*18 Jan 97*	4
Samples Upside Down by Diana Ross.				
KEEP ON KEEPIN' ON [RI]	*East West America*	27	*19 Apr 97*	2
Above hit: MC LYTE featuring XSCAPE.				
I CAN'T MAKE A MISTAKE	*East West America*	46	*5 Sep 98*	1
IT'S ALL YOURS	*East West America*	36	*19 Dec 98*	4
Above hit: MC LYTE (featuring Gina THOMPSON).				
JAMMIN'	*Tuff Gong*	42	*24 Jun 00*	2
Above hit: Bob MARLEY with MC LYTE.				

M.C. MARIO – See AMBASSADORS OF FUNK featuring M.C. MARIO

M.C. MIKER 'G' and DEEJAY SVEN — Holland

SINGLES:	HITS 1			WEEKS 7
HOLIDAY RAP	*Debut*	6	*6 Sep 86*	7
Rap over Madonna's Holiday.				

MC NEAT – See DJ LUCK and MC NEAT

M.C. NOISE – See LOVE INC featuring M.C. NOISE

MC NUMBER 6 – See F.A.B.

MC ONYX STONE – See LONYO

MC PARKER – See F.A.B.

MC SAR and the REAL McCOY – See REAL McCOY

M.C. SKAT KAT and the STRAY MOB — US

SINGLES:	HITS 1			WEEKS 2
SKAT STRUT	*Virgin America*	64	*9 Nov 91*	2
Samples Let's Groove by Earth, Wind and Fire.				

MC SKIBADEE – See PRESSURE DROP

MC SOLAAR – See Missy "Misdemeanor" ELLIOTT; URBAN SPECIES

MC SPARKS – See TEEBONE featuring MC KIE and MC SPARKS

MC SPY-D + FRIENDS — UK

SINGLES:	HITS 1			WEEKS 2
THE AMAZING SPIDER-MAN	*Parlophone*	37	*11 Mar 95*	2
From the BBC Radio 1 series on Mark Goodier's show.				

MC STYLES – See Scott GARCIA featuring MC STYLES, Scott

MC TUNES — UK

SINGLES:	HITS 3			WEEKS 19
THE ONLY RHYME THAT BITES	*ZTT*	10	*2 Jun 90*	10
TUNES SPLITS THE ATOM	*ZTT*	18	*15 Sep 90*	7
Above 2: MC TUNES versus 808 STATE.				
PRIMARY RHYMING	*ZTT*	67	*1 Dec 90*	1
THE ONLY RHYME THAT BITES 99 [RI]	*ZTT*	53	*6 Mar 99*	1
Though billed as a remix, the lead track is a longer version of the original.				
Above hit: MC TUNES vs 808 STATE.				

ALBUMS:	HITS 1			WEEKS 3
THE NORTH AT ITS HEIGHTS	*ZTT*	26	*13 Oct 90*	3

MC VIPER – See REFLEX featuring MC VIPER

MC WILDSKI — UK

SINGLES:	HITS 2			WEEKS 10
BLAME IT ON THE BASSLINE	*Go.Beat*	29	*8 Jul 89*	6
Above hit: Norman COOK featuring M.C. WILDSKI.				
WARRIOR	*Arista*	49	*3 Mar 90*	4

MDM – See Matt DAREY

ME AND YOU featuring 'WE THE PEOPLE BAND' — UK/Jamaica

SINGLES:	HITS 1			WEEKS 9
YOU NEVER KNOW WHAT YOU'VE GOT *Originally recorded by Bell and James.*	*Laser*	31	*28 Jul 79*	9

ME ME ME — UK

SINGLES:	HITS 1			WEEKS 4
HANGING AROUND	*Indolent*	19	*17 Aug 96*	4

Abigail MEAD and Nigel GOULDING — UK/US

SINGLES:	HITS 1			WEEKS 10
FULL METAL JACKET (I WANNA BE YOUR DRILL INSTRUCTOR) *From the film 'Full Metal Jacket'.*	*Warner Brothers*	2	*26 Sep 87*	10

Vaughn MEADER — US

ALBUMS:	HITS 1			WEEKS 8
THE FIRST FAMILY *Features Naomi Brossart as Jackie Kennedy.*	*London*	12	*29 Dec 62*	8

David MEASHAM - See Roger DALTREY

MEAT BEAT MANIFESTO — UK

SINGLES:	HITS 1			WEEKS 1
MINDSTREAM	*Play*	55	*20 Feb 93*	1

MEAT LOAF — US

SINGLES:	HITS 19			WEEKS 146
YOU TOOK THE WORDS RIGHT OUT OF MY MOUTH	*Epic*	33	*20 May 78*	8
TWO OUT OF THREE AIN'T BAD	*Epic*	32	*19 Aug 78*	8
BAT OUT OF HELL	*Epic*	15	*10 Feb 79*	7
I'M GONNA LOVE HER FOR BOTH OF US	*Epic*	62	*26 Sep 81*	3
DEAD RINGER FOR LOVE *Uncredited vocals by Cher.*	*Epic*	5	*28 Nov 81*	17
IF YOU REALLY WANT TO	*Epic*	59	*28 May 83*	2
MIDNIGHT AT THE LOST & FOUND	*Epic*	17	*24 Sep 83*	8
RAZOR'S EDGE *Original release reached No. 93 in 1983.*	*Epic*	41	*14 Jan 84*	3
MODERN GIRL	*Arista*	17	*6 Oct 84*	9
NOWHERE FAST	*Arista*	67	*22 Dec 84*	4
PIECE OF THE ACTION	*Arista*	47	*23 Mar 85*	5
ROCK 'N' ROLL MERCENARIES *Above hit: MEAT LOAF with John PARR.*	*Arista*	31	*30 Aug 86*	6
DEAD RINGER FOR LOVE [RI]	*Epic*	53	*22 Jun 91*	2
TWO OUT OF THREE AIN'T BAD [RI]	*Epic*	69	*27 Jun 92*	1
I'D DO ANYTHING FOR LOVE (BUT I WON'T DO THAT) *Vocals by Patti Russo.*	*Virgin*	1	*9 Oct 93*	19
BAT OUT OF HELL [RI]	*Epic*	8	*18 Dec 93*	9
ROCK AND ROLL DREAMS COME THROUGH	*Virgin*	11	*19 Feb 94*	7
OBJECTS IN THE REAR VIEW MIRROR MAY APPEAR CLOSER THAN THEY ARE	*Virgin*	26	*7 May 94*	4
I'D LIE FOR YOU (AND THAT'S THE TRUTH) *Vocals by Patti Russo.*	*Virgin*	2	*28 Oct 95*	11
NOT A DRY EYE IN THE HOUSE	*Virgin*	7	*27 Jan 96*	6
RUNNIN' FOR THE RED LIGHT (I GOTTA LIFE)	*Virgin*	21	*27 Apr 96*	3
IS NOTHING SACRED *Above hit: MEAT LOAF featuring Patti RUSSO.*	*Virgin*	15	*17 Apr 99*	4
ALBUMS:	**HITS 11**			**WEEKS 763**
COMPILATION ALBUMS:	**HITS 1**			**WEEKS 16**
BAT OUT OF HELL *Peak position reached on 23 Aug 81. Includes re-entries through to 1987.*	*Epic*	9	*11 Mar 78*	395
DEAD RINGER	*Epic*	1	*12 Sep 81*	46
MIDNIGHT AT THE LOST AND FOUND	*Epic*	7	*7 May 83*	23
BAD ATTITUDE	*Arista*	8	*10 Nov 84*	16
HITS OUT OF HELL	*Epic*	2	*26 Jan 85*	33
BLIND BEFORE I STOP	*Arista*	28	*11 Oct 86*	6
'LIVE' AT WEMBLEY	*RCA*	60	*7 Nov 87*	2
HITS OUT OF HELL [RE-1ST] *Re-released at mid-price. Chart position reached in 1993. Includes re-entries through to 1993 (1988 peak No. 77, 1991 peak No. 70).*	*Epic*	26	*16 Apr 88*	25
HEAVEN AND HELL *Features solo recordings by each artist and was thus an entry in the compilation chart.* *Above hit: MEAT LOAF/Bonnie TYLER.*	*Telstar*	9	*25 Nov 89*	12
BAT OUT OF HELL [RE] *Repackaged with additional track. Includes re-entries through to 1999. Chart position reached in 1994 (1991 peak No. 14, 1992 peak No. 24).*	*Epic*	12	*27 Jul 91*	78
BAT OUT OF HELL II - BACK INTO HELL	*Virgin*	1	*18 Sep 93*	59

HITS OUT OF HELL [RE-2ND]	*Epic*	31	*25 Dec 93*	22
Re-released. Chart position reached in 1995.				
ALIVE IN HELL	*Pure Music*	33	*22 Oct 94*	4
Live recordings from 1987.				
HEAVEN AND HELL [RI]	*Columbia*	12	*16 Sep 95*	4
Above hit: MEAT LOAF/Bonnie TYLER.				
WELCOME TO THE NEIGHBOURHOOD	*Virgin*	3	*11 Nov 95*	27
THE VERY BEST OF MEAT LOAF	*Virgin/Sony TV*	14	*14 Nov 98*	27

MECO — US

SINGLES:	HITS 1		WEEKS 9	
STAR WARS THEME/CANTINA BAND [M]	*RCA Victor*	7	*1 Oct 77*	9

Glenn MEDEIROS — US

SINGLES:	HITS 3		WEEKS 26	
NOTHING'S GONNA CHANGE MY LOVE FOR YOU	*London*	1	*18 Jun 88*	13
Originally recorded by George Benson.				
LONG AND LASTING LOVE (ONCE IN A LIFETIME)	*London*	42	*3 Sep 88*	4
SHE AIN'T WORTH IT	*London*	12	*30 Jun 90*	9
Above hit: Glenn MEDEIROS (featuring Bobby BROWN).				
ALBUMS:	**HITS 1**		**WEEKS 2**	
NOT ME	*London*	63	*8 Oct 88*	2

Paul MEDFORD – See Letitia DEAN and Paul MEDFORD

MEDIAEVAL BAEBES — International

ALBUMS:	HITS 2		WEEKS 7	
SALVA NOS	*Virgin*	62	*29 Nov 97*	6
WORLDES BLYSSE	*Venture*	73	*31 Oct 98*	1

MEDICINE HEAD — UK

SINGLES:	HITS 4		WEEKS 37	
(AND THE) PICTURES IN THE SKY	*Dandelion*	22	*26 Jun 71*	8
ONE & ONE IS ONE	*Polydor*	3	*5 May 73*	13
RISING SUN	*Polydor*	11	*4 Aug 73*	9
SLIP AND SLIDE	*Polydor*	22	*9 Feb 74*	7

MEDICINE SHOW – See DR. HOOK

Bill MEDLEY — US

SINGLES:	HITS 2		WEEKS 29	
(I'VE HAD) THE TIME OF MY LIFE (LOVE THEME FROM 'DIRTY DANCING')	*RCA*	6	*31 Oct 87*	12
From the film 'Dirty Dancing'.				
Above hit: Bill MEDLEY and Jennifer WARNES.				
HE AIN'T HEAVY, HE'S MY BROTHER	*Scotti Brothers*	25	*27 Aug 88*	6
From the film 'Rambo III'.				
(I'VE HAD) THE TIME OF MY LIFE (LOVE THEME FROM 'DIRTY DANCING') [RE]	*RCA*	8	*15 Dec 90*	11

MEDWAY — US

SINGLES:	HITS 1		WEEKS 2	
THE FAT BASTARD [EP]	*Hooj Choons*	69	*29 Apr 00*	1
Lead track: Release.				
RELEASE	*Hooj Choons*	67	*10 Mar 01*	1
Remix of track 1 from The Fat Bastard EP. Vocals by Sam Mollison.				

Michael MEDWIN, Bernard BRESSLAW, Alfie BASS and Leslie FYSON — UK

(See also Bernard Bresslaw.)

SINGLES:	HITS 1		WEEKS 9	
THE SIGNATURE TUNE OF THE ARMY GAME	*His Master's Voice*	5	*31 May 58*	9
Theme from the ITV comedy series.				

MEECHIE — US

SINGLES:	HITS 1		WEEKS 1	
YOU BRING ME JOY	*Vibe*	74	*2 Sep 95*	1

Tony MEEHAN — UK

(See also Jet Harris and Tony Meehan.)

SINGLES:	HITS 1		WEEKS 4	
SONG OF MEXICO	*Decca*	39	*18 Jan 64*	4

MEEKER — UK

SINGLES:	HITS 1			WEEKS 1
SAVE ME	*Underwater*	60	*26 Feb 00*	1

Originally recorded by Nina Simone.

MEGA CITY FOUR — UK

SINGLES:	HITS 5			WEEKS 7
WORDS THAT SAY	*Big Life*	66	*19 Oct 91*	1
STOP [EP]	*Big Life*	36	*8 Feb 92*	2
Lead track: Stop.				
SHIVERING SAND	*Big Life*	35	*16 May 92*	2
IRON SKY	*Big Life*	48	*1 May 93*	1
WALLFLOWER	*Big Life*	69	*17 Jul 93*	1

ALBUMS:	HITS 3			WEEKS 3
TRANZOPHOBIA	*Decoy*	67	*17 Jun 89*	1
SEBASTAPOL ROAD	*Big Life*	41	*7 Mar 92*	1
MAGIC BULLETS	*Big Life*	57	*22 May 93*	1

MEGABASS — UK

SINGLES:	HITS 1			WEEKS 9
TIME TO MAKE THE FLOOR BURN [M]	*Brothers Organisation*	16	*10 Nov 90*	9

Mix of dance tracks.

MEGADETH — US

SINGLES:	HITS 10			WEEKS 32
WAKE UP DEAD	*Capitol*	65	*19 Dec 87*	2
ANARCHY IN THE U.K.	*Capitol*	45	*27 Feb 88*	3
MARY JANE	*Capitol*	46	*21 May 88*	2
NO MORE MR. NICE GUY	*SBK*	13	*13 Jan 90*	6
HOLY WARS . . . THE PUNISHMENT DUE	*Capitol*	24	*29 Sep 90*	3
HANGAR 18	*Capitol*	26	*16 Mar 91*	4
SYMPHONY OF DESTRUCTION	*Capitol*	15	*27 Jun 92*	3
SKIN O' MY TEETH	*Capitol*	13	*24 Oct 92*	3
SWEATING BULLETS	*Capitol*	26	*29 May 93*	3
TRAIN OF CONSEQUENCES	*Capitol*	22	*7 Jan 95*	3

ALBUMS:	HITS 7			WEEKS 26
SO FAR, SO GOOD . . . SO WHAT!	*Capitol*	18	*26 Mar 88*	5
RUST IN PEACE	*Capitol*	8	*6 Oct 90*	4
COUNTDOWN TO EXTINCTION	*Capitol*	5	*18 Jul 92*	8
YOUTHANASIA	*Capitol*	6	*5 Nov 94*	4
YOUTHANASIA / HIDDEN TREASURE [RE]	*Capitol*	28	*25 Mar 95*	1
Hidden Treasure is the title of the 2nd disc that was repackaged with Youthanasia.				
CRYPTIC WRITINGS	*Capitol*	38	*19 Jul 97*	1
RISK	*Capitol*	29	*18 Sep 99*	2
THE WORLD NEEDS A HERO	*Metal Is*	45	*26 May 01*	1

MEGAMAN – See OXIDE and NEUTRINO

Zubin MEHTA – See 3 TENORS: José CARRERAS, Placido DOMINGO, Luciano PAVAROTTI

MEJA — Sweden

SINGLES:	HITS 2			WEEKS 14
ALL 'BOUT THE MONEY	*Columbia*	12	*24 Oct 98*	5
PRIVATE EMOTION	*Columbia*	9	*29 Apr 00*	9

Above hit: Ricky MARTIN featuring MEJA.

MEKKA — UK

SINGLES:	HITS 1			WEEKS 1
DIAMONDBACK	*Perfecto*	67	*24 Mar 01*	1

MEKON featuring Roxanne SHANTE — UK/US

SINGLES:	HITS 1			WEEKS 1
WHAT'S GOING ON?	*Wall Of Sound*	43	*23 Sep 00*	1

Samples GLOBE and Wizzkid's Play The Beat Mr DJ.

Melle MEL — US

(See also Duran Duran; Quincy Jones.)

SINGLES:	HITS 6			WEEKS 77
MESSAGE II (SURVIVAL)	*Sugar Hill*	74	*22 Jan 83*	2
Above hit: Melle MEL and Duke BOOTEE.				
WHITE LINES (DON'T DON'T DO IT)	*Sugar Hill*	60	*19 Nov 83*	3
Above hit: GRAND MASTER and Melle MEL.				
WHITE LINES (DON'T DON'T DO IT) [RE-1ST]	*Sugar Hill*	7	*11 Feb 84*	38
Peak position reached on 28 Jul 84.				

BEAT STREET BREAKDOWN *Sales combined for 7" on Atlantic and 12" on Sugar Hill. From the film 'Beat Street'.*	*Atlantic / Sugar Hill*	42	*30 Jun 84*	7
WE DON'T WORK FOR FREE *Above 2: GRANDMASTER Melle MEL and the FURIOUS FIVE.*	*Sugar Hill*	45	*22 Sep 84*	4
WHITE LINES (DON'T DON'T DO IT) [RE-2ND] *Above hit: GRAND MASTER and Melle MEL.*	*Sugar Hill*	75	*24 Nov 84*	1
STEP OFF *Above hit: GRANDMASTER Melle MEL and the FURIOUS FIVE.*	*Sugar Hill*	8	*15 Dec 84*	12
WHITE LINES (DON'T DON'T DO IT) [RE-3RD] *Above hit: GRAND MASTER and Melle MEL.*	*Sugar Hill*	73	*5 Jan 85*	1
THE MEGA MELLE MIX [M] / PUMP ME UP *The Mega Melle mix was only available on the 12" release; it was listed from 6 Apr 85, after dropping to No. 46.* *Above hit: GRANDMASTER Melle MEL and the FURIOUS FIVE.*	*Sugar Hill*	45	*16 Mar 85*	6
WHITE LINES (DON'T DO IT) [RM] *Remixed by D & S.* *Above hit: GRANDMASTER FLASH and Melle MEL.*	*WGAF*	59	*8 Jan 94*	3

ALBUMS:	**HITS 1**			**WEEKS 5**
WORK PARTY *Above hit: GRANDMASTER Melle MEL and the FURIOUS FIVE.*	*Sugar Hill*	45	*20 Oct 84*	5

MEL and KIM — UK

(See also Kim Appleby.)

SINGLES:	**HITS 4**			**WEEKS 51**
SHOWING OUT (GET FRESH AT THE WEEKEND)	*Supreme*	3	*20 Sep 86*	19
RESPECTABLE	*Supreme*	1	*7 Mar 87*	15
F.L.M.	*Supreme*	7	*11 Jul 87*	10
THAT'S THE WAY IT IS	*Supreme*	10	*27 Feb 88*	7

ALBUMS:	**HITS 1**			**WEEKS 25**
F.L.M.	*Supreme*	3	*25 Apr 87*	25

MEL and KIM - See Mel SMITH; Kim WILDE

MELACHRINO ORCHESTRA conducted by George MELACHRINO — UK

SINGLES:	**HITS 1**			**WEEKS 9**
AUTUMN CONCERTO	*His Master's Voice*	18	*13 Oct 56*	9

MELANIE — US

SINGLES:	**HITS 4**			**WEEKS 35**
RUBY TUESDAY	*Buddah*	9	*26 Sep 70*	14
RUBY TUESDAY [RE] / WHAT HAVE THEY DONE TO MY SONG MA *Ruby Tuesday was only listed on 9 January 71 when it charted at No. 43. The following week What Have They Done To My Song Ma was the side listed.*	*Buddah*	39	*9 Jan 71*	2
BRAND NEW KEY	*Buddah*	4	*1 Jan 72*	12
WILL YOU LOVE ME TOMORROW	*Neighbourhood*	37	*16 Feb 74*	5
EVERY BREATH OF THE WAY	*Neighbourhood*	70	*24 Sep 83*	2

ALBUMS:	**HITS 6**			**WEEKS 69**
CANDLES IN THE RAIN	*Buddah*	5	*19 Sep 70*	27
LEFTOVER WINE *Live recordings.*	*Buddah*	22	*16 Jan 71*	11
THE GOOD BOOK	*Buddah*	9	*29 May 71*	9
GATHER ME	*Buddah*	14	*8 Jan 72*	14
GARDEN IN THE CITY	*Buddah*	19	*1 Apr 72*	6
THE FOUR SIDES OF MELANIE	*Buddah*	23	*7 Oct 72*	2

MELBOURNE SYMPHONY ORCHESTRA - See Elton JOHN

MELISSA - See TECHNOTRONIC

MELKY SEDECK — US

(See Wyclef Jean.)

SINGLES:	**HITS 1**			**WEEKS 1**
RAW *Rap performed by Elementary and Mic Masters from Bob Foundation.*	*MCA*	50	*8 May 99*	1

John Cougar MELLENCAMP — US

SINGLES:	**HITS 4**			**WEEKS 18**
JACK AND DIANE *Above hit: John COUGAR.*	*Riva*	25	*23 Oct 82*	8
SMALL TOWN	*Riva*	53	*1 Feb 86*	4
R.O.C.K. IN THE U.S.A.	*Riva*	67	*10 May 86*	3
WILD NIGHT *Above hit: John MELLENCAMP with Me'shell NDEGEOCELLO.*	*Mercury*	34	*3 Sep 94*	3

ALBUMS:	HITS 7			WEEKS 31
AMERICAN FOOL	*Riva*	37	*6 Nov 82*	6
Above hit: John COUGAR.				
UH-HUH	*Riva*	92	*3 Mar 84*	1
THE LONESOME JUBILEE	*Mercury*	31	*3 Oct 87*	12
BIG DADDY	*Mercury*	25	*27 May 89*	4
WHENEVER WE WANTED	*Mercury*	39	*19 Oct 91*	2
HUMAN WHEELS	*Mercury*	37	*18 Sep 93*	2
THE BEST THAT I COULD DO 1978-1988	*Mercury*	25	*17 Jan 98*	4
Above 3: John MELLENCAMP.				

MELLOMEN - See Rosemary CLOONEY; Doris DAY; Frankie LAINE; Elvis PRESLEY

Will MELLOR — UK

SINGLES:	HITS 2			WEEKS 9
WHEN I NEED YOU	*Unity*	5	*28 Feb 98*	6
NO MATTER WHAT I DO	*Jive*	23	*27 Jun 98*	3

MELLOW TRAX — Germany

SINGLES:	HITS 1			WEEKS 2
OUTTA SPACE	*Substance*	41	*14 Oct 00*	2
Samples Max Romeo and Lee Perry's Chase The Devil and the Prodigy's Out Of Space.				

MELODIANS — Jamaica

SINGLES:	HITS 1			WEEKS 1
SWEET SENSATION	*Trojan*	41	*10 Jan 70*	1

MELODY MAKERS - See Ziggy MARLEY and the MELODY MAKERS

MELT featuring LITTLE MS. MARCIE — UK

SINGLES:	HITS 1			WEEKS 1
HARD HOUSE MUSIC	*WEA*	59	*8 Apr 00*	1

MELTDOWN — UK/US

SINGLES:	HITS 1			WEEKS 1
MY LIFE IS IN YOUR HANDS	*Sony*	44	*27 Apr 96*	1

Harold MELVIN and the BLUENOTES — US

SINGLES:	HITS 9			WEEKS 52
IF YOU DON'T KNOW ME BY NOW	*CBS*	9	*13 Jan 73*	9
THE LOVE I LOST	*Philadelphia International*	21	*12 Jan 74*	8
SATISFACTION GUARANTEED (OR TAKE YOUR LOVE BACK)	*Philadelphia International*	32	*13 Apr 74*	6
GET OUT (AND LET ME CRY)	*Route*	35	*31 May 75*	5
WAKE UP EVERYBODY	*Philadelphia International*	23	*28 Feb 76*	7
Above hit: Harold MELVIN and the BLUE NOTES.				
DON'T LEAVE ME THIS WAY	*Philadelphia International*	5	*22 Jan 77*	10
Above hit: Harold MELVIN and the BLUENOTES featuring Theodore PENDERGRASS.				
REACHING FOR THE WORLD	*ABC*	48	*2 Apr 77*	1
DON'T GIVE ME UP	*Philly World/London*	59	*28 Apr 84*	4
Above 2: Harold MELVIN and the BLUE NOTES.				
TODAY'S YOUR LUCKY DAY	*Philly World/London*	66	*4 Aug 84*	2
Above hit: Harold MELVIN and the BLUE NOTES featuring NIKKO.				

MEMBERS — UK

SINGLES:	HITS 2			WEEKS 14
THE SOUND OF THE SUBURBS	*Virgin*	12	*3 Feb 79*	9
OFFSHORE BANKING BUSINESS	*Virgin*	31	*7 Apr 79*	5
ALBUMS:	**HITS 1**			**WEEKS 5**
AT THE CHELSEA NIGHTCLUB	*Virgin*	45	*28 Apr 79*	5

MEMBERS OF MAYDAY — Germany

SINGLES:	HITS 1			WEEKS 3
10 IN 01	*Deviant*	31	*23 Jun 01*	3

MEMPHIS HORNS - See Robert CRAY BAND

MEN AT WORK — Australia

SINGLES:	HITS 5			WEEKS 39
WHO CAN IT BE NOW	*Epic*	45	*30 Oct 82*	5
DOWN UNDER	*Epic*	1	*8 Jan 83*	12
OVERKILL	*Epic*	21	*9 Apr 83*	10
IT'S A MISTAKE	*Epic*	33	*2 Jul 83*	6
DR. HECKYLL AND MR. JIVE	*Epic*	31	*10 Sep 83*	6

ALBUMS:	HITS 2			WEEKS 71
BUSINESS AS USUAL	*Epic*	1	*15 Jan 83*	44
CARGO	*Epic*	8	*30 Apr 83*	27

MEN OF VIZION — US

SINGLES:	HITS 1			WEEKS 2
DO YOU FEEL ME? (. . . FREAK YOU) *Rap performed by Mr. Cheeks.*	*MJJ*	36	*27 Mar 99*	2

MEN THEY COULDN'T HANG — UK

SINGLES:	HITS 1			WEEKS 4
THE COLOURS	*Magnet*	61	*2 Apr 88*	4
ALBUMS:	**HITS 5**			**WEEKS 9**
NIGHT OF A THOUSAND CANDLES	*Imp*	91	*27 Jul 85*	2
HOW GREEN IS THE VALLEY	*MCA*	68	*8 Nov 86*	2
WAITING FOR BONAPARTE	*Magnet*	41	*23 Apr 88*	2
SILVER TOWN	*Silvertone*	39	*6 May 89*	2
THE DOMINO CLUB	*Silvertone*	53	*1 Sep 90*	1

MEN WITHOUT HATS — Canada

SINGLES:	HITS 1			WEEKS 11
THE SAFETY DANCE	*Statik*	6	*8 Oct 83*	11
ALBUMS:	**HITS 1**			**WEEKS 1**
RHYTHM OF YOUTH	*Statik*	96	*12 Nov 83*	1

Sergio MENDES featuring Joe PIZZULO and Leza MILLER — Brazil

SINGLES:	HITS 1			WEEKS 5
NEVER GONNA LET YOU GO	*A&M*	45	*9 Jul 83*	5

Andrea MENDEZ — UK

SINGLES:	HITS 1			WEEKS 1
BRING ME LOVE	*AM:PM*	44	*3 Aug 96*	1

MENSWEAR — UK

SINGLES:	HITS 6			WEEKS 18
I'LL MANAGE SOMEHOW	*Laurel*	49	*15 Apr 95*	1
DAYDREAMER	*Laurel*	14	*1 Jul 95*	4
STARDUST *Based on the David Essex film of the same name.*	*Laurel*	16	*30 Sep 95*	3
SLEEPING IN	*Laurel*	24	*16 Dec 95*	3
BEING BRAVE	*Laurel*	10	*23 Mar 96*	4
WE LOVE YOU	*Laurel*	22	*7 Sep 96*	3
ALBUMS:	**HITS 1**			**WEEKS 6**
NUISANCE	*Laurel*	11	*21 Oct 95*	6

MENTAL AS ANYTHING — Australia/New Zealand

SINGLES:	HITS 1			WEEKS 13
LIVE IT UP *From the film 'Crocodile Dundee'.*	*Epic*	3	*7 Feb 87*	13

Sir Yehudi MENUHIN – See Julian LLOYD WEBBER

Natalie MERCHANT — US

ALBUMS:	HITS 2			WEEKS 3
TIGERLILY	*Elektra*	39	*1 Jul 95*	2
OPHELIA	*Elektra*	52	*13 Jun 98*	1

Freddie MERCURY — UK

(See also Freddie Mercury and Montserrat Caballe.)

SINGLES:	HITS 7			WEEKS 62
LOVE KILLS *From the film 'Metropolis'.*	*CBS*	10	*22 Sep 84*	8
I WAS BORN TO LOVE YOU	*CBS*	11	*20 Apr 85*	10
MADE IN HEAVEN	*CBS*	57	*13 Jul 85*	4
LIVING ON MY OWN	*CBS*	50	*21 Sep 85*	3
TIME	*EMI*	32	*24 May 86*	5
THE GREAT PRETENDER	*Parlophone*	4	*7 Mar 87*	9
IN MY DEFENCE *Originally from Dave Clark's musical 'Time'.*	*Parlophone*	8	*12 Dec 92*	7
THE GREAT PRETENDER [RI] *From the film 'Night In The City'.*	*Parlophone*	29	*6 Feb 93*	3

LIVING ON MY OWN [RM]	*Parlophone*	1	*31 Jul 93*	13
Rearranged and recorded by No More Brothers, initially for release only in Belgium.				
ALBUMS:	**HITS 3**			**WEEKS 57**
MR BAD GUY	*CBS*	6	*11 May 85*	23
THE FREDDIE MERCURY ALBUM	*Parlophone*	4	*28 Nov 92*	25
SOLO - THE VERY BEST OF FREDDIE MERCURY	*Parlophone*	13	*4 Nov 00*	9
3 CD set - re-issues of Mr. Bad Guy, Barcelona and a bonus CD of hits and rarities.				

Freddie MERCURY and Montserrat CABALLE — UK/Spain

(See also Placido Domingo, Jose Carreras and Montserrat Caballe; Freddie Mercury.)

SINGLES:	**HITS 1**			**WEEKS 17**
BARCELONA	*Polydor*	8	*7 Nov 87*	9
BARCELONA [RI]	*Polydor*	2	*8 Aug 92*	8
Re-issued to coincide with the 1992 Olympic Games in Barcelona.				
ALBUMS:	**HITS 1**			**WEEKS 8**
BARCELONA	*Polydor*	25	*22 Oct 88*	4
BARCELONA [RE]	*Polydor*	15	*22 Aug 92*	4
Re-entered due to the use of the title track at the 1992 Olympic Games.				

MERCURY REV — US

SINGLES:	**HITS 4**			**WEEKS 8**
GODDESS ON A HIWAY	*V2*	51	*14 Nov 98*	1
DELTA SUN BOTTLENECK STOMP	*V2*	26	*6 Feb 99*	2
OPUS 40	*V2*	31	*22 May 99*	2
GODDESS ON A HIWAY [RI]	*V2*	26	*28 Aug 99*	2
NITE AND FOG	*V2*	47	*6 Oct 01*	1
ALBUMS:	**HITS 3**			**WEEKS 17**
BOCES	*Beggars Banquet*	43	*12 Jun 93*	1
DESERTER'S SONGS	*V2*	27	*17 Oct 98*	12
ALL IS DREAM	*V2*	11	*8 Sep 01*	4

MERCY MERCY — UK

SINGLES:	**HITS 1**			**WEEKS 2**
WHAT ARE WE GONNA DO ABOUT IT?	*Ensign*	59	*21 Sep 85*	2

MERLE and ROY — UK

ALBUMS:	**HITS 1**			**WEEKS 5**
REQUESTS	*Myndd Mawr*	74	*26 Sep 87*	4
REQUESTS [RI]	*International*	93	*3 Sep 88*	1

MERLIN - See BEATMASTERS; BOMB THE BASS

MERO — UK

SINGLES:	**HITS 1**			**WEEKS 2**
IT MUST BE LOVE	*RCA*	33	*25 Mar 00*	2

Tony MERRICK — UK

SINGLES:	**HITS 1**			**WEEKS 1**
LADY JANE	*Columbia*	49	*4 Jun 66*	1
Written by Jagger and Richards.				

MERSEYBEATS — UK

SINGLES:	**HITS 7**			**WEEKS 64**
IT'S LOVE THAT REALLY COUNTS	*Fontana*	24	*14 Sep 63*	12
Originally recorded by the Shirelles in 1962.				
I THINK OF YOU	*Fontana*	5	*18 Jan 64*	17
Written by Daniel Boone.				
DON'T TURN AROUND	*Fontana*	13	*18 Apr 64*	11
WISHIN' AND HOPIN'	*Fontana*	13	*11 Jul 64*	10
Originally recorded by Dionne Warwick.				
LAST NIGHT	*Fontana*	40	*7 Nov 64*	3
I LOVE YOU, YES I DO	*Fontana*	22	*16 Oct 65*	8
I STAND ACCUSED	*Fontana*	38	*22 Jan 66*	3
Originally recorded by Tony Colton and the Big Boss Band.				
EPS:	**HITS 2**			**WEEKS 37**
I THINK OF YOU	*Fontana*	8	*21 Mar 64*	12
THE MERSEYBEATS ON STAGE	*Fontana*	2	*11 Apr 64*	25
ALBUMS:	**HITS 1**			**WEEKS 9**
THE MERSEYBEATS	*Fontana*	12	*20 Jun 64*	9

MERSEYS — UK

SINGLES:	HITS 1			WEEKS 13
SORROW	*Fontana*	4	*30 Apr 66*	13
Originally recorded by the McCoys.				

MERTON PARKAS — UK

SINGLES:	HITS 1			WEEKS 6
YOU NEED WHEELS	*Beggars Banquet*	40	*4 Aug 79*	6

MERZ — UK

SINGLES:	HITS 2			WEEKS 2
MANY WEATHERS APART	*Epic*	48	*17 Jul 99*	1
LOVELY DAUGHTER	*Epic*	60	*16 Oct 99*	1

MESCALEROS - See Joe STRUMMER

Mady MESPLE and Danielle MILLET, PARIS OPERA - COMIQUE ORCHESTRA conducted by Alain LOMBARD — France

SINGLES:	HITS 1			WEEKS 4
FLOWER DUET (FROM 'LAKME')	*EMI*	47	*6 Apr 85*	4

MESSIAH — UK

SINGLES:	HITS 3			WEEKS 13
TEMPLE OF DREAMS	*Kickin*	20	*20 Jun 92*	5
I FEEL LOVE	*Kickin*	19	*26 Sep 92*	5
Above hit: MESSIAH Vocals by Precious WILSON.				
THUNDERDOME	*WEA*	29	*27 Nov 93*	3

METAL GURUS — UK

SINGLES:	HITS 1			WEEKS 2
MERRY XMAS EVERYBODY	*Mercury*	55	*8 Dec 90*	2

METALHEADS - See GOLDIE

METALLICA — US/Denmark

SINGLES:	HITS 16			WEEKS 59
THE $5.98 E.P. - GARAGE DAYS RE-REVISITED [EP]	*Vertigo*	27	*22 Aug 87*	4
Lead track: Helpless.				
HARVESTER OF SORROW	*Vertigo*	20	*3 Sep 88*	3
ONE	*Vertigo*	13	*22 Apr 89*	7
ENTER SANDMAN	*Vertigo*	5	*10 Aug 91*	4
THE UNFORGIVEN	*Vertigo*	15	*9 Nov 91*	4
NOTHING ELSE MATTERS	*Vertigo*	6	*2 May 92*	6
WHEREVER I MAY ROAM	*Vertigo*	25	*31 Oct 92*	4
SAD BUT TRUE	*Vertigo*	20	*20 Feb 93*	3
UNTIL IT SLEEPS	*Vertigo*	5	*1 Jun 96*	4
HERO OF THE DAY	*Vertigo*	17	*28 Sep 96*	4
Dedicated to Lemmy of Motorhead.				
MAMA SAID	*Vertigo*	19	*7 Dec 96*	2
THE MEMORY REMAINS	*Vertigo*	13	*22 Nov 97*	3
Backing vocals by Marinne Faithfull.				
THE UNFORGIVEN II	*Vertigo*	15	*7 Mar 98*	4
FUEL	*Vertigo*	31	*4 Jul 98*	2
WHISKEY IN THE JAR	*Vertigo*	29	*27 Feb 99*	2
I DISAPPEAR	*Hollywood*	35	*12 Aug 00*	3
From the film Mission Impossible 2.				

ALBUMS:	HITS 11			WEEKS 116
RIDE THE LIGHTNING	*Music For Nations*	87	*11 Aug 84*	2
MASTER OF PUPPETS	*Music For Nations*	41	*15 Mar 86*	4
. . . AND JUSTICE FOR ALL	*Vertigo*	4	*17 Sep 88*	6
THE GOOD THE BAD AND THE LIVE: THE 6½ YEARS ANNIVERSARY COLLECTION	*Vertigo*	56	*19 May 90*	1
6 × 12" box set plus 4-track live EP.				
METALLICA	*Vertigo*	1	*24 Aug 91*	70
LIVE SHIT - BINGE AND PURGE	*Vertigo*	54	*11 Dec 93*	1
Package containing 3 videos/2CDs & a 72 page booklet. Live recordings from Mexico Feb 93.				
LOAD	*Vertigo*	1	*15 Jun 96*	18
HERO OF THE DAY	*Vertigo*	47	*5 Oct 96*	1
This was a 4th format release of the single. With 5 tracks and retailing at the same as a mid-price LP it was not eligible for the singles chart.				
RELOAD	*Vertigo*	4	*29 Nov 97*	9
GARAGE INC.	*Vertigo*	29	*5 Dec 98*	2
Tracks from 1987's Gararge Days Revisited EP plus B-sides and newly recorded covers.				
S&M	*Vertigo*	33	*4 Dec 99*	2
Re-recorded with the San Francisco Symphony Orchestra, conducted by Michael Kamen.				

METEORS — UK

SINGLES:	HITS 1			WEEKS 2
JOHNNY REMEMBER ME	*I.D.*	66	*26 Feb 83*	2
ALBUMS:	**HITS 1**			**WEEKS 3**
WRECKIN' CREW	*I.D.*	53	*26 Feb 83*	3

Pat METHENY GROUP – See David BOWIE

METHOD MAN — US

(See also B Real, Busta Rhymes, Coolio, LL Cool J and Method Man; Method Man and Redman.)

SINGLES:	HITS 3			WEEKS 8
RELEASE YO'DELF	*Def Jam*	46	*29 Apr 95*	1
I'LL BE THERE FOR YOU/YOU'RE ALL I NEED TO GET BY [M]	*Def Jam*	10	*29 Jul 95*	5
Above hit: METHOD MAN featuring Mary J. BLIGE.				
BREAK UPS 2 MAKE UPS	*Def Jam*	33	*22 May 99*	2
Above hit: METHOD MAN featuring D'ANGELO.				
ALBUMS:	**HITS 1**			**WEEKS 1**
TICAL 2000: JUDGEMENT DAY	*Def Jam*	49	*28 Nov 98*	1

METHOD MAN and REDMAN — US

(See also Method Man; Redman.)

ALBUMS:	HITS 1			WEEKS 3
BLACK OUT!	*Def Jam*	45	*9 Oct 99*	3

David METHREN – See MUNROS featuring David METHREN

MEZZOFORTE — Iceland

SINGLES:	HITS 2			WEEKS 10
GARDEN PARTY	*Steinar*	17	*5 Mar 83*	9
ROCKALL	*Steinar*	75	*11 Jun 83*	1
ALBUMS:	**HITS 2**			**WEEKS 10**
SURPRISE SURPRISE	*Steinar*	23	*5 Mar 83*	9
CATCHING UP WITH MEZZOFORTE	*Steinar*	95	*2 Jul 83*	1

MFSB — US

SINGLES:	HITS 3			WEEKS 18
TSOP (THE SOUND OF PHILADELPHIA)	*Philadelphia International*	22	*27 Apr 74*	9
Above hit: MFSB featuring the THREE DEGREES.				
SEXY	*Philadelphia International*	37	*26 Jul 75*	5
MYSTERIES OF THE WORLD	*The Sound Of Philadelphia*	41	*31 Jan 81*	4

MIAMI SOUND MACHINE – See Gloria ESTEFAN

George MICHAEL — UK

SINGLES:	HITS 27			WEEKS 249
CARELESS WHISPER	*Epic*	1	*4 Aug 84*	17
A DIFFERENT CORNER	*Epic*	1	*5 Apr 86*	10
I KNEW YOU WERE WAITING (FOR ME)	*Epic*	1	*31 Jan 87*	9
Above hit: Aretha FRANKLIN and George MICHAEL.				
I WANT YOUR SEX RHYTHM 1 LUST	*Epic*	3	*13 Jun 87*	10
FAITH	*Epic*	2	*24 Oct 87*	12
FATHER FIGURE	*Epic*	11	*9 Jan 88*	6
ONE MORE TRY	*Epic*	8	*23 Apr 88*	7
MONKEY	*Epic*	13	*16 Jul 88*	6
KISSING A FOOL	*Epic*	18	*3 Dec 88*	6
PRAYING FOR TIME	*Epic*	6	*25 Aug 90*	7
WAITING FOR THAT DAY	*Epic*	23	*27 Oct 90*	5
FREEDOM! 90	*Epic*	28	*15 Dec 90*	6
HEAL THE PAIN	*Epic*	31	*16 Feb 91*	4
COWBOYS AND ANGELS	*Epic*	45	*30 Mar 91*	3
DON'T LET THE SUN GO DOWN ON ME	*Epic*	1	*7 Dec 91*	10
Live recording from London, March 91.				
Above hit: George MICHAEL with Elton JOHN.				
TOOFUNKY	*Epic*	4	*13 Jun 92*	9
FIVE LIVE [EP]	*Parlophone*	1	*1 May 93*	11
Lead track: Somebody To Love, a live recording from the Freddie Mercury Tribute Concert April 92. Lisa Stansfield only sang on These Are The Days Of Our Lives. Proceeds to the Mercury Phoenix Trust.				
Above hit: George MICHAEL and QUEEN with Lisa STANSFIELD.				
FIVE LIVE [EP] [RE]	*Parlophone*	74	*24 Jul 93*	1
JESUS TO A CHILD	*Virgin*	1	*20 Jan 96*	10
JESUS TO A CHILD [RE-1ST]	*Virgin*	68	*20 Apr 96*	1
FASTLOVE	*Virgin*	1	*4 May 96*	14
Samples Patrice Rushen's Forget Me Nots.				
JESUS TO A CHILD [RE-2ND]	*Virgin*	65	*4 May 96*	2

SPINNING THE WHEEL	*Virgin*	2	*31 Aug 96*	12
OLDER / I CAN'T MAKE YOU LOVE ME	*Virgin*	3	*1 Feb 97*	8
Also credited as The Older EP, though not listed as such on the chart.				
OLDER / I CAN'T MAKE YOU LOVE ME [RE]	*Virgin*	70	*12 Apr 97*	1
STAR PEOPLE '97	*Virgin*	2	*10 May 97*	9
WALTZ AWAY DREAMING	*Aegean*	10	*7 Jun 97*	4
Dedicated to George Michael's late mother.				
Above hit: Toby BOURKE with George MICHAEL.				
STAR PEOPLE '97 [RE]	*Virgin*	59	*19 Jul 97*	4
YOU HAVE BEEN LOVED / THE STRANGEST THING '97	*Virgin*	2	*20 Sep 97*	8
The Strangest Thing '97 listed from 27 Sep 97.				
OUTSIDE	*Epic*	2	*31 Oct 98*	14
OUTSIDE [RE]	*Epic*	61	*13 Feb 99*	2
AS	*Epic*	4	*13 Mar 99*	10
Originally recorded by Stevie Wonder for his 1976 album Songs In The Key Of Life.				
Above hit: George MICHAEL – Mary J. BLIGE.				
IF I TOLD YOU THAT	*Arista*	9	*17 Jun 00*	9
Above hit: Whitney HOUSTON and George MICHAEL.				
IF I TOLD YOU THAT [RE]	*Arista*	51	*26 Aug 00*	2

ALBUMS:	**HITS 5**			**WEEKS 310**
FAITH	*Epic*	1	*14 Nov 87*	77
Includes re-entries through to 1996.				
LISTEN WITHOUT PREJUDICE VOLUME 1	*Epic*	1	*15 Sep 90*	57
OLDER / OLDER & UPPER	*Virgin*	1	*25 May 96*	99
The double-pack, Older & Upper, listed from 13 Dec 97.				
LADIES & GENTLEMEN – THE BEST OF GEORGE MICHAEL	*Epic*	1	*21 Nov 98*	60
SONGS FROM THE LAST CENTURY	*Virgin*	2	*18 Dec 99*	17

MICHAELA — UK

SINGLES:	**HITS 2**			**WEEKS 6**
-H-A-P-P-Y- RADIO	*ffrr*	62	*2 Sep 89*	4
TAKE GOOD CARE OF MY HEART	*London*	66	*28 Apr 90*	2

Lisa MICHAELIS – See Frankie KNUCKLES

Pras MICHEL – See PRAS

MICHELE – See KING BEE

Yvette MICHELE — US

SINGLES:	**HITS 1**			**WEEKS 3**
I'M NOT FEELING YOU	*Loud*	36	*5 Apr 97*	3

Keith MICHELL — Australia

SINGLES:	**HITS 3**			**WEEKS 25**
I'LL GIVE YOU THE EARTH (TOUS LES BATEAUX, TOUS LES OISEAUX)	*Spark*	43	*27 Mar 71*	1
I'LL GIVE YOU THE EARTH (TOUS LES BATEAUX, TOUS LES OISEAUX) [RE]	*Spark*	30	*17 Apr 71*	10
CAPTAIN BEAKY / WILFRED THE WEASEL	*Polydor*	5	*26 Jan 80*	10
Became popular due to airplay on Noel Edmunds BBC Radio 1 Sunday morning show.				
THE TRIAL OF HISSING SID	*Polydor*	53	*29 Mar 80*	4
Above 2: Keith MICHELL, CAPTAIN BEAKY and his BAND.				

ALBUMS:	**HITS 1**			**WEEKS 12**
CAPTAIN BEAKY AND HIS BAND	*Polydor*	28	*9 Feb 80*	12
Above hit: Keith MICHELL and VARIOUS ARTISTS.				

MICHELLE — Trinidad

SINGLES:	**HITS 1**			**WEEKS 1**
STANDING HERE ALL ALONE	*Positiva*	69	*8 Jun 96*	1

Vicki MICHELLE – See RENE and YVETTE featuring Gordon KAYE and Vicki MICHELLE

Lloyd MICHELS – See MISTURA featuring Lloyd MICHELS (trumpet)

MICK and PAT – See PAT and MICK

MICROBE — UK

SINGLES:	**HITS 1**			**WEEKS 7**
GROOVY BABY	*CBS*	29	*17 May 69*	7
Features the voice of three-year-old Ian Doody, backing singers are Lesley Duncan, Madeline Bell and Dusty Springfield.				

MICRODISNEY — Ireland

SINGLES:	**HITS 1**			**WEEKS 3**
TOWN TO TOWN	*Virgin*	55	*21 Feb 87*	3

MIDDLE OF THE ROAD — UK

SINGLES:	HITS 5			WEEKS 76
CHIRPY CHIRPY CHEEP CHEEP *Originally recorded by Lally Stott.*	*RCA Victor*	1	*5 Jun 71*	34
TWEEDLE DEE, TWEEDLE DUM	*RCA Victor*	2	*4 Sep 71*	17
SOLEY SOLEY	*RCA Victor*	5	*11 Dec 71*	12
SACRAMENTO (A WONDERFUL TOWN)	*RCA Victor*	49	*25 Mar 72*	1
SACRAMENTO (A WONDERFUL TOWN) [RE]	*RCA Victor*	23	*8 Apr 72*	6
SAMSON AND DELILAH	*RCA Victor*	26	*29 Jul 72*	6

MIDDLESBOROUGH FC featuring Bob MORTIMER and Chris REA — UK

(See also Chis Rea.)

SINGLES:	HITS 1			WEEKS 1
LET'S DANCE *Re-recorded version of Rea's hit. Charity record with proceeds to NSPCC.*	*Magnet*	44	*24 May 97*	1

MIDFIELD GENERAL featuring Linda LEWIS — UK

SINGLES:	HITS 1			WEEKS 1
REACH OUT	*Skint*	61	*19 Aug 00*	1

MIDGET — UK

SINGLES:	HITS 2			WEEKS 2
ALL FALL DOWN	*Radarscope*	57	*31 Jan 98*	1
INVISIBLE BALOON	*Radarscope*	66	*18 Apr 98*	1

MIDI XPRESS — UK

SINGLES:	HITS 1			WEEKS 1
CHASE	*Labello Dance*	73	*11 May 96*	1

Bette MIDLER — US

SINGLES:	HITS 3			WEEKS 27
WIND BENEATH MY WINGS *From the film 'Beaches'. Originally recorded by Sheena Easton in 1982.*	*Atlantic*	5	*17 Jun 89*	12
FROM A DISTANCE *Originally recorded by Nanci Griffith.*	*Atlantic*	45	*13 Oct 90*	5
FROM A DISTANCE [RE]	*Atlantic*	6	*15 Jun 91*	9
MY ONE TRUE FRIEND *From the film 'One True Thing'.*	*Warner Brothers*	58	*5 Dec 98*	1
ALBUMS:	**HITS 6**			**WEEKS 41**
THE ROSE [OST]	*Atlantic*	68	*8 Mar 80*	1
BEACHES [OST]	*Atlantic*	21	*15 Jul 89*	9
SOME PEOPLE'S LIVES	*Atlantic*	5	*13 Jul 91*	11
FOR THE BOYS [OST]	*Atlantic*	75	*15 Feb 92*	1
EXPERIENCE THE DIVINE - GREATEST HITS	*Atlantic*	3	*30 Oct 93*	15
BETTE OF ROSES	*Atlantic*	55	*25 Nov 95*	4

MIDNIGHT BLUE (A Project with) Louise TUCKER — UK

SINGLES:	HITS 1			WEEKS 5
MIDNIGHT BLUE *Originally recorded by Melissa Manchester.*	*Ariola*	59	*9 Apr 83*	5

MIDNIGHT OIL — Australia

SINGLES:	HITS 6			WEEKS 32
BEDS ARE BURNING	*CBS*	48	*23 Apr 88*	5
THE DEAD HEART	*CBS*	68	*2 Jul 88*	2
BEDS ARE BURNING [RI]	*CBS*	6	*25 Mar 89*	13
THE DEAD HEART [RI]	*CBS*	62	*1 Jul 89*	4
BLUE SKY MINE	*CBS*	66	*10 Feb 90*	2
TRUGANINI *Truganni was was supposedly the last Van Diemen's Land Aborigine, she died in 1876.*	*Columbia*	29	*17 Apr 93*	4
MY COUNTRY	*Columbia*	66	*3 Jul 93*	1
IN THE VALLEY	*Columbia*	60	*6 Nov 93*	1
ALBUMS:	**HITS 3**			**WEEKS 21**
DIESEL AND DUST	*CBS*	71	*25 Jun 88*	3
DIESEL AND DUST [RE]	*CBS*	19	*13 May 89*	13
BLUE SKY MINING	*CBS*	28	*10 Mar 90*	3
EARTH AND SUN AND MOON	*Columbia*	27	*1 May 93*	2

MIDNIGHT STAR — US

SINGLES:	HITS 5			WEEKS 26
OPERATOR	*Solar*	66	*23 Feb 85*	2
HEADLINES	*Solar*	16	*28 Jun 86*	8

MIDAS TOUCH	*Solar*	8	*4 Oct 86*	10
ENGINE NO. 9	*Solar*	64	*7 Feb 87*	3
WET MY WHISTLE	*Solar*	60	*2 May 87*	3
ALBUMS:	**HITS 2**			**WEEKS 6**
PLANETARY INVASION	*Solar*	85	*2 Feb 85*	2
HEADLINES	*Solar*	42	*5 Jul 86*	4

MIGHTY AVENGERS
UK

SINGLES:	**HITS 1**			**WEEKS 2**
SO MUCH IN LOVE	*Decca*	46	*28 Nov 64*	2

MIGHTY DUB KATZ
UK

(See also Norman Cook; Fatboy Slim.)

SINGLES:	**HITS 2**			**WEEKS 5**
JUST ANOTHER GROOVE	*ffrr*	43	*7 Dec 96*	1
MAGIC CARPET RIDE	*ffrr*	24	*2 Aug 97*	4

MIGHTY LEMON DROPS
UK

SINGLES:	**HITS 3**			**WEEKS 6**
THE OTHER SIDE OF YOU	*Blue Guitar*	67	*13 Sep 86*	1
OUT OF HAND	*Blue Guitar*	66	*18 Apr 87*	3
INSIDE OUT	*Blue Guitar*	74	*23 Jan 88*	2
ALBUMS:	**HITS 2**			**WEEKS 5**
HAPPY HEAD	*Blue Guitar*	58	*4 Oct 86*	2
THE WORLD WITHOUT END	*Blue Guitar*	34	*27 Feb 88*	3

MIGHTY MIGHTY BOSSTONES
US

SINGLES:	**HITS 2**			**WEEKS 6**
THE IMPRESSION THAT I GET	*Mercury*	12	*25 Apr 98*	5
THE RASCAL KING	*Mercury*	63	*27 Jun 98*	1
ALBUMS:	**HITS 1**			**WEEKS 2**
LET'S FACE IT	*Mercury*	40	*16 May 98*	2

MIGHTY MORPH'N POWER RANGERS
US

SINGLES:	**HITS 1**			**WEEKS 13**
POWER RANGERS	*RCA*	3	*17 Dec 94*	9
POWER RANGERS [RE-1ST]	*RCA*	57	*25 Feb 95*	2
POWER RANGERS [RE-2ND]	*RCA*	65	*25 Mar 95*	1
POWER RANGERS [RE-3RD]	*RCA*	74	*8 Apr 95*	1
ALBUMS:	**HITS 1**			**WEEKS 3**
POWER RANGERS - THE ALBUM - A ROCK ADVENTURE	*RCA*	50	*24 Dec 94*	3

MIGHTY WAH! - See WAH!

MIGIL 5
UK

SINGLES:	**HITS 2**			**WEEKS 20**
MOCKIN' BIRD HILL *Originally recorded by the Pinetoppers.*	*Pye*	10	*21 Mar 64*	13
NEAR YOU *Originally recorded by Francis Craig.*	*Pye*	31	*6 Jun 64*	7

MIG29
Italy

SINGLES:	**HITS 1**			**WEEKS 2**
MIG29	*Champion*	62	*22 Feb 92*	2

MIKAELA - See SUPERCAR

MIKE
UK

SINGLES:	**HITS 1**			**WEEKS 2**
TWANGLING THREE FINGERS IN A BOX	*Pukka*	40	*19 Nov 94*	2

MIKE and the MECHANICS
UK

(See also Mike Rutherford.)

SINGLES:	**HITS 12**			**WEEKS 67**
SILENT RUNNING (ON DANGEROUS GROUND)	*WEA*	21	*15 Feb 86*	9
ALL I NEED IS A MIRACLE	*WEA*	53	*31 May 86*	4
THE LIVING YEARS *Co-written by B.A.Robertson.*	*WEA*	2	*14 Jan 89*	11
WORD OF MOUTH	*Virgin*	13	*16 Mar 91*	10
A TIME AND A PLACE	*Virgin*	58	*15 Jun 91*	3
EVERYBODY GETS A SECOND CHANCE	*Virgin*	56	*8 Feb 92*	4
OVER MY SHOULDER	*Virgin*	12	*25 Feb 95*	9

A BEGGAR ON A BEACH OF GOLD	*Virgin*	33	*17 Jun 95*	5
ANOTHER CUP OF COFFEE	*Virgin*	51	*2 Sep 95*	4
ALL I NEED IS A MIRACLE '96 [RR]	*Virgin*	27	*17 Feb 96*	4
SILENT RUNNING [RI] *Featured in the Tennents Extra Larger TV commercial.*	*Virgin*	61	*1 Jun 96*	1
NOW THAT YOU'RE GONE	*Virgin*	35	*5 Jun 99*	2
WHENEVER I STOP	*Virgin*	73	*28 Aug 99*	1
ALBUMS:	**HITS 6**			**WEEKS 99**
MIKE AND THE MECHANICS	*WEA*	78	*15 Mar 86*	3
THE LIVING YEARS	*WEA*	2	*26 Nov 88*	19
WORD OF MOUTH	*Virgin*	11	*27 Apr 91*	7
BEGGAR ON A BEACH OF GOLD	*Virgin*	9	*18 Mar 95*	33
THE LIVING YEARS [RI] *Re-released at mid-price.*	*WEA International*	67	*2 Mar 96*	2
HITS	*Virgin*	3	*16 Mar 96*	31
MIKE AND THE MECHANICS *Both eponymous albums are different.*	*Virgin*	14	*12 Jun 99*	4

MIKI and GRIFF — UK

SINGLES:	**HITS 4**			**WEEKS 25**
HOLD BACK TOMORROW *Above hit: Lonnie Donegan Presents MIKI and GRIFF with the Lonnie DONEGAN GROUP.*	*Pye*	26	*3 Oct 59*	2
ROCKIN' ALONE (IN AN OLD ROCKING CHAIR) *Above hit: MIKI and GRIFF with the Lonnie DONEGAN GROUP.*	*Pye*	44	*15 Oct 60*	3
A LITTLE BITTY TEAR	*Pye*	16	*3 Feb 62*	13
I WANT TO STAY HERE	*Pye*	23	*24 Aug 63*	7
EPS:	**HITS 1**			**WEEKS 22**
THIS IS MIKI, THIS IS GRIFF	*Pye*	2	*3 Sep 60*	22

Buddy MILES – See Carlos SANTANA and Buddy MILES

John MILES — UK

SINGLES:	**HITS 4**			**WEEKS 30**
HIGHFLY	*Decca*	17	*18 Oct 75*	6
MUSIC	*Decca*	3	*20 Mar 76*	9
REMEMBER YESTERDAY	*Decca*	32	*16 Oct 76*	5
SLOW DOWN	*Decca*	10	*18 Jun 77*	10
ALBUMS:	**HITS 5**			**WEEKS 25**
REBEL	*Decca*	9	*27 Mar 76*	10
STRANGER IN THE CITY	*Decca*	37	*26 Feb 77*	3
ZARAGON	*Decca*	43	*1 Apr 78*	5
MORE MILES PER HOUR	*Decca*	46	*21 Apr 79*	5
MILES HIGH	*EMI*	96	*29 Aug 81*	2

Robert MILES — Italy

SINGLES:	**HITS 5**			**WEEKS 49**
CHILDREN *Import reached No. 86 a month prior to release.*	*Deconstruction*	2	*24 Feb 96*	18
FABLE *Features vocals by Fiorella Quinn.*	*Deconstruction*	7	*8 Jun 96*	7
FABLE [RE-1ST]	*Deconstruction*	71	*3 Aug 96*	1
FABLE [RE-2ND]	*Deconstruction*	69	*31 Aug 96*	1
ONE & ONE *Above hit: Robert MILES featuring Maria NAYLER.*	*Deconstruction*	3	*16 Nov 96*	17
FREEDOM *Above hit: Robert MILES featuring Kathy SLEDGE.*	*Deconstruction*	15	*29 Nov 97*	4
PATHS *Above hit: Robert MILES featuring Nina MIRANDA.*	*Salt*	74	*28 Jul 01*	1
ALBUMS:	**HITS 2**			**WEEKS 51**
DREAMLAND	*Deconstruction*	7	*22 Jun 96*	48
23AM	*Deconstruction*	42	*6 Dec 97*	3

June MILES-KINGSTON – See Jimmy SOMERVILLE

Paul MILES-KINGSTON – See Sarah BRIGHTMAN; Andrew LLOYD WEBBER

Christina MILIAN – See JA RULE

MILK – See Jason DOWNS

MILK AND HONEY featuring Gali ATARI — Israel

SINGLES:	**HITS 1**			**WEEKS 8**
HALLELUJAH *Eurovision Song Contest winner in 1979. Some copies did not credit Gali Atari.*	*Polydor*	5	*14 Apr 79*	8

MILK INCORPORATED — Belgium

SINGLES:	HITS 1			WEEKS 3
GOOD ENOUGH (LA VACHE) *Vocals by Jade 4 U.*	*Malarky*	23	*28 Feb 98*	3

MILL GIRLS – See Billy COTTON and his BAND

MILLA — US

SINGLES:	HITS 1			WEEKS 1
GENTLEMAN WHO FELL	*SBK*	65	*18 Jun 94*	1

Frankie MILLER — UK

SINGLES:	HITS 4			WEEKS 32
BE GOOD TO YOURSELF *Originally recorded by Andy Fraser.*	*Chrysalis*	27	*4 Jun 77*	6
DARLIN' *Originally recorded by Poacher.*	*Chrysalis*	6	*14 Oct 78*	15
WHEN I'M AWAY FROM YOU	*Chrysalis*	42	*20 Jan 79*	5
CALEDONIA	*MCS*	45	*21 Mar 92*	6
ALBUMS:	**HITS 1**			**WEEKS 1**
FALLING IN LOVE	*Chrysalis*	54	*14 Apr 79*	1

Gary MILLER — UK

SINGLES:	HITS 6			WEEKS 35
THE YELLOW ROSE OF TEXAS *Above hit: Gary MILLER with Dennis WILSON and his Orchestra and the Beryl STOTT CHORUS.*	*Pye Nixa*	13	*22 Oct 55*	5
ROBIN HOOD *Above hit: Gary MILLER with Tony OSBORNE and his Orchestra and the Beryl STOTT CHORUS.*	*Pye Nixa*	10	*14 Jan 56*	6
GARDEN OF EDEN	*Pye Nixa*	14	*12 Jan 57*	6
GARDEN OF EDEN [RE]	*Pye Nixa*	27	*2 Mar 57*	1
WONDERFUL, WONDERFUL *Above 4: Gary MILLER with the Tony OSBORNE ORCHESTRA and the Beryl STOTT CHORUS.*	*Pye Nixa*	29	*20 Jul 57*	1
THE STORY OF MY LIFE *Above hit: Gary MILLER with the Kim DRAKE ORCHESTRA and the Beryl STOTT CHORUS.*	*Pye Nixa*	14	*18 Jan 58*	6
THERE GOES THAT SONG AGAIN / THE NIGHT IS YOUNG (AND YOU'RE SO BEAUTIFUL) *The Night Is Young had first credit but was no longer listed from 13 Jan 62. As an AA side it peaked at No. 32.*	*Pye*	29	*23 Dec 61*	9
THERE GOES THAT SONG AGAIN [RE]	*Pye*	48	*3 Mar 62*	1

Glenn MILLER and his Orchestra — US

SINGLES:	HITS 2			WEEKS 9
MOONLIGHT SERENADE *Originally released in 1946.*	*His Master's Voice*	12	*13 Mar 54*	1
MOONLIGHT SERENADE [RI] / LITTLE BROWN JUG / IN THE MOOD	*RCA Victor Maximillion*	13	*24 Jan 76*	8
ALBUMS:	**HITS 9**			**WEEKS 80**
GLENN MILLER PLAYS SELECTIONS FROM 'THE GLENN MILLER STORY' AND OTHER HITS [OST] *Includes re-entries through to 1970.*	*RCA*	10	*28 Jan 61*	18
THE BEST OF GLENN MILLER	*RCA International*	5	*5 Jul 69*	14
NEARNESS OF YOU	*RCA International*	30	*6 Sep 69*	2
A MEMORIAL 1944-1969	*RCA Victor*	18	*25 Apr 70*	17
THE REAL GLENN MILLER AND HIS ORCHESTRA PLAY THE ORIGINAL MUSIC OF THE FILM 'THE GLENN MILLER STORY' AND OTHER HITS [OST] [RI]	*RCA International*	28	*25 Dec 71*	2
A LEGENDARY PERFORMER	*RCA Victor*	41	*14 Feb 76*	5
A LEGENDARY PERFORMER VOLUME 2	*RCA Victor*	53	*14 Feb 76*	2
THE UNFORGETTABLE GLENN MILLER	*RCA Victor*	4	*9 Apr 77*	8
THE ULTIMATE GLENN MILLER	*Bluebird*	11	*20 Mar 93*	6
THE LOST RECORDINGS *Recorded during Sep & Nov 44.*	*Happy Days*	22	*25 Feb 95*	6

Jody MILLER — US

SINGLES:	HITS 1			WEEKS 1
HOME OF THE BRAVE *Originally recorded by Bonnie and the Treasures.*	*Capitol*	49	*23 Oct 65*	1

Leza MILLER – See Sergio MENDES featuring Joe PIZZULO and Leza MILLER

Mitch MILLER with his Orchestra and Chorus — US

(See also Frankie Laine; Guy Mitchell.)

SINGLES:	HITS 1			WEEKS 13
THE YELLOW ROSE OF TEXAS	*Philips*	2	*8 Oct 55*	13

Ned MILLER — US

SINGLES:	HITS 2			WEEKS 22
FROM A JACK TO A KING	*London*	2	*16 Feb 63*	21
DO WHAT YOU DO DO WELL	*London*	48	*20 Feb 65*	1

Roger MILLER — US

SINGLES:	HITS 5			WEEKS 42
KING OF THE ROAD	*Philips*	1	*20 Mar 65*	15
ENGINE ENGINE NO. 9	*Philips*	33	*5 Jun 65*	5
KANSAS CITY STAR	*Philips*	48	*23 Oct 65*	1
ENGLAND SWINGS	*Philips*	45	*18 Dec 65*	1
ENGLAND SWINGS [RE]	*Philips*	13	*8 Jan 66*	7
LITTLE GREEN APPLES	*Mercury*	19	*30 Mar 68*	10
LITTLE GREEN APPLES [RE-1ST]	*Mercury*	48	*5 Apr 69*	1
LITTLE GREEN APPLES [RE-2ND]	*Mercury*	39	*10 May 69*	2

Steve MILLER BAND — US

SINGLES:	HITS 4			WEEKS 36
ROCK 'N' ME	*Mercury*	11	*23 Oct 76*	9
ABRACADABRA	*Mercury*	2	*19 Jun 82*	11
KEEPS ME WONDERING WHY	*Mercury*	52	*4 Sep 82*	3
THE JOKER	*Capitol*	1	*11 Aug 90*	13
Featured in the Levi's 501 Jeans commercial. Originally released in 1974, it reached No. 1 in the US.				

ALBUMS:	HITS 6			WEEKS 51
FLY LIKE AN EAGLE	*Mercury*	11	*12 Jun 76*	17
BOOK OF DREAMS	*Mercury*	12	*4 Jun 77*	12
ABRACADABRA	*Mercury*	10	*19 Jun 82*	16
STEVE MILLER BAND LIVE!	*Mercury*	79	*7 May 83*	2
Live recordings from their 1982 UK tour.				
THE BEST OF 1968-1973	*Capitol*	34	*6 Oct 90*	3
GREATEST HITS	*PolyGram TV*	58	*10 Oct 98*	1

Suzi MILLER and the JOHNSTON BROTHERS — UK

(See also Johnston Brothers.)

SINGLES:	HITS 1			WEEKS 2
HAPPY DAYS AND LONELY NIGHTS	*Decca*	14	*22 Jan 55*	2

Lisa MILLETT - See GOODFELLAS featuring Lisa MILLETT; SHEER BRONZE featuring Lisa MILLETT

MILLI VANILLI — France/Germany

SINGLES:	HITS 5			WEEKS 50
GIRL YOU KNOW IT'S TRUE	*Cooltempo*	3	*1 Oct 88*	13
Reached No. 99 when first released in Jul 1988. Originally recorded by Numarx.				
BABY DON'T FORGET MY NUMBER	*Cooltempo*	16	*17 Dec 88*	11
BLAME IT ON THE RAIN	*Cooltempo*	53	*22 Jul 89*	5
GIRL I'M GONNA MISS YOU	*Cooltempo*	2	*30 Sep 89*	15
BLAME IT ON THE RAIN [RE]	*Cooltempo*	52	*2 Dec 89*	5
ALL OR NOTHING	*Cooltempo*	74	*10 Mar 90*	1

ALBUMS:	HITS 1			WEEKS 25
ALL OR NOTHING	*Cooltempo*	37	*21 Jan 89*	6
ALL OR NOTHING / 2 X 2 [RE]	*Cooltempo*	6	*28 Oct 89*	19
2 X 2 was a remix album listed from 25 Nov 89, sales were combined.				

MILLICAN and NESBITT — UK

SINGLES:	HITS 2			WEEKS 14
VAYA CON DIOS (MAY GOD BE WITH YOU)	*Pye*	20	*1 Dec 73*	11
FOR OLD TIMES SAKE	*Pye*	38	*18 May 74*	3

ALBUMS:	HITS 2			WEEKS 24
MILLICAN AND NESBITT	*Pye*	3	*23 Mar 74*	21
EVERYBODY KNOWS MILLICAN AND NESBITT	*Pye*	23	*4 Jan 75*	3

MILLIE — Jamaica

SINGLES:	HITS 3			WEEKS 33
MY BOY LOLLIPOP	*Fontana*	2	*14 Mar 64*	18
Originally recorded by Barbie Gaye.				
SWEET WILLIAM	*Fontana*	30	*27 Jun 64*	9

BLOODSHOT EYES	*Fontana*	48	*13 Nov 65*	1
Originally recorded by Hank Penny				
MY BOY LOLLIPOP [RI]	*Island*	46	*25 Jul 87*	5

Spike MILLIGAN — UK

(See also Harry Secombe, Peter Sellers and Spike Milligan.)

ALBUMS:	HITS 2			WEEKS 5
MILLIGAN PRESERVED	*Parlophone*	11	*25 Nov 61*	4
THE SNOW GOOSE	*RCA Victor*	49	*18 Dec 76*	1
Above hit: Spike MILLIGAN with the LONDON SYMPHONY ORCHESTRA.				

MILLIONAIRE HIPPIES — UK

SINGLES:	HITS 2			WEEKS 4
I AM THE MUSIC, HEAR ME!	*Deconstruction*	52	*18 Dec 93*	3
C'MON	*Deconstruction*	59	*10 Sep 94*	1

Garry MILLS — UK

SINGLES:	HITS 3			WEEKS 31
LOOK FOR A STAR	*Top Rank*	7	*9 Jul 60*	14
From the film 'Circus Of Horrors'.				
TOP TEEN BABY	*Top Rank*	24	*22 Oct 60*	12
I'LL STEP DOWN	*Decca*	39	*24 Jun 61*	5

Hayley MILLS — UK

SINGLES:	HITS 1			WEEKS 11
LET'S GET TOGETHER	*Decca*	17	*21 Oct 61*	11
From the film 'The Parent Trap'.				
EPS:	**HITS 1**			**WEEKS 1**
IN SEARCH OF THE CASTAWAYS [OST]	*Decca*	18	*9 Feb 63*	1
Above hit: Maurice CHEVALIER and Hayley MILLS.				

Stephanie MILLS — US

SINGLES:	HITS 6			WEEKS 33
NEVER KNEW LOVE LIKE THIS BEFORE	*20th Century*	4	*18 Oct 80*	14
TWO HEARTS	*20th Century*	49	*23 May 81*	5
Above hit: Stephanie MILLS 'featuring Teddy PENDERGRASS'.				
THE MEDICINE SONG	*Club*	29	*15 Sep 84*	9
(YOU'RE PUTTIN') A RUSH ON ME	*MCA*	62	*5 Sep 87*	2
NEVER DO YOU WRONG	*MCA*	57	*1 May 93*	2
ALL DAY, ALL NIGHT	*MCA*	68	*10 Jul 93*	1

Warren MILLS — Zambia

SINGLES:	HITS 1			WEEKS 1
SUNSHINE	*Jive*	74	*28 Sep 85*	1

MILLS BROTHERS with Hal McINTRYE and his Orchestra — US

SINGLES:	HITS 1			WEEKS 1
THE GLOW WORM	*Brunswick*	10	*31 Jan 53*	1

MILLTOWN BROTHERS — UK

SINGLES:	HITS 5			WEEKS 16
WHICH WAY SHOULD I JUMP?	*A&M*	38	*2 Feb 91*	5
HERE I STAND	*A&M*	41	*13 Apr 91*	4
APPLE GREEN	*A&M*	43	*6 Jul 91*	4
Original release reached No. 82 in 1990.				
TURN OFF	*A&M*	55	*22 May 93*	1
IT'S ALL OVER NOW BABY BLUE	*A&M*	48	*17 Jul 93*	2
ALBUMS:	**HITS 1**			**WEEKS 5**
SLINKY	*A&M*	27	*23 Mar 91*	5

C.B. MILTON — Holland

SINGLES:	HITS 2			WEEKS 5
IT'S A LOVING THING	*Logic*	49	*21 May 94*	2
IT'S A LOVING THING [RM]	*Logic*	34	*25 Mar 95*	2
Remixed by Phil Wilde.				
HOLD ON - REMIXES	*Logic*	62	*19 Aug 95*	1

Garnett MIMMS and TRUCKIN' COMPANY — US

SINGLES:	HITS 1			WEEKS 1
WHAT IT IS	*Arista*	44	*25 Jun 77*	1

MIND OF KANE — UK

(See also Hope A.D.)

SINGLES:	HITS 1			WEEKS 1
STABBED IN THE BACK	*Deja Vu*	64	*27 Jul 91*	1

MINDBENDERS — UK

(See also Wayne Fontana and the Mindbenders.)

SINGLES:	HITS 4			WEEKS 34
A GROOVY KIND OF LOVE *Originally recorded by Diane and Annita in 1963.*	*Fontana*	2	*15 Jan 66*	14
CAN'T LIVE WITH YOU, CAN'T LIVE WITHOUT YOU	*Fontana*	28	*7 May 66*	7
ASHES TO ASHES	*Fontana*	14	*27 Aug 66*	9
THE LETTER	*Fontana*	42	*23 Sep 67*	4
ALBUMS:	**HITS 1**			**WEEKS 4**
THE MINDBENDERS	*Fontana*	28	*25 Jun 66*	4

MINDFUNK — US

ALBUMS:	HITS 1			WEEKS 1
DROPPED	*Megaforce*	60	*15 May 93*	1

MINDS OF MEN — UK

SINGLES:	HITS 1			WEEKS 1
BRAND NEW DAY	*Perfecto*	41	*22 Jun 96*	1

Zodiac MINDWARP and the LOVE REACTION — UK/Canada

ALBUMS:	HITS 1			WEEKS 5
PRIME MOVER	*Mercury*	18	*9 May 87*	6
BACKSEAT EDUCATION	*Mercury*	49	*14 Nov 87*	3
PLANET GIRL	*Mercury*	63	*2 Apr 88*	2
SINGLES:	**HITS 3**			**WEEKS 11**
TATTOOED BEAT MESSIAH	*Mercury*	20	*5 Mar 88*	5

Sal MINEO — US

SINGLES:	HITS 1			WEEKS 11
START MOVIN' (IN MY DIRECTION)	*Philips*	16	*13 Jul 57*	11

Marcello MINERBI E LA SUA ORCHESTRA — Italy

SINGLES:	HITS 1			WEEKS 16
ZORBA'S DANCE *From the film 'Zorba The Greek'.*	*Durium*	6	*24 Jul 65*	16

MINIMAL FUNK 2 — Italy

SINGLES:	HITS 1			WEEKS 1
THE GROOVY THANG	*Cleveland City*	65	*18 Jul 98*	1

MINIPOPS — UK

SINGLES:	HITS 1			WEEKS 2
SONGS FOR CHRISTMAS '87 [EP] *Lead track: Thanks For Giving Us Christmas.*	*Bright*	39	*26 Dec 87*	2
ALBUMS:	**HITS 2**			**WEEKS 12**
MINIPOPS	*K-Tel*	63	*26 Dec 81*	7
WE'RE THE MINIPOPS	*K-Tel*	54	*19 Feb 83*	5

MINISTERS DE-LA-FUNK featuring Jocelyn BROWN — US

SINGLES:	HITS 1			WEEKS 4
BELIEVE	*Defected*	45	*11 Mar 00*	2
BELIEVE [RM] *Remixed by Full Intention.*	*Defected*	42	*27 Jan 01*	2

MINISTRY — US

SINGLES:	HITS 1			WEEKS 3
N.W.O.	*Sire*	49	*8 Aug 92*	1
THE FALL	*Warner Brothers*	53	*6 Jan 96*	2
ALBUMS:	**HITS 2**			**WEEKS 6**
PSALM 69	*Sire*	33	*25 Jul 92*	5
FILTH PIG	*Warner Brothers*	43	*10 Feb 96*	1

MINK DEVILLE — US

SINGLES:	HITS 1			WEEKS 9
SPANISH STROLL	*Capitol*	20	*6 Aug 77*	9

MINKY — UK

SINGLES:	HITS 1			WEEKS 1
THE WEEKEND HAS LANDED	*Offbeat*	70	*30 Oct 99*	1

Liza MINNELLI — US

(See also Various Artists: Films – Original Soundtracks 'Cabaret'.)

SINGLES:	HITS 4			WEEKS 15
LOSING MY MIND	*Epic*	6	*12 Aug 89*	7
Originally recorded by Dorothy Collins in 1971.				
DON'T DROP BOMBS	*Epic*	46	*7 Oct 89*	3
SO SORRY, I SAID	*Epic*	62	*25 Nov 89*	2
LOVE PAINS	*Epic*	41	*3 Mar 90*	3

ALBUMS:	HITS 4			WEEKS 27
LIZA WITH A 'Z'	*CBS*	9	*7 Apr 73*	15
THE SINGER	*CBS*	45	*16 Jun 73*	1
RESULTS	*Epic*	6	*21 Oct 89*	10
GENTLY	*Angel*	58	*6 Jul 96*	1

Dannii MINOGUE — Australia

SINGLES:	HITS 14			WEEKS 72
LOVE AND KISSES	*MCA*	8	*30 Mar 91*	8
SUCCESS	*MCA*	11	*18 May 91*	7
JUMP TO THE BEAT	*MCA*	8	*27 Jul 91*	6
BABY LOVE	*MCA*	14	*19 Oct 91*	6
I DON'T WANNA TAKE THIS PAIN	*MCA*	40	*14 Dec 91*	5
SHOW YOU THE WAY TO GO	*MCA*	30	*1 Aug 92*	3
From the NME 40th anniversary album, Ruby Traxs.				
LOVE'S ON EVERY CORNER	*MCA*	44	*12 Dec 92*	4
THIS IS IT	*MCA*	10	*17 Jul 93*	8
THIS IS THE WAY	*MCA*	27	*2 Oct 93*	3
GET INTO YOU	*Mushroom*	36	*11 Jun 94*	2
ALL I WANT TO DO	*Eternal*	4	*23 Aug 97*	8
EVERYTHING I WANTED	*Eternal*	15	*1 Nov 97*	4
DISREMEMBRANCE	*Eternal*	21	*28 Mar 98*	3
Above 4: DANNII.				
WHO DO YOU LOVE NOW (STRINGER)?	*Double F Double R*	3	*1 Dec 01*	5
Above hit: RIVA featuring Dannii MINOGUE.				

ALBUMS:	HITS 3			WEEKS 22
LOVE AND KISSES	*MCA*	8	*15 Jun 91*	14
LOVE AND KISSES / LOVE AND KISSES AND . . . [RE]	*MCA*	51	*7 Dec 91*	6
Love And Kisses And . . . was a remix album listed from 14 Dec 91, sales were combined.				
GET INTO YOU	*MCA*	52	*16 Oct 93*	1
GIRL	*Eternal*	57	*20 Sep 97*	1
Above hit: DANNII.				

Kylie MINOGUE — Australia

(See also Visionmasters and Tony King featuring Kylie Minogue; Various Artists: Films – Original Soundtracks 'The Delinquents'.)

SINGLES:	HITS 32			WEEKS 275
I SHOULD BE SO LUCKY	*PWL*	1	*23 Jan 88*	16
GOT TO BE CERTAIN	*PWL*	2	*14 May 88*	12
THE LOCO-MOTION	*PWL*	2	*6 Aug 88*	11
Spent 7 weeks at No. 1 in Australia.				
JE NE SAIS PAS POURQUOI	*PWL*	2	*22 Oct 88*	13
ESPECIALLY FOR YOU	*PWL*	1	*10 Dec 88*	14
Above hit: Kylie MINOGUE and Jason DONOVAN.				
HAND ON YOUR HEART	*PWL*	1	*6 May 89*	11
WOULDN'T CHANGE A THING	*PWL*	2	*5 Aug 89*	9
NEVER TOO LATE	*PWL*	4	*4 Nov 89*	10
TEARS ON MY PILLOW	*PWL*	1	*20 Jan 90*	8
From the film 'The Delinquents'. Originally recorded by Little Anthony and the Imperials reached No. 4 in the US in 1958.				
BETTER THE DEVIL YOU KNOW	*PWL*	2	*12 May 90*	10
STEP BACK IN TIME	*PWL*	4	*3 Nov 90*	8
WHAT DO I HAVE TO DO	*PWL*	6	*2 Feb 91*	8
SHOCKED	*PWL*	6	*1 Jun 91*	7
WORD IS OUT	*PWL*	16	*7 Sep 91*	5
IF YOU WERE WITH ME NOW	*PWL*	4	*2 Nov 91*	7
Above hit: Kylie MINOGUE and Keith WASHINGTON.				
GIVE ME JUST A LITTLE MORE TIME	*PWL*	2	*25 Jan 92*	8
FINER FEELINGS	*PWL International*	11	*25 Apr 92*	6
WHAT KIND OF FOOL (HEARD ALL THAT BEFORE)	*PWL International*	14	*22 Aug 92*	5
CELEBRATION	*PWL International*	20	*28 Nov 92*	7
CONFIDE IN ME	*Deconstruction*	2	*10 Sep 94*	9
PUT YOURSELF IN MY PLACE	*Deconstruction*	11	*26 Nov 94*	9

WHERE IS THE FEELING? *Originally recorded by Within A Dream in 1992.*	*Deconstruction*	16	*22 Jul 95*	3
WHERE THE WILD ROSES GROW *Above hit: Nick CAVE and the BAD SEEDS + Kylie MINOGUE.*	*Mute*	11	*14 Oct 95*	4
SOME KIND OF BLISS	*Deconstruction*	22	*20 Sep 97*	5
DID IT AGAIN	*Deconstruction*	14	*6 Dec 97*	6
BREATHE	*Deconstruction*	14	*21 Mar 98*	4
GBI: GERMAN BOLD ITALIC *Above hit: Towa TEI featuring Kylie MINOGUE.*	*Arthrob*	63	*31 Oct 98*	1
SPINNING AROUND	*Parlophone*	1	*1 Jul 00*	11
ON A NIGHT LIKE THIS *Originally recorded by Pandora.*	*Parlophone*	2	*23 Sep 00*	7
KIDS *Above hit: Robbie WILLIAMS/Kylie MINOGUE.*	*Chrysalis*	2	*21 Oct 00*	15
PLEASE STAY	*Parlophone*	10	*23 Dec 00*	7
ON A NIGHT LIKE THIS [RE]	*Parlophone*	75	*13 Jan 01*	1
KIDS [RE-1ST]	*Chrysalis*	73	*10 Feb 01*	1
KIDS [RE-2ND]	*Chrysalis*	66	*24 Feb 01*	3
CAN'T GET YOU OUT OF MY HEAD *Above hit: KYLIE.*	*Parlophone*	1	*29 Sep 01*	14
ALBUMS:	**HITS 11**			**WEEKS 198**
KYLIE	*PWL*	1	*16 Jul 88*	67
ENJOY YOURSELF	*PWL*	1	*21 Oct 89*	33
RHYTHM OF LOVE	*PWL*	9	*24 Nov 90*	22
LET'S GO TO IT	*PWL*	15	*26 Oct 91*	12
KYLIE GREATEST HITS	*PWL International*	1	*5 Sep 92*	10
KYLIE MINOGUE	*Deconstruction*	4	*1 Oct 94*	15
KYLIE MINOGUE *Intended title was The Impossible Princess, but it was changed after the death of Diana, Princess Of Wales. Both eponymous albums are different.*	*Deconstruction*	10	*4 Apr 98*	4
MIXES *9 track album of mixes of 3 songs.*	*Deconstruction*	63	*15 Aug 98*	1
LIGHT YEARS	*Parlophone*	2	*7 Oct 00*	21
HITS PLUS	*Deconstruction*	41	*28 Oct 00*	1
FEVER *Above hit: KYLIE.*	*Parlophone*	1	*13 Oct 01*	12

MINT ROYALE — UK

SINGLES:	**HITS 2**			**WEEKS 5**
DON'T FALTER *Above hit: MINT ROYALE with Lauren LAVERNE.*	*Faith & Hope*	15	*5 Feb 00*	4
TAKE IT EASY *Based around Andy Kim's Rock Me Baby.*	*Faith & Hope*	66	*6 May 00*	1

Nina MIRANDA – See Robert MILES

Morris MINOR and the MAJORS — UK

SINGLES:	**HITS 1**			**WEEKS 11**
STUTTER RAP (NO SLEEP TIL BEDTIME)	*10 Records*	4	*19 Dec 87*	11

Sugar MINOTT — Jamaica

SINGLES:	**HITS 2**			**WEEKS 16**
GOOD THING GOING (WE'VE GOT A GOOD THING GOING) *Originally recorded by Michael Jackson.*	*RCA*	4	*28 Mar 81*	12
NEVER MY LOVE	*RCA*	52	*17 Oct 81*	4

MINT CONDITION — US

SINGLES:	**HITS 2**			**WEEKS 3**
WHAT KIND OF MAN WOULD I BE	*Wild Card*	38	*21 Jun 97*	2
LET ME BE THE ONE	*Wild Card*	63	*4 Oct 97*	1

MINT JULEPS — UK

SINGLES:	**HITS 2**			**WEEKS 7**
ONLY LOVE CAN BREAK YOUR HEART *Originally recorded by Neil Young reached No. 33 in the US in 1970.*	*Stiff*	62	*22 Mar 86*	2
EVERY KINDA PEOPLE	*Stiff*	58	*30 May 87*	5

MINTY — Australia

SINGLES:	**HITS 1**			**WEEKS 1**
I WANNA BE FREE *From the children's TV series 'Minty'.*	*Virgin*	67	*23 Jan 99*	1

MIRACLES — US

(See also Smokey Robinson.)

SINGLES:	HITS 8			WEEKS 81
GOING TO A GO-GO	*Tamla Motown*	44	*26 Feb 66*	5
(COME 'ROUND HERE) I'M THE ONE YOU NEED	*Tamla Motown*	45	*24 Dec 66*	2
I SECOND THAT EMOTION	*Tamla Motown*	27	*30 Dec 67*	11
IF YOU CAN WANT	*Tamla Motown*	50	*6 Apr 68*	1
THE TRACKS OF MY TEARS	*Tamla Motown*	9	*10 May 69*	13
THE TEARS OF A CLOWN	*Tamla Motown*	1	*1 Aug 70*	14
(COME ROUND HERE) I'M THE ONE YOU NEED [RI]	*Tamla Motown*	13	*30 Jan 71*	9
I DON'T BLAME YOU AT ALL	*Tamla Motown*	11	*5 Jun 71*	10
Above 6: Smokey ROBINSON and the MIRACLES.				
LOVE MACHINE	*Tamla Motown*	3	*10 Jan 76*	10
TEARS OF A CLOWN [RI]	*Tamla Motown*	34	*2 Oct 76*	6
Above hit: Smokey ROBINSON and the MIRACLES.				

ALBUMS:	HITS 1			WEEKS 2
THE GREATEST HITS	*PolyGram TV*	65	*14 Nov 92*	2
Includes both Robinson's solo and group material.				
Above hit: Smokey ROBINSON and the MIRACLES.				

MIRAGE — UK

SINGLES:	HITS 7			WEEKS 35
GIVE ME THE NIGHT [M]	*Passion*	49	*14 Jan 84*	4
Above hit: MIRAGE featuring Roy GAYLE.				
JACK MIX II [M] / JACK MIX III [M]	*Debut*	4	*9 May 87*	11
Jack Mix III was a remixed 12" version, listed on the chart from 6 Jun 87.				
SERIOUS MIX [M]	*Debut*	42	*25 Jul 87*	4
JACK MIX IV [M]	*Debut*	8	*7 Nov 87*	10
JACK MIX VII [M]	*Debut*	50	*27 Feb 88*	3
PUSH THE BEAT	*Debut*	67	*2 Jul 88*	2
LATINO HOUSE [M]	*Debut*	70	*11 Nov 89*	1
All above are medleys of current dance hits.				

ALBUMS:	HITS 3			WEEKS 33
THE BEST OF MIRAGE: JACK MIX '88	*Stylus*	7	*26 Dec 87*	15
JACK MIX IN FULL EFFECT	*Stylus*	7	*25 Jun 88*	12
ROYAL MIX '89	*Stylus*	34	*7 Jan 89*	6

MIRAGE — UK

ALBUMS:	HITS 1			WEEKS 3
CLASSIC GUITAR MOODS	*PolyGram TV*	25	*23 Sep 95*	3

Danny MIRROR — Holland

SINGLES:	HITS 1			WEEKS 9
I REMEMBER ELVIS PRESLEY (THE KING IS DEAD)	*Stone*	4	*17 Sep 77*	9
Official Elvis Presley fan club tribute disc.				

MIRRORBALL — UK

SINGLES:	HITS 2			WEEKS 5
GIVEN UP	*Multiply*	12	*13 Feb 99*	4
Samples the Three Degrees' Givin' Up Givin' In.				
BURNIN'	*Multiply*	47	*24 Jun 00*	1
Samples Don't Leave Me This Way.				

MIRWAIS — France

SINGLES:	HITS 2			WEEKS 3
DISCO SCIENCE	*Epic*	68	*20 May 00*	1
NAÏVE SONG	*Epic*	50	*23 Dec 00*	2

MISHKA — Bermuda

SINGLES:	HITS 1			WEEKS 2
(GIVE YOU ALL THE LOVE)	*Creation*	34	*15 May 99*	2

MISS JANE — UK

SINGLES:	HITS 1			WEEKS 1
IT'S A FINE DAY	*G1 Recordings*	62	*30 Oct 99*	1
Samples Jane's original vocal version, which reached No. 87 in 1983, with a dance backing by ATB.				

MISS JONES — US

SINGLES:	HITS 1			WEEKS 1
2 WAY STREET	*Motown*	49	*10 Oct 98*	1
This listed song is track 2 on the CD; track 1 is (#1 Lady).				

MISS X — UK

SINGLES:	HITS 1			WEEKS 6
CHRISTINE *Based on the Christine Keeler scandal of 1963.*	*Ember*	37	*3 Aug 63*	6

MISSA LUBA Les TROUBADOURS DU ROI BAUDOUIN — Zaire

SINGLES:	HITS 1			WEEKS 11
SANCTUS *From the film 'If . . .'*	*Philips*	28	*22 Mar 69*	6
SANCTUS [RE]	*Philips*	37	*10 May 69*	5
ALBUMS:	**HITS 1**			**WEEKS 1**
MISSA LUBA *Above hit: TROUBADOURS DU ROI BAUDOUIN.*	*Philips*	59	*22 May 76*	1

MISSION — UK

SINGLES:	HITS 16			WEEKS 58
SERPENTS KISS	*Chapter 22*	70	*14 Jun 86*	3
LIKE A HURRICANE / GARDEN OF DELIGHT	*Chapter 22*	49	*26 Jul 86*	1
STAY WITH ME	*Mercury*	30	*18 Oct 86*	4
WASTELAND	*Mercury*	11	*17 Jan 87*	6
SEVERINA	*Mercury*	25	*14 Mar 87*	5
TOWER OF STRENGTH	*Mercury*	12	*13 Feb 88*	7
BEYOND THE PALE	*Mercury*	32	*23 Apr 88*	4
BUTTERFLY ON A WHEEL	*Mercury*	12	*13 Jan 90*	4
DELIVERANCE	*Mercury*	27	*10 Mar 90*	4
INTO THE BLUE	*Mercury*	32	*2 Jun 90*	3
HANDS ACROSS THE OCEAN	*Mercury*	28	*17 Nov 90*	2
NEVER AGAIN	*Mercury*	34	*25 Apr 92*	3
LIKE A CHILD AGAIN	*Vertigo*	30	*20 Jun 92*	2
SHADES OF GREEN	*Vertigo*	49	*17 Oct 92*	2
TOWER OF STRENGTH [RM] *Remixed by Youth.*	*Vertigo*	33	*8 Jan 94*	3
AFTERGLOW	*Vertigo*	53	*26 Mar 94*	1
SWOON	*Neverland*	73	*4 Feb 95*	1
ALBUMS:	**HITS 9**			**WEEKS 48**
GOD'S OWN MEDICINE	*Mercury*	14	*22 Nov 86*	20
THE FIRST CHAPTER	*Mercury*	35	*4 Jul 87*	4
CHILDREN	*Mercury*	2	*12 Mar 88*	9
CARVED IN SAND	*Mercury*	7	*17 Feb 90*	8
GRAINS OF SAND	*Mercury*	28	*3 Nov 90*	2
MASQUE	*Vertigo*	23	*4 Jul 92*	2
SUM AND SUBSTANCE *Compilation.*	*Vertigo*	49	*19 Feb 94*	1
NEVERLAND	*Neverland*	58	*25 Feb 95*	1
BLUE	*Equator*	73	*15 Jun 96*	1

MIS-TEEQ — UK

SINGLES:	HITS 3			WEEKS 28
WHY?	*Inferno Cool*	8	*20 Jan 01*	7
ALL I WANT	*Inferno*	2	*23 Jun 01*	11
ONE MIGHT STAND	*Inferno*	5	*27 Oct 01*	10
ALBUMS:	**HITS 1**			**WEEKS 8**
LICKIN' ON BOTH SIDES	*Inferno*	3	*10 Nov 01*	8

MS DYNAMITE – See STICKY featuring MS DYNAMITE

MS. KITTIN – See FELIX DA HOUSECAT

MISS SHIVA — Germany

SINGLES:	HITS 1			WEEKS 3
DREAMS	*VC Recordings*	30	*10 Nov 01*	3

MRS. MILLS — UK

SINGLES:	HITS 1			WEEKS 5
MRS. MILLS MEDLEY [M]	*Parlophone*	18	*16 Dec 61*	5
ALBUMS:	**HITS 4**			**WEEKS 13**
COME TO MY PARTY	*Parlophone*	17	*10 Dec 66*	7
MRS. MILLS' PARTY PIECES	*Parlophone*	32	*28 Dec 68*	3
LET'S HAVE ANOTHER PARTY	*Parlophone*	23	*13 Dec 69*	2
I'M MIGHTY GLAD	*Music For Pleasure*	49	*6 Nov 71*	1

MRS WOOD — UK

SINGLES:	HITS 3			WEEKS 6
JOANNA	*React*	40	*16 Sep 95*	2
HEARTBREAK	*React*	44	*6 Jul 96*	1
Reworking of a track by Working Hard (aka Graeme Ripley of Happy Clappers).				
Above hit: MRS WOOD featuring Eve GALLAGHER.				
JOANNA [RM]	*React*	34	*4 Oct 97*	2
Samples Alison Price's Feel My Love. Remixed by Sash.				
1234	*React*	54	*15 Aug 98*	1

MISTA E featuring the AWAKENING — UK

SINGLES:	HITS 1			WEEKS 5
DON'T BELIEVE THE HYPE	*Urban*	41	*10 Dec 88*	5

MR AND MRS SMITH — UK

SINGLES:	HITS 1			WEEKS 1
GOTTA GET LOOSE	*Hooj Choons*	70	*12 Oct 96*	1

MR. BEAN and SMEAR CAMPAIGN (featuring Bruce DICKINSON) — UK

SINGLES:	HITS 1			WEEKS 5
(I WANT TO BE) ELECTED	*London*	9	*4 Apr 92*	5

MR. BIG — UK

SINGLES:	HITS 2			WEEKS 14
ROMEO	*EMI*	4	*12 Feb 77*	10
FEEL LIKE CALLING HOME	*EMI*	35	*21 May 77*	4

MR. BIG — US

SINGLES:	HITS 4			WEEKS 17
TO BE WITH YOU	*Atlantic*	3	*7 Mar 92*	11
JUST TAKE MY HEART	*Atlantic*	26	*23 May 92*	4
GREEN TINTED SIXTIES MIND	*Atlantic*	72	*8 Aug 92*	1
WILD WORLD	*Atlantic*	59	*20 Nov 93*	1
ALBUMS:	**HITS 3**			**WEEKS 14**
MR. BIG	*Atlantic*	60	*22 Jul 89*	1
LEAN INTO IT	*Atlantic*	52	*13 Apr 91*	2
LEAN INTO IT [RE]	*Atlantic*	28	*11 Apr 92*	10
BUMP AHEAD	*Atlantic*	61	*2 Oct 93*	1

MR. BLOBBY — UK

SINGLES:	HITS 2			WEEKS 16
MR BLOBBY	*Destiny Music*	1	*4 Dec 93*	12
Features the King's College School Choir, Brentwood Cathedral Choir and Shezwae Powell				
CHRISTMAS IN BLOBBYLAND	*Destiny Music*	36	*16 Dec 95*	4

MR. BLOE — UK

SINGLES:	HITS 1			WEEKS 18
GROOVIN' WITH MR. BLOE	*DJM*	2	*9 May 70*	18
Originally recorded by Wind (who was Tony Orlando under an assumed name).				

MR. BUNGLE — US

ALBUMS:	HITS 1			WEEKS 1
MR. BUNGLE	*London*	57	*21 Sep 91*	1

MR. FINGERS — US

SINGLES:	HITS 3			WEEKS 5
WHAT ABOUT THIS LOVE	*ffrr*	74	*17 Mar 90*	1
CLOSER	*MCA*	50	*7 Mar 92*	3
ON MY WAY	*MCA*	71	*23 May 92*	1

MR. FOOD — UK

SINGLES:	HITS 1			WEEKS 3
. . . AND THAT'S BEFORE ME TEA!	*Tangible*	62	*9 Jun 90*	3

MR. HANKEY POO (An Early '50s recording performed by COWBOY TIMMY) — US

SINGLES:	HITS 1			WEEKS 6
MR. HANKEY THE CHRISTMAS POO	*Columbia*	4	*25 Dec 99*	6

MR JACK — Belgium

SINGLES:	HITS 1			WEEKS 2
WIGGLY WORLD	*Extravaganza*	32	*25 Jan 97*	2

MR. LEE — US

SINGLES:	HITS 2			WEEKS 6
PUMP UP LONDON	*Breakout*	64	*6 Aug 88*	2
GET BUSY	*Jive*	71	*11 Nov 89*	1
GET BUSY [RE]	*Jive*	41	*24 Feb 90*	3

MR. MISTER — US

SINGLES:	HITS 2			WEEKS 22
BROKEN WINGS	*RCA*	4	*21 Dec 85*	13
KYRIE	*RCA*	11	*1 Mar 86*	9
ALBUMS:	**HITS 1**			**WEEKS 24**
WELCOME TO THE REAL WORLD	*RCA*	6	*15 Feb 86*	24

MR. OIZO — France

SINGLES:	HITS 1			WEEKS 15
FLAT BEAT *Featured in the Levi's jeans TV commercial.*	*F Communications*	1	*3 Apr 99*	13
FLAT BEAT [RE]	*F Communications*	60	*7 Aug 99*	2

MR. PRESIDENT — Germany

SINGLES:	HITS 3			WEEKS 13
COCO JAMBOO	*WEA*	8	*14 Jun 97*	11
I GIVE YOU MY HEART	*WEA*	52	*20 Sep 97*	1
JOJO ACTION	*WEA*	73	*25 Apr 98*	1

MR. ROY — UK

SINGLES:	HITS 2			WEEKS 6
SOMETHING ABOUT YOU	*Fresh*	74	*7 May 94*	1
SAVED	*Fresh*	24	*21 Jan 95*	4
SOMETHING ABOUT U (CAN'T BE BEAT) [RM] *Samples Nikita Warren's I Need You. Remixed by Strike.*	*Fresh*	49	*16 Dec 95*	1

MR RUMBLE – See BM DUBS presents MR RUMBLE featuring BRASSTOOTH and KEE

MR. V — UK

SINGLES:	HITS 1			WEEKS 2
GIVE ME LIFE	*Cheeky*	40	*6 Aug 94*	2

MR. VEGAS — Jamaica

SINGLES:	HITS 1			WEEKS 7
HEADS HIGH	*Greensleeves*	71	*22 Aug 98*	1
HEADS HIGH [RI] *Re-issued after he won the 1999 MOBO award for Best Reggae Act.*	*Greensleeves*	16	*13 Nov 99*	6

MISTURA featuring Lloyd MICHELS (trumpet) — US

SINGLES:	HITS 1			WEEKS 10
THE FLASHER	*Route*	23	*15 May 76*	10

Des MITCHELL — UK

SINGLES:	HITS 1			WEEKS 5
(WELCOME) TO THE DANCE	*Code Blue*	5	*29 Jan 00*	5

George MITCHELL MINSTRELS — UK

EPS:	HITS 3			WEEKS 66
CHRISTMAS WITH THE MINSTRELS	*HMV*	4	*9 Dec 61*	10
THE BLACK AND WHITE MINSTREL SHOW	*HMV*	1	*23 Jun 62*	55
THE BLACK AND WHITE MINSTREL SHOW NO. 2	*HMV*	20	*2 Mar 63*	1
ALBUMS:	**HITS 11**			**WEEKS 292**
FROM THE BLACK AND WHITE MINSTREL SHOW *Peak position reached on 29 July 61.*	*His Master's Voice*	1	*26 Nov 60*	142
FROM ANOTHER BLACK AND WHITE MINSTREL SHOW	*His Master's Voice*	1	*21 Oct 61*	64
ON STAGE WITH THE GEORGE MITCHELL MINSTRELS FROM THE BLACK AND WHITE MINSTREL SHOW *Soloists featured on the above 3: Tony Mercer, Dai Francis and John Boulter.*	*His Master's Voice*	1	*20 Oct 62*	26
ON TOUR WITH THE GEORGE MITCHELL MINSTRELS	*His Master's Voice*	6	*2 Nov 63*	18
SPOTLIGHT ON THE GEORGE MITCHELL MINSTRELS	*His Master's Voice*	6	*12 Dec 64*	7
MAGIC OF THE MINSTRELS	*His Master's Voice*	9	*4 Dec 65*	7
HERE COME THE MINSTRELS	*His Master's Voice*	11	*26 Nov 66*	11
SHOWTIME	*His Master's Voice*	26	*16 Dec 67*	2
SING THE IRVING BERLIN SONGBOOK	*Columbia*	33	*14 Dec 68*	1
THE MAGIC OF CHRISTMAS	*Columbia*	32	*19 Dec 70*	4
30 GOLDEN GREATS *Above hit: George MITCHELL MINSTRELS with the Joe LOSS ORCHESTRA.*	*EMI*	10	*19 Nov 77*	10

Guy MITCHELL — US

SINGLES:	HITS 14			WEEKS 165
FEET UP	*Columbia*	2	*15 Nov 52*	10
SHE WEARS RED FEATHERS	*Columbia*	1	*14 Feb 53*	15
PRETTY LITTLE BLACK-EYED SUSIE	*Columbia*	2	*25 Apr 53*	11
SHE WEARS RED FEATHERS [RE]	*Columbia*	12	*13 Jun 53*	1
Above 4: Guy MITCHELL with Mitch MILLER and his Orchestra and Chorus.				
LOOK AT THAT GIRL	*Philips*	1	*29 Aug 53*	14
CHICKA BOOM	*Philips*	5	*7 Nov 53*	9
From the film 'Those Redheads From Seattle'.				
CLOUD LUCKY SEVEN	*Philips*	2	*19 Dec 53*	16
CHICKA BOOM [RE]	*Philips*	4	*16 Jan 54*	6
THE CUFF OF MY SHIRT	*Philips*	9	*20 Feb 54*	1
Above 4: Guy MITCHELL with Mitch MILLER and his Orchestra and Chorus (and re-entries below).				
SIPPIN' SODA	*Philips*	11	*27 Feb 54*	1
Above entry and Cloud Lucky Seven were separate sides of the same release, each had its own chart run.				
Above hit: Guy MITCHELL with Orchestra and CHILDREN'S CHORUS conducted by Norman LUBOFF.				
THE CUFF OF MY SHIRT [RE-1ST]	*Philips*	12	*20 Mar 54*	1
THE CUFF OF MY SHIRT [RE-2ND]	*Philips*	11	*3 Apr 54*	1
A DIME AND A DOLLAR	*Philips*	8	*1 May 54*	1
From the film 'Red Garters'.				
A DIME AND A DOLLAR [RE]	*Philips*	8	*15 May 54*	4
SINGING THE BLUES	*Philips*	1	*8 Dec 56*	22
Originally recorded by Marty Robbins and features whistling by Ray Conniff.				
Above hit: Guy MITCHELL with Ray CONNIFF and his Orchestra.				
KNEE DEEP IN THE BLUES	*Philips*	3	*16 Feb 57*	12
Originally recorded by Marty Robbins.				
Above hit: Guy MITCHELL with Ray CONNIFF.				
ROCK-A-BILLY	*Philips*	1	*27 Apr 57*	14
IN THE MIDDLE OF A DARK, DARK NIGHT / SWEET STUFF	*Philips*	27	*27 Jul 57*	2
IN THE MIDDLE OF A DARK, DARK NIGHT / SWEET STUFF [RE]	*Philips*	25	*24 Aug 57*	2
Above 3: Guy MITCHELL with Jimmy CARROLL.				
CALL ROSIE ON THE PHONE	*Philips*	17	*12 Oct 57*	6
Above hit: Guy MITCHELL with Jimmy CARROLL and his Orchestra.				
HEARTACHES BY THE NUMBER	*Philips*	26	*28 Nov 59*	2
Originally recorded by Ray Price.				
HEARTACHES BY THE NUMBER [RE]	*Philips*	5	*19 Dec 59*	14

Joni MITCHELL — Canada

(See also Janet Jackson.)

SINGLES:	HITS 1			WEEKS 15
BIG YELLOW TAXI	*Reprise*	11	*13 Jun 70*	15
ALBUMS:	**HITS 16**			**WEEKS 118**
LADIES OF THE CANYON	*Reprise*	8	*6 Jun 70*	25
BLUE	*Reprise*	3	*24 Jul 71*	18
COURT AND SPARK	*Asylum*	14	*16 Mar 74*	11
MILES OF AISLES	*Asylum*	34	*1 Feb 75*	4
Live recordings with Tom Scott and the L.A. Express.				
THE HISSING OF SUMMER LAWNS	*Asylum*	14	*27 Dec 75*	10
HEJIRA	*Asylum*	11	*11 Dec 76*	5
DON JUAN'S RECKLESS DAUGHTER	*Asylum*	20	*21 Jan 78*	7
MINGUS	*Asylum*	24	*14 Jul 79*	7
A tribute to, and featuring songs by, jazz musician Charles Mingus who died on 5 Jan 79				
SHADOWS AND LIGHT	*Elektra*	63	*4 Oct 80*	3
Live recordings from Santa Barbara Country Bowl in, Sept 79.				
WILD THINGS RUN FAST	*Geffen*	32	*4 Dec 82*	8
DOG EAT DOG	*Geffen*	57	*30 Nov 85*	3
CHALK MARK IN A RAIN STORM	*Geffen*	26	*2 Apr 88*	7
NIGHT RIDE HOME	*Geffen*	25	*9 Mar 91*	5
TURBULENT INDIGO	*Reprise*	53	*5 Nov 94*	2
TAMING THE TIGER	*Reprise*	57	*10 Oct 98*	1
BOTH SIDES NOW	*Reprise*	50	*11 Mar 00*	2

Willie MITCHELL — US

SINGLES:	HITS 2			WEEKS 3
SOUL SERENADE	*London*	43	*27 Apr 68*	1
THE CHAMPION	*London*	47	*11 Dec 76*	2

MIX FACTORY — UK

SINGLES:	HITS 1			WEEKS 2
TAKE ME AWAY (PARADISE)	*All Around The World*	51	*30 Jan 93*	2

MIXMASTER

Italy

SINGLES:	HITS 1			WEEKS 10
GRAND PIANO	*BCM*	9	*4 Nov 89*	10

MIXMASTERS – See UK MIXMASTERS

MIXTURES

Australia/UK

SINGLES:	HITS 1			WEEKS 21
THE PUSHBIKE SONG *Written by original member Idris Jones in 1966.*	*Polydor*	2	*16 Jan 71*	21

Hank MIZELL

US

SINGLES:	HITS 1			WEEKS 13
JUNGLE ROCK *Originally recorded in 1957.*	*Charly*	3	*20 Mar 76*	13

MK

US

SINGLES:	HITS 2			WEEKS 3
ALWAYS *Above hit: MK featuring ALANA.*	*Activ*	69	*4 Feb 95*	1
BURNING *Chart credits 'featuring Alana Surrender' though she is not credited on the single itself.*	*Activ*	44	*27 May 95*	2

MN8

UK/Trinidad

SINGLES:	HITS 7			WEEKS 38
I'VE GOT A LITTLE SOMETHING FOR YOU	*Columbia*	2	*4 Feb 95*	13
IF YOU ONLY LET ME IN	*Columbia*	6	*29 Apr 95*	7
HAPPY	*Columbia*	8	*15 Jul 95*	7
BABY IT'S YOU	*Columbia*	22	*4 Nov 95*	2
BABY IT'S YOU [RE]	*Columbia*	59	*6 Jan 96*	1
PATHWAY TO THE MOON	*Columbia*	25	*24 Feb 96*	2
TUFF ACT TO FOLLOW	*Columbia*	15	*31 Aug 96*	3
DREAMING	*Columbia*	21	*26 Oct 96*	3
ALBUMS:	**HITS 1**			**WEEKS 4**
TO THE NEXT LEVEL	*Columbia*	13	*27 May 95*	4

MNO

Belgium

SINGLES:	HITS 1			WEEKS 2
GOD OF ABRAHAM	*A&M*	66	*28 Sep 91*	2

MOBB DEEP

US

ALBUMS:	HITS 1			WEEKS 1
HELL ON EARTH	*Loud*	67	*23 Nov 96*	1

MOBILES

UK

SINGLES:	HITS 2			WEEKS 14
DROWNING IN BERLIN	*Rialto*	9	*9 Jan 82*	10
AMOUR AMOUR	*Rialto*	45	*27 Mar 82*	4

MOBO ALLSTARS

UK/US

SINGLES:	HITS 1			WEEKS 3
AIN'T NO STOPPING US NOW *Charity record with proceeds to The Sickle Cell Society and The Royal Marsden Hospital Charity Leukaemia Research Fund.*	*PolyGram TV*	47	*26 Dec 98*	3

MOBY

US

(See also U.H.F.)

SINGLES:	HITS 16			WEEKS 63
GO *Originally appeared as a track on the US issued Mobility EP.*	*Outer Rhythm*	46	*27 Jul 91*	3
GO [RE]	*Outer Rhythm*	10	*19 Oct 91*	7
I FEEL IT / THOUSAND	*Equator*	38	*3 Jul 93*	3
MOVE *Vocals by Carole Sylvan and Roz Morehead.*	*Mute*	21	*11 Sep 93*	5
HYMN	*Mute*	31	*28 May 94*	2
FEELING SO REAL	*Mute*	30	*29 Oct 94*	2
EVERY TIME YOU TOUCH ME	*Mute*	28	*25 Feb 95*	3
INTO THE BLUE *Vocals by Mimi Goese.*	*Mute*	34	*1 Jul 95*	2
THAT'S WHEN I REACH FOR MY REVOLVER *Originally recorded by Mission Of Burma.*	*Mute*	50	*7 Sep 96*	1
JAMES BOND THEME (MOBY'S RE-VERSION) *From the James Bond film 'Tomorrow Never Dies'.*	*Mute*	8	*15 Nov 97*	7

JAMES BOND THEME (MOBY'S RE-VERSION) [RE]	*Mute*	74	*10 Jan 98*	1
HONEY	*Mute*	33	*5 Sep 98*	2
Samples Bessie Jones' Sometimes.				
RUN ON	*Mute*	33	*8 May 99*	2
BODYROCK	*Mute*	38	*24 Jul 99*	2
Samples Spoony G and the Treacherous' Love Rap.				
WHY DOES MY HEART FEEL SO BAD?	*Mute*	16	*23 Oct 99*	4
Vocals by the Shining Light Gospel Choir.				
NATURAL BLUES	*Mute*	11	*18 Mar 00*	6
Samples Vera Hall's 1937 recording of Trouble So Hard.				
PORCELAIN	*Mute*	5	*24 Jun 00*	6
Additional vocals by Pilar Basson. From the film 'The Beach'.				
WHY DOES MY HEART FEEL SO BAD? [RI]/HONEY [RR]	*Mute*	17	*28 Oct 00*	5
Honey remixed by Fafue with new vocals by Kelis.				
Above hit: MOBY/MOBY (featuring KELIS).				

ALBUMS:	**HITS 5**			**WEEKS 91**
EVERYTHING IS WRONG	*Mute*	21	*25 Mar 95*	4
EVERYTHING IS WRONG / MIXED & REMIXED [RE]	*Mute*	25	*27 Jan 96*	3
Mixed & Remixed was a remix album, sales were combined.				
ANIMAL RIGHTS	*Mute*	38	*5 Oct 96*	1
PLAY	*Mute*	33	*29 May 99*	6
PLAY [RE]	*Mute*	1	*15 Jan 00*	72
I LIKE TO SCORE	*Mute*	54	*1 Jul 00*	2
Reached No. 76 when first released in 1997.				
PLAY/THE B SIDES	*Mute*	24	*4 Nov 00*	3
Released with an additional CD of B-sides, it was listed separately from the single album.				

MOCA – See David MORALES and Albert CABRERA present MOCA featuring DEANNA

MOCHA – See Missy "Misdemeanor" ELLIOTT; NICOLE

MOCK TURTLES — UK

SINGLES:	**HITS 2**			**WEEKS 15**
CAN YOU DIG IT?	*Siren*	18	*9 Mar 91*	11
AND THEN SHE SMILES	*Siren*	44	*29 Jun 91*	4
ALBUMS:	**HITS 2**			**WEEKS 4**
TURTLE SOUP	*Imaginary*	54	*25 May 91*	1
TWO SIDES	*Siren*	33	*27 Jul 91*	3

MODERN EON — UK

ALBUMS:	**HITS 1**			**WEEKS 1**
FICTION TALES	*DinDisc*	65	*13 Jun 81*	1

MODERN LOVERS – See Jonathan RICHMAN and the MODERN LOVERS

MODERN ROMANCE — UK

SINGLES:	**HITS 8**			**WEEKS 77**
EVERYBODY SALSA	*WEA*	12	*15 Aug 81*	10
AY AY AY AY MOOSEY	*WEA*	10	*7 Nov 81*	12
QUEEN OF THE RAPPING SCENE (NOTHING EVER GOES THE WAY YOU PLAN)	*WEA*	37	*30 Jan 82*	8
CHERRY PINK AND APPLE BLOSSOM WHITE	*WEA*	15	*14 Aug 82*	8
Above hit: MODERN ROMANCE featuring John DU PREZ.				
BEST YEARS OF OUR LIVES	*WEA*	4	*13 Nov 82*	13
A special Xmas edition of the single was also released. Sales for the two were combined.				
HIGH LIFE	*WEA*	8	*26 Feb 83*	8
DON'T STOP THAT CRAZY RHYTHM	*WEA*	14	*7 May 83*	6
WALKING IN THE RAIN	*WEA*	7	*6 Aug 83*	12
ALBUMS:	**HITS 2**			**WEEKS 13**
TRICK OF THE LIGHT	*WEA*	53	*16 Apr 83*	7
PARTY TONIGHT	*Ronco*	45	*3 Dec 83*	6

MODERN TALKING — Germany

SINGLES:	**HITS 4**			**WEEKS 22**
YOU'RE MY HEART, YOU'RE MY SOUL	*Elektra*	69	*15 Jun 85*	2
YOU'RE MY HEART, YOU'RE MY SOUL [RE]	*Elektra*	56	*17 Aug 85*	5
YOU CAN WIN IF YOU WANT	*Magnet*	70	*12 Oct 85*	2
BROTHER LOUIE	*RCA*	4	*16 Aug 86*	10
ATLANTIS IS CALLING (S.O.S. FOR LOVE)	*RCA*	55	*4 Oct 86*	3
ALBUMS:	**HITS 1**			**WEEKS 3**
READY FOR ROMANCE	*RCA*	76	*11 Oct 86*	3

MODERN TONE AGE FAMILY – See Dread FLIMSTONE and the MODERN TONE AGE FAMILY

MODETTES — UK

SINGLES:	HITS 2			WEEKS 6
PAINT IT BLACK	*Deram*	42	*12 Jul 80*	5
Above hit: MO-DETTES.				
TONIGHT	*Deram*	68	*18 Jul 81*	1

MODJO — France

SINGLES:	HITS 3			WEEKS 29
LADY (HEAR ME TONIGHT)	*Sound Of Barclay*	1	*16 Sep 00*	20
Samples Chic's Soup For One.				
CHILLIN'	*Sound Of Barclay*	12	*14 Apr 01*	8
WHAT I MEAN	*Sound Of Barclay*	59	*6 Oct 01*	1

Domenico MODUGNO — Italy

SINGLES:	HITS 2			WEEKS 13
VOLARE (NEL BLU DIPINTO DI BLU)	*Oriole*	10	*6 Sep 58*	12
Italy's entry for Eurovision; it came 3rd.				
Above hit: Domenico MODUGNO with Alberto SEMPRINI and his AZZURO SEXTET.				
CIAO CIAO BAMBINA (PIOVEO)	*Oriole*	29	*28 Mar 59*	1
Italy's entry for Eurovision; it came 6th.				

MOFFATTS — Canada

SINGLES:	HITS 3			WEEKS 6
CRAZY	*Chrysalis*	16	*20 Feb 99*	3
UNTIL YOU LOVED ME	*Chrysalis*	36	*26 Jun 99*	2
From the film 'Never Been Kissed'.				
MISERY	*EMI*	47	*23 Oct 99*	1
ALBUMS:	**HITS 1**			**WEEKS 1**
CHAPTER 1: A NEW BEGINNING	*Chrysalis*	62	*6 Mar 99*	1

MOGWAI — UK

SINGLES:	HITS 3			WEEKS 3
SWEET LEAF	*Fierce Panda*	60	*4 Apr 98*	1
[AA] listed with Black Sabbath by Magoo.				
FEAR SATAN - REMIXES	*Eye-Q*	57	*11 Apr 98*	1
NO EDUCATION = NO FUTURE (FUCK THE CURFEW) [EP]	*Chemikal Underground*	68	*11 Jul 98*	1
Lead track: Xmas Steps. EP title refers to the night curfew imposed on under 16s in Glasgow.				
ROCK ACTION	*Southpaw*	23	*12 May 01*	2
ALBUMS:	**HITS 3**			**WEEKS 5**
YOUNG TEAM	*Chemikal Underground*	75	*8 Nov 97*	1
Album is largely instrumental with just one vocal track.				
COME ON, DIE YOUNG	*Chemikal Underground*	29	*10 Apr 99*	2

MOHAWKS — Jamaica

SINGLES:	HITS 1			WEEKS 2
THE CHAMP	*Pama*	58	*24 Jan 87*	2

Frank 'O MOIRAGHI featuring AMNESIA — Italy

SINGLES:	HITS 1			WEEKS 4
FEEL MY BODY	*Multiply*	39	*1 Jun 96*	2
FEEL MY BODY [RM]	*Multiply*	40	*26 Oct 96*	2
Remixed by Rollo and Sister Bliss.				

MOIST — Canada

SINGLES:	HITS 3			WEEKS 10
PUSH	*Chrysalis*	35	*12 Nov 94*	3
SILVER	*Chrysalis*	50	*25 Feb 95*	2
FREAKY BE BEAUTIFUL	*Chrysalis*	47	*29 Apr 95*	2
PUSH [RI]	*Chrysalis*	20	*19 Aug 95*	3
ALBUMS:	**HITS 1**			**WEEKS 3**
SILVER	*Chrysalis*	49	*26 Aug 95*	3

MOJO — UK

SINGLES:	HITS 1			WEEKS 3
DANCE ON [M]	*Creole*	70	*22 Aug 81*	3
Medley of Shadows hits.				

MOJOLATORS featuring CAMILLA — US

SINGLES:	HITS 1			WEEKS 1
DRIFTING	*Multiply*	52	*6 Oct 01*	1

MOJOS — UK

SINGLES:	HITS 3			WEEKS 26
EVERYTHING'S AL' RIGHT	*Decca*	9	*28 Mar 64*	11
WHY NOT TONIGHT	*Decca*	25	*13 Jun 64*	10
SEVEN DAFFODILS	*Decca*	30	*12 Sep 64*	5
Originally recorded by Lonnie Donegan.				
EPS:	**HITS 1**			**WEEKS 3**
THE MOJOS	*Decca*	12	*17 Oct 64*	3

MOKENSTEF — US

SINGLES:	HITS 1			WEEKS 1
HE'S MINE	*Def Jam*	70	*23 Sep 95*	1

MOLELLA featuring the OUTHERE BROTHERS — Italy/US

(See also Outhere Brothers.)

SINGLES:	HITS 1			WEEKS 10
IF YOU WANNA PARTY	*Eternal*	9	*16 Dec 95*	10

Sophie MOLETA – See HUMAN MOVEMENT featuring Sophie MOLETA

Ralph MOLINA and Billy TALBOT of CRAZY HORSE with Mike 'Tone' HAMILTON – See Ian McNAB

Sam MOLLISON – See SASHA

MOLLY HALF HEAD — UK

SINGLES:	HITS 1			WEEKS 1
SHINE	*Columbia*	73	*3 Jun 95*	1

MOLLY HATCHET — US

ALBUMS:	HITS 1			WEEKS 1
DOUBLE TROUBLE - LIVE	*Epic*	94	*25 Jan 86*	1

MOLOKO — UK/Ireland

SINGLES:	HITS 7			WEEKS 31
DOMINOID	*Echo*	65	*24 Feb 96*	1
FUN FOR ME	*Echo*	36	*25 May 96*	2
THE FLIPSIDE	*Echo*	53	*20 Jun 98*	1
SING IT BACK	*Echo*	45	*27 Mar 99*	2
SING IT BACK [RM]	*Echo*	4	*4 Sep 99*	9
Remixed by Boris Dlugosch and Michael Lange.				
THE TIME IS NOW	*Echo*	2	*1 Apr 00*	10
PURE PLEASURE SEEKER	*Echo*	21	*5 Aug 00*	3
INDIGO	*Echo*	51	*25 Nov 00*	1
ALBUMS:	**HITS 2**			**WEEKS 27**
I AM NOT A DOCTOR	*Echo*	64	*5 Sep 98*	1
THINGS TO MAKE AND DO	*Echo*	3	*22 Apr 00*	26

MOMBASSA — UK

SINGLES:	HITS 1			WEEKS 1
CRY FREEDOM	*Sound Proof*	63	*8 Mar 97*	1
Originally released in 1992.				

MOMENTS — US

SINGLES:	HITS 4			WEEKS 32
GIRLS	*All Platinum*	3	*8 Mar 75*	10
Above hit: MOMENTS and WHATNAUTS.				
DOLLY MY LOVE	*All Platinum*	10	*19 Jul 75*	9
LOOK AT ME (I'M IN LOVE)	*All Platinum*	42	*25 Oct 75*	4
JACK IN THE BOX	*All Platinum*	7	*22 Jan 77*	9

Tony MOMRELLE — UK

SINGLES:	HITS 1			WEEKS 1
LET ME SHOW YOU	*Art & Soul*	67	*15 Aug 98*	1

MONACO — UK

SINGLES:	HITS 3			WEEKS 11
WHAT DO YOU WANT FROM ME?	*Polydor*	11	*15 Mar 97*	6
SWEET LIPS	*Polydor*	18	*31 May 97*	4
SHINE (SOMEONE WHO NEEDS ME)	*Polydor*	55	*20 Sep 97*	1
ALBUMS:	**HITS 1**			**WEEKS 3**
MUSIC FOR PLEASURE	*Polydor*	11	*21 Jun 97*	3

Pharoahe MONCH — US

SINGLES:	HITS 4			WEEKS 10
SIMON SAYS GET THE F**K UP	*Rawkus*	24	*19 Feb 00*	2
THE LIGHT	*Rawkus*	72	*19 Aug 00*	1
LYRICIST LOUNGE VOL. 2: OH NO	*Rawkus*	24	*3 Feb 01*	4
Above hit: MOS DEF/Nate DOGG/Pharoahe MONCH.				
GOT YOU	*Priority*	27	*1 Dec 01*	3

Jay MONDI and the LIVING BASS — US

SINGLES:	HITS 1			WEEKS 3
ALL NIGHT LONG	*10 Records*	63	*24 Mar 90*	3

MONDO KANE featuring Dee LEWIS and Coral GORDON Guest star Georgie FAME — UK

SINGLES:	HITS 1			WEEKS 3
NEW YORK AFTERNOON	*Lisson*	70	*16 Aug 86*	3

MONE — US

(See also B-Crew featuring Barbara Tucker, Ultra Nate, Dajae, Mone.)

SINGLES:	HITS 2			WEEKS 2
WE CAN MAKE IT	*A&M*	64	*12 Aug 95*	1
MOVIN'	*AM:PM*	48	*16 Mar 96*	1

Zoot MONEY and the BIG ROLL BAND — UK

SINGLES:	HITS 1			WEEKS 8
BIG TIME OPERATOR	*Columbia*	25	*20 Aug 66*	8
ALBUMS:	**HITS 1**			**WEEKS 3**
ZOOT	*Columbia*	23	*15 Oct 66*	3

MONEY MARK — US

SINGLES:	HITS 2			WEEKS 3
HAND IN YOUR HEAD	*Mo Wax*	40	*28 Feb 98*	2
MAYBE I'M DEAD	*Mo Wax*	45	*6 Jun 98*	1
ALBUMS:	**HITS 2**			**WEEKS 6**
MARK'S KEYBOARD REPAIR	*Mo Wax*	35	*9 Sep 95*	2
PUSH THE BUTTON	*Mo Wax*	17	*16 May 98*	4

MONICA – See Shabba RANKS

MONICA — US

SINGLES:	HITS 7			WEEKS 37
DON'T TAKE IT PERSONAL (JUST ONE OF DEM DAYS)	*Arista*	32	*29 Jul 95*	3
Samples Back Seat (Of My Jeep) by L.L.Cool J.				
LIKE THIS AND LIKE THAT	*Arista*	33	*17 Feb 96*	2
Samples Sugarhill Gang's Spoonin' Rap. Rap performed by Malik from the Outhere Brothers.				
BEFORE YOU WALK OUT OF MY LIFE	*Arista*	22	*8 Jun 96*	3
Features backing vocals by Tony Rich.				
FOR YOU I WILL	*Atlantic*	27	*24 May 97*	2
From the film 'Space Jam'.				
THE BOY IS MINE	*Atlantic*	2	*6 Jun 98*	20
Above hit: BRANDY and MONICA.				
THE FIRST NIGHT	*Arista*	6	*17 Oct 98*	6
Samples Diana Ross' Love Hangover.				
ANGEL OF MINE	*Arista*	55	*4 Sep 99*	1
ALBUMS:	**HITS 1**			**WEEKS 10**
THE BOY IS MINE	*Arista*	52	*25 Jul 98*	10

MONIFAH — US

(See also Various Artists (EPs) 'New York Undercover 4-Track EP'.)

SINGLES:	HITS 1			WEEKS 2
TOUCH IT	*Universal*	29	*30 Jan 99*	2
Samples Laid Back's White Horse.				

MONKEES — UK/US

SINGLES:	HITS 13			WEEKS 101
I'M A BELIEVER	*RCA Victor*	1	*7 Jan 67*	17
Originally recorded by Neil Diamond.				
LAST TRAIN TO CLARKSVILLE	*RCA Victor*	23	*28 Jan 67*	7
This was their first UK release in 1966.				
A LITTLE BIT ME, A LITTLE BIT YOU	*RCA Victor*	3	*8 Apr 67*	12
Written by Neil Diamond.				
ALTERNATE TITLE	*RCA Victor*	2	*24 Jun 67*	12
Originally called Randy Scouse Git.				

PLEASANT VALLEY SUNDAY	*RCA Victor*	11	*19 Aug 67*	8
DAYDREAM BELIEVER	*RCA Victor*	5	*18 Nov 67*	17
Originally recorded by John Stewart.				
VALLERI	*RCA Victor*	12	*30 Mar 68*	8
D.W. WASHBURN	*RCA Victor*	17	*29 Jun 68*	6
Originally recorded by the Coasters.				
TEAR DROP CITY	*RCA Victor*	45	*29 Mar 69*	1
SOMEDAY MAN	*RCA Victor*	47	*28 Jun 69*	1
THE MONKEES [EP]	*Arista*	33	*15 Mar 80*	9
Lead track: I'm A Believer.				
THAT WAS THEN, THIS IS NOW	*Arista*	68	*18 Oct 86*	1
Originally recorded by The Mosquitos in 1985.				
THE MONKEES [EP]	*Arista*	62	*1 Apr 89*	2
Lead track: Daydream Believer. Both self-titled EPs are different and consist of re-issues of former releases.				
ALBUMS:	**HITS 8**			**WEEKS 118**
THE MONKEES	*RCA Victor*	1	*28 Jan 67*	36
MORE OF THE MONKEES	*RCA Victor*	1	*15 Apr 67*	25
HEADQUARTERS	*RCA Victor*	2	*8 Jul 67*	19
PISCES, AQUARIUS, CAPRICORN AND JONES LTD.	*RCA Victor*	5	*13 Jan 68*	11
THE MONKEES	*Arista*	99	*28 Nov 81*	1
Both eponymous abums are different.				
HEY HEY IT'S THE MONKEES – GREATEST HITS	*K-Tel*	12	*15 Apr 89*	9
HERE THEY COME: THE GREATEST HITS OF THE MONKEES	*warner.esp/Telstar*	15	*22 Mar 97*	10
THE DEFINITIVE MONKEES	*warner.esp*	15	*10 Mar 01*	7

MONKEY MAFIA — UK

(See also Junior Cartier.)

SINGLES:	**HITS 3**			**WEEKS 3**
WORK MI BODY	*Heavenly*	75	*10 Aug 96*	1
Above hit: MONKEY MAFIA featuring PATRA.				
15 STEPS [EP]	*Heavenly*	67	*7 Jun 97*	1
Lead track: Lion In The Hall.				
LONG AS I CAN SEE THE LIGHT	*Heavenly*	51	*2 May 98*	1
ALBUMS:	**HITS 1**			**WEEKS 1**
SHOOT THE BOSS	*Heavenly*	69	*16 May 98*	1

MONKS — UK

(See also Hudson-Ford.)

SINGLES:	**HITS 1**			**WEEKS 9**
NICE LEGS SHAME ABOUT HER FACE	*Carrere*	19	*21 Apr 79*	9

MONKS CHORUS SILOS – See CORO DE MUNJES DEL MONASTERIO BENEDICTINO DE SANTO DOMINGO DE SILOS

MONKS OF AMPLEFORTH ABBEY — UK

ALBUMS:	**HITS 1**			**WEEKS 2**
VISION OF PEACE	*Classic FM*	73	*17 Jun 95*	2

MONO — UK

SINGLES:	**HITS 1**			**WEEKS 1**
LIFE IN MONO	*Echo*	60	*2 May 98*	1
First released in 1996.				
ALBUMS:	**HITS 1**			**WEEKS 1**
FORMICA BLUES	*Echo*	71	*8 Aug 98*	1
First released in 1997, repackaged with an album of remixes.				

MONOBOY featuring DELORES — UK

SINGLES:	**HITS 1**			**WEEKS 1**
THE MUSIC IN YOU – THEME FROM AROUND THE WORLD IN 80 RAVES	*Perfecto*	50	*7 Jul 01*	1
Theme from the TV series.				

MONOCHROME SET — UK

ALBUMS:	**HITS 1**			**WEEKS 4**
STRANGE BOUTIQUE	*DinDisc*	62	*3 May 80*	4

Tony MONOPOLY — Australia

ALBUMS:	**HITS 1**			**WEEKS 4**
TONY MONOPOLY	*BUK*	25	*12 Jun 76*	4

Matt MONRO — UK

SINGLES:	**HITS 13**			**WEEKS 127**
PORTRAIT OF MY LOVE	*Parlophone*	3	*17 Dec 60*	16
MY KIND OF GIRL	*Parlophone*	5	*11 Mar 61*	12

WHY NOT NOW / CAN THIS BE LOVE *Can This Be Love? not listed on the chart of 10 June 61.*	*Parlophone*	24	*20 May 61*	9
GONNA BUILD A MOUNTAIN *From the show 'Stop The World, I Want To Get Off'.*	*Parlophone*	44	*30 Sep 61*	3
SOFTLY AS I LEAVE YOU	*Parlophone*	10	*10 Feb 62*	18
WHEN LOVE COMES ALONG	*Parlophone*	46	*16 Jun 62*	3
MY LOVE AND DEVOTION	*Parlophone*	29	*10 Nov 62*	5
FROM RUSSIA WITH LOVE *From the James Bond film of the same name.*	*Parlophone*	20	*16 Nov 63*	13
WALK AWAY (WARUM NUR WARUM) *Original version by Udo Jurgens was Austria's entry in the 1964 Eurovision Song Contest, coming 6th.*	*Parlophone*	4	*19 Sep 64*	20
FOR MAMA	*Parlophone*	36	*26 Dec 64*	4
WITHOUT YOU *Original version titled Sag Ihr, Ich Lass Sie Grussen by Udo Jurgens was Austria's entry in the 1965 Eurovision Song Contest, coming 4th.*	*Parlophone*	37	*27 Mar 65*	4
YESTERDAY	*Parlophone*	8	*23 Oct 65*	12
AND YOU SMILED (EYE LEVEL THEME FROM TV SERIES "VAN DER VALK")	*EMI*	28	*24 Nov 73*	8
EPS:	**HITS 2**			**WEEKS 7**
A SONG FOR EUROPE	*Parlophone*	16	*29 Feb 64*	6
SOMEWHERE	*Parlophone*	19	*22 May 65*	1
ALBUMS:	**HITS 4**			**WEEKS 15**
I HAVE DREAMED	*Parlophone*	20	*7 Aug 65*	1
THIS IS THE LIFE	*Capitol*	25	*17 Sep 66*	2
INVITATION TO THE MOVIES	*Capitol*	30	*26 Aug 67*	1
HEARTBREAKERS	*EMI*	5	*15 Mar 80*	11

Gerry MONROE — UK

SINGLES:	**HITS 6**			**WEEKS 57**
SALLY *Originally recorded by Gracie Fields.*	*Chapter 1*	4	*23 May 70*	20
CRY	*Chapter 1*	38	*19 Sep 70*	5
MY PRAYER	*Chapter 1*	9	*14 Nov 70*	12
IT'S A SIN TO TELL A LIE *Above 2 originally recorded by tthe Inkspots.*	*Chapter 1*	13	*17 Apr 71*	12
LITTLE DROPS OF SILVER	*Chapter 1*	37	*21 Aug 71*	6
GIRL OF MY DREAMS	*Chapter 1*	43	*12 Feb 72*	2

Hollis P. MONROE — Canada

SINGLES:	**HITS 1**			**WEEKS 1**
I'M LONELY *Samples Terence Trent D'Arby's And I Need To Be With Someone Tonight.*	*Citybeat*	51	*24 Apr 99*	1

MONSOON — UK

SINGLES:	**HITS 2**			**WEEKS 12**
EVER SO LONELY	*Mobile Suit Corporation*	12	*3 Apr 82*	9
SHAKTI (THE MEANING OF WITHIN)	*Mobile Suit Corporation*	41	*5 Jun 82*	3

MONSTA BOY featuring DENZIE — UK

SINGLES:	**HITS 1**			**WEEKS 3**
SORRY (I DIDN'T KNOW) *Original release reached No. 127 on 29 July 2000.*	*Locked On*	25	*7 Oct 00*	3

MONSTER MAGNET — US

SINGLES:	**HITS 5**			**WEEKS 6**
TWIN EARTH	*A&M*	67	*29 May 93*	1
NEGASONIC TEENAGE WARHEAD	*A&M*	49	*18 Mar 95*	1
DOPES TO INFINITY	*A&M*	58	*6 May 95*	1
POWERTRIP *From the film 'Soldiers'.*	*A&M*	39	*23 Jan 99*	2
SPACE LORD	*A&M*	45	*6 Mar 99*	1
ALBUMS:	**HITS 2**			**WEEKS 2**
DOPES TO INFINITY	*A&M*	51	*1 Apr 95*	1
POWERTRIP	*A&M*	65	*13 Jun 98*	1

MONTAGE — UK

SINGLES:	**HITS 1**			**WEEKS 1**
THERE AIN'T NOTHIN' LIKE THE LOVE	*Wild Card*	64	*15 Feb 97*	1

MONTANA SEXTET — US

SINGLES:	**HITS 1**			**WEEKS 1**
HEAVY VIBES	*Virgin*	59	*15 Jan 83*	1

MONTANO vs the TRUMPET MAN — UK

SINGLES:	HITS 1			WEEKS 1
ITZA TRUMPET THING	*Serious*	46	*18 Sep 99*	1

Hugo MONTENEGRO, his Orchestra and Chorus — US

SINGLES:	HITS 2			WEEKS 26
THE GOOD, THE BAD AND THE UGLY	*RCA Victor*	1	*14 Sep 68*	24
Originally recorded by Ennio Morricone.				
HANG 'EM HIGH	*RCA Victor*	50	*11 Jan 69*	1
Above 2 both from the films of the same name.				
THE GOOD, THE BAD AND THE UGLY [RE]	*RCA Victor*	48	*22 Mar 69*	1

Chris MONTEZ — US

SINGLES:	HITS 4			WEEKS 61
LET'S DANCE	*London*	2	*6 Oct 62*	18
SOME KINDA FUN	*London*	10	*19 Jan 63*	9
THE MORE I SEE YOU	*Pye International*	3	*2 Jul 66*	13
From the film 'Diamond Horseshoe'. Originally recorded by Dick Haymes in 1945.				
THERE WILL NEVER BE ANOTHER YOU	*Pye International*	37	*24 Sep 66*	4
Originally recorded by John Payne in 1942.				
LET'S DANCE [RI-1ST]	*London*	9	*14 Oct 72*	14
LET'S DANCE [RI-2ND]	*Lightning*	47	*14 Apr 79*	3
[AA] listed with Memphis by Lonnie Mack.				

MONTROSE — US

SINGLES:	HITS 1			WEEKS 2
SPACE STATION NUMBER 5 / GOOD ROCKIN' TONIGHT	*Warner Brothers*	71	*28 Jun 80*	2
ALBUMS:	**HITS 1**			**WEEKS 1**
MONTROSE	*Warner Brothers*	43	*15 Jun 74*	1

MONTROSE AVENUE — UK

SINGLES:	HITS 3			WEEKS 4
WHERE DO I STAND?	*Columbia*	38	*28 Mar 98*	2
SHINE	*Columbia*	58	*20 Jun 98*	1
START AGAIN	*Columbia*	59	*17 Oct 98*	1

MONTY PYTHON'S FLYING CIRCUS — UK

SINGLES:	HITS 1			WEEKS 9
ALWAYS LOOK ON THE BRIGHT SIDE OF LIFE	*Virgin*	3	*5 Oct 91*	9
From the film 'The Life Of Brian'.				
Above hit: MONTY PYTHON.				
ALBUMS:	**HITS 8**			**WEEKS 33**
ANOTHER MONTY PYTHON RECORD	*Charisma*	26	*30 Oct 71*	3
MONTY PYTHON'S PREVIOUS ALBUM	*Charisma*	39	*27 Jan 73*	3
THE MONTY PYTHON MATCHING TIE AND HANKERCHIEF	*Charisma*	49	*23 Feb 74*	2
MONTY PYTHON LIVE AT DRURY LANE	*Charisma*	19	*27 Jul 74*	8
THE ALBUM OF THE SOUNDTRACK OF THE TRAILER OF THE FILM OF MONTY PYTHON AND THE HOLY GRAIL [OST]	*Charisma*	45	*9 Aug 75*	4
MONTY PYTHON'S LIFE OF BRIAN [OST]	*Warner Brothers*	63	*24 Nov 79*	3
MONTY PYTHON'S CONTRACTUAL OBLIGATION ALBUM	*Charisma*	13	*18 Oct 80*	8
MONTY PYTHON SINGS	*Virgin*	62	*16 Nov 91*	2
Originally released in 1989.				
Above hit: MONTY PYTHON.				

MONYAKA — US/Jamaica

SINGLES:	HITS 1			WEEKS 8
GO DEH YAKA (GO TO THE TOP)	*Polydor*	14	*10 Sep 83*	8

MOOD — UK

SINGLES:	HITS 3			WEEKS 10
DON'T STOP	*RCA*	59	*6 Feb 82*	4
PARIS IS ONE DAY AWAY	*RCA*	42	*22 May 82*	5
PASSION IN DARK ROOMS	*RCA*	74	*30 Oct 82*	1

MOODSWINGS features the voice of Chrissie HYNDE — UK/US

SINGLES:	HITS 1			WEEKS 4
SPIRITUAL HIGH (STATE OF INDEPENDENCE)	*Arista*	66	*12 Oct 91*	2
SPIRITUAL HIGH (STATE OF INDEPENDENCE) [RI]	*Arista*	47	*23 Jan 93*	2
From the film 'Single White Female'.				

MOODY BLUES — UK

SINGLES:	HITS 12			WEEKS 114
GO NOW!	*Decca*	1	*12 Dec 64*	14
Originally recorded by Bessie Banks.				
I DON'T WANT TO GO ON WITHOUT YOU	*Decca*	33	*6 Mar 65*	9
FROM THE BOTTOM OF MY HEART (I LOVE YOU)	*Decca*	22	*12 Jun 65*	9
EVERYDAY	*Decca*	44	*20 Nov 65*	2
NIGHTS IN WHITE SATIN	*Deram*	19	*30 Dec 67*	11
VOICES IN THE SKY	*Deram*	27	*10 Aug 68*	10
RIDE MY SEE-SAW	*Deram*	42	*7 Dec 68*	1
QUESTION	*Threshold*	2	*2 May 70*	12
ISN'T LIFE STRANGE	*Threshold*	13	*6 May 72*	10
NIGHTS IN WHITE SATIN [RE-1ST]	*Deram*	9	*2 Dec 72*	11
I'M JUST A SINGER (IN A ROCK AND ROLL BAND)	*Threshold*	36	*10 Feb 73*	4
NIGHTS IN WHITE SATIN [RE-2ND]	*Deram*	14	*10 Nov 79*	12
BLUE WORLD	*Threshold*	35	*20 Aug 83*	5
I KNOW YOU'RE OUT THERE SOMEWHERE	*Polydor*	52	*25 Jun 88*	4
EPS:	**HITS 1**			**WEEKS 14**
THE MOODY BLUES	*Decca*	12	*12 Jun 65*	14
ALBUMS:	**HITS 18**			**WEEKS 331**
DAYS OF FUTURE PASSED	*Deram*	27	*27 Jan 68*	16
Features the London Festival Orchestra conducted by Peter Knight.				
IN SEARCH OF THE LOST CHORD	*Deram*	5	*3 Aug 68*	32
ON THE THRESHOLD OF A DREAM	*Deram*	1	*3 May 69*	73
TO OUR CHILDREN'S CHILDREN'S CHILDREN	*Threshold*	2	*6 Dec 69*	44
A QUESTION OF BALANCE	*Threshold*	1	*15 Aug 70*	19
EVERY GOOD BOY DESERVES FAVOUR	*Threshold*	1	*7 Aug 71*	21
SEVENTH SOJOURN	*Threshold*	5	*2 Dec 72*	18
THIS IS THE MOODY BLUES	*Threshold*	14	*16 Nov 74*	18
OCTAVE	*Decca*	6	*24 Jun 78*	18
OUT OF THIS WORLD	*K-Tel*	15	*10 Nov 79*	10
Compilation.				
LONG DISTANCE VOYAGER	*Threshold*	7	*23 May 81*	19
THE PRESENT	*Threshold*	15	*10 Sep 83*	8
THE OTHER SIDE OF LIFE	*Threshold*	24	*10 May 86*	6
SUR LA MER	*Polydor*	21	*25 Jun 88*	5
GREATEST HITS	*Threshold*	71	*20 Jan 90*	1
KEYS OF THE KINGDOM	*Threshold*	54	*13 Jul 91*	2
THE VERY BEST OF THE MOODY BLUES	*PolyGram TV*	13	*5 Oct 96*	15
THE VERY BEST OF THE MOODY BLUES [RI]/STRANGE TIMES	*Universal Music TV*	19	*22 Apr 00*	6
Strange Times reached No. 92 when initially released in 1999. It was repackaged with The Very Best Of The Moody Blues to promote their UK tour of 2000.				

Michael MOOG — US

SINGLES:	HITS 2			WEEKS 3
THAT SOUND	*ffrr*	32	*11 Dec 99*	2
YOU BELONG TO ME	*Strictly Rhythm*	62	*25 Aug 01*	1

MOOGWAI — Holland/Switzerland

SINGLES:	HITS 2			WEEKS 2
VIOLA	*Platipus*	55	*6 May 00*	1
THE LABYRINTH	*Platipus*	68	*26 May 01*	1

MOONMAN — Holland

SINGLES:	HITS 2			WEEKS 4
DON'T BE AFRAID	*Heat Recordings*	60	*9 Aug 97*	1
Originally released on the Sci Fi label in 1996. Vocals by Linda.				
DON'T BE AFRAID '99 [RM]	*Heat Recordings*	41	*27 Nov 99*	2
Remixed by Mick Shiney and Steve Hill (Nylon).				
GALAXIA	*Heat Recordings*	50	*7 Oct 00*	1
Original release reached No. 147 on 10 May 97. Remixed by Solar Stone.				
Above hit: MOONMAN featuring CHANTAL.				

MOONTREKKERS — UK

SINGLES:	HITS 1			WEEKS 1
NIGHT OF THE VAMPIRE	*Parlophone*	50	*4 Nov 61*	1

Ian MOOR — UK

ALBUMS:	HITS 1			WEEKS 2
NATURALLY	*BMG TV Projects*	38	*7 Oct 00*	2

Chante MOORE — US

SINGLES:	HITS 3			WEEKS 11
LOVE'S TAKEN OVER	*MCA*	54	*20 Mar 93*	3

FREE/SAIL ON [M]	*MCA*	69	*4 Mar 95*	1
STRAIGHT UP	*MCA*	11	*7 Apr 01*	6
STRAIGHT UP [RE]	*MCA*	74	*2 Jun 01*	1

Christy MOORE — Ireland

ALBUMS:	HITS 4			WEEKS 8
SMOKE AND STRONG WHISKEY	*Newbury*	49	*4 May 91*	3
THE CHRISTY MOORE COLLECTION 81-91	*East West*	69	*21 Sep 91*	1
KING PUCK	*Equator*	66	*6 Nov 93*	2
GRAFFITI TONGUE	*Grapevine*	35	*14 Sep 96*	2

Dorothy MOORE — US

SINGLES:	HITS 3			WEEKS 24
MISTY BLUE	*Contempo*	5	*19 Jun 76*	12
Originally recorded by Wilmer Burgess.				
FUNNY HOW TIME SLIPS AWAY	*Contempo*	38	*16 Oct 76*	3
Originally recorded by Willie Nelson.				
I BELIEVE YOU	*Epic*	20	*15 Oct 77*	9
Originally recorded by the Addrissi Brothers.				

Dudley MOORE — UK

(See also Peter Cook and Dudley Moore; Sir George Solti and Dudley Moore.)

ALBUMS:	HITS 2			WEEKS 19
THE OTHER SIDE OF DUDLEY MOORE	*Decca*	11	*4 Dec 65*	9
GENUINE DUD	*Decca*	13	*11 Jun 66*	10
Above hit: Dudley MOORE TRIO.				

Gary MOORE — UK

SINGLES:	HITS 21			WEEKS 103
PARISIENNE WALKWAYS	*MCA*	8	*21 Apr 79*	11
Vocals by Phil Lynott.				
HOLD ON TO LOVE	*10 Records*	65	*21 Jan 84*	3
EMPTY ROOMS	*10 Records*	51	*11 Aug 84*	5
OUT IN THE FIELDS	*10 Records*	5	*18 May 85*	10
Above hit: Gary MOORE and Phil LYNOTT.				
EMPTY ROOMS (SUMMER '85 VERSION) [RM]	*10 Records*	23	*27 Jul 85*	8
OVER THE HILLS AND FAR AWAY	*10 Records*	20	*20 Dec 86*	8
WILD FRONTIER	*10 Records*	35	*28 Feb 87*	5
FRIDAY ON MY MIND	*10 Records*	26	*9 May 87*	6
THE LONER	*10 Records*	53	*29 Aug 87*	5
TAKE A LITTLE TIME	*10 Records*	75	*5 Dec 87*	1
Double pack single.				
AFTER THE WAR	*Virgin*	37	*14 Jan 89*	4
READY FOR LOVE	*Virgin*	56	*18 Mar 89*	2
OH PRETTY WOMAN	*Virgin*	48	*24 Mar 90*	3
Above hit: Gary MOORE featuring Albert KING.				
STILL GOT THE BLUES (FOR YOU)	*Virgin*	31	*12 May 90*	7
WALKING BY MYSELF	*Virgin*	48	*18 Aug 90*	5
TOO TIRED	*Virgin*	71	*15 Dec 90*	1
Above hit: Gary MOORE featuring Albert COLLINS.				
COLD DAY IN HELL	*Virgin*	24	*22 Feb 92*	5
STORY OF THE BLUES	*Virgin*	40	*9 May 92*	4
SINCE I MET YOU BABY	*Virgin*	59	*18 Jul 92*	3
Above hit: Gary MOORE and B.B. KING.				
SEPARATE WAYS	*Virgin*	59	*24 Oct 92*	1
PARISIENNE WALKWAYS '93 [RR]	*Virgin*	32	*8 May 93*	4
Live recording from the Royal Albert Hall, Oct 92.				
NEED YOUR LOVE SO BAD	*Virgin*	48	*17 Jun 95*	2
From the film 'Mad Dogs And Englishmen'.				

ALBUMS:	HITS 16			WEEKS 104
BACK ON THE STREETS	*MCA*	70	*3 Feb 79*	1
CORRIDORS OF POWER	*Virgin*	30	*16 Oct 82*	6
VICTIMS OF THE FUTURE	*10 Records*	12	*18 Feb 84*	7
WE WANT MOORE!	*10 Records*	32	*13 Oct 84*	3
RUN FOR COVER	*10 Records*	12	*14 Sep 85*	8
ROCKIN' EVERY NIGHT	*10 Records*	99	*12 Jul 86*	1
WILD FRONTIER	*10 Records*	8	*14 Mar 87*	14
AFTER THE WAR	*Virgin*	23	*11 Feb 89*	5
STILL GOT THE BLUES	*Virgin*	13	*7 Apr 90*	26
AFTER HOURS	*Virgin*	4	*21 Mar 92*	13
BLUES ALIVE	*Virgin*	8	*22 May 93*	5
Live recordings from 1992.				
BALLADS AND BLUES 1982-1994	*Virgin*	33	*26 Nov 94*	6
BLUES FOR GREENEY	*Virgin*	14	*10 Jun 95*	5
Interpretations of Peter Green compositions.				
DARK DAYS IN PARADISE	*Virgin*	43	*7 Jun 97*	2

OUT IN THE FIELDS - THE VERY BEST OF GARY MOORE	*Virgin*	54	*31 Oct 98*	1
BACK TO THE BLUES	*Sanctuary*	53	*24 Mar 01*	1

Jackie MOORE — US

SINGLES:	HITS 1			WEEKS 5
THIS TIME BABY	*CBS*	49	*15 Sep 79*	5

Lynsey MOORE - See RAMSEY and FEN featuring Lynsey MOORE

Mandy MOORE — US

SINGLES:	HITS 2			WEEKS 18
CANDY	*Epic*	6	*6 May 00*	13
I WANNA BE WITH YOU *From the film 'Centre Stage'.*	*Epic*	21	*19 Aug 00*	5
ALBUMS:	**HITS 1**			**WEEKS 1**
I WANNA BE WITH YOU	*Epic*	52	*20 May 00*	1

Mark MOORE - See S-EXPRESS

Melba MOORE — US

SINGLES:	HITS 5			WEEKS 29
THIS IS IT	*Buddah*	9	*15 May 76*	8
PICK ME UP, I'LL DANCE	*Epic*	48	*26 May 79*	5
LOVE'S COMIN' AT YA	*EMI America*	15	*9 Oct 82*	8
MIND UP TONIGHT	*Capitol*	22	*15 Jan 83*	6
UNDERLOVE	*Capitol*	60	*5 Mar 83*	2

Pete MOORE ORCHESTRA - See Bing CROSBY

Ray MOORE — UK

SINGLES:	HITS 2			WEEKS 9
O' MY FATHER HAD A RABBIT	*Play*	24	*29 Nov 86*	7
THE BOG-EYED JOG *Backing by the Carrot Crunchers and the singers from Marlborough school, St Albans. Above 2 are charity records with proceeds to the BBC's Children In Need.*	*Play*	61	*5 Dec 87*	2
COMPILATION ALBUMS:	**HITS 1**			**WEEKS 4**
RAY MOORE - A PERSONAL CHOICE *As it featured a variety of acts, the album was only eligible for the compilation chart.* *Above hit: Ray MOORE and VARIOUS ARTISTS.*	*BBC*	7	*17 Jun 89*	4

Sam MOORE and Lou REED — US

(See also Lou Reed; Sam and Dave.)

SINGLES:	HITS 1			WEEKS 10
SOUL MAN *From the film of the same name.*	*A&M*	30	*17 Jan 87*	10

Steve MOORE - See Jim REEVES

Tina MOORE — US

SINGLES:	HITS 2			WEEKS 18
NEVER GONNA LET YOU GO	*Delirious*	7	*30 Aug 97*	15
NOBODY BETTER	*Delirious*	20	*25 Apr 98*	3

Lisa MOORISH — UK

SINGLES:	HITS 4			WEEKS 11
JUST THE WAY IT IS	*Go.Beat*	42	*7 Jan 95*	3
I'M YOUR MAN *Backing vocals by George Michael.*	*Go.Beat*	24	*19 Aug 95*	3
MR FRIDAY NIGHT	*Go.Beat*	24	*3 Feb 96*	3
LOVE FOR LIFE	*Go.Beat*	37	*18 May 96*	2

Angel MORAES — US

SINGLES:	HITS 2			WEEKS 2
HEAVEN KNOWS - DEEP DEEP DOWN	*ffrr*	72	*16 Nov 96*	1
I LIKE IT	*AM:PM*	70	*17 May 97*	1

David MORALES — US

(See also Boss; David Morales and Albert Cabrera present Moca featuring Deanna; Pulse featuring Antoinette Roberson.)

SINGLES:	HITS 4			WEEKS 19
GIMME LUV (EENIE MEENIE MINY MO) *Above hit: David MORALES and the BAD YARD CLUB featuring PAPA SAN.*	*Mercury*	37	*10 Jul 93*	3
THE PROGRAM *Above hit: David MORALES and the BAD YARD CLUB.*	*Mercury*	66	*20 Nov 93*	1

IN DE GHETTO	*Manifesto*	35	*24 Aug 96*	2
Additional vocals by Sly Dunbar (of Sly and Robbie).				
Above hit: David MORALES and the BAD YARD CLUB featuring Crystal WATERS and DELTA.				
NEEDIN' U	*Manifesto*	8	*15 Aug 98*	8
Samples Chi-Lites' My First Mistake.				
Above hit: David MORALES presents the FACE.				
NEEDIN' U II [RM]	*Manifesto*	11	*20 Jan 01*	5
Remixed by David Morales and Dancin' Danny D.				
Above hit: David MORALES presents the FACE featuring Juliet ROBERTS with James 'D Train' WILLIAMS and Sharon BRYANT.				

David MORALES and Albert CABRERA present MOCA featuring DEANNA — US

SINGLES:	HITS 1			WEEKS 2
HIGHER	*Azuli*	41	*24 Jun 00*	2

Mike MORAN - See Lyndey DE PAUL

Patrick MORAZ — Switzerland

ALBUMS:	HITS 2			WEEKS 8
PATRICK MORAZ	*Charisma*	28	*10 Apr 76*	7
OUT IN THE SUN	*Charisma*	44	*23 Jul 77*	1

MORCHEEBA — UK

SINGLES:	HITS 9			WEEKS 13
TAPE LOOP	*Indochina*	42	*13 Jul 96*	1
TRIGGER HIPPIE	*Indochina*	40	*5 Oct 96*	2
THE MUSIC THAT WE HEAR (MOOG ISLAND)	*Indochina*	47	*15 Feb 97*	1
SHOULDER HOLSTER	*Indochina*	53	*11 Oct 97*	1
BLINDFOLD	*Indochina*	56	*11 Apr 98*	1
LET ME SEE	*Indochina*	46	*20 Jun 98*	1
PART OF THE PROCESS	*China*	38	*29 Aug 98*	2
ROME WASN'T BUILT IN A DAY	*East West*	34	*5 Aug 00*	3
WORLD LOOKING IN	*East West*	48	*31 Mar 01*	1
Featured in the Ford Mondeo TV commercial.				
ALBUMS:	**HITS 3**			**WEEKS 88**
WHO CAN YOU TRUST?	*Indochina*	70	*12 Apr 97*	1
Originally released in 1996 reaching No. 94.				
BIG CALM	*Indochina*	18	*28 Mar 98*	71
WHO CAN YOU TRUST? [RE]	*Indochina*	57	*22 Jan 00*	2
FRAGMENTS OF FREEDOM	*East West*	6	*22 Jul 00*	14

MORDRED — UK

ALBUMS:	HITS 1			WEEKS 1
IN THIS LIFE	*Noise International*	70	*16 Feb 91*	1

MORE — UK

SINGLES:	HITS 1			WEEKS 2
WE ARE THE BAND	*Atlantic*	59	*14 Mar 81*	2

MOREL — US

SINGLES:	HITS 1			WEEKS 2
TRUE (THE FAGGOT IS YOU)	*Hooj Choons*	64	*12 Aug 00*	1

George MOREL featuring Heather WILDMAN — US

SINGLES:	HITS 1			WEEKS 2
LET'S GROOVE	*Positiva*	42	*26 Oct 96*	2

MORGAN — UK

SINGLES:	HITS 1			WEEKS 1
MISS PARKER	*Source*	74	*27 Nov 99*	1

Debelah MORGAN — US

SINGLES:	HITS 1			WEEKS 9
DANCE WITH ME	*Atlantic*	10	*24 Feb 01*	9
Based around Hernando's Hideaway.				

Derrick MORGAN Music backing the RUDIES — Jamaica

SINGLES:	HITS 1			WEEKS 1
MOON HOP	*Crab*	49	*17 Jan 70*	1

Jamie J. MORGAN — US

SINGLES:	HITS 1			WEEKS 6
WALK ON THE WILD SIDE	*Tabu*	27	*10 Feb 90*	6

Jane MORGAN — US

SINGLES:	HITS 3			WEEKS 22
THE DAY THE RAINS CAME *Originally recorded by Gilbert Becaud.*	*London*	1	*6 Dec 58*	16
IF ONLY I COULD LIVE MY LIFE AGAIN	*London*	27	*23 May 59*	1
ROMANTICA *Originally Italy's entry for the Eurovision Song Contest in 1960 by Renato Rascel, coming 8th.*	*London*	39	*23 Jul 60*	5

Meli'sa MORGAN — US

SINGLES:	HITS 2			WEEKS 7
FOOL'S PARADISE	*Capitol*	41	*9 Aug 86*	5
GOOD LOVE	*Capitol*	59	*25 Jun 88*	2

Ray MORGAN — UK

SINGLES:	HITS 1			WEEKS 6
LONG AND WINDING ROAD *Originally recorded by the Beatles.*	*B&C*	32	*25 Jul 70*	6

Erick "More" MORILLO Presents R.A.W. — US

SINGLES:	HITS 1			WEEKS 1
HIGHER (FEEL IT)	*A&M*	74	*4 Feb 95*	1

Alanis MORISSETTE — Canada

SINGLES:	HITS 9			WEEKS 45
YOU OUGHTA KNOW	*Maverick*	22	*5 Aug 95*	7
HAND IN MY POCKET	*Maverick*	26	*28 Oct 95*	3
YOU LEARN	*Maverick*	24	*24 Feb 96*	4
IRONIC	*Maverick*	11	*20 Apr 96*	9
HEAD OVER FEET	*Maverick*	7	*3 Aug 96*	7
ALL I REALLY WANT	*Maverick*	59	*7 Dec 96*	1
THANK U	*Maverick*	5	*31 Oct 98*	10
JOINING YOU	*Maverick*	28	*13 Mar 99*	2
SO PURE	*Maverick*	38	*31 Jul 99*	2
ALBUMS:	**HITS 3**			**WEEKS 195**
JAGGED LITTLE PILL *Peak position reached on 4 May 96.*	*Maverick*	1	*26 Aug 95*	169
SUPPOSED FORMER INFACTUATION JUNKIE	*Maverick*	3	*14 Nov 98*	21
MTV UNPLUGGED	*Maverick*	56	*4 Dec 99*	5

Giorgio MORODER — Italy

(See also Philip Oakey and Giorgio Moroder.)

SINGLES:	HITS 4			WEEKS 18
FROM HERE TO ETERNITY *Above hit: GIORGIO.*	*Oasis*	16	*24 Sep 77*	10
CHASE *From the film 'Midnight Express'.*	*Casablanca*	48	*17 Mar 79*	6
CARRY ON *Above hit: Donna SUMMER and Giorgio MORODER.*	*Almighty*	65	*11 Jul 98*	1
THE CHASE [RM] *Above hit: DJ EMPIRE presents Giorgio MORODER.*	*Logic*	46	*12 Feb 00*	1

Joseph MOROVITZ – See SOUTH BANK ORCHESTRA conducted by Joseph MOROVITZ and Laurie HOLLOWAY

Ennio MORRICONE — Italy

SINGLES:	HITS 1			WEEKS 12
CHI MAI (THEME FROM THE TV SERIES THE LIFE AND TIMES OF DAVID LLOYD GEORGE) *Theme from the BBC TV series.*	*BBC*	2	*11 Apr 81*	12
ALBUMS:	**HITS 6**			**WEEKS 36**
THE GOOD, THE BAD AND THE UGLY [OST]	*United Artists*	2	*12 Oct 68*	18
MOSES [OST]	*Pye*	43	*5 Mar 77*	2
THIS IS ENNIO MORRICONE	*EMI*	23	*2 May 81*	5
CHI MAI	*BBC*	29	*9 May 81*	6
THE MISSION [OST] *Above hit: Ennio MORRICONE with the LONDON PHILHARMONIC ORCHESTRA.*	*Virgin*	73	*7 Mar 87*	4
THE VERY BEST OF ENNIO MORRICONE	*Virgin*	48	*30 Sep 00*	1

Sarah Jane MORRIS – See COMMUNARDS

Treana MORRIS – See Roger TAYLOR

Diana MORRISON – See Michael BALL

Dorothy Combs MORRISON – See Edwin HAWKINS SINGERS. Soloist: Dorothy Combs MORRISON

Jim MORRISON – See DOORS

Mark MORRISON — UK

SINGLES:	HITS 8			WEEKS 68
CRAZY	*WEA*	19	*22 Apr 95*	4
LET'S GET DOWN	*WEA*	39	*16 Sep 95*	2
RETURN OF THE MACK	*WEA*	1	*16 Mar 96*	23
CRAZY [RM]	*WEA*	6	*27 Jul 96*	8
Mixed by Phil Chill and Clive Black.				
RETURN OF THE MACK [RE]	*WEA*	60	*31 Aug 96*	1
CRAZY [RM] [RE]	*WEA*	71	*19 Oct 96*	1
TRIPPIN'	*WEA*	8	*19 Oct 96*	6
HORNY	*WEA*	5	*21 Dec 96*	9
MOAN & GROAN	*WEA*	7	*15 Mar 97*	6
WHO'S THE MACK!	*WEA*	13	*20 Sep 97*	5
BEST FRIEND	*WEA*	23	*4 Sep 99*	3
Above hit: Mark MORRISON and Conner REEVES.				

ALBUMS:	HITS 2			WEEKS 39
RETURN OF THE MACK	*WEA*	4	*4 May 96*	38
ONLY GOD CAN JUDGE ME	*WEA*	50	*27 Sep 97*	1
Includes live recordings from Birmingham NEC and Milan, Italy and excerpts from an interview with Radio 1 DJ Lisa l'Anson.				

Van MORRISON — Ireland

(See also Van Morrison and the Chieftains; Van Morrison/Lonnie Donegan/Chris Barber.)

SINGLES:	HITS 9			WEEKS 19
BRIGHT SIDE OF THE ROAD	*Mercury*	63	*20 Oct 79*	3
HAVE I TOLD YOU LATELY	*Polydor*	74	*1 Jul 89*	1
WHENEVER GOD SHINES HIS LIGHT	*Polydor*	20	*9 Dec 89*	6
Above hit: Van MORRISON with Cliff RICHARD.				
GLORIA	*Exile*	31	*15 May 93*	3
Originally the B-side of Them's Baby Please Don't Go in 1964.				
Above hit: Van MORRISON and John Lee HOOKER.				
DAYS LIKE THIS	*Exile*	65	*10 Jun 95*	1
NO RELIGION	*Exile*	54	*2 Dec 95*	1
THE HEALING GAME	*Exile*	46	*1 Mar 97*	1
PRECIOUS TIME	*Pointblank*	36	*6 Mar 99*	2
BACK ON TOP	*Pointblank*	69	*22 May 99*	1

ALBUMS:	HITS 25			WEEKS 252
MOONDANCE	*Warner Brothers*	32	*18 Apr 70*	2
HARD NOSE THE HIGHWAY	*Warner Brothers*	22	*11 Aug 73*	3
VEEDON FLEECE	*Warner Brothers*	41	*16 Nov 74*	1
A PERIOD OF TRANSITION	*Warner Brothers*	23	*7 May 77*	5
WAVELENGTH	*Warner Brothers*	27	*21 Oct 78*	6
INTO THE MUSIC	*Vertigo*	21	*8 Sep 79*	9
THE COMMON ONE	*Mercury*	53	*20 Sep 80*	3
BEAUTIFUL VISION	*Mercury*	31	*27 Feb 82*	14
INARTICULATE SPEECH OF THE HEART	*Mercury*	14	*26 Mar 83*	8
LIVE AT THE GRAND OPERA HOUSE BELFAST	*Mercury*	47	*3 Mar 84*	4
A SENSE OF WONDER	*Mercury*	25	*9 Feb 85*	5
NO GURU, NO METHOD, NO TEACHER	*Mercury*	27	*2 Aug 86*	5
POETIC CHAMPIONS COMPOSE	*Mercury*	26	*19 Sep 87*	6
AVALON SUNSET	*Polydor*	13	*10 Jun 89*	14
THE BEST OF VAN MORRISON	*Polydor*	4	*7 Apr 90*	86
Includes re-entries through to 1999.				
ENLIGHTENMENT	*Polydor*	5	*20 Oct 90*	14
HYMNS TO THE SILENCE	*Polydor*	5	*21 Sep 91*	6
THE BEST OF VAN MORRISON VOLUME 2	*Polydor*	31	*27 Feb 93*	3
TOO LONG IN EXILE	*Exile*	4	*12 Jun 93*	9
A NIGHT IN SAN FRANCISCO	*Polydor*	8	*30 Apr 94*	5
Live recordings from Dec 93.				
DAYS LIKE THIS	*Exile*	5	*24 Jun 95*	15
THE HEALING GAME	*Exile*	10	*15 Mar 97*	7
THE PHILOSOPHER'S STONE	*Exile*	20	*27 Jun 98*	3
Compilation of rarities and unreleased tracks from 1977–81.				
BACK ON TOP	*Pontblank*	11	*20 Mar 99*	16
THE BEST OF VAN MORRISON [RE]	*Polydor*	72	*20 May 00*	1
YOU WIN AGAIN	*Pointblank*	34	*7 Oct 00*	2
Above hit: Van MORRISON and Linda Gail LEWIS.				

Van MORRISON/Lonnie DONEGAN/Chris BARBER

(See also Chris Barber/Lonnie Donegan/Van Morrison.)

ALBUMS:	HITS 1			WEEKS 3
THE SKIFFLE SESSIONS - LIVE IN BELFAST	*Venture*	14	*29 Jan 00*	3

Van MORRISON and the CHIEFTAINS — UK/Ireland

(See also Chieftains; Van Morrison.)

SINGLES:	HITS 1			WEEKS 1
HAVE I TOLD YOU LATELY THAT I LOVE YOU?	*RCA*	71	*18 Mar 95*	1
Above hit: CHIEFTAINS with Van MORRISON.				
ALBUMS:	**HITS 1**			**WEEKS 7**
IRISH HEARTBEAT	*Mercury*	18	*2 Jul 88*	7

MORRISSEY — UK

SINGLES:	HITS 24			WEEKS 74
SUEDEHEAD	*His Master's Voice*	5	*27 Feb 88*	6
EVERYDAY IS LIKE SUNDAY	*His Master's Voice*	9	*11 Jun 88*	6
THE LAST OF THE FAMOUS INTERNATIONAL PLAYBOYS	*His Master's Voice*	6	*11 Feb 89*	5
INTERESTING DRUG	*His Master's Voice*	9	*29 Apr 89*	4
Features backing vocals by Kirsty MacColl.				
OUIJA BOARD, OUIJA BOARD	*His Master's Voice*	18	*25 Nov 89*	4
NOVEMBER SPAWNED A MONSTER	*His Master's Voice*	12	*5 May 90*	4
Features vocals from Mary Margaret O'Hara.				
PICCADILLY PALARE	*His Master's Voice*	18	*20 Oct 90*	2
OUR FRANK	*His Master's Voice*	26	*23 Feb 91*	3
SING YOUR LIFE	*His Master's Voice*	33	*13 Apr 91*	2
PREGNANT FOR THE LAST TIME	*His Master's Voice*	25	*27 Jul 91*	4
MY LOVE LIFE	*His Master's Voice*	29	*12 Oct 91*	2
WE HATE IT WHEN OUR FRIENDS BECOME SUCCESSFUL	*His Master's Voice*	17	*9 May 92*	3
YOU'RE THE ONE FOR ME, FATTY	*His Master's Voice*	19	*18 Jul 92*	3
CERTAIN PEOPLE I KNOW	*His Master's Voice*	35	*19 Dec 92*	4
THE MORE YOU IGNORE ME, THE CLOSER I GET	*Parlophone*	8	*12 Mar 94*	3
HOLD ON TO YOUR FRIENDS	*Parlophone*	47	*11 Jun 94*	2
INTERLUDE	*Parlophone*	25	*20 Aug 94*	2
Originally recorded by Timi Yuro.				
Above hit: MORRISSEY and SIOUXSIE.				
BOXERS	*Parlophone*	23	*28 Jan 95*	3
DAGENHAM DAVE	*RCA Victor*	26	*2 Sep 95*	2
THE BOY RACER	*RCA Victor*	36	*9 Dec 95*	2
SUNNY	*Parlophone*	42	*23 Dec 95*	2
ALMA MATTERS	*Island*	16	*2 Aug 97*	3
ROY'S KEEN	*Island*	42	*18 Oct 97*	1
SATAN REJECTED MY SOUL	*Island*	39	*10 Jan 98*	2
ALBUMS:	**HITS 10**			**WEEKS 51**
VIVA HATE	*His Master's Voice*	1	*26 Mar 88*	20
BONA DRAG	*His Master's Voice*	9	*27 Oct 90*	4
KILL UNCLE	*His Master's Voice*	8	*16 Mar 91*	4
YOUR ARSENAL	*His Master's Voice*	4	*8 Aug 92*	5
BEETHOVEN WAS DEAF	*His Master's Voice*	13	*22 May 93*	2
Live recordings from Zenih, Paris, 22 Dec 92.				
VAUXHALL AND I	*Parlophone*	1	*26 Mar 94*	5
WORLD OF MORRISSEY	*Parlophone*	15	*18 Feb 95*	2
SOUTHPAW GRAMMAR	*RCA Victor*	4	*9 Sep 95*	3
MALADJUSTED	*Island*	8	*23 Aug 97*	3
THE BEST OF - SUEDEHEAD	*EMI*	26	*20 Sep 97*	3

MORRISSEY MULLEN — UK

ALBUMS:	HITS 3			WEEKS 11
BADNESS	*Beggars Banquet*	43	*18 Jul 81*	5
LIFE ON THE WIRE	*Beggars Banquet*	47	*3 Apr 82*	5
IT'S ABOUT TIME	*Beggars Banquet*	95	*23 Apr 83*	1

MORRISTON ORPHEUS MALE VOICE CHOIR - See ALARM

MORRISTOWN ORPHEUS CHOIR - See G.U.S. (FOOTWEAR) BAND and the MORRISTOWN ORPHEUS CHOIR

Buddy MORROW and his Orchestra — US

SINGLES:	HITS 1			WEEKS 1
NIGHT TRAIN	*His Master's Voice*	12	*21 Mar 53*	1
Originally recorded by Jimmy Forest.				

Bob MORTIMER - See MIDDLESBOROUGH FC featuring Bob MORTIMER and Chris REA; Vic REEVES

MOS DEF — US

SINGLES:	HITS 3			WEEKS 6
UMI SAYS	*Rawkus*	60	*24 Jun 00*	1
MS. FAT BOOTY PART II	*Rawkus*	64	*4 Nov 00*	1
Samples Aretha Franklin's One Step. The chart also credits Ghostface Killah although his name is only mentioned on the sleeve on the second CD format.				
LYRICIST LOUNGE VOL. 2: OH NO	*Rawkus*	24	*3 Feb 01*	4
Above hit: MOS DEF/Nate DOGG/Pharoahe MONCH.				

Mickie MOST — UK

SINGLES:	HITS 1			WEEKS 1
MR. PORTER	*Decca*	45	*27 Jul 63*	1

MOTELS — UK/US

SINGLES:	HITS 2			WEEKS 7
WHOSE PROBLEM?	*Capitol*	42	*11 Oct 80*	4
DAYS ARE OK (BUT THE NIGHTS WERE MADE FOR LOVE)	*Capitol*	41	*10 Jan 81*	3

Wendy MOTEN — US

SINGLES:	HITS 2			WEEKS 13
COME IN OUT OF THE RAIN	*EMI USA*	8	*5 Feb 94*	9
SO CLOSE TO LOVE	*EMI USA*	35	*14 May 94*	4
ALBUMS:	**HITS 1**			**WEEKS 2**
WENDY MOTEN	*EMI*	42	*19 Mar 94*	2

MOTHER — UK

SINGLES:	HITS 2			WEEKS 4
ALL FUNKED UP	*Bosting*	34	*12 Jun 93*	2
GET BACK	*Six6*	73	*1 Oct 94*	1
ALL FUNKED UP 96 [RM]	*Six6*	66	*31 Aug 96*	1
Mixed by Dobs with new vocals by Denise Johnson.				

MOTHER EARTH — UK

ALBUMS:	HITS 1			WEEKS 2
THE PEOPLE TREE	*Acid Jazz*	45	*5 Mar 94*	2

MOTHERS OF INVENTION — US

ALBUMS:	HITS 3			WEEKS 12
WE'RE ONLY IN IT FOR THE MONEY	*Verve*	32	*29 Jun 68*	5
BURNT WEENY SANDWICH	*Reprise*	17	*28 Mar 70*	3
WEASELS RIPPED MY FLESH	*Reprise*	28	*3 Oct 70*	4
Live recordings previously unreleased and studio material from 1967–70.				

MOTHERS PRIDE — UK

SINGLES:	HITS 2			WEEKS 2
FLORIBUNDA	*Heat Recordings*	42	*21 Mar 98*	1
LEARNING TO FLY	*Devolution*	54	*6 Nov 99*	1

MOTIVATION — Holland

SINGLES:	HITS 1			WEEKS 1
PARA MI	*Definitive*	71	*17 Nov 01*	1

MOTIV 8 — UK

SINGLES:	HITS 3			WEEKS 10
ROCKIN' FOR MYSELF	*Nuff Respect*	67	*17 Jul 93*	1
Above hit: MOTIV 8 featuring Angie BROWN.				
ROCKIN' FOR MYSELF [RM]	*WEA*	18	*7 May 94*	4
BREAK THE CHAIN	*Eternal*	31	*21 Oct 95*	2
SEARCHING FOR THE GOLDEN EYE	*Eternal*	40	*23 Dec 95*	3
Above hit: MOTIV 8 and Kym MAZELLE.				

MOTLEY CRUE — US

SINGLES:	HITS 9			WEEKS 28
SMOKIN' IN THE BOYS ROOM	*Elektra*	71	*24 Aug 85*	2
SMOKIN' IN THE BOYS ROOM [RI] / HOME SWEET HOME	*Elektra*	51	*8 Feb 86*	3
GIRLS, GIRLS, GIRLS	*Elektra*	26	*1 Aug 87*	6
YOU'RE ALL I NEED / WILD SIDE	*Elektra*	23	*16 Jan 88*	4
Wild Side listed from 30 Jan 88 after single dropped to No. 26.				
DR. FEELGOOD	*Elektra*	50	*4 Nov 89*	3
WITHOUT YOU	*Elektra*	39	*12 May 90*	3

PRIMAL SCREAM	*Elektra*	32	*7 Sep 91*	2
HOME SWEET HOME ('91 REMIX) [RM]	*Elektra*	37	*11 Jan 92*	2
HOOLIGAN'S HOLIDAY	*Elektra*	36	*5 Mar 94*	2
AFRAID	*East West America*	58	*19 Jul 97*	1
ALBUMS:	**HITS 5**			**WEEKS 26**
THEATRE OF PAIN	*Elektra*	36	*13 Jul 85*	3
GIRLS, GIRLS, GIRLS	*Elektra*	14	*30 May 87*	11
DR. FEELGOOD	*Elektra*	4	*16 Sep 89*	7
DECADE OF DECADENCE '81-'91	*Elektra*	20	*19 Oct 91*	3
MOTLEY CRUE	*Elektra*	17	*26 Mar 94*	2

MOTORHEAD

UK

SINGLES:	**HITS 17**			**WEEKS 81**
LOUIE LOUIE	*Bronze*	75	*16 Sep 78*	1
Originally recorded by Richard Berry and the Pharoahs in 1957.				
LOUIE LOUIE [RE]	*Bronze*	68	*30 Sep 78*	1
OVERKILL	*Bronze*	39	*10 Mar 79*	4
OVERKILL [RE]	*Bronze*	57	*14 Apr 79*	3
NO CLASS	*Bronze*	61	*30 Jun 79*	4
BOMBER	*Bronze*	34	*1 Dec 79*	7
THE GOLDEN YEARS LIVE [EP]	*Bronze*	8	*3 May 80*	7
Lead track: Leaving Here.				
ACE OF SPADES	*Bronze*	15	*1 Nov 80*	12
BEER DRINKERS AND HELL RAISERS	*Big Beat*	43	*22 Nov 80*	4
ST. VALENTINE'S DAY MASSACRE [EP]	*Bronze*	5	*21 Feb 81*	8
Lead track: Please Don't Touch.				
Above hit: HEADGIRL (MOTORHEAD and GIRLSCHOOL).				
MOTORHEAD	*Bronze*	6	*11 Jul 81*	7
Live recording from Hammersmith Odeon, 1980. Originally recorded by Hawkwind.				
IRON FIST	*Bronze*	29	*3 Apr 82*	5
I GOT MINE	*Bronze*	46	*21 May 83*	2
SHINE	*Bronze*	59	*30 Jul 83*	2
KILLED BY DEATH	*Bronze*	51	*1 Sep 84*	2
DEAF FOREVER	*GWR*	67	*5 Jul 86*	1
THE ONE TO SING THE BLUES	*Epic*	45	*5 Jan 91*	3
'92 TOUR [EP]	*Epic*	63	*14 Nov 92*	1
Lead track: Hellraiser. From the film 'Hellraiser III'.				
ACE OF SPADES [RM]	*WGAF*	23	*11 Sep 93*	5
Remixed by CCN.				
BORN TO RAISE HELL	*Fox*	47	*10 Dec 94*	2
From the film 'Airheads'.				
Above hit: MOTORHEAD with ICE-T and Whitfield CRANE.				
ALBUMS:	**HITS 16**			**WEEKS 103**
MOTORHEAD	*Chiswick*	43	*24 Sep 77*	1
OVERKILL	*Bronze*	24	*24 Mar 79*	11
BOMBER	*Bronze*	12	*27 Oct 79*	13
ON PAROLE	*United Artists*	65	*8 Dec 79*	2
Originally recorded in 1976.				
ACE OF SPADES	*Bronze*	4	*8 Nov 80*	16
NO SLEEP 'TIL HAMMERSMITH	*Bronze*	1	*27 Jun 81*	21
Live recordings from London's Hammersmith Odeon, 1980.				
MOTORHEAD [RI]	*Ace*	76	*10 Oct 81*	4
IRON FIST	*Bronze*	6	*17 Apr 82*	9
WHAT'S WORDS WORTH	*Big Beat*	71	*26 Feb 83*	2
Live recordings from London's Roundhouse, 1975.				
ANOTHER PERFECT DAY	*Bronze*	20	*4 Jun 83*	4
NO REMORSE	*Bronze*	14	*15 Sep 84*	6
ORGASMATRON	*GWR*	21	*9 Aug 86*	4
ROCK 'N' ROLL	*GWR*	34	*5 Sep 87*	3
NO SLEEP AT ALL	*GWR*	79	*15 Oct 88*	1
1916	*Epic*	24	*2 Feb 91*	4
MARCH OR DIE	*Epic*	60	*8 Aug 92*	1
THE BEST OF MOTORHEAD	*Metal Is*	52	*9 Sep 00*	1

MOTORS

UK

SINGLES:	**HITS 4**			**WEEKS 29**
DANCING THE NIGHT AWAY	*Virgin*	42	*24 Sep 77*	4
AIRPORT	*Virgin*	4	*10 Jun 78*	13
FORGET ABOUT YOU	*Virgin*	13	*19 Aug 78*	9
LOVE AND LONELINESS	*Virgin*	58	*12 Apr 80*	3
ALBUMS:	**HITS 2**			**WEEKS 6**
THE MOTORS	*Virgin*	46	*15 Oct 77*	5
APPROVED BY THE MOTORS	*Virgin*	60	*3 Jun 78*	1

MOTOWN SPINNERS – See DETROIT SPINNERS

MOTT THE HOOPLE — UK

SINGLES:	HITS 7			WEEKS 55
ALL THE YOUNG DUDES	*CBS*	3	*12 Aug 72*	11
Written, produced, rhythm guitar and backing vocals by David Bowie.				
HONALOOCHIE BOOGIE	*CBS*	12	*16 Jun 73*	9
ALL THE WAY FROM MEMPHIS	*CBS*	10	*8 Sep 73*	8
ROLL AWAY THE STONE	*CBS*	8	*24 Nov 73*	12
THE GOLDEN AGE OF ROCK 'N' ROLL	*CBS*	16	*30 Mar 74*	7
FOXY, FOXY	*CBS*	33	*22 Jun 74*	5
SATURDAY GIG	*CBS*	41	*2 Nov 74*	3

ALBUMS:	HITS 8			WEEKS 32
MOTT THE HOOPLE	*Island*	66	*2 May 70*	1
MAD SHADOWS	*Island*	48	*17 Oct 70*	2
WILD LIFE	*Island*	44	*17 Apr 71*	2
ALL THE YOUNG DUDES	*CBS*	21	*23 Sep 72*	4
MOTT	*CBS*	7	*11 Aug 73*	15
THE HOOPLE	*CBS*	11	*13 Apr 74*	5
MOTT THE HOOPLE - LIVE	*CBS*	32	*23 Nov 74*	2
Live recordings from London's Hammersmith Odeon (Nov 73) and New York (May 74).				
DRIVE ON	*CBS*	45	*4 Oct 75*	1

Bob MOULD — US

ALBUMS:	HITS 2			WEEKS 2
BOB MOULD	*Creation*	52	*11 May 96*	1
THE LAST DOG AND PONY SHOW	*Creation*	58	*5 Sep 98*	1

MOUNT RUSHMORE presents the KNACK — UK

SINGLES:	HITS 1			WEEKS 1
YOU BETTER	*Universal*	53	*3 Apr 99*	1

MOUNTAIN — US/Canada

ALBUMS:	HITS 2			WEEKS 4
NANTUCKET SLEIGHRIDE	*Island*	43	*5 Jun 71*	1
THE ROAD GOES EVER ON	*Island*	21	*8 Jul 72*	3

Nana MOUSKOURI — Greece

(See also Vladimir Cosma.)

SINGLES:	HITS 1			WEEKS 11
ONLY LOVE	*Philips/Carrere*	2	*11 Jan 86*	11
Single was released on both the Philips and Carrere record labels. Sales were combined.				

ALBUMS:	HITS 11			WEEKS 213
OVER AND OVER	*Fontana*	10	*7 Jun 69*	105
Above hit: Nana MOUSKOURI with the ATHENIANS.				
THE EXQUISITE NANA MOUSKOURI	*Fontana*	10	*4 Apr 70*	25
RECITAL '70	*Fontana*	68	*10 Oct 70*	1
TURN ON THE SUN	*Fontana*	16	*3 Apr 71*	15
BRITISH CONCERT	*Fontana*	29	*29 Jul 72*	11
SONGS FROM HER TV SERIES	*Fontana*	29	*28 Apr 73*	11
SPOTLIGHT ON NANA MOUSKOURI	*Fontana*	38	*28 Sep 74*	6
PASSPORT	*Philips*	3	*10 Jul 76*	16
ALONE	*Philips*	19	*22 Feb 86*	10
THE MAGIC OF NANA MOUSKOURI	*Philips*	44	*8 Oct 88*	8
AT HER VERY BEST	*Philips*	39	*3 Mar 01*	5

MOUSSE T — Germany

SINGLES:	HITS 2			WEEKS 27
HORNY	*AM:PM*	2	*6 Jun 98*	17
Above hit: MOUSSE T vs HOT 'N' JUICY.				
SEX BOMB	*Gut*	3	*20 May 00*	10
Above hit: Tom JONES and MOUSSE T.				

MOUTH and McNEAL — Holland

SINGLES:	HITS 1			WEEKS 10
I SEE A STAR	*Decca*	8	*4 May 74*	10
The Dutch Eurovision entry for 1974; it came 3rd.				

MOVE — UK

SINGLES:	HITS 10			WEEKS 110
NIGHT OF FEAR	*Deram*	2	*7 Jan 67*	10
Based on Tchaikovsky's 1812 Overture.				
I CAN HEAR THE GRASS GROW	*Deram*	5	*8 Apr 67*	10
FLOWERS IN THE RAIN	*Regal Zonophone*	2	*9 Sep 67*	13
The first record played on BBC Radio 1 by DJ Tony Blackburn.				

FIRE BRIGADE	*Regal Zonophone*	3	*10 Feb 68*	11
BLACKBERRY WAY	*Regal Zonophone*	1	*28 Dec 68*	12
CURLY	*Regal Zonophone*	12	*26 Jul 69*	12
BRONTOSAURUS	*Regal Zonophone*	7	*25 Apr 70*	10
TONIGHT	*Harvest*	11	*3 Jul 71*	10
CHINATOWN	*Harvest*	23	*23 Oct 71*	8
CALIFORNIA MAN	*Harvest*	7	*13 May 72*	14
ALBUMS:	**HITS 1**			**WEEKS 9**
MOVE	*Regal Zonophone*	15	*13 Apr 68*	9

MOVEMENT — US

SINGLES:	**HITS 1**			**WEEKS 2**
JUMP!	*Arista*	57	*24 Oct 92*	2

MOVEMENT. 98 featuring Carroll THOMPSON — UK

(See also Courtney Pine.)

SINGLES:	**HITS 2**			**WEEKS 8**
JOY AND HEARTBREAK	*Circa*	27	*19 May 90*	5
SUNRISE	*Circa*	58	*15 Sep 90*	3

MOVIN' MELODIES — Holland

(See also Artemesia; Ethics; Subliminal Cuts.)

SINGLES:	**HITS 3**			**WEEKS 3**
LA LUNA	*Effective*	64	*22 Oct 94*	1
Above hit: MOVIN' MELODIES PRODUCTION.				
INDICA	*Hooj Choons*	62	*29 Jun 96*	1
ROLLERBLADE	*Movin' Melodies*	71	*26 Jul 97*	1

Alison MOYET — UK

SINGLES:	**HITS 16**			**WEEKS 107**
LOVE RESURRECTION	*CBS*	10	*23 Jun 84*	11
ALL CRIED OUT	*CBS*	8	*13 Oct 84*	11
INVISIBLE	*CBS*	21	*1 Dec 84*	10
THAT OLE DEVIL CALLED LOVE	*CBS*	2	*16 Mar 85*	10
Originally recorded by Billie Holiday.				
IS THIS LOVE?	*CBS*	3	*29 Nov 86*	16
WEAK IN THE PRESENCE OF BEAUTY	*CBS*	6	*7 Mar 87*	10
Originally recorded by Floy Joy.				
ORDINARY GIRL	*CBS*	43	*30 May 87*	4
LOVE LETTERS	*CBS*	4	*28 Nov 87*	10
Originally recorded by Dick Haymes.				
IT WON'T BE LONG	*Columbia*	50	*6 Apr 91*	4
WISHING YOU WERE HERE	*Columbia*	72	*1 Jun 91*	1
THIS HOUSE	*Columbia*	40	*12 Oct 91*	5
FALLING	*Columbia*	42	*16 Oct 93*	3
WHISPERING YOUR NAME	*Columbia*	18	*12 Mar 94*	7
Originally recorded by Jules Shear in 1983.				
GETTING INTO SOMETHING	*Columbia*	51	*28 May 94*	2
ODE TO BOY	*Columbia*	59	*22 Oct 94*	1
SOLID WOOD	*Columbia*	44	*26 Aug 95*	2
ALBUMS:	**HITS 6**			**WEEKS 185**
ALF	*CBS*	1	*17 Nov 84*	84
RAINDANCING	*CBS*	2	*18 Apr 87*	52
HOODOO	*Columbia*	11	*4 May 91*	6
ESSEX	*Columbia*	24	*2 Apr 94*	4
SINGLES	*Columbia*	1	*3 Jun 95*	35
Features 3 Yazoo tracks.				
THE ESSENTIAL ALISON MOYET	*Columbia*	16	*22 Sep 01*	4
Includes 3 tracks by Yazoo.				

MOZAIC — UK

SINGLES:	**HITS 3**			**WEEKS 7**
SING IT (THE HALLELUJAH SONG)	*Perfecto*	14	*5 Aug 95*	4
RAYS OF THE RISING SUN	*Perfecto*	32	*10 Aug 96*	2
MOVING UP MOVING ON	*Perfecto*	62	*30 Nov 96*	1

MSG - See Michael SCHENKER GROUP

M3 — UK

SINGLES:	**HITS 1**			**WEEKS 2**
BAILAMOS	*Inferno*	40	*30 Oct 99*	2

MTUME — US

SINGLES:	HITS 2			WEEKS 12
JUICY FRUIT	*Epic*	34	*14 May 83*	9
PRIME TIME	*Epic*	57	*22 Sep 84*	3
ALBUMS:	**HITS 1**			**WEEKS 1**
YOU, ME AND HE	*Epic*	85	*6 Oct 84*	1

M2M — Norway

SINGLES:	HITS 1			WEEKS 6
DON'T SAY YOU LOVE ME	*Atlantic*	16	*1 Apr 00*	6

MUD — UK

SINGLES:	HITS 15			WEEKS 139
CRAZY	*RAK*	12	*10 Mar 73*	12
HYPNOSIS	*RAK*	16	*23 Jun 73*	13
DYNA-MITE	*RAK*	4	*27 Oct 73*	12
TIGER FEET	*RAK*	1	*19 Jan 74*	11
THE CAT CREPT IN	*RAK*	2	*13 Apr 74*	9
ROCKET	*RAK*	6	*27 Jul 74*	9
LONELY THIS CHRISTMAS	*RAK*	1	*30 Nov 74*	10
THE SECRETS THAT YOU KEEP	*RAK*	3	*15 Feb 75*	9
OH BOY	*RAK*	1	*26 Apr 75*	9
MOONSHINE SALLY	*RAK*	10	*21 Jun 75*	7
ONE NIGHT	*RAK*	32	*2 Aug 75*	4
L'L' LUCY	*Private Stock*	10	*4 Oct 75*	6
SHOW ME YOU'RE A WOMAN	*Private Stock*	8	*29 Nov 75*	8
SHAKE IT DOWN	*Private Stock*	12	*15 May 76*	8
LEAN ON ME	*Private Stock*	7	*27 Nov 76*	9
LONELY THIS CHRISTMAS [RI]	*EMI*	61	*21 Dec 85*	3
ALBUMS:	**HITS 4**			**WEEKS 58**
MUD ROCK	*RAK*	8	*28 Sep 74*	35
MUD ROCK VOLUME 2	*RAK*	6	*26 Jul 75*	12
MUD'S GREATEST HITS	*RAK*	25	*1 Nov 75*	6
USE YOUR IMAGINATION	*Private Stock*	33	*27 Dec 75*	5

MUDHONEY — US

SINGLES:	HITS 2			WEEKS 2
LET IT SLIDE	*Sub-Pop*	60	*17 Aug 91*	1
SUCK YOU DRY	*Reprise*	65	*24 Oct 92*	1
ALBUMS:	**HITS 3**			**WEEKS 5**
EVERY GOOD BOY DESERVES FUDGE	*Sub-Pop*	34	*31 Aug 91*	2
PIECE OF CAKE	*Reprise*	39	*17 Oct 92*	2
MY BROTHER THE COW	*Reprise*	70	*8 Apr 95*	1

MUDLARKS — UK

SINGLES:	HITS 3			WEEKS 19
LOLLIPOP	*Columbia*	2	*3 May 58*	9
Original by Ronald and Ruby reached No. 20 in the US the same year.				
BOOK OF LOVE	*Columbia*	8	*7 Jun 58*	9
Originally recorded by the Monotones.				
Above hit: MUDLARKS with the Ken JONES JIVE GROUP.				
THE LOVE GAME	*Columbia*	30	*28 Feb 59*	1
Above hit: MUDLARKS with the Ken JONES GROUP.				

Idris MUHAMMAD — US

SINGLES:	HITS 1			WEEKS 3
COULD HEAVEN EVER BE LIKE THIS	*Kudu*	42	*17 Sep 77*	3

Nick MUIR - BEDROCK

MUKKAA — UK

SINGLES:	HITS 1			WEEKS 1
BURUCHACCA	*Limbo*	74	*27 Feb 93*	1

Maria MULDAUR — US

SINGLES:	HITS 1			WEEKS 8
MIDNIGHT AT THE OASIS	*Reprise*	21	*29 Jun 74*	8

MULL HISTORICAL SOCIETY — UK

SINGLES:	HITS 1			WEEKS 1
ANIMAL CANNABUS	*Rough Trade*	53	*21 Jul 01*	1

ALBUMS:	HITS 1			WEEKS 1
LOSS	*Blanco Y Negro*	43	*27 Oct 01*	1

Arthur MULLARD - See Hylda BAKER and Arthur MULLARD

Larry MULLEN - See Adam CLAYTON and Larry MULLEN

Werner MULLER and the RIAS DANCE ORCHESTRA - See Caterina VALENTE - Werner MULLER and the RIAS DANCE ORCHESTRA

Gerry MULLIGAN and Ben WEBSTER — US

ALBUMS:	HITS 1			WEEKS 1
GERRY MULLIGAN MEETS BEN WEBSTER	*His Master's Voice*	15	*24 Sep 60*	1

Shawn MULLINS — US

SINGLES:	HITS 2			WEEKS 11
LULLABY	*Columbia*	9	*6 Mar 99*	10
Song is a tale about growing up privileged but spiritually empty in Hollywood.				
WHAT IS LIFE	*Columbia*	62	*2 Oct 99*	1
From the film 'Big Daddy'. Originally recorded by George Harrison as the B-side to My Sweet Lord.				
ALBUMS:	**HITS 1**			**WEEKS 1**
SOUL'S CORE	*Columbia*	60	*20 Mar 99*	1

MULU — UK

SINGLES:	HITS 1			WEEKS 1
PUSSYCAT	*Dedicated*	50	*2 Aug 97*	1

Samantha MUMBA — Ireland

SINGLES:	HITS 5			WEEKS 51
GOTTA TELL YOU	*Wild Card*	2	*8 Jul 00*	12
BODY II BODY	*Wild Card*	5	*28 Oct 00*	12
Samples David Bowie's Ashes To Ashes.				
ALWAYS COME BACK TO YOUR LOVE	*Wild Card*	3	*3 Mar 01*	15
BABY COME ON OVER	*Wild Card*	5	*22 Sep 01*	10
LATELY	*Wild Card*	6	*22 Dec 01*	2
ALBUMS:	**HITS 1**			**WEEKS 16**
GOTTA TELL YOU	*Wild Card*	17	*11 Nov 00*	11
GOTTA TELL YOU [RE]	*Wild Card*	9	*29 Sep 01*	5
Repackaged with 2 new tracks.				

Coati MUNDI - See Kid CREOLE and the COCONUTS

MUNDY — Ireland

SINGLES:	HITS 2			WEEKS 2
TO YOU I BESTOW	*Epic*	60	*3 Aug 96*	1
LIFE'S A CINCH	*Epic*	75	*5 Oct 96*	1

MUNGO JERRY — UK

SINGLES:	HITS 9			WEEKS 88
IN THE SUMMERTIME	*Dawn*	1	*6 Jun 70*	20
BABY JUMP	*Dawn*	32	*6 Feb 71*	1
BABY JUMP [RE]	*Dawn*	1	*20 Feb 71*	12
LADY ROSE	*Dawn*	5	*29 May 71*	12
YOU DON'T HAVE TO BE IN THE ARMY TO FIGHT IN THE WAR	*Dawn*	13	*18 Sep 71*	8
OPEN UP	*Dawn*	21	*22 Apr 72*	8
ALRIGHT, ALRIGHT, ALRIGHT	*Dawn*	3	*7 Jul 73*	12
Originally recorded by Jacques DuTronc as Et Moi Et Moi Et Moi.				
WILD LOVE	*Dawn*	32	*10 Nov 73*	5
LONG LEGGED WOMAN DRESSED IN BLACK	*Dawn*	13	*6 Apr 74*	9
SUPPORT THE TOON - IT'S YOUR DUTY [EP]	*Saraja*	57	*29 May 99*	1
Lead track: The Blaydon Races ('99). Supporters single of Newcastle FC, who reached the FA Cup Final that year.				
Above hit: MUNGO JERRY and the TOON TRAVELLERS.				
ALBUMS:	**HITS 2**			**WEEKS 14**
MUNGO JERRY	*Dawn*	13	*8 Aug 70*	6
ELECTRONICALLY TESTED	*Dawn*	14	*10 Apr 71*	8

MUNICH MACHINE — Germany

SINGLES:	HITS 2			WEEKS 9
GET ON THE FUNK TRAIN	*Oasis*	41	*10 Dec 77*	5
A WHITER SHADE OF PALE	*Oasis*	42	*4 Nov 78*	4
Above hit: MUNICH MACHINE Introducing Chris BENNETT.				

MUNICH PHILHARMONIC ORCHESTRA - See Michael NYMAN

MUNROS featuring David METHREN — UK

ALBUMS:	HITS 1			WEEKS 3
THE LONE PIPER	*Virgin*	46	*27 Jun 98*	3
Compilation of traditional Scottish melodies.				

David MUNROW – See EARLY MUSIC CONSORT, directed by David MUNROW

MUPPETS — US

SINGLES:	HITS 2			WEEKS 15
HALFWAY DOWN THE STAIRS	*Pye*	7	*28 May 77*	8
Above hit: MUPPETS Sung by Kermit's Nephew ROBIN.				
The voice of Robin was Jerry Nelson.				
THE MUPPET SHOW MUSIC HALL [EP]	*Pye*	19	*17 Dec 77*	7
Lead track: Don't Dilly Dally On The Way. (Though some weeks it was listed as an AA with Waiting At The Church).				
Above hit: MUPPETS featuring Frank OZ as Miss PIGGY Fozzie BEAR – Jim HENSON as KERMIT THE FROG with the ENTIRE CAST.				
ALBUMS:	**HITS 2**			**WEEKS 45**
THE MUPPET SHOW	*Pye*	1	*11 Jun 77*	35
THE MUPPET SHOW VOLUME 2	*Pye*	16	*25 Feb 78*	10

Lydia MURDOCK — US

SINGLES:	HITS 1			WEEKS 9
SUPERSTAR	*Korova*	14	*24 Sep 83*	9
Based on Michael Jackson's Billie Jean.				

Shirley MURDOCK — US

SINGLES:	HITS 1			WEEKS 2
TRUTH OR DARE	*Elektra*	60	*12 Apr 86*	2

Eddie MURPHY featuring Shabba RANKS — US/Jamaica

(See also Shabba Ranks.)

SINGLES:	HITS 1			WEEKS 1
I WAS A KING	*Motown*	64	*6 Mar 93*	1

Noel MURPHY — Ireland

SINGLES:	HITS 1			WEEKS 4
MURPHY AND THE BRICKS	*Murphy's*	57	*27 Jun 87*	4

Peter MURPHY — UK

ALBUMS:	HITS 1			WEEKS 1
SHOULD THE WORLD FAIL TO FALL APART	*Beggars Banquet*	82	*26 Jul 86*	1

Rosin MURPHY – See Boris DLUGOSCH

Walter MURPHY and the BIG APPLE BAND — US

SINGLES:	HITS 1			WEEKS 9
A FIFTH OF BEETHOVEN	*Private Stock*	28	*10 Jul 76*	9

Anne MURRAY — Canada

SINGLES:	HITS 5			WEEKS 40
SNOWBIRD	*Capitol*	23	*24 Oct 70*	17
DESTINY	*Capitol*	41	*21 Oct 72*	4
YOU NEEDED ME	*Capitol*	22	*9 Dec 78*	14
I JUST FALL IN LOVE AGAIN	*Capitol*	58	*21 Apr 79*	2
DAYDREAM BELIEVER	*Capitol*	61	*19 Apr 80*	3
ALBUMS:	**HITS 1**			**WEEKS 10**
THE VERY BEST OF ANNE MURRAY	*Capitol*	14	*3 Oct 81*	10

Keith MURRAY — US

SINGLES:	HITS 4			WEEKS 10
THE RHYME	*Jive*	59	*2 Nov 96*	1
SHORTY (YOU KEEP PLAYIN' WITH MY MIND)	*Jive*	22	*27 Jun 98*	3
Above hit: IMAJIN featuring Keith MURRAY.				
HOME ALONE	*Jive*	17	*14 Nov 98*	5
Above hit: R. KELLY featuring Keith MURRAY.				
INCREDIBLE	*Jive*	52	*5 Dec 98*	1
Samples James Brown's Sportin' Life.				
Above hit: Keith MURRAY featuring LL COOL J.				

Pauline MURRAY and the INVISIBLE GIRLS — UK

SINGLES:	HITS 1			WEEKS 2
DREAM SEQUENCE (ONE)	*Illusive*	67	*2 Aug 80*	2
ALBUMS:	**HITS 1**			**WEEKS 4**
PAULINE MURRAY AND THE INVISIBLE GIRLS	*Elusive*	25	*11 Oct 80*	4

Ruby MURRAY — UK

SINGLES:	HITS 9			WEEKS 114
HEARTBEAT	*Columbia*	3	*4 Dec 54*	16
SOFTLY SOFTLY	*Columbia*	1	*29 Jan 55*	22
HAPPY DAYS AND LONELY NIGHTS	*Columbia*	6	*5 Feb 55*	8
LET ME GO LOVER	*Columbia*	5	*5 Mar 55*	7
Above 2 entries were separate sides of the same release, each had its own chart run.				
Above 4: Ruby MURRAY with Ray MARTIN and his Orchestra.				
IF ANYONE FINDS THIS, I LOVE YOU	*Columbia*	4	*19 Mar 55*	11
Above hit: Ruby MURRAY and Anne WARREN with Ray MARTIN and his Orchestra.				
EVERMORE	*Columbia*	3	*2 Jul 55*	17
SOFTLY SOFTLY [RE]	*Columbia*	20	*9 Jul 55*	1
I'LL COME WHEN YOU CALL	*Columbia*	6	*15 Oct 55*	7
YOU ARE MY FIRST LOVE	*Columbia*	16	*1 Sep 56*	4
From the film 'It's Great To Be Young'.				
YOU ARE MY FIRST LOVE [RE]	*Columbia*	21	*6 Oct 56*	1
Above 5: Ruby MURRAY with Ray MARTIN and his Orchestra.				
REAL LOVE	*Columbia*	18	*13 Dec 58*	6
GOODBYE JIMMY, GOODBYE	*Columbia*	10	*6 Jun 59*	13
Above 2: Ruby MURRAY with Norrie PARAMOR and his Orchestra and Chorus.				
GOODBYE JIMMY, GOODBYE [RE]	*Columbia*	26	*10 Oct 59*	1

Junior MURVIN — Jamaica

SINGLES:	HITS 1			WEEKS 9
POLICE AND THIEVES	*Island*	23	*3 May 80*	9

MUSCLE SHOALS HORNS - See Elton JOHN

MUSE — UK

SINGLES:	HITS 9			WEEKS 27
UNO	*Mushroom*	73	*26 Jun 99*	1
CAVE	*Mushroom*	52	*18 Sep 99*	1
MUSCLE MUSEUM	*Mushroom*	43	*4 Dec 99*	2
SUNBURN	*Mushroom*	22	*4 Mar 00*	2
UNINTENDED	*Mushroom*	20	*17 Jun 00*	4
MUSCLE MUSEUM [RI]	*Mushroom*	25	*21 Oct 00*	3
PLUG IN BABY	*Mushroom*	11	*24 Mar 01*	5
NEW BORN	*Mushroom*	12	*16 Jun 01*	4
BLISS	*Mushroom*	22	*1 Sep 01*	2
FEELING GOOD/HYPER MUSIC	*Mushroom*	24	*1 Dec 01*	3
ALBUMS:	**HITS 2**			**WEEKS 38**
SHOWBIZ	*Mushroom*	29	*16 Oct 99*	16
ORIGIN OF SYMMETRY	*Mushroom*	3	*30 Jun 01*	22

MUSIC and MYSTERY featuring Gwen McCRAE — UK/US

(See also Gwen McCrae.)

SINGLES:	HITS 1			WEEKS 3
ALL THIS LOVE I'M GIVING	*KTDA*	36	*13 Feb 93*	3

MUSIC RELIEF '94 — UK

SINGLES:	HITS 1			WEEKS 1
WHAT'S GOING ON	*Jive*	70	*5 Nov 94*	1
Originally recorded by Marvin Gaye.				
Charity record with proceeds to aid Rwanda.				

MUSIC STUDENTS - See Ian DURY and the BLOCKHEADS

MUSICAL YOUTH — UK

(See also Donna Summer.)

SINGLES:	HITS 7			WEEKS 55
PASS THE DUTCHIE	*MCA*	1	*25 Sep 82*	12
Originally recorded by the Mighty Diamonds as Pass The Kutchie.				
YOUTH OF TODAY	*MCA*	13	*20 Nov 82*	9
PASS THE DUTCHIE [RE]	*MCA*	65	*8 Jan 83*	1
NEVER GONNA GIVE YOU UP	*MCA*	6	*12 Feb 83*	10
HEARTBREAKER	*MCA*	44	*16 Apr 83*	3
TELL ME WHY	*MCA*	33	*9 Jul 83*	6

007	*MCA*	26	*22 Oct 83*	6
SIXTEEN	*MCA*	23	*14 Jan 84*	8
ALBUMS:	**HITS 1**			**WEEKS 22**
THE YOUTH OF TODAY	*MCA*	24	*4 Dec 82*	22

MUSIQUE — US

SINGLES:	**HITS 1**			**WEEKS 12**
IN THE BUSH	*CBS*	16	*18 Nov 78*	12

MUSIQUE vs U2 — UK

SINGLES:	**HITS 1**			**WEEKS 5**
NEW YEAR'S DUB *Samples U2's New Year's Day.*	*Serious*	15	*2 Jun 01*	4
NEW YEAR'S DUB [RE]	*Serious*	75	*14 Jul 01*	1

MUTANT DISCO - See PHATS and SMALL

MUTINY — UK

SINGLES:	**HITS 2**			**WEEKS 3**
SECRETS *Samples First Choice's Dr. Love.*	*VC Recordings*	47	*19 May 01*	1
THE VIRUS	*VC Recordings*	42	*25 Aug 01*	2

MUTTON BIRDS — New Zealand

ALBUMS:	**HITS 1**			**WEEKS 1**
ENVY OF ANGELS	*Virgin*	64	*12 Jul 97*	1

MXM — Italy

SINGLES:	**HITS 1**			**WEEKS 1**
NOTHING COMPARES 2 U	*London*	68	*2 Jun 90*	1

MY BLOODY VALENTINE — UK/US/Ireland

SINGLES:	**HITS 2**			**WEEKS 5**
SOON	*Creation*	41	*5 May 90*	3
TO HERE KNOWS WHEN	*Creation*	29	*16 Feb 91*	2
ALBUMS:	**HITS 1**			**WEEKS 2**
LOVELESS	*Creation*	24	*23 Nov 91*	2

MY LIFE STORY — UK

(See also Marc Almond; PJ Proby.)

SINGLES:	**HITS 8**			**WEEKS 12**
12 REASONS WHY I LOVE HER	*Parlophone*	32	*17 Aug 96*	2
SPARKLE	*Parlophone*	34	*9 Nov 96*	2
THE KING OF KISSINGDOM	*Parlophone*	35	*1 Mar 97*	1
STRUMPET	*Parlophone*	27	*17 May 97*	2
DUCHESS	*Parlophone*	39	*23 Aug 97*	1
IT'S A GIRL THING	*It*	37	*19 Jun 99*	2
EMPIRE LINE	*It*	58	*30 Oct 99*	1
WALK/DON'T WALK *One song.*	*It*	48	*19 Feb 00*	1
ALBUMS:	**HITS 1**			**WEEKS 1**
THE GOLDEN MILE	*Parlophone*	36	*22 Mar 97*	1

MY VITRIOL — UK

SINGLES:	**HITS 4**			**WEEKS 6**
CEMENTED SHOES	*Infectious*	65	*22 Jul 00*	1
PIECES	*Infectious*	56	*11 Nov 00*	1
ALWAYS: YOUR WAY	*Infectious*	31	*24 Feb 01*	2
GROUNDED	*Infectious*	29	*19 May 01*	2
ALBUMS:	**HITS 1**			**WEEKS 2**
FINELINES	*Infectious*	24	*17 Mar 01*	2

MYA — US

(See also Christina Aguilera, Lil' Kim, Mya and Pink; Pras.)

SINGLES:	**HITS 4**			**WEEKS 31**
TAKE ME THERE *From the film 'The Rugrats Movie'.* *Above hit: BLACKSTREET and MYA featuring MASE and BLINKY BLINK.*	*Interscope*	7	*12 Dec 98*	9
CASE OF THE EX	*Interscope*	3	*10 Feb 01*	11
GIRLS DEM SUGAR *Above hit: BEENIE MAN featuring MYA.*	*Virgin*	13	*24 Mar 01*	5
FREE	*Interscope*	11	*9 Jun 01*	6

Tim MYCROFT - See SOUNDS NICE featuring Tim MYCROFT On Organ

Alicia MYERS — US

SINGLES:	HITS 1			WEEKS 3
YOU GET THE BEST FROM ME (SAY, SAY, SAY)	*MCA*	58	*1 Sep 84*	3

Billie MYERS — UK

SINGLES:	HITS 2			WEEKS 12
KISS THE RAIN	*Universal*	4	*11 Apr 98*	9
TELL ME	*Universal*	28	*25 Jul 98*	3
ALBUMS:	**HITS 1**			**WEEKS 9**
GROWING, PAINS	*Universal*	19	*2 May 98*	9

Richard MYHILL — UK

SINGLES:	HITS 1			WEEKS 9
IT TAKES TWO TO TANGO	*Mercury*	17	*1 Apr 78*	9

Alannah MYLES — Canada

SINGLES:	HITS 2			WEEKS 17
BLACK VELVET	*Atlantic*	2	*17 Mar 90*	15
LOVE IS	*Atlantic*	61	*16 Jun 90*	2
ALBUMS:	**HITS 1**			**WEEKS 21**
ALANNAH MYLES	*Atlantic*	3	*28 Apr 90*	21

Marie MYRIAM — France

SINGLES:	HITS 1			WEEKS 4
L'OUISEAU ET L'ENFANT	*Polydor*	42	*28 May 77*	4
Eurovision Song Contest winner in 1977.				

MYRON — US

SINGLES:	HITS 1			WEEKS 1
WE CAN GET DOWN	*Island Black Music*	74	*22 Nov 97*	1

MYSTERY — Holland

SINGLES:	HITS 1			WEEKS 1
MYSTERY	*Inferno*	56	*6 Oct 01*	1

MYSTERY GIRL - See Michael JACKSON

MYSTI - see CAMOUFLAGE featuring 'MYSTI'

MYSTIC MERLIN — US

SINGLES:	HITS 1			WEEKS 9
JUST CAN'T GIVE YOU UP	*Capitol*	20	*26 Apr 80*	9

MYSTICA — Israel

SINGLES:	HITS 2			WEEKS 2
EVER REST	*Perfecto Fluoro*	62	*24 Jan 98*	1
AFRICAN HORIZON	*Perfecto Fluoro*	59	*9 May 98*	1

MYSTIC 3 — UK/Italy

SINGLES:	HITS 1			WEEKS 1
SOMETHING'S GOIN' ON	*Rulin*	63	*24 Jun 00*	1

MYSTIKAL — US

SINGLES:	HITS 4			WEEKS 17
SHAKE YA ASS	*Jive*	30	*9 Dec 00*	5
STUTTER	*Jive*	7	*17 Feb 01*	8
Samples the Pharcyde's Passing Me By. From the film 'Double Take'.				
Above hit: JOE featuring MYSTIKAL.				
DANGER (BEEN SO LONG)	*Jive*	28	*3 Mar 01*	3
Above hit: MYSTIKAL featuring NIVEA.				
DON'T STOP (FUNKIN' 4 JAMAICA)	*Virgin*	32	*29 Dec 01*	1
Listed with its flip side Never Too Far by Mariah Carey.				
Above hit: Mariah CAREY featuring MYSTIKAL.				

MYTOWN — Ireland

SINGLES:	HITS 1			WEEKS 2
PARTY ALL NIGHT	*Universal*	22	*13 Mar 99*	2

MZ MAY - See ARTFUL DODGER; DREEM TEAM

N

N*E*R*D featuring Lee HARVEY and VITA — US

SINGLES:	HITS 1			WEEKS 2
LAPDANCE	*Virgin*	33	*9 Jun 01*	2

N-JOI — UK

SINGLES:	HITS 6			WEEKS 28
ANTHEM	*Deconstruction*	45	*27 Oct 90*	5
ADRENALIN [EP] *Lead track: Adrenalin.*	*Deconstruction*	23	*2 Mar 91*	5
ANTHEM [RI]	*Deconstruction*	8	*6 Apr 91*	8
LIVE IN MANCHESTER *This was the track title which consisted of 2 parts.*	*Deconstruction*	12	*22 Feb 92*	5
THE DRUMSTRUCK [EP] *Lead track: The Void.*	*Deconstruction*	33	*24 Jul 93*	3
PAPILLON	*Deconstruction*	70	*17 Dec 94*	1
BAD THINGS *Above hit: NJOI.*	*Deconstruction*	57	*8 Jul 95*	1

N 'N' G featuring KALLAGHAN — UK

SINGLES:	HITS 1			WEEKS 6
RIGHT BEFORE MY EYES *Originally recorded by Patti Day in 1989.*	*Urban Heat*	12	*1 Apr 00*	6

N.T. GANG — Germany

SINGLES:	HITS 1			WEEKS 1
WAM BAM	*Cooltempo*	71	*2 Apr 88*	1

N-TRANCE — UK

SINGLES:	HITS 10			WEEKS 73
SET YOU FREE *Original release reached No.81 in 1993. Features rap by T-1K.* *Above hit: N-TRANCE featuring Kelly LLORENNA.*	*All Around The World*	39	*7 May 94*	4
TURN UP THE POWER *Features vocals by Rachel McFarlane.*	*All Around The World*	23	*22 Oct 94*	3
SET YOU FREE [RM-1ST] *This was the original version although it was not the first track on the 1994 chart entry. Features uncredited vocals by Kelly Llorenna.*	*All Around The World*	2	*14 Jan 95*	15
STAYIN' ALIVE *Above hit: N-TRANCE featuring Ricardo DA FORCE.*	*All Around The World*	2	*16 Sep 95*	11
ELECTRONIC PLEASURE *Rap by Ricardo Da Force. Vocals by Gillian Wisdom*	*All Around The World*	11	*24 Feb 96*	4
D.I.S.C.O.	*All Around The World*	11	*5 Apr 97*	6
THE MIND OF THE MACHINE *Features a vocal from actor/director Steven Berkoff.*	*All Around The World*	15	*23 Aug 97*	4
DA YA THINK I'M SEXY? *Rod Stewart's vocals are sampled from his hit of the same name.* *Above hit: N-TRANCE featuring Rod STEWART.*	*All Around The World*	7	*1 Nov 97*	10
PARADISE CITY	*All Around The World*	28	*12 Sep 98*	3
TEARS IN THE RAIN	*All Around The World*	53	*19 Dec 98*	1
SHAKE YA BODY *Female vocal: Kelly Llorenna.*	*All Around The World*	37	*20 May 00*	1
SET YOU FREE [RM-2ND] *Remixed by Rob Searle.*	*All Around The World*	4	*22 Sep 01*	11

N-TYCE — UK

SINGLES:	HITS 4			WEEKS 15
HEY DJ! (PLAY THAT SONG)	*Telstar*	20	*5 Jul 97*	2
WE COME TO PARTY	*Telstar*	12	*13 Sep 97*	4
TELEFUNKIN'	*Telstar*	16	*28 Feb 98*	5
BOOM BOOM *Rap is by Dionne Warwick's son Damon Elliott.*	*Telstar*	18	*6 Jun 98*	4

ALBUMS:	HITS 1			WEEKS 1
ALL DAY EVERY DAY	*Telstar*	44	*20 Jun 98*	1

N.W.A. — US

SINGLES:	HITS 4			WEEKS 15
EXPRESS YOURSELF *Originally recorded by Charles Wright and the Watts 103rd Street Band.*	*Fourth & Broadway*	50	*9 Sep 89*	4
EXPRESS YOURSELF [RE]	*Fourth & Broadway*	26	*26 May 90*	5
GANGSTA, GANGSTA	*Fourth & Broadway*	70	*1 Sep 90*	1
100 MILES AND RUNNIN'	*Fourth & Broadway*	38	*10 Nov 90*	3
ALWAYZ INTO SOMETHIN'	*Fourth & Broadway*	60	*23 Nov 91*	2

ALBUMS:	HITS 3			WEEKS 7
STRAIGHT OUTTA COMPTON	*Fourth & Broadway*	41	*30 Sep 89*	4
EFIL4ZAGGIN	*Fourth & Broadway*	25	*15 Jun 91*	2
GREATEST HITS	*Priority*	56	*31 Aug 96*	1

N.Y.C.C. — Germany

SINGLES:	HITS 2			WEEKS 6
FIGHT FOR YOUR RIGHT (TO PARTY)	*Control*	14	*30 May 98*	5
CAN YOU FEEL IT (ROCK DA HOUSE)	*Control*	68	*19 Sep 98*	1

Jimmy NAIL — UK

SINGLES:	HITS 10			WEEKS 73
LOVE DON'T LIVE HERE ANYMORE *Produced by Queen's Roger Taylor.*	*Virgin*	3	*27 Apr 85*	11
AIN'T NO DOUBT *Co-written by Charlie Dore.*	*East West*	1	*11 Jul 92*	12
LAURA	*East West*	58	*3 Oct 92*	2
CROCODILE SHOES	*East West*	4	*26 Nov 94*	13
COWBOY DREAMS	*East West*	13	*11 Feb 95*	7
CROCODILE SHOES [RE-1ST]	*East West*	68	*11 Mar 95*	3
CROCODILE SHOES [RE-2ND]	*East West*	56	*8 Apr 95*	4
CALLING OUT YOUR NAME *Above 3 featured in the BBC1 TV series 'Crocodile Shoes'.*	*East West*	65	*6 May 95*	1
BIG RIVER *Features Mark Knopfler from Dire Straits on guitar.*	*East West*	18	*28 Oct 95*	5
LOVE	*East West*	33	*23 Dec 95*	4
BIG RIVER '96 [RM] *Remixed by Jon Kelly.*	*East West*	72	*3 Feb 96*	2
COUNTRY BOY *From the BBC1 TV series 'Crocodile Shoes II'.*	*East West*	25	*16 Nov 96*	8
THE FLAME STILL BURNS *From the film 'Still Crazy'.* *Above hit: Jimmy NAIL with STRANGE FRUIT.*	*London*	47	*21 Nov 98*	1

ALBUMS:	HITS 5			WEEKS 85
GROWING UP IN PUBLIC	*East West*	2	*8 Aug 92*	12
CROCODILE SHOES [OST-TV] *Music from the BBC1 TV series.*	*East West*	2	*3 Dec 94*	31
BIG RIVER	*East West*	8	*18 Nov 95*	15
CROCODILE SHOES II [OST-TV] *Music from the BBC1 TV series.*	*East West*	10	*30 Nov 96*	13
THE NAIL FILE - THE BEST OF JIMMY NAIL	*East West*	8	*18 Oct 97*	14

NAILBOMB — US/Brazil

ALBUMS:	HITS 1			WEEKS 1
POINT BLANK	*Roadrunner*	62	*2 Apr 94*	1

NAKATOMI — UK

SINGLES:	HITS 1			WEEKS 2
CHILDREN OF THE NIGHT (QFT REMIXES) *Original release reached No. 149 in 1996.*	*Peach*	47	*7 Feb 98*	2

NAKED EYES — UK

SINGLES:	HITS 1			WEEKS 3
ALWAYS SOMETHING THERE TO REMIND ME *Originally recorded by Lou Johnson.*	*EMI*	59	*23 Jul 83*	3

NALIN and KANE — Germany

SINGLES:	HITS 2			WEEKS 7
BEACHBALL *Vocals by Shondell Mims and Andrea Kanta.*	*ffrr*	48	*1 Nov 97*	1
PLANET VIOLET *Above hit: NALIN I.N.C.*	*Logic*	51	*28 Mar 98*	1
BEACHBALL [RM] *Remixed by Tall Paul.*	*ffrr*	17	*3 Oct 98*	5

NANA - See ARCHITECHS featuring NANA

NAPALM DEATH — UK

ALBUMS:	HITS 3			WEEKS 3
HARMONY OF CORRUPTION	*Earache*	67	*15 Sep 90*	1
UTOPIA BANISHED	*Earache*	58	*30 May 92*	1
DIATRIBES	*Earache*	74	*3 Feb 96*	1

NAPOLEON XIV — US

SINGLES:	HITS 1			WEEKS 10
THEY'RE COMING TO TAKE ME AWAY, HA-HAAA!	*Warner Brothers*	4	*6 Aug 66*	10

NARADA – See Narada Michael WALDEN

Michelle NARINE – See BIG BASS vs Michelle NARINE

NAS — US

(See also Nas Escobar, Foxy Brown, Az and Nature present the Firm featuring Dawn Robinson; QB Finest featuring Nas and Bravehearts.)

SINGLES:	HITS 7			WEEKS 29
IT AIN'T HARD TO TELL	*Columbia*	64	*28 May 94*	1
Samples Michael Jackson;'s Human Nature and N.T by Kool and the Gang.				
IF I RULED THE WORLD	*Columbia*	12	*17 Aug 96*	7
Features vocals from Lauryn Hill.				
STREET DREAMS	*Columbia*	12	*25 Jan 97*	4
Samples Sweet Dreams by the Eurythmics.				
HEAD OVER HEELS	*Epic*	18	*14 Jun 97*	3
Samples MC Shan's The Bridge.				
Above hit: ALLURE featuring NAS.				
HATE ME NOW	*Columbia*	14	*29 May 99*	6
Above hit: NAS (featuring PUFF DADDY).				
DID YOU EVER THINK	*Jive*	20	*31 Jul 99*	5
Samples Curtis Mayfield's Right On For The Darkness.				
Above hit: R. KELLY featuring NAS.				
NASTRADAMUS	*Columbia*	24	*15 Jan 00*	3
Features poetry by Jessica Care More and vocals by Ronald Isley and Ginuwine. Samples the JB Horns' It's Not The Express It's The JB Monorail.				
ALBUMS:	**HITS 2**			**WEEKS 10**
IT WAS WRITTEN	*Columbia*	38	*13 Jul 96*	6
I AM . . .	*Columbia*	31	*17 Apr 99*	4

Graham NASH — UK

(See also Crosby, Stills, Nash and Young; Graham Nash and David Crosby.)

ALBUMS:	HITS 1			WEEKS 8
SONGS FOR BEGINNERS	*Atlantic*	13	*26 Jun 71*	8

Graham NASH and David CROSBY — UK

(See also David Crosby; Crosby, Stills, Nash and Young; Graham Nash.)

ALBUMS:	HITS 1			WEEKS 5
GRAHAM NASH AND DAVID CROSBY	*Atlantic*	13	*13 May 72*	5

Johnny NASH — US

SINGLES:	HITS 10			WEEKS 106
HOLD ME TIGHT	*Regal Zonophone*	5	*10 Aug 68*	16
YOU GOT SOUL	*Major Minor*	6	*11 Jan 69*	12
Originally recorded by Bill Johnson.				
CUPID	*Major Minor*	6	*5 Apr 69*	11
CUPID [RE]	*Major Minor*	50	*28 Jun 69*	1
STIR IT UP	*CBS*	13	*1 Apr 72*	12
Originally recorded by Bob Marley & the Wailers.				
I CAN SEE CLEARLY NOW	*CBS*	5	*24 Jun 72*	15
Backing vocals by Dawn Penn and the Wailers.				
THERE ARE MORE QUESTIONS THAN ANSWERS	*CBS*	9	*7 Oct 72*	9
TEARS ON MY PILLOW (I CAN'T TAKE IT)	*CBS*	1	*14 Jun 75*	11
LET'S BE FRIENDS	*CBS*	42	*11 Oct 75*	3
(WHAT A) WONDERFUL WORLD	*Epic*	25	*12 Jun 76*	7
ROCK ME BABY	*2000 AD*	47	*9 Nov 85*	4
I CAN SEE CLEARLY NOW [RM]	*Epic*	54	*15 Apr 89*	5
ALBUMS:	**HITS 2**			**WEEKS 17**
I CAN SEE CLEARLY NOW	*CBS*	39	*5 Aug 72*	6
JOHNNY NASH COLLECTION	*Epic*	18	*10 Dec 77*	11

Leigh NASH – See DELERIUM

NASH THE SLASH — Canada

ALBUMS:	HITS 1			WEEKS 1
CHILDREN OF THE NIGHT	*DinDisc*	61	*21 Feb 81*	1

NASHVILLE TEENS — UK

SINGLES:	HITS 5			WEEKS 37
TOBACCO ROAD	*Decca*	6	*11 Jul 64*	13

GOOGLE EYE	*Decca*	10	*24 Oct 64*	11
Above 2 originally recorded by John D. Loudermilk.				
FIND MY WAY BACK HOME	*Decca*	34	*6 Mar 65*	6
THIS LITTLE BIRD	*Decca*	38	*22 May 65*	4
Originally recorded by John D.Loudermilk.				
THE HARD WAY	*Decca*	45	*5 Feb 66*	2
THE HARD WAY [RE]	*Decca*	48	*26 Feb 66*	1

NATASHA — UK

SINGLES:	HITS 2			WEEKS 16
IKO IKO	*Towerbell*	10	*5 Jun 82*	11
THE BOOM BOOM ROOM	*Towerbell*	44	*4 Sep 82*	5
ALBUMS:	**HITS 1**			**WEEKS 3**
CAPTURED	*Towerbell*	53	*9 Oct 82*	3

Ultra NATE — US

(See also B-Crew featuring Barbara Tucker, Ultra Nate, Dajae, Mone; Stars On 54: Ultra Nate, Amber, Jocelyn Enriquez; System 7.)

SINGLES:	HITS 8			WEEKS 39
IT'S OVER NOW	*Eternal*	62	*9 Dec 89*	3
IS IT LOVE?	*Eternal*	71	*23 Feb 91*	1
Above hit: BASEMENT BOYS present Ultra NATE.				
SHOW ME	*Warner Brothers*	62	*29 Jan 94*	1
FREE	*AM:PM*	4	*14 Jun 97*	17
FREE [RI]	*AM:PM*	33	*24 Jan 98*	2
CD credits Free (The Mixes), although the first track is the original radio edit.				
FOUND A CURE	*AM:PM*	6	*18 Apr 98*	7
NEW KIND OF MEDICINE	*AM:PM*	14	*25 Jul 98*	5
DESIRE	*AM:PM*	40	*22 Jul 00*	2
GET IT UP (THE FEELING)	*AM:PM*	51	*9 Jun 01*	1
Samples The Isley Brothers' Tell Me When You Need It Again.				
ALBUMS:	**HITS 1**			**WEEKS 4**
SITUATION:CRITICAL	*AM:PM*	17	*9 May 98*	4

NATIONAL BRASS BAND — UK

ALBUMS:	HITS 1			WEEKS 10
GOLDEN MEMORIES	*K-Tel*	15	*10 May 80*	10

NATIONAL PHILHARMONIC ORCHESTRA - See James GALWAY; James GALWAY and Henry MANCINI with the NATIONAL PHILHARMONIC ORCHESTRA; LONDON PHILHARMONIC CHOIR; Henri MANCINI and his Orchestra

NATIVE — UK

SINGLES:	HITS 1			WEEKS 2
FEEL THE DRUMS	*Slinky Music*	46	*10 Feb 01*	2

NATURAL BORN CHILLERS — UK

SINGLES:	HITS 1			WEEKS 3
ROCK THE FUNKY BEATS	*East West Dance*	30	*1 Nov 97*	3

NATURAL BORN GROOVES — Belgium

SINGLES:	HITS 2			WEEKS 3
FORERUNNER	*XL Recordings*	64	*2 Nov 96*	1
GROOVEBIRD	*Positiva*	21	*19 Apr 97*	2

NATURAL LIFE — UK

SINGLES:	HITS 1			WEEKS 3
NATURAL LIFE	*Tribe*	47	*7 Mar 92*	3

NATURAL SELECTION — US

SINGLES:	HITS 1			WEEKS 2
DO ANYTHING	*East West America*	69	*9 Nov 91*	2

NATURALS — UK

SINGLES:	HITS 1			WEEKS 9
I SHOULD HAVE KNOWN BETTER	*Parlophone*	24	*22 Aug 64*	9
Originally recorded by the Beatles.				

NATURE - See Nas ESCOBAR, Foxy BROWN, AZ and NATURE Present The FIRM featuring Dawn ROBINSON

David NAUGHTON — US

SINGLES:	HITS 1			WEEKS 6
MAKIN' IT	*RSO*	44	*25 Aug 79*	6
From the TV series of the same name.				

NAUGHTY BY NATURE — US

SINGLES:	HITS 5			WEEKS 17
O.P.P.	*Big Life*	73	*9 Nov 91*	1
Samples Jackson Five's ABC.				
O.P.P. [RI]	*Big Life*	35	*20 Jun 92*	3
HIP HOP HOORAY	*Big Life*	22	*30 Jan 93*	3
IT'S ON	*Big Life*	48	*19 Jun 93*	2
HIP HOP HOORAY [RI]	*Big Life*	20	*27 Nov 93*	4
Sleeve gives title as an EP: The Essential EP.				
FEEL ME FLOW	*Big Life*	23	*29 Apr 95*	3
Samples The Meters' Find Yourself.				
JAMBOREE	*Arista*	51	*11 Sep 99*	1
Samples Benny Golson's I'm Always Dancin' To The Music.				
Above hit: NAUGHTY BY NATURE (featuring ZHANE).				

ALBUMS:	HITS 2			WEEKS 5
19 NAUGHTY III	*Big Life*	40	*6 Mar 93*	2
POVERTY'S PARADISE	*Big Life*	20	*27 May 95*	3

NAVIGATOR – See FREESTYLERS

Maria NAYLER — UK

SINGLES:	HITS 5			WEEKS 26
BE AS ONE	*Deconstruction*	17	*9 Mar 96*	4
Above hit: SASHA and MARIA.				
ONE & ONE	*Deconstruction*	3	*16 Nov 96*	17
Above hit: Robert MILES featuring Maria NAYLER.				
NAKED AND SACRED	*Deconstruction*	32	*7 Mar 98*	3
WILL YOU BE WITH ME / LOVE IS THE GOD	*Deconstruction*	65	*5 Sep 98*	1
ANGRY SKIES	*Deconstruction*	42	*27 May 00*	1

NAZARETH — UK

SINGLES:	HITS 11			WEEKS 75
BROKEN DOWN ANGEL	*Mooncrest*	9	*5 May 73*	11
BAD BAD BOY	*Mooncrest*	10	*21 Jul 73*	9
THIS FLIGHT TONIGHT	*Mooncrest*	11	*13 Oct 73*	13
Originally recorded by Joni Mitchell.				
SHANGHAI'D IN SHANGHAI	*Mooncrest*	41	*23 Mar 74*	4
MY WHITE BICYCLE	*Mooncrest*	14	*14 Jun 75*	8
Originally recorded by Tomorrow in 1967.				
HOLY ROLLER	*Mountain*	36	*15 Nov 75*	4
HOT TRACKS [EP]	*Mountain*	15	*24 Sep 77*	11
Lead track: Love Hurts.				
GONE DEAD TRAIN	*Mountain*	49	*18 Feb 78*	2
PLACE IN YOUR HEART	*Mountain*	70	*13 May 78*	1
PLACE IN YOUR HEART [RE]	*Mountain*	74	*27 May 78*	1
MAY THE SUNSHINE	*Mountain*	22	*27 Jan 79*	8
STAR	*Mountain*	54	*28 Jul 79*	3

ALBUMS:	HITS 7			WEEKS 51
RAZAMANAZ	*Mooncrest*	11	*26 May 73*	25
LOUD 'N' PROUD	*Mooncrest*	10	*24 Nov 73*	7
RAMPANT	*Mooncrest*	13	*18 May 74*	3
GREATEST HITS	*Mountain*	54	*13 Dec 75*	1
NO MEAN CITY	*Mountain*	34	*3 Feb 79*	9
THE FOOL CIRCLE	*NEMS*	60	*28 Feb 81*	3
NAZARETH LIVE	*NEMS*	78	*3 Oct 81*	3

NAZLYN – See ADVENTURES OF STEVIE V; M-BEAT

Me'shell NDEGEOCELLO — US

SINGLES:	HITS 3			WEEKS 5
IF THAT'S YOUR BOYFRIEND (HE WASN'T LAST NIGHT)	*Maverick*	74	*12 Feb 94*	1
WILD NIGHT	*Mercury*	34	*3 Sep 94*	3
Above hit: John MELLENCAMP with Me'shell NDEGEOCELLO.				
NEVER MISS THE WATER	*Reprise*	59	*1 Mar 97*	1
Above hit: Chaka KHAN featuring Me'shell NDEGEOCELLO.				

Youssou N'DOUR — Senegal

SINGLES:	HITS 4			WEEKS 35
SHAKIN' THE TREE	*Virgin*	61	*3 Jun 89*	3
Above hit: Youssou N'DOUR and Peter GABRIEL.				
SHAKING THE TREE [RI]	*Virgin*	57	*22 Dec 90*	4
[AA] listed with re-issue of Solisbury Hill by Peter Gabriel.				
Above hit: Peter GABRIEL and Youssou N'DOUR.				
7 SECONDS	*Columbia*	3	*25 Jun 94*	21
Above hit: Youssou N'DOUR (featuring Neneh CHERRY).				
7 SECONDS [RE]	*Columbia*	54	*24 Dec 94*	4

UNDECIDED	*Columbia*	53	*14 Jan 95*	2
HOW COME	*Interscope*	52	*10 Oct 98*	1

From the film 'Bulworth'.
Above hit: Youssou N'DOUR and CANIBUS.

NEARLY GOD — UK

SINGLES:	HITS 1			WEEKS 2
POEMS	*Durban Poison*	28	*20 Apr 96*	2
ALBUMS:	**HITS 1**			**WEEKS 4**
NEARLY GOD - POEMS	*Durban Poison*	10	*4 May 96*	4

Martin NEARY - See Sarah BRIGHTMAN; WESTMINSTER ABBEY CHOIR/conductor: Martin NEARY

Terry NEASON — UK

SINGLES:	HITS 1			WEEKS 1
LIFEBOAT (THEME FROM THE BBC TV SERIES 'THE LIFEBOAT')	*WEA*	72	*25 Jun 94*	1

NEBULA II — UK

SINGLES:	HITS 2			WEEKS 3
SEANCE / ATHEAMA	*Reinforced*	55	*1 Feb 92*	2
FLATLINERS	*J4M*	54	*16 May 92*	1

NED'S ATOMIC DUSTBIN — UK

SINGLES:	HITS 8			WEEKS 24
KILL YOUR TELEVISION	*Chapter 22*	53	*14 Jul 90*	2
UNTIL YOU FIND OUT	*Chapter 22*	51	*27 Oct 90*	2
HAPPY	*Furtive*	16	*9 Mar 91*	4
TRUST	*Furtive*	21	*21 Sep 91*	4
NOT SLEEPING AROUND	*Furtive*	19	*10 Oct 92*	3
INTACT	*Furtive*	36	*5 Dec 92*	6
ALL I ASK OF MYSELF IS THAT I HOLD TOGETHER	*Sony S2*	33	*25 Mar 95*	2
STUCK	*Furtive*	64	*15 Jul 95*	1
ALBUMS:	**HITS 3**			**WEEKS 8**
BITE *German import.*	*Rough Trade*	72	*9 Feb 91*	1
GOD FODDER	*Furtive*	4	*13 Apr 91*	5
ARE YOU NORMAL?	*Furtive*	13	*31 Oct 92*	2

NEEDLE DAMAGE - See DJ DAN presents NEEDLE DAMAGE

Joey NEGRO — UK

(See also Li Kwan.)

SINGLES:	HITS 6			WEEKS 16
REACHIN' *Above hit: PHASE II.*	*Republic*	70	*18 Mar 89*	1
DO WHAT YOU FEEL *Above hit: Joey NEGRO - voice of Debbie FRENCH.*	*Ten Records*	36	*16 Nov 91*	3
REACHIN' [RM] *Remixed by Dave Lee.* *Above hit: Joey NEGRO presents PHASE II.*	*Republic*	70	*21 Dec 91*	1
ENTER YOUR FANTASY [EP] *Lead track: Love Fantasy (with credit: vocals by: Jannette Saul and Debbie French).*	*Ten Records*	35	*18 Jul 92*	3
WHAT HAPPENED TO THE MUSIC	*Virgin*	51	*25 Sep 93*	2
MUST BE THE MUSIC	*Incentive*	8	*19 Feb 00*	5
SATURDAY *Samples Saturday by Norma Jean (ex Chic vocalist Norma Jean Wright).* *Above 2: Joey NEGRO featuring Taka BOOM.*	*Yola*	41	*16 Sep 00*	1

neil — UK

SINGLES:	HITS 1			WEEKS 10
HOLE IN MY SHOE	*WEA*	2	*14 Jul 84*	10

Vince NEIL — US

SINGLES:	HITS 1			WEEKS 1
YOU'RE INVITED (BUT YOUR FRIEND CAN'T COME)	*Hollywood*	63	*3 Oct 92*	1
ALBUMS:	**HITS 1**			**WEEKS 1**
EXPOSED	*Warner Brothers*	44	*8 May 93*	1

NEJA — Italy

SINGLES:	HITS 1			WEEKS 1
RESTLESS (I KNOW YOU KNOW)	*Panorama*	47	*26 Sep 98*	1

NEK — Italy

SINGLES:	HITS 1			WEEKS 1
LAURA	*Coalition*	59	*29 Aug 98*	1

NELLY — US

SINGLES:	HITS 5			WEEKS 32
(HOT S+++) +++COUNTRY GRAMMAR	*Universal*	7	*11 Nov 00*	9
+++E.I.	*Universal*	11	*24 Feb 01*	5
RIDE WIT ME	*Universal*	3	*19 May 01*	12
Above hit: NELLY featuring CITY SPUD.				
BATTER UP	*Universal*	28	*15 Sep 01*	3
Above hit: NELLY and ST. LUNATICS.				
WHERE THE PARTY AT?	*Columbia*	25	*27 Oct 01*	3
Above hit: JAGGED EDGE featuring NELLY.				
ALBUMS:	**HITS 1**			**WEEKS 27**
COUNTRY GRAMMAR	*Universal*	14	*3 Feb 01*	27

NELSON — US

SINGLES:	HITS 1			WEEKS 3
(I CAN'T LIVE WITHOUT YOUR) LOVE & AFFECTION	*DGC*	54	*27 Oct 90*	3

Bill NELSON — UK

SINGLES:	HITS 4			WEEKS 12
FURNITURE MUSIC	*Harvest*	59	*24 Feb 79*	3
REVOLT INTO STYLE	*Harvest*	69	*5 May 79*	2
Above 2: Bill NELSON'S RED NOISE.				
DO YOU DREAM IN COLOUR?	*Cocteau*	52	*5 Jul 80*	4
YOUTH OF NATION ON FIRE	*Mercury*	73	*13 Jun 81*	3
ALBUMS:	**HITS 5**			**WEEKS 21**
SOUND ON SOUND	*Harvest*	33	*24 Feb 79*	5
Above hit: Bill NELSON'S RED NOISE.				
QUIT DREAMING AND GET ON THE BEAM	*Mercury*	7	*23 May 81*	6
THE LOVE THAT WHIRLS (DIARY OF A THINKING HEART)	*Mercury*	28	*3 Jul 82*	4
CHIMERA	*Mercury*	30	*14 May 83*	5
GETTING THE HOLY GHOST ACROSS	*Portrait*	91	*3 May 86*	1

Pete NELSON – See WHITE PLAINS

Phyllis NELSON — US

SINGLES:	HITS 1			WEEKS 24
MOVE CLOSER	*Carrere*	1	*23 Feb 85*	21
MOVE CLOSER [RI]	*EMI*	34	*21 May 94*	3
Featured in the Soft and Gentle anti-perspirant TV commercial.				
ALBUMS:	**HITS 1**			**WEEKS 10**
MOVE CLOSER	*Carrere*	29	*20 Apr 85*	10

Ricky NELSON — US

SINGLES:	HITS 15			WEEKS 150
STOOD UP	*London*	27	*22 Feb 58*	1
STOOD UP [RE]	*London*	29	*8 Mar 58*	1
POOR LITTLE FOOL	*London*	4	*23 Aug 58*	13
SOMEDAY	*London*	9	*8 Nov 58*	13
Originally recorded by the Mills Brothers.				
I GOT A FEELING	*London*	27	*22 Nov 58*	1
Above 2 entries were separate sides of the same release, each had its own chart run.				
POOR LITTLE FOOL [RE]	*London*	28	*29 Nov 58*	1
IT'S LATE	*London*	3	*18 Apr 59*	20
Originally recorded by Dorsey Burnette.				
NEVER BE ANYONE ELSE BUT YOU	*London*	19	*16 May 59*	1
Above 2 entries were separate sides of the same release, each had its own chart run.				
NEVER BE ANYONE ELSE BUT YOU [RE]	*London*	14	*6 Jun 59*	9
SWEETER THAN YOU	*London*	19	*5 Sep 59*	3
JUST A LITTLE TOO MUCH	*London*	11	*12 Sep 59*	8
Above 2 entries were separate sides of the same release, each had its own chart run.				
I WANNA BE LOVED	*London*	30	*16 Jan 60*	1
YOUNG EMOTIONS	*London*	48	*9 Jul 60*	1
HELLO MARY LOU / TRAVELIN' MAN	*London*	2	*3 Jun 61*	18
Travelin' Man only listed for the week of 3 Jun 61 when it entered at No. 32 and had first credit. Later copies were titled as 'Hello Marylou Goodbye Heart'.				
EVERLOVIN'	*London*	23	*18 Nov 61*	5
YOUNG WORLD	*London*	19	*31 Mar 62*	13
TEEN AGE IDOL	*London*	39	*1 Sep 62*	4
IT'S UP TO YOU	*London*	22	*19 Jan 63*	9

FOOLS RUSH IN	*Brunswick*	12	*19 Oct 63*	9
Originally recorded by Glenn Miller in 1940.				
FOR YOU	*Brunswick*	14	*1 Feb 64*	10
Originally recorded by Glenn Gray in 1933.				
GARDEN PARTY	*MCA*	41	*21 Oct 72*	4
Features the Stone Canyon Band on backing vocals.				
Above 3: Rick NELSON.				
HELLO MARY LOU (GOODBYE HEART) [RI]	*Liberty*	45	*24 Aug 91*	5

Sandy NELSON — US

SINGLES:	HITS 4			WEEKS 42
TEEN BEAT	*Top Rank*	9	*7 Nov 59*	11
Features Bruce Johnston (Beach Boys) on piano.				
TEEN BEAT [RE]	*Top Rank*	25	*6 Feb 60*	1
LET THERE BE DRUMS	*Top Rank*	3	*16 Dec 61*	16
Features Scott Walker on bass.				
DRUMS ARE MY BEAT	*London*	30	*24 Mar 62*	6
DRUMMIN' UP A STORM	*London*	39	*9 Jun 62*	8

Shara NELSON — UK

SINGLES:	HITS 7			WEEKS 23
DOWN THAT ROAD	*Cooltempo*	19	*24 Jul 93*	6
ONE GOODBYE IN TEN	*Cooltempo*	21	*18 Sep 93*	5
UPTIGHT	*Cooltempo*	19	*12 Feb 94*	5
NOBODY	*Cooltempo*	49	*4 Jun 94*	1
INSIDE OUT / DOWN THAT ROAD [RM]	*Cooltempo*	34	*10 Sep 94*	3
Down That Road remixed by David Morales.				
ROUGH WITH THE SMOOTH	*Cooltempo*	30	*16 Sep 95*	2
SENSE OF DANGER	*Pagan*	61	*5 Dec 98*	1
Above hit: PRESENCE featuring Shara NELSON.				
ALBUMS:	**HITS 2**			**WEEKS 11**
WHAT SILENCE KNOWS	*Cooltempo*	22	*2 Oct 93*	9
FRIENDLY FIRE	*Cooltempo*	44	*7 Oct 95*	2

Shelley NELSON – See TIN TIN OUT

Willie NELSON — US

SINGLES:	HITS 2			WEEKS 13
ALWAYS ON MY MIND	*CBS*	49	*31 Jul 82*	3
TO ALL THE GIRLS I'VE LOVED BEFORE	*CBS*	17	*7 Apr 84*	10
Originally recorded by Albert Hammond.				
Above hit: Julio IGLESIAS and Willie NELSON.				

NENA — Germany

SINGLES:	HITS 2			WEEKS 14
99 RED BALLOONS	*Epic*	1	*4 Feb 84*	12
JUST A DREAM	*Epic*	70	*5 May 84*	2
ALBUMS:	**HITS 1**			**WEEKS 5**
NENA	*Epic*	31	*24 Mar 84*	5

NERIO'S DUBWORK – See Darryl PANDY

Frances NERO — US

SINGLES:	HITS 1			WEEKS 9
FOOTSTEPS FOLLOWING ME	*Debut*	17	*13 Apr 91*	9

NERO and the GLADIATORS — US

SINGLES:	HITS 2			WEEKS 6
ENTRY OF THE GLADIATORS	*Decca*	50	*25 Mar 61*	1
ENTRY OF THE GLADIATORS [RE]	*Decca*	37	*8 Apr 61*	4
IN THE HALL OF THE MOUNTAIN KING	*Decca*	48	*29 Jul 61*	1

Ann NESBY — US

SINGLES:	HITS 2			WEEKS 3
WITNESS [EP]	*AM:PM*	42	*21 Dec 96*	2
Lead track: Can I Get A Witness.				
HOLD ON [EP]	*AM:PM*	75	*17 May 97*	1
Lead track: Hold On.				

Michael NESMITH — US

SINGLES:	HITS 1			WEEKS 6
RIO	*Island*	28	*26 Mar 77*	6

NETWORK — UK

SINGLES:	HITS 1			WEEKS 4
BROKEN WINGS	*Chrysalis*	46	*12 Dec 92*	4

NEVADA — UK

SINGLES:	HITS 1			WEEKS 1
IN THE BLEAK MIDWINTER	*Polydor*	71	*8 Jan 83*	1

Robbie NEVIL — US

SINGLES:	HITS 3			WEEKS 24
C'EST LA VIE *Originally recorded by Beau Williams.*	*Manhattan*	3	*20 Dec 86*	11
DOMINOES	*Manhattan*	26	*2 May 87*	6
WOT'S IT TO YA	*Manhattan*	43	*11 Jul 87*	7
ALBUMS:	**HITS 1**			**WEEKS 1**
C'EST LA VIE	*Manhattan*	93	*13 Jun 87*	1

Aaron NEVILLE – See NEVILLE BROTHERS; Linda RONSTADT

NEVILLE BROTHERS — US

SINGLES:	HITS 2			WEEKS 7
WITH GOD ON OUR SIDE	*A&M*	47	*25 Nov 89*	6
BIRD ON A WIRE	*A&M*	72	*7 Jul 90*	1
ALBUMS:	**HITS 1**			**WEEKS 3**
BROTHER'S KEEPER	*A&M*	35	*18 Aug 90*	3

Jason NEVINS — US

SINGLES:	HITS 3			WEEKS 24
IT'S LIKE THAT *German import.*	*Columbia*	63	*21 Feb 98*	3
IT'S LIKE THAT *US import.*	*Sm:)e Communications*	65	*14 Mar 98*	1
IT'S LIKE THAT	*Sm:)e Communications*	1	*21 Mar 98*	16
(IT'S) TRICKY *German import. Remixed by Jason Nevins.* *Above 4: RUN-D.M.C. vs Jason NEVINS.*	*Epidrome*	74	*18 Apr 98*	1
INSANE IN THE BRAIN *Above hit: Jason NEVINS vs. CYPRESS HILL.*	*INCredible*	19	*26 Jun 99*	3

NEW ATLANTIC — UK

SINGLES:	HITS 4			WEEKS 15
I KNOW	*3 Beat*	12	*29 Feb 92*	7
INTO THE FUTURE *Above hit: NEW ATLANTIC featuring Linda WRIGHT.*	*3 Beat*	70	*3 Oct 92*	1
TAKE OFF SOME TIME	*3 Beat*	64	*13 Feb 93*	1
THE SUNSHINE AFTER THE RAIN *Re-Issued in 1995, credited solely to Berri.* *Above hit: NEW ATLANTIC/U4EA featuring BERRI.*	*Ffrreedom*	26	*26 Nov 94*	6

NEW BOHEMIANS – See Edie BRICKELL and NEW BOHEMIANS

NEW CHRISTY MINSTRELS — US

EPS:	HITS 1			WEEKS 10
THREE WHEELS ON MY WAGON	*CBS*	5	*19 Mar 66*	10

NEW EDITION – See Mike BATT (with the NEW EDITION)

NEW EDITION — US

SINGLES:	HITS 6			WEEKS 36
CANDY GIRL	*London*	1	*16 Apr 83*	13
POPCORN LOVE	*London*	43	*13 Aug 83*	5
MR. TELEPHONE MAN *Written and produced by Ray Parker Jr.*	*MCA*	19	*23 Feb 85*	9
CRUCIAL	*MCA*	70	*15 Apr 89*	1
HIT ME OFF *Samples I Got Cha Opin by Black Moon.*	*MCA*	20	*10 Aug 96*	4
SOMETHING ABOUT YOU *Samples Edie Brickell's What I Am.*	*MCA*	16	*7 Jun 97*	4
ALBUMS:	**HITS 1**			**WEEKS 3**
HOME AGAIN	*MCA*	22	*14 Sep 96*	3

NEW FAST AUTOMATIC DAFFODILS — UK

ALBUMS:	HITS 2			WEEKS 2
PIGEON HOLE	*Play It*	49	*17 Nov 90*	1
BODY EXIT MIND	*Play It*	57	*24 Oct 92*	1

NEW FOUND GLORY — US

SINGLES:	HITS 1			WEEKS 1
HIT OR MISS (WAITED TOO LONG)	*MCA*	58	*16 Jun 01*	1

NEW GENERATION — UK

SINGLES:	HITS 1			WEEKS 5
SMOKEY BLUE'S AWAY	*Spark*	38	*29 Jun 68*	5

NEW KIDS ON THE BLOCK — US

SINGLES:	HITS 13			WEEKS 90
HANGIN' TOUGH	*CBS*	52	*16 Sep 89*	4
YOU GOT IT (THE RIGHT STUFF)	*CBS*	1	*11 Nov 89*	13
HANGIN' TOUGH [RI]	*CBS*	1	*6 Jan 90*	9
I'LL BE LOVING YOU (FOREVER)	*CBS*	5	*17 Mar 90*	8
COVER GIRL	*CBS*	4	*12 May 90*	8
STEP BY STEP	*CBS*	2	*16 Jun 90*	7
TONIGHT	*CBS*	3	*4 Aug 90*	10
LET'S TRY IT AGAIN / DIDN'T I (BLOW YOUR MIND)	*CBS*	8	*13 Oct 90*	5
THIS ONE'S FOR THE CHILDREN	*CBS*	9	*8 Dec 90*	7
Charity record with proceeds to United Cerebral Palsy.				
GAMES	*Columbia*	14	*9 Feb 91*	4
CALL IT WHAT YOU WANT	*Columbia*	12	*18 May 91*	5
Above 2: Sleeve shows group name as NKTOB.				
IF YOU GO AWAY	*Columbia*	9	*14 Dec 91*	5
DIRTY DAWG	*Columbia*	27	*19 Feb 94*	3
NEVER LET YOU GO	*Columbia*	42	*26 Mar 94*	2
Above 2: NKTOB.				

ALBUMS:	HITS 7			WEEKS 106
HANGIN' TOUGH	*CBS*	2	*9 Dec 89*	41
STEP BY STEP	*CBS*	1	*30 Jun 90*	31
NEW KIDS ON THE BLOCK	*CBS*	6	*3 Nov 90*	13
MERRY, MERRY CHRISTMAS	*CBS*	13	*15 Dec 90*	5
NO MORE GAMES/THE REMIX ALBUM	*Columbia*	15	*2 Mar 91*	11
H.I.T.S.	*Columbia*	50	*21 Dec 91*	4
FACE THE MUSIC	*Columbia*	36	*12 Mar 94*	1
Above hit: NKOTB.				

NEW MODEL ARMY — UK

SINGLES:	HITS 14			WEEKS 33
NO REST	*EMI*	28	*27 Apr 85*	5
BETTER THAN THEM / NO SENSE	*EMI*	49	*3 Aug 85*	2
Sleeve gives title as an EP:The Acoustic EP.				
BRAVE NEW WORLD	*EMI*	57	*30 Nov 85*	1
51-ST STATE	*EMI*	71	*8 Nov 86*	2
POISON STREET	*EMI*	64	*28 Feb 87*	1
WHITECOATS [EP]	*EMI*	50	*26 Sep 87*	3
Lead track: Whitecoats.				
STUPID QUESTIONS	*EMI*	31	*21 Jan 89*	3
VAGABONDS	*EMI*	37	*11 Mar 89*	3
GREEN AND GREY	*EMI*	37	*10 Jun 89*	3
GET ME OUT	*EMI*	34	*8 Sep 90*	3
PURITY	*EMI*	61	*3 Nov 90*	2
SPACE	*EMI*	39	*8 Jun 91*	2
HERE COMES THE WAR	*Epic*	25	*20 Feb 93*	2
LIVING IN THE ROSE (THE BALLADS EP) [EP]	*Epic*	51	*24 Jul 93*	1
Lead track: Living In The Rose.				

ALBUMS:	HITS 8			WEEKS 21
VENGENCE	*Abstract*	73	*12 May 84*	5
NO REST FOR THE WICKED	*EMI*	22	*25 May 85*	3
THE GHOST OF CAIN	*EMI*	45	*11 Oct 86*	3
THUNDER AND CONSOLATION	*EMI*	20	*18 Feb 89*	3
IMPURITY	*EMI*	23	*6 Oct 90*	2
RAW MELODY MEN	*EMI*	43	*22 Jun 91*	2
THE LOVE OF HOPELESS CAUSES	*Epic*	22	*10 Apr 93*	2
STRANGE BROTHERHOOD	*Eagle*	72	*25 Apr 98*	1

NEW MUSIK — UK

SINGLES:	HITS 4			WEEKS 27
STRAIGHT LINES	*GTO*	53	*6 Oct 79*	5

LIVING BY NUMBERS	*GTO*	13	*19 Jan 80*	8
THIS WORLD OF WATER	*GTO*	31	*26 Apr 80*	7
SANCTUARY	*GTO*	31	*12 Jul 80*	7
ALBUMS:	**HITS 2**			**WEEKS 11**
FROM A TO B	*GTO*	35	*17 May 80*	9
ANYWHERE	*GTO*	68	*14 Mar 81*	2

NEW ORDER UK

SINGLES:	**HITS 25**			**WEEKS 185**
CEREMONY	*Factory*	34	*14 Mar 81*	5
PROCESSION / EVERYTHING'S GONE GREEN	*Factory*	38	*3 Oct 81*	5
TEMPTATION	*Factory*	29	*22 May 82*	7
BLUE MONDAY	*Factory*	12	*19 Mar 83*	17
Available on 12" only.				
BLUE MONDAY [RE-1ST]	*Factory*	9	*13 Aug 83*	17
CONFUSION	*Factory*	12	*3 Sep 83*	7
BLUE MONDAY [RE-2ND]	*Factory*	52	*7 Jan 84*	4
THIEVES LIKE US	*Factory*	18	*28 Apr 84*	5
THE PERFECT KISS	*Factory*	46	*25 May 85*	4
SUB-CULTURE	*Factory*	63	*9 Nov 85*	4
SHELLSHOCK	*Factory*	28	*29 Mar 86*	5
STATE OF THE NATION	*Factory*	30	*27 Sep 86*	3
THE PEEL SESSIONS (1st June1982) [EP]	*Strange Fruit*	54	*27 Sep 86*	1
Lead track: Turn The Heater On. Recordings for DJ John Peel's evening show on BBC Radio 1.				
BIZARRE LOVE TRIANGLE	*Factory*	56	*15 Nov 86*	2
TRUE FAITH	*Factory*	4	*1 Aug 87*	10
TOUCHED BY THE HAND OF GOD	*Factory*	20	*19 Dec 87*	7
BLUE MONDAY 1988 [RM-1ST]	*Factory*	3	*7 May 88*	11
Issued on 7" for first time. Remixed by John Potoker.				
FINE TIME	*Factory*	11	*10 Dec 88*	8
ROUND & ROUND	*Factory*	21	*11 Mar 89*	7
RUN 2	*Factory*	49	*9 Sep 89*	2
WORLD IN MOTION . . .	*Factory*	1	*2 Jun 90*	12
The 1990 England World Cup team's official song.				
Above hit: ENGLANDNEWORDER.				
REGRET	*Centredate Co.*	4	*17 Apr 93*	7
RUINED IN A DAY	*Centredate Co.*	22	*3 Jul 93*	4
WORLD (THE PRICE OF LOVE)	*Centredate Co.*	13	*4 Sep 93*	5
SPOOKY	*Centredate Co.*	22	*18 Dec 93*	4
TRUE FAITH - 94 [RM]	*London*	9	*19 Nov 94*	8
Remixed by Stephen Hague and Mike 'Spike' Drake.				
NINETEEN63	*London*	21	*21 Jan 95*	4
Originally was the B-side of the 1987 release of True Faith.				
BLUE MONDAY-95 [RM-2ND]	*London*	17	*5 Aug 95*	4
Remixed by Hardfloor.				
CRYSTAL	*London*	8	*25 Aug 01*	4
60 MILES AN HOUR	*London*	29	*1 Dec 01*	2
ALBUMS:	**HITS 10**			**WEEKS 149**
MOVEMENT	*Factory*	30	*28 Nov 81*	10
POWER, CORRUPTION AND LIES	*Factory*	4	*14 May 83*	29
LOW-LIFE	*Factory*	7	*25 May 85*	10
BROTHERHOOD	*Factory*	9	*11 Oct 86*	5
SUBSTANCE	*Factory*	3	*29 Aug 87*	37
TECHNIQUE	*Factory*	1	*11 Feb 89*	14
BBC RADIO 1 LIVE IN CONCERT	*Windsong International*	33	*22 Feb 92*	2
REPUBLIC	*Centredate Co*	1	*15 May 93*	19
SUBSTANCE 1987 [RI]	*London*	32	*17 Jul 93*	2
? (THE BEST OF NEW ORDER)	*London*	4	*3 Dec 94*	13
? (THE BEST OF NEW ORDER) / ? (THE REST OF NEW ORDER) [RE]	*London*	5	*2 Sep 95*	4
? (The Rest Of New Order) was a remix album, sales were combined.				
GET READY	*London*	6	*8 Sep 01*	4

NEW POWER GENERATION US

(See also Prince.)

SINGLES:	**HITS 3**			**WEEKS 13**
GET WILD	*NPG*	19	*1 Apr 95*	4
Above hit: NPG.				
THE GOOD LIFE	*NPG*	29	*19 Aug 95*	3
THE GOOD LIFE [RE]	*NPG*	15	*5 Jul 97*	5
COME ON	*RCA*	65	*21 Nov 98*	1
Backing vocals by Chaka Khan.				
ALBUMS:	**HITS 2**			**WEEKS 5**
EXODUS	*NPG*	11	*8 Apr 95*	3
NEWPOWER SOUL	*NPG*	38	*11 Jul 98*	2

NEW RADICALS — US

SINGLES:	HITS 2			WEEKS 18
YOU GET WHAT YOU GIVE	*MCA*	5	*3 Apr 99*	17
SOMEDAY WE'LL KNOW	*MCA*	48	*25 Sep 99*	1
ALBUMS:	**HITS 1**			**WEEKS 14**
MAYBE YOU'VE BEEN BRAINWASHED TOO	*MCA*	10	*17 Apr 99*	14

NEW SEEKERS — UK

SINGLES:	HITS 14			WEEKS 143
WHAT HAVE THEY DONE TO MY SONG MA	*Philips*	48	*17 Oct 70*	1
Above hit: NEW SEEKERS featuring Eve GRAHAM.				
WHAT HAVE THEY DONE TO MY SONG MA [RE]	*Philips*	44	*31 Oct 70*	1
NEVER ENDING SONG OF LOVE	*Philips*	2	*10 Jul 71*	19
Originally recorded by Delaney and Bonnie.and Friends.				
I'D LIKE TO TEACH THE WORLD TO SING (IN PERFECT HARMONY)	*Polydor*	1	*18 Dec 71*	21
Featured in the Coca-Cola TV commercial.				
BEG, STEAL OR BORROW	*Polydor*	2	*4 Mar 72*	13
UK Eurovision entry in 1972, it came 2nd.				
CIRCLES	*Polydor*	4	*10 Jun 72*	16
Originally recorded by Harry Chapin.				
COME SOFTLY TO ME	*Polydor*	20	*2 Dec 72*	11
Above hit: NEW SEEKERS featuring MARTY.				
PINBALL WIZARD/SEE ME, FEEL ME [M]	*Polydor*	16	*24 Feb 73*	8
NEVERTHELESS (I'M IN LOVE WITH YOU)	*Polydor*	34	*7 Apr 73*	5
Above hit: Eve GRAHAM and the NEW SEEKERS.				
GOODBYE IS JUST ANOTHER WORD	*Polydor*	36	*16 Jun 73*	5
YOU WON'T FIND ANOTHER FOOL LIKE ME	*Polydor*	1	*24 Nov 73*	16
Above hit: NEW SEEKERS featuring Lyn PAUL.				
I GET A LITTLE SENTIMENTAL OVER YOU	*Polydor*	5	*9 Mar 74*	9
IT'S SO NICE (TO HAVE YOU HOME)	*CBS*	44	*14 Aug 76*	4
I WANNA GO BACK	*CBS*	25	*29 Jan 77*	4
ANTHEM (ONE DAY IN EVERY WEEK)	*CBS*	21	*15 Jul 78*	10
ALBUMS:	**HITS 6**			**WEEKS 49**
NEW COLOURS	*Polydor*	40	*5 Feb 72*	4
WE'D LIKE TO TEACH THE WORLD TO SING	*Polydor*	2	*1 Apr 72*	25
NEVER ENDING SONG OF LOVE	*Polydor*	35	*12 Aug 72*	4
CIRCLES	*Polydor*	23	*14 Oct 72*	5
NOW	*Polydor*	47	*21 Apr 73*	2
TOGETHER	*Polydor*	12	*30 Mar 74*	9

NEW VAUDEVILLE BAND (featuring TRISTAM VII) — UK

SINGLES:	HITS 4			WEEKS 43
WINCHESTER CATHEDRAL	*Fontana*	4	*10 Sep 66*	19
Above hit: NEW VAUDEVILLE BAND.				
PEEK-A-BOO	*Fontana*	7	*28 Jan 67*	11
FINCHLEY CENTRAL	*Fontana*	11	*13 May 67*	9
GREEN STREET GREEN	*Fontana*	37	*5 Aug 67*	4

NEW VISION — US

SINGLES:	HITS 1			WEEKS 2
(JUST) ME AND YOU	*AM:PM*	23	*29 Jan 00*	2

NEW WORLD — Australia

SINGLES:	HITS 5			WEEKS 53
ROSE GARDEN	*RAK*	15	*27 Feb 71*	11
TOM-TOM TURNAROUND	*RAK*	6	*3 Jul 71*	15
Originally recorded by Sweet.				
KARA, KARA	*RAK*	17	*4 Dec 71*	13
SISTER JANE	*RAK*	9	*13 May 72*	13
ROOFTOP SINGING	*RAK*	50	*12 May 73*	1

NEW WORLD THEATRE ORCHESTRA — UK

ALBUMS:	HITS 1			WEEKS 1
LET'S DANCE TO THE HITS OF THE 30'S AND 40'S	*Pye Golden Guinea*	20	*24 Dec 60*	1

NEW YORK CITY — US

SINGLES:	HITS 1			WEEKS 11
I'M DOIN' FINE NOW	*RCA Victor*	20	*21 Jul 73*	11

NEW YORK SKYY — US

SINGLES:	HITS 1			WEEKS 2
LET'S CELEBRATE	*Epic*	71	*16 Jan 82*	1
LET'S CELEBRATE [RE]	*Epic*	67	*30 Jan 82*	1

NEWBEATS — US

SINGLES:	HITS 2			WEEKS 22
BREAD AND BUTTER	*Hickory*	15	*12 Sep 64*	9
RUN, BABY, RUN (BACK INTO MY ARMS) / AM I NOT MY BROTHERS KEEPER	*London*	10	*23 Oct 71*	13

Booker NEWBURY III — US

SINGLES:	HITS 2			WEEKS 11
LOVE TOWN	*Polydor*	6	*28 May 83*	8
TEDDY BEAR	*Polydor*	44	*8 Oct 83*	3

Mickey NEWBURY — US

SINGLES:	HITS 1			WEEKS 5
AMERICAN TRILOGY	*Elektra*	42	*1 Jul 72*	5

NEWCLEUS — US

SINGLES:	HITS 1			WEEKS 6
JAM ON REVENGE (THE WIKKI-WIKKI SONG)	*Becket*	44	*3 Sep 83*	6
ALBUMS:	**HITS 1**			**WEEKS 2**
JAM ON REVENGE	*Sunnyview*	84	*25 Aug 84*	2

Bob NEWHART — US

EPS:	HITS 2			WEEKS 65
THE BUTTON-DOWN MIND OF BOB NEWHART	*Warner Brothers*	2	*10 Jun 61*	64
BOB NEWHART VOL. 2; THE BUTTON-DOWN MIND STRIKES BACK!	*Warner Brothers*	20	*20 Oct 62*	1
ALBUMS:	**HITS 1**			**WEEKS 37**
BUTTON-DOWN MIND OF BOB NEWHART	*Warner Brothers*	2	*1 Oct 60*	37

Anthony NEWLEY — UK

(See also Anthony Newley, Peter Sellers, Joan Collins; Various Artists: Stage Cast – London 'Stop The World – I Want To Get Off'.)

SINGLES:	HITS 12			WEEKS 130
I'VE WAITED SO LONG	*Decca*	3	*2 May 59*	15
IDLE ON PARADE [EP]	*Decca*	13	*9 May 59*	4
Lead track: I've Waited So Long. Above 2 from the film 'Idle On Parade'.				
PERSONALITY	*Decca*	6	*13 Jun 59*	12
WHY	*Decca*	1	*16 Jan 60*	18
DO YOU MIND	*Decca*	1	*26 Mar 60*	15
IF SHE SHOULD COME TO YOU (LA MONTANA)	*Decca*	4	*16 Jul 60*	15
STRAWBERRY FAIR	*Decca*	3	*[illegible] Nov 60*	11
AND THE HEAVENS CRIED	*Decca*	6	*18 Mar 61*	12
Originally recorded by Ronnie Savoy.				
POP GOES THE WEASEL / BEE BOM	*Decca*	12	*17 Jun 61*	9
Bee Bom no longer listed from 1 July 61. As an AA side it had reached No. 15.				
WHAT KIND OF FOOL AM I	*Decca*	36	*5 Aug 61*	8
From the film 'Stop The World, I Want To Get Off'.				
D-DARLING	*Decca*	25	*27 Jan 62*	6
THAT NOISE	*Decca*	34	*28 Jul 62*	5
EPS:	**HITS 1**			**WEEKS 9**
TONY'S HITS	*Decca*	6	*16 Apr 60*	9
ALBUMS:	**HITS 2**			**WEEKS 14**
LOVE IS A NOW AND THEN THING	*Decca*	19	*14 May 60*	2
TONY	*Decca*	5	*8 Jul 61*	12

Anthony NEWLEY, Peter SELLERS, Joan COLLINS — UK

(See also Anthony Newley; Peter Sellers.)

ALBUMS:	HITS 1			WEEKS 10
FOOL BRITANNIA	*Ember*	10	*28 Sep 63*	10

Tara NEWLEY – See E-ZEE POSSEE

Brad NEWMAN — UK

SINGLES:	HITS 1			WEEKS 1
SOMEBODY TO LOVE	*Fontana*	47	*24 Feb 62*	1

Dave NEWMAN — UK

SINGLES:	HITS 1			WEEKS 6
THE LION SLEEPS TONIGHT (WIMOWEH)	*Pye*	48	*15 Apr 72*	1
THE LION SLEEPS TONIGHT (WIMOWEH) [RE]	*Pye*	34	*29 Apr 72*	5

NEWS — UK

SINGLES:	HITS 1			WEEKS 3
AUDIO VIDEO	*George*	52	*29 Aug 81*	3

NEWTON — UK

SINGLES:	HITS 3			WEEKS 6
SKY HIGH	*Bags Of Fun*	56	*15 Jul 95*	2
Originally reached No. 83 in 1994.				
SOMETIMES WHEN WE TOUCH	*Dominion*	32	*15 Feb 97*	3
DON'T WORRY	*Dominion*	61	*16 Aug 97*	1

Juice NEWTON — US

SINGLES:	HITS 1			WEEKS 6
ANGEL OF THE MORNING	*Capitol*	43	*2 May 81*	6
Originally recorded by Chip Taylor.				

Olivia NEWTON-JOHN — UK

(See also Various Artists: Films - Original Soundtracks 'Grease'.)

SINGLES:	HITS 24			WEEKS 234
IF NOT FOR YOU	*Pye International*	7	*20 Mar 71*	11
Originally recorded by Bob Dylan.				
BANKS OF THE OHIO	*Pye International*	6	*23 Oct 71*	17
Originally recorded by Blue Sky Boys in 1936.				
WHAT IS LIFE	*Pye International*	16	*11 Mar 72*	8
Originally recorded by George Harrison.				
TAKE ME HOME COUNTRY ROADS	*Pye International*	15	*13 Jan 73*	13
LONG LIVE LOVE	*Pye International*	11	*16 Mar 74*	8
UK's Eurovision entry in 1974, it came 4th.				
I HONESTLY LOVE YOU	*EMI*	22	*12 Oct 74*	6
Originally recorded by Peter Allen.				
SAM	*EMI*	6	*11 Jun 77*	11
YOU'RE THE ONE THAT I WANT	*RSO*	1	*20 May 78*	26
Above hit: John TRAVOLTA and Olivia NEWTON-JOHN.				
SUMMER NIGHTS	*RSO*	1	*16 Sep 78*	19
Above hit: John TRAVOLTA, Olivia NEWTON-JOHN and CAST.				
HOPELESSLY DEVOTED TO YOU	*RSO*	2	*4 Nov 78*	11
Above 3 from the film 'Grease'.				
A LITTLE MORE LOVE	*EMI*	4	*16 Dec 78*	12
DEEPER THAN THE NIGHT	*EMI*	64	*30 Jun 79*	3
XANADU	*Jet*	1	*21 Jun 80*	11
Above hit: Olivia NEWTON-JOHN/ELECTRIC LIGHT ORCHESTRA.				
MAGIC	*Jet*	32	*23 Aug 80*	7
SUDDENLY	*Jet*	15	*25 Oct 80*	7
Above 3 from the film 'Xanadu'.				
Above hit: Olivia NEWTON-JOHN with Cliff RICHARD.				
PHYSICAL	*EMI*	7	*10 Oct 81*	16
LANDSLIDE	*EMI*	18	*16 Jan 82*	9
MAKE A MOVE ON ME	*EMI*	43	*17 Apr 82*	3
Sleeve credits just Olivia.				
HEART ATTACK	*EMI*	46	*23 Oct 82*	4
I HONESTLY LOVE YOU [RI]	*EMI*	52	*15 Jan 83*	4
TWIST OF FATE	*EMI*	57	*12 Nov 83*	2
From the film 'Two Of A Kind'.				
THE GREASE MEGAMIX [M]	*Polydor*	3	*22 Dec 90*	10
Above hit: John TRAVOLTA and Olivia NEWTON-JOHN.				
GREASE - THE DREAM MIX [M]	*Polydor*	47	*23 Mar 91*	2
Above 2 are medleys of songs from the film 'Grease'.				
Above hit: Frankie VALLI, John TRAVOLTA and Olivia NEWTON-JOHN.				
I NEED LOVE	*Mercury*	75	*4 Jul 92*	1
HAD TO BE	*EMI*	22	*9 Dec 95*	4
Above hit: Cliff RICHARD with Olivia NEWTON-JOHN.				
YOU'RE THE ONE THAT I WANT [RI]	*Polydor*	4	*25 Jul 98*	9
20th anniversary re-issue.				
Above hit: John TRAVOLTA Olivia NEWTON-JOHN.				

ALBUMS:	HITS 13			WEEKS 120
MUSIC MAKES MY DAY	*Pye*	37	*2 Mar 74*	3
LONG LIVE LOVE	*EMI*	40	*29 Jun 74*	2
HAVE YOU NEVER BEEN MELLOW	*EMI*	37	*26 Apr 75*	2
COME ON OVER	*EMI*	49	*29 May 76*	4
MAKING A GOOD THING BETTER	*EMI*	60	*27 Aug 77*	1
GREATEST HITS	*EMI*	19	*21 Jan 78*	9
TOTALLY HOT	*EMI*	30	*9 Dec 78*	9
XANADU [OST]	*Jet*	2	*19 Jul 80*	17
Album divided with one side by each artist.				
Above hit: Olivia NEWTON-JOHN/ELECTRIC LIGHT ORCHESTRA.				
PHYSICAL	*EMI*	11	*31 Oct 81*	22
The biggest selling single in the US in the 80s.				
OLIVIA'S GREATEST HITS	*EMI*	8	*23 Oct 82*	38
SOUL KISS	*Mercury*	66	*8 Mar 86*	3

BACK TO BASICS - THE ESSENTIAL COLLECTION 1971-1992	*Mercury*	12	*25 Jul 92*	6
GAIA (ONE WOMAN'S JOURNEY)	*D-Sharp*	33	*4 Feb 95*	4

NEXT — US

SINGLES:	HITS 2			WEEKS 8
TOO CLOSE	*Arista*	24	*6 Jun 98*	3
WIFEY	*Arista*	19	*16 Sep 00*	5
Vocals by Lil' Mo.				

NEXT OF KIN — UK

SINGLES:	HITS 2			WEEKS 6
24 HOURS FROM YOU	*Universal*	13	*20 Feb 99*	4
MORE LOVE	*Universal*	33	*19 Jun 99*	2

NIAGRA — UK

SINGLES:	HITS 1			WEEKS 1
CLOUDBURST	*Freeflow*	65	*27 Sep 97*	1

NICE — UK

SINGLES:	HITS 1			WEEKS 15
AMERICA	*Immediate*	21	*13 Jul 68*	15
From the film/show 'West Side Story'.				
ALBUMS:	**HITS 3**			**WEEKS 38**
NICE	*Immediate*	3	*13 Sep 69*	6
FIVE BRIDGES	*Charisma*	2	*27 Jun 70*	21
ELEGY	*Charisma*	5	*17 Apr 71*	11

Paul NICHOLAS — UK

(See also Various Artists: Stage Cast - London 'Hair'.)

SINGLES:	HITS 4			WEEKS 31
REGGAE LIKE IT USED TO BE	*RSO*	17	*17 Apr 76*	8
DANCING WITH THE CAPTAIN	*RSO*	8	*9 Oct 76*	9
GRANDMA'S PARTY	*RSO*	9	*4 Dec 76*	11
HEAVEN ON THE 7TH FLOOR	*RSO*	40	*9 Jul 77*	3
ALBUMS:	**HITS 1**			**WEEKS 8**
JUST GOOD FRIENDS	*K-Tel*	30	*29 Nov 86*	8

Sue NICHOLLS — UK

SINGLES:	HITS 1			WEEKS 8
WHERE WILL YOU BE	*Pye*	17	*6 Jul 68*	8

Stevie NICKS — US

SINGLES:	HITS 8			WEEKS 30
STOP DRAGGIN' MY HEART AROUND	*WEA*	50	*15 Aug 81*	4
Above hit: Stevie NICKS (with Tom PETTY and the HEARTBREAKERS).				
I CAN'T WAIT	*Parlophone*	54	*25 Jan 86*	4
TALK TO ME	*Parlophone*	68	*29 Mar 86*	2
ROOMS ON FIRE	*EMI*	16	*6 May 89*	7
LONG WAY TO GO	*EMI*	60	*12 Aug 89*	2
WHOLE LOTTA TROUBLE	*EMI*	62	*11 Nov 89*	2
SOMETIMES IT'S A BITCH	*EMI*	40	*24 Aug 91*	4
Written by and features Jon Bon Jovi on guitar.				
I CAN'T WAIT [RI]	*EMI*	47	*9 Nov 91*	2
MAYBE LOVE	*EMI*	42	*2 Jul 94*	3
ALBUMS:	**HITS 7**			**WEEKS 82**
BELLA DONNA	*WEA*	11	*8 Aug 81*	15
THE WILD HEART	*WEA International*	28	*2 Jul 83*	19
ROCK A LITTLE	*Modern*	30	*14 Dec 85*	22
BELLA DONNA [RI]	*Warner Brothers*	72	*28 Feb 87*	1
Re-released with different catalogue number.				
THE OTHER SIDE OF THE MIRROR	*EMI*	3	*10 Jun 89*	14
TIMESPACE - THE BEST OF STEVIE NICKS	*EMI*	15	*14 Sep 91*	6
STREET ANGEL	*EMI*	16	*4 Jun 94*	3
TROUBLE IN SHANGRI-LA	*Reprise*	43	*12 May 01*	2

Hector NICOL — UK

ALBUMS:	HITS 1			WEEKS 1
BRAVO JULIET!	*Klub*	92	*28 Apr 84*	1

NICOLE — Germany

SINGLES:	HITS 2			WEEKS 10
A LITTLE PEACE	*CBS*	1	*8 May 82*	9
Eurovision Song Contest winner in 1982. Also the 500th number one single in the UK.				
GIVE ME MORE TIME	*CBS*	75	*21 Aug 82*	1
ALBUMS:	**HITS 1**			**WEEKS 2**
A LITTLE PEACE	*CBS*	85	*2 Oct 82*	2

NICOLE — US

SINGLES:	HITS 3			WEEKS 9
NEW YORK EYES	*Portrait*	41	*28 Dec 85*	7
Above hit: NICOLE with Timmy THOMAS.				
ROCK THE HOUSE	*React*	63	*26 Dec 92*	1
Above hit: SOURCE vocals by NICOLE.				
RUNNIN' AWAY	*Ore*	69	*6 Jul 96*	1

NICOLE — US

SINGLES:	HITS 2			WEEKS 5
MAKE IT HOT	*East West America*	22	*22 Aug 98*	4
Above hit: NICOLE featuring Missy "Misdemeanor" ELLIOTT and MOCHA.				
I CAN'T SEE	*East West America*	55	*5 Dec 98*	1
Above hit: Nicole RAY (featuring MOCHA).				

NICOLETTE — UK

SINGLES:	HITS 1			WEEKS 1
NO GOVERNMENT	*Talkin Loud*	67	*23 Dec 95*	1
ALBUMS:	**HITS 1**			**WEEKS 2**
LET NO ONE LIVE RENT FREE IN YOUR HEAD	*Talkin Loud*	36	*10 Aug 96*	2

NIGHTCRAWLERS featuring John REID — UK

SINGLES:	HITS 7			WEEKS 36
PUSH THE FEELING ON	*ffrr*	22	*15 Oct 94*	5
Originally released in 1992.				
PUSH THE FEELING ON [RM]	*ffrr*	3	*4 Mar 95*	11
Remixed by MK (Marc Kinchen).				
Above 2: NIGHTCRAWLERS.				
SURRENDER YOUR LOVE	*Final Vinyl*	7	*27 May 95*	7
DON'T LET THE FEELING GO	*Final Vinyl*	13	*9 Sep 95*	4
LET'S PUSH IT	*Final Vinyl*	23	*20 Jan 96*	4
SHOULD I EVER (FALL IN LOVE)	*Arista*	34	*20 Apr 96*	2
KEEP ON PUSHING OUR LOVE	*Arista*	30	*27 Jul 96*	2
Above hit: NIGHTCRAWLERS featuring John REID and Alysha WARREN.				
NEVER KNEW LOVE	*Riverhorse*	59	*3 Jul 99*	1
Above hit: NIGHTCRAWLERS.				
ALBUMS:	**HITS 1**			**WEEKS 5**
LET'S PUSH IT	*Final Vinyl*	14	*30 Sep 95*	5

Maxine NIGHTINGALE — UK

SINGLES:	HITS 2			WEEKS 16
RIGHT BACK WHERE WE STARTED FROM	*United Artists*	8	*1 Nov 75*	8
LOVE HIT ME	*United Artists*	11	*12 Mar 77*	8
Above 2 originally recorded by J. Vincent Edwards.				

NIGHTMARES ON WAX — UK

SINGLES:	HITS 2			WEEKS 6
AFTERMATH / I'M FOR REAL	*Warp*	38	*27 Oct 90*	5
I'm For Real only listed until 17 Nov 90.				
FINER	*Warp*	63	*26 Jun 99*	1
Vocals by Sara Winton.				
ALBUMS:	**HITS 1**			**WEEKS 2**
CAR BOOT SOUL	*Warp*	71	*24 Apr 99*	2

NIGHTWRITERS — US

SINGLES:	HITS 1			WEEKS 2
LET THE MUSIC USE YOU	*Ffrreedom*	51	*23 May 92*	2

NIKKE? NICOLE! — US

SINGLES:	HITS 1			WEEKS 1
NIKKE DOES IT BETTER	*Love*	73	*1 Jun 91*	1
Features scratching by DJ Rhythm.				

NIKKO – See Harold MELVIN and the BLUENOTES

Markus NIKOLAI — Germany

SINGLES:	HITS 1			WEEKS 1
BUSHES	*Southern Fried*	74	*6 Oct 01*	1

NILSSON — US

SINGLES:	HITS 4			WEEKS 55
EVERYBODY'S TALKIN'	*RCA Victor*	50	*27 Sep 69*	1
Originally recorded by Fred Neil.				
EVERYBODY'S TALKIN' [RE-1ST]	*RCA Victor*	23	*11 Oct 69*	9
EVERYBODY'S TALKIN' [RE-2ND]	*RCA Victor*	39	*14 Mar 70*	5
WITHOUT YOU	*RCA Victor*	1	*5 Feb 72*	20
Originally recorded by Bad Finger.				
COCONUT	*RCA Victor*	42	*3 Jun 72*	5
WITHOUT YOU [RI-1ST]	*RCA Victor Maximillion*	22	*16 Oct 76*	8
ALL I THINK ABOUT IS YOU	*RCA Victor*	43	*20 Aug 77*	3
Above hit: Harry NILSSON.				
WITHOUT YOU [RI-2ND]	*RCA*	47	*19 Feb 94*	4

ALBUMS:	HITS 4			WEEKS 43
THE POINT [OST-TV]	*RCA Victor*	46	*29 Jan 72*	1
Originally released 1971. From an animated children's TV programme.				
NILSSON SCHMILSSON	*RCA Victor*	4	*5 Feb 72*	22
SON OF SCHMILSSON	*RCA Victor*	41	*19 Aug 72*	1
A LITTLE TOUCH OF SCHMILSSON IN THE NIGHT	*RCA Victor*	20	*28 Jul 73*	19

Charlotte NILSSON — Sweden

SINGLES:	HITS 1			WEEKS 4
TAKE ME TO YOUR HEAVEN	*Arista*	20	*3 Jul 99*	4
Eurovision Song Contest winner in 1999.				

NINA and FREDERIK — Denmark

SINGLES:	HITS 5			WEEKS 29
MARY'S BOY CHILD	*Columbia*	26	*19 Dec 59*	1
LISTEN TO THE OCEAN	*Columbia*	47	*12 Mar 60*	1
Above hit: NINA and FREDERIK; Jorn GRAUENGAARD and his Orchestra.				
LISTEN TO THE OCEAN [RE]	*Columbia*	46	*9 Apr 60*	1
LITTLE DONKEY	*Columbia*	3	*19 Nov 60*	10
Above hit: NINA and FREDERIK with the Jorn GRAUENGAARD QUINTET.				
LONGTIME BOY	*Columbia*	43	*30 Sep 61*	3
SUCU - SUCU	*Columbia*	23	*7 Oct 61*	13

EPS:	HITS 7			WEEKS 169
NINA AND FREDERIK	*Columbia*	2	*12 Mar 60*	113
NINA AND FREDERIK VOLUME 1	*Pye Nixa*	13	*2 Apr 60*	2
NINA AND FREDERIK VOLUME 2	*Pye Nixa*	8	*23 Apr 60*	7
NINA AND FREDERIK	*Columbia*	3	*11 Jun 60*	26
Both these self titled EPs are different.				
NINA AND FREDERIK VOLUME 3	*Columbia*	8	*26 Nov 60*	7
CHRISTMAS AT HOME WITH NINA AND FREDERIK	*Columbia*	2	*18 Nov 61*	9
WHITE CHRISTMAS	*Columbia*	11	*15 Dec 62*	3
Above hit: NINA and FREDERIK with John BARRY and his Orchestra.				

ALBUMS:	HITS 2			WEEKS 6
NINA AND FREDERIK	*Pye*	9	*13 Feb 60*	2
NINA AND FREDERIK	*Columbia*	11	*29 Apr 61*	4
Both self titled albums are different.				

9 BELOW ZERO — UK

ALBUMS:	HITS 2			WEEKS 12
DON'T POINT YOUR FINGER	*A&M*	56	*14 Mar 81*	6
THIRD DEGREE	*A&M*	38	*20 Mar 82*	6

NINE INCH NAILS — US

SINGLES:	HITS 6			WEEKS 15
HEAD LIKE A HOLE	*Island*	45	*14 Sep 91*	4
SIN	*Island*	35	*16 Nov 91*	2
MARCH OF THE PIGS	*Island*	45	*9 Apr 94*	3
CLOSER	*Island*	25	*18 Jun 94*	3
THE PERFECT DRUG	*Interscope*	43	*13 Sep 97*	1
From the film 'The Lost Highway'.				
WE'RE IN THIS TOGETHER	*Nothing*	39	*18 Dec 99*	2

ALBUMS:	HITS 4			WEEKS 12
PRETTY HATE MACHINE	*TVT*	67	*12 Oct 91*	1
BROKEN	*Interscope*	18	*17 Oct 92*	3
THE DOWNWARD SPIRAL	*Island*	9	*19 Mar 94*	4
THE FRAGILE	*Island*	10	*9 Oct 99*	4

999 — UK

SINGLES:	HITS 5			WEEKS 13
HOMICIDE	*United Artists*	40	*25 Nov 78*	3
FOUND OUT TOO LATE	*Radar*	69	*27 Oct 79*	2
OBSESSED	*Albion*	71	*16 May 81*	1
LIL RED RIDING HOOD	*Albion*	59	*18 Jul 81*	3
INDIAN RESERVATION	*Albion*	51	*14 Nov 81*	4
ALBUMS:	**HITS 1**			**WEEKS 1**
999	*United Artists*	53	*25 Mar 78*	1

911 — UK

SINGLES:	HITS 13			WEEKS 94
NIGHT TO REMEMBER	*Ginga*	38	*11 May 96*	2
LOVE SENSATION	*Ginga*	21	*10 Aug 96*	4
DON'T MAKE ME WAIT	*Virgin*	10	*9 Nov 96*	6
DON'T MAKE ME WAIT [RE]	*Virgin*	63	*4 Jan 97*	2
THE DAY WE FIND LOVE	*Virgin*	4	*22 Feb 97*	8
BODYSHAKIN'	*Virgin*	3	*3 May 97*	7
THE JOURNEY	*Virgin*	3	*12 Jul 97*	7
PARTY PEOPLE . . . FRIDAY NIGHT	*Virgin*	5	*1 Nov 97*	7
PARTY PEOPLE . . . FRIDAY NIGHT [RE]	*Virgin*	60	*3 Jan 98*	3
ALL I WANT IS YOU	*Virgin*	4	*4 Apr 98*	6
ALL I WANT IS YOU [RE]	*Virgin*	64	*20 Jun 98*	1
HOW DO YOU WANT ME TO LOVE YOU?	*Virgin*	10	*4 Jul 98*	7
HOW DO YOU WANT ME TO LOVE YOU? [RE]	*Virgin*	57	*29 Aug 98*	2
MORE THAN A WOMAN	*Virgin*	2	*24 Oct 98*	9
MORE THAN A WOMAN [RE]	*Virgin*	64	*2 Jan 99*	4
A LITTLE BIT MORE	*Virgin*	1	*23 Jan 99*	9
PRIVATE NUMBER	*Virgin*	3	*15 May 99*	7
WONDERLAND	*Virgin*	13	*23 Oct 99*	3
ALBUMS:	**HITS 4**			**WEEKS 26**
THE JOURNEY	*Virgin*	13	*8 Mar 97*	17
MOVING ON	*Virgin*	10	*18 Jul 98*	4
THERE IT IS	*Virgin*	8	*6 Feb 99*	4
THE GREATEST HITS AND A LITTLE MORE . . .	*Virgin*	40	*6 Nov 99*	1

9.9 — US

SINGLES:	HITS 1			WEEKS 3
ALL OF ME FOR ALL OF YOU	*RCA*	53	*6 Jul 85*	3

NINE YARDS — UK

SINGLES:	HITS 3			WEEKS 3
LONELINESS IS GONE	*Virgin*	70	*21 Nov 98*	1
MATTER OF TIME	*Virgin*	59	*10 Apr 99*	1
ALWAYS FIND A WAY	*Virgin*	50	*28 Aug 99*	1

1910 FRUITGUM CO. — US

SINGLES:	HITS 1			WEEKS 16
SIMON SAYS	*Pye International*	2	*23 Mar 68*	16

1927 — Australia

SINGLES:	HITS 1			WEEKS 6
THAT'S WHEN I THINK OF YOU	*WEA*	46	*22 Apr 89*	6

1999 MANCHESTER UNITED SQUAD - See MANCHESTER UNITED FOOTBALL SQUAD

98° — US

(See also Mariah Carey.)

SINGLES:	HITS 5			WEEKS 7
INVISIBLE MAN	*Motown*	66	*29 Nov 97*	1
TRUE TO YOUR HEART	*Motown*	51	*31 Oct 98*	1
From the Walt Disney film 'Mulan'. Above hit: 98° (featuring Stevie WONDER).				
BECAUSE OF YOU	*Motown*	36	*13 Mar 99*	2
THE HARDEST THING	*Universal*	29	*11 Mar 00*	2
GIVE ME JUST ONE NIGHT (UNA NOCHE)	*Universal*	61	*2 Dec 00*	1

99TH FLOOR ELEVATORS featuring Tony DE VIT — UK

(See also Tony De Vit.)

SINGLES:	HITS 2			WEEKS 5
HOOKED	*Labello Dance*	28	*12 Aug 95*	2
I'LL BE THERE	*Labello Dance*	37	*30 Mar 96*	2
Vocals by Lorraine.				

HOOKED [RM]	*Tripoli Trax*	66	*8 Apr 00*	1
Remixed by Phlash!				
Above hit: 99TH FLOOR ELEVATORS.				

Los NINOS — UK

ALBUMS:	HITS 1			WEEKS 1
FRAGILE - MYSTICAL SOUNDS OF THE PANPIPES	*Pearls*	74	*22 Jul 95*	1

NIRVANA — US

SINGLES:	HITS 1			WEEKS 6
RAINBOW CHASER	*Island*	34	*18 May 68*	6

NIRVANA — US

SINGLES:	HITS 7			WEEKS 36
SMELLS LIKE TEEN SPIRIT	*DGC*	7	*30 Nov 91*	6
COME AS YOU ARE	*DGC*	9	*14 Mar 92*	5
LITHIUM	*DGC*	11	*25 Jul 92*	6
IN BLOOM	*Geffen*	28	*12 Dec 92*	7
OH, THE GUILT	*Touch And Go*	12	*6 Mar 93*	2
[AA] listed with Puss by Jesus Lizard.				
HEART-SHAPED BOX	*Geffen*	5	*11 Sep 93*	5
ALL APOLOGIES / RAPE ME	*Geffen*	32	*18 Dec 93*	5

ALBUMS:	HITS 6			WEEKS 289
NEVERMIND	*DGC*	7	*5 Oct 91*	184
Includes re-entries through to 1999. Label change to Geffen from 12 Feb 94.				
BLEACH	*Tupelo*	33	*7 Mar 92*	7
Originally released in the US on the Sub Pop label in 1989.				
INCESTICIDE	*Geffen*	14	*26 Dec 92*	11
B-sides, demos and Radio 1 sessions.				
IN UTERO	*Geffen*	1	*25 Sep 93*	41
UNPLUGGED IN NEW YORK	*Geffen*	1	*12 Nov 94*	40
Live recordings broadcast on MTV, 18 Nov 93.				
FROM THE MUDDY BANKS OF THE WISHKAH	*Geffen*	4	*12 Oct 96*	6
Live recordings between 1989-94.				

NITRO DELUXE — US

SINGLES:	HITS 1			WEEKS 16
THIS BRUTAL HOUSE	*Cooltempo*	47	*14 Feb 87*	7
THIS BRUTAL HOUSE [RE]	*Cooltempo*	62	*13 Jun 87*	4
LET'S GET BRUTAL (ROK DA RADIO) [RM]	*Cooltempo*	24	*6 Feb 88*	5
Re-mix of This Brutal House. Not all copies had (Rok Da Radio) listed.				

NITZER EBB — UK

SINGLES:	HITS 3			WEEKS 3
GODHEAD	*Mute*	56	*11 Jan 92*	1
ASCEND	*Mute*	52	*11 Apr 92*	1
KICK IT	*Mute*	75	*4 Mar 95*	1

NIVEA – See MYSTIKAL

NKOTB – See NEW KIDS ON THE BLOCK

NO AUTHORITY — US

SINGLES:	HITS 1			WEEKS 1
DON'T STOP	*Epic*	54	*14 Mar 98*	1
Contains sample of Teddy Riley's Don't Stop.				

NO DICE — UK

SINGLES:	HITS 1			WEEKS 2
COME DANCING	*EMI*	65	*5 May 79*	2

NO DOUBT — US/UK

SINGLES:	HITS 7			WEEKS 39
JUST A GIRL	*Interscope*	38	*26 Oct 96*	2
DON'T SPEAK	*Interscope*	1	*22 Feb 97*	18
Produced by Matthew Wilder.				
JUST A GIRL [RI]	*Interscope*	3	*5 Jul 97*	7
SPIDERWEBS	*Interscope*	16	*4 Oct 97*	3
SUNDAY MORNING	*Interscope*	50	*20 Dec 97*	3
NEW	*Higher Ground*	30	*12 Jun 99*	2
From the film 'Go'.				
EX-GIRLFRIEND	*Interscope*	23	*25 Mar 00*	3
SIMPLE KIND OF LOVE	*Interscope*	69	*7 Oct 00*	1

ALBUMS:	HITS 2			WEEKS 46
TRAGIC KINGDOM	*Interscope*	3	*18 Jan 97*	44
RETURN OF SATURN	*Interscope*	31	*22 Apr 00*	2

NO MERCY — US/Cuba

SINGLES:	HITS 3			WEEKS 26
WHERE DO YOU GO *Originally recorded by La Bouche in 1995.*	*Arista*	2	*18 Jan 97*	15
PLEASE DON'T GO	*Arista*	4	*24 May 97*	7
KISS YOU ALL OVER	*Arista*	16	*6 Sep 97*	4
ALBUMS:	**HITS 1**			**WEEKS 4**
MY PROMISE	*Arista*	17	*7 Jun 97*	4

NO SWEAT — Ireland

SINGLES:	HITS 2			WEEKS 5
HEART AND SOUL	*London*	64	*13 Oct 90*	4
TEAR DOWN THE WALLS *Original release reached No. 84 in 1990.*	*London*	61	*2 Feb 91*	1

NO WAY JOSE — US

SINGLES:	HITS 1			WEEKS 6
TEQUILA	*Fourth & Broadway*	47	*3 Aug 85*	6

NO WAY SIS — UK

SINGLES:	HITS 1			WEEKS 4
I'D LIKE TO TEACH THE WORLD TO SING	*EMI*	27	*21 Dec 96*	4

NOFX — US

ALBUMS:	HITS 2			WEEKS 2
HEAVY PETTING ZOO	*Epitaph*	60	*10 Feb 96*	1
PUMP UP THE VALUUM	*Epitaph*	50	*10 Jun 00*	1

NOISE FACTORY - See VARIOUS ARTISTS (EPs) 'Fourplay Volume 1 EP'

NOLANS — Ireland

SINGLES:	HITS 9			WEEKS 90
SPIRIT, BODY AND SOUL *Above hit: NOLAN SISTERS.*	*Epic*	34	*6 Oct 79*	6
I'M IN THE MOOD FOR DANCING	*Epic*	3	*22 Dec 79*	15
DON'T MAKE WAVES	*Epic*	12	*12 Apr 80*	11
GOTTA PULL MYSELF TOGETHER	*Epic*	9	*13 Sep 80*	13
WHO'S GONNA ROCK YOU *Originally recorded by Billy Ocean.*	*Epic*	12	*6 Dec 80*	11
ATTENTION TO ME	*Epic*	9	*14 Mar 81*	13
CHEMISTRY	*Epic*	15	*15 Aug 81*	8
DON'T LOVE ME TOO HARD	*Epic*	14	*20 Feb 82*	12
I'M IN THE MOOD FOR DANCING [RR]	*Living Beat*	51	*1 Apr 95*	1
ALBUMS:	**HITS 6**			**WEEKS 84**
20 GIANT HITS *Above hit: NOLAN SISTERS.*	*Target*	3	*29 Jul 78*	12
NOLANS	*Epic*	15	*19 Jan 80*	13
MAKING WAVES	*Epic*	11	*25 Oct 80*	33
PORTRAIT	*Epic*	7	*27 Mar 82*	10
ALTOGETHER	*Epic*	52	*20 Nov 82*	8
GIRLS JUST WANNA HAVE FUN	*Towerbell*	39	*17 Nov 84*	8

NOMAD — UK

SINGLES:	HITS 5			WEEKS 22
(I WANNA GIVE YOU) DEVOTION *Above hit: NOMAD featuring MC Mikee FREEDOM.*	*Rumour*	2	*2 Feb 91*	10
JUST A GROOVE	*Rumour*	16	*4 May 91*	6
SOMETHING SPECIAL	*Rumour*	73	*28 Sep 91*	1
YOUR LOVE IS LIFTING ME	*Rumour*	60	*25 Apr 92*	2
24 HOURS A DAY	*Rumour*	61	*7 Nov 92*	1
(I WANNA GIVE YOU) DEVOTION [RM]	*Rumour*	42	*25 Nov 95*	2
ALBUMS:	**HITS 1**			**WEEKS 2**
CHANGING CABINS	*Rumour*	48	*22 Jun 91*	2

NONCHALANT — US

SINGLES:	HITS 1			WEEKS 1
5 O'CLOCK	*MCA*	44	*29 Jun 96*	1

Peter NOONE — UK

(See also Herman's Hermits.)

SINGLES:	HITS 1			WEEKS 9
OH YOU PRETTY THING *Originally recorded by David Bowie.*	*RAK*	12	*22 May 71*	9

NOOTROPIC — UK

SINGLES:	HITS 1			WEEKS 1
I SEE ONLY YOU	*Hi-Life*	42	*16 Mar 96*	1

Narration by Ken NORDENE - See Billy VAUGHN and his Orchestra

NOREAGA — US

ALBUMS:	HITS 1			WEEKS 1
N.O.R.E.	*Penalty Recordings*	72	*25 Jul 98*	1

Chris NORMAN - See Suzi QUATRO

NORTH GERMAN RADIO SYMPHONY ORCHESTRA - See Nigel KENNEDY

NORTH AND SOUTH — UK

SINGLES:	HITS 4			WEEKS 16
I'M A MAN NOT A BOY	*RCA*	7	*17 May 97*	5
TARANTINO'S NEW STAR	*RCA*	18	*9 Aug 97*	5
BREATHING	*RCA*	27	*8 Nov 97*	2
NO SWEAT '98	*RCA*	29	*4 Apr 98*	4

NORTHERN LINE — UK/South Africa

SINGLES:	HITS 3			WEEKS 12
RUN FOR YOUR LIFE	*Global Talent*	18	*9 Oct 99*	4
LOVE ON THE NORTHERN LINE	*Global Talent*	15	*11 Mar 00*	5
ALL AROUND THE WORLD	*Global Talent*	27	*17 Jun 00*	3

NORTHERN UPROAR — UK

SINGLES:	HITS 6			WEEKS 11
ROLLERCOASTER / ROUGH BOYS	*Heavenly*	41	*21 Oct 95*	2
FROM A WINDOW / THIS MORNING	*Heavenly*	17	*3 Feb 96*	3
LIVIN' IT UP *Backing vocals by James Dean Bradfield of the Manic Street Preachers.*	*Heavenly*	24	*20 Apr 96*	2
TOWN	*Heavenly*	48	*22 Jun 96*	1
ANY WAY YOU LOOK	*Heavenly*	36	*7 Jun 97*	2
A GIRL I ONCE KNEW	*Heavenly*	63	*23 Aug 97*	1
ALBUMS:	**HITS 1**			**WEEKS 2**
NORTHERN UPROAR	*Heavenly*	22	*11 May 96*	2

NORTHSIDE — UK

SINGLES:	HITS 3			WEEKS 12
SHALL WE TAKE A TRIP / MOODY PLACES	*Factory*	50	*9 Jun 90*	5
MY RISING STAR	*Factory*	32	*3 Nov 90*	3
TAKE 5	*Factory*	40	*1 Jun 91*	4
ALBUMS:	**HITS 1**			**WEEKS 3**
CHICKEN RHYTHMS	*Factory*	19	*29 Jun 91*	3

NOT THE NINE O'CLOCK NEWS CAST — UK/New Zealand

ALBUMS:	HITS 3			WEEKS 51
NOT THE NINE O'CLOCK NEWS	*BBC*	5	*8 Nov 80*	23
NOT THE NINE O'CLOCK NEWS - HEDGEHOG SANDWICH	*BBC*	5	*17 Oct 81*	24
THE MEMORY KINDA LINGERS	*BBC*	63	*23 Oct 82*	4

Freddie NOTES and the RUDIES — Jamaica

SINGLES:	HITS 1			WEEKS 2
MONTEGO BAY	*Trojan*	45	*10 Oct 70*	2

NOTORIOUS B.I.G. — US

(See also Puff Daddy.)

SINGLES:	HITS 9			WEEKS 30
JUICY	*Bad Boy*	72	*29 Oct 94*	1
BIG POPPA *Samples Between The Sheets by the Isley Brothers.*	*Puff Daddy*	63	*1 Apr 95*	1
CAN'T YOU SEE *From the film 'New Jersey Drive'.* *Above hit: TOTAL featuring the NOTORIOUS B.I.G.*	*Tommy Boy*	43	*15 Jul 95*	2
ONE MORE CHANCE/STAY WITH ME [M]	*Puff Daddy*	34	*19 Aug 95*	2

HYPNOTIZE	*Puff Daddy*	10	*3 May 97*	4
MO MONEY MO PROBLEMS *Samples Diana Ross's I'm Coming Out.* *Above hit: NOTORIOUS B.I.G. featuring PUFF DADDY and MASE.*	*Puff Daddy*	6	*9 Aug 97*	10
SKY'S THE LIMIT *Above hit: NOTORIOUS B.I.G. featuring 112.*	*Puff Daddy*	35	*14 Feb 98*	2
RUNNIN' *Above hit: 2PAC and NOTORIOUS B.I.G.*	*Black Jam*	15	*18 Jul 98*	3
NOTORIOUS B.I.G. *Samples Duran Duran's Notorious.* *Above hit: NOTORIOUS B.I.G. featuring PUFF DADDY and LIL' KIM.*	*Puff Daddy*	16	*5 Feb 00*	5
ALBUMS:	**HITS 2**			**WEEKS 17**
LIFE AFTER DEATH	*Puff Daddy*	23	*5 Apr 97*	16
BORN AGAIN *Compilation.*	*Puff Daddy*	70	*18 Dec 99*	1

NOTTING HILLBILLIES — UK

ALBUMS:	**HITS 1**			**WEEKS 14**
MISSING . . . PRESUMED HAVING A GOOD TIME	*Vertigo*	2	*17 Mar 90*	14

NOTTINGHAM FOREST with PAPER LACE — UK

(See also Paper Lace.)

SINGLES:	**HITS 1**			**WEEKS 6**
WE GOT THE WHOLE WORLD IN OUR HANDS	*Warner Brothers*	24	*4 Mar 78*	6

Heather NOVA — US

SINGLES:	**HITS 1**			**WEEKS 1**
WALK THIS WORLD	*Butterfly*	69	*25 Feb 95*	1
ALBUMS:	**HITS 2**			**WEEKS 2**
OYSTER	*Butterfly*	72	*8 Apr 95*	1
SIREN	*V2*	55	*20 Jun 98*	1

Nancy NOVA — UK

SINGLES:	**HITS 1**			**WEEKS 2**
NO, NO, NO	*EMI*	63	*4 Sep 82*	2

Tom NOVY — Germany

SINGLES:	**HITS 4**			**WEEKS 8**
SUPERSTAR *Above hit: NOVY vs. ENIAC.*	*D:disco*	32	*2 May 98*	3
PUMPIN *Mixed by Eniac.* *Above hit: NOVY vs ENIAC.*	*Positiva*	19	*3 Jun 00*	3
I ROCK *Above hit: Tom NOVY featuring VIRGINIA.*	*Rulin*	55	*2 Sep 00*	1
NOW OR NEVER *Above hit: Tom NOVY featuring LIMA.*	*Rulin*	64	*4 Aug 01*	1

NRG — UK

SINGLES:	**HITS 1**			**WEEKS 2**
NEVER LOST HIS HARDCORE	*Top Banana*	71	*29 Mar 97*	1
NEVER LOST HIS HARDCORE '98 [RM] *Remixed by Floorplay.*	*Banana Recordings*	61	*12 Dec 98*	1

*NSYNC — US

SINGLES:	**HITS 9**			**WEEKS 66**
TEARIN' UP MY HEART	*Arista*	40	*13 Sep 97*	2
I WANT YOU BACK *Above 2: 'N SYNC.*	*Arista*	62	*22 Nov 97*	1
I WANT YOU BACK [RI]	*Northwestside*	5	*27 Feb 99*	8
I WANT YOU BACK [RI] [RE]	*Northwestside*	62	*8 May 99*	2
TEARIN* UP MY HEART [RI]	*Northwestside*	9	*26 Jun 99*	8
TEARIN* UP MY HEART [RI] [RE]	*Northwestside*	73	*11 Sep 99*	2
MUSIC OF MY HEART *Above hit: 'NSYNC Gloria ESTEFAN.*	*Epic*	34	*8 Jan 00*	3
BYE BYE BYE	*Jive*	3	*11 Mar 00*	8
I'LL NEVER STOP	*Jive*	13	*22 Jul 00*	6
IT'S GONNA BE ME	*Jive*	9	*16 Sep 00*	8
THIS I PROMISE YOU	*Jive*	21	*2 Dec 00*	7
POP	*Jive*	9	*21 Jul 01*	8
GONE	*Jive*	24	*8 Dec 01*	3
ALBUMS:	**HITS 3**			**WEEKS 28**
*NSYNC	*Northwestside*	30	*17 Jul 99*	2

NO STRINGS ATTACHED	*Jive*	14	*1 Apr 00*	22
CELEBRITY	*Jive*	12	*4 Aug 01*	4

NU-BIRTH — UK

SINGLES:	HITS 1			WEEKS 2
ANYTIME	*XL Recordings*	48	*6 Sep 97*	1
Single started out as a remix of Richard Darbyshire's Wherever Love Is Found.				
ANYTIME [RI]	*Locked On*	41	*6 Jun 98*	1

NU COLOURS — UK

SINGLES:	HITS 5			WEEKS 11
TEARS	*Wild Card*	55	*6 Jun 92*	2
POWER	*Wild Card*	64	*10 Oct 92*	1
WHAT IN THE WORLD	*Wild Card*	57	*5 Jun 93*	2
POWER (THE E SMOOVE REMIXES) [RM]	*Wild Card*	40	*27 Nov 93*	2
Remixed by Eric "E-Smooth" Miller.				
DESIRE	*Wild Card*	31	*25 May 96*	2
SPECIAL KIND OF LOVER	*Wild Card*	38	*24 Aug 96*	2

NU GENERATION — UK

SINGLES:	HITS 2			WEEKS 9
IN YOUR ARMS (RESCUE ME)	*Concept*	8	*29 Jan 00*	8
Samples Fontella Bass' Rescue Me.				
GOT "NOWHERE TO RUN 2000"	*Concept*	66	*21 Oct 00*	1
Samples Martha Reeves' Nowhere To Run.				

NU-MATIC — UK

SINGLES:	HITS 1			WEEKS 1
SPRING IN MY STEP	*XL Recordings*	58	*8 Aug 92*	1

NU SHOOZ — US

SINGLES:	HITS 2			WEEKS 17
I CAN'T WAIT	*Atlantic*	2	*24 May 86*	14
POINT OF NO RETURN	*Atlantic*	48	*26 Jul 86*	3
ALBUMS:	**HITS 1**			**WEEKS 8**
POOLSIDE	*Atlantic*	32	*14 Jun 86*	8

NU SOUL featuring Kelli RICH — US

SINGLES:	HITS 1			WEEKS 2
HIDE-A-WAY	*ffrr*	27	*13 Jan 96*	2

NUANCE featuring Vikki LOVE — US

SINGLES:	HITS 1			WEEKS 3
LOVERIDE	*Fourth & Broadway*	59	*19 Jan 85*	3

NUBIAN PRINZ – See POWERCUT featuring NUBIAN PRINZ

NUCLEAR ASSAULT — US

ALBUMS:	HITS 1			WEEKS 1
HANDLE WITH CARE	*Under One Flag*	60	*7 Oct 89*	1

NUCLEUS — UK

ALBUMS:	HITS 1			WEEKS 1
ELASTIC ROCK	*Vertigo*	46	*11 Jul 70*	1

NUFF JUICE – See D-MOB

Ted NUGENT — US

ALBUMS:	HITS 6			WEEKS 14
TED NUGENT	*Epic*	56	*4 Sep 76*	1
FREE FOR ALL	*Epic*	33	*30 Oct 76*	2
CAT SCRATCH FEVER	*Epic*	28	*2 Jul 77*	5
DOUBLE LIVE GONZO!	*Epic*	47	*11 Mar 78*	2
SCREAM DREAM	*Epic*	37	*14 Jun 80*	3
IN 10 CITIES	*Epic*	75	*25 Apr 81*	1

Gary NUMAN — UK

(See also Sharpe and Numan.)

SINGLES:	HITS 29			WEEKS 148
ARE 'FRIENDS' ELECTRIC?	*Beggars Banquet*	1	*19 May 79*	16
Above hit: TUBEWAY ARMY.				

CARS	*Beggars Banquet*	1	*1 Sep 79*	11
COMPLEX	*Beggars Banquet*	6	*24 Nov 79*	9
WE ARE GLASS	*Beggars Banquet*	5	*24 May 80*	7
I DIE: YOU DIE	*Beggars Banquet*	6	*30 Aug 80*	7
THIS WRECKAGE	*Beggars Banquet*	20	*20 Dec 80*	7
SHE'S GOT CLAWS	*Beggars Banquet*	6	*29 Aug 81*	6
Features Roger Taylor from Queen on drums.				
LOVE NEEDS NO DISGUISE	*Beggars Banquet*	33	*5 Dec 81*	7
Above hit: Gary NUMAN and DRAMATIS.				
MUSIC FOR CHAMELEONS	*Beggars Banquet*	19	*6 Mar 82*	7
WE TAKE MYSTERY (TO BED)	*Beggars Banquet*	9	*19 Jun 82*	4
WHITE BOYS AND HEROES	*Beggars Banquet*	20	*28 Aug 82*	4
WARRIORS	*Beggars Banquet*	20	*3 Sep 83*	5
SISTER SURPRISE	*Beggars Banquet*	32	*22 Oct 83*	3
BERSERKER	*Numa*	32	*3 Nov 84*	5
MY DYING MACHINE	*Numa*	66	*22 Dec 84*	1
GARY NUMAN - THE LIVE [EP]	*Numa*	27	*25 May 85*	4
Lead track: Are "Friends" Electric?. Live recordings from Hammersmith Odeon, London, Dec 84.				
YOUR FASCINATION	*Numa*	46	*10 Aug 85*	5
CALL OUT THE DOGS	*Numa*	49	*21 Sep 85*	2
MIRACLES	*Numa*	49	*16 Nov 85*	3
THIS IS LOVE	*Numa*	28	*19 Apr 86*	3
I CAN'T STOP	*Numa*	27	*28 Jun 86*	4
I STILL REMEMBER	*Numa*	74	*6 Dec 86*	1
Charity record with proceeds to the R.S.P.C.A.				
RADIO HEART	*GFM*	35	*28 Mar 87*	6
LONDON TIMES	*GFM*	48	*13 Jun 87*	2
Above 2: RADIO HEART featuring Gary NUMAN.				
CARS ('E' REG MODEL) [RM-1ST] / ARE 'FRIENDS' ELECTRIC [RM]	*Beggars Banquet*	16	*19 Sep 87*	7
NEW ANGER	*Illegal*	46	*1 Oct 88*	2
AMERICA	*Illegal*	49	*3 Dec 88*	1
HEART	*I.R.S.*	43	*16 Mar 91*	2
THE SKIN GAME	*Numa*	68	*21 Mar 92*	1
MACHINE + SOUL	*Numa*	72	*1 Aug 92*	1
CARS [RM-2ND]	*Beggars Banquet*	53	*4 Sep 93*	1
Remixed by Charles Pierre and Francis Usmar of Native Soul.				
CARS (PREMIER MIX) [RM-1ST] [RI]	*PolyGram TV*	17	*16 Mar 96*	4
Featured in the Carling Premier Lager TV commercial.				

ALBUMS:	**HITS 25**			**WEEKS 143**
REPLICAS	*Beggars Banquet*	1	*9 Jun 79*	31
TUBEWAY ARMY	*Beggars Banquet*	14	*25 Aug 79*	10
Originally released in 1978.				
Above 2: TUBEWAY ARMY.				
THE PLEASURE PRINCIPLE	*Beggars Banquet*	1	*22 Sep 79*	21
TELEKON	*Beggars Banquet*	1	*13 Sep 80*	11
LIVING ORNAMENTS 1979-1980	*Beggars Banquet*	2	*2 May 81*	4
Double boxed set of the 2 separate Living Ornaments albums.				
LIVING ORNAMENTS 1980	*Beggars Banquet*	39	*2 May 81*	3
LIVING ORNAMENTS 1979	*Beggars Banquet*	47	*2 May 81*	3
DANCE	*Beggars Banquet*	3	*12 Sep 81*	8
I, ASSASSIN	*Beggars Banquet*	8	*18 Sep 82*	6
NEW MAN NUMAN - THE BEST OF GARY NUMAN	*TV Records*	45	*27 Nov 82*	7
WARRIORS	*Beggars Banquet*	12	*24 Sep 83*	6
THE PLAN 1978	*Beggars Banquet*	29	*6 Oct 84*	4
Above hit: TUBEWAY ARMY and Gary NUMAN.				
BERSERKER	*Numa*	45	*24 Nov 84*	3
WHITE NOISE - LIVE	*Numa*	29	*13 Apr 85*	5
Live recordings from 1984.				
THE FURY	*Numa*	24	*28 Sep 85*	5
STRANGE CHARM	*Numa*	59	*8 Nov 86*	2
EXHIBITION	*Beggars Banquet*	43	*3 Oct 87*	3
Compilation.				
METAL RHYTHM	*Illegal*	48	*8 Oct 88*	2
SKIN MECHANIC	*I.R.S.*	55	*28 Oct 89*	1
OUTLAND	*I.R.S.*	39	*30 Mar 91*	1
MACHINE + SOUL	*Numa*	42	*22 Aug 92*	1
BEST OF GARY NUMAN 1978-83	*Beggars Banquet*	70	*2 Oct 93*	1
THE PREMIER HITS	*PolyGram TV*	21	*30 Mar 96*	3
Above hit: Gary NUMAN/TUBEWAY ARMY.				
EXILE	*Eagle*	48	*1 Nov 97*	1
PURE	*Eagle*	58	*21 Oct 00*	1

NUMBER ONE CUP

US

SINGLES:	**HITS 1**			**WEEKS 1**
DIVEBOMB	*Blue Rose*	61	*2 Mar 96*	1
From the film 'Learning Curves'.				

Jose NUNEZ featuring OCTAHVIA — US

SINGLES:	HITS 2			WEEKS 2
IN MY LIFE	*Ministry Of Sound*	56	*5 Sep 98*	1
HOLD ON	*Sound Of Ministry*	44	*5 Jun 99*	1

Bobby NUNN — US

SINGLES:	HITS 1			WEEKS 3
DON'T KNOCK IT (UNTIL YOU TRY IT)	*Motown*	65	*4 Feb 84*	3

NUSH — UK

(See also Congress.)

SINGLES:	HITS 2			WEEKS 7
U GIRLS	*Blunted Vinyl*	58	*23 Jul 94*	1
MOVE THAT BODY	*Blunted Vinyl*	46	*22 Apr 95*	2
U GIRLS (LOOK SO SEXY) [RM]	*Blunted Vinyl*	15	*16 Sep 95*	4
This is the original Nush mix that was released before the 1994 entry above.				

NUT — UK

SINGLES:	HITS 3			WEEKS 4
BRAINS	*Epic*	64	*8 Jun 96*	1
CRAZY	*Epic*	56	*21 Sep 96*	1
SCREAM	*Epic*	43	*11 Jan 97*	2
Originally released in 1996.				

NUTTIN' NYCE — US

SINGLES:	HITS 2			WEEKS 2
DOWN 4 WHATEVA	*Jive*	62	*10 Jun 95*	1
From the film 'A Low Down Dirty Shame'. Samples Back To Life by Soul II Soul.				
FROGGY STYLE	*Jive*	68	*12 Aug 95*	1

NUYORICAN SOUL — US

(See also Masters At Work present India; River Ocean featuring India.)

SINGLES:	HITS 3			WEEKS 8
RUNAWAY	*Talkin Loud*	24	*8 Feb 97*	4
Features backing vocals from Vincent Montana of Montana Sextet. Originaly recorded by Loleatta Holloway in the early 1980s.				
Above hit: NUYORICAN SOUL featuring INDIA.				
IT'S ALRIGHT, I FEEL IT!	*Talkin Loud*	26	*10 May 97*	2
I AM THE BLACK GOLD OF THE SUN	*Talkin Loud*	31	*25 Oct 97*	2
Originally recorded by Minnie Riperton's band The Rotary Connection.				
Above 2: NUYORICAN SOUL featuring Jocelyn BROWN.				

ALBUMS:	HITS 1			WEEKS 2
NUYORICAN SOUL	*Talkin Loud*	25	*1 Mar 97*	2

Joe NYE – See DNA

NYLON MOON — Italy

SINGLES:	HITS 1			WEEKS 2
SKY PLUS	*Positiva*	43	*13 Apr 96*	2

Michael NYMAN — UK

SINGLES:	HITS 1			WEEKS 2
(THE PIANO SINGLE) THE HEART ASKS PLEASURE FIRST/THE PROMISE [M]	*Virgin*	60	*19 Mar 94*	2
From the film 'The Piano'. Features the Munich Philharmonic Orchestra.				

ALBUMS:	HITS 1			WEEKS 15
NYMAN: THE PIANO [OST]	*Venture*	31	*12 Feb 94*	15
Above hit: Michael NYMAN with the MUNICH PHILHARMONIC ORCHESTRA.				

O

O.B.I. PROJECT featuring Harry ASHER D and DJ WHAT? — UK

SINGLES:	HITS 1			WEEKS 1
BABY CAN I GET YOUR NUMBER	*East West*	75	*4 Aug 01*	1

O.R.G.A.N. — Spain

SINGLES:	HITS 1			WEEKS 2
TO THE WORLD	*Multiply*	33	*16 May 98*	2

O.R.N. UK

SINGLES:	HITS 1			WEEKS 1
SNOW	*Deconstruction*	61	*1 Mar 97*	1

O.T. QUARTET – See OUR TRIBE/ONE TRIBE/O.T. QUARTET

O-TOWN US

SINGLES:	HITS 3			WEEKS 24
LIQUID DREAMS	*J*	3	*28 Apr 01*	10
ALL OR NOTHING	*J*	4	*4 Aug 01*	10
WE FIT TOGETHER	*J*	20	*3 Nov 01*	3
WE FIT TOGETHER [RE]	*J*	74	*22 Dec 01*	1
ALBUMS:	**HITS 1**			**WEEKS 5**
O-TOWN	*J*	7	*18 Aug 01*	5

Paul OAKENFOLD presents Afrika BAMBAATAA and the SOULSONIC FORCE UK/US

SINGLES:	HITS 1			WEEKS 1
PLANET ROCK	*Tommy Boy*	47	*25 Aug 01*	1

Philip OAKEY and Giorgio MORODER UK/Italy

(See also Giorgio Moroder.)

SINGLES:	HITS 2			WEEKS 18
TOGETHER IN ELECTRIC DREAMS *From the film 'Electric Dreams'.* *Above hit: Giorgio MORODER with Philip OAKEY.*	*Virgin*	3	*22 Sep 84*	13
GOOD-BYE BAD TIMES	*Virgin*	44	*29 Jun 85*	5
ALBUMS:	**HITS 1**			**WEEKS 5**
PHILIP OAKEY AND GIORGIO MORODER	*Virgin*	52	*10 Aug 85*	5

OASIS UK

ALBUMS:	HITS 1			WEEKS 14
OASIS	*WEA*	23	*28 Apr 84*	14

OASIS UK

SINGLES:	HITS 16			WEEKS 309
SUPERSONIC	*Creation*	31	*23 Apr 94*	3
SHAKERMAKER	*Creation*	11	*2 Jul 94*	5
LIVE FOREVER	*Creation*	10	*20 Aug 94*	5
CIGARETTES AND ALCOHOL	*Creation*	7	*22 Oct 94*	6
CIGARETTES AND ALCOHOL [RE-1ST]	*Creation*	69	*31 Dec 94*	1
WHATEVER	*Creation*	3	*31 Dec 94*	10
SOME MIGHT SAY	*Creation*	1	*6 May 95*	14
SOME MIGHT SAY *Sales from 12" format which, as there were already 3 formats available was listed separately.*	*Creation*	71	*13 May 95*	1
SUPERSONIC [RE-1ST]	*Creation*	44	*24 Jun 95*	3
WHATEVER [RE-1ST]	*Creation*	48	*24 Jun 95*	3
LIVE FOREVER [RE-1ST]	*Creation*	50	*24 Jun 95*	3
SHAKERMAKER [RE-1ST]	*Creation*	52	*24 Jun 95*	3
CIGARETTES AND ALCOHOL [RE-2ND]	*Creation*	53	*24 Jun 95*	3
ROLL WITH IT *The 12" format reached No. 92.*	*Creation*	2	*26 Aug 95*	11
SOME MIGHT SAY [RE-1ST]	*Creation*	73	*26 Aug 95*	1
WONDERWALL	*Creation*	2	*11 Nov 95*	20
WIBBLING RIVALRY: A LOT OF SWEARING AND CUSSING / EVEN MORE SWEARING AND CUSSING *2 tracks of an argument between Liam and Noel Gallagher recorded after they had finished an interview for Radio One.* *Above hit: OAS*S.*	*Fierce Panda*	52	*25 Nov 95*	2
WHATEVER [RE-2ND]	*Creation*	75	*9 Dec 95*	1
SUPERSONIC [RE-2ND]	*Creation*	54	*30 Dec 95*	4
WHATEVER [RE-3RD]	*Creation*	55	*30 Dec 95*	3
CIGARETTES AND ALCOHOL [RE-3RD]	*Creation*	58	*30 Dec 95*	7
SOME MIGHT SAY [RE-2ND]	*Creation*	59	*6 Jan 96*	3
SHAKERMAKER [RE-2ND]	*Creation*	61	*6 Jan 96*	2
LIVE FOREVER [RE-2ND]	*Creation*	64	*6 Jan 96*	1
ROLL WITH IT [RE-1ST]	*Creation*	65	*6 Jan 96*	3
LIVE FOREVER [RE-3RD]	*Creation*	71	*20 Jan 96*	2
WHATEVER [RE-4TH]	*Creation*	61	*27 Jan 96*	3
WHATEVER [RE-5TH]	*Creation*	55	*24 Feb 96*	15
DON'T LOOK BACK IN ANGER	*Creation*	1	*2 Mar 96*	16
CIGARETTES AND ALCOHOL [RE-4TH]	*Creation*	62	*2 Mar 96*	4
SUPERSONIC [RE-3RD]	*Creation*	71	*2 Mar 96*	1

LIVE FOREVER [RE-4TH]	*Creation*	74	*2 Mar 96*	2
SHAKERMAKER [RE-3RD]	*Creation*	74	*2 Mar 96*	1
SOME MIGHT SAY [RE-3RD]	*Creation*	75	*16 Mar 96*	1
CIGARETTES AND ALCOHOL [RE-5TH]	*Creation*	74	*13 Apr 96*	2
CIGARETTES AND ALCOHOL [RE-6TH]	*Creation*	72	*11 May 96*	3
WHATEVER [RE-6TH]	*Creation*	62	*17 Aug 96*	4
WONDERWALL [RE-1ST]	*Creation*	60	*24 Aug 96*	5
SOME MIGHT SAY [RE-8TH]	*Creation*	70	*24 Aug 96*	1
CIGARETTES AND ALCOHOL [RE-7TH]	*Creation*	72	*24 Aug 96*	1
WHATEVER [RE-7TH]	*Creation*	66	*21 Sep 96*	1
WHATEVER [RE-8TH]	*Creation*	34	*16 Nov 96*	10
WONDERWALL [RE-2ND]	*Creation*	36	*16 Nov 96*	9
CIGARETTES AND ALCOHOL [RE-8TH]	*Creation*	38	*16 Nov 96*	5
SOME MIGHT SAY [RE-5TH]	*Creation*	40	*16 Nov 96*	4
LIVE FOREVER [RE-5TH]	*Creation*	42	*16 Nov 96*	2
SUPERSONIC [RE-4TH]	*Creation*	47	*16 Nov 96*	2
SHAKERMAKER [RE-4TH]	*Creation*	48	*16 Nov 96*	2
DON'T LOOK BACK IN ANGER [RE-1ST]	*Creation*	53	*16 Nov 96*	5
ROLL WITH IT [RE-2ND]	*Creation*	55	*16 Nov 96*	2
All the above singles re-entered on 16 Nov 96 after a promotion offering 3 singles for £10.				
DON'T LOOK BACK IN ANGER [RE-2ND]	*Creation*	53	*28 Dec 96*	3
CIGARETTES AND ALCOHOL [RE-9TH]	*Creation*	56	*28 Dec 96*	3
SOME MIGHT SAY [RE-6TH]	*Creation*	58	*28 Dec 96*	3
LIVE FOREVER [RE-6TH]	*Creation*	59	*28 Dec 96*	3
SHAKERMAKER [RE-5TH]	*Creation*	61	*4 Jan 97*	2
ROLL WITH IT [RE-3RD]	*Creation*	62	*4 Jan 97*	2
SUPERSONIC [RE-5TH]	*Creation*	63	*4 Jan 97*	1
D'YOU KNOW WHAT I MEAN?	*Creation*	1	*19 Jul 97*	18
STAND BY ME	*Creation*	2	*4 Oct 97*	18
ALL AROUND THE WORLD	*Creation*	1	*24 Jan 98*	7
Longest single to reach No.1 at 9 minutes 38 seconds.				
ALL AROUND THE WORLD [RE]	*Creation*	68	*11 Apr 98*	2
GO LET IT OUT	*Big Brother*	1	*19 Feb 00*	10
Samples Johnny Jenkins' Walk On Gilded Splinters.				
WHO FEELS LOVE?	*Big Brother*	4	*29 Apr 00*	7
GO LET IT OUT [RE]	*Big Brother*	52	*6 May 00*	2
WHO FEELS LOVE? [RE]	*Big Brother*	70	*1 Jul 00*	1
SUNDAY MORNING CALL	*Big Brother*	4	*15 Jul 00*	6

ALBUMS:	HITS 8			WEEKS 429
DEFINITELY MAYBE	*Creation*	1	*10 Sep 94*	177
Includes re-entries through to 2000.				
(WHAT'S THE STORY) MORNING GLORY?	*Creation*	1	*14 Oct 95*	145
The 2nd best selling album in the UK. Includes re-entries through to 2001.				
(WHAT'S THE STORY) MORNING GLORY? SINGLES BOX - GOLD	*Creation*	24	*16 Nov 96*	3
DEFINITELY MAYBE SINGLES BOX - SILVER	*Creation*	23	*16 Nov 96*	3
BE HERE NOW	*Creation*	1	*30 Aug 97*	36
THE MASTERPLAN	*Creation*	2	*14 Nov 98*	28
STANDING ON THE SHOULDER OF GIANTS	*Big Brother*	1	*11 Mar 00*	27
(WHAT'S THE STORY) MORNING GLORY [RI]	*Big Brother*	67	*17 Jun 00*	2
FAMILIAR TO MILLIONS	*Big Brother*	5	*25 Nov 00*	8
Live recordings from Wembley Stadium on 21 July 00.				

John OATES - See Daryl HALL and John OATES

OBERNKIRCHEN CHILDREN'S CHOIR — Germany

SINGLES:	HITS 1			WEEKS 26
THE HAPPY WANDERER (DER FROHLICHE WANDERER)	*Parlophone*	2	*23 Jan 54*	23
THE HAPPY WANDERER (DER FROHLICHE WANDERER) [RE]	*Parlophone*	8	*10 Jul 54*	3

OBITUARY — US

ALBUMS:	HITS 2			WEEKS 2
THE END COMPLETE	*Roadrunner*	52	*18 Apr 92*	1
WORLD DEMISE	*Roadrunner*	65	*17 Sep 94*	1

Dermot O'BRIEN and his CLUBMEN — Ireland

SINGLES:	HITS 1			WEEKS 2
THE MERRY PLOUGHBOY (OFF TO DUBLIN IN THE GREEN)	*Envoy*	46	*22 Oct 66*	1
THE MERRY PLOUGHBOY (OFF TO DUBLIN IN THE GREEN) [RE]	*Envoy*	50	*5 Nov 66*	1

Billy OCEAN — UK

SINGLES:	HITS 19			WEEKS 153
LOVE REALLY HURTS WITHOUT YOU	*GTO*	2	*21 Feb 76*	10
L.O.D. (LOVE ON DELIVERY)	*GTO*	19	*10 Jul 76*	8
STOP ME (IF YOU'VE HEARD IT ALL BEFORE)	*GTO*	12	*13 Nov 76*	11

RED LIGHT SPELLS DANGER *Some copies have title as Red Light.*	*GTO*	2	*19 Mar 77*	10
AMERICAN HEARTS	*GTO*	54	*1 Sep 79*	5
ARE YOU READY	*GTO*	42	*19 Jan 80*	7
CARIBBEAN QUEEN (NO MORE LOVE ON THE RUN) *Originally released as European Queen, reaching No. 82 in June 84.*	*Jive*	6	*13 Oct 84*	14
LOVERBOY	*Jive*	15	*19 Jan 85*	10
SUDDENLY	*Jive*	4	*11 May 85*	14
MYSTERY LADY	*Jive*	49	*17 Aug 85*	4
WHEN THE GOING GETS TOUGH, THE TOUGH GET GOING *From the film 'The Jewel Of The Nile'.*	*Jive*	1	*25 Jan 86*	13
THERE'LL BE SAD SONGS (TO MAKE YOU CRY)	*Jive*	12	*12 Apr 86*	13
LOVE ZONE	*Jive*	49	*9 Aug 86*	3
BITTERSWEET	*Jive*	44	*11 Oct 86*	4
LOVE IS FOREVER	*Jive*	34	*10 Jan 87*	7
GET OUTTA MY DREAMS, GET INTO MY CAR	*Jive*	3	*6 Feb 88*	11
CALYPSO CRAZY	*Jive*	35	*7 May 88*	4
THE COLOUR OF LOVE	*Jive*	65	*6 Aug 88*	3
PRESSURE	*Jive*	55	*6 Feb 93*	2
ALBUMS:	**HITS 5**			**WEEKS 142**
SUDDENLY	*Jive*	46	*24 Nov 84*	13
SUDDENLY [RE]	*Jive*	9	*11 May 85*	46
LOVE ZONE	*Jive*	2	*17 May 86*	32
TEAR DOWN THESE WALLS	*Jive*	3	*19 Mar 88*	13
GREATEST HITS	*Jive*	4	*28 Oct 89*	17
LOVE IS FOR EVER *Expanded version of the Greatest Hits album including 1993 material.*	*Jive*	7	*16 Aug 97*	21

OCEAN COLOUR SCENE — UK

(See also England United.)

SINGLES:	**HITS 15**			**WEEKS 62**
YESTERDAY TODAY	*!Phffft*	49	*23 Mar 91*	1
THE RIVERBOAT SONG *Features Paul Weller on organ.*	*MCA*	15	*17 Feb 96*	5
YOU'VE GOT IT BAD	*MCA*	7	*6 Apr 96*	4
THE DAY WE CAUGHT THE TRAIN	*MCA*	4	*15 Jun 96*	11
THE CIRCLE	*MCA*	6	*28 Sep 96*	6
HUNDRED MILE HIGH CITY	*MCA*	4	*28 Jun 97*	7
TRAVELLERS TUNE	*MCA*	5	*6 Sep 97*	5
BETTER DAY	*MCA*	9	*22 Nov 97*	5
IT'S A BEAUTIFUL THING *Above hit: OCEAN COLOUR SCENE with PP ARNOLD.*	*MCA*	12	*28 Feb 98*	4
PROFIT IN PEACE	*Island*	13	*4 Sep 99*	5
SO LOW	*Island*	34	*27 Nov 99*	2
JULY/I AM THE NEWS	*Island*	31	*8 Jul 00*	2
UP ON THE DOWN SIDE	*Island*	19	*7 Apr 01*	3
MECHANICAL WONDER	*Island*	49	*14 Jul 01*	1
CRAZY LOWDOWN WAYS	*Island*	64	*22 Dec 01*	1
ALBUMS:	**HITS 7**			**WEEKS 145**
MOSELEY SHOALS	*MCA*	2	*20 Apr 96*	73
OCEAN COLOUR SCENE *Originally released in 1992.*	*Fontana*	54	*21 Sep 96*	2
B-SIDES, SEASIDES & FREERIDES	*MCA*	4	*15 Mar 97*	14
MARCHIN' ALREADY	*MCA*	1	*27 Sep 97*	37
ONE FROM THE MODERN	*Island*	4	*25 Sep 99*	11
MECHANICAL WONDER	*Island*	7	*21 Apr 01*	4
SONGS FOR THE FRONT ROW - THE BEST OF OCEAN COLOUR SCENE	*Island*	16	*17 Nov 01*	4

OCEANIA — Australia

ALBUMS:	**HITS 1**			**WEEKS 1**
OCEANIA *Album of aboriginal chants.*	*Point Music*	70	*23 Oct 99*	1

OCEANIC — UK

SINGLES:	**HITS 4**			**WEEKS 26**
INSANITY	*Dead Dead Good*	3	*24 Aug 91*	15
WICKED LOVE	*Dead Dead Good*	25	*30 Nov 91*	3
WICKED LOVE [RE]	*Dead Dead Good*	65	*28 Dec 91*	2
CONTROLLING ME	*Dead Dead Good*	14	*13 Jun 92*	5
IGNORANCE *Above hit: OCEANIC featuring Siobhan MAHER.*	*Dead Dead Good*	72	*14 Nov 92*	1
ALBUMS:	**HITS 1**			**WEEKS 2**
THAT ALBUM BY OCEANIC	*Dead Dead Good*	49	*4 Jul 92*	2

Des O'CONNOR — UK

SINGLES:	HITS 8			WEEKS 117
CARELESS HANDS	*Columbia*	6	*4 Nov 67*	17
Originally recorded by Mel Torme.				
Above hit: Des O'CONNOR with the Mike SAMMES SINGERS and Alyn AINSWORTH and his Orchestra.				
I PRETEND	*Columbia*	1	*11 May 68*	36
ONE, TWO, THREE O'LEARY	*Columbia*	4	*23 Nov 68*	11
DICK-A-DUM-DUM (KING'S ROAD)	*Columbia*	14	*10 May 69*	10
Co-written by actor Jim Dale.				
LONELINESS (NON SONO MADDALENA)	*Columbia*	18	*29 Nov 69*	11
I'LL GO ON HOPING	*Columbia*	30	*14 Mar 70*	7
THE TIPS OF MY FINGERS	*Columbia*	15	*26 Sep 70*	15
Copies were also pressed with title 'The Tip Of My Fingers'. Original recorded by Bill Anderson.				
Above 5: Des O'CONNOR with Alyn AINSWORTH and his Orchestra.				
THE SKYE BOAT SONG	*Tembo*	10	*8 Nov 86*	10
Above hit: Roger WHITTAKER and Des O'CONNOR.				

ALBUMS:	HITS 7			WEEKS 47
I PRETEND	*Columbia*	8	*7 Dec 68*	10
WITH LOVE	*Columbia*	40	*5 Dec 70*	4
SING A FAVOURITE SONG	*Pye*	25	*2 Dec 72*	6
JUST FOR YOU	*Warwick*	17	*2 Feb 80*	7
DES O'CONNOR NOW	*Telstar*	24	*13 Oct 84*	14
PORTRAIT	*Columbia*	63	*5 Dec 92*	4
A TRIBUTE TO THE CROONERS	*Decca*	51	*17 Nov 01*	2

Hazel O'CONNOR — UK

SINGLES:	HITS 7			WEEKS 46
EIGHTH DAY	*A&M*	5	*16 Aug 80*	11
GIVE ME AN INCH	*A&M*	41	*25 Oct 80*	4
Above 2 from the film 'Breaking Glass'.				
D-DAYS	*Albion*	10	*21 Mar 81*	9
WILL YOU?	*A&M*	8	*23 May 81*	10
From the film 'Breaking Glass'. Saxophone solo by Wesley McGoogan.				
(COVER PLUS) WE'RE ALL GROWN UP	*Albion*	41	*1 Aug 81*	6
HANGING AROUND	*Albion*	45	*3 Oct 81*	3
CALLS THE TUNE	*A&M*	60	*23 Jan 82*	3
From the film 'Breaking Glass'.				

ALBUMS:	HITS 2			WEEKS 45
BREAKING GLASS [OST]	*A&M*	5	*9 Aug 80*	38
COVER PLUS	*Albion*	32	*12 Sep 81*	7

Sinead O'CONNOR — Ireland

SINGLES:	HITS 14			WEEKS 64
MANDINKA	*Ensign*	17	*16 Jan 88*	9
NOTHING COMPARES 2 U	*Ensign*	1	*20 Jan 90*	14
Written by Prince and originally recorded by The Family.				
THE EMPEROR'S NEW CLOTHES	*Ensign*	31	*21 Jul 90*	5
THREE BABIES	*Ensign*	42	*20 Oct 90*	4
MY SPECIAL CHILD	*Ensign*	42	*8 Jun 91*	3
SILENT NIGHT	*Ensign*	60	*14 Dec 91*	4
SUCCESS HAS MADE A FAILURE OF OUR HOME	*Ensign*	18	*12 Sep 92*	4
DON'T CRY FOR ME ARGENTINA	*Ensign*	53	*12 Dec 92*	4
YOU MADE ME THE THIEF OF YOUR HEART	*Island*	42	*19 Feb 94*	3
From the film 'The Name Of The Father'.				
THANK YOU FOR HEARING ME	*Ensign*	13	*26 Nov 94*	7
HAUNTED	*ZTT*	30	*29 Apr 95*	2
Above hit: Shane MacGOWAN and Sinead O'CONNOR.				
FAMINE	*Chrysalis*	51	*26 Aug 95*	1
GOSPEL OAK [EP]	*Chrysalis*	28	*17 May 97*	3
Lead track: This Is To Mother You. Features vocals by Jah Wobble.				
THIS IS A REBEL SONG	*Columbia*	60	*6 Dec 97*	1

ALBUMS:	HITS 6			WEEKS 89
THE LION AND THE COBRA	*Ensign*	27	*23 Jan 88*	20
I DO NOT WANT WHAT I HAVEN'T GOT	*Ensign*	1	*24 Mar 90*	51
AM I NOT YOUR GIRL?	*Ensign*	6	*26 Sep 92*	6
UNIVERSAL MOTHER	*Ensign*	19	*24 Sep 94*	8
SO FAR . . . THE BEST OF SINEAD O'CONNOR	*Chrysalis*	28	*22 Nov 97*	3
FAITH AND COURAGE	*Atlantic*	61	*24 Jun 00*	1

OCTAHVIA – See Jose NUNEZ featuring OCTAHVIA

OCTOPUS — UK/France

SINGLES:	HITS 3			WEEKS 5
YOUR SMILE	*Food*	42	*22 Jun 96*	2

SAVED	*Food*	40	*14 Sep 96*	2
JEALOUSY	*Food*	59	*23 Nov 96*	1

Alan O'DAY

US

SINGLES:	HITS 1			WEEKS 3
UNDERCOVER ANGEL	*Atlantic*	43	*2 Jul 77*	3

ODB - See OL' DIRTY BASTARD; PRAS

ODETTA - See Harry BELAFONTE

Daniel O'DONNELL

Ireland

SINGLES:	HITS 17			WEEKS 64
I JUST WANT TO DANCE WITH YOU	*Ritz*	20	*12 Sep 92*	7
THE THREE BELLS	*Ritz*	71	*2 Jan 93*	1
THE LOVE IN YOUR EYES	*Ritz*	47	*8 May 93*	3
WHAT EVER HAPPENED TO OLD FASHIONED LOVE *Originally recorded by B.J. Thomas.*	*Ritz*	21	*7 Aug 93*	5
SINGING THE BLUES *Originally recorded by Marty Robbins.*	*Ritz*	23	*16 Apr 94*	3
THE GIFT	*Ritz*	46	*26 Nov 94*	3
SECRET LOVE	*Ritz*	28	*10 Jun 95*	3
TIMELESS *Above 2: Daniel O'DONNELL and Mary DUFF.*	*Ritz*	32	*9 Mar 96*	3
FOOTSTEPS	*Ritz*	25	*28 Sep 96*	5
THE LOVE SONGS [EP] *Lead track: Save The Last Dance For Me.*	*Ritz*	27	*7 Jun 97*	4
GIVE A LITTLE LOVE *Charity single with proceeds to The Romanian Challenge Appeal.*	*Ritz*	7	*11 Apr 98*	5
THE MAGIC IS THERE	*Ritz*	16	*17 Oct 98*	4
THE WAY DREAMS ARE	*Ritz*	18	*20 Mar 99*	3
UNO MAS	*Ritz*	25	*24 Jul 99*	3
A CHRISTMAS KISS	*Ritz*	20	*18 Dec 99*	4
LIGHT A CANDLE (TO START A NEW DAWN)	*Ritz*	23	*15 Apr 00*	4
MORNING HAS BROKEN	*Ritz*	32	*16 Dec 00*	4

ALBUMS:	HITS 18			WEEKS 158
FROM THE HEART	*Telstar*	56	*15 Oct 88*	12
THOUGHTS OF HOME	*Telstar*	43	*28 Oct 89*	10
FAVOURITES	*Ritz*	75	*21 Apr 90*	1
THE LAST WALTZ	*Ritz*	53	*17 Nov 90*	5
THE VERY BEST OF DANIEL O'DONNELL	*Ritz*	34	*9 Nov 91*	14
FOLLOW YOUR DREAM	*Ritz*	17	*21 Nov 92*	9
A DATE WITH DANIEL - LIVE *Live recordings from The Point in Dublin.*	*Ritz*	21	*6 Nov 93*	10
THE LAST WALTZ [RE]	*Ritz*	46	*30 Jul 94*	2
FAVOURITES [RE]	*Ritz*	61	*30 Jul 94*	2
ESPECIALLY FOR YOU	*Ritz*	14	*22 Oct 94*	11
CHRISTMAS WITH DANIEL	*Ritz*	34	*3 Dec 94*	5
THE CLASSIC COLLECTION *Collection of his most popular recordings plus 7 new tracks.*	*Ritz*	34	*11 Nov 95*	9
TIMELESS *Above hit: Daniel O'DONNELL and Mary DUFF.*	*Ritz*	13	*6 Apr 96*	5
THE DANIEL O'DONNELL IRISH COLLECTION *Album of his most requested Irish songs.*	*Ritz*	35	*20 Jul 96*	3
SONGS OF INSPIRATION *Traditional ballads with a religious theme.*	*Ritz*	11	*26 Oct 96*	16
I BELIEVE	*Ritz*	11	*8 Nov 97*	11
LOVE SONGS	*Ritz*	9	*31 Oct 98*	10
GREATEST HITS	*Ritz*	10	*2 Oct 99*	8
FAITH & INSPIRATION	*Ritz*	4	*28 Oct 00*	10
LIVE LAUGH LOVE	*Rosette*	27	*1 Dec 01*	5

ODYSSEY

US

SINGLES:	HITS 9			WEEKS 82
NATIVE NEW YORKER *Originally recorded by Frankie Valli.*	*RCA Victor*	5	*24 Dec 77*	11
USE IT UP AND WEAR IT OUT	*RCA*	1	*21 Jun 80*	12
IF YOU'RE LOOKIN' FOR A WAY OUT	*RCA*	6	*13 Sep 80*	15
HANG TOGETHER	*RCA*	36	*17 Jan 81*	7
GOING BACK TO MY ROOTS *Originally recorded by Lamont Dozier.*	*RCA*	4	*30 May 81*	12
IT WILL BE ALRIGHT	*RCA*	43	*19 Sep 81*	5
INSIDE OUT	*RCA*	3	*12 Jun 82*	11
MAGIC TOUCH	*RCA*	41	*11 Sep 82*	5
(JOY) I KNOW IT	*Mirror*	51	*17 Aug 85*	4

ALBUMS:	HITS 5			WEEKS 32
HANG TOGETHER	*RCA*	38	*16 Aug 80*	3

I'VE GOT THE MELODY	*RCA*	29	*4 Jul 81*	7
HAPPY TOGETHER	*RCA*	21	*3 Jul 82*	9
THE MAGIC TOUCH OF ODYSSEY	*Telstar*	69	*20 Nov 82*	5
THE GREATEST HITS	*Stylus*	26	*26 Sep 87*	8

OEDIPUS WRECKS - See Pete WYLIE

Esther and Abi OFARIM — Israel

SINGLES:	HITS 2			WEEKS 22
CINDERELLA ROCKAFELLA *Originally recorded by Mason Williams.*	*Philips*	1	*17 Feb 68*	13
ONE MORE DANCE	*Philips*	13	*22 Jun 68*	9
ALBUMS:	**HITS 2**			**WEEKS 24**
2 IN 3	*Philips*	6	*24 Feb 68*	20
OFARIM CONCERT - LIVE '69	*Philips*	29	*12 Jul 69*	4

OFF-SHORE — UK/Germany

SINGLES:	HITS 2			WEEKS 12
I CAN'T TAKE THE POWER	*CBS*	7	*22 Dec 90*	11
I GOT A LITTLE SONG	*Dance Pool*	64	*17 Aug 91*	1

Wiston OFFICE - See Frank 'K' (featuring Wiston OFFICE)

OFFICIAL RUGBY TEAM SONG featuring Russell WATSON — UK

SINGLES:	HITS 1			WEEKS 2
SWING LOW '99 *Official song of the 1999 England World Cup team.*	*Decca*	38	*30 Oct 99*	2

OFFICIAL SCOTLAND WORLD CUP SQUAD and FRIENDS - See SCOTTISH WORLD CUP SQUAD

OFFSPRING — US

SINGLES:	HITS 11			WEEKS 56
SELF ESTEEM	*Epitaph*	37	*25 Feb 95*	3
GOTTA GET AWAY	*Out Of Step*	43	*19 Aug 95*	2
ALL I WANT	*Epitaph*	31	*1 Feb 97*	2
GONE AWAY	*Epitaph*	42	*26 Apr 97*	1
PRETTY FLY (FOR A WHITE GUY) *Samples Def Leppard's Rock Of Ages.*	*Columbia*	1	*30 Jan 99*	11
WHY DON'T YOU GET A JOB?	*Columbia*	2	*8 May 99*	8
THE KIDS AREN'T ALRIGHT	*Columbia*	11	*11 Sep 99*	6
SHE'S GOT ISSUES	*Columbia*	41	*4 Dec 99*	2
ORIGINAL PRANKSTER *Samples War's Low Rider.*	*Columbia*	6	*18 Nov 00*	8
WANT YOU BAD	*Columbia*	15	*31 Mar 01*	5
WANT YOU BAD [RE]	*Columbia*	34	*19 May 01*	4
MILLION MILES AWAY	*Columbia*	21	*7 Jul 01*	4
ALBUMS:	**HITS 4**			**WEEKS 99**
SMASH	*Epitaph*	21	*4 Mar 95*	34
IXNAY ON THE HOMBRE	*Epitaph*	17	*15 Feb 97*	3
AMERICANA	*Columbia*	10	*28 Nov 98*	44
CONSPIRACY OF ONE	*Columbia*	12	*25 Nov 00*	18

OH WELL — Germany

SINGLES:	HITS 2			WEEKS 7
OH WELL	*Parlophone*	28	*14 Oct 89*	6
RADAR LOVE	*Parlophone*	65	*3 Mar 90*	1

Mary O'HARA — UK

ALBUMS:	HITS 2			WEEKS 12
MARY O'HARA AT THE ROYAL FESTIVAL HALL	*Chrysalis*	37	*8 Apr 78*	3
TRANQUILLITY	*Warwick*	12	*1 Dec 79*	9

OHIO EXPRESS — US

SINGLES:	HITS 1			WEEKS 15
YUMMY YUMMY YUMMY	*Pye International*	5	*8 Jun 68*	15

OHIO PLAYERS — US

SINGLES:	HITS 1			WEEKS 4
WHO'D SHE COO?	*Mercury*	43	*10 Jul 76*	4

David OISTRAKH - See Herbert VON KARAJAN conducting the BERLIN PHILHARMONIC ORCHESTRA

O'JAYS — US

(See also Philadelphia International All-Stars: Lou Rawls, Billy Paul, Archie Bell, Teddy Pendergrass, O'Jays, Dee Dee Sharp, Gamble.)

SINGLES:	HITS 8			WEEKS 72
BACK STABBERS	*CBS*	14	*23 Sep 72*	9
LOVE TRAIN	*CBS*	9	*3 Mar 73*	13
I LOVE MUSIC	*Philadelphia International*	13	*31 Jan 76*	9
DARLIN' DARLIN' BABY (SWEET, TENDER, LOVE)	*Philadelphia International*	24	*12 Feb 77*	6
I LOVE MUSIC [RI]	*Philadelphia International*	36	*8 Apr 78*	3
USED TA BE MY GIRL	*Philadelphia International*	12	*17 Jun 78*	12
BRANDY	*Philadelphia International*	21	*30 Sep 78*	9
SING A HAPPY SONG	*Philadelphia International*	39	*29 Sep 79*	6
PUT OUR HEADS TOGETHER	*Philadelphia International*	45	*30 Jul 83*	5

ALBUMS:	HITS 1			WEEKS 2
THE ARTISTS VOLUME III *Compilation album with tracks by each artist.* *Above hit: WOMACK and WOMACK/O'JAYS/KLEEER/S.O.S. BAND.*	*Street Sounds*	87	*12 Oct 85*	2

John O'KANE — UK

SINGLES:	HITS 1			WEEKS 4
STAY WITH ME	*Circa*	41	*9 May 92*	4

OL' DIRTY BASTARD — US

(See also Pras.)

SINGLES:	HITS 2			WEEKS 10
SAY NOTHIN' *Above hit: OMAR featuring OL' DIRTY BASTARD of WU-TANG CLAN.*	*RCA*	29	*2 Aug 97*	2
GOT YOUR MONEY *Above hit: OL' DIRTY BASTARD featuring KELIS.*	*Elektra*	11	*8 Jul 00*	8

OLD SCHOOL JUNKIES PT. 2 – See Armand VAN HELDEN

OLD SKOOL ORCHESTRA — UK

SINGLES:	HITS 1			WEEKS 1
B-BOY HUMP *Samples Engelbert Humperdinck's Can't Take My Eyes Off You.*	*East West*	55	*23 Jan 99*	1

Mike OLDFIELD — UK

SINGLES:	HITS 19			WEEKS 113
MIKE OLDFIELD'S SINGLE (THEME FROM MIKE OLDFIELD'S ALBUM 'TUBULAR BELLS')	*Virgin*	31	*13 Jul 74*	6
IN DULCI JUBILO / ON HORSEBACK *On Horseback credited to Mike Oldfield.* *Above hit: Mike OLDFIELD; recorder: Leslie PENNING.*	*Virgin*	4	*20 Dec 75*	10
PORTSMOUTH	*Virgin*	3	*27 Nov 76*	12
TAKE 4 [EP] *Lead track: Portsmouth, which is a re-issue.*	*Virgin*	72	*23 Dec 78*	3
GUILTY	*Virgin*	22	*21 Apr 79*	8
BLUE PETER *Charity record with proceeds to the BBC TV's 'Blue Peter Cambodia Appeal'.*	*Virgin*	19	*8 Dec 79*	9
FIVE MILES OUT	*Virgin*	43	*20 Mar 82*	5
FAMILY MAN	*Virgin*	45	*12 Jun 82*	6
MOONLIGHT SHADOW *Tribute to John Lennon.*	*Virgin*	4	*28 May 83*	17
CRIME OF PASSION *Above 3 feature vocals by Maggie Reilly, though she does not have a credit on the label or front of the sleeve.*	*Virgin*	61	*14 Jan 84*	3
TO FRANCE *Above hit: Mike OLDFIELD vocals by Maggie Reilly.*	*Virgin*	48	*30 Jun 84*	7
PICTURES IN THE DARK *Above hit: Mike OLDFIELD featuring Aled JONES, Anita HEGERLAND and Barry PALMER.*	*Virgin*	50	*14 Dec 85*	6
SENTINEL (SINGLE RESTRUCTURE) TUBULAR BELLS II	*WEA*	10	*3 Oct 92*	6
TATTOO	*WEA*	33	*19 Dec 92*	5
THE BELL (MC VIV STANSHALL)	*WEA*	50	*17 Apr 93*	2
MOONLIGHT SHADOW [RI]	*Virgin*	52	*9 Oct 93*	2
HIBERNACULUM	*WEA*	47	*17 Dec 94*	3
LET THERE BE LIGHT	*WEA*	51	*2 Sep 95*	1
WOMEN OF IRELAND	*WEA*	70	*22 Nov 97*	1
FAR ABOVE THE CLOUDS	*WEA*	53	*24 Apr 99*	1

ALBUMS:	HITS 24			WEEKS 547
TUBULAR BELLS *Peak position reached on 5 Oct 74. Includes re-entries through to 1983.*	*Virgin*	1	*14 Jul 73*	264
HERGEST RIDGE *Title is the name of the hilltop where he flew his model glider.*	*Virgin*	1	*14 Sep 74*	17

THE ORCHESTRAL TUBULAR BELLS	*Virgin*	17	*8 Feb 75*	7
Live recordings from Sep 74, conducted by David Bedford.				
Above hit: Mike OLDFIELD with the ROYAL PHILHARMONIC ORCHESTRA.				
OMMADAWN	*Virgin*	4	*15 Nov 75*	23
BOXED	*Virgin*	22	*20 Nov 76*	13
4 album boxed set includes remixed versions of his three hit albums to date and a compilation of singles.				
INCANTATIONS	*Virgin*	14	*9 Dec 78*	17
EXPOSED	*Virgin*	16	*11 Aug 79*	9
Live recordings from his 1979 tour.				
PLATINUM	*Virgin*	24	*8 Dec 79*	9
Compilation.				
QE 2	*Virgin*	27	*8 Nov 80*	12
Album named after the Ocean Liner.				
FIVE MILES OUT	*Virgin*	7	*27 Mar 82*	27
CRISES	*Virgin*	6	*4 Jun 83*	29
DISCOVERY	*Virgin*	15	*7 Jul 84*	16
THE KILLING FIELDS [OST]	*Virgin*	97	*15 Dec 84*	1
THE COMPLETE MIKE OLDFIELD	*Virgin*	36	*2 Nov 85*	17
ISLANDS	*Virgin*	29	*10 Oct 87*	5
EARTH MOVING	*Virgin*	30	*22 Jul 89*	5
AMAROK	*Virgin*	49	*9 Jun 90*	2
TUBULAR BELLS II	*WEA*	1	*12 Sep 92*	30
TUBULAR BELLS [RE-1ST]	*Virgin*	43	*12 Sep 92*	10
Chart position reached in 1996 (1992 peak No. 48).				
ELEMENTS - THE BEST OF MIKE OLDFIELD	*Virgin*	5	*25 Sep 93*	10
THE SONGS OF DISTANT EARTH	*WEA*	24	*3 Dec 94*	6
Inspired by the book of the same name written by Arthur C. Clarke.				
VOYAGER	*WEA*	12	*7 Sep 96*	5
TUBULAR BELLS [RE-2ND]	*Virgin*	43	*6 Jun 98*	2
Digitally remastered 25th Anniversay edition.				
TUBULAR BELLS III	*WEA*	4	*12 Sep 98*	7
GUITARS	*WEA*	40	*5 Jun 99*	2
THE BEST OF TUBULAR BELLS	*Virgin*	60	*16 Jun 01*	2

Sally OLDFIELD — UK

SINGLES:	HITS 1			WEEKS 13
MIRRORS	*Bronze*	19	*9 Dec 78*	13

Misty OLDLAND — UK

SINGLES:	HITS 3			WEEKS 7
GOT ME A FEELING	*Columbia*	59	*16 Oct 93*	2
A FAIR AFFAIR (JE T'AIME)	*Columbia*	49	*12 Mar 94*	4
I WROTE YOU A SONG	*Columbia*	73	*9 Jul 94*	1

OLGA — Italy

SINGLES:	HITS 1			WEEKS 1
I'M A BITCH	*UMM*	68	*1 Oct 94*	1
A reworking of an old club track by A Bitch Called Joanna.				

OLIVE — UK

SINGLES:	HITS 3			WEEKS 24
YOU'RE NOT ALONE	*RCA*	42	*7 Sep 96*	4
MIRACLE	*RCA*	41	*15 Mar 97*	2
Original release reached No. 118 in 1996.				
YOU'RE NOT ALONE [RI]	*RCA*	1	*17 May 97*	13
OUTLAW	*RCA*	14	*16 Aug 97*	4
MIRACLE [RI]	*RCA*	41	*8 Nov 97*	1
ALBUMS:	**HITS 1**			**WEEKS 3**
EXTRA VIRGIN	*RCA*	15	*31 May 97*	3

OLIVER — US

SINGLES:	HITS 1			WEEKS 18
GOOD MORNING STARSHINE	*CBS*	6	*9 Aug 69*	16
From the musical 'Hair'.				
GOOD MORNING STARSHINE [RE]	*CBS*	39	*27 Dec 69*	2

Frankie OLIVER — UK

SINGLES:	HITS 1			WEEKS 1
GIVE HER WHAT SHE WANTS	*Island Jamaica*	58	*7 Jun 97*	1

OLLIE and JERRY — US

SINGLES:	HITS 2			WEEKS 14
BREAKIN' . . . THERE'S NO STOPPING US	*Polydor*	5	*23 Jun 84*	11
From the film 'Breakdance'.				
ELECTRIC BOOGALOO	*Polydor*	57	*9 Mar 85*	3

OLYMPIC ORCHESTRA — UK

SINGLES:	HITS 1			WEEKS 15
REILLY	*Red Bus*	26	*1 Oct 83*	15
Theme from the Thames ITV series 'Reilly, Ace Of Spies'.				

OLYMPIC RUNNERS — UK

SINGLES:	HITS 4			WEEKS 21
WHATEVER IT TAKES	*RCA Victor*	61	*13 May 78*	2
Above hit: OLYMPIC RUNNERS with George CHANDLER.				
GET IT WHILE YOU CAN	*Polydor*	35	*14 Oct 78*	6
SIR DANCEALOT	*Polydor*	35	*20 Jan 79*	6
THE BITCH	*Polydor*	37	*28 Jul 79*	7
From the film of the same name.				

OLYMPICS — US

SINGLES:	HITS 2			WEEKS 9
WESTERN MOVIES	*His Master's Voice*	12	*4 Oct 58*	8
I WISH I COULD SHIMMY LIKE MY SISTER KATE	*Vogue*	40	*21 Jan 61*	1

OMAR — UK

SINGLES:	HITS 7			WEEKS 18
THERE'S NOTHING LIKE THIS	*Talkin Loud*	14	*22 Jun 91*	7
Original release reached No. 78 in 1990.				
YOUR LOSS MY GAIN	*Talkin Loud*	47	*23 May 92*	2
MUSIC	*Talkin Loud*	53	*26 Sep 92*	2
OUTSIDE / SATURDAY	*RCA*	43	*23 Jul 94*	2
Outside features vocal by Nu Colours.				
KEEP STEPPIN'	*RCA*	57	*15 Oct 94*	1
SAY NOTHIN'	*RCA*	29	*2 Aug 97*	2
Above hit: OMAR featuring OL' DIRTY BASTARD Of WU-TANG CLAN.				
GOLDEN BROWN	*RCA*	37	*18 Oct 97*	2
ALBUMS:	**HITS 4**			**WEEKS 14**
THERE'S NOTHING LIKE THIS	*Kongo Dance*	54	*14 Jul 90*	4
THERE'S NOTHING LIKE THIS [RI]	*Talkin Loud*	19	*27 Jul 91*	6
MUSIC	*Talkin Loud*	37	*24 Oct 92*	2
FOR PLEASURE	*RCA*	50	*2 Jul 94*	1
THIS IS NOT A LOVE SONG	*RCA*	50	*16 Aug 97*	1

OMC — New Zealand

SINGLES:	HITS 2			WEEKS 17
HOW BIZARRE	*Polydor*	5	*20 Jul 96*	16
ON THE RUN	*Polydor*	56	*18 Jan 97*	1

OMD – See ORCHESTRAL MANOEUVRES IN THE DARK

OMNI TRIO — UK

SINGLES:	HITS 1			WEEKS 3
01.2 THE ANGELS AND SHADOWS PROJECT	*Moving Shadow*	44	*7 Jul 01*	3
ALBUMS:	**HITS 2**			**WEEKS 2**
THE DEEPEST CUT - VOLUME 1	*Moving Shadow*	60	*11 Feb 95*	1
THE HAUNTED SCIENCE	*Moving Shadow*	43	*24 Aug 96*	1

ON-U-SOUND – See Gary CLAIL ON-U SOUND SYSTEM; POP WILL EAT ITSELF; PRIMAL SCREAM

ONE — UK

SINGLES:	HITS 1			WEEKS 2
ONE MORE CHANCE	*Mercury*	31	*11 Jan 97*	2

Michie ONE – See Louchie LOU and Michie ONE

Phoebe ONE — UK

SINGLES:	HITS 2			WEEKS 3
DOIN' OUR THING / ONE MAN'S BITCH	*Mecca Recordings*	59	*12 Dec 98*	1
Above hit: Phoebe ONE featuring RED RAT, GOOFY and BUCCANEER (MAIN STREET CREW).				
GET ON IT	*Mecca Recordings*	38	*15 May 99*	2
Samples Rod Stewart's Baby Jane.				

ONE DOVE — UK

SINGLES:	HITS 3			WEEKS 9
WHITE LOVE	*Boys Own Productions*	43	*7 Aug 93*	3
BREAKDOWN	*London*	24	*16 Oct 93*	3
WHY DON'T YOU TAKE ME?	*Boys Own Productions*	30	*15 Jan 94*	3
ALBUMS:	**HITS 1**			**WEEKS 2**
MORNING DOVE WHITE	*London*	30	*25 Sep 93*	2

ONE HUNDRED TON AND A FEATHER – See Jonathan KING

ONE MINUTE SILENCE — UK/Ireland/Holland

SINGLES:	HITS 1			WEEKS 1
FISH OUT OF WATER	*V2*	56	*20 Jan 01*	1
ALBUMS:	**HITS 1**			**WEEKS 1**
BUY NOW . . . SAVED LATER	*V2*	61	*22 Apr 00*	1

ONE THE JUGGLER — UK

SINGLES:	HITS 1			WEEKS 1
PASSION KILLER	*Regard*	71	*19 Feb 83*	1

ONE TRIBE – See OUR TRIBE/ONE TRIBE/O.T. QUARTET

ONE 2 MANY — Norway

SINGLES:	HITS 1			WEEKS 11
DOWNTOWN	*A&M*	65	*12 Nov 88*	4
DOWNTOWN [RE]	*A&M*	43	*3 Jun 89*	7

ONE WAY – See Al HUDSON

ONE WORLD — UK

ALBUMS:	HITS 1			WEEKS 3
ONE WORLD ONE VOICE	*Virgin*	27	*9 Jun 90*	3

187 LOCKDOWN — UK

SINGLES:	HITS 4			WEEKS 16
GUNMAN *Samples Ennio Morricone's Sixty Seconds To What.*	*East West Dance*	16	*15 Nov 97*	4
KUNG-FU	*East West Dance*	9	*25 Apr 98*	5
GUNMAN [RI]	*East West*	17	*25 Jul 98*	4
THE DON	*East West*	29	*3 Oct 98*	2
ALL 'N' ALL *Above hit: 187 LOCKDOWN (featuring D'EMPRESS).*	*East West*	43	*13 Feb 99*	1

101 STRINGS — Germany

ALBUMS:	HITS 5			WEEKS 35
GYPSY CAMPFIRES	*Pye Golden Guinea*	9	*26 Sep 59*	7
THE SOUL OF SPAIN	*Pye Golden Guinea*	17	*26 Mar 60*	1
GRAND CANYON SUITE	*Pye Golden Guinea*	10	*16 Apr 60*	1
DOWN DRURY LANE TO MEMORY LANE *The first double album set to reach No. 1.*	*Pye Golden Guinea*	1	*27 Aug 60*	21
MORNING NOON AND NIGHT	*Ronco*	32	*15 Oct 83*	5

ONEPHATDEEVA – See A.T.F.C. presents ONEPHATDEEVA

ONES — US

SINGLES:	HITS 1			WEEKS 10
FLAWLESS	*Positiva*	7	*20 Oct 01*	9
FLAWLESS [RE]	*Positiva*	74	*29 Dec 01*	1

1000 CLOWNS — US

SINGLES:	HITS 1			WEEKS 4
(NOT THE) GREATEST RAPPER	*Elektra*	23	*22 May 99*	4

112 — US

SINGLES:	HITS 4			WEEKS 13
(See also Faith Evans; Puff Daddy.)				
ALL CRIED OUT *Originally recorded by Lisa Lisa and Cult Jam.* *Above hit: ALLURE featuring 112.*	*Epic*	12	*10 Jan 98*	5

SKY'S THE LIMIT *Above hit: NOTORIOUS B.I.G. featuring 112.*	*Puff Daddy*	35	*14 Feb 98*	2
IT'S OVER NOW *Samples Grandmaster Flash and Melle Mel's White Lines (Don't Don't Do It).* *Above hit: ONE (112) TWELVE.*	*Puff Daddy*	22	*30 Jun 01*	3
PEACHES & CREAM	*Arista*	32	*8 Sep 01*	3

Alexander O'NEAL

US

SINGLES:	HITS 22			WEEKS 107
SATURDAY LOVE *Above hit: CHERRELLE with Alexander O'NEAL.*	*Tabu*	6	*28 Dec 85*	11
IF YOU WERE HERE TONIGHT	*Tabu*	13	*15 Feb 86*	10
A BROKEN HEART CAN MEND *Original release reached No. 96 in 1985.*	*Tabu*	53	*5 Apr 86*	4
FAKE	*Tabu*	33	*6 Jun 87*	6
CRITICIZE	*Tabu*	4	*31 Oct 87*	14
NEVER KNEW LOVE LIKE THIS *Above hit: Alexander O'NEAL featuring CHERRELLE.*	*Tabu*	26	*6 Feb 88*	7
THE LOVERS	*Tabu*	28	*28 May 88*	4
(WHAT CAN I SAY) TO MAKE YOU LOVE ME	*Tabu*	27	*23 Jul 88*	5
FAKE 88 [RM] *Remixed by Keith Cohen and Steve Beltran.*	*Tabu*	16	*24 Sep 88*	7
THE CHRISTMAS SONG (CHESTNUTS ROASTING ON AN OPEN FIRE) / THANK YOU FOR A GOOD YEAR	*Tabu*	30	*10 Dec 88*	5
HEARSAY 89	*Tabu*	56	*25 Feb 89*	2
SUNSHINE	*Tabu*	72	*2 Sep 89*	1
HITMIX (THE OFFICIAL BOOTLEG MEGA-MIX) [M] *Medley of 4 tracks from his Hearsay album.*	*Tabu*	19	*9 Dec 89*	7
SATURDAY LOVE (FEELIN' LUV MIX) [RM] *Remixed by Olimar and D.J. Shapps.* *Above hit: CHERRELLE with Alexander O'NEAL.*	*Tabu*	55	*24 Mar 90*	2
ALL TRUE MAN	*Tabu*	18	*12 Jan 91*	6
WHAT IS THIS THING CALLED LOVE?	*Tabu*	53	*23 Mar 91*	2
SHAME ON ME	*Tabu*	71	*11 May 91*	1
SENTIMENTAL	*Epic*	53	*9 May 92*	2
LOVE MAKES NO SENSE	*Tabu*	26	*30 Jan 93*	3
IN THE MIDDLE	*Tabu*	32	*3 Jul 93*	3
ALL THAT MATTERS TO ME	*A&M*	67	*25 Sep 93*	1
LET'S GET TOGETHER	*EMI Premier*	38	*2 Nov 96*	2
BABY COME TO ME *Above hit: Alexander O'NEAL and CHERRELLE.*	*One World Entertainment*	56	*2 Aug 97*	1
CRITICIZE '98 MIX [RR]	*One World Entertainment*	51	*12 Dec 98*	1

ALBUMS:	HITS 6			WEEKS 162
ALEXANDER O'NEAL	*Tabu*	53	*1 Jun 85*	6
ALEXANDER O'NEAL [RE]	*Tabu*	19	*15 Mar 86*	12
HEARSAY *Peak position reached on 26 Mar 88.*	*Tabu*	4	*8 Aug 87*	96
MY GIFT TO YOU	*Tabu*	53	*17 Dec 88*	3
HEARSAY / ALL MIXED UP [RE] *All Mixed Up was a remix album, sales were combined.*	*Tabu*	60	*15 Jul 89*	7
ALL TRUE MAN	*Tabu*	2	*2 Feb 91*	16
THIS THING CALLED LOVE - THE GREATEST HITS OF ALEXANDER O'NEAL	*Tabu*	4	*30 May 92*	18
LOVE MAKES NO SENSE	*Tabu*	14	*20 Feb 93*	4

Shaquille O'NEAL

US

(See also Quincy Jones.)

SINGLES:	HITS 3			WEEKS 4
I'M OUTSTANDING *Samples Outstanding by the Gap Band, Don't Stop The Music by Yarbrough & Peoples and Funkin' For Jamaica by Tom Browne.*	*Jive*	70	*26 Mar 94*	1
YOU CAN'T STOP THE REIGN *Features Biggie Smalls (Notorious B.I.G.).*	*Interscope*	40	*1 Feb 97*	2
THE WAY IT'S GOIN' DOWN (T.W.ISM. FOR LIFE) *Above hit: Shaquille O'NEAL featuring Peter GUNZ.*	*A&M*	62	*17 Oct 98*	1

ONLY ONES

UK

SINGLES:	HITS 1			WEEKS 2
ANOTHER GIRL - ANOTHER PLANET *Originally released in 1978.*	*Columbia*	57	*1 Feb 92*	2

ALBUMS:	HITS 3			WEEKS 8
THE ONLY ONES	*CBS*	56	*3 Jun 78*	1
EVEN SERPENTS SHINE	*CBS*	42	*31 Mar 79*	2
BABY'S GOT A GUN	*CBS*	37	*3 May 80*	5

Yoko ONO — Japan

(See also John Lennon.)

SINGLES:	HITS 2			WEEKS 11
WATCHING THE WHEELS	*Geffen*	30	*4 Apr 81*	6
Above hit: John LENNON and Yoko ONO.				
WALKING ON THIN ICE	*Geffen*	35	*28 Feb 81*	5
A tribute to her husband John Lennon.				
ALBUMS:	**HITS 3**			**WEEKS 51**
DOUBLE FANTASY	*Geffen*	1	*22 Nov 80*	36
Tracks divided equally between each artist.				
Above hit: John LENNON and Yoko ONO.				
SEASON OF GLASS	*Geffen*	47	*20 Jun 81*	2
MILK AND HONEY - A HEART PLAY	*Polydor*	3	*4 Feb 84*	13
Recordings from 1980. Tracks divided equally between each artist.				
Above hit: John LENNON and Yoko ONO.				

ONSLAUGHT — UK

SINGLES:	HITS 1			WEEKS 3
LET THERE BE ROCK	*London*	50	*6 May 89*	3
ALBUMS:	**HITS 1**			**WEEKS 2**
IN SEARCH OF SANITY	*London*	46	*20 May 89*	2

ONYX — US

SINGLES:	HITS 3			WEEKS 8
SLAM	*Columbia*	31	*28 Aug 93*	4
THROW YA GUNZ	*Columbia*	34	*27 Nov 93*	3
ROC-IN-IT	*Independiente*	59	*20 Feb 99*	1
Above hit: DEEJAY PUNK-ROC vs ONYX.				
ALBUMS:	**HITS 1**			**WEEKS 3**
BACDAFUCUP	*Columbia*	59	*4 Sep 93*	3

OO LA LA — UK

SINGLES:	HITS 1			WEEKS 2
OO . . . AH . . . CANTONA	*North Speed*	64	*5 Sep 92*	2

OOBERMAN — UK

SINGLES:	HITS 4			WEEKS 5
BLOSSOMS FALLING	*Independiente*	39	*8 May 99*	2
MILLION SUNS	*Independiente*	43	*17 Jul 99*	1
TEARS FROM A WILLOW	*Independiente*	63	*23 Oct 99*	1
SHORLEY WALL	*Independiente*	47	*8 Apr 00*	1

OOE – See COLUMBO presents IN FULL ROCK-A-PHONIC SOUND featuring OOE

OPEN ARMS featuring ROWETTA — UK

SINGLES:	HITS 1			WEEKS 1
HEY MR DJ	*All Around The World*	62	*15 Jun 96*	1

OPM — US

SINGLES:	HITS 1			WEEKS 14
HEAVEN IS A HALFPIPE	*Atlantic*	4	*14 Jul 01*	14
ALBUMS:	**HITS 1**			**WEEKS 8**
MENACE TO SOBRIETY	*Atlantic*	31	*21 Jul 01*	8

OPTIMYSTIC — UK

SINGLES:	HITS 3			WEEKS 6
CAUGHT UP IN MY HEART	*WEA*	49	*17 Sep 94*	3
NOTHING BUT LOVE	*WEA*	37	*10 Dec 94*	2
BEST THING IN THE WORLD	*WEA*	70	*13 May 95*	1

OPUS — Austria

SINGLES:	HITS 1			WEEKS 15
LIVE IS LIFE	*Polydor*	6	*15 Jun 85*	15

OPUS III — UK

SINGLES:	HITS 3			WEEKS 10
IT'S A FINE DAY	*PWL International*	5	*22 Feb 92*	8
Originally recorded by Jane reaching No. 87 in 1985.				
I TALK TO THE WIND	*PWL International*	52	*27 Jun 92*	1
Originally recorded by King Crimson.				
WHEN YOU MADE THE MOUNTAIN	*PWL*	71	*11 Jun 94*	1

ORANGE — UK

SINGLES:	HITS 1			WEEKS 1
JUDY OVER THE RAINBOW	*Chrysalis*	73	*8 Oct 94*	1

ORANGE JUICE — UK

SINGLES:	HITS 9			WEEKS 34
L.O.V.E. . . LOVE	*Polydor*	65	*7 Nov 81*	2
FELICITY	*Polydor*	63	*30 Jan 82*	3
TWO HEARTS TOGETHER / HOKOYO	*Polydor*	60	*21 Aug 82*	2
I CAN'T HELP MYSELF	*Polydor*	42	*23 Oct 82*	3
RIP IT UP	*Polydor*	8	*19 Feb 83*	11
FLESH OF MY FLESH	*Polydor*	41	*4 Jun 83*	6
BRIDGE	*Polydor*	67	*25 Feb 84*	2
WHAT PRESENCE?!	*Polydor*	47	*12 May 84*	4
LEAN PERIOD	*Polydor*	74	*27 Oct 84*	1
ALBUMS:	**HITS 3**			**WEEKS 18**
YOU CAN'T HIDE YOUR LOVE FOREVER	*Polydor*	21	*6 Mar 82*	6
RIP IT UP	*Polydor*	39	*20 Nov 82*	8
TEXAS FEVER	*Polydor*	34	*10 Mar 84*	4
Mini album.				

ORB — UK

SINGLES:	HITS 8			WEEKS 32
PERPETUAL DAWN	*Big Life*	61	*15 Jun 91*	1
BLUE ROOM	*Big Life*	8	*20 Jun 92*	6
ASSASSIN	*Big Life*	12	*17 Oct 92*	5
LITTLE FLUFFY CLOUDS	*Big Life*	10	*13 Nov 93*	5
Original release reached No. 95 in 1991.				
PERPETUAL DAWN [RI]	*Big Life*	18	*5 Feb 94*	5
Though the CD is a re-issue, the cassette and 12" formats have the same catalogue numbers as the original entry.				
OXBOW LAKES	*Island*	38	*27 May 95*	2
TOXYGENE	*Island*	4	*8 Feb 97*	4
ASYLUM	*Island*	20	*24 May 97*	2
ONCE MORE . . .	*Island*	38	*24 Feb 01*	2
Samples Phan Kim's Cung Dan Dat Nuoc.				
ALBUMS:	**HITS 7**			**WEEKS 28**
THE ORB'S ADVENTURES BEYOND THE ULTRAWORLD	*Big Life*	29	*27 Apr 91*	4
THE ORB'S ADVENTURES BEYOND THE ULTRAWORLD / THE ORB'S AUBREY MIXES: THE ULTRAWORD EXCURSIONS [RE]	*Big Life*	44	*14 Dec 91*	1
Aubrey Mixes was a remix album which was deleted after 1 day, sales were combined.				
U.F. ORB	*Big Life*	1	*18 Jul 92*	9
LIVE 93	*Island*	23	*4 Dec 93*	2
Live recordings from Glastonbury, Tokyo and Copenhagen between June and September 1993.				
POMME FRITZ	*Inter-Modo*	6	*25 Jun 94*	4
ORBVS TERRARVM	*Island*	20	*1 Apr 95*	3
OBLIVION	*Island*	19	*8 Mar 97*	3
U.F.OFF - THE BEST OF THE ORB	*Island*	38	*17 Oct 98*	2

Roy ORBISON — US

SINGLES:	HITS 33			WEEKS 345
ONLY THE LONELY (KNOW HOW I FEEL)	*London*	36	*30 Jul 60*	1
Roy originally wrote the song for Elvis Presley.				
ONLY THE LONELY (KNOW HOW I FEEL) [RE]	*London*	1	*13 Aug 60*	23
BLUE ANGEL	*London*	11	*29 Oct 60*	16
RUNNIN' SCARED	*London*	9	*27 May 61*	15
CRYIN'	*London*	25	*23 Sep 61*	9
DREAM BABY	*London*	2	*10 Mar 62*	14
THE CROWD	*London*	40	*30 Jun 62*	4
WORKIN' FOR THE MAN	*London*	50	*10 Nov 62*	1
IN DREAMS	*London*	6	*2 Mar 63*	23
FALLING	*London*	9	*1 Jun 63*	11
BLUE BAYOU / MEAN WOMAN BLUES	*London*	3	*21 Sep 63*	19
Mean Woman Blues originally recorded by Elvis Presley.				
BORNE ON THE WIND	*London*	15	*22 Feb 64*	10
IT'S OVER	*London*	1	*2 May 64*	18
OH, PRETTY WOMAN	*London*	1	*12 Sep 64*	18
PRETTY PAPER	*London*	6	*21 Nov 64*	11
Originally recorded by Willie Nelson.				
GOODNIGHT	*London*	14	*13 Feb 65*	9
(SAY) YOU'RE MY GIRL	*London*	23	*24 Jul 65*	8
RIDE AWAY	*London*	34	*11 Sep 65*	6
CRAWLING BACK	*London*	19	*6 Nov 65*	9
BREAKIN' UP IS BREAKIN' MY HEART	*London*	22	*29 Jan 66*	6
TWINKLE TOES	*London*	29	*9 Apr 66*	5

LANA	*London*	15	*18 Jun 66*	9
Originally recorded by the Velvets.				
TOO SOON TO KNOW	*London*	3	*20 Aug 66*	17
Originally recorded by Don Gibson.				
THERE WON'T BE MANY COMING HOME	*London*	18	*3 Dec 66*	9
SO GOOD	*London*	32	*25 Feb 67*	6
WALK ON	*London*	39	*27 Jul 68*	10
HEARTACHE	*London*	44	*28 Sep 68*	4
MY FRIEND	*London*	35	*3 May 69*	4
PENNY ARCADE	*London*	40	*13 Sep 69*	3
PENNY ARCADE [RE]	*London*	27	*11 Oct 69*	11
YOU GOT IT	*Virgin*	3	*14 Jan 89*	10
SHE'S A MYSTERY TO ME	*Virgin*	27	*1 Apr 89*	5
Written by Bono and the Edge.				
I DROVE ALL NIGHT	*MCA*	7	*4 Jul 92*	10
CRYING [RR]	*Virgin America*	13	*22 Aug 92*	6
Originally the B-side of She's A Mystery To Me.				
Above hit: Roy ORBISON (duet with k.d Lang).				
HEARTBREAK RADIO	*Virgin America*	36	*7 Nov 92*	3
I DROVE ALL NIGHT [RI]	*Virgin*	47	*13 Nov 93*	2

EPS:	**HITS 5**			**WEEKS 101**
ONLY THE LONELY	*London*	15	*1 Jun 63*	11
IN DREAMS	*London*	6	*10 Aug 63*	44
IT'S OVER	*London*	3	*29 Aug 64*	23
OH PRETTY WOMAN	*London*	9	*9 Jan 65*	15
ROY ORBISON'S STAGE SHOW HITS	*London*	10	*27 Mar 65*	8

ALBUMS:	**HITS 21**			**WEEKS 244**
LONELY AND BLUE	*London*	15	*8 Jun 63*	8
CRYING	*London*	17	*29 Jun 63*	3
IN DREAMS	*London*	6	*30 Nov 63*	58
THE EXCITING SOUNDS OF ROY ORBISON	*Ember*	17	*25 Jul 64*	2
Compilation of early Sun recordings.				
OH PRETTY WOMAN	*London*	4	*5 Dec 64*	16
Compilation.				
THERE IS ONLY ONE ROY ORBISON	*London*	10	*25 Sep 65*	12
THE ORBISON WAY	*London*	11	*26 Feb 66*	10
THE CLASSIC ROY ORBISON	*London*	12	*24 Sep 66*	8
ORBISONGS	*Monument*	40	*22 Jul 67*	1
ROY ORBISON'S GREATEST HITS	*Monument*	40	*30 Sep 67*	1
ALL-TIME GREATEST HITS	*Monument*	39	*27 Jan 73*	3
THE BEST OF ROY ORBISON	*Arcade*	1	*29 Nov 75*	20
GOLDEN DAYS	*Monument*	63	*18 Jul 81*	1
IN DREAMS: THE GREATEST HITS	*Virgin*	86	*4 Jul 87*	2
THE LEGENDARY ROY ORBISON	*Telstar*	1	*29 Oct 88*	38
MYSTERY GIRL	*Virgin*	2	*11 Feb 89*	23
A BLACK AND WHITE NIGHT	*Virgin*	51	*25 Nov 89*	3
BALLADS - 22 CLASSIC LOVE SONGS	*Telstar*	38	*3 Nov 90*	10
KING OF HEARTS	*Virgin America*	23	*28 Nov 92*	4
THE VERY BEST OF ROY ORBISON - THE GREATEST HITS	*Virgin*	18	*16 Nov 96*	11
LOVE SONGS	*Virgin*	4	*10 Feb 01*	10

William ORBIT — UK

SINGLES:	**HITS 3**			**WEEKS 18**
WATER FROM A VINE LEAF	*Virgin*	59	*26 Jun 93*	1
BARBER'S ADAGIO FOR STRINGS	*WEA*	4	*18 Dec 99*	13
BARBER'S ADAGIO FOR STRINGS [RE]	*WEA*	69	*25 Mar 00*	2
RAVEL'S PAVANE POUR UNE INFANTE DEFUNTE	*WEA*	31	*6 May 00*	2

ALBUMS:	**HITS 1**			**WEEKS 14**
PIECES IN A MODERN STYLE	*WEA*	2	*29 Jan 00*	14
Originally released in 1995.				

ORBITAL — UK

SINGLES:	**HITS 15**			**WEEKS 53**
CHIME	*ffrr*	17	*24 Mar 90*	7
OMEN	*ffrr*	46	*22 Sep 90*	3
SATAN	*ffrr*	31	*19 Jan 91*	4
MUTATIONS [EP]	*ffrr*	24	*15 Feb 92*	3
Lead track: Chime Chime.				
RADICCIO [EP]	*Internal*	37	*26 Sep 92*	2
Lead track: Halcyon.				
LUSH 3	*Internal*	43	*21 Aug 93*	2
ARE WE HERE?	*Internal*	33	*24 Sep 94*	2
BELFAST/WASTED	*Volume*	53	*27 May 95*	1
[AA] listed with Innocent X by Therapy?				
THE BOX	*Internal*	11	*27 Apr 96*	4
Vocals by writer Grant Fulton.				

SATAN [RR]	*Internal*	3	*11 Jan 97*	6
Released on 3 CD formats. CD1 contained live recording from the Irvine Plaza, New York. CD3 was the studio recording.				
THE SAINT	*ffrr*	3	*19 Apr 97*	7
From the film of the same name. Original theme was written in 1963.				
STYLE	*ffrr*	13	*20 Mar 99*	4
Samples Suzi Quatro's Devil Gate Drive and Dollar's Mirror Mirror.				
NOTHING LEFT	*ffrr*	32	*17 Jul 99*	2
Vocals by Alison Goldfrapp.				
BEACHED	*ffrr*	36	*11 Mar 00*	3
Samples Angelo Badalamenti's The Beach Theme. From the film 'The Beach'.				
Above hit: ORBITAL and Angelo BADALAMENTI.				
FUNNY BREAK (ONE IS ENOUGH)	*ffrr*	21	*28 Apr 01*	3
ALBUMS:	**HITS 8**			**WEEKS 33**
ORBITAL	*ffrr*	71	*12 Oct 91*	1
ORBITAL	*Internal*	28	*5 Jun 93*	2
Above 2 self-titled albums are different.				
PEEL SESSIONS	*Internal*	32	*19 Mar 94*	2
4-track album recorded Sept 93 for John Peel's BBC Radio 1 show.				
SNIVILISATION	*Internal Dance*	4	*20 Aug 94*	4
IN SIDES	*Internal*	5	*11 May 96*	12
SATAN	*Internal*	48	*25 Jan 97*	1
Double-pack 12" single ineligible for the singles chart.				
THE MIDDLE OF NOWHERE	*ffrr*	4	*17 Apr 99*	7
THE ALTOGETHER	*ffrr*	11	*12 May 01*	4

ORCHESTRA e coro DELL'ACCADEMIA NAZIONALE di SANTA CECILIA conducted by Myung-Whun CHUNG – See Andrea BOCELLI

ORCHESTRA ON THE HALF SHELL — US

SINGLES:	**HITS 1**			**WEEKS 6**
TURTLE RHAPSODY	*SBK*	36	*15 Dec 90*	6
From the film 'Teenage Mutant Ninja Turtles'.				

ORCHESTRAL MANOEUVRES IN THE DARK / OMD — UK

SINGLES:	**HITS 30**			**WEEKS 201**
RED FRAME/WHITE LIGHT	*Dindisc*	67	*9 Feb 80*	2
MESSAGES	*Dindisc*	13	*10 May 80*	11
ENOLA GAY	*Dindisc*	8	*4 Oct 80*	15
Enola Gay is the name of the aeroplane that dropped the atomic bomb on Hiroshima.				
SOUVENIR	*Dindisc*	3	*29 Aug 81*	12
JOAN OF ARC	*Dindisc*	5	*24 Oct 81*	14
MAID OF ORLEANS (THE WALTZ JOAN OF ARC)	*Dindisc*	4	*23 Jan 82*	10
GENETIC ENGINEERING	*Virgin*	20	*19 Feb 83*	8
TELEGRAPH	*Virgin*	42	*9 Apr 83*	4
LOCOMOTION	*Virgin*	5	*14 Apr 84*	11
TALKING LOUD AND CLEAR	*Virgin*	11	*16 Jun 84*	10
TESLA GIRLS	*Virgin*	21	*8 Sep 84*	8
NEVER TURN AWAY	*Virgin*	70	*10 Nov 84*	2
SO IN LOVE	*Virgin*	27	*25 May 85*	7
SECRET	*Virgin*	34	*20 Jul 85*	7
LE FEMME ACCIDENT	*Virgin*	42	*26 Oct 85*	4
IF YOU LEAVE	*Virgin*	48	*3 May 86*	4
(FOREVER) LIVE AND DIE	*Virgin*	11	*6 Sep 86*	10
WE LOVE YOU	*Virgin*	54	*15 Nov 86*	5
SHAME	*Virgin*	52	*2 May 87*	3
DREAMING	*Virgin*	50	*6 Feb 88*	3
DREAMING [RE]	*Virgin*	60	*2 Jul 88*	3
SAILING ON THE SEVEN SEAS	*Virgin*	3	*30 Mar 91*	13
PANDORA'S BOX	*Virgin*	7	*6 Jul 91*	10
THEN YOU TURN AWAY	*Virgin*	50	*14 Sep 91*	4
CALL MY NAME	*Virgin*	50	*7 Dec 91*	2
STAND ABOVE ME	*Virgin*	21	*15 May 93*	4
DREAM OF ME (BASED ON LOVE'S THEME)	*Virgin*	24	*17 Jul 93*	5
EVERYDAY	*Virgin*	59	*18 Sep 93*	2
WALKING ON THE MILKY WAY	*Virgin*	17	*17 Aug 96*	5
UNIVERSAL	*Virgin*	55	*2 Nov 96*	1
THE OMD REMIXES [EP]	*Virgin*	35	*26 Sep 98*	2
Lead track: Enola Gay (remixed backing track by Sash! with re-recorded vocals).				
ALBUMS:	**HITS 12**			**WEEKS 226**
ORCHESTRAL MANOEUVRES IN THE DARK	*DinDisc*	27	*1 Mar 80*	29
ORGANISATION	*DinDisc*	6	*1 Nov 80*	25
ARCHITECTURE & MORALITY	*DinDisc*	3	*14 Nov 81*	39
DAZZLE SHIPS	*Virgin*	5	*12 Mar 83*	13
JUNK CULTURE	*Virgin*	9	*12 May 84*	27
CRUSH	*Virgin*	13	*29 Jun 85*	12
THE PACIFIC AGE	*Virgin*	15	*11 Oct 86*	7

THE BEST OF OMD	*Virgin*	2	*12 Mar 88*	33
Includes re-entries in 1991 and 1994.				
SUGAR TAX	*Virgin*	3	*18 May 91*	29
LIBERATOR	*Virgin*	14	*26 Jun 93*	6
UNIVERSAL	*Virgin*	24	*14 Sep 96*	2
THE OMD SINGLES	*Virgin*	16	*10 Oct 98*	4
Includes re-recorded versions and remixes.				

ORCHESTRE DE CHAMBRE Jean-Francois PAILLARD — France

SINGLES:	HITS 1			WEEKS 3
THEME FROM TV'S "VIETNAM" - CANON IN D MAJOR (PACHELBEL)	*Debut*	61	*20 Aug 88*	3

L'ORCHESTRE ELECTRONIQUE — UK

ALBUMS:	HITS 1			WEEKS 1
SOUND WAVES	*Nouveau Music*	75	*29 Oct 83*	1

ORCHESTRE NATIONAL DE LA RADIO DIFFUSION FRANCAISE, conducted by Sir Thomas BEECHAM — France/UK

ALBUMS:	HITS 1			WEEKS 2
CARMEN	*His Master's Voice*	18	*26 Mar 60*	2

Raul ORELLANA — Italy

SINGLES:	HITS 1			WEEKS 8
THE REAL WILD HOUSE	*BCM*	29	*30 Sep 89*	8

ORIGIN — UK

SINGLES:	HITS 1			WEEKS 1
WIDE-EYED ANGEL	*Lost Language*	73	*12 Aug 00*	1

ORIGIN UNKNOWN — UK

SINGLES:	HITS 1			WEEKS 1
VALLEY OF THE SHADOWS	*Ram*	60	*13 Jul 96*	1

ORIGINAL — US

SINGLES:	HITS 2			WEEKS 14
I LUV U BABY	*Ore*	31	*14 Jan 95*	3
I LUV U BABY [RM]	*Ore*	2	*19 Aug 95*	9
Remixed by Dancing Divaz. Extra vocals by Everett Bradley.				
B 2 GETHER	*Ore*	29	*11 Nov 95*	2

ORIGINAL MOTION PICTURE SOUNDTRACK — US

SINGLES:	HITS 1			WEEKS 4
MIDNIGHT COWBOY	*United Artists*	47	*8 Nov 80*	4
From the film of the same name.				

ORIGINAL ODC. MC. – See TZANT

ORIGINOO GUNN CLAPPAZ – See HELTAH SKELTER and ORIGINOO GUNN CLAPPAZ as the FABULOUS FIVE

ORION — UK

SINGLES:	HITS 1			WEEKS 2
ETERNITY	*Incentive*	38	*7 Oct 00*	2

ORLANDO – See VARIOUS ARTISTS (EPs) 'Fever Pitch The EP'

Tony ORLANDO — US

(See also Dawn.)

SINGLES:	HITS 1			WEEKS 11
BLESS YOU	*Fontana*	5	*7 Oct 61*	11

ORLONS — US

SINGLES:	HITS 1			WEEKS 3
DON'T HANG UP	*Cameo-Parkway*	50	*29 Dec 62*	1
DON'T HANG UP [RE]	*Cameo-Parkway*	39	*12 Jan 63*	2

Cyril ORNADEL – See LONDON SYMPHONY ORCHESTRA

Beth ORTON — UK

SINGLES:	HITS 6			WEEKS 11
TOUCH ME WITH YOUR LOVE	*Heavenly*	60	*1 Feb 97*	1
SOMEONE'S DAUGHTER	*Heavenly*	49	*5 Apr 97*	1
SHE CRIES YOUR NAME	*Heavenly*	40	*14 Jun 97*	2
Original release reached No. 96 in 1996.				

BEST BIT [EP]	*Heavenly*	36	*13 Dec 97*	3
Lead track: Best Bit. Though credited on the chart, Terry Callier only featured on 2 of the EP's tracks.				
Above hit: Beth ORTON featuring Terry CALLIER.				
STOLEN CAR	*Heavenly*	34	*13 Mar 99*	2
CENTRAL RESERVATION	*Heavenly*	37	*25 Sep 99*	8
ALBUMS:	**HITS 2**			**WEEKS 11**
TRAILER PARK	*Heavenly*	68	*26 Oct 96*	3
CENTRAL RESERVATION	*Heavenly*	17	*27 Mar 99*	8

ORVILLE – See Keith HARRIS and ORVILLE

Jeffrey OSBORNE — US

SINGLES:	**HITS 6**			**WEEKS 38**
DON'T YOU GET SO MAD	*A&M*	54	*17 Sep 83*	2
STAY WITH ME TONIGHT	*A&M*	18	*14 Apr 84*	11
Features Queen's Brian May on guitar.				
ON THE WINGS OF LOVE	*A&M*	11	*23 Jun 84*	14
DON'T STOP	*A&M*	61	*20 Oct 84*	2
SOWETO	*A&M*	44	*26 Jul 86*	5
SOWETO [RE]	*A&M*	75	*6 Sep 86*	1
LOVE POWER	*Arista*	63	*15 Aug 87*	3
Above hit: Dionne WARWICK and Jeffrey OSBORNE.				
ALBUMS:	**HITS 2**			**WEEKS 10**
STAY WITH ME TONIGHT	*A&M*	56	*5 May 84*	7
DON'T STOP	*A&M*	59	*13 Oct 84*	3

Joan OSBORNE — US

SINGLES:	**HITS 2**			**WEEKS 13**
ONE OF US	*Blue Gorilla*	6	*10 Feb 96*	10
ST TERESA	*Blue Gorilla*	33	*8 Jun 96*	3
ALBUMS:	**HITS 1**			**WEEKS 18**
RELISH	*Blue Gorilla*	5	*9 Mar 96*	18

Tony OSBORNE SOUND featuring Joanne BROWN — UK

(See also Petula Clark; Russ Conway; Gracie Fields; Edmund Hockridge; Gary Miller; Dorothy Squires; Jimmy Young.)

SINGLES:	**HITS 2**			**WEEKS 3**
THE MAN FROM MADRID	*His Master's Voice*	50	*25 Feb 61*	1
THE SHEPHERD'S SONG	*Philips*	46	*3 Feb 73*	2
Not all copies pressed credit Joanne Brown.				

Ozzy OSBOURNE — UK

SINGLES:	**HITS 11**			**WEEKS 42**
CRAZY TRAIN	*Jet*	49	*13 Sep 80*	4
MR. CROWLEY	*Jet*	46	*15 Nov 80*	3
Above 2: Ozzy OSBOURNE BLIZZARD OF OZ.				
BARK AT THE MOON	*Epic*	21	*26 Nov 83*	8
SO TIRED	*Epic*	20	*2 Jun 84*	9
SHOT IN THE DARK	*Epic*	20	*1 Feb 86*	6
THE ULTIMATE SIN / LIGHTNING STRIKES	*Epic*	72	*9 Aug 86*	1
CLOSE MY EYES FOREVER	*Dreamland*	47	*20 May 89*	3
Above hit: Lita FORD (Duet with Ozzy OSBOURNE).				
NO MORE TEARS	*Epic*	32	*28 Sep 91*	3
MAMA I'M COMING HOME	*Epic*	46	*30 Nov 91*	2
PERRY MASON	*Epic*	23	*25 Nov 95*	2
I JUST WANT YOU	*Epic*	43	*31 Aug 96*	1
Features Michael Borden of Faith No More on drums.				
ALBUMS:	**HITS 12**			**WEEKS 64**
OZZY OSBOURNE'S BLIZZARD OF OZ	*Jet*	7	*20 Sep 80*	8
Above hit: Ozzy OSBOURNE'S BLIZZARD OF OZ.				
DIARY OF A MADMAN	*Jet*	14	*7 Nov 81*	12
Also the title of his autobiography.				
TALK OF THE DEVIL	*Jet*	21	*27 Nov 82*	6
BARK AT THE MOON	*Epic*	24	*10 Dec 83*	7
THE ULTIMATE SIN	*Epic*	8	*22 Feb 86*	10
TRIBUTE	*Epic*	13	*23 May 87*	6
Live recordings from 1981. A tribute to guitarist Randy Rhoads who performs on the album.				
NO REST FOR THE WICKED	*Epic*	23	*22 Oct 88*	4
JUST SAY OZZY (LIVE)	*Epic*	69	*17 Mar 90*	1
NO MORE TEARS	*Epic*	17	*19 Oct 91*	3
OZZMOSIS	*Epic*	22	*4 Nov 95*	3
THE OZZMAN COMETH – THE BEST OF OZZY OSBOURNE	*Epic*	68	*15 Nov 97*	1
DOWN TO EARTH	*Epic*	19	*27 Oct 01*	3

OSIBISA

Ghana/Nigeria

SINGLES:	HITS 2			WEEKS 12
SUNSHINE DAY	*Bronze*	17	*17 Jan 76*	6
DANCE THE BODY MUSIC	*Bronze*	31	*5 Jun 76*	6
ALBUMS:	**HITS 2**			**WEEKS 17**
OSIBISA	*MCA*	11	*22 May 71*	10
WOYAYA	*MCA*	11	*5 Feb 72*	7

Donny OSMOND

US

(See also Donny and Marie Osmond; Osmonds.)

SINGLES:	HITS 11			WEEKS 118
PUPPY LOVE	*MGM*	1	*17 Jun 72*	17
TOO YOUNG	*MGM*	5	*16 Sep 72*	12
Originally recorded by Nat King Cole in 1951.				
PUPPY LOVE [RE-1ST]	*MGM*	45	*21 Oct 72*	2
WHY	*MGM*	3	*11 Nov 72*	20
PUPPY LOVE [RE-2ND]	*MGM*	46	*23 Dec 72*	3
TOO YOUNG [RE]	*MGM*	47	*23 Dec 72*	3
PUPPY LOVE [RE-3RD]	*MGM*	48	*27 Jan 73*	1
THE TWELFTH OF NEVER	*MGM*	1	*10 Mar 73*	14
YOUNG LOVE	*MGM*	1	*18 Aug 73*	10
WHEN I FALL IN LOVE	*MGM*	4	*10 Nov 73*	13
WHERE DID ALL THE GOOD TIMES GO	*MGM*	18	*9 Nov 74*	10
I'M IN IT FOR LOVE	*Virgin*	70	*26 Sep 87*	1
SOLDIER OF LOVE	*Virgin*	29	*6 Aug 88*	8
IF IT'S LOVE THAT YOU WANT	*Virgin*	70	*12 Nov 88*	2
MY LOVE IS A FIRE	*Capitol*	64	*9 Feb 91*	2
ALBUMS:	**HITS 7**			**WEEKS 107**
PORTRAIT OF DONNY	*MGM*	5	*23 Sep 72*	43
TOO YOUNG	*MGM*	7	*16 Dec 72*	24
ALONE TOGETHER	*MGM*	6	*26 May 73*	19
A TIME FOR US	*MGM*	4	*15 Dec 73*	13
DONNY	*MGM*	16	*8 Feb 75*	4
DISCOTRAIN	*Polydor*	59	*2 Oct 76*	1
THIS IS THE MOMENT	*Decca*	10	*21 Apr 01*	3

Donny and Marie OSMOND

US

(See also Donny Osmond; Marie Osmond; Osmonds.)

SINGLES:	HITS 4			WEEKS 37
I'M LEAVING IT (ALL) UP TO YOU	*MGM*	2	*3 Aug 74*	12
Originally recorded by Don & Dewey in 1957.				
MORNING SIDE OF THE MOUNTAIN	*MGM*	5	*14 Dec 74*	12
Originally recorded by Tommy Edwards.				
MAKE THE WORLD GO AWAY	*MGM*	18	*21 Jun 75*	6
Originally recorded by Ray Price.				
DEEP PURPLE	*MGM*	25	*17 Jan 76*	7
Originally recorded by the Larry Clinton Orchestra in 1939.				
ALBUMS:	**HITS 3**			**WEEKS 19**
I'M LEAVING IT ALL UP TO YOU	*MGM*	13	*2 Nov 74*	15
MAKE THE WORLD GO AWAY	*MGM*	30	*26 Jul 75*	3
DEEP PURPLE	*Polydor*	48	*5 Jun 76*	1

Little Jimmy OSMOND

US

SINGLES:	HITS 3			WEEKS 50
LONG HAIRED LOVER FROM LIVERPOOL	*MGM*	1	*25 Nov 72*	24
Originally recorded by the Mike Curb Congregation.				
Above hit: Little Jimmy OSMOND with the Mike CURB CONGREGATION.				
TWEEDLEE DEE	*MGM*	4	*31 Mar 73*	13
Originally recorded by Laverne Baker in 1955.				
LONG HAIRED LOVER FROM LIVERPOOL [RE]	*MGM*	41	*19 May 73*	3
I'M GONNA KNOCK ON YOUR DOOR	*MGM*	11	*23 Mar 74*	10
Originally recorded by the Isley Brothers.				
Above hit: Jimmy OSMOND.				
ALBUMS:	**HITS 1**			**WEEKS 12**
KILLER JOE	*MGM*	20	*17 Feb 73*	12

Marie OSMOND

US

(See also Donny and Marie Osmond.)

SINGLES:	HITS 1			WEEKS 15
PAPER ROSES	*MGM*	2	*17 Nov 73*	15
Originally recorded by Lola Dee.				

ALBUMS:	HITS 1			WEEKS 1
PAPER ROSES	*MGM*	46	*9 Feb 74*	1

OSMOND BOYS
US

SINGLES:	HITS 2			WEEKS 6
BOYS WILL BE BOYS	*Curb*	65	*9 Nov 91*	2
SHOW ME THE WAY	*Curb*	60	*11 Jan 92*	4

OSMONDS
US

SINGLES:	HITS 10			WEEKS 94
DOWN BY THE LAZY RIVER	*MGM*	40	*25 Mar 72*	5
CRAZY HORSES	*MGM*	2	*11 Nov 72*	18
GOIN' HOME	*MGM*	4	*14 Jul 73*	10
LET ME IN	*MGM*	2	*27 Oct 73*	14
I CAN'T STOP	*MCA*	12	*20 Apr 74*	10
LOVE ME FOR A REASON	*MGM*	1	*24 Aug 74*	9
Originally recorded by Johnny Bristol.				
HAVING A PARTY	*MGM*	28	*1 Mar 75*	8
Originally recorded by H.B.Barnum.				
THE PROUD ONE	*MGM*	5	*24 May 75*	8
Originally recorded by the Four Seasons.				
I'M STILL GONNA NEED YOU	*MGM*	32	*15 Nov 75*	4
I CAN'T LIVE A DREAM	*Polydor*	37	*30 Oct 76*	5
CRAZY HORSES [RM]	*Polydor*	50	*23 Sep 95*	1
Remixed by the Utah Saints.				
CRAZY HORSES [RI]	*Polydor*	34	*12 Jun 99*	2
Featured in the Virgin Atlantic TV commercial.				

ALBUMS:	HITS 8			WEEKS 108
OSMONDS LIVE	*MGM*	13	*18 Nov 72*	22
CRAZY HORSES	*MGM*	9	*16 Dec 72*	19
THE PLAN	*MGM*	6	*25 Aug 73*	25
OUR BEST TO YOU	*MGM*	5	*17 Aug 74*	20
LOVE ME FOR A REASON	*MGM*	13	*7 Dec 74*	9
I'M STILL GONNA NEED YOU	*MGM*	19	*14 Jun 75*	7
AROUND THE WORLD - LIVE IN CONCERT	*MGM*	41	*10 Jan 76*	1
THE VERY BEST OF THE OSMONDS	*Polydor*	17	*20 Apr 96*	5
Includes solo hits from Donny, Marie, Donny and Marie and Jimmy.				

Glenn OSSER and his Orchestra - See Georgia GIBBS

Gilbert O'SULLIVAN
Ireland

SINGLES:	HITS 16			WEEKS 145
NOTHING RHYMED	*MAM*	8	*28 Nov 70*	11
UNDERNEATH THE BLANKET GO	*MAM*	40	*3 Apr 71*	1
UNDERNEATH THE BLANKET GO [RE]	*MAM*	42	*17 Apr 71*	3
WE WILL	*MAM*	16	*24 Jul 71*	11
NO MATTER HOW I TRY	*MAM*	5	*27 Nov 71*	15
ALONE AGAIN (NATURALLY)	*MAM*	3	*4 Mar 72*	12
OOH-WAKKA-DOO-WAKKA-DAY	*MAM*	8	*17 Jun 72*	11
CLAIR	*MAM*	1	*21 Oct 72*	14
GET DOWN	*MAM*	1	*17 Mar 73*	13
OOH BABY	*MAM*	18	*15 Sep 73*	7
WHY, OH WHY, OH WHY	*MAM*	6	*10 Nov 73*	14
HAPPINESS IS ME AND YOU	*MAM*	19	*9 Feb 74*	7
A WOMAN'S PLACE	*MAM*	42	*24 Aug 74*	3
CHRISTMAS SONG	*MAM*	12	*14 Dec 74*	6
I DON'T LOVE YOU BUT I THINK I LIKE YOU	*MAM*	14	*14 Jun 75*	6
WHAT'S IN A KISS	*CBS*	19	*27 Sep 80*	9
SO WHAT	*Dover*	70	*24 Feb 90*	2

ALBUMS:	HITS 7			WEEKS 195
GILBERT O'SULLIVAN HIMSELF	*MAM*	5	*25 Sep 71*	82
BACK TO FRONT	*MAM*	1	*18 Nov 72*	64
I'M A WRITER NOT A FIGHTER	*MAM*	2	*6 Oct 73*	25
STRANGER IN MY OWN BACK YARD	*MAM*	9	*26 Oct 74*	8
GREATEST HITS	*MAM*	13	*18 Dec 76*	11
20 GOLDEN GREATS	*K-Tel*	98	*12 Sep 81*	1
NOTHING BUT THE BEST	*Castle Communication*	50	*11 May 91*	4

OTHER TWO
UK

SINGLES:	HITS 2			WEEKS 5
TASTY FISH	*Factory*	41	*9 Nov 91*	3
SELFISH	*London*	46	*6 Nov 93*	2

Johnny OTIS SHOW with Marie ADAMS — US

SINGLES:	HITS 2			WEEKS 22
MA (HE'S MAKIN' EYES AT ME)	*Capitol*	2	*23 Nov 57*	15
Originally recorded by Eddie Cantor in 1921.				
Above hit: Johnny OTIS SHOW; Johnny OTIS and his Orchestra with Marie ADAMS and the THREE TONS OF JOY.				
BYE BYE BABY	*Capitol*	20	*11 Jan 58*	7
Above hit: Johnny OTIS SHOW, vocals by Marie ADAMS and Johnny OTIS.				

OTT — Ireland

SINGLES:	HITS 4			WEEKS 18
LET ME IN	*Epic*	12	*15 Feb 97*	5
FOREVER GIRL	*Epic*	24	*17 May 97*	3
ALL OUT OF LOVE	*Epic*	11	*23 Aug 97*	4
THE STORY OF LOVE	*Epic*	11	*24 Jan 98*	6

OTTAWAN — France

SINGLES:	HITS 4			WEEKS 45
D.I.S.C.O.	*Carrere*	2	*13 Sep 80*	18
YOU'RE O.K.	*Carrere*	56	*13 Dec 80*	6
HANDS UP (GIVE ME YOUR HEART)	*Carrere*	3	*29 Aug 81*	15
HELP, GET ME SOME HELP!	*Carrere*	49	*5 Dec 81*	6
Originally recorded by Tony Ronald in 1971.				

John OTWAY and Wild Willy BARRETT — UK

SINGLES:	HITS 2			WEEKS 12
REALLY FREE	*Polydor*	27	*3 Dec 77*	8
DK 50-80	*Polydor*	45	*5 Jul 80*	4
Above hit: OTWAY and BARRETT.				
ALBUMS:	**HITS 1**			**WEEKS 1**
DEEP AND MEANINGLESS	*Polydor*	44	*1 Jul 78*	1

OUI 3 — US/UK/Switzerland

SINGLES:	HITS 6			WEEKS 21
FOR WHAT IT'S WORTH	*MCA*	28	*20 Feb 93*	6
Originally recorded by Buffalo Springfield reaching No. 7 in the US in 1967.				
ARMS OF SOLITUDE	*MCA*	54	*24 Apr 93*	2
BREAK FROM THE OLD ROUTINE	*MCA*	17	*17 Jul 93*	6
FOR WHAT IT'S WORTH [RM]	*MCA*	26	*23 Oct 93*	3
Remixed by Soulshock and Karlin.				
FACTS OF LIFE	*MCA*	38	*29 Jan 94*	2
THE JOY OF LIVING	*MCA*	55	*27 May 95*	2
ALBUMS:	**HITS 1**			**WEEKS 3**
OUI LOVE YOU	*MCA*	39	*7 Aug 93*	3

OUR DAUGHTER'S WEDDING — US

SINGLES:	HITS 1			WEEKS 6
LAWNCHAIRS	*EMI America*	49	*1 Aug 81*	6

OUR HOUSE — Australia

SINGLES:	HITS 1			WEEKS 1
FLOOR SPACE	*Perfecto*	52	*31 Aug 96*	1

OUR KID — UK

SINGLES:	HITS 1			WEEKS 11
YOU JUST MIGHT SEE ME CRY	*Polydor*	2	*29 May 76*	11

OUR LADY PEACE — Canada

SINGLES:	HITS 1			WEEKS 1
ONE MAN ARMY	*Epic*	70	*15 Jan 00*	1
Samples Terminalhead's Underfire.				

OUR TRIBE/ONE TRIBE/O.T. QUARTET — UK/US

SINGLES:	HITS 5			WEEKS 13
WHAT HAVE YOU DONE (IS THIS ALL)	*Inner Rhythm*	52	*20 Jun 92*	2
Above hit: ONE TRIBE featuring GEM.				
I BELIEVE IN YOU	*Ffreedom*	42	*27 Mar 93*	2
Above hit: OUR TRIBE.				
HOLD THAT SUCKER DOWN	*Cheeky*	24	*30 Apr 94*	3
Above hit: O.T. QUARTET.				
LOVE COME HOME	*Triangle*	73	*21 May 94*	1
Above hit: OUR TRIBE with Franke PHAROAH and Kristine W.				

HIGH AS A KITE *Above hit: ONE TRIBE featuring ROGER.*	*ffrr*	55	*13 May 95*	1
HOLD THAT SUCKER DOWN [RI-1ST] *Above hit: O.T. QUARTET.*	*Cheeky*	26	*30 Sep 95*	3
HOLD THAT SUCKER DOWN [RI-2ND] *Above hit: O.T. QUARTET.*	*Champion*	45	*9 Dec 00*	1

OUT OF MY HAIR — UK

SINGLES:	HITS 1			WEEKS 1
MISTER JONES	*RCA*	73	*1 Jul 95*	1

OUTHERE BROTHERS — US

SINGLES:	HITS 5			WEEKS 50
DON'T STOP (WIGGLE WIGGLE)	*Eternal*	1	*18 Mar 95*	15
BOOM BOOM BOOM	*Eternal*	1	*17 Jun 95*	15
LA LA LA HEY HEY	*Eternal*	7	*23 Sep 95*	7
IF YOU WANNA PARTY *Above hit: MOLELLA featuring the OUTHERE BROTHERS.*	*Eternal*	9	*16 Dec 95*	10
LET ME HEAR YOU SAY "OLE OLE"	*Eternal*	18	*25 Jan 97*	3
ALBUMS:	**HITS 2**			**WEEKS 9**
1 POLISH 2 BISCUITS AND A FISH SANDWICH	*Eternal*	56	*27 May 95*	5
PARTY ALBUM *Alternate version of their first album, without the offensive language.*	*Eternal*	41	*30 Dec 95*	4

OUTKAST — US

SINGLES:	HITS 3			WEEKS 23
B.O.B (BOMBS OVER BAGHDAD)	*LaFace*	61	*23 Dec 00*	1
MS. JACKSON *Import.*	*LaFace*	48	*3 Feb 01*	4
MS. JACKSON	*LaFace*	2	*3 Mar 01*	10
SO FRESH, SO CLEAN	*LaFace*	16	*9 Jun 01*	8
ALBUMS:	**HITS 1**			**WEEKS 13**
STANKONIA	*LaFace*	10	*20 Jan 01*	13

OUTLANDER — Belgium

SINGLES:	HITS 1			WEEKS 3
VAMP	*R&S*	51	*31 Aug 91*	2
THE VAMP (REVAMPED) [RI] *Despite the 'revamped' credit, CD1 track 1 is a straight re-issue.*	*R&S*	62	*7 Feb 98*	1

OUTLAWS — UK

(See also Mike Berry.)

SINGLES:	HITS 2			WEEKS 4
SWINGIN' LOW	*His Master's Voice*	46	*15 Apr 61*	2
AMBUSH	*His Master's Voice*	43	*10 Jun 61*	2

OUTLAWZ - See 2PAC

OUTRAGE — US

SINGLES:	HITS 1			WEEKS 2
TALL 'N' HANDSOME	*Effective*	57	*11 Mar 95*	1
TALL N HANDSOME [RM] *Remixed by Nush.*	*Positiva*	51	*23 Nov 96*	1

OVERLANDERS — UK

SINGLES:	HITS 1			WEEKS 10
MICHELLE	*Pye*	1	*15 Jan 66*	10

OVERLORD X — UK

ALBUMS:	HITS 1			WEEKS 1
WEAPON IS MY LYRIC	*Mango Street*	68	*4 Feb 89*	1

OVERWEIGHT POOCH featuring Ce Ce PENISTON — US

(See also Ce Ce Peniston.)

SINGLES:	HITS 1			WEEKS 2
I LIKE IT	*A&M*	58	*18 Jan 92*	2

Mark OWEN — UK

SINGLES:	HITS 3			WEEKS 24
CHILD	*RCA*	3	*30 Nov 96*	11

CLEMENTINE	*RCA*	3	*15 Feb 97*	6
CHILD [RE]	*RCA*	45	*22 Feb 97*	4
I AM WHAT I AM	*RCA*	29	*23 Aug 97*	3
ALBUMS:	**HITS 1**			**WEEKS 11**
GREEN MAN	*RCA*	33	*14 Dec 96*	11

Reg OWEN and his Orchestra — UK

SINGLES:	**HITS 2**			**WEEKS 10**
MANHATTAN SPIRITUAL	*Pye International*	20	*28 Feb 59*	8
OBSESSION	*Palette*	43	*29 Oct 60*	2

Sid OWEN — UK

SINGLES:	**HITS 2**			**WEEKS 6**
BETTER BELIEVE IT (CHILDREN IN NEED)	*Trinity*	60	*16 Dec 95*	1
Charity record with proceeds to BBC TV's Children In Need appeal.				
Above hit: Sid OWEN and Patsy PALMER				
GOOD THING GOING	*Mushroom*	14	*8 Jul 00*	5
Originally recorded by Michael Jackson.				
Above hit: Sid OWEN (rap performed by CHUCKLE STAR).				

Robert OWENS — US

(See also Frankie Knuckles.)

SINGLES:	**HITS 2**			**WEEKS 5**
I'LL BE YOUR FRIEND	*Perfecto*	75	*7 Dec 91*	2
I'LL BE YOUR FRIEND [RM]	*Perfecto*	25	*26 Apr 97*	2
Remixed by David Morales.				
MINE TO GIVE	*Science*	44	*24 Feb 01*	1
Above hit: PHOTEK – vocals: Robert OWENS.				

OXIDE and NEUTRONO — UK

SINGLES:	**HITS 5**			**WEEKS 35**
BOUND 4 DA RELOAD (CASUALTY)	*East West*	1	*6 May 00*	11
Based around the theme from the BBC1 TV series 'Casualty'.				
NO GOOD 4 ME	*East West*	6	*30 Dec 00*	8
Samples the Prodigy's No Good (Start The Dance).				
Above hit: OXIDE and NEUTRINO featuring MEGAMAN, ROMEO and Lisa MAFFIA.				
UP MIDDLE FINGER	*East West*	7	*26 May 01*	7
DEVIL'S NIGHTMARE	*East West*	16	*28 Jul 01*	5
RAP DIS (U CAN'T STOP DIS)/ONLY WANNA KNOW U COS URE FAMOUS	*East West*	12	*8 Dec 01*	4
OXIDE and NEUTRINO featuring SWISS, SKAT D, KAISH and HARVEY.				
ALBUMS:	**HITS 2**			**WEEKS 18**
BOUND 4 DA RELOAD (CASUALTY)	*East West*	71	*6 May 00*	1
Double-pack 12 single featuring various mixes of Bound 4 Da Reload.				
EXECUTE	*East West*	11	*9 Jun 01*	17

OZOMATLI — US

SINGLES:	**HITS 2**			**WEEKS 2**
CUT CHEMIST SUITE	*Almo Sounds*	58	*20 Mar 99*	1
Samples Jurassic 5's Unified Rebelution.				
SUPER BOWL SUNDAE	*Almo Sounds*	68	*22 May 99*	1

OZRIC TENTACLES — UK

ALBUMS:	**HITS 3**			**WEEKS 7**
STRANGEITUDE	*Dovetail*	70	*31 Aug 91*	1
JURASSIC SHIFT	*Dovetail*	11	*1 May 93*	4
ARBORESCENCE	*Dovetail*	18	*9 Jul 94*	2

P

Jazzi P — UK

(See also DNA.)

SINGLES:	**HITS 3**			**WEEKS 12**
GET LOOSE	*Breakout*	25	*8 Jul 89*	6
Above hit: L.A. MIX featuring Jazzi P.				
FEEL THE RHYTHM	*A&M USA*	51	*9 Jun 90*	2
REBEL WOMAN	*DNA*	42	*3 Aug 91*	4
Samples David Bowie's Rebel Rebel.				
Above hit: DNA rap performed by Jazzi P.				

P DIDDY – See PUFF DADDY

P.H.D — UK

SINGLES:	HITS 1			WEEKS 14
I WON'T LET YOU DOWN	*WEA*	3	*3 Apr 82*	14
ALBUMS:	**HITS 1**			**WEEKS 8**
PH.D	*WEA*	33	*1 May 82*	8

P.I.L. - See PUBLIC IMAGE LTD.

P.J. - See PJ

P.J.B. featuring HANNAH and her SISTERS — US

(See also Hannah Jones.)

SINGLES:	HITS 1			WEEKS 8
BRIDGE OVER TROUBLED WATER	*Dance Pool*	21	*14 Sep 91*	8

P.O.V. duet with JADE — US

(See also Jade.)

SINGLES:	HITS 1			WEEKS 3
ALL THRU THE NITE	*Giant*	32	*5 Feb 94*	3

Thom PACE — US

SINGLES:	HITS 1			WEEKS 15
MAYBE *Theme from the film 'The Life And Times Of Grizzly Adams'.*	*RSO*	14	*19 May 79*	15

PACIFICA — UK

SINGLES:	HITS 1			WEEKS 1
LOST IN THE TRANSLATION (HEART OF GLASS) *Samples Blondie's Heart Of Glass.*	*Wildstar*	54	*31 Jul 99*	1

PACK featuring Nigel BENN — UK

SINGLES:	HITS 1			WEEKS 2
STAND AND FIGHT	*IQ*	61	*8 Dec 90*	2

PACKABEATS — UK

SINGLES:	HITS 1			WEEKS 1
GYPSY BEAT	*Parlophone*	49	*25 Feb 61*	1

Jose PADILLA featuring Angela JOHN — Spain

SINGLES:	HITS 1			WEEKS 1
WHO DO YOU LOVE	*Manifesto*	59	*8 Aug 98*	1

PAGANINI TRAXX — Italy

SINGLES:	HITS 1			WEEKS 1
ZOE	*Sony*	47	*1 Feb 97*	1

Jimmy PAGE — UK

(See also Jimmy Page and Robert Plant.)

SINGLES:	HITS 1			WEEKS 11
COME WITH ME *US Import. Based on guitar riff from Led Zeppelin's 'Kashmir' from 1975. From the film 'Godzilla'.*	*Epic*	75	*1 Aug 98*	1
COME WITH ME *Above 2: PUFF DADDY featuring Jimmy PAGE.*	*Epic*	2	*8 Aug 98*	10
ALBUMS:	**HITS 3**			**WEEKS 14**
DEATHWISH II [OST]	*Swan Song*	40	*27 Feb 82*	4
WHATEVER HAPPENED TO JUGULA? *Above hit: Roy HARPER with Jimmy PAGE.*	*Beggars Banquet*	44	*16 Mar 85*	4
OUTRIDER	*Geffen*	27	*2 Jul 88*	6

Jimmy PAGE and the BLACK CROWeS — UK

(See also Black Crowes; Jimmy Page.)

ALBUMS:	HITS 1			WEEKS 4
LIVE AT THE GREEK *Live recordings from The Greek Theater, Los Angeles in 1999.*	*SPV Recordings*	39	*22 Jul 00*	4

Jimmy PAGE and Robert PLANT — UK

(See also Jimmy Page; Robert Plant.)

SINGLES:	HITS 2			WEEKS 5
GALLOWS POLE *This version recorded for their MTV Unledded performance.*	*Fontana*	35	*17 Dec 94*	3

MOST HIGH	*Mercury*	26	*11 Apr 98*	2
ALBUMS:	**HITS 2**			**WEEKS 19**
NO QUARTER - JIMMY PAGE AND ROBERT PLANT UNLEDDED *Live recordings for MTV.*	*Fontana*	7	*19 Nov 94*	13
WALKING INTO CLARKSDALE *Title inspired by Plant's 1988 visit around the Mississippi Delta in search of Robert Johnson contacts.*	*Mercury*	3	*2 May 98*	6

Patti PAGE — US

SINGLES:	**HITS 1**			**WEEKS 5**
(HOW MUCH IS) THAT DOGGIE IN THE WINDOW	*Oriole*	9	*28 Mar 53*	5

Tommy PAGE — US

SINGLES:	**HITS 1**			**WEEKS 3**
I'LL BE YOUR EVERYTHING *Backing vocals by New Kids On The Block*	*Sire*	53	*26 May 90*	3

Wendy PAGE - See TIN TIN OUT

PAGLIARO — Canada

SINGLES:	**HITS 1**			**WEEKS 6**
LOVIN' YOU AIN'T EASY	*Pye*	31	*19 Feb 72*	6

PAID and LIVE featuring Lauryn HILL — US

(See also Lauryn Hill.)

SINGLES:	**HITS 1**			**WEEKS 1**
ALL MY TIME	*One World Entertainment*	57	*27 Dec 97*	1

Elaine PAIGE — UK

SINGLES:	**HITS 7**			**WEEKS 41**
DON'T WALK AWAY TILL I TOUCH YOU	*EMI*	46	*21 Oct 78*	5
MEMORY *From the Andrew Lloyd Webber musical 'Cats'.*	*Polydor*	6	*6 Jun 81*	12
MEMORY [RE]	*Polydor*	67	*30 Jan 82*	3
SOMETIMES (THEME FROM 'CHAMPIONS')	*Island*	72	*14 Apr 84*	1
I KNOW HIM SO WELL *From the musical 'Chess'.* *Above hit: Elaine PAIGE and Barbara DICKSON.*	*RCA*	1	*5 Jan 85*	16
THE SECOND TIME (THEME FROM "BILITIS")	*WEA*	69	*21 Nov 87*	1
HYMNE A L'AMOUR (IF YOU LOVE ME)	*WEA*	68	*21 Jan 95*	1
MEMORY [RR] *Taken from the Soundtrack of 'Cats - The Video'. Re-recorded with a 70-piece orchestra.*	*WEA*	36	*24 Oct 98*	2
ALBUMS:	**HITS 13**			**WEEKS 155**
ELAINE PAIGE	*WEA*	56	*1 May 82*	6
STAGES	*K-Tel*	2	*5 Nov 83*	48
CINEMA	*K-Tel*	12	*20 Oct 84*	25
LOVE HURTS	*WEA*	8	*16 Nov 85*	20
CHRISTMAS	*WEA*	27	*29 Nov 86*	6
MEMORIES - THE BEST OF ELAINE PAIGE	*Telstar*	14	*5 Dec 87*	15
THE QUEEN ALBUM *Songs written by Queen.*	*Siren*	51	*19 Nov 88*	8
LOVE CAN DO THAT	*RCA*	36	*27 Apr 91*	4
THE BEST OF ELAINE PAIGE AND BARBARA DICKSON *Features their duet as well as solo recordings.* *Above hit: Elaine PAIGE and Barbara DICKSON.*	*Telstar*	22	*28 Nov 92*	9
ROMANCE AND THE STAGE	*RCA*	71	*10 Apr 93*	1
PIAF *Songs from the show 'Piaf' who Paige portrayed on stage during 1993/94.*	*WEA*	46	*19 Nov 94*	3
ENCORE	*WEA*	20	*1 Jul 95*	6
ON REFLECTION - THE VERY BEST OF ELAINE PAIGE	*Telstar TV/WEA*	60	*28 Nov 98*	4

Hal PAIGE and the WHALERS — US

SINGLES:	**HITS 1**			**WEEKS 1**
GOING BACK TO MY HOME TOWN	*Melodisc*	50	*27 Aug 60*	1

Jennifer PAIGE — US

SINGLES:	**HITS 2**			**WEEKS 13**
CRUSH	*E.A.R.*	4	*12 Sep 98*	12
SOBER	*E.A.R.*	68	*20 Mar 99*	1
ALBUMS:	**HITS 1**			**WEEKS 1**
JENNIFER PAIGE	*E.A.R.*	67	*31 Oct 98*	1

Jean-Francois PAILLARD - See ORCHESTRE DE CHAMBRE Jean-Francois PAILLARD

PALE — France

SINGLES:	HITS 1			WEEKS 2
DOGS WITH NO TAILS	*A&M*	51	*13 Jun 92*	2

PALE FOUNTAINS — UK

SINGLES:	HITS 1			WEEKS 6
THANK YOU	*Virgin*	48	*27 Nov 82*	6
ALBUMS:	**HITS 2**			**WEEKS 3**
PACIFIC STREET	*Virgin*	85	*10 Mar 84*	2
FROM ACROSS THE KITCHEN TABLE	*Virgin*	94	*16 Feb 85*	1

PALE SAINTS — UK

SINGLES:	HITS 1			WEEKS 1
KINKY LOVE	*4AD*	72	*6 Jul 91*	1
ALBUMS:	**HITS 2**			**WEEKS 3**
THE COMFORTS OF MADNESS	*4AD*	40	*24 Feb 90*	2
IN RIBBONS	*4AD*	61	*4 Apr 92*	1

PALE-X — Holland

SINGLES:	HITS 1			WEEKS 1
NITRO	*Nukleuz*	74	*3 Feb 01*	1

PALLAS — UK

ALBUMS:	HITS 2			WEEKS 4
SENTINEL	*Harvest*	41	*25 Feb 84*	3
THE WEDGE	*Harvest*	70	*22 Feb 86*	1

Narina PALLOT — UK

SINGLES:	HITS 1			WEEKS 1
PATIENCE	*Polydor*	61	*18 Aug 01*	1

Barry PALMER - See Mike OLDFIELD

Patsy PALMER - See Sid OWEN

Robert PALMER — UK

SINGLES:	HITS 23			WEEKS 128
EVERY KINDA PEOPLE	*Island*	53	*20 May 78*	4
BAD CASE OF LOVIN' YOU (DOCTOR DOCTOR)	*Island*	61	*7 Jul 79*	2
Originally recorded by Moon Martin.				
JOHNNY AND MARY	*Island*	44	*6 Sep 80*	8
LOOKING FOR CLUES	*Island*	33	*22 Nov 80*	9
SOME GUYS HAVE ALL THE LUCK	*Island*	16	*13 Feb 82*	8
Originally recorded by the Persuaders.				
YOU ARE IN MY SYSTEM	*Island*	53	*2 Apr 83*	4
Originally recorded by the System.				
YOU CAN HAVE IT (TAKE MY HEART)	*Island*	66	*18 Jun 83*	2
ADDICTED TO LOVE	*Island*	5	*10 May 86*	15
I DIDN'T MEAN TO TURN YOU ON	*Island*	9	*19 Jul 86*	9
Originally recorded by Cherrelle.				
DISCIPLINE OF LOVE	*Island*	68	*1 Nov 86*	1
Original release reached No. 95 in 1985.				
SWEET LIES	*Island*	58	*26 Mar 88*	3
SIMPLY IRRESISTIBLE	*EMI*	44	*11 Jun 88*	4
SHE MAKES MY DAY	*EMI*	6	*15 Oct 88*	12
CHANGE HIS WAYS	*EMI*	28	*13 May 89*	7
IT COULD HAPPEN TO YOU	*EMI*	71	*26 Aug 89*	1
I'LL BE YOUR BABY TONIGHT	*EMI*	6	*3 Nov 90*	10
Originally recorded by Bob Dylan.				
Above hit: Robert PALMER and UB40.				
MERCY MERCY ME/I WANT YOU [M]	*EMI*	9	*5 Jan 91*	9
Both originally recorded by Marvin Gaye.				
DREAMS TO REMEMBER	*EMI*	68	*15 Jun 91*	1
EVERY KINDA PEOPLE [RI]	*Island*	43	*7 Mar 92*	3
WITCHCRAFT	*EMI*	50	*17 Oct 92*	3
GIRL U WANT	*EMI*	57	*9 Jul 94*	2
Features Nuno Bettencourt from Extreme on guitar.				
KNOW BY NOW	*EMI*	25	*3 Sep 94*	5
YOU BLOW ME AWAY	*EMI*	38	*24 Dec 94*	4
RESPECT YOURSELF	*EMI*	45	*14 Oct 95*	2
Originally recorded by the Staple Singers.				
ALBUMS:	**HITS 13**			**WEEKS 162**
SOME PEOPLE CAN DO WHAT THEY LIKE	*Island*	46	*6 Nov 76*	1
SECRETS	*Island*	54	*14 Jul 79*	4

CLUES	*Island*	31	*6 Sep 80*	8
MAYBE IT'S LIVE	*Island*	32	*3 Apr 82*	6
Include both studio and live recordings from his concert at London's Dominion Theatre, Nov 80.				
PRIDE	*Island*	37	*23 Apr 83*	9
RIPTIDE	*Island*	69	*16 Nov 85*	2
RIPTIDE [RE]	*Island*	5	*24 May 86*	35
HEAVY NOVA	*EMI*	17	*9 Jul 88*	25
ADDICTIONS VOLUME 1	*Island*	7	*11 Nov 89*	17
DON'T EXPLAIN	*EMI*	9	*17 Nov 90*	20
ADDICTIONS VOLUME 2	*Island*	12	*4 Apr 92*	7
RIDIN' HIGH	*EMI*	32	*31 Oct 92*	3
HONEY	*EMI*	25	*24 Sep 94*	4
THE VERY BEST OF ROBERT PALMER	*EMI*	4	*28 Oct 95*	21

Suzanne PALMER – See ABSOLUTE; CLUB 69

Tyrone 'Visionary' PALMER – See SLAM

PAN POSITION — Italy/Venezuela

SINGLES:	HITS 1			WEEKS 1
ELEPHANT PAW (GET DOWN TO THE FUNK)	*Positiva*	55	*18 Jun 94*	1

PANDORA'S BOX — US

SINGLES:	HITS 1			WEEKS 3
IT'S ALL COMING BACK TO ME NOW	*Virgin*	51	*21 Oct 89*	3

Darryl PANDY — US

SINGLES:	HITS 3			WEEKS 5
LOVE CAN'T TURN AROUND	*4 Liberty*	40	*14 Dec 96*	2
This was a remix. Darryl Pandy was not credited on the original 1986 release.				
Above hit: Farley 'Jackmaster' FUNK featuring Darryl PANDY.				
RAISE YOUR HANDS	*VC Recordings*	40	*20 Feb 99*	2
Above hit: BIG ROOM GIRL featuring Darryl PANDY.				
SUNSHINE & HAPPINESS	*Azuli*	68	*2 Oct 99*	1
Above hit: Darryl PANDY meets NERIO'S DUBWORK.				

Johnny PANIC and the BIBLE OF DREAMS — UK

SINGLES:	HITS 1			WEEKS 2
JOHNNY PANIC AND THE BIBLE OF DREAMS	*Fontana*	70	*2 Feb 91*	2

PANTERA — US

SINGLES:	HITS 4			WEEKS 8
MOUTH FOR WAR	*Atco*	73	*10 Oct 92*	1
WALK	*Atco*	35	*27 Feb 93*	2
I'M BROKEN	*East West America*	19	*19 Mar 94*	2
PLANET CARAVAN	*East West America*	26	*22 Oct 94*	3
Originally recorded by Black Sabbath.				
ALBUMS:	**HITS 5**			**WEEKS 10**
VULGAR DISPLAY OF POWER	*Atco*	64	*7 Mar 92*	1
FAR BEYOND DRIVEN	*Atco*	3	*2 Apr 94*	4
THE GREAT SOUTHERN TRENDKILL	*East West*	17	*18 May 96*	3
OFFICIAL LIVE - 101 PROOF	*East West*	54	*30 Aug 97*	1
Live recordings plus 2 studio tracks.				
REINVENTING THE STEEL	*Elektra*	33	*8 Apr 00*	1

PAPA ROACH — US

SINGLES:	HITS 2			WEEKS 16
LAST RESORT	*Dreamworks*	3	*17 Feb 01*	10
BETWEEN ANGELS AND INSECTS	*Dreamworks*	17	*5 May 01*	6
ALBUMS:	**HGITS 1**			**WEEKS 36**
INFEST	*Dreamworks*	9	*13 Jan 01*	36

PAPA SAN – See David Morales

PAPER DOLLS — UK

SINGLES:	HITS 1			WEEKS 13
SOMETHING HERE IN MY HEART (KEEPS A TELLIN' ME NO)	*Pye*	11	*16 Mar 68*	13

PAPER LACE — UK

SINGLES:	HITS 4			WEEKS 41
BILLY-DON'T BE A HERO	*Bus Stop*	1	*23 Feb 74*	14
THE NIGHT CHICAGO DIED	*Bus Stop*	3	*4 May 74*	11
THE BLACK-EYED BOYS	*Bus Stop*	11	*24 Aug 74*	10
WE GOT THE WHOLE WORLD IN OUR HANDS	*Warner Brothers*	24	*04 Mar 78*	6
Above hit: NOTTINGHAM FOREST with PAPER LACE.				

PAPERDOLLS — UK

SINGLES:	HITS 1			WEEKS 1
GONNA MAKE YOU BLUSH	*MCA*	65	*12 Sep 98*	1

PAPPA BEAR featuring Van DER TOORN — Germany

SINGLES:	HITS 1			WEEKS 1
CHERISH	*Universal*	47	*16 May 98*	1

PAR-T-ONE vs INXS — Italy

(See also INXS.)

SINGLES:	HITS 1			WEEKS 6
I'M SO CRAZY *Samples Just Keep Walking by INXS.*	*Credence*	19	*3 Nov 01*	5
I'M SO CRAZY [RE]	*Credence*	71	*15 Dec 01*	1

Vanessa PARADIS — France

SINGLES:	HITS 4			WEEKS 30
JOE LE TAXI	*FA*	3	*13 Feb 88*	10
BE MY BABY	*Polydor*	6	*10 Oct 92*	15
SUNDAY MONDAYS	*Polydor*	49	*27 Feb 93*	4
JUST AS LONG AS YOU ARE THERE	*Polydor*	57	*24 Jul 93*	1
ALBUMS:	**HITS 1**			**WEEKS 2**
VANESSA PARADIS	*Remark*	45	*7 Nov 92*	2

PARADISE — UK

SINGLES:	HITS 1			WEEKS 4
ONE MIND TWO HEARTS	*Priority*	42	*10 Sep 83*	4

PARADISE LOST — UK

SINGLES:	HITS 3			WEEKS 3
THE LAST TIME	*Music For Nations*	60	*20 May 95*	1
FOREVER FAILURE	*Music For Nations*	66	*7 Oct 95*	1
SAY JUST WORDS	*Music For Nations*	53	*28 Jun 97*	1
ALBUMS:	**HITS 3**			**WEEKS 6**
DRACONIAN TIMES	*Music For Nations*	16	*24 Jun 95*	3
ONE SECOND	*Music For Nations*	31	*26 Jul 97*	2
HOST	*EMI*	61	*19 Jun 99*	1

PARADISE ORGANISATION — UK

SINGLES:	HITS 1			WEEKS 1
PRAYER TOWER	*Cowboy*	70	*23 Jan 93*	1

PARADOX — UK

SINGLES:	HITS 1			WEEKS 2
JAILBREAK	*Ronin*	66	*24 Feb 90*	2

Norrie PARAMOR ORCHESTRA — UK

(See also Tony Brent; Eddie Calvert (The Man with the Golden Trumpet); Michael Holliday; Frank Ifield; Ruby Murray; Cliff Richard; Shadows; Helen Shapiro; Norman Wisdom.)

SINGLES:	HITS 2			WEEKS 8
THEME FROM 'SUMMER PLACE' *Theme from the film of the same name.* *Above hit: Norrie PARAMOR and his Orchestra.*	*Columbia*	36	*19 Mar 60*	2
THEME FROM Z-CARS (JOHNNY TODD) *Theme from the BBC-TV series.*	*Columbia*	33	*24 Mar 62*	6

PARAMOUNT JAZZ BAND - See Mr. Acker BILK

PARAMOUNTS — UK

SINGLES:	HITS 1			WEEKS 7
POISON IVY	*Parlophone*	35	*18 Jan 64*	7

PARCHMENT — UK

SINGLES:	HITS 1			WEEKS 5
LIGHT UP THE FIRE	*Pye*	31	*16 Sep 72*	5

PARIS - See INNER CITY

PARIS — UK

SINGLES:	HITS 1			WEEKS 4
NO GETTING OVER YOU	*RCA*	49	*19 Jun 82*	4

PARIS — US

SINGLES:	HITS 1			WEEKS 2
GUERRILLA FUNK	*Virgin*	38	*21 Jan 95*	2

Mica PARIS — UK

SINGLES:	HITS 15			WEEKS 63
MY ONE TEMPTATION	*Fourth & Broadway*	7	*7 May 88*	11
LIKE DREAMERS DO	*Fourth & Broadway*	26	*30 Jul 88*	5
Above hit: Mica PARIS featuring Courtney PINE.				
BREATHE LIFE INTO ME	*Fourth & Broadway*	26	*22 Oct 88*	10
WHERE IS THE LOVE	*Fourth & Broadway*	19	*21 Jan 89*	7
Above hit: Mica PARIS and Will DOWNING.				
CONTRIBUTION	*Fourth & Broadway*	33	*6 Oct 90*	4
Above hit: Mica PARIS featuring RAKIM.				
SOUTH OF THE RIVER	*Fourth & Broadway*	50	*1 Dec 90*	2
IF I LOVE U 2 NITE	*Fourth & Broadway*	43	*23 Feb 91*	3
Written by Prince.				
YOUNG SOUL REBELS	*Big Life*	61	*31 Aug 91*	3
I NEVER FELT LIKE THIS BEFORE	*Fourth & Broadway*	15	*3 Apr 93*	5
I WANNA HOLD ON TO YOU	*Fourth & Broadway*	27	*5 Jun 93*	3
TWO IN A MILLION	*Fourth & Broadway*	51	*7 Aug 93*	2
WHISPER A PRAYER	*Fourth & Broadway*	65	*4 Dec 93*	1
ONE	*Cooltempo*	29	*8 Apr 95*	4
STAY	*Cooltempo*	40	*16 May 98*	2
BLACK ANGEL	*Cooltempo*	72	*14 Nov 98*	1

ALBUMS:	HITS 4			WEEKS 40
SO GOOD	*Fourth & Broadway*	6	*3 Sep 88*	32
CONTRIBUTION	*Fourth & Broadway*	26	*27 Oct 90*	3
WHISPER A PRAYER	*Fourth & Broadway*	20	*26 Jun 93*	4
BLACK ANGEL	*Cooltempo*	59	*22 Aug 98*	1

Ryan PARIS — Italy

SINGLES:	HITS 1			WEEKS 10
DOLCE VITA	*Carrere*	5	*3 Sep 83*	10

PARIS & SHARP — UK

SINGLES:	HITS 1			WEEKS 1
APHRODITE	*Cream*	61	*1 Dec 01*	1

PARIS ANGELS — UK

SINGLES:	HITS 3			WEEKS 5
SCOPE	*Sheer Joy*	75	*3 Nov 90*	1
PERFUME	*Virgin*	55	*20 Jul 91*	3
Original release reached No. 91 in 1990.				
FADE	*Virgin*	70	*21 Sep 91*	1

ALBUMS:	HITS 1			WEEKS 2
SUNDEW	*Virgin*	37	*17 Aug 91*	2

PARIS OPERA – COMIQUE ORCHESTRA - See Mady MESPLE and Danielle MILLET, PARIS OPERA - COMIQUE ORCHESTRA conducted by Alain LOMBARD

PARIS RED — US

SINGLES:	HITS 2			WEEKS 2
GOOD FRIEND	*Columbia*	61	*29 Feb 92*	1
PROMISES	*Columbia*	59	*15 May 93*	1

John PARISH + Polly Jean HARVEY — US

(See also PJ Harvey.)

SINGLES:	HITS 1			WEEKS 1
THAT WAS MY VEIL	*Island*	75	*23 Nov 96*	1

ALBUMS:	HITS 1			WEEKS 1
DANCE HALL AT LOUSE POINT	*Island*	46	*5 Oct 96*	1

Simon PARK ORCHESTRA — UK

SINGLES:	HITS 1			WEEKS 24
EYE LEVEL (THEME FROM THE THAMES T.V. SERIES "VAN DER VALK")	*Columbia*	41	*25 Nov 72*	2
EYE LEVEL (THEME FROM THE THAMES T.V. SERIES "VAN DER VALK") [RE]	*Columbia*	1	*15 Sep 73*	22

Graham PARKER and the RUMOUR — UK

SINGLES:	HITS 3			WEEKS 16
THE PINK PARKER [EP]	*Vertigo*	24	*19 Mar 77*	5
Lead track: Hold Back The Night.				

HEY LORD, DON'T ASK ME QUESTIONS	*Vertigo*	32	*22 Apr 78*	7
TEMPORARY BEAUTY	*RCA*	50	*20 Mar 82*	4
Above hit: Graham PARKER.				
ALBUMS:	**HITS 6**			**WEEKS 35**
HEAT TREATMENT	*Vertigo*	52	*27 Nov 76*	2
STICK TO ME	*Vertigo*	19	*12 Nov 77*	4
PARKERILLA	*Vertigo*	14	*27 May 78*	5
Live recordings.				
SQUEEZING OUT SPARKS	*Vertigo*	18	*7 Apr 79*	8
THE UP ESCALATOR	*Stiff*	11	*7 Jun 80*	10
ANOTHER GREY AREA	*RCA*	40	*27 Mar 82*	6
Above hit: Graham PARKER.				

Ray PARKER JR. — US

SINGLES:	**HITS 4**			**WEEKS 47**
GHOSTBUSTERS	*Arista*	2	*25 Aug 84*	31
Theme from the film of the same name.				
GIRLS ARE MORE FUN	*Arista*	46	*18 Jan 86*	4
I DON'T THINK THAT MAN SHOULD SLEEP ALONE	*Geffen*	13	*3 Oct 87*	10
OVER YOU	*Geffen*	65	*30 Jan 88*	2
ALBUMS:	**HITS 1**			**WEEKS 7**
AFTER DARK	*WEA*	40	*10 Oct 87*	7

Robert PARKER — US

SINGLES:	**HITS 1**			**WEEKS 8**
BAREFOOTIN'	*Island*	24	*6 Aug 66*	8

Sara PARKER — US

SINGLES:	**HITS 1**			**WEEKS 2**
MY LOVE IS DEEP	*Manifesto*	22	*12 Apr 97*	2

Jimmy PARKINSON — Australia

SINGLES:	**HITS 3**			**WEEKS 19**
THE GREAT PRETENDER	*Columbia*	9	*3 Mar 56*	13
Above hit: Jimmy PARKINSON with Ray MARTIN and his Orchestra.				
WALK HAND IN HAND	*Columbia*	30	*18 Aug 56*	1
Above hit: Jimmy PARKINSON with Ray MARTIN and his Orchestra and the Bill SHEPHERD CHORUS.				
WALK HAND IN HAND [RE]	*Columbia*	26	*6 Oct 56*	1
IN THE MIDDLE OF THE HOUSE	*Columbia*	26	*10 Nov 56*	2
Above hit: Jimmy PARKINSON with Ray MARTIN and his Orchestra.				
IN THE MIDDLE OF THE HOUSE [RE]	*Columbia*	20	*1 Dec 56*	2

PARKS and WILSON — UK

SINGLES:	**HITS 1**			**WEEKS 1**
FEEL THE DRUMS [EP]	*Hooj Choons*	71	*9 Sep 00*	1
Lead track: My Orbit.				

PARLIAMENT – See Scott GROOVES

John PARR — US

SINGLES:	**HITS 3**			**WEEKS 22**
ST. ELMO'S FIRE (MAN IN MOTION)	*London*	6	*14 Sep 85*	13
From the film 'St. Elmo's Fire'.				
NAUGHTY NAUGHTY	*London*	58	*18 Jan 86*	3
ROCK 'N' ROLL MERCENARIES	*Arista*	31	*30 Aug 86*	6
Above hit: MEAT LOAF with John PARR.				
ALBUMS:	**HITS 1**			**WEEKS 2**
JOHN PARR	*London*	60	*2 Nov 85*	2

Dean PARRISH — US

SINGLES:	**HITS 1**			**WEEKS 5**
I'M ON MY WAY	*UK USA*	*38*	*8 Feb 75*	*5*

Man PARRISH — US

SINGLES:	**HITS 3**			**WEEKS 26**
HIP HOP, BE BOP (DON'T STOP)	*Polydor*	41	*26 Mar 83*	6
BOOGIE DOWN (BRONX)	*Boiling Point*	56	*23 Mar 85*	4
MALE STRIPPER	*Bolts*	64	*13 Sep 86*	3
Above hit: MAN 2 MAN meet Man PARRISH.				
MALE STRIPPER [RE-1ST]	*Bolts*	63	*3 Jan 87*	1
MALE STRIPPER [RE-2ND]	*Bolts*	4	*7 Feb 87*	12

Alan PARSONS PROJECT — UK

SINGLES:	HITS 2			WEEKS 4
OLD AND WISE	*Arista*	74	*15 Jan 83*	1
Above hit: Alan PARSONS PROJECT lead vocals by Colin BLUNSTONE.				
DON'T ANSWER ME	*Arista*	58	*10 Mar 84*	3
ALBUMS:	**HITS 10**			**WEEKS 38**
TALES OF MYSTERY AND IMAGINATION	*Charisma*	56	*28 Aug 76*	1
Inspired by the work of Edgar Allan Poe.				
I ROBOT	*Arista*	30	*13 Aug 77*	1
Title comes from writer Isaac Asimov's science fiction book.				
PYRAMID	*Arista*	49	*10 Jun 78*	4
EVE	*Arista*	74	*29 Sep 79*	1
THE TURN OF A FRIENDLY CARD	*Arista*	38	*15 Nov 80*	4
EYE IN THE SKY	*Arista*	27	*29 May 82*	11
Title taken from a novel by Philip K. Dick.				
THE BEST OF THE ALAN PARSONS PROJECT	*Arista*	99	*26 Nov 83*	1
AMMONIA AVENUE	*Arista*	24	*3 Mar 84*	8
VULTURE CULTURE	*Arista*	40	*23 Feb 85*	5
GAUDI	*Arista*	66	*14 Feb 87*	2
Gaudi was a Spanish painter; the album is based on his life.				

Bill PARSONS — US

SINGLES:	HITS 1			WEEKS 2
THE ALL-AMERICAN BOY	*London*	22	*11 Apr 59*	2
The actual vocalist is Bobby Bare. Parson's name is on label in error.				

PARTISANS — UK

ALBUMS:	HITS 1			WEEKS 1
THE PARTISANS	*No Future*	94	*19 Feb 83*	1

PARTIZAN — UK

SINGLES:	HITS 2			WEEKS 3
DRIVE ME CRAZY	*Multiply*	36	*8 Feb 97*	2
KEEP YOUR LOVE	*Multiply*	53	*6 Dec 97*	1
Above hit: PARTIZAN featuring Natalie ROBB.				

PARTNERS – See Al HUDSON

PARTNERS IN KRYME — US

SINGLES:	HITS 1			WEEKS 10
TURTLE POWER	*SBK*	1	*21 Jul 90*	10
From the film 'Teenage Mutant Ninja Turtles'.				

David PARTON — UK

SINGLES:	HITS 1			WEEKS 9
ISN'T SHE LOVELY	*Pye*	4	*15 Jan 77*	9
Original comes from Stevie Wonder's 1976 album Songs In The Key Of Life.				

Dolly PARTON — US

(See also Dolly Parton, Linda Ronstadt and Emmylou Harris.)

SINGLES:	HITS 5			WEEKS 33
JOLENE	*RCA Victor*	7	*15 May 76*	10
9 TO 5	*RCA*	47	*21 Feb 81*	5
ISLANDS IN THE STREAM	*RCA*	7	*12 Nov 83*	15
Written by the Bee Gees.				
Above hit: Kenny ROGERS Duet with Dolly PARTON.				
HERE YOU COME AGAIN	*RCA*	75	*7 Apr 84*	1
THE DAY I FALL IN LOVE (LOVE THEME FROM BEETHOVEN'S 2ND)	*Columbia*	64	*16 Apr 94*	2
From the film 'Beethoven's 2nd'.				
Above hit: Dolly PARTON and James INGRAM.				
ALBUMS:	**HITS 7**			**WEEKS 32**
DOLLY PARTON/BOTH SIDES	*Lotus*	24	*25 Nov 78*	12
Compilation.				
GREATEST HITS	*RCA*	74	*7 Sep 85*	1
THE GREATEST HITS	*Telstar*	65	*22 Oct 94*	2
A LIFE IN MUSIC - ULTIMATE COLLECTION	*RCA*	38	*8 Nov 97*	3
HUNGRY AGAIN	*MCA Nashville*	41	*26 Sep 98*	3
LITTLE SPARROW	*Sanctuary*	30	*24 Feb 01*	6
GOLD - GREATEST HITS	*RCA*	23	*3 Mar 01*	5

Dolly PARTON, Linda RONSTADT and Emmylou HARRIS — US

(See also Emmylou Harris; Dolly Parton; Linda Ronstadt.)

ALBUMS:	HITS 1			WEEKS 4
TRIO	*Warner Brothers*	60	*14 Mar 87*	4

Stella PARTON — US

SINGLES:	HITS 1			WEEKS 4
THE DANGER OF A STRANGER	*Elektra*	35	*22 Oct 77*	4

Alan PARTRIDGE — UK

ALBUMS:	HITS 1			WEEKS 3
KNOWING ME, KNOWING YOU 3	*BBC*	41	*18 Mar 95*	3
Taken from the BBC Radio 4 show 'On The Hour' (later became 'Day To Day').				

Don PARTRIDGE — UK

SINGLES:	HITS 3			WEEKS 32
ROSIE	*Columbia*	4	*10 Feb 68*	12
BLUE EYES	*Columbia*	3	*1 Jun 68*	13
BREAKFAST ON PLUTO	*Columbia*	26	*22 Feb 69*	7

PARTRIDGE FAMILY — US

SINGLES:	HITS 5			WEEKS 53
I THINK I LOVE YOU	*Bell*	18	*13 Feb 71*	9
IT'S ONE OF THOSE NIGHTS (YES LOVE)	*Bell*	11	*26 Feb 72*	11
BREAKING UP IS HARD TO DO	*Bell*	3	*8 Jul 72*	13
Above 3: PARTRIDGE FAMILY starring Shirley JONES- featuring David CASSIDY.				
LOOKING THRU THE EYES OF LOVE	*Bell*	9	*3 Feb 73*	9
WALKING IN THE RAIN	*Bell*	10	*19 May 73*	11
Originally recorded by the Ronettes.				
Above 2: PARTRIDGE FAMILY starring David CASSIDY.				
ALBUMS:	**HITS 4**			**WEEKS 13**
UP TO DATE	*Bell*	46	*8 Jan 72*	2
THE PARTRIDGE FAMILY SOUND MAGAZINE	*Bell*	14	*22 Apr 72*	7
SHOPPING BAG	*Bell*	28	*30 Sep 72*	3
CHRISTMAS CARD	*Bell*	45	*9 Dec 72*	1

PARTY ANIMALS — Holland

SINGLES:	HITS 2			WEEKS 3
HAVE YOU EVER BEEN MELLOW?	*Mokum*	56	*1 Jun 96*	1
HAVE YOU EVER BEEN MELLOW? [EP]	*Mokum*	43	*19 Oct 96*	2
Lead track: Have You Ever Been Mellow?, which is a re-issue.				

PARTY FAITHFUL — UK

SINGLES:	HITS 1			WEEKS 1
BRASS: LET THERE BE HOUSE	*Ore*	54	*22 Jul 95*	1

PASADENAS — US

SINGLES:	HITS 10			WEEKS 57
TRIBUTE (RIGHT ON)	*CBS*	5	*28 May 88*	14
RIDING ON A TRAIN	*CBS*	13	*17 Sep 88*	9
ENCHANTED LADY	*CBS*	31	*26 Nov 88*	6
LOVE THING	*CBS*	22	*12 May 90*	5
REELING	*CBS*	75	*14 Jul 90*	1
I'M DOING FINE NOW	*Columbia*	4	*1 Feb 92*	10
MAKE IT WITH YOU	*Columbia*	20	*4 Apr 92*	4
I BELIEVE IN MIRACLES	*Columbia*	34	*6 Jun 92*	3
MOVING IN THE RIGHT DIRECTION	*Columbia*	49	*29 Aug 92*	2
LET'S STAY TOGETHER	*Columbia*	22	*21 Nov 92*	3
ALBUMS:	**HITS 2**			**WEEKS 32**
TO WHOM IT MAY CONCERN	*CBS*	3	*22 Oct 88*	21
YOURS SINCERELY	*Columbia*	6	*7 Mar 92*	11

PASSENGERS — UK/Ireland/Italy

SINGLES:	HITS 1			WEEKS 9
MISS SARAJEVO	*Island*	6	*2 Dec 95*	9
Inspired by the TV documentary that reported on a beauty pageant in the besieged Bosnian capital.				
ALBUMS:	**HITS 1**			**WEEKS 5**
ORIGINAL SOUNDTRACKS 1	*Island*	12	*18 Nov 95*	5

PASSION — UK

SINGLES:	HITS 1			WEEKS 1
SHARE YOUR LOVE (DIGGITY REMIXES)	*Charm*	62	*25 Jan 97*	1
Based on Blackstreet's No Diggity.				

PASSIONS — UK

SINGLES:	HITS 1			WEEKS 8
I'M IN LOVE WITH A GERMAN FILM STAR	*Polydor*	25	*31 Jan 81*	8
ALBUMS:	**HITS 1**			**WEEKS 1**
THIRTY THOUSAND FEET OVER CHINA	*Polydor*	92	*3 Oct 81*	1

PAT and MICK — UK

SINGLES:	HITS 5			WEEKS 27
LET'S ALL CHANT / ON THE NIGHT	*PWL*	11	*9 Apr 88*	9
On The Night listed for the week of 4 Jun 88 once single had dropped to No. 70.				
Above hit: MICK and PAT.				
I HAVEN'T STOPPED DANCING YET	*PWL*	9	*25 Mar 89*	8
USE IT UP AND WEAR IT OUT	*PWL*	22	*14 Apr 90*	6
GIMME SOME	*PWL*	53	*23 Mar 91*	2
HOT HOT HOT	*PWL International*	47	*15 May 93*	2
All singles above were to support London's Capital Radio 'Help A London Child' appeal.				

PATIENCE and PRUDENCE — US

SINGLES:	HITS 2			WEEKS 8
TONIGHT YOU BELONG TO ME	*London*	28	*3 Nov 56*	3
Originally recorded by Gene Austin in 1927.				
GONNA GET ALONG WITHOUT YA NOW	*London*	22	*2 Mar 57*	4
Originally recorded by Teresa Brewer in 1952.				
GONNA GET ALONG WITHOUT YA NOW [RE]	*London*	24	*13 Apr 57*	1

PATRA — Jamaica

(See also Shabba Ranks.)

SINGLES:	HITS 2			WEEKS 3
PULL UP TO THE BUMPER	*Epic*	50	*30 Sep 95*	2
WORK MI BODY	*Heavenly*	75	*10 Aug 96*	1
Above hit: MONKEY MAFIA featuring PATRA.				

PATRIC — UK

SINGLES:	HITS 1			WEEKS 2
LOVE ME	*Bell*	54	*9 Jul 94*	2

Dee PATTEN — UK

SINGLES:	HITS 1			WEEKS 1
WHO'S THE BAD MAN?	*Higher Ground*	42	*30 Jan 99*	1
Originally released on the Hard Hand's label in 1992.				

Kellee PATTERSON — US

SINGLES:	HITS 1			WEEKS 7
IF IT DON'T FIT DON'T FORCE IT	*EMI International*	44	*18 Feb 78*	7

Rahsaan PATTERSON — US

(See also US3.)

SINGLES:	HITS 3			WEEKS 7
CANTALOOP (FLIP FANTASIA)	*Blue Note*	23	*25 Sept 93*	5
Samples Cantaloupe Island by Herbie Hancock.				
Above hit: US3 featuring RAHSAAN.				
STOP BY	*MCA*	50	*26 Jul 97*	1
WHERE YOU ARE	*MCA*	55	*21 Mar 98*	1

Billy PAUL — US

(See also Philadelphia International All Stars: Lou Rawls, Billy Paul, Archie Bell, Teddy Pendergrass, O'Jays, Dee Dee Sharp, Gamble.)

SINGLES:	HITS 7			WEEKS 45
ME & MRS JONES	*Epic*	12	*13 Jan 73*	9
THANKS FOR SAVING MY LIFE	*Philadelphia International*	33	*12 Jan 74*	6
LET'S MAKE A BABY	*Philadelphia International*	30	*22 May 76*	5
LET 'EM IN	*Philadelphia International*	26	*30 Apr 77*	5
YOUR SONG	*Philadelphia International*	37	*16 Jul 77*	7
ONLY THE STRONG SURVIVE	*Philadelphia International*	33	*19 Nov 77*	8
Originally recorded by Jerry Butler.				
BRING THE FAMILY BACK	*Philadelphia International*	51	*14 Jul 79*	5

Chris PAUL — UK

SINGLES:	HITS 3			WEEKS 8
EXPANSIONS '86 (EXPAND YOUR MIND)	*Fourth & Broadway*	58	*31 May 86*	5
Above hit: Chris PAUL featuring the voice of David JOSEPH.				
BACK IN MY ARMS	*Syncopate*	74	*21 Nov 87*	2
TURN THE MUSIC UP	*Syncopate*	73	*13 Aug 88*	1

Frankie PAUL – See APACHIE INDIAN

Les PAUL and Mary FORD — US

SINGLES:	HITS 1			WEEKS 4
VAYA CON DIOS (MAY GOD BE WITH YOU)	*Capitol*	7	*21 Nov 53*	4

Lyn PAUL — UK

(See also New Seekers.)

SINGLES:	HITS 1			WEEKS 6
IT OUGHTA SELL A MILLION	*Polydor*	37	*28 Jun 75*	6
Featured in the Coca-Cola TV commercial.				

Owen PAUL — UK

SINGLES:	HITS 1			WEEKS 14
MY FAVOURITE WASTE OF TIME	*Epic*	3	*31 May 86*	14
Originally recorded by Marshall Crenshaw.				

PAUL and PAULA — US

SINGLES:	HITS 2			WEEKS 31
HEY PAULA	*Philips*	8	*16 Feb 63*	12
YOUNG LOVERS	*Philips*	9	*20 Apr 63*	14
HEY PAULA [RE]	*Philips*	37	*18 May 63*	5

Luciano PAVAROTTI — Italy

(See also Passengers; 3 Tenors: José Carreras, Placido Domingo, Luciano Pavarotti.)

SINGLES:	HITS 3			WEEKS 22
NESSUN DORMA	*Decca*	2	*16 Jun 90*	11
The Official BBC TV Grandstand World Cup Theme for 1990.				
MISERERE	*London*	15	*24 Oct 92*	5
Above hit: ZUCCHERO with Luciano PAVAROTTI.				
LIVE LIKE HORSES	*Rocket*	9	*14 Dec 96*	6
Above hit: Elton JOHN and Luciano PAVAROTTI.				

ALBUMS:	HITS 14			WEEKS 182
PAVAROTTI'S GREATEST HITS	*Decca*	95	*15 May 82*	1
MAMMA	*Decca*	96	*30 Jun 84*	1
Above hit: Luciano PAVAROTTI with the Henry MANCINI ORCHESTRA.				
THE PAVAROTTI COLLECTION	*Stylus*	12	*9 Aug 86*	34
THE NEW PAVAROTTI COLLECTION LIVE!	*Stylus*	63	*16 Jul 88*	8
THE ESSENTIAL PAVAROTTI	*Decca*	1	*17 Mar 90*	72
ESSENTIAL PAVAROTTI II	*Decca*	1	*20 Jul 91*	28
PAVAROTTI IN HYDE PARK	*Decca*	19	*15 Feb 92*	7
Live recordings.				
TI AMO - PUCCINI'S GREATEST LOVE SONGS	*Decca*	23	*4 Sep 93*	4
Compilation of recordings from 1972–79.				
MY HEART'S DELIGHT	*Decca*	44	*12 Feb 94*	4
Live recordings from his home town of Modena.				
Above hit: Luciano PAVAROTTI with the ROYAL PHILHARMONIC ORCHESTRA.				
TOGETHER FOR THE CHILDREN OF BOSNIA	*Decca*	11	*30 Mar 96*	6
Live recordings from the Concert in his home town of Modena, Sep 95. Features Brian Eno, Bono, The Edge, Dolores O'Riordan, Meat Loaf, Simon Le Bon, Michael Bolton, Chieftains, Zucchero, Jovanotti, Michael Kamen.				
PAVAROTTI AND FRIENDS FOR WAR CHILD	*Decca*	45	*14 Dec 96*	4
Features Elton John, Liza Minnelli, Sheryl Crow & Joan Osborne.				
Above 2: PAVAROTTI and FRIENDS.				
THE ULTIMATE COLLECTION	*Decca*	39	*25 Oct 97*	5
LOVE SONGS	*Decca*	26	*19 Jun 99*	6
AMORE - THE LOVE ALBUM	*Decca*	41	*21 Jul 01*	2

PAVEMENT — US

SINGLES:	HITS 5			WEEKS 6
WATERY, DOMESTIC [EP]	*Big Cat*	58	*28 Nov 92*	1
Lead track: Brick Wall.				
CUT YOUR HAIR	*Big Cat*	52	*12 Feb 94*	1
STEREO	*Domino*	48	*8 Feb 97*	1
SHADY LANE (KROSSFADER)	*Domino*	40	*3 May 97*	1
CARROT ROPE	*Domino*	27	*22 May 99*	2

ALBUMS:	HITS 6			WEEKS 13
SLANTED AND ENCHANTED	*Big Cat*	72	*25 Apr 92*	1
WESTING (BY MUSKET AND SEXTANT)	*Big Cat*	30	*3 Apr 93*	2
CROOKED RAIN CROOKED RAIN	*Big Cat*	15	*26 Feb 94*	3
WOWEE ZOWEE	*Big Cat*	18	*22 Apr 95*	2
BRIGHTEN THE CORNERS	*Domino*	27	*22 Feb 97*	2
TERROR TWILIGHT	*Domino*	19	*19 Jun 99*	3

Rita PAVONE — Italy

SINGLES:	HITS 2			WEEKS 19
HEART	*RCA Victor*	27	*3 Dec 66*	12
Above hit: Rita PAVONE with Charles BLACKWELL and his Orchestra.				
YOU ONLY YOU	*RCA Victor*	21	*21 Jan 67*	7
Above hit: Rita PAVONE with Geoff LOVE and his Orchestra.				

George PAXTON Orchestra and Chorus – See Adam WADE with the George PAXTON Orchestra and Chorus

Tom PAXTON — US

ALBUMS:	HITS 3			WEEKS 10
NO. 6	*Elektra*	23	*13 Jun 70*	5
THE COMPLEAT TOM PAXTON	*Elektra*	18	*3 Apr 71*	4
PEACE WILL COME	*Reprise*	47	*1 Jul 72*	1

Freda PAYNE — US

SINGLES:	HITS 3			WEEKS 30
BAND OF GOLD	*Invictus*	1	*5 Sep 70*	19
Features Ray Parker Jr on piano.				
DEEPER AND DEEPER	*Invictus*	33	*21 Nov 70*	9
CHERISH WHAT IS DEAR TO YOU (WHILE IT'S NEAR TO YOU)	*Invictus*	46	*27 Mar 71*	2

Tammy PAYNE — UK

SINGLES:	HITS 1			WEEKS 2
TAKE ME NOW	*Talkin Loud*	55	*20 Jul 91*	2

Heather PEACE — UK

SINGLES:	HITS 1			WEEKS 1
THE ROSE	*RCA*	56	*13 May 00*	1
Originally by Bette Midler reached No. 3 in the US in 1980.				

PEACE BY PIECE — UK

SINGLES:	HITS 2			WEEKS 2
SWEET SISTER	*Blanco Y Negro*	46	*21 Sep 96*	1
NOBODY'S BUSINESS	*Blanco Y Negro*	50	*25 Apr 98*	1

PEACH — UK/Belgium

SINGLES:	HITS 1			WEEKS 1
ON MY OWN	*Mute*	69	*17 Jan 98*	1

PEACHES and HERB — US

SINGLES:	HITS 2			WEEKS 23
SHAKE YOUR GROOVE THING	*Polydor*	26	*20 Jan 79*	10
REUNITED	*Polydor*	4	*21 Apr 79*	13

Mary PEARCE – See UP YER RONSON featuring Mary PEARCE

Natasha PEARL – See TASTE XPERIENCE featuring Natasha PEARL

PEARL JAM — US

SINGLES:	HITS 14			WEEKS 41
ALIVE	*Epic*	16	*15 Feb 92*	6
EVEN FLOW	*Epic*	27	*18 Apr 92*	3
JEREMY	*Epic*	15	*26 Sep 92*	4
DAUGHTER	*Epic*	18	*1 Jan 94*	5
DISSIDENT	*Epic*	14	*28 May 94*	4
SPIN THE BLACK CIRCLE	*Epic*	10	*26 Nov 94*	3
NOT FOR YOU	*Epic*	34	*25 Feb 95*	2
MERKINBALL: I GOT ID / LONG ROAD	*Epic*	25	*16 Dec 95*	3
Chart only reflected title as Merkinball which was the sleeve title.				
WHO YOU ARE	*Epic*	18	*17 Aug 96*	2
GIVEN TO FLY	*Epic*	12	*31 Jan 98*	3
WISHLIST	*Epic*	30	*23 May 98*	2
LAST KISS	*Epic*	42	*14 Aug 99*	1
Original by J. Frank Wilson and the Cavaliers reached No. 2 in the US in 1964. This was first released as a free Xmas single to their fan club.				
NOTHING AS IT SEEMS	*Epic*	22	*13 May 00*	2

LIGHT YEARS	Epic	52	22 Jul 00	1
ALBUMS:	**HITS 7**			**WEEKS 117**
TEN	Epic	18	7 Mar 92	65
VS	Epic	2	23 Oct 93	24
VITALOGY	Epic	4	3 Dec 94	11
Entered at No. 54 with first week sales only on vinyl.				
NO CODE	Epic	3	7 Sep 96	5
YIELD	Epic	7	14 Feb 98	7
LIVE - ON TWO LEGS	Epic	68	5 Dec 98	1
BINAURAL	Epic	5	27 May 00	4

PEARLS — UK

SINGLES:	**HITS 4**			**WEEKS 24**
THIRD FINGER, LEFT HAND	Bell	31	27 May 72	6
YOU CAME, YOU SAW, YOU CONQUERED	Bell	32	23 Sep 72	5
YOU ARE EVERYTHING	Bell	41	24 Mar 73	3
GUILTY	Bell	10	1 Jun 74	10

Johnny PEARSON ORCHESTRA — UK

SINGLES:	**HITS 1**			**WEEKS 15**
SLEEPY SHORES	Penny Farthing	8	18 Dec 71	15
Theme from the BBC1 TV series 'Owen M.D.'.				

David PEASTON — UK

ALBUMS:	**HITS 1**			**WEEKS 1**
INTRODUCING . . . DAVID PEASTON	Geffen	66	26 Aug 89	1

PEBBLES — US

SINGLES:	**HITS 3**			**WEEKS 17**
GIRLFRIEND	MCA	8	19 Mar 88	11
MERCEDES BOY	MCA	42	28 May 88	4
GIVING YOU THE BENEFIT	MCA	73	27 Oct 90	2
ALBUMS:	**HITS 1**			**WEEKS 4**
PEBBLES	MCA	56	14 May 88	4

PEDDLERS — UK

SINGLES:	**HITS 3**			**WEEKS 14**
LET THE SUN SHINE IN	Philips	50	9 Jan 65	1
BIRTH	CBS	17	23 Aug 69	9
GIRLIE	CBS	34	31 Jan 70	4
ALBUMS:	**HITS 2**			**WEEKS 16**
FREE WHEELERS	CBS	27	16 Mar 68	13
BIRTHDAY	CBS	16	7 Feb 70	3

PEE BEE SQUAD — UK

SINGLES:	**HITS 1**			**WEEKS 3**
RUGGED AND MEAN, BUTCH AND ON SCREEN	Project	52	5 Oct 85	3
DJ Paul Burnett with a spoof take off of Rambo.				

Ann PEEBLES — US

SINGLES:	**HITS 1**			**WEEKS 3**
I CAN'T STAND THE RAIN	London	50	20 Apr 74	1
I CAN'T STAND THE RAIN [RE]	London	41	4 May 74	2

PEECH BOYS — US

SINGLES:	**HITS 1**			**WEEKS 3**
DON'T MAKE ME WAIT	TMT Productions	49	30 Oct 82	3

Kevin PEEK — UK

(See also Kevin Peek and Rick Wakeman featuring Jeff Wayne narration Patrick Allen.)

ALBUMS:	**HITS 1**			**WEEKS 2**
AWAKENING	Ariola	52	21 Mar 81	2

Kevin PEEK and Rick WAKEMAN featuring Jeff WAYNE narration Patrick ALLEN — UK

(See also Kevin PEEK; Rick WAKEMAN; Jeff WAYNE.)

ALBUMS:	**HITS 1**			**WEEKS 6**
BEYOND THE PLANETS	Telstar	64	13 Oct 84	6

Donald PEERS — UK

SINGLES:	**HITS 2**			**WEEKS 27**
PLEASE DON'T GO	Columbia	3	21 Dec 68	18

PLEASE DON'T GO [RE]	*Columbia*	38	*3 May 69*	3
GIVE ME ONE MORE CHANCE	*Decca*	36	*24 Jun 72*	6

Above hit: Donald PEERS; The Les REED ORCHESTRA and CHORUS.

PELE — UK

SINGLES:	HITS 3			WEEKS 3
MEGALOMANIA	*M&G*	73	*15 Feb 92*	1
FAIR BLOWS THE WIND FOR FRANCE	*M&G*	62	*13 Jun 92*	1
FAT BLACK HEART	*M&G*	75	*31 Jul 93*	1

Marti PELLOW — UK

SINGLES:	HITS 2			WEEKS 8
CLOSE TO YOU	*Mercury*	9	*16 Jun 01*	6
I'VE BEEN AROUND THE WORLD	*Mercury*	28	*1 Dec 01*	2
ALBUMS:	**HITS 1**			**WEEKS 7**
SMILE	*Mercury*	7	*7 Jul 01*	7

Debbie PENDER — US

SINGLES:	HITS 1			WEEKS 2
MOVIN' ON	*AM:PM*	41	*30 May 98*	2

Teddy PENDERGRASS — US

(See also Harold Melvin And The Bluenotes; Philadelphia International All Stars: Lou Rawls, Billy Paul, Archie Bell, Teddy Pendergrass, O'Jays, Dee Dee Sharp, Gamble.)

SINGLES:	HITS 6			WEEKS 24
THE WHOLE TOWN'S LAUGHING AT ME	*Philadelphia International*	44	*21 May 77*	3
ONLY YOU / CLOSE THE DOOR	*Philadelphia International*	41	*28 Oct 78*	6
TWO HEARTS	*20th Century*	49	*23 May 81*	5
Above hit: Stephanie MILLS 'featuring Teddy PENDERGRASS'.				
HOLD ME	*Asylum*	44	*25 Jan 86*	5
Above hit: Teddy PENDERGRASS with Whitney HOUSTON.				
JOY	*Elektra*	58	*28 May 88*	3
THE MORE I GET, THE MORE I WANT	*X-Clusive*	35	*19 Nov 94*	2
He originally recorded it with Harold Melvin and the Bluenotes.				
Above hit: KWS featuring Teddy PENDERGRASS.				
ALBUMS:	**HITS 2**			**WEEKS 12**
THE ARTISTS VOLUME 2	*Street Sounds*	45	*13 Jul 85*	4
Compilation album with tracks by each artist.				
Above hit: Luther VANDROSS/Teddy PENDERGRASS/CHANGE/ATLANTIC STARR.				
JOY	*Elektra*	45	*21 May 88*	8

PENETRATION — UK

ALBUMS:	HITS 2			WEEKS 8
MOVING TARGETS	*Virgin*	22	*28 Oct 78*	4
COMING UP FOR AIR	*Virgin*	36	*6 Oct 79*	4

PENGUIN CAFE ORCHESTRA — UK

ALBUMS:	HITS 1			WEEKS 5
SIGNS OF LIFE	*EG*	49	*4 Apr 87*	5

Ce Ce PENISTON — US

SINGLES:	HITS 10			WEEKS 53
FINALLY	*A&M*	29	*12 Oct 91*	7
Rap by MC Lethal.				
WE GOT A LOVE THANG	*A&M*	6	*11 Jan 92*	8
Backing vocals by Kym Sims.				
I LIKE IT	*A&M*	58	*18 Jan 92*	2
Above hit: OVERWEIGHT POOCH featuring Ce Ce PENISTON.				
FINALLY [RI]	*A&M*	2	*21 Mar 92*	8
KEEP ON WALKIN'	*A&M*	10	*23 May 92*	6
CRAZY LOVE	*A&M*	44	*5 Sep 92*	3
INSIDE THAT I CRIED	*A&M*	42	*12 Dec 92*	2
I'M IN THE MOOD	*A&M*	16	*15 Jan 94*	4
KEEP GIVIN' ME YOUR LOVE	*A&M*	36	*2 Apr 94*	2
HIT BY LOVE	*A&M*	33	*6 Aug 94*	2
FINALLY [RM]	*AM:PM*	26	*13 Sep 97*	5
Remixed by Eric Kupper.				
SOMEBODY ELSE'S GUY	*AM:PM*	13	*7 Feb 98*	4
ALBUMS:	**HITS 2**			**WEEKS 21**
FINALLY	*A&M*	10	*8 Feb 92*	19
THOUGHT 'YA KNEW	*A&M*	31	*5 Feb 94*	2

Dawn PENN
Jamaica

SINGLES:	HITS 1			WEEKS 12
YOU DON'T LOVE ME (NO, NO, NO)	*Big Beat*	3	*11 Jun 94*	12
She wrote this song back in 1969, originally recorded by Sonny and Cher.				
ALBUMS:	**HITS 1**			**WEEKS 2**
NO, NO, NO	*Big Beat*	51	*9 Jul 94*	2

Leslie PENNING – See Mike OLDFIELD

Barbara PENNINGTON
US

SINGLES:	HITS 2			WEEKS 8
FAN THE FLAME	*Record Shack*	62	*27 Apr 85*	3
ON A CROWDED STREET	*Record Shack*	57	*27 Jul 85*	5

Tricia PENROSE
UK

SINGLES:	HITS 2			WEEKS 2
WHERE DID OUR LOVE GO	*RCA*	71	*7 Dec 96*	1
DON'T WANNA BE ALONE	*Doop*	44	*4 Mar 00*	1
Featured in the Yorkshire TV series 'Heartbeat'.				

PENTANGLE
UK

SINGLES:	HITS 2			WEEKS 4
ONCE I HAD A SWEETHEART	*Big T*	46	*31 May 69*	1
LIGHT FLIGHT (THEME FROM TAKE THREE GIRLS)	*Big T*	43	*14 Feb 70*	1
Certain copies has the title as Take Three Girls (Light Flight).				
LIGHT FLIGHT (THEME FROM TAKE THREE GIRLS) [RE]	*Big T*	45	*28 Feb 70*	2
ALBUMS:	**HITS 3**			**WEEKS 39**
THE PENTANGLE	*Transatlantic*	21	*15 Jun 68*	9
BASKET OF LIGHT	*Transatlantic*	5	*1 Nov 69*	28
CRUEL SISTER	*Transatlantic*	51	*12 Dec 70*	2

PENTHOUSE 4
UK

SINGLES:	HITS 1			WEEKS 3
BUST THIS HOUSE DOWN	*Syncopate*	56	*23 Apr 88*	3

PEOPLES CHOICE
US

SINGLES:	HITS 2			WEEKS 9
DO IT ANY WAY YOU WANNA	*Philadelphia International*	36	*20 Sep 75*	5
JAM, JAM, JAM (ALL NIGHT LONG)	*Philadelphia International*	40	*21 Jan 78*	4
Above hit: PEOPLE'S CHOICE.				

PEPE DELUXE
Finland

SINGLES:	HITS 1			WEEKS 3
BEFORE YOU LEAVE	*INCredible*	20	*26 May 01*	3
Featured in the Lee Jeans TV commercial.				

Danny PEPPERMINT and the JUMPING JACKS
US

SINGLES:	HITS 1			WEEKS 8
THE PEPPERMINT TWIST	*London*	26	*20 Jan 62*	8

PEPPERS
France

SINGLES:	HITS 1			WEEKS 12
PEPPER BOX	*Spark*	6	*26 Oct 74*	12

PEPSI and SHIRLIE
UK

SINGLES:	HITS 4			WEEKS 24
HEARTACHE	*Polydor*	2	*17 Jan 87*	12
GOODBYE STRANGER	*Polydor*	9	*30 May 87*	7
CAN'T GIVE ME LOVE	*Polydor*	58	*26 Sep 87*	3
ALL RIGHT NOW	*Polydor*	50	*12 Dec 87*	2
ALBUMS:	**HITS 1**			**WEEKS 2**
ALL RIGHT NOW	*Polydor*	69	*7 Nov 87*	2

PERCEPTION
UK

SINGLES:	HITS 1			WEEKS 2
FEED THE FEELING	*Talkin Loud*	58	*7 Mar 92*	2
[AA] listed with Three Times A Maybe by K-Creative.				

Lance PERCIVAL — UK

SINGLES:	HITS 1			WEEKS 3
SHAME AND SCANDAL IN THE FAMILY *Originally recorded by Sir Lancelot with Gerald Clark's Caribbean Serenaders.*	*Parlophone*	37	*30 Oct 65*	3

Norman PERCIVAL and his Orchestra - See Maureen EVANS

Hugo PERETTI and his Orchestra - See Valerie CARR with Hugo PERETTI and his Orchestra; Jimmy RODGERS

PERFECT - See PUFF DADDY

A PERFECT CIRCLE — US

SINGLES:	HITS 2			WEEKS 2
THE HOLLOW	*Virgin*	72	*18 Nov 00*	1
3 LIBRAS	*Virgin*	49	*13 Jan 01*	1
ALBUMS:	**HITS 1**			**WEEKS 1**
MER DE NOMS	*Virgin*	55	*3 Jun 00*	1

PERFECT DAY — UK

SINGLES:	HITS 2			WEEKS 4
LIBERTY TOWN	*London*	58	*21 Jan 89*	3
JANE	*London*	68	*1 Apr 89*	1

PERFECT PHASE — Holland

SINGLES:	HITS 1			WEEKS 2
HORNY NORNS *Samples Move Your Feet by 49ers featuring Anne Marie Smith.*	*Positiva*	21	*25 Dec 99*	7

PERFECTLY ORDINARY PEOPLE — UK

SINGLES:	HITS 1			WEEKS 3
"THEME FROM P.O.P."	*Urban*	61	*22 Oct 88*	3

PERFECTO ALLSTARZ — UK

(See also Planet Perfecto.)

SINGLES:	HITS 1			WEEKS 11
REACH UP (PAPA'S GOT A BRAND NEW PIG BAG)	*Perfecto*	6	*4 Feb 95*	11

PERFUME — UK

SINGLES:	HITS 1			WEEKS 1
HAVEN'T SEEN YOU	*Aromasound*	71	*10 Feb 96*	1

Emilio PERICOLI — Italy

SINGLES:	HITS 1			WEEKS 14
AL DI LA (THEME FROM LOVERS MUST LEARN) *Originally Italy's entry for the Eurovision Song Contest in 1961 by Betty Curtis, coming 5th.*	*Warner Brothers*	30	*30 Jun 62*	14

Nick PERITO and his Orchestra - See Julius LA ROSA with Nick PERITO and his Orchestra

Carl PERKINS — US

SINGLES:	HITS 1			WEEKS 8
BLUE SUEDE SHOES	*London*	10	*19 May 56*	8
ALBUMS:	**HITS 1**			**WEEKS 3**
OL' BLUE SUEDES IS BACK	*Jet*	38	*15 Apr 78*	3

PERPETUAL MOTION — UK

SINGLES:	HITS 1			WEEKS 5
KEEP ON DANCIN' (LET'S GO) *Samples D.O.P.s Here I Go.*	*Positiva*	12	*2 May 98*	5

Nigel PERRIN - See Cliff RICHARD

Lee 'Scratch' PERRY — Jamaica

ALBUMS:	HITS 1			WEEKS 1
ARKOLOGY *51 track, 4-CD boxed set of Perry-produced tracks.*	*Island Jamaica*	49	*26 Jul 97*	1

Steve PERRY — UK

SINGLES:	HITS 1			WEEKS 1
STEP BY STEP	*His Master's Voice*	41	*6 Aug 60*	1

Steve PERRY — US

ALBUMS:	HITS 2			WEEKS 3
STREET TALK	*CBS*	59	*14 Jul 84*	2
FOR THE LOVE OF STRANGE MEDICINE	*Columbia*	64	*27 Aug 94*	1

Nina PERSSON and David ARNOLD — Sweden/UK

SINGLES:	HITS 1			WEEKS 1
THEME FROM RANDALL AND HOPKIRK (DECEASED)	*Island*	49	*29 Apr 00*	1
Theme from the BBC1 TV series starring Vic Reeves and Bob Mortimer.				

Jon PERTWEE — UK

SINGLES:	HITS 1			WEEKS 7
WORZEL'S SONG	*Decca*	33	*1 Mar 80*	7
Worzel Gummage is the character he played in the Children's ITV series				

PESHAY — UK

SINGLES:	HITS 3			WEEKS 3
MILES FROM HOME	*Mo Wax*	75	*9 May 98*	1
SWITCH	*Island Blue*	59	*17 Jul 99*	1
TRULY	*Island Blue*	55	*19 Feb 00*	1
Above hit: PESHAY featuring Kym MAZELLE .				

ALBUMS:	HITS 1			WEEKS 1
MILES FROM HOME	*Island Blue*	63	*31 Jul 99*	1

PESTALOZZI CHILDREN'S CHOIR — International

ALBUMS:	HITS 1			WEEKS 2
SONGS OF JOY	*K-Tel*	65	*26 Dec 81*	2

PET SHOP BOYS — UK

SINGLES:	HITS 33			WEEKS 227
WEST END GIRLS	*Parlophone*	1	*23 Nov 85*	15
Original release reached No. 121 in 1984.				
LOVE COMES QUICKLY	*Parlophone*	19	*8 Mar 86*	9
OPPORTUNITIES (LET'S MAKE LOTS OF MONEY)	*Parlophone*	11	*31 May 86*	8
SUBURBIA	*Parlophone*	8	*4 Oct 86*	9
IT'S A SIN	*Parlophone*	1	*27 Jun 87*	11
WHAT HAVE I DONE TO DESERVE THIS?	*Parlophone*	2	*22 Aug 87*	9
Above hit: PET SHOP BOYS and Dusty SPRINGFIELD.				
RENT	*Parlophone*	8	*24 Oct 87*	7
ALWAYS ON MY MIND	*Parlophone*	1	*12 Dec 87*	11
Originally recorded by Brenda Lee in 1971.				
HEART	*Parlophone*	1	*2 Apr 88*	10
DOMINO DANCING	*Parlophone*	7	*24 Sep 88*	8
LEFT TO MY OWN DEVICES	*Parlophone*	4	*26 Nov 88*	8
IT'S ALRIGHT	*Parlophone*	5	*8 Jul 89*	8
Originally recorded by Sterling Void.				
SO HARD	*Parlophone*	4	*6 Oct 90*	6
BEING BORING	*Parlophone*	20	*24 Nov 90*	8
WHERE THE STREETS HAVE NO NAME (CAN'T TAKE MY EYES OFF YOU) [M] / HOW CAN YOU EXPECT TO BE TAKEN SERIOUSLY	*Parlophone*	4	*23 Mar 91*	8
JEALOUSY	*Parlophone*	12	*8 Jun 91*	5
DJ CULTURE	*Parlophone*	13	*26 Oct 91*	3
DJ CULTURE MIX [RM]	*Parlophone*	40	*23 Nov 91*	2
WAS IT WORTH IT?	*Parlophone*	24	*21 Dec 91*	4
CAN YOU FORGIVE HER?	*Parlophone*	7	*12 Jun 93*	7
GO WEST	*Parlophone*	2	*18 Sep 93*	9
I WOULDN'T NORMALLY DO THIS KIND OF THING	*Parlophone*	13	*11 Dec 93*	7
LIBERATION	*Parlophone*	14	*16 Apr 94*	5
ABSOLUTELY FABULOUS	*Parlophone*	6	*11 Jun 94*	7
Charity record to support Comic Relief. Featuring extracts by Jennifer Saunders and Joanne Lumley from the BBC1TV sitcom of the same name.				
Above hit: ABSOLUTELY FABULOUS.				
YESTERDAY, WHEN I WAS MAD	*Parlophone*	13	*10 Sep 94*	4
PANINARO '95	*Parlophone*	15	*5 Aug 95*	4
This was originally the B side to Suburbia.				
BEFORE	*Parlophone*	7	*4 May 96*	5
SE A VIDA E (THAT'S THE WAY LIFE IS)	*Parlophone*	8	*24 Aug 96*	8
SINGLE-BILINGUAL	*Parlophone*	14	*23 Nov 96*	3
Above 2 feature the Scottish female drumming troupe Sheboom.				
A RED LETTER DAY	*Parlophone*	9	*29 Mar 97*	3
Features the Choral Academy Of Moscow.				
SOMEWHERE	*Parlophone*	9	*5 Jul 97*	5
I DON'T KNOW WHAT YOU WANT BUT I CAN'T GIVE IT ANY MORE	*Parlophone*	15	*31 Jul 99*	3
NEW YORK CITY BOY	*Parlophone*	14	*9 Oct 99*	4
YOU ONLY TELL ME YOU LOVE ME WHEN YOU'RE DRUNK	*Parlophone*	8	*15 Jan 00*	4

ALBUMS:	HITS 11			WEEKS 338
PLEASE	*Parlophone*	3	*5 Apr 86*	82
DISCO	*Parlophone*	15	*29 Nov 86*	72
Features 6 12" mixes of hit singles originally on the Please album.				
PET SHOP BOYS, ACTUALLY	*Parlophone*	2	*19 Sep 87*	59
INTROSPECTIVE	*Parlophone*	2	*22 Oct 88*	39
BEHAVIOUR	*Parlophone*	2	*3 Nov 90*	14
DISCOGRAPHY - THE COMPLETE SINGLES COLLECTION	*Parlophone*	3	*16 Nov 91*	30
Includes re-entries through to 2001.				
VERY	*Parlophone*	1	*9 Oct 93*	22
DISCO 2	*Parlophone*	6	*24 Sep 94*	4
Megamix of current hits remixed by Rollo, Beatmasters, Farley and Heller, Jam and Spoon, David Morales and Brothers In Rhythm.				
ALTERNATIVE	*Parlophone*	2	*19 Aug 95*	5
Compilation featuring all their B-sides.				
BILINGUAL	*Parlophone*	4	*14 Sep 96*	8
NIGHTLIFE	*Parlophone*	7	*23 Oct 99*	3

PETER and GORDON — UK

SINGLES:	HITS 7			WEEKS 77
A WORLD WITHOUT LOVE	*Columbia*	1	*14 Mar 64*	14
Written by Lennon/McCartney.				
NOBODY I KNOW	*Columbia*	10	*6 Jun 64*	11
Above 2 written by Lennon/McCartney.				
TRUE LOVE WAYS	*Columbia*	2	*10 Apr 65*	15
TO KNOW YOU IS TO LOVE YOU	*Columbia*	5	*26 Jun 65*	10
BABY I'M YOURS	*Columbia*	19	*23 Oct 65*	9
WOMAN	*Columbia*	28	*26 Feb 66*	7
Written by Paul McCartney under the name J.Webb.				
LADY GODIVA	*Columbia*	16	*24 Sep 66*	11
Above hit: PETER and GORDON with Geoff LOVE and his Orchestra.				
EPS:	**HITS 1**			**WEEKS 1**
JUST FOR YOU	*Columbia*	20	*22 Aug 64*	1
ALBUMS:	**HITS 1**			**WEEKS 1**
PETER AND GORDON	*Columbia*	18	*20 Jun 64*	1

PETER, PAUL and MARY — US

SINGLES:	HITS 4			WEEKS 38
BLOWING IN THE WIND	*Warner Brothers*	13	*12 Oct 63*	16
Originally recorded by Bob Dylan.				
TELL IT ON THE MOUNTAIN	*Warner Brothers*	33	*18 Apr 64*	4
THE TIMES THEY ARE A-CHANGIN'	*Warner Brothers*	44	*17 Oct 64*	2
LEAVING ON A JET PLANE	*Warner Brothers*	2	*17 Jan 70*	16
Originally recorded by John Denver.				
EPS:	**HITS 4**			**WEEKS 99**
PETER, PAUL AND MARY	*Warner Brothers*	3	*30 Nov 63*	79
MOVING	*Warner Brothers*	16	*18 Apr 64*	2
BLOWIN' IN THE WIND	*Warner Brothers*	13	*28 Nov 64*	12
IN THE WIND, VOLUME 1	*Warner Brothers*	12	*8 May 65*	6
ALBUMS:	**HITS 4**			**WEEKS 26**
PETER PAUL AND MARY	*Warner Brothers*	18	*4 Jan 64*	1
IN THE WIND	*Warner Brothers*	11	*21 Mar 64*	19
IN CONCERT VOLUME 1	*Warner Brothers*	20	*13 Feb 65*	2
TEN YEARS TOGETHER	*Warner Brothers*	60	*5 Sep 70*	4

Jonathan PETERS presents LUMINAIRE — US

SINGLES:	HITS 1			WEEKS 1
FLOWER DUET	*Pelican*	75	*24 Jul 99*	1
Samples the version by Choeurs et Orchestre de Theatre National de L'Opera Comique, conducted by Georges Pretre, mezzo-soprano: Jane Berbie. seprano: Glanna d' Angelo. From the opera 'Lakme'.				

PETERS and LEE — UK

SINGLES:	HITS 5			WEEKS 57
WELCOME HOME	*Philips*	1	*26 May 73*	24
BY YOUR SIDE	*Philips*	39	*3 Nov 73*	4
DON'T STAY AWAY TOO LONG	*Philips*	3	*20 Apr 74*	15
RAINBOW	*Philips*	17	*17 Aug 74*	7
HEY, MR. MUSIC MAN	*Philips*	16	*6 Mar 76*	7
ALBUMS:	**HITS 5**			**WEEKS 166**
WE CAN MAKE IT	*Philips*	1	*30 Jun 73*	55
BY YOUR SIDE	*Philips*	9	*22 Dec 73*	48
RAINBOW	*Philips*	6	*21 Sep 74*	27
FAVOURITES	*Philips*	2	*4 Oct 75*	32
INVITATION	*Philips*	44	*18 Dec 76*	4

Ray PETERSON — US

SINGLES:	HITS 3			WEEKS 9
THE WONDER OF YOU	*RCA*	23	*5 Sep 59*	1
ANSWER ME	*RCA*	47	*26 Mar 60*	1
CORRINE, CORRINA	*London*	48	*21 Jan 61*	1
Originally recorded by Bo Carter.				
CORRINE, CORRINA [RE]	*London*	41	*4 Feb 61*	6

Tom PETTY and the HEARTBREAKERS — US

SINGLES:	HITS 11			WEEKS 43
ANYTHING THAT'S ROCK 'N' ROLL	*Shelter*	36	*25 Jun 77*	3
AMERICAN GIRL	*Shelter*	40	*13 Aug 77*	5
STOP DRAGGIN' MY HEART AROUND	*WEA*	50	*15 Aug 81*	4
Above hit: Stevie NICKS (with Tom PETTY and the HEARTBREAKERS).				
DON'T COME AROUND HERE NO MORE	*MCA*	50	*13 Apr 85*	4
I WON'T BACK DOWN	*MCA*	28	*13 May 89*	10
RUNNIN' DOWN A DREAM	*MCA*	55	*12 Aug 89*	4
FREE FALLIN'	*MCA*	64	*25 Nov 89*	2
Above 3: Tom PETTY.				
LEARNING TO FLY	*MCA*	46	*29 Jun 91*	4
TOO GOOD TO BE TRUE	*MCA*	34	*4 Apr 92*	3
SOMETHING IN THE AIR	*MCA*	53	*30 Oct 93*	2
Above hit: Tom PETTY.				
MARY JANE'S LAST DANCE	*MCA*	52	*12 Mar 94*	2
ALBUMS:	**HITS 14**			**WEEKS 104**
TOM PETTY AND THE HEARTBREAKERS	*Shelter*	24	*4 Jun 77*	12
YOU'RE GONNA GET IT	*Island*	34	*1 Jul 78*	5
DAMN THE TORPEDOES	*MCA*	57	*17 Nov 79*	4
HARD PROMISES	*MCA*	32	*23 May 81*	5
LONG AFTER DARK	*MCA*	45	*20 Nov 82*	4
SOUTHERN ACCENTS	*MCA*	23	*20 Apr 85*	6
LET ME UP (I'VE HAD ENOUGH)	*MCA*	59	*2 May 87*	2
FULL MOON FEVER	*MCA*	8	*8 Jul 89*	16
Above hit: Tom PETTY.				
INTO THE GREAT WIDE OPEN	*MCA*	3	*20 Jul 91*	18
GREATEST HITS	*MCA*	10	*13 Nov 93*	20
WILDFLOWERS	*Warner Brothers*	36	*12 Nov 94*	2
Above hit: Tom PETTY.				
SHE'S THE ONE [OST]	*Warner Brothers*	37	*24 Aug 96*	2
ECHO	*Warner Brothers*	43	*1 May 99*	2
ANTHOLOGY - THROUGH THE YEARS	*MCA*	14	*16 Jun 01*	6

PF PROJECT featuring Ewan McGREGOR — UK

SINGLES:	HITS 1			WEEKS 11
CHOOSE LIFE	*Positiva*	6	*15 Nov 97*	11
From the film 'Trainspotting'. Samples McGregor's opening monologue.				

PHANTOMS - See Johnny BRANDON with the PHANTOMS

PHARAO — Germany

SINGLES:	HITS 1			WEEKS 2
THERE IS A STAR	*Epic*	43	*4 Mar 95*	2

PHARAOHS - See SAM THE SHAM and the PHARAOHS

PHARCYDE — US

SINGLES:	HITS 3			WEEKS 6
PASSIN' ME BY	*Atlantic*	55	*31 Jul 93*	3
Samples Summer In The City by Quincy Jones.				
RUNNIN'	*Delicious Vinyl/ Go. Beat*	36	*6 Apr 96*	2
Samples Bob Marley's Running Away.				
SHE SAID	*Delicious Vinyl/ Go. Beat*	51	*10 Aug 96*	1
ALBUMS:	**HITS 2**			**WEEKS 2**
BIZARRE RIDE II THE PHARCYDE	*Atlantic*	58	*21 Aug 93*	1
LABCABINCALIFORNIA	*Delicious Vinyl/ Go. Beat*	46	*13 Apr 96*	1

Franke PHAROAH - See FRANKE; OUR TRIBE/ONE TRIBE/O.T. QUARTET

PHASE II - See Joey NEGRO

PHAT 'N' PHUNKY — UK

SINGLES:	HITS 1			WEEKS 1
LET'S GROOVE	*Chase*	61	*14 Jun 97*	1

PHATS and SMALL — UK

SINGLES:	HITS 5			WEEKS 36
TURN AROUND *Originally released on Bush Records in 1998. Samples Toney Lee's Reach Up.* *Above hit: PHATS and SMALL presents MUTANT DISCO.*	*Multiply*	2	*10 Apr 99*	16
FEEL GOOD	*Multiply*	7	*14 Aug 99*	8
TONITE *Samples Delgations Heartache No. 9.*	*Multiply*	11	*4 Dec 99*	6
THIS TIME AROUND *Samples This Time Around by S.O.U.L. featuring Larry Hancock.*	*Multiply*	15	*30 Jun 01*	5
CHANGE	*Multiply*	45	*24 Nov 01*	1

PHATT B — Holland

SINGLES:	HITS 1			WEEKS 1
AND DA DRUM MACHINE *Based around a Sweet T sample.*	*NuLife*	58	*11 Nov 00*	1

Barrington PHELOUNG — Australia

SINGLES:	HITS 1			WEEKS 2
INSPECTOR MORSE THEME *Single and album releases below are all from the Central ITV series.*	*Virgin*	61	*13 Mar 93*	2
ALBUMS:	**HITS 4**			**WEEKS 55**
INSPECTOR MORSE - ORIGINAL MUSIC FROM THE ITV SERIES	*Virgin*	4	*2 Mar 91*	30
INSPECTOR MORSE VOLUME 2 - MUSIC FROM THE TV SERIES	*Virgin Television*	18	*7 Mar 92*	12
INSPECTOR MORSE VOLUME 3 *Above hit: Barrington PHELOUNG and Janis KELLY.*	*Virgin*	20	*16 Jan 93*	11
THE MAGIC OF INSPECTOR MORSE	*Virgin*	62	*25 Nov 00*	2

PHENOMENA — UK

ALBUMS:	HITS 1			WEEKS 2
PHENOMENA	*Bronze*	63	*6 Jul 85*	2

PHILADELPHIA INTERNATIONAL ALL STARS: Lou RAWLS, Billy PAUL, Archie BELL, Teddy PENDERGRASS, O'JAYS, Dee Dee SHARP, GAMBLE — US

(See also Archie Bell and the Drells; O'Jays; Billy Paul; Teddy Pendergrass; Lou Rawls; Dee Dee Sharp.)

SINGLES:	HITS 1			WEEKS 8
LET'S CLEAN UP THE GHETTO	*Philadelphia International*	34	*13 Aug 77*	8

PHILHARMONIA ORCHESTRA conducted by Lorin MAAZEL — UK

SINGLES:	HITS 1			WEEKS 7
THEME MUSIC FROM THE FILM "2001"A SPACE ODYSSEY THUS SPAKE ZARATHUSTRA	*Columbia*	33	*2 Aug 69*	7

Arlene PHILLIPS — UK

ALBUMS:	HITS 2			WEEKS 25
KEEP IN SHAPE SYSTEM WITH ARLENE PHILLIPS *Includes music by Funk Federation.*	*Supershape*	41	*28 Aug 82*	24
KEEP IN SHAPE SYSTEM VOLUME 2	*Supershape*	100	*18 Feb 84*	1

Chynna PHILLIPS — US

(See also Wilson Phillips.)

SINGLES:	HITS 1			WEEKS 1
NAKED AND SACRED	*EMI*	62	*3 Feb 96*	1

Esther PHILLIPS — US

SINGLES:	HITS 1			WEEKS 8
WHAT A DIFFERENCE A DAY MADE *Originally recorded by the Dorsey Brothers in 1934.*	*Kudu*	6	*4 Oct 75*	8

Shola PHILLIPS - See ASTRO TRAX TEAM featuring Shola PHILLIPS

Sid PHILLIPS and his Orchestra - See DEEP RIVER BOYS with Sid PHILLIPS and his Orchestra

PHOENIX — France

SINGLES:	HITS 1			WEEKS 1
IF I EVER FEEL BETTER *Samples Toshiyuki Honda's Lament.*	*Source*	65	*3 Feb 01*	1

Paul PHOENIX (treble) with instrumental ensemble – James WATSON (trumpet), John SCOTT (organ), conducted by Barry ROSE — UK

SINGLES:	HITS 1			WEEKS 4
NUNC DIMITTIS (THEME FROM TINKER, TAILOR, SOLDIER, SPY)	*Different*	56	*3 Nov 79*	4
From the BBC TV series.				

PHOTEK — UK

SINGLES:	HITS 3			WEEKS 4
NI - TEN - ICHI - RYU (TWO SWORDS TECHNIQUE)	*Science*	37	*22 Mar 97*	2
MODUS OPERANDI	*Science*	66	*28 Feb 98*	1
MINE TO GIVE	*Science*	44	*24 Feb 01*	1
Above hit: PHOTEK – vocals: Robert OWENS.				
ALBUMS:	**HITS 3**			**WEEKS 4**
THE HIDDEN CAMERA	*Science*	39	*15 Jun 96*	1
This is an EP which due to the timing of all tracks is not eligible for the singles chart.				
MODUS OPERANDI	*Science*	30	*27 Sep 97*	2
FORM & FUNCTION	*Science*	61	*26 Sep 98*	1
Predominantly made up of tracks that appeared on his Photek 1–6 series of singles released between 1994–96.				

PHOTOS — UK

SINGLES:	HITS 1			WEEKS 4
IRENE	*Epic*	56	*17 May 80*	4
ALBUMS:	**HITS 1**			**WEEKS 9**
THE PHOTOS	*CBS*	4	*21 Jun 80*	9

PHUNKY PHANTOM — UK

SINGLES:	HITS 1			WEEKS 3
GET UP STAND UP	*Distinct'ive*	27	*16 May 98*	3

PHUTURE ASSASSINS — UK

SINGLES:	HITS 1			WEEKS 1
FUTURE SOUND [EP]	*Suburban Base*	64	*6 Jun 92*	1
Lead track: Future Sound.				

PIA – See Pia ZADORA

Edith PIAF — France

SINGLES:	HITS 1			WEEKS 15
MILORD	*Columbia*	41	*14 May 60*	4
MILORD [RE]	*Columbia*	24	*5 Nov 60*	11
ALBUMS:	**HITS 1**			**WEEKS 5**
HEART AND SOUL	*Stylus*	58	*26 Sep 87*	5

PIANOHEADZ — US

SINGLES:	HITS 1			WEEKS 2
IT'S OVER (DISTORTION)	*INCredible*	39	*11 Jul 98*	2

PIANOMAN — UK

(See also Bass Boyz.)

SINGLES:	HITS 2			WEEKS 8
BLURRED	*3 Beat*	6	*15 Jun 96*	7
Samples Blur's Girls And Boys.				
PARTY PEOPLE (LIVE YOUR LIFE BE FREE)	*3 Beat*	43	*26 Apr 97*	1
Track based on Belinda Carlisle's 1991 hit.				

Bobby (Boris) PICKETT and the CRYPT-KICKERS — US

SINGLES:	HITS 1			WEEKS 13
MONSTER MASH	*London*	3	*1 Sep 73*	13
Originally released in the US in 1962 reaching No. 1.				

Wilson PICKETT — US

SINGLES:	HITS 9			WEEKS 61
IN THE MIDNIGHT HOUR	*Atlantic*	12	*25 Sep 65*	11
DON'T FIGHT IT	*Atlantic*	29	*27 Nov 65*	8
634-5789	*Atlantic*	36	*12 Mar 66*	5
LAND OF 1000 DANCES	*Atlantic*	22	*3 Sep 66*	9
Originally written and recorded by Chris Kenner in 1963.				
MUSTANG SALLY	*Atlantic*	28	*17 Dec 66*	7
FUNKY BROADWAY	*Atlantic*	43	*30 Sep 67*	3
Originally recorded by Dyke and the Blazers.				
I'M A MIDNIGHT MOVER	*Atlantic*	38	*14 Sep 68*	6

HEY JUDE	*Atlantic*	16	*11 Jan 69*	9
IN THE MIDNIGHT HOUR (MIDNIGHT MIX - 1987 -) [RR]	*Motown*	62	*21 Nov 87*	3

PICKETTYWITCH — UK

SINGLES:	HITS 3			WEEKS 34
THAT SAME OLD FEELING	*Pye*	5	*28 Feb 70*	14
Originally recorded by Foundations				
(IT'S LIKE A) SAD OLD KINDA' MOVIE	*Pye*	16	*4 Jul 70*	10
BABY I WON'T LET YOU DOWN	*Pye*	27	*7 Nov 70*	10

Mauro PICOTTO — Italy

(See also R.A.F.)

SINGLES:	HITS 5			WEEKS 18
LIZARD (GONNA GET YOU)	*VC Recordings*	27	*12 Jun 99*	3
LIZARD GONNA GET YA (REMIXES MAURO PICOTTO) [RM]	*VC Recordings*	33	*20 Nov 99*	2
Remixed by Mauro Picotto.				
IGUANA	*VC Recordings*	33	*15 Jul 00*	3
KOMODO (SAVE A SOUL)	*VC Recordings*	13	*13 Jan 01*	5
LIKE THIS LIKE THAT	*VC Recordings*	21	*11 Aug 01*	4
VERDI	*BXR*	74	*25 Aug 01*	1

PICOTTO and Gigi D'AGOSTINO - see R.A.F.

PIGBAG — UK

SINGLES:	HITS 4			WEEKS 20
SUNNY DAY	*Y Records*	53	*7 Nov 81*	3
GETTING UP	*Y Records*	61	*27 Feb 82*	3
PAPA'S GOT A BRAND NEW PIGBAG	*Y Records*	3	*3 Apr 82*	11
Originally released 1981, constantly selling to keep appearing in the bubbling under section of the chart until its entry.				
THE BIG BEAN	*Y Records*	40	*10 Jul 82*	3
ALBUMS:	**HITS 1**			**WEEKS 14**
DR. HECKLE AND MR. JIVE	*Y Records*	18	*13 Mar 82*	14

PIGEONHED - See LO FIDELITY ALLSTARS

Nelson PIGFORD - See De Etta LITTLE and Nelson PIGFORD

PIGLETS — UK

SINGLES:	HITS 1			WEEKS 12
JOHNNY REGGAE	*Bell*	3	*6 Nov 71*	12

Dick PIKE - See Ruby WRIGHT

PIL - See PUBLIC IMAGE LTD.

PILOT — UK

SINGLES:	HITS 4			WEEKS 29
MAGIC	*EMI*	11	*2 Nov 74*	11
JANUARY	*EMI*	1	*18 Jan 75*	10
CALL ME ROUND	*EMI*	34	*19 Apr 75*	4
JUST A SMILE	*EMI*	31	*27 Sep 75*	4
ALBUMS:	**HITS 1**			**WEEKS 1**
SECOND FLIGHT	*EMI*	48	*31 May 75*	1

PILTDOWN MEN — US

SINGLES:	HITS 3			WEEKS 36
MCDONALD'S CAVE	*Capitol*	14	*10 Sep 60*	18
PILTDOWN RIDES AGAIN	*Capitol*	14	*14 Jan 61*	10
GOODNIGHT MRS. FLINTSTONE	*Capitol*	18	*11 Mar 61*	8

Courtney PINE — UK

SINGLES:	HITS 2			WEEKS 6
LIKE DREAMERS DO	*Fourth & Broadway*	26	*30 Jul 88*	5
Above hit: Mica PARIS featuring Courtney PINE.				
I'M STILL WAITING	*Mango*	66	*7 Jul 90*	1
Above hit: Courtney PINE featuring Carroll THOMPSON.				
ALBUMS:	**HITS 2**			**WEEKS 13**
JOURNEY TO THE URGE WITHIN	*Island*	39	*25 Oct 86*	11
DESTINY'S SONGS	*Antilles*	54	*6 Feb 88*	2

PING PING and Al VERLANE — Belgium

SINGLES:	HITS 1			WEEKS 4
SUCU SUCU	*Oriole*	41	*30 Sep 61*	4

PINK — US

(See also Christina Aguilera, Lil' Kim, Mya and Pink.)

SINGLES:	HITS 3			WEEKS 23
THERE YOU GO	*LaFace*	6	*10 Jun 00*	9
MOST GIRLS	*LaFace*	5	*30 Sep 00*	8
Originally recorded by Joy Enriquez.				
YOU MAKE ME SICK	*LaFace*	9	*27 Jan 01*	6
ALBUMS:	**HITS 1**			**WEEKS 35**
CAN'T TAKE ME HOME	*LaFace*	13	*27 May 00*	35

PINK FAIRIES — UK

ALBUMS:	HITS 1			WEEKS 1
WHAT A BUNCH OF SWEETIES	*Polydor*	48	*29 Jul 72*	1

PINK FLOYD — UK

SINGLES:	HITS 9			WEEKS 55
ARNOLD LAYNE	*Columbia*	20	*1 Apr 67*	8
SEE EMILY PLAY	*Columbia*	6	*24 Jun 67*	12
Above two hits: The PINK FLOYD.				
ANOTHER BRICK IN THE WALL PART II	*Harvest*	1	*1 Dec 79*	12
WHEN THE TIGERS BROKE FREE	*Harvest*	39	*7 Aug 82*	5
From the film 'The Wall'.				
NOT NOW, JOHN	*Harvest*	30	*7 May 83*	4
ON THE TURNING AWAY	*EMI*	55	*19 Dec 87*	4
ONE SLIP	*EMI*	50	*25 Jun 88*	3
TAKE IT BACK	*EMI*	23	*4 Jun 94*	4
HIGH HOPES / KEEP TALKING	*EMI*	26	*29 Oct 94*	3
ALBUMS:	**HITS 20**			**WEEKS 889**
THE PIPER AT THE GATES OF DAWN	*EMI*	6	*19 Aug 67*	14
A SAUCERFUL OF SECRETS	*Columbia*	9	*13 Jul 68*	11
Above two hits: The PINK FLOYD.				
MORE [OST]	*Columbia*	9	*28 Jun 69*	5
UMMAGUMMA	*Harvest*	5	*15 Nov 69*	21
Contains one record of live recordings and the other being solo tracks by each member of group.				
ATOM HEART MOTHER	*Harvest*	1	*24 Oct 70*	23
RELICS	*Starline*	32	*7 Aug 71*	6
Compilation.				
MEDDLE	*Harvest*	3	*20 Nov 71*	82
OBSCURED BY CLOUDS [OST]	*Harvest*	6	*17 Jun 72*	14
THE DARK SIDE OF THE MOON	*Harvest*	2	*31 Mar 73*	292
Includes re-entries through to 1982.				
A NICE PAIR [RI]	*Harvest*	21	*19 Jan 74*	20
Double re-issue of Piper At The Gates Of Dawn and A Saucerful Of Secrets.				
WISH YOU WERE HERE	*Harvest*	1	*27 Sept 75*	83
ANIMALS	*Harvest*	2	*19 Feb 77*	33
THE WALL	*Harvest*	3	*8 Dec 79*	46
Includes re-entry in 1982.				
A COLLECTION OF GREAT DANCE SONGS	*Harvest*	37	*5 Dec 81*	10
THE FINAL CUT	*Harvest*	1	*2 Apr 83*	25
THE DARK SIDE OF THE MOON [RE-1ST]	*Harvest*	69	*1 Oct 83*	9
Includes re-entries through to 1991. Peak position reached in 1990, (1983 peak No. 86, 1988 peak No. 77).				
A MOMENTARY LAPSE OF REASON	*EMI*	3	*19 Sep 87*	34
WISH YOU WERE HERE [RE]	*Harvest*	97	*20 Aug 88*	1
DELICATE SOUND OF THUNDER	*EMI*	11	*3 Dec 88*	12
THE WALL [RE]	*Harvest*	52	*4 Aug 90*	5
THE DARK SIDE OF THE MOON [RE-2ND]	*Harvest*	4	*20 Mar 93*	9
Digitally remastered 20th Anniversary edition.				
THE DIVISION BELL	*EMI*	1	*9 Apr 94*	51
THE DARK SIDE OF THE MOON [RI]	*EMI*	38	*6 Aug 94*	41
Peak position reached in 1995, (1994 peak No. 44).				
WISH YOU WERE HERE [RI]	*EMI*	52	*6 Aug 94*	5
Mid-price re-issue.				
PULSE	*EMI*	1	*10 Jun 95*	21
Live recordings from over 20 European shows.				
RELICS [RI]	*EMI*	48	*9 Mar 96*	2
First appearance on CD with new cover.				
THE PIPER AT THE GATES OF DAWN [RI]	*EMI*	44	*16 Aug 97*	2
30th Anniversary edition. The vinyl format is a remastered edition of the mono version.				
IS THERE ANYBODY OUT THERE? – THE WALL LIVE 1980-81	*EMI*	15	*8 Apr 00*	5
ECHOES – THE BEST OF PINK FLOYD	*EMI*	2	*17 Nov 01*	7

PINKEES — UK

SINGLES:	HITS 1			WEEKS 9
DANGER GAMES	*Creole*	8	*18 Sep 82*	9

PINKERTON'S 'ASSORT'. COLOURS — UK

SINGLES:	HITS 2			WEEKS 12
MIRROR, MIRROR	*Decca*	9	*15 Jan 66*	11
DON'T STOP LOVING ME BABY	*Decca*	50	*23 Apr 66*	1

PINKY and her PLAYBOYS – See Dorothy PROVINE

PINKY and PERKY — UK

SINGLES:	HITS 1			WEEKS 3
REET PETITE	*Telstar*	47	*29 May 93*	3
Featured in the HTV Childrens' series 'The Pig Attraction'. Even though not listed, this was released as an [AA] with It Only Takes A Minute Girl.				
EPS:	**HITS 1**			**WEEKS 4**
CHRISTMAS WITH PINKY AND PERKY	*Columbia*	16	*23 Dec 61*	4
COMPILATION ALBUMS:	**HITS 1**			**WEEKS 2**
THE PIG ATTRACTION FEATURING PINKY AND PERKY	*Telstar*	19	*12 Jun 93*	2
Childrens series shown on ITV. Listed on the Compilation chart as certain tracks are by other artists.				

PIONEERS — Jamaica

SINGLES:	HITS 3			WEEKS 34
LONG SHOT KICK THE BUCKET	*Trojan*	21	*18 Oct 69*	10
LONG SHOT KICK THE BUCKET [RE]	*Trojan*	40	*10 Jan 70*	1
LET YOUR YEAH BE YEAH	*Trojan*	5	*31 Jul 71*	12
Originally recorded by Jimmy Cliff.				
GIVE AND TAKE	*Trojan*	35	*15 Jan 72*	6
LONG SHOT KICK DE BUCKET [RI]	*Trojan*	42	*29 Mar 80*	5
[AA] listed with Liquidator by Harry J. All Stars.				

Billie PIPER — UK

(See also Steps Tina Cousins Cleopatra B*Witched Billie.)

SINGLES:	HITS 7			WEEKS 74
BECAUSE WE WANT TO	*Innocent*	1	*11 Jul 98*	12
GIRLFRIEND	*Innocent*	1	*17 Oct 98*	10
SHE WANTS YOU	*Innocent*	3	*19 Dec 98*	11
GIRLFRIEND [RE]	*Innocent*	71	*2 Jan 99*	2
SHE WANTS YOU [RE]	*Innocent*	54	*13 Mar 99*	2
HONEY TO THE BEE	*Innocent*	3	*3 Apr 99*	9
HONEY TO THE BEE [RE]	*Innocent*	70	*26 Jun 99*	2
Above 4: BILLIE.				
DAY & NIGHT	*Innocent*	1	*27 May 00*	11
DAY & NIGHT [RE]	*Innocent*	73	*19 Aug 00*	1
SOMETHING DEEP INSIDE	*Innocent*	4	*30 Sep 00*	8
WALK OF LIFE	*Innocent*	25	*23 Dec 00*	5
SOMETHING DEEP INSIDE [RE]	*Innocent*	67	*13 Jan 01*	1
ALBUMS:	**HITS 2**			**WEEKS 27**
HONEY TO THE B	*Innocent*	14	*31 Oct 98*	23
Above hit: BILLIE.				
WALK OF LIFE	*innocent*	14	*14 Oct 00*	4

PIPKINS — UK

SINGLES:	HITS 1			WEEKS 10
GIMME DAT DING	*Columbia*	6	*28 Mar 70*	10

PIPS – See Gladys KNIGHT and the PIPS

PIRANHAS — UK

SINGLES:	HITS 2			WEEKS 21
TOM HARK	*Sire*	6	*2 Aug 80*	12
ZAMBEZI	*Dakota*	17	*16 Oct 82*	9
Above hit: PIRANHAS featuring Boring Bob GROVER – The Man with the Golden Trumpet.				
ALBUMS:	**HITS 1**			**WEEKS 3**
PIRANHAS	*Sire*	69	*20 Sep 80*	3

PIRATES — UK

(See also Johnny Kidd and the Pirates.)

ALBUMS:	HITS 1			WEEKS 3
OUT OF THEIR SKULLS	*Warner Brothers*	57	*19 Nov 77*	3

PITCHSHIFTER — UK

SINGLES:	HITS 3			WEEKS 3
GENIUS	*Geffen*	71	*28 Feb 98*	1
MICROWAVED	*Geffen*	54	*26 Sep 98*	1
DEAD BATTERY	*MCA*	71	*21 Oct 00*	1

ALBUMS:	HITS 1			WEEKS 1
DEVIANT	*MCA*	35	*3 Jun 00*	1

Gene PITNEY — US

SINGLES:	HITS 22			WEEKS 212
(I WANNA) LOVE MY LIFE AWAY	*London*	26	*25 Mar 61*	11
TOWN WITHOUT PITY	*His Master's Voice*	32	*10 Mar 62*	6
From the film of the same name.				
TWENTY FOUR HOURS FROM TULSA	*United Artists*	5	*7 Dec 63*	19
THAT GIRL BELONGS TO YESTERDAY	*United Artists*	7	*7 Mar 64*	12
Written by Jagger/Richards.				
IT HURTS TO BE IN LOVE	*United Artists*	36	*17 Oct 64*	4
I'M GONNA BE STRONG	*Stateside*	2	*14 Nov 64*	14
Originally recorded by Frankie Laine.				
I MUST BE SEEING THINGS	*Stateside*	6	*20 Feb 65*	10
LOOKING THRU THE EYES OF LOVE	*Stateside*	3	*12 Jun 65*	12
PRINCESS IN RAGS	*Stateside*	9	*6 Nov 65*	12
Originally recorded by Tony Bennett.				
BACKSTAGE	*Stateside*	4	*19 Feb 66*	10
NOBODY NEEDS YOUR LOVE	*Stateside*	2	*11 Jun 66*	13
JUST ONE SMILE	*Stateside*	8	*12 Nov 66*	12
Above 2 originally recorded by Randy Newman.				
(IN THE) COLD LIGHT OF DAY	*Stateside*	38	*25 Feb 67*	6
SOMETHING'S GOTTEN HOLD OF MY HEART	*Stateside*	5	*18 Nov 67*	13
SOMEWHERE IN THE COUNTRY	*Stateside*	19	*6 Apr 68*	9
YOURS UNTIL TOMORROW	*Stateside*	34	*30 Nov 68*	7
MARIA ELENA	*Stateside*	25	*8 Mar 69*	6
A STREET CALLED HOPE	*Stateside*	37	*14 Mar 70*	5
SHADY LADY	*Stateside*	29	*3 Oct 70*	8
24 SYCAMORE	*Pye International*	34	*28 Apr 73*	7
Originally recorded by Wayne Fontana.				
BLUE ANGEL	*Bronze*	49	*2 Nov 74*	1
BLUE ANGEL [RE]	*Bronze*	39	*16 Nov 74*	3
SOMETHING'S GOTTEN HOLD OF MY HEART	*Parlophone*	1	*14 Jan 89*	12
Above hit: Marc ALMOND featuring special guest star Gene PITNEY.				

EPS:	HITS 3			WEEKS 26
TWENTY FOUR HOURS FROM TULSA	*United Artists*	7	*29 Feb 64*	16
THAT GIRL BELONGS TO YESTERDAY	*Stateside*	13	*27 Feb 65*	7
BACKSTAGE	*Stateside*	6	*9 Jul 66*	3

ALBUMS:	HITS 10			WEEKS 75
BLUE GENE	*United Artists*	7	*11 Apr 64*	11
GENE PITNEY'S BIG SIXTEEN	*Stateside*	12	*6 Feb 65*	6
Originally released on United Artists in 1964.				
I'M GONNA BE STRONG	*Stateside*	15	*20 Mar 65*	2
LOOKIN' THRU THE EYES OF LOVE	*Stateside*	15	*20 Nov 65*	5
NOBODY NEEDS YOUR LOVE	*Stateside*	13	*17 Sep 66*	17
YOUNG WARM AND WONDERFUL	*Stateside*	39	*4 Mar 67*	1
GENE PITNEY'S BIG SIXTEEN (VOL. 3)	*Stateside*	40	*22 Apr 67*	1
BEST OF GENE PITNEY	*Stateside*	8	*20 Sep 69*	9
HIS 20 GREATEST HITS	*Arcade*	6	*2 Oct 76*	14
BACKSTAGE - THE GREATEST HITS AND MORE	*Polydor*	17	*20 Oct 90*	7
THE ULTIMATE COLLECTION	*Sequel*	40	*22 Sep 01*	2

Mario PIU — Italy

SINGLES:	HITS 2			WEEKS 14
COMMUNICATION (SOMEBODY ANSWER THE PHONE)	*Incentive*	5	*11 Dec 99*	9
THE VISION	BXR	16	*10 Mar 01*	4
Above hit: Mario PIU presents DJ ARABESQUE.				
THE VISION [RE]	BXR	71	*21 Apr 01*	1

PIXIES — US

SINGLES:	HITS 6			WEEKS 13
MONKEY GONE TO HEAVEN	*4AD*	60	*1 Apr 89*	3
HERE COMES YOUR MAN	*4AD*	54	*1 Jul 89*	1
VELOURIA	*4AD*	28	*28 Jul 90*	3
DIG FOR FIRE	*4AD*	62	*10 Nov 90*	1
PLANET OF SOUND	*4AD*	27	*8 Jun 91*	3
DEBASER	*4AD*	23	*4 Oct 97*	2
Originally released on the album Doolittle in 1989.				

ALBUMS:	HITS 7			WEEKS 29
DOOLITTLE	*4AD*	8	*29 Apr 89*	9
BOSSANOVA	*4AD*	3	*25 Aug 90*	8
TROMPE LE MONDE	*4AD*	7	*5 Oct 91*	5
DEATH TO THE PIXIES	*4AD*	28	*18 Oct 97*	3
DEATH TO THE PIXIES - DELUXE EDITION	*4AD*	20	*18 Oct 97*	2
Same album as above plus CD of live tracks. This bonus CD therefore makes the release count as a new entry due to chart rules.				
PIXIES AT THE BBC	*4AD*	45	*18 Jul 98*	1
Material recorded for both John Peel and Mark Goodier's BBC Radio1 shows.				
COMPLETE B-SIDES	*4AD*	53	*17 Mar 01*	1

PIZZAMAN — UK

SINGLES:	HITS 4			WEEKS 18
TRIPPIN ON SUNSHINE	*Loaded*	33	*27 Aug 94*	2
Takes its chorus from Rocker's Revenge's Walking On Sunshine.				
SEX ON THE STREETS	*Loaded*	24	*10 Jun 95*	4
HAPPINESS	*Loaded*	19	*18 Nov 95*	4
SEX ON THE STREETS [RE]	*Loaded*	23	*6 Jan 96*	4
TRIPPIN' ON SUNSHINE [RI]	*Loaded*	18	*1 Jun 96*	3
HELLO HONKY TONKS (ROCK YOUR BODY)	*Loaded*	41	*14 Sep 96*	1

PIZZICATO FIVE — Japan

SINGLES:	HITS 1			WEEKS 1
MON AMOUR TOKYO	*Matador*	72	*1 Nov 97*	1

Joe PIZZULO - See Sergio MENDES featuring Joe PIZZULO and Leza MILLER

PJ — Canada

SINGLES:	HITS 1			WEEKS 2
HAPPY DAYS	*Deconstruction*	72	*20 Sep 97*	1
First released in Canada 1996.				
Above hit: P.J.				
HAPPY DAYS [RM]	*Defected*	57	*04 Sept 99*	1
Remixed by Phats and Small. Samples Northend featuring Michelle Wallace's Tee's Happy.				

PJ and DUNCAN - See ANT and DEC

PJ HARVEY - See PJ HARVEY

PKA — UK

SINGLES:	HITS 2			WEEKS 2
TEMPERATURE RISING	*Stress*	68	*20 Apr 91*	1
POWERGEN (ONLY YOUR LOVE)	*Stress*	70	*7 Mar 92*	1
Above hit: P.K.A.				

PLACEBO — US/Sweden

SINGLES:	HITS 8			WEEKS 37
TEENAGE ANGST	*Elevator Music/Hut*	30	*28 Sep 96*	3
NANCY BOY	*Elevator Music/Hut*	4	*1 Feb 97*	6
BRUISE PRISTINE	*Elevator Music/Hut*	14	*24 May 97*	3
Originally their debut release on the Fierce Panda label in 1995.				
PURE MORNING	*Elevator Music/Hut*	4	*15 Aug 98*	6
YOU DON'T CARE ABOUT US	*Elevator Music/Hut*	5	*10 Oct 98*	5
EVERY YOU EVERY ME	*Elevator Music/Hut*	11	*6 Feb 99*	5
TASTE IN MEN	*Elevator Music/Hut*	16	*29 Jul 00*	6
SLAVE TO THE WAGE	*Elevator Music/Hut*	19	*7 Oct 00*	3
Samples Pavement's Texas Never Whispers.				

ALBUMS:	HITS 3			WEEKS 35
PLACEBO	*Elevator Music*	40	*29 Jun 96*	1
PLACEBO [RE]	*Elevator Music*	5	*15 Feb 97*	12
WITHOUT YOU I'M NOTHING	*Elevator Music/Hut*	7	*24 Oct 98*	17
BLACK MARKET MUSIC	*Elevator Music/Hut*	6	*21 Oct 00*	5

PLANET PATROL — US

SINGLES:	HITS 1			WEEKS 3
CHEAP THRILLS	*Polydor*	64	*17 Sep 83*	3

PLANET PERFECTO — UK

(See also Perfecto Allstarz.)

SINGLES:	HITS 3			WEEKS 15
NOT OVER YET 99	*Code Blue*	16	*14 Aug 99*	4
Edited version of the original 1995 release which was only credited to Grace.				
Above hit: PLANET PERFECTO featuring GRACE.				
BULLET IN THE GUN	*Perfecto*	15	*13 Nov 99*	4

BULLET IN THE GUN 2000 [RM] *Remixed by Mekka.*	*Perfecto*	7	*16 Sep 00*	6
BITES DA DUST	*Perfecto*	52	*29 Sep 01*	1

PLANETFUNK — UK/Italy/Sweden

SINGLES:	HITS 1			WEEKS 9
CHASE THE SUN	*Virgin*	5	*10 Feb 01*	6
CHASE THE SUN [RE]	*Virgin*	55	*31 Mar 01*	3

PLANETS — UK

SINGLES:	HITS 2			WEEKS 8
LINES	*Rialto*	36	*18 Aug 79*	6
DON'T LOOK DOWN	*Rialto*	66	*25 Oct 80*	2

Robert PLANT — UK

(See also Jimmy Page and Robert Plant.)

SINGLES:	HITS 7			WEEKS 28
BURNING DOWN ONE SIDE	*Swan Song*	73	*9 Oct 82*	1
BIG LOG	*WEA*	11	*16 Jul 83*	10
HEAVEN KNOWS	*Es Paranza*	33	*30 Jan 88*	5
HURTING KIND (I'VE GOT MY EYES ON YOU)	*Es Paranza*	45	*28 Apr 90*	3
29 PALMS	*Es Paranza*	21	*8 May 93*	5
I BELIEVE	*Es Paranza*	64	*3 Jul 93*	2
IF I WERE A CARPENTER	*Fontana*	63	*25 Dec 93*	2
ALBUMS:	**HITS 6**			**WEEKS 57**
PICTURES AT ELEVEN	*Swan Song*	2	*10 Jul 82*	15
THE PRINCIPLE OF MOMENTS	*Atlantic*	7	*23 Jul 83*	14
SHAKEN 'N' STIRRED	*Es Paranza*	19	*1 Jun 85*	4
NOW AND ZEN	*Es Paranza*	10	*12 Mar 88*	7
MANIC NIRVANA	*Es Paranza*	15	*31 Mar 90*	9
FATE OF NATIONS	*Es*	6	*5 Jun 93*	8

PLASMATICS — US

SINGLES:	HITS 1			WEEKS 4
BUTCHER BABY	*Stiff*	55	*26 Jul 80*	4
ALBUMS:	**HITS 1**			**WEEKS 3**
NEW HOPE FOR THE WRETCHED	*Stiff*	55	*11 Oct 80*	3

PLASTIC BERTRAND — Belgium

SINGLES:	HITS 2			WEEKS 17
CA PLANE POUR MOI	*Sire*	8	*13 May 78*	12
SHA LA LA LA LEE	*Vertigo*	39	*5 Aug 78*	5

PLASTIC JAM - See BUG KANN and the PLASTIC JAM

PLASTIC ONO BAND - See John LENNON

PLASTIC PENNY — UK

SINGLES:	HITS 1			WEEKS 10
EVERYTHING I AM *Originally recorded by the Box Tops.*	*Page One*	6	*6 Jan 68*	10

PLASTIC POPULATION - See YAZZ

PLASTIK MAN — Canada

(See also Fuse.)

ALBUMS:	HITS 1			WEEKS 1
MUSIK	*Novamute*	58	*19 Nov 94*	1

PLATINUM HOOK — US

SINGLES:	HITS 1			WEEKS 1
STANDING ON THE VERGE (OF GETTING IT ON)	*Motown*	72	*2 Sep 78*	1

PLATTERS — US

SINGLES:	HITS 8			WEEKS 92
THE GREAT PRETENDER / ONLY YOU (AND YOU ALONE) *From the film 'Rock Around The Clock'.*	*Mercury*	5	*8 Sep 56*	12
MY PRAYER *Originally recorded by Glenn Miller in 1939.*	*Mercury*	4	*3 Nov 56*	10
THE GREAT PRETENDER / ONLY YOU (AND YOU ALONE) [RE-1ST]	*Mercury*	21	*8 Dec 56*	1
MY PRAYER [RE-1ST]	*Mercury*	28	*19 Jan 57*	2
YOU'LL NEVER, NEVER KNOW / IT ISN'T RIGHT	*Mercury*	23	*26 Jan 57*	1
YOU'LL NEVER, NEVER KNOW / IT ISN'T RIGHT [RE-1ST]	*Mercury*	29	*9 Feb 57*	1
MY PRAYER [RE-2ND]	*Mercury*	22	*30 Mar 57*	1

ONLY YOU (AND YOU ALONE) [RE-2ND]	*Mercury*	18	*30 Mar 57*	3
YOU'LL NEVER, NEVER KNOW / IT ISN'T RIGHT [RE-2ND]	*Mercury*	29	*13 Apr 57*	1
I'M SORRY *Originally recorded by Bobby Wayne in 1952.*	*Mercury*	18	*18 May 57*	6
I'M SORRY [RE-1ST]	*Mercury*	23	*6 Jul 57*	1
I'M SORRY [RE-2ND]	*Mercury*	22	*20 Jul 57*	1
TWILIGHT TIME *Originally recorded by the Three Suns.*	*Mercury*	3	*17 May 58*	18
SMOKE GETS IN YOUR EYES *Original recorded by Paul Whiteman in 1933.*	*Mercury*	1	*17 Jan 59*	20
REMEMBER WHEN *Above hit: PLATTERS solo vocal by Tony WILLIAMS.*	*Mercury*	25	*29 Aug 59*	2
HARBOUR LIGHTS *Originally recorded by Frances Langford in 1937.*	*Mercury*	11	*30 Jan 60*	12
ALBUMS:	**HITS 1**			**WEEKS 13**
20 CLASSIC HITS	*Mercury*	8	*8 Apr 78*	13

PLAVKA – See JAM and SPOON featuring PLAVKA

PLAYBOYS – See Dorothy PROVINE

PLAYBOYS – See Gary LEWIS and the PLAYBOYS

PLAYER — UK/US

SINGLES:	**HITS 1**			**WEEKS 7**
BABY COME BACK	*RSO*	32	*25 Feb 78*	7

PLAYERS ASSOCIATION — US

SINGLES:	**HITS 3**			**WEEKS 17**
TURN THE MUSIC UP!	*Vanguard*	8	*10 Mar 79*	9
RIDE THE GROOVE	*Vanguard*	42	*5 May 79*	5
WE GOT THE GROOVE	*Vanguard*	61	*9 Feb 80*	3
ALBUMS:	**HITS 1**			**WEEKS 4**
TURN THE MUSIC UP	*Vanguard*	54	*17 Mar 79*	4

PLAYGROUP — UK

SINGLES:	**HITS 1**			**WEEKS 9**
NUMBER ONE	*Source*	66	*24 Nov 01*	1

PLAYN JAYN — UK

ALBUMS:	**HITS 1**			**WEEKS 1**
FRIDAY THE 13TH (LIVE AT THE MARQUEE)	*A&M*	93	*1 Sep 84*	1

PLAYTHING — Italy

SINGLES:	**HITS 1**			**WEEKS 1**
INTO SPACE *Samples Sheila and B. Devotion's Spacer.*	*Manifesto*	48	*5 May 01*	1

PLUS ONE featuring SIRRON — UK

SINGLES:	**HITS 1**			**WEEKS 4**
IT'S HAPPENIN'	*MCA*	40	*19 May 90*	4

PLUTO – See Pluto SHERVINGTON

PLUX featuring Georgia JONES — US

SINGLES:	**HITS 1**			**WEEKS 2**
OVER & OVER *Samples Rufus and Chaka Khan's Ain't Nobody, Bucketheads' The Bomb and Patrick Juvet's Got A Feeling.*	*ffrr*	33	*4 May 96*	2

PM DAWN — US

SINGLES:	**HITS 10**			**WEEKS 39**
A WATCHER'S POINT OF VIEW (DON'T CHA THINK)	*Gee Street*	36	*8 Jun 91*	5
SET ADRIFT ON MEMORY BLISS *Samples Spandau Ballet's True.*	*Gee Street*	3	*17 Aug 91*	8
PAPER DOLL	*Gee Street*	49	*19 Oct 91*	3
REALITY USED TO BE A FRIEND OF MINE	*Gee Street*	29	*22 Feb 92*	4
I'D DIE WITHOUT YOU	*Gee Street*	30	*7 Nov 92*	5
LOOKING THROUGH PATIENT EYES *Samples Father Figure by George Michael and features backing vocals by Cathy Dennis.*	*Gee Street*	11	*13 Mar 93*	7
MORE THAN LIKELY *Above hit: PM DAWN featuring BOY GEORGE.*	*Gee Street*	40	*12 Jun 93*	3
DOWNTOWN VENUS *Samples Deep Purple's Hush.* *Above hit: P.M. DAWN.*	*Gee Street*	58	*30 Sep 95*	2

SOMETIMES I MISS YOU SO MUCH (DEDICATED TO THE CHRIST CONSCIOUSNESS)	*Gee Street*	58	*6 Apr 96*	1
GOTTA BE . . . MOVIN' ON UP	*Gee Street*	68	*31 Oct 98*	1
Samples Imagination's Just An Illusion.				
Above hit: P.M. DAWN featuring KY-MANI.				
ALBUMS:	**HITS 2**			**WEEKS 17**
OF THE HEART, OF THE SOUL AND OF THE CROSS - THE UTOPIAN EXPERIENCE	*Gee Street*	8	*14 Sept 91*	8
OF THE HEART, OF THE SOUL AND OF THE CROSS - THE UTOPIAN EXPERIENCE [RE]	*Gee Street*	44	*14 Mar 92*	4
Repackaged with additional tracks.				
THE BLISS ALBUM . . . ? (VIBRATIONS OF LOVE AND ANGER AND THE PONDERANCE OF LIFE AND EXISTENCE)	*Gee Street*	9	*3 Apr 93*	5

POB featuring DJ Patrick REID — UK

SINGLES:	**HITS 1**			**WEEKS 1**
BLUEBOTTLE / FLY	*Platipus*	74	*11 Dec 99*	1

POETS — UK

SINGLES:	**HITS 1**			**WEEKS 5**
NOW WE'RE THRU'	*Decca*	31	*31 Oct 64*	5

POGUES — Ireland/UK

SINGLES:	**HITS 17**			**WEEKS 70**
A PAIR OF BROWN EYES	*Stiff*	72	*6 Apr 85*	2
SALLY MACLENNANE	*Stiff*	51	*22 Jun 85*	4
DIRTY OLD TOWN	*Stiff*	62	*14 Sep 85*	3
POGUETRY IN MOTION [EP]	*Stiff*	29	*8 Mar 86*	6
Lead track: London Girl.				
HAUNTED (FROM THE MOTION PICTURE SOUNDTRACK SID AND NANCY)	*MCA*	42	*30 Aug 86*	4
THE IRISH ROVER	*Stiff*	8	*28 Mar 87*	8
Above hit: POGUES and the DUBLINERS.				
FAIRYTALE OF NEW YORK	*Pogue Mahone*	2	*5 Dec 87*	9
Above hit: POGUES featuring Kirsty MacCOLL.				
IF I SHOULD FALL FROM GRACE WITH GOD	*Pogue Mahone*	58	*5 Mar 88*	3
FIESTA	*Pogue Mahone*	24	*16 Jul 88*	5
YEAH, YEAH, YEAH, YEAH, YEAH	*Pogue Mahone*	43	*17 Dec 88*	4
MISTY MORNING, ALBERT BRIDGE	*Pogue Mahone*	41	*8 Jul 89*	3
JACK'S HEROES / WHISKEY IN THE JAR	*Pogue Mahone*	63	*16 Jun 90*	2
Above hit: POGUES and the DUBLINERS.				
SUMMER IN SIAM	*Pogue Mahone*	64	*15 Sep 90*	2
A RAINY NIGHT IN SOHO	*PM*	67	*21 Sep 91*	1
Re-Mix of track from the Poguety In Motion EP.				
FAIRYTALE OF NEW YORK [RI]	*PM*	36	*14 Dec 91*	5
Above hit: POGUES featuring Kirsty MacCOLL.				
HONKY TONK WOMEN	*PM*	56	*30 May 92*	2
TUESDAY MORNING	*PM*	18	*21 Aug 93*	5
ONCE UPON A TIME	*PM*	66	*22 Jan 94*	2
ALBUMS:	**HITS 8**			**WEEKS 72**
RED ROSES FOR ME	*Stiff*	89	*3 Nov 84*	1
RUM, SODOMY AND THE LASH	*Stiff*	13	*17 Aug 85*	14
IF I SHOULD FALL FROM GRACE WITH GOD	*Stiff*	3	*30 Jan 88*	16
PEACE AND LOVE	*Pogue Mahone*	5	*29 Jul 89*	8
HELL'S DITCH	*Pogue Mahone*	12	*13 Oct 90*	5
THE BEST OF THE POGUES	*PM*	11	*12 Oct 91*	17
WAITING FOR HERB	*PM*	20	*11 Sep 93*	3
THE VERY BEST OF THE POGUES	*warner.esp*	18	*17 Mar 01*	8

POINT BREAK — UK

SINGLES:	**HITS 5**			**WEEKS 21**
DO WE ROCK	*Eternal*	29	*9 Oct 99*	2
STAND TOUGH	*Eternal*	7	*22 Jan 00*	5
FREAKYTIME	*Eternal*	13	*22 Apr 00*	6
YOU	*Eternal*	14	*5 Aug 00*	5
WHAT ABOUT US	*Eternal*	24	*2 Dec 00*	3
ALBUMS:	**HITS 1**			**WEEKS 3**
APOCADELIC	*Eternal*	21	*19 Aug 00*	3

POINTER SISTERS — US

SINGLES:	**HITS 10**			**WEEKS 87**
EVERYBODY IS A STAR	*Planet*	61	*3 Feb 79*	3
Original by Sly and the Family Stone reached No. 1 in the US in 1970.				
FIRE	*Planet*	34	*17 Mar 79*	8
Originally recorded by Bruce Springsteen.				
SLOW HAND	*Planet*	10	*22 Aug 81*	11

SHOULD I DO IT?	*Reprise*	50	*5 Dec 81*	5
AUTOMATIC	*Planet*	2	*14 Apr 84*	15
JUMP (FOR MY LOVE)	*Planet*	6	*23 Jun 84*	10
I NEED YOU	*Planet*	25	*11 Aug 84*	9
I'M SO EXCITED	*Planet*	11	*27 Oct 84*	11
NEUTRON DANCE	*Planet*	31	*12 Jan 85*	7
From the film 'Beverley Hills Cop'.				
DARE ME	*Planet*	17	*20 Jul 85*	8
ALBUMS:	**HITS 4**			**WEEKS 88**
BLACK AND WHITE	*Planet*	21	*29 Aug 81*	13
BREAK OUT	*Planet*	9	*5 May 84*	58
CONTACT	*Planet*	34	*27 Jul 85*	7
JUMP - THE BEST OF THE POINTER SISTERS	*RCA*	11	*29 Jul 89*	10

POISON — US

SINGLES:	**HITS 10**			**WEEKS 43**
TALK DIRTY TO ME	*Music For Nations*	67	*23 May 87*	1
NOTHIN' BUT A GOOD TIME	*Capitol*	35	*7 May 88*	3
FALLEN ANGEL	*Capitol*	59	*5 Nov 88*	1
EVERY ROSE HAS ITS THORN	*Capitol*	13	*11 Feb 89*	9
YOUR MAMA DON'T DANCE	*Capitol*	13	*29 Apr 89*	7
Original by Loggins and Messina reached No. 4 in the US in 1972.				
NOTHIN' BUT A GOOD TIME [RI]	*Capitol*	48	*23 Sep 89*	3
UNSKINNY BOP	*Capitol*	15	*30 Jun 90*	7
Single (as per 7" format) starts with a 1min 26sec track called Swampjuice (Soul-O) before going into Unskinny Bop.				
SOMETHING TO BELIEVE IN	*Capitol*	35	*27 Oct 90*	4
SO TELL ME WHY	*Capitol*	25	*23 Nov 91*	2
STAND	*Capitol*	25	*13 Feb 93*	3
UNTIL YOU SUFFER SOME (FIRE AND ICE)	*Capitol*	32	*24 Apr 93*	3
ALBUMS:	**HITS 4**			**WEEKS 37**
OPEN UP AND SAY . . . AAH!	*Capitol*	18	*21 May 88*	21
FLESH AND BLOOD	*Capitol*	3	*21 Jul 90*	11
SWALLOW THIS LIVE	*Capitol*	52	*14 Dec 91*	2
NATIVE TONGUE	*Capitol*	20	*6 Mar 93*	3

POKEMON ALLSTARS - See 50 GRIND featuring POKEMON ALLSTARS

POLECATS — UK

SINGLES:	**HITS 3**			**WEEKS 18**
JOHN I'M ONLY DANCING / BIG GREEN CAR	*Mercury*	35	*7 Mar 81*	8
ROCKABILLY GUY	*Mercury*	35	*16 May 81*	6
JEEPSTER / MARIE CELESTE	*Mercury*	53	*22 Aug 81*	4
ALBUMS:	**HITS 1**			**WEEKS 2**
POLECATS	*Vertigo*	28	*4 Jul 81*	2

POLICE — UK

SINGLES:	**HITS 19**			**WEEKS 153**
CAN'T STAND LOSING YOU	*A&M*	42	*7 Oct 78*	5
ROXANNE	*A&M*	12	*28 Apr 79*	9
Originally released in 1978.				
CAN'T STAND LOSING YOU [RE]	*A&M*	2	*7 Jul 79*	11
MESSAGE IN A BOTTLE	*A&M*	1	*22 Sep 79*	11
FALL OUT	*Illegal*	47	*17 Nov 79*	4
Originally released in 1977.				
WALKING ON THE MOON	*A&M*	1	*1 Dec 79*	10
SO LONELY	*A&M*	6	*16 Feb 80*	10
SIX PACK [EP]	*A&M*	17	*14 Jun 80*	4
Lead track: The Bed's Too Big Without You. The package includes the previous 5 A&M releases to make up a 6x7" blue vinyl set.				
DON'T STAND SO CLOSE TO ME	*A&M*	1	*27 Sep 80*	10
DE DO DO DO, DE DA DA DA	*A&M*	5	*13 Dec 80*	8
INVISIBLE SUN	*A&M*	2	*26 Sep 81*	8
EVERY LITTLE THING SHE DOES IS MAGIC	*A&M*	1	*24 Oct 81*	13
SPIRITS IN THE MATERIAL WORLD	*A&M*	12	*12 Dec 81*	8
EVERY BREATH YOU TAKE	*A&M*	1	*28 May 83*	11
WRAPPED AROUND YOUR FINGER	*A&M*	7	*23 Jul 83*	7
SYNCHRONICITY II	*A&M*	17	*5 Nov 83*	4
KING OF PAIN	*A&M*	17	*14 Jan 84*	5
DON'T STAND SO CLOSE TO ME '86 [RR]	*A&M*	24	*11 Oct 86*	4
CAN'T STAND LOSING YOU (LIVE) [RR]	*A&M*	27	*13 May 95*	2
Live recording from the Orpheus, Boston, 1979.				
ROXANNE '97 [RM]	*A&M*	17	*20 Dec 97*	6
Remixed by Puff Daddy. Samples U.T.F.O.'s Roxanne Roxanne and Kool And The Gang's Kool's Back Again.				
Above hit: STING and the POLICE.				

WHEN THE WORLD IS RUNNING DOWN (YOU CAN'T GO WRONG) *Remix of a track from their 1980 album Zenyatta Mondatta.* *Above hit: DIFFERENT GEAR vs the POLICE.*	*Pagan*	28	*5 Aug 00*	3
ALBUMS:	**HITS 9**			**WEEKS 386**
OUTLANDOS D'AMOUR	*A&M*	6	*21 Apr 79*	96
REGGATTA DE BLANC	*A&M*	1	*13 Oct 79*	74
ZENYATTA MONDATTA	*A&M*	1	*11 Oct 80*	31
GHOST IN THE MACHINE	*A&M*	1	*10 Oct 81*	27
SYNCHRONICITY	*A&M*	1	*25 Jun 83*	48
EVERY BREATH YOU TAKE - THE SINGLES *Includes re-entries throught to 1992.*	*A&M*	1	*8 Nov 86*	55
GREATEST HITS	*A&M*	10	*10 Oct 92*	21
LIVE! *Live recordings of 2 complete shows from their US tours in 1979 and 1983.*	*A&M*	25	*10 Jun 95*	3
THE VERY BEST OF STING AND THE POLICE *Features both Sting's solo and group material.* *Above hit: STING/The POLICE.*	*A&M*	11	*22 Nov 97*	31

Su POLLARD — UK

SINGLES:	**HITS 2**			**WEEKS 11**
COME TO ME (I AM WOMAN)	*Rainbow*	71	*5 Oct 85*	1
STARTING TOGETHER *Theme from the BBC TV series 'The Marriage'.*	*Rainbow*	2	*1 Feb 86*	10
ALBUMS:	**HITS 1**			**WEEKS 3**
SU	*K-Tel*	86	*22 Nov 86*	3

Jimi POLO — US

SINGLES:	**HITS 2**			**WEEKS 5**
NEVER GOIN' DOWN (INCORPORATING FUTURE FREAK) *[AA] listed with Born To Be Alive! by Adamski + Soho.* *Above hit: ADAMSKI + Jimi POLO.*	*MCA*	51	*9 Nov 91*	2
EXPRESS YOURSELF	*Perfecto*	59	*1 Aug 92*	2
EXPRESS YOURSELF [RM] *Remixed by Mousse T.*	*Perfecto Red*	62	*9 Aug 97*	1

Marco POLO — Italy

SINGLES:	**HITS 1**			**WEEKS 1**
A PRAYER TO THE MUSIC	*Hi-Life*	65	*8 Apr 95*	1

POLTERGEIST — UK

SINGLES:	**HITS 1**			**WEEKS 2**
VICIOUS CIRCLES *Originally released in 1993.*	*Manifesto*	32	*6 Jul 96*	2

Peter POLYCARPOU — UK

SINGLES:	**HITS 1**			**WEEKS 4**
LOVE HURTS *Theme from the BBC TV series of the same name.*	*Soundtrack Music*	26	*20 Feb 93*	4

POLYGON WINDOW — UK

(See also Aphex Twin.)

SINGLES:	**HITS 1**			**WEEKS 1**
QUOTH	*Warp*	49	*3 Apr 93*	1

PONI-TAILS — US

SINGLES:	**HITS 2**			**WEEKS 14**
BORN TOO LATE *Certain copies reflected the artist credit as Pony-Tails.*	*His Master's Voice*	5	*20 Sep 58*	11
EARLY TO BED	*His Master's Voice*	26	*11 Apr 59*	3

Maurice PONKE and his Orchestre Fromage - See GOONS

Brian POOLE and the TREMELOES — UK

(See also Tremeloes.)

SINGLES:	**HITS 8**			**WEEKS 90**
TWIST AND SHOUT *Originally recorded by the Top Notes.*	*Decca*	4	*6 Jul 63*	14
DO YOU LOVE ME *Original by the Contours reached No. 3 in the US in 1962.*	*Decca*	1	*14 Sep 63*	14
I CAN DANCE	*Decca*	31	*30 Nov 63*	8
CANDY MAN *Originally recorded by Roy Orbison.*	*Decca*	6	*1 Feb 64*	13
SOMEONE, SOMEONE *Originally recorded by the Crickets.*	*Decca*	2	*9 May 64*	17

TWELVE STEPS TO LOVE	*Decca*	32	*22 Aug 64*	7
THREE BELLS	*Decca*	17	*9 Jan 65*	9
I WANT CANDY	*Decca*	25	*24 Jul 65*	8
Original by the Strangeloves reached No. 11 in the US in 1965.				

Glyn POOLE — UK

SINGLES:	HITS 1			WEEKS 8
MILLY MOLLY MANDY	*York*	35	*20 Oct 73*	8
He sang this on the Yorkshire ITV children's series 'Junior Showtime'.				

Ian POOLEY — Germany

SINGLES:	HITS 2			WEEKS 2
900 DEGREES	*V2*	57	*10 Mar 01*	1
Samples Rene and Angela's I Love You More.				
BALMES (A BETTER LIFE)	*V2*	65	*11 Aug 01*	1
Ian POOLEY featuring ESTHERO.				

Iggy POP — US

SINGLES:	HITS 8			WEEKS 28
REAL WILD CHILD (WILD ONE)	*A&M*	10	*13 Dec 86*	11
Originally recorded by Johnny O'Keefe.				
LIVIN' ON THE EDGE OF THE NIGHT	*Virgin America*	51	*10 Feb 90*	4
CANDY	*Virgin America*	67	*13 Oct 90*	1
WELL, DID YOU EVAH!	*Chrysalis*	42	*5 Jan 91*	4
Above hit: Deborah HARRY and Iggy POP.				
THE WILD AMERICA [EP]	*Virgin*	63	*4 Sep 93*	1
Lead track: Wild America. Features Henry Rollins.				
BESIDE YOU	*Virgin*	47	*21 May 94*	2
LUST FOR LIFE	*Virgin*	26	*23 Nov 96*	2
From the film 'Trainspotting'.				
THE PASSENGER	*Virgin*	22	*7 Mar 98*	3
Originally released in 1977. Featured in the Toyota Avensis car TV commercial.				

ALBUMS:	HITS 9			WEEKS 27
THE IDIOT	*RCA Victor*	30	*9 Apr 77*	3
RAW POWER	*Embassy*	44	*4 Jun 77*	2
Originally released in 1973.				
Above hit: IGGY and the STOOGES.				
LUST FOR LIFE	*RCA Victor*	28	*1 Oct 77*	5
NEW VALUES	*Arista*	60	*19 May 79*	4
SOLDIER	*Arista*	62	*16 Feb 80*	2
BLAH-BLAH-BLAH	*A&M*	43	*11 Oct 86*	7
INSTINCT	*A&M*	61	*2 Jul 88*	1
BRICK BY BRICK	*Virgin America*	50	*21 Jul 90*	2
AMERICAN CAESAR	*Virgin*	43	*25 Sep 93*	1

Los POP-TOPS — Spain

SINGLES:	HITS 1			WEEKS 6
MAMY BLUE	*A&M*	35	*9 Oct 71*	6

POP WILL EAT ITSELF — UK

SINGLES:	HITS 15			WEEKS 43
THERE IS NO LOVE BETWEEN US ANYMORE	*Chapter 22*	66	*30 Jan 88*	1
DEF. CON ONE	*Chapter 22*	63	*23 Jul 88*	4
CAN U DIG IT?	*RCA*	38	*11 Feb 89*	4
WISE UP! SUCKER	*RCA*	41	*22 Apr 89*	3
VERY METAL NOISE POLLUTION [EP]	*RCA*	45	*2 Sep 89*	3
Lead track: Def Con. 1989 Including The Twilight Zone.				
TOUCHED BY THE HAND OF CICCIOLINA	*RCA*	28	*9 Jun 90*	4
Above hit: PWEI.				
DANCE OF THE MAD	*RCA*	32	*13 Oct 90*	2
X, Y AND ZEE	*RCA*	15	*12 Jan 91*	4
92 DEGREES F	*RCA*	23	*1 Jun 91*	3
KARMADROME / EAT ME DRINK ME LOVE ME KILL ME	*RCA*	17	*6 Jun 92*	2
BULLETPROOF!	*RCA*	24	*29 Aug 92*	3
GET THE GIRL! KILL THE BADDIES!	*RCA*	9	*16 Jan 93*	4
Above hit: INCREDIBLE PWEI meets the ON-U-SOUND SYSTEM VOL II.				
R.S.V.P. / FAMILUS HORRIBILUS	*Infectious*	27	*16 Oct 93*	2
ICH BIN EIN AUSLANDER	*Infectious*	28	*12 Mar 94*	2
EVERYTHING'S COOL?	*Infectious*	23	*10 Sep 94*	2

ALBUMS:	HITS 7			WEEKS 14
THIS IS THE DAY . . . THIS IS THE HOUR . . . THIS IS THIS!	*RCA*	24	*13 May 89*	2
CURE FOR SANITY	*RCA*	33	*3 Nov 90*	2
THE POP WILL EAT ITSELF CURE FOR SANITY [RE]	*RCA*	58	*6 Jul 91*	1
Repackaged.				
THE LOOKS OR THE LIFESTYLE	*RCA*	15	*19 Sep 92*	3

WEIRD'S BAR AND GRILLS	*RCA*	44	*6 Mar 93*	1
16 DIFFERENT FLAVOURS OF HELL	*RCA*	73	*6 Nov 93*	1
Compilation.				
DOS DEDOS MIS AMIGOS	*Infectious*	11	*1 Oct 94*	2
TWO FINGERS MY FRIENDS!	*Infectious*	25	*18 Mar 95*	2
Remixed album of their previous chart entry.				

POPE JOHN PAUL II — Poland

ALBUMS:	HITS 2			WEEKS 8
JOHN PAUL II - THE PILGRIM POPE	*BBC*	71	*3 Jul 82*	4
THE ROSARY	*Pure Music*	50	*10 Dec 94*	4

The Rosary is a prayer recreating the 15 mysteries of the Virgin Mary and Christ's life. Pope John Paul recites in Latin while Father Colm Kilcoyne's is in English.
Above hit: POPE JOHN PAUL II/FATHER Colm KILCOYNE.

POPES – See Shane MacGOWAN

POPPERS present AURA — UK

SINGLES:	HITS 1			WEEKS 1
EVERY LITTLE TIME	*VC Recordings*	44	*25 Oct 97*	1

POPPY FAMILY (featuring Susan JACKS) — Canada

SINGLES:	HITS 1			WEEKS 14
WHICH WAY YOU GOIN' BILLY?	*Decca*	7	*15 Aug 70*	14

PORN KINGS — UK

SINGLES:	HITS 4			WEEKS 10
UP TO NO GOOD	*All Around The World*	28	*28 Sep 96*	2
AMOUR (C'MON)	*All Around The World*	17	*21 Jun 97*	3
UP TO THE WILDSTYLE	*All Around The World*	10	*16 Jan 99*	4
Above hit: PORN KINGS v's DJ SUPREME.				
SLEDGER	*All Around The World*	71	*10 Feb 01*	1
Above hit: DEEJAY DAVY T presents PORN KINGS.				

PORNO FOR PYROS — US

SINGLES:	HITS 1			WEEKS 2
PETS	*Warner Brothers*	53	*5 Jun 93*	2
ALBUMS:	**HITS 2**			**WEEKS 5**
PORNO FOR PYROS	*Warner Brothers*	13	*8 May 93*	3
GOOD GOD'S URGE	*Warner Brothers*	40	*8 Jun 96*	2

PORTISHEAD — UK

SINGLES:	HITS 5			WEEKS 20
SOUR TIMES	*Go.Beat*	57	*13 Aug 94*	1
GLORY BOX	*Go.Beat*	13	*14 Jan 95*	7
Samples Isaac Hayes' Ike's Mood.				
SOUR TIMES [RE]	*Go.Beat*	13	*22 Apr 95*	4
ALL MINE	*Go.Beat*	8	*20 Sep 97*	4
OVER	*Go.Beat*	25	*22 Nov 97*	2
ONLY YOU	*Go.Beat*	35	*14 Mar 98*	2
ALBUMS:	**HITS 3**			**WEEKS 95**
DUMMY	*Go.Beat*	32	*03 Sept 94*	5
DUMMY [RE]	*Go.Beat*	2	*24 Dec 94*	66
Peak position reached on 6 May 95. Winner of the 1995 Mercury Music Prize.				
PORTISHEAD	*Go.Beat*	2	*11 Oct 97*	22
PNYC	*Go.Beat*	40	*14 Nov 98*	2
Live recordings from the Roseland Ballroom in New York, Jul 97.				

Nick PORTLOCK – See ROYAL PHILHARMONIC ORCHESTRA

Gary PORTNOY — US

SINGLES:	HITS 1			WEEKS 3
THEME FROM CHEERS (WHERE EVERYBODY KNOWS YOUR NAME)	*Starblend*	58	*25 Feb 84*	3
Theme from the TV series.				

PORTRAIT — US

SINGLES:	HITS 3			WEEKS 6
HERE WE GO AGAIN!	*Capitol*	37	*27 Mar 93*	3
I CAN CALL YOU	*Capitol*	61	*8 Apr 95*	1
HOW DEEP IS YOUR LOVE	*Capitol*	41	*8 Jul 95*	2

PORTSMOUTH SINFONIA — UK

SINGLES:	HITS 1			WEEKS 4
CLASSICAL MUDDLY [M]	*Springtime*	38	*12 Sep 81*	4

Spoof take-off on the Royal Philharmonic Orchestra's version. Instruments are played out of tune.

Sandy POSEY — US

SINGLES:	HITS 3			WEEKS 32
BORN A WOMAN	*MGM*	24	*17 Sep 66*	11
SINGLE GIRL	*MGM*	15	*7 Jan 67*	13
WHAT A WOMAN IN LOVE WON'T DO	*MGM*	48	*15 Apr 67*	3
THE SINGLE GIRL [RI]	*MGM*	35	*6 Sep 75*	5
ALBUMS:	**HITS 1**			**WEEKS 1**
BORN A WOMAN	*MGM*	39	*11 Mar 67*	1

POSIES — US

SINGLES:	HITS 1			WEEKS 1
DEFINITE DOOR	*Geffen*	67	*19 Mar 94*	1

POSITIVE FORCE — UK

SINGLES:	HITS 1			WEEKS 9
WE GOT THE FUNK	*Sugar Hill*	18	*22 Dec 79*	9

POSITIVE GANG — UK

SINGLES:	HITS 2			WEEKS 5
SWEET FREEDOM	*PWL Continental*	34	*17 Apr 93*	4
SWEET FREEDOM PART II - (THE RETURN)	*PWL Continental*	67	*31 Jul 93*	1

POSITIVE K — US

SINGLES:	HITS 1			WEEKS 2
I GOT A MAN	*Fourth & Broadway*	43	*15 May 93*	2

Mike POST — US

SINGLES:	HITS 3			WEEKS 18
AFTERNOON OF THE RHINO *Above hit: Mike POST COALITION.*	*Warner Brothers*	48	*9 Aug 75*	1
AFTERNOON OF THE RHINO [RE]	*Warner Brothers*	47	*23 Aug 75*	1
THE THEME FROM HILL STREET BLUES *Above hit: Mike POST featuring Larry CARLTON.*	*Elektron*	25	*16 Jan 82*	11
THE A TEAM *Above 2 are themes from the TV series.*	*RCA*	45	*29 Sep 84*	5

POTTERS — UK

SINGLES:	HITS 1			WEEKS 2
WE'LL BE WITH YOU	*Pye*	34	*1 Apr 72*	2

Frank POURCEL — France

ALBUMS:	HITS 1			WEEKS 7
THIS IS POURCEL	*Studio Two*	8	*20 Nov 71*	7

POWDER — UK

SINGLES:	HITS 1			WEEKS 1
AFRODISIAC	*Parkway*	72	*24 Jun 95*	1

Bryan POWELL — UK

SINGLES:	HITS 3			WEEKS 3
IT'S ALRIGHT	*Talkin Loud*	73	*13 Mar 93*	1
I THINK OF YOU	*Talkin Loud*	61	*15 May 93*	1
NATURAL	*Talkin Loud*	73	*7 Aug 93*	1

Cozy POWELL — UK

(See also Emerson, Lake and Powell.)

SINGLES:	HITS 5			WEEKS 38
DANCE WITH THE DEVIL	*RAK*	3	*8 Dec 73*	15
THE MAN IN BLACK	*RAK*	18	*25 May 74*	8
NA NA NA	*RAK*	10	*10 Aug 74*	10
THEME ONE *Originally recorded by George Martin.*	*Ariola*	62	*10 Nov 79*	2
RESURRECTION *Above hit: Brian MAY with Cozy POWELL.*	*Parlophone*	23	*19 Jun 93*	3
ALBUMS:	**HITS 3**			**WEEKS 8**
OVER THE TOP	*Ariola*	34	*26 Jan 80*	3

TILT	*Polydor*	58	*19 Sep 81*	4
OCTOPUSS	*Polydor*	86	*28 May 83*	1

Kobie POWELL and RAHSAAN – See US3

Peter POWELL — UK

ALBUMS:	HITS 1			WEEKS 13
KEEP FIT AND DANCE	*K-Tel*	9	*20 Mar 82*	13

POWER CIRCLE – See CHICANE

POWER OF DREAMS — Ireland

SINGLES:	HITS 2			WEEKS 2
AMERICAN DREAM	*Polydor*	74	*19 Jan 91*	1
THERE I GO AGAIN	*Polydor*	65	*11 Apr 92*	1

POWER-PILL — UK

SINGLES:	HITS 1			WEEKS 3
PAC-MAN	*Ffrreedom*	43	*6 Jun 92*	3

POWER STATION — UK

SINGLES:	HITS 4			WEEKS 17
SOME LIKE IT HOT	*Parlophone*	14	*16 Mar 85*	8
GET IT ON	*Parlophone*	22	*11 May 85*	7
COMMUNICATION	*Parlophone*	75	*9 Nov 85*	1
SHE CAN ROCK IT	*Chrysalis*	63	*12 Oct 96*	1
ALBUMS:	**HITS 1**			**WEEKS 23**
THE POWER STATION	*Parlophone*	12	*6 Apr 85*	23

POWERCUT featuring NUBIAN PRINZ — US

SINGLES:	HITS 1			WEEKS 4
GIRLS	*Eternal*	50	*22 Jun 91*	4

POWERHOUSE — UK

SINGLES:	HITS 1			WEEKS 4
RHYTHM OF THE NIGHT *Samples DeBarge's song of the same title.*	*Satellite*	38	*20 Dec 97*	4

POWERHOUSE featuring Duane HARDEN — US

SINGLES:	HITS 1			WEEKS 5
WHAT YOU NEED	*Defected*	13	*22 May 99*	5

P.J. POWERS – See LADYSMITH BLACK MAMBAZO

Will POWERS — US

SINGLES:	HITS 1			WEEKS 9
KISSING WITH CONFIDENCE *Backing vocals by Carly Simon.*	*Island*	17	*1 Oct 83*	9

PPK — Russia

SINGLES:	HITS 1			WEEKS 4
RESURRECTION	*Perfecto*	3	*8 Dec 01*	4

PQM featuring CICA — US

SINGLES:	HITS 1			WEEKS 1
THE FLYING SONG	*Renaissance Recordings*	68	*9 Dec 00*	1

Perez "Prez" PRADO and his Orchestra — Cuba

SINGLES:	HITS 3			WEEKS 55
CHERRY PINK AND APPLE BLOSSOM WHITE *Trumpet solo by Billy Regis. From the film 'Under Water'.* *Above hit: Perez "Prez" PRADO and his Orchestra (The KING OF THE MAMBO).*	*His Master's Voice*	1	*26 Mar 55*	17
PATRICIA *Above hit: Perez PRADO and his Orchestra.*	*RCA*	8	*26 Jul 58*	16
GUAGLIONE *Featured in the Guinness TV commercial.*	*RCA*	41	*10 Dec 94*	4
GUAGLIONE [RE-1ST]	*RCA*	58	*8 Apr 95*	2
GUAGLIONE [RE-2ND]	*RCA*	2	*6 May 95*	16

PRAGA KHAN — Belgium

(See also Channel X; Digital Orgasm.)

SINGLES:	HITS 2			WEEKS 9
INJECTED WITH A POISON / FREE YOUR BODY	*Profile*	16	*4 Apr 92*	6
Titles were listed in reverse on 4 Apr 92.				
Above hit: Praga KHAN featuring JADE 4 U.				
RAVE ALERT!	*Profile*	39	*11 Jul 92*	2
INJECTED WITH A POISON [RM]	*Nukleuz*	52	*24 Nov 01*	1
Remixed by Krafty Kuts and Ed Solo.				

PRAISE — UK/South Africa

SINGLES:	HITS 1			WEEKS 7
ONLY YOU	*Epic*	4	*2 Feb 91*	7
Featured in the Fiat Tempra car TV commercial.				

PRAS — US

(See also Wyclef Jean; Queen.)

SINGLES:	HITS 3			WEEKS 30
GHETTO SUPASTAR (THAT IS WHAT YOU ARE)	*Interscope*	2	*27 Jun 98*	17
From the film 'Bulworth'. Interpolation of Kenny Rogers and Dolly Parton's Islands In The Stream.				
Above hit: Pras MICHEL featuring ODB and introducing MYA.				
BLUE ANGELS	*Columbia*	6	*7 Nov 98*	10
Based around the song Grease. Features Lenny Kravitz on guitar.				
MISS CALIFORNIA	*Elektra*	25	*1 Sep 01*	3
Above hit: Dante THOMAS featuring PRAS.				
ALBUMS:	**HITS 1**			**WEEKS 3**
GHETTO SUPASTAR	*Columbia*	44	*14 Nov 98*	3

Bobby PRATT – See Ted HEATH and his Music

PRATT and McLAIN with BROTHERLOVE — US

SINGLES:	HITS 1			WEEKS 6
HAPPY DAYS	*Reprise*	31	*1 Oct 77*	6
Theme from the TV series of the same name.				

PRAXIS featuring Kathy BROWN — UK

SINGLES:	HITS 1			WEEKS 5
TURN ME OUT	*Stress*	44	*25 Nov 95*	2
Original release reached No. 86 in 1994.				
TURN ME OUT (TURN TO SUGAR) [RM]	*ffrr*	35	*20 Sep 97*	3
Remixed by The Sol Brothers.				

PRAYING MANTIS — UK

SINGLES:	HITS 1			WEEKS 2
CHEATED	*Arista*	69	*31 Jan 81*	2
ALBUMS:	**HITS 1**			**WEEKS 2**
TIME TELLS NO LIES	*Arista*	60	*11 Apr 81*	2

PRECIOUS — UK

SINGLES:	HITS 4			WEEKS 20
SAY IT AGAIN	*EMI*	6	*29 May 99*	9
UK's Eurovision entry in 1999, it came 12th.				
SAY IT AGAIN [RE]	*EMI*	53	*28 Aug 99*	2
REWIND	*EMI*	11	*1 Apr 00*	5
IT'S GONNA BE MY WAY	*EMI*	27	*15 Jul 00*	3
NEW BEGINNING	*EMI*	50	*25 Nov 00*	1

PRECOCIOUS BRATS featuring KEVIN and PERRY — UK

SINGLES:	HITS 1			WEEKS 4
BIG GIRL	*Virgin*	16	*6 May 00*	4
From the film 'Kevin And Perry Go Large'.				

PREFAB SPROUT — UK

SINGLES:	HITS 16			WEEKS 60
DON'T SING	*Kitchenware*	62	*28 Jan 84*	2
FARON YOUNG	*Kitchenware*	74	*20 Jul 85*	1
WHEN LOVE BREAKS DOWN	*Kitchenware*	25	*9 Nov 85*	10
Original release reached No. 89 in 1984.				
JOHNNY JOHNNY	*Kitchenware*	64	*8 Feb 86*	2
CARS AND GIRLS	*Kitchenware*	44	*13 Feb 88*	5
THE KING OF ROCK 'N' ROLL	*Kitchenware*	7	*30 Apr 88*	10
HEY MANHATTAN!	*Kitchenware*	72	*23 Jul 88*	2

LOOKING FOR ATLANTIS	*Kitchenware*	51	*18 Aug 90*	3
WE LET THE STARS GO	*Kitchenware*	50	*20 Oct 90*	3
JORDAN: THE EP [EP]	*Kitchenware*	35	*5 Jan 91*	4
Lead track: One Of The Broken, though another track Carnival 2000 received more airplay.				
THE SOUND OF CRYING	*Kitchenware*	23	*13 Jun 92*	5
IF YOU DON'T LOVE ME	*Kitchenware*	33	*8 Aug 92*	4
ALL THE WORLD LOVES LOVERS	*Kitchenware*	61	*3 Oct 92*	2
LIFE OF SURPRISES	*Kitchenware*	24	*9 Jan 93*	4
A PRISONER OF THE PAST	*Kitchenware*	30	*10 May 97*	2
ELECTRIC GUITARS	*Kitchenware*	53	*2 Aug 97*	1
ALBUMS:	**HITS 8**			**WEEKS 106**
SWOON	*Kitchenware*	22	*17 Mar 84*	7
STEVE MCQUEEN	*Kitchenware*	21	*22 Jun 85*	35
FROM LANGLEY PARK TO MEMPHIS	*Kitchenware*	5	*26 Mar 88*	24
PROTEST SONGS	*Kitchenware*	18	*1 Jul 89*	4
JORDAN: THE COMEBACK	*Kitchenware*	7	*8 Sep 90*	17
A LIFE OF SURPRISES – THE BEST OF PREFAB SPROUT	*Kitchenware*	3	*11 Jul 92*	13
ANDROMEDA HEIGHTS	*Kitchenware*	7	*17 May 97*	5
THE GUNMAN AND OTHER STORIES	*Liberty*	60	*30 Jun 01*	1

PRELUDE — UK

SINGLES:	**HITS 4**			**WEEKS 26**
AFTER THE GOLDRUSH	*Dawn*	21	*26 Jan 74*	9
Original by Neil Young reached No. 1 in the US in 1972.				
PLATINUM BLONDE	*EMI*	45	*26 Apr 80*	7
AFTER THE GOLDRUSH [RR]	*After Hours*	28	*22 May 82*	7
ONLY THE LONELY (KNOW THE WAY I FEEL)	*After Hours*	55	*31 Jul 82*	3

PRESENCE — UK

SINGLES:	**HITS 2**			**WEEKS 2**
SENSE OF DANGER	*Pagan*	61	*5 Dec 98*	1
Above hit: PRESENCE featuring Shara NELSON.				
FUTURE LOVE	*Pagan*	66	*19 Jun 99*	1

PRESIDENT BROWN – See SABRE featuring PRESIDENT BROWN

PRESIDENTS OF THE UNITED STATES OF AMERICA — US

SINGLES:	**HITS 5**			**WEEKS 21**
LUMP	*Columbia*	15	*6 Jan 96*	7
PEACHES	*Columbia*	8	*20 Apr 96*	7
DUNE BUGGY	*Columbia*	15	*20 Jul 96*	4
MACH 5	*Columbia*	29	*2 Nov 96*	2
VIDEO KILLED THE RADIO STAR	*Maverick*	52	*1 Aug 98*	1
Originally recorded by Bruce Wooley and the Camera Club. From the film 'The Wedding Singer'.				
ALBUMS:	**HITS 2**			**WEEKS 31**
THE PRESIDENTS OF THE UNITED STATES OF AMERICA	*Columbia*	14	*13 Jan 96*	29
II	*Columbia*	36	*16 Nov 96*	2

Elvis PRESLEY — US

SINGLES:	**HITS 113**			**WEEKS 1173**
HEARTBREAK HOTEL	*His Master's Voice*	2	*12 May 56*	21
BLUE SUEDE SHOES	*His Master's Voice*	9	*26 May 56*	8
I WANT YOU I NEED YOU I LOVE YOU	*His Master's Voice*	25	*14 Jul 56*	2
I WANT YOU I NEED YOU I LOVE YOU [RE]	*His Master's Voice*	14	*4 Aug 56*	9
BLUE SUEDE SHOES [RE]	*His Master's Voice*	26	*18 Aug 56*	2
HOUND DOG	*His Master's Voice*	2	*22 Sep 56*	23
Originally recorded by Big Mama Thornton.				
HEARTBREAK HOTEL [RE]	*His Master's Voice*	23	*27 Oct 56*	1
BLUE MOON	*His Master's Voice*	9	*17 Nov 56*	11
I DON'T CARE IF THE SUN DON'T SHINE	*His Master's Voice*	29	*24 Nov 56*	1
Above 2 entries were separate sides of the same release, each had its own chart run. Originally recorded by Patti Page in 1950.				
LOVE ME TENDER	*His Master's Voice*	11	*8 Dec 56*	9
From the film of the same name.				
I DON'T CARE IF THE SUN DON'T SHINE [RE]	*His Master's Voice*	23	*22 Dec 56*	3
MYSTERY TRAIN	*His Master's Voice*	25	*16 Feb 57*	5
Originally recorded by Junior Parker. First release in the UK. This was his final Sun single in the US.				
RIP IT UP	*His Master's Voice*	27	*9 Mar 57*	1
TOO MUCH	*His Master's Voice*	6	*11 May 57*	8
Originally recorded by Bernard Hardison.				
ALL SHOOK UP	*His Master's Voice*	24	*15 Jun 57*	1
Only No.1 that Elvis gets a writing credit.				
ALL SHOOK UP [RE]	*His Master's Voice*	1	*29 Jun 57*	20
TOO MUCH [RE]	*His Master's Voice*	26	*13 Jul 57*	1

(LET ME BE YOUR) TEDDY BEAR	*RCA*	3	*13 Jul 57*	19
From the film 'Loving You'.				
Above 5 (including re-entries) Elvis PRESLEY with the JORDANAIRES.				
PARALYSED	*His Master's Voice*	8	*31 Aug 57*	10
PARTY	*RCA*	2	*5 Oct 57*	15
GOT A LOT O' LIVIN' TO DO	*RCA*	17	*19 Oct 57*	4
Above 2 entries were separate sides of the same release, each had its own chart run.				
Above 2: Elvis PRESLEY with the JORDANAIRES.				
TRYING TO GET TO YOU	*His Master's Voice*	16	*2 Nov 57*	4
LOVING YOU	*RCA*	24	*2 Nov 57*	2
Above entry and (Let Me Be Your) Teddy Bear were separate sides of the same release, each had its own chart run.				
Above 3 from the film 'Loving You'.				
Above hit: Elvis PRESLEY with the JORDANAIRES.				
LAWDY MISS CLAWDY	*His Master's Voice*	15	*9 Nov 57*	5
Above entry and Trying To Get To You were separate sides of the same release, each had its own chart run.				
SANTA BRING MY BABY BACK TO ME	*RCA*	7	*16 Nov 57*	8
I'M LEFT, YOU'RE RIGHT, SHE'S GONE	*His Master's Voice*	21	*18 Jan 58*	2
JAILHOUSE ROCK	*RCA*	1	*25 Jan 58*	14
JAILHOUSE ROCK [EP]	*RCA*	18	*1 Feb 58*	5
Lead track: Jailhouse Rock. Above 2 from the film of the same name.				
Above hit: Elvis PRESLEY with the JORDANAIRES.				
I'M LEFT, YOU'RE RIGHT, SHE'S GONE [RE]	*His Master's Voice*	29	*8 Feb 58*	1
DON'T	*RCA*	2	*1 Mar 58*	11
WEAR MY RING AROUND YOUR NECK	*RCA*	3	*3 May 58*	10
HARD HEADED WOMAN	*RCA*	2	*26 Jul 58*	11
KING CREOLE	*RCA*	2	*4 Oct 58*	15
Above 2 from the film 'King Creole'.				
Above 4: Elvis PRESLEY with the JORDANAIRES.				
ONE NIGHT / I GOT STUNG	*RCA*	1	*24 Jan 59*	12
One Night originally recorded by Smiley Lewis.				
A FOOL SUCH AS I / I NEED YOUR LOVE TONIGHT	*RCA*	1	*25 Apr 59*	15
A Fool Such As I originally recorded by Hank Snow.				
A BIG HUNK O' LOVE	*RCA*	4	*25 Jul 59*	9
Above 2: Elvis PRESLEY with the JORDANAIRES.				
STRICTLY ELVIS [EP]	*RCA*	26	*13 Feb 60*	1
Lead track: Old Shep.				
STUCK ON YOU	*RCA*	3	*9 Apr 60*	14
A MESS OF BLUES	*RCA*	2	*30 Jul 60*	18
The B-side The Girl Of My Best Friend was also popular though it was not listed on the chart.				
IT'S NOW OR NEVER (O SOLE MIO)	*RCA*	1	*5 Nov 60*	19
Originally written in 1901.				
ARE YOU LONESOME TONIGHT?	*RCA*	1	*21 Jan 61*	15
Originally recorded by Vaughn Deleath in 1927.				
Above 4: Elvis PRESLEY with the JORDANAIRES.				
WOODEN HEART	*RCA*	1	*11 Mar 61*	27
From the film 'G.I. Blues'.				
SURRENDER (TORNA A SURRIENTO)	*RCA*	1	*27 May 61*	15
WILD IN THE COUNTRY / I FEEL SO BAD	*RCA*	4	*9 Sep 61*	12
I Feel So Bad originally recorded by Chuck Willis. Wild In The Country from the film of the same name. I Feel So Bad was not listed from 7 Oct 61. The Jordanaires only credited on Wild In The Country.				
Above 2: Elvis PRESLEY with the JORDANAIRES.				
(MARIE'S THE NAME) HIS LATEST FLAME / LITTLE SISTER	*RCA*	1	*4 Nov 61*	13
Little Sister only listed for the week of 4 Nov 61 when it entered at No. 4 and had first credit. (Marie's The Name) Of His Latest Flame originally recorded by Del Shannon.				
ROCK-A-HULA-BABY ("TWIST SPECIAL") / CAN'T HELP FALLING IN LOVE	*RCA*	1	*3 Feb 62*	20
Can't Help Falling In Love listed from 3 Mar 62 and has first credit. From the film 'Blue Hawaii'.				
GOOD LUCK CHARM	*RCA*	1	*12 May 62*	17
Above 2: Elvis PRESLEY with the JORDANAIRES.				
FOLLOW THAT DREAM [EP]	*RCA*	34	*23 Jun 62*	2
Lead track: Follow That Dream. Removed from the chart due to problems with assessing returns. See also EP section. From the film of the same name.				
SHE'S NOT YOU	*RCA*	1	*1 Sep 62*	14
RETURN TO SENDER	*RCA*	1	*1 Dec 62*	14
From the film 'Girls, Girls, Girls'.				
Above 2: Elvis PRESLEY with the JORDANAIRES.				
ONE BROKEN HEART FOR SALE	*RCA Victor*	12	*2 Mar 63*	9
From the film 'It Happened At The World's Fair'.				
Above hit: Elvis PRESLEY with the MELLO MEN.				
(YOU'RE THE) DEVIL IN DISGUISE	*RCA Victor*	1	*6 Jul 63*	12
BOSSA NOVA BABY	*RCA Victor*	13	*26 Oct 63*	8
From the film 'Fun In Acapulco'. Originally recorded by Tippie and the Clovers.				
KISS ME QUICK	*RCA Victor*	14	*21 Dec 63*	10
VIVA LAS VEGAS	*RCA Victor*	17	*14 Mar 64*	12
From the film 'Love In Las Vegas'.				

Title	Label	Pos	Date	Wks
KISSIN' COUSINS *From the film of the same name.*	*RCA Victor*	10	*27 Jun 64*	11
SUCH A NIGHT *Above 6: Elvis PRESLEY with the JORDANAIRES.*	*RCA Victor*	13	*22 Aug 64*	10
AIN'T THAT LOVING YOU BABY *Originally recorded by Jimmy Reed.*	*RCA Victor*	15	*31 Oct 64*	8
BLUE CHRISTMAS	*RCA Victor*	11	*5 Dec 64*	7
DO THE CLAM *From the film 'Girl Happy'.*	*RCA Victor*	19	*13 Mar 65*	8
CRYING IN THE CHAPEL *Originally recorded by Sonny Til and the Orioles.*	*RCA Victor*	1	*29 May 65*	15
TELL ME WHY *Originally recorded in 1957 by Marie Knight.* *Above 4: Elvis PRESLEY with the JORDANAIRES.*	*RCA Victor*	15	*13 Nov 65*	10
BLUE RIVER	*RCA Victor*	22	*26 Feb 66*	7
FRANKIE AND JOHNNY *From the film of the same name.*	*RCA Victor*	21	*9 Apr 66*	9
LOVE LETTERS *Originally recorded by Dick Haymes in 1945.*	*RCA Victor*	6	*9 Jul 66*	10
ALL THAT I AM *From the film 'Spinout'.* *Above hit: Elvis PRESLEY with the JORDANAIRES.*	*RCA Victor*	18	*15 Oct 66*	8
IF EVERY DAY WAS LIKE CHRISTMAS	*RCA Victor*	13	*3 Dec 66*	7
INDESCRIBABLY BLUE *Above 2: Elvis PRESLEY with the JORDANAIRES and the IMPERIALS QUARTET.*	*RCA Victor*	21	*11 Feb 67*	5
YOU GOTTA STOP / THE LOVE MACHINE *From the film 'Easy Come, Easy Go'.*	*RCA Victor*	38	*13 May 67*	5
LONG LEGGED GIRL (WITH THE SHORT DRESS ON) *From the film 'Double Trouble'.* *Above hit: Elvis PRESLEY with the JORDANAIRES.*	*RCA Victor*	49	*19 Aug 67*	2
GUITAR MAN	*RCA Victor*	19	*24 Feb 68*	9
U.S. MALE *Above 2 originally recorded by Jerry Reed.*	*RCA Victor*	15	*18 May 68*	8
YOUR TIME HASN'T COME YET BABY *From the film 'Speedway'.*	*RCA Victor*	22	*20 Jul 68*	11
YOU'LL NEVER WALK ALONE *Above 3: Elvis PRESLEY with the JORDANAIRES.*	*RCA Victor*	44	*19 Oct 68*	3
IF I CAN DREAM	*RCA Victor*	11	*1 Mar 69*	10
IN THE GHETTO *Originally recorded by Mac Davis.*	*RCA Victor*	2	*14 Jun 69*	16
CLEAN UP YOUR OWN BACK YARD *From the film 'The Trouble With Girls (And How To Get Into It)'.*	*RCA Victor*	21	*6 Sep 69*	7
IN THE GHETTO [RE]	*RCA Victor*	50	*18 Oct 69*	1
SUSPICIOUS MINDS *Originally recorded by Mark James.*	*RCA Victor*	2	*29 Nov 69*	14
DON'T CRY DADDY *Originally recorded by Mac Davis.*	*RCA Victor*	8	*28 Feb 70*	11
KENTUCKY RAIN *Originally recorded by Eddie Rabbitt.*	*RCA Victor*	21	*16 May 70*	11
THE WONDER OF YOU *Live recording from the International Hotel, Las Vegas, Feb 70.*	*RCA Victor*	1	*11 Jul 70*	20
KENTUCKY RAIN [RE]	*RCA Victor*	46	*8 Aug 70*	1
I'VE LOST YOU	*RCA Victor*	9	*14 Nov 70*	12
YOU DON'T HAVE TO SAY YOU LOVE ME *Live recording.*	*RCA Victor*	9	*9 Jan 71*	7
THE WONDER OF YOU [RE]	*RCA Victor*	47	*23 Jan 71*	1
YOU DON'T HAVE TO SAY YOU LOVE ME [RE]	*RCA Victor*	35	*6 Mar 71*	3
THERE GOES MY EVERYTHING *Originally recorded by Jack Greene.*	*RCA Victor*	6	*20 Mar 71*	11
RAGS TO RICHES *Originally recorded by Tony Bennett.*	*RCA Victor*	9	*15 May 71*	11
HEARTBREAK HOTEL [RI-1ST] /HOUND DOG [RI]	*RCA Victor Maximillion*	10	*17 Jul 71*	12
I'M LEAVIN'	*RCA Victor*	23	*2 Oct 71*	9
I JUST CAN'T HELP BELIEVING *From the film 'Elvis: That's The Way It Is'. Originally recorded by B.J.Thomas.*	*RCA Victor*	6	*4 Dec 71*	16
JAILHOUSE ROCK [RI-1ST]	*RCA Victor Maximillion*	42	*11 Dec 71*	5
UNTIL IT'S TIME FOR YOU TO GO *Originally recorded by Buffy Saint Marie. Excluding the 2 re-issues, above 4 have vocal accompaniment by The Imperials Quartet.*	*RCA Victor*	5	*1 Apr 72*	9
AN AMERICAN TRILOGY *Live recording.*	*RCA Victor*	8	*17 Jun 72*	11
BURNING LOVE *Originally recorded by Dennis Linde.*	*RCA Victor*	7	*30 Sep 72*	9
ALWAYS ON MY MIND *Originally recorded by Brenda Lee.*	*RCA Victor*	9	*16 Dec 72*	13
POLK SALAD ANNIE *Live recording. Originally recorded by Tony Joe White.*	*RCA Victor*	23	*26 May 73*	7
FOOL *Excluding Polk Salad Annie, above 3 have vocal backing by J.D Summer and the Stamps.*	*RCA Victor*	15	*11 Aug 73*	10

Title	Label	Pos	Date	Wks
RAISED ON ROCK	*RCA Victor*	36	*24 Nov 73*	7
Originally recorded by Mark James.				
I'VE GOT A THING ABOUT YOU BABY	*RCA Victor*	33	*16 Mar 74*	5
Originally recorded by Tony Joe White.				
IF YOU TALK IN YOUR SLEEP	*RCA Victor*	40	*13 Jul 74*	3
MY BOY	*RCA Victor*	5	*16 Nov 74*	13
Originally recorded by Richard Harris.				
PROMISED LAND	*RCA Victor*	9	*18 Jan 75*	8
T.R.O.U.B.L.E.	*RCA Victor*	31	*24 May 75*	4
GREEN GREEN GRASS OF HOME	*RCA Victor*	29	*29 Nov 75*	7
HURT	*RCA Victor*	37	*1 May 76*	5
Originally recorded by Roy Hamiltion in 1954.				
THE GIRL OF MY BEST FRIEND	*RCA Victor*	9	*4 Sep 76*	12
Originally the B-side of A Mess Of Blues.				
Above hit: Elvis PRESLEY with the JORDANAIRES.				
SUSPICION	*RCA Victor*	9	*25 Dec 76*	12
Originally recorded in 1962.				
MOODY BLUE	*RCA Victor*	6	*5 Mar 77*	9
Originally recorded by Mark James.				
WAY DOWN	*RCA Victor*	1	*13 Aug 77*	13
Originally recorded by Layne Martine.				
IT'S NOW OR NEVER [RI]	*RCA Victor*	39	*3 Sep 77*	2
ALL SHOOK UP [RI]	*RCA Victor*	41	*3 Sep 77*	2
RETURN TO SENDER [RI]	*RCA Victor*	42	*3 Sep 77*	3
CRYING IN THE CHAPEL [RI]	*RCA Victor*	43	*3 Sep 77*	2
Above 4:Elvis PRESLEY with the JORDANAIRES.				
JAILHOUSE ROCK [RI-2ND]	*RCA Victor*	44	*3 Sep 77*	2
ARE YOU LONESOME TONIGHT [RI]	*RCA Victor*	46	*3 Sep 77*	1
Above hit: Elvis PRESLEY with the JORDANAIRES.				
THE WONDER OF YOU [RI]	*RCA Victor*	48	*3 Sep 77*	1
WOODEN HEART [RI]	*RCA Victor*	49	*3 Sep 77*	1
MY WAY	*RCA Victor*	9	*10 Dec 77*	8
Live recording from earlier in the year.				
DON'T BE CRUEL (TO A HEART THAT'S TRUE)	*RCA Victor*	24	*24 Jun 78*	12
Originally the B-side to Hound Dog in 1956.				
IT WON'T SEEM LIKE CHRISTMAS (WITHOUT YOU)	*RCA*	13	*15 Dec 79*	6
IT'S ONLY LOVE / BEYOND THE REEF	*RCA*	3	*30 Aug 80*	10
Beyond The Reef no longer listed from 20 Sep 80. As an AA side it peaked at No. 7.				
SANTA CLAUS IS BACK IN TOWN	*RCA*	41	*6 Dec 80*	6
Recording from 1957.				
GUITAR MAN [RR]	*RCA*	43	*14 Feb 81*	4
LOVING ARMS	*RCA*	47	*18 Apr 81*	6
ARE YOU LONESOME TONIGHT (LAUGHING VERSION) [RR]	*RCA*	25	*13 Mar 82*	7
Live recording from the International Hotel, Las Vegas, Aug 69.				
THE SOUND OF YOUR CRY	*RCA*	59	*26 Jun 82*	2
Above hit: Elvis PRESLEY with the IMPERIALS QUARTET				
JAILHOUSE ROCK [RE]	*RCA*	27	*5 Feb 83*	6
This is a 25th Anniversary re-issue with the original catalogue number.				
BABY I DON'T CARE	*RCA*	61	*7 May 83*	3
From the film 'Jailhouse Rock'. Originally appeared on the Jailhouse Rock EP.				
I CAN HELP	*RCA*	30	*3 Dec 83*	9
THE LAST FAREWELL	*RCA*	48	*10 Nov 84*	6
THE ELVIS MEDLEY [M]	*RCA*	51	*19 Jan 85*	3
Above hit: Elvis PRESLEY with the JORDANAIRES.				
ALWAYS ON MY MIND [RR]	*RCA*	59	*10 Aug 85*	4
From the film documentary 'This Is Elvis'.				
AIN'T THAT LOVIN' YOU BABY [RR] / BOSSA NOVA BABY [RR]	*RCA*	47	*11 Apr 87*	5
Above hit: Elvis PRESLEY / Elvis PRESLEY with the JORDANAIRES and the AMIGOS.				
LOVE ME TENDER [RI] / IF I CAN DREAM [RI-1ST]	*RCA Victor*	56	*22 Aug 87*	3
Re-issue to mark the 10th Anniversary of his death.				
STUCK ON YOU [RI]	*RCA*	58	*16 Jan 88*	2
Featured in a glue TV commercial.				
Above hit: Elvis PRESLEY with the JORDANAIRES.				
ARE YOU LONESOME TONIGHT (THE FAMOUS "LAUGHING VERSION") [RI]	*RCA*	68	*17 Aug 91*	2
Above hit: Elvis PRESLEY LIVE IN LAS VEGAS.				
DON'T BE CRUEL [RI]	*RCA*	42	*29 Aug 92*	2
THE TWELFTH OF NEVER	*RCA*	21	*11 Nov 95*	3
Previously unrealised track from a cassette deck recording, 16 Aug 74.				
HEARTBREAK HOTEL [RI-2ND] / I WAS THE ONE	*RCA Victor*	45	*18 May 96*	1
40th anniversary commemorative edition. I Was The One was the original B-side of Heartbreak Hotel.				
ALWAYS ON MY MIND [RI]	*RCA*	13	*24 May 97*	6
Featured in the BT TV commercial.				
Above hit: ELVIS.				
SUSPICIOUS MINDS (LIVE) [RR]	*RCA*	15	*14 Apr 01*	4
AMERICA THE BEAUTIFUL [EP]	*RCA*	69	*10 Nov 01*	1
Lead track: If I Can Dream.				

EPS:	HITS 15			WEEKS 366
STRICTLY ELVIS	*RCA*	1	*12 Mar 60*	64
A TOUCH OF GOLD	*RCA*	8	*19 Mar 60*	11
A TOUCH OF GOLD, VOLUME 2	*RCA*	10	*9 Apr 60*	13
SUCH A NIGHT	*RCA*	4	*5 Nov 60*	62
ELVIS SINGS CHRISTMAS SONGS	*RCA*	16	*26 Nov 60*	5
JAILHOUSE ROCK [OST]	*RCA*	14	*26 Aug 61*	7
PEACE IN THE VALLEY	*RCA*	12	*16 Sep 61*	10
FOLLOW THAT DREAM [OST]	*RCA*	1	*9 Jun 62*	51
KID GALAHAD [OST]	*RCA*	1	*3 Nov 62*	44
LOVE IN LAS VEGAS [OST]	*RCA Victor*	3	*18 Apr 64*	25
ELVIS FOR YOU VOLUME 1	*RCA Victor*	11	*23 May 64*	6
ELVIS FOR YOU VOLUME 2	*RCA Victor*	18	*20 Jun 64*	1
TICKLE ME [OST]	*RCA Victor*	3	*10 Jul 65*	26
TICKLE ME, VOLUME 2 [OST]	*RCA Victor*	8	*4 Sep 65*	18
EASY COME, EASY GO [OST]	*RCA Victor*	1	*1 Jul 67*	23

ALBUMS:	HITS 101			WEEKS 1155
ELVIS' GOLDEN RECORDS	*RCA*	3	*8 Nov 58*	44
Includes re-entries through to 1964.				
KING CREOLE [OST]	*RCA*	4	*8 Nov 58*	14
ELVIS (ROCK 'N' ROLL NO. 1)	*His Master's Voice*	4	*4 Apr 59*	9
Compilation.				
A DATE WITH ELVIS	*RCA*	4	*8 Aug 59*	15
ELVIS' GOLDEN RECORDS - VOLUME 2	*RCA*	4	*18 Jun 60*	20
Above hit: Elvis PRESLEY with the JORDANAIRES.				
ELVIS IS BACK!	*RCA*	1	*23 Jul 60*	27
G.I. BLUES [OST]	*RCA*	1	*10 Dec 60*	55
Above hit: Elvis PRESLEY with the JORDANAIRES.				
HIS HAND IN MINE	*RCA*	3	*20 May 61*	25
Gospel Album.				
SOMETHING FOR EVERYBODY	*RCA*	2	*4 Nov 61*	18
BLUE HAWAII [OST]	*RCA*	1	*9 Dec 61*	65
Above hit: Elvis PRESLEY with the JORDANAIRES.				
POT LUCK	*RCA*	1	*7 Jul 62*	25
ROCK 'N' ROLL NUMBER 2	*RCA Victor*	3	*8 Dec 62*	17
Originally released in 1957.				
GIRLS! GIRLS! GIRLS! [OST]	*RCA Victor*	2	*26 Jan 63*	21
IT HAPPENED AT THE WORLD'S FAIR [OST]	*RCA Victor*	4	*11 May 63*	21
FUN IN ACAPULCO [OST]	*RCA Victor*	9	*28 Dec 63*	14
ELVIS' GOLDEN RECORDS VOLUME 3	*RCA Victor*	6	*11 Apr 64*	13
KISSIN' COUSINS [OST]	*RCA Victor*	5	*4 Jul 64*	17
ROUSTABOUT [OST]	*RCA Victor*	12	*9 Jan 65*	4
GIRL HAPPY [OST]	*RCA Victor*	8	*1 May 65*	18
FLAMING STAR AND SUMMER KISSES	*RCA Victor*	11	*25 Sep 65*	4
Compilation of tracks from the album Loving You and the EP Elvis By Request.				
ELVIS FOR EVERYONE	*RCA Victor*	8	*4 Dec 65*	8
Compilation of unissued studio and film recordings.				
HAREM HOLIDAY [OST]	*RCA Victor*	11	*15 Jan 66*	5
FRANKIE AND JOHNNY [OST]	*RCA Victor*	11	*30 Apr 66*	5
PARADISE HAWAIIAN STYLE [OST]	*RCA Victor*	7	*6 Aug 66*	9
CALIFORNIA HOLIDAY [OST]	*RCA Victor*	17	*26 Nov 66*	6
HOW GREAT THOU ART	*RCA Victor*	11	*8 Apr 67*	14
Religious recordings.				
DOUBLE TROUBLE [OST]	*RCA Victor*	34	*2 Sep 67*	1
CLAMBAKE [OST]	*RCA Victor*	39	*20 Apr 68*	1
ELVIS - NBC TV SPECIAL [OST-TV]	*RCA Victor*	2	*3 May 69*	26
Transmitted on NBC TV in the US, Dec 68.				
ELVIS SINGS FLAMING STAR	*RCA International*	2	*5 Jul 69*	14
Budget Compilation.				
FROM ELVIS IN MEMPHIS	*RCA Victor*	1	*23 Aug 69*	13
PORTRAIT IN MUSIC	*RCA Victor*	36	*28 Feb 70*	1
Import.				
FROM MEMPHIS TO VEGAS - FROM VEGAS TO MEMPHIS	*RCA Victor*	3	*14 Mar 70*	16
Features live recordings from the International Hotel, Las Vegas as well as studio recordings in Memphis.				
ON STAGE, FEBRUARY 1970	*RCA Victor*	2	*1 Aug 70*	18
Live recordings from the International Hotel, Las Vegas.				
ELVIS' GOLDEN RECORDS VOLUME 1 [RI]	*RCA*	21	*5 Dec 70*	11
Original release was titled Elvis' Golden Records.				
WORLDWIDE 50 GOLD AWARD HITS VOLUME 1 - A TOUCH OF GOLD	*RCA Victor*	49	*12 Dec 70*	2
4 album box set anthologizing most of his hits.				
THAT'S THE WAY IT IS [OST]	*RCA Victor*	12	*30 Jan 71*	41
Features live recordings.				
I'M 10,000 YEARS OLD - ELVIS COUNTRY	*RCA Victor*	6	*10 Apr 71*	9
LOVE LETTERS FROM ELVIS	*RCA Victor*	7	*24 Jul 71*	5
C'MON EVERYBODY	*RCA International*	5	*7 Aug 71*	21
Budget Compilation featuring tracks from film EPs.				

YOU'LL NEVER WALK ALONE	*RCA Camden*	20	*7 Aug 71*	4
ALMOST IN LOVE	*RCA International*	38	*25 Sep 71*	2
Above 2 are budget compilations.				
ELVIS' CHRISTMAS ALBUM	*RCA International*	7	*4 Dec 71*	5
Original released in 1957. This is a budget album release.				
I GOT LUCKY	*RCA International*	26	*18 Dec 71*	3
Budget compilation featuring tracks from film EPs.				
ELVIS NOW	*RCA Victor*	12	*27 May 72*	8
ROCK AND ROLL [RI]	*RCA Victor*	34	*3 Jun 72*	4
Re-Issue of the 1959 entry Elvis (Rock 'N' Roll No. 1).				
ELVIS FOR EVERYONE	*RCA Victor*	48	*3 Jun 72*	1
This edition also has US disc. Originally released in 1965.				
ELVIS AS RECORDED AT MADISON SQUARE GARDEN	*RCA Victor*	3	*15 Jul 72*	20
Live recordings, 10 Jun 72.				
HE TOUCHED ME	*RCA Victor*	38	*12 Aug 72*	3
ALOHA FROM HAWAII VIA SATELLITE [OST-TV]	*RCA Victor*	11	*24 Feb 73*	10
Live recordings from the TV show at the Honolulu International Center on, 14 Jan 73. Benefit concert for the Kuiokalakani Lee Cancer Fund.				
ELVIS	*RCA Victor*	16	*15 Sep 73*	4
ELVIS - A LEGENDARY PERFORMER VOLUME 1	*RCA Victor*	20	*2 Mar 74*	3
Compilation including unreleased material.				
GOOD TIMES	*RCA Victor*	42	*25 May 74*	1
ELVIS AS RECORDED ON STAGE IN MEMPHIS	*RCA Victor*	44	*7 Sep 74*	1
Live recordings.				
PROMISED LAND	*RCA Victor*	21	*22 Feb 75*	4
TODAY	*RCA Victor*	48	*14 Jun 75*	3
ELVIS'S 40 GREATEST	*Arcade*	25	*5 Jul 75*	2
THE ELVIS PRESLEY SUN COLLECTION	*RCA Starcall*	16	*6 Sep 75*	13
Recordings made for the Sun record label in the 1950s.				
FROM ELVIS PRESLEY BOULEVARD, MEMPHIS, TENNESSEE	*RCA Victor*	29	*19 Jun 76*	5
ELVIS IN DEMAND	*RCA Victor*	12	*19 Feb 77*	11
Compiled by the UK fan club of hard to find recordings.				
MOODY BLUE	*RCA Victor*	3	*27 Aug 77*	15
Includes both live and studio recordings dating back to 1964.				
ELVIS'S 40 GREATEST [RE]	*Arcade*	1	*3 Sep 77*	36
WELCOME TO MY WORLD	*RCA Victor*	7	*3 Sep 77*	9
G.I. BLUES [OST][RE]	*RCA*	14	*03 Sept 77*	10
Includes re-entry in 1980.				
BLUE HAWAII [OST] [RE]	*RCA*	26	*10 Sept 77*	6
Re-released.				
ELVIS' GOLDEN RECORDS VOLUME 2 [RE]	*RCA*	27	*10 Sept 77*	4
Re-released.				
HITS OF THE 70'S	*RCA Victor*	30	*10 Sep 77*	4
ELVIS' GOLDEN RECORDS VOLUME 3 [RI]	*RCA*	49	*10 Sept 77*	2
PICTURES OF ELVIS	*RCA Starcall*	52	*10 Sep 77*	1
THE SUN YEARS	*Charly*	31	*8 Oct 77*	2
Early recordings from his time at the Sun label.				
LOVING YOU	*RCA Victor*	24	*15 Oct 77*	3
ELVIS IN CONCERT [OST-TV]	*RCA Victor*	13	*19 Nov 77*	11
Features both TV and live recordings from his last tour, Jun 77.				
HE WALKS BESIDE ME	*RCA Victor*	37	*22 Apr 78*	1
Gospel album.				
THE '56 SESSIONS VOLUME 1	*RCA Victor*	47	*3 Jun 78*	4
Compilation of early tracks.				
TV SPECIAL	*RCA Victor*	50	*2 Sep 78*	2
ELVIS'S 40 GREATEST HITS [RI]	*RCA Victor*	40	*11 Nov 78*	14
A LEGENDARY PERFORMER VOLUME 3	*RCA Victor*	43	*3 Feb 79*	3
OUR MEMORIES OF ELVIS	*RCA Victor*	72	*5 May 79*	1
LOVE SONGS	*K-Tel*	4	*24 Nov 79*	13
ELVIS PRESLEY SINGS LIEBER AND STOLLER	*RCA International*	32	*21 Jun 80*	5
Compilation.				
ELVIS ARON PRESLEY	*RCA*	21	*23 Aug 80*	4
8 LP box set including unheard material.				
PARADISE HAWAIIAN STYLE [OST] [RI]	*RCA International*	53	*23 Aug 80*	2
INSPIRATION	*K-Tel*	6	*29 Nov 80*	8
Gospel compilation.				
GUITAR MAN	*RCA*	33	*14 Mar 81*	5
THIS IS ELVIS PRESLEY [OST]	*RCA*	47	*9 May 81*	4
THE ULTIMATE PERFORMANCE	*K-Tel*	45	*28 Nov 81*	6
THE SOUND OF YOUR CRY	*RCA*	31	*13 Feb 82*	12
Compilation featuring rare recordings.				
ELVIS PRESLEY EP PACK	*RCA*	97	*6 Mar 82*	1
Box set of re-issued EPs with booklet.				
ROMANTIC ELVIS - 20 LOVE SONGS / ROCKIN' ELVIS - THE SIXTIES 20 GREAT TRACKS	*RCA*	62	*21 Aug 82*	5
IT WON'T SEEM LIKE CHRISTMAS WITHOUT YOU	*RCA International*	80	*18 Dec 82*	1
JAILHOUSE ROCK/LOVE IN LAS VEGAS	*RCA*	40	*30 Apr 83*	2
Songs from the films.				
I WAS THE ONE	*RCA*	83	*20 Aug 83*	1

A LEGENDARY PERFORMER VOLUME 4	*RCA*	91	*3 Dec 83*	1
I CAN HELP	*RCA*	71	*7 Apr 84*	3
THE FIRST LIVE RECORDINGS *Early 1950s recordings from 'The Louisiana Hayride'.*	*RCA International*	69	*21 Jul 84*	2
20 GREATEST HITS VOLUME 2	*RCA International*	98	*26 Jan 85*	1
RECONSIDER BABY *Blues recordings.*	*RCA*	92	*25 May 85*	1
ELVIS PRESLEY - BALLADS: 18 CLASSIC LOVE SONGS	*Telstar*	23	*12 Oct 85*	17
PRESLEY - THE ALL TIME GREATEST HITS	*RCA*	4	*29 Aug 87*	32
STEREO '57 (ESSENTIAL ELVIS VOLUME 2)	*RCA*	60	*28 Jan 89*	2
HITS LIKE NEVER BEFORE (ESSENTIAL ELVIS VOLUME 3)	*RCA*	71	*21 Jul 90*	1
THE GREAT PERFORMANCES	*RCA*	62	*1 Sep 90*	1
COLLECTORS GOLD	*RCA*	57	*24 Aug 91*	1
FROM THE HEART - HIS GREATEST LOVE SONGS	*RCA*	4	*22 Feb 92*	18
THE ESSENTIAL COLLECTION	*RCA*	6	*10 Sep 94*	25
ELVIS 56 *Released to celebrate the 40th anniversary of his first hit single.*	*RCA*	42	*11 May 96*	3
ALWAYS ON MY MIND - ULTIMATE LOVE SONGS *Compilation commemorating the 20th anniversary of his death.*	*RCA*	3	*7 Jun 97*	33
BLUE SUEDE SHOES *Compilation of his early hits.*	*RCA*	39	*28 Feb 98*	4
THE 50 GREATEST HITS	*RCA*	8	*2 Dec 00*	25
THE LIVE GREATEST HITS	*RCA*	50	*31 Mar 01*	3
THE 50 GREATEST LOVE SONGS	*RCA*	21	*24 Nov 01*	6

PRESSURE DROP — UK

SINGLES:	HITS 2			WEEKS 2
SILENTLY BAD MINDED *Above hit: PRESSURE DROP featuring Constantine WEIR and Martin FISHLEY.*	*Higher Ground*	53	*21 Mar 98*	1
WARRIOR SOUND *Above hit: PRESSURE DROP featuring Martin FISHLEY and MC SKIBADEE.*	*Higher Ground*	72	*17 Mar 01*	1

Billy PRESTON — US

(See also Various Artists (EPs) 'The Apple EP'.)

SINGLES:	HITS 5			WEEKS 51.
GET BACK *Above hit: BEATLES with Billy PRESTON.*	*Apple*	1	*26 Apr 69*	17
THAT'S THE WAY GOD PLANNED IT *Produced by George Harrison.*	*Apple*	11	*5 Jul 69*	10
OUTA SPACE	*A&M*	44	*16 Sep 72*	3
GET BACK [RE-1ST] *Above hit: BEATLES with Billy PRESTON.*	*Apple*	28	*3 Apr 76*	5
WITH YOU I'M BORN AGAIN *Written by Carol Connors of the Teddy Bears.*	*Motown*	2	*15 Dec 79*	11
IT WILL COME IN TIME *Above 2: Billy PRESTON and SYREETA.*	*Motown*	47	*8 Mar 80*	4
GET BACK [RE-2ND] *Above hit: BEATLES with Billy PRESTON.*	*Apple*	74	*22 Apr 89*	1

Johnny PRESTON — US

SINGLES:	HITS 5			WEEKS 46
RUNNING BEAR *Features backing vocals by the Big Bopper (who also wrote the song) and country star George Jones.*	*Mercury*	1	*13 Feb 60*	15
CRADLE OF LOVE	*Mercury*	2	*23 Apr 60*	16
RUNNING BEAR [RE]	*Mercury*	41	*4 Jun 60*	1
I'M STARTING TO GO STEADY	*Mercury*	49	*30 Jul 60*	1
FEEL SO FINE *Above 2 entries were separate sides of the same release, each had its own chart run. Originally recorded by Shirley and Lee as Feels So Good.*	*Mercury*	18	*13 Aug 60*	10
CHARMING BILLY	*Mercury*	34	*10 Dec 60*	1
CHARMING BILLY [RE]	*Mercury*	42	*24 Dec 60*	2

Mike PRESTON — UK

SINGLES:	HITS 4			WEEKS 33
MR. BLUE	*Decca*	12	*31 Oct 59*	8
I'D DO ANYTHING *From the musical 'Oliver!'.*	*Decca*	23	*27 Aug 60*	10
TOGETHERNESS	*Decca*	41	*24 Dec 60*	5
MARRY ME	*Decca*	14	*11 Mar 61*	10

PRETENDERS — US

(See also John Barry.)

SINGLES:	HITS 18			WEEKS 131
STOP YOUR SOBBING *Originally recorded by the Kinks.*	*Real*	34	*10 Feb 79*	9

KID	*Real*	33	*14 Jul 79*	7
BRASS IN POCKET	*Real*	1	*17 Nov 79*	17
TALK OF THE TOWN	*Real*	8	*5 Apr 80*	8
MESSAGE OF LOVE	*Real*	11	*14 Feb 81*	7
DAY AFTER DAY	*Real*	45	*12 Sep 81*	4
I GO TO SLEEP	*Real*	7	*14 Nov 81*	10
Written by Ray Davies and originally recorded by Peggy Lee.				
BACK ON THE CHAIN GANG	*Real*	17	*2 Oct 82*	9
2000 MILES	*Real*	15	*26 Nov 83*	9
THIN LINE BETWEEN LOVE AND HATE	*Real*	49	*9 Jun 84*	3
Originally recorded by the Persuaders and features Paul Carrack on piano and backing vocals.				
DON'T GET ME WRONG	*Realworld*	10	*11 Oct 86*	9
HYMN TO HER	*Real*	8	*13 Dec 86*	12
IF THERE WAS A MAN	*Real*	49	*15 Aug 87*	6
From the James Bond film 'The Living Daylights'.				
Above hit: PRETENDERS FOR 007.				
I'LL STAND BY YOU	*WEA*	10	*23 Apr 94*	10
NIGHT IN MY VEINS	*WEA*	25	*2 Jul 94*	5
977	*WEA*	66	*15 Oct 94*	2
KID [RR]	*WEA*	73	*14 Oct 95*	1
Acoustic version.				
HUMAN	*WEA*	33	*15 May 99*	3
ALBUMS:	**HITS 10**			**WEEKS 166**
PRETENDERS	*Real*	1	*19 Jan 80*	35
PRETENDERS II	*Real*	7	*15 Aug 81*	27
LEARNING TO CRAWL	*Real*	11	*21 Jan 84*	16
GET CLOSE	*Real*	6	*1 Nov 86*	28
THE SINGLES	*Real*	6	*7 Nov 87*	25
PACKED!	*WEA*	19	*26 May 90*	5
LAST OF THE INDEPENDENTS	*WEA*	8	*21 May 94*	13
THE ISLE OF VIEW	*WEA*	23	*28 Oct 95*	4
THE SINGLES [RI]	*WEA*	47	*31 Jan 98*	7
Mid-price reissue.				
VIVA EL AMOR	*WEA*	32	*29 May 99*	2
GREATEST HITS	*warner.esp*	21	*30 Sep 00*	4

PRETTY BOY FLOYD — US

SINGLES:	**HITS 1**			**WEEKS 1**
ROCK AND ROLL (IS GONNA SET THE NIGHT ON FIRE)	*MCA*	75	*10 Mar 90*	1

PRETTY THINGS — UK

SINGLES:	**HITS 7**			**WEEKS 41**
ROSALYN	*Fontana*	41	*20 Jun 64*	5
DON'T BRING ME DOWN	*Fontana*	10	*24 Oct 64*	11
HONEY I NEED	*Fontana*	13	*27 Feb 65*	10
CRY TO ME	*Fontana*	28	*17 Jul 65*	7
MIDNIGHT TO SIX MAN	*Fontana*	46	*22 Jan 66*	1
COME SEE ME	*Fontana*	43	*7 May 66*	5
A HOUSE IN THE COUNTRY	*Fontana*	50	*23 Jul 66*	1
Originally recorded by Kinks.				
A HOUSE IN THE COUNTRY [RE]	*Fontana*	50	*6 Aug 66*	1
EPS:	**HITS 2**			**WEEKS 37**
THE PRETTY THINGS	*Fontana*	6	*12 Dec 64*	28
RAININ' IN MY HEART	*Fontana*	12	*23 Oct 65*	9
ALBUMS:	**HITS 2**			**WEEKS 13**
PRETTY THINGS	*Fontana*	6	*27 Mar 65*	10
PARACHUTE	*Harvest*	43	*27 Jun 70*	3

Alan PRICE — UK

SINGLES:	**HITS 11**			**WEEKS 87**
I PUT A SPELL ON YOU	*Decca*	9	*2 Apr 66*	10
Originally recorded by Screaming Jay Hawkins.				
HI-LILI, HI-LO	*Decca*	11	*16 Jul 66*	12
SIMON SMITH AND THE AMAZING DANCING BEAR	*Decca*	4	*4 Mar 67*	12
Originally recorded by Randy Newman.				
THE HOUSE THAT JACK BUILT	*Decca*	4	*5 Aug 67*	10
SHAME	*Decca*	45	*18 Nov 67*	2
DON'T STOP THE CARNIVAL	*Decca*	13	*3 Feb 68*	8
Originally recorded by Sonny Rollins.				
Above 6: Alan PRICE SET.				
ROSETTA	*CBS*	11	*10 Apr 71*	10
Above hit: FAME and PRICE, PRICE and FAME TOGETHER.				
JARROW SONG	*Warner Brothers*	6	*25 May 74*	9
JUST FOR YOU	*Jet*	43	*29 Apr 78*	7
BABY OF MINE / JUST FOR YOU [RI]	*Jet*	32	*17 Feb 79*	3
CHANGES	*Ariola*	54	*30 Apr 88*	4

ALBUMS:	HITS 1			WEEKS 10
BETWEEN TODAY AND YESTERDAY	*Warner Brothers*	9	*8 Jun 74*	10

Kelly PRICE — US

(See also Whitney Houston.)

SINGLES:	HITS 2			WEEKS 5
FRIEND OF MINE	*Island Black Music*	25	*7 Nov 98*	3
SECRET LOVE	*Island Black Music*	26	*8 May 99*	2

Lloyd PRICE — US

SINGLES:	HITS 5			WEEKS 36
STAGGER LEE	*His Master's Voice*	7	*14 Feb 59*	14
Above hit: Lloyd PRICE with Don COSTA ORCHESTRA.				
WHERE WERE YOU (ON OUR WEDDING DAY)	*His Master's Voice*	15	*16 May 59*	6
PERSONALITY	*His Master's Voice*	9	*13 Jun 59*	8
Above hit: Lloyd PRICE and his Orchestra.				
PERSONALITY [RE]	*His Master's Voice*	25	*15 Aug 59*	2
I'M GONNA GET MARRIED	*His Master's Voice*	23	*12 Sep 59*	5
LADY LUCK	*His Master's Voice*	45	*23 Apr 60*	1
Above hit: Lloyd PRICE and his Orchestra.				

PRICKLY HEAT — UK

SINGLES:	HITS 1			WEEKS 1
OOOIE, OOOIE, OOOIE	*Virgin*	57	*26 Dec 98*	1
Theme to the Sky TV series 'Prickly Heat'.				

Charley PRIDE — US

ALBUMS:	HITS 4			WEEKS 17
CHARLEY PRIDE SPECIAL	*RCA Victor*	29	*10 Apr 71*	1
SHE'S JUST AN OLD LOVE TURNED MEMORY	*RCA Victor*	34	*28 May 77*	2
SOMEONE LOVES YOU HONEY	*RCA Victor*	48	*3 Jun 78*	2
GOLDEN COLLECTION	*K-Tel*	6	*26 Jan 80*	12

Dickie PRIDE — UK

SINGLES:	HITS 1			WEEKS 1
PRIMROSE LANE	*Columbia*	28	*31 Oct 59*	1

Maxi PRIEST — UK

(See also Jamaica United.)

SINGLES:	HITS 19			WEEKS 106
STROLLIN' ON	*10 Records*	32	*29 Mar 86*	9
IN THE SPRINGTIME (THE SUMMERTIME REMIX)	*10 Records*	54	*12 Jul 86*	3
CRAZY LOVE	*10 Records*	67	*8 Nov 86*	5
LET ME KNOW	*10 Records*	49	*4 Apr 87*	4
SOME GUYS HAVE ALL THE LUCK	*10 Records*	12	*24 Oct 87*	12
HOW CAN WE EASE THE PAIN	*10 Records*	41	*20 Feb 88*	6
Above hit: Maxi PRIEST featuring Beres HAMMOND.				
WILD WORLD	*10 Records*	5	*4 Jun 88*	9
Originally recorded by Cat Stevens.				
GOODBYE TO LOVE AGAIN	*10 Records*	57	*27 Aug 88*	3
CLOSE TO YOU	*10 Records*	7	*9 Jun 90*	10
PEACE THROUGHOUT THE WORLD	*10 Records*	41	*1 Sep 90*	4
Above hit: Maxi PRIEST (featuring Jazzie B.).				
HUMAN WORK OF ART	*Ten Records*	75	*1 Dec 90*	1
HUMAN WORK OF ART [RE]	*Ten Records*	71	*15 Dec 90*	3
HOUSECALL	*Epic*	31	*24 Aug 91*	7
Above hit: Shabba RANKS featuring Maxi PRIEST.				
THE MAXI PRIEST [EP]	*Ten Records*	62	*5 Oct 91*	3
Lead track: Just A Little Bit Longer.				
GROOVIN' IN THE MIDNIGHT	*Ten Records*	50	*26 Sep 92*	2
JUST WANNA KNOW / FE REAL	*Ten Records*	33	*28 Nov 92*	3
Above hit: Maxi PRIEST / Maxi PRIEST and APACHE INDIAN.				
ONE MORE CHANCE	*Ten Records*	40	*20 Mar 93*	3
HOUSECALL [RI]	*Epic*	8	*8 May 93*	8
Above hit: Shabba RANKS featuring Maxi PRIEST.				
WAITING IN VAIN	*GRP*	65	*31 Jul 93*	2
Above hit: Lee RITENOUR with Maxi PRIEST.				
THAT GIRL	*Virgin*	15	*22 Jun 96*	7
Samples Booker T. And The M.G.s Green Onions.				
Above hit: Maxi PRIEST featuring SHAGGY.				
WATCHING THE WORLD GO BY	*Virgin*	36	*21 Sep 96*	2

ALBUMS:	HITS 5			WEEKS 35
INTENTIONS	*10 Records*	96	*6 Dec 86*	1
MAXI	*10 Records*	48	*5 Dec 87*	9

MAXI [RE]	*10 Records*	25	*9 Jul 88*	6
BONAFIDE	*10 Records*	11	*14 Jul 90*	13
THE BEST OF ME	*Ten Records*	23	*9 Nov 91*	5
FE REAL	*Ten Records*	60	*14 Nov 92*	1

Louis PRIMA — US

(See also Various Artist: Films – Original Soundtracks 'Walt Disney Presents The Story And Songs Of The Jungle Book'.)

SINGLES:	HITS 1			WEEKS 1
BUONA SERA	*Capitol*	25	*22 Feb 58*	1
Above hit: Louis PRIMA with Sam BUTERA and the WITNESSES.				
EPS:	**HITS 1**			**WEEKS 2**
STRICTLY PRIMA	*Capitol*	12	*25 Jun 60*	2

PRIMA DONNA — UK

SINGLES:	HITS 1			WEEKS 4
LOVE ENOUGH FOR TWO	*Ariola*	48	*26 Apr 80*	4
UK's Eurovision Entry in 1980, it came 3rd.				

PRIMAL SCREAM — UK

SINGLES:	HITS 15			WEEKS 49
LOADED	*Creation*	16	*3 Mar 90*	9
COME TOGETHER	*Creation*	26	*18 Aug 90*	6
HIGHER THAN THE SUN	*Creation*	40	*22 Jun 91*	2
DON'T FIGHT IT, FEEL IT	*Creation*	41	*24 Aug 91*	2
Above hit: PRIMAL SCREAM featuring Denise JOHNSON.				
DIXIE-NARCO [EP]	*Creation*	11	*8 Feb 92*	6
Lead track: Movin' On Up.				
ROCKS / FUNKY JAM	*Creation*	7	*12 Mar 94*	5
JAILBIRD	*Creation*	29	*18 Jun 94*	2
(I'M GONNA) CRY MYSELF BLIND	*Creation*	49	*10 Dec 94*	2
THE BIG MAN AND THE SCREAM TEAM MEET THE BARMY ARMY UPTOWN	*Creation*	17	*15 Jun 96*	2
Above hit: PRIMAL SCREAM, Irvine WELSH and ON-U-SOUND present . . .				
KOWALSKI	*Creation*	8	*17 May 97*	3
Kowalski was the protangonist in the 70s movie 'Vanishing Point'.				
STAR	*Creation*	16	*28 Jun 97*	3
BURNING WHEEL	*Creation*	17	*25 Oct 97*	2
SWASTIKA EYES	*Creation*	22	*20 Nov 99*	2
KILL ALL HIPPIES	*Creation*	24	*1 Apr 00*	2
Samples the voice of actress Linda Manz from the film 'Out Of The Blue'.				
ACCELERATOR	*Creation*	34	*23 Sep 00*	1
The last single released on the Creation label.				
ALBUMS:	**HITS 6**			**WEEKS 70**
SONIC FLOWER GROOVE	*Elevation*	62	*17 Oct 87*	1
SCREAMADELICA	*Creation*	8	*5 Oct 91*	30
Winner of the 1992 Mercury Music Prize. Includes re-entries through to 2000.				
GIVE OUT, BUT DON'T GIVE UP	*Creation*	2	*9 Apr 94*	18
VANISHING POINT	*Creation*	2	*19 Jul 97*	10
Title taken from the cult 1970s road film.				
ECHO DEK	*Creation*	43	*8 Nov 97*	1
Dub version of 'Vanishing Point' reworked by Adrian Sherwood.				
EXTERMINATOR	*Creation*	3	*12 Feb 00*	10

PRIME MOVERS — US

SINGLES:	HITS 1			WEEKS 1
ON THE TRAIL	*Island*	74	*8 Feb 86*	1

PRIMITIVE RADIO GODS — US

SINGLES:	HITS 1			WEEKS 1
STANDING OUTSIDE A BROKEN PHONE BOOTH WITH MONEY IN MY HAND	*Columbia*	74	*30 Mar 96*	1

PRIMITIVES — UK/Australia

SINGLES:	HITS 6			WEEKS 27
CRASH	*Lazy*	5	*27 Feb 88*	10
OUT OF REACH	*Lazy*	25	*30 Apr 88*	4
WAY BEHIND ME	*Lazy*	36	*3 Sep 88*	4
SICK OF IT	*Lazy*	24	*29 Jul 89*	4
SECRETS	*Lazy*	49	*30 Sep 89*	3
YOU ARE THE WAY	*RCA*	58	*3 Aug 91*	2
ALBUMS:	**HITS 3**			**WEEKS 13**
LOVELY	*Lazy*	6	*9 Apr 88*	10
LAZY 86-88	*Lazy*	73	*2 Sep 89*	1
PURE	*RCA*	33	*28 Oct 89*	2

PRIMUS

US

ALBUMS:	HITS 1			WEEKS 1
PORK SODA	*Interscope*	56	*8 May 93*	1

PRINCE

US

SINGLES:	HITS 46			WEEKS 305
I WANNA BE YOUR LOVER	*Warner Brothers*	41	*19 Jan 80*	3
1999	*Warner Brothers*	25	*29 Jan 83*	7
LITTLE RED CORVETTE	*Warner Brothers*	54	*30 Apr 83*	6
LITTLE RED CORVETTE [RI-1ST]	*Warner Brothers*	66	*26 Nov 83*	2
WHEN DOVES CRY	*Warner Brothers*	4	*30 Jun 84*	15
PURPLE RAIN	*Warner Brothers*	8	*22 Sep 84*	9
I WOULD DIE 4 U	*Warner Brothers*	58	*8 Dec 84*	6
Above 3 from the film 'Purple Rain'.				
Above 2: PRINCE and the REVOLUTION.				
1999 [RI-1ST] / LITTLE RED CORVETTE [RI-2ND]	*Warner Brothers*	2	*19 Jan 85*	10
LET'S GO CRAZY / TAKE ME WITH YOU	*Warner Brothers*	7	*23 Feb 85*	9
PAISLEY PARK	*Paisley Park*	18	*25 May 85*	10
RASPBERRY BERET	*Paisley Park*	25	*27 Jul 85*	8
POP LIFE	*Paisley Park*	60	*26 Oct 85*	2
KISS	*Paisley Park*	6	*8 Mar 86*	9
MOUNTAINS	*Paisley Park*	45	*14 Jun 86*	4
GIRLS & BOYS	*Paisley Park*	11	*16 Aug 86*	8
ANOTHERLOVERHOLENYOHEAD	*Paisley Park*	36	*1 Nov 86*	3
Above 8: PRINCE and the REVOLUTION.				
SIGN 'O' THE TIMES	*Paisley Park*	10	*14 Mar 87*	9
IF I WAS YOUR GIRLFRIEND	*Paisley Park*	20	*20 Jun 87*	6
U GOT THE LOOK	*Paisley Park*	11	*15 Aug 87*	9
Features vocals by Sheena Easton.				
I COULD NEVER TAKE THE PLACE OF YOUR MAN	*Paisley Park*	29	*28 Nov 87*	6
ALPHABET ST.	*Paisley Park*	9	*7 May 88*	6
GLAM SLAM	*Paisley Park*	29	*23 Jul 88*	4
I WISH U HEAVEN	*Paisley Park*	24	*5 Nov 88*	5
BATDANCE	*Warner Brothers*	2	*24 Jun 89*	12
PARTYMAN	*Warner Brothers*	14	*9 Sep 89*	6
THE ARMS OF ORION	*Warner Brothers*	27	*18 Nov 89*	5
Above 3 from the film 'Batman'.				
Above hit: PRINCE with Sheena EASTON.				
THIEVES IN THE TEMPLE	*Paisley Park*	7	*4 Aug 90*	6
NEW POWER GENERATION	*Paisley Park*	26	*10 Nov 90*	4
Tevin Campbell and Mavis Staples on backing vocals.				
GETT OFF	*Paisley Park*	4	*31 Aug 91*	8
Samples Banbarra's Shack Up.				
CREAM	*Paisley Park*	15	*21 Sep 91*	7
DIAMONDS & PEARLS	*Paisley Park*	25	*7 Dec 91*	6
MONEY DON'T MATTER 2 NIGHT	*Paisley Park*	19	*28 Mar 92*	5
THUNDER	*Paisley Park*	28	*27 Jun 92*	3
SEXY MF/STROLLIN'	*Paisley Park*	4	*18 Jul 92*	7
MY NAME IS PRINCE	*Paisley Park*	7	*10 Oct 92*	5
MY NAME IS PRINCE [RM]	*Paisley Park*	51	*14 Nov 92*	1
7	*Paisley Park*	27	*5 Dec 92*	6
Samples Tramp by Lowell Fulsom.				
THE MORNING PAPERS	*Paisley Park*	52	*13 Mar 93*	3
Above 10: PRINCE and the NEW POWER GENERATION.				
PEACH	*Paisley Park*	14	*16 Oct 93*	5
CONTROVERSY	*Paisley Park*	5	*11 Dec 93*	5
THE MOST BEAUTIFUL GIRL IN THE WORLD	*NPG*	1	*9 Apr 94*	12
THE BEAUTIFUL EXPERIENCE [RM]	*NPG*	18	*4 Jun 94*	3
Consists of 7 mixes of The Most Beautiful Girl In The World.				
Above 2: [symbol]				
LETITGO	*Warner Brothers*	30	*10 Sep 94*	4
PURPLE MEDLEY [M]	*Warner Brothers*	33	*18 Mar 95*	2
EYE HATE U	*Warner Brothers*	20	*23 Sep 95*	3
GOLD	*Warner Brothers*	10	*9 Dec 95*	9
DINNER WITH DELORES	*Warner Brothers*	36	*3 Aug 96*	2
Above 3: [symbol]				
BETCHA BY GOLLY WOW!	*NPG*	11	*14 Dec 96*	7
THE HOLY RIVER	*NPG*	19	*8 Mar 97*	3
Above 2: ARTIST.				
1999 [RI-2ND]	*Warner Brothers*	10	*9 Jan 99*	4
1999 [RI-2ND] [RE]	*Warner Brothers*	49	*18 Dec 99*	5
THE GREATEST ROMANCE EVER SOLD	*NPG*	65	*26 Feb 00*	1
Above hit: ARTIST.				

ALBUMS:	HITS 21			WEEKS 434
PURPLE RAIN [OST]	*Warner Brothers*	7	*21 Jul 84*	86
Peak position reached on 16 Mar 85. Includes re-entries through to 1992.				
Above hit: PRINCE and the REVOLUTION.				

1999	*Warner Brothers*	30	*8 Sep 84*	21
Originally released in 1983.				
AROUND THE WORLD IN A DAY	*Warner Brothers*	5	*4 May 85*	20
PARADE - MUSIC FROM "UNDER THE CHERRY MOON" [OST]	*Warner Brothers*	4	*12 Apr 86*	26
Above 2: PRINCE and the REVOLUTION.				
SIGN 'O' THE TIMES	*Paisley Park*	4	*11 Apr 87*	32
LOVESEXY	*Paisley Park*	1	*21 May 88*	32
Includes re-entry in 1995.				
BATMAN [OST]	*Warner Brothers*	1	*1 Jul 89*	20
GRAFFITI BRIDGE	*Paisley Park*	1	*01 Sept 90*	8
GETT OFF	*Paisley Park*	33	*24 Aug 91*	3
US Import single. Total timing was too long to be eligible for the singles chart.				
DIAMONDS AND PEARLS	*Paisley Park*	2	*12 Oct 91*	57
SYMBOL	*Paisley Park*	1	*17 Oct 92*	21
Above 3: PRINCE and the NEW POWER GENERATION.				
THE HITS 1	*Paisley Park*	5	*25 Sep 93*	27
THE HITS 2	*Paisley Park*	5	*25 Sep 93*	28
THE HITS/THE B-SIDES	*Paisley Park*	4	*25 Sep 93*	7
COME	*Warner Brothers*	1	*27 Aug 94*	8
Above hit: PRINCE 1958–1993.				
THE BLACK ALBUM	*Warner Brothers*	36	*3 Dec 94*	3
Originally withdrawn prior to release in 1987, though widely bootlegged.				
PURPLE RAIN [OST] [RI]	*Paisley Park*	18	*18 Feb 95*	5
Mid-price reissue.				
Above hit: PRINCE and the REVOLUTION.				
THE GOLD EXPERIENCE	*Warner Brothers*	4	*7 Oct 95*	5
CHAOS AND DISORDER	*Warner Brothers*	14	*20 Jul 96*	4
Above 2: [symbol]				
EMANCIPATION	*NPG*	18	*30 Nov 96*	6
Above hit: ARTIST.				
THE VAULT . . . OLD FRIENDS 4 SALE	*Warner Brothers*	47	*4 Sept 99*	1
Previously unreleased records spanning 1985–94.				
THE VERY BEST OF PRINCE	*Warner Brothers*	2	*11 Aug 01*	14

PRINCE BUSTER and ALL STARS — Jamaica

SINGLES:	HITS 2			WEEKS 16
AL CAPONE	*Blue Beat*	18	*25 Feb 67*	13
Originally released in 1965.				
WHINE AND GRINE	*Island*	21	*4 Apr 98*	3
Featured from the Levi's Jeans TV commercial. His original recording made in 1968.				
Above hit: PRINCE BUSTER.				

PRINCE CHARLES and the CITY BEAT BAND — US

SINGLES:	HITS 1			WEEKS 2
WE CAN MAKE IT HAPPEN	*PRT*	56	*22 Feb 86*	2
ALBUMS:	**HITS 1**			**WEEKS 1**
STONE KILLERS	*Virgin*	81	*30 Apr 83*	1

PRINCE MYDAS – See SHAGGY

PRINCE NASEEM – See KALEEF

PRINCE QUICK 'MELLOW' – See Steve LAWLER; Vocal from PRINCE QUICK 'MELLOW'

PRINCESS — UK

SINGLES:	HITS 6			WEEKS 44
SAY I'M YOUR NUMBER ONE	*Supreme*	7	*3 Aug 85*	12
AFTER THE LOVE HAS GONE	*Supreme*	28	*9 Nov 85*	13
I'LL KEEP ON LOVING YOU	*Supreme*	16	*19 Apr 86*	8
TELL ME TOMORROW	*Supreme*	34	*5 Jul 86*	5
From the film 'Knights And Emeralds'.				
IN THE HEAT OF A PASSIONATE MOMENT	*Supreme*	74	*25 Oct 86*	1
RED HOT	*Polydor*	58	*13 Jun 87*	5
ALBUMS:	**HITS 1**			**WEEKS 14**
PRINCESS	*Supreme*	15	*17 May 86*	14

PRINCESS IVORI — US

SINGLES:	HITS 1			WEEKS 2
WANTED	*Supreme*	69	*17 Mar 90*	2

Patrick PRINZ – See ARTEMESIA; ETHICS; MOVIN' MELODIES; SUBLIMINAL CUTS

Maddy PRIOR from STEELEYE SPAN – See STATUS QUO; STEELEYE SPAN

PRIORY OF THE RESURRECTION — UK

ALBUMS:	HITS 1			WEEKS 1
ETERNAL LIGHT - MUSIC OF INNER PEACE	*Deutsche Grammophon*	68	*31 Mar 01*	1

PRIVATE LIVES — UK

SINGLES:	HITS 1			WEEKS 4
LIVING IN A WORLD (TURNED UPSIDE DOWN)	*EMI*	53	*11 Feb 84*	4

PRIZNA featuring the DEMOLITION MAN — UK

SINGLES:	HITS 1			WEEKS 2
FIRE	*Labello Blanco*	33	*29 Apr 95*	2

P.J. PROBY — US

SINGLES:	HITS 12			WEEKS 91
HOLD ME	*Decca*	3	*30 May 64*	15
Originally recorded by Art Hickman in 1919.				
TOGETHER	*Decca*	8	*5 Sep 64*	11
Originally recorded by Paul Whiteman Orchestra in 1928.				
SOMEWHERE	*Liberty*	6	*12 Dec 64*	12
From the show/film 'West Side Story'.				
I APOLOGISE	*Liberty*	11	*27 Feb 65*	8
Originally recorded by Billy Eckstein.				
LET THE WATER RUN DOWN	*Liberty*	19	*10 Jul 65*	8
Originally recorded by Ben E.King.				
THAT MEANS A LOT	*Liberty*	30	*2 Oct 65*	6
MARIA	*Liberty*	8	*27 Nov 65*	9
From the show/film 'West Side Story'.				
YOU'VE COME BACK	*Liberty*	25	*12 Feb 66*	7
TO MAKE A BIG MAN CRY	*Liberty*	34	*18 Jun 66*	3
I CAN'T MAKE IT ALONE	*Liberty*	37	*29 Oct 66*	5
IT'S YOUR DAY TODAY	*Liberty*	32	*9 Mar 68*	5
YESTERDAY HAS GONE	*EMI Premier*	58	*28 Dec 96*	1
Originally recorded by Little Anthony & The Imperials.				
Above hit: P.J. PROBY; Marc ALMOND featuring the MY LIFE STORY ORCHESTRA.				
YESTERDAY HAS GONE [RE]	*EMI Premier*	69	*11 Jan 97*	1
EPS:	**HITS 2**			**WEEKS 11**
P. J. PROBY	*Liberty*	13	*9 Jan 65*	6
SOMEWHERE	*Liberty*	19	*9 Oct 65*	5
ALBUMS:	**HITS 1**			**WEEKS 3**
I'M P.J. PROBY	*Liberty*	16	*27 Feb 65*	3

PROCLAIMERS — UK

SINGLES:	HITS 9			WEEKS 50
LETTER FROM AMERICA	*Chrysalis*	3	*14 Nov 87*	10
Produced by Gerry Rafferty.				
MAKE MY HEART FLY	*Chrysalis*	63	*5 Mar 88*	3
I'M GONNA BE (500 MILES)	*Chrysalis*	11	*27 Aug 88*	11
SUNSHINE ON LEITH	*Chrysalis*	41	*12 Nov 88*	5
I'M ON MY WAY	*Chrysalis*	43	*11 Feb 89*	4
KING OF THE ROAD [EP]	*Chrysalis*	9	*24 Nov 90*	8
Lead track: King Of The Road.				
LET'S GET MARRIED	*Chrysalis*	21	*19 Feb 94*	4
WHAT MAKES YOU CRY	*Chrysalis*	38	*16 Apr 94*	3
THESE ARMS OF MINE	*Chrysalis*	51	*22 Oct 94*	2
ALBUMS:	**HITS 4**			**WEEKS 55**
THIS IS THE STORY	*Chrysalis*	52	*9 May 87*	6
THIS IS THE STORY [RE]	*Chrysalis*	43	*21 Nov 87*	15
SUNSHINE ON LEITH	*Chrysalis*	6	*24 Sep 88*	27
HIT THE HIGHWAY	*Chrysalis*	8	*19 Mar 94*	6
PERSEVERE	*Persevere*	61	*9 Jun 01*	1

PROCOL HARUM — UK

SINGLES:	HITS 6			WEEKS 56
A WHITER SHADE OF PALE	*Deram*	1	*27 May 67*	15
Based on Bach's Cantata No.3 in D.				
HOMBURG	*Regal Zonophone*	6	*7 Oct 67*	10
QUITE RIGHTLY SO	*Regal Zonophone*	50	*27 Apr 68*	1
A SALTY DOG	*Regal Zonophone*	44	*21 Jun 69*	1
A SALTY DOG [RE-1ST]	*Regal Zonophone*	44	*5 Jul 69*	1
A SALTY DOG [RE-2ND]	*Regal Zonophone*	44	*19 Jul 69*	1
A WHITER SHADE OF PALE [RI]	*Fly*	13	*22 Apr 72*	13
CONQUISTADOR	*Chrysalis*	22	*5 Aug 72*	7
PANDORA'S BOX	*Chrysalis*	16	*23 Aug 75*	7
ALBUMS:	**HITS 6**			**WEEKS 11**
A SALTY DOG	*Regal Zonophone*	27	*19 Jul 69*	2
HOME	*Regal Zonophone*	49	*27 Jun 70*	1
BROKEN BARRICADES	*Chrysalis*	42	*3 Jul 71*	1

A WHITER SHADE OF PALE/A SALTY DOG	*Fly Double Back*	26	*6 May 72*	4
Double re-issue although A Whiter Shade Of Pale never charted previously.				
PROCOL HARUM LIVE IN CONCERT WITH THE EDMONTON SYMPHONY ORCHESTRA	*Chrysalis*	48	*6 May 72*	1
Live recordings from 6 Aug 71.				
PROCOL'S NINTH	*Chrysalis*	41	*30 Aug 75*	2

Michael PROCTER – See URBAN BLUES PROJECT present Michael PROCTER

PRODIGY — UK

SINGLES:	HITS 12			WEEKS 139
CHARLY	*XL Recordings*	3	*24 Aug 91*	10
EVERYBODY IN THE PLACE [EP]	*XL Recordings*	2	*4 Jan 92*	9
Lead track: Everybody In The Place.				
FIRE / JERICHO	*XL Recordings*	11	*26 Sep 92*	4
OUT OF SPACE / RUFF IN THE JUNGLE BIZNESS	*XL Recordings*	5	*21 Nov 92*	12
Ruff In The Jungle Bizness no longer listed from 5 Dec 92. As an AA side it peaked at No. 6.				
WIND IT UP (REWOUND)	*XL Recordings*	11	*17 Apr 93*	7
ONE LOVE	*XL Recordings*	8	*16 Oct 93*	6
NO GOOD (START THE DANCE)	*XL Recordings*	4	*28 May 94*	12
Samples No Good For Me by Kelly Charles.				
VOODOO PEOPLE	*XL Recordings*	13	*24 Sep 94*	5
POISON	*XL Recordings*	15	*18 Mar 95*	6
FIRESTARTER	*XL Recordings*	1	*30 Mar 96*	19
First single to feature vocals by Keith Flint. Samples Art Of Noise's Close To The Edit.				
OUT OF SPACE / RUFF IN THE JUNGLE BIZNESS [RE]	*XL Recordings*	52	*20 Apr 96*	2
NO GOOD (START THE DANCE) [RE]	*XL Recordings*	57	*20 Apr 96*	2
POISON [RE]	*XL Recordings*	62	*20 Apr 96*	1
FIRE / JERICHO [RE]	*XL Recordings*	63	*20 Apr 96*	1
CHARLY [RE]	*XL Recordings*	66	*20 Apr 96*	1
WIND IT UP (REWOUND) [RE]	*XL Recordings*	71	*20 Apr 96*	1
VOODOO PEOPLE [RE]	*XL Recordings*	75	*20 Apr 96*	1
EVERYBODY IN THE PLACE [RE]	*XL Recordings*	69	*27 Apr 96*	1
All re-entries were due to promotional offer of purchasing 3 of the singles for £10.				
BREATHE	*XL Recordings*	1	*23 Nov 96*	17
FIRESTARTER [RE-1ST]	*XL Recordings*	54	*14 Dec 96*	4
FIRESTARTER [RE-2ND]	*XL Recordings*	53	*25 Jan 97*	7
BREATHE [RE]	*XL Recordings*	71	*5 Apr 97*	1
SMACK MY BITCH UP	*XL Recordings*	8	*29 Nov 97*	10
Additional vocals by Shakim Bador.				

ALBUMS:	HITS 3			WEEKS 189
EXPERIENCE	*XL Recordings*	12	*10 Oct 92*	31
MUSIC FOR THE JILTED GENERATION	*XL Recordings*	1	*16 Jul 94*	98
THE FAT OF THE LAND	*XL Recordings*	1	*12 Jul 97*	60

PRODUCT G&B – See SANTANA

PROFESSIONALS — UK

SINGLES:	HITS 1			WEEKS 4
1-2-3	*Virgin*	43	*11 Oct 80*	4

PROFESSOR – See DJ PROFESSOR

PROFESSOR T – See SHUT UP AND DANCE

PROGRAM 2 BELTRAM – See BELTRAM

PROGRESS presents the BOY WUNDA — UK

SINGLES:	HITS 1			WEEKS 10
EVERYBODY	*Manifesto*	7	*18 Dec 99*	10
Samples the string section from Madonna's Papa Don't Preach.				

PROGRESS FUNK — Italy

SINGLES:	HITS 1			WEEKS 1
AROUND MY BRAIN	*Deconstruction*	73	*11 Oct 97*	1

PROJECT featuring GERIDEAU — US

(See also Gerideau.)

SINGLES:	HITS 1			WEEKS 1
BRING IT BACK 2 LUV	*Fruittree*	65	*27 Aug 94*	1

PROJECT D — UK

ALBUMS:	HITS 2			WEEKS 18
THE SYNTHESIZER ALBUM	*Telstar*	13	*17 Feb 90*	11
SYNTHESIZER 2	*Telstar*	25	*29 Sep 90*	7

PROJECT ONE
UK

SINGLES:	HITS 2			WEEKS 3
ROUGH NECK [EP] *Lead track: Come My Selector.*	*Rising High*	49	*16 May 92*	2
DON CARGON COMIN'	*Rising High*	64	*29 Aug 92*	1

PRONG
US

SINGLES:	HITS 1			WEEKS 1
WHOSE FIST IS THIS ANYWAY [EP] *Lead track: Prove You Wrong.*	*Epic*	58	*25 Apr 92*	1
ALBUMS:	**HITS 1**			**WEEKS 1**
CLEANSING	*Epic*	71	*12 Feb 94*	1

PROPAGANDA
Germany

SINGLES:	HITS 5			WEEKS 35
DR MABUSE	*ZTT*	27	*17 Mar 84*	9
DUEL	*ZTT*	21	*4 May 85*	12
P:MACHINERY	*ZTT*	50	*10 Aug 85*	5
HEAVEN GIVE ME WORDS	*Virgin*	36	*28 Apr 90*	5
ONLY ONE WORD	*Virgin*	71	*8 Sep 90*	4
ALBUMS:	**HITS 3**			**WEEKS 16**
SECRET WISH	*ZTT*	16	*13 Jul 85*	12
WISHFUL THINKING	*ZTT*	82	*23 Nov 85*	2
1234	*Virgin*	46	*9 Jun 90*	2

PROPELLERHEADS
UK

(See also 808 State.)

SINGLES:	HITS 5			WEEKS 15
TAKE CALIFORNIA	*Wall Of Sound*	69	*7 Dec 96*	1
SPYBREAK! *From the film 'Playing God'.*	*Wall Of Sound*	40	*17 May 97*	1
ON HER MAJESTY'S SECRET SERVICE *Above hit: PROPELLERHEADS/David ARNOLD.*	*East West*	7	*18 Oct 97*	5
HISTORY REPEATING *Above hit: PROPELLERHEADS featuring Miss Shirley BASSEY.*	*Wall Of Sound*	19	*20 Dec 97*	7
BANG ON!	*Wall Of Sound*	53	*27 Jun 98*	1
ALBUMS:	**HITS 1**			**WEEKS 13**
DECKSANDRUMSANDROCKANDROLL	*Wall Of Sound*	6	*7 Feb 98*	13

PROPHETS OF SOUND
UK

SINGLES:	HITS 1			WEEKS 1
HIGH	*Distinct'ive*	73	*14 Nov 98*	1

PROSPECT PARK featuring Carolyn HARDING
UK

SINGLES:	HITS 1			WEEKS 1
MOVIN' ON *Originally a club hit for Roach Motel in 1991.*	*AM:PM*	55	*8 Aug 98*	1

Shaila PROSPERE – See RIMES featuring Shaila PROSPERE

Brian PROTHEROE
UK

SINGLES:	HITS 1			WEEKS 6
PINBALL	*Chrysalis*	22	*7 Sep 74*	6

PROUD MARY
UK

SINGLES:	HITS 1			WEEKS 1
VERY BEST FRIEND	*Sour Mash*	75	*25 Aug 01*	1

Dorothy PROVINE
US

SINGLES:	HITS 2			WEEKS 15
DON'T BRING LULU	*Warner Brothers*	17	*9 Dec 61*	12
CRAZY WORDS CRAZY TUNES (VO-DO-DE-O) *Above 2 from the TV show 'The Roaring 20s'.* *Above hit: Dorothy PROVINE and the CHORUS GIRLS with the PLAYBOYS.*	*Warner Brothers*	45	*30 Jun 62*	3
ALBUMS:	**HITS 2**			**WEEKS 49**
THE ROARING 20'S *Music from the Warner Brothers TV show of the same name. Also features medleys by the Dixieland Band and the Band.* *Above hit: Dorothy PROVINE the CHORUS GIRLS, the TRIO and PINKY and her PLAYBOYS.*	*Warner Brothers*	3	*2 Dec 61*	42
VAMP OF THE ROARING TWENTIES *Above 2 feature medley of songs from the 1920s*	*Warner Brothers*	9	*10 Feb 62*	7

PSEUDO ECHO — Australia

SINGLES:	HITS 1			WEEKS 12
FUNKY TOWN	*RCA*	8	*18 Jul 87*	12

PSG – See COLOUR GIRL

PSYCHEDELIC FURS — UK

SINGLES:	HITS 7			WEEKS 31
DUMB WAITERS	*CBS*	59	*2 May 81*	2
PRETTY IN PINK	*CBS*	43	*27 Jun 81*	5
LOVE MY WAY	*CBS*	42	*31 Jul 82*	6
HEAVEN	*CBS*	29	*31 Mar 84*	6
THE GHOST IN YOU	*CBS*	68	*16 Jun 84*	2
PRETTY IN PINK [RR]	*CBS*	18	*23 Aug 86*	9
From the film of the same name.				
ALL THAT MONEY WANTS	*CBS*	75	*9 Jul 88*	1
ALBUMS:	**HITS 8**			**WEEKS 39**
PSYCHEDELIC FURS	*CBS*	18	*15 Mar 80*	6
TALK TALK TALK	*CBS*	30	*23 May 81*	9
FOREVER NOW	*CBS*	20	*2 Oct 82*	6
MIRROR MOVES	*CBS*	15	*19 May 84*	9
MIDNIGHT TO MIDNIGHT	*CBS*	12	*14 Feb 87*	5
ALL OF THIS AND NOTHING	*CBS*	67	*13 Aug 88*	2
BOOK OF DAYS	*CBS*	74	*18 Nov 89*	1
WORLD OUTSIDE	*East West*	68	*13 Jul 91*	1

PSYCHIC TV — UK

SINGLES:	HITS 2			WEEKS 4
GODSTAR	*Temple*	67	*26 Apr 86*	2
Above hit: PSYCHIC TV and the ANGELS OF LIGHT.				
GOOD VIBRATIONS / ROMAN P	*Temple*	65	*20 Sep 86*	2

PSYCHOTROPIC – See FREEFALL featuring PSYCHOTROPIC

PUBLIC ANNOUNCEMENT — US

(See also R. Kelly.)

SINGLES:	HITS 1			WEEKS 2
BODY BUMPIN' YIPPIE-YI-YO	*A&M*	38	*4 Jul 98*	2

PUBLIC DEMAND — UK

SINGLES:	HITS 1			WEEKS 2
INVISIBLE	*ZTT*	41	*15 Feb 97*	2

PUBLIC DOMAIN — UK

SINGLES:	HITS 2			WEEKS 16
OPERATION BLADE (BASS IN THE PLACE . . .)	*Xtrahard*	5	*2 Dec 00*	13
Samples the Pump Panel remix of New Order's Confusion from the 'Blade' soundtrack.				
ROCK DA FUNKY BEATS	*Xtrahard*	19	*23 Jun 01*	3
Above hit: PUBLIC DOMAIN featuring Chuck D.				

PUBLIC ENEMY — US

SINGLES:	HITS 16			WEEKS 53
REBEL WITHOUT A PAUSE	*Def Jam*	37	*21 Nov 87*	5
Samples The JBs The Grunt.				
REBEL WITHOUT A PAUSE [RE]	*Def Jam*	71	*2 Jan 88*	2
BRING THE NOISE	*Def Jam*	32	*9 Jan 88*	5
DON'T BELIEVE THE HYPE	*Def Jam*	18	*2 Jul 88*	5
NIGHT OF THE LIVING BASEHEADS	*Def Jam*	63	*15 Oct 88*	2
FIGHT THE POWER	*Motown*	29	*24 Jun 89*	5
WELCOME TO THE TERROR DOME	*Def Jam*	18	*20 Jan 90*	4
911 IS A JOKE	*Def Jam*	41	*7 Apr 90*	3
BROTHERS GONNA WORK IT OUT	*Def Jam*	46	*23 Jun 90*	2
CAN'T DO NUTTIN' FOR YA MAN	*Def Jam*	53	*3 Nov 90*	2
CAN'T TRUSS IT	*Def Jam*	22	*12 Oct 91*	4
SHUT 'EM DOWN	*Def Jam*	21	*25 Jan 92*	3
NIGHTTRAIN	*Def Jam*	55	*11 Apr 92*	2
GIVE IT UP	*Def Jam*	18	*13 Aug 94*	3
SO WHATCHA GONNA DO NOW?	*Def Jam*	50	*29 Jul 95*	1
HE GOT GAME	*Def Jam*	16	*6 Jun 98*	4
From the film 'He Got Game'. Samples Buffalo Springfield's For What It's Worth and features Stephen Stills on guitar and vocals.				
DO YOU WANNA GO OUR WAY???	*PLAS Recordings*	66	*25 Sept 99*	1
ALBUMS:	**HITS 7**			**WEEKS 37**
IT TAKES A NATION OF MILLIONS TO HOLD US BACK	*Def Jam*	8	*30 Jul 88*	9

FEAR OF A BLACK PLANET	*Def Jam*	4	*28 Apr 90*	10
APOCALYPSE 91 . . . THE ENEMY STRIKES BLACK	*Def Jam*	8	*19 Oct 91*	7
GREATEST MISSES	*Def Jam*	14	*3 Oct 92*	3
MUSE SICK-N-HOUR MESS AGE	*Def Jam*	12	*3 Sep 94*	3
HE GOT GAME [OST]	*Def Jam*	50	*16 May 98*	4
THERE'S A POISON GOIN ON . . .	*PLAS Recordings*	55	*31 Jul 99*	1
Previously only available from the internet US label Atomic Pop.				

PUBLIC IMAGE LTD — UK

(Certain releases below were credited to just PIL or P.I.L.)

SINGLES:	HITS 12			WEEKS 61
PUBLIC IMAGE	*Virgin*	9	*21 Oct 78*	8
DEATH DISCO	*Virgin*	20	*7 Jul 79*	7
MEMORIES	*Virgin*	60	*20 Oct 79*	2
FLOWERS OF ROMANCE	*Virgin*	24	*4 Apr 81*	7
THIS IS NOT A LOVE SONG	*Virgin*	5	*17 Sep 83*	10
BAD LIFE	*Virgin*	71	*19 May 84*	2
RISE	*Virgin*	11	*1 Feb 86*	8
HOME	*Virgin*	75	*3 May 86*	1
SEATTLE	*Virgin*	47	*22 Aug 87*	4
DISAPPOINTED	*Virgin*	38	*6 May 89*	5
DON'T ASK ME	*Virgin*	22	*20 Oct 90*	5
CRUEL	*Virgin*	49	*22 Feb 92*	2
ALBUMS:	**HITS 12**			**WEEKS 51**
PUBLIC IMAGE	*Virgin*	22	*23 Dec 78*	11
METAL BOX	*Virgin*	18	*8 Dec 79*	8
Title is due to format being available in a metal container with three 12" singles inside.				
SECOND EDITION OF PIL	*Virgin*	46	*8 Mar 80*	2
Repackage of Metal Box.				
PARIS AU PRINTEMPS (PARIS IN THE SPRING)	*Virgin*	61	*22 Nov 80*	2
Live recordings from Paris concert, Mar 80.				
FLOWERS OF ROMANCE	*Virgin*	11	*18 Apr 81*	5
PIL LIVE IN TOKYO	*Virgin*	28	*8 Oct 83*	6
THIS IS WHAT YOU WANT . . . THIS IS WHAT YOU GET	*Virgin*	56	*21 Jul 84*	2
ALBUM / CASSETTE	*Virgin*	14	*15 Feb 86*	6
Vinyl format is titled Album while the Cassette form is called the latter.				
HAPPY?	*Virgin*	40	*26 Sep 87*	2
9	*Virgin*	36	*10 Jun 89*	2
THE GREATEST HITS, SO FAR	*Virgin*	20	*10 Nov 90*	3
THAT WHAT IS NOT	*Virgin*	46	*7 Mar 92*	2

Gary PUCKETT and the UNION GAP — UK/Canada

SINGLES:	HITS 3			WEEKS 47
YOUNG GIRL	*CBS*	1	*20 Apr 68*	17
Above hit: UNION GAP featuring Gary PUCKETT.				
LADY WILLPOWER	*CBS*	5	*10 Aug 68*	16
WOMAN, WOMAN	*CBS*	48	*31 Aug 68*	1
Originally recorded by Jimmy Payne.				
Above hit: UNION GAP featuring Gary PUCKETT.				
YOUNG GIRL [RI]	*CBS*	6	*15 Jun 74*	13
ALBUMS:	**HITS 1**			**WEEKS 4**
UNION GAP	*CBS*	24	*29 Jun 68*	4

Tito PUENTE – See Tito PUENTO Jr. and the LATIN RHYTHM featuring Tito PUENTE, INDIA and Cali ALEMAN

Tito PUENTE Jr. and the LATIN RHYTHM featuring Tito PUENTE, INDIA and Cali ALEMAN — US

SINGLES:	HITS 1			WEEKS 3
OYE COMO VA	*Media*	36	*16 Mar 96*	2
Originally recorded by Tito Puente in 1962 on his album El Rey Brava. Also a No. 13 hit in the US for Santana in 1971.				
OYE COMO VA [RM]	*Nukleus*	56	*19 Jul 97*	1
Remixed by Joey Musaphia.				

PUFF DADDY — US

(See also Notorious B.I.G.)

SINGLES:	HITS 13			WEEKS 81
CAN'T NOBODY HOLD ME DOWN	*Puff Daddy*	19	*29 Mar 97*	4
Samples Grandmaster Flash and the Furious Five's The Message.				
Above hit: PUFF DADDY (featuring MASE).				
NO TIME	*Atlantic*	45	*26 Apr 97*	1
Samples Lynn Collins Take Me Just As I Am.				
Above hit: LIL' KIM featuring PUFF DADDY.				
I'LL BE MISSING YOU	*Puff Daddy*	1	*28 Jun 97*	21
Samples The Police's Every Breath You Take. Sleeve gives title as an EP: Tribute To The Notorious B.I.G.				
Above hit: PUFF DADDY and Faith EVANS (featuring 112).				

SOMEONE *Above hit: SWV featuring PUFF DADDY.*	*RCA*	34	*13 Sep 97*	2
BEEN AROUND THE WORLD *Samples the bass line from David Bowie's Let's Dance with lyrics from Lisa Stansfield's All Around The World.* *Above hit: PUFF DADDY and the FAMILY featuring the NOTORIOUS B.I.G. and MASE.*	*Puff Daddy*	20	*1 Nov 97*	4
BEEN AROUND THE WORLD [RE]	*Puff Daddy*	56	*3 Jan 98*	2
IT'S ALL ABOUT THE BENJAMINS *Above hit: PUFF DADDY and the FAMILY (featuring the NOTORIOUS B.I.G, LIL' KIM, the LOX, Dave GROHL, PERFECT, FUZZBUBBLE and Rob ZOMBIE).*	*Puff Daddy*	18	*7 Feb 98*	3
COME WITH ME *US import. Based on guitar riff from Led Zeppelin's Kashmir from 1975. From the film 'Godzilla'.*	*Epic*	75	*1 Aug 98*	1
COME WITH ME *Above 2: PUFF DADDY featuring Jimmy PAGE.*	*Epic*	2	*8 Aug 98*	10
ALL NIGHT LONG *Samples Unlimited Touch's I Hear Music In The Street.* *Above hit: Faith EVANS (featuring PUFF DADDY).*	*Puff Daddy*	23	*1 May 99*	3
HATE ME NOW *Above hit: NAS (featuring PUFF DADDY).*	*Columbia*	14	*29 May 99*	6
P.E. 2000 *Samples Public Enemy's Public Enemy No. 1.* *Above hit: PUFF DADDY [featuring HURRICANE G].*	*Puff Daddy*	13	*21 Aug 99*	4
BEST FRIEND *Samples Christopher Cross' Sailing.* *Above hit: PUFF DADDY (featuring Mario WINANS).*	*Puff Daddy*	24	*20 Nov 99*	4
SATISFY YOU *Import.* *Above hit: PUFF DADDY featuring R. KELLY.*	*Bad Boy*	73	*19 Feb 00*	1
SATISFY YOU [RE]	*Bad Boy*	73	*4 Mar 00*	1
SATISFY YOU *Samples I Got 5 On It by Luniz and Club Nouveau's Why You Treat Me So Bad.* *Above hit: PUFF DADDY (featuring R. KELLY).*	*Puff Daddy*	8	*11 Mar 00*	8
BAD BOY FOR LIFE *Above hit: P. DIDDY, BLACK ROB & Mark CURRY.*	*Puff Daddy*	13	*6 Oct 01*	6
ALBUMS:	**HITS 2**			**WEEKS 19**
NO WAY OUT *Above hit: PUFF DADDY and the FAMILY.*	*Puff Daddy*	8	*2 Aug 97*	13
FOREVER	*Puff Daddy*	9	*04 Sept 99*	6

PULP — UK

SINGLES:	**HITS 12**			**WEEKS 72**
LIP GLOSS	*Island*	50	*27 Nov 93*	2
DO YOU REMEMBER THE FIRST TIME?	*Island*	33	*2 Apr 94*	4
THE SISTERS [EP] *Lead track: Babies. This track was originally released in 1992.*	*Island*	19	*4 Jun 94*	4
COMMON PEOPLE	*Island*	2	*3 Jun 95*	13
MIS-SHAPES / SORTED FOR E'S & WIZZ	*Island*	2	*7 Oct 95*	8
DISCO 2000	*Island*	7	*9 Dec 95*	11
MIS-SHAPES / SORTED FOR E'S & WIZZ [RE]	*Island*	62	*30 Dec 95*	3
SOMETHING CHANGED	*Island*	10	*6 Apr 96*	5
SOMETHING CHANGED [RE-1ST]	*Island*	62	*8 Jun 96*	1
SOMETHING CHANGED [RE-2ND]	*Island*	61	*22 Jun 96*	1
DO YOU REMEMBER THE FIRST TIME? [RE]	*Island*	73	*7 Sep 96*	1
HELP THE AGED	*Island*	8	*22 Nov 97*	7
HELP THE AGED [RE]	*Island*	68	*24 Jan 98*	2
THIS IS HARDCORE	*Island*	12	*28 Mar 98*	4
A LITTLE SOUL	*Island*	22	*20 Jun 98*	2
PARTY HARD	*Island*	29	*19 Sep 98*	2
SUNRISE/THE TREES	*Island*	23	*20 Oct 01*	2
ALBUMS:	**HITS 5**			**WEEKS 135**
HIS 'N' HERS	*Island*	9	*30 Apr 94*	43
DIFFERENT CLASS	*Island*	1	*11 Nov 95*	62
COUNTDOWN 1992-1983 *Compilation of tracks from their 4 non charted albums If from 1983, Masters Of The Universe from 1986, Freaks in 1987 and Separations from 1992.*	*Nectar Masters*	10	*23 Mar 96*	6
THIS IS HARDCORE	*Island*	1	*11 Apr 98*	21
WE LOVE LIFE	*Island*	6	*3 Nov 01*	3

PULSE featuring Antoinette ROBERSON — US

(See also David Morales.)

SINGLES:	**HITS 1**			**WEEKS 3**
THE LOVER THAT YOU ARE	*ffrr*	22	*25 May 96*	3

PUNK CHIC — Sweden

SINGLES:	HITS 1			WEEKS 1
DJ SPINNIN'	*WEA*	69	*6 Oct 01*	1

PURE SUGAR vocals by Jennifer STARR — UK

SINGLES:	HITS 1			WEEKS 1
DELICIOUS	*Geffen*	70	*24 Oct 98*	1

PURESSENCE — UK

SINGLES:	HITS 3			WEEKS 5
THIS FEELING	*Island*	33	*23 May 98*	2
IT DOESN'T MATTER ANYMORE	*Island*	47	*8 Aug 98*	1
ALL I WANT	*Island*	39	*21 Nov 98*	2
ALBUMS:	**HITS 1**			**WEEKS 2**
ONLY FOREVER	*Island*	36	*29 Aug 98*	2

James and Bobby PURIFY — US

SINGLES:	HITS 2			WEEKS 16
I'M YOUR PUPPET *Originally recorded by Dan Penn.*	*Mercury*	12	*24 Apr 76*	10
MORNING GLORY *Originally recorded by Mac Gayden.*	*Mercury*	27	*7 Aug 76*	6

PURPLE HEARTS — UK

SINGLES:	HITS 2			WEEKS 5
MILLIONS LIKE US	*Fiction*	57	*22 Sep 79*	3
JIMMY	*Fiction*	60	*8 Mar 80*	2

PURPLE KINGS — UK

SINGLES:	HITS 1			WEEKS 3
THAT'S THE WAY YOU DO IT *Based around the guitar riff from Dire Strait's Money For Nothing.*	*Positiva*	26	*15 Oct 94*	3

PUSH — Belgium

SINGLES:	HITS 5			WEEKS 15
UNIVERSAL NATION	*Inferno*	36	*15 May 99*	2
UNIVERSAL NATION '99 [RI] *Though billed as a remix, the lead track is just a re-issue.*	*Inferno*	35	*9 Oct 99*	2
TILL WE MEET AGAIN	*Inferno*	46	*23 Sep 00*	1
STRANGE WORLD	*Inferno*	21	*12 May 01*	4
PLEASE SAVE ME *Above hit: SUNSCREEM vs PUSH.*	*Inferno*	36	*20 Oct 01*	2
THE LEGACY	*Inferno*	22	*3 Nov 01*	4

PUSSY 2000 — UK

SINGLES:	HITS 1			WEEKS 1
IT'S GONNA BE ALRIGHT *Originally recorded by Sterling Void as 'It's Alright'.*	*Ink*	70	*3 Nov 01*	1

PUSSYCAT — Holland

SINGLES:	HITS 2			WEEKS 30
MISSISSIPPI	*Sonet*	1	*28 Aug 76*	22
SMILE	*Sonet*	24	*25 Dec 76*	8

PWEI – See POP WILL EAT ITSELF

PYRAMIDS — Jamaica

SINGLES:	HITS 1			WEEKS 4
TRAIN TOUR TO RAINBOW CITY	*President*	35	*25 Nov 67*	4

PYTHON LEE JACKSON — Australia

SINGLES:	HITS 1			WEEKS 12
IN A BROKEN DREAM *Features lead vocals by Rod Stewart. Recorded in 1970.*	*Young Blood*	3	*30 Sep 72*	12

Q

Q — UK

SINGLES:	HITS 2			WEEKS 6
GET HERE	*Arista*	37	*5 Jun 93*	4
Above hit: Q-featuring Tracy ACKERMAN.				
(EVERYTHING I DO) I DO IT FOR YOU	*Bell*	47	*12 Mar 94*	2
Above hit: Q featuring Tony JACKSON.				

Soozy Q – See BIG TIME CHARLIE

Q-BASS — UK

(See also Various Artists (EPs) 'Subplates Volume 1 EP'.)

SINGLES:	HITS 1			WEEKS 1
HARDCORE WILL NEVER DIE	*Suburban Base*	64	*8 Feb 92*	1

Q-CLUB — Italy

SINGLES:	HITS 1			WEEKS 3
TELL IT TO MY HEART	*Manifesto*	28	*6 Jan 96*	3

Q TEE — UK

SINGLES:	HITS 2			WEEKS 7
AFRIKA	*SBK One*	42	*21 Apr 90*	5
Above hit: HISTORY featuring Q-TEE.				
GIMME THAT BODY	*Heavenly*	40	*10 Feb 96*	2

Q-TEX — UK

SINGLES:	HITS 4			WEEKS 7
THE POWER OF LOVE	*Stoatin'*	65	*9 Apr 94*	1
BELIEVE	*23rd Precinct*	41	*26 Nov 94*	2
LET THE LOVE	*23rd Precinct*	30	*15 Jun 96*	2
DO YOU WANT ME	*23rd Precinct*	48	*30 Nov 96*	1
POWER OF LOVE 97 [RM]	*23rd Precinct*	49	*28 Jun 97*	1
Remixed by Scott Brown and Stuart Crichton.				

Q-TIP — US

(See also De La Soul; Janet Jackson.)

SINGLES:	HITS 3			WEEKS 11
GET INVOLVED	*Hollywood*	36	*19 Jun 99*	2
Above hit: Raphael SAADIQ and Q-TIP.				
BREATHE AND STOP	*Arista*	12	*12 Feb 00*	7
Samples Kool And The Gang's N.T.				
VIVRANT THING	*Arista*	39	*6 May 00*	2
Samples Barry White's I Wanna Stay.				

Q-TIPS — UK

ALBUMS:	HITS 1			WEEKS 1
Q-TIPS	*Chrysalis*	50	*30 Aug 80*	1

Q UNIQUE – See C&C MUSIC FACTORY

QATTARA — UK

(See also Alex Whitcombe and Big C.)

SINGLES:	HITS 1			WEEKS 2
COME WITH ME	*Positiva*	31	*15 Mar 97*	2

QB FINEST featuring NAS and BRAVEHEARTS — US

SINGLES:	HITS 1			WEEKS 3
OOCHIE WALLY	*Columbia*	30	*21 Apr 01*	3

QFX — UK

SINGLES:	HITS 5			WEEKS 16
FREEDOM [EP]	*Epidemic*	41	*6 May 95*	3
Lead track: Freedom. Vocals by Moira Rankin.				
EVERY TIME YOU TOUCH ME	*Epidemic*	22	*3 Feb 96*	4
YOU GOT THE POWER	*Epidemic*	33	*3 Aug 96*	3
FREEDOM 2	*Epidemic*	21	*18 Jan 97*	4
This is a re-recording of the track from the Freedom EP. Vocals by Kerry McGregor.				
SAY YOU'LL BE MINE	*Quality Recordings*	34	*20 Mar 99*	2
Above hit: Q.F.X.				

ALBUMS:	HITS 1			WEEKS 1
ALIEN CHILD	*Epidemic*	62	*8 Mar 97*	1

QUAD CITY DJ'S — US

SINGLES:	HITS 1			WEEKS 1
SPACE JAM *From the film of the same name.*	*Atlantic*	57	*15 Nov 97*	1

QUADROPHONIA — Belgium

SINGLES:	HITS 3			WEEKS 15
QUADROPHONIA	*ARS*	14	*13 Apr 91*	9
THE WAVE OF THE FUTURE	*ARS*	40	*6 Jul 91*	3
FIND THE TIME (PART 1)	*ARS*	41	*21 Dec 91*	3

QUADS — UK

SINGLES:	HITS 1			WEEKS 2
THERE MUST BE THOUSANDS	*Big Bear*	66	*22 Sep 79*	2

QUAKE featuring Marcia RAE — UK

SINGLES:	HITS 1			WEEKS 1
THE DAY WILL COME	*ffrr*	53	*29 Aug 98*	1

QUANTUM JUMP — UK

SINGLES:	HITS 1			WEEKS 10
THE LONE RANGER	*Electric*	5	*2 Jun 79*	10

QUARTERFLASH — US

SINGLES:	HITS 1			WEEKS 5
HARDEN MY HEART	*Geffen*	49	*27 Feb 82*	5

QUARTZ — UK

SINGLES:	HITS 3			WEEKS 19
WE'RE COMIN' AT YA *Above hit: QUARTZ featuring STEPZ.*	*Mercury*	65	*17 Mar 90*	2
IT'S TOO LATE *Above hit: QUARTZ introducing Dina CARROLL.*	*Mercury*	8	*2 Feb 91*	14
NAKED LOVE (JUST SAY YOU WANT ME) *Above hit: QUARTZ and Dina CARROLL.*	*Mercury*	39	*15 Jun 91*	3

Jakie QUARTZ — France

SINGLES:	HITS 1			WEEKS 3
A LA VIE, A L'AMOUR	*PWL Continental*	55	*11 Mar 89*	3

QUARTZ LOCK featuring Lonnie GORDON — UK

(See also Lonnie Gordon.)

SINGLES:	HITS 1			WEEKS 2
LOVE EVICTION	*Xplode*	32	*7 Oct 95*	2

Suzi QUATRO — US

SINGLES:	HITS 16			WEEKS 122
CAN THE CAN	*RAK*	1	*19 May 73*	14
48 CRASH	*RAK*	3	*28 Jul 73*	9
DAYTONA DEMON	*RAK*	14	*27 Oct 73*	13
DEVIL GATE DRIVE	*RAK*	1	*9 Feb 74*	11
TOO BIG	*RAK*	14	*29 Jun 74*	6
THE WILD ONE	*RAK*	7	*9 Nov 74*	10
YOUR MAMMA WON'T LIKE ME	*RAK*	31	*8 Feb 75*	5
TEAR ME APART	*RAK*	27	*5 Mar 77*	6
IF YOU CAN'T GIVE ME LOVE	*RAK*	4	*18 Mar 78*	13
THE RACE IS ON	*RAK*	43	*22 Jul 78*	5
STUMBLIN' IN *Above hit: Suzi QUATRO and Chris NORMAN.*	*RAK*	41	*11 Nov 78*	8
SHE'S IN LOVE WITH YOU	*RAK*	11	*20 Oct 79*	9
MAMA'S BOY	*RAK*	34	*19 Jan 80*	5
I'VE NEVER BEEN IN LOVE	*RAK*	56	*5 Apr 80*	3
ROCK HARD	*Dreamland*	68	*25 Oct 80*	2
HEART OF STONE	*Polydor*	60	*13 Nov 82*	3

ALBUMS:	HITS 2			WEEKS 13
SUZI QUATRO	*RAK*	32	*13 Oct 73*	4
SUZI QUATRO'S GREATEST HITS	*RAK*	4	*26 Apr 80*	9

Finley QUAYE — UK

SINGLES:	HITS 6			WEEKS 23
SUNDAY SHINING	*Epic*	16	*21 Jun 97*	6
EVEN AFTER ALL	*Epic*	10	*13 Sep 97*	5
IT'S GREAT WHEN WE'RE TOGETHER	*Epic*	29	*29 Nov 97*	3
YOUR LOVE GETS SWEETER	*Epic*	16	*7 Mar 98*	5
ULTRA STIMULATION	*Epic*	51	*15 Aug 98*	1
SPIRITUALIZED	*Epic*	26	*23 Sep 00*	3
ALBUMS:	**HITS 2**			**WEEKS 58**
MAVERICK A STRIKE	*Epic*	3	*4 Oct 97*	56
VANGUARD	*Epic*	35	*14 Oct 00*	2

QUEDO BRASS – See CHAQUITO ORCHESTRA

QUEEN — UK

SINGLES:	HITS 49			WEEKS 420
SEVEN SEAS OF RHYE	*EMI*	10	*9 Mar 74*	10
KILLER QUEEN	*EMI*	2	*26 Oct 74*	12
NOW I'M HERE	*EMI*	11	*25 Jan 75*	7
BOHEMIAN RHAPSODY	*EMI*	1	*8 Nov 75*	17
Video to the song is established as the first to be used as a promotional tool to sell the single.				
YOU'RE MY BEST FRIEND	*EMI*	7	*3 Jul 76*	8
SOMEBODY TO LOVE	*EMI*	2	*27 Nov 76*	9
TIE YOUR MOTHER DOWN	*EMI*	31	*19 Mar 77*	4
QUEEN'S FIRST EP [EP]	*EMI*	17	*4 Jun 77*	10
Lead track: Good Old Fashioned Lover Boy. On certain weeks, the chart listed only the lead track.				
WE ARE THE CHAMPIONS	*EMI*	2	*22 Oct 77*	12
SPREAD YOUR WINGS	*EMI*	34	*25 Feb 78*	4
BICYCLE RACE / FAT BOTTOMED GIRLS	*EMI*	11	*28 Oct 78*	12
DON'T STOP ME NOW	*EMI*	9	*10 Feb 79*	12
LOVE OF MY LIFE	*EMI*	63	*14 Jul 79*	2
Live recording.				
CRAZY LITTLE THING CALLED LOVE	*EMI*	2	*20 Oct 79*	14
SAVE ME	*EMI*	11	*2 Feb 80*	6
PLAY THE GAME	*EMI*	14	*14 Jun 80*	8
ANOTHER ONE BITES THE DUST	*EMI*	7	*6 Sep 80*	9
FLASH	*EMI*	10	*6 Dec 80*	13
From the film 'Flash Gordon'.				
UNDER PRESSURE	*EMI*	1	*14 Nov 81*	11
Above hit: QUEEN and David BOWIE.				
BODY LANGUAGE	*EMI*	25	*1 May 82*	6
LAS PALABRAS DE AMOR	*EMI*	17	*12 Jun 82*	8
BACK CHAT	*EMI*	40	*21 Aug 82*	4
RADIO GA GA	*EMI*	2	*4 Feb 84*	9
I WANT TO BREAK FREE	*EMI*	3	*14 Apr 84*	15
IT'S A HARD LIFE	*EMI*	6	*28 Jul 84*	9
HAMMER TO FALL	*EMI*	13	*22 Sep 84*	7
THANK GOD IT'S CHRISTMAS	*EMI*	21	*8 Dec 84*	6
ONE VISION	*EMI*	7	*16 Nov 85*	10
A KIND OF MAGIC	*EMI*	3	*29 Mar 86*	11
From the film 'Highlander'.				
FRIENDS WILL BE FRIENDS	*EMI*	14	*21 Jun 86*	8
WHO WANTS TO LIVE FOREVER?	*EMI*	24	*27 Sep 86*	5
I WANT IT ALL	*Parlophone*	3	*13 May 89*	7
BREAKTHRU'	*Parlophone*	7	*1 Jul 89*	7
THE INVISIBLE MAN	*Parlophone*	12	*19 Aug 89*	6
SCANDAL	*Parlophone*	25	*21 Oct 89*	4
THE MIRACLE	*Parlophone*	21	*9 Dec 89*	5
INNUENDO	*Parlophone*	1	*26 Jan 91*	6
I'M GOING SLIGHTLY MAD	*Parlophone*	22	*16 Mar 91*	5
HEADLONG	*Parlophone*	14	*25 May 91*	4
THE SHOW MUST GO ON	*Parlophone*	16	*26 Oct 91*	5
THE SHOW MUST GO ON [RE]	*Parlophone*	27	*7 Dec 91*	5
BOHEMIAN RHAPSODY [RI] / THESE ARE THE DAYS OF OUR LIVES	*Parlophone*	1	*21 Dec 91*	14
Only time that the same recording has reached No. 1 on a separate issue.				
FIVE LIVE [EP]	*Parlophone*	1	*1 May 93*	11
Lead track: Somebody To Love, a live recording from the Freddie Mercury Tribute Concert, Apr 92. Lisa Stansfield only sang on These Are The Days Of Our Lives. Proceeds to the Mercury Phoenix Trust.				
Above hit: George MICHAEL and QUEEN with Lisa STANSFIELD.				
FIVE LIVE [EP] [RE]	*Parlophone*	74	*24 Jul 93*	1

HEAVEN FOR EVERYONE *Originally recorded in 1988 by Taylor's group the Cross for their Shove It album.*	*Parlophone*	2	*4 Nov 95*	12
A WINTER'S TALE	*Parlophone*	6	*23 Dec 95*	6
TOO MUCH LOVE WILL KILL YOU	*Parlophone*	15	*9 Mar 96*	6
LET ME LIVE	*Parlophone*	9	*29 Jun 96*	4
YOU DON'T FOOL ME - THE REMIXES *Lead track is the album version. The remixes are by Dancing Divaz, Jam and Spoon and David Richards.*	*Parlophone*	17	*30 Nov 96*	4
NO-ONE BUT YOU (ONLY THE GOOD DIE YOUNG) / TIE YOUR MOTHER DOWN [RI]	*Dreamworks*	13	*17 Jan 98*	4
ANOTHER ONE BITES THE DUST [RR] *From the film 'Small Soldiers'. Remix of original with additional rap.* *Above hit: QUEEN/Wyclef JEAN featuring PRAS and FREE.*	*Dreamwords*	5	*14 Nov 98*	6
UNDER PRESSURE [RM] *Remixed by Queen, Joshua J. Macrae and Justin Shirley-Smith.* *Above hit: QUEEN + David BOWIE.*	*Parlophone*	14	*18 Dec 99*	7
WE WILL ROCK YOU Above hit: FIVE + QUEEN	*RCA*	1	*29 Jul 00*	12
WE WILL ROCK YOU [RE]	*RCA*	72	*4 Nov 00*	1
ALBUMS:	**HITS 24**			**WEEKS 1200**
QUEEN 2	*EMI*	5	*23 Mar 74*	29
QUEEN *Originally released in 1973.*	*EMI*	24	*30 Mar 74*	18
SHEER HEART ATTACK	*EMI*	2	*23 Nov 74*	42
A NIGHT AT THE OPERA *Includes re-entries through to 1984.*	*EMI*	1	*13 Dec 75*	50
A DAY AT THE RACES	*EMI*	1	*25 Dec 76*	24
NEWS OF THE WORLD	*EMI*	4	*12 Nov 77*	20
JAZZ	*EMI*	2	*25 Nov 78*	27
LIVE KILLERS *Live recordings from their European Tour, Jan–Mar 79.*	*EMI*	3	*7 Jul 79*	27
THE GAME	*EMI*	1	*12 Jul 80*	18
FLASH GORDON [OST]	*EMI*	10	*20 Dec 80*	15
QUEEN GREATEST HITS *Includes re-entries through to 1991. From 12 Dec 87, label changed to Parlophone.*	*EMI*	1	*7 Nov 81*	331
HOT SPACE	*EMI*	4	*15 May 82*	19
THE WORKS	*EMI*	2	*10 Mar 84*	93
A KIND OF MAGIC	*EMI*	1	*14 Jun 86*	62
LIVE MAGIC	*EMI*	3	*13 Dec 86*	40
THE MIRACLE	*Parlophone*	1	*3 Jun 89*	32
QUEEN AT THE BEEB *Recordings made for BBC radio shows.*	*Band Of Joy*	67	*16 Dec 89*	1
INNUENDO	*Parlophone*	1	*16 Feb 91*	37
GREATEST HITS II *Includes re-entries through to 2000.*	*Parlophone*	1	*9 Nov 91*	106
QUEEN GREATEST HITS [RE-1ST]	*Parlophone*	6	*9 Nov 91*	76
LIVE MAGIC [RI]	*Parlophone*	51	*7 Dec 91*	3
A KIND OF MAGIC [RI]	*Parlophone*	66	*7 Dec 91*	1
LIVE AT WEMBLEY '86 *Live recordings from their show, Jul 86.*	*Parlophone*	2	*6 Jun 92*	15
QUEEN GREATEST HITS [RE-2ND] *Re-released at mid-price. Includes re-entries through to 2000.*	*Parlophone*	17	*30 Apr 94*	43
GREATEST HITS I AND II [RI] *Double re-issue of both their previous Greatest Hits albums.*	*EMI*	37	*19 Nov 94*	7
MADE IN HEAVEN *May, Taylor and Deacon spent 4 years working on the music to accompany Mercury's final vocal performances.*	*Parlophone*	1	*18 Nov 95*	28
QUEEN ROCKS *Compilation with one new track with vocals by May and Taylor.*	*Parlophone*	7	*15 Nov 97*	12
GREATEST HITS III *Includes solo recordings by Brian May and Freddie Mercury.*	*Parlophone*	5	*20 Nov 99*	19
THE PLATINUM COLLECTION - GREATEST HITS I, II & III	*Parlophone*	63	*25 Nov 00*	5

QUEEN LATIFAH — US

(See also De La Soul; Jungle Brothers.)

SINGLES:	**HITS 6**			**WEEKS 17**
MAMMA GAVE BIRTH TO THE SOUL CHILDREN *Above hit: QUEEN LATIFAH + DE LA SOUL.*	*Gee Street*	14	*24 Mar 90*	7
FIND A WAY *Above hit: COLDCUT featuring QUEEN LATIFAH.*	*Ahead Of Our Time*	52	*26 May 90*	2
FLY GIRL	*Gee Street*	67	*31 Aug 91*	1
WHAT'CHA GONNA DO? *Above hit: Shabba RANKS featuring QUEEN LATIFAH.*	*Epic*	21	*26 Jun 93*	4
U.N.I.T.Y. *Samples Message From The Inner City by the Crusaders.*	*Motown*	74	*26 Mar 94*	1
MR. BIG STUFF *Original by Jean Knight reached No. 2 in the US in 1971. From the film 'Te Associate'.* *Above hit: QUEEN LATIFAH, SHADES and FREE.*	*Motown*	31	*12 Apr 97*	2

QUEEN PEN — US

SINGLES:	HITS 3			WEEKS 10
MAN BEHIND THE MUSIC *Features vocals by Teddy Riley of Blackstreet.*	*Interscope*	38	*7 Mar 98*	2
ALL MY LOVE *Samples Luther Vandross' Never Too Much.* *Above hit: QUEEN PEN featuring Eric WILLIAMS of BLACKSTREET.*	*Interscope*	11	*9 May 98*	5
IT'S TRUE *Samples Spandau Ballet's True.*	*Interscope*	24	*5 Sep 98*	3

QUEENS OF THE STONE AGE — US

SINGLES:	HITS 1			WEEKS 2
THE LOST ART OF KEEPING A SECRET	*Interscope*	31	*26 Aug 00*	2
ALBUMS:	**HITS 1**			**WEEKS 2**
R	*Interscope*	54	*2 Sep 00*	2

QUEENSRYCHE — US

SINGLES:	HITS 7			WEEKS 21
EYES OF A STRANGER	*EMI USA*	59	*13 May 89*	1
EMPIRE	*EMI USA*	61	*10 Nov 90*	1
SILENT LUCIDITY	*EMI USA*	34	*20 Apr 91*	5
BEST I CAN	*EMI USA*	36	*6 Jul 91*	3
JET CITY WOMAN	*EMI USA*	39	*7 Sep 91*	2
SILENT LUCIDITY [RI]	*EMI USA*	18	*8 Aug 92*	4
I AM I	*EMI*	40	*28 Jan 95*	2
BRIDGE	*EMI*	40	*25 Mar 95*	3
ALBUMS:	**HITS 6**			**WEEKS 12**
THE WARNING	*EMI America*	100	*29 Sep 84*	1
RAGE FOR ORDER	*EMI America*	66	*26 Jul 86*	1
OPERATION MINDCRIME	*EMI Manhattan*	58	*4 Jun 88*	3
EMPIRE	*EMI USA*	13	*22 Sep 90*	3
PROMISED LAND	*EMI*	13	*22 Oct 94*	3
HEAR IN THE NOW FRONTIER	*EMI*	46	*29 Mar 97*	1

QUENCH — Australia

SINGLES:	HITS 1			WEEKS 1
DREAMS	*Infectious*	75	*17 Feb 96*	1

QUENTIN and ASH — UK

SINGLES:	HITS 1			WEEKS 3
TELL HIM	*East West*	25	*6 Jul 96*	3

? and the MYSTERIANS — US

SINGLES:	HITS 1			WEEKS 4
96 TEARS	*Cameo-Parkway*	37	*19 Nov 66*	4

QUESTIONS — UK

SINGLES:	HITS 3			WEEKS 8
PRICE YOU PAY	*Respond*	56	*23 Apr 83*	3
TEAR SOUP	*Respond*	66	*17 Sep 83*	1
TUESDAY SUNSHINE	*Respond*	46	*10 Mar 84*	4

QUICK — UK

SINGLES:	HITS 1			WEEKS 7
THE RHYTHM OF THE JUNGLE	*Epic*	41	*15 May 82*	7

Tommy QUICKLY and the REMO 4 — UK

SINGLES:	HITS 1			WEEKS 8
WILD SIDE OF LIFE	*Pye*	33	*24 Oct 64*	8

QUIET FIVE — UK

SINGLES:	HITS 2			WEEKS 3
WHEN THE MORNING SUN DRIES THE DEW	*Parlophone*	45	*15 May 65*	1
HOMEWARD BOUND	*Parlophone*	44	*23 Apr 66*	2

QUIET RIOT — US

SINGLES:	HITS 1			WEEKS 5
METAL HEALTH / CUM ON FEEL THE NOIZE *Cum On Feel The Noize listed from 10 Dec 83.*	*Epic*	45	*3 Dec 83*	5
ALBUMS:	**HITS 1**			**WEEKS 1**
CONDITION CRITICAL	*Epic*	71	*4 Aug 84*	1

Eimear QUINN — Ireland

SINGLES:	HITS 1			WEEKS 2
THE VOICE *Eurovision Song Contest winner in 1996.*	*Polydor*	40	*15 Jun 96*	2

Paul QUINN and Edwyn COLLINS — UK

SINGLES:	HITS 1			WEEKS 2
PALE BLUE EYES	*Swamplands*	72	*11 Aug 84*	2

Vanessa QUINONES – See DARIO G

QUINTESSENCE — UK/Australia

ALBUMS:	HITS 3			WEEKS 6
QUINTESSENCE	*Island*	22	*27 Jun 70*	4
DIVE DEEP	*Island*	43	*3 Apr 71*	1
SELF	*RCA Victor*	50	*27 May 72*	1

QUIREBOYS — UK

SINGLES:	HITS 6			WEEKS 27
7 O'CLOCK	*Parlophone*	36	*4 Nov 89*	4
HEY YOU	*Parlophone*	14	*6 Jan 90*	7
I DON'T LOVE YOU ANYMORE	*Parlophone*	24	*7 Apr 90*	6
THERE SHE GOES AGAIN/MISLED *Original release reached No. 87 in 1988.*	*Parlophone*	37	*8 Sep 90*	4
TRAMPS AND THIEVES	*Parlophone*	41	*10 Oct 92*	3
BROTHER LOUIE	*Parlophone*	31	*20 Feb 93*	3
ALBUMS:	**HITS 2**			**WEEKS 17**
A BIT OF WHAT YOU FANCY	*Parlophone*	2	*10 Feb 90*	15
BITTER SWEET AND TWISTED	*Parlophone*	31	*27 Mar 93*	2

QUIVER – See SUTHERLAND BROTHERS and QUIVER

QUIVVER — UK

SINGLES:	HITS 2			WEEKS 3
SAXY LADY	*A&M*	56	*5 Mar 94*	2
BELIEVE IN ME	*Perfecto*	56	*18 Nov 95*	1

QWENT CHORALE – See Bryn YEMM

QWILO and FELIX DA HOUSECAT featuring Lynn CROUCH — US

SINGLES:	HITS 1			WEEKS 1
DIRTY MOTHA	*Manifesto*	66	*6 Sep 97*	1

QUO VADIS — UK

SINGLES:	HITS 1			WEEKS 1
SONIC BOOM (LIFE'S TOO SHORT)	*Serious*	49	*16 Dec 00*	1

R

R.A.F. — Italy

(See also Mauro Picotto.)

SINGLES:	HITS 3			WEEKS 6
WE'VE GOT TO LIVE TOGETHER *Samples Enya's 'Orinoco Flow'.*	*PWL Continental*	34	*14 Mar 92*	3
TAKE ME HIGHER	*Media*	71	*5 Mar 94*	1
TAKE ME HIGHER [RM] *Remixed by Primax.*	*Media*	59	*23 Mar 96*	1
ANGEL'S SYMPHONY *Above hit: R.A.F. by PICOTTO and Gigi D'AGOSTINO.*	*Media*	73	*27 Jul 96*	1

R.A.W. – See Erick "More" MORILLO presents R.A.W.

R.E.M. — US

SINGLES:	HITS 30			WEEKS 164
THE ONE I LOVE	*I.R.S.*	51	*28 Nov 87*	8
FINEST WORKSONG	*I.R.S.*	50	*30 Apr 88*	2
STAND	*Warner Brothers*	51	*4 Feb 89*	3
ORANGE CRUSH	*Warner Brothers*	28	*3 Jun 89*	5
STAND [RI]	*Warner Brothers*	48	*12 Aug 89*	2
LOSING MY RELIGION	*Warner Brothers*	19	*9 Mar 91*	9
SHINY HAPPY PEOPLE *Features backing vocals by Kate Pierson of the B-52's.*	*Warner Brothers*	6	*18 May 91*	11

NEAR WILD HEAVEN	*Warner Brothers*	27	*17 Aug 91*	4
THE ONE I LOVE [RI]	*I.R.S.*	16	*21 Sep 91*	6
RADIO SONG	*Warner Brothers*	28	*16 Nov 91*	3
IT'S THE END OF THE WORLD AS WE KNOW IT (AND I FEEL FINE)	*I.R.S.*	39	*14 Dec 91*	4
Original release reached No. 87 in 1987.				
DRIVE	*Warner Brothers*	11	*3 Oct 92*	5
MAN ON THE MOON	*Warner Brothers*	18	*28 Nov 92*	8
Tribute to comedian Andy Kaufman.				
THE SIDEWINDER SLEEPS TONITE	*Warner Brothers*	17	*20 Feb 93*	6
EVERYBODY HURTS	*Warner Brothers*	7	*17 Apr 93*	12
NIGHTSWIMMING	*Warner Brothers*	27	*24 Jul 93*	5
FIND THE RIVER	*Warner Brothers*	54	*11 Dec 93*	1
WHAT'S THE FREQUENCY, KENNETH?	*Warner Brothers*	9	*17 Sep 94*	7
BANG AND BLAME	*Warner Brothers*	15	*12 Nov 94*	4
CRUSH WITH EYELINER	*Warner Brothers*	23	*4 Feb 95*	3
STRANGE CURRENCIES	*Warner Brothers*	9	*15 Apr 95*	4
TONGUE	*Warner Brothers*	13	*29 Jul 95*	5
E - BOW THE LETTER	*Warner Brothers*	4	*31 Aug 96*	5
Backing vocals by Patti Smith.				
BITTERSWEET ME	*Warner Brothers*	19	*2 Nov 96*	2
ELECTROLITE	*Warner Brothers*	29	*14 Dec 96*	2
DAYSLEEPER	*Warner Brothers*	6	*24 Oct 98*	6
LOTUS	*Warner Brothers*	26	*19 Dec 98*	5
AT MY MOST BEAUTIFUL	*Warner Brothers*	10	*20 Mar 99*	4
THE GREAT BEYOND	*Warner Brothers*	3	*5 Feb 00*	10
From the film 'Man On The Moon'.				
IMITATION OF LIFE	*Warner Brothers*	6	*12 May 01*	9
ALL THE WAY TO RENO (YOU'RE GONNA BE A STAR)	*Warner Brothers*	24	*4 Aug 01*	3
I'LL TAKE THE RAIN	*Warner Brothers*	44	*1 Dec 01*	1

ALBUMS:	**HITS 14**			**WEEKS 552**
RECKONING	*I.R.S.*	91	*28 Apr 84*	2
FABLES OF THE RECONSTRUCTION	*I.R.S.*	35	*29 Jun 85*	3
LIFES RICH PAGEANT	*I.R.S.*	43	*6 Sep 86*	4
DEAD LETTER OFFICE	*I.R.S.*	60	*16 May 87*	2
DOCUMENT	*I.R.S.*	28	*26 Sept 87*	3
EPONYMOUS	*I.R.S.*	69	*29 Oct 88*	3
GREEN	*Warner Brothers*	27	*19 Nov 88*	20
OUT OF TIME	*Warner Brothers*	1	*23 Mar 91*	179
Includes re-entries through to 2000.				
THE BEST OF R.E.M.	*I.R.S.*	7	*12 Oct 91*	28
Includes re-entries through to 1995.				
AUTOMATIC FOR THE PEOPLE	*Warner Brothers*	1	*10 Oct 92*	179
Includes re-entries through to 2001.				
MONSTER	*Warner Brothers*	1	*8 Oct 94*	56
DOCUMENT [RE]	*I.R.S.*	49	*4 Mar 95*	2
Re-released at mid-price.				
FABLES OF THE RECONSTRUCTION [RE]	*I.R.S.*	58	*11 Mar 95*	1
Re-released at mid-price.				
NEW ADVENTURES IN HI-FI	*Warner Brothers*	1	*21 Sep 96*	20
GREEN [RE]	*Warner Brothers*	58	*31 Jun 98*	2
Re-released at mid-price.				
UP	*Warner Brothers*	2	*7 Nov 98*	29
REVEAL	*Warner Brothers*	1	*26 May 01*	15
OUT OF TIME [RE]	*Warner Brothers*	51	*26 May 01*	4

R.H.C. — Belgium

SINGLES:	**HITS 1**			**WEEKS 1**
FEVER CALLED LOVE	*R&S*	65	*11 Jan 92*	1

R.I.P. PRODUCTIONS — UK

(See also Double 99.)

SINGLES:	**HITS 2**			**WEEKS 2**
THE CHANT (WE R) / R.I.P. PRODUCTIONS	*Satellite*	58	*29 Nov 97*	1
The Chant (We R) samples Lennie De-Ice's We Are I E.				
ALL OF THE GIRLS (ALL AI-DI GIRL DEM)	*Pepper*	51	*12 Sep 98*	1
Track recorded specifically for the Notting Hill Carnival.				
Above hit: CARNIVAL featuring R.I.P. vs. RED RAT.				

R.L. – See 2PAC

Eddie RABBITT — US

SINGLES:	**HITS 2**			**WEEKS 14**
EVERY WHICH WAY BUT LOOSE	*Elektra*	41	*27 Jan 79*	9
From the film of the same name.				
I LOVE A RAINY NIGHT	*Elektra*	53	*28 Feb 81*	5

Harry RABINOVITZ – See ROYAL PHILHARMONIC ORCHESTRA

Steve RACE and his Group — UK

SINGLES:	HITS 1			WEEKS 9
THE PIED PIPER (THE BEEJE)	*Parlophone*	29	*2 Mar 63*	9

RACEY — UK

SINGLES:	HITS 4			WEEKS 44
LAY YOUR LOVE ON ME	*RAK*	3	*25 Nov 78*	14
SOME GIRLS	*RAK*	2	*31 Mar 79*	11
BOY OH BOY	*RAK*	22	*18 Aug 79*	9
RUNAROUND SUE	*RAK*	13	*20 Dec 80*	10

RACING CARS — UK

SINGLES:	HITS 1			WEEKS 7
THEY SHOOT HORSES DON'T THEY?	*Chrysalis*	14	*12 Feb 77*	7
ALBUMS:	**HITS 1**			**WEEKS 6**
DOWNTOWN TONIGHT	*Chrysalis*	39	*19 Feb 77*	6

Jimmy RADCLIFFE — US

SINGLES:	HITS 1			WEEKS 2
LONG AFTER TONIGHT IS OVER	*Stateside*	40	*6 Feb 65*	2

RADHA KRISHNA TEMPLE (LONDON) — UK

SINGLES:	HITS 2			WEEKS 17
HARE KRISHNA MANTRA	*Apple*	12	*13 Sep 69*	9
GOVINDA	*Apple*	23	*28 Mar 70*	8
Above hit: RADHA KRISHNA TEMPLE.				

RADICAL ROB — UK

SINGLES:	HITS 1			WEEKS 1
MONKEY WAH	*R&S*	67	*11 Jan 92*	1

RADIO HEART featuring Gary NUMAN — UK

(See also Gary Numan.)

SINGLES:	HITS 2			WEEKS 8
RADIO HEART	*GFM*	35	*28 Mar 87*	6
LONDON TIMES	*GFM*	48	*13 Jun 87*	2

RADIO 1 POSSEE – See Liz KERSHAW and Bruno BROOKES

RADIO STARS — UK

SINGLES:	HITS 1			WEEKS 3
NERVOUS WRECK	*Chiswick*	39	*4 Feb 78*	3

RADIOHEAD — UK

(See also Various Artists (EPs) 'The Help EP'.)

SINGLES:	HITS 13			WEEKS 52
ANYONE CAN PLAY GUITAR	*Parlophone*	32	*13 Feb 93*	2
POP IS DEAD	*Parlophone*	42	*22 May 93*	2
CREEP	*Parlophone*	7	*18 Sep 93*	6
Original release reached No. 78 in 1992.				
MY IRON LUNG [EP]	*Parlophone*	24	*8 Oct 94*	2
Lead track: My Iron Lung.				
HIGH AND DRY / PLANET TELEX	*Parlophone*	17	*11 Mar 95*	4
FAKE PLASTIC TREES	*Parlophone*	20	*27 May 95*	4
JUST	*Parlophone*	19	*2 Sep 95*	3
STREET SPIRIT (FADE OUT)	*Parlophone*	5	*3 Feb 96*	4
PARANOID ANDROID	*Parlophone*	3	*7 Jun 97*	5
KARMA POLICE	*Parlophone*	8	*6 Sep 97*	4
NO SURPRISES	*Parlophone*	4	*24 Jan 98*	6
NO SURPRISES [RE]	*Parlophone*	74	*4 Apr 98*	1
PYRAMID SONG	*Parlophone*	5	*2 Jun 01*	5
KNIVES OUT	*Parlophone*	13	*18 Aug 01*	4
ALBUMS:	**HITS 6**			**WEEKS 346**
PABLO HONEY	*Parlophone*	25	*6 Mar 93*	65
THE BENDS	*Parlophone*	6	*25 Mar 95*	35
THE BENDS [RE]	*Parlophone*	4	*30 Dec 95*	125
OK COMPUTER	*Parlophone*	1	*28 Jun 97*	75
PABLO HONEY [RE]	*Parlophone*	22	*31 Jan 98*	17
KID A	*Parlophone*	1	*14 Oct 00*	15
AMSESIAC	*Parlophone*	1	*16 Jun 01*	12
I MIGHT BE WRONG	*Parlophone*	23	*24 Nov 01*	2
Mini live album.				

RADISH — US

SINGLES:	HITS 2			WEEKS 3
LITTLE PINK STARS	*Mercury*	32	*30 Aug 97*	2
SIMPLE SINCERITY	*Mercury*	50	*15 Nov 97*	1

Fonda RAE — US

SINGLES:	HITS 1			WEEKS 4
TUCH ME	*Streetwave*	49	*6 Oct 84*	4

Jesse RAE — UK

SINGLES:	HITS 1			WEEKS 2
OVER THE SEA	*Scotland Video*	65	*11 May 85*	2

Marcia RAE – See QUAKE featuring Marcia RAE

RAE and CHRISTIAN — UK

SINGLES:	HITS 1			WEEKS 1
ALL I ASK	*Grand Central*	67	*6 Mar 99*	1
Samples Brian and Brenda Russell's World Called Love.				
Above hit: RAE & CHRISTIAN featuring VEBA.				
ALBUMS:	**HITS 1**			**WEEKS 1**
SLEEPWALKING	*!K7*	57	*10 Mar 01*	1

RAELETS – See Ray CHARLES

Gerry RAFFERTY — UK

SINGLES:	HITS 5			WEEKS 47
BAKER STREET	*United Artists*	3	*18 Feb 78*	15
Sax solo by Raphael Ravenscroft.				
NIGHT OWL	*United Artists*	5	*26 May 79*	13
GET IT RIGHT NEXT TIME	*United Artists*	30	*18 Aug 79*	9
BRING IT ALL HOME	*United Artists*	54	*22 Mar 80*	4
ROYAL MILE	*United Artists*	67	*21 Jun 80*	2
BAKER STREET [RM]	*EMI*	53	*10 Mar 90*	4
ALBUMS:	**HITS 7**			**WEEKS 99**
CITY TO CITY	*United Artists*	6	*25 Feb 78*	37
NIGHT OWL	*United Artists*	9	*2 Jun 79*	24
SNAKES AND LADDERS	*United Artists*	15	*26 Apr 80*	9
SLEEPWALKING	*Liberty*	39	*25 Sep 82*	4
NORTH AND SOUTH	*London*	43	*21 May 88*	4
ON A WING AND A PRAYER	*A&M*	73	*13 Feb 93*	1
ONE MORE DREAM – THE VERY BEST OF GERRY RAFFERTY	*PolyGram TV*	17	*28 Oct 95*	20

RAGE — UK

SINGLES:	HITS 3			WEEKS 15
RUN TO YOU	*Pulse 8*	3	*31 Oct 92*	11
WHY DON'T YOU	*Pulse 8*	44	*27 Feb 93*	2
HOUSE OF THE RISING SUN	*Pulse 8*	41	*15 May 93*	2

RAGE AGAINST THE MACHINE — US

SINGLES:	HITS 7			WEEKS 19
KILLING IN THE NAME	*Epic*	25	*27 Feb 93*	4
Anti Ku Klux Klan song.				
BULLET IN THE HEAD	*Epic*	16	*8 May 93*	4
BOMBTRACK	*Epic*	37	*4 Sep 93*	2
BULLS ON PARADE	*Epic*	8	*13 Apr 96*	3
PEOPLE OF THE SUN	*Epic*	26	*7 Sep 96*	2
GUERRILLA RADIO	*Epic*	32	*6 Nov 99*	2
SLEEP NOW IN THE FIRE	*Epic*	43	*15 Apr 00*	2
ALBUMS:	**HITS 4**			**WEEKS 52**
RAGE AGAINST THE MACHINE	*Epic*	17	*13 Feb 93*	42
EVIL EMPIRE	*Epic*	4	*27 Apr 96*	7
THE BATTLE OF LOS ANGELES	*Epic*	23	*13 Nov 99*	2
RENEGADES	*Epic*	71	*9 Dec 00*	1
Covers album.				

RAGGA TWINS — UK

SINGLES:	HITS 6			WEEKS 12
LAMBORGHINI	*Shut Up And Dance*	55	*28 Jul 90*	2
Above hit: SHUT UP AND DANCE featuring the RAGGA TWINS.				
ILLEGAL GUNSHOT / SPLIFFHEAD	*Shut Up And Dance*	51	*10 Nov 90*	2
WIPE THE NEEDLE / JUGGLING	*Shut Up And Dance*	71	*6 Apr 91*	2
HOOLIGAN 69	*Shut Up And Dance*	56	*6 Jul 91*	2
MIXED TRUTH / BRING UP THE MIC SOME MORE	*Shut Up And Dance*	65	*7 Mar 92*	2

SHINE EYE *Above hit: RAGGA TWINS featuring Junior REID.*	*Shut Up And Dance*	63	*11 Jul 92*	2
ALBUMS:	**HITS 1**			**WEEKS 5**
REGGAE OWES ME MONEY	*Shut Up And Dance*	26	*1 Jun 91*	5

RAGING SPEEDHORN — UK

SINGLES:	**HITS 1**			**WEEKS 1**
THE GUSH	*ZTT*	47	*16 Jun 01*	1

RAGTIMERS — UK

SINGLES:	**HITS 1**			**WEEKS 8**
THE STING *Based on The Entertainer theme from the film 'The Sting'.*	*Pye*	46	*16 Mar 74*	1
THE STING [RE]	*Pye*	31	*30 Mar 74*	7

RAH BAND — UK

SINGLES:	**HITS 7**			**WEEKS 50**
THE CRUNCH	*Good Earth*	6	*9 Jul 77*	12
FALCON	*DJM*	35	*1 Nov 80*	7
SLIDE	*DJM*	50	*7 Feb 81*	7
PERFUMED GARDEN	*KR*	45	*1 May 82*	7
MESSAGES FROM THE STARS	*TMT Productions*	42	*9 Jul 83*	5
ARE YOU SATISFIED? (FUNKY NOVA)	*RCA*	70	*19 Jan 85*	2
CLOUDS ACROSS THE MOON	*RCA*	6	*30 Mar 85*	10
ALBUMS:	**HITS 1**			**WEEKS 6**
MYSTERY	*RCA*	60	*6 Apr 85*	6

RAHSAAN PATTERSON - See Rahsaan PATTERSON; US3

RAILWAY CHILDREN — UK

SINGLES:	**HITS 4**			**WEEKS 13**
EVERY BEAT OF THE HEART	*Virgin*	68	*24 Mar 90*	2
MUSIC STOP	*Virgin*	66	*2 Jun 90*	2
SO RIGHT	*Virgin*	68	*20 Oct 90*	1
EVERY BEAT OF THE HEART [RE]	*Virgin*	24	*2 Feb 91*	6
SOMETHING SO GOOD	*Virgin*	57	*20 Apr 91*	2
ALBUMS:	**HITS 2**			**WEEKS 3**
RECURRENCE	*Virgin*	96	*21 May 88*	1
NATIVE PLACE	*Virgin*	59	*16 Mar 91*	2

RAIN - See Stephanie DE SYKES

RAIN PARADE — US

ALBUMS:	**HITS 1**			**WEEKS 1**
BEYOND THE SUNSET	*Island*	78	*29 Jun 85*	1

RAIN TREE CROW — UK

(See also Japan.)

SINGLES:	**HITS 1**			**WEEKS 1**
BLACKWATER	*Virgin*	62	*30 Mar 91*	1
ALBUMS:	**HITS 1**			**WEEKS 3**
RAIN TREE CROW	*Virgin*	24	*20 Apr 91*	3

RAINBOW — UK

SINGLES:	**HITS 10**			**WEEKS 62**
KILL THE KING *Live recording.*	*Polydor*	44	*17 Sep 77*	3
LONG LIVE ROCK 'N' ROLL	*Polydor*	33	*8 Apr 78*	3
L.A. CONNECTION	*Polydor*	40	*30 Sep 78*	4
SINCE YOU BEEN GONE *Originally recorded by Russ Ballard.*	*Polydor*	6	*15 Sep 79*	10
ALL NIGHT LONG	*Polydor*	5	*16 Feb 80*	11
I SURRENDER *Originally recorded by Russ Ballard.*	*Polydor*	3	*31 Jan 81*	10
CAN'T HAPPEN HERE	*Polydor*	20	*20 Jun 81*	8
KILL THE KING [RE]	*Polydor*	41	*11 Jul 81*	4
STONE COLD	*Polydor*	34	*3 Apr 82*	4
STREET OF DREAMS	*Polydor*	52	*27 Aug 83*	3
CAN'T LET YOU GO	*Polydor*	43	*5 Nov 83*	2
ALBUMS:	**HITS 10**			**WEEKS 163**
RITCHIE BLACKMORE'S RAINBOW	*Oyster*	11	*13 Sep 75*	6
RAINBOW RISING *Above 2: Ritchie BLACKMORE'S RAINBOW.*	*Polydor*	11	*5 Jun 76*	33

ON STAGE	*Polydor*	7	*30 Jul 77*	10
Live recordings from their 1976 tour.				
LONG LIVE ROCK 'N' ROLL	*Polydor*	7	*6 May 78*	12
DOWN TO EARTH	*Polydor*	6	*18 Aug 79*	37
DIFFICULT TO CURE	*Polydor*	3	*21 Feb 81*	22
RITCHIE BLACKMORE'S RAINBOW [RI]	*Polydor*	91	*8 Aug 81*	2
Above hit: Ritchie BLACKMORE'S RAINBOW.				
THE BEST OF RAINBOW	*Polydor*	14	*21 Nov 81*	17
STRAIGHT BETWEEN THE EYES	*Polydor*	5	*24 Apr 82*	14
BENT OUT OF SHAPE	*Polydor*	11	*17 Sep 83*	6
FINYL VINYL	*Polydor*	31	*8 Mar 86*	4
Compilation including live recordings and tracks only previously available as B-sides.				

RAINBOW COTTAGE — UK

SINGLES:	HITS 1			WEEKS 4
SEAGULL	*Penny Farthing*	33	*6 Mar 76*	4

RAINDANCE — UK

(See also Blowing Free; Hypnosis; In Tune; School Of Excellence.)

ALBUMS:	HITS 1			WEEKS 7
RAINDANCE	*PolyGram TV*	15	*27 Apr 96*	7

RAINMAKERS — US

SINGLES:	HITS 1			WEEKS 11
LET MY PEOPLE GO-GO	*Mercury*	18	*7 Mar 87*	11

Marvin RAINWATER — US

SINGLES:	HITS 2			WEEKS 22
WHOLE LOTTA WOMAN	*MGM*	1	*8 Mar 58*	15
I DIG YOU BABY	*MGM*	19	*7 Jun 58*	7

RAISSA — UK

SINGLES:	HITS 1			WEEKS 1
HOW LONG DO I GET	*Polydor*	47	*12 Feb 00*	1

Bonnie RAITT — US

SINGLES:	HITS 4			WEEKS 9
I CAN'T MAKE YOU LOVE ME	*Capitol*	50	*14 Dec 91*	4
LOVE SNEAKIN' UP ON YOU	*Capitol*	69	*9 Apr 94*	1
YOU	*Capitol*	31	*18 Jun 94*	2
ROCK STEADY	*Capitol*	50	*11 Nov 95*	2
Above hit: Bonnie RAITT and Bryan ADAMS.				
ALBUMS:	**HITS 5**			**WEEKS 15**
NICK OF TIME	*Capitol*	51	*28 Apr 90*	5
LUCK OF THE DRAW	*Capitol*	38	*6 Jul 91*	3
LONGING IN THEIR HEARTS	*Capitol*	26	*16 Apr 94*	5
ROAD TESTED	*Capitol*	69	*25 Nov 95*	1
Live recordings from her 1995 world tour.				
FUNDAMENTAL	*Capitol*	52	*18 Apr 98*	1

RAJA NEE — US

SINGLES:	HITS 1			WEEKS 2
TURN IT UP	*Perspective*	42	*4 Mar 95*	2
From the film 'Low Down Dirty Shame'.				

Dionne RAKEEM — UK

SINGLES:	HITS 1			WEEKS 2
SWEETER THAN WINE	*Virgin*	46	*4 Aug 01*	2

RAKIM — US

(See also Eric B. and Rakim.)

SINGLES:	HITS 5			WEEKS 10
CONTRIBUTION	*Fourth & Broadway*	33	*6 Oct 90*	4
Above hit: Mica PARIS featuring RAKIM.				
GUESS WHO'S BACK	*Universal*	32	*27 Dec 97*	3
STAY A WHILE	*Universal*	53	*22 Aug 98*	1
Samples Loose End's Stay A Little While Child.				
BUFFALO GALS STAMPEDE	*Virgin*	65	*3 Oct 98*	1
Roger Sanchez remixed track 1 (as per CD order). Rakim appeared on track 2: Buffalo Gals (Back To Skool).				
Above hit: Malcolm McLAREN and the WORLD FAMOUS SUPREME TEAM versus RAKIM and Roger SANCHEZ.				

METAFORCE *Homage to the French poet Charles Baudelaire. Includes narration by John Hurt.* *Above hit: ART OF NOISE your forecaster: RAKIM.*	*ZTT*	53	*26 Jun 99*	1
ALBUMS:	**HITS 1**			**WEEKS 1**
18TH LETTER	*Universal*	72	*22 Nov 97*	1

Big Sound of Don RALKE – See Ed BYRNES; Connie STEVENS

Tony RALLO and the MIDNITE BAND — US/France

SINGLES:	HITS 1			WEEKS 8
HOLDIN' ON	*Calibre*	34	*23 Feb 80*	8

Sheryl Lee RALPH — US

SINGLES:	HITS 1			WEEKS 2
IN THE EVENING	*Arista*	64	*26 Jan 85*	2

RAM JAM — US

SINGLES:	HITS 1			WEEKS 20
BLACK BETTY *Originally recorded by Ledbelly.*	*Epic*	7	*10 Sep 77*	12
BLACK BETTY (ROUGH 'N READY REMIX) [RM] *Remixed by Ben Liebrand.*	*Epic*	13	*17 Feb 90*	8

RAM JAM BAND – See Geno WASHINGTON and the RAM JAM BAND

RAMBLERS – See Perry COMO

RAMBLERS (from the ABBEY HEY JUNIOR SCHOOL) — UK

SINGLES:	HITS 1			WEEKS 15
THE SPARROW	*Decca*	11	*13 Oct 79*	15

Karen RAMIREZ — UK

SINGLES:	HITS 3			WEEKS 15
TROUBLED GIRL	*Manifesto*	50	*28 Mar 98*	1
LOOKING FOR LOVE	*Manifesto*	8	*27 Jun 98*	11
IF WE TRY	*Manifesto*	23	*21 Nov 98*	3
ALBUMS:	**HITS 1**			**WEEKS 2**
DISTANT DREAMS	*Manifesto*	45	*1 Aug 98*	2

RAMONES — US

SINGLES:	HITS 8			WEEKS 32
SHEENA IS A PUNK ROCKER	*Sire*	22	*21 May 77*	7
SWALLOW MY PRIDE	*Sire*	36	*6 Aug 77*	3
DON'T COME CLOSE	*Sire*	39	*30 Sep 78*	5
ROCK 'N' ROLL HIGH SCHOOL *From the film of the same name.*	*Sire*	67	*8 Sep 79*	2
BABY, I LOVE YOU	*Sire*	8	*26 Jan 80*	9
DO YOU REMEMBER ROCK 'N' ROLL RADIO? *Sleeve credit: Rock N' Roll Radio.*	*Sire*	54	*19 Apr 80*	3
SOMETHING TO BELIEVE IN / SOMEBODY PUT SOMETHING IN MY DRINK	*Beggars Banquet*	69	*10 May 86*	1
POISON HEART	*Chrysalis*	69	*19 Dec 92*	2
ALBUMS:	**HITS 11**			**WEEKS 30**
LEAVE HOME	*Philips*	45	*23 Apr 77*	1
ROCKET TO RUSSIA	*Sire*	60	*24 Dec 77*	2
ROAD TO RUIN	*Sire*	32	*7 Oct 78*	2
IT'S ALIVE *Live recordings from London's Rainbow Theatre.*	*Sire*	27	*16 Jun 79*	8
END OF THE CENTURY	*Sire*	14	*19 Jan 80*	8
TOO TOUGH TO DIE	*Beggars Banquet*	63	*26 Jan 85*	3
ANIMAL BOY	*Beggars Banquet*	38	*31 May 86*	2
HALFWAY TO SANITY	*Beggars Banquet*	78	*10 Oct 87*	1
BRAIN DRAIN	*Chrysalis*	75	*19 Aug 89*	1
!ADIOS AMIGOS!	*Chrysalis*	62	*8 Jul 95*	1
HEY HO LET'S GO! - ANTHOLOGY	*Rhino*	74	*9 Jun 01*	1

RAMP — UK

SINGLES:	HITS 1			WEEKS 1
ROCK THE DISCOTEK '96	*Loaded*	49	*8 Jun 96*	1

RAMPAGE — UK

SINGLES:	HITS 1			WEEKS 1
THE MONKEES *Jungle version of 'The Monkees' TV theme.*	*Almo*	51	*25 Nov 95*	1

RAMPAGE featuring Billy LAWRENCE — US

SINGLES:	HITS 1			WEEKS 1
TAKE IT TO THE STREETS	*Elektra*	58	*18 Oct 97*	1

RAMRODS — US

SINGLES:	HITS 1			WEEKS 12
RIDERS IN THE SKY *Originally recorded by Stan Jones.*	*London*	8	*25 Feb 61*	12

RAMSEY and FEN featuring Lynsey MOORE — UK

SINGLES:	HITS 1			WEEKS 1
LOVE BUG *Original release reached No. 124 on 14 Feb 98.*	*Nebula*	75	*10 Jun 00*	1

RANCID — US

SINGLES:	HITS 1			WEEKS 1
TIME BOMB	*Out Of Step*	56	*7 Oct 95*	1
ALBUMS:	**HITS 3**			**WEEKS 4**
. . . AND OUT COME THE WOLVES	*Epitaph*	55	*2 Sep 95*	1
LIFE WON'T WAIT	*Epitaph*	32	*4 Jul 98*	2
RANCID	*Hellcat*	68	*5 Aug 00*	1

RANGE – See Bruce HORNSBY and the RANGE

RANI – See DELERIUM

RANK 1 — Holland

SINGLES:	HITS 1			WEEKS 5
AIRWAVE	*Manifesto*	10	*15 Apr 00*	5

RANKING ANN – See SCRITTI POLITTI

RANKING ROGER – See Pato BANTON

Cutty RANKS – See BLESSING

Shabba RANKS — Jamaica

SINGLES:	HITS 10			WEEKS 67
SHE'S A WOMAN *Above hit: SCRITTI POLITTI (featuring Shabba RANKS).*	*Virgin*	20	*16 Mar 91*	7
TRAILOR LOAD A GIRLS	*Epic*	63	*18 May 91*	2
HOUSECALL *Above hit: Shabba RANKS featuring Maxi PRIEST.*	*Epic*	31	*24 Aug 91*	7
MR. LOVERMAN *Features co-vocalist Chevelle Franklin.*	*Epic*	23	*8 Aug 92*	7
SLOW AND SEXY *Above hit: Shabba RANKS (featuring Johnny GILL).*	*Epic*	17	*28 Nov 92*	7
I WAS A KING *Above hit: Eddie MURPHY featuring Shabba RANKS.*	*Motown*	64	*6 Mar 93*	1
MR. LOVERMAN [RI] *From the film 'Deep Cover'.*	*Epic*	3	*13 Mar 93*	11
HOUSECALL [RI] *Above hit: Shabba RANKS featuring Maxi PRIEST.*	*Epic*	8	*8 May 93*	8
WHAT'CHA GONNA DO? *Above hit: Shabba RANKS featuring QUEEN LATIFAH.*	*Epic*	21	*26 Jun 93*	4
FAMILY AFFAIR *From the film 'Addams Family Values'.* *Above hit: Shabba RANKS featuring PATRA and TERRI and MONICA.*	*Polydor*	18	*25 Dec 93*	8
LET'S GET IT ON	*Epic*	22	*29 Apr 95*	3
SHINE EYE GAL *Above hit: Shabba RANKS (featuring Mykal ROSE).*	*Epic*	46	*5 Aug 95*	2
ALBUMS:	**HITS 3**			**WEEKS 10**
AS RAW AS EVER	*Epic*	51	*22 Jun 91*	2
ROUGH AND READY VOLUME 1	*Epic*	71	*22 Aug 92*	2
X-TRA NAKED	*Epic*	38	*24 Apr 93*	6

RAPINATION — Italy

SINGLES:	HITS 2			WEEKS 12
LOVE ME THE RIGHT WAY *Above hit: RAPINATION and Kym MAZELLE.*	*Logic*	22	*26 Dec 92*	10
HERE'S MY A *Above hit: RAPINATION featuring Carol KENYON.*	*Logic*	69	*10 Jul 93*	1
LOVE ME THE RIGHT WAY '96 [RM] *Remixed by the Rapino Brothers.* *Above hit: RAPINATION and Kym MAZELLE.*	*Logic*	55	*28 Sep 96*	1

RAPPIN' 4-TAY — US

SINGLES:	HITS 2			WEEKS 5
I'LL BE AROUND	*Cooltempo*	30	*24 Jun 95*	4
The (Detroit) Spinners vocals are sampled from their recording of the song.				
Above hit: RAPPIN' 4-TAY featuring the SPINNERS.				
PLAYAZ CLUB	*Cooltempo*	63	*30 Sep 95*	1

RAPSODY – See Warren G; SISSEL

RARE — UK

SINGLES:	HITS 1			WEEKS 1
SOMETHING WILD	*Equator*	57	*17 Feb 96*	1

RARE BIRD — UK

SINGLES:	HITS 1			WEEKS 8
SYMPATHY	*Charisma*	27	*14 Feb 70*	8

O. RASBURY – See Rahni HARRIS and F.L.O. vocals by T. HARRINGTON and ' O.' RASBURY

Roland RAT SUPERSTAR — UK

SINGLES:	HITS 4			WEEKS 26
RAT RAPPING (BRILLIANT ISN'T IT)	*Rodent*	14	*19 Nov 83*	12
LOVE ME TENDER	*Rodent*	32	*28 Apr 84*	7
SUMMER HOLIDAY	*Rodent*	50	*4 Aug 84*	6
Above hit: Roland RAT SUPERSTAR presents KEVIN THE GERBIL.				
NO. 1 RAT FAN	*Rodent*	72	*2 Mar 85*	1
ALBUMS:	**HITS 1**			**WEEKS 3**
THE CASSETTE OF THE ALBUM	*Rodent*	67	*15 Dec 84*	3

RATPACK — UK

SINGLES:	HITS 1			WEEKS 3
SEARCHIN' FOR MY RIZLA	*Big Giant*	58	*6 Jun 92*	3

RATT — US

ALBUMS:	HITS 4			WEEKS 5
INVASION OF YOUR PRIVACY	*Atlantic*	50	*13 Jul 85*	2
DANCING UNDERCOVER	*Atlantic*	51	*25 Oct 86*	1
REACH FOR THE SKY	*Atlantic*	82	*12 Nov 88*	1
DETONATOR	*Atlantic*	55	*8 Sep 90*	1

Simon RATTLE – See Nigel KENNEDY

RATTLES — Germany

SINGLES:	HITS 1			WEEKS 15
THE WITCH	*Decca*	8	*3 Oct 70*	15

Mark RATTRAY — UK

(See also Marti Webb and Mark Rattray.)

ALBUMS:	HITS 1			WEEKS 7
MARK RATTRAY PERFORMS THE SONGS OF THE MUSICALS	*Telstar*	46	*8 Dec 90*	7

RATTY — Germany

SINGLES:	HITS 1			WEEKS 1
SUNRISE (HERE I AM)	*Neo*	51	*24 Mar 01*	1

Nick RAUCHEN conducting the BALL'S POND ROAD near "The One-in-Harmony" – See GOONS

RAVEN — UK

ALBUMS:	HITS 1			WEEKS 3
ROCK UNTIL YOU DROP	*Neat*	63	*17 Oct 81*	3

Thurl RAVENSCROFT – See Rosemary CLOONEY

RAVESIGNAL III — UK

(See also C.J. Bolland.)

SINGLES:	HITS 1			WEEKS 2
HORSEPOWER	*R&S*	61	*14 Dec 91*	2

RAW SILK — US

SINGLES:	HITS 2			WEEKS 12
DO IT TO THE MUSIC	*KR*	18	*16 Oct 82*	9
JUST IN TIME	*West End*	49	*10 Sep 83*	3

RAW STYLUS — UK

SINGLES:	HITS 1			WEEKS 1
BELIEVE IN ME	*Wired*	66	*26 Oct 96*	1

Lou RAWLS — US

(See also Philadelphia International All Stars: Lou Rawls, Billy Paul, Archie Bell, Teddy Pendergrass, O'Jays, Dee Dee Sharp, Gamble.)

SINGLES:	HITS 1			WEEKS 10
YOU'LL NEVER FIND ANOTHER LOVE LIKE MINE	*Philadelphia International*	10	*31 Jul 76*	10

Gene Anthony RAY - See KIDS FROM "FAME"

Jimmy RAY — UK

SINGLES:	HITS 2			WEEKS 6
ARE YOU JIMMY RAY?	*Sony S2*	13	*25 Oct 97*	5
GOIN' TO VEGAS	*Sony S2*	49	*14 Feb 98*	1

Johnnie RAY — US

SINGLES:	HITS 18			WEEKS 166
WALKIN' MY BABY BACK HOME	*Columbia*	12	*15 Nov 52*	1
Above hit: Johnnie RAY with the Buddy COLE QUARTET.				
Originally recorded by Jo Stafford.				
FAITH CAN MOVE MOUNTAINS	*Columbia*	7	*20 Dec 52*	2
Above hit: Johnnie RAY with the FOUR LADS.				
FAITH CAN MOVE MOUNTAINS [RE]	*Columbia*	9	*10 Jan 53*	1
MA SAYS, PA SAYS	*Columbia*	12	*4 Apr 53*	1
Above hit: Doris DAY and Johnnie RAY.				
SOMEBODY STOLE MY GAL	*Philips*	6	*11 Apr 53*	1
Above hit: Johnnie RAY with the Buddy COLE QUARTET.				
A FULL TIME JOB	*Columbia*	11	*18 Apr 53*	1
Above entry and Ma Says Pa Says were separate sides of the same release, each had its own chart run.				
Above hit: Doris DAY and Johnnie RAY.				
SOMEBODY STOLE MY GAL [RE-1ST]	*Philips*	6	*25 Apr 53*	4
SOMEBODY STOLE MY GAL [RE-2ND]	*Philips*	12	*30 May 53*	1
LET'S WALK THAT-A WAY	*Philips*	4	*25 Jul 53*	11
Above hit: Doris DAY -Johnnie RAY with Paul WESTON and his Orchestra.				
SOMEBODY STOLE MY GAL [RE-3RD]	*Philips*	11	*8 Aug 53*	1
SUCH A NIGHT	*Philips*	1	*10 Apr 54*	18
IF YOU BELIEVE	*Philips*	15	*9 Apr 55*	1
From the film 'There's No Business Like Show Business'.				
Above hit: Johnnie RAY with Percy FAITH and his Orchestra.				
IF YOU BELIEVE [RE]	*Philips*	7	*14 May 55*	10
PATHS OF PARADISE	*Philips*	20	*21 May 55*	1
Above hit: Johnnie RAY with Joe REISMAN and his Orchestra.				
HERNANDO'S HIDEAWAY	*Philips*	11	*8 Oct 55*	5
HEY THERE	*Philips*	5	*15 Oct 55*	9
Above 2 entries were separate sides of the same release, each had its own chart run. Above 2 from the film 'The Pajama Game'.				
SONG OF THE DREAMER	*Philips*	10	*29 Oct 55*	5
Above hit: Johnnie RAY with George SIRAVO and his Orchestra.				
WHO'S SORRY NOW	*Philips*	17	*18 Feb 56*	2
Above hit: Johnnie RAY with Paul WESTON and his Orchestra.				
AIN'T MISBEHAVIN'	*Philips*	17	*21 Apr 56*	6
AIN'T MISBEHAVIN' [RE]	*Philips*	24	*9 Jun 56*	1
JUST WALKING IN THE RAIN	*Philips*	1	*13 Oct 56*	19
Originally recorded by the Prisonaires.				
Above 3: Johnnie RAY with Ray CONNIFF and his Orchestra and Chorus.				
YOU DON'T OWE ME A THING/LOOK HOMEWARD, ANGEL	*Philips*	15	*19 Jan 57*	5
You Don't Owe Me A Thing originally recorded by Marty Robbins. Look Homeward Angel originally recorded by the Four Esquires, and listed from 9 Feb 57. From 23 Feb 57 both sides had their own separate chart runs as listed below.				
LOOK HOMEWARD, ANGEL	*Philips*	7	*23 Feb 57*	14
YOU DON'T OWE ME A THING	*Philips*	12	*23 Feb 57*	10
YES TONIGHT, JOSEPHINE	*Philips*	1	*11 May 57*	16
BUILD YOUR LOVE (ON A STRONG FOUNDATION)	*Philips*	17	*7 Sep 57*	7
Above 5: Johnnie RAY with Ray CONNIFF.				
UP ABOVE MY HEAD, I HEAR MUSIC IN THE AIR / GOOD EVENING FRIENDS	*Philips*	25	*5 Oct 57*	4
Above hit: Johnnie RAY- Frankie LAINE with Ray CONNIFF and his Orchestra / Frankie LAINE- Johnnie RAY with Ray CONNIFF and his Orchestra.				
I'LL NEVER FALL IN LOVE AGAIN	*Philips*	26	*5 Dec 59*	4
I'LL NEVER FALL IN LOVE AGAIN [RE-1ST]	*Philips*	26	*9 Jan 60*	1
I'LL NEVER FALL IN LOVE AGAIN [RE-2ND]	*Philips*	28	*6 Feb 60*	1

Nicole RAY - See NICOLE

RAY-J — US

SINGLES:	HITS 3			WEEKS 12
THAT'S WHY I LIE *From the film 'Dr. Dolittle'.*	*Atlantic*	71	*17 Oct 98*	1
ANOTHER DAY IN PARADISE *Above hit: BRANDY and RAY-J.*	*WEA*	5	*16 Jun 01*	10
WAIT A MINUTE *Above hit: RAY-J featuring LIL' KIM.*	*Atlantic*	54	*11 Aug 01*	1

RAYDIO — US

SINGLES:	HITS 2			WEEKS 21
JACK AND JILL	*Arista*	11	*8 Apr 78*	12
IS THIS A LOVE THING	*Arista*	27	*8 Jul 78*	9

Simon RAYMOND – See Harold BUDD, Elizabeth FRASER, Robin GUTHRIE and Simon RAYMONDE

RAYVON – See SHAGGY

RAZE — US

(See also Doug Lazy; Legend.)

SINGLES:	HITS 4			WEEKS 41
JACK THE GROOVE	*Champion*	57	*1 Nov 86*	7
JACK THE GROOVE [RE]	*Champion*	20	*3 Jan 87*	8
LET THE MUSIC MOVE U	*Champion*	57	*28 Feb 87*	3
BREAK 4 LOVE *Originally released earlier in the year reaching No. 85.*	*Champion*	28	*31 Dec 88*	11
BREAK 4 LOVE [RE]	*Champion*	59	*2 Sep 89*	5
ALL FOR LOVE (BREAK FOR LOVE 1990) [RR] *Above hit: RAZE featuring LADY J and the SECRETARY OF ENT.*	*Champion*	30	*27 Jan 90*	5
BREAK 4 LOVE [RM]	*Champion*	44	*24 Sep 94*	2

RCA VICTOR ORCHESTRA – See Mario LANZA

RE-FLEX — UK

SINGLES:	HITS 1			WEEKS 9
THE POLITICS OF DANCING	*EMI*	28	*28 Jan 84*	9

Chris REA — UK

(See also Middlesborough FC featuring Bob Mortimer and Chris Rea.)

SINGLES:	HITS 30			WEEKS 119
FOOL (IF YOU THINK IT'S OVER)	*Magnet*	30	*7 Oct 78*	7
DIAMONDS	*Magnet*	44	*21 Apr 79*	3
LOVING YOU	*Magnet*	65	*27 Mar 82*	3
I CAN HEAR YOUR HEARTBEAT	*Magnet*	60	*1 Oct 83*	2
I DON'T KNOW WHAT IT IS BUT I LOVE IT	*Magnet*	65	*17 Mar 84*	2
STAINSBY GIRLS	*Magnet*	26	*30 Mar 85*	10
JOSEPHINE	*Magnet*	67	*29 Jun 85*	2
IT'S ALL GONE	*Magnet*	69	*29 Mar 86*	1
ON THE BEACH (SPECIAL REMIX)	*Magnet*	57	*31 May 86*	3
ON THE BEACH (SPECIAL REMIX) [RE-1ST]	*Magnet*	75	*28 Jun 86*	1
ON THE BEACH (SPECIAL REMIX) [RE-2ND]	*Magnet*	66	*12 Jul 86*	4
LET'S DANCE	*Magnet*	12	*6 Jun 87*	10
LOVING YOU AGAIN	*Magnet*	47	*29 Aug 87*	4
JOYS OF CHRISTMAS	*Magnet*	67	*5 Dec 87*	1
QUE SERA (RERECORDED '88)	*Magnet*	73	*13 Feb 88*	2
ON THE BEACH SUMMER '88 [RR]	*WEA*	12	*13 Aug 88*	6
I CAN HEAR YOUR HEARTBEAT [RR]	*WEA*	74	*22 Oct 88*	2
THE CHRISTMAS [EP] *Lead track: Driving Home For Christmas.*	*WEA*	53	*17 Dec 88*	3
WORKING ON IT	*WEA*	53	*18 Feb 89*	3
THE ROAD TO HELL (PARTS 1 & 2) *One track.*	*WEA*	10	*14 Oct 89*	9
TELL ME THERE'S A HEAVEN	*East West*	24	*10 Feb 90*	6
TEXAS	*East West*	69	*5 May 90*	1
AUBERGE	*East West*	16	*16 Feb 91*	6
HEAVEN	*East West*	57	*6 Apr 91*	2
LOOKING FOR THE SUMMER	*East West*	49	*29 Jun 91*	3
WINTER SONG	*East West*	27	*9 Nov 91*	4
NOTHING TO FEAR	*East West*	16	*24 Oct 92*	4
GOD'S GREAT BANANA SKIN	*East West*	31	*28 Nov 92*	3
SOFT TOP, HARD SHOULDER *From the film of the same name.*	*East West*	53	*30 Jan 93*	2
JULIA	*Magnet*	18	*23 Oct 93*	5
YOU CAN GO YOUR OWN WAY *Adapted from the version featured in the Ford Probe car TV commercial.*	*East West*	28	*12 Nov 94*	3
TELL ME THERE'S A HEAVEN [RI]	*East West*	70	*24 Dec 94*	1

'DISCO' LA PASSIONE	*East West*	41	*16 Nov 96*	1
From the film 'La Passione'.				
Above hit: Chris REA/Shirley BASSEY.				
ALBUMS:	**HITS 19**			**WEEKS 347**
DELTICS	*Magnet*	54	*28 Apr 79*	3
TENNIS	*Magnet*	60	*12 Apr 80*	1
CHRIS REA	*Magnet*	52	*3 Apr 82*	4
WATER SIGN	*Magnet*	64	*18 Jun 83*	2
WIRED TO THE MOON	*Magnet*	35	*21 Apr 84*	7
SHAMROCK DIARIES	*Magnet*	15	*25 May 85*	14
ON THE BEACH	*Magnet*	11	*26 Apr 86*	37
DANCING WITH STRANGERS	*Magnet*	2	*26 Sep 87*	46
ON THE BEACH [RI]	*WEA*	37	*13 Aug 88*	10
THE BEST OF CHIS REA - NEW LIGHT THROUGH OLD WINDOWS	*WEA*	5	*29 Oct 88*	49
Label change to East West from 24 Feb 90.				
THE ROAD TO HELL	*WEA*	1	*11 Nov 89*	69
Label change to East West from 17 Feb 90.				
AUBERGE	*East West*	1	*9 Mar 91*	37
GOD'S GREAT BANANA SKIN	*East West*	4	*14 Nov 92*	15
ESPRESSO LOGIC	*East West*	8	*13 Nov 93*	10
THE BEST OF CHIS REA - NEW LIGHT THROUGH OLD WINDOWS [RI]	*East West*	68	*7 May 94*	2
Re-released at mid-price.				
THE BEST OF CHRIS REA	*East West*	3	*5 Nov 94*	18
THE ROAD TO HELL [RI]	*East West*	23	*18 Feb 95*	7
Re-released at mid-price.				
LA PASSIONE [OST]	*East West*	43	*23 Nov 96*	4
THE BLUE CAFE	*East West*	10	*31 Jan 98*	7
THE ROAD TO HELL - PART 2	*East West*	54	*20 Nov 99*	1
KING OF THE BEACH	*East West*	26	*14 Oct 00*	3
THE VERY BEST OF	*East West*	69	*1 Dec 01*	1

REACT 2 RHYTHM — UK

SINGLES:	**HITS 1**			**WEEKS 1**
INTOXICATION	*Jackpot*	73	*28 Jun 97*	1
Originally released in 1991 with a remix in 1992.				

Eddi READER — UK

SINGLES:	**HITS 5**			**WEEKS 14**
PATIENCE OF ANGELS	*Blanco Y Negro*	33	*4 Jun 94*	5
JOKE (I'M LAUGHING)	*Blanco Y Negro*	42	*13 Aug 94*	3
DEAR JOHN	*Blanco Y Negro*	48	*5 Nov 94*	2
TOWN WITHOUT PITY	*Blanco Y Negro*	26	*22 Jun 96*	3
FRAGILE THING	*Track Record*	69	*21 Aug 99*	1
Above hit: BIG COUNTRY (featuring Eddi READER).				
ALBUMS:	**HITS 4**			**WEEKS 21**
MIRMAMA	*RCA*	34	*7 Mar 92*	2
EDDI READER	*Blanco Y Negro*	4	*2 Jul 94*	12
CANDYFLOSS AND MEDICINE	*Blanco Y Negro*	24	*20 Jul 96*	5
ANGELS & ELECTRICITY	*Blanco Y Negro*	49	*23 May 98*	2

READING CHOIR - See SLADE

READY FOR THE WORLD — US

SINGLES:	**HITS 2**			**WEEKS 8**
OH SHEILA	*MCA*	50	*26 Oct 85*	5
LOVE YOU DOWN	*MCA*	60	*14 Mar 87*	3

REAL EMOTION — UK

SINGLES:	**HITS 1**			**WEEKS 1**
BACK FOR GOOD	*Living Beat*	67	*1 Jul 95*	1

REAL McCOY — US/Germany

SINGLES:	**HITS 5**			**WEEKS 36**
ANOTHER NIGHT	*Logic*	61	*6 Nov 93*	1
ANOTHER NIGHT [RM]	*Logic*	2	*5 Nov 94*	12
Remixed by the Berman Brothers.				
RUN AWAY	*Logic*	6	*28 Jan 95*	10
Above 3: (MC SAR and) the REAL McCOY.				
LOVE & DEVOTION	*Logic*	11	*22 Apr 95*	8
COME AND GET YOUR LOVE	*Logic*	19	*26 Aug 95*	4
Originally by Redbone reached No. 5 in the US in 1974.				
AUTOMATIC LOVER (CALL FOR LOVE)	*Logic*	58	*11 Nov 95*	1
ALBUMS:	**HITS 1**			**WEEKS 5**
ANOTHER NIGHT - U.S. ALBUM	*Logic*	6	*20 May 95*	5

REAL PEOPLE — UK

SINGLES:	HITS 4			WEEKS 8
OPEN UP YOUR MIND (LET ME IN)	*Columbia*	70	*16 Feb 91*	1
THE TRUTH	*Columbia*	73	*20 Apr 91*	1
WINDOW PANE [EP]	*Columbia*	60	*6 Jul 91*	1
Lead track: Window Pane.				
THE TRUTH [RI]	*Columbia*	41	*11 Jan 92*	3
BELIEVER	*Columbia*	38	*23 May 92*	2
ALBUMS:	**HITS 1**			**WEEKS 1**
THE REAL PEOPLE	*Columbia*	59	*18 May 91*	1

REAL ROXANNE — US

SINGLES:	HITS 2			WEEKS 10
(BANG ZOOM) LET'S GO GO	*Cooltempo*	11	*28 Jun 86*	9
Above hit: REAL ROXANNE with HITMAN HOWIE TEE.				
RESPECT	*Cooltempo*	71	*12 Nov 88*	1
Features vocals by Dee Dee Scott.				

REAL THING — UK

SINGLES:	HITS 11			WEEKS 114
YOU TO ME ARE EVERYTHING	*Pye International*	1	*5 Jun 76*	11
CAN'T GET BY WITHOUT YOU	*Pye*	2	*4 Sep 76*	10
Originally recorded by Carl Lewis.				
YOU'LL NEVER KNOW WHAT YOU'RE MISSING	*Pye*	16	*12 Feb 77*	9
LOVE'S SUCH A WONDERFUL THING	*Pye*	33	*30 Jul 77*	5
WHENEVER YOU WANT MY LOVE	*Pye*	18	*4 Mar 78*	9
LET'S GO DISCO	*Pye*	39	*3 Jun 78*	7
From the film 'The Stud'.				
RAININ' THROUGH MY SUNSHINE	*Pye*	40	*12 Aug 78*	8
CAN YOU FEEL THE FORCE?	*Pye*	5	*17 Feb 79*	11
BOOGIE DOWN (GET FUNKY NOW)	*Pye*	33	*21 Jul 79*	6
SHE'S A GROOVY FREAK	*Calibre*	52	*22 Nov 80*	4
YOU TO ME ARE EVERYTHING (THE DECADE REMIX '76-'86) [RM]	*PRT*	5	*8 Mar 86*	12
Remixed by Froggy, Simon Harris and KC.				
CAN'T GET BY WITHOUT YOU (THE SECOND DECADE REMIX) [RM]	*PRT*	6	*24 May 86*	13
YOU TO ME ARE EVERYTHING (THE DECADE REMIX '76-'86) [RM] [RE]	*PRT*	72	*7 Jun 86*	1
CAN YOU FEEL THE FORCE? ('86 MIX) [RM]	*PRT*	24	*2 Aug 86*	6
Above 2 remixed by Bob Mallett.				
STRAIGHT TO THE HEART	*Jive*	71	*25 Oct 86*	2
ALBUMS:	**HITS 4**			**WEEKS 17**
REAL THING	*Pye*	34	*6 Nov 76*	3
CAN YOU FEEL THE FORCE	*Pye*	73	*7 Apr 79*	1
20 GREATEST HITS	*K-Tel*	56	*10 May 80*	2
THE BEST OF THE REAL THING	*West Five*	24	*12 Jul 86*	11

REAL TO REEL — US

SINGLES:	HITS 1			WEEKS 2
LOVE ME LIKE THIS	*Arista*	68	*21 Apr 84*	2

REBEL MC — UK

SINGLES:	HITS 9			WEEKS 52
JUST KEEP ROCKIN'	*Desire*	11	*27 May 89*	12
Above hit: DOUBLE TROUBLE and the REBEL MC.				
STREET TUFF	*Desire*	3	*7 Oct 89*	14
Above hit: REBEL MC DOUBLE TROUBLE.				
BETTER WORLD	*Desire*	20	*31 Mar 90*	6
REBEL MUSIC	*Desire*	53	*2 Jun 90*	2
THE WICKEDEST SOUND	*Desire*	43	*6 Apr 91*	6
Above hit: REBEL MC (featuring TENOR FLY).				
TRIBAL BASE	*Desire*	20	*15 Jun 91*	6
Above hit: REBEL M.C. featuring TENOR FLY and Barrington LEVY.				
BLACK MEANING GOOD	*Desire*	73	*31 Aug 91*	1
RICH AH GETTING RICHER	*Big Life*	48	*21 Mar 92*	4
Above hit: REBEL M.C. introducing LITTLE T.				
HUMANITY	*Big Life*	62	*8 Aug 92*	1
Above hit: REBEL M.C. featuring Prince Lincoln THOMPSON.				
ALBUMS:	**HITS 2**			**WEEKS 11**
REBEL MUSIC	*Desire*	18	*28 Apr 90*	7
BLACK MEANING GOOD	*Desire*	23	*13 Jul 91*	4

REBEL ROUSERS – See Cliff BENNETT and the REBEL ROUSERS

REBELETTES – See Duane EDDY

REBELS – See Duane EDDY

Ivan REBROFF — Russia

ALBUMS:	HITS 1			WEEKS 4
THE VERY BEST OF IVAN REBROFF	*BBC*	57	*16 Jun 90*	4

Ezz RECO and the LAUNCHERS with Boysie GRANT — Jamaica

SINGLES:	HITS 1			WEEKS 4
KING OF KINGS *Originally recorded by Jimmy Cliff.*	*Columbia*	44	*7 Mar 64*	4

RECOIL — UK

SINGLES:	HITS 1			WEEKS 1
FAITH HEALER	*Mute*	60	*21 Mar 92*	1

RED — UK

SINGLES:	HITS 1			WEEKS 1
HEAVEN & EARTH	*Slinky Music*	41	*20 Jan 01*	1

RED BOX — UK

SINGLES:	HITS 3			WEEKS 28
LEAN ON ME (AH-LI-AYO)	*Sire*	3	*24 Aug 85*	14
FOR AMERICA	*Sire*	10	*25 Oct 86*	12
HEART OF THE SUN	*Sire*	71	*31 Jan 87*	2
ALBUMS:	**HITS 1**			**WEEKS 4**
THE CIRCLE AND THE SQUARE	*Sire*	73	*6 Dec 86*	4

RED CAR AND THE BLUE CAR — UK

SINGLES:	HITS 1			WEEKS 4
HOME FOR CHRISTMAS DAY	*Virgin*	44	*14 Dec 91*	4

RED DRAGON with Brian and Tony GOLD — Jamaica

SINGLES:	HITS 1			WEEKS 15
COMPLIMENTS ON YOUR KISS	*Mango*	2	*30 Jul 94*	13
COMPLIMENTS ON YOUR KISS [RE]	*Mango*	49	*31 Dec 94*	2

RED EYE — UK

SINGLES:	HITS 1			WEEKS 1
KUT IT	*Champion*	62	*3 Dec 94*	1

RED 5 — Germany

SINGLES:	HITS 2			WEEKS 10
I LOVE YOU . . . STOP! *Vocals by Maxine Harvey.*	*Multiply*	11	*10 May 97*	5
LIFT ME UP	*Multiply*	26	*20 Dec 97*	5

RED HED - See VINYL GROOVER and the RED HED

RED HILL CHILDREN — UK

SINGLES:	HITS 1			WEEKS 2
WHEN CHILDREN RULE THE WORLD *From the Andrew Lloyd Webber musical 'Whistle Down The Wind'. Also used as the theme tune for the BBC's Children In Need appeal.*	*Really Useful*	40	*30 Nov 96*	2

RED HOT CHILI PEPPERS — US

SINGLES:	HITS 14			WEEKS 58
HIGHER GROUND	*EMI USA*	55	*10 Feb 90*	3
TASTE THE PAIN	*EMI USA*	29	*23 Jun 90*	3
HIGHER GROUND [RI]	*EMI USA*	54	*8 Sep 90*	3
UNDER THE BRIDGE	*Warner Brothers*	26	*14 Mar 92*	4
BREAKING THE GIRL	*Warner Brothers*	41	*15 Aug 92*	3
GIVE IT AWAY	*Warner Brothers*	9	*5 Feb 94*	4
UNDER THE BRIDGE [RI]	*Warner Brothers*	13	*30 Apr 94*	6
WARPED	*Warner Brothers*	31	*2 Sep 95*	2
MY FRIENDS	*Warner Brothers*	29	*21 Oct 95*	2
AEROPLANE *Child vocal from Flea's daughter Clara.*	*Warner Brothers*	11	*17 Feb 96*	3
LOVE ROLLERCOASTER *Original by the Ohio Players reached No. 1 in the US in 1976. From the film 'Beavis And Butt-Head Do America'.*	*Geffen*	7	*14 Jun 97*	8
SCAR TISSUE	*Warner Brothers*	15	*12 Jun 99*	6
AROUND THE WORLD	*Warner Brothers*	35	*4 Sept 99*	2
OTHERSIDE	*Warner Brothers*	33	*12 Feb 00*	2
CALIFORNICATION	*Warner Brothers*	16	*19 Aug 00*	5
ROAD TRIPPIN'	*Warner Brothers*	30	*13 Jan 01*	2

ALBUMS:	HITS 5			WEEKS 200
BLOOD SUGAR SEX MAGIK	*Warner Brothers*	25	*12 Oct 91*	82
Includes re-entries through to 2000.				
WHAT HITS!?	*EMI USA*	23	*17 Oct 92*	6
OUT IN LA	*EMI*	61	*19 Nov 94*	1
Demos, remixes, live recordings and previously unreleased tracks.				
ONE HOT MINUTE	*Warner Brothers*	2	*23 Sep 95*	11
CALIFORNICATION	*Warner Brothers*	5	*19 Jun 99*	100

RED HOUSE PAINTERS — US

ALBUMS:	HITS 2			WEEKS 2
RED HOUSE PAINTERS	*4AD*	63	*5 Jun 93*	1
RED HOUSE PAINTERS	*4AD*	68	*30 Oct 93*	1
Both albums are different.				

RED JERRY – See WESTBAM

RED NOISE – See Bill NELSON

RED NOSED BURGLARS – See Ivor BIGGUN

RED RAT – See Curtis LYNCH Jnr featuring Kele LE ROC and RED RAT; Phoebe ONE featuring RED RAT, GOOFY and BUCANEER (MAIN STREET CREW); R.I.P. PRODUCTIONS

RED RAW featuring 007 — UK

SINGLES:	HITS 1			WEEKS 1
OOH LA LA LA	*Media*	59	*28 Oct 95*	1

RED SNAPPER — UK

SINGLES:	HITS 1			WEEKS 1
IMAGE OF YOU	*Warp*	60	*21 Nov 98*	1
ALBUMS:	**HITS 2**			**WEEKS 2**
PRINCE BLIMEY	*Warp*	60	*21 Sep 96*	1
MAKING BONES	*Warp*	59	*10 Oct 98*	1

RED VENOM – See BIG BOSS STYLUS presents RED VENOM

REDBONE — US

SINGLES:	HITS 1			WEEKS 12
THE WITCH QUEEN OF NEW ORLEANS	*Epic*	2	*25 Sep 71*	12

Sharon REDD — US

SINGLES:	HITS 5			WEEKS 32
CAN YOU HANDLE IT	*Epic*	31	*28 Feb 81*	8
NEVER GIVE YOU UP / BEAT THE STREET	*Prelude*	20	*2 Oct 82*	9
IN THE NAME OF LOVE	*Prelude*	31	*15 Jan 83*	5
LOVE HOW YOU FEEL	*Prelude*	39	*22 Oct 83*	5
CAN YOU HANDLE IT	*EMI*	17	*1 Feb 92*	5
Above hit: DNA featuring Sharon REDD.				
ALBUMS:	**HITS 1**			**WEEKS 5**
REDD HOTT	*Prelude*	59	*23 Oct 82*	5

REDD KROSS — US

SINGLES:	HITS 3			WEEKS 4
VISIONARY	*This Way Up*	75	*5 Feb 94*	1
YESTERDAY ONCE MORE	*A&M*	45	*10 Sep 94*	2
[AA] listed with Superstar by Sonic Youth. From the 25th Anniversary tribute album to the Carpenters, If I Were A Carpenter.				
GET OUT OF MYSELF	*This Way Up*	63	*1 Feb 97*	1

Otis REDDING — US

(See also Otis Redding and Carla Thomas.)

SINGLES:	HITS 13			WEEKS 108
MY GIRL	*Atlantic*	11	*27 Nov 65*	16
(I CAN'T GET NO) SATISFACTION	*Atlantic*	33	*9 Apr 66*	4
MY LOVER'S PRAYER	*Atlantic*	37	*16 Jul 66*	6
I CAN'T TURN YOU LOOSE	*Atlantic*	29	*27 Aug 66*	8
FA-FA-FA-FA-FA (SAD SONGS)	*Atlantic*	23	*26 Nov 66*	9
TRY A LITTLE TENDERNESS	*Atlantic*	46	*28 Jan 67*	4
Originally recorded by Ted Lewis in 1933.				
DAY TRIPPER	*Stax*	43	*25 Mar 67*	6
LET ME COME ON HOME	*Stax*	48	*6 May 67*	1
SHAKE	*Stax*	28	*17 Jun 67*	10
MY GIRL [RI]	*Atlantic*	36	*17 Feb 68*	9

(SITTIN' ON) THE DOCK OF THE BAY	*Stax*	3	*24 Feb 68*	15
THE HAPPY SONG (DUM-DUM)	*Stax*	24	*1 Jun 68*	5
HARD TO HANDLE	*Atlantic*	15	*3 Aug 68*	12
LOVE MAN	*Atco*	43	*12 Jul 69*	3
ALBUMS:	**HITS 10**			**WEEKS 218**
OTIS BLUE: OTIS REDDING SINGS SOUL	*Atlantic*	6	*19 Feb 66*	21
OTIS BLUE: OTIS REDDING SINGS SOUL [RE]	*Atlantic*	7	*21 Jan 67*	54
Re-released with a new catalogue number. Peak position reached in 1968, (1967 peak No. 29).				
THE GREAT OTIS REDDING SINGS SOUL BALLADS	*Atlantic*	30	*23 Apr 66*	1
Originally released in 1965.				
THE SOUL ALBUM	*Atlantic*	22	*23 Jul 66*	9
COMPLETE AND UNBELIEVABLE. . . . THE OTIS REDDING DICTIONARY OF SOUL	*Atlantic*	23	*21 Jan 67*	16
PAIN IN MY HEART	*Atlantic*	28	*29 Apr 67*	9
THE HISTORY OF OTIS REDDING	*Stax*	2	*10 Feb 68*	43
OTIS REDDING IN EUROPE	*Stax*	14	*30 Mar 68*	16
Live recordings.				
DOCK OF THE BAY	*Stax*	1	*1 Jun 68*	15
Compilation.				
THE IMMORTAL OTIS REDDING	*Atlantic*	19	*12 Oct 68*	8
DOCK OF THE BAY - THE DEFINITIVE COLLECTION [RI]	*Atlantic*	50	*11 Sept 93*	18
Remastered CD re-issue of Dock Of The Bay, originally released in 1992. It first charted after the broadcast of 'The Atlantic Story' on Channel 4. Peak position reached in 2000, (1993 peak No. 50).				
THE VERY BEST OF OTIS REDDING	*Atco*	26	*11 Nov 00*	8

Otis REDDING and Carla THOMAS — US

(See also Otis Redding.)

SINGLES:	**HITS 2**			**WEEKS 16**
TRAMP	*Stax*	18	*22 Jul 67*	11
Originally recorded by Lowell Fulsom.				
KNOCK ON WOOD	*Stax*	35	*14 Oct 67*	5
ALBUMS:	**HITS 1**			**WEEKS 17**
THE KING AND QUEEN OF SOUL	*Stax*	18	*1 Jul 67*	17

Helen REDDY — Australia

SINGLES:	**HITS 2**			**WEEKS 18**
ANGIE BABY	*Capitol*	5	*18 Jan 75*	10
Originally recorded by Alan O'Day.				
I CAN'T SAY GOODBYE TO YOU	*MCA*	43	*28 Nov 81*	8
ALBUMS:	**HITS 2**			**WEEKS 27**
FREE AND EASY	*Capitol*	17	*8 Feb 75*	9
THE BEST OF HELEN REDDY	*Capitol*	6	*14 Feb 76*	18

REDHEAD KINGPIN and the F.B.I. — US

SINGLES:	**HITS 2**			**WEEKS 11**
DO THE RIGHT THING	*10 Records*	13	*22 Jul 89*	10
SUPERBAD SUPERSLICK	*10 Records*	68	*2 Dec 89*	1
ALBUMS:	**HITS 1**			**WEEKS 3**
A SHADE OF RED	*10 Records*	35	*9 Sep 89*	3

REDMAN — US

(See also KRS One; Method Man and Redman.)

SINGLES:	**HITS 6**			**WEEKS 27**
RAP SCHOLAR	*East West America*	42	*25 Apr 98*	1
Above hit: DAS EFX featuring REDMAN.				
HOW DEEP IS YOUR LOVE	*Island Black Music*	9	*24 Oct 98*	7
Above hit: DRU HILL (featuring REDMAN).				
HOW DEEP IS YOUR LOVE [RE]	*Island Black Music*	75	*16 Jan 99*	1
MADE IT BACK 99 [RM]	*Parlophone Rhythm Series*	19	*10 Apr 99*	5
Samples Chic's Good Times.				
Above hit: Beverley KNIGHT featuring REDMAN.				
DA GOODNESS	*Def Jam*	52	*12 Jun 99*	1
Samples Duke Ellington's Caravan.				
OOOH.	*Tommy Boy*	29	*22 Jul 00*	2
Samples Lalo Schifrin's Enter The Dragon Theme.				
Above hit: DE LA SOUL featuring REDMAN.				
SMASH SUMTHIN'	*Def Jam*	11	*15 Sep 01*	7
Above hit: REDMAN featuring Adam F.				
ALBUMS:	**HITS 1**			**WEEKS 4**
MALPRACTICE	*Def Jam*	57	*9 Jun 01*	4

REDNEX — Sweden

SINGLES:	HITS 3			WEEKS 23
COTTON EYE JOE *Originally recorded by Bob Wills and his Texas Playboys.*	*Internal Affairs*	1	*17 Dec 94*	16
OLD POP IN AN OAK	*Internal Affairs*	12	*25 Mar 95*	6
WILD 'N FREE	*Internal Affairs*	55	*21 Oct 95*	1

REDS UNITED — UK

SINGLES:	HITS 2			WEEKS 13
SING UP FOR THE CHAMPIONS! *The Official 1997 Manchester United supporters' single.*	*Music Collection International*	12	*6 Dec 97*	9
UNITED CALYPSO '98 *The Official 1998 Manchester United supporters' single. First recorded in 1954.*	*Music Collection International*	33	*9 May 98*	4

REDSKINS — UK

SINGLES:	HITS 3			WEEKS 12
KEEP ON KEEPIN' ON!	*Decca*	43	*10 Nov 84*	5
(BURN IT UP) BRING IT DOWN! (THIS INSANE THING)	*Decca*	33	*22 Jun 85*	5
THE POWER IS YOURS	*Decca*	59	*22 Feb 86*	2
ALBUMS:	**HITS 1**			**WEEKS 4**
NEITHER WASHINGTON NOR MOSCOW . . .	*Decca*	31	*22 Mar 86*	4

Alex REECE — UK

SINGLES:	HITS 3			WEEKS 7
FEEL THE SUNSHINE *Vocals by Deborah Anderson.*	*Blunted Vinyl*	69	*16 Dec 95*	1
FEEL THE SUNSHINE - REMIXES [RI] *Though listed as a remix, the first track on CD1 is the original version.*	*Fourth & Broadway*	26	*11 May 96*	3
CANDLES	*Fourth & Broadway*	33	*27 Jul 96*	2
ACID LAB	*Fourth & Broadway*	64	*16 Nov 96*	1
ALBUMS:	**HITS 1**			**WEEKS 5**
SO FAR	*Fourth & Broadway*	19	*17 Aug 96*	5

Dan REED NETWORK — US

SINGLES:	HITS 6			WEEKS 16
COME BACK BABY	*Mercury*	51	*20 Jan 90*	3
RAINBOW CHILD	*Mercury*	60	*17 Mar 90*	3
STARDATE 1990 / RAINBOW CHILD [RI] *From 4 Aug 90 titles were listed in reverse.*	*Mercury*	39	*21 Jul 90*	4
LOVER/MONEY	*Mercury*	45	*8 Sep 90*	3
MIX IT UP	*Mercury*	49	*13 Jul 91*	2
BABY NOW I	*Mercury*	65	*21 Sep 91*	1
ALBUMS:	**HITS 2**			**WEEKS 6**
SLAM	*Mercury*	66	*4 Nov 89*	2
THE HEAT	*Mercury*	15	*27 Jul 91*	4

Eileen REED - See CADETS with Eileen REED lead vocal

Jimmy REED — US

SINGLES:	HITS 1			WEEKS 2
SHAME SHAME SHAME	*Stateside*	45	*12 Sep 64*	2

Les REED ORCHESTRA and CHORUS - See Donald PEERS

Lou REED — US

SINGLES:	HITS 2			WEEKS 19
WALK ON THE WILD SIDE	*RCA Victor*	10	*12 May 73*	9
SOUL MAN *From the film of the same name.* *Above hit: Sam MOORE and Lou REED.*	*A&M*	30	*17 Jan 87*	10
ALBUMS:	**HITS 13**			**WEEKS 91**
TRANSFORMER	*RCA Victor*	13	*21 Apr 73*	25
BERLIN	*RCA Victor*	7	*20 Oct 73*	5
ROCK 'N' ROLL ANIMAL *Live recordings from New York's Academy of Music.*	*RCA Victor*	26	*16 Mar 74*	1
CONEY ISLAND BABY	*RCA Victor*	52	*14 Feb 76*	1
TRANSFORMER [RI-1ST]	*RCA International*	91	*3 Jul 82*	2
NEW SENSATIONS	*RCA*	92	*9 Jun 84*	1
MISTRIAL	*RCA*	69	*24 May 86*	1
NEW YORK	*Sire*	14	*28 Jan 89*	22
RETRO	*RCA*	29	*7 Oct 89*	5
SONGS FOR DRELLA *Above hit: Lou REED and John CALE.*	*Sire*	22	*5 May 90*	5
MAGIC AND LOSS	*Sire*	6	*25 Jan 92*	6

THE BEST OF LOU REED AND THE VELVET UNDERGROUND	*Global Television*	56	*28 Oct 95*	4
Features both Lou Reed's solo and group material.				
Above hit: Lou REED and the VELVET UNDERGROUND.				
SET THE TWILIGHT REELING	*Warner Brothers*	26	*2 Mar 96*	10
TRANSFORMER [RI-2ND]	*RCA*	16	*7 Feb 98*	8
Peak position reached in 2001, (1998 Peak No. 49).				
ECSTASY	*Reprise*	54	*15 Apr 00*	1

Natina REED – See KURUPT featuring Natina REED

Michael REED ORCHESTRA — UK

SINGLES:	HITS 1			WEEKS 10
THE MUSIC OF TORVILL AND DEAN [EP]	*Safari*	9	*25 Feb 84*	10
Lead track: Bolero. Although uncredited, the first two tracks on the EP are, in fact, by Richard Hartley.				

Don REEDMAN – See Jeff JARRATT and Don REEDMAN

REEF — UK

SINGLES:	HITS 13			WEEKS 46
GOOD FEELING	*Sony S2*	24	*15 Apr 95*	4
NAKED	*Sony S2*	11	*3 Jun 95*	5
WEIRD	*Sony S2*	19	*5 Aug 95*	3
PLACE YOUR HANDS	*Sony S2*	6	*2 Nov 96*	7
COME BACK BRIGHTER	*Sony S2*	8	*25 Jan 97*	5
CONSIDERATION	*Sony S2*	13	*5 Apr 97*	4
YER OLD	*Sony S2*	21	*2 Aug 97*	3
I'VE GOT SOMETHING TO SAY	*Sony S2*	15	*10 Apr 99*	6
SWEETY	*Sony S2*	46	*5 Jun 99*	1
NEW BIRD	*Sony S2*	73	*11 Sept 99*	1
SET THE RECORD STRAIGHT	*Sony S2*	19	*12 Aug 00*	5
SUPERHERO	*Sony S2*	55	*16 Dec 00*	1
ALL I WANT	*Sony S2*	51	*19 May 01*	1
ALBUMS:	**HITS 4**			**WEEKS 54**
REPLENISH	*Sony S2*	9	*1 Jul 95*	11
GLOW	*Sony S2*	1	*8 Feb 97*	32
RIDES	*Sony S2*	3	*1 May 99*	7
GETAWAY	*Sony S2*	15	*2 Sep 00*	4

REEL — Ireland

SINGLES:	HITS 1			WEEKS 1
LIFT ME UP	*Universal Music TV*	39	*24 Nov 01*	1

REEL 2 REAL featuring the MAD STUNTMAN — US

SINGLES:	HITS 7			WEEKS 53
I LIKE TO MOVE IT	*Positiva*	5	*12 Feb 94*	20
GO ON MOVE	*Positiva*	7	*2 Jul 94*	9
CAN YOU FEEL IT?	*Positiva*	13	*1 Oct 94*	5
Duet with Althea McQueen.				
RAISE YOUR HANDS	*Positiva*	14	*3 Dec 94*	6
CONWAY	*Positiva*	27	*1 Apr 95*	4
JAZZ IT UP	*Positiva*	7	*6 Jul 96*	7
ARE YOU READY FOR SOME MORE?	*Positiva*	24	*5 Oct 96*	2
Above 2: REEL 2 REAL.				
ALBUMS:	**HITS 1**			**WEEKS 8**
MOVE IT!	*Positiva*	8	*22 Oct 94*	8

Maureen REES — UK

SINGLES:	HITS 1			WEEKS 4
DRIVING IN MY CAR	*Eagle*	49	*20 Dec 97*	4

Tony REES and the COTTAGERS — UK

SINGLES:	HITS 1			WEEKS 1
VIVA EL FULHAM (BASED ON Y VIVA ESPANA)	*Sonet*	46	*10 May 75*	1

REESE PROJECT — US

SINGLES:	HITS 4			WEEKS 7
THE COLOUR OF LOVE	*Network*	52	*8 Aug 92*	2
I BELIEVE	*Network*	74	*12 Dec 92*	1
Featured vocals from Terrence FM.				
SO DEEP	*Network*	54	*13 Mar 93*	2
THE COLOUR OF LOVE [RM]	*Network*	55	*24 Sep 94*	1
Remixed by the Playboys (Tim Jeffrey and J. Creid).				
DIRECT-ME	*Network*	44	*6 May 95*	1
Originally recorded in 1991. Vocals by Rachel Kapp.				

Conner REEVES — UK

SINGLES:	HITS 5			WEEKS 18
MY FATHER'S SON	*Wildstar*	12	*30 Aug 97*	5
EARTHBOUND	*Wildstar*	14	*22 Nov 97*	4
READ MY MIND	*Wildstar*	19	*11 Apr 98*	4
SEARCHING FOR A SOUL	*Wildstar*	28	*3 Oct 98*	2
BEST FRIEND	*WEA*	23	*04 Sept 99*	3
Above hit: Mark MORRISON and Conner REEVES.				
ALBUMS:	**HITS 1**			**WEEKS 8**
EARTHBOUND	*Wildstar*	25	*6 Dec 97*	8

Jim REEVES — US

SINGLES:	HITS 26			WEEKS 322
HE'LL HAVE TO GO	*RCA*	36	*26 Mar 60*	1
Originally recorded by Billy Brown.				
HE'LL HAVE TO GO [RE]	*RCA*	12	*9 Apr 60*	30
WHISPERING HOPE	*RCA*	50	*18 Mar 61*	1
YOU'RE THE ONLY GOOD THING (THAT HAPPENED TO ME)	*RCA*	17	*25 Nov 61*	19
Originally recorded by Gene Autry.				
ADIOS AMIGO	*RCA*	23	*30 Jun 62*	21
I'M GONNA CHANGE EVERYTHING	*RCA*	42	*24 Nov 62*	2
WELCOME TO MY WORLD	*RCA Victor*	6	*15 Jun 63*	15
GUILTY	*RCA Victor*	29	*19 Oct 63*	7
I LOVE YOU BECAUSE	*RCA Victor*	5	*22 Feb 64*	39
Originally recorded by Leon Payne in 1950.				
I WON'T FORGET YOU	*RCA Victor*	3	*20 Jun 64*	25
THERE'S A HEARTACHE FOLLOWING ME	*RCA Victor*	6	*7 Nov 64*	13
I WON'T FORGET YOU [RE]	*RCA Victor*	47	*9 Jan 65*	1
IT HURTS SO MUCH (TO SEE YOU GO)	*RCA Victor*	8	*6 Feb 65*	10
NOT UNTIL THE NEXT TIME	*RCA Victor*	13	*17 Apr 65*	12
HOW LONG HAS IT BEEN	*RCA Victor*	45	*8 May 65*	5
THIS WORLD IS NOT MY HOME	*RCA Victor*	22	*17 Jul 65*	9
Recorded in 1962.				
IS IT REALLY OVER	*RCA Victor*	17	*13 Nov 65*	9
DISTANT DRUMS	*RCA Victor*	1	*20 Aug 66*	25
First UK No.1 written solely by a female, Cindy Walker. Originally recorded by Roy Orbison.				
I WON'T COME IN WHILE HE'S THERE	*RCA Victor*	12	*4 Feb 67*	11
TRYING TO FORGET	*RCA Victor*	33	*29 Jul 67*	5
I HEARD A HEART BREAK LAST NIGHT	*RCA Victor*	38	*25 Nov 67*	6
PRETTY BROWN EYES	*RCA Victor*	33	*30 Mar 68*	5
WHEN TWO WORLDS COLLIDE	*RCA Victor*	17	*28 Jun 69*	17
BUT YOU LOVE ME DADDY	*RCA Victor*	15	*6 Dec 69*	16
Above hit: Jim REEVES with Steve MOORE.				
NOBODY'S FOOL	*RCA Victor*	32	*21 Mar 70*	5
ANGELS DON'T LIE	*RCA Victor*	44	*12 Sep 70*	1
ANGELS DON'T LIE [RE]	*RCA Victor*	32	*26 Sep 70*	2
I LOVE YOU BECAUSE [RI] / HE'LL HAVE TO GO [RI] / MOONLIGHT AND ROSES (BRING BACK MEMORIES OF YOU)	*RCA Victor Maximillion*	34	*26 Jun 71*	8
YOU'RE FREE TO GO	*RCA Victor*	48	*19 Feb 72*	2
EPS:	**HITS 6**			**WEEKS 79**
SONGS TO WARM THE HEART	*RCA*	12	*1 Dec 62*	12
Peak position reached as a re-entry on 3 Oct 64.				
WELCOME TO MY WORLD	*RCA Victor*	6	*4 Apr 64*	25
FROM THE HEART	*RCA Victor*	4	*15 Aug 64*	26
SONGS TO WARM THE HEART, VOL. 2	*RCA Victor*	9	*12 Sep 64*	10
FROM THE HEART VOLUME 2	*RCA Victor*	14	*26 Sep 64*	1
CHRISTMAS CARD FROM JIM REEVES	*RCA Victor*	3	*3 Dec 66*	5
ALBUMS:	**HITS 28**			**WEEKS 399**
GOOD 'N' COUNTRY	*RCA Camden*	10	*28 Mar 64*	35
GENTLEMAN JIM	*RCA Victor*	3	*9 May 64*	23
A TOUCH OF VELVET	*RCA Victor*	8	*15 Aug 64*	9
INTERNATIONAL JIM REEVES	*RCA Victor*	11	*15 Aug 64*	17
HE'LL HAVE TO GO	*RCA Victor*	16	*22 Aug 64*	4
GOD BE WITH YOU	*RCA Victor*	10	*29 Aug 64*	10
THE INTIMATE JIM REEVES	*RCA Victor*	12	*29 Aug 64*	4
MOONLIGHT AND ROSES	*RCA Victor*	2	*5 Sep 64*	52
COUNTRY SIDE OF JIM REEVES	*RCA Camden*	12	*19 Sep 64*	5
WE THANK THEE	*RCA Victor*	17	*26 Sep 64*	3
TWELVE SONGS OF CHRISTMAS	*RCA Victor*	4	*28 Nov 64*	17
Includes re-entries through to 1970.				
THE BEST OF JIM REEVES	*RCA Victor*	3	*30 Jan 65*	47
HAVE I TOLD YOU LATELY THAT I LOVE YOU	*RCA Camden*	12	*10 Apr 65*	5
THE JIM REEVES WAY	*RCA Victor*	16	*22 May 65*	4
DISTANT DRUMS	*RCA Victor*	2	*5 Nov 66*	34
Compilation.				
A TOUCH OF SADNESS	*RCA Victor*	15	*18 Jan 69*	5

ACCORDING TO MY HEART	*RCA International*	1	*5 Jul 69*	14
JIM REEVES AND SOME FRIENDS	*RCA Victor*	24	*23 Aug 69*	4
ON STAGE	*RCA Victor*	13	*29 Nov 69*	4
MY CATHEDRAL	*RCA Victor*	48	*26 Dec 70*	2
JIM REEVES WRITES YOU A RECORD	*RCA Victor*	47	*3 Jul 71*	2
JIM REEVES' GOLDEN RECORDS	*RCA International*	9	*7 Aug 71*	21
THE INTIMATE JIM REEVES [RI]	*RCA International*	8	*14 Aug 71*	15
GIRLS I HAVE KNOWN	*RCA International*	35	*21 Aug 71*	5
TWELVE SONGS OF CHRISTMAS [RI]	*RCA International*	3	*27 Nov 71*	6
A TOUCH OF VELVET [RI]	*RCA International*	49	*27 Nov 71*	2
MY FRIEND	*RCA Victor*	32	*15 Apr 72*	5
40 GOLDEN GREATS	*Arcade*	1	*20 Sep 75*	25
COUNTRY GENTLEMAN	*K-Tel*	53	*6 Sep 80*	4
THE DEFINITIVE JIM REEVES	*Arcade*	9	*8 Aug 92*	10
THE ULTIMATE COLLECTION	*RCA Victor*	17	*28 Sep 96*	6

Martha REEVES and the VANDELLAS — US

SINGLES:	HITS 7			WEEKS 85
DANCING IN THE STREET	*Stateside*	28	*31 Oct 64*	8
NOWHERE TO RUN	*Tamla Motown*	26	*3 Apr 65*	8
I'M READY FOR LOVE	*Tamla Motown*	29	*3 Dec 66*	8
JIMMY MACK	*Tamla Motown*	21	*1 Apr 67*	9
Above 4: MARTHA and the VANDELLAS.				
HONEY CHILE	*Tamla Motown*	30	*20 Jan 68*	9
DANCING IN THE STREET [RI]	*Tamla Motown*	4	*18 Jan 69*	12
NOWHERE TO RUN [RI-1ST]	*Tamla Motown*	42	*19 Apr 69*	3
JIMMY MACK [RE]	*Tamla Motown*	21	*29 Aug 70*	12
Above hit: MARTHA and the VANDELLAS.				
FORGET ME NOT	*Tamla Motown*	11	*13 Feb 71*	8
BLESS YOU	*Tamla Motown*	33	*8 Jan 72*	5
NOWHERE TO RUN [RI-2ND]	*A&M*	52	*23 Jul 88*	3
[AA] listed with I Got You (I Feel Good) by James Brown.				

Vic REEVES — UK.

SINGLES:	HITS 4			WEEKS 29
BORN FREE	*Sense*	6	*27 Apr 91*	6
Above hit: Vic REEVES and the ROMAN NUMERALS.				
DIZZY	*Sense*	1	*26 Oct 91*	12
Above hit: Vic REEVES and the WONDER STUFF.				
ABIDE WITH ME	*Sense*	47	*14 Dec 91*	3
I'M A BELIEVER	*Parlophone*	3	*8 Jul 95*	8
Above hit: EMF and REEVES and MORTIMER.				
ALBUMS:	**HITS 1**			**WEEKS 9**
I WILL CURE YOU	*Sense*	16	*16 Nov 91*	9

REFLEX featuring MC VIPER — UK

SINGLES:	HITS 1			WEEKS 1
PUT YOUR HANDS UP	*Gutso*	72	*19 May 01*	1

REFUGEE ALLSTARS – See FUGEES (REFUGEE CAMP); Wyclef JEAN

REFUGEE CAMP ALLSTARS featuring Lauryn HILL – See FUGEES (REFUGEE CAMP); Lauryn HILL

REFUGEE CREW – See FUGEES (REFUGEE CAMP); Brian HARVEY

Joan REGAN — UK

(See also All Star Hit Parade.)

SINGLES:	HITS 11			WEEKS 62
RICHOCHET	*Decca*	8	*12 Dec 53*	1
Originally recorded by Teresa Brewer.				
Above hit: Joan REGAN with the SQUADRONAIRES directed by Ronnie ALDRICH.				
RICHOCHET [RE]	*Decca*	9	*9 Jan 54*	4
SOMEONE ELSE'S ROSES	*Decca*	5	*15 May 54*	8
Originally recorded by Doris Day.				
IF I GIVE MY HEART TO YOU	*Decca*	20	*2 Oct 54*	1
IF I GIVE MY HEART TO YOU [RE]	*Decca*	3	*30 Oct 54*	10
WAIT FOR ME, DARLING	*Decca*	18	*6 Nov 54*	1
Above hit: Joan REGAN and the JOHNSTON BROTHERS.				
PRIZE OF GOLD	*Decca*	6	*26 Mar 55*	8
From the film of the same name.				
Above hit: Joan REGAN with Johnny DOUGLAS and his Orchestra.				
OPEN UP YOUR HEART	*Decca*	19	*7 May 55*	1
MAY YOU ALWAYS	*His Master's Voice*	9	*2 May 59*	16
HAPPY ANNIVERSARY	*Pye*	29	*6 Feb 60*	1
HAPPY ANNIVERSARY [RE]	*Pye*	29	*20 Feb 60*	1
PAPA LOVES MAMA	*Pye*	29	*30 Jul 60*	8
ONE OF THE LUCKY ONES	*Pye*	47	*26 Nov 60*	1

MUST BE SANTA	*Pye*	42	*7 Jan 61*	1
Above hit: Joan REGAN and DR. BARNARDO'S CHILDREN with the Peter KNIGHT ORCHESTRA.				

REGENTS — UK

SINGLES:	HITS 2			WEEKS 14
7 TEEN	*Rialto*	11	*22 Dec 79*	12
SEE YOU LATER	*Arista*	55	*7 Jun 80*	2

REGGAE BOYZ — Jamaica

SINGLES:	HITS 1			WEEKS 1
KICK IT	*Universal*	59	*27 Jun 98*	1
Features reggae rhythm section of Sly and Robbie.				

REGGAE PHILHARMONIC ORCHESTRA — UK

SINGLES:	HITS 2			WEEKS 11
MINNIE THE MOOCHER	*Mango*	35	*19 Nov 88*	9
LOVELY THING	*Mango*	71	*28 Jul 90*	2
Above hit: REGGAE PHILHARMONIC ORCHESTRA featuring JAZZY JOYCE.				

REGGAE REVOLUTION - See Pato BANTON

REGGIE - See TECHNOTRONIC

REGINA — US

SINGLES:	HITS 1			WEEKS 3
BABY LOVE	*Funkin' Marvellous*	50	*1 Feb 86*	3
Features backing vocals by Siedah Garrett and sax solo by David Sanborn.				

REID — UK

SINGLES:	HITS 4			WEEKS 12
ONE WAY OUT	*Syncopate*	66	*8 Oct 88*	2
REAL EMOTION	*Syncopate*	65	*11 Feb 89*	2
GOOD TIMES	*Syncopate*	55	*15 Apr 89*	6
LOVIN' ON THE SIDE	*Syncopate*	71	*21 Oct 89*	2

Ellen REID - See CRASH TEST DUMMIES

John REID - See NIGHTCRAWLERS featuring John REID

Junior REID - See COLDCUT; RAGGA TWINS; SOUP DRAGONS

Mike REID — UK

SINGLES:	HITS 2			WEEKS 10
THE UGLY DUCKLING	*Pye*	10	*22 Mar 75*	8
THE MORE I SEE YOU	*Telstar TV*	46	*24 Apr 99*	2
Above hit: Barbara WINDSOR and Mike REID.				

Neil REID — UK

SINGLES:	HITS 2			WEEKS 26
MOTHER OF MINE	*Decca*	2	*1 Jan 72*	20
THAT'S WHAT I WANT TO BE	*Decca*	49	*8 Apr 72*	1
THAT'S WHAT I WANT TO BE [RE]	*Decca*	45	*22 Apr 72*	5
ALBUMS:	**HITS 2**			**WEEKS 18**
NEIL REID	*Decca*	1	*5 Feb 72*	16
SMILE	*Decca*	47	*2 Sep 72*	2

DJ Patrick REID - See POB featuring DJ Patrick REID

Maggie REILLY - See Mike OLDFIELD

Joe REISMAN and his Orchestra - See Johnnie RAY; Sarah VAUGHAN

Keith RELF — UK

SINGLES:	HITS 1			WEEKS 1
MR. ZERO	*Columbia*	50	*28 May 66*	1
Original written and recorded by Bob Lind.				

REMBRANDTS — US

SINGLES:	HITS 2			WEEKS 28
I'LL BE THERE FOR YOU (THEME FROM "FRIENDS")	*East West America*	3	*2 Sep 95*	12
Theme from the TV series screened on Channel 4.				
THIS HOUSE IS NOT A HOME	*East West America*	58	*20 Jan 96*	1
I'LL BE THERE FOR YOU (THEME FROM "FRIENDS") [RE]	*East West America*	5	*24 May 97*	15
ALBUMS:	**HITS 1**			**WEEKS 5**
LP	*East West America*	14	*23 Sep 95*	5

REMO 4 - See Tommy QUICKLY and the REMO 4

RENAISSANCE — UK

SINGLES:	HITS 1			WEEKS 11
NORTHERN LIGHTS	*Warner Brothers*	10	*15 Jul 78*	11
ALBUMS:	**HITS 3**			**WEEKS 10**
RENAISSANCE	*Island*	60	*21 Feb 70*	1
A SONG FOR ALL SEASONS	*Warner Brothers*	35	*19 Aug 78*	8
AZUR D'OR	*Warner Brothers*	73	*2 Jun 79*	1

RENATO - See RENEE and RENATO

RENE and ANGELA — US

SINGLES:	HITS 3			WEEKS 15
SAVE YOUR LOVE (FOR # 1)	*Club*	66	*15 Jun 85*	2
Above hit: RENE and ANGELA with Kurtis BLOW.				
I'LL BE GOOD	*Club*	22	*7 Sep 85*	10
SECRET RENDEZVOUS	*Champion*	54	*2 Nov 85*	3

RENE and YVETTE featuring Gordon KAYE and Vicki MICHELLE — UK

SINGLES:	HITS 1			WEEKS 4
JE T'AIME (ALLO ALLO) / RENE D.M.C. (DEVASTATING MACHO CHARISMA)	*Sedition*	57	*22 Nov 86*	4

Nicole RENEE — US

SINGLES:	HITS 1			WEEKS 1
STRAWBERRY	*Atlantic*	55	*12 Dec 98*	1
Samples Grover Washington Jr's Paradise.				

RENEE and RENATO — UK/Italy

SINGLES:	HITS 2			WEEKS 22
SAVE YOUR LOVE	*Hollywood*	1	*30 Oct 82*	16
JUST ONE MORE KISS	*Hollywood*	48	*12 Feb 83*	6
ALBUMS:	**HITS 1**			**WEEKS 14**
SAVE YOUR LOVE	*Lifestyle*	26	*25 Dec 82*	14
Above hit: RENATO.				

RENEGADE SOUNDWAVE — UK

SINGLES:	HITS 2			WEEKS 7
PROBABLY A ROBBERY	*Mute*	38	*3 Feb 90*	6
RENEGADE SOUNDWAVE	*Mute*	64	*5 Feb 94*	1
ALBUMS:	**HITS 1**			**WEEKS 1**
SOUNDCLASH	*Mute*	74	*24 Mar 90*	1

REO SPEEDWAGON — US

SINGLES:	HITS 3			WEEKS 38
KEEP ON LOVING YOU	*Epic*	7	*11 Apr 81*	14
TAKE IT ON THE RUN	*Epic*	19	*27 Jun 81*	14
CAN'T FIGHT THIS FEELING	*Epic*	16	*16 Mar 85*	10
ALBUMS:	**HITS 2**			**WEEKS 36**
HI INFIDELITY	*Epic*	6	*25 Apr 81*	29
GOOD TROUBLE	*Epic*	29	*17 Jul 82*	7

REPARATA and the DELRONS — US

SINGLES:	HITS 2			WEEKS 12
CAPTAIN OF YOUR SHIP	*Bell*	13	*23 Mar 68*	10
SHOES	*Dart*	43	*18 Oct 75*	2
Originally recorded by the New Settlers as 'She Didn't Forget Her Shoes'.				
Above hit: REPARATA.				

REPLAYS - See Rocky SHARPE and the REPLAYS

REPRAZENT/Roni SIZE - See Roni SIZE REPRAZENT

REPUBLICA — UK

SINGLES:	HITS 3			WEEKS 18
READY TO GO	*Deconstruction*	43	*27 Apr 96*	2
READY TO GO [RI]	*Deconstruction*	13	*1 Mar 97*	6
DROP DEAD GORGEOUS	*Deconstruction*	7	*3 May 97*	7
From the film 'Scream'.				
FROM RUSH HOUR WITH LOVE	*Deconstruction*	20	*3 Oct 98*	3
ALBUMS:	**HITS 2**			**WEEKS 38**
REPUBLICA	*Deconstruction*	4	*15 Mar 97*	36
SPEED BALLADS	*Deconstruction*	37	*17 Oct 98*	2

RESONANCE featuring the BURRELLS — US

SINGLES:	HITS 1			WEEKS 1
DJ	*Strictly Rhythm UK*	67	*26 May 01*	1

REST ASSURED — UK

SINGLES:	HITS 1			WEEKS 7
TREAT INFAMY	*ffrr*	14	*28 Feb 98*	7

Taken from the string line of Verve's Bitter Sweet Symphony, which originally comes from an orchestral version of The Rolling Stones' The Last Time by Andrew Loog Oldham.

REUNION — US

SINGLES:	HITS 1			WEEKS 4
LIFE IS A ROCK (BUT THE RADIO ROLLED ME)	*RCA Victor*	33	*21 Sep 74*	4

REVILLOS – See REZILLOS

REVIVAL 3000 — UK

SINGLES:	HITS 1			WEEKS 1
THE MIGHTY HIGH	*Hi-Life*	47	*1 Nov 97*	1

REVOLTING COCKS — US

SINGLES:	HITS 1			WEEKS 1
DO YA THINK I'M SEXY?	*Devotion*	61	*18 Sep 93*	1
ALBUMS:	**HITS 1**			**WEEKS 1**
LINGER FICKEN' GOOD	*Devotion*	39	*2 Oct 93*	1

REVOLUTION – See PRINCE

Debbie REYNOLDS — US

SINGLES:	HITS 1			WEEKS 17
TAMMY	*Vogue Coral*	2	*31 Aug 57*	17

From the film 'Tammy And The Bachelor'.

Jody REYNOLDS — US

SINGLES:	HITS 1			WEEKS 1
ENDLESS SLEEP	*Lightning*	66	*14 Apr 79*	1

[AA] listed with To Know Him Is To Love Him by the Teddy Bears. Reached No. 5 in the US in 1958.

L.J. REYNOLDS — US

SINGLES:	HITS 1			WEEKS 3
DON'T LET NOBODY HOLD YOU DOWN	*Club*	53	*30 Jun 84*	3

REYNOLDS GIRLS — UK

SINGLES:	HITS 1			WEEKS 12
I'D RATHER JACK	*PWL*	8	*25 Feb 89*	12

REZILLOS — UK

SINGLES:	HITS 4			WEEKS 21
TOP OF THE POPS	*Sire*	17	*12 Aug 78*	9
DESTINATION VENUS	*Sire*	43	*25 Nov 78*	4
I WANNA BE YOUR MAN / I CAN'T STAND MY BABY	*Sensible*	71	*18 Aug 79*	1
I WANNA BE YOUR MAN / I CAN'T STAND MY BABY [RE]	*Sensible*	75	*1 Sep 79*	1
MOTORBIKE BEAT	*Dindisc*	45	*26 Jan 80*	6
Above hit: REVILLOS.				
ALBUMS:	**HITS 2**			**WEEKS 15**
CAN'T STAND THE REZILLOS	*Sire*	16	*5 Aug 78*	10
MISSION ACCOMPLISHED BUT THE BEAT GOES ON	*Sire*	30	*28 Apr 79*	5

RHODA with the SPECIAL A.K.A. – See SPECIALS

Busta RHYMES — US

(See also B Real, Busta Rhymes, Coolio, LL Cool J and Method Man; Flipmode Squad (starring Busta Rhymes, Baby Sham, Rah Digga and Spliff Star; Fugees (Refugee Camp); Levert Sweat Gill; M.O.P.)

SINGLES:	HITS 11			WEEKS 45
WOO-HAH!! GOT YOU ALL IN CHECK	*Elektra*	8	*11 May 96*	7
IT'S A PARTY	*Elektra*	23	*21 Sep 96*	2
Above hit: Busta RHYMES featuring ZHANE.				
DO MY THING	*Elektra*	39	*3 May 97*	1
PUT YOUR HANDS WHERE MY EYES COULD SEE	*Elektra*	16	*18 Oct 97*	3
DANGEROUS	*Elektra*	32	*20 Dec 97*	4
TURN IT UP (REMIX)/FIRE IT UP [M]	*Elektra*	2	*18 Apr 98*	10

ONE	*Elektra*	23	*11 Jul 98*	3
Above hit: Busta RHYMES (featuring Erykah BADU).				
GIMME SOME MORE	*Elektra*	5	*30 Jan 99*	6
WHAT'S IT GONNA BE?!	*Elektra*	6	*1 May 99*	7
Above hit: Busta RHYMES featuring JANET.				
GET OUT	*Elektra*	57	*22 Jul 00*	1
Samples The Ugly Duckling by the Richard Wolfe Children's Chorus.				
FIRE	*Elektra*	60	*16 Dec 00*	1

ALBUMS:	**HITS 5**			**WEEKS 20**
THE COMING	*Elektra*	48	*30 Mar 96*	4
WHEN DISASTER STRIKES	*Elektra*	34	*4 Oct 97*	5
EXTINCTION LEVEL EVENT/FINAL WORLD FRONT	*Elektra*	54	*16 Jan 99*	7
ANARCHY	*Elektra*	38	*1 Jul 00*	1
TURN IT UP! - THE VERY BEST OF BUSTA RHYMES	*Elektra*	44	*29 Sep 01*	3

RHYTHM BANGERS – See Robbie RIVERA pres. RHYTHM BANGERS

RHYTHIM IS RHYTHIM — US

SINGLES:	**HITS 1**			**WEEKS 1**
STRINGS OF LIFE '89	*Kool Kat*	74	*11 Nov 89*	1

RHYTHM ETERNITY — UK

SINGLES:	**HITS 1**			**WEEKS 1**
PINK CHAMPAGNE	*Dead Dead Good*	72	*23 May 92*	1

RHYTHM FACTOR — US

SINGLES:	**HITS 1**			**WEEKS 2**
YOU BRING ME JOY	*Multiply*	53	*29 Apr 95*	2

RHYTHM MASTERS — UK

SINGLES:	**HITS 3**			**WEEKS 3**
COME ON Y'ALL	*Faze 2*	49	*16 Aug 97*	1
Samples Todd Terry and Aretha Franklin.				
ENTER THE SCENE	*Distinct'ive*	49	*6 Dec 97*	1
Above hit: DJ SUPREME vs the RHYTHM MASTERS.				
UNDERGROUND	*Black & Blue*	50	*18 Aug 01*	1

RHYTHM-N-BASS — UK

SINGLES:	**HITS 2**			**WEEKS 4**
ROSES	*Epic*	56	*19 Sep 92*	2
CAN'T STOP THIS FEELING	*Epic*	59	*3 Jul 93*	2

RHYTHM OF LIFE — UK

SINGLES:	**HITS 1**			**WEEKS 2**
YOU PUT ME IN HEAVEN WITH YOUR TOUCH	*Xtravaganza*	24	*13 May 00*	2
Samples the original version of the track by Debbie Shaw.				

RHYTHM ON THE LOOSE — UK

SINGLES:	**HITS 1**			**WEEKS 2**
BREAK OF DAWN	*Six6*	36	*19 Aug 95*	2

RHYTHM QUEST — UK

SINGLES:	**HITS 1**			**WEEKS 2**
DREAMS [EP]	*Network*	45	*20 Jun 92*	2
Lead track: Closer To All Your Dreams. The EP title was not listed for the chart of 27 Jun 92.				

RHYTHM SECTION — UK

SINGLES:	**HITS 1**			**WEEKS 1**
MIDSUMMER MADNESS [EP]	*Rhythm Section*	66	*18 Jul 92*	1
Lead track: Dreamworld.				

RHYTHM SOURCE — UK

SINGLES:	**HITS 1**			**WEEKS 1**
LOVE SHINE	*A&M*	74	*17 Jun 95*	1

RHYTHMKILLAZ — Holland

SINGLES:	**HITS 1**			**WEEKS 2**
WACK ASS M.F.	*Incentive*	32	*31 Mar 01*	2

RHYTHMATIC — UK

SINGLES:	**HITS 2**			**WEEKS 3**
TAKE ME BACK	*Network*	74	*12 May 90*	1

TAKE ME BACK [RE]	*Network*	71	*26 May 90*	1
FREQUENCY	*Network*	62	*3 Nov 90*	1

RHYTHMATIC JUNKIES — UK

SINGLES:	HITS 1			WEEKS 1
THE FEELIN' (CLAP YOUR HANDS)	*Ride Recordings*	67	*15 May 99*	1

RIALTO — UK

SINGLES:	HITS 4			WEEKS 8
MONDAY MORNING 5:19	*East West*	37	*8 Nov 97*	2
UNTOUCHABLE	*East West*	20	*17 Jan 98*	3
DREAM ANOTHER DREAM	*East West*	39	*28 Mar 98*	2
SUMMER'S OVER	*China*	60	*17 Oct 98*	1
ALBUMS:	**HITS 1**			**WEEKS 3**
RIALTO	*China*	21	*25 Jul 98*	3

RIAS DANCE ORCHESTRA – See Caterina VALENTE

Reva RICE and Greg ELLIS — UK

SINGLES:	HITS 1			WEEKS 2
NEXT TIME YOU FALL IN LOVE *From the musical 'The New Starlight Express'.*	*Really Useful*	59	*27 Mar 93*	2

Charlie RICH — US

SINGLES:	HITS 3			WEEKS 29
THE MOST BEAUTIFUL GIRL *Originally recorded by Norro Wilson.*	*Epic*	2	*16 Feb 74*	14
BEHIND CLOSED DOORS *Originally recorded by Kenny O'Dell.*	*Epic*	16	*13 Apr 74*	10
WE LOVE EACH OTHER	*Epic*	37	*1 Feb 75*	5
ALBUMS:	**HITS 2**			**WEEKS 28**
BEHIND CLOSED DOORS	*Epic*	4	*23 Mar 74*	26
VERY SPECIAL LOVE SONGS	*Epic*	34	*13 Jul 74*	2

Kelli RICH – See NU SOUL featuring Kelli RICH

Richie RICH — UK

SINGLES:	HITS 6			WEEKS 16
TURN IT UP	*Club*	48	*16 Jul 88*	3
I'LL HOUSE YOU *Above hit: Richie RICH meets JUNGLE BROTHERS.*	*Gee Street*	22	*22 Oct 88*	5
MY DJ (PUMP IT UP SOME)	*Gee Street*	74	*10 Dec 88*	1
SALSA HOUSE	*ffrr*	50	*2 Sep 89*	3
YOU USED TO SALSA *Above hit: Richie RICH'S SALSA HOUSE (featuring Ralphi ROSARIO).*	*ffrr*	52	*9 Mar 91*	3
STAY WITH ME *Above hit: Richie RICH and Esera TUAOLO.*	*Castle Communications*	58	*29 Mar 97*	1
ALBUMS:	**HITS 1**			**WEEKS 1**
I CAN MAKE YOU DANCE	*Gee Street*	65	*22 Jul 89*	1

Tony RICH PROJECT — US

SINGLES:	HITS 3			WEEKS 22
NOBODY KNOWS	*LaFace*	4	*4 May 96*	17
LIKE A WOMAN	*LaFace*	27	*31 Aug 96*	4
LEAVIN'	*LaFace*	52	*14 Dec 96*	1
ALBUMS:	**HITS 1**			**WEEKS 10**
WORDS	*LaFace*	27	*25 May 96*	10

RICH IN PARADISE – See F.P.I. PROJECT

RICH KIDS — UK

SINGLES:	HITS 1			WEEKS 5
RICH KIDS	*EMI*	24	*28 Jan 78*	5
ALBUMS:	**HITS 1**			**WEEKS 1**
GHOSTS OF PRINCES IN TOWERS	*EMI*	51	*7 Oct 78*	1

Cliff RICHARD — UK

(See also Shadows; Various Artists: Stage Cast – London 'Heathcliff Live (The Show)'.)

SINGLES:	HITS 123			WEEKS 1147
MOVE IT! *The flip side Schoolboy Crush was originally to be the A-side.*	*Columbia*	2	*13 Sep 58*	17
HIGH CLASS BABY *Label reflects 'with' instead of 'and' The Drifters.*	*Columbia*	7	*22 Nov 58*	10

LIVIN' LOVIN' DOLL	*Columbia*	20	*31 Jan 59*	6
MEAN STREAK	*Columbia*	10	*9 May 59*	9
NEVER MIND	*Columbia*	21	*16 May 59*	2
Above 2 entries were separate sides of the same release, each had its own chart run.				
LIVING DOLL	*Columbia*	1	*11 Jul 59*	21
From the film 'Serious Charge'.				
Above 6: Cliff RICHARD and the DRIFTERS.				
TRAVELLIN' LIGHT	*Columbia*	1	*10 Oct 59*	17
DYNAMITE	*Columbia*	16	*10 Oct 59*	2
Above 2 entries were separate sides of the same release, each had its own chart run.				
DYNAMITE [RE]	*Columbia*	21	*31 Oct 59*	2
Above 3: Cliff RICHARD and the SHADOWS.				
LIVING DOLL [RE-1ST]	*Columbia*	26	*12 Dec 59*	1
LIVING DOLL [RE-2ND]	*Columbia*	28	*2 Jan 60*	1
Above 2: Cliff RICHARD and the DRIFTERS.				
EXPRESSO BONGO [EP]	*Columbia*	14	*16 Jan 60*	7
Lead track: Love. This charted at No. 1 on the EP chart when it began on 12 Mar 60. See EP section.				
A VOICE IN THE WILDERNESS	*Columbia*	2	*23 Jan 60*	14
Above 2 from the film 'Expresso Bongo'. This track is also on the Expresso Bongo EP.				
FALL IN LOVE WITH YOU	*Columbia*	2	*26 Mar 60*	15
A VOICE IN THE WILDERNESS [RE]	*Columbia*	36	*7 May 60*	2
PLEASE DON'T TEASE	*Columbia*	1	*2 Jul 60*	18
Song was chosen by members of his fan club from tracks just recorded as the best bet for a hit single.				
NINE TIMES OUT OF TEN	*Columbia*	3	*24 Sep 60*	12
The fans' third choice.				
I LOVE YOU	*Columbia*	1	*3 Dec 60*	16
THEME FOR A DREAM	*Columbia*	3	*4 Mar 61*	14
GEE WHIZ IT'S YOU	*Columbia*	4	*1 Apr 61*	14
Export single which sold enough in the UK to chart.				
A GIRL LIKE YOU	*Columbia*	3	*24 Jun 61*	14
Above 10: Cliff RICHARD and the SHADOWS.				
WHEN THE GIRL IN YOUR ARMS IS THE GIRL IN YOUR HEART	*Columbia*	3	*21 Oct 61*	15
Above hit: Cliff RICHARD with Norrie PARAMOR and his Orchestra				
THE YOUNG ONES	*Columbia*	1	*13 Jan 62*	21
Above 2 from the film 'The Young Ones'.				
Above hit: Cliff RICHARD and the SHADOWS.				
I'M LOOKIN' OUT THE WINDOW / DO YOU WANT TO DANCE	*Columbia*	2	*12 May 62*	17
I'm Looking Out The Window originally recorded by Peggy Lee; Do You Want To Dance originally recorded by Bobby Freeman, it reached No. 5 in the US in 1958.				
Above hit: Cliff RICHARD with the Norrie PARAMOR ORCHESTRA / Cliff RICHARD and the SHADOWS.				
IT'LL BE ME	*Columbia*	2	*8 Sep 62*	12
Originally recorded by Jerry Lee Lewis.				
Above hit: Cliff RICHARD and the SHADOWS.				
THE NEXT TIME / BACHELOR BOY	*Columbia*	1	*8 Dec 62*	18
Bachelor Boy listed from 12 Jan 63 and only credited to Cliff Richard and the Shadows.				
Above hit: Cliff RICHARD, the SHADOWS and the Norrie PARAMOR STRINGS.				
SUMMER HOLIDAY	*Columbia*	1	*23 Feb 63*	18
Above 2 from the film 'Summer Holiday'.				
Above hit: Cliff RICHARD and the SHADOWS and the Norrie PARAMOR STRINGS.				
LUCKY LIPS	*Columbia*	4	*11 May 63*	15
Original by Ruth Brown reached No. 25 in the US in 1957.				
Above hit: Cliff RICHARD and the SHADOWS.				
IT'S ALL IN THE GAME	*Columbia:*	2	*24 Aug 63*	13
DON'T TALK TO HIM	*Columbia*	2	*9 Nov 63*	13
I'M THE LONELY ONE	*Columbia*	8	*8 Feb 64*	10
DON'T TALK TO HIM [RE]	*Columbia*	50	*15 Feb 64*	1
Above 3: Cliff RICHARD and the SHADOWS.				
CONSTANTLY (L'EDERA)	*Columbia*	4	*2 May 64*	13
ON THE BEACH	*Columbia*	7	*4 Jul 64*	13
From the film 'Wonderful Life'.				
Above hit: Cliff RICHARD and the SHADOWS.				
THE TWELFTH OF NEVER	*Columbia*	8	*10 Oct 64*	11
Original by Johnny Mathis reached No. 9 in the US in 1957.				
I COULD EASILY FALL (IN LOVE WITH YOU)	*Columbia*	9	*12 Dec 64*	11
From the Pantomime 'Aladdin'.				
Above hit: Cliff RICHARD and the SHADOWS.				
THE MINUTE YOU'RE GONE	*Columbia*	1	*13 Mar 65*	14
Originally recorded by Sonny James.				
ON MY WORD	*Columbia*	12	*12 Jun 65*	10
THE TIME IN BETWEEN	*Columbia*	22	*21 Aug 65*	8
WIND ME UP (LET ME GO)	*Columbia*	2	*6 Nov 65*	16
BLUE TURNS TO GREY	*Columbia*	15	*26 Mar 66*	9
Written By Jagger/ Richards.				
Above 3: Cliff RICHARD and the SHADOWS				
VISIONS	*Columbia*	7	*23 Jul 66*	12
Used as the closing theme to his BBC TV series.				

Title	Label	Pos	Date	Wks
TIME DRAGS BY	*Columbia*	10	*15 Oct 66*	12
From the film 'Finders Keepers'.				
IN THE COUNTRY	*Columbia*	6	*17 Dec 66*	10
From the Pantomime 'Cinderella'.				
Above 2: Cliff RICHARD and the SHADOWS.				
IT'S ALL OVER	*Columbia*	9	*18 Mar 67*	10
Originally recorded by the Everly Brothers.				
Above hit: Cliff RICHARD with Bernard EBBINGHOUSE and his Orchestra.				
I'LL COME RUNNIN'	*Columbia*	26	*10 Jun 67*	8
Originally recorded by Neil Diamond.				
THE DAY I MET MARIE	*Columbia*	10	*19 Aug 67*	14
ALL MY LOVE	*Columbia*	6	*18 Nov 67*	12
Above hit: Cliff RICHARD with Bernard EBBINGHOUSE and his Orchestra.				
CONGRATULATIONS	*Columbia*	1	*23 Mar 68*	13
UK's Eurovision entry in 1968, It came 2nd.				
I'LL LOVE YOU FOREVER TODAY	*Columbia*	27	*29 Jun 68*	6
From the film 'Two A Penny'.				
MARIANNE	*Columbia*	22	*28 Sep 68*	8
Written by actor Bill Owen.				
DON'T FORGET TO CATCH ME	*Columbia*	21	*30 Nov 68*	10
Above hit: Cliff RICHARD and the SHADOWS.				
GOOD TIMES	*Columbia*	12	*1 Mar 69*	11
BIG SHIP	*Columbia*	8	*31 May 69*	10
THROW DOWN A LINE	*Columbia*	7	*13 Sep 69*	9
Above hit: CLIFF and HANK.				
WITH THE EYES OF A CHILD	*Columbia*	20	*6 Dec 69*	11
THE JOY OF LIVING	*Columbia*	25	*21 Feb 70*	8
Theme from the TV series of the same name.				
Above hit: CLIFF and HANK.				
GOODBYE SAM, HELLO SAMANTHA	*Columbia*	6	*6 Jun 70*	15
I AIN'T GOT TIME ANYMORE	*Columbia*	21	*5 Sep 70*	7
SUNNY HONEY GIRL	*Columbia*	19	*23 Jan 71*	8
SILVERY RAIN	*Columbia*	27	*10 Apr 71*	6
FLYING MACHINE	*Columbia*	37	*17 Jul 71*	7
SING A SONG OF FREEDOM	*Columbia*	13	*13 Nov 71*	12
JESUS	*Columbia*	35	*11 Mar 72*	3
LIVING IN HARMONY	*Columbia*	12	*26 Aug 72*	10
POWER TO ALL OUR FRIENDS	*EMI*	4	*17 Mar 73*	12
UK's Eurovision entry in 1973, It came 4th.				
HELP IT ALONG / TOMORROW RISING	*EMI*	29	*12 May 73*	6
These were the only listed tracks on a 4 track EP of Eurovision entry songs for 1973.				
TAKE ME HIGH	*EMI*	27	*1 Dec 73*	12
Theme from the film of the same name.				
(YOU KEEP ME) HANGIN' ON	*EMI*	13	*18 May 74*	8
MISS YOU NIGHTS	*EMI*	15	*7 Feb 76*	10
DEVIL WOMAN	*EMI*	9	*8 May 76*	8
Originally recorded by Kristine.				
I CAN'T ASK FOR ANYMORE THAN YOU	*EMI*	17	*21 Aug 76*	8
Originally recorded by Ian Sinclair.				
HEY MR. DREAM MAKER	*EMI*	31	*4 Dec 76*	6
MY KINDA LIFE	*EMI*	15	*5 Mar 77*	8
WHEN TWO WORLDS DRIFT APART	*EMI*	46	*16 Jul 77*	3
GREEN LIGHT	*EMI*	57	*31 Mar 79*	3
WE DON'T TALK ANYMORE	*EMI*	1	*21 Jul 79*	14
HOT SHOT	*EMI*	46	*3 Nov 79*	5
CARRIE	*EMI*	4	*2 Feb 80*	10
DREAMIN'	*EMI*	8	*16 Aug 80*	10
Co-written by Leo Sayer.				
SUDDENLY	*Jet*	15	*25 Oct 80*	7
From the film 'Xanadu'.				
Above hit: Olivia NEWTON-JOHN with Cliff RICHARD.				
A LITTLE IN LOVE	*EMI*	15	*24 Jan 81*	8
WIRED FOR SOUND	*EMI*	4	*29 Aug 81*	9
DADDY'S HOME	*EMI*	2	*21 Nov 81*	12
Original by Shep and the Limelites reached No. 2 in the US in 1961. It was an answer song to the Heartbeats' A Thousand Miles Away.				
THE ONLY WAY OUT	*EMI*	10	*17 Jul 82*	9
WHERE DO WE GO FROM HERE	*EMI*	60	*25 Sep 82*	3
LITTLE TOWN	*EMI*	11	*4 Dec 82*	7
Update of the Christmas carol O Little Town Of Bethlehem.				
Above hit: Cliff RICHARD featuring Tony RIVERS and Nigel PERRIN.				
SHE MEANS NOTHING TO ME	*Capitol*	9	*19 Feb 83*	9
Above hit: Phil EVERLY / Cliff RICHARD.				
TRUE LOVE WAYS	*EMI*	8	*16 Apr 83*	8
Live recording.				
Above hit: Cliff RICHARD with the LONDON PHILHARMONIC ORCHESTRA.				
DRIFTING	*DJM*	64	*4 Jun 83*	2
Above hit: Sheila WALSH and Cliff RICHARD.				

Title	Label	Pos	Date	Wks
NEVER SAY DIE (GIVE A LITTLE BIT MORE)	*EMI*	15	*3 Sep 83*	7
PLEASE DON'T FALL IN LOVE	*EMI*	7	*26 Nov 83*	9
BABY YOU'RE DYNAMITE / OCEAN DEEP	*EMI*	27	*31 Mar 84*	6
Ocean Deep listed from 28 Apr 84 once it had dropped to No. 41.				
OCEAN DEEP / BABY YOU'RE DYNAMITE [RE]	*EMI*	72	*19 May 84*	1
SHOOTING FROM THE HEART	*EMI*	51	*3 Nov 84*	4
HEART USER	*EMI*	46	*9 Feb 85*	3
SHE'S SO BEAUTIFUL	*EMI*	17	*14 Sep 85*	9
All instruments played by Stevie Wonder.				
IT'S IN EVERY ONE OF US	*EMI*	45	*7 Dec 85*	6
Above 2 from Dave Clarke's musical 'Time'.				
LIVING DOLL	*WEA*	1	*22 Mar 86*	11
Charity record to support projects in Africa and Britain.				
Above hit: COMIC RELIEF presents Cliff RICHARD and the YOUNG ONES featuring Hank MARVIN.				
ALL I ASK OF YOU	*Polydor*	3	*4 Oct 86*	16
From the Andrew Lloyd Webber musical 'The Phantom Of The Opera'.				
Above hit: Cliff RICHARD and Sarah BRIGHTMAN with the ROYAL PHILHARMONIC ORCHESTRA conducted by David CADDICK.				
SLOW RIVERS	*Rocket*	44	*29 Nov 86*	8
Above hit: Elton JOHN and Cliff RICHARD.				
MY PRETTY ONE	*EMI*	6	*20 Jun 87*	10
Originally recorded by Jamie Rae.				
SOME PEOPLE	*EMI*	3	*29 Aug 87*	10
REMEMBER ME	*EMI*	35	*31 Oct 87*	4
TWO HEARTS	*EMI*	34	*13 Feb 88*	3
MISTLETOE AND WINE	*EMI*	1	*3 Dec 88*	8
Originally recorded by Twiggy.				
THE BEST OF ME	*EMI*	2	*10 Jun 89*	7
Cliff's 100th single. Written by Richard Marx and originally recorded by David Foster and Olivia Newton-John.				
I JUST DON'T HAVE THE HEART	*EMI*	3	*26 Aug 89*	8
Written and produced by Stock, Aitken and Waterman				
LEAN ON YOU	*EMI*	17	*14 Oct 89*	6
WHENEVER GOD SHINES HIS LIGHT	*Polydor*	20	*9 Dec 89*	6
Above hit: Van MORRISON with Cliff RICHARD.				
STRONGER THAN THAT	*EMI*	14	*24 Feb 90*	5
SILHOUETTES	*EMI*	10	*25 Aug 90*	7
FROM A DISTANCE	*EMI*	11	*13 Oct 90*	6
Above 2 are live recordings from Wembley Stadium earlier in the year.				
SAVIOURS DAY	*EMI*	1	*8 Dec 90*	7
MORE TO LIFE	*EMI*	23	*14 Sep 91*	5
Theme from the BBC1 TV series 'Trainer'.				
WE SHOULD BE TOGETHER	*EMI*	10	*7 Dec 91*	6
THIS NEW YEAR	*EMI*	30	*11 Jan 92*	2
I STILL BELIEVE IN YOU	*EMI*	7	*5 Dec 92*	6
PEACE IN OUR TIME	*EMI*	8	*27 Mar 93*	5
HUMAN WORK OF ART	*EMI*	24	*12 Jun 93*	4
NEVER LET GO	*EMI*	32	*2 Oct 93*	3
HEALING LOVE	*EMI*	19	*18 Dec 93*	5
ALL I HAVE TO DO IS DREAM / MISS YOU NIGHTS [RI]	*EMI*	14	*10 Dec 94*	6
Above hit: Cliff RICHARD (with Phil EVERLY) / Cliff RICHARD.				
ALL I HAVE TO DO IS DREAM / MISS YOU NIGHTS [RI] [RE]	*EMI*	58	*25 Feb 95*	3
MISUNDERSTOOD MAN	*EMI*	19	*21 Oct 95*	3
HAD TO BE	*EMI*	22	*9 Dec 95*	4
Above hit: Cliff RICHARD with Olivia NEWTON-JOHN.				
THE WEDDING	*EMI*	40	*30 Mar 96*	1
Above hit: Cliff RICHARD with Helen HOBSON.				
BE WITH ME ALWAYS	*EMI*	52	*25 Jan 97*	1
Above 4 from the musical 'Heathcliff'.				
CAN'T KEEP THIS FEELING IN	*EMI*	10	*24 Oct 98*	4
THE MIRACLE	*EMI*	23	*7 Aug 99*	2
Features backing vocals by James Ingram and Siedah Garrett.				
THE MILLENNIUM PRAYER	*Papillon*	1	*27 Nov 99*	16
Combines The Lord's Prayer with the tune of Auld Lang Syne. Charity record in aid of Children's Promise, The Millennium Final Hour Appeal.				
SOMEWHERE OVER THE RAINBOW/WHAT A WONDERFUL WORLD [M]	*Papillon*	11	*15 Dec 01*	3
Originally recorded by Judy Garland/Louis Armstrong.				

EPS:	**HITS 22**			**WEEKS 432**
CLIFF SINGS NO. 1	*Columbia*	4	*12 Mar 60*	18
EXPRESSO BONGO [OST]	*Columbia*	1	*12 Mar 60*	28
CLIFF SINGS NO. 2	*Columbia*	3	*19 Mar 60*	36
Above 3: Cliff RICHARD and the SHADOWS.				
CLIFF SINGS NO. 3	*Columbia*	2	*4 Jun 60*	15
CLIFF'S SILVER DISCS	*Columbia*	1	*10 Dec 60*	57
ME AND MY SHADOWS NO. 1	*Columbia*	5	*11 Feb 61*	23
ME AND MY SHADOWS NO. 2	*Columbia*	8	*29 Apr 61*	4
ME AND MY SHADOWS NO. 3	*Columbia*	6	*29 Apr 61*	11

LISTEN TO CLIFF NO. 1	*Columbia*	17	*4 Nov 61*	2
DREAM	*Columbia*	3	*18 Nov 61*	51
CLIFF'S HIT PARADE	*Columbia*	4	*10 Feb 62*	42
HITS FROM 'THE YOUNG ONES'	*Columbia*	1	*14 Apr 62*	40
CLIFF RICHARD NO. 2	*Columbia*	19	*23 Jun 62*	2
HOLIDAY CARNIVAL	*Columbia*	1	*18 May 63*	22
HITS FROM 'SUMMER HOLIDAY'	*Columbia*	4	*15 Jun 63*	21
CLIFF'S LUCKY LIPS	*Columbia*	17	*19 Oct 63*	5
Above 12: Cliff RICHARD and the SHADOWS.				
LOVE SONGS	*Columbia*	4	*16 Nov 63*	15
CLIFF SINGS 'DON'T TALK TO HIM'	*Columbia*	15	*30 May 64*	1
WONDERFUL LIFE	*Columbia*	3	*15 Aug 64*	21
CLIFF'S HITS FROM 'ALADDIN AND HIS WONDERFUL LAMP'	*Columbia*	20	*22 May 65*	1
Songs from the 1964 Pantomime.				
Above 3: Cliff RICHARD and the SHADOWS.				
LOOK IN MY EYES, MARIA	*Columbia*	15	*24 Jul 65*	1
TAKE FOUR	*Columbia*	4	*2 Oct 65*	16
Above hit: Cliff RICHARD and the SHADOWS.				
ALBUMS:	**HITS 55**			**WEEKS 799**
CLIFF	*Columbia*	4	*18 Apr 59*	31
Above hit: Cliff RICHARD and the DRIFTERS.				
CLIFF SINGS	*Columbia*	2	*14 Nov 59*	36
ME AND MY SHADOWS	*Columbia*	2	*15 Oct 60*	33
LISTEN TO CLIFF	*Columbia*	2	*22 Apr 61*	28
I'M 21 TODAY	*Columbia*	1	*21 Oct 61*	16
Above 4: Cliff RICHARD and the SHADOWS.				
THE YOUNG ONES [OST]	*Columbia*	1	*23 Dec 61*	42
Tracks also credit Robert Morley, Carole Gray, the Associated British Studio Orchestra with the Michael Sammes Singers, Norrie Paramor and his Orchestra.				
Above hit: Cliff RICHARD - the SHADOWS with Grazina FRAME.				
32 MINUTES AND 17 SECONDS	*Columbia*	3	*29 Sep 62*	21
SUMMER HOLIDAY [OST]	*Columbia*	1	*26 Jan 63*	36
Tracks also credit the Associated British Studio Orchestra conducted by Stanley Black, the Michael Sammes Singers, the Norrie Paramor Strings, Guest Singer Grazina Frame.				
CLIFF'S HIT ALBUM	*Columbia*	2	*13 Jul 63*	19
WHEN IN SPAIN	*Columbia*	8	*28 Sep 63*	10
Songs recorded in Spanish at studios located in Barcelona.				
WONDERFUL LIFE [OST]	*Columbia*	2	*11 Jul 64*	23
ALADDIN AND HIS WONDERFUL LAMP	*Columbia*	13	*9 Jan 65*	5
From the pantomime that opened at the London Palladium, Dec 63. Cast included Arthur Askey and Una Stubbs.				
Above 6: Cliff RICHARD and the SHADOWS.				
CLIFF RICHARD	*Columbia*	9	*17 Apr 65*	5
MORE HITS BY CLIFF	*Columbia*	20	*14 Aug 65*	1
LOVE IS FOREVER	*Columbia*	19	*8 Jan 66*	1
Collection of romantic ballads.				
Above 2: Cliff RICHARD and the SHADOWS.				
KINDA LATIN	*Columbia*	9	*21 May 66*	12
FINDERS KEEPERS [OST]	*Columbia*	6	*17 Dec 66*	18
CINDERELLA	*Columbia*	30	*7 Jan 67*	6
From the pantomime that opened at the London Palladium, Dec 66.				
Above 2: Cliff RICHARD and the SHADOWS.				
DON'T STOP ME NOW . . .	*Columbia*	23	*15 Apr 67*	9
GOOD NEWS	*Columbia*	37	*11 Nov 67*	1
Gospel album.				
CLIFF IN JAPAN	*Columbia*	29	*1 Jun 68*	2
Live recordings from the Sankei Hall, Tokyo.				
ESTABLISHED 1958	*Columbia*	30	*16 Nov 68*	4
Album divided between tracks recorded by Cliff and The Shadows. Released to celebrate their 10th Anniversary.				
THE BEST OF CLIFF	*Columbia*	5	*12 Jul 69*	17
Above 2: Cliff RICHARD and the SHADOWS.				
SINCERELY	*Columbia*	24	*27 Sep 69*	3
TRACKS 'N' GROOVES	*Columbia*	37	*12 Dec 70*	2
THE BEST OF CLIFF VOLUME 2	*Columbia*	49	*23 Dec 72*	2
Above hit: Cliff RICHARD and the SHADOWS.				
TAKE ME HIGH [OST]	*EMI*	41	*19 Jan 74*	4
I'M NEARLY FAMOUS	*EMI*	5	*29 May 76*	21
EVERY FACE TELLS A STORY	*EMI*	8	*26 Mar 77*	10
40 GOLDEN GREATS	*EMI*	1	*22 Oct 77*	19
Above hit: Cliff RICHARD and the SHADOWS.				
SMALL CORNERS	*EMI*	33	*4 Mar 78*	5
Gospel album.				
GREEN LIGHT	*EMI*	25	*21 Oct 78*	3
THANK YOU VERY MUCH - REUNION CONCERT AT THE LONDON PALLADIUM	*EMI*	5	*17 Feb 79*	12
Live recordings from their concerts, Feb 78.				
Above hit: Cliff RICHARD and the SHADOWS.				

ROCK 'N' ROLL JUVENILE	*EMI*	3	*15 Sep 79*	22
I'M NO HERO	*EMI*	4	*13 Sep 80*	12
LOVE SONGS	*EMI*	1	*4 Jul 81*	43
The Shadows appear on some of the tracks.				
WIRED FOR SOUND	*EMI*	4	*26 Sep 81*	25
NOW YOU SEE ME . . . NOW YOU DON'T	*EMI*	4	*4 Sep 82*	14
DRESSED FOR THE OCCASION	*EMI*	7	*21 May 83*	17
Live recordings.				
Above hit: Cliff RICHARD and the LONDON PHILHARMONIC ORCHESTRA.				
SILVER	*EMI*	7	*15 Oct 83*	18
Released as a boxed-set.				
SILVER [RE]	*EMI*	28	*7 Apr 84*	6
Re-released with standard packaging.				
20 ORIGINAL GREATS	*EMI*	43	*14 Jul 84*	6
The Shadows appear on some of the tracks.				
THE ROCK CONNECTION	*EMI*	43	*1 Dec 84*	5
ALWAYS GUARANTEED	*EMI*	5	*26 Sep 87*	25
PRIVATE COLLECTION 1979 - 1988	*EMI*	1	*19 Nov 88*	26
Compilation of his favourite tracks.				
STRONGER	*EMI*	7	*11 Nov 89*	21
FROM A DISTANCE . . . . .THE EVENT	*EMI*	3	*17 Nov 90*	15
Live recordings from Wembley Stadium earlier in the year. The first disc of the album is a collaboration with the Oh! Boy team which includes the Dallas Boys, Kalin Twins and the Vernon Girls.				
TOGETHER WITH CLIFF RICHARD	*EMI*	10	*30 Nov 91*	7
CLIFF RICHARD - THE ALBUM	*EMI*	1	*1 May 93*	15
THE HIT LIST	*EMI*	3	*15 Oct 94*	21
Compilation to celebrate his 35th Anniversary in the music business.				
SONGS FROM "HEATHCLIFF"	*EMI*	15	*11 Nov 95*	9
Musical project based on the novel by Emily Bronte.				
CLIFF AT THE MOVIES - 1959-1974	*EMI*	17	*24 Aug 96*	3
Tracks from his movies.				
THE ROCK 'N' ROLL YEARS	*EMI*	32	*2 Aug 97*	3
Features rarities and unreleased live versions.				
REAL AS I WANNA BE	*EMI*	10	*31 Oct 98*	9
THE WHOLE STORY - HIS GREATEST HITS	*EMI*	6	*21 Oct 00*	13
WANTED	*Papillon*	11	*17 Nov 01*	7

Wendy RICHARD - See Mike SARNE

Keith RICHARDS — UK

ALBUMS:	HITS 2			WEEKS 4
TALK IS CHEAP	*Virgin*	37	*15 Oct 88*	3
MAIN OFFENDER	*Virgin America*	45	*31 Oct 92*	1

Neil RICHARDSON ORCHESTRA - See Iris WILLIAMS

Lionel RICHIE — US

SINGLES:	HITS 24			WEEKS 182
ENDLESS LOVE	*Motown*	7	*12 Sep 81*	12
From the film of the same name.				
Above hit: Diana ROSS and Lionel RICHIE.				
TRULY	*Motown*	6	*20 Nov 82*	11
YOU ARE	*Motown*	43	*29 Jan 83*	7
MY LOVE	*Motown*	70	*7 May 83*	3
ALL NIGHT LONG (ALL NIGHT)	*Motown*	2	*1 Oct 83*	16
RUNNING WITH THE NIGHT	*Motown*	9	*3 Dec 83*	12
HELLO	*Motown*	1	*10 Mar 84*	15
Above 2 feature backing vocals by Richard Marx.				
STUCK ON YOU	*Motown*	12	*23 Jun 84*	12
PENNY LOVER	*Motown*	18	*20 Oct 84*	7
SAY YOU, SAY ME (TITLE SONG FROM "WHITE NIGHTS")	*Motown*	8	*16 Nov 85*	11
From the film.				
DANCING ON THE CEILING	*Motown*	7	*26 Jul 86*	11
LOVE WILL CONQUER ALL	*Motown*	45	*11 Oct 86*	5
BALLERINA GIRL / DEEP RIVER WOMAN	*Motown*	17	*20 Dec 86*	8
Deep River Woman listed from 17 Jan 87.				
Above hit: Lionel RICHIE / Lionel RICHIE Background vocals: ALABAMA.				
SELA	*Motown*	43	*28 Mar 87*	6
DO IT TO ME	*Motown*	33	*9 May 92*	6
MY DESTINY	*Motown*	7	*22 Aug 92*	13
LOVE, OH LOVE	*Motown*	52	*28 Nov 92*	3
LOVE, OH LOVE [RE]	*Motown*	73	*26 Dec 92*	1
DON'T WANNA LOSE YOU	*Mercury*	17	*6 Apr 96*	5
STILL IN LOVE	*Mercury*	66	*23 Nov 96*	1
CLOSEST THING TO HEAVEN	*Mercury*	26	*27 Jun 98*	2
ANGEL	*Mercury*	18	*21 Oct 00*	5
DON'T STOP THE MUSIC	*Mercury*	34	*23 Dec 00*	5

TENDER HEART	*Mercury*	29	*17 Mar 01*	3
I FORGOT	*Mercury*	34	*23 Jun 01*	2
ALBUMS:	**HITS 8**			**WEEKS 419**
LIONEL RICHIE	*Motown*	9	*27 Nov 82*	86
CAN'T SLOW DOWN	*Motown*	1	*29 Oct 83*	154
DANCING ON THE CEILING	*Motown*	2	*23 Aug 86*	53
BACK TO FRONT	*Motown*	1	*6 Jun 92*	74
Includes re-entries through to 2001. Includes 4 tracks with the Commodores.				
LOUDER THAN WORDS	*Mercury*	11	*20 Apr 96*	5
TRULY - THE LOVE SONGS	*Motown*	5	*31 Jan 98*	21
Includes his recordings with the Commodores and Diana Ross.				
TIME	*Mercury*	31	*11 Jul 98*	3
RENAISSANCE	*Mercury*	6	*28 Oct 00*	22

Jonathan RICHMAN and the MODERN LOVERS — US

SINGLES:	**HITS 3**			**WEEKS 27**
ROADRUNNER	*Beserkley*	11	*16 Jul 77*	9
A-side by Jonathan Richman. B-side by the Modern Lovers.				
EGYPTIAN REGGAE	*Beserkley*	5	*29 Oct 77*	14
THE MORNING OF OUR LIVES	*Beserkley*	29	*21 Jan 78*	4
Live recording. Sleeve only credits the Modern Lovers.				
ALBUMS:	**HITS 1**			**WEEKS 3**
ROCK 'N' ROLL WITH THE MODERN LOVERS	*Beserkeley*	50	*27 Aug 77*	3

RICHMOND STRINGS with the Mike SAMMES SINGERS — UK

(See also Mike Sammes Singers.)

ALBUMS:	**HITS 1**			**WEEKS 7**
MUSIC OF AMERICA	*Ronco*	18	*17 Jan 76*	7

Svatoslav RICHTER - See Herbert VON KARAJAN conducting the BERLIN PHILHARMONIC ORCHESTRA

Adam RICKITT — UK

SINGLES:	**HITS 3**			**WEEKS 19**
I BREATHE AGAIN	*Polydor*	5	*26 Jun 99*	10
EVERYTHING MY HEART DESIRES	*Polydor*	15	*16 Oct 99*	6
BEST THING	*Polydor*	25	*5 Feb 00*	3
ALBUMS:	**HITS 1**			**WEEKS 1**
GOOD TIMES	*Polydor*	41	*30 Oct 99*	1

RICO - See SPECIALS

Frank RICOTTI ALL STARS — UK

ALBUMS:	**HITS 1**			**WEEKS 3**
COMPILATION ALBUMS:	**HITS 1**			**WEEKS 5**
THE BEIDERBECKE COLLECTION	*Dormouse*	89	*24 Dec 88*	2
THE BEIDERBECKE COLLECTION	*Dormouse*	14	*14 Jan 89*	5
Incorrectly included in the Compilation chart.				
THE BEIDERBECKE COLLECTION [RE]	*Dormouse*	73	*26 Jun 93*	1

RIDDELLE SINGERS - See Ronnie HILTON

Nelson RIDDLE and his Orchestra - See Shirley BASSEY; Nat 'King' COLE; FOUR KNIGHTS; Linda RONSTADT; Frank SINATRA; Kiri TE KANAWA

RIDE — UK

SINGLES:	**HITS 10**			**WEEKS 22**
RIDE [EP]	*Creation*	71	*27 Jan 90*	2
Lead track: Chelsea Girl.				
PLAY [EP]	*Creation*	32	*14 Apr 90*	3
Lead track: Like A Daydream.				
FALL [EP]	*Creation*	34	*29 Sep 90*	3
Lead track: Dreams Burn Down.				
TODAY FOREVER [EP]	*Creation*	14	*16 Mar 91*	4
Lead track: Today Forever.				
LEAVE THEM ALL BEHIND	*Creation*	9	*15 Feb 92*	3
TWISTERELLA	*Creation*	36	*25 Apr 92*	2
BIRDMAN	*Creation*	38	*30 Apr 94*	2
HOW DOES IT FEEL TO FEEL?	*Creation*	58	*25 Jun 94*	1
Originally recorded by the Creation in 1968.				
I DON'T KNOW WHERE IT COMES FROM	*Creation*	46	*8 Oct 94*	1
Features the Christchurch Cathedral Choir.				
BLACK NITE CRASH	*Creation*	67	*24 Feb 96*	1
ALBUMS:	**HITS 4**			**WEEKS 16**
NOWHERE	*Creation*	11	*27 Oct 90*	5
GOING BLANK AGAIN	*Creation*	5	*21 Mar 92*	5

CARNIVAL OF LIGHT	*Creation*	5	*2 Jul 94*	4
TARANTULA	*Creation*	21	*23 Mar 96*	2

Andrew RIDGELEY — UK

SINGLES:	HITS 1			WEEKS 3
SHAKE	*Epic*	58	*31 Mar 90*	3

Stan RIDGWAY — US

SINGLES:	HITS 1			WEEKS 12
CAMOUFLAGE	*I.R.S.*	4	*5 Jul 86*	12

RIES - See TILLMAN and RIES

Andre RIEU — Holland

ALBUMS:	HITS 1			WEEKS 2
CELEBRATION!	*Philips*	51	*22 Apr 00*	2

RIGHEIRA — Italy

SINGLES:	HITS 1			WEEKS 3
VAMOS A LA PLAYA	*A&M*	53	*24 Sep 83*	3

RIGHT SAID FRED — UK

SINGLES:	HITS 9			WEEKS 66
I'M TOO SEXY	*Tug*	2	*27 Jul 91*	16
DON'T TALK JUST KISS	*Tug*	3	*7 Dec 91*	11
Above hit: RIGHT SAID FRED guest vocal Jocelyn BROWN.				
DEEPLY DIPPY	*Tug*	1	*21 Mar 92*	14
THOSE SIMPLE THINGS / (WHAT A DAY FOR A) DAYDREAM	*Tug*	29	*1 Aug 92*	5
STICK IT OUT	*Tug*	4	*27 Feb 93*	7
Charity Record for Comic Relief's Red Nose day (12 Mar 93). Friends are Hugh Laurie, Peter Cook, Alan Freeman, Jools Holland, Steve Coogan, Clive Anderson, Linda Robson, Pauline Quirke, Sir Basil Brush and Bernard Cribbins.				
Above hit: RIGHT SAID FRED and FRIENDS.				
BUMPED	*Tug*	32	*23 Oct 93*	4
HANDS UP (4 LOVERS)	*Tug*	60	*18 Dec 93*	3
WONDERMAN	*Tug*	55	*19 Mar 94*	1
Featured in the Sega Sonic 3 TV commercial.				
YOU'RE MY MATE	*Kingsize*	18	*13 Oct 01*	5
ALBUMS:	**HITS 2**			**WEEKS 53**
UP	*Tug*	1	*28 Mar 92*	49
SEX AND TRAVEL	*Tug*	35	*13 Nov 93*	4

RIGHTEOUS BROTHERS — US

SINGLES:	HITS 7			WEEKS 86
YOU'VE LOST THAT LOVIN' FEELIN'	*London*	1	*16 Jan 65*	10
UNCHAINED MELODY	*London*	14	*14 Aug 65*	12
Originally recorded by Alex North as an instrumental.				
EBB TIDE	*London*	48	*15 Jan 66*	2
Originally recorded by Robert Maxwell.				
(YOU'RE MY) SOUL AND INSPIRATION	*Verve*	15	*16 Apr 66*	10
THE WHITE CLIFFS OF DOVER	*London*	21	*12 Nov 66*	9
ISLAND IN THE SUN	*Verve*	36	*24 Dec 66*	5
YOU'VE LOST THAT LOVIN' FEELIN' [RI-1ST]	*London*	10	*15 Feb 69*	11
YOU'VE LOST THAT LOVIN' FEELIN' [RI-2ND]	*Phil Spector International*	42	*19 Nov 77*	4
UNCHAINED MELODY [RI]	*Verve*	1	*27 Oct 90*	14
From the film 'Ghosts'.				
YOU'VE LOST THAT LOVIN' FEELING [RI-3RD] / EBB TIDE [RI]	*Verve*	3	*15 Dec 90*	9
Ebb Tide listed from 22 Dec 90.				
ALBUMS:	**HITS 1**			**WEEKS 17**
THE VERY BEST OF THE RIGHTEOUS BROTHERS: UNCHAINED MELODY	*Verve*	11	*1 Dec 90*	17

Cheryl Pepsi RILEY — US

SINGLES:	HITS 1			WEEKS 1
THANKS FOR MY CHILD	*CBS*	75	*28 Jan 89*	1

Jeannie C. RILEY — US

SINGLES:	HITS 1			WEEKS 15
HARPER VALLEY P. T. A.	*Polydor*	12	*19 Oct 68*	15
Originally recorded by Tom T. Hall.				

Teddy RILEY featuring Tammy LUCAS — US

(See also Blackstreet.)

SINGLES:	HITS 1			WEEKS 2
IS IT GOOD TO YOU	*MCA*	53	*21 Mar 92*	2

RIMES featuring Shaila PROSPERE — UK

SINGLES:	HITS 1			WEEKS 1
IT'S OVER	*Universal*	51	*22 May 99*	1
Original by Oddyssey was the B-side of Use It Up And Wear It Out.				

LeAnn RIMES — US

SINGLES:	HITS 7			WEEKS 77
HOW DO I LIVE	*Curb*	7	*7 Mar 98*	33
LOOKING THROUGH YOUR EYES / COMMITMENT	*Curb*	38	*12 Sep 98*	2
From the film 'The Magic Sword: Quest For Camelot'.				
HOW DO I LIVE [RE]	*Curb*	72	*31 Oct 98*	1
BLUE	*Curb*	23	*12 Dec 98*	6
Written for Patsy Cline who died before she could record it				
WRITTEN IN THE STARS	*Rocket*	10	*6 Mar 99*	7
From the Walt Disney film 'Aida'.				
Above hit: Elton JOHN and LeAnn RIMES.				
WRITTEN IN THE STARS [RE]	*Rocket*	63	*22 May 99*	1
CRAZY	*Curb*	36	*18 Dec 99*	3
CAN'T FIGHT THE MOONLIGHT - THEME FROM 'COYOTE UGLY'	*Curb*	1	*25 Nov 00*	17
I NEED YOU	*Curb*	13	*31 Mar 01*	6
I NEED YOU [RE]	*Curb*	75	*19 May 01*	1

ALBUMS:	HITS 2			WEEKS 37
SITTIN' ON TOP OF THE WORLD	*Curb*	11	*6 Jun 98*	22
I NEED YOU	*Curb*	7	*14 Apr 01*	15

RIMSHOTS — US

SINGLES:	HITS 1			WEEKS 5
7-6-5-4-3-2-1 (BLOW YOUR WHISTLE)	*All Platinum*	26	*19 Jul 75*	5
Originally recorded by Blue Mink.				

RIO and MARS — UK/France

SINGLES:	HITS 1			WEEKS 3
BOY I GOTTA HAVE YOU	*Dome*	43	*28 Jan 95*	2
BOY I GOTTA HAVE YOU [RI]	*Feverpitch*	46	*13 Apr 96*	1

Miguel RIOS — Spain

SINGLES:	HITS 1			WEEKS 12
SONG OF JOY	*A&M*	16	*11 Jul 70*	12
Adapted from the last movement of Beethoven's Ninth Symphony. Conducted by Waldo de los Rios and his Orchestra.				

RIP RIG AND PANIC — UK/US

ALBUMS:	HITS 1			WEEKS 3
I AM COLD	*Virgin*	67	*26 Jun 82*	3

Minnie RIPERTON — US

SINGLES:	HITS 1			WEEKS 10
LOVIN' YOU	*Epic*	2	*12 Apr 75*	10

ALBUMS:	HITS 1			WEEKS 3
PERFECT ANGEL	*Epic*	33	*17 May 75*	3

Angela RIPPON — UK

ALBUMS:	HITS 1			WEEKS 26
SHAPE UP AND DANCE FEATURING ANGELA RIPPON (VOLUME II)	*Lifestyle*	8	*17 Apr 82*	26

RISE — UK

SINGLES:	HITS 1			WEEKS 1
THE SINGLE	*East West*	70	*3 Sep 94*	1
Features rappers Hawkeye and Anita from Yo Yo Honey.				

RITCHIE FAMILY — US

SINGLES:	HITS 3			WEEKS 19
BRAZIL	*Polydor*	41	*23 Aug 75*	4
Originally recorded by Eddy Duchin in 1942.				
THE BEST DISCO IN TOWN	*Polydor*	10	*18 Sep 76*	9
AMERICAN GENERATION	*Mercury*	49	*17 Feb 79*	6

Lee RITENOUR with Maxi PRIEST — US/UK

(See also Maxi Priest.)

SINGLES:	HITS 1			WEEKS 2
WAITING IN VAIN	GRP	65	*31 Jul 93*	2

Tex RITTER — US

SINGLES:	HITS 1			WEEKS 14
THE WAYWARD WIND	*Capitol*	8	*23 Jun 56*	14
EPS:	**HITS 1**			**WEEKS 1**
DECK OF CARDS	*Capitol*	19	*8 Dec 62*	1

RIVA featuring Dannii MONOGUE — Holland/Australia

(See also Dannii Minogue.)

SINGLES:	HITS 1			WEEKS 5
WHO DO YOU LOVE NOW? (STRINGER)	*Double F Double R*	3	*1 Dec 01*	5

Paco RIVAZ – See GAMBAFREAKS

RIVER CITY PEOPLE — UK

SINGLES:	HITS 6			WEEKS 27
(WHAT'S WRONG WITH) DREAMING?	*EMI*	70	*12 Aug 89*	3
WALKING ON ICE	*EMI*	62	*3 Mar 90*	2
CARRY THE BLAME / CALIFORNIA DREAMIN'	*EMI*	13	*30 Jun 90*	10
From 4 Aug 90 titles were listed in reverse.				
(WHAT'S WRONG WITH) DREAMING? [RI]	*EMI*	40	*22 Sep 90*	3
WHEN I WAS YOUNG	*EMI*	62	*2 Mar 91*	2
SPECIAL WAY	*EMI*	44	*28 Sep 91*	3
STANDING IN THE NEED OF LOVE	*EMI*	36	*22 Feb 92*	4
ALBUMS:	**HITS 2**			**WEEKS 10**
SAY SOMETHING GOOD	*EMI*	23	*25 Aug 90*	9
THIS IS THE WORLD	*EMI*	56	*2 Nov 91*	1

RIVER DETECTIVES — UK

SINGLES:	HITS 1			WEEKS 4
CHAINS	*WEA*	51	*29 Jul 89*	4
ALBUMS:	**HITS 1**			**WEEKS 1**
SATURDAY NIGHT SUNDAY MORNING	*WEA*	51	*23 Sep 89*	1

RIVER OCEAN featuring INDIA — UK

(See also Masters At Work present India; Nuyorican Soul.)

SINGLES:	HITS 1			WEEKS 2
LOVE AND HAPPINESS (YEMAYA Y OCHUN)	*Cooltempo*	50	*26 Feb 94*	2

Robbie RIVERA pres. RHYTHM BANGERS — US

SINGLES:	HITS 1			WEEKS 7
BANG	*Multiply*	13	*2 Sep 00*	7

Danny RIVERS — UK

SINGLES:	HITS 1			WEEKS 3
CAN'T YOU HEAR MY HEART	*Decca*	36	*14 Jan 61*	3

Tony RIVERS and Nigel PERRIN – See Cliff RICHARD

RM PROJECT — UK

SINGLES:	HITS 1			WEEKS 1
GET IT UP	*Inferno*	49	*3 Jul 99*	1
Vocals by Triple A.				

David ROACH — UK

ALBUMS:	HITS 1			WEEKS 1
I LOVE SAX	*Nouveau Music*	73	*14 Apr 84*	1

ROACH MOTEL — UK

SINGLES:	HITS 2			WEEKS 2
AFRO SLEEZE / TRANSATLANTIC	*Junior Boy's Own*	73	*21 Aug 93*	1
HAPPY BIZZNESS / WILD LUV	*Junior Boy's Own*	75	*10 Dec 94*	1

ROACHFORD — UK

SINGLES:	HITS 12			WEEKS 61
CUDDLY TOY	*CBS*	61	*18 Jun 88*	4
CUDDLY TOY [RI]	*CBS*	4	*14 Jan 89*	9

FAMILY MAN	*CBS*	25	*18 Mar 89*	6
KATHLEEN	*CBS*	43	*1 Jul 89*	5
GET READY!	*Columbia*	22	*13 Apr 91*	8
ONLY TO BE WITH YOU	*Columbia*	21	*19 Mar 94*	7
LAY YOUR LOVE ON ME	*Columbia*	36	*18 Jun 94*	5
THIS GENERATION	*Columbia*	38	*20 Aug 94*	4
CRY FOR ME	*Columbia*	46	*3 Dec 94*	2
I KNOW YOU DON'T LOVE ME	*Columbia*	42	*1 Apr 95*	2
THE WAY I FEEL	*Columbia*	20	*11 Oct 97*	4
HOW COULD I? (INSECURITY)	*Columbia*	34	*14 Feb 98*	3
NAKED WITHOUT YOU	*Columbia*	53	*11 Jul 98*	2
ALBUMS:	**HITS 4**			**WEEKS 56**
ROACHFORD	*CBS*	69	*23 Jul 88*	3
ROACHFORD [RE]	*CBS*	11	*11 Feb 89*	24
GET READY!	*Columbia*	20	*18 May 91*	5
PERMANENT SHADE OF BLUE	*Columbia*	25	*16 Apr 94*	21
FEEL	*Columbia*	19	*25 Oct 97*	3

ROB 'N' RAZ — Sweden

SINGLES:	**HITS 2**			**WEEKS 17**
GOT TO GET *Above hit: ROB 'N' RAZ featuring Leila K.*	*Arista*	8	*25 Nov 89*	14
ROK THE NATION *Above hit: ROB 'N' RAZ with Leila K.*	*Arista*	41	*17 Mar 90*	3

Natalie ROBB - See PARTIZAN

Kate ROBBINS and BEYOND — UK

SINGLES:	**HITS 1**			**WEEKS 10**
MORE THAN IN LOVE *Featured in the ATV soap 'Crossroads'.*	*RCA*	2	*30 May 81*	10

Marty ROBBINS — US

SINGLES:	**HITS 4**			**WEEKS 33**
EL PASO	*Fontana*	19	*30 Jan 60*	8
EL PASO [RE]	*Fontana*	44	*9 Apr 60*	1
BIG IRON	*Fontana*	48	*28 May 60*	1
DEVIL WOMAN	*CBS*	5	*29 Sep 62*	17
RUBY ANN	*CBS*	24	*19 Jan 63*	6
ALBUMS:	**HITS 2**			**WEEKS 15**
GUNFIGHTER BALLADS AND TRAIL SONGS	*Fontana*	20	*13 Aug 60*	1
MARTY ROBBINS COLLECTION	*Lotus*	5	*10 Feb 79*	14

Antoinette ROBERSON - See PULSE featuring Antoinette ROBERSON

Austin ROBERTS — US

SINGLES:	**HITS 1**			**WEEKS 7**
ROCKY	*Private Stock*	22	*25 Oct 75*	7

Joe ROBERTS — UK

SINGLES:	**HITS 5**			**WEEKS 17**
BACK IN MY LIFE	*London*	59	*28 Aug 93*	1
LOVER	*ffrr*	22	*29 Jan 94*	5
BACK IN MY LIFE [RI]	*ffrr*	39	*14 May 94*	3
ADORE *Prince's original version appeared on his 1987 album Sign 'O' The Times.*	*ffrr*	45	*6 Aug 94*	3
YOU ARE EVERYTHING *Original by the Stylistics reached No. 9 in the US in 1971.* *Above hit: Melanie WILLIAMS and Joe ROBERTS.*	*Columbia*	28	*18 Feb 95*	4
HAPPY DAYS *Above hit: SWEET MERCY featuring Joe ROBERTS.*	*Grass Green*	63	*24 Feb 96*	1

Juliet ROBERTS — UK

(See also David Morales.)

SINGLES:	**HITS 6**			**WEEKS 34**
CAUGHT IN THE MIDDLE	*Cooltempo*	24	*31 Jul 93*	6
FREE LOVE *Original release reached No. 83 in 1992.*	*Cooltempo*	25	*6 Nov 93*	3
AGAIN / I WANT YOU	*Cooltempo*	33	*19 Mar 94*	3
CAUGHT IN THE MIDDLE (MY HEART BEATS LIKE A DRUM) [RM] *Remixed by David Morales and Peter 'Ski' Schwartz.*	*Cooltempo*	14	*2 Jul 94*	5
I WANT YOU [RI]	*Cooltempo*	28	*15 Oct 94*	3
SO GOOD / FREE LOVE 98 [RM] *Free Love remixed by Bumpy Sunday.*	*Delirious*	15	*31 Jan 98*	4
BAD GIRLS / I LIKE	*Delirious*	17	*23 Jan 99*	5

ALBUMS:	HITS 1			WEEKS 1
NATURAL THING	*Cooltempo*	65	*2 Apr 94*	1

Malcolm ROBERTS — UK

SINGLES:	HITS 3			WEEKS 29
TIME ALONE WILL TELL	*RCA Victor*	45	*13 May 67*	2
MAY I HAVE THE NEXT DREAM WITH YOU	*Major Minor*	8	*2 Nov 68*	14
MAY I HAVE THE NEXT DREAM WITH YOU [RE]	*Major Minor*	45	*15 Feb 69*	1
LOVE IS ALL	*Major Minor*	12	*22 Nov 69*	12

Paddy ROBERTS — South Africa

EPS:	HITS 2			WEEKS 90
STRICTLY FOR GROWN-UPS	*Decca*	1	*12 Mar 60*	66
PADDY ROBERTS STRIKES AGAIN	*Decca*	1	*30 Jul 60*	24
ALBUMS:	**HITS 2**			**WEEKS 6**
STRICTLY FOR GROWN-UPS	*Decca*	8	*26 Sep 59*	5
PADDY ROBERTS TRIES AGAIN	*Decca*	16	*17 Sep 60*	1

B.A. ROBERTSON — UK

SINGLES:	HITS 6			WEEKS 60
BANG BANG	*Asylum*	2	*28 Jul 79*	12
KNOCKED IT OFF	*Asylum*	8	*27 Oct 79*	12
KOOL IN THE KAFTAN	*Asylum*	17	*1 Mar 80*	12
TO BE OR NOT TO BE	*Asylum*	9	*31 May 80*	11
HOLD ME	*Swan Song*	11	*17 Oct 81*	8
Above hit: B.A. ROBERTSON and Maggie BELL.				
TIME	*Epic*	45	*17 Dec 83*	5
Above hit: FRIDA and B.A. ROBERTSON.				
ALBUMS:	**HITS 2**			**WEEKS 10**
INITIAL SUCCESS	*Asylum*	32	*29 Mar 80*	8
BULLY FOR YOU	*Asylum*	61	*4 Apr 81*	2

Don ROBERTSON — US

SINGLES:	HITS 1			WEEKS 9
THE HAPPY WHISTLER	*Capitol*	8	*12 May 56*	9

Robbie ROBERTSON — Canada

SINGLES:	HITS 2			WEEKS 11
SOMEWHERE DOWN THE CRAZY RIVER	*Geffen*	15	*23 Jul 88*	10
TAKE YOUR PARTNER BY THE HAND	*Polydor*	74	*11 Apr 98*	1
Above hit: Howie B featuring Robbie ROBERTSON.				
ALBUMS:	**HITS 2**			**WEEKS 16**
ROBBIE ROBERTSON	*Geffen*	52	*14 Nov 87*	3
ROBBIE ROBERTSON [RE]	*Geffen*	23	*13 Aug 88*	11
STORYVILLE	*Geffen*	30	*12 Oct 91*	2

Ivo ROBIC und die SING-MASTERS — Yugoslavia

SINGLES:	HITS 1			WEEKS 1
MORGEN (ONE MORE SUNRISE) SLOW-FOX	*Polydor*	23	*7 Nov 59*	1

ROBIN – See MUPPETS

Dawn ROBINSON – See Nas ESCOBAR, Foxy BROWN, AZ and NATURE present the FIRM featuring Dawn ROBINSON

Floyd ROBINSON — US

SINGLES:	HITS 1			WEEKS 9
MAKIN' LOVE	*RCA*	9	*17 Oct 59*	9

Smokey ROBINSON — US

(See also Miracles; Diana Ross, Marvin Gaye, Smokey Robinson and Stevie Wonder.)

SINGLES:	HITS 5			WEEKS 40
JUST MY SOUL RESPONDING	*Tamla Motown*	35	*23 Feb 74*	6
BEING WITH YOU	*Motown*	1	*9 May 81*	13
TELL ME TOMORROW	*Motown*	51	*13 Mar 82*	4
JUST TO SEE HER	*Motown*	52	*28 Mar 87*	6
INDESTRUCTIBLE [RM]	*Arista*	55	*17 Sep 88*	4
Remixed by Phil Harding and Ian Curnow.				
INDESTRUCTIBLE	*Arista*	30	*25 Feb 89*	7
This was actually the original US recording, it charted after the UK mix. Smokey Robinson was only credited on the back of the sleeves of both releases.				
Above 2: FOUR TOPS featuring Smokey ROBINSON.				
ALBUMS:	**HITS 3**			**WEEKS 21**
BEING WITH YOU	*Motown*	17	*20 Jun 81*	10

LOVE SONGS	*Telstar*	69	*12 Nov 88*	9
Compilation divided between the two artists.				
Above hit: Marvin GAYE and Smokey ROBINSON.				
THE GREATEST HITS	*PolyGram TV*	65	*14 Nov 92*	2
Includes both Smokey Robinson's solo and group material.				
Above hit: Smokey ROBINSON and the MIRACLES.				

Tom ROBINSON BAND — UK

SINGLES:	HITS 7			WEEKS 41
2. 4. 6. 8. MOTORWAY	*EMI*	5	*22 Oct 77*	9
RISING FREE [EP]	*EMI*	18	*18 Feb 78*	6
Lead track: Don't Take No For An Answer. This track was listed on the chart of 18 Feb 78, EP title listed on 25 Feb 78 and the track Sing If You're Glad To Be Gay on 4 Mar 78.				
UP AGAINST THE WALL	*EMI*	33	*13 May 78*	6
BULLY FOR YOU	*EMI*	68	*17 Mar 79*	2
WAR BABY	*Panic*	6	*25 Jun 83*	9
LISTEN TO THE RADIO: ATMOSPHERICS	*Panic*	39	*12 Nov 83*	6
RIKKI DON'T LOSE THAT NUMBER	*Castaway*	58	*15 Sep 84*	3
Above 3: Tom ROBINSON.				

ALBUMS:	HITS 3			WEEKS 23
POWER IN THE DARKNESS	*EMI*	4	*3 Jun 78*	12
TRB2	*EMI*	18	*24 Mar 79*	6
HOPE AND GLORY	*Castaway*	21	*29 Sep 84*	5
Above hit: Tom ROBINSON.				

Vicki Sue ROBINSON — US

SINGLES:	HITS 1			WEEKS 1
HOUSE OF JOY	*Logic*	48	*27 Sep 97*	1

ROBO BABE - See SIR KILLALOT V ROBO BABE

ROBSON and JEROME — UK

SINGLES:	HITS 3			WEEKS 45
UNCHAINED MELODY / (THERE'LL BE BLUEBIRDS OVER) THE WHITE CLIFFS OF DOVER	*RCA*	1	*20 May 95*	17
Unchained Melody originally recorded by Alex North as an instrumental.				
Above hit: Robson GREEN and Jerome FLYNN.				
I BELIEVE / UP ON THE ROOF	*RCA*	1	*11 Nov 95*	14
WHAT BECOMES OF THE BROKEN HEARTED / SATURDAY NIGHT AT THE MOVIES / YOU'LL NEVER WALK ALONE	*RCA*	1	*9 Nov 96*	14

ALBUMS:	HITS 3			WEEKS 53
ROBSON & JEROME	*RCA*	1	*25 Nov 95*	31
TAKE TWO	*RCA*	1	*23 Nov 96*	16
HAPPY DAYS - THE BEST OF ROBSON AND JEROME	*RCA*	20	*29 Nov 97*	6

ROBYN — Sweden

SINGLES:	HITS 4			WEEKS 14
YOU'VE GOT THAT SOMETHIN'	*RCA*	54	*20 Jul 96*	1
DO YOU KNOW (WHAT IT TAKES)	*RCA*	26	*16 Aug 97*	3
SHOW ME LOVE	*RCA*	8	*7 Mar 98*	6
DO YOU REALLY WANT ME	*RCA*	20	*30 May 98*	4

John ROCCA - See FREEEZ

ROCHELLE — US

SINGLES:	HITS 1			WEEKS 6
MY MAGIC MAN	*Warner Brothers*	27	*1 Feb 86*	6

ROCK - See Wyclef JEAN

Chubb ROCK — US

SINGLES:	HITS 1			WEEKS 1
TREAT 'EM RIGHT	*Champion*	67	*19 Jan 91*	1

Pete ROCK and C.L. SMOOTH — US

ALBUMS:	HITS 1			WEEKS 1
THE MAIN INGREDIENT	*Elektra*	69	*19 Nov 94*	1

ROCK AID ARMEMIA — UK

SINGLES:	HITS 1			WEEKS 5
SMOKE ON THE WATER	*Life Aid Armenia*	39	*16 Dec 89*	5

ROCK CANDY — UK

SINGLES:	HITS 1			WEEKS 6
REMEMBER	*MCA*	32	*11 Sep 71*	6

ROCK GODDESS — UK

SINGLES:	HITS 2			WEEKS 5
MY ANGEL	*A&M*	64	*5 Mar 83*	2
I DIDN'T KNOW I LOVED YOU (TILL I SAW YOU ROCK 'N' ROLL)	*A&M*	57	*24 Mar 84*	3
ALBUMS:	**HITS 2**			**WEEKS 3**
ROCK GODDESS	*A&M*	65	*12 Mar 83*	2
HELL HATH NO FURY	*A&M*	84	*29 Oct 83*	1

Roland ROCKCAKE and his WHOLLY ROLLERS – See GOONS

ROCKERS REVENGE featuring Donnie CALVIN — US

SINGLES:	HITS 2			WEEKS 20
WALKING ON SUNSHINE *Originally recorded by Eddy Grant.*	*London*	4	*14 Aug 82*	13
THE HARDER THEY COME	*London*	30	*29 Jan 83*	7

ROCKET FROM THE CRYPT — US

SINGLES:	HITS 4			WEEKS 7
BORN IN '69	*Elemental*	68	*27 Jan 96*	1
YOUNG LIVERS	*Elemental*	67	*13 Apr 96*	1
ON A ROPE	*Elemental*	12	*14 Sep 96*	4
LIPSTICK	*Elemental*	64	*29 Aug 98*	1
ALBUMS:	**HITS 2**			**WEEKS 4**
SCREAM, DRACULA, SCREAM!	*Elemental*	41	*3 Feb 96*	3
RFTC	*Elemental*	63	*18 Jul 98*	1

ROCKETS – See Tony CROMBIE and his ROCKETS

ROCKFORD FILES — UK

SINGLES:	HITS 1			WEEKS 4
YOU SEXY DANCER	*Escapade*	34	*11 Mar 95*	3
YOU SEXY DANCER [RI]	*Escapade*	59	*6 Apr 96*	1

ROCKIN' BERRIES — UK

SINGLES:	HITS 6			WEEKS 41
I DIDN'T MEAN TO HURT YOU	*Piccadilly*	43	*3 Oct 64*	1
HE'S IN TOWN *Originally recorded by the Tokens.*	*Piccadilly*	3	*17 Oct 64*	13
WHAT IN THE WORLD'S COME OVER YOU	*Piccadilly*	23	*23 Jan 65*	7
POOR MAN'S SON *Originally recorded by the Reflections.*	*Piccadilly*	5	*15 May 65*	11
YOU'RE MY GIRL	*Piccadilly*	40	*28 Aug 65*	7
THE WATER IS OVER MY HEAD	*Piccadilly*	43	*8 Jan 66*	1
THE WATER IS OVER MY HEAD [RE]	*Piccadilly*	50	*22 Jan 66*	1
ALBUMS:	**HITS 1**			**WEEKS 1**
IN TOWN	*Pye*	15	*19 Jun 65*	1

ROCKINGBIRDS – See VARIOUS ARTISTS (EPs) 'The Fred EP'

ROCKNEY – See CHAS and DAVE

ROCKPILE — UK

(See also Dave Edmunds.)

ALBUMS:	HITS 1			WEEKS 5
SECONDS OF PLEASURE	*F-Beat*	34	*18 Oct 80*	5

ROCKSTEADY CREW — US

SINGLES:	HITS 2			WEEKS 16
(HEY YOU) THE ROCKSTEADY CREW	*Charisma*	6	*1 Oct 83*	12
UPROCK	*Charisma*	64	*5 May 84*	4
ALBUMS:	**HITS 1**			**WEEKS 1**
READY FOR BATTLE	*Charisma*	73	*16 Jun 84*	1

ROCKWELL — US

SINGLES:	HITS 1			WEEKS 11
SOMEBODY'S WATCHING ME *Backing vocals by Michael Jackson.*	*Motown*	6	*4 Feb 84*	11
ALBUMS:	**HITS 1**			**WEEKS 5**
SOMEBODY'S WATCHING ME	*Motown*	52	*25 Feb 84*	5

"ROCKY V" featuring Joey B. ELLIS and Tynetta HARE – See Joey B. ELLIS

ROCOCO — UK/Italy

SINGLES:	HITS 1			WEEKS 5
ITALO HOUSE MIX [M]	*Mercury*	54	*16 Dec 89*	5

RODEO JONES — UK/Granada

SINGLES:	HITS 2			WEEKS 2
NATURAL WORLD	*A&M*	75	*30 Jan 93*	1
SHADES OF SUMMER	*A&M*	59	*3 Apr 93*	1

Clodagh RODGERS — Ireland

SINGLES:	HITS 6			WEEKS 59
COME BACK AND SHAKE ME	*RCA Victor*	3	*29 Mar 69*	14
GOODNIGHT MIDNIGHT	*RCA Victor*	4	*12 Jul 69*	11
GOODNIGHT MIDNIGHT [RE]	*RCA Victor*	48	*4 Oct 69*	1
BILJO	*RCA Victor*	22	*8 Nov 69*	9
EVERYBODY GO HOME THE PARTY'S OVER	*RCA Victor*	47	*4 Apr 70*	2
JACK IN THE BOX	*RCA Victor*	4	*20 Mar 71*	10
UK's Eurovision entry in 1971, it came 4th.				
LADY LOVE BUG	*RCA Victor*	28	*9 Oct 71*	12
ALBUMS:	**HITS 1**			**WEEKS 1**
CLODAGH RODGERS	*RCA Victor*	27	*13 Sep 69*	1

Eric RODGERS and his ORCHESTRA – See Max BYGRAVES

Jimmy RODGERS — US

SINGLES:	HITS 5			WEEKS 37
HONEY COMB	*Columbia*	30	*2 Nov 57*	1
Originally recorded by Georgie Shaw.				
KISSES SWEETER THAN WINE	*Columbia*	7	*21 Dec 57*	11
Originally recorded by the Weavers.				
Above 2: Jimmy RODGERS with Hugo PERETTI and his Orchestra.				
OH-OH, I'M FALLING IN LOVE AGAIN	*Columbia*	18	*29 Mar 58*	6
WOMAN FROM LIBERIA	*Columbia*	18	*20 Dec 58*	6
ENGLISH COUNTRY GARDEN	*Columbia*	5	*16 Jun 62*	13

Paul RODGERS — UK

SINGLES:	HITS 1			WEEKS 2
MUDDY WATER BLUES	*Victory*	45	*12 Feb 94*	2
ALBUMS:	**HITS 2**			**WEEKS 11**
MUDDY WATER BLUES	*Victory*	9	*3 Jul 93*	7
Tribute to blues guitarist Muddy Waters.				
NOW	*SPV Recordings*	30	*15 Feb 97*	4

RODRIGUEZ – See SASH!

RODS – See EDDIE and the HOT RODS

RODS — US

ALBUMS:	HITS 1			WEEKS 4
WILD DOGS	*Arista*	75	*24 Jul 82*	4

Tommy ROE — US

SINGLES:	HITS 6			WEEKS 74
SHEILA	*His Master's Voice*	3	*8 Sep 62*	14
SUSIE DARLIN'	*His Master's Voice*	37	*8 Dec 62*	5
THE FOLK SINGER	*His Master's Voice*	4	*23 Mar 63*	13
EVERYBODY	*His Master's Voice*	9	*28 Sep 63*	11
EVERYBODY [RE]	*His Master's Voice*	49	*21 Dec 63*	3
DIZZY	*Stateside*	1	*19 Apr 69*	19
HEATHER HONEY	*Stateside*	24	*26 Jul 69*	9

ROFO — UK

SINGLES:	HITS 1			WEEKS 3
ROFO'S THEME	*PWL Continental*	44	*1 Aug 92*	3

ROGER — US

SINGLES:	HITS 3			WEEKS 8
I WANT TO BE YOUR MAN	*Reprise*	61	*17 Oct 87*	4
BOOM! THERE SHE WAS	*Virgin*	55	*12 Nov 88*	3
Above hit: SCRITTI POLITTI featuring ROGER.				
HIGH AS A KITE	*ffrr*	55	*13 May 95*	1
Above hit: ONE TRIBE featuring ROGER.				

Julie ROGERS — UK

SINGLES:	HITS 3			WEEKS 38
THE WEDDING (LA NOVIA)	*Mercury*	3	*15 Aug 64*	23
Originally recorded by Anita Bryant.				
Above hit: Julie ROGERS with Johnny ARTHEY and his Orchestra and Chorus.				
LIKE A CHILD	*Mercury*	21	*12 Dec 64*	9
HAWAIIAN WEDDING SONG	*Mercury*	31	*27 Mar 65*	6

Kenny ROGERS — US

SINGLES:	HITS 10			WEEKS 109
RUBY, DON'T TAKE YOUR LOVE TO TOWN	*Reprise*	2	*18 Oct 69*	23
Originally recorded by Johnny Darrell.				
SOMETHING'S BURNING	*Reprise*	8	*7 Feb 70*	14
Originally recorded by Mac Davis.				
Above 2: Kenny ROGERS and the FIRST EDITION.				
LUCILLE	*United Artists*	1	*30 Apr 77*	14
Originally recorded by Johnny Darrell.				
DAYTIME FRIENDS	*United Artists*	39	*17 Sep 77*	4
SHE BELIEVES IN ME	*United Artists*	42	*2 Jun 79*	7
Originally recorded by Steve Gibb.				
COWARD OF THE COUNTY	*United Artists*	1	*26 Jan 80*	12
LADY	*United Artists*	12	*15 Nov 80*	12
Written and originally recorded by Lionel Richie.				
WE'VE GOT TONIGHT	*Liberty*	28	*12 Feb 83*	7
Above hit: Kenny ROGERS and Sheena EASTON.				
EYES THAT SEE IN THE DARK	*RCA*	61	*22 Oct 83*	1
ISLANDS IN THE STREAM	*RCA*	7	*12 Nov 83*	15
Written by the Bee Gees.				
Above hit: Kenny ROGERS duet with Dolly PARTON.				

ALBUMS:	HITS 10			WEEKS 111
KENNY ROGERS	*United Artists*	14	*18 Jun 77*	7
THE KENNY ROGERS SINGLES ALBUM	*United Artists*	12	*6 Oct 79*	22
KENNY	*United Artists*	7	*9 Feb 80*	10
LADY	*Liberty*	40	*31 Jan 81*	5
EYES THAT SEE IN THE DARK	*RCA*	53	*1 Oct 83*	19
WHAT ABOUT ME?	*RCA*	97	*27 Oct 84*	1
THE KENNY ROGERS STORY	*Liberty*	4	*27 Jul 85*	29
DAYTIME FRIENDS - THE VERY BEST OF KENNY ROGERS	*EMI*	16	*25 Sep 93*	5
LOVE SONGS	*Virgin*	27	*22 Nov 97*	7
ALL THE HITS & ALL NEW LOVE SONGS	*EMI*	11	*29 May 99*	6

ROKOTTO — UK

SINGLES:	HITS 2			WEEKS 10
BOOGIE ON UP	*State*	40	*22 Oct 77*	4
FUNK THEORY	*State*	49	*10 Jun 78*	6

ROLLERGIRL — Germany

SINGLES:	HITS 1			WEEKS 3
DEAR JESSIE	*Neo*	22	*16 Sep 00*	3

ROLLING STONES — UK

SINGLES:	HITS 46			WEEKS 366
COME ON	*Decca*	21	*27 Jul 63*	14
Originally recorded by Chuck Berry.				
I WANNA BE YOUR MAN	*Decca*	12	*16 Nov 63*	16
Written by Lennon/McCartney				
NOT FADE AWAY	*Decca*	3	*29 Feb 64*	15
IT'S ALL OVER NOW	*Decca*	1	*4 Jul 64*	15
Originally recorded by the Valentinos.				
LITTLE RED ROOSTER	*Decca*	1	*21 Nov 64*	12
Originally recorded by Willie Dixon and Howlin' Wolf.				
THE LAST TIME	*Decca*	1	*6 Mar 65*	13
(I CAN'T GET NO) SATISFACTION	*Decca*	1	*28 Aug 65*	12
GET OFF OF MY CLOUD	*Decca*	1	*30 Oct 65*	12
19TH NERVOUS BREAKDOWN	*Decca*	2	*12 Feb 66*	8
PAINT IT, BLACK	*Decca*	1	*21 May 66*	10
HAVE YOU SEEN YOUR MOTHER BABY, STANDING IN THE SHADOW?	*Decca*	5	*1 Oct 66*	8
LET'S SPEND THE NIGHT TOGETHER / RUBY TUESDAY	*Decca*	3	*21 Jan 67*	10
WE LOVE YOU / DANDELION	*Decca*	8	*26 Aug 67*	8
Backing vocals by John Lennon and Paul McCartney.				
JUMPIN' JACK FLASH	*Decca*	1	*1 Jun 68*	11
HONKY TONK WOMEN	*Decca*	1	*12 Jul 69*	17
BROWN SUGAR / BITCH/LET IT ROCK	*Rolling Stones*	2	*24 Apr 71*	13
Let It Rock originally recorded by Chuck Berry.				

STREET FIGHTING MAN	*Decca*	21	*3 Jul 71*	8
TUMBLING DICE	*Rolling Stones*	5	*29 Apr 72*	8
ANGIE	*Rolling Stones*	5	*1 Sep 73*	10
Written about Angie Bowie.				
IT'S ONLY ROCK 'N ROLL	*Rolling Stones*	10	*3 Aug 74*	7
OUT OF TIME	*Decca*	45	*20 Sep 75*	2
FOOL TO CRY	*Rolling Stones*	6	*1 May 76*	10
MISS YOU / FARAWAY EYES	*Rolling Stones*	3	*3 Jun 78*	13
Faraway Eyes listed from 15 Jul 78 once single had dropped to No. 10.				
RESPECTABLE	*Rolling Stones*	23	*30 Sep 78*	9
EMOTIONAL RESCUE	*Rolling Stones*	9	*5 Jul 80*	8
SHE'S SO COLD	*Rolling Stones*	33	*4 Oct 80*	6
START ME UP	*Rolling Stones*	7	*29 Aug 81*	9
WAITING ON A FRIEND	*Rolling Stones*	50	*12 Dec 81*	6
GOING TO A GO GO (LIVE)	*Rolling Stones*	26	*12 Jun 82*	6
TIME IS ON MY SIDE (LIVE)	*Rolling Stones*	62	*2 Oct 82*	2
Above 2 are live recordings from the American Concerts in 1981.				
UNDERCOVER OF THE NIGHT	*Rolling Stones*	11	*12 Nov 83*	9
SHE WAS HOT	*Rolling Stones*	42	*11 Feb 84*	4
BROWN SUGAR [RI]	*Rolling Stones*	58	*21 Jul 84*	2
HARLEM SHUFFLE	*Rolling Stones*	13	*15 Mar 86*	7
MIXED EMOTIONS	*Rolling Stones*	36	*2 Sep 89*	5
ROCK AND A HARD PLACE	*Rolling Stones*	63	*2 Dec 89*	1
PAINT IT BLACK [RI]	*London*	61	*23 Jun 90*	3
ALMOST HEAR YOU SIGH	*Rolling Stones*	31	*30 Jun 90*	5
HIGHWIRE	*Rolling Stones*	29	*30 Mar 91*	4
RUBY TUESDAY (LIVE) [RR]	*Rolling Stones*	59	*1 Jun 91*	2
LOVE IS STRONG	*Virgin*	14	*16 Jul 94*	5
YOU GOT ME ROCKING	*Virgin*	23	*8 Oct 94*	3
OUT OF TEARS	*Virgin*	36	*10 Dec 94*	4
I GO WILD	*Virgin*	29	*15 Jul 95*	3
LIKE A ROLLING STONE	*Virgin*	12	*11 Nov 95*	5
ANYBODY SEEN MY BABY?	*Virgin*	22	*4 Oct 97*	3
SAINT OF ME	*Virgin*	26	*7 Feb 98*	2
OUT OF CONTROL	*Virgin*	51	*22 Aug 98*	1
EPS:	**HITS 3**			**WEEKS 154**
THE ROLLING STONES	*Decca*	1	*18 Jan 64*	58
FIVE BY FIVE	*Decca*	1	*22 Aug 64*	54
GOT LIVE IF YOU WANT IT!	*Decca*	1	*19 Jun 65*	42
ALBUMS:	**HITS 42**			**WEEKS 761**
COMPILATION ALBUMS:	**HITS 1**			**WEEKS 1**
THE ROLLING STONES	*Decca*	1	*25 Apr 64*	51
ROLLING STONES NUMBER 2	*Decca*	1	*23 Jan 65*	37
OUT OF OUR HEADS	*Decca*	2	*2 Oct 65*	24
AFTERMATH	*Decca*	1	*23 Apr 66*	28
BIG HITS (HIGH TIDE AND GREEN GRASS)	*Decca*	4	*12 Nov 66*	43
BETWEEN THE BUTTONS	*Decca*	3	*28 Jan 67*	22
THEIR SATANIC MAJESTIES REQUEST	*Decca*	3	*23 Dec 67*	13
BEGGARS BANQUET	*Decca*	3	*21 Dec 68*	12
THROUGH THE PAST, DARKLY (BIG HITS - VOL. 2)	*Decca*	2	*27 Sep 69*	37
LET IT BLEED	*Decca*	1	*20 Dec 69*	29
'GET YER YA-YA'S OUT!' - THE ROLLING STONES IN CONCERT	*Decca*	1	*19 Sept 70*	15
Live recordings from Madison Square Garden, New York on 27&28 Nov 69.				
STONE AGE	*Decca*	4	*3 Apr 71*	7
STICKY FINGERS	*Rolling Stones*	1	*8 May 71*	25
GIMME SHELTER	*Decca*	19	*18 Sep 71*	5
MILESTONES	*Decca*	14	*11 Mar 72*	8
EXILE ON MAIN STREET	*Rolling Stones*	1	*10 Jun 72*	16
ROCK 'N' ROLLING STONES	*Decca*	41	*11 Nov 72*	1
GOAT'S HEAD SOUP	*Rolling Stones*	1	*22 Sep 73*	14
IT'S ONLY ROCK 'N' ROLL	*Rolling Stones*	2	*2 Nov 74*	9
MADE IN THE SHADE	*Rolling Stones*	14	*28 Jun 75*	12
Compilation.				
METAMORPHOSIS	*Decca*	45	*28 Jun 75*	1
Collection of mainly Jagger/Richard songs from the 1960s which were demoed for other artists. All Decca albums above from Stone Age are re-packagings of old material.				
ROLLED GOLD - THE VERY BEST OF THE ROLLING STONES	*Decca*	7	*29 Nov 75*	50
Includes re-entry in 1982.				
BLACK AND BLUE	*Rolling Stones*	2	*8 May 76*	14
LOVE YOU LIVE	*Rolling Stones*	3	*8 Oct 77*	8
Live recordings from early 1977.				
GET STONED	*Arcade*	8	*5 Nov 77*	15
SOME GIRLS	*Rolling Stones*	2	*24 Jun 78*	25
EMOTIONAL RESCUE	*Rolling Stones*	1	*5 Jul 80*	18
TATTOO YOU	*Rolling Stones*	2	*12 Sep 81*	29
STILL LIFE (AMERICAN CONCERTS 1981)	*Rolling Stones*	4	*12 Jun 82*	18
Live recordings from the 1981 US tour.				

IN CONCERT	*Decca*	94	*31 Jul 82*	3
Dutch import.				
STORY OF THE STONES	*K-Tel*	24	*11 Dec 82*	12
UNDERCOVER	*Rolling Stones*	3	*19 Nov 83*	18
REWIND 1971-1984 (THE BEST OF THE ROLLING STONES)	*Rolling Stones*	23	*7 Jul 84*	13
DIRTY WORK	*Rolling Stones*	4	*5 Apr 86*	10
Dedicated to Ian Stewart who died from a heart-attack 12 Dec 85.				
STEEL WHEELS	*Rolling Stones*	2	*23 Sep 89*	18
HOT ROCKS - THE GREATEST HITS 1964-1971	*London*	3	*7 Jul 90*	18
REWIND 1971-1984 (THE BEST OF THE ROLLING STONES) [RE]	*Rolling Stones*	45	*7 Jul 90*	5
Re-released with a new catalogue number.				
FLASHPOINT	*Rolling Stones*	6	*20 Apr 91*	7
JUMP BACK - THE BEST OF THE ROLLING STONES 1971-93	*Virgin*	16	*4 Dec 93*	22
Includes re-entries through to 1999.				
STICKY FINGERS [RI]	*Virgin*	74	*2 Jul 94*	1
Issued for the first time on CD.				
VOODOO LOUNGE	*Virgin*	1	*23 Jul 94*	24
HOT ROCKS - THE GREATEST HITS 1964-1971 [RE]	*London*	41	*22 Jul 95*	6
Re-released with a new catalogue number. Includes re-entry in 1999.				
STRIPPED	*Virgin*	9	*25 Nov 95*	11
Live recordings from Olympia Theatre in Paris, the Paradise Club in Amsterdam and a rehearsal at the Toshiba-EMI studios in Tokyo.				
THE ROLLING STONES ROCK AND ROLL CIRCUS	*Abkco*	12	*26 Oct 96*	1
Recordings from the TV show filmed on 10 Dec 68 featuring the Who, Eric Clapton and John Lennon. This was an entry in the Compilation Chart.				
Above hit: ROLLING STONES and VARIOUS ARTISTS.				
BRIDGES TO BABYLON	*Virgin*	6	*11 Oct 97*	6
NO SECURITY	*Virgin*	67	*14 Nov 98*	1
Live recordings from shows during the Bridges To Babylon tour.				

ROLLINS BAND — US

SINGLES:	HITS 2			WEEKS 4
TEARING	*Imago*	54	*12 Sep 92*	2
LIAR/DISCONNECT	*Imago*	27	*10 Sep 94*	2
ALBUMS:	**HITS 1**			**WEEKS 2**
WEIGHT	*Imago*	22	*23 Apr 94*	2

ROLLO GOES . . . — UK

SINGLES:	HITS 3			WEEKS 8
GET OFF YOUR HIGH HORSE	*Cheeky*	43	*29 Jan 94*	2
Above hit: ROLLO GOES CAMPING.				
GET OFF YOUR HIGH HORSE [RE]	*Cheeky*	47	*1 Oct 94*	2
Above hit: ROLLO GOES CAMPING.				
LOVE, LOVE, LOVE - HERE I COME	*Cheeky*	32	*10 Jun 95*	2
Features vocals by Pauline Taylor of Gloworm.				
Above hit: ROLLO GOES MYSTIC.				
LET THIS BE A PRAYER	*Cheeky*	26	*8 Jun 96*	2
Above hit: ROLLO GOES SPIRITUAL with Pauline TAYLOR.				

ROMAN HOLLIDAY — UK

SINGLES:	HITS 3			WEEKS 19
STAND BY	*Jive*	61	*2 Apr 83*	3
DON'T TRY TO STOP IT	*Jive*	14	*2 Jul 83*	9
MOTORMANIA	*Jive*	40	*24 Sep 83*	7
ALBUMS:	**HITS 1**			**WEEKS 3**
COOKIN' ON THE ROOF	*Jive*	31	*22 Oct 83*	3

ROMAN NUMERALS – See Vic REEVES

ROMANTHONY – See DAFT PUNK

ROMANTICS – See RUBY and the ROMANTICS

ROMEO – See OXIDE and NEUTRINO

Max ROMEO — Jamaica

SINGLES:	HITS 1			WEEKS 25
WET DREAM	*Unity*	10	*31 May 69*	24
WET DREAM [RE]	*Unity*	50	*29 Nov 69*	1

Harry 'Choo Choo' ROMERO — US

SINGLES:	HITS 3			WEEKS 6
JUST CAN'T GET ENOUGH	*Almo Sounds*	39	*22 May 99*	2
Harry 'Choo Choo' ROMERO presents Inaya DAY.				
HAZIN' + PHAZIN'	*Defected*	21	*15 Jan 00*	3
Above hit: CHOO CHOO PROJECT.				
I WANT OUT (I CAN'T BELIEVE)	*Perfecto*	51	*1 Sep 01*	1

RONALDO'S REVENGE — UK

SINGLES:	HITS 1			WEEKS 2
MAS QUE MANCADA	*AM:PM*	37	*1 Aug 98*	2

RONDO VENEZIANO — Italy

SINGLES:	HITS 1			WEEKS 3
LA SERENISSIMA - THEME FROM VENICE IN PERIL	*Ferroway*	58	*22 Oct 83*	3
ALBUMS:	**HITS 2**			**WEEKS 33**
VENICE IN PERIL	*Ferroway*	59	*5 Nov 83*	3
VENICE IN PERIL [RE]	*Ferroway*	39	*31 Mar 84*	10
THE GENIUS OF VENICE	*Ferroway*	60	*10 Nov 84*	13
VENICE IN PERIL [RI]	*Fanfare*	34	*9 Jul 88*	7

RONETTES — US

SINGLES:	HITS 4			WEEKS 34
BE MY BABY *Features Cher on backing vocals.*	*London*	4	*19 Oct 63*	13
BABY, I LOVE YOU	*London*	11	*11 Jan 64*	14
(THE BEST PART OF) BREAKIN' UP	*London*	43	*29 Aug 64*	3
DO I LOVE YOU	*London*	35	*10 Oct 64*	4

RONNETTE - See FIDELFATTI featuring RONNETTE

Mick RONSON — UK

SINGLES:	HITS 1			WEEKS 1
DON'T LOOK DOWN *Above hit: Mick RONSON with Joe ELLIOTT.*	*Epic*	55	*7 May 94*	1
ALBUMS:	**HITS 2**			**WEEKS 10**
SLAUGHTER ON TENTH AVENUE	*RCA Victor*	9	*16 Mar 74*	7
PLAY DON'T WORRY	*RCA Victor*	29	*8 Mar 75*	3

Linda RONSTADT — US

(See also Dolly Parton, Linda Ronstadt and Emmylou Harris.)

SINGLES:	HITS 5			WEEKS 34
TRACKS OF MY TEARS	*Asylum*	42	*8 May 76*	3
BLUE BAYOU	*Asylum*	35	*28 Jan 78*	4
ALISON *Written and originally recorded by Elvis Costello.*	*Asylum*	66	*26 May 79*	2
SOMEWHERE OUT THERE *From the film 'An American Tail'.* *Above hit: Linda RONSTADT and James INGRAM.*	*MCA*	8	*11 Jul 87*	13
DON'T KNOW MUCH *Originally recorded by Bill Medley in 1982.* *Above hit: Linda RONSTADT featuring Aaron NEVILLE.*	*Elektra*	2	*11 Nov 89*	12
ALBUMS:	**HITS 8**			**WEEKS 39**
HASTEN DOWN THE WIND	*Asylum*	32	*4 Sep 76*	8
GREATEST HITS	*Asylum*	37	*25 Dec 76*	9
SIMPLE DREAMS	*Asylum*	15	*1 Oct 77*	5
LIVING IN THE USA	*Asylum*	39	*14 Oct 78*	2
MAD LOVE *Featuring the Cretones as backing group.*	*Asylum*	65	*8 Mar 80*	1
WHAT'S NEW	*Asylum*	31	*28 Jan 84*	5
LUSH LIFE *Above 2: Linda RONSTADT with the Nelson RIDDLE ORCHESTRA.*	*Asylum*	100	*19 Jan 85*	1
CRY LIKE A RAINSTORM - HOWL LIKE THE WIND *Above hit: Linda RONSTADT featuring Aaron NEVILLE.*	*Elektra*	43	*11 Nov 89*	8

ROOFTOP SINGERS — US

SINGLES:	HITS 1			WEEKS 12
WALK RIGHT IN *Originally recorded by Gus Cannon and the Jugstompers.*	*Fontana*	10	*2 Feb 63*	12

ROOTJOOSE — UK

SINGLES:	HITS 3			WEEKS 3
CAN'T KEEP LIVING THIS WAY	*Rage*	73	*17 May 97*	1
MR. FIXIT	*Rage*	54	*2 Aug 97*	1
LONG WAY	*Rage*	68	*4 Oct 97*	1
ALBUMS:	**HITS 1**			**WEEKS 1**
RHUBARB	*Rage*	58	*18 Oct 97*	1

ROOTS — US

SINGLES:	HITS 2			WEEKS 3
WHAT THEY DO	*Geffen*	49	*3 May 97*	1

YOU GOT ME	*MCA*	31	*6 Mar 99*	2
Above hit: ROOTS featuring Erykah BADU.				

ROOTS MANUVA ??

SINGLES:	HITS 1			WEEKS 3
DUSTED	*Hard Hands*	28	*11 Dec 99*	2
Roots Manuva recorded his vocals for the track back in 1997.				
Above hit: LEFTFIELD. ROOTS MANUVA.				
DUSTED [RE]	*Hard Hands*	75	*22 Jan 01*	1

Ralphi ROSARIO – See Richie RICH

Barry ROSE – see GUILDFORD CATHEDRAL CHOIR conductor: Barry ROSE; Paul PHOENIX (treble) with Instrumental Ensemble – James WATSON (trumpet), John SCOTT (organ), conducted by Barry ROSE

David ROSE – See Connie FRANCIS

Mykal ROSE – See Shabba RANKS

ROSE OF ROMANCE ORCHESTRA UK

SINGLES:	HITS 1			WEEKS 1
TARA'S THEME FROM 'GONE WITH THE WIND'	*BBC*	71	*9 Jan 82*	1

ROSE ROYCE US

SINGLES:	HITS 14			WEEKS 113
CAR WASH	*MCA*	9	*25 Dec 76*	12
PUT YOUR MONEY WHERE YOUR MOUTH IS	*MCA*	44	*22 Jan 77*	5
The group's first UK release in 1976.				
I WANNA GET NEXT TO YOU	*MCA*	14	*2 Apr 77*	8
Above 3 from the film 'Car Wash'. Originally recorded by Rhythm Aces.				
DO YOUR DANCE	*Whitfield*	30	*24 Sep 77*	6
WISHING ON A STAR	*Whitfield*	3	*14 Jan 78*	14
IT MAKES YOU FEEL LIKE DANCIN'	*Whitfield*	16	*6 May 78*	10
LOVE DON'T LIVE HERE ANYMORE	*Whitfield*	2	*16 Sep 78*	10
I'M IN LOVE (AND I LOVE THE FEELING)	*Whitfield*	51	*3 Feb 79*	4
IS IT LOVE YOU'RE AFTER	*Whitfield*	13	*17 Nov 79*	13
OOH BOY	*Whitfield*	46	*8 Mar 80*	7
R.R. EXPRESS	*Warner Brothers*	52	*21 Nov 81*	3
MAGIC TOUCH	*Streetwave*	43	*1 Sep 84*	8
LOVE ME RIGHT NOW	*Streetwave*	60	*6 Apr 85*	3
CAR WASH [RI] / IS IT LOVE YOU'RE AFTER [RI]	*MCA*	20	*11 Jun 88*	7
CAR WASH [RR]	*MCA*	18	*31 Oct 98*	3
Sub titled: 1998 – The Monday Night Club Mixes.				
Above hit: ROSE ROYCE featuring Gwen DICKEY.				
ALBUMS:	**HITS 6**			**WEEKS 66**
COMPILATION ALBUMS:	**HITS 1**			**WEEKS 6**
IN FULL BLOOM	*Whitfield*	18	*22 Oct 77*	13
STRIKES AGAIN	*Whitfield*	7	*30 Sep 78*	11
RAINBOW CONNECTION IV	*Atlantic*	72	*22 Sep 79*	2
ROSE ROYCE GREATEST HITS	*Whitfield*	1	*1 Mar 80*	34
MUSIC MAGIC	*Streetwave*	69	*13 Oct 84*	2
THE ARTISTS VOLUME 1	*Street Sounds*	65	*9 Mar 85*	4
Compilation album with tracks by each artist.				
Above hit: EARTH WIND AND FIRE/Jean CARN/ROSE ROYCE.				
CHIC AND ROSE ROYCE – THEIR GREATEST HITS – SIDE BY SIDE	*Dino*	8	*27 Jul 91*	6
Album contained tracks by two different recording acts and was thus ineligible for the main album chart.				
Above hit: ROSE ROYCE and CHIC.				

ROSE TATTOO Australia

SINGLES:	HITS 1			WEEKS 4
ROCK 'N' ROLL OUTLAW	*Carrere*	60	*11 Jul 81*	4
ALBUMS:	**HITS 1**			**WEEKS 4**
ASSAULT AND BATTERY	*Carrere*	40	*26 Sep 81*	4

Jimmy ROSELLI US

SINGLES:	HITS 1			WEEKS 8
WHEN YOUR OLD WEDDING RING WAS NEW	*A.1.*	51	*5 Mar 83*	5
WHEN YOUR OLD WEDDING RING WAS NEW [RI]	*First Night*	52	*20 Jun 87*	3

Diana ROSS US

(See also Placido Domingo, Diana Ross and Jose Carreras; Diana Ross and Marvin Gaye; Diana Ross and the Supremes and the Temptations; Diana Ross, Marvin Gaye, Smokey Robinson and Stevie Wonder; Supremes.)

SINGLES:	HITS 56			WEEKS 413
REACH OUT AND TOUCH	*Tamla Motown*	33	*18 Jul 70*	5

Title	Label	Pos	Date	Wks
AIN'T NO MOUNTAIN HIGH ENOUGH *Original by Marvin Gaye and Tammy Terrell reached No. 9 in the US in 1967.*	*Tamla Motown*	6	*12 Sep 70*	12
REMEMBER ME	*Tamla Motown*	7	*3 Apr 71*	12
I'M STILL WAITING	*Tamla Motown*	1	*31 Jul 71*	14
SURRENDER	*Tamla Motown*	10	*30 Oct 71*	11
DOOBEDOOD'NDOOBE, DOOBEDOOD'NDOOBE, DOOBEDOOD'NDOO	*Tamla Motown*	12	*13 May 72*	9
TOUCH ME IN THE MORNING	*Tamla Motown*	9	*14 Jul 73*	12
TOUCH ME IN THE MORNING [RE]	*Tamla Motown*	50	*13 Oct 73*	1
ALL OF MY LIFE	*Tamla Motown*	9	*5 Jan 74*	13
LAST TIME I SAW HIM	*Tamla Motown*	35	*4 May 74*	4
LOVE ME	*Tamla Motown*	38	*28 Sep 74*	5
SORRY DOESN'T ALWAYS MAKE IT RIGHT	*Tamla Motown*	23	*29 Mar 75*	9
THEME FROM MAHOGANY "DO YOU KNOW WHERE YOU'RE GOING TO" *From the film 'Mahogany'.*	*Tamla Motown*	5	*3 Apr 76*	8
LOVE HANGOVER	*Tamla Motown*	10	*24 Apr 76*	10
I THOUGHT IT TOOK A LITTLE TIME (BUT TODAY I FELL IN LOVE)	*Tamla Motown*	32	*10 Jul 76*	5
I'M STILL WAITING [RI]	*Tamla Motown*	41	*16 Oct 76*	4
GETTIN' READY FOR LOVE	*Motown*	23	*19 Nov 77*	8
LOVIN', LIVIN' AND GIVIN' *From the film 'Thank God It's Friday'.*	*Motown*	54	*22 Jul 78*	6
EASE ON DOWN THE ROAD *From the film 'The Wiz'. Originally recorded by Consumer Rapport.* *Above hit: Diana ROSS / Michael JACKSON.*	*MCA*	45	*18 Nov 78*	4
THE BOSS	*Motown*	40	*21 Jul 79*	7
NO ONE GETS THE PRIZE	*Motown*	59	*6 Oct 79*	3
IT'S MY HOUSE	*Motown*	32	*24 Nov 79*	10
UPSIDE DOWN	*Motown*	2	*19 Jul 80*	12
MY OLD PIANO	*Motown*	5	*20 Sep 80*	9
I'M COMING OUT	*Motown*	13	*15 Nov 80*	10
IT'S MY TURN *From the film of the same name.*	*Motown*	16	*17 Jan 81*	8
ONE MORE CHANCE	*Motown*	49	*28 Mar 81*	5
CRYIN' MY HEART OUT FOR YOU	*Motown*	58	*13 Jun 81*	3
ENDLESS LOVE *From the film of the same name.* *Above hit: Diana ROSS and Lionel RICHIE.*	*Motown*	7	*12 Sep 81*	12
WHY DO FOOLS FALL IN LOVE	*Capitol*	4	*7 Nov 81*	12
TENDERNESS *Originally recorded in 1980.*	*Motown*	73	*23 Jan 82*	1
MIRROR MIRROR	*Capitol*	36	*30 Jan 82*	5
TENDERNESS [RE]	*Motown*	75	*6 Feb 82*	1
WORK THAT BODY	*Capitol*	7	*29 May 82*	11
IT'S NEVER TOO LATE *Above 2 written by Dan Hartman.*	*Capitol*	41	*7 Aug 82*	4
MUSCLES *Written, produced and backing vocals by Michael Jackson.*	*Capitol*	15	*23 Oct 82*	9
SO CLOSE	*Capitol*	43	*15 Jan 83*	4
PIECES OF ICE	*Capitol*	46	*23 Jul 83*	3
ALL OF YOU *Above hit: Julio IGLESIAS and Diana ROSS.*	*CBS*	43	*7 Jul 84*	8
TOUCH BY TOUCH	*Capitol*	47	*15 Sep 84*	6
EATEN ALIVE *Co-written, produced and backing vocals by Michael Jackson.*	*Capitol*	71	*28 Sep 85*	1
CHAIN REACTION	*Capitol*	1	*25 Jan 86*	17
EXPERIENCE *Above 2 written by the Bee Gees.*	*Capitol*	47	*3 May 86*	3
DIRTY LOOKS	*EMI*	49	*13 Jun 87*	3
MR. LEE	*EMI*	58	*8 Oct 88*	2
LOVE HANGOVER [RM] *Remixed at PWL.*	*RCA*	75	*26 Nov 88*	1
WORKIN' OVERTIME	*EMI*	32	*6 May 89*	5
PARADISE *Above 2: DIANA.*	*EMI*	61	*29 Jul 89*	2
I'M STILL WAITING [RM] *Remixed by Phil Chill.*	*Motown*	21	*7 Jul 90*	6
WHEN YOU TELL ME THAT YOU LOVE ME	*EMI*	2	*30 Nov 91*	11
THE FORCE BEHIND THE POWER *Written by Stevie Wonder.*	*EMI*	27	*15 Feb 92*	3
ONE SHINING MOMENT	*EMI*	10	*20 Jun 92*	8
IF WE HOLD ON TOGETHER	*EMI*	11	*28 Nov 92*	10
HEART (DON'T CHANGE MY MIND) *Originally recorded by Barbra Streisand.*	*EMI*	31	*13 Mar 93*	3
CHAIN REACTION [RI]	*EMI*	20	*9 Oct 93*	5
YOUR LOVE	*EMI*	14	*11 Dec 93*	8
THE BEST YEARS OF MY LIFE	*EMI*	28	*2 Apr 94*	4
WHY DO FOOLS FALL IN LOVE [RI] /I'M COMING OUT (JOEY NEGRO 1994 REMIX) [RM]	*EMI*	36	*9 Jul 94*	4
TAKE ME HIGHER	*EMI*	32	*2 Sep 95*	4
I'M GONE	*EMI*	36	*25 Nov 95*	3

I WILL SURVIVE	*EMI*	14	*17 Feb 96*	4
Above hit: DIANA.				
IN THE ONES YOU LOVE	*EMI*	34	*21 Dec 96*	4
NOT OVER YOU YET	*EMI*	9	*6 Nov 99*	6
NOT OVER YOU YET [RE]	*EMI*	58	*15 Jan 00*	1

ALBUMS: **HITS 41** **WEEKS 542**

COMPILATION ALBUMS: **HITS 1** **WEEKS 2**

DIANA ROSS	*Tamla Motown*	14	*24 Oct 70*	5
EVERYTHING IS EVERYTHING	*Tamla Motown*	31	*19 Jun 71*	3
DIANA [OST-TV]	*Tamla Motown*	43	*9 Oct 71*	1
Features Bill Cosby, Danny Thomas and the Jackson 5.				
I'M STILL WAITING	*Tamla Motown*	10	*9 Oct 71*	11
GREATEST HITS	*Tamla Motown*	34	*11 Nov 72*	10
TOUCH ME IN THE MORNING	*Tamla Motown*	7	*1 Sep 73*	35
LADY SINGS THE BLUES [OST]	*Tamla Motown*	50	*27 Oct 73*	1
Ross played the role of Billie Holiday.				
LAST TIME I SAW HIM	*Tamla Motown*	41	*2 Mar 74*	1
DIANA ROSS LIVE AT CAESAR'S PALACE	*Tamla Motown*	21	*8 Jun 74*	8
Live recordings from her show in Las Vegas.				
DIANA ROSS	*Tamla Motown*	4	*27 Mar 76*	26
This self-titled album is different from the earlier chart entry.				
DIANA ROSS'GREATEST HITS / 2	*Tamla Motown*	2	*7 Aug 76*	29
AN EVENING WITH DIANA ROSS	*Motown*	52	*19 Mar 77*	1
Live recordings from the Ahmanson Theater, Los Angeles, 1976.				
THE BOSS	*Motown*	52	*4 Aug 79*	2
20 GOLDEN GREATS	*Motown*	2	*17 Nov 79*	29
DIANA	*Motown*	12	*21 Jun 80*	32
This self-titled album is different from the earlier chart entry.				
TO LOVE AGAIN	*Motown*	26	*28 Mar 81*	10
WHY DO FOOLS FALL IN LOVE	*Capital*	17	*7 Nov 81*	24
ALL THE GREAT HITS	*Motown*	21	*21 Nov 81*	31
DIANA'S DUETS	*Motown*	43	*13 Feb 82*	6
SILK ELECTRIC	*Capitol*	33	*23 Oct 82*	12
LOVE SONGS	*K-Tel*	5	*4 Dec 82*	17
ROSS	*Capitol*	44	*16 Jul 83*	5
PORTRAIT	*Telstar*	8	*24 Dec 83*	31
Compilation.				
SWEPT AWAY	*Capitol*	40	*6 Oct 84*	5
EATEN ALIVE	*Capitol*	11	*28 Sep 85*	19
DIANA . MICHAEL . GLADYS . STEVIE - THEIR VERY BEST - BACK TO BACK	*PrioriTyV*	21	*15 Nov 86*	10
Compilation featuring tracks by each act.				
Above hit: Diana ROSS/Michael JACKSON/Gladys KNIGHT/Stevie WONDER.				
RED HOT RHYTHM 'N' BLUES	*EMI*	47	*30 May 87*	4
Her versions of R&B classics.				
LOVE SONGS	*Telstar*	12	*31 Oct 87*	21
Compilation of each artist's solo recordings. When the compilation chart commenced on 14 Jan 89 it was listed there. See separate entry below.				
Above hit: Michael JACKSON and Diana ROSS.				
LOVE SONGS	*Telstar*	18	*14 Jan 89*	2
Above entry was in the compilation chart.				
Above hit: Michael JACKSON and Diana ROSS.				
WORKIN' OVERTIME	*EMI*	23	*27 May 89*	4
GREATEST HITS LIVE	*EMI*	34	*25 Nov 89*	6
THE FORCE BEHIND THE POWER	*EMI*	11	*14 Dec 91*	31
MOTOWN'S GREATEST HITS	*Motown*	20	*29 Feb 92*	11
LIVE, STOLEN MOMENTS - THE LADY SINGS THE BLUES	*EMI*	45	*24 Apr 93*	2
Live recordings from New York's Ritz club, Dec 92. Released to mark her 30th anniversary in Showbiz.				
ONE WOMAN - THE ULTIMATE COLLECTION	*EMI*	1	*30 Oct 93*	67
DIANA EXTENDED - THE REMIXES	*EMI*	58	*23 Apr 94*	1
A VERY SPECIAL SEASON	*EMI*	37	*26 Nov 94*	6
Christmas songs.				
TAKE ME HIGHER	*EMI*	10	*16 Sep 95*	3
VOICE OF LOVE	*EMI*	42	*23 Nov 96*	7
40 GOLDEN MOTOWN GREATS	*Motown*	35	*31 Oct 98*	4
Features both her solo and group recordings.				
Above hit: Diana ROSS and the SUPREMES.				
EVERY DAY IS A NEW DAY	*EMI*	71	*20 Nov 99*	1
Includes tracks recorded for the TV film 'Double Platinum'.				
LOVE & LIFE - THE VERY BEST OF DIANA ROSS	*EMI/Universal Music TV*	28	*17 Nov 01*	7
Includes tracks by the Supremes.				

Diana ROSS and Marvin GAYE — US

(See also Marvin Gaye; Diana Ross.)

SINGLES: **HITS 2** **WEEKS 20**

YOU ARE EVERYTHING	*Tamla Motown*	5	*23 Mar 74*	12
Original by the Stylistics reached No. 9 in the US in 1971.				

STOP, LOOK, LISTEN (TO YOUR HEART)	*Tamla Motown*	25	*20 Jul 74*	8
ALBUMS:	**HITS 1**			**WEEKS 45**
DIANA AND MARVIN	*Tamla Motown*	6	*19 Jan 74*	43
DIANA AND MARVIN [RI]	*Motown*	78	*29 Aug 81*	2

Diana ROSS, Marvin GAYE, Smokey ROBINSON and Stevie WONDER — US

(See also Marvin Gaye; Smokey Robinson; Diana Ross; Stevie Wonder.)

SINGLES:	**HITS 1**			**WEEKS 5**
POPS, WE LOVE YOU	*Motown*	66	*24 Feb 79*	5
Recorded to honour Berry Gordy's father's 90th birthday.				

Diana ROSS and the SUPREMES and the TEMPTATIONS — US

(See also Diana Ross; Supremes; Temptations.)

SINGLES:	**HITS 3**			**WEEKS 27**
I'M GONNA MAKE YOU LOVE ME	*Tamla Motown*	3	*1 Feb 69*	11
Originally recorded by Dee Dee Warwick.				
I'M GONNA MAKE YOU LOVE ME [RE]	*Tamla Motown*	49	*26 Apr 69*	1
I SECOND THAT EMOTION	*Tamla Motown*	18	*20 Sep 69*	8
WHY (MUST WE FALL IN LOVE)	*Tamla Motown*	31	*21 Mar 70*	7
ALBUMS:	**HITS 3**			**WEEKS 31**
DIANA ROSS AND THE SUPREMES JOIN THE TEMPTATIONS	*Tamla Motown*	1	*25 Jan 69*	15
THE ORIGINAL SOUNDTRACK FROM TCB [OST-TV]	*Tamla Motown*	11	*28 Jun 69*	12
From the TV special featuring both groups, transmitted in the US, Feb 69.				
TOGETHER	*Tamla Motown*	28	*14 Feb 70*	4

Ricky ROSS — UK

SINGLES:	**HITS 2**			**WEEKS 3**
RADIO ON	*Epic*	35	*18 May 96*	2
GOOD EVENING PHILADELPHIA	*Epic*	58	*10 Aug 96*	1
ALBUMS:	**HITS 1**			**WEEKS 1**
WHAT YOU ARE	*Epic*	36	*15 Jun 96*	1

Francis ROSSI — UK

(See also Status Quo.)

SINGLES:	**HITS 2**			**WEEKS 6**
MODERN ROMANCE (I WANT TO FALL IN LOVE AGAIN)	*Vertigo*	54	*11 May 85*	4
Above hit: Francis ROSSI and Bernard FROST.				
GIVE MYSELF TO LOVE	*Virgin*	42	*3 Aug 96*	2
Above hit: Francis ROSSI of STATUS QUO.				

Nini ROSSO — Italy

SINGLES:	**HITS 1**			**WEEKS 14**
IL SILENZIO	*Durium*	8	*28 Aug 65*	14

ROSTAL and SCHAEFER — UK

ALBUMS:	**HITS 1**			**WEEKS 2**
BEATLES CONCERTO	*Parlophone*	61	*14 Jul 79*	2

Mstilav ROSTROPOVICH – See Herbert VON KARAJAN conducting the BERLIN PHILHARMONIC ORCHESTRA

David Lee ROTH — US

SINGLES:	**HITS 6**			**WEEKS 15**
CALIFORNIA GIRLS	*Warner Brothers*	68	*23 Feb 85*	2
Features backing vocals by Carl Wilson from the Beach Boys.				
JUST LIKE PARADISE	*Warner Brothers*	27	*5 Mar 88*	7
DAMN GOOD / STAND UP	*Warner Brothers*	72	*3 Sep 88*	1
A LIL' AIN'T ENOUGH	*Warner Brothers*	32	*12 Jan 91*	3
SHE'S MY MACHINE	*Reprise*	64	*19 Feb 94*	1
NIGHT LIFE	*Reprise*	72	*28 May 94*	1
Originally recorded by Willie Nelson.				
ALBUMS:	**HITS 5**			**WEEKS 32**
CRAZY FROM THE HEAT	*Warner Brothers*	91	*2 Mar 85*	2
EAT 'EM AND SMILE	*Warner Brothers*	28	*19 Jul 86*	9
SKYSCRAPER	*Warner Brothers*	11	*6 Feb 88*	12
A LITTLE AIN'T ENOUGH	*Warner Brothers*	4	*26 Jan 91*	7
YOUR FILTHY LITTLE MOUTH	*Reprise*	28	*19 Mar 94*	2

Uli Jon ROTH and ELECTRIC SUN — Germany

ALBUMS:	**HITS 1**			**WEEKS 2**
BEYOND THE ASTRAL SKIES	*EMI*	64	*23 Feb 85*	2

ROTTERDAM TERMINATION SOURCE — Holland

SINGLES:	HITS 2			WEEKS 6
POING	*Sep*	27	*7 Nov 92*	4
MERRY X-MESS	*React*	73	*25 Dec 93*	2

ROULA – See 20 FINGERS

ROULETTES – See Adam FAITH

Thomas ROUND – See Jun BRONHILL and Thomas ROUND

Demis ROUSSOS — Greece

SINGLES:	HITS 6			WEEKS 44
HAPPY TO BE ON AN ISLAND IN THE SUN	*Philips*	5	*22 Nov 75*	10
CAN'T SAY HOW MUCH I LOVE YOU	*Philips*	35	*28 Feb 76*	5
EXCEPTS FROM THE ROUSSOS PHENOMENON [EP]	*Philips*	1	*26 Jun 76*	12
Lead track: Forever And Ever. A collection of old recordings.				
WHEN FOREVER HAS GONE	*Philips*	2	*2 Oct 76*	10
BECAUSE	*Philips*	39	*19 Mar 77*	4
KYRILA [EP]	*Philips*	33	*18 Jun 77*	3
Lead track: Kyrila				
ALBUMS:	**HITS 6**			**WEEKS 143**
FOREVER AND EVER	*Philips*	35	*22 Jun 74*	68
SOUVENIRS	*Philips*	25	*19 Apr 75*	18
HAPPY TO BE	*Philips*	4	*24 Apr 76*	34
FOREVER AND EVER [RE]	*Philips*	2	*26 Jun 76*	64
MY ONLY FASCINATION	*Philips*	39	*3 Jul 76*	6
THE MAGIC OF DEMIS ROUSSOS	*Philips*	29	*16 Apr 77*	6
LIFE AND LOVE	*Philips*	36	*28 Oct 78*	11

ROUTERS — US

SINGLES:	HITS 1			WEEKS 7
LET'S GO (PONY)	*Warner Brothers*	32	*29 Dec 62*	7
Bass and hand claps by Scott Walker.				

Maria ROWE — UK

SINGLES:	HITS 1			WEEKS 2
SEXUAL	*ffrr*	67	*20 May 95*	2

ROWETTA – See HAPPY MONDAYS; OPEN ARMS featuring ROWETTA; VARIOUS ARTISTS (EPs) 'The Further Adventures Of North – More Underground Dance EP'

Kevin ROWLAND – See DEXY'S MIDNIGHT RUNNERS

John ROWLES — New Zealand

SINGLES:	HITS 2			WEEKS 28
IF I ONLY HAD TIME	*MCA*	3	*16 Mar 68*	18
HUSH . . . NOT A WORD TO MARY	*MCA*	12	*22 Jun 68*	10

Lisa ROXANNE — UK

SINGLES:	HITS 1			WEEKS 2
NO FLOW	*Palm Pictures*	18	*9 Jun 01*	2

ROXETTE — Sweden

SINGLES:	HITS 22			WEEKS 143
THE LOOK	*EMI*	7	*22 Apr 89*	10
DRESSED FOR SUCCESS	*EMI*	48	*15 Jul 89*	5
LISTEN TO YOUR HEART	*EMI*	62	*28 Oct 89*	3
IT MUST HAVE BEEN LOVE	*EMI*	3	*2 Jun 90*	14
From the film 'Pretty Woman'.				
LISTEN TO YOUR HEART [RI] /DANGEROUS	*EMI*	6	*11 Aug 90*	9
DRESSED FOR SUCCESS [RI]	*EMI*	18	*27 Oct 90*	7
JOYRIDE	*EMI*	4	*9 Mar 91*	10
FADING LIKE A FLOWER (EVERY TIME YOU LEAVE)	*EMI*	12	*11 May 91*	6
THE BIG L	*EMI*	21	*7 Sep 91*	6
SPENDING MY TIME	*EMI*	22	*23 Nov 91*	4
CHURCH OF YOUR HEART	*EMI*	21	*28 Mar 92*	4
HOW DO YOU DO!	*EMI*	13	*1 Aug 92*	7
QUEEN OF RAIN	*EMI*	28	*7 Nov 92*	4
ALMOST UNREAL	*EMI*	7	*24 Jul 93*	9
From the film 'Super Mario Bros'.				
IT MUST HAVE BEEN LOVE [RI]	*EMI*	10	*18 Sep 93*	8
Re-issued due to first TV transmission of the film 'Pretty Woman'.				
SLEEPING IN MY CAR	*EMI*	14	*26 Mar 94*	6
CRASH! BOOM! BANG!	*EMI*	26	*4 Jun 94*	5
FIREWORKS	*EMI*	30	*17 Sep 94*	4

RUN TO YOU	*EMI*	27	*3 Dec 94*	6
VULNERABLE	*EMI*	44	*8 Apr 95*	2
THE LOOK '95 [RM] *Remixed by Chaps.*	*EMI*	28	*25 Nov 95*	3
YOU DON'T UNDERSTAND ME	*EMI*	42	*30 Mar 96*	2
JUNE AFTERNOON	*EMI*	52	*20 Jul 96*	1
WISH I COULD FLY	*EMI*	11	*20 Mar 99*	7
STARS	*EMI*	56	*9 Oct 99*	1
ALBUMS:	**HITS 6**			**WEEKS 157**
LOOK SHARP!	*EMI*	45	*17 Jun 89*	2
LOOK SHARP! [RE]	*EMI*	4	*30 Jun 90*	51
JOYRIDE	*EMI*	2	*13 Apr 91*	48
TOURISM	*EMI*	2	*12 Sep 92*	17
CRASH BOOM BANG	*EMI*	3	*23 Apr 94*	16
DON'T BORE US, GET TO THE CHORUS! - GREATEST HITS	*EMI*	5	*4 Nov 95*	20
HAVE A NICE DAY	*EMI*	28	*10 Apr 99*	3

ROXY MUSIC

UK

SINGLES:	**HITS 16**			**WEEKS 155**
VIRGINIA PLAIN	*Island*	4	*19 Aug 72*	12
PYJAMARAMA	*Island*	10	*10 Mar 73*	12
STREET LIFE	*Island*	9	*17 Nov 73*	12
ALL I WANT IS YOU	*Island*	12	*12 Oct 74*	8
LOVE IS THE DRUG	*Island*	2	*11 Oct 75*	10
BOTH ENDS BURNING	*Island*	25	*27 Dec 75*	7
VIRGINIA PLAIN [RI]	*Polydor*	11	*22 Oct 77*	6
TRASH	*Polydor*	40	*3 Mar 79*	6
DANCE AWAY	*Polydor*	2	*28 Apr 79*	14
ANGEL EYES	*Polydor*	4	*11 Aug 79*	11
OVER YOU	*Polydor*	5	*17 May 80*	9
OH YEAH (ON THE RADIO)	*Polydor*	5	*2 Aug 80*	8
THE SAME OLD SCENE	*E'G*	12	*8 Nov 80*	7
JEALOUS GUY *Tribute to John Lennon.*	*E'G*	1	*21 Feb 81*	11
MORE THAN THIS	*E'G*	6	*3 Apr 82*	8
AVALON	*E'G*	13	*19 Jun 82*	6
TAKE A CHANCE WITH ME	*E'G*	26	*25 Sep 82*	6
LOVE IS THE DRUG [RM] *Remixed by Rollo and Sister Bliss.*	*E'G*	33	*27 Apr 96*	2
ALBUMS:	**HITS 16**			**WEEKS 426**
ROXY MUSIC	*Island*	10	*29 Jul 72*	16
FOR YOUR PLEASURE	*Island*	4	*7 Apr 73*	27
STRANDED	*Island*	1	*1 Dec 73*	17
COUNTRY LIFE	*Island*	3	*30 Nov 74*	10
SIREN	*Island*	4	*8 Nov 75*	17
VIVA! ROXY MUSIC *Live recordings from 1972-75.*	*Island*	6	*31 Jul 76*	12
GREATEST HITS	*Polydor*	20	*19 Nov 77*	11
MANIFESTO	*Polydor*	7	*24 Mar 79*	34
FLESH AND BLOOD	*Polydor*	1	*31 May 80*	60
AVALON	*E'G*	1	*5 Jun 82*	57
MUSIQUE/THE HIGH ROAD *Imported mini-album. Live recordings from Glasgow's Apollo Theatre.*	*E'G*	26	*19 Mar 83*	7
ROXY MUSIC - THE ATLANTIC YEARS (1973 - 1980)	*E'G*	23	*12 Nov 83*	25
STREET LIFE - 20 GREAT HITS *Above hit: Bryan FERRY ROXY MUSIC.*	*E'G*	1	*26 Apr 86*	77
THE ULTIMATE COLLECTION	*E'G*	6	*19 Nov 88*	27
THE ULTIMATE COLLECTION [RI]	*Virgin*	26	*17 Sept 94*	8
MORE THAN THIS - THE BEST OF BRYAN FERRY AND ROXY MUSIC *Above 2: Bryan FERRY and ROXY MUSIC.*	*Virgin*	15	*4 Nov 95*	15
THE BEST OF ROXY MUSIC	*Virgin*	12	*23 Jun 01*	6

ROYA ARAB - See GROOVERIDER

Billy Joe ROYAL

US

SINGLES:	**HITS 1**			**WEEKS 4**
DOWN IN THE BOONDOCKS *Originally recorded by Joe South.*	*CBS*	38	*9 Oct 65*	4

Central Band of the ROYAL AIR FORCE

(by permission of the Air Council) cond: Wing Comdr. A.E. SIMS O.B.E. (Organising Director of Music)

UK

SINGLES:	**HITS 1**			**WEEKS 1**
THE DAM BUSTERS - MARCH *From the film of the same name.*	*His Master's Voice*	18	*22 Oct 55*	1

ROYAL CHORAL SOCIETY - See LONDON SYMPHONY ORCHESTRA

ROYAL GUARD HORNS - See Elvis COSTELLO and the ATTRACTIONS

ROYAL GUARDSMEN — US

SINGLES:	HITS 2			WEEKS 17
SNOOPY VS. THE RED BARON	*Stateside*	8	*21 Jan 67*	13
THE RETURN OF THE RED BARON	*Stateside*	37	*8 Apr 67*	4

ROYAL HOUSE — US

SINGLES:	HITS 2			WEEKS 18
CAN YOU PARTY	*Champion*	14	*10 Sep 88*	14
YEAH BUDDY	*Champion*	35	*7 Jan 89*	4

ROYAL LIVERPOOL PHILHARMONIC ORCHESTRA and CHOIR - See Carl DAVIS and the ROYAL LIVERPOOL PHILHARMONIC ORCHESTRA and CHOIR

ROYAL PHILHARMONIC ORCHESTRA — UK

(See also Sarah Brightman; Elkie Brooks; Richard Clayderman; Elvis Costello and the Attractions; Michael Crawford; Julian Lloyd-Webber; Juan Martin with the Royal Philharmonic Orchestra conducted by Louis Clark; Mike Oldfield; Cliff Richard; Andy Williams; Various Artists: Studio Cast 'Leonard Bernstein's West Side Story'.)

SINGLES:	HITS 4			WEEKS 19
HOOKED ON CLASSICS [M]	*RCA*	2	*25 Jul 81*	11
Though not credited, conductor is Louis Clark.				
HOOKED ON A CAN CAN [M]	*RCA*	47	*24 Oct 81*	3
Above 2 are segued tracks of classical songs.				
Above hit: Louis CLARK conducting the ROYAL PHILHARMONIC ORCHESTRA.				
BBC WORLD CUP GRANDSTAND	*BBC*	61	*10 Jul 82*	3
Theme from BBC sports TV coverage of the 1982 World Cup in Spain.				
IF YOU KNEW SOUSA (AND FRIENDS) [M]	*RCA*	71	*7 Aug 82*	2
Above hit: Louis CLARK conducting the ROYAL PHILHARMONIC ORCHESTRA.				
ALBUMS:	**HITS 12**			**WEEKS 131**
CLASSICAL GOLD	*Ronco*	24	*8 Jan 77*	13
CLASSIC GOLD VOLUME 2	*Ronco*	31	*23 Dec 78*	4
HOOKED ON CLASSICS	*K-Tel*	4	*19 Sep 81*	43
CAN'T STOP THE CLASSICS - HOOKED ON CLASSICS 2	*K-Tel*	13	*31 Jul 82*	26
JOURNEY THROUGH THE CLASSICS - HOOKED ON CLASSICS 3	*K-Tel*	19	*9 Apr 83*	15
Above 3: Louis CLARK conducting the ROYAL PHILHARMONIC ORCHESTRA.				
LOVE CLASSICS	*Nouveau Music*	30	*8 Oct 83*	9
Above hit: ROYAL PHILHARMONIC ORCHESTRA conducted by Nick PORTLOCK.				
THE BEST OF HOOKED ON CLASSICS	*K-Tel*	51	*10 Dec 83*	6
Above hit: ROYAL PHILHARMONIC ORCHESTRA conducted by Louis CLARK.				
AS TIME GOES BY	*Telstar*	95	*26 May 84*	2
Above hit: ROYAL PHILHARMONIC ORCHESTRA conducted by Harry RABINOVITZ.				
RHYTHM AND CLASSICS	*Telstar*	96	*26 Nov 88*	1
Above hit: Louis CLARK conducting the ROYAL PHILHARMONIC ORCHESTRA.				
MUSIC FOR THE LAST NIGHT OF THE PROMS	*Cirrus*	39	*29 Sep 90*	4
Above hit: Sir. Charles GROVES conducting the ROYAL PHILHARMONIC ORCHESTRA and CHORUS with Sarah WALKER (soprano).				
SERIOUSLY ORCHESTRAL	*Virgin*	31	*5 Oct 91*	6
Above hit: Louis CLARK conducting the ROYAL PHILHARMONIC ORCHESTRA.				
BIG SCREEN CLASSICS	*Quality Television*	49	*30 Jul 94*	2
Conducted by Richard Homes.				

Pipes and Drums and Military Band of the ROYAL SCOTS DRAGOON GUARDS — UK

SINGLES:	HITS 3			WEEKS 43
AMAZING GRACE	*RCA Victor*	1	*1 Apr 72*	24
Above hit: Pipes and Drums and Military Band of the ROYAL SCOTS DRAGOON GUARDS (CARABINIERS & GREYS) Bandmaster W.O.I.C.I. HERBERT, Pipe Major W.O.I.I.J. PRYDE.				
HEYKEN'S SERENADE (STANDCHEN) / THE DAY IS ENDED (THE DAY THOU GAVE US LORD, IS ENDED)	*RCA Victor*	30	*19 Aug 72*	7
Above hit: Pipes and Drums and Military Band of the ROYAL SCOTS DRAGOON GUARDS Bandmaster W.O.I.C.I. HERBERT Pipe Major A. CREASE.				
LITTLE DRUMMER BOY	*RCA Victor*	13	*2 Dec 72*	9
Above hit: Pipes and Drums and Military Band of the ROYAL SCOTS DRAGOON GUARDS (CARABINIERS & GREYS) Bandmaster: WOI P.STANDING, Pipe Major A.J. CREASE.				
AMAZING GRACE [RE]	*RCA Victor*	42	*23 Dec 72*	3
Above hit: Pipes and Drums and Military Band of the ROYAL SCOTS DRAGOON GUARDS (CARABINIERS & GREYS) Bandmaster W.O.I.C.I. HERBERT, Pipe Major W.O.I.I.J. PRYDE.				

ROYALLE DELITE — US

SINGLES:	HITS 1			WEEKS 6
(I'LL BE A) FREAK FOR YOU	*Streetwave*	45	*14 Sep 85*	6

ROYCE DA 5'11' - See BAD MEETS EVIL featuring EMINEM and ROYCE DA 5'11

ROYKSOPP — Norway

SINGLES:	HITS 1			WEEKS 1
POOR LENO	*Wall Of Sound*	59	*15 Dec 01*	1

Lita ROZA — UK

(See also All Star Hit Parade.)

SINGLES:	HITS 3			WEEKS 18
(HOW MUCH IS) THAT DOGGIE IN THE WINDOW *Originally recorded by Patti Page.*	*Decca*	1	*14 Mar 53*	11
HEY THERE *Originally recorded by John Raitt.*	*Decca*	17	*8 Oct 55*	2
JIMMY UNKNOWN *Originally recorded by Doris Day.* *Above 2: Lita ROZA with Bob SHARPLES and his Orchestra.*	*Decca*	15	*24 Mar 56*	5

ROZALLA — Zimbabwe

SINGLES:	HITS 10			WEEKS 48
FAITH (IN THE POWER OF LOVE)	*Pulse 8*	65	*27 Apr 91*	2
EVERYBODY'S FREE (TO FEEL GOOD)	*Pulse 8*	6	*7 Sep 91*	11
FAITH (IN THE POWER OF LOVE) [RI]	*Pulse 8*	11	*16 Nov 91*	6
ARE YOU READY TO FLY	*Pulse 8*	14	*22 Feb 92*	6
LOVE BREAKDOWN	*Pulse 8*	65	*9 May 92*	2
IN 4 CHOONS LATER [M]	*Pulse 8*	50	*15 Aug 92*	2
DON'T PLAY WITH ME	*Pulse 8*	50	*30 Oct 93*	1
I LOVE MUSIC *From the film 'Carlito's Way'.*	*Epic*	18	*5 Feb 94*	5
THIS TIME I FOUND LOVE	*Epic*	33	*6 Aug 94*	3
YOU NEVER LOVE THE SAME WAY TWICE	*Epic*	16	*29 Oct 94*	5
BABY	*Epic*	26	*4 Mar 95*	3
EVERYBODY'S FREE [RM] *Remixed by Ca$ino (Paul Gotel and Aron Friedman).*	*Pulse 8*	30	*31 Aug 96*	2
ALBUMS:	**HITS 1**			**WEEKS 4**
EVERYBODY'S FREE	*Pulse 8*	20	*4 Apr 92*	4

RTE CONCERT ORCHESTRA - See Bill WHELAN

RUBBADUBB — UK

SINGLES:	HITS 1			WEEKS 1
TRIBUTE TO OUR ANCESTORS	*Perfecto*	56	*18 Jul 98*	1

RUBETTES — UK

SINGLES:	HITS 9			WEEKS 68
SUGAR BABY LOVE	*Polydor*	1	*4 May 74*	10
TONIGHT	*Polydor*	12	*13 Jul 74*	9
JUKE BOX JIVE	*Polydor*	3	*16 Nov 74*	12
I CAN DO IT	*State*	7	*8 Mar 75*	9
FOE-DEE-O-DEE	*State*	15	*21 Jun 75*	6
LITTLE DARLING	*State*	30	*22 Nov 75*	5
YOU'RE THE REASON WHY	*State*	28	*1 May 76*	4
UNDER ONE ROOF	*State*	40	*25 Sep 76*	3
BABY I KNOW	*State*	10	*12 Feb 77*	10
ALBUMS:	**HITS 1**			**WEEKS 1**
WE CAN DO IT	*State*	41	*10 May 75*	1

Maria RUBIA — UK

SINGLES:	HITS 2			WEEKS 13
EVERYTIME YOU NEED ME *Above hit: FRAGMA featuring Maria RUBIA.*	*Positiva*	3	*13 Jan 01*	11
SAY IT	*Neo*	40	*19 May 01*	2

RUBY and the ROMANTICS — US

SINGLES:	HITS 1			WEEKS 6
OUR DAY WILL COME	*London*	38	*30 Mar 63*	6

RUDIES - See Derrick MORGAN Music backing the RUDIES; Freddie NOTES and the RUDIES

RUFF DRIVERZ — UK

SINGLES:	HITS 6			WEEKS 21
DON'T STOP	*Inferno*	30	*7 Feb 98*	2
DEEPER LOVE	*Inferno*	19	*23 May 98*	3
SHAME	*Inferno*	51	*24 Oct 98*	2
DREAMING	*Inferno*	10	*28 Nov 98*	8

LA MUSICA *Above 2: RUFF DRIVERZ presents ARROLA.*	*Inferno*	14	*24 Apr 99*	4
WAITING FOR THE SUN	*Inferno*	37	*2 Oct 99*	2

RUFF ENDZ — US

SINGLES:	HITS 1			WEEKS 5
NO MORE	*Epic*	11	*19 Aug 00*	5

Frances RUFFELLE — UK

SINGLES:	HITS 1			WEEKS 6
LONELY SYMPHONY (WE WILL BE FREE) *UK's Eurovision entry in 1994, it came 10th.*	*Virgin*	25	*16 Apr 94*	6

Bruce RUFFIN — Jamaica

SINGLES:	HITS 2			WEEKS 23
RAIN *Originally recorded by José Feliciano.*	*Trojan*	19	*1 May 71*	11
MAD ABOUT YOU	*Rhino*	9	*24 Jun 72*	12

David RUFFIN — US

(See also Daryl Hall and John Oates.)

SINGLES:	HITS 1			WEEKS 8
WALK AWAY FROM LOVE *Originally recorded by the Choice Four.*	*Tamla Motown*	10	*17 Jan 76*	8

Jimmy RUFFIN — US

SINGLES:	HITS 9			WEEKS 106
WHAT BECOMES OF THE BROKENHEARTED	*Tamla Motown*	10	*29 Oct 66*	15
I'VE PASSED THIS WAY BEFORE	*Tamla Motown*	29	*11 Feb 67*	7
GONNA GIVE HER ALL THE LOVE I'VE GOT	*Tamla Motown*	26	*22 Apr 67*	6
I'VE PASSED THIS WAY BEFORE [RI]	*Tamla Motown*	33	*9 Aug 69*	6
FAREWELL IS A LONELY SOUND	*Tamla Motown*	8	*28 Feb 70*	16
I'LL SAY FOREVER MY LOVE *Originally released in 1968.*	*Tamla Motown*	7	*4 Jul 70*	12
IT'S WONDERFUL (TO BE LOVED BY YOU)	*Tamla Motown*	6	*17 Oct 70*	14
WHAT BECOMES OF THE BROKEN HEARTED [RI]	*Tamla Motown*	4	*27 Jul 74*	12
FAREWELL IS A LONELY SOUND [RI]	*Tamla Motown*	30	*2 Nov 74*	5
TELL ME WHAT YOU WANT	*Polydor*	39	*16 Nov 74*	4
HOLD ON TO MY LOVE *Co written by Robin Gibb.*	*RSO*	7	*3 May 80*	8
THERE WILL NEVER BE ANOTHER YOU *Backing vocals by Junior Giscombe.*	*EMI*	68	*26 Jan 85*	1

ALBUMS:	HITS 2			WEEKS 10
THE JIMMY RUFFIN WAY	*Tamla Motown*	32	*13 May 67*	6
GREATEST HITS	*Tamla Motown*	41	*1 Jun 74*	4

Kim RUFFIN – See CHUBBY CHUNKS

RUFFNECK featuring YAVAHN — US

SINGLES:	HITS 2			WEEKS 6
EVERYBODY BE SOMEBODY *Samples Yello's Bostich.*	*Positiva*	13	*11 Nov 95*	4
MOVE YOUR BODY	*Positiva*	60	*7 Sep 96*	1
EVERYBODY BE SOMEBODY [RM] *Remixed by Positano.*	*Strictly Rhythm*	66	*1 Dec 01*	1

RUFUS — US

SINGLES:	HITS 1			WEEKS 21
AIN'T NOBODY *Live recording from the New York Savoy Theater, Feb 82.*	*Warner Brothers*	8	*31 Mar 84*	12
AIN'T NOBODY [RM] *Remixed by Frankie Knuckles.* *Above 2: RUFUS and Chaka KHAN.*	*Warner Brothers*	6	*8 Jul 89*	9

ALBUMS:	HITS 2			WEEKS 7
RUFUSIZED	*ABC*	48	*12 Apr 75*	2
STOMPIN' AT THE SAVOY *Live recordings from the New York Savoy Theater, Feb 82.* *Above hit: RUFUS and Chaka KHAN.*	*Warner Brothers*	64	*21 Apr 84*	5

RUKMANI – See SNAP!

RUMOUR – See Graham PARKER and the RUMOUR

RUMPLE-STILTS-SKIN — US

SINGLES:	HITS 1			WEEKS 4
I THINK I WANT TO DANCE WITH YOU	*Polydor*	51	*24 Sep 83*	4

RUN D.M.C. — US

SINGLES:	HITS 10			WEEKS 59
MY ADIDAS / PETER PIPER	*London*	62	*19 Jul 86*	2
WALK THIS WAY	*London*	8	*6 Sep 86*	10
Features Aerosmith's Steve Tyler and Joe Perry. Aerosmith's original reached No. 10 in the US in 1976.				
YOU BE ILLIN'	*London*	42	*7 Feb 87*	4
IT'S TRICKY	*London*	16	*30 May 87*	7
CHRISTMAS IN HOLLIS	*London*	56	*12 Dec 87*	4
RUN'S HOUSE	*London*	37	*21 May 88*	4
GHOSTBUSTERS	*MCA*	65	*2 Sep 89*	2
WHAT'S IT ALL ABOUT	*Profile*	48	*1 Dec 90*	3
DOWN WITH THE KING	*Profile*	69	*27 Mar 93*	2
IT'S LIKE THAT	*Columbia*	63	*21 Feb 98*	3
German import.				
IT'S LIKE THAT	*Sm:)e Communications*	65	*14 Mar 98*	1
US import.				
IT'S LIKE THAT	*Sm:)e Communications*	1	*21 Mar 98*	16
(IT'S) TRICKY [RM]	*Epidrome*	74	*18 Apr 98*	1
German import. Remixed by Jason Nevins.				
Above 4: RUN-D.M.C. vs Jason NEVINS.				

ALBUMS:	HITS 4			WEEKS 36
RAISING HELL	*Profile*	41	*26 Jul 86*	26
TOUGHER THAN LEATHER	*Profile*	13	*4 Jun 88*	5
DOWN WITH THE KING	*Profile*	44	*15 May 93*	2
TOGETHER FOREVER – GREATEST HITS 1983-1998	*Profile*	31	*6 Jun 98*	3

RUN TINGS — UK

(See also Various Artists (EPs) 'Subplates Volume 1 EP'.)

SINGLES:	HITS 1			WEEKS 1
FIRES BURNING	*Suburban Base*	58	*16 May 92*	1

Todd RUNDGREN — US

SINGLES:	HITS 2			WEEKS 8
I SAW THE LIGHT	*Bearsville*	36	*30 Jun 73*	6
Originally released in 1972.				
LOVING YOU'S A DIRTY JOB BUT SOMEBODY'S GOTTA DO IT	*CBS*	73	*14 Dec 85*	2
Above hit: Bonnie TYLER, guest vocalist Todd RUNDGREN.				

ALBUMS:	HITS 1			WEEKS 3
HERMIT OF MINK HOLLOW	*Bearsville*	42	*6 May 78*	3

RUNRIG — UK

SINGLES:	HITS 9			WEEKS 28
CAPTURE THE HEART [EP]	*Chrysalis*	49	*29 Sep 90*	2
Lead track: Stepping Down The Glory Road.				
HEARTHAMMER [EP]	*Chrysalis*	25	*7 Sep 91*	4
Lead track: Hearthammer. Not listed as an EP on the chart of 7 Sep 91.				
FLOWER OF THE WEST	*Chrysalis*	43	*9 Nov 91*	2
WONDERFUL	*Chrysalis*	29	*6 Mar 93*	3
THE GREATEST FLAME	*Chrysalis*	36	*15 May 93*	3
THIS TIME OF YEAR	*Chrysalis*	38	*7 Jan 95*	2
Live recording from an outdoor concert in Scotland, Summer '94.				
AN UBHAL AS AIRDE (THE HIGHEST APPLE)	*Chrysalis*	18	*6 May 95*	5
Featured in the Carlsberg lager TV commercial.				
THINGS THAT ARE	*Chrysalis*	40	*4 Nov 95*	2
RHYTHM OF MY HEART	*Chrysalis*	24	*12 Oct 96*	2
Recorded for the film 'Loch Ness', but it was never used.				
THE GREATEST FLAME [RM]	*Chrysalis*	30	*11 Jan 97*	3
Remixed by Pete Woodroffe.				

ALBUMS:	HITS 11			WEEKS 50
ONCE IN A LIFETIME	*Chrysalis*	61	*26 Nov 88*	2
SEARCHLIGHT	*Chrysalis*	11	*7 Oct 89*	4
THE BIG WHEEL	*Chrysalis*	4	*22 Jun 91*	15
AMAZING THINGS	*Chrysalis*	2	*27 Mar 93*	6
TRANSMITTING LIVE	*Chrysalis*	41	*26 Nov 94*	3
Live recordings from concerts in Scotland and Germany during the summer of 1994.				
THE CUTTER AND THE CLAN	*Chrysalis*	45	*20 May 95*	2
Originally released in 1988.				

MARA	*Chrysalis*	24	*18 Nov 95*	4
Mara is Gaelic for the sea. Features the Scottish National Orchestra and the Hebridean Gaelic Choir.				
LONG DISTANCE - THE BEST OF RUNRIG	*Chrysalis*	13	*19 Oct 96*	10
THE GAELIC COLLECTION 1973-1995	*Ridge*	71	*23 May 98*	1
Compilation of the band's Gaelic songs.				
IN SEARCH OF ANGELS	*Ridge*	29	*13 Mar 99*	2
THE STAMPING GROUND	*Ridge*	64	*26 May 01*	1

RUPAUL — US

SINGLES:	HITS 5			WEEKS 19
SUPERMODEL (YOU BETTER WORK)	*Union*	39	*26 Jun 93*	4
HOUSE OF LOVE / BACK TO MY ROOTS	*Union*	40	*18 Sep 93*	2
SUPERMODEL [RI] / LITTLE DRUMMER BOY	*Union*	61	*22 Jan 94*	2
DON'T GO BREAKING MY HEART	*Rocket*	7	*26 Feb 94*	7
Charity record with royalties to the Elton John AIDS Foundation.				
Above hit: Elton JOHN and RUPAUL.				
HOUSE OF LOVE [RM]	*Virgin*	68	*21 May 94*	1
Remixed by T-Empo.				
IT'S RAINING MEN . . . THE SEQUEL	*Logic*	21	*28 Feb 98*	3
Above hit: Martha WASH featuring RUPAUL.				

Kate RUSBY — UK

ALBUMS:	HITS 1			WEEKS 1
LITTLE LIGHTS	*Pure*	75	*9 Jun 01*	1

RUSH — Canada

SINGLES:	HITS 12			WEEKS 43
CLOSER TO THE HEART	*Mercury*	36	*11 Feb 78*	3
THE SPIRIT OF RADIO	*Mercury*	13	*15 Mar 80*	7
VITAL SIGNS / A PASSAGE TO BANGKOK / IN THE MOOD	*Mercury*	41	*28 Mar 81*	4
In The Mood, though listed was only available on the 12" format.				
TOM SAWYER (LIVE)	*Exit*	25	*31 Oct 81*	6
Sleeve gives title as an EP: Rush Live.				
NEW WORLD MAN	*Mercury*	42	*4 Sep 82*	3
SUBDIVISIONS	*Mercury*	53	*30 Oct 82*	2
COUNTDOWN / NEW WORLD MAN [RI]	*Vertigo*	36	*7 May 83*	3
THE BODY ELECTRIC	*Vertigo*	56	*26 May 84*	3
THE BIG MONEY	*Vertigo*	46	*12 Oct 85*	3
TIME STAND STILL	*Vertigo*	42	*31 Oct 87*	3
Vocals by Aimee Mann.				
PRIME MOVER	*Vertigo*	43	*23 Apr 88*	3
ROLL THE BONES	*Atlantic*	49	*7 Mar 92*	1

ALBUMS:	HITS 15			WEEKS 98
FAREWELL TO KINGS	*Mercury*	22	*8 Oct 77*	4
HEMISPHERES	*Mercury*	14	*25 Nov 78*	6
PERMANENT WAVES	*Mercury*	3	*26 Jan 80*	16
MOVING PICTURES	*Mercury*	3	*21 Feb 81*	11
EXIT STAGE LEFT	*Mercury*	6	*7 Nov 81*	14
Live recordings.				
SIGNALS	*Mercury*	3	*18 Sep 82*	9
GRACE UNDER PRESSURE	*Vertigo*	5	*28 Apr 84*	12
POWER WINDOWS	*Vertigo*	9	*9 Nov 85*	4
HOLD YOUR FIRE	*Vertigo*	10	*21 Nov 87*	4
A SHOW OF HANDS	*Vertigo*	12	*28 Jan 89*	4
PRESTO	*Atlantic*	27	*9 Dec 89*	2
CHRONICLES	*Vertigo*	42	*13 Oct 90*	2
ROLL THE BONES	*Atlantic*	10	*14 Sep 91*	4
COUNTERPARTS	*Atlantic*	14	*30 Oct 93*	3
TEST FOR ECHO	*Atlantic*	25	*21 Sep 96*	3

Donell RUSH — US

SINGLES:	HITS 1			WEEKS 1
SYMPHONY	ID	66	*5 Dec 92*	1

Jennifer RUSH — US

SINGLES:	HITS 5			WEEKS 58
THE POWER OF LOVE	*CBS*	1	*29 Jun 85*	32
Peak position reached on 12 Oct 85.				
RING OF ICE	*CBS*	14	*14 Dec 85*	10
THE POWER OF LOVE [RE]	*CBS*	55	*20 Dec 86*	4
FLAMES OF PARADISE	*CBS*	59	*20 Jun 87*	3
Above hit: Jennifer RUSH (duet with Elton JOHN).				
TILL I LOVED YOU	*CBS*	24	*27 May 89*	9
Above hit: Placido DOMINGO and Jennifer RUSH.				

ALBUMS:	HITS 3			WEEKS 43
JENNIFER RUSH	*CBS*	7	*16 Nov 85*	35
MOVIN'	*CBS*	32	*3 May 86*	5
HEART OVER MIND	*CBS*	48	*18 Apr 87*	3

Patrice RUSHEN — US

SINGLES:	HITS 5			WEEKS 25
HAVEN'T YOU HEARD	*Elektra*	62	*1 Mar 80*	3
NEVER GONNA GIVE YOU UP (WON'T LET YOU BE)	*Elektra*	66	*24 Jan 81*	3
FORGET ME NOTS	*Elektra*	8	*24 Apr 82*	11
I WAS TIRED OF BEING ALONE	*Elektra*	39	*10 Jul 82*	5
FEELS SO REAL (WON'T LET GO)	*Elektra*	51	*9 Jun 84*	3
ALBUMS:	**HITS 2**			**WEEKS 17**
STRAIGHT FROM THE HEART	*Elektra*	24	*1 May 82*	14
NOW	*Elektra*	73	*16 Jun 84*	3

RUSSELL — US

SINGLES:	HITS 1			WEEKS 1
FOOL FOR LOVE	*Rulin*	52	*27 May 00*	1

Brenda RUSSELL — US

SINGLES:	HITS 2			WEEKS 17
SO GOOD, SO RIGHT / IN THE THICK OF IT	*A&M*	51	*19 Apr 80*	5
PIANO IN THE DARK	*Breakout*	23	*12 Mar 88*	12
ALBUMS:	**HITS 1**			**WEEKS 4**
GET HERE	*A&M*	77	*23 Apr 88*	4

Leon RUSSELL — US

ALBUMS:	HITS 1			WEEKS 1
LEON RUSSELL AND THE SHELTER PEOPLE	*A&M*	29	*3 Jul 71*	1

Patti RUSSO – See MEAT LOAF

RUTH — UK

SINGLES:	HITS 1			WEEKS 1
I DON'T KNOW	*Arc*	66	*12 Apr 97*	1

Mike RUTHERFORD — UK

(See also Mike and the Mechanics.)

ALBUMS:	HITS 2			WEEKS 11
SMALLCREEP'S DAY	*Charisma*	13	*23 Feb 80*	7
ACTING VERY STRANGE	*WEA*	23	*18 Sep 82*	4

Paul RUTHERFORD — UK

SINGLES:	HITS 2			WEEKS 6
GET REAL	*Fourth & Broadway*	47	*8 Oct 88*	3
OH WORLD	*Fourth & Broadway*	61	*19 Aug 89*	3

RUTHLESS RAP ASSASSINS — UK

SINGLES:	HITS 2			WEEKS 2
JUST MELLOW	*Syncopate*	75	*9 Jun 90*	1
AND IT WASN'T A DREAM	*Syncopate*	75	*1 Sep 90*	1

Above hit: RUTHLESS RAP ASSASSINS featured vocalist – Tracey CARMEN.

RUTLES — UK

SINGLES:	HITS 2			WEEKS 5
I MUST BE IN LOVE	*Warner Brothers*	39	*15 Apr 78*	3
I MUST BE IN LOVE [RE]	*Warner Brothers*	64	*13 May 78*	1
SHANGRI-LA	*Virgin*	68	*16 Nov 96*	1
ALBUMS:	**HITS 1**			**WEEKS 11**
THE RUTLES	*Warner Brothers*	12	*15 Apr 78*	11

RUTS — UK

SINGLES:	HITS 4			WEEKS 28
BABYLON'S BURNING	*Virgin*	7	*16 Jun 79*	11
SOMETHING THAT I SAID	*Virgin*	29	*8 Sep 79*	5
STARING AT THE RUDE BOYS	*Virgin*	22	*19 Apr 80*	8
WEST ONE (SHINE ON ME)	*Virgin*	43	*30 Aug 80*	4
ALBUMS:	**HITS 2**			**WEEKS 10**
THE CRACK	*Virgin*	16	*13 Oct 79*	6

GRIN AND BEAR IT	*Virgin*	28	*18 Oct 80*	4
Above hit: RUTS D.C.				

Barry RYAN — UK

(See also Paul and Barry Ryan.)

SINGLES:	HITS 6			WEEKS 33
ELOISE	*MGM*	2	*26 Oct 68*	12
LOVE IS LOVE	*MGM*	25	*22 Feb 69*	4
Above 2: Barry RYAN with the MAJORITY.				
THE HUNT	*Polydor*	34	*4 Oct 69*	5
MAGICAL SPIEL	*Polydor*	49	*21 Feb 70*	1
KITSCH	*Polydor*	37	*16 May 70*	6
Above hit: Barry RYAN with the Paul RYAN ORCHESTRA.				
CAN'T LET YOU GO	*Polydor*	32	*15 Jan 72*	5

Joshua RYAN — US

SINGLES:	HITS 1			WEEKS 1
PISTOLWHIP	*NuLife*	29	*27 Jan 01*	3

Marion RYAN with the Peter KNIGHT ORCHESTRA and the Beryl STOTT CHORUS — UK

SINGLES:	HITS 1			WEEKS 11
LOVE ME FOREVER	*Pye Nixa*	5	*25 Jan 58*	11

Paul and Barry RYAN — UK

(See also Barry Ryan.)

SINGLES:	HITS 8			WEEKS 43
DON'T BRING ME YOUR HEARTACHES	*Decca*	13	*13 Nov 65*	9
HAVE PITY ON THE BOY	*Decca*	18	*5 Feb 66*	6
I LOVE HER	*Decca*	17	*14 May 66*	8
I LOVE HOW YOU LOVE ME	*Decca*	21	*16 Jul 66*	7
Originally recorded by the Paris Sisters.				
HAVE YOU EVER LOVED SOMEBODY	*Decca*	49	*1 Oct 66*	1
Originally recorded by the Hollies.				
MISSY, MISSY	*Decca*	43	*10 Dec 66*	4
KEEP IT OUT OF SIGHT	*Decca*	30	*4 Mar 67*	6
CLAIRE	*Decca*	47	*2 Jul 67*	2

Rebekah RYAN — UK

SINGLES:	HITS 3			WEEKS 5
YOU LIFT ME UP	*MCA*	26	*18 May 96*	3
Backing vocals by Carol Kenyon, Lance Ellington and Miriam Stockley.				
JUST A LITTLE BIT OF LOVE	*MCA*	51	*7 Sep 96*	1
WOMAN IN LOVE	*MCA*	64	*17 May 97*	1

Bobby RYDELL — US

SINGLES:	HITS 8			WEEKS 60
WILD ONE	*Columbia*	7	*12 Mar 60*	14
WILD ONE [RE]	*Columbia*	47	*25 Jun 60*	1
SWINGIN' SCHOOL	*Columbia*	44	*2 Jul 60*	1
From the film 'Because They're Young'.				
VOLARE	*Columbia*	46	*3 Sep 60*	1
VOLARE [RE]	*Columbia*	22	*17 Sep 60*	5
SWAY	*Columbia*	12	*17 Dec 60*	13
GOOD TIME BABY	*Columbia*	42	*25 Mar 61*	7
TEACH ME TO TWIST	*Columbia*	45	*21 Apr 62*	1
Above hit: Chubby CHECKER; Bobby RYDELL.				
JINGLE BELL ROCK	*Cameo-Parkway*	40	*22 Dec 62*	3
Above hit: Bobby RYDELL and Chubby CHECKER.				
FORGET HIM	*Cameo-Parkway*	13	*25 May 63*	14

Mark 'Ruff' RYDER; vocals by SPECIAL MC and HEIDI — UK

SINGLES:	HITS 1			WEEKS 2
JOY	*Public Demand*	34	*31 Mar 01*	2

Mitch RYDER and the DETROIT WHEELS — US

SINGLES:	HITS 1			WEEKS 5
JENNY TAKE A RIDE! [M]	*Stateside*	44	*12 Feb 66*	1
JENNY TAKE A RIDE! [M] [RE]	*Stateside*	33	*26 Feb 66*	4
This is in fact a medley of Chuck Willis' See See Rider and Little Richard's Jenny Jenny, though label does not list it as such.				

Shaun RYDER – See HEADS with Shaun RYDER; Russell WATSON

RYTHM SYNDICATE
US

SINGLES:	HITS 1			WEEKS 5
P.A.S.S.I.O.N.	*Impact American*	58	*27 Jul 91*	5

RZA
US

ALBUMS:	HITS 1			WEEKS 1
BOBBY DIGITAL IN STEREO	*Gee Street*	70	*28 Nov 98*	1
Album is an extension of the film 'Bobby Digital' in which he starred.				

S

Robin S
US

SINGLES:	HITS 7			WEEKS 37
SHOW ME LOVE	*Champion*	59	*16 Jan 93*	4
SHOW ME LOVE [RE]	*Champion*	6	*13 Mar 93*	13
LUV 4 LUV	*Champion*	11	*31 Jul 93*	7
WHAT I DO BEST	*Champion*	43	*4 Dec 93*	2
I WANT TO THANK YOU	*Champion*	48	*19 Mar 94*	1
BACK IT UP	*Champion*	43	*5 Nov 94*	2
SHOW ME LOVE [RM]	*Champion*	9	*8 Mar 97*	5
Remixed by Lisa Marie.				
IT MUST BE LOVE	*Atlantic*	37	*12 Jul 97*	2
YOU GOT THE LOVE	*Champion*	62	*4 Oct 97*	1
Above hit: T2 featuring Robin S.				

ALBUMS:	HITS 1			WEEKS 3
SHOW ME LOVE	*Champion*	34	*4 Sep 93*	3

S CLUB 7
UK

SINGLES:	HITS 8			WEEKS 115
BRING IT ALL BACK	*Polydor*	1	*19 Jun 99*	15
S CLUB PARTY	*Polydor*	2	*2 Oct 99*	12
TWO IN A MILLION / YOU'RE MY NUMBER ONE	*Polydor*	2	*25 Dec 99*	11
S CLUB PARTY [RE]	*Polydor*	68	*8 Jan 00*	2
REACH	*Polydor*	2	*3 Jun 00*	17
NATURAL	*Polydor*	3	*23 Sep 00*	13
NEVER HAD A DREAM COME TRUE	*Polydor*	1	*9 Dec 00*	16
Charity record with proceeds to the BBC's Children In Need appeal.				
NATURAL [RE]	*Polydor*	56	*6 Jan 01*	3
DON'T STOP MOVIN'	*Polydor*	1	*5 May 01*	19
NEVER HAD A DREAM COME TRUE [RE]	*Polydor*	69	*5 May 01*	2
HAVE YOU EVER	*Polydor*	1	*1 Dec 01*	5

ALBUMS:	HITS 3			WEEKS 107
S CLUB	*Polydor*	2	*16 Oct 99*	46
7	*Polydor*	1	*24 Jun 00*	24
7 [RE]	*Polydor*	7	*16 Dec 00*	33
Repackaged with an additional track.				
SUNSHINE	*Polydor*	3	*8 Dec 01*	4

S-EXPRESS
UK

SINGLES:	HITS 6			WEEKS 50
THEME FROM S-EXPRESS	*Rhythm King*	1	*16 Apr 88*	13
Samples Rose Royce's Is It Love You're After.				
SUPERFLY GUY	*Rhythm King*	5	*23 Jul 88*	9
HEY MUSIC LOVER	*Rhythm King*	6	*18 Feb 89*	10
Chart also credits featuring Eric and Billy, they are Eric Robinson and Billy Ray Martin.				
MANTRA FOR A STATE OF MIND	*Rhythm King*	21	*16 Sep 89*	8
NOTHING TO LOSE	*Rhythm King*	32	*15 Sep 90*	4
FIND 'EM, FOOL 'EM, FORGET 'EM	*Rhythm King*	43	*30 May 92*	2
Originally recorded by Dobie Gray. Above 2: Vocals by Sonique.				
THEME FROM S.EXPRESS: THE RETURN TRIP [RM]	*Rhythm King*	14	*11 May 96*	4
Remixed by Tony De Vit and Simon Parkes.				
Above hit: Mark MOORE presents S.EXPRESS.				

ALBUMS:	HITS 1			WEEKS 9
ORIGINAL SOUNDTRACK	*Rhythm King*	5	*1 Apr 89*	9

S.F.X.
UK

SINGLES:	HITS 1			WEEKS 3
LEMMINGS	*Parlophone*	51	*15 May 93*	3
Inspired by the Computer game 'Lemmings 2 – The Tribes'. Each format of this release included a different map and level solution to the game.				

S-J — UK

SINGLES:	HITS 3			WEEKS 4
FEVER	*React*	46	*11 Jan 97*	1
I FEEL DIVINE	*React*	30	*24 Jan 98*	2
SHIVER	*React*	59	*7 Nov 98*	1

S*M*A*S*H — UK

SINGLES:	HITS 1			WEEKS 1
(I WANT TO) KILL SOMEBODY	*Hi-Rise Recordings*	26	*6 Aug 94*	1
ALBUMS:	**HITS 2**			**WEEKS 4**
S*M*A*S*H	*Hi-Rise Recordings*	28	*2 Apr 94*	3
Mini-album comprising their first two singles and B-sides.				
SELF ABUSED	*Hi-Rise Recordings*	59	*17 Sep 94*	1

S.O.A.P. — Denmark

SINGLES:	HITS 1			WEEKS 2
THIS IS HOW WE PARTY	*Columbia*	36	*25 Jul 98*	2

S.O.S. BAND — US

SINGLES:	HITS 8			WEEKS 46
TAKE YOUR TIME (DO IT RIGHT)	*Tabu*	51	*19 Jul 80*	4
GROOVIN' (THAT'S WHAT WE'RE DOIN')	*Tabu*	72	*26 Feb 83*	1
JUST BE GOOD TO ME	*Tabu*	13	*7 Apr 84*	11
JUST THE WAY YOU LIKE IT	*Tabu*	32	*4 Aug 84*	7
WEEKEND GIRL	*Tabu*	51	*13 Oct 84*	5
THE FINEST	*Tabu*	17	*29 Mar 86*	10
BORROWED TIME	*Tabu*	50	*5 Jul 86*	5
NO LIES	*Tabu*	64	*2 May 87*	3
ALBUMS:	**HITS 3**			**WEEKS 21**
JUST THE WAY YOU LIKE IT	*Tabu*	29	*1 Sep 84*	10
THE ARTISTS VOLUME III	*Street Sounds*	87	*12 Oct 85*	2
Compilation album with tracks by each artist. Above hit: WOMACK and WOMACK/O'JAYS/KLEEER/S.O.S. BAND.				
SANDS OF TIME	*Tabu*	15	*17 May 86*	9

S.O.U.L. S.Y.S.T.E.M. introducing Michelle VISAGE — US

SINGLES:	HITS 1			WEEKS 5
IT'S GONNA BE A LOVELY DAY	*Arista*	17	*16 Jan 93*	5
From the film 'The Bodyguard'. Based around Bill Withers' Lovely Day.				

Raphael SAADIQ and Q-TIP — US

(See also A Tribe Called Quest.)

SINGLES:	HITS 1			WEEKS 2
GET INVOLVED	*Hollywood*	36	*19 Jun 99*	2
From the animated TV series 'The P.J.'s'. Samples the Intruders' I'll Always Love My Mama.				

SABRE featuring PRESIDENT BROWN — Jamaica

SINGLES:	HITS 1			WEEKS 1
WRONG OR RIGHT	*Greensleeves*	71	*19 Aug 95*	1

SABRES - See Denny SEYTON and the SABRES

SABRES OF PARADISE — UK

SINGLES:	HITS 3			WEEKS 8
SMOKEBELCH II	*Sabres Of Paradise*	55	*2 Oct 93*	3
THEME	*Sabres Of Paradise*	56	*9 Apr 94*	3
WILMOT	*Warp*	36	*17 Sep 94*	2
Samples a 1929 calypso record by Wilmot Houdini and the Night Owls.				
ALBUMS:	**HITS 2**			**WEEKS 3**
SABRESONIC	*Warp*	29	*23 Oct 93*	2
HAUNTED DANCEHALL	*Warp*	57	*10 Dec 94*	1

SABRINA — Italy

SINGLES:	HITS 3			WEEKS 22
BOYS (SUMMERTIME LOVE)	*Ibiza*	60	*6 Feb 88*	3
BOYS (SUMMERTIME LOVE) [RE]	*Ibiza*	3	*11 Jun 88*	11
ALL OF ME	*PWL*	25	*1 Oct 88*	7
LIKE A YO-YO	*Videogram*	72	*1 Jul 89*	1

SACRED SPIRIT — Europe

(See also Divine Works.)

SINGLES:	HITS 2			WEEKS 5
YEHA-NOHA (WISHES OF HAPPINESS AND PROSPERITY) *Featured in the Survival For Tribal People cinema advert.*	*Virgin*	71	*15 Apr 95*	1
WISHES OF HAPPINESS & PROSPERITY (YEHA-NOHA) [RI]	*Virgin*	37	*18 Nov 95*	2
WINTER CEREMONY (TOR-CHENEY-NAHANA) *Theme from the Channel 4 TV series 'Tribal Cops'.*	*Virgin*	45	*16 Mar 96*	2
ALBUMS:	**HITS 2**			**WEEKS 30**
CHANTS AND DANCES OF THE NATIVE AMERICANS *Donation of sales made to the Native American Right Fund.*	*Virgin*	62	*1 Apr 95*	3
CHANTS AND DANCES OF THE NATIVE AMERICANS [RE]	*Virgin*	9	*28 Oct 95*	24
VOLUME 2 - CULTURE CLASH *Fuses blues with classical music.*	*Virgin*	24	*26 Apr 97*	3

SAD CAFE — UK

SINGLES:	HITS 6			WEEKS 44
EVERY DAY HURTS *Produced by Eric Stewart of 10cc.*	*RCA*	3	*22 Sep 79*	12
STRANGE LITTLE GIRL	*RCA*	32	*19 Jan 80*	5
MY OH MY	*RCA*	14	*15 Mar 80*	11
NOTHING LEFT TOULOUSE	*RCA*	62	*21 Jun 80*	4
LA-DI-DA	*RCA*	41	*27 Sep 80*	6
I'M IN LOVE AGAIN	*RCA*	40	*20 Dec 80*	6
ALBUMS:	**HITS 6**			**WEEKS 36**
FANX TA RA	*RCA Victor*	56	*1 Oct 77*	1
MISPLACED IDEALS	*RCA Victor*	50	*29 Apr 78*	1
FACADES *Title is an anagram of the group's name.*	*RCA*	8	*29 Sep 79*	23
SAD CAFE	*RCA*	46	*25 Oct 80*	5
LIVE	*RCA*	37	*21 Mar 81*	4
OLE	*Polydor*	72	*24 Oct 81*	2

SADE — UK

SINGLES:	HITS 13			WEEKS 69
YOUR LOVE IS KING	*Epic*	6	*25 Feb 84*	11
YOUR LOVE IS KING [RE]	*Epic*	75	*19 May 84*	1
WHEN AM I GONNA MAKE A LIVING	*Epic*	36	*26 May 84*	5
SMOOTH OPERATOR	*Epic*	19	*15 Sep 84*	10
THE SWEETEST TABOO	*Epic*	31	*12 Oct 85*	5
IS IT A CRIME	*Epic*	49	*11 Jan 86*	3
LOVE IS STRONGER THAN PRIDE	*Epic*	44	*2 Apr 88*	3
PARADISE	*Epic*	29	*4 Jun 88*	7
NO ORDINARY LOVE	*Epic*	26	*10 Oct 92*	3
FEEL NO PAIN	*Epic*	56	*28 Nov 92*	2
KISS OF LIFE	*Epic*	44	*8 May 93*	3
NO ORDINARY LOVE [RE] *Re-entered after being featured in the film 'Indecent Proposal'.*	*Epic*	14	*5 Jun 93*	8
CHERISH THE DAY	*Epic*	53	*31 Jul 93*	2
BY YOUR SIDE	*Epic*	17	*18 Nov 00*	5
KING OF SORROW	*Epic*	59	*24 Mar 01*	1
ALBUMS:	**HITS 6**			**WEEKS 211**
DIAMOND LIFE	*Epic*	2	*28 Jul 84*	99
PROMISE	*Epic*	1	*16 Nov 85*	31
STRONGER THAN PRIDE	*Epic*	3	*14 May 88*	17
LOVE DELUXE	*Epic*	10	*7 Nov 92*	27
THE BEST OF SADE	*Epic*	6	*12 Nov 94*	16
LOVERS ROCK	*Epic*	18	*25 Nov 00*	21

Staff Sergeant Barry SADLER — US

SINGLES:	HITS 1			WEEKS 8
THE BALLAD OF THE GREEN BERETS *A tribute to the Special Forces Unit of the US army.*	*RCA Victor*	24	*26 Mar 66*	8

SAFRI DUO — Holland

SINGLES:	HITS 1			WEEKS 9
PLAYED-A-LIVE (THE BONGO SONG)	*AM:PM*	6	*3 Feb 01*	9

SAFFRON — UK

SINGLES:	HITS 1			WEEKS 2
CIRCLES	*WEA*	60	*16 Jan 93*	2

Mike SAGAR and CRESTERS — UK

SINGLES:	HITS 1			WEEKS 5
DEEP FEELING	*His Master's Voice*	44	*10 Dec 60*	5

SAGAT — US

SINGLES:	HITS 2			WEEKS 6
FUNK DAT	*ffrr*	25	*4 Dec 93*	5
LUVSTUFF	*ffrr*	71	*3 Dec 94*	1

Carole Bayer SAGER — US

SINGLES:	HITS 1			WEEKS 9
YOU'RE MOVING OUT TODAY	*Elektra*	6	*28 May 77*	9
Originally recorded by Bette Midler.				

Bally SAGOO — UK

SINGLES:	HITS 4			WEEKS 8
CHURA LIYA	*Columbia*	64	*3 Sep 94*	1
First chart hit to be sung predominantly in Hindi.				
CHOLI KE PEECHE	*Columbia*	45	*22 Apr 95*	1
Roughly translated in English as What's Behind Your Blouse?				
DIL CHEEZ (MY HEART . . .)	*Higher Ground*	12	*19 Oct 96*	3
Features vocals from Shabnam Majid, Kash Rex and K.C.				
TUM BIN JIYA	*Higher Ground*	21	*1 Feb 97*	3
ALBUMS:	**HITS 1**			**WEEKS 1**
RISING FROM THE EAST	*Higher Ground*	63	*9 Nov 96*	1

SAILOR — UK

SINGLES:	HITS 3			WEEKS 24
A GLASS OF CHAMPAGNE	*Epic*	2	*6 Dec 75*	12
GIRLS, GIRLS, GIRLS	*Epic*	7	*27 Mar 76*	8
ONE DRINK TOO MANY	*Epic*	35	*19 Feb 77*	4
ALBUMS:	**HITS 1**			**WEEKS 8**
TROUBLE	*Epic*	45	*7 Feb 76*	8

SAILORS, SOLDIERS and AIRMEN of HER MAJESTY'S FORCES – See Vera LYNN

ST. ANDREWS CHORALE — UK

SINGLES:	HITS 1			WEEKS 5
CLOUD 99 (SOLEADO)	*Decca*	31	*14 Feb 76*	5

ST. CECELIA — UK

SINGLES:	HITS 1			WEEKS 17
LEAP UP AND DOWN	*Polydor*	12	*19 Jun 71*	17
Some copies had title as Leap Up And Down (Wave Your Knickers In The Air).				

SAINT ETIENNE — UK

(See also Various Artists (EPs) 'The Fred EP'.)

SINGLES:	HITS 16			WEEKS 52
NOTHING CAN STOP US / SPEEDWELL	*Heavenly*	54	*18 May 91*	3
ONLY LOVE CAN BREAK YOUR HEART / FILTHY	*Heavenly*	39	*7 Sep 91*	4
Only Love Can Break Your Heart originally recorded and written by Neil Young. His version reached No. 33 in the US in 1970.				
JOIN OUR CLUB / PEOPLE GET REAL	*Heavenly*	21	*16 May 92*	3
AVENUE	*Heavenly*	40	*17 Oct 92*	2
YOU'RE IN A BAD WAY	*Heavenly*	12	*13 Feb 93*	5
HOBART PAVING / WHO DO YOU THINK YOU ARE	*Heavenly*	23	*22 May 93*	5
XMAS 93: I WAS BORN ON CHRISTMAS DAY	*Heavenly*	37	*18 Dec 93*	5
Vocals by Tim Burgess of the Charlatans.				
PALE MOVIE	*Heavenly*	28	*19 Feb 94*	3
LIKE A MOTORWAY	*Heavenly*	47	*28 May 94*	2
HUG MY SOUL	*Heavenly*	32	*1 Oct 94*	2
Based upon a refrain from Andrea True Connection's More More More.				
HE'S ON THE PHONE	*Heavenly*	11	*11 Nov 95*	5
Above hit: SAINT ETIENNE featuring Etienne DAHO.				
SYLVIE	*Creation*	12	*7 Feb 98*	3
THE BAD PHOTOGRAPHER	*Creation*	27	*2 May 98*	2
TELL ME WHY (THE RIDDLE)	*Deviant*	7	*20 May 00*	5
Although Saint Etienne are credited, only lead singer Sarah Cracknell appears on the track.				
Above hit: Paul VAN DYK featuring SAINT ETIENNE.				
HEART FAILED (IN THE BACK OF A TAXI)	*Mantra*	50	*24 Jun 00*	1
BOY IS CRYING	*Mantra*	34	*20 Jan 01*	2
ALBUMS:	**HITS 8**			**WEEKS 30**
FOXBASE ALPHA	*Heavenly*	34	*26 Oct 91*	3

SO TOUGH	*Heavenly*	7	*6 Mar 93*	7
TIGER BAY	*Heavenly*	8	*12 Mar 94*	4
TOO YOUNG TO DIE - THE SINGLES	*Heavenly*	17	*25 Nov 95*	9
RESERECTION *Above hit: SAINT ETIENNE DAHO.*	*Virgin*	50	*27 Jan 96*	1
CASINO CLASSICS *Remixes.*	*Heavenly*	34	*19 Oct 96*	2
GOOD HUMOR	*Creation*	18	*16 May 98*	3
SOUND OF WATER	*Mantra*	33	*3 Jun 00*	1

ST GERMAIN
France

SINGLES:	HITS 2			WEEKS 3
ALABAMA BLUES REVISITED *First appeared on the French Motherlane EP in 1993.*	*F. Communications*	50	*31 Aug 96*	1
ROSE ROUGE *Samples Marlena Shaw's Live At Montreau.*	*Blue Note*	54	*10 Mar 01*	2

ALBUMS:	HITS 1			WEEKS 1
TOURIST	*Blue Note*	73	*20 May 00*	1

Barry ST. JOHN
UK

SINGLES:	HITS 1			WEEKS 1
COME AWAY MELINDA *Originally recorded by Harry Belafonte.*	*Columbia*	47	*11 Dec 65*	1

ST. JOHN'S COLLEGE SCHOOL CHOIR and the Band of the GRENADIER GUARDS
UK

SINGLES:	HITS 1			WEEKS 3
THE QUEEN'S BIRTHDAY SONG *To commemorate Queen Elizabeth II's 60th Birthday.*	*Columbia*	40	*3 May 86*	3

ST. LOUIS UNION
UK

SINGLES:	HITS 1			WEEKS 10
GIRL *Originally recorded by the Beatles.*	*Decca*	11	*15 Jan 66*	10

ST. LUNATICS - See NELLY

ST. PAUL'S BOYS' CHOIR
UK

ALBUMS:	HITS 1			WEEKS 8
REJOICE	*K-Tel*	36	*29 Nov 80*	8

Crispian ST. PETERS
UK

SINGLES:	HITS 3			WEEKS 31
YOU WERE ON MY MIND *Originally recorded by Ian and Sylvia.*	*Decca*	2	*8 Jan 66*	14
THE PIED PIPER *Originally recorded by Changing Times.*	*Decca*	5	*2 Apr 66*	13
CHANGES	*Decca*	49	*17 Sep 66*	1
CHANGES [RE]	*Decca*	47	*1 Oct 66*	3

ST. PHILIPS CHOIR
UK

SINGLES:	HITS 1			WEEKS 4
SING FOR EVER	*BBC*	49	*12 Dec 87*	4

ST. THOMAS MORE SCHOOL CHOIR - See Scott FITZGERALD

ST. WINIFRED'S SCHOOL CHOIR
UK

SINGLES:	HITS 1			WEEKS 11
THERE'S NO ONE QUITE LIKE GRANDMA *Label only shows title as No One Quite Like Grandma.*	*Music For Pleasure*	1	*22 Nov 80*	11

Buffy SAINTE-MARIE
Canada

SINGLES:	HITS 4			WEEKS 29
SOLDIER BLUE *From the film of the same name.*	*RCA Victor*	7	*17 Jul 71*	18
I'M GONNA BE A COUNTRY GIRL AGAIN	*Vanguard*	34	*18 Mar 72*	5
THE BIG ONES GET AWAY	*Ensign*	39	*8 Feb 92*	5
FALLEN ANGELS	*Ensign*	57	*4 Jul 92*	1

ALBUMS:	HITS 1			WEEKS 2
COINCIDENCE (AND LIKELY STORIES)	*Ensign*	39	*21 Mar 92*	2

SAINTS
Australia

SINGLES:	HITS 1			WEEKS 4
THIS PERFECT DAY	*Harvest*	34	*16 Jul 77*	4

SAJA – See HAMMER

Kyu SAKAMOTO — Japan

SINGLES:	HITS 1			WEEKS 13
SUKIYAKI (UE O MUITE ARUKO)	*His Master's Voice*	6	*29 Jun 63*	13
English translation: I Look Up When I Walk.				

Riuichi SAKAMOTO — Japan

SINGLES:	HITS 3			WEEKS 15
BAMBOO HOUSES / BAMBOO MUSIC	*Virgin*	30	*7 Aug 82*	4
Above hit: SYLVIAN SAKAMOTO.				
FORBIDDEN COLOURS	*Virgin*	16	*2 Jul 83*	8
Vocal version of the theme from the film 'Merry Christmas Mr. Lawrence'.				
Above hit: David SYLVIAN and Riuichi SAKAMOTO.				
HEARTBEAT (TAINAI KAIKI II) RETURNING TO THE WOMB	*Virgin America*	58	*13 Jun 92*	3
Above hit: David SYLVIAN and Riuichi SAKAMOTO featuring Ingrid CHAVEZ.				
ALBUMS:	**HITS 1**			**WEEKS 9**
MERRY CHRISTMAS MR LAWRENCE [OST]	*Virgin*	36	*3 Sep 83*	9

SAKKARIN – See Jonathan KING

SALAD — UK/Holland

SINGLES:	HITS 5			WEEKS 5
DRINK THE ELIXIR	*Island Red*	66	*11 Mar 95*	1
MOTORBIKE TO HEAVEN	*Island Red*	42	*13 May 95*	1
GRANITE STATUE	*Island Red*	50	*16 Sep 95*	1
I WANT YOU	*Island*	60	*26 Oct 96*	1
CARDBOY KING	*Island*	65	*17 May 97*	1
ALBUMS:	**HITS 1**			**WEEKS 2**
DRINK ME	*Island Red*	16	*27 May 95*	2

SALFORD JETS — UK

SINGLES:	HITS 1			WEEKS 2
WHO YOU LOOKING AT?	*RCA*	72	*31 May 80*	2

SALSOUL ORCHESTRA – See CHARO and the SALSOUL ORCHESTRA

SALT – See GOD'S PROPERTY from Kirk FRANKLIN'S NU NATION featuring Kirk FRANKLIN and "SALT"

SALT-N-PEPA — US

SINGLES:	HITS 15			WEEKS 123
PUSH IT / I AM DOWN	*ffrr*	41	*26 Mar 88*	6
I Am Down listed from 2 Apr 88.				
PUSH IT / TRAMP	*Champion & ffrr*	2	*25 Jun 88*	13
Sales were combined with the ffrr release whch had also been repackaged to include Tramp. The Champion label had the original mix of Push It with a remixed version of Tramp by Bayside Studios, while the ffrr label had the remix of Push It by Hurby 'Lovebug' Azor with the original version of Tramp. Tramp originally recorded by Lowell Fulsom.				
SHAKE YOUR THANG (IT'S YOUR THING)	*ffrr*	22	*3 Sep 88*	8
Above hit: SALT N PEPA - featuring E.U.				
TWIST AND SHOUT	*ffrr*	4	*12 Nov 88*	9
Originally recorded by the Top Notes.				
EXPRESSION	*ffrr*	40	*14 Apr 90*	6
Sleeve subtitled The Brixton Bass Mix.				
DO YOU WANT ME	*ffrr*	5	*25 May 91*	12
Male vocalist is Herbie Luv Bug.				
LET'S TALK ABOUT SEX	*ffrr*	2	*31 Aug 91*	13
YOU SHOWED ME	*ffrr*	15	*30 Nov 91*	9
Originally recorded by the Byrds.				
EXPRESSION [RM]	*ffrr*	23	*28 Mar 92*	6
Remixed by Ben Liebrand.				
START ME UP	*ffrr*	39	*3 Oct 92*	3
SHOOP	*ffrr*	29	*9 Oct 93*	3
WHATTA MAN	*ffrr*	7	*19 Mar 94*	10
Originally recorded by Linda Lyndell.				
Above hit: SALT 'N' PEPA with EN VOGUE.				
SHOOP [RM]	*ffrr*	13	*28 May 94*	8
Remixed by Cheryl "Salt" James.				
NONE OF YOUR BUSINESS	*ffrr*	19	*12 Nov 94*	4
NONE OF YOUR BUSINESS [RE]	*ffrr*	64	*7 Jan 95*	1
CHAMPAGNE	*MCA*	23	*21 Dec 96*	6
From the film 'Bulletproof'.				
R U READY	*ffrr*	24	*29 Nov 97*	2
THE BRICK TRACK VERSUS GITTY UP	*ffrr*	22	*11 Dec 99*	4
Samples Pink Floyd's Another Brick In The Wall.				

ALBUMS:	HITS 6			WEEKS 57
A SALT WITH A DEADLY PEPA	*ffrr*	19	*6 Aug 88*	27
Above Hit: SALT N PEPA featuring SPINDERELLA.				
BLACKS' MAGIC	*ffrr*	70	*12 May 90*	1
A BLITZ OF SALT-N-PEPA HITS (THE HITS REMIXED)	*ffrr*	70	*6 Jul 91*	2
THE GREATEST HITS	*ffrr*	6	*19 Oct 91*	20
RAPPED IN REMIXES	*ffrr*	37	*25 Apr 92*	2
VERY NECESSARY	*ffrr*	36	*23 Apr 94*	5

SALT TANK — UK

SINGLES:	HITS 2			WEEKS 4
EUGINA	*Internal*	40	*11 May 96*	2
DIMENSION	*Hooj Choons*	52	*3 Jul 99*	1
EUGINA [RM]	*Lost Language*	58	*9 Dec 00*	1
Remixed by Salt Tank.				

SALVATION ARMY — UK

ALBUMS:	HITS 1			WEEKS 5
BY REQUEST	*Warwick*	16	*24 Dec 77*	5

SAM and DAVE — US

(See also Lou Reed.)

SINGLES:	HITS 4			WEEKS 39
SOOTHE ME	*Stax*	48	*18 Mar 67*	2
Originally recorded by Sam Cooke.				
SOOTHE ME [RE]	*Stax*	35	*15 Apr 67*	6
SOUL MAN	*Stax*	24	*4 Nov 67*	14
I THANK YOU	*Stax*	34	*16 Mar 68*	9
SOUL SISTER BROWN SUGAR	*Atlantic*	15	*1 Feb 69*	8
ALBUMS:	**HITS 3**			**WEEKS 20**
HOLD ON I'M A COMIN'	*Atlantic*	35	*21 Jan 67*	7
DOUBLE DYNAMITE	*Stax*	28	*22 Apr 67*	5
SOUL MEN	*Stax*	32	*23 Mar 68*	8

SAM THE SHAM and the PHARAOHS — US

SINGLES:	HITS 2			WEEKS 18
WOOLY BULLY	*MGM*	11	*26 Jun 65*	15
LIL' RED RIDING HOOD	*MGM*	48	*6 Aug 66*	1
LIL' RED RIDING HOOD [RE]	*MGM*	46	*20 Aug 66*	2

Richie SAMBORA — US

SINGLES:	HITS 3			WEEKS 4
BALLAD OF YOUTH	*Mercury*	59	*7 Sep 91*	1
HARD TIMES COME EASY	*Mercury*	37	*7 Mar 98*	2
IN IT FOR LOVE	*Mercury*	58	*1 Aug 98*	1
ALBUMS:	**HITS 2**			**WEEKS 5**
STRANGER IN THIS TOWN	*Mercury*	20	*14 Sep 91*	3
UNDISCOVERED SOUL	*Mercury*	24	*14 Mar 98*	2

Mike SAMMES SINGERS — UK

(See also Alma Cogan; Carol Deene; Michael Flanders with the Michael Sammes Singers; Ronnie Hilton; Michael Holliday; Des O'Connor; Andy Stewart; Malcolm Vaughan; Michael Ward; Jimmy Young.)

SINGLES:	HITS 1			WEEKS 38
SOMEWHERE MY LOVE	*His Master's Voice*	22	*17 Sep 66*	19
Lara's Theme from the film 'Dr. Zhivago'.				
SOMEWHERE MY LOVE [RE]	*His Master's Voice*	14	*15 Jul 67*	19

Dave SAMPSON and the HUNTERS — UK

SINGLES:	HITS 1			WEEKS 6
SWEET DREAMS	*Columbia*	48	*21 May 60*	1
SWEET DREAMS [RE]	*Columbia*	29	*4 Jun 60*	5

SAMSON — UK

SINGLES:	HITS 3			WEEKS 6
RIDING WITH THE ANGELS	*RCA*	55	*4 Jul 81*	3
LOSING MY GRIP	*Polydor*	63	*24 Jul 82*	2
RED SKIES	*Polydor*	65	*5 Mar 83*	1
ALBUMS:	**HITS 1**			**WEEKS 6**
HEAD ON	*Gem*	34	*26 Jul 80*	6

SAN JOSE featuring Rodriguez ARGENTINA — UK

(See also Argent; Silsoe.)

SINGLES:	HITS 1			WEEKS 8
ARGENTINE MELODY (CANCION DE ARGENTINA) *The BBC theme to their coverage of the 1978 World Cup.*	*MCA*	14	*17 Jun 78*	8

SAN REMO STRINGS — US

SINGLES:	HITS 1			WEEKS 8
FESTIVAL TIME	*Tamla Motown*	39	*18 Dec 71*	8

David SANBORN — US

ALBUMS:	HITS 1			WEEKS 1
A CHANGE OF HEART	*Warner Brothers*	86	*14 Mar 87*	1

Junior SANCHEZ featuring DAJAE — US

SINGLES:	HITS 1			WEEKS 2
B WITH U	*Manifesto*	31	*16 Oct 99*	2

Roger SANCHEZ — US

SINGLES:	HITS 6			WEEKS 21
RELEASE YO SELF *Above hit: Roger SANCHEZ presents TRANSATLANTIC SOUL.*	*Deconstruction*	43	*22 Mar 97*	1
BUFFALO GALS STAMPEDE *Roger Sanchez remixed track 1 (as per CD order). Rakim only appeared on track 2 titled 'Buffalo Gals (Back To Skool)'.* *Above hit: Malcolm McLAREN and the WORLD FAMOUS SUPREME TEAM versus RAKIM and Roger SANCHEZ.*	*Virgin*	65	*3 Oct 98*	1
I WANT YOUR LOVE *Above hit: Roger SANCHEZ presents TWILIGHT.*	*Perpetual*	31	*20 Feb 99*	2
I NEVER KNEW *Above Roger SANCHEZ featuring COOLY'S HOT BOX.*	*INCredible*	24	*29 Jan 00*	2
ANOTHER CHANCE *Samples Toto's I Won't Hold You Back.*	*Defected*	1	*14 Jul 01*	12
YOU CAN'T CHANGE ME *Above hit: Roger SANCHEZ featuring Armand Van HELDEN and N'Dea DAVENPORT.*	*Defected*	25	*15 Dec 01*	3

ALBUMS:	HITS 1			WEEKS 2
FIRST CONTACT	*Defected*	34	*11 Aug 01*	2

Deion SANDERS – See HAMMER

Chris SANDFORD — UK

SINGLES:	HITS 1			WEEKS 9
NOT TOO LITTLE - NOT TOO MUCH	*Decca*	17	*14 Dec 63*	9

SANDPIPERS — US

SINGLES:	HITS 4			WEEKS 33
GUANTANAMERA *Adapted to music by folk singer Pete Seeger, from a poem by Jose Marti.*	*Pye International*	7	*17 Sep 66*	17
QUANDO M'INNAMORO (A MAN WITHOUT LOVE)	*A&M*	33	*8 Jun 68*	6
KUMBAYA	*A&M*	38	*29 Mar 69*	1
KUMBAYA [RE]	*A&M*	49	*12 Apr 69*	1
HANG ON SLOOPY	*Satril*	32	*27 Nov 76*	8

SANDRA — Germany

SINGLES:	HITS 1			WEEKS 8
EVERLASTING LOVE *Original release reached No. 88 in 1987.*	*Siren*	45	*17 Dec 88*	8

Jodie SANDS — US

SINGLES:	HITS 1			WEEKS 10
SOMEDAY (YOU'LL WANT ME TO WANT YOU) *Originally recorded by Mills Brothers in 1949.*	*His Master's Voice*	14	*18 Oct 58*	10

Tommy SANDS — US

SINGLES:	HITS 1			WEEKS 7
THE OLD OAKEN BUCKET	*Capitol*	25	*6 Aug 60*	7

SANDSTORM — US

SINGLES:	HITS 1			WEEKS 1
THE RETURN OF NOTHING	*Renaissance Recordings*	54	*13 May 00*	1

Samantha SANG — Australia

SINGLES:	HITS 1			WEEKS 13
EMOTIONS	*Private Stock*	11	*4 Feb 78*	13
Written and backing vocals by Robin and Barry Gibb.				

SANTA CLAUS and the CHRISTMAS TREES — UK

SINGLES:	HITS 2			WEEKS 10
SINGALONG-A-SANTA [M]	*Polydor*	19	*11 Dec 82*	5
SINGALONG-A-SANTA AGAIN [M]	*Polydor*	39	*10 Dec 83*	5
Above 2 are medleys of Christmas songs.				

SANTA ESMERALDA and Leroy GOMEZ — US/France

SINGLES:	HITS 1			WEEKS 5
DON'T LET ME BE MISUNDERSTOOD	*Philips*	41	*12 Nov 77*	5

SANTANA — US

(See also Carlos Santana and Alice Coltrane; Carlos Santana and Buddy Miles; Carlos Santana and Mahavishnu John McLaughlin.)

SINGLES:	HITS 6			WEEKS 46
SAMBA PA TI	*CBS*	27	*28 Sep 74*	7
SHE'S NOT THERE	*CBS*	11	*15 Oct 77*	13
WELL ALL RIGHT	*CBS*	53	*25 Nov 78*	3
Originally recorded by Buddy Holly.				
ALL I EVER WANTED	*CBS*	57	*22 Mar 80*	3
SMOOTH	*Arista*	75	*23 Oct 99*	1
Above hit: SANTANA featuring Rob THOMAS.				
SMOOTH [RI]	*Arista*	3	*1 Apr 00*	10
Above hit: SANTANA (featuring Rob THOMAS).				
MARIA MARIA	*Arista*	6	*5 Aug 00*	9
Above hit: SANTANA featuring the PRODUCT G&B.				
ALBUMS:	**HITS 22**			**WEEKS 279**
SANTANA	*CBS*	26	*2 May 70*	11
ABRAXAS	*CBS*	7	*28 Nov 70*	52
SANTANA III	*CBS*	6	*13 Nov 71*	14
CARAVANSERAI	*CBS*	6	*25 Nov 72*	11
WELCOME	*CBS*	8	*8 Dec 73*	6
GREATEST HITS	*CBS*	14	*21 Sep 74*	15
BARBOLETTA	*CBS*	18	*30 Nov 74*	5
AMIGOS	*CBS*	21	*10 Apr 76*	9
FESTIVAL	*CBS*	27	*8 Jan 77*	3
MOONFLOWER	*CBS*	7	*5 Nov 77*	27
Live recordings.				
INNER SECRETS	*CBS*	17	*11 Nov 78*	16
ONENESS - SILVER DREAMS GOLDEN REALITY	*CBS*	55	*24 Mar 79*	4
Album divided between studio and live recordings from Osaska, Japan.				
Above hit: Carlos SANTANA.				
MARATHON	*CBS*	28	*27 Oct 79*	5
THE SWING OF DELIGHT	*CBS*	65	*20 Sep 80*	2
Above hit: Carlos SANTANA.				
ZEBOP!	*CBS*	33	*18 Apr 81*	4
SHANGO	*CBS*	35	*14 Aug 82*	7
HAVANA MOON	*CBS*	84	*30 Apr 83*	3
Above hit: Carlos SANTANA.				
BEYOND APPEARANCES	*CBS*	58	*23 Mar 85*	3
VIVA! SANTANA - THE VERY BEST	*K-Tel*	50	*15 Nov 86*	8
SPIRITS DANCING IN THE FLESH	*CBS*	68	*14 Jul 90*	1
THE ULTIMATE COLLECTION	*Columbia*	23	*15 Aug 98*	6
Compilation released to mark his 30th anniversary.				
SUPERNATURAL	*Arista*	33	*04 Sept 99*	2
SUPERNATURAL [RE]	*Arista*	1	*5 Feb 00*	45
THE ULTIMATE COLLECTION [RE]	*Columbia*	12	*8 Apr 00*	20

Carlos SANTANA and Alice COLTRANE — US

(See also Santana.)

ALBUMS:	HITS 1			WEEKS 1
ILLUMINATIONS	*CBS*	40	*2 Nov 74*	1

Carlos SANTANA and Mahavishnu John McLAUGHLIN — US

(See also Mahavishnu Orchestra; Santana.)

ALBUMS:	HITS 1			WEEKS 9
LOVE, DEVOTION, SURRENDER	*CBS*	7	*28 Jul 73*	9

Carlos SANTANA and Buddy MILES — US

(See also Santana.)

ALBUMS:	HITS 1			WEEKS 4
CARLOS SANTANA AND BUDDY MILES LIVE *Live recordingss from Hawaii's Diamond Head volcano, Sep 72.*	*CBS*	29	*26 Aug 72*	4

SANTO and JOHNNY — US

SINGLES:	HITS 2			WEEKS 5
SLEEP WALK	*Pye International*	22	*17 Oct 59*	4
TEARDROP	*Parlophone*	50	*2 Apr 60*	1

SANTOS — Italy

SINGLES:	HITS 1			WEEKS 6
CAMELS	*Incentive*	9	*20 Jan 01*	6

Mike SARNE — UK

SINGLES:	HITS 4			WEEKS 43
COME OUTSIDE *Above hit: Mike SARNE featuring Wendy RICHARD.*	*Parlophone*	1	*12 May 62*	19
WILL I WHAT *Above hit: Mike SARNE featuring Billie DAVIS with the Charles BLACKWELL ORCHESTRA.*	*Parlophone*	18	*1 Sep 62*	10
JUST FOR KICKS	*Parlophone*	22	*12 Jan 63*	7
CODE OF LOVE	*Parlophone*	29	*30 Mar 63*	7

Joy SARNEY — UK

SINGLES:	HITS 1			WEEKS 6
NAUGHTY NAUGHTY NAUGHTY	*Alaska*	26	*7 May 77*	6

D.C. SAROME – See D-MOB

SARR BAND — UK/Italy/France

SINGLES:	HITS 1			WEEKS 1
MAGIC MANDRAKE	*Calendar*	68	*16 Sep 78*	1

Peter SARSTEDT — UK

SINGLES:	HITS 2			WEEKS 25
WHERE DO YOU GO TO (MY LOVELY)	*United Artists*	1	*8 Feb 69*	16
FROZEN ORANGE JUICE	*United Artists*	10	*7 Jun 69*	9
ALBUMS:	**HITS 1**			**WEEKS 4**
PETER SARSTEDT	*United Artists*	8	*15 Mar 69*	4

Robin SARSTEDT — UK

SINGLES:	HITS 1			WEEKS 9
MY RESISTANCE IS LOW *Originally recorded by Hoagy Carmichael.*	*Decca*	3	*8 May 76*	9

SARTORELLO — Italy

SINGLES:	HITS 1			WEEKS 1
MOVE BABY MOVE	*Multiply*	56	*10 Aug 96*	1

SASH! — Germany

SINGLES:	HITS 10			WEEKS 103
ENCORE UNE FOIS *Vocals by Sabine Ohmes.*	*Multiply*	2	*1 Mar 97*	15
ECUADOR *Above hit: SASH! featuring RODRIGUEZ.*	*Multiply*	2	*5 Jul 97*	12
STAY *Above hit: SASH! featuring LA TREC.*	*Multiply*	2	*18 Oct 97*	14
LA PRIMAVERA	*Multiply*	3	*4 Apr 98*	12
MYSTERIOUS TIMES *Above hit: SASH! featuring Tina COUSINS.*	*Multiply*	2	*15 Aug 98*	12
MOVE MANIA *Above hit: SASH! featuring SHANNON.*	*Multiply*	8	*28 Nov 98*	10
COLOUR THE WORLD *Vocals by Finnish singer Inka and Doctor Alban.*	*Multiply*	15	*3 Apr 99*	6
ADELANTE	*Multiply*	2	*12 Feb 00*	10
JUST AROUND THE HILL *Vocals by Tina Cousins.*	*Multiply*	8	*22 Apr 00*	7
WITH MY OWN EYES *Vocals by Inka.*	*Multiply*	10	*23 Sep 00*	5

ALBUMS:	HITS 4			WEEKS 65
IT'S MY LIFE – THE ALBUM	*Multiply*	6	*19 Jul 97*	38
LIFE GOES ON	*Multiply*	5	*05 Sept 98*	19
TRILENIUM	*Multiply*	13	*29 Apr 00*	5
ENCORE UNE FOIS – THE GREATEST HITS	*Multiply*	33	*11 Nov 00*	3

SASHA — UK

SINGLES:	HITS 5			WEEKS 15
TOGETHER	*ffrr*	57	*31 Jul 93*	1
Above hit: Danny CAMPBELL and SASHA.				
HIGHER GROUND	*Deconstruction*	19	*19 Feb 94*	3
Vocals by Sam Mollison.				
MAGIC	*Deconstruction*	32	*27 Aug 94*	4
Above hit: SASHA with vocals by Sam MOLLISON.				
BE AS ONE	*Deconstruction*	17	*9 Mar 96*	4
Above hit: SASHA and MARIA.				
SCORCHIO	*Excession*	23	*23 Sep 00*	3
Above hit: SASHA/EMERSON.				

ALBUMS:	HITS 2			WEEKS 5
THE QAT COLLECTION	*Deconstruction*	55	*12 Mar 94*	2
EXPANDER [EP]	*Deconstruction*	18	*17 Jul 99*	3
This EP was too long to be eligible for the singles chart.				

Joe SATRIANI — US

SINGLES:	HITS 1			WEEKS 1
THE SATCH [EP]	*Epic*	53	*13 Feb 93*	1
Lead track: The Extremist.				

ALBUMS:	HITS 4			WEEKS 13
THE EXTREMEIST	*Epic*	13	*15 Aug 92*	6
TIME MACHINE	*Epic*	32	*6 Nov 93*	2
JOE SATRIANI	*Epic*	21	*14 Oct 95*	3
CRYSTAL PLANET	*Epic*	32	*14 Mar 98*	2

SATURDAY NIGHT BAND — US

SINGLES:	HITS 1			WEEKS 9
COME ON DANCE, DANCE	*CBS*	16	*1 Jul 78*	9

Jannette SAUL – See Joey NEGRO

Jessie SAUNDERS – See Farley "Jackmaster" FUNK

Kevin SAUNDERSON – See INNER CITY

Chantay SAVAGE — US

SINGLES:	HITS 2			WEEKS 9
I WILL SURVIVE	*RCA*	12	*4 May 96*	8
REMINDING ME (OF SEF)	*Epic*	59	*8 Nov 97*	1
Above hit: COMMON featuring Chantay SAVAGE.				

ALBUMS:	HITS 1			WEEKS 1
I WILL SURVIVE (DOIN' IT MY WAY)	*RCA*	66	*25 May 96*	1

Edna SAVAGE with CHORUS of SERVICE MEN from the NUFFIELD CENTRE, LONDON — UK

SINGLES:	HITS 1			WEEKS 1
ARRIVEDERCI DARLING	*Parlophone*	19	*14 Jan 56*	1
Originally recorded by Renato Rascel.				

SAVAGE GARDEN — Australia

SINGLES:	HITS 9			WEEKS 101
I WANT YOU	*Columbia*	11	*21 Jun 97*	7
TO THE MOON AND BACK	*Columbia*	55	*27 Sep 97*	1
TRULY MADLY DEEPLY	*Columbia*	4	*28 Feb 98*	23
TO THE MOON AND BACK [RI]	*Columbia*	3	*22 Aug 98*	16
I WANT YOU '98 [RM]	*Columbia*	12	*12 Dec 98*	10
Remix by Dave Bascombe.				
THE ANIMAL SONG	*Columbia*	16	*10 Jul 99*	6
I KNEW I LOVED YOU	*Columbia*	10	*13 Nov 99*	12
CRASH AND BURN	*Columbia*	14	*1 Apr 00*	6
AFFIRMATION	*Columbia*	8	*29 Jul 00*	10
HOLD ME	*Columbia*	16	*25 Nov 00*	5
HOLD ME [RE]	*Columbia*	61	*20 Jan 01*	2
THE BEST THING	*Columbia*	35	*31 Mar 01*	2
THE BEST THING [RE]	*Columbia*	74	*5 May 01*	1

ALBUMS:	HITS 2			WEEKS 132
SAVAGE GARDEN	*Columbia*	2	*14 Mar 98*	68
Peak position reached on 19 Sep 98.				

AFFIRMATION	*Columbia*	12	*20 Nov 99*	23
AFFIRMATION [RE]	*Columbia*	7	*15 Jul 00*	41

Telly SAVALAS — US

SINGLES:	HITS 2			WEEKS 12
IF	*MCA*	1	*22 Feb 75*	9
Original by Bread reached No. 4 in the US in 1971.				
YOU'VE LOST THAT LOVIN' FEELIN'	*MCA*	47	*31 May 75*	3
ALBUMS:	**HITS 1**			**WEEKS 10**
TELLY	*MCA*	12	*22 Mar 75*	10

SAVANNA — UK

SINGLES:	HITS 1			WEEKS 4
I CAN'T TURN AWAY	*R&B*	61	*10 Oct 81*	4

SAVOY BROWN — UK

ALBUMS:	HITS 1			WEEKS 1
LOOKIN' IN	*Decca*	50	*28 Nov 70*	1

SAVUKA – See Johnny CLEGG and SAVUKA

SAW DOCTORS — Ireland

SINGLES:	HITS 4			WEEKS 9
SMALL BIT OF LOVE	*Shamtown*	24	*12 Nov 94*	3
WORLD OF GOOD	*Shamtown*	15	*27 Jan 96*	3
TO WIN JUST ONCE	*Shamtown*	14	*13 Jul 96*	2
Inspired by former keyboardist Tony Lambert winning £1m on Irish Lottery.				
SIMPLE THINGS	*Shamtown*	56	*6 Dec 97*	1
Compilation.				
ALBUMS:	**HITS 5**			**WEEKS 12**
IF THIS IS ROCK AND ROLL, I WANT MY OLD JOB BACK	*Solid*	69	*8 Jun 91*	2
ALL THE WAY FROM TUAM	*Solid*	33	*31 Oct 92*	2
SAME OUL' TOWN	*Shamtown*	6	*24 Feb 96*	5
SONGS FROM SUN STREET	*Shamtown*	24	*24 Oct 98*	2
VILLAINS?	*Shamtown*	58	*13 Oct 01*	1

Nitin SAWHNEY — UK

SINGLES:	HITS 1			WEEKS 1
SUNSET	*V2*	65	*28 Jul 01*	1
Above hit: Nitin SAWHNEY featuring ESKA.				
ALBUMS:	**HITS 2**			**WEEKS 3**
BEYOND SKIN	*Outcaste*	44	*25 Sept 99*	2
PROPHESY	*V2*	40	*30 Jun 01*	1

SAXON — UK

SINGLES:	HITS 15			WEEKS 61
WHEELS OF STEEL	*Carrere*	20	*22 Mar 80*	11
747 (STRANGERS IN THE NIGHT)	*Carrere*	13	*21 Jun 80*	9
BACKS TO THE WALL	*Carrere*	64	*28 Jun 80*	2
BIG TEASER / RAINBOW THEME/FROZEN RAINBOW [M]	*Carrere*	66	*28 Jun 80*	2
Big Teaser originally released in 1979. Medley is only the last two tracks.				
STRONG ARM OF THE LAW	*Carrere*	63	*29 Nov 80*	3
AND THE BANDS PLAYED ON	*Carrere*	12	*11 Apr 81*	8
NEVER SURRENDER	*Carrere*	18	*18 Jul 81*	6
PRINCESS OF THE NIGHT	*Carrere*	57	*31 Oct 81*	3
POWER AND THE GLORY	*Carrere*	32	*23 Apr 83*	5
NIGHTMARE	*Carrere*	50	*30 Jul 83*	3
BACK ON THE STREETS	*Parlophone*	75	*31 Aug 85*	1
ROCK 'N' ROLL GYPSY	*Parlophone*	71	*29 Mar 86*	1
WAITING FOR THE NIGHT	*EMI*	66	*30 Aug 86*	2
RIDE LIKE THE WIND	*EMI*	52	*5 Mar 88*	4
I CAN'T WAIT ANYMORE	*EMI*	71	*30 Apr 88*	1
ALBUMS:	**HITS 9**			**WEEKS 97**
WHEELS OF STEEL	*Carrere*	5	*12 Apr 80*	29
STRONG ARM OF THE LAW	*Carrere*	11	*15 Nov 80*	13
DENIM AND LEATHER	*Carrere*	9	*3 Oct 81*	11
THE EAGLE HAS LANDED	*Carrere*	5	*22 May 82*	19
POWER AND THE GLORY	*Carrere*	15	*26 Mar 83*	9
CRUSADER	*Carrere*	18	*11 Feb 84*	7
INNOCENCE IS NO EXCUSE	*Parlophone*	36	*14 Sep 85*	4
ROCK THE NATIONS	*EMI*	34	*27 Sep 86*	3
DESTINY	*EMI*	49	*9 Apr 88*	2

Al SAXON — UK

SINGLES:	HITS 4			WEEKS 10
YOU'RE THE TOP-CHA	*Fontana*	17	*17 Jan 59*	4
ONLY SIXTEEN	*Fontana*	24	*29 Aug 59*	3
BLUE-EYED BOY	*Fontana*	39	*24 Dec 60*	2
THERE I'VE SAID IT AGAIN	*Piccadilly*	48	*9 Sep 61*	1
Above hit: Al SAXON and his Orchestra.				

Leo SAYER — UK

SINGLES:	HITS 17			WEEKS 151
THE SHOW MUST GO ON	*Chrysalis*	2	*15 Dec 73*	13
ONE MAN BAND	*Chrysalis*	6	*15 Jun 74*	9
LONG TALL GLASSES	*Chrysalis*	4	*14 Sep 74*	9
MOONLIGHTING	*Chrysalis*	2	*30 Aug 75*	8
YOU MAKE ME FEEL LIKE DANCING	*Chrysalis*	2	*30 Oct 76*	12
WHEN I NEED YOU	*Chrysalis*	1	*29 Jan 77*	13
Originally recorded by Albert Hammond.				
HOW MUCH LOVE	*Chrysalis*	10	*9 Apr 77*	8
THUNDER IN MY HEART	*Chrysalis*	22	*10 Sep 77*	8
I CAN'T STOP LOVING YOU (THOUGH I TRY)	*Chrysalis*	6	*16 Sep 78*	11
RAINING IN MY HEART	*Chrysalis*	21	*25 Nov 78*	10
MORE THAN I CAN SAY	*Chrysalis*	2	*5 Jul 80*	11
HAVE YOU EVER BEEN IN LOVE	*Chrysalis*	10	*13 Mar 82*	9
Originally recorded by Paris.				
HEART (STOP BEATING IN TIME)	*Chrysalis*	22	*19 Jun 82*	10
ORCHARD ROAD	*Chrysalis*	16	*12 Mar 83*	8
UNTIL YOU COME BACK TO ME	*Chrysalis*	51	*15 Oct 83*	3
Sleeve reflects title as Til You Come Back To Me.				
UNCHAINED MELODY	*Chrysalis*	54	*8 Feb 86*	4
WHEN I NEED YOU [RI]	*Chrysalis*	65	*13 Feb 93*	2
YOU MAKE ME FEEL LIKE DANCING [RR]	*Brothers Organisation*	32	*8 Aug 98*	3
Above hit: GROOVE GENERATION featuring Leo SAYER.				

ALBUMS:	HITS 13			WEEKS 238
SILVER BIRD	*Chrysalis*	2	*5 Jan 74*	22
JUST A BOY	*Chrysalis*	4	*26 Oct 74*	14
Line from Roger Daltrey's Giving It All Away.				
ANOTHER YEAR	*Chrysalis*	8	*20 Sep 75*	9
ENDLESS FLIGHT	*Chrysalis*	4	*27 Nov 76*	66
THUNDER IN MY HEART	*Chrysalis*	8	*22 Oct 77*	16
LEO SAYER	*Chrysalis*	15	*2 Sep 78*	25
THE VERY BEST OF LEO SAYER	*Chrysalis*	1	*31 Mar 79*	37
HERE	*Chrysalis*	44	*13 Oct 79*	4
LIVING IN A FANTASY	*Chrysalis*	15	*23 Aug 80*	9
WORLD RADIO	*Chrysalis*	30	*8 May 82*	12
HAVE YOU EVER BEEN IN LOVE	*Chrysalis*	15	*12 Nov 83*	18
ALL THE BEST	*Chrysalis*	26	*6 Mar 93*	4
THE DEFINITIVE HITS COLLECTION	*PolyGram TV*	35	*20 Feb 99*	2

Alexei SAYLE — UK

SINGLES:	HITS 1			WEEKS 8
'ULLO JOHN! GOTTA NEW MOTOR?	*Island*	15	*25 Feb 84*	8

ALBUMS:	HITS 1			WEEKS 5
THE FISH PEOPLE TAPES	*Island*	62	*17 Mar 84*	5

SCAFFOLD — UK

SINGLES:	HITS 5			WEEKS 62
THANK U VERY MUCH	*Parlophone*	4	*25 Nov 67*	12
DO YOU REMEMBER?	*Parlophone*	34	*30 Mar 68*	5
LILY THE PINK	*Parlophone*	1	*9 Nov 68*	24
GIN GAN GOOLIE	*Parlophone*	38	*1 Nov 69*	11
GIN GAN GOOLIE [RE]	*Parlophone*	50	*24 Jan 70*	1
LIVERPOOL LOU	*Warner Brothers*	7	*1 Jun 74*	9
Originally recorded by Dominic Behan.				

Boz SCAGGS — US

SINGLES:	HITS 4			WEEKS 31
LOWDOWN	*CBS*	28	*30 Oct 76*	4
WHAT CAN I SAY	*CBS*	10	*22 Jan 77*	10
LIDO SHUFFLE	*CBS*	13	*14 May 77*	9
HOLLYWOOD	*CBS*	33	*10 Dec 77*	8

ALBUMS:	HITS 3			WEEKS 29
SILK DEGREES	*CBS*	37	*12 Mar 77*	24
DOWN TWO, THEN LEFT	*CBS*	55	*17 Dec 77*	1
MIDDLE MAN	*CBS*	52	*3 May 80*	4

SCANTY SANDWICH — UK

SINGLES:	HITS 1			WEEKS 8
BECAUSE OF YOU	*Southern Fried*	3	*29 Jan 00*	8

Samples Michael Jackson's Shoo Be Doo Da Day from his 1972 album Ben.

SCARFACE — US

SINGLES:	HITS 3			WEEKS 6
HAND OF THE DEAD BODY	*Virgin*	41	*11 Mar 95*	2
Above hit: SCARFACE (featuring ICE CUBE).				
I SEEN A MAN DIE	*Virgin*	55	*5 Aug 95*	2
GAME OVER	*Virgin*	34	*5 Jul 97*	2

Samples Indeep's Last Night A DJ Saved My Life.
Above hit: SCARFACE featuring DR. DRE, ICE CUBE, TOO SHORT.

SCARFO — UK

SINGLES:	HITS 2			WEEKS 2
ALKALINE	*Deceptive*	61	*19 Jul 97*	1
COSMONAUT NO.7	*Deceptive*	67	*18 Oct 97*	1

SCARLET — UK

SINGLES:	HITS 4			WEEKS 18
INDEPENDENT LOVE SONG	*WEA*	12	*21 Jan 95*	12
I WANNA BE FREE (TO BE WITH HIM)	*WEA*	21	*29 Apr 95*	4
LOVE HANGOVER	*WEA*	54	*5 Aug 95*	1
BAD GIRL	*WEA*	54	*6 Jul 96*	1
ALBUMS:	**HITS 1**			**WEEKS 2**
NAKED	*WEA*	59	*11 Mar 95*	2

SCARLET FANTASTIC — UK

SINGLES:	HITS 2			WEEKS 12
NO MEMORY	*Arista*	24	*3 Oct 87*	10
PLUG ME IN (TO THE CENTRAL LOVE LINE)	*Arista*	67	*23 Jan 88*	2

SCARLET PARTY — UK

SINGLES:	HITS 1			WEEKS 5
101 DAM NATIONS	*Parlophone*	44	*16 Oct 82*	5

SCARS — UK

ALBUMS:	HITS 1			WEEKS 3
AUTHOR! AUTHOR!	*Pre*	67	*18 Apr 81*	3

SCATMAN JOHN — US

SINGLES:	HITS 2			WEEKS 19
SCATMAN (SKI-BA-BOP-BA-DOP BOP)	*RCA*	3	*13 May 95*	12
SCATMAN'S WORLD	*RCA*	10	*2 Sep 95*	7

SCHAEFER – See ROSTAL and SCHAEFER

Michael SCHENKER GROUP — UK/Germany

SINGLES:	HITS 3			WEEKS 9
ARMED AND READY	*Chrysalis*	53	*13 Sep 80*	3
CRY FOR THE NATIONS	*Chrysalis*	56	*8 Nov 80*	3
DANCER	*Chrysalis*	52	*11 Sep 82*	3
ALBUMS:	**HITS 7**			**WEEKS 44**
MICHAEL SCHENKER GROUP	*Chrysalis*	8	*6 Sep 80*	8
MSG	*Chrysalis*	14	*19 Sep 81*	8
ONE NIGHT AT BUDOKAN	*Chrysalis*	5	*13 Mar 82*	11
Live recordings from Japan, 12 Aug 81.				
ASSAULT ATTACK	*Chrysalis*	19	*23 Oct 82*	5
BUILT TO DESTROY	*Chrysalis*	23	*10 Sep 83*	5
ROCK WILL NEVER DIE	*Chrysalis*	24	*23 Jun 84*	5
Live recordings.				
PERFECT TIMING	*EMI*	65	*24 Oct 87*	2

Abbreviated their name to MSG after Rob McCauley had taken the place of Michael Schenker.
Above hit: MSG.

Lalo SCHIFRIN — US

SINGLES:	HITS 2			WEEKS 11
JAWS	*CTI*	14	*9 Oct 76*	9
Theme from the film of the same name.				
BULLITT	*warner.esp*	36	*25 Oct 97*	2

Theme from the film of the same name. Featured in the Ford Puma car TV commercial.

SCHILLER — Germany

SINGLES:	HITS 1			WEEKS 3
DAS GLOCKENSPIEL	*Data*	17	*28 Apr 01*	3
Original release reached No. 79 on 4 Nov 2000.				

Peter SCHILLING — Germany

SINGLES:	HITS 1			WEEKS 6
MAJOR TOM (COMING HOME)	*PSP*	42	*5 May 84*	5
MAJOR TOM (COMING HOME) [RE]	*PSP*	73	*16 Jun 84*	1

Phillip SCHOFIELD — UK

SINGLES:	HITS 1			WEEKS 6
CLOSE EVERY DOOR	*Really Useful*	27	*5 Dec 92*	6
From the musical 'Joseph And The Amazing Technicolor Dreamcoat'.				

SCHON – See HAGAR, SCHON, AARONSON, SHRIEVE

SCHOOL OF EXCELLENCE — UK

(See also Blowing Free; Harmonium; Hypnosis; In Tune; Raindance.)

ALBUMS:	HITS 1			WEEKS 2
PIANO MOODS	*Dino*	47	*28 Oct 95*	2

SCIENCE DEPT. featuring ERIRE — UK

SINGLES:	HITS 1			WEEKS 1
BREATHE	*Renaissance Recordings*	64	*10 Nov 01*	1

SCIENTIST — UK

SINGLES:	HITS 3			WEEKS 13
THE EXORCIST	*Kickin*	62	*6 Oct 90*	3
THE EXORCIST [RE] + [RM]	*Kickin*	46	*1 Dec 90*	3
From 8 Dec 90 the remixed format was listed on the chart.				
THE BEE	*Kickin*	52	*15 Dec 90*	3
THE BEE [RE]	*Kickin*	47	*26 Jan 91*	3
Re-entry was mainly due to a remixed 12" format being made available. This was listed on the chart from 2 Feb 91.				
SPIRAL SYMPHONY	*Kickin*	74	*11 May 91*	1

SCOOBIE — UK

SINGLES:	HITS 1			WEEKS 2
THE MAGNIFICENT 7	*Big Tongue*	58	*22 Dec 01*	2

SCOOCH — UK

SINGLES:	HITS 4			WEEKS 20
WHEN MY BABY	*Accolade*	29	*6 Nov 99*	4
MORE THAN I NEEDED TO KNOW	*Accolade*	5	*22 Jan 00*	5
. . . THE BEST IS YET TO COME	*Accolade*	12	*6 May 00*	4
. . . THE BEST IS YET TO COME [RE]	*Accolade*	64	*8 Jul 00*	1
FOR SURE	*Accolade*	15	*5 Aug 00*	6
ALBUMS:	**HITS 1**			**WEEKS 2**
FOUR SURE	*Accolade*	41	*19 Aug 00*	2

SCOOTER — UK/Germany

SINGLES:	HITS 5			WEEKS 14
THE MOVE YOUR ASS [EP]	*Club Tools*	23	*21 Oct 95*	4
Lead track: Move Your Ass.				
BACK IN THE U.K.	*Club Tools*	18	*17 Feb 96*	3
REBEL YELL	*Club Tools*	30	*25 May 96*	2
I'M RAVING	*Club Tools*	33	*19 Oct 96*	3
FIRE	*Club Tools*	45	*17 May 97*	2
ALBUMS:	**HITS 1**			**WEEKS 5**
OUR HAPPY HARDCORE	*Club Tools*	24	*13 Apr 96*	5

SCORPIONS — Germany

SINGLES:	HITS 10			WEEKS 35
IS THERE ANYBODY THERE? / ANOTHER PIECE OF MEAT	*Harvest*	39	*26 May 79*	4
LOVEDRIVE	*Harvest*	69	*25 Aug 79*	2
MAKE IT REAL	*Harvest*	72	*31 May 80*	2
THE ZOO	*Harvest*	75	*20 Sep 80*	1
NO ONE LIKE YOU	*Harvest*	65	*3 Apr 82*	3
NO ONE LIKE YOU [RE]	*Harvest*	64	*1 May 82*	1
CAN'T LIVE WITHOUT YOU	*Harvest*	63	*17 Jul 82*	2
RHYTHM OF LOVE	*Harvest*	59	*4 Jun 88*	2

PASSION RULES THE GAME	*Harvest*	74	*18 Feb 89*	1
WIND OF CHANGE	*Vertigo*	53	*1 Jun 91*	3
WIND OF CHANGE [RI]	*Vertigo*	2	*28 Sep 91*	9
SEND ME AN ANGEL	*Vertigo*	27	*30 Nov 91*	3
SEND ME AN ANGEL [RE]	*Vertigo*	68	*28 Dec 91*	2
ALBUMS:	**HITS 8**		**WEEKS 56**	
LOVE DRIVE	*Harvest*	36	*21 Apr 79*	11
ANIMAL MAGNETISM	*Harvest*	23	*3 May 80*	6
BLACKOUT	*Harvest*	11	*10 Apr 82*	11
LOVE AT FIRST STING	*Harvest*	17	*24 Mar 84*	6
WORLD WIDE LIVE	*Harvest*	18	*29 Jun 85*	8
SAVAGE AMUSEMENT	*Harvest*	18	*14 May 88*	6
CRAZY WORLD	*Vertigo*	51	*17 Nov 90*	1
CRAZY WORLD [RE]	*Vertigo*	27	*2 Nov 91*	6
FACE THE HEAT	*Mercury*	51	*25 Sep 93*	1

SCOT PROJECT — Germany

SINGLES:	**HITS 1**		**WEEKS 1**	
U (I GOT A FEELING)	*Positiva*	66	*27 Jul 96*	1

SCOTLAND FOOTBALL WORLD CUP SQUAD - See SCOTTISH WORLD CUP SQUAD

Band of the SCOTS GUARDS — UK

ALBUMS:	**HITS 1**		**WEEKS 2**	
BAND OF THE SCOTS GUARDS	*Fontana*	25	*28 Jun 69*	2

Jack SCOTT — Canada

SINGLES:	**HITS 4**		**WEEKS 28**	
MY TRUE LOVE	*London*	9	*11 Oct 58*	10
THE WAY I WALK	*London*	30	*26 Sep 59*	1
WHAT IN THE WORLD'S COME OVER YOU	*Top Rank*	11	*12 Mar 60*	15
BURNING BRIDGES	*Top Rank*	32	*4 Jun 60*	2
ALBUMS:	**HITS 2**		**WEEKS 12**	
I REMEMBER HANK WILLIAMS	*Top Rank*	7	*7 May 60*	11
WHAT IN THE WORLD'S COME OVER YOU	*Top Rank*	11	*3 Sep 60*	1

Jill SCOTT — US

SINGLES:	**HITS 2**		**WEEKS 4**	
GETTIN' IN THE WAY	*Epic*	30	*4 Nov 00*	3
A LONG WALK	*Epic*	54	*7 Apr 01*	1
ALBUMS:	**HITS 1**		**WEEKS 3**	
WHO IS JILL SCOTT? - WORDS AND SOUND VOL. 1	*Epic*	69	*29 Jul 00*	3

John SCOTT - See Paul PHOENIX

Johnny SCOTT and his Orchestra - See Graham BONNEY with Johnny SCOTT and his Orchestra

Linda SCOTT — US

SINGLES:	**HITS 2**		**WEEKS 14**	
I'VE TOLD EVERY LITTLE STAR *Originally recorded by Jack Denny.*	*Columbia*	7	*20 May 61*	13
DON'T BET MONEY HONEY *Above hit: Linda SCOTT with the Hutch DAVIE ORCHESTRA.*	*Columbia*	50	*16 Sep 61*	1

Mike SCOTT — UK

SINGLES:	**HITS 4**		**WEEKS 4**	
BRING 'EM ALL IN	*Chrysalis*	56	*16 Sep 95*	1
BUILDING THE CITY OF LIGHT	*Chrysalis*	60	*11 Nov 95*	1
LOVE ANYWAY	*Chrysalis*	50	*27 Sep 97*	1
RARE, PRECIOUS AND GONE	*Chrysalis*	74	*14 Feb 98*	1
ALBUMS:	**HITS 2**		**WEEKS 4**	
BRING 'EM ALL IN	*Chrysalis*	23	*30 Sep 95*	2
STILL BURNING	*Chrysalis*	34	*11 Oct 97*	2

Millie SCOTT — US

SINGLES:	**HITS 3**		**WEEKS 11**	
PRISONER OF LOVE	*Fourth & Broadway*	52	*12 Apr 86*	4
AUTOMATIC	*Fourth & Broadway*	56	*23 Aug 86*	3
EV'RY LITTLE BIT	*Fourth & Broadway*	63	*21 Feb 87*	4

Simon SCOTT and the LeROYS — UK

SINGLES:	**HITS 1**		**WEEKS 8**	
MOVE IT BABY	*Parlophone*	37	*15 Aug 64*	8

Tony SCOTT — Holland

SINGLES:	HITS 2			WEEKS 6
THAT'S HOW I'M LIVING / THE CHIEF	*Champion*	48	*15 Apr 89*	4
The Chief listed from 22 Apr 89.				
Above hit: Toni SCOTT. Name incorrectly spelt on label and sleeve.				
GET INTO IT / THAT'S HOW I'M LIVING [RI]	*Champion*	63	*10 Feb 90*	2

SCOTT and LEON — UK

SINGLES:	HITS 2			WEEKS 6
YOU USED TO HOLD ME	*AM:PM*	19	*30 Sep 00*	4
Originally recorded by Ralphi Rosario in 1989.				
SHINE ON	*AM:PM*	34	*19 May 01*	2
Above hit: SCOTT and LEON featuring Sylvia MASON-JAMES.				

SCOTTISH EURO '96 SQUAD – See SCOTTISH WORLD CUP SQUAD

SCOTTISH RUGBY TEAM with Ronnie BROWNE — UK

SINGLES:	HITS 1			WEEKS 1
FLOWER OF SCOTLAND	*Greentrax*	73	*2 Jun 90*	1

SCOTTISH WORLD CUP SQUAD — UK

SINGLES:	HITS 5			WEEKS 27
EASY EASY	*Polydor*	20	*22 Jun 74*	4
Above hit: SCOTLAND WORLD CUP SQUAD.				
OLE OLA (MUHLER BRASILEIRA)	*Riva*	4	*27 May 78*	6
Above hit: Rod STEWART and the SCOTTISH WORLD CUP SQUAD '78.				
WE HAVE A DREAM	*WEA*	5	*1 May 82*	9
Also features vocals by John Gordon Sinclair, B.A. Robertson, Willy Carson, Christian, Miss Scotland, Georgina Kearney and the Pipes and Drums of British Caledonian Airways.				
SAY IT WITH PRIDE	*RCA*	45	*9 Jun 90*	3
Friends are Fish, James Grant, Donnie Munro and Jimmy O'Neil.				
Above hit: OFFICIAL SCOTTISH WORLD CUP SQUAD and FRIENDS.				
PURPLE HEATHER	*Warner Brothers*	16	*15 Jun 96*	5
Offical Anthem for the Scottish Football Team in Euro '96. Charity single with proceeds to the Dunblaine Appeal.				
Above hit: Rod STEWART with the SCOTTISH EURO '96 SQUAD.				
ALBUMS:	**HITS 1**			**WEEKS 9**
EASY EASY	*Polydor*	3	*25 May 74*	9
Above hit: SCOTLAND FOOTBALL WORLD CUP SQUAD 1974.				

SCREAMING BLUE MESSIAHS — UK

SINGLES:	HITS 1			WEEKS 6
I WANNA BE A FLINTSTONE	*WEA*	28	*16 Jan 88*	6
ALBUMS:	**HITS 1**			**WEEKS 1**
GUN-SHY	*WEA*	90	*17 May 86*	1

SCREAMING TREES — US

SINGLES:	HITS 2			WEEKS 2
NEARLY LOST YOU	*Epic*	50	*6 Mar 93*	1
DOLLAR BILL	*Epic*	52	*1 May 93*	1
ALBUMS:	**HITS 1**			**WEEKS 4**
DUST	*Epic*	32	*20 Jul 96*	4

SCREEN II — UK

ALBUMS:	HITS 1			WEEKS 1
LET THE RECORD SPIN	*Cleveland City*	36	*9 Apr 94*	1
12" doublepack single not eligible for the singles chart.				

SCRITTI POLITTI — UK/US

SINGLES:	HITS 14			WEEKS 78
THE SWEETEST GIRL	*Rough Trade*	64	*21 Nov 81*	3
FAITHLESS	*Rough Trade*	56	*22 May 82*	4
ASYLUMS IN JERUSALEM / JACQUES DERRIDA	*Rough Trade*	43	*7 Aug 82*	5
Features Robert Wyatt on keyboards.				
WOOD BEEZ (PRAY LIKE ARETHA FRANKLIN)	*Virgin*	10	*10 Mar 84*	12
ABSOLUTE	*Virgin*	17	*9 Jun 84*	9
HYPNOTIZE	*Virgin*	68	*17 Nov 84*	2
THE WORD GIRL	*Virgin*	6	*11 May 85*	12
Above hit: SCRITTI POLITTI featuring RANKING ANN.				
PERFECT WAY	*Virgin*	48	*7 Sep 85*	5
OH PATTI (DON'T FEEL SORRY FOR LOVERBOY)	*Virgin*	13	*7 May 88*	9
FIRST BOY IN THIS TOWN (LOVE SICK)	*Virgin*	63	*27 Aug 88*	3
BOOM! THERE SHE WAS	*Virgin*	55	*12 Nov 88*	3
Above hit: SCRITTI POLITTI featuring ROGER.				

SHE'S A WOMAN	*Virgin*	20	*16 Mar 91*	7
Above hit: SCRITTI POLITTI (featuring Shabba RANKS).				
TAKE ME IN YOUR ARMS AND LOVE ME	*Virgin*	47	*3 Aug 91*	3
Above hit: SCRITTI POLITTI and Sweetie IRIE.				
TINSELTOWN TO THE BOOGIEDOWN	*Virgin*	46	*31 Jul 99*	1
ALBUMS:	**HITS 4**			**WEEKS 39**
SONGS TO REMEMBER	*Rough Trade*	12	*11 Sep 82*	7
CUPID AND PSYCHE 85	*Virgin*	5	*22 Jun 85*	19
PROVISION	*Virgin*	8	*18 Jun 88*	11
ANOMIE & BONHOMIE	*Virgin*	33	*7 Aug 99*	2

Earl SCRUGGS - See Lester FLATT and Earl SCRUGGS

SEA FRUIT — UK

SINGLES:	**HITS 1**			**WEEKS 1**
HELLO WORLD	*Electric Canyon*	59	*24 Jul 99*	1

SEA LEVEL — US

SINGLES:	**HITS 1**			**WEEKS 4**
FIFTY-FOUR	*Capricorn*	63	*17 Feb 79*	4

SEAFOOD — UK

SINGLES:	**HITS 1**			**WEEKS 1**
CLOAKING	*Infectious*	71	*28 Jul 01*	1

SEAGULLS - BRIGHTON AND HOVE ALBION FOOTBALL CLUB — UK

SINGLES:	**HITS 1**			**WEEKS 2**
THE BOYS IN THE OLD BRIGHTON BLUE	*Energy*	65	*28 May 83*	2

SEAHORSES — UK

SINGLES:	**HITS 4**			**WEEKS 26**
LOVE IS THE LAW	*Geffen*	3	*10 May 97*	7
BLINDED BY THE SUN	*Geffen*	7	*26 Jul 97*	7
LOVE ME AND LEAVE ME	*Geffen*	16	*11 Oct 97*	4
YOU CAN TALK TO ME	*Geffen*	15	*13 Dec 97*	8
ALBUMS:	**HITS 1**			**WEEKS 38**
DO IT YOURSELF	*Geffen*	2	*7 Jun 97*	38

SEAL — UK

SINGLES:	**HITS 12**			**WEEKS 70**
CRAZY	*ZTT*	2	*8 Dec 90*	15
FUTURE LOVE [EP]	*ZTT*	12	*4 May 91*	6
Lead track: Future Love Paradise.				
THE BEGINNING	*ZTT*	24	*20 Jul 91*	6
KILLER . . . ON THE LOOSE [EP]	*ZTT*	8	*16 Nov 91*	8
Lead track: Killer. 12" format is titled Killer Dance EP.				
VIOLET	*ZTT*	39	*29 Feb 92*	2
Re-recording of a track from the Future Love EP.				
PRAYER FOR THE DYING	*ZTT*	14	*21 May 94*	5
KISS FROM A ROSE	*ZTT*	20	*30 Jul 94*	5
NEWBORN FRIEND	*ZTT*	45	*5 Nov 94*	2
KISS FROM A ROSE [RI] / I'M ALIVE	*ZTT*	4	*15 Jul 95*	13
I'm Alive from the film 'Batman Forever'.				
DON'T CRY / PRAYER FOR THE DYING [RI]	*ZTT*	51	*9 Dec 95*	2
FLY LIKE AN EAGLE	*ZTT*	13	*29 Mar 97*	5
From the film 'Space Jam'.				
HUMAN BEINGS	*Warner Brothers*	50	*14 Nov 98*	1
ALBUMS:	**HITS 3**			**WEEKS 131**
SEAL	*ZTT*	1	*1 Jun 91*	65
Includes re-entres through to 1998.				
SEAL	*ZTT*	1	*4 Jun 94*	64
Both self titled albums are different.				
HUMAN BEING	*Warner Brothers*	44	*28 Nov 98*	2

SEARCHERS — UK

SINGLES:	**HITS 14**			**WEEKS 128**
SWEETS FOR MY SWEET	*Pye*	1	*29 Jun 63*	16
Original by the Drifters reached No. 16 in the US in 1961.				
SWEET NOTHIN'S	*Philips*	48	*12 Oct 63*	2
Live recording from the Star Club, Hamburg, Sep 62.				
SUGAR AND SPICE	*Pye*	2	*26 Oct 63*	13
NEEDLES AND PINS	*Pye*	1	*18 Jan 64*	15
Originally recorded by Jackie De Shannon, co-written by Sonny Bono.				

DON'T THROW YOUR LOVE AWAY *Originally recorded by the Orlons.*	*Pye*	1	*18 Apr 64*	11
SOMEDAY WE'RE GONNA LOVE AGAIN	*Pye*	11	*18 Jul 64*	8
WHEN YOU WALK IN THE ROOM *Originally recorded by Jackie De Shannon.*	*Pye*	3	*19 Sep 64*	12
WHAT HAVE THEY DONE TO THE RAIN *An anti-nuclear protest song. Originally recorded by Malvina Reynolds.*	*Pye*	13	*5 Dec 64*	11
GOODBYE MY LOVE *Originally recorded by Jimmy Hughes as Goodbye My Lover Goodbye.*	*Pye*	4	*6 Mar 65*	11
HE'S GOT NO LOVE	*Pye*	12	*10 Jul 65*	10
WHEN I GET HOME	*Pye*	35	*16 Oct 65*	3
TAKE ME FOR WHAT I'M WORTH *Originally recorded by P.F.Sloan.*	*Pye*	20	*18 Dec 65*	8
TAKE IT OR LEAVE IT *Originally recorded by Rolling Stones.*	*Pye*	31	*23 Apr 66*	6
HAVE YOU EVER LOVED SOMEBODY *Originally recorded by the Hollies.*	*Pye*	48	*15 Oct 66*	2
EPS:	**HITS 7**			**WEEKS 106**
AIN'T GONNA KISS YA	*Pye*	1	*21 Sep 63*	24
SWEETS FOR MY SWEET	*Pye*	5	*14 Dec 63*	18
HUNGRY FOR LOVE	*Pye*	4	*29 Feb 64*	19
SEARCHERS PLAY THE SYSTEM	*Pye*	4	*12 Dec 64*	18
WHEN YOU WALK IN THE ROOM	*Pye*	12	*27 Mar 65*	2
BUMBLE BEE	*Pye*	1	*8 May 65*	17
SEARCHERS '65	*Pye*	15	*25 Sep 65*	8
ALBUMS:	**HITS 4**			**WEEKS 87**
MEET THE SEARCHERS	*Pye*	2	*10 Aug 63*	44
SUGAR AND SPICE	*Pye*	5	*16 Nov 63*	21
IT'S THE SEARCHERS	*Pye*	4	*30 May 64*	17
SOUNDS LIKE THE SEARCHERS	*Pye*	8	*27 Mar 65*	5

SEASHELLS — UK

SINGLES:	**HITS 1**			**WEEKS 5**
MAYBE I KNOW *Originally recorded by Lesley Gore.*	*CBS*	32	*9 Sep 72*	5

SEB — UK

SINGLES:	**HITS 1**			**WEEKS 1**
SUGAR SHACK	*React*	61	*18 Feb 95*	1

SEBADOH — US

SINGLES:	**HITS 2**			**WEEKS 4**
BEAUTY OF THE RIDE	*Domino*	74	*27 Jul 96*	1
FLAME	*Domino*	30	*30 Jan 99*	3
ALBUMS:	**HITS 4**			**WEEKS 5**
BUBBLE AND SCRAPE	*Domino*	63	*8 May 93*	1
BAKESALE	*Domino*	40	*3 Sep 94*	2
HARMACY	*Domino*	38	*31 Aug 96*	1
THE SEBADOH	*Domino*	45	*6 Mar 99*	1

Jon SECADA — US

SINGLES:	**HITS 9**			**WEEKS 42**
JUST ANOTHER DAY *Backing vocals by Gloria Estefan.*	*SBK*	5	*18 Jul 92*	15
DO YOU BELIEVE IN US	*SBK*	30	*31 Oct 92*	4
ANGEL	*SBK*	23	*6 Feb 93*	5
DO YOU REALLY WANT ME	*SBK*	30	*17 Jul 93*	4
I'M FREE	*SBK*	50	*16 Oct 93*	2
IF YOU GO	*SBK*	39	*14 May 94*	4
IF YOU GO [RE]	*SBK*	71	*2 Jul 94*	1
MENTAL PICTURE *From the film 'The Specialist'.*	*SBK*	44	*4 Feb 95*	2
IF I NEVER KNEW YOU (LOVE THEME FROM POCAHONTAS) *From the Walt Disney film 'Pocahontas'.* *Above hit: Jon SECADA and SHANICE.*	*Walt Disney*	51	*16 Dec 95*	4
TOO LATE, TOO SOON	*SBK*	43	*14 Jun 97*	1
ALBUMS:	**HITS 2**			**WEEKS 16**
JON SECADA	*SBK*	20	*5 Sep 92*	11
HEART, SOUL AND VOICE	*SBK*	17	*4 Jun 94*	5

SECCHI featuring Orlando JOHNSON — US/Italy

SINGLES:	**HITS 1**			**WEEKS 3**
I SAY YEAH	*Epic*	46	*4 May 91*	3

Harry SECOMBE — UK

(See also Harry Secombe and Moira Anderson; Harry Secombe, Peter Sellers and Spike Milligan; Various Artists: Films – Original Soundtracks 'Oliver!'.)

SINGLES:	HITS 3			WEEKS 35
ON WITH THE MOTLEY (VESTI LA GIUBBA)	*Philips*	16	*10 Dec 55*	3
Originally recorded by Enrico Caruso.				
IF I RULED THE WORLD	*Philips*	44	*5 Oct 63*	2
From the show 'Pickwick'.				
Above hit: Harry SECOMBE with Wally STOTT and his Orchestra and Chorus.				
IF I RULED THE WORLD [RE]	*Philips*	18	*23 Nov 63*	15
THIS IS MY SONG	*Philips*	2	*25 Feb 67*	15
From the film 'A Countess From Hong Kong'. Written by Charlie Chaplin				

EPS:	HITS 6			WEEKS 68
SACRED SONGS	*Philips*	9	*2 Apr 60*	38
LAND OF MY FATHERS	*Philips*	8	*14 May 60*	22
AT YOUR REQUEST VOLUME 2	*Philips*	17	*30 Jul 60*	1
SACRED SONGS VOLUME 2	*Philips*	15	*24 Dec 60*	4
TAUBER FAVOURITES	*Philips*	18	*5 May 62*	1
SHOW SOUVENIRS	*Philips*	18	*28 Jul 62*	2

ALBUMS:	HITS 6			WEEKS 56
SACRED SONGS	*Philips*	16	*31 Mar 62*	1
SECOMBE'S PERSONAL CHOICE	*Philips*	6	*22 Apr 67*	13
IF I RULED THE WORLD	*Contour*	17	*7 Aug 71*	20
20 SONGS OF JOY	*Warwick*	8	*16 Dec 78*	12
HIGHWAY OF LIFE	*Telstar*	45	*13 Dec 86*	5
YOURS SINCERELY	*Philips*	46	*30 Nov 91*	5

Harry SECOMBE and Moira ANDERSON — UK

(See also Moira Anderson; Harry Secombe.)

ALBUMS:	HITS 1			WEEKS 5
GOLDEN MEMORIES	*Warwick*	46	*5 Dec 81*	5

Harry SECOMBE, Peter SELLERS and Spike MILLIGAN — UK

(See also Goons; Spike Milligan; Harry Secombe, Peter Sellers.)

ALBUMS:	HITS 1			WEEKS 1
HOW TO WIN AN ELECTION	*Philips*	20	*18 Apr 64*	1

SECOND CITY SOUND — UK

SINGLES:	HITS 2			WEEKS 8
TCHAIKOVSKY ONE	*Decca*	22	*22 Jan 66*	7
THE DREAM OF OLWYN	*Major Minor*	43	*5 Apr 69*	1

SECOND IMAGE — UK

SINGLES:	HITS 5			WEEKS 11
STAR	*Polydor*	60	*24 Jul 82*	2
BETTER TAKE TIME	*Polydor*	67	*2 Apr 83*	2
DON'T YOU	*MCA*	68	*26 Nov 83*	2
SING AND SHOUT	*MCA*	53	*11 Aug 84*	3
STARTING AGAIN	*MCA*	65	*2 Feb 85*	2

ALBUMS:	HITS 1			WEEKS 1
STRANGE REFLECTIONS	*MCA*	100	*30 Mar 85*	1

SECOND PHASE — US

SINGLES:	HITS 1			WEEKS 2
MENTASM	*R&S*	48	*21 Sep 91*	2

SECOND PROTOCOL — UK

SINGLES:	HITS 1			WEEKS 2
BASSLICK	*East West*	58	*23 Sep 00*	2

SECRET AFFAIR — UK

SINGLES:	HITS 5			WEEKS 34
TIME FOR ACTION	*I-Spy*	13	*1 Sep 79*	10
LET YOUR HEART DANCE	*I-Spy*	32	*10 Nov 79*	6
MY WORLD	*I-Spy*	16	*8 Mar 80*	9
SOUND OF CONFUSION	*I-Spy*	45	*23 Aug 80*	5
DO YOU KNOW	*I-Spy*	57	*17 Oct 81*	4

ALBUMS:	HITS 3			WEEKS 15
GLORY BOYS	*I-Spy*	41	*1 Dec 79*	8
BEHIND CLOSED DOORS	*I-Spy*	48	*20 Sep 80*	4
BUSINESS AS USUAL	*I-Spy*	84	*13 Mar 82*	3

SECRET KNOWLEDGE — UK/US

SINGLES:	HITS 2			WEEKS 2
LOVE ME NOW	*Deconstruction*	66	*27 Apr 96*	1
SUGAR DADDY	*Deconstruction*	75	*24 Aug 96*	1

SECRET LIFE — UK

SINGLES:	HITS 4			WEEKS 10
AS ALWAYS	*Cowboy*	45	*12 Dec 92*	4
Originally recorded by Stevie Wonder.				
LOVE SO STRONG	*Cowboy*	38	*7 Aug 93*	2
SHE HOLDS THE KEY	*Pulse 8*	63	*7 May 94*	1
I WANT YOU	*Pulse 8*	70	*29 Oct 94*	1
LOVE SO STRONG [RM]	*Pulse 8*	37	*28 Jan 95*	2
Remixed by Brothers In Rhythm. Backing vocals by Clive Griffin, Lance Ellington and Kate Kissoon				

SECRETARY OF ENT. - See RAZE

SECTION-X — France

SINGLES:	HITS 1			WEEKS 1
ATLANTIS	*Perfecto*	42	*8 Mar 97*	1

Neil SEDAKA — US

SINGLES:	HITS 18			WEEKS 190
I GO APE	*RCA*	9	*25 Apr 59*	13
OH! CAROL	*RCA*	3	*14 Nov 59*	17
Song written about his high school girlfriend Carol Klein (later to become Carole King).				
STAIRWAY TO HEAVEN	*RCA*	8	*16 Apr 60*	15
YOU MEAN EVERYTHING TO ME	*RCA*	45	*3 Sep 60*	3
CALENDAR GIRL	*RCA*	8	*4 Feb 61*	14
LITTLE DEVIL	*RCA*	9	*20 May 61*	12
Above 3: Neil SEDAKA with Stan APPLEBAUM and his Orchestra.				
HAPPY BIRTHDAY, SWEET SIXTEEN	*RCA*	3	*23 Dec 61*	18
KING OF CLOWNS	*RCA*	23	*21 Apr 62*	11
BREAKING UP IS HARD TO DO	*RCA*	7	*21 Jul 62*	16
Backing vocals by the Cookies.				
NEXT DOOR TO AN ANGEL	*RCA*	29	*24 Nov 62*	4
LET'S GO STEADY AGAIN	*RCA Victor*	42	*1 Jun 63*	1
LET'S GO STEADY AGAIN [RE]	*RCA Victor*	43	*15 Jun 63*	2
OH CAROL [RI] / BREAKING UP IS HARD TO DO[RI] / LITTLE DEVIL [RI]	*RCA Victor Maximillion*	19	*7 Oct 72*	14
Breaking Up Is Hard To Do and Little Devil have additional credit with Stan Applebaum and his Orchestra.				
BEAUTIFUL YOU	*RCA Victor*	43	*4 Nov 72*	3
THAT'S WHEN THE MUSIC TAKES ME	*RCA Victor*	18	*24 Feb 73*	10
STANDING ON THE INSIDE	*MGM*	26	*2 Jun 73*	9
OUR LAST SONG TOGETHER	*MGM*	31	*25 Aug 73*	8
Tribute to his songwriting partner Howard Greenfield.				
A LITTLE LOVIN'	*Polydor*	34	*9 Feb 74*	6
LAUGHTER IN THE RAIN	*Polydor*	15	*22 Jun 74*	9
THE QUEEN OF 1964	*Polydor*	35	*22 Mar 75*	5
ALBUMS:	**HITS 8**			**WEEKS 80**
THE TRA-LA DAYS ARE OVER	*MGM*	13	*1 Sep 73*	10
LAUGHTER IN THE RAIN	*Polydor*	17	*22 Jun 74*	10
LIVE AT THE ROYAL FESTIVAL HALL	*Polydor*	48	*23 Nov 74*	1
Live recordings with the Royal Philharmonic Orchestra.				
OVERNIGHT SUCCESS	*Polydor*	31	*1 Mar 75*	6
LAUGHTER AND TEARS - THE BEST OF NEIL SEDAKA TODAY	*Polydor*	2	*10 Jul 76*	25
TIMELESS - THE VERY BEST OF NEIL SEDAKA	*Polydor*	10	*2 Nov 91*	16
CLASSICALLY SEDAKA	*Vision*	23	*4 Nov 95*	9
Sedaka's original lyrics matched to well known classical pieces.				
THE VERY BEST OF NEIL SEDAKA	*Universal Music TV*	33	*19 Jun 99*	3

SEDUCTION — US

SINGLES:	HITS 1			WEEKS 1
HEARTBEAT	*Breakout*	75	*21 Apr 90*	1

Pete SEEGER — US

EPS:	HITS 1			WEEKS 1
IN CONCERT	*CBS*	18	*3 Oct 64*	1

SEEKERS — Australia/Sri Lanka

SINGLES:	HITS 9			WEEKS 120
I'LL NEVER FIND ANOTHER YOU	*Columbia*	1	*9 Jan 65*	23
A WORLD OF OUR OWN	*Columbia*	3	*17 Apr 65*	18

THE CARNIVAL IS OVER	*Columbia*	1	*30 Oct 65*	17
SOMEDAY, ONE DAY	*Columbia*	11	*26 Mar 66*	11
WALK WITH ME	*Columbia*	10	*10 Sep 66*	12
MORNINGTOWN RIDE	*Columbia*	2	*26 Nov 66*	15
GEORGY GIRL	*Columbia*	3	*25 Feb 67*	11
From the film of the same name. Co-written by actor Jim Dale.				
WHEN WILL THE GOOD APPLES FALL	*Columbia*	11	*23 Sep 67*	12
EMERALD CITY	*Columbia*	50	*16 Dec 67*	1
EPS:	**HITS 3**			**WEEKS 166**
THE SEEKERS	*Columbia*	1	*24 Jul 65*	50
HITS FROM THE SEEKERS	*Columbia*	1	*16 Jul 66*	73
MORNINGTOWN RIDE	*Columbia*	1	*11 Feb 67*	43
ALBUMS:	**HITS 7**			**WEEKS 283**
A WORLD OF OUR OWN	*Columbia*	5	*3 Jul 65*	36
THE SEEKERS	*Decca*	16	*3 Jul 65*	1
COME THE DAY	*Columbia*	3	*19 Nov 66*	67
SEEKERS - SEEN IN GREEN	*Columbia*	15	*25 Nov 67*	10
LIVE AT THE TALK OF THE TOWN	*Columbia*	2	*14 Sep 68*	30
THE BEST OF THE SEEKERS	*Columbia*	1	*16 Nov 68*	125
CARNIVAL OF HITS	*EMI*	7	*23 Apr 94*	14
Features both solo and group material. Includes re-entry in 2000.				
Above hit: Judith DURHAM and the SEEKERS.				

Bob SEGER and the SILVER BULLET BAND — US

SINGLES:	**HITS 7**			**WEEKS 30**
HOLLYWOOD NIGHTS	*Capitol*	42	*30 Sep 78*	6
WE'VE GOT TONITE	*Capitol*	41	*3 Feb 79*	6
Above 2: Bob SEGER.				
HOLLYWOOD NIGHTS [RR]	*Capitol*	49	*24 Oct 81*	3
WE'VE GOT TONITE [RR]	*Capitol*	60	*6 Feb 82*	4
Above 2 are live recordings.				
EVEN NOW	*Capitol*	73	*9 Apr 83*	2
WE'VE GOT TONIGHT [RI]	*Capitol*	22	*28 Jan 95*	5
NIGHT MOVES	*Capitol*	45	*29 Apr 95*	2
Reached No. 4 in the US when first released in 1977.				
HOLLYWOOD NIGHTS [RI]	*Capitol*	52	*29 Jul 95*	1
LOCK AND LOAD	*Parlophone*	57	*10 Feb 96*	1
ALBUMS:	**HITS 7**			**WEEKS 52**
STRANGER IN TOWN	*Capitol*	31	*3 Jun 78*	6
AGAINST THE WIND	*Capitol*	26	*15 Mar 80*	6
NINE TONIGHT	*Capitol*	24	*26 Sep 81*	10
Live recordings from Boston and Detroit.				
THE DISTANCE	*Capitol*	45	*8 Jan 83*	10
LIKE A ROCK	*Capitol*	35	*26 Apr 86*	6
THE FIRE INSIDE	*Capitol*	54	*21 Sep 91*	2
GREATEST HITS	*Capitol*	6	*18 Feb 95*	12

Shea SEGER — UK

SINGLES:	**HITS 1**			**WEEKS 1**
CLUTCH	*RCA*	47	*5 May 01*	1

SEIKO and Donnie WAHLBERG — Japan/US

SINGLES:	**HITS 1**			**WEEKS 5**
THE RIGHT COMBINATION	*Epic*	44	*18 Aug 90*	5

SELECTER — UK

(See also Various Artists (EPs) 'The 2 Tone EP'.)

SINGLES:	**HITS 4**			**WEEKS 28**
ON MY RADIO	*2-Tone*	8	*13 Oct 79*	9
THREE MINUTE HERO	*2-Tone*	16	*2 Feb 80*	6
MISSING WORDS	*2-Tone*	23	*29 Mar 80*	8
Some labels showed title as Nissing Words.				
THE WHISPER	*Chrysalis*	36	*23 Aug 80*	5
ALBUMS:	**HITS 2**			**WEEKS 17**
TOO MUCH PRESSURE	*2-Tone*	5	*23 Feb 80*	13
CELEBRATE THE BULLET	*Chrysalis*	41	*7 Mar 81*	4

SELENA vs X.MEN — UK

SINGLES:	**HITS 1**			**WEEKS 1**
GIVE IT UP	*Go.Beat*	61	*14 Jul 01*	1

Peter SELLERS — UK

(See also Anthony Newley, Peter Sellers, Joan Collins; Peter Sellers and Sophia Loren; Harry Secombe, Peter Sellers and Spike Milligan.)

SINGLES:	HITS 3			WEEKS 20
ANY OLD IRON	*Parlophone*	21	*3 Aug 57*	3
Above hit: Peter SELLERS presents MATE'S SPOFFLE GROUP featuring Fred SPOONS, E.P.N.S.				
ANY OLD IRON [RE]	*Parlophone*	17	*7 Sep 57*	8
A HARD DAY'S NIGHT	*Parlophone*	14	*25 Dec 65*	7
A HARD DAY'S NIGHT [EP]	*EMI*	52	*27 Nov 93*	2
Lead track: A Hard Day's Night, this itself is a re-issue.				
EPS:	**HITS 2**			**WEEKS 4**
THE BEST OF SELLERS	*Parlophone*	15	*28 May 60*	2
THE BEST OF SELLERS, NO.2	*Parlophone*	8	*27 Aug 60*	2
ALBUMS:	**HITS 2**			**WEEKS 84**
THE BEST OF SELLERS	*Parlophone*	3	*14 Feb 59*	47
SONGS FOR SWINGING SELLERS	*Parlophone*	3	*12 Dec 59*	37

Peter SELLERS and Sophia LOREN — UK/Italy

(See also Peter Sellers.)

SINGLES:	HITS 2			WEEKS 19
GOODNESS GRACIOUS ME!	*Parlophone*	4	*12 Nov 60*	14
BANGERS AND MASH	*Parlophone*	22	*14 Jan 61*	5
ALBUMS:	**HITS 1**			**WEEKS 18**
PETER AND SOPHIA	*Parlophone*	5	*3 Dec 60*	18

Michael SEMBELLO — US

SINGLES:	HITS 1			WEEKS 6
MANIAC	*Casablanca*	43	*20 Aug 83*	6
From the film 'Flashdance'.				

SEMISONIC — US

SINGLES:	HITS 4			WEEKS 20
SECRET SMILE	*MCA*	13	*10 Jul 99*	11
CLOSING TIME	*MCA*	25	*6 Nov 99*	5
SINGING IN MY SLEEP	*MCA*	39	*1 Apr 00*	2
CHEMISTRY	*MCA*	35	*3 Mar 01*	2
ALBUMS:	**HITS 2**			**WEEKS 41**
FEELING STRANGELY FINE	*MCA*	16	*24 Jul 99*	37
ALL ABOUT CHEMISTRY	*MCA*	13	*17 Mar 01*	4

SEMPRINI — UK

(See also Domenico Modugno.)

SINGLES:	HITS 1			WEEKS 8
EXODUS - MAIN THEME	*His Master's Voice*	25	*18 Mar 61*	8
Theme from the film.				

SENSATIONAL ALEX HARVEY BAND — UK

SINGLES:	HITS 3			WEEKS 25
DELILAH	*Vertigo*	7	*26 Jul 75*	7
GAMBLIN' BAR ROOM BLUES	*Vertigo*	38	*22 Nov 75*	8
BOSTON TEA PARTY	*Mountain*	13	*19 Jun 76*	10
ALBUMS:	**HITS 6**			**WEEKS 42**
THE IMPOSSIBLE DREAM	*Vertigo*	16	*26 Oct 74*	4
TOMORROW BELONGS TO ME	*Vertigo*	9	*10 May 75*	10
NEXT	*Vertigo*	37	*23 Aug 75*	5
SENSATIONAL ALEX HARVEY BAND LIVE	*Vertigo*	14	*27 Sep 75*	7
PENTHOUSE TAPES	*Vertigo*	14	*10 Apr 76*	7
SAHB STORIES	*Mountain*	11	*31 Jul 76*	9

SENSELESS THINGS — UK

SINGLES:	HITS 9			WEEKS 19
EVERYBODY'S GONE	*Epic*	73	*22 Jun 91*	1
GOT IT AT THE DELMAR	*Epic*	50	*28 Sep 91*	3
EASY TO SMILE	*Epic*	18	*11 Jan 92*	4
HOLD IT DOWN	*Epic*	19	*11 Apr 92*	4
HOMOPHOBIC ASSHOLE	*Epic*	52	*5 Dec 92*	2
PRIMARY INSTINCT	*Epic*	41	*13 Feb 93*	2
TOO MUCH KISSING	*Epic*	69	*12 Jun 93*	1
CHRISTINE KEELER	*Epic*	56	*5 Nov 94*	1
SOMETHING TO MISS	*Epic*	57	*28 Jan 95*	1

ALBUMS:	HITS 2			WEEKS 2
THE FIRST OF TOO MANY	*Epic*	66	*26 Oct 91*	1
EMPIRE OF THE SENSELESS	*Epic*	37	*13 Mar 93*	1

SENSER — UK

SINGLES:	HITS 4			WEEKS 5
THE KEY / NO COMPLY	*Ultimate*	47	*25 Sep 93*	1
SWITCH	*Ultimate*	39	*19 Mar 94*	2
AGE OF PANIC	*Ultimate*	52	*23 Jul 94*	1
CHARMING DEMONS	*Ultimate*	42	*17 Aug 96*	1

ALBUMS:	HITS 2			WEEKS 6
STACKED UP	*Ultimate*	4	*7 May 94*	5
ASYLUM	*Ultimate*	73	*2 May 98*	1

Nick SENTIENCE - See BK

SEPULTURA — Brazil

SINGLES:	HITS 6			WEEKS 12
TERRITORY	*Roadrunner*	66	*2 Oct 93*	2
REFUSE/RESIST	*Roadrunner*	51	*26 Feb 94*	2
This is just one song title.				
SLAVE NEW WORLD	*Roadrunner*	46	*4 Jun 94*	2
ROOTS BLOODY ROOTS	*Roadrunner*	19	*24 Feb 96*	2
RATAMAHATTA	*Roadrunner*	23	*17 Aug 96*	2
ATTITUDE	*Roadrunner*	46	*14 Dec 96*	2
Dedicated to Dana Wels, the son of band manager Gloria and stepson of singer Max Cavalera.				

ALBUMS:	HITS 4			WEEKS 12
ARISE	*Roadracer*	40	*6 Apr 91*	2
CHAOS A.D.	*Roadrunner*	11	*23 Oct 93*	3
CHAOS A.D. [RE]	*Roadrunner*	53	*19 Mar 94*	1
CD repackaged in tin box..				
ROOTS	*Roadrunner*	4	*9 Mar 96*	5
AGAINST	*Roadrunner*	40	*17 Oct 98*	1

SERANO - See VOODOO and SERANO

SERIAL DIVA — UK

(See also Three 'N One.)

SINGLES:	HITS 1			WEEKS 1
KEEP HOPE ALIVE	*Sound Of Ministry*	57	*18 Jan 97*	1

SERIOUS DANGER — UK

SINGLES:	HITS 2			WEEKS 4
DEEPER	*Fresh*	40	*20 Dec 97*	3
HIGH NOON	*Fresh*	54	*2 May 98*	1

SERIOUS INTENTION — US

SINGLES:	HITS 2			WEEKS 6
YOU DON'T KNOW (OH-OH-OH)	*Important/Towerbell*	75	*16 Nov 85*	1
SERIOUS	*Pow Wow*	51	*5 Apr 86*	5

SERIOUS ROPE — UK

SINGLES:	HITS 2			WEEKS 3
HAPPINESS (Medley) a) HAPPINESS b) HAPPINESS IS JUST AROUND THE BEND [M]	*Rumour*	54	*22 May 93*	2
Original by Main Ingredient reached No. 35 in the US in 1974.				
Above hit: SERIOUS ROPE presents Sharon Dee CLARKE.				
HAPPINESS/YOU MAKE ME HAPPY [M] [RR]	*Mercury*	70	*1 Oct 94*	1

Erick SERMON featuring Marvin GAYE — US

(See also Marvin Gaye.)

SINGLES:	HITS 1			WEEKS 2
MUSIC	*Polydor*	36	*6 Oct 01*	2

Eric SERRA — France

ALBUMS:	HITS 1			WEEKS 2
THE FIFTH ELEMENT [OST]	*Virgin*	58	*28 Jun 97*	2

SET THE TONE — UK

SINGLES:	HITS 2			WEEKS 4
DANCE SUCKER	*Island*	62	*22 Jan 83*	2
RAP YOUR LOVE	*Island*	67	*26 Mar 83*	2

SETTLERS — UK

SINGLES:	HITS 1			WEEKS 5
THE LIGHTNING TREE	*York*	36	*16 Oct 71*	5

Theme from the Yorkshire ITV childrens series 'Follyfoot'.

Brian SETZER ORCHESTRA — US

SINGLES:	HITS 1			WEEKS 3
JUMP JIVE AN' WAIL	*Interscope*	34	*3 Apr 99*	3

Taja SEVELLE — US

SINGLES:	HITS 2			WEEKS 13
LOVE IS CONTAGIOUS	*Paisley Park*	7	*20 Feb 88*	9
WOULDN'T YOU LOVE TO LOVE ME?	*Paisley Park*	59	*14 May 88*	4
ALBUMS:	**HITS 1**			**WEEKS 4**
TAJA SEVELLE	*Paisley Park*	48	*26 Mar 88*	4

702 — US

(See also Missy "Misdemeanor" Elliott.)

SINGLES:	HITS 4			WEEKS 10
STEELO	*Motown*	41	*14 Dec 96*	2
NO DOUBT	*Motown*	59	*29 Nov 97*	1
WHERE MY GIRLS AT?	*Motown*	22	*7 Aug 99*	4
YOU DON'T KNOW	*Motown*	36	*27 Nov 99*	3

740 BOYZ — US

SINGLES:	HITS 1			WEEKS 1
SHIMMY SHAKE	*MCA*	54	*4 Nov 95*	1

SEVEN GRAND HOUSING AUTHORITY — UK

SINGLES:	HITS 1			WEEKS 1
THE QUESTION	*Olympic*	70	*23 Oct 93*	1

7669 — US

SINGLES:	HITS 1			WEEKS 1
JOY	*Motown*	60	*18 Jun 94*	1

7TH HEAVEN — UK

SINGLES:	HITS 1			WEEKS 5
HOT FUN	*Mercury*	47	*14 Sep 85*	5

SEVERINE — France

SINGLES:	HITS 1			WEEKS 11
UN BANC, UN ARBRE, UNE RUE	*Philips*	9	*24 Apr 71*	11

Eurovision Song Contest winner for Monaco in 1971.

David SEVILLE — US

(See also Alfi and Harry; Chipmunks.)

SINGLES:	HITS 2			WEEKS 14
WITCH DOCTOR	*London*	11	*24 May 58*	6
Above hit: David SEVILLE with Orchestra and vocal accompaniment effects by the CHIPMUNKS.				
RAGTIME COWBOY JOE	*London*	11	*25 Jul 59*	8
Above hit: David SEVILLE and the CHIPMUNKS.				

Janette SEWELL – See DOUBLE TROUBLE

SEX CLUB — US

SINGLES:	HITS 1			WEEKS 1
BIG (BIG) DICK MAN	*Club Tools*	67	*28 Jan 95*	1

Features vocals by Brown Sugar. Reply record to 20 Fingers' Short Dick Man.

SEX-O-SONIQUE — UK

SINGLES:	HITS 1			WEEKS 3
I THOUGHT IT WAS YOU	*ffrr*	32	*6 Dec 97*	3

SEX PISTOLS — UK

SINGLES:	HITS 11			WEEKS 89
ANARCHY IN THE U.K.	*EMI*	38	*11 Dec 76*	5

May have climbed higher if EMI had not withdrawn the single.

GOD SAVE THE QUEEN	*Virgin*	2	*4 Jun 77*	9
Released on A&M in Mar but quickly withdrawn when label terminated their contract. It was claimed that for the week 11 Jun 77 when it peaked at No. 2, it had sold more than Rod Stewart's I Don't Want To Talk About It / First Cut Is The Deepest.				
PRETTY VACANT	*Virgin*	6	*9 Jul 77*	8
HOLIDAYS IN THE SUN	*Virgin*	8	*22 Oct 77*	6
NO ONE IS INNOCENT (A PUNK PRAYER BY RONALD BIGGS) / MY WAY	*Virgin*	7	*8 Jul 78*	10
No One Is Innocent recorded with Great Train Robber Ronald Biggs in Rio de Janeiro. Virgin refused to release single with the title Cosh The Driver.				
SOMETHING ELSE / FRIGGIN' IN THE RIGGIN'	*Virgin*	3	*3 Mar 79*	12
Above hit: SEX PISTOLS vocals: Sid VICIOUS / SEX PISTOLS vocals: Steve JONES.				
SILLY THING	*Virgin*	6	*7 Apr 79*	8
[AA] listed with Who Killed Bambi by Ten Pole Tudor.				
C'MON EVERYBODY	*Virgin*	3	*30 Jun 79*	9
Above hit: SEX PISTOLS vocals: Sid VICIOUS.				
THE GREAT ROCK 'N' ROLL SWINDLE	*Virgin*	21	*13 Oct 79*	6
[AA] listed with Rock Around The Clock by Tenpole Tudor. Above 5 from the film 'The Great Rock 'N' Roll Swindle'.				
(I'M NOT YOUR) STEPPING STONE	*Virgin*	21	*14 Jun 80*	8
Originally recorded by Paul Revere and the Raiders.				
ANARCHY IN THE UK [RI]	*Virgin*	33	*3 Oct 92*	3
PRETTY VACANT [RI]	*Virgin*	56	*5 Dec 92*	2
PRETTY VACANT LIVE [RR]	*Virgin*	18	*27 Jul 96*	3
Live recording from Finsbury Park, London, 23 Jun 96.				

ALBUMS:	**HITS 7**			**WEEKS 119**
NEVER MIND THE BOLLOCKS, HERE'S THE SEX PISTOLS	*Virgin*	1	*12 Nov 77*	48
THE GREAT ROCK 'N' ROLL SWINDLE [OST]	*Virgin*	7	*10 Mar 79*	33
Double album featuring out-takes and several songs from the film.				
SOME PRODUCT - CARRI ON SEX PISTOLS	*Virgin*	6	*11 Aug 79*	10
Non music release with commercials and the interview with Bill Grundy from the Thames ITV 'Today' programme, transmitted 1 Dec 76.				
FLOGGING A DEAD HORSE	*Virgin*	23	*16 Feb 80*	6
THE GREAT ROCK 'N' ROLL SWINDLE [OST]	*Virgin*	16	*7 Jun 80*	11
Single album including 2 tracks by Ten Pole Tudor.				
KISS THIS	*Virgin*	10	*17 Oct 92*	4
NEVER MIND THE BOLLOCKS, HERE'S THE SEX PISTOLS [RE]	*Virgin*	20	*8 Jun 96*	5
Re-packaged as a doublepack with Spunk, a live album. Peak position reached in 2000 (1996 peak No. 45).				
FILTHY LUCRE LIVE	*Virgin*	26	*10 Aug 96*	2
Live recordings from Finsbury Park, London, 23 Jun 96.				

Denny SEYTON and the SABRES — UK

SINGLES:	**HITS 1**			**WEEKS 1**
THE WAY YOU LOOK TONIGHT	*Mercury*	48	*19 Sep 64*	1

SHABOOM — UK

SINGLES:	**HITS 1**			**WEEKS 1**
SWEET SENSATION	*WEA*	64	*31 Jul 99*	1
Vocals by Chaka Khan's younger sister Taka Boom.				

SHACK — UK

SINGLES:	**HITS 3**			**WEEKS 3**
COMEDY	*London*	44	*26 Jun 99*	1
NATALIE'S PARTY	*London*	63	*14 Aug 99*	1
OSCAR	*London*	67	*11 Mar 00*	1

ALBUMS:	**HITS 1**			**WEEKS 2**
H.M.S. FABLE	*London*	25	*3 Jul 99*	2

SHADE SHEIST featuring Nate DOGG & KURUPT — US

(See also Kurupt featuring Natina Reed.)

SINGLES:	**HITS 1**			**WEEKS 7**
WHERE I WANNA BE	*London*	14	*25 Aug 01*	6
WHERE I WANNA BE [RE]	*London*	58	*13 Oct 01*	1

SHADES — US

SINGLES:	**HITS 2**			**WEEKS 3**
MR. BIG STUFF	*Motown*	31	*12 Apr 97*	2
Original by Jean Knight reached No. 2 in the US in 1971. From the film of the same name. Above hit: QUEEN LATIFAH, SHADES and FREE.				
SERENADE	*Motown*	75	*20 Sep 97*	1

SHADES OF LOVE (Junior VASQUEZ meets Johnny VICIOUS) — US

SINGLES:	**HITS 1**			**WEEKS 1**
KEEP IN TOUCH (BODY TO BODY)	*Vicious-Muzik*	64	*22 Apr 95*	1

SHADES OF RHYTHM — UK

SINGLES:	HITS 7			WEEKS 25
HOMICIDE / EXORCIST	ZTT	53	2 Feb 91	3
SWEET SENSATION	ZTT	54	13 Apr 91	4
THE SOUND OF EDEN (EVERY TIME I SEE HER)	ZTT	35	20 Jul 91	5
EXTACY	ZTT	16	30 Nov 91	7
SWEET REVIVAL (KEEP IT COMIN)	ZTT	61	20 Feb 93	1
SOUND OF EDEN [RI]	ZTT	37	11 Sep 93	3
THE WANDERING DRAGON [EP]	Public Demand	55	5 Nov 94	1
Lead track: My Love.				
PSYCHO BASE	Coalition	57	21 Jun 97	1
ALBUMS:	**HITS 1**			**WEEKS 3**
SHADES	ZTT	51	17 Aug 91	3

SHADOW - See Edwin STARR

SHADOWS — UK

(See also Cliff Richard.)

SINGLES:	HITS 31			WEEKS 359
APACHE	Columbia	1	23 Jul 60	21
Originally recorded by Bert Weedon and features Cliff Richard on bongos.				
MAN OF MYSTERY / THE STRANGER	Columbia	5	12 Nov 60	15
Man Of Mystery is the theme music of the Edgar Wallace film series. The Stranger was not listed from 11 Feb 61.				
F.B.I.	Columbia	6	11 Feb 61	19
THE FRIGHTENED CITY	Columbia	3	13 May 61	20
From the film of the same name.				
KON - TIKI	Columbia	1	9 Sep 61	10
THE SAVAGE	Columbia	10	18 Nov 61	8
From the film 'The Young Ones'.				
KON - TIKI [RE]	Columbia	37	25 Nov 61	2
WONDERFUL LAND	Columbia	1	3 Mar 62	19
GUITAR TANGO	Columbia	4	4 Aug 62	15
DANCE ON!	Columbia	1	15 Dec 62	15
FOOT TAPPER	Columbia	1	9 Mar 63	16
From the film 'Summer Holiday'.				
ATLANTIS	Columbia	2	8 Jun 63	17
Above hit: SHADOWS and the Norrie PARAMOR STRINGS.				
SHINDIG	Columbia	6	21 Sep 63	12
GERONIMO	Columbia	11	7 Dec 63	12
Above hit: SHADOWS with the Norrie PARAMOR STRINGS.				
THEME FOR YOUNG LOVERS	Columbia	12	7 Mar 64	10
From the film 'Wonderful Life'.				
THE RISE AND FALL OF FLINGEL BUNT	Columbia	5	9 May 64	14
RHYTHM AND GREENS	Columbia	22	5 Sep 64	7
Title track from the short musical comedy film.				
GENIE WITH THE LIGHT BROWN LAMP	Columbia	17	5 Dec 64	10
From the pantomine 'Aladdin'.				
MARY ANNE	Columbia	17	13 Feb 65	10
STINGRAY	Columbia	19	12 Jun 65	7
DON'T MAKE MY BABY BLUE	Columbia	10	7 Aug 65	10
Original by Frankie Laine in 1963.				
THE WAR LORD	Columbia	18	27 Nov 65	9
Theme from the film of the same name.				
I MET A GIRL	Columbia	22	19 Mar 66	5
A PLACE IN THE SUN	Columbia	24	9 Jul 66	6
THE DREAMS I DREAM	Columbia	42	5 Nov 66	6
MAROC 7	Columbia	24	15 Apr 67	8
Theme from the film of the same name.				
LET ME BE THE ONE	EMI	12	8 Mar 75	9
UK's Eurovision entry in 1975, it came 2nd.				
DON'T CRY FOR ME ARGENTINA	EMI	5	16 Dec 78	14
From the Tim Rice/Andrew Lloyd Webber musical 'Evita'.				
THEME FROM THE DEER HUNTER (CAVATINA)	EMI	9	28 Apr 79	14
RIDERS IN THE SKY	EMI	12	26 Jan 80	12
EQUINOXE (PART V)	Polydor	50	23 Aug 80	3
THE THIRD MAN	Polydor	44	2 May 81	4
Originally recorded by Anton Karas. Theme from the film of the same name.				
EPS:	**HITS 19**			**WEEKS 461**
THE SHADOWS	Columbia	1	21 Jan 61	86
THE SHADOWS TO THE FORE	Columbia	1	10 Jun 61	81
SPOTLIGHT ON THE SHADOWS	Columbia	1	10 Feb 62	59
THE SHADOWS NO. 2	Columbia	12	9 Jun 62	16
THE SHADOWS NO. 3	Columbia	13	11 Aug 62	4
THE WONDERFUL LAND OF THE SHADOWS	Columbia	6	22 Sep 62	34
THE BOYS	Columbia	1	13 Oct 62	46
Songs from the film of the same name.				

OUT OF THE SHADOWS	*Columbia*	3	*23 Feb 63*	21
DANCE ON WITH THE SHADOWS	*Columbia*	16	*9 Mar 63*	5
OUT OF THE SHADOWS NO. 2	*Columbia*	20	*22 Jun 63*	1
LOS SHADOWS	*Columbia*	4	*21 Sep 63*	18
Features Spanish tunes recorded in Barcelona.				
FOOT TAPPING WITH THE SHADOWS	*Columbia*	7	*12 Oct 63*	10
SHINDIG WITH THE SHADOWS	*Columbia*	9	*14 Dec 63*	4
THOSE BRILLIANT SHADOWS	*Columbia*	6	*20 Jun 64*	14
RHYTHM AND GREENS [OST]	*Columbia*	8	*24 Oct 64*	14
THEMES FROM "ALADDIN AND HIS WONDERFUL LAMP"	*Columbia*	14	*27 Mar 65*	2
From the pantomine 'Aladdin'.				
DANCE WITH THE SHADOWS NO. 3	*Columbia*	16	*5 Jun 65*	2
THOSE TALENTED SHADOWS	*Columbia*	9	*1 Oct 66*	2
THUNDERBIRDS ARE GO [OST]	*Columbia*	6	*19 Nov 66*	7
From the Gerry Anderson film (where The Shadows feature as puppets). One track is by Cliff Richard.				

ALBUMS:	HITS 29			WEEKS 475
THE SHADOWS	*Columbia*	1	*16 Sep 61*	57
OUT OF THE SHADOWS	*Columbia*	1	*13 Oct 62*	38
THE SHADOWS' GREATEST HITS	*Columbia*	2	*22 Jun 63*	49
DANCE WITH THE SHADOWS	*Columbia*	2	*9 May 64*	27
THE SOUND OF THE SHADOWS	*Columbia*	4	*17 Jul 65*	17
SHADOW MUSIC	*Columbia*	5	*21 May 66*	17
JIGSAW	*Columbia*	8	*15 Jul 67*	16
SHADES OF ROCK	*Columbia*	30	*24 Oct 70*	4
ROCKIN' WITH CURLY LEADS	*EMI*	45	*13 Apr 74*	1
THE SHADOWS' GREATEST HITS [RE]	*Columbia*	48	*11 May 74*	6
Re-released with a new catalogue number.				
SPECS APPEAL	*EMI*	30	*29 Mar 75*	5
As well as new material, it includes the 6 songs picked for Eurovision that year.				
SHADOWS 20 GOLDEN GREATS	*EMI*	1	*12 Feb 77*	43
Includes re-entries through to 1983.				
STRING OF HITS	*EMI*	1	*15 Sep 79*	43
ANOTHER STRING OF HITS	*EMI*	16	*26 Jul 80*	8
CHANGE OF ADDRESS	*Polydor*	17	*13 Sep 80*	6
HITS RIGHT UP YOUR STREET	*Polydor*	15	*19 Sep 81*	16
LIFE IN THE JUNGLE/LIVE AT ABBEY ROAD	*Polydor*	24	*25 Sep 82*	6
Live At Abbey Road recorded in front of a studio audience.				
XXV	*Polydor*	34	*22 Oct 83*	6
Released to celebrate their 25th anniversary.				
GUARDIAN ANGEL	*Polydor*	98	*17 Nov 84*	1
MOONLIGHT SHADOWS	*Polydor*	6	*24 May 86*	19
SIMPLY SHADOWS	*Polydor*	11	*24 Oct 87*	17
STEPPIN' TO THE SHADOWS	*Polydor*	11	*20 May 89*	9
AT THEIR VERY BEST	*Polydor*	12	*16 Dec 89*	9
REFLECTION	*Polydor*	5	*13 Oct 90*	15
THEMES AND DREAMS	*Polydor*	21	*16 Nov 91*	11
SHADOWS IN THE NIGHT - 16 CLASSIC TRACKS	*PolyGram TV*	22	*15 May 93*	4
Compilation of cover versions.				
THE BEST OF HANK MARVIN AND THE SHADOWS	*PolyGram TV*	19	*22 Oct 94*	11
PLAY ANDREW LLOYD WEBBER AND TIM RICE	*PolyGram TV*	41	*22 Nov 97*	6
VERY BEST OF HANK MARVIN AND THE SHADOWS - THE FIRST 40 YEARS	*PolyGram TV*	56	*14 Nov 98*	5
Above 3 includes both solo and group material.				
Above 3:Hank MARVIN and the SHADOWS.				
50 GOLDEN GREATS	*EMI*	35	*12 Aug 00*	3

SHAFT — UK

SINGLES:	HITS 2			WEEKS 9
ROOBARB AND CUSTARD	*Ffrreedom*	7	*21 Dec 91*	8
Roobarb and Custard are characters from the BBC TV children's show.				
MONKEY	*Ffrreedom*	61	*25 Jul 92*	1

SHAFT — UK

SINGLES:	HITS 3			WEEKS 19
(MUCHO MAMBO) SWAY	*Wonderboy*	2	*4 Sep 99*	12
Shaft first recorded the track using samples from Rosemary Clooney's version. Permission to use the sample was withheld and so the vocals were recreated by Claire Vaughan.				
MAMBO ITALIANO	*Wonderboy*	12	*20 May 00*	6
KIKI RIRI BOOM	*Wonderboy*	62	*21 Jul 01*	1

SHAG - See Jonathan KING

SHAGGY — Jamaica

(See also Jamaica United.)

SINGLES:	HITS 12			WEEKS 120
OH CAROLINA	*Greensleeves*	1	*6 Feb 93*	19
Originally recorded by the Folkes Brothers.				

SOON BE DONE	*Greensleeves*	46	*10 Jul 93*	3
IN THE SUMMERTIME	*Virgin*	5	*8 Jul 95*	9
Above hit: SHAGGY featuring RAYVON.				
BOOMBASTIC	*Virgin*	1	*23 Sep 95*	12
Featured in the Levi's Jeans TV commercial. Samples Baby Let Me Kiss You by King Floyd.				
WHY YOU TREAT ME SO BAD	*Virgin*	11	*13 Jan 96*	5
Samples Bob Marley's Mr. Brown.				
Above hit: SHAGGY featuring GRAND PUBA.				
SOMETHING DIFFERENT / THE TRAIN IS COMING	*Virgin*	21	*23 Mar 96*	5
Something Different samples First Choice's Love Thang and Stetsasonic's Go Stetsa. The Train Is Coming from the film 'Money Train'.				
Above hit: SHAGGY featuring Wayne WONDER / SHAGGY.				
THAT GIRL	*Virgin*	15	*22 Jun 96*	7
Samples Booker T. and The M.G.s Green Onions.				
Above hit: Maxi PRIEST featuring SHAGGY.				
PIECE OF MY HEART	*Virgin*	7	*19 Jul 97*	6
Samples Erma Franklin's version.				
Above hit: SHAGGY (featuring MARSHA).				
IT WASN'T ME	*MCA*	31	*17 Feb 01*	3
Import.				
Above hit: SHAGGY featuring Ricardo Rikrok DUCENT.				
IT WASN'T ME	*MCA*	1	*10 Mar 01*	20
ANGEL	*MCA*	1	*9 Jun 01*	16
Based around The Joker and Angel Of The Morning.				
Above hit: SHAGGY featuring RAYVON.				
LUV ME LUV ME	*MCA*	5	*29 Sep 01*	10
DANCE & SHOUT/HOPE	*MCA*	19	*1 Dec 01*	5
SHAGGY/SHAGGY featuring PRINCE MYDAS.				
ALBUMS:	**HITS 3**			**WEEKS 53**
PURE PLEASURE	*Greensleeves*	67	*24 Jul 93*	1
BOOMBASTIC	*Virgin*	37	*14 Oct 95*	6
HOT SHOT	*MCA*	1	*17 Feb 01*	46

SHAH — UK

SINGLES:	**HITS 1**			**WEEKS 1**
SECRET LOVE	*Evocative*	69	*6 Jun 98*	1

SHAI — US

SINGLES:	**HITS 1**			**WEEKS 6**
IF I EVER FALL IN LOVE	*MCA*	36	*19 Dec 92*	6

SHAKATAK — UK

SINGLES:	**HITS 14**			**WEEKS 85**
FEELS LIKE THE RIGHT TIME	*Polydor*	41	*8 Nov 80*	5
LIVING IN THE U.K.	*Polydor*	52	*7 Mar 81*	4
BRAZILIAN DAWN	*Polydor*	48	*25 Jul 81*	3
EASIER SAID THAN DONE	*Polydor*	12	*21 Nov 81*	17
NIGHT BIRDS	*Polydor*	9	*3 Apr 82*	8
STREETWALKIN'	*Polydor*	38	*19 Jun 82*	6
INVITATIONS	*Polydor*	24	*4 Sep 82*	7
STRANGER	*Polydor*	43	*6 Nov 82*	3
DARK IS THE NIGHT	*Polydor*	15	*4 Jun 83*	8
IF YOU COULD SEE ME NOW	*Polydor*	49	*27 Aug 83*	4
DOWN ON THE STREET	*Polydor*	9	*7 Jul 84*	11
DON'T BLAME IT ON LOVE	*Polydor*	55	*15 Sep 84*	3
DAY BY DAY	*Polydor*	53	*16 Nov 85*	3
Above hit: SHAKATAK with Al JARREAU.				
MR. MANIC AND SISTER COOL	*Polydor*	56	*24 Oct 87*	3
ALBUMS:	**HITS 7**			**WEEKS 73**
DRIVIN' HARD	*Polydor*	35	*30 Jan 82*	17
NIGHT BIRDS	*Polydor*	4	*15 May 82*	28
INVITATIONS	*Polydor*	30	*27 Nov 82*	11
OUT OF THIS WORLD	*Polydor*	30	*22 Oct 83*	4
DOWN ON THE STREET	*Polydor*	17	*25 Aug 84*	9
LIVE!	*Polydor*	82	*23 Feb 85*	3
THE COOLEST CUTS	*K-Tel*	73	*22 Oct 88*	1
Compilation.				

Johnny SHAKER – See THREE 'N ONE

SHAKESPEARS SISTER — UK/US

SINGLES:	**HITS 9**			**WEEKS 52**
YOU'RE HISTORY	*ffrr*	7	*29 Jul 89*	9
RUN SILENT	*ffrr*	54	*14 Oct 89*	3
DIRTY MIND	*ffrr*	71	*10 Mar 90*	1

GOODBYE CRUEL WORLD	*London*	59	*12 Oct 91*	2
The sleeves of the above 4 credited Shakespear's Sister'.				
STAY	*London*	1	*25 Jan 92*	16
I DON'T CARE	*London*	7	*16 May 92*	7
GOODBYE CRUEL WORLD [RI]	*London*	32	*18 Jul 92*	4
HELLO (TURN YOUR RADIO ON)	*London*	14	*7 Nov 92*	6
MY 16TH APOLOGY [EP]	*London*	61	*27 Feb 93*	1
Lead track: My 16th Apology. Other 3 are live tracks recorded by the BBC and broadcast 16 Apr 92.				
I CAN DRIVE	*London*	30	*22 Jun 96*	3
ALBUMS:	**HITS 2**			**WEEKS 63**
SACRED HEART	*London*	9	*2 Sep 89*	8
HORMONALLY YOURS	*London*	3	*29 Feb 92*	55

SHAKIN' PYRAMIDS — UK

ALBUMS:	**HITS 1**			**WEEKS 4**
SKIN 'EM UP	*Cuba Libra*	48	*4 Apr 81*	4

SHAKY - See Shakin' STEVENS

SHAKY and BONNIE - See Shakin' STEVENS; Bonnie TYLER

SHALAMAR — US

SINGLES:	**HITS 17**			**WEEKS 134**
UPTOWN FESTIVAL [M]	*Soul Train*	30	*14 May 77*	5
Medley of Motown songs.				
TAKE THAT TO THE BANK	*RCA Victor*	20	*9 Dec 78*	12
THE SECOND TIME AROUND	*Solar*	45	*24 Nov 79*	9
RIGHT IN THE SOCKET	*Solar*	44	*9 Feb 80*	6
I OWE YOU ONE	*Solar*	13	*30 Aug 80*	10
MAKE THAT MOVE	*Solar*	30	*28 Mar 81*	10
I CAN MAKE YOU FEEL GOOD	*Solar*	7	*27 Mar 82*	11
A NIGHT TO REMEMBER	*Solar*	5	*12 Jun 82*	12
THERE IT IS	*Solar*	5	*4 Sep 82*	10
FRIENDS	*Solar*	12	*27 Nov 82*	10
DEAD GIVEAWAY	*Solar*	8	*11 Jun 83*	10
DISAPPEARING ACT	*Solar*	18	*13 Aug 83*	8
OVER AND OVER	*Solar*	23	*15 Oct 83*	6
DANCING IN THE SHEETS	*CBS*	41	*24 Mar 84*	3
From the film 'Footloose'.				
DEADLINE U.S.A.	*MCA*	52	*31 Mar 84*	3
From the film 'Street Fleet'.				
AMNESIA	*Solar*	61	*24 Nov 84*	2
MY GIRL LOVES ME	*Solar*	45	*2 Feb 85*	3
A NIGHT TO REMEMBER (THE M AND M MIX) [RM]	*Solar*	52	*26 Apr 86*	4
ALBUMS:	**HITS 4**			**WEEKS 121**
FRIENDS	*Solar*	6	*27 Mar 82*	72
Peak position reached on 15 Jan 83.				
GREATEST HITS	*Solar*	71	*11 Sep 82*	5
THE LOOK	*Solar*	7	*30 Jul 83*	20
THE GREATEST HITS	*Stylus*	5	*12 Apr 86*	24

SHAM ROCK — Ireland

SINGLES:	**HITS 1**			**WEEKS 11**
TELL ME MA	*Jive*	13	*7 Nov 98*	11

SHAM 69 — UK

SINGLES:	**HITS 7**			**WEEKS 53**
ANGELS WITH DIRTY FACES	*Polydor*	19	*13 May 78*	10
IF THE KIDS ARE UNITED	*Polydor*	9	*29 Jul 78*	9
HURRY UP HARRY	*Polydor*	10	*14 Oct 78*	8
QUESTIONS AND ANSWERS	*Polydor*	18	*24 Mar 79*	9
HERSHAM BOYS	*Polydor*	6	*4 Aug 79*	9
YOU'RE A BETTER MAN THAN I	*Polydor*	49	*27 Oct 79*	5
Originally recorded by Yardbirds.				
TELL THE CHILDREN	*Polydor*	45	*12 Apr 80*	3
ALBUMS:	**HITS 3**			**WEEKS 27**
TELL US THE TRUTH	*Polydor*	25	*11 Mar 78*	8
THAT'S LIFE	*Polydor*	27	*2 Dec 78*	11
THE ADVENTURES OF THE HERSHAM BOYS	*Polydor*	8	*29 Sep 79*	8

SHAMEN — UK

SINGLES:	**HITS 12**			**WEEKS 77**
PRO-GEN	*One Little Indian*	55	*7 Apr 90*	4
MAKE IT MINE	*One Little Indian*	42	*22 Sep 90*	5
HYPERREAL	*One Little Indian*	29	*6 Apr 91*	5

MOVE ANY MOUNTAIN - PROGEN 91 [RM-1ST]	*One Little Indian*	4	*27 Jul 91*	10
Remixed by the Beatmasters.				
L.S.I.	*One Little Indian*	6	*18 Jul 92*	8
EBENEEZER GOODE	*One Little Indian*	1	*5 Sep 92*	10
BOSS DRUM	*One Little Indian*	4	*7 Nov 92*	7
BOSS DRUM [RM]	*One Little Indian*	58	*7 Nov 92*	1
5th format (a 12" remix) which, due to chart rules, had its own chart run.				
PHOREVER PEOPLE	*One Little Indian*	5	*19 Dec 92*	10
RE:EVOLUTION	*One Little Indian*	18	*6 Mar 93*	2
Terence McKenna is a new age author whose books have influenced the band.				
Above hit: SHAMEN with Terence McKENNA.				
THE SHAMEN S.O.S. [EP]	*One Little Indian*	14	*6 Nov 93*	4
Lead track: Comin' On.				
DESTINATION ESCHATON	*One Little Indian*	15	*19 Aug 95*	4
TRANSAMAZONIA	*One Little Indian*	28	*21 Oct 95*	2
Above 2 feature former Soul II Soul vocalist Victoria Wilson James.				
HEAL (THE SEPARATION)	*One Little Indian*	31	*10 Feb 96*	2
MOVE ANY MOUNTAIN '96 [RM-2ND]	*One Little Indian*	35	*21 Dec 96*	3
Remixed by the Beatmasters.				

ALBUMS:	**HITS 6**			**WEEKS 54**
EN-TACT	*One Little Indian*	31	*3 Nov 90*	10
PROGNEY	*One Little Indian*	23	*28 Sep 91*	2
BOSS DRUM	*One Little Indian*	3	*26 Sept 92*	30
ON AIR - BBC SESSIONS	*Band Of Joy*	61	*20 Nov 93*	1
Compilation of their In Session recordings for BBC Radio 1.				
BOSS DRUM / DIFFERENT DRUM [RE]	*One Little Indian*	51	*18 Dec 93*	5
Different Drum was a remix album, sales were combined.				
AXIS MUTATIS	*One Little Indian*	27	*4 Nov 95*	2
THE SHAMEN COLLECTION	*One Little Indian*	26	*2 May 98*	4
2 album set. First features their radio edit hits while the second includes remixes by Mr. C.				

SHAMPOO — UK

SINGLES:	**HITS 5**			**WEEKS 28**
TROUBLE	*Food*	11	*30 Jul 94*	12
VIVA LA MEGABABES	*Food*	27	*15 Oct 94*	4
DELICIOUS	*Food*	21	*18 Feb 95*	4
TROUBLE [RI]	*Food*	36	*5 Aug 95*	3
From the film 'Mighty Morphin Power Rangers: The Movie'.				
GIRL POWER	*Food*	25	*13 Jul 96*	4
I KNOW WHAT BOYS LIKE	*Food*	42	*21 Sep 96*	1
Originally recorded by The Waitresses.				

ALBUMS:	**HITS 1**			**WEEKS 2**
WE ARE SHAMPOO	*Food*	45	*5 Nov 94*	2

Jimmy SHAND and his Band — UK

SINGLES:	**HITS 1**			**WEEKS 2**
BLUEBELL POLKA	*Parlophone*	20	*24 Dec 55*	2
Sub titled: Scottish Country Dance In Strict Tempo.				

EPS:	**HITS 1**			**WEEKS 3**
DANCE WITH JIMMY SHAND (NO. 2)	*Parlophone*	15	*6 Jan 62*	3
Above hit: Jimmy SHAND.				

ALBUMS:	**HITS 1**			**WEEKS 2**
FIFTY YEARS ON WITH JIMMY SHAND	*Ross*	97	*24 Dec 83*	2
Above hit: Jimmy SHAND, his Band and Guests.				

Paul SHANE and the YELLOWCOATS — UK

SINGLES:	**HITS 1**			**WEEKS 5**
HI-DE-HI (HOLIDAY ROCK)	*EMI*	36	*16 May 81*	5
Theme from the BBC1 TV sitcom 'Hi-Di-Hi'.				

SHANGRI-LAS — US

SINGLES:	**HITS 2**			**WEEKS 48**
REMEMBER (WALKIN' IN THE SAND)	*Red Bird*	14	*10 Oct 64*	13
LEADER OF THE PACK	*Red Bird*	11	*16 Jan 65*	9
Features Billy Joel on piano.				
LEADER OF THE PACK [RI-1ST]	*Kama Sultra*	3	*14 Oct 72*	14
LEADER OF THE PACK [RI-2ND]	*Charly*	7	*5 Jun 76*	11
LEADER OF THE PACK [RI-3RD]	*Contempo*	7	*12 Jun 76*	10
On 12 Jun 76 there were 2 separate entries on the chart. (Charly issue at No. 43, Contempo at No. 47). From 19 Jun 76 sales were combined.				

SHANICE — US

SINGLES:	**HITS 5**			**WEEKS 24**
I LOVE YOUR SMILE	*Motown*	55	*23 Nov 91*	4

I LOVE YOUR SMILE [RM]	*Motown*	2	*22 Feb 92*	10
Remixed by Driza Bone.				
LOVIN' YOU	*Motown*	54	*14 Nov 92*	1
SAVING FOREVER FOR YOU	*Giant*	42	*16 Jan 93*	3
From the film 'Beverley Hills 90210'.				
I LIKE	*Motown*	49	*13 Aug 94*	2
IF I NEVER KNEW YOU (LOVE THEME FROM POCAHONTAS)	*Walt Disney*	51	*16 Dec 95*	4
From the Walt Disney film 'Pocahontas'.				
Above hit: Jon SECADA and SHANICE.				
ALBUMS:	**HITS 1**			**WEEKS 4**
INNER CHILD	*Motown*	21	*21 Mar 92*	4

SHANKS and BIGFOOT — UK

(See also Doolally.)

SINGLES:	**HITS 2**			**WEEKS 24**
SWEET LIKE CHOCOLATE	*Pepper*	1	*29 May 99*	15
Vocals by Sharon Woolf.				
SWEET LIKE CHOCOLATE [RE]	*Pepper*	66	*2 Oct 99*	1
SING-A-LONG	*Pepper*	12	*29 Jul 00*	7
SING-A-LONG [RE]	*Pepper*	52	*23 Sep 00*	1

SHANNON — US

SINGLES:	**HITS 6**			**WEEKS 54**
LET THE MUSIC PLAY	*Club*	51	*19 Nov 83*	3
LET THE MUSIC PLAY [RE]	*Club*	14	*28 Jan 84*	12
GIVE ME TONIGHT	*Club*	24	*7 Apr 84*	7
SWEET SOMEBODY	*Club*	25	*30 Jun 84*	8
STRONGER TOGETHER	*Club*	46	*20 Jul 85*	6
IT'S OVER LOVE	*Manifesto*	16	*6 Dec 97*	8
Above hit: Todd TERRY presents SHANNON.				
MOVE MANIA	*Multiply*	8	*28 Nov 98*	10
Above hit: SASH! featuring SHANNON.				
ALBUMS:	**HITS 1**			**WEEKS 12**
LET THE MUSIC PLAY	*Club*	52	*10 Mar 84*	12

Del SHANNON — US

SINGLES:	**HITS 14**			**WEEKS 147**
RUNAWAY	*London*	1	*29 Apr 61*	22
Musitron (electric organ) solo by Max Crook.				
HATS OFF TO LARRY	*London*	6	*16 Sep 61*	12
SO LONG BABY	*London*	10	*9 Dec 61*	11
HEY! LITTLE GIRL	*London*	2	*17 Mar 62*	15
CRY MYSELF TO SLEEP	*London*	29	*8 Sep 62*	6
THE SWISS MAID	*London*	2	*13 Oct 62*	17
Originally recorded by Roger Miller.				
LITTLE TOWN FLIRT	*London*	4	*19 Jan 63*	13
TWO KINDS OF TEARDROPS	*London*	5	*27 Apr 63*	13
TWO SILHOUETTES	*London*	23	*24 Aug 63*	8
SUE'S GONNA BE MINE	*London*	21	*26 Oct 63*	8
MARY JANE	*Stateside*	35	*14 Mar 64*	5
HANDY MAN	*Stateside*	36	*1 Aug 64*	4
KEEP SEARCHIN' (WE'LL FOLLOW THE SUN)	*Stateside*	3	*16 Jan 65*	11
STRANGER IN TOWN	*Stateside*	40	*20 Mar 65*	2
EPS:	**HITS 2**			**WEEKS 21**
DEL SHANNON	*London*	14	*27 Jan 62*	2
DEL SHANNON NO. 2	*London*	9	*11 May 63*	19
ALBUMS:	**HITS 2**			**WEEKS 23**
HATS OFF TO DEL SHANNON	*London*	9	*11 May 63*	17
Compilation.				
LITTLE TOWN FLIRT	*London*	15	*2 Nov 63*	6

Roxanne SHANTE — US

SINGLES:	**HITS 4**			**WEEKS 11**
HAVE A NICE DAY	*Cold Chillin'*	58	*1 Aug 87*	3
Samples King Erricsson's Well, Have A Nice Day.				
GO ON GIRL	*Breakout*	55	*4 Jun 88*	3
SHARP AS A KNIFE	*Club*	45	*29 Oct 88*	3
Above hit: Brandon COOKE featuring Roxanne SHANTE.				
GO ON GIRL (THE HIP HOP MIX) [RM]	*Breakout*	74	*14 Apr 90*	1
Remixed by C.J. MacKintosh.				
WHAT'S GOING ON?	*Wall Of Sound*	43	*23 Sep 00*	1
Above hit: MEKON featuring Roxanne SHANTE.				

Helen SHAPIRO — UK

SINGLES:	HITS 11			WEEKS 119
DON'T TREAT ME LIKE A CHILD	*Columbia*	3	*25 Mar 61*	20
YOU DON'T KNOW	*Columbia*	1	*1 Jul 61*	23
WALKIN' BACK TO HAPPINESS	*Columbia*	1	*30 Sep 61*	19
TELL ME WHAT HE SAID	*Columbia*	2	*17 Feb 62*	15
Above hit: Helen SHAPIRO with the Martin SLAVIN ORCHESTRA.				
LET'S TALK ABOUT LOVE	*Columbia*	23	*5 May 62*	7
From the film 'It's Trad Dad'.				
Above hit: Helen SHAPIRO with Norrie PARAMOR and his Orchestra.				
LITTLE MISS LONELY	*Columbia*	8	*14 Jul 62*	11
Above hit: Helen SHAPIRO with Martin SLAVIN and his Orchestra.				
KEEP AWAY FROM OTHER GIRLS	*Columbia*	40	*20 Oct 62*	6
Originally recorded by Babs Tino.				
QUEEN FOR TONIGHT	*Columbia*	33	*9 Feb 63*	5
Above hit: Helen SHAPIRO with Martin SLAVIN and his Orchestra.				
WOE IS ME	*Columbia*	35	*27 Apr 63*	6
LOOK WHO IT IS	*Columbia*	47	*26 Oct 63*	3
FEVER	*Columbia*	38	*25 Jan 64*	4
EPS:	**HITS 3**			**WEEKS 92**
HELEN	*Columbia*	1	*25 Nov 61*	43
HELEN'S HIT PARADE	*Columbia*	1	*10 Feb 62*	41
MORE HITS FROM HELEN	*Columbia*	12	*6 Oct 62*	8
ALBUMS:	**HITS 1**			**WEEKS 25**
'TOPS' WITH ME	*Columbia*	2	*10 Mar 62*	25
Collection of her own personal favourites.				

SHARADA HOUSE GANG — Italy

SINGLES:	HITS 3			WEEKS 4
KEEP IT UP	*Media*	36	*12 Aug 95*	2
LET THE RHYTHM MOVE YOU	*Media*	50	*11 May 96*	1
Original release reached No. 90 in 1993.				
GYPSY BOY, GYPSY GIRL	*Gut*	52	*18 Oct 97*	1

SHARKEY — UK

SINGLES:	HITS 1			WEEKS 1
REVOLUTIONS [EP]	*React*	53	*8 Mar 97*	1
EP consists of various mixes of one song: Revolution.				

Feargal SHARKEY — UK

(See also Undertones.)

SINGLES:	HITS 7			WEEKS 58
LISTEN TO YOUR FATHER	*Zarjazz*	23	*13 Oct 84*	7
LOVING YOU	*Virgin*	26	*29 Jun 85*	10
Features Roger Taylor who also co-produced the single.				
A GOOD HEART	*Virgin*	1	*12 Oct 85*	16
Written by Maria McKee.				
YOU LITTLE THIEF	*Virgin*	5	*4 Jan 86*	9
Written by Tom Petty's drummer Benmont Tench about Maria McKee.				
SOMEBODY TO SOMEBODY	*Virgin*	64	*5 Apr 86*	3
MORE LOVE	*Virgin*	44	*16 Jan 88*	5
I'VE GOT NEWS FOR YOU	*Virgin*	12	*16 Mar 91*	8
ALBUMS:	**HITS 2**			**WEEKS 24**
FEARGAL SHARKEY	*Virgin*	12	*23 Nov 85*	20
SONGS FROM THE MARDI GRAS	*Virgin*	27	*20 Apr 91*	4

SHARONETTES — US

SINGLES:	HITS 2			WEEKS 8
PAPA OOM MOW MOW	*Black Magic*	26	*26 Apr 75*	5
Original by the Rivingtons reached No. 48 in the US in 1962.				
GOING TO A GO-GO	*Black Magic*	46	*12 Jul 75*	3

SHARP – See PARIS & SHARP

Debbie SHARP – See DREAM FREQUENCY

Dee Dee SHARP — US

(See also Philadelphia International All Stars: Lou Rawls, Billy Paul, Archie Bell, Teddy Pendergrass, O'Jays, Dee Dee Sharp, Gamble.)

SINGLES:	HITS 1			WEEKS 2
DO THE BIRD	*Cameo-Parkway*	46	*27 Apr 63*	2

Barrie K. SHARPE – See Diana BROWN and Barrie K. SHARPE

Rocky SHARPE and the REPLAYS — UK

SINGLES:	HITS 7			WEEKS 41
RAMA LAMA DING DONG *Original by the Edsels released in 1958, reaching No. 21 in the US in1961.*	*Chiswick*	17	*16 Dec 78*	10
IMAGINATION *Originally recorded by Harry Reser's Orchestra.*	*Chiswick*	39	*24 Mar 79*	6
LOVE WILL MAKE YOU FAIL IN SCHOOL *Originally recorded by Mickey and Sylvia.*	*Chiswick*	60	*25 Aug 79*	4
MARTIAN HOP *Original by the Ran-Dells reached No. 16 in the US in 1963.* *Above 2: Rocky SHARPE and the REPLAYS featuring the TOP LINERS.*	*Chiswick*	55	*9 Feb 80*	4
SHOUT! SHOUT! (KNOCK YOURSELF OUT) *Original by Ernie Maresca reached No. 6 in the US in 1962.*	*Chiswick*	19	*17 Apr 82*	9
CLAP YOUR HANDS *Originally recorded by Beau-Marks in 1960.*	*RAK*	54	*7 Aug 82*	3
IF YOU WANNA BE HAPPY	*Polydor*	46	*26 Feb 83*	5

SHARPE and NUMAN — UK

(See also Gary Numan; Radio Heart featuring Gary Numan.)

SINGLES:	HITS 4			WEEKS 16
CHANGE YOUR MIND	*Polydor*	17	*9 Feb 85*	8
NEW THING FROM LONDON TOWN	*Numa*	52	*4 Oct 86*	3
NO MORE LIES	*Polydor*	34	*30 Jan 88*	3
I'M ON AUTOMATIC	*Polydor*	44	*3 Jun 89*	2
ALBUMS:	**HITS 1**			**WEEKS 1**
AUTOMATIC	*Polydor*	59	*8 Jul 89*	1

Bob SHARPLES and his Orchestra - See JOHNSTON BROTHERS, Lita ROZA; Jimmy YOUNG

Ben SHAW featuring Adele HOLNESS — UK

SINGLES:	HITS 1			WEEKS 1
SO STRONG	*Fire Recordings*	72	*14 Jul 01*	1

Mark SHAW — UK

SINGLES:	HITS 1			WEEKS 1
LOVE SO BRIGHT	*EMI*	54	*17 Nov 90*	1

Roland SHAW ORCHESTRA - See BEVERLEY SISTERS; Don CORNELL; JOHNSTON BROTHERS; Dave KING; MANTOVANI and his Orchestra; Al MARTINO; David WHITFIELD

Sandie SHAW — UK

SINGLES:	HITS 20			WEEKS 165
(THERE'S) ALWAYS SOMETHING THERE TO REMIND ME *Originally recorded by Lou Johnson.*	*Pye*	1	*10 Oct 64*	11
GIRL DON'T COME	*Pye*	3	*12 Dec 64*	12
I'LL STOP AT NOTHING *Originally written for Adam Faith.*	*Pye*	4	*20 Feb 65*	11
LONG LIVE LOVE	*Pye*	1	*15 May 65*	14
MESSAGE UNDERSTOOD	*Pye*	6	*25 Sep 65*	10
HOW CAN YOU TELL	*Pye*	21	*20 Nov 65*	9
TOMORROW	*Pye*	9	*29 Jan 66*	9
NOTHING COMES EASY	*Pye*	14	*21 May 66*	9
RUN	*Pye*	32	*10 Sep 66*	5
THINK SOMETIMES ABOUT ME	*Pye*	32	*26 Nov 66*	4
I DON'T NEED ANYTHING *Originally recorded by Maxine Brown.*	*Pye*	50	*21 Jan 67*	1
PUPPET ON A STRING *UK's Eurovision entry in 1967, it came 1st.*	*Pye*	1	*18 Mar 67*	18
TONIGHT IN TOKYO	*Pye*	21	*15 Jul 67*	6
YOU'VE NOT CHANGED	*Pye*	18	*7 Oct 67*	12
TODAY	*Pye*	27	*10 Feb 68*	7
MONSIEUR DUPONT	*Pye*	6	*15 Feb 69*	15
THINK IT ALL OVER	*Pye*	42	*17 May 69*	4
HAND IN GLOVE *Collaboration with the Smiths.*	*Rough Trade*	27	*21 Apr 84*	5
ARE YOU READY TO BE HEARTBROKEN? *Originally recorded by Lloyd Cole & The Commotions.*	*Polydor*	68	*14 Jun 86*	1
NOTHING LESS THAN BRILLIANT	*Virgin*	66	*12 Nov 94*	2
EPS:	**HITS 2**			**WEEKS 26**
(THERE'S) ALWAYS SOMETHING THERE TO REMIND ME	*Pye*	9	*30 Jan 65*	12
TELL THE BOYS	*Pye*	4	*22 Apr 67*	14
ALBUMS:	**HITS 2**			**WEEKS 14**
SANDIE	*Pye*	3	*6 Mar 65*	13
NOTHING LESS THAN BRILLIANT *Compilation to celebrate 30th anniversary of her first No. 1 single.*	*Virgin*	64	*19 Nov 94*	1

Tracy SHAW — UK

SINGLES:	HITS 1			WEEKS 1
HAPPENIN' ALL OVER AGAIN	*Recognition*	46	*4 Jul 98*	1
She first performed the song on the Coronation Street special 'Viva Las Vegas'.				

Winifred SHAW — US

SINGLES:	HITS 1			WEEKS 4
LULLABY OF BROADWAY	*United Artists*	42	*14 Aug 76*	4
From the film 'Gold Diggers Of 1935'.				

SHAWNA - See LUDACRIS

SHE - See URBAN DISCHARGE featuring SHE

SHE ROCKERS — UK

SINGLES:	HITS 1			WEEKS 2
JAM IT JAM	*Jive*	58	*13 Jan 90*	2

George SHEARING QUINTET with strings — UK

(See also Nat King Cole/The George Shearing Quintet; Peggy Lee and George Shearing.)

SINGLES:	HITS 1			WEEKS 1
BAUBLES, BANGLES AND BEADS	*Capitol*	49	*6 Oct 62*	1

Gary SHEARSTON — Australia

SINGLES:	HITS 1			WEEKS 8
I GET A KICK OUT OF YOU	*Charisma*	7	*5 Oct 74*	8
Written by Cole Porter.				

SHED SEVEN — UK

SINGLES:	HITS 14			WEEKS 48
DOLPHIN	*Polydor*	28	*25 Jun 94*	4
SPEAKEASY	*Polydor*	24	*27 Aug 94*	3
OCEAN PIE	*Polydor*	33	*12 Nov 94*	2
WHERE HAVE YOU BEEN TONIGHT?	*Polydor*	23	*13 May 95*	2
GETTING BETTER	*Polydor*	14	*27 Jan 96*	3
GOING FOR GOLD	*Polydor*	8	*23 Mar 96*	5
BULLY BOY	*Polydor*	22	*18 May 96*	3
ON STANDBY	*Polydor*	12	*31 Aug 96*	4
CHASING RAINBOWS	*Polydor*	17	*23 Nov 96*	5
SHE LEFT ME ON FRIDAY	*Polydor*	11	*14 Mar 98*	4
THE HEROES	*Polydor*	18	*23 May 98*	3
DEVIL IN YOUR SHOES (WALKING ALL OVER)	*Polydor*	37	*22 Aug 98*	2
DISCO DOWN	*Polydor*	13	*5 Jun 99*	6
Above hit: SHED 7.				
CRY FOR HELP	*Artful*	30	*5 May 01*	2
ALBUMS:	**HITS 5**			**WEEKS 46**
CHANGE GIVER	*Polydor*	16	*17 Sep 94*	2
A MAXIMUM HIGH	*Polydor*	8	*13 Apr 96*	26
LET IT RIDE	*Polydor*	9	*13 Jun 98*	7
GOING FOR GOLD - THE GREATEST HITS	*Polydor*	7	*12 Jun 99*	10
TRUTH BE TOLD	*Artful*	42	*19 May 01*	1

SHEEP ON DRUGS — UK

SINGLES:	HITS 3			WEEKS 5
15 MINUTES OF FAME	*Island*	44	*27 Mar 93*	2
FROM A TO H AND BACK AGAIN	*Island*	40	*30 Oct 93*	2
LET THE GOOD TIMES ROLL	*Island*	56	*14 May 94*	1
ALBUMS:	**HITS 1**			**WEEKS 1**
GREATEST HITS	*Island*	55	*10 Apr 93*	1

SHEER BRONZE featuring Lisa MILLETT — UK

SINGLES:	HITS 1			WEEKS 1
WALKIN' ON	*Go.Beat*	63	*3 Sep 94*	1

SHEER ELEGANCE — UK

SINGLES:	HITS 3			WEEKS 23
MILKY WAY	*Pye International*	18	*20 Dec 75*	10
LIFE IS TOO SHORT GIRL	*Pye International*	9	*3 Apr 76*	9
IT'S TEMPTATION	*Pye International*	41	*24 Jul 76*	4

SHEILA B. DEVOTION — France

SINGLES:	HITS 3			WEEKS 33
SINGIN' IN THE RAIN	*Carrere*	11	*11 Mar 78*	13

YOU LIGHT MY FIRE	*Carrere*	44	*22 Jul 78*	6
SPACER	*Carrere*	18	*24 Nov 79*	14

Above hit: SHEILA and B. DEVOTION

Doug SHELDON — UK

SINGLES:	HITS 3			WEEKS 15
RUN AROUND SUE	*Decca*	36	*11 Nov 61*	3
YOUR MA SAID YOU CRIED IN YOUR SLEEP LAST NIGHT	*Decca*	29	*6 Jan 62*	6
I SAW LINDA YESTERDAY	*Decca*	36	*9 Feb 63*	6

Originally recorded by Dickey Lee.

Michelle SHELLERS - See SOUL PROVIDERS featuring Michelle SHELLERS

Pete SHELLEY — UK

SINGLES:	HITS 1			WEEKS 1
TELEPHONE OPERATOR	*Genetic*	66	*12 Mar 83*	1
ALBUMS:	**HITS 1**			**WEEKS 4**
XL - 1	*Genetic*	42	*2 Jul 83*	4

Peter SHELLEY — UK

SINGLES:	HITS 2			WEEKS 20
GEE BABY	*Magnet*	4	*14 Sep 74*	10
LOVE ME LOVE MY DOG	*Magnet*	3	*22 Mar 75*	10

Anne SHELTON — UK

SINGLES:	HITS 5			WEEKS 31
ARRIVEDERCI DARLING	*His Master's Voice*	17	*17 Dec 55*	4
Originally recorded by Renato Rascel.				
Above hit: Anne SHELTON with Geoff LOVE and his Orchestra.				
SEVEN DAYS	*Philips*	20	*14 Apr 56*	4
LAY DOWN YOUR ARMS	*Philips*	1	*25 Aug 56*	14
THE VILLAGE OF ST. BERNADETTE	*Philips*	27	*21 Nov 59*	1
SAILOR	*Philips*	10	*28 Jan 61*	8

Above 4: Anne SHELTON with Wally STOTT and his Orchestra and Chorus.

SHENA — UK

SINGLES:	HITS 2			WEEKS 3
LET THE BEAT HIT 'EM	*VC Recordings*	28	*2 Aug 97*	2
I'LL BE WAITING	*Rulin*	44	*1 Sep 01*	1

Above hit: FULL INTENTION presents SHENA.

Vikki SHEPARD - See SLEAZESISTERS

Vonda SHEPARD — US

SINGLES:	HITS 1			WEEKS 9
SEARCHIN' MY SOUL	*Epic*	10	*5 Dec 98*	9
Theme from the TV series 'Ally McBeal'.				
COMPILATION ALBUMS:	**HITS 1**			**WEEKS 2**
ALBUMS:	**HITS 3**			**WEEKS 49**
SONGS FROM 'ALLY MCBEAL' [OST-TV]	*Epic*	3	*17 Oct 98*	34
BY 7.30	*Epic*	39	*12 Jun 99*	2
HEART & SOUL - NEW SONGS FROM ALLY MCBEAL [OST-TV]	*Epic*	9	*20 Nov 99*	13
ALLY MCBEAL - FOR ONCE IN MY LIFE [OST-TV]	*Epic*	10	*5 May 01*	2

Shepard sings on 9 of the 16 tracks. Album was listed in the compilation chart.

Bill SHEPHERD CHORUS - See Jimmy PARKINSON

SHEPHERD SINGERS — US

SINGLES:	HITS 1			WEEKS 6
ALONE (WHY MUST I BE ALONE)	*His Master's Voice*	14	*16 Nov 57*	5
ALONE (WHY MUST I BE ALONE) [RE]	*His Master's Voice*	22	*4 Jan 58*	1

SHERBET — Australia

SINGLES:	HITS 1			WEEKS 10
HOWZAT	*Epic*	4	*25 Sep 76*	10

Tony SHERIDAN and the BEATLES — UK

(See also Beatles.)

SINGLES:	HITS 1			WEEKS 1
MY BONNIE	*Polydor*	48	*8 Jun 63*	1

Originally released in 1962.

Allan SHERMAN — US

SINGLES:	HITS 1			WEEKS 10
HELLO MUDDAH! HELLO FADDUH! (A LETTER FROM CAMP) *Novelty song with music addapted from Ponchielli's Dance Of The Hours.*	*Warner Brothers*	14	*14 Sep 63*	10

Bim SHERMAN – See Gary CLAIL ON-U SOUND SYSTEM

Bobby SHERMAN — US

SINGLES:	HITS 1			WEEKS 4
JULIE, DO YA LOVE ME	*CBS*	28	*31 Oct 70*	4

SHERRICK — US

SINGLES:	HITS 2			WEEKS 10
JUST CALL	*Warner Brothers*	23	*1 Aug 87*	8
LET'S BE LOVERS TONIGHT	*Warner Brothers*	63	*21 Nov 87*	2
ALBUMS:	**HITS 1**			**WEEKS 6**
SHERRICK	*Warner Brothers*	27	*29 Aug 87*	6

Pluto SHERVINGTON — Jamaica

SINGLES:	HITS 3			WEEKS 20
DAT	*Opal*	6	*7 Feb 76*	8
RAM GOAT RIVER	*Trojan*	43	*10 Apr 76*	4
YOUR HONOUR *Above hit: PLUTO.*	*KR*	19	*6 Mar 82*	8

Holly SHERWOOD — US

SINGLES:	HITS 1			WEEKS 7
DAY BY DAY (INCORPORATING "PREPARE YE THE WAY OF THE LORD") *From the musical 'Godspell'.*	*Bell*	29	*5 Feb 72*	7

Tony SHEVETON — UK

SINGLES:	HITS 1			WEEKS 1
MILLION DRUMS	*Orole*	49	*15 Feb 64*	1

SHIMMON and WOOLFSON — UK

(See also Sundance.)

SINGLES:	HITS 1			WEEKS 1
WELCOME TO THE FUTURE	*React*	69	*10 Jan 98*	1

SHIMON and Andy C — UK

SINGLES:	HITS 1			WEEKS 2
BODY ROCK	*Ram*	58	*15 Sep 01*	2

Brendan SHINE — Ireland

ALBUMS:	HITS 4			WEEKS 29
THE BRENDAN SHINE COLLECTION	*Play*	51	*12 Nov 83*	12
WITH LOVE	*Play*	74	*3 Nov 84*	4
MEMORIES	*Play*	81	*16 Nov 85*	7
MAGIC MOMENTS	*Stylus*	62	*18 Nov 89*	6

SHINEHEAD — Jamaica

SINGLES:	HITS 2			WEEKS 6
JAMAICAN IN NEW YORK *Based on Sting's An Englishman In New York.*	*Elektra*	30	*3 Apr 93*	5
LET 'EM IN	*Elektra*	70	*26 Jun 93*	1

SHIREHORSES — UK

ALBUMS:	HITS 2			WEEKS 8
THE WORST ALBUM IN THE WORLD EVER . . . EVER! *Features the Shirehorses' group incarnations (Charley Twins, Baby Bloke, Creeper, Doofergrass, Po-Fasis).*	*East West*	22	*15 Nov 97*	4
OUR KID EH	*Columbia*	20	*26 May 01*	4

SHIRELLES — US

SINGLES:	HITS 3			WEEKS 29
WILL YOU LOVE ME TOMORROW	*Top Rank*	4	*11 Feb 61*	15
SOLDIER BOY	*His Master's Voice*	23	*2 Jun 62*	9
FOOLISH LIITLE GIRL	*Stateside*	38	*25 May 63*	5

SHIRLEY and COMPANY — US

SINGLES:	HITS 1			WEEKS 9
SHAME, SHAME, SHAME	*All Platinum*	6	*8 Feb 75*	9
Male vocal by Jesus Alvarez.				

SHIRLEY and LEE — US

EPS:	HITS 1			WEEKS 5
SHIRLEY AND LEE	*Vogue*	16	*25 Jun 60*	5

SHIVA — UK

SINGLES:	HITS 2			WEEKS 5
WORK IT OUT	*ffrr*	36	*13 May 95*	2
FREEDOM	*ffrr*	18	*19 Aug 95*	3

SHIVAREE — US

SINGLES:	HITS 1			WEEKS 1
GOODNIGHT MOON	*Capitol*	63	*17 Feb 01*	1

SHO NUFF — US

SINGLES:	HITS 1			WEEKS 4
IT'S ALRIGHT	*Ensign*	53	*24 May 80*	4

Michelle SHOCKED — US

SINGLES:	HITS 3			WEEKS 10
ANCHORAGE	*Cooking Vinyl*	60	*8 Oct 88*	4
IF LOVE WAS A TRAIN	*Cooking Vinyl*	63	*14 Jan 89*	3
WHEN I GROW UP	*Cooking Vinyl*	67	*11 Mar 89*	3
ALBUMS:	**HITS 3**			**WEEKS 24**
SHORT SHARP SHOCKED	*Cooking Vinyl*	33	*10 Sep 88*	19
CAPTAIN SWING	*Cooking Vinyl*	31	*18 Nov 89*	3
ARKANSAS TRAVELER	*London*	46	*11 Apr 92*	2

SHOCKING BLUE — Holland

SINGLES:	HITS 2			WEEKS 14
VENUS	*Penny Farthing*	8	*17 Jan 70*	11
MIGHTY JOE	*Penny Farthing*	43	*25 Apr 70*	3

SHOCKING PINKS - See Neil YOUNG

Troy SHONDELL — US

SINGLES:	HITS 1			WEEKS 11
THIS TIME	*London*	22	*4 Nov 61*	11
Originally recorded by Thomas Wayne.				

SHONDELLS - See Tommy JAMES and the SHONDELLS

SHOOTING PARTY — UK

SINGLES:	HITS 1			WEEKS 2
LET'S HANG ON	*Lisson*	66	*31 Mar 90*	2

SHOP ASSISTANTS — UK

ALBUMS:	HITS 1			WEEKS 1
SHOP ASSISTANTS	*Blue Guitar*	100	*29 Nov 86*	1

SHORTIE vs BLACK LEGEND — ??

(See also Black Legend.)

SINGLES:	HITS 1			WEEKS 2
SOMEBODY	*WEA*	37	*4 Aug 01*	2

SHOWADDYWADDY — UK

SINGLES:	HITS 23			WEEKS 209
HEY ROCK AND ROLL	*Bell*	2	*18 May 74*	14
ROCK 'N' ROLL LADY	*Bell*	15	*17 Aug 74*	9
HEY MISTER CHRISTMAS	*Bell*	13	*30 Nov 74*	8
Accompanied by the National Childrens Home Harpenden Choir.				
SWEET MUSIC	*Bell*	14	*22 Feb 75*	9
THREE STEPS TO HEAVEN	*Bell*	2	*17 May 75*	11
HEARTBEAT	*Bell*	7	*6 Sep 75*	7
HEAVENLY	*Bell*	34	*15 Nov 75*	6
TROCADERO	*Bell*	32	*29 May 76*	3
UNDER THE MOON OF LOVE	*Bell*	1	*6 Nov 76*	15
Originally recorded by Curtis Lee.				

WHEN	*Arista*	3	*5 Mar 77*	11
YOU GOT WHAT IT TAKES	*Arista*	2	*23 Jul 77*	10
DANCIN' PARTY	*Arista*	4	*5 Nov 77*	11
I WONDER WHY	*Arista*	2	*25 Mar 78*	11
A LITTLE BIT OF SOAP	*Arista*	5	*24 Jun 78*	12
Original by the Jarmels reached No. 12 in the US in 1961.				
PRETTY LITTLE ANGEL EYES	*Arista*	5	*4 Nov 78*	12
Originally recorded by Curtis Lee.				
REMEMBER THEN	*Arista*	17	*31 Mar 79*	8
Original by the Earls reached No. 24 in the US in 1963.				
SWEET LITTLE ROCK 'N' ROLLER	*Arista*	15	*28 Jul 79*	9
A NIGHT AT DADDY GEES	*Arista*	39	*10 Nov 79*	5
Originally recorded by Curtis Lee in 1962.				
WHY DO LOVERS BREAK EACH OTHERS' HEARTS	*Arista*	22	*27 Sep 80*	10
Originally recorded by Bob B. Soxx and The Blue Jeans.				
BLUE MOON	*Arista*	32	*29 Nov 80*	9
MULTIPLICATION	*Arista*	39	*13 Jun 81*	4
FOOTSTEPS	*Bell*	31	*28 Nov 81*	9
WHO PUT THE BOMP (IN THE BOMP-A-BOMP-A-BOMP)	*RCA*	37	*28 Aug 82*	6
ALBUMS:	**HITS 10**			**WEEKS 126**
SHOWADDYWADDY	*Bell*	9	*7 Dec 74*	19
STEP TWO	*Bell*	7	*12 Jul 75*	17
TROCADERO	*Bell*	41	*29 May 76*	3
SHOWADDYWADDY'S GREATEST HITS	*Arista*	4	*25 Dec 76*	26
RED STAR	*Arista*	20	*3 Dec 77*	10
GREATEST HITS (1976-1978)	*Arista*	1	*9 Dec 78*	17
CREPES AND DRAPES	*Arista*	8	*10 Nov 79*	14
BRIGHT LIGHTS	*Arista*	33	*20 Dec 80*	8
THE VERY BEST OF SHOWADDYWADDY	*Arista*	33	*7 Nov 81*	11
THE BEST STEPS TO HEAVEN	*Tiger*	90	*5 Dec 87*	1

SHOWDOWN — US

SINGLES:	**HITS 1**			**WEEKS 4**
KEEP DOIN' IT	*State*	41	*17 Dec 77*	4

SHOWDOWN – See Garry LEE and SHOWDOWN

SHOWSTOPPERS — US

SINGLES:	**HITS 2**			**WEEKS 25**
AIN'T NOTHING BUT A HOUSEPARTY	*Beacon*	11	*16 Mar 68*	15
EENY MEENY	*MGM*	33	*16 Nov 68*	7
AIN'T NOTHING BUT A HOUSEPARTY [RI]	*Beacon*	43	*30 Jan 71*	1
AIN'T NOTHING BUT A HOUSEPARTY [RI] [RE-1ST]	*Beacon*	33	*13 Feb 71*	1
AIN'T NOTHING BUT A HOUSEPARTY [RI] [RE-2ND]	*Beacon*	36	*27 Feb 71*	1

SHRI – See DJ BADMARSH & SHRI featuring UK APACHE

SHRIEKBACK — UK

SINGLES:	**HITS 1**			**WEEKS 4**
HAND ON MY HEART	*Arista*	52	*28 Jul 84*	4
ALBUMS:	**HITS 1**			**WEEKS 1**
JAM SCIENCE	*Arista*	85	*11 Aug 84*	1

SHRIEVE – See HAGAR, SCHON, AARONSON, SHRIEVE

SHRINK — Holland

SINGLES:	**HITS 2**			**WEEKS 4**
(NERVOUS.(.BREAKDOWN)	*VC Recordings*	42	*10 Oct 98*	2
ARE YOU READY TO PARTY?	*NuLife*	39	*19 Aug 00*	2
Samples Don't Miss The Partyline by Bizz Nizz.				

SHUT UP AND DANCE — UK

SINGLES:	**HITS 7**			**WEEKS 14**
£20 TO GET IN	*Shut Up And Dance*	56	*21 Apr 90*	3
This track was actually the second track on this 12" only release. Track 1 was called Raps My Occupation.				
LAMBORGHINI	*Shut Up And Dance*	55	*28 Jul 90*	2
Above hit: SHUT UP AND DANCE featuring the RAGGA TWINS.				
AUTOBIOGRAPHY OF A CRACKHEAD / THE GREEN MAN	*Shut Up And Dance*	43	*8 Feb 92*	2
RAVING I'M RAVING	*Shut Up And Dance*	2	*30 May 92*	2
Samples Marc Cohn's Walking In Memphis. As copyright clearance was not given it was deleted, with an order that proceeds from the sales of those released be given to charity.				
Above hit: SHUT UP AND DANCE featuring Peter BOUNCER.				
THE ART OF MOVING BUTTS	*Shut Up And Dance*	69	*15 Aug 92*	1
Above hit: SHUT UP AND DANCE featuring ERIN.				
SAVE IT 'TIL THE MOURNING AFTER	*Pulse 8*	25	*1 Apr 95*	3
Samples Duran Duran's Save A Prayer.				

I LOVE U	*Pulse 8*	68	*8 Jul 95*	1
Samples Perez Prado's Guaglione.				
Above hit: SHUT UP AND DANCE featuring Richie DAVIS and PROFESSOR T.				
ALBUMS:	**HITS 1**			**WEEKS 2**
DEATH IS NOT THE END	*Shut Up And Dance*	38	*27 Jun 92*	2

SHY — UK

SINGLES:	**HITS 1**			**WEEKS 3**
GIRL (IT'S ALL I HAVE)	*Gallery*	60	*19 Apr 80*	3
ALBUMS:	**HITS 1**			**WEEKS 2**
EXCESS ALL AREAS	*RCA*	74	*11 Apr 87*	2

SHY FX — UK

(See UK Apachi with Shy FX.)

SINGLES:	**HITS 2**			**WEEKS 4**
ORIGINAL NUTTAH	*Sound Of Underground*	39	*1 Oct 94*	3
Samples Cypress Hill's I Ain't Going Out Like That and vocal introduction from the film 'Goodfellas'.				
Above hit: UK APACHI with SHY FX.				
BAMBAATA 2012	*Ebony*	60	*20 Mar 99*	1
Original release reached No. 120 in 1998.				

SHYHEIM — US

SINGLES:	**HITS 1**			**WEEKS 1**
THIS IZ REAL	*Noo Trybe*	61	*8 Jun 96*	1

SIA — Australia

(See also Zero 7.)

SINGLES:	**HITS 1**			**WEEKS 5**
TAKEN FOR GRANTED	*Long Lost Brother*	10	*3 Jun 00*	5

Labi SIFFRE — UK

SINGLES:	**HITS 5**			**WEEKS 44**
IT MUST BE LOVE	*Pye International*	14	*27 Nov 71*	12
CRYING, LAUGHING, LOVING, LYING	*Pye International*	11	*25 Mar 72*	9
WATCH ME	*Pye International*	29	*29 Jul 72*	6
(SOMETHING INSIDE) SO STRONG	*China*	4	*4 Apr 87*	13
A protest song against apartheid in South Africa.				
NOTHING'S GONNA CHANGE	*China*	52	*21 Nov 87*	4
ALBUMS:	**HITS 2**			**WEEKS 2**
SINGER AND THE SONG	*Pye*	47	*24 Jul 71*	1
CRYING, LAUGHING, LOVING, LYING	*Pye*	46	*14 Oct 72*	1

SIGNUM — Holland

SINGLES:	**HITS 2**			**WEEKS 2**
WHAT YA GOT 4 ME	*Tidy Trax*	70	*28 Nov 98*	1
COMING ON STRONG	*Tidy Trax*	66	*31 Jul 99*	1
Above hit: SIGNUM featuring Scott MAC.				

SIGUE SIGUE SPUTNIK — UK

SINGLES:	**HITS 5**			**WEEKS 20**
LOVE MISSILE F1-11	*Parlophone*	3	*1 Mar 86*	9
21ST CENTURY BOY	*Parlophone*	20	*7 Jun 86*	5
SUCCESS	*Parlophone*	31	*19 Nov 88*	3
DANCERAMA	*Parlophone*	50	*1 Apr 89*	2
ALBINONI VS STAR WARS	*Parlophone*	75	*20 May 89*	1
ALBUMS:	**HITS 2**			**WEEKS 7**
FLAUNT IT	*Parlophone*	10	*9 Aug 86*	6
DRESS FOR EXCESS	*Parlophone*	53	*15 Apr 89*	1

SIGUR ROS — Iceland

ALBUMS:	**HITS 1**			**WEEKS 1**
AGAETIS BYRJUN	*Fat Cat*	52	*26 Aug 00*	1
English translation: A New Beginning.				

SIL — Holland

SINGLES:	**HITS 1**			**WEEKS 1**
WINDOWS '98	*Hooj Choons*	58	*11 Apr 98*	1
Originally released in Holland in 1992.				

SILENCERS — UK

SINGLES:	HITS 3			WEEKS 7
PAINTED MOON	*RCA*	57	*25 Jun 88*	4
SCOTTISH RAIN	*RCA*	71	*27 May 89*	2
I CAN FEEL IT	*RCA*	62	*15 May 93*	1
ALBUMS:	**HITS 2**			**WEEKS 3**
DANCE TO THE HOLY MAN	*RCA*	39	*23 Mar 91*	2
SECONDS OF PLEASURE	*RCA*	52	*5 Jun 93*	1

SILENT UNDERDOG — UK

(See also Paul Hardcastle.)

SINGLES:	HITS 1			WEEKS 1
PAPA'S GOT A BRAND NEW PIGBAG	*Kaz*	73	*16 Feb 85*	1

SILICONE SOUL featuring Louise Clare MARSHALL — UK

SINGLES:	HITS 1			WEEKS 5
RIGHT ON!	*VC Recordings*	15	*6 Oct 01*	4
RIGHT ON! [RE]	*VC Recordings*	68	*24 Nov 01*	1

SILJE — Norway

SINGLES:	HITS 1			WEEKS 6
TELL ME WHERE YOU'RE GOING	*EMI*	55	*15 Dec 90*	6

Original release reached No. 85 earlier in the year.

SILK — US

SINGLES:	HITS 3			WEEKS 10
FREAK ME	*Elektra*	46	*24 Apr 93*	5
GIRL U FOR ME	*Elektra*	67	*5 Jun 93*	2
BABY IT'S YOU	*Elektra*	44	*9 Oct 93*	2
FREAK ME [RE]	*Elektra*	72	*26 Feb 94*	1

SILKIE — UK

SINGLES:	HITS 1			WEEKS 6
YOU'VE GOT TO HIDE YOUR LOVE AWAY	*Fontana*	28	*25 Sep 65*	6

SILSOE — UK

(See also Argent; San Jose featuring Rodriguez Argentina.)

SINGLES:	HITS 1			WEEKS 4
AZTEC GOLD - THE OFFICIAL ITV THEME FOR THE WORLD CUP	*CBS*	48	*21 Jun 86*	4

SILVAH BULLET - See Jonny L

Lucie SILVAS — UK

SINGLES:	HITS 1			WEEKS 1
IT'S TOO LATE	*EMI*	62	*17 Jun 00*	1

SILVER BULLET — UK

SINGLES:	HITS 3			WEEKS 20
BRING FORTH THE GUILLOTINE	*Tam Tam*	70	*2 Sep 89*	1
20 SECONDS TO COMPLY	*Tam Tam*	11	*9 Dec 89*	10
BRING FORTH THE GUILLOTINE [RE]	*Tam Tam*	45	*3 Mar 90*	5
UNDERCOVER ANARCHIST	*Parlophone*	33	*13 Apr 91*	4
ALBUMS:	**HITS 1**			**WEEKS 2**
BRING DOWN THE WALLS NO LIMIT SQUAD RETURNS	*Parlophone*	38	*4 May 91*	2

SILVER BULLET BAND - See Bob SEGER and the SILVER BULLET BAND

SILVER CITY — UK

SINGLES:	HITS 1			WEEKS 1
LOVE INFINITY	*Silver City*	62	*30 Oct 93*	1

SILVER CONVENTION — US/Germany

SINGLES:	HITS 5			WEEKS 35
SAVE ME	*Magnet*	30	*5 Apr 75*	7
FLY ROBIN FLY	*Magnet*	28	*15 Nov 75*	8
GET UP AND BOOGIE	*Magnet*	7	*3 Apr 76*	11
TIGER BABY / NO, NO JOE	*Magnet*	41	*19 Jun 76*	4
EVERYBODY'S TALKING 'BOUT LOVE	*Magnet*	25	*29 Jan 77*	5
ALBUMS:	**HITS 1**			**WEEKS 3**
SILVER CONVENTION: GREATEST HITS	*Magnet*	34	*25 Jun 77*	3

SILVER SUN — UK

SINGLES:	HITS 6			WEEKS 13
LAVA	*Polydor*	54	*2 Nov 96*	1
LAST DAY	*Polydor*	48	*22 Feb 97*	1
GOLDEN SKIN	*Polydor*	32	*3 May 97*	2
JULIA	*Polydor*	51	*5 Jul 97*	1
LAVA [RI]	*Polydor*	35	*18 Oct 97*	2
TOO MUCH, TOO LITTLE, TOO LATE	*Polydor*	20	*20 Jun 98*	4
I'LL SEE YOU AROUND	*Polydor*	26	*26 Sep 98*	2
ALBUMS:	**HITS 2**			**WEEKS 2**
SILVER SUN	*Polydor*	30	*24 May 97*	1
NEO WAVE	*Polydor*	74	*17 Oct 98*	1

SILVERCHAIR — Australia

SINGLES:	HITS 5			WEEKS 8
PURE MASSACRE	*Murmur*	71	*29 Jul 95*	1
TOMORROW	*Murmur*	59	*9 Sep 95*	2
FREAK	*Murmur*	34	*5 Apr 97*	2
ABUSE ME	*Murmur*	40	*19 Jul 97*	2
ANA'S SONG (OPEN FIRE)	*Murmur*	45	*15 May 99*	1
ALBUMS:	**HITS 3**			**WEEKS 5**
FROGSTOMP	*Murmur*	49	*23 Sep 95*	1
FREAK SHOW	*Murmur*	38	*15 Feb 97*	2
NEON BALLROOM	*Murmur*	29	*27 Mar 99*	2

SILVERFISH — US

ALBUMS:	HITS 1			WEEKS 1
ORGAN FAN	*Creation*	65	*27 Jun 92*	1

Dooley SILVERSPOON — US

SINGLES:	HITS 1			WEEKS 3
LET ME BE THE NO. 1 (LOVE OF YOUR LIFE)	*Seville*	44	*31 Jan 76*	3

Harry SIMEONE CHORALE — US

SINGLES:	HITS 2			WEEKS 14
THE LITTLE DRUMMER BOY	*Top Rank*	13	*14 Feb 59*	7
ONWARD CHRISTIAN SOLDIERS	*Ember*	35	*24 Dec 60*	1
ONWARD CHRISTIAN SOLDIERS [RE-1ST]	*Ember*	38	*7 Jan 61*	1
ONWARD CHRISTIAN SOLDIERS [RE-2ND]	*Ember*	36	*23 Dec 61*	3
ONWARD CHRISTIAN SOLDIERS [RI]	*Ember*	38	*22 Dec 62*	2
EPS:	**HITS 1**			**WEEKS 7**
GOLDEN HITS OF THE HARRY SIMEONE CHORALE	*Ember*	8	*9 Dec 61*	7

Gene SIMMONS — US

SINGLES:	HITS 1			WEEKS 4
RADIOACTIVE	*Casablanca*	41	*27 Jan 79*	4

SIMON — UK

SINGLES:	HITS 1			WEEKS 2
FREE AT LAST	*Positiva*	36	*31 Mar 01*	2
Samples Martin Luther King's civil rights speech 'I Have A Dream', given on 28 Aug 63 at the Lincoln Memorial in Washington DC, and Soft Cell's Tainted Love.				

SIMON – See TREVOR and SIMON

Carly SIMON — US

(See also Will Powers.)

SINGLES:	HITS 7			WEEKS 78
YOU'RE SO VAIN	*Elektra*	3	*16 Dec 72*	15
Backing vocals by Mick Jagger.				
THE RIGHT THING TO DO	*Elektra*	17	*31 Mar 73*	9
MOCKINGBIRD	*Elektra*	34	*16 Mar 74*	5
Duet with James Taylor.				
NOBODY DOES IT BETTER	*Elektra*	7	*6 Aug 77*	12
From the James Bond film 'The Spy Who Loved Me'.				
WHY	*WEA*	10	*21 Aug 82*	13
From the film 'Soup For One'.				
COMING AROUND AGAIN	*Arista*	10	*24 Jan 87*	12
From the film 'Heartburn'.				
WHY [RI]	*WEA*	56	*10 Jun 89*	5
YOU'RE SO VAIN [RI]	*Elektra*	41	*20 Apr 91*	5
SON OF A GUN (I BETCHA THINK THIS SONG IS ABOUT YOU)	*Virgin*	13	*22 Dec 01*	2
Above hit: JANET featuring Carly SIMON.				

ALBUMS:	HITS 5			WEEKS 67
NO SECRETS	*Elektra*	3	*20 Jan 73*	26
HOT CAKES	*Elektra*	19	*16 Mar 74*	9
COMING AROUND AGAIN	*Arista*	25	*9 May 87*	20
GREATEST HITS LIVE	*Arista*	49	*3 Sep 88*	6
Live recordings from the Gay Head harbour in Massachusetts.				
NOBODY DOES IT BETTER - THE VERY BEST OF CARLY SIMON	*warner.esp/Global TV*	22	*20 Mar 99*	6

Joe SIMON — US

SINGLES:	HITS 1			WEEKS 10
STEP BY STEP	*Mojo*	14	*16 Jun 73*	10

Paul SIMON — US

(See also Simon and Garfunkel.)

SINGLES:	HITS 11			WEEKS 86
MOTHER AND CHILD REUNION	*CBS*	5	*19 Feb 72*	12
Written after eating egg fried rice and chicken in a chinese restaurant.				
ME AND JULIO DOWN BY THE SCHOOLYARD	*CBS*	15	*29 Apr 72*	9
TAKE ME TO THE MARDI GRAS	*CBS*	7	*16 Jun 73*	11
LOVE ME LIKE A ROCK	*CBS*	39	*22 Sep 73*	5
Above hit: Paul SIMON (with the DIXIE HUMMINGBIRDS).				
50 WAYS TO LEAVE YOUR LOVER	*CBS*	23	*10 Jan 76*	6
Backing vocals by Patti Austin, Phoebe Snow and Valerie Simpson.				
SLIP SLIDIN' AWAY	*CBS*	36	*3 Dec 77*	6
Oak Ridge Boys on backing vocals.				
LATE IN THE EVENING	*Warner Brothers*	58	*6 Sep 80*	4
From the film 'One-Trick Pony'.				
YOU CAN CALL ME AL	*Warner Brothers*	4	*13 Sep 86*	13
THE BOY IN THE BUBBLE	*Warner Brothers*	26	*13 Dec 86*	8
THE OBVIOUS CHILD	*Warner Brothers*	15	*6 Oct 90*	10
SOMETHING SO RIGHT	*RCA*	44	*9 Dec 95*	2
Originally appeared on Simon's 1973 album There Goes Rhymin' Simon.				
Above hit: Annie LENNOX featuring Paul SIMON on guitar and vocals.				

ALBUMS:	HITS 12			WEEKS 291
PAUL SIMON	*CBS*	1	*26 Feb 72*	26
THERE GOES RHYMIN' SIMON	*CBS*	4	*2 Jun 73*	22
STILL CRAZY AFTER ALL THESE YEARS	*CBS*	6	*1 Nov 75*	31
GREATEST HITS, ETC.	*CBS*	6	*3 Dec 77*	15
ONE-TRICK PONY [OST]	*Warner Brothers*	17	*30 Aug 80*	12
HEARTS AND BONES	*Warner Brothers*	34	*12 Nov 83*	8
GRACELAND	*Warner Brothers*	1	*13 Sept 86*	101
Includes re-entries through to 1993.				
GREATEST HITS, ETC. [RE]	*CBS*	73	*24 Jan 87*	2
Re-released at mid-price.				
NEGOTIATIONS AND LOVE SONGS 1971-1986	*Warner Brothers*	17	*05 Nov 88*	15
THE RHYTHM OF THE SAINTS	*Warner Brothers*	1	*27 Oct 90*	28
PAUL SIMON'S CONCERT IN THE PARK - AUGUST 15TH, 1991	*Warner Brothers*	60	*23 Nov 91*	1
GRACELAND [RE]	*Warner Brothers*	27	*9 Aug 97*	14
Re-released at mid-price. Charted after being featured on BBC TV's 'Classic Albums' series.				
GREATEST HITS - SHINING LIKE A NATIONAL GUITAR	*Warner Brothers*	6	*27 May 00*	12
YOU'RE THE ONE	*Warner Brothers*	20	*14 Oct 00*	4

Ronni SIMON — UK

SINGLES:	HITS 2			WEEKS 2
B GOOD 2 ME	*Network*	73	*13 Aug 94*	1
TAKE YOU THERE	*Network*	58	*10 Jun 95*	1

Tito SIMON — Jamaica

SINGLES:	HITS 1			WEEKS 4
THIS MONDAY MORNING FEELING	*Horse*	45	*8 Feb 75*	4

SIMON and GARFUNKEL — US

(See also Art Garfunkel; Paul Simon.)

SINGLES:	HITS 8			WEEKS 87
HOMEWARD BOUND	*CBS*	9	*26 Mar 66*	12
Written on Widnes railway station.				
I AM A ROCK	*CBS*	17	*18 Jun 66*	10
Originally a solo Paul Simon recording from 1964.				
MRS. ROBINSON	*CBS*	4	*13 Jul 68*	12
From the film 'The Graduate'.				
MRS. ROBINSON [EP]	*CBS*	9	*11 Jan 69*	5
Lead track: Mrs. Robinson, which is a re-issue. Its chart life of 5 weeks would have been longer but for a decision not to allow EPs in the singles chart.				
THE BOXER	*CBS*	6	*3 May 69*	14

BRIDGE OVER TROUBLED WATER	*CBS*	1	*21 Feb 70*	19
Piano by Larry Knetchel.				
BRIDGE OVER TROUBLED WATER [RE]	*CBS*	45	*15 Aug 70*	1
AMERICA	*CBS*	25	*7 Oct 72*	7
SEVEN O'CLOCK NEWS/SILENT NIGHT [M] / A HAZY SHADE OF WINTER	*Columbia*	30	*7 Dec 91*	6
A Hazy Shade Of Winter listed from 28 Dec 91 and had first credit on the chart.				
THE BOXER [RI]	*Columbia*	75	*15 Feb 92*	1

EPS:	HITS 1			WEEKS 11
I AM A ROCK	*CBS*	4	*18 Jun 66*	11

ALBUMS:	HITS 11			WEEKS 1107
SOUNDS OF SILENCE	*CBS*	13	*16 Apr 66*	104
Includes re-entries through to 1971.				
BOOKENDS	*CBS*	1	*3 Aug 68*	77
PARSLEY, SAGE, ROSEMARY AND THYME	*CBS*	15	*31 Aug 68*	24
Originally released in 1966.				
THE GRADUATE [OST]	*CBS*	3	*26 Oct 68*	71
WEDNESDAY MORNING 3 A.M.	*CBS*	24	*9 Nov 68*	6
Their debut album, originally released in 1964.				
PARSLEY, SAGE, ROSEMARY AND THYME [RE]	*CBS*	13	*1 Mar 69*	42
BRIDGE OVER TROUBLED WATER	*CBS*	1	*21 Feb 70*	303
SIMON AND GARFUNKEL'S GREATEST HITS	*CBS*	2	*22 Jul 72*	280
Includes re-entries through to 1981.				
THE SIMON AND GARFUNKEL COLLECTION – 17 OF THEIR ALL-TIME GREATEST RECORDINGS	*CBS*	4	*21 Nov 81*	80
Includes re-entries through to 1987.				
THE CONCERT IN CENTRAL PARK	*Geffen*	6	*20 Mar 82*	43
Live recordings from 19 Sep 81.				
SOUNDS OF SILENCE [RE]	*CBS*	68	*4 Apr 81*	1
Re-released with a new catalogue number.				
SIMON AND GARFUNKEL'S GREATEST HITS [RE]	*CBS*	78	*24 Jul 82*	3
Peak position reached in 1984, (1982 peak No. 81).				
THE DEFINITIVE SIMON AND GARFUNKEL	*Columbia*	8	*30 Nov 91*	27
THE DEFINITIVE SIMON AND GARFUNKEL [RE]	*Columbia*	12	*30 Apr 94*	30
Re-released. Chart position reached in 1997, (1994 peak No. 24).				
BRIDGE OVER TROUBLED WATER [RI]	*Columbia*	56	*23 Sept 95*	4
Peak position reached in 1996, (1995 peak No. 63).				
TALES FROM NEW YORK – THE VERY BEST OF SIMON AND GARFUNKEL	*Columbia*	8	*5 Feb 00*	12

SIMONE — US

SINGLES:	HITS 1			WEEKS 1
MY FAMILY DEPENDS ON ME	*Strictly Rhythm*	75	*23 Nov 91*	1

Nina SIMONE — US

SINGLES:	HITS 5			WEEKS 46
I PUT A SPELL ON YOU	*Philips*	49	*7 Aug 65*	1
AIN'T GOT NO-I GOT LIFE / DO WHAT YOU GOTTA DO	*RCA Victor*	2	*19 Oct 68*	18
Do What You Gotta Do no longer listed from 14 Dec 68. As an AA side it peaked at No. 7.				
I PUT A SPELL ON YOU [RI]	*Philips*	28	*18 Jan 69*	4
TO LOVE SOMEBODY	*RCA Victor*	5	*18 Jan 69*	9
MY BABY JUST CARES FOR ME	*Charly*	5	*31 Oct 87*	11
Original release reached No. 82 in 1985. Originally recorded by Eddie Cantor in 1930.				
FEELING GOOD	*Mercury*	40	*9 Jul 94*	3
Featured in the VW car TV commercial.				

ALBUMS:	HITS 5			WEEKS 30
I PUT A SPELL ON YOU	*Philips*	18	*24 Jul 65*	3
'NUFF SAID	*RCA Victor*	11	*15 Feb 69*	1
MY BABY JUST CARES FOR ME	*Charly*	56	*14 Nov 87*	8
FEELING GOOD – THE VERY BEST OF NINA SIMONE	*PolyGram TV*	9	*16 Jul 94*	8
BLUE FOR YOU – THE VERY BEST OF NINA SIMONE	*Global Television*	12	*7 Feb 98*	10

Victor SIMONELLI presents SOLUTION — US

SINGLES:	HITS 1			WEEKS 1
FEELS SO RIGHT	*MCA*	63	*2 Nov 96*	1

SIMPLE MINDS — UK

SINGLES:	HITS 28			WEEKS 187
LIFE IN A DAY	*Zoom*	62	*12 May 79*	2
THE AMERICAN	*Virgin*	59	*23 May 81*	3
LOVE SONG	*Virgin*	47	*15 Aug 81*	4
SWEAT IN BULLET	*Virgin*	52	*7 Nov 81*	3
PROMISED YOU A MIRACLE	*Virgin*	13	*10 Apr 82*	11
GLITTERING PRIZE	*Virgin*	16	*28 Aug 82*	11
SOMEONE SOMEWHERE (IN SUMMERTIME)	*Virgin*	36	*13 Nov 82*	5
WATERFRONT	*Virgin*	13	*26 Nov 83*	10
SPEED YOUR LOVE TO ME	*Virgin*	20	*28 Jan 84*	4

UP ON THE CATWALK	*Virgin*	27	*24 Mar 84*	5
DON'T YOU (FORGET ABOUT ME)	*Virgin*	7	*20 Apr 85*	11
From the film 'The Breakfast Club'. Originally written for Roxy Music who turned it down.				
DON'T YOU (FORGET ABOUT ME) [RE-1ST]	*Virgin*	61	*17 Aug 85*	8
ALIVE & KICKING	*Virgin*	7	*12 Oct 85*	9
DON'T YOU (FORGET ABOUT ME) [RE-2ND]	*Virgin*	74	*28 Dec 85*	1
ALIVE & KICKING [RE]	*Virgin*	60	*4 Jan 86*	2
SANCTIFY YOURSELF	*Virgin*	10	*1 Feb 86*	7
DON'T YOU (FORGET ABOUT ME) [RE-3RD]	*Virgin*	62	*15 Feb 86*	3
DON'T YOU (FORGET ABOUT ME) [RE-4TH]	*Virgin*	68	*15 Mar 86*	1
ALL THE THINGS SHE SAID	*Virgin*	9	*12 Apr 86*	8
ALL THE THINGS SHE SAID [RE]	*Virgin*	73	*14 Jun 86*	1
GHOSTDANCING	*Virgin*	13	*15 Nov 86*	6
Live recording.				
GHOSTDANCING [RE]	*Virgin*	68	*3 Jan 87*	2
PROMISED YOU A MIRACLE [RR]	*Virgin*	19	*20 Jun 87*	7
Live recording from Le Zenith, Paris, France, Aug 86.				
Above hit: SIMPLE MINDS LIVE				
BELFAST CHILD	*Virgin*	1	*18 Feb 89*	11
Sleeve gives title as an EP: Ballad Of The Streets, though the 7" format only had 2 tracks.				
THIS IS YOUR LAND	*Virgin*	13	*22 Apr 89*	4
KICK IT IN	*Virgin*	15	*29 Jul 89*	5
THE AMSTERDAM [EP]	*Virgin*	18	*9 Dec 89*	6
Lead track: Sign O' The Times.				
LET THERE BE LOVE	*Virgin*	6	*23 Mar 91*	7
SEE THE LIGHTS	*Virgin*	20	*25 May 91*	4
STAND BY LOVE	*Virgin*	13	*31 Aug 91*	4
REAL LIFE	*Virgin*	34	*26 Oct 91*	3
LOVE SONG [RM] / ALIVE AND KICKING [RI]	*Virgin*	6	*10 Oct 92*	6
Love Song remixed by Greg Jackman.				
SHE'S A RIVER	*Virgin*	9	*28 Jan 95*	5
HYPNOTISED	*Virgin*	18	*8 Apr 95*	5
GLITTERBALL	*Chrysalis*	18	*14 Mar 98*	2
WAR BABIES	*Chrysalis*	43	*30 May 98*	1

ALBUMS:	**HITS 14**			**WEEKS 354**
A LIFE IN THE DAY	*Zoom*	30	*5 May 79*	6
EMPIRES AND DANCE	*Arista*	41	*27 Sep 80*	3
SONS AND FASCINATIONS / SISTERS FEELINGS CALL	*Virgin*	11	*12 Sep 81*	7
Double package of 2 earlier album releases.				
CELEBRATION	*Arista*	45	*27 Feb 82*	7
Compilation of early recordings.				
NEW GOLD DREAM (81,82,83,84)	*Virgin*	3	*25 Sep 82*	52
Includes re-entries through to 1987.				
SPARKLE IN THE RAIN	*Virgin*	1	*18 Feb 84*	57
ONCE UPON A TIME	*Virgin*	1	*2 Nov 85*	83
LIVE IN THE CITY OF LIGHT	*Virgin*	1	*6 Jun 87*	23
Live recordings from Le Zenith, Paris, France, Aug 86 (apart from 1 track which is from the Sydney Entertainment Centre, Australia).				
STREET FIGHTING YEARS	*Virgin*	1	*13 May 89*	28
LIVE IN THE CITY OF LIGHT [RE]	*Virgin*	66	*5 Aug 89*	3
Re-released at mid-price.				
REAL LIFE	*Virgin*	2	*20 Apr 91*	25
GLITTERING PRIZE 81/92	*Virgin*	1	*24 Oct 92*	39
Compilation.				
GOOD NEWS FROM THE NEXT WORLD	*Virgin*	2	*11 Feb 95*	14
NEAPOLIS	*Chrysalis*	19	*28 Mar 98*	3
THE BEST OF SIMPLE MINDS	*Virgin*	34	*17 Nov 01*	4

SIMPLICIOUS — US

(See also Eugene Wilde.)

SINGLES:	**HITS 1**			**WEEKS 3**
LET HER FEEL IT	*Fourth & Broadway*	65	*29 Sep 84*	3

SIMPLY RED — UK

SINGLES:	**HITS 30**			**WEEKS 354**
MONEY'S TOO TIGHT (TO MENTION)	*Elektra*	13	*15 Jun 85*	12
Originally recorded by the Valentine Brothers.				
COME TO MY AID	*Elektra*	66	*21 Sep 85*	2
HOLDING BACK THE YEARS	*Elektra*	51	*16 Nov 85*	4
Originally recorded by Mick Hucknell's previous group the Frantic Elevators.				
JERICHO	*WEA*	53	*8 Mar 86*	3
HOLDING BACK THE YEARS [RI]	*WEA*	2	*17 May 86*	13
OPEN UP THE RED BOX	*WEA*	61	*9 Aug 86*	4
THE RIGHT THING	*WEA*	11	*14 Feb 87*	10
INFIDELITY	*WEA*	31	*23 May 87*	5

EV'RY TIME WE SAY GOODBYE	*WEA*	11	*28 Nov 87*	9
I WON'T FEEL BAD	*WEA*	68	*12 Mar 88*	3
IT'S ONLY LOVE	*WEA*	13	*28 Jan 89*	8
IF YOU DON'T KNOW ME BY NOW	*WEA*	2	*8 Apr 89*	10
A NEW FLAME	*WEA*	17	*8 Jul 89*	8
YOU'VE GOT IT	*WEA*	46	*28 Oct 89*	3
SOMETHING GOT ME STARTED	*East West*	11	*21 Sep 91*	8
STARS	*East West*	8	*30 Nov 91*	10
FOR YOUR BABIES	*East West*	9	*8 Feb 92*	8
THRILL ME	*East West*	33	*2 May 92*	5
YOUR MIRROR	*East West*	17	*25 Jul 92*	4
MONTREUX [EP]	*East West*	11	*21 Nov 92*	10
Live recordings from the 26th Montreux Jazz Festival, 8 Jul 92. Lead track: Love For Sale, written by Cole Porter, though the track Lady Godiva's Room also received airplay.				
FAIRGROUND	*East West*	1	*30 Sep 95*	14
REMEMBERING THE FIRST TIME	*East West*	22	*16 Dec 95*	6
NEVER NEVER LOVE	*East West*	18	*24 Feb 96*	4
WE'RE IN THIS TOGETHER	*East West*	11	*22 Jun 96*	6
Official theme song for football's Euro '96.				
ANGEL	*East West*	4	*9 Nov 96*	13
NIGHT NURSE	*East West*	13	*20 Sep 97*	8
Originally recorded by Gregory Isaacs in 1982.				
Above hit: SLY and ROBBIE featuring SIMPLY RED.				
SAY YOU LOVE ME	*East West*	7	*16 May 98*	7
Features the Pro Arte Orchestra Of London conducted by David Sinclair Whitaker.				
THE AIR THAT I BREATHE	*East West*	6	*22 Aug 98*	7
GHETTO GIRL	*East West*	34	*12 Dec 98*	2
AIN'T THAT A LOT OF LOVE	*East West*	14	*30 Oct 99*	6
Orginally recorded by Horner Banks in 1966.				
YOUR EYES	*East West*	26	*19 Feb 00*	2

ALBUMS:	HITS 9			WEEKS 566
PICTURE BOOK	*Elektra*	33	*26 Oct 85*	13
PICTURE BOOK [RE]	*Elektra*	2	*8 Mar 86*	109
Includes re-entries through to 1992.				
MEN AND WOMEN	*WEA*	2	*21 Mar 87*	56
A NEW FLAME	*WEA*	1	*25 Feb 89*	84
STARS	*East West*	1	*12 Oct 91*	134
Includes re-entries through to 2000.				
PICTURE BOOK [RI]	*East West*	33	*21 Mar 92*	13
Digitally remastered. Peak position reached in 1996, (1992 peak No. 39).				
MEN AND WOMEN [RI]	*East West*	20	*4 Mar 95*	7
Re-released at mid-price.				
LIFE	*East West*	1	*21 Oct 95*	47
A NEW FLAME [RI]	*East West*	28	*24 Feb 96*	6
Re-released at mid-price.				
GREATEST HITS	*East West*	1	*19 Oct 96*	48
Includes re-entries through to 2001.				
BLUE	*East West*	1	*30 May 98*	26
LOVE AND THE RUSSIAN WINTER	*East West*	6	*13 Nov 99*	17
IT'S ONLY LOVE'	*East West*	27	*25 Nov 00*	6

SIMPLY RED AND WHITE — UK

SINGLES:	HITS 1			WEEKS 4
DAYDREAM BELIEVER (CHEER UP PETER REID)	*Ropery*	41	*6 Apr 96*	3
Peter Reid is Sunderland FC's manager.				
DAYDREAM BELIEVER (CHEER UP PETER REID) [RE]	*Ropery*	74	*4 May 96*	1

SIMPLY SMOOTH — US

SINGLES:	HITS 1			WEEKS 1
LADY (YOU BRING ME UP)	*Big Bang*	70	*17 Oct 98*	1

Fay SIMPSON – See Ronny JORDAN

Michael SIMPSON and John KING – See DUST BROTHERS (Michael SIMPSON and John KING) featuring Tyler DURDEN

Paul SIMPSON featuring ADEVA — US

(See also Adeva.)

SINGLES:	HITS 1			WEEKS 8
MUSICAL FREEDOM (MOVING ON UP)	*Cooltempo*	22	*25 Mar 89*	8

Jessica SIMPSON — US

SINGLES:	HITS 3			WEEKS 24
I WANNA LOVE YOU FOREVER	*Columbia*	7	*22 Apr 00*	9
I WANNA LOVE YOU FOREVER [RE]	*Columbia*	68	*8 Jul 00*	2
I THINK I'M IN LOVE WITH YOU	*Columbia*	15	*15 Jul 00*	7
Samples John Cougar (Mellencamp's) Jack & Diane.				

IRRESISTABLE	*Columbia*	11	*14 Jul 01*	6
ALBUMS:	**HITS 1**			**WEEKS 2**
SWEET KISSES	*Columbia*	36	*6 May 00*	2

Vida SIMPSON — US

SINGLES:	**HITS 1**			**WEEKS 1**
OOHHH BABY	*Hi-Life*	70	*18 Feb 95*	1

SIMPSONS — US

SINGLES:	**HITS 2**			**WEEKS 19**
DO THE BARTMAN	*Geffen*	1	*26 Jan 91*	12
DEEP, DEEP TROUBLE	*Geffen*	7	*6 Apr 91*	7
Above hit: SIMPSONS featuring BART and HOMER.				
ALBUMS:	**HITS 1**			**WEEKS 30**
COMPILATION ALBUMS:	**HITS 1**			**WEEKS 2**
THE SIMPSONS SING THE BLUES	*Geffen*	6	*2 Feb 91*	30
THE SIMPSONS - SONGS IN THE KEY OF SPRINGFIELD	*Rhino*	18	*12 Sep 98*	2
Above entry was in the compilation chart.				

A.E. SIMS - see Central Band of the ROYAL AIR FORCE (by permission of the Air Council) cond: Wing Comdr. A.E. SIMS O.B.E. (Organising director of music)

Joyce SIMS — US

SINGLES:	**HITS 6**			**WEEKS 36**
ALL AND ALL	*London*	16	*19 Apr 86*	10
LIFETIME LOVE	*London*	34	*13 Jun 87*	6
COME INTO MY LIFE	*London*	7	*9 Jan 88*	9
WALK AWAY	*London*	24	*23 Apr 88*	6
LOOKING FOR A LOVE	*ffrr*	39	*17 Jun 89*	4
Title as per sleeve and chart. Label only has Looking For Love.				
COME INTO MY LIFE [RR]	*Club Tools*	72	*27 May 95*	1
ALBUMS:	**HITS 2**			**WEEKS 25**
COME INTO MY LIFE	*London*	5	*9 Jan 88*	24
ALL ABOUT LOVE	*ffrr*	64	*16 Sep 89*	1

Kym SIMS — US

SINGLES:	**HITS 4**			**WEEKS 23**
TOO BLIND TO SEE IT	*Atco*	5	*7 Dec 91*	12
TAKE MY ADVICE	*Atco*	13	*28 Mar 92*	7
A LITTLE BIT MORE	*Atco*	30	*27 Jun 92*	3
WE GOTTA LOVE	*Pulse 8*	58	*8 Jun 96*	1
ALBUMS:	**HITS 1**			**WEEKS 2**
TOO BLIND TO SEE IT	*Atco*	39	*18 Apr 92*	2

SIN WITH SEBASTIAN — Germany

SINGLES:	**HITS 1**			**WEEKS 2**
SHUT UP (AND SLEEP WITH ME)	*Sing Sing*	44	*16 Sep 95*	1
SHUT UP (AND SLEEP WITH ME) [RM]	*Sing Sing*	46	*27 Jan 96*	1
Remixed by George Morel.				

Frank SINATRA — US

(See also Frank Sinatra and Count Basie and his Orchestra; Various Artists: Films - Original Soundtracks 'Can Can', 'Pal Joey', 'High Society'.)

SINGLES:	**HITS 35**			**WEEKS 433**
YOUNG-AT-HEART	*Capitol*	12	*10 Jul 54*	1
From the film of the same name.				
THREE COINS IN THE FOUNTAIN	*Capitol*	1	*17 Jul 54*	19
From the film of the same name.				
YOU MY LOVE	*Capitol*	13	*11 Jun 55*	3
From the film 'Young At Heart'.				
YOU MY LOVE [RE-1ST]	*Capitol*	17	*23 Jul 55*	2
LEARNIN' THE BLUES	*Capitol*	2	*6 Aug 55*	13
Above hit: Frank SINATRA with Nelson RIDDLE and his Orchestra.				
YOU MY LOVE [RE-2ND]	*Capitol*	17	*13 Aug 55*	2
NOT AS A STRANGER	*Capitol*	18	*3 Sep 55*	1
LOVE AND MARRIAGE ("OUR TOWN")	*Capitol*	3	*14 Jan 56*	8
From the American TV series 'Our Town'.				
(LOVE IS) THE TENDER TRAP	*Capitol*	2	*21 Jan 56*	9
From the film 'The Tender Trap'.				
SONGS FOR SWINGIN' LOVERS [LP]	*Capitol*	12	*16 Jun 56*	8
15 track LP, first track: You Make Me Feel So Young. In 1958 it entered the album chart. See album section below.				

ALL THE WAY / CHICAGO	*Capitol*	3	*23 Nov 57*	20
All The Way was listed on 23 Nov 57 at No. 29, the following week Chicago was listed at No. 25, and on 7 Dec 57 both sides were listed together at No. 21. From 14 Dec 57 All The Way was the only side listed.				
WITCHCRAFT	*Capitol*	12	*8 Feb 58*	8
MR. SUCCESS	*Capitol*	29	*15 Nov 58*	1
MR. SUCCESS [RE-1ST]	*Capitol*	25	*13 Dec 58*	2
MR. SUCCESS [RE-2ND]	*Capitol*	26	*3 Jan 59*	1
FRENCH FOREIGN LEGION	*Capitol*	18	*11 Apr 59*	5
COME DANCE WITH ME! [LP]	*Capitol*	30	*16 May 59*	1
12 track LP, first track: Come Dance With Me. This also entered the album chart the same week. See album section below.				
Above hit: Frank SINATRA with Billy MAY and his Orchestra.				
HIGH HOPES	*Capitol*	28	*29 Aug 59*	1
From the film 'A Hole In The Head'. Backing vocals and hand claps by Eddie Hodges.				
HIGH HOPES [RE-1ST]	*Capitol*	6	*12 Sep 59*	13
HIGH HOPES [RE-2ND]	*Capitol*	42	*12 Mar 60*	1
IT'S NICE TO GO TRAV'LING	*Capitol*	48	*9 Apr 60*	2
RIVER STAY 'WAY FROM MY DOOR	*Capitol*	18	*18 Jun 60*	9
Originally recorded by Kate Smith and Guy Lombardo.				
NICE 'N' EASY	*Capitol*	15	*10 Sep 60*	12
OL' MAC DONALD	*Capitol*	11	*26 Nov 60*	8
MY BLUE HEAVEN	*Capitol*	33	*22 Apr 61*	7
The majority of the singles listed above had backing orchestra conducted by Nelson Riddle.				
GRANADA	*Reprise*	15	*30 Sep 61*	8
Originally recorded by Frankie Laine.				
Above hit: Frank SINATRA with Billy MAY and his Orchestra.				
THE COFFEE SONG	*Reprise*	39	*25 Nov 61*	3
EVERYBODY'S TWISTIN'	*Reprise*	22	*7 Apr 62*	12
ME AND MY SHADOW	*Reprise*	20	*15 Dec 62*	7
Originally recorded by Whispering Jack Smith in 1927.				
Above hit: Frank SINATRA and Sammy DAVIS Jnr.				
ME AND MY SHADOW [RE]	*Reprise*	47	*9 Feb 63*	2
STRANGERS IN THE NIGHT	*Reprise*	1	*14 May 66*	20
From the film 'A Man Could Get Killed'.				
SUMMER WIND	*Reprise*	36	*1 Oct 66*	5
THAT'S LIFE	*Reprise*	46	*17 Dec 66*	5
Originally recorded by O.C.Smith.				
SOMETHIN' STUPID	*Reprise*	1	*25 Mar 67*	18
Above hit: Nancy SINATRA and Frank SINATRA.				
Originally recorded by C. Carson Parkes.				
THE WORLD WE KNEW (OVER AND OVER)	*Reprise*	33	*26 Aug 67*	11
MY WAY	*Reprise*	5	*5 Apr 69*	42
The single with most weeks on the singles chart, 124 weeks in total. Originally recorded by Claude Francois with English lyric by Paul Anka.				
LOVE'S BEEN GOOD TO ME	*Reprise*	8	*4 Oct 69*	18
Originally recorded by Rod McKuen.				
MY WAY [RE-1ST]	*Reprise*	49	*31 Jan 70*	1
MY WAY [RE-2ND]	*Reprise*	30	*28 Feb 70*	5
MY WAY [RE-3RD]	*Reprise*	33	*11 Apr 70*	9
MY WAY [RE-4TH]	*Reprise*	28	*27 Jun 70*	21
MY WAY [RE-5TH]	*Reprise*	18	*28 Nov 70*	16
I WILL DRINK THE WINE	*Reprise*	16	*6 Mar 71*	12
MY WAY [RE-6TH]	*Reprise*	22	*27 Mar 71*	19
MY WAY [RE-7TH]	*Reprise*	39	*4 Sep 71*	8
MY WAY [RE-8TH]	*Reprise*	50	*1 Jan 72*	1
I BELIEVE I'M GONNA LOVE YOU	*Reprise*	34	*20 Dec 75*	7
THEME FROM NEW YORK, NEW YORK	*Reprise*	59	*9 Aug 80*	4
THEME FROM NEW YORK, NEW YORK [RE]	*Reprise*	4	*22 Feb 86*	10
I'VE GOT YOU UNDER MY SKIN	*Island*	4	*4 Dec 93*	9
[AA] listed with Stay (Faraway, So Close) by U2. It was not available on the 2nd CD format.				
Above hit: Frank SINATRA with BONO.				
MY WAY [RI]	*Reprise*	45	*16 Apr 94*	2
Featured in the Dulux Paint TV commercial.				
THEY ALL LAUGHED	*Reprise*	41	*30 Jan 99*	1
Featured in the Carlsberg lager TV commercial. Originally recorded by Fred Astaire and Ginger Rogers in 1937, Sinatra's recording is from 1980.				

EPS:	**HITS 7**			**WEEKS 49**
COME DANCE WITH ME NO. 1	*Capitol*	11	*26 Mar 60*	2
THE SONG IS YOU	*Fontana*	19	*2 Apr 60*	1
SONGS FOR SWINGIN' LOVERS NO. 1	*Capitol*	20	*16 Apr 60*	1
THE LADY IS A TRAMP	*Capitol*	7	*23 Apr 60*	19
I'VE GOT A CRUSH ON YOU	*Fontana*	14	*9 Jul 60*	1
COME DANCE WITH ME NO. 2	*Capitol*	13	*26 Nov 60*	10
ALL THE WAY	*Capitol*	6	*14 Jan 61*	15

COMPILATION ALBUMS:	HITS 1			WEEKS 4
ALBUMS:	**HITS 53**			**WEEKS 732**
COME FLY WITH ME	*Capitol*	2	*8 Nov 58*	18
Above hit: Frank SINATRA with Billy MAY and his Orchestra.				
SONGS FOR SWINGING LOVERS	*Capitol*	8	*15 Nov 58*	8
First entered the singles chart in 1956. See singles section above.				
FRANK SINATRA STORY	*Fontana*	8	*29 Nov 58*	1
FRANK SINATRA SINGS FOR ONLY THE LONELY	*Capitol*	5	*13 Dec 58*	13
COME DANCE WITH ME!	*Capitol*	2	*16 May 59*	30
Also entered the singles chart the same week. See singles section above.				
Above hit: Frank SINATRA with Billy MAY and his Orchestra.				
LOOK TO YOUR HEART	*Capitol*	5	*22 Aug 59*	8
COME BACK TO SORRENTO	*Fontana*	6	*11 Jun 60*	9
SWING EASY	*Capitol*	5	*29 Oct 60*	17
NICE 'N EASY	*Capitol*	4	*21 Jan 61*	28
SINATRA SOUVENIR	*Fontana*	18	*15 Jul 61*	1
WHEN YOUR LOVER HAS GONE	*Encore*	6	*19 Aug 61*	10
SINATRA'S SWINGING SESSION!!!	*Capitol*	6	*23 Sep 61*	8
SINATRA SWINGS	*Reprise*	8	*28 Oct 61*	8
SINATRA PLUS	*Fontana*	7	*25 Nov 61*	9
RING-A-DING-DING	*Reprise*	8	*16 Dec 61*	9
COME SWING WITH ME	*Capitol*	13	*17 Feb 62*	4
I REMEMBER TOMMY . . .	*Reprise*	10	*7 Apr 62*	12
Songs first performed by Tommy Dorsey.				
SINATRA AND STRINGS	*Reprise*	6	*9 Jun 62*	20
GREAT SONGS FROM GREAT BRITAIN	*Reprise*	12	*27 Oct 62*	9
SINATRA WITH SWINGING BRASS	*Reprise*	14	*29 Dec 62*	11
CONCERT SINATRA	*Reprise*	8	*27 Jul 63*	18
SINATRA'S SINATRA	*Reprise*	9	*5 Oct 63*	24
SOFTLY AS I LEAVE YOU	*Reprise*	20	*20 Mar 65*	1
A MAN AND HIS MUSIC	*Reprise*	9	*22 Jan 66*	19
Compilation with narration by Sinatra.				
MOONLIGHT SINATRA	*Reprise*	18	*21 May 66*	8
STRANGERS IN THE NIGHT	*Reprise*	4	*2 Jul 66*	18
IN CONCERT: SINATRA AT 'THE SANDS'	*Reprise*	7	*1 Oct 66*	18
Live recordings featuring backing by Count Basie and his Orchestra.				
FRANK SINATRA SINGS SONGS FOR PLEASURE	*Music For Pleasure*	26	*3 Dec 66*	2
THAT'S LIFE	*Reprise*	22	*25 Feb 67*	12
FRANK SINATRA	*Reprise*	28	*7 Oct 67*	5
GREATEST HITS	*Reprise*	8	*19 Oct 68*	38
BEST OF FRANK SINATRA	*Capitol*	17	*7 Dec 68*	10
MY WAY	*Reprise*	2	*7 Jun 69*	59
A MAN ALONE - THE WORDS AND MUSIC OF ROD MCKUEN	*Reprise*	18	*4 Oct 69*	7
WATERTOWN	*Reprise*	14	*9 May 70*	9
GREATEST HITS VOLUME 2	*Reprise*	6	*12 Dec 70*	40
SINATRA AND COMPANY	*Reprise*	9	*5 Jun 71*	9
FRANK SINATRA SINGS RODGERS AND HART	Starline	35	*27 Nov 71*	1
GREATEST HITS VOLUME 2 [RE]	*Reprise*	29	*8 Jan 72*	3
Re-released with new catalogue number.				
MY WAY [RE]	*Reprise*	35	*8 Jan 72*	1
Re-released with new catalogue number.				
OL' BLUE EYES IS BACK	*Warner Brothers*	12	*1 Dec 73*	13
SOME NICE THINGS I'VE MISSED	*Reprise*	35	*17 Aug 74*	3
SINATRA - THE MAIN EVENT LIVE [OST-TV]	*Reprise*	30	*15 Feb 75*	2
Live recordings from Madison Square Garden. Featured backing from Woody Herman and the Young Thundering Herd.				
THE BEST OF OL' BLUE EYES	*Reprise*	30	*14 Jun 75*	3
PORTRAIT OF SINATRA	*Reprise*	1	*19 Mar 77*	18
Compilation.				
20 GOLDEN GREATS	*Capitol*	4	*13 May 78*	11
L.A. IS MY LADY	*Qwest*	41	*18 Aug 84*	8
Above hit: Frank SINATRA with the Quincy JONES ORCHESTRA.				
NEW YORK, NEW YORK (GREATEST HITS)	*Warner Brothers*	13	*22 Mar 86*	12
THE FRANK SINATRA COLLECTION	*Capitol*	40	*4 Oct 86*	5
DUETS	*Capitol*	5	*6 Nov 93*	14
DUETS II	*Capitol*	29	*26 Nov 94*	6
Above 2, as the titles suggest are collaborations with various artists.				
THIS IS FRANK SINATRA 1953 - 1957	*Music For Pleasure*	56	*11 Mar 95*	1
SINATRA 80TH - ALL THE BEST	*Capitol*	49	*2 Dec 95*	5
MY WAY - THE BEST OF FRANK SINATRA	*Reprise*	13	*16 Aug 97*	14
Sales combined of either a single 20 track album or a double 46 track.				
MY WAY - THE BEST OF FRANK SINATRA [RE]	*Reprise*	7	*23 May 98*	73
SONGS FOR SWINGING LOVERS [RE]	*Capitol*	63	*30 May 98*	2
Re-released with new catalogue number.				
CLASSIC SINATRA - HIS GREATEST PERFORMANCES 1953-1960	*Capitol*	10	*24 Jun 00*	7
EEE- O 11 - THE BEST OF THE RAT PACK	*Capitol*	2	*8 Dec 01*	4
Solo recordings and 2 duets. Above entry listed in the compilation chart.				
Above hit: Frank SINATRA Dean MARTIN Sammy DAVIS Jr.				

Frank SINATRA and Count BASIE and his Orchestra — US

(See also Count Basie and his Orchestra; Frank Sinatra.)

SINGLES:	HITS 2			WEEKS 7
MY KIND OF GIRL	*Reprise*	35	*9 Mar 63*	6
HELLO DOLLY	*Reprise*	47	*26 Sep 64*	1
From the musical of the same name.				

ALBUMS:	HITS 2			WEEKS 27
SINATRA - BASIE	*Reprise*	2	*23 Feb 63*	23
IT MIGHT AS WELL BE SWING	*Reprise*	17	*19 Sep 64*	4

Nancy SINATRA — US

(See also Nancy Sinatra and Lee Hazlewood.)

SINGLES:	HITS 6			WEEKS 79
THESE BOOTS ARE MADE FOR WALKIN'	*Reprise*	1	*29 Jan 66*	14
Originally recorded by Lee Hazelwood.				
HOW DOES THAT GRAB YOU, DARLIN'?	*Reprise*	19	*30 Apr 66*	8
SUGAR TOWN	*Reprise*	8	*21 Jan 67*	10
SOMETHIN' STUPID	*Reprise*	1	*25 Mar 67*	18
Originally recorded by C. Carson Parkes.				
Above hit: Nancy SINATRA and Frank SINATRA.				
YOU ONLY LIVE TWICE	*Reprise*	11	*8 Jul 67*	19
From the James Bond film of the same name. [AA] listed with Jackson by Nancy Sinatra and Lee Hazlewood.				
THE HIGHWAY SONG	*Reprise*	21	*29 Nov 69*	10

ALBUMS:	HITS 3			WEEKS 15
BOOTS	*Reprise*	12	*16 Apr 66*	9
HOW DOES THAT GRAB YOU	*Reprise*	17	*18 Jun 66*	3
NANCY'S GREATEST HITS	*Reprise*	39	*10 Oct 70*	3

Nancy SINATRA and Lee HAZLEWOOD — US

(See also Nancy Sinatra.)

SINGLES:	HITS 3			WEEKS 38
JACKSON	*Reprise*	11	*15 Jul 67*	18
[AA] listed with You Only Live Twice by Nancy Sinatra.				
LADY BIRD	*Reprise*	47	*11 Nov 67*	1
DID YOU EVER	*Reprise*	2	*21 Aug 71*	19
Originally recorded by Charles Louvin and Melba Mongomery.				

ALBUMS:	HITS 2			WEEKS 17
NANCY AND LEE	*Reprise*	17	*29 Jun 68*	12
NANCY AND LEE [RE]	*Reprise*	42	*25 Sept 71*	1
Re-released with new catalogue number.				
DID YOU EVER	*RCA Victor*	31	*29 Jan 72*	4

SINCLAIR — UK

SINGLES:	HITS 3			WEEKS 8
AIN'T NO CASANOVA	*Dome*	28	*21 Aug 93*	5
(I WANNA KNOW) WHY	*Dome*	58	*26 Feb 94*	2
DON'T LIE	*Dome*	70	*6 Aug 94*	1

Bob SINCLAR — France

SINGLES:	HITS 3			WEEKS 7
MY ONLY LOVE	*East West*	56	*20 Mar 99*	1
Above hit: Bob SINCLAR featuring Lee A. GENESIS.				
I FEEL FOR YOU	*Defected*	9	*19 Aug 00*	5
Samples Cerrone's Look For Love.				
DARLIN'	*Defected*	46	*7 Apr 01*	1
Above hit: Bob SINCLAR featuring James D-Train WILLIAMS.				

SINDY — UK

SINGLES:	HITS 1			WEEKS 1
SATURDAY NIGHT	*Love This*	70	*5 Oct 96*	1

SINE — US

SINGLES:	HITS 1			WEEKS 9
JUST LET ME DO MY THING	*CBS*	33	*10 Jun 78*	9

SINFONIA OF LONDON - Howard BLAKE conducting the SINFONIA OF LONDON; SNOWMAN

Talvin SINGH — UK

SINGLES:	HITS 1			WEEKS 4
KISS THEM FOR ME	*Wonderland*	32	*25 May 91*	4
Above hit: SIOUXSIE and the BANSHEES featuring Talvin SINGH.				

ALBUMS:	HITS 2			WEEKS 5
OK	*Island*	41	*18 Sept 99*	4
Originally released in 1998, charted after winning the 1999 Mercury Music Prize.				
HA	*Island*	57	*7 Apr 01*	1

SINGING CORNER meets DONOVAN — UK

SINGLES:	HITS 1			WEEKS 1
JENNIFER JUNIPER	*Fontana*	68	*1 Dec 90*	1

SINGING DOGS - See Don CHARLES presents the SINGING DOGS

SINGING NUN (SOEUR SOURIRE) — Belgium

SINGLES:	HITS 1			WEEKS 14
DOMINIQUE (SOEUR SOURIRE)	*Philips*	7	*7 Dec 63*	14

SINGING SHEEP — Denmark

SINGLES:	HITS 1			WEEKS 5
BAA BAA BLACK SHEEP	*Sheep*	42	*18 Dec 82*	5

Maxine SINGLETON — US

SINGLES:	HITS 1			WEEKS 3
YOU CAN'T RUN FROM LOVE	*Creole*	57	*2 Apr 83*	3

SINITTA — US

SINGLES:	HITS 12			WEEKS 104
SO MACHO / CRUISING	*Fanfare*	47	*8 Mar 86*	11
SO MACHO / CRUISING [RE]	*Fanfare*	2	*28 Jun 86*	17
FEELS LIKE THE FIRST TIME	*Fanfare*	45	*11 Oct 86*	5
TOY BOY	*Fanfare*	4	*25 Jul 87*	14
G.T.O.	*Fanfare*	15	*12 Dec 87*	9
CROSS MY BROKEN HEART	*Fanfare*	6	*19 Mar 88*	9
I DON'T BELIEVE IN MIRACLES	*Fanfare*	22	*24 Sep 88*	8
RIGHT BACK WHERE WE STARTED FROM	*Fanfare*	4	*3 Jun 89*	10
Originally recorded by J.Vincent Edwards.				
LOVE ON A MOUNTAIN TOP	*Fanfare*	20	*7 Oct 89*	6
HITCHIN' A RIDE	*Fanfare*	24	*21 Apr 90*	6
LOVE AND AFFECTION	*Fanfare*	62	*22 Sep 90*	3
SHAME, SHAME, SHAME	*Arista*	28	*4 Jul 92*	4
THE SUPREME [EP]	*Arista*	49	*17 Apr 93*	2
Lead track: Where Did Our Love Go?				

ALBUMS:	HITS 2			WEEKS 23
SINITTA!	*Fanfare*	34	*26 Dec 87*	19
WICKED!	*Fanfare*	52	*9 Dec 89*	4

SINNAMON — US

SINGLES:	HITS 1			WEEKS 1
I NEED YOU NOW	*Worx*	70	*28 Sep 96*	1

SIOUXSIE and the BANSHEES — UK

SINGLES:	HITS 30			WEEKS 150
HONG KONG GARDEN	*Polydor*	7	*26 Aug 78*	10
THE STAIRCASE (MYSTERY)	*Polydor*	24	*31 Mar 79*	8
PLAYGROUND TWIST	*Polydor*	28	*7 Jul 79*	6
MITTAGEISEN (METAL POSTCARD)	*Polydor*	47	*29 Sep 79*	3
HAPPY HOUSE	*Polydor*	17	*15 Mar 80*	8
CHRISTINE	*Polydor*	22	*7 Jun 80*	8
ISRAEL	*Polydor*	41	*6 Dec 80*	8
SPELLBOUND	*Polydor*	22	*30 May 81*	8
ARABIAN KNIGHTS	*Polydor*	32	*1 Aug 81*	7
FIRE WORKS	*Polydor*	22	*29 May 82*	6
SLOWDIVE	*Polydor*	41	*9 Oct 82*	4
MELT / IL EST NE LE DIVIN ENFANT	*Polydor*	49	*4 Dec 82*	5
Il Est Ne Le Divin Enfant is a French Christmas song.				
DEAR PRUDENCE	*Wonderland*	3	*1 Oct 83*	8
Originally recorded by the Beatles, written about Mia Farrow's sister.				
SWIMMING HORSES	*Wonderland*	28	*24 Mar 84*	4
DAZZLE	*Wonderland*	33	*2 Jun 84*	3
THE THORN [EP]	*Wonderland*	47	*27 Oct 84*	3
Lead track: Overground, features the Chandos Players.				
CITIES IN DUST	*Wonderland*	21	*26 Oct 85*	6
CANDYMAN	*Wonderland*	34	*8 Mar 86*	5
THIS WHEEL'S ON FIRE	*Wonderland*	14	*17 Jan 87*	6
THE PASSENGER	*Wonderland*	41	*28 Mar 87*	6
Originally recorded by Iggy Pop.				

SONG FROM THE EDGE OF THE WORLD	*Wonderland*	59	*25 Jul 87*	3
PEEK A BOO	*Wonderland*	16	*30 Jul 88*	6
THE KILLING JAR	*Wonderland*	41	*8 Oct 88*	3
THE LAST BEAT OF MY HEART	*Wonderland*	44	*3 Dec 88*	1
KISS THEM FOR ME	*Wonderland*	32	*25 May 91*	4
Above hit: SIOUXSIE and the BANSHEES featuring Talvin SINGH.				
SHADOWTIME	*Wonderland*	57	*13 Jul 91*	1
FACE TO FACE	*Wonderland*	21	*25 Jul 92*	4
INTERLUDE	*Parlophone*	25	*20 Aug 94*	2
Originally recorded by Timi Yuro in 1968.				
Above hit: MORRISSEY and SIOUXSIE.				
O BABY	*Wonderland*	34	*7 Jan 95*	3
STARGAZER	*Wonderland*	64	*18 Feb 95*	1
ALBUMS:	**HITS 14**			**WEEKS 119**
THE SCREAM	*Polydor*	12	*2 Dec 78*	11
JOIN HANDS	*Polydor*	13	*22 Sep 79*	5
KALEIDOSCOPE	*Polydor*	5	*16 Aug 80*	6
JU JU	*Polydor*	7	*27 Jun 81*	17
ONCE UPON A TIME - THE SINGLES	*Polydor*	21	*12 Dec 81*	26
A KISS IN THE DREAMHOUSE	*Polydor*	11	*13 Nov 82*	11
NOCTURNE	*Wonderland*	29	*3 Dec 83*	10
Live recordings.				
HYENA	*Wonderland*	15	*16 Jun 84*	6
TINDERBOX	*Wonderland*	13	*26 Apr 86*	6
THROUGH THE LOOKING GLASS	*Wonderland*	15	*14 Mar 87*	8
Album of covers.				
PEEPSHOW	*Wonderland*	20	*17 Sep 88*	5
SUPERSTITION	*Wonderland*	25	*22 Jun 91*	4
TWICE UPON A TIME - THE SINGLES	*Wonderland*	26	*17 Oct 92*	2
THE RAPTURE	*Wonderland*	33	*28 Jan 95*	2

SIR DOUGLAS QUINTET — US

SINGLES:	**HITS 1**			**WEEKS 10**
SHE'S ABOUT A MOVER	*London*	15	*19 Jun 65*	10

SIR KILLALOT V ROBO BABE — UK

SINGLES:				
ROBOT WARS (ANDROID LOVE)	*Polydor*	51	*30 Dec 00*	3
Inspired by the BBC2 series 'Robot Wars'.				

SIR MIX-A-LOT — US

SINGLES:	**HITS 1**			**WEEKS 2**
BABY GOT BACK	*Def American*	56	*8 Aug 92*	2

George SIRAVO and his Orchestra – See Johnnie RAY

SIRRON – See PLUS ONE featuring SIRRON

SISQO — US

SINGLES:	**HITS 5**			**WEEKS 43**
GOT TO GET IT	*Def Soul*	14	*12 Feb 00*	4
THONG SONG	*Def Soul*	3	*22 Apr 00*	14
Samples Ricky Martin's Livin' La Vida Loca.				
UNLEASH THE DRAGON	*Def Soul*	6	*30 Sep 00*	7
INCOMPLETE	*Def Soul*	13	*16 Dec 00*	8
DANCE FOR ME	*Def Soul*	6	*28 Jul 01*	10
ALBUMS:	**HITS 2**			**WEEKS 41**
UNLEASH THE DRAGON	*Def Soul*	15	*26 Feb 00*	36
RETURN OF DRAGON	*Def Soul*	22	*4 Aug 01*	5

SISSEL — US/Norway

SINGLES:	**HITS 1**			**WEEKS 7**
PRINCE IGOR	*Def Jam*	15	*10 Jan 98*	7
Based on music composed by Borodin.				
Above hit: RAPSODY: Warren G and SISSEL.				
ALBUMS:	**HITS 1**			**WEEKS 1**
DEEP WITHIN MY SOUL	*Mercury*	58	*20 May 95*	1
Nordic electronic folk songs.				

SISTA featuring Craig MACK – See VARIOUS ARTISTS (EPs) 'Dangerous Minds EP'

SISTER BLISS — UK

SINGLES:	**HITS 5**			**WEEKS 11**
CANTGETAMAN, CANTGETAJOB (LIFE'S A BITCH!)	*Go.Beat*	31	*15 Oct 94*	4
Above hit: SISTER BLISS with COLETTE.				

OH! WHAT A WORLD	*Go.Beat*	40	*15 Jul 95*	2
Colette, though the vocalist, is not credited on this release.				
BAD MAN	*Junk Dog*	51	*29 Jun 96*	1
SISTER SISTER	*Multiply*	34	*7 Oct 00*	2
DELIVER ME	*Multiply*	31	*24 Mar 01*	2
Originally recorded by the Beloved for their 1996 album X.				
Above hit: SISTER BLISS featuring John MARTYN.				

SISTER SLEDGE — US

(See also Kathy Sledge.)

SINGLES:	HITS 9			WEEKS 111
MAMA NEVER TOLD ME	*Atlantic*	20	*21 Jun 75*	6
HE'S THE GREATEST DANCER	*Atlantic*	6	*17 Mar 79*	11
WE ARE FAMILY	*Atlantic*	8	*26 May 79*	10
Backing vocals by Luther Vandross.				
LOST IN MUSIC	*Atlantic*	17	*11 Aug 79*	10
GOT TO LOVE SOMEBODY	*Atlantic*	34	*19 Jan 80*	4
ALL AMERICAN GIRLS	*Atlantic*	41	*28 Feb 81*	5
THINKING OF YOU	*Atlantic*	11	*26 May 84*	13
Originally recorded in 1979.				
LOST IN MUSIC [RI]	*Atlantic*	4	*8 Sep 84*	12
WE ARE FAMILY [RM-1ST]	*Atlantic*	33	*17 Nov 84*	4
FRANKIE	*Atlantic*	1	*1 Jun 85*	16
DANCING ON THE JAGGED EDGE	*Atlantic*	50	*31 Aug 85*	3
WE ARE FAMILY ('93 MIXES) [RM-2ND]	*Atlantic*	5	*23 Jan 93*	8
LOST IN MUSIC (SURE IS PURE REMIXES) [RM]	*Atlantic*	14	*13 Mar 93*	5
Above 2 remixed by Sure Is Pure.				
THINKING OF YOU ('93 REMIXES) [RM]	*Atlantic*	17	*12 Jun 93*	4
Remixed by Ramp.				

ALBUMS:	HITS 4			WEEKS 58
WE ARE FAMILY	*Atlantic*	15	*12 May 79*	23
WE ARE FAMILY [RE]	*Atlantic*	7	*29 Sept 84*	16
WHEN THE BOYS MEET THE GIRLS	*Atlantic*	19	*22 Jun 85*	11
FREAK OUT	*Telstar*	72	*5 Dec 87*	3
Compilation of hits by both groups.				
Above hit: CHIC and SISTER SLEDGE.				
THE VERY BEST OF SISTER SLEDGE 1973 - 1993	*Atlantic*	19	*20 Feb 93*	5
Includes originals and remixes.				

SISTERHOOD — UK

ALBUMS:	HITS 1			WEEKS 1
GIFT	*Merciful Release*	90	*26 Jul 86*	1

SISTERS OF MERCY — UK

SINGLES:	HITS 10			WEEKS 40
BODY AND SOUL / TRAIN	*Merciful Release*	46	*16 Jun 84*	3
WALK AWAY	*Merciful Release*	45	*20 Oct 84*	3
NO TIME TO CRY	*Merciful Release*	63	*9 Mar 85*	2
THIS CORROSION	*Merciful Release*	7	*3 Oct 87*	6
DOMINION	*Merciful Release*	13	*27 Feb 88*	6
LUCRETIA MY REFLECTION	*Merciful Release*	20	*18 Jun 88*	4
MORE	*Merciful Release*	14	*13 Oct 90*	4
DOCTOR JEEP	*Merciful Release*	37	*22 Dec 90*	4
TEMPLE OF LOVE (1992) TOUCHED BY THE HAND OF OFRA HAZA	*Merciful Release*	3	*2 May 92*	5
Original recording was released in 1983.				
UNDER THE GUN	*Merciful Release*	19	*28 Aug 93*	3
Vocals provided by Terri Nunn of Berlin.				

ALBUMS:	HITS 5			WEEKS 42
FIRST AND LAST AND ALWAYS	*Merciful Release*	14	*23 Mar 85*	8
FLOODLAND	*Merciful Release*	9	*28 Nov 87*	20
VISION THING	*Merciful Release*	11	*3 Nov 90*	4
SOME GIRLS WANDER BY MISTAKE	*Merciful Release*	5	*9 May 92*	5
GREATEST HITS VOLUME 1	*Merciful Release*	14	*4 Sep 93*	5

SISTERS OF SOUL - See Steve WRIGHT

SISTER2SISTER — Australia

SINGLES:	HITS 2			WEEKS 5
SISTER	*Mushroom*	18	*22 Apr 00*	4
WHAT'S A GIRL TO DO?	*Mushroom*	61	*28 Oct 00*	1

SIVUCA — Brazil

SINGLES:	HITS 1			WEEKS 3
AIN'T NO SUNSHINE	*London*	56	*28 Jul 84*	3

SIX BY SEVEN — UK

SINGLES:	HITS 1			WEEKS 1
CANDLELIGHT	*Mantra*	70	*9 May 98*	1

6 BY SIX — UK

SINGLES:	HITS 1			WEEKS 1
INTO YOUR HEART	*Six6*	51	*4 May 96*	1
A re-mix of the 1995 club hit by Rozzo.				

SIX CHIX — UK

SINGLES:	HITS 1			WEEKS 1
ONLY THE WOMEN KNOW	*EMI*	72	*26 Feb 00*	1
Unsuccessful contender in the UK's Song For Europe competition.				

666 — Germany

SINGLES:	HITS 2			WEEKS 5
ALARMA	*Danceteria*	58	*3 Oct 98*	1
D.E.V.I.L.	*Echo*	18	*25 Nov 00*	4

SIXPENCE NONE THE RICHER — US

SINGLES:	HITS 2			WEEKS 17
KISS ME	*Elektra*	4	*29 May 99*	12
THERE SHE GOES	*Elektra*	14	*18 Sept 99*	5
ALBUMS:	**HITS 1**			**WEEKS 3**
SIXPENCE NONE THE RICHER	*Elektra*	27	*26 Jun 99*	3

60FT DOLLS — UK

SINGLES:	HITS 4			WEEKS 4
STAY	*Indolent*	48	*3 Feb 96*	1
TALK TO ME	*Indolent*	37	*11 May 96*	1
HAPPY SHOPPER	*Indolent*	38	*20 Jul 96*	1
ALISON'S ROOM	*Indolent*	61	*9 May 98*	1
ALBUMS:	**HITS 1**			**WEEKS 2**
THE BIG 3	*Indolent*	36	*8 Jun 96*	2

Roni SIZE REPRAZENT — UK

SINGLES:	HITS 7			WEEKS 16
SHARE THE FALL	*Talkin Loud*	37	*14 Jun 97*	2
Above hit: REPRAZENT/Roni SIZE.				
HEROES	*Talkin Loud*	31	*13 Sep 97*	2
BROWN PAPER BAG	*Talkin Loud*	20	*15 Nov 97*	3
WATCHING WINDOWS	*Talkin Loud*	28	*14 Mar 98*	2
WHO TOLD YOU	*Talkin Loud*	17	*7 Oct 00*	3
DIRTY BEATS	*Talkin Loud*	32	*24 Mar 01*	3
LUCKY PRESSURE	*Talkin Loud*	58	*23 Jun 01*	1
ALBUMS:	**HITS 2**			**WEEKS 38**
NEW FORMS	*Talkin Loud*	8	*5 Jul 97*	34
Climbed to its peak position after winning the 1997 Mercury Music Prize.				
IN THE MODE	*Talkin Loud*	15	*21 Oct 00*	4

SIZE 9 — US

(See also Josh Wink.)

SINGLES:	HITS 1			WEEKS 4
I'M READY	*Virgin*	52	*17 Jun 95*	1
Samples B-Beat Girls' For The Same Man and Raw Silk's Do It To The Music.				
I'M READY [RI]	*VC Recordings*	30	*11 Nov 95*	3
Lead track on the CD is a radio edit of the original chart entry. The lead track of that entry was the full version of 11 minutes 54 seconds.				
Above hit: Josh WINK'S SIZE 9.				

SIZZLA — Jamaica

SINGLES:	HITS 1			WEEKS 2
RAIN SHOWERS	*Xterminator*	51	*17 Apr 99*	2

SKANDAL — UK

SINGLES:	HITS 1			WEEKS 1
CHAMPAGNE HIGHWAY	*Prestige Management*	53	*14 Oct 00*	1

SKAT D – See OXIDE and NEUTRINO

SKATALITES — Jamaica

SINGLES:	HITS 1			WEEKS 6
GUNS OF NAVARONE	*Island*	36	*22 Apr 67*	6
Originally recorded by Joe Reisman.				

SKEE-LO — US

SINGLES:	HITS 2			WEEKS 10
I WISH	*Wild Card*	15	*9 Dec 95*	8
TOP OF THE STAIRS	*Wild Card*	38	*27 Apr 96*	2
From the film 'Money Train'.				

Beverli SKEETE - See DE-CODE featuring Beverli SKEETE

Peter SKELLERN — UK

SINGLES:	HITS 3			WEEKS 24
YOU'RE A LADY	*Decca*	3	*23 Sep 72*	11
HOLD ON TO LOVE	*Decca*	14	*29 Mar 75*	9
LOVE IS THE SWEETEST THING	*Mercury*	60	*28 Oct 78*	4
Above hit: Peter SKELLERN featuring the GRIMETHORPE COLLIERY BAND.				
ALBUMS:	**HITS 4**			**WEEKS 31**
SKELLERN	*Mercury*	48	*9 Sep 78*	3
ASTAIRE	*Mercury*	23	*8 Dec 79*	20
A STRING OF PEARLS	*Mercury*	67	*4 Dec 82*	5
STARDUST MEMORIES	*WEA*	50	*1 Apr 95*	3
Tribute album to the Ink Spots and Hoagy Carmichael.				

SKID ROW — UK

ALBUMS:	HITS 1			WEEKS 3
SKID	*CBS*	30	*17 Oct 70*	3

SKID ROW — US

SINGLES:	HITS 8			WEEKS 27
YOUTH GONE WILD	*Atlantic*	42	*18 Nov 89*	3
18 AND LIFE	*Atlantic*	12	*3 Feb 90*	6
I REMEMBER YOU	*Atlantic*	36	*31 Mar 90*	4
MONKEY BUSINESS	*Atlantic*	19	*15 Jun 91*	3
SLAVE TO THE GRIND	*Atlantic*	43	*14 Sep 91*	2
WASTED TIME	*Atlantic*	20	*23 Nov 91*	3
YOUTH GONE WILD [RI] / DELIVERING THE GOODS	*Atlantic*	22	*29 Aug 92*	4
Delivering The Goods is a live recording from Phoenix, Arizona, 17 Mar 92 featuring Rob Halford of Judas Priest.				
BREAKIN' DOWN	*Atlantic*	48	*18 Nov 95*	2
From the film 'The Phrophecy'.				
ALBUMS:	**HITS 3**			**WEEKS 28**
SKID ROW	*Atlantic*	30	*2 Sep 89*	16
SLAVE TO THE GRIND	*Atlantic*	5	*22 Jun 91*	9
SUBHUMAN RACE	*Atlantic*	8	*8 Apr 95*	3

SKIDS — UK

SINGLES:	HITS 10			WEEKS 60
SWEET SUBURBIA	*Virgin*	70	*23 Sep 78*	1
SWEET SUBURBIA [RE]	*Virgin*	71	*7 Oct 78*	2
THE SAINTS ARE COMING	*Virgin*	48	*4 Nov 78*	3
INTO THE VALLEY	*Virgin*	10	*17 Feb 79*	11
MASQUERADE	*Virgin*	14	*26 May 79*	9
CHARADE	*Virgin*	31	*29 Sep 79*	6
WORKING FOR THE YANKEE DOLLAR	*Virgin*	20	*24 Nov 79*	11
ANIMATION	*Virgin*	56	*1 Mar 80*	3
CIRCUS GAMES	*Virgin*	32	*16 Aug 80*	7
GOODBYE CIVILIAN	*Virgin*	52	*18 Oct 80*	4
WOMEN IN WINTER	*Virgin*	49	*6 Dec 80*	3
ALBUMS:	**HITS 3**			**WEEKS 20**
SCARED TO DANCE	*Virgin*	19	*17 Mar 79*	10
DAYS IN EUROPA	*Virgin*	32	*27 Oct 79*	5
THE ABSOLUTE GAME	*Virgin*	9	*27 Sep 80*	5

SKIN — UK/Germany

SINGLES:	HITS 9			WEEKS 19
THE SKIN UP [EP]	*Parlophone*	67	*25 Dec 93*	2
Lead track: Look But Don't Touch.				
HOUSE OF LOVE	*Parlophone*	45	*12 Mar 94*	2
THE MONEY EP [EP]	*Parlophone*	18	*30 Apr 94*	3
Lead track: Money.				
TOWER OF STRENGTH	*Parlophone*	19	*23 Jul 94*	3

LOOK BUT DON'T TOUCH [EP]	*Parlophone*	33	*15 Oct 94*	3
Lead track: Look But Don't Touch. A re-issue from The Skin Up EP.				
TAKE ME DOWN THE RIVER	*Parlophone*	26	*20 May 95*	2
HOW LUCKY YOU ARE	*Parlophone*	32	*23 Mar 96*	2
PERFECT DAY	*Parlophone*	33	*18 May 96*	2
ALBUMS:	**HITS 3**			**WEEKS 5**
SKIN	*Parlophone*	9	*14 May 94*	3
LUCKY	*Parlophone*	38	*6 Apr 96*	1
EXPERIENCE ELECTRIC	*Recall*	72	*13 Sep 97*	1
Originally released in Japan in 1996 with the title Big Fat Slice Of Life.				

SKIN UP — UK

SINGLES:	**HITS 3**			**WEEKS 9**
IVORY	*Love*	48	*7 Sep 91*	3
A JUICY RED APPLE	*Love*	32	*14 Mar 92*	4
ACCELERATE	*Love*	45	*18 Jul 92*	2

SKINNY — UK

SINGLES:	**HITS 1**			**WEEKS 2**
FAILURE	*Cheeky*	31	*11 Apr 98*	2

SKIP RAIDERS featuring JADA — ??

SINGLES:	**HITS 1**			**WEEKS 1**
ANOTHER DAY	*Perfecto*	46	*15 Jul 00*	1
Based around Barber's Adagio For Strings. Released after being featured in a party political broadcast by the Green Party.				

SKIPWORTH and TURNER — US

SINGLES:	**HITS 2**			**WEEKS 12**
THINKING ABOUT YOUR LOVE	*Fourth & Broadway*	24	*27 Apr 85*	10
MAKE IT LAST	*Fourth & Broadway*	60	*21 Jan 89*	2

Nick SKITZ - See FUNKY CHOAD featuring Nick SKITZ

SKUNK ANANSIE — UK

SINGLES:	**HITS 11**			**WEEKS 41**
SELLING JESUS	*One Little Indian*	46	*25 Mar 95*	1
I CAN DREAM	*One Little Indian*	41	*17 Jun 95*	2
CHARITY	*One Little Indian*	40	*2 Sep 95*	2
WEAK	*One Little Indian*	20	*27 Jan 96*	5
CHARITY [RI]	*One Little Indian*	20	*27 Apr 96*	3
ALL I WANT	*One Little Indian*	14	*28 Sep 96*	4
TWISTED (EVERYDAY HURTS)	*One Little Indian*	26	*30 Nov 96*	4
HEDONISM (JUST BECAUSE YOU FEEL GOOD)	*One Little Indian*	13	*1 Feb 97*	6
BRAZEN 'WEEP'	*One Little Indian*	11	*14 Jun 97*	5
CHARLIE BIG POTATO	*Virgin*	17	*13 Mar 99*	3
SECRETLY	*Virgin*	16	*22 May 99*	4
LATELY	*Virgin*	33	*7 Aug 99*	2
ALBUMS:	**HITS 3**			**WEEKS 101**
PARANOID & SUNBURNT	*One Little Indian*	8	*30 Sep 95*	32
STOOSH	*One Little Indian*	9	*19 Oct 96*	55
Stoosh is Jamaican slang for street posh.				
POST ORGASMIC CHILL	*Virgin*	16	*3 Apr 99*	14

SKY — UK/Australia

SINGLES:	**HITS 1**			**WEEKS 11**
TOCCATA	*Ariola*	5	*5 Apr 80*	11
Written by J.S. Bach.				
ALBUMS:	**HITS 8**			**WEEKS 202**
SKY	*Ariola*	9	*2 Jun 79*	56
SKY 2	*Ariola*	1	*26 Apr 80*	53
SKY 3	*Ariola*	3	*28 Mar 81*	23
SKY 4 - FORTHCOMING	*Ariola*	7	*3 Apr 82*	22
SKY FIVE LIVE	*Ariola*	14	*22 Jan 83*	14
CADMIUM	*Ariola*	44	*3 Dec 83*	10
MASTERPIECES - THE VERY BEST OF SKY	*Telstar*	15	*12 May 84*	18
THE GREAT BALLOON RACE	*Epic*	63	*13 Apr 85*	6

SKYHOOKS — Australia

SINGLES:	**HITS 1**			**WEEKS 1**
WOMEN IN UNIFORM	*United Artists*	73	*9 Jun 79*	1

SKYY

US

ALBUMS:	HITS 1			WEEKS 1
FROM THE LEFT SIDE	*Capitol*	85	*21 Jun 86*	1

SLACKER

UK

SINGLES:	HITS 2			WEEKS 4
SCARED	*XL Recordings*	36	*26 Apr 97*	2
YOUR FACE	*XL Recordings*	33	*30 Aug 97*	2
Samples Roberta Flack's First Time Ever I Saw Your Face.				

SLADE

UK

SINGLES:	HITS 35			WEEKS 279
GET DOWN AND GET WITH IT	*Polydor*	16	*19 Jun 71*	14
Originally recorded by Bobby Marchan.				
COZ I LUV YOU	*Polydor*	1	*30 Oct 71*	15
LOOK WOT YOU DUN	*Polydor*	4	*5 Feb 72*	10
TAKE ME BAK 'OME	*Polydor*	1	*3 Jun 72*	13
MAMA WEER ALL CRAZEE NOW	*Polydor*	1	*2 Sep 72*	10
GUDBUY T'JANE	*Polydor*	2	*25 Nov 72*	13
CUM ON FEEL THE NOIZE	*Polydor*	1	*3 Mar 73*	12
SKWEEZE ME, PLEEZE ME	*Polydor*	1	*30 Jun 73*	10
MY FRIEND STAN	*Polydor*	2	*6 Oct 73*	8
MERRY XMAS EVERYBODY	*Polydor*	1	*15 Dec 73*	9
EVERYDAY	*Polydor*	3	*6 Apr 74*	7
THE BANGIN MAN	*Polydor*	3	*6 Jul 74*	7
FAR FAR AWAY	*Polydor*	2	*19 Oct 74*	6
HOW DOES IT FEEL?	*Polydor*	15	*15 Feb 75*	7
Above 2 from the film 'Slade In Flame'.				
THANKS FOR THE MEMORY (WHAM BAM THANK YOU MAM)	*Polydor*	7	*17 May 75*	7
IN FOR A PENNY	*Polydor*	11	*22 Nov 75*	8
LET'S CALL IT QUITS	*Polydor*	11	*7 Feb 76*	7
GYPSY ROADHOG	*Barn*	48	*5 Feb 77*	2
MY BABY LEFT ME/THAT'S ALL RIGHT [M]	*Barn*	32	*29 Oct 77*	4
SLADE - ALIVE AT READING '80 [EP]	*Cheapskate*	44	*18 Oct 80*	5
Lead track: When I'm Dancin' I Ain't Fightin'.				
MERRY XMAS EVERYBODY [RR]	*Cheapskate*	70	*27 Dec 80*	2
Above 2 are live recordings from the Reading Rock Festival, Aug 80.				
Above hit: SLADE and the READING CHOIR.				
WE'LL BRING THE HOUSE DOWN	*Cheapskate*	10	*31 Jan 81*	9
WHEELS AIN'T COMING DOWN	*Cheapskate*	60	*4 Apr 81*	3
LOCK UP YOUR DAUGHTERS	*RCA*	29	*19 Sep 81*	8
MERRY XMAS EVERYBODY [RE-1ST]	*Polydor*	32	*19 Dec 81*	4
RUBY RED	*RCA*	51	*27 Mar 82*	3
(AND NOW - THE WALTZ) C'EST LA VIE	*RCA*	50	*27 Nov 82*	6
MERRY XMAS EVERYBODY [RE-2ND]	*Polydor*	67	*25 Dec 82*	3
MY OH MY	*RCA*	2	*19 Nov 83*	11
MERRY XMAS EVERYBODY [RE-3RD]	*Polydor*	20	*10 Dec 83*	5
RUN RUNAWAY	*RCA*	7	*4 Feb 84*	10
ALL JOIN HANDS	*RCA*	15	*17 Nov 84*	9
MERRY XMAS EVERYBODY [RE-4TH]	*Polydor*	47	*15 Dec 84*	4
7 YEAR BITCH	*RCA*	60	*26 Jan 85*	3
MYZSTERIOUS MIZSTER JONES	*RCA*	50	*23 Mar 85*	5
DO YOU BELIEVE IN MIRACLES	*RCA*	54	*30 Nov 85*	6
MERRY XMAS EVERYBODY [RI]	*Polydor*	48	*21 Dec 85*	3
MERRY XMAS EVERYBODY [RI] [RE]	*Polydor*	71	*27 Dec 86*	1
STILL THE SAME	*RCA*	73	*21 Feb 87*	2
RADIO WALL OF SOUND	*Polydor*	21	*19 Oct 91*	5
Backing DJ vocals from Mike Read.				
MERRY XMAS EVERYBODY '98 [RM]	*Polydor*	30	*26 Dec 98*	3
Though labelled as a remix by Stefan Runqvist and Sven Oslen (aka Flush), the only vocals come from the chorus of the original.				
Above hit: SLADE vs. FLUSH.				

ALBUMS:	HITS 17			WEEKS 212
SLADE ALIVE!	*Polydor*	2	*8 Apr 72*	58
Live recordings from the Command Theatre Studio.				
SLAYED?	*Polydor*	1	*9 Dec 72*	34
SLADEST	*Polydor*	1	*6 Oct 73*	24
Compilation.				
OLD NEW BORROWED AND BLUE	*Polydor*	1	*23 Feb 74*	16
SLADE IN FLAME [OST]	*Polydor*	6	*14 Dec 74*	18
NOBODY'S FOOL	*Polydor*	14	*27 Mar 76*	4
SLADE SMASHES	*Polydor*	21	*22 Nov 80*	15
WE'LL BRING THE HOUSE DOWN	*Cheapskate*	25	*21 Mar 81*	4
TILL DEAF US DO PART	*RCA*	68	*28 Nov 81*	2
SLADE ON STAGE	*RCA*	58	*18 Dec 82*	3
Live recordings.				

THE AMAZING KAMIKAZE SYNDROME	*RCA*	49	*24 Dec 83*	13
SLADE'S GREATZ	*Polydor*	89	*9 Jun 84*	1
ROGUES GALLERY	*RCA*	60	*6 Apr 85*	2
"CRACKERS" - THE SLADE CHRISTMAS PARTY ALBUM	*Telstar*	34	*30 Nov 85*	7
YOU BOYZ MAKE BIG NOIZE	*RCA*	98	*9 May 87*	1
Named after a comment made by the tea lady at the recording studio.				
WALL OF HITS	*Polydor*	34	*23 Nov 91*	5
GREATEST HITS - FEEL THE NOIZE	*Polydor*	19	*25 Jan 97*	5

SLAM — UK

SINGLES:	HITS 3			WEEKS 4
POSITIVE EDUCATION	*VC Recordings*	44	*17 Feb 01*	2
Original release on the Soma label reached No. 87 on 28 Aug 93.				
NARCO TOURISTS	*Soma Recordings*	66	*17 Mar 01*	1
Above hit: SLAM versus UNKLE.				
LIFETIMES	*Soma Recordings*	61	*7 Jul 01*	1
Above hit: SLAM featuring Tyrone 'Visionary' PALMER.				

SLAMM — UK

SINGLES:	HITS 4			WEEKS 6
ENERGIZE	*PWL International*	57	*17 Jul 93*	2
VIRGINIA PLAIN	*PWL International*	60	*23 Oct 93*	1
THAT'S WHERE MY MIND GOES	*PWL International*	68	*22 Oct 94*	1
CAN'T GET BY	*PWL International*	47	*4 Feb 95*	2

SLARTA JOHN - See BASEMENT JAXX; HATIRAS featuring SLARTA JOHN

SLASH'S SNAKEPIT — US

(See also Michael Jackson.)

ALBUMS:	HITS 1			WEEKS 4
IT'S FIVE O'CLOCK SOMEWHERE	*Geffen*	15	*25 Feb 95*	4

Luke SLATER — UK

SINGLES:	HITS 1			WEEKS 1
ALL EXHALE	*Novamute*	74	*16 Sep 00*	1

SLAUGHTER — US

SINGLES:	HITS 2			WEEKS 2
UP ALL NIGHT	*Chrysalis*	62	*29 Sep 90*	1
FLY TO THE ANGELS	*Chrysalis*	55	*2 Feb 91*	1
ALBUMS:	**HITS 1**			**WEEKS 1**
THE WILD LIFE	*Chrysalis*	64	*23 May 92*	1

SLAVE — US

SINGLES:	HITS 1			WEEKS 3
JUST A TOUCH OF LOVE	*Atlantic*	64	*8 Mar 80*	3

Martin SLAVIN ORCHESTRA - See Helen SHAPIRO

Frank SLAY and his Orchestra - See Freddie CANNON

SLAYER — US

SINGLES:	HITS 3			WEEKS 3
CRIMINALLY INSANE	*London*	64	*13 Jun 87*	1
SEASONS IN THE ABYSS	*Def American*	51	*26 Oct 91*	1
SERENITY IN MURDER	*American Recordings*	50	*9 Sep 95*	1
ALBUMS:	**HITS 8**			**WEEKS 21**
REIGN IN BLOOD	*London*	47	*2 May 87*	3
SOUTH OF HEAVEN	*London*	25	*23 Jul 88*	4
SEASONS IN THE ABYSS	*Def American*	18	*6 Oct 90*	3
DECADE OF AGGRESSION - LIVE	*Def American*	29	*2 Nov 91*	2
DIVINE INTERVENTION	*American Recordings*	15	*15 Oct 94*	4
UNDISPUTED ATTITUDE	*American Recordings*	31	*1 Jun 96*	2
Consists mainly of punk rock covers.				
DIABOLUS IN MUSICA	*American Recordings*	27	*20 Jun 98*	2
GOD HATES US ALL	*Mercury*	31	*22 Sep 01*	1

SLEAZESISTERS — UK

SINGLES:	HITS 3			WEEKS 3
SEX	*Pulse 8*	53	*29 Jul 95*	1
Vocals by Jeanie Tracy.				
LET'S WHIP IT UP (YOU GO GIRL)	*Pulse 8*	46	*30 Mar 96*	1
Above 2: SLEAZESISTERS with Vikki SHEPARD.				
WORK IT UP	*Logic*	74	*26 Sep 98*	1

Kathy SLEDGE — US

(See also Sister Sledge.)

SINGLES:	HITS 3			WEEKS 7
TAKE ME BACK TO LOVE AGAIN	*Epic*	62	*16 May 92*	2
ANOTHER STAR	*NRC*	54	*18 Feb 95*	1
FREEDOM	*Deconstruction*	15	*29 Nov 97*	4

Above hit: Robert MILES featuring Kathy SLEDGE.

Percy SLEDGE — US

SINGLES:	HITS 2			WEEKS 34
WHEN A MAN LOVES A WOMAN	*Atlantic*	4	*14 May 66*	17
WARM AND TENDER LOVE	*Atlantic*	34	*6 Aug 66*	7
WHEN A MAN LOVES A WOMAN [RI]	*Atlantic*	2	*14 Feb 87*	10

Featured in the Levi's 501 Jeans commercial.

ALBUMS:	HITS 1			WEEKS 4
WHEN A MAN LOVES A WOMAN (THE ULTIMATE COLLECTION)	*Atlantic*	36	*14 Mar 87*	4

SLEEPER — UK

SINGLES:	HITS 9			WEEKS 29
DELICIOUS	*Indolent*	75	*21 May 94*	1
INBETWEENER	*Indolent*	16	*21 Jan 95*	4
VEGAS	*Indolent*	33	*8 Apr 95*	3
WHAT DO I DO NOW?	*Indolent*	14	*7 Oct 95*	4
SALE OF THE CENTURY	*Indolent*	10	*4 May 96*	5
NICE GUY EDDIE	*Indolent*	10	*13 Jul 96*	5
STATUESQUE	*Indolent*	17	*5 Oct 96*	3
SHE'S A GOOD GIRL	*Indolent*	28	*4 Oct 97*	2
ROMEO ME	*Indolent*	39	*6 Dec 97*	2

ALBUMS:	HITS 3			WEEKS 48
SMART	*Indolent*	5	*25 Feb 95*	11
THE IT GIRL	*Indolent*	5	*18 May 96*	34
PLEASED TO MEET YOU	*Indolent*	7	*25 Oct 97*	3

SLEIGHRIDERS — UK

ALBUMS:	HITS 1			WEEKS 1
A VERY MERRY DISCO	*Warwick*	100	*17 Dec 83*	1

SLICK — US

SINGLES:	HITS 2			WEEKS 15
SPACE BASS	*Fantasy*	16	*16 Jun 79*	10
SEXY CREAM	*Fantasy*	47	*15 Sep 79*	5

Above hit: SLICK (featuring Doris JAMES).

Grace SLICK — US

SINGLES:	HITS 1			WEEKS 4
DREAMS	*RCA*	50	*24 May 80*	4

ALBUMS:	HITS 1			WEEKS 6
DREAMS	*RCA*	28	*31 May 80*	6

SLICK RICK – See Montell JORDAN; Al B SURE!

SLIK — UK

SINGLES:	HITS 2			WEEKS 18
FOREVER AND EVER *Originally recorded by Kenny.*	*Bell*	1	*17 Jan 76*	9
REQUIEM	*Bell*	24	*8 May 76*	9

ALBUMS:	HITS 1			WEEKS 1
SLIK	*Bell*	58	*12 Jun 76*	1

SLIM CHANCE – See Ronnie LANE and the Band SLIM CHANCE

SLIPKNOT — US

SINGLES:	HITS 3			WEEKS 9
WAIT AND BLEED	*Roadrunner*	27	*11 Mar 00*	3
SPIT IT OUT	*Roadrunner*	28	*16 Sep 00*	2
LEFT BEHIND	*Roadrunner*	24	*10 Nov 01*	4

ALBUMS:	HITS 2			WEEKS 12
SLIPKNOT	*Roadrunner*	37	*10 Jul 99*	5
IOWA	*Roadrunner*	1	*8 Sep 01*	7

SLIPSTREEM — UK

SINGLES:	HITS 1			WEEKS 7
WE ARE RAVING – THE ANTHEM *Based on Rod Stewart's Sailing.*	*Boogie Food*	18	*19 Dec 92*	7

SLITS — UK

SINGLES:	HITS 1			WEEKS 3
TYPICAL GIRLS /I HEARD IT THROUGH THE GRAPEVINE	*Island*	60	*13 Oct 79*	3
ALBUMS:	**HITS 1**			**WEEKS 5**
CUT	*Island*	30	*22 Sep 79*	5

SLO MOSHUN — UK

SINGLES:	HITS 2			WEEKS 4
BELLS OF NY	*Six6*	29	*5 Feb 94*	3
HELP MY FRIEND	*Six6*	52	*30 Jul 94*	1

P.F. SLOAN — US

SINGLES:	HITS 1			WEEKS 3
SINS OF THE FAMILY	*RCA Victor*	38	*6 Nov 65*	3

SLOWDIVE — UK

SINGLES:	HITS 2			WEEKS 2
CATCH THE BREEZE / SHINE	*Creation*	52	*15 Jun 91*	1
OUTSIDE YOUR ROOM [EP] *Lead track: Outside Your Room.*	*Creation*	69	*29 May 93*	1
ALBUMS:	**HITS 2**			**WEEKS 3**
JUST FOR A DAY	*Creation*	32	*14 Sep 91*	2
SOUVLAKI	*Creation*	51	*12 Jun 93*	1

SL2 — UK

SINGLES:	HITS 3			WEEKS 25
DJS TAKE CONTROL / WAY IN MY BRAIN	*XL Recordings*	11	*2 Nov 91*	5
DJS TAKE CONTROL / WAY IN MY BRAIN [RE]	*XL Recordings*	71	*4 Jan 92*	1
ON A RAGGA TIP	*XL Recordings*	2	*18 Apr 92*	11
WAY IN MY BRAIN [RM] / DRUMBEATS	*XL Recordings*	26	*19 Dec 92*	6
ON A RAGGA TIP '97 [RM] *Remixed by Goodfello's.*	*XL Recordings*	31	*15 Feb 97*	2

SLUSNIK LUNA — Finland

SINGLES:	HITS 1			WEEKS 2
SUN	*Incentive*	40	*1 Sep 01*	2

SLY and the FAMILY STONE — US

SINGLES:	HITS 5			WEEKS 42
DANCE TO THE MUSIC	*Direction*	7	*13 Jul 68*	14
M'LADY	*Direction*	32	*5 Oct 68*	7
EVERYDAY PEOPLE	*Direction*	36	*22 Mar 69*	1
EVERYDAY PEOPLE [RE]	*Direction*	37	*12 Apr 69*	4
FAMILY AFFAIR	*Epic*	15	*8 Jan 72*	8
RUNNIN' AWAY	*Epic*	17	*15 Apr 72*	8
ALBUMS:	**HITS 1**			**WEEKS 2**
THERE'S A RIOT GOIN' ON	*Epic*	31	*5 Feb 72*	2

SLY FOX — US

SINGLES:	HITS 1			WEEKS 16
LET'S GO ALL THE WAY	*Capitol*	3	*31 May 86*	16

SLY and ROBBIE — Jamaica

SINGLES:	HITS 4			WEEKS 32
SMILE *Above hit: Audrey HALL featuring Sly DUNBAR and Robert SHAKESPEARE.*	*Germain*	14	*5 Jul 86*	9
BOOPS (HERE TO GO)	*Fourth & Broadway*	12	*4 Apr 87*	11
FIRE	*Fourth & Broadway*	60	*25 Jul 87*	4
NIGHT NURSE *Originally recorded by Gregory Isaacs in 1982.* *Above hit: SLY and ROBBIE featuring SIMPLY RED.*	*East West*	13	*20 Sep 97*	8
ALBUMS:	**HITS 1**			**WEEKS 5**
RHYTHM KILLERS	*Fourth & Broadway*	35	*9 May 87*	5

Heather SMALL — UK

(See also M People.)

SINGLES:	HITS 3			WEEKS 9
PROUD	*Arista*	16	*20 May 00*	5
HOLDING ON	*Arista*	58	*19 Aug 00*	1
YOU NEED LOVE LIKE I DO	*Gut*	24	*18 Nov 00*	3
Original by Gladys Knight aand the Pips reached No. 25 in the US in 1970.				
Above hit: Tom JONES and Heather SMALL.				

ALBUMS:	HITS 2			WEEKS 12
PROUD	*Arista*	12	*10 Jun 00*	4

SMALL ADS — UK

SINGLES:	HITS 1			WEEKS 3
SMALL ADS	*Bronze*	63	*18 Apr 81*	3

SMALL FACES — UK

SINGLES:	HITS 12			WEEKS 137
WHATCHA GONNA DO ABOUT IT?	*Decca*	14	*4 Sep 65*	12
SHA-LA-LA-LA-LEE	*Decca*	3	*12 Feb 66*	11
Co-written by Kenny Lynch.				
HEY GIRL	*Decca*	10	*14 May 66*	9
ALL OR NOTHING	*Decca*	1	*13 Aug 66*	12
MY MIND'S EYE	*Decca*	4	*19 Nov 66*	11
Part of its melody is from the Christmas carol Angels From The Realms Of Glory.				
I CAN'T MAKE IT	*Decca*	26	*11 Mar 67*	7
HERE COMES THE NICE	*Immediate*	12	*10 Jun 67*	10
ITCHYCOO PARK	*Immediate*	3	*12 Aug 67*	14
TIN SOLDIER	*Immediate*	9	*9 Dec 67*	12
LAZY SUNDAY	*Immediate*	2	*20 Apr 68*	11
THE UNIVERSAL	*Immediate*	16	*13 Jul 68*	11
AFTERGLOW OF YOUR LOVE	*Immediate*	36	*22 Mar 69*	1
ITCHYCOO PARK [RI]	*Immediate*	9	*13 Dec 75*	11
LAZY SUNDAY [RI]	*Immediate*	39	*20 Mar 76*	5

ALBUMS:	HITS 5			WEEKS 67
SMALL FACES	*Decca*	3	*14 May 66*	25
FROM THE BEGINNING	*Decca*	17	*17 Jun 67*	5
Compilation.				
SMALL FACES	*Immediate*	21	*1 Jul 67*	17
Both self titled albums are different.				
OGDEN'S NUT GONE FLAKE	*Immediate*	1	*15 Jun 68*	19
Features comedian Stanley Unwin speaking between tracks on one side of the album.				
THE DECCA ANTHOLOGY 1965-1967	*Deram*	66	*11 May 96*	1

SMALLER — UK

SINGLES:	HITS 2			WEEKS 2
WASTED	*Better*	72	*28 Sep 96*	1
IS	*Better*	55	*29 Mar 97*	1
Noel Gallagher on guitar.				

SMART E'S — UK

SINGLES:	HITS 1			WEEKS 9
SESAME'S TREET	*Suburban Base*	2	*11 Jul 92*	9
Based on the theme from the Children's TV series 'Sesame Street'.				

SMASH MOUTH — US

SINGLES:	HITS 2			WEEKS 9
WALKIN' ON THE SUN	*Interscope*	19	*25 Oct 97*	4
ALL STAR	*Interscope*	24	*31 Jul 99*	5
From the film 'Mystery Man'.				

SMASHING PUMPKINS — US

SINGLES:	HITS 13			WEEKS 36
I AM ONE	*Hut*	73	*5 Sep 92*	1
CHERUB ROCK	*Hut*	31	*3 Jul 93*	2
TODAY	*Hut*	44	*25 Sep 93*	2
DISARM	*Hut*	11	*5 Mar 94*	3
BULLET WITH BUTTERFLY WINGS	*Virgin*	20	*28 Oct 95*	3
1979	*Hut*	16	*10 Feb 96*	3
TONIGHT, TONIGHT	*Virgin*	7	*18 May 96*	6
THIRTY THREE	*Virgin*	21	*23 Nov 96*	2
THE END IS THE BEGINNING IS THE END	*Warner Brothers*	10	*14 Jun 97*	4
From the film 'Batman And Robin'.				
THE END IS THE BEGINNING IS THE END [RM]	*Warner Brothers*	72	*23 Aug 97*	1
Remixed by Fluke.				

AVA ADORE	*Hut*	11	*30 May 98*	4
PERFECT	*Hut*	24	*19 Sep 98*	2
STAND INSIDE YOUR LOVE	*Hut*	23	*4 Mar 00*	2
TRY, TRY, TRY	*Hut*	73	*23 Sep 00*	1
ALBUMS:	**HITS 5**			**WEEKS 71**
SIAMESE DREAM	*Hut*	4	*31 Jul 93*	15
MELLON COLLIE AND THE INFINITE SADNESS	*Virgin*	4	*4 Nov 95*	37
Double album, the first is titled Dawn To Dust and the second From Starlight To Twilight.				
ADORE	*Hut*	5	*13 Jun 98*	12
MACHINA/THE MACHINES OF GOD	*Hut*	7	*11 Mar 00*	4
ROTTEN APPLES - THE SMASHING PUMPKINS GREATEST HITS	*Hut*	28	*1 Dec 01*	3

SMELLS LIKE HEAVEN — Italy

SINGLES:	**HITS 1**			**WEEKS 1**
LONDRES STRUTT	*Deconstruction*	57	*10 Jul 93*	1
Originally an underground dance hit in 1991.				

Allan SMETHURST — UK

EPS:	**HITS 2**			**WEEKS 12**
THE SINGING POSTMAN	*Ralph*	20	*5 Jun 65*	2
FIRST DELIVERY	*Parlophone*	7	*10 Dec 66*	10

Ann-Marie SMITH — UK

SINGLES:	**HITS 3**			**WEEKS 5**
MUSIC	*Synthetic*	34	*23 Jan 93*	2
Above hit: FARGETTA and Anne-Marie SMITH.				
ROCKIN' MY BODY	*Media*	31	*18 Mar 95*	2
Above hit: 49ERS featuring Ann-Marie SMITH.				
(YOU'RE MY ONE AND ONLY) TRUE LOVE	*Media*	46	*15 Jul 95*	1

Brian SMITH and his HAPPY PIANO — UK

ALBUMS:	**HITS 1**			**WEEKS 1**
PLAY IT AGAIN	*Deram*	97	*19 Sep 81*	1

"Fast" Eddie SMITH - See DJ FAST EDDIE; Kenny "Jammin" JASON and "Fast" Eddie SMITH

Elliott SMITH — US

SINGLES:	**HITS 3**			**WEEKS 3**
WALTZ #2 (XO)	*Dreamworks*	52	*19 Dec 98*	1
BABY BRITAIN	*Dreamworks*	55	*1 May 99*	1
SON OF SAM	*Dreamworks*	55	*8 Jul 00*	1
ALBUMS:	**HITS 1**			**WEEKS 2**
FIGURE 8	*Dreamworks*	37	*29 Apr 00*	2

Hurricane SMITH — UK

SINGLES:	**HITS 3**			**WEEKS 35**
DON'T LET IT DIE	*Columbia*	2	*12 Jun 71*	12
OH BABE, WHAT WOULD YOU SAY	*Columbia*	4	*29 Apr 72*	16
WHO WAS IT	*Columbia*	23	*2 Sep 72*	7
Originally recorded by Gilbert O'Sullivan.				

Whistling Jack SMITH — UK

SINGLES:	**HITS 1**			**WEEKS 12**
I WAS KAISER BILL'S BATMAN	*Deram*	5	*4 Mar 67*	12

Jimmy SMITH — US

SINGLES:	**HITS 1**			**WEEKS 3**
GOT MY MOJO WORKING	*Verve*	48	*30 Apr 66*	2
GOT MY MOJO WORKING [RE]	*Verve*	48	*21 May 66*	1
EPS:	**HITS 1**			**WEEKS 3**
SWINGING WITH THE INCREDIBLE JIMMY SMITH	*Verve*	10	*23 Jul 66*	1
ALBUMS:	**HITS 1**			**WEEKS 1**
GOT MY MOJO WORKING	*Verve*	19	*18 Jun 66*	3

Keely SMITH — US

SINGLES:	**HITS 1**			**WEEKS 10**
YOU'RE BREAKING MY HEART	*Reprise*	14	*20 Mar 65*	10
Originally recorded by Vic Damone.				
ALBUMS:	**HITS 1**			**WEEKS 9**
LENNON-McCARTNEY SONGBOOK	*Reprise*	12	*16 Jan 65*	9

Lonnie Liston SMITH - See WAG YA TAIL featuring Lonnie Liston SMITH

Mandy SMITH — UK

SINGLES:	HITS 1			WEEKS 2
DON'T YOU WANT ME BABY	*PWL*	59	*20 May 89*	2

Mark E. SMITH – See D.O.S.E. featuring Mark E. SMITH; INSPIRAL CARPETS

Mel SMITH — UK

(See also Smith and Jones.)

SINGLES:	HITS 2			WEEKS 10
ROCKIN' AROUND THE CHRISTMAS TREE *To support Comic Relief Red Nose Day, 5 Feb 88.* *Above hit: COMIC RELIEF presents MEL and KIM performed by Kim WILDE and Mel SMITH.*	*10 Records*	3	*5 Dec 87*	7
ANOTHER BLOOMING CHRISTMAS *From the animated film 'Father Christmas'.*	*Epic*	59	*21 Dec 91*	3

Muriel SMITH with Wally STOTT and his Orchestra — UK

SINGLES:	HITS 1			WEEKS 17
HOLD ME, THRILL ME, KISS ME	*Philips*	3	*16 May 53*	17

O. C. SMITH — US

SINGLES:	HITS 2			WEEKS 23
THE SON OF HICKORY HOLLER'S TRAMP *Originally recorded by Johnny Darrell.*	*CBS*	2	*1 Jun 68*	15
TOGETHER *Features his wife on backing vocals.*	*Caribou*	25	*26 Mar 77*	8
ALBUMS:	**HITS 1**			**WEEKS 1**
HICKORY HOLLER REVISITED	*CBS*	40	*17 Aug 68*	1

Patti SMITH GROUP — US

SINGLES:	HITS 3			WEEKS 16
BECAUSE THE NIGHT *Co-written by Bruce Springstreen.*	*Arista*	5	*29 Apr 78*	12
PRIVILEGE (SET ME FREE)	*Arista*	72	*19 Aug 78*	1
FREDERICK	*Arista*	63	*2 Jun 79*	3
ALBUMS:	**HITS 4**			**WEEKS 23**
EASTER	*Arista*	16	*1 Apr 78*	14
WAVE	*Arista*	41	*19 May 79*	6
DREAM OF LIFE	*Arista*	70	*16 Jul 88*	1
GONE AGAIN *Above 2: Patti SMITH.*	*Arista*	44	*13 Jul 96*	2

Rex SMITH and Rachel SWEET — US

(See also Rachel Sweet.)

SINGLES:	HITS 1			WEEKS 7
EVERLASTING LOVE	*CBS*	35	*22 Aug 81*	7

Richard Jon SMITH — South Africa

SINGLES:	HITS 1			WEEKS 2
SHE'S THE MASTER (OF THE GAME)	*Jive*	63	*16 Jul 83*	2

Roger SMITH CHORALE – See LONDON SYMPHONY ORCHESTRA

Rose SMITH – See DELAKOTA

Sheila SMITH – See Cevin FISHER

Steven SMITH and FATHER — UK

ALBUMS:	HITS 1			WEEKS 3
STEVEN SMITH AND FATHER AND 16 GREAT SONGS	*Decca*	17	*13 May 72*	3

Will SMITH — US

SINGLES:	HITS 9			WEEKS 100
MEN IN BLACK *From the film of the same name. Samples Patrice Rushen's Forget Me Nots.*	*Columbia*	1	*16 Aug 97*	16
JUST CRUISIN' *Samples Al Johnson's I'm Back For More.*	*Columbia*	23	*13 Dec 97*	6
GETTIN' JIGGY WIT IT *Samples Sister Sledge's He's The Greatest Dancer.*	*Columbia*	3	*7 Feb 98*	10
JUST THE TWO OF US *Dedicated to his son Tre.*	*Columbia*	2	*1 Aug 98*	10
MIAMI *Samples The Whispers' And The Beat Goes On.*	*Columbia*	3	*5 Dec 98*	14

BOY YOU KNOCK ME OUT	*MJJ*	3	*13 Feb 99*	8
Samples Bobby Caldwell's What You Won't Do For Love.				
Above hit: Tatyana ALI featuring Will SMITH.				
BOY YOU KNOCK ME OUT [RE]	*MJJ*	69	*15 May 99*	1
WILD WILD WEST	*Columbia*	2	*10 Jul 99*	16
Samples Stevie Wonder's I Wish. From the film of the same name.				
Above hit: Will SMITH (featuring DRU HILL).				
WILL 2K	*Columbia*	2	*20 Nov 99*	11
Based on the Clash's Rock The Casbah.				
Above hit: Will SMITH (featuring K-CI).				
FREAKIN' IT	*Columbia*	15	*25 Mar 00*	7
Samples Diana Ross' Love Hangover and the Sugarhill Gang's Rapper's Delight.				
ALBUMS:	**HITS 2**			**WEEKS 85**
BIG WILLIE STYLE	*Columbia*	11	*6 Dec 97*	39
BIG WILLIE STYLE [RE]	*Columbia*	9	*5 Dec 98*	31
WILLENNIUM	*Columbia*	10	*27 Nov 99*	15

SMITH and JONES — UK

(See also Mel Smith.)

ALBUMS:	**HITS 1**			**WEEKS 8**
SCRATCH AND SNIFF	*10 Records*	62	*15 Nov 86*	8

SMITHS — UK

SINGLES:	**HITS 17**			**WEEKS 105**
THIS CHARMING MAN	*Rough Trade*	25	*12 Nov 83*	12
WHAT DIFFERENCE DOES IT MAKE?	*Rough Trade*	12	*28 Jan 84*	9
HEAVEN KNOWS I'M MISERABLE NOW	*Rough Trade*	10	*2 Jun 84*	8
WILLIAM, IT WAS REALLY NOTHING	*Rough Trade*	17	*1 Sep 84*	6
HOW SOON IS NOW?	*Rough Trade*	24	*9 Feb 85*	6
SHAKESPEARE'S SISTER	*Rough Trade*	26	*30 Mar 85*	4
THAT JOKE ISN'T FUNNY ANYMORE	*Rough Trade*	49	*13 Jul 85*	3
THE BOY WITH THE THORN IN HIS SIDE	*Rough Trade*	23	*5 Oct 85*	5
BIG MOUTH STRIKES AGAIN	*Rough Trade*	26	*31 May 86*	4
PANIC	*Rough Trade*	11	*2 Aug 86*	8
ASK	*Rough Trade*	14	*1 Nov 86*	5
SHOPLIFTERS OF THE WORLD UNITE	*Rough Trade*	12	*7 Feb 87*	4
SHEILA TAKE A BOW	*Rough Trade*	10	*25 Apr 87*	5
GIRLFRIEND IN A COMA	*Rough Trade*	13	*22 Aug 87*	5
I STARTED SOMETHING I COULDN'T FINISH	*Rough Trade*	23	*14 Nov 87*	4
LAST NIGHT I DREAMT THAT SOMEBODY LOVED ME	*Rough Trade*	30	*19 Dec 87*	4
THIS CHARMING MAN [RI]	*WEA*	8	*15 Aug 92*	5
HOW SOON IS NOW? [RI]	*WEA*	16	*12 Sep 92*	4
THERE IS A LIGHT THAT NEVER GOES OUT	*WEA*	25	*24 Oct 92*	3
Originally from their 1986 album, The Queen Is Dead.				
ASK [RI]	*WEA*	62	*18 Feb 95*	1
ALBUMS:	**HITS 12**			**WEEKS 205**
THE SMITHS	*Rough Trade*	2	*3 Mar 84*	33
HATFUL OF HOLLOW	*Rough Trade*	7	*24 Nov 84*	46
BBC radio sessions and B-sides.				
MEAT IS MURDER	*Rough Trade*	1	*23 Feb 85*	13
THE QUEEN IS DEAD	*Rough Trade*	2	*28 Jun 86*	22
THE WORLD WON'T LISTEN	*Rough Trade*	2	*7 Mar 87*	15
Compilation.				
LOUDER THAN BOMBS	*Rough Trade*	38	*30 May 87*	5
Import compilation.				
STRANGEWAYS, HERE WE COME	*Rough Trade*	2	*10 Oct 87*	17
RANK	*Rough Trade*	2	*17 Sep 88*	7
Live recordings from the National Ballroom, Kilburn, London, Oct 86.				
BEST . . . I	*WEA*	1	*29 Aug 92*	9
BEST . . . II	*WEA*	29	*14 Nov 92*	5
SINGLES	*WEA*	5	*4 Mar 95*	8
HATFUL OF HOLLOW [RI]	*WEA*	26	*4 Mar 95*	3
THE QUEEN IS DEAD [RI]	*WEA*	30	*4 Mar 95*	4
STRANGEWAYS, HERE WE COME [RI]	*WEA*	38	*4 Mar 95*	4
MEAT IS MURDER [RI]	*WEA*	39	*4 Mar 95*	2
THE SMITHS [RI]	*WEA*	42	*4 Mar 95*	4
THE WORLD WON'T LISTEN [RI]	*WEA*	52	*4 Mar 95*	2
Above 5 were re-issued at mid-price.				
LOUDER THAN BOMBS [RI]	*WEA*	52	*14 Oct 00*	2
THE VERY BEST OF THE SMITHS	*WEA*	30	*16 Jun 01*	4

SMOKE — UK

SINGLES:	**HITS 1**			**WEEKS 3**
MY FRIEND JACK	*Columbia*	45	*11 Mar 67*	3

SMOKE CITY — UK/Brazil

SINGLES:	HITS 1			WEEKS 5
UNDERWATER LOVE *Featured in the Levi's Jeans TV commercial.*	*Jive*	4	*12 Apr 97*	5

SMOKED – See Oliver LIEB presents SMOKED

SMOKIE — UK

SINGLES:	HITS 13			WEEKS 125
IF YOU THINK YOU KNOW HOW TO LOVE ME	*RAK*	3	*19 Jul 75*	9
DON'T PLAY YOUR ROCK 'N' ROLL TO ME *Above 2: SMOKEY.*	*RAK*	8	*4 Oct 75*	7
SOMETHING'S BEEN MAKING ME BLUE	*RAK*	17	*31 Jan 76*	8
I'LL MEET YOU AT MIDNIGHT	*RAK*	11	*25 Sep 76*	9
LIVING NEXT DOOR TO ALICE *Originally recorded by New World.*	*RAK*	5	*4 Dec 76*	11
LAY BACK IN THE ARMS OF SOMEONE	*RAK*	12	*19 Mar 77*	9
IT'S YOUR LIFE	*RAK*	5	*16 Jul 77*	9
NEEDLES AND PINS	*RAK*	10	*15 Oct 77*	9
FOR A FEW DOLLARS MORE	*RAK*	17	*28 Jan 78*	6
OH CAROL	*RAK*	5	*20 May 78*	13
MEXICAN GIRL	*RAK*	19	*23 Sep 78*	9
TAKE GOOD CARE OF MY BABY	*RAK*	34	*19 Apr 80*	7
LIVING NEXT DOOR TO ALICE (WHO THE F**K IS ALICE?) [RR] *Altered lyrics to the original. Proceeds to the family of Alan Barton who was lead singer at the time of his death in Mar of that year.* *Above hit: SMOKIE featuring Roy Chubby BROWN.*	*N.O.W.*	64	*13 May 95*	2
LIVING NEXT DOOR TO ALICE (WHO THE F**K IS ALICE?) [RR] [RE]	*N.O.W.*	3	*26 Aug 95*	17
ALBUMS:	**HITS 5**			**WEEKS 45**
SMOKIE/CHANGING ALL THE TIME	*RAK*	18	*1 Nov 75*	5
GREATEST HITS	*RAK*	6	*30 Apr 77*	22
THE MONTREUX ALBUM	*RAK*	52	*4 Nov 78*	2
SMOKIE'S HITS	*RAK*	23	*11 Oct 80*	13
UNCOVERED – THE VERY BEST OF SMOKIE	*Universal Music TV*	63	*17 Mar 01*	3

SMOKIN BEATS featuring Lyn EDEN — UK

SINGLES:	HITS 1			WEEKS 3
DREAMS	*AM:PM*	23	*17 Jan 98*	3

SMOKIN' MOJO FILTERS — UK/US

SINGLES:	HITS 1			WEEKS 5
COME TOGETHER (WAR CHILD) *Charity record to support aid for the children of Bosnia.*	*Go! Discs*	19	*23 Dec 95*	5

SMOOTH — US

SINGLES:	HITS 5			WEEKS 7
MIND BLOWIN'	*Jive*	36	*22 Jul 95*	2
IT'S SUMMERTIME (LET IT GET INTO YOU)	*Jive*	46	*7 Oct 95*	1
LOVE GROOVE (GROOVE WITH YOU)	*Jive*	46	*16 Mar 96*	1
WE GOT IT *Above hit: IMMATURE (featuring SMOOTH).*	*MCA*	26	*16 Mar 96*	2
UNDERCOVER LOVER	*Jive*	41	*6 Jul 96*	1

C.L. SMOOTH – See Pete ROCK and C.L. SMOOTH

Joe SMOOTH — US

SINGLES:	HITS 1			WEEKS 4
PROMISED LAND	*DJ International*	56	*4 Feb 89*	4

SMOOTH TOUCH — US

SINGLES:	HITS 1			WEEKS 1
HOUSE OF LOVE (IN MY HOUSE)	*Six6*	58	*2 Apr 94*	1

Jean Jacques SMOOTHIE — UK

SINGLES:				
2 PEOPLE	*Echo*	12	*13 Oct 01*	7

SMURFS — Holland

SINGLES:	HITS 5			WEEKS 52
THE SMURF SONG	*Decca*	2	*3 Jun 78*	17
DIPPETY DAY *Above 2: FATHER ABRAHAM.*	*Decca*	13	*30 Sep 78*	12
CHRISTMAS IN SMURFLAND *Above hit: FATHER ABRAHAM and the SMURFS.*	*Decca*	19	*2 Dec 78*	7

I'VE GOT A LITTLE PUPPY	*EMI TV*	4	*7 Sep 96*	10
Based on Teeboheuil's I Want To Be A Hippy.				
YOUR CHRISTMAS WISH	*EMI TV*	8	*21 Dec 96*	6
ALBUMS:	**HITS 6**			**WEEKS 77**
FATHER ABRAHAM IN SMURFLAND	*Decca*	19	*25 Nov 78*	11
Above hit: FATHER ABRAHAM and the SMURFS.				
THE SMURFS GO POP!	*EMI TV*	2	*6 Jul 96*	33
SMURF'S CHRISTMAS PARTY	*EMI TV*	8	*16 Nov 96*	9
Alternative versions of Xmas classics.				
THE SMURFS HITS '97 – VOLUME 1	*EMI TV*	2	*22 Feb 97*	11
GO POP! AGAIN	*EMI*	15	*6 Sep 97*	7
GREATEST HITS	*EMI*	28	*18 Apr 98*	6

Patty SMYTH with Don HENLEY — US

(See also Don Henley.)

SINGLES:	**HITS 1**			**WEEKS 6**
SOMETIMES LOVE JUST AIN'T ENOUGH	*MCA*	22	*3 Oct 92*	6

SNAKEBITE — Italy

SINGLES:	**HITS 1**			**WEEKS 2**
THE BIT GOES ON	*Multiply*	25	*9 Aug 97*	2

SNAP! — US/Germany

SINGLES:	**HITS 14**			**WEEKS 115**
THE POWER	*Arista*	1	*24 Mar 90*	15
Samples Loleatta Holloway's Love's Gonna Get You.				
OOOPS UP	*Arista*	5	*16 Jun 90*	12
CULT OF SNAP	*Arista*	8	*22 Sep 90*	7
MARY HAD A LITTLE BOY	*Arista*	8	*8 Dec 90*	10
SNAP MEGAMIX [M]	*Arista*	10	*30 Mar 91*	6
COLOUR OF LOVE	*Arista*	54	*21 Dec 91*	3
RHYTHM IS A DANCER	*Logic*	1	*4 Jul 92*	19
Features vocals by Thea Austin.				
EXTERMINATE!	*Logic*	2	*9 Jan 93*	11
DO YOU SEE THE LIGHT (LOOKING FOR)	*Logic*	10	*12 Jun 93*	8
Above 2: SNAP! featuring Niki HARIS.				
WELCOME TO TOMORROW (ARE YOU READY?)	*Arista*	6	*17 Sep 94*	13
WELCOME TO TOMORROW (ARE YOU READY?) [RE]	*Arista*	75	*14 Jan 95*	1
THE FIRST THE LAST ETERNITY (TIL THE END)	*Arista*	15	*1 Apr 95*	7
THE WORLD IN MY HANDS	*Arista*	44	*28 Oct 95*	1
Above 4: SNAP! featuring SUMMER				
RAME	*Arista*	50	*13 Apr 96*	1
Above hit: SNAP! featuring 'RUKMANI'.				
THE POWER 96 [RR]	*Arista*	42	*24 Aug 96*	1
Above hit: SNAP! featuring EINSTEIN.				
ALBUMS:	**HITS 4**			**WEEKS 56**
WORLD POWER	*Arista*	21	*26 May 90*	23
WORLD POWER [RE]	*Arista*	10	*22 Dec 90*	16
THE MADMAN'S RETURN	*Logic*	20	*8 Aug 92*	8
THE MADMAN'S RETURN [RE]	*Logic*	8	*13 Feb 93*	7
Repackaged from 20 Feb 93.				
WELCOME TO TOMORROW	*Ariola*	69	*15 Oct 94*	1
SNAP! ATTACK – THE BEST OF SNAP! / SNAP! ATTACK – THE REMIXES	*Ariola*	47	*7 Sep 96*	1
Available as either a single album or double album including the remixes.				

SNEAKER PIMPS — UK

SINGLES:	**HITS 5**			**WEEKS 19**
6 UNDERGROUND	*Clean Up*	15	*19 Oct 96*	4
SPIN SPIN SUGAR	*Clean Up*	21	*15 Mar 97*	3
SIX UNDERGROUND [RI]	*Clean Up*	9	*7 Jun 97*	4
From the film 'The Saint'.				
POST MODERN SLEAZE	*Clean Up*	22	*30 Aug 97*	3
SPIN SPIN SUGAR [RM]	*Clean Up*	46	*7 Feb 98*	2
Remixed by Armand Van Helden.				
LOW FIVE	*Clean Up*	39	*21 Aug 99*	2
TEN TO TWENTY	*Clean Up*	56	*30 Oct 99*	1
ALBUMS:	**HITS 1**			**WEEKS 7**
BECOMING X	*Clean Up*	72	*31 Aug 96*	1
BECOMING X [RE]	*Clean Up*	27	*21 Jun 97*	6

SNIFF N' THE TEARS — UK

SINGLES:	**HITS 1**			**WEEKS 5**
DRIVER'S SEAT	*Chiswick*	42	*23 Jun 79*	5

SNIFFLE GROUP – See Stan FREBERG

Miss SNOB and CLASS 3C - See WIZZARD

SNOOP DOGGY DOGG — US

SINGLES:	HITS 12			WEEKS 56
WHAT'S MY NAME?	*Death Row*	20	*4 Dec 93*	8
GIN AND JUICE *Samples Watching You by Slave.*	*Death Row*	39	*12 Feb 94*	3
DOGGY DOGG WORLD *Features backing vocals by the Dramatics.*	*Death Row*	32	*20 Aug 94*	3
SNOOP'S UPSIDE YA HEAD *Above hit: SNOOP DOGGY DOGG featuring Charlie WILSON.*	*Interscope*	12	*14 Dec 96*	7
WANTED DEAD OR ALIVE *From the film 'Gridlock'd'.* *Above hit: 2 PAC and SNOOP DOGGY DOGG.*	*Def Jam*	16	*26 Apr 97*	3
VAPORS *Original was by rapper Biz Markie.* *Above hit: SNOOP DOGGY DOGG featuring Charlie WILSON and Teena MARIE.*	*Interscope*	18	*3 May 97*	2
WE JUST WANNA PARTY WITH YOU *From the film 'Men In Black'.* *Above hit: SNOOP DOGGY DOGG featuring JD.*	*Columbia*	21	*20 Sep 97*	2
THA DOGGFATHER *Above hit: SNOOP DOGGY DOGG.*	*Interscope*	36	*24 Jan 98*	2
COME AND GET WITH ME *Above hit: Keith SWEAT featuring SNOOP DOGG.*	*Elektra*	58	*12 Dec 98*	1
STILL D.R.E. *Above hit: DR. DRE featuring SNOOP DOGG.*	*Interscope*	6	*25 Mar 00*	10
THE NEXT EPISODE *Above hit: DR DRE featuring SNOOP DOGG.*	*Interscope*	3	*3 Feb 01*	10
SNOOP DOGG	*Priority*	13	*28 Apr 01*	5
ALBUMS:	**HITS 5**			**WEEKS 44**
DOGGYSTYLE	*Death Row*	38	*11 Dec 93*	27
THA DOGGFATHER	*Interscope*	15	*23 Nov 96*	11
DA GAMES IS TO BE SOLD, NOT TO BE TOLD	*Priority*	28	*15 Aug 98*	3
TOP DOGG	*Priority*	48	*5 Jun 99*	1
THA LAST MEAL *Above 3: SNOOP DOGG.*	*Priority*	62	*5 May 01*	2

Sid SNOT - See Kenny EVERETT

SNOW — Canada

SINGLES:	HITS 3			WEEKS 18
INFORMER	*East West America*	2	*13 Mar 93*	15
GIRL, I'VE BEEN HURT	*East West America*	48	*5 Jun 93*	2
UHH IN YOU	*Atlantic*	67	*4 Sep 93*	1
ALBUMS:	**HITS 1**			**WEEKS 4**
12 INCHES OF SNOW	*East West America*	41	*17 Apr 93*	4

Mark SNOW — UK

SINGLES:	HITS 1			WEEKS 15
THE X FILES *Theme from the TV series of the same name.*	*Warner Brothers*	2	*30 Mar 96*	15
ALBUMS:	**HITS 1**			**WEEKS 2**
TRUTH AND THE LIGHT: MUSIC FROM THE X-FILES *Includes themes used in the X-Files interspersed with dialogue.*	*Warner Brothers*	42	*12 Oct 96*	2

Phoebe SNOW — US

SINGLES:	HITS 1			WEEKS 7
EVERY NIGHT *Originally recorded by Paul McCartney.*	*CBS*	37	*6 Jan 79*	7

SNOWMAN — UK

(See also Howard Blake conducting the Sinfonia Of London, narration: Bernard Cribbins; Digital Dream Baby.)

SINGLES:	HITS 1			WEEKS 9
WALKING IN THE AIR *Original release reached No. 99 in 1984.* *Above hit: SNOWMAN featuring Peter AUTY.*	*Stiff*	42	*14 Dec 85*	5
WALKING IN THE AIR (FROM THE SNOWMAN) [RI] *Peter Auty is not credited on this issue.*	*CBS*	37	*19 Dec 87*	4

SNOWMEN — UK

SINGLES:	HITS 2			WEEKS 12
HOKEY COKEY	*Slack*	18	*12 Dec 81*	8
XMAS PARTY [M]	*Solid*	44	*18 Dec 82*	4

SNUG — UK

SINGLES:	HITS 1			WEEKS 1
BEATNIK GIRL	*WEA*	55	*18 Apr 98*	1

SO — UK

SINGLES:	HITS 1			WEEKS 3
ARE YOU SURE	*Parlophone*	62	*13 Feb 88*	3

SO SOLID CREW — UK

SINGLES:	HITS 2			WEEKS 22
21 SECONDS	*Relentless*	1	*18 Aug 01*	13
THEY DON'T KNOW	*Relentless*	3	*17 Nov 01*	7
21 SECONDS [RE]	*Relentless*	64	*24 Nov 01*	2
ALBUMS:	**HITS 1**			**WEEKS 5**
THEY DON'T KNOW	*Relentless*	6	*1 Dec 01*	5

SOAPY — UK

SINGLES:	HITS 1			WEEKS 2
HORNY AS FUNK	*WEA*	35	*14 Sep 96*	2

Gino SOCCIO — Canada

SINGLES:	HITS 1			WEEKS 5
DANCER	*Warner Brothers*	46	*28 Apr 79*	5

SOEUR SOURIRE – See SINGING NUN (SOEUR SOURIRE)

SOFT CELL — UK

SINGLES:	HITS 10			WEEKS 107
TAINTED LOVE	*Some Bizzare*	1	*1 Aug 81*	16
Originally recorded by Gloria Jones in 1965.				
BEDSITTER	*Some Bizzare*	4	*14 Nov 81*	12
TAINTED LOVE [RE-1ST]	*Some Bizzare*	43	*9 Jan 82*	10
SAY HELLO WAVE GOODBYE	*Some Bizzare*	3	*6 Feb 82*	9
TORCH	*Some Bizzare*	2	*29 May 82*	9
TAINTED LOVE [RE-2ND]	*Some Bizzare*	50	*24 Jul 82*	4
WHAT	*Some Bizzare*	3	*21 Aug 82*	8
Originally recorded by Judy Street in 1978.				
WHERE THE HEART IS	*Some Bizzare*	21	*4 Dec 82*	7
NUMBERS / BARRIERS	*Some Bizzare*	25	*5 Mar 83*	4
SOUL INSIDE	*Some Bizzare*	16	*24 Sep 83*	5
DOWN IN THE SUBWAY	*Some Bizzare*	24	*25 Feb 84*	6
Originally recorded by Jack Hammer.				
TAINTED LOVE [RE-3RD]	*Some Bizzare*	43	*9 Feb 85*	6
SAY HELLO WAVE GOODBYE '91 [RR]	*Mercury*	38	*23 Mar 91*	3
TAINTED LOVE [RI]	*Mercury*	5	*18 May 91*	8
Above 2: SOFT CELL Marc ALMOND.				
ALBUMS:	**HITS 6**			**WEEKS 101**
NON-STOP EROTIC CABARET	*Some Bizzare*	5	*12 Dec 81*	46
NON-STOP ECSTATIC DANCING	*Some Bizzare*	6	*26 Jun 82*	18
Dance remixes of tracks from their previous album.				
THE ART OF FALLING APART	*Some Bizzare*	5	*22 Jan 83*	10
THIS LAST NIGHT IN SODOM	*Some Bizzare*	12	*31 Mar 84*	5
THE SINGLES ALBUM	*Some Bizzare*	58	*20 Dec 86*	9
MEMORABILIA - THE SINGLES	*Mercury*	8	*1 Jun 91*	13
Includes both Almond's solo and group material.				
Above hit: SOFT CELL Marc ALMOND.				

SOFT MACHINE — UK

ALBUMS:	HITS 2			WEEKS 8
THIRD	*CBS*	18	*4 Jul 70*	6
FOURTH	*CBS*	32	*3 Apr 71*	2

SOFT PARADE – See ELECTRIC SOFT PARADE

SOHO — UK

SINGLES:	HITS 2			WEEKS 11
HIPPYCHICK	*S&M*	67	*5 May 90*	1
Samples How Soon is Now by the Smiths.				
HIPPYCHICK [RE]	*S&M*	8	*19 Jan 91*	8
BORN TO BE ALIVE!	*MCA*	51	*9 Nov 91*	2
[AA] listed with Never Goin' Down (Incorporating Future Freak) by Adamski + Jimi Polo.				
Above hit: ADAMSKI + SOHO.				

SOLAR STONE — UK

SINGLES:	HITS 2			WEEKS 3
THE IMPRESSIONS [EP] *Lead track: The Calling.*	*Hooj Choons*	75	*21 Feb 98*	1
SEVEN CITIES	*Hooj Choons*	39	*6 Nov 99*	2

SOLID GOLD CHARTBUSTERS — UK

SINGLES:	HITS 1			WEEKS 1
I WANNA 1-2-1 WITH YOU *Based around the Grand Valse mobile phone ringing tone.*	*Virgin*	62	*25 Dec 99*	1

SOLID HARMONIE — UK/US

SINGLES:	HITS 4			WEEKS 11
I'LL BE THERE FOR YOU	*Jive*	18	*31 Jan 98*	3
I WANT YOU TO WANT ME	*Jive*	16	*18 Apr 98*	3
I WANNA LOVE YOU	*Jive*	20	*15 Aug 98*	4
TO LOVE ONCE AGAIN	*Jive*	55	*21 Nov 98*	1

SOLID SENDERS — UK

ALBUMS:	HITS 1			WEEKS 3
SOLID SENDERS	*Virgin*	42	*23 Sep 78*	3

SOLO — UK

SINGLES:	HITS 2			WEEKS 4
RAINBOW (SAMPLE-FREE) *Based on the theme of the Children's ITV programme.*	*Reverb*	59	*20 Jul 91*	2
COME ON!	*Reverb*	75	*18 Jan 92*	1
COME ON! [RM] *Remix has replaced the vocals of Jasmine Rennie with Mary Kiani's.*	*Stoatin'*	63	*11 Sep 93*	1

SOLO (US) — US

SINGLES:	HITS 2			WEEKS 3
HEAVEN *Samples Isley Brothers' Between The Sheets.*	*Perspective*	35	*3 Feb 96*	2
WHERE DO U WANT ME TO PUT IT *Above hit: SOLO U.S.*	*Perspective*	45	*30 Mar 96*	1

Sal SOLO — UK

SINGLES:	HITS 2			WEEKS 13
SAN DAMIANO (HEART AND SOUL)	*MCA*	15	*15 Dec 84*	10
MUSIC AND YOU *Above hit: Sal SOLO with the LONDON COMMUNITY GOSPEL CHOIR.*	*MCA*	52	*6 Apr 85*	3

Diane SOLOMON — UK

ALBUMS:	HITS 1			WEEKS 6
TAKE TWO	*Philips*	26	*9 Aug 75*	6

Sir Georg SOLTI and Dudley MOORE — UK

(See also Dudley Moore.)

ALBUMS:	HITS 1			WEEKS 5
ORCHESTRA!	*Decca*	38	*26 Jan 91*	5

SOLUTION - See Victor SIMONELLI presents SOLUTION

Belouis SOME — UK

SINGLES:	HITS 3			WEEKS 26
IMAGINATION	*Parlophone*	50	*27 Apr 85*	7
IMAGINATION [RI]	*Parlophone*	17	*18 Jan 86*	10
SOME PEOPLE *Original release reached No. 83 in 1985.*	*Parlophone*	33	*12 Apr 86*	7
LET IT BE WITH YOU	*Parlophone*	53	*16 May 87*	2

Glen SOMERS and his Orchestra - See Eve BOSWELL with Glenn SOMERS and his Orchestra

Jimmy SOMERVILLE — UK

(See also Bronski Beat; Communards.)

SINGLES:	HITS 9			WEEKS 49
COMMENT TE DIRE ADIEU *Originally recorded by Francois Hardy.* *Above hit: Jimmy SOMERVILLE featuring June MILES KINGSTON.*	*London*	14	*11 Nov 89*	9
YOU MAKE ME FEEL (MIGHTY REAL)	*London*	5	*13 Jan 90*	8
READ MY LIPS (ENOUGH IS ENOUGH)	*London*	26	*17 Mar 90*	6
TO LOVE SOMEBODY	*London*	8	*3 Nov 90*	11

RUN FROM LOVE	*London*	52	*10 Aug 91*	2
HEARTBEAT	*London*	24	*28 Jan 95*	4
HURT SO GOOD	*London*	15	*27 May 95*	6
BY YOUR SIDE	*London*	41	*28 Oct 95*	2
DARK SKY	*Gut*	66	*13 Sep 97*	1
ALBUMS:	**HITS 4**			**WEEKS 46**
READ MY LIPS	*London*	29	*9 Dec 89*	14
THE SINGLES COLLECTION 1984/1990	*London*	4	*24 Nov 90*	26
Includes his recordings with Bronski Beat and the Communards as well as his own solo material.				
DARE TO LOVE	*London*	38	*24 Jun 95*	2
THE VERY BEST OF JIMMY SOMERVILLE – BRONSKI BEAT AND THE COMMUNARDS	*London*	29	*22 Sep 01*	4
17 track compilation. 5 solo tracks, 4 with Bronski Beat, 8 with Communards.				
Above hit: Jimmy SOMERVILLE – BRONSKI BEAT and the COMMUNARDS.				

SOMETHIN' FOR THE PEOPLE featuring TRINA and TAMARA — US

(See also Trina and Tamara.)

SINGLES:	**HITS 1**			**WEEKS 1**
MY LOVE IS THE SHHH!	*Warner Brothers*	64	*7 Feb 98*	1

SOMORE featuring Damon TRUEITT — US

SINGLES:	**HITS 1**			**WEEKS 2**
I REFUSE (WHAT YOU WANT)	*XL Recordings*	21	*24 Jan 98*	2

SON'Z OF A LOOP DA LOOP ERA — UK

(See also Various Artists (EPs) 'Subplates Volume 1 EP'.)

SINGLES:	**HITS 2**			**WEEKS 4**
FAR OUT	*Suburban Base*	36	*15 Feb 92*	3
PEACE + LOVEISM	*Suburban Base*	60	*17 Oct 92*	1

SONGSTRESS — US

SINGLES:	**HITS 1**			**WEEKS 1**
SEE LINE WOMAN '99	*Locked On*	64	*27 Feb 99*	1
Samples Nina Simone's See Line Woman.				

SONIA — UK

SINGLES:	**HITS 12**			**WEEKS 78**
YOU'LL NEVER STOP ME LOVING YOU	*Chrysalis*	1	*24 Jun 89*	13
CAN'T FORGET YOU	*Chrysalis*	17	*7 Oct 89*	6
LISTEN TO YOUR HEART	*Chrysalis*	10	*9 Dec 89*	10
COUNTING EVERY MINUTE	*Chrysalis*	16	*7 Apr 90*	7
YOU'VE GOT A FRIEND	*Jive*	14	*23 Jun 90*	6
Charity record in aid of Childline.				
Above hit: BIG FUN and SONIA featuring Gary BARNACLE on saxophone.				
END OF THE WORLD	*Chrysalis*	18	*25 Aug 90*	7
ONLY FOOLS (NEVER FALL IN LOVE)	*IQ*	10	*1 Jun 91*	8
BE YOUNG, BE FOOLISH, BE HAPPY	*IQ*	22	*31 Aug 91*	5
YOU TO ME ARE EVERYTHING	*IQ*	13	*16 Nov 91*	5
BOOGIE NIGHTS	*Arista*	30	*12 Sep 92*	3
BETTER THE DEVIL YOU KNOW	*Arista*	15	*1 May 93*	7
UK's Eurovision entry in 1993, it came 2nd.				
HOPELESSLY DEVOTED TO YOU	*Cockney*	61	*30 Jul 94*	1
From the musical 'Grease'.				
ALBUMS:	**HITS 3**			**WEEKS 14**
EVERYBODY KNOWS	*Chrysalis*	7	*5 May 90*	10
SONIA	*IQ*	33	*19 Oct 91*	2
BETTER THE DEVIL YOU KNOW	*Arista*	32	*29 May 93*	2

SONIC BOOM — UK

ALBUMS:	**HITS 1**			**WEEKS 1**
SPECTRUM	*Silvertone*	65	*17 Mar 90*	1

SONIC The HEDGEHOG – See H.W.A. featuring SONIC The HEDGEHOG

SONIC SOLUTION — UK

SINGLES:	**HITS 1**			**WEEKS 1**
BEATSTIME	*R&S*	59	*4 Apr 92*	1

SONIC SURFERS — Holland

SINGLES:	**HITS 2**			**WEEKS 2**
TAKE ME UP	*A&M*	61	*20 Mar 93*	1
Above hit: SONIC SURFERS featuring Jocelyn BROWN.				
DON'T GIVE IT UP	*Brilliant*	54	*30 Jul 94*	1

SONIC YOUTH — US

SINGLES:	HITS 6			WEEKS 14
100%	*DGC*	28	*11 Jul 92*	4
YOUTH AGAINST FASCISM	*Geffen*	52	*7 Nov 92*	2
SUGAR KANE	*Geffen*	26	*3 Apr 93*	3
BULL IN THE HEATHER	*Geffen*	24	*7 May 94*	2
SUPERSTAR	*A&M*	45	*10 Sep 94*	2
[AA] listed with Yesterday Once More by Redd Kross. From the Various Artists 25th anniversary tribute album to the Carpenters, If I Were A Carpenter.				
SUNDAY	*Geffen*	72	*11 Jul 98*	1
ALBUMS:	**HITS 8**			**WEEKS 14**
DAYDREAM NATION	*Blast First*	99	*29 Oct 88*	1
THE WHITEY ALBUM	*Blast First*	63	*4 Feb 89*	1
Above hit: CICCONE YOUTH.				
"GOO"	*DGC*	32	*7 Jul 90*	2
THE DIRTY BOOTS EP - PLUS 5 LIVE TRACKS	*DGC*	69	*4 May 91*	1
DIRTY	*DGC*	6	*1 Aug 92*	5
EXPERIMENTAL JET SET, TRASH AND NO STAR	*Geffen*	10	*21 May 94*	2
WASHING MACHINE	*Geffen*	39	*14 Oct 95*	1
A THOUSAND LEAVES	*Geffen*	38	*23 May 98*	1

SONIQUE — UK

SINGLES:	HITS 3			WEEKS 42
I PUT A SPELL ON YOU	*Serious*	36	*13 Jun 98*	2
IT FEELS SO GOOD	*Serious*	24	*5 Dec 98*	3
IT FEELS SO GOOD [RM]	*Serious*	1	*3 Jun 00*	17
SKY	*Serious*	2	*16 Sep 00*	10
I PUT A SPELL ON YOU [RI]	*Serious*	8	*9 Dec 00*	10
ALBUMS:	**HITS 1**			**WEEKS 37**
HEAR MY CRY	*Serious*	6	*24 Jun 00*	37

SONNY — US

(See also Sonny and Cher.)

SINGLES:	HITS 1			WEEKS 11
LAUGH AT ME	*Atlantic*	9	*21 Aug 65*	11

SONNY and CHER — US

(See Cher; Sonny.)

SINGLES:	HITS 9			WEEKS 78
I GOT YOU BABE	*Atlantic*	1	*14 Aug 65*	12
BABY DON'T GO	*Reprise*	11	*18 Sep 65*	9
Originally released earlier in the year.				
BUT YOU'RE MINE	*Atlantic*	17	*23 Oct 65*	8
WHAT NOW MY LOVE	*Atlantic*	13	*19 Feb 66*	11
HAVE I STAYED TOO LONG	*Atlantic*	42	*2 Jul 66*	3
LITTLE MAN	*Atlantic*	4	*10 Sep 66*	10
LIVING FOR YOU	*Atlantic*	44	*19 Nov 66*	4
THE BEAT GOES ON	*Atlantic*	29	*4 Feb 67*	8
ALL I EVER NEED IS YOU	*MCA*	8	*15 Jan 72*	12
Originally recorded by Ray Sanders.				
I GOT YOU BABE [RI]	*Epic*	66	*22 May 93*	1
From the film 'Groundhog Day'.				
ALBUMS:	**HITS 2**			**WEEKS 20**
LOOK AT US	*Atlantic*	7	*16 Oct 65*	13
THE WONDEROUS WORLD OF SONNY AND CHER	*Atlantic*	15	*14 May 66*	7

SONO — Germany

SINGLES:	HITS 1			WEEKS 1
KEEP CONTROL	*Code Blue*	66	*16 Jun 01*	1

SOPHIE – See ZERO 7

SORROWS — UK

SINGLES:	HITS 1			WEEKS 8
TAKE A HEART	*Piccadilly*	21	*18 Sep 65*	8

Aaron SOUL — UK

SINGLES:	HITS 1			WEEKS 4
RING RING RING	*Def Soul UK*	14	*2 Jun 01*	4
From the film 'Bridget Jones's Diary'.				

David SOUL — US

SINGLES:	HITS 5			WEEKS 56
DON'T GIVE UP ON US	*Private Stock*	1	*18 Dec 76*	16
GOING IN WITH MY EYES OPEN	*Private Stock*	2	*26 Mar 77*	8
SILVER LADY	*Private Stock*	1	*27 Aug 77*	14
LET'S HAVE A QUIET NIGHT IN	*Private Stock*	8	*17 Dec 77*	9
IT SURE BRINGS OUT THE LOVE IN YOUR EYES	*Private Stock*	12	*27 May 78*	9
ALBUMS:	**HITS 2**			**WEEKS 51**
DAVID SOUL	*Private Stock*	2	*27 Nov 76*	28
PLAYING TO AN AUDIENCE OF ONE	*Private Stock*	8	*17 Sep 77*	23

Jimmy SOUL — US

SINGLES:	HITS 1			WEEKS 5
IF YOU WANNA BE HAPPY *Based on a calypso tune called Ugly Woman.*	*Stateside*	39	*13 Jul 63*	2
IF YOU WANNA BE HAPPY [RI]	*Epic*	68	*15 Jun 91*	3

SOUL ASYLUM — US

SINGLES:	HITS 5			WEEKS 33
RUNAWAY TRAIN	*Columbia*	37	*19 Jun 93*	8
SOMEBODY TO SHOVE	*Columbia*	34	*4 Sep 93*	3
RUNAWAY TRAIN [RE]	*Columbia*	7	*13 Nov 93*	11
BLACK GOLD	*Columbia*	26	*22 Jan 94*	4
SOMEBODY TO SHOVE [RI]	*Columbia*	32	*26 Mar 94*	3
MISERY	*Columbia*	30	*15 Jul 95*	3
JUST LIKE ANYONE	*Columbia*	52	*2 Dec 95*	1
ALBUMS:	**HITS 2**			**WEEKS 29**
GRAVE DANCERS UNION	*Columbia*	27	*31 Jul 93*	25
LET YOUR DIM LIGHT SHINE	*Columbia*	22	*1 Jul 95*	4

SOUL BROTHERS — UK

SINGLES:	HITS 1			WEEKS 3
I KEEP RINGING MY BABY	*Decca*	43	*24 Apr 65*	3

SOUL CITY ORCHESTRA — UK

SINGLES:	HITS 1			WEEKS 1
IT'S JURASSIC (VERSION OF THE THEME TO JURASSIC PARK)	*London*	70	*11 Dec 93*	1

SOUL CITY SYMPHONY - See Van McCOY

SOUL FAMILY SENSATION — UK/US

SINGLES:	HITS 1			WEEKS 4
I DON'T EVEN KNOW IF I SHOULD CALL YOU BABY	*One Little Indian*	49	*11 May 91*	4

SOUL FOR REAL — US

SINGLES:	HITS 2			WEEKS 4
CANDY RAIN	*Uptown*	23	*8 Jul 95*	2
EVERY LITTLE THING I DO	*Uptown*	31	*23 Mar 96*	2

SOUL PROVIDERS featuring Michelle SHELLERS — US

SINGLES:	HITS 1			WEEKS 1
RISE *Original release reached No. 142 on 4 Mar 2000.*	*AM:PM*	59	*14 Jul 01*	1

SOUL SONIC FORCE - See Afrika BAMBAATAA

SOUL II SOUL — UK

SINGLES:	HITS 15			WEEKS 89
FAIRPLAY *Above hit: SOUL II SOUL featuring Rose WINDROSS.*	*10 Records*	63	*21 May 88*	3
FEEL FREE *Above hit: SOUL II SOUL featuring DO'REEN.*	*10 Records*	64	*17 Sep 88*	2
KEEP ON MOVIN' *Features the Reggae Philharmonic Orchestra.*	*10 Records*	5	*18 Mar 89*	12
BACK TO LIFE (HOWEVER DO YOU WANT ME) *Certain copies did not credit Caron Wheeler on either the sleeve or the label.* *Above 2: SOUL II SOUL featuring Caron WHEELER.*	*10 Records*	1	*10 Jun 89*	14
GET A LIFE *The B-side was called Jazzie's Groove, which was also popular.*	*10 Records*	3	*9 Dec 89*	13
A DREAMS A DREAM *Vocals by Victoria Wilson James.*	*10 Records*	6	*5 May 90*	6
MISSING YOU *Above hit: SOUL II SOUL (vocals: Kym MAZELLE).*	*Ten Records*	22	*24 Nov 90*	7

JOY *Richie Stephens on lead vocals.*	*Ten Records*	4	*4 Apr 92*	7
MOVE ME NO MOUNTAIN *Above hit: SOUL II SOUL; Lead vocal by KOFI.*	*Ten Records*	31	*13 Jun 92*	4
JUST RIGHT	*Ten Records*	38	*26 Sep 92*	2
WISH	*Virgin*	24	*6 Nov 93*	4
LOVE ENUFF *Vocals by Penny Ford.*	*Virgin*	12	*22 Jul 95*	6
I CARE (SOUL II SOUL)	*Virgin*	17	*21 Oct 95*	4
KEEP ON MOVIN' [RI] *Featured in the Renault Clio car TV commercial.*	*Virgin*	31	*19 Oct 96*	2
REPRESENT *Vocals by Paul Johnson.*	*Island*	39	*30 Aug 97*	2
PLEASURE DOME	*Island*	51	*8 Nov 97*	1
ALBUMS:	**HITS 5**			**WEEKS 108**
CLUB CLASSICS - VOLUME ONE	*10 Records*	1	*22 Apr 89*	60
VOLUME II (1990 A NEW DECADE)	*10 Records*	1	*2 Jun 90*	20
VOLUME III JUST RIGHT	*Ten Records*	3	*25 Apr 92*	11
VOLUME IV THE CLASSICS SINGLES 88-93	*Virgin*	10	*27 Nov 93*	13
VOLUME V - BELIEVE	*Virgin*	13	*12 Aug 95*	4

SOUL U*NIQUE — UK

SINGLES:	**HITS 2**			**WEEKS 2**
BE MY FRIEND	*M&J*	53	*19 Feb 00*	1
3IL (THRILL)	*M&J*	66	*29 Jul 00*	1

SOUL VISION - See EVERYTHING BUT THE GIRL

SOULED OUT — UK/US/Italy

SINGLES:	**HITS 1**			**WEEKS 1**
IN MY LIFE	*Columbia*	75	*9 May 92*	1

SOULFLY — US/Brazil

ALBUMS:	**HITS 2**			**WEEKS 5**
SOULFLY	*Roadrunner*	16	*2 May 98*	2
PRIMITIVE	*Roadrunner*	45	*7 Oct 00*	1

SOULSEARCHER — US

SINGLES:	**HITS 2**			**WEEKS 9**
CAN'T GET ENOUGH *Vocals by Thea Austin. Samples Gary's Gang's Let Love Dance Tonight.*	*Defected*	8	*13 Feb 99*	7
DO IT TO ME AGAIN	*Defected*	32	*8 Apr 00*	2

SOULWAX — Belgium

SINGLES:	**HITS 3**			**WEEKS 5**
CONVERSATION INTERCOM	*PIAS Recordings*	65	*25 Mar 00*	1
MUCH AGAINST EVERYONE'S ADVICE	*PIAS Recordings*	56	*24 Jun 00*	1
TOO MANY DJ'S	*PIAS Recordings*	40	*30 Sep 00*	2
CONVERSATION INTERCOM [RM] *Remixed by Dave Bascombe.*	*PIAS Recordings*	50	*3 Mar 01*	1

SOUND DE-ZIGN — Holland

SINGLES:	**HITS 1**			**WEEKS 5**
HAPPINESS *Samples Shena's Let The Beat Hit 'Em.*	*NuLife*	19	*14 Apr 01*	5

SOUND FACTORY — Sweden

SINGLES:	**HITS 1**			**WEEKS 1**
2 THE RHYTHM	*Logic*	72	*5 Jun 93*	1

SOUND 5 — UK

SINGLES:	**HITS 1**			**WEEKS 1**
ALA KABOO	*Gut*	69	*24 Apr 99*	1

SOUND 9418 - See Jonathan KING

SOUND OF ONE featuring GLADEZZ — US

SINGLES:	**HITS 1**			**WEEKS 1**
AS I AM	*Cooltempo*	65	*20 Nov 93*	1

SOUNDGARDEN — US

SINGLES:	**HITS 10**			**WEEKS 24**
JESUS CHRIST POSE	*A&M*	30	*11 Apr 92*	3
RUSTY CAGE	*A&M*	41	*20 Jun 92*	1

OUTSHINED	*A&M*	50	*21 Nov 92*	1
SPOONMAN	*A&M*	20	*26 Feb 94*	3
Written about a Seattle resident who has written books on the philosophy of spoon-playing.				
THE DAY I TRIED TO LIVE	*A&M*	42	*30 Apr 94*	2
BLACK HOLE SUN	*A&M*	12	*20 Aug 94*	5
FELL ON BLACK DAYS	*A&M*	24	*28 Jan 95*	2
PRETTY NOOSE	*A&M*	14	*18 May 96*	3
BURDEN IN MY HAND	*A&M*	33	*28 Sep 96*	2
BLOW UP THE OUTSIDE WORLD	*A&M*	40	*28 Dec 96*	2
ALBUMS:	**HITS 3**			**WEEKS 32**
BADMOTORFINGER	*A&M*	39	*25 Apr 92*	2
SUPERUNKNOWN	*A&M*	4	*19 Mar 94*	24
DOWN ON THE UPSIDE	*A&M*	7	*1 Jun 96*	6

SOUNDMAN and Don LLOYDIE with Elisabeth TROY — UK

SINGLES:	**HITS 1**			**WEEKS 2**
GREATER LOVE	*Sound Of Underground*	49	*25 Feb 95*	2

SOUNDS INCORPORATED — UK

(See also Gene Vincent.)

SINGLES:	**HITS 2**			**WEEKS 11**
THE SPARTANS	*Columbia*	30	*25 Apr 64*	6
SPANISH HARLEM	*Columbia*	35	*1 Aug 64*	5

SOUNDS NICE featuring Tim MYCROFT on organ — UK

SINGLES:	**HITS 1**			**WEEKS 11**
LOVE AT FIRST SIGHT (JE T'AIME . . . MOI NON PLUS)	*Parlophone*	18	*6 Sep 69*	11

SOUNDS OF BLACKNESS — US

SINGLES:	**HITS 7**			**WEEKS 32**
OPTIMISTIC	*Perspective*	45	*22 Jun 91*	4
THE PRESSURE PT 1	*Perspective*	71	*28 Sep 91*	1
OPTIMISTIC [RI]	*Perspective*	28	*15 Feb 92*	4
THE PRESSURE PART 1 [RM 1ST]	*Perspective*	49	*25 Apr 92*	2
Remixed by C.J. Macintosh.				
I'M GOING ALL THE WAY	*Perspective*	27	*8 May 93*	3
I BELIEVE	*A&M*	17	*26 Mar 94*	4
GLORYLAND	*Mercury*	36	*2 Jul 94*	4
Offical theme song of the 1994 World Cup in the US and used by ITV Sport for their coverage of the games.				
Above hit: Daryl HALL and SOUNDS OF BLACKNESS.				
EVERYTHING IS GONNA BE ALRIGHT	*A&M*	29	*20 Aug 94*	3
Samples Isaac Hayes' Walk On By.				
I'M GOING ALL THE WAY [RI]	*A&M*	14	*14 Jan 95*	4
SPIRIT	*A&M*	35	*7 Jun 97*	2
Above hit: SOUNDS OF BLACKNESS featuring Craig MACK.				
THE PRESSURE [RM-2ND]	*AM:PM*	46	*14 Feb 98*	1
Remixed by Marc Pomeroy and Brian Tappert.				
ALBUMS:	**HITS 1**			**WEEKS 6**
AFRICA TO AMERICA: THE JOURNEY OF THE DRUM	*A&M*	28	*30 Apr 94*	6

SOUNDS ORCHESTRAL — UK

SINGLES:	**HITS 2**			**WEEKS 18**
CAST YOUR FATE TO THE WIND	*Piccadilly*	5	*5 Dec 64*	16
Original by Vince Guaraldi Trio in 1962, reached No. 22 in the US the following year.				
MOONGLOW (INTRODUCING THEME FROM PICNIC)	*Piccadilly*	43	*10 Jul 65*	2
ALBUMS:	**HITS 1**			**WEEKS 1**
CAST YOUR FATE TO THE WIND	*Piccadilly*	17	*12 Jun 65*	1

SOUNDSATION — UK

SINGLES:	**HITS 1**			**WEEKS 1**
PEACE AND JOY	*Ffreedom*	48	*14 Jan 95*	1
Originally featured a guitar sample from Lenny Kravitz's Are You Gonna Go My Way but clearance was denied.				

SOUNDSCAPE — UK

SINGLES:	**HITS 1**			**WEEKS 1**
DUBPLATE CULTURE	*Satellite*	61	*14 Feb 98*	1

SOUNDSOURCE — UK/Sweden

SINGLES:	**HITS 1**			**WEEKS 1**
TAKE ME UP	*ffrr*	62	*11 Jan 92*	1

SOUP DRAGONS — UK

SINGLES:	HITS 5			WEEKS 23
CAN'T TAKE NO MORE	*Raw TV Products*	65	*20 Jun 87*	1
SOFT AS YOUR FACE	*Raw TV Products*	66	*5 Sep 87*	2
I'M FREE *Originally recorded by the Rolling Stones.* *Above hit: SOUP DRAGONS featuring Junior REID.*	*Raw TV Products*	5	*14 Jul 90*	12
MOTHER UNIVERSE *Original release reached No. 94 earlier in the year.*	*Big Life*	26	*20 Oct 90*	5
DIVINE THING	*Big Life*	53	*11 Apr 92*	3
ALBUMS:	**HITS 3**			**WEEKS 17**
THIS IS OUR ART	*Siren*	60	*7 May 88*	1
LOVEGOD	*Raw TV Products*	60	*5 May 90*	1
LOVEGOD [RE] *Re-released with additional track.*	*Raw TV Products*	7	*18 Aug 90*	14
HOTWIRED	*Big Life*	74	*16 May 92*	1

SOURCE — UK

SINGLES:	HITS 3			WEEKS 22
YOU GOT THE LOVE *Original release reached No. 95 in 1986. Original vocal version of the song was by Jamie Principal and was called Your Love.* *Above hit: SOURCE featuring Candi STATON.*	*Truelove*	4	*2 Feb 91*	11
ROCK THE HOUSE *Above hit: SOURCE vocals by NICOLE.*	*React*	63	*26 Dec 92*	1
YOU GOT THE LOVE [RM] *Remixed by Now Voyager (AKA John Truelove).* *Above hit: SOURCE featuring Candi STATON.*	*React*	3	*1 Mar 97*	8
CLOUDS *Original recording was by Chaka Khan in 1980.*	*XL Recordings*	38	*23 Aug 97*	2

SOURMASH — UK

SINGLES:	HITS 1			WEEKS 1
PILGRIMAGE/MESCALITO	*Hooj Choons*	73	*23 Dec 00*	1

SOUTH — UK

SINGLES:	HITS 1			WEEKS 1
PAINT THE SILENCE	*Mo Wax*	69	*17 Mar 01*	1

Joe SOUTH — US

SINGLES:	HITS 1			WEEKS 11
GAMES PEOPLE PLAY	*Capitol*	6	*8 Mar 69*	11

SOUTH BANK ORCHESTRA conducted by Joseph MOROVITZ and Laurie HOLLOWAY — UK

ALBUMS:	HITS 1			WEEKS 6
LILLIE [OST-TV]	*Sounds*	47	*2 Dec 78*	6

SOUTH ST. PLAYER — US

SINGLES:	HITS 1			WEEKS 1
WHO KEEPS CHANGING YOUR MIND	*Cream*	49	*2 Sep 00*	1

Jeri SOUTHERN — US

SINGLES:	HITS 1			WEEKS 3
FIRE DOWN BELOW	*Brunswick*	22	*22 Jun 57*	3

SOUTHERN DEATH CULT - See CULT

SOUTHLANDERS — UK

SINGLES:	HITS 1			WEEKS 10
ALONE	*Decca*	17	*23 Nov 57*	10

SOUTHSIDE SPINNERS — Holland

SINGLES:	HITS 1			WEEKS 7
LUVSTRUCK *Original release on the Infusion label reached No. 85 on 17 Jul 99. From the film 'Kevin & Perry Go Large'.*	*AM:PM*	9	*27 May 00*	7

SOUVLAKI — UK

(See also Mark Summers.)

SINGLES:	HITS 2			WEEKS 4
INFERNO	*Wonderboy*	24	*15 Feb 97*	3
MY TIME	*Wonderboy*	63	*8 Aug 98*	1

SOVEREIGN COLLECTION — UK

SINGLES:	HITS 1			WEEKS 6
MOZART 40	*Capitol*	27	*3 Apr 71*	6

Red SOVINE — US

SINGLES:	HITS 1			WEEKS 8
TEDDY BEAR	*Starday*	4	*13 Jun 81*	8
Originally reached No. 40 in the US in 1976.				

SOX — UK

SINGLES:	HITS 1			WEEKS 1
GO FOR THE HEART	*Living Beat*	47	*15 Apr 95*	1
One of the contenders for Eurovision's A Song For Europe, it came 4th (out of 8).				

Bob B SOXX and the BLUE JEANS — US

SINGLES:	HITS 1			WEEKS 2
ZIP-A-DEE-DOO-DAH	*London*	45	*2 Feb 63*	2
Originally recorded by Johnny Mercer.				

SPACE — France

SINGLES:	HITS 1			WEEKS 12
MAGIC FLY	*Pye International*	2	*13 Aug 77*	12
ALBUMS:	**HITS 1**			**WEEKS 9**
MAGIC FLY	*Pye International*	11	*17 Sep 77*	9

SPACE — UK

(See also England United.)

SINGLES:	HITS 9			WEEKS 51
NEIGHBOURHOOD	*Gut*	56	*6 Apr 96*	1
FEMALE OF THE SPECIES	*Gut*	14	*8 Jun 96*	10
ME AND YOU VERSUS THE WORLD	*Gut*	9	*7 Sep 96*	6
NEIGHBOURHOOD [RI]	*Gut*	11	*2 Nov 96*	6
DARK CLOUDS	*Gut*	14	*22 Feb 97*	4
AVENGING ANGELS	*Gut*	6	*10 Jan 98*	8
THE BALLAD OF TOM JONES	*Gut*	4	*7 Mar 98*	8
Above hit: SPACE with CERYS of CATATONIA.				
BEGIN AGAIN	*Gut*	21	*4 Jul 98*	4
THE BAD DAYS [EP]	*Gut*	20	*5 Dec 98*	3
Lead track: Bad Days. The track on CD1, We Gotta Get Out Of This Place was featured in the Honda Accord car TV commercial				
DIARY OF A WIMP	*Gut*	49	*8 Jul 00*	1
ALBUMS:	**HITS 2**			**WEEKS 67**
SPIDERS	*Gut*	5	*28 Sep 96*	42
TIN PLANET	*Gut*	3	*21 Mar 98*	25

SPACE BROTHERS — UK

SINGLES:	HITS 4			WEEKS 19
SHINE	*Manifesto*	23	*17 May 97*	3
FORGIVEN (I FEEL YOU LOVE)	*Manifesto*	27	*13 Dec 97*	7
LEGACY [SHOW ME LOVE]	*Manifesto*	31	*10 Jul 99*	3
HEAVEN WILL COME	*Manifesto*	25	*9 Oct 99*	2
Vocals by Kate Cameron.				
SHINE 2000 [RM]	*Manifesto*	18	*5 Feb 00*	4
Remixed by Commie. Vocals by Joanna Law.				

SPACE KITTENS — UK

SINGLES:	HITS 1			WEEKS 1
STORM	*Hooj Choons*	58	*13 Apr 96*	1

SPACE MANOEUVRES — UK

SINGLES:	HITS 1			WEEKS 2
STAGE ONE	*Hooj Choons*	25	*29 Jan 00*	2

SPACE MONKEY — UK

SINGLES:	HITS 1			WEEKS 4
CAN'T STOP RUNNING	*Inner Vision*	53	*8 Oct 83*	4

SPACE RAIDERS — UK

SINGLES:	HITS 1			WEEKS 1
GLAM RAID	*Skint*	68	*28 Mar 98*	1
Samples Kenny's The Bump.				

SPACE 2000 — UK

SINGLES:	HITS 1			WEEKS 1
DO U WANNA FUNK?	*Wired*	50	*12 Aug 95*	1

SPACEBABY — UK

SINGLES:	HITS 1			WEEKS 1
FREE YOUR MIND	*Hooj Choons*	55	*8 Jul 95*	1

SPACECORN — Sweden

SINGLES:	HITS 1			WEEKS 1
AXEL F	*69*	74	*28 Apr 01*	1

SPACEDUST — UK

SINGLES:	HITS 2			WEEKS 12
GYM AND TONIC	*East West Dance*	1	*24 Oct 98*	8
Originally recorded by Bob Sinclar. Contains sample from Jane Fonda's Workout record.				
GYM AND TONIC [RE]	*East West*	55	*9 Jan 99*	2
LET'S GET DOWN	*East West*	20	*27 Mar 99*	2
Samples Chic's I Want Your Love. Vocals by Lisa Millet.				

SPACEHOG — UK

SINGLES:	HITS 2			WEEKS 8
IN THE MEANTIME	*Sire*	70	*11 May 96*	1
IN THE MEANTIME [RE]	*Sire*	29	*28 Dec 96*	6
CARRY ON	*Sire*	43	*7 Feb 98*	1
ALBUMS:	**HITS 1**			**WEEKS 2**
RESIDENT ALIEN	*Sire*	40	*15 Feb 97*	2

SPACEMAID — UK

SINGLES:	HITS 1			WEEKS 1
BABY COME ON	*Big Star*	70	*5 Apr 97*	1

SPACEMEN 3 — UK

ALBUMS:	HITS 1			WEEKS 1
RECURRING	*Fire*	46	*9 Mar 91*	1

SPAGHETTI SURFERS — UK

SINGLES:	HITS 1			WEEKS 1
MISIRLOU (THEME TO THE MOTION PICTURE 'PULP FICTION')	*Tempo*	55	*22 Jul 95*	1

SPAGNA — Italy

SINGLES:	HITS 3			WEEKS 23
CALL ME	*CBS*	2	*25 Jul 87*	12
EASY LADY	*CBS*	62	*17 Oct 87*	3
EVERY GIRL AND BOY	*CBS*	23	*20 Aug 88*	8

SPANDAU BALLET — UK

SINGLES:	HITS 20			WEEKS 159
TO CUT A LONG STORY SHORT	*Reformation*	5	*15 Nov 80*	11
THE FREEZE	*Reformation*	17	*24 Jan 81*	8
MUSCLE BOUND / GLOW	*Reformation*	10	*4 Apr 81*	10
CHANT NO.1 (I DON'T NEED THIS PRESSURE ON)	*Reformation*	3	*18 Jul 81*	10
Features backing from Beggar And Co.				
PAINT ME DOWN	*Reformation*	30	*14 Nov 81*	5
SHE LOVED LIKE DIAMOND	*Reformation*	49	*30 Jan 82*	4
INSTINCTION	*Reformation*	10	*10 Apr 82*	11
LIFELINE	*Reformation*	7	*2 Oct 82*	9
COMMUNICATION	*Reformation*	12	*12 Feb 83*	10
TRUE	*Reformation*	1	*23 Apr 83*	12
GOLD	*Reformation*	2	*13 Aug 83*	9
ONLY WHEN YOU LEAVE	*Reformation*	3	*9 Jun 84*	9
ONLY WHEN YOU LEAVE [RE]	*Reformation*	74	*18 Aug 84*	1
I'LL FLY FOR YOU	*Reformation*	9	*25 Aug 84*	9
HIGHLY STRUNG	*Reformation*	15	*20 Oct 84*	5
ROUND AND ROUND	*Reformation*	18	*8 Dec 84*	8
FIGHT FOR OURSELVES	*Reformation*	15	*26 Jul 86*	7
THROUGH THE BARRICADES	*Reformation*	6	*8 Nov 86*	10
HOW MANY LIES?	*Reformation*	34	*14 Feb 87*	4
RAW	*CBS*	47	*3 Sep 88*	3
BE FREE WITH YOUR LOVE	*CBS*	42	*26 Aug 89*	4
ALBUMS:	**HITS 9**			**WEEKS 271**
JOURNEY TO GLORY	*Reformation*	5	*14 Mar 81*	29

DIAMOND	*Reformation*	15	*20 Mar 82*	18
TRUE	*Reformation*	1	*12 Mar 83*	90
PARADE	*Reformation*	2	*7 Jul 84*	39
THE SINGLES COLLECTION	*Chrysalis*	3	*16 Nov 85*	50
THROUGH THE BARRICADES	*Reformation*	7	*29 Nov 86*	19
HEART LIKE A SKY	*CBS*	31	*30 Sep 89*	3
THE BEST OF SPANDAU BALLET	*Chrysalis*	44	*28 Sep 91*	3
GOLD - THE BEST OF SPANDAU BALLET	*Chrysalis*	7	*16 Sep 00*	17
THE SINGLES COLLECTION [RE]	*Chrysalis*	56	*28 Apr 01*	3

SPARKLE — US

SINGLES:	HITS 3			WEEKS 10
BE CAREFUL	*Jive*	7	*18 Jul 98*	6
Above hit: SPARKLE featuring R. KELLY.				
BE CAREFUL [RE]	*Jive*	75	*5 Sep 98*	1
TIME TO MOVE ON	*Jive*	40	*7 Nov 98*	2
LOVIN' YOU	*Jive*	65	*28 Aug 99*	1
Even though not listed, this was released as an [AA] with What About.				

ALBUMS:	HITS 1			WEEKS 1
SPARKLE	*Jive*	57	*1 Aug 98*	1

SPARKLEHORSE — US

SINGLES:	HITS 2			WEEKS 2
RAINMAKER	*Capitol*	61	*31 Aug 96*	1
SICK OF GOODBYES	*Parlophone*	57	*17 Oct 98*	1

ALBUMS:	HITS 3			WEEKS 4
VIVADIXIESUBMARINETRANSMISSIONPLOT	*Capitol*	58	*18 May 96*	1
GOOD MORNING SPIDER	*Parlophone*	30	*1 Aug 98*	2
IT'S A WONDERFUL LIFE	*Capitol*	49	*23 Jun 01*	1

SPARKS — US

SINGLES:	HITS 14			WEEKS 81
THIS TOWN AIN'T BIG ENOUGH FOR BOTH OF US	*Island*	2	*4 May 74*	10
AMATEUR HOUR	*Island*	7	*20 Jul 74*	9
NEVER TURN YOUR BACK ON MOTHER EARTH	*Island*	13	*19 Oct 74*	7
SOMETHING FOR THE GIRL WITH EVERYTHING	*Island*	17	*18 Jan 75*	7
GET IN THE SWING	*Island*	27	*19 Jul 75*	7
LOOKS, LOOKS, LOOKS	*Island*	26	*1 Oct 75*	4
THE NUMBER ONE SONG IN HEAVEN	*Virgin*	14	*21 Apr 79*	12
BEAT THE CLOCK	*Virgin*	10	*21 Jul 79*	9
TRYOUTS FOR THE HUMAN RACE	*Virgin*	45	*27 Oct 79*	5
WHEN DO I GET TO SING "MY WAY"	*Logic*	38	*29 Oct 94*	3
WHEN I KISS YOU (I HEAR CHARLIE PARKER PLAYING)	*Logic*	36	*11 Mar 95*	2
WHEN DO I GET TO SING "MY WAY" [RI]	*Logic*	32	*20 May 95*	2
NOW THAT I OWN THE BBC	*Logic*	60	*9 Mar 96*	1
THE NUMBER ONE SONG IN HEAVEN [RR]	*Roadrunner*	70	*25 Oct 97*	1
THIS TOWN AIN'T BIG ENOUGH FOR BOTH OF US [RR]	*Roadrunner*	40	*13 Dec 97*	2
Above hit: SPARKS vs. FAITH NO MORE.				

ALBUMS:	HITS 4			WEEKS 42
KIMONO MY HOUSE	*Island*	4	*1 Jun 74*	24
PROPAGANDA	*Island*	9	*23 Nov 74*	13
INDISCREET	*Island*	18	*18 Oct 75*	4
NUMBER ONE IN HEAVEN	*Virgin*	73	*8 Sep 79*	1

Bubba SPARXXX — US

SINGLES:	HITS 1			WEEKS 6
UGLY	*Interscope*	7	*24 Nov 01*	5

SPEAR OF DESTINY — UK

SINGLES:	HITS 10			WEEKS 43
THE WHEEL	*Epic*	59	*21 May 83*	5
PRISONER OF LOVE	*Epic*	59	*21 Jan 84*	3
LIBERATOR	*Epic*	67	*14 Apr 84*	2
ALL MY LOVE (ASK NOTHING)	*Epic*	61	*15 Jun 85*	3
COME BACK	*Epic*	55	*10 Aug 85*	3
STRANGERS IN OUR TOWN	*10 Records*	49	*7 Feb 87*	4
NEVER TAKE ME ALIVE	*10 Records*	14	*4 Apr 87*	11
WAS THAT YOU?	*10 Records*	55	*25 Jul 87*	4
THE TRAVELLER	*10 Records*	44	*3 Oct 87*	3
SO IN LOVE WITH YOU	*Virgin*	36	*24 Sep 88*	5

ALBUMS:	HITS 6			WEEKS 35
GRAPES OF WRATH	*Epic*	62	*23 Apr 83*	2
ONE EYED JACKS	*Epic*	22	*28 Apr 84*	7
WORLD SERVICE	*Epic*	11	*7 Sep 85*	7

OUTLAND	*10 Records*	16	*2 May 87*	13
S.O.D. THE EPIC YEARS *Compilation.*	*Epic*	53	*16 May 87*	3
THE PRICE YOU PAY	*Virgin*	37	*22 Oct 88*	3

SPEARHEAD — US

SINGLES:	HITS 4			WEEKS 5
OF COURSE YOU CAN	*Capitol*	74	*17 Dec 94*	1
HOLE IN THE BUCKET	*Capitol*	55	*22 Apr 95*	1
PEOPLE IN THA MIDDLE	*Capitol*	49	*15 Jul 95*	2
WHY OH WHY *Samples Isaac Hayes The End Theme (Tough Guys).*	*Capitol*	45	*15 Mar 97*	1

ALBUMS:	HITS 1			WEEKS 1
CHOCOLATE SUPA HIGHWAY	*Capitol*	68	*29 Mar 97*	1

Billie Jo SPEARS — US

SINGLES:	HITS 4			WEEKS 40
BLANKET ON THE GROUND	*United Artists*	6	*12 Jul 75*	13
WHAT I'VE GOT IN MIND	*United Artists*	4	*17 Jul 76*	13
SING ME AN OLD FASHIONED SONG	*United Artists*	34	*11 Dec 76*	9
I WILL SURVIVE	*United Artists*	47	*21 Jul 79*	5

ALBUMS:	HITS 3			WEEKS 28
WHAT I'VE GOT IN MIND	*United Artists*	47	*11 Sep 76*	2
THE BILLIE JO SPEARS SINGLES ALBUM	*United Artists*	7	*19 May 79*	17
COUNTRY GIRL	*Warwick*	17	*21 Nov 81*	9

Britney SPEARS — US

SINGLES:	HITS 9			WEEKS 114
... BABY ONE MORE TIME	*Jive*	1	*27 Feb 99*	22
SOMETIMES	*Jive*	3	*26 Jun 99*	16
(YOU DRIVE ME) CRAZY (THE STOP REMIX!) *From the film of the same name.*	*Jive*	5	*2 Oct 99*	11
BORN TO MAKE YOU HAPPY	*Jive*	1	*29 Jan 00*	12
OOPS! ... I DID IT AGAIN	*Jive*	1	*13 May 00*	14
LUCKY	*Jive*	5	*26 Aug 00*	11
STRONGER	*Jive*	7	*16 Dec 00*	10
DON'T LET ME BE THE LAST TO KNOW	*Jive*	12	*7 Apr 01*	8
I'M A SLAVE 4 U	*Jive*	4	*27 Oct 01*	10

ALBUMS:	HITS 3			WEEKS 131
... BABY ONE MORE TIME *Peak position reached on 05 Feb 00.*	*Jive*	2	*20 Mar 99*	81
OOPS! ... I DID IT AGAIN	*Jive*	2	*27 May 00*	43
BRITNEY	*Jive*	4	*17 Nov 01*	7

SPECIAL MC - See Mark 'Ruff' RYDER; Vocals by SPECIAL MC and HEIDI

SPECIALS — UK

(See also Various Artists (EPs) 'The 2 Tone EP'.)

SINGLES:	HITS 12			WEEKS 101
GANGSTERS *Tribute to the Prince Buster's 1965 ska recording Al Capone.* *Above hit: SPECIAL A.K.A.*	*2-Tone*	6	*28 Jul 79*	12
A MESSAGE TO YOU RUDY / NITE KLUB *A Message To You Rudy originally recorded by Dandy Livingstone.* *Above hit: SPECIALS featuring RICO +.*	*2-Tone*	10	*27 Oct 79*	14
THE SPECIAL A.K.A. LIVE! [EP] *Live recordings from the Lyceum, London on side 1 and Tiffany's, Coventry on side 2. Lead track: Too Much Too Young. Other tracks are covers of ska and reggae songs.* *Above hit: SPECIALS featuring RICO.*	*2-Tone*	1	*26 Jan 80*	10
RAT RACE / RUDE BUOYS OUTA JAIL'	*2-Tone*	5	*24 May 80*	9
STEREOTYPE / INTERNATIONAL JET SET	*2-Tone*	6	*20 Sep 80*	8
DO NOTHING / MAGGIE'S FARM *Maggie's Farm listed from 10 Jan 81.* *Above hit: SPECIALS featuring RICO with the ICE RINK STRING SOUNDS / SPECIALS*	*2-Tone*	4	*13 Dec 80*	11
GHOST TOWN	*2-Tone*	1	*20 Jun 81*	14
THE BOILER *Above hit: RHODA with the SPECIAL A.K.A.*	*2-Tone*	35	*23 Jan 82*	5
RACIST FRIEND / BRIGHT LIGHT	*2-Tone*	60	*3 Sep 83*	3
NELSON MANDELA *Nelson Mandela was imprisoned for treason in 1964. This song demanded his release.*	*2-Tone*	9	*17 Mar 84*	10
WHAT I LIKE MOST ABOUT YOU IS YOUR GIRLFRIEND *Above 3: SPECIAL AKA.*	*2-Tone*	51	*8 Sep 84*	4
HYPOCRITE *Originally recorded by Bob Marley in 1967.*	*Kuff*	66	*10 Feb 96*	1

ALBUMS:	HITS 4			WEEKS 82
SPECIALS	*2-Tone*	4	*3 Nov 79*	45
MORE SPECIALS	*2-Tone*	5	*4 Oct 80*	19
IN THE STUDIO	*2-Tone*	34	*23 Jun 84*	6
Above hit: SPECIAL AKA.				
THE SPECIALS SINGLES	*2-Tone*	10	*7 Sep 91*	9
SPECIALS [RI]	*Chrysalis*	22	*7 Jul 01*	3

Phil SPECTOR — US

ALBUMS:	HITS 3			WEEKS 29
PHIL SPECTOR'S CHRISTMAS ALBUM	*Apple*	21	*23 Dec 72*	3
PHIL SPECTOR'S ECHOES OF THE 60'S	*Phil Spector International*	21	*15 Oct 77*	10
PHIL SPECTOR'S CHRISTMAS ALBUM [RI-1ST]	*Phil Spector International*	96	*25 Dec 82*	2
PHIL SPECTOR'S GREATEST HITS / PHIL SPECTOR'S CHRISTMAS ALBUM [RI-2ND]	*Impression*	19	*10 Dec 83*	8
THE PHIL SPECTOR CHRISTMAS ALBUM [RI-3RD]	*Chrysalis*	69	*12 Dec 87*	6

Phil Spector is only the producer, all the above compilations are by various artists.

SPECTRUM — UK

SINGLES:	HITS 1			WEEKS 1
TRUE LOVE WILL FIND YOU IN THE END	*Silvertone*	70	*26 Sep 92*	1

Chris SPEDDING — UK

SINGLES:	HITS 1			WEEKS 8
MOTOR BIKIN'	*RAK*	14	*23 Aug 75*	8

SPEECH — US

SINGLES:	HITS 1			WEEKS 2
LIKE MARVIN GAYE SAID (WHAT'S GOING ON)	*Cooltempo*	35	*17 Feb 96*	2

SPEEDY — UK

SINGLES:	HITS 1			WEEKS 1
BOY WONDER	*Boiler House!*	56	*9 Nov 96*	1

SPEEDY J — Holland

ALBUMS:	HITS 1			WEEKS 1
GINGER	*Warp*	68	*10 Jul 93*	1

SPELLBOUND — India

SINGLES:	HITS 1			WEEKS 1
HEAVEN ON EARTH	*East West*	73	*31 May 97*	1

Johnny SPENCE and his Orchestra — UK

SINGLES:	HITS 1			WEEKS 15
THE DR. KILDARE THEME	*Parlophone*	15	*3 Mar 62*	15
Theme from the TV series.				

Don SPENCER — UK

SINGLES:	HITS 1			WEEKS 12
FIREBALL	*His Master's Voice*	32	*23 Mar 63*	11
Theme from the Gerry Anderson children's animated TV series 'Fireball XL5'.				
FIREBALL [RE]	*His Master's Voice*	49	*15 Jun 63*	1

Jon SPENCER BLUES EXPLOSION — US

SINGLES:	HITS 1			WEEKS 1
WAIL	*Mute*	66	*10 May 97*	1
ALBUMS:	**HITS 2**			**WEEKS 2**
NOW I GOT WORRY	*Mute*	50	*12 Oct 96*	1
ACME	*Mute*	72	*31 Oct 98*	1

Tracie SPENCER — US

SINGLES:	HITS 2			WEEKS 3
THIS HOUSE	*Capitol*	65	*4 May 91*	2
IT'S ALL ABOUT YOU (NOT ABOUT ME)	*Parlophone Rhythm Series*	65	*6 Nov 99*	1

SPHINX — UK/US

SINGLES:	HITS 1			WEEKS 2
WHAT HOPE HAVE I	*Champion*	43	*25 Mar 95*	2

SPICE GIRLS — UK

(See also England United.)

SINGLES:	HITS 10			WEEKS 179
WANNABE	*Virgin*	1	*20 Jul 96*	26
SAY YOU'LL BE THERE	*Virgin*	1	*26 Oct 96*	17
2 BECOME 1	*Virgin*	1	*28 Dec 96*	19
MAMA / WHO DO YOU THINK YOU ARE	*Virgin*	1	*15 Mar 97*	15
Charity record for Comic Relief's Red Nose day, 14 Mar 97.				
2 BECOME 1 [RE]	*Virgin*	54	*17 May 97*	4
SPICE UP YOUR LIFE	*Virgin*	1	*25 Oct 97*	15
TOO MUCH	*Virgin*	1	*27 Dec 97*	15
First act to have their first six releases top the chart.				
STOP	*Virgin*	2	*21 Mar 98*	15
STOP [RE]	*Virgin*	52	*11 Jul 98*	2
VIVA FOREVER	*Virgin*	1	*1 Aug 98*	13
GOODBYE	*Virgin*	1	*26 Dec 98*	21
HOLLER/LET LOVE LEAD THE WAY	*Virgin*	1	*4 Nov 00*	17
ALBUMS:	**HITS 3**			**WEEKS 135**
SPICE	*Virgin*	1	*16 Nov 96*	72
SPICEWORLD	*Virgin*	1	*15 Nov 97*	55
FOREVER	*Virgin*	2	*18 Nov 00*	8

SPIDER — UK

SINGLES:	HITS 2			WEEKS 5
WHY D'YA LIE TO ME	*RCA*	65	*5 Mar 83*	2
HERE WE GO ROCK 'N' ROLL	*A&M*	57	*10 Mar 84*	3
ALBUMS:	**HITS 2**			**WEEKS 2**
ROCK 'N' ROLL GYPSIES	*RCA*	75	*23 Oct 82*	1
ROUGH JUSTICE	*A&M*	96	*7 Apr 84*	1

SPIKEY TEE – See BOMB THE BASS

SPILLER; Lead vocals by Sophie ELLIS-BEXTOR — Italy/UK

SINGLES:	HITS 1			WEEKS 24
GROOVEJET (IF THIS AIN'T LOVE)	*Positiva*	1	*26 Aug 00*	24
Based on Love Is You by Carol Williams in 1977.				

SPIN CITY — UK/Ireland

SINGLES:	HITS 1			WEEKS 3
LANDSLIDE	*Glow Worm*	30	*26 Aug 00*	3

SPIN DOCTORS — US

SINGLES:	HITS 8			WEEKS 28
TWO PRINCES	*Epic*	3	*15 May 93*	15
LITTLE MISS CAN'T BE WRONG	*Epic*	23	*14 Aug 93*	5
Original release reached No. 80 earlier that year.				
JIMMY OLSEN'S BLUES	*Epic*	40	*9 Oct 93*	2
Jimmy Olsen was the photographer at the Daily Planet in 'Superman'.				
WHAT TIME IS IT?	*Epic*	56	*4 Dec 93*	1
CLEOPATRA'S CAT	*Epic*	29	*25 Jun 94*	2
YOU LET YOUR HEART GO TOO FAST	*Epic*	66	*30 Jul 94*	1
MARY JANE	*Epic*	55	*29 Oct 94*	1
SHE USED TO BE MINE	*Epic*	55	*8 Jun 96*	1
ALBUMS:	**HITS 2**			**WEEKS 57**
POCKET FULL OF KRYPTONITE	*Epic*	2	*20 Mar 93*	48
Re-released from 12 Feb 94 with additional track.				
TURN IT UPSIDE DOWN	*Epic*	3	*9 Jul 94*	9

SPINAL TAP — UK/US

SINGLES:	HITS 2			WEEKS 3
BITCH SCHOOL	*MCA*	35	*28 Mar 92*	2
THE MAJESTY OF ROCK	*MCA*	61	*2 May 92*	1
ALBUMS:	**HITS 1**			**WEEKS 2**
BREAK LIKE THE WIND	*MCA*	51	*11 Apr 92*	2

SPINNERS — UK

ALBUMS:	HITS 4			WEEKS 24
THE SPINNERS ARE IN TOWN	*Fontana*	40	*5 Sep 70*	5
SPINNERS LIVE PERFORMANCE	*Contour*	14	*7 Aug 71*	12
THE SWINGING CITY	*Philips*	20	*13 Nov 71*	3
LOVE IS TEASING	*Columbia*	33	*8 Apr 72*	4

SPINNERS – See DETROIT SPINNERS; RAPPIN' 4-TAY

SPIRAL TRIBE — UK

SINGLES:	HITS 2			WEEKS 2
BREACH THE PEACE	*Butterfly*	66	*29 Aug 92*	1
FORWARD THE REVOLUTION	*Butterfly*	70	*21 Nov 92*	1

SPIRIT — US

ALBUMS:	HITS 1			WEEKS 2
POTATO LAND	*Beggars Banquet*	40	*18 Apr 81*	2
Originally recorded in the early 1970s.				

SPIRITS — UK

SINGLES:	HITS 2			WEEKS 5
DON'T BRING ME DOWN	*MCA*	31	*19 Nov 94*	3
SPIRIT INSIDE	*MCA*	39	*8 Apr 95*	2

SPIRITUAL COWBOYS – See David A. STEWART

SPIRITUALIZED — UK

SINGLES:	HITS 10			WEEKS 16
ANYWAY THAT YOU WANT ME / STEP INTO THE BREEZE	*Dedicated*	75	*30 Jun 90*	1
RUN	*Dedicated*	59	*17 Aug 91*	1
MEDICATION	*Dedicated*	55	*25 Jul 92*	1
ELECTRIC MAINLINE [EP]	*Dedicated*	49	*23 Oct 93*	1
Lead track: Good Times.				
LET IT FLOW	*Dedicated*	30	*4 Feb 95*	2
Above hit: SPIRITUALIZED ELECTRIC MAINLINE.				
ELECTRICITY	*Dedicated*	32	*9 Aug 97*	2
I THINK I'M IN LOVE	*Dedicated*	27	*14 Feb 98*	2
THE ABBEY ROAD [EP]	*Deconstruction*	39	*6 Jun 98*	2
Lead track: Come Together.				
STOP YOUR CRYING	*Spaceman*	18	*15 Sep 01*	3
OUT OF SIGHT	*Spaceman*	65	*8 Dec 01*	1
ALBUMS:	**HITS 5**			**WEEKS 24**
LAZER GUIDED MELODIES	*Dedicated*	27	*11 Apr 92*	2
PURE PHASE	*Dedicated*	20	*18 Feb 95*	2
Features contributions from Michael Nyman's string section, the Balanescu Quartet.				
Above hit: SPIRITUALIZED ELECTRIC MAINLINE.				
LADIES & GENTLEMEN WE ARE FLOATING IN SPACE	*Dedicated*	4	*28 Jun 97*	15
CD comes foil wrapped in a pill box. A second CD format contains 12 × 3" CDs, one for each track.				
LIVE AT THE ROYAL ALBERT HALL	*Deconstruction*	38	*7 Nov 98*	1
Live recordings from London's Royal Albert Hall, 10 Oct 97.				
LET IT COME DOWN	*Spaceman*	3	*29 Sep 01*	4

SPIRO and WIX — UK

SINGLES:	HITS 1			WEEKS 2
TARA'S THEME	*EMI Premier*	29	*10 Aug 96*	2
Theme from the BBC's coverage of the 1996 Olympic Games.				

SPITTING IMAGE — UK

SINGLES:	HITS 2			WEEKS 18
THE CHICKEN SONG	*Virgin*	1	*10 May 86*	10
THE CHICKEN SONG [RE]	*Virgin*	67	*26 Jul 86*	1
SANTA CLAUS IS ON THE DOLE / 1ST ATHEIST TABERNACLE CHOIR	*Virgin*	22	*6 Dec 86*	7
ALBUMS:	**HITS 1**			**WEEKS 3**
SPIT IN YOUR EAR	*Virgin*	55	*18 Oct 86*	3

SPLINTER — UK

SINGLES:	HITS 1			WEEKS 10
COSTAFINE TOWN	*Dark Horse*	17	*2 Nov 74*	10
Features George Harrison on bass guitar.				

SPLIT ENZ — UK/New Zealand

SINGLES:	HITS 2			WEEKS 15
I GOT YOU	*A&M*	12	*16 Aug 80*	11
HISTORY NEVER REPEATS	*A&M*	63	*23 May 81*	4
ALBUMS:	**HITS 2**			**WEEKS 9**
TRUE COLOURS	*A&M*	42	*30 Aug 80*	8
TIME AND TIDE	*A&M*	71	*8 May 82*	1

A SPLIT SECOND — Italy/Belgium

SINGLES:	HITS 1			WEEKS 1
FLESH	*ffrr*	68	*14 Dec 91*	1

SPLODGENESSABOUNDS — UK

SINGLES:	HITS 3			WEEKS 17
SIMON TEMPLER / TWO PINTS OF LAGER AND A PACKET OF CRISPS PLEASE	*Deram*	7	*14 Jun 80*	8
TWO LITTLE BOYS / HORSE	*Deram*	26	*6 Sep 80*	7
Two Little Boys originally written in 1903 about the American Civil War.				
COWPUNK MEDLUM	*Deram*	69	*13 Jun 81*	2

SPOILED and ZIGO — Israel

SINGLES:	HITS 1			WEEKS 3
MORE & MORE	*Manifesto*	31	*12 Aug 00*	3

SPONGE — US

SINGLES:	HITS 1			WEEKS 1
PLOWED	*Columbia*	74	*19 Aug 95*	1

SPOOKS — US

SINGLES:	HITS 3			WEEKS 17
THINGS I'VE SEEN	*Epic*	6	*27 Jan 01*	10
KARMA HOTEL	*Epic*	15	*5 May 01*	6
SWEET REVENGE	*Epic*	67	*15 Sep 01*	1
ALBUMS:	**HITS 1**			**WEEKS 12**
S.I.O.S.O.S. VOLUME 1	*Epic*	25	*17 Feb 01*	12
Title is an acronym for Spooks Is On Some Other Shit.				

SPOOKY — UK

SINGLES:	HITS 1			WEEKS 1
SCHMOO	*Guerilla*	72	*13 Mar 93*	1
Backing vocals by Heather Sian Wildman.				

Fred SPOONS, E.P.N.S – See Peter SELLERS

SPORTY THIEVZ — US

SINGLES:	HITS 1			WEEKS 6
NO PIGEONS	*Columbia*	21	*10 Jul 99*	6
Answer record to TLC's No Scrubs. Samples Sporty Thievz's Cheapskate and TLC's No Scrubs.				

SPOTNICKS — Sweden

SINGLES:	HITS 4			WEEKS 37
ORANGE BLOSSOM SPECIAL	*Oriole*	29	*16 Jun 62*	10
THE ROCKET MAN	*Oriole*	38	*8 Sep 62*	9
HAVA NAGILA	*Oriole*	13	*2 Feb 63*	12
JUST LISTEN TO MY HEART	*Oriole*	36	*27 Apr 63*	6
EPS:	**HITS 1**			**WEEKS 27**
ON THE AIR	*Oriole*	2	*30 Mar 63*	27
ALBUMS:	**HITS 1**			**WEEKS 1**
OUT-A-SPACE	*Oriole*	20	*9 Feb 63*	1

Dusty SPRINGFIELD — UK

(See also Springfields.)

SINGLES:	HITS 26			WEEKS 211
I ONLY WANT TO BE WITH YOU	*Philips*	4	*23 Nov 63*	18
The first song played on BBC TV's 'Top Of The Pops', 1 Jan 64.				
STAY AWHILE	*Philips*	13	*22 Feb 64*	10
I JUST DON'T KNOW WHAT TO DO WITH MYSELF	*Philips*	3	*4 Jul 64*	12
Originally recorded by Tommy Hunt.				
LOSING YOU	*Philips*	9	*24 Oct 64*	13
YOUR HURTIN' KINDA LOVE	*Philips*	37	*20 Feb 65*	4
IN THE MIDDLE OF NOWHERE	*Philips*	8	*3 Jul 65*	10
SOME OF YOUR LOVIN'	*Philips*	8	*18 Sep 65*	12
Backing vocals by Madeleine Bell and Doris Troy.				
LITTLE BY LITTLE	*Philips*	17	*29 Jan 66*	9
YOU DON'T HAVE TO SAY YOU LOVE ME (IO CHE NO VIVO SENZA TE)	*Philips*	1	*2 Apr 66*	13
GOIN' BACK	*Philips*	10	*9 Jul 66*	10
ALL I SEE IS YOU	*Philips*	9	*17 Sep 66*	12
I'LL TRY ANYTHING	*Philips*	13	*25 Feb 67*	9
GIVE ME TIME	*Philips*	24	*27 May 67*	6
I CLOSE MY EYES AND COUNT TO TEN	*Philips*	4	*13 Jul 68*	12
SON-OF-A PREACHER MAN	*Philips*	9	*7 Dec 68*	9
AM I THE SAME GIRL	*Philips*	43	*20 Sep 69*	3
Originally recorded by Barbara Acklin.				
AM I THE SAME GIRL [RE]	*Philips*	46	*18 Oct 69*	1
HOW CAN I BE SURE	*Philips*	36	*19 Sep 70*	4

BABY BLUE	*Mercury*	61	*20 Oct 79*	5
WHAT HAVE I DONE TO DESERVE THIS?	*Parlophone*	2	*22 Aug 87*	9
Above hit: PET SHOP BOYS and Dusty SPRINGFIELD.				
NOTHING HAS BEEN PROVED	*Parlophone*	16	*25 Feb 89*	7
From the film 'Scandal'.				
IN PRIVATE	*Parlophone*	14	*2 Dec 89*	10
REPUTATION	*Parlophone*	38	*26 May 90*	6
Originally recorded by Brian Spence.				
ARRESTED BY YOU	*Parlophone*	70	*24 Nov 90*	2
HEART AND SOUL	*Columbia*	75	*30 Oct 93*	1
Above hit: Cilla BLACK and Dusty SPRINGFIELD.				
WHEREVER WOULD I BE	*Columbia*	44	*10 Jun 95*	3
Above hit: Dusty SPRINGFIELD and Daryl HALL.				
ROLL AWAY	*Columbia*	68	*4 Nov 95*	1

EPS:	**HITS 4**			**WEEKS 51**
I ONLY WANT TO BE WITH YOU	*Philips*	8	*28 Mar 64*	19
DUSTY	*Philips*	3	*19 Sep 64*	20
DUSTY IN NEW YORK	*Philips*	13	*8 May 65*	9
MADEMOISELLE DUSTY	*Philips*	17	*7 Aug 65*	3

ALBUMS:	**HITS 12**			**WEEKS 134**
A GIRL CALLED DUSTY	*Philips*	6	*25 Apr 64*	23
EVERYTHING'S COMING UP DUSTY	*Philips*	6	*23 Oct 65*	12
GOLDEN HITS	*Philips*	2	*22 Oct 66*	36
WHERE AM I GOING?	*Philips*	40	*11 Nov 67*	1
DUSTY . . . DEFINITELY	*Philips*	30	*21 Dec 68*	6
FROM DUSTY . . . WITH LOVE	*Philips*	35	*2 May 70*	2
IT BEGINS AGAIN	*Mercury*	41	*4 Mar 78*	2
DUSTY – THE SILVER COLLECTION	*Phonogram*	14	*30 Jan 88*	10
REPUTATION	*Parlophone*	18	*7 Jul 90*	6
GOIN' BACK – THE VERY BEST OF DUSTY SPRINGFIELD 1962–1994	*Philips*	5	*14 May 94*	11
This compilation includes her recordings with the Springfields and the Pet Shop Boys as well as her own solo material.				
A VERY FINE LOVE	*Columbia*	43	*8 Jul 95*	1
THE BEST OF DUSTY SPRINGFIELD	*Mercury/PolyGram TV*	19	*7 Nov 98*	24
From 27 Mar 99 label changed to Mercury/Universal Music TV.				

Rick SPRINGFIELD — US

SINGLES:	**HITS 2**			**WEEKS 13**
HUMAN TOUCH / SOULS	*RCA*	23	*14 Jan 84*	7
Souls listed from 11 Feb 84 once single had dropped to No. 24.				
JESSIE'S GIRL	*RCA*	43	*24 Mar 84*	6
Originally released in 1981 reaching No. 1 in the US.				

ALBUMS:	**HITS 3**			**WEEKS 8**
LIVING IN OZ	*RCA*	41	*11 Feb 84*	4
TAO	*RCA*	68	*25 May 85*	3
ROCK OF LIFE	*RCA*	80	*26 Mar 88*	1

SPRINGFIELDS — UK

(See also Dusty Springfield.)

SINGLES:	**HITS 5**			**WEEKS 66**
BREAKAWAY	*Philips*	31	*2 Sep 61*	8
BAMBINO	*Philips*	16	*18 Nov 61*	11
ISLAND OF DREAMS	*Philips*	5	*15 Dec 62*	26
SAY I WON'T BE THERE	*Philips*	5	*30 Mar 63*	15
COME ON HOME	*Philips*	31	*27 Jul 63*	6

Bruce SPRINGSTEEN — US

SINGLES:	**HITS 23**			**WEEKS 147**
HUNGRY HEART	*CBS*	44	*22 Nov 80*	4
Howard Kaylan and Mark Volman of the Turtles on backing vocals.				
THE RIVER	*CBS*	35	*13 Jun 81*	6
JOLE BLON	*EMI America*	51	*22 Aug 81*	3
Above hit: Gary U.S. BONDS with Bruce SPRINGSTEEN.				
DANCING IN THE DARK	*CBS*	28	*26 May 84*	7
COVER ME	*CBS*	38	*6 Oct 84*	5
DANCING IN THE DARK [RE]	*CBS*	4	*12 Jan 85*	16
COVER ME [RE]	*CBS*	16	*23 Mar 85*	8
I'M ON FIRE / BORN IN THE U.S.A.	*CBS*	5	*15 Jun 85*	12
GLORY DAYS	*CBS*	17	*3 Aug 85*	6
SANTA CLAUS IS COMIN' TO TOWN / MY HOMETOWN	*CBS*	9	*14 Dec 85*	5
Santa Claus Is Comin' To Town is a live recording from C.W. Post College, Greenvale, New York,12 Dec 75, and was originally recorded by George Hall in 1934.				
WAR	*CBS*	18	*29 Nov 86*	7
FIRE	*CBS*	54	*7 Feb 87*	2
Above 2: Bruce SPRINGSTEEN and the E STREET BAND.				
BORN TO RUN (LIVE)	*CBS*	16	*23 May 87*	4

BRILLIANT DISGUISE	*CBS*	20	*3 Oct 87*	5
TUNNEL OF LOVE	*CBS*	45	*12 Dec 87*	4
TOUGHER THAN THE REST	*CBS*	13	*18 Jun 88*	8
SPARE PARTS	*CBS*	32	*24 Sep 88*	3
HUMAN TOUCH	*Columbia*	11	*21 Mar 92*	5
BETTER DAYS	*Columbia*	34	*23 May 92*	3
57 CHANNELS (AND NOTHIN' ON)	*Columbia*	32	*25 Jul 92*	4
LEAP OF FAITH	*Columbia*	46	*24 Oct 92*	3
LUCKY TOWN (LIVE)	*Columbia*	48	*10 Apr 93*	3
Live recording for TV channel MTV.				
STREETS OF PHILADELPHIA	*Columbia*	2	*19 Mar 94*	12
From the film 'Philadelphia'.				
SECRET GARDEN	*Columbia*	44	*22 Apr 95*	3
HUNGRY HEART [RI]	*Columbia*	28	*11 Nov 95*	3
THE GHOST OF TOM JOAD	*Columbia*	26	*4 May 96*	2
Tom Joad is a character in the novel 'The Grapes Of Wrath' by John Steinbeck.				
SECRET GARDEN [RI]	*Columbia*	17	*19 Apr 97*	4
From the film 'Jerry Maguire'.				
ALBUMS:	**HITS 17**			**WEEKS 486**
BORN TO RUN	*CBS*	36	*1 Nov 75*	29
Includes re-entries through to 1985.				
DARKNESS ON THE EDGE OF TOWN	*CBS*	16	*17 Jun 78*	12
THE RIVER	*CBS*	2	*25 Oct 80*	88
Includes re-entries through to 1985.				
NEBRASKA	*CBS*	3	*2 Oct 82*	19
BORN IN THE U.S.A.	*CBS*	1	*16 Jun 84*	126
Peak position reached on 16 Feb 85.				
DARKNESS ON THE EDGE OF TOWN [RE]	*CBS*	24	*26 Jan 85*	28
Re-released with a new catalogue number.				
BORN TO RUN [RE]	*CBS*	17	*27 Apr 85*	21
GREETING FROM ASBURY PARK, N.J.	*CBS*	41	*15 Jun 85*	10
Originally released in 1973.				
THE WILD, THE INNOCENT AND THE E. STREET SHUFFLE	*CBS*	33	*15 Jun 85*	12
Originally released in 1973.				
LIVE/1975-1985	*CBS*	4	*22 Nov 86*	9
Boxed set of live recordings.				
Above hit: Bruce SPRINGSTEEN and the E STREET BAND.				
TUNNEL OF LOVE	*CBS*	1	*17 Oct 87*	33
HUMAN TOUCH	*Columbia*	1	*4 Apr 92*	17
LUCKY TOWN	*Columbia*	2	*4 Apr 92*	11
BORN IN THE U.S.A. [RI]	*Columbia*	41	*11 Jul 92*	2
IN CONCERT - MTV PLUGGED	*Columbia*	4	*24 Apr 93*	7
Live recordings for TV channel MTV.				
GREATEST HITS	*Columbia*	1	*11 Mar 95*	34
Includes re-entries through to 2001.				
THE GHOST OF TOM JOAD	*Columbia*	16	*25 Nov 95*	14
TRACKS	*Columbia*	50	*21 Nov 98*	1
4CD set.				
18 TRACKS	*Columbia*	23	*24 Apr 99*	7
Highlights from the 1998 boxed set Tracks.				
LIVE IN NEW YORK CITY	*Columbia*	12	*14 Apr 01*	6
Above hit: Bruce SPRINGSTEEN and the E STREET BAND.				

SPRINGWATER — UK

SINGLES:	**HITS 1**			**WEEKS 12**
I WILL RETURN	*Polydor*	5	*23 Oct 71*	12

SPRINKLER — UK/US

SINGLES:	**HITS 1**			**WEEKS 2**
LEAVE 'EM SOMETHING TO DESIRE	*Island*	45	*11 Jul 98*	2

SPURLING - See BELL & SPURLING

SPYRO GYRA — US

SINGLES:	**HITS 1**			**WEEKS 10**
MORNING DANCE	*Infinity*	17	*21 Jul 79*	10
ALBUMS:	**HITS 2**			**WEEKS 22**
MORNING DANCE	*Infinity*	11	*14 Jul 79*	16
CATCHING THE SUN	*MCA*	31	*23 Feb 80*	6

SQUADRONAIRES directed by Ronnie ALDRICH - See Joan REGAN

SQUEEZE — UK

SINGLES:	**HITS 21**			**WEEKS 123**
TAKE ME I'M YOURS	*A&M*	19	*8 Apr 78*	9
Was originally to be released on the BTM label in 1977 but it was withdrawn.				
BANG BANG	*A&M*	49	*10 Jun 78*	5

GOODBYE GIRL	*A&M*	63	*18 Nov 78*	2
COOL FOR CATS	*A&M*	2	*24 Mar 79*	11
UP THE JUNCTION	*A&M*	2	*2 Jun 79*	11
SLAP & TICKLE	*A&M*	24	*8 Sep 79*	8
ANOTHER NAIL IN MY HEART	*A&M*	17	*1 Mar 80*	9
PULLING MUSSELS (FROM THE SHELL)	*A&M*	44	*10 May 80*	6
IS THAT LOVE	*A&M*	35	*16 May 81*	8
TEMPTED	*A&M*	41	*25 Jul 81*	5
Lead vocals by Paul Carrack.				
LABELLED WITH LOVE	*A&M*	4	*10 Oct 81*	10
BLACK COFFEE IN BED	*A&M*	51	*24 Apr 82*	4
Features backing vocals from Elvis Costello and Paul Young.				
ANNIE GET YOUR GUN	*A&M*	43	*23 Oct 82*	4
LAST TIME FOREVER	*A&M*	45	*15 Jun 85*	5
HOURGLASS	*A&M*	16	*8 Aug 87*	10
TRUST ME TO OPEN MY MOUTH	*A&M*	72	*17 Oct 87*	1
COOL FOR CATS [RI]	*A&M*	62	*25 Apr 92*	2
Featured in the milk TV commercial.				
THIRD RAIL	*A&M*	39	*24 Jul 93*	3
SOME FANTASTIC PLACE	*A&M*	73	*11 Sep 93*	1
THIS SUMMER	*A&M*	36	*9 Sep 95*	3
ELECTRIC TRAINS	*A&M*	44	*18 Nov 95*	2
HEAVEN KNOWS	*A&M*	27	*15 Jun 96*	2
From the film 'Hackers'.				
THIS SUMMER [RM]	*A&M*	32	*24 Aug 96*	2
Remixed by Mark Stent.				

ALBUMS:	**HITS 13**			**WEEKS 124**
COOL FOR CATS	*A&M*	45	*28 Apr 79*	11
ARGY BARGY	*A&M*	32	*16 Feb 80*	15
EAST SIDE STORY	*A&M*	19	*23 May 81*	26
SWEETS FROM A STRANGER	*A&M*	20	*15 May 82*	7
SINGLES - 45'S AND UNDER	*A&M*	3	*6 Nov 82*	29
COSI FAN TUTTI FRUTTI	*A&M*	31	*7 Sep 85*	7
BABYLON AND ON	*A&M*	14	*19 Sep 87*	8
FRANK	*A&M*	58	*23 Sep 89*	1
A ROUND AND A BOUT	*I.R.S.*	50	*7 Apr 90*	1
PLAY	*Reprise*	41	*7 Sep 91*	1
GREATEST HITS	*A&M*	6	*23 May 92*	13
SOME FANTASTIC PLACE	*A&M*	26	*25 Sep 93*	4
RIDICULOUS	*A&M*	50	*25 Nov 95*	1

Billy SQUIER — US

SINGLES:	**HITS 1**			**WEEKS 3**
THE STROKE	*Capitol*	52	*3 Oct 81*	3

Chris SQUIRE — UK

ALBUMS:	**HITS 1**			**WEEKS 7**
FISH OUT OF WATER	*Atlantic*	25	*6 Dec 75*	7

Dorothy SQUIRES — UK

SINGLES:	**HITS 5**			**WEEKS 56**
I'M WALKING BEHIND YOU	*Polygon*	12	*6 Jun 53*	1
SAY IT WITH FLOWERS	*Columbia*	23	*26 Aug 61*	10
Above hit: Dorothy SQUIRES/Russ CONWAY with Tony OSBORNE and his Orchestra.				
FOR ONCE IN MY LIFE	*President*	24	*20 Sep 69*	10
FOR ONCE IN MY LIFE [RE]	*President*	48	*20 Dec 69*	1
TILL	*President*	25	*21 Feb 70*	10
TILL [RE]	*President*	48	*9 May 70*	1
MY WAY (COMME D'HABITUDE)	*President*	40	*8 Aug 70*	5
MY WAY (COMME D'HABITUDE) [RE-1ST]	*President*	34	*19 Sep 70*	8
MY WAY (COMME D'HABITUDE) [RE-2ND]	*President*	25	*28 Nov 70*	10

STABBS — US/Finland/Cameroon

SINGLES:	**HITS 1**			**WEEKS 1**
JOY AND HAPPINESS	*Hi-Life*	65	*24 Dec 94*	1

STACCATO — UK/Holland

SINGLES:	**HITS 1**			**WEEKS 1**
I WANNA KNOW	*Multiply*	65	*20 Jul 96*	1

Jim STAFFORD — US

SINGLES:	**HITS 2**			**WEEKS 16**
SPIDERS & SNAKES	*MGM*	14	*27 Apr 74*	8
Originally recorded by the Bellamy Brothers.				
MY GIRL BILL	*MGM*	20	*6 Jul 74*	8

Jo STAFFORD — US

SINGLES:	HITS 4			WEEKS 28
YOU BELONG TO ME	*Columbia*	1	*15 Nov 52*	19
Above hit: Jo STAFFORD with Paul WESTON and his Orchestra				
JAMBALAYA (ON THE BAYOU)	*Columbia*	11	*20 Dec 52*	2
Originally recorded by Hank Williams.				
Above hit: Jo STAFFORD with Paul WESTON and his Orchestra and the Norman LUBOFF CHOIR.				
MAKE LOVE TO ME!	*Philips*	8	*8 May 54*	1
Above hit: Jo STAFFORD with Paul WESTON and his Orchestra.				
SUDDENLY THERE'S A VALLEY	*Philips*	12	*10 Dec 55*	5
Above hit: Jo STAFFORD with Paul WESTON and his Orchestra and the Norman LUBOFF CHOIR.				
SUDDENLY THERE'S A VALLEY [RE]	*Philips*	19	*4 Feb 56*	1

Terry STAFFORD — US

SINGLES:	HITS 1			WEEKS 9
SUSPICION	*London*	31	*9 May 64*	9
Originally recorded by Elvis Presley in 1962.				

STAIFFI et Ses MUSTAFA'S — France

SINGLES:	HITS 1			WEEKS 1
MUSTAFA - CHA CHA ORIENTAL	*Pye International*	43	*30 Jul 60*	1

STAIND — US

SINGLES:	HITS 2			WEEKS 8
IT'S BEEN AWHILE	*Elektra*	15	*15 Sep 01*	6
OUTSIDE	*Elektra*	33	*1 Dec 01*	2
ALBUMS:	**HITS 1**			**WEEKS 18**
BREAK THE CYCLE	*East West*	1	*1 Sep 01*	18

STAKKA BO — Sweden

SINGLES:	HITS 2			WEEKS 12
HERE WE GO	*Polydor*	13	*25 Sep 93*	8
DOWN THE DRAIN	*Polydor*	64	*18 Dec 93*	4

Frank STALLONE — US

(See also Various Artists: Films - Original Soundtracks 'Rocky III'.)

SINGLES:	HITS 1			WEEKS 2
FAR FROM OVER	*RSO*	68	*22 Oct 83*	2
From the film 'Staying Alive'.				

STAMFORD BRIDGE — UK

SINGLES:	HITS 1			WEEKS 1
CHELSEA	*Penny Farthing*	47	*16 May 70*	1

STAN — UK

SINGLES:	HITS 1			WEEKS 3
SUNTAN	*Hug*	40	*31 Jul 93*	3

Chuck STANLEY – See Alyson WILLIAMS

Lisa STANSFIELD — UK

(See also George Michael; Queen.)

SINGLES:	HITS 18			WEEKS 115
PEOPLE HOLD ON	*Ahead Of Our Time*	11	*25 Mar 89*	9
Above hit: COLDCUT featuring Lisa STANSFIELD.				
THIS IS THE RIGHT TIME	*Arista*	13	*12 Aug 89*	8
ALL AROUND THE WORLD	*Arista*	1	*28 Oct 89*	14
LIVE TOGETHER	*Arista*	10	*10 Feb 90*	6
WHAT DID I DO TO YOU? [EP]	*Arista*	25	*12 May 90*	4
Lead track: What Did I Do To You?				
CHANGE	*Arista*	10	*19 Oct 91*	7
ALL WOMAN	*Arista*	20	*21 Dec 91*	8
TIME TO MAKE YOU MINE	*Arista*	14	*14 Mar 92*	8
SET YOUR LOVING FREE	*Arista*	28	*6 Jun 92*	4
SOMEDAY (I'M COMING BACK)	*Arista*	10	*19 Dec 92*	9
From the film 'The Bodyguard'.				
IN ALL THE RIGHT PLACES	*MCA*	8	*5 Jun 93*	11
From the film 'Indecent Proposal'.				
SO NATURAL	*Arista*	15	*23 Oct 93*	5
LITTLE BIT OF HEAVEN	*Arista*	32	*11 Dec 93*	4

PEOPLE HOLD ON (THE BOOTLEG MIXES) [RR]	*Arista*	4	*18 Jan 97*	6
Features same bassline as Armand Van Helden's mix of Tori Amos' Professional Widow.				
Above hit: Lisa STANSFIELD vs the DIRTY ROTTEN SCOUNDRELS.				
THE REAL THING	*Arista*	9	*22 Mar 97*	7
NEVER, NEVER GONNA GIVE YOU UP	*Arista*	25	*21 Jun 97*	3
THE LINE	*Arista*	64	*4 Oct 97*	1
LET'S JUST CALL IT LOVE	*Arista*	48	*23 Jun 01*	1
ALBUMS:	**HITS 5**			**WEEKS 116**
AFFECTION	*Arista*	2	*2 Dec 89*	31
REAL LOVE	*Arista*	3	*23 Nov 91*	51
SO NATURAL	*Arista*	6	*20 Nov 93*	14
LISA STANSFIELD	*Arista*	2	*5 Apr 97*	18
FACE UP	*Arista*	38	*7 Jul 01*	2

STANTON WARRIORS — UK

SINGLES:	**HITS 1**			**WEEKS 1**
DA ANTIDOTE	*Mob*	69	*22 Sep 01*	1

STAPLE SINGERS — US

SINGLES:	**HITS 2**			**WEEKS 14**
I'LL TAKE YOU THERE	*Stax*	30	*10 Jun 72*	8
IF YOU'RE READY (COME GO WITH ME)	*Stax*	34	*8 Jun 74*	6

Cyril STAPLETON and his Orchestra — UK

(See also David Whitfield.)

SINGLES:	**HITS 5**			**WEEKS 27**
ELEPHANT TANGO	*Decca*	20	*28 May 55*	2
ELEPHANT TANGO [RE-1ST]	*Decca*	20	*2 Jul 55*	1
ELEPHANT TANGO [RE-2ND]	*Decca*	19	*23 Jul 55*	1
BLUE STAR (THE "MEDIC" THEME)	*Decca*	2	*24 Sep 55*	12
Above hit: Cyril STAPLETON and his Orchestra featuring Julie DAWN.				
THE ITALIAN THEME	*Decca*	18	*7 Apr 56*	2
THE HAPPY WHISTLER	*Decca*	22	*2 Jun 56*	4
Above hit: Cyril STAPLETON and his Orchestra featuring Desmond LANE – The penny whistle boy.				
FORGOTTEN DREAMS	*Decca*	27	*20 Jul 57*	5

Robin STAPLETON – See Aled JONES

STAR SOUND — Holland

SINGLES:	**HITS 4**			**WEEKS 37**
STARS ON 45 [M]	*CBS*	2	*18 Apr 81*	14
Consists mainly of Beatles songs.				
STARS ON 45 VOLUME 2 [M]	*CBS*	2	*4 Jul 81*	10
Consists mainly of Abba songs.				
STARS ON 45 (3) [M]	*CBS*	17	*19 Sep 81*	6
Consists of instrumental intros.				
STARS ON STEVIE [M]	*CBS*	14	*27 Feb 82*	7
Consists of Stevie Wonder songs.				
ALBUMS:	**HITS 3**			**WEEKS 28**
STARS ON 45	*CBS*	1	*16 May 81*	21
Side one is a medley of Beatles songs. Side two features 2 medleys by Long Tall Ernie and the Shakers.				
STARS ON 45 VOLUME 2	*CBS*	18	*19 Sep 81*	6
STARS MEDLEY	*CBS*	94	*3 Apr 82*	1

STARDUST — Sweden

SINGLES:	**HITS 1**			**WEEKS 3**
ARIANA	*Satril*	42	*8 Oct 77*	3

STARDUST — France

SINGLES:	**HITS 1**			**WEEKS 26**
MUSIC SOUNDS BETTER WITH YOU	*Roule*	55	*1 Aug 98*	3
French import on 12" vinyl only.				
MUSIC SOUNDS BETTER WITH YOU	*Virgin*	2	*22 Aug 98*	23
Samples Chaka Khan's Fate.				

Alvin STARDUST — UK

(See also Shane Fenton and the Fentones.)

SINGLES:	**HITS 13**			**WEEKS 119**
MY COO CA CHOO	*Magnet*	2	*3 Nov 73*	21
Vocals by Peter Shelley.				
JEALOUS MIND	*Magnet*	1	*16 Feb 74*	11
RED DRESS	*Magnet*	7	*4 May 74*	8

YOU YOU YOU	*Magnet*	6	*31 Aug 74*	10
TELL ME WHY	*Magnet*	16	*30 Nov 74*	8
GOOD LOVE CAN NEVER DIE	*Magnet*	11	*1 Feb 75*	9
SWEET CHEATIN' RITA	*Magnet*	37	*12 Jul 75*	4
PRETEND	*Stiff*	4	*5 Sep 81*	10
A WONDERFUL TIME UP THERE *Originally recorded by Sister Rosetta Tharpe.*	*Stiff*	56	*21 Nov 81*	8
I FEEL LIKE BUDDY HOLLY	*Chrysalis*	7	*5 May 84*	11
I WON'T RUN AWAY	*Chrysalis*	7	*27 Oct 84*	13
SO NEAR TO CHRISTMAS	*Chrysalis*	29	*15 Dec 84*	4
GOT A LITTLE HEARTACHE	*Chrysalis*	55	*23 Mar 85*	2

ALBUMS:	HITS 3			WEEKS 17
THE UNTOUCHABLE	*Magnet*	4	*16 Mar 74*	12
ALVIN STARDUST	*Magnet*	37	*21 Dec 74*	3
ROCK WITH ALVIN	*Magnet*	52	*4 Oct 75*	2

STARFIGHTER

Belgium

SINGLES:	HITS 1			WEEKS 3
APACHE	*Sound Of Ministry*	31	*5 Feb 00*	3

STARGARD

US

SINGLES:	HITS 3			WEEKS 14
THEME SONG FROM "WHICH WAY IS UP" *Theme from the film.*	*MCA*	19	*28 Jan 78*	7
LOVE IS SO EASY	*MCA*	45	*15 Apr 78*	1
WHAT YOU WAITIN' FOR	*MCA*	39	*9 Sep 78*	6

STARGAZERS

UK

SINGLES:	HITS 9			WEEKS 68
BROKEN WINGS *Originally recorded by Art and Dotty Todd.*	*Decca*	11	*14 Feb 53*	1
BROKEN WINGS [RE]	*Decca*	1	*28 Feb 53*	11
I SEE THE MOON *Above hit: STARGAZERS with Syd DEAN and his Orchestra.* *Originally recorded by The Mariners.*	*Decca*	1	*20 Feb 54*	15
THE HAPPY WANDERER *Above hit: STARGAZERS with Syd DEAN and his Band.*	*Decca*	12	*10 Apr 54*	1
THE FINGER OF SUSPICION *Above hit: Dickie VALENTINE with the STARGAZERS.*	*Decca*	1	*18 Dec 54*	15
SOMEBODY *Above hit: STARGAZERS with Sonny FARRAR and his Banjo Band.*	*Decca*	20	*5 Mar 55*	1
THE CRAZY OTTO RAG	*Decca*	18	*4 Jun 55*	3
CLOSE THE DOOR *Above hit: STARGAZERS with Johnnie GRAY and the Band of the Day.* *Originally recorded by Jim Lowe.*	*Decca*	6	*10 Sep 55*	9
TWENTY TINY FINGERS *Above hit: STARGAZERS with Syd DEAN and his Band.*	*Decca*	4	*12 Nov 55*	11
HOT DIGGITY (DOG ZIGGITY BOOM) *Above hit: STARGAZERS with Johnnie GRAY and his Band of the Day.*	*Decca*	28	*23 Jun 56*	1

STARGAZERS

UK

SINGLES:	HITS 1			WEEKS 3
GROOVE BABY GROOVE [EP] *Lead track: Groove Baby Groove.*	*Epic*	56	*6 Feb 82*	3

Ed STARINK

US

ALBUMS:	HITS 2			WEEKS 11
SYNTHESIZER GREATEST	*Arcade*	22	*27 Oct 90*	5
SYNTHESIZER GOLD	*Arcada*	29	*9 Jan 93*	6

STARJETS

UK

SINGLES:	HITS 1			WEEKS 5
WAR STORIES	*Epic*	51	*8 Sep 79*	5

STARLAND VOCAL BAND

US

SINGLES:	HITS 1			WEEKS 10
AFTERNOON DELIGHT	*RCA Victor*	18	*7 Aug 76*	10

STARLIGHT

Italy

SINGLES:	HITS 1			WEEKS 11
NUMERO UNO	*Citybeat*	9	*19 Aug 89*	11

STARLITERS – See Joey DEE and the STARLITERS

STARPARTY — Holland

SINGLES:	HITS 1			WEEKS 2
I'M IN LOVE	*Incentive*	26	*26 Feb 00*	2
Samples Gwen Guthrie's Peanut Butter.				

Edwin STARR — US

SINGLES:	HITS 10			WEEKS 72
STOP HER ON SIGHT (SOS)	*Polydor*	35	*14 May 66*	8
HEADLINE NEWS	*Polydor*	39	*20 Aug 66*	3
STOP HER ON SIGHT (SOS) [RI] / HEADLINE NEWS [RI]	*Polydor*	11	*14 Dec 68*	11
Headline News no longer listed from 25 Jan 69. As an AA side it peaked at No. 16.				
25 MILES	*Tamla Motown*	36	*13 Sep 69*	6
WAR	*Tamla Motown*	3	*24 Oct 70*	12
Originally recorded by the Temptations.				
STOP THE WAR NOW	*Tamla Motown*	33	*20 Feb 71*	1
CONTACT	*20th Century*	6	*27 Jan 79*	12
H.A.P.P.Y. RADIO	*20th Century*	9	*26 May 79*	11
IT AIN'T FAIR	*Hippodrome*	56	*1 Jun 85*	4
WAR [RR]	*Weekend*	69	*30 Oct 93*	2
The instrumental version was used to accompany the ITV series 'Gladiators'. [AA] listed with Wild Thing by The Troggs and Wolf.				
Above hit: Edwin STARR and SHADOW.				
FUNKY MUSIC - SHO NUFF TURNS ME ON	*Echo*	23	*20 May 00*	2
Above hit: UTAH SAINTS Special guest vocal by Edwin STARR.				

Freddie STARR — UK

SINGLES:	HITS 2			WEEKS 14
IT'S YOU	*Tiffany*	9	*23 Feb 74*	10
WHITE CHRISTMAS	*Thunderbird*	41	*20 Dec 75*	4
Recorded as an impressionist of people from his TV show.				
ALBUMS:	**HITS 2**			**WEEKS 16**
AFTER THE LAUGHTER	*Dover*	10	*18 Nov 89*	9
THE WANDERER	*Dover*	33	*17 Nov 90*	7

Jennifer STARR - See PURE SUGAR vocals by Jennifer STARR

Kay STARR — US

SINGLES:	HITS 5			WEEKS 58
COMES A-LONG A-LOVE	*Capitol*	1	*6 Dec 52*	16
SIDE BY SIDE	*Capitol*	7	*25 Apr 53*	4
CHANGING PARTNERS	*Capitol*	4	*20 Mar 54*	14
AM I A TOY OR TREASURE	*Capitol*	17	*16 Oct 54*	3
AM I A TOY OR TREASURE [RE]	*Capitol*	20	*13 Nov 54*	1
ROCK AND ROLL WALTZ	*His Master's Voice*	1	*18 Feb 56*	20
Above hit: Kay STARR with Hugo WINTERHALTER'S ORCHESTRA and CHORUS.				
ALBUMS:	**HITS 1**			**WEEKS 1**
MOVIN'	*Capitol*	16	*26 Mar 60*	1

Ringo STARR — UK

SINGLES:	HITS 6			WEEKS 56
IT DON'T COME EASY	*Apple*	4	*17 Apr 71*	11
Features both George Harrison and Stephen Stills on guitar and Badfinger on backing vocals.				
BACK OFF BOOGALOO	*Apple*	2	*1 Apr 72*	10
PHOTOGRAPH	*Apple*	8	*27 Oct 73*	13
Features George Harrison on backing vocal and guitar.				
YOU'RE SIXTEEN	*Apple*	4	*23 Feb 74*	10
Features backing vocals from Harry Nilsson and Paul McCartney.				
ONLY YOU	*Apple*	28	*30 Nov 74*	11
WEIGHT OF THE WORLD	*Private Music*	74	*6 Jun 92*	1
ALBUMS:	**HITS 3**			**WEEKS 28**
SENTIMENTAL JOURNEY	*Apple*	7	*18 Apr 70*	6
RINGO	*Apple*	7	*8 Dec 73*	20
GOODNIGHT VIENNA	*Apple*	30	*7 Dec 74*	2

STARS ON 54: Ultra NATE, AMBER, Jocelyn ENRIQUEZ — US

SINGLES:	HITS 1			WEEKS 3
IF YOU COULD READ MY MIND	*Tommy Boy*	23	*28 Nov 98*	3

STARSAILOR — UK

SINGLES:	HITS 4			WEEKS 17
FEVER	*Chrysalis*	18	*17 Feb 01*	3
GOOD SOULS	*Chrysalis*	12	*5 May 01*	6
ALCOHOLIC	*Chrysalis*	10	*29 Sep 01*	6
LULLABY	*Chrysalis*	36	*22 Dec 01*	2

ALBUMS:	HITS 1			WEEKS 10
LOVE IS HERE	*Chrysalis*	2	*20 Oct 01*	10

STARSHIP — US

SINGLES:	HITS 4			WEEKS 41
JANE	*Grunt*	21	*26 Jan 80*	9
Above hit: JEFFERSON STARSHIP.				
WE BUILT THIS CITY	*RCA*	12	*16 Nov 85*	12
SARA	*RCA*	66	*8 Feb 86*	3
NOTHING'S GONNA STOP US NOW	*Grunt*	1	*11 Apr 87*	17
From the film 'Manniquin'.				

ALBUMS:	HITS 7			WEEKS 28
BLESS ITS POINTED LITTLE HEAD	*RCA Victor*	38	*28 Jun 69*	1
Live recordings.				
VOLUNTEERS	*RCA Victor*	34	*7 Mar 70*	7
BARK	*Grunt*	42	*2 Oct 71*	1
LONG JOHN SILVER	*Grunt*	30	*2 Sep 72*	1
Above 4: JEFFERSON AIRPLANE.				
SPITFIRE	*Grunt*	30	*31 Jul 76*	2
FREEDOM AT POINT ZERO	*Grunt*	22	*9 Feb 80*	11
Above 2: JEFFERSON STARSHIP.				
NO PROTECTION	*Grunt*	26	*18 Jul 87*	5

STARSHIP TROOPERS - See Sarah BRIGHTMAN

STARTRAX — UK

SINGLES:	HITS 1			WEEKS 8
STARTRAX CLUB DISCO [M]	*Picksy*	18	*1 Aug 81*	8
Consists of Bee Gees' songs.				

ALBUMS:	HITS 1			WEEKS 7
STARTRAX CLUB DISCO	*Picksy*	26	*1 Aug 81*	7

STARTURN ON 45 (PINTS) — UK

SINGLES:	HITS 2			WEEKS 9
STARTURN ON 45 (PINTS) [M]	*V Tone*	45	*24 Oct 81*	4
Parody of the influx of medleys charting during 1981.				
PUMP UP THE BITTER (BRUTAL MIX)	*Pacific*	12	*30 Apr 88*	5
Parody of M/A/R/R/S' Pump Up The Volume and Bomb The Bass' Beat Dis.				

STARVATION/TAM-TAM POUR L'ETHIOPIE — Multi-National

SINGLES:	HITS 1			WEEKS 6
STARVATION / TAM-TAM POUR L'ETHIOPIE	*Zarjazz*	33	*9 Mar 85*	6
Charity record in aid of African famine charities: Oxfam, War On Want and Medecins Sans Frontieres.				

STARVING SOULS — UK

SINGLES:	HITS 1			WEEKS 1
I BE THE PROPHET [EP]	*Durban Poison*	66	*21 Oct 95*	1
Lead track: I Be The Prophet, which features vocals by Terry Hall.				

STATE OF MIND — UK

SINGLES:	HITS 2			WEEKS 3
THIS IS IT	*Sound Of Ministry*	30	*18 Apr 98*	2
TAKE CONTROL	*Sound Of Ministry*	46	*25 Jul 98*	1

STATE OF THE HEART — UK

ALBUMS:	HITS 2			WEEKS 9
PURE SAX	*Virgin*	18	*16 Mar 96*	7
SAX AT THE MOVIES	*Virgin*	62	*12 Oct 96*	2

STATIC REVENGER — US

SINGLES:	HITS 1			WEEKS 3
HAPPY PEOPLE	*Incentive*	23	*7 Jul 01*	3

STATIC-X — US

SINGLES:	HITS 1			WEEKS 1
BLACK AND WHITE	*Warner Brothers*	65	*6 Oct 01*	1

ALBUMS:	HITS 1			WEEKS 2
MACHINE	*Warner Brothers*	56	*23 Jun 01*	2

STATLER BROTHERS — US

(See also Johnny Cash.)

SINGLES:	HITS 1			WEEKS 4
FLOWERS ON THE WALL	*CBS*	38	*26 Feb 66*	4

Candi STATON — US

SINGLES:	HITS 8			WEEKS 71
YOUNG HEARTS RUN FREE	*Warner Brothers*	2	*29 May 76*	13
DESTINY	*Warner Brothers*	41	*18 Sep 76*	3
NIGHTS ON BROADWAY	*Warner Brothers*	6	*23 Jul 77*	12
Original by the Bee Gees reached No. 7 in the US in 1975.				
HONESTLY I DO LOVE YOU	*Warner Brothers*	48	*3 Jun 78*	5
SUSPICIOUS MINDS	*Sugar Hill*	31	*24 Apr 82*	9
YOUNG HEARTS RUN FREE [RI]	*Warner Brothers*	47	*31 May 86*	5
YOU GOT THE LOVE	*Truelove*	4	*2 Feb 91*	11
Original release reached No. 95 in 1986. Original vocal version of the song was by Jamie Principal and was called Your Love.				
YOU GOT THE LOVE [RM]	*React*	3	*1 Mar 97*	8
Remixed by Now Voyager (AKA John Truelove).				
Above 2: SOURCE featuring Candi STATON.				
LOVE ON LOVE	*React*	27	*17 Apr 99*	3
YOUNG HEARTS RUN FREE [RR]	*React*	29	*7 Aug 99*	2

ALBUMS:	HITS 1			WEEKS 3
YOUNG HEARTS RUN FREE	*Warner Brothers*	34	*24 Jul 76*	3

STATUS IV — US

SINGLES:	HITS 1			WEEKS 3
YOU AIN'T REALLY DOWN	*TMT Productions*	56	*9 Jul 83*	3

STATUS QUO — UK

(See also Francis Rossi.)

SINGLES:	HITS 56			WEEKS 413
PICTURES OF MATCHSTICK MEN	*Pye*	7	*27 Jan 68*	12
ICE IN THE SUN	*Pye*	8	*24 Aug 68*	12
Written by Marty Wilde.				
ARE YOU GROWING TIRED OF MY LOVE	*Pye*	46	*31 May 69*	2
Originally recorded by Nancy Sinatra.				
ARE YOU GROWING TIRED OF MY LOVE [RE]	*Pye*	50	*21 Jun 69*	1
DOWN THE DUSTPIPE	*Pye*	12	*2 May 70*	17
IN MY CHAIR	*Pye*	21	*7 Nov 70*	14
PAPER PLANE	*Vertigo*	8	*13 Jan 73*	11
MEAN GIRL	*Pye*	20	*14 Apr 73*	11
CAROLINE	*Vertigo*	5	*8 Sep 73*	13
Originally written in 1970.				
BREAK THE RULES	*Vertigo*	8	*4 May 74*	8
DOWN DOWN	*Vertigo*	1	*7 Dec 74*	11
ROLL OVER LAY DOWN	*Vertigo*	9	*17 May 75*	8
RAIN	*Vertigo*	7	*14 Feb 76*	7
MYSTERY SONG	*Vertigo*	11	*10 Jul 76*	9
WILD SIDE OF LIFE	*Vertigo*	9	*11 Dec 76*	12
Originally recorded by Hank Thompson.				
ROCKIN' ALL OVER THE WORLD	*Vertigo*	3	*8 Oct 77*	16
Original by John Fogerty reached No. 27 in the US in 1975.				
AGAIN AND AGAIN	*Vertigo*	13	*2 Sep 78*	9
ACCIDENT PRONE	*Vertigo*	36	*25 Nov 78*	8
WHATEVER YOU WANT	*Vertigo*	4	*22 Sep 79*	9
LIVING ON AN ISLAND	*Vertigo*	16	*24 Nov 79*	10
WHAT YOU'RE PROPOSING	*Vertigo*	2	*11 Oct 80*	11
LIES / DON'T DRIVE MY CAR	*Vertigo*	11	*6 Dec 80*	10
Don't Drive My Car listed from 20 Dec 80.				
SOMETHING 'BOUT YOU BABY I LIKE	*Vertigo*	9	*28 Feb 81*	7
ROCK N' ROLL	*Vertigo*	8	*28 Nov 81*	11
DEAR JOHN	*Vertigo*	10	*27 Mar 82*	8
SHE DON'T FOOL ME	*Vertigo*	36	*12 Jun 82*	5
CAROLINE (LIVE AT THE N.E.C.) [RR]	*Vertigo*	13	*30 Oct 82*	7
OL' RAG BLUES	*Vertigo*	9	*10 Sep 83*	8
A MESS OF BLUES	*Vertigo*	15	*5 Nov 83*	6
MARGUERITA TIME	*Vertigo*	3	*10 Dec 83*	11
GOING DOWN TOWN TONIGHT	*Vertigo*	20	*19 May 84*	6
THE WANDERER	*Vertigo*	7	*27 Oct 84*	11
ROLLIN' HOME	*Vertigo*	9	*17 May 86*	6
RED SKY	*Vertigo*	19	*26 Jul 86*	8
IN THE ARMY NOW	*Vertigo*	2	*4 Oct 86*	14
Originally recorded by Bolland and Bolland.				

DREAMIN'	*Vertigo*	15	*6 Dec 86*	8
AIN'T COMPLAINING	*Vertigo*	19	*26 Mar 88*	6
WHO GETS THE LOVE?	*Vertigo*	34	*21 May 88*	4
RUNNING ALL OVER THE WORLD [RR]	*Vertigo*	17	*20 Aug 88*	6
Alternative wording to support the Sport Aid '88 charity. The worldwide run took place 11 Sep 88.				
BURNING BRIDGES (ON AND OFF AND ON AGAIN)	*Vertigo*	5	*3 Dec 88*	10
NOT AT ALL	*Vertigo*	50	*28 Oct 89*	2
THE ANNIVERSARY WALTZ - PART ONE [M]	*Vertigo*	2	*29 Sep 90*	9
THE ANNIVERSARY WALTZ (PART TWO) [M]	*Vertigo*	16	*15 Dec 90*	7
Above 2 medleys of rock 'n' roll classics were live recordings from Bray.				
CAN'T GIVE YOU MORE	*Vertigo*	37	*7 Sep 91*	3
ROCK 'TIL YOU DROP	*Vertigo*	38	*18 Jan 92*	3
ROADHOUSE MEDLEY (ANNIVERSARY WALTZ PART 25) [M]	*Polydor*	21	*10 Oct 92*	4
I DIDN'T MEAN IT	*Polydor*	21	*6 Aug 94*	4
SHERRI DON'T FAIL ME NOW!	*Polydor*	38	*22 Oct 94*	2
RESTLESS	*Polydor*	39	*3 Dec 94*	2
Originally recorded by Jennifer Warnes.				
WHEN YOU WALK IN THE ROOM	*PolyGram TV*	34	*4 Nov 95*	2
FUN FUN FUN	*PolyGram TV*	24	*2 Mar 96*	4
Above hit: STATUS QUO with the BEACH BOYS.				
DON'T STOP	*PolyGram TV*	35	*13 Apr 96*	2
ALL AROUND MY HAT	*PolyGram TV*	47	*9 Nov 96*	1
Above hit: STATUS QUO with Maddy PRIOR from STEELEYE SPAN.				
THE WAY IT GOES	*Eagle*	39	*20 Mar 99*	2
LITTLE WHITE LIES	*Eagle*	47	*12 Jun 99*	1
TWENTY WILD HORSES	*Eagle*	53	*2 Oct 99*	1
MONY MONY	*Universal Music TV*	48	*13 May 00*	1

ALBUMS:	**HITS 31**			**WEEKS 459**
PILEDRIVER	*Vertigo*	5	*20 Jan 73*	37
THE BEST OF STATUS QUO	*Pye*	32	*9 Jun 73*	7
HELLO	*Vertigo*	1	*6 Oct 73*	28
QUO	*Vertigo*	2	*18 May 74*	16
ON THE LEVEL	*Vertigo*	1	*1 Mar 75*	27
DOWN THE DUSTPIPE	*Golden Hour*	20	*8 Mar 75*	6
Material recorded for Pye records during 1970/71.				
BLUE FOR YOU	*Vertigo*	1	*20 Mar 76*	30
STATUS QUO - LIVE	*Vertigo*	3	*12 Mar 77*	14
ROCKIN' ALL OVER THE WORLD	*Vertigo*	5	*26 Nov 77*	15
IF YOU CAN'T STAND THE HEAT	*Vertigo*	3	*11 Nov 78*	14
WHATEVER YOU WANT	*Vertigo*	3	*20 Oct 79*	14
12 GOLD BARS	*Vertigo*	3	*22 Mar 80*	48
Compilation.				
JUST SUPPOSIN'	*Vertigo*	4	*25 Oct 80*	18
NEVER TOO LATE	*Vertigo*	2	*28 Mar 81*	13
FRESH QUOTA	PRT	74	*10 Oct 81*	1
Compilation of rarities from late 1960s/early 1970s.				
1982	*Vertigo*	1	*24 Apr 82*	20
"FROM THE MAKERS OF . . . "	*Vertigo*	4	*13 Nov 82*	18
Compilation which includes album of live recordings from the Birmingham N.E.C.				
BACK TO BACK	*Vertigo*	9	*3 Dec 83*	22
STATUS QUO LIVE AT THE N.E.C.	*Vertigo*	83	*4 Aug 84*	3
Dutch import.				
12 GOLD BARS VOLUME TWO - (AND ONE)	*Vertigo*	12	*1 Dec 84*	18
New compilation including the 1980 package.				
IN THE ARMY NOW	*Vertigo*	7	*6 Sep 86*	23
AIN'T COMPLAINING	*Vertigo*	12	*18 Jun 88*	5
PERFECT REMEDY	*Vertigo*	49	*2 Dec 89*	2
ROCKING ALL OVER THE YEARS	*Vertigo*	2	*20 Oct 90*	25
Compilation.				
ROCK 'TIL YOU DROP	*Vertigo*	10	*5 Oct 91*	7
LIVE ALIVE QUO	*Polydor*	37	*14 Nov 92*	1
THIRSTY WORK	*Polydor*	13	*3 Sep 94*	3
DON'T STOP - THE 30TH ANNIVERSARY ALBUM	*PolyGram TV*	2	*17 Feb 96*	11
Cover versions.				
WHATEVER YOU WANT - THE VERY BEST OF STATUS QUO	*Mercury TV*	13	*25 Oct 97*	6
UNDER THE INFLUENCE	*Eagle*	26	*10 Apr 99*	2
FAMOUS IN THE LAST CENTURY	*Universal Music TV*	19	*29 Apr 00*	5
Covers of rock'n'roll standards.				

STAXX — UK

SINGLES:	**HITS 2**			**WEEKS 11**
JOY	*Champion*	25	*2 Oct 93*	6
YOU	*Champion*	50	*20 May 95*	1
JOY [RM]	*Champion*	14	*13 Sep 97*	4
Remixed by Mondo.				

STEALERS WHEEL — UK

SINGLES:	HITS 3			WEEKS 22
STUCK IN THE MIDDLE	*A&M*	8	*26 May 73*	10
Some copies have title in full as Stuck In The Middle With You.				
EVERYTHING'L TURN OUT FINE	*A&M*	33	*1 Sep 73*	6
STAR	*A&M*	25	*26 Jan 74*	6

STEAM — US

SINGLES:	HITS 1			WEEKS 14
NA NA HEY HEY KISS HIM GOODBYE	*Fontana*	9	*31 Jan 70*	14

STEEL – See UNITONE ROCKERS featuring STEEL

Anthony STEEL with the RADIO REVELLERS and Jackie BROWN and his Music — UK

SINGLES:	HITS 1			WEEKS 6
WEST OF ZANZIBAR	*Polygon*	11	*11 Sep 54*	6

STEEL HORSES – See TRUMAN and WOLFF featuring STEEL HORSES

STEEL PULSE — UK

SINGLES:	HITS 3			WEEKS 12
KU KLUX KLAN	*Island*	41	*1 Apr 78*	4
PRODIGAL SON	*Island*	35	*8 Jul 78*	6
SOUND SYSTEM	*Island*	71	*23 Jun 79*	2
ALBUMS:	**HITS 2**			**WEEKS 18**
HANDSWORTH REVOLUTION	*Island*	9	*5 Aug 78*	12
TRIBUTE TO MARTYRS	*Island*	42	*14 Jul 79*	6

Tommy STEELE and the STEELMEN — UK

(See also All Star Hit Parade.)

SINGLES:	HITS 17			WEEKS 147
ROCK WITH THE CAVEMAN	*Decca*	13	*27 Oct 56*	4
ROCK WITH THE CAVEMAN [RE]	*Decca*	23	*1 Dec 56*	1
SINGING THE BLUES	*Decca*	1	*15 Dec 56*	13
KNEE DEEP IN THE BLUES	*Decca*	15	*16 Feb 57*	9
SINGING THE BLUES [RE-1ST]	*Decca*	24	*20 Apr 57*	1
BUTTERFINGERS	*Decca*	25	*4 May 57*	1
From the film 'The Tommy Steele Story'.				
BUTTERFINGERS [RE]	*Decca*	8	*18 May 57*	17
SINGING THE BLUES [RE-2ND]	*Decca*	29	*18 May 57*	1
WATER, WATER / A HANDFUL OF SONGS	*Decca*	5	*17 Aug 57*	16
A Handful Of Songs listed from 24 Aug 57. From the film 'The Tommy Steele Story'. A Handful Of Songs was also used as the theme to his TV show.				
SHIRALEE	*Decca*	11	*31 Aug 57*	4
From the film of the same name.				
HEY, YOU!	*Decca*	28	*23 Nov 57*	1
A HANDFUL OF SONGS / WATER, WATER [RE]	*Decca*	28	*14 Dec 57*	1
NAIROBI	*Decca*	3	*8 Mar 58*	11
Originally recorded by Bob Merrill.				
HAPPY GUITAR	*Decca*	20	*26 Apr 58*	5
From the film 'The Duke Wore Jeans'.				
THE ONLY MAN ON THE ISLAND	*Decca*	16	*19 Jul 58*	8
COME ON, LET'S GO	*Decca*	10	*15 Nov 58*	13
Original by Richie Valens reached No. 42 in the US.				
TALLAHASSEE LASSIE	*Decca*	16	*15 Aug 59*	4
GIVE! GIVE! GIVE!	*Decca*	28	*29 Aug 59*	2
Above 2 entries were separate sides of the same release, each had its own chart run.				
TALLAHASSEE LASSIE [RE]	*Decca*	25	*26 Sep 59*	1
LITTLE WHITE BULL	*Decca*	6	*5 Dec 59*	12
From the film 'Tommy The Toreador'.				
LITTLE WHITE BULL [RE]	*Decca*	30	*12 Mar 60*	5
WHAT A MOUTH (WHAT A NORTH AND SOUTH)	*Decca*	5	*25 Jun 60*	11
MUST BE SANTA	*Decca*	40	*31 Dec 60*	1
THE WRITING ON THE WALL	*Decca*	30	*19 Aug 61*	5
Original by Adam Wade reached No. 5 in the US in 1961.				
Above 9: Tommy STEELE.				
EPS:	**HITS 1**			**WEEKS 14**
TOMMY THE TOREADOR [OST]	*Decca*	4	*12 Mar 60*	14
Above hit: Tommy STEELE.				

STEELEYE SPAN — UK

SINGLES:	HITS 2			WEEKS 18
GAUDETE	*Chrysalis*	14	*8 Dec 73*	9
Originally released in 1972.				
ALL AROUND MY HAT	*Chrysalis*	5	*15 Nov 75*	9

ALBUMS:	HITS 7			WEEKS 48
PLEASE TO SEE THE KING	*B&C*	45	*10 Apr 71*	2
BELOW THE SALT	*Chrysalis*	43	*14 Oct 72*	1
PARCEL OF ROGUES	*Chrysalis*	26	*28 Apr 73*	5
NOW WE ARE SIX	*Chrysalis*	13	*23 Mar 74*	13
COMMONER'S CROWN	*Chrysalis*	21	*15 Feb 75*	4
ALL AROUND MY HAT	*Chrysalis*	7	*25 Oct 75*	20
ROCKET COTTAGE	*Chrysalis*	41	*16 Oct 76*	3

STEELY DAN — US

SINGLES:	HITS 4			WEEKS 21
DO IT AGAIN	*ABC*	39	*30 Aug 75*	4
HAITIAN DIVORCE	*ABC*	17	*11 Dec 76*	9
FM (NO STATIC AT ALL)	*MCA*	49	*29 Jul 78*	4
From the film 'FM'.				
FM (NO STATIC AT ALL) [RE]	*MCA*	75	*2 Sep 78*	1
RIKKI DON'T LOSE THAT NUMBER	*ABC*	58	*10 Mar 79*	3
ALBUMS:	**HITS 13**			**WEEKS 88**
PRETZEL LOGIC	*Probe*	37	*30 Mar 74*	2
KATY LIED	*ABC*	13	*3 May 75*	6
CAN'T BUY A THRILL	*ABC*	38	*20 Sep 75*	1
Originally released in 1973.				
ROYAL SCAM	*ABC*	11	*22 May 76*	13
AJA	*ABC*	5	*8 Oct 77*	10
GREATEST HITS	*ABC*	41	*2 Dec 78*	18
GAUCHO	*MCA*	27	*29 Nov 80*	12
GOLD	*MCA*	44	*3 Jul 82*	6
Compilation.				
REELIN' IN THE YEARS - VERY BEST OF STEELY DAN	*MCA*	43	*26 Oct 85*	5
DO IT AGAIN - THE VERY BEST OF STEELY DAN	*Telstar*	64	*10 Oct 87*	4
REMASTERED - THE BEST OF STEELY DAN	*MCA*	42	*20 Nov 93*	5
ALIVE IN AMERICA	*Giant*	62	*28 Oct 95*	1
Live recordings from their 1993/94 tour.				
TWO AGAINST NATURE	*Giant*	11	*11 Mar 00*	5

Wout STEENHUIS — Holland

ALBUMS:	HITS 1			WEEKS 7
HAWAIIAN PARADISE/CHRISTMAS	*Warwick*	28	*21 Nov 81*	7

Gwen STEFANI - See EVE

Jim STEINMAN — US

SINGLES:	HITS 2			WEEKS 9
ROCK AND ROLL DREAMS COME THROUGH	*Epic*	52	*4 Jul 81*	7
Features vocals by Rory Dodd.				
TONIGHT IS WHAT IT MEANS TO BE YOUNG	*MCA*	67	*23 Jun 84*	2
Above hit: Jim STEINMAN and FIRE INC.				
ALBUMS:	**HITS 1**			**WEEKS 25**
BAD FOR GOOD	*Epic*	7	*9 May 81*	25

STEINSKI and MASS MEDIA — US

SINGLES:	HITS 1			WEEKS 2
WE'LL BE RIGHT BACK	*Fourth & Broadway*	63	*31 Jan 87*	2

STELLA BROWNE — UK

SINGLES:	HITS 1			WEEKS 1
EVERY WOMAN NEEDS LOVE	*Perfecto*	55	*20 May 00*	1

Doreen STEPHENS - See Billy COTTON and his BAND

Richie STEPHENS featuring GENERAL DEGREE — Jamaica

SINGLES:	HITS 2			WEEKS 2
LEGACY	*Columbia*	64	*15 May 93*	1
Above hit: MAD COBRA featuring Richie STEPHENS.				
COME GIVE ME YOUR LOVE	*Delirious*	61	*9 Aug 97*	1
Features Sly and Robbie's Taxi Gang.				

Martin STEPHENSON and the DAINTEES — UK

SINGLES:	HITS 3			WEEKS 7
BOAT TO BOLIVIA	*Kitchenware*	70	*8 Nov 86*	2
TROUBLE TOWN	*Kitchenware*	58	*17 Jan 87*	3
Above hit: DAINTEES.				
BIG SKY NEW LIGHT	*Kitchenware*	71	*27 Jun 92*	2

ALBUMS:	HITS 4			WEEKS 11
BOAT TO BOLIVIA	*Kitchenware*	85	*17 May 86*	3
GLADSOME, HUMOUR AND BLUE	*Kitchenware*	39	*16 Apr 88*	4
SALUTATION ROAD	*Kitchenware*	35	*19 May 90*	3
THE BOY'S HEART	*Kitchenware*	68	*25 Jul 92*	1

STEPPENWOLF — US/Canada

SINGLES:	HITS 1			WEEKS 14
BORN TO BE WILD	*Stateside*	30	*14 Jun 69*	7
Originally released in 1968. From the film 'Easy Rider'.				
BORN TO BE WILD [RE]	*Stateside*	50	*9 Aug 69*	2
BORN TO BE WILD [RI]	*Universal*	18	*27 Feb 99*	5
Featured in the Ford Cougar TV commercial.				
ALBUMS:	**HITS 3**			**WEEKS 20**
MONSTER	*Stateside*	43	*28 Feb 70*	4
STEPPENWOLF	*Stateside*	59	*25 Apr 70*	2
Originally released in 1968.				
STEPPENWOLF LIVE	*Stateside*	16	*4 Jul 70*	14

STEPS — UK

(See also Steps Tina Cousins Cleopatra B*Witched Billie.)

SINGLES:	HITS 15			WEEKS 196
5,6,7,8	*Jive*	14	*22 Nov 97*	17
LAST THING ON MY MIND	*Jive*	6	*2 May 98*	14
Originally recorded by Bananarama.				
ONE FOR SORROW	*Jive*	2	*5 Sep 98*	11
HEARTBEAT / TRAGEDY	*Jive*	1	*21 Nov 98*	30
BETTER BEST FORGOTTEN	*Jive*	2	*20 Mar 99*	15
BETTER BEST FORGOTTEN [RE]	*Jive*	49	*10 Jul 99*	2
LOVE'S GOT A HOLD ON MY HEART	*Jive*	2	*24 Jul 99*	11
AFTER THE LOVE HAS GONE	*Jive*	5	*23 Oct 99*	9
LOVE'S GOT A HOLD ON MY HEART [RE]	*Jive*	73	*23 Oct 99*	1
SAY YOU'LL BE MINE/BETTER THE DEVIL YOU KNOW	*Jive*	4	*25 Dec 99*	17
AFTER THE LOVE HAS GONE [RE]	*Jive*	60	*1 Jan 00*	2
DEEPER SHADE OF BLUE	*Jive*	4	*15 Apr 00*	9
Originally recorded in 1998 by Tina Cousins.				
WHEN I SAID GOODBYE/SUMMER OF LOVE	*Jive*	5	*15 Jul 00*	11
STOMP	*Jive*	1	*28 Oct 00*	11
THE WAY YOU MAKE ME FEEL/TOO BUSY THINKING ABOUT MY BABY	*Jive*	2	*6 Jan 01*	11
HERE AND NOW/YOU'LL BE SORRY	*Jive*	4	*16 Jun 01*	10
CHAIN REACTION/ONE FOR SORROW [RM]	*Jive*	2	*6 Oct 01*	12
WORDS ARE NOT ENOUGH/I KNOW HIM SO WELL	*Jive*	5	*15 Dec 01*	3
ALBUMS:	**HITS 4**			**WEEKS 160**
STEP ONE	*Jive*	2	*26 Sept 98*	62
STEPTACULAR	*Jive*	1	*6 Nov 99*	62
BUZZ	*Jive*	4	*11 Nov 00*	26
GOLD - THE GREATEST HITS	*Jive*	1	*27 Oct 01*	10

STEPS Tina COUSINS CLEOPATRA B*WITCHED BILLIE — UK/Ireland

(See also B*Witched; Billie; Cleopatra; Tina Cousins; Steps.)

SINGLES:	HITS 1			WEEKS 13
THANK ABBA FOR THE MUSIC [M]	*Epic*	4	*10 Apr 99*	13
Charity record in aid of the BRIT trust.				

STEPZ – See QUARTZ

STEREO MC'S — UK

SINGLES:	HITS 8			WEEKS 37
ELEVATE MY MIND	*Fourth & Broadway*	74	*29 Sep 90*	1
LOST IN MUSIC	*Fourth & Broadway*	46	*9 Mar 91*	3
CONNECTED	*Fourth & Broadway*	18	*26 Sep 92*	6
Samples Jimmy "Bo" Horne's Let Me (Let Me Be Your Lover). Featured in the Carphone warehouse Radio commercials.				
STEP IT UP	*Fourth & Broadway*	12	*5 Dec 92*	12
GROUND LEVEL	*Fourth & Broadway*	19	*20 Feb 93*	5
CREATION	*Fourth & Broadway*	19	*29 May 93*	4
DEEP DOWN & DIRTY	*Island*	17	*26 May 01*	4
DEEP DOWN & DIRTY [RE]	*Island*	62	*30 Jun 01*	1
WE BELONG IN THIS WORLD TOGETHER	*Island*	59	*1 Sep 01*	1
ALBUMS:	**HITS 2**			**WEEKS 55**
CONNECTED	*Fourth & Broadway*	2	*17 Oct 92*	52
DEEP DOWN & DIRTY	*Island*	17	*9 Jun 01*	3

STEREO NATION — UK

SINGLES:	HITS 2			WEEKS 3
I'VE BEEN WAITING	*EMI Premier*	53	*17 Aug 96*	1
LAILA	*Wizard*	44	*27 Oct 01*	2
Above hit: TAZ/STEREO NATION.				

STEREOLAB — UK/France

SINGLES:	HITS 5			WEEKS 6
JENNY ONDIOLINE / FRENCH DISKO	*Duophonic Ultra High Frequency*	75	*8 Jan 94*	1
Originally released in 1993.				
PING PONG	*Duophonic Ultra High Frequency*	45	*30 Jul 94*	2
WOW AND FLUTTER	*Duophonic Ultra High Frequency*	70	*12 Nov 94*	1
CYBELE'S REVERIE	*Duophonic Ultra High Frequency*	62	*2 Mar 96*	1
MISS MODULAR	*Duophonic Ultra High Frequency*	60	*13 Sep 97*	1
ALBUMS:	**HITS 6**			**WEEKS 11**
TRANSIENT RANDOM NOISE BURSTS	*Duophonic Ultra High Frequency*	62	*18 Sep 93*	1
MARS AUDIAC QUINTET	*Duophonic Ultra High Frequency*	16	*20 Aug 94*	3
MUSIC FOR AMORPHOUS BODY STUDY CENTRE	*Duophonic Ultra High Frequency*	59	*29 Apr 95*	1
Music set to accompany sculptor Charle's Long's exhibition in New York.				
REFRIED ECTOPLASM (SWITCHED ON - VOLUME 2)	*Duophonic Ultra High Frequency*	30	*16 Sep 95*	2
Collection of early limited edition singles.				
EMPEROR TOMATO KETCHUP	*Duophonic Ultra High Frequency*	27	*30 Mar 96*	2
DOTS AND LOOPS	*Duophonic Ultra High Frequency*	19	*4 Oct 97*	2

STEREOPHONICS — UK

SINGLES:	HITS 14			WEEKS 94
LOCAL BOY IN THE PHOTOGRAPH	*V2*	51	*29 Mar 97*	1
MORE LIFE IN A TRAMPS VEST	*V2*	33	*31 May 97*	2
A THOUSAND TREES	*V2*	22	*23 Aug 97*	3
TRAFFIC	*V2*	20	*8 Nov 97*	3
LOCAL BOY IN THE PHOTOGRAPH [RI]	*V2*	14	*21 Feb 98*	4
THE BARTENDER AND THE THIEF	*V2*	3	*21 Nov 98*	12
JUST LOOKING	*V2*	4	*6 Mar 99*	8
PICK A PART THAT'S NEW	*V2*	4	*15 May 99*	9
JUST LOOKING [RE]	*V2*	73	*29 May 99*	1
I WOULDN'T BELIEVE YOUR RADIO	*V2*	11	*4 Sept 99*	6
I WOULDN'T BELIEVE YOUR RADIO [RE]	*V2*	71	*30 Oct 99*	1
HURRY UP AND WAIT	*V2*	11	*20 Nov 99*	5
HURRY UP AND WAIT [RE]	*V2*	53	*1 Jan 00*	3
MAMA TOLD ME NOT TO COME	*Gut*	4	*18 Mar 00*	7
Written and originally recorded by Randy Newman.				
Above hit: Tom JONES and STEREOPHONICS.				
MR. WRITER	*V2*	5	*31 Mar 01*	12
HAVE A NICE DAY	*V2*	5	*23 Jun 01*	9
STEP ON MY OLD SIZE NINES	*V2*	16	*6 Oct 01*	5
HANDBAGS AND GLADRAGS	*V2*	4	*15 Dec 01*	3
Originally recorded by Mike D'Abo.				
ALBUMS:	**HITS 3**			**WEEKS 245**
WORD GETS AROUND	*V2*	6	*6 Sep 97*	116
PERFORMANCE AND COCKTAILS	*V2*	1	*20 Mar 99*	93
JUST ENOUGH EDUCATION TO PERFORM	*V2*	1	*21 Apr 01*	32
JUST ENOUGH EDUCATION TO PERFORM [RE]	*V2*	14	*8 Dec 01*	4
Repackaged with additional track.				

STETSASONIC — US

SINGLES:	HITS 1			WEEKS 3
TALKIN' ALL THAT JAZZ	*Breakout*	73	*24 Sep 88*	2
Samples Donald Byrd's Dominoes and Banbarra's Shack Up.				
TALKIN ALL THAT JAZZ [RM]	*Tommy Boy*	54	*7 Nov 98*	1
Remixed by Dimiti From Paris.				

STEVE and EYDIE - See Eydie GORME; Steve LAWRENCE

April STEVENS - See Nino TEMPO and April STEVENS

Cat STEVENS — UK

SINGLES:	HITS 11			WEEKS 96
I LOVE MY DOG	*Deram*	28	*22 Oct 66*	7
MATTHEW AND SON	*Deram*	2	*14 Jan 67*	10
I'M GONNA GET ME A GUN	*Deram*	6	*1 Apr 67*	10
A BAD NIGHT	*Deram*	20	*5 Aug 67*	8
KITTY	*Deram*	47	*23 Dec 67*	1
LADY D'ARBANVILLE	*Island*	8	*27 Jun 70*	13
Dedicated to his ex-girlfriend Patti D'Arbanville. Flute by Peter Gabriel.				
MOON SHADOW	*Island*	22	*28 Aug 71*	11

MORNING HAS BROKEN	*Island*	9	*1 Jan 72*	13
His version of Eleanor Fareon's children's hymn featuring Rick Wakeman on piano.				
CAN'T KEEP IT IN	*Island*	13	*9 Dec 72*	12
ANOTHER SATURDAY NIGHT	*Island*	19	*24 Aug 74*	8
(REMEMBER THE DAYS OF THE) OLD SCHOOL YARD	*Island*	44	*2 Jul 77*	3
Features backing vocals by Elkie Brooks.				

ALBUMS:	**HITS 11**			**WEEKS 265**
MATTHEW AND SON	*Deram*	7	*25 Mar 67*	16
MONA BONE JAKON	*Island*	63	*11 Jul 70*	4
TEA FOR THE TILLERMAN	*Island*	20	*28 Nov 70*	39
TEASER AND THE FIRECAT	*Island*	3	*2 Oct 71*	93
CATCH BULL AT FOUR	*Island*	2	*7 Oct 72*	27
FOREIGNER	*Island*	3	*21 Jul 73*	10
BUDDAH AND THE CHOCOLATE BOX	*Island*	3	*6 Apr 74*	15
GREATEST HITS	*Island*	2	*19 Jul 75*	24
IZITSO	*Island*	18	*14 May 77*	15
THE VERY BEST OF CAT STEVENS	*Island*	4	*3 Feb 90*	16
REMEMBER CAT STEVENS - THE ULTIMATE COLLECTION	*Island*	31	*27 Nov 99*	6

Connie STEVENS — US

SINGLES:	**HITS 2**			**WEEKS 20**
SIXTEEN REASONS	*Warner Brothers*	9	*7 May 60*	11
Above hit: Connie STEVENS with the Big Sound of Don RALKE.				
KOOKIE, KOOKIE (LEND ME YOUR COMB)	*Warner Brothers*	27	*7 May 60*	8
From the TV series '77 Sunset Strip'.				
Above hit: Edward BYRNES and Connie STEVENS with the Big Sound of Don RALKE.				
SIXTEEN REASONS [RE]	*Warner Brothers*	45	*6 Aug 60*	1

Ray STEVENS — US

SINGLES:	**HITS 7**			**WEEKS 64**
EVERYTHING IS BEAUTIFUL	*CBS*	6	*16 May 70*	16
Children on the intro are Susie and Timmy Ragsdale (Ray Stevens' children) and Julie Shacklett (Brenda Lee's daughter).				
BRIDGET THE MIDGET (THE QUEEN OF THE BLUES)	*CBS*	2	*13 Mar 71*	14
TURN YOUR RADIO ON	*CBS*	33	*25 Mar 72*	4
THE STREAK	*Janus*	1	*25 May 74*	12
MISTY	*Janus*	2	*21 Jun 75*	10
INDIAN LOVE CALL	*Janus*	34	*27 Sep 75*	4
Originally recorded by Paul Whiteman Orchestra.				
IN THE MOOD	*Warner Brothers*	31	*5 Mar 77*	4
Billed in the US as Henhouse Five Plus Too.				

ALBUMS:	**HITS 2**			**WEEKS 8**
EVERYTHING IS BEAUTIFUL	*CBS*	62	*26 Sep 70*	1
MISTY	*Janus*	23	*13 Sep 75*	7

Ricky STEVENS with the Rita WILLIAMS SINGERS and Geoff LOVE and his Orchestra — UK

SINGLES:	**HITS 1**			**WEEKS 7**
I CRIED FOR YOU	*Columbia*	34	*16 Dec 61*	7

Shakin' STEVENS — UK

SINGLES:	**HITS 37**			**WEEKS 277**
HOT DOG	*Epic*	24	*16 Feb 80*	9
Originally recorded by Buck Owens.				
MARIE MARIE	*Epic*	19	*16 Aug 80*	10
Originally recorded by the Blasters.				
THIS OLE HOUSE	*Epic*	1	*28 Feb 81*	17
Originally recorded by Stuart Hamblen in 1949.				
YOU DRIVE ME CRAZY	*Epic*	2	*2 May 81*	12
GREEN DOOR	*Epic*	1	*25 Jul 81*	12
IT'S RAINING	*Epic*	10	*10 Oct 81*	9
Originally recorded by Irma Thomas.				
OH JULIE	*Epic*	1	*16 Jan 82*	10
SHIRLEY	*Epic*	6	*24 Apr 82*	6
Originally recorded by John Fred and the Playboys in 1959.				
GIVE ME YOUR HEART TONIGHT	*Epic*	11	*21 Aug 82*	10
I'LL BE SATISFIED	*Epic*	10	*16 Oct 82*	8
Original by Jackie Wilson reached No. 20 in the US in 1959.				
THE SHAKIN' STEVENS [EP]	*Epic*	2	*11 Dec 82*	7
Lead track: Blue Christmas.				
IT'S LATE	*Epic*	11	*23 Jul 83*	7
Originally recorded by Dorsey Burnette.				
CRY JUST A LITTLE BIT	*Epic*	3	*5 Nov 83*	12
A ROCKIN' GOOD WAY	*Epic*	5	*7 Jan 84*	9
Originally recorded by Priscilla Bowman.				
Above hit: SHAKY and BONNIE.				

A LOVE WORTH WAITING FOR	*Epic*	2	*24 Mar 84*	10
A LETTER TO YOU	*Epic*	10	*15 Sep 84*	8
Originally recorded by Dennis Linde.				
TEARDROPS	*Epic*	5	*24 Nov 84*	9
BREAKING UP MY HEART	*Epic*	14	*2 Mar 85*	7
LIPSTICK POWDER AND PAINT	*Epic*	11	*12 Oct 85*	9
Originally recorded by Joe Turner in 1957.				
MERRY CHRISTMAS EVERYONE	*Epic*	1	*7 Dec 85*	8
TURNING AWAY	*Epic*	15	*8 Feb 86*	7
BECAUSE I LOVE YOU	*Epic*	14	*1 Nov 86*	10
MERRY CHRISTMAS EVERYONE [RE]	*Epic*	58	*20 Dec 86*	3
A LITTLE BOOGIE WOOGIE (IN THE BACK OF MY MIND)	*Epic*	12	*27 Jun 87*	10
COME SEE ABOUT ME	*Epic*	24	*19 Sep 87*	6
WHAT DO YOU WANT TO MAKE THOSE EYES AT ME FOR	*Epic*	5	*28 Nov 87*	8
FEEL THE NEED IN ME	*Epic*	26	*23 Jul 88*	5
HOW MANY TEARS CAN YOU HIDE	*Epic*	47	*15 Oct 88*	4
TRUE LOVE	*Epic*	23	*10 Dec 88*	6
JEZEBEL	*Epic*	58	*18 Feb 89*	2
LOVE ATTACK	*Epic*	28	*13 May 89*	4
I MIGHT	*Epic*	18	*24 Feb 90*	6
YES I DO	*Epic*	60	*12 May 90*	2
PINK CHAMPAGNE	*Epic*	59	*18 Aug 90*	2
MY CUTIE CUTIE	*Epic*	75	*13 Oct 90*	1
THE BEST CHRISTMAS OF THEM ALL	*Epic*	19	*15 Dec 90*	4
I'LL BE HOME THIS CHRISTMAS	*Epic*	34	*7 Dec 91*	5
RADIO	*Epic*	37	*10 Oct 92*	3
Above hit: SHAKY featuring Roger TAYLOR.				

ALBUMS:	**HITS 12**			**WEEKS 158**
TAKE ONE!	*Epic*	62	*15 Mar 80*	2
THIS OLE HOUSE	*Epic*	2	*4 Apr 81*	28
SHAKIN' STEVENS	*Hallmark*	34	*8 Aug 81*	5
Mid-price release of early material from the 1970s.				
SHAKY	*Epic*	1	*19 Sep 81*	28
GIVE ME YOUR HEART TONIGHT	*Epic*	3	*9 Oct 82*	18
THE BOP WON'T STOP	*Epic*	21	*26 Nov 83*	27
SHAKIN' STEVENS GREATEST HITS VOLUME 1	*Epic*	8	*17 Nov 84*	22
LIPSTICK POWDER AND PAINT	*Epic*	37	*16 Nov 85*	9
LET'S BOOGIE	*Epic*	59	*31 Oct 87*	7
A WHOLE LOTTA SHAKY	*Epic*	42	*19 Nov 88*	8
THERE'S TWO KINDS OF MUSIC: ROCK 'N' ROLL!	*Telstar*	65	*20 Oct 90*	2
THE EPIC YEARS	*Epic*	57	*31 Oct 92*	2
Above hit: SHAKY.				

STEVENSON'S ROCKET — UK

SINGLES:	**HITS 1**			**WEEKS 5**
ALRIGHT BABY	*Magnet*	37	*29 Nov 75*	2
ALRIGHT BABY [RE]	*Magnet*	45	*20 Dec 75*	3

Al STEWART — UK

SINGLES:	**HITS 1**			**WEEKS 6**
YEAR OF THE CAT	*RCA Victor*	31	*29 Jan 77*	6
Written about comedian Tony Hancock.				

ALBUMS:	**HITS 5**			**WEEKS 20**
ZERO SHE FLIES	*CBS*	40	*11 Apr 70*	4
YEAR OF THE CAT	*RCA Victor*	38	*5 Feb 77*	7
TIME PASSAGES	*RCA Victor*	39	*21 Oct 78*	1
24 CARAT	*RCA*	55	*6 Sep 80*	6
RUSSIANS AND AMERICANS	*RCA*	83	*9 Jun 84*	2

Amii STEWART — US

SINGLES:	**HITS 7**			**WEEKS 61**
KNOCK ON WOOD	*Atlantic*	6	*7 Apr 79*	12
LIGHT MY FIRE/137 DISCO HEAVEN [M]	*Atlantic*	5	*16 Jun 79*	11
JEALOUSY	*Atlantic*	58	*3 Nov 79*	3
PARADISE BIRD / THE LETTER	*Atlantic*	39	*19 Jan 80*	4
MY GUY - MY GIRL [M]	*Atlantic*	39	*19 Jul 80*	5
Above hit: Amii STEWART and Johnny BRISTOL.				
FRIENDS	*RCA*	12	*29 Dec 84*	11
KNOCK ON WOOD [RM] / LIGHT MY FIRE/137 DISCO HEAVEN [M] [RM]	*Sedition*	7	*17 Aug 85*	12
Remixed by Barry Leng and Alan Coulthard.				
MY GUY, MY GIRL [M] [RR]	*Sedition*	63	*25 Jan 86*	3
Above hit: Amii STEWART and Dion ESTUS.				

Andy STEWART UK

SINGLES:	HITS 4			WEEKS 67
DONALD WHERE'S YOUR TROOSERS	*Top Rank*	37	*17 Dec 60*	1
A SCOTTISH SOLDIER (GREEN HILLS OF TYROL)	*Top Rank*	19	*14 Jan 61*	38
THE BATTLE'S O'ER	*Top Rank*	28	*3 Jun 61*	13
A SCOTTISH SOLDIER (GREEN HILLS OF TYROL) [RE]	*Top Rank*	43	*14 Oct 61*	2
Above 3: Andy STEWART with the Michael SAMMES SINGERS.				
DR. FINLAY	*His Master's Voice*	50	*14 Aug 65*	1
DR. FINLAY [RE]	*His Master's Voice*	43	*28 Aug 65*	4
DONALD WHERE'S YOUR TROOSERS? [RI]	*Stone*	4	*9 Dec 89*	8
Made popular again due to constant airplay on Simon Mayo's BBC Radio 1 breakfast show.				
EPS:	**HITS 2**			**WEEKS 54**
ANDY SINGS	*Top Rank*	3	*17 Jun 61*	48
ANDY STEWART SINGS	*Top Rank*	12	*27 Jan 62*	6
ALBUMS:	**HITS 1**			**WEEKS 2**
ANDY STEWART	*Top Rank*	13	*3 Feb 62*	2

Billy STEWART US

SINGLES:	HITS 1			WEEKS 2
SUMMERTIME	*Chess*	39	*10 Sep 66*	2
From the film 'Porgy And Bess'. Originally recorded by Billie Holiday in 1936.				

Dave STEWART UK

SINGLES:	HITS 4			WEEKS 30
WHAT BECOMES OF THE BROKEN HEARTED?	*Stiff*	13	*14 Mar 81*	10
Above hit: Dave STEWART Guest vocals Colin BLUNSTONE.				
IT'S MY PARTY	*Stiff*	1	*19 Sep 81*	13
Above hit: Dave STEWART with Barbara GASKIN.				
BUSY DOING NOTHING	*Broken*	49	*13 Aug 83*	4
THE LOCOMOTION	*Broken*	70	*14 Jun 86*	3
Above 2: Dave STEWART and Barbara GASKIN.				

David A. STEWART UK

SINGLES:	HITS 4			WEEKS 23
LILY WAS HERE	*AnXious*	6	*24 Feb 90*	12
From the film of the same name.				
Above hit: David A. STEWART featuring Candy DULFER.				
JACK TALKING	*RCA*	69	*18 Aug 90*	2
Above hit: Dave STEWART and the SPIRITUAL COWBOYS.				
ALL YOU NEED IS LOVE	*Childline*	19	*6 Feb 93*	4
Charity record for the Childline Appeal. Backing vocals by Kiki Dee.				
Above hit: Tom JONES and Dave STEWART.				
HEART OF STONE	*East West*	36	*3 Sep 94*	5
Above hit: Dave STEWART.				
ALBUMS:	**HITS 2**			**WEEKS 7**
LILY WAS HERE [OST]	*Anxious*	35	*7 Apr 90*	5
Features Candy Dulfer and Various Artists.				
DAVE STEWART AND THE SPIRITUAL COWBOYS	*RCA*	38	*15 Sep 90*	2
Above hit: Dave STEWART and the SPIRITUAL COWBOYS.				

Jermaine STEWART US

SINGLES:	HITS 5			WEEKS 42
WE DON'T HAVE TO . . .	*10 Records*	2	*9 Aug 86*	14
JODY	*10 Records*	50	*1 Nov 86*	4
SAY IT AGAIN	*10 Records*	7	*16 Jan 88*	12
GET LUCKY	*Siren*	13	*2 Apr 88*	9
DON'T TALK DIRTY TO ME	*Siren*	61	*24 Sep 88*	3
ALBUMS:	**HITS 2**			**WEEKS 12**
FRANTIC ROMANTIC	*10 Records*	49	*4 Oct 86*	4
SAY IT AGAIN	*Siren*	32	*5 Mar 88*	8

John STEWART US

SINGLES:	HITS 1			WEEKS 6
GOLD	*RSO*	43	*30 Jun 79*	6

Patrick STEWART – See Rick WAKEMAN

Rod STEWART UK

(See also Jeff Beck; Faces; Glass Tiger; N-Trance; Python Lee Jackson.)

SINGLES:	HITS 58			WEEKS 462
MAGGIE MAY / REASON TO BELIEVE	*Mercury*	1	*4 Sep 71*	21
Reason To Believe was listed for 4 Sep 71 and 11 Sep 71 reaching No. 19. From 18 Sep 71, Maggie May was listed, and became the official A-side. Reason To Believe originally recorded by Tim Hardin. Maggie May features Ron Wood on guitar and Pete Sears of Jefferson Airplane on piano.				
YOU WEAR IT WELL	*Mercury*	1	*12 Aug 72*	12
ANGEL / WHAT MADE MILWAUKEE FAMOUS (HAS MADE A LOSER OUT OF ME)	*Mercury*	4	*18 Nov 72*	11
Angel originally recorded by Jimi Hendrix. What Made Milwaukee Famous originally recorded by Jerry Lee Lewis in 1968.				
OH! NO NOT MY BABY	*Mercury*	6	*8 Sep 73*	9
Original by The Shirelles reached No. 24 in the US in 1964.				
FAREWELL / BRING IT ON HOME TO ME / YOU SEND ME	*Mercury*	7	*5 Oct 74*	7
SAILING	*Warner Brothers*	1	*16 Aug 75*	11
Originally recorded by the Sutherland Brothers.				
THIS OLD HEART OF MINE	*Riva*	4	*15 Nov 75*	9
TONIGHT'S THE NIGHT	*Riva*	5	*5 Jun 76*	9
Whispers by Britt Eckland.				
THE KILLING OF GEORGIE PARTS 1 & 2	*Riva*	2	*21 Aug 76*	10
SAILING [RE-1ST]	*Warner Brothers*	3	*4 Sep 76*	20
Re-entered after being used by BBC TV as the theme to their documentary 'Sailor'.				
GET BACK	*Riva*	11	*20 Nov 76*	9
From the film 'All This And World War II'.				
MAGGIE MAY [RI]	*Mercury*	31	*4 Dec 76*	7
I DON'T WANT TO TALK ABOUT IT / FIRST CUT IS THE DEEPEST	*Riva*	1	*23 Apr 77*	13
I Don't Want To Talk About It originally recorded by Crazy Horse, First Cut Is The Deepest originally recorded by Cat Stevens.				
YOU'RE IN MY HEART	*Riva*	3	*15 Oct 77*	10
HOT LEGS / I WAS ONLY JOKING	*Riva*	5	*28 Jan 78*	8
OLE OLA (MUHLER BRASILEIRA)	*Riva*	4	*27 May 78*	6
Above hit: Rod STEWART and the SCOTTISH WORLD CUP SQUAD '78.				
DO 'YA' THINK I'M SEXY?	*Riva*	1	*18 Nov 78*	13
Royalties from the song donated to the United Nations' UNICEF children's charity.				
AIN'T LOVE A BITCH	*Riva*	11	*3 Feb 79*	8
BLONDES (HAVE MORE FUN)	*Riva*	63	*5 May 79*	3
IF LOVING YOU IS WRONG (I DON'T WANT TO BE RIGHT)	*Riva*	23	*31 May 80*	9
Originally recorded by Luther Ingram.				
PASSION	*Riva*	17	*8 Nov 80*	10
MY GIRL	*Riva*	32	*20 Dec 80*	7
TONIGHT I'M YOURS (DON'T HURT ME)	*Riva*	8	*17 Oct 81*	13
YOUNG TURKS	*Riva*	11	*12 Dec 81*	9
HOW LONG	*Riva*	41	*27 Feb 82*	4
BABY JANE	*Warner Brothers*	1	*4 Jun 83*	14
WHAT AM I GONNA DO (I'M SO IN LOVE WITH YOU)	*Warner Brothers*	3	*27 Aug 83*	8
SWEET SURRENDER	*Warner Brothers*	23	*10 Dec 83*	9
INFATUATION	*Warner Brothers*	27	*26 May 84*	7
Features guitar by Jeff Beck.				
SOME GUYS HAVE ALL THE LUCK	*Warner Brothers*	15	*28 Jul 84*	10
Original by the Persuaders reached No. 39 in the US in 1973.				
LOVE TOUCH (FROM THE MOTION PICTURE 'LEGAL EAGLES')	*Warner Brothers*	27	*24 May 86*	5
LOVE TOUCH (FROM THE MOTION PICTURE 'LEGAL EAGLES') [RE]	*Warner Brothers*	69	*5 Jul 86*	3
EVERY BEAT OF MY HEART	*Warner Brothers*	2	*12 Jul 86*	9
ANOTHER HEARTACHE	*Warner Brothers*	54	*20 Sep 86*	2
Co-written by Bryan Adams.				
SAILING [RE-2ND]	*Warner Brothers*	41	*28 Mar 87*	3
Proceeds from this entry went to the Zeebrugge Channel Ferry Disaster Fund.				
LOST IN YOU	*Warner Brothers*	21	*28 May 88*	6
FOREVER YOUNG	*Warner Brothers*	57	*13 Aug 88*	3
Above 2 feature Duran Duran's Andy Taylor on guitar.				
MY HEART CAN'T TELL YOU NO	*Warner Brothers*	49	*6 May 89*	4
THIS OLD HEART OF MINE [RR]	*Warner Brothers*	51	*11 Nov 89*	3
Above hit: Rod STEWART featuring Ronald ISLEY.				
DOWNTOWN TRAIN	*Warner Brothers*	10	*13 Jan 90*	12
Originally recorded by Tom Waits on his 1983 album Rain Dogs.				
IT TAKES TWO	*Warner Brothers*	5	*24 Nov 90*	8
Above hit: Rod STEWART and Tina TURNER.				
RHYTHM OF MY HEART	*Warner Brothers*	3	*16 Mar 91*	11
THE MOTOWN SONG	*Warner Brothers*	10	*15 Jun 91*	8
Above hit: Rod STEWART (with the TEMPTATIONS).				
BROKEN ARROW	*Warner Brothers*	54	*7 Sep 91*	3
Originally recorded by Robbie Robertson.				
PEOPLE GET READY	*Epic*	49	*7 Mar 92*	3
Above hit: Jeff BECK and Rod STEWART.				

YOUR SONG / BROKEN ARROW [RI]	*Warner Brothers*	41	*18 Apr 92*	4
Rod's version of Your Song was a tribute to Freddie Mercury.				
TOM TRAUBERT'S BLUES (WALTZING MATILDA)	*Warner Brothers*	6	*5 Dec 92*	9
Originally recorded by Tom Waits.				
RUBY TUESDAY	*Warner Brothers*	11	*20 Feb 93*	6
SHOTGUN WEDDING	*Warner Brothers*	21	*17 Apr 93*	4
HAVE I TOLD YOU LATELY	*Warner Brothers*	5	*26 Jun 93*	9
Originally recorded by Van Morrison.				
REASON TO BELIEVE (LIVE VERSION) [RR]	*Warner Brothers*	51	*21 Aug 93*	3
Above hit: Rod STEWART with special guest Ronnie WOOD.				
PEOPLE GET READY (LIVE VERSION) [RR]	*Warner Brothers*	45	*18 Dec 93*	4
This also features Ronnie Wood, though credit is only reflected in the small print on the label. Above 2 are live recordings from Los Angeles, 5 Feb 93.				
ALL FOR LOVE	*A&M*	2	*15 Jan 94*	13
From the film 'The Three Musketeers'.				
Above hit: Bryan ADAMS, Rod STEWART and STING.				
YOU'RE THE STAR	*Warner Brothers*	19	*20 May 95*	5
LADY LUCK	*Warner Brothers*	56	*19 Aug 95*	1
PURPLE HEATHER	*Warner Brothers*	16	*15 Jun 96*	5
Offical anthem for the Scottish Football Team in Euro '96. Charity single with proceeds to the Dunblane Appeal.				
Above hit: Rod STEWART with the SCOTTISH EURO '96 SQUAD.				
IF WE FALL IN LOVE TONIGHT	*Warner Brothers*	58	*14 Dec 96*	1
OOH LA LA	*Warner Brothers*	16	*30 May 98*	5
Original was the title track of the Faces 1973 album with vocals by Ronnie Lane. This release was dedicated to him after he died in 1996 of multiple sclerosis.				
ROCKS	*Warner Brothers*	55	*5 Sep 98*	1
FAITH OF THE HEART	*Universal*	60	*17 Apr 99*	1
From the film 'Patch Adams'.				
I CAN'T DENY IT	*Atlantic*	26	*24 Mar 01*	2

ALBUMS:	**HITS 28**			**WEEKS 812**
GASOLINE ALLEY	*Vertigo*	62	*3 Oct 70*	1
EVERY PICTURE TELLS A STORY	*Mercury*	1	*24 Jul 71*	81
NEVER A DULL MOMENT	*Philips*	1	*5 Aug 72*	36
SING IT AGAIN ROD	*Mercury*	1	*25 Aug 73*	30
Compilation.				
SMILER	*Mercury*	1	*19 Oct 74*	20
ATLANTIC CROSSING	*Warner Brothers*	1	*30 Aug 75*	88
A NIGHT ON THE TOWN	*Riva*	1	*3 Jul 76*	47
THE BEST OF ROD STEWART	*Mercury*	18	*16 Jul 77*	22
FOOT LOOSE & FANCY FREE	*Riva*	3	*19 Nov 77*	26
Label reads as Footloose 'N' Fancy Free.				
ATLANTIC CROSSING [RI]	*Riva*	60	*24 Jun 78*	1
BLONDES HAVE MORE FUN	*Riva*	3	*9 Dec 78*	31
ROD STEWART - GREATEST HITS VOL. 1	*Riva*	1	*10 Nov 79*	47
FOOLISH BEHAVIOUR	*Riva*	4	*22 Nov 80*	13
TONIGHT I'M YOURS	*Riva*	8	*14 Nov 81*	21
ABSOLUTELY LIVE	*Riva*	35	*13 Nov 82*	5
BODY WISHES	*Warner Brothers*	5	*18 Jun 83*	27
ROD STEWART - GREATEST HITS VOL. 1 [RE]	*Riva*	62	*21 Jan 84*	27
Re-released. Charts credited label as Warner Brothers from 2 Jun 84 until 9 Feb 85. Peak position reached in 1987, (1984 peak No. 66).				
CAMOUFLAGE	*Warner Brothers*	8	*23 Jun 84*	17
EVERY BEAT OF MY HEART	*Warner Brothers*	5	*5 Jul 86*	17
OUT OF ORDER	*Warner Brothers*	11	*4 Jun 88*	8
THE BEST OF ROD STEWART	*Warner Brothers*	3	*25 Nov 89*	74
VAGABOND HEART	*Warner Brothers*	2	*6 Apr 91*	27
THE BEST OF ROD STEWART AND THE FACES 1971-1975	*Mercury*	58	*7 Nov 92*	1
Features both Rod Stewart's solo and group material.				
Above hit: Rod STEWART and the FACES.				
THE BEST OF ROD STEWART [RE]	*Warner Brothers*	22	*27 Feb 93*	53
Re-released at mid price. Includes re-entries through to 2000. Peak position reached in 1994, (1993 peak No. 44).				
ROD STEWART, LEAD VOCALIST	*Warner Brothers*	3	*6 Mar 93*	9
Features old tracks with Faces, Jeff Beck Group as well as new cover versions.				
UNPLUGGED . . . AND SEATED	*Warner Brothers*	2	*5 Jun 93*	27
Acoustic set recorded in Los Angeles, 5 Feb 95.				
A SPANNER IN THE WORKS	*Warner Brothers*	4	*10 Jun 95*	12
IF WE FALL IN LOVE TONIGHT	*Warner Brothers*	8	*16 Nov 96*	19
Compilation of hit ballads spanning 1975-93.				
WHEN WE WERE THE NEW BOYS	*Atlantic*	2	*13 Jun 98*	11
HUMAN	*Atlantic*	9	*7 Apr 01*	8
THE STORY SO FAR: THE VERY BEST OF ROD STEWART	*Warner Brothers*	7	*24 Nov 01*	6

STEX — UK

SINGLES:	**HITS 1**			**WEEKS 2**
STILL FEEL THE RAIN	*Some Bizzare*	63	*19 Jan 91*	2

STICKY featuring MS DYNAMITE — UK

SINGLES:	HITS 1			WEEKS 6
BOOO!	*ffrr*	12	*23 Jun 01*	6

STIFF LITTLE FINGERS — UK

SINGLES:	HITS 8			WEEKS 39
STRAW DOGS	*Chrysalis*	44	*29 Sep 79*	4
AT THE EDGE	*Chrysalis*	15	*16 Feb 80*	9
NOBODY'S HERO / TIN SOLDIERS	*Chrysalis*	36	*24 May 80*	5
BACK TO FRONT	*Chrysalis*	49	*2 Aug 80*	4
JUST FADE AWAY	*Chrysalis*	47	*28 Mar 81*	6
SILVER LINING	*Chrysalis*	68	*30 May 81*	3
LISTEN [EP]	*Chrysalis*	33	*23 Jan 82*	6
Lead track: Listen.				
BITS OF KIDS	*Chrysalis*	73	*18 Sep 82*	2
ALBUMS:	**HITS 6**			**WEEKS 57**
INFLAMMABLE MATERIAL	*Rough Trade*	14	*3 Mar 79*	19
NOBODY'S HEROES	*Chrysalis*	8	*15 Mar 80*	10
HANX	*Chrysalis*	9	*20 Sep 80*	5
GO FOR IT	*Chrysalis*	14	*25 Apr 81*	8
NOW THEN . . .	*Chrysalis*	24	*2 Oct 82*	6
ALL THE BEST	*Chrysalis*	19	*12 Feb 83*	9

Curtis STIGERS — US

SINGLES:	HITS 6			WEEKS 34
I WONDER WHY	*Arista*	5	*18 Jan 92*	10
YOU'RE ALL THAT MATTERS TO ME	*Arista*	6	*28 Mar 92*	12
SLEEPING WITH THE LIGHTS ON	*Arista*	53	*11 Jul 92*	4
NEVER SAW A MIRACLE	*Arista*	34	*17 Oct 92*	4
THIS TIME	*Arista*	28	*3 Jun 95*	3
KEEP ME FROM THE COLD	*Arista*	57	*2 Dec 95*	1
ALBUMS:	**HITS 2**			**WEEKS 52**
CURTIS STIGERS	*Arista*	7	*29 Feb 92*	50
TIME WAS	*Arista*	34	*1 Jul 95*	2

Stephen STILLS — US

(See also Crosby, Stills, Nash and Young; Stephen Stills' Manassas; Stills-Young Band.)

SINGLES:	HITS 1			WEEKS 4
LOVE THE ONE YOU'RE WITH	*Atlantic*	37	*13 Mar 71*	4
Backing vocals by John Sebastian, Rita Coolidge, David Crosby and Graham Nash.				
ALBUMS:	**HITS 4**			**WEEKS 7**
STEPHEN STILLS	*Atlantic*	30	*19 Dec 70*	1
STEPHEN STILLS 2	*Atlantic*	22	*14 Aug 71*	3
STILLS	*CBS*	31	*26 Jul 75*	1
ILLEGAL STILLS	*CBS*	54	*29 May 76*	2

Stephen STILLS' MANASSAS — US

(See also Stephen Stills.)

ALBUMS:	HITS 2			WEEKS 7
MANASSAS	*Atlantic*	30	*20 May 72*	5
DOWN THE ROAD	*Atlantic*	33	*19 May 73*	2

STILLS-YOUNG BAND — US

(See also Crosby, Stills, Nash and Young; Stephen Stills; Neil Young.)

ALBUMS:	HITS 1			WEEKS 5
LONG MAY YOU RUN	*Reprise*	12	*9 Oct 76*	5

STILTSKIN — UK

SINGLES:	HITS 2			WEEKS 15
INSIDE	*White Water*	1	*7 May 94*	13
Featured in the Levi's 501 Jeans TV commercial.				
FOOTSTEPS	*White Water*	34	*24 Sep 94*	2
ALBUMS:	**HITS 1**			**WEEKS 4**
THE MIND'S EYE	*White Water*	17	*29 Oct 94*	4

STING — UK

(See also Police; Various Artists: Films – Original Soundtracks 'Brimstone And Treacle'.)

SINGLES:	HITS 31			WEEKS 146
SPREAD A LITTLE HAPPINESS	*A&M*	16	*14 Aug 82*	8
From the film 'Brimstone And Treacle'. Originally recorded by Binnie Hale.				
IF YOU LOVE SOMEBODY SET THEM FREE	*A&M*	26	*8 Jun 85*	7

LOVE IS THE SEVENTH WAVE (NEW MIX)	*A&M*	41	*24 Aug 85*	5
FORTRESS AROUND YOUR HEART	*A&M*	49	*19 Oct 85*	3
RUSSIANS	*A&M*	12	*7 Dec 85*	11
MOON OVER BOURBIN STREET	*A&M*	44	*15 Feb 86*	4
RUSSIANS [RE]	*A&M*	71	*1 Mar 86*	1
WE'LL BE TOGETHER	*A&M*	41	*7 Nov 87*	4
ENGLISHMAN IN NEW YORK	*A&M*	51	*20 Feb 88*	3
Written about Quentin Crisp.				
FRAGILE	*A&M*	70	*9 Apr 88*	2
AN ENGLISHMAN IN NEW YORK [RM]	*A&M*	15	*11 Aug 90*	7
Remixed by Ben Liebrand.				
ALL THIS TIME	*A&M*	22	*12 Jan 91*	4
MAD ABOUT YOU	*A&M*	56	*9 Mar 91*	2
THE SOUL CAGES	*A&M*	57	*4 May 91*	1
IT'S PROBABLY ME	*A&M*	30	*29 Aug 92*	5
From the film 'Lethal Weapon 3'.				
Above hit: STING with Eric CLAPTON.				
IF I EVER LOSE MY FAITH IN YOU	*A&M*	14	*13 Feb 93*	6
SEVEN DAYS	*A&M*	25	*24 Apr 93*	4
FIELDS OF GOLD	*A&M*	16	*19 Jun 93*	6
SHAPE OF MY HEART	*A&M*	57	*4 Sep 93*	1
DEMOLITION MAN	*A&M*	21	*20 Nov 93*	4
From the film of the same name.				
ALL FOR LOVE	*A&M*	2	*15 Jan 94*	13
From the film 'The Three Musketeers'.				
Above hit: Bryan ADAMS, Rod STEWART and STING.				
NOTHING 'BOUT ME	*A&M*	32	*26 Feb 94*	3
WHEN WE DANCE	*A&M*	9	*29 Oct 94*	7
THIS COWBOY SONG	*A&M*	15	*11 Feb 95*	6
Jimmy Nail on backing vocals.				
Above hit: STING (featuring Pato BANTON).				
SPIRITS IN THE MATERIAL WORLD	*MCA*	36	*20 Jan 96*	2
From the film 'Ace Ventura When Nature Calls'.				
Above hit: Pato BANTON with STING.				
LET YOUR SOUL BE YOUR PILOT	*A&M*	15	*2 Mar 96*	4
YOU STILL TOUCH ME	*A&M*	27	*11 May 96*	3
LIVE AT T.F.I. FRIDAY [EP]	*A&M*	53	*22 Jun 96*	2
Lead track: You Still Touch Me. Live recordings from Chris Evans' Channel 4 TV show.				
I WAS BROUGHT TO MY SENSES	*A&M*	31	*14 Sep 96*	2
I'M SO HAPPY I CAN'T STOP CRYING	*A&M*	54	*30 Nov 96*	1
BRAND NEW DAY	*A&M*	13	*25 Sept 99*	5
DESERT ROSE	*A&M*	15	*29 Jan 00*	6
Above hit: STING featuring CHEB MAMI.				
AFTER THE RAIN HAS FALLEN	*A&M*	31	*22 Apr 00*	4

ALBUMS:	**HITS 10**			**WEEKS 349**
THE DREAM OF THE BLUE TURTLES	*A&M*	3	*29 Jun 85*	64
BRING ON THE NIGHT	*A&M*	16	*28 Jun 86*	12
Live recordings from the documentary film of his 1985 tour in Paris, France.				
. . . NOTHING LIKE THE SUN	*A&M*	1	*24 Oct 87*	47
THE SOUL CAGES	*A&M*	1	*2 Feb 91*	16
TEN SUMMONER'S TALES	*A&M*	2	*13 Mar 93*	60
FIELDS OF GOLD – THE BEST OF STING 1984-1994	*A&M*	2	*19 Nov 94*	41
MERCURY FALLING	*A&M*	4	*16 Mar 96*	27
THE VERY BEST OF STING AND THE POLICE	*A&M*	11	*22 Nov 97*	30
Features both Sting's solo and group material.				
Above hit: STING/The POLICE.				
BRAND NEW DAY	*A&M*	5	*9 Oct 99*	44
ALL THIS TIME	*A&M*	3	*17 Nov 01*	7
Live recordings from Italy.				

Byron STINGILY — US

SINGLES:	**HITS 5**			**WEEKS 14**
GET UP (EVERYBODY)	*Manifesto*	14	*25 Jan 97*	5
Based around Sylvester's Dance (Disco Heat).				
SING A SONG	*Manifesto*	38	*1 Nov 97*	2
YOU MAKE ME FEEL (MIGHTY REAL)	*Manifesto*	13	*31 Jan 98*	4
TESTIFY	*Manifesto*	48	*13 Jun 98*	1
THAT'S THE WAY LOVE IS	*Manifesto*	32	*12 Feb 00*	2

STINX — UK

WHY DO YOU KEEP ON RUNNING BOY?	*HEBS*	49	*24 Mar 01*	3
Anti-smoking song featured in a Health Education Board of Scotland TV commercial.				

STIX 'N' STONED — UK

SINGLES:	**HITS 1**			**WEEKS 2**
OUTRAGEOUS	*Positiva*	39	*20 Jul 96*	2

Catherine STOCK — UK

SINGLES:	HITS 1			WEEKS 6
TO HAVE AND TO HOLD (THEME SONG FROM THE LWT SERIES)	*Sierra*	17	*18 Oct 86*	6

STOCK AITKEN WATERMAN — UK

(See also Christians, Holly Johnson, Paul McCartney, Gerry Marsden and Stock Aitken Waterman.)

SINGLES:	HITS 4			WEEKS 19
ROADBLOCK	*Breakout*	13	*25 Jul 87*	9
PACKJAMMED (WITH THE PARTY POSSE)	*Breakout*	41	*12 Dec 87*	6
Features samples from tracks they had produced.				
ALL THE WAY	*MCA*	64	*21 May 88*	2
Above hit: ENGLAND FOOTBALL TEAM with the 'sound' of STOCK, AITKEN and WATERMAN.				
S.S. PAPARAZZI	*PWL*	68	*3 Dec 88*	2

STOCKLAND GREEN BILATERAL SCHOOL FIRST YEAR CHOIR – See WIZZARD

Miriam STOCKLEY – See ADIEMUS; ATLANTIS vs AVATAR featuring Miriam STOCKLEY

Rhet STOLLER — UK

SINGLES:	HITS 1			WEEKS 8
CHARIOT	*Decca*	26	*14 Jan 61*	8

Morris STOLOFF conducting the COLUMBIA PICTURES ORCHESTRA — US

SINGLES:	HITS 1			WEEKS 11
MOONGLOW/THEME FROM "PICNIC" [M]	*Brunswick*	7	*2 Jun 56*	11

Angie STONE — US

SINGLES:	HITS 2			WEEKS 4
LIFE STORY	*Arista*	22	*15 Apr 00*	3
KEEP YOUR WORRIES	*Virgin*	57	*16 Dec 00*	1
Above hit: GURU'S JAZZMATAZZ featuring Angie STONE.				

ALBUMS:	HITS 1			WEEKS 3
BLACK DIAMOND	*Arista*	62	*11 Mar 00*	3

R and J STONE — UK/US

SINGLES:	HITS 1			WEEKS 9
WE DO IT	*RCA Victor*	5	*10 Jan 76*	9

STONE FREE — UK

SINGLES:	HITS 1			WEEKS 1
CAN'T SAY 'BYE	*Ensign*	73	*23 May 87*	1

STONE ROSES — UK

SINGLES:	HITS 12			WEEKS 77
SHE BANGS THE DRUMS	*Silvertone*	36	*29 Jul 89*	3
FOOLS GOLD / WHAT THE WORLD IS WAITING FOR	*Silvertone*	8	*25 Nov 89*	14
The chart for 25 Nov 89 had titles listed in reverse.				
SALLY CINNAMON	*Black/FM-Revolver*	75	*6 Jan 90*	1
Originally released in 1987.				
SALLY CINNAMON [RE]	*Black/FM-Revolver*	46	*20 Jan 90*	4
ELEPHANT STONE	*Silvertone*	8	*3 Mar 90*	6
Originally released in 1988.				
MADE OF STONE	*Silvertone*	20	*17 Mar 90*	4
Original release reached No. 90 in 1989.				
SHE BANGS THE DRUMS [RE]	*Silvertone*	34	*31 Mar 90*	3
ONE LOVE	*Silvertone*	4	*14 Jul 90*	7
FOOLS GOLD / WHAT THE WORLD IS WAITING FOR [RE-1ST]	*Silvertone*	22	*15 Sep 90*	5
I WANNA BE ADORED	*Silvertone*	20	*14 Sep 91*	3
WATERFALL	*Silvertone*	27	*11 Jan 92*	4
I AM THE RESURRECTION	*Silvertone*	33	*11 Apr 92*	2
FOOLS GOLD [RE-2ND]	*Silvertone*	73	*30 May 92*	1
12" and CD releases have the 9.53 extended version.				
LOVE SPREADS	*Geffen*	2	*3 Dec 94*	8
TEN STORY LOVE SONG	*Geffen*	11	*11 Mar 95*	3
FOOLS GOLD '95 [RI]	*Silvertone*	25	*29 Apr 95*	3
Though listed as Fool's Gold '95, the first track of the CD was the original version.				
BEGGING YOU	*Geffen*	15	*11 Nov 95*	3
FOOLS GOLD [RM]	*Jive Electro*	25	*6 Mar 99*	3
Remixed by the Grooverider.				

ALBUMS:	HITS 7			WEEKS 148
THE STONE ROSES	*Silvertone*	32	*13 May 89*	17
THE STONE ROSES [RE-1ST]	*Silvertone*	19	*2 Dec 89*	50
TURNS INTO STONE	*Silvertone*	32	*1 Aug 92*	3

SECOND COMING *Includes re-entries through to 1999.*	*Geffen*	4	*17 Dec 94*	28
THE STONE ROSES [RE-2ND] *Re-released with additional tracks. Peak position reached in 1998, (1995 peak No. 69, 1997 peak No. 37).*	*Silvertone*	23	*29 Apr 95*	19
THE COMPLETE STONE ROSES *Includes re-entries through to 2000.*	*Silvertone*	4	*27 May 95*	25
GARAGE FLOWER *Contains previously unreleased songs and early B-sides.*	*Silvertone*	58	*7 Dec 96*	1
STONE ROSES - 10TH ANNIVERSARY EDITION *Reissue of their first album plus a second enhanced CD.*	*Silvertone*	26	*16 Oct 99*	3
THE REMIXES	*Silvertone*	41	*11 Nov 00*	2

STONE TEMPLE PILOTS — US

SINGLES:	HITS 4		WEEKS 11	
SEX TYPE THING	*Atlantic*	60	*27 Mar 93*	2
PLUSH	*Atlantic*	23	*4 Sep 93*	4
SEX TYPE THING [RI]	*Atlantic*	55	*27 Nov 93*	2
VASOLINE	*Atlantic*	48	*20 Aug 94*	2
INTERSTATE LOVE SONG	*Atlantic*	53	*10 Dec 94*	1
ALBUMS:	**HITS 3**		**WEEKS 19**	
CORE *Originally released in 1992.*	*Atlantic*	27	*4 Sep 93*	8
PURPLE	*Atlantic*	10	*18 Jun 94*	9
TINY MUSIC . . . SONGS FROM THE VATICAN GIFT SHOP	*Atlantic*	31	*6 Apr 96*	2

STONE THE CROWS — UK

ALBUMS:	HITS 1		WEEKS 3	
CONTINUOUS PERFORMANCE	*Polydor*	33	*7 Oct 72*	3

STONEBRIDGE McGUINNESS — UK

SINGLES:	HITS 1		WEEKS 2	
OO-EEH BABY	*RCA Victor*	54	*14 Jul 79*	2

STONEPROOF° — UK

SINGLES:	HITS 1		WEEKS 1	
EVERYTHING'S NOT YOU	*VC Recordings*	68	*15 May 99*	1

STONKERS - See HALE and PACE and the STONKERS

STOOGES - See Iggy POP

STOP THE VIOLENCE MOVEMENT — US

SINGLES:	HITS 1		WEEKS 1	
SELF-DESTRUCTION	*Jive*	75	*18 Feb 89*	1

Axel STORDAHL - See June HUTTON and Axel STORDAHL with the BOYS NEXT DOOR

STORM — UK

SINGLES:	HITS 1		WEEKS 10	
IT'S MY HOUSE	*Scope*	36	*17 Nov 79*	10

STORM — Germany

(See also Jam and Spoon featuring Plavka.)

SINGLES:	HITS 3		WEEKS 19	
STORM	*Positiva*	32	*29 Aug 98*	2
TIME TO BURN	*Data*	3	*12 Aug 00*	10
STORM ANIMAL	*Data*	21	*23 Dec 00*	5
STORM [RM] *Remixed by BK and Nick Sentience.*	*Positiva*	32	*26 May 01*	2

Danny STORM — UK

SINGLES:	HITS 1		WEEKS 4	
HONEST I DO	*Piccadilly*	42	*14 Apr 62*	4

Rebecca STORM — UK

SINGLES:	HITS 1		WEEKS 13	
THE SHOW (THEME FROM CONNIE) *Theme from the Central region ITV series.*	*Towerbell*	22	*13 Jul 85*	13

STORYVILLE JAZZMEN - See Bob WALLIS and his STORYVILLE JAZZMEN

Beryl STOTT CHORUS - See Petula CLARK; Joe "Mr. Piano" HENDERSON; Edmund HOCKRIDGE; George FORMBY with the Beryl STOTT CHORUS; David MacBETH - Kim DRAKE MUSIC - Beryl STOTT GROUP; Gary MILLER; Marion RYAN with the Peter KNIGHT ORCHESTRA and the Beryl STOTT CHORUS

Wally STOTT and his Orchestra – see Winifred ATWELL; Shirley BASSEY; Ronnie CARROLL; Roy CASTLE; Lonnie DONEGAN; Robert EARL; David HUGHES with the Wally STOTT ORCHESTRA; KAYE SISTERS; Susan MAUGHAN; Harry SECOMBE; Anne SHELTON; Muriel SMITH with Wally STOTT and his Orchestra; Dickie VALENTINE; Frankie VAUGHAN

Izzy STRADLIN' — US

SINGLES:	HITS 1			WEEKS 2
PRESSURE DROP	*Geffen*	45	*26 Sep 92*	2
ALBUMS:	**HITS 1**			**WEEKS 1**
IZZY STRADLIN' AND THE JU JU HOUNDS	*Geffen*	52	*24 Oct 92*	1
Above hit: Izzy STRADLIN' and the JU JU HOUNDS.				

Nick STRAKER BAND — UK

SINGLES:	HITS 2			WEEKS 15
A WALK IN THE PARK	*CBS*	20	*2 Aug 80*	12
LEAVING ON THE MIDNIGHT TRAIN	*CBS*	61	*15 Nov 80*	3

Peter STRAKER – The HANDS OF DOCTOR TELENY — UK

SINGLES:	HITS 1			WEEKS 4
THE SPIRIT IS WILLING	*RCA Victor*	40	*19 Feb 72*	4

STRANGE BEHAVIOUR – See Jane KENNAWAY and STRANGE BEHAVIOUR

STRANGE FRUIT – See Jimmy NAIL

STRANGELOVE — UK

SINGLES:	HITS 6			WEEKS 8
LIVING WITH THE HUMAN MACHINES	*Food*	53	*20 Apr 96*	1
BEAUTIFUL ALONE	*Food*	35	*15 Jun 96*	2
SWAY	*Food*	47	*19 Oct 96*	1
THE GREATEST SHOW ON EARTH	*Food*	36	*26 Jul 97*	2
FREAK	*Food*	43	*11 Oct 97*	1
ANOTHER NIGHT IN	*Food*	46	*21 Feb 98*	1
ALBUMS:	**HITS 3**			**WEEKS 3**
TIME FOR THE REST OF YOUR LIFE	*Food*	69	*13 Aug 94*	1
LOVE AND OTHER DEMONS	*Food*	44	*29 Jun 96*	1
STRANGELOVE	*Food*	67	*18 Oct 97*	1

STRANGLERS — UK

SINGLES:	HITS 31			WEEKS 194
(GET A) GRIP (ON YOURSELF)	*United Artists*	44	*19 Feb 77*	4
PEACHES / GO BUDDY GO	*United Artists*	8	*21 May 77*	14
Go Buddy Go listed from 11 Jun 77.				
SOMETHING BETTER CHANGE / STRAIGHTEN OUT	*United Artists*	9	*30 Jul 77*	8
Straighten Out listed from 13 Aug 77.				
NO MORE HEROES	*United Artists*	8	*24 Sep 77*	9
5 MINUTES	*United Artists*	11	*4 Feb 78*	9
NICE 'N' SLEAZY	*United Artists*	18	*6 May 78*	8
WALK ON BY	*United Artists*	21	*12 Aug 78*	8
DUCHESS	*United Artists*	14	*18 Aug 79*	9
NUCLEAR DEVICE (THE WIZARD OF AUS)	*United Artists*	36	*20 Oct 79*	4
DON'T BRING HARRY [EP]	*United Artists*	41	*1 Dec 79*	3
Lead track: Don't Bring Harry.				
BEAR CAGE	*United Artists*	36	*22 Mar 80*	5
WHO WANTS THE WORLD	*United Artists*	39	*7 Jun 80*	4
THROWN AWAY	*Liberty*	42	*31 Jan 81*	4
LET ME INTRODUCE YOU TO THE FAMILY	*United Artists*	42	*14 Nov 81*	3
GOLDEN BROWN	*Liberty*	2	*9 Jan 82*	12
LA FOLIE	*Liberty*	47	*24 Apr 82*	3
STRANGE LITTLE GIRL	*Liberty*	7	*24 Jul 82*	9
EUROPEAN FEMALE	*Epic*	9	*8 Jan 83*	6
MIDNIGHT SUMMER DREAM	*Epic*	35	*26 Feb 83*	4
PARADISE	*Epic*	48	*6 Aug 83*	3
SKIN DEEP	*Epic*	15	*6 Oct 84*	7
NO MERCY	*Epic*	37	*1 Dec 84*	7
LET ME DOWN EASY	*Epic*	48	*16 Feb 85*	4
NICE IN NICE	*Epic*	30	*23 Aug 86*	5
ALWAYS THE SUN	*Epic*	30	*18 Oct 86*	5
BIG IN AMERICA	*Epic*	48	*13 Dec 86*	6
SHAKIN' LIKE A LEAF	*Epic*	58	*7 Mar 87*	4
ALL DAY AND ALL OF THE NIGHT	*Epic*	7	*9 Jan 88*	7
GRIP '89 (GET A) GRIP (ON YOURSELF) [RM]	*EMI*	33	*28 Jan 89*	3
Remixed by Taff B. Dylan and Barry Cooder.				
96 TEARS	*Epic*	17	*17 Feb 90*	6
SWEET SMELL OF SUCCESS	*Epic*	65	*21 Apr 90*	2
ALWAYS THE SUN [RM]	*Epic*	29	*5 Jan 91*	5
GOLDEN BROWN [RM]	*Epic*	68	*30 Mar 91*	2

HEAVEN OR HELL	*Psycho*	46	*22 Aug 92*	2
ALBUMS:	**HITS 19**			**WEEKS 219**
STRANGLERS IV (RATTUS NORVEGICUS)	*United Artists*	4	*30 Apr 77*	34
NO MORE HEROES	*United Artists*	2	*8 Oct 77*	19
BLACK AND WHITE	*United Artists*	2	*3 Jun 78*	18
LIVE (X CERT)	*United Artists*	7	*10 Mar 79*	10
Live recordings from the Roundhouse and Battersea Park, London.				
THE RAVEN	*United Artists*	4	*6 Oct 79*	8
THEMENINBLACK	*Liberty*	8	*21 Feb 81*	5
LA FOLIE	*Liberty*	11	*21 Nov 81*	18
THE COLLECTION 1977 - 1982	*Liberty*	12	*25 Sep 82*	16
FELINE	*Epic*	4	*22 Jan 83*	11
AURAL SCULPTURE	*Epic*	14	*17 Nov 84*	10
OFF THE BEATEN TRACK	*Liberty*	80	*20 Sep 86*	2
Compilation of early recordings.				
DREAMTIME	*Epic*	16	*8 Nov 86*	6
ALL LIVE AND ALL OF THE NIGHT	*Epic*	12	*20 Feb 88*	6
Consists mainly of live recordings from 1987.				
THE SINGLES - THE UA YEARS	*EMI*	57	*18 Feb 89*	2
10	*Epic*	15	*17 Mar 90*	4
GREATEST HITS 1977-1990	*Epic*	47	*1 Dec 90*	3
GREATEST HITS 1977-1990 [RE]	*Epic*	4	*12 Jan 91*	44
Peak position reached on 6 Jul 91.				
STRANGLERS IN THE NIGHT	*Psycho*	33	*19 Sep 92*	1
ABOUT TIME	*When!*	31	*27 May 95*	1
Album of demos recorded in 1975.				
WRITTEN IN RED	*When!*	52	*8 Feb 97*	1

STRAW — UK

SINGLES:	**HITS 3**			**WEEKS 4**
THE AEROPLANE SONG	*WEA*	37	*6 Feb 99*	2
MOVING TO CALIFORNIA	*WEA*	50	*24 Apr 99*	1
SAILING OFF THE EDGE OF THE WORLD	*Columbia*	52	*3 Mar 01*	1

STRAWBERRY SWITCHBLADE — UK

SINGLES:	**HITS 3**			**WEEKS 26**
SINCE YESTERDAY	*Korova*	5	*17 Nov 84*	17
LET HER GO	*Korova*	59	*23 Mar 85*	5
JOLENE	*Korova*	53	*21 Sep 85*	4
ALBUMS:	**HITS 1**			**WEEKS 4**
STRAWBERRY SWITCHBLADE	*Korova*	25	*13 Apr 85*	4

STRAWBS — UK

SINGLES:	**HITS 3**			**WEEKS 27**
LAY DOWN	*A&M*	12	*28 Oct 72*	13
PART OF THE UNION	*A&M*	2	*27 Jan 73*	11
SHINE ON SILVER SUN	*A&M*	34	*6 Oct 73*	3
ALBUMS:	**HITS 5**			**WEEKS 31**
JUST A COLLECTION OF ANTIQUES AND CURIOS	*A&M*	27	*21 Nov 70*	2
FROM THE WITCHWOOD	*A&M*	39	*17 Jul 71*	2
GRAVE NEW WORLD	*A&M*	11	*26 Feb 72*	12
BUSTING AT THE SEAMS	*A&M*	2	*24 Feb 73*	12
HERO AND HEROINE	*A&M*	35	*27 Apr 74*	3

STRAY CATS — US

SINGLES:	**HITS 7**			**WEEKS 49**
RUNAWAY BOYS	*Arista*	9	*29 Nov 80*	10
ROCK THIS TOWN	*Arista*	9	*7 Feb 81*	8
STRAY CAT STRUT	*Arista*	11	*25 Apr 81*	10
THE RACE IS ON	*Swan Song*	34	*20 Jun 81*	6
Originally recorded by George Jones.				
Above hit: Dave EDMUNDS and the STRAY CATS.				
YOU DON'T BELIEVE ME	*Arista*	57	*7 Nov 81*	3
(SHE'S) SEXY AND 17	*Arista*	29	*6 Aug 83*	9
BRING IT BACK AGAIN	*EMI USA*	64	*4 Mar 89*	3
ALBUMS:	**HITS 4**			**WEEKS 32**
STRAY CATS	*Arista*	6	*28 Feb 81*	22
GONNA BALL	*Arista*	48	*21 Nov 81*	4
RANT 'N' RAVE WITH THE STRAY CATS	*Arista*	51	*3 Sep 83*	5
BLAST OFF	*EMI*	58	*8 Apr 89*	1

STREETBAND — UK

SINGLES:	**HITS 1**			**WEEKS 6**
TOAST / HOLD ON	*Logo*	18	*4 Nov 78*	6

STREETS — UK

SINGLES:	HITS 1			WEEKS 5
HAS IT COME TO THIS?	*679 Recordings*	18	*20 Oct 01*	4
HAS IT COME TO THIS? [RE]	*679 Recordings*	55	*1 Dec 01*	1

STREETWALKERS — UK

ALBUMS:	HITS 1			WEEKS 6
RED CARD	*Vertigo*	16	*12 Jun 76*	6

Barbra STREISAND — US

SINGLES:	HITS 18			WEEKS 155
SECOND HAND ROSE	*CBS*	14	*22 Jan 66*	13
STONEY END	*CBS*	46	*30 Jan 71*	1
Originally recorded by Laura Nyro.				
STONEY END [RE]	*CBS*	27	*13 Feb 71*	10
THE WAY WE WERE	*CBS*	31	*30 Mar 74*	6
From the film of the same name.				
LOVE THEME FROM "A STAR IS BORN" (EVERGREEN)	*CBS*	3	*9 Apr 77*	19
Theme from the film.				
YOU DON'T BRING ME FLOWERS	*CBS*	5	*25 Nov 78*	12
Above hit: BARBRA and NEIL.				
NO MORE TEARS (ENOUGH IS ENOUGH)	*CBS & Casablanca*	3	*3 Nov 79*	13
Sales combined for the 7" on Casablanca and the 12" on CBS.				
Above hit: Donna SUMMER/Barbra STREISAND.				
WOMAN IN LOVE	*CBS*	1	*4 Oct 80*	16
Written by Barry Gibb.				
GUILTY	*CBS*	34	*6 Dec 80*	10
Above hit: Barbra STREISAND and Barry GIBB.				
COMIN' IN AND OUT OF YOUR LIFE	*CBS*	66	*30 Jan 82*	3
MEMORY	*CBS*	34	*20 Mar 82*	6
From the Andrew Lloyd Webber musical 'Cats'.				
TILL I LOVED YOU (THE LOVE THEME FROM GOYA)	*CBS*	16	*5 Nov 88*	7
From the film 'Goya'.				
Above hit: Barbra STREISAND and Don JOHNSON.				
PLACES THAT BELONG TO YOU	*Columbia*	17	*7 Mar 92*	5
From the film 'The Prince Of Tides'.				
WITH ONE LOOK	*Columbia*	30	*5 Jun 93*	3
From the musical 'Sunset Boulevard'.				
THE MUSIC OF THE NIGHT	*Columbia*	54	*15 Jan 94*	3
From the Andrew Lloyd Webber musical 'The Phantom Of The Opera'.				
Above hit: Barbra STREISAND (duet with Michael CRAWFORD).				
AS IF WE NEVER SAID GOODBYE (FROM SUNSET BOULEVARD)	*Columbia*	20	*30 Apr 94*	3
From the musical.				
I FINALLY FOUND SOMEONE	*A&M*	10	*8 Feb 97*	7
From the film 'The Mirror Has Two Faces'.				
Above hit: Barbra STREISAND and Bryan ADAMS.				
TELL HIM	*Columbia*	3	*15 Nov 97*	15
Above hit: Barbra STREISAND/Celine DION.				
IF YOU EVER LEAVE ME	*Columbia*	26	*30 Oct 99*	3
Above hit: Barbra STREISAND / Vince GILL.				

EPS:	HITS 2			WEEKS 14
MY MAN	*CBS*	8	*15 Jan 66*	13
EN FRANCAIS	*CBS*	10	*11 Jun 66*	1

ALBUMS:	HITS 24			WEEKS 516
MY NAME IS BARBRA, TWO	*CBS*	6	*22 Jan 66*	22
FUNNY GIRL	*Capitol*	19	*30 Apr 66*	3
London cast recording.				
FUNNY GIRL [OST]	*CBS*	11	*10 May 69*	22
Includes track by Mae Questal and Kay Medford.				
HELLO DOLLY! [OST]	*EMI Stateside*	45	*14 Mar 70*	2
Includes tracks by Michael Crawford, Marianne McAndrew and Walter Matthau.				
BARBRA STREISAND'S GREATEST HITS	*CBS*	44	*4 Apr 70*	2
STONEY END	*CBS*	28	*17 Apr 71*	2
THE WAY WE WERE	*CBS*	49	*15 Jun 74*	1
A STAR IS BORN [OST]	*CBS*	1	*9 Apr 77*	54
Kris Kristofferson appears on 5 tracks, Streisand on 8 of which 2 are as duets.				
Above hit: Barbra STREISAND Kris KRISTOFFERSON				
STREISAND SUPERMAN	*CBS*	32	*23 Jul 77*	9
SONGBIRD	*CBS*	50	*15 Jul 78*	1
BARBRA STREISAND GREATEST HITS VOLUME 2	*CBS*	1	*17 Mar 79*	30
WET	*CBS*	25	*17 Nov 79*	13
GUILTY	*CBS*	1	*11 Oct 80*	82
LOVE SONGS	*CBS*	1	*16 Jan 82*	128
YENTL [OST]	*CBS*	21	*19 Nov 83*	35
EMOTION	*CBS*	15	*27 Oct 84*	12

THE BROADWAY ALBUM *Songs from the musicals.*	*CBS*	3	*18 Jan 86*	16
ONE VOICE *Live recordings in front of 500 invited guests at her home in Malibu.*	*CBS*	27	*30 May 87*	7
TILL I LOVED YOU	*CBS*	29	*3 Dec 88*	13
A COLLECTION - GREATEST HITS . . . AND MORE	*CBS*	22	*25 Nov 89*	20
BACK TO BROADWAY *Sequel to the 1986 album.*	*Columbia*	4	*10 Jul 93*	17
A COLLECTION - GREATEST HITS . . . AND MORE [RI]	*Columbia*	37	*30 Apr 94*	3
BARBRA - THE CONCERT *Live recordings of her New York Madison Square Garden concert.*	*Columbia*	63	*29 Oct 94*	1
HIGHER GROUND	*Columbia*	12	*22 Nov 97*	12
A LOVE LIKE OURS	*Columbia*	12	*2 Oct 99*	9
TIMELESS - LIVE IN CONCERT *Live recordings from the MGM Grand, Las Vegas on 31 Dec 99.*	*Columbia*	54	*30 Sep 00*	1

STRESS — UK

SINGLES:	HITS 1			WEEKS 1
BEAUTIFUL PEOPLE	*Eternal*	74	*13 Oct 90*	1

STRETCH — UK

SINGLES:	HITS 1			WEEKS 9
WHY DID YOU DO IT	*Anchor*	16	*8 Nov 75*	9

STRETCH and VERN present "MADDOG" — UK

SINGLES:	HITS 2			WEEKS 14
I'M ALIVE *Samples Earth, Wind And Fire and the Emotions' Boogie Wonderland.*	*ffrr*	6	*14 Sep 96*	9
GET UP! GO INSANE! *Samples House Of Pain's Jump Around.* *Above hit: STRETCH 'N' VERN present "MADDOG".*	*ffrr*	17	*9 Aug 97*	5

STRICT INSTRUCTOR — Russia

SINGLES:	HITS 1			WEEKS 1
STEP-TWO-THREE-FOUR *Based around Bob Sinclair's Jane Fonda work-out inspired disc Gymtonic.*	*All Around The World*	49	*24 Oct 98*	1

STRIKE — UK/Australia

SINGLES:	HITS 5			WEEKS 24
U SURE DO *Vocals by Australian singer Vicky Newton from the group Eden.*	*Fresh*	31	*24 Dec 94*	5
U SURE DO [RE]	*Fresh*	4	*1 Apr 95*	9
THE MORNING AFTER (FREE AT LAST)	*Fresh*	38	*23 Sep 95*	1
INSPIRATION	*Fresh*	27	*29 Jun 96*	2
MY LOVE IS FOR REAL	*Fresh*	35	*16 Nov 96*	2
I HAVE PEACE *Features rapper K-Gee.*	*Fresh*	17	*31 May 97*	4
U SURE DO '99 [RM] *Remixed by Jono Grant.*	*Fresh*	53	*25 Sept 99*	1

STRIKERS — US

SINGLES:	HITS 1			WEEKS 5
BODY MUSIC	*Epic*	45	*6 Jun 81*	5

STRING-A-LONGS — US

SINGLES:	HITS 1			WEEKS 16
WHEELS	*London*	8	*25 Feb 61*	16

STRINGS FOR PLEASURE — UK

ALBUMS:	HITS 1			WEEKS 1
THE BEST OF BACHARACH	*Music For Pleasure*	49	*4 Dec 71*	1

STRINGS OF LOVE — Italy

SINGLES:	HITS 1			WEEKS 2
NOTHING HAS BEEN PROVED	*Breakout*	59	*3 Mar 90*	2

STROKES — US

SINGLES:	HITS 3			WEEKS 13
HARD TO EXPLAIN/NEW YORK CITY COPS	*Rough Trade*	16	*7 Jul 01*	5
THE MODERN AGE *Original release peaked at No. 79 when first released in February 2001.*	*Rough Trade*	74	*7 Jul 01*	1
THE MODERN AGE [RE-1ST]	*Rough Trade*	68	*21 Jul 01*	1
THE MODERN AGE [RE-2ND]	*Rough Trade*	71	*11 Aug 01*	1
LAST NITE	*Rough Trade*	14	*17 Nov 01*	5

ALBUMS:	HITS 1			WEEKS 17
IS THIS IT?	*Rough Trade*	2	*8 Sep 01*	17

Joe STRUMMER — UK

(See also Black Grape.)

SINGLES:	HITS 2			WEEKS 9
LOVE KILLS	*CBS*	69	*2 Aug 86*	1
JUST THE ONE	*China*	12	*23 Dec 95*	8

Above hit: LEVELLERS Special guest Joe STRUMMER on piano.

ALBUMS:	HITS 3			WEEKS 3
EARTHQUAKE WEATHER	*Epic*	58	*14 Oct 89*	1
ROCK ART AND THE X-RAY STYLE	*Mercury*	71	*30 Oct 99*	1
GLOBAL A GO GO	*Hellcat*	68	*28 Jul 01*	1

Above 2: Joe STRUMMER and the MESCALEROS.

STRYKER – See MANCHESTER UNITED FOOTBALL SQUAD

Chad STUART and Jeremy CLYDE — UK

SINGLES:	HITS 1			WEEKS 7
YESTERDAY'S GONE	*Ember*	37	*30 Nov 63*	7

STUDIO 45 — Germany

SINGLES:	HITS 1			WEEKS 2
FREAK IT!	*Azuli*	36	*20 Feb 99*	2

STUDIO 2 — Jamaica

SINGLES:	HITS 1			WEEKS 1
TRAVELLING MAN	*Multiply*	40	*27 Jun 98*	1

STUMP — UK

SINGLES:	HITS 1			WEEKS 1
CHARLTON HESTON	*Ensign*	72	*13 Aug 88*	1

Cupid STUNT – See Kenny EVERETT

STUNTMASTERZ — UK

SINGLES:	HITS 1			WEEKS 9
THE LADYBOY IS MINE	*East West*	10	*3 Mar 01*	9

A fusion of Modjo's Lady and Brandy & Monica's The Boy Is Mine, it also samples Chic's Soup For One.

STUTZ BEAR CATS — UK

SINGLES:	HITS 1			WEEKS 6
THE SONG THAT I SING	*Multi-Media Tapes*	36	*24 Apr 82*	6

Vocal version of the theme to the LWT ITV series 'We'll Meet Again'. [AA] listed with The Theme From "We'll Meet Again" by Denis King and his Orchestra.

STYLE COUNCIL — UK

SINGLES:	HITS 17			WEEKS 103
SPEAK LIKE A CHILD	*Polydor*	4	*19 Mar 83*	8
MONEY GO ROUND (PART ONE)	*Polydor*	11	*28 May 83*	6
LONG HOT SUMMER / THE PARIS MATCH	*Polydor*	3	*13 Aug 83*	9
The Paris Match listed from 3 Sep 83 once single had dropped to No 7. Sleeve gives title as an EP: A Paris.				
MONEY GO ROUND (PART 1) [RE]	*Polydor*	74	*20 Aug 83*	1
A SOLID BOND IN YOUR HEART	*Polydor*	11	*19 Nov 83*	8
Was planned as the Jam's last single.				
MY EVER CHANGING MOODS	*Polydor*	5	*18 Feb 84*	7
GROOVIN' (YOU'RE THE BEST THING) / GROOVIN' (THE BIG BOSS GROOVE)	*Polydor*	5	*26 May 84*	8
SHOUT TO THE TOP	*Polydor*	7	*13 Oct 84*	8
WALLS COME TUMBLING DOWN!	*Polydor*	6	*11 May 85*	7
COME TO MILTON KEYNES	*Polydor*	23	*6 Jul 85*	5
THE LODGERS	*Polydor*	13	*28 Sep 85*	6
Above hit: STYLE COUNCIL featuring Dee C. LEE.				
HAVE YOU EVER HAD IT BLUE	*Polydor*	14	*5 Apr 86*	6
From the film 'Absolute Beginners'.				
IT DIDN'T MATTER	*Polydor*	9	*17 Jan 87*	5
WAITING	*Polydor*	52	*14 Mar 87*	3
WANTED	*Polydor*	20	*31 Oct 87*	4
LIFE AT A TOP PEOPLES HEALTH FARM	*Polydor*	28	*28 May 88*	3
HOW SHE THREW IT ALL AWAY	*Polydor*	41	*23 Jul 88*	2
PROMISED LAND	*Polydor*	27	*18 Feb 89*	5
LONG HOT SUMMER '89 [RM]	*Polydor*	48	*27 May 89*	2

ALBUMS:	HITS 9			WEEKS 99
CAFE BLEU	*Polydor*	2	*24 Mar 84*	38
OUR FAVOURITE SHOP	*Polydor*	1	*8 Jun 85*	22
HOME AND ABROAD	*Polydor*	8	*17 May 86*	8
THE COST OF LOVING	*Polydor*	2	*14 Feb 87*	7
CONFESSIONS OF A POP GROUP	*Polydor*	15	*2 Jul 88*	3
THE SINGULAR ADVENTURES OF THE STYLE COUNCIL GREATEST HITS VOLUME 1	*Polydor*	3	*18 Mar 89*	15
HERE'S SOME THAT GOT AWAY	*Polydor*	39	*10 Jul 93*	1
Compilation of B-sides, demos, cover versions and previously unavailable tracks.				
THE STYLE COUNCIL COLLECTION	*Polydor*	60	*2 Mar 96*	1
GREATEST HITS	*Polydor*	28	*2 Sep 00*	4

STYLISTICS — US

SINGLES:	HITS 16			WEEKS 143
BETCHA BY GOLLY, WOW	*Avco*	13	*24 Jun 72*	12
Above hit: STYLISTICS featuring Russell THOMPKINS, JR.				
I'M STONE IN LOVE WITH YOU	*Avco*	9	*4 Nov 72*	10
BREAK UP TO MAKE UP	*Avco*	34	*17 Mar 73*	5
PEEK-A-BOO	*Avco*	35	*30 Jun 73*	6
ROCKIN' ROLL BABY	*Avco*	6	*19 Jan 74*	9
YOU MAKE ME FEEL BRAND NEW	*Avco*	2	*13 Jul 74*	14
Above hit: STYLISTICS (featuring Airrion LOVE and Russell THOMPKINS, Jr.).				
LET'S PUT IT ALL TOGETHER	*Avco*	9	*19 Oct 74*	9
STAR ON A TV SHOW	*Avco*	12	*25 Jan 75*	8
SING BABY SING	*Avco*	3	*10 May 75*	10
CAN'T GIVE YOU ANYTHING (BUT MY LOVE)	*Avco*	1	*26 Jul 75*	11
NA-NA IS THE SADDEST WORD	*Avco*	5	*15 Nov 75*	10
FUNKY WEEKEND	*Avco*	10	*14 Feb 76*	7
CAN'T HELP FALLING IN LOVE	*H&L*	4	*24 Apr 76*	7
SIXTEEN BARS	*H&L*	7	*7 Aug 76*	9
YOU'LL NEVER GET TO HEAVEN [EP]	*H&L*	24	*27 Nov 76*	9
Lead track: You'll Never Get To Heaven (If You Break My Heart).				
$7000 AND YOU	*H&L*	24	*26 Mar 77*	7
ALBUMS:	**HITS 9**			**WEEKS 142**
ROCKIN' ROLL BABY	*Avco*	42	*24 Aug 74*	3
LET'S PUT IT ALL TOGETHER	*Avco*	26	*21 Sep 74*	14
FROM THE MOUNTAIN	*Avco*	36	*1 Mar 75*	1
Title was 'Heavy' in the US.				
THE BEST OF THE STYLISTICS	*Avco*	1	*5 Apr 75*	63
THANK YOU BABY	*Avco*	5	*5 Jul 75*	23
YOU ARE BEAUTIFUL	*Avco*	26	*6 Dec 75*	9
FABULOUS	*H&L*	21	*12 Jun 76*	5
BEST OF THE STYLISTICS VOLUME 2	*H&L*	1	*18 Sep 76*	21
THE GREATEST HITS OF THE STYLISTICS	*Mercury*	34	*17 Oct 92*	3

STYLUS TROUBLE — UK

SINGLES:	HITS 1			WEEKS 1
SPUTNIK ONE	*Junior*	63	*23 Jun 01*	1

STYX — US

SINGLES:	HITS 3			WEEKS 18
BABE	*A&M*	6	*5 Jan 80*	10
THE BEST OF TIMES	*A&M*	42	*24 Jan 81*	5
Labelled as the world's first laser-etched single.				
DON'T LET IT END	*A&M*	56	*18 Jun 83*	3
ALBUMS:	**HITS 4**			**WEEKS 24**
CORNERSTONE	*A&M*	36	*3 Nov 79*	8
PARADISE THEATER	*A&M*	8	*24 Jan 81*	8
KILROY WAS HERE	*A&M*	67	*12 Mar 83*	6
CAUGHT IN THE ACT	*A&M*	44	*5 May 84*	2
Live recordings.				

SUB.MERGE featuring Jan JOHNSTON — US

SINGLES:	HITS 1			WEEKS 2
TAKE ME BY THE HAND	*AM:PM*	28	*8 Feb 97*	2

SUB SUB — UK

SINGLES:	HITS 2			WEEKS 12
AIN'T NO LOVE (AIN'T NO USE)	*Rob's Records*	3	*10 Apr 93*	11
Above hit: SUB SUB featuring Melanie WILLIAMS.				
RESPECT	*Rob's Records*	49	*19 Feb 94*	1
Samples the Fatback Band's Double Dutch.				

SUBCIRCUS — UK/Denmark

SINGLES:	HITS 2			WEEKS 2
YOU LOVE YOU	*Echo*	61	*26 Apr 97*	1
86'D	*Echo*	56	*12 Jul 97*	1

Original release reached No. 88 earlier in the year.

SUBLIME — US

SINGLES:	HITS 1			WEEKS 1
WHAT I GOT	*MCA*	71	*5 Jul 97*	1

SUBLIMINAL CUTS — Holland

(See also Artemesia; Ethics; Movin' Melodies.)

SINGLES:	HITS 1			WEEKS 3
LE VOIE LE SOLEIL	*XL Recordings*	69	*15 Oct 94*	1
LE VOIE LE SOLEIL [RM]	*XL Recordings*	23	*20 Jul 96*	2

Remixed by Way Out West.

SUBSONIC 2 — UK

SINGLES:	HITS 1			WEEKS 3
UNSUNG HEROES OF HIP HOP	*Unity*	63	*13 Jul 91*	3

SUBTERRANIA featuring Ann CONSUELO — Sweden

SINGLES:	HITS 1			WEEKS 1
DO IT FOR LOVE	*Champion*	68	*5 Jun 93*	1

SUEDE — UK

SINGLES:	HITS 17			WEEKS 68
THE DROWNERS / TO THE BIRDS	*Nude*	49	*23 May 92*	2
METAL MICKEY	*Nude*	17	*26 Sep 92*	3
ANIMAL NITRATE	*Nude*	7	*6 Mar 93*	7
SO YOUNG	*Nude*	22	*29 May 93*	3
STAY TOGETHER	*Nude*	3	*26 Feb 94*	6
WE ARE THE PIGS	*Nude*	18	*24 Sep 94*	3
Brass accompaniment by The Kick Horns.				
THE WILD ONES	*Nude*	18	*19 Nov 94*	4
NEW GENERATION	*Nude*	21	*11 Feb 95*	3
NEW GENERATION [RE]	*Nude*	75	*11 Mar 95*	1
TRASH	*Nude*	3	*10 Aug 96*	6
BEAUTIFUL ONES	*Nude*	8	*26 Oct 96*	5
SATURDAY NIGHT	*Nude*	6	*25 Jan 97*	4
LAZY	*Nude*	9	*19 Apr 97*	3
FILMSTAR	*Nude*	9	*23 Aug 97*	4
ELECTRICITY	*Nude*	5	*24 Apr 99*	5
SHE'S IN FASHION	*Nude*	13	*3 Jul 99*	5
EVERYTHING WILL FLOW	*Nude*	24	*18 Sept 99*	2
CAN'T GET ENOUGH	*Nude*	23	*20 Nov 99*	2
ALBUMS:	**HITS 5**			**WEEKS 101**
SUEDE	*Nude*	1	*10 Apr 93*	22
DOG MAN STAR	*Nude*	3	*22 Oct 94*	16
COMING UP	*Nude*	1	*14 Sep 96*	44
SCI-FI LULLABIES	*Nude*	9	*18 Oct 97*	3
Compilation containing all the B-sides of their singles to date.				
HEAD MUSIC	*Nude*	1	*15 May 99*	16

SUEDETTES – See WIZZARD

SUENO LATINO featuring Carolina DAMAS — Italy

SINGLES:	HITS 1			WEEKS 6
SUENO LATINO	*BCM*	47	*23 Sep 89*	5
SUENO LATINO [RM]	*Distinct'ive*	68	*11 Nov 00*	1

Remixed by Kayestone.
Above hit: SUENO LATINO.

SUGABABES — UK

SINGLES:	HITS 4			WEEKS 26
OVERLOAD	*London*	6	*23 Sep 00*	8
NEW YEAR	*London*	12	*30 Dec 00*	9
RUN FOR COVER	*London*	13	*21 Apr 01*	7
SOUL SOUND	*London*	30	*28 Jul 01*	2
ALBUMS:	**HITS 1**			**WEEKS 15**
ONE TOUCH	*London*	26	*23 Dec 00*	15

SUGAR — US

SINGLES:	HITS 5			WEEKS 7
A GOOD IDEA	*Creation*	65	*31 Oct 92*	1
IF I CAN'T CHANGE YOUR MIND	*Creation*	30	*30 Jan 93*	2
TILTED	*Creation*	48	*21 Aug 93*	1
YOUR FAVORITE THING	*Creation*	40	*3 Sep 94*	2
BELIEVE WHAT YOU'RE SAYING	*Creation*	73	*29 Oct 94*	1
ALBUMS:	**HITS 3**			**WEEKS 19**
COPPER BLUE	*Creation*	10	*19 Sep 92*	11
BEASTER	*Creation*	3	*17 Apr 93*	5
FILE UNDER EASY LISTENING	*Creation*	7	*17 Sep 94*	3

SUGAR CANE — US

SINGLES:	HITS 1			WEEKS 5
MONTEGO BAY	*Ariola Hansa*	54	*30 Sep 78*	5

SUGAR RAY — US

SINGLES:	HITS 3			WEEKS 12
FLY	*Atlantic*	58	*31 Jan 98*	1
Above hit: SUGAR RAY (featuring SUPER CAT).				
EVERY MORNING	*Atlantic*	10	*29 May 99*	9
WHEN IT'S OVER	*Atlantic*	32	*20 Oct 01*	2
ALBUMS:	**HITS 1**			**WEEKS 1**
14:59	*Atlantic*	60	*19 Jun 99*	1

SUGARCUBES — Iceland

SINGLES:	HITS 6			WEEKS 22
BIRTHDAY	*One Little Indian*	65	*14 Nov 87*	3
COLD SWEAT	*One Little Indian*	56	*30 Jan 88*	4
DEUS	*One Little Indian*	51	*16 Apr 88*	3
BIRTHDAY [RR]	*One Little Indian*	65	*3 Sep 88*	3
REGINA	*One Little Indian*	55	*16 Sep 89*	2
HIT	*One Little Indian*	17	*11 Jan 92*	6
BIRTHDAY [RM]	*One Little Indian*	64	*3 Oct 92*	1
Remixed by Justin Robertson				
ALBUMS:	**HITS 4**			**WEEKS 14**
LIFE'S TOO GOOD	*One Little Indian*	14	*7 May 88*	6
HERE TODAY, TOMORROW, NEXT WEEK	*One Little Indian*	15	*14 Oct 89*	3
STICK AROUND FOR JOY	*One Little Indian*	16	*22 Feb 92*	4
IT'S IT	*One Little Indian*	47	*17 Oct 92*	1

SUGARHILL GANG — US

SINGLES:	HITS 2			WEEKS 16
RAPPER'S DELIGHT	*Sugar Hill*	3	*1 Dec 79*	11
The first rap record to chart. Based around Chic's Good Times.				
THE LOVER IN YOU	*Sugar Hill*	54	*11 Sep 82*	3
RAPPERS DELIGHT '89 [RM]	*Sugar Hill*	58	*25 Nov 89*	2

SUGGS — UK

SINGLES:	HITS 7			WEEKS 46
I'M ONLY SLEEPING / OFF ON HOLIDAY	*WEA*	7	*12 Aug 95*	6
I'm Only Sleeping originally recorded by the Beatles on their 1966 album Revolver.				
CAMDEN TOWN	*WEA*	14	*14 Oct 95*	6
THE TUNE	*WEA*	33	*16 Dec 95*	3
Sleeve gives title as an EP: The Christmas EP.				
CECILIA	*WEA*	4	*13 Apr 96*	17
Originally recorded by Simon and Garfunkel from their 1970 album Bridge Over Troubled Water.				
CECILIA [RE-1ST]	*WEA*	65	*24 Aug 96*	1
CECILIA [RE-2ND]	*WEA*	59	*7 Sep 96*	1
NO MORE ALCOHOL	*WEA*	24	*21 Sep 96*	4
Samples the Champs' Tequila.				
Above 4: SUGGS featuring Louchie LOU and Michie ONE.				
BLUE DAY	*WEA*	22	*17 May 97*	5
Above hit: SUGGS and CO. featuring the CHELSEA TEAM.				
I AM	*WEA*	38	*5 Sep 98*	3
From the film 'The Avengers'.				
ALBUMS:	**HITS 1**			**WEEKS 5**
THE LONE RANGER	*WEA*	14	*28 Oct 95*	5

SUICIDAL TENDENCIES — UK

ALBUMS:	HITS 2			WEEKS 2
JOIN THE ARMY	*Virgin*	81	*9 May 87*	1
LIGHTS . . . CAMERA . . . REVOLUTION	*Epic*	59	*21 Jul 90*	1

SULTANA
Italy

SINGLES:	HITS 1			WEEKS 1
TE AMO	*Union*	57	*26 Mar 94*	1

SULTANS OF PING
Ireland

SINGLES:	HITS 7			WEEKS 12
WHERE'S ME JUMPER?	*Divine*	67	*8 Feb 92*	2
STUPID KID	*Divine*	67	*9 May 92*	1
VERONICA	*Divine*	69	*10 Oct 92*	1
YOU TALK TOO MUCH	*Rhythm King*	26	*9 Jan 93*	3
Above 4: SULTANS OF PING F.C.				
TEENAGE PUNKS	*Epic*	49	*11 Sep 93*	2
MICHIKO	*Epic*	43	*30 Oct 93*	2
WAKE UP AND SCRATCH ME	*Epic*	50	*19 Feb 94*	1
ALBUMS:	**HITS 2**			**WEEKS 3**
CASUAL SEX IN THE CINEPLEX	*Rhythm King*	26	*13 Feb 93*	2
Above hit: SULTANS OF PING F.C.				
TEENAGE DRUG	*Epic*	57	*5 Mar 94*	1

SUM 41
Canada

SINGLES:	HITS 2			WEEKS 12
FAT LIP	*Island*	8	*13 Oct 01*	9
IN TOO DEEP	*Island*	13	*15 Dec 01*	3
ALBUMS:	**HITS 1**			**WEEKS 21**
ALL KILLER NO FILLER	*Island*	18	*11 Aug 01*	21

SUMMER - See SNAP!

Donna SUMMER
US

SINGLES:	HITS 39			WEEKS 299
LOVE TO LOVE YOU BABY	*GTO*	4	*17 Jan 76*	9
COULD IT BE MAGIC	*GTO*	40	*29 May 76*	7
WINTER MELODY	*GTO*	27	*25 Dec 76*	6
I FEEL LOVE	*GTO*	1	*9 Jul 77*	11
DOWN DEEP INSIDE (THEME FROM THE DEEP)	*Casablanca*	5	*20 Aug 77*	10
From the film 'The Deep'.				
I REMEMBER YESTERDAY	*GTO*	14	*24 Sep 77*	7
LOVE'S UNKIND	*GTO*	3	*3 Dec 77*	13
I LOVE YOU	*Casablanca*	10	*10 Dec 77*	9
RUMOUR HAS IT	*Casablanca*	19	*25 Feb 78*	8
BACK IN LOVE AGAIN	*GTO*	29	*22 Apr 78*	7
LAST DANCE	*Casablanca*	70	*10 Jun 78*	1
From the film 'Thank God It's Friday'.				
LAST DANCE [RE]	*Casablanca*	51	*24 Jun 78*	8
MACARTHUR PARK	*Casablanca*	5	*14 Oct 78*	10
HEAVEN KNOWS	*Casablanca*	34	*17 Feb 79*	8
Features Brooklyn Dreams.				
HOT STUFF	*Casablanca*	11	*12 May 79*	10
BAD GIRLS	*Casablanca*	14	*7 Jul 79*	10
DIM ALL THE LIGHTS	*Casablanca*	29	*1 Sep 79*	9
NO MORE TEARS (ENOUGH IS ENOUGH)	*Casablanca & CBS*	3	*3 Nov 79*	13
Sales combined for the 7" on Casablanca & the 12" on CBS.				
Above hit: Donna SUMMER/Barbra STREISAND.				
ON THE RADIO	*Casablanca*	32	*16 Feb 80*	6
SUNSET PEOPLE	*Casablanca*	46	*21 Jun 80*	5
THE WANDERER	*Geffen*	48	*27 Sep 80*	6
COLD LOVE	*Geffen*	44	*17 Jan 81*	3
LOVE IS IN CONTROL (FINGER ON THE TRIGGER)	*Warner Brothers*	18	*10 Jul 82*	11
STATE OF INDEPENDENCE	*Warner Brothers*	14	*6 Nov 82*	11
Features an All-Star Chorus (see later remix entry for details when they got a full artist credit on the sleeve).				
I FEEL LOVE [RM]	*Casablanca*	21	*4 Dec 82*	10
Remixed by Patrick Cowley.				
THE WOMAN IN ME	*Warner Brothers*	62	*5 Mar 83*	2
SHE WORKS HARD FOR THE MONEY	*Mercury*	25	*18 Jun 83*	8
UNCONDITIONAL LOVE	*Mercury*	14	*24 Sep 83*	12
Featuring backing vocals by Musical Youth.				
STOP, LOOK AND LISTEN	*Mercury*	57	*21 Jan 84*	2
DINNER WITH GERSHWIN	*Warner Brothers*	13	*24 Oct 87*	11
Originally recorded by Brenda Russell.				
ALL SYSTEMS GO	*Warner Brothers*	54	*23 Jan 88*	3
THIS TIME I KNOW IT'S FOR REAL	*Warner Brothers*	3	*25 Feb 89*	14
I DON'T WANNA GET HURT	*Warner Brothers*	7	*27 May 89*	9
LOVE'S ABOUT TO CHANGE MY HEART	*Warner Brothers*	20	*26 Aug 89*	6
WHEN LOVE TAKES OVER YOU	*Warner Brothers*	72	*25 Nov 89*	1
STATE OF INDEPENDENCE [RI]	*Warner Brothers*	45	*17 Nov 90*	3

BREAKAWAY	*Warner Brothers*	49	*12 Jan 91*	4
WORK THAT MAGIC	*Warner Brothers*	74	*30 Nov 91*	1
MELODY OF LOVE (WANNA BE LOVED)	*Mercury*	21	*12 Nov 94*	3
I FEEL LOVE [RR]	*Manifesto*	8	*9 Sep 95*	5
Re-recorded as the record label lost the original multi-track.				
STATE OF INDEPENDENCE [RM] -	*Manifesto*	13	*6 Apr 96*	5
Remix programmed by Phil Ramacon and edited by Bruno Morelli.				
Above hit: Donna SUMMER; ALL STAR CHOIR featuring Dara BERNARD, Dylan CANNON, Christopher CROSS, James INGRAM, Michael JACKSON, Peggy Lipton JONES, Quincy JONES, Kenny LOGGINS, Michael McDONALD, Lionel RICHIE, Brenda RUSSELL, Donna SUMMER, Dionne WARWICK and Stevie WONDER.				
CARRY ON	*Almighty*	65	*11 Jul 98*	1
Above hit: Donna SUMMER and Giorgio MORODER.				
I WILL GO WITH YOU (CON TE PARTIRO)	*Epic*	44	*30 Oct 99*	1
ALBUMS:	**HITS 15**			**WEEKS 198**
LOVE TO LOVE YOU BABY	*GTO*	16	*31 Jan 76*	9
A LOVE TRILOGY	*GTO*	41	*22 May 76*	10
I REMEMBER YESTERDAY	*GTO*	3	*25 Jun 77*	23
ONCE UPON A TIME	*Casablanca*	24	*26 Nov 77*	13
GREATEST HITS	*GTO*	4	*7 Jan 78*	18
LIVE AND MORE	*Casablanca*	16	*21 Oct 78*	16
Three sides are live recordings.				
BAD GIRLS	*Casablanca*	23	*2 Jun 79*	23
ON THE RADIO - GREATEST HITS VOLUMES 1 & 2	*Casablanca*	24	*10 Nov 79*	22
THE WANDERER	*Geffen*	55	*1 Nov 80*	2
DONNA SUMMER	*Warner Brothers*	13	*31 Jul 82*	16
SHE WORKS HARD FOR THE MONEY	*Mercury*	28	*16 Jul 83*	5
CATS WITHOUT CLAWS	*Warner Brothers*	69	*15 Sep 84*	2
ANOTHER PLACE AND TIME	*Warner Brothers*	17	*25 Mar 89*	28
THE BEST OF DONNA SUMMER	*Warner Brothers*	24	*24 Nov 90*	9
ENDLESS SUMMER - GREATEST HITS	*Mercury*	37	*26 Nov 94*	2

SUMMER DAZE — UK

SINGLES:	**HITS 1**			**WEEKS 1**
SAMBA MAGIC	*VC Recordings*	61	*26 Oct 96*	1
Originaly released in 1995.				

Mark SUMMERS — UK

(See also Souvlaki.)

SINGLES:	**HITS 1**			**WEEKS 6**
SUMMERS MAGIC	*Fourth & Broadway*	27	*26 Jan 91*	6
Samples the theme from BBC1 children's programme 'The Magic Roundabout'.				

SUNBURST — UK

SINGLES:	**HITS 1**			**WEEKS 1**
EYEBALL (EYEBALL PAUL'S THEME)	*Virgin*	48	*8 Jul 01*	1
From the film 'Kevin And Perry Go Large'.				

SUNDANCE - See DJ FAST EDDIE

SUNDANCE — UK

(See also Shimmon and Woolfson.)

SINGLES:	**HITS 3**			**WEEKS 7**
SUNDANCE	*React*	33	*8 Nov 97*	2
Uses composer Lamont Booker's piano line from Smokebelch.				
SUNDANCE '98 [RM]	*React*	37	*3 Oct 98*	2
Remixed by Shimmon and Woolfson.				
THE LIVING DREAM	*React*	56	*27 Feb 99*	1
WON'T LET THIS FEELING GO	*Inferno*	40	*5 Feb 00*	2
Samples A Man Called Adam's Barefoot In The Head.				

SUNDAYS — UK

SINGLES:	**HITS 4**			**WEEKS 12**
CAN'T BE SURE	*Rough Trade*	45	*11 Feb 89*	5
GOODBYE	*Parlophone*	27	*3 Oct 92*	2
SUMMERTIME	*Parlophone*	15	*20 Sep 97*	4
CRY	*Parlophone*	43	*22 Nov 97*	1
ALBUMS:	**HITS 3**			**WEEKS 15**
READING WRITING AND ARITHMETIC	*Rough Trade*	4	*27 Jan 90*	8
BLIND	*Parlophone*	15	*31 Oct 92*	3
STATIC & SILENCE	*Parlophone*	10	*4 Oct 97*	4

SUNDRAGON — UK

SINGLES:	**HITS 1**			**WEEKS 1**
GREEN TAMBOURINE	*MGM*	50	*24 Feb 68*	1

SUNFIRE — US

SINGLES:	HITS 1			WEEKS 11
YOUNG, FREE AND SINGLE	*Warner Brothers*	20	*12 Mar 83*	11

SUNKIDS featuring CHANCE — US

SINGLES:	HITS 1			WEEKS 2
RESCUE ME	*A&M*	50	*13 Nov 99*	2

SUNNY — UK

SINGLES:	HITS 1			WEEKS 10
DOCTOR'S ORDERS	*CBS*	7	*30 Mar 74*	10

SUNSCREEM — UK

SINGLES:	HITS 10			WEEKS 35
PRESSURE	*Sony S2*	60	*29 Feb 92*	2
LOVE U MORE	*Sony S2*	23	*18 Jul 92*	6
PERFECT MOTION	*Sony S2*	18	*17 Oct 92*	5
BROKEN ENGLISH	*Sony S2*	13	*9 Jan 93*	5
Originally recorded by Marianne Faithfull in 1979.				
PRESSURE US [RM]	*Sony S2*	19	*27 Mar 93*	5
WHEN	*Sony S2*	47	*2 Sep 95*	2
EXODUS	*Sony S2*	40	*18 Nov 95*	2
WHITE SKIES	*Sony S2*	25	*20 Jan 96*	3
SECRETS	*Sony S2*	36	*23 Mar 96*	2
CATCH	*Pulse 8*	55	*6 Sep 97*	1
PLEASE SAVE ME	*Inferno*	36	*20 Oct 01*	2
Above hit: SUNSCREEM vs PUSH.				
ALBUMS:	**HITS 2**			**WEEKS 6**
O3	*Sony S2*	33	*13 Feb 93*	5
CHANGE OR DIE	*Sony S2*	53	*30 Mar 96*	1

Monty SUNSHINE – See Chris BARBER'S JAZZ BAND

SUNSHIP featuring M.C.R.B — UK

SINGLES:	HITS 1			WEEKS 1
CHEQUE ONE TWO	*Filter*	75	*1 Apr 00*	1

SUPER FURRY ANIMALS — UK

SINGLES:	HITS 15			WEEKS 36
HOMETOWN UNICORN	*Creation*	47	*9 Mar 96*	1
GOD! SHOW ME MAGIC	*Creation*	33	*11 May 96*	2
SOMETHING 4 THE WEEKEND	*Creation*	18	*13 Jul 96*	3
IF YOU DON'T WANT ME TO DESTROY YOU	*Creation*	18	*12 Oct 96*	2
THE MAN DON'T GIVE A FUCK	*Creation*	22	*14 Dec 96*	2
HERMANN LOVES PAULINE	*Creation*	26	*24 May 97*	2
Hermann and Pauline were the parents of Albert Einstein.				
THE INTERNATIONAL LANGUAGE OF SCREAMING	*Creation*	24	*26 Jul 97*	2
PLAY IT COOL	*Creation*	27	*4 Oct 97*	2
DEMONS	*Creation*	27	*6 Dec 97*	2
ICE HOCKEY HAIR	*Creation*	12	*6 Jun 98*	3
NORTHERN LITES	*Creation*	11	*22 May 99*	4
FIRE IN MY HEART	*Creation*	25	*21 Aug 99*	3
DO OR DIE	*Creation*	20	*29 Jan 00*	2
JUXTAPOZED WITH U	*Epic*	14	*21 Jul 01*	4
(DRAWING) RINGS AROUND THE WORLD	*Epic*	28	*20 Oct 01*	2
ALBUMS:	**HITS 6**			**WEEKS 28**
FUZZY LOGIC	*Creation*	23	*1 Jun 96*	6
RADIATOR	*Creation*	8	*6 Sep 97*	3
OUT SPACED	*Creation*	44	*5 Dec 98*	1
Includes early singles recorded for the Ankst label, B-sides and BBC sessions.				
GUERRILLA	*Creation*	10	*26 Jun 99*	9
MWNG	*Placid Casual*	11	*27 May 00*	2
Welsh for Mane.				
RINGS AROUND THE WORLD	*Epic*	3	*4 Aug 01*	7

SUPERCAR — Italy

SINGLES:	HITS 2			WEEKS 6
TONITE	*Pepper*	15	*13 Feb 99*	5
COMPUTER LOVE	*Pepper*	67	*21 Aug 99*	1
Above hit: SUPERCAR featuring MIKAELA.				

SUPERCAT — Jamaica

SINGLES:	HITS 4			WEEKS 8
IT FE DONE	*Columbia*	66	*1 Aug 92*	1

ALRIGHT *Samples Slave's Just A Touch Of Love.* *Above hit: KRISS KROSS featuring SUPERCAT*	*Columbia*	47	*11 Sep 93*	2
MY GIRL JOSEPHINE *From the film 'Pret-A-Porter'.* *Above hit: SUPER CAT featuring JACK RADICS.*	*Columbia*	22	*6 May 95*	4
FLY *Above hit: SUGAR RAY (featuring SUPER CAT).*	*Atlantic*	58	*31 Jan 98*	1

SUPERFUNK — France

SINGLES:	HITS 2			WEEKS 2
LUCKY STAR *Samples Chris Rea's Josephine.* *Above hit: SUPERFUNK featuring Ron CARROLL.*	*Virgin*	42	*4 Mar 00*	1
THE YOUNG MC *Samples Musical Youth's Pass The Dutchie.*	*Virgin*	62	*10 Jun 00*	1

SUPERGRASS — UK

SINGLES:	HITS 12			WEEKS 54
CAUGHT BY THE FUZZ	*Parlophone*	43	*29 Oct 94*	2
MANSIZE ROOSTER	*Parlophone*	20	*18 Feb 95*	3
LOSE IT	*Sub-Pop*	75	*25 Mar 95*	1
LENNY	*Parlophone*	10	*13 May 95*	3
ALRIGHT / TIME	*Parlophone*	2	*15 Jul 95*	10
GOING OUT	*Parlophone*	5	*9 Mar 96*	6
RICHARD III	*Parlophone*	2	*12 Apr 97*	5
SUN HITS THE SKY	*Parlophone*	10	*21 Jun 97*	4
LATE IN THE DAY	*Parlophone*	18	*18 Oct 97*	4
PUMPING ON YOUR STEREO	*Parlophone*	11	*5 Jun 99*	6
PUMPING ON YOUR STEREO [RE]	*Parlophone*	74	*21 Aug 99*	1
MOVING	*Parlophone*	9	*18 Sept 99*	5
MARY	*Parlophone*	36	*4 Dec 99*	3
MARY [RE]	*Parlophone*	72	*22 Jan 00*	1
ALBUMS:	**HITS 3**			**WEEKS 86**
I SHOULD COCO	*Parlophone*	1	*27 May 95*	36
IN IT FOR THE MONEY	*Parlophone*	2	*3 May 97*	25
SUPERGRASS	*Parlophone*	3	*2 Oct 99*	25

SUPERMEN LOVERS featuring Mani HOFFMAN — France

SINGLES:	HITS 1			WEEKS 14
STARLIGHT	*Independiente*	2	*15 Sep 01*	14

SUPERNATURALS — UK

SINGLES:	HITS 8			WEEKS 15
LAZY LOVER	*Food*	34	*26 Oct 96*	2
THE DAY BEFORE YESTERDAY'S MAN	*Food*	25	*8 Feb 97*	3
SMILE	*Food*	23	*26 Apr 97*	2
LOVE HAS PASSED AWAY	*Food*	38	*12 Jul 97*	2
PREPARE TO LAND	*Food*	48	*25 Oct 97*	1
I WASN'T BUILT TO GET UP	*Food*	25	*1 Aug 98*	3
SHEFFIELD SONG (I LOVE HER MORE THAN I LOVE YOU)	*Food*	45	*24 Oct 98*	1
EVEREST	*Food*	52	*13 Mar 99*	1
ALBUMS:	**HITS 2**			**WEEKS 7**
IT DOESN'T MATTER ANYMORE	*Food*	9	*17 May 97*	4
A TUNE A DAY	*Food*	21	*22 Aug 98*	3

SUPERNOVA — UK

SINGLES:	HITS 1			WEEKS 1
SOME MIGHT SAY	*Sing Sing*	55	*11 May 96*	1

SUPERSISTER — UK

SINGLES:	HITS 3			WEEKS 8
COFFEE	*Gut*	16	*14 Oct 00*	5
SHOPPING	*Gut*	36	*25 Aug 01*	2
SUMMER GONNA COME AGAIN	*Gut*	51	*17 Nov 01*	1

SUPERSTAR — UK

SINGLES:	HITS 2			WEEKS 2
EVERY DAY I FALL APART	*Camp Fabulous*	66	*7 Feb 98*	1
SUPERSTAR	*Camp Fabulous*	49	*25 Apr 98*	1

SUPERTRAMP — UK

SINGLES:	HITS 6			WEEKS 52
DREAMER	*A&M*	13	*15 Feb 75*	10
GIVE A LITTLE BIT	*A&M*	29	*25 Jun 77*	7
THE LOGICAL SONG	*A&M*	7	*31 Mar 79*	11
BREAKFAST IN AMERICA	*A&M*	9	*30 Jun 79*	10
GOODBYE STRANGER	*A&M*	57	*27 Oct 79*	3
IT'S RAINING AGAIN	*A&M*	26	*30 Oct 82*	11
Above hit: SUPERTRAMP featuring vocals by Roger HODGSON.				

ALBUMS:	HITS 11			WEEKS 181
CRIME OF THE CENTURY	*A&M*	4	*23 Nov 74*	22
CRISIS? WHAT CRISIS?	*A&M*	20	*6 Dec 75*	15
EVEN IN THE QUIETEST MOMENTS . . .	*A&M*	12	*23 Apr 77*	22
BREAKFAST IN AMERICA	*A&M*	3	*31 Mar 79*	53
PARIS	*A&M*	7	*4 Oct 80*	17
Live recordings from the Paris Pavilion, 29 Nov 79.				
". . . FAMOUS LAST WORDS . . ."	*A&M*	6	*6 Nov 82*	16
BROTHER WHERE YOU BOUND	*A&M*	20	*25 May 85*	5
THE AUTOBIOGRAPHY OF SUPERTRAMP	*A&M*	9	*18 Oct 86*	19
FREE AS A BIRD	*A&M*	93	*31 Oct 87*	1
THE VERY BEST OF SUPERTRAMP	*A&M*	24	*15 Aug 92*	4
SOME THINGS NEVER CHANGE	*Chrysalis*	74	*3 May 97*	1
THE VERY BEST OF SUPERTRAMP [RI]	*PolyGram TV*	8	*27 Sep 97*	6

SUPREMES — US

(See also Diana Ross and the Supremes and the Temptations; Supremes and Four Tops.)

SINGLES:	HITS 24			WEEKS 259
WHERE DID OUR LOVE GO	*Stateside*	3	*5 Sep 64*	14
Song was originally written for the Marvelettes, but they rejected it.				
BABY LOVE	*Stateside*	1	*24 Oct 64*	15
COME SEE ABOUT ME	*Stateside*	27	*23 Jan 65*	6
STOP! IN THE NAME OF LOVE	*Tamla Motown*	7	*27 Mar 65*	12
BACK IN MY ARMS AGAIN	*Tamla Motown*	40	*12 Jun 65*	5
I HEAR A SYMPHONY	*Tamla Motown*	50	*11 Dec 65*	1
I HEAR A SYMPHONY [RE]	*Tamla Motown*	39	*25 Dec 65*	4
YOU CAN'T HURRY LOVE	*Tamla Motown*	3	*10 Sep 66*	12
YOU KEEP ME HANGIN' ON	*Tamla Motown*	8	*3 Dec 66*	10
LOVE IS HERE AND NOW YOU'RE GONE	*Tamla Motown*	17	*4 Mar 67*	10
THE HAPPENING	*Tamla Motown*	6	*13 May 67*	12
From the film of the same name.				
REFLECTIONS	*Tamla Motown*	5	*2 Sep 67*	14
IN AND OUT OF LOVE	*Tamla Motown*	13	*2 Dec 67*	13
FOREVER CAME TODAY	*Tamla Motown*	28	*13 Apr 68*	8
SOME THINGS YOU NEVER GET USED TO	*Tamla Motown*	34	*6 Jul 68*	6
LOVE CHILD	*Tamla Motown*	15	*23 Nov 68*	14
Co-written by R. Dean Taylor.				
I'M LIVIN' IN SHAME	*Tamla Motown*	14	*26 Apr 69*	9
I'M LIVIN' IN SHAME [RE]	*Tamla Motown*	50	*5 Jul 69*	1
NO MATTER WHAT SIGN YOU ARE	*Tamla Motown*	37	*19 Jul 69*	7
SOMEDAY WE'LL BE TOGETHER	*Tamla Motown*	13	*13 Dec 69*	13
Originally recorded by Johnny (Bristol) & Jackie (Beavers).				
Above 9: Diana ROSS and the SUPREMES.				
UP THE LADDER TO THE ROOF	*Tamla Motown*	6	*2 May 70*	15
STONED LOVE	*Tamla Motown*	3	*16 Jan 71*	13
NATHAN JONES	*Tamla Motown*	5	*21 Aug 71*	11
FLOY JOY	*Tamla Motown*	9	*4 Mar 72*	10
Written and produced by Smokey Robinson.				
AUTOMATICALLY SUNSHINE	*Tamla Motown*	10	*15 Jul 72*	9
BAD WEATHER	*Tamla Motown*	37	*21 Apr 73*	4
Written and produced by Stevie Wonder.				
BABY LOVE [RI]	*Tamla Motown*	12	*24 Aug 74*	10
STOP! IN THE NAME OF LOVE [RI]	*Motown*	62	*18 Feb 89*	1
Above 2: Diana ROSS and the SUPREMES.				

EPS:	HITS 1			WEEKS 12
THE SUPREMES	*Tamla Motown*	6	*1 May 65*	12

ALBUMS:	HITS 12			WEEKS 184
MEET THE SUPREMES	*Stateside*	8	*5 Dec 64*	6
SUPREMES A GO-GO	*Tamla Motown*	15	*17 Dec 66*	21
THE SUPREMES SING MOTOWN	*Tamla Motown*	15	*13 May 67*	16
THE SUPREMES SING RODGERS AND HART	*Tamla Motown*	25	*30 Sep 67*	7
DIANA ROSS AND THE SUPREMES GREATEST HITS	*Tamla Motown*	1	*20 Jan 68*	60
'LIVE' AT LONDON'S TALK OF THE TOWN	*Tamla Motown*	6	*30 Mar 68*	18
REFLECTIONS	*Tamla Motown*	30	*20 Jul 68*	2
LOVE CHILD	*Tamla Motown*	8	*1 Feb 69*	6
Above 4: Diana ROSS and the SUPREMES.				
TOUCH	*Tamla Motown*	40	*25 Sep 71*	1

DIANA ROSS & THE SUPREMES 20 GOLDEN GREATS	*Motown*	1	*17 Sep 77*	34
LOVE SUPREME	*Motown*	10	*21 Jan 89*	9
40 GOLDEN MOTOWN GREATS	*Motown*	35	*31 Oct 98*	4

Features both her solo and group recordings.
Above 3: Diana ROSS and the SUPREMES.

SUPREMES and FOUR TOPS — US

(See also Four Tops; Supremes.)

SINGLES:	HITS 2			WEEKS 20
RIVER DEEP - MOUNTAIN HIGH	*Tamla Motown*	11	*26 Jun 71*	10
YOU GOTTA HAVE LOVE IN YOUR HEART	*Tamla Motown*	25	*20 Nov 71*	10

ALBUMS:	HITS 1			WEEKS 11
THE MAGNIFICENT SEVEN	*Tamla Motown*	6	*29 May 71*	11

Al B. SURE! — US

(See also Quincy Jones.)

SINGLES:	HITS 4			WEEKS 12
NITE AND DAY	*Uptown*	44	*16 Apr 88*	5
OFF ON YOUR OWN (GIRL)	*Uptown*	70	*30 Jul 88*	2
IF I'M NOT YOUR LOVER	*Uptown*	54	*10 Jun 89*	3
Above hit: Al B. SURE! featuring SLICK RICK.				
BLACK TIE WHITE NOISE	*Arista*	36	*12 Jun 93*	2
Above hit: David BOWIE featuring Al B. SURE!				

SuREAL — UK

SINGLES:	HITS 1			WEEKS 4
YOU TAKE MY BREATH AWAY	*Cream*	15	*7 Oct 00*	4

SURFACE — US

SINGLES:	HITS 4			WEEKS 14
FALLING IN LOVE	*Salsoul*	67	*23 Jul 83*	3
WHEN YOUR 'EX' WANTS YOU BACK	*Salsoul*	52	*23 Jun 84*	4
HAPPY	*CBS*	56	*28 Feb 87*	5
THE FIRST TIME	*Columbia*	60	*12 Jan 91*	2

SURFACE NOISE — UK

SINGLES:	HITS 2			WEEKS 11
THE SCRATCH	*WEA*	26	*31 May 80*	8
DANCIN' ON A WIRE	*Groove*	59	*30 Aug 80*	3

SURFARIS — US

SINGLES:	HITS 1			WEEKS 14
WIPE OUT	*London*	5	*27 Jul 63*	14
The laugh at the start is by their manager Dale Smallin.				

SURPRISE SISTERS — UK

SINGLES:	HITS 1			WEEKS 3
LA BOOGA ROOGA	*Good Earth*	38	*13 Mar 76*	3

SURVIVOR — US

(See also Various Artists: Films – Original Soundtracks 'Rocky III', 'Rocky IV'.)

SINGLES:	HITS 2			WEEKS 26
EYE OF THE TIGER	*Scotti Brothers*	1	*31 Jul 82*	15
From the film 'Rocky III'.				
BURNING HEART	*Scotti Brothers*	5	*1 Feb 86*	11
From the film 'Rocky IV'. While this was still in the Top 40 in March, it was also released as an [AA] with I Can't Hold Back which reached No. 80.				

ALBUMS:	HITS 1			WEEKS 10
EYE OF THE TIGER	*Scotti Brothers*	12	*21 Aug 82*	10

Peter SUSSKIND – See LONDON PHILHARMONIC CHOIR

SUTHERLAND BROTHERS and QUIVER — UK

SINGLES:	HITS 3			WEEKS 20
ARMS OF MARY	*CBS*	5	*3 Apr 76*	12
SECRETS	*CBS*	35	*20 Nov 76*	4
EASY COME, EASY GO	*CBS*	50	*2 Jun 79*	4
Above hit: SUTHERLAND BROTHERS.				

ALBUMS:	HITS 2			WEEKS 11
REACH FOR THE SKY	*CBS*	26	*15 May 76*	8
SLIPSTREAM	*CBS*	49	*9 Oct 76*	3

Pat SUZUKI — US

SINGLES:	HITS 1			WEEKS 1
I ENJOY BEING A GIRL	*RCA*	49	*16 Apr 60*	1

SVENSON & GIELEN — Belgium

(See also Johann Gielen featuring Abnea.)

SINGLES:	HITS 1			WEEKS 2
THE BEAUTY OF SILENCE	*Xtrahard*	41	*22 Sep 01*	2

Billy SWAN — US

SINGLES:	HITS 2			WEEKS 13
I CAN HELP	*Monument*	6	*14 Dec 74*	9
DON'T BE CRUEL	*Monument*	42	*24 May 75*	4

SWAN LAKE — US

SINGLES:	HITS 1			WEEKS 4
IN THE NAME OF LOVE	*Champion*	53	*17 Sep 88*	4

SWANS WAY — UK

SINGLES:	HITS 2			WEEKS 12
SOUL TRAIN	*Exit*	20	*4 Feb 84*	7
ILLUMINATIONS	*Balgier*	57	*26 May 84*	5
ALBUMS:	**HITS 1**			**WEEKS 1**
THE FUGITIVE KIND	*Balgier*	88	*3 Nov 84*	1

Patrick SWAYZE featuring Wendy FRASER — US

SINGLES:	HITS 1			WEEKS 11
SHE'S LIKE THE WIND	*RCA*	17	*26 Mar 88*	11
From the film 'Dirty Dancing'.				

Keith SWEAT — US

SINGLES:	HITS 8			WEEKS 23
I WANT HER	*Elektra*	26	*20 Feb 88*	10
SOMETHING JUST AIN'T RIGHT	*Elektra*	55	*14 May 88*	3
HOW DO YOU LIKE IT?	*Elektra*	71	*14 May 94*	1
Features rap by Lisa Lopes of TLC.				
TWISTED	*Elektra*	39	*22 Jun 96*	2
Features vocals by Kut Klose.				
JUST A TOUCH	*Elektra*	35	*23 Nov 96*	2
NOBODY	*Elektra*	30	*3 May 97*	2
Above hit: Keith SWEAT featuring Athena CAGE.				
I WANT HER [RM]	*Elektra*	44	*6 Dec 97*	1
Remixed by Femi Fem.				
COME AND GET WITH ME	*Elektra*	58	*12 Dec 98*	1
Above hit: Keith SWEAT featuring SNOOP DOGG.				
I'M NOT READY	*Elektra*	53	*27 Mar 99*	1
ALBUMS:	**HITS 5**			**WEEKS 32**
MAKE IT LAST FOREVER	*Elektra*	41	*16 Jan 88*	21
I'LL GIVE ALL MY LOVE TO YOU	*Elektra*	47	*23 Jun 90*	4
GET UP ON IT	*Elektra*	20	*9 Jul 94*	4
KEITH SWEAT	*Elektra*	36	*29 Jun 96*	2
STILL IN THE GAME	*Elektra*	62	*3 Oct 98*	1

Michelle SWEENEY — US

SINGLES:	HITS 1			WEEKS 1
THIS TIME	*Big Beat*	57	*29 Oct 94*	1

SWEET — UK

SINGLES:	HITS 17			WEEKS 159
FUNNY, FUNNY	*RCA Victor*	13	*13 Mar 71*	14
CO-CO	*RCA Victor*	2	*12 Jun 71*	15
ALEXANDER GRAHAM BELL	*RCA Victor*	33	*16 Oct 71*	5
POPPA JOE	*RCA Victor*	11	*5 Feb 72*	12
LITTLE WILLY	*RCA Victor*	4	*10 Jun 72*	14
WIG-WAM BAM	*RCA Victor*	4	*9 Sep 72*	13
BLOCK BUSTER!	*RCA Victor*	1	*13 Jan 73*	15
HELL RAISER	*RCA Victor*	2	*5 May 73*	11
THE BALLROOM BLITZ	*RCA Victor*	2	*22 Sep 73*	9
TEENAGE RAMPAGE	*RCA Victor*	2	*19 Jan 74*	8
THE SIX TEENS	*RCA Victor*	9	*13 Jul 74*	7
TURN IT DOWN	*RCA Victor*	41	*9 Nov 74*	2
FOX ON THE RUN	*RCA Victor*	2	*15 Mar 75*	10

ACTION	*RCA Victor*	15	*12 Jul 75*	6
THE LIES IN YOUR EYES	*RCA Victor*	35	*24 Jan 76*	4
LOVE IS LIKE OXYGEN *From the film 'The Bitch'.*	*Polydor*	9	*28 Jan 78*	9
IT'S IT'S THE SWEET MIX [M] *Mixed together by Sanny X.*	*Anagram*	45	*26 Jan 85*	5
ALBUMS:	**HITS 3**			**WEEKS 14**
SWEET FANNY ADAMS	*RCA Victor*	27	*18 May 74*	2
SWEET SIXTEEN - IT'S IT'S . . . SWEET'S HITS	*Anagram*	49	*22 Sep 84*	6
BALLROOM HITZ - THE VERY BEST OF SWEET	*PolyGram TV*	15	*20 Jan 96*	6

Rachel SWEET — US

SINGLES:	**HITS 2**			**WEEKS 15**
B-A-B-Y *Original by Carla Thomas reached No. 14 in the US in 1966.*	*Stiff*	35	*9 Dec 78*	8
EVERLASTING LOVE *Above hit: Rex SMITH and Rachel SWEET.*	*CBS*	35	*22 Aug 81*	7

SWEET DREAMS — UK

SINGLES:	**HITS 1**			**WEEKS 12**
HONEY HONEY *Originally recorded by Abba.*	*Bradley's*	10	*20 Jul 74*	12

SWEET DREAMS — UK

SINGLES:	**HITS 1**			**WEEKS 7**
I'M NEVER GIVING UP *UK's Eurovision in 1983, it came 6th.*	*Ariola*	21	*9 Apr 83*	7

SWEET FEMALE ATTITUDE — UK

SINGLES:	**HITS 2**			**WEEKS 14**
FLOWERS	*WEA*	2	*15 Apr 00*	12
8 DAYS A WEEK	*WEA*	43	*7 Oct 00*	2

SWEET MERCY featuring Joe ROBERTS — UK

SINGLES:	**HITS 1**			**WEEKS 1**
HAPPY DAYS	*Grass Green*	63	*24 Feb 96*	1

SWEET PEOPLE — France

SINGLES:	**HITS 1**			**WEEKS 10**
AND THE BIRDS WERE SINGING (ET LES OISEAUX CHANTAIENT)	*Polydor*	4	*4 Oct 80*	8
AND THE BIRDS WERE SINGING (ET LES OISEAUX CHANTAIENT) [RE]	*Polydor*	73	*29 Aug 87*	2

SWEET PUSSY PAULINE - See CANDY GIRLS

SWEET SENSATION — UK

SINGLES:	**HITS 2**			**WEEKS 17**
SAD SWEET DREAMER *Written by David Parton under the name Des Parton.*	*Pye*	1	*14 Sep 74*	10
PURELY BY COINCIDENCE	*Pye*	11	*18 Jan 75*	7

SWEET TEE — US

(See also Tin Tin Out.)

SINGLES:	**HITS 1**			**WEEKS 6**
I GOT DA FEELIN' / IT'S LIKE THAT Y'ALL	*Cooltempo*	31	*16 Jan 88*	6

SWEETBACK featuring Amel LARRIEUX from GROOVE THEORY — UK

SINGLES:	**HITS 1**			**WEEKS 1**
YOU WILL RISE	*Epic*	64	*29 Mar 97*	1

SWEETBOX — US/Germany

SINGLES:	**HITS 1**			**WEEKS 12**
EVERYTHING'S GONNA BE ALRIGHT *Based around Bach's Air On A 'G' String. Featured in the Lancome Oui! fragrance TV commercial.*	*RCA*	5	*22 Aug 98*	12

Sally SWEETLAND - See Eddie FISHER

SWERVEDRIVER — UK

SINGLES:	**HITS 3**			**WEEKS 3**
SANDBLASTED [EP] *Lead track: Sandblaster.*	*Creation*	67	*10 Aug 91*	1
NEVER LOSE THAT FEELING	*Creation*	62	*30 May 92*	1
DUEL	*Creation*	60	*14 Aug 93*	1

ALBUMS:	HITS 2			WEEKS 2
RAISE	*Creation*	44	*12 Oct 91*	1
MEZCAL HEAD	*Creation*	55	*9 Oct 93*	1

SWIMMING WITH SHARKS — Germany

SINGLES:	HITS 1			WEEKS 3
CARELESS LOVE	*WEA*	63	*7 May 88*	3

SWING featuring DR. ALBAN — US/Nigeria

(See also Dr. Alban.)

SINGLES:	HITS 1			WEEKS 1
SWEET DREAMS	*Logic*	59	*29 Apr 95*	1

SWING 52 — US

SINGLES:	HITS 1			WEEKS 1
COLOR OF MY SKIN	*ffrr*	60	*25 Feb 95*	1

SWING KIDS - See K7

SWING OUT SISTER — UK

SINGLES:	HITS 9			WEEKS 55
BREAKOUT	*Mercury*	4	*25 Oct 86*	14
SURRENDER	*Mercury*	7	*10 Jan 87*	8
TWILIGHT WORLD	*Mercury*	32	*18 Apr 87*	6
FOOLED BY A SMILE	*Mercury*	43	*11 Jul 87*	4
YOU ON MY MIND	*Fontana*	28	*8 Apr 89*	9
WHERE IN THE WORLD	*Fontana*	47	*8 Jul 89*	4
AM I THE SAME GIRL	*Fontana*	21	*11 Apr 92*	6
Originally recorded by Barbara Acklin.				
NOTGONNACHANGE	*Fontana*	49	*20 Jun 92*	2
LA LA (MEANS I LOVE YOU)	*Fontana*	37	*27 Aug 94*	2
From the film 'Four Weddings And A Funeral'.				
ALBUMS:	**HITS 3**			**WEEKS 36**
IT'S BETTER TO TRAVEL	*Mercury*	1	*23 May 87*	21
KALEIDOSCOPE WORLD	*Fontana*	9	*20 May 89*	11
GET IN TOUCH WITH YOURSELF	*Fontana*	27	*16 May 92*	4

SWINGING BLUE JEANS — UK

SINGLES:	HITS 5			WEEKS 57
IT'S TOO LATE NOW	*His Master's Voice*	30	*22 Jun 63*	6
IT'S TOO LATE NOW [RE]	*His Master's Voice*	46	*10 Aug 63*	3
HIPPY HIPPY SHAKE	*His Master's Voice*	2	*14 Dec 63*	17
Originally recorded by Chan Romero in 1959.				
GOOD GOLLY MISS MOLLY	*His Master's Voice*	11	*21 Mar 64*	10
YOU'RE NO GOOD	*His Master's Voice*	3	*6 Jun 64*	13
Originally recorded by Betty Everett the same year.				
DON'T MAKE ME OVER	*His Master's Voice*	31	*22 Jan 66*	8
Original by Dionne Warwick reached No. 21 in the US in 1963.				
EPS:	**HITS 1**			**WEEKS 8**
SHAKE WITH THE SWINGING BLUE JEANS	*His Master's Voice*	13	*18 Apr 64*	8

SWINGLE SINGERS — US/France

EPS:	HITS 1			WEEKS 18
JAZZ SEBASTIAN BACH	*Philips*	11	*16 May 64*	14
ALBUMS:	**HITS 1**			**WEEKS 14**
JAZZ SEBASTIAN BACH	*Philips*	13	*1 Feb 64*	18

SWIRL 360 — US

SINGLES:	HITS 1			WEEKS 1
HEY NOW NOW	*Mercury*	61	*14 Nov 98*	1

SWISS - See OXIDE and NEUTRINO

SWITCH — US

SINGLES:	HITS 1			WEEKS 3
KEEPING SECRETS	*Total Experience*	61	*10 Nov 84*	3

SWV — US

SINGLES:	HITS 9			WEEKS 43
I'M SO INTO YOU	*RCA*	17	*1 May 93*	6
WEAK	*RCA*	33	*26 Jun 93*	3
RIGHT HERE	*RCA*	3	*28 Aug 93*	12
Samples Michael Jackson's Human Nature from his 1982 album Thriller.				

DOWNTOWN	*RCA*	19	*26 Feb 94*	5
ANYTHING	*RCA*	24	*11 Jun 94*	3
From the film 'Above The Rim'.				
YOU'RE THE ONE	*RCA*	13	*25 May 96*	3
IT'S ALL ABOUT U	*RCA*	36	*21 Dec 96*	5
CAN WE	*Jive*	18	*12 Apr 97*	4
From the film 'Booty Call'.				
SOMEONE	*RCA*	34	*13 Sep 97*	2
Above hit: SWV featuring PUFF DADDY.				

ALBUMS:	**HITS 3**			**WEEKS 27**
IT'S ABOUT TIME	*RCA*	17	*17 Jul 93*	17
NEW BEGINNING	*RCA*	26	*4 May 96*	5
RELEASE SOME TENSION	*RCA*	19	*16 Aug 97*	5

SYBIL — US

SINGLES:	**HITS 12**			**WEEKS 69**
FALLING IN LOVE	*Champion*	68	*1 Nov 86*	3
LET YOURSELF GO	*Champion*	32	*25 Apr 87*	6
MY LOVE IS GUARANTEED	*Champion*	42	*29 Aug 87*	5
DON'T MAKE ME OVER	*Champion*	59	*22 Jul 89*	5
Original by Dionne Warwick reached No. 21 in the US in 1963.				
DON'T MAKE ME OVER [RE]	*Champion*	19	*14 Oct 89*	6
WALK ON BY	*PWL*	6	*27 Jan 90*	9
CRAZY FOR YOU	*PWL*	71	*21 Apr 90*	1
THE LOVE I LOST	*PWL Sanctuary*	3	*16 Jan 93*	13
Above hit: WEST END featuring SYBIL.				
WHEN I'M GOOD AND READY	*PWL International*	5	*20 Mar 93*	13
BEYOND YOUR WILDEST DREAMS	*PWL International*	41	*26 Jun 93*	2
STRONGER TOGETHER	*PWL International*	41	*11 Sep 93*	2
MY LOVE IS GUARANTEED [RM]	*PWL International*	48	*11 Dec 93*	1
Remixed by Tony King.				
SO TIRED OF BEING ALONE	*PWL International*	53	*9 Mar 96*	1
WHEN I'M GOOD AND READY [RM]	*Next Plateau*	66	*8 Mar 97*	1
Remixed by Love To Infinity.				
STILL A THRILL	*Coalition*	55	*26 Jul 97*	1

ALBUMS:	**HITS 3**			**WEEKS 12**
LET YOURSELF GO	*Champion*	92	*5 Sep 87*	1
WALK ON BY	*PWL*	21	*24 Feb 90*	5
GOOD 'N' READY	*PWL International*	13	*12 Jun 93*	6

SYLK 130 — US

SINGLES:	**HITS 1**			**WEEKS 2**
LAST NIGHT A DJ SAVED MY LIFE	*Sony S2*	33	*25 Apr 98*	2

SYLVESTER — US

SINGLES:	**HITS 6**			**WEEKS 45**
YOU MAKE ME FEEL (MIGHTY REAL)	*Fantasy*	8	*19 Aug 78*	15
DANCE (DISCO HEAT)	*Fantasy*	29	*18 Nov 78*	12
I (WHO HAVE NOTHING)	*Fantasy*	46	*31 Mar 79*	5
STARS	*Fantasy*	47	*7 Jul 79*	3
DO YA WANNA FUNK	*London*	32	*11 Sep 82*	8
Above hit: SYLVESTER with Patrick COWLEY.				
BAND OF GOLD	*London*	67	*3 Sep 83*	2

ALBUMS:	**HITS 1**			**WEEKS 3**
MIGHTY REAL	*Fantasy*	62	*23 Jun 79*	3

SYLVIA — US

SINGLES:	**HITS 1**			**WEEKS 11**
PILLOW TALK	*London*	14	*23 Jun 73*	11
She wrote it for Al Green but he rejected it.				

SYLVIA (VRETHAMMAR) — Sweden

SINGLES:	**HITS 2**			**WEEKS 33**
Y VIVA ESPANA	*Sonet*	4	*10 Aug 74*	19
Appeared in the breakers section under the chart from February of that year before finally charting.				
Y VIVA ESPANA [RE]	*Sonet*	35	*4 Jan 75*	9
HASTA LA VISTA	*Sonet*	38	*26 Apr 75*	5
Above hit: SYLVIA.				

David SYLVIAN — UK

(See also David Sylvian and Robert Fripp.)

SINGLES:	**HITS 11**			**WEEKS 34**
BAMBOO HOUSES / BAMBOO MUSIC	*Virgin*	30	*7 Aug 82*	4
Above hit: SYLVIAN SAKAMOTO.				

FORBIDDEN COLOURS *Vocal version of the theme from the film 'Mr. Christmas Mr. Lawrence'.* *Above hit: David SYLVIAN and Riuichi SAKAMOTO.*	*Virgin*	16	*2 Jul 83*	8
RED GUITAR	*Virgin*	17	*2 Jun 84*	5
THE INK IN THE WELL	*Virgin*	36	*18 Aug 84*	3
PULLING PUNCHES	*Virgin*	56	*3 Nov 84*	2
WORDS WITH THE SHAMAN	*Virgin*	72	*14 Dec 85*	1
TAKING THE VEIL *Sleeve has title as A Little Girl Dreams Of Taking The Veil.*	*Virgin*	53	*9 Aug 86*	3
BUOY *Above hit: Mick KARN featuring David SYLVIAN.*	*Virgin*	63	*17 Jan 87*	2
LET THE HAPPINESS IN	*Virgin*	66	*10 Oct 87*	1
HEARTBEAT (TAINAI KAIKI II) RETURNING TO THE WOMB *Above hit: David SYLVIAN and Riuichi SAKAMOTO featuring Ingrid CHAVEZ.*	*Virgin America*	58	*13 Jun 92*	3
I SURRENDER	*Virgin*	40	*27 Mar 99*	2
ALBUMS:	**HITS 6**			**WEEKS 25**
BRILLIANT TREES	*Virgin*	4	*7 Jul 84*	14
GONE TO EARTH	*Virgin*	24	*13 Sep 86*	5
SECRETS OF THE BEEHIVE	*Virgin*	37	*7 Nov 87*	2
PLIGHT AND PREMONITION *Above hit: David SYLVIAN and Holgar CZUKAY.*	*Virgin*	71	*2 Apr 88*	1
DEAD BEES ON A CAKE	*Virgin*	31	*10 Apr 99*	2
EVERYTHING AND NOTHING	*Virgin*	57	*21 Oct 00*	1

David SYLVIAN and Robert FRIPP — UK

(See also Robert Fripp; David Sylvian.)

SINGLES:	**HITS 1**			**WEEKS 2**
JEAN THE BIRDMAN	*Virgin*	68	*28 Aug 93*	2
ALBUMS:	**HITS 1**			**WEEKS 2**
THE FIRST DAY	*Virgin*	21	*17 Jul 93*	2

SYMARIP — UK

SINGLES:	**HITS 1**			**WEEKS 3**
SKINHEAD MOONSTOMP	*Trojan*	54	*2 Feb 80*	3

SYMBOLS — UK

SINGLES:	**HITS 2**			**WEEKS 15**
BYE BYE BABY	*President*	44	*5 Aug 67*	3
(THE BEST PART OF) BREAKING UP	*President*	25	*6 Jan 68*	12

Terri SYMON — UK

SINGLES:	**HITS 1**			**WEEKS 1**
I WANT TO KNOW WHAT LOVE IS	*A&M*	54	*10 Jun 95*	1

SYMPHONIQUE — UK

ALBUMS:	**HITS 1**			**WEEKS 4**
MOODS SYMPHONIQUE 95	*Vision*	21	*1 Apr 95*	4

SYMPOSIUM — UK

SINGLES:	**HITS 6**			**WEEKS 10**
FAREWELL TO TWILIGHT	*Infectious*	25	*22 Mar 97*	2
THE ANSWER TO WHY I HATE YOU	*Infectious*	32	*31 May 97*	2
FAIRWEATHER FRIEND	*Infectious*	25	*30 Aug 97*	3
AVERAGE MAN	*Infectious*	45	*14 Mar 98*	1
BURY YOU	*Infectious*	41	*16 May 98*	1
BLUE	*Infectious*	48	*18 Jul 98*	1
ALBUMS:	**HITS 2**			**WEEKS 3**
ONE DAY AT A TIME	*Infectious*	29	*8 Nov 97*	2
ON THE OUTSIDE	*Infectious*	32	*30 May 98*	1

SYNTHPHONIC VARIATIONS — UK

ALBUMS:	**HITS 1**			**WEEKS 1**
SEASONS	*CBS*	84	*1 Nov 86*	1

SYREETA — US

SINGLES:	**HITS 5**			**WEEKS 30**
SPINNIN' AND SPINNIN'	*Tamla Motown*	49	*21 Sep 74*	3
YOUR KISS IS SWEET *Written by Stevie Wonder.*	*Tamla Motown*	12	*1 Feb 75*	8
HARMOUR LOVE	*Tamla Motown*	32	*12 Jul 75*	4
WITH YOU I'M BORN AGAIN	*Motown*	2	*15 Dec 79*	11
IT WILL COME IN TIME *Above 2: Billy PRESTON and SYREETA.*	*Motown*	47	*8 Mar 80*	4

Stanislas SYREWICZ – See Anthony WAY

SYSTEM — US

SINGLES:	HITS 1			WEEKS 2
I WANNA MAKE YOU FEEL GOOD	*Polydor*	73	*9 Jun 84*	2

SYSTEM F — Holland

SINGLES:	HITS 2			WEEKS 10
OUT OF THE BLUE	*Essential Recordings*	14	*3 Apr 99*	6
CRY	*Essential Recordings*	19	*6 May 00*	4

SYSTEM OF A DOWN — US

SINGLES:	HITS 1			WEEKS 4
CHOP SUEY	*Columbia*	17	*3 Nov 01*	4
ALBUMS:	**HITS 1**			**WEEKS 11**
TOXICITY	*Columbia*	13	*8 Sep 01*	11

SYSTEM 7 — UK/France

SINGLES:	HITS 2			WEEKS 2
7:7 EXPANSION	*Big Life*	39	*13 Feb 93*	1
SINBAD / QUEST	*Big Life*	74	*17 Jul 93*	1
ALBUMS:	**HITS 2**			**WEEKS 3**
ALTITUDE	*Ten Records*	75	*20 Jun 92*	1
12" single with 8 mixes.				
Above hit: SYSTEM 7 featuring Ultra NATE.				
777	*WAU*	30	*20 Mar 93*	2

T

T.A.F.K.A.P. – See PRINCE

T-BOZ — US

SINGLES:	HITS 1			WEEKS 1
TOUCH MYSELF	*LaFace*	48	*23 Nov 96*	1
From the film 'Fled'.				

T-CONNECTION — US

SINGLES:	HITS 5			WEEKS 27
DO WHAT YOU WANNA DO	*TK*	11	*18 Jun 77*	8
ON FIRE	*TK*	16	*14 Jan 78*	5
LET YOURSELF GO	*TK*	52	*10 Jun 78*	3
AT MIDNIGHT	*TK*	53	*24 Feb 79*	5
SATURDAY NIGHT	*TK*	41	*5 May 79*	6

T-COY – See VARIOUS ARTISTS (EPs) 'The Further Adventures Of North – More Underground Dance EP'

T-EMPO — UK

SINGLES:	HITS 2			WEEKS 4
SATURDAY NIGHT, SUNDAY MORNING	*ffrr*	19	*7 May 94*	3
Original by Thelma Houston reached No. 34 in the US in 1979.				
THE LOOK OF LOVE / THE BLUE ROOM	*ffrr*	71	*9 Nov 96*	1
The Look Of Love samples New Order's Blue Monday.				
Above hit: T-EMPO featuring FEEBI / T-EMPO featuring Doreen EDWARDS.				

T.H.S. – THE HORNE SECTION — US

SINGLES:	HITS 1			WEEKS 3
LADY SHINE (SHINE ON)	*Fourth & Broadway*	54	*18 Aug 84*	3

T'PAU — UK

SINGLES:	HITS 10			WEEKS 77
HEART AND SOUL	*Siren*	4	*8 Aug 87*	13
CHINA IN YOUR HAND	*Siren*	1	*24 Oct 87*	15
VALENTINE	*Siren*	9	*30 Jan 88*	8
SEX TALK (LIVE)	*Siren*	23	*2 Apr 88*	7
Live recording from the Scottish Exhibition Centre, 29 Oct 87. Originally titled Intimate Strangers when studio version was first released in 1987.				
I WILL BE WITH YOU	*Siren*	14	*25 Jun 88*	6
SECRET GARDEN	*Siren*	18	*1 Oct 88*	7
ROAD TO OUR DREAM	*Siren*	42	*3 Dec 88*	6
ONLY THE LONELY	*Siren*	28	*25 Mar 89*	6
WHENEVER YOU NEED ME	*Siren*	16	*18 May 91*	6

WALK ON AIR	*Siren*	62	*27 Jul 91*	2
VALENTINE [RI]	*Virgin*	53	*20 Feb 93*	1
ALBUMS:	**HITS 4**			**WEEKS 85**
BRIDGE OF SPIES	*Siren*	1	*26 Sep 87*	59
RAGE	*Siren*	4	*5 Nov 88*	17
THE PROMISE	*Siren*	10	*22 Jun 91*	7
HEART AND SOUL - THE VERY BEST OF T'PAU	*Virgin*	35	*27 Feb 93*	2

T.POWER

UK

SINGLES:	**HITS 1**			**WEEKS 1**
POLICE STATE *Comment on the Criminal Justice Bill.*	*Sour*	63	*13 Apr 96*	1

T. REX

UK

SINGLES:	**HITS 26**			**WEEKS 236**
DEBORA	*Regal Zonophone*	34	*11 May 68*	7
ONE INCH ROCK	*Regal Zonophone*	28	*7 Sep 68*	7
KING OF THE RUMBLING SPIRES *Above 3: TYRANNOSAURUS REX.*	*Regal Zonophone*	44	*9 Aug 69*	1
RIDE A WHITE SWAN	*Fly*	2	*24 Oct 70*	20
HOT LOVE	*Fly*	1	*27 Feb 71*	17
GET IT ON *Howard Kaylan and Mark Volman of the Turtles on backing vocals.*	*Fly*	1	*10 Jul 71*	13
JEEPSTER	*Fly*	2	*13 Nov 71*	15
TELEGRAM SAM	*T.Rex*	1	*29 Jan 72*	12
DEBORA [RI] / ONE INCH ROCK [RI] *Above hit: TYRANNOSAURUS REX.*	*Magnifly*	7	*1 Apr 72*	10
METAL GURU	*EMI*	1	*13 May 72*	14
CHILDREN OF THE REVOLUTION	*EMI*	2	*16 Sep 72*	10
SOLID GOLD EASY ACTION	*EMI*	2	*9 Dec 72*	11
20TH CENTURY BOY	*EMI*	3	*10 Mar 73*	9
THE GROOVER	*EMI*	4	*16 Jun 73*	9
TRUCK ON (TYKE)	*EMI*	12	*24 Nov 73*	11
TEENAGE DREAM *Above hit: Marc BOLAN and T. REX.*	*EMI*	13	*9 Feb 74*	5
LIGHT OF LOVE	*EMI*	22	*13 Jul 74*	5
ZIP GUN BOOGIE *Above hit: Marc BOLAN/T.REX.*	*EMI*	41	*16 Nov 74*	3
NEW YORK CITY	*EMI*	15	*12 Jul 75*	8
DREAMY LADY *Above hit: T. REX DISCO PARTY.*	*EMI*	30	*11 Oct 75*	5
LONDON BOYS	*EMI*	40	*6 Mar 76*	3
I LOVE TO BOOGIE *Based on Teenage Boogie by Webb Pierce.*	*EMI*	13	*19 Jun 76*	9
LASER LOVE	*EMI*	41	*2 Oct 76*	4
THE SOUL OF MY SUIT	*EMI*	42	*2 Apr 77*	3
RETURN OF THE ELECTRIC WARRIOR [EP] *Lead track: Sing Me A Song.*	*Rarn*	50	*9 May 81*	4
YOU SCARE ME TO DEATH *Above 2: Marc BOLAN.*	*Cherry Red*	51	*19 Sep 81*	4
TELEGRAM SAM [RI]	*EMI*	69	*27 Mar 82*	2
MEGAREX [M] *Mixed by Sanny X of Disco Mix Club (UK).*	*Marc On Wax*	72	*18 May 85*	2
GET IT ON [RM]	*Marc On Wax*	54	*9 May 87*	4
20TH CENTURY BOY [RI] *Featured in the Levi's 501 Jeans TV commercial.* *Above hit: Marc BOLAN and T-REX.*	*Marc On Wax*	13	*24 Aug 91*	8
GET IT ON [RM] *Above hit: BUS STOP featuring T-REX.*	*All Around The World*	59	*7 Oct 00*	1
ALBUMS:	**HITS 21**			**WEEKS 222**
MY PEOPLE WERE FAIR AND HAD SKY IN THEIR HAIR BUT NOW THEY'RE CONTENT TO WEAR STARS ON THEIR BROWS	*Regal Zonophone*	15	*13 Jul 68*	9
UNICORN	*Regal Zonophone*	12	*7 Jun 69*	3
A BEARD OF STARS *Above 3: TYRANNOSAURUS REX.*	*Regal Zonophone*	21	*14 Mar 70*	6
T. REX	*Fly*	13	*16 Jan 71*	24
THE BEST OF T. REX *Consists mainly of material from when they were Tyrannosaurus Rex.*	*Flyback*	21	*7 Aug 71*	7
ELECTRIC WARRIOR	*Fly*	1	*9 Oct 71*	44
PROPHETS, SEERS AND SAGES, THE ANGELS OF THE AGES / MY PEOPLE WERE FAIR AND HAD SKY IN THEIR HAIR BUT NOW THEY'RE CONTENT TO WEAR STARS ON THEIR BROWS [RI] *Prophets, Seers And Sages was originally released in 1968.* *Above hit: TYRANNOSAURUS REX.*	*Fly Double Back*	1	*29 Apr 72*	12
BOLAN BOOGIE *Compilation.*	*Fly*	1	*20 May 72*	19

THE SLIDER	*EMI*	4	*5 Aug 72*	18
A BEARD OF STARS / UNICORN [RI]	*Cube*	44	*9 Dec 72*	2
Above hit: TYRANNOSAURUS REX.				
TANX	*EMI*	4	*31 Mar 73*	12
GREAT HITS	*EMI*	32	*10 Nov 73*	3
ZINC ALLOY AND THE HIDDEN RIDERS OF TOMORROW	*EMI*	12	*16 Mar 74*	3
Above hit: Marc BOLAN and T. REX.				
FUTURISTIC DRAGON	*EMI*	50	*21 Feb 76*	1
DANDY IN THE UNDERWORLD	*EMI*	26	*9 Apr 77*	3
SOLID GOLD	*EMI*	51	*30 Jun 79*	3
T. REX IN CONCERT	*Marc*	35	*12 Sep 81*	6
Live recordings.				
YOU SCARE ME TO DEATH	*Cherry Red*	88	*7 Nov 81*	1
DANCE IN THE MIDNIGHT	*Marc On Wax*	83	*24 Sep 83*	3
Above 2: Marc BOLAN.				
BEST OF THE 20TH CENTURY BOY	*K-Tel*	5	*4 May 85*	21
THE ULTIMATE COLLECTION	*Telstar*	4	*28 Sep 91*	16
THE ESSENTIAL COLLECTION	*PolyGram TV*	24	*7 Oct 95*	3
Released to coincide with the 18th anniversary of his death.				
Above 3: Marc BOLAN and T. REX.				
THE ESSENTIAL COLLECTION [RI]	*Universe/Music TV*	34	*28 Oct 00*	3

T.S. MONK — US

SINGLES:	HITS 2			WEEKS 6
BON BON VIE	*Mirage*	63	*7 Mar 81*	2
CANDIDATE FOR LOVE	*Mirage*	58	*25 Apr 81*	4

T-SHIRT — UK

SINGLES:	HITS 1			WEEKS 1
YOU SEXY THING	*Eternal*	63	*13 Sep 97*	1

T-SPOON — Holland

SINGLES:	HITS 2			WEEKS 15
SEX ON THE BEACH	*Control*	2	*19 Sep 98*	13
TOM'S PARTY	*Control*	27	*23 Jan 99*	2
Adapted around 10CC's Dreadlock Holiday and Suzanne Vega's Tom's Diner.				

TABERNACLE — UK

SINGLES:	HITS 1			WEEKS 2
I KNOW THE LORD	*Good Groove*	62	*4 Mar 95*	1
Track rearranged around Bessie Griffin's recording of the song from the 1940s.				
I KNOW THE LORD [RM]	*Good Groove*	55	*3 Feb 96*	1
Remixed by Tabernacle.				

TACK HEAD — US

SINGLES:	HITS 1			WEEKS 3
DANGEROUS SEX	*SBK One*	48	*30 Jun 90*	3
Features Mark E. Smith of the Fall.				

TAFFY — UK

SINGLES:	HITS 2			WEEKS 14
I LOVE MY RADIO [MIDNIGHT RADIO]	*Transglobal*	6	*10 Jan 87*	10
A 7" remix was sub credited [Dee Jay's Radio] instead.				
STEP BY STEP	*Transglobal*	59	*18 Jul 87*	4

TAG TEAM — US

SINGLES:	HITS 2			WEEKS 8
WHOOMP! (THERE IT IS)	*Club Tools*	34	*8 Jan 94*	5
Samples I'm Ready by Kano.				
ADDAMS FAMILY (WHOOMP!) [RR]	*Atlas*	53	*29 Jan 94*	1
From the film 'Addams Family Values'. This is an alternative recording of Whoomp! (There It Is).				
WHOOMP! (THERE IT IS) [RM]	*Club Tools*	48	*10 Sep 94*	2
Sales of the remix were combined with sales of the 3 original formats released earlier in the year.				

TAK TIX — US

SINGLES:	HITS 1			WEEKS 2
FEEL LIKE SINGING	*A&M*	33	*20 Jan 96*	2

TAKE 5 — US

SINGLES:	HITS 2			WEEKS 4
I GIVE	*Edel*	70	*7 Nov 98*	1
NEVER HAD IT SO GOOD	*Edel*	34	*27 Mar 99*	3

TAKE THAT — UK

SINGLES:	HITS 16			WEEKS 158
PROMISES	*RCA*	38	*23 Nov 91*	2
ONCE YOU'VE TASTED LOVE	*RCA*	47	*8 Feb 92*	3
IT ONLY TAKES A MINUTE	*RCA*	7	*6 Jun 92*	8
I FOUND HEAVEN	*RCA*	15	*15 Aug 92*	6
A MILLION LOVE SONGS - THE LOVE SONGS [EP]	*RCA*	7	*10 Oct 92*	9
Lead track: A Million Love Songs.				
COULD IT BE MAGIC	*RCA*	3	*12 Dec 92*	12
Inspired by Prelude in C Minor by F. Chopin.				
WHY CAN'T I WAKE UP WITH YOU?	*RCA*	2	*20 Feb 93*	10
PRAY	*RCA*	1	*17 Jul 93*	11
RELIGHT MY FIRE	*RCA*	1	*9 Oct 93*	14
Originally recorded by Dan Hartman.				
Above hit: TAKE THAT featuring LULU.				
BABE	*RCA*	1	*18 Dec 93*	10
EVERYTHING CHANGES	*RCA*	1	*9 Apr 94*	10
LOVE AIN'T HERE ANYMORE	*RCA*	3	*9 Jul 94*	10
LOVE AIN'T HERE ANYMORE [RE]	*RCA*	55	*15 Oct 94*	2
SURE	*RCA*	1	*15 Oct 94*	15
BACK FOR GOOD	*RCA*	1	*8 Apr 95*	13
NEVER FORGET	*RCA*	1	*5 Aug 95*	9
Charity record in aid of the Nordoff Robbins Music Therapy charity.				
HOW DEEP IS YOUR LOVE	*RCA*	1	*9 Mar 96*	13
HOW DEEP IS YOUR LOVE [RE]	*RCA*	74	*15 Jun 96*	1
ALBUMS:	**HITS 5**			**WEEKS 228**
TAKE THAT AND PARTY	*RCA*	2	*5 Sep 92*	73
EVERYTHING CHANGES	*RCA*	1	*23 Oct 93*	78
NOBODY ELSE	*RCA*	1	*13 May 95*	33
NOBODY ELSE (US VERSION)	*Arista*	26	*26 Aug 95*	4
US import version with different track listing to the UK release.				
GREATEST HITS	*RCA*	1	*6 Apr 96*	40

Billy TALBOT - See Ian McNABB

TALISMAN P. meets Barrington LEVY — UK/Jamaica

SINGLES:	HITS 1			WEEKS 2
HERE I COME (SING DJ)	*NuLife*	37	*13 Oct 01*	2

TALK TALK — UK

SINGLES:	HITS 9			WEEKS 73
TALK TALK	*EMI*	52	*24 Apr 82*	4
TODAY	*EMI*	14	*24 Jul 82*	13
TALK TALK [RI]	*EMI*	23	*13 Nov 82*	10
MY FOOLISH FRIEND	*EMI*	57	*19 Mar 83*	3
IT'S MY LIFE	*EMI*	46	*14 Jan 84*	5
SUCH A SHAME	*EMI*	49	*7 Apr 84*	6
DUM DUM GIRL	*EMI*	74	*11 Aug 84*	1
LIFE'S WHAT YOU MAKE IT	*EMI*	16	*18 Jan 86*	9
LIVING IN ANOTHER WORLD	*EMI*	48	*15 Mar 86*	4
GIVE IT UP	*Parlophone*	59	*17 May 86*	3
IT'S MY LIFE [RI]	*Parlophone*	13	*19 May 90*	9
LIFE'S WHAT YOU MAKE IT [RI]	*Parlophone*	23	*1 Sep 90*	6
ALBUMS:	**HITS 8**			**WEEKS 86**
THE PARTY'S OVER	*EMI*	21	*24 Jul 82*	25
IT'S MY LIFE	*EMI*	35	*25 Feb 84*	8
THE COLOUR OF SPRING	*EMI*	8	*1 Mar 86*	21
SPIRIT OF EDEN	*Parlophone*	19	*24 Sep 88*	5
THE VERY BEST OF TALK TALK - NATURAL HISTORY	*Parlophone*	3	*9 Jun 90*	21
HISTORY REVISITED - THE REMIXES	*Parlophone*	35	*6 Apr 91*	2
LAUGHING STOCK	*Verve*	26	*28 Sep 91*	2
THE VERY BEST OF TALK TALK	*EMI*	54	*8 Feb 97*	2

TALKING HEADS — UK/US

(See also Heads with Shaun Ryder.)

SINGLES:	HITS 10			WEEKS 54
ONCE IN A LIFETIME	*Sire*	14	*7 Feb 81*	10
HOUSES IN MOTION	*Sire*	50	*9 May 81*	3
THIS MUST BE THE PLACE (NAIVE MELODY)	*Sire*	51	*21 Jan 84*	3
SLIPPERY PEOPLE (LIVE VERSION)	*EMI*	68	*3 Nov 84*	2
Live recording from the Pantages Theatre, Hollywood, Dec 83.				
ROAD TO NOWHERE	*EMI*	6	*12 Oct 85*	16
AND SHE WAS	*EMI*	17	*8 Feb 86*	8
WILD WILD LIFE	*EMI*	43	*6 Sep 86*	4
RADIO HEAD (LP VERSION)	*EMI*	52	*16 May 87*	2

BLIND	*EMI*	59	*13 Aug 88*	3
LIFETIME PILING UP	*EMI*	50	*10 Oct 92*	3
ALBUMS:	**HITS 11**			**WEEKS 232**
TALKING HEADS '77	*Sire*	60	*25 Feb 78*	1
MORE SONGS ABOUT BUILDINGS AND FOOD	*Sire*	21	*29 Jul 78*	3
FEAR OF MUSIC	*Sire*	33	*15 Sep 79*	5
REMAIN IN LIGHT	*Sire*	21	*1 Nov 80*	17
THE NAME OF THIS BAND IS TALKING HEADS	*Sire*	22	*10 Apr 82*	5
Live recordings and out-takes.				
SPEAKING IN TONGUES	*Sire*	21	*18 Jun 83*	12
STOP MAKING SENSE	*EMI*	37	*27 Oct 84*	81
Live recordings from the Pantages Theatre, Hollywood, Dec 83.				
LITTLE CREATURES	*EMI*	10	*29 Jun 85*	65
TRUE STORIES	*EMI*	7	*27 Sep 86*	9
NAKED	*EMI*	3	*26 Mar 88*	15
ONCE IN A LIFETIME - THE BEST OF TALKING HEADS/ SAND IN THE VASELINE	*EMI*	7	*24 Oct 92*	16
Both albums sold separately, but sales combined.				
STOP MAKING SENSE [RE]	*EMI*	24	*18 Sept 99*	3
Re-released to celebrate the re-issue of Jonathan Demme's live concert film. It was remixed/remastered and included extra tracks. Peak position reached in 2000 (1999 peak: No. 74).				

TALL PAUL — UK

(See also Grifters featuring Tall Paul and Brandon Block.)

SINGLES:	**HITS 4**			**WEEKS 14**
ROCK DA HOUSE	*VC Recordings*	12	*29 Mar 97*	4
BE THERE	*Duty Free*	45	*29 May 99*	1
FREEBASE	*Duty Free*	43	*8 Apr 00*	2
ROCK DA HOUSE [RM]	*VC Recordings*	29	*2 Jun 01*	2
Remixed by Fergie. Samples Turn It Out by the Homeboys.				
PRECIOUS HEART	*Duty Free*	14	*18 Aug 01*	4
Above hit: TALL PAUL vs INXS.				
PRECIOUS HEART [RE]	*Duty Free*	57	*29 Sep 01*	1

TAM-TAM POUR L'ETHIOPIE - See STARVATION / TAM-TAM POUR L'ETHIOPIE

TAMARA - See TRINA and TAMARA

TAMARA - See MARVIN and TAMARA

TAMBA TRIO — Argentina

SINGLES:	**HITS 1**			**WEEKS 2**
MAS QUE NADA	*Talkin Loud*	34	*18 Jul 98*	2
Featured in the Nike TV commercial.				

TAMPERER featuring MAYA — US/Italy

SINGLES:	**HITS 3**			**WEEKS 38**
FEEL IT	*Pepper*	1	*25 Apr 98*	17
Samples the Jacksons' Can You Feel It.				
IF YOU BUY THIS RECORD YOUR LIFE WILL BE BETTER	*Pepper*	3	*14 Nov 98*	14
Samples Madonna's Material Girl.				
HAMMER TO THE HEART	*Pepper*	6	*12 Feb 00*	5
HAMMER TO THE HEART [RE]	*Pepper*	68	*25 Mar 00*	2

TAMS — US

SINGLES:	**HITS 3**			**WEEKS 31**
BE YOUNG BE FOOLISH, BE HAPPY	*Stateside*	32	*14 Feb 70*	7
HEY GIRL DON'T BOTHER ME	*Probe*	1	*31 Jul 71*	17
THERE AIN'T NOTHING LIKE SHAGGIN'	*Virgin*	21	*21 Nov 87*	7

Norma TANEGA — US

SINGLES:	**HITS 1**			**WEEKS 8**
WALKIN' MY CAT NAMED DOG	*Stateside*	22	*9 Apr 66*	8

TANGERINE DREAM — Germany

ALBUMS:	**HITS 16**			**WEEKS 77**
PHAEDRA	*Virgin*	15	*20 Apr 74*	15
RUBYCON	*Virgin*	12	*5 Apr 75*	14
RICOCHET	*Virgin*	40	*20 Dec 75*	2
STRATOSFEAR	*Virgin*	39	*13 Nov 76*	4
SORCERER [OST]	*MCA*	25	*23 Jul 77*	7
ENCORE	*Virgin*	55	*19 Nov 77*	1
CYCLONE	*Virgin*	37	*1 Apr 78*	4
FORCE MAJEURE	*Virgin*	26	*17 Feb 79*	7
TANGRAM	*Virgin*	36	*7 Jun 80*	5

THIEF [OST]	*Virgin*	43	*18 Apr 81*	3
EXIT	*Virgin*	43	*19 Sep 81*	5
WHITE EAGLE	*Virgin*	57	*10 Apr 82*	5
HYPERBOREA	*Virgin*	45	*5 Nov 83*	2
POLAND	*Jive Electro*	90	*10 Nov 84*	1
UNDERWATER SUNLIGHT	*Jive Electro*	97	*26 Jul 86*	1
TYGER	*Jive*	88	*27 Jun 87*	1

TANK — UK

ALBUMS:	HITS 1			WEEKS 5
FILTH HOUNDS OF HADES	*Kamaflage*	33	*13 Mar 82*	5

Children of TANSLEY SCHOOL — UK

SINGLES:	HITS 1			WEEKS 4
MY MUM IS ONE IN A MILLION	*EMI*	27	*28 Mar 81*	4

Jimmy TARBUCK — UK

SINGLES:	HITS 1			WEEKS 2
AGAIN	*Safari*	74	*16 Nov 85*	1
AGAIN [RE]	*Safari*	68	*30 Nov 85*	1

Bill TARMEY — UK

SINGLES:	HITS 3			WEEKS 9
ONE VOICE	*Arista*	16	*3 Apr 93*	4
Featuring backing vocals by St. Winifred's School Choir.				
THE WIND BENEATH MY WINGS	*EMI*	40	*19 Feb 94*	3
I.O.U.	*EMI*	55	*19 Nov 94*	2
ALBUMS:	**HITS 3**			**WEEKS 25**
A GIFT OF LOVE	*EMI*	15	*27 Nov 93*	14
TIME FOR LOVE	*EMI*	28	*5 Nov 94*	9
AFTER HOURS	*EMI Premier*	61	*18 May 96*	2

TARRIERS — US

SINGLES:	HITS 2			WEEKS 6
CINDY OH CINDY	*London*	26	*15 Dec 56*	1
Above hit: Vince MARTIN and the TARRIERS.				
THE BANANA BOAT SONG	*Columbia*	15	*2 Mar 57*	5

TARTAN ARMY featuring the WEE'IST PIPE BAND IN THE WORLD — UK

SINGLES:	HITS 1			WEEKS 4
SCOTLAND BE GOOD (JOCK & ROLL)	*Precious Organisation*	54	*6 Jun 98*	4

TASTE — Ireland

ALBUMS:	HITS 2			WEEKS 12
ON THE BOARDS	*Polydor*	18	*7 Feb 70*	11
TASTE - LIVE AT THE ISLE OF WIGHT	*Polydor*	41	*9 Sep 72*	1

A TASTE OF HONEY — US

SINGLES:	HITS 1			WEEKS 19
BOOGIE OOGIE OOGIE	*Capitol*	3	*17 Jun 78*	16
BOOGIE OOGIE OOGIE [RM]	*Capitol*	59	*18 May 85*	3
Remixed by John Luongo.				

TASTE XPERIENCE featuring Natasha PEARL — UK

SINGLES:	HITS 1			WEEKS 1
SUMMERSAULT	*Manifesto*	66	*6 Nov 99*	1

TATA BOX INHIBITORS — Holland

SINGLES:	HITS 1			WEEKS 1
FREET	*Hooj Choons*	67	*3 Feb 01*	1

Jeffrey TATE – See Nigel KENNEDY

TATJANA — Croatia

SINGLES:	HITS 1			WEEKS 2
SANTA MARIA	*Love This*	40	*21 Sep 96*	2
Original release reached No. 102 in 1995.				

TAVARES — US

SINGLES:	HITS 9			WEEKS 77
HEAVEN MUST BE MISSING AN ANGEL	*Capitol Soul*	4	*10 Jul 76*	11
DON'T TAKE AWAY THE MUSIC	*Capitol Soul*	4	*9 Oct 76*	10

THE MIGHTY POWER OF LOVE	*Capitol*	25	*5 Feb 77*	6
WHODUNIT	*Capitol*	5	*9 Apr 77*	10
ONE STEP AWAY	*Capitol*	16	*2 Jul 77*	7
THE GHOST OF LOVE	*Capitol*	29	*18 Mar 78*	6
MORE THAN A WOMAN	*Capitol*	7	*6 May 78*	11
From the film 'Saturday Night Fever'. Originally recorded by the Bee Gees.				
SLOW TRAIN TO PARADISE	*Capitol*	62	*12 Aug 78*	3
HEAVEN MUST BE MISSING AN ANGEL [RM]	*Capitol*	12	*22 Feb 86*	9
Remixed by Ben Liebrand.				
IT ONLY TAKES A MINUTE	*Capitol*	46	*3 May 86*	4
Original release reached No. 10 in the US in 1975.				

ALBUMS:	HITS 2			WEEKS 15
SKY HIGH	*Capitol Soul*	22	*21 Aug 76*	13
THE BEST OF TAVARES	*Capitol*	39	*1 Apr 78*	2

TAXI GANG – See BEENIE MAN; Chaka DEMUS and PLIERS

TAXMAN – See KICKING BACK with TAXMAN

TAYLOR – See LIBRA presents TAYLOR

Andy TAYLOR — UK

SINGLES:	HITS 1			WEEKS 2
LOLA	*A&M*	60	*20 Oct 90*	2
ALBUMS:	**HITS 1**			**WEEKS 1**
THUNDER	*MCA*	61	*30 May 87*	1

Becky TAYLOR — UK

SINGLES:	HITS 1			WEEKS 1
SONG OF DREAMS	*EMI Classics*	60	*16 Jun 01*	1
Charity record for the Daily Mail Farm Aid appeal.				
ALBUMS:	**HITS 1**			**WEEKS 1**
A DREAM COME TRUE	*EMI Classics*	67	*23 Jun 01*	1

Felice TAYLOR — US

SINGLES:	HITS 1			WEEKS 13
I FEEL LOVE COMIN' ON	*President*	11	*28 Oct 67*	13

James TAYLOR — US

(See also Carly Simon.)

SINGLES:	HITS 2			WEEKS 18
FIRE AND RAIN	*Warner Brothers*	42	*21 Nov 70*	3
YOU'VE GOT A FRIEND	*Warner Brothers*	4	*28 Aug 71*	15
Originally recorded by Carole King from her 1971 album Tapestry.				
ALBUMS:	**HITS 5**			**WEEKS 112**
SWEET BABY JAMES	*Warner Brothers*	7	*21 Nov 70*	53
MUD SLIDE SLIM AND THE BLUE HORIZON	*Warner Brothers*	4	*29 May 71*	41
SWEET BABY JAMES [RE]	*Warner Brothers*	34	*8 Jan 72*	6
MUD SLIDE SLIM AND THE BLUE HORIZON [RE]	*Warner Brothers*	49	*18 Mar 72*	1
Above 2 were re-released with new catalogue numbers.				
ONE MAN DOG	*Warner Brothers*	27	*9 Dec 72*	5
CLASSIC SONGS	*CBS/WEA*	53	*4 Apr 87*	5
HOURGLASS	*Columbia*	46	*21 Jun 97*	1

James TAYLOR QUARTET — UK

SINGLES:	HITS 3			WEEKS 6
LOVE THE LIFE	*Big Life*	34	*3 Apr 93*	3
SEE A BRIGHTER DAY	*Big Life*	49	*3 Jul 93*	2
Above 2: JTQ with Noel McKOY.				
LOVE WILL KEEP US TOGETHER	*Acid Jazz*	63	*25 Feb 95*	1
Above hit: James TAYLOR QUARTET featuring Alison LIMERICK.				
ALBUMS:	**HITS 3**			**WEEKS 5**
SUPERNATURAL FEELING	*Big Life*	36	*1 May 93*	3
Above hit: JTQ with Noel McKOY.				
EXTENDED PLAY	*Acid Jazz*	70	*29 Oct 94*	1
IN THE HAND OF THE INEVITABLE	*Acid Jazz*	63	*11 Mar 95*	1

John TAYLOR — UK

SINGLES:	HITS 1			WEEKS 4
I DO WHAT I DO (THEME FOR 9½ WEEKS)	*Parlophone*	42	*15 Mar 86*	4
Theme from the film.				

Johnnie TAYLOR — US

SINGLES:	HITS 1			WEEKS 7
DISCO LADY	*CBS*	25	*24 Apr 76*	7

J.T. TAYLOR — US

SINGLES:	HITS 3			WEEKS 5
LONG HOT SUMMER NIGHT	*MCA*	63	*24 Aug 91*	2
FEEL THE NEED	*MCA*	57	*30 Nov 91*	1
FOLLOW ME	*MCA*	59	*18 Apr 92*	2

Pauline TAYLOR — UK

SINGLES:	HITS 2			WEEKS 3
LET THIS BE A PRAYER	*Cheeky*	26	*8 Jun 96*	2
Above hit: ROLLO GOES SPIRITUAL with Pauline TAYLOR.				
CONSTANTLY WAITING	*Cheeky*	51	*9 Nov 96*	1

R. Dean TAYLOR — Canada

SINGLES:	HITS 4			WEEKS 48
GOTTA SEE JANE	*Tamla Motown*	17	*22 Jun 68*	12
INDIANA WANTS ME	*Tamla Motown*	2	*3 Apr 71*	15
THERE'S A GHOST IN MY HOUSE	*Tamla Motown*	3	*11 May 74*	12
WINDOW SHOPPING	*Polydor*	36	*31 Aug 74*	5
GOTTA SEE JANE [RI]	*Tamla Motown*	41	*21 Sep 74*	4

Roger TAYLOR — UK

SINGLES:	HITS 8			WEEKS 18
FUTURE MANAGEMENT	*EMI*	49	*18 Apr 81*	4
MAN ON FIRE	*EMI*	66	*16 Jun 84*	2
RADIO	*Epic*	37	*10 Oct 92*	3
Above hit: SHAKY featuring Roger TAYLOR.				
NAZIS 1994	*Parlophone*	22	*14 May 94*	2
FOREIGN SAND	*Parlophone*	26	*1 Oct 94*	2
Above hit: Roger TAYLOR and YOSHIKI.				
HAPPINESS	*Parlophone*	32	*26 Nov 94*	2
PRESSURE ON	*Parlophone*	45	*10 Oct 98*	1
SURRENDER	*Parlophone*	38	*10 Apr 99*	2
Above hit: Roger TAYLOR featuring Treana MORRIS.				

ALBUMS:	HITS 4			WEEKS 11
FUN IN SPACE	*EMI*	18	*18 Apr 81*	5
STRANGE FRONTIER	*EMI*	30	*7 Jul 84*	4
HAPPINESS?	*Parlophone*	22	*17 Sep 94*	1
ELECTRIC FIRE	*Parlophone*	53	*10 Oct 98*	1

TAZ/STEREO NATION — UK

(See also Stereo Nation.)

SINGLES:	HITS 1			WEEKS 2
LAILA	*Wizard*	44	*27 Oct 01*	2

TC — Italy

SINGLES:	HITS 3			WEEKS 5
BERRY (THE REMIXES)	*Union City*	73	*14 Mar 92*	1
Above hit: TC 1991.				
FUNKY GUITAR	*Union City*	40	*21 Nov 92*	2
Above hit: TC 1992.				
HARMONY	*Union*	51	*10 Jul 93*	2
Samples the Temptations' Undisputed Truth.				
Above hit: TC 1993.				

Kiri TE KANAWA — New Zealand

(See also Various Artists: Studio Cast 'West Side Story', 'South Pacific', 'My Fair Lady'.)

SINGLES:	HITS 1			WEEKS 11
WORLD IN UNION	*Columbia*	4	*28 Sep 91*	11
Theme from the ITV Rugby World Cup broadcasts. Based around Gustav Holst's Planet Suite.				

ALBUMS:	HITS 8			WEEKS 53
CHANTS D'AUVERGNE VOLUME 1	*Decca*	57	*2 Apr 83*	1
Above hit: Kiri TE KANAWA with the ENGLISH CHAMBER ORCHESTRA.				
BLUE SKIES	*London*	41	*26 Oct 85*	18
Above hit: Kiri TE KANAWA with Nelson RIDDLE and his ORCHESTRA.				
BLUE SKIES [RE]	*London*	40	*17 May 86*	11
CHRISTMAS WITH KIRI	*Decca*	47	*13 Dec 86*	4
KIRI	*K-Tel*	70	*17 Dec 88*	3
THE ESSENTIAL KIRI	*Decca*	23	*29 Feb 92*	10
KIRI SIDETRACKS – THE JAZZ ALBUM	*Philips*	73	*23 May 92*	1

KIRI!	*PolyGram TV*	16	*9 Apr 94*	4
Live recordings from the Royal Albert Hall, 10 Mar 94 to celebrate her 50th birthday.				
KIRI - THE DEFINITIVE COLLECTION	*EMI Classics*	73	*10 Nov 01*	1

TEACH-IN — Holland

SINGLES:	HITS 1			WEEKS 7
DING-A-DONG	*Polydor*	13	*12 Apr 75*	7
Eurovision Song Contest winner in 1975.				

TEAM — UK

SINGLES:	HITS 1			WEEKS 5
WICKI WACKY HOUSE PARTY	*EMI*	55	*1 Jun 85*	5

TEAM DEEP — Belgium

SINGLES:	HITS 1			WEEKS 1
MORNINGLIGHT	*Multiply*	42	*17 May 97*	1

TEARDROP EXPLODES — UK

SINGLES:	HITS 7			WEEKS 50
WHEN I DREAM	*Mercury*	47	*27 Sep 80*	6
REWARD	*Mercury*	6	*31 Jan 81*	13
Trumpet played by "Hurricane" Smith.				
TREASON (IT'S JUST A STORY)	*Mercury*	18	*2 May 81*	8
Originally released in 1980.				
PASSIONATE FRIEND	*Zoo/Mercury*	25	*29 Aug 81*	10
COLOURS FLY AWAY	*Mercury*	54	*21 Nov 81*	3
TINY CHILDREN	*Mercury*	44	*19 Jun 82*	7
YOU DISAPPEAR FROM VIEW	*Mercury*	41	*19 Mar 83*	3
ALBUMS:	**HITS 4**			**WEEKS 45**
KILIMANJARO	*Mercury*	35	*18 Oct 80*	4
KILIMANJARO [RE]	*Mercury*	24	*14 Mar 81*	31
WILDER	*Mercury*	29	*5 Dec 81*	6
EVERBODY WANTS TO SHAG . . . THE TEARDROP EXPLODES	*Fontana*	72	*14 Apr 90*	1
FLOORED GENIUS - THE BEST OF JULIAN COPE AND THE TEARDROP EXPLODES	*Island*	22	*15 Aug 92*	3
Features both Julian Cope's solo and group material.				
Above hit: Julian COPE and the TEARDROP EXPLODES.				

TEARS FOR FEARS — UK

SINGLES:	HITS 19			WEEKS 143
MAD WORLD	*Mercury*	3	*2 Oct 82*	16
CHANGE	*Mercury*	4	*5 Feb 83*	9
PALE SHELTER	*Mercury*	5	*30 Apr 83*	8
Originally released in 1982.				
THE WAY YOU ARE	*Mercury*	24	*3 Dec 83*	8
MOTHERS TALK	*Mercury*	14	*18 Aug 84*	8
SHOUT	*Mercury*	4	*1 Dec 84*	16
EVERYBODY WANTS TO RULE THE WORLD	*Mercury*	2	*30 Mar 85*	14
HEAD OVER HEELS	*Mercury*	12	*22 Jun 85*	9
SUFFER THE CHILDREN	*Mercury*	52	*31 Aug 85*	4
This was their first single release in 1981.				
PALE SHELTER [RI]	*Mercury*	73	*7 Sep 85*	2
I BELIEVE (A SOULFUL RE-RECORDING)	*Mercury*	23	*12 Oct 85*	4
EVERYBODY WANTS TO RULE THE WORLD [RE]	*Mercury*	73	*22 Feb 86*	1
EVERYBODY WANTS TO RUN THE WORLD [RR]	*Mercury*	5	*31 May 86*	6
Re-written version to support Sport Aid's Race Against Time on 15 May 86.				
EVERYBODY WANTS TO RUN THE WORLD [RR] [RE]	*Mercury*	73	*19 Jul 86*	1
SOWING THE SEEDS OF LOVE	*Fontana*	5	*2 Sep 89*	9
WOMAN IN CHAINS	*Fontana*	26	*18 Nov 89*	8
Vocals by Oleta Adams and Phil Collins on drums.				
ADVICE FOR THE YOUNG AT HEART	*Fontana*	36	*3 Mar 90*	4
LAID SO LOW (TEARS ROLL DOWN)	*Fontana*	17	*22 Feb 92*	5
WOMAN IN CHAINS [RI]	*Fontana*	57	*25 Apr 92*	1
Above hit: TEARS FOR FEARS featuring Oleta ADAMS.				
BREAK IT DOWN AGAIN	*Mercury*	20	*29 May 93*	5
COLD	*Mercury*	72	*31 Jul 93*	1
RAOUL AND THE KINGS OF SPAIN	*Epic*	31	*7 Oct 95*	3
GOD'S MISTAKE	*Epic*	61	*29 Jun 96*	1
ALBUMS:	**HITS 6**			**WEEKS 211**
THE HURTING	*Mercury*	1	*19 Mar 83*	65
SONGS FROM THE BIG CHAIR	*Mercury*	2	*9 Mar 85*	81
Includes re-entry in 1991.				
THE SEEDS OF LOVE	*Fontana*	1	*7 Oct 89*	30
TEARS ROLL DOWN (GREATEST HITS 1982-1992)	*Fontana*	2	*14 Mar 92*	27
ELEMENTAL	*Mercury*	5	*19 Jun 93*	7

RAOUL AND THE KINGS OF SPAIN *A tribute to Roland Orzabal's Spanish father.*	*Epic*	41	*28 Oct 95*	1

TECHNATION — UK

SINGLES:	HITS 1			WEEKS 1
SEA OF BLUE *Vocals by Kelly Jones.*	*Slinky Music*	56	*7 Apr 01*	1

TECHNICIAN 2 featuring Georgia LEWIS — UK

SINGLES:	HITS 1			WEEKS 1
PLAYING WITH THE BOY	*MCA*	70	*14 Nov 92*	1

TECHNIQUE — UK

SINGLES:	HITS 2			WEEKS 2
SUN IS SHINING	*Creation*	64	*10 Apr 99*	1
YOU + ME	*Creation*	56	*28 Aug 99*	1

TECHNO TWINS — UK

SINGLES:	HITS 1			WEEKS 2
FALLING IN LOVE AGAIN	*PRT*	75	*16 Jan 82*	1
FALLING IN LOVE AGAIN [RE]	*PRT*	70	*30 Jan 82*	1

TECHNOCAT featuring Tom WILSON - See Tom WILSON

TECHNOHEAD — UK

(See also G.T.O.; Tricky Disco.)

SINGLES:	HITS 3			WEEKS 20
I WANNA BE A HIPPY	*Mokum*	6	*3 Feb 96*	14
HAPPY BIRTHDAY	*Mokum*	18	*27 Apr 96*	5
BANANA-NA-NA (DUMB DIDDY DUMB) *Vocals by Dutch ragga artist Whoops.*	*Mokum*	64	*12 Oct 96*	1

TECHNOTRONIC — UK/Belgium

SINGLES:	HITS 8			WEEKS 66
PUMP UP THE JAM *Though single credits Felly, vocals are actually by Ya Kid K.* *Above hit: TECHNOTRONIC featuring FELLY.*	*Swanyard*	2	*2 Sep 89*	15
GET UP (BEFORE THE NIGHT IS OVER) *Above hit: TECHNOTRONIC featuring YA KID K.*	*Swanyard*	2	*3 Feb 90*	10
THIS BEAT IS TECHNOTRONIC *Above hit: TECHNOTRONIC featuring MC ERIC.*	*Swanyard*	14	*7 Apr 90*	7
ROCKIN' OVER THE BEAT *Above hit: TECHNOTRONIC featuring YA KID K.*	*Swanyard*	9	*14 Jul 90*	9
MEGAMIX [M] *Mix of their previous hits.*	*Swanyard*	6	*6 Oct 90*	8
TURN IT UP *Above hit: TECHNOTRONIC featuring MELISSA and EINSTEIN.*	*Swanyard*	42	*15 Dec 90*	4
MOVE THAT BODY *Above hit: TECHNOTRONIC featuring REGGIE.*	*ARS*	12	*25 May 91*	7
WORK *Above 2: TECHNOTRONIC featuring REGGIE.*	*ARS*	40	*3 Aug 91*	4
PUMP UP THE JAM '96 [RM] *Remixed by Tin Tin Out.*	*Worx*	36	*14 Dec 96*	2
ALBUMS:	**HITS 3**			**WEEKS 62**
PUMP UP THE JAM	*Swanyard*	2	*6 Jan 90*	44
TRIP ON THIS - REMIXES *Above hit: TECHNOTRONIC and HI TEK 3.*	*Telstar*	7	*3 Nov 90*	14
BODY TO BODY	ARS	27	*15 Jun 91*	4

TEDDY BEARS — US

SINGLES:	HITS 1			WEEKS 17
TO KNOW HIM, IS TO LOVE HIM *Inspired by the epitaph on Phil Spector's father's tombstone. Features Sandy Nelson on drums.*	*London*	2	*20 Dec 58*	16
TO KNOW HIM IS TO LOVE HIM [RI] *[AA] listed with Endless Sleep by Jody Reynolds.*	*Lightning*	66	*14 Apr 79*	1

TEEBONE featuring MC KIE and MC SPARKS — UK

SINGLES:	HITS 1			WEEKS 2
FLY BI	*East West*	43	*5 Aug 00*	2

TEENAGE FANCLUB — UK

SINGLES:	HITS 14			WEEKS 21
STAR SIGN	*Creation*	44	*24 Aug 91*	2
THE CONCEPT	*Creation*	51	*2 Nov 91*	1

WHAT YOU DO TO ME [EP]	*Creation*	31	*8 Feb 92*	2
Lead track: What You Do To Me.				
RADIO	*Creation*	31	*26 Jun 93*	2
NORMAN 3	*Creation*	50	*2 Oct 93*	1
FALLIN'	*Epic*	59	*2 Apr 94*	1
From the film 'Judgement Night'. Samples Tom Petty's Free Fallin.				
Above hit: TEENAGE FANCLUB and DE LA SOUL.				
MELLOW DOUBT	*Creation*	34	*8 Apr 95*	2
SPARKY'S DREAM	*Creation*	40	*27 May 95*	2
NEIL JUNG	*Creation*	62	*2 Sep 95*	1
HAVE LOST IT [EP]	*Creation*	53	*16 Dec 95*	1
Lead track: Don't Look Back.				
AIN'T THAT ENOUGH	*Creation*	17	*12 Jul 97*	3
I DON'T WANT CONTROL OF YOU	*Creation*	43	*30 Aug 97*	1
START AGAIN	*Creation*	54	*29 Nov 97*	1
I NEED DIRECTION	*Columbia*	48	*28 Oct 00*	1
ALBUMS:	**HITS 6**			**WEEKS 23**
THE KING	*Creation*	53	*7 Sep 91*	2
BANDWAGONESQUE	*Creation*	22	*16 Nov 91*	7
THIRTEEN	*Creation*	14	*16 Oct 93*	3
Title refers to the number of tracks on the album.				
GRAND PRIX	*Creation*	7	*10 Jun 95*	4
SONGS FROM NORTHERN BRITAIN	*Creation*	3	*2 Aug 97*	5
HOWDY!	*Columbia*	33	*4 Nov 00*	2

TEENAGERS - See Frankie LYMON and the TEENAGERS

Towa TEI featuring Kylie MINOGUE — Japan/Australia

(See also Kylie Minogue.)

SINGLES:	**HITS 1**			**WEEKS 1**
GBI: GERMAN BOLD ITALIC	*Arthrob*	63	*31 Oct 98*	1

TEKNO TOO — UK

SINGLES:	**HITS 1**			**WEEKS 2**
JET-STAR	*D-Zone*	56	*13 Jul 91*	2

TELETUBBIES — UK

SINGLES:	**HITS 1**			**WEEKS 32**
TELETUBBIES SAY "EH-OH!"	*BBC Worldwide Music*	1	*13 Dec 97*	29
TELETUBBIES SAY "EH-OH!" [RE-1ST]	*BBC Worldwide Music*	66	*18 Jul 98*	2
TELETUBBIES SAY "EH-OH!" [RE-2ND]	*BBC Worldwide Music*	72	*15 Aug 98*	1
ALBUMS:	**HITS 1**			**WEEKS 4**
THE ALBUM	*BBC Worldwide Music*	31	*4 Apr 98*	4

TELEVISION — US

SINGLES:	**HITS 3**			**WEEKS 10**
MARQUEE MOON	*Elektra*	30	*16 Apr 77*	4
PROVE IT	*Elektra*	25	*30 Jul 77*	4
FOXHOLE	*Elektra*	36	*22 Apr 78*	2
ALBUMS:	**HITS 2**			**WEEKS 17**
MARQUEE MOON	*Elektra*	28	*26 Mar 77*	13
ADVENTURE	*Elektra*	7	*29 Apr 78*	4

TELEX — Belgium

SINGLES:	**HITS 1**			**WEEKS 7**
ROCK AROUND THE CLOCK	*Sire*	34	*21 Jul 79*	7

Sylvia TELLA - See BLOW MONKEYS

TEMPERANCE SEVEN vocal refrain by Mr. Paul MACDOWELL — UK

SINGLES:	**HITS 4**			**WEEKS 45**
YOU'RE DRIVING ME CRAZY	*Parlophone*	1	*1 Apr 61*	16
George Martin's first No.1 as a producer. Originally recorded by Guy Lombardo in 1930.				
PASADENA	*Parlophone*	4	*17 Jun 61*	17
Originally recorded by Murray and Smalle in 1924.				
HARD HEARTED HANNAH / CHILI BOM BOM	*Parlophone*	28	*30 Sep 61*	4
Chili Bom Bom listed from 12 Oct 61.				
THE CHARLESTON	*Parlophone*	22	*9 Dec 61*	8
EPS:	**HITS 2**			**WEEKS 57**
THE MUSICK	*Argo*	2	*13 May 61*	21
THE TEMPERANCE SEVEN	*Parlophone*	3	*23 Sep 61*	36
ALBUMS:	**HITS 2**			**WEEKS 10**
TEMPERANCE SEVEN PLUS ONE	Argo	19	*13 May 61*	1
TEMPERANCE SEVEN 1961	*Parlophone*	8	*25 Nov 61*	9

TEMPLE CHURCH CHOIR — UK

ALBUMS:	HITS 1			WEEKS 3
CHRISTMAS CAROLS	*His Master's Voice*	8	*16 Dec 61*	3

TEMPLE OF THE DOG — US

SINGLES:	HITS 1			WEEKS 2
HUNGER STRIKE	*A&M*	51	*24 Oct 92*	2

Nino TEMPO and April STEVENS — US

SINGLES:	HITS 2			WEEKS 19
DEEP PURPLE *Originally recorded by Larry Clinton Orchestra in 1939.*	*London*	17	*9 Nov 63*	11
WHISPERING *Originally recorded by Paul Whiteman Orchestra in 1920.*	*London*	20	*18 Jan 64*	8

TEMPTATIONS — US

(See also Diana Ross and the Supremes and the Temptations; Bruce Willis.)

SINGLES:	HITS 24			WEEKS 184
MY GIRL	*Stateside*	43	*20 Mar 65*	1
IT'S GROWING	*Tamla Motown*	49	*3 Apr 65*	1
IT'S GROWING [RE]	*Tamla Motown*	45	*17 Apr 65*	1
AIN'T TOO PROUD TO BEG	*Tamla Motown*	21	*16 Jul 66*	11
BEAUTY IS ONLY SKIN DEEP	*Tamla Motown*	18	*8 Oct 66*	10
(I KNOW) I'M LOSING YOU	*Tamla Motown*	19	*17 Dec 66*	9
YOU'RE MY EVERYTHING	*Tamla Motown*	26	*9 Sep 67*	15
I WISH IT WOULD RAIN	*Tamla Motown*	45	*9 Mar 68*	1
I COULD NEVER LOVE ANOTHER (AFTER LOVING YOU)	*Tamla Motown*	47	*15 Jun 68*	1
GET READY *Original release reached No. 29 in the US in 1966.*	*Tamla Motown*	10	*8 Mar 69*	9
CLOUD NINE	*Tamla Motown*	15	*23 Aug 69*	10
I CAN'T GET NEXT TO YOU	*Tamla Motown*	13	*17 Jan 70*	9
PSYCHEDELIC SHACK	*Tamla Motown*	33	*13 Jun 70*	7
BALL OF CONFUSION (THAT'S WHAT THE WORLD IS TODAY)	*Tamla Motown*	7	*19 Sep 70*	12
BALL OF CONFUSION (THAT'S WHAT THE WORLD IS TODAY) [RE]	*Tamla Motown*	48	*19 Dec 70*	3
JUST MY IMAGINATION (RUNNING AWAY WITH ME)	*Tamla Motown*	8	*22 May 71*	16
SUPERSTAR (REMEMBER HOW YOU GOT WHERE YOU ARE)	*Tamla Motown*	32	*5 Feb 72*	5
TAKE A LOOK AROUND	*Tamla Motown*	13	*15 Apr 72*	10
PAPA WAS A ROLLIN' STONE	*Tamla Motown*	14	*13 Jan 73*	8
LAW OF THE LAND *Above 2 originally recorded by Undisputed Truth.*	*Tamla Motown*	41	*29 Sep 73*	4
STANDING ON THE TOP (PART 1) *Above hit: TEMPTATIONS featuring Rick JAMES.*	*Motown*	53	*12 Jun 82*	3
TREAT HER LIKE A LADY	*Motown*	12	*17 Nov 84*	10
PAPA WAS A ROLLIN' STONE [RM] *Remixed by Freddy Bastone.*	*Motown*	31	*15 Aug 87*	6
LOOK WHAT YOU STARTED	*Motown*	63	*6 Feb 88*	2
ALL I WANT FROM YOU	*Motown*	71	*21 Oct 89*	1
THE MOTOWN SONG *Above hit: Rod STEWART (with the TEMPTATIONS).*	*Warner Brothers*	10	*15 Jun 91*	8
MY GIRL [RI] *From the film of the same name.*	*Epic*	2	*15 Feb 92*	10
THE JONES'	*Motown*	69	*22 Feb 92*	1

EPS:	HITS 2			WEEKS 3
THE TEMPTATIONS	*Tamla Motown*	18	*3 Apr 65*	1
IT'S THE TEMPTATIONS	*Tamla Motown*	8	*18 Feb 67*	2

ALBUMS:	HITS 14			WEEKS 113
GETTING READY	*Tamla Motown*	40	*24 Dec 66*	2
TEMPTATIONS GREATEST HITS	*Tamla Motown*	26	*11 Feb 67*	17
THE TEMPTATIONS LIVE!	*Tamla Motown*	20	*22 Jul 67*	4
TEMPTATIONS GREATEST HITS [RE]	*Tamla Motown*	17	*20 Jan 68*	23
WITH A LOT O'SOUL	*Tamla Motown*	19	*18 Nov 67*	18
CLOUD NINE	*Tamla Motown*	32	*20 Sep 69*	1
PUZZLE PEOPLE	*Tamla Motown*	20	*14 Feb 70*	4
PSYCHEDELIC SHACK	*Tamla Motown*	56	*11 Jul 70*	1
GREATEST HITS VOLUME 2	*Tamla Motown*	35	*26 Dec 70*	12
SOLID ROCK	*Tamla Motown*	34	*29 Apr 72*	2
ALL DIRECTIONS	*Tamla Motown*	19	*20 Jan 73*	7
MASTERPIECE	*Tamla Motown*	28	*7 Jul 73*	3
TRULY FOR YOU	*Motown*	75	*8 Dec 84*	5
MOTOWN'S GREATEST HITS	*Motown*	8	*11 Apr 92*	9
AT THEIR VERY BEST	*Universal Music TV*	28	*27 Jan 01*	5

10 C.C. — UK

SINGLES:	HITS 14			WEEKS 133
DONNA	*UK*	2	*23 Sep 72*	13

RUBBER BULLETS	*UK*	1	*19 May 73*	15
THE DEAN AND I	*UK*	10	*25 Aug 73*	8
THE WALL STREET SHUFFLE	*UK*	10	*15 Jun 74*	10
SILLY LOVE	*UK*	24	*14 Sep 74*	7
LIFE IS A MINESTRONE	*Mercury*	7	*5 Apr 75*	8
I'M NOT IN LOVE	*Mercury*	1	*31 May 75*	11
ART FOR ARTS SAKE	*Mercury*	5	*29 Nov 75*	10
I'M MANDY FLY ME	*Mercury*	6	*20 Mar 76*	9
THE THINGS WE DO FOR LOVE	*Mercury*	6	*11 Dec 76*	11
GOOD MORNING JUDGE	*Mercury*	5	*16 Apr 77*	12
DREADLOCK HOLIDAY	*Mercury*	1	*12 Aug 78*	13
Song written about the experiences of Justin Hayward's Caribbean holiday.				
RUN AWAY	*Mercury*	50	*7 Aug 82*	4
I'M NOT IN LOVE (ACOUSTIC SESSION '95) [RR]	*Avex UK*	29	*18 Mar 95*	2
ALBUMS:	**HITS 13**			**WEEKS 219**
10 C.C.	*UK*	36	*1 Sep 73*	5
SHEET MUSIC	*UK*	9	*15 Jun 74*	24
THE ORIGINAL SOUNDTRACK	*Mercury*	4	*22 Mar 75*	40
GREATEST HITS OF 10 C.C.	*Decca*	9	*7 Jun 75*	18
HOW DARE YOU!	*Mercury*	5	*31 Jan 76*	31
DECEPTIVE BENDS	*Mercury*	3	*14 May 77*	21
LIVE AND LET LIVE	*Mercury*	14	*10 Dec 77*	15
Live recordings from their UK tour, May 77.				
BLOODY TOURISTS	*Mercury*	3	*23 Sep 78*	15
GREATEST HITS 1972-1978	*Mercury*	5	*6 Oct 79*	21
LOOK HEAR?	*Mercury*	35	*5 Apr 80*	5
WINDOW IN THE JUNGLE	*Mercury*	70	*15 Oct 83*	2
CHANGING FACES - THE VERY BEST OF 10CC AND GODLEY AND CREME	*ProTV*	4	*29 Aug 87*	18
Features both Godley and Creme's material as a duo and with 10CC.				
Above hit: 10 CC and GODLEY and CRÈME.				
THE VERY BEST OF 10CC	*Mercury TV*	37	*5 Apr 97*	4
Also includes 3 hits from Godley and Creme.				

TEN CITY — US

SINGLES:	**HITS 6**			**WEEKS 21**
THAT'S THE WAY LOVE IS	*Atlantic*	8	*21 Jan 89*	10
DEVOTION	*Atlantic*	29	*8 Apr 89*	4
WHERE DO WE GO?	*Atlantic*	60	*22 Jul 89*	1
WHATEVER MAKES YOU HAPPY	*Atlantic*	60	*27 Oct 90*	2
ONLY TIME WILL TELL / MY PEACE OF HEAVEN	*East West America*	63	*15 Aug 92*	2
FANTASY	*Columbia*	45	*11 Sep 93*	2
ALBUMS:	**HITS 1**			**WEEKS 12**
FOUNDATION	*Atlantic*	22	*18 Feb 89*	12

TEN SHARP — Holland

SINGLES:	**HITS 2**			**WEEKS 15**
YOU	*Columbia*	10	*21 Mar 92*	13
AIN'T MY BEATING HEART	*Columbia*	63	*20 Jun 92*	2
ALBUMS:	**HITS 1**			**WEEKS 2**
UNDER THE WATER-LINE	*Columbia*	46	*9 May 92*	2

10,000 MANIACS — US

SINGLES:	**HITS 3**			**WEEKS 7**
THESE ARE DAYS	*Elektra*	58	*12 Sep 92*	3
CANDY EVERYBODY WANTS	*Elektra*	47	*10 Apr 93*	3
BECAUSE THE NIGHT	*Elektra*	65	*23 Oct 93*	1
ALBUMS:	**HITS 3**			**WEEKS 12**
BLIND MAN'S ZOO	*Elektra*	18	*27 May 89*	8
OUR TIME IN EDEN	*Elektra*	33	*10 Oct 92*	2
UNPLUGGED	*Elektra*	40	*6 Nov 93*	2
Live recordings for the MTV channel.				

TEN YEARS AFTER — UK

SINGLES:	**HITS 1**			**WEEKS 18**
LOVE LIKE A MAN	*Deram*	10	*6 Jun 70*	18
ALBUMS:	**HITS 8**			**WEEKS 73**
UNDEAD	*Deram*	26	*21 Sep 68*	7
STONEDHENGE	*Deram*	6	*22 Feb 69*	5
SSSSH	*Deram*	4	*4 Oct 69*	18
CRICKLEWOOD GREEN	*Deram*	4	*2 May 70*	27
WATT	*Deram*	5	*9 Jan 71*	12
A SPACE IN TIME	*Chrysalis*	36	*13 Nov 71*	1
ROCK & ROLL MUSIC TO THE WORLD	*Chrysalis*	27	*7 Oct 72*	1
RECORDED LIVE	*Chrysalis*	36	*28 Jul 73*	2

Danny TENAGLIA — US

SINGLES:	HITS 2			WEEKS 5
MUSIC IS THE ANSWER (DANCIN' AND PRANCIN') *Above hit: Danny TENAGLIA + CELEDA.*	*Twisted UK*	36	*5 Sep 98*	3
TURN ME ON *Above hit: Danny TENAGLIA featuring Liz TORRES.*	*Twisted UK*	53	*10 Apr 99*	1
MUSIC IS THE ANSWER '99 (DANCIN' AND PRANCIN') [RM] *Remixed by Future Shock.* *Above hit: Danny TENAGLIA + CELEDA.*	*Twisted UK*	50	*23 Oct 99*	1

TENNESSEE THREE – See Johnny CASH

Klaus TENNSTEDT – See Nigel KENNEDY

TENOR FLY — UK

(See also Rebel MC.)

SINGLES:	HITS 3			WEEKS 11
THE WICKEDEST SOUND *Above hit: REBEL MC (featuring TENOR FLY).*	*Desire*	43	*6 Apr 91*	6
BRIGHT SIDE OF LIFE *Samples Nina Simone's My Baby Just Cares For Me.*	*Mango*	51	*7 Jan 95*	2
B-BOY STANCE *Above hit: FREESTYLERS featuring TENOR FLY.*	*Freskanova*	23	*7 Feb 98*	3

TENPOLE TUDOR — UK

SINGLES:	HITS 5			WEEKS 40
WHO KILLED BAMBI *[AA] listed with Silly Thing by the Sex Pistols.* *Above hit: TEN POLE TUDOR.*	*Virgin*	6	*7 Apr 79*	8
ROCK AROUND THE CLOCK *[AA] listed with The Great Rock 'N' Roll Swindle by the Sex Pistols. Above 2 from the film 'The Great Rock 'N' Roll Swindle'.*	*Virgin*	21	*13 Oct 79*	6
SWORDS OF A THOUSAND MEN	*Stiff*	6	*25 Apr 81*	12
WUNDERBAR	*Stiff*	16	*1 Aug 81*	9
THROWING MY BABY OUT WITH THE BATH WATER	*Stiff*	49	*14 Nov 81*	5
ALBUMS:	**HITS 1**			**WEEKS 8**
EDDIE, OLD BOB, DICK & GARRY	*Stiff*	44	*9 May 81*	8

TENTH PLANET — UK

SINGLES:	HITS 1			WEEKS 1
GHOSTS	*Nebula*	59	*14 Apr 01*	1

TEPHLON – See M.O.P.

Bryn TERFEL — UK

SINGLES:	HITS 1			WEEKS 3
WORLD IN UNION *Official ITV theme to the 1999 Rugby World Cup. Features The Morriston Rugby Club Choir and the City of Prague Philharmonic Orchestra.* *Above hit: Shirley BASSEY, Bryn TERFEL and the BLACK MOUNTAIN MALE CHORUS.*	*Decca*	35	*23 Oct 99*	3
ALBUMS:	**HITS 3**			**WEEKS 13**
SOMETHING WONDERFUL *Interpretations of Rodgers and Hammerstein songs.*	*Deutsche Grammophon*	72	*16 Nov 96*	1
WE'LL KEEP A WELCOME – THE WELSH ALBUM *Above hit: Bryn TERFEL; the ORCHESTRA OF WELSH NATIONAL OPERA; Gareth JONES.*	*Deutsche Grammophon*	33	*28 Oct 00*	10
SOME ENCHANTED EVENING – THE BEST OF THE MUSICALS	*Deutsche Grammophon*	49	*3 Nov 01*	2

Max TERR CHOIR – See Bing CROSBY

TERRA FERMA — Italy

SINGLES:	HITS 1			WEEKS 1
FLOATING	*Platipus*	64	*18 May 96*	1

TERRAPLANE — UK

ALBUMS:	HITS 1			WEEKS 1
BLACK AND WHITE	*Epic*	74	*25 Jan 86*	1

TERRAR – See KELIS

Tammi TERRELL – See Marvin GAYE and Tammi TERRELL

TERRI and MONICA – See Shabba RANKS

TERRIS — UK

SINGLES:	HITS 1			WEEKS 1
FABRICATED LUNACY	*Blanco Y Negro*	62	*17 Mar 01*	1

TERRORIZE — UK

SINGLES:	HITS 2			WEEKS 6
IT'S JUST A FEELING	*Hamster*	52	*2 May 92*	3
FEEL THE RHYTHM	*Hamster*	69	*22 Aug 92*	1
IT'S JUST A FEELING [RI]	*Hamster*	47	*14 Nov 92*	2

TERRORVISION — UK

SINGLES:	HITS 16			WEEKS 55
AMERICAN T.V.	*Total Vegas*	63	*19 Jun 93*	1
NEW POLICY ONE	*Total Vegas*	42	*30 Oct 93*	2
MY HOUSE	*Total Vegas*	29	*8 Jan 94*	4
Originally released in 1992.				
OBLIVION	*Total Vegas*	21	*9 Apr 94*	5
MIDDLEMAN	*Total Vegas*	25	*25 Jun 94*	4
PRETEND BEST FRIEND	*Total Vegas*	25	*3 Sep 94*	3
ALICE WHAT'S THE MATTER?	*Total Vegas*	24	*29 Oct 94*	4
SOME PEOPLE SAY	*Total Vegas*	22	*18 Mar 95*	3
PERSEVERANCE	*Total Vegas*	5	*2 Mar 96*	4
CELEBRITY HIT LIST	*Total Vegas*	20	*4 May 96*	3
BAD ACTRESS	*Total Vegas*	10	*20 Jul 96*	3
EASY	*Total Vegas*	12	*11 Jan 97*	4
JOSEPHINE	*Total Vegas*	23	*3 Oct 98*	2
TEQUILA	*Total Vegas*	2	*30 Jan 99*	10
III WISHES	*Total Vegas*	42	*15 May 99*	1
D'YA WANNA GO FASTER?	*Papillon*	28	*27 Jan 01*	2
ALBUMS:	**HITS 5**			**WEEKS 41**
FORMALDEHYDE	*Total Vegas*	75	*15 May 93*	1
HOW TO MAKE FRIENDS AND INFLUENCE PEOPLE	*Total Vegas*	18	*30 Apr 94*	25
REGULAR URBAN SURVIVORS	*Total Vegas*	8	*23 Mar 96*	12
SHAVING PEACHES	*Total Vegas*	34	*17 Oct 98*	2
GOOD TO GO	*Papillon*	48	*17 Feb 01*	1

Helen TERRY — UK

SINGLES:	HITS 1			WEEKS 6
LOVE LIES LOST	*Virgin*	34	*12 May 84*	6

Todd TERRY — US

(See also Gypsymen.)

SINGLES:	HITS 7			WEEKS 36
WEEKEND *Above hit: Todd TERRY PROJECT.*	*Sleeping Bag*	56	*12 Nov 88*	3
A DAY IN THE LIFE / WARLOCK *A Day In The Life not listed until 10 Dec 88.* *Above hit: Todd TERRY presents BLACK RIOT.*	*Champion*	68	*3 Dec 88*	3
WEEKEND [RM] *Remixed by Mike Gray and Jon Pearn for DMC (UK).* *Above hit: Todd TERRY PROJECT.*	*Ore*	28	*14 Oct 95*	3
KEEP ON JUMPIN' *Originally recorded by Musique as the B-side to the US release of In The Bush.*	*Manifesto*	8	*13 Jul 96*	6
SOMETHING GOIN' ON *Above 2: Todd TERRY featuring Martha WASH and Jocelyn BROWN.*	*Manifesto*	5	*12 Jul 97*	10
IT'S OVER LOVE *Above hit: Todd TERRY presents SHANNON.*	*Manifesto*	16	*6 Dec 97*	8
READY FOR A NEW DAY *Above hit: Todd TERRY features Martha WASH.*	*Manifesto*	20	*11 Apr 98*	2
LET IT RIDE *Above 2 with vocals by Antoinette Robertson.*	*Arrested*	58	*3 Jul 99*	1
ALBUMS:	**HITS 1**			**WEEKS 1**
THE MINISTRY OF SOUNDS PRESENTS A DAY IN THE LIFE OF TODD TERRY	*Sound Of Ministry*	73	*5 Aug 95*	1

Tony TERRY — US

SINGLES:	HITS 1			WEEKS 6
LOVEY DOVEY	*Epic*	44	*27 Feb 88*	6

TERRY, BLAIR and ANOUCHKA - See Terry HALL

TESLA — US

SINGLES:	HITS 1			WEEKS 1
SIGNS	*Geffen*	70	*27 Apr 91*	1

ALBUMS:	HITS 4			WEEKS 6
THE GREAT RADIO CONTROVERSY	*Geffen*	34	*11 Feb 89*	2
FIVE MAN ACOUSTICAL JAM	*Geffen*	59	*2 Mar 91*	1
PSYCHOTIC SUPPER	*Geffen*	44	*21 Sep 91*	2
BUST A NUT	*Geffen*	51	*3 Sep 94*	1

TESTAMENT

US

ALBUMS:	HITS 4			WEEKS 6
THE NEW ORDER	*Megaforce*	81	*28 May 88*	1
PRACTICE WHAT YOU PREACH	*Atlantic*	40	*19 Aug 89*	2
SOULS OF BLACK	*Megaforce*	35	*6 Oct 90*	2
THE RITUAL	*Atlantic*	48	*30 May 92*	1

Joe TEX

US

SINGLES:	HITS 1			WEEKS 11
AIN'T GONNA BUMP NO MORE (WITH NO BIG FAT WOMAN)	*Epic*	2	*23 Apr 77*	11

TEXAS

UK

SINGLES:	HITS 21			WEEKS 127
I DON'T WANT A LOVER	*Mercury*	8	*4 Feb 89*	11
THRILL HAS GONE	*Mercury*	60	*6 May 89*	3
EVERYDAY NOW	*Mercury*	44	*5 Aug 89*	5
PRAYER FOR YOU	*Mercury*	73	*2 Dec 89*	1
WHY BELIEVE IN YOU	*Mercury*	66	*7 Sep 91*	1
IN MY HEART	*Mercury*	74	*26 Oct 91*	1
ALONE WITH YOU	*Mercury*	32	*8 Feb 92*	4
TIRED OF BEING ALONE	*Mercury*	19	*25 Apr 92*	6
SO CALLED FRIEND	*Vertigo*	30	*11 Sep 93*	3
Used on the opening titles of the US TV comedy show 'Ellen'.				
YOU OWE IT ALL TO ME	*Vertigo*	39	*30 Oct 93*	3
SO IN LOVE WITH YOU	*Vertigo*	28	*12 Feb 94*	2
SAY WHAT YOU WANT	*Mercury*	3	*18 Jan 97*	10
HALO	*Mercury*	10	*19 Apr 97*	7
BLACK EYED BOY	*Mercury*	5	*9 Aug 97*	6
PUT YOUR ARMS AROUND ME	*Mercury*	10	*15 Nov 97*	5
PUT YOUR ARMS AROUND ME [RE-1ST]	*Mercury*	75	*3 Jan 98*	1
PUT YOUR ARMS AROUND ME [RE-2ND]	*Mercury*	64	*17 Jan 98*	2
SAY WHAT YOU WANT (ALL DAY EVERY DAY) [RR] / INSANE	*Mercury*	4	*21 Mar 98*	7
They first sang this together at the 1998 Brit Awards on 9 Feb 98. Insane is only credited to Texas.				
Above hit: TEXAS featuring the WU TANG CLAN.				
IN OUR LIFETIME	*Mercury*	4	*1 May 99*	9
SUMMER SON	*Mercury*	5	*28 Aug 99*	9
WHEN WE ARE TOGETHER	*Mercury*	12	*27 Nov 99*	9
IN DEMAND	*Mercury*	6	*14 Oct 00*	8
IN DEMAND [RE]	*Mercury*	62	*13 Jan 01*	2
INNER SMILE	*Mercury*	6	*20 Jan 01*	8
I DON'T WANT A LOVER [RM]	*Mercury*	16	*21 Jul 01*	4
Remixed by Stargate.				

ALBUMS:	HITS 6			WEEKS 229
SOUTHSIDE	*Mercury*	3	*25 Mar 89*	29
Named after a district of Glasgow. Includes re-entry in 1997.				
MOTHERS HEAVEN	*Mercury*	32	*5 Oct 91*	4
RICKS ROAD	*Vertigo*	18	*13 Nov 93*	2
Title came from the pathway that led to the Bearsville Studios, New York where they recorded the album.				
WHITE ON BLONDE	*Mercury*	1	*15 Feb 97*	102
THE HUSH	*Mercury*	1	*22 May 99*	47
SOUTHSIDE [RE]	*Mercury*	45	*22 May 99*	1
THE GREATEST HITS	*Mercury*	1	*4 Nov 00*	44

THA DOGG POUND

US

ALBUMS:	HITS 1			WEEKS 2
DOGG FOOD	*Death Row*	66	*11 Nov 95*	2

THAT KID CHRIS

US

SINGLES:	HITS 1			WEEKS 1
FEEL THA VIBE	*Manifesto*	52	*22 Feb 97*	1

THAT PETROL EMOTION

UK/US

SINGLES:	HITS 7			WEEKS 24
BIG DECISION	*Polydor*	43	*11 Apr 87*	7
DANCE	*Polydor*	64	*11 Jul 87*	2
GENIUS MOVE	*Virgin*	65	*17 Oct 87*	2
ABANDON	*Virgin*	73	*31 Mar 90*	1
HEY VENUS	*Virgin*	49	*1 Sep 90*	4

TINGLE	*Virgin*	49	*9 Feb 91*	4
SENSITIZE	*Virgin*	55	*27 Apr 91*	4

Original release reached No. 99 in 1990.

ALBUMS:	**HITS 4**			**WEEKS 8**
MANIC POP THRILL	*Demon*	84	*10 May 86*	2
BABBLE	*Polydor*	30	*23 May 87*	3
END OF MILLENNIUM PSYCHOSIS BLUES	*Virgin*	53	*24 Sep 88*	2
CHEMICRAZY	*Virgin*	62	*21 Apr 90*	1

The THE — UK

SINGLES:	**HITS 15**			**WEEKS 52**
UNCERTAIN SMILE	*Epic*	68	*4 Dec 82*	3
THIS IS THE DAY	*Epic*	71	*17 Sep 83*	3
HEARTLAND	*Some Bizzare*	29	*9 Aug 86*	10
INFECTED	*Some Bizzare*	48	*25 Oct 86*	5
SLOW TRAIN TO DAWN	*Some Bizzare*	64	*24 Jan 87*	2
SWEET BIRD OF TRUTH	*Epic*	55	*23 May 87*	2
THE BEAT(EN) GENERATION	*Epic*	18	*1 Apr 89*	5
GRAVITATE TO ME	*Epic*	63	*22 Jul 89*	3
ARMAGEDDON DAYS ARE HERE (AGAIN)	*Epic*	70	*7 Oct 89*	2
SHADES OF BLUE [EP]	*Epic*	54	*2 Mar 91*	1
Lead track: Jealous Of Youth.				
DOGS OF LUST	*Epic*	25	*16 Jan 93*	4
SLOW MOTION REPLAY	*Epic*	35	*17 Apr 93*	3
LOVE IS STRONGER THAN DEATH	*Epic*	39	*19 Jun 93*	3
DIS-INFECTED [EP]	*Epic*	17	*15 Jan 94*	4
Lead track: That Was The Day, which is a re-recording of This Is The Day.				
I SAW THE LIGHT	*Epic*	31	*4 Feb 95*	2
Originally recorded by Hank Williams in 1953.				

ALBUMS:	**HITS 7**			**WEEKS 52**
SOUL MINING	*Epic*	27	*29 Oct 83*	5
INFECTED	*Some Bizzare*	14	*29 Nov 86*	30
MIND BOMB	*Epic*	4	*27 May 89*	9
DUSK	*Epic*	2	*6 Feb 93*	4
BURNING BLUE SOUL	*4AD*	65	*19 Jun 93*	1
Originally released in 1981 credited to Matt Johnson.				
HANKY PANKY	*Epic*	28	*25 Feb 95*	2
Tribute to Hank Willams.				
NAKED SELF	*Nothing*	45	*11 Mar 00*	1

THEATRE OF HATE — UK

SINGLES:	**HITS 2**			**WEEKS 9**
DO YOU BELIEVE IN THE WESTWORLD	*Burning Rome*	40	*23 Jan 82*	7
THE HOP	*Burning Rome*	70	*29 May 82*	2

ALBUMS:	**HITS 2**			**WEEKS 9**
WESTWORLD	*Burning Rome*	17	*13 Mar 82*	6
REVOLUTION	*Burning Rome*	67	*18 Aug 84*	3

THEAUDIENCE — UK

SINGLES:	**HITS 3**			**WEEKS 5**
IF YOU CAN'T DO IT WHEN YOU'RE YOUNG; WHEN CAN YOU DO IT?	*ElleFre*	48	*7 Mar 98*	1
A PESSIMIST IS NEVER DISAPPOINTED	*ElleFre*	27	*23 May 98*	2
I KNOW ENOUGH (I DON'T GET ENOUGH)	*ElleFre*	25	*8 Aug 98*	2

ALBUMS:	**HITS 1**			**WEEKS 2**
THEAUDIENCE	*ElleFre*	22	*29 Aug 98*	2

THEM — UK

SINGLES:	**HITS 2**			**WEEKS 23**
BABY PLEASE DON'T GO	*Decca*	10	*9 Jan 65*	9
Originally recorded by Big Joe Williams.				
HERE COMES THE NIGHT	*Decca*	2	*27 Mar 65*	12
Originally recorded by Lulu.				
BABY PLEASE DON'T GO [RI]	*London*	65	*9 Feb 91*	2
From the film 'Wild At Heart'. Featured in the Peugeot 205 TV commercial.				

EPS:	**HITS 1**			**WEEKS 18**
THEM	*Decca*	5	*20 Mar 65*	18

THEN JERICO — UK

SINGLES:	**HITS 6**			**WEEKS 36**
LET HER FALL	*London*	65	*31 Jan 87*	3
THE MOTIVE	*London*	18	*25 Jul 87*	12
MUSCLE DEEP	*London*	48	*24 Oct 87*	4
Original release reached No. 85 in 1986.				
BIG AREA	*London*	13	*28 Jan 89*	7

WHAT DOES IT TAKE?	*London*	33	*8 Apr 89*	4
SUGAR BOX	*London*	22	*12 Aug 89*	6
ALBUMS:	**HITS 2**			**WEEKS 24**
FIRST (THE SOUND OF MUSIC)	*London*	35	*3 Oct 87*	7
THE BIG AREA	*London*	4	*4 Mar 89*	17

THERAPY?

UK

SINGLES:	**HITS 13**			**WEEKS 33**
TEETHGRINDER	*A&M*	30	*31 Oct 92*	2
SHORTSHARPSHOCK [EP] *Lead track: Screamager.*	*A&M*	9	*20 Mar 93*	4
FACE THE STRANGE [EP] *Lead track: Turn.*	*A&M*	18	*12 Jun 93*	3
OPAL MANTRA	*A&M*	13	*28 Aug 93*	3
NOWHERE	*A&M*	18	*29 Jan 94*	4
TRIGGER INSIDE	*A&M*	22	*12 Mar 94*	3
DIE LAUGHING	*A&M*	29	*11 Jun 94*	2
INNOCENT X *[AA] listed with Belfast/Wasted by Orbital.*	*Volume*	53	*27 May 95*	1
STORIES	*A&M*	14	*3 Jun 95*	3
LOOSE	*A&M*	25	*29 Jul 95*	3
DIANE *Originally recorded by Husker Du.*	*A&M*	26	*18 Nov 95*	2
CHURCH OF MOISE	*A&M*	29	*14 Mar 98*	2
LONELY, CRYIN', ONLY	*A&M*	32	*30 May 98*	1
ALBUMS:	**HITS 6**			**WEEKS 24**
PLEASURE DEATH	*Wiiija*	52	*8 Feb 92*	1
NURSE	*A&M*	38	*14 Nov 92*	3
TROUBLEGUM	*A&M*	5	*19 Feb 94*	11
INFERNAL LOVE	*A&M*	9	*24 Jun 95*	7
SEMI-DETACHED	*A&M*	21	*11 Apr 98*	1
SUICIDE PACT – YOU FIRST	*Ark 21*	61	*30 Oct 99*	1

THESE ANIMAL MEN

UK

SINGLES:	**HITS 3**			**WEEKS 3**
THIS IS THE SOUND OF YOUTH *Originally appeared on the Fierce Panda label release Shagging In The Streets EP.*	*Hi-Rise Recordings*	72	*24 Sep 94*	1
LIFE SUPPORT MACHINE	*Hut*	62	*8 Feb 97*	1
LIGHT EMITTING ELECTRICAL WAVE	*Hut*	72	*12 Apr 97*	1
ALBUMS:	**HITS 3**			**WEEKS 4**
TOO SUSSED?	*Hi-Rise Recordings*	39	*2 Jul 94*	2
(COME ON, JOIN) THE HIGH SOCIETY	*Hi-Rise Recordings*	62	*8 Oct 94*	1
TAXI FOR THESE ANIMAL MEN *6-track mini album.*	*Hi-Rise Recordings*	64	*25 Mar 95*	1

THEY MIGHT BE GIANTS

US

SINGLES:	**HITS 3**			**WEEKS 18**
BIRDHOUSE IN YOUR SOUL	*Elektra*	6	*3 Mar 90*	11
ISTANBUL (NOT CONSTANTINOPLE)	*Elektra*	61	*2 Jun 90*	2
BOSS OF ME *Theme to the Sky TV show 'Malcolm In The Middle'.*	*PIAS Recordings*	21	*28 Jul 01*	5
ALBUMS:	**HITS 1**			**WEEKS 12**
FLOOD	*Elektra*	14	*7 Apr 90*	12

THIN LIZZY

UK/Ireland

SINGLES:	**HITS 18**			**WEEKS 128**
WHISKY IN THE JAR	*Decca*	6	*20 Jan 73*	12
THE BOYS ARE BACK IN TOWN	*Vertigo*	8	*29 May 76*	10
JAILBREAK	*Vertigo*	31	*14 Aug 76*	4
DON'T BELIEVE A WORD	*Vertigo*	12	*15 Jan 77*	7
DANCING IN THE MOONLIGHT (IT'S CAUGHT ME IN IT'S SPOTLIGHT)	*Vertigo*	14	*13 Aug 77*	8
ROSALIE/ (COWGIRLS' SONG) [M] *Live recording from the Hammersmith Odeon, London, 14 Nov 76. Originally recorded by Bob Seger.*	*Vertigo*	20	*13 May 78*	13
WAITING FOR AN ALIBI	*Vertigo*	9	*3 Mar 79*	8
DO ANYTHING YOU WANT TO	*Vertigo*	14	*16 Jun 79*	9
SARAH	*Vertigo*	24	*20 Oct 79*	13
CHINATOWN	*Vertigo*	21	*24 May 80*	9
KILLER ON THE LOOSE	*Vertigo*	10	*27 Sep 80*	7
KILLERS LIVE [EP] *Lead track: Are You Ready.*	*Vertigo*	19	*2 May 81*	7
TROUBLE BOYS	*Vertigo*	53	*8 Aug 81*	4
HOLLYWOOD (DOWN ON YOUR LUCK)	*Vertigo*	53	*6 Mar 82*	3
COLD SWEAT	*Vertigo*	27	*12 Feb 83*	5
THUNDER AND LIGHTNING	*Vertigo*	39	*7 May 83*	2

THE SUN GOES DOWN	*Vertigo*	52	*6 Aug 83*	3
DEDICATION	*Vertigo*	35	*26 Jan 91*	3
THE BOYS ARE BACK IN TOWN [RI]	*Vertigo*	63	*23 Mar 91*	1
ALBUMS:	**HITS 14**			**WEEKS 250**
FIGHTING	*Vertigo*	60	*27 Sep 75*	1
JAILBREAK	*Vertigo*	10	*10 Apr 76*	50
JOHNNY THE FOX	*Vertigo*	11	*6 Nov 76*	24
BAD REPUTATION	*Vertigo*	4	*1 Oct 77*	9
LIVE AND DANGEROUS	*Vertigo*	2	*17 Jun 78*	62
Live recordings from the Hammersmith Odeon, London, 14 Nov 76 and the Seneca College Fieldhouse, Toronto, 28 Oct 77.				
BLACK ROSE (A ROCK LEGEND)	*Vertigo*	2	*5 May 79*	21
CHINATOWN	*Vertigo*	7	*18 Oct 80*	7
THE ADVENTURES OF THIN LIZZY	*Vertigo*	6	*11 Apr 81*	13
RENEGADE	*Vertigo*	38	*5 Dec 81*	8
THUNDER AND LIGHTNING	*Vertigo*	4	*12 Mar 83*	11
LIFE - LIVE	*Vertigo*	29	*26 Nov 83*	6
SOLDIER OF FORTUNE - THE BEST OF PHIL LYNOTT AND THIN LIZZY	*Telstar*	55	*14 Nov 87*	10
Features Lynott's solo and group material.				
Above hit: Phil LYNOTT and THIN LIZZY.				
DEDICATION - THE VERY BEST OF THIN LIZZY	*Vertigo*	8	*16 Feb 91*	17
WILD ONE - THE VERY BEST OF THIN LIZZY	*Vertigo*	18	*13 Jan 96*	11

3RD BASS — US

SINGLES:	**HITS 3**			**WEEKS 5**
THE GAS FACE	*Def Jam*	71	*10 Feb 90*	1
BROOKLYN QUEENS	*Def Jam*	61	*7 Apr 90*	2
POP GOES THE WEASEL	*Def Jam*	64	*22 Jun 91*	2
Samples Sledgehammer by Peter Gabriel and You Haven't Done Nothin' by Stevie Wonder.				
ALBUMS:	**HITS 1**			**WEEKS 1**
DERELICTS OF DIALECT	*Def Jam*	46	*20 Jul 91*	1

THIRD DIMENSION featuring Julie McDERMOTT — UK

SINGLES:	**HITS 1**			**WEEKS 2**
DON'T GO	*Sound Proof*	34	*12 Oct 96*	2

THIRD EAR BAND — UK

ALBUMS:	**HITS 1**			**WEEKS 2**
AIR, EARTH, FIRE, WATER	*Harvest*	49	*27 Jun 70*	2

THIRD EYE BLIND — US

SINGLES:	**HITS 2**			**WEEKS 6**
SEMI-CHARMED LIFE	*Elektra*	33	*27 Sep 97*	5
HOW'S IT GOING TO BE	*Elektra*	51	*21 Mar 98*	1

3RD STOREE — US

SINGLES:	**HITS 1**			**WEEKS 1**
IF EVER	*Elektra*	53	*5 Jun 99*	1
Samples Unlimited Touch's I Hear Music In The Street.				

THIRD WORLD — Jamaica

SINGLES:	**HITS 5**			**WEEKS 53**
NOW THAT WE'VE FOUND LOVE	*Island*	10	*23 Sep 78*	9
Originally recorded by the O'Jays.				
COOL MEDITATION	*Island*	17	*6 Jan 79*	10
TALK TO ME	*Island*	56	*16 Jun 79*	5
DANCING ON THE FLOOR (HOOKED ON LOVE)	*CBS*	10	*6 Jun 81*	15
TRY JAH LOVE	*CBS*	47	*17 Apr 82*	6
Written by Stevie Wonder.				
NOW THAT WE'VE FOUND LOVE [RI]	*Island*	22	*9 Mar 85*	8
ALBUMS:	**HITS 3**			**WEEKS 18**
JOURNEY TO ADDIS	*Island*	30	*21 Oct 78*	6
ROCKS THE WORLD	*CBS*	37	*11 Jul 81*	9
YOU'VE GOT THE POWER	*CBS*	87	*15 May 82*	3

THIRST — UK

SINGLES:	**HITS 1**			**WEEKS 2**
THE ENEMY WITHIN	*Ten Records*	61	*6 Jul 91*	2

1300 DRUMS featuring the UNJUSTIFIED ANCIENTS OF MU — UK

SINGLES:	**HITS 1**			**WEEKS 4**
OOH! AAH! CANTONA	*Dynamo*	11	*18 May 96*	4

THIS ISLAND EARTH — UK

SINGLES:	HITS 1			WEEKS 5
SEE THAT GLOW	*Magnet*	47	*5 Jan 85*	5

THIS MORTAL COIL — UK

SINGLES:	HITS 1			WEEKS 3
SONG TO THE SIREN *When it appeared in the Breakers section 2 weeks before charting, the flip side 16 Days was listed instead. Originally recorded by Tim Buckley.*	*4AD*	66	*22 Oct 83*	2
SONG TO THE SIREN [RE]	*4AD*	75	*12 Nov 83*	1
ALBUMS:	**HITS 3**			**WEEKS 10**
IT'LL END IN TEARS	*4AD*	38	*20 Oct 84*	4
FILIGREE AND SHADOW	*4AD*	53	*11 Oct 86*	3
BLOOD	*4AD*	28	*4 May 91*	3

THIS WAY UP — UK

SINGLES:	HITS 1			WEEKS 2
TELL ME WHY	*Virgin*	72	*22 Aug 87*	2

THIS YEAR'S BLONDE — UK

SINGLES:	HITS 2			WEEKS 8
PLATINUM POP [M] *Medley covering hits of Blondie.*	*Creole*	46	*10 Oct 81*	5
WHO'S THAT MIX [M] *Medley covering hits of Madonna.*	*Debut*	62	*14 Nov 87*	3

B. J. THOMAS — US

SINGLES:	HITS 1			WEEKS 4
RAINDROPS KEEP FALLIN' ON MY HEAD *From the film 'Butch Cassidy And The Sundance Kid'.*	*Wand*	38	*21 Feb 70*	3
RAINDROPS KEEP FALLIN' ON MY HEAD [RE]	*Wand*	49	*2 May 70*	1

Carla THOMAS – See Otis REDDING and Carla THOMAS

Dante THOMAS featuring PRAS — US

(See also Pras.)

SINGLES:	HITS 1			WEEKS 3
MISS CALIFORNIA	*Elektra*	25	*1 Sep 01*	3

Evelyn THOMAS — US

SINGLES:	HITS 4			WEEKS 29
WEAK SPOT	*20th Century*	26	*24 Jan 76*	7
DOOMSDAY	*20th Century*	41	*17 Apr 76*	1
DOOMSDAY [RE]	*20th Century*	45	*1 May 76*	1
HIGH ENERGY	*Record Shack*	5	*21 Apr 84*	17
MASQUERADE	*Record Shack*	60	*25 Aug 84*	3

Jamo THOMAS and his PARTY BROTHERS ORCHESTRA — US

SINGLES:	HITS 1			WEEKS 3
I SPY (FOR THE FBI)	*Polydor*	48	*1 Mar 69*	1
I SPY (FOR THE FBI) [RE-1ST]	*Polydor*	44	*15 Mar 69*	1
I SPY (FOR THE FBI) [RE-2ND]	*Polydor*	50	*29 Mar 69*	1

John Hugh THOMAS – See Aled JONES

Kenny THOMAS — UK

SINGLES:	HITS 9			WEEKS 54
OUTSTANDING *Original release reached No. 79 in 1990.*	*Cooltempo*	12	*26 Jan 91*	10
THINKING ABOUT YOUR LOVE	*Cooltempo*	4	*1 Jun 91*	13
BEST OF YOU *Originally recorded by Booker T Jones.*	*Cooltempo*	11	*5 Oct 91*	7
TENDER LOVE	*Cooltempo*	26	*30 Nov 91*	6
STAY *Originally recorded by the Controllers.*	*Cooltempo*	22	*10 Jul 93*	6
TRIPPIN' ON YOUR LOVE *Originally recorded by the Staple Singers.*	*Cooltempo*	17	*4 Sep 93*	5
PIECE BY PIECE	*Cooltempo*	36	*6 Nov 93*	3
DESTINY	*Cooltempo*	59	*14 May 94*	1
WHEN I THINK OF YOU	*Cooltempo*	27	*2 Sep 95*	3
ALBUMS:	**HITS 2**			**WEEKS 28**
VOICES	*Cooltempo*	3	*26 Oct 91*	23
WAIT FOR ME	*Cooltempo*	10	*25 Sep 93*	5

Lillo THOMAS — US

SINGLES:	HITS 3			WEEKS 10
SETTLE DOWN	*Capitol*	66	*27 Apr 85*	2
SEXY GIRL	*Capitol*	23	*21 Mar 87*	5
I'M IN LOVE	*Capitol*	54	*30 May 87*	3
ALBUMS:	**HITS 1**			**WEEKS 7**
LILLO	*Capitol*	43	*2 May 87*	7

Millard THOMAS – See Harry BELAFONTE

Nicky THOMAS — Jamaica

SINGLES:	HITS 1			WEEKS 14
LOVE OF THE COMMON PEOPLE	*Trojan*	9	*13 Jun 70*	14
Originally recorded by the Four Preps.				

Ray THOMAS — UK

ALBUMS:	HITS 1			WEEKS 3
FROM MIGHTY OAKS	*Threshold*	23	*26 Jul 75*	3

Rob THOMAS – See SANTANA

Rufus THOMAS — US

SINGLES:	HITS 1			WEEKS 12
DO THE FUNKY CHICKEN	*Stax*	18	*11 Apr 70*	12

Steve THOMAS – See VARIOUS ARTISTS (EPs) 'Trade EP 2'

Tasha THOMAS — US

SINGLES:	HITS 1			WEEKS 3
SHOOT ME (WITH YOUR LOVE)	*Atlantic*	59	*20 Jan 79*	3

Timmy THOMAS — US

SINGLES:	HITS 2			WEEKS 20
WHY CAN'T WE LIVE TOGETHER	*Mojo*	12	*24 Feb 73*	11
NEW YORK EYES	*Portrait*	41	*28 Dec 85*	7
Above hit: NICOLE with Timmy THOMAS.				
WHY CAN'T WE LIVE TOGETHER (1990 REMIX) [RM]	*T.K.*	54	*14 Jul 90*	2
Remixed by Pluto.				

THOMAS and TAYLOR — US

SINGLES:	HITS 1			WEEKS 5
YOU CAN'T BLAME LOVE	*Cooltempo*	53	*17 May 86*	5

Russell THOMPKINS, JR – See STYLISTICS

Amanda THOMPSON – Lesley GARRETT

Carroll THOMPSON – See MOVEMENT. 98 featuring Carroll THOMPSON; Courtney PINE

Chris THOMPSON — UK

SINGLES:	HITS 1			WEEKS 5
IF YOU REMEMBER ME	*Planet*	42	*27 Oct 79*	5
From the film 'The Champ'.				

Danny THOMPSON – See Richard THOMPSON

Gina THOMPSON – See MC LYTE

Prince Lincoln THOMPSON – See REBEL MC

Richard THOMPSON — UK

ALBUMS:	HITS 8			WEEKS 15
ACROSS A CROWDED ROOM	*Polydor*	80	*27 Apr 85*	2
DARING ADVENTURES	*Polydor*	92	*18 Oct 86*	1
AMNESIA	*Capitol*	89	*29 Oct 88*	1
RUMOR AND SIGH	Capital	32	*25 May 91*	3
MIRROR BLUE	*Capitol*	23	*29 Jan 94*	3
Title taken from the poem by Tennyson 'The Lady Of Shalott'.				
YOU? ME? US?	*Capitol*	32	*20 Apr 96*	2
INDUSTRY	*Parlophone*	69	*24 May 97*	1
Above hit: Richard and Danny THOMPSON.				
MOCK TUDOR	*Capitol*	28	*4 Sept 99*	2

Sue THOMPSON — US

SINGLES:	HITS 2			WEEKS 9
SAD MOVIES	*Polydor*	46	*4 Nov 61*	1

SAD MOVIES [RE]	*Polydor*	48	*18 Nov 61*	1
PAPER TIGER	*Hickory*	50	*23 Jan 65*	1
Both hits written by John D. Loudermilk.				
PAPER TIGER [RE]	*Hickory*	30	*13 Feb 65*	6

THOMPSON TWINS — UK/New Zealand

SINGLES:	HITS 16			WEEKS 110
LIES	*Arista*	67	*6 Nov 82*	3
LOVE ON YOUR SIDE	*Arista*	9	*29 Jan 83*	12
WE ARE DETECTIVE	*Arista*	7	*16 Apr 83*	9
WATCHING	*Arista*	33	*16 Jul 83*	6
HOLD ME NOW	*Arista*	4	*19 Nov 83*	15
DOCTOR DOCTOR	*Arista*	3	*4 Feb 84*	10
YOU TAKE ME UP	*Arista*	2	*31 Mar 84*	9
SISTER OF MERCY	*Arista*	11	*7 Jul 84*	8
SISTER OF MERCY [RE]	*Arista*	66	*8 Sep 84*	1
LAY YOUR HANDS ON ME	*Arista*	13	*8 Dec 84*	9
DON'T MESS WITH DOCTOR DREAM	*Arista*	15	*31 Aug 85*	6
KING FOR A DAY	*Arista*	22	*19 Oct 85*	6
REVOLUTION	*Arista*	56	*7 Dec 85*	3
Originally recorded by the Beatles on the B-side of Hey Jude.				
REVOLUTION [RE]	*Arista*	75	*4 Jan 86*	1
GET THAT LOVE	*Arista*	68	*21 Mar 87*	2
GET THAT LOVE [RE]	*Arista*	66	*11 Apr 87*	1
IN THE NAME OF LOVE '88	*Arista*	46	*15 Oct 88*	3
Original release in 1982 appeared in the Bubbling Under section of the chart.				
COME INSIDE	*Warner Brothers*	56	*28 Sep 91*	4
THE SAINT	*Warner Brothers*	53	*25 Jan 92*	2

ALBUMS:	HITS 6			WEEKS 128
SET	*Tee*	48	*13 Mar 82*	3
QUICK STEP & SIDE KICK	*Arista*	2	*26 Feb 83*	56
INTO THE GAP	*Arista*	1	*25 Feb 84*	51
HERE'S TO FUTURE DAYS	*Arista*	5	*28 Sep 85*	9
CLOSE TO THE BONE	*Arista*	90	*2 May 87*	1
THOMPSON TWINS - THE GREATEST HITS	*Stylus*	23	*10 Mar 90*	8

Tracey THORN – See MASSIVE ATTACK

David THORNE with Richard WOLFF and his Orchestra — US

SINGLES:	HITS 1			WEEKS 8
THE ALLEY CAT SONG	*Stateside*	21	*26 Jan 63*	8

Ken THORNE and his Orchestra; trumpet solo: Ray DAVIES — UK

SINGLES:	HITS 1			WEEKS 15
THEME FROM FILM "THE LEGION'S LAST PATROL" (CONCERTO DISPERATO)	*His Master's Voice*	4	*20 Jul 63*	15

George THOROGOOD and the DESTROYERS — US

ALBUMS:	HITS 1			WEEKS 1
GEORGE THOROGOOD AND THE DESTROYERS	*Sonet*	67	*2 Dec 78*	1

THOSE 2 GIRLS — UK

SINGLES:	HITS 2			WEEKS 4
WANNA MAKE YOU GO . . . UUH!	*Final Vinyl*	74	*5 Nov 94*	1
ALL I WANT	*Final Vinyl*	36	*4 Mar 95*	3

THOUSAND YARD STARE — UK

SINGLES:	HITS 4			WEEKS 5
SEASONSTREAM [EP]	*Stifled Aardvark*	65	*26 Oct 91*	1
Lead track: O-O-AET.				
COMEUPPANCE [EP]	*Stifled Aardvark*	37	*8 Feb 92*	2
Lead track: Comeuppance.				
SPINDRIFT [EP]	*Stifled Aardvark*	58	*11 Jul 92*	1
Lead track: Wideshire Two.				
VERSION OF ME	*Polydor*	57	*8 May 93*	1

ALBUMS:	HITS 1			WEEKS 2
HANDS ON	*Polydor*	38	*7 Mar 92*	2

THRASHING DOVES — UK

SINGLES:	HITS 1			WEEKS 3
BEAUTIFUL IMBALANCE	*A&M*	50	*24 Jan 87*	3

THREE AMIGOS

UK

SINGLES:	HITS 2			WEEKS 8
LOUIE LOUIE *From the film 'American Pie'.*	*Inferno*	15	*3 Jul 99*	6
25 MILES 2001 *Samples Edwin Starr's 25 Miles.*	*Wonderboy*	30	*24 Mar 01*	2

3 COLOURS RED

UK

SINGLES:	HITS 7			WEEKS 17
NUCLEAR HOLIDAY	*Creation*	22	*18 Jan 97*	2
SIXTY MILE SMILE	*Creation*	20	*15 Mar 97*	3
PURE	*Creation*	28	*10 May 97*	1
COPPER GIRL	*Creation*	30	*12 Jul 97*	2
THIS IS MY HOLLYWOOD *Original release reached No. 162 in 1996.*	*Creation*	48	*8 Nov 97*	1
BEAUTIFUL DAY	*Creation*	11	*23 Jan 99*	6
THIS IS MY TIME	*Creation*	36	*29 May 99*	2
ALBUMS:	**HITS 2**			**WEEKS 4**
PURE	*Creation*	16	*24 May 97*	2
REVOLT	*Creation*	17	*20 Feb 99*	2

THREE DEGREES

US

SINGLES:	HITS 15			WEEKS 113
YEAR OF DECISION	*Philadelphia International*	13	*13 Apr 74*	10
TSOP (THE SOUND OF PHILADELPHIA) *Above hit: MFSB featuring the THREE DEGREES.*	*Philadelphia International*	22	*27 Apr 74*	9
WHEN WILL I SEE YOU AGAIN	*Philadelphia International*	1	*13 Jul 74*	16
GET YOUR LOVE BACK	*Philadelphia International*	34	*2 Nov 74*	4
TAKE GOOD CARE OF YOURSELF	*Philadelphia International*	9	*12 Apr 75*	9
LONG LOST LOVER	*Philadelphia International*	40	*5 Jul 75*	4
TOAST OF LOVE	*Epic*	36	*1 May 76*	4
GIVING UP, GIVING IN	*Ariola*	12	*7 Oct 78*	10
WOMAN IN LOVE	*Ariola*	3	*13 Jan 79*	11
THE RUNNER	*Ariola*	10	*24 Mar 79*	10
THE GOLDEN LADY *From the film of the same name.*	*Ariola*	56	*23 Jun 79*	3
JUMP THE GUN	*Ariola*	48	*29 Sep 79*	5
MY SIMPLE HEART *Originally recorded by the Dukes.*	*Ariola*	9	*24 Nov 79*	11
THE HEAVEN I NEED	*Supreme*	42	*5 Oct 85*	5
LAST CHRISTMAS *Above hit: ALIEN VOICES featuring the THREE DEGREES.*	*Wildstar*	54	*26 Dec 98*	2
ALBUMS:	**HITS 6**			**WEEKS 91**
THREE DEGREES	*Philadelphia International*	12	*10 Aug 74*	22
TAKE GOOD CARE OF YOURSELF	*Philadelphia International*	6	*17 May 75*	16
NEW DIMENSIONS	*Ariola*	34	*24 Feb 79*	13
A COLLECTION OF THEIR 20 GREATEST HITS	*Epic*	8	*3 Mar 79*	18
3D	*Ariola*	61	*15 Dec 79*	7
GOLD	*Ariola*	9	*27 Sep 80*	15

THREE DOG NIGHT

US

SINGLES:	HITS 2			WEEKS 23
MAMA TOLD ME NOT TO COME *Written by Randy Newman. Originally recorded by the Animals.*	*Stateside*	3	*8 Aug 70*	14
JOY TO THE WORLD	*Probe*	24	*29 May 71*	9

THREE DRIVES

Holland

SINGLES:	HITS 2			WEEKS 7
GREECE 2000	*Hooj Choons*	44	*27 Jun 98*	1
GREECE 2000 [RI] *Original version with vocal by Julie Harrington added.*	*Hooj Choons*	12	*30 Jan 99*	4
SUNSET ON IBIZA *Above hit: THREE DRIVES (ON A VINYL).*	*Xtravaganza*	44	*17 Nov 01*	2

THREE GOOD REASONS

UK

SINGLES:	HITS 1			WEEKS 3
NOWHERE MAN *Originally recorded by the Beatles.*	*Mercury*	47	*12 Mar 66*	3

3 JAYS

UK

SINGLES:	HITS 1			WEEKS 5
FEELING IT TOO	*Multiply*	17	*31 Jul 99*	5

THREE KAYES – See KAYE SISTERS

3LW — US

SINGLES:	HITS 2			WEEKS 12
NO MORE (BABY I'M A DO RIGHT)	*Epic*	6	*2 Jun 01*	8
NO MORE (BABY I'M A DO RIGHT) [RE]	*Epic*	74	*4 Aug 01*	1
PLAYAS GON' PLAY	*Epic*	21	*8 Sep 01*	3
ALBUMS:	**HITS 1**			**WEEKS 1**
3LW	*Epic*	75	*16 Jun 01*	1

THREE 'N ONE — Germany

SINGLES:	HITS 2			WEEKS 3
REFLECT	*ffrr*	66	*7 Jun 97*	1
PEARL RIVER	*Low Sense*	32	*15 May 99*	2

Originally released as an instrumental in 1997.
Above hit: THREE 'N ONE presents Johnny SHAKER [featuring SERIAL DIVA].

3T — US

SINGLES:	HITS 5			WEEKS 45
ANYTHING	*Epic*	2	*27 Jan 96*	14
24/7	*Epic*	11	*4 May 96*	7
WHY	*Epic*	2	*24 Aug 96*	9
Above hit: 3T featuring Michael JACKSON.				
I NEED YOU	*Epic*	3	*7 Dec 96*	10
Backing vocals by Michael Jackson.				
GOTTA BE YOU	*Epic*	10	*5 Apr 97*	5
Above hit: 3T (featuring HERBIE).				
ALBUMS:	**HITS 1**			**WEEKS 15**
BROTHERHOOD	*Epic*	11	*24 Feb 96*	15

3 TENORS: José CARRERAS, Placido DOMINGO, Luciano PAVAROTTI — Spain/Italy

(See also José Carreras; Placido Domingo; Luciano Pavarotti.)

SINGLES:	HITS 2			WEEKS 8
LIBIAMO, NE' LIETI CALICI FROM VERDI LA TRAVIATA / LA DONNA E MOBILE FROM VERDI RIGOLETTO	*Teldec*	21	*30 Jul 94*	4
Live recording from Monte Carlo, 9 Jun 94.				
Above hit: THREE TENORS IN CONCERT 1994 – CARRERAS DOMINGO PAVAROTTI with MEHTA.				
YOU'LL NEVER WALK ALONE	*Decca*	35	*25 Jul 98*	4
Above hit: Tibor RUDAS presents the 3 TENORS PARIS 1988: Jose CARRERAS, Placido DOMINGO, Luciano PAVAROTTI.				
COMPILATION ALBUMS:	**HITS 1**			**WEEKS 1**
ALBUMS:	**HITS 4**			**WEEKS 112**
IN CONCERT	*Decca*	1	*1 Sep 90*	78
Live recordings before the 1990 World Cup Final at Terme di Caracalla, Roma, 7 Jul 90.				
Above hit: CARRERAS DOMINGO PAVAROTTI Orchestra del Maggio Musicale Fiorentino Orchestra del Teatro dell'Opera di Roma Zubin MEHTA.				
THE 3 TENORS IN CONCERT 1994	*Teldec*	1	*10 Sep 94*	26
Live recordings before the 1994 World Cup Final at Los Angeles' Dodger Stadium, 16 Jul 94.				
Above hit: CARRERAS DOMINGO PAVAROTTI with Orchestra conducted by Zubin MEHTA.				
THE 3 TENORS PARIS 1998	*Decca*	14	*29 Aug 98*	6
Live recordings at the Effiel Tower, Paris, France, 10 Jul 98.				
Above hit: CARRERAS DOMINGO PAVAROTTI with James LEVINE.				
THE THREE TENORS CHRISTMAS	*Sony Classical*	57	*23 Dec 00*	2
Above hit: Jose CARRERAS, Placido DOMINGO, Luciano PAVAROTTI featuring Zubin MEHTA.				
LUCIANO PAVAROTTI JOSE CARRERAS PLACIDO DOMINGO - THREE LEGENDS IN ONE COLLECTION	*Emporio*	14	*16 Jun 01*	1
3CDs, one artist per disc. Above entry was listed in the compilation chart.				
Above hit: Luciano PAVAROTTI Jose CARRERAS Placido DOMINGO.				

THREE TONS OF JOY - See Johnny OTIS SHOW with Marie ADAMS

THRILLSEEKERS featuring Sheryl DEANE — UK

SINGLES:	HITS 1			WEEKS 2
SYNAESTHESIA (FLY AWAY)	*Neo*	28	*17 Feb 01*	2

Original instrumental version reached No. 90 on 14 Aug 99.

THROWING MUSES — US

SINGLES:	HITS 4			WEEKS 6
COUNTING BACKWARDS	*4AD*	70	*9 Feb 91*	2
FIREPILE [EP]	*4AD*	46	*1 Aug 92*	1
Lead track: Firepile.				
BRIGHT YELLOW GUN	*4AD*	51	*24 Dec 94*	2
SHARK	*4AD*	53	*10 Aug 96*	1

ALBUMS:	HITS 6			WEEKS 13
HUNKPAPA	*4AD*	59	*4 Feb 89*	1
THE REAL RAMONA	*4AD*	26	*2 Mar 91*	4
RED HEAVEN	*4AD*	13	*22 Aug 92*	3
THE CURSE	*4AD*	74	*28 Nov 92*	1
UNIVERSITY	*4AD*	10	*28 Jan 95*	3
LIMBO	*4AD*	36	*31 Aug 96*	1

Harry THUMANN — Germany

SINGLES:	HITS 1			WEEKS 6
UNDERWATER	*Decca*	41	*21 Feb 81*	6

THUNDER — UK

SINGLES:	HITS 18			WEEKS 52
DIRTY LOVE	*EMI*	32	*17 Feb 90*	4
BACKSTREET SYMPHONY	*EMI*	25	*12 May 90*	4
GIMME SOME LOVIN'	*EMI*	36	*14 Jul 90*	3
SHE'S SO FINE	*EMI*	34	*29 Sep 90*	3
LOVE WALKED IN	*EMI*	21	*23 Feb 91*	4
LOW LIFE IN HIGH PLACES	*EMI*	22	*15 Aug 92*	5
EVERYBODY WANTS HER	*EMI*	36	*10 Oct 92*	4
A BETTER MAN	*EMI*	18	*13 Feb 93*	4
LIKE A SATELLITE [EP]	*EMI*	28	*19 Jun 93*	2
Lead track: Like A Satellite.				
STAND UP	*EMI*	23	*7 Jan 95*	4
RIVER OF PAIN	*EMI*	31	*25 Feb 95*	2
CASTLES IN THE SAND	*EMI*	30	*6 May 95*	3
IN A BROKEN DREAM	*EMI*	26	*23 Sep 95*	2
DON'T WAIT UP	*Raw Power*	27	*25 Jan 97*	2
LOVE WORTH DYING FOR	*Raw Power*	60	*5 Apr 97*	1
THE ONLY ONE	*Eagle*	31	*7 Feb 98*	2
PLAY THAT FUNKY MUSIC	*Eagle*	39	*27 Jun 98*	2
YOU WANNA KNOW	*Eagle*	49	*20 Mar 99*	1

ALBUMS:	HITS 7			WEEKS 39
BACK STREET SYMPHONY	*EMI*	21	*17 Mar 90*	16
LAUGHING ON JUDGEMENT DAY	*EMI*	2	*5 Sep 92*	10
BEHIND CLOSED DOORS	*EMI*	5	*4 Feb 95*	5
BEST OF THUNDER - THEIR FINEST HOUR (AND A BIT)	*EMI*	22	*7 Oct 95*	3
THE THRILL OF IT ALL	*Raw Power*	14	*15 Feb 97*	3
LIVE	*Eagle*	35	*28 Feb 98*	1
Live recordings from their 1997 UK tour.				
GIVING THE GAME AWAY	*Eagle*	49	*27 Mar 99*	1

THUNDERBUGS — UK/France/Germany

SINGLES:	HITS 2			WEEKS 15
FRIENDS FOREVER	*Epic*	5	*18 Sept 99*	9
FRIENDS FOREVER [RE]	*Epic*	71	*11 Dec 99*	1
IT'S ABOUT TIME YOU WERE MINE	*Epic*	43	*18 Dec 99*	5

THUNDERCLAP NEWMAN — UK

SINGLES:	HITS 2			WEEKS 13
SOMETHING IN THE AIR	*Track*	1	*14 Jun 69*	12
ACCIDENTS	*Track*	46	*27 Jun 70*	1
Above 2 hits produced by the Who's Pete Townshend.				

THUNDERTHIGHS — UK

SINGLES:	HITS 1			WEEKS 5
CENTRAL PARK ARREST	*Philips*	30	*22 Jun 74*	5
Originally recorded by Lynsey De Paul for the B-side to No Honestly.				

Bobby THURSTON — US

SINGLES:	HITS 1			WEEKS 10
CHECK OUT THE GROOVE	*Epic*	10	*29 Mar 80*	10

TIDY GIRLS presents Lisa LASHES — UK

SINGLES:	HITS 1			WEEKS 1
UNBELIEVABLE	*Tidy Trax*	63	*8 Jul 00*	1
Track 1 on the CD format is Dance 2 The House (Don't Go). Track 2 is Unbelievable which was listed on the chart.				

TIFFANY — US

SINGLES:	HITS 6			WEEKS 45
I THINK WE'RE ALONE NOW	*MCA*	1	*16 Jan 88*	13
Original by Tommy James and the Shondells reached No. 4 in the US in 1967.				

COULD'VE BEEN	*MCA*	4	*19 Mar 88*	9
I SAW HIM STANDING THERE	*MCA*	8	*4 Jun 88*	7
Female version of the Beatles' I Saw Her Standing There				
FEELINGS OF FOREVER	*MCA*	52	*6 Aug 88*	2
RADIO ROMANCE	*MCA*	13	*12 Nov 88*	11
ALL THIS TIME	*MCA*	47	*11 Feb 89*	3
ALBUMS:	**HITS 2**			**WEEKS 27**
TIFFANY	*MCA*	5	*27 Feb 88*	21
HOLD AN OLD FRIEND'S HAND	*MCA*	56	*17 Dec 88*	6

TIGER — UK/Ireland

SINGLES:	**HITS 4**			**WEEKS 5**
RACE	*Trade 2*	37	*31 Aug 96*	2
MY PUPPET PAL	*Trade 2*	62	*16 Nov 96*	1
ON THE ROSE	*Trade 2*	57	*22 Feb 97*	1
FRIENDS	*Trade 2*	72	*22 Aug 98*	1

TIGERTAILZ — US

SINGLES:	**HITS 2**			**WEEKS 2**
LOVE BOMB BABY	*Music For Nations*	75	*24 Jun 89*	1
HEAVEN	*Music For Nations*	71	*16 Feb 91*	1
ALBUMS:	**HITS 1**			**WEEKS 2**
BEZERK	*Music For Nations*	36	*7 Apr 90*	2

TIGHT FIT — UK

SINGLES:	**HITS 5**			**WEEKS 49**
BACK TO THE 60'S [M]	*Jive*	4	*18 Jul 81*	11
BACK TO THE 60'S (PART II) [M]	*Jive*	33	*26 Sep 81*	5
Above 2 are medleys of 1960s hits.				
THE LION SLEEPS TONIGHT	*Jive*	1	*23 Jan 82*	15
Originally recorded by Solomon Linda and the Evening Birds as Mbube in 1939.				
FANTASY ISLAND	*Jive*	5	*1 May 82*	12
SECRET HEART	*Jive*	41	*31 Jul 82*	6
ALBUMS:	**HITS 2**			**WEEKS 6**
BACK TO THE SIXTIES	*Jive*	38	*26 Sep 81*	4
TIGHT FIT	*Jive*	87	*4 Sep 82*	2

TIJUANA BRASS - See Herb ALPERT and the TIJUANA BRASS

TIK and TOK — UK

SINGLES:	**HITS 1**			**WEEKS 2**
COOL RUNNING	*Survival*	69	*8 Oct 83*	2
ALBUMS:	**HITS 1**			**WEEKS 2**
INTOLERANCE	*Survival*	89	*4 Aug 84*	2

Tanita TIKARAM — UK

SINGLES:	**HITS 9**			**WEEKS 31**
GOOD TRADITION	*WEA*	10	*30 Jul 88*	10
TWIST IN MY SOBRIETY	*WEA*	22	*22 Oct 88*	8
CATHEDRAL SONG	*WEA*	48	*14 Jan 89*	3
WORLD OUTSIDE YOUR WINDOW	*WEA*	58	*18 Mar 89*	2
WE ALMOST GOT IT TOGETHER	*WEA*	52	*13 Jan 90*	3
ONLY THE ONES WE LOVE	*East West*	69	*9 Feb 91*	1
I MIGHT BE CRYING	*East West*	64	*4 Feb 95*	2
STOP LISTENING	*Mother*	67	*6 Jun 98*	1
I DON'T WANNA LOSE AT LOVE	*Mother*	73	*29 Aug 98*	1
ALBUMS:	**HITS 5**			**WEEKS 62**
ANCIENT HEART	*WEA*	3	*24 Sep 88*	49
THE SWEET KEEPER	*East West*	3	*10 Feb 90*	7
EVERYBODY'S ANGEL	*East West*	19	*16 Feb 91*	4
LOVERS IN THE CITY	*East West*	75	*25 Feb 95*	1
THE CAPPUCCINO SONGS	*Mother*	69	*19 Sep 98*	1

TILLMAN and RIES — Germany

SINGLES:	**HITS 1**			**WEEKS 1**
BASSFLY	*Liquid Asset*	70	*16 Sep 00*	1

Johnny TILLOTSON — US

SINGLES:	**HITS 6**			**WEEKS 50**
POETRY IN MOTION	*London*	1	*3 Dec 60*	15
JIMMY'S GIRL	*London*	50	*4 Feb 61*	1
JIMMY'S GIRL [RE]	*London*	43	*18 Feb 61*	1
IT KEEPS RIGHT ON A-HURTIN'	*London*	31	*14 Jul 62*	10

SEND ME THE PILLOW YOU DREAM ON *Originally recorded by Hank Locklin.*	*London*	21	*6 Oct 62*	10
I CAN'T HELP IT *Originally recorded by Hank Williams in 1952.*	*London*	42	*29 Dec 62*	1
I CAN'T HELP IT [RE-1ST]	*London*	47	*12 Jan 63*	1
I CAN'T HELP IT [RE-2ND]	*London*	41	*26 Jan 63*	4
OUT OF MY MIND	*London*	34	*11 May 63*	5
POETRY IN MOTION [RI] / PRINCESS PRINCESS *Princess Princess was the original B-side of Poetry in Motion in 1960.*	*Lightning*	67	*14 Apr 79*	2

TILT — UK

SINGLES:	HITS 7			WEEKS 8
I DREAM	*Perfecto*	69	*2 Dec 95*	1
MY SPIRIT	*Perfecto*	61	*10 May 97*	1
PLACES	*Perfecto*	64	*13 Sep 97*	1
BUTTERFLY *Above hit: TILT featuring ZEE.*	*Perfecto Mainline*	41	*7 Feb 98*	1
CHILDREN	*Deconstruction*	51	*27 Mar 99*	1
INVISIBLE	*Hollywood*	20	*8 May 99*	2
DARK SCIENCE [EP] *Lead track: 36.*	*Hooj Choons*	55	*12 Feb 00*	1

TIMBALAND — US

SINGLES:	HITS 4			WEEKS 13
GET ON THE BUS *From the film 'Why Do Fools Fall In Love'.* *Above hit: DESTINY'S CHILD (featuring TIMBALAND).*	*East West*	15	*23 Jan 99*	5
HERE WE COME *Samples the melody from the Spiderman cartoon series.* *Above hit: TIMBALAND featuring Missy "Misdemeanor" ELLIOTT and MAGOO.*	*Virgin*	43	*13 Mar 99*	1
LOBSTER & SCRIMP *Above hit: TIMBALAND featuring JAY-Z.*	*Virgin*	48	*19 Jun 99*	1
WE NEED A RESOLUTION *Above hit: AALIYAH featuring TIMBALAND.*	*Virgin*	20	*21 Jul 01*	4
WE NEED A RESOLUTION [RE]	*Virgin*	65	*1 Sep 01*	2

TIMBUK 3 — US

SINGLES:	HITS 1			WEEKS 7
THE FUTURE'S SO BRIGHT I GOTTA WEAR SHADES	*I.R.S.*	21	*31 Jan 87*	7
ALBUMS:	**HITS 1**			**WEEKS 4**
GREETINGS FROM TIMBUK 3	*I.R.S.*	51	*14 Feb 87*	4

TIME — US

ALBUMS:	HITS 1			WEEKS 1
PANDEMONIUM	*Paisley Park*	66	*28 Jul 90*	1

TIME FREQUENCY — UK

SINGLES:	HITS 6			WEEKS 33
REAL LOVE	*Jive*	60	*6 Jun 92*	1
NEW EMOTION [EP] *Lead track: New Emotion.*	*Internal Affairs*	36	*9 Jan 93*	6
THE POWER ZONE [EP] *Lead track: The Ultimate High.*	*Internal Affairs*	17	*12 Jun 93*	11
REAL LOVE '93 [RM] *Remixed by the Time Frenquency.*	*Internal Affairs*	8	*6 Nov 93*	6
REAL LOVE '93 [RM] [RE]	*Internal Affairs*	71	*1 Jan 94*	2
SUCH A PHANTASY [EP] *Lead track: Such A Fantasy.*	*Internal Affairs*	25	*28 May 94*	4
DREAMSCAPE '94	*Internal Affairs*	32	*8 Oct 94*	3
ALBUMS:	**HITS 1**			**WEEKS 4**
DOMINATOR	*Internal Affairs*	23	*18 Jun 94*	4

TIME OF THE MUMPH — UK

SINGLES:	HITS 1			WEEKS 1
CONTROL	*Fresh*	69	*11 Feb 95*	1

TIME UK — UK

SINGLES:	HITS 1			WEEKS 3
THE CABARET	*Red Bus*	63	*8 Oct 83*	3

TIME ZONE featuring John LYDON and Afrika BAMBAATAA — UK/US

(See also Afrika Bambaataa, John Lydon.)

SINGLES:	HITS 1			WEEKS 9
WORLD DESTRUCTION	*Virgin*	44	*19 Jan 85*	9

TIMEBOX — UK

SINGLES:	HITS 1			WEEKS 4
BEGGIN'	*Deram*	38	*27 Jul 68*	4
Original by the Four Seasons reached No. 16 in the US in 1967.				

TIMELORDS — UK

(See also Justified Ancients Of Mu Mu; KLF; 2K.)

SINGLES:	HITS 1			WEEKS 9
DOCTORIN' THE TARDIS	*KLF Communications*	1	*4 Jun 88*	9
Based around Gary Glitter's Rock And Roll and the theme to Dr. Who.				

TIMEX SOCIAL CLUB — US

SINGLES:	HITS 1			WEEKS 9
RUMORS	*Cooltempo*	13	*13 Sep 86*	9

TIN MACHINE — UK/US

SINGLES:	HITS 4			WEEKS 10
UNDER THE GOD	*EMI USA*	51	*1 Jul 89*	2
TIN MACHINE / MAGGIE'S FARM (LIVE)	*EMI USA*	48	*9 Sep 89*	2
Maggie's Farm (Live) only listed on the chart for 16 Sep 89.				
YOU BELONG IN ROCK N' ROLL	*London*	33	*24 Aug 91*	3
BABY UNIVERSAL	*London*	48	*2 Nov 91*	3
ALBUMS:	**HITS 2**			**WEEKS 12**
TIN MACHINE	*EMI USA*	3	*3 Jun 89*	9
TIN MACHINE II	*London*	23	*14 Sep 91*	3

TIN TIN – See Stephen 'Tin Tin' DUFFY

TIN TIN OUT — UK

SINGLES:	HITS 9			WEEKS 42
THE FEELING	*Deep Distraxion*	32	*13 Aug 94*	2
Sweet Tee's vocals are sampled from her 1988 single I Got Da Feelin.				
Above hit: TIN TIN OUT featuring SWEET TEE.				
ALWAYS SOMETHING THERE TO REMIND ME	*WEA*	14	*25 Mar 95*	5
Started out as a solo Espiritu track in 1994 but was never released.				
Above hit: TIN TIN OUT featuring ESPIRITU.				
ALL I WANNA DO	*VC Recordings*	31	*8 Feb 97*	2
DANCE WITH ME	*VC Recordings*	35	*10 May 97*	2
Above hit: TIN TIN OUT featuring Tony HADLEY.				
STRINGS FOR YASMIN	*VC Recordings*	31	*20 Sep 97*	3
HERE'S WHERE THE STORY ENDS	*VC Recordings*	7	*28 Mar 98*	10
Originally recorded by the Sundays on their 1990 album Reading, Writing And Arithmetic.				
Above hit: TIN TIN OUT featuring Shelley NELSON.				
SOMETIMES	*VC Recordings*	20	*12 Sep 98*	4
Above hit: TIN TIN OUT with Shelley NELSON.				
ELEVEN TO FLY	*VC Recordings*	26	*11 Sept 99*	2
Above hit: TINTINOUT featuring Wendy PAGE.				
WHAT I AM	*VC Recordings*	2	*13 Nov 99*	12
Above hit: TIN TIN OUT featuring Emma BUNTON.				
ALBUMS:	**HITS 1**			**WEEKS 1**
ADVENTURES IN TIN TIN OUT LAND	*VC Recordings*	65	*5 Oct 96*	1
12" double-pack single.				

TINA – See Tina TURNER

TINDERSTICKS — UK

SINGLES:	HITS 6			WEEKS 6
KATHLEEN [EP]	*This Way Up*	61	*5 Feb 94*	1
Lead track: Kathleen, originally recorded by Townes Van Zandt.				
NO MORE AFFAIRS	*This Way Up*	58	*18 Mar 95*	1
TRAVELLING LIGHT	*This Way Up*	51	*12 Aug 95*	1
BATHTIME	*This Way Up*	38	*7 Jun 97*	1
RENTED ROOMS	*This Way Up*	56	*1 Nov 97*	1
CAN WE START AGAIN?	*Island*	54	*4 Sept 99*	1
ALBUMS:	**HITS 6**			**WEEKS 9**
TINDERSTICKS	*This Way Up*	56	*23 Oct 93*	1
THE SECOND TINDERSTICKS ALBUM	*This Way Up*	13	*15 Apr 95*	3
LIVE AT THE BLOOMSBURY THEATRE 12.3.95	*This Way Up*	32	*28 Oct 95*	1
Live recordings with backing Orchestra.				

CURTAINS	*This Way Up*	37	*21 Jun 97*	2
SIMPLE PLEASURE	*Island*	36	*18 Sept 99*	1
CAN OUR LOVE . . .	*Beggars Banquet*	47	*2 Jun 01*	1

TINGO TANGO — UK

SINGLES:	HITS 1			WEEKS 2
IT IS JAZZ	*Champion*	68	*21 Jul 90*	2

TINMAN — UK

(See also James Brown.)

SINGLES:	HITS 2			WEEKS 9
EIGHTEEN STRINGS *Recorded earlier in the year with a sample from Nirvana's Smells Like Teen Spirit. Clearance was refused so Tinman sampled the Monkees' (I'm Not Your) Steppin' Stone.*	*ffrr*	9	*20 Aug 94*	8
GUDVIBE *Samples Yello's The Race.*	*ffrr*	49	*3 Jun 95*	1

TINY TIM — US

SINGLES:	HITS 1			WEEKS 1
GREAT BALLS OF FIRE	*Reprise*	45	*8 Feb 69*	1

TITANIC — UK/Norway

SINGLES:	HITS 1			WEEKS 12
SULTANA	*CBS*	5	*25 Sep 71*	12

TITIYO — Sweden

SINGLES:	HITS 3			WEEKS 6
AFTER THE RAIN	*Arista*	60	*3 Mar 90*	3
FLOWERS	*Arista*	71	*6 Oct 90*	1
TELL ME (I'M NOT DREAMING)	*Arista*	45	*5 Feb 94*	2

Cara TIVEY – See Billy BRAGG

TJR featuring XAVIER — UK

SINGLES:	HITS 1			WEEKS 2
JUST GETS BETTER	*Multiply*	28	*27 Sep 97*	2

TLC — US

(See also Tionne "T Boz" Watkins of TLC.)

SINGLES:	HITS 10			WEEKS 83
AIN'T 2 PROUD 2 BEG *Samples James Brown's Escapeism, Kool and the Gang's Jungle Boogie, Average White Band's School Boy Crush and Silver Convention's Fly Robin Fly.*	*LaFace*	13	*20 Jun 92*	5
BABY-BABY-BABY	*LaFace*	55	*22 Aug 92*	3
WHAT ABOUT YOUR FRIENDS	*LaFace*	59	*24 Oct 92*	2
CREEP *Samples Hey Young World by Slick Rick.*	*LaFace*	22	*21 Jan 95*	4
RED LIGHT SPECIAL	*LaFace*	18	*22 Apr 95*	4
WATERFALLS	*LaFace*	4	*5 Aug 95*	14
DIGGIN' ON YOU	*LaFace*	18	*4 Nov 95*	5
CREEP 96 [RI] *Though issued as a remix, the first track of the CD is the original.*	*LaFace*	6	*13 Jan 96*	7
NO SCRUBS	*LaFace*	3	*3 Apr 99*	19
UNPRETTY	*LaFace*	6	*28 Aug 99*	11
DEAR LIE	*LaFace*	31	*18 Dec 99*	9
ALBUMS:	**HITS 2**			**WEEKS 96**
CRAZYSEXYCOOL	*LaFace*	4	*20 May 95*	39
FANMAIL	*LaFace*	7	*6 Mar 99*	57

T99 — Belgium

SINGLES:	HITS 2			WEEKS 10
ANASTHASIA	*XL Recordings*	14	*11 May 91*	6
NOCTURINE	*Emphasis*	33	*19 Oct 91*	4

TOADS – See Stan FREBERG

Art and Dotty TODD — US

SINGLES:	HITS 1			WEEKS 7
BROKEN WINGS	*His Master's Voice*	6	*14 Feb 53*	7

TOGETHER — UK

SINGLES:	HITS 1			WEEKS 8
HARDCORE UPROAR	*ffrr*	12	*4 Aug 90*	8

TOKENS — US

SINGLES:	HITS 1			WEEKS 12
THE LION SLEEPS TONIGHT (WIMOWEH)	*RCA*	11	*23 Dec 61*	12

TOKYO GHETTO PUSSY — Germany

(See also Jam and Spoon featuring Plavka.)

SINGLES:	HITS 2			WEEKS 4
EVERYBODY ON THE FLOOR (PUMP IT) *Vocals by Joan Faulkner.*	*Epic*	26	*16 Sep 95*	2
I KISS YOUR LIPS	*Epic*	55	*16 Mar 96*	2

TOL and TOL — Holland

SINGLES:	HITS 1			WEEKS 2
ELENI	*Dover*	73	*14 Apr 90*	2

TOM TOM CLUB — US

SINGLES:	HITS 3			WEEKS 20
WORDY RAPPINGHOOD	*Island*	7	*20 Jun 81*	9
GENIUS OF LOVE	*Island*	65	*10 Oct 81*	2
UNDER THE BOARDWALK	*Island*	22	*7 Aug 82*	9
ALBUMS:	**HITS 1**			**WEEKS 1**
TOM TOM CLUB	*Island*	78	*24 Oct 81*	1

TOMBA VIRA — Holland

SINGLES:	HITS 1			WEEKS 1
THE SOUND OF: OH YEAH *Samples OMD's Enola Gay.*	*VC Recordings*	51	*16 Jun 01*	1

TOMCAT — UK

SINGLES:	HITS 1			WEEKS 1
CRAZY	*Virgin*	48	*14 Oct 00*	1

Satoshi TOMIIE - See Frankie KNUCKLES

TOMITA — Japan

ALBUMS:	HITS 4			WEEKS 33
SNOWFLAKES ARE DANCING	*RCA Red Seal*	17	*7 Jun 75*	20
PICTURES AT AN EXHIBITION	*RCA Red Seal*	42	*16 Aug 75*	5
HOLST: THE PLANETS	*RCA Red Seal*	41	*7 May 77*	6
TOMITA'S GREATEST HITS	*RCA Red Seal*	66	*9 Feb 80*	2

Ricky TOMLINSON — UK

SINGLES:	HITS 1			WEEKS 3
ARE YOU LOOKIN' AT ME? *Originally recorded by The Popes.*	*All Around The World*	28	*10 Nov 01*	3

TOMSKI — UK

SINGLES:	HITS 2			WEEKS 3
14 HOURS TO SAVE THE EARTH *Includes sample from the 1980 film 'Flash Gordon'.*	*Xtravaganza*	42	*18 Apr 98*	1
LOVE WILL COME *Above hit: TOMSKI featuring Jan JOHNSTON.*	*Xtravaganza*	31	*12 Feb 00*	2

TONETTES - See Russ HAMILTON

TONGUE 'N' CHEEK — UK

SINGLES:	HITS 5			WEEKS 28
NOBODY (CAN LOVE ME) *Above hit: TONGUE IN CHEEK.*	*Criminal*	59	*27 Feb 88*	6
ENCORE	*Syncopate*	41	*25 Nov 89*	4
TOMORROW	*Syncopate*	20	*14 Apr 90*	7
NOBODY	*Syncopate*	37	*4 Aug 90*	5
FORGET ME NOTS	*Syncopate*	26	*19 Jan 91*	6
ALBUMS:	**HITS 1**			**WEEKS 3**
THIS IS TONGUE 'N' CHEEK	*Syncopate*	45	*22 Sep 90*	3

TONIGHT — UK

SINGLES:	HITS 2			WEEKS 10
DRUMMER MAN	*TDS Records*	14	*28 Jan 78*	8
MONEY THAT'S YOUR PROBLEM	*TDS Records*	66	*20 May 78*	2

TONY! TONI! TONE! — US

SINGLES:	HITS 4			WEEKS 12
OAKLAND STROKE	*Wing*	50	*30 Jun 90*	5
IT NEVER RAINS (IN SOUTHERN CALIFORNIA) *Original by Albert Hammond reached No. 5 in the US in 1972.*	*Wing*	69	*9 Mar 91*	2
IF I HAD NO LOOT *Above hit: TONY TONI TONE.*	*Polydor*	44	*4 Sep 93*	3
LET'S GET DOWN *Above hit: TONY TONI TONE featuring DJ QUIK.*	*Mercury*	33	*3 May 97*	2
ALBUMS:	**HITS 1**			**WEEKS 1**
SONS OF SOUL	*Polydor*	66	*2 Oct 93*	1

TOO SHORT – See SCARFACE

TOO TOUGH TEE – See DYNAMIX II featuring: TOO TOUGH TEE

TOOL — US/UK

ALBUMS:	HITS 1			WEEKS 3
LATERALUS	*Tool Dissrectional*	16	*26 May 01*	3

TOON TRAVELLERS – See MUNGO JERRY

TOP — UK

SINGLES:	HITS 1			WEEKS 2
NUMBER ONE DOMINATOR	*Island*	67	*20 Jul 91*	2

TOP CAT – See DOUBLE 99

TOP LINERS – See Rocky SHARPE and the REPLAYS

TOPLOADER — UK

SINGLES:	HITS 5			WEEKS 49
ACHILLES HEEL	*Sony S2*	64	*22 May 99*	1
LET THE PEOPLE KNOW	*Sony S2*	52	*7 Aug 99*	1
DANCING IN THE MOONLIGHT *Originally recorded by Boffalongo in 1970.*	*Sony S2*	19	*4 Mar 00*	7
ACHILLES HEEL [RI]	*Sony S2*	8	*13 May 00*	7
JUST HOLD ON	*Sony S2*	20	*2 Sep 00*	4
DANCING IN THE MOONLIGHT [RI]	*Sony S2*	7	*25 Nov 00*	25
ONLY FOR A WHILE	*Sony S2*	19	*21 Apr 01*	4
ALBUMS:	**HITS 1**			**WEEKS 61**
ONKA'S BIG MOKA	*Sony S2*	4	*3 Jun 00*	61

TOPOL — Israel

(See also Various Artists: Films – Original Soundtracks 'Fiddler On The Roof'; Stage Cast – London 'Fiddler On The Roof'.)

SINGLES:	HITS 1			WEEKS 20
IF I WERE A RICH MAN *From the musical 'Fiddler On The Roof'. Originally recorded by Zero Mostel.*	*CBS*	9	*22 Apr 67*	20
ALBUMS:	**HITS 1**			**WEEKS 1**
TOPOL'S ISRAEL	*BBC*	80	*11 May 85*	1

Bernie TORME — UK

ALBUMS:	HITS 1			WEEKS 3
TURN OUT THE LIGHTS	*Kamaflage*	50	*3 Jul 82*	3

Mel TORME — US

SINGLES:	HITS 2			WEEKS 32
MOUNTAIN GREENERY *Originally recorded by Frank Crumit in 1929.*	*Vogue Coral*	15	*28 Apr 56*	11
MOUNTAIN GREENERY [RE]	*Vogue Coral*	4	*28 Jul 56*	13
COMIN' HOME BABY	*London*	13	*5 Jan 63*	8

TORNADOS — UK

(See also Various Artists: Films – Original Soundtracks 'Just For Fun').

SINGLES:	HITS 5			WEEKS 59
TELSTAR *Title was the name of the world's first communications satellite, launched on 10 Jul 62.*	*Decca*	1	*1 Sep 62*	25
GLOBETROTTER	*Decca*	5	*12 Jan 63*	11
ROBOT	*Decca*	17	*23 Mar 63*	12
THE ICE CREAM MAN *From the film 'Farewell Performance'.*	*Decca*	18	*8 Jun 63*	9
DRAGONFLY	*Decca*	41	*12 Oct 63*	2
EPS:	**HITS 5**			**WEEKS 88**
THE SOUNDS OF THE TORNADOS	*Decca*	2	*15 Dec 62*	26

TELSTAR	*Decca*	4	*2 Feb 63*	22
MORE SOUNDS FROM THE TORNADOS	*Decca*	8	*13 Apr 63*	11
BILLY FURY AND THE TORNADOS	*Decca*	2	*25 May 63*	16
Above hit: Billy FURY and the TORNADOS.				
TORNADO ROCK	*Decca*	7	*17 Aug 63*	13

Mitchell TOROK — US

SINGLES:	HITS 2			WEEKS 19
WHEN MEXICO GAVE UP THE RHUMBA	*Brunswick*	6	*29 Sep 56*	17
RED LIGHT, GREEN LIGHT	*Brunswick*	29	*12 Jan 57*	1
Above hit: Mitchell TOROK and the TULANE SISTERS.				
WHEN MEXICO GAVE UP THE RHUMBA [RE]	*Brunswick*	30	*2 Feb 57*	1

Liz TORRES - See Danny TENAGLIA

Emiliana TORRINI — Italy

SINGLES:	HITS 3			WEEKS 3
EASY	*One Little Indian*	63	*10 Jun 00*	1
UNEMPLOYED IN SUMMERTIME	*One Little Indian*	63	*9 Sep 00*	1
TO BE FREE	*One Little Indian*	44	*3 Feb 01*	1

Peter TOSH — US

SINGLES:	HITS 2			WEEKS 12
(YOU GOTTA WALK) DON'T LOOK BACK	*Rolling Stones*	43	*21 Oct 78*	7
Mick Jagger on backing vocals.				
JOHNNY B. GOODE	*Radic*	48	*2 Apr 83*	5
Original by Chuck Berry reached No. 8 in the US in 1958.				
ALBUMS:	**HITS 1**			**WEEKS 1**
LEGALIZE IT	*Virgin*	54	*25 Sep 76*	1

TOTAL — US

SINGLES:	HITS 5			WEEKS 11
CAN'T YOU SEE	*Tommy Boy*	43	*15 Jul 95*	2
From the film 'New Jersey Drive'.				
Above hit: TOTAL featuring the NOTORIOUS B.I.G.				
KISSIN' YOU	*Puff Daddy*	29	*14 Sep 96*	2
DO YOU THINK ABOUT US	*Puff Daddy*	49	*15 Feb 97*	1
WHAT YOU WANT	*Puff Daddy*	15	*18 Apr 98*	5
Above hit: MASE featuring TOTAL.				
I WONDER WHY HE'S THE GREATEST DJ	*Tommy Boy*	68	*30 Sep 00*	1
Samples Sister Sledge's He's The Greatest Dancer.				
Above hit: Tony TOUCH featuring TOTAL.				

TOTAL CONTRAST — UK

SINGLES:	HITS 4			WEEKS 22
TAKES A LITTLE TIME	*London*	17	*3 Aug 85*	10
HIT AND RUN	*London*	41	*19 Oct 85*	5
THE RIVER	*London*	44	*1 Mar 86*	3
WHAT YOU GONNA DO ABOUT IT	*London*	63	*10 May 86*	4
ALBUMS:	**HITS 1**			**WEEKS 3**
TOTAL CONTRAST	*London*	66	*8 Mar 86*	3

TOTO — US

SINGLES:	HITS 5			WEEKS 35
HOLD THE LINE	*CBS*	14	*10 Feb 79*	11
AFRICA	*CBS*	3	*5 Feb 83*	10
ROSANNA	*CBS*	12	*9 Apr 83*	8
Originally released in 1982. Written about actress Rosanna Arquette who at the time was dating keyboard player Steve Porcaro.				
I WON'T HOLD YOU BACK	*CBS*	37	*18 Jun 83*	5
I WILL REMEMBER	*Columbia*	64	*18 Nov 95*	1
ALBUMS:	**HITS 5**			**WEEKS 39**
TOTO	*CBS*	37	*31 Mar 79*	5
TOTO IV	*CBS*	4	*26 Feb 83*	30
ISOLATION	*CBS*	67	*17 Nov 84*	2
FAHRENHEIT	*CBS*	99	*20 Sep 86*	1
THE SEVENTH ONE	*CBS*	73	*9 Apr 88*	1

TOTO COELO — UK

SINGLES:	HITS 2			WEEKS 14
I EAT CANNIBALS (PART ONE)	*Radialchoice*	8	*7 Aug 82*	10
DRACULA'S TANGO (SUCKER FOR YOUR LOVE) / MUCHO MACHO	*Radialchoice*	54	*13 Nov 82*	4

TOTTENHAM HOTSPUR F.A. CUP FINAL SQUAD — UK

SINGLES:	HITS 4			WEEKS 23
OSSIE'S DREAM . . . (SPURS ARE ON THEIR WAY TO WEMBLEY) *Above hit: TOTTENHAM HOTSPUR F.A. CUP FINAL SQUAD SEASON 1980/81.*	*Shelf*	5	*9 May 81*	8
TOTTENHAM, TOTTENHAM *Above hit: TOTTENHAM HOTSPUR F.A. CUP FINAL SQUAD 1981/82 SEASON.*	*Shelf*	19	*1 May 82*	7
HOT SHOT TOTTENHAM! *Above hit: TOTTENHAM HOTSPUR F.A. CUP FINAL SQUAD 1986/87 SEASON with CHAS and DAVE.*	*Rainbow*	18	*9 May 87*	5
WHEN THE YEAR ENDS IN 1 *New lyrics composed by Chas 'N' Dave to the music of their 1983 hit London Girls.* *Above hit: TOTTENHAM HOTSPUR with CHAS 'N' DAVE.*	*A.1.*	44	*11 May 91*	3
EPS:	**HITS 1**			**WEEKS 3**
SPURS GO MARCHING ON *Above hit: TOTTENHAM HOTSPUR F.A. CUP SQUAD.*	*Columbia*	6	*10 Jun 67*	3

Tony TOUCH featuring TOTAL — US

SINGLES:	HITS 1			WEEKS 1
I WONDER WHY HE'S THE GREATEST DJ *Samples Sister Sledge's He's The Greatest Dancer.*	*Tommy Boy*	68	*30 Sep 00*	1

TOUCH AND GO — UK/Japan

SINGLES:	HITS 1			WEEKS 12
WOULD YOU . . . ?	*V2*	3	*7 Nov 98*	12

TOUCH OF SOUL — UK

SINGLES:	HITS 1			WEEKS 3
WE GOT THE LOVE	*Cooltempo*	46	*19 May 90*	3

TOUR DE FORCE — UK

SINGLES:	HITS 1			WEEKS 1
CATALAN	*East West Dance*	71	*16 May 98*	1

Ali Farka TOURE and Ry COODER — Mali/US

(See also Ry Cooder.)

ALBUMS:	HITS 1			WEEKS 3
TALKING TIMBUKTU	*World Circuit*	44	*9 Apr 94*	3

TOURISTS — UK

SINGLES:	HITS 5			WEEKS 40
BLIND AMONG THE FLOWERS	*Logo*	52	*9 Jun 79*	5
THE LONELIEST MAN IN THE WORLD	*Logo*	32	*8 Sep 79*	7
I ONLY WANT TO BE WITH YOU	*Logo*	4	*10 Nov 79*	14
SO GOOD TO BE BACK HOME AGAIN	*Logo*	8	*9 Feb 80*	9
DON'T SAY I TOLD YOU SO	*RCA*	40	*18 Oct 80*	5
ALBUMS:	**HITS 3**			**WEEKS 18**
THE TOURISTS	*Logo*	72	*14 Jul 79*	1
REALITY EFFECT	*Logo*	23	*3 Nov 79*	16
LUMINOUS BASEMENT	*RCA*	75	*22 Nov 80*	1

TOUTES LES FILLES — UK

SINGLES:	HITS 1			WEEKS 1
THAT'S WHAT LOVE CAN DO *Original by Boy Krazy reached No. 18 in the US in 1993.*	*London*	44	*4 Sept 99*	1

Carol Lynn TOWNES — US

SINGLES:	HITS 2			WEEKS 7
99½	*Polydor*	47	*4 Aug 84*	4
BELIEVE IN THE BEAT	*Polydor*	56	*19 Jan 85*	3

Fuzz TOWNSHEND — UK

SINGLES:	HITS 1			WEEKS 1
HELLO DARLIN *Originally released in Jul on the Fidelity Lo label reaching No. 131.*	*Echo*	51	*6 Sep 97*	1

Pete TOWNSHEND — UK

(See also Pete Townshend and Ronnie Lane.)

SINGLES:	HITS 3			WEEKS 17
ROUGH BOYS	*Atco*	39	*5 Apr 80*	6

LET MY LOVE OPEN THE DOOR	*Atco*	46	*21 Jun 80*	6
UNIFORMS (CORPS D'ESPRIT)	*Atco*	48	*21 Aug 82*	5
ALBUMS:	**HITS 4**			**WEEKS 25**
WHO CAME FIRST	*Track*	30	*21 Oct 72*	2
EMPTY GLASS	*Atco*	11	*3 May 80*	14
ALL THE BEST COWBOYS HAVE CHINESE EYES	*Acto*	32	*3 Jul 82*	8
WHITE CITY	*Atco*	70	*30 Nov 85*	1

Pete TOWNSHEND and Ronnie LANE — UK

(See also Ronnie Lane and the Band Slim Chance; Pete Townshend.)

ALBUMS:	**HITS 1**			**WEEKS 3**
ROUGH MIX	*Polydor*	44	*15 Oct 77*	3

TOXIC TWO — US

SINGLES:	**HITS 1**			**WEEKS 6**
RAVE GENERATOR	*PWL International*	13	*7 Mar 92*	6

TOY-BOX — Denmark

SINGLES:	**HITS 1**			**WEEKS 2**
BEST FRIEND	*Edel*	41	*18 Sept 99*	2

TOY DOLLS — UK

SINGLES:	**HITS 1**			**WEEKS 12**
NELLIE THE ELEPHANT *Originally recorded by Mandy Miller.*	*Volume*	4	*1 Dec 84*	12
ALBUMS:	**HITS 1**			**WEEKS 1**
A FAR OUT DISC	*Volume*	71	*25 May 85*	1

TOYAH — UK

SINGLES:	**HITS 12**			**WEEKS 87**
FOUR FROM TOYAH [EP] *Lead track: It's A Mystery.*	*Safari*	4	*14 Feb 81*	14
I WANT TO BE FREE	*Safari*	8	*16 May 81*	11
THUNDER IN THE MOUNTAINS	*Safari*	4	*3 Oct 81*	9
FOUR MORE FROM TOYAH [EP] *Lead track: Good Morning Universe.*	*Safari*	14	*28 Nov 81*	9
BRAVE NEW WORLD	*Safari*	21	*22 May 82*	8
IEYA *Originally released in 1981.*	*Safari*	48	*17 Jul 82*	5
BE PROUD BE LOUD (BE HEARD)	*Safari*	30	*9 Oct 82*	7
REBEL RUN	*Safari*	24	*24 Sep 83*	5
THE VOW	*Safari*	50	*19 Nov 83*	5
DON'T FALL IN LOVE (I SAID)	*Portrait*	22	*27 Apr 85*	6
SOUL PASSING THROUGH SOUL	*Portrait*	57	*29 Jun 85*	3
ECHO BEACH	*E'G*	54	*25 Apr 87*	5
ALBUMS:	**HITS 8**			**WEEKS 97**
THE BLUE MEANING	*Safari*	40	*14 Jun 80*	4
TOYAH! TOYAH! TOYAH!	*Safari*	22	*17 Jan 81*	14
ANTHEM *Side 1 is titled Once Upon A Time . . . ;side 2 Happy Ever After?*	*Safari*	2	*30 May 81*	46
THE CHANGELING	*Safari*	6	*19 Jun 82*	12
WARRIOR ROCK - TOYAH ON TOUR *Live recordings.*	*Safari*	20	*13 Nov 82*	6
LOVE IS THE LAW	*Safari*	28	*5 Nov 83*	7
TOYAH! TOYAH! TOYAH! *Compilation. This is a different album to the 1981 entry.*	*K-Tel*	43	*25 Feb 84*	4
MINX	*Portrait*	24	*3 Aug 85*	4

TOYS — US

SINGLES:	**HITS 2**			**WEEKS 17**
A LOVER'S CONCERTO *Adapted from Bach's Minuet In G.*	*Stateside*	5	*6 Nov 65*	13
ATTACK	*Stateside*	36	*29 Jan 66*	4

TQ — US

SINGLES:	**HITS 6**			**WEEKS 35**
WESTSIDE *Dedicated to Tupac Shakur and NWA's Easy-E.*	*Epic*	4	*30 Jan 99*	9
BYE BYE BABY	*Epic*	7	*1 May 99*	7
BETTER DAYS	*Epic*	32	*21 Aug 99*	2
SUMMERTIME *Above hit: ANOTHER LEVEL featuring TQ.*	*Northwestside*	7	*04 Sept 99*	7
DAILY	*Epic*	14	*29 Apr 00*	5

LET'S GET BACK TO BED – BOY	*Epic*	16	*13 Oct 01*	5
Above hit: Sarah CONNOR featuring TQ				
ALBUMS:	**HITS 2**			**WEEKS 9**
THEY NEVER SAW ME COMING	*Epic*	27	*8 May 99*	7
Originally released in 1998.				
THE SECOND COMING	*Epic*	32	*20 May 00*	2

Ian TRACEY with the LIVERPOOL CATHEDRALS' CHOIRS — UK

ALBUMS:	**HITS 1**			**WEEKS 3**
YOUR FAVOURITE HYMNS	*Virgin Classics*	62	*21 Mar 92*	3

TRACIE — UK

SINGLES:	**HITS 5**			**WEEKS 24**
THE HOUSE THAT JACK BUILT	*Respond*	9	*26 Mar 83*	8
GIVE IT SOME EMOTION	*Respond*	24	*16 Jul 83*	9
SOUL'S ON FIRE	*Respond*	73	*14 Apr 84*	2
(I LOVE YOU) WHEN YOU SLEEP	*Respond*	59	*9 Jun 84*	3
I CAN'T LEAVE YOU ALONE	*Respond*	60	*17 Aug 85*	2
Above hit: Tracie YOUNG.				
ALBUMS:	**HITS 1**			**WEEKS 2**
FAR FROM THE HURTING KIND	*Respond*	64	*30 Jun 84*	2

TRACY – See MASSIVO featuring TRACY

Jeanie TRACY — US

SINGLES:	**HITS 3**			**WEEKS 3**
IF THIS IS LOVE	*Pulse 8*	73	*11 Jun 94*	1
DO YOU BELIEVE IN THE WONDER	*Pulse 8*	57	*5 Nov 94*	1
IT'S A MAN'S MAN'S MAN'S WORLD	*Pulse 8*	73	*13 May 95*	1
Above hit: Jeanie TRACY and Bobby WOMACK.				

TRAFFIC — UK

SINGLES:	**HITS 4**			**WEEKS 40**
PAPER SUN	*Island*	5	*3 Jun 67*	10
HOLE IN MY SHOE	*Island*	2	*9 Sep 67*	14
HERE WE GO ROUND THE MULBERRY BUSH	*Island*	8	*2 Dec 67*	12
From the film of the same name.				
NO FACE, NO NAME, NO NUMBER	*Island*	40	*9 Mar 68*	4
ALBUMS:	**HITS 6**			**WEEKS 41**
MR. FANTASY	*Island*	8	*30 Dec 67*	16
TRAFFIC	*Island*	9	*26 Oct 68*	8
JOHN BARLEYCORN MUST DIE	*Island*	11	*8 Aug 70*	9
TRAFFIC – ON THE ROAD	*Island*	40	*24 Nov 73*	3
Live recordings from their 1973 World Tour.				
WHEN THE EAGLE FLIES	*Island*	31	*28 Sep 74*	1
FAR FROM HOME	*Virgin*	29	*21 May 94*	4

TRAIN — US

SINGLES:	**HITS 1**			**WEEKS 8**
DROPS OF JUPITER (TELL ME)	*Columbia*	10	*11 Aug 01*	8
ALBUMS:	**HITS 1**			**WEEKS 9**
DROPS OF JUPITER	*Columbia*	8	*18 Aug 01*	9

TRAMAINE — US

SINGLES:	**HITS 1**			**WEEKS 2**
FALL DOWN (SPIRIT OF LOVE)	*A&M*	60	*5 Oct 85*	2

TRAMMPS — US

SINGLES:	**HITS 7**			**WEEKS 56**
ZING WENT THE STRINGS OF MY HEART	*Buddah*	29	*23 Nov 74*	10
Originally recorded by Judy Garland in 1943.				
SIXTY MINUTE MAN	*Buddah*	40	*1 Feb 75*	4
Originally recorded by Billy Ward and the Dominoes in 1951.				
HOLD BACK THE NIGHT	*Buddah*	5	*11 Oct 75*	8
THAT'S WHERE THE HAPPY PEOPLE GO	*Atlantic*	35	*13 Mar 76*	8
SOUL SEARCHING TIME	*Atlantic*	42	*24 Jul 76*	3
DISCO INFERNO	*Atlantic*	16	*14 May 77*	7
DISCO INFERNO [RI]	*Atlantic*	47	*24 Jun 78*	10
From the film 'Saturday Night Fever'.				
HOLD BACK THE NIGHT [RR]	*Network*	30	*12 Dec 92*	6
Above hit: KWS features guest vocals from the TRAMMPS.				

TRANCESETTERS ??

SINGLES:	HITS 2			WEEKS 2
ROACHES	*Hooj Choons*	55	*4 Mar 00*	1
SYNERGY	*Hooj Choons*	72	*9 Jun 01*	1

TRANS-X Canada

SINGLES:	HITS 1			WEEKS 9
LIVING ON VIDEO ('85 RE-MIX)	*Boiling Point*	9	*13 Jul 85*	9
Original release reached No. 77 in 1984.				

TRANSA UK

SINGLES:	HITS 2			WEEKS 2
PROPHASE	*Perfecto Fluoro*	65	*30 Aug 97*	1
ENERVATE	*Perfecto Fluoro*	42	*21 Feb 98*	1

TRANSATLANTIC SOUL - See Roger SANCHEZ

TRANSFER UK

SINGLES:	HITS 1			WEEKS 1
POSESSION	*Multiply*	54	*3 Nov 01*	1

TRANSFORMER 2 Holland/Belgium

SINGLES:	HITS 1			WEEKS 1
JUST CAN'T GET ENOUGH	*Positiva*	45	*24 Feb 96*	1

TRANSGLOBAL UNDERGROUND UK

ALBUMS:	HITS 3			WEEKS 3
DREAM OF 100 NATIONS	*Nation*	45	*30 Oct 93*	1
INTERNATIONAL TIMES	*Nation*	40	*29 Oct 94*	1
PSYCHIC KARAOKE	*Nation*	62	*25 May 96*	1

TRANSISTOR UK/US

SINGLES:	HITS 1			WEEKS 1
LOOK WHO'S PERFECT NOW	*Virgin*	56	*28 Mar 98*	1

TRANSVISION VAMP UK

SINGLES:	HITS 10			WEEKS 59
TELL THAT GIRL TO SHUT UP	*MCA*	45	*16 Apr 88*	3
Originally recorded by Holly and the Italians.				
I WANT YOUR LOVE	*MCA*	5	*25 Jun 88*	13
REVOLUTION BABY	*MCA*	30	*17 Sep 88*	5
Original release reached No. 77 in 1987.				
SISTER MOON	*MCA*	41	*19 Nov 88*	5
BABY I DON'T CARE	*MCA*	3	*1 Apr 89*	11
THE ONLY ONE	*MCA*	15	*10 Jun 89*	6
LANDSLIDE OF LOVE	*MCA*	14	*5 Aug 89*	5
BORN TO BE SOLD	*MCA*	22	*4 Nov 89*	4
(I JUST WANNA) B WITH U	*MCA*	30	*13 Apr 91*	4
IF LOOKS COULD KILL	*MCA*	41	*22 Jun 91*	3
ALBUMS:	**HITS 2**			**WEEKS 58**
POP ART	*MCA*	4	*15 Oct 88*	32
VELVETEEN	*MCA*	1	*8 Jul 89*	26

TRASH UK

SINGLES:	HITS 1			WEEKS 3
GOLDEN SLUMBERS/CARRY THAT WEIGHT [M]	*Apple*	35	*25 Oct 69*	3
Both tracks originally recorded by the Beatles.				

TRASH CAN SINATRAS UK

SINGLES:	HITS 1			WEEKS 1
HAYFEVER	*Go! Discs*	61	*24 Apr 93*	1
ALBUMS:	**HITS 2**			**WEEKS 2**
CAKE	*Go! Discs*	74	*7 Jul 90*	1
I'VE SEEN EVERYTHING	*Go! Discs*	50	*15 May 93*	1

TRAVEL France

SINGLES:	HITS 1			WEEKS 2
BULGARIAN	*Tidy Trax*	67	*24 Apr 99*	2

TRAVELING WILBURYS UK/US

SINGLES:	HITS 3			WEEKS 19
HANDLE WITH CARE	*Wilbury*	21	*29 Oct 88*	13

END OF THE LINE	*Wilbury*	52	*11 Mar 89*	4
NOBODY'S CHILD	*Wilbury*	44	*30 Jun 90*	2
ALBUMS:	**HITS 2**			**WEEKS 44**
THE TRAVELING WILBURYS VOLUME 1	*Wilbury*	16	*5 Nov 88*	35
THE TRAVELING WILBURYS VOLUME 3	*Wilbury*	14	*10 Nov 90*	9

Pat TRAVERS — US

ALBUMS:	**HITS 1**			**WEEKS 3**
MAKIN' MAGIC	*Polydor*	40	*2 Apr 77*	3

TRAVIS — UK

SINGLES:	**HITS 12**			**WEEKS 72**
U16 GIRLS	*Independiente*	40	*12 Apr 97*	2
ALL I WANT TO DO IS ROCK	*Independiente*	39	*28 Jun 97*	2
First issued in 1996 as a 500 copy limited edition 10" on the Red Telephone Box Records label.				
TIED TO THE 90'S	*Independiente*	30	*23 Aug 97*	2
HAPPY	*Independiente*	38	*25 Oct 97*	2
MORE THAN US [EP]	*Independiente*	16	*11 Apr 98*	3
Lead track: More Than Us, with Anne Dudley.				
WRITING TO REACH YOU	*Independiente*	14	*20 Mar 99*	5
DRIFTWOOD	*Independiente*	13	*29 May 99*	5
WHY DOES IT ALWAYS RAIN ON ME?	*Independiente*	10	*14 Aug 99*	8
TURN	*Independiente*	8	*20 Nov 99*	11
COMING AROUND	*Independiente*	5	*17 Jun 00*	7
COMING AROUND [RE-1ST]	*Independiente*	55	*12 Aug 00*	2
COMING AROUND [RE-2ND]	*Independiente*	75	*2 Sep 00*	1
SING	*Independiente*	3	*9 Jun 01*	14
SIDE	*Independiente*	14	*29 Sep 01*	8
ALBUMS:	**HITS 3**			**WEEKS 135**
GOOD FEELING	*Independiente*	9	*20 Sept 97*	16
THE MAN WHO	*Independiente*	1	*5 Jun 99*	91
THE INVISIBLE BAND	*Independiente*	1	*23 Jun 01*	28

Randy TRAVIS — US

SINGLES:	**HITS 1**			**WEEKS 6**
FOREVER AND EVER, AMEN	*Warner Brothers*	55	*21 May 88*	6
ALBUMS:	**HITS 1**			**WEEKS 2**
OLD 8 X 10	*Warner Brothers*	64	*6 Aug 88*	2

John TRAVOLTA — US

(See also Various Artists: Films - Original Soundtracks 'Grease'.)

SINGLES:	**HITS 6**			**WEEKS 90**
YOU'RE THE ONE THAT I WANT	*RSO*	1	*20 May 78*	26
Above hit: John TRAVOLTA and Olivia NEWTON-JOHN.				
SUMMER NIGHTS	*RSO*	1	*16 Sep 78*	19
Above hit: John TRAVOLTA, Olivia NEWTON-JOHN and CAST.				
SANDY	*Midsong*	2	*7 Oct 78*	15
GREASED LIGHTNING	*Midsong/Polydor*	11	*2 Dec 78*	9
Above 4 from the film 'Grease'.				
THE GREASE MEGAMIX [M]	*Polydor*	3	*22 Dec 90*	10
Above hit: John TRAVOLTA and Olivia NEWTON-JOHN.				
GREASE - THE DREAM MIX [M]	*Polydor*	47	*23 Mar 91*	2
Above 2 are medleys of songs from the film 'Grease'.				
Above hit: Frankie VALLI, John TRAVOLTA and Olivia NEWTON-JOHN.				
YOU'RE THE ONE THAT I WANT [RI]	*Polydor*	4	*25 Jul 98*	9
20th anniversary re-issue.				
Above hit: John TRAVOLTA Olivia NEWTON-JOHN.				
ALBUMS:	**HITS 1**			**WEEKS 6**
SANDY	*Midsong*	40	*23 Dec 78*	6
Apart from the title track, all others are earlier recordings from 1976/77.				

TREMELOES — UK

(See also Brian Poole and the Tremeloes.)

SINGLES:	**HITS 13**			**WEEKS 131**
HERE COMES MY BABY	*CBS*	4	*4 Feb 67*	11
Originally recorded by Cat Stevens.				
SILENCE IS GOLDEN	*CBS*	1	*29 Apr 67*	15
Originally recorded by the Four Seasons for the B-side of Rag Doll.				
EVEN THE BAD TIMES ARE GOOD	*CBS*	4	*5 Aug 67*	13
BE MINE (MI SEGUIRAI)	*CBS*	39	*11 Nov 67*	2
SUDDENLY YOU LOVE ME	*CBS*	6	*20 Jan 68*	11
HELULE HELULE	*CBS*	14	*11 May 68*	9
MY LITTLE LADY	*CBS*	6	*21 Sep 68*	12

I SHALL BE RELEASED	*CBS*	29	*14 Dec 68*	5
Above hit: TREMELOES with the Keith MANSFIELD STRINGS.				
HELLO WORLD	*CBS*	14	*22 Mar 69*	8
(CALL ME) NUMBER ONE	*CBS*	2	*1 Nov 69*	14
BY THE WAY	*CBS*	35	*21 Mar 70*	6
ME AND MY LIFE	*CBS*	4	*12 Sep 70*	18
HELLO BUDDY	*CBS*	32	*10 Jul 71*	7
ALBUMS:	**HITS 1**			**WEEKS 7**
HERE COMES THE TREMELOES	*CBS*	15	*3 Jun 67*	7

Jackie TRENT — UK

SINGLES:	**HITS 3**			**WEEKS 17**
WHERE ARE YOU NOW	*Pye*	1	*24 Apr 65*	11
WHEN SUMMERTIME IS OVER	*Pye*	39	*3 Jul 65*	2
I'LL BE THERE	*Pye*	38	*5 Apr 69*	4

Ralph TRESVANT — US

(See also Janet Jackson; Luther Vandross.)

SINGLES:	**HITS 1**			**WEEKS 8**
SENSITIVITY	*MCA*	18	*12 Jan 91*	8
ALBUMS:	**HITS 1**			**WEEKS 3**
RALPH TRESVANT	*MCA*	37	*23 Feb 91*	3

TREVOR and SIMON — UK

SINGLES:	**HITS 1**			**WEEKS 5**
HANDS UP	*Substance*	12	*10 Jun 00*	5
Samples Put Your Hands Up by the Black and White Brothers.				

TRI — UK

SINGLES:	**HITS 1**			**WEEKS 1**
WE GOT THE LOVE	*Epic*	61	*2 Sep 95*	1

TRIBAL HOUSE — US

SINGLES:	**HITS 1**			**WEEKS 2**
MOTHERLAND -A-FRI-CA-	*Cooltempo*	57	*3 Feb 90*	2

Tony TRIBE — Jamaica

SINGLES:	**HITS 1**			**WEEKS 2**
RED, RED WINE	*Downtown*	50	*19 Jul 69*	1
RED, RED WINE [RE]	*Downtown*	46	*9 Aug 69*	1

A TRIBE CALLED QUEST — US

(See also Fugees (Refugee Camp); Jungle Brothers.)

SINGLES:	**HITS 7**			**WEEKS 18**
BONITA APPLEBUM	*Jive*	47	*18 Aug 90*	3
Samples Rotary Connections' Memory Band.				
CAN I KICK IT?	*Jive*	15	*19 Jan 91*	7
Samples Lou Reed's Walk On The Wild Side.				
OH MY GOD	*Jive*	68	*11 Jun 94*	1
1NCE AGAIN	*Jive*	34	*13 Jul 96*	2
Vocals by Tammy Lucas.				
STRESSED OUT	*Jive*	33	*23 Nov 96*	2
Above hit: A TRIBE CALLED QUEST featuring Faith EVANS and Raphael SAADIQ.				
THE JAM [EP]	*Jive*	61	*23 Aug 97*	1
Lead track: Jam (Samples Dirty Old Bossa Nova). 2 other tracks on the EP, Mardi Fras At Midnight and Same Ol' Thing, are from the film 'Men In Black'.				
FIND A WAY	*Jive*	41	*29 Aug 98*	2
Samples Towa Tei's Dubnova (Parts 1 & 2).				
ALBUMS:	**HITS 5**			**WEEKS 9**
PEOPLE'S INSTINCTIVE TRAVELS . . .	*Jive*	54	*19 May 90*	2
THE LOW END THEORY	*Jive*	58	*12 Oct 91*	1
MIDNIGHT MARAUDERS	*Jive*	70	*27 Nov 93*	1
BEATS, RHYMES AND LIFE	*Jive*	28	*10 Aug 96*	4
THE LOVE MOVEMENT	*Jive*	38	*10 Oct 98*	1

A TRIBE OF TOFFS — UK

SINGLES:	**HITS 1**			**WEEKS 5**
JOHN KETTLEY (IS A WEATHERMAN)	*Completely Different*	21	*24 Dec 88*	5

TRICKBABY — UK

SINGLES:	**HITS 1**			**WEEKS 2**
INDIE-YARN	*Logic*	47	*12 Oct 96*	2

TRICKSTER (CMV'S) — UK

SINGLES:	HITS 1			WEEKS 3
MOVE ON UP	*AM:PM*	19	*4 Apr 98*	3

TRICKY — UK

SINGLES:	HITS 11			WEEKS 29
AFTERMATH	*Fourth & Broadway*	69	*5 Feb 94*	1
OVERCOME	*Fourth & Broadway*	34	*28 Jan 95*	3
BLACK STEEL	*Fourth & Broadway*	28	*15 Apr 95*	3
Originally recorded by Public Enemy from their 1988 album It Takes A Nation Of Millions To Hold Us Back.				
THE HELL [EP]	*Fourth & Broadway*	12	*5 Aug 95*	3
Lead track: Hell Is Around The Corner. The Gravediggaz appear on the EP's other tracks.				
Above hit: TRICKY vs. the GRAVEDIGGAZ.				
PUMPKIN	*Fourth & Broadway*	26	*11 Nov 95*	2
Vocals by Alison Goldfrapp.				
CHRISTIANSANDS	*Fourth & Broadway*	36	*9 Nov 96*	2
Vocals by Martina.				
MILK	*Mushroom*	10	*23 Nov 96*	7
Though credited on the chart, Tricky's contribution was only as a remixer of a secondary track of the CD.				
Above hit: GARBAGE featuring TRICKY.				
TRICKY KID	*Fourth & Broadway*	28	*11 Jan 97*	2
Samples the Commodores' The Zoo (The Human Zoo).				
MILK [RE]	*Mushroom*	74	*18 Jan 97*	1
MAKES ME WANNA DIE	*Fourth & Broadway*	29	*3 May 97*	2
Vocals by Martina. Samples Eric B and Rakim's To The Listeners.				
MONEY GREEDY / BROKEN HOMES	*Island*	25	*30 May 98*	2
Above hit: TRICKY / TRICKY featuring Polly Jean HARVEY.				
FOR REAL	*Island*	45	*21 Aug 99*	1
Vocals by Kioka Williams and Mad Dog.				
ALBUMS:	**HITS 5**			**WEEKS 43**
MAXINQUAYE	*Fourth & Broadway*	3	*4 Mar 95*	35
PRE-MILLENNIUM TENSION	*Fourth & Broadway*	30	*23 Nov 96*	2
ANGELS WITH DIRTY FACES	*Island*	23	*6 Jun 98*	2
JUXTAPOSE	*Island*	22	*28 Aug 99*	2
Above hit: TRICKY with DJ MUGGS and GREASE.				
BLOWBACK	*Anti*	34	*14 Jul 01*	2

TRICKY DISCO — UK

(See also G.T.O.; Technohead.)

SINGLES:	HITS 2			WEEKS 10
TRICKY DISCO	*Warp*	14	*28 Jul 90*	8
HOUSE FLY	*Warp*	55	*20 Apr 91*	2

TRIFFIDS — Australia

SINGLES:	HITS 1			WEEKS 1
A TRICK OF THE LIGHT	*Island*	73	*6 Feb 88*	1
ALBUMS:	**HITS 1**			**WEEKS 1**
THE BLACK SWAN	*Island*	63	*22 Apr 89*	1

TRILOGY – See C&C MUSIC FACTORY

TRINA and TAMARA — US

SINGLES:	HITS 2			WEEKS 3
MY LOVE IS THE SHHH!	*Warner Brothers*	64	*7 Feb 98*	1
Above hit: SOMETHIN' FOR THE PEOPLE featuring TRINA and TAMARA.				
WHAT'D YOU COME HERE FOR?	*Columbia*	46	*12 Jun 99*	2

TRINIDAD OIL COMPANY — Trinidad

SINGLES:	HITS 1			WEEKS 5
THE CALENDAR SONG (JANUARY, FEBRUARY, MARCH, APRIL, MAY)	*Harvest*	34	*21 May 77*	5

TRINIDAD SINGERS – See Murray HEAD

TRINITY – See Julie DRISCOLL, Brian AUGER and the TRINITY

TRIO – See Dorothy PROVINE

TRIO — Germany

SINGLES:	HITS 1			WEEKS 10
DA DA DA	*Mobile Suit Corporation*	2	*3 Jul 82*	10

TRIPLE X — Italy

SINGLES:	HITS 1			WEEKS 2
FEEL THE SAME *Samples Delegations' You & I.*	*Sound Of Ministry*	32	*30 Oct 99*	2

TRIPPING DAISY — US

SINGLES:	HITS 1			WEEKS 1
PIRANHA	*Island*	72	*30 Mar 96*	1

TRISCO — UK

SINGLES:	HITS 1			WEEKS 2
MUZAK	*Positiva*	28	*30 Jun 01*	2

TRISTRAM VII – See NEW VAUDEVILLE BAND

TRIUMPH — Canada

SINGLES:	HITS 1			WEEKS 2
I LIVE FOR THE WEEKEND	*RCA*	59	*22 Nov 80*	2
ALBUMS:	**HITS 2**			**WEEKS 8**
PROGRESSIONS OF POWER	*RCA*	61	*10 May 80*	5
ALLIED FORCES	*RCA*	64	*3 Oct 81*	3

TROGGS — UK

SINGLES:	HITS 10			WEEKS 87
WILD THING *Originally recorded by Chip Taylor.*	*Fontana*	2	*7 May 66*	12
WITH A GIRL LIKE YOU	*Fontana*	1	*16 Jul 66*	12
I CAN'T CONTROL MYSELF	*Page One*	2	*1 Oct 66*	14
ANY WAY THAT YOU WANT ME	*Page One*	8	*17 Dec 66*	10
GIVE IT TO ME	*Page One*	12	*18 Feb 67*	10
NIGHT OF THE LONG GRASS	*Page One*	17	*3 Jun 67*	6
HI HI HAZEL	*Page One*	42	*29 Jul 67*	3
LOVE IS ALL AROUND	*Page One*	5	*21 Oct 67*	14
LITTLE GIRL	*Page One*	37	*2 Mar 68*	4
WILD THING [RR] *Instrumental version used to accompany the ITV series 'Gladiators'. [AA] listed with War by Edwin Starr and Shadow.* *Above hit: TROGGS and WOLF.*	*Weekend*	69	*30 Oct 93*	2
EPS:	**HITS 1**			**WEEKS 4**
TROGGS TOPS	*Page One*	8	*25 Mar 67*	4
ALBUMS:	**HITS 4**			**WEEKS 35**
FROM NOWHERE . . . THE TROGGS	*Fontana*	6	*30 Jul 66*	16
TROGGLODYNAMITE	*Page One*	10	*25 Feb 67*	11
THE BEST OF THE TROGGS	*Page One*	24	*5 Aug 67*	5
GREATEST HITS	*PolyGram TV*	27	*16 Jul 94*	3

TRONIKHOUSE — US

SINGLES:	HITS 1			WEEKS 1
UP TEMPO	*KMS UK*	68	*14 Mar 92*	1

John Scott TROTTER and his Orchestra – See Bing CROSBY

TROUBLE FUNK — US

SINGLES:	HITS 1			WEEKS 3
WOMAN OF PRINCIPLE	*Fourth & Broadway*	65	*27 Jun 87*	3
ALBUMS:	**HITS 2**			**WEEKS 4**
SAY WHAT!	*Fourth & Broadway*	75	*8 Nov 86*	2
TROUBLE OVER HERE, TROUBLE OVER THERE	*Fourth & Broadway*	54	*5 Sep 87*	2

Robin TROWER — UK

ALBUMS:	HITS 5			WEEKS 16
FOR EARTH BELOW	*Chrysalis*	26	*1 Mar 75*	4
ROBIN TROWER LIVE	*Chrysalis*	15	*13 Mar 76*	6
LONG MISTY DAYS	*Chrysalis*	31	*30 Oct 76*	1
IN CITY DREAMS	*Chrysalis*	58	*29 Oct 77*	1
VICTIMS OF THE FURY	*Chrysalis*	61	*16 Feb 80*	4

Doris TROY — US

SINGLES:	HITS 1			WEEKS 12
WHAT'CHA GONNA DO ABOUT IT?	*Atlantic*	37	*21 Nov 64*	7
WHAT'CHA GONNA DO ABOUT IT? [RE]	*Atlantic*	38	*23 Jan 65*	5

Elisabeth TROY - See MJ COLE; SOUNDMAN and Don LLOYDIE with Elisabeth TROY; Y TRIBE featuring Elisabeth TROY

TRU FAITH and DUB CONSPIRACY — UK

SINGLES:	HITS 1			WEEKS 5
FREAK LIKE ME *Vocals by Imaani. Samples Parliament's I'd Rather Be With You.*	*Positiva*	12	*9 Sep 00*	5

TRUBBLE — UK

SINGLES:	HITS 1			WEEKS 5
DANCING BABY (OOGA - CHAKA) *As seen on the TV series 'Ally McBeal'. Samples Blue Swede's Hooked On A Feeling.*	*Yum! Yum! Boogie Food*	21	*26 Dec 98*	5

TRUCE — UK

SINGLES:	HITS 4			WEEKS 6
THE FINEST	*Big Life*	54	*2 Sep 95*	1
CELEBRATION OF LIFE	*Big Life*	51	*30 Mar 96*	1
NOTHIN' BUT A PARTY	*Big Life*	71	*29 Nov 97*	1
EYES DON'T LIE	*Big Life*	20	*5 Sep 98*	3

Andrea TRUE CONNECTION — US

SINGLES:	HITS 2			WEEKS 16
MORE, MORE, MORE	*Buddah*	5	*17 Apr 76*	10
WHAT'S YOUR NAME, WHAT'S YOUR NUMBER	*Buddah*	34	*4 Mar 78*	6

TRUE FAITH and Bridgette GRACE with FINAL CUT — US

SINGLES:	HITS 1			WEEKS 4
TAKE ME AWAY	*Network*	51	*2 Mar 91*	4

TRUE IMAGE - See Monie LOVE

TRUE PARTY — UK

SINGLES:	HITS 1			WEEKS 6
WHAZZUP? *Inspired by the Budweiser TV commercial.*	*Positiva*	13	*2 Dec 00*	6

TRUE PLAYAZ - See DJ HYPE; DJ ZINC

TRUE STEPPERS — UK

SINGLES:	HITS 3			WEEKS 31
BUGGIN *Above hit: TRUE STEPPERS featuring Dane BOWERS from ANOTHER LEVEL.*	*NuLife*	6	*29 Apr 00*	8
OUT OF YOUR MIND *Above hit: TRUE STEPPERS and Dane BOWERS featuring Victoria BECKHAM.*	*NuLife*	2	*26 Aug 00*	16
TRUE STEP TONIGHT *Above hit: TRUE STEPPERS featuring Brian HARVEY and Donell JONES.*	*NuLife*	25	*2 Dec 00*	3
OUT OF YOUR MIND [RE]	*NuLife*	58	*6 Jan 01*	4

Damon TRUEITT - See SOMORE featuring Damon TRUEITT

TRUMAN and WOLFF featuring STEEL HORSES — UK

SINGLES:	HITS 1			WEEKS 1
COME AGAIN	*Multiply*	57	*22 Aug 98*	1

TRUMPET MAN - See MONTANO vs the TRUMPET MAN

TRUSSEL — US

SINGLES:	HITS 1			WEEKS 4
LOVE INJECTION	*Elektra*	43	*8 Mar 80*	4

TRUTH — UK

SINGLES:	HITS 1			WEEKS 6
GIRL *Originally recorded by the Beatles.*	*Pye*	27	*5 Feb 66*	6

TRUTH — UK

SINGLES:	HITS 3			WEEKS 16
CONFUSION (HITS US EVERYTIME)	*Formation*	22	*11 Jun 83*	7
A STEP IN THE RIGHT DIRECTION	*Formation*	32	*27 Aug 83*	7
NO STONE UNTURNED	*Formation*	66	*4 Feb 84*	2

TSD — UK

SINGLES:	HITS 2			WEEKS 2
HEART & SOUL	*Avex UK*	69	*17 Feb 96*	1
BABY I LOVE YOU	*Avex UK*	64	*30 Mar 96*	1

T2 featuring Robin S — US

(See also Robin S.)

SINGLES:	HITS 1			WEEKS 1
YOU GOT THE LOVE	*Champion*	62	*4 Oct 97*	1

Esera TUAOLO - See Richie RICH

TUBES — US

SINGLES:	HITS 3			WEEKS 18
WHITE PUNKS ON DOPE	*A&M*	28	*19 Nov 77*	4
PRIME TIME	*A&M*	34	*28 Apr 79*	10
DON'T WANT TO WAIT ANYMORE	*Capitol*	60	*12 Sep 81*	4
ALBUMS:	**HITS 3**			**WEEKS 7**
WHAT DO YOU WANT FROM LIFE	*A&M*	38	*4 Mar 78*	1
Live recordings.				
REMOTE CONTROL	*A&M*	40	*2 Jun 79*	5
OUTSIDE INSIDE	*Capitol*	77	*4 Jun 83*	1

TUBEWAY ARMY - See Gary NUMAN

Barbara TUCKER — US

(See also B-Crew featuring Barbara Tucker, Ultra Nate, Dajae, Mone.)

SINGLES:	HITS 5			WEEKS 12
BEAUTIFUL PEOPLE	*Positiva*	23	*5 Mar 94*	3
Backing vocals from Byron Stingley of Ten City, Michael Watford and India.				
I GET LIFTED	*Positiva*	33	*26 Nov 94*	2
STAY TOGETHER	*Positiva*	46	*23 Sep 95*	1
EVERYBODY DANCE (THE HORN SONG)	*Positiva*	28	*8 Aug 98*	2
STOP PLAYING WITH MY MIND	*Positiva*	17	*18 Mar 00*	4
Above hit: Barbara TUCKER featuring Darryl D'BONNEAU.				

Junior TUCKER — UK

SINGLES:	HITS 1			WEEKS 2
DON'T TEST	*10 Records*	54	*2 Jun 90*	2

Louise TUCKER - See MIDNIGHT BLUE (A project with) Louise TUCKER

Tommy TUCKER — US

SINGLES:	HITS 1			WEEKS 10
HI-HEEL SNEEKERS	*Pye*	23	*28 Mar 64*	10

TUFF JAM — UK

SINGLES:	HITS 1			WEEKS 1
NEED GOOD LOVE	*Locked On*	44	*10 Oct 98*	1

TUKAN — Holland/Slovakia

SINGLES:	HITS 1			WEEKS 3
LIGHT A RAINBOW	*Incentive*	38	*15 Dec 01*	3

TULANE SISTERS - See Mitchell TOROK

TURIN BREAKS — UK

SINGLES:	HITS 4			WEEKS 6
THE DOOR	*Source*	67	*3 Mar 01*	1
UNDERDOG (SAVE ME)	*Source*	39	*12 May 01*	2
MIND OVER MONEY	*Source*	31	*11 Aug 01*	2
72	*Source*	41	*27 Oct 01*	1
ALBUMS:	**HITS 1**			**WEEKS 18**
THE OPTIMIST LP	*Source*	27	*17 Mar 01*	18

Ike and Tina TURNER — US

(See also Tina Turner.)

SINGLES:	HITS 4			WEEKS 44
RIVER DEEP - MOUNTAIN HIGH	*London*	3	*11 Jun 66*	13
TELL HER I'M NOT HOME	*Warner Brothers*	48	*30 Jul 66*	1
A LOVE LIKE YOURS	*London*	16	*29 Oct 66*	10
Originally recorded by Martha Reeves and the Vandellas.				
RIVER DEEP MOUNTAIN HIGH [RI]	*London*	33	*15 Feb 69*	7

NUTBUSH CITY LIMITS	*United Artists*	4	*8 Sep 73*	13

ALBUMS:	**HITS 1**			**WEEKS 1**
RIVER DEEP - MOUNTAIN HIGH	*London*	27	*1 Oct 66*	1

Ruby TURNER — UK

SINGLES:	**HITS 7**			**WEEKS 31**
IF YOU'RE READY (COME GO WITH ME)	*Jive*	30	*25 Jan 86*	7
Above hit: Ruby TURNER featuring Jonathan BUTLER.				
I'M IN LOVE	*Jive*	61	*29 Mar 86*	4
BYE BABY	*Jive*	52	*13 Sep 86*	3
I'D RATHER GO BLIND	*Jive*	24	*14 Mar 87*	8
Originally recorded by Etta James.				
I'M IN LOVE [RI]	*Jive*	57	*16 May 87*	2
IT'S GONNA BE ALRIGHT	*Jive*	57	*13 Jan 90*	3
STAY WITH ME BABY	*M&G*	39	*5 Feb 94*	3
Theme from the Channel 4 TV series 'Comics'. Originally recorded by Lorraine Ellison in 1966.				
SHAKABOOM!	*Telstar*	64	*9 Dec 95*	1
Featured on 'Junior Gladiators' from TV's 'Scratchy And Co.'.				
Above hit: HUNTER featuring Ruby TURNER.				

ALBUMS:	**HITS 3**			**WEEKS 19**
WOMEN HOLD UP HALF THE SKY	*Jive*	47	*18 Oct 86*	11
THE MOTOWN SONG BOOK	*Jive*	22	*8 Oct 88*	6
PARADISE	*Jive*	74	*17 Feb 90*	2

Sammy TURNER — US

SINGLES:	**HITS 1**			**WEEKS 2**
ALWAYS	*London*	26	*14 Nov 59*	2

Tina TURNER — US

(See also Ike and Tina Turner.)

SINGLES:	**HITS 36**			**WEEKS 224**
LET'S STAY TOGETHER	*Capitol*	6	*19 Nov 83*	13
HELP	*Capitol*	40	*25 Feb 84*	6
WHAT'S LOVE GOT TO DO WITH IT	*Capitol*	3	*16 Jun 84*	16
BETTER BE GOOD TO ME	*Capitol*	45	*15 Sep 84*	5
PRIVATE DANCER	*Capitol*	26	*17 Nov 84*	9
Written by Mark Knopfler and features Jeff Beck on guitar.				
I CAN'T STAND THE RAIN	*Capitol*	57	*2 Mar 85*	3
Original by Ann Peebles reached No. 38 in the US in 1973				
WE DON'T NEED ANOTHER HERO (THUNDERDOME)	*Capitol*	3	*20 Jul 85*	12
From the film 'Mad Max: Beyond Thunderdome'.				
ONE OF THE LIVING	*Capitol*	55	*12 Oct 85*	2
IT'S ONLY LOVE	*A&M*	29	*2 Nov 85*	6
Above hit: Bryan ADAMS and Tina TURNER.				
TYPICAL MALE	*Capitol*	33	*23 Aug 86*	6
TWO PEOPLE	*Capitol*	43	*8 Nov 86*	4
WHAT YOU GET IS WHAT YOU SEE	*Capitol*	30	*14 Mar 87*	7
BREAK EVERY RULE	*Capitol*	43	*13 Jun 87*	3
TEARING US APART	*Duck*	56	*20 Jun 87*	3
Above hit: Eric CLAPTON and Tina TURNER.				
ADDICTED TO LOVE (LIVE)	*Capitol*	71	*19 Mar 88*	2
THE BEST	*Capitol*	5	*2 Sep 89*	12
Edgar Winter on sax, originally recorded by Bonnie Tyler.				
I DON'T WANNA LOSE YOU	*Capitol*	8	*18 Nov 89*	11
STEAMY WINDOWS	*Capitol*	13	*17 Feb 90*	6
Originally recorded by Tony Joe White.				
LOOK ME IN THE HEART	*Capitol*	31	*11 Aug 90*	6
BE TENDER WITH ME BABY	*Capitol*	28	*13 Oct 90*	4
IT TAKES TWO	*Warner Brothers*	5	*24 Nov 90*	8
Above hit: Rod STEWART and Tina TURNER.				
NUTBUSH CITY LIMITS (THE 90'S VERSION)	*Capitol*	23	*21 Sep 91*	5
WAY OF THE WORLD	*Capitol*	13	*23 Nov 91*	7
LOVE THING	*Capitol*	29	*15 Feb 92*	4
I WANT YOU NEAR ME	*Capitol*	22	*6 Jun 92*	4
I DON'T WANNA FIGHT	*Parlophone*	7	*22 May 93*	9
Originally recorded by Lulu.				
DISCO INFERNO	*Parlophone*	12	*28 Aug 93*	6
WHY MUST WE WAIT UNTIL TONIGHT	*Parlophone*	16	*30 Oct 93*	4
Above 3 from the film 'What's Love Got To Do With It'.				
GOLDENEYE	*Parlophone*	10	*18 Nov 95*	9
From the James Bond film of the same name.				
WHATEVER YOU WANT	*Parlophone*	23	*23 Mar 96*	6
ON SILENT WINGS	*Parlophone*	13	*8 Jun 96*	6
Features backing vocals by Sting.				
MISSING YOU	*Parlophone*	12	*27 Jul 96*	5
SOMETHING BEAUTIFUL REMAINS	*Parlophone*	27	*19 Oct 96*	2

IN YOUR WILDEST DREAMS	*Parlophone*	32	*21 Dec 96*	3
Above hit: Tina TURNER featuring Barry WHITE.				
WHEN THE HEARTACHE IS OVER	*Parlophone*	10	*30 Oct 99*	7
WHATEVER YOU NEED	*Parlophone*	27	*12 Feb 00*	3
Above 2: TINA.				
ALBUMS:	**HITS 8**			**WEEKS 521**
PRIVATE DANCER	*Capitol*	2	*30 Jun 84*	147
Includes re-entries through to 1990.				
BREAK EVERY RULE	*Capitol*	2	*20 Sep 86*	49
LIVE IN EUROPE	*Capitol*	8	*2 Apr 88*	13
Live recordings from the European leg of her world tour, 1987.				
FOREIGN AFFAIR	*Capitol*	1	*30 Sep 89*	78
SIMPLY THE BEST	*Capitol*	2	*12 Oct 91*	141
Compilation. Includes re-entries through to 1997.				
WHAT'S LOVE GOT TO DO WITH IT [OST]	*Parlophone*	1	*19 Jun 93*	33
WILDEST DREAMS	*Parlophone*	4	*13 Apr 96*	41
TWENTY FOUR SEVEN	*Parlophone*	9	*13 Nov 99*	19

TURNTABLE ORCHESTRA — US

SINGLES:	**HITS 1**			**WEEKS 4**
YOU'RE GONNA MISS ME	*Republic*	52	*21 Jan 89*	4

TURTLES — US

SINGLES:	**HITS 3**			**WEEKS 39**
HAPPY TOGETHER	*London*	12	*25 Mar 67*	12
SHE'D RATHER BE WITH ME	*London*	4	*17 Jun 67*	15
ELENORE	*London*	7	*2 Nov 68*	12
ALBUMS:	**HITS 1**			**WEEKS 9**
HAPPY TOGETHER	*London*	18	*22 Jul 67*	9

TWA featuring LADY JOJO, Queen of the GoGo — UK

SINGLES:	**HITS 1**			**WEEKS 1**
NASTY GIRLS	*Mercury*	51	*16 Sep 95*	1

Shania TWAIN — Canada

SINGLES:	**HITS 6**			**WEEKS 72**
YOU'RE STILL THE ONE	*Mercury*	10	*28 Feb 98*	10
WHEN	*Mercury*	18	*13 Jun 98*	4
FROM THIS MOMENT ON	*Mercury*	9	*28 Nov 98*	8
Features the Brooklyn Philharmonic Orchestra.				
THAT DON'T IMPRESS ME MUCH	*Mercury*	3	*22 May 99*	21
MAN! I FEEL LIKE A WOMAN!	*Mercury*	3	*2 Oct 99*	18
DON'T BE STUPID (YOU KNOW I LOVE YOU)	*Mercury*	5	*26 Feb 00*	9
The B-side to Man I Feel Like A Woman!				
DON'T BE STUPID (YOU KNOW I LOVE YOU) [RE]	*Mercury*	60	*13 May 00*	2
ALBUMS:	**HITS 3**			**WEEKS 155**
COME ON OVER	*Mercury*	15	*21 Mar 98*	36
COME ON OVER [RE]	*Mercury*	1	*17 Apr 99*	92
From 5 Jun 99 re-released with additional track. Peak position reached on 11 Sep 99.				
THE WOMAN IN ME	*Mercury*	7	*18 Mar 00*	25
WILD & WICKED	*RWP*	62	*15 Jul 00*	2

TWEENIES — UK

SINGLES:	**HITS 4**			**WEEKS 44**
NO.1	*BBC Music*	5	*11 Nov 00*	18
NO.1 [RE]	*BBC Music*	72	*24 Mar 01*	5
BEST FRIENDS FOREVER	*BBC Music*	12	*31 Mar 01*	7
BEST FRIENDS FOREVER [RE]	*BBC Music*	56	*26 May 01*	3
DO THE LOLLIPOP	*BBC Music*	17	*4 Aug 01*	8
I BELIEVE IN CHRISTMAS	*BBC Music*	9	*15 Dec 01*	3
ALBUMS:	**HITS 2**			**WEEKS 9**
FRIENDS FOREVER	*BBC Music*	56	*25 Nov 00*	4
THE CHRISTMAS ALBUM	*BBC Music*	34	*1 Dec 01*	5

TWEETS — UK

SINGLES:	**HITS 2**			**WEEKS 34**
BIRDIE SONG (BIRDIE DANCE)	*PRT*	2	*12 Sep 81*	23
Originally recorded by Cash And Carry with Bobby Setter & Co as 'Tchip Tchip'. Certain copies were released with title reflecting only Birdie Song.				
LET'S ALL SING LIKE THE BIRDIES SING	*PRT*	44	*5 Dec 81*	6
BIRDIE SONG (BIRDIE DANCE) [RE]	*PRT*	46	*18 Dec 82*	5

TWELFTH NIGHT — UK

ALBUMS:	HITS 1			WEEKS 2
ART AND ILLUSION	*Music For Nations*	83	*27 Oct 84*	2

20 FINGERS — US

SINGLES:	HITS 2			WEEKS 14
SHORT DICK MAN	*Multiply*	21	*26 Nov 94*	4
SHORT SHORT MAN [RM]	*Multiply*	11	*30 Sep 95*	7
Remixed by Strike.				
Above 2: 20 FINGERS featuring GILLETTE.				
LICK IT	*ZYX*	48	*30 Sep 95*	3
Above hit: 20 FINGERS featuring ROULA.				

21ST CENTURY GIRLS — UK

SINGLES:	HITS 1			WEEKS 4
21ST CENTURY GIRLS	*19 Recordings*	16	*12 Jun 99*	4

TWENTY 4 SEVEN featuring CAPTAIN HOLLYWOOD — Germany/US

(See also Captain Hollywood Project.)

SINGLES:	HITS 2			WEEKS 20
I CAN'T STAND IT	*BCM*	7	*22 Sep 90*	10
ARE YOU DREAMING?	*BCM*	17	*24 Nov 90*	10
ALBUMS:	**HITS 1**			**WEEKS 2**
STREET MOVES	*BCM*	69	*19 Jan 91*	2

TWICE AS MUCH — UK

SINGLES:	HITS 1			WEEKS 9
SITTIN' ON A FENCE	*Immediate*	25	*18 Jun 66*	9

TWIGGY — UK

SINGLES:	HITS 1			WEEKS 10
HERE I GO AGAIN	*Mercury*	17	*14 Aug 76*	10
ALBUMS:	**HITS 2**			**WEEKS 11**
TWIGGY	*Mercury*	33	*21 Aug 76*	8
PLEASE GET MY NAME RIGHT	*Mercury*	35	*30 Apr 77*	3

TWILIGHT – See Roger SANCHEZ

TWIN HYPE — US

SINGLES:	HITS 1			WEEKS 2
DO IT TO THE CROWD	*Profile*	65	*15 Jul 89*	2

TWINKLE — UK

SINGLES:	HITS 2			WEEKS 20
TERRY	*Decca*	4	*28 Nov 64*	15
GOLDEN LIGHTS	*Decca*	21	*27 Feb 65*	5

TWISTED SISTER — US

SINGLES:	HITS 5			WEEKS 28
I AM (I'M ME)	*Atlantic*	18	*26 Mar 83*	9
THE KIDS ARE BACK	*Atlantic*	32	*28 May 83*	6
YOU CAN'T STOP ROCK 'N' ROLL	*Atlantic*	43	*20 Aug 83*	4
WE'RE NOT GONNA TAKE IT	*Atlantic*	58	*2 Jun 84*	6
LEADER OF THE PACK	*Atlantic*	47	*18 Jan 86*	3
ALBUMS:	**HITS 5**			**WEEKS 20**
UNDER THE BLADE	*Secret*	70	*25 Sep 82*	3
YOU CAN'T STOP ROCK 'N' ROLL	*Atlantic*	14	*7 May 83*	9
STAY HUNGRY	*Atlantic*	34	*16 Jun 84*	5
COME OUT AND PLAY	*Atlantic*	95	*14 Dec 85*	1
LOVE IS FOR SUCKERS	*Atlantic*	57	*25 Jul 87*	2

Conway TWITTY — US

SINGLES:	HITS 5			WEEKS 36
IT'S ONLY MAKE BELIEVE	*MGM*	1	*15 Nov 58*	15
THE STORY OF MY LOVE	*MGM*	30	*28 Mar 59*	1
MONA LISA	*MGM*	5	*22 Aug 59*	14
IS A BLUE BIRD BLUE	*MGM*	43	*23 Jul 60*	3
C'EST SI BON (IT'S SO GOOD)	*MGM*	40	*25 Feb 61*	3
Originally recorded by Danny Kaye in 1950.				

2 BAD MICE — UK

SINGLES:	HITS 2			WEEKS 4
HOLD IT DOWN	*Moving Shadow*	70	*15 Feb 92*	1
HOLD IT DOWN [RE]	*Moving Shadow*	48	*8 Aug 92*	2
BOMBSCARE	*Arista*	46	*7 Sep 96*	1

Vocals by Lady Mouse Brucella.

TWO COWBOYS — Italy

SINGLES:	HITS 1			WEEKS 11
EVERYBODY GONFI GON	*3 Beat*	7	*9 Jul 94*	11

2 EIVISSA — Germany

SINGLES:	HITS 1			WEEKS 6
OH LA LA LA	*Club Tools*	13	*4 Oct 97*	6

Samples Crystal Waters' Gypsy Woman.

2 FOR JOY — UK

SINGLES:	HITS 2			WEEKS 3
IN A STATE	*Mercury*	61	*1 Dec 90*	1
Above hit: 2 FOR JOY featuring Addell BENJAMIN.				
LET THE BASS KICK	*All Around The World*	67	*9 Nov 91*	2

2-4 FAMILY — UK/US/Korea

SINGLES:	HITS 1			WEEKS 1
LEAN ON ME (WITH THE FAMILY)	*Epic*	69	*29 May 99*	1

2 FUNKY 2 featuring Kathryn DION — UK

SINGLES:	HITS 1			WEEKS 4
BROTHERS AND SISTERS	*Logic*	56	*6 Nov 93*	2
Above hit: 2 FUNKY 2 starring Kathryn DION.				
BROTHERS AND SISTERS [RM]	*All Around The World*	36	*30 Nov 96*	2

Remixed by the Porn Kings.

2 HOUSE — US

SINGLES:	HITS 1			WEEKS 1
GO TECHNO	*Atlantic*	65	*21 Mar 92*	1

2 IN A ROOM — US

SINGLES:	HITS 6			WEEKS 15
SOMEBODY IN THE HOUSE SAY YEAH!	*Big Life*	66	*18 Nov 89*	1
WIGGLE IT	*SBK*	3	*26 Jan 91*	8
SHE'S GOT ME GOING CRAZY	*SBK*	54	*6 Apr 91*	2
EL TRAGO (THE DRINK)	*Positiva*	34	*22 Oct 94*	2
AHORA ES (NOW IS THE TIME)	*Positiva*	43	*8 Apr 95*	1
GIDDY-UP	*Encore*	74	*17 Aug 96*	1
ALBUMS:	**HITS 1**			**WEEKS 1**
WIGGLE IT	*SBK*	73	*2 Mar 91*	1

2 IN A TENT — UK

SINGLES:	HITS 2			WEEKS 7
WHEN I'M CLEANING WINDOWS (TURNED OUT NICE AGAIN)	*Silly Money*	25	*17 Dec 94*	5
Samples George Formby's 1936 recording of the song.				
BOOGIE WOOGIE BUGLE BOY (DON'T STOP)	*Bald Cat*	48	*13 May 95*	1
Marrying together recordings from the Andrew Sisters with the Outhere Brothers.				
Above hit: 2 IN A TANK.				
WHEN I'M CLEANING WINDOWS (TURNED OUT NICE AGAIN) [RE]	*Silly Money*	62	*6 Jan 96*	1

2 MAD — UK

SINGLES:	HITS 1			WEEKS 4
THINKIN' ABOUT YOUR BODY	*Big Life*	43	*9 Feb 91*	4

TWO MAN SOUND — Belgium

SINGLES:	HITS 1			WEEKS 7
QUE TAL AMERICA	*Miracle/Gull*	46	*20 Jan 79*	7

TWO MEN, A DRUM MACHINE AND A TRUMPET — UK

SINGLES:	HITS 2			WEEKS 17
I'M TIRED OF GETTING PUSHED AROUND	*London*	18	*9 Jan 88*	8
The label credits act as Two Guys, while the sleeve credits Two Men.				
HEAT IT UP	*Jive*	21	*25 Jun 88*	9

Above hit: WEE PAPA GIRL RAPPERS featuring TWO MEN AND A DRUM MACHINE.

TWO NATIONS — UK

SINGLES:	HITS 1			WEEKS 1
THAT'S THE WAY IT FEELS	*10 Records*	74	*20 Jun 87*	1

TWO PEOPLE — UK

SINGLES:	HITS 1			WEEKS 2
HEAVEN	*Polydor*	63	*31 Jan 87*	2

2WO THIRD3 — UK

SINGLES:	HITS 4			WEEKS 15
HEAR ME CALLING	*Epic*	48	*19 Feb 94*	3
EASE THE PRESSURE	*Epic*	45	*11 Jun 94*	2
I WANT THE WORLD *Backing vocals by Helen Terry.*	*Epic*	20	*8 Oct 94*	5
I WANT TO BE ALONE	*Epic*	29	*17 Dec 94*	5

2 UNLIMITED — Holland

SINGLES:	HITS 14			WEEKS 112
GET READY FOR THIS	*PWL Continental*	2	*5 Oct 91*	15
TWILIGHT ZONE	*PWL Continental*	2	*25 Jan 92*	10
WORKAHOLIC	*PWL Continental*	4	*2 May 92*	7
THE MAGIC FRIEND	*PWL Continental*	11	*15 Aug 92*	7
NO LIMIT	*PWL Continental*	1	*30 Jan 93*	16
TRIBAL DANCE	*PWL Continental*	4	*8 May 93*	11
FACES	*PWL Continental*	8	*4 Sep 93*	7
MAXIMUM OVERDRIVE	*PWL Continental*	15	*20 Nov 93*	8
LET THE BEAT CONTROL YOUR BODY	*PWL Continental*	6	*19 Feb 94*	9
THE REAL THING	*PWL Continental*	6	*21 May 94*	7
NO ONE	*PWL Continental*	17	*1 Oct 94*	6
HERE I GO	*PWL Continental*	22	*25 Mar 95*	3
DO WHAT'S GOOD FOR ME	*PWL Continental*	16	*21 Oct 95*	4
WANNA GET UP	*Big Life*	38	*11 Jul 98*	2
ALBUMS:	**HITS 4**			**WEEKS 38**
GET READY	*PWL Continental*	37	*7 Mar 92*	3
NO LIMITS	*PWL Continental*	1	*22 May 93*	21
REAL THINGS	*PWL Continental*	1	*18 Jun 94*	9
HITS UNLIMITED	*PWL International*	27	*11 Nov 95*	5

2K — UK

(See also Justified Ancients Of Mu Mu; KLF; Timelords.)

SINGLES:	HITS 1			WEEKS 2
***K THE MILLENNIUM *Samples The KLF's Kick Out The Jams and Isaac Hayes' Theme From Shaft.*	*Blast First*	28	*25 Oct 97*	2

2PAC — US

SINGLES:	HITS 15			WEEKS 75
CALIFORNIA LOVE *Samples Roger's So Ruff So Tuff and Joe Cocker's Woman To Woman.* *Above hit: 2PAC featuring DR DRE.*	*Death Row*	6	*13 Apr 96*	8
HOW DO YOU WANT IT *Samples Body Heat by Quincy Jones.* *Above hit: 2PAC (featuring KC and JOJO).*	*Death Row*	17	*27 Jul 96*	4
I AIN'T MAD AT CHA	*Death Row*	13	*30 Nov 96*	9
TO LIVE & DIE IN LA *Above hit: MAKAVELI (2 PAC is MAKAVELI).*	*Interscope*	10	*12 Apr 97*	4
WANTED DEAD OR ALIVE *From the film 'Gridlock'd'.* *Above hit: 2 PAC and SNOOP DOGGY DOGG.*	*Def Jam*	16	*26 Apr 97*	3
TOSS IT UP *Above hit: MAKAVELI.*	*Interscope*	15	*9 Aug 97*	3
I WONDER IF HEAVEN GOT A GHETTO *Vocals by Charmayne Maxee of Brownstone. Samples Cameo's The Two Of Us.*	*Jive*	21	*10 Jan 98*	4
HAIL MARY *Above hit: MAKAVELI.*	*Interscope*	43	*14 Feb 98*	1
DO FOR LOVE *Samples Bobby Caldwell's What You Can't Do For Love.* *Above hit: 2PAC featuring Eric WILLIAMS of BLACKSTREET.*	*Jive*	12	*13 Jun 98*	4
RUNNIN' *Originally recorded in 1995.* *Above hit: 2PAC and NOTORIOUS B.I.G.*	*Black Jam*	15	*18 Jul 98*	3
HAPPY HOME	*Eagle*	17	*28 Nov 98*	2
CHANGES *Samples Bruce Hornsby And The Range's The Way It Is.*	*Jive*	3	*20 Feb 99*	12

DEAR MAMA	*Jive*	27	*3 Jul 99*	3
Tribute to his mother Afeni Shakur.				
UNTIL THE END OF TIME	*Interscope*	4	*23 Jun 01*	11
Samples Mr. Mister's Broken Wings.				
Above hit: 2PAC featuring R.L.				
LETTER 2 MY UNBORN	*Interscope*	21	*10 Nov 01*	5
ALBUMS:	**HITS 7**			**WEEKS 61**
ALL EYEZ ON ME	*Death Row*	32	*9 Mar 96*	5
THE DON KILLUMINATI - THE SEVEN DAY THEORY	*Death Row*	53	*16 Nov 96*	1
Above hit: MAKAVELI.				
R U STILL DOWN? (REMEMBER ME)	*Jive*	44	*6 Dec 97*	1
Album of previously unreleased songs.				
IN HIS OWN WORDS	*Eagle*	65	*8 Aug 98*	1
Consists of studio interviews at KMEL Radio.				
GREATEST HITS	*Jive*	17	*12 Dec 98*	35
STILL I RISE	*Interscope*	75	*8 Jan 00*	1
Above hit: 2PAC and the OUTLAWZ				
UNTIL THE END OF TIME	*Interscope*	31	*21 Apr 01*	17

Tommy TYCHO - See David GRAY and Tommy TYCHO

TYGERS OF PAN TANG — UK

SINGLES:	**HITS 4**			**WEEKS 15**
HELLBOUND	*MCA*	48	*14 Feb 81*	3
LOVE POTION NO. 9	*MCA*	45	*27 Mar 82*	6
Original by the Clovers reached No. 23 in the US in 1959.				
RENDEZVOUS	*MCA*	49	*10 Jul 82*	4
PARIS BY AIR	*MCA*	63	*11 Sep 82*	2
ALBUMS:	**HITS 4**			**WEEKS 20**
WILD CAT	*MCA*	18	*30 Aug 80*	5
SPELLBOUND	*MCA*	33	*18 Apr 81*	4
CRAZY NIGHTS	*MCA*	51	*21 Nov 81*	3
THE CAGE	*MCA*	13	*28 Aug 82*	8

Bonnie TYLER — UK

SINGLES:	**HITS 11**			**WEEKS 82**
LOST IN FRANCE	*RCA Victor*	9	*30 Oct 76*	11
MORE THAN A LOVER	*RCA Victor*	27	*19 Mar 77*	6
IT'S A HEARTACHE	*RCA Victor*	4	*3 Dec 77*	12
Features Mike Gibbins from Badfinger on drums.				
Above hit: Bonnie TYLER and the Bonnie TYLER BAND.				
MARRIED MEN	*RCA Victor*	35	*30 Jun 79*	6
From the film 'The World Is Full Of Married Men'.				
TOTAL ECLIPSE OF THE HEART	*CBS*	1	*19 Feb 83*	12
Male vocalist is Rory Dodd.				
FASTER THAN THE SPEED OF LIGHT	*CBS*	43	*7 May 83*	4
HAVE YOU EVER SEEN THE RAIN	*CBS*	47	*25 Jun 83*	3
A ROCKIN' GOOD WAY	*Epic*	5	*7 Jan 84*	9
Originally recorded by Priscilla Bowman.				
Above hit: SHAKY and BONNIE.				
HOLDING OUT FOR A HERO	*CBS*	2	*31 Aug 85*	13
From the film 'Footloose'. Original release reached No. 96 in 1984.				
LOVING YOU'S A DIRTY JOB BUT SOMEBODY'S GOTTA DO IT	*CBS*	73	*14 Dec 85*	2
Above hit: Bonnie TYLER, guest vocalist Todd RUNDGREN.				
HOLDING OUT FOR A HERO [RI]	*Total*	69	*28 Dec 91*	2
MAKING LOVE (OUT OF NOTHING AT ALL)	*East West*	45	*27 Jan 96*	2
Original by Air Supply reached No. 2 in the US in 1983.				
ALBUMS:	**HITS 5**			**WEEKS 79**
COMPILATION ALBUMS:	**HITS 1**			**WEEKS 16**
FASTER THAN THE SPEED OF NIGHT	*CBS*	1	*16 Apr 83*	45
SECRET DREAMS AND FORBIDDEN FIRE	*CBS*	24	*17 May 86*	12
THE GREATEST HITS	*Telstar*	24	*29 Nov 86*	17
HIDE YOUR HEART	*CBS*	78	*21 May 88*	1
HEAVEN AND HELL	*Telstar*	9	*25 Nov 89*	12
Features solo recordings by each artist and was thus an entry in the compilation chart.				
Above hit: MEAT LOAF/Bonnie TYLER.				
HEAVEN AND HELL [RI]	*Columbia*	12	*16 Sep 95*	4
THE GREATEST HITS	*Sanctuary*	18	*14 Jul 01*	4

TYMES — US

SINGLES:	**HITS 5**			**WEEKS 41**
SO MUCH IN LOVE	*Cameo-Parkway*	21	*27 Jul 63*	8
PEOPLE	*Direction*	16	*18 Jan 69*	10
From the film 'Funny Girl'.				
YOU LITTLE TRUSTMAKER	*RCA Victor*	18	*21 Sep 74*	9

M/S GRACE	*RCA Victor*	1	*21 Dec 74*	11
GOD'S GONNA PUNISH YOU	*RCA Victor*	41	*17 Jan 76*	3

TYMES 4 — UK

SINGLES:	HITS 2			WEEKS 5
BODYROCK	*Edel*	23	*25 Aug 01*	3
SHE GOT GAME	*Edel*	40	*15 Dec 01*	2

TYPE O NEGATIVE — US

ALBUMS:	HITS 2			WEEKS 2
OCTOBER RUST	*Roadrunner*	26	*14 Sep 96*	1
WORLD COMING DOWN	*Roadrunner*	49	*2 Oct 99*	1

TYPICALLY TROPICAL — UK

SINGLES:	HITS 1			WEEKS 11
BARBADOS	*Gull*	1	*5 Jul 75*	11

TYRANNOSAURUS REX - See T. REX

TYREE — US

SINGLES:	HITS 3			WEEKS 10
TURN UP THE BASS	*ffrr*	12	*25 Feb 89*	7
Above hit: TYREE Rap by KOOL ROCK STEADY.				
HARDCORE HIP HOUSE	*DJ International*	70	*6 May 89*	2
MOVE YOUR BODY	*DJ International*	72	*2 Dec 89*	1
Above hit: TYREE featuring J.M.D.				

TYRESE — US

SINGLES:	HITS 2			WEEKS 2
NOBODY ELSE	*RCA*	59	*31 Jul 99*	1
SWEET LADY	*RCA*	55	*25 Sept 99*	1

TYRREL CORPORATION — UK

SINGLES:	HITS 5			WEEKS 9
THE BOTTLE	*Volante*	71	*14 Mar 92*	1
GOING HOME	*Volante*	58	*15 Aug 92*	2
WAKING WITH A STRANGER / ONE DAY	*Volante*	59	*10 Oct 92*	1
YOU'RE NOT HERE	*Cooltempo*	42	*24 Sep 94*	2
Backing vocals by Juliet Roberts				
BETTER DAYS AHEAD	*Cooltempo*	29	*14 Jan 95*	3

TZANT — UK

SINGLES:	HITS 3			WEEKS 10
HOT & WET (BELIEVE IT)	*Logic*	36	*7 Sep 96*	2
SOUNDS OF WICKEDNESS	*Logic*	11	*25 Apr 98*	6
Above hit: TZANT featuring the ORIGINAL ODC MC.				
BOUNCE WITH THE MASSIVE	*Logic*	39	*22 Aug 98*	2

Judie TZUKE — UK

SINGLES:	HITS 1			WEEKS 10
STAY WITH ME TILL DAWN	*Rocket*	16	*14 Jul 79*	10
ALBUMS:	**HITS 8**			**WEEKS 61**
WELCOME TO THE CRUISE	*Rocket*	14	*4 Aug 79*	17
SPORTS CAR	*Rocket*	7	*10 May 80*	11
I AM PHOENIX	*Rocket*	17	*16 May 81*	10
SHOOT THE MOON	*Chrysalis*	19	*17 Apr 82*	10
ROAD NOISE - THE OFFICIAL BOOTLEG	*Chrysalis*	39	*30 Oct 82*	4
RITMO	*Chrysalis*	26	*1 Oct 83*	5
THE CAT IS OUT	*Legacy*	35	*15 Jun 85*	3
TURNING STONES	*Polydor*	57	*29 Apr 89*	1

U

U.C.C. - See URBAN COOKIE COLLECTIVE

U.F.O. — UK/Germany

SINGLES:	HITS 7			WEEKS 31
ONLY YOU CAN ROCK ME	*Chrysalis*	50	*5 Aug 78*	4
DOCTOR DOCTOR	*Chrysalis*	35	*27 Jan 79*	6
SHOOT, SHOOT	*Chrysalis*	48	*31 Mar 79*	5
Above 2 are live recordings. The studio recording of Doctor Doctor was originally released in 1974.				

YOUNG BLOOD	*Chrysalis*	36	*12 Jan 80*	5
Produced by George Martin.				
LONELY HEART	*Chrysalis*	41	*17 Jan 81*	5
LET IT RAIN	*Chrysalis*	62	*30 Jan 82*	3
WHEN IT'S TIME TO ROCK	*Chrysalis*	70	*19 Mar 83*	3

ALBUMS: **HITS 9** **WEEKS 48**

LIGHTS OUT	*Chrysalis*	54	*4 Jun 77*	2
OBSESSION	*Chrysalis*	26	*15 Jul 78*	7
STRANGERS IN THE NIGHT	*Chrysalis*	8	*10 Feb 79*	11
Live recordings.				
NO PLACE TO RUN	*Chrysalis*	11	*19 Jan 80*	7
THE WILD, THE WILLING AND THE INNOCENT	*Chrysalis*	19	*24 Jan 81*	5
MECHANIX	*Chrysalis*	8	*20 Feb 82*	6
MAKING CONTACT	*Chrysalis*	32	*12 Feb 83*	4
HEADSTONE - THE BEST OF UFO	*Chrysalis*	39	*3 Sep 83*	4
MISDEMEANOR	*Chrysalis*	74	*16 Nov 85*	2

U.H.F. — US

(See also Moby.)

SINGLES: **HITS 1** **WEEKS 4**

U.H.F. / EVERYTHING	*XL Recordings*	46	*14 Dec 91*	4

U.K. — UK

SINGLES: **HITS 1** **WEEKS 2**

NOTHING TO LOSE	*Polydor*	67	*30 Jun 79*	2

ALBUMS: **HITS 1** **WEEKS 3**

U.K.	*Polydor*	43	*27 May 78*	3

U.K. SUBS — UK

SINGLES: **HITS 7** **WEEKS 39**

STRANGLEHOLD	*Gems*	26	*23 Jun 79*	8
TOMORROW'S GIRLS	*Gems*	28	*8 Sep 79*	6
SHE'S NOT THERE/KICKS [EP]	*Gems*	36	*1 Dec 79*	7
Lead track: She's Not There.				
WARHEAD	*Gems*	30	*8 Mar 80*	4
TEENAGE	*Gems*	32	*17 May 80*	5
PARTY IN PARIS	*Gems*	37	*25 Oct 80*	4
KEEP ON RUNNING (TILL YOU BURN)	*Gems*	41	*18 Apr 81*	5

ALBUMS: **HITS 4** **WEEKS 26**

ANOTHER KIND OF BLUES	*Gem*	21	*13 Oct 79*	6
BRAND NEW AGE	*Gem*	18	*19 Apr 80*	9
CRASH COURSE	*Gem*	8	*27 Sep 80*	6
DIMINISHED RESPONSIBILITY	*Gem*	18	*21 Feb 81*	5

U.S.U.R.A. - See USURA

U.T.F.O. — US

ALBUMS: **HITS 1** **WEEKS 1**

ROXANNE ROXANNE (6 TRACK VERSION)	*Streetwave*	72	*16 Mar 85*	1
12" single ineligible for the singles chart.				

UB40 — UK

SINGLES: **HITS 47** **WEEKS 330**

KING / FOOD FOR THOUGHT	*Graduate*	4	*8 Mar 80*	13
King is dedicated to Martin Luther King.				
MY WAY OF THINKING / I THINK IT'S GOING TO RAIN TODAY	*Graduate*	6	*14 Jun 80*	10
I Think It's Going To Rain Today was originally recorded by Randy Newman in 1968.				
Above 2: U.B.40.				
THE EARTH DIES SCREAMING / DREAM A LIE	*Graduate*	10	*1 Nov 80*	12
DON'T LET IT PASS YOU BY / DON'T SLOW DOWN	*DEP International*	16	*23 May 81*	9
ONE IN TEN	*DEP International*	7	*8 Aug 81*	10
Written about the unemployment situation in the UK at the time.				
I WON'T CLOSE MY EYES	*DEP International*	32	*13 Feb 82*	6
LOVE IS ALL IS ALRIGHT	*DEP International*	29	*15 May 82*	7
SO HERE I AM	*DEP International*	25	*28 Aug 82*	9
I'VE GOT MINE	*DEP International*	45	*5 Feb 83*	4
RED RED WINE	*DEP International*	1	*20 Aug 83*	14
Originally recorded by Neil Diamond in 1968.				
PLEASE DON'T MAKE ME CRY	*DEP International*	10	*15 Oct 83*	8
Originally recorded by Winston Groovy.				
MANY RIVERS TO CROSS	*DEP International*	16	*10 Dec 83*	8
Originally recorded by Jimmy Cliff.				
CHERRY OH BABY	*DEP International*	12	*17 Mar 84*	8
Originally recorded by Eric Donaldson.				
IF IT HAPPENS AGAIN	*DEP International*	9	*22 Sep 84*	8

RIDDLE ME	*DEP International*	59	*1 Dec 84*	2
I GOT YOU BABE	*DEP International*	1	*3 Aug 85*	13
Above hit: UB40 Guest vocals by Chrissie HYNDE.				
DON'T BREAK MY HEART	*DEP International*	3	*26 Oct 85*	13
SING OUR OWN SONG	*DEP International*	5	*12 Jul 86*	9
Released to support black activists in South Africa.				
ALL I WANT TO DO	*DEP International*	41	*27 Sep 86*	4
RAT IN MI KITCHEN	*DEP International*	12	*17 Jan 87*	7
WATCHDOGS	*DEP International*	39	*9 May 87*	4
MAYBE TOMORROW	*DEP International*	14	*10 Oct 87*	8
RECKLESS	*EMI*	17	*27 Feb 88*	8
Above hit: Afrika BAMBAATAA and FAMILY featuring UB40.				
BREAKFAST IN BED	*DEP International*	6	*18 Jun 88*	11
Originally recorded by Dusty Springfield.				
Above hit: UB40 with Chrissie HYNDE.				
WHERE DID I GO WRONG	*DEP International*	26	*20 Aug 88*	6
I WOULD DO FOR YOU	*DEP International*	45	*17 Jun 89*	4
HOMELY GIRL	*DEP International*	6	*18 Nov 89*	10
HERE I AM (COME AND TAKE ME)	*DEP International*	46	*27 Jan 90*	3
Original by Al Green reached No. 10 in the US in 1973.				
KINGSTON TOWN	*DEP International*	4	*31 Mar 90*	12
Originally recorded by Lord Creator.				
WEAR YOU TO THE BALL	*DEP International*	35	*28 Jul 90*	6
I'LL BE YOUR BABY TONIGHT	*EMI*	6	*3 Nov 90*	10
Above hit: UB40 PALMER and UB40.				
IMPOSSIBLE LOVE	*DEP International*	47	*1 Dec 90*	2
THE WAY YOU DO THE THINGS YOU DO	*DEP International*	49	*2 Feb 91*	3
Originally recorded by The Temptations.				
ONE IN TEN [RM]	*ZTT*	17	*12 Dec 92*	8
Though classed as a remix by 808 State, they have only utilised the chorus and the saxophone intro.				
Above hit: 808 STATE UB40.				
(I CAN'T HELP) FALLING IN LOVE WITH YOU	*DEP International*	1	*22 May 93*	16
From the film 'Sliver'.				
HIGHER GROUND	*DEP International*	8	*21 Aug 93*	9
BRING ME YOUR CUP	*DEP International*	24	*11 Dec 93*	6
C'EST LA VIE	*DEP International*	37	*2 Apr 94*	3
REGGAE MUSIC	*DEP International*	28	*27 Aug 94*	2
UNTIL MY DYING DAY	*DEP International*	15	*4 Nov 95*	6
TELL ME IS IT TRUE	*DEP International*	14	*30 Aug 97*	4
From the film 'Speed 2'.				
ALWAYS THERE	*DEP International*	53	*15 Nov 97*	1
COME BACK DARLING	*DEP International*	10	*10 Oct 98*	6
Originally recorded by Johnny Osborne in 1969.				
HOLLY HOLY	*DEP International*	31	*19 Dec 98*	3
Original by Neil Diamond reached No. 6 in the US in 1969.				
THE TRAIN IS COMING	*DEP International*	30	*1 May 99*	2
Originally recorded by Ken Boothe in 1973.				
LIGHT MY FIRE	*DEP International*	63	*9 Dec 00*	1
SINCE I MET YOU LADY/SPARKLE OF MY EYES	*DEP International*	40	*20 Oct 01*	2
Since I Met You Lady originally recorded by Ivory Joe Hunter in 1956.				
Above hit: UB40 featuring LADY SAW.				

ALBUMS:	**HITS 19**			**WEEKS 588**
SIGNING OFF	*Graduate*	2	*6 Sep 80*	71
PRESENT ARMS	*DEP International*	2	*6 Jun 81*	38
PRESENT ARMS IN DUB	*DEP International*	38	*10 Oct 81*	7
Reworking of tracks from the last studio album.				
THE SINGLES ALBUM	*Graduate*	17	*28 Aug 82*	8
UB 44	*DEP International*	4	*9 Oct 82*	8
UB40 LIVE	*DEP International*	44	*26 Feb 83*	5
LABOUR OF LOVE	*DEP International*	1	*24 Sep 83*	76
This album plus the later editions consist of cover versions.				
GEFFERY MORGAN . . .	*DEP International*	3	*20 Oct 84*	14
BAGGARIDDIM	*DEP International*	14	*14 Sep 85*	23
Dub versions from the last 2 studio albums.				
RAT IN THE KITCHEN	*DEP International*	8	*9 Aug 86*	20
THE BEST OF UB40 - VOLUME ONE	*DEP International*	3	*7 Nov 87*	132
Includes re-entries through to 1996.				
UB40	*DEP International*	12	*23 Jul 88*	12
LABOUR OF LOVE II	*DEP International*	3	*9 Dec 89*	69
PROMISES AND LIES	*DEP International*	1	*24 Jul 93*	37
LABOUR OF LOVE - VOLUMES I AND II [RI]	*DEP International*	5	*12 Nov 94*	15
Combined repackage of both previous Labour Of Love albums.				
THE BEST OF UB40 - VOLUME TWO	*DEP International*	12	*11 Nov 95*	11
GUNS IN THE GHETTO	*DEP International*	7	*12 Jul 97*	9
LABOUR OF LOVE III	*DEP International*	8	*24 Oct 98*	12
THE VERY BEST OF UB40 1980-2000	*DEP International*	7	*4 Nov 00*	19
COVER UP	*DEP International*	29	*3 Nov 01*	2

UBM — Germany

SINGLES:	HITS 1			WEEKS 1
LOVIN' YOU	*Logic*	46	*23 May 98*	1

U4EA featuring BERRI – See NEW ATLANTIC

UGK – See JAY-Z

UGLY DUCKLING — US

SINGLES:	HITS 1			WEEKS 3
A LITTLE SAMBA	*XL Recordings*	70	*13 Oct 01*	1

UGLY KID JOE — US

SINGLES:	HITS 6			WEEKS 28
EVERYTHING ABOUT YOU	*Mercury*	3	*16 May 92*	9
From the film 'Wayne's World'.				
NEIGHBOR	*Mercury*	28	*22 Aug 92*	4
SO DAMN COOL	*Mercury*	44	*31 Oct 92*	2
CATS IN THE CRADLE	*Mercury*	7	*13 Mar 93*	9
Original by Harry Chapin reached No. 1 in the US in 1974. From the film 'Wayne's World'.				
BUSY BEE	*Mercury*	39	*19 Jun 93*	2
MILKMAN'S SON	*Mercury*	39	*8 Jul 95*	2
ALBUMS:	**HITS 3**			**WEEKS 42**
AS UGLY AS THEY WANNA BE	*Mercury*	9	*13 Jun 92*	13
AMERICA'S LEAST WANTED	*Vertigo*	11	*12 Sep 92*	24
MENACE TO SOBRIETY	*Mercury*	25	*17 Jun 95*	5

UK — Canada/Spain

SINGLES:	HITS 1			WEEKS 1
SMALL TOWN BOY	*Media*	74	*3 Aug 96*	1

UK APACHI with SHY FX — UK

(See also DJ Badmarsh & Shri featuring UK Apache; Shy FX.)

SINGLES:	HITS 1			WEEKS 3
ORIGINAL NUTTAH	*Sound Of Underground*	39	*1 Oct 94*	3
Samples Cypress Hill's I Ain't Going Out Like That and vocal introduction from the film 'Goodfellas'.				

UK MIXMASTERS — UK

SINGLES:	HITS 3			WEEKS 15
THE NIGHT FEVER MEGAMIX [M]	*IQ*	23	*2 Feb 91*	5
Songs from Saturday Night Fever.				
Above hit: MIXMASTERS.				
THE LUCKY 7 MEGAMIX [M]	*IQ*	43	*27 Jul 91*	3
Songs that were hits for Kylie Minogue.				
THE BARE NECESSITIES MEGAMIX [M]	*Connect*	14	*7 Dec 91*	7
Features the songs from The Jungle Book– I Wanna Be Like You and Bare Necessities.				

UK PLAYERS — UK

SINGLES:	HITS 1			WEEKS 3
LOVE'S GONNA GET YOU	*RCA*	52	*14 May 83*	3

Tracey ULLMAN — UK

SINGLES:	HITS 6			WEEKS 49
BREAKAWAY	*Stiff*	4	*19 Mar 83*	11
Originally recorded by Jackie De Shannon.				
THEY DON'T KNOW	*Stiff*	2	*24 Sep 83*	11
Originally recorded by Kirsty MacColl in 1979.				
MOVE OVER DARLING	*Stiff*	8	*3 Dec 83*	9
MY GUY'S MAD AT ME	*Stiff*	23	*3 Mar 84*	6
Cover of Madness' My Girl.				
SUNGLASSES	*Stiff*	18	*28 Jul 84*	9
Originally recorded by John D. Loudermilk.				
HELPLESS	*Stiff*	61	*27 Oct 84*	3
ALBUMS:	**HITS 2**			**WEEKS 22**
YOU BROKE MY HEART IN 17 PLACES	*Stiff*	14	*3 Dec 83*	20
YOU CAUGHT ME OUT	*Stiff*	92	*8 Dec 84*	2

ULTIMATE KAOS — UK

SINGLES:	HITS 6			WEEKS 28
SOME GIRLS	*Wild Card*	9	*22 Oct 94*	8
SOME GIRLS [RE]	*Wild Card*	67	*7 Jan 95*	1
HOOCHIE BOOTY	*Wild Card*	17	*21 Jan 95*	4

SHOW A LITTLE LOVE	*Wild Card*	23	*1 Apr 95*	5
RIGHT HERE	*Wild Card*	18	*1 Jul 95*	4
CASANOVA	*Polydor*	24	*8 Mar 97*	3
CASANOVA [RI]	*Mercury*	29	*18 Jul 98*	2
ANYTHING YOU WANT (I'VE GOT IT)	*Mercury*	52	*5 Jun 99*	1
ALBUMS:	**HITS 1**			**WEEKS 1**
ULTIMATE KAOS	*Wild Card*	51	*29 Apr 95*	1

ULTRA — UK

SINGLES:	**HITS 4**			**WEEKS 22**
SAY YOU DO	*East West*	11	*18 Apr 98*	7
SAY IT ONCE	*East West*	16	*4 Jul 98*	6
THE RIGHT TIME	*East West*	28	*10 Oct 98*	2
THE RIGHT TIME [RE]	*East West*	74	*31 Oct 98*	1
RESCUE ME	*East West*	8	*16 Jan 99*	6
ALBUMS:	**HITS 1**			**WEEKS 2**
ULTRA	*East West*	37	*6 Feb 99*	2

ULTRA HIGH — UK

SINGLES:	**HITS 2**			**WEEKS 3**
STAY WITH ME	*MCA*	36	*2 Dec 95*	2
ARE YOU READY FOR LOVE	*MCA*	45	*20 Jul 96*	1

ULTRA-SONIC — UK

SINGLES:	**HITS 2**			**WEEKS 2**
OBSESSION	*Clubscene*	75	*3 Sep 94*	1
DO YOU BELIEVE IN LOVE	*Clubscene*	47	*21 Sep 96*	1
ALBUMS:	**HITS 1**			**WEEKS 1**
GLOBALTEKNO	*Clubscene*	58	*11 Nov 95*	1

ULTRA VIVID SCENE — US

ALBUMS:	**HITS 1**			**WEEKS 1**
JOY 1967-1990	*4AD*	58	*19 May 90*	1

ULTRACYNIC — UK

SINGLES:	**HITS 1**			**WEEKS 3**
NOTHING IS FOREVER	*380 PEW*	50	*20 Aug 92*	2
NOTHING IS FOREVER [RM]	*All Around The World*	47	*19 Apr 97*	1

Remixed by Ultracynic.

ULTRAMARINE — UK

SINGLES:	**HITS 3**			**WEEKS 4**
KINGDOM	*Blanco Y Negro*	46	*24 Jul 93*	2
BAREFOOT [EP]	*Blanco Y Negro*	61	*29 Jan 94*	1

Lead track: Happy Land, this track and the previous hit feature vocals by Robert Wyatt.

HYMN	*Blanco Y Negro*	65	*27 Apr 96*	1

Above hit: ULTRAMARINE (featuring David McALMONT).

ALBUMS:	**HITS 1**			**WEEKS 1**
UNITED KINGDOMS	*Blanco Y Negro*	49	*4 Sep 93*	1

ULTRASOUND — UK

SINGLES:	**HITS 3**			**WEEKS 5**
BEST WISHES	*Nude*	68	*7 Mar 98*	1
STAY YOUNG	*Nude*	30	*13 Jun 98*	2
FLOODLIT WORLD	*Nude*	39	*10 Apr 99*	2
ALBUMS:	**HITS 1**			**WEEKS 1**
EVERYTHING PICTURE	*Nude*	23	*1 May 99*	1

ULTRAVIBE – See DEAD DRED featuring ASEND and ULTRAVIBE

ULTRAVOX — UK/Canada

(See also Midge Ure.)

SINGLES:	**HITS 17**			**WEEKS 142**
SLEEPWALK	*Chrysalis*	29	*5 Jul 80*	11
PASSING STRANGERS	*Chrysalis*	57	*18 Oct 80*	4
VIENNA	*Chrysalis*	2	*17 Jan 81*	14
SLOW MOTION	*Island*	33	*28 Mar 81*	4

Originally released in 1978.

ALL STOOD STILL	*Chrysalis*	8	*6 Jun 81*	10
THE THIN WALL	*Chrysalis*	14	*22 Aug 81*	8
THE VOICE	*Chrysalis*	16	*7 Nov 81*	12
REAP THE WILD WIND	*Chrysalis*	12	*25 Sep 82*	9

HYMN	*Chrysalis*	11	*27 Nov 82*	11
VISIONS IN BLUE	*Chrysalis*	15	*19 Mar 83*	6
WE CAME TO DANCE	*Chrysalis*	18	*4 Jun 83*	7
Above 4 produced by George Martin.				
ONE SMALL DAY	*Chrysalis*	27	*11 Feb 84*	6
DANCING WITH TEARS IN MY EYES	*Chrysalis*	3	*19 May 84*	10
LAMENT	*Chrysalis*	22	*7 Jul 84*	6
DANCING WITH TEARS IN MY EYES [RE]	*Chrysalis*	74	*4 Aug 84*	1
LAMENT [RE]	*Chrysalis*	73	*25 Aug 84*	1
LOVE'S GREAT ADVENTURE	*Chrysalis*	12	*20 Oct 84*	9
SAME OLD STORY	*Chrysalis*	31	*27 Sep 86*	4
ALL FALL DOWN	*Chrysalis*	30	*22 Nov 86*	5
VIENNA [RI]	*Chrysalis*	13	*6 Feb 93*	4
ALBUMS:	**HITS 9**			**WEEKS 233**
VIENNA	*Chrysalis*	14	*19 Jul 80*	12
VIENNA [RE]	*Chrysalis*	3	*24 Jan 81*	60
RAGE IN EDEN	*Chrysalis*	4	*19 Sep 81*	23
QUARTET	*Chrysalis*	6	*23 Oct 82*	30
MONUMENT - THE SOUNDTRACK	*Chrysalis*	9	*22 Oct 83*	15
LAMENT	*Chrysalis*	8	*14 Apr 84*	26
THE COLLECTION	*Chrysalis*	2	*10 Nov 84*	53
U-VOX	*Chrysalis*	9	*25 Oct 86*	6
IF I WAS: THE VERY BEST OF MIDGE URE AND ULTRAVOX	*Chrysalis*	10	*6 Mar 93*	6
Includes tracks with Band Aid, Visage, Phil Lynott and Mick Karn.				
Above hit: Midge URE/ULTRAVOX.				
THE VERY BEST OF MIDGE URE AND ULTRAVOX	*EMI*	45	*10 Nov 01*	2
Includes Midge Ure's solo and group material.				
Above hit: Midge URE and ULTRAVOX.				

UMBOZA — UK

SINGLES:	**HITS 2**			**WEEKS 9**
CRY INDIA	*Positiva*	19	*23 Sep 95*	4
Samples Lionel Ritchie's All Night Long.				
SUNSHINE	*Positiva*	14	*20 Jul 96*	5
Samples the Gipsy Kings' Bomboleo.				

Piero UMILIANI — Italy

SINGLES:	**HITS 1**			**WEEKS 8**
MAH-NA, MAH-NA	*EMI International*	8	*30 Apr 77*	8
Originally released in the US in 1969.				

UNATION — UK

SINGLES:	**HITS 2**			**WEEKS 3**
HIGHER AND HIGHER	*MCA*	42	*5 Jun 93*	2
Features 16-piece string section arranged by Barrington Pheloung.				
DO YOU BELIEVE IN LOVE?	*MCA*	75	*7 Aug 93*	1

UNBELIEVABLE TRUTH — UK

SINGLES:	**HITS 3**			**WEEKS 5**
HIGHER THAN REASON	*Virgin*	38	*14 Feb 98*	2
SOLVED	*Virgin*	39	*9 May 98*	2
SETTLE DOWN / DUNE SEA	*Virgin*	46	*18 Jul 98*	1
ALBUMS:	**HITS 1**			**WEEKS 2**
ALMOST HERE	*Virgin*	21	*23 May 98*	2

UNCANNY ALLIANCE — US

SINGLES:	**HITS 1**			**WEEKS 5**
I GOT MY EDUCATION	*A&M*	39	*19 Dec 92*	5

UNCLE SAM — US

SINGLES:	**HITS 1**			**WEEKS 2**
I DON'T EVER WANT TO SEE YOU AGAIN	*Epic*	30	*16 May 98*	2

UNCLE KRACKER — US

SINGLES:	**HITS 1**			**WEEKS 17**
FOLLOW ME	*Atlantic*	3	*8 Sep 01*	17
ALBUMS:	**HITS 1**			**WEEKS 3**
DOUBLE WIDE	*Atlantic*	40	*22 Sep 01*	3

UNDERCOVER — UK

SINGLES:	**HITS 4**			**WEEKS 29**
BAKER STREET	*PWL International*	2	*15 Aug 92*	14
NEVER LET HER SLIP AWAY	*PWL International*	5	*14 Nov 92*	11

I WANNA STAY WITH YOU	*PWL International*	28	*6 Feb 93*	3
LOVESICK	*PWL International*	62	*14 Aug 93*	1
Above hit: UNDERCOVER featuring John MATTHEWS.				
ALBUMS:	**HITS 1**			**WEEKS 9**
CHECK OUT THE GROOVE	*PWL International*	26	*5 Dec 92*	9

UNDERTAKERS — UK

SINGLES:	**HITS 1**			**WEEKS 1**
JUST A LITTLE BIT	*Pye*	49	*11 Apr 64*	1

UNDERTONES — UK

SINGLES:	**HITS 10**			**WEEKS 67**
TEENAGE KICKS	*Sire*	31	*21 Oct 78*	6
Originally released on the Good Vibrations record label earlier in the year.				
GET OVER YOU	*Sire*	57	*3 Feb 79*	4
JIMMY JIMMY	*Sire*	16	*28 Apr 79*	10
HERE COMES THE SUMMER	*Sire*	34	*21 Jul 79*	6
YOU'VE GOT MY NUMBER (WHY DON'T YOU USE IT!)	*Sire*	32	*20 Oct 79*	6
MY PERFECT COUSIN	*Sire*	9	*5 Apr 80*	10
WEDNESDAY WEEK	*Sire*	11	*5 Jul 80*	9
IT'S GOING TO HAPPEN!	*Ardeck*	18	*2 May 81*	9
JULIE OCEAN	*Ardeck*	41	*25 Jul 81*	5
TEENAGE KICKS [EP]	*Ardeck*	60	*9 Jul 83*	2
Lead track: Teenage Kicks, which itself is a re-issue.				
ALBUMS:	**HITS 7**			**WEEKS 50**
THE UNDERTONES	*Sire*	13	*19 May 79*	21
HYPNOTISED	*Sire*	6	*26 Apr 80*	10
POSITIVE TOUCH	*Ardeck*	17	*16 May 81*	6
THE SIN OF PRIDE	*Ardeck*	43	*19 Mar 83*	5
ALL WRAPPED UP	*Ardeck*	67	*10 Dec 83*	4
Compilation.				
CHER O'BOWLIES - PICK OF THE UNDERTONES	*Ardeck*	96	*14 Jun 86*	1
Above hit: UNDERTONES featuring Feargal SHARKEY.				
THE BEST OF THE UNDERTONES - TEENAGE KICKS	*Castle Communications*	45	*25 Sep 93*	3
Released to celebrate 15th anniversary of the release of Teenage Kicks.				

UNDERWORLD — UK

SINGLES:	**HITS 8**			**WEEKS 41**
SPIKEE / DOGMAN GO WOOF	*Junior Boy's Own*	63	*18 Dec 93*	1
DARK AND LONG	*Junior Boy's Own*	57	*25 Jun 94*	1
BORN SLIPPY	*Junior Boy's Own*	52	*13 May 95*	2
PEARL'S GIRL	*Junior Boy's Own*	24	*18 May 96*	2
BORN SLIPPY [RM]	*Junior Boy's Own*	2	*13 Jul 96*	16
From the film 'Trainspotting'. This remix was actually the 2nd track on the original CD release.				
PEARL'S GIRL [RI]	*Junior Boy's Own*	22	*9 Nov 96*	3
BORN SLIPPY [RM] [RE]	*Junior Boy's Own*	58	*28 Dec 96*	5
PUSH UPSTAIRS	*JBO*	12	*27 Mar 99*	4
JUMBO	*JBO*	21	*5 Jun 99*	2
KING OF SNAKE	*JBO*	17	*28 Aug 99*	3
Based around Donna Summer's I Feel Love.				
COWGIRL	*JBO*	24	*2 Sep 00*	2
ALBUMS:	**HITS 4**			**WEEKS 47**
DUB NO BASS WITH MY HEAD MAN	*Junior Boy's Own*	12	*5 Feb 94*	4
SECOND TOUGHEST IN THE INFANTS	*Junior Boy's Own*	9	*23 Mar 96*	28
BEAUCOUP FISH	*JBO*	3	*13 Mar 99*	12
EVERYTHING EVERYTHING	*JBO*	22	*16 Sep 00*	3
Live album.				

UNDISPUTED TRUTH — US

SINGLES:	**HITS 1**			**WEEKS 4**
YOU + ME = LOVE	*Warner Brothers*	43	*22 Jan 77*	4

U96 — Germany

SINGLES:	**HITS 3**			**WEEKS 7**
DAS BOOT	*M&G*	18	*29 Aug 92*	5
INSIDE YOUR DREAMS	*Logic*	44	*4 Jun 94*	1
CLUB BIZARRE	*Urban*	70	*29 Jun 96*	1

UNION — UK/Holland

SINGLES:	**HITS 1**			**WEEKS 7**
SWING LOW (RUN WITH THE BALL)	*Columbia*	16	*12 Oct 91*	7
Above hit: UNION featuring the ENGLAND RUGBY WORLD CUP SQUAD.				

ALBUMS:	HITS 1			WEEKS 6
WORLD IN UNION *Features Various Artists.*	*Columbia*	17	*26 Oct 91*	6

UNION GAP - See Gary PUCKETT and the UNION GAP

UNION STATION - See Alison KRAUSS and UNION STATION

UNIQUE — US

SINGLES:	HITS 1			WEEKS 7
WHAT I GOT IS WHAT YOU NEED	*Prelude*	27	*10 Sep 83*	7

UNIQUE 3 — UK

SINGLES:	HITS 4			WEEKS 12
THE THEME	*10 Records*	61	*4 Nov 89*	3
MUSICAL MELODY / WEIGHT FOR THE BASS	*10 Records*	29	*14 Apr 90*	5
RHYTHM TAKES CONTROL *Above hit: UNIQUE 3 (featuring KARIN).*	*Ten Records*	41	*10 Nov 90*	3
NO MORE	*Ten Records*	74	*16 Nov 91*	1

UNIT FOUR PLUS TWO — UK

SINGLES:	HITS 4			WEEKS 29
GREEN FIELDS	*Decca*	48	*15 Feb 64*	2
CONCRETE AND CLAY	*Decca*	1	*27 Feb 65*	15
(YOU'VE) NEVER BEEN IN LOVE LIKE THIS BEFORE	*Decca*	14	*15 May 65*	11
BABY NEVER SAY GOODBYE	*Decca*	49	*19 Mar 66*	1
EPS:	**HITS 1**			**WEEKS 5**
UNIT FOUR PLUS TWO	*Decca*	11	*5 Jun 65*	5

UNITED CITIZEN FEDERATION featuring Sarah BRIGHTMAN — UK

(See also Sarah Brightman.)

SINGLES:	HITS 1			WEEKS 1
STARSHIP TROOPERS	*Coalition*	58	*14 Feb 98*	1

UNITED KINGDOM SYMPHONY ORCHESTRA conducted by Donald GOULD — UK

SINGLES:	HITS 1			WEEKS 4
SHADES (THEME FROM THE CROWN PAINT TELEVISION COMMERCIAL)	*Food For Thought*	68	*27 Jul 85*	4

UNITONE - See Laurel AITKEN and the UNITONE

UNITONE ROCKERS featuring STEEL — UK

SINGLES:	HITS 1			WEEKS 1
CHILDREN OF THE REVOLUTION	*The Hit Label*	60	*26 Jun 93*	1

UNITY — UK

SINGLES:	HITS 1			WEEKS 2
UNITY	*Cardiac*	64	*31 Aug 91*	2

UNIVERSAL — Australia

SINGLES:	HITS 2			WEEKS 6
ROCK ME GOOD	*London*	19	*2 Aug 97*	4
MAKE IT WITH YOU	*London*	33	*18 Oct 97*	2

UNJUSTIFIED ANCIENTS OF M U - See 1300 DRUMS featuring the UNJUSTIFIED ANCIENTS OF M U

UNKLE — UK

SINGLES:	HITS 2			WEEKS 7
BE THERE *Above hit: UNKLE featuring Ian BROWN.*	*Mo Wax*	8	*20 Feb 99*	6
NARCO TOURISTS *Above hit: SLAM versus UNKLE.*	*Soma Recordings*	66	*17 Mar 01*	1
ALBUMS:	**HITS 2**			**WEEKS 10**
THE TIME HAS COME [EP] *12" double-pack of remixes.* *Above hit: U.N.K.L.E.*	*Mo Wax*	73	*21 Jan 95*	1
PSYENCE FICTION	*Mo Wax*	4	*5 Sept 98*	9

UNO CLIO featuring Martine McCUTCHEON — UK

(See also Martine McCutcheon.)

SINGLES:	HITS 1			WEEKS 1
ARE YOU MAN ENOUGH	*Avex UK*	62	*18 Nov 95*	1

UNTOUCHABLES — US

SINGLES:	HITS 2			WEEKS 16
FREE YOURSELF	*Stiff*	26	*6 Apr 85*	11
(I SPY FOR THE) FBI	*Stiff*	59	*27 Jul 85*	5
ALBUMS:	**HITS 1**			**WEEKS 7**
WILD CHILD	*Stiff*	51	*13 Jul 85*	7

UP YER RONSON featuring Mary PEARCE — UK

SINGLES:	HITS 3			WEEKS 7
LOST IN LOVE	*Hi-Life*	27	*5 Aug 95*	3
ARE YOU GONNA BE THERE? *Originally recorded by Shay Jones in 1991.*	*Hi-Life*	27	*30 Mar 96*	2
I WILL BE RELEASED	*Hi-Life*	32	*19 Apr 97*	2

Phil UPCHURCH COMBO — US

SINGLES:	HITS 1			WEEKS 2
YOU CAN'T SIT DOWN	*Sue*	39	*7 May 66*	2

UPSETTERS — Jamaica

SINGLES:	HITS 1			WEEKS 15
RETURN OF DJANGO / DOLLAR IN THE TEETH	*Upsetter*	5	*4 Oct 69*	15

Dawn UPSHAW (soprano)/The LONDON SINFONIETTA/David ZINMAN (conductor) — US/UK/US

ALBUMS:	HITS 1			WEEKS 18
GORECKI: SYMPHONY NO. 3 *First released in 1992, charted after extensive airplay on radio station Classic FM.*	*Elektra Nonsuch*	6	*23 Jan 93*	18

UPSIDE DOWN — UK

SINGLES:	HITS 4			WEEKS 16
CHANGE YOUR MIND *Originally recorded by Bad Boys Inc.*	*World*	11	*20 Jan 96*	7
EVERY TIME I FALL IN LOVE	*World*	18	*13 Apr 96*	3
EVERY TIME I FALL IN LOVE [RE]	*World*	71	*8 Jun 96*	1
NEVER FOUND A LOVE LIKE THIS BEFORE	*World*	19	*29 Jun 96*	3
IF YOU LEAVE ME NOW	*World*	27	*23 Nov 96*	2

URBAN ALL STARS — UK/US

SINGLES:	HITS 1			WEEKS 2
IT BEGAN IN AFRICA FEATURING I BELIEVE IN MIRACLES & CROSS THE TRACK [M]	*Urban*	64	*27 Aug 88*	2

URBAN BLUES PROJECT present Michael PROCTER — US

SINGLES:	HITS 1			WEEKS 1
LOVE DON'T LIVE	*AM:PM*	55	*10 Aug 96*	1

URBAN COOKIE COLLECTIVE — UK

SINGLES:	HITS 8			WEEKS 37
THE KEY: THE SECRET	*Pulse 8*	2	*10 Jul 93*	16
FEELS LIKE HEAVEN	*Pulse 8*	5	*13 Nov 93*	9
SAIL AWAY	*Pulse 8*	18	*19 Feb 94*	4
HIGH ON A HAPPY VIBE	*Pulse 8*	31	*23 Apr 94*	3
BRING IT ON HOME	*Pulse 8*	56	*15 Oct 94*	1
SPEND THE DAY	*Pulse 8*	59	*27 May 95*	1
REST OF MY LOVE	*Pulse 8*	67	*9 Sep 95*	1
SO BEAUTIFUL	*Pulse 8*	68	*16 Dec 95*	1
THE KEY, THE SECRET [RM] *Remixed by Dancing Divaz.* *Above hit: U.C.C.*	*Pulse 8*	52	*24 Aug 96*	1
ALBUMS:	**HITS 1**			**WEEKS 2**
HIGH ON A HAPPY VIBE	*Pulse 8*	28	*26 Mar 94*	2

URBAN DISCHARGE featuring SHE — US

SINGLES:	HITS 1			WEEKS 1
WANNA DROP A HOUSE (ON THAT BITCH)	*MCA*	51	*27 Jan 96*	1

URBAN HYPE — UK

SINGLES:	HITS 3			WEEKS 12
A TRIP TO TRUMPTON *Samples from the BBC Children's TV show 'Trumpton'.*	*Faze 2*	6	*11 Jul 92*	8
THE FEELING	*Faze 2*	67	*17 Oct 92*	1
LIVING IN A FANTASY	*Faze 2*	57	*9 Jan 93*	3

URBAN SHAKEDOWN featuring Micky FINN — UK/Italy

SINGLES:	HITS 3			WEEKS 8
SOME JUSTICE *Samples vocals of Ce Ce Rogers.*	*Urban Shakedown*	23	*27 Jun 92*	5
BASS SHAKE	*Urban Shakedown*	59	*12 Sep 92*	2
SOME JUSTICE '95 [RR] *Above hit: URBAN SHAKEDOWN featuring D.BO GENERAL.*	*Urban Shakedown*	49	*10 Jun 95*	1

URBAN SOUL — UK

SINGLES:	HITS 3			WEEKS 11
ALRIGHT	*Cooltempo*	60	*30 Mar 91*	4
ALRIGHT (THE SASHA MIXES) [RM] *Remixed by Sasha.*	*Cooltempo*	43	*21 Sep 91*	3
ALWAYS	*Cooltempo*	41	*28 Mar 92*	3
LOVE IS SO NICE	*VC Recordings*	75	*13 Jun 98*	1

URBAN SPECIES — UK

SINGLES:	HITS 4			WEEKS 10
SPIRITUAL LOVE	*Talkin Loud*	35	*12 Feb 94*	4
BROTHER	*Talkin Loud*	40	*16 Apr 94*	3
LISTEN *Original release reached No. 79 in 1993.* *Above hit: URBAN SPECIES featuring MC SOLAAR.*	*Talkin Loud*	47	*20 Aug 94*	2
BLANKET *Above hit: URBAN SPECIES featuring Imogen HEAP.*	*Talkin Loud*	56	*6 Mar 99*	1
ALBUMS:	**HITS 1**			**WEEKS 2**
LISTEN	*Talkin Loud*	43	*7 May 94*	2

Midge URE — UK

SINGLES:	HITS 10			WEEKS 56
NO REGRETS *Originally recorded by Tom Rush.*	*Chrysalis*	9	*12 Jun 82*	10
AFTER A FASHION *Above hit: Midge URE and Mick KARN.*	*Musicfest*	39	*9 Jul 83*	4
IF I WAS	*Chrysalis*	1	*14 Sep 85*	11
THAT CERTAIN SMILE	*Chrysalis*	28	*16 Nov 85*	4
WASTELANDS	*Chrysalis*	46	*8 Feb 86*	3
CALL OF THE WILD	*Chrysalis*	27	*7 Jun 86*	8
ANSWERS TO NOTHING	*Chrysalis*	49	*20 Aug 88*	4
DEAR GOD	*Chrysalis*	55	*19 Nov 88*	4
COLD, COLD HEART	*Arista*	17	*17 Aug 91*	7
BREATHE	*Arista*	70	*25 May 96*	1
ALBUMS:	**HITS 5**			**WEEKS 28**
THE GIFT	*Chrysalis*	2	*19 Oct 85*	15
ANSWERS TO NOTHING	*Chrysalis*	30	*10 Sep 88*	3
PURE	*Arista*	36	*28 Sep 91*	2
IF I WAS: THE VERY BEST OF MIDGE URE AND ULTRAVOX *Includes tracks with Band Aid, Visage, Phil Lynott and Mick Karn.* *Above hit: Midge URE/ULTRAVOX.*	*Chrysalis*	10	*6 Mar 93*	6
THE VERY BEST OF MIDGE URE AND ULTRAVOX *Includes Midge Ure's solo and group material.* *Above hit: Midge URE and ULTRAVOX.*	*EMI*	45	*10 Nov 01*	2

URGE OVERKILL — US

SINGLES:	HITS 3			WEEKS 6
SISTER HAVANA	*Geffen*	67	*21 Aug 93*	1
POSITIVE BLEEDING	*Geffen*	61	*16 Oct 93*	1
GIRL, YOU'LL BE A WOMAN SOON *From the film 'Pulp Fiction'. Original by Neil Diamond reached No. 10 in the US in 1967.*	*MCA*	37	*19 Nov 94*	4

URIAH HEEP — UK

ALBUMS:	HITS 12			WEEKS 51
LOOK AT YOURSELF	*Island*	39	*13 Nov 71*	1
DEMONS AND WIZARDS	*Bronze*	20	*10 Jun 72*	11
THE MAGICIAN'S BIRTHDAY	*Bronze*	28	*2 Dec 72*	3
URIAH HEEP LIVE	*Island*	23	*19 May 73*	8
SWEET FREEDOM	*Island*	18	*29 Sep 73*	3
WONDERWORLD	*Bronze*	23	*29 Jun 74*	3
RETURN TO FANTASY	*Bronze*	7	*5 Jul 75*	6
HIGH AND MIGHTY	*Island*	55	*12 Jun 76*	1
CONQUEST	*Bronze*	37	*22 Mar 80*	3
ABOMINOG	*Bronze*	34	*17 Apr 82*	6
HEAD FIRST	*Bronze*	46	*18 Jun 83*	4
EQUATOR	*Portrait*	79	*6 Apr 85*	2

URUSEI YATSURA — UK

SINGLES:	HITS 4			WEEKS 4
STATEGIC HAMLETS	*Che*	64	*22 Feb 97*	1
FAKE FUR	*Che*	58	*28 Jun 97*	1
HELLO TIGER	*Che*	40	*21 Feb 98*	1
SLAIN BY ELF	*Che*	63	*6 Jun 98*	1
ALBUMS:	**HITS 1**			**WEEKS 1**
SLAIN BY	*Che*	64	*14 Mar 98*	1

USA FOR AFRICA — US

SINGLES:	HITS 1			WEEKS 9
WE ARE THE WORLD *Charity record in aid of famine relief in Africa. 5,000 radio stations globally aired the song on 5 Apr 95 at 3.50pm GMT.*	*CBS*	1	*13 Apr 85*	9
ALBUMS:	**HITS 1**			**WEEKS 5**
WE ARE THE WORLD *Contains previously unreleased tracks from Bruce Springsteen, Prince, Huey Lewis and the News, Chicago, Tina Turner, Pointer Sisters, Kenny Rodgers, Steve Perry plus the Canadian charity ensemble Northern Lights.*	*CBS*	31	*25 May 85*	5

USHER — US

SINGLES:	HITS 6			WEEKS 45
THINK OF YOU *Rap by Biz Marke, backing vocals by Faith Evans and samples Tidal Wave by Ronnie Laws.*	*LaFace*	70	*18 Mar 95*	1
YOU MAKE ME WANNA . . .	*LaFace*	1	*31 Jan 98*	12
NICE & SLOW	*LaFace*	24	*2 May 98*	5
YOU MAKE ME WANNA . . . [RE]	*LaFace*	72	*2 May 98*	1
POP YA COLLAR	*LaFace*	2	*3 Feb 01*	9
U REMIND ME	*LaFace*	3	*7 Jul 01*	9
U GOT IT BAD	*LaFace*	5	*20 Oct 01*	8
ALBUMS:	**HITS 2**			**WEEKS 42**
MY WAY	*LaFace*	16	*17 Jan 98*	18
8701	*LaFace*	1	*21 Jul 01*	24

US3 — UK

SINGLES:	HITS 4			WEEKS 15
RIDDIM *Above hit: US3 featuring Tukka YOOT.*	*Blue Note*	34	*10 Jul 93*	6
CANTALOOP (FLIP FANTASIA) *Samples Cantaloupe Island by Herbie Hancock.* *Above hit: US3 featuring RAHSAAN.*	*Blue Note*	23	*25 Sep 93*	5
I GOT IT GOIN' ON *Above hit: US3 featuring Kobie POWELL and RAHSAAN.*	*Blue Note*	52	*28 May 94*	2
COME ON EVERYBODY (GET DOWN)	*Blue Note*	38	*1 Mar 97*	2
ALBUMS:	**HITS 1**			**WEEKS 6**
HAND ON THE TORCH	*Blue Note*	40	*31 Jul 93*	5
HAND ON THE TORCH / JAZZ MIXES [RE] *Jazz Mixes was a remix album, sales were combined.*	*Blue Note*	54	*11 Jun 94*	1

USURA — Italy

SINGLES:	HITS 2			WEEKS 15
OPEN YOUR MIND	*Deconstruction*	7	*23 Jan 93*	9
SWEAT	*Deconstruction*	29	*10 Jul 93*	3
OPEN YOUR MIND '97 [RM] *Remixed by DJ Quicksilver.* *Above hit: U.S.U.R.A.*	*Malarky*	21	*6 Dec 97*	3

UTAH SAINTS — UK

SINGLES:	HITS 8			WEEKS 39
WHAT CAN YOU DO FOR ME *Samples Eurythmics' There Must Be An Angel (Playing With My Heart) and Gwen Guthrie's Ain't Nothing Goin' On But The Rent.*	*ffrr*	10	*24 Aug 91*	11
SOMETHING GOOD *Samples Kate Bush's Cloudbusting.*	*ffrr*	4	*6 Jun 92*	9
BELIEVE IN ME *Samples Crown Heights Affair's You Gave Me Love and the Human League's Love Action (I Believe In Love).*	*ffrr*	8	*8 May 93*	6
I WANT YOU *Samples Slayer's War Ensemble.*	*ffrr*	25	*17 Jul 93*	5
I STILL THINK OF YOU *A re-working of an album track Too Much To Swallow. From the film 'Shopping'.*	*ffrr*	32	*25 Jun 94*	2
OHIO *Samples Jocelyn Brown's Somebody Else's Guy.*	*ffrr*	42	*2 Sep 95*	2

LOVE SONG	*Echo*	37	*5 Feb 00*	2
Samples Average White Band's Pick Up The Pieces.				
FUNKY MUSIC - SHO NUFF TURNS ME ON	*Echo*	23	*20 May 00*	2
Above hit: UTAH SAINTS Special guest vocal by Edwin STARR.				
ALBUMS:	**HITS 1**			**WEEKS 15**
UTAH SAINTS	*ffrr*	10	*5 Jun 93*	15

UTOPIA — UK

ALBUMS:	**HITS 3**			**WEEKS 9**
RA	*Bearsville*	27	*29 Jan 77*	6
OOPS! SORRY WRONG PLANET	*Bearsville*	59	*1 Oct 77*	1
ADVENTURES IN UTOPIA	*Island*	57	*16 Feb 80*	2

U2 — Ireland

SINGLES:	**HITS 33**			**WEEKS 254**
FIRE	*Island*	35	*8 Aug 81*	6
GLORIA	*Island*	55	*17 Oct 81*	4
A CELEBRATION	*Island*	47	*3 Apr 82*	4
NEW YEAR'S DAY	*Island*	10	*22 Jan 83*	8
TWO HEARTS BEAT AS ONE	*Island*	18	*2 Apr 83*	5
PRIDE (IN THE NAME OF LOVE)	*Island*	3	*15 Sep 84*	11
Dedicated to Martin Luther King Jr.				
THE UNFORGETTABLE FIRE	*Island*	6	*4 May 85*	6
WITH OR WITHOUT YOU	*Island*	4	*28 Mar 87*	11
I STILL HAVEN'T FOUND WHAT I'M LOOKING FOR	*Island*	6	*6 Jun 87*	11
WHERE THE STREETS HAVE NO NAME	*Island*	4	*12 Sep 87*	6
IN GOD'S COUNTRY	*Island*	48	*26 Dec 87*	4
Import.				
DESIRE	*Island*	1	*1 Oct 88*	8
ANGEL OF HARLEM	*Island*	9	*17 Dec 88*	6
Tribute to Billie Holiday.				
WHEN LOVE COMES TO TOWN	*Island*	6	*15 Apr 89*	7
Above hit: U2 with B.B. KING.				
ALL I WANT IS YOU	*Island*	4	*24 Jun 89*	6
THE FLY	*Island*	1	*2 Nov 91*	5
MYSTERIOUS WAYS	*Island*	13	*14 Dec 91*	7
THE FLY [RE]	*Island*	62	*4 Jan 92*	1
ONE	*Island*	7	*7 Mar 92*	6
EVEN BETTER THAN THE REAL THING	*Island*	12	*20 jJun 92*	7
EVEN BETTER THAN THE REAL THING (THE PERFECTO MIX) [RM]	*Island*	8	*11 Jul 92*	7
Remixed by Paul Oakenfold and Steve Osborne.				
WHO'S GONNA RIDE YOUR WILD HORSES	*Island*	14	*5 Dec 92*	8
STAY (FARAWAY, SO CLOSE!)	*Island*	4	*4 Dec 93*	9
[AA] listed with I've Got You Under My Skin by Frank Sinatra with Bono, although that track was not available on the 2nd CD format.				
HOLD ME, THRILL ME, KISS ME, KILL ME	*Atlantic*	2	*17 Jun 95*	14
From the film 'Batman Forever'.				
DISCOTHEQUE	*Island*	1	*15 Feb 97*	9
STARING AT THE SUN	*Island*	3	*26 Apr 97*	6
DISCOTHEQUE [RE]	*Island*	72	*17 May 97*	2
LAST NIGHT ON EARTH	*Island*	10	*2 Aug 97*	4
LAST NIGHT ON EARTH [RE]	*Island*	68	*6 Sep 97*	1
PLEASE	*Island*	7	*4 Oct 97*	4
IF GOD WILL SEND HIS ANGELS	*Island*	12	*20 Dec 97*	6
Second CD format has Mofo as the lead track.				
SWEETEST THING	*Island*	3	*31 Oct 98*	13
A new mix of the original 'B' side of Where The Streets Have No Name.				
BEAUTIFUL DAY	*Island*	1	*21 Oct 00*	16
STUCK IN A MOMENT YOU CAN'T GET OUT OF	*Island*	2	*10 Feb 01*	8
NEW YEAR'S DUB	*Serious*	15	*2 Jun 01*	4
Samples New Year's Day.				
Above hit: MUSIQUE vs U2				
NEW YEAR'S DUB [RE]	*Serious*	75	*14 Jul 01*	1
ELEVATION	*Island*	3	*28 Jul 01*	8
WALK ON	*Island*	5	*1 Dec 01*	5
ALBUMS:	**HITS 15**			**WEEKS 1068**
BOY	*Island*	52	*29 Aug 81*	31
Originally released in 1980.				
OCTOBER	*Island*	11	*24 Oct 81*	41
WAR	*Island*	1	*12 Mar 83*	145
U2 LIVE "UNDER A BLOOD RED SKY"	*Island*	2	*3 Dec 83*	203
Includes re-entries through to 1992. Live recordings from Boston in Massachusetts, Red Rocks festival in Colorado and West Germany.				
THE UNFORGETTABLE FIRE	*Island*	1	*13 Oct 84*	130
Includes re-entries through to 1992.				
WIDE AWAKE IN AMERICA	*Island*	11	*27 Jul 85*	16
US import EP.				

THE JOSHUA TREE	*Island*	1	*21 Mar 87*	130
Includes re-entries through to 1996.				
THE JOSHUA TREE SINGLES	*Island*	100	*20 Feb 88*	1
Release is 4 x 7" singles set.				
RATTLE AND HUM	*Island*	1	*22 Oct 88*	54
Live recordings between 1986–88 and rare studio tracks. Includes re-entries through to 1993.				
ACHTUNG BABY	*Island*	2	*30 Nov 91*	87
Includes re-entries through to 2001.				
WAR [RE-1ST]	*Island*	38	*13 Jun 92*	4
Chart Position reached in 1993, (1992 peak No. 51).				
OCTOBER [RE]	*Island*	72	*13 Jun 92*	1
ZOOROPA	*Island*	1	*17 Jul 93*	31
POP	*Island*	1	*15 Mar 97*	35
THE JOSHUA TREE [RE]	*Island*	20	*26 Jul 97*	26
Peak position reached on 28 Apr 01 (1997 peak: No. 46).				
THE BEST OF 1980-1990 & B-SIDES	*Island*	1	*14 Nov 98*	9
THE BEST OF 1980-1990	*Island*	4	*21 Nov 98*	62
Both compilations listed above had separate chart entries due to chart rules. The first entry had additional CD of B-sides.				
ALL THAT YOU CAN'T LEAVE BEHIND	*Island*	1	*11 Nov 00*	57
RATTLE AND HUM [RE]	*Island*	53	*3 Mar 01*	7

Verna V. - See HELIOTROPIC featuring Verna V.

V.D.C. - See BLAST featuring V.D.C.

V.I.M. — UK

SINGLES:	HITS 1			WEEKS 1
MAGGIE'S LAST PARTY	*Boz*	68	*26 Jan 91*	1

V.I.P.'S — UK

SINGLES:	HITS 1			WEEKS 4
THE QUARTER MOON	*Gems*	55	*6 Sep 80*	4

VAGABONDS - See Jimmy JAMES and the VAGABONDS

Steve VAI — US

ALBUMS:	HITS 4			WEEKS 20
PASSION AND WARFARE	*Food*	8	*2 Jun 90*	10
SEX AND RELIGION	*Relativity*	17	*7 Aug 93*	6
Above hit: VAI.				
ALIEN LOVE SECRETS	*Relativity*	39	*15 Apr 95*	2
FIRE GARDEN	*Epic*	41	*28 Sep 96*	2

Ricky VALANCE — UK

SINGLES:	HITS 1			WEEKS 16
TELL LAURA I LOVE HER	*Columbia*	1	*27 Aug 60*	16
Original by Ray Peterson reached No. 7 in the US in 1960.				

Ritchie VALENS — US

SINGLES:	HITS 2			WEEKS 5
DONNA	*London*	29	*7 Mar 59*	1
LA BAMBA	*RCA*	49	*1 Aug 87*	4
Originally the B-side of Donna in 1959. Re-issued after the release of the biopic of the same name.				

Caterina VALENTE - Werner MULLER and the RIAS DANCE ORCHESTRA — France

SINGLES:	HITS 1			WEEKS 14
THE BREEZE AND I (ANDALUCIA)	*Polydor*	5	*20 Aug 55*	14
Originally recorded by Jimmy Dorsey in 1940.				

Dickie VALENTINE — UK

(See also All Star Hit Parade.)

SINGLES:	HITS 14			WEEKS 92
BROKEN WINGS	*Decca*	12	*21 Feb 53*	1
ALL THE TIME AND EV'RYWHERE	*Decca*	9	*14 Mar 53*	3
IN A GOLDEN COACH (THERE'S A HEART OF GOLD)	*Decca*	7	*6 Jun 53*	1
ENDLESS	*Decca*	19	*6 Nov 54*	1
MISTER SANDMAN	*Decca*	5	*18 Dec 54*	12
Above hit: Dickie VALENTINE with Johnny DOUGLAS and his Orchestra.				

THE FINGER OF SUSPICION	*Decca*	1	*18 Dec 54*	15
Above hit: Dickie VALENTINE with the STARGAZERS.				
A BLOSSOM FELL	*Decca*	9	*19 Feb 55*	9
A BLOSSOM FELL [RE]	*Decca*	18	*30 Apr 55*	1
I WONDER	*Decca*	4	*4 Jun 55*	15
CHRISTMAS ALPHABET	*Decca*	1	*26 Nov 55*	7
Above 4: Dickie VALENTINE with Johnny DOUGLAS and his Orchestra.				
THE OLD PI-ANNA RAG	*Decca*	15	*17 Dec 55*	5
CHRISTMAS ISLAND	*Decca*	8	*8 Dec 56*	5
Above hit: Dickie VALENTINE with Johnny DOUGLAS and his Orchestra.				
SNOWBOUND FOR CHRISTMAS	*Decca*	28	*28 Dec 57*	1
VENUS	*Pye Nixa*	28	*14 Mar 59*	1
VENUS [RE-1ST]	*Pye Nixa*	25	*4 Apr 59*	1
VENUS [RE-2ND]	*Pye Nixa*	20	*18 Apr 59*	4
VENUS [RE-3RD]	*Pye Nixa*	25	*23 May 59*	1
VENUS [RE-4TH]	*Pye Nixa*	28	*20 Jun 59*	1
ONE MORE SUNRISE (MORGEN)	*Pye Nixa*	14	*24 Oct 59*	8
Above hit: Dickie VALENTINE; Wally STOTT ORCHESTRA and Chorus.				

VALENTINE BROTHERS — US

SINGLES:	HITS 1			WEEKS 1
MONEY'S TOO TIGHT (TO MENTION)	*Energy*	73	*23 Apr 83*	1

Joe VALINO — US

SINGLES:	HITS 1			WEEKS 2
THE GARDEN OF EDEN	*His Master's Voice*	23	*19 Jan 57*	2

Frankie VALLI — US

(See also Four Seasons.)

SINGLES:	HITS 6			WEEKS 52
YOU'RE READY NOW	*Philips*	11	*12 Dec 70*	13
Originally released in 1966.				
MY EYES ADORED YOU	*Private Stock*	5	*1 Feb 75*	11
SWEARIN' TO GOD	*Private Stock*	31	*21 Jun 75*	5
FALLEN ANGEL	*Private Stock*	11	*17 Apr 76*	7
Originally recorded by Rogue.				
GREASE	*RSO*	3	*26 Aug 78*	14
From the film of the same name. Written by Barry Gibb.				
GREASE - THE DREAM MIX [M]	*Polydor*	47	*23 Mar 91*	2
Medley of songs from the film 'Grease'.				
Above hit: Frankie VALLI, John TRAVOLTA and Olivia NEWTON-JOHN.				

ALBUMS:	HITS 3			WEEKS 28
THE COLLECTION - THE 20 GREATEST HITS	*Telstar*	38	*21 May 88*	9
CD format is titled The 22 Greatest Hits.				
THE VERY BEST OF FRANKIE VALLI AND THE FOUR SEASONS	*PolyGram TV*	7	*7 Mar 92*	15
Above 2 contain Frankie Valli's solo and group material.				
THE DEFINITIVE FRANKIE VALLI AND THE FOUR SEASONS	*WSM*	26	*13 Oct 01*	4
Above 3 contain Frankie Valli's solo and group material.				
Above 3: Frankie VALLI and the FOUR SEASONS.				

Ian VAN DAHL — Belgium

SINGLES:	HITS 2			WEEKS 18
CASTLES IN THE SKY	*NuLife*	3	*21 Jul 01*	16
WILL I?	*NuLife*	5	*22 Dec 01*	2

Mark VAN DALE with ENRICO — Belgium

SINGLES:	HITS 1			WEEKS 1
WATER WAVE	*Club Tools*	71	*3 Oct 98*	1
Raved-up version of the Verve's Bittersweet Symphony.				

David VAN DAY — UK

SINGLES:	HITS 1			WEEKS 3
YOUNG AMERICANS TALKING	*WEA*	43	*14 May 83*	3

VAN DER GRAAF GENERATOR — UK

ALBUMS:	HITS 1			WEEKS 2
THE LEAST WE CAN DO IS WAVE TO EACH OTHER	*Charisma*	47	*25 Apr 70*	2

George VAN DUSEN — UK

SINGLES:	HITS 1			WEEKS 4
IT'S PARTY TIME AGAIN	*Bri-Tone*	43	*17 Dec 88*	4

Paul VAN DYK — Germany

SINGLES:	HITS 6			WEEKS 24
FORBIDDEN FRUIT	*Deviant*	69	*17 May 97*	1
WORDS	*Deviant*	54	*15 Nov 97*	1
Above hit: Paul VAN DYK featuring Toni HALLIDAY.				
FOR AN ANGEL	*Deviant*	28	*5 Sep 98*	4
ANOTHER WAY / AVENUE	*Deviant*	13	*20 Nov 99*	5
ANOTHER WAY/AVENUE [RE]	*Deviant*	69	*8 Jan 00*	2
TELL ME WHY (THE RIDDLE)	*Deviant*	7	*20 May 00*	5
Although Saint Etienne are credited, only lead singer Sarah Cracknell appears on the track.				
Above hit: Paul VAN DYK featuring SAINT ETIENNE.				
WE ARE ALIVE	*Deviant*	15	*2 Dec 00*	6
Vocals by Jennifer Brown.				

ALBUMS:	HITS 1			WEEKS 3
OUT THERE AND BACK	*Deviant*	12	*17 Jun 00*	3

Leroy VAN DYKE — US

SINGLES:	HITS 2			WEEKS 20
WALK ON BY	*Mercury*	5	*6 Jan 62*	17
BIG MAN IN A BIG HOUSE	*Mercury*	34	*28 Apr 62*	3

Niels VAN GOGH — Germany

SINGLES:	HITS 1			WEEKS 1
PULVERTURM	*Kosmo*	75	*10 Apr 99*	1

VAN HALEN — US

SINGLES:	HITS 12			WEEKS 51
RUNNIN' WITH THE DEVIL	*Warner Brothers*	52	*28 Jun 80*	3
JUMP	*Warner Brothers*	7	*4 Feb 84*	13
PANAMA	*Warner Brothers*	61	*19 May 84*	2
WHY CAN'T THIS BE LOVE	*Warner Brothers*	8	*5 Apr 86*	14
DREAMS	*Warner Brothers*	62	*12 Jul 86*	2
WHEN IT'S LOVE	*Warner Brothers*	28	*6 Aug 88*	7
FEELS SO GOOD	*Warner Brothers*	63	*1 Apr 89*	1
POUNDCAKE	*Warner Brothers*	74	*22 Jun 91*	1
TOP OF THE WORLD	*Warner Brothers*	63	*19 Oct 91*	1
JUMP (LIVE VERSION) [RE]	*Warner Brothers*	26	*27 Mar 93*	3
DON'T TELL ME	*Warner Brothers*	27	*21 Jan 95*	2
CAN'T STOP LOVIN' YOU	*Warner Brothers*	33	*1 Apr 95*	2

ALBUMS:	HITS 13			WEEKS 102
VAN HALEN	*Warner Brothers*	34	*27 May 78*	11
VAN HALEN II	*Warner Brothers*	23	*14 Apr 79*	7
WOMEN AND CHILDREN FIRST	*Warner Brothers*	15	*5 Apr 80*	7
FAIR WARNING	*Warner Brothers*	49	*23 May 81*	4
DIVER DOWN	*Warner Brothers*	36	*1 May 82*	5
1984	*Warner Brothers*	15	*4 Feb 84*	23
5150	*Warner Brothers*	16	*5 Apr 86*	18
OU812	*Warner Brothers*	16	*4 Jun 88*	12
FOR UNLAWFUL CARNAL KNOWLEDGE	*Warner Brothers*	12	*29 Jun 91*	5
LIVE: RIGHT HERE, RIGHT NOW	*Warner Brothers*	24	*6 Mar 93*	4
BALANCE	*Warner Brothers*	8	*4 Feb 95*	3
1984 [RE]	*Warner Brothers*	75	*11 Mar 95*	1
Re-released at mid-price.				
THE BEST OF VAN HALEN - VOLUME 1	*Warner Brothers*	45	*9 Nov 96*	1
VAN HALEN 3	*Warner Brothers*	43	*28 Mar 98*	1

Armand VAN HELDEN — US

(See also Roger Sanchez.)

SINGLES:	HITS 6			WEEKS 29
THE FUNK PHENOMENA	*ZYX*	38	*8 Mar 97*	2
Above hit: Armand VAN HELDEN presents OLD SCHOOL JUNKIES PT. 2.				
ULTRAFUNKULA	*ffrr*	46	*8 Nov 97*	1
YOU DON'T KNOW ME	*ffrr*	1	*6 Feb 99*	11
Originally appeared on the 2 Future 4U EP which reached No. 92 on the album charts in 1998.				
Above hit: Armand VAN HELDEN featuring Duane HARDEN.				
FLOWERS	*ffrr*	18	*1 May 99*	5
Above hit: Armand VAN HELDEN featuring Roland CLARK.				
YOU DON'T KNOW ME [RE]	*ffrr*	72	*15 May 99*	1
KOOCHY	*ffrr*	4	*20 May 00*	7
Samples Gary Numan's Cars.				
WHY CAN'T U FREE SOME TIME	*ffrr*	34	*3 Nov 01*	2

ALBUMS:	HITS 2			WEEKS 7
2 FUTURE 4 U	*ffrr*	22	*10 Apr 99*	6
KILLING PURITANS	*ffrr*	38	*10 Jun 00*	1

Paul VAN KEMPEN — Holland

EPS:	HITS 1			WEEKS 20
1812 OVERTURE	*Philips*	11	*19 Mar 60*	20

VAN TWIST — Belgium/Zaire

SINGLES:	HITS 1			WEEKS 2
SHAFT	*Polydor*	57	*16 Feb 85*	2

VANDELLAS - See Martha REEVES and the VANDELLAS

Luther VANDROSS — US

SINGLES:	HITS 26			WEEKS 148
NEVER TOO MUCH	*Epic*	44	*19 Feb 83*	6
Originally released in 1981 reaching No. 33 in the US.				
GIVE ME THE REASON	*Epic*	60	*26 Jul 86*	3
From the film 'Ruthless People'.				
GIVE ME THE REASON [RI-1ST]	*Epic*	71	*21 Feb 87*	2
SEE ME	*Epic*	60	*28 Mar 87*	4
I REALLY DIDN'T MEAN IT	*Epic*	16	*11 Jul 87*	10
STOP TO LOVE	*Epic*	24	*5 Sep 87*	7
SO AMAZING	*Epic*	33	*7 Nov 87*	6
GIVE ME THE REASON [RI-2ND]	*Epic*	26	*23 Jan 88*	6
I GAVE IT UP (WHEN I FELL IN LOVE)	*Epic*	28	*16 Apr 88*	5
THERE'S NOTHING BETTER THAN LOVE	*Epic*	72	*9 Jul 88*	1
Above hit: Luther VANDROSS (duet with Gregory HINES).				
ANY LOVE	*Epic*	31	*8 Oct 88*	4
SHE WON'T TALK TO ME	*Epic*	34	*4 Feb 89*	4
COME BACK	*Epic*	53	*22 Apr 89*	3
NEVER TOO MUCH - REMIX '89 [RM]	*Epic*	13	*28 Oct 89*	7
Remixed by Justin Strauss.				
HERE AND NOW	*Epic*	43	*6 Jan 90*	3
POWER OF LOVE/LOVE POWER [M]	*Epic*	46	*27 Apr 91*	5
Backing vocals by Darlene Love and Cissy Houston.				
THE RUSH	*Epic*	53	*18 Jan 92*	3
THE BEST THINGS IN LIFE ARE FREE	*Perspective*	2	*15 Aug 92*	13
From the film 'Mo'Money'.				
Above hit: Luther VANDROSS and Janet JACKSON with special guests BBD and Ralph TRESVANT.				
LITTLE MIRACLES (HAPPEN EVERY DAY)	*Epic*	28	*22 May 93*	3
HEAVEN KNOWS	*Epic*	34	*18 Sep 93*	3
LOVE IS ON THE WAY (REAL LOVE)	*Epic*	38	*4 Dec 93*	2
ENDLESS LOVE	*Epic*	3	*17 Sep 94*	10
Above hit: Luther VANDROSS and Mariah CAREY.				
LOVE THE ONE YOU'RE WITH	*Epic*	31	*26 Nov 94*	4
ENDLESS LOVE [RE-1ST]	*Epic*	70	*7 Jan 95*	2
ALWAYS AND FOREVER	*Epic*	20	*4 Feb 95*	5
ENDLESS LOVE [RE-2ND]	*Epic*	55	*4 Feb 95*	4
AIN'T NO STOPPIN' US NOW	*Epic*	22	*15 Apr 95*	3
POWER OF LOVE/LOVE POWER [M] [RM]	*Epic*	31	*11 Nov 95*	3
Remixed by Frankie Knuckles.				
THE BEST THINGS IN LIFE ARE FREE [RM]	*A&M*	7	*16 Dec 95*	7
Remixed by K-Klass.				
Above hit: Luther VANDROSS and Janet JACKSON.				
EVERY YEAR, EVERY CHRISTMAS	*Epic*	43	*23 Dec 95*	2
YOUR SECRET LOVE	*Epic*	14	*12 Oct 96*	5
I CAN MAKE IT BETTER	*Epic*	44	*28 Dec 96*	2
TAKE YOU OUT	*J*	59	*20 Oct 01*	1

ALBUMS:	HITS 15			WEEKS 269
BUSY BODY	*Epic*	42	*21 Jan 84*	8
THE NIGHT I FELL IN LOVE	*Epic*	19	*6 Apr 85*	10
THE ARTISTS VOLUME 2	*Street Sounds*	45	*13 Jul 85*	4
Compilation album with tracks by each artist.				
Above hit: Luther VANDROSS/Teddy PENDERGRASS/CHANGE/ATLANTIC STARR.				
GIVE ME THE REASON	*Epic*	13	*1 Nov 86*	10
GIVE ME THE REASON [RE]	*Epic*	3	*31 Jan 87*	89
Peak position reached on 5 Mar 88.				
NEVER TOO MUCH	*Epic*	79	*21 Feb 87*	30
Originally released in 1981.				
NEVER TOO MUCH [RE]	*Epic*	41	*20 Jun 87*	23
FOREVER, FOR ALWAYS, FOR LOVE	*Epic*	23	*4 Jul 87*	16
BUSY BODY [RE]	*Epic*	78	*16 Apr 88*	4
Re-released with a new catalogue number.				
ANY LOVE	*Epic*	3	*29 Oct 88*	22
BEST OF LUTHER VANDROSS - BEST OF LOVE	*Epic*	14	*11 Nov 89*	13
POWER OF LOVE	*Epic*	9	*25 May 91*	9

NEVER LET ME GO	*Epic*	11	*12 Jun 93*	5
SONGS	*Epic*	1	*1 Oct 94*	28
GREATEST HITS 1981–1995	*Epic*	12	*28 Oct 95*	14
YOUR SECRET LOVE	*Epic*	14	*19 Oct 96*	4
ONE NIGHT WITH YOU – THE BEST OF LOVE	*Epic*	56	*11 Oct 97*	2
Compilation of love songs.				
I KNOW	*EMI*	42	*22 Aug 98*	1

VANESSA-MAE — UK

SINGLES:	HITS 8			WEEKS 21
TOCCATA AND FUGUE IN D MINOR	*EMI Classics*	16	*28 Jan 95*	10
RED HOT	*EMI*	37	*20 May 95*	2
She performed the song in front of Queen Elizabeth II at the V.E. Day anniversary celebrations, 8 May 95.				
CLASSICAL GAS	*EMI*	41	*18 Nov 95*	2
I'M A DOUN FOR LACK O'JOHNNIE' (A LITTLE SCOTTISH FANTASY)	*EMI*	28	*26 Oct 96*	2
Modern arrangement of an old Scottish folk song.				
STORM	*EMI*	54	*25 Oct 97*	1
I FEEL LOVE	*EMI*	41	*20 Dec 97*	2
DEVIL'S TRILL / REFLECTION	*EMI*	53	*5 Dec 98*	1
Devil's Trill featured in the Siemens "Be Inspired" TV commercial. Reflection is from the Walt Disney film 'Mulan'.				
WHITE BIRD	*EMI*	66	*28 Jul 01*	1
Originally recorded by It's A Beautiful Day in 1969.				

ALBUMS:	HITS 5			WEEKS 33
THE VIOLIN PLAYER	*EMI*	11	*25 Feb 95*	21
CLASSICAL ALBUM 1	*EMI Premier*	47	*2 Nov 96*	2
Features Russian conductor Viktor Fadov and the London Symphony Orchestra.				
STORM	*EMI*	27	*8 Nov 97*	5
CHINA GIRL – THE CLASSICAL ALBUM 2	*EMI Classics*	56	*7 Feb 98*	3
Features the London Philharmonic Orchestra and the Orchestra of the Royal Opera House.				
SUBJECT TO CHANGE	*EMI*	58	*26 May 01*	2

VANGELIS — Greece

(See also Jon and Vangelis.)

SINGLES:	HITS 3			WEEKS 25
CHARIOTS OF FIRE – TITLES	*Polydor*	12	*9 May 81*	10
Theme from the film.				
HEAVEN AND HELL 3RD MOVEMENT (THEME FROM THE TV SERIES COSMOS)	*BBC*	48	*11 Jul 81*	6
Theme from Carl Sagan's BBC TV series.				
CHARIOTS OF FIRE – TITLES [RE]	*Polydor*	41	*24 Apr 82*	7
CONQUEST OF PARADISE	*East West*	60	*31 Oct 92*	2
From the film '1492 – Conquest Of Paradise'.				

ALBUMS:	HITS 10			WEEKS 157
HEAVEN AND HELL	*RCA Victor*	31	*10 Jan 76*	7
ALBEDO 0.39	*RCA Victor*	18	*9 Oct 76*	6
CHARIOTS OF FIRE [OST]	*Polydor*	5	*18 Apr 81*	97
CHARIOTS OF FIRE [OST] [RE]	*Polydor*	39	*5 May 84*	9
Re-released with a new catalogue number.				
SOIL FESTIVITIES	*Polydor*	55	*13 Oct 84*	4
MASK	*Polydor*	69	*30 Mar 85*	2
THEMES	*Polydor*	11	*22 Jul 89*	13
1492 – THE CONQUEST OF PARADISE [OST]	*East West*	33	*24 Oct 92*	6
BLADERUNNER [OST]	*East West*	20	*18 Jun 94*	6
Film was originally released in 1982.				
VOICES	*East West*	58	*2 Mar 96*	1
PORTRAIT (SO LONG AGO, SO CLEAR)	*Polydor*	14	*20 Apr 96*	6
Compilation featuring 5 tracks with Jon Anderson.				

VANILLA — UK

SINGLES:	HITS 2			WEEKS 10
NO WAY NO WAY	*EMI*	75	*22 Nov 97*	1
NO WAY NO WAY [RE]	*EMI*	14	*27 Dec 97*	7
TRUE TO US	*EMI*	36	*23 May 98*	2

VANILLA FUDGE — US

SINGLES:	HITS 1			WEEKS 11
YOU KEEP ME HANGING ON	*Atlantic*	18	*12 Aug 67*	11

ALBUMS:	HITS 1			WEEKS 3
VANILLA FUDGE	*Atlantic*	31	*4 Nov 67*	3

VANILLA ICE — US

SINGLES:	HITS 5			WEEKS 32
ICE ICE BABY *Samples Queen and David Bowie's Under Pressure.*	*SBK*	1	*24 Nov 90*	13
PLAY THAT FUNKY MUSIC	*SBK*	10	*2 Feb 91*	6
I LOVE YOU	*SBK*	45	*30 Mar 91*	5
ROLLIN' IN MY 5.0	*SBK*	27	*29 Jun 91*	4
SATISFACTION	*SBK*	22	*10 Aug 91*	4
ALBUMS:	**HITS 2**			**WEEKS 23**
TO THE EXTREME	*SBK*	4	*15 Dec 90*	20
EXTREMELY LIVE	*SBK*	35	*6 Jul 91*	3

VANITY FARE — UK

SINGLES:	HITS 3			WEEKS 34
I LIVE FOR THE SUN *Originally recorded by the Sunrays in 1967.*	*Page One*	20	*31 Aug 68*	9
EARLY IN THE MORNING	*Page One*	8	*26 Jul 69*	12
HITCHIN' A RIDE	*Page One*	16	*27 Dec 69*	13

Joe T. VANNELLI PROJECT — Italy

SINGLES:	HITS 1			WEEKS 2
SWEETEST DAY OF MAY *Features the Harambee Gospel Choir from New Jersey.*	*Positiva*	45	*17 Jun 95*	2

Randy VANWARMER — US

SINGLES:	HITS 1			WEEKS 11
JUST WHEN I NEEDED YOU MOST	*Bearsville*	8	*4 Aug 79*	11

VAPORS — UK

SINGLES:	HITS 3			WEEKS 23
TURNING JAPANESE	*United Artists*	3	*9 Feb 80*	13
NEWS AT TEN	*United Artists*	44	*5 Jul 80*	4
JIMMIE JONES	*Liberty*	44	*11 Jul 81*	6
ALBUMS:	**HITS 1**			**WEEKS 6**
NEW CLEAR DAYS	*United Artists*	44	*7 Jun 80*	6

VARDIS — UK

SINGLES:	HITS 1			WEEKS 4
LET'S GO	*Logo*	59	*27 Sep 80*	4
ALBUMS:	**HITS 1**			**WEEKS 1**
100 MPH	*Logo*	52	*1 Nov 80*	1

Halo VARGA — US

SINGLES:	HITS 1			WEEKS 1
FUTURE	*Hooj Choons*	67	*9 Dec 00*	1

VARIOUS ARTISTS — Multi-National

SINGLES:	HITS 2			WEEKS 22
THE BRITS 1990 (DANCE MEDLEY) [M] *Mix of 8 dance hits by British acts chosen by Jonathan King. It was performed at the Brit Awards, Feb 90.*	*RCA*	2	*3 Mar 90*	7
PERFECT DAY *Charity record with proceeds to BBC Children In Need. Originally recorded by Lou Reed and appeared on the B-side of his 1973 hit Walk On The Wild Side.*	*Chrysalis*	1	*29 Nov 97*	19
PERFECT DAY [RE]	*Chrysalis*	68	*18 Apr 98*	2
PERFECT DAY 2000 [RR] *Re-recorded for BBC Music Live, all profits to BBC's Children in Need.*	*Chrysalis*	69	*17 Jun 00*	1

VARIOUS ARTISTS (EPs)

SINGLES:	HITS 13			WEEKS 20
THE FOOD CHRISTMAS EP 1989 [EP] *Tracks: Like Princes Do (Crazyhead)/ I Don't Want That Kind Of Love (Jesus Jones)/ Info Freako (Diesel Park West).*	*Food*	63	*9 Dec 89*	1
THE FURTHER ADVENTURES OF NORTH - MORE UNDERGROUND DANCE [EP] *Tracks: Dream 17 (Annette)/ Carino 90 (T-Coy)/ The Way I Feel (Frequency 9)/ Stop This Thing (Dynasty Of Two featuring Rowetta).*	*Deconstruction*	64	*20 Jan 90*	2
THE APPLE [EP] *Tracks: Those Were The Days (Mary Hopkin)/ That's The Way God Planned It (Billy Preston)/ Sour Milk Tea (Jackie Lomax)/ Come And Get It (Badfinger).*	*Apple*	60	*2 Nov 91*	1
FOURPLAY VOLUME 1 [EP] *Tracks: DJ's Unite (DJ's Unite)/ Alright (Glide)/ Be Free (Noise Factory)/ True Devotion (EQ).*	*XL Recordings*	45	*11 Jul 92*	2

THE FRED [EP] *Charity Record with Proceeds to The Terrence Higgins Trust (for AIDS research). Tracks: Deeply Dippy (Rockingbirds)/ Don't Talk Just Kiss (Flowered Up)/ I'm Too Sexy (St Etienne).*	*Heavenly*	26	*7 Nov 92*	3
GIMME SHELTER [EP] *Charity release for the 'Putting Our House In Order' project to support the homeless. Only common track available on all formats: Gimme Shelter – Interview. All other tracks on the 4 formats available were by various acts recording their versions of the Rolling Stone song Gimme Shelter.*	*Food*	23	*24 Apr 93*	4
SUBPLATES VOLUME 1 [EP] *Tracks: Style Warz (Son'z Of A Loop Da Loop Era) / Funky Dope Bass (Q Bass)/ The Chopper (DJ Hype)/ Look No Further (Run Tings).*	*Suburban Base*	69	*5 Jun 93*	1
2 TONE [EP] *Tracks: Gangsters (Special A.K.A.)/ The Prince (Madness) / On My Radio (Selecter) / Tears Of A Clown (Beat).*	*2-Tone*	30	*9 Oct 93*	3
HELP [EP] *Charity Record with Proceeds to 'War Child' (to help Bosnian refugee children). Tracks: Lucky (Radiohead)/ 50ft Queenie (Live) (PJ Harvey)/ Momentum (Guru's Jazzmatazz) (Guru)/ Untitled (no artist credit). The last track was used as incidental music for the Help TV documentary.*	*Go! Discs*	51	*4 Nov 95*	2
NEW YORK UNDERCOVER 4-TRACK EP [EP] *From the film of the same name. Tracks: Tell Me What You Like (Guy)/ Dom Perignon (Little Shawn) / I Miss You (Monifah)/ Jeeps, Lex Coups, Bimaz & Benz (Lost Boyz).*	*Uptown*	39	*16 Mar 96*	1
DANGEROUS MINDS [EP] *From the film of the same name. Tracks: Curiosity (Aaron Hall)/ Gin & Juice (De Vante)/ It's Alright (Sista featuring Craig Mack).*	*MCA*	35	*30 Mar 96*	1
FEVER PITCH THE EP [EP] *From the film of the same name. Tracks: Goin' Back (Pretenders)/ There She Goes (La's)/ How Can We Hang On To A Dream (Orlando)/ Football (Nick Hornby).*	*Blanco Y Negro*	65	*10 May 97*	1
TRADE EP 2 [EP] *Tracks: Put Your House In Order (Steve Thomas)/ The Dawn (Tony De Vit). This was sales of a 12" only. The CD format had 6 tracks, including the two above, and was not eligible for the charts. The other 4 tracks were available on two other 12" singles. Trade EP 1 charted at No. 103, and Trade EP 3 at No. 96.*	*Tidy Trax*	75	*26 Sep 98*	1
HARD BEAT EP 19 *Tracks: Eternal Rhythm (Eternal 99)/Tragic (BK)/Please F**k Me (BK)/Don't Give Up (BK).*	*Nukleuz*	71	*10 Nov 01*	1

VARIOUS ARTISTS FOR CHILDREN'S PROMISE — UK/US

SINGLES:	HITS 1			WEEKS 2
IT'S ONLY ROCK 'N' ROLL *Charity record in aid of The Children's Promise (The Millennium Final Hour Appeal)*	*Universal Music TV*	19	*25 Dec 99*	8
IT'S ONLY ROCK 'N' ROLL [RE]	*Universal Music TV*	67	*26 Feb 00*	2

Junior VASQUEZ — US

(See also Shades Of Love (Junior Vasquez meets Johnny Vicious).)

SINGLES:	HITS 2			WEEKS 5
GET YOUR HANDS OFF MY MAN!	*Positiva*	22	*15 Jul 95*	3
IF MADONNA CALLS *Madonna's voice from a phone message left on his answering machine.*	*Multiply*	24	*31 Aug 96*	2

Elaine VASSELL – See BEATMASTERS; DEFINITION OF SOUND

VAST — US/Australia

SINGLES:	HITS 1			WEEKS 1
FREE	*Mushroom*	55	*16 Sep 00*	1

Sven VATH — Germany

SINGLES:	HITS 3			WEEKS 5
L'ESPERANZA	*Eye-Q*	63	*24 Jul 93*	2
AN ACCIDENT IN PARADISE (REMIXES)	*Eye-Q*	57	*6 Nov 93*	2
HARLEQUIN – THE BEAUTY AND THE BEAST	*Eye-Q*	72	*22 Oct 94*	1

Frankie VAUGHAN — UK

SINGLES:	HITS 31			WEEKS 232
ISTANBUL (NOT CONSTANTINOPLE) *Above hit: Frankie VAUGHAN with the Peter KNIGHT SINGERS.*	*His Master's Voice*	11	*30 Jan 54*	1
HAPPY DAYS AND LONELY NIGHTS *Above hit: Frankie VAUGHAN with Geoff LOVE and his Orchestra.*	*His Master's Voice*	12	*29 Jan 55*	3
TWEEDLE DEE *Above hit: Frankie VAUGHAN with Wally STOTT and his Orchestra and Chorus.*	*Philips*	17	*23 Apr 55*	1
SEVENTEEN *Above hit: Frankie VAUGHAN with Wally STOTT and his Orchestra.*	*Philips*	18	*3 Dec 55*	3
MY BOY FLAT TOP *Original by Boyd Bennett reached No. 39 in the US in 1955.*	*Philips*	20	*4 Feb 56*	2
THE GREEN DOOR	*Philips*	2	*10 Nov 56*	15
THE GARDEN OF EDEN	*Philips*	1	*12 Jan 57*	13

MAN ON FIRE / WANDERIN' EYES *Man On Fire from the film of the same name and originally recorded by Bing Crosby.* *Above 4: Frankie VAUGHAN with Wally STOTT and his Orchestra and Chorus.*	*Philips*	6	*5 Oct 57*	12
GOT-TA HAVE SOMETHING IN THE BANK, FRANK *Originally recorded by Bob Jaxon.* *Above hit: Frankie VAUGHAN and the KAYE SISTERS with Wally STOTT and his Orchestra.*	*Philips*	8	*2 Nov 57*	11
KISSES SWEETER THAN WINE *Originally recorded by The Weavers in 1951.* *Above hit: Frankie VAUGHAN with Wally STOTT and his Orchestra and Chorus.*	*Philips*	8	*21 Dec 57*	11
CAN'T GET ALONG WITHOUT YOU / WE ARE NOT ALONE *Certain pressings had title as We're Not Alone.* *Above hit: Frankie VAUGHAN with Ray ELLIS and his Orchestra and Chorus.*	*Philips*	11	*8 Mar 58*	6
KEWPIE DOLL *Above hit: Frankie VAUGHAN with Wally STOTT and his Orchestra and Chorus.*	*Philips*	10	*10 May 58*	12
WONDERFUL THINGS *From the film of the same name.* *Above hit: Frankie VAUGHAN with Wally STOTT and his Orchestra.*	*Philips*	22	*2 Aug 58*	3
WONDERFUL THINGS [RE]	*Philips*	27	*13 Sep 58*	3
AM I WASTING MY TIME ON YOU *Above hit: Frankie VAUGHAN with Ray ELLIS and his Orchestra.*	*Philips*	25	*11 Oct 58*	2
AM I WASTING MY TIME ON YOU [RE]	*Philips*	27	*10 Jan 59*	2
THAT'S MY DOLL *From the film 'The Lady Is A Square'.* *Above hit: Frankie VAUGHAN with Wally STOTT and his Orchestra.*	*Philips*	28	*31 Jan 59*	2
COME SOFTLY TO ME *Above hit: Frankie VAUGHAN and the KAYE SISTERS with Wally STOTT and his Orchestra.*	*Philips*	9	*2 May 59*	9
THE HEART OF A MAN *From the film of the same name.* *Above hit: Frankie VAUGHAN with Wally STOTT and his Orchestra and Chorus.*	*Philips*	5	*25 Jul 59*	14
WALKIN' TALL	*Philips*	28	*19 Sep 59*	1
WALKIN' TALL [RE]	*Philips*	29	*3 Oct 59*	1
WHAT MORE DO YOU WANT	*Philips*	25	*30 Jan 60*	2
KOOKIE LITTLE PARADISE	*Philips*	31	*24 Sep 60*	5
MILORD *Above hit: Frankie VAUGHAN with Wally STOTT and his Orchestra and Chorus.*	*Philips*	34	*29 Oct 60*	6
TOWER OF STRENGTH *Originally recorded by Gene McDaniels.*	*Philips*	1	*11 Nov 61*	13
DON'T STOP - TWIST!	*Philips*	22	*3 Feb 62*	7
HERCULES	*Philips*	42	*29 Sep 62*	4
LOOP DE LOOP *Original by Johnny Thunder reached No. 4 in the US in 1963.*	*Philips*	5	*26 Jan 63*	12
HEY MAMA	*Philips*	21	*22 Jun 63*	9
HELLO DOLLY *From the musical of the same name.*	*Philips*	18	*6 Jun 64*	11
SOMEONE MUST HAVE HURT YOU A LOT	*Philips*	46	*13 Mar 65*	1
THERE MUST BE A WAY	*Columbia*	7	*26 Aug 67*	19
SO TIRED	*Columbia*	21	*18 Nov 67*	9
THERE MUST BE A WAY	*Columbia*	30	*6 Jan 68*	2
NEVERTHELESS *Above 3: Frankie VAUGHAN with Alyn AINSWORTH and his Orchestra.*	*Columbia*	29	*2 Mar 68*	5
ALBUMS:	**HITS 4**			**WEEKS 20**
FRANKIE VAUGHAN AT THE LONDON PALLADIUM	*Philips*	6	*5 Sep 59*	2
FRANKIE VAUGHAN SONGBOOK	*Philips*	40	*4 Nov 67*	1
THERE MUST BE A WAY	*Columbia*	22	*25 Nov 67*	8
100 GOLDEN GREATS	*Ronco*	24	*12 Nov 77*	9

Malcolm VAUGHAN — UK

SINGLES:	**HITS 9**			**WEEKS 106**
EV'RY DAY OF MY LIFE	*His Master's Voice*	5	*2 Jul 55*	16
WITH YOUR LOVE *Above hit: Malcolm VAUGHAN with the Peter KNIGHT SINGERS.*	*His Master's Voice*	20	*28 Jan 56*	1
WITH YOUR LOVE [RE-1ST]	*His Master's Voice*	18	*11 Feb 56*	1
WITH YOUR LOVE [RE-2ND]	*His Master's Voice*	20	*3 Mar 56*	1
ST. THERESE OF THE ROSES	*His Master's Voice*	27	*27 Oct 56*	1
ST. THERESE OF THE ROSES [RE]	*His Master's Voice*	3	*17 Nov 56*	19
THE WORLD IS MINE	*His Master's Voice*	30	*13 Apr 57*	1
THE WORLD IS MINE [RE-1ST]	*His Master's Voice*	29	*4 May 57*	2
CHAPEL OF THE ROSES	*His Master's Voice*	13	*11 May 57*	8
THE WORLD IS MINE [RE-2ND]	*His Master's Voice*	26	*1 Jun 57*	1
MY SPECIAL ANGEL	*His Master's Voice*	3	*30 Nov 57*	14
TO BE LOVED	*His Master's Voice*	14	*22 Mar 58*	12
MORE THAN EVER (COME PRIMA) *Above 2: Malcolm VAUGHAN with the Michael SAMMES SINGERS.*	*His Master's Voice*	5	*18 Oct 58*	14
WAIT FOR ME (TI DIRO) / WILLINGLY (MELODIE PERDUE)	*His Master's Voice*	28	*28 Feb 59*	1
WAIT FOR ME (TI DIRO) [RE] *Majority of hits listed above had Orchestra conducted by Frank Cordell.*	*His Master's Voice*	13	*14 Mar 59*	14

Norman VAUGHAN with the "CORONA SCHOOL CHILDREN" — UK

SINGLES:	HITS 1			WEEKS 5
SWINGING IN THE RAIN (SINGIN' IN THE RAIN)	*Pye*	34	*19 May 62*	5
Originally recorded by Cliff Edwards.				

Sarah VAUGHAN — US

(See also Various Artists: Studio Cast 'South Pacific'.)

SINGLES:	HITS 3			WEEKS 34
PASSING STRANGERS	*Mercury*	22	*28 Sep 57*	2
Above hit: Sarah VAUGHAN and Billy ECKSTINE.				
BROKEN-HEARTED MELODY	*Mercury*	7	*12 Sep 59*	13
LET'S / SERENATA	*Columbia*	37	*31 Dec 60*	3
Serenata does not credit the Chorus. Serenata originally recorded as an instrumental by Leroy Anderson.				
Above hit: Sarah VAUGHAN with Joe REISMAN'S ORCHESTRA and Chorus.				
SERENATA [RE]	*Columbia*	47	*4 Feb 61*	1
PASSING STRANGERS [RI]	*Mercury*	20	*15 Mar 69*	15
Above hit: Sarah VAUGHAN and Billy ECKSTINE.				
EPS:	**HITS 1**			**WEEKS 2**
SMOOTH SARAH	*Mercury*	11	*26 Mar 60*	2
ALBUMS:	**HITS 1**			**WEEKS 1**
NO COUNT - SARAH	*Mercury*	19	*26 Mar 60*	1

Stevie Ray VAUGHAN and DOUBLE TROUBLE — US

ALBUMS:	HITS 1			WEEKS 1
IN STEP	*Epic*	63	*15 Jul 89*	1

VAUGHAN BROTHERS — US

ALBUMS:	HITS 1			WEEKS 1
FAMILY STYLE	*Epic*	63	*20 Oct 90*	1

Billy VAUGHN and his Orchestra — US

(See also Pat Boone; Tab Hunter; Hilltoppers.)

SINGLES:	HITS 2			WEEKS 8
THE SHIFTING WHISPERING SANDS	*London*	20	*28 Jun 56*	1
Above hit: Billy VAUGHN and his Orchestra and Chorus, narration by Ken NORDENE.				
A THEME FROM THE 'THREEPENNY OPERA' (MACK THE KNIFE)	*London*	12	*24 Mar 56*	7

VEBA - See RAE and CHRISTIAN

Bobby VEE — US

(See also Bobby Vee and the Crickets.)

SINGLES:	HITS 10			WEEKS 134
RUBBER BALL	*London*	4	*21 Jan 61*	11
Written by Gene Pitney.				
MORE THAN I CAN SAY / STAYIN' IN	*London*	4	*15 Apr 61*	16
Stayin' In no longer listed from 13 May 61. As an AA side it peaked at No. 13.				
HOW MANY TEARS	*London*	10	*5 Aug 61*	13
TAKE GOOD CARE OF MY BABY	*London*	3	*28 Oct 61*	16
Originally recorded by Dion.				
RUN TO HIM	*London*	6	*23 Dec 61*	15
PLEASE DON'T ASK ABOUT BARBARA	*Liberty*	29	*10 Mar 62*	9
SHARING YOU	*Liberty*	10	*9 Jun 62*	13
Above hit: Bobby VEE with the Johnny MANN SINGERS.				
A FOREVER KIND OF LOVE	*Liberty*	13	*29 Sep 62*	19
THE NIGHT HAS A THOUSAND EYES	*Liberty*	3	*9 Feb 63*	12
From the film 'Just For Fun'.				
BOBBY TOMORROW	*Liberty*	21	*22 Jun 63*	10
The B-side Charms was the official A-side in the US.				
Above hit: Bobby VEE with the Johnny MANN SINGERS.				
EPS:	**HITS 4**			**WEEKS 31**
BOBBY VEE NO. 1	*London*	19	*26 Aug 61*	1
SINCERELY	*Liberty*	8	*22 Dec 62*	24
A FOREVER KIND OF LOVE	*Liberty*	14	*29 Jun 63*	4
BOBBY VEE'S BIGGEST HITS	*Stateside*	16	*5 Oct 63*	2
ALBUMS:	**HITS 6**			**WEEKS 46**
TAKE GOOD CARE OF MY BABY	*London*	7	*24 Feb 62*	8
HITS OF THE ROCKIN' 50'S	*London*	20	*31 Mar 62*	1
A BOBBY VEE RECORDING SESSION	*Liberty*	10	*12 Jan 63*	11
BOBBY VEE'S GOLDEN GREATS	*Liberty*	10	*20 Apr 63*	14
THE NIGHT HAS A THOUSAND EYES	*Liberty*	15	*5 Oct 63*	2
THE BOBBY VEE SINGLES ALBUM	*United Artists*	5	*19 Apr 80*	10

Bobby VEE and the CRICKETS — US

(See also Crickets; Bobby Vee.)

EPS:	HITS 1			WEEKS 16
JUST FOR FUN	*Liberty*	1	*20 Apr 63*	16
ALBUMS:	**HITS 1**			**WEEKS 27**
BOBBY VEE MEETS THE CRICKETS	*Liberty*	2	*27 Oct 62*	27

Little Louie VEGA and Marc ANTHONY — US

SINGLES:	HITS 1			WEEKS 4
RIDE ON THE RHYTHM	*Atlantic*	71	*5 Oct 91*	1
RIDE ON THE RHYTHM [RI]	*Atlantic*	70	*23 May 92*	1
Above hit: Louie VEGA and Marc ANTHONY.				
RIDE ON THE RHYTHM [RM]	*Perfecto Red*	36	*31 Jan 98*	2
Remixed by Mr. Roy.				
Above hit: "Little" LOUIE and Marc ANTHONY.				

Suzanne VEGA — US

SINGLES:	HITS 11			WEEKS 52
SMALL BLUE THING	*A&M*	65	*18 Jan 86*	3
MARLENE ON THE WALL	*A&M*	21	*22 Mar 86*	9
Original release reached No. 83 in 1985. Written about Marlene Dietrich.				
LEFT OF CENTRE	*A&M*	32	*7 Jun 86*	9
Label has British spelling; the sleeve the US variant 'Center'. From the film 'Pretty In Pink'.				
Above hit: Suzanne VEGA featuring Joe JACKSON on piano.				
LUKA	*A&M*	23	*23 May 87*	8
TOM'S DINER	*A&M*	58	*18 Jul 87*	3
BOOK OF DREAMS	*A&M*	66	*19 May 90*	1
TOM'S DINER [RM]	*A&M*	2	*28 Jul 90*	10
Though this credits her as a featuring artist, this is actually a remix by DNA of her earlier hit.				
Above hit: DNA featuring Suzanne VEGA.				
IN LIVERPOOL	*A&M*	52	*22 Aug 92*	2
99.9° F	*A&M*	46	*24 Oct 92*	2
BLOOD MAKES NOISE	*A&M*	60	*19 Dec 92*	3
WHEN HEROES GO DOWN	*A&M*	58	*6 Mar 93*	1
NO CHEAP THRILL	*A&M*	40	*22 Feb 97*	1
ALBUMS:	**HITS 6**			**WEEKS 127**
SUZANNE VEGA	*A&M*	55	*19 Oct 85*	14
SUZANNE VEGA [RE]	*A&M*	11	*12 Apr 86*	57
SOLITUDE STANDING	*A&M*	2	*9 May 87*	39
DAYS OF OPEN HAND	*A&M*	7	*28 Apr 90*	7
99.9° F	*A&M*	20	*19 Sep 92*	4
NINE OBJECTS OF DESIRE	*A&M*	43	*8 Mar 97*	3
TRIED AND TRUE - THE BEST OF SUZANNE VEGA	*A&M*	46	*31 Oct 98*	3

Tata VEGA — US

SINGLES:	HITS 1			WEEKS 4
GET IT UP FOR LOVE / I JUST KEEP THINKING ABOUT YOU BABY	*Motown*	52	*26 May 79*	4

VEGAS — UK

SINGLES:	HITS 3			WEEKS 10
POSSESSED	*RCA*	32	*19 Sep 92*	4
SHE	*RCA*	43	*28 Nov 92*	4
WALK INTO THE WIND	*RCA*	65	*3 Apr 93*	2
Features vocals by Siobhan Fahey of Shakespears Sister.				

Rosie VELA — US

SINGLES:	HITS 1			WEEKS 7
MAGIC SMILE	*A&M*	27	*17 Jan 87*	7
ALBUMS:	**HITS 1**			**WEEKS 11**
ZAZU	*A&M*	20	*31 Jan 87*	11

Wil. VELOZ - See LOS DEL MAR featuring Wil. VELOZ

VELVELETTES — US

SINGLES:	HITS 1			WEEKS 7
THESE THINGS WILL KEEP ME LOVING YOU	*Tamla Motown*	34	*31 Jul 71*	7

VELVET UNDERGROUND — UK/US

SINGLES:	HITS 1			WEEKS 1
VENUS IN FURS (LIVE)	*Sire*	71	*12 Mar 94*	1
Featured in the Dunlop Tyres TV commercial. Live recording from the Olympia in Paris, Jun 93.				

ALBUMS:	HITS 3			WEEKS 9
V.U.	*Polydor*	47	*23 Feb 85*	4
Remix album of previously unreleased material.				
LIVE MCMXCIII	*Sire*	70	*13 Nov 93*	1
Live recordings from the Olympia in Paris, Jun 93.				
THE BEST OF LOU REED AND THE VELVET UNDERGROUND	*Global Television*	56	*28 Oct 95*	4
Features both Lou Reed's solo and group material.				
Above hit: Lou REED and the VELVET UNDERGROUND.				

VELVETS — US

SINGLES:	HITS 2			WEEKS 2
THAT LUCKY OLD SUN	*London*	46	*13 May 61*	1
TONIGHT (COULD BE THE NIGHT)	*London*	50	*19 Aug 61*	1

VENGABOYS — Holland/Hungary/Brazil/Spain/Trinidad

SINGLES:	HITS 9			WEEKS 99
UP AND DOWN	*Positiva*	4	*28 Nov 98*	15
WE LIKE TO PARTY! (THE VENGABUS)	*Positiva*	3	*13 Mar 99*	14
BOOM, BOOM, BOOM, BOOM!!	*Positiva*	1	*26 Jun 99*	15
WE'RE GOING TO IBIZA!	*Jive*	69	*11 Sept 99*	1
Import. Based around Typically Tropical's Barbados.				
Above hit: DANSKI and DJ DELMUNDO present VENGABOYS.				
WE'RE GOING TO IBIZA!	*Positiva*	1	*18 Sept 99*	12
KISS (WHEN THE SUN DON'T SHINE)	*Positiva*	3	*18 Dec 99*	18
SHALALA LALA	*Positiva*	5	*11 Mar 00*	10
Originally recorded by the Walkers.				
UNCLE JOHN FROM JAMAICA	*Positiva*	6	*8 Jul 00*	7
CHEEKAH BOW-BOW (THAT COMPUTER SONG)	*Positiva*	19	*14 Oct 00*	5
Above hit: VENGABOYS featuring CHEEKAH				
FOREVER AS ONE	*Positiva*	28	*24 Feb 01*	2
ALBUMS:	**HITS 2**			**WEEKS 77**
THE PARTY ALBUM!	*Positiva*	6	*3 Apr 99*	49
THE PLATINUM ALBUM	*Positiva*	9	*25 Mar 00*	28

VENOM — UK

ALBUMS:	HITS 2			WEEKS 2
AT WAR WITH SATAN	*Neat*	64	*21 Apr 84*	1
POSSESSED	*Neat*	99	*13 Apr 85*	1

VENT 414 — UK

SINGLES:	HITS 1			WEEKS 1
FIXER	*Polydor*	71	*28 Sep 96*	1

Anthony VENTURA ORCHESTRA — Switzerland

ALBUMS:	HITS 1			WEEKS 4
DREAM LOVER	*Lotus*	44	*20 Jan 79*	4

VENTURES — US

SINGLES:	HITS 4			WEEKS 31
WALK DON'T RUN	*Top Rank*	8	*10 Sep 60*	13
Originally recorded by Johnny Smith.				
PERFIDIA	*London*	4	*3 Dec 60*	13
Originally recorded by Xavier Cugat in 1941.				
RAM-BUNK-SHUSH	*London*	45	*11 Mar 61*	1
Originally recorded by Bill Doggett in 1957.				
LULLABY OF THE LEAVES	*London*	43	*13 May 61*	4
Originally recorded by George Olsen in 1932.				
EPS:	**HITS 1**			**WEEKS 1**
THE VENTURES	*London*	20	*13 May 61*	1

VERACOCHA — Holland

SINGLES:	HITS 1			WEEKS 4
CARTE BLANCHE	*Positiva*	22	*15 May 99*	4

Tom VERLAINE — US

ALBUMS:	HITS 1			WEEKS 1
FLASH LIGHT	*Fontana*	99	*14 Mar 87*	1

Al VERLANE – See PING PING and Al VERLANE

VERNONS GIRLS — UK

SINGLES:	HITS 4			WEEKS 31
LOVER PLEASE *Originally recorded by Mirt Merley and his Rhythm Steppers.*	*Decca*	16	*19 May 62*	9
LOVER PLEASE [RE] / YOU KNOW WHAT I MEAN *You Know What I Mean listed from 1 Sep 62.*	*Decca*	39	*25 Aug 62*	7
THE LOCO-MOTION	*Decca*	47	*8 Sep 62*	1
YOU KNOW WHAT I MEAN [RE-1ST]	*Decca*	37	*20 Oct 62*	3
YOU KNOW WHAT I MEAN [RE-2ND]	*Decca*	50	*17 Nov 62*	1
FUNNY ALL OVER	*Decca*	31	*5 Jan 63*	8
DO THE BIRD	*Decca*	50	*20 Apr 63*	1
DO THE BIRD [RE]	*Decca*	44	*4 May 63*	1

VERNONS WONDERLAND — Germany

SINGLES:	HITS 1			WEEKS 1
VERNONS WONDERLAND *First released in Germany, 1993. Used on the TV series 'Baywatch' as incidental music.*	*Eye-Q Classics*	59	*25 May 96*	1

Runnig VERRELL – See Ted HEATH and his Music

VERTICAL HORIZON — US

SINGLES:	HITS 1			WEEKS 2
EVERYTHING YOU WANT	*RCA*	42	*26 Aug 00*	2

VERUCA SALT — US

SINGLES:	HITS 4			WEEKS 5
SEETHER	*Scared Hitless*	61	*2 Jul 94*	1
SEETHER [RI]	*Hi-Rise Recordings*	73	*3 Dec 94*	1
NUMBER ONE BLIND	*Hi-Rise Recordings*	68	*4 Feb 95*	1
VOLCANO GIRLS	*Outpost Recordings*	56	*22 Feb 97*	1
BENJAMIN	*Outpost Recordings*	75	*30 Aug 97*	1
ALBUMS:	**HITS 1**			**WEEKS 2**
AMERICAN THIGHS *Named after a line in AC/DC's You Shook Me All Night Long.*	*Hi-Rise Recordings*	47	*15 Oct 94*	2

VERVE — UK

SINGLES:	HITS 9			WEEKS 50
SHE'S A SUPERSTAR	*Hut*	66	*4 Jul 92*	1
BLUE	*Hut*	69	*22 May 93*	1
THIS IS MUSIC	*Hut*	35	*13 May 95*	3
ON YOUR OWN	*Hut*	28	*24 Jun 95*	2
HISTORY	*Hut*	24	*30 Sep 95*	3
BITTER SWEET SYMPHONY *Samples an orchestral version of the Rolling Stones' The Last Time by Andrew Loog Oldham.*	*Hut*	2	*28 Jun 97*	11
THE DRUGS DON'T WORK	*Hut*	1	*13 Sep 97*	12
LUCKY MAN	*Hut*	7	*6 Dec 97*	13
BITTER SWEET SYMPHONY [RE]	*Hut*	70	*3 Jan 98*	2
THE DRUGS DON'T WORK [RE]	*Hut*	66	*3 Jan 98*	1
SONNET *Import.*	*Hut*	74	*30 May 98*	1
ALBUMS:	**HITS 3**			**WEEKS 97**
A STORM IN HEAVEN	*Hut*	27	*3 Jul 93*	2
A NORTHERN SOUL	*Hut*	13	*15 Jul 95*	11
URBAN HYMNS	*Hut*	1	*11 Oct 97*	84

A VERY GOOD FRIEND OF MINE featuring JOY — Italy

SINGLES:	HITS 1			WEEKS 1
JUST ROUND *Samples Stevie Wonder's Uptight.*	*Positiva*	55	*3 Jul 99*	1

VIBRATIONS – See Tony JACKSON and the VIBRATIONS

VIBRATORS — UK

SINGLES:	HITS 2			WEEKS 8
AUTOMATIC LOVER	*Epic*	35	*18 Mar 78*	5
JUDY SAYS (KNOCK YOU IN THE HEAD)	*Epic*	70	*17 Jun 78*	3
ALBUMS:	**HITS 2**			**WEEKS 7**
PURE MANIA	*Epic*	49	*25 Jun 77*	5
V2	*Epic*	33	*29 Apr 78*	2

VICE SQUAD — UK

SINGLES:	HITS 1			WEEKS 1
OUT OF REACH	*Riot City*	68	*13 Feb 82*	1

ALBUMS:	HITS 2			WEEKS 10
NO CAUSE FOR CONCERN	*Zonophone*	32	*24 Oct 81*	5
STAND STRONG STAND PROUD	*Riot City*	47	*22 May 82*	5

Johnny VICIOUS - See SHADES OF LOVE (Junior VASQUEZ meets Johnny VICIOUS)

Sid VICIOUS — UK

(See also Sex Pistols.)

ALBUMS:	HITS 1			WEEKS 8
SID SINGS	*Virgin*	30	*15 Dec 79*	8

VICIOUS CIRCLES — UK

SINGLES:	HITS 1			WEEKS 1
VICIOUS CIRCLES	*Platipus*	68	*16 Dec 00*	1

VICIOUS PINK — UK

SINGLES:	HITS 1			WEEKS 4
CCCAN'T YOU SEE...	*Parlophone*	67	*15 Sep 84*	4

Mike VICKERS - See Kenny EVERETT

Maria VIDAL — US

SINGLES:	HITS 1			WEEKS 13
BODY ROCK *From the film of the same name.*	*EMI America*	11	*24 Aug 85*	13

VIDEO KIDS — Holland

SINGLES:	HITS 1			WEEKS 1
WOODPECKERS FROM SPACE *Original release reached No. 89 earlier that year.*	*Epic*	72	*5 Oct 85*	1

VIDEO SYMPHONIC — UK

SINGLES:	HITS 1			WEEKS 3
THE FLAME TREES OF THIKA *Theme from the Thames ITV series of the same name.*	*EMI*	42	*24 Oct 81*	3

VIENNA PHILHARMONIC ORCHESTRA conducted by Aram KHACHATURIAN — Austria

SINGLES:	HITS 1			WEEKS 14
THE 'ONEDIN LINE' THEME *Music from Spartacus, adapted for the theme of the BBC1 TV series.*	*Decca*	15	*18 Dec 71*	14
ALBUMS:	**HITS 1**			**WEEKS 15**
SPARTACUS	*Decca*	16	*22 Jan 72*	15

VIENNA SYMPHONY ORCHESTRA — Austria

ALBUMS:	HITS 1			WEEKS 4
SYMPHONIC ROCK WITH THE VIENNA SYMPHONY ORCHESTRA	*Stylus*	43	*4 Apr 87*	4

VIEW FROM THE HILL — UK

SINGLES:	HITS 2			WEEKS 6
NO CONVERSATION	*EMI*	58	*19 Jul 86*	3
I'M NO REBEL	*EMI*	59	*21 Feb 87*	3

VIKKI — UK

SINGLES:	HITS 1			WEEKS 3
LOVE IS . . . *UKs Eurovision entry in 1983, it came 4th.*	*PRT*	49	*4 May 85*	3

VILLAGE PEOPLE — US

SINGLES:	HITS 6			WEEKS 67
SAN FRANCISCO (YOU'VE GOT ME)	*DJM*	45	*3 Dec 77*	6
Y.M.C.A.	*Mercury*	1	*25 Nov 78*	16
IN THE NAVY	*Mercury*	2	*17 Mar 79*	9
GO WEST	*Mercury*	15	*16 Jun 79*	8
CAN'T STOP THE MUSIC *From the film of the same name.*	*Mercury*	11	*9 Aug 80*	11
SEX OVER THE PHONE	*Record Shack*	59	*9 Feb 85*	5
Y.M.C.A. '93 REMIX [RM-1ST] *Remixed by Dave Ford.*		12	*4 Dec 93*	7
IN THE NAVY - 1994 REMIXES [RM] *Remixed by Mr. Hyder and Mr. Kalif.*	*Bell*	36	*28 May 94*	2
YMCA MILLENNIUM MIX [RM-2ND] *Remixed by Almighty.*	*Wrasse*	35	*27 Nov 99*	3

ALBUMS:	HITS 4			WEEKS 37
CRUISIN'	*Mercury*	24	*27 Jan 79*	9
GO WEST	*Mercury*	14	*12 May 79*	19
CAN'T STOP THE MUSIC [OST]	*Mercury*	9	*16 Aug 80*	8
Includes tracks by Ritchie Family and David London.				
THE BEST OF THE VILLAGE PEOPLE	*Bell*	72	*18 Dec 93*	1

Gene VINCENT — US

SINGLES:	HITS 8			WEEKS 51
BE BOP A LULA	*Capitol*	30	*14 Jul 56*	2
From the film 'The Girl Can't Help It'.				
BE BOP A LULA [RE-1ST]	*Capitol*	16	*25 Aug 56*	3
BE BOP A LULA [RE-2ND]	*Capitol*	23	*29 Sep 56*	2
RACE WITH THE DEVIL	*Capitol*	28	*13 Oct 56*	1
Above 4: Gene VINCENT and the BLUE CAPS.				
BLUEJEAN BOP	*Capitol*	16	*20 Oct 56*	5
Above hit: Gene VINCENT and his BLUE CAPS.				
WILD CAT	*Capitol*	21	*9 Jan 60*	3
MY HEART	*Capitol*	16	*12 Mar 60*	6
Above hit: Gene VINCENT and the BLUE CAPS.				
WILD CAT [RE]	*Capitol*	39	*12 Mar 60*	3
MY HEART [RE-1ST]	*Capitol*	47	*30 Apr 60*	1
MY HEART [RE-2ND]	*Capitol*	36	*21 May 60*	1
PISTOL PACKIN' MAMA	*Capitol*	15	*18 Jun 60*	9
Originally recorded by Al Dexter.				
Above hit: Gene VINCENT with the BEAT BOYS.				
SHE SHE LITTLE SHEILA	*Capitol*	22	*3 Jun 61*	10
Recording from 1959.				
SHE SHE LITTLE SHEILA [RE]	*Capitol*	44	*19 Aug 61*	1
I'M GOING HOME (TO SEE MY BABY)	*Capitol*	36	*2 Sep 61*	4
Above hit: Gene VINCENT with SOUNDS INCORPORATED.				
EPS:	**HITS 1**			**WEEKS 1**
RACE WITH THE DEVIL	*Capitol*	19	*6 Oct 62*	1
ALBUMS:	**HITS 1**			**WEEKS 2**
CRAZY TIMES	*Capitol*	12	*16 Jul 60*	2

Vinnie VINCENT — US

ALBUMS:	HITS 1			WEEKS 2
ALL SYSTEMS GO	*Chrysalis*	51	*28 May 88*	2

VINDALOO SUMMER SPECIAL — UK

SINGLES:	HITS 1			WEEKS 3
ROCKIN' WITH RITA (HEAD TO TOE)	*Vindaloo*	56	*19 Jul 86*	3

Bobby VINTON — US

SINGLES:	HITS 3			WEEKS 29
ROSES ARE RED (MY LOVE)	*Columbia*	15	*4 Aug 62*	8
THERE! I'VE SAID IT AGAIN	*Columbia*	34	*21 Dec 63*	10
Originally recorded by the Benny Carter Orchestra in 1941.				
BLUE VELVET	*Epic*	2	*29 Sep 90*	10
Featured in the Nivea Lotion TV commercial. Originally recorded by Tony Bennett in 1951.				
ROSES ARE RED (MY LOVE) [RI]	*Epic*	71	*17 Nov 90*	1
ALBUMS:	**HITS 1**			**WEEKS 2**
BLUE VELVET	*Epic*	67	*17 Nov 90*	2
Compilation.				

VINYL GROOVER and the RED HED — UK

SINGLES:	HITS 1			WEEKS 1
ROK DA HOUSE	*Nukleuz*	72	*27 Jan 01*	1

VIOLENT FEMMES — US

ALBUMS:	HITS 1			WEEKS 1
THE BLIND LEADING THE NAKED	*Slash*	81	*1 Mar 86*	1

VIOLINSKI — UK

SINGLES:	HITS 1			WEEKS 9
CLOG DANCE	*Jet*	17	*17 Feb 79*	9
ALBUMS:	**HITS 1**			**WEEKS 1**
NO CAUSE FOR ALARM	*Jet*	49	*26 May 79*	1

VIPER — Belgium

SINGLES:	HITS 1			WEEKS 1
THE TWISTER *Samples Nina Simone's Feeling Good.*	*Hooj Choons*	55	*7 Feb 98*	1

VIPERS SKIFFLE GROUP — UK

SINGLES:	HITS 3			WEEKS 18
DON'T YOU ROCK ME DADDY-O	*Parlophone*	10	*26 Jan 57*	9
THE CUMBERLAND GAP	*Parlophone*	10	*23 Mar 57*	6
STREAMLINE TRAIN	*Parlophone*	23	*1 Jun 57*	3

VIRGINIA – See Tom NOVY

VIRUS — UK

SINGLES:	HITS 2			WEEKS 3
SUN	*Perfecto*	62	*26 Aug 95*	1
MOON *Based on U2's Lemon.*	*Perfecto*	36	*25 Jan 97*	2

VISAGE — UK

(See also Midge Ure.)

SINGLES:	HITS 7			WEEKS 56
FADE TO GREY	*Polydor*	8	*20 Dec 80*	15
MIND OF A TOY	*Polydor*	13	*14 Mar 81*	8
VISAGE	*Polydor*	21	*11 Jul 81*	7
THE DAMNED DON'T CRY	*Polydor*	11	*13 Mar 82*	8
NIGHT TRAIN	*Polydor*	12	*26 Jun 82*	10
PLEASURE BOYS	*Polydor*	44	*13 Nov 82*	3
LOVE GLOVE	*Polydor*	54	*1 Sep 84*	3
FADE TO GREY [RM] *Remixed by Bassheads and Andy Stevenson.*	*Polydor*	39	*28 Aug 93*	2

ALBUMS:	HITS 4			WEEKS 58
VISAGE	*Polydor*	13	*24 Jan 81*	29
THE ANVIL	*Polydor*	6	*3 Apr 82*	16
FADE TO GREY - THE SINGLES COLLECTION	*Polydor*	38	*19 Nov 83*	11
BEAT BOY	*Polydor*	79	*3 Nov 84*	2

Michelle VISAGE – See S.O.U.L. S.Y.S.T.E.M. introducing Michelle VISAGE

VISCOUNTS — UK

SINGLES:	HITS 2			WEEKS 18
SHORT'NIN' BREAD	*Pye*	16	*15 Oct 60*	8
WHO PUT THE BOMP	*Pye*	21	*16 Sep 61*	10

VISION — UK

SINGLES:	HITS 1			WEEKS 1
LOVE DANCE	*MVM*	74	*9 Jul 83*	1

VISION MASTERS and Tony KING featuring Kylie MINOGUE — UK/Australia

(See also Kylie Minogue.)

SINGLES:	HITS 1			WEEKS 1
KEEP ON PUMPIN' IT	*PWL*	49	*30 Nov 91*	1

VITA – See N*E*R*D featuring Lee HARVEY and VITA

VIXEN — US

SINGLES:	HITS 6			WEEKS 21
EDGE OF A BROKEN HEART *Written and produced by Richard Marx.*	*Manhattan*	51	*3 Sep 88*	4
CRYIN'	*EMI Manhattan*	27	*4 Mar 89*	4
LOVE MADE ME	*EMI USA*	36	*3 Jun 89*	4
EDGE OF A BROKEN HEART [RI]	*EMI USA*	59	*2 Sep 89*	2
HOW MUCH LOVE	*EMI USA*	35	*28 Jul 90*	3
LOVE IS A KILLER	*EMI USA*	41	*20 Oct 90*	2
NOT A MINUTE TOO SOON	*EMI USA*	37	*16 Mar 91*	2

ALBUMS:	HITS 2			WEEKS 5
VIXEN	*Manhattan*	66	*8 Oct 88*	1
REV IT UP	*EMI USA*	20	*18 Aug 90*	4

VOGGUE — Canada

SINGLES:	HITS 1			WEEKS 6
DANCIN' THE NIGHT AWAY	*Mercury*	39	*18 Jul 81*	6

VOICE OF LIFE — US

SINGLES:	HITS 1			WEEKS 2
THE WORD IS LOVE (SAY THE WORD)	*AM:PM*	26	*21 Mar 98*	2

VOICE OF THE BEEHIVE — UK/US

SINGLES:	HITS 6			WEEKS 51
I SAY NOTHING	*London*	45	*14 Nov 87*	5
I WALK THE EARTH	*London*	42	*5 Mar 88*	4
DON'T CALL ME BABY	*London*	15	*14 May 88*	10
I SAY NOTHING [RI]	*London*	22	*23 Jul 88*	6
I WALK THE EARTH [RI]	*London*	46	*22 Oct 88*	4
MONSTERS AND ANGELS	*London*	17	*13 Jul 91*	10
I THINK I LOVE YOU	*London*	25	*28 Sep 91*	6
PERFECT PLACE	*London*	37	*11 Jan 92*	6
ALBUMS:	**HITS 2**			**WEEKS 26**
LET IT BEE	*London*	13	*2 Jul 88*	13
HONEY LINGERS	*London*	17	*24 Aug 91*	13

Sterling VOID — UK

SINGLES:	HITS 1			WEEKS 3
RUNAWAY GIRL / IT'S ALL RIGHT	*ffrr*	53	*4 Feb 89*	3

VOLCANO — UK/Norway

SINGLES:	HITS 2			WEEKS 4
MORE TO LOVE	*Deconstruction*	32	*23 Jul 94*	3
THAT'S THE WAY LOVE IS	*Exp*	72	*18 Nov 95*	1
Above hit: VOLCANO with Sam CARTWRIGHT.				

VOLATILE AGENTS featuring Simone BENN — UK

SINGLES:	HITS 1			WEEKS 3
HOOKED ON YOU	*Melting Pot*	54	*15 Dec 01*	3

Herbert VON KARAJAN conducting the BERLIN PHILHARMONIC ORCHESTRA — Austria/Germany

ALBUMS:	HITS 5			WEEKS 18
BEETHOVEN TRIPLE CONCERTO	*His Master's Voice*	51	*26 Sep 70*	2
Above hit: BERLIN PHILHARMONIC ORCHESTRA conducted by Herbert VON KARAJAN – Soloist: David OISTRAKH (violin), Mstislav ROSTROPOVICH (cello), Sviatoslau RICHTER (piano).				
THE ESSENTIAL KARAJAN	*Deutsche Grammophon*	51	*16 Apr 88*	5
Above hit: Herbert VON KARAJAN.				
HOLST: THE PLANETS	*Deutsche Grammophon*	52	*3 Aug 91*	2
KARAJAN: ADAGIO	*Deutsche Grammophon*	30	*7 Oct 95*	8
ADAGIO 2	*Deutsche Grammophon*	63	*13 Apr 96*	1
Compilation of material from 1964-1986.				

Anne VON OTTER meets Elvis COSTELLO — Sweden/UK

(See also Elvis Costello.)

ALBUMS:	HITS 1			WEEKS 1
FOR THE STARS	*Deutsche Grammophon*	67	*31 Mar 01*	1

VOODOO and SERANO — Germany

SINGLES:	HITS 1			WEEKS 4
BLOOD IS PUMPIN'	*Xtrahard*	19	*3 Feb 01*	4

VOW WOW — US/Japan

ALBUMS:	HITS 1			WEEKS 1
HELTER SKELTER	*Arista*	75	*18 Mar 89*	1

VOYAGE — UK/France

SINGLES:	HITS 3			WEEKS 27
FROM EAST TO WEST / SCOTS MACHINE	*GTO*	13	*17 Jun 78*	13
Scots Machine listed from 24 Jun 78.				
SOUVENIRS	*GTO*	56	*25 Nov 78*	7
LET'S FLY AWAY	*GTO*	38	*24 Mar 79*	7
ALBUMS:	**HITS 1**			**WEEKS 1**
VOYAGE	*GTO*	59	*9 Sep 78*	1

VOYAGER — UK

SINGLES:	HITS 1			WEEKS 8
HALFWAY HOTEL	*Mountain*	33	*26 May 79*	8

VYBE — US

SINGLES:	HITS 1			WEEKS 1
WARM SUMMER DAZE *Samples William Bell and Judy Clay's Private Number.*	*Fourth & Broadway*	60	*7 Oct 95*	1

W

Kristine W — US

(See also Our Tribe/One Tribe/O.T. Quartet.)

SINGLES:	HITS 3			WEEKS 7
FEEL WHAT YOU WANT	*Champion*	33	*25 Jun 94*	3
ONE MORE TRY	*Champion*	41	*25 May 96*	1
LAND OF THE LIVING	*Champion*	57	*21 Dec 96*	1
FEEL WHAT YOU WANT [RM] *Remixed by Peter Ries.*	*Champion*	40	*5 Jul 97*	2

W.A.S.P. — US

SINGLES:	HITS 12			WEEKS 38
WILD CHILD	*Capitol*	71	*31 May 86*	2
95 - NASTY	*Capitol*	70	*11 Oct 86*	1
SCREAM UNTIL YOU LIKE IT (THEME FROM 'GHOULIES II') *Theme from the film.*	*Capitol*	32	*29 Aug 87*	5
I DON'T NEED NO DOCTOR *Live recording from Long Beach Arena, California.*	*Capitol*	31	*31 Oct 87*	5
ANIMAL (F**K LIKE A BEAST) *Original release reached No. 83 in 1984.*	*Music For Nations*	61	*20 Feb 88*	3
MEAN MAN	*Capitol*	21	*4 Mar 89*	5
THE REAL ME	*Capitol*	23	*27 May 89*	5
FOREVER FREE	*Capitol*	25	*9 Sep 89*	5
CHAINSAW CHARLIE (MURDERS IN THE NEW MORGUE)	*Parlophone*	17	*4 Apr 92*	2
THE IDOL	*Parlophone*	41	*6 Jun 92*	2
I AM ONE	*Parlophone*	56	*31 Oct 92*	1
SUNSET AND BABYLON	*Capitol*	38	*23 Oct 93*	2

ALBUMS:	HITS 8			WEEKS 24
W.A.S.P.	*Capitol*	51	*8 Sep 84*	2
THE LAST COMMAND	*Capitol*	48	*9 Nov 85*	1
INSIDE THE ELECTRIC CIRCUS	*Capitol*	53	*8 Nov 86*	3
LIVE . . . IN THE RAW	*Capitol*	23	*26 Sep 87*	4
THE HEADLESS CHILDREN	*Capitol*	8	*15 Apr 89*	10
THE CRIMSON IDOL	*Parlophone*	21	*20 Jun 92*	2
FIRST BLOOD . . . LAST CUTS *Compilation.*	*Capitol*	69	*6 Nov 93*	1
STILL NOT BLACK ENOUGH	*Raw Power*	52	*1 Jul 95*	1

Andrew W.K. — US

SINGLES:				
PARTY HARD	*Mercury*	19	*10 Nov 01*	4

ALBUMS:				
I GET WET	*Mercury*	71	*24 Nov 01*	1

W.O.S.P. — UK

SINGLES:	HITS 1			WEEKS 1
GETTIN' INTO U	*Data*	48	*17 Nov 01*	1

Bill WADDINGTON – See CORONATION STREET CAST

Adam WADE with the George PAXTON Orchestra and Chorus — US

SINGLES:	HITS 1			WEEKS 6
TAKE GOOD CARE OF HER	*His Master's Voice*	38	*10 Jun 61*	1
TAKE GOOD CARE OF HER [RE]	*His Master's Voice*	38	*24 Jun 61*	5

WAG YA TAIL featuring Lonnie Liston SMITH — UK

SINGLES:	HITS 1			WEEKS 1
XPAND YA MIND (EXPANSIONS)	*PWL Sanctuary*	49	*3 Oct 92*	1

WAH! — UK

SINGLES:	HITS 3			WEEKS 26
THE STORY OF THE BLUES	*Eternal*	3	*25 Dec 82*	12
HOPE (I WISH YOU'D BELIEVE ME)	*WEA*	37	*19 Mar 83*	5

COME BACK	*Beggars Banquet*	20	*30 Jun 84*	9
Above hit: MIGHTY WAH!				
ALBUMS:	**HITS 2**			**WEEKS 11**
NAH=POO-THE ART OF BLUFF	*Eternal*	33	*18 Jul 81*	5
A WORD TO THE WISE GUY	*Beggars Banquet*	28	*4 Aug 84*	6
Above hit: MIGHTY WAH!				

Donny WAHLBERG – See SEIKO and Donnie WAHLBERG

WAIKIKIS — Belgium

SINGLES:	**HITS 1**			**WEEKS 2**
HAWAII TATTOO	*Pye International*	41	*13 Mar 65*	2

WAILERS – See Bob MARLEY and the WAILERS

John WAITE — UK

SINGLES:	**HITS 1**			**WEEKS 13**
MISSING YOU	*EMI America*	9	*29 Sep 84*	11
MISSING YOU [RI]	*Chrysalis*	56	*13 Feb 93*	2
ALBUMS:	**HITS 1**			**WEEKS 3**
NO BRAKES	*EMI America*	64	*10 Nov 84*	3

Terry WAITE – See Carol KIDD featuring Terry WAITE

WAITRESSES — UK

SINGLES:	**HITS 1**			**WEEKS 4**
CHRISTMAS WRAPPING	*Ze*	45	*18 Dec 82*	4
Originally released 1981 appearing in the Bubbling Under section of the chart.				

Tom WAITS — US

ALBUMS:	**HITS 8**			**WEEKS 25**
SWORDFISHTROMBONES	*Island*	62	*8 Oct 83*	3
RAIN DOGS	*Island*	29	*19 Oct 85*	5
FRANKS WILD YEARS	*Island*	20	*5 Sep 87*	5
Contains songs from his musical of the same name that was staged in Chicago and New York during 1986.				
BIG TIME	*Island*	84	*8 Oct 88*	1
BONE MACHINE	*Island*	26	*19 Sep 92*	3
THE BLACK RIDER	*Island*	47	*20 Nov 93*	2
BEAUTIFUL MALADIES 1983-1993: THE ISLAND YEARS	*Island*	63	*27 Jun 98*	1
MULE VARIATIONS	*Epitaph*	9	*1 May 99*	5

Johnny WAKELIN — UK

SINGLES:	**HITS 2**			**WEEKS 20**
BLACK SUPERMAN (MUHAMMAD ALI)	*Pye*	7	*18 Jan 75*	10
Above hit: Johnny WAKELIN and the KINSHASA BAND.				
IN ZAIRE	*Pye*	4	*24 Jul 76*	10
Above 2 are tribute songs to Boxing champion Muhammad Ali. Zaire is where he regained his world heavyweight title on 29 Oct 74, knocking out George Foreman.				

Rick WAKEMAN — UK

(See also Anderson Bruford Wakeman Howe; Kevin Peek and Rick Wakeman featuring Jeff Wayne narration Patrick Allen.)

ALBUMS:	**HITS 10**			**WEEKS 125**
THE SIX WIVES OF HENRY VIII	*A&M*	7	*24 Feb 73*	22
JOURNEY TO THE CENTRE OF THE EARTH	*A&M*	1	*18 May 74*	30
Live recordings from the Royal Festival Hall, London, 18 Jan 74. Conducted by David Measham and narrated by David Hemmings.				
Above hit: Rick WAKEMAN with the LONDON SYMPHONY ORCHESTRA and ENGLISH CHAMBER CHOIR.				
THE MYTHS AND LEGENDS OF KING ARTHUR & THE KNIGHTS OF THE ROUND TABLE	*A&M*	2	*12 Apr 75*	28
Above hit: Rick WAKEMAN with the ENGLISH CHAMBER CHOIR and ORCHESTRA.				
NO EARTHLY CONNECTION	*A&M*	9	*24 Apr 76*	9
WHITE ROCK [OST]	*A&M*	14	*12 Feb 77*	9
RICK WAKEMAN'S CRIMINAL RECORD	*A&M*	25	*3 Dec 77*	5
RHAPSODIES	*A&M*	25	*2 Jun 79*	10
1984	*Charisma*	24	*27 Jun 81*	9
THE GOSPELS	*Stylus*	94	*16 May 87*	1
RETURN TO THE CENTRE OF THE EARTH	*EMI Classics*	34	*27 Mar 99*	2
Features Katrina Leskanich of Katrina and the Waves, Ozzy Osbourne, Justin Hayward and Bonnie Tyler.				
Above hit: Rick WAKEMAN; LONDON SYMPHONY ORCHESTRA; ENGLISH CHAMBER CHOIR; narrated by Patrick STEWART.				

Narada Michael WALDEN — US

SINGLES:	HITS 3			WEEKS 28
TONIGHT I'M ALRIGHT	*Atlantic*	34	*23 Feb 80*	9
I SHOULDA LOVED YA	*Atlantic*	8	*26 Apr 80*	9
DIVINE EMOTIONS	*Reprise*	8	*23 Apr 88*	10
Above hit: NARADA.				
ALBUMS:	**HITS 1**			**WEEKS 5**
DIVINE EMOTION	*Reprise*	60	*14 May 88*	5
Above hit: NARADA.				

Gary WALKER — US

(See also Walker Brothers.)

SINGLES:	HITS 2			WEEKS 12
YOU DON'T LOVE ME	*CBS*	26	*26 Feb 66*	6
Originally recorded by Sonny and Cher.				
TWINKIE-LEE	*CBS*	26	*28 May 66*	6

John WALKER — US

(See also Walker Brothers.)

SINGLES:	HITS 1			WEEKS 6
ANNABELLA	*Philips*	48	*8 Jul 67*	1
ANNABELLA [RE]	*Philips*	24	*22 Jul 67*	5
EPS:	**HITS 1**			**WEEKS 7**
SOLO JOHN - SOLO SCOTT	*Philips*	4	*10 Dec 66*	7

Jr. WALKER and the ALL STARS — US

SINGLES:	HITS 6			WEEKS 59
HOW SWEET IT IS (TO BE LOVED BY YOU)	*Tamla Motown*	22	*20 Aug 66*	10
ROAD RUNNER	*Tamla Motown*	12	*5 Apr 69*	12
WHAT DOES IT TAKE (TO WIN YOUR LOVE)	*Tamla Motown*	13	*18 Oct 69*	12
WALK IN THE NIGHT	*Tamla Motown*	16	*26 Aug 72*	11
TAKE ME GIRL, I'M READY	*Tamla Motown*	16	*27 Jan 73*	9
WAY BACK HOME	*Tamla Motown*	35	*30 Jun 73*	5
Originally recorded by the Jazz Crusaders. Above 2 were released in the US in 1971 reaching No. 50 and No. 52 respectively.				

Sarah WALKER – See ROYAL PHILHARMONIC ORCHESTRA

Scott WALKER — US

(See also Walker Brothers.)

SINGLES:	HITS 3			WEEKS 30
JACKIE	*Philips*	22	*9 Dec 67*	9
Originally recorded by Jacques Brel.				
JOANNA	*Philips*	7	*4 May 68*	11
Originally recorded by Tony Hatch and Jackie Trent.				
LIGHTS OF CINCINNATI	*Philips*	13	*14 Jun 69*	10
EPS:	**HITS 1**			**WEEKS 7**
SOLO JOHN - SOLO SCOTT	*Philips*	4	*10 Dec 66*	7
ALBUMS:	**HITS 7**			**WEEKS 58**
SCOTT	*Philips*	3	*16 Sep 67*	17
SCOTT 2	*Philips*	1	*20 Apr 68*	18
SCOTT 3	*Philips*	3	*5 Apr 69*	4
SCOTT WALKER SINGS SONGS FROM HIS TV SERIES	*Philips*	7	*5 Jul 69*	3
CLIMATE OF HUNTER	*Virgin*	60	*31 Mar 84*	2
NO REGRETS - THE BEST OF SCOTT WALKER AND THE WALKER BROTHERS 1965-1976	*Fontana*	4	*25 Jan 92*	12
Contains both Scott Walker's solo and group material. Includes re-entries through to 2000. Above hit: Scott WALKER and the WALKER BROTHERS.				
TILT	*Fontana*	27	*20 May 95*	1
Tracks were written between 1991/92.				
NO REGRETS - THE BEST OF SCOTT WALKER AND THE WALKER BROTHERS [RI]	*Universal Music TV*	55	*15 Jul 00*	1

WALKER BROTHERS — US

(See also Gary Walker; John Walker; Scott Walker.)

SINGLES:	HITS 10			WEEKS 93
LOVE HER	*Philips*	20	*1 May 65*	13
Originally by The Everly Brothers on the B-side of their 1963 hit The Girl Sang The Blues.				
MAKE IT EASY ON YOURSELF	*Philips*	1	*21 Aug 65*	14
Original by Jerry Butler reached No. 20 in the US in 1962.				
MY SHIP IS COMING IN	*Philips*	3	*4 Dec 65*	12
Originally recorded by Jimmy Radcliffe in 1964.				

THE SUN AIN'T GONNA SHINE ANYMORE	*Philips*	1	*5 Mar 66*	11
Originally recorded by Frankie Valli.				
(BABY) YOU DON'T HAVE TO TELL ME	*Philips*	13	*16 Jul 66*	8
ANOTHER TEAR FALLS	*Philips*	12	*24 Sep 66*	8
Originally recorded by Gene McDaniels in 1962 as the B-side to his single Chip Chip.				
DEADLIER THAN THE MALE	*Philips*	34	*17 Dec 66*	6
From the film of the same name.				
STAY WITH ME BABY	*Philips*	26	*11 Feb 67*	6
Originally recorded by Lorraine Ellison in 1966.				
WALKING IN THE RAIN	*Philips*	26	*20 May 67*	6
Original by the Ronettes reachied No. 23 in the US in 1964.				
NO REGRETS	*GTO*	7	*17 Jan 76*	12
Originally recorded by Tom Rush in 1968.				
EPS:	**HITS 1**			**WEEKS 25**
I NEED YOU	*Philips*	1	*18 Jun 66*	25
ALBUMS:	**HITS 6**			**WEEKS 109**
TAKE IT EASY WITH THE WALKER BROTHERS	*Philips*	3	*18 Dec 65*	36
PORTRAIT	*Philips*	3	*3 Sep 66*	23
IMAGES	*Philips*	6	*18 Mar 67*	15
THE WALKER BROTHERS' STORY	*Philips*	9	*16 Sep 67*	19
NO REGRETS	*GTO*	49	*21 Feb 76*	3
NO REGRETS - THE BEST OF SCOTT WALKER AND THE WALKER BROTHERS 1965-1976	*Fontana*	4	*25 Jan 92*	12
Contains both Scott Walker's solo and group material. Includes re-entries through to 2000. Above hit: Scott WALKER and the WALKER BROTHERS.				
NO REGRETS - THE BEST OF SCOTT WALKER AND THE WALKER BROTHERS [RI]	*Universal Music TV*	55	*15 Jul 00*	1

WALL OF SOUND featuring Gerald LETHAN — US

SINGLES:	**HITS 1**			**WEEKS 1**
CRITICAL (IF YOU ONLY KNEW)	*Positiva*	73	*31 Jul 93*	1

WALL OF VOODOO — US

SINGLES:	**HITS 1**			**WEEKS 3**
MEXICAN RADIO	*Illegal*	64	*19 Mar 83*	3

Jerry WALLACE — US

SINGLES:	**HITS 1**			**WEEKS 1**
YOU'RE SINGING OUR LOVE SONG TO SOMEBODY ELSE	*London*	46	*25 Jun 60*	1

Fats WALLER — US

EPS:	**HITS 1**			**WEEKS 2**
FATS WALLER	*RCA*	14	*3 Sep 60*	2

WALLFLOWERS — US

SINGLES:	**HITS 1**			**WEEKS 1**
ONE HEADLIGHT	*Interscope*	54	*12 Jul 97*	1
ALBUMS:	**HITS 1**			**WEEKS 2**
BRINGING DOWN THE HORSE	*Interscope*	58	*21 Jun 97*	2

Bob WALLIS and his STORYVILLE JAZZMEN — UK

SINGLES:	**HITS 2**			**WEEKS 7**
I'M SHY MARY ELLEN I'M SHY	*Pye Jazz Today*	44	*8 Jul 61*	2
COME ALONG PLEASE	*Pye Jazz Today*	33	*6 Jan 62*	5
ALBUMS:	**HITS 1**			**WEEKS 1**
EVERYBODY LOVES SATURDAY NIGHT	*Top Rank*	20	*11 Jun 60*	1

Joe WALSH — US

SINGLES:	**HITS 2**			**WEEKS 15**
ROCKY MOUNTAIN WAY [EP]	*ABC*	39	*16 Jul 77*	4
Lead track: Rocky Mountain Way.				
LIFE'S BEEN GOOD	*Asylum*	14	*8 Jul 78*	11
ALBUMS:	**HITS 2**			**WEEKS 20**
YOU CAN'T ARGUE WITH A SICK MIND	*Anchor*	28	*17 Apr 76*	3
Live recordings.				
BUT SERIOUSLY FOLKS . . .	*Asylum*	16	*10 Jun 78*	17

Maureen WALSH – See MAUREEN

Sheila WALSH and Cliff RICHARD — UK

(See also Cliff Richard.)

SINGLES:	HITS 1			WEEKS 2
DRIFTING	*DJM*	64	*4 Jun 83*	2

Steve WALSH — UK

SINGLES:	HITS 3			WEEKS 18
I FOUND LOVIN'	*A.1*	74	*18 Jul 87*	1
I FOUND LOVIN' [RE]	*A.1*	9	*29 Aug 87*	12
LET'S GET TOGETHER TONITE	*A.1*	74	*12 Dec 87*	1
AIN'T NO STOPPIN' US NOW (PARTY FOR THE WORLD)	*A.1*	44	*30 Jul 88*	4

Trevor WALTERS — UK

SINGLES:	HITS 3			WEEKS 22
LOVE ME TONIGHT	*Magnet*	27	*24 Oct 81*	8
STUCK ON YOU	*I&S*	9	*21 Jul 84*	12
NEVER LET HER SLIP AWAY	*Polydor*	73	*1 Dec 84*	2

WAMDUE PROJECT — US

SINGLES:	HITS 2			WEEKS 19
KING OF MY CASTLE	*Orange*	61	*20 Nov 99*	1
Import.				
KING OF MY CASTLE	*AM:PM*	1	*27 Nov 99*	15
KING OF MY CASTLE [RE]	*AM:PM*	74	*25 Mar 00*	1
YOU'RE THE REASON	*AM:PM*	39	*15 Apr 00*	2

WANG CHUNG — UK

SINGLES:	HITS 1			WEEKS 12
DANCE HALL DAYS	*Geffen*	21	*28 Jan 84*	12
ALBUMS:	**HITS 1**			**WEEKS 5**
POINTS ON THE CURVE	*Geffen*	34	*21 Apr 84*	5

WANNADIES — Sweden

SINGLES:	HITS 7			WEEKS 12
MIGHT BE STARS	*Indolent*	51	*18 Nov 95*	2
HOW DOES IT FEEL?	*Indolent*	53	*24 Feb 96*	1
YOU & ME SONG	*Indolent*	18	*20 Apr 96*	3
Originally released 1995 reaching No. 119.				
SOMEONE SOMEWHERE	*Indolent*	38	*7 Sep 96*	1
HIT	*Indolent*	20	*26 Apr 97*	2
Originally released in 1996.				
SHORTY	*Indolent*	41	*5 Jul 97*	2
YEAH	*RCA*	56	*4 Mar 00*	1
ALBUMS:	**HITS 2**			**WEEKS 4**
BAGSY ME	*Indolent*	37	*17 May 97*	3
YEAH	*RCA*	73	*18 Mar 00*	1

Dexter WANSELL — US

SINGLES:	HITS 1			WEEKS 3
ALL NIGHT LONG	*Philadelphia International*	59	*20 May 78*	3

WAR — US

(See also Eric Burdon and War.)

SINGLES:	HITS 6			WEEKS 32
LOW RIDER	*Island*	12	*24 Jan 76*	7
ME AND BABY BROTHER	*Island*	21	*26 Jun 76*	7
Original release reached No. 15 in the US in 1973.				
GALAXY	*MCA*	14	*14 Jan 78*	7
HEY SENORITA	*MCA*	40	*15 Apr 78*	2
YOU GOT THE POWER	*RCA*	58	*10 Apr 82*	4
GROOVIN'	*BlueBird*	43	*6 Apr 85*	5

Stephen WARBECK — UK

ALBUMS:	HITS 1			WEEKS 5
CAPTAIN CORELLI'S MANDOLIN [OST]	*Decca*	30	*19 May 01*	5

Anita WARD — US

SINGLES:	HITS 1			WEEKS 11
RING MY BELL	*TK*	1	*2 Jun 79*	11

Originally recorded by Frederick Knight who also plays all instruments on Anita's version.

Billy WARD and the DOMINOES — US

SINGLES:	HITS 2			WEEKS 13
STARDUST	*London*	13	*14 Sep 57*	11
Originally recorded by Irving Mills in 1930.				
DEEP PURPLE	*London*	30	*30 Nov 57*	1
Above hit: Billy WARD and his DOMINOES.				
STARDUST [RE]	*London*	26	*4 Jan 58*	1

Chrissy WARD — US

SINGLES:	HITS 1			WEEKS 2
RIGHT AND EXACT	*Ore*	62	*24 Jun 95*	1
RIGHT AND EXACT [RM]	*Ore*	59	*8 Feb 97*	1
Remixed by Stonebridge and Nick Nice.				

Clifford T. WARD — UK

SINGLES:	HITS 2			WEEKS 16
GAYE	*Charisma*	8	*30 Jun 73*	11
SCULLERY	*Charisma*	37	*26 Jan 74*	5
ALBUMS:	**HITS 2**			**WEEKS 5**
HOME THOUGHTS	*Charisma*	40	*21 Jul 73*	3
MANTLE PIECES	*Charisma*	42	*16 Feb 74*	2

Michael WARD — UK

SINGLES:	HITS 1			WEEKS 13
LET THERE BE PEACE ON EARTH (LET IT BEGIN WITH ME)	*Philips*	15	*29 Sep 73*	10
Above hit: Michael WARD with the Mike SAMMES SINGERS.				
LET THERE BE PEACE ON EARTH (LET IT BEGIN WITH ME) [RE]	*Philips*	50	*15 Dec 73*	3
ALBUMS:	**HITS 1**			**WEEKS 3**
INTRODUCING MICHAEL WARD	*Philips*	26	*5 Jan 74*	3

WARD BROTHERS — UK

SINGLES:	HITS 1			WEEKS 8
CROSS THAT BRIDGE	*Siren*	32	*10 Jan 87*	8

Justin WARFIELD – See BOMB THE BASS

WARLOCK — Germany

ALBUMS:	HITS 1			WEEKS 2
TRIUMPH AND AGONY	*Vertigo*	54	*14 Nov 87*	2

WARM JETS — UK/Canada

SINGLES:	HITS 2			WEEKS 4
NEVER NEVER	*This Way Up*	37	*14 Feb 98*	2
Original release reached No. 97 in 1997.				
HURRICANE	*Island*	34	*25 Apr 98*	2
Original release reached No. 79 in 1997.				
ALBUMS:	**HITS 1**			**WEEKS 1**
FUTURE SIGNS	*Island*	40	*7 Mar 98*	1

WARM SOUNDS — UK

SINGLES:	HITS 1			WEEKS 6
BIRDS AND BEES	*Deram*	27	*6 May 67*	6

Toni WARNE — UK

SINGLES:	HITS 1			WEEKS 4
BEN	*Mint*	50	*25 Apr 87*	4

Jennifer WARNES — US

SINGLES:	HITS 3			WEEKS 37
UP WHERE WE BELONG	*Island*	7	*15 Jan 83*	13
From the film 'An Officer And A Gentleman'.				
Above hit: Joe COCKER and Jennifer WARNES.				
FIRST WE TAKE MANHATTAN	*RCA*	74	*25 Jul 87*	1
Originally recorded by Leonard Cohen.				
(I'VE HAD) THE TIME OF MY LIFE (LOVE THEME FROM 'DIRTY DANCING')	*RCA*	6	*31 Oct 87*	12
From the film 'Dirty Dancing'.				
Above hit: Bill MEDLEY and Jennifer WARNES.				
(I'VE HAD) THE TIME OF MY LIFE (LOVE THEME FROM 'DIRTY DANCING') [RE]	*RCA*	8	*15 Dec 90*	11
ALBUMS:	**HITS 1**			**WEEKS 12**
FAMOUS BLUE RAINCOAT	*RCA*	33	*18 Jul 87*	12
Covers consists of Leonard Cohen songs.				

WARP BROTHERS — Germany

SINGLES:	HITS 3			WEEKS 16
PHATT BASS	*Dos Or Die*	58	*11 Nov 00*	3
Import. From the film 'The Blade'.				
Above hit: WARP BROTHERS vs. AQUAGEN.				
PHATT BASS	*NuLife*	9	*9 Dec 00*	8
WE WILL SURVIVE	*NuLife*	19	*17 Feb 01*	4
Samples Josh Wink's Higher State Of Conciousness.				
BLAST THE SPEAKERS	*NuLife*	40	*29 Dec 01*	1

WARRANT — US

SINGLES:	HITS 1			WEEKS 7
CHERRY PIE	*CBS*	59	*17 Nov 90*	2
CHERRY PIE [RI]	*Columbia*	35	*9 Mar 91*	5
ALBUMS:	**HITS 1**			**WEEKS 1**
DOG EAT DOG	*Columbia*	74	*19 Sep 92*	1

Alysha WARREN — UK

SINGLES:	HITS 3			WEEKS 4
I'M SO IN LOVE	*Wild Card*	61	*24 Sep 94*	1
I THOUGHT I MEANT THE WORLD TO YOU	*Wild Card*	40	*25 Mar 95*	1
KEEP ON PUSHING OUR LOVE	*Arista*	30	*27 Jul 96*	2
Above hit: NIGHTCRAWLERS featuring John REID and Alysha WARREN.				

Anne WARREN – See Ruby MURRAY

Nikita WARREN — Italy

SINGLES:	HITS 1			WEEKS 1
I NEED YOU	*VC Recordings*	48	*13 Jul 96*	1
Originally released in 1991.				

K- WARREN featuring LEE-O — UK

SINGLES:	HITS 1			WEEKS 2
COMING HOME	*Go.Beat*	32	*5 May 01*	2

WARRIOR — UK

SINGLES:	HITS 2			WEEKS 6
WARRIOR	*Incentive*	19	*21 Oct 00*	4
VOODOO	*Incentive*	37	*30 Jun 01*	2

WARSAW PHILHARMONIA – See Anthony WAY

Dionne WARWICK — US

(See also Dionne Warwick Placido Domingo; Stevie Wonder.)

SINGLES:	HITS 14			WEEKS 101
ANYONE WHO HAD A HEART	*Pye International*	42	*15 Feb 64*	3
WALK ON BY	*Pye International*	9	*18 Apr 64*	14
YOU'LL NEVER GET TO HEAVEN (IF YOU BREAK MY HEART)	*Pye International*	20	*1 Aug 64*	8
REACH OUT FOR ME	*Pye International*	23	*10 Oct 64*	7
YOU CAN HAVE HIM	*Pye International*	37	*3 Apr 65*	5
(THEME FROM) VALLEY OF THE DOLLS	*Pye International*	28	*16 Mar 68*	8
Theme from the film.				
DO YOU KNOW THE WAY TO SAN JOSE	*Pye International*	8	*18 May 68*	10
THEN CAME YOU	*Atlantic*	29	*19 Oct 74*	6
Above hit: Dionne WARWICKE and the DETROIT SPINNERS.				
HEARTBREAKER	*Arista*	2	*23 Oct 82*	13
Features backing vocals by Barry Gibb.				
ALL THE LOVE IN THE WORLD	*Arista*	10	*11 Dec 82*	10
Above 2 written by the Bee Gees.				
YOURS	*Arista*	66	*26 Feb 83*	2
I'LL NEVER LOVE THIS WAY AGAIN	*Arista*	62	*28 May 83*	3
Produced by Barry Manilow. Reached No. 5 in the US when first released in 1979.				
THAT'S WHAT FRIENDS ARE FOR	*Arista*	16	*9 Nov 85*	9
Charity record with proceeds donated to the American Foundation for AIDS research. Originally recorded by Rod Stewart.				
Above hit: DIONNE and FRIENDS featuring Elton JOHN, Gladys KNIGHT and Stevie WONDER.				
LOVE POWER	*Arista*	63	*15 Aug 87*	3
Above hit: Dionne WARWICK and Jeffrey OSBORNE.				
EPS:	**HITS 2**			**WEEKS 10**
IT'S LOVE THAT REALLY COUNTS	*Pye International*	18	*15 Aug 64*	1
DON'T MAKE ME OVER	*Pye International*	13	*3 Oct 64*	9
ALBUMS:	**HITS 12**			**WEEKS 148**
PRESENTING DIONNE WARWICK	*Pye International*	14	*23 May 64*	10

BEST OF DIONNE WARWICK	*Pye International*	8	*7 May 66*	11
HERE WHERE THERE IS LOVE	*Pye International*	39	*4 Feb 67*	2
VALLEY OF THE DOLLS	*Pye International*	10	*18 May 68*	13
GREATEST HITS VOLUME 1	*Wand*	31	*23 May 70*	26
GREATEST HITS VOLUME 2	*Wand*	28	*6 Jun 70*	14
HEARTBREAKER	*Arista*	3	*30 Oct 82*	33
THE DIONNE WARWICK COLLECTION	*Starblend*	11	*21 May 83*	17
SO AMAZING	*Arista*	60	*29 Oct 83*	3
WITHOUT YOUR LOVE	*Arista*	86	*23 Feb 85*	2
LOVE SONGS	*Arista*	6	*6 Jan 90*	13
THE ESSENTIAL COLLECTION	*Global Television*	58	*14 Dec 96*	4

Dionne WARWICK Placido DOMINGO — US/Spain

(See also Placido Domingo; Dionne Warwick.)

ALBUMS:	HITS 1			WEEKS 2
CHRISTMAS IN VIENNA II *Live recordings from the Hofburg, Vienna, 21 Dec 93.*	*Sony Classical*	60	*10 Dec 94*	2

WAS (NOT WAS) — US

SINGLES:	HITS 10			WEEKS 58
OUT COME THE FREAKS	*Ze*	41	*3 Mar 84*	5
SPY IN THE HOUSE OF LOVE	*Fontana*	51	*18 Jul 87*	7
WALK THE DINOSAUR	*Fontana*	10	*3 Oct 87*	10
SPY IN THE HOUSE OF LOVE [RE]	*Fontana*	21	*6 Feb 88*	8
OUT COME THE FREAKS (AGAIN) [RR]	*Fontana*	44	*7 May 88*	3
ANYTHING CAN HAPPEN	*Fontana*	67	*16 Jul 88*	3
PAPA WAS A ROLLING STONE	*Fontana*	12	*26 May 90*	7
HOW THE HEART BEHAVES	*Fontana*	53	*11 Aug 90*	3
LISTEN LIKE THIEVES	*Fontana*	58	*23 May 92*	2
SHAKE YOUR HEAD *Features vocals by Ozzy Osbourne and Kim Basinger.*	*Fontana*	4	*11 Jul 92*	9
SOMEWHERE IN AMERICA (THERE'S A STREET NAMED AFTER MY DAD)	*Fontana*	57	*26 Sep 92*	1
ALBUMS:	**HITS 3**			**WEEKS 15**
WHAT UP DOG?	*Fontana*	47	*9 Apr 88*	6
ARE YOU OKAY?	*Fontana*	35	*21 Jul 90*	6
HELLO DAD . . . I'M IN JAIL	*Fontana*	61	*13 Jun 92*	3

Martha WASH — US

(See also Todd Terry.)

SINGLES:	HITS 7			WEEKS 16
CARRY ON	*RCA*	74	*28 Nov 92*	1
GIVE IT TO YOU	*RCA*	37	*6 Mar 93*	4
RUNAROUND / CARRY ON [RM-1ST]	*RCA*	49	*10 Jul 93*	2
CARRY ON [RM-2ND] *Remixed by Full Intention.*	*Delirious*	49	*25 Oct 97*	1
IT'S RAINING MEN . . . THE SEQUEL *Above hit: Martha WASH featuring RUPAUL.*	*Logic*	21	*28 Feb 98*	3
READY FOR A NEW DAY *Background vocals by Antoinette Robertson.* *Above hit: Todd TERRY features Martha WASH.*	*Manifesto*	20	*11 Apr 98*	2
CATCH THE LIGHT	*Logic*	45	*15 Aug 98*	1
COME	*Logic*	64	*3 Jul 99*	1
IT'S RAINING MEN [RM] *Remixed by James Kharti. RuPaul's vocals have been removed from the mix.*	*Logic*	56	*5 Feb 00*	1

Dinah WASHINGTON — US

SINGLES:	HITS 2			WEEKS 8
SEPTEMBER IN THE RAIN *Originally recorded by James Melton.*	*Mercury*	35	*2 Dec 61*	3
SEPTEMBER IN THE RAIN [RE]	*Mercury*	49	*20 Jan 62*	1
MAD ABOUT THE BOY *Featured in the Levi's 501 Jeans TV commercial.*	*Mercury*	41	*4 Apr 92*	4

Geno WASHINGTON and the RAM JAM BAND — US

SINGLES:	HITS 4			WEEKS 20
WATER	*Piccadilly*	39	*21 May 66*	8
HI! HI! HAZEL	*Piccadilly*	45	*23 Jul 66*	3
HI! HI! HAZEL [RE]	*Piccadilly*	48	*27 Aug 66*	1
QUE SERA SERA	*Piccadilly*	43	*8 Oct 66*	3
MICHAEL	*Piccadilly*	39	*4 Feb 67*	5
EPS:	**HITS 1**			**WEEKS 3**
HI!	*Piccadilly*	7	*4 Feb 67*	3

ALBUMS:	HITS 2			WEEKS 51
HAND CLAPPIN' - FOOT STOMPIN' - FUNKY-BUTT - LIVE!	*Piccadilly*	5	*10 Dec 66*	38
Live recording recorded in a studio in front of an audience.				
HIPSTERS, FLIPSTERS, FINGER-POPPIN' DADDIES	*Piccadilly*	8	*23 Sep 67*	13
Live recordings.				

Grover WASHINGTON JR. — US

SINGLES:	HITS 1			WEEKS 7
JUST THE TWO OF US	*Elektra*	34	*16 May 81*	7
Vocals by Bill Withers.				

ALBUMS:	HITS 2			WEEKS 10
WINELIGHT	*Elektra*	34	*9 May 81*	9
COME MORNING	*Elektra*	98	*19 Dec 81*	1

Keith WASHINGTON – See Kylie MINOGUE

Sarah WASHINGTON — UK

SINGLES:	HITS 4			WEEKS 13
I WILL ALWAYS LOVE YOU	*Almighty*	12	*14 Aug 93*	7
CARELESS WHISPER	*Almighty*	45	*27 Nov 93*	2
HEAVEN	*AM:PM*	28	*25 May 96*	2
EVERYTHING	*AM:PM*	30	*12 Oct 96*	2

WASP STAR – See XTC

WATERBOYS — UK

SINGLES:	HITS 5			WEEKS 33
THE WHOLE OF THE MOON	*Ensign*	26	*2 Nov 85*	7
FISHERMAN'S BLUES	*Ensign*	32	*14 Jan 89*	6
AND A BANG ON THE EAR	*Ensign*	51	*1 Jul 89*	4
THE WHOLE OF THE MOON [RI]	*Ensign*	3	*6 Apr 91*	9
FISHERMAN'S BLUES [RI]	*Ensign*	75	*8 Jun 91*	1
THE RETURN OF PAN	*Geffen*	24	*15 May 93*	3
GLASTONBURY SONG	*Geffen*	29	*24 Jul 93*	3
Released to celebrate the festival which has been staged by Michael and Jean Eavis at Worthy Farm, Glastonbury almost every summer since 1970.				

ALBUMS:	HITS 7			WEEKS 71
A PAGAN PLACE	*Ensign*	100	*16 Jun 84*	1
THIS IS THE SEA	*Ensign*	37	*28 Sep 85*	12
THIS IS THE SEA [RE]	*Ensign*	73	*23 Aug 86*	5
Re-released with a new catalogue number.				
FISHERMAN'S BLUES	*Ensign*	13	*29 Oct 88*	19
ROOM TO ROAM	*Ensign*	5	*29 Sep 90*	6
THE BEST OF THE WATERBOYS '81-'90	*Ensign*	2	*11 May 91*	16
DREAM HARDER	*Geffen*	5	*5 Jun 93*	10
A ROCK IN THE WEARY LAND	*RCA*	47	*7 Oct 00*	1
THIS IS THE SEA [RE-2ND]	*Ensign*	57	*21 Jul 01*	1

WATERFRONT — UK

SINGLES:	HITS 3			WEEKS 19
BROKEN ARROW	*Polydor*	63	*15 Apr 89*	2
CRY	*Polydor*	17	*27 May 89*	13
NATURE OF LOVE	*Polydor*	63	*9 Sep 89*	4
Original release reached No. 78 earlier in the year.				

ALBUMS:	HITS 1			WEEKS 3
WATERFRONT	*Polydor*	45	*12 Aug 89*	3

WATERGATE — Turkey

(See also DJ Quicksilver.)

SINGLES:	HITS 1			WEEKS 10
HEART OF ASIA	*Positiva*	3	*13 May 00*	10
Samples Ryuichi Sakamoto's Merry Christmas Mr. Lawrence.				

Dennis WATERMAN — UK

SINGLES:	HITS 2			WEEKS 17
I COULD BE SO GOOD FOR YOU	*EMI*	3	*25 Oct 80*	12
Theme from the Thames ITV series 'Minder'. Originally recorded by Gerard Kenny.				
Above hit: Dennis WATERMAN with the Dennis WATERMAN BAND.				
WHAT ARE WE GONNA GET 'ER INDOORS? (INTERPOL. IN THE BLEAK MID-WINTER)	*EMI*	21	*17 Dec 83*	5
Sung in the role of their characters in 'Minder', Terry McCann and Arthur Daley.				
Above hit: Dennis WATERMAN and George COLE.				

Crystal WATERS — US

(See also David Morales.)

SINGLES:	HITS 7			WEEKS 33
GYPSY WOMAN (LA DA DEE)	*A&M*	2	*18 May 91*	10
MAKIN' HAPPY	*A&M*	18	*7 Sep 91*	6
MEGAMIX [M]	*A&M*	39	*11 Jan 92*	3
GYPSY WOMAN [RM]	*Epic*	35	*3 Oct 92*	2
[AA] listed with remix of Peace by Sabrina Johnston. Remixed by Joey Negro. From the Red Hot & Dance album (to benefit AIDS research and relief).				
100% PURE LOVE	*A&M*	15	*23 Apr 94*	7
GHETTO DAY / WHAT I NEED	*A&M*	40	*2 Jul 94*	2
RELAX	*Manifesto*	37	*25 Nov 95*	2
SAY . . . IF YOU FEEL ALRIGHT	*Mercury*	45	*19 Apr 97*	1
Based around Earth, Wind And Fire's September.				

Jan WATERS - See David WHITFIELD

Latanza WATERS – See E-SMOOVE featuring Latanza WATERS

Muddy WATERS — US

SINGLES:	HITS 1			WEEKS 6
MANNISH BOY	*Epic*	51	*16 Jul 88*	6
Featured in the Levi's 501 Jeans TV commercial. Originally recorded in 1955.				

Roger WATERS — UK

SINGLES:	HITS 3			WEEKS 8
RADIO WAVES	*Harvest*	74	*30 May 87*	1
THE TIDE IS TURNING (AFTER LIVE AID)	*EMI*	54	*26 Dec 87*	4
WHAT GOD WANTS GOD GETS (PART 1)	*Columbia*	35	*5 Sep 92*	3
ALBUMS:	**HITS 4**			**WEEKS 25**
THE PROS AND CONS OF HITCH-HIKING	*Harvest*	13	*12 May 84*	11
RADIO K.A.O.S.	*EMI*	25	*27 Jun 87*	7
THE WALL - LIVE IN BERLIN	*Mercury*	27	*29 Sep 90*	3
Live recordings, 21 Jul 90. Songs from Pink Floyd's 1979 album The Wall performed with 12 other acts.				
Proceeds to the Memorial Fund for Disaster Relief.				
Above hit: Roger WATERS and VARIOUS ARTISTS.				
AMUSED TO DEATH	*Columbia*	8	*19 Sep 92*	4

Michael WATFORD — US

SINGLES:	HITS 1			WEEKS 2
SO INTO YOU	*East West America*	53	*26 Feb 94*	2

Tionne "T-Boz" WATKINS of TLC — US

(See also TLC.)

SINGLES:	HITS 1			WEEKS 1
MY GETAWAY	*Maverick*	44	*14 Apr 01*	1
From the film 'Rugrats In Paris – The Movie'.				

Adam WATKISS — UK

ALBUMS:	HITS 1			WEEKS 3
THIS IS THE MOMENT	*Decca*	65	*15 Dec 01*	3

Jody WATLEY — US

(See also Babyface.)

SINGLES:	HITS 8			WEEKS 35
LOOKING FOR A NEW LOVE	*MCA*	13	*9 May 87*	11
DON'T YOU WANT ME	*MCA*	55	*17 Oct 87*	3
REAL LOVE	*MCA*	31	*8 Apr 89*	7
FRIENDS	*MCA*	21	*12 Aug 89*	6
Above hit: Jody WATLEY with Eric B. and RAKIM.				
EVERYTHING	*MCA*	74	*10 Feb 90*	2
I'M THE ONE YOU NEED (DRIZA BONE MIX)	*MCA*	50	*11 Apr 92*	3
WHEN A MAN LOVES A WOMAN	*MCA*	33	*21 May 94*	2
OFF THE HOOK	*Atlantic*	51	*25 Apr 98*	1
ALBUMS:	**HITS 2**			**WEEKS 4**
JODY WATLEY	*MCA*	62	*5 Sep 87*	2
LARGER THAN LIFE	*MCA*	39	*27 May 89*	2

James WATSON – See Paul PHOENIX

Johnny Guitar WATSON — US

SINGLES:	HITS 2			WEEKS 8
I NEED IT	*DJM*	35	*28 Aug 76*	5
A REAL MOTHER FOR YA	*DJM*	44	*23 Apr 77*	3

Nigel WATSON and the SPLINTER GROUP – See Peter GREEN

Russell WATSON — UK

SINGLES:	HITS 2			WEEKS 3
SWING LOW '99 *The official song of the 1999 England World Cup Team.* *Above hit: OFFICIAL RUGBY TEAM SONG featuring Russell WATSON.*	*Decca*	38	*30 Oct 99*	2
BARCELONA (FRIENDS UNTIL THE END) *Above hit: Russell WATSON and Shaun RYDER.*	*Decca*	68	*22 Jul 00*	1
ALBUMS:	**HITS 2**			**WEEKS 44**
THE VOICE	*Decca*	5	*7 Oct 00*	36
THE VOICE - ENCORE	*Decca*	6	*10 Nov 01*	8

WAVELENGTH — UK

SINGLES:	HITS 1			WEEKS 12
HURRY HOME	*Ariola*	17	*10 Jul 82*	12

WAVES – See KATRINA and the WAVES

WAX — UK/US

SINGLES:	HITS 2			WEEKS 16
RIGHT BETWEEN THE EYES	*RCA*	60	*12 Apr 86*	5
BRIDGE TO YOUR HEART	*RCA*	12	*1 Aug 87*	11
ALBUMS:	**HITS 1**			**WEEKS 3**
AMERICAN ENGLISH	*RCA*	59	*12 Sep 87*	3

Anthony WAY — UK

SINGLES:	HITS 1			WEEKS 2
PANIS ANGELICUS *From the BBC1 TV series 'The Choir'.* *Above hit: Anthony WAY and the WARSAW PHILHARMONIA.*	*Decca*	55	*15 Apr 95*	2
ALBUMS:	**HITS 4**			**WEEKS 19**
THE CHOIR - MUSIC FROM THE BBC TV SERIES *Features the Choir of Gloucester Catherdral.* *Above hit: Anthony WAY and Stanislas SYREWICZ.*	*Decca*	3	*8 Apr 95*	12
THE CHOIRBOY	*Permanent*	61	*9 Dec 95*	3
THE CHOIRBOY'S CHRISTMAS	*Decca*	59	*14 Dec 96*	3
WINGS OF A DOVE *Recorded with his friends and teachers at his school in Uppingham.*	*Decca*	69	*15 Mar 97*	1

A WAY OF LIFE — US

SINGLES:	HITS 1			WEEKS 3
TRIPPIN' ON YOUR LOVE *Originally recorded by the Staple Singers.*	*Eternal*	55	*21 Apr 90*	3

WAY OF THE WEST — UK

SINGLES:	HITS 1			WEEKS 5
DON'T SAY THAT'S JUST FOR WHITE BOYS	*Mercury*	54	*25 Apr 81*	5

WAY OUT WEST — UK

SINGLES:	HITS 6			WEEKS 14
AJARE	*Deconstruction*	52	*3 Dec 94*	1
DOMINATION	*Deconstruction*	38	*2 Mar 96*	2
THE GIFT *Samples Joanna Law's First Time Ever.* *Above hit: WAY OUT WEST featuring Miss Joanna LAW.*	*Deconstruction*	15	*14 Sep 96*	5
BLUE *Samples the pianos and chords from the film soundtrack of 'Withnail & I'.*	*Deconstruction*	41	*30 Aug 97*	2
AJARE [RI]	*Deconstruction*	36	*29 Nov 97*	2
THE FALL *Samples Coldcut's Autumn Leaves.*	*Wow*	61	*9 Dec 00*	1
INTENSIFY	*Distinctive Breaks*	46	*18 Aug 01*	1
ALBUMS:	**HITS 2**			**WEEKS 2**
WAY OUT WEST	*Deconstruction*	42	*13 Sep 97*	1
INTENSIFY	*Distinctive Breaks*	61	*1 Sep 01*	1

Bruce WAYNE — Germany

SINGLES:	HITS 2			WEEKS 2
READY *Originally released earlier in the year.*	*Logic*	44	*13 Dec 97*	1
NO GOOD FOR ME	*Logic*	70	*4 Jul 98*	1

Jeff WAYNE — US

(See also Kevin Peek and Rick Wakeman featuring Jeff Wayne narration Patrick Allen.)

SINGLES:	HITS 4			WEEKS 37
FOREVER AUTUMN *Originally recorded by Vigrass and Osborne.* *Above hit: From Jeff WAYNE'S "WAR OF THE WORLDS" featuring Justin HAYWARD.*	*CBS*	5	*8 Jul 78*	13
THE EVE OF THE WAR *Above hit: Jeff WAYNE'S "THE WAR OF THE WORLDS".*	*CBS*	36	*9 Sep 78*	8
BRAVE NEW WORLD *Above hit: featuring the vocal performance of David ESSEX from Jeff WAYNE'S "The WAR OF THE WORLDS'.*	*CBS*	55	*21 Oct 78*	3
MATADOR *ITV theme for their 1982 World Cup coverage in Spain.*	*CBS*	57	*10 Jul 82*	3
THE EVE OF THE WAR (BEN LIEBRAND REMIX) [RM] *This remix by Ben Liebrand features narration by Richard Burton.*	*CBS*	3	*25 Nov 89*	10

ALBUMS:	HITS 4			WEEKS 261
JEFF WAYNE'S MUSICAL VERSION OF THE WAR OF THE WORLDS *Includes re-entries through to 1984. Features Richard Burton, Julie Covington, David Essex, Justin Hayward, Phil Lynott, Jo Partridge and Chris Thompson.*	*CBS*	5	*1 Jul 78*	226
JEFF WAYNE'S MUSICAL VERSION OF THE WAR OF THE WORLDS [RE]	*CBS*	54	*9 Dec 89*	6
JEFF WAYNE'S MUSICAL VERSION OF SPARTACUS *Features Fish, Bill Fredericks, Jimmy Helms, Anthony Hopkins, Incantation, Catherine Zeta Jones, Alan King, Ladysmith Black Mambazo, Jo Partridge and Chris Thompson.*	*Columbia*	36	*3 Oct 92*	2
HIGHLIGHTS FROM JEFF WAYNE'S MUSICAL VERSION OF THE WAR OF THE WORLDS *This highlighted edition was originally released in 1981, it charted after being made available at mid-price.*	*Columbia*	64	*19 Oct 96*	2
JEFF WAYNE'S MUSICAL VERSION OF THE WAR OF THE WORLDS [RI] *Digitally remastered with new remixes. Peak position reached in 1997 (1995 peak No. 26, 1996 peak No. 24)*	*Columbia*	23	*2 Sep 95*	24
JEFF WAYNE'S MUSICAL VERSION OF THE WAR OF THE WORLDS – ULLADUBULLA THE REMIX ALBUM *Remix album released to mark the 100 year anniversary of War Of The Worlds author H.G. Wells.*	*Columbia*	64	*22 Apr 00*	1

WAYSTED — UK

ALBUMS:	HITS 2			WEEKS 5
VICES	*Chrysalis*	78	*8 Oct 83*	3
WAYSTED	*Music For Nations*	73	*22 Sep 84*	2

WE THE PEOPLE BAND – See ME AND YOU featuring "WE THE PEOPLE BAND"

WEATHER GIRLS — US

SINGLES:	HITS 1			WEEKS 14
IT'S RAINING MEN	*CBS*	73	*27 Aug 83*	3
IT'S RAINING MEN [RE]	*CBS*	2	*3 Mar 84*	11

WEATHER PROPHETS — UK

SINGLES:	HITS 1			WEEKS 2
SHE COMES FROM THE RAIN	*Elevation*	62	*28 Mar 87*	2
ALBUMS:	**HITS 1**			**WEEKS 2**
MAYFLOWER	*Elevation*	67	*9 May 87*	2

WEATHER REPORT — US

ALBUMS:	HITS 4			WEEKS 12
HEAVY WEATHER	*CBS*	43	*23 Apr 77*	6
MR. GONE	*CBS*	47	*11 Nov 78*	3
WEATHER REPORT	*CBS*	88	*27 Feb 82*	2
DOMINO THEORY	*CBS*	54	*24 Mar 84*	1

WEATHERMEN – See Jonathan KING

Geoffrey WEBB — UK

EPS:	HITS 1			WEEKS 1
FOLLOW THAT GIRL	*Oriole*	19	*4 Jun 60*	1

Marti WEBB — UK

(See also Marti Webb and Mark Rattray.)

SINGLES:	HITS 6			WEEKS 42
TAKE THAT LOOK OFF YOUR FACE	*Polydor*	3	*9 Feb 80*	12
TELL ME ON A SUNDAY	*Polydor*	67	*19 Apr 80*	2
YOUR EARS SHOULD BE BURNING NOW	*Polydor*	61	*20 Sep 80*	4
Above 3 from the Andrew Lloyd Webber show 'Tell Me On A Sunday'.				
BEN	*Starblend*	5	*8 Jun 85*	11
Charity record with proceeds to the Ben Hardwick Memorial Fund.				
ALWAYS THERE	*BBC*	13	*20 Sep 86*	12
Theme from the BBC1 TV series 'Howard's Way'.				
Above hit: Marti WEBB with the Simon May ORCHESTRA.				
I CAN'T LET GO	*Rainbow*	65	*6 Jun 87*	1

ALBUMS:	HITS 3			WEEKS 32
TELL ME ON A SUNDAY	*Polydor*	2	*16 Feb 80*	23
Songs from the show.				
ENCORE	*Starblend*	55	*28 Sep 85*	4
ALWAYS THERE	*BBC*	65	*6 Dec 86*	5

Marti WEBB and Mark RATTRAY — UK

(See also Mark Rattray; Marti Webb.)

ALBUMS:	HITS 1			WEEKS 1
THE MAGIC OF THE MUSICALS	*Quality Television*	55	*10 Oct 92*	1

WEBB BROTHERS — US

SINGLES:	HITS 1			WEEKS 1
I CAN'T BELIEVE YOU'RE GONE	*WEA*	69	*17 Feb 01*	1

Joan WEBER — US

SINGLES:	HITS 1			WEEKS 1
LET ME GO LOVER	*Philips*	16	*19 Feb 55*	1
Originally recorded by Georgie Shaw as Let Me Go Devil.				

Bert WEBSTER – See Gerry MULLIGAN and Ben WEBSTER

WEDDING PRESENT — UK

SINGLES:	HITS 23			WEEKS 38
NOBODY'S TWISTING YOUR ARM	*Reception*	46	*5 Mar 88*	2
WHY ARE YOU BEING SO REASONABLE NOW?	*Reception*	42	*1 Oct 88*	2
KENNEDY	*RCA*	33	*7 Oct 89*	3
BRASSNECK	*RCA*	24	*17 Feb 90*	3
3 SONGS [EP]	*RCA*	25	*29 Sep 90*	4
Lead track: Corduroy, though the track Make Me Smile (Come Up And See Me) received more airplay.				
DALLIANCE	*RCA*	29	*11 May 91*	3
LOVENEST	*RCA*	58	*27 Jul 91*	1
BLUE EYES	*RCA*	26	*18 Jan 92*	2
GO-GO DANCER	*RCA*	20	*15 Feb 92*	1
THREE	*RCA*	14	*14 Mar 92*	2
SILVER SHORTS	*RCA*	14	*18 Apr 92*	1
COME PLAY WITH ME	*RCA*	10	*16 May 92*	2
CALIFORNIA	*RCA*	16	*13 Jun 92*	1
FLYING SAUCER	*RCA*	22	*18 Jul 92*	1
BOING!	*RCA*	19	*15 Aug 92*	1
LOVE SLAVE	*RCA*	17	*19 Sep 92*	1
STICKY	*RCA*	17	*17 Oct 92*	1
THE QUEEN OF OUTER SPACE	*RCA*	23	*14 Nov 92*	1
NO CHRISTMAS	*RCA*	25	*19 Dec 92*	1
All above 12 hits were limited edition 7" formats only.				
YEAH YEAH YEAH YEAH YEAH	*Island*	51	*10 Sep 94*	2
IT'S A GAS	*Island*	71	*26 Nov 94*	1
2, 3, GO	*Cooking Vinyl*	67	*31 Aug 96*	1
MONTREAL	*Cooking Vinyl*	40	*25 Jan 97*	1

ALBUMS:	HITS 10			WEEKS 21
GEORGE BEST	*Reception*	47	*24 Oct 87*	2
TOMMY	*Reception*	42	*23 Jul 88*	3
UKRAINSKI VISTUIP V JOHNA PEELA	*RCA*	22	*29 Apr 89*	3
BIZZARO	*RCA*	22	*4 Nov 89*	3
SEA MONSTERS	*RCA*	13	*8 Jun 91*	3
HIT PARADE 1	*RCA*	22	*20 Jun 92*	2
HIT PARADE 2	*RCA*	19	*16 Jan 93*	2
Above 2 consist of the A and B-side of their 12 singles that charted during 1992. Hit Parade 1, from January–June and Hit Parade 2, from July–December.				
WATUSI	*Island*	47	*24 Sep 94*	1

MINI	*Cooking Vinyl*	40	*3 Feb 96*	1
Not listed in the chart published in Music Week as incorrectly logged as a budget release. Chart was amended the following week.				
SATURNALIA	*Cooking Vinyl*	36	*21 Sep 96*	1

Fred WEDLOCK — UK

SINGLES:	HITS 1			WEEKS 10
OLDEST SWINGER IN TOWN	*Rocket*	6	*31 Jan 81*	10
Became popular due to airplay on the Noel Edmunds BBC Radio 1 Sunday morning show.				

WEE PAPA GIRL RAPPERS — UK

SINGLES:	HITS 5			WEEKS 27
FAITH	*Jive*	60	*12 Mar 88*	4
HEAT IT UP	*Jive*	21	*25 Jun 88*	9
Above hit: WEE PAPA GIRL RAPPERS featuring TWO MEN AND A DRUM MACHINE.				
WEE RULE	*Jive*	6	*1 Oct 88*	9
SOULMATE	*Jive*	45	*24 Dec 88*	4
BLOW THE HOUSE DOWN	*Jive*	65	*25 Mar 89*	1
ALBUMS:	**HITS 1**			**WEEKS 3**
THE BEAT, THE RHYME, THE NOISE	*Jive*	39	*5 Nov 88*	3

Bert WEEDON — UK

SINGLES:	HITS 8			WEEKS 38
GUITAR BOOGIE SHUFFLE	*Top Rank*	10	*16 May 59*	9
Originally recorded by Arthur Smith as Guitar Boogie in 1945.				
NASHVILLE BOOGIE	*Top Rank*	29	*21 Nov 59*	2
BIG BEAT BOOGIE	*Top Rank*	37	*12 Mar 60*	3
BIG BEAT BOOGIE [RE]	*Top Rank*	49	*9 Apr 60*	1
TWELFTH STREET RAG	*Top Rank*	47	*11 Jun 60*	2
Above hit: Bert WEEDON and his "Honky Tonk" Guitar.				
APACHE	*Top Rank*	44	*30 Jul 60*	1
APACHE [RE]	*Top Rank*	24	*13 Aug 60*	3
SORRY ROBBIE	*Top Rank*	28	*29 Oct 60*	11
GINCHY	*Top Rank*	35	*4 Feb 61*	5
MR. GUITAR	*Top Rank*	47	*6 May 61*	1
ALBUMS:	**HITS 2**			**WEEKS 26**
KING SIZE GUITAR	*Top Rank*	18	*16 Jul 60*	1
22 GOLDEN GUITAR GREATS	*Warwick*	1	*23 Oct 76*	25

WEE'IST PIPE BAND IN THE WORLD – See TARTAN ARMY featuring the WEE'IST PIPE BAND IN THE WORLD

WEEKEND — Multi-National

SINGLES:	HITS 1			WEEKS 5
CHRISTMAS MEDLEY (SHORT VERSION) [M] / AULD LANG SYNE	*Lifestyle*	47	*14 Dec 85*	*5*

WEEKEND PLAYERS — UK

SINGLES:	HITS 1			WEEKS 4
21ST CENTURY	*Multiply*	22	*8 Sep 01*	4

Michelle WEEKS — US

SINGLES:	HITS 3			WEEKS 6
MOMENT OF MY LIFE	*Ministry Of Sound*	23	*2 Aug 97*	3
Originally recorded by Inner Life featuring Jocelyn Brown in 1982.				
Above hit: Bobby D'AMBROSIO featuring Michelle WEEKS.				
DON'T GIVE UP	*Ministry Of Sound*	28	*8 Nov 97*	2
GIVE ME LOVE	*VC Recordings*	59	*11 Jul 98*	1
Above hit: DJ DADO vs Michelle WEEKS.				

WEEN — US

SINGLES:	HITS 1			WEEKS 3
BEACON LIGHT	*Elektra*	20	*29 Aug 98*	3
[AA] listed with Walking After You by the Foo Fighters. From the film 'The X Files'.				

WEEZER — US

SINGLES:	HITS 6			WEEKS 17
UNDONE - THE SWEATER SONG	*Geffen*	35	*11 Feb 95*	2
BUDDY HOLLY	*Geffen*	12	*6 May 95*	7
SAY IT AIN'T SO	*Geffen*	37	*22 Jul 95*	2
EL SCORCHO	*Geffen*	50	*5 Oct 96*	1
HASH PIPE	*Geffen*	21	*14 Jul 01*	3
ISLAND IN THE SUN	*Geffen*	31	*3 Nov 01*	2
ALBUMS:	**HITS 3**			**WEEKS 16**
WEEZER	*Geffen*	23	*4 Mar 95*	11

PINKERTON	*Geffen*	43	*12 Oct 96*	1
THE GREEN ALBUM	*Geffen*	31	*26 May 01*	4

Constantine WEIR – See PRESSURE DROP

Frank WEIR and his Orchestra

UK

(See also Vera Lynn.)

SINGLES:	HITS 1			WEEKS 4
CARIBBEAN HONEYMOON	*Oriole*	42	*17 Sep 60*	4

WEIRD SCIENCE

UK

SINGLES:	HITS 1			WEEKS 1
FEEL THE NEED	*NuLife*	62	*1 Jul 00*	1

Eric WEISSBERG – See 'DELIVERANCE' SOUNDTRACK

WELCH – See MARVIN, WELCH and FARRAR

Denise WELCH

UK

SINGLES:	HITS 1			WEEKS 3
YOU DON'T HAVE TO SAY YOU LOVE ME / CRY ME A RIVER	*Virgin*	23	*4 Nov 95*	3
From the Central ITV series 'Soldier, Soldier'.				

Paul WELLER

UK

SINGLES:	HITS 18			WEEKS 62
INTO TOMORROW	*Freedom High*	36	*18 May 91*	3
Above hit: Paul WELLER MOVEMENT.				
UH HUH OH YEH	*Go! Discs*	18	*15 Aug 92*	5
ABOVE THE CLOUDS	*Go! Discs*	47	*10 Oct 92*	2
SUNFLOWER	*Go! Discs*	16	*17 Jul 93*	5
WILD WOOD	*Go! Discs*	14	*4 Sep 93*	3
THE WEAVER [EP]	*Go! Discs*	18	*13 Nov 93*	3
Lead track: The Weaver.				
HUNG UP	*Go! Discs*	11	*9 Apr 94*	3
OUT OF THE SINKING	*Go! Discs*	20	*5 Nov 94*	1
THE CHANGINGMAN	*Go! Discs*	7	*6 May 95*	4
Backing vocals by Carleen Anderson.				
YOU DO SOMETHING TO ME	*Go! Discs*	9	*22 Jul 95*	6
BROKEN STONES	*Go! Discs*	20	*30 Sep 95*	4
OUT OF THE SINKING [RR]	*Go! Discs*	16	*9 Mar 96*	2
Backing vocals by Carleen Anderson				
PEACOCK SUIT	*Go! Discs*	5	*17 Aug 96*	5
BRUSHED	*Island*	14	*9 Aug 97*	3
FRIDAY STREET	*Island*	21	*11 Oct 97*	2
Above 2 had sleeves giving title as an EP:A Heavy Soul.				
MERMAIDS	*Island*	30	*6 Dec 97*	2
BRAND NEW START	*Island*	16	*14 Nov 98*	3
WILD WOOD [RI]	*Island*	22	*9 Jan 99*	3
SWEET PEA, MY SWEET PEA	*Island*	44	*2 Sep 00*	1

ALBUMS:	HITS 8			WEEKS 201
PAUL WELLER	*Go! Discs*	8	*12 Sep 92*	7
WILD WOOD	*Go! Discs*	2	*18 Sep 93*	51
LIVE WOOD	*Go! Discs*	13	*24 Sep 94*	5
Live recordings from his UK and European tours, 1993/94.				
STANLEY ROAD	*Go! Discs*	1	*27 May 95*	87
HEAVY SOUL	*Island*	2	*5 Jul 97*	13
MODERN CLASSICS - THE GREATEST HITS	*Island*	7	*21 Nov 98*	19
HELIOCENTRIC	*Island*	2	*22 Apr 00*	8
DAYS OF SPEED	*Independiente*	3	*20 Oct 01*	11

Brandi WELLS

US

SINGLES:	HITS 1			WEEKS 1
WATCH OUT	*WMOT*	74	*20 Feb 82*	1

Houston WELLS and the MARKSMEN

UK

SINGLES:	HITS 1			WEEKS 10
ONLY THE HEARTACHES	*Parlophone*	22	*3 Aug 63*	10

Mary WELLS

US

SINGLES:	HITS 2			WEEKS 25
MY GUY	*Stateside*	5	*23 May 64*	14
ONCE UPON A TIME	*Stateside*	50	*1 Aug 64*	1
Above hit: Marvin GAYE and Mary WELLS.				
MY GUY [RI]	*Tamla Motown*	14	*8 Jul 72*	10

Terri WELLS — US

SINGLES:	HITS 2			WEEKS 9
YOU MAKE IT HEAVEN	*Philly World*	53	*2 Jul 83*	2
I'LL BE AROUND	*Philly World/London*	17	*5 May 84*	7

Original by the Detroit Spinners reached No. 3 in the US in 1972.

Alex WELSH — UK

SINGLES:	HITS 1			WEEKS 4
TANSY	*Columbia*	45	*12 Aug 61*	4

Irvine WELSH and ON-U-SOUND presents . . . – See PRIMAL SCREAM

WENDY and LISA — US

SINGLES:	HITS 7			WEEKS 31
WATERFALL	*Virgin*	66	*5 Sep 87*	4
SIDESHOW	*Virgin*	49	*16 Jan 88*	5
ARE YOU MY BABY?	*Virgin*	70	*18 Feb 89*	3
LOLLY LOLLY (ACCORDING TO PRINCE)	*Virgin*	64	*29 Apr 89*	3
SATISFACTION	*Virgin*	27	*8 Jul 89*	8
WATERFALL '89 [RM]	*Virgin*	69	*18 Nov 89*	2
Remixed by Wendy and Lisa.				
STRUNG OUT	*Virgin*	44	*30 Jun 90*	5
RAINBOW LAKE	*Virgin*	70	*10 Nov 90*	1
ALBUMS:	**HITS 3**			**WEEKS 7**
WENDY AND LISA	*Virgin*	84	*10 Oct 87*	2
FRUIT AT THE BOTTOM	*Virgin*	45	*18 Mar 89*	2
EROICA	*Virgin*	33	*4 Aug 90*	3

WES — Cameroon

SINGLES:	HITS 2			WEEKS 7
ALANE	*Epic*	11	*14 Feb 98*	6
I LOVE FOOTBALL	*Epic*	75	*27 Jun 98*	1

Official song for the Cameroon 1998 World Cup Squad.

Dodie WEST — UK

SINGLES:	HITS 1			WEEKS 4
GOIN' OUT OF MY HEAD	*Decca*	39	*16 Jan 65*	4

Keith WEST — UK

SINGLES:	HITS 2			WEEKS 18
EXCERPT FROM "A TEENAGE OPERA"	*Parlophone*	2	*12 Aug 67*	15
SAM	*Parlophone*	38	*25 Nov 67*	3

Kit WEST – See DEGREES OF MOTION featuring BITI

WEST END featuring SYBIL — UK

(See also Sybil.)

SINGLES:	HITS 1			WEEKS 13
THE LOVE I LOST	*PWL Sanctuary*	3	*16 Jan 93*	13

WEST END — UK

SINGLES:	HITS 1			WEEKS 2
LOVE RULES	*RCA*	44	*19 Aug 95*	2

WEST HAM UNITED CUP SQUAD — UK

SINGLES:	HITS 1			WEEKS 2
I'M FOREVER BLOWING BUBBLES	*Pye*	31	*10 May 75*	2

WEST STREET MOB — US

SINGLES:	HITS 1			WEEKS 3
BREAK DANCIN' - ELECTRIC BOOGIE	*Sugar Hill*	71	*8 Oct 83*	1
BREAK DANCIN' - ELECTRIC BOOGIE [RE]	*Sugar Hill*	64	*22 Oct 83*	2

WESTBAM — Germany

SINGLES:	HITS 5			WEEKS 9
CELEBRATION GENERATION	*Urban*	48	*9 Jul 94*	2
BAM BAM BAM	*Urban*	57	*19 Nov 94*	1
WIZARDS OF THE SONIC	*Urban*	32	*3 Jun 95*	2
ALWAYS MUSIC	*Low Spirit*	51	*23 Mar 96*	1
Above hit: WESTBAM/KOON + STEPHENSON.				
WIZARDS OF THE SONIC [RM]	*Wonderboy*	43	*13 Jun 98*	2
Mixed by Matt Darey.				
Above hit: WESTBAM vs. RED JERRY.				

ROOF IS ON FIRE	*Logic*	58	*28 Nov 98*	1
Above hit: WESTBAM'S.				

WESTLIFE — Ireland

SINGLES:	HITS 10			WEEKS 124
SWEAR IT AGAIN	*RCA*	1	*1 May 99*	12
SWEAR IT AGAIN [RE]	*RCA*	71	*14 Aug 99*	1
IF I LET YOU GO	*RCA*	1	*21 Aug 99*	11
FLYING WITHOUT WINGS	*RCA*	1	*30 Oct 99*	13
I HAVE A DREAM / SEASONS IN THE SUN	*RCA*	1	*25 Dec 99*	17
FOOL AGAIN	*RCA*	1	*8 Apr 00*	10
FOOL AGAIN [RE]	*RCA*	60	*1 Jul 00*	2
AGAINST ALL ODDS (TAKE A LOOK AT ME NOW)	*Columbia*	1	*30 Sep 00*	11
Above hit: Mariah CAREY and WESTLIFE.				
MY LOVE	*RCA*	1	*11 Nov 00*	10
WHAT MAKES A MAN	*RCA*	2	*30 Dec 00*	13
AGAINST ALL ODDS (TAKE A LOOK AT ME NOW) [RE]	*Columbia*	68	*13 Jan 01*	1
UPTOWN GIRL	*RCA*	1	*17 Mar 01*	16
Charity record in aid of Comic Relief.				
QUEEN OF MY HEART	*RCA*	1	*17 Nov 01*	7

ALBUMS:	HITS 3			WEEKS 103
WESTLIFE	*RCA*	2	*13 Nov 99*	69
COAST TO COAST	*RCA*	1	*18 Nov 00*	28
WORLD OF OUR OWN	*RCA*	1	*24 Nov 01*	6

WESTMINSTER ABBEY CHOIR/ conductor: Martin NEARY — UK

ALBUMS:	HITS 2			WEEKS 7
JOHN TAVENER: INNOCENCE	*Sony Classical*	34	*20 Sep 97*	4
PERFECT PEACE	*Sony Classical*	58	*12 Sep 98*	3
Features songs performed at the funeral service of Diana, Princess Of Wales on 6 Sep 97.				

Kim WESTON – See Marvin GAYE

Paul WESTON and his Orchestra – See Doris DAY; Frankie LAINE; Johnnie RAY, Jo STAFFORD

WESTWORLD — UK/US

SINGLES:	HITS 5			WEEKS 23
SONIC BOOM BOY	*RCA*	11	*21 Feb 87*	7
BA-NA-NA-BAM-BOO	*RCA*	37	*2 May 87*	5
WHERE THE ACTION IS	*RCA*	54	*25 Jul 87*	4
SILVERMAC	*RCA*	42	*17 Oct 87*	5
EVERYTHING GOOD IS BAD	*RCA*	72	*15 Oct 88*	2

ALBUMS:	HITS 1			WEEKS 2
WHERE THE ACTION IS	*RCA*	49	*5 Sep 87*	2

WET WET WET — UK

SINGLES:	HITS 26			WEEKS 209
WISHING I WAS LUCKY	*Precious Organisation*	6	*11 Apr 87*	14
A 12" double pack reached No. 96 on 13 Jun 87.				
SWEET LITTLE MYSTERY	*Precious Organisation*	5	*25 Jul 87*	12
ANGEL EYES (HOME AND AWAY)	*Precious Organisation*	5	*5 Dec 87*	12
TEMPTATION	*Precious Organisation*	12	*19 Mar 88*	8
WITH A LITTLE HELP FROM MY FRIENDS	*Childline*	1	*14 May 88*	11
Charity record in aid of Childline. [AA] listed with She's Leaving Home by Billy Bragg with Cara Tivey.				
SWEET SURRENDER	*Precious Organisation*	6	*30 Sep 89*	8
BROKE AWAY	*Precious Organisation*	19	*9 Dec 89*	7
HOLD BACK THE RIVER	*Precious Organisation*	31	*10 Mar 90*	4
STAY WITH ME HEARTACHE / I FEEL FINE	*Precious Organisation*	30	*11 Aug 90*	4
MAKE IT TONIGHT	*Precious Organisation*	37	*14 Sep 91*	3
PUT THE LIGHT ON	*Precious Organisation*	56	*2 Nov 91*	2
GOODNIGHT GIRL	*Precious Organisation*	1	*4 Jan 92*	11
MORE THAN LOVE	*Precious Organisation*	19	*21 Mar 92*	5
THE LIP SERVICE [EP]	*Precious Organisation*	15	*11 Jul 92*	5
Lead track: Lip Service. Chart only listed as an EP from 1 Aug 92.				
BLUE FOR YOU / THIS TIME (LIVE)	*Precious Organisation*	38	*8 May 93*	2
Charity record with proceeds to Nordoff Robbins Music Therapy. Live recordings from the Royal Albert Hall, London, 3 Nov 92.				
SHED A TEAR	*Precious Organisation*	22	*6 Nov 93*	5
COLD COLD HEART	*Precious Organisation*	20	*8 Jan 94*	4
LOVE IS ALL AROUND	*Precious Organisation*	1	*21 May 94*	37
From the film 'Four Weddings And A Funeral'.				
JULIA SAYS	*Precious Organisation*	3	*25 Mar 95*	9
DON'T WANT TO FORGIVE ME NOW	*Precious Organisation*	7	*17 Jun 95*	8
SOMEWHERE SOMEHOW	*Precious Organisation*	7	*30 Sep 95*	7
SHE'S ALL ON MY MIND	*Precious Organisation*	17	*2 Dec 95*	7
MORNING	*Precious Organisation*	16	*30 Mar 96*	4

IF I NEVER SEE YOU AGAIN	*Precious Organisation*	3	*22 Mar 97*	8
STRANGE	*Precious Organisation*	13	*14 Jun 97*	4
IF I NEVER SEE YOU AGAIN [RE]	*Precious Organisation*	72	*21 Jun 97*	1
STRANGE [RE]	*Precious Organisation*	74	*19 Jul 97*	1
YESTERDAY	*Precious Organisation*	4	*16 Aug 97*	6

ALBUMS:	HITS 8			WEEKS 278
POPPED IN SOULED OUT	*Precious Organisation*	1	*3 Oct 87*	72
Includes re-entry in 1997.				
THE MEMPHIS SESSIONS	*Precious Organisation*	3	*19 Nov 88*	13
HOLDING BACK THE RIVER	*Precious Organisation*	2	*11 Nov 89*	26
HIGH ON THE HAPPY SIDE	*Precious Organisation*	1	*8 Feb 92*	25
LIVE AT THE ROYAL ALBERT HALL	*Precious Organisation*	10	*29 May 93*	4
Live recordings from 3 Nov 92 in aid of Nordoff Robbins Music Therapy.				
Above hit: WET WET WET with the WREN ORCHESTRA.				
END OF PART ONE (THEIR GREATEST HITS)	*Precious Organisation*	4	*20 Nov 93*	17
END OF PART ONE (THEIR GREATEST HITS) [RE]	*Precious Organisation*	1	*30 Apr 94*	50
PICTURE THIS	*Precious Organisation*	1	*22 Apr 95*	45
10	*Precious Organisation*	2	*12 Apr 97*	26

WE'VE GOT A FUZZBOX AND WE'RE GONNA USE IT — UK

SINGLES:	HITS 6			WEEKS 39
RULES AND REGULATIONS [EP]	*Vindaloo*	41	*26 Apr 86*	7
Lead track: X X Sex. The chart for 26 Apr 86 only listed entry as an [AA] with Rules And Regulations.				
LOVE IS THE SLUG	*Vindaloo*	31	*15 Nov 86*	4
WHAT'S THE POINT	*Vindaloo*	51	*7 Feb 87*	2
Above hit: FUZZBOX.				
INTERNATIONAL RESCUE	*WEA*	11	*25 Feb 89*	10
PINK SUNSHINE	*WEA*	14	*20 May 89*	10
SELF!	*WEA*	24	*5 Aug 89*	6
Above hit: FUZZBOX.				

ALBUMS:	HITS 1			WEEKS 6
BIG BANG	*WEA*	5	*26 Aug 89*	6

WHALE — Sweden

SINGLES:	HITS 3			WEEKS 8
HOBO HUMPIN SLOBO BABE	*East West*	46	*19 Mar 94*	2
I'LL DO YA	*Hut*	53	*15 Jul 95*	1
HOBO HUMPIN' SLOBO BABE [RI]	*Hut*	15	*25 Nov 95*	4
FOUR BIG SPEAKERS	*Hut*	69	*4 Jul 98*	1
Above hit: WHALE featuring BUS75.				

ALBUMS:	HITS 1			WEEKS 2
WE CARE	*Hut*	42	*12 Aug 95*	2

WHALERS – See Hal PAGE and the WHALERS

WHAM! — UK

SINGLES:	HITS 10			WEEKS 137
YOUNG GUNS (GO FOR IT)	*Inner Vision*	3	*16 Oct 82*	17
WHAM RAP! (ENJOY WHAT YOU DO)	*Inner Vision*	8	*15 Jan 83*	11
Originally released in 1982 appearing in the Bubbling Under section of the chart.				
BAD BOYS	*Inner Vision*	2	*14 May 83*	14
CLUB TROPICANA	*Inner Vision*	4	*30 Jul 83*	11
CLUB FANTASTIC MEGAMIX [M]	*Inner Vision*	15	*3 Dec 83*	8
Mix of tracks from their album 'Fantastic'.				
WAKE ME UP BEFORE YOU GO GO	*Epic*	1	*26 May 84*	16
FREEDOM	*Epic*	1	*13 Oct 84*	14
LAST CHRISTMAS / EVERYTHING SHE WANTS	*Epic*	2	*15 Dec 84*	13
A repackaged edition was listed from 5 Jan 85 with a remixed version of Everything She Wants as the first track.				
Charity record with proceeds to Famine relief in Ethiopia.				
I'M YOUR MAN	*Epic*	1	*23 Nov 85*	12
LAST CHRISTMAS [RI-1ST]	*Epic*	6	*14 Dec 85*	7
THE EDGE OF HEAVEN / WHERE DID YOUR HEART GO?	*Epic*	1	*21 Jun 86*	10
Where Did Your Heart Go? listed from 2 Aug 86 once single had dropped to No. 28. The Edge Of Heaven features Elton John on piano.				
LAST CHRISTMAS [RI-2ND]	*Epic*	45	*20 Dec 86*	4

ALBUMS:	HITS 4			WEEKS 259
FANTASTIC	*Inner*	1	*9 Jul 83*	116
MAKE IT BIG	*Epic*	1	*17 Nov 84*	72
THE FINAL	*Epic*	2	*19 Jul 86*	45
Compilation.				
THE BEST OF WHAM! . . . IF YOU WERE THERE	*Epic*	4	*6 Dec 97*	24
THE FINAL [RE]	*Epic*	27	*10 Jul 99*	2

WHATNAUTS – See MOMENTS

Rebecca WHEATLEY — UK

SINGLES:	HITS 1			WEEKS 8
STAY WITH ME (BABY)	*BBC Music*	10	*26 Feb 00*	7
Featured in the BBC1 TV series 'Casualty'. Originally recorded by Lorraine Ellison in 1966.				
STAY WITH ME (BABY) [RE]	*BBC Music*	71	*13 May 00*	1

WHEATUS — US

SINGLES:	HITS 2			WEEKS 32
TEENAGE DIRTBAG	*Columbia*	2	*17 Feb 01*	20
From the film 'Loser'.				
A LITTLE RESPECT	*Columbia*	3	*14 Jul 01*	12
ALBUMS:	**HITS 1**			**WEEKS 29**
WHEATUS	*Columbia*	7	*3 Mar 01*	29

Caron WHEELER — UK

SINGLES:	HITS 7			WEEKS 42
KEEP ON MOVIN'	*10 Records*	5	*18 Mar 89*	12
Above hit: SOUL II SOUL (featuring Caron WHEELER).				
BACK TO LIFE (HOWEVER DO YOU WANT ME)	*10 Records*	1	*10 Jun 89*	14
Certain copies did not credit Caron Wheeler on either the sleeve or the label.				
Above hit: SOUL II SOUL featuring Caron WHEELER.				
LIVIN' IN THE LIGHT	*RCA*	14	*8 Sep 90*	6
UK BLAK	*RCA*	40	*10 Nov 90*	4
DON'T QUIT	*RCA*	53	*9 Feb 91*	3
I ADORE YOU	*A&M*	59	*7 Nov 92*	2
From the film 'Mo'Money'.				
BEACH OF THE WAR GODDESS	*EMI*	75	*11 Sep 93*	1
ALBUMS:	**HITS 1**			**WEEKS 5**
UK BLAK	*RCA*	14	*13 Oct 90*	5

Bill WHELAN — Ireland

SINGLES:	HITS 1			WEEKS 16
RIVERDANCE	*Son*	9	*17 Dec 94*	16
Originally reached No. 95 in June 94. Charted after being performed at the Royal Command Performance which was screened on BBC1 TV.				
Above hit: Bill WHELAN featuring ANUNA and the RTE CONCERT ORCHESTRA.				
ALBUMS:	**HITS 1**			**WEEKS 38**
MUSIC FROM RIVERDANCE - THE SHOW	*Atlantic*	31	*25 Mar 95*	38
Label changed to Celtic Heartbeat from 17 Jun 95.				

WHEN IN ROME — UK

SINGLES:	HITS 1			WEEKS 3
THE PROMISE	*10 Records*	58	*28 Jan 89*	3

WHIGFIELD — Denmark

SINGLES:	HITS 6			WEEKS 52
SATURDAY NIGHT	*Systematic*	1	*17 Sep 94*	18
First debut artist to enter at No. 1. Originally released in Italy, 1993.				
ANOTHER DAY	*Systematic*	7	*10 Dec 94*	10
THINK OF YOU	*Systematic*	7	*10 Jun 95*	11
CLOSE TO YOU	*Systematic*	13	*9 Sep 95*	7
LAST CHRISTMAS / BIG TIME	*Systematic*	21	*16 Dec 95*	5
SEXY EYES - REMIXES	*ZYX*	68	*10 Oct 98*	1
ALBUMS:	**HITS 1**			**WEEKS 7**
WHIGFIELD	*Systematic*	13	*1 Jul 95*	7

WHIPPING BOY — Ireland

SINGLES:	HITS 3			WEEKS 4
WE DON'T NEED NOBODY ELSE	*Columbia*	51	*14 Oct 95*	1
WHEN WE WERE YOUNG	*Columbia*	46	*3 Feb 96*	2
TWINKLE	*Columbia*	55	*25 May 96*	1
Original release reached No. 83 in 1995.				

Nancy WHISKEY – See Chas McDEVITT SKIFFLE GROUP (featuring Nancy WHISKEY)

WHISPERS — US

SINGLES:	HITS 8			WEEKS 52
AND THE BEAT GOES ON	*Solar*	2	*2 Feb 80*	12
LADY	*Solar*	55	*10 May 80*	3
MY GIRL	*Solar*	26	*12 Jul 80*	6
IT'S A LOVE THING	*Solar*	9	*14 Mar 81*	11
I CAN MAKE IT BETTER	*Solar*	44	*13 Jun 81*	5
CONTAGIOUS	*Solar*	56	*19 Jan 85*	3

AND THE BEAT GOES ON [RI]	*Solar*	45	*28 Mar 87*	4
ROCK STEADY	*Solar*	38	*23 May 87*	6
SPECIAL F./X	*Solar*	69	*15 Aug 87*	2
ALBUMS:	**HITS 2**			**WEEKS 9**
IMAGINATION	*Solar*	42	*14 Mar 81*	5
JUST GETS BETTER WITH TIME	*Solar*	63	*6 Jun 87*	4

WHISTLE — US

SINGLES:	**HITS 1**			**WEEKS 8**
(NOTHING SERIOUS) JUST BUGGIN'	*Champion*	7	*1 Mar 86*	8

Alex WHITCOMBE and BIG C — UK

(See also Qattara.)

SINGLES:	**HITS 1**			**WEEKS 1**
ICE RAIN	*Xtravaganza*	44	*23 May 98*	1
Original release reached No. 188 in 1996. Vocals by Luciana.				

Alan WHITE — UK

ALBUMS:	**HITS 1**			**WEEKS 4**
RAMSHACKLED	*Atlantic*	41	*13 Mar 76*	4

Barry WHITE — US

(See also Quincy Jones.)

SINGLES:	**HITS 18**			**WEEKS 138**
I'M GONNA LOVE YOU JUST A LITTLE BIT MORE BABY	*Pye International*	23	*9 Jun 73*	7
NEVER, NEVER GONNA GIVE YA UP	*Pye International*	14	*26 Jan 74*	11
CAN'T GET ENOUGH OF YOUR LOVE, BABE	*Pye International*	8	*17 Aug 74*	12
YOU'RE THE FIRST, THE LAST, MY EVERYTHING	*20th Century*	1	*2 Nov 74*	14
WHAT AM I GONNA DO WITH YOU?	*20th Century*	5	*8 Mar 75*	8
FOR YOU I'LL DO ANYTHING YOU WANT ME TO	*20th Century*	20	*24 May 75*	6
LET THE MUSIC PLAY	*20th Century*	9	*27 Dec 75*	8
YOU SEE THE TROUBLE WITH ME	*20th Century*	2	*6 Mar 76*	10
BABY, WE BETTER TRY TO GET IT TOGETHER	*20th Century*	15	*21 Aug 76*	7
DON'T MAKE ME WAIT TOO LONG	*20th Century*	17	*13 Nov 76*	9
I'M QUALIFIED TO SATISFY YOU	*20th Century*	37	*5 Mar 77*	5
IT'S ECSTASY WHEN YOU LAY DOWN NEXT TO ME	*20th Century*	40	*15 Oct 77*	3
JUST THE WAY YOU ARE	*20th Century*	12	*16 Dec 78*	12
SHA LA LA MEANS I LOVE YOU	*20th Century*	55	*24 Mar 79*	6
SHO' YOU RIGHT	*Breakout*	14	*7 Nov 87*	7
NEVER NEVER GONNA GIVE YA UP [RM]	*Club*	63	*16 Jan 88*	2
PRACTICE WHAT YOU PREACH / LOVE IS THE ICON	*A&M*	20	*21 Jan 95*	4
I ONLY WANT TO BE WITH YOU	*A&M*	36	*8 Apr 95*	2
IN YOUR WILDEST DREAMS	*Parlophone*	32	*21 Dec 96*	3
Above hit: Tina TURNER featuring Barry WHITE.				
LET THE MUSIC PLAY [RM]	*Wonderboy*	45	*4 Nov 00*	2
Remixed by Funkstar De Luxe.				
ALBUMS:	**HITS 11**			**WEEKS 228**
STONE GON'	*Pye*	18	*9 Mar 74*	17
CAN'T GET ENOUGH	*20th Century*	4	*2 Nov 74*	34
JUST ANOTHER WAY TO SAY I LOVE YOU	*20th Century*	12	*26 Apr 75*	15
GREATEST HITS	*20th Century*	18	*22 Nov 75*	12
LET THE MUSIC PLAY	*20th Century*	22	*21 Feb 76*	14
BARRY WHITE'S GREATEST HITS VOLUME 2	*20th Century*	17	*9 Apr 77*	7
THE MAN	*20th Century*	46	*10 Feb 79*	4
HEART AND SOUL	*K-Tel*	34	*21 Dec 85*	10
Compilation.				
THE RIGHT NIGHT AND BARRY WHITE	*Breakout*	74	*17 Oct 87*	6
THE COLLECTION	*Mercury*	5	*2 Jul 88*	29
THE BARRY WHITE COLLECTION [RI-1ST]	*PolyGram TV*	36	*19 Feb 94*	5
Re-issue of The Collection.				
THE ICON IS LOVE	*A&M*	44	*11 Feb 95*	3
Originally released in 1994.				
THE BARRY WHITE COLLECTION [RI-2ND]	*Universal Music TV*	6	*11 Dec 99*	72

Chris WHITE — UK

SINGLES:	**HITS 1**			**WEEKS 4**
SPANISH WINE	*Charisma*	37	*20 Mar 76*	4

Jesse WHITE – See Stan FREBERG

Karyn WHITE — US

SINGLES:	**HITS 6**			**WEEKS 38**
THE WAY YOU LOVE ME	*Warner Brothers*	42	*5 Nov 88*	5
SECRET RENDEZVOUS	*Warner Brothers*	52	*18 Feb 89*	3

SUPERWOMAN	*Warner Brothers*	11	*10 Jun 89*	13
SECRET RENDEZVOUS [RI]	*Warner Brothers*	22	*9 Sep 89*	9
ROMANTIC	*Warner Brothers*	23	*17 Aug 91*	5
THE WAY I FEEL ABOUT YOU	*Warner Brothers*	65	*18 Jan 92*	2
HUNGAH	*Warner Brothers*	69	*24 Sep 94*	1
ALBUMS:	**HITS 2**			**WEEKS 30**
KARYN WHITE	*Warner Brothers*	20	*11 Mar 89*	27
RITUAL OF LOVE	*Warner Brothers*	31	*21 Sep 91*	3

Snowy WHITE — UK

SINGLES:	**HITS 2**			**WEEKS 12**
BIRD OF PARADISE	*Towerbell*	6	*24 Dec 83*	10
FOR YOU	*R4*	65	*28 Dec 85*	1
FOR YOU [RE]	*R4*	72	*18 Jan 86*	1
ALBUMS:	**HITS 2**			**WEEKS 5**
WHITE FLAMES	*Towerbell*	21	*11 Feb 84*	4
SNOWY WHITE	*Towerbell*	88	*9 Feb 85*	1

Tam WHITE — UK

SINGLES:	**HITS 1**			**WEEKS 4**
WHAT IN THE WORLD'S COME OVER YOU	*RAK*	36	*15 Mar 75*	4

Tony Joe WHITE — US

SINGLES:	**HITS 1**			**WEEKS 10**
GROUPY GIRL	*Monument*	22	*6 Jun 70*	10
ALBUMS:	**HITS 1**			**WEEKS 1**
TONY JOE	*CBS*	63	*26 Sep 70*	1

WHITE and TORCH — UK

SINGLES:	**HITS 1**			**WEEKS 4**
PARADE	*Chrysalis*	54	*2 Oct 82*	4

WHITE LION — US

ALBUMS:	**HITS 2**			**WEEKS 3**
BIG GAME	*Atlantic*	47	*1 Jul 89*	1
MANE ATTRACTION	*Atlantic*	31	*20 Apr 91*	2

WHITE PLAINS — UK

SINGLES:	**HITS 5**			**WEEKS 56**
MY BABY LOVES LOVIN'	*Deram*	9	*7 Feb 70*	11
I'VE GOT YOU ON MY MIND	*Deram*	17	*18 Apr 70*	11
JULIE DO YA LOVE ME	*Deram*	8	*24 Oct 70*	14
Above hit: WHITE PLAINS with Pete NELSON.				
WHEN YOU ARE A KING	*Deram*	13	*12 Jun 71*	11
STEP INTO A DREAM	*Deram*	21	*17 Feb 73*	9
Above hit: WHITE PLAINS with Gerry BUTLER STRINGS.				

WHITE STRIPES — US

SINGLES:	**HITS 1**			**WEEKS 2**
HOTEL YORBA	*XL Recordings*	26	*24 Nov 01*	2
ALBUMS:	**HITS 1**			**WEEKS 5**
WHITE BLOOD CELLS	*Sympathy For The Record Industry*	58	*18 Aug 01*	5

WHITE TOWN — UK

SINGLES:	**HITS 2**			**WEEKS 10**
YOUR WOMAN	*Chrysalis*	1	*25 Jan 97*	9
Based on Al Bowlly's My Woman from 1932.				
UNDRESSED	*Chrysalis*	57	*24 May 97*	1

WHITE ZOMBIE — US

SINGLES:	**HITS 2**			**WEEKS 4**
MORE HUMAN THAN HUMAN	*Geffen*	51	*20 May 95*	2
ELECTRIC HEAD PT.2 (THE ECSTASY)	*Geffen*	31	*18 May 96*	2
ALBUMS:	**HITS 1**			**WEEKS 6**
ASTRO CREEP 2000	*Geffen*	25	*27 May 95*	3
ASTRO CREEP 2000 / SUPERSEXY SWINGIN' SOUNDS [RE]	*Geffen*	32	*31 Aug 96*	3
Supersexy Swingin' Sounds' is a remix album. Sales were combined.				

WHITEHEAD BROS. — US

SINGLES:	HITS 2			WEEKS 5
YOUR LOVE IS A 187	*Motown*	32	*14 Jan 95*	3
FORGET I WAS A G	*Motown*	40	*13 May 95*	2

WHITEHOUSE — UK/US

SINGLES:	HITS 1			WEEKS 1
AIN'T NO MOUNTAIN HIGH ENOUGH	*Beautiful Noise*	60	*15 Aug 98*	1

WHITEOUT — UK

SINGLES:	HITS 2			WEEKS 2
DETROIT	*Silvertone*	73	*24 Sep 94*	1
JACKIE'S RACING	*Silvertone*	72	*18 Feb 95*	1
ALBUMS:	**HITS 1**			**WEEKS 1**
BITE IT	*Silvertone*	71	*1 Jul 95*	1

WHITESNAKE — UK

SINGLES:	HITS 21			WEEKS 112
SNAKE BITE [EP]	*EMI International*	61	*24 Jun 78*	3
Lead track: Bloody Mary.				
Above hit: David COVERDALE'S WHITESNAKE.				
LONG WAY FROM HOME	*United Artists*	55	*10 Nov 79*	2
FOOL FOR YOUR LOVING	*United Artists*	13	*26 Apr 80*	9
READY AN' WILLING (SWEET SATISFACTION)	*United Artists*	43	*12 Jul 80*	4
AIN'T NO LOVE IN THE HEART OF THE CITY	*Liberty*	51	*22 Nov 80*	4
Live recording from the Hammersmith Odeon, London, Jun 80. A studio version originally appeared on the Snake Bite EP. Originally recorded by Bobby Bland in 1974.				
DON'T BREAK MY HEART AGAIN	*Liberty*	17	*11 Apr 81*	9
WOULD I LIE TO YOU	*Liberty*	37	*6 Jun 81*	6
HERE I GO AGAIN / BLOODY LUXURY	*Liberty*	34	*6 Nov 82*	10
GUILTY OF LOVE	*Liberty*	31	*13 Aug 83*	5
GIVE ME MORE TIME	*Liberty*	29	*14 Jan 84*	4
STANDING IN THE SHADOW	*Liberty*	62	*28 Apr 84*	2
LOVE AIN'T NO STRANGER	*Liberty*	44	*9 Feb 85*	4
STILL OF THE NIGHT	*EMI*	16	*28 Mar 87*	8
IS THIS LOVE	*EMI*	9	*6 Jun 87*	11
HERE I GO AGAIN (USA REMIX) [RR]	*EMI*	9	*31 Oct 87*	11
GIVE ME ALL YOUR LOVE	*EMI*	18	*6 Feb 88*	6
FOOL FOR YOUR LOVING [RR]	*EMI*	43	*2 Dec 89*	2
THE DEEPER THE LOVE	*EMI*	35	*10 Mar 90*	3
NOW YOU'RE GONE	*EMI*	31	*25 Aug 90*	4
IS THIS LOVE [RI] / SWEET LADY LUCK	*EMI*	25	*6 Aug 94*	4
TOO MANY TEARS	*EMI*	46	*7 Jun 97*	1
Above hit: David COVERDALE and WHITESNAKE.				
ALBUMS:	**HITS 11**			**WEEKS 159**
TROUBLE	*EMI International*	50	*18 Nov 78*	2
LOVE HUNTER	*United Artists*	29	*13 Oct 79*	7
READY AND WILLING	*United Artists*	6	*7 Jun 80*	15
LIVE IN THE HEART OF THE CITY	*United Artists*	5	*8 Nov 80*	15
Live recordings from the 1978 and 1980 Hammersmith Odeon shows in London.				
COME AND GET IT	*Liberty*	2	*18 Apr 81*	23
SAINTS 'N' SINNERS	*Liberty*	9	*27 Nov 82*	9
SLIDE IT IN	*Liberty*	9	*11 Feb 84*	7
WHITESNAKE 1987	*EMI*	8	*11 Apr 87*	57
SLIP OF THE TONGUE	*EMI*	10	*25 Nov 89*	10
WHITESNAKE'S GREATEST HITS	*EMI*	4	*16 Jul 94*	12
RESTLESS HEART	*EMI*	34	*21 Jun 97*	2
Above hit: David COVERDALE and WHITESNAKE.				

David WHITFIELD — UK

(See also All Star Hit Parade.)

SINGLES:	HITS 17			WEEKS 190
THE BRIDGE OF SIGHS	*Decca*	9	*3 Oct 53*	1
ANSWER ME	*Decca*	1	*17 Oct 53*	13
RAGS TO RICHES	*Decca*	12	*12 Dec 53*	1
Above 2: David WHITFIELD with Stanley BLACK and his Orchestra.				
RAGS TO RICHES [RE]	*Decca*	3	*9 Jan 54*	10
ANSWER ME [RE]	*Decca*	12	*30 Jan 54*	1
THE BOOK	*Decca*	5	*20 Feb 54*	12
Above hit: David WHITFIELD with Stanley BLACK and his Orchestra with Chorus.				
THE BOOK [RE]	*Decca*	10	*29 May 54*	3
CARA MIA	*Decca*	1	*19 Jun 54*	25
Above hit: David WHITFIELD with MANTOVANI and his Orchestra and Chorus.				
SANTO NATALE (MERRY CHRISTMAS)	*Decca*	2	*13 Nov 54*	10
Above hit: David WHITFIELD with Stanley BLACK and his Orchestra.				

BEYOND THE STARS	*Decca*	8	*12 Feb 55*	9
Above hit: David WHITFIELD with MANTOVANI and his Orchestra.				
MAMA	*Decca*	20	*28 May 55*	1
MAMA [RE-1ST]	*Decca*	19	*25 Jun 55*	2
EV'RYWHERE	*Decca*	3	*9 Jul 55*	20
Above 2 entries were separate sides of the same release, each had its own chart run.				
MAMA [RE-2ND]	*Decca*	12	*30 Jul 55*	8
Above 4: David WHITFIELD with the Roland SHAW ORCHESTRA.				
WHEN YOU LOSE THE ONE YOU LOVE	*Decca*	7	*26 Nov 55*	11
Above hit: David WHITFIELD with MANTOVANI and his Orchestra and Chorus.				
MY SEPTEMBER LOVE	*Decca*	19	*3 Mar 56*	2
MY SEPTEMBER LOVE [RE-1ST]	*Decca*	18	*24 Mar 56*	1
MY SEPTEMBER LOVE [RE-2ND]	*Decca*	3	*7 Apr 56*	20
MY SON JOHN	*Decca*	22	*25 Aug 56*	4
MY UNFINISHED SYMPHONY	*Decca*	29	*1 Sep 56*	1
Above 2 entries were separate sides of the same release, each had its own chart run.				
MY SEPTEMBER LOVE [RE-3RD]	*Decca*	25	*8 Sep 56*	1
THE ADORATION WALTZ	*Decca*	9	*26 Jan 57*	11
I'LL FIND YOU	*Decca*	28	*6 Apr 57*	2
From the film 'Sea Wife'.				
I'LL FIND YOU [RE]	*Decca*	27	*8 Jun 57*	2
Above 9: David WHITFIELD with the Roland SHAW ORCHESTRA.				
CRY MY HEART	*Decca*	22	*15 Feb 58*	3
Above hit: David WHITFIELD with MANTOVANI and his Orchestra and Chorus.				
ON THE STREET WHERE YOU LIVE	*Decca*	16	*17 May 58*	14
From the show 'My Fair Lady'.				
Above hit: David WHITFIELD with Cyril STAPLETON and his Orchestra.				
THE RIGHT TO LOVE	*Decca*	30	*9 Aug 58*	1
I BELIEVE	*Decca*	49	*26 Nov 60*	1

EPS:	**HITS 2**			**WEEKS 3**
ROSE MARIE (SELECTION)	*Decca*	15	*24 Jun 61*	2
EXCERPTS FROM THE DESERT SONG	*Decca*	16	*28 Apr 62*	1
Above hit: David WHITFIELD with Jan WATERS.				

Slim WHITMAN — US

SINGLES:	**HITS 7**			**WEEKS 77**
ROSE MARIE	*London*	1	*16 Jul 55*	19
Originally recorded by Nelson Eddy and Jeanette MacDonald.				
INDIAN LOVE CALL	*London*	7	*30 Jul 55*	12
Above 2 from the film 'Rose Marie' and originally written in 1924.				
CHINA DOLL	*London*	15	*24 Sep 55*	2
Above 2 entries were separate sides of the same release, each had its own chart run.				
TUMBLING TUMBLEWEEDS	*London*	19	*10 Mar 56*	2
I'M A FOOL	*London*	16	*14 Apr 56*	3
I'M A FOOL [RE]	*London*	29	*12 May 56*	1
SERENADE	*London*	24	*23 Jun 56*	3
From the film of the same name.				
SERENADE [RE]	*London*	8	*28 Jul 56*	12
I'LL TAKE YOU HOME AGAIN KATHLEEN	*London*	7	*13 Apr 57*	13
HAPPY ANNIVERSARY	*United Artists*	14	*5 Oct 74*	10

ALBUMS:	**HITS 7**			**WEEKS 61**
HAPPY ANNIVERSARY	*United Artists*	44	*14 Dec 74*	2
THE VERY BEST OF SLIM WHITMAN	*United Artists*	1	*31 Jan 76*	17
RED RIVER VALLEY	*United Artists*	1	*15 Jan 77*	14
HOME ON THE RANGE	*United Artists*	2	*15 Oct 77*	13
GHOST RIDERS IN THE SKY	*United Artists*	27	*13 Jan 79*	6
SLIM WHITMAN'S 20 GREATEST LOVE SONGS	*United Artists*	18	*22 Dec 79*	7
THE VERY BEST OF SLIM WHITMAN - 50TH ANNIVERSARY COLLECTION	*EMI*	54	*27 Sep 97*	2

Roger WHITTAKER — UK

SINGLES:	**HITS 7**			**WEEKS 85**
DURHAM TOWN (THE LEAVIN')	*Columbia*	12	*8 Nov 69*	18
I DON'T BELIEVE IN IF ANY MORE	*Columbia*	8	*11 Apr 70*	18
NEW WORLD IN THE MORNING	*Columbia*	17	*10 Oct 70*	14
WHY	*Columbia*	47	*3 Apr 71*	1
MAMY BLUE	*Columbia*	31	*2 Oct 71*	10
THE LAST FAREWELL	*EMI*	2	*26 Jul 75*	14
THE SKYE BOAT SONG	*Tembo*	10	*8 Nov 86*	10
Above hit: Roger WHITTAKER and Des O'CONNOR.				

ALBUMS:	**HITS 11**			**WEEKS 111**
I DON'T BELIEVE IN IF ANYMORE	*Columbia*	23	*27 Jun 70*	1
NEW WORLD IN THE MORNING	*Columbia*	45	*3 Apr 71*	2
THE VERY BEST OF ROGER WHITTAKER	*Columbia*	5	*6 Sep 75*	42
THE SECOND ALBUM OF THE VERY BEST OF ROGER WHITTAKER	*EMI*	27	*15 May 76*	7
ROGER WHITTAKER SINGS THE HITS	*Columbia*	52	*9 Dec 78*	5
20 ALL TIME GREATS	*Polydor*	24	*4 Aug 79*	9

THE ROGER WHITTAKER ALBUM	*K-Tel*	18	*7 Feb 81*	14
SKYE BOAT SONG AND OTHER GREAT SONGS	*Tembo*	89	*27 Dec 86*	1
HIS FINEST COLLECTION	*Tembo*	15	*23 May 87*	19
HOME LOVIN' MAN	*Tembo*	20	*23 Sep 89*	10
A PERFECT DAY - HIS GREATEST HITS & MORE	*RCA*	74	*11 May 96*	1
Collection of old hits, songs from stage and screen plus new songs.				

WHO — UK

(See also High Numbers; Various Artists: Films – Original Soundtracks 'Tommy'.)

SINGLES:	**HITS 28**			**WEEKS 247**
I CAN'T EXPLAIN	*Brunswick*	8	*20 Feb 65*	13
Backing vocals by the Ivy League and Jimmy Page on guitar.				
ANYWAY ANYHOW ANYWHERE	*Brunswick*	10	*29 May 65*	12
Theme to the ITV programme 'Ready Steady Go'.				
MY GENERATION	*Brunswick*	2	*6 Nov 65*	13
SUBSTITUTE	*Reaction*	5	*12 Mar 66*	13
A LEGAL MATTER	*Brunswick*	32	*26 Mar 66*	6
I'M A BOY	*Reaction*	2	*3 Sep 66*	13
THE KIDS ARE ALRIGHT	*Brunswick*	41	*3 Sep 66*	2
THE KIDS ARE ALRIGHT [RE]	*Brunswick*	48	*24 Sep 66*	1
HAPPY JACK	*Reaction*	3	*17 Dec 66*	11
PICTURES OF LILY	*Track*	4	*29 Apr 67*	10
THE LAST TIME / UNDER MY THUMB	*Track*	44	*29 Jul 67*	3
Both tracks originally recorded by the Rolling Stones.				
I CAN SEE FOR MILES	*Track*	10	*21 Oct 67*	12
DOGS	*Track*	25	*22 Jun 68*	5
MAGIC BUS	*Track*	26	*26 Oct 68*	6
PINBALL WIZARD	*Track*	4	*22 Mar 69*	13
THE SEEKER	*Track*	19	*4 Apr 70*	11
SUMMERTIME BLUES	*Track*	38	*8 Aug 70*	4
Live recording from Leeds University, 14 Feb 70.				
WON'T GET FOOLED AGAIN	*Track*	9	*10 Jul 71*	12
LET'S SEE ACTION	*Track*	16	*23 Oct 71*	12
JOIN TOGETHER	*Track*	9	*24 Jun 72*	9
RELAY	*Track*	21	*13 Jan 73*	5
5:15	*Track*	20	*13 Oct 73*	6
SQUEEZE BOX	*Polydor*	10	*24 Jan 76*	9
SUBSTITUTE [RI]	*Polydor*	7	*30 Oct 76*	7
WHO ARE YOU	*Polydor*	18	*22 Jul 78*	12
LONG LIVE ROCK	*Polydor*	48	*28 Apr 79*	5
YOU BETTER YOU BET	*Polydor*	9	*7 Mar 81*	8
DON'T LET GO THE COAT	*Polydor*	47	*9 May 81*	4
ATHENA	*Polydor*	40	*2 Oct 82*	4
READY STEADY WHO [EP]	*Polydor*	58	*26 Nov 83*	2
Lead track: Disguises. Originally charted in the EP chart. See EP section below.				
MY GENERATION [RI-1ST]	*Polydor*	68	*20 Feb 88*	2
MY GENERATION [RI-2ND]	*Polydor*	31	*27 Jul 96*	2
Featured in the Calippo TV Commercial.				

EPS:	**HITS 1**			**WEEKS 20**
READY STEADY WHO	*Reaction*	1	*26 Nov 66*	20
Re-recordings of their performance on 'Ready Steady Go', Oct 66.				

ALBUMS:	**HITS 25**			**WEEKS 231**
MY GENERATION	*Brunswick*	5	*25 Dec 65*	11
A QUICK ONE	*Reaction*	4	*17 Dec 66*	17
THE WHO SELL-OUT	*Track*	13	*13 Jan 68*	11
TOMMY	*Track*	2	*7 Jun 69*	9
LIVE AT LEEDS	*Track*	3	*6 Jun 70*	21
Live recordings from Leeds University, 14 Feb 70.				
WHO'S NEXT	*Track*	1	*11 Sep 71*	13
MEATY, BEATY, BIG AND BOUNCY	*Track*	9	*18 Dec 71*	8
Compilation.				
QUADROPHENIA	*Track*	2	*17 Nov 73*	13
ODDS AND SODS	*Track*	10	*26 Oct 74*	4
Collection of unreleased material from 1964–72.				
TOMMY [OST]	*Track*	30	*23 Aug 75*	2
THE WHO BY NUMBERS	*Polydor*	7	*18 Oct 75*	6
THE STORY OF THE WHO	*Polydor*	2	*9 Oct 76*	18
WHO ARE YOU	*Polydor*	6	*9 Sep 78*	9
THE KIDS ARE ALRIGHT [OST]	*Polydor*	26	*30 Jun 79*	13
Compilation of live recordings and interviews from their career.				
QUADROPHENIA [OST]	*Polydor*	23	*6 Oct 79*	16
Selected remixed tracks from the original 1973 studio album plus various 1960s tracks from other artists.				
MY GENERATION [RI]	*Virgin*	20	*25 Oct 80*	7
FACE DANCES	*Polydor*	2	*28 Mar 81*	9
IT'S HARD	*Polydor*	11	*11 Sep 82*	6

WHO'S LAST *Live recordings from their concert at Maple Leaf Gardens, Toronto, Canada, 17 Dec 82.*	*MCA*	48	*17 Nov 84*	4
THE WHO COLLECTION	*Impression*	44	*12 Oct 85*	6
WHO'S BETTER, WHO'S BEST	*Polydor*	10	*19 Mar 88*	11
THE WHO COLLECTION *This album is different to the earlier entry.*	*Stylus*	71	*19 Nov 88*	4
JOIN TOGETHER *Live recordings from their Las Vegas tour of 1989.*	*Virgin*	59	*24 Mar 90*	1
30 YEARS OF MAXIMUM R&B *4CD boxed set containing unreleased tracks, live cuts, rarities, commercials and studio dialogue.*	*Polydor*	48	*16 Jul 94*	1
LIVE AT LEEDS [RI] *Includes bonus tracks.*	*Polydor*	59	*4 Mar 95*	1
QUADROPHENIA [RI] *Digitally remastered.*	*Polydor*	47	*6 Jul 96*	2
MY GENERATION - THE VERY BEST OF THE WHO *Same track listing as 1988's Who's Better, Who's Best plus 2 other tracks.*	*Polydor*	11	*24 Aug 96*	6
BBC SESSIONS *Recorded between 1965-1973.*	*BBC Music*	24	*26 Feb 00*	2

WHO WANTS TO BE A MILLIONAIRE — UK

SINGLES:	HITS 1			WEEKS 2
IS THAT YOUR FINAL ANSWER? *Performed by Amoure. Based on the theme to the ITV show.*	*Celador*	33	*27 May 00*	2

WHODINI — US

SINGLES:	HITS 2			WEEKS 10
MAGIC'S WAND	*Jive*	47	*25 Dec 82*	6
MAGIC'S WAND (THE WHODINI ELECTRIC EP) [EP] *Lead track: Jive Magic Wand.*	*Jive*	63	*17 Mar 84*	4

WHOOLIGANZ — US

SINGLES:	HITS 1			WEEKS 2
PUT YOUR HANDZ UP	*Positiva*	53	*13 Aug 94*	2

WHOOSH — UK

SINGLES:	HITS 1			WEEKS 1
WHOOSH	*Wonderboy*	72	*13 Sep 97*	1

WHYCLIFFE — UK

SINGLES:	HITS 2			WEEKS 2
HEAVEN	*MCA*	56	*20 Nov 93*	1
ONE MORE TIME	*MCA*	72	*2 Apr 94*	1

WIDEBOYS featuring Dennis G — UK

SINGLES:	HITS 1			WEEKS 6
SAMBUCA	*679 Recordings*	15	*27 Oct 01*	6

Jane WIEDLIN — US

SINGLES:	HITS 2			WEEKS 14
RUSH HOUR	*Manhattan*	12	*6 Aug 88*	11
INSIDE A DREAM	*Manhattan*	64	*29 Oct 88*	3
ALBUMS:	**HITS 1**			**WEEKS 3**
FUR	*Manhattan*	48	*24 Sep 88*	3

WIGAN'S CHOSEN FEW — Canada

SINGLES:	HITS 1			WEEKS 11
FOOTSEE (INSTRUMENTAL)	*Pye Disco Demand*	9	*18 Jan 75*	11

WIGAN'S OVATION — UK

SINGLES:	HITS 3			WEEKS 19
SKIING IN THE SNOW *Originally recorded by the Invitations.*	*Spark*	12	*15 Mar 75*	10
PER-SO-NAL-LY *Originally recorded by Bobby Paris.*	*Spark*	38	*28 Jun 75*	6
SUPER LOVE *Originally recorded by David and the Giants.*	*Spark*	41	*29 Nov 75*	3

WILCO — US

(See also Billy Bragg and Wilco.)

SINGLES:	HITS 1			WEEKS 1
CAN'T STAND IT	*Reprise*	67	*17 Apr 99*	1

ALBUMS:	HITS 1			WEEKS 2
SUMMERTEETH	*Reprise*	38	*20 Mar 99*	2

Jack WILD UK

SINGLES:	HITS 1			WEEKS 2
SOME BEAUTIFUL	*Capitol*	46	*2 May 70*	2

WILD BOYS – See HEINZ

WILD CHERRY US

SINGLES:	HITS 1			WEEKS 11
PLAY THAT FUNKY MUSIC	*Epic*	7	*9 Oct 76*	11

WILD COLOUR UK

SINGLES:	HITS 1			WEEKS 2
DREAMS	*Perfecto*	25	*14 Oct 95*	2

WILD HORSES UK

ALBUMS:	HITS 1			WEEKS 4
WILD HORSES	*EMI*	38	*26 Apr 80*	4

WILD PAIR – See Paula ABDUL

WILD WEEKEND UK

SINGLES:	HITS 2			WEEKS 2
BREAKIN' UP BREAKIN' DOWN	*Parlophone*	74	*29 Apr 89*	1
WHO'S AFRAID OF THE BIG BAD LOVE?	*Parlophone*	70	*5 May 90*	1

WILDCATS – See KREW-KATS, Marty WILDE

WILDCHILD UK

SINGLES:	HITS 3			WEEKS 20
LEGENDS OF THE DARK BLACK - PT 2	*Hi-Life*	34	*22 Apr 95*	3
RENEGADE MASTER [RI]	*Hi-Life*	11	*21 Oct 95*	4
A re-issue of the the first chart hit with a different title.				
JUMP TO MY BEAT	*Hi-Life*	30	*23 Nov 96*	2
Samples Mark Ryder's Get Down, Aretha Franklin's Jump To It and Lisa Lisa's Let The Beat Hit 'Em.				
RENEGADE MASTER 98 [RM]	*Hi-Life*	3	*17 Jan 98*	10
Remixed by Fatboy Slim.				
BAD BOY	*Polydor*	38	*25 Apr 98*	1
Above hit: WILDCHILD featuring JOMALSKI.				

Eugene WILDE US

SINGLES:	HITS 2			WEEKS 15
GOTTA GET YOU HOME TONIGHT	*Fourth & Broadway*	18	*13 Oct 84*	9
PERSONALITY / LET HER FEEL IT	*Fourth & Broadway*	34	*2 Feb 85*	6
Though Let Her Feel It is credited to Eugene Wilde, it is actually by Simplicious.				

ALBUMS:	HITS 1			WEEKS 4
EUGENE WILDE	*Fourth & Broadway*	67	*8 Dec 84*	4

Kim WILDE UK

SINGLES:	HITS 30			WEEKS 194
KIDS IN AMERICA	*RAK*	2	*21 Feb 81*	13
CHEQUERED LOVE	*RAK*	4	*9 May 81*	9
WATER ON GLASS / BOYS	*RAK*	11	*1 Aug 81*	8
CAMBODIA	*RAK*	12	*14 Nov 81*	12
VIEW FROM A BRIDGE	*RAK*	16	*17 Apr 82*	7
CHILD COME AWAY	*RAK*	43	*16 Oct 82*	4
LOVE BLONDE	*RAK*	23	*30 Jul 83*	8
DANCING IN THE DARK	*RAK*	67	*12 Nov 83*	2
THE SECOND TIME	*MCA*	29	*13 Oct 84*	6
THE TOUCH	*MCA*	56	*8 Dec 84*	3
RAGE TO LOVE	*MCA*	19	*27 Apr 85*	8
YOU KEEP ME HANGIN' ON	*MCA*	2	*25 Oct 86*	14
ANOTHER STEP (CLOSER TO YOU)	*MCA*	6	*4 Apr 87*	11
Above hit: Kim WILDE and JUNIOR.				
SAY YOU REALLY WANT ME	*MCA*	29	*8 Aug 87*	5
ROCKIN' AROUND THE CHRISTMAS TREE	*10 Records*	3	*5 Dec 87*	7
To support Comic Relief Red Nose Day (5 Feb 88).				
Above hit: COMIC RELIEF presents MEL and KIM performed by Kim WILDE and Mel SMITH.				
HEY MISTER HEARTACHE	*MCA*	31	*14 May 88*	5
YOU CAME	*MCA*	3	*16 Jul 88*	11
NEVER TRUST A STRANGER	*MCA*	7	*1 Oct 88*	9

FOUR LETTER WORD	*MCA*	6	*3 Dec 88*	12
LOVE IN THE NATURAL WAY	*MCA*	32	*4 Mar 89*	6
IT'S HERE	*MCA*	42	*14 Apr 90*	4
TIME	*MCA*	71	*16 Jun 90*	3
I CAN'T SAY GOODBYE	*MCA*	51	*15 Dec 90*	3
LOVE IS HOLY	*MCA*	16	*2 May 92*	6
HEART OVER MIND	*MCA*	34	*27 Jun 92*	3
WHO DO YOU THINK YOU ARE?	*MCA*	49	*12 Sep 92*	3
IF I CAN'T HAVE YOU	*MCA*	12	*10 Jul 93*	8
IN MY LIFE	*MCA*	54	*13 Nov 93*	1
BREAKIN' AWAY	*MCA*	43	*14 Oct 95*	2
THIS I SWEAR	*MCA*	46	*10 Feb 96*	1
ALBUMS:	**HITS 10**			**WEEKS 88**
KIM WILDE	*RAK*	3	*11 Jul 81*	14
SELECT	*RAK*	19	*22 May 82*	11
CATCH AS CATCH CAN	*RAK*	90	*26 Nov 83*	1
TEASES AND DARES	*MCA*	66	*17 Nov 84*	2
THE VERY BEST OF KIM WILDE	*RAK*	78	*18 May 85*	4
ANOTHER STEP	*MCA*	88	*15 Nov 86*	3
ANOTHER STEP [RI]	*MCA*	73	*26 Sep 87*	2
Re-released with bonus disc.				
CLOSE	*MCA*	44	*25 Jun 88*	19
CLOSE [RE]	*MCA*	8	*24 Dec 88*	19
LOVE MOVES	*MCA*	37	*26 May 90*	3
LOVE IS	*MCA*	21	*30 May 92*	3
THE SINGLES COLLECTION 1981-1993	*MCA*	11	*25 Sep 93*	7

Marty WILDE — UK

SINGLES:	**HITS 13**			**WEEKS 117**
ENDLESS SLEEP	*Philips*	4	*12 Jul 58*	14
Original by Jody Reynolds reached No. 5 in the US in 1958.				
Above hit: Marty WILDE and his WILDCATS.				
DONNA	*Philips*	3	*7 Mar 59*	16
A TEENAGER IN LOVE	*Philips*	2	*6 Jun 59*	17
DONNA [RE]	*Philips*	25	*4 Jul 59*	2
SEA OF LOVE	*Philips*	3	*26 Sep 59*	12
Original by Phil Phillips reached No. 2 in the US In 1959.				
BAD BOY	*Philips*	7	*12 Dec 59*	8
JOHNNY ROCCO	*Philips*	30	*12 Mar 60*	1
THE FIGHT	*Philips*	47	*21 May 60*	1
LITTLE GIRL	*Philips*	16	*24 Dec 60*	9
RUBBER BALL	*Philips*	9	*28 Jan 61*	9
Written by Gene Pitney.				
HIDE AND SEEK	*Philips*	47	*29 Jul 61*	2
TOMORROW'S CLOWN	*Philips*	33	*11 Nov 61*	5
JEZEBEL	*Philips*	19	*26 May 62*	11
Originally recorded by Frankie Laine in 1951.				
EVER SINCE YOU SAID GOODBYE	*Philips*	31	*27 Oct 62*	7

Matthew WILDER — US

SINGLES:	**HITS 1**			**WEEKS 11**
BREAK MY STRIDE	*Epic*	4	*21 Jan 84*	11

WILDHEARTS — UK

SINGLES:	**HITS 10**			**WEEKS 24**
TV TAN	*Bronze*	53	*20 Nov 93*	2
CAFFEINE BOMB	*Bronze*	31	*19 Feb 94*	3
SUCKERPUNCH	*Bronze*	38	*9 Jul 94*	2
IF LIFE IS LIKE A LOVE BANK, I WANT AN OVERDRAFT / GEORDIE IN WONDERLAND	*Bronze*	31	*28 Jan 95*	3
I WANNA GO WHERE THE PEOPLE GO	*Bronze*	16	*6 May 95*	3
JUST IN LUST	*Bronze*	28	*29 Jul 95*	2
SICK OF DRUGS	*Round*	14	*20 Apr 96*	3
RED LIGHT - GREEN LIGHT [EP]	*Round*	30	*29 Jun 96*	2
Lead track: Red Light - Green Light.				
ANTHEM	*Mushroom*	21	*16 Aug 97*	2
URGE	*Mushroom*	26	*18 Oct 97*	2
ALBUMS:	**HITS 4**			**WEEKS 8**
EARTH VS THE WILDHEARTS	*East West*	46	*11 Sep 93*	1
P.H.U.Q.	*East West*	6	*3 Jun 95*	4
FISHING FOR LUCKIES	*East West*	16	*1 Jun 96*	2
Originally released in 1994 to the fan club only.				
ENDLESS, NAMELESS	*Mushroom*	41	*8 Nov 97*	1

Heather WILDMAN – See George MOREL featuring Heather WILDMAN

Jonathan WILKES — UK

SINGLES:	HITS 1			WEEKS 2
JUST ANOTHER DAY	*Innocent*	24	*17 Mar 01*	2

Arthur WILKINSON ORCHESTRA — UK

EPS:	HITS 1			WEEKS 14
BEATLE CRACKER MUSIC	*His Master's Voice*	7	*8 Jan 66*	14

Colm WILKINSON — Ireland

ALBUMS:	HITS 1			WEEKS 6
STAGE HEROES	*RCA*	27	*10 Jun 89*	6

Sue WILKINSON — UK

SINGLES:	HITS 1			WEEKS 8
YOU GOTTA BE A HUSTLER IF YOU WANNA GET ON	*Cheapskate*	25	*2 Aug 80*	8

WILL TO POWER — US

SINGLES:	HITS 2			WEEKS 18
BABY I LOVE YOUR WAY / FREE BIRD [M]	*Epic*	6	*7 Jan 89*	9
I'M NOT IN LOVE	*Epic*	29	*22 Dec 90*	9

Alyson WILLIAMS — US

SINGLES:	HITS 4			WEEKS 28
SLEEP TALK	*Def Jam*	17	*4 Mar 89*	9
MY LOVE IS SO RAW	*Def Jam*	34	*6 May 89*	5
Above hit: Alyson WILLIAMS featuring NIKKI-D.				
I NEED YOUR LOVIN'	*Def Jam*	8	*19 Aug 89*	11
I SECOND THAT EMOTION	*Def Jam*	44	*18 Nov 89*	3
Above hit: Alyson WILLIAMS featuring Chuck STANLEY.				
ALBUMS:	**HITS 1**			**WEEKS 21**
RAW	*Def Jam*	29	*25 Mar 89*	21

Andy WILLIAMS — US

SINGLES:	HITS 21			WEEKS 234
BUTTERFLY	*London*	1	*20 Apr 57*	15
I LIKE YOUR KIND OF LOVE	*London*	16	*22 Jun 57*	10
Vocals by Peggy Powers. Originally recorded by Melvin Endsley in 1957.				
BUTTERFLY [RE]	*London*	29	*31 Aug 57*	1
STRANGER ON THE SHORE	*CBS*	30	*16 Jun 62*	10
CAN'T GET USED TO LOSING YOU	*CBS*	2	*23 Mar 63*	18
A FOOL NEVER LEARNS	*CBS*	40	*29 Feb 64*	4
Originally recorded by Sonny Curtis.				
ALMOST THERE	*CBS*	2	*18 Sep 65*	17
MAY EACH DAY	*CBS*	19	*26 Feb 66*	8
IN THE ARMS OF LOVE	*CBS*	33	*24 Sep 66*	7
From the film 'What Did You Do In The War Daddy?'.				
MUSIC TO WATCH GIRLS BY	*CBS*	33	*6 May 67*	6
Original instrumental version by Bob Crewe was featured in a US TV commercial for Diet Pepsi and reached No. 15 over there.				
MORE AND MORE	*CBS*	45	*5 Aug 67*	1
CAN'T TAKE MY EYES OFF YOU	*CBS*	5	*16 Mar 68*	18
HAPPY HEART	*CBS*	47	*10 May 69*	1
HAPPY HEART [RE]	*CBS*	19	*24 May 69*	9
CAN'T HELP FALLING IN LOVE	*CBS*	3	*14 Mar 70*	17
IT'S SO EASY	*CBS*	13	*1 Aug 70*	13
IT'S SO EASY [RE]	*CBS*	49	*7 Nov 70*	1
HOME LOVIN' MAN	*CBS*	7	*21 Nov 70*	12
(WHERE DO I BEGIN) LOVE STORY	*CBS*	4	*20 Mar 71*	17
From the film 'Love Story'.				
(WHERE DO I BEGIN) LOVE STORY [RE]	*CBS*	49	*24 Jul 71*	1
LOVE THEME FROM "THE GODFATHER" (SPEAK SOFTLY LOVE)	*CBS*	50	*5 Aug 72*	1
From the film.				
LOVE THEME FROM "THE GODFATHER" (SPEAK SOFTLY LOVE) [RE-1ST]	*CBS*	44	*2 Sep 72*	*3*
LOVE THEME FROM "THE GODFATHER" (SPEAK SOFTLY LOVE) [RE-2ND]	*CBS*	42	*30 Sep 72*	*5*
SOLITAIRE	*CBS*	4	*8 Dec 73*	18
Originally recorded by Neil Sedaka.				
GETTING OVER YOU	*CBS*	35	*18 May 74*	5
YOU LAY SO EASY ON MY MIND	*CBS*	32	*31 May 75*	7
THE OTHER SIDE OF ME	*CBS*	42	*6 Mar 76*	3
MUSIC TO WATCH GIRLS BY [RI]	*Columbia*	9	*27 Mar 99*	6
Featured in the Fiat Punto car TV commercial.				
EPS:	**HITS 3**			**WEEKS 55**
ANDY WILLIAMS FAVOURITES, VOLUME 1	*CBS*	3	*7 Aug 65*	38
ANDY WILLIAMS FAVOURITES, VOLUME 2	*CBS*	17	*4 Dec 65*	2

ANDY'S NEWEST HITS	*CBS*	6	*14 Jan 67*	15
ALBUMS:	**HITS 27**			**WEEKS 452**
ALMOST THERE	*CBS*	4	*26 Jun 65*	46
CAN'T GET USED TO LOSING YOU	*CBS*	16	*7 Aug 65*	1
MAY EACH DAY	*CBS*	11	*19 Mar 66*	6
GREAT SONGS FROM MY FAIR LADY	*CBS*	30	*30 Apr 66*	1
SHADOW OF YOUR SMILE	*CBS*	24	*23 Jul 66*	4
BORN FREE	*CBS*	22	*29 Jul 67*	11
LOVE ANDY	*CBS*	1	*11 May 68*	22
HONEY	*CBS*	4	*6 Jul 68*	17
HAPPY HEART	*CBS*	22	*26 Jul 69*	9
GET TOGETHER WITH ANDY WILLIAMS	*CBS*	13	*27 Dec 69*	12
Includes 3 tracks with the Osmonds.				
ANDY WILLIAMS' SOUND OF MUSIC	*CBS*	22	*24 Jan 70*	10
ANDY WILLIAMS' GREATEST HITS	*CBS*	1	*11 Apr 70*	116
Peak position reached on 5 Dec 70.				
CAN'T HELP FALLING IN LOVE	*CBS*	7	*20 Jun 70*	48
ANDY WILLIAMS SHOW	*CBS*	10	*5 Dec 70*	6
HOME LOVIN' MAN	*CBS*	1	*3 Apr 71*	25
LOVE STORY	*CBS*	11	*31 Jul 71*	11
THE IMPOSSIBLE DREAM	*CBS*	26	*29 Apr 72*	3
LOVE THEME FROM 'THE GODFATHER'	*CBS*	11	*29 Jul 72*	16
GREATEST HITS VOLUME 2	*CBS*	23	*16 Dec 72*	10
SOLITAIRE	*CBS*	3	*22 Dec 73*	26
THE WAY WE WERE	*CBS*	7	*15 Jun 74*	11
THE OTHER SIDE OF ME	*CBS*	60	*11 Oct 75*	1
REFLECTIONS	*CBS*	2	*28 Jan 78*	17
GREATEST LOVE CLASSICS	*EMI*	22	*27 Oct 84*	10
Above hit: Andy WILLIAMS and the ROYAL PHILHARMONIC ORCHESTRA.				
THE BEST OF ANDY WILLIAMS	*Dino*	51	*7 Nov 92*	3
IN THE LOUNGE WITH . . . ANDY WILLIAMS	*Columbia*	39	*10 Apr 99*	3
Compilation originally released in 1996.				
THE VERY BEST OF ANDY WILLIAMS	*Columbia*	27	*19 Feb 00*	7

Andy and David WILLIAMS — US

SINGLES:	**HITS 1**			**WEEKS 5**
I DON'T KNOW WHY (I JUST DO)	*MCA*	37	*24 Mar 73*	5

Billy WILLIAMS — US

SINGLES:	**HITS 1**			**WEEKS 9**
I'M GONNA SIT RIGHT DOWN AND WRITE MYSELF A LETTER	*Vogue Coral*	22	*3 Aug 57*	*8*
I'M GONNA SIT RIGHT DOWN AND WRITE MYSELF A LETTER [RE]	*Vogue Coral*	28	*19 Oct 57*	*1*

Danny WILLIAMS — US

SINGLES:	**HITS 8**			**WEEKS 74**
WE WILL NEVER BE AS YOUNG AS THIS AGAIN	*His Master's Voice*	44	*27 May 61*	3
Above hit: Danny WILLIAMS with the Rita WILLIAMS SINGERS and Geoff LOVE and his Orchestra.				
THE MIRACLE OF YOU	*His Master's Voice*	41	*8 Jul 61*	8
MOON RIVER	*His Master's Voice*	1	*4 Nov 61*	19
From the film 'Breakfast At Tiffany's'.				
Above hit: Danny WILLIAMS with Geoff LOVE and his Orchestra and the Rita WILLIAMS SINGERS.				
JEANNIE	*His Master's Voice*	14	*20 Jan 62*	14
Above hit: Danny WILLIAMS with the Rita WILLIAMS SINGERS and Geoff LOVE and his Orchestra.				
THE WONDERFUL WORLD OF THE YOUNG	*His Master's Voice*	8	*14 Apr 62*	13
TEARS	*His Master's Voice*	22	*7 Jul 62*	7
Above 2: Danny WILLIAMS with Geoff LOVE and his Orchestra.				
MY OWN TRUE LOVE	*His Master's Voice*	45	*2 Mar 63*	3
DANCIN' EASY	*Ensign*	30	*30 Jul 77*	7
Tune was featured in the Martini TV commercial.				

Deniece WILLIAMS — US

(See also Johnny Mathis and Deniece Williams.)

SINGLES:	**HITS 4**			**WEEKS 39**
FREE	*CBS*	1	*2 Apr 77*	10
THAT'S WHAT FRIENDS ARE FOR	*CBS*	8	*30 Jul 77*	11
BABY, BABY MY LOVE'S ALL FOR YOU	*CBS*	32	*12 Nov 77*	5
LET'S HEAR IT FOR THE BOY	*CBS*	2	*5 May 84*	12
From the film 'Footloose'.				
LET'S HEAR IT FOR THE BOY [RE]	*CBS*	75	*4 Aug 84*	1
ALBUMS:	**HITS 1**			**WEEKS 12**
THIS IS NIECEY	*CBS*	31	*21 May 77*	12

Diana WILLIAMS — US

SINGLES:	HITS 1			WEEKS 3
TEDDY BEAR'S LAST RIDE	*Capitol*	54	*25 Jul 81*	3
Answer song to Red Sovine's Teddy Bear.				

Don WILLIAMS — US

SINGLES:	HITS 2			WEEKS 16
I RECALL A GYPSY WOMAN	*ABC*	13	*19 Jun 76*	10
YOU'RE MY BEST FRIEND	*ABC*	35	*23 Oct 76*	6
ALBUMS:	**HITS 14**			**WEEKS 136**
GREATEST HITS VOLUME 1	*ABC*	29	*10 Jul 76*	15
VISIONS	*ABC*	13	*19 Feb 77*	20
COUNTRY BOY	*ABC*	27	*15 Oct 77*	5
IMAGES	*K-Tel*	2	*5 Aug 78*	38
YOU'RE MY BEST THING	*ABC*	58	*5 Aug 78*	1
EXPRESSIONS	*ABC*	28	*4 Nov 78*	8
NEW HORIZONS	*K-Tel*	29	*22 Sep 79*	12
PORTRAIT	*MCA*	58	*15 Dec 79*	4
I BELIEVE IN YOU	*MCA*	36	*6 Sep 80*	5
ESPECIALLY FOR YOU	*MCA*	33	*18 Jul 81*	7
LISTEN TO THE RADIO	*MCA*	69	*17 Apr 82*	3
YELLOW MOON	*MCA*	52	*23 Apr 83*	1
LOVE STORIES	*K-Tel*	22	*15 Oct 83*	13
CAFE CAROLINA	*MCA*	65	*26 May 84*	4

Eric WILLIAMS of BLACKSTREET – See BLACKSTREET; QUEEN PEN; 2PAC

Freedom WILLIAMS — US

SINGLES:	HITS 4			WEEKS 31
GONNA MAKE YOU SWEAT (EVERYBODY DANCE NOW)	*CBS*	3	*15 Dec 90*	12
HERE WE GO	*Columbia*	20	*30 Mar 91*	7
THINGS THAT MAKE YOU GO HMMM . . .	*Columbia*	4	*6 Jul 91*	11
Above 3: C&C MUSIC FACTORY (featuring Freedom WILLIAMS).				
VOICE OF FREEDOM	*Columbia*	62	*5 Jun 93*	1
Samples George Michael's Freedom.				

Geoffrey WILLIAMS — UK

SINGLES:	HITS 4			WEEKS 8
IT'S NOT A LOVE THING	*EMI*	63	*11 Apr 92*	2
SUMMER BREEZE	*EMI*	56	*22 Aug 92*	3
DRIVE	*Hands On*	52	*18 Jan 97*	2
SEX LIFE	*Hands On*	71	*19 Apr 97*	1
Original release reached No. 96 in 1995.				

Iris WILLIAMS — UK

SINGLES:	HITS 1			WEEKS 8
HE WAS BEAUTIFUL (CAVATINA) THE THEME FROM 'DEER HUNTER'	*Columbia*	18	*27 Oct 79*	8
From the film.				
Above hit: Iris WILLIAMS with the Neil RICHARDSON ORCHESTRA.				
ALBUMS:	**HITS 1**			**WEEKS 4**
HE WAS BEAUTIFUL	*Columbia*	69	*22 Dec 79*	4

James 'D Train' WILLIAMS – See David MORALES; Bob SINCLAR

John WILLIAMS — Australia

(See also Cleo Laine and John Williams.)

SINGLES:	HITS 1			WEEKS 11
CAVATINA	*Cube*	13	*19 May 79*	11
Theme from the film 'The Deerhunter'.				
ALBUMS:	**HITS 6**			**WEEKS 43**
PLAYS SPANISH MUSIC	*CBS*	46	*3 Oct 70*	1
RODRIGO: CONCERTO DE ARANJUEZ	*CBS*	20	*7 Feb 76*	9
Above hit: John WILLIAMS with the ENGLISH CHAMBER ORCHESTRA conducted by Daniel BARENBOIM.				
TRAVELLING	*Cube*	23	*17 Jun 78*	5
BRIDGES	*Lotus*	5	*30 Jun 79*	22
CAVATINA	*Cube*	64	*4 Aug 79*	3
JOHN WILLIAMS PLAYS THE MOVIES	*Sony Classical*	54	*26 Oct 96*	3
Released to mark a century of Cinema. Double album consists of 1 disc classical and the other pop.				

John WILLIAMS — US

SINGLES:	HITS 3			WEEKS 17
THEME FROM SUPERMAN (MAIN TITLE)	*Warner Brothers*	32	*6 Jan 79*	5
Above hit: Composed and conducted by John WILLIAMS performed by the LONDON SYMPHONY ORCHESTRA.				
THEME FROM E.T. (THE EXTRA-TERRESTRIAL)	*MCA*	17	*18 Dec 82*	10
THEME FROM JURASSIC PARK	*MCA*	45	*14 Aug 93*	2
Above 2 are from the films of the respective titles.				

ALBUMS:	HITS 9			WEEKS 62
JAWS [OST]	*MCA*	55	*31 Jan 76*	1
Above hit: Composed and conducted by John WILLIAMS.				
STAR WARS [OST]	*20th Century*	21	*21 Jan 78*	12
Above hit: Composed and conducted by John WILLIAMS; performed by the LONDON SYMPHONY ORCHESTRA.				
CLOSE ENCOUNTERS OF THE THIRD KIND [OST]	*Arista*	40	*29 Apr 78*	6
Above hit: Composed and conducted by John WILLIAMS.				
E.T. - THE EXTRATERRESTRIAL [OST]	*MCA*	47	*25 Dec 82*	10
RETURN OF THE JEDI [OST]	*RSO*	85	*25 Jun 83*	5
Above hit: Composed and conducted by John WILLIAMS; performed by the LONDON SYMPHONY ORCHESTRA.				
JURASSIC PARK [OST]	*MCA*	42	*31 Jul 93*	5
SCHINDLER'S LIST [OST]	*MCA*	59	*2 Apr 94*	2
STAR WARS - THE PHANTOM MENACE [OST]	*Sony Classical*	8	*15 May 99*	17
Above hit: Composed and conducted by John WILLIAMS; performed by the LONDON SYMPHONY ORCHESTRA.				
HARRY POTTER AND THE PHILOSOPHER'S STONE [OST]	*Atlantic*	19	*10 Nov 01*	4

Kathryn WILLIAMS — UK

ALBUMS:	HITS 1			WEEKS 1
LITTLE BLACK NUMBERS	*East West*	70	*15 Sep 01*	1

Kenny WILLIAMS — US

SINGLES:	HITS 1			WEEKS 8
(YOU'RE) FABULOUS BABE	*Decca*	35	*19 Nov 77*	8

Larry WILLIAMS — US

SINGLES:	HITS 2			WEEKS 18
SHORT FAT FANNIE	*London*	21	*21 Sep 57*	8
BONY MORONIE	*London*	11	*18 Jan 58*	10

Lenny WILLIAMS — US

SINGLES:	HITS 2			WEEKS 7
SHOO DOO FU FU OOH!	*ABC*	38	*5 Nov 77*	4
YOU GOT ME RUNNING	*ABC*	67	*16 Sep 78*	3

Lucinda WILLIAMS — US

ALBUMS:	HITS 1			WEEKS 1
ESSENCE	*Lost Highway*	63	*16 Jun 01*	1

Mark WILLIAMS – See Karen BODDINGTON and Mark WILLIAMS

Mason WILLIAMS — US

SINGLES:	HITS 1			WEEKS 13
CLASSICAL GAS	*Warner Brothers*	9	*31 Aug 68*	13

Maurice WILLIAMS and the ZODIACS — US

SINGLES:	HITS 1			WEEKS 9
STAY	*Top Rank*	14	*7 Jan 61*	9

Melanie WILLIAMS — UK

SINGLES:	HITS 5			WEEKS 21
AIN'T NO LOVE (AIN'T NO USE)	*Rob's Records*	3	*10 Apr 93*	11
Above hit: SUB SUB featuring Melanie WILLIAMS.				
ALL CRIED OUT	*Columbia*	60	*9 Apr 94*	2
EVERYDAY THANG	*Columbia*	38	*11 Jun 94*	3
NOT ENOUGH?	*Columbia*	65	*17 Sep 94*	1
YOU ARE EVERYTHING	*Columbia*	28	*18 Feb 95*	4
Original version by the Stylistics reached No. 9 in the US in 1971.				
Above hit: Melanie WILLIAMS and Joe ROBERTS.				

Rita WILLIAMS SINGERS – See Shirley BASSEY; Alma COGAN; Russ CONWAY; Gracie FIELDS; KING BROTHERS; Ricky STEVENS with the Rita WILLIAMS SINGERS and Geoff LOVE and his Orchestra; Danny WILLIAMS

Robbie WILLIAMS — UK

SINGLES:	HITS 16			WEEKS 214
FREEDOM	*Chrysalis*	2	*10 Aug 96*	10
FREEDOM [RE]	*Chrysalis*	56	*26 Oct 96*	4
OLD BEFORE I DIE	*Chrysalis*	2	*26 Apr 97*	9
OLD BEFORE I DIE [RE-1ST]	*Chrysalis*	72	*5 Jul 97*	1
OLD BEFORE I DIE [RE-2ND]	*Chrysalis*	69	*19 Jul 97*	1
LAZY DAYS	*Chrysalis*	8	*26 Jul 97*	5
SOUTH OF THE BORDER	*Chrysalis*	14	*27 Sep 97*	4
ANGELS	*Chrysalis*	4	*13 Dec 97*	20
LET ME ENTERTAIN YOU	*Chrysalis*	3	*28 Mar 98*	12
MILLENNIUM	*Chrysalis*	1	*19 Sep 98*	20
Samples theme from the James Bond film 'You Only Live Twice'.				
NO REGRETS	*Chrysalis*	4	*12 Dec 98*	13
Features vocals by Neil Tennant (Pet Shop Boys) and Neil Hannon (Divine Comedy). Though issued as an [AA], Antmusic was not listed.				
ANGELS [RE-1ST]	*Chrysalis*	57	*2 Jan 99*	4
ANGELS [RE-2ND]	*Chrysalis*	75	*27 Feb 99*	1
ANGELS [RE-3RD]	*Chrysalis*	75	*20 Mar 99*	1
STRONG	*Chrysalis*	4	*27 Mar 99*	9
SHE'S THE ONE / IT'S ONLY US	*Chrysalis*	1	*20 Nov 99*	16
She's The One originally recorded by World Party on their 1997 album Egyptology.				
ANGELS [RE-4TH]	*Chrysalis*	71	*1 Jan 00*	1
MILLENNIUM [RE]	*Chrysalis*	74	*8 Jan 00*	1
SHE'S THE ONE/IT'S ONLY US [RE]	*Chrysalis*	57	*18 Mar 00*	4
ROCK DJ	*Chrysalis*	1	*12 Aug 00*	17
Based around Barry White's It's Ecstasy When You Lay Down Next To Me.				
KIDS	*Chrysalis*	2	*21 Oct 00*	15
Above hit: Robbie WILLIAMS/Kylie MINOGUE.				
ROCK DJ [RE]	*Chrysalis*	60	*16 Dec 00*	3
SUPREME	*Chrysalis*	4	*23 Dec 00*	10
KIDS [RE-1ST]	*Chrysalis*	73	*10 Feb 01*	1
KIDS [RE-2ND]	*Chrysalis*	66	*24 Feb 01*	3
LET LOVE BE YOUR ENERGY	*Chrysalis*	10	*21 Apr 01*	9
ETERNITY/THE ROAD TO MANDALAY	*Chrysalis*	1	*21 Jul 01*	16
LET LOVE BE YOUR ENERGY [RE]	*Chrysalis*	73	*21 Jul 01*	2
SOMETHIN' STUPID	*Chrysalis*	1	*22 Dec 01*	2
Originally recorded by C. Carson Parkes.				
Above hit: Robbie WILLIAMS and Nicole KIDMAN.				

ALBUMS:	HITS 4			WEEKS 279
LIFE THRU A LENS	*Chrysalis*	11	*11 Oct 97*	4
LIFE THRU A LENS [RE]	*Chrysalis*	1	*13 Dec 97*	119
Peak position reached on 18 Apr 98.				
I'VE BEEN EXPECTING YOU	*Chrysalis*	1	*7 Nov 98*	97
SING WHEN YOU'RE WINNING	*Chrysalis*	1	*9 Sep 00*	54
SWING WHEN YOU'RE WINNING	*Chrysalis*	1	*1 Dec 01*	5

Saul WILLIAMS – See KRUST featuring Saul WILLIAMS

Vanessa WILLIAMS — US

SINGLES:	HITS 6			WEEKS 24
THE RIGHT STUFF	*Wing*	71	*20 Aug 88*	1
DREAMIN'	*Wing*	74	*25 Mar 89*	2
THE RIGHT STUFF [RM]	*Wing*	62	*19 Aug 89*	2
Remixed by Norman Cook.				
SAVE THE BEST FOR LAST	*Polydor*	3	*21 Mar 92*	11
THE SWEETEST DAYS	*Mercury*	41	*8 Apr 95*	2
THE WAY THAT YOU LOVE	*Mercury*	52	*8 Jul 95*	1
COLOURS OF THE WIND	*Walt Disney*	21	*16 Sep 95*	5
From the film 'Pocahontas'.				

ALBUMS:	HITS 1			WEEKS 4
THE COMFORT ZONE	*Polydor*	24	*25 Apr 92*	4

Vesta WILLIAMS — US

SINGLES:	HITS 1			WEEKS 13
ONCE BITTEN TWICE SHY	*A&M*	14	*20 Dec 86*	13

Wendell WILLIAMS — US

SINGLES:	HITS 2			WEEKS 6
EVERYBODY (RAP)	*Deconstruction*	30	*6 Oct 90*	4
Above hit: CRIMINAL ELEMENT ORCHESTRA featuring Wendell WILLIAMS.				
SO GROOVY	*Deconstruction*	74	*18 May 91*	2

Wendy O. WILLIAMS US

ALBUMS:	HITS 1			WEEKS 1
W.O.W.	*Music For Nations*	100	*30 Jun 84*	1

WILLIAMS SINGERS – Russ CONWAY

Ann WILLIAMSON UK

ALBUMS:	HITS 2			WEEKS 13
PRECIOUS MEMORIES	*Emerald*	16	*15 Feb 86*	9
COUNT YOUR BLESSINGS	*Emerald Gem*	58	*6 Feb 88*	4

Sonny Boy WILLIAMSON US

ALBUMS:	HITS 1			WEEKS 1
DOWN AND OUT BLUES	*Pye*	20	*20 Jun 64*	1

WILLING SINNERS – See Marc ALMOND

Bruce WILLIS US

SINGLES:	HITS 4			WEEKS 30
RESPECT YOURSELF	*Motown*	7	*7 Mar 87*	10
UNDER THE BOARDWALK	*Motown*	2	*30 May 87*	15
Backing vocals by the Temptations.				
SECRET AGENT MAN/JAMES BOND IS BACK [M]	*Motown*	43	*12 Sep 87*	4
COMIN' RIGHT UP	*Motown*	73	*23 Jan 88*	1
ALBUMS:	**HITS 1**			**WEEKS 28**
THE RETURN OF BRUNO	*Motown*	4	*18 Apr 87*	28

Chill WILLS – See LAUREL and HARDY

Viola WILLS US

SINGLES:	HITS 2			WEEKS 16
GONNA GET ALONG WITHOUT YOU NOW	*Ariola Hansa*	8	*6 Oct 79*	10
Originally recorded by Teresa Brewer in 1952.				
DARE TO DREAM / BOTH SIDES NOW	*Streetwave*	35	*15 Mar 86*	6

WILSATIONS – See Mari WILSON

Al WILSON US

SINGLES:	HITS 1			WEEKS 5
THE SNAKE	*Bell*	41	*23 Aug 75*	5

Brian WILSON US

ALBUMS:	HITS 2			WEEKS 3
I JUST WASN'T MADE FOR THESE TIMES	*MCA*	59	*16 Sep 95*	1
Wilson's compositions re-recorded for Don Was' TV documentary about him.				
IMAGINATION	*Giant*	30	*27 Jun 98*	2

Charlie WILSON – See SNOOP DOGGY DOGG

Dennis WILSON and his Orchestra – See Gary MILLER

Dooley WILSON with the voices of Humphrey BOGART and Ingrid BERGMAN US

SINGLES:	HITS 1			WEEKS 9
AS TIME GOES BY	*United Artists*	15	*3 Dec 77*	9
From the 1943 film 'Casablanca'. Originally recorded by Jacques Renard in 1931.				

Jackie WILSON US

SINGLES:	HITS 6			WEEKS 97
REET PETITE	*Coral*	6	*16 Nov 57*	14
From the film 'The Sweetest Girl In Town'.				
TO BE LOVED	*Coral*	27	*15 Mar 58*	1
TO BE LOVED [RE-1ST]	*Coral*	23	*29 Mar 58*	6
TO BE LOVED [RE-2ND]	*Coral*	23	*17 May 58*	1
(YOU WERE MADE FOR) ALL MY LOVE	*Coral*	33	*17 Sep 60*	6
(YOU WERE MADE FOR) ALL MY LOVE [RE]	*Coral*	47	*5 Nov 60*	1
ALONE AT LAST	*Coral*	50	*24 Dec 60*	1
Based on Tchaikovsky's Piano Concerto in B flat.				
(YOUR LOVE KEEPS LIFTING ME) HIGHER AND HIGHER	*MCA*	11	*17 May 69*	11
Higher And Higher originally recorded by The Dells in 1967.				
I GET THE SWEETEST FEELING	*MCA*	9	*29 Jul 72*	13
Originally released in the US in 1968 reaching No. 34.				
I GET THE SWEETEST FEELING [RI-1ST] / (YOUR LOVE KEEPS LIFTING ME) HIGHER AND HIGHER [RI 1ST]	*Brunswick*	25	*3 May 75*	8
(Your Love Keeps Lifting Me) Higher And Higher listed from 17 May 75.				
REET PETITE (THE SWEETEST GIRL IN TOWN) [RI]	*SMP*	1	*29 Nov 86*	17

I GET THE SWEETEST FEELING [RI-2ND]	*SMP*	3	*28 Feb 87*	11
This re-issue originally reached No. 98 in 1983.				
(YOUR LOVE KEEPS LIFTING ME) HIGHER AND HIGHER [RI-2ND]	*SMP*	15	*4 Jul 87*	7

Mari WILSON — UK

SINGLES:	HITS 6			WEEKS 34
BEAT THE BEAT	*Compact Organisation*	59	*6 Mar 82*	3
Above hit: Mari WILSON and the IMAGINATIONS.				
BABY IT'S TRUE	*Compact Organisation*	42	*8 May 82*	6
JUST WHAT I ALWAYS WANTED	*Compact Organisation*	8	*11 Sep 82*	10
(BEWARE) BOYFRIEND	*Compact Organisation*	51	*13 Nov 82*	4
CRY ME A RIVER	*Compact Organisation*	27	*19 Mar 83*	7
WONDERFUL	*Compact Organisation*	47	*11 Jun 83*	4
Above hit: Mari WILSON with the WILSATIONS.				
ALBUMS:	**HITS 1**			**WEEKS 9**
SHOW PEOPLE	*Compact Organisation*	24	*26 Feb 83*	9
Above hit: Mari WILSON with the WILSATIONS.				

Meri WILSON — US

SINGLES:	HITS 1			WEEKS 10
TELEPHONE MAN	*Pye International*	6	*27 Aug 77*	10

Mike 'Hitman' WILSON featuring Shawn CHRISTOPHER — US

(See also Shawn Christopher.)

SINGLES:	HITS 1			WEEKS 1
ANOTHER SLEEPLESS NIGHT	*Arista*	74	*22 Sep 90*	1
This single was re-issued in 1991 crediting just Shawn Christopher.				

Precious WILSON – See ERUPTION; MESSIAH

Richard WILSON – See Eric IDLE featuring Richard WILSON

Tom WILSON — UK

SINGLES:	HITS 2			WEEKS 4
TECHNOCAT	*Pukka*	33	*2 Dec 95*	3
Above hit: TECHNOCAT featuring Tom WILSON.				
LET YOUR BODY GO	*Clubscene*	60	*16 Mar 96*	1

Victoria WILSON JAMES — US

SINGLES:	HITS 1			WEEKS 1
REACH 4 THE MELODY	*Sony*	72	*9 Aug 97*	1

WILSON PHILLIPS — US

SINGLES:	HITS 6			WEEKS 33
HOLD ON	*SBK*	6	*26 May 90*	12
RELEASE ME	*SBK*	36	*18 Aug 90*	5
IMPULSIVE	*SBK*	42	*10 Nov 90*	3
YOU'RE IN LOVE	*SBK*	29	*11 May 91*	5
YOU WON'T SEE ME CRY	*SBK*	18	*23 May 92*	5
GIVE IT UP	*SBK*	36	*22 Aug 92*	3
ALBUMS:	**HITS 2**			**WEEKS 38**
WILSON PHILLIPS	*SBK*	7	*30 Jun 90*	32
SHADOWS AND LIGHT	*SBK*	6	*13 Jun 92*	6

WILT — Ireland

SINGLES:	HITS 2			WEEKS 2
RADIO DISCO	*Mushroom*	56	*8 Apr 00*	1
OPEN ARMS	*Mushroom*	59	*8 Jul 00*	1

Chris WILTSHIRE – See CLASS ACTION featuring Chris WILTSHIRE

WIMBLEDON CHORAL SOCIETY — UK

(See also Read by Des Lynam performed by the Wimbledon Choral Society.)

SINGLES:	HITS 1			WEEKS 5
WORLD CUP '98 - PAVANE BY FAURE	*Telstar*	20	*4 Jul 98*	5
BBC TV's theme for the coverage of the 1998 World Cup in France. Originally written in the 19th century.				

WIN — UK

SINGLES:	HITS 1			WEEKS 3
SUPER POPOID GROOVE	*Swamplands*	63	*4 Apr 87*	3
ALBUMS:	**HITS 1**			**WEEKS 1**
UH! TEARS BABY	*London*	51	*25 Apr 87*	1

WINANS — US

SINGLES:	HITS 1			WEEKS 1
LET MY PEOPLE GO	*Qwest*	71	*30 Nov 85*	1

BeBe WINANS – See ETERNAL

CeCe WINANS – See Whitney HOUSTON

Mario WINANS – See PUFF DADDY

WINCHESTER CATHEDRAL CHOIR – See Andrew LLOYD WEBBER

WINDJAMMER — US

SINGLES:	HITS 1			WEEKS 12
TOSSING AND TURNING	*MCA*	18	*30 Jun 84*	12
ALBUMS:	**HITS 1**			**WEEKS 1**
WINDJAMMER II	*MCA*	82	*25 Aug 84*	1

Rose WINDROSS – See SOUL II SOUL

Barbara WINDSOR — UK

SINGLES:	HITS 1			WEEKS 2
THE MORE I SEE YOU	*Telstar TV*	46	*24 Apr 99*	2
Originally recorded by Dick Haymes.				
Above hit: Barbara WINDSOR and Mike REID.				
ALBUMS:	**HITS 1**			**WEEKS 2**
YOU'VE GOT A FRIEND	*Telstar TV*	45	*3 Apr 99*	2

WING AND A PRAYER FIFE AND DRUM CORPS — US

SINGLES:	HITS 1			WEEKS 7
BABY FACE	*Atlantic*	12	*24 Jan 76*	7
Originally recorded by Jan Garber in 1926.				

WINGER — US

SINGLES:	HITS 1			WEEKS 3
MILES AWAY	*Atlantic*	56	*19 Jan 91*	3

Pete WINGFIELD — UK

SINGLES:	HITS 1			WEEKS 7
EIGHTEEN WITH A BULLET	*Island*	7	*28 Jun 75*	7

WINGS – See Paul McCARTNEY

Josh WINK — US

(See also Size 9.)

SINGLES:	HITS 4			WEEKS 29
DON'T LAUGH	*XL Recordings*	38	*6 May 95*	2
Above hit: WINX.				
HIGHER STATE OF CONSCIOUSNESS	*Manifesto*	8	*21 Oct 95*	8
HIGHER STATE OF CONSCIOUSNESS [RE]	*Manifesto*	60	*30 Dec 95*	4
HYPNOTIZIN'	*XL Recordings*	35	*2 Mar 96*	2
Originally released in the US in 1990.				
Above hit: WINX.				
HIGHER STATE OF CONSCIOUSNESS '96 REMIXES [RM]	*Manifesto*	7	27 Jul 96	10
Remixed by Dex and Jonesey. Other remixes are by Mr. Spring and Itty Bitty Boozy Woozy.				
Above hit: WINK.				
HOW'S YOUR EVENING SO FAR?	*ffrr*	23	*12 Aug 00*	3
A re-recorded version of Lil' Louis' French Kiss.				
Above hit: Josh WINK and LIL' LOUIS.				
ALBUMS:	**HITS 1**			**WEEKS 1**
LEFT ABOVE THE CLOUDS	*XL Recordings*	43	*21 Sep 96*	1
Above hit: WINX.				

Kate WINSLET — UK

SINGLES:	HITS 1			WEEKS 4
WHAT IF	*Liberty*	6	*8 Dec 01*	4

Edgar WINTER GROUP — US

SINGLES:	HITS 1			WEEKS 9
FRANKENSTEIN	*Epic*	18	*26 May 73*	9

Johnny WINTER — US

ALBUMS:	HITS 3			WEEKS 12
SECOND WINTER	*CBS*	59	*16 May 70*	2

JOHNNY WINTER AND . . . *Features the McCoys as backing group.*	*CBS*	29	*31 Oct 70*	4
JOHNNY WINTER AND . . . LIVE	*CBS*	20	*15 May 71*	6

Hugo WINTERHALTER and his Orchestra – See AMES BROTHERS with Hugo WINTERHALTER and his Orchestra; Perry COMO; Eddie FISHER; Tony MARTIN with Hugo WINTERHALTER's Orchestra and Chorus; Kay STARR

Ruby WINTERS — US

SINGLES:	HITS 4			WEEKS 35
I WILL! *Originally recorded by Vic Dana.*	*Creole*	4	*5 Nov 77*	13
COME TO ME!	*Creole*	11	*29 Apr 78*	12
I WON'T MENTION IT AGAIN	*Creole*	45	*26 Aug 78*	5
BABY LAY DOWN	*Creole*	43	*16 Jun 79*	5
ALBUMS:	**HITS 2**			**WEEKS 16**
RUBY WINTERS	*Creole*	27	*10 Jun 78*	7
SONGBIRD	*K-Tel*	31	*23 Jun 79*	9

Steve WINWOOD — UK

SINGLES:	HITS 6			WEEKS 33
WHILE YOU SEE A CHANCE	*Island*	45	*17 Jan 81*	5
VALERIE	*Island*	51	*9 Oct 82*	4
HIGHER LOVE *Backing vocals by Chaka Khan.*	*Island*	13	*28 Jun 86*	9
FREEDOM OVERSPILL *Features Joe Walsh on guitar.*	*Island*	69	*13 Sep 86*	1
BACK IN THE HIGH LIFE AGAIN *James Taylor on backing vocals.*	*Island*	53	*24 Jan 87*	2
VALERIE [RM] *Remixed by Tom Lord Alge.*	*Island*	19	*19 Sep 87*	8
ROLL WITH IT	*Virgin*	53	*11 Jun 88*	4
ALBUMS:	**HITS 8**			**WEEKS 122**
STEVE WINWOOD	*Island*	12	*9 Jul 77*	9
ARC OF A DIVER	*Island*	13	*10 Jan 81*	20
TALKING BACK TO THE NIGHT	*Island*	6	*14 Aug 82*	13
BACK IN THE HIGH LIFE	*Island*	8	*12 Jul 86*	42
CHRONICLES *Compilation.*	*Island*	12	*7 Nov 87*	17
ROLL WITH IT	*Virgin*	4	*2 Jul 88*	16
REFUGEES OF THE HEART	*Virgin*	26	*17 Nov 90*	3
JUNCTION SEVEN	*Virgin*	32	*14 Jun 97*	2

WINX – See Josh WINK

WIRE — UK

SINGLES:	HITS 2			WEEKS 4
OUTDOOR MINER	*Harvest*	51	*27 Jan 79*	3
EARDRUM BUZZ	*Mute*	68	*13 May 89*	1
ALBUMS:	**HITS 3**			**WEEKS 3**
CHAIRS MISSING	*Harvest*	48	*7 Oct 78*	1
154	*Harvest*	39	*13 Oct 79*	1
THE IDEAL COPY	*Mute*	87	*9 May 87*	1

WIRED — Holland/Finland

SINGLES:	HITS 1			WEEKS 1
TRANSONIC *Samples Yazoo's Don't Go.*	*Future Groove*	73	*20 Feb 99*	1

WIRELESS — UK

SINGLES:	HITS 2			WEEKS 2
I NEED YOU	*Chrysalis*	68	*28 Jun 97*	1
IN LOVE WITH THE FAMILIAR	*Chrysalis*	69	*7 Feb 98*	1

Norman WISDOM — UK

SINGLES:	HITS 2			WEEKS 20
DON'T LAUGH AT ME ('CAUSE I'M A FOOL) *Above hit: Norman WISDOM with Norrie PARAMOR and his Orchestra.*	*Columbia*	3	*20 Feb 54*	15
THE WISDOM OF A FOOL *Above hit: Norman WISDOM with Eric JUPP and his Orchestra.*	*Columbia*	13	*16 Mar 57*	5

WISDOME — Italy

SINGLES:	HITS 1			WEEKS 2
OFF THE WALL	*Positiva*	33	*11 Mar 00*	2

WISEGUYS — UK

SINGLES:	HITS 2			WEEKS 13
OOH LA LA	*Wall Of Sound*	55	*6 Jun 98*	1
START THE COMMOTION	*Wall Of Sound*	66	*12 Sep 98*	1
OOH LA LA [RI]	*Wall Of Sound*	2	*5 Jun 99*	10
Featured in the Budweiser TV commercial.				
START THE COMMOTION [RI]	*Wall Of Sound*	47	*11 Sep 99*	1
Samples The Ventures' Wild Child.				

WISHBONE ASH — UK

ALBUMS:	HITS 13			WEEKS 75
WISHBONE ASH	*MCA*	34	*23 Jan 71*	2
PILGRIMAGE	*MCA*	14	*9 Oct 71*	9
ARGUS	*MCA*	3	*20 May 72*	20
WISHBONE FOUR	*MCA*	12	*26 May 73*	10
THERE'S THE RUB	*MCA*	16	*30 Nov 74*	5
LOCKED IN	*MCA*	36	*3 Apr 76*	2
NEW ENGLAND	*MCA*	22	*27 Nov 76*	3
FRONT PAGE NEWS	*MCA*	31	*29 Oct 77*	4
NO SMOKE WITHOUT FIRE	*MCA*	43	*28 Oct 78*	3
JUST TESTING	*MCA*	41	*2 Feb 80*	4
LIVE DATES II	*MCA*	40	*1 Nov 80*	3
Live recordings between 1976–80.				
NUMBER THE BRAVE	*MCA*	61	*25 Apr 81*	5
TWIN BARRELS BURNING	*AVM*	22	*16 Oct 82*	5

Bill WITHERS — US

SINGLES:	HITS 3			WEEKS 29
LEAN ON ME	*A&M*	18	*12 Aug 72*	9
LOVELY DAY	*CBS*	7	*14 Jan 78*	8
OH YEAH!	*CBS*	60	*25 May 85*	3
LOVELY DAY (SUNSHINE MIX) [RM]	*CBS*	4	*10 Sep 88*	9
Remixed by Ben Liebrand.				
ALBUMS:	**HITS 3**			**WEEKS 10**
MENAGERIE	*CBS*	27	*11 Feb 78*	5
WATCHING YOU, WATCHING ME	*CBS*	60	*15 Jun 85*	1
GREATEST HITS	*CBS*	90	*17 Sep 88*	4

WITNESS — UK

SINGLES:	HITS 2			WEEKS 2
SCARS	*Island*	71	*13 Mar 99*	1
AUDITION	*Island*	71	*19 Jun 99*	1
ALBUMS:	**HITS 2**			**WEEKS 2**
BEFORE THE CALM	*Island*	59	*24 Jul 99*	1
UNDER A SUN	*Island*	62	*4 Aug 01*	1

WITNESSES – See Louis PRIMA

WIX – See SPIRO and WIX

WIZZARD — UK

SINGLES:	HITS 7			WEEKS 77
BALL PARK INCIDENT	*Harvest*	6	*9 Dec 72*	12
SEE MY BABY JIVE	*Harvest*	1	*21 Apr 73*	17
Above hit: WIZZARD vocal backing – the SUEDETTES.				
ANGEL FINGERS (A TEEN BALLAD)	*Harvest*	1	*1 Sep 73*	10
Above hit: WIZZARD vocal backing – the SUEDETTES and the BLEACH BOYS.				
I WISH IT COULD BE CHRISTMAS EVERYDAY	*Harvest*	4	*8 Dec 73*	9
Above hit: WIZZARD vocal backing by the SUEDETTES, plus the STOCKLAND GREEN BILATERAL SCHOOL FIRST CHOIR additional noises MISS SNOB and CLASS 3C				
ROCK N' ROLL WINTER (LOONY'S TUNE)	*Warner Brothers*	6	*27 Apr 74*	7
THIS IS THE STORY OF MY LOVE (BABY)	*Warner Brothers*	34	*10 Aug 74*	4
ARE YOU READY TO ROCK	*Warner Brothers*	8	*21 Dec 74*	10
I WISH IT COULD BE CHRISTMAS EVERYDAY [RI]	*Harvest*	41	*19 Dec 81*	4
I WISH IT COULD BE CHRISTMAS EVERYDAY [RI] [RE]	*Harvest*	23	*15 Dec 84*	4
Above 2: WIZZARD vocal backing by the SUEDETTES, plus the STOCKLAND GREEN BILATERAL SCHOOL FIRST CHOIR additional noises MISS SNOB and CLASS 3C.				
ALBUMS:	**HITS 2**			**WEEKS 11**
WIZZARD BREW	*Harvest*	29	*19 May 73*	7
INTRODUCING EDDY AND THE FALCONS	*Warner Brothers*	19	*17 Aug 74*	4

Jah WOBBLE'S INVADERS OF THE HEART — UK

(See also Brian Eno and Jah Wobble.)

SINGLES:	HITS 3			WEEKS 10
VISIONS OF YOU	*Oval*	35	*1 Feb 92*	5
Features vocals by Sinead O'Connor.				
BECOMING MORE LIKE GOD	*Island*	36	*30 Apr 94*	2
Vocals by Anneli M. Decker.				
THE SUN DOES RISE	*Island*	41	*25 Jun 94*	3
Above hit: Jah WOBBLE'S INVADERS OF THE HEART featuring DOLORES from the CRANBERRIES.				
ALBUMS:	**HITS 1**			**WEEKS 5**
TAKE ME TO GOD	*Island*	13	*28 May 94*	5

Terry WOGAN — Ireland

SINGLES:	HITS 1			WEEKS 5
THE FLORAL DANCE	*Philips*	21	*7 Jan 78*	5

WOLF – See TROGGS

Richard WOLFF and his Orchestra – See David THORNE with Richard WOLFF and his Orchestra

WOLFGANG PRESS — UK

ALBUMS:	HITS 1			WEEKS 1
FUNKY LITTLE DEMONS	*4AD*	75	*4 Feb 95*	1

WOLFSBANE — US

SINGLES:	HITS 1			WEEKS 1
EZY	*Def American*	68	*5 Oct 91*	1
ALBUMS:	**HITS 3**			**WEEKS 3**
LIVE FAST, DIE FAST	*Def American*	48	*5 Aug 89*	1
ALL HELL'S BREAKING LOOSE . . .	*Def American*	48	*20 Oct 90*	1
DOWN FALL THE GOOD GUYS	*Def American*	53	*19 Oct 91*	1

Bobby WOMACK — US

(See also Wilton Felder; Living In A Box.)

SINGLES:	HITS 5			WEEKS 13
TELL ME WHY	*Motown*	60	*16 Jun 84*	3
I WISH HE DIDN'T TRUST ME SO MUCH	*MCA*	64	*5 Oct 85*	2
LIVING IN A BOX	*MCA*	70	*7 Nov 87*	2
I'M BACK FOR MORE	*Dome*	27	*3 Apr 93*	5
Originally recorded by Al Johnson and Jean Carn.				
Above hit: LULU and Bobby WOMACK.				
IT'S A MAN'S MAN'S MAN'S WORLD	*Pulse 8*	73	*13 May 95*	1
Above hit: Jeanie TRACY and Bobby WOMACK.				
ALBUMS:	**HITS 2**			**WEEKS 15**
THE POET II	*Motown*	31	*28 Apr 84*	8
SO MANY RIVERS	*MCA*	28	*28 Sep 85*	7

Lee Ann WOMACK — US

SINGLES:	HITS 1			WEEKS 2
I HOPE YOU DANCE	*MCA Nashville*	40	*9 Jun 01*	2

WOMACK and WOMACK — US

SINGLES:	HITS 7			WEEKS 51
LOVE WARS	*Elektra*	14	*28 Apr 84*	10
BABY I'M SCARED OF YOU	*Elektra*	72	*30 Jun 84*	2
SOUL LOVE / SOUL MAN [M]	*Manhattan*	58	*6 Dec 86*	6
TEARDROPS	*Fourth & Broadway*	3	*6 Aug 88*	17
LIFE'S JUST A BALLGAME	*Fourth & Broadway*	32	*12 Nov 88*	5
CELEBRATE THE WORLD	*Fourth & Broadway*	19	*25 Feb 89*	8
SECRET STAR	*Warner Brothers*	46	*5 Feb 94*	3
Above hit: HOUSE OF ZEKKARIYAS Aka WOMACK and WOMACK.				
ALBUMS:	**HITS 4**			**WEEKS 54**
LOVE WARS	*Elektra*	45	*21 Apr 84*	13
RADIO M.U.S.C. MAN	*Elektra*	56	*22 Jun 85*	2
THE ARTISTS VOLUME III	*Street Sounds*	87	*12 Oct 85*	2
Compilation album with tracks by each artist.				
Above hit: WOMACK and WOMACK/O'JAYS/KLEEER/S.O.S. BAND.				
CONSCIENCE	*Fourth & Broadway*	4	*27 Aug 88*	37

WOMBLES — UK

SINGLES:	HITS 9			WEEKS 98
THE WOMBLING SONG	*CBS*	4	*26 Jan 74*	23
Theme from the BBC1 children's TV series 'The Wombles'.				
REMEMBER YOU'RE A WOMBLE	*CBS*	3	*6 Apr 74*	16
BANANA ROCK	*CBS*	9	*22 Jun 74*	13
MINUETTO ALLEGRETTO	*CBS*	16	*12 Oct 74*	9
WOMBLING MERRY CHRISTMAS	*CBS*	2	*7 Dec 74*	8
WOMBLING WHITE TIE AND TAILS (FOX TROT)	*CBS*	22	*10 May 75*	7
SUPER WOMBLE	*CBS*	20	*9 Aug 75*	6
LET'S WOMBLE TO THE PARTY TONIGHT	*CBS*	34	*13 Dec 75*	5
REMEMBER YOU'RE A WOMBLE [RI]	*Columbia*	13	*21 Mar 98*	5
THE WOMBLING SONG (UNDERGROUND OVERGROUND) [RI]	*Columbia*	27	*13 Jun 98*	3
I WISH IT COULD BE A WOMBLING MERRY CHRISTMAS EVERY DAY	*Dramatico*	22	*30 Dec 00*	3
Combines Wizzard's I Wish It Could Be Christmas Everyday and the Wombles' Wombling Merry Christmas.				
Above hit: WOMBLES with Roy WOOD.				

ALBUMS:	HITS 5			WEEKS 58
WOMBLING SONGS	*CBS*	19	*2 Mar 74*	17
REMEMBER YOU'RE A WOMBLE	*CBS*	18	*13 Jul 74*	31
KEEP ON WOMBLING	*CBS*	17	*21 Dec 74*	6
20 WOMBLING GREATS	*Warwick*	29	*8 Jan 77*	1
THE BEST WOMBLES ALBUM SO FAR - VOLUME 1	*Columbia*	26	*18 Apr 98*	3

Stevie WONDER — US

(See also Diana Ross, Marvin Gaye, Smokey Robinson and Stevie Wonder; Dionne Warwick.)

SINGLES:	HITS 51			WEEKS 401
UPTIGHT (EVERYTHING'S ALRIGHT)	*Tamla Motown*	14	*5 Feb 66*	10
BLOWIN' IN THE WIND	*Tamla Motown*	36	*20 Aug 66*	5
Featuring vocals by Henry Cosby.				
A PLACE IN THE SUN	*Tamla Motown*	20	*7 Jan 67*	5
I WAS MADE TO LOVE HER	*Tamla Motown*	5	*29 Jul 67*	15
I'M WONDERING	*Tamla Motown*	22	*28 Oct 67*	8
SHOO BE DOO BE DOO DA DAY	*Tamla Motown*	46	*11 May 68*	4
FOR ONCE IN MY LIFE	*Tamla Motown*	3	*21 Dec 68*	13
Originally recorded by Tony Bennett.				
DON'T KNOW WHY I LOVE YOU	*Tamla Motown*	14	*22 Mar 69*	10
DON'T KNOW WHY I LOVE YOU [RE] / MY CHERIE AMOUR	*Tamla Motown*	4	*12 Jul 69*	16
Don't Know Why I Love You only listed for the week of 12 Jul 69 at No.43. From 19 Jul 69, My Cherie Amour was listed instead.				
YESTER-ME, YESTER-YOU, YESTERDAY	*Tamla Motown*	2	*15 Nov 69*	13
Produced by Johnny Bristol.				
NEVER HAD A DREAM COME TRUE	*Tamla Motown*	6	*28 Mar 70*	12
SIGNED SEALED DELIVERED I'M YOURS	*Tamla Motown*	15	*18 Jul 70*	9
SIGNED SEALED DELIVERED I'M YOURS [RE]	*Tamla Motown*	49	*26 Sep 70*	1
HEAVEN HELP US ALL	*Tamla Motown*	29	*21 Nov 70*	11
WE CAN WORK IT OUT	*Tamla Motown*	27	*15 May 71*	7
IF YOU REALLY LOVE ME	*Tamla Motown*	20	*22 Jan 72*	7
SUPERSTITION	*Tamla Motown*	11	*3 Feb 73*	9
YOU ARE THE SUNSHINE OF MY LIFE	*Tamla Motown*	7	*19 May 73*	11
Introduction vocals are by Jim Gilstrap and Gloria Barley.				
HIGHER GROUND	*Tamla Motown*	29	*13 Oct 73*	5
LIVING FOR THE CITY	*Tamla Motown*	15	*12 Jan 74*	9
HE'S MISSTRA KNOW IT ALL	*Tamla Motown*	10	*13 Apr 74*	9
YOU HAVEN'T DONE NOTHIN'	*Tamla Motown*	30	*19 Oct 74*	5
Above hit: Stevie WONDER doo doo wopsssss by the JACKSON FIVE.				
BOOGIE ON REGGAE WOMAN	*Tamla Motown*	12	*11 Jan 75*	8
I WISH	*Motown*	5	*18 Dec 76*	10
SIR DUKE	*Motown*	2	*9 Apr 77*	9
Tribute to Duke Ellington.				
ANOTHER STAR	*Motown*	29	*10 Sep 77*	5
SEND ONE YOUR LOVE	*Motown*	52	*24 Nov 79*	3
BLACK ORCHID	*Motown*	63	*26 Jan 80*	3
OUTSIDE MY WINDOW	*Motown*	52	*29 Mar 80*	4
MASTERBLASTER (JAMMIN')	*Motown*	2	*13 Sep 80*	10
Inspired by Bob Marley's hit Jamming.				
I AIN'T GONNA STAND FOR IT	*Motown*	10	*27 Dec 80*	10
LATELY	*Motown*	3	*7 Mar 81*	13
HAPPY BIRTHDAY	*Motown*	2	*25 Jul 81*	11
Song was part of Wonder's campaign to have Martin Luther King's birthday (15th January) marked as a US holiday.				
THAT GIRL	*Motown*	39	*23 Jan 82*	6
EBONY AND IVORY	*Parlophone*	1	*10 Apr 82*	10
Above hit: Paul McCARTNEY with additional vocals by Stevie WONDER.				
DO I DO	*Motown*	10	*5 Jun 82*	7
Features Dizzy Gillespie on trumpet.				
RIBBON IN THE SKY	*Motown*	45	*25 Sep 82*	4

I JUST CALLED TO SAY I LOVE YOU	*Motown*	1	*25 Aug 84*	24
LOVE LIGHT IN FLIGHT	*Motown*	44	*1 Dec 84*	5
Above 2 from the film 'The Woman In Red'.				
DON'T DRIVE DRUNK	*Motown*	71	*29 Dec 84*	1
DON'T DRIVE DRUNK [RE]	*Motown*	62	*12 Jan 85*	2
PART-TIME LOVER	*Motown*	3	*7 Sep 85*	12
Features Luther Vandross on backing vocals.				
GO HOME	*Motown*	67	*23 Nov 85*	2
I JUST CALLED TO SAY I LOVE YOU [RE]	*Motown*	64	*28 Dec 85*	2
OVERJOYED	*Motown*	17	*8 Mar 86*	8
STRANGER ON THE SHORE OF LOVE	*Motown*	55	*17 Jan 87*	3
SKELETONS	*Motown*	59	*31 Oct 87*	3
GET IT	*Motown*	37	*28 May 88*	4
Above hit: Stevie WONDER and Michael JACKSON.				
MY LOVE	*CBS*	5	*6 Aug 88*	11
Above hit: Julio IGLESIAS featuring Stevie WONDER.				
FREE	*Motown*	49	*20 May 89*	5
FUN DAY	*Motown*	63	*12 Oct 91*	1
From the film 'Jungle Fever'.				
FOR YOUR LOVE	*Motown*	23	*25 Feb 95*	4
TOMORROW ROBINS WILL SING	*Motown*	71	*22 Jul 95*	1
HOW COME, HOW LONG	*Epic*	10	*19 Jul 97*	5
Above hit: BABYFACE featuring Stevie WONDER.				
TRUE TO YOUR HEART	*Motown*	51	*31 Oct 98*	1
From the Walt Disney film 'Mulan'.				
Above hit: 98° (featuring Stevie WONDER).				

ALBUMS:	**HITS 18**			**WEEKS 353**
STEVIE WONDER'S GREATEST HITS	*Tamla Motown*	25	*7 Sep 68*	10
MY CHERIE AMOUR	*Tamla Motown*	17	*13 Dec 69*	2
GREATEST HITS VOLUME 2	*Tamla Motown*	30	*12 Feb 72*	4
TALKING BOOK	*Tamla Motown*	16	*3 Feb 73*	48
INNERVISIONS	*Tamla Motown*	8	*1 Sep 73*	55
FULFILLINGNESS' FIRST FINALE	*Tamla Motown*	5	*17 Aug 74*	16
SONGS IN THE KEY OF LIFE	*Tamla Motown*	2	*16 Oct 76*	54
JOURNEY THROUGH THE SECRET LIFE OF PLANTS	*Motown*	8	*10 Nov 79*	15
HOTTER THAN JULY	*Motown*	2	*8 Nov 80*	55
Dedicated to Martin Luther King Jr.				
ORIGINAL MUSIQUARIUM 1	*Motown*	8	*22 May 82*	17
Compilation plus some new tracks.				
THE WOMAN IN RED [OST]	*Motown*	2	*22 Sep 84*	19
Above hit: Stevie WONDER and featuring Dionne WARWICK.				
LOVE SONGS - 16 CLASSIC HITS	*Telstar*	20	*24 Nov 84*	10
IN SQUARE CIRCLE	*Motown*	5	*28 Sep 85*	16
DIANA . MICHAEL . GLADYS . STEVIE - THEIR VERY BEST - BACK TO BACK	*PrioriTyV*	21	*15 Nov 86*	10
Compilation featuring hits by each artist.				
Above hit: Diana ROSS/Michael JACKSON/Gladys KNIGHT/Stevie WONDER.				
CHARACTERS	*RCA*	33	*28 Nov 87*	4
JUNGLE FEVER [OST]	*Motown*	56	*8 Jun 91*	1
CONVERSATION PEACE	*Motown*	8	*25 Mar 95*	4
SONG REVIEW - A GREATEST HITS COLLECTION	*Motown*	19	*23 Nov 96*	12
SONGS IN THE KEY OF LIFE [RI]	*Motown*	66	*23 Aug 97*	1
Charted after being featured on BBC1's 'Classic Albums' series.				

Wayne WONDER – See SHAGGY

WONDER DOG

UK

SINGLES:	**HITS 1**			**WEEKS 7**
RUFF MIX	*Flip*	31	*21 Aug 82*	7

WONDER STUFF

UK

SINGLES:	**HITS 16**			**WEEKS 66**
GIVE GIVE GIVE ME MORE MORE MORE	*Polydor*	72	*30 Apr 88*	2
A WISH AWAY	*Polydor*	43	*16 Jul 88*	5
IT'S YER MONEY I'M AFTER BABY	*Polydor*	40	*24 Sep 88*	3
WHO WANTS TO BE THE DISCO KING?	*Polydor*	28	*11 Mar 89*	3
DON'T LET ME DOWN GENTLY	*Polydor*	19	*23 Sep 89*	4
GOLDEN GREEN / GET TOGETHER	*Polydor*	33	*11 Nov 89*	3
CIRCLESQUARE	*Polydor*	20	*12 May 90*	4
THE SIZE OF A COW	*Polydor*	5	*13 Apr 91*	7
CAUGHT IN MY SHADOW	*Polydor*	18	*25 May 91*	3
SLEEP ALONE	*Polydor*	43	*7 Sep 91*	2
DIZZY	*Sense*	1	*26 Oct 91*	12
Above hit: Vic REEVES and the WONDER STUFF.				
WELCOME TO THE CHEAP SEATS - THE ORIGINAL SOUNDTRACK [EP]	*Polydor*	8	*25 Jan 92*	5
Lead track: Welcome To The Cheap Seats.				
ON THE ROPES [EP]	*Polydor*	10	*25 Sep 93*	4
Lead track: On The Ropes.				
FULL OF LIFE (HAPPY NOW)	*Polydor*	28	*27 Nov 93*	3

HOT LOVE NOW! [EP]	*Polydor*	19	*26 Mar 94*	3
Lead track: Hot Love Now!				
UNBEARABLE	*Polydor*	16	*10 Sep 94*	3
Originally released in 1987 on the Far Out label.				
ALBUMS:	**HITS 6**			**WEEKS 48**
THE EIGHT LEGGED GROOVE MACHINE	*Polydor*	18	*27 Aug 88*	7
HUP	*Polydor*	5	*14 Oct 89*	8
NEVER LOVED ELVIS	*Polydor*	3	*8 Jun 91*	23
CONSTRUCTION FOR THE MODERN IDIOT	*Polydor*	4	*16 Oct 93*	5
IF THE BEATLES HAD READ HUNTER . . . THE SINGLES	*Polydor*	8	*8 Oct 94*	4
Compilation.				
LIVE IN MANCHESTER	*Windsong*	74	*29 Jul 95*	1
Live recordings from the G-Mex, Manchester, Nov 91.				

WONDERS — US

SINGLES:	**HITS 1**			**WEEKS 3**
THAT THING YOU DO!	*Play-Tone*	22	*22 Feb 97*	3
From the film of the same name.				

WONDRESS – See MANTRONIX

Brenton WOOD — UK

SINGLES:	**HITS 1**			**WEEKS 14**
GIMME LITTLE SIGN	*Liberty*	8	*30 Dec 67*	14

Ronnie WOOD – See Rod STEWART

Roy WOOD — UK

(See also Doctor and the Medics.)

SINGLES:	**HITS 6**			**WEEKS 40**
DEAR ELAINE	*Harvest*	18	*11 Aug 73*	8
FOREVER	*Harvest*	8	*1 Dec 73*	13
GOIN' DOWN THE ROAD (A SCOTTISH REGGAE SONG)	*Harvest*	13	*15 Jun 74*	7
OH WHAT A SHAME	*Jet*	13	*31 May 75*	7
I WISH IT COULD BE CHRISTMAS EVERYDAY	*Woody*	59	*23 Dec 95*	2
Live recording.				
Above hit: Roy WOOD BIG BAND LIVE.				
I WISH IT COULD BE A WOMBLING MERRY CHRISTMAS EVERY DAY	*Dramatico*	22	*30 Dec 00*	3
Combines Wizzard's I Wish It Could Be Christmas Everyday and the Wombles' Wombling Merry Christmas.				
Above hit: WOMBLES with Roy WOOD.				
ALBUMS:	**HITS 2**			**WEEKS 14**
BOULDERS	*Harvest*	15	*18 Aug 73*	8
THE SINGLES	*Speed*	37	*24 Jul 82*	6

WOODENTOPS — UK/New Zealand

SINGLES:	**HITS 1**			**WEEKS 1**
EVERYDAY LIVING	*Rough Trade*	72	*11 Oct 86*	1
ALBUMS:	**HITS 2**			**WEEKS 6**
GIANT	*Rough Trade*	35	*12 Jul 86*	4
WOODEN FOOT COPS ON THE HIGHWAY	*Rough Trade*	48	*5 Mar 88*	2

Marcella WOODS – See Matt DAREY

Edward WOODWARD — UK

SINGLES:	**HITS 1**			**WEEKS 2**
THE WAY YOU LOOK TONIGHT	*DJM*	50	*16 Jan 71*	1
THE WAY YOU LOOK TONIGHT [RE]	*DJM*	42	*30 Jan 71*	1
ALBUMS:	**HITS 2**			**WEEKS 12**
THIS MAN ALONE	*DJM*	53	*6 Jun 70*	2
THE EDWARD WOODWARD ALBUM	*Jam*	20	*19 Aug 72*	10

WOOKIE — UK

SINGLES:	**HITS 3**			**WEEKS 11**
WHAT'S GOING ON?	*S2s*	45	*3 Jun 00*	1
BATTLE	*S2s*	10	*12 Aug 00*	7
BACK UP (TO ME)	*S2s*	38	*12 May 01*	3
Above 2: WOOKIE featuring LAIN.				

Sheb WOOLEY — UK

SINGLES:	**HITS 1**			**WEEKS 8**
THE PURPLE PEOPLE EATER	*MGM*	12	*21 Jun 58*	8

WOOLFSON – See SHIMMON and WOOLFSON

WOOLPACKERS — UK

SINGLES:	HITS 2			WEEKS 24
HILLBILLY ROCK HILLBILLY ROLL	*RCA*	5	*16 Nov 96*	14
LINE DANCE PARTY	*RCA*	25	*29 Nov 97*	10

Above 2 were featured in the Yorkshire ITV soap 'Emmerdale'.

ALBUMS:	HITS 2			WEEKS 13
EMMERDANCE	*RCA*	26	*14 Dec 96*	10
THE GREATEST LINE DANCING PARTY ALBUM	*RCA*	48	*29 Nov 97*	3

WORKING WEEK — UK

SINGLES:	HITS 1			WEEKS 2
VENCEREMOS - WE WILL WIN	*Virgin*	64	*9 Jun 84*	2

ALBUMS:	HITS 2			WEEKS 10
WORKING NIGHTS	*Virgin*	23	*6 Apr 85*	9
COMPANEROS	*Virgin*	72	*27 Sep 86*	1

WORLD – See LIL' LOUIS

WORLD OF TWIST — UK

SINGLES:	HITS 4			WEEKS 12
THE STORM	*Circa*	42	*24 Nov 90*	3
THE STORM [RE]	*Circa*	74	*5 Jan 91*	2
SONS OF THE STAGE	*Circa*	47	*23 Mar 91*	3
SWEETS	*Circa*	58	*12 Oct 91*	2
SHE'S A RAINBOW	*Circa*	62	*22 Feb 92*	2

ALBUMS:	HITS 1			WEEKS 1
QUALITY STREET	*Circa*	50	*9 Nov 91*	1

WORLD PARTY — UK/Ireland

SINGLES:	HITS 8			WEEKS 29
SHIP OF FOOLS	*Ensign*	42	*14 Feb 87*	6
MESSAGE IN THE BOX	*Ensign*	39	*16 Jun 90*	6
WAY DOWN NOW	*Ensign*	66	*15 Sep 90*	2
THANK YOU WORLD	*Ensign*	68	*18 May 91*	1
IS IT LIKE TODAY?	*Ensign*	19	*10 Apr 93*	6
GIVE IT ALL AWAY	*Ensign*	43	*10 Jul 93*	3
ALL I GAVE	*Ensign*	37	*2 Oct 93*	3
BEAUTIFUL DREAM	*Chrysalis*	31	*7 Jun 97*	2

ALBUMS:	HITS 5			WEEKS 25
PRIVATE REVOLUTION	*Chrysalis*	56	*21 Mar 87*	4
GOODBYE JUMBO	*Ensign*	36	*19 May 90*	10
BANG!	*Ensign*	2	*8 May 93*	8
EGYPTOLOGY	*Chrysalis*	34	*28 Jun 97*	2
DUMBING UP	*Papillon*	64	*2 Sep 00*	1

WORLD PREMIERE — UK

SINGLES:	HITS 1			WEEKS 4
SHARE THE NIGHT	*Epic*	64	*28 Jan 84*	4

WORLD WARRIOR — UK

(See also Simon Harris.)

SINGLES:	HITS 1			WEEKS 1
STREET FIGHTER II	*Living Beat*	70	*16 Apr 94*	1

Tie-in release with the computer game of the same name.

WORLDS APART — UK/France/Cuba/Jamaica/Bangladesh

SINGLES:	HITS 5			WEEKS 17
HEAVEN MUST BE MISSING AN ANGEL	*Arista*	29	*27 Mar 93*	3
WONDERFUL WORLD	*Arista*	51	*3 Jul 93*	1
EVERLASTING LOVE	*Bell*	20	*25 Sep 93*	4
COULD IT BE I'M FALLING IN LOVE	*Bell*	15	*26 Mar 94*	6
BEGGIN' TO BE WRITTEN	*Bell*	29	*4 Jun 94*	3

WORLD'S FAMOUS SUPREME TEAM — US

(See also Malcolm McLaren.)

SINGLES:	HITS 2			WEEKS 6
HEY DJ	*Charisma*	52	*25 Feb 84*	5
OPERAA HOUSE	*Virgin*	75	*8 Dec 90*	1

Above hit: Malcolm McLAREN presents the WORLD FAMOUS SUPREME TEAM SHOW.

WRECKLESS ERIC — UK

ALBUMS:	HITS 2			WEEKS 5
WRECKLESS ERIC	*Stiff*	46	*1 Apr 78*	1
BIG SMASH	*Stiff*	30	*8 Mar 80*	4

WRECKX-N-EFFECT — US

SINGLES:	HITS 3			WEEKS 18
JUICY	*Motown*	29	*13 Jan 90*	7
Above hit: WRECKS-N-EFFECT.				
RUMP SHAKER	*MCA*	24	*5 Dec 92*	7
Samples Back To The Hotel by N2Deep.				
WRECKX SHOP	*MCA*	26	*7 May 94*	2
Above hit: WRECKX 'N' EFFECT (featuring APACHE INDIAN).				
RUMP SHAKER [RI]	*MCA*	40	*13 Aug 94*	2

WREN ORCHESTRA – See WET WET WET

Betty WRIGHT — US

(See also Peter Brown.)

SINGLES:	HITS 4			WEEKS 23
SHOO-RAH! SHOO-RAH!	*RCA Victor*	27	*25 Jan 75*	7
WHERE IS THE LOVE	*RCA Victor*	25	*19 Apr 75*	7
PAIN	*Cooltempo*	42	*8 Feb 86*	6
KEEP LOVE NEW	*Sure Delight*	71	*9 Sep 89*	3

Ian WRIGHT — UK

SINGLES:	HITS 1			WEEKS 2
DO THE RIGHT THING	*M&G*	43	*28 Aug 93*	2
Originally titled Keep The Peace by DTRT when promoed to DJ's.				

LInda WRIGHT – See NEW ATLANTIC

Rick WRIGHT — UK

ALBUMS:	HITS 1			WEEKS 1
BROKEN CHINA	*EMI*	61	*19 Oct 96*	1

Ruby WRIGHT — US

SINGLES:	HITS 2			WEEKS 15
BIMBO	*Parlophone*	7	*17 Apr 54*	4
BIMBO [RE]	*Parlophone*	12	*22 May 54*	1
THREE STARS	*Parlophone*	19	*23 May 59*	10
Tribute to Buddy Holly, the Big Bopper and Ritchie Valens who were killed in a plane crash 3 Feb 59. Original by Tommy Dee reached No. 11 in the US in 1959.				
Above hit: Ruby WRIGHT (narration by Dick PIKE).				

Steve WRIGHT — UK

SINGLES:	HITS 3			WEEKS 10
I'M ALRIGHT	*RCA*	40	*27 Nov 82*	6
Above hit: YOUNG STEVE and the AFTERNOON BOYS.				
GET SOME THERAPY	*RCA*	75	*15 Oct 83*	1
Above hit: Steve WRIGHT and the SISTERS Of SOUL.				
THE GAY CAVALIEROS (THE STORY SO FAR . . .)	*MCA*	61	*1 Dec 84*	3

WU-TANG CLAN — US

(See also Omar.)

SINGLES:	HITS 3			WEEKS 21
TRIUMPH	*Loud*	46	*16 Aug 97*	1
Above hit: WU-TANG CLAN (featuring CAPPADONNA).				
SAY WHAT YOU WANT (ALL DAY EVERY DAY)	*Mercury*	4	*21 Mar 98*	7
[AA] listed with Insane by Texas.				
Above hit: TEXAS featuring the WU TANG CLAN.				
GRAVEL PIT/PROTECT YA NECK	*Epic*	6	*25 Nov 00*	13

ALBUMS:	HITS 2			WEEKS 23
WU-TANG FOREVER	*Loud*	1	*14 Jun 97*	10
THE W	*Epic*	19	*2 Dec 00*	13

WUBBLE-U — UK

SINGLES:	HITS 1			WEEKS 1
PETAL	*Indolent*	55	*7 Mar 98*	1

Klaus WUNDERLICH — Germany

ALBUMS:	HITS 4			WEEKS 19
THE HIT WORLD OF KLAUS WUNDERLICH	*Decca*	27	*30 Aug 75*	8

THE UNIQUE KLAUS WUNDERLICH SOUND	*Decca*	28	*20 May 78*	4
THE FANTASTIC SOUND OF KLAUS WUNDERLICH	*Lotus*	43	*26 May 79*	5
ON THE SUNNY SIDE OF THE STREET	*Polydor*	81	*17 Mar 84*	2

WURZELS — UK

SINGLES:	HITS 4			WEEKS 30
DRINK UP THY ZIDER	*Columbia*	45	*4 Feb 67*	1
Above hit: Adge CUTLER and the WURZELS.				
THE COMBINE HARVESTER (BRAND NEW KEY)	*EMI*	1	*15 May 76*	13
I AM A CIDER DRINKER (PALOMA BLANCA)	*EMI*	3	*11 Sep 76*	9
FARMER BILL'S COWMAN (I WAS KAISER BILL'S BATMAN)	*EMI*	32	*25 Jun 77*	5
Above 3 are paradies of the respective songs in brackets.				
COMBINE HARVESTER 2001 [RM]	*EMI Gold*	39	*11 Aug 01*	2
Remixed by Humpafunk.				
ALBUMS:	**HITS 3**			**WEEKS 29**
ADGE CUTLER AND THE WURZELS	*Columbia*	38	*11 Mar 67*	4
Above hit: Adge CUTLER and the WURZELS.				
COMBINE HARVESTER	*One Up*	15	*3 Jul 76*	20
GOLDEN DELICIOUS	*EMI*	32	*2 Apr 77*	5

WWF SUPERSTARS — UK/US

SINGLES:	HITS 3			WEEKS 15
SLAM JAM	*Arista*	4	*12 Dec 92*	8
SLAM JAM [RE]	*Arista*	75	*13 Feb 93*	1
WRESTLEMANIA	*Arista*	14	*3 Apr 93*	5
U.S.A.	*Arista*	71	*10 Jul 93*	1
Above hit: WWF SUPERSTARS featuring HACKSAW Jim DUGGAN.				
ALBUMS:	**HITS 1**			**WEEKS 5**
WRESTLEMANIA - THE ALBUM	*Arista*	10	*17 Apr 93*	5

Robert WYATT — UK

SINGLES:	HITS 2			WEEKS 11
I'M A BELIEVER	*Virgin*	29	*28 Sep 74*	5
SHIPBUILDING	*Rough Trade*	35	*7 May 83*	6
Writtten by Elvis Costello as a protest against the Falklands War.				

Michael WYCOFF — US

SINGLES:	HITS 1			WEEKS 2
(DO YOU REALLY LOVE ME) TELL ME LOVE	*RCA*	60	*23 Jul 83*	2

Pete WYLIE — UK

SINGLES:	HITS 3			WEEKS 18
SINFUL	*Eternal*	13	*3 May 86*	10
Above hit: Pete WYLIE and the OEDIPUS WRECKS.				
DIAMOND GIRL	*Eternal*	57	*13 Sep 86*	3
Above hit: Pete WYLIE featuring the FABULOUS Josie JONES.				
SINFUL! (SCARY JIGGIN' WITH DOCTOR LOVE)	*Siren*	28	*13 Apr 91*	5
Above hit: Pete WYLIE (and the FARM).				

Bill WYMAN — UK

SINGLES:	HITS 2			WEEKS 13
(SI SI) JE SUIS UN ROCK STAR	*A&M*	14	*25 Jul 81*	9
A NEW FASHION	*A&M*	37	*20 Mar 82*	4
ALBUMS:	**HITS 3**			**WEEKS 8**
MONKEY GRIP	*Rolling Stones*	39	*8 Jun 74*	1
BILL WYMAN	*A&M*	55	*10 Apr 82*	6
GROOVIN'	*Papillon*	52	*27 May 00*	1
Above hit: Bill WYMAN'S RHYTHM KINGS.				

Jane WYMAN – See Bing CROSBY

Tammy WYNETTE — US

SINGLES:	HITS 4			WEEKS 35
STAND BY YOUR MAN	*Epic*	1	*26 Apr 75*	12
Reached No. 19 in the US in 1968.				
D.I.V.O.R.C.E.	*Epic*	12	*28 Jun 75*	7
I DON'T WANNA PLAY HOUSE	*Epic*	37	*12 Jun 76*	4
Above 3 originally recorded and released in the U.S. in 1968.				
JUSTIFIED AND ANCIENT	*KLF Commuications*	2	*7 Dec 91*	12
Above hit: KLF (lead vocals: "The First Lady of Country" Miss Tammy WYNETTE).				
ALBUMS:	**HITS 5**			**WEEKS 49**
THE BEST OF TAMMY WYNETTE	*Epic*	4	*17 May 75*	23
STAND BY YOUR MAN	*Epic*	13	*21 Jun 75*	7
20 COUNTRY CLASSICS	*CBS*	3	*17 Dec 77*	11

COUNTRY GIRL MEETS COUNTRY BOY	*Warwick*	43	*4 Feb 78*	3
ANNIVERSARY - 20 YEARS OF HITS	*Epic*	45	*6 Jun 87*	5

Mark WYNTER — UK

SINGLES:	HITS 9			WEEKS 80
IMAGE OF A GIRL	*Decca*	11	*27 Aug 60*	10
KICKIN' UP THE LEAVES	*Decca*	24	*12 Nov 60*	10
DREAM GIRL	*Decca*	27	*11 Mar 61*	5
EXCLUSIVELY YOURS	*Decca*	32	*10 Jun 61*	7
VENUS IN BLUE JEANS	*Pye*	4	*6 Oct 62*	15
Original by Jimmy Clanton reached No. 7 in the US in 1962.				
GO AWAY, LITTLE GIRL	*Pye*	6	*15 Dec 62*	11
SHY GIRL	*Pye*	28	*8 Jun 63*	6
IT'S ALMOST TOMORROW	*Decca*	12	*16 Nov 63*	12
ONLY YOU (AND YOU ALONE)	*Pye*	38	*11 Apr 64*	4

X

Malcolm X, music by Keith LeBLANC — US

SINGLES:	HITS 1			WEEKS 4
NO SELL OUT	*Tommy Boy*	60	*7 Apr 84*	4
Malcolm X's voice is taken from various speeches during the early 1960s.				

X MAL DEUTSCHLAND — UK/Germany

ALBUMS:	HITS 1			WEEKS 1
TOCSIN	*4AD*	86	*7 Jul 84*	1

X.MEN – See SELENA vs X.MEN

X-PRESS 2 — UK

SINGLES:	HITS 8			WEEKS 10
LONDON X-PRESS	*Junior Boy's Own*	59	*5 Jun 93*	1
SAY WHAT!	*Junior Boy's Own*	32	*16 Oct 93*	2
ROCK 2 HOUSE / HIP HOUSIN'	*Junior Boy's Own*	55	*30 Jul 94*	2
Above hit: X-PRESS 2 featuring LO-PRO.				
THE SOUND	*Junior Boy's Own*	38	*9 Mar 96*	1
TRANZ EURO XPRESS	*Junior Boy's Own*	45	*12 Oct 96*	1
AC/DC	*Skint*	60	*30 Sep 00*	1
MUZIKIZUM	*Skint*	52	*28 Apr 01*	1
SMOKE MACHINE	*Skint*	43	*20 Oct 01*	1

X-RAY SPEX — UK

SINGLES:	HITS 4			WEEKS 33
THE DAY THE WORLD TURNED DAYGLO	*EMI International*	23	*29 Apr 78*	8
IDENTITY	*EMI International*	24	*22 Jul 78*	10
GERM FREE ADOLESCENCE	*EMI International*	19	*4 Nov 78*	11
HIGHLY INFLAMMABLE	*EMI International*	45	*21 Apr 79*	4
ALBUMS:	**HITS 1**			**WEEKS 14**
GERM FREE ADOLESCENTS	*EMI International*	30	*9 Dec 78*	14

XSTASIA — UK

SINGLES:	HITS 1			WEEKS 1
SWEETNESS	*Liquid Asset*	65	*17 Mar 01*	1

X-STATIC — Italy

SINGLES:	HITS 1			WEEKS 2
I'M STANDING (HIGHER)	*Positiva*	41	*4 Feb 95*	2

XAVIER featuring George CLINTON and Bootsy COLLINS — US

(See also George Clinton.)

SINGLES:	HITS 1			WEEKS 3
WORK THAT SUCKER TO DEATH / LOVE IS ON THE ONE	*Liberty*	53	*20 Mar 82*	3

XAVIER – See TJR featuring XAVIER

XPANSIONS — UK

SINGLES:	HITS 2			WEEKS 20
ELEVATION	*Optimism*	49	*6 Oct 90*	5
MOVE YOUR BODY (ELEVATION) [RE]	*Optimism*	7	*23 Feb 91*	9

The label was pressed with a different song title on this re-entry, though the sleeve was the original packaging.

WHAT YOU WANT	*Arista*	55	*15 Jun 91*	2
Above hit: XPANSIONS featuring Dale JOYNER.				
MOVE YOUR BODY [RM]	*Arista*	14	*26 Aug 95*	4
Remixed by Tony De Vit and Simon Parkes.				
Above hit: XPANSIONS 95.				

XSCAPE

US

SINGLES:	HITS 5			WEEKS 15
JUST KICKIN' IT	*Columbia*	49	*20 Nov 93*	2
JUST KICKIN' IT [RI]	*Columbia*	54	*5 Nov 94*	2
FEELS SO GOOD	*Columbia*	34	*7 Oct 95*	2
WHO CAN I RUN TO	*Columbia*	31	*27 Jan 96*	3
Originally recorded by the Jones Girls in 1979. Samples Teddy Pendergrass' Love TKO.				
KEEP ON, KEEPIN' ON	*East West America*	39	*29 Jun 96*	2
From the film 'Sunset Park'. Samples Michael Jackson's Liberian Girl.				
KEEP ON KEEPIN' ON [RI]	*East West America*	27	*19 Apr 97*	2
Above 2: MC LYTE featuring XSCAPE.				
THE ARMS OF THE ONE WHO LOVES YOU	*Columbia*	46	*22 Aug 98*	2

XTC

UK

SINGLES:	HITS 12			WEEKS 70
LIFE BEGINS AT THE HOP	*Virgin*	54	*12 May 79*	4
MAKING PLANS FOR NIGEL	*Virgin*	17	*22 Sep 79*	11
GENERALS AND MAJORS / DON'T LOSE YOUR TEMPER	*Virgin*	32	*6 Sep 80*	8
TOWERS OF LONDON	*Virgin*	31	*18 Oct 80*	5
SGT. ROCK (IS GOING TO HELP ME)	*Virgin*	16	*24 Jan 81*	9
SENSES WORKING OVERTIME	*Virgin*	10	*23 Jan 82*	9
BALL AND CHAIN	*Virgin*	58	*27 Mar 82*	4
LOVE ON A FARMBOY'S WAGES	*Virgin*	50	*15 Oct 83*	4
ALL YOU PRETTY GIRLS	*Virgin*	55	*29 Sep 84*	5
MAYOR OF SIMPLETON	*Virgin*	46	*28 Jan 89*	5
THE DISAPPOINTED	*Virgin*	33	*4 Apr 92*	5
THE BALLAD OF PETER PUMPKINHEAD	*Virgin*	71	*13 Jun 92*	1
ALBUMS:	**HITS 14**			**WEEKS 51**
WHITE MUSIC	*Virgin*	38	*11 Feb 78*	4
GO 2	*Virgin*	21	*28 Oct 78*	3
DRUMS AND WIRES	*Virgin*	34	*1 Sep 79*	7
BLACK SEA	*Virgin*	16	*20 Sep 80*	7
ENGLISH SETTLEMENT	*Virgin*	5	*20 Feb 82*	11
WAXWORKS - SOME SINGLES (1977-1982)	*Virgin*	54	*13 Nov 82*	3
MUMMER	*Virgin*	51	*10 Sep 83*	4
THE BIG EXPRESS	*Virgin*	38	*27 Oct 84*	2
SKYLARKING	*Virgin*	90	*8 Nov 86*	1
ORANGES AND LEMONS	*Virgin*	28	*11 Mar 89*	3
NONSUCH	*Virgin*	28	*9 May 92*	2
FOSSIL FUEL - THE XTC SINGLES COLLECTION 1977-1992	*Virgin*	33	*28 Sep 96*	2
APPLE VENUS - VOLUME 1	*Cooking Vinyl*	42	*6 Mar 99*	1
APPLE VENUS - VOLUME 2	*Cooking Vinyl*	40	*3 Jun 00*	1
Above hit: XTC + WASP STAR.				

XZIBIT

US

SINGLES:	HITS 1			WEEKS 7
X	*Epic*	14	*17 Mar 01*	7
ALBUMS:	**HITS 1**			**WEEKS 11**
RESTLESS	*Epic*	27	*10 Feb 01*	11

Y

Y & T

US

SINGLES:	HITS 1			WEEKS 4
MEAN STREAK	*A&M*	41	*13 Aug 83*	4
ALBUMS:	**HITS 3**			**WEEKS 15**
BLACK TIGER	*A&M*	53	*11 Sep 82*	8
MEAN STREAK	*A&M*	35	*10 Sep 83*	4
IN ROCK WE TRUST	*A&M*	33	*18 Aug 84*	3

Y?N-VEE

US

SINGLES:	HITS 1			WEEKS 1
CHOCOLATE	*RAL*	65	*17 Dec 94*	1

Y-TRAXX — Belgium

SINGLES:	HITS 1			WEEKS 1
MYSTERY LAND [EP] *Lead track: Mystery Land.*	*ffrr*	63	*24 May 97*	1

Y TRIBE featuring Elisabeth TROY — UK

SINGLES:	HITS 1			WEEKS 3
ENOUGH IS ENOUGH *Originally released in 1998 as an instrumental titled 10th Night. Samples the guitar from a recording of Shakespeare's Twelth Night.*	*Northwest 10*	49	*18 Dec 99*	2
ENOUGH IS ENOUGH [RE]	*Northwest 10*	75	*8 Jan 00*	1

YA KID K – See HI TEK 3 featuring YA KID K; TECHNOTRONIC

"Weird Al" YANKOVIC — US

SINGLES:	HITS 2			WEEKS 8
EAT IT *Parody of Michael Jackson's Beat It.*	*Scotti Brothers*	36	*7 Apr 84*	7
SMELLS LIKE NIRVANA *Parody of Nirvana's Smells Like Teen Spirit.*	*Scotti Brothers*	58	*4 Jul 92*	1

YANNI — Greece

ALBUMS:	HITS 1			WEEKS 2
TRIBUTE	*Virgin*	40	*4 Apr 98*	2

YARBROUGH and PEOPLES — US

SINGLES:	HITS 4			WEEKS 20
DON'T STOP THE MUSIC	*Mercury*	7	*27 Dec 80*	12
DON'T WASTE YOUR TIME	*Total Experience*	60	*5 May 84*	3
GUILTY	*Total Experience*	53	*11 Jan 86*	3
I WOULDN'T LIE	*Total Experience*	61	*5 Jul 86*	2

YARDBIRDS — UK

SINGLES:	HITS 7			WEEKS 62
GOOD MORNING LITTLE SCHOOLGIRL	*Columbia*	44	*14 Nov 64*	4
FOR YOUR LOVE	*Columbia*	3	*20 Mar 65*	12
HEART FULL OF SOUL *Above 2 written by Graham Gouldman of 10cc.*	*Columbia*	2	*19 Jun 65*	13
EVIL HEARTED YOU / STILL I'M SAD	*Columbia*	3	*16 Oct 65*	10
SHAPES OF THINGS	*Columbia*	3	*5 Mar 66*	9
OVER UNDER SIDEWAYS DOWN	*Columbia*	10	*4 Jun 66*	9
HAPPENINGS TEN YEARS TIME AGO	*Columbia*	43	*29 Oct 66*	5
EPS:	**HITS 1**			**WEEKS 33**
FIVE YARDBIRDS	*Columbia*	5	*28 Aug 65*	33
ALBUMS:	**HITS 1**			**WEEKS 8**
YARDBIRDS	*Columbia*	20	*23 Jul 66*	8

YAVAHN – See RUFFNECK featuring YAVAHN

YAZOO — UK

(See also Alison Moyet.)

SINGLES:	HITS 5			WEEKS 55
ONLY YOU	*Mute*	2	*17 Apr 82*	14
DON'T GO	*Mute*	3	*17 Jul 82*	11
THE OTHER SIDE OF LOVE	*Mute*	13	*20 Nov 82*	9
NOBODY'S DIARY	*Mute*	3	*21 May 83*	11
SITUATION *Originally the B-side of Don't Go, remixed by Francois Kevorkian.*	*Mute*	14	*8 Dec 90*	8
ONLY YOU - 1999 MIX [RM] *Remixed by Richard Stannard and Julian Gallagher.*	*Mute*	38	*4 Sep 99*	2
ALBUMS:	**HITS 3**			**WEEKS 86**
UPSTAIRS AT ERIC'S	*Mute*	2	*4 Sep 82*	63
YOU AND ME BOTH	*Mute*	1	*16 Jul 83*	20
ONLY YAZOO - THE BEST OF YAZOO	*Mute*	22	*18 Sep 99*	3

YAZZ — UK

SINGLES:	HITS 12			WEEKS 69
DOCTORIN' THE HOUSE *Above hit: COLDCUT featuring YAZZ and the PLASTIC POPULATION.*	*Ahead Our Our Time*	6	*20 Feb 88*	9
THE ONLY WAY IS UP *Originally recorded by Otis Clay.* *Above hit: YAZZ and the PLASTIC POPULATION.*	*Big Life*	1	*23 Jul 88*	15
STAND UP FOR YOUR LOVE RIGHTS	*Big Life*	2	*29 Oct 88*	12

FINE TIME	*Big Life*	9	*4 Feb 89*	8
WHERE HAS ALL THE LOVE GONE	*Big Life*	16	*29 Apr 89*	6
TREAT ME GOOD	*Big Life*	20	*23 Jun 90*	5
ONE TRUE WOMAN	*Polydor*	60	*28 Mar 92*	2
HOW LONG	*Polydor*	31	*31 Jul 93*	5
Above hit: YAZZ and ASWAD.				
HAVE MERCY	*Polydor*	42	*2 Apr 94*	3
EVERYBODY'S GOT TO LEARN SOMETIME	*Polydor*	56	*9 Jul 94*	2
GOOD THING GOING	*East West*	53	*28 Sep 96*	1
Features Sugar Minott. Originally recorded by Michael Jackson				
NEVER CAN SAY GOODBYE	*East West*	61	*22 Mar 97*	1
ALBUMS:	**HITS 1**			**WEEKS 32**
WANTED	*Big Life*	3	*26 Nov 88*	30
WANTED / WANTED - THE REMIXES [RE]	*Big Life*	53	*25 Nov 89*	2
Wanted – The Remixes was a remix album, sales were combined.				

Trisha YEARWOOD — US

SINGLES:	**HITS 1**			**WEEKS 1**
HOW DO I LIVE	*MCA*	66	*9 Aug 97*	1
From the film 'Con Air'.				
ALBUMS:	**HITS 1**			**WEEKS 2**
WHERE YOUR ROAD LEADS	*MCA Nashville*	36	*25 Jul 98*	2

YELL! — UK

SINGLES:	**HITS 1**			**WEEKS 8**
INSTANT REPLAY	*Fanfare*	10	*20 Jan 90*	8

YELLO — Switzerland

SINGLES:	**HITS 12**			**WEEKS 42**
I LOVE YOU	*Stiff*	41	*25 Jun 83*	4
LOST AGAIN	*Stiff*	73	*26 Nov 83*	1
GOLDRUSH	*Mercury*	54	*9 Aug 86*	3
THE RHYTHM DIVINE	*Mercury*	54	*22 Aug 87*	2
Above 2: Backing vocals by Billy MacKenzie of the Associates.				
Above hit: YELLO featuring Shirley BASSEY.				
THE RACE	*Mercury*	7	*27 Aug 88*	11
TIED UP	*Mercury*	60	*17 Dec 88*	5
OF COURSE I'M LYING	*Mercury*	23	*25 Mar 89*	8
Features vocals by Billy MacKenzie.				
BLAZING SADDLES	*Mercury*	47	*22 Jul 89*	2
RUBBERBANDMAN	*Mercury*	58	*8 Jun 91*	2
Features vocals by Billy MacKenzie.				
JUNGLE BILL	*Mercury*	61	*5 Sep 92*	2
THE RACE [RI] / BOSTICH	*Mercury*	55	*7 Nov 92*	1
HOW HOW	*Mercury*	59	*15 Oct 94*	1
ALBUMS:	**HITS 5**			**WEEKS 15**
YOU GOTTA SAY YES TO ANOTHER EXCESS	*Stiff*	65	*21 May 83*	2
STELLA	*Elektra*	92	*6 Apr 85*	1
ONE SECOND	*Mercury*	48	*4 Jul 87*	3
FLAG	*Mercury*	56	*10 Dec 88*	7
BABY	*Mercury*	37	*29 Jun 91*	2

YELLOW DOG — UK/US

SINGLES:	**HITS 2**			**WEEKS 13**
JUST ONE MORE NIGHT	*Virgin*	8	*4 Feb 78*	9
WAIT UNTIL MIDNIGHT	*Virgin*	54	*22 Jul 78*	4

YELLOW MAGIC ORCHESTRA — Japan

SINGLES:	**HITS 1**			**WEEKS 11**
COMPUTER GAME (THEME FROM THE INVADERS) / FIRECRACKER / TECHNOPOLIS	*A&M*	17	*14 Jun 80*	11
Adapted from the computer game 'Space Invaders'. Computer Game was only a 22 second intro before the track Firecracker.				

YELLOWCOATS – See Paul SHANE and the YELLOWCOATS

Bryn YEMM — UK

ALBUMS:	**HITS 4**			**WEEKS 14**
HOW DO I LOVE THEE	*Lifestyle*	57	*9 Jun 84*	2
HOW GREAT THOU ART	*Lifestyle*	67	*7 Jul 84*	8
THE BRYN YEMM CHRISTMAS COLLECTION	*Bay*	95	*22 Dec 84*	2
MY TRIBUTE - BRYN YEMM INSPIRATIONAL ALBUM	*Word*	85	*26 Oct 85*	2
Above hit: Bryn YEMM and the GWENT CHORALE.				

YES — UK

SINGLES:	HITS 6			WEEKS 31
WONDEROUS STORIES	*Atlantic*	7	*17 Sep 77*	9
GOING FOR THE ONE	*Atlantic*	24	*26 Nov 77*	4
DON'T KILL THE WHALE	*Atlantic*	36	*9 Sep 78*	4
OWNER OF A LONELY HEART	*Atco*	28	*12 Nov 83*	9
LEAVE IT	*Atco*	56	*31 Mar 84*	4
LOVE WILL FIND A WAY	*Atco*	73	*3 Oct 87*	1
ALBUMS:	**HITS 21**			**WEEKS 214**
TIME AND A WORD	*Atlantic*	45	*1 Aug 70*	3
THE YES ALBUM	*Atlantic*	7	*3 Apr 71*	29
FRAGILE	*Atlantic*	7	*4 Dec 71*	17
CLOSE TO THE EDGE	*Atlantic*	4	*23 Sep 72*	13
YESSONGS	*Atlantic*	7	*26 May 73*	13
Live recordings from 1972.				
TALES FROM TOPOGRAPHIC OCEANS	*Atlantic*	1	*22 Dec 73*	15
Inspired by the Shastric scriptures.				
RELAYER	*Atlantic*	4	*21 Dec 74*	11
YESTERDAYS	*Atlantic*	27	*29 Mar 75*	7
Compilation including tracks from their early album releases Yes (from 1969) and Time And A Word.				
GOING FOR THE ONE	*Atlantic*	1	*30 Jul 77*	28
TORMATO	*Atlantic*	8	*7 Oct 78*	11
DRAMA	*Atlantic*	2	*30 Aug 80*	8
YESSHOWS	*Atlantic*	22	*10 Jan 81*	9
Live recordings from 1976–78.				
90125	*Atco*	16	*26 Nov 83*	28
Title is the assigned international catalogue number.				
9012 LIVE: THE SOLOS	*Atco*	44	*29 Mar 86*	3
Mini album of live recordings.				
BIG GENERATOR	*Atco*	17	*10 Oct 87*	5
UNION	*Arista*	7	*11 May 91*	6
TALK	*London*	20	*2 Apr 94*	4
KEYS TO ASCENSION	*Essential*	48	*9 Nov 96*	1
Live recordings from March 96.				
KEYS TO ASCENSION 2	*Essential!*	62	*15 Nov 97*	1
Documents the 3 day concert they played at California in 1996.				
THE LADDER	*Eagle*	36	*2 Oct 99*	1
MAGNIFICATION	*Eagle*	71	*22 Sep 01*	1

Melissa YIANNAKOU – See DESIYA featuring Melissa YIANNAKOU

YIN and YAN — UK

SINGLES:	HITS 1			WEEKS 5
IF	*EMI*	25	*29 Mar 75*	5
Spoof take-off based around Telly Savalas' version of the song.				

YO-HANS – See JODE featuring YO-HANS

YO-YO – See Quincy JONES

Dwight YOAKAM — US

SINGLES:	HITS 1			WEEKS 2
CRAZY LITTLE THING CALLED LOVE	*Reprise*	43	*10 Jul 99*	2
Featured in the Gap clothing TV commercial.				
ALBUMS:	**HITS 2**			**WEEKS 4**
HILLBILLY DELUXE	*Reprise*	51	*9 May 87*	3
BUENAS NOCHES FROM A LONELY ROOM	*Reprise*	87	*13 Aug 88*	1

YOMANDA — UK

SINGLES:	HITS 3			WEEKS 18
SYNTH & STRINGS	*Manifesto*	8	*24 Jul 99*	10
Samples Liquid Gold's Dance Yourself Dizzy.				
SUNSHINE	*Manifesto*	16	*11 Mar 00*	6
ON THE LEVEL	*Manifesto*	28	*2 Sep 00*	2

Tukka YOOT – See US3

YORK — Germany

SINGLES:	HITS 4			WEEKS 21
THE AWAKENING	*Manifesto*	11	*9 Oct 99*	5
ON THE BEACH/REACHERS OF CIVILISATION	*Manifesto*	4	*10 Jun 00*	10
On The Beach samples Chris Rea's original.				
FAREWELL TO THE MOON	*Manifesto*	37	*18 Nov 00*	2
THE FIELDS OF LOVE	*Club Tools*	16	*27 Jan 01*	4
Above hit: ATB featuring YORK.				

YOSH presents LOVEDEEJAY AKEMI — Holland

SINGLES:	HITS 2			WEEKS 5
IT'S WHAT'S UPFRONT THAT COUNTS *Vocals by Loletta Holloway.*	*Limbo*	69	*29 Jul 95*	1
IT'S WHAT'S UPFRONT THAT COUNTS [RM] *Remixed by Umboza (Stuart Crichton and Michael Kilkie).*	*Limbo*	31	*2 Dec 95*	2
THE SCREAMER	*Limbo*	38	*20 Apr 96*	2

YOSHIKI – See Roger TAYLOR

YOTHU YINDI — Australia

SINGLES:	HITS 1			WEEKS 1
TREATY	*Hollywood*	72	*15 Feb 92*	1

Faron YOUNG — US

SINGLES:	HITS 1			WEEKS 23
IT'S FOUR IN THE MORNING *Vocal accompaniment by the Nashville Edition.*	*Mercury*	3	*15 Jul 72*	23
ALBUMS:	**HITS 1**			**WEEKS 5**
IT'S FOUR IN THE MORNING	*Mercury*	27	*28 Oct 72*	5

Jimmy YOUNG — UK

(See also All Star Hit Parade.)

SINGLES:	HITS 11			WEEKS 88
FAITH CAN MOVE MOUNTAINS	*Decca*	11	*10 Jan 53*	1
ETERNALLY (THE THEME FROM "LIMELIGHT") *From the film.*	*Decca*	8	*22 Aug 53*	9
UNCHAINED MELODY *From the film 'Unchained'. Originally recorded by Alex North as an instrumental.*	*Decca*	1	*7 May 55*	19
THE MAN FROM LARAMIE *From the film of the same name.*	*Decca*	1	*17 Sep 55*	12
SOMEONE ON YOUR MIND	*Decca*	13	*24 Dec 55*	5
CHAIN GANG *Original by Bobby Scott reached No. 13 in the US in 1956.*	*Decca*	9	*17 Mar 56*	6
THE WAYWARD WIND	*Decca*	27	*9 Jun 56*	1
RICH MAN, POOR MAN *Above 2 entries were separate sides of the same release, each had its own chart run.*	*Decca*	25	*23 Jun 56*	1
MORE *Above 7: Jimmy YOUNG with Bob SHARPLES and his Music.*	*Decca*	4	*29 Sep 56*	17
ROUND AND ROUND *Above hit: Jimmy YOUNG with the Michael SAMMES SINGERS.*	*Decca*	30	*4 May 57*	1
MISS YOU *Above hit: Jimmy YOUNG with Tony OSBORNE and his Orchestra.*	*Columbia*	15	*12 Oct 63*	13
UNCHAINED MELODY [RR] *Above hit: Jimmy YOUNG with the Mike SAMMES SINGERS.*	*Columbia*	43	*28 Mar 64*	3

John Paul YOUNG — UK

SINGLES:	HITS 1			WEEKS 16
LOVE IS IN THE AIR	*Ariola*	5	*29 Apr 78*	13
LOVE IS IN THE AIR (BALLROOM MIX) [RM] *From the film 'Strictly Ballroom'.*	*Columbia*	49	*14 Nov 92*	3

Karen YOUNG — UK

SINGLES:	HITS 1			WEEKS 21
NOBODY'S CHILD	*Major Minor*	6	*6 Sep 69*	21

Karen YOUNG — US

SINGLES:	HITS 1			WEEKS 9
HOT SHOT	*Atlantic*	34	*19 Aug 78*	7
HOT SHOT [RI]	*Atlantic*	75	*24 Feb 79*	1
HOT SHOT '97 [RM] *Remixed by Rollercoaster.*	*Distinct'ive*	68	*15 Nov 97*	1

Leon YOUNG STRING CHORALE – See Mr. Acker BILK

Neil YOUNG — Canada

(See also Crosby, Stills, Nash and Young; Stills-Young Band.)

SINGLES:	HITS 6			WEEKS 22
HEART OF GOLD *Backing vocals by Linda Rondstadt and James Taylor.*	*Reprise*	10	*11 Mar 72*	11
FOUR STRONG WINDS *Features vocals by Nicolette Larson. Originally recorded by Ian and Sylvia.*	*Reprise*	57	*6 Jan 79*	4
HARVEST MOON	*Reprise*	36	*27 Feb 93*	3

THE NEEDLE AND THE DAMAGE DONE *Recording made for MTV's Unplugged series. Originally appeared on his 1972 album Harvest.*	*Reprise*	75	*17 Jul 93*	1
LONG MAY YOU RUN (LIVE) *Acoustic version originally recorded with Stephen Stills in 1976.*	*Reprise*	71	*30 Oct 93*	1
PHILADELPHIA *From the film of the same name.*	*Reprise*	62	*9 Apr 94*	2

ALBUMS:	**HITS 30**			**WEEKS 235**
AFTER THE GOLD RUSH	*Reprise*	7	*31 Oct 70*	68
HARVEST	*Reprise*	1	*4 Mar 72*	33
TIME FADES AWAY *Features David Crosby and Graham Nash.*	*Warner Brothers*	20	*27 Oct 73*	2
ON THE BEACH	*Reprise*	42	*10 Aug 74*	2
TONIGHT'S THE NIGHT *Dedicated to Crazy Horse member Danny Whitten who died from a heroin overdose on 18 Nov 72.*	*Reprise*	48	*5 Jul 75*	1
ZUMA	*Reprise*	44	*27 Dec 75*	2
AMERICAN STARS 'N' BARS *Features unissued studio tracks from previous 3 years.*	*Reprise*	17	*9 Jul 77*	8
DECADE *Compilation including both solo and group material with Buffalo Springfield and Crosby, Stills, Nash and Young.*	*Reprise*	46	*17 Dec 77*	4
COMES A TIME	*Reprise*	42	*28 Oct 78*	3
RUST NEVER SLEEPS *Identically titled film documentary of their 1978 tour was released simultaneously.*	*Reprise*	13	*14 Jul 79*	13
RUST *Live recordings from his 1978 tour.* *Above 2: Neil YOUNG and CRAZY HORSE.*	*Reprise*	55	*1 Dec 79*	3
HAWKS AND DOVES	*Reprise*	34	*15 Nov 80*	3
RE-AC-TOR *Above hit: Neil YOUNG and CRAZY HORSE.*	*Reprise*	69	*14 Nov 81*	3
TRANS	*Geffen*	29	*5 Feb 83*	5
EVERYBODY'S ROCKIN' *Above hit: Neil YOUNG and the SHOCKING PINKS.*	*Geffen*	50	*3 Sep 83*	3
OLD WAYS	*Geffen*	39	*14 Sep 85*	3
LANDING ON WATER	*Geffen*	52	*2 Aug 86*	2
LIFE *Above hit: Neil YOUNG and CRAZY HORSE.*	*Geffen*	71	*4 Jul 87*	1
THIS NOTE'S FOR YOU *Above hit: Neil YOUNG and the BLUE NOTES.*	*WEA*	56	*30 Apr 88*	3
FREEDOM	*Reprise*	17	*21 Oct 89*	5
RAGGED GLORY	*Reprise*	15	*22 Sep 90*	5
WELD *Live recordings.* *Above 2: Neil YOUNG and CRAZY HORSE.*	*Reprise*	20	*2 Nov 91*	3
HARVEST MOON	*Reprise*	9	*14 Nov 92*	18
LUCKY THIRTEEN *Live recordings and unreleased material from 1982–88.*	*Geffen*	69	*23 Jan 93*	1
UNPLUGGED *Live recordings made for MTV, Feb 93.*	*Reprise*	4	*26 Jun 93*	13
HARVEST [RE] *Re-released with a new catalogue number.*	*Reprise*	41	*9 Apr 94*	1
SLEEPS WITH ANGELS *Above hit: Neil YOUNG and CRAZY HORSE.*	*Reprise*	2	*27 Aug 94*	7
MIRROR BALL *Features Pearl Jam as his backing band.*	*Reprise*	4	*8 Jul 95*	9
BROKEN ARROW	*Reprise*	17	*6 Jul 96*	5
YEAR OF THE HORSE *Live recordings from Young's back catalogue.* *Above 2: Neil YOUNG and CRAZY HORSE.*	*Reprise*	36	*28 Jun 97*	2
SILVER AND GOLD	*Reprise*	10	*6 May 00*	4

Paul YOUNG — UK

SINGLES:	**HITS 21**			**WEEKS 134**
WHEREVER I LAY MY HAT (THAT'S MY HOME) *Originally recorded by Marvin Gaye in 1963 and was the B-side to his single 'Too Busy Thinking About My Baby' in 1969.*	*CBS*	1	*18 Jun 83*	15
COME BACK AND STAY *Originally recorded by Jack Lee.*	*CBS*	4	*10 Sep 83*	9
LOVE OF THE COMMON PEOPLE *Originally recorded by the Four Preps.*	*CBS*	2	*19 Nov 83*	13
I'M GONNA TEAR YOUR PLAYHOUSE DOWN *Originally recorded by Ann Peebles in 1973.*	*CBS*	9	*13 Oct 84*	7
EVERYTHING MUST CHANGE	*CBS*	9	*8 Dec 84*	11
EVERY TIME YOU GO AWAY *Originally recorded by Hall and Oates.*	*CBS*	4	*9 Mar 85*	11
TOMB OF MEMORIES	*CBS*	16	*22 Jun 85*	7
TOMB OF MEMORIES [RE]	*CBS*	74	*17 Aug 85*	1
WONDERLAND *Originally recorded by Betsy Cook.*	*CBS*	24	*4 Oct 86*	5

SOME PEOPLE	*CBS*	56	*29 Nov 86*	3
WHY DOES A MAN HAVE TO BE STRONG?	*CBS*	63	*7 Feb 87*	2
SOFTLY WHISPERING I LOVE YOU	*CBS*	21	*12 May 90*	6
Originally recorded by David and Jonathan.				
OH GIRL	*CBS*	25	*7 Jul 90*	6
HEAVEN CAN WAIT	*CBS*	71	*6 Oct 90*	2
CALLING YOU	*Columbia*	57	*12 Jan 91*	2
SENZA UNA DONNA (WITHOUT A WOMAN)	*London*	4	*30 Mar 91*	12
Originally recorded by Zucchero.				
Above hit: ZUCCHERO featuring Paul YOUNG.				
BOTH SIDES NOW	*MCA*	74	*10 Aug 91*	1
Above hit: CLANNAD and Paul YOUNG.				
DON'T DREAM IT'S OVER	*Columbia*	20	*26 Oct 91*	5
NOW I KNOW WHAT MADE OTIS BLUE	*Columbia*	14	*25 Sep 93*	7
HOPE IN A HOPELESS WORLD	*Columbia*	42	*27 Nov 93*	3
IT WILL BE YOU	*Columbia*	34	*23 Apr 94*	4
I WISH YOU LOVE	*East West*	33	*17 May 97*	2
ALBUMS:	**HITS 8**			**WEEKS 229**
NO PARLEZ	*CBS*	1	*30 Jul 83*	119
THE SECRET OF ASSOCIATION	*CBS*	1	*6 Apr 85*	49
BETWEEN TWO FIRES	*CBS*	4	*1 Nov 86*	17
OTHER VOICES	*CBS*	4	*16 Jun 90*	11
FROM TIME TO TIME - THE SINGLES COLLECTION	*Columbia*	1	*14 Sep 91*	27
THE CROSSING	*Columbia*	27	*23 Oct 93*	2
REFLECTIONS	*Vision*	64	*26 Nov 94*	2
PAUL YOUNG	*East West*	39	*31 May 97*	2

Retta YOUNG — US

SINGLES:	**HITS 1**			**WEEKS 7**
(SENDING OUT AN) S.O.S.	*All Platinum*	28	*24 May 75*	7

Tracie YOUNG – See TRACIE

Victor YOUNG and his Orchestra and Chorus – See Charlie APPLEWHITE

YOUNG AND MOODY BAND — UK

SINGLES:	**HITS 1**			**WEEKS 4**
DON'T DO THAT	*Bronze*	63	*10 Oct 81*	4

YOUNG BLACK TEENAGERS — US

SINGLES:	**HITS 1**			**WEEKS 3**
TAP THE BOTTLE	*MCA*	39	*9 Apr 94*	3

YOUNG and COMPANY — US

SINGLES:	**HITS 1**			**WEEKS 12**
I LIKE (WHAT YOU'RE DOING TO ME)	*Excaliber*	20	*1 Nov 80*	12

YOUNG DISCIPLES — UK

SINGLES:	**HITS 3**			**WEEKS 17**
GET YOURSELF TOGETHER	*Talkin Loud*	68	*13 Oct 90*	1
APPARENTLY NOTHIN'	*Talkin Loud*	46	*23 Feb 91*	4
APPARENTLY NOTHIN' [RE]	*Talkin Loud*	13	*3 Aug 91*	7
GET YOURSELF TOGETHER [RI]	*Talkin Loud*	65	*5 Oct 91*	2
YOUNG DISCIPLES [EP]	*Talkin Loud*	48	*5 Sep 92*	3
Lead track: Move On.				
ALBUMS:	**HITS 1**			**WEEKS 5**
ROAD TO FREEDOM	*Talkin Loud*	21	*31 Aug 91*	5

YOUNG GODS — Switzerland

ALBUMS:	**HITS 1**			**WEEKS 1**
T.V. SKY	*Play It*	54	*15 Feb 92*	1

YOUNG IDEA — UK

SINGLES:	**HITS 1**			**WEEKS 6**
WITH A LITTLE HELP FROM MY FRIENDS	*Columbia*	10	*2 Jul 67*	6

YOUNG M.C. — US

SINGLES:	**HITS 3**			**WEEKS 7**
BUST A MOVE	*Delicious Vinyl/Fourth & Broadway*	73	*15 Jul 89*	2
PRINCIPAL'S OFFICE	*Delicious Vinyl/Fourth & Broadway*	54	*17 Feb 90*	3
THAT'S THE WAY LOVE GOES	*Capitol*	65	*17 Aug 91*	2

YOUNG OFFENDERS — Ireland

SINGLES:	HITS 1			WEEKS 1
THAT'S WHY WE LOSE CONTROL	*Columbia*	60	*7 Mar 98*	1

YOUNG ONES – See Cliff RICHARD

YOUNG RASCALS — US/Canada

SINGLES:	HITS 2			WEEKS 17
GROOVIN'	*Atlantic*	8	*27 May 67*	13
A GIRL LIKE YOU	*Atlantic*	37	*19 Aug 67*	4

YOUNG STEVE and the AFTERNOON BOYS – See Steve WRIGHT

Sydney YOUNGBLOOD — US

SINGLES:	HITS 5			WEEKS 31
IF ONLY I COULD	*Circa*	3	*26 Aug 89*	14
SIT AND WAIT	*Circa*	16	*9 Dec 89*	8
I'D RATHER GO BLIND	*Circa*	44	*31 Mar 90*	5
HOOKED ON YOU	*Circa*	72	*29 Jun 91*	2
ANYTHING	*RCA*	48	*20 Mar 93*	2
ALBUMS:	**HITS 1**			**WEEKS 17**
FEELING FREE	*Circa*	23	*28 Oct 89*	17

YOUNGER YOUNGER 28'S — UK

SINGLES:	HITS 1			WEEKS 1
WE'RE GOING OUT	*V2*	61	*5 Jun 99*	1

Z

Z FACTOR — UK

SINGLES:	HITS 2			WEEKS 2
GOTTA KEEP PUSHIN'	*ffrr*	47	*21 Feb 98*	1
RIDE THE RHYTHM	*Direction*	52	*17 Nov 01*	1

Helmut ZACHARIAS and his ORCHESTRA — Germany

SINGLES:	HITS 1			WEEKS 11
TOKYO MELODY *Theme to the 1964 Olympic Games held in Tokyo.*	*Polydor*	9	*31 Oct 64*	11

Pia ZADORA — US

SINGLES:	HITS 2			WEEKS 6
WHEN THE RAIN BEGINS TO FALL *From the film 'Voyage Of The Rock Aliens'.* *Above hit: Jermaine JACKSON and Pia ZADORA.*	*Arista*	68	*27 Oct 84*	2
DANCE OUT OF MY HEAD *Above hit: PIA.*	*Epic*	65	*12 Nov 88*	4

Michael ZAGER BAND — US

SINGLES:	HITS 1			WEEKS 12
LET'S ALL CHANT	*Private Stock*	8	*1 Apr 78*	12

ZAGER and EVANS — US

SINGLES:	HITS 1			WEEKS 13
IN THE YEAR 2525 (EXORDIUM AND TERMINUS) *Written by Rick Evans in 1964 while in a band called the Eccentrics.*	*RCA Victor*	1	*9 Aug 69*	13

Gheorghe ZAMFIR — Romania

SINGLES:	HITS 1			WEEKS 9
THE LIGHT OF EXPERIENCE 'DOINA DE JALE' *Theme from the BBC TV series.*	*Epic*	4	*21 Aug 76*	9

Tommy ZANG — US

SINGLES:	HITS 1			WEEKS 1
HEY GOOD LOOKING *Originally recorded by Hank Williams.*	*Polydor*	45	*18 Feb 61*	1

ZAPP — US

SINGLES:	HITS 2			WEEKS 6
IT DOESN'T REALLY MATTER	*Warner Brothers*	57	*25 Jan 86*	3
COMPUTER LOVE (PART 1)	*Warner Brothers*	64	*24 May 86*	3

Frank ZAPPA — US

ALBUMS:	HITS 13			WEEKS 57
HOT RATS	*Reprise*	9	*28 Feb 70*	27
CHUNGA'S REVENGE	*Reprise*	43	*19 Dec 70*	1
ZAPPA IN NEW YORK	*Discreet*	55	*6 May 78*	1
Live recordings.				
SHEIK YERBOUTI	*CBS*	32	*10 Mar 79*	7
JOE'S GARAGE ACT I	*CBS*	62	*13 Oct 79*	3
JOE'S GARAGE ACTS II & III	*CBS*	75	*19 Jan 80*	1
TINSEL TOWN REBELLION	*CBS*	55	*16 May 81*	4
YOU ARE WHAT YOU IS	*CBS*	51	*24 Oct 81*	2
Above 2 are live recordings.				
SHIP ARRIVING TOO LATE TO SAVE A DROWNING WITCH	*CBS*	61	*19 Jun 82*	4
THE MAN FROM UTOPIA	*CBS*	87	*18 Jun 83*	1
THEM OR US	*EMI*	53	*27 Oct 84*	2
GUITAR	*Zappa*	82	*30 Apr 88*	2
Compilation.				
STRICTLY COMMERCIAL - THE BEST OF FRANK ZAPPA	*Rykodisc*	45	*2 Sep 95*	2

Francesco ZAPPALA — Italy

SINGLES:	HITS 2			WEEKS 3
WE GOTTA DO IT	*Fourth & Broadway*	57	*10 Aug 91*	2
Above hit: D.J. PROFESSOR and Francesco ZAPPALA.				
NO WAY OUT	*PWL Continental*	69	*2 May 92*	1

Lena ZAVARONI — UK

SINGLES:	HITS 2			WEEKS 14
MA! (HE'S MAKING EYES AT ME)	*Philips*	10	*9 Feb 74*	11
Originally recorded by Eddie Cantor in 1921.				
(YOU'VE GOT) PERSONALITY	*Philips*	33	*1 Jun 74*	3
ALBUMS:	**HITS 1**			**WEEKS 5**
MA	*Philips*	8	*23 Mar 74*	5

ZED BIAS — UK

SINGLES:	HITS 1			WEEKS 4
NEIGHBOURHOOD	*Locked On*	25	*15 Jul 00*	4

ZEE — UK

SINGLES:	HITS 3			WEEKS 4
DREAMTIME	*Perfecto*	31	*6 Jul 96*	2
SAY MY NAME	*Perfecto*	36	*22 Mar 97*	1
BUTTERFLY	*Perfecto Mainline*	41	*7 Feb 98*	1
Above hit: TILT featuring ZEE.				

ZEITIA – See ARIZONA featuring ZEITIA; Zeitia MASSIAH

ZEPHYRS — UK

SINGLES:	HITS 1			WEEKS 1
SHE'S LOST YOU	*Columbia*	48	*20 Mar 65*	1

ZERO B — UK

SINGLES:	HITS 3			WEEKS 6
THE E.P. (BRAND NEW MIXES) [EP]	*Ffrreedom*	32	*22 Feb 92*	4
Lead track: Lock Up.				
RECONNECTION [EP]	*Internal*	54	*24 Jul 93*	2
Lead track: Lock-Up. This is a remix of the track on the previous EP.				

ZERO 7 — UK

SINGLES:	HITS 2			WEEKS 4
DESTINY	*Ultimate Dilemma*	30	*18 Aug 01*	3
Above hit: ZERO 7 featuring SIA & SOPHIE.				
IN THE WAITING LINE	*Ultimate Dilemma*	47	*17 Nov 01*	1
ALBUMS:	**HITS 1**			**WEEKS 19**
SIMPLE THINGS	*Ultimate Dilemma*	28	*5 May 01*	19

ZERO VU featuring Lorna B — UK

SINGLES:	HITS 1			WEEKS 1
FEELS SO GOOD	*Avex UK*	69	*15 Mar 97*	1

ZERO ZERO — UK

SINGLES:	HITS 1			WEEKS 1
ZEROXED	*Kickin*	71	*10 Aug 91*	1

ZHANE — US

SINGLES:	HITS 9			WEEKS 18
HEY MR. D.J.	*Epic*	26	*11 Sep 93*	3
Samples Looking Up To You by Michael Wycoff.				
HEY MR. D.J. [RE]	*Epic*	50	*4 Dec 93*	2
GROOVE THANG	*Motown*	34	*19 Mar 94*	3
VIBE	*Motown*	67	*20 Aug 94*	1
SHAME	*Jive*	66	*25 Feb 95*	1
From the film 'A Low Down Dirty Shame'.				
IT'S A PARTY	*Elektra*	23	*21 Sep 96*	2
Features vocals by SWV.				
Above hit: Busta RHYMES featuring ZHANE.				
4 MORE	*Tommy Boy*	52	*8 Mar 97*	1
Recreates Sharon Redd's Never Give You Up.				
Above hit: DE LA SOUL featuring ZHANE.				
REQUEST LINE	*Motown*	22	*26 Apr 97*	3
CRUSH	*Motown*	44	*30 Aug 97*	1
JAMBOREE	*Arista*	51	*11 Sep 99*	1
Samples Benny Golson's I'm Always Dancin' To The Music.				
Above hit: NAUGHTY BY NATURE (featuring ZHANE).				

ALBUMS:	HITS 1			WEEKS 1
SATURDAY NIGHT	*Motown*	52	*10 May 97*	1
Previously released in 1994 with the title Zhane Pronounced Jah-Nay, peaked at No. 89.				

ZIG and ZAG — Ireland

SINGLES:	HITS 2			WEEKS 12
THEM GIRLS/THEM GIRLS	*RCA*	5	*24 Dec 94*	9
HANDS UP! HANDS UP!	*RCA*	21	*1 Jul 95*	3

ZIGO – See SPOILED and ZIGO

Hans ZIMMER — US

ALBUMS:	HITS 3			WEEKS 20
GLADIATOR [OST]	*Decca*	17	*27 May 00*	16
Above hit: Hans ZIMMER and Lisa GERRARD				
HANNIBAL [OST]	*Decca*	74	*3 Mar 01*	2
PEARL HARBOR [OST]	*Hollywood*	50	*16 Jun 01*	2
Above hit: Hans ZIMMER, Orchestra conducted by Gavin GREENAWAY.				

David ZINMAN – See Dawn UPSHAW (soprano)/the LONDON SINFONIETTA/David ZINMAN (conductor)

ZION TRAIN — UK

SINGLES:	HITS 1			WEEKS 1
RISE	*China*	61	*27 Jul 96*	1
Track created using Soundpool – an on-line bank of royalty-free samples.				

ALBUMS:	HITS 1			WEEKS 1
GROW TOGETHER	*China*	56	*13 Jul 96*	1

ZODIACS – See Maurice WILLIAMS and the ZODIACS

ZOE — UK

SINGLES:	HITS 3			WEEKS 22
SUNSHINE ON A RAINY DAY	*M&G*	53	*10 Nov 90*	5
SUNSHINE ON A RAINY DAY [RM]	*M&G*	4	*24 Aug 91*	11
Remixed by Youth and Mark Stent.				
LIGHTNING	*M&G*	37	*2 Nov 91*	4
HOLY DAYS	*M&G*	72	*29 Feb 92*	2

ALBUMS:	HITS 1			WEEKS 1
SCARLET, RED AND BLUE	*M&G*	67	*7 Dec 91*	1

Rob ZOMBIE — US

(See also Puff Daddy.)

SINGLES:	HITS 1			WEEKS 2
DRAGULA	*Geffen*	44	*26 Dec 98*	2

ALBUMS:	HITS 1			WEEKS 2
HELLBILLY DELUXE	*Geffen*	37	*5 Sep 98*	2

ZOMBIE NATION — Germany

SINGLES:	HITS 1			WEEKS 16
KERNKRAFT 400	*Transk*	61	*2 Sep 00*	1
Import.				
KERNKRAFT 400	*Data*	2	*30 Sep 00*	15

ZOMBIES — UK

SINGLES:	HITS 2			WEEKS 16
SHE'S NOT THERE	*Decca*	12	*15 Aug 64*	11
TELL HER NO	*Decca*	42	*13 Feb 65*	5

ZOO EXPERIENCE – featuring DESTRY — UK/US

SINGLES:	HITS 1			WEEKS 1
LOVE'S GOT A HOLD ON ME	*Cooltempo*	66	*22 Aug 92*	1

Z2 — UK

SINGLES:	HITS 1			WEEKS 1
I WANT YOU	*Platipus*	61	*26 Feb 00*	1

ZUCCHERO — Italy

SINGLES:	HITS 3			WEEKS 24
SENZA UNA DONNA (WITHOUT A WOMAN)	*London*	4	*30 Mar 91*	12
Originally recorded by Zucchero.				
Above hit: ZUCCHERO featuring Paul YOUNG.				
DIAMANTE	*London*	44	*18 Jan 92*	7
Above hit: ZUCCHERO with Randy CRAWFORD.				
MISERERE	*London*	15	*24 Oct 92*	5
Above hit: ZUCCHERO with Luciano PAVAROTTI.				
ALBUMS:	**HITS 1**			**WEEKS 4**
ZUCCHERO	*London*	29	*18 May 91*	4

ZZ TOP — US

(See also Martay featuring ZZ Top.)

SINGLES:	HITS 15			WEEKS 92
GIMME ALL YOUR LOVIN'	*Warner Brothers*	61	*3 Sep 83*	3
SHARP DRESSED MAN	*Warner Brothers*	53	*26 Nov 83*	3
TV DINNERS	*Warner Brothers*	67	*31 Mar 84*	3
GIMME ALL YOUR LOVIN' [RE]	*Warner Brothers*	10	*6 Oct 84*	15
SHARP DRESSED MAN [RE]	*Warner Brothers*	22	*15 Dec 84*	10
LEGS (SPECIAL US REMIX)	*Warner Brothers*	16	*23 Feb 85*	7
THE ZZ TOP SUMMER HOLIDAY [EP]	*Warner Brothers*	51	*13 Jul 85*	5
Lead track: Tush. EP of old tracks. Tush was originally released in 1975 and reached No. 20 in the US.				
SLEEPING BAG	*Warner Brothers*	27	*19 Oct 85*	5
STAGES	*Warner Brothers*	43	*15 Feb 86*	3
ROUGH BOY	*Warner Brothers*	23	*19 Apr 86*	9
VELCRO FLY ('86 REMIX)	*Warner Brothers*	54	*4 Oct 86*	3
DOUBLEBACK	*Warner Brothers*	29	*21 Jul 90*	6
From the film 'Back To The Future III'.				
MY HEAD'S IN MISSISSIPPI	*Warner Brothers*	37	*13 Apr 91*	5
VIVA LAS VEGAS	*Warner Brothers*	10	*11 Apr 92*	7
ROUGH BOY [RI]	*Warner Brothers*	49	*20 Jun 92*	3
PINCUSHION	*RCA*	15	*29 Jan 94*	3
BREAKAWAY	*RCA*	60	*7 May 94*	1
WHATS UP WITH THAT	*RCA*	58	*29 Jun 96*	1
ALBUMS:	**HITS 8**			**WEEKS 211**
FANDANGO!	*London*	60	*12 Jul 75*	1
One side live, the other has studio recordings.				
EL LOCO	*Warner Brothers*	88	*8 Aug 81*	2
ELIMINATOR	*Warner Brothers*	43	*30 Apr 83*	24
Chart position reached in 1984 (1983 peak No. 67)				
ELIMINATOR [RE-1ST]	*Warner Brothers*	3	*7 Jul 84*	111
Peak position reached on 26 Jan 85.				
AFTERBURNER	*Warner Brothers*	2	*9 Nov 85*	40
RECYCLER	*Warner Brothers*	8	*27 Oct 90*	7
GREATEST HITS	*Warner Brothers*	5	*25 Apr 92*	17
ANTENNA	*RCA*	3	*5 Feb 94*	5
Tribute to the Mexican border rock'n'roll radio stations of the 1950s/60s.				
RHYTHMEEN	*RCA*	32	*21 Sep 96*	2
ELIMINATOR [RE]	*Warner Brothers*	28	*8 Jul 00*	2

VARIOUS ARTISTS

This section lists all entries which do not constitute an entry under a respective individual artist. This includes compilations, soundtracks and cast recordings. From 14 Jan 89 a Top 20 Compilation chart was established, removing all albums with tracks by more than one artist form the main chart. Totals have been segregated between the two charts.

ANONYMOUS

Album Chart entries in this section during 1971 were all budget releases. They only charted between 7 Aug 71 through to 1 Jan 72 when the Budget chart was combined with the Full Price album chart.

Aral

EPS:	HITS 4			WEEKS 12
TOP TEN RECORD	*Aral*	15	*27 Apr 63*	6
TOP TEN RECORD	*Aral*	16	*23 Nov 63*	3
TOP TEN RECORD	*Aral*	17	*15 Feb 64*	2
The above 3 albums are different.				
TOP TEN RECORD CLUB	*Aral*	17	*21 Mar 64*	1

Hallmark

ALBUMS:	HITS 4			WEEKS 32
TOP OF THE POPS VOLUME 18	*Hallmark*	1	*7 Aug 71*	12
TOP OF THE POPS VOLUME 17	*Hallmark*	16	*7 Aug 71*	3
TOP OF THE POPS VOLUME 19	*Hallmark*	3	*2 Oct 71*	9
TOP OF THE POPS VOLUME 20	*Hallmark*	1	*13 Nov 71*	8

K-Tel

ALBUMS:	HITS 1			WEEKS 7
40 SINGALONG PUB SONGS	*K-Tel*	21	*27 Sep 75*	7

Music For Pleasure

ALBUMS:	HITS 8			WEEKS 30
HOT HITS 6	*Music For Pleasure*	1	*7 Aug 71*	7
MILLION SELLER HITS	*Music For Pleasure*	46	*7 Aug 71*	2
HOT HITS 5	*Music For Pleasure*	48	*7 Aug 71*	1
SMASH HIT SUPREMES STYLE	*Music For Pleasure*	36	*21 Aug 71*	3
HOT HITS 7	*Music For Pleasure*	3	*23 Oct 71*	9
SMASH HITS COUNTRY STYLE	*Music For Pleasure*	38	*6 Nov 71*	1
SMASH HITS '71	*Music For Pleasure*	21	*4 Dec 71*	3
HOT HITS 8	*Music For Pleasure*	2	*11 Dec 71*	4

Plexium

ALBUMS:	HITS 1			WEEKS 2
NON STOP 20 VOLUME 4	*Plexium*	35	*27 Nov 71*	2

Ronco

ALBUMS:	HITS 1			WEEKS 6
FORTY MANIA	*Ronco*	21	*6 Nov 76*	6

Top Six

EPS:	HITS 3			WEEKS 10
TOP SIX	*Top Six*	10	*22 Feb 64*	4
TOP SIX VOLUME 2	*Top Six*	10	*21 Mar 64*	4
TOP SIX VOLUME 3	*Top Six*	16	*11 Apr 64*	2
ALBUMS:	**HITS 1**			**WEEKS 2**
BEATLEMANIA	*Top Six*	19	*29 Feb 64*	2

CHRISTMAS

ALBUMS:	HITS 6			WEEKS 18
A CHRISTMAS GIFT	*Ronco*	39	*13 Dec 75*	5
THE CHRISTMAS CAROL COLLECTION	*Fame*	75	*8 Dec 84*	3
MERRY CHRISTMAS TO YOU	*Warner Brothers*	64	*22 Dec 84*	2
CHRISTMAS AT THE COUNTRY STORE	*Country Store/Starblend*	94	*21 Dec 85*	1
SPECIAL OLYMPICS - A VERY SPECIAL CHRISTMAS	*A&M*	40	*5 Dec 87*	5
NOEL - CHRISTMAS SONGS AND CAROLS	*Trax*	89	*17 Dec 88*	2
COMPILATION ALBUMS:	**HITS 8**			**WEEKS 56**
SPECIAL OLYMPICS - A VERY SPECIAL CHRISTMAS	*A&M*	19	*23 Dec 89*	1
Benefit album with proceeds to the Special Olympics charity.				
IT'S CHRISTMAS	*EMI*	3	*9 Dec 89*	5

IT'S CHRISTMAS [RE]	*EMI*	2	*8 Dec 90*	11
CHRISTMAS GREATEST HITS	*Legends In*	16	*22 Dec 90*	1
A CLASSIC CHRISTMAS	*EMI*	14	*30 Nov 91*	7
CHRISTMAS LOVE SONGS	*Arcade*	11	*14 Dec 91*	6
IT'S CHRISTMAS TIME	*EMI*	3	*21 Nov 92*	15
THAT'S CHRISTMAS	*EMI*	10	*10 Dec 94*	4
THAT'S CHRISTMAS [RI]	*EMI TV*	15	*16 Dec 95*	2
Re-released.				
THE CHRISTMAS ALBUM	*warner.esp/Global TV/Sony TV*	13	*12 Dec 98*	4

COMPILATIONS

From 18 Aug 73, the BPI had requested that TV advertised Compilations were to be removed from the main Full Price chart and placed in the Mid-Price chart. As such, entries in the latter are not listed. They did not appear in the main chart again until 1 Nov 75.

A&M

COMPILATION ALBUMS:	HITS 4			WEEKS 31
SLAMMIN'	*A&M*	1	*29 Sep 90*	6
RAGE - MAKE SOME NOISE VOLUME 1	*A&M*	12	*20 Apr 91*	3
WINGS OF LOVE	*A&M*	1	*29 Jun 91*	21
THE HACIENDA COLLECTION - PLAY BY 01/96	*A&M*	18	*4 Nov 95*	1

Abstract

ALBUMS:	HITS 1			WEEKS 8
PUNK AND DISORDERLY	*Abstract*	48	*27 Mar 82*	8

Ace Of Hearts

ALBUMS:	HITS 1			WEEKS 1
OUT CAME THE BLUES	*Ace Of Hearts*	19	*16 May 64*	1

Acid Jazz

COMPILATION ALBUMS:	HITS 1			WEEKS 1
BEST OF ACID JAZZ VOLUME 2	*Acid Jazz*	16	*29 May 93*	1

Alternative Tentacles

COMPILATION ALBUMS:	HITS 1			WEEKS 1
VIRUS 100 - ALTERNATIVE TENTACLES	*Alternative Tentacles*	15	*9 May 92*	1

Anagram

ALBUMS:	HITS 1			WEEKS 2
PUNK AND DISORDERLY (FURTHER CHARGES)	*Anagram*	91	*4 Sep 82*	2

Arcade

ALBUMS:	HITS 8			WEEKS 85
20 FANTASTIC HITS	*Arcade*	1	*29 Jul 72*	24
20 FANTASTIC HITS VOLUME 2	*Arcade*	2	*25 Nov 72*	14
40 FANTASTIC HITS FROM THE 50'S AND 60'S	*Arcade*	2	*7 Apr 73*	15
20 FANTASTIC HITS VOLUME 3	*Arcade*	3	*26 May 73*	8
DISCO HITS '75	*Arcade*	5	*15 Nov 75*	11
ROCK ON	*Arcade*	16	*26 Mar 77*	10
RULE BRITANNIA	*Arcade*	56	*2 Jul 77*	1
FIRST LOVE	*Arcade*	58	*23 Feb 80*	2
COMPILATION ALBUMS:	**HITS 14**			**WEEKS 73**
POP CLASSICS - 28 CLASSIC TRACKS	*Arcade*	19	*12 Jan 91*	2
SOFT METAL BALLADS	*Arcade*	5	*30 Mar 91*	10
IT STARTED WITH A KISS	*Arcade*	9	*8 Jun 91*	8
THE HEAT IS ON!	*Arcade*	4	*13 Jul 91*	9
DANCE CLASSICS VOLUME 2	*Arcade*	7	*31 Aug 91*	5
DANCE CLASSICS VOLUME 1	*Arcade*	8	*31 Aug 91*	4
GROOVY GHETTO	*Arcade*	1	*21 Sep 91*	6
GROOVY GHETTO - ALL THE RAGE	*Arcade*	15	*2 Nov 91*	2
GROOVY GHETTO 2	*Arcade*	8	*29 Feb 92*	4
THE ESSENTIAL CHILL	*Arcade*	16	*4 Apr 92*	2
ONE LOVE - THE VERY BEST OF REGGAE	*Arcade*	7	*18 Jul 92*	6
ROCK ROMANCE - 18 MOMENTS OF PURE LOVE	*Arcade*	9	*13 Feb 93*	5
WOW! - LET THE MUSIC LIFT YOU UP	*Arcade*	13	*7 May 94*	3
COMMITTED TO SOUL	*Arcade*	11	*13 Aug 94*	7

Ariola

ALBUMS:	HITS 1			WEEKS 5
BROTHERS IN RHYTHM	*Ariola*	35	*8 Oct 88*	5

Arista

ALBUMS:	HITS 1			WEEKS 1
MODS MAYDAY 79	*Arista*	75	*3 Nov 79*	1

Atlantic

ALBUMS:	HITS 9			WEEKS 107
SOLID GOLD SOUL	*Atlantic*	12	*2 Apr 66*	27
MIDNIGHT SOUL	*Atlantic*	22	*5 Nov 66*	19
THIS IS SOUL	*Atlantic*	16	*14 Jun 69*	15
THE NEW AGE OF ATLANTIC	*Atlantic*	25	*25 Mar 72*	1
ATLANTIC BLACK GOLD	*Atlantic*	23	*22 Jun 74*	7
BY INVITATION ONLY	*Atlantic*	17	*3 Apr 76*	6
THIS IS SOUL	*Atlantic/Starblend*	78	*2 Feb 85*	7
ATLANTIC SOUL CLASSICS - 16 HITS	*Atlantic*	9	*6 Jun 87*	23
ATLANTIC SOUL BALLADS	*Atlantic*	84	*18 Jun 88*	2

Azuli

COMPILATION ALBUMS:	HITS 1			WEEKS 1
BLACKMARKET PRESENTS 2 STEP - THE BEST OF UNDERGROUND GARAGE	*Azuli*	17	*19 Feb 00*	1

Beechwood Music

COMPILATION ALBUMS:	HITS 14			WEEKS 23
THE BEST OF INDIE TOP 20	*Beechwood Music*	10	*11 May 91*	3
THIS IS . . . SWING	*Beechwood Music*	20	*9 Mar 96*	1
THIS IS . . . HOUSE	*Beechwood Music*	18	*13 Jul 96*	1
THIS IS . . . CLUB NATION	*Beechwood Music*	19	*12 Jul 97*	1
THIS IS . . . IBIZA	*Beechwood Music*	13	*11 Oct 97*	3
THIS IS . . . SPEED GARAGE	*Beechwood Music*	10	*31 Jan 98*	3
THIS IS . . . CLUB NATION 2	*Beechwood Music*	19	*21 Mar 98*	1
THIS IS . . . IBIZA 98	*Beechwood Music*	16	*26 Sep 98*	2
THIS IS . . . R&B	*Beechwood Music*	14	*30 Jan 99*	2
THIS IS . . . IBIZA 2000	*Beechwood Music*	17	*5 Jun 99*	1
THIS IS . . . TRANCE	*Beechwood Music*	19	*17 Jul 99*	1
THIS IS . . . TRANCELIFE	*Beechwood Music*	19	*5 Feb 00*	1
SLINKY - TECH-NIQUE	*Beechwood Music*	10	*19 Feb 00*	2
SLINKY FACTOR 3	*Beechwood Music*	20	*1 Jul 00*	1

Beggars Banquet

ALBUMS:	HITS 3			WEEKS 8
SLIP STREAM (BEST BRITISH JAZZ FUNK)	*Beggars Banquet*	72	*21 Nov 81*	3
SEX, SWEAT AND BLOOD	*Beggars Banquet*	88	*15 May 82*	1
THE BEST OF BRITISH JAZZ FUNK VOLUME TWO	*Beggars Banquet*	44	*11 Sep 82*	4

Beyond

COMPILATION ALBUMS:	HITS 1			WEEKS 1
AMBIENT DUB VOLUME 2 - EARTH JUICE	*Beyond*	20	*6 Mar 93*	1

Big Beat

ALBUMS:	HITS 1			WEEKS 3
ROCKABILLY PSYCHOS AND THE GARAGE DISEASE	*Big Beat*	88	*21 Jul 84*	3

BMG/Telstar TV

COMPILATION ALBUMS:	HITS 5			WEEKS 16
ULTIMATE SIXTIES COLLECTION	*BMG Commercial/Telstar*	19	*23 Dec 00*	1
LOVE UNLIMITED - THE SOULFUL SOUND OF LOVE	*BMG/Telstar TV*	9	*17 Feb 01*	2
THE ULTIMATE SOUL COLLECTION	*BMG Commercial/Telstar TV*	10	*24 Mar 01*	3
ESSENTIAL TRACKS	*BMG/Telstar TV*	15	*9 Jun 01*	2
FUNKY DIVAS - THE VERY BEST IN SOUL DANCE AND R&B	*BMG/Telstar TV*	5	*30 Jun 01*	8

BMG/Telstar TV/Sony Music TV

COMPILATION ALBUMS:	HITS 1			WEEKS 3
PURE HIP HOP - MIXED BY SHORTEE BLITZ	*BMG/Telstar TV/Sony Music TV*	9	*7 Jul 01*	3

Break Down

COMPILATION ALBUMS:	HITS 2			WEEKS 6
DRUM AND BASS SELECTION 2	*Break Down*	14	*17 Sep 94*	3
MAX POWER - MAX BASS	*Break Down*	13	*13 Jul 96*	3

Breakout

ALBUMS:	HITS 1			WEEKS 2
HOUSE HALLUCINATIONS (PUMP UP LONDON VOLUME 1)	*Breakout*	90	*3 Sep 88*	2

Business

COMPILATION ALBUMS:	HITS 1			WEEKS 1
LOVERS FOR LOVERS VOLUME 3	*Business*	18	*16 Jun 90*	1

Cactus

ALBUMS:	HITS 1			WEEKS 1
REGGAE CHARTBUSTERS 75	*Cactus*	53	*31 Jan 76*	1

Capitol

COMPILATION ALBUMS:	HITS 1			WEEKS 2
CAPITOL CLASSICS VOLUME 1	*Capitol*	16	*18 Feb 89*	2

Castle Communications

COMPILATION ALBUMS:	HITS 7			WEEKS 41
THE ULTIMATE 60'S COLLECTION	*Castle Communications*	4	*7 Jul 90*	11
THE ULTIMATE BLUES COLLECTION	*Castle Communications*	14	*12 Jan 91*	6
JAZZ ON A SUMMER'S DAY	*Castle Classics*	4	*8 Aug 92*	8
BLOCKBUSTER! - THE SENSATIONAL 70'S	*Castle Communications*	6	*10 Oct 92*	6
ONE ORIGINAL STEP BEYOND - STORY . . .	*Castle Communications*	7	*5 Jun 93*	5
MONSTER HITS OF DANCE	*Castle Communications*	13	*3 Jul 93*	3
GOING UNDERGROUND	*Castle Communications*	18	*30 Oct 93*	2

CBS

ALBUMS:	HITS 15			WEEKS 258
THRILL TO THE SENSATIONAL SOUNDS OF SUPER STEREO	*CBS*	20	*20 May 67*	30
ROCK MACHINE I LOVE YOU	*CBS*	15	*28 Jun 69*	5
THE ROCK MACHINE TURNS YOU ON	*CBS*	18	*28 Jun 69*	7
THE MUSIC PEOPLE	*CBS*	10	*20 May 72*	9
SATIN CITY	*CBS*	10	*21 Oct 78*	11
THIS IS IT	*CBS*	6	*2 Jun 79*	12
FIRST LADIES OF COUNTRY	*CBS*	37	*19 Apr 80*	6
KILLER WATTS	*CBS*	27	*21 Jun 80*	6
BITTER SUITE	*CBS*	55	*4 Apr 81*	3
REFLECTIONS	*CBS*	4	*16 Oct 82*	92
IMAGINATIONS	*CBS*	15	*22 Oct 83*	21
CLUB CLASSICS VOLUME 2	*CBS*	90	*20 Apr 85*	2
MOVE CLOSER	*CBS*	4	*14 Mar 87*	19
THE HOLIDAY ALBUM	*CBS*	13	*27 Jun 87*	9
NITE FLITE	*CBS*	1	*30 Apr 88*	26

COMPILATION ALBUMS:	HITS 4			WEEKS 75
CHEEK TO CHEEK	*CBS*	2	*4 Mar 89*	32
NITE FLITE 2	*CBS*	1	*13 May 89*	26
LAMBADA	*CBS*	15	*30 Dec 89*	6
NITE FLITE 3 - BEING WITH YOU	*CBS*	3	*9 Jun 90*	11

Champagne

ALBUMS:	HITS 1			WEEKS 5
RE-MIXTURE	*Champagne*	32	*4 Apr 81*	5

Champion

ALBUMS:	HITS 3			WEEKS 6
ULTIMATE TRAX - VOLUME 1	*Champion*	66	*8 Nov 86*	2
ULTIMATE TRAX - VOLUME 2 - BATTLE OF THE D.J.'S	*Champion*	50	*7 Mar 87*	2
ULTIMATE TRAX 3 - BATTLE OF THE DJ'S	*Champion*	69	*18 Jul 87*	2

Charm

COMPILATION ALBUMS:	HITS 8			WEEKS 16
PURE LOVERS VOLUME 1	*Charm*	14	*21 Apr 90*	4
PURE LOVERS VOLUME 2	*Charm*	12	*22 Sep 90*	3
PURE LOVERS VOLUME 3	*Charm*	16	*6 Apr 91*	2
PURE LOVERS VOLUME 4	*Charm*	19	*2 Nov 91*	1
JUST RAGGA	*Charm*	17	*25 Jul 92*	1
PURE LOVERS VOLUME 5	*Charm*	13	*29 Aug 92*	3
JUST RAGGA VOLUME III	*Charm*	19	*27 Feb 93*	1
PURE LOVERS VOLUME 6	*Charm*	17	*1 May 93*	1

Chrysalis

COMPILATION ALBUMS:	HITS 1			WEEKS 3
RED, HOT AND BLUE	*Chrysalis*	6	*3 Nov 90*	3

Benefit album with proceeds to AIDS research. Tracks recorded are also a tribute to Carl Porter.

Club

ALBUMS:	HITS 1			WEEKS 2
COME WITH CLUB (CLUB TRACKS VOLUME 2)	*Club*	55	*3 Sep 83*	2

Columbia

COMPILATION ALBUMS:	HITS 52			WEEKS 344
THINKING OF YOU . . .	*Columbia*	1	*2 Feb 91*	23
THE FISH AND THE TREE AND THE BIRD AND THE BELL	*Columbia*	9	*2 Feb 91*	3
EVERYBODY DANCE NOW	*Columbia*	12	*30 Mar 91*	3
FREE SPIRIT - 17 CLASSIC ROCK BALLADS	*Columbia*	4	*20 Apr 91*	23
YOU'RE THE INSPIRATION - 16 ROMATIC LOVE SONGS	*Columbia*	10	*20 Apr 91*	5
SIMPLY. LOVE	*Columbia*	3	*10 Aug 91*	10
THE SOUND OF THE SUBURBS	*Columbia*	1	*17 Aug 91*	25
THE SOUND OF THE CITY	*Columbia*	11	*29 Feb 92*	5
HARD FAX	*Columbia*	3	*27 Jun 92*	6

THE BOYS ARE BACK IN TOWN	*Columbia*	11	*4 Jul 92*	6
SOMETHING IN THE AIR	*Columbia*	10	*3 Oct 92*	5
THE ULTIMATE COUNTRY COLLECTION	*Columbia*	1	*31 Oct 92*	23
HARD FAX 2 - TWICE THE VICE!	*Columbia*	6	*21 Nov 92*	2
ORIGINALS	*Columbia*	1	*29 May 93*	23
AFTER DARK	*Columbia*	8	*21 Aug 93*	4
TRUE LOVE WAYS	*Columbia*	14	*15 Jan 94*	2
SECRET LOVERS	*Columbia*	8	*12 Feb 94*	4
ORIGINALS 2	*Columbia*	4	*19 Mar 94*	10
SOUL SEARCHING	*Columbia*	6	*23 Jul 94*	5
MUNDO LATINO	*Columbia*	3	*1 Jul 95*	5
PURE ATTRACTION	*Columbia*	5	*8 Jul 95*	3
RAP FLAVAS	*Columbia*	6	*15 Jun 96*	3
TAKE A BREAK	*Columbia*	10	*2 Nov 96*	2
WHAT A FEELING!	*Columbia*	4	*17 May 97*	12
BOYS	*Columbia*	15	*31 May 97*	2
IT'S A SIXTIES PARTY	*Columbia*	12	*18 Oct 97*	3
OH! WHAT A NIGHT	*Columbia*	4	*21 Mar 98*	9
PERFECT DAY	*Columbia*	7	*28 Mar 98*	6
ALLEZ! OLA! OLE!	*Columbia*	8	*27 Jun 98*	3
SUMMER DANCE '98	*Columbia*	12	*25 Jul 98*	3
ANOTHER PERFECT DAY	*Columbia*	13	*8 Aug 98*	2
THIS IS NOIZE	*Columbia*	17	*27 Feb 99*	1
ESPECIALLY FOR YOU	*Columbia*	1	*20 Mar 99*	2
THE NEW SOUL ALBUM	*Columbia*	9	*8 May 99*	4
MUSIC TO WATCH GIRLS BY	*Columbia*	2	*5 Jun 99*	27
VIVA! LATINO	*Columbia*	11	*4 Sep 99*	4
MORE MUSIC TO WATCH GIRLS BY	*Columbia*	10	*20 Nov 99*	4
FOR YOU . . . 20 SONGS ESPECIALLY FOR YOU	*Columbia*	4	*8 Apr 00*	4
CIGARETTES AND ALCOHOL - 40 MODERN ANTHEMS	*Columbia*	7	*24 Jun 00*	10
IBIZA: THE STORY SO FAR . . . MIXED BY MATT CASSAR	*Columbia*	17	*1 Jul 00*	1
SUMMER BREEZE	*Columbia*	14	*29 Jul 00*	1
CAFE MAMBO - THE REAL SOUND OF IBIZA	*Columbia*	19	*29 Jul 00*	1
R&B MASTERS	*Columbia*	4	*20 Jan 01*	5
CORROSION	*Columbia*	17	*3 Mar 01*	1
MUSIC TO WATCH GIRLS BY - VOLUME 3	*Columbia*	20	*5 May 01*	1
First Entered Top 50 on 9 Dec 00 peaking at No. 21				
LET THE MUSIC PLAY - 80S GROOVE	*Columbia*	18	*9 Jun 01*	1
INDEPENDENT WOMAN	*Columbia*	7	*7 Jul 01*	5
R&B MASTERS 2	*Columbia*	12	*14 Jul 01*	2
THE CLASSIC CHILLOUT ALBUM - A COLLECTION OF CLASSICS FOR A MODERN WORLD	*Columbia*	1	*11 Aug 01*	18
CIGARETTES AND ALCOHOL VOLUME II - 40 MODERN ANTHEMS	*Columbia*	10	*15 Sep 01*	5
SCHOOL DISCO.COM - THE BEST DAYS OF YOUR LIFE	*Columbia*	9	*3 Nov 01*	3
40 Rock Pop Disco Anthems. School Disco.com is a retro club.				
THE CLASSIC CHILLOUT ALBUM 2 - ANOTHER COLLECTION OF CLASSICS FOR A MODERN WORLD	*Columbia*	13	*8 Dec 01*	4

Concept

COMPILATION ALBUMS:	HITS 1			WEEKS 7
RAP ATTACK	*Concept*	9	*12 Mar 94*	7

Concrete

COMPILATION ALBUMS:	HITS 1			WEEKS 1
BRIT HOP AND AMYL HOUSE	*Concrete*	16	*10 Feb 96*	1

Conifer Classics

COMPILATION ALBUMS:	HITS 1			WEEKS 1
ONLY CLASSICAL ALBUM YOU'LL EVER NEED	*Conifer Classics*	17	*21 Nov 98*	1

Cookie Jar

COMPILATION ALBUMS:	HITS 10			WEEKS 66
STEAMIN! - HARDCORE '92	*Cookie Jar*	3	*14 Dec 91*	8
TECHNOSTATE - 20 SERIOUS TECHNO AND GARAGE RAVES	*Cookie Jar*	2	*21 Mar 92*	9
THE RAVE GENER8TOR	*Cookie Jar*	1	*23 May 92*	8
THE RAVE GENER8TOR 2	*Cookie Jar*	2	*5 Sep 92*	7
RAVE 92	*Cookie Jar*	3	*28 Nov 92*	11
UNDERGROUND VOLUME 1	*Cookie Jar*	6	*27 Mar 93*	5
JAMMIN'	*Cookie Jar*	7	*7 Aug 93*	5
FULL ON DANCE	*Cookie Jar*	12	*11 Sep 93*	2
SOUL BEAT	*Cookie Jar*	8	*6 Nov 93*	2
FULL ON DANCE '93	*Cookie Jar*	3	*27 Nov 93*	9

Cooltempo

ALBUMS:	HITS 1			WEEKS 6
FIERCE	*Cooltempo*	37	*1 Aug 87*	6
COMPILATION ALBUMS:	**HITS 1**			**WEEKS 2**
THIS IS GARAGE	*Cooltempo*	18	*1 Jul 89*	2

Cowboy

COMPILATION ALBUMS:	HITS 1			WEEKS 1
COWBOY COMPILATION - THE ALBUM VOLUME 1	*Cowboy*	18	*8 May 93*	1

Creole

ALBUMS:	HITS 1			WEEKS 6
20 HOLIDAY HITS	*Creole*	48	*24 Aug 85*	6

Dance Pool

COMPILATION ALBUMS:	HITS 1			WEEKS 2
IBIZA: THE CLOSING PARTY	*Dance Pool*	19	*25 Sep 99*	2

Debut

COMPILATION ALBUMS:	HITS 1			WEEKS 1
JUNGLE TEKNO VOLUME 1	*Debut*	18	*27 Jun 92*	1

Decca

ALBUMS:	HITS 1			WEEKS 17
FORMULA 30	*Decca*	6	*26 Nov 83*	17
COMPILATION ALBUMS:	**HITS 7**			**WEEKS 69**
THE ESSENTIAL MOZART	*Decca*	1	*1 Jun 91*	23
ESSENTIAL OPERA	*Decca*	2	*16 Nov 91*	28
ESSENTIAL BALLET	*Decca*	9	*26 Sep 92*	4
ESSENTIAL OPERA 2	*Decca*	17	*6 Nov 93*	2
THE GREATEST CLASSICAL STARS ON EARTH	*Decca*	13	*6 Jun 98*	4
CALM	*Decca*	14	*2 Sep 00*	2
CLASSICS 2002	*Decca*	2	*24 Nov 01*	6

Deconstruction

COMPILATION ALBUMS:	HITS 3			WEEKS 9
ITALIA - DANCE MUSIC FROM ITALY	*Deconstruction*	4	*14 Oct 89*	6
FULL ON - A YEAR IN THE LIFE OF HOUSE	*Deconstruction*	18	*27 Feb 93*	2
DECONSTRUCTION CLASSICS - A HISTORY OF DANCE MUSIC	*Deconstruction*	17	*26 Aug 95*	1

Def Jam

ALBUMS:	HITS 1			WEEKS 7
KICK IT - THE DEF JAM SAMPLER VOLUME 1	*Def Jam*	19	*8 Aug 87*	7
COMPILATION ALBUMS:	**HITS 1**			**WEEKS 5**
WESTWOOD	*Def Jam UK*	7	*7 Apr 01*	5

Deram/Oi

ALBUMS:	HITS 1			WEEKS 5
STRENGTH THROUGH OI!	*Deram*	51	*30 May 81*	5

Deutsche Grammophon

COMPILATION ALBUMS:	HITS 2			WEEKS 14
ESSENTIAL CLASSICS	*Deutsche Grammophon*	6	*13 Oct 90*	9
LIVING CLASSICS	*Deutsche Grammophon*	7	*28 Mar 92*	5

Dino

COMPILATION ALBUMS:	HITS 70			WEEKS 518
LEATHER AND LACE. THE MEN AND WOMEN OF ROCK	*Dino*	3	*23 Jun 90*	8
THE SUMMER OF LOVE	*Dino*	9	*11 Aug 90*	9
LEATHER AND LACE - THE SECOND CHAPTER	*Dino*	14	*10 Nov 90*	4
ROCK 'N' ROLL LOVE SONGS	*Dino*	4	*24 Nov 90*	29
BACHARACH AND DAVID - THEY WRITE THE SONGS	*Dino*	16	*29 Dec 90*	3
THE TRACKS OF MY TEARS - THE BEST OF SMOKEY ROBINSON: WRITER AND PERFORMER	*Dino*	6	*9 Feb 91*	8
HARDCORE UPROAR	*Dino*	2	*30 Mar 91*	9
LOVE SUPREME	*Dino*	4	*1 Jun 91*	5
THE RHYTHM DIVINE	*Dino*	1	*15 Jun 91*	15
HARDCOAR DANCEFLOOR	*Dino*	2	*13 Jul 91*	10
L.A. FREEWAY	*Dino*	6	*3 Aug 91*	7
WE WILL ROCK YOU	*Dino*	3	*12 Oct 91*	6
HARDCORE ECSTASY	*Dino*	1	*2 Nov 91*	16
RHYTHM DIVINE 2	*Dino*	6	*2 Nov 91*	5
MORE ROCK 'N' ROLL LOVE SONGS	*Dino*	6	*23 Nov 91*	23
PARTY MIX	*Dino*	8	*7 Dec 91*	9
ESSENTIAL HARDCORE	*Dino*	1	*28 Dec 91*	10
HEAVENLY HARDCORE	*Dino*	2	*14 Mar 92*	9
BREAKING HEARTS	*Dino*	3	*28 Mar 92*	10
COLD SWEAT	*Dino*	2	*18 Apr 92*	7
HEARTLANDS	*Dino*	4	*2 May 92*	11
LET'S TALK ABOUT LOVE	*Dino*	3	*20 Jun 92*	4
PRECIOUS	*Dino*	11	*11 Jul 92*	2
MIDNIGHT CRUISING	*Dino*	10	*18 Jul 92*	6
UNDER SPANISH SKIES	*Dino*	5	*1 Aug 92*	7

THE ORIGINALS!	*Dino*	8	*22 Aug 92*	6
TRANCE DANCE	*Dino*	7	*29 Aug 92*	5
SIXTIES BEAT	*Dino*	1	*19 Sep 92*	13
THE GREATEST VOICES	*Dino*	5	*24 Oct 92*	6
SWING HITS	*Dino*	19	*14 Nov 92*	1
ROCK 'N' ROLL IS HERE TO STAY	*Dino*	16	*28 Nov 92*	2
STOMPIN' PARTY	*Dino*	10	*5 Dec 92*	7
MEMORIES . . . ARE MADE OF THIS	*Dino*	8	*12 Dec 92*	12
BLUES BROTHER SOUL SISTER	*Dino*	1	*13 Feb 93*	38
ROCK 'N' ROLL IS HERE TO STAY [RE]	*Dino*	14	*3 Jul 93*	3
HEART FULL OF SOUL	*Dino*	9	*10 Jul 93*	8
BLUES BROTHER SOUL SISTER VOLUME 2	*Dino*	8	*17 Jul 93*	8
RAVE GENERATION	*Dino*	2	*18 Sep 93*	7
MORE THAN UNPLUGGED	*Dino*	11	*25 Sep 93*	3
PLANET ROCK	*Dino*	8	*16 Oct 93*	2
FUTURESHOCK - 20 FURIOUS DANCE TUNES	*Dino*	4	*23 Oct 93*	4
COUNTRY WOMEN	*Dino*	11	*23 Oct 93*	3
AS TIME GOES BY	*Dino*	14	*27 Nov 93*	5
KEEP ON DANCING	*Dino*	14	*4 Dec 93*	6
LOVE IN THE SIXTIES	*Dino*	11	*25 Dec 93*	9
RAVE GENERATION 2	*Dino*	5	*29 Jan 94*	3
SOUL MATE	*Dino*	6	*19 Feb 94*	3
IT'S ELECTRIC	*Dino*	2	*9 Apr 94*	12
BLUES BROTHER SOUL SISTER VOLUME 3	*Dino*	5	*7 May 94*	12
WONDERFUL WORLD	*Dino*	8	*4 Jun 94*	6
THE BEST OF ROCK 'N' ROLL LOVE SONGS	*Dino*	9	*23 Jul 94*	5
START - THE BEST OF BRITISH	*Dino*	13	*30 Jul 94*	3
DANCE MASSIVE	*Dino*	3	*3 Sep 94*	8
WHEN A MAN LOVES A WOMAN	*Dino*	7	*17 Sep 94*	6
ROCK ANTHEMS	*Dino*	3	*10 Dec 94*	17
DANCE MASSIVE 2	*Dino*	8	*17 Dec 94*	6
THE ULTIMATE JUNGLE COLLECTION	*Dino*	17	*7 Jan 95*	2
SKA MANIA	*Dino*	4	*27 May 95*	5
DANCE MASSIVE '95	*Dino*	2	*10 Jun 95*	5
REGGAE MASSIVE	*Dino*	19	*24 Jun 95*	1
RAVE ANTHEMS	*Dino*	7	*15 Jul 95*	5
THE AMERICAN DINER	*Dino*	7	*19 Aug 95*	5
THE GREATEST DANCE ALBUM OF ALL TIME	*Dino*	7	*21 Oct 95*	4
SPIRITUALLY IBIZA	*Dino*	17	*28 Oct 95*	1
VERY BEST OF BLUES BROTHER SOUL SISTER	*Dino*	11	*25 Nov 95*	7
THE GREATEST SOUL ALBUM OF ALL TIME	*Dino*	16	*9 Dec 95*	4
EIGHTIES SOUL WEEKENDER	*Dino*	7	*30 Mar 96*	7
ROCK ANTHEMS - VOLUME 2	*Dino*	10	*11 May 96*	4
PURE JAZZ MOODS - COOL JAZZ FOR A SUMMERS DAY	*Dino*	9	*22 Jun 96*	3
THE VERY BEST OF CAJUN - 40 HOT CAJUN CLASSICS	*Dino*	16	*7 Sep 96*	3
THE VERY BEST OF BRASS	*Dino*	18	*17 May 97*	1

Disco Diamond

ALBUMS:	HITS 1			WEEKS 1
SOLID SOUL SENSATIONS	*Disco Diamond*	30	*15 Mar 75*	1

DJ International

ALBUMS:	HITS 4			WEEKS 26
THE "HOUSE" SOUND OF CHICAGO	*DJ International*	52	*20 Sep 86*	12
THE "HOUSE" SOUND OF CHICAGO - VOL II	*Trax*	38	*18 Apr 87*	7

Label shows as Trax, though this was one of DJ International's releases.

JACKMASTER VOLUME 1	*DJ International*	36	*31 Oct 87*	4
JACKMASTER VOLUME 2	*DJ International*	38	*13 Feb 88*	3

DMC

COMPILATION ALBUMS:	HITS 2			WEEKS 2
GROOVE ARMADA - BACK TO MINE	*DMC*	16	*18 Mar 00*	1
BACK TO MINE - FAITHLESS	*DMC*	19	*28 Oct 00*	1

Dover

COMPILATION ALBUMS:	HITS 7			WEEKS 58
AND ALL BECAUSE THE LADY LOVES . . .	*Dover*	2	*4 Mar 89*	10

Issued in conjuction with Cadbury's Milk Tray chocolate.

ALL BY MYSELF	*Dover*	2	*10 Feb 90*	15
A TON OF HITS - THE BEST OF STOCK AITKEN WATERMAN	*Dover*	7	*24 Nov 90*	8
RED HOT METAL - 18 ROCK CLASSICS	*Dover*	4	*20 Apr 91*	6
ALL BY MYSELF VOLUME 2	*Dover*	13	*8 Jun 91*	5
MOMENTS IN SOUL	*Dover*	2	*14 Sep 91*	7
THE GREATEST MOMENTS IN SOUL	*Dover*	4	*16 May 92*	7

Dreamscape

COMPILATION ALBUMS:	HITS 1			WEEKS 1
RADIO DREAMSCAPE - VOLUME 1	*Dreamscape*	20	*17 Jun 95*	1

Earth

COMPILATION ALBUMS:	HITS 1			WEEKS 1
LTJ BUKEM PRESENTS EARTH - VOLUME ONE	*Earth*	19	*16 Nov 96*	1

East West

COMPILATION ALBUMS:	HITS 2			WEEKS 3
I'M YOUR FAN - THE SONGS OF LEONARD COHEN	*East West*	16	*12 Oct 91*	2
DISCO INFERNO	*East West*	17	*26 Jun 93*	1

Elevate

COMPILATION ALBUMS:	HITS 3			WEEKS 8
RAVE 2 - STRICTLY HARDCORE!	*Elevate*	11	*11 Apr 92*	3
RAVING MAD	*Elevate*	17	*8 Aug 92*	2
THE WIND DOWN ZONE	*Elevate*	17	*27 Feb 93*	3

ELF

COMPILATION ALBUMS:	HITS 1			WEEKS 6
EARTHRISE - THE RAINFOREST ALBUM	*ELF*	1	*13 Jun 92*	6

EMI

ALBUMS:	HITS 12			WEEKS 133
IMPACT	*EMI*	15	*21 Jun 69*	14
PURE GOLD	*EMI*	1	*2 Jun 73*	11
DON'T WALK - BOOGIE	*EMI*	1	*18 Nov 78*	23
COUNTRY LIFE	*EMI*	2	*21 Apr 79*	14
KNUCKLE SANDWICH	*EMI International*	19	*2 Jun 79*	6
ALL ABOARD	*EMI*	13	*15 Dec 79*	8
METAL FOR MUTHAS	*EMI*	16	*23 Feb 80*	7
METAL FOR MUTHAS VOLUME 2	*EMI*	58	*14 Jun 80*	1
20 WITH A BULLET	*EMI*	11	*13 Mar 82*	8
THEN CAME ROCK 'N' ROLL	*EMI*	5	*26 May 84*	15
UNFORGETTABLE	*EMI*	5	*5 Mar 88*	21
HELLO CHILDREN . . . EVERYWHERE	*EMI*	59	*3 Dec 88*	5

COMPILATION ALBUMS:	HITS 46			WEEKS 246
UNFORGETTABLE	*EMI*	18	*28 Jan 89*	1
UNFORGETTABLE 2	*EMI*	1	*18 Mar 89*	15
IS THIS LOVE	*EMI*	2	*30 Sep 89*	10
THE 80'S - THE ALBUM OF THE DECADE	*EMI*	1	*18 Nov 89*	12
THE WILD ONE	*EMI*	8	*4 Aug 90*	7
MISSING YOU - AN ALBUM OF LOVE	*EMI*	1	*20 Oct 90*	18
TRULY UNFORGETTABLE	*EMI*	6	*17 Nov 90*	9
MISSING YOU 2 - AN ALBUM OF LOVE	*EMI*	2	*16 Feb 91*	11
SEXUAL HEALING	*EMI*	7	*26 Oct 91*	6
TENDER LOVE - 17 ROMANTIC LOVE SONGS	*EMI*	2	*22 Feb 92*	11
THE CLASSIC ROMANCE	*EMI*	5	*22 Feb 92*	7
MAXIMUM RAVE	*EMI*	2	*22 Aug 92*	9
WICKED!!	*EMI*	2	*17 Oct 92*	5
SMASHIE AND NICEY PRESENT LET'S ROCK!	*EMI*	8	*31 Oct 92*	4
FOREVER	*EMI*	17	*5 Dec 92*	2
SOUL MOODS	*EMI*	4	*20 Feb 93*	8
INNA DANCEHALL STYLE	*EMI*	11	*3 Jul 93*	4
BACK TO THE 70'S	*EMI*	8	*18 Sep 93*	6
LET'S GO DISCO	*EMI*	12	*6 Nov 93*	3
IT TAKES TWO - LOVE'S GREATEST DUETS	*EMI*	17	*27 Nov 93*	1
TRANQUILITY	*EMI*	14	*25 Jun 94*	5
CLUB TOGETHER *Joint label with EMI catalogue prefix.*	*React/EMI*	10	*8 Oct 94*	4
MISSING YOU	*EMI*	8	*29 Oct 94*	5
THE BEST COUNTRY ALBUM IN THE WORLD . . . EVER!	*EMI*	4	*26 Nov 94*	12
UNLACED	*EMI*	8	*11 Mar 95*	4
CLUB TOGETHER 2 *Joint label with EMI catalogue prefix.*	*React/EMI*	9	*29 Apr 95*	4
THE BEST CLASSICAL ALBUM IN THE WORLD . . . EVER!	*EMI*	6	*15 Jul 95*	6
MOST EXCELLENT DANCE	EDI	8	*22 Jul 95*	4
DEDICATED TO PLEASURE	*EMI*	18	*29 Jul 95*	3
TECHNO NIGHTS AMBIENT DAWN	*EMI*	16	*23 Sep 95*	3
THAT'S ROCK 'N' ROLL	*EMI*	12	*28 Oct 95*	2
THAT'S COUNTRY	*EMI*	11	*4 Nov 95*	6
THE GREATEST PARTY ALBUM UNDER THE SUN!	*EMI TV*	1	*11 Nov 95*	7
THE GREATEST DANCE ALBUM UNDER THE SUN!	*EMI TV*	8	*2 Mar 96*	4
THE BEST OF THE NINETIES . . . SO FAR	*EMI TV*	9	*9 Mar 96*	5
BABY LOVE	*EMI TV*	11	*16 Mar 96*	2
MIX'O'MATIC	*EMI TV*	8	*11 May 96*	3
LOST PROPERTY	*EMI TV*	12	*18 May 96*	2
COMMON GROUND	*EMI Premier*	17	*1 Jun 96*	2
CLUB TOGETHER 3	*EMI TV*	7	*8 Jun 96*	3
LOVERMAN	*EMI TV*	17	*15 Jun 96*	2
EASY MOODS	*EMI TV*	15	*9 Nov 96*	1

GREATEST NON-STOP PARTY UNDER THE SUN	*EMI TV*	13	*30 Nov 96*	4
THE DOG'S . . . .!	*EMI TV*	20	*28 Dec 96*	2
TWENTIETH CENTURY BLUES	*EMI*	14	*25 Apr 98*	1
A SONG FOR EUROTRASH	*EMI*	19	*16 May 98*	1

EMI/Virgin/Polygram

COMPILATION ALBUMS:	HITS 5			WEEKS 43
THE ULTIMATE RAVE	*EMI/Virgin/PolyGram*	1	*25 Jan 92*	15
THE MEGA RAVE	*EMI/Virgin/PolyGram*	2	*30 Jan 93*	8
MEGA DANCE - THE POWER ZONE	*EMI/Virgin/PolyGram*	2	*13 Mar 93*	8
LOADED	*EMI/Virgin/PolyGram*	6	*10 Apr 93*	6
MEGA DANCE 2 - THE ENERGY ZONE	*EMI/Virgin/PolyGram*	3	*17 Apr 93*	6

Epic

ALBUMS:	HITS 3			WEEKS 37
ELECTRO SHOCK VOLTAGE ONE	*Epic*	73	*3 Mar 84*	1
AMERICAN HEARTBEAT	*Epic*	4	*16 Jun 84*	22
HITS FOR LOVERS - 16 OF TODAY'S GREAT LOVE SONGS	*Epic*	2	*8 Mar 86*	14

COMPILATION ALBUMS:	HITS 6			WEEKS 60
JUST THE TWO OF US	*Epic*	1	*24 Mar 90*	37
MELLOW MADNESS	*Epic*	14	*9 Nov 91*	2
RED HOT + DANCE	*Epic*	6	*18 Jul 92*	5
Benefit album with proceeds to AIDS research. Consists of remixed dance tracks.				
ROMANCING THE SCREEN	*Epic*	5	*29 Aug 92*	11
MIX HEAVEN '97	*Epic*	19	*6 Sep 97*	1
DIVAS LIVE	*Epic*	3	*17 Oct 98*	4
Tracks by Maria Carey, Celine Dion, Aretha Franklin, Gloria Estefan and Shania Twain.				

Erato

COMPILATION ALBUMS:	HITS 1			WEEKS 5
THE ULTIMATE OPERA COLLECTION	*Erato*	14	*11 Jul 92*	5

Expansion

COMPILATION ALBUMS:	HITS 1			WEEKS 1
WINNER'S CIRCLE	*Expansion*	20	*24 Apr 93*	1

Fanfare/PWL

ALBUMS:	HITS 1			WEEKS 9
THE HIT FACTORY VOLUME 2	*Fanfare/PWL*	16	*12 Nov 88*	9

COMPILATION ALBUMS:	HITS 2			WEEKS 13
THE HIT FACTORY VOLUME 2	*Fanfare/PWL*	13	*14 Jan 89*	3
THE HIT FACTORY VOLUME 3	*Fanfare/PWL*	3	*15 Jul 89*	10

Fantazia

COMPILATION ALBUMS:	HITS 12			WEEKS 71
FANTAZIA - THE FIRST TASTE	*Fantazia*	13	*5 Dec 92*	5
FANTAZIA - TWICE AS NICE	*Fantazia*	17	*24 Jul 93*	3
FANTAZIA III - MADE IN HEAVEN	*Fantazia*	16	*25 Jun 94*	2
THE HOUSE COLLECTION - VOLUME 2	*Fantazia*	6	*29 Apr 95*	6
THE HOUSE COLLECTION - VOLUME 3	*Fantazia*	4	*30 Sep 95*	7
THE HOUSE COLLECTION - CLUB CLASSICS	*Fantazia*	3	*17 Feb 96*	10
FANTAZIA PRESENT THE HOUSE COLLECTION 4	*Fantazia*	2	*29 Jun 96*	9
THE HOUSE COLLECTION CLUB CLASSICS - 2	*Fantazia*	4	*14 Sep 96*	8
THE HOUSE COLLECTION - VOLUME 5	*Fantazia*	3	*8 Mar 97*	7
CLUB CLASSICS - VOLUME 3	*Fantazia*	4	*7 Jun 97*	6
THE HOUSE COLLECTION 6 - PAUL OKENFOLD/PAUL COSFORD	*Fantazia*	10	*27 Sep 97*	3
FANTAZIA - BRITISH ANTHEMS	*Fantazia*	2	*21 Feb 98*	5

Feverpitch

COMPILATION ALBUMS:	HITS 4			WEEKS 8
TRADE	*Feverpitch*	14	*16 Sep 95*	2
TRADE - VOLUME TWO	*Feverpitch*	11	*20 Apr 96*	3
TRADE - VOLUME THREE	*Feverpitch*	19	*9 Nov 96*	1
TRADE - VOLUME FOUR	*Feverpitch*	15	*12 Apr 97*	2

ffrr

ALBUMS:	HITS 3			WEEKS 13
THE HOUSE SOUND OF CHICAGO VOLUME 3	*ffrr*	40	*30 Jan 88*	4
THE HOUSE SOUND OF LONDON VOLUME 4	*ffrr*	70	*27 Aug 88*	7
BALEARIC BEATS VOLUME 1	*ffrr*	58	*1 Oct 88*	2

COMPILATION ALBUMS:	HITS 7			WEEKS 19
ESSENTIAL MIX - TONG COX SASHA OAKENFOLD	*ffrr*	12	*20 Jan 96*	3
LTJ BUKEM PRESENTS LOGICAL PROGRESSION	*ffrr*	14	*20 Apr 96*	1
ESSENTIAL MIX 2 - TONG, MACKINTOSH . . .	*ffrr*	6	*11 May 96*	3
METALHEADZ - PLATINUM BREAKZ	*ffrr*	12	*10 Aug 96*	2
ESSENTIAL MIX 3 - TONG, SEAMAN, JULES ETC	*ffrr*	12	*7 Sep 96*	3

CARL COX - NON STOP 98/01	*ffrr*	8	*8 Aug 98*	5
CARL COX - NON STOP 2000	*ffrr*	13	*30 Oct 99*	2

Firm

COMPILATION ALBUMS:	HITS 1			WEEKS 4
WORLD DANCE - THE DRUM + BASS EXPERIENCE	*Firm*	10	*11 Jan 97*	4

Four Beat

COMPILATION ALBUMS:	HITS 4			WEEKS 7
UNITED DANCE - VOLUME 3	*Fourbeat*	11	*20 Jan 96*	2
UNITED DANCE - VOLUME FOUR	*4 Beat*	17	*25 May 96*	1
UNITED DANCE - VOLUME 5	*4 Beat*	20	*9 Nov 96*	1
UNITED DANCE - VOLUME 6	*Fourbeat*	10	*26 Apr 97*	3

4AD

ALBUMS:	HITS 1			WEEKS 2
LONELY IS AN EYESORE	*4AD*	53	*11 Jul 87*	2

Fourth & Broadway

COMPILATION ALBUMS:	HITS 2			WEEKS 6
THE REBIRTH OF COOL, TOO	*Fourth & Broadway*	13	*7 Mar 92*	2
THE REBIRTH OF COOL III	*Fourth & Broadway*	9	*15 May 93*	4

Freestyle

COMPILATION ALBUMS:	HITS 1			WEEKS 3
BROTHER'S GONNA WORK IT OUT	*Freestyle*	7	*3 Oct 98*	3
Remix album by the Chenical Brothers, includes 1 disc of their own material.				

Fresh

COMPILATION ALBUMS:	HITS 1			WEEKS 1
FRESHEN UP VOLUME 1	*Fresh*	20	*3 Jun 95*	1

Global Television

COMPILATION ALBUMS:	HITS 84			WEEKS 380
SOUNDS OF THE SEVENTIES	*Global Television*	11	*17 Dec 94*	5
HITS, HITS AND MORE DANCE HITS	*Global Television*	13	*17 Dec 94*	4
SOFT REGGAE	*Global Television*	2	*21 Jan 95*	7
NEW SOUL REBELS	*Global Television*	6	*18 Feb 95*	6
ON A DANCE TIP	*Global Television*	1	*25 Feb 95*	9
GIRLS AND GUITARS	*Global Television*	8	*4 Mar 95*	4
FIFTY NUMBER ONES OF THE '60S	*Global Television*	8	*15 Apr 95*	4
CLUB CLASS	*Global Television*	4	*22 Apr 95*	5
INTO THE EIGHTIES	*Global Television*	5	*22 Apr 95*	5
ON A DANCE TIP 2	*Global Television*	1	*20 May 95*	7
DANCE BUZZ	*Global Television*	3	*17 Jun 95*	4
CHARTBUSTERS	*Global Television*	2	*1 Jul 95*	6
GREAT SEX	*Global Television*	13	*1 Jul 95*	2
THEMES AND DREAMS	*Global Television*	11	*15 Jul 95*	2
NATURAL WOMAN	*Global Television*	7	*29 Jul 95*	8
SUMMER DANCE PARTY	*Global Television*	2	*12 Aug 95*	5
HITZ BLITZ	*Global Television*	2	*26 Aug 95*	5
DANCE TIP 3	*Global Television*	2	*23 Sep 95*	6
DRIVING ROCK	*Global Television*	9	*30 Sep 95*	6
NIGHTFEVER	*Global Television*	7	*28 Oct 95*	5
DANCE TIP '95	*Global Television*	3	*18 Nov 95*	12
VYBIN' - YOUNG SOUL REBELS	*Global Television*	9	*17 Feb 96*	4
COUNTRY GOLD	*Global Television*	12	*6 Apr 96*	3
UNTITLED	*Global Television*	6	*27 Apr 96*	4
VYBIN' 3 - NEW SOUL REBELS	*Global Television*	2	*4 May 96*	5
DANCE MIX UK	*Global Television*	6	*11 May 96*	4
NATURAL WOMAN - VOLUME 2	*Global Television*	10	*25 May 96*	3
THE BEST OF ACID JAZZ	*Global Television*	5	*15 Jun 96*	5
NO GREATER LOVE	*Global Television*	4	*13 Jul 96*	6
SHADES OF SOUL	*Global Television*	15	*20 Jul 96*	1
VYBIN' 4	*Global Television*	7	*27 Jul 96*	5
UNTITLED 2	*Global Television*	6	*3 Aug 96*	6
THE ULTIMATE LINE DANCING ALBUM	*Global Television*	9	*17 Aug 96*	6
DANCE MIX UK 2	*Global Television*	10	*14 Sep 96*	4
UNTITLED 3	*Global Television*	20	*16 Nov 96*	1
THE ULTIMATE PARTY ANIMAL	*Global Television*	4	*30 Nov 96*	10
THE ULTIMATE LINE DANCING ALBUM	*Global Television*	7	*8 Feb 97*	8
This Album is different from previous chart entry.				
BEST OF ACID JAZZ - VOLUME 2	*Global TV / PolyGram TV*	13	*15 Feb 97*	4
GIRL POWER	*Global Television*	9	*15 Mar 97*	5
THE OLD SKOOL	*PolyGram TV / Global TV*	6	*5 Apr 97*	7
KLUBHOPPIN'	*Global Television*	6	*19 Apr 97*	4
CHARTBUSTERS	*Global Television*	4	*24 May 97*	6
This Album is different from previous chart entry.				
MODROPHENIA	*Global Television*	14	*31 May 97*	3

THE ULTIMATE SUMMER PARTY ANIMAL	*Global Television*	2	*28 Jun 97*	8
THE OLD SKOOL REUNION	*PolyGram TV / Global TV*	12	*26 Jul 97*	2
DRIVE ON	*Global Television*	10	*30 Aug 97*	3
THE BEST DANCE ALBUM OF THE YEAR	*Global Television*	6	*6 Sep 97*	5
PURE REGGAE	*Global Television*	12	*20 Sep 97*	3
SPEED GARAGE ANTHEMS	*Global Television*	5	*18 Oct 97*	4
FUNKY DIVAS	*Global Television*	3	*27 Dec 97*	13
THE EIGHTIES MIX	*Global TV / PolyGram TV*	1	*17 Jan 98*	7
SHADES OF SOUL	*Global Television*	9	*17 Jan 98*	3
This Album is different from previous chart entry.				
ONE WORLD	*Global Television*	8	*31 Jan 98*	3
DROP DEAD GORGEOUS	*Global Television*	4	*21 Feb 98*	7
SPEED GARAGE ANTHEMS - VOLUME 2	*Global Television*	5	*21 Feb 98*	8
CLUB CULTURE EXPOSED!!	*Global Television*	5	*4 Apr 98*	4
URBAN RHYMES	*Global TV / PolyGram TV*	5	*18 Apr 98*	5
THE BEST DANCE ALBUM OF THE YEAR	*Global Television*	13	*23 May 98*	3
This Album is different from previous chart entry.				
DROP DEAD GORGEOUS 2	*Global Television*	10	*30 May 98*	3
SPEED GARAGE ANTHEMS IN IBIZA	*Global Television*	7	*1 Aug 98*	4
FUNKY DIVAS 2	*Global Television*	16	*5 Dec 98*	8
THE GREATEST ROCK 'N' ROLL LOVE SONGS	*Global Television*	6	*13 Feb 99*	4
DISCO HOUSE	*Global Television*	7	*6 Mar 99*	2
THE VERY BEST OF LATIN JAZZ - 2	*Global Television*	15	*15 May 99*	3
FAT DANCE HITS	*Global Television*	5	*12 Jun 99*	5
MIDSUMMER CLASSICS	*Global Television*	20	*26 Jun 99*	2
UNDER LATIN SKIES	*Global Television*	14	*17 Jul 99*	2
IBIZA 99 - THE YEAR OF TRANCE	*Global Television*	2	*24 Jul 99*	5
SALSA FEVER!	*Global Television*	12	*31 Jul 99*	4
IBIZA DEL MAR	*Global Television*	11	*28 Aug 99*	2
SPEED GARAGE ANTHEMS 99	*Global Television*	13	*11 Sep 99*	3
FAT POP HITS	*Global Television*	6	*2 Oct 99*	5
IBIZA 99 - THE YEAR OF TRANCE - VOLUME TWO	*Global Television*	11	*9 Oct 99*	2
ROCK THE WORLD	*Global Television*	9	*9 Oct 99*	4
AYIA NAPA - CLUBBERS PARADISE	*Global Television*	14	*23 Oct 99*	2
FUNK SOUL BROTHER - THE BEST OF DANCE SOUL & SWING	*Global Television*	19	*20 Nov 99*	1
THE BIGGEST CLUB ALBUM OF THE YEAR	*Global Television*	20	*20 Nov 99*	1
DISCO FEVER	*Global Television*	19	*8 Jan 00*	1
FUNKY DIVAS 3	*Global Television*	18	*15 Jan 00*	3
SOUNDTRACK TO THE WEEKEND	*Global Television*	8	*13 May 00*	4
CRUISIN' - THE BEST OF DRIVETIME	*Global Television*	5	*3 Jun 00*	3
ALL YOU NEED IS . . . LOVE	*Global Television*	18	*17 Jun 00*	1
HEADRUSH	*Global Television*	10	*8 Jul 00*	5
CD1 (Trance) mixed by Hyperlogic; CD2 (Hard House) mixed by the Tidy Boys.				
TRASHED IN IBIZA	*Global Television*	16	*29 Jul 00*	2

Global Underground

COMPILATION ALBUMS:	HITS 8			WEEKS 11
JOHN DIGWEED SYDNEY	*Global Underground*	16	*25 Apr 98*	1
PAUL OAKENFOLD - NEW YORK	*Global Underground*	12	*6 Jun 98*	3
SASHA - SAN FRANCISCO	*Global Underground*	18	*21 Nov 98*	1
DANNY TENAGLIA LIVE IN ATHENS	*Global Underground*	16	*27 Feb 99*	1
NICK WARREN - BUDAPEST	*Global Underground*	20	*19 Jun 99*	1
SASHA - IBIZA	*Global Underground*	12	*2 Oct 99*	2
DARREN EMERSON - URUGUAY	*Global Underground*	20	*27 May 00*	1
019 JOHN DIGWEED - LOS ANGELES	*Global Underground*	14	*10 Mar 01*	1

Go! Discs

COMPILATION ALBUMS:	HITS 1			WEEKS 7
HELP - WAR CHILD	*Go! Discs*	1	*16 Sep 95*	7
Charity album in aid of children caught up in the Bosnian war.				

Good Looking

COMPILATION ALBUMS:	HITS 3			WEEKS 4
BLAME PRESENT LOGICAL PROGRESSION LEVEL 2	*Good Looking*	12	*10 May 97*	2
LTJ BUKEM PRESENTS EARTH - VOLUME TWO	*Good Looking*	18	*11 Oct 97*	1
INTENSE PRESENTS LOGICAL PROGRESSION LEVEL 3	*Good Looking*	18	*16 May 98*	1

GTO

ALBUMS:	HITS 1			WEEKS 5
NEVER TOO YOUNG TO ROCK	*GTO*	30	*16 Aug 75*	5

Guerilla

COMPILATION ALBUMS:	HITS 1			WEEKS 1
DUB HOUSE DISCO 2000	*Guerilla*	18	*17 Apr 93*	1

Happy Days

COMPILATION ALBUMS:	HITS 1			WEEKS 1
YOU MUST REMEMBER THIS . . .	*Happy Days*	16	*13 May 95*	1

Harvest

ALBUMS:	HITS 1			WEEKS 12
A MONUMENT TO BRITISH ROCK	*Harvest*	13	*26 May 79*	12

Heart And Soul

COMPILATION ALBUMS:	HITS 4			WEEKS 47
HEART AND SOUL - 18 CLASSIC SOUL CUTS	*Heart & Soul*	2	*19 Aug 89*	12
BODY AND SOUL - HEART AND SOUL II	*Heart & Soul*	2	*17 Feb 90*	14
HEART AND SOUL III - HEART FULL OF SOUL	*Heart & Soul*	4	*4 Aug 90*	9
SOUL REFLECTION	*Heart & Soul*	2	*16 Feb 91*	12

Heaven Music

COMPILATION ALBUMS:	HITS 5			WEEKS 13
HARDCORE HEAVEN - VOLUME ONE	*Heaven Music*	12	*5 Apr 97*	4
HARDCORE HEAVEN - VOLUME 2	*Heaven Music*	13	*9 Aug 97*	2
HARDCORE HEAVEN - VOLUME 3	*Heaven Music*	12	*14 Feb 98*	2
HARDCORE HEAVEN - VOLUME 4	*Heaven Music*	17	*8 Aug 98*	1
HARDCORE HEAVEN - VOLUME 5	*Heaven Music*	17	*13 Feb 99*	4

Heavenly

COMPILATION ALBUMS:	HITS 1			WEEKS 1
LIVE AT THE SOCIAL - VOLUME 1	*Heavenly*	19	*25 May 96*	1

Hi-Life/Polydor

COMPILATION ALBUMS:	HITS 1			WEEKS 1
THE SUMMER OF NINETY SIX - UP YER RONSON	*Hi-Life/Polydor*	17	*2 Nov 96*	1

Higher Ground

COMPILATION ALBUMS:	HITS 1			WEEKS 1
GROOVERIDER PRESENTS THE PROTOTYPE YEARS	*Higher Ground*	19	*12 Apr 97*	1

The Hit Label

COMPILATION ALBUMS:	HITS 11			WEEKS 43
BIG! DANCE HITS OF 92	*The Hit Label*	11	*28 Nov 92*	7
REMEMBER WHEN SINGERS COULD SING	*The Hit Label*	16	*5 Dec 92*	2
THE LEGENDARY JOE BLOGGS DANCE ALBUM	*The Hit Label*	3	*8 May 93*	8
GET IT ON - GREATEST HITS OF THE 70'S	*The Hit Label*	12	*31 Jul 93*	5
THE LEGENDARY JOE BLOGGS ALBUM 2	*The Hit Label*	15	*30 Oct 93*	2
IT MUST BE LOVE	*The Hit Label*	11	*13 Nov 93*	4
THE BOYZ WHO SOULED THE WORLD	*The Hit Label*	9	*5 Mar 94*	4
THE ULTIMATE GOLD COLLECTION	*The Hit Label*	12	*27 Aug 94*	4
ULTIMATE LOVE	*The Hit Label*	13	*4 Feb 95*	4
FEEL LIKE MAKING LOVE	*The Hit Label*	17	*18 Feb 95*	2
REGGAE GROOVE	*The Hit Label*	12	*8 Jul 95*	1

Ignition

COMPILATION ALBUMS:	HITS 1			WEEKS 1
FIRE & SKILL - THE SONGS OF THE JAM *Tribute album to the Jam.*	*Ignition*	12	*13 Nov 99*	1

Immediate

ALBUMS:	HITS 1			WEEKS 1
BLUES ANYTIME	*Immediate*	40	*11 May 68*	1

IMP Classics & Pickwick

Both labels sales were combined.

COMPILATION ALBUMS:	HITS 2			WEEKS 6
DISCOVER THE CLASSICS VOLUME 2	*IMP Classics / Pickwick*	12	*11 Apr 92*	3
DISCOVER THE CLASSICS VOLUME 1	*IMP Classics / Pickwick*	15	*11 Apr 92*	3

Impression

ALBUMS:	HITS 7			WEEKS 51
BEST FRIENDS	*Impression*	28	*16 Oct 82*	21
SUNNY AFTERNOON	*Impression*	13	*3 Sep 83*	8
PRECIOUS MOMENTS	*Impression*	77	*26 Nov 83*	5
ALWAYS AND FOREVER - THE COLLECTION	*Impression*	24	*7 Apr 84*	12
WIPEOUT - 20 INSTRUMENTAL GREATS	*Impression*	37	*21 Jul 84*	3
SUNNY AFTERNOON VOLUME TWO	*Impression*	90	*28 Jul 84*	1
FRIENDS AGAIN	*Impression*	91	*22 Dec 84*	1

INCredible

COMPILATION ALBUMS:	HITS 11			WEEKS 37
GATECRASHER	*INCredible*	7	*31 Oct 98*	2
NORTHERN EXPOSURE - SASHA + JON DIGWEED *Sales of vinyl format had its own entry reaching No. 37.*	*INCredible*	6	*6 Mar 99*	2
INCREDIBLE SOUND OF TREVOR NELSON	*INCredible*	14	*20 Mar 99*	3

GATECRASHER RED	*INCredible*	4	*10 Apr 99*	8
INCREDIBLE SOUND OF DRUM'N'BASS: MIXED BY GOLDIE	*INCredible*	16	*8 May 99*	2
GATECRASHER.WET	*INCredible*	3	*7 Aug 99*	6
GATECRASHER DISCO-TECH	*INCredible*	6	*20 Nov 99*	3
SASHA & DIGWEED, 'COMMUNICATE'	*INCredible*	13	*8 Jul 00*	2
INCREDIBLE SOUND OF THE DREEM TEAM	*INCredible*	14	*19 Aug 00*	2
CD1 is mixes of current dance tracks. CD2 are old tracks.				
GARAGE NATION - SUMMER 2001 - MIXED BY JASON KAYE & STICKY	*INCredible*	11	*15 Sep 01*	4
GODS KITCHEN - THE TRUE SOUND OF A CLUBBING SUMMER	*INCredible*	17	*29 Sep 01*	1
Gods Kitchen is a Midland's Superclub.				

Inspired

COMPILATION ALBUMS:	HITS 8			WEEKS 21
LOVED UP	*Inspired*	8	*12 Feb 00*	4
ULTIMATE AGIA NAPA	*Inspired*	7	*27 May 00*	3
ULTIMATE IBIZA: MIXED BY BRANDON BLOCK & ALEX P	*Inspired*	14	*7 Oct 00*	3
CD1 is Alex's Night Life Mix; CD2 is Brandon Block's Beach Life Mix.				
FEELS SO GOOD	*Inspired*	13	*3 Feb 01*	2
DANCESTAR 2001	*Inspired*	12	*9 Jun 01*	3
DREAMSTATES	*Inspired*	18	*21 Jul 01*	1
BIG CLUBHITS	*Inspired*	5	*22 Sep 01*	3
RAVE NATION - 40 MASSIVE OLD SKOOL ANTHEMS	*Inspired*	16	*3 Nov 01*	2

Inspired/INCredible

COMPILATION ALBUMS:	HITS 2			WEEKS 11
LOVIN' IT - THE CREAM OF R&B AND UK GARAGE	*Inspired/INCredible*	3	*25 Aug 01*	9
LOVIN' IT 2 - THE CREAM OF R&B AND UK GARAGE	*Inspired/INCredible*	16	*22 Dec 01*	2

Island

ALBUMS:	HITS 5			WEEKS 51
CLUB SKA '67	*Island*	37	*26 Aug 67*	19
YOU CAN ALL JOIN IN	*Island*	18	*14 Jun 69*	10
CLUB SKA '67 [RE]	*Island*	53	*29 Mar 80*	6
Re-released with a new catalogue number.				
CREW CUTS	*Island*	71	*16 Jun 84*	4
CREW CUTS - LESSON 2	*Island*	95	*27 Oct 84*	2
THE ISLAND STORY	*Island*	9	*18 Jul 87*	10
COMPILATION ALBUMS:	**HITS 4**			**WEEKS 17**
HAPPY DAZE . . . VOLUME 1	*Island*	7	*3 Nov 90*	4
HAPPY DAZE VOLUME 2	*Island*	17	*6 Apr 91*	2
REGGAE 93	*PolyGram TV*	5	*30 Oct 93*	6
PURE REGGAE - VOLUME 1	*Island*	10	*27 Aug 94*	5

Jack Trax

ALBUMS:	HITS 3			WEEKS 8
JACK TRAX - THE FIRST ALBUM	*Jack Trax*	83	*18 Jul 87*	2
JACK TRAX - THE SECOND ALBUM	*Jack Trax*	61	*3 Oct 87*	2
JACK TRAX - THE FOURTH ALBUM	*Jack Trax*	49	*5 Mar 88*	4

JDJ

COMPILATION ALBUMS:	HITS 1			WEEKS 2
DANCE WARS - JUDGE JULES VS. JOHN KELLY	*JDJ*	11	*30 Mar 96*	2

Jetstar

ALBUMS:	HITS 4			WEEKS 21
REGGAE HITS VOLUME ONE	*Jetstar*	32	*30 Mar 85*	11
REGGAE HITS VOLUME 2	*Jetstar*	86	*26 Oct 85*	2
REGGAE HITS VOLUME 4	*JetStar*	56	*4 Jun 88*	7
REGGAE HITS VOLUME 5	*JetStar*	96	*17 Dec 88*	1
COMPILATION ALBUMS:	**HITS 7**			**WEEKS 39**
REGGAE HITS VOLUME 6	*JetStar*	13	*5 Aug 89*	6
REGGAE HITS VOLUME 7	*Jetstar*	13	*23 Dec 89*	6
REGGAE HITS VOLUME 8	*Jetstar*	7	*30 Jun 90*	5
REGGAE HITS VOLUME 10	*Jetstar*	6	*20 Jul 91*	7
REGGAE HITS VOLUME 12	*Jetstar*	5	*18 Apr 92*	6
REGGAE HITS VOLUME 14	*Jetstar*	13	*28 Aug 93*	1
JUNGLE HITS VOLUME 1	*Jetstar*	9	*3 Sep 94*	8

Jive

ALBUMS:	HITS 1			WEEKS 2
THE WORD VOLUME 2	*Jive*	70	*26 Mar 88*	2

Jumpin' And Pumpin'

COMPILATION ALBUMS:	HITS 2			WEEKS 4
NOISE	*Jumpin' & Pumpin'*	20	*18 Jan 92*	1
NOISE 2	*Jumpin' & Pumpin'*	11	*16 May 92*	3

Junior Boy's Own

COMPILATION ALBUMS:	HITS 1			WEEKS 1
JUNIOR BOY'S OWN COLLECTION	*Junior Boy's Own*	20	*13 Aug 94*	1

Kasino

ALBUMS:	HITS 1			WEEKS 3
STARGAZERS	*Kasino*	69	*16 Feb 85*	3

Knight

COMPILATION ALBUMS:	HITS 1			WEEKS 2
SOUTHERN NIGHTS	*Knight*	13	*18 May 91*	2

K-Tel

ALBUMS:	HITS 113			WEEKS 1147
20 DYNAMIC HITS	*K-Tel*	1	*10 Jun 72*	28
20 ALL TIME GREATS OF THE 50'S	*K-Tel*	1	*7 Oct 72*	22
25 DYNAMIC HITS VOLUME 2	*K-Tel*	2	*25 Nov 72*	12
25 ROCKIN' AND ROLLIN' GREATS	*K-Tel*	1	*2 Dec 72*	18
20 FLASHBACK GREATS OF THE SIXTIES	*K-Tel*	1	*31 Mar 73*	11
BELIEVE IN MUSIC	*K-Tel*	2	*21 Apr 73*	8
40 SUPER GREATS	*K-Tel*	9	*13 Dec 75*	8
MUSIC EXPRESS	*K-Tel*	3	*31 Jan 76*	10
JUKE BOX JIVE	*K-Tel*	3	*10 Apr 76*	13
GREAT ITALIAN LOVE SONGS	*K-Tel*	17	*17 Apr 76*	14
HIT MACHINE	*K-Tel*	4	*15 May 76*	10
SUMMER CRUISING	*K-Tel*	30	*2 Oct 76*	1
SOUL MOTION	*K-Tel*	1	*16 Oct 76*	14
COUNTRY COMFORT	*K-Tel*	8	*16 Oct 76*	12
DISCO ROCKET	*K-Tel*	3	*4 Dec 76*	14
44 SUPERSTARS	*K-Tel*	14	*11 Dec 76*	10
HEARTBREAKERS	*K-Tel*	2	*12 Feb 77*	18
DANCE TO THE MUSIC	*K-Tel*	5	*19 Feb 77*	9
HIT ACTION	*K-Tel*	15	*7 May 77*	9
SOUL CITY	*K-Tel*	12	*29 Oct 77*	7
FEELINGS	*K-Tel*	3	*12 Nov 77*	24
DISCO FEVER	*K-Tel*	1	*26 Nov 77*	20
40 NUMBER ONE HITS	*K-Tel*	15	*21 Jan 78*	7
DISCO STARS	*K-Tel*	6	*4 Mar 78*	8
DISCO DOUBLE	*K-Tel*	10	*10 Jun 78*	6
ROCK RULES	*K-Tel*	12	*8 Jul 78*	11
THE WORLD'S WORST RECORD SHOW *Release was collaboration with Kenny Everett.*	*Yuk/K-Tel*	47	*8 Jul 78*	2
STAR PARTY	*K-Tel*	4	*19 Aug 78*	9
EMOTIONS	*K-Tel*	2	*4 Nov 78*	17
MIDNIGHT HUSTLE	*K-Tel*	2	*25 Nov 78*	13
ACTION REPLAY	*K-Tel*	1	*20 Jan 79*	14
DISCO INFERNO	*K-Tel*	11	*7 Apr 79*	9
HI ENERGY	*K-Tel*	17	*5 May 79*	7
HOT TRACKS	*K-Tel*	31	*22 Sep 79*	8
NIGHT MOVES	*K-Tel*	10	*24 Nov 79*	10
TOGETHER	*K-Tel*	35	*24 Nov 79*	8
VIDEO STARS	*K-Tel*	5	*12 Jan 80*	10
THE SUMMIT	*K-Tel*	17	*26 Jan 80*	5
STAR TRACKS	*K-Tel*	6	*29 Mar 80*	8
GOOD MORNING AMERICA	*K-Tel*	15	*26 Apr 80*	12
MAGIC REGGAE	*K-Tel*	9	*17 May 80*	17
HAPPY DAYS	*K-Tel*	32	*17 May 80*	6
HOT WAX	*K-Tel*	3	*14 Jun 80*	10
MOUNTING EXCITEMENT	*K-Tel*	2	*27 Sep 80*	8
THE LOVE ALBUM	*K-Tel*	6	*11 Oct 80*	16
AXE ATTACK	*K-Tel*	15	*25 Oct 80*	14
CHART EXPLOSION	*K-Tel*	6	*15 Nov 80*	17
NIGHTLIFE	*K-Tel*	25	*27 Dec 80*	10
HIT MACHINE *This album is different from previous chart entry.*	*K-Tel*	17	*14 Feb 81*	6
RHYTHM 'N' REGGAE	*K-Tel*	42	*21 Mar 81*	4
CHART BLASTERS 81	*K-Tel*	3	*25 Apr 81*	9
AXE ATTACK 2	*K-Tel*	31	*2 May 81*	6
THEMES	*K-Tel*	6	*23 May 81*	15
CALIFORNIA DREAMING	*K-Tel*	27	*29 Aug 81*	11
DANCE DANCE DANCE	*K-Tel*	29	*19 Sep 81*	5
THE PLATINUM ALBUM	*K-Tel*	32	*3 Oct 81*	11
LOVE IS . . .	*K-Tel*	10	*10 Oct 81*	15
CHART HITS '81	*K-Tel*	1	*21 Nov 81*	17
MODERN DANCE	*K-Tel*	6	*9 Jan 82*	10
DREAMING	*K-Tel*	2	*6 Feb 82*	12
ACTION TRAX	*K-Tel*	2	*6 Mar 82*	12
MIDNIGHT HOUR	*K-Tel*	98	*1 May 82*	1

TURBO TRAX	*K-Tel*	17	*3 Jul 82*	7
THE NO. 1 SOUNDS OF THE SEVENTIES	*K-Tel*	83	*4 Sep 82*	1
CHARTBEAT/CHARTHEAT	*K-Tel*	2	*11 Sep 82*	14
THE LOVE SONGS ALBUM	*K-Tel*	28	*30 Oct 82*	8
CHART HITS '82	*K-Tel*	11	*6 Nov 82*	17
DISCO DANCER	*K-Tel*	26	*6 Nov 82*	8
STREETSCENE	*K-Tel*	42	*18 Dec 82*	6
VISIONS	*K-Tel*	5	*15 Jan 83*	21
HEAVY	*K-Tel*	46	*12 Feb 83*	12
HOTLINE	*K-Tel*	3	*5 Mar 83*	9
CHART STARS	*K-Tel*	7	*11 Jun 83*	9
COOL HEAT	*K-Tel*	79	*20 Aug 83*	3
HEADLINE HITS	*K-Tel*	5	*10 Sep 83*	6
THE TWO OF US	*K-Tel*	3	*8 Oct 83*	16
IMAGES	*K-Tel*	33	*8 Oct 83*	6
CHART HITS '83 VOLUMES 1 AND 2	*K-Tel*	6	*12 Nov 83*	11
NIGHT MOVES	*K-Tel*	90	*24 Mar 84*	1
This album is different from previous chart entry.				
HUNGRY FOR HITS	*K-Tel*	4	*26 May 84*	11
THE THEMES ALBUM	*K-Tel*	43	*23 Jun 84*	3
BREAKDANCE, YOU CAN DO IT!	*K-Tel*	18	*28 Jul 84*	12
NIGHT MOVES [RE]	*K-Tel*	15	*15 Sep 84*	10
ALL BY MYSELF	*K-Tel*	7	*22 Sep 84*	16
HOOKED ON NUMBER ONES - 100 NON-STOP HITS	*K-Tel*	25	*1 Dec 84*	15
FOUR STAR COUNTRY	*K-Tel*	52	*2 Feb 85*	6
MODERN LOVE - 24 LOVE SONGS FOR TODAY	*K-Tel*	13	*2 Mar 85*	7
EXPRESSIONS - 24 BEAUTIFUL BALLADS	*K-Tel*	11	*5 Oct 85*	8
ROCK ANTHEMS	*K-Tel*	10	*9 Nov 85*	11
THE BEST OF ANDREW LLOYD WEBBER - OVATION	*K-Tel*	34	*9 Nov 85*	12
Features tracks by Barbara Dickson, Paul Nicholas and Rebecca Storm.				
MASTERS OF METAL	*K-Tel*	38	*22 Mar 86*	4
HEART TO HEART - 24 LOVE SONG DUETS	*K-Tel*	8	*12 Apr 86*	15
ROCK ANTHEMS - VOLUME 2	*K-Tel*	43	*19 Apr 86*	9
RAP IT UP - RAP'S GREATEST HITS	*K-Tel*	50	*5 Jul 86*	4
DRIVE TIME USA - 22 SUMMER CRUISING GREATS	*K-Tel*	20	*19 Jul 86*	8
DANCE HITS '86	*K-Tel*	35	*18 Oct 86*	7
TOGETHER	*K-Tel*	20	*1 Nov 86*	10
This album is different from previous chart entry.				
IMPRESSIONS - 15 INSTRUMENTAL IMAGES	*K-Tel*	15	*7 Feb 87*	14
RHYTHM OF THE NIGHT	*K-Tel*	36	*21 Mar 87*	7
HITS REVIVAL	*K-Tel (Holland)*	63	*21 Mar 87*	1
Holland import.				
FRIENDS AND LOVERS	*K-Tel*	10	*13 Jun 87*	10
HITS REVIVAL	*K-Tel*	10	*27 Jun 87*	9
TRUE LOVE	*K-Tel*	38	*17 Oct 87*	5
FROM MOTOWN WITH LOVE	*K-Tel*	9	*31 Oct 87*	21
ALWAYS	*K-Tel*	65	*14 Nov 87*	4
WOW WHAT A PARTY	*K-Tel*	97	*19 Dec 87*	2
HORIZONS	*K-Tel*	13	*5 Mar 88*	10
HITS REVIVAL 2: REPLAY	*K-Tel*	45	*30 Apr 88*	3
TSOP - THE SOUND OF PHILADELPHIA	*K-Tel*	26	*14 May 88*	9
THE HITS OF HOUSE ARE HERE	*K-Tel*	12	*11 Jun 88*	12
MOTOWN IN MOTION	*K-Tel*	28	*15 Oct 88*	13
THE RETURN OF SUPERBAD	*K-Tel*	83	*15 Oct 88*	4
THE LOVERS	*K-Tel*	50	*5 Nov 88*	5
RAPPIN' UP THE HOUSE	*K-Tel*	43	*26 Nov 88*	7

COMPILATION ALBUMS:	HITS 10			WEEKS 61
FROM MOTOWN WITH LOVE	*K-Tel*	6	*4 Feb 89*	7
RAPPIN' UP THE HOUSE	*K-Tel*	19	*14 Jan 89*	1
HIP HOUSE - THE DEEPEST BEATS IN TOWN	*K-Tel*	10	*25 Mar 89*	5
GLAM SLAM	*K-Tel*	5	*29 Jul 89*	8
LOVE HOUSE	*K-Tel*	5	*23 Sep 89*	7
ETERNAL LOVE	*K-Tel*	5	*30 Sep 89*	7
RAP ATTACK	*K-Tel*	6	*21 Oct 89*	7
SEDUCTION	*K-Tel*	15	*25 Nov 89*	4
CAN U FEEL IT? - THE CHAMPION LEGEND	*K-Tel*	12	*10 Mar 90*	3
HOOKED ON COUNTRY	*K-Tel*	6	*21 Apr 90*	12

Life Aid Armenia

COMPILATION ALBUMS:	HITS 1			WEEKS 10
THE EARTHQUAKE ALBUM . . . ROCK AID ARMENIA	*Life Aid Armenia*	3	*21 Apr 90*	10
Charity album to support victims of the Armenian Earthquake.				

Limbo

COMPILATION ALBUMS:	HITS 1			WEEKS 1
THE TUNNEL MIXES	*Limbo*	17	*18 May 96*	1

London

COMPILATION ALBUMS:	HITS 7			WEEKS 25
FFRR - SILVER ON BLACK	*London*	8	*10 Jun 89*	5
DANCE DECADE - DANCE HITS OF THE 80'S	*London*	8	*11 Nov 89*	7
THE NORTHERN BEAT	*London*	4	*16 Jun 90*	8
MASSIVE 4	*London*	20	*7 Jul 90*	2
ONLY FOR THE HEADSTRONG	*London*	10	*8 Feb 92*	1
ONLY FOR THE HEADSTRONG II	*London*	18	*20 Jun 92*	1
G-A-Y	*London*	18	*15 Jul 00*	1

Loose End

ALBUMS:	HITS 1			WEEKS 5
CHUNKS OF FUNK	*Loose Ends*	46	*11 Aug 84*	5

Lotus

ALBUMS:	HITS 1			WEEKS 6
ECSTACY	*Lotus*	24	*28 Oct 78*	6

Mango

COMPILATION ALBUMS:	HITS 1			WEEKS 9
ON A REGGAE TIP	*Mango*	3	*3 Jul 93*	9

Marble Arch

ALBUMS:	HITS 1			WEEKS 3
STARS OF '68	*Marble Arch*	23	*10 Feb 68*	3

Marquee

COMPILATION ALBUMS:	HITS 1			WEEKS 6
MARQUEE METAL	*Marquee*	5	*4 May 91*	6

Massive Music

COMPILATION ALBUMS:	HITS 2			WEEKS 7
101% SPEED GARAGE VOLUME 2	*Massive Music*	16	*25 Apr 98*	2
101% SPEED GARAGE ANTHEMS	*Massive Music*	14	*17 Apr 99*	5

Mastercuts

COMPILATION ALBUMS:	HITS 12			WEEKS 27
CLASSIC MELLOW MASTERCUTS VOLUME 1	*Mastercuts*	18	*28 Sep 91*	2
NEW JACK SWING MASTERCUTS VOLUME 1	*Mastercuts*	8	*21 Mar 92*	5
CLASSIC FUNK MASTERCUTS VOLUME 1	*Mastercuts*	14	*16 May 92*	3
CLASSIC JAZZ-FUNK MASTERCUTS VOLUME 3	*Mastercuts*	18	*4 Jul 92*	1
CLASSIC MELLOW MASTERCUTS VOLUME 2	*Mastercuts*	12	*15 Aug 92*	3
CLASSIC SALSOUL MASTERCUTS VOLUME 1	*Mastercuts*	16	*6 Mar 93*	3
CLASSIC RARE GROOVE MASTERCUTS VOLUME 1	*Mastercuts*	14	*24 Apr 93*	3
CLASSIC P-FUNK MASTERCUTS VOLUME 1	*Mastercuts*	16	*22 May 93*	1
CLASSIC JAZZ FUNK MASTERCUTS VOLUME 4	*Mastercuts*	19	*22 Jan 94*	2
NEW JACK SWING VOLUME 3	*Mastercuts*	18	*26 Mar 94*	1
CLASSIC ELECTRO MASTERCUTS VOLUME 1	*Mastercuts*	18	*14 May 94*	1
CLASSIC HOUSE MASTERCUTS VOLUME 1	*Mastercuts*	11	*18 Jun 94*	2

Mastersound

ALBUMS:	HITS 1			WEEKS 1
HEAT OF SOUL VOLUME 1	*Mastersound*	96	*28 Mar 87*	1

Masterworks

COMPILATION ALBUMS:	HITS 1			WEEKS 3
TAKE 2: OPERA FAVOURITES/ORCHESTRAL CLASSICS	*Masterworks*	18	*5 Dec 92*	3

Mawson And Wareham

COMPILATION ALBUMS:	HITS 1			WEEKS 3
PETER HETHERINGTON: SONGS FROM THE HEART	*Mawson And Wareham*	10	*16 Mar 91*	3

Had 3 chart runs of 1 week each at the same period of time for 3 consecutive years.

MCA

ALBUMS:	HITS 1			WEEKS 2
PRECIOUS METAL	*MCA*	60	*24 May 80*	2

COMPILATION ALBUMS:	HITS 3			WEEKS 6
RHYTHM COUNTRY AND BLUES	*MCA*	19	*23 Apr 94*	2
MORE BUMP N' GRIND	*MCA*	9	*27 May 95*	3
THE TARANTTINO COLLECTION	*MCA*	18	*2 Nov 96*	1

MCI Music

COMPILATION ALBUMS:	HITS 1			WEEKS 1
BORN TO BE WILD	*MCI Music*	20	*4 Mar 95*	1

Mercury

ALBUMS:	HITS 3			WEEKS 9
WIRED FOR CLUBS (CLUB TRACKS VOLUME 1)	*Mercury*	58	*2 Jul 83*	4

BEAT RUNS WILD	*Mercury*	70	*14 Jun 86*	2
FORMULA THIRTY - 2	*Mercury*	80	*1 Nov 86*	3
COMPILATION ALBUMS:	**HITS 1**			**WEEKS 21**
TWO ROOMS - CELEBRATING THE SONGS OF ELTON JOHN AND BERNIE TAUPIN	*Mercury*	1	*26 Oct 91*	21

Metropole Music

COMPILATION ALBUMS:	**HITS 3**			**WEEKS 7**
DANNY RAMPLING - LOVE GROOVE DANCE PARTY	*Metropole Music*	10	*25 May 96*	3
DANNY RAMPLING - LOVE GROOVE DANCE PARTY *This album is different from previous chart entry.*	*Metropole Music*	17	*8 Feb 97*	2
DANNY RAMPLING/LOVE GROOVE PARTY 5 & 6	*Metropole Music*	12	*7 Jun 97*	2

Ministry Of Sound

Ministry Of Sound is an established nightclub in South London.

COMPILATION ALBUMS:	**HITS 24**			**WEEKS 118**
MINISTRY OF SOUND: THE SESSIONS VOLUME 1	*Ministry Of Sound*	16	*11 Sep 93*	2
MINISTRY OF SOUND - THE SESSIONS VOLUME 2	*Ministry Of Sound*	6	*30 Apr 94*	5
MINISTRY OF SOUND - THE SESSIONS VOLUME 3	*Ministry Of Sound*	8	*22 Oct 94*	3
THE FUTURE SOUND OF NEW YORK	*Sound Of Ministry*	19	*1 Apr 95*	1
MINISTRY OF SOUND - THE SESSIONS 4	*Sound Of Ministry*	9	*6 May 95*	5
MINISTRY OF SOUND SESSIONS - VOLUME 5	*Ministry Of Sound*	15	*30 Sep 95*	5
MINISTRY OF SOUND SESSION SIX - FRANKIE KNUCKLES	*Ministry Of Sound*	8	*16 Mar 96*	4
ONE HALF OF A WHOLE DECADE - 5 YEARS . . .	*Ministry Of Sound*	9	*21 Sep 96*	6
NORTHERN EXPOSURE - SASHA & JOHN DIGWEED	*Ministry Of Sound*	7	*12 Oct 96*	4
SESSIONS SEVEN	*Ministry Of Sound*	4	*1 Mar 97*	4
MINISTRY OF SOUND CLASSICS MIXED BY JUDGE JULES	*Ministry Of Sound*	12	*21 Jun 97*	3
SESSIONS EIGHT - TODD TERRY	*Ministry Of Sound*	11	*26 Jul 97*	3
NORTHERN EXPOSURE 2 - SASHA & DIGWEED	*Ministry Of Sound*	15	*27 Sep 97*	2
SESSIONS NINE - ERICK MORILLO	*Ministry Of Sound*	17	*14 Mar 98*	1
CLUBBER'S GUIDE TO . . . IBIZA - JULES/TONG	*Ministry Of Sound*	2	*4 Jul 98*	9
THE IBIZA ANNUAL	*Ministry Of Sound*	1	*5 Sep 98*	9
CLUBBER'S GUIDE TO . . . NINETY NINE	*Ministry Of Sound*	1	*30 Jan 99*	7
GALAXY WEEKEND: MIXED BY BOY GEORGE & ALLISTER WHITEHEAD	*Ministry Of Sound*	6	*15 May 99*	4
TRANCE NATION: MIXED BY SYSTEM F	*Ministry Of Sound*	1	*29 May 99*	9
CLUBBERS GUIDE TO IBIZA - SUMMER '99	*Ministry Of Sound*	1	*19 Jun 99*	10
CLUBBER'S GUIDE TO . . . TRANCE: MIXED BY ATB	*Ministry Of Sound*	4	*7 Aug 99*	5
THE IBIZA ANNUAL: MIXED BY JUDGE JULES + TALL PAUL	*Ministry Of Sound*	1	*28 Aug 99*	8
TRANCE NATION 2: MIXED BY FERRY CORSTEN	*Ministry Of Sound*	1	*9 Oct 99*	6
GALAXY MIX - BOY GEORGE	*Ministry Of Sound*	8	*30 Oct 99*	3
GALAXY HIT MIX	*Ministry Of Sound*	14	*27 May 00*	2
HEADLINERS: 01 - TALL PAUL LIVE AT THE GALLERY *Live recordings at DJ Tall Paul's club The Gallery.*	*Ministry Of Sound*	20	*15 Jul 00*	1
AYIA NAPA THE ALBUM - MIXED BY SHANKS & BIGFOOT	*Ministry Of Sound*	5	*22 Jul 00*	7
UK GARAGE - THE ALBUM - THE SOUND OF 2000	*Ministry Of Sound*	9	*2 Dec 00*	7
THE CHILLOUT SESSION	*Ministry Of Sound*	1	*17 Feb 01*	18
REAL GARAGE - MIXED LIVE BY MASTERSTEPZ	*Relentless/Ministry Of Sound*	6	*24 Feb 01*	5
HARD ENERGY: MIXED BY FERGIE AND YOMANDA	*Ministry Of Sound*	10	*3 Mar 01*	3
AYIA NAPA - THE ALBUM 2001: MIXED BY MASTERSTEPZ	*Relentless/Ministry Of Sound*	9	*16 Jun 01*	3
THE CHILLOUT SESSION 2	*Ministry Of Sound*	2	*23 Jun 01*	11
IBIZA CHILLOUT SESSION	*Ministry Of Sound*	12	*8 Sep 01*	3
CLUB NATION 2001	*Ministry Of Sound*	4	*6 Oct 01*	4
BACK TO THE OLD SKOOL	*Ministry Of Sound*	2	*13 Oct 01*	7
BACK TO THE OLD SKOOL 2	*Ministry Of Sound*	11	*1 Dec 01*	2

Miracle

COMPILATION ALBUMS:	**HITS 1**			**WEEKS 4**
LOVE ETERNAL	*Miracle*	5	*4 Feb 95*	4

Miss Moneypenny's

COMPILATION ALBUMS:	**HITS 1**			**WEEKS 1**
GLAMOROUS ONE	*Miss Moneypeny's*	12	*22 Mar 97*	1

More Protein

COMPILATION ALBUMS:	**HITS 1**			**WEEKS 1**
CLOSET CLASSICS VOLUME 1 - MORE PROTEIN SAMPLER	*More Protein*	20	*1 Feb 92*	1

Motown

ALBUMS:	**HITS 14**			**WEEKS 175**
A COLLECTION OF TAMLA MOTOWN HITS	*Tamla Motown*	16	*3 Apr 65*	4
16 ORIGINAL BIG HITS - VOLUME 4	*Tamla Motown*	33	*4 Mar 67*	3
TAMLA MOTOWN HITS VOLUME 5	*Tamla Motown*	11	*17 Jun 67*	40
MOTOWN MEMORIES	*Tamla Motown*	21	*10 Feb 68*	13
TAMLA MOTOWN HITS VOLUME 6	*Tamla Motown*	32	*24 Aug 68*	2
COLLECTION OF BIG HITS VOLUME 8	*Tamla Motown*	56	*21 Feb 70*	1
MOTOWN MEMORIES *This album is different from previous chart entry.*	*Tamla Motown*	22	*26 Feb 72*	4
MOTOWN STORY	*Tamla Motown*	21	*18 Mar 72*	8

MOTOWN GOLD	*Tamla Motown*	8	*1 Nov 75*	35
MOTOWN GOLD VOLUME 2	*Motown*	28	*5 Nov 77*	4
BIG WHEELS OF MOTOWN	*Motown*	2	*7 Oct 78*	18
THE LAST DANCE	*Motown*	1	*2 Feb 80*	23
THE 20TH ANNIVERSARY ALBUM	*Motown*	53	*2 Aug 80*	2
MOTOWN DANCE PARTY	*Motown*	3	*21 May 88*	18
COMPILATION ALBUMS:	**HITS 6**			**WEEKS 38**
MOTOWN DANCE PARTY 2	*Motown*	10	*19 May 90*	7
SOUL DECADE; THE SIXTIES	*Motown/Atlantic*	3	*6 Oct 90*	10
MOTOWN'S GREATEST LOVE SONGS	*Motown*	5	*24 Oct 92*	5
MOTOWN - THE ULTIMATE HITS COLLECTION	*Motown*	6	*12 Nov 94*	13
MOTOWN - THE HITS COLLECTION - VOLUME 2	*Motown*	19	*4 Nov 95*	1
MOTOWN 40 FOREVER	*Motown*	15	*12 Sep 98*	2

Mountain

ALBUMS:	**HITS 1**			**WEEKS 2**
GOLDEN FIDDLE AWARDS 1976	*Mountain*	45	*3 Jul 76*	2

Music For Pleasure

ALBUMS:	**HITS 1**			**WEEKS 1**
BREAKTHROUGH	*Music For Pleasure*	49	*4 Dec 71*	1

Music Unites

COMPILATION ALBUMS:	**HITS 1**			**WEEKS 1**
JOURNEYS BY DJ VOLUME 4	*Music Unites*	19	*12 Mar 94*	1

Needle

ALBUMS:	**HITS 3**			**WEEKS 14**
DANCE MANIA VOLUME 1	*Needle*	46	*4 Jul 87*	4
MAD ON HOUSE VOLUME 1	*Needle*	81	*20 Feb 88*	2
HOUSE HITS	*Needle*	25	*14 May 88*	8

Nems

ALBUMS:	**HITS 1**			**WEEKS 2**
LIVE AND HEAVY	*NEMS*	100	*12 Dec 81*	2

Network

COMPILATION ALBUMS:	**HITS 2**			**WEEKS 3**
RENAISSANCE - MIX COLLECTION - PART 2	*Network*	16	*20 Jan 96*	2
BACK TO BASICS - CUT THE CRAP	*Network*	20	*13 Apr 96*	1

Nice

COMPILATION ALBUMS:	**HITS 1**			**WEEKS 1**
TRIBUTE TO THE SMALL FACES - LONG AGOS/WORLDS APART	*Nice*	20	*14 Sep 96*	1

Nouveau Music

ALBUMS:	**HITS 3**			**WEEKS 4**
CLASSIC THEMES	*Nouveau Music*	61	*24 Sep 83*	2
ESSENTIAL DISCO AND DANCE	*Nouveau Music*	96	*2 Jun 84*	1
DREAM MELODIES	*Nouveau Music*	91	*30 Mar 85*	1

NPG

COMPILATION ALBUMS:	**HITS 1**			**WEEKS 1**
1-800 NEW FUNK	*NPG*	15	*20 Aug 94*	1

Numa

ALBUMS:	**HITS 1**			**WEEKS 1**
NUMA RECORDS YEAR 1	*Numa*	94	*22 Mar 86*	1

Old Gold

COMPILATION ALBUMS:	**HITS 1**			**WEEKS 1**
LET'S DANCE - SOUND OF THE SIXTIES PART 1	*Old Gold*	18	*7 Apr 90*	1

Oriole

ALBUMS:	**HITS 1**			**WEEKS 5**
THE MERSEY BEAT VOLUME 1	*Oriole*	17	*24 Aug 63*	5

Parkfield

COMPILATION ALBUMS:	**HITS 1**			**WEEKS 2**
NOTHING COMPARES TO THIS	*Parkfield*	13	*28 Jul 90*	2

Parlophone

COMPILATION ALBUMS:	**HITS 2**			**WEEKS 12**
IT'S COOL	*Parlophone*	3	*22 Jun 91*	7
60'S SOUL 90'S SOUL	*Parlophone*	6	*3 Sep 94*	5

Perfecto

COMPILATION ALBUMS:	HITS 5			WEEKS 9
HARDCORE DJS . . . TAKE CONTROL	*Perfecto*	15	*1 Aug 92*	4
PERFECTO FLUORO: OAKENFOLD	*Perfecto*	18	*9 Nov 96*	1
PERFECTO PRESENTS . . . PAUL OAKENFOLD - TRAVELLING	*Perfecto*	12	*4 Nov 00*	2
PERFECTO PRESENTS . . . TIMO MAAS - CONNECTED	*Perfecto*	20	*19 May 01*	1
PERFECTO PRESENTS . . . PAUL OAKENFOLD - IBIZA	*Perfecto*	13	*25 Aug 01*	1

Philips

ALBUMS:	HITS 3			WEEKS 24
20 ORIGINAL CHART HITS	*Philips*	9	*2 Jun 73*	11
NICE 'N' EASY	*Philips*	36	*2 Jun 73*	1
NEW WAVE	*Philips*	11	*6 Aug 77*	12
COMPILATION ALBUMS:	**HITS 1**			**WEEKS 3**
UTOPIA - CHILLED CLASSICS	*Philips*	10	*3 Nov 01*	3

Polydor

ALBUMS:	HITS 4			WEEKS 14
STEREO MUSICALE SHOWCASE	*Polydor*	26	*10 Dec 66*	2
THE A-Z OF EASY LISTENING	*Polydor*	24	*9 Oct 71*	4
20 OF ANOTHER KIND	*Polydor*	45	*24 Feb 79*	3
MONSTERS OF ROCK	*Polydor*	16	*18 Oct 80*	5
COMPILATION ALBUMS:	**HITS 2**			**WEEKS 26**
THE MARQUEE - 30 LEGENDARY YEARS	*Polydor*	1	*4 Feb 89*	21
ABSOLUTION - ROCK THE ALTERNATIVE WAY	*Polydor*	6	*5 Oct 91*	5

Polydor/EMI

COMPILATION ALBUMS:	HITS 1			WEEKS 13
PURPLE RAINBOWS	*Polydor/EMI*	1	*13 Jul 91*	13

Polydor/Universal Music TV

COMPILATION ALBUMS:	HITS 1			WEEKS 7
ABBAMANIA *Tribute album to Abba.*	*Polydor/Universal Music TV*	2	*20 Nov 99*	7

PolyGram TV

After Seagram's merger of PolyGram with Universal, charts from 13 March 99 reflected change of label to Universal Music TV on all entries.

COMPILATION ALBUMS:	HITS 97			WEEKS 488
SOUL EMOTION	*PolyGram TV*	1	*21 Mar 92*	10
COUNTRY MOODS	*PolyGram TV*	2	*2 May 92*	10
BEATS RHYMES AND BASSLINES - THE BEST OF RAP	*PolyGram TV*	7	*30 May 92*	3
POWER CUTS - ROCK'S GREATEST HITS	*PolyGram TV*	5	*6 Jun 92*	9
MODERN LOVE	*PolyGram TV*	1	*20 Jun 92*	20
DANCING ON SUNSHINE	*PolyGram TV/Virgin*	4	*18 Jul 92*	11
BLAME IT ON THE BOOGIE	*PolyGram TV*	5	*1 Aug 92*	8
READING - THE INDIE ALBUM	*PolyGram TV*	5	*5 Sep 92*	5
COUNTRY ROADS	*PolyGram TV*	3	*27 Mar 93*	10
MEGA-LO-MANIA	*PolyGram TV*	8	*17 Apr 93*	6
UNDER THE COVERS	*PolyGram TV*	11	*24 Apr 93*	5
MIDNIGHT MOODS - THE LIGHTER SIDE OF JAZZ	*Verve/PolyGram TV*	3	*8 May 93*	8
WOMAN TO WOMAN	*PolyGram TV*	5	*5 Jun 93*	10
THE GIFT OF SONG	*PolyGram TV*	7	*19 Jun 93*	4
SOUL INSPIRATION	*PolyGram TV*	4	*26 Jun 93*	7
THE BLUES EXPERIENCE	*PolyGram TV*	7	*3 Jul 93*	6
TEMPTED	*PolyGram TV*	10	*24 Jul 93*	4
LEADERS OF THE PACK	*PolyGram TV*	9	*14 Aug 93*	9
ALL NIGHT LONG	*PolyGram TV*	15	*14 Aug 93*	3
PROGRESSION	*PolyGram TV*	9	*4 Sep 93*	3
'ROUND MIDNIGHT	*Verve/PolyGram TV*	16	*2 Oct 93*	2
DISCO DIVAS	*PolyGram TV*	4	*9 Oct 93*	5
DANCE DIVAS	*PolyGram TV*	11	*19 Feb 94*	3
FACE THE MUSIC - TORVILL AND DEAN	*PolyGram TV*	8	*5 Mar 94*	3
SOUL DEVOTION	*PolyGram TV*	1	*12 Mar 94*	14
I KNOW THEM SO WELL - TIM RICE	*PolyGram TV*	2	*19 Mar 94*	7
WOMAN 2 WOMAN TWO	*PolyGram TV*	9	*9 Apr 94*	4
ACOUSTIC MOODS	*PolyGram TV*	4	*23 Apr 94*	8
REMEMBER THEN - 30 DOO-WOP GREATS	*PolyGram TV*	10	*21 May 94*	3
ROCK THERAPY	*PolyGram TV*	9	*2 Jul 94*	6
POWER AND SOUL	*PolyGram TV*	5	*23 Jul 94*	10
GROOVIN'	*PolyGram TV*	2	*27 Aug 94*	7
SATIN AND STEEL - WOMEN IN ROCK	*PolyGram TV*	3	*10 Sep 94*	7
SOUL NIGHTS	*PolyGram TV*	3	*17 Sep 94*	6
SENSES	*PolyGram TV*	5	*1 Oct 94*	5
AFTER MIDNIGHT	*PolyGram TV*	17	*15 Oct 94*	1
ENDLESS LOVE	*PolyGram TV*	3	*11 Feb 95*	6
ELECTRIC DREAMS	*PolyGram TV*	3	*25 Feb 95*	8

THE ESSENTIAL GROOVE	*PolyGram TV*	11	*11 Mar 95*	3
EMERALD ROCK	*PolyGram TV*	14	*25 Mar 95*	3
TOGETHER	*PolyGram TV*	2	*1 Apr 95*	5
EVERY SONG TELLS A STORY	*PolyGram TV*	17	*8 Apr 95*	1
ROCKS OFF	*PolyGram TV*	4	*15 Apr 95*	5
LET'S HEAR IT FOR THE GIRLS	*PolyGram TV*	8	*6 May 95*	5
SILK AND STEEL	*PolyGram TV*	3	*20 May 95*	6
TEENAGE KICKS	*PolyGram TV*	8	*3 Jun 95*	3
WORLD IN UNION - ANTHEMS	*PolyGram TV*	8	*10 Jun 95*	4
SUNNY AFTERNOONS	*PolyGram TV*	6	*1 Jul 95*	3
ACOUSTIC FREEWAY	*PolyGram TV*	7	*19 Aug 95*	4
SUMMERTIME SOUL	*PolyGram TV*	5	*26 Aug 95*	4
ACOUSTIC ROCK	*PolyGram TV*	7	*23 Sep 95*	5
SOFT ROCK	*PolyGram TV*	3	*10 Feb 96*	6
PASS THE VIBES	*PolyGram TV*	4	*10 Feb 96*	3
THE LOOK OF LOVE	*PolyGram TV*	6	*10 Feb 96*	7
CLASSIC MOODS	*PolyGram TV*	7	*10 Feb 96*	8
FREEWAY	*PolyGram TV*	17	*2 Mar 96*	1
AMBIENT MOODS	*PolyGram TV*	7	*9 Mar 96*	5
THE BEST OF WOMAN TO WOMAN	*PolyGram TV*	3	*23 Mar 96*	5
GO WITH THE FLOW - ESSENTIAL ACID JAZZ	*PolyGram TV*	9	*27 Apr 96*	2
BOYZ OF SWING	*PolyGram TV*	1	*11 May 96*	5
LADYKILLERS	*PolyGram TV*	3	*1 Jun 96*	4
FUNKMASTER MIX	*PolyGram TV*	16	*8 Jun 96*	2
TRUEBRIT	*PolyGram TV*	7	*15 Jun 96*	4
MIX ZONE	*PolyGram TV*	2	*22 Jun 96*	5
SUMMER VYBES	*PolyGram TV*	8	*29 Jun 96*	3
HORIZONS - 12 DREAMHOUSE ANTHEMS	*PolyGram TV*	17	*6 Jul 96*	1
PURE DANCE '96	*PolyGram TV*	5	*7 Sep 96*	4
THE SAX ALBUM	*PolyGram TV*	6	*7 Sep 96*	4
BOYZ OF SWING II	*PolyGram TV*	6	*14 Sep 96*	5
HITS ZONE '97	*PolyGram TV*	11	*14 Dec 96*	5
WIRED	*PolyGram TV*	2	*1 Feb 97*	6
CRUSH	*PolyGram TV*	5	*8 Feb 97*	5
DRUM & BASS MIX 97	*PolyGram TV*	11	*22 Mar 97*	2
FUSED	*PolyGram TV*	14	*17 May 97*	2
TRACKSPOTTING	*PolyGram TV*	12	*24 May 97*	4
LADYKILLERS 2	*PolyGram TV*	15	*7 Jun 97*	2
MIXED EMOTIONS	*PolyGram TV*	6	*21 Jun 97*	5
SUGAR HITS!	*PolyGram TV*	9	*12 Jul 97*	3
HITS ZONE SUMMER '97	*PolyGram TV*	8	*30 Aug 97*	4
DANGER ZONE	*PolyGram TV*	15	*30 Aug 97*	2
PURE DANCE 97	*PolyGram TV*	9	*18 Oct 97*	3
HEART & SOUL	*PolyGram TV*	17	*8 Nov 97*	1
HITS ZONE - THE BEST OF '97	*PolyGram TV*	18	*15 Nov 97*	1
LOVE - 39 ALL-TIME LOVE CLASSICS	*PolyGram TV*	1	*14 Feb 98*	4
PURE ROCK BALLADS	*PolyGram TV*	10	*21 Feb 98*	4
INTO THE BLUE	*PolyGram TV*	10	*28 Mar 98*	3
UNDISPUTED	*PolyGram TV*	6	*11 Apr 98*	3
FRIDAY NIGHT FEVER	*PolyGram TV*	6	*25 Apr 98*	4
CONNECTED	*PolyGram TV*	18	*2 May 98*	1
MIXED EMOTIONS II	*PolyGram TV*	3	*4 Jul 98*	8
COOL GROOVES	*PolyGram TV*	12	*5 Sep 98*	3
POWER & SOUL	*PolyGram TV*	5	*12 Sep 98*	5
MOBO 1998 - MUSIC OF BLACK ORIGIN	*PolyGram TV*	13	*24 Oct 98*	2
THE BEST OF DRIVE TIME	*PolyGram TV*	12	*31 Oct 98*	1
SOUL	*PolyGram TV*	10	*7 Nov 98*	3
MUSIC OF THE NIGHT	*PolyGram TV*	5	*12 Dec 98*	20
PARTY	*PolyGram TV*	19	*9 Jan 99*	1

PolyGram TV/Sony TV

COMPILATION ALBUMS:	HITS 4			WEEKS 26
MUNDO AFRIKA	*Sony TV/PolyGram TV*	17	*13 Jul 96*	1
THE FIRST SUMMER OF LOVE	*Sony TV/PolyGram TV*	6	*2 Aug 97*	7
THE SUMMER OF LOVE GOES ON - SIXTIES	*Sony TV/PolyGram TV*	16	*1 Aug 98*	1
WOMAN	*PolyGram TV/Sony TV*	5	*21 Nov 98*	17

PolyGram TV/warner.esp

COMPILATION ALBUMS:	HITS 2			WEEKS 16
ALL MY LOVE	*warner.esp/PolyGram TV*	7	*1 Nov 97*	4
LOVE SONGS	*PolyGram TV/warner.esp*	1	*13 Feb 99*	12

Polystar

ALBUMS:	HITS 7			WEEKS 72
BOOGIE BUS	*Polystar*	23	*19 May 79*	11
CHAMPAGNE AND ROSES	*Polystar*	7	*3 May 80*	14
I AM WOMAN	*Polystar*	11	*30 Aug 80*	13
COUNTRY ROUND UP	*Polystar*	64	*11 Oct 80*	3
THE HITMAKERS	*Polystar*	45	*6 Dec 80*	10

ROLL ON	*Polystar*	3	*4 Apr 81*	13
MONSTER TRACKS	*Polystar*	20	*17 Oct 81*	8

Portrait

ALBUMS:	**HITS 2**			**WEEKS 18**
THE HEAT IS ON - 16 TRACKS	*Portrait*	9	*16 Aug 86*	12
SUMMER DAYS, BOOGIE NIGHTS - 16 TRACKS	*Portrait*	40	*16 Aug 86*	6

Positiva

COMPILATION ALBUMS:	**HITS 2**			**WEEKS 4**
PHASE ONE	*Positiva*	15	*2 Apr 94*	1
ACCESS ALL AREAS	*Positiva*	11	*26 Apr 97*	3

Priority

COMPILATION ALBUMS:	**HITS 1**			**WEEKS 8**
WORLD WRESTLING FEDERATION AGGRESSION	*Priority*	13	*15 Apr 00*	8
Rap versions of the Official World Wrestling Federation Superstar Themes.				

Proto

ALBUMS:	**HITS 1**			**WEEKS 1**
TWELVE INCHES OF PLEASURE	*Proto*	100	*26 Nov 83*	1

Prototype

COMPILATION ALBUMS:	**HITS 2**			**WEEKS 3**
SEB FONTAINE - PROTOTYPE	*Prototype*	14	*8 May 99*	2
PROTOTYPE 3 - SEB FONTAINE	*Prototype/Global Underground*	19	*22 Apr 00*	1

Pump

COMPILATION ALBUMS:	**HITS 4**			**WEEKS 12**
EIGHTIES SOUL WEEKENDER 2	*Pump*	11	*20 Jul 96*	4
THE VERY BEST OF PURE SWING	*Pump*	17	*7 Dec 96*	3
SLOW JAMS	*Pump*	10	*8 Feb 97*	3
EIGHTIES SOUL WEEKENDER 3	*Pump*	15	*10 May 97*	2

Pure Music

COMPILATION ALBUMS:	**HITS 7**			**WEEKS 50**
THE LADY SINGS THE BLUES	*Pure Music*	9	*22 Oct 94*	4
THE GREATEST NUMBER ONES OF THE EIGHTIES	*Pure Music*	11	*5 Nov 94*	4
DANCE MANIA 95 - VOLUME 1	*Pure Music*	1	*11 Feb 95*	11
DANCE MANIA 95 - VOLUME 2	*Pure Music*	1	*8 Apr 95*	9
DANCE MANIA 95 - VOLUME 3	*Pure Music*	1	*15 Jul 95*	7
DANCE MANIA 95 - VOLUME 4	*Pure Music*	7	*30 Sep 95*	4
THE BEST OF DANCE MANIA 95	*Pure Music*	5	*11 Nov 95*	11

Pure Silk

COMPILATION ALBUMS:	**HITS 5**			**WEEKS 13**
PURE SILK - A NEW DIMENSION	*Pure Silk*	15	*6 Nov 99*	2
PURE SILK - THE THIRD DIMENSION - MIXED BY TIMMY MAGIC	*Pure Silk*	12	*26 Feb 00*	3
Garage compilation.				
PURE SILK IN AYIA NAPA - THE HOME OF UK GARAGE	*Pure Silk*	8	*1 Jul 00*	Q6
Mixed by Mikee B of the Dreem Teem and DJ S with MC GKP.				
GARAGE VIBES	*Pure Silk*	20	*11 Nov 00*	1
Mixed by Frankie "Fabulous" Foncett.				
PURE SILK IN AYIA NAPA 2	*Pure Silk*	20	*9 Jun 01*	1
Mixed by Karl 'Tuff Enuff' Brown & DJ S featuring Ms Dynamite & CKP.				

Pye

ALBUMS:	**HITS 9**			**WEEKS 39**
CURTAIN UP	*Pye Nixa*	4	*9 May 59*	13
HONEY HIT PARADE	*Pye Golden Guinea*	13	*23 Jun 62*	7
ALL THE HITS BY ALL THE STARS	*Pye Golden Guinea*	19	*1 Dec 62*	2
HITSVILLE	*Pye Golden Guinea*	11	*7 Sep 63*	6
HITSVILLE VOLUME 2	*Pye Golden Guinea*	20	*23 Nov 63*	1
THE BLUES VOLUME 1	*Pye*	15	*4 Jan 64*	3
THE BLUES VOLUME 2	*Pye*	16	*30 May 64*	3
PYE CHARTBUSTERS	*Pye*	36	*16 Oct 71*	1
PYE CHARTBUSTERS VOLUME 2	*Pye*	29	*18 Dec 71*	3

Quality Price Music

COMPILATION ALBUMS:	**HITS 2**			**WEEKS 3**
CLUB IBIZA	*Quality Price Music*	15	*4 Nov 95*	1
CLUB IBIZA SILVER EDITION [RE]	*Quality Price Music*	19	*30 Mar 96*	1
Special repackaged edition.				
CLUB IBIZA - VOLUME 2	*Quality Price Music*	19	*19 Oct 96*	1

Quality Television

COMPILATION ALBUMS:	**HITS 13**			**WEEKS 79**
HIT THE DECKS VOLUME 1 - BATTLE OF THE DJS	*Quality Television*	3	*15 Feb 92*	7
TEMPTATION	*Quality Television*	3	*2 May 92*	8

THE SOUND OF SKA	*Quality Television*	4	*6 Jun 92*	6
TO HAVE AND TO HOLD - THE WEDDING ALBUM	*Quality Television*	7	*20 Jun 92*	4
HIT THE DECKS VOLUME 2 - BATTLE OF THE DJS	*Quality Television*	3	*4 Jul 92*	6
CELEBRATION - THE BEST OF REGGAE - 25 YEARS OF TROJAN	*Quality Television*	5	*11 Jul 92*	8
DANGER ZONE VOLUME 1	*Quality Television*	16	*18 Jul 92*	3
THREE STEPS TO HEAVEN - ROCK 'N' ROLL LEGENDS	*Quality Television*	6	*12 Sep 92*	5
HIT THE DECKS VOLUME III	*Quality Television*	3	*7 Nov 92*	4
THE POWER OF LOVE	*Quality Television*	4	*7 Nov 92*	7
RARE GROOVE - DYNAMIC DISCO HITS	*Quality Television*	7	*21 Nov 92*	14
THE NASHVILLE DREAM	*Quality Television*	10	*30 Jan 93*	3
GLAM MANIA	*Quality Television*	10	*8 May 93*	4

R&S

COMPILATION ALBUMS:	HITS 2			WEEKS 2
R & S RECORDS - ORDER TO DANCE	*R&S*	18	*16 Nov 91*	1
IN ORDER TO DANCE 5	*R&S*	16	*24 Sep 94*	1

RCA

ALBUMS:	HITS 1			WEEKS 5
GET ON UP	*RCA*	35	*28 May 83*	5
COMPILATION ALBUMS:	**HITS 5**			**WEEKS 31**
RAINBOW WARRIORS	*RCA*	2	*24 Jun 89*	10
Benefit album to support Greenpeace.				
CELTIC HEART	*RCA*	6	*13 Feb 93*	10
PRIDE - THE VERY BEST OF SCOTLAND	*RCA*	13	*1 Jul 95*	4
THE BEAUTIFUL GAME - EUFA EURO '96	*RCA*	10	*1 Jun 96*	6
EVERY WOMAN	*RCA*	19	*11 Apr 98*	1

Reachin'

COMPILATION ALBUMS:	HITS 1			WEEKS 2
RAVE	*Reachin'*	18	*9 Nov 91*	2

React

COMPILATION ALBUMS:	HITS 4			WEEKS 6
FRESKA!	*React*	20	*4 Jun 94*	1
HOUSE NATION 1	*React*	20	*24 Sep 94*	1
LAURENT GARNIER - LABORATOIRE MIX	*React*	16	*2 Nov 96*	1
TWICE AS NICE IN AYIA NAPA - DJ SPOONY	*React*	18	*16 Oct 99*	3

Really Useful/Polydor

ALBUMS:	HITS 1			WEEKS 9
ANDREW LLOYD WEBBER - THE PREMIERE COLLECTION	*Really Useful/Polydor*	3	*12 Nov 88*	9
COMPILATION ALBUMS:	**HITS 5**			**WEEKS 96**
ANDREW LLOYD WEBBER - THE PREMIERE COLLECTION	*Really Useful/Polydor*	1	*14 Jan 89*	55
SKINBEAT - THE FIRST TOUCH	*Really Useful/Polydor*	6	*31 Mar 90*	8
THE PREMIERE COLLECTION - ENCORE (ANDREW LLOYD WEBBER)	*Really Useful/Polydor*	2	*28 Nov 92*	11
THE VERY BEST OF ANDREW LLOYD WEBBER	*Really Useful/Polydor*	3	*5 Nov 94*	18
SONGS FROM WHISTLE DOWN THE WIND	*Really Useful/Polydor*	3	*31 Oct 98*	4
Re-recording of songs from the Stage Show.				

Record Shack

ALBUMS:	HITS 1			WEEKS 4
RECORD SHACK PRESENTS - VOLUME ONE	*Record Shack*	41	*8 Sep 84*	4

Reinforced

COMPILATION ALBUMS:	HITS 1			WEEKS 1
INFORCERS 3	*Reinforced*	18	*29 May 93*	1

Renaissance Recordings

COMPILATION ALBUMS:	HITS 5			WEEKS 10
RENAISSANCE WORLDWIDE LONDON	*Renaissance Recordings*	16	*18 Oct 97*	2
RENAISSANCE - AWAKENING - DAVE SEAMAN	*Renaissance Recordings*	18	*1 Apr 00*	1
RENAISSANCE IBIZA - MIXED BY DEEP DISH	*Renaissance Recordings*	20	*19 Aug 00*	1
Sleeve reads title as 'The Master Series Part Two: Ibiza'.				
PROGRESSION VOLUME ONE	*Renaissance Recordings*	17	*17 Mar 01*	1
RENAISSANCE IBIZA 2001	*Renaissance Recordings*	2	*28 Jul 01*	5
3CD box set. CD1-Bar Life, CD2-Club Life, CD3-Beach Life.				

Respond

ALBUMS:	HITS 1			WEEKS 3
RESPOND PACKAGE - LOVE THE REASON	*Respond*	50	*15 Oct 83*	3

Rhythm King

ALBUMS:	HITS 1			WEEKS 2
CHICAGO JACKBEAT VOLUME 2	*Rhythm King*	67	*6 Jun 87*	2

Ritz

ALBUMS:	HITS 1			WEEKS 6
TEARDROPS	*Ritz*	37	*18 Jun 83*	6

Ronco

ALBUMS:	HITS 44			WEEKS 408
20 STAR TRACKS	*Ronco*	2	*21 Oct 72*	13
BLAZING BULLETS	*Ronco*	17	*8 Nov 75*	8
STAR TRACKIN' 76	*Ronco*	9	*24 Jan 76*	5
SUPERGROUPS	*Ronco*	57	*16 Jul 77*	1
BLACK JOY	*Ronco*	26	*26 Nov 77*	13
BOOGIE NIGHTS	*Ronco*	5	*18 Mar 78*	7
BOOGIE FEVER	*Ronco*	15	*18 Nov 78*	11
ROCK LEGENDS	*Ronco*	54	*9 Jun 79*	3
ROCK 'N' ROLLER DISCO	*Ronco*	3	*3 Nov 79*	11
PEACE IN THE VALLEY	*Ronco*	6	*8 Dec 79*	18
MILITARY GOLD	*Ronco*	62	*22 Dec 79*	3
STREET LEVEL	*Ronco*	29	*25 Oct 80*	5
COUNTRY LEGENDS	*Ronco*	9	*8 Nov 80*	12
RADIOACTIVE	*Ronco*	13	*15 Nov 80*	9
SPACE INVADERS	*Ronco*	47	*29 Nov 80*	3
THE LEGENDARY BIG BANDS	*Ronco*	24	*6 Dec 80*	6
DISCO DAZE AND DISCO NITES	*Ronco*	1	*9 May 81*	23
SUPER HITS 1 & 2	*Ronco*	2	*19 Sep 81*	17
COUNTRY SUNRISE/COUNTRY SUNSET	*Ronco*	27	*24 Oct 81*	11
ROCK HOUSE	*Ronco*	44	*14 Nov 81*	9
MISTY MORNINGS	*Ronco*	44	*12 Dec 81*	5
MEMORIES ARE MADE OF THIS	*Ronco*	84	*12 Dec 81*	4
HITS, HITS, HITS	*Ronco*	2	*26 Dec 81*	10
DISCO UK AND DISCO USA	*Ronco*	7	*24 Apr 82*	10
CHARTBUSTERS	*Ronco*	3	*15 May 82*	10
OVERLOAD	*Ronco*	10	*3 Jul 82*	8
SOUL DAZE/SOUL NITES	*Ronco*	25	*28 Aug 82*	10
BREAKOUT	*Ronco*	4	*11 Sep 82*	8
MUSIC FOR THE SEASONS	*Ronco*	41	*30 Oct 82*	10
CHART WARS	*Ronco*	30	*27 Nov 82*	7
THE GREAT COUNTRY MUSIC SHOW	*Ronco*	38	*27 Nov 82*	7
THE BEST OF THE COMPOSERS: BEETHOVEN/STRAUSS/TCHAIKOWSKY/ MOZART	*Ronco*	49	*18 Dec 82*	10
RAIDERS OF THE POP CHARTS	*Ronco*	1	*25 Dec 82*	17
CHART RUNNERS	*Ronco*	4	*19 Mar 83*	13
CHART ENCOUNTERS OF THE HIT KIND	*Ronco*	5	*21 May 83*	10
LOVERS ONLY	*Ronco*	12	*18 Jun 83*	13
HITS ON FIRE	*Ronco*	11	*16 Jul 83*	10
THE HIT SQUAD - CHART TRACKING	*Ronco*	4	*17 Sep 83*	9
THE HIT SQUAD - NIGHT CLUBBING	*Ronco*	28	*17 Sep 83*	7
THE HIT SQUAD - HITS OF '83	*Ronco*	12	*12 Nov 83*	11
CHART TREK VOLUMES 1 AND 2	*Ronco*	20	*7 Jan 84*	9
SOMETIMES WHEN WE TOUCH	*Ronco*	8	*21 Jan 84*	14
BABY LOVE	*Ronco*	47	*24 Mar 84*	6
DREAMS AND THEMES	*Ronco*	75	*7 Apr 84*	2

Ronco & Telstar

ALBUMS:	HITS 1			WEEKS 27
GREEN VELVET	*Ronco*	6	*17 Dec 83*	17
GREEN VELVET [RI]	*Telstar*	10	*15 Dec 84*	10

Ronco/Charisma

ALBUMS:	HITS 1			WEEKS 9
WE ARE MOST AMUSED (THE BEST OF BRITISH COMEDY)	*Ronco/Charisma*	30	*19 Dec 81*	9

Rough Trade

ALBUMS:	HITS 1			WEEKS 3
SOWETO	*Rough Trade*	66	*14 Aug 82*	3

Rumour

COMPILATION ALBUMS:	HITS 5			WEEKS 6
BREAKS, BASS AND BLEEPS 2	*Rumour*	20	*20 Jul 91*	1
BREAKS, BASS AND BLEEPS 4	*Rumour*	20	*18 Apr 92*	1
MOVIN' ON	*Rumour*	20	*27 Jun 92*	1
TRANCE	*Rumour*	18	*26 Sep 92*	1
MOVIN' ON 2	*Rumour*	15	*24 Oct 92*	2

Satellite

COMPILATION ALBUMS:	HITS 2			WEEKS 3
TUFF JAM PRESENTS UNDERGROUND FREQUENCIES - 1	*Satellite*	20	*19 Jul 97*	1
TUFF JAM PRESENTS UNDERGROUND FREQUENCIES - 2	*Satellite*	14	*23 May 98*	2

Save The Children Fund

ALBUMS:	HITS 1			WEEKS 16
STARS CHARITY FANTASIA SAVE THE CHILDREN FUND	*SCF*	6	*10 Sep 66*	16

Secret

ALBUMS:	HITS 2			WEEKS 8
CARRY ON OI!	*Secret*	60	*31 Oct 81*	4
OI! OI! THAT'S YER LOT	*Secret*	54	*25 Sep 82*	4

Serious

ALBUMS:	HITS 10			WEEKS 41
SERIOUS HIP-HOP 2	*Serious*	95	*28 Mar 87*	1
THE BEST OF HOUSE VOLUME 1	*Serious*	55	*1 Jul 87*	12
BEST OF HOUSE VOLUME 2	*Serious*	30	*12 Sep 87*	7
HIP-HOP '87	*Serious*	81	*17 Oct 87*	1
BEST OF HOUSE VOLUME 3	*Serious*	61	*14 Nov 87*	3
BEST OF HOUSE MEGAMIX	*Serious*	77	*12 Dec 87*	4
DANCE MANIA VOLUME 2	*Serious*	59	*20 Feb 88*	2
BEST OF HOUSE VOLUME 4	*Serious*	27	*12 Mar 88*	8
BEST OF HOUSE MEXAMIX VOLUME 2	*Serious*	73	*14 May 88*	2
ACID TRAX MEGAMIX VOLUME 1	*Serious*	93	*29 Oct 88*	1

Shut Up And Dance

COMPILATION ALBUMS:	HITS 1			WEEKS 1
SHUT UP AND DANCE/FUCK OFF AND DIE	*Shut Up And Dance*	20	*22 Feb 92*	1

Six6

COMPILATION ALBUMS:	HITS 2			WEEKS 8
RENAISSANCE	*Six6*	9	*1 Oct 94*	5
RENAISSANCE THE MIX COLLECTION - PART 3	*Six6*	12	*6 Jul 96*	3

Slinky Music

COMPILATION ALBUMS:	HITS 1			WEEKS 1
SLINKY PRESENTS SUPERCLUB DJ'S - GUY ORNADEL	*Slinky Music*	17	*17 Feb 01*	1

Solar

ALBUMS:	HITS 1			WEEKS 1
THE SOLAR SYSTEM	*Solar*	70	*30 May 87*	1

Solid State

COMPILATION ALBUMS:	HITS 2			WEEKS 3
HIP HOP DON'T STOP - 20 CLASSIC HIP HOP SUPERJAMS	*Solid State*	16	*8 Feb 97*	1
HOUSE OF HANDBAG - NUOVO DISCO COLLECTION	*Solid State*	17	*29 Mar 97*	2

Some Bizarre

ALBUMS:	HITS 1			WEEKS 1
THE SOME BIZZARRE ALBUM	*Some Bizzare*	58	*14 Mar 81*	1

Sony TV

COMPILATION ALBUMS:	HITS 1			WEEKS 5
ABSOLUTE GOLD	*Sony TV*	3	*1 Feb 97*	5

Sony TV/Global TV

COMPILATION ALBUMS:	HITS 4			WEEKS 26
THIS YEAR'S LOVE IS FOREVER	*Sony TV/Global TV*	4	*25 Nov 95*	11
IT TAKES TWO	*Sony TV/Global TV*	6	*13 Apr 96*	6
THE BEST OF VYBIN'	*Sony TV/Global TV*	12	*16 Nov 96*	2
THIS YEAR'S LOVE (WILL LAST FOREVER) XXX	*Sony TV/Global TV*	12	*30 Nov 96*	7

Sony TV/MCI

COMPILATION ALBUMS:	HITS 1			WEEKS 1
LOVE TRAIN - THE SOUND OF PHILADELPHIA	*Sony TV/MCI*	18	*18 Apr 98*	1

Sony Music TV/Universal Music TV

COMPILATION ALBUMS:	HITS 4			WEEKS 20
COUNTRY	*Sony Music TV/Universal Music TV*	8	*17 Jul 99*	8
LATIN FEVER	*Sony Music TV/Universal Music TV*	3	*5 Aug 00*	9
WOMAN	*Universal Music TV/Sony Music TV*	10	*18 Nov 00*	2
FEMALE	*Sony Music TV/Universal Music TV*	14	*17 Nov 01*	1

Sony TV/warner.esp

COMPILATION ALBUMS:	HITS 2			WEEKS 4
LIVE 4 EVER	*Sony TV/warner.esp*	11	*11 Jul 98*	3
AMERICAN DREAM - 36 DRIVETIME CLASSICS	*Sony Music TV/warner.esp*	17	*24 Jun 00*	1

Sound Dimension

COMPILATION ALBUMS:	HITS 7			WEEKS 28
A RETROSPECTIVE OF HOUSE '91-'95 - VOLUME 1	*Sound Dimension*	10	*5 Aug 95*	10

A RETROSPECTIVE OF HOUSE '91-'95 - VOLUME 2	*Sound Dimension*	15	*13 Jan 96*	3
A RETROSPECTIVE OF HOUSE '91-'96 - VOLUME 3: JAY/KELLY/ANDERSON	*Sound Dimension*	9	*1 Jun 96*	2
A RETROSPECTIVE OF HOUSE '91-'96 - VOLUME 4	*Sound Dimension*	7	*7 Sep 96*	5
AN INTROSPECTIVE OF HOUSE: 1ST DIMENSION	*Sound Dimension*	18	*1 Feb 97*	2
AN INTROSPECTIVE OF HOUSE: 2ND DIMENSION	*Sound Dimension*	9	*14 Jun 97*	4
AN INTROSPECTIVE OF HOUSE: 3RD DIMENSION	*Sound Dimension*	14	*13 Sep 97*	2

Starblend

ALBUMS:	HITS 7			WEEKS 31
IN TOUCH	*Starblend*	89	*12 Nov 83*	2
BROKEN DREAMS	*Starblend*	48	*23 Jun 84*	7
12 X 12 MEGA MIXES	*Starblend*	77	*27 Apr 85*	2
AMERICAN DREAMS	*Starblend*	43	*3 Aug 85*	8
DISCOVER COUNTRY/DISCOVER NEW COUNTRY	*Starblend*	60	*12 Jul 86*	3
HEARTBREAKERS - 18 CLASSIC LOVE HITS	*Starblend*	38	*16 Aug 86*	8
ABSOLUTE ROCK 'N' ROLL	*Starblend*	88	*20 Sep 86*	1

Start

COMPILATION ALBUMS:	HITS 1			WEEKS 5
THE SONGS OF BOB DYLAN	*Start*	13	*15 Apr 89*	5

Stax

ALBUMS:	HITS 1			WEEKS 16
HIT THE ROAD STAX	*Stax*	10	*8 Apr 67*	16

Stiff

ALBUMS:	HITS 1			WEEKS 7
STIFF'S LIVE STIFFS	*Stiff*	28	*11 Mar 78*	7

Stoic

ALBUMS:	HITS 1			WEEKS 14
EMERALD CLASSICS	*Stoic*	35	*16 Jun 84*	14

Street Sounds

ALBUMS:	HITS 54			WEEKS 259
STREET SOUNDS EDITION 2	*Street Sounds*	35	*19 Feb 83*	6
STREET SOUNDS EDITION 3	*Street Sounds*	21	*23 Apr 83*	5
STREET SOUNDS EDITION 4	*Street Sounds*	14	*25 Jun 83*	8
STREET SOUNDS EDITION 5	*Street Sounds*	16	*13 Aug 83*	8
STREET SOUNDS EDITION 6	*Street Sounds*	23	*8 Oct 83*	5
STREET SOUNDS ELECTRO 1	*Street Sounds*	18	*22 Oct 83*	8
STREET SOUNDS EDITION 7	*Street Sounds*	48	*17 Dec 83*	4
STREET SOUNDS ELECTRO 2	*Street Sounds*	49	*7 Jan 84*	7
STREET SOUNDS HI-ENERGY NO 1	*Street Sounds*	71	*3 Mar 84*	1
STREET SOUNDS EDITION 8	*Street Sounds*	22	*10 Mar 84*	7
STREET SOUNDS CRUCIAL ELECTRO	*Street Sounds*	24	*10 Mar 84*	10
STREET SOUNDS ELECTRO 3	*Street Sounds*	25	*7 Apr 84*	9
STREET SOUNDS EDITION 9	*Street Sounds*	22	*12 May 84*	5
STREET SOUNDS ELECTRO 4	*Street Sounds*	25	*9 Jun 84*	9
STREET SOUNDS UK ELECTRO	*Street Sounds*	60	*30 Jun 84*	4
LET THE MUSIC SCRATCH	*Street Sounds*	91	*21 Jul 84*	3
STREET SOUNDS CRUCIAL ELECTRO 2	*Street Sounds*	35	*11 Aug 84*	6
STREET SOUNDS EDITION 10	*Street Sounds*	24	*18 Aug 84*	6
STREET SOUNDS ELECTRO 5	*Street Sounds*	17	*6 Oct 84*	6
STREET SOUNDS EDITION 11	*Street Sounds*	48	*10 Nov 84*	4
STREET SOUNDS ELECTRO 6	*Street Sounds*	24	*9 Mar 85*	10
STREET SOUNDS ELECTRO 7	*Street Sounds*	12	*18 May 85*	7
STREET SOUNDS EDITION 12	*Street Sounds*	23	*18 May 85*	4
STREET SOUNDS ELECTRO 8	*Street Sounds*	23	*13 Jul 85*	5
STREET SOUNDS EDITION 13	*Street Sounds*	19	*17 Aug 85*	9
STREET SOUNDS N.Y. VS. L.A. BEATS	*Street Sounds*	65	*17 Aug 85*	4
STREET SOUNDS ELECTRO 9	*Street Sounds*	18	*5 Oct 85*	6
STREET SOUNDS EDITION 14	*Street Sounds*	43	*16 Nov 85*	3
STREET SOUNDS EDITION 15	*Street Sounds*	58	*21 Dec 85*	8
STREET SOUNDS ELECTRO 10	*Street Sounds*	72	*21 Dec 85*	6
STREET SOUNDS HIP-HOP ELECTRO 11	*Street Sounds*	19	*29 Mar 86*	5
STREET SOUNDS EDITION 16	*Street Sounds*	17	*5 Apr 86*	7
JAZZ JUICE 2	*Street Sounds*	96	*21 Jun 86*	1
STREET SOUNDS HIP-HOP ELECTRO 12	*Street Sounds*	28	*28 Jun 86*	4
STREET SOUNDS EDITION 17	*Street Sounds*	35	*19 Jul 86*	5
STREET SOUNDS HIP-HOP ELECTRO 13	*Street Sounds*	23	*6 Sep 86*	5
STREET SOUNDS EDITION 18	*Street Sounds*	20	*11 Oct 86*	5
STREET SOUNDS HIP HOP ELECTRO 14	*Street Sounds*	40	*11 Oct 86*	3
JAZZ JUICE 3	*Street Sounds*	88	*11 Oct 86*	1
STREET SOUNDS HIP-HOP ELECTRO 15	*Street Sounds*	46	*15 Nov 86*	2
STREET SOUNDS EDITION 19	*Street Sounds*	61	*6 Dec 86*	3
STREET SOUNDS CRUCIAL ELECTRO - 3	*Street Sounds*	41	*24 Jan 87*	3
STREET SOUNDS ANTHEMS - VOLUME 1	*Street Sounds*	61	*7 Feb 87*	3
STREET SOUNDS EDITION 20	*Street Sounds*	25	*14 Feb 87*	4

STREET SOUNDS HIP-HOP ELECTRO 16	*Street Sounds*	40	*13 Jun 87*	3
STREET SOUNDS DANCE MUSIC '87	*Street Sounds*	40	*4 Jul 87*	5
STREET SOUNDS HIP-HOP 17	*Street Sounds*	38	*15 Aug 87*	3
JAZZ JUICE 5	*Street Sounds*	97	*15 Aug 87*	1
STREET SOUNDS 87 VOLUME 2	*Street Sounds*	47	*12 Sep 87*	3
BEST OF WEST COAST HIP HOP	*Street Sounds*	80	*12 Sep 87*	2
STREET SOUNDS HIP HOP 18	*Street Sounds*	67	*24 Oct 87*	1
STREET SOUNDS HIP HOP 20	*Street Sounds*	39	*19 Mar 88*	4
STREET SOUNDS 88-1	*Street Sounds*	73	*19 Mar 88*	2
STREET SOUNDS HIP HOP 21	*Street Sounds*	87	*4 Jun 88*	1

Streetwave

ALBUMS:	HITS 1			WEEKS 4
STREETNOISE VOLUME 1	*Streetwave*	51	*23 Oct 82*	4

Strictly Underground

COMPILATION ALBUMS:	HITS 1			WEEKS 1
ILLEGAL RAVE	*Strictly Underground*	20	*19 Sep 92*	1

Studio Two

ALBUMS:	HITS 3			WEEKS 27
BREAKTHROUGH	*Studio Two*	2	*21 Oct 67*	19
TOTAL SOUND	*Studio Two*	39	*4 Sep 71*	4
STUDIO TWO CLASSICS	*Studio Two*	16	*30 Oct 71*	4

Stylus

ALBUMS:	HITS 25			WEEKS 267
THE MAGIC OF TORVILL AND DEAN	*Stylus*	35	*3 Aug 85*	9
NIGHT BEAT	*Stylus*	15	*17 Aug 85*	8
DISCO BEACH PARTY	*Stylus*	29	*24 Aug 85*	10
VELVET WATERS	*Stylus*	54	*14 Dec 85*	4
CHOICES OF THE HEART	*Stylus*	87	*28 Dec 85*	2
NIGHT BEAT II	*Stylus*	7	*8 Mar 86*	9
LET'S HEAR IT FOR THE GIRLS	*Stylus*	17	*17 May 86*	10
BLACK MAGIC	*Stylus*	26	*1 Nov 86*	9
HIT MIX '86	*Stylus*	10	*8 Nov 86*	14
CLASSICS BY CANDLELIGHT	*Stylus*	74	*22 Nov 86*	4
BANDS OF GOLD - THE SWINGING SIXTIES	*Stylus*	48	*14 Mar 87*	6
BANDS OF GOLD - THE SENSATIONAL SEVENTIES	*Stylus*	75	*21 Mar 87*	4
BANDS OF GOLD - THE ELECTRIC EIGHTIES	*Stylus*	82	*28 Mar 87*	1
SIXTIES MIX - 60 SEQUENCED HITS FROM THE SIXTIES	*Stylus*	3	*11 Jul 87*	44
THE HIT FACTORY: THE BEST OF STOCK AITKEN WATERMAN	*Stylus*	18	*24 Oct 87*	17
HIT MIX - HITS OF THE YEAR	*Stylus*	29	*21 Nov 87*	11
HIP HOP AND RAPPING IN THE HOUSE	*Stylus*	5	*2 Apr 88*	13
SIXTIES MIX 2	*Stylus*	14	*7 May 88*	20
BACK ON THE ROAD	*Stylus*	29	*4 Jun 88*	11
THE GREATEST EVER ROCK 'N' ROLL MIX	*Stylus*	8	*30 Jul 88*	15
RAP TRAX	*Stylus*	3	*3 Sep 88*	13
RARE GROOVE MIX - 70 SMASH HITS OF THE 70'S	*Stylus*	20	*1 Oct 88*	10
SOFT METAL	*Stylus*	7	*22 Oct 88*	12
HIT MIX '88	*Stylus*	48	*26 Nov 88*	7
THE GREATEST HITS OF HOUSE	*Stylus*	26	*17 Dec 88*	4

COMPILATION ALBUMS:	HITS 21			WEEKS 222
SOFT METAL	*Stylus*	7	*14 Jan 89*	27
HIT MIX '88	*Stylus*	15	*14 Jan 89*	2
THE GREATEST HITS OF HOUSE	*Stylus*	5	*14 Jan 89*	9
BEAT THIS - 20 HITS OF RHYTHM KING	*Stylus*	9	*18 Feb 89*	8
NEW ROOTS	*Stylus*	18	*11 Mar 89*	1
HIP HOUSE	*Stylus*	3	*25 Mar 89*	8
THE SINGER AND THE SONG	*Stylus*	5	*22 Apr 89*	11
PRECIOUS METAL	*Stylus*	2	*27 May 89*	29
DON'T STOP THE MUSIC	*Stylus*	7	*24 Jun 89*	6
HOT SUMMER NIGHTS	*Stylus*	4	*15 Jul 89*	11
SUNSHINE MIX	*Stylus*	9	*19 Aug 89*	7
THE GREATEST EVER ROCK 'N' ROLL MIX	*Stylus*	5	*26 Aug 89*	9
MIDNIGHT LOVE	*Stylus*	7	*2 Sep 89*	6
LEGENDS AND HEROES	*Stylus*	6	*16 Sep 89*	10
THE RIGHT STUFF - REMIX '89	*Stylus*	2	*21 Oct 89*	11
JUKE BOX JIVE MIX - ROCK 'N' ROLL GREATS	*Stylus*	13	*25 Nov 89*	8
WARE'S THE HOUSE?	*Stylus*	2	*30 Dec 89*	10
PURE SOFT METAL	*Stylus*	1	*13 Jan 90*	23
THE RIGHT STUFF 2 - NOTHING BUT A HOUSE PARTY	*Stylus*	2	*10 Mar 90*	15
SIXTIES MIX 3	*Stylus*	4	*26 May 90*	9
MOMENTS IN SOUL	*Stylus*	9	*20 Oct 90*	2

Supreme Underground

COMPILATION ALBUMS:	HITS 1			WEEKS 1
HARDCORE EXPLOSION '97	*Supreme Underground*	20	*8 Mar 97*	1

Talkin Loud

COMPILATION ALBUMS:	HITS 1			WEEKS 3
TALKIN LOUD TWO	*Talkin Loud*	6	*30 Jan 93*	3

Teldec

COMPILATION ALBUMS:	HITS 1			WEEKS 2
SENSUAL CLASSICS	*Teldec*	19	*21 Nov 92*	2

Telstar

ALBUMS:	HITS 36			WEEKS 327
CHART ATTACK	*Telstar*	7	*16 Oct 82*	6
MIDNIGHT IN MOTOWN	*Telstar*	34	*6 Nov 82*	16
DIRECT HITS	*Telstar*	89	*18 Dec 82*	1
DANCIN' - 20 ORIGINAL MOTOWN MOVERS	*Telstar*	97	*8 Jan 83*	1
INSTRUMENTAL MAGIC	*Telstar*	68	*5 Feb 83*	5
20 GREAT ITALIAN LOVE SONGS	*Telstar*	28	*30 Apr 83*	6
IN THE GROOVE - THE 12 INCH DISCO PARTY	*Telstar*	20	*4 Jun 83*	12
ROOTS REGGAE 'N' REGGAE ROCK	*Telstar*	34	*12 Nov 83*	6
SUPERCHART '83	*Telstar*	22	*19 Nov 83*	9
THE VERY BEST OF MOTOWN LOVE SONGS	*Telstar*	10	*4 Feb 84*	22
DON'T STOP DANCING	*Telstar*	11	*26 May 84*	12
HITS, HITS, HITS - 18 SMASH ORIGINALS	*Telstar*	6	*13 Oct 84*	9
LOVE SONGS - 16 CLASSIC LOVE SONGS	*Telstar*	20	*8 Dec 84*	12
OPEN TOP CARS AND GIRLS IN T'SHIRTS	*Telstar*	13	*7 Sep 85*	9
THE LOVE ALBUM - 16 CLASSIC LOVE SONGS	*Telstar*	7	*16 Nov 85*	18
PERFORMANCE - THE VERY BEST OF TIM RICE AND ANDREW LLOYD WEBBER	*Telstar*	33	*7 Dec 85*	7
Includes tracks by David Essex abd Elaine Paige.				
MORE GREEN VELVET	*Telstar*	42	*7 Dec 85*	5
THE CHART	*Telstar*	6	*18 Oct 86*	12
ROCK LEGENDS	*Telstar*	54	*1 Nov 86*	7
LOVERS	*Telstar*	14	*8 Nov 86*	16
SIXTIES MANIA	*Telstar*	19	*22 Nov 86*	22
MOTOWN CHARTBUSTERS	*Telstar*	25	*6 Dec 86*	12
THE DANCE CHART	*Telstar*	23	*28 Mar 87*	8
TRACKS OF MY TEARS	*Telstar*	27	*3 Oct 87*	7
DANCE MIX '87	*Telstar*	39	*28 Nov 87*	10
ALWAYS AND FOREVER THE LOVE ALBUM	*Telstar*	41	*28 Nov 87*	10
SIXTIES PARTY MEGAMIX ALBUM	*Telstar*	46	*28 Nov 87*	7
LIFE IN THE FAST LANE	*Telstar*	10	*26 Dec 87*	12
. . . AND THE BEAT GOES ON	*Telstar*	12	*1 Oct 88*	8
THE HEART AND SOUL OF ROCK AND ROLL	*Telstar*	60	*5 Nov 88*	6
THE LOVE ALBUM '88	*Telstar*	51	*12 Nov 88*	9
BEST OF HOUSE '88	*Telstar*	33	*19 Nov 88*	8
INSTRUMENTAL GREATS	*Telstar*	79	*19 Nov 88*	5
BACK TO THE SIXTIES	*Telstar*	47	*3 Dec 88*	6
HYPERACTIVE	*Telstar*	78	*3 Dec 88*	4
MORNING HAS BROKEN	*Telstar*	88	*17 Dec 88*	2
COMPILATION ALBUMS:	**HITS 144**			**WEEKS 836**
BEST OF HOUSE '88	*Telstar*	11	*14 Jan 89*	5
BACK TO THE SIXTIES	*Telstar*	14	*14 Jan 89*	4
PROTECT THE INNOCENT	*Telstar*	9	*15 Jul 89*	9
RHYTHM OF THE SUN	*Telstar*	12	*15 Jul 89*	4
THIS IS SKA	*Telstar*	6	*22 Jul 89*	10
MOTOWN HEARTBREAKERS	*Telstar*	4	*14 Oct 89*	10
NUMBER ONES OF THE EIGHTIES	*Telstar*	2	*18 Nov 89*	19
SOFT ROCK	*Telstar*	15	*9 Dec 89*	5
NEW TRADITIONS	*Telstar*	13	*3 Feb 90*	4
MILESTONES - 20 ROCK OPERAS	*Telstar*	6	*10 Feb 90*	11
PRODUCT 2378	*Telstar*	16	*17 Mar 90*	3
GET ON THIS! - 30 DANCE HITS VOLUME 1	*Telstar*	2	*12 May 90*	12
A NIGHT AT THE OPERA	*Telstar*	2	*19 May 90*	12
MEGABASS	*Telstar*	1	*18 Aug 90*	12
GET ON THIS!!! 2	*Telstar*	3	*25 Aug 90*	9
MOLTEN METAL	*Telstar*	13	*25 Aug 90*	5
COUNTRY'S GREATEST HITS	*Telstar*	9	*15 Sep 90*	7
THE FINAL COUNTDOWN - THE VERY BEST OF SOFT METAL	*Telstar*	9	*27 Oct 90*	6
RAVE	*Telstar*	10	*3 Nov 90*	4
THE MOTOWN COLLECTION	*Telstar*	8	*24 Nov 90*	12
60 NUMBER ONES OF THE SIXTIES	*Telstar*	7	*1 Dec 90*	11
MEGABASS 2	*Telstar*	6	*8 Dec 90*	8
UNCHAINED MELODIES	*Telstar*	1	*23 Feb 91*	20
DON'T STOP . . . DOOWOP!	*Telstar*	15	*23 Mar 91*	4
THIN ICE - THE FIRST STEP	*Telstar*	2	*30 Mar 91*	9
AFTER THE DANCE	*Telstar*	16	*13 Apr 91*	3
MASSIVE HITS	*Telstar*	2	*11 May 91*	6
UNCHAINED MELODIES - II	*Telstar*	3	*18 May 91*	8
MEGABASS 3	*Telstar*	3	*8 Jun 91*	8

THIN ICE 2 - THE SECOND SHIVER	*Telstar*	1	*3 Aug 91*	9
MAKE YOU SWEAT	*Telstar*	4	*28 Sep 91*	6
BORN TO BE WILD	*Telstar*	8	*12 Oct 91*	5
BURNING HEARTS	*Telstar*	7	*2 Nov 91*	10
PUNK AND DISORDERLY - NEW WAVE 1976-1981	*Telstar*	18	*23 Nov 91*	2
CLASSICAL MASTERS	*Telstar*	13	*30 Nov 91*	15
LEGENDS OF SOUL - A WHOLE STACK OF SOUL	*Telstar*	15	*7 Dec 91*	10
KAOS THEORY	*Telstar*	2	*15 Feb 92*	7
ALL THE BEST - LOVE DUETS VOLUME 1	*Telstar*	5	*15 Feb 92*	6
GOLD - 18 EPIC SPORTING ANTHEMS	*Telstar*	15	*29 Feb 92*	3
THE ULTIMATE HARDCORE	*Telstar*	1	*7 Mar 92*	10
CLUB FOR HEROES	*Telstar*	3	*11 Apr 92*	10
KAOS THEORY 2	*Telstar*	2	*2 May 92*	8
INDIE HITS	*Telstar*	13	*2 May 92*	3
FLIGHT OF THE CONDOR	*Telstar*	11	*9 May 92*	6
GARAGE CITY	*Telstar*	8	*23 May 92*	5
RAVING WE'RE RAVING	*Telstar*	2	*6 Jun 92*	6
KT3 - KAOS THEORY 3	*Telstar*	1	*18 Jul 92*	8
THE DIVAS OF DANCE	*Telstar*	9	*1 Aug 92*	4
RAVE ALERT	*Telstar*	2	*8 Aug 92*	10
BLUE EYED SOUL	*Telstar*	4	*19 Sep 92*	6
KAOS THEORY 4	*Telstar*	2	*10 Oct 92*	5
RAVE NATION	*Telstar*	2	*17 Oct 92*	6
MORE THAN LOVE	*Telstar*	4	*17 Oct 92*	9
CLASSIC LOVE	*Telstar*	4	*14 Nov 92*	15
ROCK N ROLL HEARTBEATS	*Telstar*	13	*21 Nov 92*	1
MY GENERATION	*Telstar*	16	*21 Nov 92*	1
SONIC SYSTEM	*Telstar*	17	*19 Dec 92*	3
COUNTRY LOVE	*Telstar*	5	*27 Feb 93*	15
RAGGA HEAT REGGAE BEAT	*Telstar*	4	*3 Jul 93*	14
FRESH DANCE 93	*Telstar*	4	*17 Jul 93*	7
DANCE ADRENALIN	*Telstar*	1	*18 Sep 93*	7
LOVE IS RHYTHM	*Telstar*	5	*9 Oct 93*	5
COUNTRY LOVE 2	*Telstar*	11	*9 Oct 93*	4
THE ALL TIME GREATEST HITS OF DANCE	*Telstar*	11	*20 Nov 93*	7
A HEART OF GOLD	*Telstar*	9	*18 Dec 93*	4
NO 1'S OF DANCE	*Telstar*	16	*8 Jan 94*	3
DANCE HITS 94 - VOLUME 1	*Telstar*	1	*19 Feb 94*	10
LOVE OVER GOLD	*Telstar*	2	*19 Feb 94*	6
LOVE ON FILM	*Telstar*	17	*9 Apr 94*	2
AWESOME DANCE	*Telstar*	2	*7 May 94*	7
DANCE HITS '94 VOLUME 2	*Telstar*	1	*11 Jun 94*	8
JAZZ MOODS	*Telstar*	3	*2 Jul 94*	8
IT'S THE ULTIMATE DANCE ALBUM	*Telstar*	1	*23 Jul 94*	11
JUNGLE MANIA 94	*Telstar*	7	*29 Oct 94*	6
ULTIMATE REGGAE PARTY ALBUM!	*Telstar*	14	*29 Oct 94*	2
JAZZ MOODS 2	*Telstar*	18	*29 Oct 94*	1
JUNGLE MANIA 2	*Telstar*	5	*24 Dec 94*	8
JUNGLE MANIA 3	*Telstar*	5	*25 Mar 95*	6
WARNING! DANCE BOOM	*Telstar*	2	*6 May 95*	6
CLUB ZONE	*Telstar*	4	*5 Aug 95*	5
WARNING! DANCE BOOM 2	*Telstar*	7	*2 Sep 95*	4
CLUB ZONE 2	*Telstar*	10	*7 Oct 95*	3
BEST SWING '95	*Telstar*	10	*4 Nov 95*	3
BEST SWING 96	*Telstar*	2	*6 Jan 96*	7
OUR FRIENDS ELECTRIC	*Telstar*	8	*17 Feb 96*	5
THE GREATEST 90S DANCE HITS	*Telstar*	16	*24 Feb 96*	2
BEST SWING 96 - VOLUME 2	*Telstar*	6	*9 Mar 96*	5
LOVE OVER GOLD 2	*Telstar*	19	*13 Apr 96*	1
TECHNOHEDZ - 20 FIRESTARTIN' TECHO ANTHEMS	*Telstar*	12	*20 Apr 96*	3
LOVE II SWING	*Telstar*	10	*27 Apr 96*	3
SWING MIX 96	*Telstar*	3	*25 May 96*	6
CAFE LATINO	*Telstar*	18	*29 Jun 96*	1
BEST SWING '96 - VOLUME 3	*Telstar*	20	*13 Jul 96*	1
F1 ROCK	*Telstar*	20	*20 Jul 96*	1
MAD FOR IT	*Telstar*	12	*28 Sep 96*	3
THE MOTHER OF ALL SWING ALBUMS	*Telstar*	9	*9 Nov 96*	4
THE GREATEST CLASSICAL MOVIE ALBUM	*Telstar*	15	*18 Jan 97*	3
THE MOTHER OF ALL SWING MIX ALBUMS	*Telstar*	7	*22 Feb 97*	5
ONCE IN A LIFETIME	*Telstar*	13	*8 Mar 97*	3
SOUL SURVIVORS - 40 NORTHERN SOUL ANTHEMS	*Telstar*	10	*10 May 97*	7
CLUB CUTS 97	*Telstar*	5	*17 May 97*	7
CLUBLAND	*Telstar TV*	3	*14 Jun 97*	7
SIXTIES SUMMER MIX	*Telstar TV*	5	*21 Jun 97*	10
A DECADE OF IBIZA - 1987-1997	*Telstar TV*	5	*5 Jul 97*	10
CLUB CUTS 97 - VOLUME 2	*Telstar TV*	2	*19 Jul 97*	7
THE MOTHER OF ALL SWING II	*Telstar TV*	11	*2 Aug 97*	5
PURE HITS '97	*Telstar TV*	13	*16 Aug 97*	2
THE GREATEST DANCE ALBUM EVER MADE	*Telstar TV*	5	*30 Aug 97*	5

MOONDANCE - THE ALBUM	*Telstar TV*	16	*20 Sep 97*	4
CLUBLAND - VOLUME 2	*Telstar TV*	6	*27 Sep 97*	4
CLUB CUTS 97 - VOLUME 3	*Telstar TV*	5	*11 Oct 97*	4
CLUBLIFE	*Telstar TV*	3	*7 Mar 98*	5
NON-STOP DANCE ANTHEMS	*Telstar TV*	5	*4 Apr 98*	6
CLUB HITS 98	*Telstar TV*	2	*2 May 98*	7
FANTAZIA - BRITISH ANTHEMS - SUMMERTIME	*Telstar TV*	3	*23 May 98*	6
SMILE JAMAICA	*Telstar TV*	20	*20 Jun 98*	2
NON STOP HITS	*Telstar TV*	4	*4 Jul 98*	5
IBIZA ANTHEMS	*Telstar TV*	5	*11 Jul 98*	7
SIXTIES SUMMER MIX 2	*Telstar TV*	19	*15 Aug 98*	1
CLUBLIFE 2	*Telstar TV*	13	*22 Aug 98*	2
ULTIMATE COUNTRY: 40 COUNTRY GREATS	*Telstar TV*	8	*29 Aug 98*	9
NON STOP HITS - VOLUME 2	*Telstar TV*	19	*5 Sep 98*	1
SOUL SURVIVORS 2	*Telstar TV*	17	*19 Sep 98*	2
SUNDANCE - CHAPTER ONE	*Telstar TV*	9	*10 Oct 98*	3
CARWASH	*Telstar TV*	15	*31 Oct 98*	1
CHRIS TARRANT PRESENTS ULTIMATE PARTY MEGAMIX	*Telstar TV*	17	*5 Dec 98*	1
EUPHORIA	*Telstar TV*	1	*6 Feb 99*	17
BORN TO BE WILD	*Telstar TV*	15	*13 Mar 99*	1
THE CHILLOUT ALBUM	*Telstar TV*	4	*3 Apr 99*	10
BEST DANCE 99	*Telstar TV*	10	*10 Apr 99*	5
FUNKY HOUSE	*Telstar TV*	9	*24 Apr 99*	3
DEEPER - EUPHORIA II: MIXED BY RED JERRY	*Telstar TV*	2	*29 May 99*	6
NATIONAL ANTHEMS 99: MIXED BY RUFF DRIVERZ	*Telstar TV*	3	*5 Jun 99*	5
IBIZA ANTHEMS 2	*Telstar TV*	7	*3 Jul 99*	4
CHRIS TARRANT'S ULTIMATE SUMMER PARTY	*Telstar TV*	15	*10 Jul 99*	2
ADRENALIN	*Telstar TV*	10	*24 Jul 99*	3
THE CHILL OUT ALBUM - 2	*Telstar TV*	14	*31 Jul 99*	4
SUMMER DANCE ANTHEMS 99	*Telstar TV*	10	*14 Aug 99*	3
NATIONAL ANTHEMS 99 - VOLUME 2	*Telstar TV*	11	*4 Sep 99*	2
IBIZA EUPHORIA	*Telstar TV*	5	*11 Sep 99*	5
CLUB HITS 99	*Telstar TV*	16	*9 Oct 99*	1
EUPHORIA - LEVEL 3	*Telstar TV*	18	*25 Dec 99*	2
GARAGE ANTHEMS - MIXED BY CRAIG DAVID - THE VERY BEST OF GARAGE 2000	*Telstar TV*	6	*18 Mar 00*	6
BIG TUNES 2000 - 42 MASSIVE DANCE TUNES	*Telstar TV*	9	*27 May 00*	3
GARAGE NATION - LIVE MIX BY JASON KAYE *Sub titled: Garage Music For A Garage Nation.*	*Telstar TV*	10	*10 Jun 00*	3
LOVE ON A SUMMER'S DAY	*Telstar TV*	14	*24 Jun 00*	2
THE COOL SOUND OF THE 70S	*Telstar TV*	9	*30 Sep 00*	4
LOVE 2 DANCE - 36 ALL-TIME DANCE FLOOR CLASSICS	*Telstar TV*	18	*7 Oct 00*	1

Telstar TV/PolyGram TV

COMPILATION ALBUMS:	HITS 1			WEEKS 3
STREET JAMS	*Telstar TV / PolyGram TV*	14	*23 May 98*	3

Telstar/warner.esp

COMPILATION ALBUMS:	HITS 1			WEEKS 4
POWER OF A WOMAN	*Telstar/ warner.esp*	13	*7 Mar 98*	4

Telstar/4 Liberty

COMPILATION ALBUMS:	HITS 1			WEEKS 3
THE DREEM TEEM IN SESSION - UK GARAGE - PAST - PRESENT AND FUTURE	*Telstar/4 Liberty*	12	*17 Feb 01*	3

Tommy Boy/Island

ALBUMS:	HITS 1			WEEKS 6
TOMMY BOY GREATEST BEATS	*Tommy Boy*	44	*6 Apr 85*	6

Topaz

ALBUMS:	HITS 2			WEEKS 8
A TOUCH OF COUNTRY	*Topaz*	7	*22 May 76*	7
A TOUCH OF CLASS	*Topaz*	57	*3 Jul 76*	1

Touchdown

COMPILATION ALBUMS:	HITS 1			WEEKS 4
D-FROST - 20 GLOBAL DANCE WARNINGS	*Touchdown*	8	*13 Mar 93*	4

Towerbell

ALBUMS:	HITS 6			WEEKS 45
THE DANCE HITS ALBUM	*Towerbell*	10	*8 Feb 86*	11
SISTERS ARE DOIN' IT	*Towerbell*	27	*17 May 86*	9
TWO'S COMPANY	*Towerbell*	51	*7 Jun 86*	5
DANCE HITS II	*Towerbell*	25	*28 Jun 86*	8
THE ORIGINALS: 32 ALL-TIME CLASSIC GREATS	*Towerbell*	15	*2 Aug 86*	9
YOU'VE GOT TO LAUGH	*Towerbell*	51	*9 Aug 86*	3

Trax

COMPILATION ALBUMS:	HITS 5			WEEKS 25
DREAMS OF IRELAND	*Trax*	19	*22 Jul 89*	1
ROCK OF AMERICA	*Trax*	7	*17 Feb 90*	6
FREEDOM TO PARTY - FIRST LEGAL RAVE	*Trax*	4	*19 May 90*	10
SUMMER CHART PARTY	*Trax*	9	*28 Jul 90*	6
FREEDOM 2 - THE ULTIMATE RAVE	*Trax*	16	*3 Nov 90*	2

Trojan

ALBUMS:	HITS 3			WEEKS 12
TIGHTEN UP VOLUME 4	*Trojan*	20	*7 Aug 71*	7
CLUB REGGAE	*Trojan*	25	*21 Aug 71*	4
20 REGGAE CLASSICS	*Trojan*	89	*16 Jun 84*	1

TV Records

ALBUMS:	HITS 4			WEEKS 25
MODERN HEROES	*TV Records*	24	*2 Oct 82*	7
ENDLESS LOVE	*TV Records*	26	*9 Oct 82*	8
FLASH TRACKS	*TV Records*	19	*6 Nov 82*	7
PARTY FEVER/DISCO MANIA	*TV Records*	71	*25 Dec 82*	3

TVD Entertainment/Life On Mars

COMPILATION ALBUMS:	HITS 1			WEEKS 3
OFF YER NUT!!	*TVD Entertainment/Life On Mars*	12	*9 May 98*	3

2 Tone

ALBUMS:	HITS 1			WEEKS 9
THIS ARE TWO TONE	*2-Tone*	51	*26 Nov 83*	9
COMPILATION ALBUMS:	**HITS 2**			**WEEKS 9**
THE 2 TONE STORY	*2-Tone*	16	*5 Aug 89*	5
THE BEST OF 2 TONE	*Chrysalis*	10	*23 Oct 93*	4

Ultrasound

COMPILATION ALBUMS:	HITS 2			WEEKS 5
THE HOUSE OF HANDBAG	*Ultrasound*	13	*15 Jul 95*	3
THE HOUSE OF HANDBAG - AUTUMN/WINTER COLLECTION	*Ultrasound*	16	*4 Nov 95*	2

United Dance

COMPILATION ALBUMS:	HITS 2			WEEKS 5
THE ANTHEMS '92-'97	*United Dance*	8	*18 Jan 97*	3
UNITED DANCE PRESENTS ANTHEMS 2 - '88-'92	*United Dance*	17	*12 Jul 97*	2

Universe

COMPILATION ALBUMS:	HITS 3			WEEKS 5
UNIVERSE - WORLD TECHNO TRIBE	*Universe*	13	*15 May 93*	2
UNIVERSE PRESENTS THE TRIBAL GATHERING	*Universe*	19	*10 Jun 95*	1
TRIBAL GATHERING '96	*Universe*	15	*19 Oct 96*	2

Universal Classics & Jazz/Virgin/EMI

COMPILATION ALBUMS:	HITS 2			WEEKS 17
THE CLASSICAL ALBUM	*Universal Classics And Jazz/ Virgin/EMI*	6	*29 Apr 00*	7
THE CLASSICAL ALBUM 2001	*Universal Classics & Jazz/ Virgin/EMI*	4	*2 Dec 00*	10

Universal Music TV

COMPILATION ALBUMS:	HITS 34			WEEKS 121
THE LOVE SONGS OF BURT BACHARACH	*Universal Music TV*	5	*20 Mar 99*	3
BLUES BROTHER SOUL SISTER CLASSICS	*Universal Music TV*	8	*27 Mar 99*	3
DANCING IN THE STREET - 43 MOTOWN DANCE CLASSICS	*Universal Music TV*	13	*29 May 99*	2
THE SOUND OF MAGIC	*Universal Music TV*	10	*12 Jun 99*	5
SIXTIES SUMMER LOVE	*Universal Music TV*	16	*19 Jun 99*	2
AFRODISIAC	*Universal Music TV*	14	*31 Jul 99*	3
THE SOUND OF MAGIC LOVE	*Universal Music TV*	5	*2 Oct 99*	5
MOBO 1999	*Universal Music TV*	10	*16 Oct 99*	2
Based around the award show that took place on 7 Oct 99.				
LAND OF MY FATHERS	*Decca/Universal Music TV*	1	*16 Oct 99*	6
Official album of the Rugby Word Cup 1999.				
THE 90'S	*Universal Music TV*	20	*6 Nov 99*	1
CELEBRATION 2000	*Universal Music TV*	14	*8 Jan 00*	1
THAT OLE DEVIL CALLED LOVE	*Universal Music TV*	5	*1 Apr 00*	4
RELOADED	*Universal Music TV*	3	*15 Apr 00*	7
DJ LUCK & MC NEAT PRESENTS	*Universal Music TV*	6	*10 Jun 00*	3
UEFA EURO 2000 - THE OFFICIAL ALBUM	*Universal Music TV*	15	*24 Jun 00*	1
THE SOUND OF AGIA NAPA - MIXED BY ARCHITECHS	*Universal Music TV*	11	*12 Aug 00*	3
SUMMERTIME - THE PERFECT PARTNER TO SUMMER	*Universal Music TV*	15	*19 Aug 00*	2
HOT POP!	*Universal Music TV*	11	*23 Sep 00*	2
THE LATE NIGHT MIX	*Universal Music TV*	15	*30 Sep 00*	2

THE HIT FACTORY - PETE WATERMAN'S GREATEST HITS	*Universal Music TV*	3	*28 Oct 00*	5
RELOADED 2	*Universal Music TV*	2	*3 Feb 01*	7
THE NATURAL BLUES ALBUM	*Universal Music TV*	11	*10 Mar 01*	3
CLUBBED VOLUME ONE - MIXED BY JUDGE JULES	*Universal Music TV*	6	*31 Mar 01*	4
DJ LUCK & MC. NEAT PRESENTS . . . II	*Universal Music TV*	4	*14 Apr 01*	8
DISCO FEVER	*Universal Music TV*	4	*5 May 01*	7
SUNSET IBIZA	*Universal Music TV*	7	*26 May 01*	4
PURE & SIMPLE	*Universal Music TV*	7	*2 Jun 01*	3
RELOADED 3	*Universal Music TV*	9	*23 Jun 01*	4
R&B SELECTOR	*Universal Music TV*	11	*23 Jun 01*	3
CLUBBED VOLUME TWO: SUMMER COLLECTION - MIXED BY JUDGE JULES	*Universal Music TV*	8	*4 Aug 01*	3
ATOMIC80S - THE DEFINITIVE EIGHTIES ALBUM	*Universal Music TV*	11	*11 Aug 01*	4
DISCO FEVER VOLUME 2	*Universal Music TV*	9	*1 Sep 01*	2
CLOSE TO YOU	*Universal Music TV*	5	*8 Sep 01*	7
DJ LUCK & MC. NEAT PRESENTS . . . III	*Universal Music TV*	7	*6 Oct 01*	4
URBAN CHILL	*Universal Music TV*	15	*13 Oct 01*	2
PUMP UP THE VOLUME	*Universal Music TV*	11	*17 Nov 01*	2
TAMLA MOTOWN GOLD - THE SOUND OF YOUNG AMERICA *Hits from the 60's on 3CD's.*	*Universal Music TV*	7	*1 Dec 01*	5
R&B HITS	*Universal Music TV*	16	*1 Dec 01*	1

Universal Music TV/Ministry Of Sound

COMPILATION ALBUMS:	HITS 2			WEEKS 9
CLUB 2K	*Universal Music TV/ Ministry Of Sound*	2	*11 Mar 00*	6
CLUB 2K VOLUME 2	*Universal Music TV/ Ministry Of Sound*	7	*12 Aug 00*	3

Universal Music TV/Sony TV/Global TV

COMPILATION ALBUMS:	HITS 1			WEEKS 19
WOMAN II	*Universal Music/ Sony TV/ Global TV*	4	*13 Nov 99*	19

Urban

ALBUMS:	HITS 3			WEEKS 12
URBAN CLASSICS	*Urban*	96	*14 Nov 87*	1
URBAN ACID	*Urban*	51	*24 Sep 88*	8
ACID JAZZ AND OTHER ILLICIT GROOVES	*Urban*	86	*8 Oct 88*	3

Vertigo

ALBUMS:	HITS 2			WEEKS 16
HEAR 'N' AID	*Vertigo*	50	*21 Jun 86*	2
HOT CITY NIGHTS	*Vertigo*	1	*27 Aug 88*	14
COMPILATION ALBUMS:	**HITS 2**			**WEEKS 23**
ROCK CITY NIGHTS	*Vertigo*	3	*4 Nov 89*	14
THE POWER AND THE GLORY	*Vertigo*	2	*28 Sep 91*	9

Virgin

ALBUMS:	HITS 3			WEEKS 10
CASH COWS *Deleted from chart as it was below retailer price required.*	*Virgin*	49	*22 Nov 80*	1
MUSIC OF QUALITY AND DISTINCTION (VOLUME 1)	*Virgin*	25	*17 Apr 82*	6
MASSIVE - AN ALBUM OF REGGAE HITS	*Virgin*	61	*1 Jun 85*	3
COMPILATION ALBUMS:	**HITS 33**			**WEEKS 218**
MOODS	*Virgin Television*	2	*19 Oct 91*	22
THREE MINUTE HEROES	*Virgin Television*	4	*29 Feb 92*	10
MOODS 2	*Virgin Television*	3	*16 May 92*	8
THE GREATEST DANCE ALBUM IN THE WORLD!	*Virgin*	2	*25 Jul 92*	12
NEW ROMANTIC CLASSICS	*Virgin*	7	*31 Oct 92*	5
THE SINGER AND THE SONG	*Virgin*	5	*23 Oct 93*	6
SWEET SOUL HARMONIES	*Virgin*	1	*29 Jan 94*	9
DANCE TO THE MAX	*Virgin*	2	*26 Feb 94*	10
RAP TO THE MAX	*Virgin*	10	*12 Mar 94*	4
IN THE AIR TONIGHT *Released to celebrate 21 years of Virgin records.*	*Virgin*	8	*30 Apr 94*	10
PURE MOODS	*Virgin*	1	*7 May 94*	31
DANCE TO THE MAX 2	*Virgin*	4	*28 May 94*	8
SUPERFUNK	*Virgin*	8	*9 Jul 94*	5
SWEET SOUL HARMONIES 2	*Virgin*	10	*20 Aug 94*	2
DANCE TO THE MAX 3	*Virgin*	12	*3 Sep 94*	3
DANCE '95	*Virgin*	8	*18 Feb 95*	5
CELTIC MOODS	*Virgin*	8	*25 Mar 95*	2
STREET SOUL	*Virgin*	2	*6 May 95*	9
DANCE HEAT '95	*Virgin*	8	*10 Jun 95*	3
CELTIC MOODS 2	*Virgin*	6	*17 Jun 95*	5
THE BLUES ALBUM	*Virgin*	8	*15 Jul 95*	3
SUMMER SWING	*Virgin*	18	*29 Jul 95*	1
SERVE CHILLED	*Virgin*	16	*19 Aug 95*	1

THIS IS CULT FICTION	*Virgin*	9	*2 Sep 95*	4
INSTRUMENTAL MOODS	*Virgin*	14	*18 Nov 95*	5
SHARPE - OVER THE HILLS & FAR AWAY	*Virgin*	14	*18 May 96*	3
SPIRITS OF NATURE	*Virgin*	5	*15 Jun 96*	5
THE BIG HIT MIX	*Virgin*	16	*29 Jun 96*	2
THIS IS THE RETURN OF CULT FICTION	*Virgin*	15	*21 Sep 96*	3
THE BEST OF MASTERCUTS	*Virgin*	11	*28 Sep 96*	3
WIPEOUT 2097: THE SOUNDTRACK	*Virgin*	16	*12 Oct 96*	1
THE SOUL ALBUM	*Virgin*	1	*15 Feb 97*	11
GORGEOUS	*Virgin*	2	*29 Mar 97*	7

Virgin/EMI

COMPILATION ALBUMS:	HITS 36			WEEKS 168
ELECTRONICA (FULL-ON BIG BEATS)	*Virgin/EMI*	11	*24 May 97*	3
CAFE MAMBO	*Virgin/EMI*	17	*30 Aug 97*	2
MORE! GIRLS' NIGHT OUT	*Virgin/EMI*	10	*6 Sep 97*	3
CLUB HITS 97/98: SOUNDTRACK TO A SEASON	*Virgin/EMI*	5	*20 Sep 97*	7
NEW PURE MOODS	*Virgin/EMI*	16	*22 Nov 97*	3
MAXIMUM SPEED	*Virgin/EMI*	3	*10 Jan 98*	6
THE SOUL ALBUM II	*Virgin/EMI*	3	*7 Feb 98*	8
CARIBBEAN UNCOVERED	*Virgin/EMI*	10	*7 Mar 98*	5
SUPERWOMAN	*Virgin/EMI*	2	*21 Mar 98*	7
CLUB NATION	*Virgin/EMI*	3	*4 Apr 98*	6
R.I.P. PRESENTS THE REAL SOUND OF UNDERGROUND	*Virgin/EMI*	18	*2 May 98*	2
WORLD MOODS	*Virgin/EMI*	17	*5 Sep 98*	2
CLUB NATION 2	*Virgin/EMI*	8	*7 Nov 98*	2
DISCO:1999	*Virgin/EMI*	13	*6 Mar 99*	2
MAXIMUM SPEED 99	*Virgin/EMI*	13	*10 Apr 99*	4
TRANCEFORMER	*Virgin/EMI*	3	*15 May 99*	5
21ST CENTURY ROCK	*Virgin/EMI*	9	*29 May 99*	3
NEW WOMAN	*Virgin/EMI*	14	*28 Aug 99*	4
CLUB ANTHEMS 99	*Virgin/EMI*	4	*4 Sep 99*	4
TRANCEMIX 99 - A SPIRITUAL JOURNEY THROUGH TIME AND SPACE	*Virgin/EMI*	8	*25 Sep 99*	3
THE CHILLOUT MIX	*Virgin/EMI*	7	*16 Oct 99*	4
THE SIXTIES	*Virgin/EMI*	16	*27 Nov 99*	2
UNDERGROUND EXPLOSION - THE REAL GARAGE MIX	*Virgin/EMI*	10	*25 Mar 00*	4
MELTDOWN 2000 - BEST NEW TRANCE	*Virgin/EMI*	6	*1 Apr 00*	4
GIRLS 2K: 43 MASSIVE HITS FROM THE GIRLS ON TOP!	*Virgin/EMI*	1	*22 Apr 00*	5
DECADES - THE STORY OF THE 60'S/70'S/80'S	*Virgin/EMI*	13	*18 Nov 00*	2
THE NEW LOVE ALBUM	*Virgin/EMI*	4	*25 Nov 00*	14
DANCE MASTERS	*Virgin/EMI*	4	*17 Feb 01*	6
A FRENCH AFFAIR *Classic French Love Songs.*	*Virgin/EMI*	19	*24 Feb 01*	1
THE ALBUM	*Virgin/EMI*	3	*28 Apr 01*	11
CLUBBED OUT - CHILLED BEATS & LAID-BACK HOUSE	*Virgin/EMI*	5	*26 May 01*	4
THE CHILLOUT	*Virgin/EMI*	19	*14 Jul 01*	1
UNBELIEVABLE	*Virgin/EMI*	3	*28 Jul 01*	6
CLASSICAL CHILLOUT	*Virgin/EMI*	4	*22 Sep 01*	15
IT'S A . . . GIRL THING	*Virgin/EMI*	4	*13 Oct 01*	5
THE OPERA ALBUM 2002	*Virgin/EMI*	7	*17 Nov 01*	6
PURE CHILLOUT	*Virgin/EMI*	11	*8 Dec 01*	4

Vision

COMPILATION ALBUMS:	HITS 4			WEEKS 18
FLARED HITS AND PLATFORM SOUL	*Vision*	13	*4 Mar 95*	5
DANCE NATION '95	*Vision*	6	*13 May 95*	5
LOVE WITH A REGGAE RHYTHM	*Vision*	18	*10 Jun 95*	2
THE BEST DANCE ALBUM OF THE YEAR!	*Vision*	5	*9 Sep 95*	6

Vital Sounds

COMPILATION ALBUMS:	HITS 3			WEEKS 6
RED HOT AND WHITE LABELS	*Vital Sounds*	17	*4 Jul 92*	2
RED HOT AND WHITE 2	*Vital Sounds*	13	*26 Sep 92*	2
STRICTLY RAGGA	*Vital Sounds*	12	*29 May 93*	2

Volume

COMPILATION ALBUMS:	HITS 3			WEEKS 6
VOLUME SIX	*Volume*	19	*1 May 93*	1
TRANCE EUROPE EXPRESS	*Volume*	14	*2 Oct 93*	3
TRANCE EUROPE EXPRESS 2	*Volume*	17	*11 Jun 94*	2

V2

COMPILATION ALBUMS:	HITS 2			WEEKS 2
LOADED LOCK IN	*V2*	20	*24 May 97*	1
YOU'LL NEVER WALK ALONE	*V2*	18	*14 Jun 97*	1

Warner Brothers

COMPILATION ALBUMS:	HITS 3			WEEKS 9
NOBODY'S CHILD - ROMANIAN ANGEL APPEAL *Benefit album with proceeds to orphans in Romania.*	*Warner Brothers*	18	*4 Aug 90*	3
BARCELONA GOLD	*Warner Brothers*	15	*15 Aug 92*	2
SONGS IN THE KEY OF X	*Warner Brothers*	8	*6 Apr 96*	4

warner.esp

COMPILATION ALBUMS:	HITS 14			WEEKS 58
DISCO MIX 96	*warner.esp*	7	*2 Nov 96*	4
SUMMER GROOVE	*warner.esp*	14	*7 Jun 97*	2
CLUBBIN'	*warner.esp*	6	*16 May 98*	5
CLUB CLASS	*warner.esp*	9	*15 Aug 98*	2
MUSIC FOR LIFE	*warner.esp*	17	*19 Jun 99*	1
CLUB IBIZA	*warner.esp*	4	*10 Jul 99*	5
DANCEMIX.UK.V1	*warner.esp*	13	*4 Sep 99*	3
THIS YEAR IN IBIZA	*warner.esp*	5	*25 Sep 99*	5
THE DEFINITIVE SOUND OF ATLANTIC SOUL	*warner.esp*	18	*2 Oct 99*	1
TWICE AS NICE - SEXY & STYLISH - DJ SPOONY & STEVE 'SMOOTH' SUTHERLAND	*warner.esp*	5	*13 May 00*	7
SPACE - IBIZA DANCE	*warner.esp*	8	*2 Sep 00*	3
CHILLED IBIZA *Re-entered 12 May 01 on WSM label. See WSM section.*	*warner.esp*	7	*9 Sep 00*	5
TWICE AS NICE - SUMMER OF LOVE - MIXED LIVE BY DJ SPOONY & STEVE 'SMOOTH' SUNDERLAND	*warner.esp*	6	*23 Sep 00*	7
HARD HOUSE NATION *Mixed by Lisa Pin-Up and Andy Farley.*	*warner.esp*	4	*30 Sep 00*	8

warner.esp/Columbia

COMPILATION ALBUMS:	HITS 1			WEEKS 3
THE CELTIC COLLECTION	*warner.esp/Columbia*	14	*26 Jun 99*	3

warner.esp/Global TV

COMPILATION ALBUMS:	HITS 12			WEEKS 62
DANCE TIP 4	*warner.esp TV/Global TV*	7	*2 Mar 96*	3
TWELVE	*warner.esp TV/Global TV*	10	*6 Apr 96*	5
VIVA! EUROPOP	*warner.esp TV/Global TV*	4	*8 Jun 96*	5
DANCE TIP 2000	*warner.esp/Global TV*	7	*21 Dec 96*	7
A PERFECT LOVE	*warner.esp/Global TV*	4	*22 Nov 97*	15
A LITTLE BLUES IN YOUR SOUL	*warner.esp/Global TV*	5	*7 Mar 98*	4
HEART FULL OF SOUL	*warner.esp/Global TV*	8	*8 Aug 98*	3
THE FEMALE TOUCH	*warner.esp/Global TV*	2	*24 Oct 98*	5
A PERFECT LOVE II	*warner.esp/Global TV*	9	*21 Nov 98*	3
THE FEMALE TOUCH 2	*warner.esp/Global TV*	9	*10 Apr 99*	7
HEART FULL OF SOUL - 2	*warner.esp/Global TV*	12	*1 May 99*	4
CRAZY LITTLE THING CALLED LOVE	*warner.esp/Global TV*	17	*25 Sep 99*	1

warner.esp/Global TV/Sony Music TV

COMPILATION ALBUMS:	HITS 5			WEEKS 24
TOTALLY WICKED	*warner.esp/Global TV/ Sony Music TV*	4	*22 Aug 98*	6
STREET VIBES	*warner.esp/Global TV/ Sony Music TV*	6	*22 Aug 98*	7
STREET VIBES 2	*warner.esp/Global TV/ Sony Music TV*	5	*16 Jan 99*	4
TOTALLY WICKED TOO!	*warner.esp/Global TV/ Sony Music TV*	7	*6 Feb 99*	2
STREET VIBES 3	*warner.esp/Global TV/ Sony Music TV*	6	*12 Jun 99*	5

warner.esp/Universal Music TV

COMPILATION ALBUMS:	HITS 2			WEEKS 10
RESPECT - THE SOUNDTRACK TO THE SOUL GENERATION	*warner.esp/Universal Music TV*	15	*29 Jul 00*	3
PASSION - SONGS FOR LOVERS	*warner.esp/Universal Music TV*	2	*10 Feb 01*	7

warner.esp/Universal TV/Global TV

COMPILATION ALBUMS:	HITS 2			WEEKS 13
THE LOVE SONGS ALBUM	*warner.esp/Universal Music TV/ Global TV*	1	*12 Feb 00*	7
A PERFECT LOVE III	*warner.esp/Universal Music TV/ Global TV*	5	*29 Apr 00*	6

Warner Music

COMPILATION ALBUMS:	HITS 3			WEEKS 12
THE ULTIMATE SOUL COLLECTION - 45 SOUL CLASSICS	*Warner Music*	4	*18 Feb 95*	9
DISCO INFERNO	*Warner Music UK*	16	*5 Aug 95*	1
THE ULTIMATE SOUL COLLECTION - VOLUME 2	*Warner Music*	11	*28 Oct 95*	2

Warp

COMPILATION ALBUMS:	HITS 1			WEEKS 2
ARTIFICIAL INTELLIGENCE II	*Warp*	16	*11 Jun 94*	2

Warwick

ALBUMS:	HITS 11			WEEKS 83
ALL-TIME PARTY HITS	*Warner Brothers*	21	*29 Nov 75*	8
INSTRUMENTAL GOLD	*Warner Brothers*	3	*17 Apr 76*	24
SONGS OF PRAISE	*Warner Brothers*	31	*8 Jan 77*	2
HIT SCENE	*Warner Brothers*	19	*29 Jan 77*	5
LOVE SONGS	*Warner Brothers*	47	*25 Nov 78*	7
BLACK VELVET	*Warner Brothers*	72	*2 Dec 78*	3
COUNTRY PORTRAITS	*Warner Brothers*	14	*7 Apr 79*	10
COUNTRY GUITAR	*Warner Brothers*	46	*16 Feb 80*	3
DISCO EROTICA	*Warner Brothers*	35	*14 Nov 81*	8
PS I LOVE YOU	*Warner Brothers*	68	*10 Apr 82*	3
HITS OF THE SCREAMING 60'S	*Warner Brothers*	24	*6 Nov 82*	10

WEA

ALBUMS:	HITS 2			WEEKS 33
THE BEST DISCO ALBUM IN THE WORLD	*WEA*	1	*21 Jul 79*	17
THE LAUGHTER AND TEARS COLLECTION	*WEA*	19	*14 May 83*	16

COMPILATION ALBUMS:	HITS 1			WEEKS 1
URBAN RENEWAL FEATURING THE SONGS BY PHIL COLLINS	*WEA*	16	*30 Jun 01*	1

West Five

ALBUMS:	HITS 1			WEEKS 7
THE POWER OF LOVE	*West Five*	33	*18 Oct 86*	7

Westmoor

COMPILATION ALBUMS:	HITS 1			WEEKS 2
EMERALD CLASSICS VOLUMES I AND II	*Westmoor*	14	*24 Mar 90*	2

Westway Dance

COMPILATION ALBUMS:	HITS 1			WEEKS 3
ELEMENTS - SEB FONTAINE/TONY DE VIT	*Westway Dance*	15	*18 Jul 98*	3

Worlds End

COMPILATION ALBUMS:	HITS 1			WEEKS 1
VOLUME FOUR	*Worlds End*	17	*26 Sep 92*	1

Worldwide Ultimatumn

COMPILATION ALBUMS:	HITS 1			WEEKS 2
CARL COX - FACT 2	*Worldwide Ultimation*	13	*15 Mar 97*	2

WSM

COMPILATION ALBUMS:	HITS 11			WEEKS 59
60 NUMBER ONES OF THE SIXTIES - THE ULTIMATE SIXTIES COLECTION	*WSM*	13	*25 Nov 00*	2
HARD HOUSE NATION - 2	*WSM*	5	*16 Dec 00*	6
HARD HOUSE THREE	*WSM*	7	*17 Mar 01*	3
Above 2 mixed by Lisa Pin-Up and Andy Farley.				
TWICE AS NICE - SEXY & STYLISH - MIXED LIVE BY DJ SPOONY & STEVE 'SMOOTH' SUTHERLAND	*WSM*	11	*28 Apr 01*	4
CHILLED IBIZA [RI]	*warner.esp*	3	*12 May 01*	20
Originally charted 9 Sep 00 on the warner.esp label. See warner.esp section.				
FUNKOLOGY - ONE NATION UNDER A GROOVE	*WSM*	14	*12 May 01*	4
FRANTIC - THE FUTURE SOUND OF HARD DANCE: MIXED BY ED REAL & PHIL REYNOLDS	*WSM*	17	*16 Jun 01*	3
Frantic is the UK's Premier Hard Dance Club Night.				
THE GREATEST 80'S SOUL WEEKENDER	*WSM*	9	*4 Aug 01*	8
CHILLED IBIZA II	*WSM*	5	*8 Sep 01*	6
TEENDREEM - THE ULTIMATE CLUB NIGHT	*WSM*	19	*27 Oct 01*	1
HARD DANCE ANTHEMS - MIXED BY PUBLIC DOMAIN	*WSM*	19	*24 Nov 01*	2

WSM/Universal Music TV

COMPILATION ALBUMS:	HITS 3			WEEKS 22
THE LOOK OF LOVE - THE BURT BACHARACH COLLECTION	*WSM/Universal Music TV*	4	*19 May 01*	17
PURE HIP HOP - EXPLICIT BEATS - MIXED BY DJ SWERVE	*WSM/Universal Music TV*	10	*14 Jul 01*	3
DANCE PARADE IBIZA	*WSM/Universal Music TV*	14	*28 Jul 01*	2

XL Recordings

COMPILATION ALBUMS:	HITS 3			WEEKS 20
XL - RECORDINGS - THE SECOND CHAPTER	*XL Recordings*	5	*14 Sep 91*	9
THE THIRD CHAPTER	*XL Recordings*	6	*25 Apr 92*	8
PRODIGY PRESENTS THE DIRTCHAMBER SESSIONS 1	*XL Recordings*	3	*6 Mar 99*	3

Zomba

ALBUMS:	HITS 1			WEEKS 1
THE WORD	*Zomba*	86	*24 Oct 87*	1

ZTT/Island

ALBUMS:	HITS 1			WEEKS 3
IQ 6: ZANG TUMB TUM SAMPLED	*ZTT/Island*	40	*19 Oct 85*	3

CONCERTS AND FESTIVALS

ALBUMS:	HITS 13			WEEKS 91
ALL STAR FESTIVAL	*Philips*	4	*9 Mar 63*	19
FOLK FESTIVAL OF THE BLUES (LIVE RECORDING)	*Pye*	16	*22 Feb 64*	4
WOODSTOCK [OST]	*Atlantic*	35	*18 Jul 70*	19
Music that appeared in the film of the festival during 15+17 Aug 69.				
CONCERT FOR BANGLADESH (RECORDED LIVE)	*Apple*	1	*22 Jan 72*	13
Live recordings from Madison Square Garden, New York, 1 Aug 71 featuring Bob Dylan, Eric Clapton, George Harrison and Ringo Starr. Proceeds to aid victims of the war.				
THE ROXY LONDON WC2 (JAN-APR 77)	*Harvest*	24	*16 Jul 77*	5
HOPE AND ANCHOR FRONT ROW FESTIVAL	*Warner Brothers*	28	*25 Mar 78*	3
THE SECRET POLICEMAN'S BALL	*Island*	33	*5 Jan 80*	6
CONCERTS FOR THE PEOPLE OF KAMPUCHEA	*Atlantic*	39	*11 Apr 81*	2
Live recordings from Hammersmith Odeon, London, over 4 days in Dec 79. Features the Who, Wings, Queen, Clash, Specials, Elvis Costello.				
THE SECRET POLICEMAN'S OTHER BALL	*Springtime*	69	*12 Dec 81*	4
THE SECRET POLICEMAN'S OTHER BALL (THE MUSIC)	*Springtime*	29	*20 Mar 82*	5
Live recordings from the Amnesty International Benefit Concert, London, May 81. Features Jeff Beck, Eric Clapton, Phil Collins, Donovan, Bob Geldof, Sting.				
THE PRINCE'S TRUST COLLECTION	*Telstar*	64	*30 Nov 85*	5
THE PRINCE'S TRUST TENTH ANNIVERSARY BIRTHDAY PARTY	*A&M*	76	*2 May 87*	3
Live recordings from Wembley Arena, London, 20 June 86.				
THE PRINCE'S TRUST CONCERT 1987	*A&M*	44	*22 Aug 87*	3

COMPILATION ALBUMS:	HITS 1			WEEKS 10
KNEBWORTH - THE ALBUM	*Polydor*	1	*18 Aug 90*	10
Live recordings 30 Jun 90 with proceeds to Nordoff-Robbins Music Therapy and the Brit School for the Performing Arts. Featuring Genesis, Paul McCartney, Pink Floyd, Robert Plant, Cliff Richard and the Shadows, Status Quo, Tears For Fears				

EDINBURGH TATTOO

ALBUMS:	HITS 2			WEEKS 5
EDINBURGH MILITARY TATTOO 1970	*Warner Brothers*	34	*12 Sep 70*	4
EDINBURGH MILITARY TATTOO 1971	*Warner Brothers*	44	*18 Sep 71*	1

FILMS

(See also Soundtracks under following artists: AC/DC; David Arnold; Burt Bacharach his Orchestra and chorus; Backbeat Band; Band; John Barry Orchestra, Beatles; Blues Brothers; Jon Bon Jovi; Roy Budd; Commitments; Roger Daltrey; Neil Diamond; Doors; Bob Dylan; Electric Light Orchestra; Adam Faith; Brad Fiedel; Grimthorpe Colliery Band; Marvin Hamlisch; Chesney Hawkes; Jimi Hendrix; David Hirschfelder; James Horner; Whitney Houston; Maurice Jarre; Trevor Jones; Mark Knopfler; kd lang; Mario Lanza; Los Lobos; Madonna; Neville Marriner and the Academy of St. Martin In The Fields, Paul McCartney; Bette Midler; Monty Python's Flying Circus; Ennio Morricone; Olivia Newton-John; Michael Nyman; Hazel O'Connor; Mike Oldfield; Jimmy Page; Tom Petty and the Heartbreakers; Pink Floyd; Elvis Presley; Prince; Public Enemy; Queen; Chris Rea; Cliff Richard; Riuichi Sakamoto; Eric Serra; Sex Pistols; Simon And Garfunkel; Frank Sinatra; Barbra Streisand; Tangerine Dream; Tina Turner; Vangelis; Village People; Rick Wakeman; Stephen Warbeck; Who; John Williams; Stevie Wonder; Hans Zimmer.)

Original Soundtracks

SINGLES:	HITS 1			WEEKS 2
CAROUSEL [LP]	*Capitol*	27	*16 Jun 56*	1
Features Gordon MacRae, Shirley Jones, Cameron Mitchell. This album appeared in the singles chart as there was no album chart at that period of time. See 1958 entry in album section below.				
CAROUSEL [LP] [RE]	*Capitol*	26	*7 Jul 56*	1

EPS:	HITS 7			WEEKS 150
CAROUSEL NO. 1	*Capitol*	12	*14 May 60*	11
SOUTH PACIFIC NO. 1	*RCA*	1	*6 Aug 60*	86
SEVEN BRIDES FOR SEVEN BROTHERS	*MGM*	9	*6 Aug 60*	15
THE KING AND I	*Capitol*	12	*1 Oct 60*	5
NEVER ON SUNDAY	*London*	8	*17 Jun 61*	11
SEVEN BRIDES FOR SEVEN BROTHERS VOLUME 2	*MGM*	18	*1 Jul 61*	1
SOME PEOPLE	*Pye*	2	*25 Aug 62*	21

ALBUMS:	HITS 90			WEEKS 2726
SOUTH PACIFIC	*RCA*	1	*8 Nov 58*	286
Features Rossano Brazzi, Mitzi Gaynor, John Kerr. The first Number One Album. Includes re-entries through to 1965.				
THE KING AND I	*Capitol*	4	*8 Nov 58*	103
Features Deborrah Kerr, Yul Brynner, Rita Moreno.				

OKLAHOMA!	*Capitol*	4	*8 Nov 58*	90
Features Gordon MacRae, Gloria Grahame, Gene Nelson, Charlotte Greenwood, James Whitmore, Shirley Jones.				
CAROUSEL	*Capitol*	8	*6 Dec 58*	15
See also singles section above.				
GIGI	*MGM*	2	*31 Jan 59*	88
Features Leslie Caron, Maurice Chevalier, Louis Jourdan.				
PORGY AND BESS	*Philips*	7	*10 Oct 59*	5
Features Sidney Poitier, Dorothy Dandrige.				
THE FIVE PENNIES	*London*	2	*23 Jan 60*	15
Features Danny Kaye, Louis Armstrong, Barbara Bel Geddes.				
CAN CAN	*Capitol*	2	*7 May 60*	31
Features Frank Sinatra, Shirley MacLaine.				
PAL JOEY	*Capitol*	20	*28 May 60*	1
Features Frank Sinatra.				
HIGH SOCIETY	*Capitol*	16	*23 Jul 60*	1
Features Bing Crosby, Grace Kelly, Frank Sinatra. Originally released in 1956. Based around the play 'Philadelphia Story'.				
BEN-HUR	*MGM*	15	*5 Nov 60*	3
NEVER ON SUNDAY	*London*	17	*21 Jan 61*	1
Composed and conducted by Manos Hadjildakis.				
SONG WITHOUT END	*Pye Golden Guinea*	9	*18 Feb 61*	10
SEVEN BRIDES FOR SEVEN BROTHERS	*MGM*	6	*29 Apr 61*	22
EXODUS	*RCA*	17	*3 Jun 61*	1
Composed and conducted by Ernest Gold.				
GLENN MILLER STORY	*Ace Of Hearts*	12	*11 Nov 61*	7
WEST SIDE STORY	*Philips*	1	*24 Mar 62*	175
Features Natalie Wood, Richard Beymer, Russ Tamblyn, Rita Moreno, George Chakiris. Re-issued on the CBS label during its chart run.				
IT'S TRAD DAD	*Columbia*	3	*28 Apr 62*	21
THE MUSIC MAN	*Warner Brothers*	14	*22 Sep 62*	9
Features Robert Preston, Shirley Jones, Buddy Hackett.				
PORGY AND BESS	*CBS*	14	*3 Nov 62*	7
JUST FOR FUN	*Decca*	20	*15 Jun 63*	2
Features the Tornados.				
MY FAIR LADY	*CBS*	12	*31 Oct 64*	14
Features Audrey Hepburn, Rex Harrison, Stanley Holloway.				
MARY POPPINS	*His Master's Voice*	2	*16 Jan 65*	82
Features Julie Andrews, Dick Van Dyke, David Tomlinson, Glynis Johns, Ed Wynn.				
MY FAIR LADY [RE]	*CBS*	9	*3 Apr 65*	37
THE SOUND OF MUSIC	*RCA Victor*	1	*10 Apr 65*	381
Features Julie Andrews, Christopher Plummer. Includes re-entries through to 1972.				
A MAN AND A WOMAN	*United Artists*	35	*29 Jul 67*	3
THOROUGHLY MODERN MILLIE	*Brunswick*	9	*28 Oct 67*	19
Features Julie Andrews.				
THE JUNGLE BOOK	*Disney*	5	*9 Mar 68*	51
A MAN AND A WOMAN [RE]	*United Artists*	31	*17 Aug 68*	8
STAR!	*Stateside*	36	*21 Sep 68*	1
Features Julie Andrews, Richard Crenna, Michael Craig.				
OLIVER!	*RCA Victor*	7	*23 Nov 68*	9
Features Ron Moody, Harry Secombe, Shani Wallis, Mark Lester, & Jack Wild.				
CAMELOT	*Warner Brothers*	37	*23 Nov 68*	1
Features Richard Harris, Vanessa Redgrave.				
CHITTY CHITTY BANG BANG	*United Artists*	10	*8 Feb 69*	4
Features Dick Van Dyke, Sally Ann Howes, Lionel Jeffries, Gert Frobe.				
OLIVER! [RE]	*RCA Victor*	4	*12 Apr 69*	98
2001 - A SPACE ODYSSEY	*MGM*	3	*14 Jun 69*	67
EASY RIDER	*Stateside*	2	*20 Dec 69*	67
THE JUNGLE BOOK [RE]	*Disney*	25	*24 Jan 70*	26
Re-released.				
PAINT YOUR WAGON	*Paramount*	2	*7 Feb 70*	102
Features Lee Marvin, Clint Eastwood, Jean Seberg, Harve Presnell.				
LOVE STORY	*Paramount*	10	*24 Apr 71*	33
Composed and conducted by Francis Lai.				
CLOCKWORK ORANGE	*Warner Brothers*	4	*12 Feb 72*	46
Composed and conducted by Walter Carlos.				
FIDDLER ON THE ROOF	*United Artists*	26	*8 Apr 72*	2
Features Topol, Norma Crane.				
2001 - A SPACE ODYSSEY [RE]	*MGM*	20	*13 May 72*	2
Re-released.				
SOUTH PACIFIC [RI]	*RCA Victor*	25	*25 Nov 72*	2
CABARET	*Probe*	13	*31 Mar 73*	22
Features Liza Minnelli.				
LOST HORIZON	*Bell*	36	*14 Apr 73*	3
THAT'LL BE THE DAY	*Ronco*	1	*23 Jun 73*	7
JESUS CHRIST SUPERSTAR	*MCA*	23	*22 Sep 73*	18
Features Ted Neely, Yvonne Elliman, Carl Anderson. Barry Dennen.				
AMERICAN GRAFFITI	*MCA*	37	*27 Apr 74*	1
A TOUCH OF CLASS	*Philips*	32	*8 Jun 74*	1

Title	Label	Pos	Date	Wks
SUNSHINE	*MCA*	47	*5 Oct 74*	3
TOMMY	*Polydor*	21	*5 Apr 75*	9
Features the Who.				
ALL THIS AND WORLD WAR II	*Riva*	23	*27 Nov 76*	7
Covers of Beatles songs.				
SATURDAY NIGHT FEVER	*RSO*	1	*11 Mar 78*	65
Features the Bee Gees.				
THE STUD	*Ronco*	2	*22 Apr 78*	19
THANK GOD IT'S FRIDAY	*Casablanca*	40	*20 May 78*	5
FM	*MCA*	37	*27 May 78*	7
GREASE	*RSO*	1	*8 Jul 78*	47
Features Olivia Newton-John, John Travolta.				
SGT. PEPPER'S LONELY HEARTS CLUB BAND	*A&M*	38	*12 Aug 78*	2
Based around the Beatles classic album from 1967. Features Bee Gees, Earth, Wind And Fire, Peter Frampton.				
CONVOY	*Capitol*	52	*7 Oct 78*	1
LEMON POPSICLE	*Warner Brothers*	42	*31 Mar 79*	6
THAT SUMMER	*Arista*	36	*9 Jun 79*	8
THE WORLD IS FULL OF MARRIED MEN	*Ronco*	25	*30 Jun 79*	9
THE WARRIORS	*A&M*	53	*14 Jul 79*	7
SUNBURN	*Warner Brothers*	45	*9 Feb 80*	7
GOING STEADY	*Warner Brothers*	25	*16 Feb 80*	10
THE WANDERERS	Gem	48	*8 Mar 80*	7
FAME	*RSO*	21	*6 Sep 80*	7
DANCE CRAZE	*2-Tone*	5	*14 Feb 81*	15
FAME [RE]	*RSO*	1	*3 Jul 82*	18
Recharted after the showing of the TV series on BBC TV.				
THE SOUND OF MUSIC [RI]	*RCA International*	98	*17 Jul 82*	1
ROCKY III	*Liberty*	42	*4 Sep 82*	7
Composed and conducted by Bill Conti, features Frank Stallone, Survivor.				
ANNIE	*CBS*	83	*4 Sep 82*	2
BRIMSTONE AND TREACLE	*A&M*	67	*11 Sep 82*	3
Features Sting.				
AN OFFICER AND A GENTLEMAN	*Island*	40	*12 Feb 83*	14
FLASHDANCE	*Casablanca*	9	*2 Jul 83*	30
STAYING ALIVE	*RSO*	14	*1 Oct 83*	8
Majority of the tracks are by the Bee Gees.				
FOOTLOOSE	*CBS*	7	*21 Apr 84*	25
AGAINST ALL ODDS	*Virgin*	29	*21 Apr 84*	10
BREAKDANCE	*Polydor*	6	*16 Jun 84*	29
BEAT STREET	*Atlantic*	30	*7 Jul 84*	13
ELECTRIC DREAMS	*Virgin*	46	*18 Aug 84*	7
GHOSTBUSTERS	*Arista*	24	*29 Sep 84*	25
BREAKDANCE 2 - ELECTRIC BOOGALOO	*Polydor*	34	*12 Jan 85*	20
BEVERLY HILLS COP	*MCA*	24	*16 Feb 85*	32
BACK TO THE FUTURE	*MCA*	66	*11 Jan 86*	8
ROCKY IV	*Scotti Brothers*	3	*1 Feb 86*	22
Features Survivor.				
ABSOLUTE BEGINNERS	*Virgin*	19	*5 Apr 86*	9
TOP GUN	*CBS*	4	*11 Oct 86*	46
PLATOON	*WEA*	90	*2 May 87*	2
BEVERLY HILLS COP II	*MCA*	71	*18 Jul 87*	5
WHO'S THAT GIRL	*Sire*	4	*1 Aug 87*	25
Features tracks by Madonna.				
FULL METAL JACKET	*Warner Brothers*	60	*3 Oct 87*	4
DIRTY DANCING	*RCA*	4	*31 Oct 87*	63
Peak position reached on 7 May 88.				
FLASHDANCE [RI]	*Mercury*	93	*16 Jan 88*	2
Re-issued at mid-price.				
CRY FREEDOM	*MCA*	73	*20 Feb 88*	2
MORE DIRTY DANCING	*RCA*	3	*14 May 88*	27
BUSTER	*Virgin*	6	*24 Sep 88*	16
Features Phil Collins.				
GOOD MORNING VIETNAM	*A&M*	50	*22 Oct 88*	9
COMPILATION ALBUMS:	**HITS 88**			**WEEKS 1180**
DIRTY DANCING	*RCA*	3	*14 Jan 89*	96
BUSTER	*Virgin*	2	*14 Jan 89*	36
GOOD MORNING VIETNAM	*A&M*	7	*21 Jan 89*	28
Peak position reached on 8 Jul 89.				
THE LOST BOYS	*Atlantic*	13	*28 Jan 89*	15
COCKTAIL	*Elektra*	2	*4 Feb 89*	15
MORE DIRTY DANCING	*RCA*	14	*4 Feb 89*	17
SCANDAL	*Parlophone*	13	*18 Mar 89*	3
TOP GUN	*CBS*	12	*22 Apr 89*	17
LICENCE TO KILL	*MCA*	17	*15 Jul 89*	2
GHOSTBUSTERS II	*MCA*	15	*22 Jul 89*	4
THE DELIQUENTS	*PWL*	16	*10 Mar 90*	1
Features Kylie Minogue.				
PRETTY WOMAN	*EMI USA*	2	*26 May 90*	72

TEENAGE MUTANT NINJA TURTLES	*SBK*	6	*23 Jun 90*	18
DAYS OF THUNDER	*Epic*	4	*11 Aug 90*	15
TOP GUN [RE]	*CBS*	4	*13 Oct 90*	17
GHOST	*Milan*	15	*27 Oct 90*	4
DIRTY DANCING [RE]	*RCA*	1	*5 Jan 91*	52
THE LOST BOYS [RE-1ST]	*Atlantic*	1	*12 Jan 91*	44
Above 2 re-charted after they were first transmitted on British TV.				
ROCKY V	*Capitol*	9	*2 Feb 91*	9
GREASE	*Polydor*	8	*2 Mar 91*	11
THE GODFATHER PART III	*Columbia*	19	*23 Mar 91*	1
Composed and conducted by Carmine Coppola and Nina Rota, features Al Martino.				
NEW JACK CITY	*Giant*	16	*27 Apr 91*	5
MERMAIDS	*Epic*	6	*1 Jun 91*	15
Features Cher.				
ROBIN HOOD: PRINCE OF THIEVES	*Polydor*	3	*27 Jul 91*	14
Composed and conducted by Michael Kamen, features Brian Adams, Jeff Lynne.				
BILL AND TED'S BOGUS JOURNEY	*Interscope*	3	*18 Jan 92*	8
MY GIRL	*Epic*	13	*29 Feb 92*	7
WAYNE'S WORLD	*Reprise*	5	*30 May 92*	11
MO' MONEY	*Perspective*	16	*19 Sep 92*	1
BOOMERANG	*LaFace*	17	*14 Nov 92*	2
THE BODYGUARD	*Arista*	1	*28 Nov 92*	80
Features Whitney Houston.				
SISTER ACT	*Hollywood*	14	*30 Jan 93*	4
BRAM STOKER'S DRACULA	*Columbia*	10	*13 Feb 93*	6
RESERVOIR DOGS	*MCA*	16	*20 Mar 93*	3
GOOD MORNING VIETNAM [RE]	*A&M*	19	*8 May 93*	1
Re-released at mid-price.				
INDECENT PROPOSAL	*MCA*	13	*5 Jun 93*	3
THE LAST ACTION HERO	*Columbia*	16	*24 Jul 93*	6
SLIVER	*Virgin*	20	*18 Sep 93*	1
SLEEPLESS IN SEATTLE	*Epic*	10	*16 Oct 93*	6
JUDGEMENT NIGHT	*Epic*	16	*16 Oct 93*	3
ALADDIN	*Pickwick*	11	*8 Jan 94*	5
WAYNE'S WORLD 2	*Pinnacle*	17	*5 Mar 94*	1
PHILADELPHIA	*Epic*	5	*12 Mar 94*	14
THE LOST BOYS [RE-2ND]	*Atlantic*	17	*2 Apr 94*	2
Re-released at mid-price.				
ABOVE THE RIM	*Interscope*	18	*7 May 94*	1
FOUR WEDDINGS AND A FUNERAL	*Vertigo*	5	*28 May 94*	21
THE CROW	*Atlantic*	13	*25 Jun 94*	5
THE FLINTSTONES	*MCA*	18	*6 Aug 94*	1
THE LION KING	*Mercury*	4	*22 Oct 94*	20
Features tracks by Elton John.				
FORREST GUMP	*Epic*	5	*22 Oct 94*	13
PULP FICTION	*MCA*	5	*5 Nov 94*	56
NATURAL BORN KILLERS	*Interscope*	10	*11 Mar 95*	6
BAD BOYS	*Work*	19	*8 Jul 95*	1
BATMAN FOREVER	*Atlantic*	11	*29 Jul 95*	4
WAITING TO EXHALE	*Arista*	8	*3 Feb 96*	5
Features Whitney Houston.				
DANGEROUS MINDS	*MCA*	13	*3 Feb 96*	2
TRAINSPOTTING	*EMI Premier*	2	*2 Mar 96*	66
MISSION: IMPOSSIBLE	*Mother*	18	*20 Jul 96*	1
THE NUTTY PROFESSOR	*Def Jam*	20	*19 Oct 96*	1
SPACE JAM	*Atlantic*	5	*29 Mar 97*	10
ROMEO + JULIET	*Premier Soundtracks*	3	*5 Apr 97*	24
THE SAINT	*Virgin*	15	*3 May 97*	1
MEN IN BLACK - THE ALBUM	*Columbia*	5	*2 Aug 97*	13
SPRAWN - THE ALBUM	*Epic*	18	*9 Aug 97*	1
THE FULL MONTY	*RCA Victor*	1	*13 Sep 97*	43
TRAINSPOTTING #2	*Premier Soundtracks*	11	*27 Sep 97*	5
BOOGIE NIGHTS	*Premier Soundtracks*	19	*31 Jan 98*	1
JACKIE BROWN	*Maverick*	11	*18 Apr 98*	7
An import cataloge number was listed on the first 2 weeks charts.				
THE WEDDING SINGER	*Maverick*	15	*27 Jun 98*	4
CITY OF ANGELS	*Reprise*	18	*4 Jul 98*	3
GREASE [RE]	*Polydor*	2	*18 Jul 98*	15
20th Anniversary re-release including CD-ROM with 3 videos.				
GODZILLA - THE ALBUM	*Epic*	13	*25 Jul 98*	4
LOCK, STOCK & TWO SMOKING BARRELS	*Island*	7	*12 Sep 98*	23
ARMAGEDDON	*Columbia*	19	*26 Sep 98*	2
NOTTING HILL	*Island*	4	*5 Jun 99*	19
HUMAN TRAFFIC	*London*	14	*19 Jun 99*	3
THE MATRIX (ORIGINAL SOUNDTRACK)	*Maverick*	16	*26 Jun 99*	5
AUSTIN POWERS - THE SPY WHO SHAGGED ME	*Maverick*	6	*17 Jul 99*	11
SOUTH PARK: BIGGER, LONGER & UNCUT	*Atlantic*	9	*11 Sep 99*	5
MANUMISSION - THE MOVIE	*Telstar TV*	17	*2 Oct 99*	1
THE BEACH (ORIGINAL SOUNDTRACK)	*London*	1	*4 Mar 00*	8

THE MILLION DOLLAR HOTEL	*Island*	13	*25 Mar 00*	1
POKEMON – THE FIRST MOVIE	*Atlantic*	8	*8 Apr 00*	5
KEVIN AND PERRY 'GO LARGE'	*Virgin/EMI*	4	*29 Apr 00*	7
MISSION: IMPOSSIBLE 2	*Hollywood*	12	*1 Jul 00*	8
SNATCH	*Universal Soundtracks*	11	*16 Sep 00*	3
BILLY ELLIOT	*Polydor*	10	*21 Oct 00*	4
COYOTE UGLY	*Curb/London*	16	*4 Nov 00*	3
DIRTY DANCING [RE-2ND]	*RCA:*	6	*10 Feb 01*	5
SAVE THE LAST DANCE	*Hollywood*	5	*14 Apr 01*	8
BRIDGET JONES'S DIARY	*Mercury*	1	*28 Apr 01*	30
LARA CROFT TOMB RAIDER	*Elektra*	13	*21 Jul 01*	2
MOULIN ROUGE	*Twentieth Century Fox Film Corp/ Interscope*	2	*15 Sep 01*	12
THE FAST AND THE FURIOUS	*Murder Inc/Def Jam*	20	*29 Sep 01*	2
AMERICAN PIE 2	*Republic/Universal*	17	*27 Oct 01*	2
BRIDGET JONES'S DIARY 2	*Mercury*	8	*10 Nov 01*	2

Related Compilations

ALBUMS:	HITS 5			WEEKS 29
GREAT MOTION PICTURE THEMES	*His Master's Voice*	19	*10 Mar 62*	1
THE BEST OF CAR WASH	*MCA*	59	*2 Jul 77*	1
20 SMASH DISCO HITS (THE BITCH)	*Warner Brothers*	42	*10 Nov 79*	5
JAMES BOND'S GREATEST HITS	*Liberty*	4	*27 Mar 82*	13
THE CINEMA HITS ALBUM	*Towerbell*	44	*15 Mar 86*	9

COMPILATION ALBUMS:	HITS 16			WEEKS 88
DIRTY DANCING – LIVE IN CONCERT	*RCA*	19	*13 May 89*	2
THE BEST FROM THE M.G.M. MUSICALS	*EMI*	12	*1 Dec 90*	4
LOVE AT THE MOVIES	*Telstar*	6	*23 Nov 91*	14
THE BEST OF JAMES BOND – 30TH ANNIVERSARY COLLECTION	*EMI*	2	*12 Sep 92*	11
MOVIE HITS	*Telstar*	19	*23 Jan 93*	2
THE MOVIES' GREATEST LOVE SONGS	*PolyGram TV*	4	*19 Feb 94*	6
THE LION KING SING-ALONG	*Pickwick/Disney*	16	*5 Nov 94*	3
MOVIE KILLERS	*Telstar*	4	*29 Jun 96*	16
LOVE AT THE MOVIES . . . THE ALBUM	*EMI TV/Sony TV*	16	*7 Dec 96*	3
MOVIE LOVERS	*Telstar*	17	*21 Feb 98*	1
ESSENTIAL SOUNDTRACKS	*Telstar TV*	4	*10 Apr 99*	10
THE BEST OF BOND . . . JAMES BOND	*Capitol*	6	*13 Nov 99*	10
ESSENTIAL SOUNDTRACKS – 40 TRACKS – THE NEW MOVIE COLLECTION *In conjunction with the Channel 4 FilmFour series of films broadcast.*	*Telstar TV*	8	*15 Apr 00*	3
MUSIC TO WATCH MOVIES BY	*Columbia*	18	*23 Jun 01*	1
THE ULTIMATE MOVIE ALBUM	*Decca*	16	*10 Nov 01*	1
THE ARISTOCATS – READ ALONG	*Walt Disney*	60	*8 Apr 00*	1

KARAOKE

COMPILATION ALBUMS:	HITS 2			WEEKS 10
KARAOKE PARTY	*Trax*	20	*17 Nov 90*	1
KARAOKE PARTY II	*Trax*	7	*16 Mar 91*	9

MAGAZINE RELATED

ALBUMS:	HITS 2			WEEKS 10
KERRANG! KOMPILATION – 24 ROCK MONSTERS *Kerrang is a Rock Magazine.*	*EMI/Virgin*	84	*13 Jul 85*	2
SERGEANT PEPPER KNEW MY FATHER *Charity album to support Childline. Issued in conunction with the music paper New Musical Express.*	*NME/Island*	37	*9 Apr 88*	8

COMPILATION ALBUMS:	HITS 13			WEEKS 55
JUST SEVENTEEN – HEARTBEATS	*Fanfare*	3	*23 Sep 89*	6
JUST SEVENTEEN – GET KICKIN'	*Dover*	2	*22 Sep 90*	6
FAST FORWARD *Just Seventeen and Fast Forward are teen magazines.*	*Telstar*	4	*22 Jun 91*	8
Q – THE ALBUM VOLUME 1	*Telstar*	10	*14 Sep 91*	4
Q THE BLUES	*The Hit Label*	6	*27 Jun 92*	5
Q RHYTHM AND BLUES	*The Hit Label*	14	*10 Apr 93*	4
Q COUNTRY	*The Hit Label*	20	*21 May 94*	1
KERRANG! THE ALBUM	*The Hit Label*	12	*18 Jun 94*	5
Q AWARDS: THE ALBUM	*Virgin/EMI/Universal Music TV*	6	*18 Nov 00*	4
KERRANG! – THE ALBUM	*WSM/Universal Music TV*	9	*14 Jul 01*	5
Q ANTHEMS	*Virgin/EMI/Universal Music TV*	10	*20 Oct 01*	2
MIXMAG PRESENTS BIG TUNES! *Mixmag is a Dance/Clubbing magazine.*	*Virgin/EMI*	12	*27 Oct 01*	1
KERRANG! 2 – THE ALBUM	*WSM/Universal Music TV*	8	*24 Nov 01*	4

MISCELLANEOUS

ALBUMS:	HITS 2			WEEKS 2
ELECTRONIC ORGANS TODAY	*Ad-Rhythm*	48	*11 Dec 71*	1
STRINGS OF SCOTLAND	*Philips*	50	*27 Dec 75*	1
COMPILATION ALBUMS:	**HITS 1**			**WEEKS 1**
TRIVIAL PURSUIT - THE MUSIC MASTER GAME	*Telstar*	20	*28 Dec 91*	1

RADIO

Related Compilations

ALBUMS:	HITS 9			WEEKS 66
THE BEST OF RADIO LUXEMBOURG	*Pye Golden Guinea*	14	*14 Sep 63*	2
THE WORLD OF YOUR 100 BEST TUNES *100 Best Tunes was a programme on BBC Radio 2.*	*Decca*	10	*7 Aug 71*	22
THE WORLD OF YOUR 100 BEST TUNES VOLUME 2	*Decca*	9	*9 Oct 71*	13
THE WORLD OF YOUR 100 BEST TUNES VOLUME 10	*Decca*	41	*27 Sep 75*	4
THE TOP 25 FROM YOUR 100 BEST TUNES	*Decca*	21	*13 Dec 75*	5
HAMILTON'S HOT SHOTS *David Hamiltion was a DJ on BBC Radio 1 and 2.*	*Warner Brothers*	15	*29 May 76*	5
10 YEARS OF HITS - RADIO ONE	*Super Beeb*	39	*22 Oct 77*	3
SIMON BATES - OUR TUNE *BBC Radio 1 Morning DJ with 'Our Tune' being a daily feature.*	*Polydor*	58	*1 Nov 86*	5
ONES ON 1 *Released to coincide with Radio One's 21st anniversary.*	*BBC*	10	*8 Oct 88*	7
COMPILATION ALBUMS:	**HITS 26**			**WEEKS 150**
32 ONES ON ONE - RADIO 1'S 25TH BIRTHDAY	*Connoisseur Collection*	8	*25 Jul 92*	10
BEST OF CAPITAL GOLD - 24 CARAT CLASSIC HITS *Capitol Gold is a London basis Oldies Radio station.*	*The Hit Label*	20	*17 Oct 92*	1
ROAD SHOW HITS (21 YEARS OF RADIO 1 FM ROAD SHOW)	*Connoisseur Collection*	18	*3 Jul 93*	2
HALL OF FAME	*Classic FM*	13	*20 Apr 96*	4
EVENING SESSION - PRIORITY TUNES	*Virgin*	11	*17 Aug 96*	4
DAVE PEARCE PRESENTS DANCE ANTHEMS *Dave Pearce is a Dance DJ who's 'Dance Anthems' show was on BBC Radio1.*	*PolyGram TV*	4	*30 May 98*	7
ROCK THE DANCEFLOOR *Based around Preston's Rock RM radio station.*	*All Around The World*	9	*22 Aug 98*	2
DAVE PEARCE PRESENTS DANCE ANTHEMS VOLUME 2	*PolyGram TV*	5	*17 Oct 98*	3
THE HEART OF THE 80S & 90S *In conjunction with Heart FM radio.*	*Universal*	9	*17 Oct 98*	3
ROCK THE DANCEFLOOR 2	*All Around The World*	7	*3 Apr 99*	1
CLUBZONE - DANCING IN THE CITY	*warner.esp/Radio City/3 Beat*	20	*10 Apr 99*	1
DAVE PEARCE PRESENTS 40 CLASSIC DANCE ANTHEMS	*Universal Music TV*	5	*24 Jul 99*	6
RELAX . . . *Issued in conjunction with the radio station.*	*Classic FM*	11	*16 Oct 99*	7
DAVE PEARCE PRESENTS 40 CLASSIC DANCE ANTHEMS 2	*Universal Music TV*	7	*23 Oct 99*	3
RADIO 2 - SONGS OF THE CENTURY	*Global TV*	9	*18 Dec 99*	8
TREVOR NELSON'S RHYTHM NATION	*INCredible*	9	*29 Apr 00*	4
HALL OF FAME 2000	*Classic FM*	10	*6 May 00*	8
PEPSI CHART 2001 *Sponsers of the Commercial Radio Top 40 chart transmitted on Sundays.*	*Virgin/EMI*	2	*7 Oct 00*	8
BBC RADIO 2 COUNTRY HITS	*BMG TV/Telstar TV*	20	*14 Oct 00*	1
CLASSIC FM - RELAX MORE	*Classic FM*	7	*4 Nov 00*	8
STEVE WRIGHT'S SUNDAY LOVE SONGS *BBC Radio 2 DJ.*	*BBC Music/Universal Music TV*	6	*11 Nov 00*	19
THE NEW PEPSI CHART ALBUM	*Virgin/EMI*	2	*3 Mar 01*	7
THE SOUND OF CLASSIC FM	*Classic FM*	16	*14 Apr 01*	3
CAPITAL GOLD LEGENDS	*Virgin/EMI*	1	*23 Jun 01*	20
RTD 5 ROCK THE DANCEFLOOR 5 *Disc One titled Planet Dance, Disc Two titled Sunday Selection.*	*All Around The World*	19	*30 Jun 01*	1
95.8 CAPITAL FM'S PARTY IN THE PARK FOR THE PRINCE'S TRUST *Party In The Park is an open air concert organised by London's Capital Radio.*	*Universal Music TV*	2	*7 Jul 01*	5
PEPSI CHART 2002	*Virgin/EMI*	1	*20 Oct 01*	7
CLASSIC FM - TIME TO RELAX	*Classic FM*	9	*27 Oct 01*	6
CAPITAL GOLD LEGENDS II	*Virgin/EMI*	2	*17 Nov 01*	7
STEVE WRIGHT'S SUNDAY LOVE SONGS - VOLUME 2	*BBC/Universal Music TV*	12	*24 Nov 01*	3

Soundtracks

ALBUMS:	HITS 3			WEEKS 4
VICTORY IN EUROPE - BROADCASTS AND REPORTS FROM BBC CORRESPONDENTS *World War II news broadcasts.*	*BBC*	61	*18 May 85*	1
DOCTOR WHO - THE PARADISE OF DEATH *30th Anniversary recording for radio starring Jon Pertwee and Elizabeth Sladen.*	*BBC*	48	*18 Sep 93*	1
INDEPENDENCE DAY UK *BBC Radio 1 broadcast on 4 Aug 96. An amended script based around the film 'Independence Day'. Features Nicky Campbell, Patrick Moore, Toyah Wilcox, Colin Baker and Mark Goodier.*	*Speaking Volume*	66	*17 Aug 96*	2

ROYALTY

ALBUMS:	HITS 4			WEEKS 19
MUSIC FOR A ROYAL WEDDING *Music from the wedding of Princess Anne to Mark Philips, 14 Nov 73.*	*BBC*	7	*8 Dec 73*	6
THE OFFICAL BBC ALBUM OF THE ROYAL WEDDING *Music from the wedding of Prince Charles to Diana Spencer, 29 Jul 81.*	*BBC*	1	*8 Aug 81*	11
ROYAL ROMANCE	*Windsor*	84	*8 Aug 81*	1
ROYAL WEDDING *Music from the wedding of Prince Andrew to Sarah Ferguson, 23 Jul 86.*	*BBC*	55	*9 Aug 86*	1

COMPILATION ALBUMS:	HITS 3			WEEKS 16
DIANA PRINCESS OF WALES 1961-1997 - FUNERAL SERVICE *Music from the service at Westminster Abbey, 6 Sep 97.*	*BBC Worldwide Classics*	3	*27 Sep 97*	5
DIANA PRINCESS OF WALES - TRIBUTE	*Diana Memorial Fund*	1	*13 Dec 97*	10
HAPPY & GLORIOUS *The Official Album of H.M. The Queen Mother's 100th Birthday Celebrations on Horse Guards. Features various Orchestra, Choirs and Military Bands, plus Dame Vera Lynn and commentary from Sir Winston Churchill, Angela Rippon and Sir Trevor McDonald.*	*Decca*	20	*22 Jul 00*	1

SELECTED SERIES

All Time Greatest

COMPILATION ALBUMS:	HITS 11			WEEKS 80
THE ALL TIME GREATEST LOVE SONGS . . .	*Columbia*	4	*2 Nov 96*	17
THE ALL TIME GREATEST COUNTRY SONGS	*Columbia*	5	*29 Mar 97*	6
THE ALL TIME GREATEST LOVE SONGS - VOLUME II	*Columbia*	4	*1 Nov 97*	14
THE ALL TIME GREATEST ROCK SONGS	*Sony TV/warner.esp*	7	*8 Nov 97*	4
THE ALL TIME GREATEST MOVIE SONGS	*Sony TV/PolyGram TV*	3	*7 Nov 98*	8
THE ALL TIME GREATEST LOVE SONGS OF THE 60'S, 70'S, 80'S & 90'S VOLUME III	*Columbia*	6	*28 Nov 98*	14
THE ALL TIME GREATEST POP ALBUM	*Columbia*	12	*10 Jul 99*	3
ALL TIME GREATEST MOVIE SONGS - VOLUME TWO	*Sony TV/Universal Music TV*	7	*13 Nov 99*	4
THE ALL TIME GREATEST LOVE SONGS *Chart reads title as 'All Time Greatest Love Album - Volume 4'.*	*Sony TV/Universal Music TV*	9	*27 Nov 99*	8
THE ALL TIME GREATEST LOVE SONGS V	*Sony Music TV/Universal Music TV*	20	*2 Dec 00*	1
ALL TIME GREATEST MOVIE SONGS 2001	*Columbia*	18	*28 Apr 01*	1

All Woman

COMPILATION ALBUMS:	HITS 6			WEEKS 51
ALL WOMAN	*Quality Television*	1	*4 Apr 92*	15
ALL WOMAN 2	*Quality Television*	1	*10 Oct 92*	7
ALL WOMAN - THE COMPLETE WOMAN	*Quality Television*	19	*16 Jan 93*	1
ALL WOMAN 3	*Quality Television*	2	*19 Mar 94*	11
ALL WOMAN 4	*Quality Television*	18	*3 Dec 94*	4
THE BEST OF ALL WOMAN	*Quality Television*	6	*7 Oct 95*	13

Andrew Lloyd Webber

COMPILATION ALBUMS:	HITS 4			WEEKS 88
ANDREW LLOYD WEBBER - GOLD	*Really Useful/Polydor*	5	*8 Dec 01*	4

The Annual

COMPILATION ALBUMS:	HITS 12			WEEKS 135
THE ANNUAL	*Ministry Of Sound*	13	*25 Nov 95*	6
THE ANNUAL II - PETE TONG & BOY GEORGE	*Ministry Of Sound*	1	*23 Nov 96*	24
THE ANNUAL III - PETE TONG & BOY GEORGE	*Ministry Of Sound*	1	*15 Nov 97*	15
THE ANNUAL IV - JUDGE JULES & BOY GEORGE	*Ministry Of Sound*	1	*14 Nov 98*	15
THE ANNUAL - MILLENNIUM EDITION - MIXED BY JUDGE JULES & TALL PAUL	*Ministry Of Sound*	2	*13 Nov 99*	15
THE IBIZA ANNUAL - MIXED BY JUDGE JULES AND TALL PAUL - SUMMER 2000	*Ministry Of Sound*	1	*2 Sep 00*	10
THE ANNUAL 2000 - MIXED BY JUDGE JULES & TALL PAUL	*Ministry Of Sound*	1	*11 Nov 00*	12
THE ANNUAL - SPRING 2001	*Ministry Of Sound*	1	*7 Apr 01*	9
IBIZA ANNUAL - SUMMER 2001	*Ministry Of Sound*	3	*1 Sep 01*	5
THE ANNUAL 2002 - LIMITED EDITION BOX SET	*Ministry Of Sound*	1	*17 Nov 01*	7

Artful Dodger . . . Rewind

COMPILATION ALBUMS:	HITS 3			WEEKS 15
REWIND - THE SOUND OF UK GARAGE - MIXED BY THE ARTFUL DODGER	*Ministry Of Sound*	1	*26 Feb 00*	7
THE ARTFUL DODGER PRESENTS RE-REWIND BACK BY PUBLIC DEMAND	*Public Demand/ffrr*	6	*26 Aug 00*	4
THE ARTFUL DODGER PRESENTS REWIND 2001 - LESSONS FROM THE UNDERGROUND	*Public Demand/ffrr/WSM*	12	*7 Jul 01*	4

Awesome

COMPILATION ALBUMS:	HITS 2			WEEKS 23
AWESOME!! - 20 MASSIVE HITS	*EMI*	1	*23 Feb 91*	12
AWESOME 2	*EMI/Virgin/PolyGram*	2	*2 Nov 91*	11

Best . . . Ever!

COMPILATION ALBUMS:	HITS 105			WEEKS 796
THE BEST DANCE ALBUM IN THE WORLD . . . EVER!	*Virgin*	1	*17 Jul 93*	19
THE BEST DANCE ALBUM IN THE WORLD . . . EVER! 2	*Virgin*	3	*20 Nov 93*	12
THE BEST CHRISTMAS ALBUM IN THE WORLD . . . EVER!	*Virgin*	2	*4 Dec 93*	9
THE BEST REGGAE ALBUM IN THE WORLD . . . EVER!	*Virgin*	4	*4 Jun 94*	10
THE BEST DANCE ALBUM IN THE WORLD . . . EVER! 3	*Virgin*	2	*30 Jul 94*	11
THE BEST ROCK ALBUM IN THE WORLD . . . EVER!	*Virgin*	1	*3 Sep 94*	24
THE BEST ROCK 'N' ROLL ALBUM IN THE WORLD . . . EVER!	*Virgin*	2	*29 Oct 94*	10
THE BEST DANCE ALBUM IN THE WORLD . . . EVER! 4	*Virgin*	5	*19 Nov 94*	4
THE BEST PUNK ALBUM IN THE WORLD . . . EVER!	*Virgin*	1	*4 Feb 95*	13
THE BEST FUNK ALBUM IN THE WORLD . . . EVER!	*Virgin*	11	*4 Mar 95*	3
THE BEST ROCK ALBUM IN THE WORLD . . . EVER! II	*Virgin*	3	*15 Apr 95*	8
THE BEST DANCE ALBUM IN THE WORLD . . . EVER! 5	*Virgin*	4	*15 Jul 95*	7
THE BEST SUMMER ALBUM IN THE WORLD . . . EVER!	*Virgin*	1	*22 Jul 95*	11
THE BEST ROCK BALLADS ALBUM IN THE WORLD . . . EVER!	*Virgin*	2	*2 Sep 95*	23
THE BEST . . . ALBUM IN THE WORLD . . . EVER!	*Virgin*	2	*16 Sep 95*	8
THE BEST DANCE ALBUM IN THE WORLD . . . 95!	*Virgin*	3	*21 Oct 95*	4
THE BEST 80'S ALBUM IN THE WORLD . . . EVER!	*Virgin*	7	*11 Nov 95*	4
THE BEST PARTY . . . EVER!	*Virgin*	5	*25 Nov 95*	8
THE BEST SIXTIES ALBUM IN THE WORLD . . . EVER!	*Virgin*	2	*2 Dec 95*	17
THE BEST . . . ALBUM IN THE WORLD . . . EVER! 2	*Virgin*	1	*10 Feb 96*	12
THE BEST RAP ALBUM IN THE WORLD . . . EVER!	*Virgin*	2	*23 Mar 96*	10
THE BEST PUNK ALBUM IN THE WORLD . . . EVER! 2	*Virgin*	16	*13 Apr 96*	2
THE BEST . . . ALBUM IN THE WORLD . . . EVER! 3	*Virgin*	2	*27 Apr 96*	7
THE BEST ROCK ANTHEMS ALBUM IN THE WORLD . . . EVER!	*Virgin*	8	*1 Jun 96*	4
THE BEST SWING ALBUM IN THE WORLD . . . EVER!	*Virgin*	3	*15 Jun 96*	10
THE BEST FOOTIE ANTHEMS IN THE WORLD . . . EVER!	*Virgin*	5	*29 Jun 96*	5
THE BEST DANCE ALBUM IN THE WORLD . . . EVER! 6	*Virgin*	1	*17 Aug 96*	13
THE BEST JAZZ ALBUM IN THE WORLD . . . EVER!	*Virgin*	8	*17 Aug 96*	5
THE BEST . . . ALBUM IN THE WORLD . . . EVER! 4	*Virgin*	2	*26 Oct 96*	6
THE BEST OPERA ALBUM IN THE WORLD . . . EVER!	*Virgin*	10	*9 Nov 96*	10
THE BEST IRISH ALBUM IN THE WORLD . . . EVER!	*Virgin*	11	*9 Nov 96*	9
THE BEST SIXTIES ALBUM IN THE WORLD . . . EVER! II	*Virgin*	2	*23 Nov 96*	15
THE BEST MIX ALBUM IN THE WORLD . . . EVER!	*Virgin*	9	*23 Nov 96*	3
THE BEST CHRISTMAS ALBUM IN THE WORLD . . . EVER! *Same tracks that appeared on the 1993 issue plus additional tracks.*	*Virgin*	2	*30 Nov 96*	19
THE BEST . . . ALBUM IN THE WORLD . . . EVER! 5	*Virgin/EMI*	1	*22 Mar 97*	7
SPICE GIRLS PRESENT THE BEST GIRL POWER ALBUM IN THE WORLD . . . EVER!	*Virgin/EMI*	2	*17 May 97*	9
THE BEST CLUB ANTHEMS IN THE WORLD . . . EVER!	*Virgin/EMI*	1	*14 Jun 97*	9
THE BEST SCOTTISH ALBUM IN THE WORLD . . . EVER!	*Virgin/EMI*	9	*21 Jun 97*	6
THE BEST SUMMER ALBUM IN THE WORLD . . . EVER!	*Virgin/EMI*	3	*5 Jul 97*	9
THE BEST DISCO ALBUM IN THE WORLD . . . EVER!	*Virgin/EMI*	1	*12 Jul 97*	15
THE BEST . . . ALBUM IN THE WORLD . . . EVER! 6	*Virgin/EMI*	8	*19 Jul 97*	4
THE BEST DANCE ALBUM IN THE WORLD . . . EVER! 7	*Virgin/EMI*	2	*16 Aug 97*	11
THE BEST LATINO CARNIVAL IN THE WORLD . . . EVER!	*Virgin/EMI*	5	*16 Aug 97*	6
THE BEST . . . ANTHEMS . . . EVER!	*Virgin/EMI*	1	*25 Oct 97*	10
THE MOST RELAXING CLASSICAL ALBUM IN THE WORLD . . . EVER!	*Virgin/EMI*	10	*8 Nov 97*	16
THE BEST SIXTIES ALBUM IN THE WORLD . . . EVER! III	*Virgin/EMI*	3	*22 Nov 97*	12
THE BEST SEVENTIES ALBUM IN THE WORLD . . . EVER!	*Virgin/EMI*	13	*22 Nov 97*	9
THE BEST ROCK BALLADS ALBUM IN THE WORLD . . . EVER! II	*Virgin/EMI*	7	*29 Nov 97*	11
THE BEST CLUB ANTHEMS IN THE WORLD . . . EVER! 2	*Virgin/EMI*	6	*6 Dec 97*	11
THE BEST PARTY IN THE WORLD . . . EVER! 2	*Virgin/EMI*	7	*6 Dec 97*	6
THE BEST . . . ANTHEMS . . . EVER! 2	*Virgin/EMI*	3	*18 Apr 98*	10
THE BEST HIP HOP ANTHEMZ IN THE WORLD . . . EVER!	*Virgin/EMI*	6	*25 Apr 98*	5
THE BEST CLUB ANTHEMS IN THE WORLD . . . EVER! III	*Virgin/EMI*	3	*16 May 98*	6
THE BEST DISCO ALBUM IN THE WORLD . . . EVER! 2	*Virgin/EMI*	7	*30 May 98*	5
THE BEST SIXTIES SUMMER ALBUM IN THE WORLD . . . EVER!	*Virgin/EMI*	2	*27 Jun 98*	11
ALL NEW - THE BEST FOOTIE ANTHEMS IN THE WORLD . . . EVER!	*Virgin/EMI*	6	*27 Jun 98*	3
THE BEST SUMMER PARTY ALBUM IN THE WORLD . . . EVER!	*Virgin/EMI*	6	*11 Jul 98*	6
THE BEST ALBUM . . . IN THE WORLD . . . EVER! 7	*Virgin/EMI*	11	*18 Jul 98*	3
THE BEST DANCE ALBUM IN THE WORLD . . . EVER! 8	*Virgin/EMI*	2	*25 Jul 98*	9
THE BEST RAVE ANTHEMS IN THE WORLD . . . EVER!	*Virgin/EMI*	11	*15 Aug 98*	3
THE BEST CHART HITS ALBUM IN THE WORLD . . . EVER!	*Virgin/EMI*	1	*31 Oct 98*	5
THE MOST RELAXING CLASSICAL ALBUM IN THE WORLD . . . EVER! II	*Virgin/EMI*	12	*7 Nov 98*	9
THE BEST COUNTRY BALLADS IN THE WORLD . . . EVER!	*Virgin/EMI*	14	*14 Nov 98*	3
THE BEST . . . ANTHEMS . . . EVER! 3	*Virgin/EMI*	19	*14 Nov 98*	1
THE BEST ROCK ANTHEMS . . . EVER!	*Virgin/EMI*	10	*21 Nov 98*	2
THE BEST SIXTIES ALBUM IN THE WORLD . . . EVER! IV	*Virgin/EMI*	11	*21 Nov 98*	7
BIGGEST 80'S HITS IN THE WORLD . . . EVER!	*Virgin/EMI*	16	*28 Nov 98*	2
THE BEST CLUB ANTHEMS 99 IN THE WORLD . . . EVER!	*Virgin/EMI*	1	*23 Jan 99*	11
THE BEST SIXTIES LOVE ALBUM . . . EVER!	*Virgin/EMI*	2	*13 Feb 99*	6
THE BEST CHART HITS IN THE WORLD . . . EVER! 99	*Virgin/EMI*	5	*27 Feb 99*	4
THE BEST HOUSE ANTHEMS . . . EVER!	*Virgin/EMI*	5	*8 May 99*	4
THE BEST TRANCE ANTHEMS . . . EVER!	*Virgin/EMI*	7	*10 Jul 99*	4
THE BEST DANCE ALBUM IN THE WORLD . . . EVER! 9	*Virgin/EMI*	1	*24 Jul 99*	9
THE BEST IBIZA ANTHEMS . . . EVER!	*Virgin/EMI*	2	*7 Aug 99*	11

THE BEST PEPSI CHART ALBUM IN THE WORLD . . . EVER!	*Virgin/EMI*	2	*23 Oct 99*	4
THE BEST CLASSICAL ALBUM OF THE MILLENNIUM . . . EVER!	*Virgin/EMI*	10	*6 Nov 99*	3
THE BEST LOVESONGS . . . EVER!	*Virgin/EMI*	8	*20 Nov 99*	15
THE BEST . . . AND FRIENDS ALBUM IN THE WORLD . . . EVER!	*Virgin/EMI*	8	*4 Dec 99*	12
THE BEST MILLENNIUM PARTY . . . EVER!	*Virgin/EMI*	5	*4 Dec 99*	6
THE BEST CLUB ANTHEMS 2000 . . . EVER!	*Virgin/EMI*	8	*11 Dec 99*	10
THE BEST MUSICALS ALBUM IN THE WORLD . . . EVER!	*Virgin/EMI*	12	*11 Dec 99*	7
THE BEST DANCE ALBUM IN THE WORLD . . . EVER! 2000	*Virgin/EMI*	4	*26 Feb 00*	5
THE BEST PEPSI CHART ALBUM IN THE WORLD . . . EVER! 2000	*Virgin/EMI*	7	*18 Mar 00*	4
THE BEST JAZZ ALBUM IN THE WORLD . . . EVER! (Second Album)	*Virgin/EMI*	11	*15 Apr 00*	3
THE BEST TV ADS . . . EVER!	*Virgin/EMI*	10	*13 May 00*	4
THE BEST CLUB ANTHEMS . . . EVER! 2K	*Virgin/EMI*	2	*3 Jun 00*	7
THE BEST SUMMER HOLIDAY . . . EVER!	*Virgin/EMI*	6	*17 Jun 00*	9
THE BEST FOOTIE ANTHEMS . . . EVER!	*Virgin/EMI*	4	*17 Jun 00*	3
Updated version of the 1996 release.				
THE BEST EASY ALBUM . . . EVER!	*Virgin/EMI*	10	*17 Jun 00*	4
THE BEST PUB JUKEBOX IN THE WORLD . . . EVER!	*Virgin/EMI*	9	*24 Jun 00*	8
THE BEST IBIZA ANTHEMS . . . EVER! 2K	*Virgin/EMI*	2	*12 Aug 00*	8
THE BEST DANCE ALBUM IN THE WORLD . . . EVER! PART 10	*Virgin/EMI*	3	*2 Sep 00*	6
THE BEST PROMS ALBUM IN THE WORLD . . . EVER!	*Virgin/EMI*	16	*9 Sep 00*	3
THE BEST GARAGE ANTHEMS . . . EVER!	*Virgin/EMI*	8	*30 Sep 00*	5
THE BEST . . . AND FRIENDS ALBUM IN THE WORLD . . . EVER! VOL. 2	*Virgin/EMI*	20	*25 Nov 00*	1
THE BEST CHRISTMAS ALBUM IN THE WORLD . . . EVER!	*Virgin/EMI*	6	*9 Dec 00*	4
New Edition of the previous 2 releases.				
THE BEST CLUB ANTHEMS 2001 . . . EVER!	*Virgin/EMI*	12	*9 Dec 00*	6
THE BEST PARTY IN TOWN . . . EVER!	*Virgin/EMI*	19	*6 Jan 01*	1
THE BEST HARD HOUSE . . . EVER!	*Virgin/EMI*	10	*12 May 01*	3
THE BEST NORTHERN SOUL ALL-NIGHTER . . . EVER!	*Virgin/EMI*	17	*19 May 01*	2
THE BEST SUMMER HOLIDAY 2001 . . . EVER!	*Virgin/EMI*	2	*7 Jul 01*	8
THE BEST DANCE ALBUM IN THE WORLD . . . EVER! PART 11	*Virgin/EMI*	4	*21 Jul 01*	4
THE BEST IBIZA ANTHEMS . . . EVER! 2001	*Virgin/EMI*	5	*18 Aug 01*	4
CD1 titled Club Ibiza, CD2 titled Chilled Ibiza.				
THE BEST CARNIVAL ALBUM . . . EVER!	*Virgin/EMI*	11	*1 Sep 01*	2
THE BEST AIR GUITAR ALBUM IN THE WORLD . . . EVER!	*Virgin/EMI/Universal Music TV*	5	*17 Nov 01*	7
THE BEST CHRISTMAS ALBUM IN THE WORLD . . . EVER! [RE]	*Virgin/EMI*	4	*15 Dec 01*	3

Best Of Dance

COMPILATION ALBUMS:	HITS 7			WEEKS 60
THE BEST OF DANCE '91	*Telstar*	2	*9 Nov 91*	15
THE BEST OF DANCE '92 - 32 PUMPIN' CLUB HITS	*Telstar*	1	*7 Nov 92*	17
THE BEST OF DANCE '93	*Telstar*	1	*6 Nov 93*	11
THE BEST OF DANCE 94	*Telstar*	10	*5 Nov 94*	5
THE BEST OF DANCE 96	*Telstar*	13	*9 Nov 96*	3
THE BEST OF DANCE 97	*Telstar TV*	6	*8 Nov 97*	4
THE BEST OF DANCE 98	*Telstar TV*	9	*7 Nov 98*	2

Big Mix

COMPILATION ALBUMS:	HITS 4			WEEKS 24
BIG MIX 96	*EMI TV/warner.esp*	1	*20 Jul 96*	8
BIG MIX '96 - VOLUME 2	*EMI TV/warner.esp*	7	*28 Sep 96*	4
BIG MIX '97	*Warner/Virgin/EMI*	1	*24 May 97*	7
BIG MIX '97 - VOLUME 2	*Virgin/EMI/warner.esp*	1	*11 Oct 97*	5

Bonkers

COMPILATION ALBUMS:	HITS 6			WEEKS 17
BONKERS 2	*React*	10	*10 May 97*	3
BONKERS 3 - JOURNEY INTO MADNESS	*React*	9	*1 Nov 97*	3
BONKERS 4 - WORLD FRENZY	*React*	8	*30 May 98*	4
BONKERS 5 - ANARCHY IN THE UNIVERSE	*React*	12	*7 Nov 98*	2
BONKERS 6 (WHEEL CRAZY)	*React*	10	*1 May 99*	4
BONKERS 7 - MILLENNIUM MADNESS	*React*	18	*16 Oct 99*	1

The Box

The Box is a cable TV station which plays music videos selected by viewers.

COMPILATION ALBUMS:	HITS 8			WEEKS 32
THE BOX HITS 98	*Telstar TV*	2	*21 Mar 98*	5
THE BOX HITS 98 - VOLUME 2	*Telstar TV*	1	*13 Jun 98*	6
BOX HITS 98 - VOLUME 3	*Telstar TV*	2	*17 Oct 98*	4
THE BOX R&B HITS ALBUM	*Telstar TV*	6	*9 Jan 99*	6
THE BOX - DANCE HITS	*Universal Music TV*	2	*10 Jul 99*	4
THE BOX DANCE HITS - VOLUME 2	*Universal Music TV*	5	*13 Nov 99*	3
THE BOX DANCE HITS 2000 - 41 HUGE DANCE HITS!	*Universal Music TV*	5	*15 Apr 00*	2
THE BOX - 41 MASSIVE HITS FOR 2000	*Universal Music TV*	12	*9 Sep 00*	2

Brit Awards

The Brits are the Music Industry's Award Presentations in the U.K.

COMPILATION ALBUMS:	HITS 13			WEEKS 79
THE BRITS - THE AWARDS 1989	*Telstar*	1	*25 Feb 89*	8
THE AWARDS 1990	*Telstar*	3	*24 Feb 90*	10

THE BRITS 1991 - THE MAGIC OF BRITISH MUSIC	*Telstar*	7	*16 Feb 91*	6
THE AWARDS 1992	*PolyGram TV*	1	*22 Feb 92*	9
THE AWARDS 1993	*PolyGram TV*	3	*20 Feb 93*	7
THE BRIT AWARDS	*EMI*	6	*26 Feb 94*	3
THE AWARDS 1995	*Columbia*	10	*4 Mar 95*	2
BRIT AWARDS '96	*Columbia*	6	*17 Feb 96*	4
THE '97 BRIT AWARDS	*Columbia*	2	*22 Feb 97*	6
THE BRIT AWARDS 1998	*Columbia*	11	*7 Feb 98*	5
THE 1999 BRIT AWARDS	*Columbia*	3	*13 Feb 99*	7
THE 2000 BRIT AWARDS - THE ALBUM OF THE YEAR	*Columbia*	3	*4 Mar 00*	5
BRIT AWARDS WITH MASTERCARD 2001 - ALBUM OF THE YEAR	*Columbia*	3	*24 Feb 01*	7

Café Del Mar

COMPILATION ALBUMS:	HITS 7			WEEKS 13
CAFE DEL MAR IBIZA - VOLUMEN DOS	*React*	17	*12 Aug 95*	1
CAFE DEL MAR IBIZA - VOLUMEN TRES	*React*	16	*10 Aug 96*	1
CAFE DEL MAR - VOLUMEN CUATRO	*Manifesto*	18	*23 Aug 97*	1
CAFE DEL MAR - VOLUMEN CINCO	*Manifesto*	16	*25 Jul 98*	2
CAFE DEL MAR - VOLUMEN SEIS	*Manifesto*	15	*21 Aug 99*	2
CAFE DEL MAR - VOLUMEN SIETE	*Manifesto*	14	*8 Jul 00*	3
CAFE DEL MAR - VOLUMEN OCHO	*Manifesto*	12	*30 Jun 01*	3

Classic Experience

ALBUMS:	HITS 1			WEEKS 12
THE CLASSIC EXPERIENCE	*EMI*	27	*22 Oct 88*	12
COMPILATION ALBUMS:	**HITS 5**			**WEEKS 111**
THE CLASSIC EXPERIENCE	*EMI*	12	*14 Jan 89*	14
THE CLASSIC EXPERIENCE [RE]	*EMI*	8	*11 Nov 89*	44
CLASSIC EXPERIENCE II	*EMI*	1	*26 May 90*	32
CLASSIC EXPERIENCE III	*EMI*	3	*11 May 91*	14
CLASSIC EXPERIENCE IV	*EMI*	9	*27 Mar 93*	6
THE VERY BEST OF CLASSICAL EXPERIENCE	*Virgin/EMI*	18	*18 Sep 99*	1

Club Mix

COMPILATION ALBUMS:	HITS 14			WEEKS 92
CLUB MIX 96	*PolyGram TV*	2	*6 Apr 96*	7
CLUB MIX 96 - VOLUME 2	*PolyGram TV*	2	*3 Aug 96*	8
CLUB MIX 97	*PolyGram TV*	7	*21 Dec 96*	8
CLUB MIX 97 - VOLUME 2	*PolyGram TV*	1	*1 Mar 97*	6
CLUB MIX 97 - VOLUME 3	*PolyGram TV*	4	*28 Jun 97*	5
ULTIMATE CLUB MIX	*PolyGram TV*	1	*7 Feb 98*	7
ULTIMATE CLUB MIX 2	*PolyGram TV*	5	*15 Aug 98*	5
ULTIMATE CLUB MIX - 98	*PolyGram TV*	13	*7 Nov 98*	1
CLUB MIX 99	*Universal Music TV*	3	*21 Aug 99*	7
CLUBMIX 2000	*Universal Music TV*	2	*5 Feb 00*	6
CLUB MIX IBIZA 2000	*Universal Music TV*	1	*24 Jun 00*	11
CLUBMIX 2000 2	*Universal Music TV*	1	*21 Oct 00*	5
CLUB MIX 2001	*Universal Music TV*	3	*24 Feb 01*	8
CLUBMIX IBIZA	*Ministry Of Sound/ Universal Music TV*	2	*11 Aug 01*	8

Clubber's Guide To

COMPILATION ALBUMS:	HITS 8			WEEKS 56
CLUBBER'S GUIDE TO . . . 2000	*Ministry Of Sound*	1	*29 Jan 00*	8
CLUBBER'S GUIDE . . . TO IBIZA - SUMMER 2000 - MIXED BY JUDGE JULES	*Ministry Of Sound*	1	*10 Jun 00*	7
CLUBBER'S GUIDE TO . . . 2001: MIXED BY TALL PAUL	*Ministry Of Sound*	1	*20 Jan 01*	5
CLUBBER'S GUIDE TO . . . IBIZA - SUMMER 2001	*Ministry Of Sound*	4	*9 Jun 01*	5

CD1 titled Beach Life, CD2 titled Night Life.

Cream

Cream is a major nightclub in Liverpool.

COMPILATION ALBUMS:	HITS 18			WEEKS 101
CREAM LIVE	*Deconstruction*	3	*6 May 95*	17
CREAM ANTHEMS	*Deconstruction*	2	*11 Nov 95*	3
CREAM LIVE - TWO	*Deconstruction*	3	*6 Jul 96*	5
CREAM SEPARATES - THE COLLECTION	*Deconstruction*	16	*29 Mar 97*	1
CREAM ANTHEMS '97	*Deconstruction*	11	*15 Nov 97*	2
CREAM ANTHEMS MIXED BY TALL PAUL AND SEB FONTAINE	*Virgin/EMI*	15	*28 Nov 98*	1
RESIDENT - 2 YEARS OF OAKENFOLD AT CREAM	*Virgin/EMI*	2	*27 Mar 99*	6
CREAM IBIZA - ARRIVALS	*Virgin/EMI*	2	*12 Jun 99*	7
CREAM IBIZA - DEPARTURES	*Virgin/EMI*	13	*18 Sep 99*	2
CREAM ANTHEMS 2000	*Virgin/EMI*	2	*27 Nov 99*	14
CREAM LIVE	*Virgin/EMI*	2	*29 Apr 00*	8
This is different album to 1995 release.				
CREAM IBIZA ARRIVALS	*Virgin/EMI*	4	*1 Jul 00*	5
CREAM RESIDENT - SEB FONTAINE	*Virgin/EMI*	18	*29 Jul 00*	2
CREAMFIELDS	*Virgin/EMI*	5	*9 Sep 00*	4
CREAM ANTHEMS 2001	*Virgin/EMI*	1	*25 Nov 00*	12

CREAM LIVE *This is a different album to previous releases.*	*Virgin/EMI*	5	*14 Apr 01*	8
CREAM IBIZA	*Virgin/EMI*	7	*1 Sep 01*	3
CREAM ANTHEMS 2002	*Virgin/EMI*	18	*24 Nov 01*	1

Dance Energy

COMPILATION ALBUMS:	HITS 4			WEEKS 17
DANCE ENERGY	*Virgin Television*	20	*19 Jan 91*	2
DANCE ENERGY 2	*Virgin Television*	6	*1 Jun 91*	5
DANCE ENERGY 3	*Virgin Television*	10	*30 Nov 91*	6
DANCE ENERGY 4 - FEEL THE RHYTHM	*Parlophone*	6	*4 Jul 92*	4

Dance Mix

ALBUMS:	HITS 4			WEEKS 7
DANCE MIX - DANCE HITS VOLUME 1	*Epic*	85	*2 Jul 83*	2
DANCE MIX - DANCE HITS VOLUME 2	*Epic*	51	*24 Sep 83*	3
DANCE MIX - DANCE HITS VOLUME 3	*Epic*	70	*3 Mar 84*	1
DANCE MIX - DANCE HITS VOLUME 4	*Epic*	99	*16 Jun 84*	1

Dance Nation

COMPILATION ALBUMS:	HITS 7			WEEKS 57
DANCE NATION	*Ministry Of Sound*	5	*13 Apr 96*	6
MINISTRY OF SOUND - DANCE NATION PART 2	*Ministry Of Sound*	4	*20 Jul 96*	8
DANCE NATION 3 - PETE TONG & JUDGE JULES	*Ministry Of Sound*	1	*29 Mar 97*	10
DANCE NATION 4 - PETE TONG/BOY GEORGE	*Ministry Of Sound*	2	*13 Sep 97*	8
PETE TONG/BOY GEORGE - DANCE NATION 5	*Ministry Of Sound*	2	*28 Mar 98*	9
DANCE NATION SIX - TALL PAUL & BRANDON BLOCK	*Ministry Of Sound*	1	*27 Mar 99*	11
DANCE NATION - BRANDON BLOCK TALL PAUL	*Ministry Of Sound*	1	*8 Apr 00*	5

Dave Pearce Presents

COMPILATION ALBUMS:	HITS 5			WEEKS 23
DAVE PEARCE PRESENTS - 40 CLASSIC DANCE ANTHEMS VOL 3	*Manifesto/Universal Music TV*	7	*20 May 00*	4

Dance Zone

COMPILATION ALBUMS:	HITS 11			WEEKS 75
DANCE ZONE - LEVEL ONE	*PolyGram TV*	1	*7 May 94*	8
DANCE ZONE - LEVEL TWO	*PolyGram TV*	1	*16 Jul 94*	6
DANCE ZONE - LEVEL THREE	*PolyGram TV*	1	*8 Oct 94*	6
DANCE ZONE '94	*PolyGram TV*	2	*12 Nov 94*	12
DANCE ZONE - LEVEL FOUR	*PolyGram TV*	1	*25 Mar 95*	8
DANCE ZONE - LEVEL FIVE	*PolyGram TV*	1	*24 Jun 95*	10
DANCE ZONE - LEVEL SIX	*PolyGram TV*	1	*2 Sep 95*	7
DANCE ZONE '95	*PolyGram TV*	8	*11 Nov 95*	4
DANCE ZONE - LEVEL SEVEN	*PolyGram TV*	1	*4 May 96*	5
DANCE ZONE - LEVEL EIGHT	*PolyGram TV*	4	*21 Sep 96*	6
DANCE ZONE - LEVEL NINE	*PolyGram TV*	7	*31 May 97*	3

Deep Heat

COMPILATION ALBUMS:	HITS 14			WEEKS 149
DEEP HEAT - 26 HOTTEST HOUSE HITS	*Telstar*	1	*4 Mar 89*	15
DEEP HEAT - THE SECOND BURN	*Telstar*	2	*22 Apr 89*	13
DEEP HEAT 3 - THE THIRD DEGREE	*Telstar*	2	*22 Jul 89*	13
DEEP HEAT 4 - PLAY WITH FIRE	*Telstar*	1	*23 Sep 89*	11
DEEP HEAT 1989 - FIGHT THE FLAME	*Telstar*	4	*25 Nov 89*	17
DEEP HEAT 5 - FEED THE FEVER - 32 HOTTEST CLUB HITS	*Telstar*	1	*3 Feb 90*	11
DEEP HEAT 6 - THE SIXTH SENSE	*Telstar*	1	*31 Mar 90*	14
DEEP HEAT 7 - SEVENTH HEAVEN	*Telstar*	1	*7 Jul 90*	9
DEEP HEAT 8 - THE HAND OF FATE	*Telstar*	3	*27 Oct 90*	5
DEEP HEAT 90	*Telstar*	3	*24 Nov 90*	12
DEEP HEAT 9 - NINTH LIFE - KISS THE BLISS	*Telstar*	1	*26 Jan 91*	7
DEEP HEAT 10 - THE AWAKENING	*Telstar*	2	*1 Jun 91*	7
DEEP HEAT 11 - SPIRIT OF ECSTASY	*Telstar*	3	*21 Dec 91*	8
DEEP HEAT 93 VOLUME 1	*Telstar*	2	*10 Apr 93*	7

Disney

ALBUMS:	HITS 2			WEEKS 19
GOOFY GREATS	*K-Tel*	19	*8 Nov 75*	7
GREATEST HITS OF WALT DISNEY	*Ronco*	11	*6 Dec 75*	12

COMPILATION ALBUMS:	HITS 5			WEEKS 25
THE VERY BEST OF DISNEY	*Pickwick*	4	*20 Nov 93*	12
THE VERY BEST OF DISNEY 2	*Pickwick/Disney*	9	*19 Nov 94*	4
DISNEY'S HIT SINGLES & MORE!	*Walt Disney*	9	*22 Nov 97*	4
THE DISNEY EXPERIENCE	*Walt Disney*	12	*28 Nov 98*	4
DISNEY'S GREATEST HITS	*Telstar TV/BMG*	19	*2 Dec 00*	1

Drive Time

COMPILATION ALBUMS:	HITS 4			WEEKS 24
DRIVE TIME - 36 OF THE GREATEST RADIO ANTHEMS . . .	*Dino*	5	*8 Apr 95*	8

DRIVE TIME 2	*Dino*	4	*22 Jul 95*	7
DRIVETIME 3	*Dino*	4	*6 Jan 96*	6
DRIVE TIME 4	*Dino*	8	*31 Aug 96*	3

Energy Rush

COMPILATION ALBUMS:	HITS 14			WEEKS 99
ENERGY RUSH	*Dino*	1	*17 Oct 92*	6
ENERGY RUSH II	*Dino*	7	*12 Dec 92*	7
ENERGY RUSH LEVEL 3	*Dino*	3	*30 Jan 93*	6
ENERGY RUSH PRESENTS DANCE HITS 93	*Dino*	1	*10 Apr 93*	12
ENERGY RUSH PHASE 4	*Dino*	2	*5 Jun 93*	6
ENERGY RUSH DANCE HITS 93 (2ND DIMENSION)	*Dino*	2	*24 Jul 93*	8
ENERGY RUSH FACTOR 5	*Dino*	3	*11 Sep 93*	5
ENERGY RUSH PRESENTS DANCE HITS OF THE YEAR	*Dino*	3	*16 Oct 93*	13
ENERGY RUSH - SAFE SIX	*Dino*	5	*4 Dec 93*	7
ENERGY RUSH - EURO DANCE HITS 94	*Dino*	5	*12 Mar 94*	4
ENERGY RUSH 7	*Dino*	2	*2 Apr 94*	5
ENERGY RUSH - XTERMIN8	*Dino*	1	*28 May 94*	8
ENERGY RUSH DANCE HITS 94	*Dino*	3	*6 Aug 94*	8
ENERGY RUSH K9	*Dino*	3	*11 Feb 95*	4

Essential Selection

COMPILATION ALBUMS:	HITS 17			WEEKS 80
PETE TONG ESSENTIAL SELECTION - SUMMER 97	*PolyGram TV*	4	*23 Aug 97*	5
Pete Tong is a DJ who has the show 'Essential Selection' on BBC Radio 1.				
PETE TONG ESSENTIAL SELECTION - WINTER 97	*ffrr*	10	*15 Nov 97*	2
PETE TONG ESSENTIAL SELECTION	*ffrr*	4	*18 Apr 98*	7
PETE TONG ESSENTIAL SELECTION - SUMMER 1998 (3CD issue)	*ffrr*	2	*29 Aug 98*	7
PETE TONG ESSENTIAL SELECTION - SUMMER 1998	*ffrr*	4	*29 Aug 98*	9
ESSENTIAL SELECTION '98 - PETE TONG/PAUL OAKENFOLD (3CD issue)	*ffrr*	11	*5 Dec 98*	6
ESSENTIAL SELECTION '98 - PETE TONG/PAUL OAKENFOLD	*ffrr*	13	*9 Jan 99*	5
PETE TONG - ESSENTIAL SECTION - SPRING 1999 (3CD issue)	*ffrr*	3	*20 Mar 99*	6
PETE TONG - ESSENTIAL SECTION - SPRING 1999	*ffrr*	13	*20 Mar 99*	3
PETE TONG ESSENTIAL SELECTION - IBIZA 99	*ffrr*	11	*31 Jul 99*	5
PETE TONG ESSENTIAL SELECTION - IBIZA 99 (3CD issue)	*ffrr*	7	*31 Jul 99*	3
Due to chart rules, sales of the 3CD issues listed above could not be combined with the standard packages.				
ESSENTIAL MILLENNIUM - PETE TONG FATBOY SLIM PAUL OAKENFOLD	*ffrr*	10	*13 Nov 99*	3
PETE TONG ESSENTIAL SELECTION SPRING 2000	*Essential Recordings*	8	*6 May 00*	4
ESSENTIAL SELECTION IBIZA 2000 - THE SOUNDTRACK TO YOUR SUMMER	*Essential Recordings*	11	*9 Sep 00*	3
ESSENTIAL SELECTION PRESENTS THE CLUBBER'S BIBLE - YOUR SOUNDTRACK TO THE WEEKEND	*WSM*	11	*9 Dec 00*	6
ESSENTIAL SELECTION PRESENTS THE CLUBBER'S BIBLE II - THE SECOND COMING	*WSM*	6	*5 May 01*	5
ESSENTIAL SELECTION PRESENTS THE CLUBBER'S BIBLE WINTER 2002	*WSM*	17	*8 Dec 01*	1

Euphoria

COMPILATION ALBUMS:	HITS 19			WEEKS 131
EUPHORIA - LEVEL 3	*Telstar TV*	5	*25 Dec 99*	12
BREAKDOWN - THE VERY BEST OF EUPHORIC DANCE (First Album)	*Telstar TV*	4	*15 Jan 00*	11
PURE EUPHORIA - LEVEL 4 - DIGITALLY MIXED BY MATT DAREY	*Telstar TV*	3	*29 Apr 00*	6
CHILLED EUPHORIA - DIGITALLY MIXED BY RED JERRY	*Telstar TV*	4	*10 Jun 00*	7
IBIZA EUPHORIA - MIXED BY ALEX GOLD AND AGNELLI & NELSON	*Telstar TV*	4	*19 Aug 00*	5
BREAKDOWN - THE VERY BEST OF EUPHORIC DANCE	*Telstar TV*	4	*2 Sep 00*	7
This is a different album to the previous release.				
TRANSCENDENTAL EUPHORIA	*BMG/Telstar TV*	6	*2 Dec 00*	8
HARD HOUSE EUPHORIA - MIXED BY LISA LASHES	*BMG/Telstar TV*	6	*16 Dec 00*	8
DEEP & CHILLED EUPHORIA: DIGITALLY MIXED BY RED JERRY	*BMG/Telstar TV*	5	*27 Jan 01*	6
BREAKDOWN - THE VERY BEST OF EUPHORIC DANCE	*BMG/Telstar TV*	1	*3 Feb 01*	8
This is a different album to the previous releases.				
THE VERY BEST EUPHORIC CHILLOUT MIXES - BREAKDOWN	*BMG/Telstar TV*	8	*31 Mar 01*	5
TRUE EUPHORIA - MIXED BY DAVE PEARCE	*BMG/Telstar TV*	3	*14 Apr 01*	6
THE VERY BEST OF EUPHORIC DANCE - BREAKDOWN IBIZA	*BMG/Telstar TV*	2	*4 Aug 01*	4
CHILLED OUT EUPHORIA: DIGITALLY MIXED BY SOLAR STONE	*Telstar TV/BMG*	8	*25 Aug 01*	2
IBIZA EUPHORIA MIXED BY DAVE PEARCE	*BMG/Telstar TV*	3	*15 Sep 01*	6
HARD HOUSE EUPHORIA - MIXED BY TIDY BOYS VS LISA PIN-UP	*BMG/Telstar TV*	12	*3 Nov 01*	2

Fantastic

COMPILATION ALBUMS:	HITS 6			WEEKS 31
FANTASTIC 80'S!	*Columbia*	1	*7 Mar 98*	13
FANTASTIC 80'S! - 2	*Columbia*	4	*23 May 98*	7
FANTASTIC DANCE!	*Columbia*	14	*29 Aug 98*	2
FANTASTIC 70'S!	*Columbia*	8	*3 Oct 98*	4
FANTASTIC 80'S! - 3	*Columbia*	11	*14 Nov 98*	2
FANTASTIC 80S! - GO FOR IT!	*Columbia*	10	*2 Sep 00*	3

Gatecrasher

Gatecrasher is a major nightclub in Sheffield.

COMPILATION ALBUMS:	HITS 8			WEEKS 31
GATECRASHER: GLOBAL SOUND SYSTEM	*INCredible*	3	*12 Aug 00*	4

GATECRASHER - NATIONAL ANTHEMS	*INCredible*	13	*9 Dec 00*	2
GATECRASHER DISCOTECH GENERATION	*INCredible*	10	*7 Apr 01*	2
GATECRASHER DIGITAL	*Gatecrasher Music*	6	*20 Oct 01*	4

Greatest Hits Of

ALBUMS:	HITS 4			WEEKS 49
THE GREATEST HITS OF 1985	*Telstar*	1	*16 Nov 85*	17
THE GREATEST HITS OF 1986	*Telstar*	8	*8 Nov 86*	13
THE GREATEST HITS OF 1987	*Telstar*	12	*21 Nov 87*	11
THE GREATEST HITS OF 1988	*Telstar*	11	*19 Nov 88*	8

COMPILATION ALBUMS:	HITS 15			WEEKS 139
THE GREATEST HITS OF 1988	*Telstar*	8	*14 Jan 89*	8
THE GREATEST HITS OF 1989	*Telstar*	4	*18 Nov 89*	11
THE GREATEST HITS OF 1990	*Telstar*	4	*17 Nov 90*	14
THE GREATEST HITS OF 1991	*Telstar*	4	*16 Nov 91*	13
THE GREATEST HITS OF 1992	*Telstar*	4	*14 Nov 92*	16
THE GREATEST HITS OF DANCE	*Telstar*	5	*28 Nov 92*	11
THE GREATEST HITS OF 1993	*Telstar*	4	*13 Nov 93*	13
THE GREATEST HITS OF 1994	*Telstar*	9	*12 Nov 94*	5
THE GREATEST HITS OF THE 90'S - PART 1	*Telstar*	19	*28 Jan 95*	2
THE GREATEST HITS OF 1995	*Telstar*	8	*18 Nov 95*	9
THE GREATEST HITS OF 1996 - THE STORY OF THE YEAR	*Telstar*	4	*16 Nov 96*	9
THE GREATEST HITS OF 1997	*Telstar TV*	2	*15 Nov 97*	12
THE GREATEST HITS OF 1998	*Telstar TV*	3	*14 Nov 98*	12
THE GREATEST HITS OF THE NINETIES	*Telstar TV*	19	*6 Nov 99*	1
THE GREATEST HITS OF 1999 - THE STORY SO FAR	*Telstar TV*	8	*13 Nov 99*	3

Greatest Love

ALBUMS:	HITS 2			WEEKS 42
THE GREATEST LOVE	*Telstar*	11	*26 Dec 87*	40
THE GREATEST LOVE 2	*Telstar*	37	*31 Dec 88*	2

COMPILATION ALBUMS:	HITS 9			WEEKS 134
THE GREATEST LOVE	*Telstar*	7	*14 Jan 89*	31
THE GREATEST LOVE 2	*Telstar*	3	*14 Jan 89*	23
THE GREATEST LOVE 3	*Telstar*	4	*11 Nov 89*	18
THE GREATEST LOVE 4	*Telstar*	4	*27 Oct 90*	19
THE VERY BEST OF GREATEST LOVE	*Telstar*	5	*8 Dec 90*	17
IN LOVE - GREATEST LOVE 5	*Telstar*	5	*19 Oct 91*	11
THE GREATEST LOVE VI - WITH LOVE FROM THE STARS	*Telstar*	16	*20 Nov 93*	8
THE GREATEST LOVE EVER	*Telstar*	6	*7 Jan 95*	5
THE GREATEST LOVE	*Telstar TV*	14	*30 Jan 99*	2

Heartbeat

Heartbeat was a TV series by Yorkshire Television set in the 1960's.

COMPILATION ALBUMS:	HITS 7			WEEKS 87
HEARTBEAT (MUSIC FROM THE TV SERIES)	*Columbia*	1	*27 Jun 92*	14
THE BEST OF HEARTBEAT	*Columbia*	1	*28 Jan 95*	16
HEARTBEAT - FOREVER YOURS	*Columbia*	1	*30 Sep 95*	17
HEARTBEAT - NUMBER 1 LOVE SONGS OF THE '60S	*RCA/Global TV*	2	*19 Oct 96*	21
HEARTBEAT - LOVE ME TENDER	*RCA/Global TV*	6	*1 Nov 97*	5
HEARTBEAT - THE 60'S GOLD COLLECTION	*RCA/Global TV*	7	*28 Nov 98*	12
HEARTBEAT - THE OFFICIAL 10TH ANNIVERSARY	*BMG TV Projects*	17	*25 Nov 00*	2

Hits

ALBUMS:	HITS 9			WEEKS 177
THE HITS ALBUM/THE HITS TAPE - 32 ORIGINAL HITS	*CBS/WEA*	1	*1 Dec 84*	36
THE HITS ALBUM 2/THE HITS TAPE 2	*CBS/WEA*	1	*13 Apr 85*	21
HITS 3	*CBS/WEA*	2	*7 Dec 85*	21
HITS 4	*CBS/WEA/RCA/Ariola*	1	*29 Mar 86*	21
HITS 5	*CBS/RCA/Ariola/WEA*	1	*22 Nov 86*	25
HITS 6	*CBS/WEA/BMG*	1	*25 Jul 87*	19
HITS 7	*CBS/WEA/RCA/Arista*	2	*5 Dec 87*	17
HITS 8	*CBS/WEA/BMG*	2	*30 Jul 88*	13
THE HITS ALBUM	*CBS/WEA/BMG*	5	*17 Dec 88*	4

COMPILATION ALBUMS:	HITS 43			WEEKS 397
THE HITS ALBUM	*CBS/WEA/BMG*	4	*14 Jan 89*	7
THE HITS ALBUM 10	*CBS/WEA/BMG*	1	*3 Jun 89*	13
MONSTER HITS	*CBS/WEA/BMG*	2	*2 Dec 89*	14
SNAP! IT UP - MONSTER HITS 2	*CBS/WEA/BMG*	2	*11 Aug 90*	10
THE HIT PACK: THE BEST OF CHART MUSIC	*CBS/WEA/BMG*	2	*29 Dec 90*	8
From 12 Jan 91 tha labels changed to Sony/WEA/BMG.				
THE HITS ALBUM	*Sony/BMG*	1	*10 Aug 91*	9
This album is different to an earlier chart entry.				
HITS 93 VOLUME 1	*Telstar/BMG*	1	*20 Feb 93*	15
HITS 93 VOLUME 2	*Telstar*	2	*29 May 93*	8
HITS 93 VOLUME 3	*Telstar*	2	*14 Aug 93*	9
HITS 93 VOLUME 4	*Telstar*	2	*20 Nov 93*	9

HITS 94 VOLUME 1	*Telstar/BMG*	3	*19 Mar 94*	7
THE ULTIMATE HITS ALBUM	*Telstar/BMG*	11	*15 Oct 94*	2
HITS 96	*Global TV/Warner TV*	1	*23 Dec 95*	14
NEW HITS 96	*warner.esp/Global TV/Sony TV*	1	*18 May 96*	16
FRESH HITS 96	*warner.esp/Global TV/Sony TV*	2	*31 Aug 96*	10
HUGE HITS 1996	*warner.esp/Global TV/Sony TV*	1	*9 Nov 96*	12
HITS 97	*warner.esp/Global TV/Sony TV*	2	*21 Dec 96*	13
THE HITS ALBUM 1997	*Telstar*	4	*15 Mar 97*	3
NEW HITS 1997	*warner.esp/Global TV/Sony TV*	1	*26 Apr 97*	11
FRESH HITS 1997	*warner.esp/Global TV/Sony TV*	1	*16 Aug 97*	12
HUGE HITS 1997	*warner.esp/Global TV/Sony TV*	1	*1 Nov 97*	7
BIG HITS	*warner.esp/Global TV/Sony TV*	4	*20 Dec 97*	7
NEW HITS 98	*warner.esp/Global TV/Sony TV*	1	*4 Apr 98*	12
FRESH HITS 98	*warner.esp/Global TV/Sony TV*	1	*4 Jul 98*	17
BIG HITS 98	*warner.esp/Global TV/Sony TV*	1	*19 Sep 98*	9
HUGE HITS 1998	*warner.esp/Global TV/Sony TV*	1	*7 Nov 98*	11
HITS 99	*warner.esp/Global TV/Sony TV*	2	*19 Dec 98*	14
NEW HITS 99	*warner.esp/Global TV/Sony TV*	1	*3 Apr 99*	12
FRESH HITS 99	*warner.esp/Global Music TV/Sony Music TV*	1	*3 Jul 99*	9
BIG HITS 99	*warner.esp/Global TV/Sony TV*	1	*4 Sep 99*	11
HUGE HITS 99	*warner.esp/Global TV/Sony TV*	1	*6 Nov 99*	13
MASSIVE DANCE HITS 2000	*warner.esp/Global TV/Universal Music TV*	11	*11 Dec 99*	4
HITS 2000	*warner.esp/Global TV/Sony TV*	2	*18 Dec 99*	12
DANCE HITS 2000	*warner.esp/Global TV/Sony TV*	4	*4 Mar 00*	5
NEW HITS 2000	*warner.esp/Global TV/Sony TV*	1	*25 Mar 00*	8
FRESH HITS - VOLUME 1	*warner.esp/Global TV/Sony TV*	1	*15 Jul 00*	7
FRESH HITS - VOLUME 2	*warner.esp/Global TV/Sony TV*	2	*16 Sep 00*	7
HUGE HITS 2000	*WSM/Global TV/Sony Music TV*	2	*4 Nov 00*	5
HITS 2001	*WSM/Sony Music TV/Telstar TV/BMG*	2	*16 Dec 00*	9
MUSIC - THE DEFINITIVE HITS COLLECTION - VOLUME 1	*BMG/Telstar TV/Sony Music TV/WSM*	4	*31 Mar 01*	5
MUSIC! - TODAY'S DEFINITIVE HITS COLLECTION - VOLUME 2	*BMG/Telstar TV/Sony Music/WSM*	7	*23 Jun 01*	3
HITS 50: 50 TRACKS - 50 HITS	*BMG/Telstar TV/Sony Music/WSM*	1	*29 Sep 01*	6
CHRISTMAS HITS - 50 FESTIVE FAVOURITES	*BMG/Telstar TV/Sony Music/WSM*	11	*15 Dec 01*	3
HITS 51: 50 TRACKS - 50 HITS!	*BMG/Telstar TV/Sony Music/WSM*	13	*15 Dec 01*	3

I Love

Based around the BBC's 'I Love' TV series.

COMPILATION ALBUMS:	HITS 5			WEEKS 22
I LOVE 80S	*BBC/Virgin/EMI*	3	*17 Feb 01*	10
I LOVE 70S	*BBC/Virgin/EMI*	9	*2 Jun 01*	3
I LOVE IBIZA	*BBC/Virgin/EMI*	10	*9 Jun 01*	3
I LOVE 90S	*BBC/Virgin/EMI*	11	*6 Oct 01*	3
I LOVE 2 PARTY	*BBC/Virgin/EMI*	2	*15 Dec 01*	3

In The Mix

COMPILATION ALBUMS:	HITS 12			WEEKS 84
IN THE MIX 96	*Virgin*	1	*24 Feb 96*	12
IN THE MIX 96 - 2	*Virgin*	2	*25 May 96*	14
IN THE MIX - 90'S HITS	*Virgin*	3	*27 Jul 96*	6
IN THE MIX 96 - 3	*Virgin*	1	*12 Oct 96*	6
IN THE MIX 97	*Virgin*	1	*8 Feb 97*	11
IN THE MIX 97 - 2	*Virgin/EMI*	2	*26 Apr 97*	7
IN THE MIX 97 - 3	*Virgin/EMI*	2	*2 Aug 97*	6
IN THE MIX 98	*Virgin/EMI*	1	*14 Feb 98*	7
IN THE MIX 98	*Virgin/EMI*	6	*4 Jul 98*	4
IN THE MIX IBIZA	*Virgin/EMI*	1	*24 Oct 98*	4
IN THE MIX 2000	*Virgin/EMI*	3	*13 Mar 99*	4
IN THE MIX 2000 - THE ULTIMATE CLUB EXPERIENCE	*Virgin/EMI*	11	*18 Mar 00*	3

Kiss

Kiss FM is a London based radio station.

COMPILATION ALBUMS:	HITS 33			WEEKS 190
THE SOUND OF KISS 100FM	*PolyGram TV*	1	*22 Jan 94*	4
KISS IN IBIZA '95	*PolyGram TV*	3	*14 Oct 95*	5
KISSMIX '96	*PolyGram TV*	5	*13 Jul 96*	3
KISS IN IBIZA '96	*PolyGram TV*	1	*19 Oct 96*	8
KISS ANTHEMS	*PolyGram TV*	2	*19 Apr 97*	7
KISS 100FM - SMOOTH GROOVES	*PolyGram TV*	3	*5 Jul 97*	8
KISS MIX '97	*PolyGram TV*	3	*9 Aug 97*	6
KISS IN IBIZA '97	*PolyGram TV*	1	*27 Sep 97*	7
KISS ANTHEMS '97	*PolyGram TV*	6	*29 Nov 97*	7
KISS SMOOTH GROOVES '98	*PolyGram TV*	2	*28 Feb 98*	7
KISS GARAGE	*PolyGram TV*	3	*9 May 98*	7
KISS MIX '98	*PolyGram TV*	4	*25 Jul 98*	4
KISS IN IBIZA '98	*PolyGram TV*	2	*19 Sep 98*	7
KISS ANTHEMS '98	*PolyGram TV*	8	*28 Nov 98*	9
KISS SMOOTH GROOVES '99	*PolyGram TV*	3	*6 Feb 99*	6
KISS HOUSE NATION	*PolyGram TV*	1	*27 Feb 99*	9

Above 2: Label changed to Universal Music TV from 13 Mar 99.

KISS CLUBLIFE	*Universal Music TV*	2	*8 May 99*	7
KISS SMOOTH GROOVES - SUMMER '99	*Universal Music TV*	7	*26 Jun 99*	4
KISS IBIZA '99	*Universal Music TV*	1	*18 Sep 99*	8
KISS CLUBLIFE 2000	*Universal Music TV*	6	*27 Nov 99*	11
KISS UK GARAGE - MIXED BY KARL BROWN	*Universal Music TV*	3	*1 Apr 00*	4
KISS HOUSE NATION 2000	*Universal Music TV*	2	*6 May 00*	7
KISS SMOOTH GROOVES 2000	*Universal Music TV*	3	*3 Jun 00*	5
KISS CLUBLIFE SUMMER 2000	*Universal Music TV*	1	*22 Jul 00*	7
KISS IBIZA 2000	*Universal Music TV*	1	*23 Sep 00*	7
KISS GARAGE PRESENTED BY . . . DJ LUCK & MC. NEAT	*Universal Music TV*	3	*4 Nov 00*	4
KISS HOUSE NATION 2001 - MIXED BY ALEX & BRANDON BLOCK	*Universal Music TV*	8	*18 Nov 00*	2
KISS SMOOTH GROOVES 2001	*Universal Music TV*	2	*17 Mar 01*	6
KISS CLUBLIFE 2001	*Universal Music TV*	12	*21 Apr 01*	2
KISS SMOOTH GROOVES SUMMER 2001	*Universal Music TV*	7	*11 Aug 01*	4
KISS IBIZA 2001	*Universal Music TV*	6	*29 Sep 01*	4
URBAN KISS *Mixed by DJ Pied Piper (CD1) and Matt White (CD2).*	*Universal Music TV*	5	*27 Oct 01*	3
KISS HITLIST 2002	*EMI/Virgin/Universal Music TV*	19	*29 Dec 01*	1

Love Album

COMPILATION ALBUMS:	HITS 6			WEEKS 83
THE LOVE ALBUM	*Virgin*	1	*19 Nov 94*	23
THE LOVE ALBUM II	*Virgin*	2	*18 Nov 95*	16
THE LOVE ALBUM III	*Virgin*	2	*16 Nov 96*	13
THE LOVE ALBUM IV	*Virgin/EMI*	11	*15 Nov 97*	9
THE VERY BEST OF THE LOVE ALBUM	*Virgin/EMI*	3	*14 Nov 98*	18
THE '80S LOVE ALBUM	*Virgin/EMI*	6	*13 Mar 99*	4

Love Groove Dance Party

COMPILATION ALBUMS:	HITS 4			WEEKS 9
DANNY RAMPLING - LOVE GROOVE DANCE PARTY	*Universal Music TV*	15	*23 Jun 01*	2

Magic

COMPILATION ALBUMS:	HITS 4			WEEKS 15
THE SOUND OF MAGIC *This album is different from previous release.*	*Universal Music TV*	9	*10 Jun 00*	2
MAGIC	*Universal Music TV*	7	*24 Mar 01*	3

Massive Dance

COMPILATION ALBUMS:	HITS 7			WEEKS 46
MASSIVE DANCE MIX 96	*Telstar*	9	*8 Jun 96*	4
MASSIVE DANCE: 98	*warner.esp/PolyGram TV/Global TV*	8	*13 Dec 97*	9
MASSIVE DANCE: 98 - VOLUME 2	*PolyGram TV/warner.esp/Global TV*	2	*13 Jun 98*	6
MASSIVE DANCE: 99	*warner.esp/PolyGram TV/Global TV*	5	*12 Dec 98*	9
MASSIVE DANCE 99 - VOLUME 2	*warner.esp/Universal Music TV/Global TV*	3	*3 Apr 99*	5
MASSIVE DANCE HITS 2000	*warner.esp/Global TV/Universal Music TV*	9	*11 Dec 99*	10
MASSIVE DANCE 2001	*Universal Music TV/BMG/warner.esp/ Ministry Of Sound*	18	*9 Dec 00*	3

MOBO

The MOBOs are the Music Of Black Origin awards.

COMPILATION ALBUMS:	HITS 4			WEEKS 12
MOBO 2000	*Universal Music TV*	3	*14 Oct 00*	5
MOBO 2001 - THE ALBUM	*Sony Music TV/Columbia/BMG/Telstar TV*	13	*13 Oct 01*	3

MTV

COMPILATION ALBUMS:	HITS 6			WEEKS 14
MTV IBIZA 2000 - THE PARTY	*White Island*	13	*14 Oct 00*	3
MTV SELECT	*Universal Music TV*	6	*7 Apr 01*	3
MTV DANCE	*Manifesto/Universal Music TV*	18	*7 Jul 01*	1
MTV IBIZA 2001	*WSM*	18	*18 Aug 01*	2
MTV HITS	*Universal Music TV*	15	*8 Sep 01*	2

Motown Chartbusters

ALBUMS:	HITS 9			WEEKS 316
BRITISH MOTOWN CHARTBUSTERS	*Tamla Motown*	2	*21 Oct 67*	54
BRITISH MOTOWN CHARTBUSTERS VOLUME 2	*Tamla Motown*	8	*30 Nov 68*	11
MOTOWN CHARTBUSTERS VOLUME 3	*Tamla Motown*	1	*25 Oct 69*	93
MOTOWN CHARTBUSTERS VOLUME 4	*Tamla Motown*	1	*24 Oct 70*	40
MOTOWN CHARTBUSTERS VOLUME 5	*Tamla Motown*	1	*17 Apr 71*	36
MOTOWN CHARTBUSTERS VOLUME 6	*Tamla Motown*	2	*23 Oct 71*	36
MOTOWN CHARTBUSTERS VOLUME 7	*Tamla Motown*	9	*25 Nov 72*	16
MOTOWN CHARTBUSTERS VOLUME 8	*Tamla Motown*	9	*3 Nov 73*	15
MOTOWN CHARTBUSTERS VOLUME 9	*Tamla Motown*	14	*26 Oct 74*	15

New Woman

COMPILATION ALBUMS:	HITS 5			WEEKS 27
NEW WOMAN 2000	*Virgin/EMI*	1	*1 Apr 00*	7
NEW WOMAN SUMMER 2000	*Virgin/EMI*	5	*19 Aug 00*	6

NEW WOMAN 2001	*Virgin/EMI*	1	*24 Mar 01*	8
NEW WOMAN - LOVE SONGS	*Virgin/EMI*	14	*24 Nov 01*	2

Now!

The longest running Compilation series.

ALBUMS:	HITS 19			WEEKS 425
NOW, THAT'S WHAT I CALL MUSIC	*EMI/Virgin*	1	*10 Dec 83*	50
NOW THAT'S WHAT I CALL MUSIC II	*Virgin/EMI*	1	*7 Apr 84*	38
NOW, THAT'S WHAT I CALL MUSIC III	*Virgin/EMI*	1	*11 Aug 84*	30
NOW, THAT'S WHAT I CALL MUSIC 4 - 32 CHART HITS	*Virgin/EMI*	2	*8 Dec 84*	43
NOW DANCE - THE 12" MIXES	*EMI/Virgin*	3	*1 Jun 85*	14
NOW, THAT'S WHAT I CALL MUSIC 5	*Virgin/EMI*	1	*17 Aug 85*	21
NOW - THE CHRISTMAS ALBUM	*Virgin/EMI*	1	*30 Nov 85*	22
NOW, THAT'S WHAT I CALL MUSIC 6	*Virgin/EMI*	1	*7 Dec 85*	40
NOW - THE SUMMER ALBUM - 30 SUMMER HITS	*EMI/Virgin*	7	*19 Jul 86*	9
NOW, THAT'S WHAT I CALL MUSIC 7	*Virgin/EMI*	1	*23 Aug 86*	21
NOW DANCE '86	*EMI/Virgin*	2	*8 Nov 86*	13
NOW, THAT'S WHAT I CALL MUSIC '86	*Virgin/EMI*	65	*29 Nov 86*	4
The first CD only compilation album to chart.				
NOW, THAT'S WHAT I CALL MUSIC 8	*EMI/Virgin/PolyGram*	1	*6 Dec 86*	23
NOW, THAT'S WHAT I CALL MUSIC 9	*Virgin/EMI/PolyGram*	1	*4 Apr 87*	26
NOW! SMASH HITS	*EMI/Virgin/PolyGram*	5	*3 Oct 87*	10
Issued in conjunction with the teen magazine 'Smash Hits'.				
NOW THAT'S WHAT I CALL MUSIC 10	*EMI/Virgin/PolyGram*	1	*5 Dec 87*	21
NOW THAT'S WHAT I CALL MUSIC 11	*EMI/Virgin/PolyGram*	1	*2 Apr 88*	17
NOW THAT'S WHAT I CALL MUSIC 12	*EMI/Virgin/PolyGram*	1	*23 Jul 88*	17
NOW THAT'S WHAT I CALL MUSIC 13	*EMI/Virgin/PolyGram*	1	*3 Dec 88*	6

COMPILATION ALBUMS:	HITS 70			WEEKS 791
NOW THAT'S WHAT I CALL MUSIC 13	*EMI/Virgin/PolyGram*	1	*14 Jan 89*	15
NOW THAT'S WHAT I CALL MUSIC 14	*EMI/Virgin/PolyGram*	1	*1 Apr 89*	18
NOW DANCE '89 - THE 12" MIXES	*EMI/Virgin*	1	*15 Jul 89*	14
NOW THAT'S WHAT I CALL MUSIC 15	*EMI/Virgin/PolyGram*	1	*26 Aug 89*	13
NOW THAT'S WHAT I CALL MUSIC 16	*EMI/Virgin/PolyGram*	1	*2 Dec 89*	15
NOW DANCE 901 - 20 SMASH DANCE HITS - THE 12" MIXES	*EMI/Virgin/PolyGram*	1	*10 Mar 90*	14
NOW THAT'S WHAT I CALL MUSIC 17	*EMI/Virgin/PolyGram*	1	*5 May 90*	15
NOW DANCE 902	*EMI/Virgin/PolyGram*	1	*28 Jul 90*	13
NOW DANCE 903 - THE 12" MIXES	*EMI/Virgin/PolyGram*	1	*10 Nov 90*	9
NOW! THAT'S WHAT I CALL MUSIC 18	*EMI/Virgin/PolyGram*	1	*1 Dec 90*	18
NOW! THAT'S WHAT I CALL MUSIC 19	*EMI/Virgin/PolyGram*	1	*6 Apr 91*	16
NOW DANCE 91	*EMI/Virgin/PolyGram*	1	*5 Oct 91*	9
NOW THAT'S WHAT I CALL MUSIC! 20	*EMI/Virgin/PolyGram*	1	*30 Nov 91*	18
NOW THAT'S WHAT I CALL MUSIC! 21	*EMI/Viurgin/PolyGram*	1	*25 Apr 92*	13
NOW THAT'S WHAT I CALL MUSIC! 22	*EMI/Virgin/PolyGram*	1	*8 Aug 92*	14
NOW DANCE 92	*EMI/Virgin/PolyGram*	3	*14 Nov 92*	11
NOW THAT'S WHAT I CALL MUSIC! 23	*EMI/Virgin/PolyGram*	1	*28 Nov 92*	18
NOW THAT'S WHAT I CALL MUSIC! 24	*EMI/Virgin/PolyGram*	1	*8 May 93*	13
NOW DANCE 93	*EMI/Virgin/PolyGram*	1	*26 Jun 93*	9
NOW THAT'S WHAT I CALL MUSIC! 25	*EMI/Virgin/PolyGram*	1	*14 Aug 93*	10
NOW THAT'S WHAT I CALL MUSIC! 1983	*EMI/Virgin/PolyGram*	10	*4 Sep 93*	5
NOW THAT'S WHAT I CALL MUSIC! 1984	*EMI/Virgin/PolyGram*	13	*4 Sep 93*	4
NOW THAT'S WHAT I CALL MUSIC! 1985	*EMI/Virgin/PolyGram*	15	*4 Sep 93*	4
NOW THAT'S WHAT I CALL MUSIC! 1986	*EMI/Virgin/PolyGram*	16	*4 Sep 93*	2
NOW THAT'S WHAT I CALL MUSIC! 1987	*EMI/Virgin/PolyGram*	17	*4 Sep 93*	2
NOW THAT'S WHAT I CALL MUSIC! 1992	*EMI/Virgin/PolyGram*	14	*25 Sep 93*	2
NOW THAT'S WHAT I CALL MUSIC! 1988	*EMI/Virgin/PolyGram*	20	*25 Sep 93*	1
NOW THAT'S WHAT I CALL MUSIC! 1993	*EMI/Virgin/PolyGram*	1	*9 Oct 93*	8
NOW DANCE - THE BEST OF '93	*EMI/Virgin/PolyGram*	1	*30 Oct 93*	6
NOW THAT'S WHAT I CALL MUSIC! 26	*EMI/Virgin/PolyGram*	1	*27 Nov 93*	15
NOW DANCE 94 VOLUME 1	*EMI/Virgin/PolyGram*	1	*29 Jan 94*	7
NOW! THAT'S WHAT I CALL LOVE	*EMI/Virgin/PolyGram*	6	*19 Mar 94*	6
NOW! DANCE 94 VOLUME 2	*EMI/Virgin/PolyGram*	8	*19 Mar 94*	5
NOW THAT'S WHAT I CALL MUSIC! 27	*EMI/Virgin/PolyGram*	1	*9 Apr 94*	15
NOW DANCE - SUMMER 94	*EMI/Virgin*	1	*2 Jul 94*	8
NOW THAT'S WHAT I CALL MUSIC! 28	*EMI/Virgin/PolyGram*	1	*13 Aug 94*	13
NOW THAT'S WHAT I CALL MUSIC! 1994	*EMI/Virgin/PolyGram*	1	*15 Oct 94*	8
NOW THAT'S WHAT I CALL MUSIC! 29	*EMI/Virgin/PolyGram*	1	*26 Nov 94*	13
NOW DANCE - THE BEST OF '94	*EMI/Virgin*	4	*10 Dec 94*	9
NOW DANCE 95	*EMI/Virgin*	3	*1 Apr 95*	6
NOW THAT'S WHAT I CALL MUSIC! 30	*EMI/Virgin/PolyGram*	1	*22 Apr 95*	12
NOW DANCE SUMMER 95	*EMI/Virgin/PolyGram*	3	*29 Jul 95*	5
NOW THAT'S WHAT I CALL MUSIC! 31	*EMI/Virgin/PolyGram*	1	*12 Aug 95*	12
NOW THAT'S WHAT I CALL MUSIC! 1995	*EMI/Virgin/PolyGram*	2	*14 Oct 95*	6
NOW THAT'S WHAT I CALL MUSIC! 32	*EMI/Virgin/PolyGram*	1	*25 Nov 95*	15
NOW THAT'S WHAT I CALL MUSIC! 33	*EMI/Virgin/PolyGram*	1	*30 Mar 96*	13
NOW THAT'S WHAT I CALL MUSIC! 34	*EMI/Virgin/PolyGram*	1	*24 Aug 96*	15
NOW THAT'S WHAT I CALL MUSIC! 35	*EMI/Virgin/PolyGram*	1	*30 Nov 96*	18
NOW THAT'S WHAT I CALL MUSIC! 36	*EMI/Virgin/PolyGram*	1	*5 Apr 97*	16
NOW THAT'S WHAT I CALL MUSIC! 37	*EMI/Virgin/PolyGram*	1	*26 Jul 97*	16

NOW DANCE 97	*Virgin/EMI*	1	*1 Nov 97*	6
NOW THAT'S WHAT I CALL MUSIC! 38	*EMI/Virgin/PolyGram*	1	*29 Nov 97*	17
NOW THAT'S WHAT I CALL MUSIC! 39	*EMI/Virgin/PolyGram*	1	*18 Apr 98*	17
NOW DANCE 98	*Virgin/EMI*	3	*7 Nov 98*	5
NOW THAT'S WHAT I CALL MUSIC! 40	*EMI/Virgin/PolyGram*	1	*15 Aug 98*	14
NOW THAT'S WHAT I CALL MUSIC! 41	*EMI/Virgin/PolyGram*	1	*5 Dec 98*	18
NOW THAT'S WHAT I CALL MUSIC! 42	*EMI/Virgin/Universal Music TV*	1	*10 Apr 99*	16
NOW THAT'S WHAT I CALL MUSIC! 43	*EMI/Virgin/Universal Music TV*	1	*31 Jul 99*	15
NOW DANCE 2000	*Virgin/EMI*	1	*30 Oct 99*	8
NOW THAT'S WHAT I CALL MUSIC! 44	*EMI/Virgin/Universal Music TV*	1	*4 Dec 99*	18
NOW THAT'S WHAT I CALL MUSIC! 45	*Virgin/EMI/Universal*	1	*29 Apr 00*	15
NOW THAT'S WHAT I CALL MUSIC! 46	*Virgin/EMI/Universal*	1	*5 Aug 00*	16
NOW DANCE 2001	*Virgin/EMI*	1	*4 Nov 00*	13
NOW THAT'S WHAT I CALL MUSIC! 47	*Virgin/EMI/Universal*	1	*2 Dec 00*	18
NOW! THE CHRISTMAS ALBUM	*Virgin/EMI/Universal*	2	*9 Dec 00*	8
NOW DANCE 2001 PART 2	*Virgin/EMI*	2	*31 Mar 01*	6
NOW THAT'S WHAT I CALL MUSIC! 48	*Virgin/EMI/Universal*	1	*21 Apr 01*	15
NOW THAT'S WHAT I CALL MUSIC! 49	*Virgin/EMI/Universal*	1	*11 Aug 01*	14
NOW DANCE 2002	*Virgin/EMI*	1	*3 Nov 01*	5
NOW THAT'S WHAT I CALL MUSIC! 50	*Virgin/EMI/Universal*	1	*1 Dec 01*	5

Nukleuz Presentz

COMPILATION ALBUMS:	HITS 5			WEEKS 14
NUKLEUZ PRESENTS HARDHOUSE ANTHEMS	*Virgin/EMI*	14	*18 Mar 00*	3
NUKLEUZ PRESENTZ . . . HARDHOUSE ANTHEMS 2 – SUMMER EDITION *Mixed by Andy Farley and Ed Real.*	*Virgin/EMI*	16	*1 Jul 00*	2
NUKLEUZ PRESENTZ . . . HARDHOUSE ANTHEMS 3 – AUTUMN COLLECTION MIXED BY ED REAL *CD1 mixed by Ed Real; CD2 mixes by BK.*	*Virgin/EMI*	13	*7 Oct 00*	4
NUKLEUZ PRESENTZ . . . BIG ROOM DJ'S: MIXED BY MARIO PIU & NICK SENTIENCE	*Virgin/EMI*	6	*27 Jan 01*	3
NUKLEUZ PRESENTZ . . . HARDHOUSE ANTHEMS 2001: MIXED BY BK & ED REAL	*Virgin/EMI*	13	*3 Mar 01*	2

The Number One

COMPILATION ALBUMS:	HITS 22			WEEKS 102
THE NUMBER ONE CLASSIC SOUL ALBUM	*PolyGram TV*	5	*15 Jul 95*	7
THE NUMBER ONE REGGAE ALBUM	*PolyGram TV*	14	*22 Jul 95*	2
THE NUMBER ONE '70S ROCK ALBUM	*PolyGram TV*	3	*26 Aug 95*	5
THE NUMBER ONE MOVIES ALBUM	*PolyGram TV*	2	*4 Nov 95*	12
THE NUMBER ONE ALL TIME ROCK ALBUM	*PolyGram TV*	16	*11 Nov 95*	2
THE NUMBER ONE CHRISTMAS ALBUM	*PolyGram TV*	4	*9 Dec 95*	9
THE NUMBER ONE LOVE ALBUM	*PolyGram TV*	1	*17 Feb 96*	6
THE NUMBER ONE EIGHTIES ALBUM	*PolyGram TV*	10	*27 Jul 96*	4
THE NUMBER ONE SUMMER ALBUM	*PolyGram TV*	12	*27 Jul 96*	3
THE NUMBER ONE COUNTRY ALBUM	*PolyGram TV*	16	*17 Aug 96*	2
THE NUMBER ONE ACOUSTIC ROCK ALBUM	*PolyGram TV*	6	*12 Oct 96*	4
THE NUMBER ONE RAP ALBUM	*PolyGram TV*	12	*2 Nov 96*	1
THE NUMBER ONE ROCK BALLADS ALBUM	*PolyGram TV*	18	*16 Nov 96*	2
THE NUMBER ONE MOTOWN ALBUM	*PolyGram TV*	2	*18 Jan 97*	10
THE NUMBER ONE SCIFI ALBUM	*PolyGram TV*	13	*29 Mar 97*	4
THE NUMBER ONE SKA ALBUM	*PolyGram TV*	9	*5 Apr 97*	5
THE NUMBER ONE DRIVE ALBUM	*PolyGram TV*	14	*6 Sep 97*	2
THE NUMBER ONE JAZZ ALBUM	*PolyGram TV*	13	*20 Sep 97*	3
THE NUMBER ONE LINE DANCING ALBUM	*PolyGram TV*	10	*4 Oct 97*	4
THE NUMBER ONE ROCK 'N' ROLL ALBUM	*PolyGram TV*	20	*11 Oct 97*	1
THE NUMBER ONE SEVENTIES ALBUM	*PolyGram TV*	13	*1 Nov 97*	2
THE NUMBER ONE CHRISTMAS ALBUM [RE] *Re-released with a new catalogue number.*	*PolyGram TV*	7	*13 Dec 97*	4
THE NUMBER ONE DANCE PARTY ALBUM	*Universal Music TV*	17	*20 Nov 99*	2
THE NO. 1 MOTOWN ALBUM [RI]	*Universal Music TV*	15	*30 Dec 00*	6

100%

COMPILATION ALBUMS:	HITS 29			WEEKS 195
100% DANCE	*Telstar*	1	*26 Jun 93*	15
100% DANCE VOLUME 2	*Telstar*	1	*2 Oct 93*	9
100% REGGAE	*Telstar*	2	*11 Dec 93*	17
100% DANCE VOLUME 3	*Telstar*	7	*11 Dec 93*	9
100% RAP	*Telstar*	3	*12 Mar 94*	10
100% DANCE VOLUME 4	*Telstar*	2	*23 Apr 94*	7
100% REGGAE VOLUME 2	*Telstar*	4	*30 Apr 94*	14
100% SUMMER	*Telstar*	4	*23 Jul 94*	7
100% REGGAE VOLUME 3	*Telstar*	6	*6 Aug 94*	7
100% HITS	*Telstar*	2	*24 Sep 94*	8
100% ACID JAZZ	*Telstar*	5	*8 Oct 94*	14
100% PURE LOVE	*Telstar*	7	*5 Nov 94*	7
100% CHRISTMAS	*Telstar*	9	*10 Dec 94*	6
THE BEST OF 100% DANCE	*Telstar*	11	*7 Jan 95*	3
100% CLASSICS	*Telstar*	8	*14 Jan 95*	6

100% HOUSE CLASSICS - VOLUME 1	*Telstar*	16	*18 Feb 95*	4
100% ACID JAZZ - VOLUME 2	*Telstar*	14	*17 Jun 95*	4
100% SUMMER '95	*Telstar*	7	*8 Jul 95*	2
100% SUMMER JAZZ	*Telstar*	11	*5 Aug 95*	4
100% CARNIVAL!	*Telstar*	16	*2 Sep 95*	2
100% CLASSICS - VOLUME 2	*Telstar*	20	*20 Jan 96*	1
100% PURE GROOVE	*Telstar*	4	*23 Mar 96*	8
100% PURE GROOVE 2	*Telstar*	12	*8 Jun 96*	3
100% SUMMER MIX 96	*Telstar*	7	*6 Jul 96*	9
100% DANCE HITS 96	*Telstar*	11	*21 Sep 96*	3
100% DRUM & BASS	*Telstar*	11	*5 Oct 96*	4
100% SUMMER MIX 97	*Telstar TV*	8	*26 Jul 97*	6
BEST OF 100% PURE GROOVES	*Telstar TV*	13	*27 Jun 98*	2
100% SUMMER MIX 98	*Telstar TV*	13	*18 Jul 98*	4

Out Now!

ALBUMS:	HITS 2			WEEKS 28
OUT NOW! 28 HOT HITS	*Chrysalis/MCA*	2	*25 May 85*	16
OUT NOW!! 2 - 28 HOT HITS	*Chrysalis/MCA*	3	*26 Oct 85*	12

Pure Garage

COMPILATION ALBUMS:	HITS 5			WEEKS 45
PURE GARAGE (MIXED LIVE BY EZ)	*warner.esp*	2	*12 Feb 00*	15
PURE GARAGE II: (MIXED LIVE BY: EZ):	*warner.esp*	2	*15 Jul 00*	11
PURE GARAGE III: (MIXED LIVE BY EZ:)	*WSM*	2	*25 Nov 00*	11
PURE GARAGE IV :(MIXED LIVE BY: EZ):	*WSM*	3	*17 Mar 01*	6
LP vinyl format had its own chart entry at No. 41.				
PURE GARAGE V: (MXED LIVE BY: EZ):	*WSM*	7	*10 Nov 01*	2

Pure R&B

COMPILATION ALBUMS:	HITS 3			WEEKS 15
PURE R&B - THE FINEST CUTS FOR TODAY'S R&B GENERATION	*Telstar TV*	6	*2 Sep 00*	8
PURE R&B 2	*BMG Commercial/Telstar TV*	11	*25 Nov 00*	3
PURE R&B 3: REPRESENTING R&B AT ITS FINEST	*BMG/Telstar TV/Sony Music TV*	8	*9 Jun 01*	4

Pure Swing

COMPILATION ALBUMS:	HITS 6			WEEKS 39
PURE SWING	*Dino*	2	*11 Mar 95*	9
PURE SWING TWO	*Dino*	4	*10 Jun 95*	5
PURE SWING III	*Dino*	3	*2 Sep 95*	8
PURE SWING IV	*Dino*	1	*18 Nov 95*	9
PURE SWING 5	*Dino*	6	*6 Jan 96*	5
PURE SWING 96	*Dino*	9	*13 Apr 96*	3

Rare

ALBUMS:	HITS 2			WEEKS 2
RARE	*RCA*	80	*5 Sep 87*	1
RARE 2	*RCA*	88	*23 Apr 88*	1

COMPILATION ALBUMS:	HITS 1			WEEKS 2
RARE 3	*Ariola*	15	*11 Feb 89*	2

Reactivate

COMPILATION ALBUMS:	HITS 7			WEEKS 16
REACTIVATE VOLUME 1 - THE BELGIAN TECHNO ANTHEMS	*React*	13	*22 Jun 91*	4
REACTIVATE VOLUME 2 - PHASERS ON FULL	*React*	9	*5 Oct 91*	4
REACTIVATE VOLUME 4 - TECHNOVATION	*React*	16	*16 May 92*	2
REACTIVATE VOLUME 5 - PURE TRANCE AND TECHNO	*React*	18	*5 Sep 92*	2
REACTIVATE 10	*React*	14	*3 Jun 95*	1
REACTIVATE 11 - STINGER BEAT AND TECHNO RAYS	*React*	14	*26 Oct 96*	1
REACTIVATE 12	*React*	17	*21 Jun 97*	2

Sessions

COMPILATION ALBUMS:	HITS 10			WEEKS 33
SESSIONS TEN - SUBLIMINAL SESSIONS	*Subliminal/Defected*	18	*25 Mar 00*	1

Shine

COMPILATION ALBUMS:	HITS 11			WEEKS 56
SHINE: 20 BRILLIANT INDIE HITS	*PolyGram TV*	4	*13 May 95*	5
SHINE TOO	*PolyGram TV*	4	*2 Sep 95*	5
SHINE 3	*PolyGram TV*	13	*18 Nov 95*	6
SHINE FOUR	*PolyGram TV*	3	*9 Mar 96*	6
SHINE 5	*PolyGram TV*	2	*20 Jul 96*	9
SHINE 6	*PolyGram TV*	2	*5 Oct 96*	5
SHINE 7	*PolyGram TV*	13	*7 Dec 96*	7
SHINE 8	*PolyGram TV*	6	*3 May 97*	5
SHINE 9	*PolyGram TV*	7	*13 Sep 97*	4
SHINE - BEST OF 97	*PolyGram TV*	20	*17 Jan 98*	1
SHINE 10	*PolyGram TV*	10	*29 Aug 98*	3

Simply The Best

COMPILATION ALBUMS:	HITS 7			WEEKS 28
SIMPLY THE BEST LOVE SONGS	*warner.esp*	2	*15 Feb 97*	6
SIMPLY THE BEST - CLASSIC SOUL	*warner.esp*	7	*5 Apr 97*	6
SIMPLY THE BEST LOVE SONGS 2	*warner.esp*	2	*14 Feb 98*	6
SIMPLY THE BEST DISCO	*warner.esp*	9	*28 Mar 98*	3
SIMPLY THE BEST CLASSICAL ANTHEMS	*warner.esp*	14	*31 Oct 98*	2
SIMPLY THE BEST RADIO HITS	*warner.esp*	17	*14 Nov 98*	2
SIMPLY THE BEST REGGAE ALBUM	*WSM*	12	*4 Aug 01*	3

Sisters Of Swing

COMPILATION ALBUMS:	HITS 5			WEEKS 25
SISTERS OF SWING	*PolyGram TV*	1	*3 Feb 96*	10
SISTERS OF SWING 2	*PolyGram TV*	4	*1 Jun 96*	3
SISTERS OF SWING III	*PolyGram TV/Global TV*	7	*10 May 97*	4
SISTERS OF SWING 98	*PolyGram TV*	5	*11 Jul 98*	5
SISTERS OF SWING 99	*Universal Music TV*	9	*4 Sep 99*	3

Smash Hits

Smash Hits is a teen magazine. Since 1988 they have held a televised awards show.

ALBUMS:	HITS 1			WEEKS 11
SMASH HITS PARTY '88	*Dover*	6	*29 Oct 88*	11
COMPILATION ALBUMS:	**HITS 23**			**WEEKS 177**
SMASH HITS PARTY '88	*Dover*	12	*14 Jan 89*	5
SMASH HITS PARTY '89 - 30 SMASH HITS	*Dover*	1	*28 Oct 89*	14
SMASH HITS - RAVE!	*Dover*	1	*14 Jul 90*	10
SMASH HITS 1990	*Dover*	2	*3 Nov 90*	14
SMASH HITS - MASSIVE!	*Dover*	1	*25 May 91*	9
SMASH HITS 1991	*Dover*	3	*26 Oct 91*	16
SMASH HITS - PARTY ON!	*The Hit Label*	9	*22 Aug 92*	5
SMASH HITS '92 - 40 BIG HITS! SORTED!	*Chrysalis*	5	*12 Dec 92*	8
SMASH HITS '93 - 40 TOP CHARTIN' GROOVES	*Chrysalis*	4	*13 Nov 93*	10
SMASH HITS '94	*Telstar*	9	*3 Dec 94*	7
SMASH HITS '95 - VOLUME 1	*Telstar*	1	*18 Mar 95*	7
SMASH HITS '95 - VOLUME 2	*Telstar*	4	*24 Jun 95*	5
SMASH HITS MIX '97	*Virgin*	8	*14 Dec 96*	7
SMASH HITS - SUMMER '97	*Virgin/EMI*	1	*7 Jun 97*	8
SMASH HITS '98	*Virgin/EMI*	9	*13 Dec 97*	7
SMASH HITS - SUMMER '98	*Virgin/EMI*	2	*30 May 98*	6
SMASH HITS '99!	*Virgin/EMI*	10	*26 Dec 98*	4
SMASH HITS - SUMMER '99	*Virgin/EMI*	3	*5 Jun 99*	5
SMASH HITS 2000	*Virgin/EMI*	7	*25 Dec 99*	7
SMASH HITS SUMMER 2000	*Virgin/EMI*	3	*22 Jul 00*	7
SMASH HITS 2001	*Virgin/EMI*	5	*16 Dec 00*	7
SMASH! HITS SUMMER 2001 - NON STOP POP!	*Virgin/EMI/Universal Music TV*	2	*9 Jun 01*	7
SMASH HITS 2002 - NON-STOP POP!	*Virgin/EMI/Universal Music TV*	5	*22 Dec 01*	2

Street Vibes

COMPILATION ALBUMS:	HITS 8			WEEKS 46
STREET VIBES 4	*warner.esp/Global TV/Sony TV*	4	*18 Mar 00*	6
STREET VIBES 5	*Sony Music TV/Global TV*	2	*24 Jun 00*	8
STREET VIBES 6	*Sony Music TV/BMG TV*	6	*28 Oct 00*	4
STREET VIBES 7	*BMG/Telstar TV/Sony Music TV*	7	*28 Apr 01*	6
STREET VIBES 8	*BMG/Telstar TV/Sony Music TV*	4	*8 Sep 01*	6

That Loving Feeling

COMPILATION ALBUMS:	HITS 8			WEEKS 140
THAT LOVING FEELING	*Dino*	11	*2 Dec 89*	11
THAT LOVING FEELING VOLUME 2	*Dino*	5	*3 Mar 90*	26
THAT LOVING FEELING VOLUME 3	*Dino*	1	*6 Oct 90*	31
THAT LOVING FEELING VOLUME IV	*Dino*	3	*6 Apr 91*	14
THAT LOVING FEELING VOLUME V	*Dino*	2	*19 Oct 91*	15
THAT LOVING FEELING VOLUME VI	*Dino*	3	*4 Sep 93*	12
THE VERY BEST OF THAT LOVING FEELING	*Dino*	2	*4 Dec 93*	21
THAT LOVING FEELING VOLUME VII	*Dino*	4	*13 Aug 94*	10

Top Of The Pops

BBC TV's 'Top Of The Pops' is the longest running pop music programme. First transmitted 1 Jan 64.

ALBUMS:	HITS 1			WEEKS 5
BBC TV'S BEST OF TOP OF THE POPS	*Super Beeb*	21	*4 Jan 75*	5
COMPILATION ALBUMS:	**HITS 16**			**WEEKS 81**
TOP OF THE POPS 1	*Columbia*	1	*10 Jun 95*	6
TOP OF THE POPS 2	*Columbia*	14	*2 Dec 95*	7
TOP OF THE POPS - THE CUTTING EDGE	*Columbia*	10	*28 Sep 96*	3
TOP OF THE POPS 1998 - VOLUME 1	*PolyGram TV*	2	*16 May 98*	7
TOP OF THE POPS 1998 - VOLUME 2	*PolyGram TV/BBC Music*	3	*26 Sep 98*	6

TOP OF THE POPS - BEST OF 1998	*PolyGram TV*	11	*28 Nov 98*	2
TOP OF THE POPS '99 - VOLUME ONE	*BBC/Universal Music TV*	2	*22 May 99*	6
TOP OF THE POPS '99 - VOLUME TWO	*Universal Music TV*	1	*25 Sep 99*	8
TOP OF THE POPS 2000 VOLUME 1	*Universal Music TV*	3	*4 Mar 00*	6
TOP OF THE POPS 2	*Universal Music TV*	15	*29 Apr 00*	2
Based on the Nostalga TV music show broadcast on BBC2.				
TOP OF THE POPS 2000 - VOLUME TWO	*BBC Music/Universal Music TV*	1	*17 Jun 00*	11
TOP OF THE POPS 2000 VOLUME THREE	*BBC Music/Universal Music TV*	4	*11 Nov 00*	4
TOP OF THE POPS 2 - 70S ROCK	*BBC Music/Universal Music TV*	10	*3 Feb 01*	2
TOP OF THE POPS 2001 - VOLUME ONE	*BBC Music/Universal Music TV*	4	*3 Mar 01*	4
TOP OF THE POPS - SUMMER 2001	*BBC Music/Universal Music TV*	4	*14 Jul 01*	4
TOP OF THE POPS - AUTUMN 2001	*BBC Music/Universal Music TV*	8	*3 Nov 01*	3

Trance Nation

COMPILATION ALBUMS:	HITS 5			WEEKS 33
TRANCE NATION THREE - FERRY CORSTEN SYSTEM F	*Ministry Of Sound*	2	*13 May 00*	6
TRANCE NATION 4: FERRY CORSTEN; SYSTEM F	*Ministry Of Sound*	1	*7 Oct 00*	7
TRANCE NATION 5: FERRY CORSTEN SYSTEM F	*Ministry Of Sound*	4	*12 May 01*	5

Ultimate

COMPILATION ALBUMS:	HITS 8			WEEKS 43
THE ULTIMATE EIGHTIES	*PolyGram TV*	2	*25 Jun 94*	9
THE ULTIMATE 80'S BALLADS	*PolyGram TV*	5	*29 Oct 94*	3
AMOUR - THE ULTIMATE LOVE COLLECTION	*PolyGram TV*	3	*15 Feb 97*	5
ULTIMATE DISCO MIX	*PolyGram TV*	15	*4 Apr 98*	2
THE ULTIMATE SUMMER PARTY ALBUM	*PolyGram TV*	7	*27 Jun 98*	3
RELAX! THE ULTIMATE 80'S MIX	*PolyGram TV*	4	*8 Aug 98*	11
THE ULTIMATE CHRISTMAS COLLECTION	*PolyGram TV*	11	*12 Dec 98*	4
RELAX: - THE ULTIMATE 80'S MIX - VOLUME 2	*PolyGram TV*	8	*6 Feb 99*	3
THE ULTIMATE CHRISTMAS COLLECTION [RI]	*Universal Music TV*	15	*4 Dec 99*	3

Uncovered

COMPILATION ALBUMS:	HITS 6			WEEKS 39
IBIZA UNCOVERED II	*Virgin/EMI*	5	*23 Sep 00*	6
UNCOVERED	*Virgin/EMI*	10	*28 Jul 01*	2

Upfront

ALBUMS:	HITS 10			WEEKS 54
UPFRONT 1 - 14 DANCE TRACKS	*Serious*	17	*7 Jun 86*	10
UPFRONT 2 - 14 DANCE TRACKS	*Serious*	27	*23 Aug 86*	6
UPFRONT 3	*Serious*	37	*1 Nov 86*	5
UPFRONT 4	*Serious*	21	*31 Jan 87*	5
UPFRONT 5	*Serious*	21	*28 Mar 87*	6
UPFRONT 6	*Serious*	22	*23 May 87*	6
UPFRONT 7	*Serious*	31	*15 Aug 87*	4
UPFRONT 8	*Serious*	22	*17 Oct 87*	6
UPFRONT 9	*Serious*	92	*19 Dec 87*	1
UPFRONT 10	*Serious*	45	*9 Apr 88*	5

COMPILATION ALBUMS:	HITS 1			WEEKS 1
UPFRONT 89	*Serious*	15	*18 Feb 89*	1

Warehouse Raves

COMPILATION ALBUMS:	HITS 6			WEEKS 16
WAREHOUSE RAVES	*Rumour*	15	*16 Sep 89*	4
WAREHOUSE RAVES 3	*Rumour*	12	*31 Mar 90*	5
WAREHOUSE RAVES 4	*Rumour*	13	*29 Sep 90*	3
WAREHOUSE RAVES 5	*Rumour*	18	*11 May 91*	1
WAREHOUSE RAVES 6	*Rumour*	16	*21 Mar 92*	2
WAREHOUSE RAVES 7	*Rumour*	20	*29 Aug 92*	1

The World Of

ALBUMS:	HITS 5			WEEKS 26
THE WORLD OF BLUES POWER	*Decca*	24	*28 Jun 69*	6
THE WORLD OF BRASS BANDS	*Decca*	13	*5 Jul 69*	11
THE WORLD OF HITS VOLUME 2	*Decca*	7	*6 Sep 69*	5
THE WORLD OF PROGRESSIVE MUSIC (WOWIE ZOWIE)	*Decca*	17	*20 Sep 69*	2
THE WORLD OF PHASE 4 STEREO	*Decca*	29	*20 Sep 69*	2

STAGE CAST

Broadway

EPS:	HITS 4			WEEKS 37
MY FAIR LADY NO. 4	*Philips*	20	*10 Sep 60*	2
THE SOUND OF MUSIC	*Philips*	13	*14 Oct 61*	4
WEST SIDE STORY	*Philips*	5	*19 May 62*	26
WEST SIDE STORY	*CBS*	15	*26 Jan 63*	5
Above 2 entries are different casts to the show.				

ALBUMS:	HITS 10			WEEKS 239
MY FAIR LADY	*Philips*	2	*8 Nov 58*	129
Features Rex Harrison, Julie Andrews, Stanley Holloway, Robert Coote. Adapted from Bernard Shaw's 'Pygmalion'.				
WEST SIDE STORY	*Philips*	3	*24 Jan 59*	27
FLOWER DRUM SONG	*Philips*	2	*2 Apr 60*	27
MOST HAPPY FELLA	*Philips*	6	*21 May 60*	13
WEST SIDE STORY	*Philips*	14	*30 Jul 60*	1
This is a different cast recording than the original.				
THE SOUND OF MUSIC	*Philips*	4	*24 Jun 61*	19
MY FAIR LADY	*CBS*	19	*4 Jan 64*	1
This is a different cast recording than the original.				
CAMELOT	*CBS*	10	*3 Oct 64*	12
HAIR	*RCA*	29	*6 Sep 69*	3
MACK AND MABEL	*MCA*	38	*6 Nov 82*	7

London

EPS:	HITS 3			WEEKS 23
SALAD DAYS	*Oriole*	19	*21 May 60*	1
OLIVER	*Decca*	5	*18 Nov 61*	21
THE SOUND OF MUSIC	*HMV*	19	*21 Apr 62*	1

ALBUMS:	HITS 38			WEEKS 741
FINGS AIN'T WOT THEY USED TO BE	*Decca*	5	*26 Mar 60*	11
FOLLOW THAT GIRL	*His Master's Voice*	5	*7 May 60*	9
MAKE ME AN OFFER	*His Master's Voice*	18	*21 May 60*	1
FLOWER DRUM SONG	*His Master's Voice*	10	*28 May 60*	3
MOST HAPPY FELLA	*His Master's Voice*	19	*9 Jul 60*	1
OLIVER!	*Decca*	6	*10 Sep 60*	31
Features Ron Moody, Georgia Brown, Paul Whitsun-Jones.				
MUSIC MAN	*His Master's Voice*	8	*6 May 61*	13
OLIVER! [RE]	*Decca*	4	*13 May 61*	60
BEYOND THE FRINGE	*Parlophone*	13	*22 Jul 61*	17
BYE BYE BIRDIE	*Philips*	17	*22 Jul 61*	3
THE SOUND OF MUSIC	*His Master's Voice*	4	*29 Jul 61*	68
STOP THE WORLD – I WANT TO GET OFF	*Decca*	8	*9 Sep 61*	14
Features Anthony Newley.				
BLITZ	*His Master's Voice*	7	*14 Jul 62*	21
HALF A SIXPENCE	*Decca*	20	*18 May 63*	2
PICKWICK	*Philips*	12	*3 Aug 63*	10
CAMELOT	*His Master's Voice*	19	*16 Jun 63*	1
FIDDLER ON THE ROOF	*CBS*	4	*11 Mar 67*	50
Features Topol.				
HAIR	*Polydor*	3	*28 Dec 68*	94
Features Paul Nicholas, Vince Edward, Oliver Tobias, Michael Feast.				
THE WORLD OF OLIVER [RI]	*Decca*	23	*30 Aug 69*	4
Re-release of the 1960 cast recording.				
GODSPELL	*Arista*	25	*19 Feb 72*	17
EVITA	*MCA*	24	*18 Nov 78*	18
Features Julie Covington.				
CATS	*Polydor*	6	*1 Aug 81*	26
STARLIGHT EXPRESS	*Starlight*	21	*4 Aug 84*	9
LES MISERABLES	*First Night*	72	*15 Feb 86*	4
THE PHANTOM OF THE OPERA	*Really Useful*	1	*21 Feb 87*	141
Features Sarah Brightman, Michael Crawford.				
ASPECTS OF LOVE	*Really Useful/Polydor*	1	*16 Sep 89*	29
Features Michael Ball.				
MISS SAIGON	*Geffen*	4	*24 Feb 90*	11
FIVE GUYS NAMED MOE	*First Night*	59	*29 Jun 91*	1
JOSEPH AND THE AMAZING TECHNICOLOR DREAMCOAT	*Really Useful/Polydor*	1	*31 Aug 91*	38
Features Jason Donovan.				
THE NEW STARLIGHT EXPRESS	*Really Useful/Polydor*	42	*10 Apr 93*	2
SUNSET BOULEVARD	*Really Useful/Polydor*	11	*11 Sep 93*	4
GREASE	*Epic*	20	*2 Oct 93*	3
Features Debbie Gibson, Craig McLachlan.				
OLIVER! (1994 LONDON CAST)	*First Night*	36	*1 Apr 95*	3
LES MISERABLES – 10TH ANNIVERSARY CONCERT	*First Night*	32	*11 May 96*	7
Live recordings from the Royal Albert Hall, 8 Oct 95 with the Royal Philharmonic Orchestra.				
MARTIN GUERRE	*First Night*	58	*16 Nov 96*	1
HEATHCLIFF LIVE (THE SHOW)	*EMI*	41	*14 Dec 96*	4
Features Cliff Richard.				
CHICAGO – THE MUSICAL	*RCA Victor*	61	*27 Jun 98*	1
SATURDAY NIGHT FEVER	*Polydor*	17	*22 Aug 98*	6
MAMMA MIA!	*Polydor*	56	*13 Nov 99*	2
Features Siobhan McCarthy, Hilton McCrae, Lisa Stokke, Andrew Langtree, Jenny Galloway, Louise Plowright.				
MY FAIR LADY (2001 LONDON CAST RECORDING)	*First Night*	73	*4 Aug 01*	1
Features Jonathan Pryce, Martin McCutcheon, Dennis Waterman, Nicholas Le Prevost, Mark Umbers, Patsy Rowlands, Caroline Blakiston.				

South Africa

ALBUMS:	HITS 1			WEEKS 8
KING KONG	*Decca*	12	*11 Mar 61*	8

STUDIO CAST

ALBUMS:	HITS 14			WEEKS 170
SHOWBOAT	*His Master's Voice*	12	*25 Jun 60*	1
JESUS CHRIST SUPERSTAR	*MCA*	6	*8 Jan 72*	20
EVITA	*MCA*	4	*22 Jan 77*	35
WHITE MANSIONS	*A&M*	51	*17 Jun 78*	3
CHESS	*RCA*	10	*10 Nov 84*	16
WEST SIDE STORY *Features Leonard Bernstein, Kiri Te Kanawa, Jose Carreras, Tatiana Troyanos.*	*Deutsche Grammophon*	11	*18 May 85*	32
CHESS PIECES	*Telstar*	87	*2 Nov 85*	3
HIGHLIGHTS FROM WEST SIDE STORY	*Deutsche Grammophon*	72	*10 May 86*	6
DAVE CLARK'S TIME THE ALBUM	*EMI*	21	*17 May 86*	6
SOUTH PACIFIC *Features Kiri Te Kanawa, Jose Carreras, Sarah Vaughan.*	*CBS*	5	*11 Oct 86*	24
MATADOR *Features Tom Jones.*	*Epic*	26	*13 Jun 87*	5
MY FAIR LADY *Features Kiri Te Kanawa and Jeremy Irons.*	*Decca*	41	*21 Nov 87*	12
THE KING AND I *Features John Mauceri, Julie Andrews, Ben Kingsley, The Hollywood Bowl Orchestra.*	*Philips*	57	*10 Oct 92*	2
LEONARD BERNSTEIN'S WEST SIDE STORY *Features Michael Ball, Barbra Bonny, Barry Wordsworth, Royal Philharmonic Orchestra.*	*IMG*	33	*10 Apr 93*	5

TELEVISION

(See also Television Soundtracks or related compilations under the following artists: John Barry; Geoffrey Burgon; Clannad; Eric Clapton; Enya; Gladiators; Inti Illimani-Guamary; Aled Jones; Nana Mouskouri; Barrington Pheloung; Elvis Presley; Vonda Shepherd; Simpsons; Frank Sinatra; Scott Walker; Anthony Way.)

Related Compilations

ALBUMS:	HITS 20			WEEKS 121
JACK GOOD'S 'OH BOY!'	*Parlophone*	9	*13 Dec 58*	14
READY STEADY GO *Above 2 were music programmes on ITV.*	*Decca*	20	*8 Feb 64*	1
STARS FROM STARS AND GARTERS	*Pye Golden Guinea*	17	*28 Mar 64*	2
SUPERSONIC *Music programme on ITV.*	*Stallion*	21	*6 Dec 75*	6
FONZIE'S FAVOURITES *Fonzie is character in the American sitcom 'Happy Day's' set in the 1950's.*	*Warner Brothers*	8	*11 Mar 78*	16
STARS ON SUNDAY BY REQUEST *Religious programme on ITV.*	*Curzon Sounds*	65	*9 Dec 78*	3
THE TUBE *Music programme on Channel 4.*	*K-Tel*	30	*18 Feb 84*	6
THE TV HITS ALBUM	*Towerbell*	26	*28 Sep 85*	13
THE EASTENDERS SING-ALONG ALBUM *BBC1 TV soap, album features the Original BBC TV cast.*	*BBC*	33	*16 Nov 85*	10
TELLYHITS - 16 TOP TV THEMES	*Stylus/BBC*	34	*23 Nov 85*	6
JONATHAN KING'S ENTERTAINMENT FROM THE U.S.A. *BBC programme reflecting the news and music in the US.*	*Stylus*	6	*15 Feb 86*	11
THE T.V. HITS ALBUM TWO - 16 ORIGINAL HIT TV THEMES	*Towerbell*	19	*12 Apr 86*	7
TELLYHITS 2 - 16 TOP TV THEMES	*Stylus/BBC*	68	*5 Jul 86*	2
THE VERY BEST OF ENTERTAINMENT FROM THE USA VOLUME 2	*PrioriTyV*	44	*18 Oct 86*	4
THE ROCK 'N' ROLL YEARS 1964-1967 *BBC TV series that each edition reflects a particular years news and music.*	*BBC*	71	*27 Jun 87*	2
THE ROCK 'N' ROLL YEARS 1968-1971	*BBC*	77	*27 Jun 87*	1
THE ROCK 'N' ROLL YEARS 1956-1959	*BBC*	80	*27 Jun 87*	2
THE ROCK 'N' ROLL YEARS 1960-1963	*BBC*	84	*27 Jun 87*	1
THE CHART SHOW - DANCE HITS 1987 *Music video show, first transmitted on Channel 4 in 1986 before moving to ITV.*	*Chrysalis*	39	*28 Nov 87*	6
THE CHART SHOW ROCK THE NATION	*Dover*	16	*26 Mar 88*	8

COMPILATION ALBUMS:	HITS 44			WEEKS 206
THE CHART SHOW - ROCK THE NATION 2	*Dover*	8	*20 May 89*	4
THE CHART SHOW - DANCE MASTERS	*Dover*	4	*3 Jun 89*	7
TV TUNES	*K-Tel*	17	*23 Sep 89*	3
THE OLD GREY WHISTLE TEST - BEST OF THE TEST *BBC2 music programme from the 1970s.*	*Windsong International*	13	*21 Sep 91*	3
THE BEST OF THE CLASSICAL BITS *Classical music featured in TV commercials.*	*Philips*	7	*30 Jan 93*	10
THE CHART SHOW - THE ULTIMATE ROCK ALBUM	*The Hit Label*	4	*17 Apr 93*	11
CLASSIC COMMERCIALS	*Decca*	8	*12 Jun 93*	6
THE BIG BREAKFAST ALBUM *Breakfast show on Channel 4.*	*Arcade*	8	*7 Aug 93*	5
THE CHART SHOW: ULTIMATE ROCK 2	*The Hit Label*	10	*2 Oct 93*	3

TALES FROM THE CITY	*PolyGram TV*	17	*23 Oct 93*	2
RETURN OF THE GLADIATORS	*PolyGram TV*	20	*20 Nov 93*	1
TOP GEAR	*Epic*	3	*4 Jun 94*	13
BBC2 TV programme on cars.				
CHART SHOW - ULTIMATE BLUES ALBUM	*The Hit Label*	13	*16 Jul 94*	3
DR. HILARY JONES' CLASSIC RELAXATION	*PolyGram TV*	13	*22 Oct 94*	2
THE CHART SHOW PRESENTS THE CHART MACHINE	*PolyGram TV*	18	*20 May 95*	2
TOP GEAR 2	*Columbia*	4	*27 May 95*	6
TOP GEAR CLASSICS - TURBO CLASSICS	*Deutsche Grammophon*	17	*24 Jun 95*	1
THE CHART SHOW DANCE ALBUM	*PolyGram TV*	6	*5 Aug 95*	3
THE CORONATION STREET ALBUM	*EMI Premier*	20	*18 Nov 95*	1
Granada ITV region soap, album features the Original cast.				
TOP GEAR 3	*Columbia*	11	*9 Mar 96*	4
TOP GEAR - ON THE ROAD AGAIN	*EMI TV*	12	*9 Nov 96*	3
AFTER THE BREAK	*Columbia*	17	*2 Aug 97*	1
IBIZA UNCOVERED	*Virgin/EMI*	1	*13 Sep 97*	10
Based around the Sky TV holiday documentary.				
READY STEADY GO! - NUMBER ONE SIXTIES ALBUM	*PolyGram TV*	10	*8 Nov 97*	2
READY STEADY GO! - SIXTIES MOTOWN SOUND	*PolyGram TV*	5	*21 Mar 98*	5
IBIZA UNCOVERED 2	*Virgin/EMI*	2	*22 Aug 98*	9
TOP GEAR ANTHEMS	*Virgin/EMI*	6	*26 Sep 98*	6
STARSKY AND HUTCH PRESENTS	*Virgin/EMI*	13	*3 Oct 98*	2
TV cop series from the 1970's.				
LIVE & KICKING - VIEWERS CHOICE PART 1	*Virgin/EMI*	12	*3 Apr 99*	3
MTV IBIZA 99	*Columbia*	10	*28 Aug 99*	3
IBIZA UNCOVERED - THE RETURN	*Virgin/EMI*	2	*2 Oct 99*	7
ABBAMANIA	*Polydor/Universal Music TV*	2	*20 Nov 99*	14
MUSIC OF THE MILLENNIUM	*Universal/Virgin/EMI*	2	*27 Nov 99*	16
Based around the Channel 4 programme of the same name.				
SWITCHED ON - THE COOL SOUND OF TV ADVERTISING	*Telstar TV*	9	*8 Apr 00*	4
TV 2000	*Columbia*	16	*29 Apr 00*	2
ALAN TITCHMARSH - IN A COUNTRY GARDEN	*Sony Classical*	20	*20 May 00*	1
From BBC TV's Ground Force and Gardener's World. Works associated with the countryside and gardens.				
YOUNG GUNS GO FOR IT - HEROES OF THE 80'S	*Virgin/EMI*	10	*30 Sep 00*	4
Based on the BBC2 TV series focusing on music from the eighties.				
CD:UK - 40 WICKED HITS - YOU KNOW WHERE IT'S AT!	*Universal/BMG/Sony Music TV*	7	*14 Oct 00*	4
Music show hosted by Ant, Dec and Kat on ITV Saturday mornings.				
JAMIE OLIVER'S COOKIN' - MUSIC TO COOK BY	*Columbia*	14	*18 Nov 00*	1
Music inspired by his BBC TV series 'The Naked Chef'.				
MUSIC OF THE MILLENNIUM 2	*Universal/EMI/Virgin*	6	*2 Dec 00*	10
CONTENDERS FOR THE RECORD OF THE YEAR 2000	*BMG Commercial/Telstar*	13	*23 Dec 00*	3
MOTOWN MANIA	*Universal Music TV/BMG*	9	*30 Dec 00*	2
Based around the ITV tribute show to Motown artists				
THE GREATEST NO. 1 SINGLES	*Virgin/EMI/Universal Music TV*	2	*20 Jan 01*	12
Companion release of the Channel 4 programme of the same name.				
THE LICK - PRESENTED BY TREVOR NELSON	*Universal Music TV/Def Soul*	3	*3 Feb 01*	7
Companion to the MTV show.				
CD: UK - MORE WICKED HITS	*Universal/BMG/Sony Music TV*	9	*3 Feb 01*	3
TRIGGER HAPPY TV - SOUNDTRACK TO SERIES 2	*Channel 4 Music*	15	*26 May 01*	2
From the Channel 4 TV series.				
PURE FLAVA - MIXED BY STEVE 'SMOOTH' SUTHERLAND	*WSM/Universal Music TV*	10	*1 Sep 01*	4
Companion to the Channel 4 TV series.				
ALL TOGETHER NOW - CHILDREN'S FAVOURITE TV THEMES	*Universal Music TV*	11	*17 Nov 01*	5

Soundtracks

ALBUMS:	HITS 20			WEEKS 159
HUCKLEBERRY HOUND	*Pye Golden Guinea*	10	*4 Mar 61*	12
Animated character.				
THAT WAS THE WEEK THAT WAS	*Parlophone*	11	*2 Mar 63*	9
ROCK FOLLIES	*Island*	1	*10 Apr 76*	15
ITV musical drama series Julie Covington, Charlotte Cornwell and Rula Lenska.				
PENNIES FROM HEAVEN	*World Records*	10	*8 Apr 78*	17
ITV musical drama series.				
MORE PENNIES FROM HEAVEN	*World Records*	31	*1 Jul 78*	4
FAWLTY TOWERS	*BBC*	25	*15 Dec 79*	10
FAWLTY TOWERS VOLUME 2 (TV ORIGINAL CAST)	*BBC*	26	*7 Feb 81*	7
Above 2 are from the BBC sitcom starring John Cleese, Prunella Scales, Andrew Sachs and Connie Booth.				
THE HITCHHIKERS GUIDE TO THE GALAXY VOLUME 2	*Original*	47	*14 Feb 81*	4
BBC comedy series.				
THE MUSIC OF THE COSMOS	*RCA*	43	*1 Aug 81*	10
Carl Sagan's TV series broadcast on BBC1.				
REILLY ACE OF THEMES	*Red Bus*	54	*26 Nov 83*	6
ORIGINAL MUSIC FROM AUF WIEDERSEHEN PET	*Towerbell*	21	*4 Feb 84*	6
Above 2 are ITV drama series'.				
SONG AND DANCE	*RCA*	46	*8 Sep 84*	4
BBC series featuring Sarah Brightman and Wayne Sleep.				
MUSIC FROM THE TELEVISION SERIES 'MIAMI VICE'	*BBC*	11	*26 Oct 85*	8

MUSIC FROM THE TELEVISION SERIES 'MIAMI VICE' [RI]	*MCA*	94	*26 Jul 86*	1
MUSIC FROM THE BBC-TV SERIES 'THE SINGING DETECTIVE'	*BBC*	10	*6 Dec 86*	24
MOONLIGHTING "THE TV SOUNDTRACK ALBUM"	*MCA*	50	*3 Oct 87*	6
MIAMI VICE 2	*MCA*	71	*17 Oct 87*	4
MOONLIGHTING 2	*WEA*	5	*1 Oct 88*	9
MIAMI VICE III	*MCA*	95	*1 Oct 88*	1
DOCTOR WHO - THE EVIL OF THE DALEKS *Featuring Tom Baker.*	*BBC*	72	*18 Jul 92*	1
DOCTOR WHO - THE POWER OF THE DALEKS *Featuring Patrick Troughton.*	*BBC*	71	*14 Aug 93*	1

COMPILATION ALBUMS:	**HITS 17**			**WEEKS 98**
PENNIES FROM HEAVEN *This is a different album to the previous 1989 chart entry.*	*BBC*	8	*17 Feb 90*	13
HEAD OVER HEELS	*Telstar*	3	*13 Feb 93*	9
LIPSTICK ON YOUR COLLAR - 28 ORIGINAL HITS OF THE 50S *Above 2 are ITV musical drama series'.*	*PolyGram TV*	2	*13 Mar 93*	13
CHEF AID - THE SOUTH PARK ALBUM *South Park is an adult animated series broadcast by Channel 4.*	*Columbia*	2	*5 Dec 98*	14
QUEER AS FOLK - THE WHOLE THING. SORTED	*Almighty*	2	*17 Apr 99*	9
SONGS FROM DAWSON'S CREEK *Above 2 are Channel 4 drama series'.*	*Columbia*	3	*12 Jun 99*	11
SEX, CHIPS & ROCK N' ROLL *BBC drama series.*	*Virgin/EMI*	12	*23 Oct 99*	1
BUFFY THE VAMPIRE SLAYER - THE ALBUM *Songs from the series broadcast on Sky One and the BBC.*	*Columbia*	7	*20 Nov 99*	2
AGIA NAPA - FANTASY ISLAND - THE BEST UPFRONT & CLASSIC UK GARAGE *Soundtrack to the Channel 4 docusoap. Mixes by DJ Spoony from Dreem Team.*	*Telstar TV*	1	*12 Feb 00*	6
QUEER AS FOLK 2 - SAME MEN. NEW TRACKS	*Channel 4 Music*	5	*26 Feb 00*	5
THE GRIMLEYS - ORIGINAL TV SOUNDTRACK	*Global Television*	17	*11 Mar 00*	1
POKEMON - 2 B A MASTER	*Koch*	20	*22 Apr 00*	1
BIG BROTHER - THE ORIGINAL SOUNDTRACK	*Bazal/Channel 4 Music*	17	*26 Aug 00*	3
SONGS FROM DAWSON'S CREEK - VOLUME 2	*Columbia*	5	*28 Oct 00*	3
MORE COLD FEET *ITV drama series.*	*BMG TV Projects*	18	*30 Dec 00*	1
AYIA NAPA - RETURN TO FANTASY ISLAND *Mixed by Heartless Crew.*	*BMG/Telstar TV*	18	*31 Mar 01*	2
COLD FEET	*Universal Music TV*	13	*8 Dec 01*	4

TELEVISION AND RADIO COMBINED

ALBUMS:	**HITS 2**			**WEEKS 10**
THE BBC 1922-1972 (TV AND RADIO EXTRACTS)	*BBC*	16	*4 Nov 72*	7
ON THE AIR - 60 YEARS OF BBC THEME MUSIC	*BBC*	85	*23 Oct 82*	3

TITLE INDEX OF CHART ENTRIES

The index has been divided into three sections: singles, EPs and albums. Within each section the title is given first, followed by the artist credit as appears on the release, then year of chart entry and highest position attained.

Where a single has charted again as a re-issue or re-mix, a separate year and position is shown.

A song with more than one charted version is listed once, with the name of each artist who had a hit with it listed below. Occasionally versions of the same song have slightly different titles (e.g. UB40's cover of Can't Help Falling In Love was titled (I Can't Help) Falling In Love With You). In these instances the song is listed twice, an asterisk marking the title that differs from the release.

Double A sides are given two separate entries.

EPs in the singles chart are listed by the title of the EP and also by the lead track (e.g. Erasure's Crackers International is listed, as is the main track Stop!).

The EP section contains only those discs that appeared in the separate EP chart of the Sixties.

The album section also includes entries from the compilation charts.

SINGLE

AMERICA THE BEAUTIFUL [EP], Elvis Presley, 01-69
AMERICA: WHAT TIME IS LOVE? [RR], KLF, 92-4
THE AMERICAN, Simple Minds, 81-59
AMERICAN BAD ASS, Kid Rock, 00-25
AMERICAN DREAM, Crosby Stills Nash and Young, 89-55
AMERICAN DREAM, Power Of Dreams, 91-74
AMERICAN DREAM, Jakatta, 01-3, 01-63
AMERICAN GENERATION, Ritchie Family, 79-49
AMERICAN GIRL, Tom Petty and The Heartbreakers, 77-40
AMERICAN HEARTS, Billy Ocean, 79-54
AMERICAN PIE:
Don McLean, 72-2, 91-12
Chupito, 95-54
Just Luis, 95-31, 96-70
Madonna, 00-1
AMERICAN T.V., Terrorvision, 93-63
AN AMERICAN TRILOGY:
Elvis Presley, 72-8
Mickey Newbury, 72-42
AMERICAN TRILOGY, Delgados, 00-61
AMERICAN WOMAN, Guess Who, 70-19
AMERICANOS, Holly Johnson, 89-4
AMIGO, Black Slate, 80-9
AMIGOS PARA SIEMPRE (FRIENDS FOR LIFE), Jose Carreras and Sarah Brightman, 92-11
AMITYVILLE (THE HOUSE ON THE HILL), Lovebug Starski, 86-12
AMNESIA, Shalamar, 84-61
AMNESIA, Chumbawamba, 98-10
AMONG MY SOUVENIRS, Connie Francis, 59-11
AMOR, Julio Iglesias, 82-32
AMOR, AMOR, Ben E. King, 61-38
AMOUR AMOUR, Mobiles, 82-45
AMOUR (C'MON), Porn Kings, 97-17
AMOUREUSE, Kiki Dee, 73-13, 76-13
THE AMSTERDAM (EP), Simple Minds, 89-18
AN UBHAL AS AIRDE (THE HIGHEST APPLE), Runrig, 95-18
ANA'S SONG (OPEN FIRE), Silverchair, 99-45
ANARCHY IN THE U.K.:
Sex Pistols, 76-38, 92-33
Megadeth, 88-45
Green Jelly, 93-27
ANASTHASIA, T99, 91-14
ANCHORAGE, Michelle Shocked, 88-60
ANCODIA (from THE EXTENDED PLEASURE OF DANCE [EP]), 808 State, 90-56
AND A BANG ON THE EAR, Waterboys, 89-51
AND DA DRUM MACHINE, Phatt B, 00-58
AND I LOVE YOU SO, Perry Como, 73-3
AND I'M TELLING YOU I'M NOT GOING:
Jennifer Holliday, 82-32
Donna Giles, 94-43, 96-27
AND I WISH, Dooleys, 81-52
AND IT HURTS, Dayeene, 99-63
AND IT WASN'T A DREAM, Ruthless Rap Assassins featured vocalist – Tracey Carmen, 90-75
(AND NOW – THE WALTZ) C'EST LA VIE, Slade, 82-50
AND SHE WAS, Talking Heads, 86-17
AND SO I WILL WAIT FOR YOU, Dee Fredrix, 93-56
AND SO IS LOVE, Kate Bush, 94-26
. . . AND STONES, Blue Aeroplanes, 90-63
. . . AND THAT'S BEFORE ME TEA!, Mr. Food, 90-62
. . . (AND THAT'S NO LIE), Heaven 17, 85-52
AND THE BAND PLAYED ON (DOWN AMONG THE DEAD MEN), Flash And The Pan, 78-54
AND THE BANDS PLAYED ON, Saxon, 81-12
AND THE BEAT GOES ON, Whispers, 80-2, 87-45
AND THE BIRDS WERE SINGING (ET LES OISEAUX CHANTAIENT), Sweet People, 80-4, 87-73
AND THE HEAVENS CRIED, Anthony Newley, 61-6
AND THE LEADER ROCKS ON [M], Gary Glitter, 92-58
(AND THE) PICTURES IN THE SKY, Medicine Head, 71-22
AND THE SUN WILL SHINE, Jose Feliciano, 69-25
AND THEN SHE KISSED ME, Gary Glitter, 81-39
AND THEN SHE SMILES, Mock Turtles, 91-44
AND THEN THE RAIN FALLS, Blue Amazon, 97-53
AND YOU SMILED (EYE LEVEL THEME FROM TV SERIES "VAN DER VALK"), Matt Monro, 73-28
ANDRES, L7, 94-34
ANDROGYNY, Garbage, 01-24
ANFIELD RAP (RED MACHINE IN FULL EFFECT), Liverpool F.C., 88-3
ANGEL, Rod Stewart, 72-4
ANGEL:
Aretha Franklin, 73-37
Simply Red, 96-4
ANGEL, Madonna, 85-5
ANGEL, Aerosmith, 88-69
ANGEL, Eurythmics, 90-23
ANGEL, Jon Secada, 93-23
ANGEL, A-Ha, 93-41
ANGEL, Goldie, 95-41
ANGEL, Ralph Fridge, 00-20
ANGEL, Shaggy featuring Rayvon, 01-1
AN ANGEL, Kelly Family, 95-69
ANGEL, Massive Attack, 98-30
ANGEL, Tina Cousins, 99-46
ANGEL, Lionel Richie, 00-18
THE ANGEL AND THE GAMBLER, Iron Maiden, 98-18
ANGEL EYES, Roxy Music, 79-4
ANGEL EYES (HOME AND AWAY), Wet Wet Wet, 87-5
ANGEL FACE, Glitter Band, 74-4
ANGEL FINGERS (A TEEN BALLAD), Wizzard vocal backing – The Suedettes and the Bleach Boys, 73-1
ANGEL IN BLUE, J. Geils Band, 82-55
ANGEL INTERCEPTOR, Ash, 95-14
ANGEL (LADADI O-HEYO), Jam and Spoon featuring Plavka, 95-26
ANGEL OF HARLEM, U2, 88-9
ANGEL OF MINE:
Eternal, 97-4
Monica, 99-55
ANGEL OF THE MORNING:
P.P. Arnold, 68-29
Juice Newton, 81-43
ANGEL OF THE MORNING/ANY WAY THAT YOU WANT ME [M], Mary Mason, 77-27
ANGEL ST, M People, 98-8
ANGEL'S HEAP, Finn, 95-41
ANGEL'S SYMPHONY, R.A.F. by Picotto and Gigi D'Agostino, 96-73
ANGELA JONES, Michael Cox; Charles Blackwell's Orchestra, 60-7
ANGELEYES, Abba, 79-3
ANGELIA, Richard Marx, 89-45
ANGELO, Brotherhood Of Man, 77-1
ANGELS, Robbie Williams, 97-4, 99-57, 00-71
ANGELS DON'T LIE, Jim Reeves, 70-32
ANGELS GO BALD: TOO, Howie B, 97-36
ANGELS OF THE SILENCES, Counting Crows, 96-41
ANGELS WITH DIRTY FACES, Sham 69, 78-19
ANGIE, Rolling Stones, 73-5
ANGIE BABY, Helen Reddy, 75-5
ANGRY AT THE BIG OAK TREE, Frank Ifield, 64-25
ANGRY CHAIR, Alice In Chains, 93-33
ANGRY SKIES, Maria Nayler, 00-42
ANIMAL, Def Leppard, 87-6
ANIMAL, Lost It.Com, 01-70
ANIMAL ARMY, Babylon Zoo, 96-17
ANIMAL CANNABUS, Mull Historical Society, 01-53
ANIMAL (FK LIKE A BEAST),** W.A.S.P., 88-61
ANIMAL INSTINCT, Commodores, 85-74
ANIMAL INSTINCT, Cranberries, 99-54
ANIMAL NITRATE, Suede, 93-7
THE ANIMAL SONG, Savage Garden, 99-16
ANIMATION, Skids, 80-56
A9, Ariel, 00-28
ANITINA (THE FIRST TIME I SEE SHE DANCE), M/A/R/R/S, 87-1
ANNABELLA, John Walker, 67-24
ANNIE GET YOUR GUN, Squeeze, 82-43
ANNIE, I'M NOT YOUR DADDY, Kid Creole and the Coconuts, 82-2
ANNIE'S SONG, James Galway, flute; National Philharmonic Orchestra Charles Gerhart, conductor, 78-3
ANNIE'S SONG, John Denver, 74-1
ANNIVERSARY WALTZ, Anita Harris, 68-21
THE ANNIVERSARY WALTZ – PART ONE [M], Status Quo, 90-2
THE ANNIVERSARY WALTZ (PART TWO) [M], Status Quo, 90-16
ANOMALY – CALLING YOUR NAME, Libra presents Taylor, 96-71, 00-43
ANOTHER BLOOMING CHRISTMAS, Mel Smith, 91-59
ANOTHER BODY MURDERED, Faith No More and the Boo-Yaa Tribe, 93-26
ANOTHER BRICK IN THE WALL PART II, Pink Floyd, 79-1
ANOTHER CHANCE, Roger Sanchez, 01-1
ANOTHER CUP OF COFFEE, Mike and the Mechanics, 95-51
ANOTHER DAY, Paul McCartney, 71-2
ANOTHER DAY, Whigfield, 94-7
ANOTHER DAY, Buckshot Lefonque, 97-65
ANOTHER DAY, Skip Raiders Featuring Jada, 00-46
ANOTHER DAY (ANOTHER GIRL), Lambrettas, 80-49
ANOTHER DAY IN PARADISE:
Phil Collins, 89-2
Jam Tronik, 90-19
Brandy and Ray J, 01-5
ANOTHER FUNNY HONEYMOON, David Dundas, 77-29
ANOTHER GIRL – ANOTHER PLANET, Only Ones, 92-57
ANOTHER HEARTACHE, Rod Stewart, 86-54
ANOTHER KIND OF LOVE, Hugh Cornwell, 88-71
ANOTHER LONELY NIGHT IN NEW YORK, Robin Gibb, 84-71
ANOTHER LOVER, Dane, 01-9
ANOTHER MAN, Barbara Mason, 84-45
ANOTHER MONSTERJAM, Simon Harris featuring Einstein, 89-65
ANOTHER NAIL IN MY HEART, Squeeze, 80-17
ANOTHER NIGHT, Aretha Franklin, 86-54
ANOTHER NIGHT, Jason Donovan, 90-18
ANOTHER NIGHT, (MC Sar) and the Real McCoy, 93-61, 94-2
ANOTHER NIGHT IN, Strangelove, 98-46
ANOTHER ONE BITES THE DUST:
Queen, 80-7
Queen/Wyclef Jean featuring Pras and Free, 98-5
ANOTHER PART OF ME, Michael Jackson, 88-15
ANOTHER PEARL, Badly Drawn Boy, 00-41
ANOTHER PIECE OF MEAT, Scorpions, 79-39
ANOTHER ROCK AND ROLL CHRISTMAS, Gary Glitter, 84-7
ANOTHER SAD LOVE SONG, Toni Braxton, 93-51, 94-15
ANOTHER SATURDAY NIGHT:
Sam Cooke, 63-23, 86-75
Cat Stevens, 74-19
ANOTHER SILENT DAY, Adventures, 84-71
ANOTHER SLEEPLESS NIGHT, Jimmy Clanton, 60-50
ANOTHER SLEEPLESS NIGHT, Mike 'Hitman' Wilson featuring Shawn Christopher, 90-74, 91-50
ANOTHER STAR:
Stevie Wonder, 77-29
Kathy Sledge, 95-54
ANOTHER STEP (CLOSER TO YOU), Kim Wilde and Junior, 87-6
ANOTHER SUITCASE IN ANOTHER HALL:
Barbara Dickson, 77-18
Madonna, 97-7
ANOTHER TEAR FALLS, Walker Brothers, 66-12
ANOTHER TIME, ANOTHER PLACE, Engelbert Humperdinck, 71-13
ANOTHER WAY, Paul Van Dyk, 99-13
ANOTHER WEEKEND, Five Star, 88-18
ANOTHERLOVERHOLENYOHEAD, Prince and the Revolution, 86-36
ANSWER ME:
David Whitfield with Stanley Black and his Orchestra, 53-1
Frankie Laine, 53-1
Ray Peterson, 60 47
Barbara Dickson, 76-9
THE ANSWER TO WHY I HATE YOU, Symposium, 97-32
ANSWERS TO NOTHING, Midge Ure, 88-49
ANT RAP, Adam and the Ants, 81-3
ANTE UP – REMIX, M.O.P. (featuring Busta Rhymes, Tephlon and Remy Martin), 01-7
ANTHEM, N-Joi, 90-45, 91-8
ANTHEM, Wildhearts, 97-21
ANTHEM (ONE DAY IN EVERY WEEK), New Seekers, 78-21
ANTI-SOCIAL, Anthrax, 89-44
ANTMUSIC, Adam and the Ants, 80-2
THE ANTMUSIC (EP) (THE B-SIDES) [EP], Adam and the Ants, 82-46
ANY DREAM WILL DO, Jason Donovan, 91-1
ANY LOVE, Luther Vandross, 88-31
ANY OLD IRON, Peter Sellers presents Mate's Spoffle Group featuring Fred Spoons, E.P.N.S., 57-17

ATLANTIS, Donovan, 68-23
ATLANTIS, Section-X, 97-42
ATLANTIS IS CALLING (S.O.S. FOR LOVE), Modern Talking, 86-55
ATMOSPHERE, Russ Abbot, 84-7
ATMOSPHERE, Joy Division, 88-34
ATMOSPHERE, Kayestone, 00-55
ATMOSPHERIC ROAD, Family Cat, 93-69
ATOM BOMB, Fluke, 96-20
ATOM POWERED ACTION! [EP], Bis, 96-54
ATOMIC, Blondie, 80-1, 94-19
ATOMIC CITY, Holly Johnson, 89-18
ATTACK, Toys, 66-36
ATTACK, Exploited, 82-50
ATTACK ME WITH YOUR LOVE, Cameo, 85-65
ATTENTION TO ME, Nolans, 81-9
ATTITUDE, Sepultura, 96-46
AUBERGE, Chris Rea, 91-16
AUDIO VIDEO, News, 81-52
AUDITION, Witness, 99-71
AUF WIEDERSEH'N SWEETHEART, Vera Lynn with Soldiers and Airmen of Her Majesty's Forces, 52-10
AUGUST OCTOBER, Robin Gibb, 70-45
AULD LANG SYNE, Weekend, 85-47
AUSLANDER, Living Colour, 93-53
AUSTRALIA, Manic Street Preachers, 96-7
AUTOBAHN, Kraftwerk, 75-11
AUTOBIOGRAPHY OF A CRACKHEAD, Shut Up And Dance, 92-43
AUTODRIVE, Herbie Hancock, 83-33
AUTOMATIC, Pointer Sisters, 84-2
AUTOMATIC, Millie Scott, 86-56
AUTOMATIC, Floorplay, 96-50
AUTOMATIC LOVER, Vibrators, 78-35
AUTOMATIC LOVER, Dee D. Jackson, 78-4
AUTOMATIC LOVER (CALL FOR LOVE), Real McCoy, 95-58
AUTOMATICALLY SUNSHINE, Supremes, 72-10
AUTOMATIK, Beat Renegades, 01-73
AUTOPHILIA OR HOW I LEARNED TO STOP WORRYING AND LOVE MY CAR, Bluetones, 00-18
AUTUMN ALMANAC, Kinks, 67-3
AUTUMN CONCERTO, Melachrino Orchestra conducted by George Melachrino, 56-18
AUTUMN LEAVES, Coldcut, 94-50
AUTUMN LOVE, Electra, 89-51
AUTUMN TACTICS, Chicane, 00-44
AVA ADORE, Smashing Pumpkins, 98-11
AVALON, Roxy Music, 82-13
AVE MARIA:
Shirley Bassey, 62-31
Lesley Garrett with Amanda Thompson, 93-16
Andrea Bocelli and the Orchestra E Coro Dell'accademia Nazionale Di Santa Cecilia conducted by Myung- Whun Chung, 99-65
AVENGING ANGELS, Space, 98-6
AVENUE, Saint Etienne, 92-40
AVENUE, Paul Van Dyk, 99-13
AVENUES AND ALLEYWAYS, Tony Christie, 73-37
AVERAGE MAN, Symposium, 98-45
THE AWAKENING, York, 99-11
AWAY FROM HOME, Dr. Alban, 94-42
AWFUL, Hole, 99-42
AXEL F:
Harold Faltermeyer, 85-2
Clock, 95-7
Spacecorn, 01-74

AY AY AY AY MOOSEY, Modern Romance, 81-10
AYLA, Ayla, 99-22
AZTEC GOLD – THE OFFICIAL ITV THEME FOR THE WORLD CUP, Silsoe, 86-48
AZTEC LIGHTNING – THEME FROM BBC WORLD CUP GRANDSTAND, Heads, 86-45
B-A-B-Y, Rachel Sweet, 78-35
B-BOY HUMP, Old Skool Orchestra, 99-55
B-BOY STANCE, Freestylers featuring Tenor Fly, 98-23
B.E.T.A., Empirion, 97-75
B GOOD 2 ME, Ronni Simon, 94-73
B LINE, Lamb, 99-52
B.O.B (BOMBS OVER BAGHDAD), Outkast, 00-61
B 2 GETHER, Original, 95-29
B WITH U, Junior Sanchez featuring Dajae, 99-31
B.Y.O.F. (BRING YOUR OWN FUNK), Fantastic Four, 79-62
BA-BA-BANKROBBERY (ENGLISH VERSION??), EAV (Erste Allgemeine Verunsicherung), 86-63
BA-NA-NA-BAM-BOO, Westworld, 87-37
BAA BAA BLACK SHEEP, Singing Sheep, 82-42
BAAL'S HYMN [EP] + lead track title, David Bowie, 82-29
BABARABATIRI, Gypsymen, 01-32
BABE, Styx, 80-6
BABE, Take That, 93-1
BABES IN THE WOOD, Matchbox, 81-46
BABETTE, Tommy Bruce, 62-50
BABIES, Ashford and Simpson, 85-56
BABIES (from THE SISTERS [EP]), Pulp, 94-19
BABOOSHKA, Kate Bush, 80-5
THE BABY, Hollies, 72-26
BABY, Halo James, 90-43
BABY, Rozalla, 95-26
BABY, BABY, Frankie Lymon and the Teenagers, 57-4
BABY BABY, Eighth Wonder, 88-65
BABY BABY, Amy Grant, 91-2
BABY BABY, Corona, 95-5
BABY-BABY-BABY, TLC, 92-55
BABY BABY BYE BYE, Jerry Lee Lewis, 60-47
BABY, BABY MY LOVE'S ALL FOR YOU, Deniece Williams, 77-32
BABY BE MINE, Blackstreet featuring Teddy Riley, 93-37
BABY BLUE, Dusty Springfield, 79-61
BABY BRITAIN, Elliott Smith, 99-55
BABY, CAN I GET YOUR NUMBER, OBI Project featuring Harry Asher D and DJ What?, 01-75
BABY CAN I HOLD YOU, Boyzone, 97-2
BABY COME BACK:
Equals, 68-1
Pato Banton featuring Ali and Robin Campbell of UB40, 94-1
BABY COME BACK, Player, 78-32
BABY COME ON, Spacemaid, 97-70
BABY COME ON OVER, Samantha Mumba, 01-5
BABY COME TO ME, Alexander O'Neal and Cherrelle, 97-56
BABY, COME TO ME, Patti Austin and James Ingram, 83-11
BABY DID A BAD BAD THING, Chris Isaak, 99-44
BABY DON'T CHANGE YOUR MIND, Gladys Knight and the Pips, 77-4
BABY DON'T CRY, Lalah Hathaway, 91-54
BABY DON'T CRY, Inxs, 92-20
BABY DON'T FORGET MY NUMBER, Milli Vanilli, 88-16
BABY DON'T GET HOOKED ON ME, Mac Davis, 72-29
BABY DON'T GO, 4mandu, 96-47

BABY DON'T GO, Sonny and Cher, 65-11
BABY FACE:
Little Richard, 59-2
Bobby Darin, 62-40
Wing And A Prayer Fife and Drum Corps, 76-12
BABY GOT BACK, Sir Mix-A-Lot, 92-56
BABY I DON'T CARE:
Buddy Holly, 61-12
Elvis Presley, 83-61
BABY I DON'T CARE, Transvision Vamp, 89-3
BABY I KNOW, Rubettes, 77-10
BABY, I LOVE YOU:
Ronettes, 64-11
Dave Edmunds, 73-8
Ramones, 80-8
TSD, 96-64
BABY I LOVE YOU, Aretha Franklin, 67-39
BABY I LOVE YOU, OK!, Kenny, 75-12
BABY I LOVE YOUR WAY:
Peter Frampton, 76-43
Big Mountain, 94-2
BABY I LOVE YOUR WAY / FREE BIRD [M], Will To Power, 89-6
BABY I'M-A WANT YOU, Bread, 72-14
BABY I'M SCARED OF YOU, Womack and Womack, 84-72
BABY I'M YOURS:
Peter and Gordon, 65-19
Linda Lewis, 76-33
BABY I NEED YOUR LOVING, Fourmost, 64-24
BABY I WON'T LET YOU DOWN, Pickettywitch, 70-27
BABY, IT'S COLD OUTSIDE, Tom Jones and Cerys Of Catatonia, 99-17
BABY IT'S TRUE, Mari Wilson, 82-42
BABY IT'S YOU:
Dave Berry, 64-24
Beatles, 95-7
BABY IT'S YOU, Silk, 93-44
BABY IT'S YOU, MN8, 95-22
BABY JANE, Rod Stewart, 83-1
BABY JUMP, Mungo Jerry, 71-1
BABY LAY DOWN, Ruby Winters, 79-43
BABY LEE, John Lee Hooker with Robert Cray, 96-65
BABY LET ME TAKE YOU HOME, Animals, 64-21
BABY LOVE:
Supremes, 64-1, 74-12
Honey Bane, 81-58
BABY LOVE:
Regina, 86-50
Dannii Minogue, 91-14
BABY LOVER, Petula Clark and the Beryl Stott Group, 58-12
BABY MAKE IT SOON, Marmalade, 69-9
BABY MY HEART, Crickets, 60-33
BABY NEVER SAY GOODBYE, Unit Four Plus Two, 66-49
BABY NOW I, Dan Reed Network, 91-65
BABY, NOW THAT I'VE FOUND YOU, Foundations, 67-1
BABY OF MINE, Alan Price, 79-32
. . . BABY ONE MORE TIME, Britney Spears, 99-1
BABY PLAYS AROUND [EP] + lead track title, Elvis Costello, 89-65
BABY PLEASE DON'T GO, Them, 65-10, 91-65
BABY ROO, Connie Francis, 61-5
BABY'S COMING BACK, Jellyfish, 91-51
BABY'S FIRST CHRISTMAS, Connie Francis, 61-30
BABY'S REQUEST, Wings, 79-60
BABY SITTIN', Bobby Angelo and the Tuxedos, 61-30
BABY SITTIN' BOOGIE, Buzz Clifford, 61-17
BABY STOP CRYING, Bob Dylan, 78-13

BABY TAKE A BOW, Adam Faith, 62-22
BABY TALK, Alisha, 86-67
BABY U LEFT ME (IN THE COLD), Marilyn, 85-70
BABY UNIVERSAL, Tin Machine, 91-48
BABY WANTS TO RIDE, Hani, 00-70
BABY, WE BETTER TRY TO GET IT TOGETHER, Barry White, 76-15
BABY WE CAN'T GO WRONG, Cilla Black, 74-36
BABY, WHAT A BIG SURPRISE, Chicago, 77-41
BABY WHAT I MEAN, Drifters, 67-49
(BABY) YOU DON'T HAVE TO TELL ME, Walker Brothers, 66-13
BABY YOU'RE DYNAMITE, Cliff Richard, 84-27
BABYLON, Black Dog featuring Ofra Haza, 99-65
BABYLON, David Gray, 00-5
BABYLON'S BURNING, Ruts, 79-7
BACHELOR BOY, Cliff Richard, the Shadows and the Norrie Paramor Strings, 62-1
BACHELORETTE, Bjork, 97-21
BACK AND FORTH, Cameo, 87-11
BACK AND FORTH, Aaliyah, 94-16
BACK BY DOPE DEMAND, King Bee, 91-61
BACK CHAT, Queen, 82-40
BACK FOR GOOD:
Take That, 95-1
Real Emotion, 95-67
BACK FROM THE EDGE, Bruce Dickinson, 96-68
BACK HERE, Bbmak, 99-37, 01-5
BACK HOME, England World Cup Squad "70", 70-1
BACK IN LOVE AGAIN, Donna Summer, 78-29
BACK IN MY ARMS, Chris Paul, 87-74
BACK IN MY ARMS AGAIN, Supremes, 65-40
BACK IN MY ARMS (ONCE AGAIN), Hazell Dean, 84-41
BACK IN MY LIFE, Joe Roberts, 93-59, 94-39
BACK IN MY LIFE, Alice Deejay, 99-4
BACK IN THE DAY, Ahmad, 94-64
BACK IN THE HIGH LIFE AGAIN, Steve Winwood, 87-53
BACK IN THE U.K., Scooter, 96-18
BACK IN THE U.S.S.R., Beatles, 76-19
BACK IT UP, Robin S, 94-43
THE BACK OF LOVE, Echo and the Bunnymen, 82-19
BACK OF MY HAND, Jags, 79-17
BACK OFF BOOGALOO, Ringo Starr, 72-2
BACK ON MY FEET AGAIN, Foundations, 68-18
BACK ON THE CHAIN GANG, Pretenders, 82-17
BACK ON THE ROAD, Earth, Wind And Fire, 80-63
BACK ON THE ROAD, Marmalade, 71-35
BACK ON THE STREETS, Saxon, 85-75
BACK ON TOP, Van Morrison, 99-69
THE BACK SEAT OF MY CAR, Paul and Linda McCartney, 71-39
BACK STABBERS, O'Jays, 72-14
BACK STREET LUV, Curved Air, 71-4
BACK TO EARTH, Yves Deruyter, 01-63
BACK TO FRONT, Stiff Little Fingers, 80-49
BACK TO FRONT, Adamski, 92-63
BACK TO LIFE (HOWEVER DO YOU WANT ME), Soul Ii Soul featuring Caron Wheeler, 89-1

BACK TO LOVE, Evelyn King, 82-40
BACK TO LOVE, Brand New Heavies, 94-23
BACK TO MY ROOTS, RuPaul, 93-40
BACK TO REALITY, Intelligent Hoodlum, 90-55
BACK TO SCHOOL AGAIN, Four Tops, 82-62
BACK TO THE LIGHT, Brian May, 92-19
BACK TO THE OLD SCHOOL, Bassheads, 92-12
BACK TO THE 60'S [M], Tight Fit, 81-4
BACK TO THE 60'S (PART II) [M], Tight Fit, 81-33
BACK TO YOU, Bryan Adams, 97-18
BACK TOGETHER, Babybird, 99-22
BACK TOGETHER AGAIN:
Roberta Flack and Donny Hathaway, 80-3
Inner City, 93-49
BACK UP (TO ME), Wookie featuring Lain., 01-38
BACK WITH THE BOYS AGAIN, Joe Fagin, 86-53
BACK WITH THE KILLER (EP), Auteurs, 96-45
BACKAROUND, Elevator Suite, 00-71
BACKFIELD IN MOTION, J.B.'S All Stars, 84-48
BACKFIRED, Debbie Harry, 81-32
BACKS TO THE WALL, Saxon, 80-64
BACKSEAT EDUCATION, Zodiac Mindwarp and the Love Reaction, 87-49
BACKSTAGE, Gene Pitney, 66-4
BACKSTREET SYMPHONY, Thunder, 90-25
BACKSTROKIN', Fatback, 80-41
BAD, Michael Jackson, 87-3
BAD ACTRESS, Terrorvision, 96-10
BAD AMBASSADOR, Divine Comedy, 01-34
BAD BAD BOY, Nazareth, 73-10
BAD BOY, Marty Wilde, 59-7
BAD BOY, Adicts, 83-75
BAD BOY, Miami Sound Machine, 86-16
BAD BOY, Wildchild featuring Jomalski, 98-38
BAD BOY FOR LIFE, P. Diddy, Black Rob and Mark Curry, 01-13
BAD BOYS, Wham!, 83-2
BAD BOYS, Inner Circle, 93-52
BAD CASE OF LOVIN' YOU (DOCTOR DOCTOR), Robert Palmer, 79-61
BAD DAY, Carmel, 83-15
THE BAD DAYS [EP] + lead track title, Space, 98-20
BAD GIRL, Madonna, 93-10
BAD GIRL, Scarlet, 96-54
BAD GIRL, DJ Rap, 98-32
BAD GIRLS:
Donna Summer, 79-14
Juliet Roberts, 99-17
BAD HABIT, ATFC presents Onephatdeeva featuring Lisa Millett, 00-17
BAD HABITS, Jenny Burton, 85-68
BAD LIFE, PIL, 84-71
BAD LOVE, Eric Clapton, 90-25
BAD LUCK, FM, 89-54
BAD MAN, Sister Bliss, 96-51
BAD MEDICINE, Bon Jovi, 88-17
BAD MOON RISING, Creedence Clearwater Revival, 69-1, 92-71
A BAD NIGHT, Cat Stevens, 67-20
BAD OLD DAYS, Co-Co, 78-13
BAD OLD MAN, Babybird, 98-31
BAD PENNY BLUES, Humphrey Lyttelton and his Band, 56-19
THE BAD PHOTOGRAPHER, Saint Etienne, 98-27
BAD THING, Cry Of Love, 94-60
BAD THINGS, Njoi, 95-57
BAD TIME, Jayhawks, 95-70
BAD TO ME, Billy J. Kramer with the Dakotas, 63-1
THE BAD TOUCH, Bloodhound Gang, 00-4
A BAD TOWN, Big Sound Authority, 85-54
BAD WEATHER, Supremes, 73-37
BAD YOUNG BROTHER, Derek B, 88-16
BADDER BADDER SCHWING, Freddy Fresh (featuring Fatboy Slim), 99-34
BADDEST RUFFEST, Backyard Dog, 01-15
BADGE, Cream, 69-18, 72-42
BADMAN, Cockney Rejects, 80-65
THE BADMAN IS ROBBIN', Hijack, 90-56
BAG IT UP, Geri Halliwell, 00-1
BAGGY TROUSERS, Madness, 80-3
THE BAGUIO TRACK, Luzon, 01-67
BAILAMOS, Enrique Iglesias, 99-4
BAILAMOS, M3, 99-40
BAILANDO CON LOBOS, Cabana, 95-65
BAKER STREET:
Gerry Rafferty, 78-3, 90-53
Undercover, 92-2
BAKERMAN, Laid Back, 90-44
BALL AND CHAIN, XTC, 82-58
BALL OF CONFUSION (THAT'S WHAT THE WORLD IS TODAY), Temptations, 70-7
BALL PARK INCIDENT, Wizzard, 72-6
BALLAD OF A LANDLORD, Terry Hall, 97-50
THE BALLAD OF BONNIE AND CLYDE, Georgie Fame, 67-1
THE BALLAD OF CHASEY LAIN, Bloodhound Gang, 00-15
BALLAD OF DAVY CROCKETT:
Bill Hayes with Archie Bleyer's Orchestra, 56-2
Tennessee Ernie Ford, 56-3
Dick James with Stephen James and his Chums, 56-29
Max Bygraves with Children's Chorus, 56-20
THE BALLAD OF JAYNE, L.A. Guns, 91-53
THE BALLAD OF JOHN AND YOKO, Beatles, 69-1
THE BALLAD OF LUCY JORDAN, Marianne Faithfull, 79-48
BALLAD OF PALADIN, Duane Eddy, 62-10
THE BALLAD OF PETER PUMPKINHEAD:
XTC, 92-71
Crash Test Dummies featuring Ellen Reid, 95-30
THE BALLAD OF SPOTTY MULDOON, Peter Cook with the Dudley Moore Trio, 65-34
THE BALLAD OF THE GREEN BERETS, Staff Sergeant Barry Sadler, 66-24
THE BALLAD OF TOM JONES, Space with Cerys of Catatonia, 98-4
BALLAD OF YOUTH, Richie Sambora, 91-59
BALLERINA (PRIMA DONNA), Steve Harley and Cockney Rebel, 83-51
BALLERINA GIRL, Lionel Richie, 86-17
BALLOON, Catherine Wheel, 92-59
THE BALLROOM BLITZ:
Sweet, 73-2
Tia Carrere, 92-26
THE BALLROOM OF ROMANCE, Chris De Burgh, 86-40
BALMES (A BETTER LIFE), Ian Pooley featuring Esthero, 01-65
BAM BAM BAM, Westbam, 94-57
BAMA BOOGIE WOOGIE, Cleveland Eaton, 78-35
BAMA LAMA BAMA LOO, Little Richard, 64-20
BAMBAATA 2012, Shy Fx, 99-60
BAMBINO, Springfields, 61-16
BAMBOO HOUSES, Sylvian Sakamoto, 82-30
BAMBOO MUSIC, Sylvian Sakamoto, 82-30
BAMBOOGIE, Bamboo, 98-2
BANANA BANANA, King Kurt, 84-54
THE BANANA BOAT SONG:
Shirley Bassey with Wally Stott and his Orchestra and Chorus, 57-8
Harry Belafonte with Tony Scott's Orchestra and Chorus, 57-2
Tarriers, 57-15
BANANA-NA-NA (DUMB DIDDY DUMB), Technohead, 96-64
BANANA REPUBLIC, Boomtown Rats, 80-3
BANANA ROCK, Wombles, 74-9
THE BANANA SONG, GSP, 92-37
BANANA SPLITS (THE TRA LA LA SONG), Dickies, 79-7
BAND OF GOLD, Don Cherry with Ray Conniff and his Orchestra, 56-6
BAND OF GOLD:
Freda Payne, 70-1
Sylvester, 83-67
BAND ON THE RUN, Paul McCartney and Wings, 74-3
THE BAND PLAYED THE BOOGIE, C.C.S., 73-36
BANG, Blur, 91-24
BANG, Robbie Rivera pres. Rhythm Bangers, 00-13
BANG AND BLAME, R.E.M., 94-15
BANG BANG, Squeeze, 78-49
BANG BANG, B.A. Robertson, 79-2
BANG BANG (MY BABY SHOT ME DOWN), Cher, 66-3
BANG ON!, Propellerheads, 98-53
BANG YOUR HEAD (from SIX FEET DEEP [EP]), Gravediggaz, 95-64
(BANG ZOOM) LET'S GO GO, Real Roxanne with Hitman Howie Tee, 86-11
BANGERS AND MASH, Peter Sellers and Sophia Loren, 61-22
BANGIN' BASS, Da Techno Bohemian, 97-63
THE BANGIN MAN, Slade, 74-3
BANGLA-DESH, George Harrison, 71-10
BANJO BOY:
George Formby with the Beryl Stott Chorus, 60-40
Jan and Kjeld with Gert Wilden's Orchestra, 60-36
THE BANJO'S BACK IN TOWN, Alma Cogan, 55-17
BANKROBBER, Audioweb, 97-19
BANKROBBER, Clash, 80-12
BANKS OF THE OHIO, Olivia Newton John, 71-6
THE BANNER MAN, Blue Mink, 71-3
BARBADOS, Typically Tropical, 75-1
BARBARA ANN, Beach Boys, 66-3
BARBARELLA, Alisha's Attic, 99-34
BARBER'S ADAGIO FOR STRINGS, William Orbit, 99-4
BARBIE GIRL, Aqua, 97-1
BARCELONA:
Freddie Mercury and Montserrat Caballe, 87-8, 92-2
Russell Watson / Shaun Ryder*, 00-68
THE BARE NECESSITIES MEGAMIX [M], UK Mixmasters, 91-14
BAREFOOT [EP], Ultramarine, 94-61
BAREFOOT IN THE HEAD, A Man Called Adam, 90-60
BAREFOOTIN', Robert Parker, 66-24
BARK AT THE MOON, Ozzy Osbourne, 83-21
BARMY LONDON ARMY, Charlie Harper, 80-68
BARNEY (. . . AND ME), Boo Radleys, 94-48
BARREL OF A GUN, Depeche Mode, 97-4
BARRIERS, Soft Cell, 83-25
THE BARTENDER AND THE THIEF, Stereophonics, 98-3
BASKET CASE, Green Day, 94-55, 95-7
BASS (HOW LOW CAN YOU GO), Simon Harris, 88-12
BASS SHAKE, Urban Shakedown featuring Micky Finn, 92-59
BASSCAD, [EP], Autechre, 94-56
BASSCADETMXS (from BASSCAD, [EP]), Autechre, 94-56
BASSFLY, Tillman and Ries, 00-70
BASSLICK, Second Protocol, 00-58
BASSLINE, Mantronix, 86-34
BAT OUT OF HELL, Meat Loaf, 79-15, 93-8
BATDANCE, Prince, 89-2
BATHTIME, Tindersticks, 97-38
BATMAN THEME, Neal Hefti, 88-55
BATTER UP, Nelly and St. Lunatics, 01-28
BATTLE, Wookie featuring Lain., 00-10
BATTLE OF NEW ORLEANS:
Lonnie Donegan and his Skiffle Group, 59-2
Johnny Horton, 59-16
BATTLE OF THE SEXES, Faith Hope and Charity, 90-53
BATTLE OF WHO COULD CARE LESS, Ben Folds Five, 97-26
THE BATTLE'S O'ER, Andy Stewart with the Michael Sammes Singers, 61-28
BATTLEFLAG, Lo Fidelity Allstars featuring Pigeonhed, 98-36
BATTLESHIP CHAINS, Georgia Satellites, 87-44
BAUBLES, BANGLES AND BEADS, George Shearing Quintet with Strings, 62-49
BAUHAUS, Cappella, 88-60
BAWITDABA (DAH WIT DA-DAH), Kid Rock, 01-41
BBC WORLD CUP GRANDSTAND, Royal Philharmonic Orchestra, 82-61
BE AGGRESSIVE, Faith No More, 93-3
BE ALONE NO MORE, Another Level, 98-6, 99-11
BE AS ONE, Sasha and Maria, 96-17
BE BOP A LULA, Gene Vincent and the Blue Caps, 56-16
BE CAREFUL, Sparkle featuring R. Kelly, 98-7
BE FREE WITH YOUR LOVE, Spandau Ballet, 89-42
BE GOOD TO YOURSELF, Frankie Miller, 77-27
BE HAPPY, Mary J. Blige, 94-30
BE MINE, Charlotte, 98-59
BE MINE (ALLE MADCHEN WOLLEN KUSSEN), Lance Fortune, 60-4
BE MINE (MI SEGUIRAI), Tremeloes, 67-39
BE MINE TONIGHT, Jammers, 83-65
BE MY BABY, Ronettes, 63-4
BE MY BABY, Vanessa Paradis, 92-6
BE MY BABY, Cappella, 97-53
BE MY DOWNFALL, Del Amitri, 92-30
BE MY FRIEND, Soul U*nique, 00-53
BE MY GIRL, Jim Dale, 57-2
BE MY GUEST, Fats Domino, 59-11
BE MY LIGHT, BE MY GUIDE, Gene, 94-54
BE MY LOVER, La Bouche, 95-27, 96-25
BE MY NUMBER TWO, Joe Jackson, 84-70
BE MY TWIN, Brother Beyond, 89-14
BE NEAR ME, ABC, 85-26
BE PROUD BE LOUD (BE HEARD), Toyah, 82-30

BE QUICK OR BE DEAD, Iron Maiden, 92-2
BE QUITE AND DRIVE (FAR AWAY), Deftones, 98-50
BE STIFF, Devo, 78-71
BE TENDER WITH ME BABY, Tina Turner, 90-28
BE THANKFUL FOR WHAT YOU GOT:
William Devaughn, 74-31
William De Vaughn, 80-44
BE THE FIRST TO BELIEVE, A1, 99-6
BE THERE, Unkle featuring Ian Brown, 99-8
BE THERE, Tall Paul, 99-45
BE WITH ME ALWAYS, Cliff Richard, 97-52
BE WITH YOU, Bangles, 89-23
BE YOUNG BE FOOLISH, BE HAPPY:
Tams, 70-32
Sonia, 91-22
BE YOURSELF, Celeda, 99-61
BEACH BABY, First Class, 74-13
BEACH BOY GOLD [M], Gidea Park, 81-11
BEACH BOYS MEDLEY [M], Beach Boys, 81-47
BEACH BUMP, Baby Ford, 90-68
BEACH OF THE WAR GODDESS, Caron Wheeler, 93-75
BEACHBALL, Nalin and Kane, 97-48, 98-17
BEACHED, Orbital and Angelo Badalamenti, 00-36
BEACON LIGHT, Foo Fighters, 98-20
BEAR CAGE, Stranglers, 80-36
BEAT BOX, Art Of Noise, 85-51
A BEAT CALLED LOVE, Grid, 90-64
BEAT DIS, Bomb The Bass, 88-2
BEAT FOR BEATNIKS, John Barry and his Orchestra, 60-40
THE BEAT GOES ON:
Sonny and Cher, 67-29
All Seeing I, 98-11
BEAT IT, Michael Jackson, 83-3
BEAT MAMA, Cast, 99-9
BEAT STREET BREAKDOWN, Grandmaster Melle Mel and the Furious Five, 84-42
BEAT SURRENDER, Jam, 82-1
BEAT THE BEAT, Mari Wilson and the Imaginations, 82-59
BEAT THE CLOCK, Sparks, 79-10
BEAT THE STREET, Sharon Redd, 82-20
THE BEAT(EN) GENERATION, The, 89-18
BEATIN' THE HEAT, Jack 'N' Chill, 88-42
BEATLES AND THE STONES, House Of Love, 90-36
BEATLES MOVIE MEDLEY [M], Beatles, 82-10
BEATNIK FLY, Johnny and the Hurricanes, 60-8
BEATNIK GIRL, Snug, 98-55
BEATSTIME, Sonic Solution, 92-59
BEAUTIFUL, Marillion, 95-29
BEAUTIFUL, Matt Darey's Mash Up featuring Marcella Woods, 00-21
BEAUTIFUL ALONE, Strangelove, 96-35
BEAUTIFUL DAY, 3 Colours Red, 99-11
BEAUTIFUL DAY, U2, 00-1
BEAUTIFUL DREAM, World Party, 97-31
THE BEAUTIFUL EXPERIENCE [EP], Symbol (The Artist Formerly Known As Prince), 94-18
BEAUTIFUL GIRL, Inxs, 93-23
BEAUTIFUL IMBALANCE, Thrashing Doves, 87-50
BEAUTIFUL IN MY EYES, Joshua Kadison, 94-65, 95-37
BEAUTIFUL INSIDE, Louise, 00-13
BEAUTIFUL LIFE, Ace Of Base, 96-15
BEAUTIFUL LOVE, Adeva, 89-57
BEAUTIFUL LOVE, Julian Cope, 91-32
BEAUTIFUL LOVER, Brotherhood Of Man, 78-15
BEAUTIFUL NIGHT, Paul McCartney, 97-25
BEAUTIFUL NOISE, Neil Diamond, 76-13
BEAUTIFUL ONES, Suede, 96-8
BEAUTIFUL PEOPLE, Stress, 90-74
BEAUTIFUL PEOPLE, Big Country, 91-72
BEAUTIFUL PEOPLE, Barbara Tucker, 94-23
THE BEAUTIFUL PEOPLE, Marilyn Manson, 97-18
BEAUTIFUL SON, Hole, 93-54
BEAUTIFUL STRANGER, Madonna, 99-2
BEAUTIFUL SUNDAY, Daniel Boone, 72-21
BEAUTIFUL YOU, Neil Sedaka, 72-43
BEAUTY AND THE BEAST, David Bowie, 78-39
BEAUTY AND THE BEAST, Celine Dion and Peabo Bryson, 92-9
BEAUTY DIES YOUNG, Lowgold, 00-67, 01-40
BEAUTY IS ONLY SKIN DEEP:
Temptations, 66-18
Aswad *, 89-31
THE BEAUTY OF SILENCE, Svenson and Gielen, 01-41
BEAUTY OF THE RIDE, Sebadoh, 96-74
BECAUSE, Demis Roussos, 77-39
BECAUSE, Julian Lennon, 85-40
BECAUSE I GOT HIGH, Afroman, 01-45, 01-1
BECAUSE I GOT IT LIKE THAT, Jungle Brothers, 98-32
BECAUSE I LOVE YOU, Georgie Fame, 67-15
BECAUSE I LOVE YOU, Shakin' Stevens, 86-14
BECAUSE I LOVE YOU (THE POSTMAN SONG), Stevie B, 91-6
BECAUSE OF LOVE, Billy Fury, 62-18
BECAUSE OF LOVE, Janet Jackson, 94-19
BECAUSE OF YOU, Kevin Rowland featuring Dexy's Midnight Runners, 86-13
BECAUSE OF YOU, Gabrielle, 94-24
BECAUSE OF YOU, 98°, 99-36
BECAUSE OF YOU, Scanty Sandwich, 00-3
BECAUSE THE NIGHT:
Patti Smith Group, 78-5
Co.Ro featuring Tarlisa, 92-61
10,000 Maniacs, 93-65
BECAUSE THEY'RE YOUNG:
Duane Eddy, 60-2
James Darren, 60-29
BECAUSE WE WANT TO, Billie, 98-1
BECAUSE YOU LOVED ME (THEME FROM "UP CLOSE & PERSONAL"), Celine Dion, 96-5
BECAUSE YOU'RE MINE:
Mario Lanza-tenor with RCA Victor Orchestra and the Jeff Alexander Choir Cond. by Constantine Callinicos, 52-3
Nat "King" Cole, 52-6
BECAUSE YOU'RE YOUNG, Classix Nouveaux, 82-43
BECOMING MORE LIKE ALFIE, Divine Comedy, 96-27
BECOMING MORE LIKE GOD, Jah Wobble's Invaders Of The Heart, 94-36
BED OF NAILS, Alice Cooper, 89-38
BED OF ROSES, Bon Jovi, 93-13
THE BED'S TOO BIG WITHOUT YOU :
Police (from Six Pack [EP]), 80-17
Sheila Hylton, 81-35
BEDS ARE BURNING, Midnight Oil, 88-48, 89-6
BEDSI'TTER, Soft Cell, 81-4
BEDSIDE RADIO (from INDUSTRIAL STRENGTH [EP]), Krokus, 81-62
BEDTIME STORY, Madonna, 95-4
THE BEE, Scientist, 90-52, 91-47
BEE-BOM, Anthony Newley, 61-15
BEE STING, Camouflage featuring 'Mysti', 77-48
BEEF, Gary Clail On-U Sound System featuring Bim Sherman, 90-64
BEEN A LONG TIME, Fog, 94-44, 98-27
BEEN AROUND THE WORLD, Puff Daddy and the Family featuring the Notorious B.I.G. and Mase, 97-20
BEEN CAUGHT STEALING, Jane's Addiction, 91-34
BEEN IT, Cardigans, 96-56
BEEN THINKING ABOUT YOU, Martine Girault, 95-63
BEEP ME 911, Missy Misdemeanor Elliott (featuring 702 and Magoo), 98-14
BEER DRINKERS AND HELL RAISERS, Motorhead, 80-43
BEETHOVEN (I LOVE TO LISTEN TO), Eurythmics, 87-25
BEETLEBUM, Blur, 97-1
BEFORE, Pet Shop Boys, 96-7
BEFORE TODAY, Everything But The Girl, 97-25
BEFORE YOU LEAVE, Pepe Deluxe, 01-20
BEFORE YOU LOVE ME, Alsou, 01-27
BEFORE YOU WALK OUT OF MY LIFE, Monica, 96-22
BEG, STEAL OR BORROW, New Seekers, 72-2
A BEGGAR ON A BEACH OF GOLD, Mike and the Mechanics, 95-33
BEGGIN', Timebox, 68-38
BEGGIN' TO BE WRITTEN, Worlds Apart, 94-29
BEGGING YOU, Stone Roses, 95-15
BEGIN AGAIN, Space, 98-21
BEGIN THE BEGUINE (VOLVER A EMPEZAR), Julio Iglesias, 81-1
THE BEGINNING, Seal, 91-24
BEHIND A PAINTED SMILE, Isley Brothers, 69-5
BEHIND CLOSED DOORS, Charlie Rich, 74-16
BEHIND THE COUNTER [EP] + lead track title, Fall, 93-75
BEHIND THE GROOVE, Teena Marie, 80-6
BEHIND THE MASK, Eric Clapton, 87-15
BEHIND THE WHEEL, Depeche Mode, 88-21
BEING A GIRL (PART ONE) (from NINE [EP]), Mansun, 98-13
BEING AROUND, Lemonheads, 92-19
BEING BOILED :
Human League (from Holiday 80 [EP]), 80-56
Human League *, 82-6
BEING BORING, Pet Shop Boys, 90-20
BEING BRAVE, Menswear, 96-10
BEING WITH YOU, Smokey Robinson, 81-1
BEL AMOUR, Bel Amour, 01-23
BELARUSE, Levellers, 93-12
BELFAST, Boney M, 77-8
BELFAST, Barnbrack, 85-45
BELFAST, Energy Orchard, 90-52
BELFAST BOY, Don Fardon, 70-32
BELFAST CHILD, Simple Minds, 89-1
BELFAST WASTED, Orbital, 95-53
BELIEVE, Lenny Kravitz, 93-30
BELIEVE, Q Tex, 94-41
BELIEVE, Elton John, 95-15
BELIEVE, Goldie, 98-36
BELIEVE, Cher, 98-1
BELIEVE, Ministers De-La-Funk featuring Jocelyn Brown, 00-45, 01-42
BELIEVE IN ME, Utah Saints, 93-8
BELIEVE IN ME, Quivver, 95-56
BELIEVE IN ME, Raw Stylus, 96-66
BELIEVE IN ME, Mankey, 96-74
BELIEVE IN THE BEAT, Carol Lynn Townes, 85-56
BELIEVE WHAT YOU'RE SAYING, Sugar, 94-73
BELIEVER, Real People, 92-38
BELIEVERS, Baz, 01-36
THE BELL (MC VIV STANSHALL), Mike Oldfield, 93-50
BELL BOTTOM BLUES, Alma Cogan, 54-4
BELL BOTTOMED TEAR, Beautiful South, 92-16
THE BELLE OF ST. MARK, Sheila E., 85-18
BELLISSIMA, DJ Quicksilver, 97-4
THE BELLS OF AVIGNON, Max Bygraves with the Corona Children, 61-36
BELLS OF NY, Slo Moshun, 94-29
BELO HORIZONTI, Heartists, 97-42, 98-40
BEN:
Michael Jackson, 72-7
Marti Webb, 85-5
Toni Warne, 87-50
BEND IT!, Dave Dee, Dozy, Beaky, Mick and Tich, 66-2
BEND ME SHAPE ME:
Amen Corner, 68-3
American Breed, 68-24
BENEDICTUS, Brainbug, 97-24
BENJAMIN, Veruca Salt, 97-75
BENNY AND THE JETS, Elton John, 76-37
BENNY'S THEME, Paul Henry and the Mayson Glen Orchestra, 78-39
BENTLEYS GONNA SORT YOU OUT!, Bentley Rhythm Ace, 97-17
BERMUDA TRIANGLE, Barry Manilow, 81-15
BERNADETTE, Four Tops, 67-8, 72-23
BERRY (THE REMIXES), TC 1991, 92-73
BERSERKER, Gary Numan, 84-32
BESAME MUCHO, Jet Harris, 62-22
BESIDE YOU, Iggy Pop, 94-47
THE BEST, Tina Turner, 89-5
BEST BIT (EP) + lead track title, Beth Orton featuring Terry Callier, 97-36
THE BEST CHRISTMAS OF THEM ALL, Shakin' Stevens, 90-19
BEST DAYS, Juice, 98-28
THE BEST DISCO IN TOWN, Ritchie Family, 76-10
BEST FRIEND, Beat, 80-22
BEST FRIEND, Mark Morrison and Conner Reeves, 99-23
BEST FRIEND, Toy-Box, 99-41
BEST FRIEND, Puff Daddy (featuring Mario Winans), 99-24
BEST FRIEND'S GIRL, Electrasy, 98-41
BEST FRIENDS, Allstars, 01-20
BEST FRIENDS FOREVER, Tweenies, 01-12
BEST I CAN, Queensryche, 91-36
BEST IN ME, Let Loose, 95-8
. . . THE BEST IS YET TO COME, Scooch, 00-12
BEST KEPT SECRET, China Crisis, 87-36
BEST LOVE, Course, 97-51
THE BEST OF EVERYTHING, Johnny Mathis, 59-30
THE BEST OF LOVE, Michael Bolton, 97-14
THE BEST OF ME, Cliff Richard, 89-2

BLACK HEART, Marc and the Mambas, 83-49
THE BLACK HILLS OF DAKOTA, Doris Day with Orchestra and vocal quartet, 54-7
BLACK HOLE SUN, Soundgarden, 94-12
BLACK IS BLACK:
Los Bravos, 66-2
La Belle Epoque, 77-2
BLACK IS BLACK, Jungle Brothers, 89-72
BLACK JESUS, Everlast, 01-37
BLACK LODGE, Anthrax, 93-53
BLACK MAGIC WOMAN, Fleetwood Mac, 68-37
BLACK MAN RAY, China Crisis, 85-14
BLACK MEANING GOOD, Rebel MC, 91-73
BLACK METALLIC [EP] + lead track title, Catherine Wheel, 91-68
BLACK NIGHT:
Deep Purple, 70-2, 80-43, 95-66
Deep Purple (from New Live and Rare [EP]), 77-31
BLACK NITE CRASH, Ride, 96-67
BLACK OR WHITE, Michael Jackson, 91-1, 92-14
BLACK ORCHID, Stevie Wonder, 80-63
BLACK PEARL, Horace Faith, 70-13
BLACK PUDDING BERTHA (THE QUEEN OF NORTHERN SOUL), Goodies, 75-19
BLACK SABBATH, Magoo, 98-60
BLACK SKIN BLUE EYED BOYS, Equals, 70-9
BLACK STATIONS/WHITE STATIONS, M + M, 84-46
BLACK STEEL, Tricky, 95-28
BLACK STOCKINGS, John Barry Seven, 60-27
BLACK SUPERMAN (MUHAMMAD ALI), Johnny Wakelin and the Kinshasa Band, 75-7
BLACK TIE WHITE NOISE, David Bowie featuring Al B. Sure!, 93-36
BLACK VELVET, Alannah Myles, 90-2
BLACK VELVET BAND, Dubliners, 67-15
BLACK WHITE, Asiandubfoundation, 98-52
BLACKBERRY WAY, Move, 68-1
BLACKBIRD ON THE WIRE, Beautiful South, 97-23
BLACKBOARD JUMBLE [M], Barron Knights, 81-52
BLACKER THAN BLACK, Goodbye Mr MacKenzie, 90-61
BLACKERTHREETRACKER [EP], Curve, 93-39
BLACKWATER, Rain Tree Crow, 91-62
BLAH, Heltah Skelter and Originoo Gunn Clappaz as the Fabulous Five, 96-60
BLAME IT ON ME, D:Ream, 94-25
BLAME IT ON THE BASSLINE, Norman Cook featuring M.C. Wildski, 89-29
BLAME IT ON THE BOOGIE:
Jacksons, 78-8
Mick Jackson, 78-15
Big Fun, 89-4
Clock, 98-16
BLAME IT ON THE BOSSA NOVA, Eydie Gorme, 63-32
(BLAME IT) ON THE PONY EXPRESS, Johnny Johnson and his Bandwagon, 70-7
BLAME IT ON THE RAIN, Milli Vanilli, 89-52
BLAME IT ON THE WEATHERMAN, B*Witched, 99-1
BLANKET, Urban Species featuring Imogen Heap, 99-56
BLANKET ON THE GROUND, Billie Jo Spears, 75-6
BLASPHEMOUS RUMOURS, Depeche Mode, 84-16
BLAST THE SPEAKERS, Warp Brothers, 01-40
THE BLAYDON RACES ('99) (from SUPPORT THE TOON – IT'S YOUR DUTY [EP]), Mungo Jerry and the Toon Travellers, 99-57
BLAZE OF GLORY, Jon Bon Jovi, 90-13
BLAZING SADDLES, Yello, 89-47
BLEED, Catatonia, 96-46
BLEED ME WHITE, Eat, 93-73
BLESS YOU, Tony Orlando, 61-5
BLESS YOU, Martha Reeves and the Vandellas, 72-33
BLIND, Talking Heads, 88-59
BLIND AMONG THE FLOWERS, Tourists, 79-52
BLIND MAN, Aerosmith, 94-23
BLIND VISION, Blancmange, 83-10
BLINDED BY THE LIGHT, Manfred Mann's Earth Band, 76-6
BLINDED BY THE SUN, Seahorses, 97-7
BLINDFOLD, Morcheeba, 98-56
THE BLINDFOLD [EP], Curve, 91-68
BLISS, Muse, 01-22
BLOCK BUSTER!, Sweet, 73-1
THE BLOCK PARTY, Lisa "Left Eye" Lopes, 01-16
BLOCK ROCKIN' BEATS, Chemical Brothers, 97-1
BLONDE HAIR, BLUE JEANS, Chris De Burgh, 94-51
BLONDES (HAVE MORE FUN), Rod Stewart, 79-63
BLOOD IS PUMPIN', Voodoo and Serano, 01-19
BLOOD MAKES NOISE, Suzanne Vega, 92-60
BLOOD MUSIC [EP], Earthling, 96-69
BLOOD OF EDEN, Peter Gabriel, 93-43
BLOOD ON THE DANCE FLOOR, Michael Jackson, 97-1
THE BLOOD THAT MOVES THE BODY, A-Ha, 88-25
BLOODNOK'S ROCK'N'ROLL CALL, Goons featuring Major Dennis Bloodnok, 43RD Deserters (Rtd.), with Roland Rockcake and his Wholly Rollers directed by Maestro Ponke, 56-3
BLOODSHOT EYES, Millie, 65-48
BLOODSPORTS FOR ALL, Carter – The Unstoppable Sex Machine, 91-48
BLOODY LUXURY, Whitesnake, 82-34
BLOODY MARY (from SNAKE BITE [EP]), David Coverdale's Whitesnake, 78-61
A BLOSSOM FELL:
Dickie Valentine, 55-9
Nat 'King' Cole, 55-3
Ronnie Hilton, 55-10
BLOSSOMS FALLING, Ooberman, 99-39
BLOW AWAY, George Harrison, 79-51
BLOW THE HOUSE DOWN, Living In A Box, 89-10
BLOW THE HOUSE DOWN, Wee Papa Girl Rappers, 89-65
BLOW UP THE OUTSIDE WORLD, Soundgarden, 96-40
BLOW YA MIND, Lock 'N' Load, 00-6
BLOW YOUR MIND, Jamiroquai, 93-12
BLOW YOUR WHISTLE, DJ Duke, 94-15
BLOWING IN THE WIND:
Peter, Paul and Mary, 63-13
Stevie Wonder *, 66-36
BLOWING WILD (THE BALLAD OF BLACK GOLD), Frankie Laine (Carl Fischer: Piano), 54-2
BLUE, Fine Young Cannibals, 85-41
BLUE, Verve, 93-69
BLUE, Way Out West, 97-41
BLUE, Symposium, 98-48
BLUE, Leann Rimes, 98-23
BLUE ANGEL, Roy Orbison, 60-11
BLUE ANGEL, Gene Pitney, 74-39
BLUE ANGELS, Pras, 98-6
BLUE BAYOU:
Roy Orbison, 63-3
Linda Ronstadt, 78-35
BLUE BLUE HEARTACHE, Johnny Duncan and the Blue Grass Boys, 57-27
BLUE CHRISTMAS:
Elvis Presley with the Jordanaires, 64-11
Shakin' Stevens (from The Shakin' Stevens [EP]), 82-2
BLUE [DA BA DEE], Eiffel 65, 99-39, 99-1
BLUE DAY, Suggs and Co. featuring The Chelsea Team, 97-22
BLUE EMOTION, Fiat Lux, 84-59
BLUE-EYED BOY, Al Saxon, 60-39
BLUE EYES, Don Partridge, 68-3
BLUE EYES, Elton John, 82-8
BLUE EYES, Wedding Present, 92-26
BLUE FEAR, Armin, 98-45
BLUE FLOWERS, Dr. Octagon, 96-66
BLUE FOR YOU, Wet Wet Wet, 93-38
BLUE GIRL, Bruisers, 63-31
BLUE GUITAR, Justin Hayward and John Lodge, 75-8
BLUE HAT FOR A BLUE DAY, Nick Heyward, 83-14
BLUE HOTEL, Chris Isaak, 91-17
BLUE IS THE COLOUR, Chelsea Football Team, 72-5
BLUE JEAN, David Bowie, 84-6
BLUE LIGHT, RED LIGHT (SOMEONE'S THERE), Harry Connick, Jr., 91-54
BLUE LOVE (CALL MY NAME), Dna featuring Joe Nye, 92-66
BLUE MONDAY, Fats Domino, 57-23
BLUE MONDAY, New Order, 83-9, 88-3, 95-17
BLUE MOON:
Elvis Presley, 56-9
Marcels, 61-1
Showaddywaddy, 80-32
John Alford, 96-9
BLUE MORNING, BLUE DAY, Foreigner, 79-45
BLUE PETER, Mike Oldfield, 79-19
BLUE RIVER, Elvis Presley, 66-22
BLUE ROOM, Orb, 92-8
THE BLUE ROOM, T-Empo featuring Doreen Edwards, 96-71
BLUE SAVANNAH, Erasure, 90-3
BLUE SKIES, John Dummer and Helen April, 82-54
BLUE SKIES, Jets, 83-53
BLUE SKIES, BT featuring Tori Amos, 96-26
BLUE SKIES, Longpigs, 99-21
BLUE SKY MINE, Midnight Oil, 90-66
BLUE STAR (THE "MEDIC" THEME):
Cyril Stapleton and his Orchestra featuring Julie Dawn, 55-2
Charlie Applewhite with Victor Young and his Orchestra and Chorus, 55-20
Ron Goodwin and his Concert Orchestra, 55-20
BLUE SUEDE SHOES:
Carl Perkins, 56-10
Elvis Presley, 56-9
BLUE TANGO, Ray Martin and his Concert Orchestra, 52-8
BLUE TOMORROW, Chelsea and Co, 00-22
BLUE TURNS TO GREY, Cliff Richard and the Shadows, 66-15
BLUE VELVET, Bobby Vinton, 90-2
BLUE WATER, Fields Of The Nephilim, 87-75
BLUE WEEK-END, Karl Denver, 62-33
BLUE WORLD, Moody Blues, 83-35
BLUEBEARD, Cocteau Twins, 94-33
BLUEBELL POLKA, Jimmy Shand and his Band, 55-20
BLUEBERRY HILL:
Fats Domino, 56-6, 76-41
John Barry Orchestra, 60-34
BLUEBIRDS OVER THE MOUNTAIN, Beach Boys, 68-33
BLUEBOTTLE, POB featuring DJ Patrick Reid, 99-74
THE BLUEBOTTLE BLUES, Goons with Maurice Ponke and his Orchestre Fromage, 56-4
BLUEJEAN BOP, Gene Vincent and his Blue Caps, 56-16
BLUER THAN BLUE, Rolf Harris, 69-30
THE BLUES BAND [EP], Blues Band, 80-68
BLUES FROM A GUN, Jesus And Mary Chain, 89-32
BLUETONIC, Bluetones, 95-19
BLURRED, Pianoman, 96-6
BO DIDDLEY, Buddy Holly, 63-4
THE BOAT THAT I ROW, Lulu, 67-6
BOAT TO BOLIVIA, Martin Stephenson and the Daintees, 86-70
BOBBY'S GIRL, Susan Maughan with Wally Stott and his Orchestra and Chorus, 62-3
BOBBY TOMORROW, Bobby Vee with the Johnny Mann Singers, 63-21
BODY, Funky Green Dogs, 99-46
BODY AND SOUL, Sisters Of Mercy, 84-46
BODY AND SOUL, Mai Tai, 85-9
BODY AND SOUL, Anita Baker, 94-48
BODY BUMPIN' YIPPIE-YI-YO, Public Announcement, 98-38
THE BODY ELECTRIC, Rush, 84-56
BODY GROOVE, Architechs featuring Nana, 00-3
BODY IN MOTION, Atlantic Ocean, 94-15
BODY LANGUAGE, Detroit Spinners, 80-40
BODY LANGUAGE, Dooleys, 80-46
BODY LANGUAGE, Queen, 82-25
BODY LANGUAGE, Adventures Of Stevie V, 90-29
THE BODY MOVIN', Beastie Boys, 98-15
BODY MUSIC, Strikers, 81-45
BODY ROCK, Original Motion Picture Soundtrack "Body Rock" vocal: Maria Vidal, 85-11
BODY ROCK, Shimon and Andy C, 01-58
BODY ROCKIN', Errol Brown, 87-51
THE BODY SHINE [EP] + lead track title, Billy Hendrix, 98-55
BODY TALK, Imagination, 81-4
BODY II BODY, Samantha Mumba, 00-5
BODY WORK, Hot Streak, 83-19
BODYHEAT, James Brown, 77-36
BODYROCK, Moby, 99-38
BODYROCK, Tymes 4, 01-23
BODYSHAKIN', 911, 97-3
THE BOG-EYED JOG, Ray Moore, 87-61
BOHEMIAN LIKE YOU, Dandy Warhols, 00-42, 01-5
BOHEMIAN RHAPSODY:
Queen, 75-1, 91-1
Bad News, 87-44
Rolf Harris, 96-50
Braids, 96-21
THE BOILER, Rhoda with the Special A.K.A., 82-35
BOILER, Limp Bizkit, 01-18
BOING!, Wedding Present, 92-19
BOLERO (from THE MUSIC OF TORVILL AND DEAN [EP]), Michael Reed Orchestra, 84-9
THE BOLL WEEVIL SONG, Brook Benton, 61-30

BREAKAWAY, Tracey Ullman, 83-4
BREAKAWAY, Donna Summer, 91-49
BREAKAWAY, Kim Appleby, 93-56
BREAKAWAY, ZZ Top, 94-60
BREAKBEAT ERA, Breakbeat Era, 98-38
BREAKDANCE PARTY, Break Machine, 84-9
BREAKDOWN (track from SPIRAL SCRATCH [EP]), Buzzcocks with Howard Devoto, 79-31
BREAKDOWN, One Dove, 93-24
BREAKDOWN, Double Six, 99-59
BREAKFAST, Associates, 85-49
BREAKFAST AT TIFFANY'S, Deep Blue Something, 96-1
BREAKFAST IN AMERICA, Supertramp, 79-9
BREAKFAST IN BED:
Sheila Hylton, 79-57
UB40 with Chrissie Hynde, 88-6
BREAKFAST ON PLUTO, Don Partridge, 69-26
BREAKIN' AWAY, Kim Wilde, 95-43
BREAKIN' DOWN, Skid Row, 95-48
BREAKIN' DOWN (SUGAR SAMBA), Julia and Company, 84-15
BREAKIN' DOWN THE WALLS OF HEARTACHE, Bandwagon, 68-4
BREAKIN' IN A BRAND NEW BROKEN HEART, Connie Francis, 61-12
BREAKIN' . . . THERE'S NO STOPPING US, Ollie and Jerry, 84-5
BREAKIN' UP BREAKIN' DOWN, Wild Weekend, 89-74
BREAKIN' UP IS BREAKIN' MY HEART, Roy Orbison, 66-22
BREAKING AWAY, Jaki Graham, 86-16
BREAKING GLASS [EP] + lead track title, David Bowie, 78-54
BREAKING HEARTS (AIN'T WHAT IT USED TO BE), Elton John, 85-59
BREAKING POINT, Bourgie Bourgie, 84-48
BREAKING THE GIRL, Red Hot Chili Peppers, 92-41
BREAKING THE LAW, Judas Priest, 80-12
BREAKING UP IS HARD TO DO:
Neil Sedaka, 62-7, 72-19
Partridge Family starring Shirley Jones – featuring David Cassidy, 72-3
BREAKING UP MY HEART, Shakin' Stevens, 85-14
BREAKING US IN TWO, Joe Jackson, 83-59
BREAKOUT, Swing Out Sister, 86-4
BREAKOUT, Foo Fighters, 00-29
THE BREAKS, Kurtis Blow, 80-47
BREAKTHRU', Queen, 89-7
BREATH OF LIFE, Erasure, 92-8
BREATHE, Maria McKee, 91-59
BREATHE, Midge Ure, 96-70
BREATHE, Prodigy, 96-1
BREATHE, Kylie Minogue, 98-14
BREATHE, Faith Hill, 00-33, 01-36
BREATHE, Blue Amazon, 00-73
BREATHE, Science Dept. featuring Erire, 01-64
BREATHE (A LITTLE DEEPER), Blameless, 96-27
BREATHE A SIGH, Def Leppard, 96-43
BREATHE AGAIN, Toni Braxton, 94-2
BREATHE AND STOP, Q-Tip, 00-12
BREATHE LIFE INTO ME (RADIO REMIX), Mica Paris, 88-26
BREATHING, Kate Bush, 80-16
BREATHING, North and South, 97-27
BREATHING IS E-ZEE, E-Zee Possee featuring Tara Newley, 91-72
BREATHLESS, Jerry Lee Lewis, 58-8
BREATHLESS, Corrs, 00-1
THE BREEZE AND I (ANDALUCIA):
Caterina Valente – Werner Muller and the Rias Dance Orchestra, 55-5
Fentones, 62-48
BRIAN WILSON (2000), Barenaked Ladies, 99-73
BRICK, Ben Folds Five, 98-26
BRICK HOUSE, Commodores, 77 32
THE BRICK TRACK VERSUS GITTY UP, Saltnpepa, 99-22
BRICK WALL (from WATERY, DOMESTIC [EP]), Pavement, 92-58
BRIDESHEAD THEME, Geoffrey Burgon, 81-48
BRIDGE, Orange Juice, 84-67
THE BRIDGE, Cactus World News, 86-74
BRIDGE, Queensryche, 95-40
THE BRIDGE OF SIGHS, David Whitfield, 53-9
BRIDGE OVER TROUBLED WATER:
Simon and Garfunkel, 70-1
Linda Clifford, 79-28
P.J.B. featuring Hannah and her Sisters, 91-21
BRIDGE TO YOUR HEART, Wax, 87-12
BRIDGET THE MIDGET (THE QUEEN OF THE BLUES), Ray Stevens, 71-2
BRIGHT EYES:
Art Garfunkel, 79-1
Stephen Gately, 00-3
THE BRIGHT LIGHT, Tanya Donelly, 97-64
BRIGHT SIDE OF LIFE, Tenor Fly, 95-51
BRIGHT SIDE OF THE ROAD, Van Morrison, 79-63
BRIGHT YELLOW GUN, Throwing Muses, 94-51
BRIGHTER DAY, Kelly Llorenna, 96-43
BRIGHTEST STAR, Drizabone, 94-45
BRILLIANT DISGUISE, Bruce Springsteen, 87-20
BRILLIANT FEELING, Full Monty Allstars featuring T.J. Davis, 96-72
BRILLIANT MIND, Furniture, 86-21
BRIMFUL OF ASHA, Cornershop, 97-60, 98-1
BRING A LITTLE WATER, SYLVIE, Lonnie Donegan and his Skiffle Group, 56-7
BRING 'EM ALL IN, Mike Scott, 95-56
BRING FORTH THE GUILLOTINE, Silver Bullet, 89-70, 90-45
BRING IT ALL BACK, S Club 7, 99-1
BRING IT ALL HOME, Gerry Rafferty, 80-54
BRING IT BACK AGAIN, Stray Cats, 89-64
BRING IT BACK 2 LUV, Project featuring Gerideau, 94-65
BRING IT DOWN! (THIS INSANE THING), Redskins, 85-33
BRING IT ON, N'Dea Davenport, 98-52
BRING IT ON, Gomez, 99-21
BRING IT ON . . . BRING IT ON, James Brown, 83-45
BRING IT ON DOWN, Jesus Jones, 89-46
BRING IT ON HOME, Urban Cookie Collective, 94-56
BRING IT ON HOME TO ME:
Animals, 65-7
Rod Stewart, 74-7
BRING ME CLOSER, Altered Images, 83-29
BRING ME EDELWEISS, Edelweiss, 89-5
BRING ME LOVE, Andrea Mendez, 96-44
BRING ME YOUR CUP, UB40, 93-24
BRING MY FAMILY BACK, Faithless, 99-14
BRING ON THE DANCING HORSES, Echo and the Bunnymen, 85-21
BRING THE FAMILY BACK, Billy Paul, 79-51
BRING THE NOISE:
Public Enemy, 88-32
Anthrax featuring Chuck D from Public Enemy, 91-14
BRING UP THE MIC SOME MORE, Ragga Twins, 92-65
BRING YOUR DAUGHTER . . . TO THE SLAUGHTER, Iron Maiden, 91-1
BRINGING ON BACK THE GOOD TIMES, Love Affair, 69-9
BRISTOL STOMP, Late Show, 79-40
BRITE SIDE, Deborah Harry, 89-59
BRITISH HUSTLE, Hi Tension, 78-8
THE BRITISH WAY OF LIFE, Chords, 80-54
THE BRITS 1990 (DANCE MEDLEY) [M], Various Artists, 90-2
BRITTANNIA RAG, Winifred Atwell and her Other Piano with Rhythm, 52-5
BROKE, Beta Band, 01-30
BROKE AWAY, Wet Wet Wet, 89-19
BROKEN ARROW, Waterfront, 89-63
BROKEN ARROW, Rod Stewart, 91-54, 92-41
BROKEN DOLL, Tommy Bruce and the Bruisers, 60-36
BROKEN DOWN ANGEL, Nazareth, 73-9
BROKEN ENGLISH, Sunscreem, 93-13
A BROKEN HEART CAN MEND, Alexander O'Neal, 86-53
BROKEN HEART (THIRTEEN VALLEYS), Big Country, 88-47
BROKEN-HEARTED MELODY, Sarah Vaughan, 59-7
BROKEN HOMES, Tricky featuring Polly Jean Harvey, 98-25
BROKEN LAND, Adventures, 88-20
BROKEN NOSE, Catherine Wheel, 98-48
BROKEN STONES, Paul Weller, 95-20
BROKEN WINGS:
Stargazers, 53-1
Art and Dotty Todd, 53-6
Dickie Valentine, 53-12
BROKEN WINGS:
Mr. Mister, 85-4
Network, 92-46
THE BROKEN YEARS, Hipsway, 85-72
BROKENHEARTED, Ken Dodd, 70-15
BRONTOSAURUS, Move, 70-7
BROOKLYN BEATS, Scotti Deep, 97-67
BROOKLYN-QUEENS, 3RD Bass, 90-61
BROTHER, C C S, 72-25
BROTHER, Urban Species, 94-40
BROTHER BRIGHT, Ca Va Ca Va, 83-65
BROTHER LOUIE, Hot Chocolate, 73-7
BROTHER LOUIE, Modern Talking, 86-4
BROTHER LOUIE, Quireboys, 93-31
BROTHER OF MINE, Anderson Bruford Wakeman Howe, 89-63
BROTHERS AND SISTERS, 2 Funky 2 Starring Kathryn Dion, 93-56, 96-36
BROTHERS GONNA WORK IT OUT, Public Enemy, 90-46
BROTHERS IN ARMS, Dire Straits, 85-16
BROWN EYED HANDSOME MAN:
Buddy Holly, 63-3
Paul McCartney, 99-42
BROWN GIRL IN THE RING, Boney M, 78-2, 93-38
BROWN PAPER BAG, Roni Size Reprazent, 97-20
BROWN SKIN, India.Arie, 01-29
BROWN SUGAR, D'Angelo, 95-24
BROWN SUGAR, Rolling Stones, 71-2, 84-58
BRUISE PRISTINE, Placebo, 97-14
BRUSHED, Paul Weller, 97-14
BRUTAL-8-E, Altern 8, 92-43
BUBBLE, Fluke, 94-37
BUBBLING HOT, Pato Banton with Ranking Roger, 95-15
BUCK ROGERS, Feeder, 01-5
THE BUCKET OF WATER SONG, Four Bucketeers, 80-26
BUDDHA OF SUBURBIA, David Bowie (featuring Lenny Kravitz on Guitar), 93-35
BUDDY, De La Soul featuring The Jungle Brothers, Monie Love, Queen Latifah and Q-Tip, 89-8
BUDDY HOLLY, Weezer, 95-12
BUDDY X:
Neneh Cherry, 93-35
Dreem Teem 'V' Neneh Cherry, 99-15
BUFFALO BILL'S LAST SCRATCH, Barron Knights, 83-49
BUFFALO GALS:
Malcolm McLaren and the World's Famous Supreme Team, 82-9
Malcolm McLaren and the World Famous Supreme Team Versus Rakim and Roger Sanchez, 98-65
BUFFALO SOLDIER, Bob Marley and the Wailers, 83-4
BUFFALO STANCE, Neneh Cherry, 88-3
THE BUG, Dire Straits, 92-67
BUG A BOO, Destiny's Child, 99-9
BUG IN THE BASSBIN, Innerzone Orchestra, 96-68
BUG POWDER DUST, Bomb The Bass featuring Justin Warfield, 94-24
BUGGIN, True Steppers featuring Dane Bowers from Another Level, 00-6
BUGS, Hepburn, 99-14
BUILD, Housemartins, 87-15
BUILD, Innocence, 92-72
BUILD ME UP BUTTERCUP, Foundations, 68-2, 98-71
BUILD YOUR LOVE (ON A STRONG FOUNDATION), Johnnie Ray with Ray Conniff, 57-17
BUILDING THE CITY OF LIGHT, Mike Scott, 95-60
BULGARIAN, Travel, 99-67
BULL IN THE HEATHER, Sonic Youth, 94-24
BULLDOG NATION, Kevin Kennedy, 00-70
BULLET, Fluke, 95-23
BULLET COMES, Charlatans, 95-32
BULLET IN THE GUN, Planet Perfecto, 99-15, 00-7
BULLET IN THE HEAD, Rage Against The Machine, 93-16
BULLET WITH BUTTERFLY WINGS, Smashing Pumpkins, 95-20
BULLETPROOF!, Pop Will Eat Itself, 92-24
BULLFROG, G.T.O., 91-72
BULLITPROOF, Breakbeat Era, 00-65
BULLITT, Lalo Schifrin, 97-36
BULLS ON PARADE, Rage Against The Machine, 96-8

CAN'T DO NUTTIN' FOR YA MAN, Public Enemy, 90-53
CAN'T FAKE THE FEELING, Geraldine Hunt, 80-44
CAN'T FIGHT THE MOONLIGHT – THEME FROM 'COYOTE UGLY', Leann Rimes, 00-1
CAN'T FIGHT THIS FEELING, Reo Speedwagon, 85-16
CAN'T FORGET YOU, Sonia, 89-17
CAN'T GET ALONG WITHOUT YOU, Frankie Vaughan with Ray Ellis and his Orchestra and Chorus, 58-11
CAN'T GET ANY HARDER, James Brown, 93-59
CAN'T GET BY, Slamm, 95-47
CAN'T GET BY WITHOUT YOU, Real Thing, 76-2, 86-6
CAN'T GET ENOUGH, Bad Company, 74-15
CAN'T GET ENOUGH, Soulsearcher, 99-8
CAN'T GET ENOUGH, Suede, 99-23
CAN'T GET ENOUGH OF YOU, Eddy Grant, 81-13
CAN'T GET ENOUGH OF YOUR LOVE, Darts, 79-43
CAN'T GET ENOUGH OF YOUR LOVE, BABE:
Barry White, 74-8
KWS *, 93-71
Taylor Dayne *, 93-14
CAN'T GET OUT OF BED, Charlatans, 94-24
CAN'T GET OUT OF MY HEAD (from THE ELO EP [EP]), Electric Light Orchestra, 78-34
CAN'T GET THE BEST OF ME, Cypress Hill, 00-35
CAN'T GET USED TO LOSING YOU:
Andy Williams, 63-2
Beat, 83-3
Colour Girl, 00-31
CAN'T GET YOU OFF MY MIND, Lenny Kravitz, 96-54
CAN'T GET YOU OUT OF MY HEAD, Kylie, 01-1
CAN'T GET YOU OUT OF MY THOUGHTS, Dum Dums, 00-18
CAN'T GIVE ME LOVE, Pepsi and Shirlie, 87-58
CAN'T GIVE YOU ANYTHING (BUT MY LOVE), Stylistics, 75-1
CAN'T GIVE YOU MORE, Status Quo, 91-37
CAN'T HAPPEN HERE, Rainbow, 81-20
CAN'T HAVE YOU, Lyte Funkie Ones, 99-54
CAN'T HELP FALLING IN LOVE:
Elvis Presley with the Jordanaires, 62-1
Andy Williams, 70-3
Stylistics, 76-4
Lick The Tins, 86-42
UB40 *, 93-1
CAN'T HELP IT, Happy Clappers, 96-18
CAN'T HELP MYSELF, Linx, 81-55
CAN'T I, Nat "King" Cole and Billy May and his Orchestra, 53-6
CAN'T KEEP IT IN, Cat Stevens, 72-13
CAN'T KEEP LIVING THIS WAY, Rootjoose, 97-73
CAN'T KEEP ME SILENT, Angelic, 01-12
CAN'T KEEP THIS FEELING IN, Cliff Richard, 98-10
CAN'T KNOCK THE HUSTLE, Jay-Z featuring Mary J. Blige, 97-30
CAN'T LET GO, Earth, Wind And Fire, 79-46
CAN'T LET GO, Mariah Carey, 92-20
CAN'T LET HER GO, Boyz II Men, 98-23
CAN'T LET YOU GO, Barry Ryan, 72-32
CAN'T LET YOU GO, Rainbow, 83-43
CAN'T LIVE WITH YOU, CAN'T LIVE WITHOUT YOU, Mindbenders, 66-28
CAN'T LIVE WITHOUT YOU, Scorpions, 82-63
CAN'T NOBODY HOLD ME DOWN, Puff Daddy (featuring Mase), 97-19
CAN'T SAY 'BYE, Stone Free, 87-73
CAN'T SAY HOW MUCH I LOVE YOU, Demis Roussos, 76-35
CAN'T SEE ME, Ian Brown, 98-21
CAN'T SET RULES ABOUT LOVE, Adam Ant, 90-47
CAN'T SHAKE LOOSE, Agnetha Faltskog, 83-63
CAN'T SHAKE THE FEELING, Big Fun, 89-8
CAN'T SMILE WITHOUT YOU:
Barry Manilow, 78-43
James Buller, 99-51
CAN'T STAND IT, Wilco, 99-67
CAN'T STAND LOSING YOU:
Police, 78-42
Police, 95-27
CAN'T STAY AWAY FROM YOU, Gloria Estefan and Miami Sound Machine, 89-7
CAN'T STOP, After 7, 90-54
CAN'T STOP LOVIN' YOU, Van Halen, 95-33
CAN'T STOP RUNNING, Space Monkey, 83-53
CAN'T STOP THE MUSIC, Village People, 80-11
CAN'T STOP THESE THINGS, China Drum, 96-65
CAN'T STOP THIS FEELING, Rhythm N Bass, 93-59
CAN'T STOP THIS THING WE STARTED, Bryan Adams, 91-12
CAN'T TAKE MY EYES OFF YOU:
Andy Williams, 68-5
Boystown Gang, 82-4
CAN'T TAKE NO MORE, Soup Dragons, 87-65
CAN'T TAKE YOUR LOVE, Pauline Henry, 94-30
CAN'T TRUSS IT, Public Enemy, 91-22
CAN'T WAIT ANOTHER MINUTE, Five Star, 86-7
CAN'T WAIT TO BE WITH YOU, Jazzy Jeff and the Fresh Prince, 94-29
CAN'T YOU HEAR MY HEART, Danny Rivers, 61-36
CAN'T YOU HEAR MY HEARTBEAT?, Goldie and the Gingerbreads, 65-25
CAN'T YOU HEAR THE BEAT OF A BROKEN HEART, Iain Gregory, 62-39
CAN'T YOU SEE, Total featuring The Notorious B.I.G., 95-43
CAN'T YOU SEE THAT SHE'S MINE, Dave Clark Five, 64-10
(CAN'T YOU) TRIP LIKE I DO, Filter and the Crystal Method, 97-39
CANCER FOR THE CURE, Eels, 98-60
CANDIDA, Dawn, 71-9
CANDIDATE FOR LOVE, T.S. Monk, 81-58
CANDLE IN THE WIND:
Elton John, 74-11
Elton John, 88-5
Elton John *, 97-1
CANDLEFIRE, Dawn Of The Replicants, 98-52
CANDLELAND (THE SECOND COMING), Ian McCulloch featuring Elizabeth Fraser, 90-75
CANDLELIGHT, Six by Seven, 98-70
CANDLES, Alex Reece, 96-33
CANDY, Cameo, 86-27
CANDY, Iggy Pop, 90-67
CANDY, Mandy Moore, 00-6
CANDY, Ash, 01-20
CANDY EVERYBODY WANTS, 10,000 Maniacs, 93-47
CANDY GIRL, New Edition, 83-1
CANDY GIRL, Babybird, 97-14
CANDY MAN, Brian Poole and the Tremeloes, 64-6
CANDY MAN, Mary Jane Girls, 83-60
CANDY RAIN, Soul For Real, 95-23
CANDYBAR EXPRESS, Love and Money, 86-56
CANDYMAN, Siouxsie and the Banshees, 86-34
CANED AND UNABLE, Hi-Gate, 00-12
CANNED HEAT, Jamiroquai, 99-4
CANNIBALS, Mark Knopfler, 96-42
CANNONBALL, Duane Eddy, his "Twangy" Guitar and the Rebels, 59-22
CANNONBALL [EP] + lead track title, Breeders, 93-40
CANTALOOP (FLIP FANTASIA), US3 featuring Rahsaan, 93-23
CANTGETAMAN, CANTGETAJOB (LIFE'S A BITCH!), Sister Bliss with Colette, 94-31
CANTO DELLA TERRA, Andrea Bocelli, 99-25, 00-24
CANTON (LIVE), Japan, 83-42
CANTONESE BOY, Japan, 82-24
CAPSTICK COMES HOME, Tony Capstick-Carlton Main/Frickley Colliery Band, 81-3
CAPTAIN BEAKY, Keith Michell Captain Beaky and his Band, 80-5
CAPTAIN DREAD, Dreadzone, 95-49
CAPTAIN KREMMEN (RETRIBUTION), Kenny Everett and Mike Vickers, 77-32
THE CAPTAIN OF HER HEART, Double, 86-8
CAPTAIN OF YOUR SHIP, Reparata and the Delrons, 68-13
CAPTAIN SCARLET THEME, Barry Gray Orchestra featuring Keyboards by Peter Beckett, 86-53
CAPTURE THE HEART [EP], Runrig, 90-49
CAR BOOT SALE, Bill, 93-73
CAR 67, Driver 67, 78-7
CAR SONG, Madder Rose, 94-68
CAR WASH:
Rose Royce, 76-9, 88-20
Gwen Dickey, 90-72
Rose Royce featuring Gwen Dickey, 98-18
CARA MIA, David Whitfield with Mantovani and his Orchestra and Chorus, 54-1
CARAVAN, Duane Eddy, 61-42
CARAVAN, Inspiral Carpets, 91-30
CARAVAN OF LOVE:
Isley Jasper Isley, 85-52
Housemartins, 86-1
CARAVAN SONG, Song from the film "Caravans" featuring Barbara Dickson, 80-41
CARDBOY KING, Salad, 97-65
CARDIAC ARREST, Madness, 82-14
CAREFUL, Horse, 90-52, 97-44
CARELESS HANDS, Des O'Connor with the Mike Sammes Singers and Alyn Ainsworth and his Orchestra, 67-6
CARELESS LOVE, Swimming with Sharks, 88-63
CARELESS MEMORIES, Duran Duran, 81-37
CARELESS WHISPER:
George Michael, 84-1
Sarah Washington, 93-45
CARIBBEAN BLUE, Enya, 91-13
THE CARIBBEAN DISCO SHOW [M], Lobo, 81-8
CARIBBEAN HONEYMOON, Frank Weir, 60-42
CARIBBEAN QUEEN (NO MORE LOVE ON THE RUN), Billy Ocean, 84-6
CARMEN QUEASY, Maxim, 00-33
CARNATION, Liam Gallagher and Steve Cradock, 99-6
CARNAVAL DE PARIS, Dario G, 98-5
CARNIVAL, Cardigans, 95-35
CARNIVAL [EP], Lionrock, 93-34
CARNIVAL IN HEAVEN, Malandra Burrows, 97-49
THE CARNIVAL IS OVER, Seekers, 65-1
CAROLINA MOON, Connie Francis, 58-1
CAROLINE:
Status Quo, 73-5
Status Quo, 82-13
CAROLINE, Kirsty MacColl, 95-58
CAROUSEL [LP], Various Artists: Films – Original Soundtracks, 56-26
THE CAROUSEL WALTZ, Ray Martin, 56-24
CARRIE, Cliff Richard, 80-4
CARRIE, Europe, 87-22
CARRIE ANNE, Hollies, 67-3
CARROT ROPE, Pavement, 99-27
CARRY ME HOME, Gloworm, 94-9
CARRY ON, Martha Wash, 92-74, 93-49, 97-49
CARRY ON, Spacehog, 98-43
CARRY ON, Donna Summer and Giorgio Moroder, 98-65
CARRY ON WAYWARD SON, Kansas, 78-51
CARRY THE BLAME, River City People, 90-13
CARRYING A TORCH, Tom Jones, 91-57
CARS:
Gary Numan, 79-1, 87-16, 93-53, 96-17
Fear Factory, 99-57
CARS AND GIRLS, Prefab Sprout, 88-44
CARTE BLANCHE, Veracocha, 99-22
CARTOON HEROES, Aqua, 00-7
CARTROUBLE, Adam and the Ants, 81-33
CASABLANCA, Kenny Ball and his Jazzmen, 63-21
CASANOVA, Petula Clark with the Henry Mayer Orchestra, 63-39
CASANOVA:
Coffee, 80-13
Baby D, 94-67
CASANOVA:
Levert, 87-9
Ultimate Kaos, 97-24, 98-29
CASCADE, Future Sound Of London, 93-27
CASE OF THE EX, Mya, 01-3
CASINO ROYALE, Herb Alpert and the Tijuana Brass, 67-27
CASINO ROYALE, True Playaz present DJ Zinc, 01-58
CASSIUS 99, Cassius, 99-7
CAST YOUR FATE TO THE WIND, Sounds Orchestral, 64-5
CASTE SYSTEM (from NUFF VIBES [EP]), Apache Indian, 93-5
CASTLE ROCK, Bluetones, 96-7
CASTLES IN SPAIN, Armoury Show, 84-69
CASTLES IN THE AIR, Don McLean, 82-47
CASTLES IN THE AIR, Colourfield, 85-51
CASTLES IN THE SAND, Thunder, 95-30
CASTLES IN THE SKY, Ian Van Dahl, 01-3
CASUAL SUB (BURNING SPEAR), ETA, 97-28, 98-28
CAT AMONG THE PIGEONS, Bros, 88-2
THE CAT CAME BACK, Sonny James, 56-30
THE CAT CREPT IN, Mud, 74-2
CAT PEOPLE (PUTTING OUT FIRE), David Bowie, 82-26

CHILDREN, EMF, 91-19
CHILDREN:
Robert Miles, 96-2
Tilt, 99-51
CHILDREN OF PARADISE, Boney M, 81-66
CHILDREN OF THE NIGHT, Richard Marx, 90-54
CHILDREN OF THE NIGHT (QFT REMIXES), Nakatomi, 98-47
CHILDREN OF THE REVOLUTION:
T.Rex, 72-2
Baby Ford, 89-53
Unitone Rockers featuring Steel, 93-60
CHILDREN SAY, Level 42, 87-22
A CHILD'S PRAYER, Hot Chocolate, 75-7
CHILI BOM BOM, Temperance Seven vocal refrain by Mr. Paul MacDowell, 61-28
CHILL OUT (THINGS GONNA CHANGE), John Lee Hooker, 95-45
CHILL TO THE PANIC, Deep C featuring Dezz The Dezz and Shola, 91-73
CHILLIN', Modjo, 01-12
CHILLIN' OUT, Curtis Hairston, 86-57
CHIME, Orbital, 90-17
CHIME CHIME (from MUTATIONS [EP]), Orbital, 92-24
CHINA, Tori Amos, 92-51
CHINA DOLL, Slim Whitman, 55-15
CHINA DOLL, Julian Cope, 89-53
CHINA GIRL, David Bowie, 83-2
CHINA IN YOUR HAND, T'Pau, 87-1
CHINA TEA, Russ Conway, 59-5
CHINATOWN, Move, 71-23
CHINATOWN, Thin Lizzy, 80-21
CHINESE BAKERY, Auteurs, 94-42
CHINESE BURN, Heavy Stereo, 96-45
THE CHINESE WAY, Level 42, 83-24
CHIQUITITA, Abba, 79-2
CHIRPY CHIRPY CHEEP CHEEP:
Middle Of The Road, 71-1
Mac and Katie Kissoon, 71-41
THE CHISELLERS, Fall, 96-60
CHOC ICE, Long And The Short, 64-49
CHOCOLATE, Y?N-Vee, 94-65
CHOCOLATE BOX, Bros, 89-9
CHOCOLATE CAKE, Crowded House, 91-69
CHOCOLATE GIRL, Deacon Blue, 88-43
CHOCOLATE SALTY BALLS (P.S. I LOVE YOU), Chef, 98-1
CHOCOLATE SENSATION, Lenny Fontana and DJ Shorty, 00-39
CHOICE?, Blow Monkeys featuring Sylvia Tella, 89-22
CHOK THERE, Apache Indian, 93-30
CHOLI KE PEECHE, Bally Sagoo, 95-45
CHOOSE, Color Me Badd, 94-65
CHOOSE LIFE, PF Project featuring Ewan McGregor, 97-6
CHOOSE ME (RESCUE ME), Loose Ends, 84-59
CHOP SUEY, System Of A Down, 01-17
CHORUS, Erasure, 91-3
THE CHOSEN FEW, Dooleys, 79-7
CHRISTIAN, China Crisis, 83-12
CHRISTIANSANDS, Tricky, 96-36
CHRISTINE, Miss X, 63-37
CHRISTINE, Siouxsie and the Banshees, 80-22
CHRISTINE KEELER, Senseless Things, 94-56
CHRISTMAS ALPHABET, Dickie Valentine with Johnny Douglas and his Orchestra, 55-1
CHRISTMAS AND YOU, Dave King, 56-23
CHRISTMAS COUNTDOWN, Frank Kelly, 83-26, 84-54
THE CHRISTMAS [EP], Chris Rea, 88-53
CHRISTMAS IN BLOBBYLAND, Mr. Blobby, 95-36
CHRISTMAS IN DREADLAND, Judge Dread, 75-14
CHRISTMAS IN HOLLIS, Run D.M.C., 87-56
CHRISTMAS IN SMURFLAND, Father Abraham and the Smurfs, 78-19
CHRISTMAS ISLAND, Dickie Valentine with Johnny Douglas and his Orchestra, 56-8
A CHRISTMAS KISS, Daniel O'Donnell, 99-20
CHRISTMAS MEDLEY (SHORT VERSION) [M], Weekend, 85-47
CHRISTMAS ON 45 [M], Holly and the Ivys, 81-40
CHRISTMAS RAPPIN, Kurtis Blow, 79-30
CHRISTMAS RAPPING, Dizzy Heights, 82-49
CHRISTMAS SONG, Gilbert O'Sullivan, 74-12
THE CHRISTMAS SONG (CHESTNUTS ROASTING ON AN OPEN FIRE):
Alexander O'Neal, 88-30
Nat King Cole, 91-69
CHRISTMAS SPECTRE, Jingle Belles, 83-37
CHRISTMAS THROUGH YOUR EYES, Gloria Estefan, 92-8
CHRISTMAS TIME, Bryan Adams, 85-55
CHRISTMAS WILL BE JUST ANOTHER LONELY DAY, Brenda Lee, 64-29
CHRISTMAS WRAPPING, Waitresses, 82-45
CHRONOLOGIE PART 4, Jean Michel Jarre, 93-55, 93-56
CHUCK E.'S IN LOVE, Rickie Lee Jones, 79-18
CHUNG KUO (REVISITED), Addams and Gee, 91-72
CHURA LIYA, Bally Sagoo, 94-64
CHURCH OF FREEDOM, Amos, 95-54
CHURCH OF MOISE, Therapy?, 98-29
THE CHURCH OF THE HOLY SPOOK, Shane MacGowan and the Popes, 94-74
CHURCH OF THE POISON MIND, Culture Club, 83-2
CHURCH OF YOUR HEART, Roxette, 92-21
CIAO CIAO BAMBINA:
Marino Marini and his Quartet, 59-24
Domenico Modugno, 59-29
CIGARETTES AND ALCOHOL, Oasis, 94-7, 95-53, 96-38
CINDERELLA ROCKAFELLA, Esther and Abi Ofarim, 68-1
CINDY INCIDENTALLY, Faces, 73-2
CINDY, OH CINDY:
Eddie Fisher with Hugo Winterhalter's Orchestra and Chorus, 56-5
Tony Brent with Eric Jupp and his Orchestra, 56-16
Vince Martin and the Tarriers, 56-26
CINDY'S BIRTHDAY, Shane Fenton and the Fentones, 62-19
CIRCLE, Edie Brickell and New Bohemians, 89-74
THE CIRCLE, Ocean Colour Scene, 96-6
CIRCLE IN THE SAND, Belinda Carlisle, 88-4
CIRCLE OF LIFE, Elton John, 94-11
CIRCLE OF ONE, Oleta Adams, 91-73
CIRCLES, New Seekers, 72-4
CIRCLES, Saffron, 93-60
CIRCLES, Adam F, 97-20
CIRCLESQUARE, Wonder Stuff, 90-20
THE CIRCUS, Erasure, 87-6
CIRCUS, Lenny Kravitz, 95-54
CIRCUS, Eric Clapton, 98-39
CIRCUS GAMES, Skids, 80-32
CITIES IN DUST, Siouxsie and the Banshees, 85-21
THE CITY IS MINE, Jay-Z featuring Blackstreet, 98-38
CITY LIGHTS, David Essex, 76-24
CITYSONG, Luscious Jackson, 95-69
THE "CIVIL WAR" [EP] + lead track ttle, Guns N' Roses, 93 11
CLAIR, Gilbert O'Sullivan, 72-1
CLAIRE, Paul and Barry Ryan, 67-47
THE CLAIRVOYANT, Iron Maiden, 88-6
CLAP CLAP SOUND, Klaxons, 83-45
CLAP YOUR HANDS, Rocky Sharpe and the Replays, 82-54
CLAP YOUR HANDS, Camisra, 99-34
THE CLAPPING SONG:
Shirley Ellis, 65-6, 78-59
Belle Stars, 82-11
THE CLAPPING SONG [EP] + lead track title, Shirley Ellis, 78-59
CLARE, Fairground Attraction, 89-49
CLASH CITY ROCKERS, Clash, 78-35
CLASSIC, Adrian Gurvitz, 82-8
CLASSIC GIRL, Jane's Addiction, 91-60
CLASSICAL GAS:
Mason Williams, 68-9
Vanessa-Mae, 95-41
CLASSICAL MUDDLY [M], Portsmouth Sinfonia, 81-38
CLAUDETTE, Everly Brothers, 58-1
CLEAN, CLEAN, Buggles, 80-38
CLEAN UP YOUR OWN BACK YARD, Elvis Presley, 69-21
CLEMENTINE, Bobby Darin, 60-8
CLEMENTINE, Mark Owen, 97-3
CLEOPATRA'S CAT, Spin Doctors, 94-29
CLEOPATRA'S THEME, Cleopatra, 98-3
THE CLICHES ARE TRUE, Manchild featuring Kelly Jones, 00-60
CLIMB EV'RY MOUNTAIN, Shirley Bassey with Geoff Love and his Orchestra, 61-1
CLINT EASTWOOD, Gorillaz, 01-4
CLIPPED, Curve, 91-36
CLOAKING, Seafood, 01-71
CLOG DANCE, Violinski, 79-17
CLOSE . . . BUT, Echobelly, 94-59
CLOSE BUT NO CIGAR, Thomas Dolby, 92-22
CLOSE EVERY DOOR, Phillip Schofield, 92-27
CLOSE MY EYES FOREVER, Lita Ford (duet with Ozzy Osbourne), 89-47
CLOSE THE DOOR, Stargazers with Johnnie Gray and the Band Of The Day, 55-6
CLOSE THE DOOR, Teddy Pendergrass, 78-41
CLOSE TO ME, Cure, 85-24, 90-13
CLOSE TO PERFECTION, Miquel Brown, 85-63
CLOSE (TO THE EDIT), Art Of Noise, 84-8
CLOSE TO YOU, Maxi Priest, 90-7
CLOSE TO YOU, Brand New Heavies, 95-38
CLOSE TO YOU, Whigfield, 95-13
CLOSE TO YOU, Marti Pellow, 01-9
CLOSE TO YOUR HEART, JX, 97-18
CLOSE YOUR EYES, Tony Bennett, 55-18
CLOSED FOR BUSINESS (from SEVEN [EP]), Mansun, 97-10
CLOSER, Mr. Fingers, 92-50
CLOSER, Nine Inch Nails, 94-25
CLOSER, Liquid, 95-47
THE CLOSER I GET TO YOU, Roberta Flack with Donny Hathaway, 78-42
CLOSER THAN CLOSE, Rosie Gaines, 97-4
CLOSER THAN MOST, Beautiful South, 00-22
CLOSER TO ALL YOUR DREAMS (from DREAMS [EP]), Rhythm Quest, 92-45
CLOSER TO ME (REMIX), Five, 01-4
CLOSER TO THE HEART, Rush, 78-36
CLOSEST THING TO HEAVEN, Kane Gang, 84-12
CLOSEST THING TO HEAVEN, Lionel Richie, 98-26
CLOSING TIME, Deacon Blue, 91-42
CLOSING TIME, Semisonic, 99-25
CLOUD 8, Frazier Chorus, 90-52
CLOUD LUCKY SEVEN, Guy Mitchell with Mitch Miller and his Orchestra and Chorus, 53-2
CLOUD NINE, Temptations, 69-15
CLOUD 99 (SOLEADO), St. Andrews Chorale, 76-31
CLOUD #9, Bryan Adams, 99-6
CLOUDBURST, Don Lang with the Mairants-Langhorn Big Six, 55-16
CLOUDBURST, Niagra, 97-65
CLOUDBUSTING, Kate Bush, 85-20
CLOUDS, Source, 97-38
CLOUDS ACROSS THE MOON, Rah Band, 85-6
THE CLOUDS WILL SOON ROLL BY, Tony Brent, 58-20
CLOWN SHOES, Johnny Burnette, 62-35
CLUB AT THE END OF THE STREET, Elton John, 90-47
CLUB BIZARRE, U96, 96-70
CLUB COUNTRY, Associates, 82-13
CLUB FANTASTIC MEGAMIX [M], Wham!, 83-15
CLUB FOR LIFE '98, Chris and James, 98-66
CLUB LONELY, Groove Connektion 2, 98-54
CLUB TROPICANA, Wham!, 83-4
CLUBLAND, Elvis Costello and the Attractions, 80-60
CLUNK CLICK, Laurel and Hardy, 83-65
CLUTCH, Shea Seger, 01-47
C'MON, Millionaire Hippies, 94-59
C'MON AND GET MY LOVE, D Mob introducing Cathy Dennis, 89-15
C'MON BILLY, PJ Harvey, 95-29
C'MON CINCINNATI, Delakota featuring Rose Smith, 98-55
C'MON EVERY BEATBOX, Big Audio Dynamite, 86-51
C'MON EVERYBODY:
Eddie Cochran, 59-6, 86-14
Sex Pistols vocals: Sid Vicious, 79-3
C'MON KIDS, Boo Radleys, 96-18
C'MON LET'S GO, Girlschool, 81-42
C'MON MARIANNE, Grapefruit, 68-31
C'MON PEOPLE, Paul McCartney, 93-41
C'MON PEOPLE (WE'RE MAKING IT NOW), Richard Ashcroft, 00-21
CO-CO, Sweet, 71-2
COAST IS CLEAR, Curve, 91-34
COCK A DOODLE DO IT, Eggs On Legs, 95-42
COCKNEY TRANSLATION, Smiley Culture, 85-71
COCO JAMBOO, Mr. President, 97-8
COCOMOTION, El Coco, 78-31
COCONUT, Nilsson, 72-42
CODE OF LOVE, Mike Sarne, 63-29
CODE RED ('94 REMIX), Conquering Lion, 94-53

CODED LANGUAGE, Krust featuring Saul Williams, 99-66
COFFEE, Supersister, 00-16
COFFEE + TV, Blur, 99-11
THE COFFEE SONG, Frank Sinatra, 61-39
COGNOSCENTI VS INTELLIGENTSIA, Cuban Boys, 99-4
COISICH A RUIN (WALK MY BELOVED) [from A PRINCE AMONG ISLAND [EP]), Capercaillie, 92-39
COLD, Annie Lennox, 92-26
COLD, Tears For Fears, 93-72
COLD AS CHRISTMAS (IN THE MIDDLE OF THE YEAR), Elton John, 83-33
COLD AS ICE,
Foreigner, 78-24, 85-64
M.O.P., 01-4
COLD, COLD HEART, Midge Ure, 91-17
COLD COLD HEART, Wet Wet Wet, 94-20
COLD DAY IN HELL, Gary Moore, 92-24
COLD HEARTED, Paula Abdul, 90-46
COLD LOVE, Donna Summer, 81-44
COLD ROCK A PARTY (BAD BOY REMIX), MC Lyte, 97-15
COLD SHOULDER, Culture Club, 99-43
COLD SWEAT, Thin Lizzy, 83-27
COLD SWEAT, Sugarcubes, 88-56
COLD TURKEY, Plastic Ono Band, 69-14
COLD WORLD, Genius/Gza featuring D'Angelo and Inspektah Deck A.K.A. Rollie Fingers, 96-40
COLDCUT'S CHRISTMAS BREAK, Coldcut, 89-67
COLLETTE, Billy Fury, 60-9
COLOR OF MY SKIN, Swing 52, 95-60
THE COLOUR FIELD, Colour Field, 84-43
COLOUR MY LIFE, M People, 92-35
THE COLOUR OF LOVE, Billy Ocean, 88-65
COLOUR OF LOVE, Snap!, 91-54
THE COLOUR OF LOVE, Reese Project, 92-52, 94-55
THE COLOUR OF MY LOVE, Jefferson, 69-22
COLOUR THE WORLD, Sash!, 99-15
COLOURED KISSES, Martika, 92-41
COLOURS, Donovan, 65-4
THE COLOURS, Men They Couldn't Hang, 88-61
COLOURS FLY AWAY, Teardrop Explodes, 81-54
COLOURS OF THE WIND, Vanessa Williams, 95-21
COMA AROMA, Inaura, 96-57
THE COMANCHEROS, Lonnie Donegan, 62-14
COMBAT DANCING [EP], 4 Hero, 90-73
THE COMBINE HARVESTER (BRAND NEW KEY), Wurzels, 76-1, 01-39
COME, Martha Wash, 99-64
COME AGAIN, Truman and Wolff Feat. Steel Horses, 98-57
COME ALONG PLEASE, Bob Wallis and his Storyville Jazzmen, 62-33
COME AND GET IT, Badfinger, 70-4
COME AND GET ME, Cleopatra, 00-29
COME AND GET WITH ME, Keith Sweat featuring Snoop Dogg, 98-58
COME AND GET YOUR LOVE, Real McCoy, 95-19
COME AND STAY WITH ME, Marianne Faithfull, 65-4
COME AS YOU ARE, Nirvana, 92-9
COME AWAY MELINDA, Barry St. John, 65-47
COME BABY COME, K7, 93-3
COME BACK, Mighty Wah!, 84-20
COME BACK, Spear Of Destiny, 85-55
COME BACK, Luther Vandross, 89-53
COME BACK, Londonbeat, 95-69
COME BACK (FOR REAL LOVE), Alison Limerick, 91-53
COME BACK AND FINISH WHAT YOU STARTED, Gladys Knight and the Pips, 78-15
COME BACK AND SHAKE ME, Clodagh Rodgers, 69-3
COME BACK AND STAY (SINGLE REMIX VERSION), Paul Young, 83-4
COME BACK BABY, Dan Reed Network, 90-51
COME BACK BRIGHTER, Reef, 97-8
COME BACK DARLING, UB40, 98-10
COME BACK JONEE, Devo, 78-60
COME BACK MY LOVE, Darts, 78-2
COME BACK TO ME, Janet Jackson, 90-20
COME BACK TO ME, Angelheart featuring Rochelle Harris, 96-68
COME BACK TO WHAT YOU KNOW, Embrace, 98-6
COME DANCE WITH ME! [LP], Frank Sinatra with Billy May and his Orchestra, 59-30
COME DANCING, No Dice, 79-65
COME DANCING, Kinks, 83-12
COME DIG IT, Machel, 96-56
COME GET MY LOVIN', Dionne, 89-69
COME GIVE ME YOUR LOVE, Richie Stephens featuring General Degree, 97-61
COME HELL OR WATERS HIGH, Dee C. Lee, 86-46
COME HOME, Dave Clark Five, 65-16
COME HOME, James, 90-32
COME HOME, Lil' Devious, 01-[illegible]
COME HOME WITH ME BABY, Dead Or Alive, 89-62
COME IN OUT OF THE RAIN, Wendy Moten, 94-8
COME INSIDE, Thompson Twins, 91-56
COME INTO MY LIFE:
Joyce Sims, 88-7
Joyce Sims, 95-72
COME INTO MY LIFE, Gala, 98-38
COME LIVE WITH ME, Heaven 17, 83-5
COME NEXT SPRING, Tony Bennett, 56-29
COME ON, Rolling Stones, 63-21
COME ON!, Solo, 92-75, 93-63
COME ON, DJ Seduction, 92-37
COME ON, Jesus And Mary Chain, 94-52
COME ON, New Power Generation, 98-65
COME ON (AND DO IT), FPI Project, 93-59
COME ON AND GET SOME (SUPERFLY MIX), Cookie Crew, 89-42
COME ON BABY (ALL I WANT IS YOU), Christina Aguilera, 00-8
(COME ON) BE MY GIRL, Dennisons, 63-46
COME ON,COME ON, Bronski Beat, 86-20
COME ON DANCE, DANCE, Saturday Night Band, 78-16
COME ON EILEEN, Dexys Midnight Runners and the Emerald Express, 82-1
COME ON ENGLAND!, England's Barmy Army, 99-45
COME ON EVERYBODY (GET DOWN), US3, 97-38
COME ON HOME, Springfields, 63-31
COME ON HOME, Wayne Fontana, 66-16
COME ON HOME, Everything But The Girl, 86-44
COME ON HOME, Cyndi Lauper, 95-39
COME ON, LET'S GO:
Tommy Steele, 58-10
Los Lobos, 87-18
COME ON OVER TO MY PLACE, Drifters, 65-40, 72-9
COME ON Y'ALL, Rhythm Masters, 97-49
COME ON YOU REDS, Manchester United Football Squad, 94-1
COME OUTSIDE:
Mike Sarne featuring Wendy Richard, 62-1
Judge Dread, 75-14
COME PLAY WITH ME, Wedding Present, 92-10
COME PRIMA:
Marino Marini and his Quartet, 58-2
Malcolm Vaughan with the Michael Sammes Singers *, 58-5
Robert Earl with Wally Stott and his Orchestra and Chorus *, 58-26
(COME 'ROUND HERE) I'M THE ONE YOU NEED, Miracles, 66-45, 71-13
COME SEE ABOUT ME:
Supremes, 65-27
Shakin' Stevens, 87-24
COME SEE ME, Pretty Things, 66-43
COME SOFTLY TO ME:
Fleetwoods, 59-6
Frankie Vaughan and the Kaye Sisters with Wally Stott and his Orchestra., 59-9
New Seekers featuring Marty, 72-20
COME TO DADDY, Aphex Twin, 97-36
COME TO ME, Julie Grant, 64-31
COME TO ME!, Ruby Winters, 78-11
COME TO ME (I AM WOMAN), Su Pollard, 85-71
COME TO MILTON KEYNES, Style Council, 85-23
COME TO MY AID, Simply Red, 85-66
COME TO MY PARTY, Keith Harris and Orville with Dippy, 83-44
COME TO THE DANCE, Barron Knights with Duke D'Mond, 64-42
COME TOGETHER:
Beatles, 69-4
Michael Jackson, 92-10
Spiritualized (from The Abbey Road [EP]), 98-39
Smokin' Mojo Filters *, 95-19
COME TOGETHER, Primal Scream, 90-26
COME TOGETHER AS ONE, Will Downing, 90-48
COME TOMORROW, Manfred Mann; vocal: Paul Jones, 65-4
COME UNDONE, Duran Duran, 93-13
COME WHAT MAY, Nicole Kidman and Ewan McGregor, 01-27
COME WHAT MAY (APRES – TOI), Vicky Leandros, 72-2
COME WITH ME, Jesse Green, 77-29
COME WITH ME, Ronny Jordan (Guest vocalist Fay Simpson), 94-63
COME WITH ME, Qattara, 97-31
COME WITH ME, Puff Daddy featuring Jimmy Page, 98-75, 98-2
COMEDY, Shack, 99-44
COMES A-LONG A-LOVE, Kay Starr, 52-1
COMEUPPANCE (EP)+ lead track title, Thousand Yard Stare, 92-37
COMIN' BACK, Crystal Method, 98-73
COMIN' HOME, Delaney and Bonnie and Friends featuring Eric Clapton, 69-16
COMIN' HOME, Danger Danger, 92-75
COMIN' HOME BABY, Mel Torme, 63-13
COMIN' IN AND OUT OF YOUR LIFE, Barbra Streisand, 82-66
COMIN' ON (from THE SHAMEN S.O.S. [EP]), Shamen, 93-14
COMIN' ON STRONG, Broken English, 87-18
COMIN' ON STRONG, Desiya featuring Melissa Yiannakou, 92-74
COMIN' RIGHT UP, Bruce Willis, 88-73
COMING AROUND, Travis, 00-5
COMING AROUND AGAIN, Carly Simon, 87-10
COMING BACK, DJ Dado, 98-63
COMING BACK FOR MORE, Jellybean featuring Richard Darbyshire, 88-41
COMING BACK FOR MORE, La Mix, 90-50
COMING DOWN, Cult, 94-50
COMING HOME, David Essex, 76-24
COMING HOME, Marshall, Hain, 78-39
COMING HOME, K- Warren featuring Lee-O, 01-32
COMING HOME NOW, Boyzone, 96-4
COMING ON STRONG, Signum featuring Scott Mac, 99-66
COMING OUT OF THE DARK, Gloria Estefan, 91-25
COMING UP, Paul McCartney, 80-2
COMING UP ROSES, Curve, 98-51
COMMENT TE DIRE ADIEU, Jimmy Somerville featuring June Miles Kingston, 89-14
COMMITMENT, Leann Rimes, 98-38
COMMON PEOPLE, Pulp, 95-2
COMMUNICATION, David McCallum, 66-32
COMMUNICATION, Spandau Ballet, 83-12
COMMUNICATION, Power Station, 85-75
COMMUNICATION, Armin, 00-18
COMMUNICATION BREAKDOWN, Junior, 83-57
COMMUNICATION (SOMEBODY ANSWER THE PHONE), Mario Piu, 99-5
THE COMPASS, Dave Clarke, 01-46
COMPLETE CONTROL, Clash, 77-28
THE COMPLETE DOMINATOR [RM], Human Resource, 91-18
THE COMPLETE STELLA [RM], Jam and Spoon, 92-66
COMPLEX, Gary Numan, 79-6
COMPLIMENTS ON YOUR KISS, Red Dragon with Brian and Tony Gold, 94-2
COMPUTER GAME (THEME FROM THE INVADERS) FIRECRACKER, Yellow Magic Orchestra, 80-17
COMPUTER LOVE, Kraftwerk, 81-36, 81-1
COMPUTER LOVE, Zapp, 86-64
COMPUTER LOVE, Supercar featuring Mikaela, 99-67
CON LOS ANOS QUE ME QUEDAN, Gloria Estefan, 93-40
CON TE PARTIRO:
Sarah Brightman and Andrea Bocelli *, 97-2
Donna Summer *, 99-44
DJVisage featuring Clarissa *, 00-58
THE CONCEPT, Teenage Fanclub, 91-51
CONCRETE AND CLAY:
Unit Four Plus Two, 65-1
Randy Edelman, 76-11

CONCRETE SCHOOLYARD, Jurassic 5, 98-35
CONDEMNATION [EP] + lead track title, Depeche Mode, 93-9
CONFESSIN' (THAT I LOVE YOU), Frank Ifield, 63-1
CONFETTI, Lemonheads, 93-44
CONFIDE IN ME, Kylie Minogue, 94-2
CONFUSION, Lee Dorsey, 66-38
CONFUSION, Electric Light Orchestra, 79-8
CONFUSION, New Order, 83-12
CONFUSION (HITS US EVERYTIME), Truth, 83-22
CONGO, Boss, 94-54
CONGO, Genesis, 97-29
CONGO SQUARE, Great White, 91-62
CONGRATULATIONS, Cliff Richard, 68-1
CONNECTED, Stereo MC's, 92-18
CONNECTION, Elastica, 94-17
CONQUEST OF PARADISE, Vangelis, 92-60
CONQUISTADOR, Procol Harum, 72-22
CONQUISTADOR, Espiritu, 93-47
CONSCIENCE, James Darren, 62-30
CONSCIOUS MAN, Jolly Brothers, 79-46
CONSIDER YOURSELF, Max Bygraves, 60-50
CONSIDERATION, Reef, 97-13
A CONSPIRACY, Black Crowes, 95-25
CONSTANT CRAVING, K.d. lang, 92-52, 93-15
CONSTANTLY (L'EDERA), Cliff Richard, 64-4
CONSTANTLY WAITING, Pauline Taylor, 96-51
CONTACT, Edwin Starr, 79-6
CONTACT . . ., Eat Static, 98-67
CONTAGIOUS, Whispers, 85-56
THE CONTINENTAL, Maureen McGovern, 76-16
CONTRIBUTION, Mica Paris featuring Rakim, 90-33
CONTROL, Janet Jackson, 86-42
CONTROL, Time Of The Mumph, 95-69
CONTROLLING ME, Oceanic, 92-14
CONTROVERSY, Prince, 93-5
CONVERSATION INTERCOM, Soulwax, 00-65, 01-50
CONVERSATIONS, Cilla Black, 69-7
CONVOY, C.W. McCall, 76-2
CONVOY G.B., Laurie Lingo and the Dipsticks, 76-4
CONWAY, Reel 2 Real featuring The Mad Stuntman, 95-27
COOCHY COO, En-Core featuring Eska and Stephen Emmanuel, 00-32
COOKIN' UP YAH BRAIN, 4 Hero, 92-59
COOL BABY, Charlie Gracie, 58-26
COOL FOR CATS, Squeeze, 79-2, 92-62
COOL JERK, Go-Go's, 91-60
COOL MEDITATION, Third World, 79-17
COOL OUT TONIGHT, David Essex, 77-23
COOL RUNNING, Tik and Tok, 83-69
COOL WATER, Frankie Laine with Paul Weston and his Orchestra and the Mellomen, 55-2
COPACABANA (AT THE COPA), Barry Manilow, 78-42, 93-22
COPPER GIRL, 3 Colours Red, 97-30
COPPERHEAD ROAD, Steve Earle, 88-45
CORDUROY (from 3 SONGS [EP]), Wedding Present, 90-25
CORNERSHOP, Babybird, 97-37
CORNFLAKE GIRL, Tori Amos, 94-4
CORONATION RAG, Winifred Atwell and Her Other Piano, 53-5
THE CORONATION STREET SINGLE, Coronation Street Cast, 95-35
CORPSES, Ian Brown, 98-14
CORRINE CORRINA, Ray Peterson, 61-41
COSMIC GIRL, Jamiroquai, 96-6
COSMONAUT NO.7, Scarfo, 97-67
THE COST OF LIVING [EP], Clash, 79-22
COSTAFINE TOWN, Splinter, 74-17
COTTON EYE JOE, Rednex, 94-1
COTTONFIELDS, Beach Boys, 70-5
COULD HAVE TOLD YOU SO, Halo James, 89-6
COULD HEAVEN EVER BE LIKE THIS, Idris Muhammad, 77-42
COULD I HAVE THIS KISS FOREVER, Whitney Houston and Enrique Iglesias, 00-7
COULD IT BE, Jaheim, 01-33
COULD IT BE FOREVER :
David Cassidy, 72-2
Gemini, 96-38
COULD IT BE I'M FALLING IN LOVE:
Detroit Spinners, 73-11, 77-32
David Grant and Jaki Graham, 85-5
Worlds Apart, 94-15
COULD IT BE I'M FALLING IN LOVE [EP] + lead track title, Detroit Spinners, 77-32
COULD IT BE MAGIC:
Donna Summer, 76-40
Barry Manilow, 78-25
Take That, 92-3
Barry Manilow, 93-36
COULD YOU BE LOVED, Bob Marley and the Wailers, 80-5, 84-71
COULDN'T GET IT RIGHT, Climax Blues Band, 76-10
COULDN'T SAY GOODBYE, Tom Jones, 91-51
COULD'VE BEEN, Tiffany, 88-4
COULD'VE BEEN ME, Billy Ray Cyrus, 92-24
COULD'VE BEEN YOU, Cher, 92-31
COUNT MY SELECTOR (from ROUGH NECK [EP]), Project One, 92-49
COUNT ON ME, Julie Grant, 63-24
COUNT ON ME, Whitney Houston and Cece Winans, 96-12
COUNT YOUR BLESSINGS INSTEAD OF SHEEP, Bing Crosby, 55-11
COUNTDOWN, Rush, 83-36
COUNTEFEIT, Lowgold, 01-52
COUNTING BACKWARDS, Throwing Muses, 91-70
COUNTING EVERY MINUTE, Sonia, 90-16
COUNTING SHEEP, Airhead, 91-35
COUNTING TEARDROPS, Emile Ford and the Checkmates, 60-4
COUNTING THE DAYS, Abi, 98-44
COUNTRY BOY, Fats Domino, 60-19
COUNTRY BOY, Heinz, 63-26
COUNTRY BOY, Jimmy Nail, 96-25
COUNTRY HOUSE, Blur's, 95-1
THE COUNTRY OF THE BLIND, Faith Brothers, 85-63
COUNTRY ROADS, Hermes House Band, 01-7
COURSE BRUV, Genius Cru, 01-39
COUSIN NORMAN, Marmalade, 71-6
COVER FROM THE SKY, Deacon Blue, 91-31
COVER GIRL, New Kids On The Block, 90-4
COVER ME, Bruce Springsteen, 84-38, 85-16
COVER MY EYES (PAIN AND HEAVEN), Marillion, 91-34
(COVER PLUS) WE'RE ALL GROWN UP, Hazel O'Connor, 81-41
COVERS [EP], Everything But The Girl, 92-13
COWARD OF THE COUNTY, Kenny Rogers, 80-1
COWBOY, Kid Rock, 99-36
COWBOY DREAMS, Jimmy Nail, 95-13
COWBOY JIMMY JOE, Alma Cogan with Geoff Love and his Orchestra and the Rita Williams Singers, 61-37
COWBOYS AND ANGELS, George Michael, 91-45
COWBOYS & KISSES, Anastacia, 01-28
COWBOYS AND INDIANS, Cross, 87-74
COWGIRL, Underworld, 00-24
COWPUNCHER'S CANTATA [M], Max Bygraves, 52-6
COWPUNK MEDLUM, Splodgenessabounds, 81-69
COZ I LUV YOU, Slade, 71-1
CRACKERS INTERNATIONAL [EP], Erasure, 88-2
CRACKIN' UP, Tommy Hunt, 75-39
CRACKING UP, Nick Lowe, 79-34
CRACKING UP, Jesus And Mary Chain, 98-35
CRACKLIN' ROSIE, Neil Diamond, 70-3
CRADLE OF LOVE, Johnny Preston, 60-2
CRADLE OF LOVE, Billy Idol, 90-34
CRANK, Catherine Wheel, 93-66
CRASH, Primitives, 88-5
CRASH, Feeder, 97-48
CRASH AND BURN, Savage Garden, 00-14
CRASH! BOOM! BANG!, Roxette, 94-26
CRASHIN' IN, Charlatans, 95-31
CRAWL, Headswim, 95-64
CRAWLING, Linkin Park, 01-16
CRAWLING BACK, Roy Orbison, 65-19
CRAWLING FROM THE WRECKAGE, Dave Edmunds, 79-59
CRAYZY MAN, Blast featuring V.D.C., 94-22
CRAZY, Mud, 73-12
CRAZY, Manhattans, 83-63
CRAZY, Icehouse, 87-74, 88-38
CRAZY, Boys, 90-57
CRAZY, Seal, 90-2
CRAZY:
Patsy Cline, 90-14
Julio Iglesias, 94-43
Leann Rimes, 99-36
CRAZY, Bob Geldof, 94-65
CRAZY, Aerosmith, 94-23
CRAZY, Eternal, 94-15
CRAZY, Mark Morrison, 95-19, 96-6
CRAZY, Nut, 96-56
CRAZY, Awesome, 98-63
CRAZY, Moffatts, 99-16
CRAZY, Lucid, 99-14
CRAZY, Tomcat, 00-48
CRAZY, K-Ci and Jojo, 01-35
CRAZY CHANCE:
Kavana, 96-35
Kavana, 97-16
CRAZY CRAZY NIGHTS, Kiss, 87-4
CRAZY CUTS, Grandmixer D.St, 83-71
CRAZY DREAM, Jim Dale, 58-24
CRAZY (FOR ME), Freddie Jackson, 88-41
CRAZY FOR YOU, Madonna, 85-2, 91-2
CRAZY FOR YOU, Sybil, 90-71
CRAZY FOR YOU, Incognito featuring Chyna, 91-59
CRAZY FOR YOU, Let Loose, 93-44, 94-2
CRAZY HORSES, Osmonds, 72-2, 95-50, 99-34
CRAZY LITTLE PARTY GIRL, Aaron Carter, 98-7
CRAZY LITTLE THING CALLED LOVE:
Queen, 79-2
Dwight Yoakam, 99-43
CRAZY LOVE, Paul Anka, 58-26
CRAZY LOVE, Maxi Priest, 86-67
CRAZY LOVE, Ce Ce Peniston, 92-44
CRAZY LOVE, MJ Cole, 00-10
CRAZY LOWDOWN WAYS, Ocean Colour Scene, 01-64
THE CRAZY OTTO RAG, Stargazers, 55-18
THE CRAZY PARTY MIXES [M], Jive Bunny and the Mastermixers, 90-13
CRAZY TRAIN, Ozzy Osbourne Blizzard Of Oz, 80-49
CRAZY WATER, Elton John, 77-27
CRAZY WORDS CRAZY TUNES (V0-DO-DE-O), Dorothy Provine, 62-45
CRAZY YOU, G.U.N., 97-21
CREAM, Prince and the New Power Generation, 91-15
CREAM, Blank and Jones, 99-24
CREAM (ALWAYS RISES TO THE TOP), Gregg Diamond Bionic Boogie, 79-61
CREATION, Stereo MC's, 93-19
CREATURES OF THE NIGHT, Kiss, 83-34
CREDO, Fish, 92-38
CREEP, TLC, 95-22, 96-6
THE CREEP, Ken Mackintosh, his Saxophone and his Orchestra, 54-10
CREEP, Radiohead, 93-7
CREEQUE ALLEY, Mama's and the Papa's, 67-9
CREOLE JAZZ, Mr. Acker Bilk and his Paramount Jazz Band, 61-22
CRESCENT MOON, Lynden David Hall, 98-45
CRIME OF PASSION, Mike Oldfield featuring Maggie Reilly, 84-61
CRIMINALLY INSANE, Slayer, 87-64
CRIMSON AND CLOVER, Joan Jett and the Blackhearts, 82-60
CRISPY BACON, Laurent Garnier, 97-60
CRITICAL (IF YOU ONLY KNEW), Wall Of Sound featuring Gerald Lethan, 93-73
CRITICIZE:
Alexander O'Neal, 87-4
Alexander O'Neal, 98-51
CROCKETT'S THEME, Jan Hammer, 87-2, 91-47
CROCODILE ROCK, Elton John, 72-5
CROCODILE SHOES, Jimmy Nail, 94-4
CROCODILES, Echo and the Bunnymen, 81-37
CROSS MY BROKEN HEART, Sinitta, 88-6
CROSS MY HEART, Eighth Wonder, 88-13
CROSS THAT BRIDGE, Ward Brothers, 87-32
CROSS THE TRACK (WE BETTER GO BACK), Maceo and the Macks, 87-54
CROSSROADS, Tracy Chapman, 89-61
CROSSTOWN TRAFFIC, Jimi Hendrix Experience, 69-37, 90-61
THE CROWD, Roy Orbison, 62-40
THE CROWN, Gary Byrd and the GB Experience, 83-6
CRUCIAL, New Edition, 89-70
CRUCIFIED, Army Of Lovers, 91-47, 92-31
CRUCIFY, Tori Amos, 92-15
CRUEL, P.I.L., 92-49
THE CRUEL SEA, Dakotas, 63-18
CRUEL SUMMER:
Bananarama, 83-8, 89-19
Ace Of Base, 98-8
CRUEL TO BE KIND, Nick Lowe, 79-12
CRUISE INTO CHRISTMAS [M], Jane McDonald, 98-10
CRUISIN', D'Angelo, 96-31
CRUISING, Sinitta, 86-2
THE CRUNCH, Rah Band, 77-6
CRUSH, Zhane, 97-44

DANCING WITH TEARS IN MY EYES, Ultravox, 84-3
DANCING WITH THE CAPTAIN, Paul Nicholas, 76-8
DANDELION, Rolling Stones, 67-8
DANGER, AC/DC, 85-48
DANGER, Blahzay Blahzay, 96-56
DANGER (BEEN SO LONG), Mystikal featuring Nivea, 01-28
DANGER GAMES, Pinkees, 82-8
THE DANGER OF A STRANGER, Stella Parton, 77-35
DANGER ZONE, Kenny Loggins, 86-45
DANGEROUS, Pennye Ford, 85-43
DANGEROUS, Roxette, 90-6
DANGEROUS, Busta Rhymes, 97-32
DANGEROUS MINDS [EP], Various Artists (EPs), 96-35
DANGEROUS SEX, Tack Head, 90-48
DANIEL, Elton John, 73-4
DARE ME, Pointer Sisters, 85-17
DARE TO DREAM, Viola Wills, 86-35
DARK ALAN (AILEIN DUINN), Capercaillie, 95-65
DARK AND LONG, Underworld, 94-57
DARK CLOUDS, Space, 97-14
DARK IS THE NIGHT, Shakatak, 83-15
DARK IS THE NIGHT, A-Ha, 93-19
DARK LADY, Cher, 74-36
DARK MOON, Tony Brent with Eric Jupp and his Orchestra, 57-17
DARK NIGHT, Gorky's Zygotic Mynci, 97-49
DARK SCIENCE (EP), Tilt, 00-55
DARK SKY, Jimmy Somerville, 97-66
DARK THERAPY, Echobelly, 96-20
DARKHEART, Bomb The Bass featuring Spikey Tee, 94-35
DARKLANDS, Jesus And Mary Chain, 87-33
THE DARKTOWN STRUTTERS BALL, Joe Brown and the Bruvvers, 60-34
DARLIN':
Beach Boys, 68-11
David Cassidy, 75-16
DARLIN', Frankie Miller, 78-6
DARLIN', Bob Sinclar featuring James "D-Train" Williams, 01-46
DARLIN' DARLIN' BABY (SWEET, TENDER, LOVE), O'Jays, 77-24
DARLING BE HOME SOON:
Lovin' Spoonful, 67-44
Let Loose, 96-65
DARLING PRETTY, Mark Knopfler, 96-33
DAS BOOT, U96, 92-18
DAS GLOCKENSPIEL, Schiller, 01-17
DAT, Pluto Shervington, 76-6
DAUGHTER, Pearl Jam, 94-18
DAUGHTER OF DARKNESS, Tom Jones, 70-5
DAVID WATTS, Jam, 78-25, 80-54, 83-50
DAVID'S SONG (MAIN THEME FROM "KIDNAPPED"):
Arranged and conducted by Vladimi Cosma, 79-64
DJ Sakin and Friends *, 99-14
DAVY'S ON THE ROAD AGAIN, Manfred Mann's Earth Band, 78-6
DAWN, Flintlock, 76-30
THE DAWN, Tony De Vit, 00-56
DAY AFTER DAY, Badfinger, 72-10
DAY AFTER DAY, Pretenders, 81-45
DAY AFTER DAY, Julian Lennon, 98-66
DAY & NIGHT, Billie Piper, 00-1
THE DAY BEFORE YESTERDAY'S MAN, Supernaturals, 97-25
THE DAY BEFORE YOU CAME:
Abba, 82-32
Blancmange, 84-22
DAY BY DAY, Shakatak with Al Jarreau, 85-53
DAY BY DAY (INCORPORATING "PREPARE YE THE WAY OF THE LORD"), Holly Sherwood, 72-29
THE DAY I FALL IN LOVE (LOVE THEME FROM BEETHOVEN'S 2ND), Dolly Parton and James Ingram, 94-64
THE DAY I MET MARIE, Cliff Richard, 67-10
THE DAY I TRIED TO LIVE, Soundgarden, 94-42
DAY-IN DAY-OUT, David Bowie, 87-17
DAY IN DAY OUT, Feeder, 99-31
A DAY IN THE LIFE, Todd Terry presents Black Riot, 88-68
A DAY IN THE LIFE OF VINCE PRINCE [M], Russ Abbot, 82-61
THE DAY IS ENDED (THE DAY THOU GAVE LORD, IS ENDED, Pipes and Drums and Military Band Of The Royal Scots Dragoon Guards, 72-30
THE DAY THAT CURLY BILLY SHOT CRAZY SAM MCGEE, Hollies, 73-24
THE DAY THE EARTH CAUGHT FIRE, City Boy, 79-67
THE DAY THE RAINS CAME, Jane Morgan, 58-1
THE DAY THE WORLD TURNED DAYGLO, X-Ray Spex, 78-23
DAY TIME, 4 Strings, 00-48
DAY TRIPPER:
Beatles, 65-1
Otis Redding, 67-43
THE DAY WE CAUGHT THE TRAIN, Ocean Colour Scene, 96-4
THE DAY WE FIND LOVE, 911, 97-4
THE DAY WILL COME, Quake featuring Marcia Rae, 98-53
A DAY WITHOUT LOVE, Love Affair, 68-6
DAYDREAM:
Lovin' Spoonful, 66-2
Right Said Fred *, 92-29
DAYDREAM, Back To The Planet, 93-52
DAYDREAM BELIEVER:
Monkees, 67-5, 89-62
Anne Murray, 80-61
Simply Red And White *, 96-41
DAYDREAM IN BLUE, I Monster, 01-20
DAYDREAMER, David Cassidy, 73-1
DAYDREAMER, Menswear, 95-14
DAYDREAMIN', Tatyana Ali, 98-6
DAYDREAMING, Penny Ford, 93-43
DAYLIGHT FADING, Counting Crows, 97-54
DAYLIGHT KATY, Gordon Lightfoot, 78-41
DAYS:
Kirsty MacColl, 89-12, 95-42
Kinks, 68-12, 97-35
DAYS ARE OK (BUT THE NIGHTS WERE MADE FOR LOVE), Motels, 81-41
THE DAYS [EP] + lead track title, Kinks, 97-35
DAYS GO BY, Dirty Vegas, 01-27
DAYS LIKE THAT, Fierce, 99-11
DAYS LIKE THESE, Billy Bragg, 85-43
DAYS LIKE THIS, Sheena Easton, 89-43
DAYS LIKE THIS, Van Morrison, 95-65
DAYS OF NO TRUST, Magnum, 88-32
DAYS OF OUR LIVEZ, Bone Thugs-N-Harmony, 97-37
THE DAYS OF PEARLY SPENCER, Marc Almond, 92-4
DAYS OF YOUTH, Laurnea, 97-36
DAYSLEEPER, R.E.M., 98-6
DAYTIME FRIENDS, Kenny Rogers, 77-39
DAYTONA DEMON, Suzi Quatro, 73-14
DAYTRIP TO BANGOR (DIDN'T WE HAVE A LOVELY TIME), Fiddler's Dram, 79-3
DAZZ, Brick, 77-36
DAZZLE, Siouxsie and the Banshees, 84-33
DE DAH DAH (SPICE OF LIFE), Keith Mac Project, 94-66
DE DO DO DO, DE DA DA DA, Police, 80-5
DE-LUXE (from MAD LOVE [EP]), Lush, 90-55
DE NIRO, Disco Evangelists, 93-59
DEAD A'S, DJ Hype, 01-58
DEAD BATTERY, Pitchshifter, 00-71
DEAD CITIES, Exploited, 81-31
DEAD END STREET, Kinks, 66-5
DEAD FROM THE WAIST DOWN, Catatonia, 99-7
DEAD GIVEAWAY, Shalamar, 83-8
THE DEAD HEART, Midnight Oil, 88-68, 89-62
DEAD HUSBAND, Deejay Punk-Roc, 98-71
DEAD MAN WALKING, David Bowie, 97-32
DEAD OR ALIVE, Lonnie Donegan and his Skiffle Group, 56-7
DEAD POP STARS, Altered Images, 81-67
DEAD RINGER FOR LOVE, Meat Loaf, 81-5, 91-53
DEADLIER THAN THE MALE, Walker Brothers, 66-34
DEADLINE, Dutch Force, 00-35
DEADLINE U.S.A., Shalamar, 84-52
DEADWEIGHT, Beck, 97-23
DEAF FOREVER, Motorhead, 86-67
THE DEAL, Pat Campbell, 69-31
THE DEAN AND I, 10 C.C., 73-10
DEAR ADDY, Kid Creole and the Coconuts, 82-29
DEAR BOOPSIE, Pam Hall, 86-54
DEAR DELILAH, Grapefruit, 68-21
DEAR ELAINE, Roy Wood, 73-18
DEAR GOD, Midge Ure, 88-55
DEAR JESSIE:
Madonna, 89-5
Rollergirl, 00-22
DEAR JOHN, Status Quo, 82-10
DEAR JOHN, Eddi Reader, 94-48
DEAR LIE, TLC, 99-31
DEAR LONELY HEARTS, Nat King Cole, 62-37
DEAR MAMA, 2pac, 99-27
DEAR MISS LONELY HEARTS, Philip Lynott, 80-32
DEAR MRS. APPLEBEE, David Garrick, 66-22
DEAR PRUDENCE, Siouxsie and the Banshees, 83-3
DEATH DISCO, PIL, 79-20
DEATH OF A CLOWN, Dave Davies, 67-3
DEBASER, Pixies, 97-23
DEBORA, Tyrannosaurus Rex, 68-34, 72-7
DECADENCE DANCE, Extreme, 91-36
THE DECEIVER, Alarm, 84-51
DECEMBER, All About Eve, 89-34
DECEMBER, 1963 (OH, WHAT A NIGHT):
Four Seasons, 76-1, 88-49
Clock *, 96-13
DECEMBER WILL BE MAGIC AGAIN, Kate Bush, 80-29
DECEPTION, Fergie, 00-47
DECK OF CARDS:
Wink Martindale, 59-18, 60-28, 63-5, 73-22
Max Bygraves, 73-13
DEDICATED FOLLOWER OF FASHION, Kinks, 66-4
DEDICATED TO THE ONE I LOVE:
Mama's and the Papa's, 67-2
Bitty McLean, 94-6
DEDICATION, Thin Lizzy, 91-35
DEEE-LITE THEME, Deee-Lite, 90-25
DEEP, East 17, 93-5
THE DEEP, Global Communication, 97-51
DEEP & WIDE & TALL, Aztec Camera, 88-55
DEEP DEEP DOWN, Hepburn, 00-16
DEEP, DEEP TROUBLE, Simpsons featuring Bart and Homer, 91-7
DEEP DOWN & DIRTY, Stereo MC's, 01-17
DEEP FEELING, Mike Sagar and Cresters, 60-44
DEEP FOREST, Deep Forest, 94-20
DEEP HEAT '89 [M], Latino Rave, 89-12
DEEP (I'M FALLING DEEPER), Ariel, 97-47
DEEP IN MY HEART, Clubhouse, 91-55
DEEP IN THE HEART OF TEXAS, Duane Eddy, 62-19
DEEP IN YOU, Livin' Joy, 97-17
DEEP INSIDE, Mary J. Blige, 99-42
DEEP MENACE (SPANK), D'Menace, 98-20
DEEP PURPLE:
Nino Tempo and April Stevens, 63-17
Donny and Marie Osmond, 76-25
DEEP PURPLE, Billy Ward and his Dominoes, 57-30
DEEP RIVER WOMAN, Lionel Richie Background vocals: Alabama, 86-17
DEEP SHAG, Luscious Jackson, 95-69
DEEPER, Escrima, 95-27
DEEPER, Delirious?, 97-20, 97-36
DEEPER, Serious Danger, 97-40
DEEPER AND DEEPER, Freda Payne, 70-33
DEEPER AND DEEPER, Madonna, 92-6
A DEEPER LOVE:
Clivilles and Cole, 92-15
Aretha Franklin, 94-5
DEEPER LOVE, Ruff Driverz, 98-19
DEEPER LOVE (SYMPHONIC PARADISE), B.B.E., 98-19
DEEPER SHADE OF BLUE, Steps, 00-4
DEEPER THAN THE NIGHT, Olivia Newton-John, 79-64
THE DEEPER THE LOVE, Whitesnake, 90-35
DEEPER UNDERGROUND, Jamiroquai, 98-1
DEEPLY DIPPY:
Right Said Fred, 92-1
Rockingbirds – See Various Artists (EPs) (from The Fred [EP]), 92-26
DEF. CON ONE:
Pop Will Eat Itself, 88-63
Pop Will Eat Itself * (from Very Metal Noise Pollution [EP]), 89-45
DEFINITE DOOR, Posies, 94-67
DEJA VU, E-Smoove featuring Latanza Waters, 98-63
DEJA VU (UPTOWN BABY), Lord Tariq and Peter Gunz, 98-21
DELAWARE, Perry Como with Mitchell Ayres and his Orchestra and the Ray Charles Singers, 60-3
DELICATE, Terence Trent D'Arby featuring Des'ree, 93-14
DELICIOUS, Sleeper, 94-75
DELICIOUS, Shampoo, 95-21
DELICIOUS, Catherine Wheel, 97-53
DELICIOUS, Deni Hines featuring Don-E, 98-52
DELICIOUS, Kulay, 98-73
DELICIOUS, Pure Sugar vocals by Jennifer Starr, 98-70
DELILAH:
Tom Jones, 68-2, 92-68
Sensational Alex Harvey Band, 75-7

DO IT FOR LOVE, 4mandu, 96-45
DO IT NOW, Brain Bashers, 00-64
DO IT PROPERLY ("NO WAY BACK"), Adonis (featuring 2 Puerto Ricans, A Blackman and A Dominican), 87-47
DO IT TO ME, Lionel Richie, 92-33
DO IT TO ME AGAIN, Soulsearcher, 00-32
DO IT TO THE CROWD, Twin Hype, 89-65
DO IT TO THE MUSIC, Raw Silk, 82-18
DO ME, Bell Biv Devoe, 90-56
DO ME RIGHT, Inner City, 96-47
DO MY THING, Busta Rhymes, 97-39
DO NOT DISTURB, Bananarama, 85-31
DO NOT PASS ME BY, Hammer (featuring Tremaine Hawkins introducing Trina Johnson and Voices), 92-14
DO NOTHING, Specials Featuring Rico with the Ice Rirk Strirg Sourds, 80-4
DO OR DIE, Super Furry Animals, 00-20
DO RE ME, SO FAR SO GOOD, Carter – The Unstoppable Sex Machine, 92-22
DO SOMETHING, Macy Gray, 99-51
DO THAT TO ME, Lisa Marie Experience, 96-33
DO THAT TO ME ONE MORE TIME, Captain and Tennille, 80-7
DO THE BARTMAN, Simpsons, 91-1
DO THE BIRD:
Vernons Girls, 63-44
Dee Dee Sharp, 63-46
DO THE CLAM, Elvis Presley, 65-19
DO THE CONGA, Black Lace, 84-10
DO THE FUNKY CHICKEN, Rufus Thomas, 70-18
(DO) THE HUCKLEBUCK, Coast To Coast, 81-5
DO THE LOLLIPOP, Tweenies, 01-17
DO THE RIGHT THING, Redhead Kingpin and the F.B.I., 89-13
DO THE RIGHT THING, Ian Wright, 93-43
(DO THE) SPANISH HUSTLE, Fatback Band, 76-10
DO THEY KNOW IT'S CHRISTMAS?:
Band Aid, 84-1, 85-3
Band Aid II, 89-1
DO THIS MY WAY, Kid 'N' Play, 88-48
DO U FEEL 4 ME, Eden, 93-51
DO U KNOW WHERE YOU'RE COMING FROM, M-Beat featuring Jamiroquai, 96-12
DO U STILL?, East 17, 96-7
DO U WANNA FUNK?, Space 2000, 95-50
DO WAH DIDDY DIDDY:
Manfred Mann, 64-1
Blue Melons, 96-70
DJ Otzi*, 01-9
DO WATCHA DO, Hyper Go Go and Adeva, 96-54, 97-60
DO WE ROCK, Point Break, 99-29
DO WHAT WE WOULD, Aczess, 01-65
DO WHAT YOU DO, Jermaine Jackson, 85-6
DO WHAT YOU DO, Annabella Lwin, 95-61
DO WHAT YOU DO DO WELL, Ned Miller, 65-48
DO WHAT YOU DO (EARWORM SONG), Clint Boon Experience!, 00-63
DO WHAT YOU FEEL, Joey Negro – voice of Debbie French, 91-36
DO WHAT YOU FEEL, Johnna, 96-43
DO WHAT YOU GOTTA DO:
Nina Simone, 68-2
Four Tops, 69-11
DO WHAT YOU WANNA DO, T – Connection, 77-11
DO WHAT'S GOOD FOR ME, 2 Unlimited, 95-16
DO YA, Inner City, 94-44
DO YA DO YA (WANNA PLEASE ME), Samantha Fox, 86-10
DO 'YA' THINK I'M SEXY?:
Rod Stewart, 78-1
Revolting Cocks, 93-61
N-Trance featuring Rod Stewart, 97-7
DO YA WANNA FUNK, Sylvester with Patrick Cowley, 82-32
DO YA WANNA GET FUNKY WITH ME, Peter Brown, 78-43
DO YOU BELIEVE IN LOVE, Huey Lewis and the News, 86-9
DO YOU BELIEVE IN LOVE?, Unation, 93-75
DO YOU BELIEVE IN LOVE, Ultra-Sonic, 96-47
DO YOU BELIEVE IN MIRACLES, Slade, 85-54
DO YOU BELIEVE IN SHAME?, Duranduran, 89-30
DO YOU BELIEVE IN THE WESTWORLD, Theatre Of Hate, 82-40
DO YOU BELIEVE IN THE WONDER, Jeanie Tracy, 94-57
DO YOU BELIEVE IN US, Jon Secada, 92-30
DO YOU DREAM IN COLOUR?, Bill Nelson, 80-52
DO YOU FEEL LIKE I FEEL?, Belinda Carlisle, 91-29
DO YOU FEEL LIKE WE DO, Peter Frampton, 76-39
DO YOU FEEL ME? (. . . FREAK YOU), Men Of Vizion, 99-36
DO YOU FEEL MY LOVE?, Eddy Grant, 80-8, 83-47
DO YOU KNOW, Secret Affair, 81-57
DO YOU KNOW, Michelle Gayle, 97-6
DO YOU KNOW THE WAY TO SAN JOSE, Dionne Warwick, 68-8
DO YOU KNOW (WHAT IT TAKES), Robyn, 97-26
DO YOU LIKE IT, Kingdom Come, 89-73
DO YOU LOVE ME:
Brian Poole and the Tremeloes, 63-1
Dave Clark Five, 63-30
Deep Feeling, 70-34
Duke Baysee, 95-46
DO YOU LOVE ME?, Nick Cave and the Bad Seeds, 94-68
DO YOU LOVE ME?, Mademoiselle, 01-56
DO YOU LOVE ME BOY?, Kerri-Ann, 98-58
DO YOU LOVE ME LIKE YOU SAY?, Terence Trent D'Arby, 93-14
DO YOU LOVE ME NOW (from SAFARI [EP]), Breeders, 92-69
DO YOU LOVE WHAT YOU FEEL, Inner City, 89-16
DO YOU MIND, Anthony Newley, 60-1
DO YOU REALLY LIKE IT?, DJ Pied Piper and the Masters Of Ceremonies, 01-1
(DO YOU REALLY LOVE ME) TELL ME LOVE, Michael Wycoff, 83-60
DO YOU REALLY LOVE ME TOO (FOOL'S ERRAND), Billy Fury, 64-13
DO YOU REALLY WANT ME, Jon Secada, 93-30
DO YOU REALLY WANT ME, Robyn, 98-20
DO YOU REALLY (WANT MY LOVE), Junior, 85-47
DO YOU REALLY WANT TO HURT ME, Culture Club, 82-1
DO YOU REMEMBER?, Scaffold, 68-34
DO YOU REMEMBER (LIVE), Phil Collins, 90-57
DO YOU REMEMBER ROCK 'N' ROLL RADIO?, Ramones, 80-54
DO YOU REMEMBER THE FIRST TIME?, Pulp, 94-33, 96-73
DO YOU SEE, Warren G, 95-29
DO YOU SEE THE LIGHT (LOOKING FOR), Snap! featuring Niki Haris, 93-10
DO YOU SLEEP?, Lisa Loeb and Nine Stories, 95-45
DO YOU THINK ABOUT US, Total, 97-49
DO YOU UNDERSTAND, Almighty, 96-38
DO YOU WANNA DANCE?, Barry Blue, 73-7
DO YOU WANNA GET FUNKY, C&C Music Factory, 94-27
DO YOU WANNA GO OUR WAY???, Public Enemy, 99-66
DO YOU WANNA HOLD ME?, Bow Wow Wow, 83-47
DO YOU WANNA PARTY, DJ Scott featuring Lorna B, 95-36
DO YOU WANNA TOUCH ME? (OH YEAH!), Gary Glitter, 73-2
DO YOU WANT IT RIGHT NOW, Degrees Of Motion featuring Biti, 92-31, 94-26
DO YOU WANT ME, Salt-N-Pepa, 91-5
DO YOU WANT ME, Q Tex, 96-48
DO YOU WANT ME?, Leilani, 99-40
DO YOU WANT ME TO, Four Pennies, 64-47
DO YOU WANT TO DANCE, Cliff Richard and the Shadows, 62-2
DO YOU WANT TO KNOW A SECRET, Billy J. Kramer with the Dakotas, 63-2
DO YOUR DANCE, Rose Royce, 77-30
THE DOCTOR, Doobie Brothers, 89-73
DR. BEAT, Miami Sound Machine, 84-6
DOCTOR DOCTOR, U.F.O., 79-35
DOCTOR DOCTOR, Thompson Twins, 84-3
DR. FEELGOOD, Motley Crue, 89-50
DR. FINLAY, Andy Stewart, 65-43
DR. GREENTHUMB, Cypress Hill, 99-34
DR. HECKYLL AND MR. JIVE, Men At Work, 83-31
DOCTOR JACKYLL AND MISTER FUNK, Jackie McLean, 79-53
DOCTOR JEEP, Sisters Of Mercy, 90-37
DOCTOR JONES, Aqua, 98-1
THE DR. KILDARE THEME:
Johnny Spence and his Orchestra, 62-15
Richard Chamberlain *, 62-12
DOCTOR KISS – KISS, 5000 Volts, 76-8
DR. LOVE, Tina Charles, 76-4
DR MABUSE, Propaganda, 84-27
DOCTOR MY EYES, Jackson 5, 73-9
DR STEIN, Helloween, 88-57
DR. WHO, Mankind, 78-25
DOCTOR'S ORDERS, Sunny, 74-7
DOCTORIN' THE HOUSE, Coldcut featuring Yazz and the Plastic Population, 88-6
DOCTORIN' THE TARDIS, Timelords, 88-1
DOES HE LOVE YOU, Reba McEntire, 99-62
DOES IT FEEL GOOD, B.T. Express, 80-52
DOES IT FEEL GOOD TO YOU, DJ Carl Cox, 92-35
DOES SHE HAVE A FRIEND?, Gene Chandler, 80-28
DOES THAT RING A BELL, Dynasty, 83-53
DOES THIS HURT?, Boo Radleys, 92-67
DOES YOUR CHEWING GUM LOSE ITS FLAVOUR (ON THE BEDPOST OVERNIGHT), Lonnie Donegan and his Skiffle Group, 59-3
DOES YOUR HEART GO BOOM, Helen Love, 97-71
DOES YOUR MOTHER KNOW, Abba, 79-4
DOESN'T ANYBODY KNOW MY NAME?, Vince Hill, 69-50
DOESN'T REALLY MATTER, Janet Jackson, 00-5
DOG, Dada, 93-71
DOG EAT DOG, Adam and the Ants, 80-4
DOG ON WHEELS, Belle And Sebastian, 97-59
DOG TRAIN, Levellers, 97-24
DOGGY DOGG WORLD, Snoop Doggy Dogg, 94-32
DOGMAN GO WOOF, Underworld, 93-63
DOGMONAUT 2000 (IS THERE ANYBODY OUT THERE?), Frigid Vinegar, 99-53
DOGS, Who, 68-25
DOGS OF LUST, The, 93-25
DOGS OF WAR, Exploited, 81-63
DOGS WITH NO TAILS, Pale, 92-51
DOIN IT, Ll Cool J (Guest vocalist Leshaun), 96-15
DOIN' IT, Liberty, 01-14
DOIN' IT IN A HAUNTED HOUSE, Yvonne Gage, 84-45
DOIN' OUR OWN DANG, Jungle Brothers featuring De La Soul, Monie Love, Tribe Called Quest and Queen Latifah, 90-33
DOIN' OUR THING, Phoebe One featuring Red Rat, Goofy and Buccaneer (Main Street Crew), 98-59
DOIN' THE DO, Betty Boo, 90-7
DOING ALL RIGHT WITH THE BOYS, Gary Glitter, 75-6
DOLCE VITA, Ryan Paris, 83-5
DOLL HOUSE, King Brothers and the Rita Williams Singers, 61-21
DOLL PARTS, Hole, 95-16
DOLLAR BILL, Screaming Trees, 93-52
DOLLAR IN THE TEETH, Upsetters, 69-5
DOLLARS, C.J. Lewis, 94-34
DOLLARS IN THE HEAVENS, Geneva, 99-59
DOLLY MY LOVE, Moments, 75-10
DOLPHIN, Shed Seven, 94-28
THE DOLPHIN'S CRY, Live, 00-62
DOLPHINS MAKE ME CRY, Martyn Joseph, 92-34
DOLPHINS WERE MONKEYS, Ian Brown, 00-5
DOMINATION, Way Out West, 96-38
DOMINATOR, Human Resource, 91-36, 91-18
DOMINION, Sisters Of Mercy, 88-13
DOMINIQUE (SOEUR SOURIRE), Singing Nun (Soeur Sourire), 63-7
DOMINO DANCING, Pet Shop Boys, 88-7
DOMINOES, Robbie Nevil, 87-26
DOMINOID, Moloko, 96-65
THE DON, 187 Lockdown, 98-29
DON CARGON COMIN', Project One, 92-64
DON JUAN, Dave Dee, Dozy, Beaky, Mick and Tich, 69-23
DON QUIXOTE, Nik Kershaw, 85-10
DON'T, Elvis Presley with the Jordanaires, 58-2

DON'T ANSWER ME, Cilla Black, 66-6
DON'T ANSWER ME, Alan Parsons Project, 84-58
DON'T ARGUE, Cabaret Voltaire, 87-69
DON'T ASK ME, Public Image Limited, 90-22
DON'T ASK ME WHY, Eurythmics, 89-25
DON'T BE A DUMMY, John Du Cann, 79-33
DON'T BE A FOOL, Loose Ends, 90-13
DON'T BE A STRANGER, Dina Carroll, 93-3
DON'T BE AFRAID, Aaron Hall, 92-56
DON'T BE AFRAID, Moonman, 97-60, 99-41
DON'T BE ANGRY, Bad Manners, 81-34
DON'T BE CRUEL:
Bill Black's Combo, 60-32
Billy Swan, 75-42
Elvis Presley *, 78-24, 92-42
DON'T BE CRUEL, Bobby Brown, 88-42, 89-13
DON'T BE STUPID (YOU KNOW I LOVE YOU), Shania Twain, 00-5
DON'T BELIEVE A WORD, Thin Lizzy, 77-12
DON'T BELIEVE THE HYPE, Public Enemy, 88-18
DON'T BELIEVE THE HYPE, Mista E featuring the Awakening, 88-41
DON'T BET MONEY HONEY, Linda Scott with the Hutch Davie Orchestra, 61-50
DON'T BLAME IT ON LOVE, Shakatak, 84-55
DON'T BLAME IT ON THAT GIRL, Matt Bianco, 88-11
DON'T BLAME ME:
Everly Brothers, 61-20
Frank Ifield with Norrie Paramor and his Orchestra, 64-8
DON'T BREAK MY HEART, UB40, 85-3
DON'T BREAK MY HEART AGAIN, Whitesnake, 81-17
DON'T BREAK THE HEART THAT LOVES YOU, Connie Francis, 62-39
DON'T BRING HARRY [EP] + lead track title, Stranglers, 79-41
DON'T BRING LULU, Dorothy Provine, 61-17
DON'T BRING ME DOWN, Pretty Things, 64-10
DON'T BRING ME DOWN, Animals, 66-6
DON'T BRING ME DOWN, Electric Light Orchestra, 79-3
DON'T BRING ME DOWN, Spirits, 94-31
DON'T BRING ME YOUR HEARTACHES, Paul and Barry Ryan, 65-13
DON'T CALL IT LOVE (from WILDLIFE [EP]), Girlschool, 82-58
DON'T CALL ME BABY, Voice Of The Beehive, 88-15
DON'T CALL ME BABY, Madison Avenue, 99-30, 00-1
DON'T CARE, Klark Kent, 78-48
DON'T COME AROUND HERE NO MORE, Tom Petty and the Heartbreakers, 85-50
DON'T COME CLOSE, Ramones, 78-39
DON'T COME HOME TOO SOON (OFFICIAL TEAM SCOTLAND SONG WORLD CUP '98), Del Amitri, 98-15
DON'T COME TO STAY, Hot House, 87-74, 88-70
DON'T CRY, Asia, 83-33
DON'T CRY, Boy George, 88-60
DON'T CRY, Guns N' Roses, 91-8
DON'T CRY, Seal, 95-51
DON'T CRY DADDY, Elvis Presley, 70-8
DON'T CRY FOR ME ARGENTINA:
Julie Covington, 76-1, 78-63
Shadows, 78-5
Sinead O'Connor, 92-53
Madonna, 96-2
Mike Flowers Pops, 96-30
DON'T CRY OUT LOUD, Elkie Brooks, 78-12
DON'T DIE JUST YET, David Holmes, 98-33
DON'T DILLY DALLY ON THE WAY (from THE MUPPET SHOW MUSIC HALL [EP]), Muppets, 77-19
DON'T DO IT BABY, Mac and Katie Kissoon, 75-9
DON'T DO THAT, Geordie, 72-32
DON'T DO THAT, Young and Moody Band, 81-63
DON'T DON'T TELL ME NO, Sophie B. Hawkins, 94-36
DON'T DREAM IT'S OVER:
Crowded House, 87-27, 96-25
Paul Young, 91-20
Dove *, 99-37
DON'T DRIVE DRUNK, Stevie Wonder, 84-62
DON'T DRIVE MY CAR, Status Quo, 80-11
DON'T DROP BOMBS, Liza Minnelli, 89-46
DON'T EVER CHANGE, Crickets, 62-5
DON'T FALL IN LOVE (I SAID), Toyah, 85-22
DON'T FALTER, Mint Royale with Lauren Laverne, 00-15
(DON'T FEAR) THE REAPER:
Blue Oyster Cult, 78-16
Apollo 440, 95-35
DON'T FIGHT IT, Wilson Pickett, 65-29
DON'T FIGHT IT, FEEL IT, Primal Scream featuring Denise Johnson, 91-41
DON'T FORBID ME, Pat Boone, 57-2
DON'T FORGET ME (WHEN I'M GONE), Glass Tiger, 86-29
DON'T FORGET TO CATCH ME, Cliff Richard and the Shadows, 68-21
DON'T FORGET TO DANCE, Kinks, 83-58
DON'T FORGET TO REMEMBER, Bee Gees featuring Barry Gibb, Maurice Gibb and Colin Peterson, 69-2
DON'T GET ME WRONG, Pretenders, 86-10
DON'T GIVE IT UP, Sonic Surfers, 94-54
DON'T GIVE ME UP, Harold Melvin and the Blue Notes, 84-59
DON'T GIVE ME YOUR LIFE, Alex Party, 95-2
DON'T GIVE UP, Peter Gabriel and Kate Bush, 86-9
DON'T GIVE UP, Michelle Weeks, 97-28
DON'T GIVE UP, Chicane featuring Bryan Adams, 00-1
DON'T GIVE UP ON US, David Soul, 76-1
DON'T GO, Judas Priest, 81-51
DON'T GO:
Yazoo, 82-3
Lizzy Mack, 95-52
DON'T GO, Hothouse Flowers, 88-11
DON'T GO:
Awesome 3, 92-75, 94-45, 96-27
Third Dimension featuring Julie McDermott, 96-34
DON'T GO BREAKING MY HEART:
Elton John and Kiki Dee, 76-1
Elton John and Rupaul, 94-7
DON'T GO MESSIN' WITH MY HEART, Mantronix, 91-22
DON'T HANG UP, Orlons, 62-39
DON'T HOLD BACK, Chanson, 79-33
DON'T IT MAKE MY BROWN EYES BLUE, Crystal Gayle, 77-5
DON'T IT MAKE YOU FEEL GOOD, Stefan Dennis, 89-16
DON'T JUMP OFF THE ROOF DAD, Tommy Cooper, 61-40
DON'T KILL IT CAROL, Manfred Mann's Earth Band, 79-45
DON'T KILL THE WHALE, Yes, 78-36
DON'T KNOCK IT (UNTIL YOU TRY IT), Bobby Nunn, 84-65
DON'T KNOCK THE ROCK, Bill Haley and his Comets, 57-7
DON'T KNOW MUCH, Linda Ronstadt featuring Aaron Neville, 89-2
DON'T KNOW WHAT YOU GOT (TIL IT'S GONE), Cinderella, 89-54
DON'T KNOW WHY I LOVE YOU, Stevie Wonder, 69-14
DON'T LAUGH, Winx, 95-38
DON'T LAUGH AT ME ('CAUSE I'M A FOOL), Norman Wisdom with Norrie Paramor and his Orchestra, 54-3
DON'T LEAVE, Faithless, 96-34, 97-21
DON'T LEAVE ME, Blackstreet, 97-6
DON'T LEAVE ME, Malandra Burrows, 98-54
DON'T LEAVE ME BEHIND, Everything But The Girl, 86-72
DON'T LEAVE ME THIS WAY:
Harold Melvin and the Bluenotes featuring Theodore Pendergrass, 77-5
Thelma Houston, 77-13
Communards with Sarah Jane Morris, 86-1
Thelma Houston, 95-35
DON'T LET 'EM GRIND YOU DOWN EP (EXTRACTS FROM THE EDINBURGH LIVE NITE, Exploited / Anti-Pasti, 81-70
DON'T LET GO, Manhattan Transfer, 77-32
DON'T LET GO (LOVE), En Vogue, 97-5
DON'T LET GO THE COAT, Who, 81-47
DON'T LET HIM STEAL YOUR HEART AWAY, Phil Collins with the Martyn Ford Orchestra, 83-45
DON'T LET HIM TOUCH YOU, Angelettes, 72-35
DON'T LET IT DIE, Hurricane Smith, 71-2
DON'T LET IT END, Styx, 83-56
DON'T LET IT FADE AWAY, Darts, 78-18
DON'T LET IT GET YOU DOWN, Echo and the Bunnymen, 97-50
DON'T LET IT GO TO YOUR HEAD, Brand New Heavies featuring N'dea Davenport, 92-24
DON'T LET IT PASS YOU BY, UB40, 81-16
DON'T LET IT SHOW ON YOUR FACE, Adeva, 92-34
DON'T LET LOVE GET YOU DOWN, Archie Bell and the Drells, 86-49
DON'T LET ME BE MISUNDERSTOOD:
Animals, 65-3
Santa Esmeralda and Leroy Gomez, 77-41
Costello Show featuring The Confederates, 86-33
Joe Cocker, 96-53
DON'T LET ME BE THE LAST TO KNOW, Britney Spears, 01-12
DON'T LET ME DOWN, Farm, 91-36
DON'T LET ME DOWN GENTLY, Wonder Stuff, 89-19
DON'T LET NOBODY HOLD YOU DOWN, L.J. Reynolds, 84-53
DON'T LET THE FEELING GO, Nightcrawlers featuring John Reid, 95-13
DON'T LET THE RAIN COME DOWN (CROOKED LITTLE MAN), Ronnie Hilton with the Michael Sammes Singers, 64-21
DON'T LET THE STARS GET IN YOUR EYES, Perry Como with the Ramblers, 53-1
DON'T LET THE SUN CATCH YOU CRYING, Gerry and the Pacemakers, 64-6
DON'T LET THE SUN GO DOWN ON ME:
Elton John, 74-16
Oleta Adams, 91-33
George Michael with Elton John, 91-1
DON'T LET THIS MOMENT END, Gloria!, 99-28
DON'T LIE, Sinclair, 94-70
DON'T LOOK ANY FURTHER:
Dennis Edwards featuring Siedah Garrett, 84-45, 87-55
Kane Gang, 88-52
M People, 93-9
DON'T LOOK AT ME THAT WAY, Chaka Khan, 93-73
DON'T LOOK BACK, Boston, 78-43
DON'T LOOK BACK, Fine Young Cannibals, 89-34
DON'T LOOK BACK, Lloyd Cole, 90-59
DON'T LOOK BACK (from HAVE LOST IT [EP]), Teenage Fanclub, 95-53
DON'T LOOK BACK IN ANGER, Oasis, 96-1
DON'T LOOK DOWN, Planets, 80-66
DON'T LOOK DOWN, Mick Ronson with Joe Elliott, 94-55
DON'T LOOK DOWN – THE SEQUEL, Go West, 85-13
DON'T LOSE THE MAGIC, Shawn Christopher, 92-30
DON'T LOSE YOUR TEMPER, XTC, 80-32
DON'T LOVE ME TOO HARD, Nolans, 82-14
DON'T MAKE ME (FALL IN LOVE WITH YOU), Babbity Blue, 65-48
DON'T MAKE ME OVER:
Swinging Blue Jeans, 66-31
Sybil, 89-19
DON'T MAKE ME WAIT, Peech Boys, 82-49
DON'T MAKE ME WAIT, Bomb The Bass featuring Lorraine, 88-6
DON'T MAKE ME WAIT, Loveland featuring the voice of Rachel McFarlane, 95-22
DON'T MAKE ME WAIT, 911, 96-10
DON'T MAKE ME WAIT TOO LONG:
Barry White, 76-17
Roberta Flack, 80-44
DON'T MAKE MY BABY BLUE, Shadows, 65-10
DON'T MAKE WAVES, Nolans, 80-12
DON'T MARRY HER, Beautiful South, 96-8
DON'T MESS WITH DOCTOR DREAM, Thompson Twins, 85-15
DON'T MESS WITH MY MAN, Lucy Pearl, 00-20
DON'T MISS THE PARTYLINE, Bizz Nizz, 90-7
DON'T NEED A GUN, Billy Idol, 87-26
DON'T NEED THE SUN TO SHINE (TO MAKE ME SMILE), Gabrielle, 01-9
DON'T PANIC, Liquid Gold, 81-42
DON'T PANIC, Logo featuring Dawn Joseph, 01-42

DON'T PAY THE FERRYMAN, Chris De Burgh, 82-48
DON'T PLAY THAT SONG, Aretha Franklin, 70-13
DON'T PLAY THAT SONG AGAIN, Nicki French, 00-34
DON'T PLAY WITH ME, Rozalla, 93-50
DON'T PLAY YOUR ROCK 'N' ROLL TO ME, Smokey, 75-8
DON'T PULL YOUR LOVE, Sean Maguire, 96-14
DON'T PUSH IT, Ruth Joy, 89-66
DON'T PUSH IT DON'T FORCE IT, Leon Haywood, 80-12
DON'T PUT YOUR SPELL ON ME, Ian McNabb, 96-72
DON'T QUIT, Caron Wheeler, 91-53
DON'T RUSH (TAKE LOVE SLOWLY), K-Ci and Jojo, 98-16
DON'T SAY I TOLD YOU SO, Tourists, 80-40
DON'T SAY IT'S LOVE, Johnny Hates Jazz, 88-48
DON'T SAY IT'S OVER, Gun, 94-19
DON'T SAY THAT'S JUST FOR WHITE BOYS, Way Of The West, 81-54
DON'T SAY YOU LOVE ME, M2M, 00-16
DON'T SAY YOUR LOVE IS KILLING ME, Erasure, 97-23
DON'T SET ME FREE, Ray Charles, 63-37
DON'T SHED A TEAR, Paul Carrack, 89-60
DON'T SING, Prefab Sprout, 84-62
DON'T SLEEP IN THE SUBWAY, Petula Clark, 67-12
DON'T SLOW DOWN, UB40, 81-16
DON'T SPEAK:
No Doubt, 97-1
Clueless, 97-61
DON'T STAND SO CLOSE TO ME:
Police, 80-1
Police, 86-24
DON'T STAY AWAY TOO LONG, Peters and Lee, 74-3
DON'T STOP:
Fleetwood Mac, 77-32
Status Quo, 96-35
DON'T STOP, K.I.D., 81-49
DON'T STOP, Mood, 82-59
DON'T STOP, Jeffrey Osborne, 84-61
DON'T STOP, K-Klass, 92-32
DON'T STOP, Hammer, 94-72
DON'T STOP, Ruff Driverz, 98-30
DON'T STOP, No Authority, 98-54
DON'T STOP, ATB, 99-61, 99-3
DON'T STOP BELIEVIN', Journey, 82-62
DON'T STOP (FUNKIN' 4 JAMAICA), Mariah Carey featuring Mystikal, 01-32
DON'T STOP IT NOW, Hot Chocolate, 76-11
DON'T STOP (JAMMIN'), L.A. Mix, 87-47
DON'T STOP LOVING ME BABY, Pinkerton's 'Assort'. Colours, 66-50
DON'T STOP ME NOW, Queen, 79-9
DON'T STOP MOVIN', Livin' Joy, 96-5
DON'T STOP MOVIN', S Club 7, 01-1
DON'T STOP NOW, Gene Farrow with the G.F. Band, 78-71
DON'T STOP THAT CRAZY RHYTHM, Modern Romance, 83-14
DON'T STOP THE CARNIVAL, Alan Price Set, 68-13
DON'T STOP THE DANCE, Bryan Ferry, 85-21
DON'T STOP THE FEELING, Roy Ayers, 80-56
DON'T STOP THE MUSIC, Yarbrough and Peoples, 80-7
DON'T STOP THE MUSIC, Lionel Richie, 00-34
DON'T STOP TIL YOU GET ENOUGH (MICHAEL JACKSON MEDLEY) [M], Ashaye, 83-45
DON'T STOP 'TILL YOU GET ENOUGH, Michael Jackson, 79-3
DON'T STOP – TWIST!, Frankie Vaughan, 62-22
DON'T STOP (WIGGLE WIGGLE), Outhere Brothers, 95-1
DON'T TAKE AWAY THE MUSIC, Tavares, 76-4
DON'T TAKE IT LYIN' DOWN, Dooleys, 78-60
DON'T TAKE IT PERSONAL, Jermaine Jackson, 89-69
DON'T TAKE IT PERSONAL (JUST ONE OF DEM DAYS), Monica, 95-32
DON'T TAKE MY KINDNESS FOR WEAKNESS, Heads with Shaun Ryder, 96-60
DON'T TAKE MY MIND ON A TRIP, Boy George, 89-68
DON'T TAKE NO FOR AN ANSWER (from RISING FREE [EP]), Tom Robinson Band, 78-18
DON'T TALK, Hank Marvin, 82-49
DON'T TALK, Jon B, 01-29
DON'T TALK ABOUT LOVE, Bad Boys Inc, 93-19
DON'T TALK DIRTY TO ME, Jermaine Stewart, 88-61
DON'T TALK JUST KISS, Right Said Fred Guest vocal Jocelyn Brown, 91-3
DON'T TALK TO HIM, Cliff Richard and the Shadows, 63-2
DON'T TALK TO ME ABOUT LOVE, Altered Images, 83-7
DON'T TELL ME, Central Line, 82-55
DON'T TELL ME, Blancmange, 84-8
DON'T TELL ME, Van Halen, 95-27
DON'T TELL ME, Madonna, 00-4
DON'T TELL ME LIES, Breathe, 89-45
DON'T TEST, Junior Tucker, 90-54
DON'T THAT BEAT ALL, Adam Faith with Johnny Keating and his Orchestra, 62-8
DON'T THINK I'M NOT, Kandi, 00-9
DON'T THROW AWAY ALL THOSE TEARDROPS, Frankie Avalon, 60-37
DON'T THROW IT ALL AWAY, Gary Benson, 75-20
DON'T THROW YOUR LOVE AWAY, Searchers, 64-1
DON'T TREAT ME BAD, Firehouse, 91-71
DON'T TREAT ME LIKE A CHILD, Helen Shapiro, 61-3
DON'T TRY TO CHANGE ME, Crickets, 63-37
DON'T TRY TO STOP IT, Roman Holliday, 83-14
DON'T TURN AROUND, Merseybeats, 64-13
DON'T TURN AROUND:
Aswad, 88-1
Ace Of Base, 94-5
DON'T WAIT UP, Thunder, 97-27
DON'T WALK, Big Supreme, 86-58
DON'T WALK AWAY, Electric Light Orchestra, 80-21
DON'T WALK AWAY, Four Tops, 81-16
DON'T WALK AWAY, Pat Benatar, 88-42
DON'T WALK AWAY, Toni Childs, 89-53
DON'T WALK AWAY, Jade, 93-7
DON'T WALK AWAY TILL I TOUCH YOU, Elaine Paige, 78-46
DON'T WANNA BE A PLAYER, Joe, 97-16
DON'T WANNA BE ALONE, Tricia Penrose, 00-44
DON'T WANNA FALL IN LOVE, Jane Child, 90-22
DON'T WANNA LET YOU GO, Five, 00-9
DON'T WANNA LOSE YOU, Gloria Estefan, 89-6
DON'T WANNA LOSE YOU, Lionel Richie, 96-17
DON'T WANNA SAY GOODNIGHT, Kandidate, 78-47
DON'T WANT TO FORGIVE ME NOW, Wet Wet Wet, 95-7
DON'T WANT TO WAIT ANYMORE, Tubes, 81-60
DON'T WANT YOU BACK, Ellie Campbell, 01 50
DON'T WASTE MY TIME, Paul Hardcastle Lead vocals – Carol Kenyon, 86-8
DON'T WASTE YOUR TIME, Yarbrough and Peoples, 84-60
DON'T WORRY, Johnny Brandon, 55-18
DON'T WORRY, Billy Fury and the Four Kestrels, 61-40
DON'T WORRY, Kim Appleby, 90-2
DON'T WORRY, Newton, 97-61
DON'T WORRY BABY, Los Lobos, 85-57
DON'T WORRY BE HAPPY, Bobby McFerrin, 88-2
DON'T YOU, Second Image, 83-68
DON'T YOU (FORGET ABOUT ME):
Simple Minds, 85-7, 86-62
Best Company, 93-65
DON'T YOU GET SO MAD, Jeffrey Osborne, 83-54
DON'T YOU JUST KNOW IT, Amazulu, 85-15
DON'T YOU KNOW IT?, Adam Faith, 61-12
DON'T YOU KNOW (SHE SAID HELLO), Butterscotch, 70-17
DON'T YOU LOVE ME, 49ers, 90-12
DON'T YOU LOVE ME, Eternal, 97-3
DON'T YOU ROCK ME DADDY-O:
Lonnie Donegan and his Skiffle Group, 57-4
Vipers Skiffle Group, 57-10
DON'T YOU THINK IT'S TIME, Mike Berry with the Outlaws, 63-6
DON'T YOU WANT ME:
Human League 100, 81-1, 95-16
Mandy Smith *, 89-59
Farm, 92-18
DON'T YOU WANT ME, Jody Watley, 87-55
DON'T YOU WANT ME, Felix, 92-6, 95-10, 96-17
DON'T YOU WORRY, Madasun, 00-14
DON'T YOU WORRY 'BOUT A THING, Incognito, 92-19
DONALD WHERE'S YOUR TROOSERS?, Andy Stewart, 60-37, 89-4
THE DONKEY CART, Frank Chacksfield and his Orchestra, 56-26
DONNA:
Ritchie Valens, 59-29
Marty Wilde, 59-3
DONNA, 10C.C., 72-2
DOO WOP (THAT THING), Lauryn Hill, 98-3
DOOBEDOOD'NDOOBE, DOOBEDOOD'NDOOBE, DOOBEDOOD'NDOO, Diana Ross, 72-12
DOODAH!, Cartoons, 99-7
DOOMS NIGHT, Azzido Da Bass, 00-58, 00-46, 00-8
DOOMSDAY, Evelyn Thomas, 76-41
DOOP, Doop, 94-1
THE DOOR, Turin Brakes, 01-67
THE DOOR IS STILL OPEN TO MY HEART, Dean Martin, 64-42
DOOR #1, Levert Sweat Gill, 98-45
DOORS OF YOUR HEART, Beat, 81-33
DOOT DOOT, Freur, 83-59
THE DOPE SHOW, Marilyn Manson, 98-12
DOPES TO INFINITY, Monster Magnet, 95-58
DOUBLE BARREL, Dave and Ansil Collins, 71-1
DOUBLE DUTCH, Fatback Band, 77-31
DOUBLE DUTCH:
Malcolm McLaren, 83-3
Dope Smugglaz, 99-15
DOUBLE TROUBLE, Lynyrd Skynyrd, 76-31
DOUBLEBACK, ZZ Top, 90-29
DOV'E L'AMOURE, Cher, 99-21
DOWN AT THE DOCTORS, Dr. Feelgood, 78-48
DOWN BY THE LAZY RIVER, Osmonds, 72-40
DOWN BY THE WATER, P J Harvey, 95-38
DOWN DEEP INSIDE (THEME FROM THE DEEP), Donna Summer, 77-5
DOWN DOWN, Status Quo, 74-1
DOWN DOWN DOWN, Gambafreaks, 00-57
DOWN FOR THE ONE, Beverley Knight, 95-55
DOWN 4 WHATEVA, Nuttin' Nyce, 95-62
DOWN IN A HOLE, Alice In Chains, 93-36
DOWN IN THE BOONDOCKS, Billy Joe Royal, 65-38
DOWN IN THE SUBWAY, Soft Cell, 84-24
DOWN IN THE TUBE STATION AT MIDNIGHT, Jam, 78-15, 83-30
DOWN LOW (NOBODY HAS TO KNOW) THE MOVIE, R. Kelly featuring Ronald Isley, 96-23
DOWN ON THE BEACH TONIGHT, Drifters, 74-7
DOWN ON THE CORNER, Creedence Clearwater Revival, 70-31
DOWN ON THE STREET, Shakatak, 84-9
DOWN SO LONG, Jewel, 99-38
DOWN THAT ROAD, Shara Nelson, 93-19, 94-34
DOWN THE DRAIN, Stakka Bo, 93-64
DOWN THE DUSTPIPE, Status Quo, 70-12
DOWN THE HALL, Four Seasons, 77-34
DOWN THE RIVER NILE, John Leyton, 62-42
DOWN THE WIRE, A.S.A.P., 90-67
DOWN TO EARTH, Curiosity Killed The Cat, 86-3
DOWN TO EARTH, Monie Love, 90-31
DOWN TO EARTH, Grace, 96-20, 97-29
DOWN TO THE WIRE, Ghost Dance, 89-66
DOWN UNDER, Men At Work, 83-1
DOWN WITH THE CLIQUE, Aaliyah (Ah-Lee-Yah), 95-33
DOWN WITH THE KING, Run-D.M.C., 93-69
DOWN YONDER, Johnny and the Hurricanes, 60-8
DOWNHEARTED, Eddie Fisher with Hugo Winterhalter and his Orchestra, 53-3
DOWNTOWN, Petula Clark, 64-2, 88-10
DOWNTOWN, One 2 Many, 88-65, 89-43
DOWNTOWN, SWV, 94-19
THE DOWNTOWN LIGHTS, Blue Nile, 89-67
DOWNTOWN TRAIN, Rod Stewart, 90-10

EATEN ALIVE, Diana Ross, 85-71
EATING ME ALIVE, Diana Brown and Barrie K. Sharpe, 92-53
EBB TIDE:
Frank Chacksfield and his Orchestra, 54-9
Righteous Brothers, 66-48, 90-3
EBENEEZER GOODE, Shamen, 92-1
EBONY AND IVORY, Paul McCartney with additional vocals by Stevie Wonder, 82-1
EBONY EYES, Everly Brothers, 61-1
ECHO BEACH:
Martha and the Muffins, 80-10
Toyah, 87-54
ECHO CHAMBER, Beats International, 91-60
ECHO MY HEART, Lindy Layton, 91-42
ECHO ON MY MIND PART II, Earthling, 95-61
ECHOES IN A SHALLOW BAY [EP], Cocteau Twins, 85-65
ECUADOR, Sash! featuring Rodriguez, 97-2
ED'S FUNKY DINER (FRIDAY NIGHT, SATURDAY MORNING), It's Immaterial, 86-65
EDDY VORTEX, Steve Gibbons Band, 78-56
EDELWEISS, Vince Hill with the Eddie Lester Singers, 67-2
EDEN, Sarah Brightman, 99-68
EDGE OF A BROKEN HEART, Vixen, 88-51, 89-59
EDGE OF DARKNESS, Eric Clapton with Michael Kamen, 86-65
THE EDGE OF HEAVEN, Wham!, 86-1
EDIE (CIAO BABY), Cult, 89-32
EENY MEENY, Showstoppers, 68-33
EGG RUSH, Flowered Up, 91-38
EGG SHAPED FRED (from ONE [EP]), Mansun, 96-37
EGO, Elton John, 78-34
EGYPTIAN REGGAE, Jonathan Richman and the Modern Lovers, 77-5
EIGHT [EP], Mansun, 98-7
EIGHT BY TEN, Ken Dodd, 64-22
8 DAYS A WEEK, Sweet Female Attitude, 00-43
EIGHT MILES HIGH, Byrds, 66-24
808, Blaque Ivory, 99-31
18 AND LIFE, Skid Row, 90-12
18 CARAT LOVE AFFAIR, Associates, 82-21
EIGHTEEN STRINGS, Tinman, 94-9
18 TILL I DIE, Bryan Adams, 97-22
EIGHTEEN WITH A BULLET, Pete Wingfield, 75-7
EIGHTEEN YELLOW ROSES, Bobby Darin, 63-37
EIGHTH DAY, Hazel O'Connor, 80-5
EIGHTIES, Killing Joke, 84-60
80'S ROMANCE, Belle Stars, 84-71
86'D, Subcircus, 97-56
EINSTEIN A GO-GO, Landscape, 81-5
EL BIMBO, Bimbo Jet, 75-12
(EL CONDOR PASA) IF I COULD, Julie Felix, 70-19
EL LUTE, Boney M, 79-22
EL NINO, Agnelli and Nelson, 98-21
EL PARAISCO RICO, Deet-Ah, 99-39
EL PASO, Marty Robbins, 60-19
EL PRESIDENT, Drugstore, 98-20
EL SCORCHO, Weezer, 96-50
EL TRAGO (THE DRINK), 2 In A Room, 94-34
EL VINO COLLAPSO, Black Lace, 85-42
ELDORADO (REMIX), Drum Theatre, 87-44
ELEANOR RIGBY:
Beatles, 66-1, 86-63
Ray Charles, 68-36
ELECTED:
Alice Cooper, 72-4
Mr. Bean and Smear Campaign (featuring Bruce Dickinson) *, 92-9
ELECTION DAY, Arcadia, 85-7
ELECTRIC AVENUE, Eddy Grant, 83-2, 01-5
ELECTRIC BARBARELLA, Duran Duran, 99-23
ELECTRIC BLUE, Icehouse, 88-53
ELECTRIC BOOGALOO, Ollie and Jerry, 85-57
ELECTRIC GUITAR, Fluke, 93-58
ELECTRIC GUITARS, Prefab Sprout, 97-53
ELECTRIC HEAD PT.2 (THE ECSTASY), White Zombie, 96-31
ELECTRIC LADY, Geordie, 73-32
ELECTRIC MAINLINE [EP], Spiritualized, 93-49
ELECTRIC MAN (from THIRTEEN [EP]), Mansun, 00-23
ELECTRIC TRAINS, Squeeze, 95-44
ELECTRIC YOUTH, Debbie Gibson, 89-14
ELECTRICITY, Spiritualized, 97-32
ELECTRICITY, Suede, 99-5
ELECTROLITE, R.E.M., 96-29
ELECTRONIC PLEASURE, N-Trance, 96-11
ELEGANTLY AMERICAN EP, M People, 94-31
ELEGANTLY WASTED, Inxs, 97-20
ELEKTROBANK, Chemical Brothers, 97-17
ELENI, Tol and Tol, 90-73
ELENORE, Turtles, 68-7
ELEPHANT PAW (GET DOWN TO THE FUNK), Pan Position, 94-55
ELEPHANT STONE, Stone Roses, 90-8
ELEPHANT TANGO, Cyril Stapleton and his Orchestra, 55-19
THE ELEPHANTS GRAVEYARD (GUILTY), Boomtown Rats, 81-26
ELEVATE MY MIND, Stereo MC's, 90-74
ELEVATION, Xpansions, 90-49, 91-7
ELEVATION, G.T.O., 92-59
ELEVATION, U2, 01-3
ELEVATOR SONG – THE MIXES, Dubstar, 96-25
ELEVEN [EP], Mansun, 99-16
ELEVEN TO FLY, Tintinout featuring Wendy Page, 99-26
ELISABETH SERENADE, Gunter Kallman Choir, 64-45
ELIZABETHAN REGGAE, Boris Gardner, 70-14
ELMO JAMES, Chairmen Of The Board, 72-21
THE ELO EP [EP], Electric Light Orchestra, 78-34
ELOISE:
Barry Ryan with the Majority, 68-2
Damned, 86-3
ELSTREE, Buggles, 80-55
ELUSIVE BUTTERFLY:
Bob Lind, 66-5
Val Doonican, 66-5
THE ELVIS MEDLEY [M], Elvis Presley with the Jordanaires, 85-51
EMBRACE, Agnelli and Nelson, 00-35
EMBARRASSMENT, Madness, 80-4
EMERALD CITY, Seekers, 67-50
EMERGENCY, Kool And The Gang, 85-50
EMERGENCY (DIAL 999), Loose Ends, 84-41
EMERGENCY ON PLANET EARTH, Jamiroquai, 93-32
EMMA, Hot Chocolate, 74-3
EMOTIONAL RESCUE, Rolling Stones, 80-9
AN EMOTIONAL TIME, Hothouse Flowers, 93-38
EMOTIONS, Brenda Lee, 61-45
EMOTIONS:
Samantha Sang, 78-11
Destiny's Child *, 01-3
EMOTIONS, Mariah Carey, 91-17
THE EMPEROR'S NEW CLOTHES, Sinead O'Connor, 90-31
EMPIRE, Queensryche, 90-61
EMPIRE LINE, My Life Story, 99-58
EMPIRE SONG, Killing Joke, 82-43
EMPIRE STATE HUMAN, Human League, 80-62
EMPTY AT THE END, Soft Parade, 01-65
EMPTY GARDEN, Elton John, 82-51
EMPTY ROOMS, Gary Moore, 84-51, 85-23
EMPTY SKIES, Kosheen, 00-73
EMPTY WORLD, Dogs D'Amour, 90-61
EMRACING THE SUNSHINE, B.T., 95-34
ENCHANTED LADY, Pasadenas, 88-31
ENCORE:
Cheryl Lynn, 84-68
Tongue 'N' Cheek, 89-41
ENCORE UNE FOIS, Sash!, 97-2
ENCORES [EP], Dire Straits, 93-31
THE END IS THE BEGINNING IS THE END, Smashing Pumpkins, 97-10
END OF A CENTURY, Blur, 94-19
THE END OF THE INNOCENCE, Don Henley, 89-48
END OF THE LINE, Traveling Wilburys, 89-52
END OF THE LINE, Honeyz, 98-5
END OF THE ROAD, Boyz Ii Men, 92-1
THE END OF THE WORLD:
Skeeter Davis, 63-18
Sonia, 90-18
THE END . . . OR THE BEGINNING?, Classix Nouveaux, 82-60
ENDLESS, Dickie Valentine, 54-19
ENDLESS ART, A House, 92-46
ENDLESS LOVE:
Diana Ross and Lionel Richie, 81-7
Luther Vandross and Mariah Carey, 94-3
ENDLESS SLEEP:
Marty Wilde and his Wildcats, 58-4
Jody Reynolds, 79-66
ENDLESS SUMMER NIGHTS, Richard Marx, 88-50, 90-60
ENDLESSLY, Brook Benton, 59-28
ENDLESSLY, John Foxx, 83-66
ENDS, Everlast, 99-47
ENEMY MAKER, Dub War, 96-41
THE ENEMY WITHIN, Thirst, 91-61
ENERGIZE, Slamm, 93-57
THE ENERGY (FEEL THE VIBE), Astro Trax Team featuring Shola Phillips, 98-74
ENERGY FLASH [EP] + lead track title, Beltram, 91-52
ENERGY IS EUROBEAT, Man To Man, 87-43
ENERVATE, Transa, 98-42
ENGINE ENGINE NO. 9, Roger Miller, 65-33
ENGINE NO. 9, Midnight Star, 87-64
ENGLAND SWINGS, Roger Miller, 65-13
ENGLAND, WE'LL FLY THE FLAG, England World Cup Squad, 82-2
ENGLAND'S IRIE, Black Grape featuring Joe Strummer and Keith Allen, 96-6
ENGLISH CIVIL WAR (JOHNNY COMES MARCHING HOME), Clash, 79-25
ENGLISH COUNTRY GARDEN, Jimmy Rodgers, 62-5
ENGLISH COUNTRY GARDEN, Dandys, 98-57
ENGLISHMAN IN NEW YORK:
Sting, 88-51, 90-15
Shinehead *, 93-30
ENJOY THE SILENCE, Depeche Mode, 90-6
ENJOY YOURSELF, Jacksons, 77-42
ENJOY YOURSELF, A+, 99-5
ENOLA GAY:
Orchestral Manoeuvres In The Dark, 80-8
Orchestral Manoeuvres In The Dark (from The Omd Remixes [EP]), 98-35
ENOUGH IS ENOUGH, Chumbawamba and Credit To The Nation, 93-56
ENOUGH IS ENOUGH, Y Tribe featuring Elisabeth Troy, 99-49
ENTER SANDMAN, Metallica, 91-5
ENTER THE SCENE, DJ Supreme vs the Rhythm Masters, 97-49
ENTER YOUR FANTASY [EP], Joey Negro, 92-35
THE ENTERTAINER – MUSIC FROM "THE STING", Featuring Marvin Hamlisch on Piano, 74-25
ENTRY OF THE GLADIATORS, Nero and the Gladiators, 61-37
EP THREE [EP], Hundred Reasons, 01-37
EP TWO [EP], Hundred Reasons, 01-47
EPIC, Faith No More, 90-37, 90-25
EQUINOXE PART 5, Jean-Michel Jarre, 79-45
EQUINOXE (PART V), Shadows, 80-50
ERASE/REWIND, Cardigans, 99-7
ERASURE-ISH – (A LITTLE RESPECT/STOP!) (EP), Bjorn Again, 92-25
ERNIE (THE FASTEST MILKMAN IN THE WEST), Benny Hill, 71-1, 92-29
EROTICA, Madonna, 92-3
ESCAPADE, Janet Jackson, 90-17
ESCAPE, Gary Clail On-U Sound System (additional vocals by Akabu), 91-44
ESCAPE (THE PINA COLADA SONG), Rupert Holmes, 80-23
ESCAPE TO ALCATRAZ (from EOLUTIONDANCE PART ONE [EP]), Evolution, 94-52
ESCAPING:
Asia Blue, 92-50
Dina Carroll, 96-3
ESPECIALLY FOR YOU:
Kylie Minogue and Jason Donovan, 88-1
Denise and Johnny, 98-3
THE ESSENTIAL WALLY PARTY MEDLEY [M], Gay Gordon and the Mince Pies, 86-60
ETERNAL FLAME:
Bangles, 89-1
Atomic Kitten, 01-1
ETERNAL LOVE, PJ and Duncan AKA, 94-12
ETERNAL 99 (PAUL GLAZBY MIX) (from HARD BEAT EP 19 [EP]), Eternal Rhythm – See Various Artists (EPs), 01-71
ETERNALLY (THE THEME FROM "LIMELIGHT"), Jimmy Young, 53-8
ETERNITY, Orion, 00-38
ETERNITY, Robbie Williams, 01-1
ETHNIC PRAYER, Havana, 93-71
THE ETON RIFLES, Jam, 79-3, 83-54
EUGINA, Salt Tank, 96-40, 00-58
EURODISCO, Bis, 98-37
EUROPA AND THE PIRATE TWINS, Thomas Dolby, 81-48
EUROPE AFTER THE RAIN, John Foxx, 81-40
EUROPEAN FEMALE, Stranglers, 83-9

EUROPEAN SON, Japan, 82-31
EVANGELINE, Icicle Works, 87-53
EVANGELINE, Cocteau Twins, 93-34
EVAPOR 8, Altern 8 Guest vocal P.P. Arnold, 92-6
EVE OF DESTRUCTION, Barry McGuire, 65-3
THE EVE OF THE WAR, Jeff Wayne's "The War Of The Worlds", 78-36, 89-3
EVEN AFTER ALL, Finley Quaye, 97-10
EVEN BETTER THAN THE REAL THING, U2, 92-8
EVEN FLOW, Pearl Jam, 92-27
EVEN MORE PARTY POPS [M], Russ Conway, 60-27
EVEN MORE SWEARING AND CUSSING (from WIBBLING RIVALRY), Oas*s, 95-52
EVEN NOW, Bob Seger and the Silver Bullet Band, 83-73
EVEN THE BAD TIMES ARE GOOD, Tremeloes, 67-4
EVEN THE NIGHTS ARE BETTER, Air Supply, 82-44
EVEN THOUGH YOU BROKE MY HEART, Gemini, 95-40
EVEN THOUGH YOU'VE GONE, Jacksons, 78-31
EVENING FALLS . . ., Enya, 88-20
EVENING STAR, Judas Priest, 79-53
EVER FALLEN IN LOVE (WITH SOMEONE YOU SHOULDN'T'VE):
Buzzcocks, 78-12
Fine Young Cannibals *, 87-9
EVER REST, Mystica, 98-62
EVER SINCE YOU SAID GOODBYE, Marty Wilde, 62-31
EVER SO LONELY, Monsoon, 82-12
EVEREST, Supernaturals, 99-52
EVERGLADE, L7, 92-27
EVERGREEN, Hazell Dean, 84-63
EVERLASTING, Natalie Cole, 88-28
THE EVERLASTING, Manic Street Preachers, 98-11
EVERLASTING LOVE:
Love Affair, 68-1
Robert Knight, 68-40, 74-19
Rex Smith and Rachel Sweet, 81-35
Sandra, 88-45
Worlds Apart, 93-20
Gloria Estefan, 95-19
Cast from Casualty, 98-5
AN EVERLASTING LOVE, Andy Gibb, 78-10
EVERLASTING LOVE, Howard Jones, 89-62
EVERLONG, Foo Fighters, 97-18
EVERLOVIN', Ricky Nelson, 61-23
EVERMORE, Ruby Murray with Ray Martin and his Orchestra, 55-3
EVERY ANGEL, All About Eve, 88-30
EVERY BEAT OF MY HEART, Rod Stewart, 86-2
EVERY BEAT OF THE HEART, Railway Children, 90-68, 91-24
EVERY BREATH OF THE WAY, Melanie, 83-70
EVERY BREATH YOU TAKE, Police, 83-1
EVERY DAY, Don McLean, 73-38
EVERY DAY HURTS, Sad Cafe, 79-3
EVERY DAY I FALL APART, Superstar, 98-66
EVERY DAY I LOVE YOU, Boyzone, 99-3
EVERY DAY (I LOVE YOU MORE), Jason Donovan, 89-2
EVERY DAY OF THE WEEK, Jade, 95-19
EVERY DAY SHOULD BE A HOLIDAY, Dandy Warhols, 98-29
EVERY GIRL AND BOY, Spagna, 88-23
EVERY HEARTBEAT, Amy Grant, 91-25
EVERY KINDA PEOPLE:
Robert Palmer, 78-53, 92-43
Mint Juleps, 87-58
Chaka Demus and Pliers, 96-47
EVERY LITTLE BIT HURTS, Spencer Davis Group, 65-41
EVERY LITTLE STEP, Bobby Brown, 89-6, 96-25
EVERY LITTLE TEARDROP, Gallagher and Lyle, 77-32
EVERY LITTLE THING, Jeff Lynne, 90-59
EVERY LITTLE THING HE DOES IS MAGIC, Shawn Colvin, 94-65
EVERY LITTLE THING I DO, Soul For Real, 96-31
EVERY LITTLE THING SHE DOES IS MAGIC:
Police, 81-1
Shawn Colvin *, 94-65
Chaka Demus and Pliers, 97-51
EVERY LITTLE TIME, Poppers present Aura, 97-44
EVERY LOSER WINS, Nick Berry, 86-1
EVERY MAN MUST HAVE A DREAM, Liverpool Express, 76-17
EVERY MORNING, Sugar Ray, 99-10
EVERY NIGHT, Phoebe Snow, 79-37
EVERY NITE'S A SATURDAY NIGHT WITH YOU, Drifters, 76-29
EVERY 1'S A WINNER, Hot Chocolate, 78-12, 87-69
EVERY ROSE HAS ITS THORN, Poison, 89-13
EVERY SINGLE DAY, Dodgy, 98-32
EVERY TIME, Janet, 98-46
EVERY TIME I FALL, Gina G, 97-52
EVERY TIME I FALL IN LOVE, Upside Down, 96-18
EVERY TIME YOU GO AWAY, Paul Young, 85-4
EVERY TIME YOU TOUCH ME:
Moby, 95-28
QFX, 96-22
EVERY WHICH WAY BUT LOOSE, Eddie Rabbitt, 79-41
EVERY WOMAN KNOWS, Lulu, 94-44
EVERY WOMAN NEEDS LOVE, Stella Browne, 00-55
EVERY YEAR, EVERY CHRISTMAS, Luther Vandross, 95-43
EVERY YOU EVERY ME, Placebo, 99-11
EVERYBODY, Tommy Roe, 63-9
EVERYBODY, Cappella, 91-66
EVERYBODY, Altern 8, 93-58
EVERYBODY, D.J. Bobo, 94-47
EVERYBODY, Clock, 95-6
EVERYBODY, Kinky, 96-71
EVERYBODY, Progress presents the Boy Wunda, 99-7
EVERYBODY, Hear'say, 01-4
EVERYBODY (ALL OVER THE WORLD), F.P.I. Project, 91-65, 99-67
EVERYBODY (BACKSTREET'S BACK), Backstreet Boys, 97-3
EVERYBODY BE SOMEBODY, Ruffneck featuring Yavahn, 95-13, 01-66
EVERYBODY DANCE:
Chic, 78-9
Evolution, 93-19
EVERYBODY DANCE (THE HORN SONG), Barbara Tucker, 98-28
EVERYBODY EVERYBODY, Black Box, 90-16
(EVERYBODY) GET DANCIN', Bombers, 79-37
EVERYBODY GET TOGETHER, Dave Clark Five, 70-8
EVERYBODY GET UP, Five, 98-2
EVERYBODY GET UP, Capriccio, 99-44
EVERYBODY GETS A SECOND CHANCE, Mike and the Mechanics, 92-56
EVERYBODY GO HOME THE PARTY'S OVER, Clodagh Rodgers, 70-47
EVERYBODY GONFI GON, Two Cowboys, 94-7
EVERYBODY HAVE A GOOD TIME, Archie Bell and the Drells, 77-43
EVERYBODY HERE WANTS YOU, Jeff Buckley, 98-43
EVERYBODY HURTS, R.E.M., 93-7
EVERYBODY IN THE PLACE [EP] + lead track title, Prodigy, 92-2, 96-69
EVERYBODY IS A STAR, Pointer Sisters, 79-61
EVERYBODY KNOWS, Dave Clark Five, 65-37
EVERYBODY KNOWS, Dave Clark Five, 67-2
EVERYBODY KNOWS (EXCEPT YOU), Divine Comedy, 97-14
EVERYBODY LET'S SOMEBODY LOVE, Frank 'K' (featuring Wiston Office), 91-61
EVERYBODY LOVES A LOVER, Doris Day, 58-25
EVERYBODY LOVES SOMEBODY, Dean Martin, 64-11
EVERYBODY MOVE, Cathy Dennis, 91-25
EVERYBODY (MOVE YOUR BODY), Diva, 96-44
EVERYBODY MUST PARTY, Georgie Porgie, 95-61
EVERYBODY NEEDS A 303, Fatboy Slim, 97-34
EVERYBODY NEEDS SOMEBODY, Birdland, 91-44
EVERYBODY NEEDS SOMEBODY, Nick Howard, 95-64
EVERYBODY NEEDS SOMEBODY TO LOVE, Blues Brothers, 90-12
EVERYBODY ON THE FLOOR (PUMP IT), Tokyo Ghetto Pussy, 95-26
EVERYBODY PUMP, DJ Power, 92-46
EVERYBODY (RAP), Criminal Element Orchestra featuring Wendell Williams, 90-30
EVERYBODY SALSA, Modern Romance, 81-12
EVERYBODY SAY EVERYBODY DO, Let Loose, 95-29
EVERYBODY THINKS THEY'RE GOING TO GET THEIRS, Bis, 97-64
EVERYBODY UP!, Glam Metal Detectives, 95-29
EVERYBODY WANTS HER, Thunder, 92-36
EVERYBODY WANTS TO RULE THE WORLD:
Tears For Fears, 85-2, 86-73
Tears For Fears *, 86-5
EVERYBODY WANTS TO RUN THE WORLD [RR], Tears For Fears, 86-5
EVERYBODY'S FREE (TO FEEL GOOD), Rozalla, 91-6
EVERYBODY'S FREE (TO WEAR SUNSCREEN) THE SUNSCREEN SONG (CLASS OF '99), Baz Luhrmann presents, 99-1
EVERYBODY'S GONE, Senseless Things, 91-73
EVERYBODY'S GONNA BE HAPPY, Kinks, 65-17
EVERYBODY'S GOT SUMMER, Atlantic Starr, 94-36
EVERYBODY'S GOT TO LEARN SOMETIME:
Korgis, 80-5
Yazz, 94-56
Baby D *, 95-3
Marc Et Claude*, 00-12
EVERYBODY'S HAPPY NOWADAYS, Buzzcocks, 79-29
EVERYBODY'S LAUGHING, Phil Fearon and Galaxy, 84-10
EVERYBODY'S SOMEBODY'S FOOL, Connie Francis, 60-5
EVERYBODY'S TALKIN':
Nilsson, 69-23, 70-39
Beautiful South, 94-12
EVERYBODY'S TALKING 'BOUT LOVE, Silver Convention, 77-25
EVERYBODY'S TWISTIN', Frank Sinatra, 62-22
EVERYDAY, Moody Blues, 65-44
EVERYDAY, Slade, 74-3
EVERYDAY, Jam Machine, 89-68
EVERYDAY, Anticappella, 92-45
EVERYDAY, Orchestral Manoeuvres In The Dark, 93-59
EVERYDAY, Phil Collins, 94-15
EVERYDAY, Incognito, 95-23
EVERYDAY, Craig McLachlan and the Culprits, 95-65
EVERYDAY, Agnelli and Nelson, 99-17
EVERYDAY GIRL, DJ Rap, 99-47
EVERYDAY I WRITE THE BOOK, Elvis Costello and the Attractions, 83-28
EVERYDAY IS A WINDING ROAD, Sheryl Crow, 96-12
EVERYDAY IS LIKE SUNDAY, Morrissey, 88-9
EVERYDAY LIVING, Woodentops, 86-72
EVERYDAY NOW, Texas, 89-44
EVERYDAY OF MY LIFE, House Traffic, 97-24
EVERYDAY PEOPLE:
Sly and the Family Stone, 69-36
Aretha Franklin, 91-69
EVERYDAY SUNSHINE, Fishbone, 92-60
EVERYDAY THANG, Melanie Williams, 94-38
EVERYONE SAYS YOU'RE SO FRAGILE, Idlewild, 98-47
EVERYONE'S GONE TO THE MOON, Jonathan King, 65-4
EVERYTHING, Jody Watley, 90-74
EVERYTHING, Kicking Back with Taxman, 90-54
EVERYTHING, U.H.F., 91-46
EVERYTHING, Hysterix, 95-65
EVERYTHING, Sarah Washington, 96-30
EVERYTHING, Inxs, 97-71
EVERYTHING, Mary J. Blige, 97-6
EVERYTHING, Dum Dums, 00-21
EVERYTHING A MAN COULD EVER NEED, Glen Campbell, 70-32
EVERYTHING ABOUT YOU, Ugly Kid Joe, 92-3
EVERYTHING CHANGES, Take That, 94-1
EVERYTHING COUNTS:
Depeche Mode, 83-6
Depeche Mode, 89-22
EVERYTHING GOOD IS BAD, Westworld, 88-72
EVERYTHING I AM, Plastic Penny, 68-6
EVERYTHING I DO (I DO IT FOR YOU):
Bryan Adams, 91-1
Fatima Mansions, 92-7
Q featuring Tony Jackson, 94-47
EVERYTHING I HAVE IS YOURS, Eddie Fisher, 53-8
EVERYTHING I OWN:
Bread, 72-32
Ken Boothe, 74-1
Boy George, 87-1
EVERYTHING I WANTED, Dannii, 97-15
EVERYTHING IS ALRIGHT (UPTIGHT), C.J. Lewis, 94-10
EVERYTHING IS BEAUTIFUL, Ray Stevens, 70-6
EVERYTHING IS EVERYTHING, Lauryn Hill, 99-19

EVERYTHING IS GONNA BE ALRIGHT, Sounds Of Blackness, 94-29
EVERYTHING IS GREAT, Inner Circle, 79-37
EVERYTHING'L TURN OUT FINE, Stealers Wheel, 73-33
EVERYTHING MUST CHANGE, Paul Young, 84-9
EVERYTHING MUST GO, Manic Street Preachers, 96-5
EVERYTHING MY HEART DESIRES, Adam Rickitt, 99-15
EVERYTHING SHE WANTS, Wham!, 84-2
EVERYTHING STARTS WITH AN 'E', E-Zee Possee, 89-69, 90-15
EVERYTHING TO EVERYONE, Everclear, 98-41
EVERYTHING WILL FLOW, Suede, 99-24
EVERYTHING YOU NEED, Madison Avenue, 01-33
EVERYTHING YOU WANT, Vertical Horizon, 00-42
EVERYTHING'S AL' RIGHT, Mojos, 64-9
EVERYTHING'S COOL?, Pop Will Eat Itself, 94-23
EVERYTHING'S GONE GREEN, New Order, 81-38
EVERYTHING'S GONNA BE ALRIGHT, Sweetbox, 98-5
EVERYTHING'S NOT YOU, Stoneproof, 99-68
EVERYTHING'S RUINED, Faith No More, 92-28
EVERYTHING'S TUESDAY, Chairmen Of The Board, 71-12
EVERYTIME, Lustral, 97-60, 99-30
EVERYTIME, Tatyana Ali, 99-20
EVERYTIME, A1, 99-3
EVERYTIME I CLOSE MY EYES, Babyface, 97-13
EVERYTIME I THINK OF YOU, FM, 90-73
EVERYTIME IT RAINS, Ace Of Base, 99-22
EVERYTIME YOU NEED ME, Fragma featuring Maria Rubia, 01-3
EVERYTIME YOU SLEEP, Deaconblue, 01-64
EVERYWHERE, Fleetwood Mac, 88-4
EVERYWHERE I GO, Isotonik, 92-25
EVERYWHERE I GO, Jackson Browne, 94-67
EVERYWHERE I LOOK, Daryl Hall and John Oates, 91-74
EVE'S VOLCANO (COVERED IN SIN), Julian Cope, 87-41
EVIDENCE, Faith No More, 95-32
EVIL HEARTED YOU, Yardbirds, 65-3
EVIL MAN, Fatima Mansions, 92-59
THE EVIL THAT MEN DO, Iron Maiden, 88-5
EVIL TWIN, Love/Hate, 91-59
EVIL WOMAN, Electric Light Orchestra, 76-10
EVOLUTIONDANCE PART ONE [EP], Evolution, 94-52
EV'RY DAY OF MY LIFE, Malcolm Vaughan, 55-5
EV'RY LITTLE BIT, Millie Scott, 87-63
EV'RY TIME WE SAY GOODBYE, Simply Red, 87-11
EV'RYWHERE, David Whitfield with the Roland Shaw Orchestra, 55-3
EX-FACTOR, Lauryn Hill, 99-4
EX-GIRLFRIEND, No Doubt, 00-23
EXCERPT FROM "A TEENAGE OPERA", Keith West, 67-2
EXCITABLE, Amazulu, 85-12
EXCITED, M-People, 92-29
EXCLUSIVE, Apollo presents House Of Virginism, 96-67
EXCLUSIVELY YOURS, Mark Wynter, 61-32
EXCUSE ME BABY, Magic Lanterns, 66-44
EXHALE (SHOOP SHOOP), Whitney Houston, 95-11
EXODUS:
Bob Marley and the Wailers, 77-14
Bob Marley and the Wailers, 92-53
EXODUS, Sunscreem, 95-40
EXODUS – LIVE, Levellers, 96-24
EXODUS (THEME FROM "EXODUS"):
Ferrante and Teicher, 61-6
Semprini *, 61-25
THE EXORCIST, Scientist, 90-62
EXORCIST, Shades Of Rhythm, 91-53
EXPANDER, Future Sound Of London, 94-72
EXPANSIONS '86 (EXPAND YOUR MIND):
Chris Paul featuring the voice of David Joseph, 86-58
Wag Ya Tail *, 92-49
Scott Grooves featuring Roy Ayers *, 98-68
EXPERIENCE, Diana Ross, 86-47
EXPERIMENT IV, Kate Bush, 86-23
EXPERIMENTS WITH MICE, Johnny Dankworth and his Orchestra, 56-7
EXPLAIN THE REASONS, First Light, 83-65
EXPO2000, Kraftwerk, 00-27
EXPRESS, B.T. Express, 75-34, 94-67
EXPRESS (WEST END REMIX), Dina Carroll, 93-12
EXPRESS YOUR FREEDOM, Anticappella, 95-31
EXPRESS YOURSELF, Madonna, 89-5
EXPRESS YOURSELF, N.W.A., 89-50, 90-26
EXPRESS YOURSELF, Jimi Polo, 92-59, 97-62
EXPRESSION, Salt-N-Pepa, 90-40, 92-23
EXPRESSLY (EP), Edwyn Collins, 94-42
EXPRESSO BONGO [EP], Cliff Richard and the Shadows, 60-14
EXTACY, Shades Of Rhythm, 91-16
EXTENDED PLAY [EP], Bryan Ferry, 76-7
THE EXTENDED PLEASURE OF DANCE [EP], 808 State, 90-56
EXTERMINATE!, Snap! featuring Niki Haris!, 93-2
EXTREMIS, Hal featuring Gillian Anderson, 97-23
THE EXTREMIST (from THE SATCH [EP]), Joe Satriani, 93-53
EYE BEE M, Commander Tom, 00-75
EYE HATE U, Symbol (The Artist Formerly Known As Prince), 95-20
EYE KNOW, De La Soul, 89-14
EYE LEVEL (THEME FROM THE THAMES T.V. SERIES "VAN DER VALK")
Simon Park Orchestra, 72-41, 73-1
Matt Monro *, 73-28
EYE OF THE TIGER:
Survivor, 82-1
Frank Bruno, 95-28
EYE TALK, Fashion, 84-69
EYE TO EYE, Chaka Khan, 85-16
EYE WONDER, Apples, 91-75
EYEBALL (EYEBALL PAUL'S THEME), Sunburst, 00-48
EYES DON'T LIE, Truce, 98-20
THE EYES HAVE IT, Karel Fialka, 80-52
EYES OF A STRANGER, Queensryche, 89-59
EYES OF BLUE, Paul Carrack, 96-40, 96-45
EYES OF SORROW, A Guy Called Gerald, 89-52
THE EYES OF TRUTH, Enigma, 94-21
EYES THAT SEE IN THE DARK, Kenny Rogers, 83-61
EYES WITHOUT A FACE, Billy Idol, 84-18
EZY, Wolfsbane, 91-68
F.B.I., Shadows, 61-6
F.E.A.R., Ian Brown, 01-13
F.L.M., Mel and Kim, 87-7
THE F-WORD, Babybird, 00-35
FA-FA-FA-FA-FA (SAD SONG), Otis Redding, 66-23
FABLE, Robert Miles, 96-7
FABRICATED LUNACY, Terris, 01-62
FABULOUS, Charlie Gracie, 57-8
THE FACE, And Why Not?, 90-13
FACE THE STRANGE (LP], Therapy?, 93-18
FACE TO FACE, Siouxsie and the Banshees, 92-21
FACES, 2 Unlimited, 93-8
THE FACES [EP], Faces, 77-41
FACTS + FIGURES, Hugh Cornwell, 87-61
THE FACTS OF LIFE, Danny Madden, 90-72
FACTS OF LIFE, Oui 3, 94-38
THE FACTS OF LIFE, Black Box Recorder, 00-20
FACTS OF LOVE, Climie Fisher, 89-50
FADE, Paris Angels, 91-70
FADE INTO YOU, Mazzy Star, 94-48
FADE TO GREY, Visage, 80-8, 93-39
FADED, Ben Harper, 98-54
FADER, Drugstore, 95-72
FADING LIKE A FLOWER (EVERY TIME YOU LEAVE), Roxette, 91-12
FAILURE, Skinny, 98-31
FAILURE, Kings Of Convenience, 01-63
A FAIR AFFAIR (JE T'AIME), Misty Oldland, 94-49
FAIR BLOWS THE WIND FOR FRANCE, Pele, 92-62
FAIRGROUND, Simply Red, 95-1
FAIRPLAY, Soul II Soul featuring Rose Windross, 88-63
FAIRWEATHER FRIEND, Symposium, 97-25
FAIRYTALE, Dana, 76-13
FAIRYTALE OF NEW YORK, Pogues featuring Kirsty MacColl, 87-2, 91-36
FAIT ACCOMPLI, Curve, 92-22
FAITH:
George Michael, 87-2
Limp Bizkit, 01-18
FAITH, Wee Papa Girl Rappers, 88-60
FAITH (IN THE POWER OF LOVE), Rozalla, 91-65, 91-11
FAITH CAN MOVE MOUNTAINS:
Johnnie Ray with the Four Lads, 52-7
Nat "King" Cole, 53-10
Jimmy Young, 53-11
FAITH HEALER, Recoil, 92-60
FAITH OF THE HEART, Rod Stewart, 99-60
FAITHFUL, Go West, 92-13
THE FAITHFUL HUSSAR:
Ted Heath and his Music, 56-18
Louis Armstrong with his All Stars, 56-27
Vera Lynn *, 57-29
FAITHLESS, Scritti Politti, 82-56
FAKE, Alexander O'Neal, 87-33, 88-16
FAKE FUR, Urusei Yatsura, 97-58
FAKE PLASTIC TREES, Radiohead, 95-20
FAKER, Audioweb, 97-70
FALCON, Rah Band, 80-35
THE FALL, Ministry, 96-53
THE FALL, Way Out West, 00-61
FALL AT YOUR FEET, Crowded House, 91-17
FALL DOWN (SPIRIT OF LOVE), Tramaine, 85-60
FALL [EP], Ride, 90-34
FALL FROM GRACE, Eskimos And Egypt, 93-51
FALL IN LOVE WITH ME, Earth, Wind And Fire, 83-47
FALL IN LOVE WITH ME, Booth and the Bad Angel featuring Tim Booth Of James, 98-57
FALL IN LOVE WITH YOU, Cliff Richard and the Shadows, 60-2
FALL OUT, Police, 79-47
FALL TO LOVE, Diesel Park West, 92-48
FALLEN ANGEL, Frankie Valli, 76-11
FALLEN ANGEL, Poison, 88-59
FALLEN ANGEL, Traci Lords, 95-72
FALLEN ANGELS, Buffy Sainte-Marie, 92-57
FALLIN', Connie Francis, 58-20
FALLIN', Teenage Fanclub and De La Soul, 94-59
FALLIN', Alicia Keys, 01-3
FALLIN' IN LOVE, Hamilton, Joe Frank and Reynolds, 75-33
FALLING, Roy Orbison, 63-9
FALLING, Julee Cruise, 90-7
FALLING (THE PM DAWN VERSION), Cathy Dennis, 93-32
FALLING, Alison Moyet, 93-42
FALLING, Ant and Dec, 97-14
FALLING, Boom!, 01-11
FALLING ANGELS RIDING, David Essex, 85-29
FALLING APART AT THE SEAMS, Marmalade, 76-9
FALLING AWAY FROM ME, Korn, 00-24
FALLING IN AND OUT OF LOVE, Femme Fatale, 89-69
FALLING IN LOVE, Surface, 83-67
FALLING IN LOVE, Sybil, 86-68
FALLING IN LOVE, La Bouche, 95-43
FALLING IN LOVE AGAIN, Techno Twins, 82-70
FALLING IN LOVE AGAIN, Londonbeat, 89-60
FALLING IN LOVE AGAIN, Eagle-Eye Cherry, 98-8
FALLING IN LOVE (IS HARD ON THE KNEES), Aerosmith, 97-22
FALLING INTO YOU, Celine Dion, 96-10
FALLING TO PIECES, Faith No More, 90-41
FAME, David Bowie, 75-17, 90-28
FAME, Irene Cara, 82-1
FAMILUS HORRIBILUS, Pop Will Eat Itself, 93-27
FAMILY AFFAIR:
Sly and the Family Stone, 72-15
B.E.F. featuring Lalah Hathaway, 91-37
Shabba Ranks featuring Patra and Terri and Monica, 93-18
FAMILY AFFAIR, Mary J Blige, 01-8
FAMILY MAN:
Mike Oldfield featuring Maggie Reilly, 82-45
Daryl Hall and John Oates, 83-15
FAMILY MAN, Fleetwood Mac, 87-54
FAMILY MAN, Roachford, 89-25
FAMILY OF MAN, Farm, 90-58
FAMINE, Sinead O'Connor, 95-51
FAN' DABI' DOZI, Krankies, 81-46
FAN MAIL, Dickies, 80-57
FAN THE FLAME, Barbara Pennington, 85-62
FANCY PANTS, Kenny, 75-4
FANFARE FOR THE COMMON MAN, Emerson Lake and Palmer, 77-2
FANFARE PASSOMEZO DU ROY, GAILLARDE D'ESCOSSE (from HENRY VIII SUITE: THE SIX WIVES OF HENRY VIII [OST-TV]), Early Music Consort, directed by David Munrow, 71-49
FANLIGHT FANNY, Clinton Ford with the George Chisholm All-Stars, 62-22

FANTASTIC DAY, Haircut One Hundred, 82-9
FANTASTIC VOYAGE, Coolio, 94-41
FANTASY:
Earth, Wind And Fire, 78-14
Black Box, 90-5
FANTASY, Gerard Kenny, 80-34
FANTASY, Fantasy U.F.O., 90-56
FANTASY, Ten City, 93-45
FANTASY, Mariah Carey, 95-4
FANTASY, Levellers, 95-16
FANTASY ISLAND, Tight Fit, 82-5
FANTASY ISLAND, M People, 97-33
FANTASY REAL, Phil Fearon and Galaxy, 83-41
FAR, Longpigs, 96-37
FAR ABOVE THE CLOUDS, Mike Oldfield, 99-53
FAR AND AWAY, A I D A, 00-58
FAR AWAY, Shirley Bassey with Geoff Love and his Orchestra, 62-24
FAR FAR AWAY, Slade, 74-2
FAR FROM HOME, Levellers, 91-71
FAR FROM OVER, Frank Stallone, 83-68
FAR GONE AND OUT, Jesus And Mary Chain, 92-23
FAR OUT, Son'z Of A Loop Da Loop Era, 92-36
FAR OUT, Deejay Punk-Roc, 98-43
FAR-OUT SON OF LUNG AND THE RAMBLINGS OF A MADMAN, Future Sound Of London, 95-22
FARAWAY EYES, Rolling Stones, 78-3
FARAWAY PLACES, Bachelors, 63-36
FAREWELL, Rod Stewart, 74-7
FAREWELL ANGELINA, Joan Baez, 65-35
FAREWELL IS A LONELY SOUND, Jimmy Ruffin, 70-8, 74-30
FAREWELL MR SORROW, All About Eve, 91-36
FAREWELL MY SUMMER LOVE:
Michael Jackson, 84-7
Chaos, 92-55
FAREWELL TO THE MOON, York, 00-37
FAREWELL TO TWILIGHT, Symposium, 97-25
FARMER BILL'S COWMAN (I WAS KAISER BILL'S BATMAN), Wurzels, 77-32
FARON YOUNG, Prefab Sprout, 85-74
FASCINATED, Lisa B, 93-35
FASCINATING RHYTHM, Bass-O-Matic, 90-9
FASHION:
David Bowie, 80-5
Glamma Kid, 98-49
FASHION CRISIS HITS NEW YORK, Frank And Walters, 93-42
FAST AS YOU CAN, Fiona Apple, 00-33
FAST CAR, Tracy Chapman, 88-5
FASTER, Manic Street Preachers, 94-16
FASTER THAN THE SPEED OF LIGHT, Bonnie Tyler, 83-43
FASTLOVE, George Michael, 96-1
THE FAT BASTARD [EP], Medway, 00-69
FAT BLACK HEART, Pele, 93-75
FAT BOTTOMED GIRLS, Queen, 78-11
FAT LIP, Sum 41, 01-8
FAT NECK, Black Grape, 96-10
FATAL HESITATION, Chris De Burgh, 86-44
FATHER, Christians, 92-55
FATHER, LL Cool J, 98-10
FATHER AND SON, Boyzone, 95-2
FATHER CHRISTMAS DO NOT TOUCH ME, Goodies, 74-7
FATHER FIGURE, George Michael, 88-11
FATTIE BUM BUM:
Carl Malcolm, 75-8
Diversions, 75-34
FAVOURITE SHIRTS (BOY MEETS GIRL), Haircut One Hundred, 81-4
FE REAL, Maxi Priest and Apache Indian, 92-33
FEAR LOVES THIS PLACE, Julian Cope, 92-42
FEAR OF THE DARK, Gordon Giltrap Band, 79-58
FEAR OF THE DARK (LIVE), Iron Maiden, 93-8
FEAR (PROLOGUE) (from FEAR: THE MINDKILLER [EP]), Eon, 91-63
FEAR SATAN – REMIXES, Mogwai, 98-57
FEAR: THE MINDKILLER [EP], Eon, 91-63
FED UP, House Of Pain, 96-68
FEDORA (I'LL BE YOUR DAWG), Caramba, 83-56
FEE FI FO FUM, Candy Girls featuring Sweet Pussy Pauline, 95-23
FEED MY FRANKENSTEIN, Alice Cooper, 92-27
FEED THE FEELING, Perception, 92-58
FEED THE TREE, Belly, 93-32
FEEDING TIME, Look, 81-50
FEEL, Ruth Joy, 92-67
FEEL, House Of Love, 92-45
FEEL EVERY BEAT, Electronic, 91-39
FEEL FREE, Soul II Soul featuring Do'reen, 88-64
FEEL GOOD, Phats and Small, 99-7
FEEL GOOD, Madasun, 00-29
FEEL IT, Hi-Lux, 95-41, 95-58
FEEL IT, Carol Bailey, 95-41
FEEL IT, Neneh Cherry, 97-68
FEEL IT, Tamperer featuring Maya, 98-1
FEEL IT, Inaya Day, 00-51
FEEL LIKE CALLING HOME, Mr. Big, 77-35
FEEL LIKE CHANGE, Black, 91-56
FEEL LIKE MAKIN' LOVE:
Roberta Flack, 74-34
George Benson, 83-28
FEEL LIKE MAKIN' LOVE:
Bad Company, 75-20
Pauline Henry *, 93-12
FEEL LIKE SINGIN':
Sandy B, 93-60
Tak Tix *, 96-33
FEEL ME, Blancmange, 82-46
FEEL ME FLOW, Naughty By Nature, 95-23
FEEL MY BODY, Frank 'O Moiraghi featuring Amnesia, 96-39, 96-40
FEEL NO PAIN, Sade, 92-56
FEEL SO FINE, Johnny Preston, 60-18
FEEL SO GOOD, Mase, 97-10
FEEL SO GOOD, Jon The Dentist vs Ollie Jaye, 00-72
FEEL SO HIGH, Des'ree, 91-51, 92-13
FEEL SO REAL, Steve Arrington, 85-5
FEEL SO REAL, Dream Frequency featuring Debbie Sharp, 92-23
FEEL SURREAL, Freefall featuring Psychotropic, 91-63
FEEL THA VIBE, That Kid Chris, 97-52
FEEL THE BEAT, Camisra, 98-32
FEEL THE BEAT, Darude, 00-5
FEEL THE DRUMS, Native, 01-46
FEEL THE DRUMS [EP], Parks And Wilson, 00-71
FEEL THE MUSIC, Guru: Jazzamatazz Vol. II The New Reality, 95-34
FEEL THE NEED, J.T. Taylor, 91-57
FEEL THE NEED, Weird Science, 00-62
FEEL THE NEED IN ME:
Detroit Emeralds, 73-4
Detroit Emeralds, 77-12
Leif Garrett *, 79-38
Forrest, 83-17
Shakin' Stevens, 88-26
G Nation featuring Rosie *, 97-58
FEEL THE PAIN, Dinosaur Jr, 94-25
FEEL THE RAINDROPS, Adventures, 85-58
FEEL THE REAL, David Bendeth, 79-44
FEEL THE RHYTHM, Jazzi P, 90-51
FEEL THE RHYTHM, Terrorize, 92-69
FEEL THE RHYTHM, Jinny, 93-74
FEEL THE SAME, Triple X, 99-32
FEEL THE SUNSHINE, Alex Reece, 95-69, 96-26
FEEL WHAT YOU WANT, Kristine W, 94-33, 97-40
FEELIN', La's, 91-43
FEELIN' ALRIGHT, E.Y.C., 93-16
THE FEELIN' (CLAP YOUR HANDS), Rhythmatic Junkies, 99-67
FEELIN' INSIDE, Bobby Brown, 97-40
FEELIN' SO GOOD, Jennifer Lopez (featuring Big Pun and Fat Joe), 00-15
FEELIN' YOU, Ali, 98-63
THE FEELING, Urban Hype, 92-67
THE FEELING, Tin Tin Out featuring Sweet Tee, 94-32
FEELING FOR YOU, Cassius, 99-16
FEELING GOOD:
Nina Simone, 94-40
Huff and Herb, 97-31, 98-69
Muse, 01-24
FEELING IT TOO, 3 Jays, 99-17
FEELING SO REAL, Moby, 94-30
FEELING THIS WAY, Conductor and the Cowboy, 00-35
FEELINGS, Morris Albert, 75-4
FEELINGS OF FOREVER, Tiffany, 88-52
FEELS LIKE FOREVER, Joe Cocker, 92-25
(FEELS LIKE) HEAVEN, Fiction Factory, 84-6
FEELS LIKE HEAVEN, Urban Cookie Collective, 93-5
FEELS LIKE I'M IN LOVE, Kelly Marie, 80-1
FEELS LIKE THE FIRST TIME, Foreigner, 78-39
FEELS LIKE THE FIRST TIME, Sinitta, 86-45
FEELS LIKE THE RIGHT TIME, Shakatak, 80-41
FEELS SO GOOD, Van Halen, 89-63
FEELS SO GOOD, Xscape, 95-34
FEELS SO GOOD, Zero Vu featuring Lorna B, 97-69
FEELS SO GOOD, Melanie B, 01-5
FEELS SO REAL (WON'T LET GO), Patrice Rushen, 84-51
FEELS SO RIGHT, Victor Simonelli Presents Solution, 96-63
FEENIN', Jodeci, 94-18
FEET LIKE FINS (from OTHERNESS [EP]), Cocteau Twins, 95-59
FEET UP, Guy Mitchell with Mitch Miller and his Chorus and Orchestra, 52-2
FELICITY, Orange Juice, 82-63
FELL ON BLACK DAYS, Soundgarden, 95-24
FEMALE INTUITION, Mai-Tai, 86-54
FEMALE OF THE SPECIES, Space, 96-14
FERGUS SINGS THE BLUES, Deacon Blue, 89-14
FERNANDO, Abba, 76-1
THE FERRIS WHEEL, Everly Brothers, 64-22
FERRY CROSS THE MERSEY:
Gerry and the Pacemakers, 64-8
Christians, Holly Johnson, Paul McCartney, Gerry Marsden, Stock Aitken Waterman, 89-1
FESTIVAL TIME, San Remo Strings, 71-39
FEVER:
Peggy Lee with Jack Marshall's Music, 58-5, 92-75
Helen Shapiro, 64-38
McCoys, 65-44
Madonna, 93-6
FEVER, S-J, 97-46
FEVER, Starsailor, 01-18
FEVER CALLED LOVE, R.H.C., 92-65
FEVER PITCH THE EP [EP], Various Artists (EPs), 97-65
FICTION OF LIFE, China Drum, 97-65
FIELDS OF FIRE (400 MILES), Big Country, 83-10
FIELDS OF GOLD, Sting, 93-16
THE FIELDS OF LOVE, A1B featuring York, 01-16
FIESTA, Pogues, 88-24
FIESTA, R. Kelly featuring Jay-Z and Boo and Gotti, 01-23
¡FIESTA FATAL!, B-Tribe, 93-64
FIFTEEN FEET OF PURE WHITE SNOW, Nick Cave and the Bad Seeds, 01-52
15 MINUTES OF FAME, Sheep On Drugs, 93-44
15 STEPS [EP], Monkey Mafia, 97-67
15 WAYS, Fall, 94-65
15 YEARS [EP] + lead track title, Levellers, 92-11
5TH ANNIVERSARY [EP], Judge Dread, 77-31
A FIFTH OF BEETHOVEN, Walter Murphy and the Big Apple Band, 76-28
50 WAYS TO LEAVE YOUR LOVER, Paul Simon, 76-23
50 FT QUEENIE, PJ Harvey, 93-27
51ST STATE, New Model Army, 86-71
FIFTY-FOUR, Sea Level, 79-63
54-46 (WAS MY NUMBER), Aswad, 84-70
57 CHANNELS (AND NOTHIN' ON), Bruce Springsteen, 92-32
59TH STREET BRIDGE SONG (FEELIN' GROOVY), Harpers Bizarre, 67-34
FIGARO, Brotherhood Of Man, 78-1
THE FIGHT, Marty Wilde, 60-47
FIGHT, McKoy, 93-54
FIGHT FOR OURSELVES, Spandau Ballet, 86-15
FIGHT FOR YOUR RIGHT (TO PARTY), N.Y.C.C., 98-14
FIGHT MUSIC, D12, 01-11
THE FIGHT SONG, Marilyn Manson, 01-24
FIGHT THE POWER, Public Enemy, 89-29
FIGHT THE POWER 95 (from MAXIMUM [EP]), Dreadzone, 95-56
FIGHT THE YOUTH, Fishbone, 92-60
FIGHTING FIT, Gene, 96-22
FIGURE OF EIGHT, Paul McCartney, 89-42
FIGURE OF EIGHT, Grid, 92-50
FIJI, Atlantis vs Avatar featuring Miriam Stockley, 00-52
FILL HER UP, Gene, 99-36
FILL ME IN, Craig David, 00-1
FILLING UP WITH HEAVEN, Human League, 95-36
A FILM FOR THE FUTURE, Idlewild, 98-53
FILMSTAR, Suede, 97-9
FILTHY, St. Etienne, 91-39
THE FINAL COUNTDOWN:
Europe, 86-1
Europe, 99-36
FINALLY, Ce Ce Peniston, 91-29, 92-2, 97-26
FINALLY, Kings Of Tomorrow featuring Julie Mc Knight, 01-54, 01-24

FINALLY FOUND, Honeyz, 98-4
FINCHLEY CENTRAL, New Vaudeville Band (featuring Tristam Vii), 67-11
FIND A WAY, Coldcut featuring Queen Latifah, 90-52
FIND A WAY, A Tribe Called Quest, 98-41
FIND 'EM, FOOL 'EM, FORGET 'EM, S'Express, 92-43
FIND ME (ODYSSEY TO ANYOONA), Jam and Spoon featuring Plavka, 94-37, 95-22
FIND MY LOVE, Fairground Attraction, 88-7
FIND MY WAY BACK HOME, Nashville Teens, 65 34
FIND THE ANSWER WITHIN, Boo Radleys, 95-37
FIND THE RIVER, R.E.M., 93-54
FIND THE TIME, Five Star, 86-7
FIND THE TIME (PART 1), Quadrophonia, 91-41
FINDERS KEEPERS, Chairmen Of The Board, 73-21
FINE DAY, Rolf Harris, 00-24
FINE TIME, New Order, 88-11
FINE TIME, Yazz, 89-9
FINER, Nightmares On Wax, 99-63
FINER FEELINGS, Kylie Minogue, 92-11
THE FINEST:
S.O.S. Band, 86-17
Truce, 95-54
FINEST WORKSONG, R.E.M., 88-50
FINETIME, Cast, 95-17
THE FINGER OF SUSPICION, Dickie Valentine with the Stargazers, 54-1
FINGERS & THUMBS (COLD SUMMER'S DAY), Erasure, 95-20
FINGERS OF LOVE, Crowded House, 94-25
FINGS AIN'T WOT THEY USED T'BE:
Max Bygraves with chorus from the Gang Show, 60-5
Russ Conway, 60-47
FINISHED SYMPHONY, Hybrid, 99-58
FIRE!, Crazy World Of Arthur Brown, 68-1
FIRE:
Pointer Sisters, 79-34
Bruce Springsteen and the E Street Band, 87-54
FIRE, U2, 81-35
FIRE, Sly and Robbie, 87-60
FIRE, Prodigy, 92-11, 96-63
FIRE, Prizna featuring the Demolition Man, 95-33
FIRE, Scooter, 97-45
FIRE, Busta Rhymes, 00-60
FIRE AND RAIN, James Taylor, 70-42
FIRE BRIGADE, Move, 68-3
FIRE DOWN BELOW:
Jeri Southern, 57-22
Shirley Bassey with Wally Stott and his Orchestra, 57-30
FIRE IN MY HEART, Super Furry Animals, 99-25
FIRE ISLAND, Fire Island, 92-66
FIRE OF LOVE, Jungle High with Blue Pearl, 93-71
FIRE UP THE SHOESAW, Lionrock, 96-43
FIRE WIRE, Cosmic Gate, 01-9
FIRE WOMAN, Cult, 89-15
FIRE WORKS, Siouxsie and the Banshees, 82-22
FIREBALL, Don Spencer, 63-32
FIREBALL, Deep Purple, 71-15
FIRED UP, Elevatorman, 95-44
FIRED UP!, Funky Green Dogs, 97-17
FIREPILE [(EP] + lead track title, Throwing Muses, 92-46
FIRES BURNING, Run Tings, 92-58
FIRESTARTER, Prodigy, 96-1, 97-53
FIREWORKS, Roxette, 94-30
FIREWORKS [EP], Embrace, 97-34
FIRM BIZ, Nas Escobar, Foxy Brown, Az and Nature present the Firm featuring Dawn Robinson, 97-18
1ST ATHEIST TABERNACLE CHOIR, Spitting Image, 86-22
FIRST BOY IN THIS TOWN (LOVE SICK), Scritti Politti, 88-63
THE FIRST CUT IS THE DEEPEST:
P. P. Arnold, 67-18
Rod Stewart, 77-1
FIRST DATE, Blink-182, 01-31
THE FIRST DAY (HORIZON), Man with No Name, 98-72
FIRST IMPRESSIONS, Impressions, 75-16
1ST MAN IN SPACE, All Seeing I, 99-28
THE FIRST MAN YOU REMEMBER, Michael Ball and Diana Morrison, 89-68
THE FIRST NIGHT, Monica, 98-6
FIRST OF MAY, Bee Gees, 69-6
1ST OF THA MONTH, Bone Thugs-N-Harmony, 95-32, 96-1
THE FIRST PICTURE OF YOU, Lotus Eaters, 83-15
FIRST TASTE OF LOVE, Ben E. King, 61-27
THE FIRST THE LAST ETERNITY (TIL THE END), Snap! featuring Summer, 95-15
FIRST THING IN THE MORNING, Kiki Dee, 77-32
THE FIRST TIME, Adam Faith with the Roulettes, 63-5
FIRST TIME, Robin Beck, 88-1
THE FIRST TIME, Surface, 91-60
THE FIRST TIME EVER I SAW YOUR FACE:
Roberta Flack, 72-14
Joanna Law *, 90-67
Celine Dion, 00-19
1ST TRANSMISSION (from BLOOD MUSIC [EP]), Earthling, 96-69
FIRST WE TAKE MANHATTAN, Jennifer Warnes, 87-74
FISH OUT OF WATER, One Minute Silence, 01-56
FISHERMAN'S BLUES, Waterboys, 89-32, 91-75
FIVE [EP], Mansun, 97-9
THE $5.98 E.P.-GARAGE DAYS RE-REVISITED [EP], Metallica, 87-27
FIVE FATHOMS, Everything But The Girl, 99-27
5:15, Who, 73-20
555, Delakota, 99-42
5-4-3-2-1, Manfred Mann, 64-5
FIVE GET OVER EXCITED, Housemartins, 87-11
500 (SHAKE BABY SHAKE), Lush, 96-21
FIVE LITTLE FINGERS, Frankie McBride, 67-19
FIVE LIVE (EP), George Michael and Queen with Lisa Stansfield, 93-1
FIVE MILES OUT, Mike Oldfield: Maggie Reilly – vocals, 82-43
5 MILES TO EMPTY, Brownstone, 97-12
5 MINUTES, Stranglers, 78-11
5 MINUTES, Lil' Mo featuring Missy "Misdemeanor" Elliott, 98-72
5 O'CLOCK, Nonchalant, 96-44
5 O'CLOCK WORLD, Julian Cope, 89-42
5.7.0.5., City Boy, 78-8
5,6,7,8, Steps, 97-14
5 STEPS, Dru Hill, 97-22
FIX, Blackstreet, 97-7
FIXATION, Andy Ling, 00-55
FIXER, Vent 414, 96-71
FLAGPOLE SITTA, Harvey Danger, 98-57
THE FLAME, Arcadia, 86-58
THE FLAME, Fine Young Cannibals, 96-17
FLAME, Sebadoh, 99-30
THE FLAME STILL BURNS, Jimmy Nail with Strange Fruit, 98-47
THE FLAME TREES OF THIKA, Video Symphonic, 81-42
FLAMES OF PARADISE, Jennifer Rush (Duet with Elton John), 87-59
FLAMING JUNE, BT, 97-19, 98-28
FLAMING SWORD, Care, 83-48
FLASH, Queen, 80-10
FLASH:
B.B.E., 97-5
BK and Nick Sentience, 01-67
FLASH, Grifters featuring Tall Paul and Brandon Block, 99-63
FLASHBACK, Imagination, 81-16
FLASHBACK JACK, Adamski, 90-46
FLASHDANCE . . . WHAT A FEELING:
Irene Cara, 83-2
Bjorn Again, 93-65
THE FLASHER, Mistura featuring Lloyd Michels (trumpet), 76-23
FLAT BEAT, Mr. Oizo, 99-1
FLATLINERS, Nebula II, 92-54
FLAVA, Peter Andre, 96-1
FLAVA, Imajin, 00-64
FLAVA IN YA EAR, Craig Mack, 94-57
FLAVOR OF THE WEAK, American Hi-Fi, 01-31
FLAVOUR OF THE OLD SCHOOL, Beverley Knight, 95-50, 95-33
FLAWLESS, Ones, 01-7
FLEE FLY FLO, Fe-M@il, 00-46
FLESH, A Split Second, 91-68
FLESH, Jan Johnston, 01-36
FLESH FOR FANTASY, Billy Idol, 84-54
FLESH OF MY FLESH, Orange Juice, 83-41
"FLETCH" THEME, Harold Faltermeyer, 85-74
FLIGHT OF ICARUS, Iron Maiden, 83-11
FLIGHT 643, DJ Tiesto, 01-56
FLIP, Jesse Green, 76-26
THE FLIPSIDE, Moloko, 98-53
FLIRT!, Jonathan King, 72-22
FLIRTATION WALTZ, Winifred Atwell and her piano, 53-10
FLOAT ON, Floaters, 77-1
FLOATATION, Grid, 90-60
FLOATING, Terra Ferma, 96-64
FLOATING IN THE WIND, Hudson-Ford, 74-35
FLOODLIT WORLD, Ultrasound, 99-39
THE FLOOR, Johnny Gill, 93-53
FLOOR-ESSENCE, Man With No Name, 95-68
FLOOR SPACE, Our House, 96-52
THE FLORAL DANCE:
Brighouse and Rastrick Brass Band, 77-2
Terry Wogan, 78-21
FLORIBUNDA, Mothers Pride, 98-42
FLOWER DUET (FROM 'LAKME'):
Mady Mesple and Danielle Millet, Paris Opera – Comique Orchestra conducted by Alain Lombard, 85-47
Jonathan Peters presents Luminaire, 99-75
FLOWER OF SCOTLAND, Scottish Rugby Team with Ronnie Browne, 90-73
FLOWER OF THE WEST, Runrig, 91-43
FLOWERS, Titiyo, 90-71
FLOWERS, Armand Van Helden featuring Roland Clark, 99-18
FLOWERS, Sweet Female Attitude, 00-2
FLOWERS IN DECEMBER, Mazzy Star, 96-40
FLOWERS IN THE RAIN, Move, 67-2
FLOWERS OF ROMANCE, Public Image Ltd., 81-24
FLOWERS ON THE WALL, Statler Brothers, 66-38
FLOWTATION, Vincent De Moor, 97-54
FLOY JOY, Supremes, 72-9
THE FLY, U2, 91-1
FLY, Sugar Ray (featuring Super Cat), 98-58
FLY, POB featuring DJ Patrick Reid, 99-74
FLY BI, Teebone featuring MC Kie and MC Sparks, 00-43
FLY AWAY, Haddaway, 95-20
FLY AWAY, Lenny Kravitz, 99-1
FLY AWAY, Vincent De Moor, 01-30
FLY AWAY (BYE BYE), Eyes Cream, 99-53
FLY GIRL, Queen Latifah, 91-67
FLY LIFE, Basement Jaxx, 97-19
FLY LIKE AN EAGLE, Seal, 97-13
FLY ROBIN FLY, Silver Convention, 75-28
FLY TO THE ANGELS, Slaughter, 91-55
FLY TOO HIGH, Janis Ian, 79-44
FLYING, Cast, 96-4
FLYING ELVIS, Leilani, 00-73
FLYING HIGH, Commodores, 78-37
FLYING HIGH, Freeez, 81-35
FLYING HIGH, Captain Hollywood Project, 95-58
FLYING MACHINE, Cliff Richard, 71-37
FLYING SAUCER, Wedding Present, 92-22
THE FLYING SONG, PQM featuring Cica, 00-68
FLYING WITHOUT WINGS, Westlife, 99-1
FLYSWATTER, Eels, 00-55
FM (NO STATIC AT ALL), Steely Dan, 78-49
FOE-DEE-O-DEE, Rubettes, 75-15
FOG ON THE TYNE (REVISITED), Gazza and Lindisfarne, 90-2
FOGGY MOUNTAIN BREAKDOWN, Lester Flatt and Earl Scruggs, 67-39
FOGHORN, A, 98-63
THE FOLK SINGER, Tommy Roe, 63-4
FOLLOW ME, J.T. Taylor, 92-59
FOLLOW ME, Aly-Us, 92-43
FOLLOW ME, Atomic Kitten, 00-20
FOLLOW ME, Uncle Kracker, 01-3
FOLLOW THAT DREAM [EP] + lead track title, Elvis Presley, 62-34
FOLLOW THE LEADER, Eric B. and Rakim, 88-21
FOLLOW THE LEADERS, Killing Joke, 81-55
FOLLOW THE RULES, Livin' Joy, 96-9
FOLLOW YOU DOWN, Gin Blossoms, 96-30
FOLLOW YOU FOLLOW ME:
Genesis, 78-7
Sonny Jones featuring Tara Chase, 00-42
FOLLOWING, Bangles, 87-55
THE FOOD CHRISTMAS EP 1989 [EP], Various Artists (EPs), 89-63
FOOD FOR THOUGHT, U.B.40, 80-4
FOOD FOR THOUGHT [M], Barron Knights, 79-46
FOOL, Elvis Presley, 73-15
FOOL, Al Matthews, 75-16
FOOL (track from FOURTEEN [EP]), Mansun, 01-28
FOOL AGAIN (2000 REMIX), Westlife, 00-1
A FOOL AM I (DIMMELO PARLAMI), Cilla Black, 66-13
FOOL FOR LOVE, Russell, 00-52
FOOL FOR YOUR LOVING:
Whitesnake, 80-13
Whitesnake, 89-43
FOOL (IF YOU THINK IT'S OVER):
Chris Rea, 78-30
Elkie Brooks, 82-17

FREE YOUR BODY
Praga Khan featuring Jade 4 U, 92-16
FREE YOUR MIND, En Vogue, 92-16
FREE YOUR MIND, Spacebaby, 95-55
FREE YOURSELF, Untouchables, 85-26
FREEBASE, Tall Paul, 00-43
FREED FROM DESIRE, Gala, 97-2
FREEDOM, Wham!, 84-1
FREEDOM, Alice Cooper, 88-50
FREEDOM, A Homeboy, A Hippie and A Funki Dredd, 90-68
FREEDOM, London Boys, 91-54
FREEDOM:
QFX (from Freedom [EP]), 95-41
QFX, 97-21
FREEDOM, Michelle Gayle, 95-16
FREEDOM, Shiva, 95-18
FREEDOM, Robert Miles featuring Kathy Sledge, 97-15
FREEDOM, Erasure, 00-27
FREEDOM COME, FREEDOM GO, Fortunes, 71-6
FREEDOM [EP] + lead track title, Qfx, 95-41
FREEDOM GOT AN A.K., Da Lench Mob, 93-51
FREEDOM (MAKE IT FUNKY), Black Magic: A Lil Louis Painting, 96-41
FREEDOM! 90:
George Michael, 90-28
Robbie Williams, 96-2
FREEDOM OVERSPILL, Steve Winwood, 86-69
FREEDOM'S PRISONER, Steve Harley, 79-58
FREEFLOATING, Gary Clark, 93-50
FREEK 'N YOU, Jodeci, 95-17
FREELOVE, Depeche Mode, 01-19
FREESTYLER, Bomfunk MC's, 00-2
FREET, Tata Box Inhibitors, 01-67
FREEWAY OF LOVE, Aretha Franklin, 85-68, 86-51
FREEWHEEL BURNIN', Judas Priest, 84-42
THE FREEZE, Spandau Ballet, 81-17
FREEZE-FRAME, J. Geils Band, 82-27
FREEZE THE ATLANTIC, Cable, 97-44
FREIGHT TRAIN, Chas McDevitt Skiffle Group (featuring Nancy Whiskey), 57-5
FRENCH DISKO, Stereolab, 94-75
FRENCH FOREIGN LEGION, Frank Sinatra, 59-18
FRENCH KISS, Lil Louis, 89-2
FRENCH KISSIN' IN THE USA, Debbie Harry, 86-8
FREQUENCY, Rhythmatic, 90-62
FREQUENCY, Altern 8, 92-41
FRESH, Kool And The Gang, 84-11
FRESH!, Gina G, 97-6
FRIDAY I'M IN LOVE, Cure, 92-6
FRIDAY NIGHT (LIVE VERSION), Kids From Fame featuring Carlo Imperato and "The Waters", 83-13
FRIDAY ON MY MIND:
Easybeats, 66-6
Gary Moore, 87-26
FRIDAY STREET, Paul Weller, 97-21
FRIDAY THE THIRTEENTH [EP], Damned, 81-50
FRIDAYS ANGELS, Generation X, 79-62
A FRIEND, Krs-One featuring Redman and Angie Martinez, 97-66
FRIEND OF MINE, Kelly Price, 98-25
FRIEND OR FOE, Adam Ant, 82-9
FRIENDLY PERSUASION (THEE I LOVE):
Pat Boone, 56-3
Four Aces featuring Al Roberts, 57-29
FRIENDLY PRESSURE, Jhelisa, 95-75
FRIENDS, Beach Boys, 68-25
FRIENDS, Arrival, 70-8
FRIENDS (from THE ANTMUSIC (EP) (THE B-SIDES) [EP]), Adam and the Ants, 82-46
FRIENDS, Shalamar, 82-12
FRIENDS, Amii Stewart, 84-12
FRIENDS, Jody Watley with Eric B. and Rakim, 89-21
FRIENDS, Tiger, 98-72
THE FRIENDS AGAIN [EP], Friends Again, 84-59
FRIENDS AND NEIGHBOURS, Billy Cotton and his Band featuring The Bandits, 54-3
FRIENDS FOREVER, Thunderbugs, 99-5
FRIENDS IN LOW PLACES, Garth Brooks, 95-36
FRIENDS WILL BE FRIENDS, Queen, 86-14
FRIENDSHIP, Sabrina Johnston, 91-58
FRIGGIN' IN THE RIGGIN', Sex Pistols vocals: Steve Jones, 79-3
THE FRIGHTENED CITY, Shadows, 61-3
THE FROG PRINCESS, Divine Comedy, 96-15
FROGGY MIX [M], James Brown, 85-50
FROGGY STYLE, Nuttin' Nyce, 95-68
FROM A DISTANCE:
Cliff Richard, 90-11
Bette Midler, 90-45, 91-6
FROM A JACK TO A KING, Ned Miller, 63-2
FROM A LOVER TO A FRIEND, Paul McCartney, 01-45
FROM A TO H AND BACK AGAIN, Sheep On Drugs, 93-40
FROM A WINDOW, Billy J. Kramer with the Dakotas, 64-10
FROM A WINDOW, Northern Uproar, 96-17
FROM DESPAIR TO WHERE, Manic Street Preachers, 93-25
FROM EAST TO WEST, Voyage, 78-13
FROM HEAD TO TOE, Elvis Costello and the Attractions, 82-43
FROM HERE TO ETERNITY, Giorgio, 77-16
FROM HERE TO ETERNITY, Iron Maiden, 92-21
FROM HERE TO ETERNITY, Michael Ball, 94-36
FROM HERE TO THERE TO YOU, Hank Locklin, 62-44
FROM ME TO YOU, Beatles, 63-1, 83-40
FROM NEW YORK TO L.A., Patsy Gallant, 77-6
FROM NOW ON, Jaki Graham, 89-73
FROM OUT OF NOWHERE, Faith No More, 90-23
FROM RUSH HOUR WITH LOVE, Republica, 98-20
FROM RUSSIA WITH LOVE:
Matt Monro, 63-20
John Barry Seven and Orchestra, 63-39
FROM RUSSIA WITH LOVE, Matt Darey presents DSP, 00-40
FROM THE BENCH AT BELVIDERE, Boo Radleys, 95-24
FROM THE BOTTOM OF MY HEART (I LOVE YOU), Moody Blues, 65-22
FROM THE GHETTO, Dread Flimstone and the New Tone Age Family, 91-66
FROM THE HEART, Another Level, 99-6
FROM THE HIP [EP] + lead track title, Lloyd Cole and the Commotions, 88-59
FROM THE UNDERWORLD, Herd, 67-6
FROM THIS DAY, Machine Head, 99-74
FROM THIS MOMENT ON, Shania Twain, 98-9
FRONTIER PSYCHIATRIST, Avalanches, 01-18
FROSTY THE SNOWMAM, Cocteau Twins, 93-58
FROZEN, Madonna, 98-1
FROZEN HEART, FM, 87-64
FROZEN METAL HEAD [EP], Beastie Boys, 92-55
FROZEN ORANGE JUICE, Peter Sarstedt, 69-10
FU-GEE-LA, Fugees (Refugee Camp), 96-21
FUEL, Metallica, 98-31
FULL METAL JACKET (I WANNA BE YOUR DRILL INSTRUCTOR), Abigail Mead and Nigel Goulding, 87-2
THE FULL MONTY MONSTER MIX [M], Full Monty, 98-62
FULL OF LIFE (HAPPY NOW), Wonder Stuff, 93-28
FULL TERM LOVE, Monie Love, 92-34
A FULL TIME JOB, Doris Day and Johnnie Ray, 53-11
FUN, Da Mob featuring Jocelyn Brown, 98-33
FUN DAY, Stevie Wonder, 91-63
FUN FOR ME, Moloko, 96-36
FUN FUN FUN, Status Quo with the Beach Boys, 96-24
THE FUN LOVIN' CRIMINAL, Fun Lovin' Criminals, 96-26
FUNERAL PYRE, Jam, 81-4
THE FUNERAL (SEPTEMBER 25, 1977), Cry Freedom (Solo voice:Thuli Dumakude), 88-75
FUNGI MAMA (BEBOPAFUNKADISCOLYPSO), Tom Browne, 82-58
FUNK AND DRIVE, Elevatorman, 95-37
FUNK DAT, Sagat, 93-25
FUNK ON AH ROLL, James Brown, 99-40, 00-63
THE FUNK PHENOMENA, Armand Van Helden presents Old School Junkies Pt. 2, 97-38
FUNK THEORY, Rokotto, 78-49
FUNKATARIUM, Jump, 97-56
FUNKDAFIED, Da Brat, 94-65
FUNKIN' FOR JAMAICA (N.Y.), Tom Browne, 80-10, 92-45
FUNKY BROADWAY, Wilson Pickett, 67-43
FUNKY COLD MEDINA, Tone Loc, 89-13
THE FUNKY GIBBON, Goodies, 75-4
FUNKY GUITAR, TC 1992, 92-40
FUNKY JAM, Primal Scream, 94-7
FUNKY LOVE, Kavana, 98-32
FUNKY LOVE VIBRATIONS, Bass-O-Matic, 91-71
FUNKY MOPED, Jasper Carrott, 75-5
FUNKY MUSIC – SHO NUFF TURNS ME ON, Utah Saints special guest vocal by Edwin Starr, 00-23
FUNKY NASSAU, Beginning Of The End, 74-31
FUNKY SENSATION, Ladies Choice, 86-41
FUNKY STREET, Arthur Conley, 68-46
FUNKY STUFF, Kool And The Gang, 81-17
FUNKY WEEKEND, Stylistics, 76-10
FUNKYTOWN:
Lipps Inc., 80-2
Pseudo Echo *, 87-8
FUNNY ALL OVER, Vernons Girls, 63-31
FUNNY BREAK (ONE IS ENOUGH), Orbital, 01-21
FUNNY FAMILIAR FORGOTTEN FEELINGS, Tom Jones, 67-7
FUNNY, FUNNY, Sweet, 71-13
FUNNY HOW, Airhead, 91-57
FUNNY HOW LOVE CAN BE, Ivy League, 65-8
FUNNY HOW LOVE IS, Fine Young Cannibals, 86-58
FUNNY HOW TIME FLIES (WHEN YOU'RE HAVING FUN), Janet Jackson, 87-59
FUNNY HOW TIME SLIPS AWAY, Dorothy Moore, 76-38
FUNNY WAY OF LAUGHIN', Burl Ives, 62-29
FUNTIME, Boy George, 95-45
FURIOUS ANGELS, Rob Dougan, 98-62
FURNITURE, Fugazi, 01-61
FURNITURE MUSIC, Bill Nelson's Red Noise, 79-59
THE FURTHER ADVENTURES OF NORTH – MORE UNDERGROUND DANCE [EP], Various Artists (EPs), 90-64
FUTURE, Halo Varga, 00-67
FUTURE LOVE, Presence, 99-66
FUTURE LOVE [EP], Seal, 91-12
FUTURE LOVE PARADISE (from FUTURE LOVE [EP]), Seal, 91-12
FUTURE MANAGEMENT, Roger Taylor, 81-49
THE FUTURE MUSIC [EP], Liquid, 92-59
THE FUTURE OF THE FUTURE (STAY GOLD) [RM], Deep Dish with Everything But The Girl, 98-31
FUTURE SHOCK, Herbie Hancock, 84-54
FUTURE SOUND [EP] + lead track title, Phuture Assassins, 92-64
THE FUTURE'S SO BRIGHT I GOTTA WEAR SHADES, Timbuk 3, 87-21
FX, A Guy Called Gerald, 89-52
G.H.E.T.T.O.U.T., Changing Faces, 97-10
G.L.A.D., Kim Appleby, 91-10
G SPOT [RM], Wayne Marshall, 96-50
G.T.O., Sinitta, 87-15
GABRIEL, Roy Davis Jr. featuring Peven Everett, 97-22
GAINESVILLE ROCK CITY, Less Than Jake, 01-57
GAL WINE, Chaka Demus and Pliers, 94-20
THE GAL WITH THE YALLER SHOES, Michael Holliday with Norrie Paramor and his Orchestra and the Four Shepherd Boys, 56-13
GALAXIA, Moonman featuring Chantal, 00-50
GALAXIE, Blind Melon, 95-37
GALAXY, War, 78-14
GALAXY OF LOVE, Crown Heights Affair, 78-24
GALLOPING HOME, London String Chorale, 73-49, 74-31
GALLOWS POLE, Jimmy Page and Robert Plant, 94-35
GALVESTON, Glen Campbell, 69-14
GALVESTON BAY, Lonnie Hill, 86-51
GAMBLER, Madonna, 85-4
GAMBLIN' MAN, Lonnie Donegan and his Skiffle Group, 57-1
GAMBLIN'BAR ROOM BLUES, Sensational Alex Harvey Band, 75-38
THE GAME, Echo and the Bunnymen, 87-28
THE GAME, Nichola Holt, 00-72
GAME BOY, K.W.S., 92-1
THE GAME OF LOVE, Wayne Fontana and the Mindbenders, 65-2
THE GAME OF LOVE, Tony Hadley, 93-72
GAME ON, Catatonia, 98-33
GAME OVER, Scarface featuring Dr. Dre, Ice Cube, Too Short, 97-34
GAMEMASTER, Lost Tribe, 99-24

GHETTO DAY, Crystal Waters, 94-40
GHETTO GIRL, Simply Red, 98-34
GHETTO HEAVEN, Family Stand, 90-10, 98-30
GHETTO ROMANCE, Damage, 00-7
GHETTO SUPASTAR (THAT IS WHAT YOU ARE), Pras Michel featuring ODB and introducing Mya, 98-2
THE GHOST AT NUMBER ONE, Jellyfish, 93-43
GHOST DANCER, Addrisi Brothers, 79-57
GHOST HOUSE, House Engineers, 87-69
THE GHOST IN YOU, Psychedelic Furs, 84-68
THE GHOST OF LOVE, Tavares, 78-29
GHOST OF LOVE, Fiction Factory, 84-64
THE GHOST OF TOM JOAD, Bruce Springsteen, 96-26
GHOST TOWN, Specials, 81-1
GHOSTBUSTERS:
Ray Parker Jr., 84-2
Run Dmc, 89-65
GHOSTDANCING, Simple Minds, 86-13
GHOSTS:
Japan, 82-5
Tenth Planet, 01-59
GHOSTS, Michael Jackson, 97-5
GIDDY-UP, 2 In A Room, 96-74
GIDDY-UP-A DING DONG, Freddie Bell and the Bell Boys, 56-4
THE GIFT, Inxs, 93-11
THE GIFT, Daniel O'Donnell, 94-46
THE GIFT, Way Out West featuring Miss Joanna Law, 96-15
THE GIFT OF CHRISTMAS, Childliners, 95-9
GIGANTOR, Dickies, 80-72
GIGI, Billy Eckstine, 59-8
GIGOLO, Damned, 87-29
GILLY GILLY OSSENFEFFER KATZENELLENBOGEN BY THE SEA, Max Bygraves with Children's Chorus, 54-7
GIMME ALL YOUR LOVIN':
ZZ Top, 83-61, 84-10
Jocelyn Brown and Kym Mazelle, 94-22
Martay featuring ZZ Top *, 99-28
GIMME DAT BANANA, Black Gorilla, 77-29
GIMME DAT DING, Pipkins, 70-6
GIMME, GIMME, GIMME (A MAN AFTER MIDNIGHT), Abba, 79-3
GIMME GIMME GOOD LOVIN', Crazy Elephant, 69-12
GIMME HOPE JO'ANNA, Eddy Grant, 88-7
GIMME LITTLE SIGN:
Brenton Wood, 67-8
Danielle Brisebois, 95-75
GIMME LOVE, Alexia, 98-17
GIMME LUV (EENIE MEENIE MINY MO), David Morales and the Bad Yard Club, 93-37
GIMME SHELTER [EP] + lead track title, Various Artists (EPs), 93-23
GIMME SOME:
Brendon, 77-14
Pat and Mick, 91-53
GIMME SOME LOVE, Gina G, 97-25
GIMME SOME LOVING:
Spencer Davis Group, 66-2
Thunder *, 90-36
GIMME SOME MORE, Busta Rhymes, 99-5
GIMME THAT BODY, Q Tee, 96-40
GIMME THE SUNSHINE, Curiosity, 93-73
GIMME YOUR LUVIN', Atlantic Starr, 78-66
| **GIMMIX ! PLAY LOUD,** John Cooper Clarke, 79-39
GIN AND JUICE, Snoop Doggy Dogg, 94-39
GIN GAN GOOLIE, Scaffold, 69-38
GIN HOUSE BLUES, Amen Corner, 67-12
GIN SOAKED BOY, Divine Comedy, 99-38
GINCHY, Bert Weedon, 61-35
GINGER, David Devant And His Spirit Wife, 97-54
GINGER BREAD, Frankie Avalon, 58-30
GINNY COME LATELY, Brian Hyland, 62-5
GIRL, St. Louis Union, 66-11
GIRL, Truth, 66-27
GIRL/BOY [EP] + lead track title, Aphex Twin, 96-64
THE GIRL CAN'T HELP IT, Little Richard and his Band, 57-9
GIRL CRAZY, Hot Chocolate, 82-7
GIRL DON'T COME, Sandie Shaw, 64-3
THE GIRL FROM IPANEMA (GAROTA DE IPANEMA):
Stan Getz Joao Gilberto vocal by Astrud Gilberto, 64-29
Astrud Gilberto, 84-55
GIRL FROM MARS, Ash, 95-11
A GIRL I ONCE KNEW, Northern Uproar, 97-63
THE GIRL I USED TO KNOW, Brother Beyond, 91-48
GIRL I'M GONNA MISS YOU, Milli Vanilli, 89-2
THE GIRL IN THE WOOD, Frankie Laine with Paul Weston and his Orchestra and the Norman Luboff Choir (Carl Fischer at the Piano), 53-11
THE GIRL IS MINE, Michael Jackson and Paul McCartney, 82-8
GIRL (IT'S ALL I HAVE), Shy, 80-60
GIRL, I'VE BEEN HURT, Snow, 93-48
A GIRL LIKE YOU, Cliff Richard and the Shadows, 61-3
A GIRL LIKE YOU, Young Rascals, 67-37
A GIRL LIKE YOU (first entry from EXPRESSLY [EP]), Edwyn Collins, 94-42, 95-4
THE GIRL OF MY BEST FRIEND:
Elvis Presley with the Jordanaires, 76-9
Bryan Ferry, 93-57
GIRL OF MY DREAMS:
Tony Brent with Eric Jupp and his Orchestra, 58-16
Gerry Monroe, 72-43
GIRL ON TV, Lyte Funkie Ones, 00-6
GIRL POWER, Shampoo, 96-25
GIRL'S LIFE, Girlfriend, 93-68
THE GIRL SANG THE BLUES, Everly Brothers, 63-25
GIRL TO GIRL, 49ers, 90-31
GIRL U FOR ME, Silk, 93-67
GIRL U WANT, Robert Palmer, 94-57
THE GIRL WITH THE LONELIEST EYES, House Of Love, 91-58
GIRL YOU KNOW IT'S TRUE:
Milli Vanilli, 88-3
Keith 'N' Shane, 00-36
GIRL, YOU'LL BE A WOMAN SOON, Urge Overkill, 94-37
GIRL YOU'RE SO TOGETHER, Michael Jackson, 84-33
GIRLFRIEND, Michael Jackson, 80-41
GIRLFRIEND, Pebbles, 88-8
GIRLFRIEND, Billie, 98-1
GIRLFRIEND / BOYFRIEND, Blackstreet featuring Janet, 99-11
GIRLFRIEND IN A COMA, Smiths, 87-13
GIRLIE, Peddlers, 70-34
GIRLIE GIRLIE, Sophia George, 85-7
GIRLS, Johnny Burnette, 61-37
GIRLS:
Moments and Whatnauts, 75-3
Powercut featuring Nubian Prinz, 91-50
GIRLS, Beastie Boys, 87-34
GIRLS AIN'T NOTHIN BUT TROUBLE, D.J. Jazzy Jeff and Fresh Prince, 86-21
GIRLS & BOYS, Prince and the Revolution, 86-11
GIRLS AND BOYS, Blur, 94-5
GIRLS + BOYS, Hed Boys, 94-21, 95-36
GIRLS ARE MORE FUN, Ray Parker Jr., 86-46
GIRLS ARE OUT TO GET YOU, Fascinations, 71-32
GIRLS CAN GET IT, Dr. Hook, 80-40
GIRLS DEM SUGAR, Beenie Man featuring Mya, 01-13
GIRLS GIRLS GIRLS, Steve Lawrence, 60-49
GIRLS GIRLS GIRLS, Fourmost, 65-33
GIRLS, GIRLS, GIRLS, Sailor, 76-7
GIRLS GIRLS GIRLS, Kandidate, 79-34
GIRLS, GIRLS, GIRLS, Motley Crue, 87-26
(GIRLS GIRLS GIRLS) MADE TO LOVE, Eddie Hodges, 62-37
GIRLS JUST WANT TO HAVE FUN:
Cyndi Lauper, 84-2
Cyndi Lauper *, 94-4
Lolly*, 00-14
GIRLS LIKE US, B-15 Project featuring Crissy D and Lady G, 00-7
GIRLS NIGHT OUT, Alda, 98-20
THE GIRLS OF SUMMER [EP], Arab Strap, 97-74
GIRLS ON FILM, Duran Duran, 81-5
GIRLS ON MY MIND, Fatback, 85-69
GIRLS ON TOP, Girl Thing, 00-25
GIRLS SCHOOL, Wings, 77-1
GIRLS TALK, Dave Edmunds, 79-4
GIT DOWN (SHAKE YOUR THANG), Gaye Bykers On Acid, 87-54
GIT ON UP, Fast Eddie featuring Sundance, 89-49
GITTIN' FUNKY, Kid 'N' Play, 88-55
GIVE A LITTLE BIT, Supertramp, 77-29
GIVE A LITTLE LOVE, Bay City Rollers, 75-1
GIVE A LITTLE LOVE, Aswad, 88-11
GIVE A LITTLE LOVE, Daniel O'Donnell, 98-7
GIVE A LITTLE LOVE, Invisible Man, 99-48
GIVE A LITTLE LOVE BACK TO THE WORLD, Emma, 90-33
GIVE AND TAKE, Pioneers, 72-35
GIVE AND TAKE, Brass Construction, 85-62
GIVE! GIVE! GIVE!, Tommy Steele, 59-28
GIVE GIVE GIVE ME MORE MORE MORE, Wonder Stuff, 88-72
GIVE HER MY LOVE, Johnston Brothers, 57-27
GIVE HER WHAT SHE WANTS, Frankie Oliver, 97-58
GIVE IN TO ME, Michael Jackson featuring special guitar performance by Slash, 93-2
GIVE IRELAND BACK TO THE IRISH, Wings, 72-16
GIVE IT ALL AWAY, World Party, 93-43
GIVE IT AWAY, Red Hot Chili Peppers, 94-9
GIVE IT SOME EMOTION, Tracie, 83-24
GIVE IT TO ME, Troggs, 67-12
GIVE IT TO ME, Bam-Bam, 88-65
GIVE IT TO ME BABY, Rick James, 81-47
GIVE IT TO ME NOW, Kenny, 73-38
GIVE IT TO YOU, Martha Wash, 93-37
GIVE IT TO YOU, Jordan Knight, 99-5
GIVE IT UP:
KC and the Sunshine Band, 83-1
Cut 'N' Move, 93-61
GIVE IT UP, Talk Talk, 86-59
GIVE IT UP, Hothouse Flowers, 90-30
GIVE IT UP, Wilson Phillips, 92-36
GIVE IT UP, Goodmen, 93-5
GIVE IT UP, Public Enemy, 94-18
GIVE IT UP, Selena vs X.Men, 01-61
GIVE IT UP, TURN IT LOOSE, En Vogue, 93-22
GIVE ME A LITTLE MORE TIME, Gabrielle, 96-5
GIVE ME A REASON, Corrs, 01-27
GIVE ME ALL YOUR LOVE, Whitesnake, 88-18
GIVE ME ALL YOUR LOVE, Magic Affair, 94-30
GIVE ME AN INCH, Hazel O'Connor, 80-41
GIVE ME BACK ME BRAIN, Duffo, 79-60
GIVE ME BACK MY HEART, Dollar, 82-4
GIVE ME BACK MY MAN, B-52'S, 80-61
GIVE ME FIRE, Charged G.B.H., 82-69
GIVE ME JUST A LITTLE MORE TIME:
Chairmen Of The Board, 70-3
Kylie Minogue, 92-2
GIVE ME JUST ONE NIGHT (UNA NOCHE), 98°, 00-61
GIVE ME LIFE, Mr. V, 94-40
GIVE ME LOVE, Diddy, 94-52, 97-23
GIVE ME LOVE, DJ Dado vs Michelle Weeks, 98-59
GIVE ME LOVE (GIVE ME PEACE ON EARTH), George Harrison, 73-8
GIVE ME LUV, Alcatraz, 96-12
GIVE ME MORE TIME, Nicole, 82-75
GIVE ME MORE TIME, Whitesnake, 84-29
GIVE ME ONE MORE CHANCE, Donald Peers; The Les Reed Orchestra and Chorus, 72-36
GIVE ME ONE MORE CHANCE, Luke Goss and the Band Of Thieves, 93-68
GIVE ME RHYTHM, Black Connection, 98-32
GIVE ME SOME KINDA MAGIC, Dollar, 82-34
GIVE ME SOME MORE, DJ Gert, 01-50
GIVE ME STRENGTH, Jon Of The Pleased Wimmin, 96-30
GIVE ME THE NIGHT:
George Benson, 80-7
Randy Crawford, 97-60
GIVE ME THE NIGHT [M], Mirage featuring Roy Gayle, 84-49
GIVE ME THE REASON, Luther Vandross, 86-60, 87-71, 88-26
GIVE ME TIME, Dusty Springfield, 67-24
GIVE ME TONIGHT, Shannon, 84-24
GIVE ME YOU, Mary J. Blige, 00-19
GIVE ME YOUR BODY, Chippendales, 92-28
GIVE ME YOUR HEART TONIGHT, Shakin' Stevens, 82-11
GIVE ME YOUR WORD:
Tennessee Ernie Ford, 55-1
Billy Fury, 66-27
GIVE MYSELF TO LOVE, Francis Rossi of Status Quo, 96-42

GOOD MORNING BRITAIN, Aztec Camera and Mick Jones, 90-19
GOOD MORNING FREEDOM, Blue Mink, 70-10
GOOD MORNING JUDGE, 10cc, 77-5
GOOD MORNING LITTLE SCHOOLGIRL, Yardbirds, 64-44
GOOD MORNING STARSHINE, Oliver, 69-6
GOOD MORNING SUNSHINE, Aqua, 98-18
GOOD MORNING UNIVERSE (from FOUR MORE FROM TOYAH [EP]), Toyah, 81-14
GOOD OLD ARSENAL, Arsenal 1st Team Squad, 71-16
GOOD OLD FASHIONED LOVER BOY (from QUEEN'S FIRST EP [EP]), Queen, 77-17
GOOD OLD ROCK 'N' ROLL [M], Dave Clark Five, 69-7
GOOD RHYMES, Da Click, 99-14
GOOD ROCKIN' TONIGHT, Montrose, 80-71
GOOD SIGN, Emilia, 99-54
GOOD SOULS, Starsailor, 01-12
GOOD STUFF, B-52'S, 92-21
GOOD STUFF, Kelis featuring Terrar, 00-19
GOOD SWEET LOVIN', Louchie Lou and Michie One, 96-34
THE GOOD, THE BAD AND THE UGLY, Hugo Montenegro, his Orchestra and Chorus, 68-1
GOOD THING, Fine Young Cannibals, 89-7
GOOD THING, Eternal, 96-8
GOOD THING GOING (WE'VE GOT A GOOD THING GOING):
Sugar Minott, 81-4
Yazz *, 96-53
Sid Owen rap performed by Chuckle Star*, 00-14
GOOD TIME BABY, Bobby Rydell, 61-42
GOOD TIMES, Eric Burdon and the Animals, 67-20
GOOD TIMES, Cliff Richard, 69-12
GOOD TIMES, Chic, 79-5
GOOD TIMES, Matt Bianco, 88-55
GOOD TIMES, Reid, 89-55
GOOD TIMES, Jimmy Barnes and Inxs, 91-18
GOOD TIMES (from ELECTRIC MAINLINE [EP]), Spiritualized, 93-49
GOOD TIMES, Dream Frequency, 94-67
GOOD TIMES, Edie Brickell, 94-40
GOOD TIMIN', Jimmy Jones, 60-1
GOOD TO BE ALIVE, DJ Rap, 98-36
GOOD TO GO LOVER, Gwen Guthrie, 87-37
GOOD TRADITION, Tanita Tikaram, 88-10
GOOD VIBRATIONS:
Beach Boys, 66-1, 76-18
Psychic TV, 86-65
GOOD VIBRATIONS, Marky Mark and the Funky Bunch (featuring Loletta Holloway), 91-14
GOOD VIBRATIONS, Brothers Like Outlaw featuring Alison Evelyn, 93-74
A GOOD YEAR FOR THE ROSES, Elvis Costello and the Attractions, 81-6
GOODBYE, Mary Hopkin, 69-2
A GOODBYE, Cameo, 86-65
GOODBYE, Sundays, 92-27
GOODBYE, Air Supply, 93-66
GOODBYE, Spice Girls, 98-1
GOODBYE, Def Leppard, 99-54
GOODBYE BABY AND AMEN, Lulu, 94-40
GOODBYE BLUEBIRD, Wayne Fontana, 66-49
GOODBYE CIVILIAN, Skids, 80-52
GOODBYE CRUEL WORLD, James Darren, 61-28
GOODBYE CRUEL WORLD, Shakespear's Sister, 91-59, 92-32
GOODBYE GIRL, Squeeze, 78-63
GOODBYE GIRL, Go West, 85-25
GOODBYE HEARTBREAK, Lighthouse Family, 96-14
GOODBYE IS JUST ANOTHER WORD, New Seekers, 73-36
GOODBYE JIMMY, GOODBYE, Ruby Murray with Norrie Paramor and his Orchestra and Chorus, 59-10
GOODBYE MR. MACKENZIE, Goodbye Mr. MacKenzie, 88-62
GOODBYE MY LOVE, Searchers, 65-4
GOODBYE MY LOVE, Glitter Band, 75-2
GOODBYE NOTHIN' TO SAY, Javells featuring Nosmo King, 74-26
GOODBYE SAM, HELLO SAMANTHA, Cliff Richard, 70-6
GOODBYE STRANGER, Supertramp, 79-57
GOODBYE STRANGER, Pepsi and Shirlie, 87-9
GOODBYE SWEET PRINCE, Mr. Acker Bilk and his Paramount Jazz Band, 60-50
GOODBYE TO LOVE, Carpenters, 72-9
GOODBYE TO LOVE AGAIN, Maxi Priest, 88-57
GOODBYE YELLOW BRICK ROAD, Elton John, 73-6
GOODBYEEE, Peter Cook and Dudley Moore with the Dudley Moore Trio, 65-18
GOODGROOVE, Derek B, 88-16
GOODNESS GRACIOUS ME!, Peter Sellers and Sophia Loren, 60-4
GOODNIGHT, Roy Orbison, 65-14
GOODNIGHT, Babybird, 96-28
GOODNIGHT GIRL, Wet Wet Wet, 92-1
GOODNIGHT MIDNIGHT, Clodagh Rodgers, 69-4
GOODNIGHT MRS. FLINTSTONE, Piltdown Men, 61-18
GOODNIGHT MOON, Shivaree, 01-63
GOODNIGHT SAIGON, Billy Joel, 84-29
GOODNIGHT TONIGHT, Wings, 79-5
GOODWILL CITY, Goodbye Mr. MacKenzie, 89-49
GOODY GOODY, Frankie Lymon and the Teenagers, 57-24
GOODY TWO SHOES, Adam Ant, 82-1
GOOGLE EYE, Nashville Teens, 64-10
GORECKI, Lamb, 97-30
GORGEOUS, Gene Loves Jezebel, 87-68
GOSP, L.W.S., 94-65
GOSPEL OAK [EP], Sinead O'Connor, 97-28
GOSSIP CALYPSO, Bernard Cribbins, 62-25
GOT A FEELING, Patrick Juvet, 78-34
GOT A GIRL, Four Preps, 60-28
GOT A LITTLE HEARTACHE, Alvin Stardust, 85-55
GOT A LOT O' LIVIN' TO DO, Elvis Presley with the Jordanaires, 57-17
GOT A LOVE FOR YOU, Jomanda, 91-43
GOT A MATCH, Russ Conway, 58-30
GOT FUNK, Funk Junkeez, 98-57
GOT IT AT THE DELMAR, Senseless Things, 91-50
GOT ME A FEELING, Misty Oldland, 93-59
GOT MY MIND MADE UP, Instant Funk, 79-46
GOT MY MIND SET ON YOU, George Harrison, 87-2
GOT MY MOJO WORKING, Jimmy Smith, 66-48
GOT MYSELF TOGETHER, Kenny "Dope" presents The Bucketheads, 96-12
GOT NO BRAINS, Bad Manners, 82-44
GOT "NOWHERE TO RUN 2000", Nu Generation, 00-66
GOT THE FEELIN', 5, 98-3
GOT THE LIFE, Korn, 98-23
GOT THE TIME, Anthrax, 91-16
GOT 'TIL IT'S GONE, Janet (featuring Q-Tip and Joni Mitchell), 97-6
GOT TO BE CERTAIN, Kylie Minogue, 88-2
GOT TO BE FREE, 49ers, 92-46
GOT TO BE REAL, Erik, 94-42
GOT TO BE THERE, Michael Jackson, 72-5
GOT TO GET, Rob 'N' Raz featuring Leila K, 89-8
GOT TO GET IT, Culture Beat, 93-4
GOT TO GET IT, Sisqo, 00-14
GOT TO GET UP [RM], Afrika Bambaataa vs. Carpe Diem, 98-22
GOT TO GET YOU BACK, Kym Mazelle, 89-29
GOT TO GET YOU INTO MY LIFE:
Cliff Bennett and the Rebel Rousers, 66-6
Earth, Wind And Fire, 78-33
GOT TO GIVE IT UP:
Marvin Gaye, 77-7
Aaliyah, 96-37
GOT TO GIVE ME LOVE, Dana Dawson, 95-27
GOT TO HAVE YOUR LOVE, Mantronix featuring Wondress, 90-4
GOT TO KEEP ON, Cookie Crew, 89-17
GOT TO LOVE SOMEBODY, Sister Sledge, 80-34
GOT YOU – MUSIC FROM THE MOTION PICTURE TRAINING DAY THE SOUNDTRACK, Pharoahe Monch, 01-27
GOT YOU ON MY MIND, Tony Brent, 53-12
GOT YOUR MONEY, Ol' Dirty Bastard featuring Kelis, 00-11
GOTHAM CITY, R. Kelly, 97-9
GOTTA BE A SIN, Adam Ant, 95-48
GOTTA BE . . . MOVIN' ON UP, P.M. Dawn featuring Ky-Mani, 98-68
GOTTA BE YOU, 3T (featuring Herbie), 97-10
GOTTA CATCH 'EM ALL, 50.Grind featuring Pokemon All-Stars, 01-57
GOTTA GET A DATE, Frank Ifield, 60-49
GOTTA GET AWAY, Offspring, 95-43
GOTTA GET IT RIGHT, Lena Fiagbe, 93-20
GOTTA GET LOOSE, Mr And Mrs Smith, 96-70
GOTTA GET THRU THIS, Daniel Bedingfield, 01-1
GOTTA GET YOU HOME TONIGHT, Eugene Wilde, 84-18
GOTTA GO HOME, Boney M, 79-12
GOTTA HAVE HOPE, Blackout, 99-46
GOTTA HAVE RAIN, Max Bygraves, 58-28
GOT-TA HAVE SOMETHING IN THE BANK, FRANK, Frankie Vaughan and the Kaye Sisters with Wally Stott and his Orchestra, 57-8
GOTTA KEEP PUSHIN', Z Factor, 98-47
GOTTA KNOW (YOUR NAME), Malaika, 93-68
GOTTA LOTTA LOVE, Ice-T, 94-24
GOTTA PULL MYSELF TOGETHER, Nolans, 80-9
GOTTA SEE BABY TONIGHT, Mr. Acker Bilk and his Paramount Jazz Band (vocal by Mr. Acker Bilk), 62-24
GOTTA SEE JANE, R. Dean Taylor, 68-17, 74-41
GOTTA TELL YOU, Samantha Mumba, 00-2
GOURYELLA, Gouryella, 99-15
GOVINDA, Radha Krishna Temple, 70-23
GOVINDA, Kula Shaker, 96-7
GRACE, Band A.K.A., 82-41
GRACEADELICA, Dark Star, 00-25
GRACELAND, Bible, 89-51
GRANADA:
Frankie Laine with Paul Weston and his Orchestra (Carl Fischer: piano), 54-9
Frank Sinatra with Billy May and his Orchestra, 61-15
THE GRAND COOLIE DAM, Lonnie Donegan and his Skiffle Group, 58-6
GRAND PIANO, Mixmaster, 89-9
GRANDAD, Clive Dunn, 70-1
GRANDMA'S PARTY, Paul Nicholas, 76-9
GRANDPA'S PARTY, Monie Love, 89-16
GRANITE STATUE, Salad, 95-50
GRAPEVYNE, Brownstone, 95-16
GRATEFUL WHEN YOU'RE DEAD/JERRY WAS THERE [M], Kula Shaker, 96-35
THE GRAVE AND THE CONSTANT, Fun Lovin' Criminals, 96-72
GRAVEL PIT, Wu-Tang Clan presents, 00-6
GRAVITATE TO ME, The, 89-63
GRAVITY, James Brown, 86-65
GREASE:
Frankie Valli, 78-3
Craig McLachlan, 93-44
GREASE – THE DREAM MIX [M], Frankie Valli, John Travolta and Olivia Newton-John, 91-47
THE GREASE MEGAMIX [M], John Travolta and Olivia Newton-John, 90-3
GREASED LIGHTNING, John Travolta, 78-11
GREAT BALLS OF FIRE:
Jerry Lee Lewis, 57-1
Tiny Tim, 69-45
THE GREAT BEYOND, R.E.M., 00-3
THE GREAT ESCAPE:
England Supporters Band, 98-46
England Supporters Band *, 00-26
GREAT GOSH A'MIGHTY (IT'S A MATTER OF TIME), Little Richard, 86-62
GREAT INDIFFERENCE (from RAGING [EP]), Beyond, 91-68
THE GREAT PRETENDER:
Jimmy Parkinson with Ray Martin and his Orchestra, 56-9
Platters, 56-5
Freddie Mercury, 87-4, 93-29
THE GREAT ROCK 'N' ROLL SWINDLE, Sex Pistols, 79-21
THE GREAT SNOW MAN, Bob Luman, 61-49
THE GREAT SONG OF INDIFFERENCE, Bob Geldof, 90-15
GREAT SPANGLED FRITILLARY (from ECHOES IN A SHALLOW BAY [EP]), Cocteau Twins, 85-65
GREAT THINGS, Echobelly, 95-13
THE GREAT TRAIN ROBBERY, Black Uhuru, 86-62
GREATER LOVE, Soundman and Don Lloydie with Elisabeth Troy, 95-49
THE GREATEST COCKNEY RIP-OFF, Cockney Rejects, 80-21

GREATEST DAY, Beverley Knight, 99-14
THE GREATEST FLAME, Runrig, 93-36, 97-30
THE GREATEST HIGH, Hurricane #1, 99-43
THE GREATEST LOVE OF ALL:
George Benson, 77-27
Whitney Houston, 86-8
THE GREATEST LOVE YOU'LL NEVER KNOW, Lutricia McNeal, 98-17
THE GREATEST ROMANCE EVER SOLD, Artist, 00-65
THE GREATEST SHOW ON EARTH, Strangelove, 97-36
THE GREATNESS AND PERFECTION OF LOVE, Julian Cope, 84-52
GREECE 2000, Three Drives, 98-44, 99-12
GREED, Laurent Garnier, 00-36
GREEDY FLY, Bush, 97-22
THE GREEDY UGLY PEOPLE, Hefner, 00-64
GREEN AND GREY, New Model Army, 89-37
THE GREEN DOOR:
Jim Lowe with the High Fives, 56-8
Frankie Vaughan with Wally Stott and his Orchestra and Chorus, 56-2
Glen Mason, 56-24
Shakin' Stevens, 81-1
GREEN FIELDS:
Beverley Sisters, 60-29
Brothers Four *, 60-40
GREEN FIELDS, Unit Four Plus Two, 64-48
GREEN, GREEN GRASS OF HOME:
Tom Jones, 66-1
Elvis Presley, 75-29
GREEN JEANS, Fabulous Flee-Rakkers, 60-23
THE GREEN LEAVES OF SUMMER, Kenny Ball and his Jazzmen, 62-7
GREEN LIGHT, Cliff Richard, 79-57
THE GREEN MAN, Shut Up And Dance, 92-43
THE GREEN MANALISHI (WITH THE TWO PRONG CROWN), Fleetwood Mac, 70-10
GREEN ONIONS, Booker T. and the MGs, 79-7
GREEN RIVER, Creedence Clearwater Revival, 69-19
GREEN SHIRT, Elvis Costello and the Attractions, 85-68
GREEN STREET GREEN, New Vaudeville Band (featuring Tristam Vii), 67-37
GREEN TAMBOURINE:
Lemon Pipers, 68-7
Sundragon, 68-50
GREEN TINTED SIXTIES MIND, Mr. Big, 92-72
GREENBACK DOLLAR, Chas McDevitt Skiffle Group (featuring Nancy Whiskey), 57-28
GREENBACK DRIVE, Christians, 90-63
GREENFIELDS, Brothers Four, 60-40
GREETINGS TO THE NEW BRUNETTE, Billy Bragg with Johnny Marr and Kirsty MacColl, 86-58
GREY DAY, Madness, 81-4
GRIMLY FIENDISH, Damned, 85-21
GRIND, Alice In Chains, 95-23
GRIP '89 (GET A) GRIP (ON YOURSELF) [RM], Stranglers, 89-33
GRITTY SHAKER, David Holmes, 97-53
THE GROOVE, Rodney Franklin, 80-7
GROOVE BABY GROOVE [EP] + lead track title, Stargazers, 82-56
GROOVE IS IN THE HEART, Deee-Lite, 90-2, 91-52
THE GROOVE LINE:
Heatwave, 78-12
Blockster *, 99-18
GROOVE MACHINE, Marvin and Tamara, 99-11
GROOVE OF LOVE, E.V.E., 94-30
GROOVE THANG, Zhane, 94-34
GROOVE TO MOVE, Channel X, 91-67
GROOVEBIRD, Natural Born Grooves, 97-21
GROOVEJET (IF THIS AIN'T LOVE), Spiller; Lead vocals by Sophie Ellis-Bextor, 00-1
GROOVELINE, Blockster, 99-18
THE GROOVER, T.Rex, 73-4
GROOVIN':
Young Rascals, 67-8
War, 85-43
Pato Banton and the Reggae Revolution, 96-14
GROOVIN' (THE BIG BOSS GROOVE), Style Council, 84-5
GROOVIN' IN THE MIDNIGHT, Maxi Priest, 92-50
GROOVIN' (THAT'S WHAT WE'RE DOIN'), S.O.S. Band, 83-72
GROOVIN' WITH MR. BLOE, Mr. Bloe, 70-2
GROOVIN' (YOU'RE THE BEST THING), Style Council, 84-5
GROOVY BABY, Microbe, 69-29
GROOVY BEAT, D.O.P., 96-54
GROOVY FEELING, Fluke, 93-45
A GROOVY KIND OF LOVE:
Mindbenders, 66-2
Les Gray, 77-32
Phil Collins, 88-1
THE GROOVY THANG, Minimal Funk 2, 98-65
GROOVY TRAIN, Farm, 90-6
GROUND LEVEL, Stereo MC's, 93-19
GROUNDED, My Vitriol, 01-29
GROUPY GIRL, Tony Joe White, 70-22
GUAGLIONE:
Dean Martin *, 57-21
Perez 'Prez' Prado and his Orchestra, 94-41, 95-2
GUANTANAMERA:
Sandpipers, 66-7
Wyclef Jean featuring Refugee Allstars, 97-25
GUARANTEED, Level 42, 91-17
GUARDIAN ANGEL, Nino De Angelo, 84-57
GUARDIANS OF THE LAND, George Bowyer and William McClintock Bunbury, 98-33
GUDBUY T'JANE, Slade, 72-2
GUDVIBE, Tinman, 95-49
GUERRILLA FUNK, Paris, 95-38
GUERRILLA RADIO, Rage Against The Machine, 99-32
GUESS I WAS A FOOL, Another Level, 98-5
GUESS WHO'S BACK, Rakim, 97-32
GUIDING STAR, Cast, 97-9
GUILTY, Jim Reeves, 63-29
GUILTY, Pearls, 74-10
GUILTY, Mike Oldfield, 79-22
GUILTY, Barbra Streisand and Barry Gibb, 80-34
GUILTY, Classix Nouveaux, 81-43
GUILTY, Paul Hardcastle, 84-55
GUILTY, Yarbrough and Peoples, 86-53
GUILTY CONSCIENCE, Eminem featuring Dr. Dre, 99-5
GUILTY OF LOVE, Whitesnake, 83-31
GUITAR BOOGIE SHUFFLE, Bert Weedon, 59-10
GUITAR MAN:
Elvis Presley, 68-19
Elvis Presley, 81-43
THE GUITAR MAN, Bread, 72-16
GUITAR TANGO, Shadows, 62-4
GUITARRA G, Banda Sonora, 01-50
GUN LAW, Kane Gang, 85-53
GUNMAN, 187 Lockdown, 97-16, 98-17
GUNS FOR HIRE, AC/DC, 83-37
GUNS OF NAVARONE, Skatalites, 67-36
GUNSLINGER, Frankie Laine, 61-50
GUNZ AND PIANOZ, Bass Boyz, 96-74
GURNEY SLADE, Max Harris with his Group, 60-11
THE GUSH, Raging Speedhorn, 01-47
GUSTA (from STOP STARTING TO START STOPPING [EP]), D.O.P., 96-58
GYM AND TONIC, Spacedust, 98-1
GYPSY, Fleetwood Mac, 82-46
GYPSY BEAT, Packabeats, 61-49
GYPSY BOY, GYPSY GIRL, Sharada House Gang, 97-52
GYPSY EYES, Jimi Hendrix Experience, 71-35
GYPSY ROAD, Cinderella, 88-54
GYPSY ROADHOG, Slade, 77-48
GYPSY ROVER (THE WHISTLING GYPSY), Highwaymen, 61-41
GYPSY WOMAN, Brian Hyland, 71-42
GYPSY WOMAN (LA DA DEE), Crystal Waters, 91-2, 92-35
GYPSYS, TRAMPS AND THIEVES, Cher, 71-4
H.A.P.P.Y. RADIO:
Edwin Starr, 79-9
Michaela, 89-62
HA CHA CHA (FUNKTION), Brass Construction, 77-37
HA! HA! SAID THE CLOWN, Manfred Mann, 67-4
HAD TO BE, Cliff Richard with Olivia Newton-John, 95-22
HAIL CAESAR, AC/DC, 96-56
HAIL HAIL ROCK 'N' ROLL, Garland Jeffreys, 92-72
HAIL MARY, Makaveli, 98-43
HAITIAN DIVORCE, Steely Dan, 76-17
HALCYON (from RADICCIO [EP]), Orbital, 92-37
HALCYON, Chicane, 00-28
HALE BOPP, Der Dritte Raum, 99-75
HALEY'S GOLDEN MEDLEY [M], Bill Haley and his Comets, 81-50
HALF A BOY AND HALF A MAN, Nick Lowe, 84-53
HALF A MINUTE, Matt Bianco, 84-23
HALF AS MUCH, Rosemary Clooney with Percy Faith and his Orchestra, 52-3
HALF OF MY HEART, Emile Ford and the Checkmates, 61-42
HALF ON A BABY, R. Kelly, 98-16
HALF THE DAY'S GONE AND WE HAVEN'T EARNE'D A PENNY, Kenny Lynch, 83-50
HALF THE MAN, Jamiroquai, 94-15
HALF THE WORLD, Belinda Carlisle, 92-35
HALFWAY AROUND THE WORLD, A*Teens, 01-30
HALFWAY DOWN THE STAIRS, Muppets Sung by Kermit's Nephew Robin, 77-7
HALFWAY HOTEL, Voyager, 79-33
HALFWAY TO HEAVEN, Europe, 92-42
HALFWAY TO PARADISE, Billy Fury, 61-3
HALFWAY UP, HALFWAY DOWN, Dennis Brown, 82-56
HALLELUJAH, Milk and Honey featuring Gail Atari, 79-5
HALLELUJAH (from MADCHESTER RAVE ON [EP]), Happy Mondays, 89-19
HALLELUJAH DAY, Jackson 5, 73-20
HALLELUJAH FREEDOM, Junior Campbell, 72-10
HALLELUJAH, I LOVE HER SO:
Eddie Cochran, 60-22
Dick Jordan, 60-47
HALLELUJAH MAN, Love and Money, 88-63
HALLELUJAH '92, Inner City, 92-22
HALLO SPACEBOY, David Bowie, 96-12
HALLOWED BE THY NAME (LIVE), Iron Maiden, 93-9
HALLS OF ILLUSIONS, Insane Clown Posse, 98-56
HALO, Texas, 97-10
(HAMMER HAMMER) THEY PUT ME IN THE MIX, M.C. Hammer, 91-20
HAMMER HORROR, Kate Bush, 78-44
HAMMER TO FALL, Queen, 84-13
HAMMER TO THE HEART, Tamperer featuring Maya, 00-6
HAND A HANDKERCHIEF TO HELEN, Susan Maughan, 63-41
HAND HELD IN BLACK AND WHITE, Dollar, 81-19
HAND IN GLOVE, Sandie Shaw, 84-27
HAND IN HAND, Grace, 97-38
HAND IN MY POCKET, Alanis Morissette, 95-26
HAND IN YOUR HEAD, Money Mark, 98-40
HAND OF THE DEAD BODY, Scarface (featuring Ice Cube), 95-41
HAND ON MY HEART, Shriekback, 84-52
HAND ON YOUR HEART, Kylie Minogue, 89-1
HANDBAGS AND GLADRAGS:
Chris Farlowe, 67-33
Stereophonics, 01-4
HANDFUL OF PROMISES, Big Fun, 90-21
A HANDFUL OF SONGS, Tommy Steele and the Steelmen, 57-5
HANDLE WITH CARE, Traveling Wilburys, 88-21
HANDS, Jewel, 98-41
HANDS ACROSS THE OCEAN, Mission, 90-28
HANDS OFF . . . SHE'S MINE, Beat, 80-9
HANDS TO HEAVEN, Breathe, 88-4
HANDS UP, Clubzone, 94-50
HANDS UP, Trevor and Simon, 00-12
HANDS UP (4 LOVERS), Right Said Fred, 93-60
HANDS UP (GIVE ME YOUR HEART), Ottawan, 81-3
HANDS UP! HANDS UP!, Zig and Zag, 95-21
HANDY MAN:
Jimmy Jones, 60-3
Del Shannon, 64-36
HANG 'EM HIGH, Hugo Montenegro, his Orchestra and Chorus, 69-50
HANG IN LONG ENOUGH, Phil Collins, 90-34
HANG MYSELF ON YOU, Candyskins, 97-65
HANG ON IN THERE BABY:
Johnny Bristol, 74-3
Curiosity, 92-3
HANG ON NOW, Kajagoogoo, 83-13
HANG ON SLOOPY:
McCoys, 65-5
Sandpipers, 76-32
HANG ON TO A DREAM, Tim Hardin, 67-50
HANG ON TO YOUR LOVE, Jason Donovan, 90-8
HANG TOGETHER, Odyssey, 81-36
HANG YOUR HEAD [EP] + lead track title, Deacon Blue, 93-21
HANGAR 18, Megadeth, 91-26
HANGIN', Chic, 83-64
HANGIN' ON A STRING (CONTEMPLATING), Loose Ends, 85-13, 92-25
HANGIN' OUT, Kool And The Gang, 80-52
HANGIN' TOUGH, New Kids On The Block, 89-52, 90-1

HANGINAROUND, Counting Crows, 99-46
HANGING AROUND, Hazel O'Connor, 81-45
HANGING AROUND, Me Me Me, 96-19
HANGING AROUND, Cardigans, 99-17
HANGING AROUND WITH THE BIG BOYS, Bloomsbury Set, 83-56
HANGING BY A MOMENT, Lifehouse, 01-25
THE HANGING GARDEN, Cure, 82-34
HANGING ON THE TELEPHONE, Blondie, 78-5
HANGOVER, Betty Boo, 93-50
HANKY PANKY, Tommy James and the Shondells, 66-38
HANKY PANKY, Madonna, 90-2
HANNA HANNA, China Crisis, 84-44
HAPPENIN' ALL OVER AGAIN:
Lonnie Gordon, 90-4
Tracy Shaw, 98-46
THE HAPPENING, Supremes, 67-6
HAPPENINGS TEN YEARS TIME AGO, Yardbirds, 66-43
HAPPINESS, Ken Dodd, 64-31
HAPPINESS, Roger Taylor, 94-32
HAPPINESS, Pizzaman, 95-19
HAPPINESS, Kamasultra featuring Jocelyn Brown, 97-45
HAPPINESS, Bini and Martini, 00-53
HAPPINESS, Sound De-Zign, 01-19
HAPPINESS HAPPENING, Lost Witness, 99-18
HAPPINESS (Medley) a) HAPPINESS b) HAPPINESS IS JUST AROUND THE BEND [M]:
Serious Rope presents Sharon Dee Clarke, 93-54
Serious Rope *, 94-70
HAPPINESS IS JUST AROUND THE BEND, Cuba Gooding, 83-72
HAPPINESS IS ME AND YOU, Gilbert O'Sullivan, 74-19
HAPPINESS/YOU MAKE ME HAPPY [M] [RR], Serious Rope, 94-70
HAPPY, Ned's Atomic Dustbin, 91-16
HAPPY:
Surface, 87-56
MN8, 95-8
Pauline Henry, 96-46
HAPPY, Travis, 97-38
HAPPY ANNIVERSARY, Joan Regan; Peter Knight Orchestra and Chorus, 60-29
HAPPY ANNIVERSARY, Slim Whitman, 74-14
HAPPY BIRTHDAY, Stevie Wonder, 81-2
HAPPY BIRTHDAY, Altered Images, 81-2
HAPPY BIRTHDAY, Technohead, 96-18
HAPPY BIRTHDAY REVOLUTION, Levellers, 00-57
HAPPY BIRTHDAY, SWEET SIXTEEN, Neil Sedaka, 61-3
HAPPY BIZZNESS, Roach Motel, 94-75
HAPPY BUSMAN, Frank And Walters, 92-49
HAPPY DAY, Blink, 94-57
HAPPY DAYS, Pratt and McLain with Brotherlove, 77-31
HAPPY DAYS, Sweet Mercy featuring Joe Roberts, 96-63
HAPPY DAYS, P.J., 97-72, 99-57
HAPPY DAYS AND LONELY NIGHTS:
Suzi Miller and the Johnston Brothers, 55-14
Frankie Vaughan with Geoff Love and his Orchestra, 55-12
Ruby Murray with Ray Martin and his Orchestra, 55-6
HAPPY ENDING, Joe Jackson, 84-58
HAPPY ENDINGS (GIVE YOURSELF A PINCH), Lionel Bart, 89-68
HAPPY EVER AFTER, Julia Fordham, 88-27
HAPPY FEELING, Hamilton Bohannon, 75-49
HAPPY GO LUCKY ME, George Formby with the Beryl Stott Chorus, 60-40
HAPPY GUITAR, Tommy Steele and the Steelmen, 58-20
HAPPY HEART, Andy Williams, 69-19
HAPPY HOME, 2 Pac, 98-17
HAPPY HOUR, Housemartins, 86-3
HAPPY HOUSE, Siouxsie and the Banshees, 80-17
HAPPY JACK, Who, 66-3
HAPPY JUST TO BE WITH YOU, Michelle Gayle, 95-11
HAPPY LAND (from BAREFOOT [EP]), Ultramarine, 94-61
HAPPY (LOVE THEME FROM 'LADY SINGS THE BLUES'), Michael Jackson, 83-52
THE HAPPY MAN, Thomas Lang, 88-67
HAPPY NATION, Ace Of Base, 93-42, 94-40
HAPPY PEOPLE, Static Revenger, 01-23
HAPPY SHOPPER, 60ft Dolls, 96-38
THE HAPPY SONG (DUM-DUM), Otis Redding, 68-24
HAPPY TALK, Captain Sensible, 82-1
HAPPY TO BE ON AN ISLAND IN THE SUN, Demis Roussos, 75-5
HAPPY TO MAKE YOUR ACQUAINTANCE, Sammy Davis Jr. and Carmen McRae, 60-46
HAPPY TOGETHER:
Turtles, 67-12
Jason Donovan, 91-10
THE HAPPY WANDERER (DER FROHLICHE WANDERER):
Obernkirchen Children's Choir, 54-2
Stargazers with Syd Dean and his Band *, 54-12
HAPPY WHEN IT RAINS, Jesus And Mary Chain, 87-25
THE HAPPY WHISTLER:
Don Robertson, 56-8
Cyril Stapleton and his Orchestra featuring Desmond Lane – The Penny Whistle Boy, 56-22
HAPPY XMAS (WAR IS OVER), John and Yoko/Plastic Ono Band with the Harlem Community Choir, 72-4, 75-48, 80-2, 81-28, 82-56, 88-45
HARBOUR LIGHTS, Platters, 60-11
HARD AS A ROCK, AC/DC, 95-33
HARD BEAT EP 19 [EP], Various Artists (EPs), 01-71
A HARD DAY'S NIGHT:
Beatles, 64-1, 84-52
Peter Sellers, 65-14, 93-52
A HARD DAY'S NIGHT [EP] + lead track title, Peter Sellers, 93-52
HARD HABIT TO BREAK, Chicago, 84-8
HARD HEADED WOMAN, Elvis Presley with the Jordanaires, 58-2
HARD HEARTED HANNAH, Temperance Seven Vocal refrain by Mr. Paul MacDowell, 61-28
HARD HOUSE MUSIC, Melt featuring Little Ms. Marcie, 00-59
HARD KNOCK LIFE (GHETTO ANTHEM), Jay-Z, 98-2
A HARD RAIN'S A-GONNA FALL, Bryan Ferry, 73-10
HARD ROAD, Black Sabbath, 78-33
HARD TIMES COME EASY, Richie Sambora, 98-37
HARD TO EXPLAIN, Strokes, 01-16
HARD TO HANDLE:
Otis Redding, 68-15
Black Crowes, 90-45, 91-39
HARD TO MAKE A STAND, Sheryl Crow, 97-22
HARD TO SAY I'M SORRY:
Chicago, 82-4
AZ Yet featuring Peter Cetera, 97-7
HARD UP, Awesome 3, 90-55
THE HARD WAY, Nashville Teens, 66-45
THE HARDCORE [EP], Hypnotist, 91-68
HARDCORE HEAVEN, DJ Seduction, 92-26
HARDCORE HIP HOUSE, Tyree, 89-70
HARDCORE – THE FINAL CONFLICT, Hardcore Rhythm Team, 92-69
HARDCORE U KNOW THE SCORE (from THE HARDCORE [EP]), Hypnotist, 91-68
HARDCORE UPROAR, Together, 90-12
HARDCORE WILL NEVER DIE, Q-Bass, 92-64
HARDEN MY HEART, Quarterflash, 82-49
HARDER BETTER FASTER STRONGER, Daft Punk, 01-25
THE HARDER I TRY, Brother Beyond, 88-2
THE HARDER THEY COME:
Rockers Revenge featuring Donnie Calvin, 83-30
Madness, 92-44
HARDEST PART IS THE NIGHT, Bon Jovi, 85-68
THE HARDEST THING, 98°, 00-29
HARDROCK, Herbie Hancock, 84-65
HARDTRANCE ACPERIENCE [EP], Hardfloor, 92-56
HARE KRISHNA MANTRA, Radha Krishna Temple (London), 69-12
HARLEM DESIRE, London Boys, 89-17
HARLEM SHUFFLE:
Bob and Earl, 69-7
Rolling Stones, 86-13
HARLEQUIN – THE BEAUTY AND THE BEAST, Sven Vath, 94-72
HARMONICA MAN, Bravado, 94-37
HARMONY, TC 1993, 93-51
HARMONY IN MY HEAD, Buzzcocks, 79-32
HARMOUR LOVE, Syreeta, 75-32
HARPER VALLEY P. T. A., Jeannie C. Riley, 68-12
HARVEST FOR THE WORLD:
Isley Brothers, 76-10
Christians, 88-8
Terry Hunter, 97-48
HARVEST MOON, Neil Young, 93-36
THE HARVEST OF LOVE, Benny Hill with the Kestrels, 63-20
HARVESTER OF SORROW, Metallica, 88-20
HAS IT COME TO THIS, Streets, 01-18
HASH PIPE, Weezer, 01-21
HASTA LA VISTA, Sylvia, 75-38
HATE ME NOW, Nas (featuring Puff Daddy), 99-14
HATS OFF TO LARRY, Del Shannon, 61-6
HAUNTED:
Pogues, 86-42
Shane MacGowan and Sinead O'Connor, 95-30
HAUNTED BY YOU, Gene, 95-32
HAVA NAGILA, Spotnicks, 63-13
HAVE A DRINK ON ME, Lonnie Donegan and his Group, 61-8
HAVE A GOOD FOREVER..., Cool Notes, 85-73
HAVE A LITTLE FAITH, Joe Cocker, 95-67
HAVE A NICE DAY, Roxanne Shante, 87-58
HAVE A NICE DAY, Stereophonics, 01-5
HAVE FUN, GO MAD!, Blair, 95-37
HAVE I STAYED TOO LONG, Sonny and Cher, 66-42
HAVE I THE RIGHT?:
Honeycombs, 64-1
Dead End Kids, 77-6
HAVE I TOLD YOU LATELY:
Van Morrison, 89-74
Rod Stewart, 93-5
Chieftains with Van Morrison *, 95-71
HAVE LOST IT [EP], Teenage Fanclub, 95-53
HAVE LOVE, WILL TRAVEL [EP] + lead track title, Crazyhead, 89-68
HAVE MERCY, Yazz, 94-42
HAVE PITY ON THE BOY, Paul and Barry Ryan, 66-18
HAVE YOU EVER?, Brandy, 98-13
HAVE YOU EVER, S Club 7, 01-1
HAVE YOU EVER BEEN IN LOVE, Leo Sayer, 82-10
HAVE YOU EVER BEEN MELLOW?, Party Animals, 96-56, 96-43
HAVE YOU EVER BEEN MELLOW? [EP] + lead track title, Party Animals, 96-43
HAVE YOU EVER HAD IT BLUE, Style Council, 86-14
HAVE YOU EVER LOVED SOMEBODY:
Paul and Barry Ryan, 66-49
Searchers, 66-48
HAVE YOU EVER LOVED SOMEBODY, Freddie Jackson, 87-33
HAVE YOU EVER NEEDED SOMEONE SO BAD, Def Leppard, 92-16
HAVE YOU EVER REALLY LOVE A WOMAN?, Bryan Adams, 95-4
HAVE YOU EVER SEEN THE RAIN:
Creedence Clearwater Revival, 71-36
Bonnie Tyler, 83-47
HAVE YOU SEEN HER:
Chi-Lites, 72-3, 75-5
M.C. Hammer, 90-8
HAVE YOU SEEN YOUR MOTHER BABY, STANDING IN THE SHADOW?, Rolling Stones, 66-5
HAVEN'T SEEN YOU, Perfume, 96-71
HAVEN'T STOPPED DANCING YET, Gonzalez, 79-15
HAVEN'T YOU HEARD, Patrice Rushen, 80-62
HAVING A PARTY, Osmonds, 75-28
HAWAII TATTOO, Waikikis, 65-41
HAWAIIAN WEDDING SONG, Julie Rogers, 65-31
HAWK-EYE, Frankie Laine with Ray Conniff and his Orchestra, 55-7
HAYFEVER, Trash Can Sinatras, 93-61
HAZARD, Richard Marx, 92-3
HAZEL, Loop Da Loop, 99-20
HAZELL, Maggie Bell, 78-37
HAZIN' + PHAZIN', Choo Choo Project, 00-21
HAZY SHADE OF WINTER:
Bangles, 88-11
Simon and Garfunkel *, 91-30
HE AIN'T HEAVY . . . HE'S MY BROTHER:
Hollies, 69-3, 88-1
Bill Medley, 88-25
HE AIN'T NO COMPETITION, Brother Beyond, 88-6
HE DOESN'T LOVE YOU LIKE I DO, Nick Heyward, 93-58
HE DON'T LOVE YOU, Human Nature, 01-18

HOLDING ON:
Clock, 93-66
Clock *, 96-27
HOLDING ON, DJ Manta, 99-47
HOLDING ON, Heather Small, 00-58
HOLDING ON 4 U (RR], Clock, 96-27
HOLDING ON TO YOU, Terence Trent D'Arby's, 95-20
HOLDING ON (WHEN LOVE IS GONE), L.T.D., 78-70
HOLDING OUT FOR A HERO, Bonnie Tyler, 85-2, 91-69
HOLE HEARTED, Extreme, 91-12
HOLE IN MY SHOE:
Traffic, 67-2
neil, 84-2
HOLE IN MY SOUL, Aerosmith, 97-29
HOLE IN THE BUCKET, Spearhead, 95-55
THE HOLE IN THE GROUND, Bernard Cribbins, 62-9
HOLE IN THE ICE, Neil Finn, 01-43
HOLIDAY, Madonna, 84-6, 85-2, 91-5
HOLIDAY 80 [EP], Human League, 80-56, 82-46
HOLIDAY RAP, M.C. Miker 'G' and Deejay Sven, 86-6
HOLIDAYS IN THE SUN, Sex Pistols, 77-8
HOLLER, Ginuwine, 98-13
HOLLER, Spice Girls, 00-1
HOLLIEDAZE (A MEDLEY) [M], Hollies, 81-28
THE HOLLOW, A Perfect Circle, 00-72
HOLLOW HEART, Birdland, 89-70
THE HOLLOW MAN, Marillion, 94-30
HOLLY HOLY, UB40, 98-31
HOLLYWOOD, Boz Scaggs, 77-33
HOLLYWOOD (DOWN ON YOUR LUCK), Thin Lizzy, 82-53
HOLLYWOOD NIGHTS:
Bob Seger, 78-42, 95-52
Bob Seger and the Silver Bullet Band *, 81-49
HOLLYWOOD SWINGING, Kool And The Gang, 81-17
HOLLYWOOD TEASE, Girl, 80-50
THE HOLY CITY, Moira Anderson, 69-43
HOLY COW, Lee Dorsey, 66-6
HOLY DAYS, Zoe, 92-72
HOLY DIVER, Dio, 83-72
HOLY JOE, Haysi Fantayzee, 82-51
THE HOLY RIVER, Artist, 97-19
HOLY ROLLER, Nazareth, 75-36
HOLY SMOKE, Iron Maiden, 90-3
HOLY WARS . . . THE PUNISHMENT DUE, Megadeth, 90-24
HOMBURG, Procol Harum, 67-6
HOME, Public Image Limited, 86-75
HOME, God Machine, 93-65
HOME, Depeche Mode, 97-23
HOME, Chakra, 97-46, 00-47
HOME, Sheryl Crow, 97-25
HOME, Coast 2 Coast featuring Discovery, 01-44
HOME ALONE, R. Kelly featuring Keith Murray, 98-17
HOME AND AWAY, Karen Boddington and Mark Williams, 89-73
HOME FOR CHRISTMAS DAY, Red Car And The Blue Car, 91-44
HOME IS WHERE THE HEART IS, Gladys Knight and the Pips, 77-35
HOME LOVIN' MAN, Andy Williams, 70-7
HOME OF THE BRAVE, Jody Miller, 65-49
HOME SWEET HOME, Motley Crue, 86-51, 92-37
HOMELY GIRL:
Chi-Lites, 74-5
UB40, 89-6
HOMETOWN UNICORN, Super Furry Animals, 96-47
HOMEWARD BOUND:
Simon and Garfunkel, 66-9
Quiet Five, 66-44
HOMICIDE, 999, 78-40
HOMICIDE, Shades Of Rhythm, 91-53
THE HOMING WALTZ, Vera Lynn with Sailors, Soldiers and Airmen Of Her Majesty's Forces, 52-9
HOMOPHOBIC ASSHOLE, Senseless Things, 92-52
HONALOOCHIE BOOGIE, Mott The Hoople, 73-12
HONDY (NO ACCESS), Hondy, 97-26
HONEST I DO, Danny Storm, 62-42
HONEST MEN, Electric Light Orchestra Part Two, 91-60
HONESTLY I DO LOVE YOU, Candi Staton, 78-48
HONEY, Bobby Goldsboro, 68-2, 75-2
HONEY, Mariah Carey, 97-3
HONEY:
Moby, 98-33
Moby (featuring Kelis), 00-17
HONEY, Billie Ray Martin, 99-54
HONEY BE GOOD, Bible, 89-54
HONEY CHILE, Fats Domino, 57-29
HONEY CHILE, Martha Reeves and the Vandellas, 68-30
HONEY COMB, Jimmy Rodgers with Hugo Peretti and his Orchestra, 57-30
HONEY COME BACK, Glen Campbell, 70-4
HONEY HONEY, Sweet Dreams, 74-10
HONEY I, George McCrae, 76-33
HONEY I'M LOST, Dooleys, 79-24
HONEY I NEED, Pretty Things, 65-13
HONEY TO THE BEE, Billie, 99-3
THE HONEYDRIPPER, Jets, 82-58
THE HONEYMOON SONG, Manuel and the Music Of The Mountains, 59-22
THE HONEYTHIEF, Hipsway, 86-17
HONG KONG GARDEN, Siouxsie and the Banshees, 78-7
HONKY CAT, Elton John, 72-31
THE HONKY DOODLE DAY [EP], Honky, 93-61
HONKY TONK TRAIN BLUES, Keith Emerson, 76-21
HONKY TONK WOMEN:
Rolling Stones, 69-1
Pogues, 92-56
HOOCHIE BOOTY, Ultimate Kaos, 95-17
HOOKED, 99th Floor Elevators featuring Tony De Vit, 95-28, 00-66
HOOKED ON A CAN CAN [M], Louis Clark conducting The Royal Philharmonic Orchestra, 81-47
HOOKED ON A FEELING, Jonathan King, 71-23
HOOKED ON CLASSICS [M], Royal Philharmonic Orchestra, 81-2
HOOKED ON LOVE, Dead Or Alive, 87-69
HOOKED ON YOU, Sydney Youngblood, 91-72
HOOKED ON YOU, Volatile Agents featuring Simone Benn, 01-54
HOOKS IN YOU, Marillion, 89-30
HOOLIGAN, Embrace, 99-18
HOOLIGAN 69, Ragga Twins, 91-56
HOOLIGAN'S HOLIDAY, Motley Crue, 94-36
HOORAY HOORAY, IT'S A HOLI – HOLIDAY, Boney M, 79-3
HOOTIN', Nigel Gee, 01-57
HOOTS MON, Jack Good presents Lord Rockingham's XI, 58-1, 93-60
HOOVERS AND HORNS, Fergie and BK, 00-57
HOOVERVILLE (AND THEY PROMISED US THE WORLD), Christians, 87-21
THE HOP, Theatre Of Hate, 82-70
HOPE, Shaggy featuring Prince Mydas, 01-19
HOPE (I WISH YOU'D BELIEVE ME), Wah!, 83-37
HOPE IN A HOPELESS WORLD, Paul Young, 93-42
HOPE (NEVER GIVE UP), Loveland featuring Rachel McFarlane, 94-37
HOPE OF DELIVERANCE, Paul McCartney, 93-18
HOPE ST., Levellers, 95-12
HOPELESS, Dionne Farris, 97-42
HOPELESSLY, Rick Astley, 93-33
HOPELESSLY DEVOTED TO YOU:
Olivia Newton-John, 78-2
Sonia, 94-61
THE HORN TRACK, Egyptian Empire, 92-61
HORNY, Mark Morrison, 96-5
HORNY, Mousse T vs Hot 'N' Juicy, 98-2
HORNY AS FUNK, Soapy, 96-35
HORNY HORNS, Perfect Phase, 99-21
HORROR HEAD, Curve, 92-31
HORSE, Splodgenessabounds, 80-26
HORSE & CARRIAGE, Cam'ron featuring Mase, 98-12
A HORSE WITH NO NAME, America, 71-3
HORSEPOWER, Ravesignal III, 91-61
HOSTAGE IN A FROCK, Cecil, 97-68
HOT, Ideal, 94-49
HOT & WET (BELIEVE IT), Tzant, 96-36
HOT BLOODED, Foreigner, 78-42
HOT BOYZ, Missy Misdemeanor Elliott, 00-18
HOT DIGGITY (DOG ZIGGITY BOOM):
Perry Como with Mitchell Ayers and his Orchestra and the Ray Charles Singers, 56-4
Michael Holliday with Norrie Paramor and his Orchestra and the Four Shepherd Boys, 56-14
Stargazers with Johnnie Gray and his Band Of The Day, 56-28
HOT DOG, Shakin' Stevens, 80-24
HOT FUN, 7th Heaven, 85-47
HOT-HOT-HOT:
Arrow, 84-59, 94-38
Pat and Mick, 93-47
HOT HOT HOT!!!, Cure, 88-45
HOT IN THE CITY, Billy Idol, 82-58, 88-13
HOT LEGS, Rod Stewart, 78-5
HOT LIKE FIRE, Aaliyah, 97-30
HOT LINE TO HEAVEN, Bananarama, 84-58
HOT LOVE, T. Rex, 71-1
HOT LOVE, David Essex, 80-57
HOT LOVE, Kelly Marie, 81-22
HOT LOVE, Five Star, 90-68
HOT LOVE NOW! [EP] + lead track title, Wonder Stuff, 94-19
HOT PEPPER, Floyd Cramer, 62-46
HOT ROCKIN', Judas Priest, 81-60
(HOT S+++) +++COUNTRY GRAMMAR, Nelly, 00-7
HOT SHOT, Barry Blue, 74-23
HOT SHOT, Karen Young, 78-34, 79-75, 97-68
HOT SHOT, Cliff Richard, 79-46
HOT SHOT TOTTENHAM!, Tottenham Hotspur F.A. Cup Final Squad 1986/87 Season with Chas and Dave, 87-18
HOT SPOT, Foxy Brown, 99-31
HOT STUFF:
Donna Summer, 79-11
Arsenal F.C., 98-9
HOT SUMMER SALSA [M], Jive Bunny and the Mastermixers, 91-43
HOT TODDY, Ted Heath and his Music, 53-6
HOT TRACKS [EP], Nazareth, 77-15
HOT VALVES [EP], Be Bop Deluxe, 76-36
HOT WATER, Level 42, 84-18
HOTEL CALIFORNIA:
Eagles, 77-8
Jam On The Mutha, 90-62
HOTEL ILLNESS, Black Crowes, 92-47
HOTEL YORBA, White Stripes, 01-26
HOTELLOUNGE (BE THE DEATH OF ME), Deus, 95-55
HOUND DOG, Elvis Presley, 56-2, 71-10
HOUND DOG MAN, Fabian, 60-46
HOUNDS OF LOVE, Kate Bush, 86-18
HOURGLASS, Squeeze, 87-16
HOUSE ARREST, Krush, 87-3
HOUSE ENERGY REVENGE, Cappella, 89-73
HOUSE FLY, Tricky Disco, 91-55
A HOUSE IN THE COUNTRY, Pretty Things, 66-50
THE HOUSE IS HAUNTED (BY THE ECHO OF YOUR LAST GOODBYE), Marc Almond, 86-55
THE HOUSE IS MINE, Hypnotist, 91-65
HOUSE IS NOT A HOME, Charles and Eddie, 93-29
HOUSE MUSIC, Eddie Amador, 98-37
HOUSE NATION, House Master Boyz and the Rude Boy Of House, 87-8
HOUSE OF BROKEN LOVE, Great White, 90-44
HOUSE OF FIRE, Alice Cooper, 89-65
HOUSE OF FUN, Madness, 82-1, 92-40
HOUSE OF JOY, Vicki Sue Robinson, 97-48
HOUSE OF LOVE, East 17, 92-10
HOUSE OF LOVE, Rupaul, 93-40, 94-68
HOUSE OF LOVE, Skin, 94-45
HOUSE OF LOVE, Amy Grant with Vince Gill, 95-46
HOUSE OF LOVE (IN MY HOUSE), Smooth Touch, 94-58
HOUSE OF THE BLUE DANUBE, Malcolm McLaren and the Bootzilla Orchestra, 89-73
THE HOUSE OF THE RISING SUN:
Animals, 64-1, 72-25, 82-11
Frijid Pink, 70-4
Rage, 93-41
HOUSE ON FIRE, Boomtown Rats, 82-24
HOUSE ON FIRE, Arkarna, 97-33
HOUSE SOME MORE, Lock 'N' Load, 01-45
THE HOUSE THAT JACK BUILT, Alan Price Set, 67-4
THE HOUSE THAT JACK BUILT, Tracie, 83-9
A HOUSE WITH LOVE IN IT, Vera Lynn, 56-17
HOUSECALL, Shabba Ranks featuring Maxi Priest, 91-31, 93-8
HOUSES IN MOTION, Talking Heads, 81-50
HOW ABOUT THAT!, Adam Faith with John Barry and his Orchestra, 60-4
HOW AM I SUPPOSED TO LIVE WITHOUT YOU, Michael Bolton, 90-3
HOW BIZARRE, OMC, 96-5
HOW 'BOUT US:
Champaign, 81-5
Lulu, 93-46

I BELIEVE:
Frankie Laine with Paul Weston and his Orchestra, 53-1
David Whitfield, 60-49
Bachelors, 64-2
Robson and Jerome, 95-1
I BELIEVE (A SOULFUL RE-RECORDING), Tears For Fears, 85-23
I BELIEVE, EMF, 91-6
I BELIEVE, Reese Project, 92-74
I BELIEVE, Robert Plant, 93-64
I BELIEVE, Bon Jovi, 93-11
I BELIEVE, Marcella Detroit, 94-11
I BELIEVE, Sounds Of Blackness, 94-17
I BELIEVE, Blessid Union Of Souls, 95-29
I BELIEVE, Happy Clappers, 95-21, 95-7, 97-28
I BELIEVE, Booth and the Bad Angel, 96-25
I BELIEVE, Absolute featuring Suzanne Palmer, 97-38
I BELIEVE, Jamestown featuring Jocelyn Brown, 99-62
I BELIEVE, Lange, 99-68
I BELIEVE, Stephen Gately, 00-11
I BELIEVE I CAN FLY, R. Kelly, 97-1
I BELIEVE I'M GONNA LOVE YOU, Frank Sinatra, 75-34
I BELIEVE IN CHRISTMAS, Tweenies, 01-9
I BELIEVE IN FATHER CHRISTMAS, Greg Lake, 75-2, 82-72, 83-65
I BELIEVE (IN LOVE), Hot Chocolate, 71-8
I BELIEVE IN MIRACLES:
Jackson Sisters, 87-72
Pasadenas, 92-34
I BELIEVE IN YOU, Our Tribe, 93-42
I BELIEVE IN YOU AND ME, Whitney Houston, 97-16
(I BELIEVE) LOVE'S A PRIMA DONNA, Steve Harley and Cockney Rebel, 76-41
I BELIEVE YOU, Dorothy Moore, 77-20
I BELONG, Kathy Kirby, 65-36
I BELONG TO YOU, Whitney Houston, 91-54
I BELONG TO YOU, Gina G, 96-6
I BELONG TO YOU, Lenny Kravitz, 98-75
I BREATHE AGAIN, Adam Rickitt, 99-5
I CALL YOUR NAME, A-Ha, 90-44
I CALLED U, Lil Louis and the World, 90-16
I CAN BUY YOU, A Camp, 01-46
I CAN CALL YOU, Portrait, 95-61
I CAN CAST A SPELL, Disco Tex presents Cloudburst, 01-35
I CAN DANCE, Brian Poole and the Tremeloes, 63-31
I CAN DANCE, DJ Fast Eddie, 89-47
I CAN DO IT, Rubettes, 75-7
I CAN DO THIS, Monie Love, 89-37
I CAN DREAM, Skunk Anansie, 95-41
I CAN DREAM ABOUT YOU, Dan Hartman, 85-12
I CAN DRIVE, Shakespears Sister, 96-30
I CAN FEEL IT, Silencers, 93-62
I CAN HEAR MUSIC, Beach Boys, 69-10
I CAN HEAR THE GRASS GROW, Move, 67-5
I CAN HEAR VOICES, Hi-Gate, 00-12
I CAN HEAR YOUR HEARTBEAT:
Chris Rea, 83-60
Chris Rea, 88-74
I CAN HELP:
Billy Swan, 74-6
Elvis Presley, 83-30
I CAN LOVE YOU LIKE THAT, All-4-One, 95-33
I CAN MAKE IT BETTER, Whispers, 81-44
I CAN MAKE IT BETTER, Luther Vandross, 96-44
I CAN MAKE YOU FEEL GOOD:
Shalamar, 82-7
Kavana, 97-8
I CAN MAKE YOU FEEL LIKE, Maxx, 95-56
I CAN ONLY DISAPPOINT U, Mansun, 00-8
I CAN PROVE IT:
Tony Etoria, 77-21
Phil Fearon, 86-8
I CAN SEE CLEARLY, Deborah Harry, 93-23
I CAN SEE CLEARLY NOW:
Johnny Nash, 72-5, 89-54
Hothouse Flowers, 90-23
Jimmy Cliff, 94-23
I CAN SEE FOR MILES, Who, 67-10
I CAN SEE HER NOW, Dramatis, 82-57
I CAN SEE IT, Blancmange, 86-71
I CAN TAKE OR LEAVE YOUR LOVING, Herman's Hermits, 68-11
I CAN'T ASK FOR ANYMORE THAN YOU, Cliff Richard, 76-17
I CAN'T BE WITH YOU, Cranberries, 95-23
I CAN'T BELIEVE YOU'RE GONE, Webb Brothers, 01-69
I CAN'T CONTROL MYSELF, Troggs, 66-2
I CAN'T DANCE, Genesis, 92-7
I CAN'T DENY IT, Rod Stewart, 01-26
I CAN'T EXPLAIN, Who, 65-8
I CAN'T FACE THE WORLD, Lemon Trees, 93-52
(I CAN'T GET ME NO) SATISFACTION, Devo, 78-41
I CAN'T GET NEXT TO YOU, Temptations, 70-13
(I CAN'T GET NO) SATISFACTION:
Rolling Stones, 65-1
Otis Redding, 66-33
Aretha Franklin *, 67-37
Bubblerock, 74-29
Devo *, 78-41
Vanilla Ice *, 91-22
I CAN'T GET NO SLEEP '95, Masters At Work present India, 95-44
I CAN'T GET YOU OUTA MY MIND, Yvonne Elliman, 77-17
I CAN'T GO FOR THAT (NO CAN DO), Daryl Hall and John Oates, 82-8
(I CAN'T HELP) FALLING IN LOVE WITH YOU, UB40, 93-1
I CAN'T HELP IT, Johnny Tillotson, 62-42, 63-41
I CAN'T HELP IT, Junior, 82-53
I CAN'T HELP IT, Bananarama, 88-20
I CAN'T HELP MYSELF:
Four Tops, 65-23, 70-10
Donnie Elbert, 72-11
I CAN'T HELP MYSELF, Orange Juice, 82-42
I CAN'T HELP MYSELF, Joey Lawrence, 93-27
I CAN'T HELP MYSELF, Julia Fordham, 94-62
I CAN'T HELP MYSELF, Lucid, 98-7
I CAN'T IMAGINE THE WORLD WITHOUT ME, Echobelly, 94-39
I CAN'T LEAVE YOU ALONE:
George McCrae, 74-9
Tracie Young, 85-60
I CAN'T LET GO, Hollies, 66-2
I CAN'T LET GO, Marti Webb, 87-65
I CAN'T LET MAGGIE GO, Honeybus, 68-8
I CAN'T LET YOU GO, Haywoode, 84-63, 86-50
I CAN'T LET YOU GO, 52nd Street, 86-57
I CAN'T LET YOU GO, Mack Vibe featuring Jacqueline, 95-53
I CAN'T LIVE A DREAM, Osmonds, 76-37
(I CAN'T LIVE WITHOUT YOUR) LOVE & AFFECTION, Nelson, 90-54
I CAN'T MAKE A MISTAKE, MC Lyte, 98-46
I CAN'T MAKE IT, Small Faces, 67-26
I CAN'T MAKE IT ALONE:
P.J. Proby, 66-37
Maria McKee, 93-74
I CAN'T MAKE YOU LOVE ME:
Bonnie Raitt, 91-50
George Michael, 97-3
I CAN'T READ, David Bowie, 98-73
I CAN'T SAY GOODBYE, Kim Wilde, 90-51
I CAN'T SAY GOODBYE TO YOU, Helen Reddy, 81-43
I CAN'T SEE, Nicole Ray [featuring Mocha], 98-55
I CAN'T SLEEP BABY, R. Kelly, 00-24
I CAN'T STAND IT, Spencer Davis Group, 64-47
I CAN'T STAND IT, Twenty 4 Seven featuring Captain Hollywood, 90-7
I CAN'T STAND IT (from OBLIVION (HEAD IN THE CLOUDS) [EP]), Manix, 92-43
I CAN'T STAND MY BABY, Rezillos, 79-71
I CAN'T STAND THE RAIN:
Ann Peebles, 74-41
Eruption featuring Precious Wilson, 78-5
Tina Turner, 85-57
I CAN'T STAND UP FOR FALLING DOWN, Elvis Costello and the Attractions, 80-4
I CAN'T STOP, Osmonds, 74-12
I CAN'T STOP, Gary Numan, 86-27
I CAN'T STOP LOVING YOU, Ray Charles, 62-1
I CAN'T STOP LOVING YOU (THOUGH I TRY), Leo Sayer, 78-6
I CAN'T TAKE THE POWER, Off-Shore, 90-7
I CAN'T TELL A WALTZ FROM A TANGO, Alma Cogan, 54-6
I CAN'T TELL THE BOTTOM FROM THE TOP, Hollies, 70-7
I CAN'T TELL YOU WHY, Brownstone, 95-27
I CAN'T TURN AROUND, J.M. Silk, 86-62
I CAN'T TURN AWAY, Savanna, 81-61
I CAN'T TURN YOU LOOSE, Otis Redding, 66-29
I CAN'T WAIT, Stevie Nicks, 86-54, 91-47
I CAN'T WAIT, Nu Shooz, 86-2
I CAN'T WAIT ANYMORE, Saxon, 88-71
I CARE (SOUL II SOUL), Soul Ii Soul, 95-17
I CAUGHT YOU OUT, Rebecca De Ruvo, 94-72
I CLOSE MY EYES AND COUNT TO TEN, Dusty Springfield, 68-4
I COME FROM ANOTHER PLANET, BABY, Julian Cope, 96-34
I CONFESS, Beat, 82-54
I COULD BE HAPPY, Altered Images, 81-7
I COULD BE SO GOOD FOR YOU, Dennis Waterman with the Dennis Waterman Band, 80-3
I COULD EASILY FALL (IN LOVE WITH YOU), Cliff Richard and the Shadows, 64-9
I COULD HAVE BEEN A DREAMER, Dio, 87-69
I COULD NEVER LOVE ANOTHER (AFTER LOVING YOU), Temptations, 68-47
I COULD NEVER MISS YOU (MORE THAN I DO), Lulu, 81-62
I COULD NEVER TAKE THE PLACE OF YOUR MAN, Prince, 87-29
I COULD NOT LOVE YOU MORE, Bee Gees, 97-14
I COULD SING OF YOUR LOVE FOREVER, Delirious?, 01-40
I COULDN'T LIVE WITHOUT YOUR LOVE, Petula Clark, 66-6
I COUNT THE TEARS, Drifters, 61-28
I CRIED FOR YOU, Ricky Stevens with the Rita Williams Singers and Geoff Love and his Orchestra, 61-34
I DID WHAT I DID FOR MARIA, Tony Christie, 71-2
I DIDN'T KNOW I LOVED YOU (TILL I SAW YOU ROCK AND ROLL):
Gary Glitter, 72-4
Rock Goddess, 84-57
I DIDN'T KNOW I WAS LOOKING FOR LOVE:
Everything But The Girl (from EP of the same name), 93-72
Karen Ramirez *, 98-8
I DIDN'T MEAN IT, Status Quo, 94-21
I DIDN'T MEAN TO HURT YOU, Rockin' Berries, 64-43
I DIDN'T MEAN TO TURN YOU ON, Robert Palmer, 86-9
I DIDN'T WANT TO NEED YOU, Heart, 90-47
I DIE: YOU DIE, Gary Numan, 80-6
I DIG YOU BABY, Marvin Rainwater, 58-19
I DISAPPEAR, Metallica, 00-35
I DO, Jamelia, 99-36
I DO, I DO, I DO, I DO, I DO, Abba, 75-38
I DO WHAT I DO (THEME FOR 9½ WEEKS), John Taylor, 86-42
I DON'T BELIEVE IN IF ANY MORE, Roger Whittaker, 70-8
I DON'T BELIEVE IN MIRACLES, Colin Blunstone, 72-31
I DON'T BELIEVE IN MIRACLES, Sinitta, 88-22
I DON'T BLAME YOU AT ALL, Smokey Robinson and the Miracles, 71-11
I DON'T CARE, Los Bravos, 66-16
I DON'T CARE, Shakespears Sister, 92-7
I DON'T CARE (AS LONG AS YOU CARE FOR ME), Liberace, 56-28
I DON'T CARE IF THE SUN DON'T SHINE, Elvis Presley, 56-23
I DON'T EVEN KNOW IF I SHOULD CALL YOU BABY:
Soul Family Sensation, 91-49
Rozalla *, 95-26
I DON'T EVER WANT TO SEE YOU AGAIN, Uncle Sam, 98-30
I DON'T KNOW, Ruth, 97-66
I DON'T KNOW, Honeyz, 01-28
I DON'T KNOW ANYBODY ELSE, Black Box, 90-4
I DON'T KNOW HOW TO LOVE HIM:
Petula Clark, 72-47
Yvonne Elliman/Various Artists, 72-47
I DON'T KNOW IF IT'S RIGHT, Evelyn "Champagne" King, 79-67
I DON'T KNOW WHAT IT IS BUT I LOVE IT, Chris Rea, 84-65
I DON'T KNOW WHAT YOU WANT BUT I CAN'T GIVE IT ANY MORE, Pet Shop Boys, 99-15

I KNOW A PLACE, Petula Clark, 65-17
I KNOW A PLACE, Kim English, 95-52
I KNOW ENOUGH (I DON'T GET ENOUGH), Theaudience, 98-25
I KNOW HIM SO WELL:
Elaine Paige and Barbara Dickson, 85-1
Steps, 01-5
(I KNOW) I'M LOSING YOU, Temptations, 66-19
I KNOW MY LOVE, Chieftains featuring the Corrs, 99-37
I KNOW THE LORD, Tabernacle, 95-62, 96-55
I KNOW THERE'S SOMETHING GOING ON, Frida, 82-43
I KNOW WHAT BOYS LIKE, Shampoo, 96-42
I KNOW WHAT I LIKE (IN YOUR WARDROBE), Genesis, 74-21
I KNOW WHAT I'M HERE FOR, James, 99-22
I KNOW WHERE I'M GOIN', George Hamilton IV, 58-23
I KNOW WHERE I'M GOING, Countrymen, 62-45
I KNOW WHERE IT'S AT, All Saints, 97-4
I KNOW YOU DON'T LOVE ME, Roachford, 95-42
I KNOW YOU GOT SOUL (THE DOUBLE TROUBLE REMIX), Eric B. and Rakim, 88-13
I KNOW YOU'RE OUT THERE SOMEWHERE, Moody Blues, 88-52
I LEARNED FROM THE BEST, Whitney Houston, 99-19
(I LEFT MY HEART) IN SAN FRANCISCO, Tony Bennett, 65-25
I LIFT MY CUP, Gloworm, 93-20, 94-46
I LIKE, Shanice, 94-49
I LIKE, Kut Klose, 95-72
I LIKE, Montell Jordan featuring Slick Rick, 96-24
I LIKE, Juliet Roberts, 99-17
I LIKE IT, Gerry and the Pacemakers, 63-1
I LIKE IT, D.J.H. featuring Stefy, 91-16
I LIKE IT, Overweight Pooch featuring Ce Ce Peniston, 92-58
I LIKE IT, Jomanda, 93-67
I LIKE IT, D:Ream, 93-26
I LIKE IT, Angel Moraes, 97-70
I LIKE THE WAY, Deni Hines, 97-37
I LIKE THE WAY (THE KISSING GAME):
Hi-Five, 91-43
Kaleef, 97-58
I LIKE TO MOVE IT, Reel 2 Real featuring the Mad Stuntman, 94-5
I LIKE TO ROCK, April Wine, 80-41
I LIKE (WHAT YOU'RE DOING TO ME), Young and Company, 80-20
I LIKE YOUR KIND OF LOVE, Andy Williams, 57-16
I LIVE FOR THE SUN, Vanity Fare, 68-20
I LIVE FOR THE WEEKEND, Triumph, 80-59
I LIVE FOR YOUR LOVE, Natalie Cole, 88-23
I LOST MY HEART TO A STARSHIP TROOPER, Sarah Brightman and Hot Gossip, 78-6
I LOVE A MAN IN UNIFORM, Gang Of Four, 82-65
I LOVE A RAINY NIGHT, Eddie Rabbitt, 81-53
I LOVE AMERICA:
Patrick Juvet, 78-12
Full Intention *, 96-32, 97-56
I LOVE BEING IN LOVE WITH YOU, Adam Faith with the Roulettes, 64-33
I LOVE FOOTBALL, Wes, 98-75
I LOVE HER, Paul and Barry Ryan, 66-17
I LOVE HOW YOU LOVE ME:
Jimmy Crawford, 61-18
Maureen Evans, 64-34
Paul and Barry Ryan, 66-21
I LOVE I HATE, Neil Arthur, 94-50
I LOVE LAKE TAHOE, A, 99-59
I LOVE MEN, Eartha Kitt, 84-50
I LOVE MUSIC:
O'Jays, 76-13, 78-36
Rozalla, 94-18
I LOVE MUSIC [M], Enigma, 81-25
I LOVE MY DOG, Cat Stevens, 66-28
I LOVE MY RADIO [MIDNIGHT RADIO], Taffy, 87-6
I LOVE ROCK 'N ROLL, Joan Jett and the Blackhearts, 82-4, 94-75
I LOVE SATURDAY, Erasure, 94-20
I LOVE THE NIGHT LIFE (DISCO 'ROUND), Alicia Bridges, 78-32, 94-61
I LOVE THE SOUND OF BREAKING GLASS, Nick Lowe, 78-7
I LOVE THE WAY YOU LOVE, Marv Johnson, 60-35
I LOVE THE WAY YOU LOVE ME, Boyzone, 98-2
I LOVE TO BOOGIE, T.Rex, 76-13
I LOVE TO LOVE (BUT MY BABY LOVES TO DANCE), Tina Charles, 76-1, 86-67
(I LOVE TO PLAY) MY UKELELE, Max Bygraves, 59-19
I LOVE U, Shut Up and Dance featuring Richie Davis and Professor T, 95-68
I LOVE YOU, Cliff Richard and the Shadows, 60-1
I LOVE YOU, Donna Summer, 77-10
I LOVE YOU, Yello, 83-41
I LOVE YOU, Vanilla Ice, 91-45
I LOVE YOU ALWAYS FOREVER, Donna Lewis, 96-5
I LOVE YOU, BABY, Paul Anka, 57-3
I LOVE YOU BABY, Freddie and the Dreamers, 64-16
I LOVE YOU BECAUSE:
Al Martino, 63-48
Jim Reeves, 64-5, 71-34
I LOVE YOU GOODBYE, Thomas Dolby, 92-36
I LOVE YOU LOVE ME LOVE, Gary Glitter, 73-1
I LOVE YOU SO MUCH IT HURTS, Charlie Gracie, 57-14
I LOVE YOU . . . STOP!, Red 5, 97-11
(I LOVE YOU) WHEN YOU SLEEP, Tracie, 84-59
I LOVE YOU, YES I DO, Merseybeats, 65-22
I LOVE YOU, YES I LOVE YOU, Eddy Grant, 81-37
I LOVE YOUR SMILE, Shanice, 91-55, 92-2
I LUV U BABY, Original, 95-31, 95-2
I MADE IT THROUGH THE RAIN, Barry Manilow, 81-37
I MAY NEVER PASS THIS WAY AGAIN:
Ronnie Hilton with the Michael Sammes Singers, 58-27
Robert Earl, 58-14
Perry Como with Mitchell Ayres' Orchestra and the Ray Charles Singers, 58-15
I MET A GIRL, Shadows, 66-22
I MIGHT, Shakin' Stevens, 90-18
I MIGHT BE CRYING, Tanita Tikaram, 95-64
I MIGHT BE LYING, Eddie and the Hotrods, 77-44
I MISS YOU, 4 Of Us, 93-62
I MISS YOU, Haddaway, 93-9
I MISS YOU, Bjork, 97-36
I MISS YOU BABY (HOW I MISS YOU), Marv Johnson, 69-25
I MISSED AGAIN, Phil Collins, 81-14
I MISSED THE BUS, Kris Kross, 92-57
I MUST BE IN LOVE, Rutles, 78-39
I MUST BE SEEING THINGS, Gene Pitney, 65-6
I MUST STAND, Ice T, 96-23
I NEED, Meredith Brooks, 97-28
I NEED A LOVER TONIGHT (from NAKASAKI EP (I NEED A LOVER TONIGHT) [EP]), Ken Doh, 96-7
I NEED A MAN, Man To Man, 87-43
I NEED A MAN, Eurythmics, 88-26
I NEED A MAN, Li Kwan, 94-51
I NEED A MIRACLE, Coco, 97-39
I NEED ANOTHER [EP] + lead track title, Dodgy, 93-67
I NEED DIRECTION, Teenage Fanclub, 00-48
I NEED IT, Johnny Guitar Watson, 76-35
I NEED LOVE, L.L. Cool J, 87-8
I NEED LOVE, Olivia Newton-John, 92-75
I NEED SOMEBODY, Loveland featuring the voice of Rachel McFarlane, 95-21, 95-38
I NEED TO BE IN LOVE, Carpenters, 76-36
I NEED TO KNOW, Marc Anthony, 99-28
I NEED YOU, Joe Dolan, 77-43
I NEED YOU, Pointer Sisters, 84-25
I NEED YOU, B.V.S.M.P., 88-3
I NEED YOU, Deuce, 95-10
I NEED YOU, Nikita Warren, 96-48
I NEED YOU, 3T, 96-3
I NEED YOU, Wireless, 97-68
I NEED YOU, Leann Rimes, 01-13
I NEED YOU NOW, Eddie Fisher with Hugo Winterhalter and his Orchestra, 54-13
I NEED YOU NOW, Sinnamon, 96-70
I NEED YOU TONIGHT, Junior M.A.F.I.A. featuring Aaliyah, 96-66
I NEED YOUR LOVE TONIGHT, Elvis Presley with the Jordanaires, 59-1
I NEED YOUR LOVIN':
Teena Marie, 80-28
Curiosity, 92-47
I NEED YOUR LOVIN', Alyson Williams, 89-8
I NEED YOUR LOVIN' (LIKE THE SUNSHINE), Marc Et Claude, 00-12
I NEED YOUR LOVING, Human League Red, 86-72
I NEVER FELT LIKE THIS BEFORE, Mica Paris, 93-15
I NEVER GO OUT IN THE RAIN, High Society, 80-53
I NEVER KNEW, Roger Sanchez featuring Cooly's Hot Box, 00-24
I NEVER LOVED YOU ANYWAY, Corrs, 97-43
I NEVER WANT AN EASY LIFE IF ME AND HE WERE EVER TO GET THERE, Charlatans, 94-38
I.O.I.O., Bee Gees featuring Barry and Maurice Gibb, 70-49
I.O.U., Jane Kennaway and Strange Behaviour, 81-65
I.O.U., Freeez, 83-2, 87-23
I.O.U., Bill Tarmey, 94-55
I ONLY HAVE EYES FOR YOU, Art Garfunkel, 75-1
I ONLY LIVE TO LOVE YOU, Cilla Black, 67-26
I ONLY WANT TO BE WITH YOU:
Dusty Springfield, 63-4
Bay City Rollers *, 76-4
Tourists, 79-4
Samantha Fox *, 89-16
I ONLY WANT TO BE WITH YOU, Barry White, 95-36
I OWE YOU NOTHING, Bros, 88-1
I OWE YOU ONE, Shalamar, 80-13
I PRETEND, Des O'Connor, 68-1
I PROMISE YOU (GET READY), Samantha Fox, 87-58
I PROMISED MYSELF, Nick Kamen, 90-50
I PRONOUNCE YOU, Madness, 88-44
I PUT A SPELL ON YOU:
Nina Simone, 65-49, 69-28
Alan Price Set, 66-9
Bryan Ferry, 93-18
Sonique, 98-36, 00-8
I QUIT, Bros, 88-4
I QUIT, Hepburn, 99-8
I RAN, A Flock Of Seagulls, 82-43
I REALLY DIDN'T MEAN IT, Luther Vandross, 87-16
I RECALL A GYPSY WOMAN, Don Williams, 76-13
I REFUSE, Hue And Cry, 88-47
I REFUSE (WHAT YOU WANT), Somore featuring Damon Trueitt, 98-21
I REMEMBER, Coolio, 94-73
I REMEMBER ELVIS PRESLEY (THE KING IS DEAD), Danny Mirror, 77-4
I REMEMBER YESTERDAY, Donna Summer, 77-14
I REMEMBER YOU, Frank Ifield, 62-1
I REMEMBER YOU, Skid Row, 90-36
I ROCK, Tom Novy featuring Virginia, 00-55
I SAVED THE WORLD TODAY, Eurythmics, 99-11
I SAW HER STANDING THERE:
Elton John Band featuring John Lennon and the Muscle Shoals Horns, 81-40
Tiffany *, 88-8
I SAW HERE AGAIN, Mama's and the Papa's, 66-11
I SAW HIM STANDING THERE, Tiffany, 88-8
I SAW LINDA YESTERDAY, Doug Sheldon, 63-36
I SAW MOMMY KISSING SANTA CLAUS:
Jimmy Boyd, 53-3
Beverley Sisters, 53-6
Billy Cotton and his Band featuring the Mill Girls and the Bandits, 53-11
I SAW THE LIGHT, Todd Rundgren, 73-36
I SAW THE LIGHT, The, 95-31
I SAY A LITTLE PRAYER:
Aretha Franklin, 68-4
Bomb The Bass featuring Maureen *, 88-10
Diana King, 97-17
I SAY NOTHING, Voice Of The Beehive, 87-45, 88-22
I SAY YEAH, Secchi featuring Orlando Johnson, 91-46
I SCARE MYSELF, Thomas Dolby, 84-46
I SECOND THAT EMOTION:
Smokey Robinson and the Miracles, 67-27
Diana Ross and the Supremes and the Temptations, 69-18
Japan, 82-9
Alyson Williams featuring Chuck Stanley, 89-44
I SEE A STAR, Mouth and McNeal, 74-8
I SEE ONLY YOU, Nootropic, 96-42
I SEE THE MOON, Stargazers with Syd Dean and his Orchestra, 54-1
I SEE YOU BABY, Groove Armada featuring Gram'ma Funk, 99-17
I SEE YOUR SMILE, Gloria Estefan, 93-48
I SEEN A MAN DIE, Scarface, 95-55
I SHALL BE RELEASED, Tremeloes with the Keith Mansfield Strings, 68-29

I WAS TIRED OF BEING ALONE, Patrice Rushen, 82-39
I WASN'T BUILT TO GET UP, Supernaturals, 98-25
I (WHO HAVE NOTHING) (UNO DEI TANTI):
Shirley Bassey, 63-6
Tom Jones, 70-16
Sylvester, 79-46
I WILL:
Billy Fury, 64-14
Ruby Winters, 77-4
I WILL ALWAYS LOVE YOU:
Whitney Houston, 92-1, 93-25
Sarah Washington, 93-12
I WILL BE RELEASED, Up Yer Ronson featuring Mary Pearce, 97-32
I WILL BE WITH YOU, T'Pau, 88-14
I WILL BE YOUR GIRLFRIEND, Dubstar, 98-28
I WILL COME TO YOU, Hanson, 97-5
I WILL DRINK THE WINE, Frank Sinatra, 71-16
I WILL GO WITH YOU (CON TE PARTIRO), Donna Summer, 99-44
I WILL LOVE AGAIN, Lara Fabian, 00-63
I WILL LOVE YOU ALL MY LIFE, Foster and Allen, 83-49
I WILL LOVE YOU (EVERYTIME WHEN WE ARE GONE), Fureys, 82-54
I WILL REMEMBER, Toto, 95-64
I WILL RETURN, Springwater, 71-5
I WILL SURVIVE, Arrival, 70-16
I WILL SURVIVE:
Gloria Gaynor, 79-1, 93-5
Billie Jo Spears, 79-47
Diana, 96-14
Chantay Savage, 96-12
Cake, 97-29
I WILL WAIT, Hootie And The Blowfish, 98-57
I WISH, Stevie Wonder, 76-5
I WISH, Gabrielle, 93-26
I WISH, Skee-Lo, 95-15
I WISH, R. Kelly, 00-12
I WISH HE DIDN'T TRUST ME SO MUCH, Bobby Womack, 85-64
I WISH I COULD SHIMMY LIKE MY SISTER KATE, Olympics, 61-40
(I WISH I KNEW HOW IT WOULD FEEL TO BE) FREE/ONE, Lighthouse Family, 01-6
I WISH IT COULD BE A WOMBLING CHRISTMAS EVERY DAY, Wombles with Roy Wood, 00-22
I WISH IT COULD BE CHRISTMAS EVERYDAY:
Wizzard vocal backing by the Suedettes, plus the Stockland Green Bilateral School First Choir additional noises Miss Snob and Class 3C, 73-4, 81-41, 84-23
Roy Wood Big Band Live, 95-59
I WISH IT WOULD RAIN:
Temptations, 68-45
Faces *, 73-8
I WISH IT WOULD RAIN DOWN, Phil Collins, 90-7
I WISH U HEAVEN, Prince, 88-24
I WISH YOU LOVE, Paul Young, 97-33
I WISH YOU WOULD, Jocelyn Brown, 84-51
I WON'T BACK DOWN, Tom Petty, 89-28
I WON'T BLEED FOR YOU, Climie Fisher, 88-35
I WON'T CLOSE MY EYES, UB40, 82-32
I WON'T COME IN WHILE HE'S THERE, Jim Reeves, 67-12
I WON'T CRY, Glen Goldsmith, 87-34
I WON'T FEEL BAD, Simply Red, 88-68
I WON'T FORGET YOU, Jim Reeves, 64-3
I WON'T HOLD YOU BACK, Toto, 83-37
I WON'T LAST A DAY WITHOUT YOU, Carpenters, 72-49, 74-32
I WON'T LET THE SUN GO DOWN ON ME, Nik Kershaw, 83-47, 84-2
I WON'T LET YOU DOWN, P.H.D, 82-3
I WON'T MENTION IT AGAIN, Ruby Winters, 78-45
I WON'T RUN AWAY, Alvin Stardust, 84-7
I WONDER:
Dickie Valentine with Johnny Douglas and his Orchestra, 55-4
Jane Froman, 55-14
I WONDER, Brenda Lee, 63-14
I WONDER, Crystals, 64-36
I WONDER IF HEAVEN GOT A GHETTO, 2Pac, 98-21
I WONDER IF I TAKE YOU HOME, Lisa Lisa and Cult Jam with Full Force, 85-12
I WONDER WHO'S KISSING HER NOW, Emile Ford and the Checkmates, 62-43
I WONDER WHY, Showaddywaddy, 78-2
I WONDER WHY, Curtis Stigers, 92-5
I WONDER WHY HE'S THE GREATEST DJ, Tony Touch featuring Total, 00-68
I WOULD DIE 4 U, Prince and the Revolution, 84-58
I WOULD DO FOR YOU, UB40, 89-45
I WOULD FIX YOU, Kenickie, 98-36
I WOULDN'T BELIEVE YOUR RADIO, Stereophonics, 99-11
I WOULDN'T LIE, Yarbrough and Peoples, 86-61
I WOULDN'T NORMALLY DO THIS KIND OF THING, Pet Shop Boys, 93-13
I WOULDN'T TRADE YOU FOR THE WORLD, Bachelors, 64-4
I WOULDN'T WANNA HAPPEN TO YOU, Embrace, 00-23
I WRITE THE SONGS :
David Cassidy, 75-11
Big Daddy (from Dancing In The Dark [EP]), 85-21
I WROTE YOU A SONG, Misty Oldland, 94-73
I'D BE SURPRISINGLY GOOD FOR YOU, Linda Lewis, 79-40
I'D DIE WITHOUT YOU, PM Dawn, 92-30
I'D DO ANYTHING, Mike Preston, 60-23
I'D DO ANYTHING FOR LOVE (BUT I WON'T DO THAT), Meat Loaf, 93-1
I'D LIE FOR YOU (AND THAT'S THE TRUTH), Meat Loaf, 95-2
I'D LIKE TO TEACH THE WORLD TO SING (IN PERFECT HARMONY):
New Seekers, 71-1
No Way Sis, 96-27
I'D LOVE YOU TO WANT ME, Lobo, 74-5
I'D NEVER FIND ANOTHER YOU, Billy Fury, 61-5
I'D RATHER GO BLIND:
Chicken Shack, 69-14
Ruby Turner, 87-24
Sydney Youngblood, 90-44
I'D RATHER JACK, Reynolds Girls, 89-8
I'D REALLY LOVE TO SEE YOU TONIGHT, England Dan and John Ford Coley, 76-26
I'LL ALWAYS BE AROUND, C+C Music Factory, 95-42
I'LL ALWAYS BE IN LOVE WITH YOU, Michael Holliday, 58-27
I'LL ALWAYS LOVE MY MAMA, Intruders, 74-32
I'LL ALWAYS LOVE YOU, Taylor Dayne, 88-41
I'LL BE, Foxy Brown featuring Jay Z, 97-9
(I'LL BE A) FREAK FOR YOU, Royalle Delite, 85-45
I'LL BE AROUND:
Terri Wells, 84-17
Rappin' 4-Tay featuring the Spinners, 95-30
I'LL BE BACK, Arnee and the Terminaters, 91-5
I'LL BE GOOD, Rene and Angela, 85-22
I'LL BE GOOD TO YOU, Quincy Jones featuring Ray Charles and Chaka Khan, 90-21
I'LL BE HOME, Pat Boone, 56-1
I'LL BE HOME THIS CHRISTMAS, Shakin' Stevens, 91-34
I'LL BE LOVING YOU (FOREVER), New Kids On The Block, 90-5
I'LL BE MISSING YOU, Puff Daddy and Faith Evans (featuring 112), 97-1
I'LL BE SATISFIED, Shakin' Stevens, 82-10
I'LL BE THERE, Gerry and the Pacemakers, 65-15
I'LL BE THERE, Jackie Trent, 69-38
I'LL BE THERE:
Jackson 5, 70-4
Mariah Carey, 92-2
I'LL BE THERE, Innocence, 92-26
I'LL BE THERE, 99th Floor Elevators featuring Tony De Vit, 96-37
I'LL BE THERE FOR YOU, Bon Jovi, 89-18
I'LL BE THERE FOR YOU, Solid Harmonie, 98-18
I'LL BE THERE FOR YOU (DOYA DODODO DOYA), House Of Virginism, 93-29
I'LL BE THERE FOR YOU (THEME FROM "FRIENDS"), Rembrandts, 95-3, 97-5
I'LL BE THERE FOR YOU/YOU'RE ALL I NEED TO GET BY [M], Method Man featuring Mary J. Blige, 95-10
I'LL BE WAITING, Clive Griffin, 91-56
I'LL BE WAITING, Full Intention presents Shena, 01-44
"I'LL BE WITH YOU" IN APPLE BLOSSOM TIME, Rosemary June, 59-14
I'LL BE YOUR BABY TONIGHT, Robert Palmer and UB40, 90-6
I'LL BE YOUR EVERYTHING, Tommy Page, 90-53
I'LL BE YOUR FRIEND, Robert Owens, 91-75, 97-25
I'LL BE YOUR SHELTER, Taylor Dayne, 90-43
I'LL COME RUNNIN', Cliff Richard, 67-26
I'LL COME RUNNIN', Juice, 98-48
I'LL COME WHEN YOU CALL, Ruby Murray with Ray Martin and his Orchestra, 55-6
I'LL CRY FOR YOU, Europe, 92-28
I'LL CUT YOUR TAIL OFF, John Leyton, 63-36
I'LL DO ANYTHING – TO MAKE YOU MINE, Holloway and Co., 99-58
I'LL DO ANYTHING YOU WANT ME TO, Barry White, 75-20
I'LL DO YA, Whale, 95-53
I'LL FIND MY WAY HOME, Jon and Vangelis, 81-6
I'LL FIND YOU, David Whitfield with the Roland Shaw Orchestra, 57-27
I'LL FIND YOU, Michelle Gayle, 94-26
I'LL FIND YOU (from EP THREE [EP]), Hundred Reasons, 01-37
I'LL FLY FOR YOU, Spandau Ballet, 84-9
I'LL GET BY:
Connie Francis, 58-19
Shirley Bassey with the Williams Singers and Geoff Love and his Orchestra, 61-10
I'LL GIVE YOU THE EARTH (TOUS LES BATEAUX, TOUS LES OISEAUX), Keith Michell, 71-30
I'LL GO ON HOPING, Des O'Connor with Alyn Ainsworth and Orchestra, 70-30
I'LL GO WHERE YOUR MUSIC TAKES ME:
Jimmy James and the Vagabonds, 76-23
Tina Charles, 78-27
I'LL HOUSE YOU:
Richie Rich meets Jungle Brothers, 88-22
Jungle Brothers, 98-26
I'LL KEEP ON LOVING YOU, Princess, 86-16
I'LL KEEP YOU SATISFIED, Billy J. Kramer with the Dakotas, 63-4
I'LL KEEP YOUR DREAMS ALIVE, George Benson and Patti Austin, 92-68
I'LL LOVE YOU FOREVER TODAY, Cliff Richard, 68-27
I'LL MAKE LOVE TO YOU, Boyz II Men, 94-5
I'LL MANAGE SOMEHOW, Menswear, 95-49
I'LL MEET YOU AT MIDNIGHT, Smokie, 76-11
I'LL NEVER BREAK YOUR HEART, Backstreet Boys, 95-42, 96-8
I'LL NEVER FALL IN LOVE AGAIN, Johnnie Ray with Richard Maltby and his Orchestra, 59-26
I'LL NEVER FALL IN LOVE AGAIN, Tom Jones, 67-2
I'LL NEVER FALL IN LOVE AGAIN:
Bobbie Gentry, 69-1
Deacon Blue (from Four Bacharach And David Songs [EP]), 90-2
I'LL NEVER FIND ANOTHER YOU, Seekers, 65-1
I'LL NEVER GET OVER YOU, Johnny Kidd and the Pirates, 63-4
I'LL NEVER GET OVER YOU, Everly Brothers, 65-35
I'LL NEVER GET OVER YOU (GETTING OVER ME), Expose, 93-75
I'LL NEVER LOVE THIS WAY AGAIN, Dionne Warwick, 83-62
I'LL NEVER QUITE GET OVER YOU, Billy Fury, 66-35
I'LL NEVER STOP, *Nsync, 00-13
I'LL NEVER STOP LOVING YOU, Doris Day, 55-17
I'LL PICK A ROSE FOR MY ROSE, Marv Johnson, 69-10
I'LL PUT YOU TOGETHER AGAIN (FROM DEAR ANYONE), Hot Chocolate, 78-13
I'LL REMEMBER (THEME FROM 'WITH HONOURS'), Madonna, 94-7
I'LL REMEMBER TONIGHT, Pat Boone, 59-18
I'LL SAIL THIS SHIP ALONE, Beautiful South, 89-31
I'LL SAY FOREVER MY LOVE, Jimmy Ruffin, 70-7
I'LL SEE YOU ALONG THE WAY, Rick Clarke, 88-63
I'LL SEE YOU AROUND, Silver Sun, 98-26
I'LL SEE YOU IN MY DREAMS, Pat Boone, 62-27

I'M SHY MARY ELLEN I'M SHY, Bob Wallis and his Storyville Jazz Band, 61-44
I'M SICK OF YOU, Goodbye Mr. MacKenzie, 89-49
I'M SO BEAUTIFUL, Divine, 84-52
I'M SO CRAZY, Par-T-One vs Inxs, 01-19
I'M SO CRAZY (BOUT YOU), KC and the Sunshine Band, 75-34
I'M SO EXCITED, Pointer Sisters, 84-11
I'M SO GLAD I'M STANDING HERE TODAY, Crusaders, featured vocalist Joe Cocker, 81-61
I'M SO HAPPY, Light Of The World, 81-35
I'M SO HAPPY, Julia and Co, 85-56
I'M SO HAPPY, Walter Beasley, 88-70
I'M SO HAPPY I CAN'T STOP CRYING, Sting, 96-54
I'M SO IN LOVE, Alysha Warren, 94-61
I'M SO INTO YOU, SWV, 93-17
I'M SO LONELY, Cast, 97-14
I'M SORRY, Platters, 57-18
I'M SORRY, Brenda Lee, 60-12
I'M SORRY, Hothouse Flowers, 88-53
I'M SORRY I MADE YOU CRY, Connie Francis, 58-11
I'M STANDING (HIGHER), X-Static, 95-41
I'M STARTING TO GO STEADY, Johnny Preston, 60-49
I'M STILL GONNA NEED YOU, Osmonds, 75-32
I'M STILL IN LOVE WITH YOU, Al Green, 72-35
I'M STILL STANDING, Elton John, 83-4
I'M STILL WAITING:
Diana Ross, 71-1, 76-41, '90-21
Courtney Pine featuring Carroll Thompson, 90-66
I'M STILL WAITING, Angelheart featuring Aletia Bourne, 97-74
I'M STONE IN LOVE WITH YOU:
Stylistics, 72-9
Johnny Mathis, 75-10
I'M TELLIN YOU, Kentish Man presents Chubby Chunks featuring Kim Ruffin, 99-61
I'M TELLIN' YOU NOW, Freddie and the Dreamers, 63-2
I'M THAT TYPE OF GUY, L.L. Cool J, 89-43
I'M THE FACE, High Numbers, 80-49
I'M THE LEADER OF THE GANG (I AM!):
Gary Glitter, 73-1, 80-57
Hulk Hogan with Green Jelly and the Wrestling Boot Trash Can Band, 93-25
I'M THE LONELY ONE, Cliff Richard and the Shadows, 64-8
I'M THE MAN, Anthrax, 87-20
I'M THE ONE, Gerry and the Pacemakers, 64-2
I'M THE ONE FOR YOU, Adeva, 92-51
I'M THE ONE YOU NEED (DRIZA BONE MIX), Jody Watley, 92-50
I'M THE URBAN SPACEMAN, Bonzo Dog Doo-Dah Band, 68-5
I'M TIRED OF GETTING PUSHED AROUND, Two Men, A Drum Machine and A Trumpet, 88-18
I'M TOO SCARED, Steven Dante, 88-34
I'M TOO SEXY, Right Said Fred, 91-2
I'M WAKING UP TO US, Belle and Sebastian, 01-39
I'M WALKIN', Fats Domino, 57-19
I'M WALKING BACKWARDS FOR CHRISTMAS, Goons with Nick Rauchen conducting The Ball's Pond Road Near "The One-In-Harmony", 56-4
I'M WALKING BEHIND YOU:
Eddie Fisher with Hugo Winterhalter and his Orchestra and Sally Sweetland, 53-1
Dorothy Squires, 53-12
I'M WONDERING, Stevie Wonder, 67-22
I'M YOUR ANGEL, Celine Dion and R. Kelly, 98-3
I'M YOUR BABY TONIGHT, Whitney Houston, 90-5
I'M YOUR BOOGIE MAN, K.C. and the Sunshine Band, 77-41
I'M YOUR MAN, Blue Zoo, 82-55
I'M YOUR MAN:
Wham!, 85-1
Lisa Moorish, 95-24
I'M YOUR PUPPET, James and Bobby Purify, 76-12
I'M YOUR TOY, Elvis Costello and the Attractions with Royal Philharmonic Orchestra, 82-51
I'VE BEEN A BAD, BAD BOY, Paul Jones with Mike Leander and his Orchestra, 67-5
I'VE BEEN AROUND THE WORLD, Marti Pellow, 01-28
I'VE BEEN DRINKING, Jeff Beck Group vocal: Rod Stewart, 73-27
I'VE BEEN HURT, Guy Darrell, 73-12
I'VE BEEN IN LOVE BEFORE, Cutting Crew, 86-31, 87-24
I'VE BEEN LONELY FOR SO LONG, Frederick Knight, 72-22
I'VE BEEN LOSING YOU, A-Ha, 86-8
I'VE BEEN THINKING ABOUT YOU, Londonbeat, 90-2
I'VE BEEN TO A MARVELLOUS PARTY, Divine Comedy, 98-28
I'VE BEEN WAITING, Stereo Nation, 96-53
I'VE BEEN WATCHIN', Joe Public, 92-75
I'VE BEEN WRONG BEFORE, Cilla Black, 65-17
I'VE DONE EVERYTHING FOR YOU, Sammy Hagar, 80-36
I'VE GOT A LITTLE PUPPY, Smurfs, 96-4
I'VE GOT A LITTLE SOMETHING FOR YOU, MN8, 95-2
I'VE GOT A THING ABOUT YOU BABY, Elvis Presley, 74-33
I'VE GOT MINE, UB40, 83-45
I'VE GOT NEWS FOR YOU, Feargal Sharkey, 91-12
I'VE GOT SOMETHING TO SAY, Reef, 99-15
I'VE GOT THIS FEELING, Mavericks, 98-27
I'VE GOT TO LEARN TO SAY NO!, Richard 'Dimples' Fields, 82-56
I'VE GOT YOU, Martine McCutcheon, 99-6
I'VE GOT YOU ON MY MIND:
Dorian Gray, 68-36
White Plains, 70-17
I'VE GOT YOU UNDER MY SKIN:
4 Seasons featuring the "Sound" Of Frankie Valli, 66-12
Neneh Cherry, 90-25
Frank Sinatra with Bono, 93-4
(I'VE GOT YOUR) PLEASURE CONTROL, Simon Harris featuring Lonnie Gordon, 89-60
I'VE GOTTA GET A MESSAGE TO YOU, Bee Gees, 68-1
I'VE HAD ENOUGH, Wings, 78-42
I'VE HAD ENOUGH, Earth, Wind And Fire, 82-29
I'VE HAD ENOUGH, Ivan Matias, 96-69
I'VE HAD ENOUGH, Hillman Minx, 98-72
(I'VE HAD) THE TIME OF MY LIFE (LOVE THEME FROM 'DIRTY DANCING'), Bill Medley and Jennifer Warnes, 87-6, 90-08
I'VE JUST BEGUN TO LOVE YOU, Dynasty, 80-51
I'VE LOST YOU, Elvis Presley, 70-9
I'VE NEVER BEEN IN LOVE, Suzi Quatro, 80-56
I'VE NEVER BEEN TO ME, Charlene, 82-1
I'VE PASSED THIS WAY BEFORE, Jimmy Ruffin, 67-29, 69-33
I'VE SEEN THE WORD, Blancmange, 82-65
I'VE TOLD EVERY LITTLE STAR, Linda Scott, 61-7
I'VE WAITED SO LONG:
Anthony Newley, 59-3
Anthony Newley (from Idle On Parade [EP]), 59-13
IBIZA, Maxima featuring Lily, 93-55
THE ICE CREAM MAN, Tornados, 63-18
ICE HOCKEY HAIR, Super Furry Animals, 98-12
ICE ICE BABY, Vanilla Ice, 90-1
ICE IN THE SUN, Status Quo, 68-8
ICE RAIN, Alex Whitcombe and Big C, 98-44
ICEBLINK LUCK, Cocteau Twins, 90-38
ICH BIN EIN AUSLANDER, Pop Will Eat Itself, 94-28
ICING ON THE CAKE, Stephen 'Tin Tin' Duffy, 85-14
IDEAL WORLD, Christians, 87-14
IDENTITY, X-Ray Spex, 78-24
IDIOTS AT THE WHEEL [EP], Kingmaker, 92-30
IDLE GOSSIP, Perry Como with Hugo Winterhalter and his Orchestra, 54-3
IDLE ON PARADE [EP], Anthony Newley, 59-13
THE IDOL, Wasp, 92-41
THE IDOL, Marc Almond, 95-44
IDOL, Amanda Ghost, 00-63
IEYA, Toyah, 82-48
IF:
Telly Savalas, 75-1
Yin and Yan, 75-25
John Alford, 96-24
IF, Janet Jackson, 93-14
IF . . ., Bluetones, 98-13
IF A MAN ANSWERS, Bobby Darin, 62-24
IF ANYONE FINDS THIS, I LOVE YOU, Ruby Murray and Anne Warren with Ray Martin and his Orchestra, 55-4
IF DREAMS CAME TRUE, Pat Boone, 58-16
IF EVER, 3rd Storee, 99-53
IF EVERY DAY WAS LIKE CHRISTMAS, Elvis Presley with the Jordanaires and the Imperials Quartet, 66-13
IF EVERYBODY LOOKED THE SAME, Groove Armada, 99-25
IF EYE LOVE U 2 NIGHT, Mayte, 95-67
IF GOD WILL SEND HIS ANGELS, U2, 97-12
IF HE TELLS YOU, Adam Faith with the Roulettes, 64-25
IF I CAN DREAM (3rd entry from AMERICA THE BEAUTIFUL [EP]):
Elvis Presley, 69-11, 87-56, 01-69
Michael Ball (from EP of the same name), 92-51
IF I CAN'T CHANGE YOUR MIND, Sugar, 93-30
IF I CAN'T HAVE YOU:
Yvonne Elliman, 78-4
Kim Wilde, 93-12
IF I COULD, David Essex, 75-13
IF I COULD BUILD MY WHOLE WORLD AROUND YOU, Marvin Gaye and Tammi Terrell, 68-41
IF I COULD FLY, Grace, 96-29
IF I COULD ONLY MAKE YOU CARE, Mike Berry, 80-37
IF I COULD ONLY SAY GOODBYE, David Hasselhoff, 93-35
IF I COULD TALK I'D TELL YOU, Lemonheads, 96-39
IF I COULD TURN BACK THE HANDS OF TIME, R. Kelly, 99-57, 99-2
IF I COULD TURN BACK TIME, Cher, 89-6
IF I DIDN'T CARE, David Cassidy, 74-9
IF I EVER FALL IN LOVE, Shai, 92-36
IF I EVER FEEL BETTER, Phoenix, 01-65
IF I EVER LOSE MY FAITH IN YOU, Sting, 93-14
IF I GIVE MY HEART TO YOU:
Joan Regan, 54-3
Doris Day with the Mellomen, 54-4
IF I GIVE YOU MY NUMBER, PJ and Duncan A.K.A, 94-15
IF I HAD A HAMMER, Trini Lopez, 63-4
IF I HAD NO LOOT, Tony Toni Tone, 93-44
IF I HAD WORDS, Scott Fitzgerald and Yvonne Keely (with St. Thomas More School Choir), 78-3
IF I HAD YOU, Korgis, 79-13
IF I HAVE TO GO AWAY, Jigsaw, 77-36
IF I HAVE TO STAND ALONE, Lonnie Gordon, 90-68
IF I KNEW THEN WHAT I KNOW NOW, Val Doonican, 68-14
IF I LET YOU GO, Westlife, 99-1
IF I LOVE U 2 NITE, Mica Paris, 91-43
IF I LOVE YA, THEN I NEED YA, IF I NEED YA, I WANT'CHA AROUND, Eartha Kitt, 94-43
IF I LOVED YOU, Richard Anthony, 64-18
IF I NEEDED SOMEONE, Hollies, 65-20
IF I NEVER KNEW YOU (LOVE THEME FROM POCAHONTAS), Jon Secada and Shanice, 95-51
IF I NEVER SEE YOU AGAIN, Wet Wet Wet, 97-3
IF I ONLY HAD TIME, John Rowles, 68-3
IF I ONLY KNEW, Tom Jones, 94-11
IF I REMEMBER, Benz, 97-59
IF I RULED THE WORLD:
Harry Secombe with Wally Stott and his Orchestra and Chorus, 63-18
Tony Bennett with the Will Bronson Chorus conducted by Don Costa, 65-40
IF I RULED THE WORLD:
Kurtis Blow, 86-24
Nas, 96-12
IF I SAID YOU HAVE A BEAUTIFUL BODY WOULD YOU HOLD IT AGAINST ME, Bellamy Brothers, 79-3
IF I SAY YES, Five Star, 86-15
IF I SHOULD FALL FROM GRACE WITH GOD, Pogues, 88-58
IF I SHOULD LOVE AGAIN, Barry Manilow, 82-66
IF I SURVIVE, Hybrid featuring Julee Cruise, 99-52
IF I THOUGHT YOU'D EVER CHANGE YOUR MIND, Cilla Black, 69-20
IF I TOLD YOU THAT, Whitney Houston and George Michael, 00-9
IF I WAS, Midge Ure, 85-1
IF I WAS, Aswad, 95-58
IF I WAS A RIVER, Tina Arena, 98-43
IF I WAS YOUR GIRLFRIEND, Prince, 87-20
IF I WERE A CARPENTER:
Bobby Darin, 66-9
Four Tops, 68-7
Robert Plant, 93-63

IF I WERE A RICH MAN, Topol, 67-9
IF I WERE YOU, k.d. lang, 95-53
IF I'M NOT YOUR LOVER, Al B. Sure! featuring Slick Rick, 89-54
IF IT DON'T FIT DON'T FORCE IT, Kellee Patterson, 78-44
IF IT HAPPENS AGAIN, UB40, 84-9
IF IT MAKES YOU HAPPY, Sheryl Crow, 96-9
IF IT WASN'T FOR THE REASON THAT I LOVE YOU, Miki Antony, 73-27
IF IT'S ALRIGHT WITH YOU BABY, Korgis, 80-56
IF IT'S LOVE THAT YOU WANT, Donny Osmond, 88-70
IF: KIPLING'S POEM WITH THE BBC WORLD CUP '98 THEME – PAVANE, Read by Des Lynam; performed by the Wimbledon Choral Society, 98-45
IF LEAVING ME IS EASY, Phil Collins, 81-17
IF LIFE IS LIKE A LOVE BANK, I WANT AN OVERDRAFT, Wildhearts, 95-31
IF LOOKS COULD KILL, Transvision Vamp, 91-41
IF LOVE WAS A TRAIN, Michelle Shocked, 89-63
IF LOVE WAS LIKE GUITARS, Ian McNabb, 93-67
IF LOVING YOU IS WRONG (I DON'T WANT TO BE RIGHT), Rod Stewart, 80-23
IF MADONNA CALLS, Junior Vasquez, 96-24
IF MY FRIENDS COULD SEE ME NOW, Linda Clifford, 78-50
IF NOT FOR YOU, Olivia Newton-John, 71-7
IF NOT YOU, Dr. Hook, 76-5
IF ONLY, Hanson, 00-15
IF ONLY I COULD, Sydney Youngblood, 89-3
IF ONLY I COULD LIVE MY LIFE AGAIN, Jane Morgan, 59-27
IF ONLY TOMORROW (COULD BE LIKE TODAY), Ronnie Carroll, 62-33
(IF PARADISE IS) HALF AS NICE, Amen Corner, 69-1, 76-34
IF SHE KNEW WHAT SHE WANTS, Bangles, 86-31
IF SHE SHOULD COME TO YOU (LA MONTANA), Anthony Newley, 60-4
IF 60'S WERE 90'S, Beautiful People, 94-74
IF THAT WERE ME, Melanie C, 00-18
IF THAT'S YOUR BOYFRIEND (HE WASN'T LAST NIGHT), Me'shell Ndegeocello, 94-74
IF THE KIDS ARE UNITED, Sham 69, 78-9
IF THE RIVER CAN BEND, Elton John, 98-32
IF THE WHOLE WORLD STOPPED LOVIN', Val Doonican, 67-3
IF THERE WAS A MAN, Pretenders For 007, 87-49
IF THIS IS IT, Huey Lewis and the News, 84-39
IF THIS IS LOVE, J.J., 91-55
IF THIS IS LOVE, Jeanie Tracy, 94-73
IF WE FALL IN LOVE TONIGHT, Rod Stewart, 96-58
IF WE HOLD ON TOGETHER, Diana Ross, 92-11
IF WE TRY, Karen Ramirez, 98-23
IF WE WERE LOVERS, Gloria Estefan, 93-40
IF YA GETTIN' DOWN, Five, 99-2
IF YOU ASKED ME TO, Celine Dion, 92-57
IF YOU BELIEVE, Johnnie Ray with Percy Faith and his Orchestra, 55-7
IF YOU BUY THIS RECORD YOUR LIFE WILL BE BETTER, Tamperer featuring Maya, 98-3
IF YOU CAN WANT, Smokey Robinson and the Miracles, 68-50
IF YOU CAN'T DO IT WHEN YOU'RE YOUNG; WHEN CAN YOU DO IT?, Theaudience, 98-48
IF YOU CAN'T GIVE ME LOVE, Suzi Quatro, 78-4
IF YOU CAN'T SAY NO, Lenny Kravitz, 98-48
IF YOU CAN'T STAND THE HEAT, Bucks Fizz, 82-10
IF YOU CARED, Kim Appleby, 91-44
IF YOU COME BACK, Blue, 01-1
IF YOU COULD READ MY MIND:
Gordon Lightfoot, 71-30
Stars On 54: Ultra Nate, Amber, Jocelyn Enriquez, 98-23
IF YOU COULD SEE ME NOW, Shakatak, 83-49
IF YOU DON'T KNOW ME BY NOW:
Harold Melvin and the Bluenotes, 73-9
Simply Red, 89-2
IF YOU DON'T LOVE ME, Prefab Sprout, 92-33
IF YOU DON'T WANT ME TO DESTROY YOU, Super Furry Animals, 96-18
IF YOU DON'T WANT MY LOVE, Robert John, 68-42
IF YOU EVER, East Seventeen featuring Gabrielle, 96-2
IF YOU EVER LEAVE ME, Barbra Streisand / Vince Gill, 99-26
IF YOU FEEL IT, Thelma Houston, 81-48
IF YOU GO, Jon Secada, 94-39
IF YOU GO AWAY, Terry Jacks, 74-8
IF YOU GO AWAY, New Kids On The Block, 91-9
IF YOU GOTTA GO, GO NOW:
Manfred Mann, 65-2
Fairport Convention *, 69-21
IF YOU GOTTA MAKE A FOOL OF SOMEBODY, Freddie and the Dreamers, 63-3
IF YOU HAD MY LOVE, Jennifer Lopez, 99-4
IF YOU HAVE TO GO, Geneva, 00-69
IF YOU KNEW SOUSA (AND FRIENDS), Louis Clark conducting The Royal Philharmonic Orchestra, 82-71
IF YOU KNOW WHAT I MEAN, Neil Diamond, 76-35
IF YOU LEAVE, Orchestral Manoeuvres In The Dark, 86-48
IF YOU LEAVE ME NOW:
Chicago, 76-1
Upside Down, 96-27
IF YOU LET ME STAY, Terence Trent D'Arby, 87-7
IF YOU LOVE HER, Dick Emery, 69-32
IF YOU LOVE ME, Brownstone, 95-8
IF YOU LOVE ME (I WON'T CARE):
Mary Hopkin, 76-32
Elaine Paige *, 95-68
IF YOU LOVE SOMEBODY SET THEM FREE, Sting, 85-26
IF YOU ONLY LET ME IN, MN8, 95-6
IF YOU REALLY CARED, Gabrielle, 96-15
IF YOU REALLY LOVE ME, Stevie Wonder, 72-20
IF YOU REALLY WANNA KNOW, Marc Dorsey, 99-58
IF YOU REALLY WANT TO, Meat Loaf, 83-59
IF YOU REMEMBER ME, Chris Thompson, 79-42
IF YOU SHOULD NEED A FRIEND, Fire Island featuring Mark Anthoni, 95-51
IF YOU TALK IN YOUR SLEEP, Elvis Presley, 74-40
IF YOU THINK YOU KNOW HOW TO LOVE ME, Smokey, 75-3
(IF YOU THINK) YOU'RE GROOVY, P.P. Arnold, 68-41
IF YOU TOLERATE THIS YOUR CHILDREN WILL BE NEXT, Manic Street Preachers, 98-1
IF YOU WALK AWAY, Peter Cox, 97-24
IF YOU WANNA BE HAPPY:
Jimmy Soul, 63-39, 91-68
Rocky Sharpe and the Replays, 83-46
IF YOU WANNA PARTY, Molella featuring the Outhere Brothers, 95-9
IF YOU WANT, Luciana, 94-47
IF YOU WANT ME, Hinda Hicks, 98-25
IF YOU WANT MY LOVE, Cheap Trick, 82-57
IF YOU WANT MY LOVIN', Evelyn King, 81-43
IF YOU WERE HERE TONIGHT:
Alexander O'Neal, 86-13
Matt Goss, 96-23
IF YOU WERE MINE, MARY, Eddy Arnold, 66-49
IF YOU WERE THE ONLY BOY IN THE WORLD, Stevie Marsh, 59-24
IF YOU WERE WITH ME NOW, Kylie Minogue and Keith Washington, 91-4
IF YOU'LL BE MINE, Babybird, 98-28
IF YOUR GIRL ONLY KNEW, Aaliyah, 96-21, 97-15
IF YOUR HEART ISN'T IN IT, Atlantic Starr, 86-48
IF YOU'RE GONE, Matchbox Twenty, 01-50
IF YOU'RE LOOKIN' FOR A WAY OUT, Odyssey, 80-6
IF YOU'RE READY (COME GO WITH ME):
Staple Singers, 74-34
Ruby Turner featuring Jonathan Butler, 86-30
IF YOU'RE THINKING OF ME, Dodgy, 96-11
IGGIN' ME, Chico Debarge, 98-50
IGNORANCE, Oceanic featuring Siobhan Maher, 92-72
IGUANA, Mauro Picotto, 00-33
IKO IKO:
Dixie Cups, 65-23
Natasha, 82-10
Belle Stars, 82-35
IL ADORE, Boy George, 95-50
IL EST NE LE DIVIN ENFANT, Siouxsie and the Banshees, 82-49
IL NOSTRO CONCERTO (OUR CONCERTO), Umberto Bindi, 60-47
IL SILENZIO, Nini Rosso, 65-8
ILLEGAL ALIEN, Genesis, 84-46
ILLEGAL GUNSHOT, Ragga Twins, 90-51
ILLUMINATIONS, Swans Way, 84-57
ILLUSIONS, Cypress Hill, 96-23
ILOVEROCKNROLL, Jesus And Mary Chain, 98-38
I'M A LITTLE CHRISTMAS CRACKER, Bouncing Czecks featuring Charlene Ducall, 84-72
IMAGE, Hank Levine, 61-45
IMAGE OF A GIRL:
Mark Wynter, 60-11
Nelson Keene, 60-37
IMAGE OF YOU, Red Snapper, 98-60
IMAGINATION, Rocky Sharpe and the Replays, 79-39
IMAGINATION, Belouis Some, 85-50, 86-17
IMAGINATION, Jon The Dentist vs Ollie Jaye, 99-72
IMAGINE:
John Lennon, 75-6, 80-1, 88-45, 99-3
Randy Crawford, 82-60
IMAGINE, Shola Ama, 00-24
IMAGINE ME IMAGINE YOU, Fox, 75-15
IMITATION OF LIFE, Billie Ray Martin, 96-29
IMITATION OF LIFE, R.E.M., 01-6
IMMACULATE FOOLS, Immaculate Fools, 85-51
IMMORTALITY, Celine Dion with Special Guests the Bee Gees, 98-5
IMPERIAL WIZARD, David Essex, 79-32
THE IMPORTANCE OF YOUR LOVE (L'IMPORTANT, C'EST LA ROSE), Vince Hill with the Eddie Lester Singers, 68-32
IMPOSSIBLE, Captain Hollywood Project, 94-29
IMPOSSIBLE, Charlatans, 00-15
THE IMPOSSIBLE DREAM, Carter – The Unstoppable Sex Machine, 92-21
IMPOSSIBLE LOVE, UB40, 90-47
THE IMPRESSION THAT I GET, Mighty Mighty Bosstones, 98-12
THE IMPRESSIONS [EP], Solar Stone, 98-75
IMPULSIVE, Wilson Phillips, 90-42
IN A BIG COUNTRY, Big Country, 83-17
IN A BROKEN DREAM:
Python Lee Jackson, 72-3
Thunder, 95-26
IN A GOLDEN COACH (THERE'S A HEART OF GOLD):
Billy Cotton and his Band with Doreen Stephens and Chorus, 53-3
Dickie Valentine, 53-7
IN A LIFETIME, Clannad/additional vocals: Bono, 86-20, 89-17
IN A LITTLE SPANISH TOWN ('TWAS ON A NIGHT LIKE THIS), Bing Crosby wth the Buddy Cole Trio, 56-22
IN A PERSIAN MARKET, Sammy Davis, 56-28
IN A ROOM, Dodgy, 96-12
IN A STATE, 2 For Joy featuring Addell Benjamin, 90-61
IN A WORD OR 2, Monie Love, 93-33
IN ALL THE RIGHT PLACES, Lisa Stansfield, 93-8
IN AND OUT, Willie Hutch, 82-51
IN AND OUT OF LOVE, Diana Ross and the Supremes, 67-13
IN AND OUT OF LOVE, Imagination, 81-16
IN AND OUT OF MY LIFE, Tonja Dantzler, 94-66
IN AND OUT OF MY LIFE, A.T.F.C. Presents Onephatdeeva, 99-11
IN BETWEEN DAYS, Cure, 85-15
IN BLOOM, Nirvana, 92-28
THE IN CROWD:
Dobie Gray, 65-25
Bryan Ferry, 74-13
IN DE GHETTO, David Morales and the Bad Yard Club featuring Crystal Waters and Delta, 96-35
IN DEMAND, Texas, 00-6
IN DREAMS, Roy Orbison, 63-6
IN DULCE DECORUM, Damned, 87-72
IN DULCI JUBILO, Mike Oldfield; Recorder: Leslie Penning, 75-4
IN FOR A PENNY, Slade, 75-11
IN 4 CHOONS LATER [M], Rozalla, 92-50
IN GOD'S COUNTRY, U2, 87-48
IN IT FOR LOVE, Richie Sambora, 98-58
IN LIVERPOOL, Suzanne Vega, 92-52

IN LOVE, Michael Holliday, 58-26
IN LOVE WITH LOVE, Debbie Harry, 87-45
IN LOVE WITH THE FAMILIAR, Wireless, 98-69
IN MY ARMS, Erasure, 97-13
IN MY BED, Dru Hill, 97-16
IN MY CHAIR, Status Quo, 70-21
IN MY DEFENCE, Freddie Mercury, 92-8
IN MY DREAMS, Will Downing, 88-34
IN MY DREAMS, Johnna, 96-66
IN MY HEART, Texas, 91-74
IN MY LIFE, Souled Out, 92-75
IN MY LIFE, Kim Wilde, 93-54
IN MY LIFE, Jose Nunez featuring Octahvia, 98-56
IN MY OWN TIME, Family, 71-4
IN MY STREET, Chords, 80-50
IN MY WORLD, Anthrax, 90-29
IN OLD LISBON, Frank Chacksfield and his Orchestra, 56-15
IN OUR LIFETIME, Texas, 99-4
IN PRIVATE, Dusty Springfield, 89-14
IN SPIRIT, Dilemma, 96-42
IN SUMMER, Billy Fury, 63-5
IN THE AIR TONIGHT, Phil Collins, 81-2, 88-4
IN THE AIR TONITE, Lil' Kim featuring Phil Collins, 01-26
IN THE ARMS OF LOVE, Andy Williams, 66-33
IN THE ARMS OF LOVE, Catherine Zeta Jones, 95-72
IN THE ARMY NOW, Status Quo, 86-2
IN THE BACK OF MY MIND, Fleetwood Mac, 90-58
IN THE BAD, BAD OLD DAYS (BEFORE YOU LOVED ME), Foundations, 69-8
IN THE BEGINNING, Frankie Laine with Paul Weston his Orchestra and the Norman Luboff Choir, 55-20
IN THE BEGINNING, EYC, 95-41
IN THE BEST POSSIBLE TASTE (PART 2), Kingmaker, 95-41
IN THE BLEAK MIDWINTER, Nevada, 83-71
IN THE BOTTLE, C.O.D., 83-54
IN THE BROWNIES, Billy Connolly, 79-38
IN THE BUSH, Musique, 78-16
IN THE CAULDRON OF LOVE, Icicle Works, 84-53
IN THE CHAPEL IN THE MOONLIGHT, Bachelors, 65-27
IN THE CITY, Jam, 77-40, 80-40, 83-47
IN THE CLOSET, Michael Jackson and Mystery Girl: Duet, 92-8
IN THE CLOUDS, All About Eve, 87-47
(IN THE) COLD LIGHT OF DAY, Gene Pitney, 67-38
IN THE COUNTRY:
Cliff Richard and the Shadows, 66-6
Farmer's Boys, 84-44
IN THE END, Linkin Park, 01-8
IN THE EVENING, Sheryl Lee Ralph, 85-64
IN THE FOREST, Baby O, 80-46
IN THE GHETTO:
Elvis Presley, 69-2
Beats International, 91-44
IN THE HALL OF THE MOUNTAIN KING, Nero and the Gladiators, 61-48
IN THE HEAT OF A PASSIONATE MOMENT, Princess, 86-74
IN THE HEAT OF THE NIGHT, Diamond Head, 82-67
IN THE HEAT OF THE NIGHT, Imagination, 82-22
IN THE HOUSE, Clock, 95-23
IN THE MEANTIME, Georgie Fame and the Blue Flames, 65-22
IN THE MEANTIME, Spacehog, 96-29
IN THE MIDDLE, Alexander O'Neal, 93-32
IN THE MIDDLE OF A DARK, DARK NIGHT, Guy Mitchell with Jimmy Carroll, 57-25
IN THE MIDDLE OF AN ISLAND, King Brothers with Geoff Love and his Orchestra and the Rita Williams Singers, 57-19
IN THE MIDDLE OF NOWHERE, Dusty Springfield, 65-8
IN THE MIDDLE OF THE HOUSE:
Alma Cogan, 56-20
Jimmy Parkinson with Ray Martin and his Orchestra, 56-20
Johnston Brothers and the Keynotes, 56-27
IN THE MIDDLE OF THE NIGHT, Magic Affair, 94-38
IN THE MIDNIGHT HOUR:
Wilson Pickett, 65-12
Wilson Pickett, 87-62
IN THE MOOD:
Ernie Field's Orchestra, 59-13
Glenn Miller and his Orchestra, 76-13
Sound 9418, 76-46
Ray Stevens, 77-31
IN THE MOOD, Rush, 81-41
IN THE NAME OF LOVE, Sharon Redd, 83-31
IN THE NAME OF LOVE, Swan Lake, 88-53
IN THE NAME OF LOVE '88, Thompson Twins, 88-46
IN THE NAME OF THE FATHER, Bono and Gavin Friday, 94-46
IN THE NAME OF THE FATHER, Black Grape, 95-8
IN THE NAVY, Village People, 79-2, 94-36
IN THE NIGHT, Barbara Dickson, 80-48
IN THE ONES YOU LOVE, Diana Ross, 96-34
IN THE REALM OF THE SENSES, Bass-O-Matic, 90-66
IN THE SHAPE OF A HEART, Jackson Browne, 86-66
IN THE SPRINGTIME, Maxi Priest, 86-54
IN THE STILL OF THE NITE (I'LL REMEMBER), Boyz II Men, 93-27
IN THE STONE, Earth Wind And Fire, 80-53
IN THE SUMMERTIME:
Mungo Jerry, 70-1
Shaggy featuring Rayvon, 95-5
IN THE THICK OF IT, Brenda Russell, 80-51
IN THE VALLEY, Midnight Oil, 93-60
IN THE WAITING LINE, Zero 7 featuring Sophie Barker, 01-47
IN THE YEAR 2525 (EXORDIUM AND TERMINUS), Zager and Evans, 69-1
IN THESE ARMS, Bon Jovi, 93-9
IN THOUGHTS OF YOU, Billy Fury, 65-9
IN TOO DEEP, Dead Or Alive, 85-14
IN TOO DEEP (FROM THE FILM 'MONA LISA'), Genesis, 86-19
IN TOO DEEP, Belinda Carlisle, 96-6
IN TOO DEEP, Sum 41, 01-13
IN WALKED LOVE, Louise, 96-17
IN YER FACE, 808 State, 91-9
IN YOUR ARMS (RESCUE ME), Nu Generation, 00-8
IN YOUR BONES, Fire Island, 92-66
IN YOUR CAR, Cool Notes, 85-13
IN YOUR CAR, Kenickie, 97-24
IN YOUR CARE, Tasmin Archer, 93-16
IN YOUR DANCE, E-Lustrious, 94-69
IN YOUR EYES, George Benson, 83-7
IN YOUR EYES, Niamh Kavanagh, 93-24
IN YOUR ROOM, Bangles, 88-35
IN YOUR ROOM, Depeche Mode, 94-8
IN YOUR WILDEST DREAMS, Tina Turner featuring Barry White, 96-32
IN ZAIRE, Johnny Wakelin, 76-4
IN ZAIRE, African Business, 90-73
INBETWEENER, Sleeper, 95-16
THE INBETWEENIES, Goodies, 74-7
THE INCIDENTALS, Alisha's Attic, 98-13
INCOMMUNICADO, Marillion, 87-6
INCOMPLETE, Sisqo, 00-13
INCREDIBLE, Keith Murray featuring LL Cool J, 98-52
INCREDIBLE, M-Beat featuring General Levy, 94-39, 94-8
INDEPENDENCE, Lulu, 93-11
INDEPENDENCE DAY, Comsat Angels, 84-71
INDEPENDENT LOVE SONG, Scarlet, 95-12
INDEPENDENT WOMEN PART 1, Destiny's Child, 00-1
INDESCRIBABLY BLUE, Elvis Presley, 67-21
INDESTRUCTIBLE, Four Tops featuring Smokey Robinson, 88-55, 89-30
INDESTRUCTIBLE, Alisha's Attic, 97-12
INDIAN LOVE CALL:
Slim Whitman, 55-7
Karl Denver, 63-32
Ray Stevens, 75-34
INDIAN RESERVATION:
Don Fardon, 70-3
999, 81-51
INDIAN ROPE, Charlatans, 91-57
INDIAN SUMMER, Belle Stars, 83-52
INDIANA, Freddie Cannon, 60-42
INDIANA WANTS ME, R. Dean Taylor, 71-2
INDIANS, Anthrax, 87-44
INDICA, Movin' Melodies, 96-62
INDIE-YARN, Trickbaby, 96-47
INDIGO, Moloko, 00-51
INDUSTRIAL STRENGTH [EP], Krokus, 81-62
INDUSTRY STANDARD VOL. 1 (WHAT YOU WANT), Industry Standard, 98-34
INFATUATION, Rod Stewart, 84-27
INFECTED, The, 86-48
INFERNO, Souvlaki, 97-24
INFIDELITY, Simply Red, 87-31
INFILTRATE 202, Altern 8, 91-28
INFINITE DREAMS (LIVE), Iron Maiden, 89-6
INFINITY (1990'S: TIME FOR THE GURU), Guru Josh, 90-5
INFO-FREAKO, Jesus Jones, 89-42
INFORMER, Snow, 93-2
INHERIT THE WIND, Wilton Felder, 80-39
INJECTED WITH A POISON, Praga Khan featuring Jade 4 U, 92-16, 01-52
THE INK IN THE WELL, David Sylvian, 84-36
INKANYEZI NEZAZI (THE STAR AND THE WISEMAN), Ladysmith Black Mambazo, 97-33, 98-63
INNA CITY MAMMA, Neneh Cherry, 89-31
INNAMORATA, Dean Martin, 56-21
INNER CITY LIFE, Goldie Presents Metalheads, 94-49, 95-39
INNER SMILE, Texas, 01-6
INNOCENT, Addis Black Widow, 96-42
AN INNOCENT MAN, Billy Joel, 84-8
INNOCENT X, Therapy?, 95-53
INNOCENTE (FALLING IN LOVE), Delerium featuring Leigh Nash (of Sixpence None The Richer), 01-32
INNUENDO, Queen, 91-1
INSANE, Texas featuring The Wu Tang Clan, 98-4
INSANE IN THE BRAIN:
Cypress Hill, 93-32, 94-21
Jason Nevins vs. Cypress Hill, 99-19
INSANITY, Oceanic, 91-3
INSENSITIVE, Jann Arden, 96-40
INSIDE, Stiltskin, 94-1
INSIDE A DREAM, Jane Wiedlin, 88-64
INSIDE AMERICA, Juggy Jones, 76-39
INSIDE-LOOKING OUT:
Animals, 66-12
Grand Funk Railroad, 71-40
INSIDE LOVE (SO PERSONAL), George Benson, 83-57
INSIDE OUT, Odyssey, 82-3
INSIDE OUT, Mighty Lemon Drops, 88-74
INSIDE OUT, Gun, 89-57
INSIDE OUT, Shara Nelson, 94-34
INSIDE OUT, Culture Beat, 96-32
INSIDE OUTSIDE, Classix Nouveaux, 81-45
INSIDE THAT I CRIED, Ce Ce Peniston, 92-42
INSIDE YOUR DREAMS, U96, 94-44
INSOMNIA, Faithless, 95-27, 96-3
INSOMNIA, Feeder, 99-22
INSOMNIAC, Echobelly, 94-47
INSPECTOR GADGET, Kartoon Krew, 85-58
INSPECTOR MORSE THEME, Barrington Pheloung, 93-61
INSPIRATION, Strike, 96-27
INSSOMNIAK, DJPC, 91-62, 92-64
INSTANT KARMA, Lennon/Ono with the Plastic Ono Band, 70-5
INSTANT REPLAY:
Dan Hartman, 78-8
Yell!, 90-10
Gambafreaks featuring Paco Rivaz, 98-57
INSTANT STREET, Deus, 99-49
INSTINCT, Crowded House, 96-12
INSTINCTION, Spandau Ballet, 82-10
INSTINCTUAL, Imagination, 88-62
INSTRUMENTS OF DARKNESS (ALL OF US ARE ONE PEOPLE), Art Of Noise, 92-45
INTACT, Ned's Atomic Dustbin, 92-36
INTENSIFY, Way Out West, 01-46
INTERCEPTOR, Eat Static, 97-44
INTERESTING DRUG, Morrissey, 89-9
..INTERGALACTIC.., Beastie Boys, 98-5
INTERLUDE, Morrissey and Siouxsie, 94-25
INTERNAL EXILE, Fish, 91-37
INTERNATIONAL, Brass Construction, 84-70
INTERNATIONAL BRIGHT YOUNG THING, Jesus Jones, 91-7
INTERNATIONAL JET SET, Specials, 80-6
THE INTERNATIONAL LANGUAGE OF SCREAMING, Super Furry Animals, 97-24
INTERNATIONAL RESCUE, We've Got A Fuzzbox and We're Gonna Use It, 89-11
INTERSTATE LOVE SONG, Stone Temple Pilots, 94-53
INTERVENTION, Lavine Hudson, 88-57
INTO MY ARMS, Nick Cave and the Bad Seeds, 97-53
INTO MY WORLD, Audioweb, 96-42
INTO SPACE, Plaything, 01-48
INTO THE BLUE, Mission, 90-32
INTO THE BLUE, Moby, 95-34
INTO THE BLUE, Geneva, 97-26

INTO THE FUTURE, New Atlantic featuring Linda Wright, 92-70
INTO THE GROOVE, Madonna, 85-1
INTO THE MOTION, Cool Notes, 86-66
INTO THE VALLEY, Skids, 79-10
INTO TOMORROW, Paul Weller Movement, 91-36
INTO YOUR ARMS, Lemonheads, 93-14
INTO YOUR HEART, 6 By Six, 96-51
INTOXICATION, React 2 Rhythm, 97-73
"INTRO", Alan Braxe and Fred Falke presents, 00-35
INTUITION, Linx, 81-7
INVALID LETTER DEPT., At The Drive-In, 01-50
INVASION (LIVE) (from MAGNUM LIVE [EP]), Magnum, 80-47
INVINCIBLE (THEME FROM 'THE LEGEND OF BILLIE JEAN'), Pat Benatar, 85-53
INVISIBLE, Alison Moyet, 84-21
INVISIBLE, Public Demand, 97-41
INVISIBLE, Tilt, 99-20
INVISIBLE BALOON, Midget, 98-66
THE INVISIBLE MAN, Queen, 89-12
INVISIBLE MAN, 98°, 97-66
INVISIBLE SUN, Police, 81-2
INVISIBLE TOUCH:
Genesis, 86-15
Genesis, 92-7
INVITATIONS, Shakatak, 82-24
IRE FEELINGS (SKANGA), Rupie Edwards, 74-9
IRENE, Photos, 80-56
IRIS, Goo Goo Dolls, 98-50, 99-26
THE IRISH ROVER, Pogues and the Dubliners, 87-8
IRON FIST, Motorhead, 82-29
IRON HORSE, Christie, 72-47
IRON LION ZION, Bob Marley and the Wailers, 92-5
IRON SKY, Mega City Four, 93-48
IRONIC, Alanis Morissette, 96-11
IRRESISTIBLE, Cathy Dennis, 92-24
IRRESISTIBLE, Corrs, 00-20
IRRESISTIBLE, Jessica Simpson, 01-11
IS, Smaller, 97-55
IS A BLUE BIRD BLUE, Conway Twitty, 60-43
IS IT A CRIME, Sade, 86-49
IS IT A DREAM, Classix Nouveaux, 82-11
IS IT A DREAM "WILD WEST END MIX", Damned, 85-34
IS IT BECAUSE?, Honeycombs, 64-38
IS IT GOOD TO YOU:
Heavy D and the Boyz, 91-46
Teddy Riley featuring Tammy Lucas, 92-53
IS IT LIKE TODAY?, World Party, 93-19
IS IT LOVE?, Basement Boys Present Ultra Nate, 91-71
IS IT LOVE?, Chili Hi Fly, 00-37
IS IT LOVE YOU'RE AFTER, Rose Royce, 79-13, 88-20
IS IT REALLY OVER, Jim Reeves, 65-17
IS IT TRUE, Brenda Lee, 64-17
IS NOTHING SACRED, Meat Loaf featuring Patti Russo, 99-15
IS SHE REALLY GOING OUT WITH HIM?, Joe Jackson, 79-13
IS THAT LOVE, Squeeze, 81-35
IS THAT YOUR FINAL ANSWER?, Who Wants To Be A Millionaire, 00-33
IS THERE ANY LOVE IN YOUR HEART, Lenny Kravitz, 93-52
IS THERE ANYBODY OUT THERE?, Bassheads, 91-5, 95-24
IS THERE ANYBODY THERE, Scorpions, 79-39
IS THERE SOMEONE OUT THERE?, Code Red, 97-34
IS THERE SOMETHING I SHOULD KNOW?:
Duran Duran, 83-1
Allstars, 01-12
IS THIS A DREAM? [RR], Love Decade, 96-39
IS THIS A LOVE THING, Raydio, 78-27
IS THIS LOVE, Bob Marley and the Wailers, 78-9
IS THIS LOVE?, Alison Moyet, 86-3
IS THIS LOVE, Whitesnake, 87-9, 94-25
(IS THIS THE WAY TO) AMARILLO, Tony Christie, 71-18
IS THIS WHAT I GET FROM LOVING YOU?, Marianne Faithfull, 67-43
IS VIC THERE?, Department S, 81-22
IS YOUR LOVE IN VAIN?, Bob Dylan, 78-56
IS YOUR LOVE STRONG ENOUGH, Bryan Ferry, 86-22
ISLAND GIRL, Elton John, 75-14
ISLAND HEAD [EP], Inspiral Carpets, 90-21
ISLAND IN THE SUN:
Harry Belafonte, 57-3
Righteous Brothers, 66-36
ISLAND IN THE SUN, Weezer, 01-31
ISLAND OF DREAMS, Springfields, 62-5
ISLAND OF LOST SOULS, Blondie, 82-11
ISLANDS IN THE STREAM, Kenny Rogers Duet with Dolly Parton, 83-7
THE ISLE OF INNISFREE, Bing Crosby with John Scott Trotter and his Orchestra, 52-3
ISMS, Dog Eat Dog, 96-43
ISN'T IT A WONDER, Boyzone, 97-2
ISN'T IT AMAZING, Hothouse Flowers, 93-46
ISN'T IT MIDNIGHT, Fleetwood Mac, 88-60
ISN'T IT TIME, Babys, 78-45
ISN'T LIFE STRANGE, Moody Blues, 72-13
ISN'T SHE LOVELY, David Parton, 77-4
ISOBEL, Bjork, 95-23
ISRAEL, Siouxsie and the Banshees, 80-41
ISRAELITES, Desmond Dekker and the Aces, 69-1, 75-10
ISTANBUL (NOT CONSTANTINOPLE):
Frankie Vaughan with the Peter Knight Singers, 54-11
They Might Be Giants, 90-61
IT AIN'T A CRIME, House Of Pain, 94-37
IT AIN'T ENOUGH, Dreem Teem vs Artful Dodger featuring MZ May and MC Alistair, 01-20
IT AIN'T FAIR, Edwin Starr, 85-56
IT AIN'T GONNA BE ME, CJ Bolland, 99-35
IT AIN'T HARD TO TELL, Nas, 94-64
IT AIN'T ME BABE, Johnny Cash, 65-28
IT AIN'T NECESSARILY SO, Bronski Beat, 84-16
IT AIN'T OVER 'TIL IT'S OVER, Lenny Kravitz, 91-11
IT AIN'T WHAT YOU DO IT'S THE WAY THAT YOU DO IT, Fun Boy Three with Bananarama, 82-4
IT BEGAN IN AFRICA FEATURING I BELIEVE IN MIRACLES & CROSS THE TRACK [M], Urban All Stars, 88-64
IT BEGAN IN AFRIKA, Chemical Brothers, 01-8
IT COULD HAPPEN TO YOU, Robert Palmer, 89-71
IT DIDN'T MATTER, Style Council, 87-9
IT DOESN'T HAVE TO BE, Erasure, 87-12
IT DOESN'T HAVE TO BE THIS WAY, Blow Monkeys, 87-5
IT DOESN'T MATTER, Wyclef Jean featuring the Rock and Melky Sedeck, 00-3
IT DOESN'T MATTER ANYMORE, Buddy Holly, 59-1
IT DOESN'T MATTER ANYMORE, Puressence, 98-47
IT DOESN'T REALLY MATTER, Zapp, 86-57
IT DON'T COME EASY, Ringo Starr, 71-4
IT FE DONE, Supercat, 92-66
IT FEELS SO GOOD, Sonique, 98-24, 00-1
IT HAD TO BE YOU, Harry Connick, Jr., 91-32
IT HURTS SO MUCH (TO SEE YOU GO), Jim Reeves, 65-8
IT HURTS TO BE IN LOVE, Gene Pitney, 64-36
IT IS JAZZ, Tingo Tango, 90-68
IT IS TIME TO GET FUNKY, D. Mob featuring LRS and D.C. Sarome, 89-9
IT ISN'T, IT WASN'T, IT AIN'T NEVER GONNA BE, Aretha and Whitney, 89-29
IT ISN'T RIGHT, Platters, 57-23
IT KEEPS RAININ':
Fats Domino, 61-49
Bitty McLean *, 93-2
IT KEEPS RIGHT ON A-HURTIN', Johnny Tillotson, 62-31
IT'LL BE ME, Cliff Richard and the Shadows, 62-2
IT MAKES ME WONDER, Bruce Foxton, 84-74
IT MAKES YOU FEEL LIKE DANCIN', Rose Royce, 78-16
IT MAY BE WINTER OUTSIDE (BUT IN MY HEART IT'S SPRING), Love Unlimited, 75-11
IT MIEK, Desmond Dekker and the Aces, 69-7
IT MIGHT AS WELL RAIN UNTIL SEPTEMBER, Carole King, 62-3, 72-43
IT MUST BE HIM (SEUL SUR SON E TOILE), Vikki Carr, 67-2
IT MUST BE LOVE:
Labi Siffre, 71-14
Madness, 81-4, 92-6
IT MUST BE LOVE, Robin S., 97-37
IT MUST BE LOVE, Mero, 00-33
IT MUST HAVE BEEN LOVE, Magnum, 88-33
IT MUST HAVE BEEN LOVE, Roxette, 90-3, 93-10
IT NEVER RAINS (IN SOUTHERN CALIFORNIA), Tony! Toni! Tone!, 91-69
IT ONLY TAKES A MINUTE:
One Hundred Ton and A Feather, 76-9
Tavares, 86-46
Take That, 92-7
IT ONLY TOOK A MINUTE, Joe Brown and the Bruvvers, 62-6
IT OUGHTA SELL A MILLION, Lyn Paul, 75-37
IT SEEMS TO HANG ON:
Ashford and Simpson, 78-48
KWS, 94-58
IT SHOULD HAVE BEEN ME:
Yvonne Fair, 76-5
Adeva *, 91-48
IT STARTED ALL OVER AGAIN, Brenda Lee, 62-15
IT STARTED WITH A KISS, Hot Chocolate, 82-5, 93-31, 98-18
IT SURE BRINGS OUT THE LOVE IN YOUR EYES, David Soul, 78-12
IT TAKES ALL NIGHT LONG, Gary Glitter, 77-25
IT TAKES TWO:
Marvin Gaye and Kim Weston, 67-16
Liz Kershaw, Bruno Brookes, Jive Bunny and Londonbeat *, 89-53
Rod Stewart and Tina Turner, 90-5
IT TAKES TWO, Rob Base and D.J. E-Z Rock, 88-24, 89-49
IT TAKES TWO TO TANGO, Richard Myhill, 78-17
IT WAS A GOOD DAY, Ice Cube, 93-27
IT WAS EASIER TO HURT HER, Wayne Fontana, 65-36
IT WASN'T ME, Shaggy featuring Ricardo "Rikrok" Ducent, 01-31, 01-1
IT WILL BE ALRIGHT, Odyssey, 81-43
IT WILL BE YOU, Paul Young, 94-34
IT WILL COME IN TIME, Billy Preston and Syreeta, 80-47
IT WILL MAKE ME CRAZY, Felix, 92-11
IT WON'T BE LONG, Alison Moyet, 91-50
IT WON'T SEEM LIKE CHRISTMAS (WITHOUT YOU), Elvis Presley, 79-13
IT'S A BEAUTIFUL THING, Ocean Colour Scene with PP Arnold, 98-12
IT'S A BETTER THAN GOOD TIME, Gladys Knight and the Pips, 78-59
IT'S A DISCO NIGHT (ROCK DON'T STOP), Isley Brothers, 79-14
IT'S A FINE DAY:
Opus III, 92-5
Miss Jane, 99-62
IT'S A GAME, Bay City Rollers, 77-16
IT'S A GAS, Wedding Present, 94-71
IT'S A GIRL THING, My Life Story, 99-37
IT'S A GOOD LIFE, Cevin Fisher featuring Ramona Keller, 01-54
IT'S A HARD LIFE, Queen, 84-6
IT'S A HEARTACHE, Bonnie Tyler and the Bonnie Tyler Band, 77-4
IT'S A LONG WAY TO THE TOP (IF YOU WANNA ROCK 'N' ROLL), AC/DC, 80-55
IT'S A LOVE THING, Whispers, 81-9
IT'S A LOVING THING, C B Milton, 94-49, 95-34
IT'S A MAN'S MAN'S MAN'S WORLD:
James Brown and the Famous Flames, 66-13
Brilliant, 85-58
Jeanie Tracy and Bobby Womack, 95-73
IT'S A MIRACLE, Culture Club, 84-4
IT'S A MISTAKE, Men At Work, 83-33
IT'S A MYSTERY (FOUR FROM TOYAH [EP]), Toyah, 81-4
IT'S A PARTY, Busta Rhymes featuring Zhane, 96-23
IT'S A PARTY, Bounty Killer (featuring Cocoa Brovaz, Nona Hendryx and Free), 99-65
IT'S A RAGGY WALTZ, Dave Brubeck Quartet, 62-36
IT'S A RAINY DAY, Ice MC, 95-73
IT'S A SHAME:
Motown Spinners, 70-20
Monie Love (featuring True Image) *, 90-12
IT'S A SHAME, Kris Kross, 92-31
IT'S A SHAME ABOUT RAY, Lemonheads, 92-70, 93-31
IT'S A SHAME (MY SISTER), Monie Love (featuring True Image), 90-12
IT'S A SIN, Pet Shop Boys, 87-1
IT'S A SIN TO TELL A LIE, Gerry Monroe, 71-13
IT'S A TRIP (TUNE IN, TURN ON, DROP OUT), Children Of The Night, 88-52

IT'S ABOUT TIME, Lemonheads, 93-57
IT'S ABOUT TIME YOU WERE MINE, Thunderbugs, 99-43
IT'S ALL ABOUT THE BENJAMINS, Puff Daddy and the Family [featuring The Notorious B.I.G Lil' Kim, The Lox, Dave Grohl, Perfect, Fuzzbubble and Rob Zombie], 98-18
IT'S ALL ABOUT U, SWV, 96-36
IT'S ALL ABOUT YOU, Justin, 99-34
IT'S ALL ABOUT YOU (NOT ABOUT ME), Tracie Spencer, 99 65
IT'S ALL BEEN DONE, Barenaked Ladies, 99-28
IT'S ALL COMING BACK TO ME NOW:
Pandora's Box, 89-51
Celine Dion, 96-3
IT'S ALL GONE, Chris Rea, 86-69
IT'S ALL GOOD, Hammer, 94-52
IT'S ALL GOOD, Da Mob featuring Jocelyn Brown, 99-54
IT'S ALL IN THE GAME:
Tommy Edwards, 58-1
Cliff Richard, 63-2
Four Tops, 70-5
IT'S ALL OVER, Cliff Richard with Bernard Ebbinghouse and his Orchestra, 67-9
IT'S ALL OVER NOW, Shane Fenton and the Fentones, 62-29
IT'S ALL OVER NOW, Rolling Stones, 64-1
IT'S ALL OVER NOW, BABY BLUE:
Joan Baez, 65-22
Milltown Brothers, 93-48
IT'S ALL RIGHT:
Sterling Void, 89-53
Pet Shop Boys *, 89-5
Hyper Go-Go *, 94-49
IT'S ALL THE WAY LIVE (NOW), Coolio, 96-34
IT'S ALL TRUE, Lemonheads, 96-61
IT'S ALL UP TO YOU, Jim Capaldi, 74-27
IT'S ALL YOURS, MC Lyte (featuring Gina Thompson), 98-36
IT'S ALMOST TOMORROW:
Dream Weavers, 56-1
Mark Wynter, 63-12
IT'S ALRIGHT, Sho Nuff, 80-53
IT'S ALRIGHT:
Pet Shop Boys, 89-5
Hyper Go-Go, 94-49
IT'S ALRIGHT, Bryan Powell, 93-73
IT'S ALRIGHT, East 17, 93-3
IT'S ALRIGHT, Deni Hines, 97-35
IT'S ALRIGHT, Echo and the Bunnymen, 01-41
IT'S ALRIGHT (BABY'S COMING BACK), Eurythmics, 86-12
IT'S ALRIGHT, I FEEL IT!, Nuyorican Soul featuring Jocelyn Brown, 97-26
IT'S ALRIGHT NOW, Beloved, 90-48
IT'S AN OPEN SECRET, Joy Strings, 64-32
IT'S BEEN AWHILE, Staind, 01-15
IT'S BEEN NICE (GOODNIGHT), Everly Brothers, 63-26
IT'S BEEN SO LONG, George McCrae, 75-4
IT'S BETTER TO HAVE (AND DON'T NEED), Don Covay, 74-29
IT'S CALLED A HEART, Depeche Mode, 85-18
IT'S DIFFERENT FOR GIRLS, Joe Jackson, 80-5
IT'S ECSTASY WHEN YOU LAY DOWN NEXT TO ME, Barry White, 77-40
IT'S FOR YOU, Cilla Black, 64-7
IT'S FOUR IN THE MORNING, Faron Young, 72-3
IT'S GETTING BETTER, Mama Cass, 69-8
IT'S GOING TO HAPPEN!, Undertones, 81-18
IT'S GONNA BE A COLD COLD CHRISTMAS, Dana, 75-4
IT'S GONNA BE A LOVELY DAY, S.O.U.L. S.Y.S.T.E.M. introducing Michelle Visage, 93-17
IT'S GONNA BE ALL RIGHT, Gerry and the Pacemakers, 64-24
IT'S GONNA BE ALRIGHT, Ruby Turner, 90-57
IT'S GONNA BE ALRIGHT, Pussy 2000, 01-70
IT'S GONNA BE ME, *Nsync, 00 9
IT'S GONNA BE MY WAY, Precious, 00-27
IT'S GOOD NEWS WEEK, Hedgehoppers Anonymous, 65-5
IT'S GREAT WHEN WE'RE TOGETHER, Finley Quaye, 97-29
IT'S GRIM UP NORTH, Justified Ancients Of Mu Mu, 91-10
IT'S GROWING, Temptations, 65-45
IT'S HAPPENIN', Plus One featuring Sirron, 90-40
IT'S HARD SOMETIME, Frankie Knuckles featuring Shelton Becton, 91-67
IT'S HARD TO BE HUMBLE, Mac Davis, 80-27
IT'S HERE, Kim Wilde, 90-42
IT'S IMPOSSIBLE, Perry Como, 71-4
IT'S IN EVERY ONE OF US, Cliff Richard, 85-45
IT'S IN HIS KISS (THE SHOOP SHOOP SONG):
Betty Everett, 68-34
Linda Lewis *, 75-6
Cher *, 91-1
IT'S IN YOUR EYES, Phil Collins, 96-30
IT'S IT'S THE SWEET MIX [M], Sweet, 85-45
IT'S JURASSIC (VERSION OF THE THEME TO JURASSIC PARK), Soul City Orchestra, 93-70
IT'S JUST A FEELING, Terrorize, 92-52, 92-47
IT'S JUST A LITTLE BIT TOO LATE, Wayne Fontana and the Mindbenders, 65-20
(IT'S JUST) THE WAY THAT YOU LOVE ME, Paula Abdul, 89-74
IT'S LATE:
Ricky Nelson, 59-3
Shakin' Stevens, 83-11
(IT'S LIKE A) SAD OLD KINDA' MOVIE, Pickettywitch, 70-16
IT'S LIKE THAT, Run-D.M.C. vs Jason Nevins, 98-63, 98-65, 98-1
IT'S LIKE THAT Y'ALL, Sweet Tee, 88-31
IT'S LOVE (IN UN FIORE), Ken Dodd with Brian Fahey and his Orchestra, 66-36
IT'S LOVE THAT REALLY COUNTS, Merseybeats, 63-24
IT'S LULU, Boo Radleys, 95-25
IT'S ME, Alice Cooper, 94-34
IT'S MY HOUSE:
Storm, 79-36
Diana Ross, 79-32
IT'S MY LIFE, Animals, 65-7
IT'S MY LIFE, Talk Talk, 84-46, 90-13
IT'S MY LIFE, Dr. Alban, 92-2
IT'S MY LIFE, Bon Jovi, 00-3
IT'S MY PARTY:
Lesley Gore, 63-9
Dave Stewart with Barbara Gaskin, 81-1
IT'S MY PARTY, Chaka Khan, 89-71
IT'S MY TIME, Everly Brothers, 68-39
IT'S MY TURN, Diana Ross, 81-16
IT'S MY TURN, Angelic, 00-11
IT'S NATURE'S WAY (NO PROBLEM), Dollar, 88-58
IT'S NEVER TOO LATE, Diana Ross, 82-41
IT'S NICE TO GO TRAV'LING, Frank Sinatra, 60-48
IT'S NO GOOD, Depeche Mode, 97-5
IT'S NOT A LOVE THING, Geoffrey Williams, 92-63
IT'S NOT RIGHT BUT IT'S OKAY, Whitney Houston, 99-3
IT'S NOT UNUSUAL, Tom Jones, 65-1, 87-17
IT'S NOW OR NEVER (O SOLE MIO), Elvis Presley with the Jordanaires, 60-1, 77-39
IT'S OH SO QUIET, Bjork, 95-4
IT'S OK, Delirious?, 00-18
IT'S ON, Flowered Up, 90-54, 91-38
IT'S ON, Naughty By Nature, 93-48
IT'S ON YOU (SCAN ME), Eurogroove, 95-25
IT'S ONE OF THOSE NIGHTS (YES LOVE), Partridge Family starring Shirley Jones and featuring David Cassidy, 72-11
IT'S ONLY LOVE, Tony Blackburn with the Majority, 69-41
IT'S ONLY LOVE, Elvis Presley, 80-3
IT'S ONLY LOVE, Gary U.S. Bonds, 81-43
IT'S ONLY LOVE, Bryan Adams and Tina Turner, 85-29
IT'S ONLY LOVE, Simply Red, 89-13
IT'S ONLY MAKE BELIEVE:
Conway Twitty, 58-1
Billy Fury, 64-10
Glen Campbell, 70-4
Child, 78-10
IT'S ONLY NATURAL, Crowded House, 92-24
IT'S ONLY ROCK 'N ROLL: 74-10
Rolling Stones, 74-10
Various Artists For Children's Promise, 99-19
IT'S ONLY US, Robbie Williams, 99-1
IT'S 'ORRIBLE BEING IN LOVE (WHEN YOU'RE 8 1/2), Claire and Friends, 86-13
IT'S OVER, Roy Orbison, 64-1
IT'S OVER:
Funk Master, 83-8
Clock, 97-10
IT'S OVER, Level 42, 87-10
IT'S OVER, Rimes featuring Shaila Prospere, 99-51
IT'S OVER, Kurupt (featuring Natina Reed), 01-21
IT'S OVER (DISTORTION), Pianoheadz, 98-39
IT'S OVER LOVE, Todd Terry presents Shannon, 97-16
IT'S OVER NOW, Ultra Nate, 89-62
IT'S OVER NOW, Deborah Cox, 99-49
IT'S OVER NOW, One (112) Twelve, 01-22
IT'S PARTY TIME AGAIN, George Van Dusen, 88-43
IT'S PROBABLY ME, Sting with Eric Clapton, 92-30
IT'S RAINING, Darts, 78-2
IT'S RAINING, Shakin' Stevens, 81-10
IT'S RAINING AGAIN, Supertramp featuring vocals by Roger Hodgson, 82-26
IT'S RAINING MEN:
Weather Girls, 83-73, 84-2
Martha Wash featuring Rupaul, 98-21
Martha Wash, 00-56
Geri Halliwell, 01-1
IT'S SO EASY, Andy Williams, 70-13
IT'S SO HIGH, Matt Fretton, 83-50
IT'S SO NICE (TO HAVE YOU HOME), New Seekers, 76-44
IT'S STILL ROCK AND ROLL TO ME, Billy Joel, 80-14
IT'S STILL YOU, Michael Ball, 91-58
IT'S SUMMERTIME (LET IT GET INTO YOU), Smooth, 95-46
IT'S TEMPTATION, Sheer Elegance, 76-41
IT'S THE END OF THE WORLD AS WE KNOW IT (AND I FEEL FINE), R.E.M., 91-39
IT'S THE SAME OLD SONG:
Four Tops, 65-34
Weathermen, 71-19
KC and the Sunshine Band, 78-47
IT'S THE WAY YOU MAKE ME FEEL, Steps, 01-2
IT'S TIME, Elvis Costello and the Attractions, 96-58
IT'S TIME FOR LOVE, Chi – Lites, 75-5
IT'S TIME TO CRY, Paul Anka, 60-28
IT'S TOO LATE:
Carole King, 71-6
Quartz Introducing Dina Carroll, 91-8
IT'S TOO LATE, Lucie Silvas, 00-62
IT'S TOO LATE NOW, Swinging Blue Jeans, 63-30
IT'S TOO LATE NOW, Long John Baldry, 69-21
IT'S TOO SOON TO KNOW, Pat Boone, 58-7
IT'S TRICKY:
Run-D.M.C., 87-16
Run-D.M.C. vs Jason Nevins, 98-74
IT'S TRUE, Queen Pen, 98-24
IT'S UP TO YOU, Rick Nelson, 63-22
IT'S UP TO YOU PETULA, Edison Lighthouse, 71-49
IT'S WHAT UPFRONT THAT COUNTS, Yosh presents Lovedeejay Akemi, 95-69, 95-31
IT'S WONDERFUL (TO BE LOVED BY YOU), Jimmy Ruffin, 70-6
IT'S WRITTEN ON YOUR BODY, Ronnie Bond, 80-52
IT'S YER MONEY I'M AFTER BABY, Wonder Stuff, 88-40
IT'S YOU, Freddie Starr, 74-9
IT'S YOU, Manhattans, 77-43
IT'S YOU, EMF, 92-23
IT'S YOU, ONLY YOU (MEIN SCHMERZ), Lene Lovich, 82-68
IT'S YOUR DAY TODAY, P. J. Proby, 68-32
IT'S YOUR DESTINY, Electra, 89-51
IT'S YOUR LIFE, Smokie, 77-5
IT'S YOUR THING:
Isley Brothers, 69-30
Salt N Pepa – featuring E.U. *, 88-22
IT'S YOUR TIME, Arthur Baker and the Backbeat Disciples featuring Shirley Lewis, 89-64
THE ITALIAN THEME, Stapleton and his Orchestra, 56-18
ITALO HOUSE MIX [M], Rococo, 89-54
ITCHYCOO PARK:
Small Faces, 67-3, 75-9
M People, 95-11
ITSY BITSY TEENIE WEENIE YELLOW POLKADOT BIKINI:
Brian Hyland, 60-8
Bombalurina, 90-1
ITZA TRUMPET THING, Montano vs the Trumpet Man, 99-46
IVORY, Skin Up, 91-48
IVORY TOWER, Three Kayes, 56-20
IZZO (H.O.V.A.), Jay-Z, 01-21
J.J. TRIBUTE, Asha, 95-38
JA-DA, Johnny and the Hurricanes, 61-14
JACK AND DIANE, John Cougar, 82-25
JACK AND JILL, Raydio, 78-11
JACK IN THE BOX, Clodagh Rodgers, 71-4
JACK IN THE BOX, Moments, 77-7
JACK LE FREAK [RM], Chic, 87-19

JOY, Mark 'Ruff' Ryder; vocals by Special MC and Heidi, 01-34
JOY AND HAPPINESS, Stabbs, 94-65
JOY AND HEARTBREAK, Movement. 98 featuring Carroll Thompson, 90-27
JOY AND PAIN, Rob Base and D.J. E-Z Rock, 89-47
JOY AND PAIN:
Maze, 89-57
Donna Allen, 89-10
(JOY) I KNOW IT, Odyssey, 85-51
THE JOY OF LIVING, Cliff and Hank, 70-25
THE JOY OF LIVING, Oui 3, 95-55
JOY TO THE WORLD, Three Dog Night, 71-24
JOYBRINGER, Manfred Mann's Earth Band, 73-9
JOYENERGISER, Joy Kitikonti, 01-57
JOYRIDE, Roxette, 91-4
JOYRIDER (YOU'RE PLAYING WITH FIRE), Colour Girl, 00-51
JOYS OF CHRISTMAS, Chris Rea, 87-67
JOYS OF LIFE, David Joseph, 84-61
JUDGE FUDGE, Happy Mondays, 91-24
THE JUDGEMENT IS THE MIRROR, Dali's Car, 84-66
JUDY IN DISGUISE (WITH GLASSES), John Fred and his Playboy Band, 68-3
JUDY OVER THE RAINBOW, Orange, 94-73
JUDY SAYS (KNOCK YOU IN THE HEAD), Vibrators, 78-70
JUDY TEEN, Cockney Rebel, 74-5
JUGGLING, Ragga Twins, 91-71
JUICY, Notorious B.I.G., 94-72
JUICY FRUIT:
Mtume, 83-34
Wrecks-N-Effect *, 90-29
A JUICY RED APPLE, Skin Up, 92-32
JUKE BOX BABY, Perry Como, 56-22
JUKE BOX GYPSY, Lindisfarne, 78-56
JUKE BOX HERO, Foreigner, 81-48
JUKE BOX JIVE, Rubettes, 74-3
JULIA, Eurythmics, 85-44
JULIA, Chris Rea, 93-18
JULIA, Silver Sun, 97-51
JULIA SAYS, Wet Wet Wet, 95-3
JULIE (NEW VERSION) (from THE JULIE [EP]), Levellers, 94-17
JULIE ANNE, Kenny, 75-10
JULIE DO YA LOVE ME:
White Plains with Pete Nelson, 70-8
Bobby Sherman, 70-28
JULIE OCEAN, Undertones, 81-41
JULIET, Four Pennies, 64-1
JULY, Ocean Colour Scene, 00-31
JUMBO, Bee Gees, 68-25
JUMBO, Underworld, 99-21
JUMP:
Van Halen, 84-7
Aztec Camera, 84-37
Van Halen, 93-26
Bus Stop, 99-23
JUMP, Kris Kross, 92-2
JUMP!, Movement, 92-57
JUMP AROUND, House Of Pain, 92-32, 93-8
JUMP BACK (SET ME FREE), Dhar Braxton, 86-32
JUMP DOWN, B*Witched, 00-16
JUMP (FOR MY LOVE), Pointer Sisters, 84-6
JUMP JIVE AN' WAIL, Brian Setzer Orchestra, 99-34
JUMP N' SHOUT, Basement Jaxx featuring Slarta John, 99-12
JUMP START, Natalie Cole, 87-44, 88-36
JUMP THE GUN, Three Degrees, 79-48
JUMP THEY SAY, David Bowie, 93-9
JUMP TO IT, Aretha Franklin, 82-42
JUMP TO MY BEAT, Wildchild, 96-30
JUMP TO MY LOVE, Incognito, 96-29
JUMP TO THE BEAT:
Stacy Lattisaw, 80-3
Dannii Minogue, 91-8
JUMPIN' JACK FLASH:
Rolling Stones, 68-1
Aretha Franklin, 86-58
JUMPIN' JIVE, Joe Jackson's Jumpin' Jive, 81-43
JUMPIN' JUMPIN', Destiny's Child, 00-5
JUNE AFTERNOON, Roxette, 96-52
JUNGLE BILL, Yello, 92-61
THE JUNGLE BOOK GROOVE, Jungle Book Disney Cast, 93-14
JUNGLE BROTHER, Jungle Brothers, 97-56, 98-18
JUNGLE FEVER, Chakachas, 72-29
JUNGLE HIGH, Juno Reactor, 97-45
JUNGLE ROCK, Hank Mizell, 76-3
JUNIOR'S FARM, Paul McCartney and Wings, 74-16
JUPITER, Earth, Wind And Fire, 78-41
JUS' COME, Cool Jack, 96-44
JUS 1 KISS, Basement Jaxx, 01-23
JUS' REACH (RECYCLED), Galliano, 92-66
JUST, Radiohead, 95-19
JUST A DAY [EP] + lead track title, Feeder, 01-12
JUST A DAY AWAY, Barclay James Harvest, 83-68
JUST A DREAM, Nena, 84-70
JUST A DREAM, Donna De Lory, 93-71
JUST A FEELING, Bad Manners, 81-13
JUST A FRIEND, Biz Markie, 90-55
JUST A GIRL, No Doubt, 96-38, 97-3
JUST A GROOVE, Nomad, 91-16
JUST A LITTLE BIT, Undertakers, 64-49
JUST A LITTLE BIT BETTER, Herman's Hermits, 65-15
JUST A LITTLE BIT LONGER (from THE MAXI PRIEST [EP]), Maxi Priest, 91-62
JUST A LITTLE BIT OF LOVE, Rebekah Ryan, 96-51
JUST A LITTLE MISUNDERSTANDING, Contours, 70-31
JUST A LITTLE MORE, Deluxe, 89-74
JUST A LITTLE TOO MUCH, Ricky Nelson, 59-11
JUST A MIRAGE, Jellybean featuring Adele Bertei, 88-13
JUST A SHADOW, Big Country, 85-26
JUST A SMILE, Pilot, 75-31
JUST A STEP FROM HEAVEN, Eternal, 94-8
JUST A TOUCH, Keith Sweat, 96-35
JUST A TOUCH OF LOVE, Slave, 80-64
JUST A TOUCH OF LOVE (EVERYDAY), C&C Music Factory featuring Zelma Davis, 91-31
JUST AN ILLUSION, Imagination, 82-2
JUST ANOTHER BROKEN HEART, Sheena Easton, 81-33
JUST ANOTHER DAY, Jon Secada, 92-5
JUST ANOTHER DAY, Jonathan Wilkes, 01-24
JUST ANOTHER DREAM, Cathy Dennis, 91-13
JUST ANOTHER GROOVE, Mighty Dub Katz, 96-43
JUST ANOTHER ILLUSION, Hurricane #1, 97-35
JUST ANOTHER NIGHT, Mick Jagger, 85-32
JUST AROUND THE HILL, Sash!, 00-8
JUST AS LONG AS YOU ARE THERE, Vanessa Paradis, 93-57
JUST AS MUCH AS EVER, Nat King Cole, 60-18
JUST BE GOOD TO ME:
S.O.S. Band, 84-13
Beats International featuring Lindy *, 90-1
JUST BE TONIGHT, Bbg featuring Erin, 97-45
JUST BETWEEN YOU AND ME, April Wine, 81-52
JUST BORN (TO BE YOUR BABY), Jim Dale, 58-27
JUST CALL, Sherrick, 87-23
JUST CALL ME, Good Girls, 93-75
JUST CAN'T GET ENOUGH, Depeche Mode, 81-8
JUST CAN'T GET ENOUGH, Transformer 2, 96-45
JUST CAN'T GET ENOUGH, Harry 'Choo Choo' Romero presents Inaya Day, 99-39
JUST CAN'T GET ENOUGH (NO NO NO NO), Eye To Eye featuring Taka Boom, 01-36
JUST CAN'T GIVE YOU UP, Mystic Merlin, 80-20
JUST CAN'T STAND IT, Matt Bianco, 86-66
JUST CHECKIN', Beautiful South, 00-59
JUST CRUISIN', Will Smith, 97-23
JUST DON'T WANT TO BE LONELY:
Main Ingredient, 74-27
Freddie McGregor, 87-9
JUST FADE AWAY, Stiff Little Fingers, 81-47
JUST FOR KICKS, Mike Sarne, 63-22
JUST FOR MONEY, Paul Hardcastle, 85-19
JUST FOR OLD TIME'S SAKE, Foster and Allen, 84-47
JUST FOR YOU, Freddie and the Dreamers, 64-41
JUST FOR YOU, Glitter Band, 74-10
JUST FOR YOU, Alan Price, 78-43, 79-32
JUST FOR YOU, M People, 97-8
JUST GET UP AND DANCE:
Afrika Bambaataa, 91-45
Afrika Bambaataa vs. Carpe Diem *, 98-22
JUST GETS BETTER, TJR featuring Xavier, 97-28
JUST GIVE THE DJ A BREAK, Dynamix Ii featuring: Too Tough Tee, 87-50
JUST GOOD FRIENDS, Fish featuring Sam Brown, 95-63
JUST GOT LUCKY, Joboxers, 83-7
JUST GOT PAID, Johnny Kemp, 88-68
JUST HOLD ON, Toploader, 00-20
JUST IN CASE, Jaheim, 01-34
JUST IN LUST, Wildhearts, 95-28
JUST IN TIME, Raw Silk, 83-49
JUST KEEP IT UP AND SEE WHAT HAPPENS, Dee Clark, 59-26
JUST KEEP ME MOVING, k.d. lang, 93-59
JUST KEEP ROCKIN', Double Trouble and the Rebel MC, 89-11
JUST KICKIN' IT, Xscape, 93-49, 94-54
JUST LET ME DO MY THING, Sine, 78-33
JUST LIKE A MAN, Del Amitri, 92-25
JUST LIKE A WOMAN, Manfred Mann, 66-10
JUST LIKE ANYONE, Soul Asylum, 95-52
JUST LIKE EDDIE, Heinz, 63-5
JUST LIKE FRED ASTAIRE, James, 99-17
JUST LIKE HEAVEN, Cure, 87-29
JUST LIKE HONEY, Jesus And Mary Chain, 85-45
JUST LIKE JESSE JAMES, Cher, 90-11
JUST LIKE PARADISE, David Lee Roth, 88-27
(JUST LIKE) STARTING OVER, John Lennon, 80-1
JUST LISTEN TO MY HEART, Spotnicks, 63-36
JUST LOOKIN', Charlatans, 95-32
JUST LOOKING, Stereophonics, 99-4
JUST LOVING YOU, Anita Harris, 67-6
(JUST) ME AND YOU, New Vision, 00-23
JUST MELLOW, Ruthless Rap Assassins, 90-75
JUST MY IMAGINATION (RUNNING AWAY WITH ME):
Temptations, 71-8
McGanns *, 98-59
JUST MY SOUL RESPONDING, Smokey Robinson, 74-35
JUST ONE LOOK:
Hollies, 64-2
Faith Hope and Charity, 76-38
JUST ONE MORE KISS, Renee and Renato, 83-48
JUST ONE MORE NIGHT, Yellow Dog, 78-8
JUST ONE SMILE, Gene Pitney, 66-8
JUST OUT OF REACH (OF MY TWO EMPTY ARMS), Ken Dodd, 72-29
JUST OUTSIDE OF HEAVEN, H2O, 83-38
JUST PLAY MUSIC!, Big Audio Dynamite, 88-51
JUST PLAYIN', JT Playaz, 97-30
JUST RIGHT, Soul II Soul, 92-38
JUST ROUND, A Very Good Friend Of Mine featuring Joy, 99-55
JUST SAY NO, Grange Hill Cast (Rap: Mmoloki Chrystie), 86-5
JUST SEVEN NUMBERS (CAN STRAIGHTEN OUT MY LIFE), Four Tops, 71-36
JUST SHOW ME HOW TO LOVE YOU, Sarah Brightman and the London Symphony Orchestra featuring Jose Cura, 97-54
JUST TAH LET U KNOW, Eazy-E, 96-30
JUST TAKE MY HEART, Mr. Big, 92-26
JUST THE ONE, Levellers special guest Joe Strummer on piano, 95-12
JUST THE TWO OF US:
Grover Washington, 81-34
Will Smith, 98-2
JUST THE WAY, Alfonzo Hunter, 97-38
JUST THE WAY IT IS, Lisa Moorish, 95-42
JUST THE WAY YOU ARE:
Billy Joel, 78-19, 86-53
Barry White, 78-12
JUST THE WAY YOU LIKE IT, S.O.S. Band, 84-32
JUST THIRTEEN, Lurkers, 79-66
JUST THIS SIDE OF LOVE, Malandra Burrows, 90-11
JUST TO BE CLOSE TO YOU, Commodores, 78-62
JUST TO SEE HER, Smokey Robinson, 87-52
JUST WALK IN MY SHOES, Gladys Knight and the Pips, 72-35
JUST WALKING IN THE RAIN, Johnnie Ray with Ray Conniff and his Orchestra and Chorus, 56-1
JUST WANNA KNOW, Maxi Priest, 92-33
JUST WANNA TOUCH ME, Fidelfatti featuring Ronnette, 90-65
JUST WAVE HELLO, Charlotte Church, 99-31
JUST WHAT I ALWAYS WANTED, Mari Wilson, 82-8

JUST WHAT I NEEDED, Cars, 79-17
JUST WHEN I NEEDED YOU MOST:
Randy Vanwarmer, 79-8
Barbara Jones, 81-31
JUST WHEN YOU'RE THINKIN' THINGS OVER, Charlatans, 95-12
JUST WHO IS THE 5 O'CLOCK HERO, Jam, 82-8
JUSTIFIED AND ANCIENT, KLF (Lead vocals: "The First Lady of Country" Miss Tammy Wynette), 91-2
JUSTIFY MY LOVE, Madonna, 90-2
JUXTAPOZED WITH U, Super Furry Animals, 01-14
K.K.K. (BOOM BOOM TRA LA LA LA) (from THE HONKY DOODLE DAY [EP]), Honky, 93-61
*****K THE MILLENNIUM,** 2K, 97-28
KALEIDOSCOPE SKIES, Jam and Spoon featuring Plavka, 97-48
KANDY POP (from THE SECRET VAMPIRE SOUNDTRACK [EP]), Bis, 96-25
KANSAS CITY:
Little Richard, 59-26
Trini Lopez, 63-35
KANSAS CITY STAR, Roger Miller, 65-48
KARA, KARA, New World, 71-17
KARAOKE QUEEN, Catatonia, 99-36
KARMA CHAMELEON, Culture Club, 83-1
KARMA HOTEL, Spooks, 01-15
KARMA POLICE, Radiohead, 97-8
THE KARMACOMA [EP] + lead track title, Massive Attack, 95-28
KARMADROME, Pop Will Eat Itself, 92-17
KATE, Ben Folds Five, 97-39
KATE BUSH ON STAGE [EP], Kate Bush, 79-10
KATHLEEN, Roachford, 89-43
KATHLEEN [EP] + lead track title, Tindersticks, 94-61
KAYLEIGH, Marillion, 85-2
KEEEP YOUR BODY WORKING, Kleeer, 79-51
KEEP A KNOCKIN', Little Richard, 57-21
KEEP AWAY FROM OTHER GIRLS, Helen Shapiro, 62-40
KEEP COMING BACK, Richard Marx, 91-55
KEEP CONTROL, Sono, 01-66
KEEP DOIN' IT, Showdown, 77-41
KEEP EACH OTHER WARM, Bucks Fizz, 86-45
(KEEP FEELING) FASCINATION, Human League, 83-2
KEEP GIVIN' ME YOUR LOVE, Ce Ce Peniston, 94-36
KEEP GIVING ME LOVE, D Train, 83-65
KEEP GIVING ME LOVE, Bomb The Bass, 92-62
KEEP HOPE ALIVE, Serial Diva, 97-57
KEEP HOPE ALIVE, Crystal Method, 98-71
KEEP IN TOUCH, Freeez, 80-49
KEEP IN TOUCH (BODY TO BODY), Shades Of Love (Junior Vasquez meets Johnny Vicious), 95-64
KEEP IT COMIN' (DANCE TIL YOU CAN'T DANCE NO MORE), C&C Music Factory featuring Q Unique and Deborah Cooper, 92-34
KEEP IT COMIN' LOVE, KC and the Sunshine Band, 76-31
KEEP IT DARK, Genesis, 81-33
KEEP IT ON, Hannah Jones, 93-67
KEEP IT OUT OF SIGHT, Paul and Barry Ryan, 67-30
KEEP IT TOGETHER, David Grant, 90-56
KEEP IT UP, Sharada House Gang, 95-36
KEEP LOVE NEW, Betty Wright, 89-71
KEEP LOVE TOGETHER, Love To Infinity, 95-38
KEEP ME FROM THE COLD, Curtis Stigers, 95-57
KEEP ME IN MIND, Boy George, 87-29
KEEP ON, Bruce Channel, 68-12
KEEP ON, Cabaret Voltaire, 90-55
KEEP ON BELIEVING, Grand Prix, 82-75
KEEP ON BURNING, Edwyn Collins, 96-45
KEEP ON DANCIN', Gary's Gang, 79-8
KEEP ON DANCIN' (LET'S GO), Perpetual Motion, 98-12
KEEP ON DANCING, Bay City Rollers, 71-9
KEEP ON JAMMIN', Willie Hutch, 85-73
KEEP ON JUMPIN':
Lisa Marie Experience, 96-7
Todd Terry featuring Martha Wash and Jocelyn Brown, 96-8
KEEP ON KEEPIN' ON!, Redskins, 84-43
KEEP ON, KEEPIN' ON, MC Lyte featuring Xscape, 96-39, 97-27
KEEP ON LOVING YOU, Reo Speedwagon, 81-7
KEEP ON MOVIN', Soul II Soul (featuring Caron Wheeler), 89-5, 96-31
KEEP ON MOVIN', Five, 99-1
KEEP ON MOVING, Bob Marley and the Wailers, 95-17
KEEP ON PUMPIN' IT, Vision Masters and Tony King featuring Kylie Minogue, 91-49
KEEP ON PUSHING OUR LOVE, Nightcrawlers featuring John Reid and Alysha Warren, 96-30
KEEP ON RUNNING:
Spencer Davis Group, 65-1
John Alford, 96-21
KEEP ON RUNNING (TIL YOU BURN), U.K. Subs, 81-41
(KEEP ON) SHINING, Loveland featuring Rachel McFarlane, 94-37
KEEP ON TRUCKIN', Eddie Kendricks, 73-18
KEEP ON WALKIN', Ce Ce Peniston, 92-10
KEEP PUSHIN', Clock, 95-7
KEEP PUSHIN', Boris Dlugosch presents Booom!, 96-41
KEEP REACHING OUT FOR LOVE, Liner, 79-49
KEEP SEARCHIN' (WE'LL FOLLOW THE SUN), Del Shannon, 65-3
KEEP STEPPIN', Omar, 94-57
KEEP TALKING, Pink Floyd, 94-26
KEEP THE CUSTOMER SATISFIED, Marsha Hunt, 70-41
KEEP THE FAITH, Bon Jovi, 92-5
KEEP THE FIRE BURNIN', Dan Hartman starring Loleatta Holloway, 95-49
KEEP THE FIRES BURNING, Clock, 94-36
KEEP THE HOME FIRES BURNING, Bluetones, 00-13
KEEP THE MUSIC STRONG, Bizarre Inc, 96-33
KEEP THEIR HEADS RINGIN', Dr. Dre, 95-25
KEEP THIS FREQUENCY CLEAR, DTI, 88-73
KEEP WARM, Jinny, 91-68, 95-11
KEEP YOUR EYE ON ME – SPECIAL MIX, Herb Alpert, 87-19
KEEP YOUR HANDS OFF MY BABY, Little Eva, 63-30
KEEP YOUR HANDS TO YOURSELF, Georgia Satellites, 87-69
KEEP YOUR LOVE, Partizan featuring Natalie Robb, 97-53
KEEP YOUR WORRIES, Guru's Jazzmatazz featuring Angie Stone, 00-57
KEEPER OF THE CASTLE, Four Tops, 72-18
KEEPIN' LOVE NEW, Howard Johnson, 82-64
KEEPIN' THE FAITH, De La Soul, 91-50
KEEPING A RENDEZVOUS, Budgie, 81-71
KEEPING SECRETS, Switch, 84-61
KEEPING THE DREAM ALIVE, Freiheit, 88-14
KEEPS ME WONDERING WHY, Steve Miller Band, 82-52
KELLY, Wayne Gibson, 64-48
KELLY WATCH THE STARS, Air (French Band), 98-18
KELLY'S HEROES, Black Grape, 95-17
KENNEDY, Wedding Present, 89-33
KENTUCKY RAIN, Elvis Presley, 70-21
KERNKRAFT 400, Zombie Nation, 00-61,00-2
KERRY KERRY, Cinerama, 98-71
KEVIN CARTER, Manic Street Preachers, 96-9
KEWPIE DOLL:
Perry Como with Mitchell Ayres Orchestra and the Ray Charles Singers, 58-9
Frankie Vaughan with Wally Stott and his Orchestra and Chorus, 58-10
THE KEY, Senser, 93-47
THE KEY, Matt Goss, 95-40
KEY LARGO, Bertie Higgins, 82-60
THE KEY: THE SECRET, Urban Cookie Collective, 93-2, 96-52
KEY TO MY LIFE, Boyzone, 95-3
KICK IN THE EYE, Bauhaus, 81-59, 82-45
KICK IN THE EYE – SEARCHING FOR SATORI [EP] + lead track title, Bauhaus, 82-45
KICK IT, Nitzer Ebb, 95-75
KICK IT, Reggae Boyz, 98-59
KICK IT IN, Simple Minds, 89-15
KICKIN' HARD, Klubbheads, 98-36
KICKIN' IN THE BEAT, Pamela Fernandez, 94-43, 95-59
KICKIN' UP THE LEAVES, Mark Wynter, 60-24
KICKING MY HEART AROUND, Black Crowes, 98-55
KICKING UP DUST, Little Angels, 90-46
KID:
Pretenders, 79-33
Pretenders, 95-73
Hybrid Featuring Chrissie Hynde *, 00-32
KIDDIO, Brook Benton, 60-41
KIDS, Robbie Williams / Kylie Minogue, 00-2
THE KIDS ARE ALRIGHT, Who, 66-41
THE KIDS ARE BACK, Twisted Sister, 83-32
THE KIDS AREN'T ALRIGHT, Offspring, 99-11
KIDS IN AMERICA, Kim Wilde, 81-2
THE KID'S LAST FIGHT, Frankie Laine with Carl Fischer at the upright and the Norman Luboff Choir, 54-3
KIDS OF THE CENTURY, Helloween, 91-56
KIDS ON THE STREET, Angelic Upstarts, 81-57
KILL ALL HIPPIES, Prml Scrm, 00-24
KILL THE KING, Rainbow, 77-44, 81-41
KILL THE POOR, Dead Kennedys, 80-49
KILL YOUR TELEVISION, Ned's Atomic Dustbin, 90-53
KILLED BY DEATH, Motorhead, 84-51
KILLER:
Adamski, 90-1
Seal (from Killer . . . On The Loose [EP]), 91-8
ATB, 00-4
KILLER ON THE LOOSE, Thin Lizzy, 80-10
KILLER . . . ON THE LOOSE [EP], Seal, 91-8
KILLER QUEEN, Queen, 74-2
KILLERS LIVE [EP], Thin Lizzy, 81-19
KILLIN' TIME, Tina Cousins, 99-15
KILLING IN THE NAME, Rage Against The Machine, 93-25
THE KILLING JAR, Siouxsie and the Banshees, 88-41
KILLING ME SOFTLY WITH HIS SONG:
Roberta Flack, 73-6
Fugees (Refugee Camp) *, 96-1
THE KILLING MOON, Echo and the Bunnymen, 84-9
THE KILLING OF GEORGIE PARTS 1 & 2, Rod Stewart, 76-2
A KIND OF CHRISTMAS CARD, Morten Harket, 95-53
A KIND OF MAGIC, Queen, 86-3
KINETIC, Golden Girls, 98-38, 99-56
KING, U.B.40, 80-4
THE KING AND QUEEN OF AMERICA, Eurythmics, 90-29
KING CREOLE, Elvis Presley with the Jordanaires, 58-2
KING FOR A DAY, Thompson Twins, 85-22
KING FOR A DAY, Jamiroquai, 99-20
KING IN A CATHOLIC STYLE (WAKE UP), China Crisis, 85-19
THE KING IS DEAD, Go West, 87-67
THE KING IS HALF UNDRESSED, Jellyfish, 91-39
THE KING IS HERE, 45 King, 89-60
KING KONG, Terry Lightfoot's New Orleans Jazzmen, 61-29
KING MIDAS IN REVERSE, Hollies, 67-18
KING OF CLOWNS, Neil Sedaka, 62-23
KING OF DREAMS, Deep Purple, 90-70
KING OF EMOTION, Big Country, 88-16
KING OF KINGS, Ezz Reco and the Launchers with Boysie Grant, 64-44
THE KING OF KISSINGDOM, My Life Story, 97-35
KING OF LOVE, Dave Edmunds, 90-68
KING OF MISERY, Honeycrack, 96-32
KING OF MY CASTLE, Wamdue Project, 99-61, 99-1
KING OF NEW YORK, Fun Lovin' Criminals, 97-28
KING OF PAIN, Police, 84-17
THE KING OF ROCK 'N' ROLL, Prefab Sprout, 88-7
KING OF SNAKE, Underworld, 99-17
KING OF SORROW, Sade, 01-59
KING OF THE COPS, Billy Howard, 75-6
KING OF THE KERB, Echobelly, 95-25
KING OF THE NEW YORK STREETS, Dion, 89-74
KING OF THE ROAD:
Roger Miller, 65-1
Proclaimers (from EP of the same name), 90-9
KING OF THE RUMBLING SPIRES, Tyrannosaurus Rex, 69-44
THE KING OF WISHFUL THINKING, Go West, 90-18

KING ROCKER, Generation X, 79-11
KING WITHOUT A CROWN, ABC, 87-44
KINGS AND QUEENS, Killing Joke, 85-58
KING'S CALL, Philip Lynott, 80-35, 87-68
KINGS OF THE WILD FRONTIER, Adam and the Ants, 80-48, 81-2
KINGDOM, Ultramarine, 93-46
KINGSTON TOWN, UB40, 90-4
KINKY AFRO, Happy Mondays, 90-5
KINKY BOOTS, Patrick MacNee and Honor Blackman, 90-5
KINKY LOVE, Pale Saints, 91-72
KIRI RIRI BOOM, Shaft, 01-62
KISS, Dean Martin, 53-5
KISS:
Prince and the Revolution, 86-6
Age Of Chance, 87-50
Art Of Noise featuring Tom Jones, 88-5
KISS AND SAY GOODBYE, Manhattans, 76-4
KISS AND TELL, Bryan Ferry, 88-41
KISS AND TELL, Brownstone, 97-21
KISS FROM A ROSE, Seal, 94-20, 95-4
KISS LIKE ETHER, Claudia Brucken, 91-63
KISS ME, Stephen 'Tintin' Duffy, 85-4
KISS ME, Sixpence None The Richer, 99-4
KISS ME ANOTHER, Georgia Gibbs, 56-24
KISS ME DEADLY, Lita Ford, 88-75
KISS ME GOODBYE, Petula Clark, 68-50
KISS ME, HONEY HONEY, KISS ME, Shirley Bassey with Wally Stott and his Orchestra and Chorus, 58-3
KISS ME QUICK, Elvis Presley with the Jordanaires, 63-14
KISS OF LIFE, Sade, 93-44
KISS ON MY LIST, Daryl Hall and John Oates, 80-33
KISS THAT FROG, Peter Gabriel, 93-46
KISS THE BRIDE, Elton John, 83-20
KISS THE DIRT (FALLING DOWN THE MOUNTAIN), Inxs, 86-54
KISS THE GIRL, Peter Andre, 98-9
KISS THE RAIN, Billie Myers, 98-4
KISS THEM FOR ME, Siouxsie and the Banshees featuring Talvin Singh, 91-32
KISS THIS THING GOODBYE, Del Amitri, 89-59, 90-43
KISS (WHEN THE SUN DON'T SHINE), Vengaboys, 99-3
KISS YOU ALL OVER:
Exile, 78-6
No Mercy, 97-16
KISSES IN THE MOONLIGHT, George Benson, 86-60
KISSES ON THE WIND, Neneh Cherry, 89-20
KISSES SWEETER THAN WINE:
Jimmy Rodgers with Hugo Peretti and his Orchestra, 57-7
Frankie Vaughan with Wally Stott and his Orchestra and Chorus, 57-8
KISSIN' COUSINS, Elvis Presley with the Jordanaires, 64-10
KISSIN' IN THE BACK ROW OF THE MOVIES, Drifters, 74-2
KISSIN' YOU, Total, 96-29
KISSING A FOOL, George Michael, 88-18
KISSING GATE, Sam Brown, 90-23
KISSING WITH CONFIDENCE, Will Powers, 83-17
KITE, Nick Heyward, 93-44
KITES, Simon Dupree and the Big Sound, 67-9
KITSCH, Barry Ryan with the Paul Ryan Orchestra, 70-37
KITTY, Cat Stevens, 67-47
KLACTOVEESEDSTEIN, Blue Rondo A La Turk, 82-50
KLUBBHOPPING, Klubbheads, 96-10
KNEE DEEP IN THE BLUES:
Guy Mitchell with Ray Conniff, 57-3
Tommy Steele and the Steelmen, 57-15
KNIFE EDGE, Alarm, 86-43
KNIVES OUT, Radiohead, 01-13
KNOCK, KNOCK WHO'S THERE?, Mary Hopkin, 70-2
KNOCK ME OUT, Gary's Gang, 82-45
KNOCK ON WOOD:
Eddie Floyd, 67-19
Otis Redding and Carla Thomas, 67-35
Bowie, 74-10
Amii Stewart, 79-6, 85-07
KNOCK THREE TIMES, Dawn, 71-1
KNOCKED IT OFF, B.A. Robertson, 79-8
KNOCKED OUT, Paula Abdul, 89-45, 90-21
KNOCKIN' ON HEAVEN'S DOOR:
Bob Dylan, 73-14
Eric Clapton, 75-38
Guns N' Roses, 92-2
Dunblane, 96-1
KNOCKING AT YOUR BACK DOOR, Deep Purple, 85-68
KNOCKS ME OFF MY FEET, Donell Jones, 97-58
KNOW BY NOW, Robert Palmer, 94-25
KNOW YOUR RIGHTS, Clash, 82-43
KNOWING ME, KNOWING YOU, Abba, 77-1
KOKOMO, Beach Boys, 88-25
KOMMOTION, Duane Eddy, 60-13
KOMODO (SAVE A SOUL), Mauro Picotto, 01-13
KON – TIKI, Shadows, 61-1
KOOCHIE RYDER, Freaky Realistic, 93-52
KOOCHY, Armand Van Helden, 00-4
KOOKIE, KOOKIE (LEND ME YOUR COMB), Edward Byrnes and Connie Stevens with the Big Sound of Don Ralke, 60-27
KOOKIE LITTLE PARADISE, Frankie Vaughan, 60-31
KOOL IN THE KAFTAN, B.A. Robertson, 80-17
KOOTCHI, Neneh Cherry, 96-38
KOREAN BODEGA, Fun Lovin' Criminals, 99-15
KOWALSKI, Primal Scream, 97-8
KRUPA, Apollo Four Forty, 96-23
KU KLUX KLAN, Steel Pulse, 78-41
KUMBAYA, Sandpipers, 69-38
KUNG FU, Ash, 95-57
KUNG-FU, 187 Lockdown, 98-9
KUNG FU FIGHTING:
Carl Douglas, 74-1
Bus Stop featuring Carl Douglas, 98-8
KUT IT, Red Eye, 94-62
KYRIE, Mr. Mister, 86-11
KYRILA [EP] + lead track title, Demis Roussos, 77-33
L.A. CONNECTION, Rainbow, 78-40
THE L.A. RUN, Carvells, 77-31
L.A. WOMAN, Billy Idol, 90-70
L'ESPERANZA, Airscape, 99-33
L'L' LUCY, Mud, 75-10
L.O.D. (LOVE ON DELIVERY), Billy Ocean, 76-19
L.O.V.E. (LOVE):
Al Green, 75-24
Orange Juice, 81-65
L.S.D. [EP], Kaotic Chemistry, 92-68
L.S.I., Shamen, 92-6
LA, Marc Et Claude, 98-28
LA BAMBA, Ritchie Valens, 87-49
LA BAMBA, Los Lobos, 87-1
LA BOOGA ROOGA, Surprise Sisters, 76-38
LA DEE DAH, Jackie Dennis, 58-4
LA DERNIERE VALSE (THE LAST WALTZ), Mireille Mathieu, 67-26
LA DI DA, Sad Cafe, 80-41
LA DONNA E MOBILE FROM VERDI RIGOLETTO, Three Tenors In Concert 1994 – Carreras Domingo Pavarotti with Mehta, 94-21
LA FOLIE, Stranglers, 82-47
LA ISLA BONITA, Madonna, 87-1
LA LA LA, Massiel, 68-35
LA LA LA HEY HEY, Outhere Brothers, 95-7
LA-LA MEANS I LOVE YOU:
Delfonics, 71-19
Swing Out Sister, 94-37
LA LUNA, Belinda Carlisle, 89-38
LA LUNA, Movin' Melodies Production, 94-64
LA MER (BEYOND THE SEA):
Bobby Darin, 60-8
George Benson *, 85-60
LA MOUCHE, Cassius, 99-53
LA MUSICA, Ruff Driverz Presents Arrola, 99-14
LA PLUME DE MA TANTE, Hugo and Luigi their Orchestra and Children's Chorus, 59-29
LA PRIMAVERA, Sash!, 98-3
LA SERENISSIMA – THEME FROM VENICE IN PERIL:
Rondo Veneziano, 83-58
DNA, 90-34
LA TRISTESSE DURERA (SCREAM TO A SIGH), Manic Street Preachers, 93-22
LA VIE EN ROSE, Grace Jones, 86-12
LA YENKA, Johnny and Charley, 65-49
LABELLED WITH LOVE, Squeeze, 81-4
LABOUR OF LOVE, Hue And Cry, 87-6, 93-25
THE LABYRINTH, Moogwai, 01-68
LADIES, Mantronix, 86-55
LADIES NIGHT, Kool And The Gang, 79-9
LADY, Whispers, 80-55
LADY, Kenny Rogers, 80-12
LADY, D'Angelo, 96-21
LADY BARBARA, Peter Noone and Herman's Hermits, 70-13
LADY BIRD, Nancy Sinatra and Lee Hazlewood, 67-47
LADY D'ARBANVILLE, Cat Stevens, 70-8
LADY ELEANOR, Lindisfarne, 72-3
LADY GODIVA, Peter and Gordon with Geoff Love and his Orchestra, 66-16
LADY (HEAR ME TONIGHT), Modjo, 00-1
THE LADY IN RED, Chris De Burgh, 86-1
THE LADY IS A TRAMP, Buddy Greco, 60-26
LADY JANE:
Tony Merrick, 66-49
David Garrick, 66-28
LADY LET IT LIE, Fish, 94-46
LADY LOVE BUG, Clodagh Rodgers, 71-28
LADY LOVE ME (ONE MORE TIME), George Benson, 83-11
LADY LUCK, Lloyd Price and his Orchestra, 60-45
LADY LUCK, Rod Stewart, 95-56
LADY LYNDA, Beach Boys, 79-6
LADY MADONNA, Beatles, 68-1, 88-67
LADY MARMALADE (VOULEZ-VOUS COUCHER AVEC MOI CE SOIR?):
Labelle, 75-17
All Saints *, 98-1
Christina Aguilera, Lil' Kim, Mya and Pink *, 01-1
LADY ROSE, Mungo Jerry, 71-5
LADY SHINE (SHINE ON), T.H.S. – The Horne Section, 84-54
LADY WILLPOWER, Gary Puckett and the Union Gap, 68-5
LADY WRITER, Dire Straits, 79-51
LADY (YOU BRING ME UP):
Commodores, 81-56
Simply Smooth, 98-70
THE LADYBOY IS MINE, Stuntmasterz, 01-10
LADYFINGERS, Luscious Jackson, 99-43
LADYKILLERS, Lush, 96-22
LADYSHAVE, Gusgus, 99-64
LAGARTIJA NICK, Bauhaus, 83-44
LAID, James, 93-25
LAID SO LOW (TEARS ROLL DOWN), Tears For Fears, 92-17
LAILA, Taz / Stereo Nation, 01-44
LAKINI'S JUICE, Live, 97-29
LAMBADA, Kaoma, 89-4
LAMBORGHINI, Shut Up and Dance featuring the Ragga Twins, 90-55
LAMENT, Ultravox, 84-22
LAMPLIGHT, David Essex, 73-7
LANA, Roy Orbison, 66-15
LAND OF CONFUSION, Genesis, 86-14
LAND OF HOPE AND GLORY, Ex Pistols, 85-69
THE LAND OF MAKE BELIEVE, Bucks Fizz, 81-1
LAND OF 1000 DANCES, Wilson Pickett, 66-22
THE LAND OF RING DANG DO, King Kurt, 87-67
LAND OF THE LIVING, Kristine W, 96-57
LANDSLIDE, Olivia Newton-John, 82-18
LANDSLIDE, Harmonix, 96-28
LANDSLIDE, Spin City, 00-30
LANDSLIDE OF LOVE, Transvision Vamp, 89-14
THE LANE, Ice-T, 96-18
LANGUAGE OF LOVE, John D. Loudermilk, 62-13
LANGUAGE OF VIOLENCE, Disposable Heroes Of Hiphoprisy, 92-68
LAP OF LUXURY, Jethro Tull, 84-70
LAPDANCE, N*E*R*D featuring Lee Harvey and Vita, 01-33
LARGER THAN LIFE, Backstreet Boys, 99-5
LAS PALABRAS DE AMOR, Queen, 82-17
LAS VEGAS, Tony Christie, 71-21
LASER LOVE, T. Rex, 76-41
LASER LOVE, After The Fire, 79-62
THE LAST BEAT OF MY HEART, Siouxsie and the Banshees, 88-44
LAST CHANCE, China Drum, 96-60
LAST CHRISTMAS:
Wham!, 84-2, 85-6, 86-45
Whigfield, 95-21
Alien Voices featuring the Three Degrees, 98-54
LAST CUP OF SORROW, Faith No More, 97-51
LAST DANCE, Donna Summer, 78-51
LAST DAY, Silver Sun, 97-48
THE LAST FAREWELL:
Roger Whittaker, 75-2
Ship's Company and Royal Marine Band of H.M.S. Ark Royal, 78-46
Elvis Presley, 84-48
LAST FILM, Kissing The Pink, 83-19
THE LAST GAS (from FIREWORKS [EP]), Embrace, 97-34
LAST GOODBYE, Jeff Buckley, 95-54
LAST HORIZON, Brian May, 93-51
THE LAST KISS, David Cassidy, 85-6
LAST KISS, Pearl Jam, 99-42
LAST NIGHT, Merseybeats, 64-40
LAST NIGHT, Kid 'N Play, 87-71

LET ME GO, Heaven 17, 82-41
LET ME GO LOVER:
Teresa Brewer with the Lancers, 55-9
Joan Weber, 55-16
Dean Martin, 55-3
Ruby Murray with Ray Martin and his Orchestra, 55-5
Kathy Kirby, 64-10
LET ME HEAR YOU SAY "OLE OLE", Outhere Brothers, 97-18
LET ME IN:
Osmonds, 73-2
OTT, 97-12
LET ME INTRODUCE YOU TO THE FAMILY, Stranglers, 81-42
LET ME KNOW, Junior, 82-53
LET ME KNOW, Maxi Priest, 87-49
LET ME KNOW (I HAVE A RIGHT), Gloria Gaynor, 79-32
LET ME LET GO, Faith Hill, 99-72
LET ME LIVE, Queen, 96-9
LET ME LOVE YOU FOR TONIGHT, Kariya, 89-44
LET ME RIDE, Dr. Dre, 94-31
LET ME ROCK YOU, Kandidate, 80-58
LET ME SEE, Morcheeba, 98-46
LET ME SHOW YOU, K-Klass, 93-13
LET ME SHOW YOU, Camisra, 98-5
LET ME SHOW YOU, Tony Momrelle, 98-67
LET ME TAKE YOU THERE, Betty Boo, 92-12
LET ME TALK, Earth, Wind And Fire, 80-29
LET ME TRY AGAIN, Tammy Jones, 75-5
LET ME WAKE UP IN YOUR ARMS, Lulu, 93-51
LET MY LOVE OPEN THE DOOR, Pete Townshend, 80-46
LET MY NAME BE SORROW, Mary Hopkin, 71-46
LET MY PEOPLE GO, Winans, 85-71
LET MY PEOPLE GO-GO, Rainmakers, 87-18
LET ROBESON SING, Manic Street Preachers, 01-19
LET SOMEBODY LOVE YOU, Keni Burke, 81-59
LET THE BASS KICK, 2 For Joy, 91-67
LET THE BEAT CONTROL YOUR BODY, 2 Unlimited, 94-6
LET THE BEAT HIT 'EM:
Lisa Lisa and Cult Jam, 91-17, 91-49
Shena, 97-28
LET THE BEAT HIT 'EM PART 2 [RM], Lisa Lisa and Cult Jam, 91-49
LET THE CABLES SLEEP, Bush, 00-51
LET THE DAY BEGIN, Call, 89-42
LET THE FLAME BURN BRIGHTER, Graham Kendrick, 89-55
LET THE FREAK, Big Ron, 00-57
LET THE GOOD TIMES ROLL, Sheep On Drugs, 94-56
LET THE HAPPINESS IN, David Sylvian, 87-66
LET THE HEALING BEGIN, Joe Cocker, 94-32
LET THE HEARTACHES BEGIN, Long John Baldry, 67-1
LET THE LITTLE GIRL DANCE, Billy Bland, 60-15
LET THE LOVE, Q Tex, 96-30
LET THE MUSIC HEAL YOUR SOUL, Bravo All Stars, 98-36
LET THE MUSIC (LIFT YOU UP), Loveland featuring Rachel McFarlane vs. Darlene Lewis, 94-16
LET THE MUSIC MOVE U, Raze, 87-57
LET THE MUSIC PLAY, Barry White, 75-9, 00-45
LET THE MUSIC PLAY, Charles Earland, 78-46
LET THE MUSIC PLAY:
Shannon, 83-51, 84-14
BBG featuring Erin, 96-46
Mary Kiani, 96-19
LET THE MUSIC TAKE CONTROL, J.M. Silk, 87-47
LET THE MUSIC USE YOU, Nightwriters, 92-51
LET THE PEOPLE KNOW, Toploader, 99-52
LET THE RHYTHM MOVE YOU, Sharada House Gang, 96-50
LET THE RHYTHM PUMP, Doug Lazy, 89-45, 90-63
LET THE SUN SHINE IN, Peddlers, 65-50
LET THE WATER RUN DOWN, P.J. Proby, 65-19
LET THEM ALL TALK, Elvis Costello and the Attractions, 83-59
LET THERE BE DRUMS, Sandy Nelson, 61-3
LET THERE BE HOUSE, Deskee, 90-52
LET THERE BE LIGHT, Mike Oldfield, 95-51
LET THERE BE LOVE, Nat King Cole/The George Shearing Quintet, 62-11
LET THERE BE LOVE, Simple Minds, 91-6
LET THERE BE PEACE ON EARTH (LET IT BEGIN WITH ME), Michael Ward with the Mike Sammes Singers, 73-15
LET THERE BE ROCK, Onslaught, 89-50
LET THIS BE A PRAYER, Rollo Goes Spiritual with Pauline Taylor, 96-26
LET THIS FEELING, Simone Angel, 93-60
LET TRUE LOVE BEGIN, Nat King Cole, 61-29
LET U GO, ATB, 01-34
LET YOUR BODY GO, Tom Wilson, 96-60
LET YOUR BODY GO DOWNTOWN, Martyn Ford Orchestra, 77-38
LET YOUR HEART DANCE, Secret Affair, 79-32
LET YOUR LOVE FLOW, Bellamy Brothers, 76-7
LET YOUR SOUL BE YOUR PILOT, Sting, 96-15
LET YOUR YEAH BE YEAH:
Pioneers, 71-5
Ali Campbell, 95-25
LET YOURSELF GO, T-Connection, 78-52
LET YOURSELF GO, Sybil, 87-32
LET'S, Sarah Vaughan with Joe Reisman's Orchestra and Chorus, 60-37
LET'S ALL CHANT:
Michael Zager Band, 78-8
Mick and Pat, 88-11
Gusto, 96-21
(LET'S ALL GO BACK) DISCO NIGHTS, Jazz and the Brothers Grimm, 88-57
LET'S ALL GO (TO THE FIRE DANCES), Killing Joke, 83-51
LET'S ALL GO TOGETHER, Marion, 95-37
LET'S ALL SING LIKE THE BIRDIES SING, Tweets, 81-44
LET'S BE FRIENDS, Johnny Nash, 75-42
LET'S BE LOVERS TONIGHT, Sherrick, 87-63
LET'S CALL IT QUITS, Slade, 76-11
LET'S CELEBRATE, New York Skyy, 82-67
LET'S CLEAN UP THE GHETTO, Philadelphia International All Stars: Lou Rawls, Billy Paul, Archie Bell, Teddy Pendergrass, O'Jays, Dee Dee Sharp, Gamble, 77-34
LET'S DANCE:
Chris Montez, 62-2, 72-9, 79-47
Bruno and Liz and the Radio 1 DJ Posse, 90-54
LET'S DANCE, Bombers, 79-58
LET'S DANCE, David Bowie, 83-1
LET'S DANCE:
Chris Rea, 87-12
Middlesborough FC featuring Bob Mortimer and Chris Rea, 97-44
LET'S DANCE, Five, 01-1
LET'S DO IT AGAIN:
George Benson, 88-56
Lynden David Hall, 00-69
LETS DO ROCK STEADY, Bodysnatchers, 80-22
LET'S DO THE LATIN HUSTLE:
Eddie Drennon and B.B.S. Unlimited, 76-20
M. and O. Band, 76-16
LET'S FACE THE MUSIC AND DANCE, Nat King Cole, 94-30
LET'S FLY AWAY, Voyage, 79-38
LET'S FUNK TONIGHT, Blue Feather, 82-50
LET'S GET BACK TO BED – BOY!, Sarah Connor featuring TQ, 01-16
LET'S GET BRUTAL (ROK DA RADIO) [RM], Nitro Deluxe, 88-24
LET'S GET DIRTY (I CAN'T GET IN DA CLUB), Redman (featuring DJ Kool), 01-11
LET'S GET DOWN, Isotonik, 92-25
LET'S GET DOWN, Mark Morrison, 95-39
LET'S GET DOWN, Tony Toni Tone featuring DJ Quik, 97-33
LET'S GET DOWN, JT Playaz, 98-64
LET'S GET DOWN, Spacedust, 99-20
LET'S GET FUNKTIFIED, Boiling Point, 78-41
LET'S GET HAPPY, Mass Order, 92-45
LET'S GET IT ON, Marvin Gaye, 73-31
LET'S GET IT ON, Shabba Ranks, 95-22
LET'S GET IT ON, Big Boss Stylus presents Red Venom, 99-72
LET'S GET IT UP, AC/DC, 82-13
LET'S GET MARRIED, Proclaimers, 94-21
LET'S GET READY TO RHUMBLE, PJ and Duncan A.K.A., 94-9
LET'S GET ROCKED, Def Leppard, 92-2
LET'S GET SERIOUS, Jermaine Jackson, 80-8
LET'S GET TATTOOS, Carter – The Unstoppable Sex Machine, 94-30
LET'S GET THIS STRAIGHT (FROM THE START), Kevin Rowland and Dexys Midnight Runners, 82-17
LET'S GET TOGETHER, Hayley Mills, 61-17
LET'S GET TOGETHER, Alexander O'Neal, 96-38
LET'S GET TOGETHER AGAIN, Glitter Band, 74-8
LET'S GET TOGETHER AGAIN – NO. 1 [M], Big Ben Banjo Band, 55-18
LET'S GET TOGETHER (IN OUR MINDS), Gorky's Zygotic Mynci, 98-43
LET'S GET TOGETHER NO. 1 [M], Big Ben Banjo Band, 54-6
LET'S GET TOGETHER (SO GROOVY NOW), Krush Perspective, 93-61
LET'S GET TOGETHER TONITE, Steve Walsh, 87-74
LET'S GO, Cars, 79-51
LET'S GO, Vardis, 80-59
LET'S GO ALL THE WAY, Sly Fox, 86-3
LET'S GO CRAZY, Prince and the Revolution, 85-7
LET'S GO DISCO, Real Thing, 78-39
LET'S GO (PONY), Routers, 62-32
LET'S GO ROUND AGAIN:
Average White Band, 80-12, 94-56
Louise, 97-10
LET'S GO ROUND THERE, Darling Buds, 89-49
LET'S GO STEADY AGAIN, Neil Sedaka, 63-42
LET'S GO TO BED, Cure, 82-44
LET'S GO TO SAN FRANCISCO, Flower Pot Men, 67-4
LET'S GO TOGETHER, Change, 85-37
LET'S GROOVE:
Earth, Wind And Fire, 81-3
Phat 'N' Phunky, 97-61
LET'S GROOVE, George Morel featuring Heather Wildman, 96-42
LET'S HANG ON!:
4 Seasons featuring The "Sound" of Frankie Valli, 65-4
Bandwagon, 69-36
Darts, 80-11
Barry Manilow, 81-12
Shooting Party, 90-66
LET'S HAVE A BALL [M], Winifred Atwell and her Other Piano, 57-4
LET'S HAVE A DING DONG [M], Winifred Atwell and her Other Piano, 55-3
LET'S HAVE A PARTY:
Elvis Presley with the Jordanaires*, 57-2
Wanda Jackson, 60-32
LET'S HAVE A PARTY [M], Winifred Atwell and her "Other Piano", 53-2, 54-14
LET'S HAVE A QUIET NIGHT IN, David Soul, 77-8
LET'S HAVE ANOTHER PARTY [M], Winifred Atwell and her "Other Piano", 54-1
LET'S HEAR IT FOR THE BOY, Deniece Williams, 84-2
LET'S JUMP THE BROOMSTICK:
Brenda Lee, 61-12
Coast To Coast, 81-28
LET'S JUST CALL IT LOVE, Lisa Stansfield, 01-48
LET'S KILL MUSIC, Cooper Temple Clause, 01-41
LET'S LIVE IT UP (NITE PEOPLE), David Joseph, 83-26
LET'S LOVEDANCE TONIGHT, Gary's Gang, 79-49
LET'S MAKE A BABY, Billy Paul, 76-30
LET'S MAKE A NIGHT TO REMEMBER, Bryan Adams, 96-10
LET'S PARTY [M], Jive Bunny and the Mastermixers, 89-1
LET'S PLAY HOUSE, Kraze, 89-71
LET'S PRETEND, Lulu, 67-11
LET'S PUSH IT, Innocence, 90-25
LET'S PUSH IT, Nightcrawlers featuring John Reid, 96-23
LET'S PUT IT ALL TOGETHER, Stylistics, 74-9
LET'S RIDE, Montell Jordan featuring Master P and Silkk "The Shocker", 98-25
LET'S ROCK, E-Trax, 01-60
LET'S ROCK 'N' ROLL [M], Winifred Atwell and her Other Piano, 57-24
LET'S SEE ACTION, Who, 71-16
LET'S SLIP AWAY, Cleo Laine, 60-42
LET'S SPEND THE NIGHT TOGETHER :
Rolling Stones, 67-3
Mash!, 95-66
LET'S START OVER, Pamela Fernandez, 95-59
LET'S START THE DANCE, Hamilton Bohannon, 78-56
LET'S START TO DANCE AGAIN, Hamilton Bohannon, 82-49

LIQUID COOL, Apollo 440, 94-35
LIQUID DREAMS, O-Town, 01-3
LIQUID IS LIQUID (from THE FUTURE MUSIC [EP]), Liquid, 92-59
LIQUIDATOR, Harry J. All Stars, 69-9, 80-42
LISTEN, Urban Species featuring MC Solaar, 94-47
LISTEN [EP] + lead track title, Stiff Little Fingers, 82-33
LISTEN LIKE THIEVES:
Inxs, 86-46
Was (Not Was), 92-58
LISTEN LITTLE GIRL, Keith Kelly, 60-47
LISTEN TO ME, Buddy Holly, 58-16, 62-48
LISTEN TO ME, Hollies, 68-11
LISTEN TO THE MUSIC, Doobie Brothers, 74-29, 94-37
LISTEN TO THE OCEAN, Nina and Frederik; Jorn Grauengaard and his Orchestra, 60-46
LISTEN TO THE RADIO: ATMOSPHERICS, Tom Robinson, 83-39
LISTEN TO THE RHYTHM, K3m, 92-71
LISTEN TO THE RHYTHM FLOW, G.T.O., 91-72
LISTEN TO WHAT THE MAN SAID, Wings, 75-6
LISTEN TO YOUR FATHER, Feargal Sharkey, 84-23
LISTEN TO YOUR HEART, Roxette, 89-62
LISTEN TO YOUR HEART, Sonia, 89-10, 90-6
LITHIUM, Nirvana, 92-11
LITTLE ARITHMETICS, Deus, 96-44
LITTLE ARROWS, Leapy Lee, 68-2
LITTLE BABY NOTHING, Manic Street Preachers, 92-29, 97-50
LITTLE BAND OF GOLD, James Gilreath, 63-29
LITTLE BERNADETTE, Belafonte, 58-16
LITTLE BIRD, Annie Lennox, 93-3
A LITTLE BIT FURTHER AWAY, Kokomo, 82-45
A LITTLE BIT ME, A LITTLE BIT YOU, Monkees, 67-3
A LITTLE BIT MORE:
Dr. Hook, 76-2, 92-47
911, 99-1
A LITTLE BIT MORE, Kym Sims, 92-30
LITTLE BIT OF HEAVEN, Lisa Stansfield, 93-32
LITTLE BIT OF LOVE, Free, 72-13
LITTLE BIT OF LOVIN', Kele Le Roc, 98-8
A LITTLE BIT OF LUCK, DJ Luck and MC Neat, 99-9
LITTLE BIT OF SNOW, Howard Jones, 87-70
A LITTLE BIT OF SOAP, Showaddywaddy, 78-5
A LITTLE BITTY TEAR:
Burl Ives, 62-9
Miki and Griff, 62-16
LITTLE BLACK BOOK, Jimmy Dean, 62-33
LITTLE BLACK BOOK, Belinda Carlisle, 92-28
LITTLE BLUEBIRD, Vince Hill, 69-42
A LITTLE BOOGIE WOOGIE IN THE BACK OF MY MIND:
Gary Glitter, 77-31
Shakin' Stevens, 87-12
LITTLE BOY LOST, Michael Holliday, 60-50
LITTLE BOY SAD, Johnny Burnette, 61-12
LITTLE BRITAIN, Dreadzone, 96-20
LITTLE BROTHER, Blue Pearl, 90-31
LITTLE BROWN JUG, Glenn Miller and his Orchestra, 76-13
LITTLE BY LITTLE, Dusty Springfield, 66-17
LITTLE CHILD, Des'ree, 94-69
LITTLE CHILDREN, Billy J. Kramer with the Dakotas, 64-1
LITTLE CHRISTINE, Dick Jordan, 60-39
LITTLE DARLIN', Diamonds, 57-3
LITTLE DARLIN' (I NEED YOU), Marvin Gaye, 66-50
LITTLE DARLING, Rubettes, 75-30
LITTLE DEVIL, Neil Sedaka with Stan Applebaum and his Orchestra, 61-9, 72-19
LITTLE DISCOURAGE, Idlewild, 99-24
LITTLE DOES SHE KNOW, Kursaal Flyers, 76-14
LITTLE DONKEY:
Gracie Fields with the Rita Williams Singers, 59-21
Beverley Sisters, 59-14
Nina and Frederik with the Jorn Grauengaard Quintet, 60-3
LITTLE DROPS OF SILVER, Gerry Monroe, 71-37
THE LITTLE DRUMMER BOY:
Beverley Sisters, 59-6
Harry Simeone Chorale, 59-13
Michael Flanders with the Michael Sammes Singers, 59-20
Pipes and Drums and Military Band of the Royal Scots Dragoon Guards, 72-13
Rupaul, 94-61
LITTLE 15, Depeche Mode, 88-60
LITTLE FLUFFY CLOUDS, Orb, 93-10
LITTLE GIRL, Marty Wilde, 60-16
LITTLE GIRL, Troggs, 68-37
LITTLE GIRL, Banned, 77-36
LITTLE GIRL LOST, Icicle Works, 88-59
LITTLE GREEN APPLES, Roger Miller, 68-19
A LITTLE IN LOVE, Cliff Richard, 81-15
LITTLE JEANIE, Elton John, 80-33
LITTLE L, Jamiroquai, 01-5
LITTLE LADY, Aneka, 81-50
LITTLE LIES, Fleetwood Mac, 87-5
LITTLE LOST SOMETIMES, Almighty, 91-42
A LITTLE LOVE, A LITTLE KISS, Karl Denver, 62-19
A LITTLE LOVE AND UNDERSTANDING, Gilbert Becaud, 75-10
A LITTLE LOVIN', Neil Sedaka, 74-34
A LITTLE LOVING, Fourmost, 64-6
LITTLE MAN, Sonny and Cher, 66-4
LITTLE MIRACLES (HAPPEN EVERY DAY), Luther Vandross, 93-28
LITTLE MISS CAN'T BE WRONG, Spin Doctors, 93-23
LITTLE MISS LONELY, Helen Shapiro with Martin Slavin and his Orchestra, 62-8
A LITTLE MORE LOVE, Olivia Newton-John, 78-4
A LITTLE PEACE, Nicole, 82-1
A LITTLE PIECE OF LEATHER, Donnie Elbert, 72-27
LITTLE PINK STARS, Radish, 97-32
LITTLE RED CORVETTE, Prince, 83-54, 83-66, 85-2
LITTLE RED MONKEY, Frank Chacksfield's Tunesmiths with Jack Jordan (Clavioline), 53-10
LITTLE RED ROOSTER, Rolling Stones, 64-1
A LITTLE RESPECT:
Erasure, 88-4
Bjorn Again (from Erasure-Ish – (A Little Respect/Stop!)), 92-25
Wheatus, 01-3
A LITTLE SAMBA, Ugly Duckling, 01-70
LITTLE SERENADE (PICCOLISSIMA SERENATA), Eddie Calvert (The Man with the Golden Trumpet), 58-28
THE LITTLE SHOEMAKER (LE PETIT CORDONNIER), Petula Clark with Malcolm Lockyer and his Orchestra, 54-7
LITTLE SISTER, Elvis Presley, 61-1
A LITTLE SOUL, Pulp, 98-22
LITTLE STAR, Elegants, 58-25
LITTLE STAR, Madonna, 98-6
LITTLE THINGS, Dave Berry, 65-5
LITTLE THINGS MEAN A LOT:
Kitty Kallen, 54-1
Alma Cogan, 54-11
A LITTLE TIME, Beautiful South, 90-1
LITTLE TOWN, Cliff Richard featuring Tony Rivers and Nigel Perrin, 82-11
LITTLE TOWN FLIRT, Del Shannon, 63-4
LITTLE TRAIN, Max Bygraves, 58-28
LITTLE WHITE BERRY, Roy Castle, 60-40
LITTLE WHITE BULL, Tommy Steele, 59-6
LITTLE WHITE LIES, Status Quo, 99-47
LITTLE WILLY, Sweet, 72-4
LITTLE WONDER, David Bowie, 97-14
A LITTLE YOU, Freddie and the Dreamers, 65-26
LIVE AND LEARN, Joe Public, 92-43
LIVE AND LET DIE:
Wings, 73-9
Guns N' Roses, 91-5
LIVE AT T.F.I. FRIDAY [EP], Sting, 96-53
LIVE AT THE MARQUEE [EP], Eddie and the Hotrods, 76-43
LIVE [EP], Barclay James Harvest, 77-49
LIVE FOR LOVING YOU, Gloria Estefan, 91-33
LIVE FOR THE ONE I LOVE, Tina Arena, 00-63
LIVE FOREVER, Oasis, 94-10, 95-50, 96-42
LIVE IN MANCHESTER, N-Joi, 92-12
LIVE IN THE SKY, Dave Clark Five, 68-39
LIVE IN TROUBLE [M], Barron Knights, 77-7
LIVE IS LIFE, Opus, 85-6
LIVE IT UP, Mental As Anything, 87-3
LIVE LIKE HORSES, Elton John and Luciano Pavarotti, 96-9
LIVE MY LIFE, Boy George, 88-62
LIVE THE DREAM, Cast, 97-7
LIVE TO TELL, Madonna, 86-2
LIVE TOGETHER, Lisa Stansfield, 90-10
LIVE YOUR LIFE BE FREE, Belinda Carlisle, 91-12
LIVELY, Lonnie Donegan and his Group, 60-13
LIVERPOOL (ANTHEM), Liverpool Football Club, 83-54
LIVERPOOL LOU, Scaffold, 74-7
LIVERPOOL (WE'RE NEVER GONNA STOP), Liverpool Football Club, 83-54
LIVIN' IN THE LIGHT, Caron Wheeler, 90-14
LIVIN' IN THE WORLD, Guru, 96-61
LIVIN' IT UP, Northern Uproar, 96-24
LIVIN' IT UP, Ja Rule (featuring Case), 01-27
LIVIN' IT UP (FRIDAY NIGHT), Bell and James, 79-59
LIVIN' LA VIDA LOCA, Ricky Martin, 99-1
LIVIN' LOVIN' DOLL, Cliff Richard and the Drifters, 59-20
LIVIN' ON A PRAYER, Bon Jovi, 86-4
LIVIN' ON THE EDGE, Aerosmith, 93-19
LIVIN' ON THE EDGE OF THE NIGHT, Iggy Pop, 90-51
LIVIN' THING, Electric Light Orchestra, 76-4
LIVING AFTER MIDNIGHT, Judas Priest, 80-12
LIVING BY NUMBERS, New Musik, 80-13
THE LIVING DAYLIGHTS, A-Ha, 87-5
LIVING DOLL:
Cliff Richard and the Drifters, 59-1
Comic Relief presents Cliff Richard and the Young Ones featuring Hank Marvin, 86-1
THE LIVING DREAM, Sundance, 99-56
LIVING FOR THE CITY:
Stevie Wonder, 74-15
Gillan, 82-50
LIVING FOR YOU, Sonny and Cher, 66-44
LIVING IN A BOX:
Living In A Box, 87-5
Bobby Womack, 87-70
LIVING IN A FANTASY, Urban Hype, 93-57
LIVING IN A WORLD (TURNED UPSIDE DOWN), Private Lives, 84-53
LIVING IN AMERICA, James Brown, 86-5
LIVING IN ANOTHER WORLD, Talk Talk, 86-48
LIVING IN DANGER, Ace Of Base, 95-18
LIVING IN HARMONY, Cliff Richard, 72-12
LIVING IN SIN, Bon Jovi, 89-35
LIVING IN THE PAST:
Jethro Tull, 69-3
Jethro Tull *, 93-32
LIVING IN THE PAST, Drum Theatre, 86-67
LIVING IN THE ROSE (THE BALLADS EP) [EP] + lead track title, New Model Army, 93-51
LIVING IN THE SUNSHINE, Clubhouse featuring Carl, 94-21
LIVING IN THE U.K., Shakatak, 81-52
LIVING NEXT DOOR TO ALICE:
Smokie, 76-5
Smokie featuring Roy Chubby Brown *, 95-3
Gompie *, 95-17
LIVING ON AN ISLAND, Status Quo, 79-16
LIVING ON MY OWN, Freddie Mercury, 85-50, 93-1
LIVING ON THE CEILING, Blancmange, 82-7
LIVING ON THE FRONT LINE, Eddy Grant, 79-11, 83-47
LIVING ON VIDEO ('85 RE-MIX), Trans-X, 85-9
LIVING WITH THE HUMAN MACHINES, Strangelove, 96-53
THE LIVING YEARS, Mike and the Mechanics, 89-2
LIZARD (GONNA GET YOU), Mauro Picotto, 99-27, 99-33
LOADED, Primal Scream, 90-16
LOADED, Ricky Martin, 01-19
LOADSAMONEY (DOIN' UP THE HOUSE), Harry Enfield, 88-4
LOBSTER & SCRIMP, Timbaland featuring Jay-Z, 99-48
LOCAL BOY IN THE PHOTOGRAPH, Stereophonics, 97-51, 98-14
LOC'ED AFTER DARK, Tone Loc, 89-21
LOCK AND LOAD, Bob Seger and the Silver Bullet Band, 96-57
LOCK UP (first entry from THE E.P. (BRAND NEW MIXES) [EP]; second entry from RECONNECTION [EP]), Zero B, 92-32, 93-54

LOST IN MUSIC, Stereo MC's, 91-46
LOST IN SPACE, Electrasy, 98-60
LOST IN SPACE, Lighthouse Family, 98-6
LOST IN SPACE (THEME), Apollofourforty, 98-4
LOST IN THE TRANSLATION (HEART OF GLASS), Pacifica, 99-54
LOST IN YOU, Rod Stewart, 88-21
LOST IN YOU, Garth Brooks as Chris Gaines, 99-70
LOST IN YOUR EYES, Debbie Gibson, 89-34
LOST IN YOUR LOVE, Tony Hadley, 92-42
LOST JOHN, Lonnie Donegan Skiffle Group, 56-2
LOST MYSELF, Longpigs, 96-22
LOST WEEKEND, Lloyd Cole and the Commotions, 85-17
LOST WITHOUT YOU, Jayn Hanna, 97-44
LOST WITHOUT YOUR LOVE, Bread, 76-27
LOST YOU SOMEWHERE, Chicane, 97-35
A LOT OF SWEARING AND CUSSING (from WIBBLING RIVALRY), Oas*s, 95-52
LOTUS, R.E.M., 98-26
LOUIE LOUIE:
Kingsmen, 64-26
Motorhead, 78-68
Fat Boys, 88-46
Three Amigos, 99-15
LOUIS QUATORZE (first entry from YOUR CASSETTE PET [EP]), Bow Wow Wow, 80-58, 82-66
LOUISE, Phil Everly, 82-47
LOUISE, Human League, 84-13
L'OUISEAU ET L'ENFANT, Marie Myriam, 77-42
LOUNGIN, LL Cool J, 96-7
LOVE (from EXPRESSO BONGO [EP]), Cliff Richard and the Shadows, 60-14
LOVE:
John Lennon, 82-41
Jimmy Nail, 95-33
LOVE ACTION (I BELIEVE IN LOVE), Human League Red, 81-3
LOVE AIN'T HERE ANYMORE, Take That, 94-3
LOVE AIN'T NO STRANGER, Whitesnake, 85-44
LOVE ALL DAY, Nick Heyward, 84-31
LOVE ALL THE HURT AWAY, Aretha Franklin and George Benson, 81-49
LOVE AND AFFECTION:
Joan Armatrading, 76-10
Sinitta, 90-62
LOVE AND ANGER, Kate Bush, 90-38
LOVE AND DESIRE, Arpeggio, 79-63
LOVE & DEVOTION, Real McCoy, 95-11
LOVE AND HAPPINESS (YEMAYA Y OCHUN), River Ocean featuring India, 94-50
LOVE AND KISSES, Dannii Minogue, 91-8
LOVE AND LONELINESS, Motors, 80-58
LOVE AND MARRIAGE ("OUR TOWN"), Frank Sinatra, 56-3
LOVE AND MONEY, Love and Money, 87-68
LOVE AND PAIN, Carlton, 91-56
LOVE AND PRIDE, King, 85-2
LOVE AND REGRET, Deacon Blue, 89-28
LOVE AND TEARS, Naomi Campbell, 94-40
LOVE AND UNDERSTANDING, Cher, 91-10
LOVE ANYWAY, Mike Scott, 97-50
LOVE AT FIRST SIGHT (JE T'AIME . . . MOI NON PLUS), Sounds Nice featuring Tim Mycroft On Organ, 69-18
LOVE ATTACK, Shakin' Stevens, 89-28
LOVE BALLAD, George Benson, 79-29
LOVE BITES, Def Leppard, 88-11
LOVE BLONDE, Kim Wilde, 83-23
LOVE BOMB BABY, Tigertailz, 89-75
LOVE BREAKDOWN, Rozalla, 92-65
LOVE BUG, Ramsey and Fen featuring Lynsey Moore, 00-75
LOVE BUG – SWEETS FOR MY SWEET [M], Tina Charles, 77-26
LOVE CAN BUILD A BRIDGE:
Children For Rwanda, 94-57
Cher, Chrissie Hynde and Neneh Cherry with Eric Clapton, 95-1
LOVE CAN MOVE MOUNTAINS, Celine Dion, 92-46
LOVE CAN'T TURN AROUND:
Farley "Jackmaster" Funk and Jessie Saunders, 86-10, 96-40
Heavy Weather, 96-56
THE LOVE CATS, Cure, 83-7
LOVE CHANGES (EVERYTHING), Climie Fisher, 87-67, 88-2
LOVE CHANGES EVERYTHING, Michael Ball, 89-2
LOVE CHILD, Diana Ross and the Supremes, 68-15
LOVE CHILD, Goodbye Mr. MacKenzie, 90-52
LOVE CITY GROOVE, Love City Groove, 95-7
LOVE COME DOWN:
Evelyn King, 82-7
Alison Limerick, 94-36
LOVE COME DOWN:
Eve Gallagher, 90-61
Eve Gallagher, 95-57
LOVE COME HOME, Our Tribe with Franke Pharoah and Kristine W, 94-73
LOVE COME RESCUE ME, Lovestation, 95-42
LOVE COMES QUICKLY, Pet Shop Boys, 86-19
LOVE COMES TO MIND, Chimes, 90-49
LOVE COMMANDMENTS, Gisele Jackson, 97-54
LOVE CONQUERS ALL, Deep Purple, 91-57
LOVE CONQUERS ALL, ABC, 91-47
LOVE DANCE, Vision, 83-74
LOVE DETECTIVE – MOTION PICTURE SOUNDTRACK, Arab Strap, 01-66
LOVE DISCO STYLE, Erotic Drum Band, 79-47
LOVE DON'T COME EASY, Alarm, 90-48
LOVE DON'T COST A THING, Jennifer Lopez, 01-1
LOVE DON'T LIVE, Urban Blues Project present Michael Procter, 96-55
LOVE DON'T LIVE HERE ANYMORE:
Rose Royce, 78-2
Jimmy Nail, 85-3
Double Trouble vocals – Janette Sewell voice-overs – Carl Brown, 90-21
LOVE DON'T LOVE YOU, En Vogue, 93-64
LOVE ENOUGH FOR TWO, Prima Donna, 80-48
LOVE ENUFF, Soul II Soul, 95-12
LOVE EVICTION, Quartz Lock featuring Lonnie Gordon, 95-32
LOVE FANTASY (from ENTER YOUR FANTASY [EP]), Joey Negro vocals by: Jannette Saul and Debbie French, 92-35
LOVE FOR LIFE, Lisa Moorish, 96-37
LOVE FOR SALE (from MONTREUX [EP]), Simply Red, 92-11
THE LOVE GAME, Mudlarks with the Ken Jones Group, 59-30
LOVE GAMES, Drifters, 75-33
LOVE GAMES, Level 42, 81-38
LOVE GAMES, Belle and the Devotions, 84-11
LOVE GLOVE, Visage, 84-54
LOVE GROOVE (GROOVE WITH YOU), Smooth, 96-46
LOVE GROWS (WHERE MY ROSEMARY GOES), Edison Lighthouse, 70-1
LOVE GUARANTEED, Damage, 97-7
LOVE HANGOVER:
Diana Ross, 76-10, 88-75
Associates, 82-21
Pauline Henry, 95-37
LOVE HANGOVER, Scarlet, 95-54
LOVE HAS COME AGAIN, Human Movement featuring Sophie Moleta, 01-53
LOVE HAS COME AROUND, Donald Byrd, 81-41
LOVE HAS FOUND ITS WAY, Dennis Brown, 82-47
LOVE HAS PASSED AWAY, Supernaturals, 97-38
LOVE HER, Walker Bros., 65-20
LOVE HERE I COME, Bad Boys Inc, 94-26
LOVE HIT ME, Maxine Nightingale, 77-11
LOVE HOUSE, Samantha Fox, 88-32
LOVE HOW YOU FEEL, Sharon Redd, 83-39
LOVE HURTS:
Jim Capaldi, 75-4
Nazareth (from Hot Tracks [EP]), 77-15
Cher, 91-43
LOVE HURTS, Peter Polycarpou, 93-26
THE LOVE I LOST:
Harold Melvin and the Bluenotes, 74-21
West End featuring Sybil, 93-3
LOVE IN A PEACEFUL WORLD, Level 42, 94-31
LOVE IN AN ELEVATOR, Aerosmith, 89-13
LOVE IN ANGER, Armoury Show, 87-63
LOVE IN 'C' MINOR, Cerrone, 77-31
LOVE IN ITSELF . 2, Depeche Mode, 83-21
LOVE IN THE FIRST DEGREE, Bananarama, 87-3
LOVE IN THE KEY OF C, Belinda Carlisle, 96-20
LOVE IN THE NATURAL WAY, Kim Wilde, 89-32
LOVE IN THE SUN, Glitter Band, 75-15
THE LOVE IN YOUR EYES:
Vicky Leandros, 72-40
Daniel O'Donnell, 93-47
LOVE INFINITY, Silver City, 93-62
LOVE INJECTION, Trussel, 80-43
LOVE INSIDE, Sharon Forrester, 95-50
LOVE IS . . ., Vikki, 85-49
LOVE IS, Alannah Myles, 90-61
LOVE IS A BATTLEFIELD, Pat Benatar, 84-49, 85-17
LOVE IS A BEAUTIFUL THING, Al Green, 93-56
LOVE IS A GOLDEN RING, Frankie Laine with the Easy Riders, 57-19
LOVE IS A KILLER, Vixen, 90-41
LOVE IS A MANY SPLENDOURED THING, Four Aces featuring Al Alberts, 55-2
LOVE IS A STRANGER, Eurythmics, 82-54, 83-6, 91-46
LOVE IS A WONDERFUL THING, Michael Bolton, 91-23
LOVE IS ALL:
Malcolm Roberts, 69-12
Engelbert Humperdinck, 73-44
LOVE IS ALL AROUND:
Troggs, 67-5
Wet Wet Wet, 94-1
LOVE IS ALL AROUND, D.J. Bobo, 95-49
LOVE IS ALL IS ALRIGHT, UB40, 82-29
LOVE IS ALL THAT MATTERS, Human League, 88-41
LOVE IS ALL WE NEED, Mary J. Blige, 97-15
LOVE IS BLUE, Edward Ball, 97-59
LOVE IS BLUE (L'AMOUR EST BLEU):
Paul Mauriat and his Orchestra, 68-12
Jeff Beck, 68-23
LOVE IS CONTAGIOUS, Taja Sevelle, 88-7
LOVE IS EVERYWHERE, Cicero, 92-19
LOVE IS FOREVER, Billy Ocean, 87-34
LOVE IS HERE AND NOW YOU'RE GONE, Supremes, 67-17
LOVE IS HOLY, Kim Wilde, 92-16
LOVE IS IN CONTROL (FINGER ON THE TRIGGER), Donna Summer, 82-18
LOVE IS IN THE AIR, John Paul Young, 78-5, 92-49
LOVE IS IN YOUR EYES, Lemon Trees, 92-75
LOVE IS JUST THE GREAT PRETENDER '85, Animal Nightlife, 85-28
LOVE IS LIFE, Hot Chocolate, 70-6
LOVE IS LIKE A VIOLIN, Ken Dodd, 60-8
LOVE IS LIKE OXYGEN, Sweet, 78-9
LOVE IS LOVE, Barry Ryan with the Majority, 69-25
LOVE IS NOT A GAME, J. Malik featuring Kathy Brown, 01-34
LOVE IS ON THE ONE, Xavier featuring George Clinton and Bootsy Collins, 82-53
LOVE IS ON THE WAY (REAL LOVE), Luther Vandross, 93-38
LOVE IS SO EASY, Stargard, 78-45
LOVE IS SO NICE, Urban Soul, 98-75
LOVE IS STRANGE:
Everly Brothers, 65-11
Everything But The Girl (from Covers [EP]), 92-13
LOVE IS STRONG, Rolling Stones, 94-14
LOVE IS STRONGER THAN DEATH, The, 93-39
LOVE IS STRONGER THAN PRIDE, Sade, 88-44
LOVE IS SUCH A WONDERFUL COLOUR, Icicle Works, 83-15
LOVE IS THE ANSWER, England Dan and John Ford Coley, 79-45
LOVE IS THE ART, Living In A Box, 88-45
LOVE IS THE DRUG:
Roxy Music, 75-2, 96-33
Grace Jones, 86-35
LOVE IS THE GOD, Maria Nayler, 98-65
LOVE IS THE GUN, Blue Mercedes, 88-46
LOVE IS THE ICON, Barry White, 95-20
LOVE IS THE KEY, Charlatans, 01-16
LOVE IS THE LAW, Seahorses, 97-3
LOVE IS THE MESSAGE, Love Inc featuring M.C. Noise, 91-59
LOVE IS THE SEVENTH WAVE (NEW MIX), Sting, 85-41
LOVE IS THE SLUG, We've Got A Fuzzbox and We're Gonna Use It, 86-31
LOVE IS THE SWEETEST THING, Peter Skellern featuring The Grimethorpe Colliery Band, 78-60

LOVE YOU DOWN, Ready For The World, 87-60
LOVE YOU INSIDE OUT, Bee Gees, 79-13
LOVE YOU MORE, Buzzcocks, 78-34
THE LOVE YOU SAVE, Jackson 5, 70-7
LOVE YOU SOME MORE, Cevin Fisher featuring Sheila Smith, 01-60
LOVE YOUR MONEY, Daisy Chainsaw, 92-26
LOVE YOUR SEXY . . .!!, Byker Grooove!, 94-48
LOVE'S A LOADED GUN, Alice Cooper, 91-38
LOVE'S ABOUT TO CHANGE MY HEART, Donna Summer, 89-20
LOVE'S BEEN GOOD TO ME, Frank Sinatra, 69-8
LOVE'S COMIN' AT YA, Melba Moore, 82-15
LOVE'S CRASHING WAVES, Difford and Tilbrook, 84-57
LOVE'S EASY TEARS, Cocteau Twins, 86-53
LOVE'S GONNA GET YOU, UK Players, 83-52
LOVE'S GONNA GET YOU, Jocelyn Brown, 86-70
LOVE'S GOT A HOLD ON ME, Zoo Experience – featuring Destry, 92-66
LOVE'S GOT A HOLD ON MY HEART, Steps, 99-2
LOVE'S GOT ME, Loose Ends, 90-40
LOVE'S GOT ME ON A TRIP SO HIGH, Loni Clark, 94-59
LOVE'S GOTTA HOLD ON ME, Dollar, 79-4
LOVE'S GREAT ADVENTURE, Ultravox, 84-12
LOVE'S JUST A BROKEN HEART, Cilla Black, 66-5
LOVE'S MADE A FOOL OF YOU:
Crickets, 59-26
Buddy Holly, 64-39
Matchbox, 81-63
LOVE'S ON EVERY CORNER, Dannii Minogue, 92-44
LOVE'S SUCH A WONDERFUL THING, Real Thing, 77-33
LOVE'S SWEET EXILE, Manic Street Preachers, 91-26, 97-55
LOVE'S TAKEN OVER, Chante Moore, 93-54
LOVE'S THEME, Love Unlimited Orchestra, 74-10
LOVE'S UNKIND:
Donna Summer, 77-3
Sophie Lawrence, 91-21
LOVE ZONE, Billy Ocean, 86-49
LOVEBIRDS, Dodgy, 93-65
LOVEDRIVE, Scorpions, 79-69
LOVEFOOL, Cardigans, 96-21, 97-2
LOVELIGHT (RIDE ON A LOVE TRAIN), Jayn Hanna, 96-42
LOVELY DAUGHTER, Merz, 99-60
LOVELY DAY:
Bill Withers, 78-7, 88-4
S.O.U.L. S.Y.S.T.E.M. introducing Michelle Visage *, 93-17
Jazzy Jeff and Fresh Prince *, 98-37
LOVELY DAZE, Jazzy Jeff and Fresh Prince, 98-37
LOVELY HEAD, Goldfrapp, 01-68
LOVELY MONEY, Damned, 82-42
LOVELY ONE, Jacksons, 80-29
LOVELY THING, Reggae Philharmonic Orchestra featuring Jazzy Joyce, 90-71
LOVENEST, Wedding Present, 91-58
LOVER, Dan Reed Network, 90-45
LOVER, Joe Roberts, 94-22
LOVER, Rachel McFarlane, 98-38
LOVER BOY, Chairmen Of The Board featuring General Johnson, 86-56
LOVER COME BACK TO ME, Dead Or Alive, 85-11
THE LOVER IN ME, Sheena Easton, 89-15
THE LOVER IN YOU, Sugarhill Gang, 82-54
LOVER LOVER LOVER, Ian McCulloch, 92-47
LOVER PLEASE, Vernons Girls, 62-16
A LOVER SPURNED, Marc Almond, 90-29
THE LOVER THAT YOU ARE, Pulse featuring Antoinette Roberson, 96-22
A LOVER'S CONCERTO, Toys, 65-5
A LOVER'S HOLIDAY, Change, 80-14
LOVER'S LANE, Georgio, 88-54
LOVERBOY, Billy Ocean, 85-15
LOVERBOY, Mariah Carey featuring Cameo, 01-12
LOVERIDE, Nuance featuring Vikki Love, 85-59
THE LOVERS, Alexander O'Neal, 88-28
LOVERS OF THE WORLD UNITE, David and Jonathan, 66-7
THE LOVERS WE WERE, Michael Ball, 94-63
LOVESICK, Gang Starr, 91-50
LOVESICK, Undercover featuring John Matthews, 93-62
LOVESICK BLUES, Frank Ifield with Norrie Paramor and his Orchestra, 62-1
LOVESONG, Cure, 89-18
LOVESTRUCK, Madness, 99-10
LOVETOWN, Peter Gabriel, 94-49
LOVEY DOVEY, Tony Terry, 88-44
LOVIN', CRW, 00-49
LOVIN' EACH DAY, Ronan Keating, 01-2
LOVIN' (LET ME LOVE YOU), Apache Indian, 97-53
LOVIN' ON THE SIDE, Reid, 89-71
LOVIN' THINGS, Marmalade, 68-6
LOVIN' UP A STORM, Jerry Lee Lewis, 59-28
LOVIN' YOU:
Minnie Riperton, 75-2
Massivo featuring Tracy, 90-25
Shanice, 92-54
UBM, 98-46
Sparkle, 99-65
LOVIN' YOU AIN'T EASY, Pagliaro, 72-31
LOVIN', LIVIN' AND GIVIN', Diana Ross, 78-54
LOVING AND FREE, Kiki Dee, 76-13
LOVING ARMS, Elvis Presley, 81-47
LOVING EVERY MINUTE, Lighthouse Family, 96-20
LOVING JUST FOR FUN, Kelly Marie, 80-21
LOVING ON THE LOSING SIDE, Tommy Hunt, 76-28
LOVING THE ALIEN, David Bowie, 85-19
LOVING YOU, Elvis Presley with the Jordanaires, 57-24
LOVING YOU, Donald Byrd, 81-41
LOVING YOU, Chris Rea, 82-65
LOVING YOU, Feargal Sharkey, 85-26
LOVING YOU AGAIN, Chris Rea, 87-47
LOVING YOU HAS MADE ME BANANAS, Guy Marks, 78-25
LOVING YOU IS SWEETER THAN EVER:
Four Tops, 66-21
Nick Kamen, 87-16
LOVING YOU MORE, B.T. featuring Vincent Covello, 95-28, 96-14
LOVING YOU (OLE OLE OLE), Brian Harvey and the Refugee Crew, 01-20
LOVING YOU'S A DIRTY JOB BUT SOMEBODY'S GOTTA DO IT, Bonnie Tyler, Guest vocalist Todd Rundgren, 85-73
LOW, Cracker, 94-43
LOW FIVE, Sneaker Pimps, 99-39
LOW LIFE IN HIGH PLACES, Thunder, 92-22
LOW RIDER, War, 76-12
LOWDOWN:
Boz Scaggs, 76-28
Hindsight, 87-62
LOWDOWN, Electrafixion, 95-54
LOWRIDER, Cypress Hill, 01-33
THE LOYALISER, Fatima Mansions, 94-58
LUCAS WITH THE LID OFF, Lucas, 94-37
LUCHINI AKA (THIS IS IT), Camp Lo, 97-74
LUCILLE:
Little Richard and his Band, 57-10
Everly Brothers, 60-4
LUCILLE, Kenny Rogers, 77-1
LUCKY (from HELP [EP]), Radiohead – See Various Artists (EPs), 95-51
LUCKY, Britney Spears, 00-5
LUCKY DEVIL:
Frank Ifield, 60-22
Carl Dobkins Jr., 60-44
LUCKY FIVE, Russ Conway, 60-14
LUCKY LIPS, Cliff Richard and the Shadows, 63-4
LUCKY LOVE, Ace Of Base, 95-20
LUCKY LUCKY ME, Marvin Gaye, 94-67
LUCKY MAN, Verve, 97-7
LUCKY NUMBER, Lene Lovich, 79-3
THE LUCKY ONE, Laura Branigan, 84-56
LUCKY ONE, Amy Grant, 94-60
LUCKY PRESSURE, Roni Size Reprazent, 01-58
THE LUCKY 7 MEGAMIX [M], UK Mixmasters, 91-43
LUCKY STAR, Madonna, 84-14
LUCKY STAR, Superfunk featuring Ron Carroll, 00-42
LUCKY STARS, Dean Friedman, 78-3
LUCKY TOWN (LIVE), Bruce Springsteen, 93-48
LUCKY YOU, Lightning Seeds, 94-43, 95-15
LUCRETIA MY REFLECTION, Sisters Of Mercy, 88-20
LUCY, Habit, 88-56
LUCY IN THE SKY WITH DIAMONDS, Elton John, 74-10
LUDI, Dream Warriors, 91-39
LUKA, Suzanne Vega, 87-23
LULLABY, Cure, 89-5
LULLABY, Shawn Mullins, 99-9
LULLABY, Melanie B, 01-13
LULLABY, Starsailor, 01-36
LULLABY NO. 2 LOVE ON BOARD (from THE FRIENDS AGAIN [EP]), Friends Again, 84-59
LULLABY OF BROADWAY, Winifred Shaw, 76-42
LULLABY OF THE LEAVES, Ventures, 61-43
LUMBERED, Lonnie Donegan and his Group, 61-6
LUMP, Presidents Of The United States Of America, 96-15
THE LUNATICS (HAVE TAKEN OVER THE ASYLUM), Fun Boy Three, 81-20
LUNCH OR DINNER, Sunshine Anderson, 01-57
LUSH 3, Orbital, 93-43
LUST FOR LIFE, Iggy Pop, 96-26
LUTON AIRPORT, Cats U.K., 79-22
LUV DUP, High Fidelity, 98-70
LUV 4 LUV, Robin S, 93-11
LUV ME, LUV ME, Shaggy, 01-5
LUV'D UP, Crush, 96-45
LUVSTRUCK, Southside Spinners, 00-9
LUVSTUFF, Sagat, 94-71
LYDIA, Dean Friedman, 78-31
LYIN' EYES, Eagles, 75-23
LYRICIST LOUNGE VOL. 2 [EP], Mos Def Nate Dogg Pharoahe Monch, 01-24
M'LADY, Sly and the Family Stone, 68-32
M.O.R., Blur, 97-15
MA BAKER, Boney M, 77-2
MA BAKER / SOMEBODY SCREAM [M], Boney M vs Horny United, 99-22
MA (HE'S MAKIN' EYES AT ME):
Johnny Otis Show; Johnny Otis and his Orchestra with Marie Adams and the Three Tons of Joy, 57-2
Lena Zavaroni, 74-10
MA-MA-MA-BELLE, Electric Light Orchestra, 74-22
MA SAYS, PA SAYS, Doris Day and Johnnie Ray, 53-12
MA SOLITUDA, Catherine Wheel, 98-53
MACARENA:
Los Del Rio, 96-2
Los Del Mar featuring Wil. Veloz, 96-43
Los Del Chipmunks, 96-65
MACARTHUR PARK:
Richard Harris, 68-4, 72-38
Donna Summer, 78-5
MACH 5, Presidents Of The United States Of America, 96-29
MACHINE + SOUL, Gary Numan, 92-72
MACHINE GUN, Commodores, 74-20
MACHINEHEAD, Bush, 96-48
MACHINERY, Sheena Easton, 82-38
MACK THE KNIFE:
Billy Vaughn and his Orchestra *, 56-12
"Unforgettable" Sound of the Dick Hyman Trio *, 56-9
Louis Armstrong and his All Stars *, 56-8, 59-24
Bobby Darin, 59-1, 79-64
Ella Fitzgerald, 60-19
King Kurt, 84-55
MAD ABOUT THE BOY, Dinah Washington, 92-41
MAD ABOUT YOU, Bruce Ruffin, 72-9
MAD ABOUT YOU, Belinda Carlisle, 88-67
MAD ABOUT YOU, Sting, 91-56
MAD DOG, Elastica, 00-44
MAD EYED SCREAMER, Creatures, 81-24
MAD IF YA DON'T!, Gayle And Gillian, 93-75
MAD LOVE [EP], Lush, 90-55
MAD PASSIONATE LOVE, Bernard Bresslaw, 58-6
MAD WORLD, Tears For Fears, 82-3
MADAGASGA, Art Of Trance, 98-69, 99-48
MADAM BUTTERFLY (UN BEL DI VEDREMO), Malcolm McLaren, 84-13
MADCHESTER RAVE ON [EP], Happy Mondays, 89-19
MADE FOR LOVIN' YOU, Anastacia, 01-27
MADE IN ENGLAND, Elton John, 95-18
MADE IN HEAVEN, Freddie Mercury, 85-57
MADE IN TWO MINUTES, Bug Kann and the Plastic Jam featuring Patti Low and Doogie, 91-70, 94-64
MADE IT BACK, Beverley Knight featuring Redman, 98-21, 99-19
MADE OF STONE, Stone Roses, 90-20
MADE YOU, Adam Faith with John Barry and his Orchestra, 60-5
THE MADISON, Ray Ellington with Tony Crombie, his Orchestra and Chorus, 62-36
MADLY IN LOVE, Bros, 90-14
MADNESS IS ALL IN THE MIND, Madness, 83-8
MADNESS THING, Leilani, 99-19
MAGGIE, Foster and Allen, 83-27
MAGGIE MAY, Rod Stewart, 71-1, 76-31

MARBLEHEAD JOHNSON, Bluetones, 96-7
MARBLES, Black Grape, 98-46
MARCH OF THE MODS (FINNJENKA DANCE), Joe Loss and his Orchestra, 64-31
MARCH OF THE PIGS, Nine Inch Nails, 94-45
MARCH OF THE SIAMESE CHILDREN, Kenny Ball and his Jazzmen, 62-4
MARCHETA, Karl Denver, 61-8
MARCO TOURISTS, Slam versus Unkle, 01-66
MARGATE, Chas and Dave, 82-46
MARGIE, Fats Domino, 59-18
MARGO, Billy Fury, 59-28
MARGUERITA TIME, Status Quo, 83-3
MARIA, P.J. Proby, 65-8
MARIA, Blondie, 99-1
MARIA ELENA, Los Indios Tabajaras, 63-5
MARIA ELENA, Gene Pitney, 69-25
MARIA MARIA, Santana featuring the Product G&B, 00-6
MARIANA, Gibson Brothers, 80-11
MARIANNE, Hilltoppers with Billy Vaughn's Orchestra, 57-20
MARIANNE, Cliff Richard, 68-22
MARIE, Bachelors, 65-9
MARIE CELESTE, Polecats, 81-53
MARIE MARIE, Shakin Stevens, 80-19
(MARIE'S THE NAME) HIS LATEST FLAME, Elvis Presley, 61-1
MARJORINE, Joe Cocker, 68-48
MARKET SQUARE HEROES, Marillion, 82-60, 83-53
MARLENE ON THE WALL, Suzanne Vega, 86-21
MAROC 7, Shadows, 67-24
MARQUEE MOON, Television, 77-30
MARQUIS, Linoleum, 97-73
MARRAKESH EXPRESS, Crosby, Stills and Nash, 69-17
MARRIED MEN, Bonnie Tyler, 79-35
MARRY ME, Mike Preston, 61-14
MARTA, Bachelors, 67-20
MARTA'S SONG, Deep Forest, 95-26
MARTHA'S HARBOUR, All About Eve, 88-10
MARTIAN HOP, Rocky Sharpe and the Replays featuring the Top Liners, 80-55
MARTIKA'S KITCHEN, Martika, 91-17
MARVELLOUS, Lightning Seeds, 95-24
MARVIN, Marvin, The Paranoid Android, 81-53
MARY, Supergrass, 99-36
MARY ANN, Black Lace, 79-42
MARY ANNE, Shadows, 65-17
MARY HAD A LITTLE BOY, Snap!, 90-8
MARY HAD A LITTLE LAMB, Wings, 72-9
MARY JANE, Del Shannon, 64-35
MARY JANE, Megadeth, 88-46
MARY JANE, Spin Doctors, 94-55
MARY JANE (ALL NIGHT LONG), Mary J. Blige, 95-17
MARY JANE'S LAST DANCE, Tom Petty and the Heartbreakers, 94-52
MARY OF THE 4TH FORM, Boomtown Rats, 77-15
MARY'S BOY CHILD:
Harry Belafonte, 57-1, 58-10, 59-30
Nina and Frederik, 59-26
Boney M *, 78-1, 88-52
MARY'S PRAYER, Danny Wilson, 87-42, 88-3
MAS QUE MANCADA, Ronaldo's Revenge, 98-37
MAS QUE NADA:
Tamba Trio, 98-34
Echobeatz, 98-10
Colour Girl featuring PSG, 01-57
MASH IT UP, MDM, 01-66
MASQUERADE, Skids, 79-14
MASQUERADE, Evelyn Thomas, 84-60
MASQUERADE, Fall, 98-69
MASQUERADE, Gerideau, 98-63
MASSACHUSETTS (THE LIGHTS WENT OUT IN), Bee Gees, 67-1
THE MASSES AGAINST THE CLASSES, Manic Street Preachers, 00-1
MASSIVE ATTACK [EP], Massive Attack, 92-27
MASTER AND SERVANT, Depeche Mode, 84-9
MASTERBLASTER (JAMMIN'):
Stevie Wonder, 80-2
DJ Luck And MC Neat featuring JJ *, 00-5
THE MASTERPLAN, Diana Brown and Barrie K. Sharpe, 90-39
MATADOR, Jeff Wayne, 82-57
MATCH OF THE DAY (from SPOT THE PIGEON [EP]), Genesis, 77-14
MATCHSTALK MEN AND MATCHSTALK CATS AND DOGS (LOWRY'S SONG), Brian and Michael (Burke and Jerk), 78-1
MATED, David Grant and Jaki Graham, 85-20
MATERIAL GIRL, Madonna, 85-3
MATHAR, Indian Vibes, 94-68, 98-52
A MATTER OF FACT, Innocence, 90-37
MATTER OF TIME, Nine Yards, 99-59
A MATTER OF TRUST, Billy Joel, 86-52
MATTHEW AND SON, Cat Stevens, 67-2
MATT'S MOOD:
Matt Bianco, 84-44
Breekout Krew, 84-51
MAX DON'T HAVE SEX WITH YOUR EX, E – Rotic, 95-45
THE MAXI PRIEST [EP], Maxi Priest, 91-62
MAXIMUM EP, Dreadzone, 95-56
MAXIMUM OVERDRIVE, 2 Unlimited, 93-15
MAY EACH DAY, Andy Williams, 66-19
MAY I HAVE THE NEXT DREAM WITH YOU, Malcolm Roberts, 68-8
MAY THE SUNSHINE, Nazareth, 79-22
MAY YOU ALWAYS:
Joan Regan, 59-9
McGuire Sisters, 59-15
MAYBE, Thom Pace, 79-14
MAYBE BABY, Crickets, 58-4
MAYBE I KNOW:
Lesley Gore, 64-20
Seashells, 72-32
MAYBE I'M AMAZED:
Wings, 77-28
Carleen Anderson, 98-24
MAYBE I'M DEAD, Money Mark, 98-45
MAYBE LOVE, Stevie Nicks, 94-42
MAYBE TOMORROW, Billy Fury, 59-18
MAYBE TOMORROW, Chords, 80-40
MAYBE TOMORROW, UB40, 87-14
MAYBE (WE SHOULD CALL IT A DAY), Hazell Dean, 88-15
MAYOR OF SIMPLETON, XTC, 89-46
MCDONALD'S CAVE, Piltdown Men, 60-14
ME AND BABY BROTHER, War, 76-21
ME AND JULIO DOWN BY THE SCHOOLYARD, Paul Simon, 72-15
ME & MRS JONES:
Billy Paul, 73-12
Freddie Jackson, 92-32
ME AND MR. SANCHEZ, Blue Rondo A La Turk, 81-40
ME AND MY GIRL (NIGHT-CLUBBING), David Essex, 82-13
ME AND MY LIFE, Tremeloes, 70-4
ME AND MY SHADOW, Frank Sinatra and Sammy Davis Jnr., 62-20
ME AND THE FARMER, Housemartins, 87-15
ME AND YOU AND A DOG NAMED BOO, Lobo, 71-4
ME AND YOU VERSUS THE WORLD, Space, 96-9
ME. IN TIME, Charlatans, 91-28
ME' ISRAELITES, Chops-Emc and Extensive, 92-60
ME MYSELF AND I, De La Soul, 89-22
ME MYSELF I, Joan Armatrading, 80-21
ME NO POP I, Kid Creole and the Coconuts present Coati Mundi, 81-32
ME OR YOU?, Killing Joke, 83-57
ME, THE PEACEFUL HEART, Lulu, 68-9
MEA CULPA PART II, Enigma, 91-55
MEAN GIRL, Status Quo, 73-20
MEAN MAN, W.A.S.P., 89-21
MEAN MEAN MAN, Wanda Jackson, 61-40
MEAN STREAK, Cliff Richard and the Drifters, 59-10
MEAN STREAK, Y and T, 83-41
MEAN TO ME, Shaye Cogan, 60-40
MEAN WOMAN BLUES, Roy Orbison, 63-3
THE MEANING OF CHRISTMAS, Boris Gardiner, 86-69
THE MEANING OF LOVE, Depeche Mode, 82-12
MEAT PIE SAUSAGE ROLL (COME ON ENGLAND GI'S A GOAL), Grandad Roberts and his son Elvis, 98-67
MECCA, Cheetahs, 64-36
MECHANICAL WONDER, Ocean Colour Scene, 01-49
THE MEDAL SONG, Culture Club, 84-32
MEDICATION, Spiritualized, 92-55
MEDICINE SHOW, Big Audio Dynamite, 86-29
THE MEDICINE SONG, Stephanie Mills, 84-29
MEET EL PRESIDENTE, Duran Duran, 87-24
MEET HER AT THE LOVE PARADE, Da Hool, 98-15, 01-11
MEET ME ON THE CORNER, Max Bygraves, 55-2
MEET ME ON THE CORNER, Lindisfarne, 72-5
(MEET) THE FLINTSTONES, BC-52'S, 94-3
THE MEGA MELLE MIX [M], Grandmaster Melle Mel and the Furious Five, 85-46
MEGABLAST, Bomb The Bass featuring Merlin and Antonia, 88-6
MEGALOMANIA, Pele, 92-73
MEGAMIX [M], Corona, 97-36
MEGAMIX [M], Boney M, 88-52
MEGAMIX [M], Technotronic, 90-6
MEGAMIX [M], Crystal Waters, 92-39
MEGAREX [M], T. Rex, 85-72
MEISO, DJ Krush, 96-52
MELANCHOLY ROSE, Marc Almond, 87-71
MELLOW DOUBT, Teenage Fanclub, 95-34
MELLOW MELLOW RIGHT ON, Lowrell, 79-37
MELLOW YELLOW, Donovan, 67-8
THE MELOD-E.P. [EP], Dodgy, 94-53
MELODIES HAUNT YOU (from THE MELOD-E.P. [EP]), Dodgy, 94-53
MELODY OF LOVE, Ink Spots, 55-10
MELODY OF LOVE (WANNA BE LOVED), Donna Summer, 94-21
MELT, Siouxsie and the Banshees, 82-49
MELTING POT, Blue Mink, 69-3
MEMO FROM TURNER, Mick Jagger, 70-32
MEMORIES, PIL, 79-60
MEMORIES, Mike Berry, 81-55
MEMORIES, Beverley Craven, 91-68
MEMORIES ARE MADE OF THIS:
Dean Martin, 56-1
Dave King with the Roland Shaw Orchestra and the Keynotes, 56-5
Val Doonican, 67-11
MEMORY:
Elaine Paige, 81-6, 82-67
Barbra Streisand, 82-34
Aled Jones with the London Symphony Orchestra *, 85-42
Elaine Paige, 98-36
THE MEMORY REMAINS, Metallica, 97-13
MEMPHIS :
Faces (From The Faces [EP]), 77-41
Lonnie Mack, 79-47
MEMPHIS TENNESSEE:
Dave Berry and the Cruisers, 63-19
Chuck Berry, 63-6
MEN IN BLACK, Frank Black, 96-37
MEN IN BLACK, Will Smith, 97-1
MENTAL, Manic MC's featuring Sara Carlson, 89-30
MENTAL PICTURE, Jon Secada, 95-44
MENTASM, Second Phase, 91-48
MERCEDES BOY, Pebbles, 88-42
MERCI CHERI, Vince Hill, 66-36
MERCURY, Lowgold, 01-48
MERCURY AND SOLACE, BT featuring vocals by Jan Johnston, 99-38
MERCY MERCY ME/I WANT YOU [M], Robert Palmer, 91-9
MERKINBALL, Pearl Jam, 95-25
MERMAIDS, Paul Weller, 97-30
MERRY CHRISTMAS DARLING, Carpenters, 72-45, 90-25
MERRY CHRISTMAS EVERYONE, Shakin' Stevens, 85-1, 86-58
MERRY GENTLE POPS [M], Barron Knights with Duke D'Mond, 65-9
A MERRY JINGLE, Greedies, 79-28
THE MERRY PLOUGHBOY (OFF TO DUBLIN IN THE GREEN), Dermot O'Brien and his Clubmen, 66-46
MERRY X-MESS, Rotterdam Termination Source, 93-73
MERRY XMAS EVERYBODY:
Slade, 73-1, 81-32, 82-67, 83-20, 84-47, 85-48, 86-71
Slade and the Reading Choir *, 80-70
Metal Gurus, 90-55,
Slade vs. Flush, 98-30
MERSEYBEAST, Ian McNabb, 96-74
MESCALITO, Sourmash, 00-73
MESMERISE, Chapterhouse, 91-60
A MESS OF BLUES:
Elvis Presley with the Jordanaires, 60-2
Status Quo, 83-15
THE MESSAGE, Grandmaster Flash and the Furious Five, 82-8
THE MESSAGE, 49ers, 92-68
MESSAGE IN A BOTTLE:
Police, 79-1
Dance Floor Virus, 95-49
MESSAGE IN THE BOX, World Party, 90-39
THE MESSAGE IS LOVE, Arthur Baker and the Backbeat Disciples featuring Al Green, 89-38
MESSAGE OF LOVE, Pretenders, 81-11

MR. SLEAZE, Bananarama, 87-3
MR. SOFT, Cockney Rebel, 74-8
MR. SOLITARE, Animal Nightlife, 84-25
MR. SUCCESS, Frank Sinatra, 58-25
MR. TAMBOURINE MAN, Byrds, 65-1
MR. TELEPHONE MAN, New Edition, 85-19
MR. VAIN, Culture Beat, 93-1
MR. WENDAL, Arrested Development, 93-4
MR. WONDERFUL, Peggy Lee, 57-5
MR. WRITER, Stereophonics, 01-5
MR. ZERO, Keith Relf, 66-50
MISTLETOE AND WINE, Cliff Richard, 88-1
MISTY:
Johnny Mathis, 60-12
Ray Stevens, 75-2
MISTY BLUE, Dorothy Moore, 76-5
MISTY MORNING, ALBERT BRIDGE, Pogues, 89-41
MISUNDERSTANDING, Genesis, 80-42
MISUNDERSTOOD MAN, Cliff Richard, 95-19
MITCH, Biscuit Boy A.K.A Crackerman, 01-75
MITTAGEISEN (METAL POSTCARD), Siouxsie and the Banshees, 79-47
MIX IT UP, Dan Reed Network, 91-49
MIXED BIZNESS, Beck, 00-34
MIXED EMOTIONS, Rolling Stones, 89-36
MIXED TRUTH, Ragga Twins, 92-65
MIYAKO HIDEAWAY, Marion, 98-45
MMM MMM MMM MMM, Crash Test Dummies, 94-2
MMMBOP, Hanson, 97-1
MO MONEY MO PROBLEMS, Notorious B.I.G. featuring Puff Daddy and Mase, 97-6
MOAN & GROAN, Mark Morrison, 97-7
MOANIN', Chris Farlowe, 67-46
MOB RULES, Black Sabbath, 81-46
MOBILE, Ray Burns with Eric Jupp and his Orchestra, 55-4
MOCKIN' BIRD HILL, Migil 5, 64-10
MOCKINGBIRD:
Inez and Charlie Foxx, 69-33
Carly Simon, 74-34
Belle Stars, 82-51
THE MODEL, Kraftwerk, 81-36, 81-1
THE MODERN AGE, Strokes, 01-68
MODERN GIRL, Sheena Easton, 80-56, 80-8
MODERN GIRL, Meat Loaf, 84-17
MODERN LOVE, David Bowie, 83-2
MODERN ROMANCE (I WANT TO FALL IN LOVE AGAIN), Francis Rossi and Bernard Frost, 85-54
THE MODERN WORLD, Jam, 77-36, 80-52, 83-51
MODUS OPERANDI, Photek, 98-66
MOIRA JANE'S CAFE, Definition Of Sound, 92-34
MOLLIE'S SONG, Beverley Craven, 93-61
MOLLY, Carrie, 98-56
MOMENT OF MY LIFE, Bobby D'Ambrosio featuring Michelle Weeks, 97-23
MOMENTS IN LOVE, Art Of Noise, 85-51
MOMENTS IN SOUL, J.T. and the Big Family, 90-7
MOMENTS OF PLEASURE, Kate Bush, 93-26
MON AMI, Giresse, 01-61
MON AMOUR TOKYO, Pizzicato Five, 97-72
MONA, Craig McLachlan and Check 1-2, 90-2
MONA LISA, Conway Twitty, 59-5
MONDAY MONDAY, Mama's and the Papa's, 66-3
MONDAY MORNING, Candyskins, 97-34
MONDAY MORNING 5:19, Rialto, 97-37
MONEY:
Bern Elliott and the Fenmen, 63-14
Flying Lizards, 79-5
Backbeat Band, 94-48
MONEY, Dan Reed Network, 90-45
MONEY, Charli Baltimore, 98-12
MONEY, Jamelia featuring Beenie Man, 00-5
(MONEY CAN'T) BUY ME LOVE, Blackstreet, 97-18
MONEY DON'T MATTER 2 NIGHT, Prince and the New Power Generation, 92-19
THE MONEY EP [EP], Skin, 94-18
MONEY (EVERYBODY LOVES HER), Gun, 89-73
MONEY FOR NOTHING, Dire Straits, 85-4
MONEY GO ROUND (PART ONE), Style Council, 83-11
MONEY GREEDY, Tricky, 98-25
MONEY HONEY, Bay City Rollers, 75-3
MONEY IN MY POCKET, Dennis Brown, 79-14
MONEY LOVE, Neneh Cherry, 92-23
MONEY, MONEY, MONEY, Abba, 76-3
MONEY THAT'S YOUR PROBLEM, Tonight, 78-66
MONEY TO BURN, Richard Ashcroft, 00-17
MONEY'S TOO TIGHT (TO MENTION):
Valentine Brothers, 83-73
Simply Red, 85-13
MONEYTALKS, AC/DC, 90-36
MONIE IN THE MIDDLE, Monie Love, 90-46
THE MONKEES, Rampage, 95-51
THE MONKEES [EP], Monkees, 80-33
THE MONKEES [EP], Monkees, 89-62
MONKEY, George Michael, 88-13
MONKEY, Shaft, 92-61
MONKEY BUSINESS, Skid Row, 91-19
MONKEY BUSINESS, Danger Danger, 92-42
MONKEY CHOP, Dan-I, 79-30
MONKEY GONE TO HEAVEN, Pixies, 89-60
MONKEY MAN:
Maytals, 70-47
General Levy, 93-75
MONKEY SPANNER, Dave and Ansil Collins, 71-7
MONKEY WAH, Radical Rob, 92-67
MONKEY WRENCH, Foo Fighters, 97-12
MONSIEUR DUPONT, Sandie Shaw, 69-6
MONSTER, L7, 92-33
MONSTER MASH, Bobby (Boris) Pickett and the Crypt-Kickers, 73-3
MONSTERS AND ANGELS, Voice Of The Beehive, 91-17
MONTEGO BAY:
Bobby Bloom, 70-3
Freddie Notes and the Rudies, 70-45
Sugar Cane, 78-54
Amazulu, 86-16
MONTREAL, Wedding Present, 97-40
MONTREUX [EP], Simply Red, 92-11
MONTUNO, Gloria Estefan, 93-55
MONY MONY:
Tommy James and the Shondells, 68-1
Billy Idol, 87-7
Amazulu, 87-38
Status Quo, 00-48
THE MOOD CLUB, Firstborn, 99-69
MOODY BLUE, Elvis Presley, 77-6
MOODY PLACES, Northside, 90-50
MOODY RIVER, Pat Boone, 61-18
MOOG ERUPTION, Digital Orgasm, 92-62
MOON, Virus, 97-36
MOON HOP, Derrick Morgan Music backing the Rudies, 70-49
MOON OVER BOURBIN STREET, Sting, 86-44
MOON RIVER:
Danny Williams with Geoff Love and his Orchestra and the Rita Williams Singers, 61-1
Henry Mancini and his Orchestra, 61-44
Greyhound, 72-12
MOON SHADOW, Cat Stevens, 71-22
MOON TALK, Perry Como with Mitchell Ayres' Orchestra and the Ray Charles Singers, 58-17
MOONCHILD, Fields Of The Nephilim, 88-28
MOONGLOW/THEME FROM "PICNIC" [M]:
Morris Stoloff conducting the Columbia Pictures Orchestra, 56-7
Sounds Orchestral, 65-43
MOONLIGHT AND MUZAK, M, 79-33
MOONLIGHT AND ROSES (BRING BACK MEMORIES OF YOU), Jim Reeves, 71-34
MOONLIGHT GAMBLER, Frankie Laine with Ray Conniff and his Orchestra, 56-13
MOONLIGHT SERENADE, Glenn Miller and his Orchestra, 54-12, 76-13
MOONLIGHT SHADOW, Mike Oldfield, 83-4, 93-52
MOONLIGHTING, Leo Sayer, 75-2
MOONLIGHTING "THEME", Al Jarreau, 87-8
MOONSHINE SALLY, Mud, 75-10
MORE:
Perry Como and the Ray Charles Singers with Mitchell Ayres and his Orchestra, 56-10
Jimmy Young with Bob Sharples and his Music, 56-4
MORE, Sisters Of Mercy, 90-14
MORE . . ., High, 91-67
MORE AND MORE, Andy Williams, 67-45
MORE AND MORE, Captain Hollywood Project, 93-23
MORE & MORE, Spoiled and Zigo, 00-31
MORE AND MORE PARTY POPS [M], Russ Conway, 59-5
MORE BEATS + PIECES, Coldcut, 97-37
MORE GOOD OLD ROCK 'N ROLL [M], Dave Clark Five, 70-34
MORE HUMAN THAN HUMAN, White Zombie, 95-51
THE MORE I GET, THE MORE I WANT, KWS featuring Teddy Pendergrass, 94-35
THE MORE I SEE (THE LESS I BELIEVE), Fun Boy Three, 83-68
THE MORE I SEE YOU:
Joy Marshall, 66-34
Chris Montez, 66-3
Barbara Windsor and Mike Reid, 99-46
MORE LIFE IN A TRAMPS VEST, Stereophonics, 97-33
MORE LIKE THE MOVIES, Dr. Hook, 78-14
MORE LOVE, Feargal Sharkey, 88-44
MORE LOVE, Next Of Kin, 99-33
MORE MONEY FOR YOU AND ME [M], Four Preps, 61-39
MORE, MORE, MORE:
Andrea True Connection, 76-5
Bananarama, 93-24
MORE, MORE, MORE, Carmel, 84-23
MORE PARTY POPS [M], Russ Conway, 58-10
MORE THAN A FEELING, Boston, 77-22
MORE THAN A LOVER, Bonnie Tyler, 77-27
MORE THAN A WOMAN:
Tavares, 78-7
911, 98-2
MORE THAN EVER (COME PRIMA):
Malcolm Vaughan with the Michael Sammes Singers, 58-5
Robert Earl with Wally Stott and his Orchestra and Chorus, 58-26
MORE THAN I CAN BEAR, Matt Bianco, 85-50
MORE THAN I CAN SAY:
Crickets, 60-42
Bobby Vee, 61-4
Leo Sayer, 80-2
MORE THAN I NEEDED TO KNOW, Scooch, 00-5
MORE THAN IN LOVE, Kate Robbins and Beyond, 81-2
MORE THAN LIKELY, PM Dawn featuring Boy George, 93-40
MORE THAN LOVE, Ken Dodd with Johnny Pearson and his Orchestra, 66-14
MORE THAN LOVE, Wet Wet Wet, 92-19
MORE THAN ONE KIND OF LOVE, Joan Armatrading, 90-75
MORE THAN PHYSICAL, Bananarama, 86-41
MORE THAN THAT, Backstreet Boys, 01-12
MORE THAN THIS:
Roxy Music, 82-6
Emmie, 99-5
MORE THAN US [EP] + lead track title, Travis, 98-16
MORE THAN WORDS, Extreme, 91-2
MORE THAN YOU KNOW, Martika, 90-15
THE MORE THEY KNOCK THE MORE I LOVE YOU, Gloria D. Brown, 85-57
MORE TO LIFE, Cliff Richard, 91-23
MORE TO LOVE, Volcano, 94-32
MORE TO THIS WORLD, Bad Boys Inc., 94-8
THE MORE YOU IGNORE ME, THE CLOSER I GET, Morrissey, 94-8
THE MORE YOU LIVE, THE MORE YOU LOVE, A Flock Of Seagulls, 84-26
MORGEN (ONE MORE SUNRISE) SLOW-FOX, Ivo Robic und die Sing-Masters, 59-23
MORNIN', Al Jarreau, 83-28
MORNING, Val Doonican, 71-12
MORNING, Wet Wet Wet, 96-16
THE MORNING AFTER (FREE AT LAST), Strike, 95-38
MORNING AFTERGLOW, Electrasy, 98-19
MORNING DANCE, Spyro Gyra, 79-17
MORNING GLORY, James and Bobby Purify, 76-27
MORNING HAS BROKEN:
Cat Stevens, 72-9
Neil Diamond, 92-36
Daniel O'Donnell, 00-32
THE MORNING OF OUR LIVES, Jonathan Richman and the Modern Lovers, 78-29
THE MORNING PAPERS, Prince and the New Power Generation, 93-52
MORNING SIDE OF THE MOUNTAIN, Donny and Marie Osmond, 74-5
MORNINGLIGHT, Team Deep, 97-42
MORNINGTOWN RIDE, Seekers, 66-2
THE MOST BEAUTIFUL GIRL, Charlie Rich, 74-2

MY BOY, Elvis Presley, 74-5
MY BOY FLAT TOP, Frankie Vaughan, 56-20
MY BOY LOLLIPOP:
Millie, 64-2, 87-46
Bad Manners *, 82-9
MY BOYFRIEND'S BACK, Angels, 63-50
MY BRAVE FACE, Paul McCartney, 89-18
MY BROTHER JAKE, Free, 71-4
MY CAMERA NEVER LIES, Bucks Fizz, 82-1
MY CHERIE AMOUR, Stevie Wonder, 69-4
MY CHILD, Connie Francis, 65-26
MY COO CA CHOO, Alvin Stardust, 73-2
MY COUNTRY, Midnight Oil, 93-66
MY CUTIE CUTIE, Shakin' Stevens, 90-75
MY DEFINITION OF A BOOMBASTIC JAZZ STYLE, Dream Warriors, 90-13
MY DESIRE, Amira, 97-51, 98-46, 01-20
MY DESTINY, Lionel Richie, 92-7
MY DING-A-LING, Chuck Berry, 72-1
MY DIXIE DARLING, Lonnie Donegan and his Skiffle Group, 57-10
MY DJ (PUMP IT UP SOME), Richie Rich, 88-74
MY DOCS, Kiss Amc, 90-66
MY DRUG BUDDY, Lemonheads, 93-44
MY DYING MACHINE, Gary Numan, 84-66
MY EVER CHANGING MOODS, Style Council, 84-5
MY EYES ADORED YOU, Frankie Valli, 75-5
MY FAMILY DEPENDS ON ME, Simone, 91-75
MY FATHER'S EYES, Eric Clapton, 98-33
MY FATHER'S SHOES, Level 42, 92-55
MY FATHER'S SON, Conner Reeves, 97-12
MY FAVORITE MISTAKE, Sheryl Crow, 98-9
MY FAVOURITE GAME, Cardigans, 98-14
MY FAVOURITE WASTE OF TIME, Owen Paul, 86-3
MY FEELING, Junior Jack, 00-31
MY FEET KEEP DANCING, Chic, 79-21
MY FIRST NIGHT WITH YOU, Cyndi Lauper, 89-53
MY FOOLISH FRIEND, Talk Talk, 83-57
MY FORBIDDEN LOVER:
Chic, 79-15
Romina Johnson featuring Luci Martin and Norma Jean from Chic, 00-59
MY FRIEND, Frankie Laine with Paul Weston and his Orchestra and the Norman Luboff Choir, 54-3
MY FRIEND, Roy Orbison, 69-35
MY FRIEND, Groove Armada, 01-36
MY FRIEND JACK:
Smoke, 67-45
Boney M, 80-57
MY FRIEND STAN, Slade, 73-2
MY FRIEND THE SEA, Petula Clark, 61-7
MY FRIENDS, Red Hot Chili Peppers, 95-29
MY GENERATION, Who, 65-2, 88-68, 96-31
MY GENERATION, Limp Bizkit, 00-15
MY GETAWAY, Tionne "T-Boz" Watkins of [Tlc], 01-44
MY GIRL:
Temptations, 65-43, 92-2
Otis Redding, 65-11, 68-36
Whispers, 80-26
MY GIRL:
Madness, 80-3, 92-27
Tracey Ullman *, 84-23
MY GIRL, Rod Stewart, 80-32
MY GIRL BILL, Jim Stafford, 74-20
MY GIRL JOSEPHINE:
Fats Domino, 61-32
Super Cat featuring Jack Radics, 95-22
MY GIRL LOLLIPOP (MY BOY LOLLIPOP), Bad Manners, 82-9
MY GIRL LOVES ME, Shalamar, 85-45
MY GUY, Mary Wells, 64-5, 72-14
MY GUY – MY GIRL [M]:
Amii Stewart and Johnny Bristol, 80-39
Amii Stewart and Dion Estus, 86-63
MY GUY'S MAD AT ME, Tracey Ullman, 84-23
MY HAND OVER MY HEART, Marc Almond, 92-33
MY HAPPINESS, Connie Francis; David Rose and his Orchestra, 59-4
MY HEAD'S IN MISSISSIPPI, ZZ Top, 91-37
MY HEART, Gene Vincent and the Blue Caps, 60-16
MY HEART CAN'T TELL YOU NO, Rod Stewart, 89-49
MY HEART GOES BANG (GET ME TO THE DOCTOR), Dead Or Alive, 85-23
MY HEART GOES BOOM, French Affair, 00-44
MY HEART HAS A MIND OF ITS OWN, Connie Francis, 60-3
MY HEART, THE BEAT, D-Shake, 91-42
MY HEART WILL GO ON (LOVE THEME FROM TITANIC), Celine Dion, 98-1
MY HEART'S BEATING WILD (TIC TAC TIC TAC), Gibson Brothers, 83-56
MY HEART'S SYMPHONY, Gary Lewis and the Playboys, 75-36
MY HERO, Foo Fighters, 98-21
MY HOMETOWN, Bruce Springsteen, 85-9
MY HOUSE, Terrorvision, 94-29
MY IRON LUNG [EP] + lead track title, Radiohead, 94-24
MY JAMAICAN GUY, Grace Jones, 83-56
MY KIND OF GIRL:
Matt Monro, 61-5
Frank Sinatra and Count Basie and his Orchestra, 63-35
MY KINDA LIFE, Cliff Richard, 77-15
MY KINGDOM, Future Sound Of London, 96-13
MY LAST NIGHT WITH YOU, Arrows, 75-25
MY LIFE, Billy Joel, 78-12
MY LIFE IS IN YOUR HANDS, Meltdown, 96-44
MY LITTLE BABY, Mike Berry with the Outlaws, 63-34
MY LITTLE CORNER OF THE WORLD, Anita Bryant, 60-48
MY LITTLE GIRL, Crickets, 63-17
MY LITTLE GIRL, Autumn, 71-37
MY LITTLE LADY, Tremeloes, 68-6
MY LITTLE ONE, Marmalade, 71-15
MY LOVE, Petula Clark, 66-4
MY LOVE, Paul McCartney and Wings, 73-9
MY LOVE, Lionel Richie, 83-70
MY LOVE, Julio Iglesias featuring Stevie Wonder, 88-5
MY LOVE, London Boys, 89-46
MY LOVE, Mary J. Blige, 94-29
MY LOVE (from THE WANDERING DRAGON [EP]), Shades Of Rhythm, 94-55
MY LOVE, Kele Le Roc, 99-8
MY LOVE, Westlife, 00-1
MY LOVE, Kluster featuring Ron Carroll, 01-73
MY LOVE AND DEVOTION:
Doris Day with Percy Faith and his Orchestra, 52-10
Matt Monro, 62-29
MY LOVE FOR YOU, Johnny Mathis, 60-9
MY LOVE IS A FIRE, Donny Osmond, 91-64
MY LOVE IS DEEP, Sara Parker, 97-22
MY LOVE IS FOR REAL, Paula Abdul, 95-28
MY LOVE IS FOR REAL, Strike, 96-35
MY LOVE IS GUARANTEED, Sybil, 87-42, 93-48
MY LOVE IS MAGIC, Bas Noir, 89-73
MY LOVE IS SO RAW, Alyson Williams featuring Nikki-D, 89-34
MY LOVE IS THE SHHH!, Somethin' For The People featuring Trina and Tamara, 98-64
MY LOVE IS WAITING, Marvin Gaye, 83-34
MY LOVE IS YOUR LOVE, Whitney Houston, 99-2
MY LOVE LIFE, Morrissey, 91-29
MY LOVER'S PRAYER, Otis Redding, 66-37
MY LOVIN', En Vogue, 92-69, 92-4
MY MAGIC MAN, Rochelle, 86-27
MY MAMMY, Happenings, 67-34
MY MAN A SWEET MAN, Millie Jackson, 72-50
MY MAN AND ME, Lynsey De Paul, 75-40
MY MARIE, Engelbert Humperdinck, 70-31
MY MATE PAUL, David Holmes, 98-39
MY MELANCHOLY BABY:
Tommy Edwards, 59-29
Chas and Dave, 83-51
MY MIND'S EYE, Small Faces, 66-4
MY MUM IS ONE IN A MILLION, Children Of Tansley School, 81-27
MY NAME IS, Eminem, 99-2
MY NAME IS JACK, Manfred Mann, 68-8
MY NAME IS NOT SUSAN, Whitney Houston, 91-29
MY NAME IS PRINCE, Prince and the New Power Generation, 92-7
MY OH MY, Sad Cafe, 80-14
MY OH MY, Slade, 83-2
MY OH MY, Aqua, 98-6
MY OLD MAN'S A DUSTMAN (BALLAD OF A REFUSE DISPOSAL OFFICER), Lonnie Donegan and his Group, 60-1
MY OLD PIANO, Diana Ross, 80-5
MY ONE SIN (IN LIFE), Nat 'King' Cole, 55-17
MY ONE TEMPTATION, Mica Paris, 88-7
MY ONE TRUE FRIEND, Bette Midler, 98-58
MY ONLY LOVE, Bob Sinclar featuring Lee A. Genesis, 99-56
MY ORBIT (from FEEL THE DRUMS [EP]), Parks and Wilson, 00-71
MY OWN SUMMER (SHOVE IT), Deftones, 98-29
MY OWN TRUE LOVE, Danny Williams, 63-45
MY OWN WAY, Duran Duran, 81-14
MY OWN WORST ENEMY, Lit, 99-16
MY PEACE OF HEAVEN, Ten City, 92-63
MY PERFECT COUSIN, Undertones, 80-9
MY PERSONAL POSSESSION, Nat "King" Cole and the Four Knights with Nelson Riddle's Music, 57-21
MY PHILOSOPHY, Boogie Down Productions, 88-69
MY PRAYER:
Platters, 56-4
Gerry Monroe, 70-9
MY PREROGATIVE, Bobby Brown, 88-6, 95-17
MY PRETTY ONE, Cliff Richard, 87-6
MY PUPPET PAL, Tiger, 96-62
MY REMEDY, Hinda Hicks, 00-61
MY RESISTANCE IS LOW, Robin Sarstedt, 76-3
MY RISING STAR, Northside, 90-32
MY SALT HEART, Hue And Cry, 91-47
MY SENTIMENTAL FRIEND, Herman's Hermits, 69-2
MY SEPTEMBER LOVE, David Whitfield with the Roland Shaw Orchestra, 56-3
MY SHARONA, Knack, 79-6
MY SHIP IS COMING IN, Walker Brothers, 65-3
MY SIDE OF THE BED, Susanna Hoffs, 91-44
MY SIMPLE HEART, Three Degrees, 79-9
MY SISTER, Juliana Hatfield Three, 93-71
MY 16TH APOLOGY [EP] + lead track title, Shakespears Sister, 93-61
MY SON JOHN, David Whitfield, 56-22
MY SON, MY SON, Vera Lynn and Frank Weir and his Saxophone, his Chorus and Orchestra, 54-1
MY SPECIAL ANGEL:
Malcolm Vaughan, 57-3
Bobby Helms, 57-22
MY SPECIAL CHILD, Sinead O'Connor, 91-42
MY SPECIAL DREAM (THEME FROM "THE VICTORS"), Shirley Bassey, 64-32
MY SPIRIT, Tilt, 97-61
MY STAR, Ian Brown, 98-5
MY SUNDAY BABY (UN TELEGRAMA), Dale Sisters, 61-36
MY SUPERSTAR, Dimestars, 01-72
MY SWEET JANE, G.U.N., 97-51
MY SWEET LORD, George Harrison, 71-1
MY SWEET ROSALIE, Brotherhood Of Man, 76-30
MY TELPHONE, Coldcut, 89-52
MY TIME, Souvlaki, 98-63
MY TOOT TOOT, Denise Lasalle, 85-6
MY TOWN, Glass Tiger, 91-33
MY TRUE LOVE, Jack Scott, 58-9
MY UNFINISHED SYMPHONY, David Whitfield, 56-29
MY UNKNOWN LOVE, Count Indigo, 96-59
MY WAY, Eddie Cochran, 63-23
MY WAY:
Frank Sinatra, 69-5, 70-18, 71-22, 72-50, 94-45
Dorothy Squires *, 70-25
Elvis Presley, 77-9
Sex Pistols, 78-7
Shane MacGowan, 96-29
MY WAY, Limp Bizkit, 01-6
MY WAY OF GIVING IN, Chris Farlowe, 67-48
MY WAY OF THINKING, U.B.40, 80-6
MY WEAKNESS IS NONE OF YOUR BUSINESS, Embrace, 98-9
MY WHITE BICYCLE, Nazareth, 75-14
MY WOMAN'S MAN, Dave Dee, 70-42
MY WORLD, Cupids Inspiration, 68-33
MY WORLD, Bee Gees, 72-16
MY WORLD, Secret Affair, 80-16
MY WORLD OF BLUE, Karl Denver, 64-29
MYFANWY, David Essex, 87-41
MYSTERIES OF LOVE, La Mix, 91-46

NEVER SAY DIE, Black Sabbath, 78-21
NEVER SAY DIE (GIVE A LITTLE BIT MORE), Cliff Richard, 83-15
NEVER SAY GOODBYE, Bon Jovi, 87-21
NEVER STOP, Echo and the Bunnymen, 83-15
NEVER STOP (second entry from ULTIMATE TRUNK FUNK – THE EP [EP]), Brand New Heavies featuring N'dea Davenport, 91-43, 92-19
NEVER SURRENDER, Saxon, 81-18
NEVER TAKE ME ALIVE, Spear Of Destiny, 87-14
NEVER TEAR US APART, Inxs, 88-24
NEVER THERE, Cake, 99-66
NEVER TOO FAR, Mariah Carey, 01-32
NEVER TOO LATE, Kylie Minogue, 89-4
NEVER TOO MUCH, Luther Vandross, 83-44, 89-13
NEVER TRUST A STRANGER, Kim Wilde, 88-7
NEVER TURN AWAY, Orchestral Manoeuvres In The Dark, 84-70
NEVER TURN YOUR BACK ON MOTHER EARTH, Sparks, 74-13
NEVER UNDERSTAND, Jesus and Mary Chain, 85-47
NEVERTHELESS:
Frankie Vaughan with Alyn Ainsworth and his Orchestra, 68-29
Eve Graham and the New Seekers *, 73-34
NEW, No Doubt, 99-30
NEW AMSTERDAM, Elvis Costello, 80-36
NEW ANGER, Gary Numan, 88-46
NEW BEGINNING, Stephen Gately, 00-3
NEW BEGINNING, Precious . . ., 00-50
NEW BEGINNING (MAMBA SEYRA), Bucks Fizz, 86-8
NEW BIRD, Reef, 99-73
NEW BORN, Muse, 01-12
NEW BORN, Elbow, 01-42
A NEW DAY, Killing Joke, 84-56
NEW DAY, Wyclef Jean featuring Bono, 99-23
NEW DIMENSION, Imagination, 83-56
NEW DIRECTION, Freak Power, 96-60
NEW EMOTION [EP] + lead track title, Time Frequency, 93-36
A NEW ENGLAND, Kirsty MacColl, 85-7
A NEW FASHION, Bill Wyman, 82-37
A NEW FLAME, Simply Red, 89-17
NEW GENERATION, Suede, 95-21
NEW GRANGE, Clannad, 83-65
NEW GUITAR IN TOWN, Lurkers, 79-72
NEW KICKS, Johann, 96-54
NEW KID IN TOWN, Eagles, 77-20
NEW KIND OF MEDICINE, Ultra Nate, 98-14
NEW LIFE, Depeche Mode, 81-11
NEW LIVE AND RARE [EP], Deep Purple, 77-31
NEW LIVE AND RARE VOL. II [EP], Deep Purple, 78-45
NEW LIVE AND RARE VOLUME 3 [EP], Deep Purple, 80-48
NEW MISTAKE, Jellyfish, 93-55
NEW MOON ON MONDAY, Duran Duran, 84-9
NEW ORLEANS:
U.S. Bonds, 61-16
Bern Elliott and the Fenmen, 64-24
Harley Quinne, 72-19
Gillan, 81-17
NEW POLICY ONE, Terrorvision, 93-42
THE NEW POLLUTION, Beck, 97-14
NEW POWER GENERATION, Prince, 90-26
NEW SENSATION, Inxs, 88-25
NEW SONG, Howard Jones, 83-3
A NEW SOUTH WALES, Alarm, 89-31
NEW THING FROM LONDON TOWN, Sharpe and Numan, 86-52
NEW TOY, Lene Lovich, 81-53
NEW WAY, NEW LIFE, Asian Dub Foundation, 00-49
NEW WORLD IN THE MORNING, Roger Whittaker, 70-17
NEW WORLD MAN, Rush, 82-42, 83-36
NEW YEAR, Sugababes, 00-12
NEW YEAR'S DAY, U2, 83-10
NEW YEARS DUB, Musique vs U2, 01-15
NEW YORK AFTERNOON, Mondo Kane featuring Dee Lewis and Coral Gordon guest star Georgie Fame, 86-70
NEW YORK CITY, T.Rex, 75-15
NEW YORK CITY BOY, Pet Shop Boys, 99-14
NEW YORK CITY COPS, Strokes, 01-16
NEW YORK EYES, Nicole with Timmy Thomas, 85-41
NEW YORK GROOVE, Hello, 75-9
NEW YORK MINING DISASTER 1941, Bee Gees, 67-12
NEW YORK, NEW YORK, Gerard Kenny, 78-43
NEW YORK NEW YORK, Ryan Adams, 01-53
NEW YORK UNDERCOVER 4-TRACK EP [EP], Various Artists (EPs), 96-39
NEWBORN FRIEND, Seal, 94-45
NEWS AT TEN, Vapors, 80-44
NEWS OF THE WORLD, Jam, 78-27, 80-53, 83-39
THE NEXT BIG THING, Jesus Jones, 97-49
NEXT DOOR TO AN ANGEL, Neil Sedaka, 62-29
THE NEXT EPISODE, Dr. Dre featuring Snoop Dogg, 01-3
NEXT LIFETIME, Erykah Badu, 97-30
THE NEXT TIME, Cliff Richard, the Shadows and the Norrie Paramor Strings, 62-1
NEXT TIME YOU FALL IN LOVE, Reva Rice and Greg Ellis, 93-59
NEXT TO YOU, Aswad, 90-24
NEXT YEAR, Foo Fighters, 00-42
NI – TEN – ICHI – RYU (TWO SWORDS TECHNIQUE), Photek, 97-37
NIALL QUINN'S DISCO PANTS, A Love Supreme, 99-59
NICE 'N' EASY, Frank Sinatra, 60-15
NICE 'N' SLEAZY, Stranglers, 78-18
NICE & SLOW, Jesse Green, 76-17
NICE AND SLOW, Freddie Jackson, 88-56
NICE & SLOW, Usher, 98-24
NICE GUY EDDIE, Sleeper, 96-10
NICE IN NICE, Stranglers, 86-30
NICE LEGS SHAME ABOUT HER FACE, Monks, 79-19
NICE ONE CYRIL, Cockerel Chorus, 73-14
THE NIGHT:
Frankie Valli and the Four Seasons, 75-7
Intastella, 95-60
A NIGHT AT DADDY GEES, Showaddywaddy, 79-39
NIGHT BIRDS, Shakatak, 82-9
NIGHT BOAT TO CAIRO (first entry from WORK REST AND PLAY [EP]), Madness, 80-6, 93-56
THE NIGHT CHICAGO DIED, Paper Lace, 74-3
NIGHT CRAWLER, Judas Priest, 93-63
NIGHT DANCING, Joe Farrell, 78-57
NIGHT FEVER, Fatback Band, 76-38
NIGHT FEVER:
Bee Gees, 78-1
Carol Douglas, 78-66
Adam Garcia, 98-15
THE NIGHT FEVER MEGAMIX [M], Mixmasters, 91-23
NIGHT GAMES, Graham Bonnet, 81-6
THE NIGHT HAS A THOUSAND EYES, Bobby Vee, 63-3
NIGHT IN MOTION, Cubic 22, 91-15
NIGHT IN MY VEINS, Pretenders, 94-25
A NIGHT IN NEW YORK, Elbow Bones and the Racketeers, 84-33
THE NIGHT IS YOUNG (AND YOU'RE SO BEAUTIFUL), Gary Miller, 61-29
NIGHT LADIES, Crusaders, 84-55
NIGHT LIFE, David Lee Roth, 94-72
NIGHT MOVES, Bob Seger and the Silver Bullet Band, 95-45
NIGHT NURSE, Sly and Robbie featuring Simply Red, 97-13
NIGHT OF FEAR, Move, 67-2
NIGHT OF THE LIVING BASEHEADS, Public Enemy, 88-63
NIGHT OF THE LONG GRASS, Troggs, 67-17
NIGHT OF THE VAMPIRE, Moontrekkers, 61-50
NIGHT OWL, Gerry Rafferty, 79-5
THE NIGHT THE EARTH CRIED, Gravediggaz, 98-44
THE NIGHT, THE WINE AND THE ROSES, Liquid Gold, 80-32
THE NIGHT THEY DROVE OLD DIXIE DOWN, Joan Baez, 71-6
A NIGHT TO REMEMBER:
Shalamar, 82-5, 86-52
911, 96-38
NIGHT TRAIN:
Buddy Morrow and his Orchestra, 53-12
Kadoc *, 96-14
NIGHT TRAIN, Visage, 82-12
THE NIGHT YOU MURDERED LOVE, ABC, 87-31
NIGHTBIRD, Convert, 92-39, 98-45
THE NIGHTFLY, Blank and Jones, 00-55
NIGHTLIFE, Kenickie, 97-27
NIGHTLINE, Randy Crawford, 83-51
NIGHTMARE, Gillan, 81-36
NIGHTMARE, Saxon, 83-50
NIGHTMARE, Kid Unknown, 92-64
NIGHTMARE, Brainbug, 97-11, 97-24
NIGHTMARES, A Flock Of Seagulls, 83-53
NIGHTPORTER, Japan, 82-29
NIGHTRAIN, Guns N' Roses, 88-24, 89-17
NIGHTS IN WHITE SATIN:
Moody Blues, 67-19, 72-9, 79-14
Dickies, 79-39
Elkie Brooks, 82-33
NIGHTS OF PLEASURE, Loose Ends, 86-42
NIGHTS ON BROADWAY, Candi Staton, 77-6
NIGHTS OVER EGYPT, Incognito, 99-56
NIGHTSHIFT, Commodores, 85-3
NIGHTSWIMMING, R.E.M., 93-27
NIGHTTRAIN, Public Enemy, 92-55
THE NIGHTRAIN, Kadoc, 96-14
NIKITA, Elton John, 85-3
NIKKE DOES IT BETTER, Nikke? Nicole!, 91-73
NIMBUS, 808 State, 92-59
NINE [EP], Mansun, 98-13
9 A.M. (THE COMFORT ZONE), Londonbeat, 88-19
900 DEGREES, Ian Pooley, 01-57
THE 900 NUMBER, 45 King, 89-60, 90-73
911, Wyclef Jean featuring Mary J. Blige, 00-9
911 IS A JOKE, Public Enemy, 90-41
977, Pretenders, 94-66
(9PM) 'TIL I COME, ATB, 99-68, '99-47, 99-63, 99-1
NINE TIMES OUT OF TEN, Cliff Richard and the Shadows, 60-3
9 TO 5, Sheena Easton, 80-3
9 TO 5, Dolly Parton, 81-47
NINE WAYS, JDS, 97-61, 01-47
19, Paul Hardcastle, 85-1
19/2000, Gorillaz, 01-6
1962, Grass-Show, 97-53
NINETEEN63, New Order, 95-21
1979, Smashing Pumpkins, 96-16
1998 / 1999, Binary Finary, 98-24, 99-11
1999, Prince, 83-25, 85-2, 99-10, 99-40
19TH NERVOUS BREAKDOWN, Rolling Stones, 66-2
90'S GIRL, Blackgirl, 94-23
92° F, Pop Will Eat Itself, 91-23
92 TOUR [EP], Motorhead, 92-63
95 – NASTY, W.A.S.P., 86-70
96 TEARS:
? and the Mysterians, 66-37
Eddie and the Hotrods (from Live At The Marquee [EP]), 76-43
Stranglers, 90-17
98.6:
Keith, 67-24
Bystanders, 67-45
99 RED BALLOONS, Nena, 84-1
NINETY-NINE WAYS, Tab Hunter with Billy Vaughn's Orchestra, 57-5
99½, Carol Lynn Townes, 84-47
99.9° F, Suzanne Vega, 92-46
NIPPLE TO THE BOTTLE, Grace Jones, 82-50
NITE AND DAY, Al B. Sure!, 88-44
NITE AND FOG, Mercury Rev, 01-47
A NITE AT THE APOLLO LIVE! [M], Daryl Hall and John Oates, 85-58
NITE KLUB, Specials featuring Rico +, 79-10
NITE LIFE, Kim English, 94-35, 96-35
NITRO, Pale – X, 01-74
NO, Chuck D, 96-55
NO-ONE BUT YOU (ONLY THE GOOD DIE YOUNG), Queen, 98-13
NO-ONE DRIVING, John Foxx, 80-32
NO ALIBIS, Eric Clapton, 90-53
NO ARMS CAN EVER HOLD YOU, Bachelors, 64-7
NO BLUE SKIES, Lloyd Cole, 90-42
NO CHANCE (NO CHARGE), Billy Connolly, 76-24
NO CHARGE:
J.J. Barrie, 76-1
Billy Connolly *, 76-24
NO CHEAP THRILL, Suzanne Vega, 97-40
NO CHRISTMAS, Wedding Present, 92-25
NO CLASS, Motorhead, 79-61
NO CLAUSE 28, Boy George, 88-57
NO COMPLY, Senser, 93-47
NO CONVERSATION, View From The Hill, 86-58
NO DIGGITY, Blackstreet (featuring Dr. Dre), 96-9
NO DISTANCE LEFT TO RUN, Blur, 99-14
NO DOUBT, 702, 97-59
NO DOUBT, Imajin, 99-42
NO DOUBT ABOUT IT, Hot Chocolate, 80-2
NO DREAM IMPOSSIBLE, Lindsay, 01-33

NOTHIN' AT ALL, Heart, 88-38
NOTHIN' BUT A GOOD TIME, Poison, 88-35, 89-48
NOTHIN' BUT A PARTY, Truce, 97-71
NOTHIN' MY LOVE CAN'T FIX, Joey Lawrence, 93-13
NOTHIN' PERSONAL, Dust Junkys, 98-62
NOTHIN (THAT COMPARES 2 U), Jacksons, 89-33
NOTHIN' TO DO, Michael Holliday with Norrie Paramor and his Orchestra and Chorus, 56-20
NOTHING, Frazier Chorus, 90-51
NOTHING, Fluffy, 96-52
NOTHING AS IT SEEMS, Pearl Jam, 00-22
NOTHING 'BOUT ME, Sting, 94-32
NOTHING BUT LOVE, Optimystic, 94-37
NOTHING CAN CHANGE THIS LOVE, Bitty McLean, 95-55
NOTHING CAN DIVIDE US, Jason Donovan, 88-5
NOTHING CAN STOP ME, Gene Chandler, 68-41
NOTHING CAN STOP US, Saint Etienne, 91-54
NOTHING COMES EASY, Sandie Shaw, 66-14
NOTHING COMPARES 2 U:
Sinead O'Connor, 90-1
MXM, 90-68
NOTHING ELSE MATTERS, Metallica, 92-6
NOTHING EVER HAPPENS, Del Amitri, 90-11
NOTHING HAS BEEN PROVED:
Dusty Springfield, 89-16
Strings Of Love, 90-59
NOTHING IN PARTICULAR, Brotherhood, 96-55
NOTHING IS FOREVER, Ultracynic, 92-50, 97-47
NOTHING IS REAL BUT THE GIRL, Blondie, 99-26
NOTHING LASTS FOREVER, Echo and the Bunnymen, 97-8
NOTHING LEFT, Orbital, 99-32
NOTHING LEFT TOULOUSE, Sad Cafe, 80-62
NOTHING LESS THAN BRILLIANT, Sandie Shaw, 94-66
NOTHING NATURAL, Lush, 91-43
NOTHING REALLY MATTERS, Madonna, 99-7
NOTHING RHYMED, Gilbert O'Sullivan, 70-8
(NOTHING SERIOUS) JUST BUGGIN', Whistle, 86-7
NOTHING TO DECLARE, Laptop, 99-74
NOTHING TO FEAR, Chris Rea, 92-16
NOTHING TO LOSE, S*Express, 90-32
NOTHING TO LOSE, U.K., 79-67
NOTHING WITHOUT ME, Manchild, 01-40
NOTHING'S GONNA CHANGE, Labi Siffre, 87-52
NOTHING'S GONNA CHANGE MY LOVE FOR YOU, Glenn Medeiros, 88-1
NOTHING'S GONNA STOP ME NOW, Samantha Fox, 87-8
NOTHING'S GONNA STOP US NOW, Starship, 87-1
NOTORIOUS, Duran Duran, 86-7
NOTORIOUS B.I.G., Notorious B.I.G. featuring Puff Daddy and Lil' Kim, 00-16
NOVELTY WAVES, Biosphere, 95-51
NOVEMBER RAIN, Guns N' Roses, 92-4, 92-8
NOVEMBER SPAWNED A MONSTER, Morrissey, 90-12
NOVOCAINE FOR THE SOUL, Eels, 97-10
NOW, Al Martino, 53-3
NOW, Val Doonican, 68-43
NOW ALWAYS AND FOREVER, Gay Dad, 01-41
NOW AND FOREVER, Richard Marx, 94-13
NOW I KNOW WHAT MADE OTIS BLUE, Paul Young, 93-14
NOW I'M HERE, Queen, 75-11
NOW I'VE FOUND YOU, Sean Maguire, 95-22
NOW IS THE TIME, Jimmy James and the Vagabonds, 76-5
NOW IS TOMORROW, Definition Of Sound (vocals by Elaine Vassell), 91-46
NOW IT'S GONE, Chords, 79-63
NOW OR NEVER, Tom Novy featuring Lima, 01-64
NOW SHE KNOWS SHE'S WRONG (from THE SCARY-GO-ROUND [EP]), Jellyfish, 91-49
NOW THAT I OWN THE BBC, Sparks, 96-60
NOW THAT THE MAGIC HAS GONE, Joe Cocker, 92-28
NOW THAT WE'VE FOUND LOVE:
Third World, 78-10, 85-22
Heavy D and the Boyz, 91-2
NOW THAT YOU'RE GONE, Mike and the Mechanics, 99-35
NOW THEY'LL SLEEP, Belly, 95-28
NOW THOSE DAYS ARE GONE, Bucks Fizz, 82-8
NOW WE'RE THRU', Poets, 64-31
NOW YOU'RE GONE, Black, 89-66
NOW YOU'RE GONE, Whitesnake, 90-31
NOW YOU'RE IN HEAVEN, Julian Lennon, 89-59
NOWHERE, Therapy?, 94-18
NOWHERE FAST, Meat Loaf, 84-67
NOWHERE GIRL, B-Movie, 82-67
NOWHERE LAND, Clubhouse featuring Carl, 95-56
NOWHERE MAN, Three Good Reasons, 66-47
NOWHERE TO RUN:
Martha and the Vandellas, 65-26, 69-42, 88-52
Nu Generation *, 00-66
NUCLEAR DEVICE (THE WIZARD OF AUS), Stranglers, 79-36
NUCLEAR HOLIDAY, 3 Colours Red, 97-22
NUFF VIBES [EP], Apache Indian, 93-5
#9 DREAM, John Lennon, 75-23
THE NUMBER OF THE BEAST, Iron Maiden, 82-18
NUMBER ONE, E.Y.C., 94-27
NUMBER ONE, A, 98-47
NO.1, Tweenies, 00-5
NUMBER ONE, Playgroup, 01-66
NUMBER ONE BLIND, Veruca Salt, 95-68
#1 DEE JAY, Goody Goody, 78-55
NUMBER ONE DOMINATOR, Top, 91-67
NO. 1 RAT FAN, Roland Rat Superstar, 85-72
THE NUMBER ONE SONG IN HEAVEN:
Sparks, 79-14
Sparks, 97-70
NUMBERS, Soft Cell, 83-25
NUMERO UNO, Starlight, 89-9
NUNC DIMITTIS (THEME FROM TINKER, TAILOR, SOLDIER, SPY), Paul Phoenix (treble) with instrumental ensemble – James Watson (trumpet), John Scott (organ), conducted by Barry Rose, 79-56
NURSERY RHYMES, Iceberg Slimm, 00-37
NURTURE, LFO, 91-47
NUT ROCKER, B. Bumble and the Stingers, 62-1, 72-19
NUTBUSH CITY LIMITS:
Ike and Tina Turner, 73-4
Tina Turner, 91-23
NUTHIN' BUT A 'G' THANG, Dr. Dre, 94-31
O BABY, Siouxsie and the Banshees, 95-34
O.K?, Julie Covington, Charlotte Cornwell, Rula Lenska, Sue Jones-Davies, 77-10
O.K. FRED, Errol Dunkley, 79-11
O L'AMOUR, Dollar, 87-7
O' MY FATHER HAD A RABBIT, Ray Moore, 86-24
O-O AET (from SEASONSTREAM [EP]), Thousand Yard Stare, 91-65
O-O-O, Adrenalin M.O.D., 88-49
O.P.P., Naughty By Nature, 91-73, 92-35
O SUPERMAN, Laurie Anderson, 81-2
OAKLAND STROKE, Tony! Toni! Tone!, 90-50
OB-LA-DI OB-LA-DA:
Marmalade, 68-1
Bedrocks, 68-20
OBJECTS IN THE REAR VIEW MIRROR MAY APPEAR CLOSER THAN THEY ARE, Meat Loaf, 94-26
OBLIVION, Terrorvision, 94-21
OBLIVION (HEAD IN THE CLOUDS) [EP], Manix, 92-43
OBLIVIOUS, Aztec Camera, 83-47, 83-18
OBSESSED, 999, 81-71
OBSESSION, Reg Owen and his Orchestra, 60-43
OBSESSION, Animotion, 85-5
OBSESSION, Army Of Lovers, 91-67
OBSESSION, Ultra-Sonic, 94-75
THE OBVIOUS CHILD, Paul Simon, 90-15
OCEAN BLUE, ABC, 86-51
OCEAN DEEP, Cliff Richard, 84-41
OCEAN DRIVE, Lighthouse Family, 95-34, 96-11
OCEAN PIE, Shed Seven, 94-33
OCEAN SPRAY, Manic Street Preachers, 01-15
OCTOBER SWIMMER, JJ72, 00-29
ODE TO BILLY JOE, Bobbie Gentry, 67-13
ODE TO BOY, Alison Moyet, 94-59
ODE TO JOY (FROM BEETHOVEN SYMPHONY NO. 9), BBC Concert Orchestra/BBC Symphony Chorus conducted by Stephen Jackson, 96-36
ODE TO MY FAMILY, Cranberries, 94-26
OF COURSE I'M LYING, Yello, 89-23
OF COURSE YOU CAN, Spearhead, 94-74
OFF ON HOLIDAY, Suggs, 95-7
OFF ON YOUR OWN (GIRL), Al B. Sure!, 88-70
OFF THE HOOK, Jody Watley, 98-51
OFF THE WALL:
Michael Jackson, 79-7
Wisdome, 00-33
OFFICIAL SECRETS, M, 80-64
OFFSHORE, Chicane, 96-14, 97-17
OFFSHORE BANKING BUSINESS, Members, 79-31
OH-OH, I'M FALLING IN LOVE AGAIN, Jimmy Rodgers, 58-18
OH BABE, WHAT WOULD YOU SAY, Hurricane Smith, 72-4
OH BABY I . . ., Eternal, 94-4
OH, BOY:
Crickets, 57-3
Mud, 75-1
OH BOY, Fabulous Baker Boys, 97-34
OH BOY (THE MOOD I'M IN), Brotherhood Of Man, 77-8
OH! CAROL:
Neil Sedaka, 59-3, 72-19
General Saint featuring Don Campbell, 94-54
OH CAROL, Smokie, 78-5
OH CAROLINA, Shaggy, 93-1
OH DIANE, Fleetwood Mac, 82-9
OH FATHER, Madonna, 96-16
OH GIRL:
Chi-Lites, 72-14, 75-5
Paul Young, 90-25
OH HAPPY DAY, Johnston Brothers, 53-4
OH HAPPY DAY:
Edwin Hawkins Singers. Soloist: Dorothy Combs Morrison, 69-2
Beat System *, 93-70
OH HOW I MISS YOU, Bachelors, 67-30
OH JIM, Gay Dad, 99-47
OH JULIE, Shakin' Stevens, 82-1
OH LA LA LA, 2 Eivissa, 97-13
OH, LONESOME ME, Craig Douglas, 62-15
OH, LORI, Alessi, 77-8
OH LOUISE, Junior, 85-74
OH ME OH MY (I'M A FOOL FOR YOU BABY), Lulu, 69-47
OH, MEIN PAPA:
Eddie Calvert (The Man with the Golden Trumpet) with Norrie Paramor and his Orchestra, 53-1
Eddie Fisher with Hugo Winterhalter's Orchestra and Chorus *, 54-9
OH MY GOD, A Tribe Called Quest, 94-68
OH NO, Commodores, 81-44
OH NO (track from LYRICIST LOUNGE VOL. 2 [EP]), Mos Def Nate Dogg Pharoahe Monch, 01-24
OH NO NOT MY BABY:
Manfred Mann, 65-11
Rod Stewart, 73-6
Cher, 92-33
OH NO WON'T DO [EP] + lead track title, Cud, 91-49
OH PATTI (DON'T FEEL SORRY FOR LOVERBOY), Scritti Politti, 88-13
OH, PEOPLE, Patti Labelle, 86-26
OH, PRETTY WOMAN, Roy Orbison, 64-1
OH PRETTY WOMAN, Gary Moore featuring Albert King, 90-48
OH ROMEO, Mindy McCready, 98-41
OH SHEILA, Ready For The World, 85-50
OH SUSANNA, Don Charles presents The Singing Dogs, 55-13
OH, THE GUILT, Nirvana, 93-12
OH WELL:
Fleetwood Mac, 69-2
Oh Well, 89-28
OH WHAT A CIRCUS, David Essex, 78-3
OH! WHAT A DAY, Craig Douglas, 60-43
OH WHAT A FEELING, Change, 85-56
OH WHAT A NIGHT, Clock, 96-13
OH WHAT A SHAME, Roy Wood, 75-13
OH! WHAT A WORLD, Sister Bliss, 95-40
OH WORLD, Paul Rutherford, 89-61
OH YEAH!, Bill Withers, 85-60
OH YEAH, Ash, 96-6
OH YEAH, Caprice, 99-24
OH YEAH, Foxy Brown (featuring Spragga Benz), 01-27
OH YEAH, BABY, Dweeb, 97-70
OH YEAH (ON THE RADIO), Roxy Music, 80-5
OH YES! YOU'RE BEAUTIFUL, Gary Glitter, 74-2
OH YOU PRETTY THING, Peter Noone, 71-12
OHIO, Utah Saints, 95-42
OKAY!, Dave Dee, Dozy, Beaky, Mick and Tich, 67-4
OL' MAC DONALD, Frank Sinatra, 60-11
OL' RAG BLUES, Status Quo, 83-9
OLD, Kevin Rowland and Dexys Midnight Runners, 82-17

OLD, Machine Head, 95-43
OLD AND WISE, Alan Parsons Project lead vocals by Colin Blunstone, 83-74
OLD BEFORE I DIE, Robbie Williams, 97-2
THE OLD FASHIONED WAY (LES PLAISIRS DEMODES), Charles Aznavour, 73-38, 74-47
OLD FLAMES, Foster and Allen, 82-51
OLD FOLKS, A, 99-54
OLD MAN & ME (WHEN I GET TO HEAVEN), Hootie and the Blowfish, 96-57
THE OLD MAN AND THE ANGEL, It Bites, 87-72
THE OLD OAKEN BUCKET, Tommy Sands, 60-25
THE OLD PAYOLA ROLL BLUES, Stan Freberg, 60-40
THE OLD PI-ANNA RAG, Dickie Valentine, 55-15
OLD POP IN AN OAK, Rednex, 95-12
OLD RED EYES IS BACK, Beautiful South, 92-22
OLD RIVERS, Walter Brennan with the Johnny Mann Singers, 62-38
THE OLD RUGGED CROSS, Ethna Campbell, 75-33
OLD SHEP:
Clinton Ford, 59-27
Elvis Presley (from Strictly Elvis [EP]), 60-26
OLD SIAM, SIR, Wings, 79 35
OLD SMOKIE, Johnny and the Hurricanes, 61-24
THE OLD SONGS, Barry Manilow, 81-48
OLDER, George Michael, 97-3
OLDEST SWINGER IN TOWN, Fred Wedlock, 81-6
OLE OLA (MUHLER BRASILEIRA), Rod Stewart and the Scottish World Cup Squad '78, 78-4
THE OLIVE TREE, Judith Durham, 67-33
OLIVER'S ARMY, Elvis Costello and the Attractions, 79-2
OLYMPIAN, Gene, 95-18
OLYMPIC, 808 State, 90-10
AN OLYMPIC RECORD [M], Barron Knights, 68-35
THE OMD REMIXES [EP], Orchestral Manoeuvres In The Dark, 98-35
OMEN, Orbital, 90-46
THE OMEN, Program 2 Beltram, 91 53
OMEN III, Magic Affair, 94-17
ON, Aphex Twin, 93-32
ON A CAROUSEL, Hollies, 67-4
ON A CROWDED STREET, Barbara Pennington, 85-57
ON A DAY LIKE TODAY, Bryan Adams, 98-13
ON A LITTLE STREET IN SINGAPORE, Manhattan Transfer, 78-20
ON A MISSION, Aloof, 92-64
ON A NIGHT LIKE THIS, Kylie Minogue, 00-2
ON A RAGGA TIP, SL2, 92-2, 97-31
ON A ROPE, Rocket From The Crypt, 96-12
ON A SATURDAY NIGHT, Terry Dactyl and the Dinosaurs, 73-45
ON A SLOW BOAT TO CHINA, Emile Ford and the Checkmates, 60-3
ON A SUN-DAY, Benz, 97-73
ON A SUNDAY, Nick Heyward, 83-52
ON & ON, Erykah Badu, 97-12
ON AND ON, Aswad, 89-25
ON AND ON, Longpigs, 96-16
ON BENDED KNEE, Boyz II Men, 94-20
ON EVERY STREET, Dire Straits, 92-42
ON FIRE, T-Connection, 78-16
ON FIRE, Tone Loc, 89-13
ON HER MAJESTY'S SECRET SERVICE, Propellerheads/David Arnold, 97-7
ON HORSEBACK, Mike Oldfield, 75-4
ON MOTHER KELLY'S DOORSTEP, Danny La Rue, 68-33
ON MY OWN, Patti Labelle and Michael McDonald, 86-2
ON MY OWN, Craig McLachlan, 92-59
ON MY OWN, Peach, 98-69
ON MY RADIO, Selecter, 79-8
ON MY WAY, Mr. Fingers, 92-71
ON MY WAY, Mike Koglin featuring Beatrice, 99-28
ON MY WAY HOME, Enya, 96-26
ON MY WORD, Cliff Richard, 65-12
ON OUR OWN, Bobby Brown, 89-4
ON POINT, House Of Pain, 94-19
ON SILENT WINGS, Tina Turner, 96-13
ON STANDBY, Shed Seven, 96-12
ON THE BEACH, Cliff Richard and the Shadows, 64-7
ON THE BEACH :
Chris Rea, 86-57
Chris Rea, 88-12
York, 00-4
ON THE BEAT, B.B. and Q. Band, 81-41
ON THE BIBLE, Deuce, 95-13
ON THE DANCEFLOOR, DJ Disciple, 94 67
ON THE INSIDE (THEME FROM 'PRISONER CELL BLOCK H'), Lynne Hamilton, 89-3
ON THE LEVEL, Yomanda, 00-28
ON THE MOVE, Barthezz, 01-18
ON THE NIGHT, Mick and Pat, 88-70
ON THE ONE, Lukk featuring Felicia Collins, 85-72
ON THE RADIO:
Donna Summer, 80-32
Martine Mccutcheon, 01-7
ON THE REBOUND, Floyd Cramer, 61-1
ON THE ROAD AGAIN, Canned Heat, 68-8
ON THE ROPES [EP] + lead track title, Wonder Stuff, 93-10
ON THE ROSE, Tiger, 97-57
ON THE RUN, OMC, 97-56
ON THE RUN, De Bos, 97-51
ON THE RUN, Big Time Charlie, 99-22
ON THE STREET WHERE YOU LIVE:
Vic Damone with Percy Faith and his Orchestra and Chorus, 58-1
David Whitfield with Cyril Stapleton and his Orchestra, 58-16
ON THE TOP OF THE WORLD, Diva Surprise featuring Georgia Jones, 98-29
ON THE TRAIL, Prime Movers, 86-74
ON THE TURNING AWAY, Pink Floyd, 87-55
ON THE WINGS OF A NIGHTINGALE, Everly Brothers, 84-41
ON THE WINGS OF LOVE, Jeffrey Osborne, 84-11
ON WITH THE MOTLEY (VESTI LA GIUBBA), Harry Secombe, 55-16
ON YA WAY, Helicopter, 94-32, 96-37
ON YOUR OWN, Verve, 95-28
ON YOUR OWN, Blur, 97-5
ONCE, Geneveve, 66-43
ONCE AGAIN, Cud, 92-45
1NCE AGAIN, A Tribe Called Quest, 96-34
ONCE AROUND THE BLOCK, Badly Drawn Boy, 99-46, 00-27
ONCE AROUND THE SUN, Caprice, 01-24
ONCE BITTEN TWICE SHY, Ian Hunter, 75-14
ONCE BITTEN TWICE SHY, Vesta Williams, 86-14
ONCE I HAD A SWEETHEART, Pentangle, 69-46
ONCE IN A LIFETIME, Talking Heads, 81-14
ONCE IN EVERY LIFETIME, Ken Dodd, 61-28
ONCE MORE . . ., Orb, 01-38
ONCE THERE WAS A TIME, Tom Jones, 66-18
ONCE UPON A DREAM, Billy Fury, 62-7
ONCE UPON A LONG AGO, Paul McCartney, 87-10
ONCE UPON A TIME, Marvin Gaye and Mary Wells, 64-50
ONCE UPON A TIME, Tom Jones, 65-32
ONCE UPON A TIME, Pogues, 94-66
ONCE YOU'VE TASTED LOVE, Take That, 92-47
ONE, Metallica, 89-13
ONE, Bee Gees, 89-71
ONE:
U2, 92-7
Mica Paris, 95-29
THE ONE, Elton John, 92-10
ONE, Busta Rhymes (featuring Erykah Badu), 98-23
THE ONE, Backstreet Boys, 00-8
ONE [EP], Mansun, 96-37
ONE & ONE, Robert Miles featuring Maria Nayler, 96-3
ONE & ONE IS ONE, Medicine Head, 73-3
THE ONE AND ONLY, Gladys Knight and the Pips, 78-32
THE ONE AND ONLY, Chesney Hawkes, 91-1
ONE ARMED SCISSOR, At The Drive-In, 00-64
ONE BETTER DAY, Madness, 84-17
ONE BETTER WORLD, ABC, 89-32
ONE BIG FAMILY [EP] + lead track title, Embrace, 97-21
ONE BROKEN HEART FOR SALE, Elvis Presley with the Mello Men, 63-12
ONE BY ONE, Cher, 96-7
ONE COOL REMOVE, Shawn Colvin with Mary Chapin Carpenter, 95-40
ONE DANCE WON'T DO, Audrey Hall, 86-20
ONE DAY, Tyrrel Corporation, 92-59
ONE DAY, Danny D Presents D:Mob, 94-41
ONE DAY AT A TIME, Lena Martell, 79-1
ONE DAY AT A TIME, Alice Band, 01-52
ONE DAY I'LL FLY AWAY, Randy Crawford, 80-2
ONE DAY IN YOUR LIFE, Michael Jackson, 81-1
ONE DRINK TOO MANY, Sailor, 77-35
ONE FINE DAY, Chiffons, 63-29
ONE FINE MORNING, Tommy Hunt, 76-44
ONE FOOT IN THE GRAVE, Eric Idle featuring Richard Wilson, 94-50
THE ONE FOR ME, Joe, 94-34
ONE FOR SORROW, Steps, 98-2, 01-2
ONE FOR THE MOCKINGBIRD, Cutting Crew, 87-52
ONE FOR THE MONEY, Horace Brown, 96-12
ONE FOR YOU, ONE FOR ME:
Jonathan King, 78-29
La Bionda, 78-54
ONE GIANT LOVE, Cud, 94-52
ONE GIFT OF LOVE, Dear Jon, 95-68
ONE GOODBYE IN TEN, Shara Nelson, 93-21
ONE GREAT THING, Big Country, 86-19
ONE HEADLIGHT, Wallflowers, 97-54
ONE HEART BETWEEN TWO, Dave Berry, 64-41
ONE HELLO, Randy Crawford, 82-48
100 MILES AND RUNNIN', N.W.A., 90-38
100%, Sonic Youth, 92-28
100%, Mary Kiani, 97-23
100% PURE LOVE, Crystal Waters, 94-15
101, Sheena Easton, 89-54
101-DAM – NATIONS, Scarlet Party, 82-44
138 TREK, DJ Zinc, 00-27
THE ONE I GAVE MY HEART TO, Aaliyah, 97-30
THE ONE I LOVE, R.E.M., 87-51, 91-16
ONE IN A MILLION, Aaliyah, 97-15
ONE IN TEN:
UB40, 81-7
808 State; UB40, 92-17
ONE INCH ROCK, Tyrannosaurus Rex, 68-28, 72-7
ONE KISS FROM HEAVEN, Louise, 96-9
ONE LAST KISS, J. Geils Band, 79-74
ONE LAST LOVE SONG, Beautiful South, 94-14
ONE LOVE, Atlantic Starr, 85-58
ONE LOVE, Pat Benatar, 89-59
ONE LOVE, Stone Roses, 90-4
ONE LOVE, Dr. Alban, 92-45
ONE LOVE, Prodigy, 93-8
ONE LOVE FAMILY, Liquid, 95-14
ONE LOVE IN MY LIFETIME, Innocence, 92-40
ONE LOVE/PEOPLE GET READY [M], Bob Marley and the Wailers, 84-5, 91-42
ONE LOVER AT A TIME, Atlantic Starr, 87-57
ONE LOVER (DON'T STOP THE SHOW), Forrest, 83-67
ONE MAN, Chanelle, 89-16, 94-50
ONE MAN ARMY, Our Lady Peace, 00-70
ONE MAN BAND, Leo Sayer, 74-6
ONE MAN IN MY HEART, Human League, 95-13
ONE MAN WOMAN, Sheena Easton, 80-14
ONE MAN'S BITCH, Phoebe One featuring Red Rat, Goofy and Buccaneer (Main Street Crew), 98-59
ONE MIND TWO HEARTS, Paradise, 83-42
ONE MINUTE MAN, Missy "Misdemeanor" Elliott featuring Ludacris, 01-10
ONE MIRROR TOO MANY, Black Crowes, 96-51
ONE MOMENT IN TIME, Whitney Houston, 88-1
ONE MORE, Haziza, 01-75
ONE MORE CHANCE, Diana Ross, 81-49
ONE MORE CHANCE, Maxi Priest, 93-40
ONE MORE CHANCE, E.Y.C., 94-25
ONE MORE CHANCE, Madonna, 96-11
ONE MORE CHANCE, One, 97-31
ONE MORE CHANCE/STAY WITH ME [M], Notorious Big, 95-34
ONE MORE DANCE, Esther and Abi Ofarim, 68-13
ONE MORE GOOD NIGHT WITH THE BOYS, Tasmin Archer, 96-45
ONE MORE NIGHT, Phil Collins, 85-4
ONE MORE RIVER, Luciana, 94-67
ONE MORE SATURDAY NIGHT, Matchbox, 82-63

ONE MORE SUNRISE (MORGEN):
Dickie Valentine; Wally Stott Orchestra and Chorus, 59-14
Ivo Robic und die Sing-Masters *, 59-23
ONE MORE TIME, Whycliffe, 94-72
ONE MORE TIME, Daft Punk vocals performed by Romanthony, 00-2
ONE MORE TRY, George Michael, 88-8
ONE MORE TRY, Kristine W, 96-41
ONE NATION, Masquerade, 86-54
ONE NATION UNDER A GROOVE, Funkadelic, 78-9
ONE NIGHT:
Elvis Presley, 59-1
Mud, 75-32
ONE NIGHT IN BANGKOK, Murray Head, 84-12
ONE NIGHT IN HEAVEN (second entry from ELEGANTLY AMERICAN [EP]), M-People, 93-6, 94-31
ONE NIGHT STAND, Let Loose, 95-12
ONE NIGHT STAND, Aloof, 96-30
ONE NIGHT STAND, Mis-Teeq, 01-5
ONE-NINE FOR SANTA, Fogwell Flax and the Ankle Biters from Freehold Junior School, 81-68
ONE OF THE BROKEN (from JORDAN: THE EP [EP]), Prefab Sprout, 91-35
ONE OF THE LIVING, Tina Turner, 85-55
ONE OF THE LUCKY ONES, Joan Regan, 60-47
ONE OF THE PEOPLE, Adamski's Thing, 98-56
ONE OF THESE DAYS, Ambassador, 00-67
ONE OF THESE NIGHTS, Eagles, 75-23
ONE OF THOSE NIGHTS, Bucks Fizz, 81-20
ONE OF US, Abba, 81-3
ONE OF US, Joan Osborne, 96-6
ONE OF US MUST KNOW (SOONER OR LATER), Bob Dylan, 66-33
ONE ON ONE, Daryl Hall and John Oates, 83-63
ONE PIECE AT A TIME, Johnny Cash and the Tennessee Three, 76-32
ONE REASON WHY, Craig McLachlan, 92-29
ONE ROAD, Love Affair, 69-16
ONE RULE FOR YOU, After The Fire, 79-40
ONE SHINING MOMENT, Diana Ross, 92-10
ONE SHOT, Brotherhood, 96-55
ONE SLIP, Pink Floyd, 88-50
ONE SMALL DAY, Ultravox, 84-27
ONE STEP, Killah Priest, 98-45
ONE STEP AHEAD, Nik Kershaw, 89-55
ONE STEP AWAY, Tavares, 77-16
ONE STEP BEYOND . . ., Madness, 79-7
ONE STEP CLOSER, Linkin Park, 01-24
ONE STEP CLOSER (TO LOVE), George McCrae, 84-57
ONE STEP FURTHER, Bardo, 82-2
ONE STEP OUT OF TIME, Michael Ball, 92-20
ONE SWEET DAY, Mariah Carey and Boyz II Men, 95-6
1000%, Fatima Mansions, 92-61
1234, Mrs Wood, 98-54
ONE TO ANOTHER, Charlatans, 96-3
THE ONE TO CRY, Escorts, 64-49
1 TO 1 RELIGION, Bomb The Bass featuring Carlton, 95-53
THE ONE TO SING THE BLUES, Motorhead, 91-45
ONE TONGUE, Hothouse Flowers, 93-45
ONE TRUE WOMAN, Yazz, 92-60
1-2-3, Len Barry, 65-3
1-2-3, Professionals, 80-43
1-2-3, Gloria Estefan and Miami Sound Machine, 88-9
1-2-3, Chimes, 89-60
ONE, TWO, THREE, Dina Carroll, 98-16
ONE, TWO, THREE O'LEARY, Des O'Connor with Alyn Ainsworth and his Orchestra, 68-4
1.2.3.4 GET WITH THE WICKED, Richard Blackwood featuring Deetah, 00-10
1, 2, 3, 4 (SUMPIN' NEW), Coolio, 96-13
ONE VISION, Queen, 85-7
ONE VOICE, Bill Tarmey, 93-16
ONE WAY:
Levellers, 91-51
Levellers, 99-33
ONE WAY LOVE, Cliff Bennett and the Rebel Rousers, 64-9
ONE WAY OUT, Reid, 88-66
ONE WAY TICKET, Eruption, 79-9
ONE WEEK, Barenaked Ladies, 99-5
ONE WILD NIGHT (2001 VERSION), Bon Jovi, 01-10
ONE WOMAN, Jade, 93-22
THE 'ONEDIN LINE' THEME, Vienna Philharmonic Orchestra conducted by Aram Khachaturian, 71-15
THE ONES YOU LOVE, Rick Astley, 93-48
THE ONION SONG, Marvin Gaye and Tammi Terrell, 69-9
ONLY, Anthrax, 93-36
ONLY CRYING, Keith Marshall, 81-12
THE ONLY FLAME IN TOWN, Elvis Costello and the Attractions, 84-71
ONLY FOOLS (NEVER FALL IN LOVE), Sonia, 91-10
ONLY FOR A WHILE, Toploader, 01-19
ONLY FOR LOVE, Limahl, 83-16
ONLY HAPPY WHEN IT RAINS, Garbage, 95-29
ONLY HUMAN, Dina Carroll, 96-33
ONLY IF . . ., Enya, 97-43
ONLY IN MY DREAMS, Debbie Gibson, 87-54, 88-11
THE ONLY LIVING BOY IN NEW CROSS, Carter – The Unstoppable Sex Machine, 92-7
THE ONLY LIVING BOY IN NEW YORK [EP] + lead track title, Everything But The Girl, 93-42
ONLY LOVE, Nana Mouskouri, 86-2
ONLY LOVE CAN BREAK YOUR HEART:
Elkie Brooks, 78-43
Mint Juleps, 86-62
St. Etienne, 91-39
ONLY LOVE REMAINS, Paul McCartney, 86-34
ONLY LOVING DOES IT, Guys 'N' Dolls, 78-42
THE ONLY MAN ON THE ISLAND:
Tommy Steele and the Steelmen, 58-16
Vic Damone with Frank De Vol and his Orchestra, 58-24
ONLY ME, Hyperlogic, 95-35, 98-48
THE ONLY ONE, Transvision Vamp, 89-15
THE ONLY ONE, Gun, 95-29
ONLY ONE, Peter Andre, 96-16
THE ONLY ONE, Thunder, 98-31
THE ONLY ONE I KNOW, Charlatans, 90-9
ONLY ONE ROAD, Celine Dion, 95-8
ONLY ONE WOMAN, Marbles, 68-5
ONLY ONE WORD, Propaganda, 90-71
THE ONLY RHYME THAT BITES, MC Tunes versus 808 State, 90-10, 99-53
ONLY SAW TODAY/INSTANT KARMA [M], Amos, 94-48
ONLY SIXTEEN:
Craig Douglas, 59-1
Sam Cooke, 59-23
Al Saxon, 59-24
ONLY TENDER LOVE, Deacon Blue, 93-22
ONLY THE HEARTACHES, Houston Wells and the Marksmen, 63-22
ONLY THE LONELY, T'Pau, 89-28
ONLY THE LONELY (KNOW HOW I FEEL):
Roy Orbison, 60-1
Prelude *, 82-55
ONLY THE LOOT CAN MAKE ME HAPPY, R. Kelly, 00-24
ONLY THE MOMENT, Marc Almond, 89-45
ONLY THE ONES WE LOVE, Tanita Tikaram, 91-69
ONLY THE STRONG SURVIVE, Billy Paul, 77-33
ONLY THE STRONG SURVIVE, DJ Krush, 96-71
ONLY THE STRONGEST SURVIVE, Hurricane #1, 98-19
ONLY THE WOMEN KNOW, Six Chix, 00-72
THE ONLY THING THAT LOOKS GOOD ON ME IS YOU, Bryan Adams, 96-6
ONLY TIME, Enya, 00-32
ONLY TIME WILL TELL, Asia, 82-54
ONLY TIME WILL TELL, Ten City, 92-63
ONLY TO BE WITH YOU, Roachford, 94-21
ONLY WANNA KNOW U COS URE FAMOUS (REMIX), Oxide and Neutrino (featuring Swiss, Skat D, Kaish, Harvey), 01-12
THE ONLY WAY IS UP, Yazz and the Plastic Population, 88-1
THE ONLY WAY OUT, Cliff Richard, 82-10
ONLY WHEN I LOSE MYSELF, Depeche Mode, 98-17
ONLY WHEN I SLEEP, Corrs, 97-58
ONLY WHEN YOU LEAVE, Spandau Ballet, 84-3
ONLY WITH YOU, Captain Hollywood Project, 93-67, 94-61
ONLY WOMEN BLEED, Julie Covington, 77-12
ONLY YESTERDAY, Carpenters, 75-7
ONLY YOU, Teddy Pendergrass, 78-41
ONLY YOU:
Yazoo, 82-2, 99-38
Flying Pickets, 83-1
ONLY YOU, Praise, 91-4
ONLY YOU, Portishead, 98-35
ONLY YOU, Casino, 99-72
ONLY YOU (AND YOU ALONE):
Hilltoppers, 56-3
Platters, 56-5, 57-18
Mark Wynter, 64-38
Jeff Collins *, 72-40
Ringo Starr *, 74-28
Child, 79-33
John Alford *, 96-9
ONLY YOU CAN, Fox, 75-3
ONLY YOU CAN ROCK ME, U.F.O., 78-50
ONLY YOUR LOVE, Bananarama, 90-27
ONWARD CHRISTIAN SOLDIERS, Harry Simeone Chorale, 60-35, 61-36, 62-38
OO . . . AH . . . CANTONA, Oo La La, 92-64
OO-EEH BABY, Stonebridge McGuinness, 79-54
OOCHIE WALLY, QB Finest featuring Nas and Bravehearts, 01-30
OOCHY KOOCHY, Baby Ford, 88-58
OOH AAH (G-SPOT), Wayne Marshall, 94-29, 96-50
OOH! AAH! CANTONA, 1300 Drums featuring The Unjustified Ancients Of M U, 96-11
OOH AAH.. JUST A LITTLE BIT, Gina G, 96-1
OOH-AH-AA (I FEEL IT), E.Y.C., 95-33
OOH BABY, Gilbert O'Sullivan, 73-18
OOH BOY, Rose Royce, 80-46
OOH I DO, Lynsey De Paul, 74-25
OOH I LIKE IT, Jonny L, 93-73
OOH LA LA, Joe 'Mr. Piano' Henderson, 60-46
OOH LA LA, Coolio, 97-14
OOH LA LA, Rod Stewart, 98-16
OOH LA LA, Wiseguys, 98-55, 99-2
OOH LA LA LA, Red Raw featuring 007, 95-59
OOH LA LA LA (LET'S GO DANCIN'), Kool And The Gang, 82-6
OOH! MY SOUL, Little Richard, 58-22
OOH STICK YOU!, Daphne and Celeste, 00-8
OOH TO BE AH, Kajagoogoo, 83-7
OOH-WAKKA-DOO-WAKKA-DAY, Gilbert O'Sullivan, 72-8
OOH! WHAT A LIFE, Gibson Brothers, 79-10
OOHHH BABY, Vida Simpson, 95-70
OOO LA LA LA, Teena Marie, 88-74
OOOH., De La Soul featuring Redman, 00-29
OOOIE, OOOIE, OOOIE, Prickly Heat, 98-57
OOOPS, 808 State featuring Bjork, 91-42
OOOPS UP, Snap!, 90-5
OOPS! . . . I DID IT AGAIN, Britney Spears, 00-1
OOPS UP SIDE YOUR HEAD, Gap Band, 80-6, 87-20
007 (SHANTY TOWN):
Desmond Dekker and the Aces, 67-14
Musical Youth *, 83-26
OPAL MANTRA, Therapy?, 93-13
OPEN ARMS, Mariah Carey, 96-4
OPEN ARMS, Wilt, 00-59
OPEN ROAD, Gary Barlow, 97-7
OPEN SESAME, Leila K, 93-23
OPEN UP, Mungo Jerry, 72-21
OPEN UP, Leftfield Lydon, 93-13
OPEN UP THE RED BOX, Simply Red, 86-61
OPEN UP YOUR HEART, Joan Regan, 55-19
OPEN UP YOUR MIND (LET ME IN), Real People, 91-70
OPEN YOUR EYES, Black Box, 91-48
OPEN YOUR HEART, Human League Blue, 81-6
OPEN YOUR HEART, M People, 95-9
OPEN YOUR HEART, Madonna, 86-4
OPEN YOUR MIND, 808 State, 91-38
OPEN YOUR MIND, Usura, 93-7, 97-21
THE OPERA HOUSE, Jack E. Makossa, 87-48
OPERAA HOUSE, Malcolm McLaren presents the World Famous Supreme Team Show, 90-75
OPERATION BLADE (BASS IN THE PLACE . . .), Public Domain, 00-5
OPERATOR, Midnight Star, 85-66
OPERATOR, Little Richard, 86-67
OPIUM SCUMBAGZ, Olav Basoski, 00-56

OPPORTUNITIES (LET'S MAKE LOTS OF MONEY), Pet Shop Boys, 86-11
OPPOSITES ATTRACT, Paula Abdul (duet with the Wild Pair), 90-2
OPTIMISTIC, Sounds Of Blackness, 91-45, 92-28
OPUS 40, Mercury Rev, 99-31
OPUS 17 (DON'T YOU WORRY 'BOUT ME), 4 Seasons featuring the "Sound" Of Frankie Valli, 66-20
ORANGE BLOSSOM SPECIAL, Spotnicks, 62-29
ORANGE CRUSH, R.E.M., 89-28
THE ORANGE THEME, Cygnus X, 00-43
ORCHARD ROAD, Leo Sayer, 83-16
ORDINARY ANGEL, Hue And Cry, 88-42
ORDINARY DAY, Curiosity Killed The Cat, 87-11
ORDINARY GIRL, Alison Moyet, 87-43
ORDINARY LIVES, Bee Gees, 89-54
ORDINARY WORLD:
Duran Duran, 93-6
Aurora featuring Naimee Coleman, 00-5
ORIGINAL, Leftfield Halliday, 95-18
THE ORIGINAL BIRD DANCE, Electronica's, 81-22
ORIGINAL NUTTAH, UK Apachi with Shy Fx, 94-39
ORIGINAL PRANKSTER, Offspring, 00-6
ORIGINAL SIN (THEME FROM THE SHADOW), Taylor Dayne, 95-63
ORINOCO FLOW (SAIL AWAY), Enya, 88-1
ORLANDO DAWN, Liquid, 00-53
ORVILLE'S SONG, Keith Harris and Orville, 82-4
OSCAR, Shaft, 00-67
OSSIE'S DREAM . . . (SPURS ARE ON THEIR WAY TO WEMBLEY), Tottenham Hotspur F.A. Cup Final Squad Season 1980/81, 81-5
THE OTHER MAN'S GRASS (IS ALWAYS GREENER), Petula Clark, 67-20
THE OTHER SIDE, Aerosmith, 90-46
THE OTHER SIDE OF LOVE, Yazoo, 82-13
THE OTHER SIDE OF ME, Andy Williams, 76-42
THE OTHER SIDE OF SUMMER, Elvis Costello, 91-43
THE OTHER SIDE OF THE SUN, Janis Ian, 80-44
THE OTHER SIDE OF YOU, Mighty Lemon Drops, 86-67
THE OTHER WOMAN, THE OTHER MAN, Gerard Kenny, 84-69
OTHERNESS [EP], Cocteau Twins, 95-59
OTHERSIDE, Red Hot Chili Peppers, 00-33
OUIJA BOARD, OUIJA BOARD, Morrissey, 89-18
OUR DAY WILL COME, Ruby and the Romantics, 63-38
OUR FAVOURITE MELODIES, Craig Douglas with Harry Robinson and his Orchestra, 62-9
OUR FRANK, Morrissey, 91-26
OUR GOAL, Arsenal F.C., 00-46
OUR HOUSE, Madness, 82-5
OUR KIND OF LOVE, Hannah, 00-41
OUR LAST SONG TOGETHER, Neil Sedaka, 73-31
OUR LIPS ARE SEALED:
Go-Go's, 82-47
Fun Boy Three, 83-7
OUR LOVE, Elkie Brooks, 82-43
(OUR LOVE) DON'T THROW IT ALL AWAY, Andy Gibb, 79-32
OUR RADIO ROCKS, PJ and Duncan AKA, 95-15
OUR WORLD, Blue Mink, 70-17
OUT COME THE FREAKS:
Was (Not Was), 84-41
Was (Not Was) *, 88-44
OUT DEMONS OUT, Edgar Broughton Band, 70-39
OUT HERE ON MY OWN, Irene Cara, 82-58
OUT IN THE DARK, Lurkers, 79-72
OUT IN THE FIELDS, Gary Moore and Phil Lynott, 85-5
OUT OF CONTROL, Angelic Upstarts, 80-58
OUT OF CONTROL, Rolling Stones, 98-51
OUT OF CONTROL, Chemical Brothers, 99-21
OUT OF CONTROL (BACK FOR MORE), Darude, 01-13
OUT OF HAND, Mighty Lemon Drops, 87-66
OUT OF MY HEAD, Marradona, 94-38, 97-39
OUT OF MY MIND, Johnny Tillotson, 63-34
OUT OF MY MIND, Duran Duran, 97-21
OUT OF REACH, Vice Squad, 82-68
OUT OF REACH, Primitives, 88-25
OUT OF REACH, Gabrielle, 01-4
OUT OF SEASON, Almighty, 93-41
OUT OF SIGHT, Babybird, 00-58
OUT OF SIGHT, Spiritualized, 01-65
OUT OF SIGHT.OUT OF MIND, Level 42, 83-41
OUT OF SPACE, Prodigy, 92-6, 96-52
OUT OF TEARS, Rolling Stones, 94-36
OUT OF THE BLUE, Debbie Gibson, 88-19
OUT OF THE BLUE, System F, 99-14
OUT OF THE SILENT PLANET, Iron Maiden, 00-20
OUT OF THE SINKING:
Paul Weller, 94-20
Paul Weller, 96-16
OUT OF THE STORM, Incognito, 96-57
OUT OF THE VOID, Grass-Show, 97-75
OUT OF THIS WORLD, Tony Hatch, 62-50
OUT OF TIME:
Chris Farlowe, 66-1, 75-44
Dan McCafferty, 75-41
Rolling Stones, 75-45
OUT OF TOUCH, Daryl Hall and John Oates, 84-48, 85-62
OUT OF TOWN, Max Bygraves, 56-18
OUT OF YOUR MIND, True Steppers and Dane Bowers featuring Victoria Beckham, 00-2
OUT ON THE FLOOR, Dobie Gray, 75-42
OUT THERE, Dinosaur Jr, 93-44
OUT THERE, Friends Of Matthew, 99-61
OUT WITH HER, Blow Monkeys, 87-30
OUTA SPACE, Billy Preston, 72-44
OUTDOOR MINER, Wire, 79-51
OUTERSPACE GIRL, Beloved, 93-38
OUTLAW, Olive, 97-14
OUTRAGEOUS, Stix 'N' Stoned, 96-39
OUTSHINED, Soundgarden, 92-50
OUTSIDE, Omar, 94-43
OUTSIDE, George Michael, 98-2
OUTSIDE, Staind, 01-33
OUTSIDE IN THE RAIN, Gwen Guthrie, 87-37
OUTSIDE MY WINDOW, Stevie Wonder, 80-52
OUTSIDE OF HEAVEN, Eddie Fisher with Hugo Winterhalter's Orchestra and Chorus, 53-1
OUTSIDE YOUR ROOM [EP] + lead track title, Slowdive, 93-69
OUTSTANDING:
Gap Band, 83-68
Kenny Thomas, 91-12
Andy Cole, 99-68
OUTTA SPACE, Mellow Trax, 00-41
OVER, Portishead, 97-25
OVER AND OVER, Dave Clark Five, 65-45
OVER AND OVER, James Boys, 73-39
OVER AND OVER, Shalamar, 83-23
OVER & OVER, Plux featuring Georgia Jones, 96-33
OVER AND OVER, Puff Johnson, 97-20
OVER MY HEAD – MUSIC FROM THE MOTION PICTURE TITAN A.E., Lit, 00-37
OVER MY SHOULDER, Mike and the Mechanics, 95-12
OVER RISING, Charlatans, 91-15
OVER THE EDGE, Almighty, 93-38
OVER THE HILLS AND FAR AWAY, Gary Moore, 86-20
OVER THE RAINBOW:
Sam Harris, 85-67
Eva Cassidy, 01-42
OVER THE RAINBOW/YOU BELONG TO ME [M], Matchbox, 80-15
OVER THE RIVER, Bitty McLean, 95-27
OVER THE SEA, Jesse Rae, 85-65
OVER THE WEEKEND, Nick Heyward, 86-43
OVER THERE (I DON'T CARE), House Of Pain, 95-20
OVER TO YOU JOHN (HERE WE GO AGAIN) [M], Jive Bunny and the Mastermixers, 91-28
OVER UNDER SIDEWAYS DOWN, Yardbirds, 66-10
OVER YOU, Freddie and the Dreamers, 64-13
OVER YOU, Roxy Music, 80-5
OVER YOU, Ray Parker Jr., 80-65
OVER YOU, Justin, 99-11
OVER YOU, Warren Clarke featuring Kathy Brown, 01-42
OVERCOME, Tricky, 95-34
OVERDRIVE, DJ Sandy vs Housetrap, 00-32
OVERGROUND (from THE THORN [EP]), Siouxsie and the Banshees, 84-47
OVERJOYED, Stevie Wonder, 86-17
OVERKILL, Motorhead, 79-39
OVERKILL, Men At Work, 83-21
OVERLOAD, Sugababes, 00-6
OVERTHROWN, Libido, 98-53
OVERTIME, Level 42, 91-62
OWNER OF A LONELY HEART, Yes, 83-28
OXBOW LAKES, Orb, 95-38
OXYGEN, Blaggers I*T*A, 93-51
OXYGEN, JJ72, 00-23
OXYGENE (PART 4), Jean Michel Jarre, 77-4, 89-65
OXYGENE 8, Jean Michel Jarre, 97-17
OXYGENE 10, Jean Michel Jarre, 97-21
OYE, Gloria!, 98-33
OYE COMO VA, Tito Puente Jr. and the Latin Rhythm featuring Tito Puente, India and Cali Aleman, 96-36, 97-56
OYE MI CANTO (HEAR MY VOICE), Gloria Estefan, 89-16
P.A.S.S.I.O.N., Rythm Syndicate, 91-58
P.C.P., Manic Street Preachers, 94-16
P.E. 2000, Puff Daddy [featuring Hurricane G], 99-13
P:MACHINERY, Propaganda, 85-50
P.OWER OF A.MERICAN N.ATIVES, Dance 2 Trance, 93-25
P.Y.T. (PRETTY YOUNG THING), Michael Jackson, 84-11
PABLO, Russ Conway, 61-45
PAC-MAN, Power-Pill, 92-43
PACIFIC -, 808 State, 89-10, 98-21
PACIFIC MELODY, Airscape, 97-27
PACK UP YOUR SORROWS, Joan Baez, 66-50
PACKET OF PEACE, Lionrock, 93-32
PACKJAMMED (WITH THE PARTY POSSE), Stock Aitken Waterman, 87-41
PAGAN POETRY, Bjork, 01-38
PAID IN FULL, Eric B. and Rakim, 87-15
PAID MY DUES, Anastacia, 01-14
PAIN, Betty Wright, 86-42
THE PAIN INSIDE, Cosmic Rough Riders, 01-36
PAIN KILLER, Judas Priest, 90-74
PAINT A PICTURE, Man With No Name featuring Hannah, 96-42
PAINT IT, BLACK:
Rolling Stones, 66-1, 90-61
Mo-Dettes, 80-42
PAINT ME DOWN, Spandau Ballet, 81-30
PAINT THE SILENCE, South, 01-69
PAINTED MOON, Silencers, 88-57
PAINTER MAN:
Creation, 66-36
Boney M, 79-10
A PAIR OF BROWN EYES, Pogues, 85-72
PAISLEY PARK, Prince and the Revolution, 85-18
PAL OF MY CRADLE DAYS, Ann Breen, 83-69, 84-74
PALE BLUE EYES, Paul Quinn and Edwyn Collins, 84-72
PALE MOVIE, Saint Etienne, 94-28
PALE RED, Jerry Burns, 92-64
PALE SHELTER, Tears For Fears, 83-5, 85-73
PALISADES PARK, Freddy Cannon with Frank Slay and his Orchestra, 62-20
PALOMA BLANCA, George Baker Selection, 75-10
PAMELA, PAMELA, Wayne Fontana, 66-11
PANAMA, Van Halen, 84-61
THE PANDEMONIUM SINGLE [EP] + lead track title, Killing Joke, 94-28
PANDORA'S BOX, Procol Harum, 75-16
PANDORA'S BOX, Orchestral Manoeuvres In The Dark, 91-7
PANIC, Smiths, 86-11
PANIC ON, Madder Rose, 94-65
PANINARO '95, Pet Shop Boys, 95-15
PANIS ANGELICUS, Anthony Way and the Warsaw Philharmonia, 95-55
PANTHER PARTY, Mad Moses, 97-50
PAPA DON'T PREACH, Madonna, 86-1
PAPA LOVES MAMA, Joan Regan, 60-29
PAPA LOVES MAMBO, Perry Como and the Ray Charles Singers, 54-16
PAPA OOM MOW MOW:
Sharonettes, 75-26
Gary Glitter, 75-38
PAPA WAS A ROLLIN' STONE, Temptations, 73-14, 87-13
PAPA WAS A ROLLING STONE, Was Not Was, 90-12
PAPA'S GOT A BRAND NEW BAG, James Brown and the Famous Flames, 65-25
PAPA'S GOT A BRAND NEW PIGBAG:
Pigbag, 82-3
Silent Underdog, 85-73
Perfecto Allstarz *, 95-6
PAPER DOLL, Don Estelle and Windsor Davies, 75-41
PAPER DOLL, PM Dawn, 91-49
PAPER PLANE, Status Quo, 73-8

PAPER ROSES:
Anita Bryant, 60-24
Maureen Evans, 60-40
Kaye Sisters, 60-7
Marie Osmond, 73-2
PAPER SUN, Traffic, 67-5
PAPER TIGER, Sue Thompson, 65-30
PAPERBACK WRITER, Beatles, 66-1, 76-23
PAPERCUT, Linkin Park, 01-14
PAPERFACES, Feeder, 99-41
PAPERLATE (from 3 X 3 [EP]), Genesis, 82-10
PAPILLON, N-Joi, 94-70
PAPUA NEW GUINEA, Future Sound Of London, 92-22, 01-28
PARA MI, Motivation, 01-71
PARADE, White and Torch, 82-54
PARADISE, Frank Ifield, 65-26
PARADISE, Stranglers, 83-48
PARADISE, Black, 88-38
PARADISE, Sade, 88-29
PARADISE, Birdland, 89-70
PARADISE, Diana Ross, 89-61
PARADISE, Ralph Fridge, 99-68
PARADISE, Kaci, 01-11
PARADISE BIRD, Amii Stewart, 80-39
PARADISE CITY :
Guns N' Roses, 89-6
N-Trance, 98-28
PARADISE LOST, Herd, 67-15
PARADISE SKIES, Max Webster, 79-43
PARALYSED, Elvis Presley, 57-8
PARANOID:
Black Sabbath, 70-4, 80-14
Dickies, 79-45
PARANOID ANDROID, Radiohead, 97-3
PARANOIMIA, Art Of Noise with Max Headroom, 86-12
PARDON ME, Incubus, 00-61
PARIS BY AIR, Tygers Of Pan Tang, 82-63
PARIS IS ONE DAY AWAY, Mood, 82-42
THE PARIS MATCH, Style Council, 83-7
PARISIENNE GIRL, Incognito, 80-73
PARISIENNE WALKWAYS:
Gary Moore, 79-8
Gary Moore, 93-32
PARKLIFE, Blur starring Phil Daniels, 94-10
PART OF THE PROCESS, Morcheeba, 98-38
PART OF THE UNION, Strawbs, 73-2
PART TIME LOVE, Gladys Knight and the Pips, 75-30
PART TIME LOVE, Elton John, 78-15
PART-TIME LOVER, Stevie Wonder, 85-3
PARTAY FEELING, B-Crew featuring Barbara Tucker, Ultra Nate, Dajae, Mone, 97-45
PARTY, Elvis Presley with the Jordanaires, 57-2
THE PARTY, Kraze, 88-29
PARTY ALL NIGHT, Kreuz, 95-75
PARTY ALL NIGHT, Mytown, 99-22
PARTY DOLL:
Buddy Knox with the Rhythm Orchids, 57-29
Jets, 84-72
PARTY FEARS TWO, Associates, 82-9
PARTY FOUR [EP], Mad Jocks featuring Jockmaster B.A., 93-57
PARTY FREAK, Cashflow, 86-15
PARTY HARD, Pulp, 98-29
PARTY HARD, Andrew W.K., 01-19
PARTY IN PARIS, U.K. Subs, 80-37
PARTY LIGHTS, Gap Band, 80-30
PARTY PARTY, Elvis Costello and the Attractions with the Royal Guard Horns, 82-48
PARTY PEOPLE . . . FRIDAY NIGHT, 911, 97-5
PARTY PEOPLE (LIVE YOUR LIFE BE FREE), Pianoman, 97-43
PARTY POPS [M], Russ Conway, 57-24
PARTY TIME, Fatback Band, 76-41
PARTY TIME (THE GO-GO EDIT), Kurtis Blow, 85-67
PARTY UP THE WORLD, D:Ream, 95-20
PARTY ZONE, Daffy Duck featuring The Groove Gang, 91-58
PARTYLINE, Brass Construction, 84-56
PARTYMAN, Prince, 89-14
THE PARTY'S OVER, Lonnie Donegan, 62-9
PASADENA, Temperance Seven vocal refrain by Mr. Paul MacDowell, 61-4
PASILDA, Afro Medusa, 00-31
PASS & MOVE (IT'S THE LIVERPOOL GROOVE), Liverpool FC and the Boot Room Boyz, 96-4
PASS IT ON, Bitty McLean, 93-35
PASS THE DUTCHIE, Musical Youth, 82-1
PASS THE MIC, Beastie Boys, 92-47
PASS THE VIBES, Definition Of Sound, 95-23
A PASSAGE TO BANGKOK, Rush, 81-41
THE PASSENGER:
Siouxsie and the Banshees, 87-41
Iggy Pop, 98-22
PASSENGERS, Elton John, 84-5
PASSIN' ME BY, Pharcyde, 93-55
PASSING BREEZE, Russ Conway with Tony Osborne and his Orchestra, 60-16
PASSING STRANGERS:
Sarah Vaughan and Billy Eckstine, 57-22, 69-20
Joe Longthorne and Liz Dawn, 94-34
PASSING STRANGERS, Ultravox, 80-57
PASSION, Rod Stewart, 80-17
PASSION, Gat Decor, 92-29, 96-6
PASSION, Jon Of The Pleased Wimmin, 95-27
PASSION, Amen! UK, 97-15
PASSION IN DARK ROOMS, Mood, 82-74
PASSION KILLER, One The Juggler, 83-71
THE PASSION OF LOVERS + also (from THE SINGLES 1981-1983 [EP]), Bauhaus, 81-56
PASSION RULES THE GAME, Scorpions, 89-74
PASSIONATE FRIEND, Teardrop Explodes, 81-25
PAST, PRESENT AND FUTURE, Cindy and the Saffrons, 83-56
PAST THE MISSION, Tori Amos, 94-31
PAT-A-CAKE, PAT-A-CAKE/THREE BLIND MICE/JINGLE BELLS [M], Don Charles presents the Singing Dogs, 55-13
PATCHES, Clarence Carter, 70-2
PATHS, Robert Miles featuring Nina Miranda, 01-74
PATHS OF PARADISE, Johnnie Ray, 55-20
PATHWAY TO THE MOON, MN8, 96-25
PATIENCE, Guns N' Roses, 89-10
PATIENCE, Nerina Pallot, 01-61
PATIENCE OF ANGELS, Eddi Reader, 94-33
PATIO SONG, Gorky's Zygotic Mynci, 96-41
PATRICIA, Perez Prado and his Orchestra, 58-8
THE PAY-OFF (A MOI DE PAYER), Kenny Ball and his Jazzmen; Clarinet-Dave Jones, 62-23
PAY TO THE PIPER, Chairmen Of The Board, 71-34
THE PAYBACK MIX PART ONE [M], James Brown, 88-12
PAYING THE PRICE OF LOVE, Bee Gees, 93-23
PEACE, Sabrina Johnston, 91-8, 92-35
PEACE AND JOY, Soundsation, 95-48
PEACE + LOVEISM, Son'z Of A Loop Da Loop Era, 92-60
PEACE IN OUR TIME, Imposter, 84-48
PEACE IN OUR TIME, Big Country, 89-39
PEACE IN OUR TIME, Cliff Richard, 93-8
PEACE IN THE WORLD, Don-E, 92-41
PEACE ON EARTH, Hi Tension, 78-8
PEACE ON EARTH – LITTLE DRUMMER BOY [M], David Bowie and Bing Crosby, 82-3
PEACE THROUGHOUT THE WORLD, Maxi Priest (featuring Jazzie B.), 90-41
PEACEFUL, Georgie Fame, 69-16
PEACH, Prince, 93-14
PEACHES, Stranglers, 77-8
PEACHES, Darts, 80-66
PEACHES, Presidents Of The United States Of America, 96-8
PEACHES & CREAM, One (112) Twelve, 01-32
PEACOCK SUIT, Paul Weller, 96-5
PEAKIN', Bleachin', 00-32
PEARL, Chapterhouse, 91-67
PEARL IN THE SHELL, Howard Jones, 84-7
PEARL RIVER, Three 'N One presents Johnny Shaker [featuring Serial Diva], 99-32
PEARL'S A SINGER, Elkie Brooks, 77-8
PEARL'S GIRL, Underworld, 96-24, 96-22
PEARLY-DEWDROPS DROPS, Cocteau Twins, 84-29
PEEK-A-BOO, New Vaudeville Band (featuring Tristam Vii), 67-7
PEEK-A-BOO, Stylistics, 73-35
PEEK A BOO, Siouxsie and the Banshees, 88-16
THE PEEL SESSIONS (1ST JUNE 1982) [EP], New Order, 86-54
PEGGY SUE, Buddy Holly, 57-6, 68-32
PEGGY SUE GOT MARRIED, Buddy Holly, 59-13
PENNIES FROM HEAVEN, Inner City, 92-24
PENNY ARCADE, Roy Orbison, 69-27
PENNY LANE, Beatles, 67-2, 87-65
PENNY LOVER, Lionel Richie, 84-18
PENTHOUSE AND PAVEMENT, Heaven 17, 81-57, 93-54
PEOPLE, Tymes, 69-16
PEOPLE, Intastella, 91-74
PEOPLE ARE PEOPLE, Depeche Mode, 84-4
PEOPLE ARE STILL HAVING SEX, Latour, 91-15
PEOPLE ARE STRANGE, Echo and the Bunnymen, 88-29, 91-34
PEOPLE EVERYDAY, Arrested Development, 92-2
PEOPLE GET READY:
Jeff Beck and Rod Stewart, 92-49
Rod Stewart, 93-45
PEOPLE GET REAL, Saint Etienne, 92-21
PEOPLE HOLD ON:
Coldcut featuring Lisa Stansfield, 89-11
Lisa Stansfield vs the Dirty Rotten Scoundrels, 97-4
PEOPLE IN THA MIDDLE, Spearhead, 95-49
PEOPLE LIKE YOU AND PEOPLE LIKE ME, Glitter Band, 76-5
PEOPLE OF LOVE, Amen! UK, 97-36
PEOPLE OF THE SUN, Rage Against The Machine, 96-26
PEPE:
Duane Eddy, 61-2
Russ Conway with John Barry and his Orchestra, 61-19
PEPPER, Butthole Surfers, 96-59
PEPPER BOX, Peppers, 74-6
THE PEPPERMINT TWIST, Danny Peppermint and the Jumping Jacks, 62-26
PEPPERMINT TWIST, Joey Dee and the Starliters, 62-33
PER SEMPRE AMORE (FOREVER IN LOVE), Lolly, 00-11
PER-SO-NAL-LY, Wigans Ovation, 75-38
PERFECT, Fairground Attraction, 88-1
PERFECT, Lightning Seeds, 95-18
PERFECT, PJ and Duncan, 95-16
PERFECT, Smashing Pumpkins, 98-24
PERFECT BLISS, Bellefire, 01-18
PERFECT DAY, EMF, 95-27
PERFECT DAY:
Duran Duran, 95-28
Kirsty MacColl and Evan Dando, 95-75
Various Artists, 97-1
Various Artists, 00-69
PERFECT DAY, Skin, 96-33
A PERFECT DAY ELISE, P J Harvey, 98-25
THE PERFECT DRUG, Nine Inch Nails, 97-43
PERFECT GENTLEMEN, Wyclef Jean, 01-4
THE PERFECT KISS, New Order, 85-46
PERFECT LOVESONG, Divine Comedy, 01-42
PERFECT MOMENT, Martine McCutcheon, 99-1
PERFECT MOTION, Sunscreem, 92-18
PERFECT PLACE, Voice Of The Beehive, 92-37
PERFECT SKIN, Lloyd Cole and the Commotions, 84-71
PERFECT STRANGERS, Deep Purple, 85-48, 85-68
PERFECT 10, Beautiful South, 98-2
PERFECT TIMING, Kiki Dee, 81-66
PERFECT WAY, Scritti Politti, 85-48
PERFECT WORLD, Huey Lewis and the News, 88-48
THE PERFECT YEAR, Dina Carroll, 93-5
PERFIDIA, Ventures, 60-4
PERFUME, Paris Angels, 91-55
PERFUMED GARDEN, Rah Band, 82-45
PERHAPS LOVE, Placido Domingo and John Denver, vocal duet – John Denver, guitar, 81-46
PERMANENT TEARS, Eagle-Eye Cherry, 99-43
PERPETUAL DAWN, Orb, 91-61, 94-18
PERRY MASON, Ozzy Osbourne, 95-23
PERSEVERANCE, Terrorvision, 96-5
PERSONAL FEELING, Audioweb, 98-65
PERSONAL JESUS, DM, 89-13
PERSONAL TOUCH, Errol Brown, 87-25
PERSONALITY:
Anthony Newley, 59-6
Lloyd Price and his Orchestra, 59-9
Lena Zavaroni *, 74-33
PERSONALITY, Eugene Wilde, 85-34
PERSUASION, Tim Finn, 93-43
A PESSIMIST IS NEVER DISAPPOINTED, Theaudience, 98-27
PETAL, Wubble-U, 98-55
PETER AND THE WOLF, Clyde Valley Stompers, 62-25

POOR MAN'S SON, Rockin' Berries, 65-5
POOR ME, Adam Faith, 60-1
THE POOR PEOPLE OF PARIS, Winifred Atwell and her Other Piano, 56-1
POP, *Nsync, 01-9
POP COP, Gyres, 96-71
POP GO THE WORKERS [M], Barron Knights with Duke D'Mond, 65-5
POP GOES MY LOVE, Freeez, 83-26
POP GOES THE WEASEL, Anthony Newley, 61-12
POP GOES THE WEASEL, 3rd Bass, 91-64
POP IS DEAD, Radiohead, 93-42
POP LIFE, Prince and the Revolution, 85-60
POP MUZIK:
M, 79-2, 89-15
All Systems Go, 88-63
THE POP SINGER'S FEAR OF THE POLLEN COUNT, Divine Comedy, 99-17
POP YA COLLAR, Usher, 01-2
POPCORN, Hot Butter, 72-5
POPCORN LOVE, New Edition, 83-43
POPPA JOE, Sweet, 72-11
POPPA PICCOLINO, Diana Decker, 53-2
POPPED!!, Fool Boona, 99-52
POPS, WE LOVE YOU, Diana Ross, Marvin Gaye, Smokey Robinson and Stevie Wonder, 79-66
POPSCENE, Blur, 92-32
PORCELAIN, Moby, 00-5
PORT-AU-PRINCE, Winifred Atwell and Frank Chacksfield, 56-18
PORTRAIT OF MY LOVE, Matt Monro, 60-3
PORTSMOUTH (second entry from TAKE 4 [EP]), Mike Oldfield, 76-3, 78-72
PORTUGUESE WASHERWOMAN, Joe 'Fingers' Carr, 56-20
POSITIVE BLEEDING, Urge Overkill, 93-61
POSITIVE EDUCATION, Slam, 01-44
A POSITIVE VIBRATION, Blackbox, 96-21
POSITIVELY 4TH STREET, Bob Dylan, 65-8
POSSESSED, Vegas, 92-32
POSSESSION, Transfer, 01-54
POSSIBLY MAYBE, Bjork, 96-13
POST MODERN SLEAZE, Sneaker Pimps, 97-22
POSTCARDS FROM HEAVEN, Lighthouse Family, 99-24
POSTMAN PAT, Ken Barrie, 82-44, 83-59
POUNDCAKE, Van Halen, 91-74
POUR SOME SUGAR ON ME, Def Leppard, 87-18
POW POW POW, Fontana featuring Darryl D'Bonneau, 01-62
POWDER BLUE, Elbow, 01-41
THE POWER:
Snap!, 90-1
Snap! featuring Einstein, 96-42
POWER:
Nu Colours, 92-64, 93-40
Monie Love, 93-33
POWER AND THE GLORY, Saxon, 83-32
THE POWER IS YOURS, Redskins, 86-59
POWER OF A WOMAN, Eternal, 95-5
THE POWER (OF ALL THE LOVE IN THE WORLD), D:Ream, 95-40
THE POWER OF GOOD-BYE, Madonna, 98-6
THE POWER OF LOVE:
Frankie Goes To Hollywood, 84-1, 93-10, 00-6
Holly Johnson, 99-56,
THE POWER OF LOVE, Celine Dion, 94-4
THE POWER OF LOVE, Jennifer Rush, 85-1, 86-55
POWER OF LOVE, Huey Lewis and the News, 85-11, 86-9
POWER OF LOVE, Deee-Lite, 90-25
THE POWER OF LOVE, Q-Tex, 94-65, 97-49
THE POWER OF LOVE, Fits Of Gloom featuring Lizzy Mack, 94-49
POWER OF LOVE/LOVE POWER [M], Luther Vandross, 91-46, 95-31
POWER RANGERS, Mighty Morph'n Power Rangers, 94-3
POWER TO ALL OUR FRIENDS, Cliff Richard, 73-4
POWER TO THE PEOPLE, John Lennon/Plastic Ono Band, 71-7
THE POWER ZONE [EP], Time Frequency, 93-17
POWERGEN (ONLY YOUR LOVE), P.K.A., 92-70
POWERTRIP, Monster Magnet, 99-39
PRACTICE WHAT YOU PREACH, Barry White, 95-20
PRAISE, Inner City, 92-59
PRAISE YOU, Fatboy Slim, 99-1
PRANCE ON, Eddie Henderson, 78-44
PRAY, M.C. Hammer, 90-8
PRAY, Take That, 93-1
PRAY, Tina Cousins, 98-20
PRAY FOR LOVE, Love To Infinity, 96-69
PRAYER FOR THE DYING, Seal, 94-14, 95-51
PRAYER FOR YOU, Texas, 89-73
A PRAYER TO THE MUSIC, Marco Polo, 95-65
PRAYER TOWER, Paradise Organisation, 93-70
PRAYING FOR TIME, George Michael, 90-6
PREACHER MAN, Bananarama, 91-20
PREACHER, PREACHER, Animal Nightlife, 85-67
PRECIOUS, Jam, 82-1, 83-73
PRECIOUS, Annie Lennox, 92-23
PRECIOUS HEART, Tall Paul vs Inxs, 01-14
PRECIOUS TIME, Van Morrison, 99-36
PREGNANT FOR THE LAST TIME, Morrissey, 91-25
PREPARE TO LAND, Supernaturals, 97-48
PRESENCE OF LOVE (LAUGHARNE), Alarm, 88-44
PRESS, Paul McCartney, 86-25
PRESSURE, Sunscreem, 92-60, 93-19
PRESSURE, Billy Ocean, 93-55
PRESSURE, Driza Bone, 94-33
PRESSURE DROP, Izzy Stradlin', 92-45
PRESSURE ON, Roger Taylor, 98-45
THE PRESSURE PT 1, Sounds Of Blackness, 91-71, 92-49, 98-46
PRESSURE US [RM], Sunscreem, 93-19
PRETEND:
Nat "King" Cole, 53-2
Alvin Stardust, 81-4
PRETEND BEST FRIEND, Terrorvision, 94-25
PRETEND WE'RE DEAD, L7, 92-21, 92-50
PRETENDER GOT MY HEART, Presenting . . . Alisha's Attic, 01-43
PRETENDERS TO THE THRONE, Beautiful South, 95-18
PRETTIEST EYES, Beautiful South, 94-37
PRETTY BLUE EYES, Craig Douglas, 60-4
PRETTY BROWN EYES, Jim Reeves, 68-33
PRETTY DEEP, Tanya Donelly, 97-55
PRETTY FLAMINGO, Manfred Mann, 66-1
PRETTY FLY (FOR A WHITE GUY), Offspring, 99-1
PRETTY GOOD YEAR, Tori Amos, 94-7
PRETTY IN PINK:
Psychedelic Furs, 81-43
Psychedelic Furs, 86-18
PRETTY JENNY, Jess Conrad, 62-50
PRETTY LITTLE ANGEL EYES:
Curtis Lee, 61-47
Showaddywaddy, 78-5
PRETTY LITTLE BLACK-EYED SUSIE, Guy Mitchell with Mitch Miller and his Orchestra and Chorus, 53-2
PRETTY NOOSE, Soundgarden, 96-14
PRETTY PAPER, Roy Orbison, 64-6
PRETTY THING, Bo Diddley, 63-34
PRETTY VACANT:
Sex Pistols, 77-6, 92-56
Sex Pistols, 96-18
PRETTY WOMAN, Juicy Lucy, 70-44
THE PRICE OF LOVE:
Everly Brothers, 65-2
Bryan Ferry (from Extended Play [EP]), 76-7, 89-49
PRICE YOU PAY, Questions, 83-56
PRIDE (IN THE NAME OF LOVE):
U2, 84-3
Clivilles and Cole, 92-15
PRIMAL SCREAM, Motley Crue, 91-32
PRIMARY, Cure, 81-43
PRIMARY INSTINCT, Senseless Things, 93-41
PRIMARY RHYMING, MC Tunes, 90-67
PRIME MOVER, Zodiac Mindwarp and the Love Reaction, 87-18
PRIME MOVER, Rush, 88-43
PRIME TIME, Tubes, 79-34
PRIME TIME, Haircut One Hundred, 83-46
PRIME TIME, Mtume, 84-57
PRIMROSE LANE, Dickie Pride, 59-28
THE PRINCE, Madness, 79-16
A PRINCE AMONG ISLANDS [EP], Capercaillie, 92-39
PRINCE CHARMING, Adam and the Ants, 81-1
PRINCE IGOR, Rapsody Warren G and Sissel, 98-15
PRINCE OF DARKNESS, Bow Wow Wow, 81-58
PRINCE OF PEACE, Galliano, 92-47
PRINCES OF THE NIGHT, Blast featuring V.D.C., 94-40
PRINCESS IN RAGS, Gene Pitney, 65-9
PRINCESS OF THE NIGHT, Saxon, 81-57
PRINCESS PRINCESS, Johnny Tillotson, 79-67
PRINCIPAL'S OFFICE, Young M.C., 90-54
PRINCIPLES OF LUST, Enigma, 91-59
THE PRISONER, F.A.B. featuring MC Number 6, 90-56
PRISONER, All Blue, 99-73
PRISONER OF LOVE, Spear Of Destiny, 84-59
PRISONER OF LOVE, Millie Scott, 86-52
A PRISONER OF THE PAST, Prefab Sprout, 97-30
PRIVATE DANCER, Tina Turner, 84-26
PRIVATE EMOTION, Ricky Martin featuring Meja, 00-9
PRIVATE EYES, Daryl Hall and John Oates, 82-32
PRIVATE INVESTIGATIONS, Dire Straits, 82-2
PRIVATE LIFE, Grace Jones, 80-17
PRIVATE NUMBER:
Judy Clay and William Bell, 68-8
911, 99-3
PRIVATE PARTY, Wally Jump Jr. and the Criminal Element, 88-57
PRIVILEGE (SET ME FREE), Patti Smith Group, 78-72
PRIX CHOC, Etienne De Crecy, 98-60
PRIZE OF GOLD, Joan Regan with Johnny Douglas and his Orchestra, 55-6
PRO-GEN, Shamen, 90-55, 91-5, 96-35
PROBABLY A ROBBERY, Renegade Soundwave, 90-38
PROBLEMS, Everly Brothers, 59-6
PROCESS OF ELIMINATION, Eric Gable, 94-63
PROCESSION, New Order, 81-38
PRODIGAL BLUES, Billy Idol, 90-47
PRODIGAL SON, Steel Pulse, 78-35
PRODUCT OF THE WORKING CLASS, Little Angels, 91-40
PROFESSIONAL WIDOW, Tori Amos, 96-20, 97-1
PROFIT IN PEACE, Ocean Colour Scene, 99-13
PROFOUNDLY IN LOVE WITH PANDORA, Ian Dury, 85-45
PROFOUNDLY YOURS, Hue And Cry, 92-74
THE PROGRAM, David Morales and the Bad Yard Club, 93-66
A PROMISE, Echo and the Bunnymen, 81-49
THE PROMISE, Arcadia, 86-37
THE PROMISE, When In Rome, 89-58
PROMISE, Delirious?, 97-20
THE PROMISE, Essence, 98-27
PROMISE ME, Beverley Craven, 91-3
THE PROMISE OF A NEW DAY, Paula Abdul, 91-52
THE PROMISE YOU MADE, Cock Robin, 86-28
THE PROMISED LAND:
Chuck Berry, 65-26
Elvis Presley, 75-9
PROMISED LAND:
Joe Smooth, 89-56
Style Council, 89-27
PROMISED YOU A MIRACLE:
Simple Minds, 82-13
Simple Minds Live, 87-19
PROMISES, Ken Dodd with Geoff Love and his Orchestra, 66-6
PROMISES, Eric Clapton, 78-37
PROMISES, Buzzcocks, 78-20
PROMISES (FRENCH MIX), Basia, 88-48
PROMISES, Take That, 91-38
PROMISES, Paris Red, 93-59
PROMISES, Cranberries, 99-13
PROMISES, Def Leppard, 99-41
PROPHASE, Transa, 97-65
THE PROPHET, CJ Bolland, 97-19
PROTECT YOUR MIND (FOR THE LOVE OF A PRINCESS), DJ Sakin and Friends, 99-4
PROTECTION, Massive Attack with Tracey Thorn, 95-14
PROUD, Heather Small, 00-16
PROUD MARY:
Creedence Clearwater Revival, 69-8
Checkmates Ltd., featuring Sonny Charles, 69-30
THE PROUD ONE, Osmonds, 75-5
PROUD TO FALL, Ian McCulloch, 89-51
PROVE IT, Television, 77-25
PROVE YOU WRONG (from WHOSE FIST IS THIS ANYWAY [EP]), Prong, 92-58
PROVE YOUR LOVE, Taylor Dayne, 88-8
PSYCHE ROCK, Pierre Henry/Michel Colombier, 97-58
PSYCHEDELIC SHACK, Temptations, 70-33
PSYCHO BASE, Shades Of Rhythm, 97-57

THE RAIN (SUPA DUPA FLY), Missy 'Misdemeanor' Elliott, 97-16
RAINBOW, Marmalade, 70-3
RAINBOW, Peters and Lee, 74-17
RAINBOW CHASER, Nirvana, 68-34
RAINBOW CHILD, Dan Reed Network, 90-60, 90-39
RAINBOW COUNTRY, Bob Marley vs. Funkstar De Luxe, 00-11
RAINBOW IN THE DARK, Dio, 83-46
RAINBOW LAKE, Wendy and Lisa, 90-70
RAINBOW PEOPLE, Manix, 92-57
RAINBOW (SAMPLE-FREE), Solo, 91-59
RAINBOW THEME/FROZEN RAINBOW [M], Saxon, 80-66
RAINBOW VALLEY, Love Affair with the Keith Mansfield Orchestra, 68-5
RAINBOWS [EP], Terry Hall, 95-62
RAINBOWS OF COLOUR, Grooverider with guest vocalist Roya Arab, 98-40
RAINCLOUD, Lighthouse Family, 97-6
THE RAINDANCE, Dare, 89-62
RAINDROPS KEEP FALLING ON MY HEAD:
Sacha Distel, 70-10
B. J. Thomas *, 70-38
Bobbie Gentry, 70-40
RAININ' THROUGH MY SUNSHINE, Real Thing, 78-40
RAINING ALL OVER THE WORLD, Adventures, 92-68
RAINING IN MY HEART, Leo Sayer, 78-21
RAINMAKER, Sparklehorse, 96-61
RAINY DAY WOMEN NOS. 12 & 35, Bob Dylan, 66-7
RAINY DAYS AND MONDAYS, Carpenters, 93-63
RAINY NIGHT IN GEORGIA, Randy Crawford, 81-18
A RAINY NIGHT IN SOHO, Pogues, 91-67
RAISE, Hyper Go-Go, 94-36
RAISE YOUR HAND, Eddie Floyd, 67-42
RAISE YOUR HANDS, Reel 2 Real featuring The Mad Stuntman, 94-14
RAISE YOUR HANDS, Big Room Girl featuring Darryl Pandy, 99-40
RAISED ON ROCK, Elvis Presley, 73-36
RAM-BUNK-SHUSH, Ventures, 61-45
RAM GOAT RIVER, Pluto Shervington, 76-43
RAMA LAMA DING DONG, Rocky Sharpe and the Replays, 78-17
RAMBLIN' ROSE, Nat King Cole, 62-5
RAME, Snap! featuring 'Rukmani', 96-50
RAMONA, Bachelors, 64-4
RANDY, Blue Mink, 73-9
RANKING FULL STOP, Beat, 79-6
RAOUL AND THE KINGS OF SPAIN, Tears For Fears, 95-31
RAP DIS (U CAN'T STOP DIS ST),** Oxide and Neutrino (featuring Swiss, Skat D, Kaish, Harvey), 01-12
RAP SCHOLAR, Das Efx featuring Redman, 98-42
RAP SUMMARY, Big Daddy Kane, 89-52
(RAP) SUPERSTAR, Cypress Hill, 00-13
RAP YOUR LOVE, Set The Tone, 83-67
RAPE ME, Nirvana, 93-32
RAPP PAYBACK (WHERE IZ MOSES ?), James Brown, 81-39
RAPPAZ R.N. DAINJA, Krs One, 96-47
RAPPER'S DELIGHT, Sugarhill Gang, 79-3, 89-58
RAPTURE, Blondie, 81-5
RAPTURE, IIO, 01-2
RARE, PRECIOUS AND GONE, Mike Scott, 98-74
THE RASCAL KING, Mighty Mighty Bosstones, 98-63
RASPBERRY BERET, Prince and the Revolution, 85-25
RASPUTIN, Boney M, 78-2
RAT IN MI KITCHEN, UB40, 87-12
RAT RACE, Specials, 80-5
RAT RAPPING (BRILLIANT ISN'T IT), Roland Rat Superstar, 83-14
RAT TRAP, Boomtown Rats, 78-1
RATAMAHATTA, Sepultura, 96-23
THE RATTLER, Goodbye Mr. MacKenzie, 89-37
RATTLESNAKES, Lloyd Cole and the Commotions, 84-65
RAUNCHY:
Bill Justis, 58-11
Ken Mackintosh, his Saxophone and his Orchestra, 58-19
RAVE ALERT!, Praga Khan, 92-39
THE RAVE DIGGER, MC Lethal, 92-66
RAVE GENERATOR, Toxic Two, 92-13
RAVE ON, Buddy Holly, 58-5, 68-32
RAVEL'S PAVANE POUR UNE INFANTE DEFUNTE, William Orbit, 00-31
RAVING I'M RAVING, Shut Up And Dance featuring Peter Bouncer, 92-2
RAW, Spandau Ballet, 88-47
RAW, Alarm, 91-51
RAW, Melky Sedeck, 99-50
RAW POWER, Apollo Four Forty, 97-32
RAWHIDE, Frankie Laine with Jimmy Carroll and his Orchestra, 59-6
RAY OF LIGHT, Madonna, 98-2
RAYS OF THE RISING SUN:
Denise Johnson, 94-45
Mozaic, 96-32
RAZOR'S EDGE, Meat Loaf, 84-41
RAZZAMATAZZ, Quincy Jones, 81-11
RAZZLE DAZZLE, Bill Haley and his Comets, 56-13
RAZZLE DAZZLE, Heatwave, 79-43
RE:EVOLUTION, Shamen with Terence McKenna, 93-18
RE-REWIND THE CROWD SAY BO SELECTA, Artful Dodger, 99-2
RE:VOLUTION, Coldcut and the Guilty Party, 01-67
REACH, Judy Cheeks, 94-17, 96-22
REACH, Lil Mo' Yin Yang, 96-28
REACH, Gloria Estefan, 96-15
REACH, S Club 7, 00-2
REACH FOR THE STARS, Shirley Bassey with Geoff Love and his Orchestra, 61-1
REACH 4 THE MELODY, Victoria Wilson James, 97-72
REACH OUT, Midfield General featuring Linda Lewis, 00-61
REACH OUT AND TOUCH (SOMEBODY'S HAND), Diana Ross, 70-33
REACH OUT FOR ME, Dionne Warwick, 64-23
REACH OUT I'LL BE THERE:
Four Tops, 66-1, 88-11
Gloria Gaynor, 75-14
Michael Bolton, 93-37
REACH UP, Toney Lee, 83-64
REACH UP (PAPA'S GOT A BRAND NEW PIG BAG), Perfecto Allstarz, 95-6
REACHERS OF CIVILISATION, York, 00-4
REACHIN':
Phase II, 89-70, 91-70
House Of Virginism, 94-35
REACHING FOR THE BEST, Exciters, 75-31
REACHING FOR THE WORLD, Harold Melvin and the Blue Notes, 77-48
READ 'EM AND WEEP, Barry Manilow, 83-17
READ MY LIPS, DSK, 91-51
READ MY LIPS, Alex Party, 93-49, 94-29, 96-28
READ MY LIPS (ENOUGH IS ENOUGH), Jimmy Somerville, 90-26
READ MY MIND, Conner Reeves, 98-19
READY, Bruce Wayne, 97-44
READY AN' WILLING (SWEET SATISFACTION), Whitesnake, 80-43
READY FOR A NEW DAY, Todd Terry features Martha Wash, 98-20
READY FOR LOVE, Jimmy Jones, 60-46
READY FOR LOVE, Gary Moore, 89-56
READY OR NOT, Lightning Seeds, 96-20
READY OR NOT:
Fugees (Refugee Camp), 96-1
Course, 97-5
READY OR NOT, DJ Dado and Simone Jay, 99-51
READY OR NOT, A1, 99-3
READY OR NOT HERE I COME (CAN'T HIDE FROM LOVE):
Delfonics, 71-41
Fugees (Refugee Camp) *, 96-1
Course *, 97-5
READY STEADY GO, Generation X, 78-47
READY STEADY WHO [EP], Who, 83-58
READY TO GO, Republica, 96-43, 97-13
READY TO RECEIVE, Animalhouse, 00-61
READY TO RUN, Dixie Chicks, 99-53
READY, WILLING AND ABLE, Doris Day with Buddy Cole and his Orchestra, 55-7
REAL, Donna Allen, 95-34
REAL COOL WORLD, David Bowie, 92-53
REAL EMOTION, Reid, 89-65
REAL FASHION REGGAE STYLE, Carey Johnson, 87-19
REAL GONE KID, Deacon Blue, 88-8
REAL GOOD, Double Six, 98-66
REAL GOOD TIME, Alda, 98-7
REAL GREAT BRITAIN, Asian Dub Foundation, 00-41
REAL LIFE, Simple Minds, 91-34
REAL LIFE, Bon Jovi, 99-21
THE REAL LIFE, Raven Maize, 01-12
REAL LOVE, Ruby Murray with the Norrie Paramor Orchestra, 58-18
REAL LOVE, Jody Watley, 89-31
REAL LOVE:
Driza – Bone, 91-16
Drizabone, 95-24
REAL LOVE, Dare, 91-67
REAL LOVE, Time Frequency, 92-60, 93-8
REAL LOVE, Mary J. Blige, 92-68, 93-26
REAL LOVE, Beatles, 96-4
THE REAL ME, W.A.S.P., 89-23
A REAL MOTHER FOR YA, Johnny 'Guitar' Watson, 77-44
REAL PEOPLE, Apache Indian, 97-66
REAL REAL REAL, Jesus Jones, 90-19
THE REAL SLIM SHADY, Eminem, 00-1
THE REAL THING, Brothers Johnson, 81-50
THE REAL THING, Jellybean featuring Steven Dante, 87-13
THE REAL THING, ABC, 89-68
THE REAL THING, Tony Di Bart, 94-1, 98-51
THE REAL THING, 2 Unlimited, 94-6
THE REAL THING, Lisa Stansfield, 97-9
REAL VIBRATION (WANT LOVE), Express Of Sound, 96-45
REAL WILD CHILD (WILD ONE), Iggy Pop, 86-10
THE REAL WILD HOUSE, Raul Orellana, 89-29
REALITY USED TO BE A FRIEND OF MINE, PM Dawn, 92-29
REALLY DOE, Ice Cube, 93-66
REALLY FREE, John Otway and Wild Willy Barrett, 77-27
REALLY SAYING SOMETHING (HE WAS REALLY SAYIN' SOMETHIN'):
Bananarama and the Fun Boy Three, 82-5
Buffalo G*, 00-17
REALLY SCRAP THE SKY (from IDIOTS AT THE WHEEL [EP]), Kingmaker, 92-30
REAP THE WILD WIND, Ultravox, 82-12
THE REASON, Celine Dion, 97-11
REASON FOR LIVING, Roddy Frame, 98-45
REASON TO BELIEVE:
Rod Stewart, 71-19
Rod Stewart with special guest Ronnie Wood, 93-51
REASON TO LIVE, Kiss, 87-33
REASONS, Kleshay, 98-33
REASONS TO BE CHEERFUL, PART 3, Ian Dury and the Blockheads, 79-3
REBEL MUSIC, Rebel MC, 90-53
REBEL REBEL, David Bowie, 74-5
REBEL-ROUSER, Duane Eddy and his Twangy Guitar, 58-19
REBEL RUN, Toyah, 83-24
REBEL WITHOUT A PAUSE, Public Enemy, 87-37
REBEL WOMAN, DNA rap performed by Jazzi P, 91-42
REBEL YELL:
Billy Idol, 84-62, 85-6
Scooter, 96-30
REBIRTH OF SLICK (COOL LIKE DAT), Digable Planets, 93-67
RECIPE FOR LOVE, Harry Connick, Jr., 91-32
RECKLESS, Afrika Bambaataa and Family featuring UB40, 88-17
RECONNECTION [EP], Zero B, 93-54
RECOVER YOUR SOUL, Elton John, 98-16
RECOVERY, Fontella Bass, 66-32
RED, Elbow, 01-36
RED ALERT, Basement Jaxx, 99-5
THE RED BALLOON, Dave Clark Five, 68-7
RED DRESS, Alvin Stardust, 74-7
RED FRAME/WHITE LIGHT, Orchestral Manoeuvres In The Dark, 80-67
RED GUITAR, David Sylvian, 84-17
RED HOT, Princess, 87-58
RED HOT, Vanessa-Mae, 95-37
A RED LETTER DAY, Pet Shop Boys, 97-9
RED LIGHT, Billy Ocean, 77-2
RED LIGHT, GREEN LIGHT, Mitchell Torok and the Tulane Sisters, 57-29
RED LIGHT – GREEN LIGHT [EP] + lead track title, Wildhearts, 96-30
RED LIGHT SPECIAL, TLC, 95-18
RED RAIN :
Peter Gabriel, 87-46
Peter Gabriel (from SW Live [EP]), 94-39
RED RED WINE:
Jimmy James and the Vagabonds, 68-36
Tony Tribe, 69-46
UB40, 83-1

RIDE MY SEE-SAW, Moody Blues, 68-42
RIDE-O-ROCKET, Brothers Johnson, 78-50
RIDE ON BABY, Chris Farlowe, 66-31
RIDE ON THE RHYTHM, Little Louie Vega and Marc Anthony, 91-71, 92-70, 98-36
RIDE ON TIME, Black Box, 89-1
RIDE THE BULLET, Army Of Lovers, 92-67
RIDE THE GROOVE, Players Association, 79-42
RIDE THE LOVE TRAIN, Light Of The World, 81-49
RIDE THE RHYTHM, Z Factor, 01-52
RIDE THE STORM (JOEY NEGRO & AUDIO SOUL PROJECT MIXES), Akabu featuring Linda Clifford (A Joey Negro Production), 01-69
RIDE THE TIGER, Boo Radleys, 97-38
RIDE WIT ME, Nelly featuring City Spud, 01-3
RIDERS IN THE SKY:
Ramrods, 61-8
Shadows, 80-12
RIDERS ON THE STORM:
Doors, 71-22, 76-33, 91-68
Annabel Lamb, 83-27
RIDICULOUS THOUGHTS, Cranberries, 95-20
RIDING ON A TRAIN, Pasadenas, 88-13
RIDING ON THROUGH, Deee-Lite, 91-53
RIDING WITH THE ANGELS, Samson, 81-55
RIGHT AND EXACT, Chrissy Ward, 95-62, 97-59
RIGHT BACK WHERE WE STARTED FROM:
Maxine Nightingale, 75-8
Sinitta, 89-4
RIGHT BEFORE MY EYES:
Patti Day, 89-69
N 'n' G Featuring Kallaghan, 00-12
RIGHT BESIDE YOU, Sophie B. Hawkins, 94-13
RIGHT BETWEEN THE EYES, Wax, 86-60
RIGHT BY YOUR SIDE, Eurythmics, 83-10
THE RIGHT COMBINATION, Seiko and Donnie Wahlberg, 90-44
THE RIGHT DECISION, Jesus Jones, 93-36
RIGHT HERE, SWV, 93-3
RIGHT HERE, Ultimate Kaos, 95-18
RIGHT HERE, RIGHT NOW, Jesus Jones, 90-31, 91-31
RIGHT HERE RIGHT NOW, Disco Citizens, 95-40
RIGHT HERE RIGHT NOW, Fierce, 99-25
RIGHT HERE RIGHT NOW, Fatboy Slim, 99-2
RIGHT HERE WAITING, Richard Marx, 89-2
RIGHT IN THE NIGHT (FALL IN LOVE WITH MUSIC), Jam and Spoon featuring Plavka, 94-31, 95-10
RIGHT IN THE SOCKET, Shalamar, 80-44
THE RIGHT KINDA LOVER, Patti Labelle, 94-50
RIGHT NEXT DOOR (BECAUSE OF ME), Robert Cray Band, 87-50
RIGHT NOW, Creatures, 83-14
RIGHT NOW, Airhead, 92-50
RIGHT NOW, Atomic Kitten, 99-10
RIGHT ON, Silicone Soul featuring Louise Clare Marshall, 01-15
RIGHT ON TRACK, Breakfast Club, 87-54
RIGHT, SAID FRED, Bernard Cribbins, 62-10
THE RIGHT STUFF, Bryan Ferry, 87-37
THE RIGHT STUFF, Vanessa Williams, 88-71, 89-62
THE RIGHT THING, Simply Red, 87-11
THE RIGHT THING TO DO, Carly Simon, 73-17
THE RIGHT THING TO SAY, Nat King Cole, 62-42
THE RIGHT TIME, Ultra, 98-28
THE RIGHT TO LOVE, David Whitfield, 58-30
RIKKI DON'T LOSE THAT NUMBER:
Steely Dan, 79-58
Tom Robinson, 84-58
RILKEAN HEART (from TWINLIGHTS [EP]), Cocteau Twins, 95-59
RING-A-DING GIRL, Ronnie Carroll with Wally Stott and his Orchestra and Chorus, 62-46
RING MY BELL, Anita Ward, 79-1
RING MY BELL, Monie Love vs Adeva, 91-20
RING MY BELL, D.J. Jazzy Jeff and the Fresh Prince, 91-53
RING OF BRIGHT WATER, Val Doonican, 69-48
RING OF FIRE, Duane Eddy, 61-17
RING OF FIRE, Eric Burdon and the Animals, 69-35
RING OF ICE, Jennifer Rush, 85-14
RING OUT SOLSTICE BELLS [EP] + lead track title, Jethro Tull, 76-28
RING RING, Abba (Bjorn, Benny, Anna and Frida), 74-32
RING RING, Dollar, 82-61
RING RING RING, Aaron Soul, 01-14
RING RING RING (HA HA HEY), De La Soul, 91-10
RING THE BELLS, James, 92-37
RINGO, Lorne Greene, 64-22
RIO, Michael Nesmith, 77-28
RIO, Duran Duran, 82-9
RIP IT UP:
Bill Haley and his Comets, 56-4
Little Richard, 56-30
Elvis Presley, 57-27
Little Richard, 77-37
RIP IT UP, Orange Juice, 83-8
RIPGROOVE, Double 99, 97-31, 97-14
RIPPED IN 2 MINUTES, A Vs B, 98-49
RISE, Herb Alpert, 79-13
RISE, Public Image Ltd., 86-11
RISE, Zion Train, 96-61
RISE, Eddie Amador, 00-19
RISE, Gabrielle, 00-1
RISE, Soul Providers featuring Michelle Shellers, 01-59
THE RISE AND FALL OF FLINGEL BUNT, Shadows, 64-5
RISE & SHINE, Cardigans, 96-29
RISE 'IN, Steve Lawler; vocal from Prince Quick 'Mellow', 00-50
RISE TO THE OCCASION, Climie Fisher, 87-10
RISE UP, Jamaica United starring Ziggy Marley, Buju Banton, Diana King, Shaggy, Maxi Priest, Ini Kamoze, Toots Hibber, 98-54
RISIN' TO THE TOP, Keni Burke, 92-70
RISING FREE [EP], Tom Robinson Band, 78-18
RISING SIGN, Hurricane #1, 98-47
RISING SUN, Medicine Head, 73-11
RISING SUN, Farm, 92-48
RISINGSON, Massive Attack, 97-11
THE RIVER, Bruce Springsteen, 81-35
RIVER, King Trigger, 82-57
THE RIVER, Total Contrast, 86-44
THE RIVER, Beautiful South, 00-59
RIVER DEEP – MOUNTAIN HIGH:
Ike and Tina Turner, 66-3, 69-33
Supremes and Four Tops, 71-11
THE RIVER (LE COLLINE SONO IN FIORE), Ken Dodd with Geoff Love and his Orchestra, 65-3
THE RIVER OF DREAMS, Billy Joel, 93-3
RIVER OF PAIN, Thunder, 95-31
RIVER STAY 'WAY FROM MY DOOR, Frank Sinatra, 60-18
THE RIVERBOAT SONG, Ocean Colour Scene, 96-15
RIVERDANCE, Bill Whelan featuring Anuna and the RTE Concert Orchestra, 94-9
RIVERS OF BABYLON, Boney M, 78-1
THE RIVERS OF BELIEF, Enigma, 92-68
THE RIVER'S RUN DRY, Vince Hill, 62-41
ROACHES, Trancesetters, 00-55
ROAD RAGE, Catatonia, 98-5
ROAD RUNNER, Jnr. Walker and the All Stars, 69-12
THE ROAD TO HELL (PARTS 1 & 2), Chris Rea, 89-10
THE ROAD TO MANDALAY, Robbie Williams, 01-1
ROAD TO NOWHERE, Talking Heads, 85-6
ROAD TO OUR DREAM, T'Pau, 88-42
ROAD TO YOUR SOUL, All About Eve, 89-37
ROAD TRIPPIN', Red Hot Chili Peppers, 01-30
ROADBLOCK, Stock Aitken Waterman, 87-13
ROADHOUSE MEDLEY (ANNIVERSARY WALTZ PART 25) [M], Status Quo, 92-21
ROADRUNNER, Jonathan Richman / Modern Lovers, 77-11
ROAM, B-52'S, 90-17
ROBERT DE NIRO'S WAITING, Bananarama, 84-3
ROBIN HOOD:
Gary Miller with Tony Osborne and his Orchestra and the Beryl Stott Chorus, 56-10
Dick James with Stephen James and his Chums, 56-14
ROBIN (THE HOODED MAN), Clannad, 84-42
THE ROBIN'S RETURN, Neville Dickie, 69-33
ROBOT, Tornados, 63-17
ROBOT MAN, Connie Francis, 60-2
ROBOT WARS [ANDROID LOVE], Sir Killalot v Robo Babe, 00-51
THE ROBOTS, Kraftwerk, 91-20
ROC-IN-IT, Deejay Punk-Roc vs Onyx, 99-59
ROCCO, Death In Vegas, 97-51
ROCHDALE COWBOY, Mike Harding, 75-22
THE ROCK, Alarm, 89-31
THE ROCK, Delakota, 98-60
ROCK-A-BEATIN' BOOGIE, Bill Haley and his Comets, 55-4
ROCK-A-BILLY, Guy Mitchell with Jimmy Carroll, 57-1
ROCK-A-BYE YOUR BABY WITH A DIXIE MELODY, Jerry Lewis, 57-12
ROCK A DOODLE DOO, Linda Lewis, 73-15
ROCK-A-HULA-BABY ("TWIST SPECIAL"), Elvis Presley with the Jordanaires, 62-1
ROCK AND A HARD PLACE, Rolling Stones, 89-63
ROCK AND ROLL DREAMS COME THROUGH:
Jim Steinman, 81-52
Meat Loaf, 94-11
ROCK AND ROLL (I GAVE YOU THE BEST YEARS OF MY LIFE), Kevin Johnson, 75-23
ROCK AND ROLL IS DEAD, Lenny Kravitz, 95-22
ROCK AND ROLL (IS GONNA SET THE NIGHT ON FIRE), Pretty Boy Floyd, 90-75
ROCK AND ROLL MUSIC, Beach Boys, 76-36
ROCK AND ROLL NIGGER, Birdland, 90-47
ROCK AND ROLL PART 1 AND 2, Gary Glitter, 72-2
ROCK AND ROLL WALTZ, Kay Starr with Hugo Winterhalter's Orchestra and Chorus, 56-1
ROCK AROUND THE CLOCK:
Bill Haley and his Comets *, 55-1, 68-20, 74-12
Telex, 79-34
Tenpole Tudor, 79-21
ROCK BOTTOM, Lynsey De Paul and Mike Moran, 77-19
ROCK BOTTOM, Babyface, 94-50
ROCK DA FUNKY BEATS, Public Domain featuring Chuck D, 01-19
ROCK DA HOUSE, Tall Paul, 97-12, 01-29
ROCK DJ, Robbie Williams, 00-1
ROCK HARD, Suzi Quatro, 80-68
ROCK IS DEAD, Marilyn Manson, 99-23
ROCK ISLAND LINE:
Lonnie Donegan Skiffle Group, 56-8
Stan Freberg and his Sniffle Group interruptions by Peter Leeds, 56-24
ROCK LOBSTER, B-52S, 79-37, 86-12
ROCK ME AMADEUS, Falco, 86-1
ROCK ME BABY, David Cassidy, 72-11
ROCK ME BABY, Johnny Nash, 85-47
ROCK ME BABY, Baby Roots, 92-71
ROCK ME GENTLY, Andy Kim, 74-2
ROCK ME GOOD, Universal, 97-19
ROCK ME STEADY, DJ Professor, 92-49
ROCK ME TONIGHT (FOR OLD TIME'S SAKE), Freddie Jackson, 86-18
ROCK MY HEART, Haddaway, 94-9
ROCK MY WORLD, Five Star, 88-28
ROCK 'N' ME, Steve Miller Band, 76-11
ROCK N' ROLL, Status Quo, 81-8
ROCK 'N' ROLL, John McEnroe and Pat Cash with the Full Metal Rackets, 91-66
ROCK 'N' ROLL AIN'T NOISE POLLUTION, AC/DC, 80-15
ROCK 'N' ROLL CHILDREN, Dio, 85-26
ROCK 'N' ROLL DAMNATION, AC/DC, 78-24
ROCK 'N' ROLL DANCE PARTY [M], Jive Bunny and the Mastermixers, 91-48
ROCK 'N' ROLL (DOLE), J.Pac, 95-51
ROCK 'N' ROLL GYPSY, Saxon, 86-71
ROCK 'N' ROLL HIGH SCHOOL, Ramones, 79-67
ROCK 'N' ROLL IS KING, Electric Light Orchestra, 83-13
ROCK 'N' ROLL LADY, Showaddywaddy, 74-15
ROCK 'N' ROLL MERCENARIES, Meat Loaf with John Parr, 86-31
ROCK 'N' ROLL OUTLAW, Rose Tattoo, 81-60
ROCK 'N' ROLL STAGE SHOW [LP], Bill Haley and his Comets, 56-30
ROCK 'N ROLL STAR (from LIVE [EP]), Barclay James Harvest, 77-49
ROCK 'N' ROLL SUICIDE, Bowie, 74-22
ROCK N' ROLL WINTER (LOONY'S TUNE), Wizzard, 74-6
ROCK OF AGES, Def Leppard, 83-41
ROCK ON, David Essex, 73-3

ROCK ON BROTHER, Chequers, 75-21
THE ROCK SHOW, Blink-182, 01-14
ROCK STEADY, Whispers, 87-38
ROCK STEADY, Bonnie Raitt and Bryan Adams, 95-50
(ROCK) SUPERSTAR, Cypress Hill, 00-13
ROCK THE BELLS, Kadoc, 97-34
ROCK THE BOAT:
Hues Corporation, 74-6
Forrest, 83-4
Delage, 90-63
ROCK THE CASBAH, Clash, 82-30, 91-15
ROCK THE DISCOTEK '96, Ramp, 96-49
ROCK THE FUNKY BEATS, Natural Born Chillers, 97-30
ROCK THE HOUSE, Source vocals by Nicole, 92-63
ROCK THE HOUSE, Gorillaz, 01-18
ROCK THE JOINT, Bill Haley and his Comets, 57-20
ROCK THE MIDNIGHT, David Grant, 83-46
ROCK THE NIGHT, Europe, 87-12
ROCK THIS TOWN, Stray Cats, 81-9
ROCK 'TIL YOU DROP, Status Quo, 92-38
ROCK 2 HOUSE, X-Press 2 featuring Lo-Pro, 94-55
ROCK WIT'CHA, Bobby Brown, 89-33
ROCK WITH THE CAVEMAN, Tommy Steele and the Steelmen, 56-13
ROCK WITH YOU:
Michael Jackson, 80-7
D'Influence, 98-30
ROCK YOUR BABY:
George McCrae, 74-1
K.W.S., 92-8
ROCK YOUR BODY, Clock, 98-30
ROCKABILLY BOB, Columbo presents In Full Rock-A-Phonic Sound featuring Ooe, 99-59
ROCKABILLY GUY, Polecats, 81-35
ROCKABILLY REBEL, Matchbox, 79-18
THE ROCKAFELLER SKANK, Fatboy Slim, 98-6
ROCKALL, Mezzoforte, 83-75
ROCKARIA!, Electric Light Orchestra, 77-9
ROCKET, Mud, 74-6
ROCKET, Def Leppard, 89-15
THE ROCKET MAN, Spotnicks, 62-38
ROCKET MAN (I THINK IT'S GOING TO BE A LONG LONG TIME):
Elton John, 72-2
Kate Bush, 91-12
ROCKET 2 U, Jets, 88-69
ROCKIN' ALL OVER THE WORLD:
Status Quo, 77-3
Status Quo *, 88-17
ROCKIN' ALONE (IN AN OLD ROCKING CHAIR), Miki and Griff with the Lonnie Donegan Group, 60-44
ROCKIN' AROUND THE CHRISTMAS TREE:
Brenda Lee, 62-6
Jets, 83-62
Comic Relief presents Mel and Kim performed by Kim Wilde and Mel Smith, 87-3
ROCKIN' BACK INSIDE MY HEART, Julee Cruise, 91-66
ROCKIN' CHAIR, Magnum, 90-27
ROCKIN' FOR MYSELF, Motiv 8 featuring Angie Brown, 93-67, 94-18
ROCKIN' GOOD CHRISTMAS, Roy Chubby Brown, 96-51
A ROCKIN' GOOD WAY, Shaky and Bonnie, 84-5
ROCKIN' ME, Professor, 94-56
ROCKIN' MY BODY, 49ers featuring Ann-Marie Smith, 95-31
ROCKIN' OVER THE BEAT, Technotronic featuring Ya Kid K, 90-9
ROCKIN' RED WING, Sammy Masters, 60-36
ROCKIN' ROBIN:
Bobby Day, 58-29
Michael Jackson, 72-3
Lolly, 99-10
ROCKIN' ROLL BABY, Stylistics, 74-6
ROCKIN' SOUL, Hues Corporation, 74-24
ROCKIN' THE SUBURBS, Ben Folds, 01-53
ROCKIN' THROUGH THE RYE, Bill Haley and his Comets, 56-3, 57-19
ROCKIN' TO THE MUSIC, Black Box, 93-39
ROCKIN' TO THE RHYTHM, Convert, 93-42
ROCKIN' WITH RITA (HEAD TO TOE), Vindaloo Summer Special, 86-56
ROCKING GOOSE, Johnny and the Hurricanes, 60-3
ROCKIT, Herbie Hancock, 83-8
ROCKS:
Primal Scream, 94-7
Rod Stewart, 98-55
ROCKS ON THE ROAD, Jethro Tull, 92-47
ROCKY, Austin Roberts, 75-22
ROCKY MOUNTAIN WAY [EP] + lead track title, Joe Walsh, 77-39
THE RODEO SONG, Garry Lee and Showdown, 93-44
RODRIGO'S GUITAR CONCERTO DE ARANJUEZ (THEME FROM 2ND MOVEMENT), Manuel and the Music Of The Mountains, 76-3
ROFO'S THEME, Rofo, 92-44
ROK DA HOUSE, Beatmasters featuring The Cookie Crew, 88-5
ROK DA HOUSE, Vinyl Groover and the Red Hed, 01-72
ROK THE NATION, Rob 'N' Raz with Leila K, 90-41
ROLL AWAY, Dusty Springfield, 95-68
ROLL AWAY THE STONE, Mott The Hoople, 73-8
ROLL ON DOWN THE HIGHWAY, Bachman-Turner Overdrive, 75-22
ROLL OVER BEETHOVEN, Electric Light Orchestra, 73-6
ROLL OVER LAY DOWN, Status Quo, 75-9
ROLL THE BONES, Rush, 92-49
ROLL TO ME, Del Amitri, 95-22
ROLL WITH IT, Steve Winwood, 88-53
ROLL WITH IT, Oasis, 95-2, 96-55, 97-62
A ROLLER SKATING JAM NAMED 'SATURDAYS', De La Soul, 91-22
ROLLERBLADE, Nick Heyward, 96-37
ROLLERBLADE, Movin' Melodies, 97-71
ROLLERCOASTER, Grid, 94-19
ROLLERCOASTER, Northern Uproar, 95-41
ROLLERCOASTER, B*Witched, 98-1
ROLLERCOASTER [EP] + lead track title, Jesus And Mary Chain, 90-46
ROLLERCOASTER [EP] + lead track title, Everything But The Girl, 94-65
ROLLIN', Limp Bizkit, 01-1
ROLLIN' HOME, Status Quo, 86-9
ROLLIN' IN MY 5.0, Vanilla Ice, 91-27
ROLLIN' ON, Cirrus, 78-62
ROLLING STONE, David Essex, 75-5
ROLODEX PROPAGANDA, At The Drive-In, 00-54
ROMAN P, Psychic TV, 86-65
ROMANCE (LET YOUR HEART GO), David Cassidy, 85-54
ROMANCING THE STONE, Eddy Grant, 84-52
ROMANTIC, Karyn White, 91-23
ROMANTICA, Jane Morgan, 60-39
ROME WASN'T BUILT IN A DAY, Morcheeba, 00-34
ROMEO, Petula Clark, 61-3
ROMEO, Mr. Big, 77-4
ROMEO, Basement Jaxx, 01-6
ROMEO AND JULIET, Dire Straits, 81-8
ROMEO ME, Sleeper, 97-39
ROMEO WHERE'S JULIET?, Collage, 85-46
RONDO (BASED ON MOZART'S "RONDO A LA TURK"), Kenny Ball and his Jazzmen, 63-24
RONI, Bobby Brown, 89-21
ROOBARB AND CUSTARD, Shaft, 91-7
ROOF IS ON FIRE, Westbam's, 98-58
ROOFTOP SINGING, New World, 73-50
ROOM AT THE TOP, Adam Ant, 90-13
ROOM ELEVEN, Daisy Chainsaw, 92-65
ROOM IN YOUR HEART, Living In A Box, 89-5
ROOMS ON FIRE, Stevie Nicks, 89-16
THE ROOT OF ALL EVIL, Beautiful South, 01-50
ROOTS BLOODY ROOTS, Sepultura, 96-19
ROSALIE/ (COWGIRLS' SONG) [M], Thin Lizzy, 78-20
ROSALYN, Pretty Things, 64-41
ROSANNA, Toto, 83-12
THE ROSE:
Michael Ball, 95-42
Heather Peace, 00-56
ROSE GARDEN:
Lynn Anderson, 71-3
New World, 71-15
A ROSE HAS TO DIE, Dooleys, 78-11
A ROSE IS STILL A ROSE, Aretha Franklin, 98-22
ROSE MARIE, Slim Whitman, 55-1
ROSE ROUGE, St Germain, 01-54
ROSEABILITY, Idlewild, 00-38
ROSES, Haywoode, 85-65, 86-11
ROSES, Rhythm-N-Bass, 92-56
ROSES, Deus, 97-56
ROSES ARE RED, Mac Band featuring the McCampbell Brothers, 88-8
ROSES ARE RED (MY LOVE):
Ronnie Carroll with Wally Stott and his Orchestra and Chorus, 62-3
Bobby Vinton, 62-15, 90-71
ROSES IN THE HOSPITAL, Manic Street Preachers, 93-15
ROSES OF PICARDY, Vince Hill with the Eddie Lester Singers, 67-13
ROSETTA, Fame and Price, Price and Fame Together, 71-11
ROSIE, Don Partridge, 68-4
ROSIE, Joan Armatrading, 80-49
ROTATION, Herb Alpert, 80-46
ROTTERDAM, Beautiful South, 96-5
ROUGH BOY, ZZ Top, 86-23, 92-49
ROUGH BOYS, Pete Townshend, 80-39
ROUGH BOYS, Northern Uproar, 95-41
ROUGH JUSTICE, Bananarama, 84-23
ROUGH WITH THE SMOOTH, Shara Nelson, 95-30
ROUGHNECK [EP], Project One, 92-49
ROULETTE, Russ Conway, 59-1
ROUND AND AROUND, Jaki Graham, 85-9
ROUND AND ROUND, Jimmy Young with the Michael Sammes Singers, 57-30
ROUND AND ROUND, Spandau Ballet, 84-18
ROUND & ROUND, New Order, 89-21
ROUND & ROUND, Hi-Tek featuring Jonell, 01-73
ROUND EVERY CORNER, Petula Clark, 65-43
ROUND HERE, Counting Crows, 94-70
ROUND OF BLUES, Shawn Colvin, 94-73
THE ROUSSOS PHENOMENON [EP], Demis Roussos, 76-1
ROXANNE, Police, 79-12, 97-17
ROYAL EVENT, Russ Conway, 60-15
ROYAL MILE, Gerry Rafferty, 80-67
ROY'S KEEN, Morrissey, 97-42
RUB-A-DUB, Double Trouble, 91-66
RUB A DUB DUB, Equals, 69-34
RUBBER BALL:
Bobby Vee, 61-4
Marty Wilde, 61-9
Avons, 61-30
RUBBER BULLETS, 10C.C., 73-1
RUBBERBAND GIRL, Kate Bush, 93-12
THE RUBBERBAND MAN, Detroit Spinners, 76-16
RUBBERBANDMAN, Yello, 91-58
RUBBISH, Carter – The Unstoppable Sex Machine, 92-14
THE RUBETTES, Auteurs, 99-66
RUBY ANN, Marty Robbins, 63-24
RUBY, DON'T TAKE YOUR LOVE TO TOWN, Kenny Rogers and the First Edition, 69-2
RUBY RED, Slade, 82-51
RUBY RED, Marc Almond, 86-47
RUBY TUESDAY:
Rolling Stones, 67-3
Melanie, 70-9
Rolling Stones, 91-59
Rod Stewart, 93-11
RUDE BOY ROCK, Lionrock, 98-20
RUDE BUOYS OUTA JAIL', Specials, 80-5
RUDI GOT MARRIED, Laurel Aitken and the Unitone, 80-60
RUDI'S IN LOVE, Locomotive, 68-25
RUDY'S ROCK, Bill Haley and his Comets, 56-26
RUFF IN THE JUNGLE BIZNESS, Prodigy, 92-5, 96-52
RUFF MIX, Wonder Dog, 82-31
RUFFNECK, MC Lyte, 94-67
RUGGED AND MEAN, BUTCH AND ON SCREEN, Pee Bee Squad, 85-52
RUINED IN A DAY, New Order, 93-22
RULES AND REGULATIONS [EP], We've Got A Fuzzbox And We're Gonna Use It, 86-41
RULES OF THE GAME, Bucks Fizz, 83-57
RUMBLE IN THE JUNGLE, Fugees featuring A Tribe Called Quest, Busta Rhymes and Forte, 97-3
RUMORS:
Timex Social Club, 86-13
Awesome *, 97-58
RUMOUR HAS IT, Donna Summer, 78-19
RUMOURS, Hot Chocolate, 73-44
RUMOURS, Damage, 00-22
RUMP SHAKER, Wreckx-N-Effect, 92-24, 94-40
RUN, Sandie Shaw, 66-32
RUN, Spiritualized, 91-59
RUN AWAY, 10 C.C., 82-50
RUN AWAY, (Mc Sar and) the Real McCoy, 95-6
RUN, BABY, RUN, Sheryl Crow, 95-24

RUN, BABY, RUN (BACK INTO MY ARMS), Newbeats, 71-10
RUN BACK, Carl Douglas, 77-25
RUN DADDY RUN, Fun Lovin' Criminals, 01-50
RUN FOR COVER, Sugababes, 01-13
RUN FOR HOME, Lindisfarne, 78-10
RUN FOR YOUR LIFE, Bucks Fizz, 83-14
RUN FOR YOUR LIFE, Northern Line, 99-18
RUN FROM LOVE, Jimmy Somerville, 91-52
RUN ON, Moby, 99-33
RUN RUDOLPH RUN, Chuck Berry, 63-36
RUN RUN RUN, Jo Jo Gunne, 72-6
RUN RUNAWAY, Slade, 84-7
RUN SILENT, Shakespear's Sister, 89-54
RUN TO HIM, Bobby Vee, 61-6
RUN TO ME, Bee Gees, 72-9
RUN TO MY LOVIN' ARMS, Billy Fury, 65-25
RUN TO THE DOOR, Clinton Ford, 67-25
RUN TO THE HILLS:
Iron Maiden, 82-7
Iron Maiden, 85-26
RUN TO THE SUN, Erasure, 94-6
RUN TO YOU:
Bryan Adams, 85-11
Rage, 92-3
RUN TO YOU, Whitney Houston, 93-15
RUN TO YOU, Roxette, 94-27
RUN 2, New Order, 89-49
RUN'S HOUSE, Run D.M.C., 88-37
RUNAGROUND, James, 98-29
RUNAROUND, Martha Wash, 93-49
RUNAROUND SUE:
Dion, 61-11
Doug Sheldon, 61-36
Racey, 80-13
RUNAWAY, Del Shannon, 61-1
THE RUNAWAY, Elkie Brooks, 79-50
RUNAWAY, Deee-Lite, 92-45
RUNAWAY, Janet Jackson, 95-6
RUNAWAY, E'voke, 95-30
RUNAWAY, Corrs, 96-49, 96-60, 97-62, 99-2
RUNAWAY, Nuyorican Soul featuring India, 97-24
RUNAWAY BOYS, Stray Cats, 80-9
RUNAWAY GIRL, Sterling Void, 89-53
RUNAWAY HORSES, Belinda Carlisle, 90-40
RUNAWAY LOVE, En Vogue, 93-36
RUNAWAY SKIES, Celetia, 98-66
RUNAWAY TRAIN, Elton John and Eric Clapton, 92-31
RUNAWAY TRAIN, Soul Asylum, 93-7
THE RUNNER, Three Degrees, 79-10
RUNNIN', Bass Bumpers, 93-68
RUNNIN', Pharcyde, 96-36
RUNNIN', 2Pac and Notorious B.I.G., 98-15
RUNNIN, Basstoy, 00-62
RUNNIN' AWAY:
Sly and the Family Stone, 72-17
Nicole, 96-69
RUNNIN' DOWN A DREAM, Tom Petty, 89-55
RUNNIN' FOR THE RED LIGHT (I GOTTA LIFE), Meat Loaf, 96-21
RUNNIN' SCARED, Roy Orbison, 61-9
RUNNIN' WITH THE DEVIL, Van Halen, 80-52
RUNNING ALL OVER THE WORLD [RR], Status Quo, 88-17
RUNNING AROUND TOWN, Billie Ray Martin, 95-29
RUNNING BEAR, Johnny Preston, 60-1
RUNNING FREE:
Iron Maiden, 80-34
Iron Maiden, 85-19
RUNNING FROM PARADISE, Daryl Hall and John Oates, 80-41
RUNNING IN THE FAMILY, Level 42, 87-6
RUNNING OUT OF TIME, Digital Orgasm, 91-16
RUNNING UP THAT HILL, Kate Bush, 85-3
RUNNING WITH THE NIGHT, Lionel Richie, 83-9
RUPERT, Jackie Lee, 71-14
THE RUSH, Luther Vandross, 92-53
RUSH, Freak Power, 94-62
RUSH, Kleshay, 99-19
RUSH HOUR:
Jane Wiedlin, 88-12
Joyrider, 96-22
RUSH RUSH, Paula Abdul, 91-6
RUSHING, Loni Clark, 93-37
RUSSIANS, Sting, 85-12
RUST, Echo and the Bunnymen, 99-22
RUSTY CAGE, Soundgarden, 92-41
S CLUB PARTY, S Club 7, 99-2
S.M.D.U., Brock Landars, 98-49
S.O.S., ABC, 84-39
S.S. PAPARAZZI, Stock Aitken Waterman, 88-68
S-S-S-SINGLE BED, Fox, 76-4
SABOTAGE, Beastie Boys, 94-19
SABRE DANCE, Love Sculpture, 68-5
SACRAMENTO (A WONDERFUL TOWN), Middle Of The Road, 72-23
SACRED CYCLES, Pete Lazonby, 00-49
SACRIFICE, Elton John, 89-55, 90-1
SAD BUT TRUE, Metallica, 93-20
SAD EYES, Robert John, 79-31
SAD MOVIES:
Carol Deene, 61-44
Sue Thompson, 61-46
SAD SONGS (SAY SO MUCH), Elton John, 84-7
SAD SWEET DREAMER, Sweet Sensation, 74-1
SADDLE UP, David Christie, 82-9
SADIE'S SHAWL (SANTIE SE KOPDOEK), Frank Cordell and his Orchestra, 56-29
SADNESS PART 1, Enigma, 90-1
SAFARI [EP], Breeders, 92-69
SAFE FROM HARM, Massive Attack, 91-25
THE SAFETY DANCE, Men Without Hats, 83-6
SAID I LOVED YOU, BUT I LIED, Michael Bolton, 93-15
SAID SHE WAS A DANCER, Jethro Tull, 88-55
SAIL AWAY, Little Angels, 93-45
SAIL AWAY, Urban Cookie Collective, 94-18
SAIL AWAY, David Gray, 01-26
SAIL ON, Commodores, 79-8
SAILING, Rod Stewart, 75-1, 76-3. 87-41
SAILING, Christopher Cross, 81-48
SAILING OFF THE EDGE OF THE WORLD, Straw, 01-52
SAILING ON THE SEVEN SEAS, Orchestral Manoeuvres In The Dark, 91-3
SAILOR:
Petula Clark; Peter Knight Orchestra and Chorus, 61-1
Anne Shelton with Wally Stott and his Orchestra and Chorus, 61-10
SAILORTOWN, Energy Orchard, 90-73
THE SAINT, Thompson Twins, 92-53
THE SAINT, Orbital, 97-3
ST. ELMO'S FIRE (MAN IN MOTION), John Parr, 85-6
SAINT OF ME, Rolling Stones, 98-26
ST TERESA, Joan Osborne, 96-33
ST. THERESE OF THE ROSES, Malcolm Vaughan, 56-3
ST. VALENTINE'S DAY MASSACRE [EP], Headgirl (Motorhead and Girlschool), 81-5
THE SAINTS ARE COMING, Skids, 78-48
THE SAINTS ROCK 'N ROLL, Bill Haley and his Comets, 56-5
SAL'S GOT A SUGAR LIP, Lonnie Donegan and his Skiffle Group, 59-13
SALE OF THE CENTURY, Sleeper, 96-10
SALLY, Gerry Monroe, 70-4
SALLY, Carmel, 86-60
SALLY, Kerbdog, 96-69
SALLY ANN, Joe Brown and the Bruvvers, 63-28
SALLY CINNAMON, Stone Roses, 90-46
SALLY DON'T YOU GRIEVE/BETTY BETTY BETTY, Lonnie Donegan and his Skiffle Group, 58-11
SALLY MACLENNANE, Pogues, 85-51
SALSA HOUSE, Richie Rich, 89-50
SALSOUL NUGGET (IF U WANNA), M&S presents the Girl Next Door, 01-6
SALT SWEAT SUGAR, Jimmy Eat World, 01-60
SALTWATER, Julian Lennon, 91-6
SALTWATER, Chicane (featuring Maire Brennan of Clannad), 99-6
A SALTY DOG, Procol Harum, 69-44
SALVA MEA (SAVE ME), Faithless, 95-30, 96-9
SALVATION, Cranberries, 96-13
SAM, Keith West, 67-38
SAM, Olivia Newton-John, 77-6
SAMANTHA, Kenny Ball and his Jazzmen Vocal: Kenny Ball, 61-13
SAMBA DE JANEIRO, Bellini, 97-8
SAMBA MAGIC, Summer Daze, 96-61
SAMBA PA TI, Santana, 74-27
SAMBUCA, Wideboys featuring Dennis G, 01-15
SAME OLD BRAND NEW YOU, A1, 00-1
THE SAME OLD SCENE, Roxy Music, 80-12
SAME OLD STORY, Ultravox, 86-31
SAME SONG, Digital Underground, 91-52
SAME TEMPO, Changing Faces, 98-53
SAME THING IN REVERSE, Boy George, 95-56
(THE SAME THINGS HAPPEN WITH) THE BIRDS AND THE BEES, Alma Cogan with Vocal Group, 56-25
SAMSON AND DELILAH, Middle Of The Road, 72-26
SAMSON AND DELILAH, Bad Manners, 82-58
SAN ANTONIO ROSE, Floyd Cramer, 61-36
SAN BERNADINO, Christie, 70-7
SAN DAMIANO (HEART AND SOUL), Sal Solo, 84-15
SAN FRANCISCAN NIGHTS, Eric Burdon and the Animals, 67-7
SAN FRANCISCO (BE SURE TO WEAR SOME FLOWERS IN YOUR HAIR), Scott McKenzie, 67-1
SAN FRANCISCO DAYS, Chris Isaak, 93-62
SAN FRANCISCO (YOU'VE GOT ME), Village People, 77-45
SAN MIGUEL:
Lonnie Donegan and his Skiffle Group, 59-19
Kingston Trio, 59-29
SANCTIFIED LADY, Marvin Gaye, 85-51
SANCTIFY YOURSELF, Simple Minds, 86-10
SANCTUARY, Iron Maiden, 80-29
SANCTUARY, New Musik, 80-31
SANCTUS, Missa Luba Les Troubadours Du Roi Baudouin, 69-28
SANDBLASTED EP, Swervedriver, 91-67
SANDBLASTER (from SANDBLASTED [EP]), Swervedriver, 91-67
SANDCASTLES, Bomb The Bass featuring Bernard Fowler, 95-54
SANDMAN, Blueboy, 97-25
SANDS OF TIME, Kaleef, 98-26
SANDSTORM, Cast, 96-8
SANDSTORM, Darude, 00-3
SANDWICHES, Detroit Grand Pu Bahs, 00-29
SANDY, John Travolta, 78-2
SANITY, Killing Joke, 86-70
SANTA BRING MY BABY BACK TO ME, Elvis Presley, 57-7
SANTA CLAUS IS BACK IN TOWN, Elvis Presley, 80-41
SANTA CLAUS IS COMIN' TO TOWN:
Jackson 5, 72-43
Carpenters, 75-37
Bruce Springsteen, 85-9
Bjorn Again, 92-55
SANTA CLAUS IS ON THE DOLE, Spitting Image, 86-22
SANTA MARIA:
Tatjana, 96-40
DJ Milano featuring Samantha Fox, 98-31
SANTA MONICA (WATCH THE WORLD DIE), Everclear, 96-40
SANTO NATALE (MERRY CHRISTMAS), David Whitfield with Stanley Black and his Orchestra, 54-2
SARA, Fleetwood Mac, 79-37
SARA, Starship, 86-66
SARAH, Thin Lizzy, 79-24
SARTORIAL ELOQUENCE, Elton John, 80-44
SAT IN YOUR LAP, Kate Bush, 81-11
SATAN:
Orbital, 91-31
Orbital, 97-3
SATAN REJECTED MY SOUL, Morrissey, 98-39
THE SATCH [EP], Joe Satriani, 93-53
SATELLITE, Hooters, 87-22
SATELLITE, Beloved, 96-19
SATELLITE KID, Dogs D'Amour, 89-26
SATIN SHEETS, Bellamy Brothers, 76-43
SATISFACTION:
Aretha Franklin, 67-37
Vanilla Ice, 91-22
SATISFACTION, Wendy and Lisa, 89-27
SATISFACTION GUARANTEED (OR TAKE YOUR LOVE BACK), Harold Melvin and the Bluenotes, 74-32
SATISFIED, Richard Marx, 89-52
SATISFIED (TAKE ME HIGHER), H2O, 97-66
SATISFY MY LOVE, Exoterix, 94-62
SATISFY MY LOVE, Sabrina Johnston, 94-62
SATISFY MY SOUL, Bob Marley and the Wailers, 78-21
SATISFY YOU, Puff Daddy (featuring R. Kelly), 00-73, 00-8
SATURDAY, Omar, 94-43
SATURDAY:
East 57th St featuring Donna Allen, 97-29
Joey Negro featuring Taka Boom, 00-41
SATURDAY GIG, Mott The Hoople, 74-41
SATURDAY LOVE:
Cherrelle with Alexander O'Neal, 85-6, 90-55
Illegal Motion featuring Simone Chapman, 93-67
SATURDAY NIGHT, T-Connection, 79-41
SATURDAY NIGHT, Blue Nile, 91-50

THE SECRET VAMPIRE SOUNDTRACK [EP], Bis, 96-25
SECRETLY, Skunk Anansie, 99-16
SECRETS, Sutherland Brothers and Quiver, 76-35
SECRETS, Fiat Lux, 84-65
SECRETS, Primitives, 89-49
SECRETS, Sunscreem, 96-36
SECRETS, Eternal, 96-9
SECRETS, Mutiny, 01-47
SECRETS IN THE STREET, Nils Lofgren, 85-53
SECRETS (OF SUCCESS), Cookie Crew featuring Danny D, 91-53
SECRETS OF THE HEART, Chesney Hawkes, 91-57
THE SECRETS THAT YOU KEEP, Mud, 75-3
THE SEDUCTION (LOVE THEME), James Last Band, 80-48
SEE A BRIGHTER DAY, JTQ with Noel McKoy, 93-49
SEE EMILY PLAY, Pink Floyd, 67-6
SEE JUNGLE! (JUNGLE BOY), Bow Wow Wow, 82-45
SEE LINE WOMAN '99, Songstress, 99-64
SEE ME, Luther Vandross, 87-60
SEE MY BABY JIVE, Wizzard vocal backing – the Suedettes, 73-1
SEE MY FRIEND, Kinks, 65-10
SEE THAT GLOW, This Island Earth, 85-47
SEE THE DAY, Dee C. Lee, 85-3
SEE THE LIGHTS, Simple Minds, 91-20
SEE THE STAR, Delirious?, 99-16
SEE THOSE EYES, Altered Images, 82-11
SEE WANT MUST HAVE, Blue Mercedes, 88-57
SEE YA, Atomic Kitten, 00-6
SEE YOU, Depeche Mode, 82-6
SEE YOU LATER, Regents, 80-55
SEE YOU LATER, ALLIGATOR, Bill Haley and his Comets, 56-7
SEEING THINGS, Black Crowes, 91-72
THE SEEKER, Who, 70-19
SEETHER, Veruca Salt, 94-61, 94-73
SEIZE THE DAY, FKW, 93-45
SELA, Lionel Richie, 87-43
SELF!, Fuzzbox, 89-24
SELF CONTROL, Laura Branigan, 84-5
SELF-DESTRUCTION, Stop The Violence Movement, 89-75
SELF ESTEEM, Offspring, 95-37
SELFISH, Other Two, 93-46
SELLING JESUS, Skunk Anansie, 95-46
SELLING THE DRAMA, Live, 95-30
SEMI-CHARMED LIFE, Third Eye Blind, 97-33
SEMI-DETACHED, SUBURBAN MR. JAMES, Manfred Mann, 66-2
SEND HIS LOVE TO ME, PJ Harvey, 95-34
SEND IN THE CLOWNS, Judy Collins, 75-6
SEND ME AN ANGEL, Blackfoot, 83-66
SEND ME AN ANGEL, Scorpions, 91-27
SEND ME THE PILLOW YOU DREAM ON, Johnny Tillotson, 62-21
SEND MY HEART, Adventures, 84-62
SEND ONE YOUR LOVE, Stevie Wonder, 79-52
(SENDING OUT AN) S.O.S., Retta Young, 75-28
SENSATION, Electroset, 95-69
SENSATIONAL, Michelle Gayle, 97-14
SENSE:
Lightning Seeds, 92-31
Terry Hall, 94-54
SENSE OF DANGER, Presence featuring Shara Nelson, 98-61
SENSES WORKING OVERTIME, XTC, 82-10
SENSITIVITY, Ralph Tresvant, 91-18
SENSITIZE, That Petrol Emotion, 91-55
SENSUAL SOPHIS-TI-CAT/THE PLAYER, Carl Cox, 96-25
THE SENSUAL WORLD, Kate Bush, 89-12
SENSUALITY, Lovestation, 98-16
SENTIMENTAL, Alexander O'Neal, 92-53
SENTIMENTAL, Deborah Cox, 95-34
SENTIMENTAL FOOL, Lloyd Cole, 95-73
SENTINEL (SINGLE RESTRUCTURE) TUBULAR BELLS II, Mike Oldfield, 92-10
SENZA UNA DONNA (WITHOUT A WOMAN), Zucchero featuring Paul Young, 91-4
SEPARATE LIVES, Phil Collins and Marilyn Martin, 85-4
SEPARATE TABLES, Chris De Burgh, 92-30
SEPARATE WAYS, Gary Moore, 92-59
SEPTEMBER, Earth, Wind And Fire, 78-3, 99-25
SEPTEMBER IN THE RAIN, Dinah Washington, 61-35
SEPTEMBER SONG, Ian McCulloch, 84-51
SERENADE, Mario Lanza, 55-15
SERENADE:
Slim Whitman, 56-8
Mario Lanza, 56-25
SERENADE, Shades, 97-75
SERENATA, Sarah Vaughan with Joe Reisman's Orchestra and Chorus, 60-37
SERENITY IN MURDER, Slayer, 95-50
SGT. PEPPER'S LONELY HEARTS CLUB BAND/WITH A LITTLE HELP FROM MY FRIENDS [M], Beatles, 78-63
SGT. ROCK (IS GOING TO HELP ME), XTC, 81-16
SERIOUS, Billy Griffin, 84-64
SERIOUS, Serious Intention, 86-51
SERIOUS, Donna Allen, 87-8
SERIOUS, Deja, 87-75
SERIOUS, Duran Duran, 90-48
SERIOUS, Maxwell D, 01-38
SERIOUS MIX [M], Mirage, 87-42
SERPENTS KISS, Mission, 86-70
SESAME'S TREET, Smart-E's, 92-2
SET ADRIFT ON MEMORY BLISS, PM Dawn, 91-3
SET FIRE TO ME, Willie Colon, 86-41
SET IN STONE, John Digweed and Nick Muir present Bedrock, 97-71
SET IT OFF (BUNKER '88 MIX), Bunker Kru/Harlequin 4'S, 88-55
SET ME FREE, Kinks, 65-9
SET ME FREE, Jaki Graham, 86-7
SET ME FREE, Brit Pack, 00-41
SET THE RECORD STRAIGHT, Reef, 00-19
SET THEM FREE, Aswad, 88-70
SET YOU FREE, N-Trance featuring Kelly Llorenna, 94-39, 95-2, 01-4
SET YOUR LOVING FREE, Lisa Stansfield, 92-28
SETTING SUN, Chemical Brothers, 96-1
SETTLE DOWN, Lillo Thomas, 85-66
SETTLE DOWN, Unbelievable Truth, 98-46
7, Prince and the New Power Generation, 92-27
SEVEN [EP] + lead track title, James, 92-46
SEVEN [EP], Mansun, 97-10
SEVEN, David Bowie, 00-32
SEVEN AND SEVEN IS (LIVE VERSION), Alice Cooper, 82-62
SEVEN CITIES, Solar Stone, 99-39
7 COLOURS, Lost Witness, 00-28
SEVEN DAFFODILS:
Cherokees, 64-33
Mojos, 64-30
SEVEN DAYS, Anne Shelton with Wally Stott and his Orchestra, 56-20
SEVEN DAYS, Sting, 93-25
SEVEN DAYS, Mary J. Blige featuring George Benson, 98-22
7 DAYS, Craig David, 00-1
SEVEN DAYS AND ONE WEEK, B.B.E., 96-3
SEVEN DAYS IN THE SUN, Feeder, 01-14
SEVEN DRUNKEN NIGHTS, Dubliners, 67-7
747, Kent, 99-61
747 (STRANGERS IN THE NIGHT), Saxon, 80-13
SEVEN LITTLE GIRLS SITTING IN THE BACK SEAT:
Avons, 59-3
Paul Evans and the Curls, 59-25
Bombalurina featuring Timmy Mallett, 90-18
SEVEN LONELY DAYS, Gisele MacKenzie, 53-6
SEVEN O'CLOCK NEWS/SILENT NIGHT [M], Simon and Garfunkel, 91-30
7 O'CLOCK, Quireboys, 89-36
7-ROOMS OF GLOOM, Four Tops, 67-12
SEVEN SEAS, Echo and the Bunnymen, 84-16
SEVEN SEAS OF RHYE, Queen, 74-10
7 SECONDS, Youssou N'dour (featuring Neneh Cherry), 94-3
7:7 EXPANSION, System 7, 93-39
7-6-5-4-3-2-1 (BLOW YOUR WHISTLE), Rimshots, 75-26
SEVEN TEARS, Goombay Dance Band, 82-1
7 WAYS TO LOVE, Cola Boy, 91-8
SEVEN WONDERS, Fleetwood Mac, 87-56
7 YEAR BITCH, Slade, 85-60
SEVEN YEARS IN TIBET, David Bowie, 97-61
SEVENTEEN:
Frankie Vaughan with Wally Stott and his Orchestra and Chorus, 55-18
Boyd Bennett and his Rockets (vocal by Big Moe), 55-16
7 TEEN, Regents, 79-11
SEVENTEEN, Let Loose, 94-44, 94-11
17 AGAIN, Eurythmics, 00-27
SEVENTH SON, Georgie Fame, 69-25
$7000 AND YOU, Stylistics, 77-24
72, Turin Brakes, 01-41
'74-'75, Connells, 95-14, 96-21
SEVENTY – SIX TROMBONES, King Brothers with the Rita Williams Singers and Geoff Love and his Orchestra, 61-19
78 STONE WOBBLE, Gomez, 98-44
SEVERINA, Mission, 87-25
SEX, Sleazesisters with Vikki Shepard, 95-53
SEX AND CANDY, Marcy Playground, 98-29
SEX AS A WEAPON, Pat Benatar, 86-67
SEX BOMB, Tom Jones and Mousse T., 00-3
SEX CRIME (NINETEEN EIGHTY-FOUR), Eurythmics, 84-4
SEX LIFE, Geoffrey Williams, 97-71
SEX ME, R. Kelly and Public Announcement, 93-75
THE SEX OF IT, Kid Creole and the Coconuts, 90-29
SEX ON THE BEACH, T-Spoon, 98-2
SEX ON THE STREETS, Pizzaman, 95-24, 96-23
SEX OVER THE PHONE, Village People, 85-59
SEX TALK (LIVE), T'Pau, 88-23
SEX TYPE THING, Stone Temple Pilots, 93-60, 93-55
SEXOMATIC, Bar – Kays, 85-51
SEXUAL, Maria Rowe, 95-67
SEXUAL, Amber, 00-34
SEXUAL HEALING, Marvin Gaye, 82-4
SEXUAL REVOLUTION, Macy Gray, 01-45
SEXUALITY, Billy Bragg, 91-27
SEXX LAWS, Beck, 99-27
SEXY, MFSB, 75-37
SEXY BOY, Air (French Band), 98-13
SEXY CINDERELLA, Lynden David Hall, 97-45, 98-17
SEXY CREAM, Slick (featuring Doris James), 79-47
SEXY EYES, Dr. Hook, 80-4
SEXY EYES – REMIXES, Whigfield, 98-68
SEXY GIRL, Lillo Thomas, 87-23
SEXY MF, Prince and the New Power Generation, 92-4
SH-BOOM (LIFE COULD BE A DREAM):
Crew Cuts, 54-12
Stan Freberg with the Toads, 54-15
Darts, 80-48
SHA LA LA, Manfred Mann, 64-3
SHA-LA-LA-LA-LEE:
Small Faces, 66-3
Plastic Bertrand, 78-39
SHA-LA-LA (MAKE ME HAPPY), Al Green, 74-20
SHA LA LA MEANS I LOVE YOU, Barry White, 79-55
SHACKLES (PRAISE YOU), Mary Mary, 00-5
SHADDAP YOU FACE, Joe Dolce Music Theatre, 81-1
SHADES OF BLUE [EP], The, 91-54
SHADES OF GREEN, Mission, 92-49
SHADES OF PARANOIMIA, Art Of Noise, 92-53
SHADES OF SUMMER, Rodeo Jones, 93-59
SHADES (THEME FROM THE CROWN PAINT TELEVISION COMMERCIAL), United Kingdom Symphony Orchestra conducted by Donald Gould, 85-68
SHADOW DANCING, Andy Gibb, 78-42
THE SHADOW OF LOVE (EDITION PREMIERE), Damned, 85-25
SHADOWS OF THE NIGHT, Pat Benatar, 85-50
SHADOWTIME, Siouxsie and the Banshees, 91-57
SHADY LADY, Gene Pitney, 70-29
SHADY LANE (KROSSFADER), Pavement, 97-40
SHAFT, Van Twist, 85-57
SHAKABOOM!, Hunter featuring Ruby Turner, 95-64
SHAKE, Otis Redding, 67-28
SHAKE, Andrew Ridgeley, 90-58
SHAKE! (HOW ABOUT A SAMPLING, GENE?), Gene And Jim Are Into Shakes, 88-68
SHAKE IT DOWN, Mud, 76-12
SHAKE ME I RATTLE, Kaye Sisters with Wally Stott and his Orchestra, 58-27
SHAKE, RATTLE AND ROLL, Bill Haley and his Comets, 54-4
(SHAKE, SHAKE, SHAKE) SHAKE YOUR BOOTY, KC and the Sunshine Band, 76-22
SHAKE THE DISEASE, Depeche Mode, 85-18
SHAKE THIS MOUNTAIN, Horse, 93-52
SHAKE YA ASS, Mystikal, 00-30
SHAKE YA BODY, N-Trance, 00-37

SHINOBI V DRAGON NINJA, Lostprophets, 01-41
SHINY HAPPY PEOPLE, R.E.M., 91-6
SHINY SHINY, Haysi Fantayzee, 83-16
SHIP AHOY, Marxman, 93-64
SHIP OF FOOLS, World Party, 87-42
SHIP OF FOOLS, Erasure, 88-6
SHIPBUILDING:
Robert Wyatt, 83-35
Tasmin Archer, 94-40
SHIPS IN THE NIGHT, Be-Bop Deluxe, 76-23
SHIPS (WHERE WERE YOU?), Big Country, 93-29
SHIPWRECKED, Genesis, 97-54
SHIRALEE, Tommy Steele and the Steelmen, 57-11
SHIRLEY, Shakin' Stevens, 82-6
SH!T ON YOU, D12: Eminem.Kon Artis.Bizarre.Kuniva.Proof.Swift, 01-10
SHIVER, George Benson, 86-19
SHIVER, S-J, 98-59
SHIVER, Coldplay, 00-35
SHIVERING SAND, Mega City Four, 92-35
SHO' YOU RIGHT, Barry White, 87-14
SHOCK THE MONKEY, Peter Gabriel, 82-58
SHOCK TO THE SYSTEM, Billy Idol, 93-30
SHOCK YOUR MAMA, Debbie Gibson, 93-74
SHOCKAHOLIC, Kinky Machine, 93-70
SHOCKED, Kylie Minogue, 91-6
SHOES, Reparata, 75-43
SHOO BE DOO BE DOO DA DAY, Stevie Wonder, 68-46
SHOO DOO FU FU OOH!, Lenny Williams, 77-38
SHOO-RAH! SHOO-RAH!, Betty Wright, 75-27
SHOOP, Salt 'N' Pepa, 93-29, 94-13
THE SHOOP SHOOP SONG (IT'S IN HIS KISS), Cher, 91-1
SHOOT ALL THE CLOWNS, Bruce Dickinson, 94-37
SHOOT ME (WITH YOUR LOVE), Tasha Thomas, 79-59
SHOOT ME WITH YOUR LOVE, D:Ream, 95-7
SHOOT, SHOOT, U.F.O., 79-48
SHOOTING FROM MY HEART, Big Bam Boo, 89-61
SHOOTING FROM THE HEART, Cliff Richard, 84-51
SHOOTING STAR, Dollar, 78-14
SHOOTING STAR, Boyzone, 97-2
SHOPLIFTERS OF THE WORLD UNITE, Smiths, 87-12
SHOPPING, Supersister, 01-36
SHORLEY WALL, Ooberman, 00-47
SHORT DICK MAN, 20 Fingers featuring Gillette, 94-21, 95-11
SHORT FAT FANNIE, Larry Williams, 57-21
SHORT SHORT MAN [RM], 20 Fingers featuring Gillette, 95-11
SHORT SKIRT/LONG JACKET, Cake, 01-63
SHORTCUT TO SOMEWHERE, Fish and Tony Banks, 86-75
SHORTNIN' BREAD, Viscounts, 60-16
SHORT'NIN' BREAD ROCK, Tony Crombie and his Rockets, 56-25
SHORTSHARPSHOCK [EP], Therapy?, 93-9
SHORTY, Wannadies, 97-41
SHORTY (GOT HER EYES ON ME), Donell Jones, 00-19
SHORTY (YOU KEEP PLAYIN' WITH MY MIND), Imajin featuring Keith Murray, 98-22
SHOT BY BOTH SIDES, Magazine, 78-41
SHOT DOWN IN THE NIGHT, Hawkwind, 80-59
SHOT IN THE DARK, Ozzy Osbourne, 86-20
SHOT IN THE DARK, DJ Hype, 93-63
SHOT OF POISON, Lita Ford, 92-63
A SHOT OF RHYTHM AND BLUES, Johnny Kidd and the Pirates, 63-48
SHOTGUN WEDDING:
Roy "C", 66-6, 72-8
Rod Stewart, 93-21
SHOULD I DO IT?, Pointer Sisters, 81-50
SHOULD I EVER (FALL IN LOVE), Nightcrawlers featuring John Reid, 96-34
SHOULD I STAY, Gabrielle, 00-13
SHOULD I STAY OR SHOULD I GO, Clash, 82-17, 91-1
SHOULDER HOLSTER, Morcheeba, 97-53
SHOULDN'T DO THAT, Kaja, 85-63
SHOULD'VE KNOWN BETTER, Richard Marx, 88-50
SHOUT:
Lulu and the Luvvers, 64-7, 86-8
Louchie Lou and Michie One, 93-7
Lulu, 86-8
SHOUT, Tears For Fears, 84-4
SHOUT, Ant and Dec, 97-10
SHOUT! SHOUT! (KNOCK YOURSELF OUT), Rocky Sharpe and the Replays, 82-19
SHOUT TO THE TOP:
Style Council, 84-7
Fire Island featuring Loleatta Holloway, 98-23
SHOUTING FOR THE GUNNERS, Arsenal F.A. Cup Final Squad '93 featuring Tippa Irie and Peter Hunningdale, 93-34
THE SHOW, Doug E. Fresh and the Get Fresh Crew, 85-7
SHOW A LITTLE LOVE, Ultimate Kaos, 95-23
SHOW ME, Dexys Midnight Runners, 81-16
SHOW ME, Lindy Layton, 93-47
SHOW ME, Ultra Nate, 94-62
SHOW ME, Dana Dawson, 96-28
SHOW ME GIRL, Herman's Hermits, 64-19
SHOW ME HEAVEN:
Maria McKee, 90-1
Tina Arena, 95-29
Chimira, 97-70
SHOW ME LOVE, Robin S, 93-6, 97-9
SHOW ME LOVE, Robyn, 98-8
SHOW ME MARY, Catherine Wheel, 93-62
SHOW ME THE MEANING OF BEING LONELY, Backstreet Boys, 00-66, 00-3
SHOW ME THE MONEY, Architechs, 01-20
SHOW ME THE WAY, Peter Frampton, 76-10
SHOW ME THE WAY, Osmond Boys, 92-60
SHOW ME YOU'RE A WOMAN, Mud, 75-8
THE SHOW MUST GO ON, Leo Sayer, 73-2
THE SHOW MUST GO ON, Queen, 91-16
THE SHOW (THEME FROM CONNIE), Rebecca Storm, 85-22
SHOW YOU THE WAY TO GO:
Jacksons, 77-1
Dannii Minogue, 92-30
SHOWDOWN, Electric Light Orchestra, 73-12
SHOWER YOUR LOVE, Kula Shaker, 99-14
SHOWING OUT (GET FRESH AT THE WEEKEND), Mel and Kim, 86-3
SHOWROOM DUMMIES, Kraftwerk, 82-25
THE SHUFFLE, Van McCoy, 77-4
SHUT 'EM DOWN, Public Enemy, 92-21
SHUT UP, Madness, 81-7
SHUT UP AND DANCE, Aerosmith, 94-24
SHUT UP . . . AND FORGET ABOUT IT, Dane, 01-9
SHUT UP AND KISS ME, Mary Chapin Carpenter, 95-35
SHUT UP (AND SLEEP WITH ME), Sin With Sebastian, 95-44, 96-46
SHUT YOUR MOUTH, Made In London, 00-74
SHY BOY, Bananarama, 82-4
SHY GIRL, Mark Wynter, 63-28
SHY GUY, Diana King, 95-2
(SI SI) JE SUIS UN ROCK STAR, Bill Wyman, 81-14
SI TU DOIS PARTIR (IF YOU GOTTA GO, GO NOW), Fairport Convention, 69-21
SICK AND TIRED, Fats Domino, 58-26
SICK & TIRED, Cardigans, 95-34
SICK-MAN BLUES, Goodies, 75-4
SICK OF DRUGS, Wildhearts, 96-14
SICK OF GOODBYES, Sparklehorse, 98-57
SICK OF IT, Primitives, 89-24
SIDE, Travis, 01-14
SIDE BY SIDE, Kay Starr, 53-7
SIDE SADDLE, Russ Conway, 59-1
SIDE SHOW, Barry Biggs, 76-3
THE SIDEBOARD SONG (GOT MY BEER IN THE SIDEBOARD HERE), Chas and Dave, 79-55
SIDESHOW, Chanter Sisters, 76-43
SIDESHOW, Wendy and Lisa, 88-49
SIDEWALK TALK, Jellybean featuring Catherine Buchanan, 86-47
SIDEWALKING, Jesus and Mary Chain, 88-30
THE SIDEWINDER SLEEPS TONITE, R.E.M., 93-17
SIGHT FOR SORE EYES, M People, 94-6
THE SIGN, Ace Of Base, 94-2
SIGN 'O' THE TIMES:
Prince, 87-10
Simple Minds (from The Amsterdam [EP]), 89-18
A SIGN OF THE TIMES, Petula Clark, 66-49
SIGN OF THE TIMES, Bryan Ferry, 78-37
SIGN OF THE TIMES, Belle Stars, 83-3
SIGN OF THE TIMES, Grandmaster Flash, 85-72
SIGN YOUR NAME, Terence Trent D'Arby, 88-2
THE SIGNATURE TUNE OF THE ARMY GAME, Michael Medwin, Bernard Bresslaw, Alfie Bass and Leslie Fyson, 58-5
SIGNED SEALED DELIVERED I'M YOURS:
Stevie Wonder, 70-15
Boystown Gang, 82-50
SIGNS, Tesla, 91-70
SIGNS . . ., Blameless, 96-49
SIGNS, DJ Badmarsh and Shri featuring UK Apache, 01-63
THE SILENCE, Mike Koglin, 98-20
SILENCE:
Delerium, 99-73
Delerium featuring Sarah Mclachlan, 00-3
SILENCE IS GOLDEN, Tremeloes, 67-1
SILENT ALL THESE YEARS, Tori Amos, 91-51, 92-26
SILENT LUCIDITY, Queensryche, 91-34, 92-18
SILENT NIGHT, HOLY NIGHT:
Bing Crosby; vocal with the Max Terr Choir and John Scott Trotter and his Orchestra, 52-8
Dickies *, 78-47
Bros *, 88-2
Sinead O'Connor *, 91-60
SILENT RUNNING (ON DANGEROUS GROUND), Mike and the Mechanics, 86-21, 96-61
SILENT SCREAM, Richard Marx, 94-32
SILENT VOICE, Innocence, 90-37
SILENT WORDS, Jan Johnston, 01-57
SILENTLY BAD MINDED, Pressure Drop featuring Constantine Weir and Martin Fishley, 98-53
SILHOUETTES, Herman's Hermits, 65-3
SILHOUETTES, Cliff Richard, 90-10
SILK PYJAMAS, Thomas Dolby, 92-62
SILLY GAMES:
Janet Kay, 79-2, 90-62
Lindy Layton featuring Janet Kay, 90-22
SILLY LOVE, 10 C.C., 74-24
SILLY LOVE SONGS, Wings, 76-2
SILLY THING, Sex Pistols, 79-6
SILVER, Echo and the Bunnymen, 84-30
SILVER, Moist, 95-50
SILVER AND GOLD, A S A P, 89-60
SILVER DREAM MACHINE, David Essex, 80-4
SILVER LADY, David Soul, 77-1
SILVER LINING, Stiff Little Fingers, 81-68
SILVER MACHINE, Hawkwind, 72-3, 78-34, 83-67
SILVER SCREEN SHOWER SCENE, Felix Da Housecat featuring Ms Kittin, 01-55
SILVER SHADOW, Atlantic Starr, 85-41
SILVER SHORTS, Wedding Present, 92-14
SILVER STAR, Four Seasons, 76-3
SILVER THUNDERBIRD, Marc Cohn, 91-54
SILVERMAC, Westworld, 87-42
SILVERY RAIN, Cliff Richard, 71-27
SIMBA GROOVE, Hi Power, 90-73
SIMON SAYS, 1910 Fruitgum Co., 68-2
SIMON SAYS GET THE FK UP,** Pharoahe Monch, 00-24
SIMON SMITH AND THE AMAZING DANCING BEAR, Alan Price Set, 67-4
SIMON TEMPLER, Splodgenessabounds, 80-7
SIMPLE AS THAT, Huey Lewis and the News, 87-47
SIMPLE GAME, Four Tops, 71-3
SIMPLE KIND OF LOVE, No Doubt, 00-69
SIMPLE LIFE, Elton John, 93-44
SIMPLE SIMON (YOU GOTTA REGARD), Mantronix, 88-72
SIMPLE SINCERITY, Radish, 97-50
THE SIMPLE THINGS, Joe Cocker, 94-17
SIMPLE THINGS, Saw Doctors, 97-56
THE SIMPLE TRUTH (A CHILD IS BORN), Chris De Burgh, 87-55, 91-36
SIMPLY IRRESISTIBLE, Robert Palmer, 88-44
SIN, Nine Inch Nails, 91-35
SINBAD, System 7, 93-74
SINCE DAY ONE, Teena Marie, 90-69
SINCE I DON'T HAVE YOU:
Art Garfunkel, 79-38
Guns N' Roses, 94-10
SINCE I LEFT YOU, Avalanches, 01-16
SINCE I MET YOU BABY, Gary Moore and B.B. King, 92-59
SINCE I MET YOU LADY, UB40 featuring Lady Saw, 01-40
SINCE YESTERDAY, Strawberry Switchblade, 84-5
SINCE YOU BEEN GONE, Rainbow, 79-6
SINCE YOU'RE GONE, Cars, 82-37
SINCERE, MJ Cole, 98-38, 00-13

SMASH IT UP, Damned, 79-35
SMASH SUMTHIN', Redman (featuring Adam F), 01-11
SMELLS LIKE NIRVANA, "Weird Al" Yankovic, 92-58
SMELLS LIKE TEEN SPIRIT:
Nirvana, 91-7
Abigail, 94-29
SMILE:
Nat "King" Cole, 54-2
Robert Downey Jr., 93-68
SMILE, Pussycat, 76-24
THE SMILE, David Essex, 83-52
SMILE, Audrey Hall featuring Sly Dunbar and Robert Shakespeare, 86-14
SMILE, Aswad featuring Sweetie Irie, 90-53
SMILE, Supernaturals, 97-23
SMILE, Lonestar, 00-55
SMILE, Future Breeze, 01-67
A SMILE IN A WHISPER, Fairground Attraction, 88-75
SMILER, Heavy Stereo, 95-46
SMOKE, Natalie Imbruglia, 98-5
SMOKE GETS IN YOUR EYES:
Platters, 59-1
Blue Haze, 72-32
Bryan Ferry, 74-17
John Alford, 96-13
SMOKE MACHINE, X-Press 2, 01-43
SMOKE ON THE WATER:
Deep Purple, 77-21
Deep Purple (from New Live and Rare Volume 3 [EP]), 80-48
Rock Aid Armemia, 89-39
SMOKEBELCH II, Sabres Of Paradise, 93-55
SMOKESTACK LIGHTNIN', Howlin' Wolf, 64-42
SMOKEY BLUE'S AWAY, New Generation, 68-38
SMOKIN' IN THE BOY'S ROOM:
Brownsville Station, 74-27
Motley Crue, 85-71, 86-51
SMOKIN' ME OUT, Warren G featuring Ron Isley, 97-14
SMOOTH, Santana (featuring Rob Thomas), 99-75, 00-3
SMOOTH CRIMINAL:
Michael Jackson, 88-8
Alien Ant Farm, 01-74, 01-3
SMOOTH OPERATOR, Sade, 84-19
SMOOTH OPERATOR, Big Daddy Kane, 89-65
SMOOTHIN' GROOVIN', Ingram, 83-56
SMOULDER, King Adora, 00-62
SMUGGLER'S BLUES, Glenn Frey, 85-22
THE SMURF, Tyrone Brunson, 82-52
THE SMURF SONG, Father Abraham, 78-2
THE SNAKE, Al Wilson, 75-41
SNAKE BITE [EP], David Coverdale's Whitesnake, 78-61
SNAKE IN THE GRASS, Dave Dee, Dozy, Beaky, Mick and Tich, 69-23
SNAKEDRIVER (from SOUND OF SPEED [EP]), Jesus And Mary Chain, 93-30
SNAP MEGAMIX [M], Snap!, 91-10
SNAP YOUR FINGAZ, Kumara, 00-70
SNAPPINESS, BBG, 90-28, 96-50
SNEAKIN' SUSPICION, Dr. Feelgood, 77-47
SNEAKING OUT THE BACK DOOR, Matt Bianco, 84-44
SNOBBERY AND DECAY, Act, 87-60
SNOOKER LOOPY, Matchroom Mob with Chas and Dave, 86-6
SNOOP DOGG, No Limit Records present Snoop Dogg, 01-13
SNOOP'S UPSIDE YA HEAD, Snoop Doggy Dogg featuring Charlie Wilson, 96-12
SNOOPY VS, THE RED BARON:
Royal Guardsmen, 67-8
Hotshots, 73-4
SNOT RAP, Kenny Everett featuring Sid Snot and Cupid Stunt, 83-9
SNOW, O.R.N., 97-61
SNOW, JJ72, 01-21
SNOW COACH, Russ Conway, 59-7
SNOWBIRD, Anne Murray, 70-23
SNOWBOUND FOR CHRISTMAS, Dickie Valentine, 57-28
THE SNOWS OF NEW YORK, Chris De Burgh, 95-60
SO AMAZING, Luther Vandross, 87-33
SO BEAUTIFUL, Urban Cookie Collective, 95-68
SO BEAUTIFUL, Chris De Burgh, 97-29
SO CALLED FRIEND, Texas, 93-30
SO CLOSE, Diana Ross, 83-43
SO CLOSE, Hall and Oates, 90-69
SO CLOSE, Dina Carroll, 92-20
SO CLOSE TO LOVE, Wendy Moten, 94-35
SO COLD THE NIGHT, Communards, 86-8
SO DAMN COOL, Ugly Kid Joe, 92-44
SO DEEP, Reese Project, 93-54
SO DEEP IS THE NIGHT, Ken Dodd, 64-31
SO DO I, Kenny Ball and his Jazzmen vocal: Kenny Ball, 62-14
SO EMOTIONAL, Whitney Houston, 87-5
SO FAR AWAY, Dire Straits, 85-20
SO FINE, Howard Johnson, 82-45
SO FINE, Kinane, 98-63
SO FRESH, SO CLEAN, Outkast, 01-16
SO GOOD, Roy Orbison, 67-32
SO GOOD, Eternal, 94-13
SO GOOD, Boyzone, 95-3
SO GOOD, Juliet Roberts, 98-15
SO GOOD, SO RIGHT/IN THE THICK OF IT, Brenda Russell, 80-51
SO GOOD TO BE BACK HOME AGAIN, Tourists, 80-8
SO GOOD (TO COME HOME TO), Ivan Matias, 96-69
SO GROOVY, Wendell Williams, 91-74
SO HARD, Pet Shop Boys, 90-4
SO HELP ME GIRL, Gary Barlow, 97-11
SO HERE I AM, UB40, 82-25
SO HOT, J.C., 98-74
SO IN LOVE, Orchestral Manoeuvres In The Dark, 85-27
SO IN LOVE (THE REAL DEAL), Judy Cheeks, 93-27
SO IN LOVE WITH YOU, Freddy Breck, 74-44
SO IN LOVE WITH YOU, Spear Of Destiny, 88-36
SO IN LOVE WITH YOU, Texas, 94-28
SO IN LOVE WITH YOU, Duke, 96-66, 96-22, 00-65
SO INTO YOU, Michael Watford, 94-53
(SO IT WAS . . . SO IT IS) SO IT WILL ALWAYS BE, Everly Brothers, 63-23
SO LET ME GO FAR, Dodgy, 95-30
SO LITTLE TIME, Arkarna, 97-46
SO LONELY, Police, 80-6
SO LONG, Fischer-Z, 80-72
SO LONG, Fierce, 99-15
SO LONG BABY, Del Shannon, 61-10
SO LOW, Ocean Colour Scene, 99-34
SO MACHO, Sinitta, 86-2
SO MANY WAYS, Braxtons, 97-32
SO MANY WAYS, Ellie Campbell, 99-26
SO MUCH IN LOVE:
Tymes, 63-21
All-4-One, 94-60, 94-49
SO MUCH IN LOVE, Mighty Avengers, 64-46
SO MUCH LOVE, Tony Blackburn, 68-31
SO MUCH TROUBLE IN THE WORLD, Bob Marley and the Wailers, 79-56
SO NATURAL, Lisa Stansfield, 93-15
SO NEAR TO CHRISTMAS, Alvin Stardust, 84-29
SO PURE, Baby D, 96-3
SO PURE, Alanis Morissette, 99-38
SO REAL, Love Decade, 91-14
SO RIGHT, Railway Children, 90-68
SO RIGHT, K-Klass, 92-20
SO SAD THE SONG, Gladys Knight and the Pips, 76-20
SO SAD (TO WATCH GOOD LOVE GO BAD), Everly Brothers, 60-4
SO SORRY, I SAID, Liza Minnelli, 89-62
SO STRONG, Ben Shaw featuring Adele Holness, 01-72
SO TELL ME WHY, Poison, 91-25
SO THE STORY GOES, Living In A Box, 87-34
SO THIS IS ROMANCE, Linx, 81-15
SO TIRED, Frankie Vaughan with Alyn Ainsworth and his Orchestra, 67-21
SO TIRED, Ozzy Osbourne, 84-20
SO TIRED OF BEING ALONE, Sybil, 96-53
SO WHAT, Gilbert O'Sullivan, 90-70
SO WHAT!, Ronny Jordan, 92-32
SO WHAT IF I, Damage, 01-12
SO WHATCHA GONNA DO NOW?, Public Enemy, 95-50
SO WHY SO SAD, Manic Street Preachers, 01-8
SO YOU WIN AGAIN, Hot Chocolate, 77-1
SO YOU'D LIKE TO SAVE THE WORLD, Lloyd Cole, 93-72
SO YOUNG, Suede, 93-22
SO YOUNG, Corrs, 98-6
SOAPBOX, Little Angels, 93-33
SOBER, Drugstore, 98-68
SOBER, Jennifer Paige, 99-68
SOCKIT2ME, Missy Misdemeanor Elliott featuring Da Brat, 97-33
SOFT AS YOUR FACE, Soup Dragons, 87-66
SOFT TOP, HARD SHOULDER, Chris Rea, 93-53
SOFTLY AS I LEAVE YOU, Matt Monro, 62-10
SOFTLY SOFTLY, Ruby Murray and Ray Martin and his Orchestra, 55-1
SOFTLY SOFTLY, Equals, 68-48
SOFTLY WHISPERING I LOVE YOU:
Congregation, 71-4
Paul Young, 90-21
SOLACE OF YOU, Living Colour, 91-33
SOLD, Boy George, 87-24
SOLD ME DOWN THE RIVER, Alarm, 89-43
SOLD MY ROCK 'N' ROLL (GAVE IT FOR FUNKY SOUL), Linda and the Funky Boys, 76-36
SOLDIER BLUE, Buffy Sainte-Marie, 71-7
SOLDIER BOY:
Shirelles, 62-23
Cheetahs, 65-39
SOLDIER OF LOVE, Donny Osmond, 88-29
SOLDIER'S SONG, Hollies, 80-58
SOLEADO [CLOUD 99/WHEN A CHILD IS BORN]:
St. Andrews Chorale *, 76-31
Johnny Mathis *, 76-1
Johnny Mathis and Gladys Knight and the Pips *, 81-74
SOLEY SOLEY, Middle Of The Road, 71-5
SOLID, Ashford and Simpson, 85-3
A SOLID BOND IN YOUR HEART, Style Council, 83-11
SOLID GOLD EASY ACTION, T.Rex, 72-2
SOLID ROCK (LIVE), Dire Straits, 84-50
SOLID WOOD, Alison Moyet, 95-44
SOLITAIRE:
Andy Williams, 73-4
Carpenters, 75-32
SOLOMON BITES THE WORM, Bluetones, 98-10
SOLSBURY HILL, Peter Gabriel, 77-13, 90-57
(SOLUTION TO) THE PROBLEM, Masquerade, 86-64
SOLVED, Unbelievable Truth, 98-39
SOME BEAUTIFUL, Jack Wild, 70-46
SOME CANDY TALKING, Jesus And Mary Chain, 86-13
SOME FANTASTIC PLACE, Squeeze, 93-73
SOME FINER DAY, All About Eve, 92-57
SOME GIRLS, Racey, 79-2
SOME GIRLS, Ultimate Kaos, 94-9
SOME GUYS HAVE ALL THE LUCK:
Robert Palmer, 82-16
Rod Stewart, 84-15
Maxi Priest, 87-12
SOME JUSTICE:
Urban Shakedown featuring Micky Finn, 92-23
Urban Shakedown featuring D.Bo General, 95-49
SOME KIND-A EARTHQUAKE, Duane Eddy, 59-12
SOME KIND OF A SUMMER, David Cassidy, 73-3
SOME KIND OF BLISS, Kylie Minogue, 97-22
SOME KIND OF FRIEND, Barry Manilow, 83-48
SOME KIND OF HEAVEN, BBG, 90-65
SOME KIND OF WONDERFUL, Blow Monkeys, 87-67
SOME KINDA FUN, Chris Montez, 63-10
SOME LIE 4 LOVE, L.A. Guns, 91-61
SOME LIKE IT HOT, Power Station, 85-14
SOME MIGHT SAY:
Oasis, 95-1, 96-40
Supernova, 96-55
De-Code featuring Beverli Skeete, 96-69
SOME OF YOUR LOVIN', Dusty Springfield, 65-8
SOME OTHER GUY, Big Three, 63-37
SOME OTHER SUCKER'S PARADE, Del Amitri, 97-46
SOME PEOPLE, Carol Deene, 62-25
SOME PEOPLE, Belouis Some, 86-33
SOME PEOPLE, Paul Young, 86-56
SOME PEOPLE, Cliff Richard, 87-3
SOME PEOPLE SAY, Terrorvision, 95-22
SOME THINGS YOU NEVER GET USED TO, Diana Ross and the Supremes, 68-34
SOMEBODY, Stargazers with Sonny Farrar and his Banjo Band, 55-20
SOMEBODY, Junior, 84-64
SOMEBODY, Depeche Mode, 84-16
SOMEBODY, Bryan Adams, 85-35
SOMEBODY, Brilliant, 86-67
SOMEBODY, Shortie vs Black Legend, 01-37
SOMEBODY ELSE'S GIRL, Billy Fury, 63-18
SOMEBODY ELSE'S GUY:
Jocelyn Brown, 84-13
CeCe Peniston, 98-13
SOMEBODY ELSE'S GUY (ME DID LOVE YOU), Louchie Lou and Michie One, 93-54
SOMEBODY HELP ME, Spencer Davis Group, 66-1
(SOMEBODY) HELP ME OUT, Beggar and Co., 81-15
SOMEBODY IN THE HOUSE SAY YEAH!, 2 In A Room, 89-66
SOMEBODY LIKE YOU, Elate, 97-38

SONG OF DREAMS, Becky Taylor, 01-60
SONG OF JOY, Miguel Rios, 70-16
SONG OF LIFE, Leftfield, 92-59
SONG OF MEXICO, Tony Meehan, 64-39
THE SONG OF MY LIFE, Petula Clark, 71-32
SONG OF THE DREAMER, Johnnie Ray with George Siravo and his Orchestra, 55-10
SONG SUNG BLUE, Neil Diamond, 72-14
THE SONG THAT I SING, Stutz Bear Cats, 82-36
SONG TO THE SIREN, This Mortal Coil, 83-66
SONG 2, Blur, 97-2
SONGBIRD, Kenny G, 87-22
SONGS FOR CHRISTMAS '87 [EP], Mini Pops, 87-39
SONGS FOR SWINGIN' LOVERS [LP], Frank Sinatra, 56-12
SONIC BOOM BOY, Westworld, 87-11
SONIC BOOM (LIFE'S TOO SHORT), Quo Vadis, 00-49
SONNET, Verve, 98-74
"SONS AND DAUGHTERS" THEME, Kerri and Mick, 84-68
SONS OF THE STAGE, World Of Twist, 91-47
SOON, My Bloody Valentine, 90-41
SOON BE DONE, Shaggy, 93-46
SOONER OR LATER, Larry Graham, 82-54
SOOTHE ME, Sam and Dave, 67-35
SORRENTO MOON (I REMEMBER), Tina Arena, 96-22
SORROW:
Merseys, 66-4
David Bowie, 73-3
SORRY BUT I'M GONNA HAVE TO PASS, Coasters, 94-41
SORRY DOESN'T ALWAYS MAKE IT RIGHT, Diana Ross, 75-23
SORRY (I DIDN'T KNOW), Monsta Boy featuring. Denzie, 00-25
SORRY (I RAN ALL THE WAY HOME), Impalas, 59-28
SORRY I'M A LADY, Baccara, 78-8
SORRY ROBBIE, Bert Weedon, 60-28
SORRY SEEMS TO BE THE HARDEST WORD, Elton John, 76-11
SORRY SUZANNE, Hollies, 69-3
SORTED FOR E'S & WIZZ, Pulp, 95-2
SOS, Abba, 75-6
SOUL BOSSA NOVA, Cool, The Fab And The Groovy present Quincy Jones, 98-47
THE SOUL CAGES, Sting, 91-57
SOUL CHA CHA, Van McCoy, 77-34
THE SOUL CITY WALK, Archie Bell and the Drells, 76-13
SOUL CLAP '69, Booker T. and the M.G.'S, 69-35
SOUL COAXING, Raymond Lefevre, 68-46
SOUL DEEP:
Box Tops, 69-22
Gary U.S. Bonds, 82-59
SOUL DEEP, Council Collective, 84-24
SOUL DRACULA, Hot Blood, 76-32
SOUL FINGER, Bar-Kays, 67-33
SOUL FREEDOM – FREE YOUR SOUL, Degrees Of Motion featuring Biti, 92-64
SOUL HEAVEN, Goodfellas featuring Lisa Millett, 01-27
SOUL INSIDE, Soft Cell, 83-16
SOUL INSPIRATION, Simon Climie, 92-60
SOUL LIMBO:
Booker T. and the M.G.'S, 68-30
England's Barmy Army *, 99-45
SOUL LOVE, Blessing featuring Cutty Ranks, 94-73
SOUL LOVE / SOUL MAN [M], Womack and Womack, 86-58
SOUL MAN:
Sam and Dave, 67-24
Sam Moore and Lou Reed, 87-30
SOUL OF MY SOUL, Michael Bolton, 94-32
THE SOUL OF MY SUIT, T.Rex, 77-42
SOUL PASSING THROUGH SOUL, Toyah, 85-57
SOUL PROVIDER, Michael Bolton, 96-35
SOUL SEARCHING TIME, Trammps, 76-42
SOUL SERENADE, Willie Mitchell, 68-43
SOUL SISTER BROWN SUGAR, Sam and Dave, 69-15
SOUL SOUND, Sugababes, 01-30
SOUL TRAIN, Swansway, 84-20
SOULJACKER PART 1, Eels, 01-30
SOULMATE, Wee Papa Girl Rappers, 88-45
SOULS, Rick Springfield, 84-24
THE SOULSHAKER, Max Linen, 01-55
SOUL'S ON FIRE, Tracie, 84-73
SOUND, James, 91-9
THE SOUND, X-Press 2, 96-38
SOUND AND VISION, David Bowie, 77-3
SOUND BWOY BURIAL, Gant, 97-67
SOUND CLASH (CHAMPION SOUND), Kick Squad, 90-59
THE SOUND OF BAMBOO, Flickman, 00-11
SOUND OF CONFUSION, Secret Affair, 80-45
THE SOUND OF CRYING, Prefab Sprout, 92-23
SOUND OF DRUMS, Kula Shaker, 98-3
THE SOUND OF EDEN (EVERY TIME I SEE HER):
Shades Of Rhythm, 91-35, 93-37
Casino *, 97-52
THE SOUND OF MUSIC, Dayton, 83-75
THE SOUND OF MUSIK, Falco, 86-61
THE SOUND OF: OH YEAH, Tomba Vira, 01-51
THE SOUND OF SILENCE, Bachelors, 66-3
SOUND OF SPEED [EP], Jesus And Mary Chain, 93-30
THE SOUND OF THE CROWD, Human League Red, 81-12
THE SOUND OF THE SUBURBS, Members, 79-12
THE SOUND OF YOUR CRY, Elvis Presley with the Imperials Quartet, 82-59
SOUND SYSTEM, Steel Pulse, 79-71
SOUND SYSTEM, Drum Club, 93-62
SOUND YOUR FUNKY HORN, K C and the Sunshine Band, 74-17
SOUNDS OF WICKEDNESS, Tzant featuring the Original ODC. MC., 98-11
SOUR TIMES, Portishead, 94-57, 95-13
SOUTH AFRICAN MAN, Hamilton Bohannon, 75-22
SOUTH OF THE BORDER, Robbie Williams, 97-14
SOUTH OF THE RIVER, Mica Paris, 90-50
SOUTHERN COMFORT, Berni Flint, 77-48
SOUTHERN FREEEZ, Freeez, 81-8, 87-63
SOUTHERN NIGHTS, Glen Campbell, 77-28
SOUTHSIDE, Dave Clarke, 96-34
SOUVENIR, OMD, 81-3
SOUVENIRS, Voyage, 78-56
SOWETO, Malcolm McLaren with the McLarenettes, 83-32
SOWETO, Jeffrey Osborne, 86-44
SOWING THE SEEDS OF HATRED, Credit To The Nation, 94-72
SOWING THE SEEDS OF LOVE, Tears For Fears, 89-5
SPACE, New Model Army, 91-39
SPACE AGE LOVE SONG, A Flock Of Seagulls, 82-34
SPACE BASS, Slick, 79-16
THE SPACE BETWEEN, Dave Matthews Band, 01-35
SPACE CAKES (from L.S.D. [EP]), Kaotic Chemistry, 92-68
SPACE COWBOY, Jamiroquai, 94-17
SPACE JAM, Quad City DJ's, 97-57
THE SPACE JUNGLE, Adamski, 90-7
SPACE LORD, Monster Magnet, 99-45
SPACE OASIS, Billie Ray Martin, 96-66
SPACE ODDITY, David Bowie, 69-5, 75-1
SPACE RIDER, Shaun Escoffery, 01-52
SPACE STATION NO. 5:
Sammy Hagar, 79-52
Montrose, 80-71
SPACED INVADER, Hatiras featuring Slarta John, 01-14
SPACEMAN, 4 Non Blondes, 93-53
SPACEMAN, Babylon Zoo, 96-1
A SPACEMAN CAME TRAVELLING, Chris De Burgh, 86-40
SPACER, Sheila and B. Devotion, 79-18
SPANISH DANCE TROUPE, Gorky's Zygotic Mynci, 99-47
SPANISH EYES, Al Martino, 70-49, 73-5
SPANISH FLEA, Herb Alpert and the Tijuana Brass, 65-3
SPANISH HARLEM:
Jimmy Justice, 62-20
Sounds Incorporated, 64-35
Aretha Franklin, 71-14
SPANISH HORSES, Aztec Camera, 92-52
SPANISH STROLL, Mink Deville, 77-20
SPANISH WINE, Chris White, 76-37
SPARE PARTS, Bruce Springsteen, 88-32
SPARK, Tori Amos, 98-16
SPARKLE, My Life Story, 96-34
SPARKLE OF MY EYES, UB40 featuring Lady Saw, 01-40
SPARKY'S DREAM, Teenage Fanclub, 95-40
THE SPARROW, Ramblers (from the Abbey Hey Junior School), 79-11
THE SPARTANS, Sounds Incorporated, 64-30
SPEAK LIKE A CHILD, Style Council, 83-4
SPEAK TO ME PRETTY, Brenda Lee, 62-3
SPEAK TO ME SOMEONE, Gene, 97-30
THE "SPEAK UP" MUSICAL – UP WITH PEOPLE!, Lambchop presents . . ., 00-66
SPEAKEASY, Shed Seven, 94-24
SPECIAL, Garbage, 98-15
THE SPECIAL A.K.A. LIVE! [EP], Specials featuring Rico, 80-1
SPECIAL BREW, Bad Manners, 80-3
SPECIAL F./X, Whispers, 87-69
SPECIAL KIND OF LOVE, Dina Carroll, 92-16
SPECIAL KIND OF LOVER, Nu Colours, 96-38
SPECIAL KIND OF SOMETHING, Kavana, 98-13
SPECIAL WAY, River City People, 91-44
THE SPECIAL YEARS, Val Doonican, 65-7
SPEED, Billy Idol, 94-47
SPEED AT THE SOUND OF LONELINESS, Alabama 3, 97-72
SPEED YOUR LOVE TO ME, Simple Minds, 84-20
SPEEDWELL, Saint Etienne, 91-54
SPEEDY GONZALES, Pat Boone, 62-2
THE SPELL!, Funky Worm, 88-61
SPELLBOUND, Siouxsie and the Banshees, 81-22
SPEND SOME TIME, Brand New Heavies, 94-26
SPEND THE DAY, Urban Cookie Collective, 95-59
SPEND THE NIGHT, Cool Notes, 85-11
SPEND THE NIGHT, Danny J Lewis, 98-29
SPENDING MY TIME, Roxette, 91-22
SPICE OF LIFE, Manhattan Transfer, 84-19
SPICE UP YOUR LIFE, Spice Girls, 97-1
SPIDERS & SNAKES, Jim Stafford, 74-14
SPIDERWEBS, No Doubt, 97-16
SPIES LIKE US, Paul McCartney, 85-13
SPIKEE, Underworld, 93-63
SPILLER FROM RIO (DO IT EASY), Laguna, 97-40
SPIN SPIN SUGAR, Sneaker Pimps, 97-21, 98-46
SPIN THAT WHEEL TURTLES GET REAL, Hi Tek 3 featuring Ya Kid K, 90-69, 90-15
SPIN THE BLACK CIRCLE, Pearl Jam, 94-10
SPINDRIFT [EP], Thousand Yard Stare, 92-58
SPINNIN' AND SPINNIN', Syreeta, 74-49
SPINNING AROUND, Kylie Minogue, 00-1
SPINNING ROCK BOOGIE, Hank C. Burnette, 76-21
SPINNING THE WHEEL, George Michael, 96-2
SPIRAL SCRATCH [EP], Buzzcocks with Howard Devoto, 79-31
SPIRAL SYMPHONY, Scientist, 91-74
SPIRIT, Bauhaus, 82-42
SPIRIT, Wayne Marshall, 95-58
SPIRIT, Sounds Of Blackness featuring Craig Mack, 97-35
SPIRIT, BODY AND SOUL, Nolan Sisters, 79-34
SPIRIT IN THE SKY:
Norman Greenbaum, 70-1
Doctor and the Medics, 86-1
SPIRIT INSIDE, Spirits, 95-39
THE SPIRIT IS WILLING, Peter Straker – The Hands Of Doctor Teleny, 72-40
THE SPIRIT OF RADIO, Rush, 80-13
SPIRIT OF 76, Alarm, 86-22
SPIRITS (HAVING FLOWN), Bee Gees, 80-16
SPIRITS IN THE MATERIAL WORLD:
Police, 81-12
Pato Banton with Sting, 96-36
SPIRITUAL HIGH (STATE OF INDEPENDENCE), Moodswings (features the voice of Chrissie Hynde), 91-66, 93-47
SPIRITUAL LOVE, Urban Species, 94-35
SPIRITUAL THANG, Eric Benet, 97-62
SPIRITUALIZED, Finley Quaye, 00-26
SPIT IN THE RAIN, Del Amitri, 90-21
SPIT IT OUT, Slipknot, 00-28
SPITTING IN THE WIND, Badly Drawn Boy, 01-22
SPLIFFHEAD, Ragga Twins, 90-51
SPLISH SPLASH:
Bobby Darin, 58-18
Charlie Drake, 58-7

STEP BY STEP, Whitney Houston, 96-13
A STEP IN THE RIGHT DIRECTION, Truth, 83-32
STEP INSIDE LOVE, Cilla Black, 68-8
STEP INTO A DREAM, White Plains with Gerry Butler Strings, 73-21
STEP INTO A WORLD (RAPTURE'S DELIGHT), Krs One, 97-24
STEP INTO CHRISTMAS, Elton John, 73-24
STEP INTO MY WORLD, Hurricane #1, 97-29, 97-19
STEP INTO THE BREEZE, Spiritualized, 90-75
STEP IT UP, Stereo MC's, 92-12
STEP OFF, Junior Giscombe, 90-63
STEP OFF, Grandmaster Melle Mel and the Furious Five, 84-8
STEP ON, Happy Mondays Guest vocal: Rowetta, 90-5
STEP ON MY OLD SIZE NINES, Stereophonics, 01-16
STEP RIGHT UP, Jaki Graham, 86-15
STEP TO ME (DO ME), Mantronix, 91-59
STEP-TWO-THREE-FOUR, Strict Instructor, 98-49
STEPPIN' OUT, Kool And The Gang, 81-12
STEPPIN' OUT, Joe Jackson, 83-6
STEPPING DOWN THE GLORY ROAD (from CAPTURE THE HEART [EP]), Runrig, 90-49
STEPPING STONE:
Farm, 90-58
PJ and Duncan, 96-11
STEPTOE & SON AT BUCKINGHAM PALACE, Wilfred Brambell and Harry H. Corbett, 63-25
STEREO, Pavement, 97-48
STEREOTYPE, Specials, 80-6
STEREOTYPES, Blur, 96-7
STEWBALL, Lonnie Donegan Skiffle Group, 56-7
STICK IT OUT, Right Said Fred and Friends, 93-4
STICKS AND STONES, Cud, 94-68
STICKY, Wedding Present, 92-17
STIFF UPPER LIP, AC/DC, 00-65
STILL:
Karl Denver, 63-13
Ken Dodd with Geoff Love and his Orchestra, 63-35
STILL, Commodores, 79-4
STILL, Macy Gray, 00-18
STILL A FRIEND OF MINE, Incognito, 93-47
STILL A THRILL, Sybil, 97-55
STILL BE LOVIN' YOU, Damage, 01-11
STILL BELIEVE, Shola Ama, 99-26
STILL D.R.E., Dr. Dre featuring Snoop Dogg, 00-6
STILL FEEL THE RAIN, Stex, 91-63
STILL GOT THE BLUES (FOR YOU), Gary Moore, 90-31
STILL I'M SAD, Yardbirds, 65-3
STILL IN LOVE, Go West, 93-43
STILL IN LOVE, Lionel Richie, 96-66
STILL OF THE NIGHT, Whitesnake, 87-16
STILL ON YOUR SIDE, BBMak, 01-8
STILL THE SAME, Slade, 87-73
STILL TOO YOUNG TO REMEMBER, It Bites, 89-66, 90-66
STILL WATER (LOVE), Four Tops, 70-10
STILL WATERS (RUN DEEP), Bee Gees, 97-18
STILLNESS IN TIME, Jamiroquai, 95-9
THE STING, Ragtimers, 74-31
STING ME, Black Crowes, 92-42
STINGRAY, Shadows, 65-19
THE STINGRAY MEGAMIX, F.A.B. featuring Aqua Marina, 90-66
STINKIN' THINKIN', Happy Mondays, 92-31
STIR IT UP, Johnny Nash, 72-13
STOLEN CAR, Beth Orton, 99-34
STOMP:
Brothers Johnson, 80-6
Quincy Jones featuring: Melle Mel/Coolio/Yo-Yo/Shaquille O'Neal/Luniz, 96-28
STOMP, God's Property from Kirk Franklin's Nu Nation featuring Kirk Franklin and "Salt", 97-60
STOMP, Steps, 00-1
STONE BY STONE, Catatonia, 01-19
STONE COLD, Rainbow, 82-34
STONE LOVE, Kool And The Gang, 87-45
STONED LOVE, Supremes, 71-3
STONEY END, Barbra Streisand, 71-27
STONEY GROUND, Guys 'N' Dolls, 76-38
THE STONK, Hale and Pace and the Stonkers, 91-1
STOOD ON GOLD, Gorky's Zygotic Mynci, 01-65
STOOD UP, Ricky Nelson, 58-27
STOOL PIGEON, Kid Creole and the Coconuts, 82-7
STOP, Sam Brown, 88-52, 89-4
STOP! :
Erasure (from Crackers International [EP]), 88-2
Bjorn Again, 92-25
STOP, Spice Girls, 98-2
STOP [EP] + lead track title, Mega City Four, 92-36
STOP AND GO, David Grant, 83-19
STOP BAJON . . . PRIMAVERA, Tullio De Piscopo, 87-58
STOP BREAKING MY HEART, Inner Circle, 79-50
STOP BY, Rahsaan Patterson, 97-50
STOP DRAGGIN' MY HEART AROUND, Stevie Nicks (with Tom Petty and the Heartbreakers), 81-50
STOP FEELING SORRY FOR YOURSELF, Adam Faith, 65-23
STOP HER ON SIGHT (SOS), Edwin Starr, 66-35, 68-11
STOP! IN THE NAME OF LOVE, Supremes, 65-7, 89-62
STOP LISTENING, Tanita Tikaram, 98-67
STOP, LOOK AND LISTEN, Donna Summer, 84-57
STOP LOOK AND LISTEN, Wayne Fontana and the Mindbenders, 64-37
STOP, LOOK, LISTEN (TO YOUR HEART), Diana Ross and Marvin Gaye, 74-25
STOP LOVING ME, STOP LOVING YOU, Daryl Hall, 94-30
STOP ME (IF YOU'VE HEARD IT ALL BEFORE), Billy Ocean, 76-12
STOP PLAYING WITH MY MIND, Barbara Tucker featuring Darryl D'Bonneau, 00-17
STOP STARTING TO START STOPPING [EP], D.O.P., 96-58
STOP STOP STOP, Hollies, 66-2
STOP THAT GIRL, Chris Andrews, 66-36
STOP THE CAVALRY, Jona Lewie, 80-3
STOP THE ROCK, Apollo Four Forty, 99-10
STOP THE VIOLENCE, Boogie Down Productions, 88-69
STOP THE WAR NOW, Edwin Starr, 71-33
STOP THE WORLD, Extreme, 92-22
STOP THIS CRAZY THING, Coldcut featuring Junior Reid and the Ahead Of Our Time Orchestra, 88-21
STOP TO LOVE, Luther Vandross, 87-24
STOP YOUR CRYING, Spiritualized, 01-18
STOP YOUR SOBBING, Pretenders, 79-34
STORIES, Izit, 89-52
STORIES, Therapy?, 95-14
STORIES OF JOHNNY, Marc Almond, 85-23
THE STORM, World Of Twist, 90-42
STORM, Space Kittens, 96-58
STORM, Vanessa-Mae, 97-54
STORM, Storm, 98-32, 01-32
STORM ANIMAL, Storm, 00-21
STORM IN A TEACUP, Fortunes, 72-7
THE STORM IS OVER NOW, R. Kelly, 01-18
STORMS IN AFRICA (PART II), Enya, 89-41
STORMTROOPER IN DRAG, Paul Gardiner, 81-49
THE STORY OF LOVE, OTT, 98-11
THE STORY OF MY LIFE:
Michael Holliday, 58-1
Gary Miller with the Kim Drake Orchestra and the Beryl Stott Group, 58-14
Dave King and the Roland Shaw Orchestra, 58-20
Alma Cogan, 58-25
THE STORY OF MY LOVE, Conway Twitty, 59-30
THE STORY OF THE BLUES, Wah!, 82-3
STORY OF THE BLUES, Gary Moore, 92-40
THE STORY OF TINA:
Ronnie Harris, 54-12
Al Martino, 54-10
STOWAWAY, Barbara Lyon with Ray Martin and his Orchestra, 55-12
STRAIGHT AHEAD, Kool And The Gang, 83-15
STRAIGHT AT YER HEAD, Lionrock, 96-33
STRAIGHT FROM THE HEART, Bryan Adams, 86-51
STRAIGHT FROM THE HEART, Doolally, 98-20, 99-9
STRAIGHT LINES, New Musik, 79-53
STRAIGHT OUT OF THE JUNGLE, Jungle Brothers, 89-72
STRAIGHT TO HELL, Clash, 82-17
STRAIGHT TO MY FEET, Hammer/Deion Sanders, 95-57
STRAIGHT TO THE HEART, Real Thing, 86-71
STRAIGHT TO YOU, Nick Cave and the Bad Seeds, 92-68
STRAIGHT UP, Paula Abdul, 89-3
STRAIGHT UP, Chante Moore, 01-11
STRAIGHT UP NO BENDS, Brian Harvey, 01-26
STRAIGHTEN OUT, Stranglers, 77-9
STRANDED, Heart, 90-60
STRANDED, Deep Dish, 97-60
STRANDED, Lutricia McNeal, 98-3
STRANGE, Wet Wet Wet, 97-13
STRANGE BAND: THE WEAVERS ANSWER, Family, 70-11
STRANGE BREW, Cream, 67-17
STRANGE CURRENCIES, R.E.M., 95-9
STRANGE GLUE, Catatonia, 98-11
STRANGE KIND OF LOVE, Love And Money, 89-45
STRANGE KIND OF WOMAN, Deep Purple, 71-8
STRANGE LADY IN TOWN, Frankie Laine with Mitch Miller and his Orchestra and Chorus, 55-6
STRANGE LITTLE GIRL, Sad Cafe, 80-32
STRANGE LITTLE GIRL, Stranglers, 82-7
STRANGE MAGIC, Electric Light Orchestra, 76-38
STRANGE TOWN, Jam, 79-15, 80-44, 83-42
STRANGE WAY, All About Eve, 91-50
STRANGE WORLD, Ke, 96-73
STRANGE WORLD, Push, 01-21
STRANGELOVE, Depeche Mode, 87-16
THE STRANGER, Shadows, 60-5
STRANGER, Shakatak, 82-43
STRANGER IN A STRANGE LAND, Iron Maiden, 86-22
STRANGER IN MOSCOW, Michael Jackson, 96-4
STRANGER IN PARADISE:
Tony Bennett with Percy Faith and his Orchestra and Chorus, 55-1
Tony Martin with Hugo Winterhalter's Orchestra and Chorus, 55-6
Don Cornell with the Roland Shaw Orchestra, 55-19
Bing Crosby, 55-17
Eddie Calvert (The Man with the Golden Trumpet) with Norrie Paramor and his Orchestra, 55-14
Four Aces featuring Al Alberts, 55-6
STRANGER IN TOWN, Del Shannon, 65-40
A STRANGER ON HOME GROUND, Faith Brothers, 85-69
STRANGER ON THE SHORE:
Mr. Acker Bilk with the Leon Young String Chorale, 61-2
Andy Williams, 62-30
STRANGER ON THE SHORE OF LOVE, Stevie Wonder, 87-55
STRANGER THINGS, ABC, 97-57
STRANGERS IN OUR TOWN, Spear Of Destiny, 87-49
STRANGERS IN THE NIGHT, Frank Sinatra, 66-1
STRANGERS WHEN WE MEET, David Bowie, 95-39
THE STRANGEST PARTY (THESE ARE THE TIMES), Inxs, 94-15
THE STRANGEST THING '97, George Michael, 97-2
STRANGLEHOLD, U.K. Subs, 79-26
STRAW DOGS, Stiff Little Fingers, 79-44
STRAWBERRY, Nicole Renee, 98-55
STRAWBERRY BLONDE (THE BAND ROCKED ON), Frank D'Rone, 60-24
STRAWBERRY FAIR, Anthony Newley, 60-3
STRAWBERRY FIELDS FOREVER:
Beatles, 67-2, 87-65, 76-32
Candy Flip, 90-3
STRAWBERRY LETTER 23, Brothers Johnson, 77-35
STRAY CAT STRUT, Stray Cats, 81-11
THE STREAK, Ray Stevens, 74-1
STREAMLINE TRAIN, Vipers Skiffle Group, 57-23
STREET CAFE, Icehouse, 83-62
A STREET CALLED HOPE, Gene Pitney, 70-37
STREET DANCE, Break Machine, 84-3
STREET DREAMS, Nas, 97-12
STREET FIGHTER II, World Warrior, 94-70
STREET FIGHTING MAN, Rolling Stones, 71-21
STREET GANG, A.R.E. Weapons, 01-72
STREET LIFE, Roxy Music, 73-9
STREET LIFE, Crusaders, 79-5
STREET OF DREAMS, Rainbow, 83-52
STREET SPIRIT (FADE OUT), Radiohead, 96-5
STREET TUFF, Rebel MC and Double Trouble, 89-3

SUN OF JAMAICA, Goombay Dance Band, 82-50
THE SUN RISING, Beloved, 89-26, 97-31
SUN SHINING DOWN, Circa featuring Destry, 99-70
SUN STREET, Katrina and the Waves, 86-22
SUN WORSHIPPERS (POSITIVE THINKING), Diana Brown and Barrie K. Sharpe, 90-61
SUNBURN, Graham Gouldman, 79-52
SUNBURN, Michelle Collins, 99-28
SUNBURN, Muse, 00-22
SUNCHYME, Dario G, 97-2
SUNDANCE, Sundance, 97-33, 98-37
SUNDAY, Buster, 76-49
SUNDAY, Sonic Youth, 98-72
SUNDAY GIRL, Blondie, 79-1
SUNDAY MONDAYS, Vanessa Paradis, 93-49
SUNDAY MORNING, No Doubt, 97-50
SUNDAY MORNING CALL, Oasis, 00-4
SUNDAY SHINING, Finley Quaye, 97-16
SUNDAY SHOUTIN', Johnny Corporate, 00-45
SUNDAY SUNDAY, Blur, 93-26
SUNDOWN:
Gordon Lightfoot, 74-33
Elwood, 00-72
SUNFLOWER, Paul Weller, 93-16
SUNGLASSES, Tracey Ullman, 84-18
SUNMACHINE, Dario G, 98-17
SUNNY:
Bobby Hebb, 66-12
Georgie Fame, 66-13
Cher, 66-32
Boney M, 77-3
SUNNY, Morrissey, 95-42
SUNNY AFTERNOON, Kinks, 66-1
SUNNY CAME HOME, Shawn Colvin, 98-29
SUNNY DAY, Pigbag, 81-53
SUNNY HONEY GIRL, Cliff Richard, 71-19
SUNRISE, Movement. 98 featuring Carroll Thompson, 90-58
SUNRISE, Goldenscan, 00-52
SUNRISE, Pulp, 01-23
SUNSET, Nitin Sawhney featuring Eska, 01-65
SUNSET & BABYLON, W.A.S.P., 93-38
SUNSET [BIRD OF PREY], Fatboy Slim, 00-9
SUNSET BOULEVARD, Michael Ball, 93-72
SUNSET ON IBIZA, Three Drives (On A Vinyl), 01-44
SUNRISE (HERE I AM), Ratty, 01-51
SUNSET NOW, Heaven 17, 84-24
SUNSET PEOPLE, Donna Summer, 80-46
SUNSHINE, Warren Mills, 85-74
SUNSHINE, Alexander O'Neal, 89-72
SUNSHINE, Umboza, 96-14
SUNSHINE, Jay-Z featuring Babyface and Foxy Brown, 97-25
SUNSHINE, Gabrielle, 99-9
SUNSHINE, Yomanda, 00-16
SUNSHINE AFTER THE RAIN:
Elkie Brooks, 77-10
New Atlantic/U4ea featuring Berri, 94-26, 95-4
SUNSHINE & HAPPINESS, Darryl Pandy meets Nerio's Dubwork, 99-68
SUNSHINE AND LOVE, Happy Mondays, 92-62
SUNSHINE DAY:
Osibisa, 76-17
Clock, 99-58
SUNSHINE GIRL, Herman's Hermits, 68-8
THE SUNSHINE OF LOVE, Louis Armstrong, 68-41
SUNSHINE OF YOUR LOVE, Cream, 68-25
THE SUNSHINE OF YOUR SMILE, Mike Berry, 80-9
SUNSHINE ON A RAINY DAY, Zoe, 90-53, 91-4
SUNSHINE ON LEITH, Proclaimers, 88-41
SUNSHINE PLAYROOM, Julian Cope, 83-64
SUNSHINE SUPERMAN, Donovan, 66-2
SUNSTORM FEATURING 'SONG FOR GUY', Hurley and Todd, 00-38
SUNSTROKE, Chicane, 97-21
SUNTAN, Stan, 93-40
SUPER BOWL SUNDAE, Ozomatli, 99-68
SUPER GIRL, Graham Bonney with Johnny Scott and his Orchestra, 66-19
SUPER GRAN (THEME), Billy Connolly, 85-32
SUPER LOVE, Wigan's Ovation, 75-41
SUPER POPOID GROOVE, Win, 87-63
SUPER TROUPER:
Abba, 80-1
A*Teens, 99-21
SUPER WOMBLE, Wombles, 75-20
SUPERBAD SUPERSLICK, Redhead Kingpin and the F.B.I., 89-68
SUPERFLY 1990, Curtis Mayfield and Ice-T, 90-48
SUPERFLY GUY, S-Express, 88-5
SUPERHERO, Reef, 00-55
SUPERMAN (GIOCA JOUER), Black Lace, 83-9
SUPERMARIOLAND, Ambassadors Of Funk featuring M.C. Mario, 92-8
SUPERMARKET SWEEP (WILL YOU DANCE WITH ME), Bar-Codes featuring Alison Brown, 94-72
SUPERMODEL (YOU BETTER WORK), Rupaul, 93-39, 94-61
SUPERNATURAL, Kim English, 97-50
SUPERNATURAL GIVER, Kinky Machine, 93-70
SUPERNATURE, Cerrone, 78-8, 96-66
SUPERNOVA, Five Thirty, 91-75
SUPERSHIP, George 'Bad' Benson, 75-30
SUPERSONIC, H.W.A. featuring Sonic The Hedgehog, 92-33
SUPERSONIC, Oasis, 94-31, 95-44, 96-47, 97-63
SUPERSONIC, Jamiroquai, 99-22
SUPERSONIC ROCKET SHIP, Kinks, 72-16
SUPERSTAR:
Carpenters, 71-18
Sonic Youth, 94-45
SUPERSTAR, Murray Head with the Trinidad Singers, 72-47
SUPERSTAR, Lydia Murdock, 83-14
SUPERSTAR, Superstar, 98-49
SUPERSTAR, Novy vs. Eniac, 98-32
SUPERSTAR (REMEMBER HOW YOU GOT WHERE YOU ARE), Temptations, 72-32
SUPERSTITION, Stevie Wonder, 73-11
SUPERSTITION / GOOD TIMES [M], Club House, 83-59
SUPERSTITIOUS, Europe, 88-34
SUPERSTRING, Cygnus X, 01-33
SUPERSTYLIN', Groove Armada, 01-12
SUPERWOMAN, Karyn White, 89-11
SUPPORT THE TOON – IT'S YOUR DUTY [EP], Mungo Jerry and the Toon Travellers, 99-57
SUPREME, Robbie Williams, 00-4
THE SUPREME (EP), Sinitta, 93-49
SURE, Take That, 94-1
SURE SHOT, Beastie Boys, 94-27
SURE THING, Darling Buds, 92-71
SURF CITY, Jan and Dean, 63-26
SURFIN' U.S.A.:
Beach Boys, 63-34
Aaron Carter, 98-18
SURGERY (from N.H.S. [EP]), DJ Doc Scott, 92-64
SURPRISE, Bizarre Inc, 96-21
SURPRISE SURPRISE, Central Line, 83-48
SURRENDER, Diana Ross, 71-10
SURRENDER, Swing Out Sister, 87-7
SURRENDER, Roger Taylor featuring Treana Morris, 99-38
SURRENDER (TORNA A SURRIENTO), Elvis Presley with the Jordanaires, 61-1
SURRENDER YOUR LOVE, Nightcrawlers featuring John Reid, 95-7
SURROUND YOURSELF WITH SORROW, Cilla Black, 69-3
SURVIVAL CAR, Fountains Of Wayne, 97-53
SURVIVE, David Bowie, 00-28
SURVIVOR, Destiny's Child, 01-1
SUSANNA, Art Company, 84-12
SUSAN'S HOUSE, Eels, 97-9
SUSIE DARLIN':
Robin Luke, 58-23
Tommy Roe, 62-37
SUSPICION:
Terry Stafford, 64-31
Elvis Presley, 76-9
SUSPICIOUS MINDS:
Elvis Presley, 69-2
Candi Staton, 82-31
Fine Young Cannibals, 86-8
Elvis Presley *, 01-15
SUSSUDIO, Phil Collins, 85-12
SUZANAH'S STILL ALIVE, Dave Davies, 67-20
SUZANNE BEWARE OF THE DEVIL, Dandy Livingstone, 72-14
SVEN SVEN SVEN (COME ON ENGLAND!!), Bell and Spurling, 01-7
SW LIVE [EP], Peter Gabriel, 94-39
SWALLOW MY PRIDE, Ramones, 77-36
SWALLOWED, Bush, 97-7
SWAMP THING, Grid, 94-3
SWAN LAKE, Cats, 69-48
SWASTIKA EYES, Primal Scream, 99-22
SWAY:
Dean Martin, 75-31,
Bobby Rydell, 60-12
Shaft *, 99-2
SWAY, Strangelove, 96-47
SWEAR IT AGAIN, Westlife, 99-1
SWEARIN' TO GOD, Frankie Valli, 75-31
SWEAT, Usura, 93-29
SWEAT (A LA LA LA LA LONG), Inner Circle,
SWEAT IN BULLET, Simple Minds, 81-52
SWEATING BULLETS, Megadeth, 93-26
SWEDISH RHAPSODY:
Mantovani and his Orchestra, 53-2
Ray Martin and his Concert Orchestra, 53-4
SWEET AND LOW, Deborah Harry, 90-57
SWEET BABY, Macy Gray (featuring Erykah Badu), 01-23
SWEET BIRD OF TRUTH, The, 87-55
SWEET CAROLINE, Neil Diamond, 71-8
SWEET CATATONIA, Catatonia, 96-61
SWEET CHEATIN' RITA, Alvin Stardust, 75-37
SWEET CHILD O' MINE:
Guns N' Roses, 88-24, 89-6
Sheryl Crow, 99-30
SWEET DANGER, Angelwitch, 80-75
SWEET DREAM, Jethro Tull, 69-7
SWEET DREAMS, Dave Sampson and the Hunters, 60-29
SWEET DREAMS:
Tommy McLain, 66-49
Roy Buchanan, 73-40
Elvis Costello and the Attractions, 81-42
SWEET DREAMS, La Bouche, 94-63, 96-44
SWEET DREAMS:
DJ Scott featuring Lorna B, 95-37
Swing featuring Dr. Alban, 95-59
SWEET DREAMS (ARE MADE OF THIS):
Eurythmics, 83-2, 91-48
DJ Scott featuring Lorna B *, 95-37
Swing featuring Dr. Alban *, 95-59
SWEET EMOTION, Aerosmith, 94-74
SWEET FREEDOM, Michael McDonald, 86-12
SWEET FREEDOM, Positive Gang, 93-34
SWEET FREEDOM PART II (THE RETURN), Positive Gang, 93-67
SWEET HARMONY, Beloved, 93-8
SWEET HARMONY [EP] + lead track title, Liquid, 92-15, 95-14
SWEET HEART CONTRACT, Magazine, 80-54
SWEET HITCH-HIKER, Creedence Clearwater Revival, 71-36
SWEET HOME ALABAMA, Lynyrd Skynyrd, 76-31, 79-43, 82-21
SWEET ILLUSION, Junior Campbell, 73-15
SWEET IMPOSSIBLE YOU, Brenda Lee, 63-28
SWEET INSPIRATION, Johnny Johnson and the Bandwagon, 70-10
SWEET INVISIBILITY, Hue And Cry, 89-55
SWEET JOHNNY, Gorky's Zygotic Mynci, 98-60
SWEET LADY, Tyrese, 99-55
SWEET LADY LUCK, Whitesnake, 94-25
SWEET LEAF, Mogwai, 98-60
SWEET LIES, Robert Palmer, 88-58
SWEET LIES, Ellie Campbell, 99-42
SWEET LIKE CHOCOLATE, Shanks and Bigfoot, 99-1
SWEET LIPS, Monaco, 97-18
SWEET LITTLE MYSTERY, Wet Wet Wet, 87-5
SWEET LITTLE ROCK 'N' ROLLER, Showaddywaddy, 79-15
SWEET LITTLE SIXTEEN:
Chuck Berry, 58-16
Jerry Lee Lewis, 62-38
SWEET LOVE, Commodores, 77-32
SWEET LOVE:
Anita Baker, 86-13
M-Beat featuring Nazlyn, 94-18
Fierce *, 00-3
SWEET LUI-LOUISE, Ironhorse, 79-60
SWEET LULLABY, Deep Forest, 94-10
SWEET MEMORY, Belle Stars, 83-22
SWEET MUSIC, Showaddywaddy, 75-14
SWEET NUTHIN'S:
Brenda Lee, 60-4
Searchers *, 63-48
A SWEET OLD FASHIONED GIRL, Teresa Brewer, 56-3
SWEET PEA, Manfred Mann, 67-36
SWEAT PEA, MY SWEAT PEA, Paul Weller, 00-44
SWEET POTATOE PIE, Domino, 94-42
SWEET REVENGE, Spooks, 01-67
SWEET REVIVAL (KEEP IT COMIN), Shades Of Rhythm, 93-61
SWEET SENSATION, Melodians, 70-41
SWEET SENSATION, Shades Of Rhythm, 91-54

TAKE THE LONG WAY HOME, Faithless, 98-15
TAKE THESE CHAINS FROM MY HEART, Ray Charles with the Jack Halloran Singers, 63-5
TAKE THIS HEART, Richard Marx, 92-13
TAKE THIS TIME, Sean Maguire, 94-27
TAKE TO THE MOUNTAINS, Richard Barnes, 70-35
TAKE YOU OUT, Luther Vandross, 01-59
TAKE YOU THERE, Ronni Simon, 95-58
TAKE YOUR MAMA FOR A RIDE, Lulu, 75-37
TAKE YOUR PARTNER BY THE HAND, Howie B featuring Robbie Robertson, 98-74
TAKE YOUR TIME, Mantronix featuring Wondress, 90-10
TAKE YOUR TIME, High, 90-56
TAKE YOUR TIME, Love Bite, 00-56
TAKE YOUR TIME (DO IT RIGHT), S.O.S. Band, 80-51
TAKEN FOR GRANTED, S.I.A, 00-10
TAKES A LITTLE TIME, Total Contrast, 85-17
TAKES TWO TO TANGO, Louis Armstrong, 52-6
TAKIN' A CHANCE ON YOU, Dollar, 80-62
TAKING ON THE WORLD, Gun, 90-50
TAKING THE VEIL, David Sylvian, 86-53
TALES FROM A DANCEOGRAPHIC OCEAN [EP], Jam and Spoon, 92-49
TALES FROM THE HARD SIDE, Biohazard, 94-47
TALK ABOUT IT IN THE MORNING, Martyn Joseph, 95-43
TALK BACK, Double Trouble featuring Janette Sewell, 90-71
TALK DIRTY TO ME, Poison, 87-67
TALK OF THE TOWN, Pretenders, 80-8
TALK TALK, Talk Talk, 82-52, 82-23
TALK TO ME, Third World, 79-56
TALK TO ME, Stevie Nicks, 86-68
TALK TO ME, Anita Baker, 90-68
TALK TO ME, 60ft Dolls, 96-37
TALKIN' ALL THAT JAZZ, Stetsasonic, 88-73, 98-54
TALKING IN YOUR SLEEP:
Crystal Gayle, 78-11
Martine McCutcheon, 99-6
TALKING IN YOUR SLEEP, Bucks Fizz, 84-15
TALKING LOUD AND CLEAR, Orchestral Manoeuvres In The Dark, 84-11
TALKING OF LOVE, Anita Dobson, 87-43
TALKING WITH MYSELF, Electribe 101, 90-23, 98-39
TALL DARK STRANGER, Rose Brennan, 61-31
TALL 'N' HANDSOME, Outrage, 95-57, 96-51
TALLAHASSEE LASSIE:
Freddy Cannon, 59-17
Tommy Steele, 59-16
TALLYMAN, Jeff Beck, 67-30
TALULA, Tori Amos, 96-22
TAM-TAM POUR L'ETHIOPIE, Tam-Tam Pour L'ethiopie, 85-33
TAMMY, Debbie Reynolds, 57-2
TAN TA RA (from WHAT IS HOUSE [EP]), LFO, 92-62
TANGERINE, Feeder, 97-60
TANGO IN MONO, Expressos, 81-70
TANSY, Alex Welsh, 61-45
TANTALISE (WO WO EE YEH YEH), Jimmy The Hoover, 83-18
TAP THE BOTTLE, Young Black Teenagers, 94-39
TAP TURNS ON THE WATER, C.C.S., 71-5
TAPE LOOP, Morcheeba, 96-42
TARA'S THEME FROM 'GONE WITH THE WIND':
Rose Of Romance Orchestra, 82-71
Spiro and Wix *, 96-29
TARANTINO'S NEW STAR, North and South, 97-18
TARANTULA, Faithless, 01-29
TARZAN BOY, Baltimora, 85-3
TASTE IN MEN, Placebo, 00-16
TASTE IT, Inxs, 92-21
A TASTE OF AGGRO [M], Barron Knights, 78-3
TASTE OF BITTER LOVE, Gladys Knight and the Pips, 80 35
A TASTE OF HONEY, Mr. Acker Bilk with the Leon Young String Chorale, 63-16
THE TASTE OF YOUR TEARS, King, 85-11
TASTE THE PAIN, Red Hot Chili Peppers, 90-29
TASTE YOUR LOVE, Horace Brown, 95-58
TASTY FISH, Other Two, 91-41
TASTY LOVE, Freddie Jackson, 86-73
TATTOO, Mike Oldfield, 92-33
TATTOOED MILLIONAIRE, Bruce Dickinson, 90-18
TATTVA, Kula Shaker, 96-4
TAVERN IN THE TOWN, Terry Lightfoot and his New Orleans Jazzmen, 62-49
TAXI, J. Blackfoot, 84-48
TAXLOSS (from SIX [EP]), Mansun, 97-15
TCHAIKOVSKY ONE, Second City Sound, 66-22
TE AMO, Sultana, 94-57
TEA FOR TWO CHA CHA, Tommy Dorsey Orchestra starring Warren Covington, 58-3
TEACH ME TO TWIST, Chubby Checker; Bobby Rydell, 62-45
TEACH ME TONIGHT, De Castro Sisters – vocal with the Skip Martin Orchestra, 55-20
TEACH YOU TO ROCK, Tony Crombie and his Rockets, 56-25
TEACHER, Jethro Tull, 70-4
TEACHER, I-Level, 83-56
THE TEACHER, Big Country, 86-28
TEACHER, TEACHER, Johnny Mathis, 58-27
TEAR DOWN THE WALLS, No Sweat, 91-61
TEAR DROP, Massive Attack, 98-10
TEAR DROP CITY, Monkees, 69-45
A TEAR FELL, Teresa Brewer, 56-2
TEAR ME APART, Suzi Quatro, 77-27
TEAR SOUP, Questions, 83-66
TEARDROP, Santo and Johnny, 60-50
TEARDROPS, Shakin' Stevens, 84-5
TEARDROPS :
Womack and Womack, 88-3
Lovestation, 98-14, 00-24
TEARIN' UP MY HEART, 'N Sync, 97-40, 99-9
TEARING, Rollins Band, 92-54
TEARING US APART, Eric Clapton and Tina Turner, 87-56
TEARS, Danny Williams with Geoff Love and his Orchestra, 62-22
TEARS, Ken Dodd with Geoff Love and his Orchestra, 65-1
TEARS:
Frankie Knuckles presents Satoshi Tomiie featuring Robert Owens, 89-50
Nu Colours, 92-55
TEARS ARE FALLING, Kiss, 85-57
TEARS ARE NOT ENOUGH, ABC, 81-19
TEARS DON'T LIE, Mark' Oh, 95-24
TEARS FROM A WILLOW, Ooberman, 99-63
TEARS FROM HEAVEN, Heartbeat, 87-32
THE TEARS I CRIED, Glitter Band, 75-8
TEARS IN HEAVEN, Eric Clapton, 92-5
TEARS IN THE RAIN, N-Trance, 98-53
TEARS IN THE WIND, Chicken Shack, 69-29
THE TEARS OF A CLOWN:
Smokey Robinson and the Miracles, 70-1, 76-34
Beat, 79-6
TEARS OF THE DRAGON, Bruce Dickinson, 94-28
TEARS ON MY PILLOW, Kylie Minogue, 90-1
TEARS ON MY PILLOW (I CAN'T TAKE IT), Johnny Nash, 75-1
TEARS ON THE TELEPHONE, Claude Francois; girl vocal: Kathy Barnet, 76-35
TEARS ON THE TELEPHONE, Hot Chocolate, 83-37
TEARS RUN RINGS, Marc Almond, 88-26
TEARS WON'T WASH AWAY THESE HEARTACHES, Ken Dodd, 69-22
TEASE ME, Chaka Demus and Pliers, 93-3
TEASER, George Benson, 87-45
TECHNARCHY, Cybersonik, 90-73
TECHNO TRANCE, D-Shake, 90-20
TECHNOCAT, Technocat featuring Tom Wilson, 95-33
TECHNOFUNK, Lost, 91-75
TECHNOPOLIS, Yellow Magic Orchestra, 80-17
TEDDY BEAR, Red Sovine, 81-4
TEDDY BEAR, Booker Newbury III, 83-44
TEDDY BEAR'S LAST RIDE, Diana Williams, 81-54
TEEN AGE IDOL, Ricky Nelson, 62-39
TEEN ANGEL, Mark Dinning, 60-37
TEEN BEAT, Sandy Nelson, 59-9
TEENAGE, U.K. Subs, 80-32
TEENAGE ANGST, Placebo, 96-30
TEENAGE DEPRESSION; Eddie and the Hot Rods, 76-35
TEENAGE DIRTBAG, Wheatus, 01-2
TEENAGE DREAM, Marc Bolan and T. Rex, 74-13
TEENAGE KICKS, Undertones, 78-31, 83-60
TEENAGE LAMENT '74, Alice Cooper, 74-12
TEENAGE PUNKS, Sultans Of Ping, 93-49
TEENAGE RAMPAGE, Sweet, 74-2
TEENAGE SENSATION, Credit To The Nation, 94-24
TEENAGE TURTLES, Back To The Planet, 93-52
TEENAGE WARNING, Angelic Upstarts, 79-29
A TEENAGER IN LOVE:
Marty Wilde, 59-2
Craig Douglas, 59-13
Dion and the Belmonts, 59-28
TEENSVILLE, Chet Atkins, 60-46
TEETHGRINDER, Therapy?, 92-30
TELEFUNKIN', N-Tyce, 98-16
TELEGRAM SAM, T. Rex, 72-1, 82-69
TELEGRAPH, Orchestral Manoeuvres In The Dark, 83-42
THE TELEPHONE ALWAYS RINGS, Fun Boy Three, 82-17
TELEPHONE LINE, Electric Light Orchestra, 77-8
TELEPHONE MAN, Meri Wilson, 77-6
TELEPHONE OPERATOR, Pete Shelley, 83-66
TELEPHONE THING, Fall, 90-58
TELEPORT, Man With No Name, 96-55
TELETUBBIES SAY "EH-OH!", Teletubbies, 97-1
TELEVISION, THE DRUG OF THE NATION, Disposable Heroes Of Hiphoprisy, 92-57, 92-44
TELL HER ABOUT IT, Billy Joel, 83-4
TELL HER I'M NOT HOME, Ike and Tina Turner, 66-48
TELL HER NO, Zombies, 65-42
TELL HER THIS, Del Amitri, 95-32
TELL HIM:
Billie Davis, 63-10
Exciters, 63-46
Hello, 74-6
Quentin and Ash, 96-25
TELL HIM, Barbra Streisand/Celine Dion, 97-3
TELL IT LIKE IT T-I-IS, B-52'S, 92-61
TELL IT ON THE MOUNTAIN, Peter, Paul and Mary, 64-33
TELL IT TO MY HEART:
Taylor Dayne, 88-3, 96-23
Q-Club, 96-28
TELL IT TO THE RAIN, 4 Seasons featuring the "Sound" Of Frankie Valli, 67-37
TELL LAURA I LOVE HER, Ricky Valance, 60-1
TELL ME, Nick Kamen, 88-40
TELL ME, Groove Theory, 95-31
TELL ME, Dru Hill, 97-30
TELL ME, Billie Myers, 98-28
TELL ME, Melanie B, 00-4
TELL ME A STORY, Jimmy Boyd-Frankie Laine, 53-5
TELL ME DO U WANNA, Ginuwine, 97-16
TELL ME (HOW IT FEELS), 52nd Street, 85-54
TELL ME (I'M NOT DREAMING), Titiyo, 94-45
TELL ME IS IT TRUE, UB40, 97-14
TELL ME IT'S REAL, K-Ci and Jojo, 99-40, 00-16
TELL ME MA, Sham Rock, 98-13
TELL ME ON A SUNDAY, Marti Webb, 80-67
TELL ME THAT YOU LOVE ME, Paul Anka, 57-25
TELL ME THE WAY, Cappella, 95-17
TELL ME THERE'S A HEAVEN, Chris Rea, 90-24, 94-70
TELL ME TO MY FACE, Keith, 67-50
TELL ME TOMORROW, Smokey Robinson, 82-51
TELL ME TOMORROW, Princess, 86-34
TELL ME WHAT HE SAID, Helen Shapiro with the Martin Slavin Orchestra, 62-2
TELL ME WHAT YOU LIKE (from NEW YORK UNDERCOVER 4-TRACK EP [EP]), Guy – See Various Artists (EPs), 96-39
TELL ME WHAT YOU WANT, Jimmy Ruffin, 74-39
TELL ME WHAT YOU WANT, Loose Ends, 84-74
TELL ME WHAT YOU WANT, Blu Peter, 98-70
TELL ME WHAT YOU WANT ME TO DO, Tevin Campbell, 92-63
TELL ME WHEN, Applejacks, 64-7
TELL ME WHEN, Human League, 95-6
TELL ME WHEN THE FEVER ENDED, Electribe 101, 89-32
TELL ME WHERE YOU'RE GOING, Silje, 90-55
TELL ME WHY, Elvis Presley with the Jordanaires, 65-15
TELL ME WHY, Alvin Stardust, 74-16
TELL ME WHY, Musical Youth, 83-33

TELL ME WHY, Bobby Womack, 84-60
TELL ME WHY, This Way Up, 87-72
TELL ME WHY, Genesis, 93-40
TELL ME WHY (THE RIDDLE), Paul Van Dyk featuring Saint Etienne, 00-7
TELL THAT GIRL TO SHUT UP, Transvision Vamp, 88-45
TELL THE CHILDREN, Sham 69, 80-45
TELLIN' STORIES, Charlatans, 97-16
TELSTAR, Tornados, 62-1
TEMMA HARBOUR, Mary Hopkin, 70-6
TEMPER TEMPER, Goldie, 98-13
TEMPERAMENTAL, Everything But The Girl, 00-72
TEMPERATURE RISING, PKA, 91-68
TEMPLE OF DREAMS, Messiah, 92-20
TEMPLE OF LOVE (1992) TOUCHED BY THE HAND OF OFRA HAZA, Sisters Of Mercy, 92-3
TEMPO FIESTA (PARTY TIME), Itty Bitty Boozy Woozy, 95-34
TEMPORARY BEAUTY, Graham Parker, 82-50
TEMPTATION, Everly Brothers, 61-1
TEMPTATION, New Order, 82-29
TEMPTATION, Heaven 17, 83-2, 92-4
TEMPTATION, Joan Armatrading, 85-65
TEMPTATION, Wet Wet Wet, 88-12
TEMPTED, Squeeze, 81-41
TEN [EP], Mansun, 98-27
10IN01, Members Of Mayday, 01-31
TEN LITTLE GIRLS (from THE BLINDFOLD [EP]), Curve, 91-68
TEN MILES HIGH, Little Angels, 94-18
10 SECOND BIONIC MAN, Kinky Machine, 94-66
TEN STORY LOVE SONG, Stone Roses, 95-11
10 X 10, 808 State, 93-67
TEN TO TWENTY, Sneaker Pimps, 99-56
10 YEARS ASLEEP, Kingmaker, 93-15
TEN THOUSAND MILES, Michael Holliday, 56-24
10538 OVERTURE, Electric Light Orchestra, 72-9
TENDER, Blur, 99-2
TENDER HANDS, Chris De Burgh, 89-43
TENDER HEART, Lionel Richie, 01-29
TENDER LOVE:
Force M.D.'s, 86-23
Kenny Thomas, 91-26
TENDERLY, Nat "King" Cole, 54-10
TENDERNESS, Diana Ross, 82-73
TENNESSEE, Arrested Development, 92-46, 93-18
TENNESSEE WIG WALK, Bonnie Lou, 54-4
TENSHI, Gouryella, 00-45
TEQUILA:
Champs, 58-5
Ted Heath and his Music, 58-21
No Way Jose, 85-47
TEQUILA, Terrorvision, 99-2
TEQULA SUNRISE, Cypress Hill, 98-23
TERESA, Joe Dolan, 69-20
TERRITORY, Sepultura, 93-66
TERRY, Twinkle, 64-4
TERRY'S THEME FROM "LIMELIGHT", Frank Chacksfield and his Orchestra, 53-2
TESLA GIRLS, O.M.D., 84-21
TEST OF TIME, Will Downing, 89-67
TEST THE THEORY, Audioweb, 99-56
TESTAMENT 4, Chubby Chunks Volume II, 94-52
TESTIFY, Byron Stingily, 98-48
TESTIFY, M People, 98-12
TETRIS, Doctor Spin, 92-6
TEXAS, Chris Rea, 90-69
TEXAS COWBOYS, Grid, 93-21, 94-17
THA CROSSROADS, Bone Thugs-N-Harmony, 96-8
THA DOGGFATHER, Snoop Doggy Dogg, 98-36
THA HORNS OF JERICHO, DJ Supreme, 98-29
THA WILDSTYLE:
DJ Supreme, 96-39, 97-24
Porn Kings V's DJ Supreme *, 99-10
THANK ABBA FOR THE MUSIC [M], Steps Tina Cousins Cleopatra B*Witched Billie, 99-4
THANK GOD I FOUND YOU, Mariah featuring Joe and 98°, 00-10
THANK GOD IT'S CHRISTMAS, Queen, 84-21
THANK GOD IT'S FRIDAY, R. Kelly, 96-14
THANK U, Alanis Morissette, 98-5
THANK U VERY MUCH, Scaffold, 67-4
THANK YOU, Pale Fountains, 82-48
THANK YOU, Boyz II Men, 95-26
THANK YOU, Dido, 01-3
THANK YOU FOR A GOOD YEAR, Alexander O'Neal, 88-30
THANK YOU FOR BEING A FRIEND, Andrew Gold, 78-42
THANK YOU FOR HEARING ME, Sinead O'Connor, 94-13
THANK YOU FOR LOVING ME, Bon Jovi, 00-12
THANK YOU FOR THE MUSIC, Abba, 83-33
THANK YOU FOR THE PARTY, Dukes (Bugatti and Musker), 82-53
THANK YOU MY LOVE, Imagination, 84-22
THANK YOU WORLD, World Party, 91-68
THANKS A LOT, Brenda Lee, 65-41
THANKS FOR GIVING US CHRISTMAS) (from SONGS FOR CHRISTMAS '87 [EP]), Minipops, 87-39
THANKS FOR MY CHILD, Cheryl Pepsi Riley, 89-75
THANKS FOR SAVING MY LIFE, Billy Paul, 74-33
THANKS FOR THE MEMORY (WHAM BAM THANK YOU MAM), Slade, 75-7
THANKS FOR THE NIGHT, Damned, 84-43
THAT CERTAIN SMILE, Midge Ure, 85-28
THAT DAY, Natalie Imbruglia, 01-11
THAT DON'T IMPRESS ME MUCH, Shania Twain, 99-3
THAT GIRL, Stevie Wonder, 82-39
THAT GIRL, Maxi Priest featuring Shaggy, 96-15
THAT GIRL BELONGS TO YESTERDAY, Gene Pitney, 64-7
THAT GIRL (GROOVY SITUATION), Freddie McGregor, 87-47
THAT JOKE ISN'T FUNNY ANYMORE, Smiths, 85-49
THAT LADY, Isley Brothers, 73-14
THAT LOOK, De'lacy, 96-19
THAT LOOK IN YOUR EYE, Ali Campbell, 95-5
THAT LOVING FEELING, Cicero, 92-46
THAT LUCKY OLD SUN, Velvets, 61-46
THAT MAN (HE'S ALL MINE), Inner City, 90-42
THAT MEANS A LOT, P.J. Proby, 65-30
THAT NOISE, Anthony Newley, 62-34
THAT OLD BLACK MAGIC, Sammy Davis, 55-16
THAT OLE DEVIL CALLED LOVE, Alison Moyet, 85-2
THAT SAME OLD FEELING, Pickettywitch, 70-5
THAT SOUND, Michael Moog, 99-32
THAT SOUNDS GOOD TO ME [M], Jive Bunny and the Mastermixers, 90-4
THAT THING YOU DO!, Wonders, 97-22
THAT WAS MY VEIL, John Parish + Polly Jean Harvey, 96-75
THAT WAS THE DAY [RR] (from DIS-INFECTED [EP]), The, 94-17
THAT WAS THEN BUT THIS IS NOW, ABC, 83-18
THAT WAS THEN, THIS IS NOW, Monkees, 86-68
THAT WAS YESTERDAY, Foreigner, 85-28
THAT WOMAN'S GOT ME DRINKING, Shane MacGowan and the Popes, 94-34
THAT ZIPPER TRACK, DJ Dan presents Needle Damage, 01-53
THAT'LL BE THE DAY:
Crickets, 57-1
Everly Brothers, 65-30
THAT'LL DO NICELY, Bad Manners, 83-49
THAT'S ALL, Genesis, 83-16
THAT'S AMORE, Dean Martin with Dick Stabile and his Orchestra, 54-2, 96-43
THAT'S ENTERTAINMENT, Jam, 81-21, 83-60, 91-57
THAT'S HOW A LOVE SONG WAS BORN, Ray Burns with the Coronets, 55-14
THAT'S HOW I FEEL ABOUT YOU, Londonbeat, 92-69
THAT'S HOW I'M LIVIN', Ice-T, 93-21
THAT'S HOW I'M LIVING, Toni Scott, 89-48, 90-63
THAT'S HOW STRONG MY LOVE IS, In Crowd, 65-48
THAT'S JUST THE WAY IT IS, Phil Collins, 90-26
THAT'S LIFE, Frank Sinatra, 66-46
THAT'S LIVIN' ALRIGHT, Joe Fagin, 84-3
THAT'S LOVE, Billy Fury with the Four Jays, 60-19
THAT'S LOVE, THAT IT IS, Blancmange, 83-33
THAT'S MY DOLL, Frankie Vaughan with Wally Stott and his Orchestra, 59-28
THAT'S MY HOME, Mr. Acker Bilk and his Paramount Jazz Band (Vocal Mr. Acker Bilk), 61-7
THAT'S NICE, Neil Christian, 66-14
THAT'S RIGHT, Deep River Boys, 56-29
THAT'S THE WAY, Honeycombs, 65-12
THAT'S THE WAY GOD PLANNED IT, Billy Preston, 69-11
THAT'S THE WAY (I LIKE IT):
K C and the Sunshine Band, 75-4, 91-59
Dead Or Alive, 84-22
Clock, 98-11
THAT'S THE WAY I WANNA ROCK N ROLL, AC/DC, 88-22
THAT'S THE WAY IT FEELS, Two Nations, 87-74
THAT'S THE WAY IT IS, Mel and Kim, 88-10
THAT'S THE WAY IT IS, Celine Dion, 99-12
THAT'S THE WAY LOVE GOES, Charles Dickens, 65-37
THAT'S THE WAY LOVE GOES, Young M.C., 91-65
THAT'S THE WAY LOVE GOES, Janet Jackson, 93-2
THAT'S THE WAY LOVE IS:
Ten City, 89-8
Volcano with Sam Cartwright, 95-72
Byron Stingily, 00-32
THAT'S THE WAY LOVE IS, Bobby Brown, 93-56
THAT'S THE WAY OF THE WORLD, D Mob featuring Cathy Dennis, 90-48
THAT'S THE WAY THE MONEY GOES, M, 80-45
THAT'S THE WAY YOU DO IT, Purple Kings, 94-26
THAT'S WHAT FRIENDS ARE FOR, Deniece Williams, 77-8
THAT'S WHAT FRIENDS ARE FOR, Dionne and Friends featuring Elton John, Gladys Knight and Stevie Wonder, 85-16
THAT'S WHAT I LIKE [M], Jive Bunny and the Mastermixers, 89-1
THAT'S WHAT I THINK, Cyndi Lauper, 93-31
THAT'S WHAT I WANT, Marauders, 63-43
THAT'S WHAT I WANT TO BE, Neil Reid, 72-45
THAT'S WHAT LIFE IS ALL ABOUT, Bing Crosby with the Pete Moore Orchestra, 75-41
THAT'S WHAT LOVE CAN DO, Toutes Les Filles, 99-44
THAT'S WHAT LOVE IS FOR, Amy Grant, 91-60
THAT'S WHAT LOVE WILL DO, Joe Brown and the Bruvvers, 63-3
THAT'S WHEN I REACH FOR MY REVOLVER, Moby, 96-50
THAT'S WHEN I THINK OF YOU, 1927, 89-46
THAT'S WHEN THE MUSIC TAKES ME, Neil Sedaka, 73-18
THAT'S WHERE MY MIND GOES, Slamm, 94-68
THAT'S WHERE THE HAPPY PEOPLE GO, Trammps, 76-35
THAT'S WHY I LIE, Ray-J, 98-71
THAT'S WHY I'M CRYING, Ivy League, 65-22
THAT'S WHY WE LOSE CONTROL, Young Offenders, 98-60
THAT'S YOU, Nat King Cole with the music of Nelson Riddle, 60-10
THE WAY WE WERE/TRY TO REMEMBER [M], Gladys Knight and the Pips, 75-4
THEM BONES, Alice In Chains, 93-26
THEM GIRLS/THEM GIRLS, Zig and Zag, 94-5
THEM HEAVY PEOPLE (from KATE BUSH ON STAGE [EP]), Kate Bush, 79-10
THEM THERE EYES, Emile Ford; Johnny Keating Music; Babs Knight Group, 60-18
THE THEME, Unique 3, 89-61
THEME, Sabres Of Paradise, 94-56
THE THEME, Dreem Teem, 97-34
THEME FOR A DREAM, Cliff Richard and the Shadows, 61-3
THEME FOR YOUNG LOVERS, Shadows, 64-12
THE THEME FROM "A SUMMER PLACE":
Percy Faith and his Orchestra, 60-2
Norrie Paramor and his Orchestra, 60-36
THEME FROM 'CADE'S COUNTY', Henry Mancini and his Orchestra, 72-42
THEME FROM 'CHEERS' (WHERE EVERYBODY KNOWS YOUR NAME), Gary Portnoy, 84-58
THEME FROM "COME SEPTEMBER", Bobby Darin and his Orchestra, 61-50

THEME FROM DIXIE, Duane Eddy, 61-7
THEME FROM DR. KILDARE (THREE STARS WILL SHINE TONIGHT), Richard Chamberlain, 62-12
THEME FROM E.T. (THE EXTRA-TERRESTRIAL), John Williams, 82-17
THEME FROM "EXODUS":
Ferrante and Teicher, 61-6
Semprini *, 61-25
THEME FROM FILM "THE LEGION'S LAST PATROL" (CONCERTO DISPERATO), Ken Thorne and his Orchestra; trumpet solo: Ray Davies, 63-4
THE THEME FROM GET CARTER, Roy Budd, 99-68
THEME FROM GUTBUSTER, Bentley Rhythm Ace, 00-29
THEME FROM HARRY'S GAME, Clannad, 82-5
THE THEME FROM HILL STREET BLUES, Mike Post featuring Larry Carlton, 82-25
THEME FROM 'HONG KONG BEAT', Richard Denton and Martin Cook, 78-25
THEME FROM JURASSIC PARK:
John Williams, 93-45
Soul City Orchestra *, 93-70
THEME FROM M*A*S*H* (SUICIDE IS PAINLESS):
Mash, 80-1
Manic Street Preachers, 92-7
THEME FROM MAHOGANY "DO YOU KNOW WHERE YOU'RE GOING TO", Diana Ross, 76-5
THEME FROM MISSION: IMPOSSIBLE:
Adam Clayton and Larry Mullen, 96-7
Limp Bizkit*, 00-3
THEME FROM NEW YORK, NEW YORK, Frank Sinatra, 80-59, 86-4
"THEME FROM P.O.P.", Perfectly Ordinary People, 88-61
THEME FROM RANDALL AND HOPKIRK (DECEASED), Nina Persson and David Arnold, 00-49
THEME FROM S-EXPRESS, S-Express, 88-1, 96-14
THEME FROM "SHAFT":
Isaac Hayes, 71-4, 00-53
Van Twist *, 85-57
Eddy and the Soulband, 85-13
THEME FROM SUPERMAN (MAIN TITLE), London Symphony Orchestra conducted by John Williams, 79-32
THEME FROM 'THE APARTMENT', Ferrante and Teicher, 60-44
THEME FROM THE DEER HUNTER (CAVATINA), Shadows, 79-9
THE THEME FROM THE FILM "LIMELIGHT":
Ron Goodwin and his Orchestra, 53-3
Frank Chacksfield and his Orchestra *, 53-2
Jimmy Young *, 53-8
THEME FROM 'THE MAGNIFICENT SEVEN', Al Caiola and his Orchestra, 61-34
THEME FROM "THE PERSUADERS", John Barry, 71-13
THEME FROM THE PROFESSIONALS, Laurie Johnson's London Big Band, 97-36
A THEME FROM THE 'THREEPENNY OPERA' (MACK THE KNIFE):
Billy Vaughn and his Orchestra, 56-12
"Unforgettable" sound of the Dick Hyman Trio, 56-9
Louis Armstrong and his All Stars, 56-8, 59-24
THEME FROM TRAVELLING MAN, Duncan Browne, 84-68
THEME FROM TURNPIKE [EP] + lead track title, Deus, 96-68
THEME FROM TV'S "VIETNAM" – CANON IN D MAJOR (PACHEBEL), Orchestre De Chambre Jean-Francois Paillard, 88-61
(THEME FROM) VALLEY OF THE DOLLS, Dionne Warwick, 68-28
THE THEME FROM "WE'LL MEET AGAIN", Denis King and his Orchestra, 82-36
THEME FROM Z-CARS (JOHNNY TODD):
Johnny Keating, 62-8
Norrie Paramor Orchestra, 62-33
THE THEME: IT'S PARTY TIME, Tracey Lee, 97-51
THEME MUSIC FROM THE FILM "2001" A SPACE ODYSSEY THUS SPAKE ZARATHUSTRA:
Philharmonia Orchestra conducted by Lorin Maazel, 69-33
Deodato arranged and conducted by Eumir Deodato *, 73-7
THEME ONE, Cozy Powell, 79-62
THEME SONG FROM "WHICH WAY IS UP", Stargard, 78-19
THEN, Charlatans, 90-12
THEN CAME YOU:
Dionne Warwicke and the Detroit Spinners, 74-29
Junior Giscombe, 92-32
THEN HE KISSED ME:
Crystals, 63-2
Beach Boys *, 67-4
Gary Glitter *, 81-39
THEN I FEEL GOOD, Katherine E, 92-56
THEN I KISSED HER, Beach Boys, 67-4
THEN YOU CAN TELL ME GOODBYE, Casinos, 67-28
THEN YOU TURN AWAY, Orchestral Manoeuvres In The Dark, 91-50
THERE AIN'T NOTHIN' LIKE THE LOVE, Montage, 97-64
THERE AIN'T NOTHING LIKE SHAGGIN', Tams, 87-21
THERE ARE MORE QUESTIONS THAN ANSWERS, Johnny Nash, 72-9
THERE ARE MORE SNAKES THAN LADDERS, Captain Sensible, 84-57
THERE BUT FOR FORTUNE, Joan Baez, 65-8
THERE BUT FOR THE GRACE OF GOD, Fire Island featuring: Love Nelson, 94-32
THERE GOES MY EVERYTHING:
Engelbert Humperdinck, 67-2
Elvis Presley, 71-6
THERE GOES MY FIRST LOVE, Drifters, 75-3
THERE GOES THAT SONG AGAIN, Gary Miller, 61-32
THERE GOES THE NEIGHBORHOOD, Sheryl Crow, 98-19
THERE I GO AGAIN, Power Of Dreams, 92-65
THERE I GO (SE PER TE C'E SOLTANTO QUELL'UOMO), Vikki Carr, 67-50
THERE I'VE SAID IT AGAIN:
Al Saxon and his Orchestra, 61-48
Bobby Vinton, 63-34
THERE IS A LIGHT THAT NEVER GOES OUT, Smiths, 92-25
THERE IS A MOUNTAIN, Donovan, 67-8
THERE IS A STAR, Pharao, 95-43
THERE IS ALWAYS SOMETHING THERE TO REMIND ME, Housemartins, 88-35
THERE IS NO LOVE BETWEEN US ANYMORE, Pop Will Eat Itself, 88-66
THERE IT IS, Shalamar, 82-5
THERE MUST BE A REASON, Frankie Laine with Paul Weston and his Orchestra (Carl Fischer: piano), 54-9
THERE MUST BE A WAY:
Joni James, 59-24
Frankie Vaughan with Alyn Ainsworth and his Orchestra, 67-7
THERE MUST BE AN ANGEL (PLAYING WITH MY HEART), Eurythmics, 85-1
THERE MUST BE THOUSANDS, Quads, 79-66
THERE SHE GOES:
La's, 89-59, 90-13, 99-65
Sixpence None The Richer, 99-14
THERE SHE GOES AGAIN, Quireboys, 90-37
THERE THERE MY DEAR, Dexy's Midnight Runners, 80-7
THERE WILL NEVER BE ANOTHER TONIGHT, Bryan Adams, 91-32
THERE WILL NEVER BE ANOTHER YOU, Chris Montez, 66-37
THERE WILL NEVER BE ANOTHER YOU, Jimmy Ruffin, 85-68
THERE WON'T BE MANY COMING HOME, Roy Orbison, 66-18
THERE YOU GO, Pink, 00-6
THERE YOU'LL BE, Faith Hill, 01-3
(THERE'LL BE BLUEBIRDS OVER)THE WHITE CLIFFS OF DOVER, Robson Green and Jerome Flynn, 95-1
THERE'LL BE SAD SONGS (TO MAKE YOU CRY), Billy Ocean, 86-12
THERE'S A BRAND NEW WORLD, Five Star, 88-61
THERE'S A GHOST IN MY HOUSE:
R. Dean Taylor, 74-3
Fall, 87-30
THERE'S A GOLD MINE IN THE SKY, Pat Boone with Billy Vaughn's Orchestra, 57-23
THERE'S A GUY WORKS DOWN THE CHIP SHOP, SWEARS HE'S ELVIS, Kirsty MacColl, 81-14
THERE'S A HEARTACHE FOLLOWING ME, Jim Reeves, 64-6
THERE'S A HOLE IN THE BUCKET, Harry Belafonte and Odetta, 61-32
THERE'S A KIND OF HUSH (ALL OVER THE WORLD):
Herman's Hermits *, 67-7
Carpenters, 76-22
THERE'S A SILENCE, Electric Soft Parade, 01-52
THERE'S A WHOLE LOT OF LOVING, Guys and Dolls, 75-2
(THERE'S) ALWAYS SOMETHING THERE TO REMIND ME:
Sandie Shaw, 64-1
Naked Eyes*, 83-59
Tin Tin Out featuring Espiritu*, 95-14
(THERE'S GONNA BE) A SHOWDOWN, Archie Bell and the Drells, 73-36
THERE'S GOT TO BE A WAY, Mariah Carey, 91-54
THERE'S MORE TO LOVE, Communards, 88-20
THERE'S NO LIVING WITHOUT YOU, Will Downing, 93-67
THERE'S NO ONE QUITE LIKE GRANDMA, St. Winifred's School Choir, 80-1
THERE'S NO OTHER WAY, Blur, 91-8
THERE'S NOTHING BETTER THAN LOVE, Luther Vandross (Duet with Gregory Hines), 88-72
THERE'S NOTHING I WON'T DO, JX, 96-4
THERE'S NOTHING LIKE THIS, Omar, 91-14
THERE'S SOMETHING WRONG IN PARADISE, Kid Creole and the Coconuts, 83-35
THERE'S THE GIRL, Heart, 87-34
THERE'S YOUR TROUBLE, Dixie Chicks, 99-26
THESE ARE DAYS, 10,000 Maniacs, 92-58
THESE ARE THE DAYS OF OUR LIVES, Queen, 91-1
THESE ARE THE TIMES, Dru Hill, 99-4
THESE ARMS OF MINE, Proclaimers, 94-51
THESE BOOTS ARE MADE FOR WALKIN':
Nancy Sinatra, 66-1
Billy Ray Cyrus, 92-63
THESE DAYS, Bon Jovi, 96-7
THESE DREAMS, Heart, 86-62, 88-8
THESE EARLY DAYS, Everything But The Girl, 88-75
THESE THINGS ARE WORTH FIGHTING FOR, Gary Clail On-U Sound System, 93-45
THESE THINGS WILL KEEP ME LOVING YOU, Velvelettes, 71-34
THESE WOODEN IDEAS, Idlewild, 00-32
THEY ALL LAUGHED, Frank Sinatra, 99-41
(THEY CALL HER) LA BAMBA, Crickets, 64-21
THEY DON'T CARE ABOUT US, Michael Jackson, 96-4
THEY DON'T KNOW, Tracey Ullman, 83-2
THEY DON'T KNOW, Jon B, 98-32
THEY DON'T KNOW, So Solid Crew featuring in order of appearance Asher D. Megaman. G-Man, 01-3
THEY LONG TO BE CLOSE TO YOU:
Carpenters, 70-6, 90-25
Gwen Guthrie, 86-25
THEY SAY IT'S GONNA RAIN, Hazell Dean, 85-58
THEY SHOOT HORSES DON'T THEY?, Racing Cars, 77-14
THEY'RE COMING TO TAKE ME AWAY, HA-HAAA!, Napoleon XIV, 66-4
THEY'RE HERE, EMF, 92-29
THIEVES IN THE TEMPLE, Prince, 90-7
THIEVES LIKE US, New Order, 84-18
THIGHS HIGH (GRIP YOUR HIPS AND MOVE), Tom Browne, 80-45
THIN LINE BETWEEN LOVE AND HATE, Pretenders, 84-49
THE THIN WALL, Ultravox, 81-14
A THING CALLED LOVE, Johnny Cash and the Evangel Temple Choir, 72-4
THE THING I LIKE, Aaliyah, 95-33
THINGS, Bobby Darin, 62-2
THINGS CAN ONLY GET BETTER, Howard Jones, 85-6
THINGS CAN ONLY GET BETTER, D:Ream, 93-24, 94-1, 97-19
THINGS GET BETTER, Eddie Floyd, 67-31
THINGS HAVE CHANGED, Bob Dylan, 00-58
THINGS I'VE SEEN, Spooks, 01-6
THINGS THAT ARE, Runrig, 95-40
THINGS THAT GO BUMP IN THE NIGHT, Allstars, 01-12

THREE COINS IN THE FOUNTAIN:
Frank Sinatra, 54-1
Four Aces featuring Al Alberts, 54-5
3 IS FAMILY, Dana Dawson, 95-9
3 LIBRAS, A Perfect Circle, 01-49
THREE LIONS (THE OFFICIAL SONG OF THE ENGLAND FOOTBALL TEAM), Baddiel and Skinner and Lightning Seeds, 96-1
3 LIONS '98 [RR], Baddiel, Skinner and the Lightning Seeds, 98-1
THREE LITTLE BIRDS, Bob Marley and the Wailers, 80-17
THREE LITTLE PIGS, Green Jelly, 93-5
THREE LITTLE WORDS (I LOVE YOU), Applejacks, 64-23
3 MCS & 1 DJ, Beastie Boys, 99-21
THREE MINUTE HERO, Selecter, 80-16
THREE NIGHTS A WEEK, Fats Domino, 60-45
THREE RING CIRCUS, Barry Biggs, 77-22
3.. 6.. 9 SECONDS OF LIGHT [EP], Belle And Sebastian, 97-32
3 SONGS [EP], Wedding Present, 90-25
THREE STARS, Ruby Wright (Narration by Dick Pike), 59-19
THREE STEPS TO HEAVEN:
Eddie Cochran, 60-1
Showaddywaddy, 75-2
THREE TIMES A LADY, Commodores, 78-1
THREE TIMES A MAYBE, K-Creative, 92-58
3 X 3 [EP], Genesis, 82-10
III WISHES, Terrorvision, 99-42
3AM, Matchbox 20, 98-64
3IL (THRILL), Soul U*Nique, 00-66
THRILL HAS GONE, Texas, 89-60
THRILL ME, Simply Red, 92-33
THRILLER, Michael Jackson, 83-10
THROUGH THE BARRICADES, Spandau Ballet, 86-6
THROUGH THE ROOF, Cud, 92-44
THROUGH THE STORM, Aretha Franklin and Elton John, 89-41
THROUGH THE YEARS, Gary Glitter, 92-49
THROUGH THE YEARS, Cilla Black, 93-54
THROW AWAY THE KEY, Linx, 81-21
THROW DOWN A LINE, Cliff and Hank, 69-7
THROW THESE GUNS AWAY, Dunblane, 96-1
THROW YA GUNZ, Onyx, 93-34
THROW YOUR HANDS UP, L.V., 95-24
THROW YOUR SET IN THE AIR, Cypress Hill, 95-15
THROWING IT ALL AWAY, Genesis, 87-22
THROWING MY BABY OUT WITH THE BATH WATER, Tenpole Tudor, 81-49
THROWN AWAY, Stranglers, 81-42
THRU' THESE WALLS, Phil Collins, 82-56
THUNDER, Prince and the New Power Generation, 92-28
THUNDER (from RED THREE [EP]), Dave Clarke presents . . ., 95-45
THUNDER, E.17, 95-4
THUNDER AND LIGHTNING, Thin Lizzy, 83-39
THUNDER IN MY HEART, Leo Sayer, 77-22
THUNDER IN THE MOUNTAINS, Toyah, 81-4
THUNDERBALL, Tom Jones, 66-35
THUNDERBIRDS, Barry Gray Orchestra, 81-61
THUNDERBIRDS ARE GO, F.A.B. featuring M.C. Parker, 90-5
THUNDERDOME, Messiah, 93-29
THUNDERSTRUCK, AC/DC, 90-13
THURSDAY'S CHILD, David Bowie, 99-16
TI AMO, Gina G, 97-11
TIC, TIC TAC, Chilli featuring Carrapicho, 97-59
TICKET TO RIDE, Beatles, 65-1, 85-70
TICKET TO THE MOON, ELO, 82-24
THE TIDE IS HIGH, Blondie, 80-1
THE TIDE IS TURNING (AFTER LIVE AID), Roger Waters, 87-54
TIE A YELLOW RIBBON ROUND THE OLE OAK TREE, Dawn featuring Tony Orlando, 73-1
TIE ME KANGAROO DOWN SPORT, Rolf Harris with his Wobble Board and the Rhythm Spinners, 60-9
TIE YOUR MOTHER DOWN, Queen, 77-31, 98-13
TIED TO THE 90'S, Travis, 97-30
TIED UP, Yello, 88-60
TIGER BABY, Silver Convention, 76-41
TIGER FEET, Mud, 74-1
TIGER RAG (from TAKE IT SATCH [EP]), Louis Armstrong with His All Stars, 56-29
TIGHTEN UP/I JUST CAN'T STOP DANCIN', Wally Jump Jr. and the Criminal Element, 87-24
TIJUANA TAXI, Herb Alpert and the Tijuana Brass, 66-37
TIL I HEAR IT FROM YOU, Gin Blossoms, 96-39
('TIL) I KISSED YOU, Everly Brothers, 59-2
TIL TEARS DO US PART, Heavens Cry, 01-68
. . . TIL THE COPS COME KNOCKIN' THE OPUS, Maxwell, 96-63
TILL:
Tony Bennett, 61-35
Dorothy Squires, 70-25
Tom Jones, 71-2
TILL I CAN'T TAKE LOVE NO MORE, Eddy Grant, 83-42
TILL I LOVED YOU (THE LOVE THEME FROM GOYA):
Barbra Streisand and Don Johnson, 88-16
Placido Domingo and Jennifer Rush *, 89-24
TILL THE END OF THE DAY, Kinks, 65-8
TILL THERE WAS YOU, Peggy Lee with Jack Marshall's Music, 61-30
TILL WE MEET AGAIN, Inner City, 91-47, 93-55
TILL WE MEET AGAIN, Push, 00-46
TILTED, Sugar, 93-48
TIME, Craig Douglas with Harry Robinson and his Orchestra, 61-9
TIME, Light Of The World, 81-35
TIME, Frida and B.A. Robertson, 83-45
TIME, Freddie Mercury, 86-32
TIME, Kim Wilde, 90-71
TIME, Supergrass, 95-2
TIME, Marion, 96-29
TIME AFTER TIME:
Cyndi Lauper, 84-3
Hyperstate featuring Janey Lee Grace, 93-71
Changing Faces (featuring Jay-Z), 98-35
TIME AFTER TIME, Beloved, 90-46
TIME ALONE WILL TELL, Malcolm Roberts, 67-45
A TIME AND A PLACE, Mike and the Mechanics, 91-58
TIME AND CHANCE, Color Me Badd, 93-62
TIME AND THE RIVER, Nat King Cole, 60-23
TIME AND TIDE, Basia, 88-61
TIME BOMB, 808 State, 92-59
TIME BOMB, Rancid, 95-56
TIME (CLOCK OF THE HEART), Culture Club, 82-3
TIME DRAGS BY, Cliff Richard and the Shadows, 66-10
TIME FOR ACTION, Secret Affair, 79-13
TIME FOR LIVIN', Association, 68-23
TIME FOR LOVE, Kim English, 95-48
THE TIME HAS COME, Adam Faith, 61-4
THE TIME HAS COME, P.P. Arnold, 67-47
TIME HAS TAKEN IT'S TOLL ON YOU, Crazyhead, 88-65
THE TIME IN BETWEEN, Cliff Richard and the Shadows, 65-22
THE TIME IS NOW, Moloko, 00-2
TIME IS ON MY SIDE (LIVE), Rolling Stones, 82-62
TIME IS TIGHT, Booker T. and the M.G.'S, 69-4
A TIME LIKE THIS, Haywoode, 83-48
TIME, LOVE AND TENDERNESS, Michael Bolton, 91-28
TIME OF OUR LIVES, Alison Limerick, 94-36
TIME OF YOUR LIFE (GOOD RIDDANCE), Green Day, 98-11
TIME SELLER, Spencer Davis Group, 67-30
TIME STAND STILL, Rush, 87-42
TIME TO BURN, Storm, 00-3
TIME TO GET BACK, Hysteric Ego, 99-50
TIME TO GET UP, Liquid, 93-46
TIME TO MAKE THE FLOOR BURN [M], Megabass, 90-16
TIME TO MAKE YOU MINE, Lisa Stansfield, 92-14
TIME TO MOVE ON, Sparkle, 98-40
TIME TO SAY GOODBYE (CON TE PARTIRO):
Sarah Brightman and Andrea Bocelli, 97-2
DJ Visage featuring Clarissa*, 00-58
THE TIME WARP :
Damian, 87-51, 88-64, 89-7
Cast of the New Rocky Horror Show, 98-57
TIME WILL CRAWL, David Bowie, 87-33
TIMEBOMB, Chumbawamba, 93-59
TIMELESS, Daniel O'Donnell and Mary Duff, 96-32
TIMELESS MELODY, La's, 90-57
THE TIMES THEY ARE A-CHANGIN':
Peter, Paul and Mary, 64-44
Bob Dylan, 65-9
Ian Campbell Folk Group, 65-42
TIN MACHINE, Tin Machine, 89-48
TIN SOLDIER, Small Faces, 67-9
TIN SOLDIERS, Stiff Little Fingers, 80-36
TINA MARIE, Perry Como and the Ray Charles Singers with Mitchell Ayres and his Orchestra, 55-24
TINGLE, That Petrol Emotion, 91-49
TINSEL TOWN, Ronny Jordan, 94-64
TINSELTOWN TO THE BOOGIEDOWN, Scritti Politti, 99-46
TINY CHILDREN, Teardrop Explodes, 82-44
TINY DYNAMINE [EP], Cocteau Twins, 85-52
TINY MACHINE, Darling Buds, 90-60
THE TIP OF MY FINGERS, Des O'Connor with Alyn Ainsworth and his Orchestra, 70-15
TIPP CITY, Amps, 95-61
TIRED OF BEING ALONE:
Al Green, 71-4
Texas, 92-19
TIRED OF TOEIN' THE LINE, Rocky Burnette, 79-58
TIRED OF WAITING FOR YOU, Kinks, 65-1
TISHBITE, Cocteau Twins, 96-34
TO A BRIGHTER DAY (O'HAPPY DAY), Beat System, 93-70
TO ALL THE GIRLS I'VE LOVED BEFORE, Julio Iglesias and Willie Nelson, 84-17
TO BE A LOVER, Billy Idol, 86-22
TO BE FREE, Emiliana Torrini, 01-44
TO BE IN LOVE, MAW presents India, 99-23
TO BE LOVED:
Jackie Wilson, 58-23
Malcolm Vaughan with the Michael Sammes Singers, 58-14
TO BE OR NOT TO BE, B.A. Robertson, 80-9
TO BE OR NOT TO BE (THE HITLER RAP), Mel Brooks, 84-12
TO BE REBORN, Boy George, 87-13
TO BE WITH YOU, Mr. Big, 92-3
TO BE WITH YOU AGAIN, Level 42, 87-10
TO CUT A LONG STORY SHORT, Spandau Ballet, 80-5
TO DIE FOR, Luke Galliana, 01-42
TO EARTH WITH LOVE, Gay Dad, 99-10
TO FRANCE, Mike Oldfield vocals by Maggie Reilly, 84-48
TO HAVE AND TO HOLD (THEME SONG FROM THE LWT SERIES), Catherine Stock, 86-17
TO HERE KNOWS WHEN, My Bloody Valentine, 91-29
TO KNOW HIM, IS TO LOVE HIM:
Teddy Bears, 58-2, 79-66
Peter and Gordon *, 65-5
TO KNOW SOMEONE DEEPLY IS TO KNOW SOMEONE SOFTLY, Terence Trent D'Arby, 90-55
TO KNOW YOU IS TO LOVE YOU, Peter and Gordon, 65-5
TO LIVE & DIE IN LA, Makaveli (2 Pac is Makaveli), 97-10
TO LOVE ONCE AGAIN, Solid Harmonie, 98-55
TO LOVE SOMEBODY:
Bee Gees, 67-41
Nina Simone, 69-5
Jimmy Somerville, 90-8
Michael Bolton, 92-16
TO MAKE A BIG MAN CRY, P.J. Proby, 66-34
TO THE BEAT OF THE DRUM (LA LUNA), Ethics, 95-13
TO THE BIRDS, Suede, 92-49
TO THE END, Blur, 94-16
TO THE LIMIT, Tony De Vit, 95-44
TO THE MOON AND BACK, Savage Garden, 97-55, 98-3
TO THE WORLD, O.R.G.A.N, 98-33
TO WHOM IT CONCERNS, Chris Andrews, 65-13
TO WIN JUST ONCE, Saw Doctors, 96-14
TO YOU I BELONG, B*Witched, 98-1
TO YOU I BESTOW, Mundy, 96-60
TOAST, Streetband, 78-18
TOAST OF LOVE, Three Degrees, 76-36
TOBACCO ROAD, Nashville Teens, 64-6
TOCA ME, Fragma, 99-11
TOCA'S MIRACLE, Fragma, 00-1
TOCCATA, Sky, 80-5
TOCCATA AND FUGUE IN D MINOR, Vanessa-Mae, 95-16
TODAY, Sandie Shaw, 68-27
TODAY, Talk Talk, 82-14

TOWN, Northern Uproar, 96-48
TOWN CALLED MALICE, Jam, 82-1, 83-73
TOWN CLOWNS, Blameless, 95-56
TOWN CRIER, Craig Douglas, 63-36
TOWN OF PLENTY, Elton John, 88-74
TOWN TO TOWN, Microdisney, 87-55
TOWN WITHOUT PITY:
Gene Pitney, 62-32
Eddi Reader, 96-26
TOXIC GIRL, Kings Of Convenience, 01-44
TOXYGENE, Orb, 97-4
TOY, Casuals, 68-30
TOY BALLOONS, Russ Conway, 61-7
TOY BOY, Sinitta, 87-4
TOY SOLDIERS, Martika, 89-5
TOYS FOR BOYS, Marion, 95-57
TRACEY IN MY ROOM, EBTG vs Soul Vision, 01-34
TRACIE, Level 42, 89-25
THE TRACKS OF MY TEARS:
Smokey Robinson and the Miracles, 69-9
Linda Ronstadt, 76-42
Colin Blunstone, 82-60
Go West, 93-16
TRACY, Cuff-Links, 69-4
TRADE EP 2 [EP], Various Artists (EPs), 98-75
TRAFFIC, Stereophonics, 97-20
TRAGEDY, Argent, 72-34
TRAGEDY:
Bee Gees, 79-1
Steps, 98-1
TRAGEDY AND MYSTERY, China Crisis, 83-46
TRAGIC COMIC, Extreme, 93-15
TRAIL OF TEARS, Dogs D'Amour, 89-47
THE TRAIL OF THE LONESOME PINE, Laurel and Hardy with the Avalon Boys featuring Chill Wills, 75-2
TRAILOR LOAD A GIRLS, Shabba Ranks, 91-63
TRAIN, Sisters Of Mercy, 84-46
THE TRAIN IS COMING, Shaggy, 96-21
THE TRAIN IS COMING, UB40, 99-30
TRAIN OF CONSEQUENCES, Megadeth, 95-22
THE TRAIN OF LOVE, Alma Cogan with the Michael Sammes Singers, 60-27
TRAIN OF THOUGHT, A-Ha, 86-8
TRAIN OF THOUGHT, Escrima, 95-36
TRAIN TO SKAVILLE, Ethiopians, 67-40
TRAIN TOUR TO RAINBOW CITY, Pyramids, 67-35
TRAINS AND BOATS AND PLANES:
Burt Bacharach His Orchestra and Chorus, 65-4
Billy J. Kramer and the Dakotas, 65-12
TRAMBONE, Krew-Kats, 61-33
TRAMP:
Otis Redding and Carla Thomas, 67-18
Salt-N-Pepa, 88-2
TRAMPOLENE, Julian Cope, 87-31
TRAMPS AND THIEVES, Quireboys, 92-41
TRANCESCRIPT, Hardfloor, 93-72
TRANQUILLIZER, Geneva, 97-24
TRANSAMAZONIA, Shamen, 95-28
TRANSATLANTIC, Roach Motel, 93-73
TRANSFER AFFECTION, A Flock Of Seagulls, 83-38
TRANSISTOR RADIO, Benny Hill, 61-24
TRANSMISSION, Gay Dad, 01-58
TRANSONIC, Wired, 99-73
TRANZ EURO XPRESS, X-Press 2, 96-45
TRAPPED, Colonel Abrams, 85-3
TRASH, Roxy Music, 79-40
TRASH, Suede, 96-3
TRAVELIN' BAND, Creedence Clearwater Revival, 70-8
TRAVELIN' MAN, Ricky Nelson, 61-2
THE TRAVELLER, Spear Of Destiny, 87-44
TRAVELLERS TUNE, Ocean Colour Scene, 97-5
TRAVELLIN' HOME, Vera Lynn, 57-20
TRAVELLIN' LIGHT, Cliff Richard and the Shadows, 59-1
TRAVELLING LIGHT, Tindersticks, 95-51
TRAVELLING MAN, Studio 2, 98-40
TREASON (IT'S JUST A STORY), Teardrop Explodes, 81-18
TREASURE OF LOVE, Clyde McPhatter, 56-27
TREAT 'EM RIGHT, Chubb Rock, 91-67
TREAT HER LIKE A LADY, Temptations, 84-12
TREAT HER LIKE A LADY, Celine Dion, 99-29
TREAT HER LIKE A LADY, Joe, 00-60
TREAT HER RIGHT, Roy Head, 65-30
TREAT INFAMY, Rest Assured, 98-14
TREAT ME GOOD, Yazz, 90-20
TREAT ME LIKE A LADY, Five Star, 90-54
TREAT ME RIGHT, Adeva, 90-62
TREATY, Yothu Yindi, 92-72
TREBLE CHANCE, Joe "Mr. Piano" Henderson, 59-28
TREE FROG, Hope A.D., 94-73
THE TREES, Pulp, 01-23
TREMELO SONG [EP] + lead track ttle., Charlatans, 92-44
THE TRIAL OF HISSING SID, Keith Michell, Captain Beaky and his Band, 80-53
TRIALS OF LIFE, Kaleef, 97-75
TRIBAL BASE, Rebel M.C. featuring Tenor Fly and Barrington Levy, 91-20
TRIBAL DANCE, 2 Unlimited, 93-4
TRIBUTE (RIGHT ON), Pasadenas, 88-5
A TRIBUTE TO A KING, William Bell, 68-31
TRIBUTE TO BUDDY HOLLY, Mike Berry with the Outlaws, 61-24
TRIBUTE TO JIM REEVES, Larry Cunningham and the Mighty Avons, 64-40
TRIBUTE TO OUR ANCESTORS, Rubbadubb, 98-56
A TRICK OF THE LIGHT, Triffids, 88-73
TRICK OF THE NIGHT, Bananarama, 87-32
TRICKY DISCO, Tricky Disco, 90-14
TRICKY KID, Tricky, 97-28
TRIGGER HIPPIE, Morcheeba, 96-40
TRIGGER INSIDE, Therapy?, 94-22
TRINI-TRAX [M], Trini Lopez, 81-59
TRIP II THE MOON, Acen, 92-38, 92-71
A TRIP TO TRUMPTON, Urban Hype, 92-6
TRIPPIN', Mark Morrison, 96-8
TRIPPIN ON SUNSHINE, Pizzaman, 94-33, 96-18
TRIPPIN' ON YOUR LOVE:
A Way Of Life, 90-55
Kenny Thomas, 93-17
TRIPPY, Arab Strap, 98-48
TRIPWIRE, Lionrock, 94-44
TRIUMPH, Wu-Tang Clan (featuring Cappadonna), 97-46
TROCADERO, Showaddywaddy, 76-32
THE TROOPER, Iron Maiden, 83-12
TROPICALIA, Beck, 98-39
TROUBLE, Gillan, 80-14
TROUBLE, Lindsey Buckingham, 82-31
TROUBLE, Heaven 17, 87-51
TROUBLE, Shampoo, 94-11, 95-36
TROUBLE, Coldplay, 00-10
TROUBLE, Cypress Hill, 01-33
TROUBLE BOYS, Thin Lizzy, 81-53
TROUBLE IN PARADISE, Al Jarreau, 83-36
TROUBLE IS MY MIDDLE NAME:
Brook Brothers, 63-38
Four Pennies, 66-32
TROUBLE TOWN, Daintees, 87-58
TROUBLE WITH HARRY, Alfi and Harry, 56-15
TROUBLED GIRL, Karen Ramirez, 98-50
TRUCK ON (TYKE), T.Rex, 73-12
TRUDIE, Joe "Mr. Piano" Henderson with the Beryl Stott Chorus, 58-14
TRUE, Spandau Ballet, 83-1
TRUE BLUE, Madonna, 86-1
TRUE COLORS:
Cyndi Lauper, 86-12
Phil Collins, 98-26
TRUE COLOURS, Go West, 86-48
TRUE DEVOTION, Samantha Fox, 87-62
TRUE FAITH, New Order, 87-4, 94-9
TRUE LOVE:
Bing Crosby and Grace Kelly, 56-4, 83-70
Terry Lightfoot's New Orleans Jazzmen, 61-33
Richard Chamberlain, 63-30
Shakin' Stevens, 88-23
Elton John – duet with Kiki Dee, 93-2
TRUE LOVE, Chimes, 90-48
TRUE LOVE FOR EVERMORE, Bachelors, 65-34
TRUE LOVE NEVER DIES, Flip&Fill featuring Kelly Llorenna, 01-34
TRUE LOVE WAYS:
Buddy Holly, 60-25, 88-65
Peter and Gordon, 65-2
Cliff Richard with the London Philharmonic Orchestra, 83-8
David Essex and Catherine Zeta Jones, 94-38
TRUE LOVE WILL FIND YOU IN THE END, Spectrum, 92-70
TRUE SPIRIT, Carleen Anderson, 94-24
TRUE STEP TONIGHT, True Steppers featuring Brian Harvey and Donell Jones, 00-25
TRUE (THE FAGGOT IS YOU), Morel, 00-64
TRUE TO US, Vanilla, 98-36
TRUE TO YOUR HEART, 98° (featuring Stevie Wonder), 98-51
TRUGANINI, Midnight Oil, 93-29
TRULY:
Lionel Richie, 82-6
Steven Houghton, 98-23
TRULY, Hinda Hicks, 98-31
TRULY, Peshay featuring Kym Mazelle, 00-55
TRULY MADLY DEEPLY, Savage Garden, 98-4
TRUST, Brother Beyond, 90-53
TRUST, Ned's Atomic Dustbin, 91-21
TRUST ME, Guru featuring N'dea Davenport, 93-34
TRUST ME TO OPEN MY MOUTH, Squeeze, 87-72
THE TRUTH, Colonel Abrams, 85-53
THE TRUTH, Real People, 91-73, 92-41
TRUTH OR DARE, Shirley Murdock, 86-60
TRY, Bros, 91-27
TRY A LITTLE KINDNESS, Glen Campbell, 70-45
TRY A LITTLE TENDERNESS, Otis Redding, 67-46
TRY AGAIN, Aaliyah, 00-5
TRY JAH LOVE, Third World, 82-47
TRY ME OUT, Corona, 95-6
TRY MY WORLD, Georgie Fame, 67-37
TRY TO UNDERSTAND, Lulu, 65-25
TRY TRY TRY, Julian Cope, 95-24
TRY, TRY, TRY, Smashing Pumpkins, 00-73
TRYIN' TO GET THE FEELING AGAIN, Carpenters, 94-44
TRYIN' TO GET TO YOU, Elvis Presley, 57-16
TRYING, Hilltoppers, 56-30
TRYING TO FORGET, Jim Reeves, 67-33
TRYOUTS FOR THE HUMAN RACE, Sparks, 79-45
TSOP (THE SOUND OF PHILADELPHIA), MFSB featuring the Three Degrees, 74-22
TSUNAMI, Manic Street Preachers, 99-11
TU AMOR, Kaci, 01-24
TU M'AIMES ENCORE (TO LOVE ME AGAIN), Celine Dion, 95-7
TUBTHUMPING, Chumbawamba, 97-2
TUBULAR BELLS, Champs Boys, 76-41
TUCH ME, Fonda Rae, 84-49
TUESDAY AFTERNOON, Jennifer Brown, 99-57
TUESDAY MORNING, Pogues, 93-18
TUESDAY SUNSHINE, Questions, 84-46
TUFF ACT TO FOLLOW, MN8, 96-15
TUG OF WAR, Paul McCartney, 82-53
TULANE, Steve Gibbons Band, 77-12
TULIPS FROM AMSTERDAM, Max Bygraves with Eric Rodgers and his Orchestra, 58-3
TUM BIN JIYA, Bally Sagoo, 97-21
TUMBLING DICE, Rolling Stones, 72-5
TUMBLING TUMBLEWEEDS, Slim Whitman, 56-19
THE TUNE, Suggs, 95-33
TUNES SPLITS THE ATOM, MC Tunes versus 808 State, 90-18
TUNNEL OF LOVE, Dire Straits, 81-54
TUNNEL OF LOVE, Fun Boy Three, 83-10
TUNNEL OF LOVE, Bruce Springsteen, 87-45
TURANDOT 'NESSUM DORMA', Luis Cobos featuring Placido Domingo, 90-59
TURN (from FACE THE STRANGE [EP]), Therapy?, 93-18
TURN, Travis, 99-8
TURN, Feeder, 01-27
TURN AROUND, Fab!, 98-59
TURN AROUND, Phats and Small presents Mutant Disco, 99-3
TURN AROUND AND COUNT 2 TEN, Dead Or Alive, 88-70
TURN BACK THE CLOCK, Johnny Hates Jazz, 87-12
TURN BACK TIME, Aqua, 98-1
TURN IT AROUND, Alena, 99-14
TURN IT DOWN, Sweet, 74-41
TURN IT INTO LOVE, Hazell Dean, 88-21
TURN IT ON, Level 42, 81-57
TURN IT ON AGAIN, Genesis, 80-8
TURN IT UP, Conway Brothers, 85-11
TURN IT UP, Richie Rich, 88-48
TURN IT UP, Technotronic featuring Melissa and Einstein, 90-42

WALKIN' TALL, Frankie Vaughan, 59-28
WALKIN' TALL, Adam Faith with Johnny Keating and his Orchestra, 63-23
WALKIN' THE LINE, Brass Construction, 83-47
WALKIN' TO MISSOURI, Tony Brent with Norrie Paramor, his Chorus and Orchestra, 52-7
WALKING, C.C.S., 71-7
WALKING AFTER YOU, Foo Fighters, 98-20
WALKING ALONE, Richard Anthony, 63-37
WALKING AWAY, Craig David, 00-3
WALKING BY MYSELF, Gary Moore, 90-48
WALKING DOWN MADISON, Kirsty MacColl, 91-23
WALKING DOWN YOUR STREET, Bangles, 87-16
WALKING IN MEMPHIS:
Marc Cohn, 91-66, 91-22
Cher, 95-11
WALKING IN MY SHOES, Depeche Mode, 93-14
WALKING IN MY SLEEP, Roger Daltrey, 84-56
WALKING IN RHYTHM, Blackbyrds, 75-23
WALKING IN THE AIR (FROM THE SNOWMAN):
Aled Jones, 85-5
Snowman featuring Peter Auty, 85-42, 87-37
Digital Dream Baby, 91-49
WALKING IN THE RAIN:
Walker Brothers, 67-26
Partridge Family starring David Cassidy, 73-10
WALKING IN THE RAIN, Modern Romance, 83-7
WALKING IN THE SUNSHINE, Bad Manners, 81-10
WALKING INTO SUNSHINE, Central Line, 81-42
WALKING ON AIR, Frazier Chorus, 91-60
WALKING ON AIR, Bad Boys Inc, 93-24
WALKING ON BROKEN GLASS, Annie Lennox, 92-8
WALKING ON ICE, River City People, 90-62
WALKING ON SUNSHINE:
Rockers Revenge featuring Donnie Calvin, 82-4
Eddy Grant, 89-63, 01-57
Krush, 92-71
WALKING ON SUNSHINE, Katrina and the Waves, 85-8, 96-53
WALKING ON THE CHINESE WALL, Philip Bailey, 85-34
WALKING ON THE MILKY WAY, OMD, 96-17
WALKING ON THE MOON, Police, 79-1
WALKING ON THIN ICE, Yoko Ono, 81-35
WALKING ON WATER, Madasun, 00-14
WALKING THE DOG, Dennisons, 64-36
WALKING THE FLOOR OVER YOU, Pat Boone, 60-39
WALKING TO NEW ORLEANS, Fats Domino, 60-19
WALKING WOUNDED, Everything But The Girl, 96-6
THE WALL STREET SHUFFLE, 10 C.C., 74-10
WALLFLOWER, Mega City Four, 93-69
WALLS COME TUMBLING DOWN!, Style Council, 85-6
THE WALLS FELL DOWN, Marbles, 69-28
WALTZ AWAY DREAMING, Toby Bourke with George Michael, 97-10
WALTZ DARLING, Malcolm McLaren and the Bootzilla Orchestra, 89-31
WALTZ #2 (XO), Elliott Smith, 98-52
WALTZING ALONE, James, 97-23
WAM BAM, Handley Family, 73-30
WAM BAM, N.T. Gang, 88-71
THE WANDERER:
Dion, 62-10, 76-16
Status Quo, 84-7
THE WANDERER, Donna Summer, 80-48
THE WANDERING DRAGON [EP], Shades Of Rhythm, 94-55
WANDERING EYES:
Charlie Gracie, 57-6
Frankie Vaughan with Wally Stott and his Orchestra and Chorus *, 57-6
WAND'RIN' STAR, Lee Marvin, 70-1
WANNA BE STARTIN' SOMETHIN', Michael Jackson, 83-8
WANNA BE WITH YOU, Jinny, 95-30
WANNA BE YOUR LOVER, Gayle and Gillian, 94-62
WANNA DROP A HOUSE (ON THAT BITCH), Urban Discharge featuring She, 96-51
WANNA GET UP, 2 Unlimited, 98-38
WANNA MAKE YOU GO . . . UUH!, Those 2 Girls, 94-74
WANNABE, Spice Girls, 96-1
WANT LOVE, Hysteric Ego, 96-28, 98-46
WANT YOU BAD, Offspring, 01-15
WANTED:
Perry Como with Hugo Winterhalter's Orchestra and Chorus, 54-4
Al Martino, 54-4
WANTED, Dooleys, 79-3
WANTED, Style Council, 87-20
WANTED, Halo James, 89-45
WANTED, Princess Ivori, 90-69
WANTED DEAD OR ALIVE, Bon Jovi, 87-13
WANTED DEAD OR ALIVE, 2 Pac and Snoop Doggy Dogg, 97-16
WANTED IT ALL, Claytown Troupe, 92-74
WAP-BAM-BOOGIE, Matt Bianco, 88-11, 89-59
WAR:
Edwin Starr, 70-3
Bruce Springsteen and the E Street Band, 86-18
Edwin Starr and Shadow, 93-69
WAR BABIES, Simple Minds, 98-43
WAR BABY, Tom Robinson, 83-6
WAR CHILD, Blondie, 82-39
THE WAR LORD, Shadows, 65-18
WAR OF NERVES, All Saints, 98-7
WAR PARTY, Eddy Grant, 83-42
THE WAR SONG, Culture Club, 84-2
WAR STORIES, Starjets, 79-51
WARFAIR, Clawfinger, 94-54
WARHEAD, U.K. Subs, 80-30
WARLOCK, Todd Terry presents Black Riot, 88-68
WARM AND TENDER LOVE, Percy Sledge, 66-34
WARM IT UP, Kris Kross, 92-16
WARM LOVE, Beatmasters featuring Claudia Fontaine, 89-51
WARM MACHINE, Bush, 00-45
WARM SUMMER DAZE, Vybe, 95-60
WARM WET CIRCLES, Marillion, 87-22
WARMED OVER KISSES (LEFT OVER LOVE), Brian Hyland, 62-28
WARNING!, Adeva, 89-17
WARNING, A.K.A., 96-43
WARNING, Freestylers featuring Navigator, 98-68
WARNING, Green Day, 00-27
WARNING SIGN, Nick Heyward, 84-25
WARPAINT, Brook Brothers with the Tony Hatch Group, 61-5
WARPED, Red Hot Chili Peppers, 95-31
WARRIOR, M.C. Wildski, 90-49
WARRIOR, Dance 2 Trance, 95-56
WARRIOR, Warrior, 00-19
WARRIOR GROOVE, D.S.M., 85-68
WARRIOR SOUND, Pressure Drop featuring Martin Fishley and MC Skibadee, 01-72
WARRIORS, Gary Numan, 83-20
WARRIORS, Aswad, 94-33
WARRIORS (OF THE WASTELAND), Frankie Goes To Hollywood, 86-19
WAS IT WORTH IT?, Pet Shop Boys, 91-24
WAS THAT ALL IT WAS, Kym Mazelle, 90-33
WAS THAT YOU?, Spear Of Destiny, 87-55
WASH YOUR FACE IN MY SINK, Dream Warriors, 90-16
WASSUUP!, Da Muttz, 00-11
WASTED, Def Leppard, 79-61
WASTED, Smaller, 96-72
WASTED IN AMERICA, Love/Hate, 92-38
WASTED TIME, Skid Row, 91-20
WASTED YEARS, Iron Maiden, 86-18
WASTELAND, Mission, 87-11
WASTELANDS, Midge Ure, 86-46
WATCH ME, Labi Siffre, 72-29
WATCH OUT, Brandi Wells, 82-74
WATCH THE MIRACLE START, Pauline Henry, 94-54
WATCH WHAT YOU SAY, Guru featuring Chaka Khan, 95-28
WATCHDOGS, UB40, 87-39
A WATCHER'S POINT OF VIEW (DON'T CHA THINK), PM Dawn, 91-36
WATCHING, Thompson Twins, 83-33
WATCHING THE DETECTIVES, Elvis Costello, 77-15
WATCHING THE RIVER FLOW, Bob Dylan, 71-24
WATCHING THE WHEELS, John Lennon and Yoko Ono, 81-30
WATCHING THE WILDLIFE, Frankie Goes To Hollywood, 87-28
WATCHING THE WORLD GO BY, Maxi Priest, 96-36
WATCHING WINDOWS, Roni Size Reprazent, 98-28
WATCHING YOU, Ether, 98-74
WATCHING YOU, WATCHING ME, David Grant, 83-10
WATER, Geno Washington and the Ram Jam Band, 66-39
WATER, Martika, 90-59
WATER FROM A VINE LEAF, William Orbit, 93-59
THE WATER IS OVER MY HEAD, Rockin' Berries, 66-43
THE WATER MARGIN:
Pete Mac Junior, 77-37
Godiego, 77-37
WATER ON GLASS/BOYS, Kim Wilde, 81-11
WATER RUNS DRY, Boyz II Men, 95-24
WATER, WATER, Tommy Steele and the Steelmen, 57-5
WATER WAVE, Mark Van Dale with Enrico, 98-71
WATERFALL, Wendy and Lisa, 87-66, 89-69
WATERFALL, Stone Roses, 92-27
WATERFALL, Atlantic Ocean, 94-22, 96-21
WATERFALLS, Paul McCartney, 80-9
WATERFALLS, TLC, 95-4
WATERFRONT, Simple Minds, 83-13
WATERLOO, Stonewall Jackson, 59-24
WATERLOO:
Abba (Bjorn, Benny, Anna and Frida), 74-1
Doctor and the Medics with Roy Wood starring the Anadin Brothers, 86-45
WATERLOO SUNSET:
Kinks, 67-2
Cathy Dennis, 97-11
WATERY, DOMESTIC [EP], Pavement, 92-58
THE WAVE OF THE FUTURE, Quadrophonia, 91-40
WAVES, Blancmange, 83-19
WAX THE VAN, Lola, 87-65
THE WAY, Global Communication, 97-51
THE WAY, Funky Green Dogs, 97-43
THE WAY, Fastball, 98-21
WAY BACK HOME, Junior Walker and the All-Stars, 73-35
WAY BEHIND ME, Primitives, 88-36
WAY DOWN, Elvis Presley, 77-1
WAY DOWN NOW, World Party, 90-66
WAY DOWN YONDER IN NEW ORLEANS, Freddie Cannon, 60-3
THE WAY DREAMS ARE, Daniel O'Donnell, 99-18
THE WAY I AM, Eminem, 00-8
THE WAY I FEEL, Lemon Trees, 92-62
THE WAY I FEEL, Roachford, 97-20
THE WAY I FEEL ABOUT YOU, Karyn White, 92-65
THE WAY I WALK, Jack Scott, 59-30
THE WAY I WANT TO TOUCH YOU, Captain and Tennille, 76-28
WAY IN MY BRAIN, SL2, 91-11, 92-26
THE WAY IT GOES, Status Quo, 99-39
THE WAY IT IS:
Bruce Hornsby and the Range, 86-15
Chameleon, 96-34
THE WAY IT USED TO BE, Engelbert Humperdinck, 69-3
THE WAY IT'S GOIN' DOWN (T.W.ISM. FOR LIFE), Shaquille O'Neal featuring Peter Gunz, 98-62
A WAY OF LIFE, Family Dogg, 69-6
WAY OF THE WORLD, Cheap Trick, 80-73
WAY OF THE WORLD, Tina Turner, 91-13
THE WAY SHE LOVES ME, Richard Marx, 94-38
THE WAY THAT YOU FEEL, Adeva, 97-54
THE WAY THAT YOU LOVE, Vanessa Williams, 95-52
THE WAY TO YOUR LOVE, Hear'say, 01-1
THE WAY WE WERE, Barbra Streisand, 74-31
THE WAY YOU ARE, Tears For Fears, 83-24
THE WAY YOU DO THE THINGS YOU DO, UB40, 91-49
THE WAY YOU LOOK TONIGHT:
Lettermen, 61-36
Denny Seyton and the Sabres, 64-48
Edward Woodward, 71-42
THE WAY YOU LOVE ME, Karyn White, 88-42
THE WAY YOU LOVE ME – LOVE TO INFINITY MIX, Faith Hill, 01-15
THE WAY YOU MAKE ME FEEL, Michael Jackson, 87-3
THE WAY YOU MAKE ME FEEL, Ronan Keating, 00-6
THE WAY YOU WORK IT, E.Y.C., 94-14
WAYDOWN, Catherine Wheel, 95-67
WAYS OF LOVE, Claytown Troupe, 90-57

WELCOME TO THE FUTURE, Shimmon and Woolfson, 98-69
WELCOME TO THE JUNGLE, Guns N' Roses, 87-67, 88-24
WELCOME TO THE PLEASURE DOME, Frankie Goes To Hollywood, 85-2, 93-18, 00-45
WELCOME TO THE REAL WORLD, Gun, 92-43
WELCOME TO THE TERROR DOME, Public Enemy, 90-18
WELCOME TO TOMORROW (ARE YOU READY?), Snap! featuring Summer, 94-6
WELL ALL RIGHT, Santana, 78-53
WELL, DID YOU EVAH!, Deborah Harry and Iggy Pop, 91-42
WELL I ASK YOU, Eden Kane, 61-1
WEST END GIRLS:
Pet Shop Boys, 85-1
East 17, 93-11
WEST END PAD, Cathy Dennis, 96-25
WEST OF ZANZIBAR, Anthony Steel with the Radio Revellers and Jackie Brown and his Music, 54-11
WEST ONE (SHINE ON ME), Ruts, 80-43
WESTERN MOVIES, Olympics, 58-12
WESTSIDE, TQ, 99-4
WET DREAM, Max Romeo, 69-10
WET MY WHISTLE, Midnight Star, 87-60
WHADDA U WANT (FROM ME), Frankie Knuckles featuring Adeva, 95-36
WHAM BAM, Candy Girls featuring Sweet Pussy Pauline, 96-20
WHAM RAP! (ENJOY WHAT YOU DO), Wham!, 83-8
WHAT, Soft Cell, 82-3
WHAT A BEAUTIFUL DAY, Levellers, 97-13
WHAT A CRAZY WORLD WE'RE LIVING IN, Joe Brown and the Bruvvers, 62-37
(WHAT A DAY FOR A) DAYDREAM, Right Said Fred, 92-29
WHAT A DIFFERENCE A DAY MADE, Esther Phillips, 75-6
WHAT A FOOL BELIEVES:
Doobie Brothers, 79-31, 87-57
Aretha Franklin, 80-46
Peter Cox, 98-39
WHAT A GIRL WANTS, Christina Aguilera, 00-3
WHAT A MOUTH (WHAT A NORTH AND SOUTH), Tommy Steele, 60-5
WHAT A NIGHT, City Boy, 78-39
WHAT A PARTY, Fats Domino, 61-43
WHAT A WASTE, Ian Dury and the Blockheads and Jankel and Jenner and Latham, 78-9
WHAT A WOMAN IN LOVE WON'T DO, Sandy Posey, 67-48
WHAT A WONDERFUL WORLD:
Louis Armstrong Orchestra and Chorus, 68-1, 88-53
Nick Cave and Shane MacGowan, 92-72
(WHAT A) WONDERFUL WORLD, Johnny Nash, 76-25
WHAT ABOUT LOVE, Heart, 88-14
WHAT ABOUT THIS LOVE, Mr. Fingers, 90-74
WHAT ABOUT US, Point Break, 00-24
WHAT ABOUT YOUR FRIENDS, TLC, 92-59
WHAT AM I GONNA DO, Emile Ford and the Checkmates, 61-33
WHAT AM I GONNA DO (I'M SO IN LOVE WITH YOU), Rod Stewart, 83-3
WHAT AM I GONNA DO WITH YOU?, Barry White, 75-5
WHAT AM I TO YOU, Kenny Lynch, 64-37
WHAT ARE WE GONNA DO ABOUT IT?, Mercy Mercy, 85-59
WHAT ARE WE GONNA GET 'ER INDOORS? (INTERPOL. IN THE BLEAK MID-WINTER), Dennis Waterman and George Cole, 83-21
WHAT ARE YOU DOING SUNDAY, Dawn, 71-3
WHAT ARE YOU UNDER, Definition Of Sound, 92-68
WHAT BECOMES OF THE BROKENHEARTED:
Jimmy Ruffin, 66-10, 74-4
Dave Stewart Guest vocals Colin Blunstone, 81-13
Robson and Jerome, 96-1
WHAT CAN I DO, Corrs, 98-53, 98-3
WHAT CAN I SAY, Boz Scaggs, 77-10
(WHAT CAN I SAY) TO MAKE YOU LOVE ME, Alexander O'Neal, 88-27
WHAT CAN YOU DO FOR ME, Utah Saints, 91-10
WHAT DID I DO TO YOU? [EP] + lead track title, Lisa Stansfield, 90-25
WHAT DIFFERENCE DOES IT MAKE?, Smiths, 84-12
WHAT DO I DO?, Phil Fearon and Galaxy, 84-5
WHAT DO I DO NOW?, Sleeper, 95-14
WHAT DO I GET?, Buzzcocks, 78-37
WHAT DO I HAVE TO DO, Kylie Minogue, 91-6
WHAT DO YA SAY, Chubby Checker, 63-37
WHAT DO YOU WANT?, Adam Faith, 59-1
WHAT DO YOU WANT FROM ME?, Monaco, 97-11
WHAT DO YOU WANT TO MAKE THOSE EYES AT ME FOR?:
Emile Ford and the Checkmates, 59-1
Shakin' Stevens, 87-5
WHAT DOES IT TAKE?, Then Jerico, 89-33
WHAT DOES IT TAKE (TO WIN YOUR LOVE):
Jr. Walker and the All Stars, 69-13
Kenny G, 86-64
WHAT DOES YOUR SOUL LOOK LIKE, DJ Shadow, 95-59, 98-54
WHAT EVER HAPPENED TO OLD FASHIONED LOVE, Daniel O'Donnell, 93-21
WHAT GOD WANTS GOD GETS (PART 1), Roger Waters, 92-35
WHAT GOES AROUND, Bitty McLean, 94-36
WHAT GOES AROUND, Luciana, 94-67
WHAT GOES AROUND COMES AROUND, Bob Marley, 96-42
WHAT GOES ON, Bryan Ferry, 78-67
WHAT GOOD AM I?, Cilla Black, 67-24
WHAT HAPPENED TO THE MUSIC, Joey Negro, 93-51
WHAT HAVE I DONE TO DESERVE THIS?, Pet Shop Boys and Dusty Springfield, 87-2
WHAT HAVE THEY DONE TO MY SONG MA:
New Seekers, 70-44
Melanie, 71-39
WHAT HAVE THEY DONE TO THE RAIN, Searchers, 64-13
WHAT HAVE YOU DONE FOR ME LATELY, Janet Jackson, 86-3
WHAT HAVE YOU DONE (IS THIS ALL), One Tribe featuring Gem, 92-52
WHAT HOPE HAVE I, Sphinx, 95-43
WHAT I AM:
Edie Brickell and New Bohemians, 89-31
Tin Tin Out featuring Emma Bunton, 99-2
WHAT I CAN DO FOR YOU, Sheryl Crow, 95-43
WHAT I DO BEST, Robin S, 93-43
WHAT I GOT, Sublime, 97-71
WHAT I GOT IS WHAT YOU NEED, Unique, 83-27
WHAT I LIKE MOST ABOUT YOU IS YOUR GIRLFRIEND, Special A.K.A., 84-51
WHAT I MEAN, Modjo, 01-59
WHAT I MISS THE MOST, Aloof, 98-70
WHAT I NEED, Crystal Waters, 94-40
WHAT I'VE GOT IN MIND, Billie Jo Spears, 76-4
WHAT IF . . ., Lightning Seeds, 96-14
WHAT IF, Kate Winslet, 01-6
WHAT IN THE WORLD, Nu Colours, 93-57
WHAT IN THE WORLD'S COME OVER YOU:
Jack Scott, 60-11
Tam White, 75-36
WHAT IN THE WORLD'S COME OVER YOU, Rockin' Berries, 65-23
WHAT IS A MAN, Four Tops, 69-16
WHAT IS HOUSE [EP], LFO, 92-62
WHAT IS LIFE:
Olivia Newton-John, 72-16
Shawn Mullins, 99-62
WHAT IS LIFE?, Black Uhuru, 84-56
WHAT IS LOVE?, Howard Jones, 83-2
WHAT IS LOVE?, Deee-Lite, 90-2
WHAT IS LOVE, Haddaway, 93-2
WHAT IS THIS THING CALLED LOVE?, Alexander O'Neal, 91-53
WHAT IS TRUTH, Johnny Cash, 70-21
WHAT IT FEELS LIKE FOR A GIRL, Madonna, 01-7
WHAT IT IS, Garnett Mimms and Truckin' Company, 77-44
WHAT IT IS, Freddy Fresh, 99-63
WHAT IT'S LIKE, Everlast, 99-34
WHAT KIND OF FOOL, All About Eve, 88-29
WHAT KIND OF FOOL AM I:
Anthony Newley, 61-36
Sammy Davis Jr., 62-26
Shirley Bassey with Frank Barber and his Orchestra, 63-47
WHAT KIND OF FOOL (HEARD ALL THAT BEFORE), Kylie Minogue, 92-14
WHAT KIND OF MAN WOULD I BE, Mint Condition, 97-38
WHAT KINDA BOY YOU'RE LOOKIN' FOR (GIRL), Hot Chocolate, 83-10
WHAT MADE MILWAUKEE FAMOUS (HAS MADE A LOSER OUT OF ME), Rod Stewart, 72-4
WHAT MAKES A MAN (SINGLE REMIX), Westlife, 00-2
WHAT MAKES A MAN A MAN (LIVE), Marc Almond, 93-60
WHAT MAKES YOU CRY, Proclaimers, 94-38
WHAT MORE DO YOU WANT, Frankie Vaughan, 60-25
WHAT NOW, Adam Faith with Johnny Keating and his Orchestra, 63-31
WHAT NOW MY LOVE?:
Shirley Bassey with Nelson Riddle and his Orchestra, 62-5
Sonny and Cher, 66-13
WHAT PRESENCE?!, Orange Juice, 84-47
WHAT THE WORLD IS WAITING FOR/FOOLS GOLD, Stone Roses, 89-8, 90-22
WHAT THEY DO, Roots, 97-49
WHAT TIME IS IT?, Spin Doctors, 93-56
WHAT.TIME.IS.IT.?, Dust Junkys, 98-39
WHAT TIME IS LOVE? (LIVE AT TRANCENTRAL):
KLF featuring the Children Of The Revolution, 90-5
KLF *, 92-4
WHAT TO DO:
Buddy Holly, 61-34
Buddy Holly, 63-27
WHAT TOOK YOU SO LONG?, Emma Bunton, 01-1
WHAT U DO, Colours featuring Stephen Emmanuel and Eska, 99-51
WHAT "U" WAITIN' "4"?, Jungle Brothers, 90-35
WHAT WILL I DO WITHOUT YOU, Lene Lovich, 80-58
WHAT WILL MARY SAY, Johnny Mathis, 63-49
WHAT WOULD HAPPEN, Meredith Brooks, 98-49
WHAT WOULD I BE, Val Doonican, 66-2
WHAT WOULD WE DO, DSK, 91-46, 97-55
WHAT WOULD YOU DO?, City High, 01-3
WHAT WOULD YOU DO IF . . .?, Code Red, 98-55
WHAT YA GOT 4 ME, Signum, 98-70
WHAT YA LOOKIN' AT?, Crow, 01-60
WHAT YOU DO, Big Bass vs Michelle Narine, 00-67
WHAT YOU DO TO ME [EP] + lead track title, Teenage Fanclub, 92-31
WHAT YOU GET IS WHAT YOU SEE, Tina Turner, 87-30
WHAT YOU GONNA DO ABOUT IT, Total Contrast, 86-63
WHAT YOU NEED, Inxs, 86-51
WHAT YOU NEED, Powerhouse featuring Duane Harden, 99-13
WHAT YOU SAY, Lightning Seeds, 97-41
WHAT YOU SEE IS WHAT YOU GET, Glen Goldsmith, 88-33
WHAT YOU THINK OF THAT, Memphis Bleek featuring Jay-Z, 99-58
WHAT YOU WAITIN' FOR, Stargard, 78-39
WHAT YOU WANT, Xpansions featuring Dale Joyner, 91-55
WHAT YOU WANT, Future Force, 96-47
WHAT YOU WANT, Mase featuring Total, 98-15
WHAT YOU WON'T DO FOR LOVE, Go West, 93-15
WHAT YOU'RE MISSING, K-Klass, 94-24
WHAT YOU'RE PROPOSING, Status Quo, 80-2
WHAT'D I SAY, Jerry Lee Lewis, 61-10
WHAT'D YOU COME HERE FOR?, Trina and Tamara, 99-46
WHAT'LL I DO, Janet Jackson, 95-9
WHAT'S A GIRL TO DO?, Sister2sister, 00-61
WHAT'S ANOTHER YEAR, Johnny Logan, 80-1
WHAT'S GOIN DOWN, Honky, 96-49
WHAT'S GOING ON:
Cyndi Lauper, 87-57
Music Relief '94, 94-70
Artists Against Aids Worldwide featuring Ja Rule, 01-6
WHAT'S GOING ON?, Wookie, 00-45
WHAT'S GOING ON?, Mekon featuring Roxanne Shante, 00-43

WHEN YOU BELIEVE (FROM THE PRINCE OF EGYPT), Mariah Carey and Whitney Houston, 98-4
WHEN YOU COME BACK TO ME, Jason Donovan, 89-2
WHEN YOU GET RIGHT DOWN TO IT, Ronnie Dyson, 71-34
WHEN YOU GONNA LEARN?, Jamiroquai, 92-52, 93-28
WHEN YOU LOSE THE ONE YOU LOVE, David Whitfield with Mantovani and his Orchestra and Chorus, 55-7
WHEN YOU MADE THE MOUNTAIN, Opus III, 94-71
WHEN YOU SAY NOTHING AT ALL, Ronan Keating, 99-1
(WHEN YOU SAY YOU LOVE SOMEBODY) IN THE HEART, Kool And The Gang, 84-7
WHEN YOU TELL ME THAT YOU LOVE ME, Diana Ross, 91-2
WHEN YOU WALK IN THE ROOM:
Searchers, 64-3
Child, 78-38
Paul Carrack, 87-48
Status Quo, 95-34
WHEN YOU WERE SWEET SIXTEEN, Fureys and Davey Arthur, 81-14
WHEN YOU WERE YOUNG, Del Amitri, 93-20
WHEN YOUR 'EX' WANTS YOU BACK, Surface, 84-52
WHEN YOUR OLD WEDDING RING WAS NEW, Jimmy Roselli, 83-51, 87-52
WHEN YOU'RE GONE, Bryan Adams featuring Melanie C., 98-3
WHEN YOU'RE IN LOVE WITH A BEAUTIFUL WOMAN, Dr. Hook, 79-1, 92-44
WHEN YOU'RE NUMBER 1, Gene Chandler, 79-43
WHEN YOU'RE YOUNG, Jam, 79-17, 83-53
WHEN YOU'RE YOUNG AND IN LOVE:
Marvelettes, 67-13
Flying Pickets, 84-7
WHENEVER GOD SHINES HIS LIGHT, Van Morrison with Cliff Richard, 89-20
WHENEVER I STOP, Mike and the Mechanics, 99-73
WHENEVER YOU NEED ME, T'Pau, 91-16
WHENEVER YOU NEED SOMEBODY, Rick Astley, 87-3
WHENEVER YOU NEED SOMEONE, Bad Boys Inc, 93-26
WHENEVER YOU WANT MY LOVE, Real Thing, 78-18
WHENEVER YOU'RE NEAR, Cher, 93-72
WHENEVER YOU'RE READY, Five Star, 87-11
WHERE ARE THEY NOW?, Gene, 97-22
WHERE ARE YOU, Kavana, 96-26
WHERE ARE YOU, Imaani, 98-15
WHERE ARE YOU BABY?, Betty Boo, 90-3
WHERE ARE YOU GOING TO MY LOVE, Brotherhood Of Man, 70-22
WHERE ARE YOU NOW, Jackie Trent, 65-1
WHERE ARE YOU NOW?, Generator, 99-60
WHERE CAN I FIND LOVE, Livin' Joy, 97-12
WHERE DID ALL THE GOOD TIMES GO, Donny Osmond, 74-18
WHERE DID I GO WRONG, UB40, 88-26
WHERE DID OUR LOVE GO:
Supremes, 64-3
Donnie Elbert, 72-8
Sinitta (from The Supreme [EP]), 93-49
Tricia Penrose, 96-71
Manhattan Transfer, 78-40
WHERE DID WE GO WRONG, Liquid Gold, 82-56
WHERE DID YOUR HEART GO?, Wham!, 86-28
WHERE DO BROKEN HEARTS GO, Whitney Houston, 88-14
(WHERE DO I BEGIN) LOVE STORY:
Andy Williams, 71-4
Shiley Bassey, 71-34
WHERE DO I STAND?, Montrose Avenue, 98-38
WHERE DO U WANT ME TO PUT IT, Solo U.S., 96-45
WHERE DO WE GO?, Ten City, 89-60
WHERE DO WE GO FROM HERE, Cliff Richard, 82-60
WHERE DO YOU GO, No Mercy, 97-2
WHERE DO YOU GO TO (MY LOVELY), Peter Sarstedt, 69-1
WHERE DOES MY HEART BEAT NOW, Celine Dion, 93-72
WHERE DOES THE TIME GO?, Julia Fordham, 89-41
WHERE EAGLES FLY, Crystal Palace FC 1990 FA Cup Final Squad featuring the "Fab Four", 90-50
WHERE HAS ALL THE LOVE GONE, Yazz, 89-16
WHERE HAS ALL THE LOVE GONE, Maureen, 91-51
WHERE HAS LOVE GONE?, Holly Johnson, 90-73
WHERE HAVE ALL THE COWBOYS GONE?, Paula Cole, 97-15
WHERE HAVE YOU BEEN TONIGHT?, Shed Seven, 95-23
WHERE I FIND MY HEAVEN, Gigolo Aunts, 95-29
WHERE I WANNA BE, Shade Sheist featuring Nate Dogg and Kurupt, 01-14
WHERE I'M HEADED, Lene Marlin, 01-31
WHERE IN THE WORLD, Swing Out Sister, 89-47
WHERE IN THE WORLD, BBM, 94-57
WHERE IS MY MAN, Eartha Kitt, 83-36
WHERE IS THE FEELING?, Kylie Minogue, 95-16
WHERE IS THE LOVE:
Roberta Flack and Donny Hathaway, 72-29
Mica Paris and Will Downing, 89-19
WHERE IS THE LOVE, Betty Wright, 75-25
WHERE IS THE LOVE?, Adeva, 97-54
WHERE IS THE LOVE (WE USED TO KNOW), Delegation, 77-22
WHERE IS TOMORROW?, Cilla Black, 68-39
WHERE IT'S AT, Beck, 96-35
WHERE LOVE LIVES (COME ON IN), Alison Limerick, 91-27, 96-9
WHERE MY GIRLS AT?, 702, 99-22
WHERE THE ACTION IS, Westworld, 87-54
WHERE THE BOYS ARE, Connie Francis, 61-5
WHERE THE HEART IS, Soft Cell, 82-21
WHERE THE PARTY AT, Jagged Edge featuring Nelly, 01-25
WHERE THE POOR BOYS DANCE, Lulu, 00-24
WHERE THE ROSE IS SOWN, Big Country, 84-29
WHERE THE STREETS HAVE NO NAME, U2, 87-4
WHERE THE STREETS HAVE NO NAME (CAN'T TAKE MY EYES OFF YOU) [M], Pet Shop Boys, 91-4
WHERE THE WILD ROSES GROW, Nick Cave and the Bad Seeds + Kylie Minogue, 95-11
WHERE THE WINDS BLOW, Frankie Laine; Carl Fischer-piano, 53-2
WHERE WERE YOU, Adult Net, 89-66
WHERE WERE YOU HIDING WHEN THE STORM BROKE, Alarm, 84-22
WHERE WERE YOU (ON OUR WEDDING DAY), Lloyd Price, 59-15
WHERE WILL THE DIMPLE BE?, Rosemary Clooney and the Mellomen with the Buddy Cole Quartet Bass solo: Thurl Ravenscroft, 55-6
WHERE WILL YOU BE, Sue Nicholls, 68-17
WHERE YOU ARE, Rahsaan Patterson, 98-55
WHERE YOU GONNA BE TONIGHT?, Willie Collins, 86-46
WHERE'S JACK THE RIPPER?, Grooverider, 99-61
WHERE'S ME JUMPER?, Sultans Of Ping F.C., 92-67
WHERE'S ROMEO?, Ca Va Ca Va, 82-49
WHERE'S THE LOVE, Hanson, 97-4
WHERE'S YOUR HEAD AT?, Basement Jaxx, 01-9
WHERE'S YOUR LOVE BEEN, Heliocentric World, 95-71
WHEREVER I LAY MY HAT (THAT'S MY HOME), Paul Young, 83-1
WHEREVER I MAY ROAM, Metallica, 92-25
WHEREVER WOULD I BE, Dusty Springfield and Daryl Hall, 95-44
WHEREVER YOU ARE, Neil Finn, 01-32
WHICH WAY SHOULD I JUMP?, Milltown Brothers, 91-38
WHICH WAY YOU GOIN' BILLY?, Poppy Family (featuring Susan Jacks), 70-7
WHIGGLE IN LINE, Black Duck, 94-33
WHILE I LIVE, Kenny Damon, 66-48
WHILE YOU SEE A CHANCE, Steve Winwood, 81-45
WHINE AND GRINE, Prince Buster, 98-21
WHIP IT, Devo, 80-51
WHIPPIN' PICCADILLY, Gomez, 98-35
WHISKY IN THE JAR:
Thin Lizzy, 73-6
Pogues and the Dubliners *, 90-63
Metallica *, 99-29
THE WHISPER, Selecter, 80-36
WHISPER A PRAYER, Mica Paris, 93-65
WHISPER YOUR NAME, Human Nature, 97-53
WHISPERING:
Bachelors, 63-18
Nino Tempo and April Stevens, 64-20
WHISPERING GRASS, Windsor Davies as B.S.M. Williams and Don Estelle as Gunner Sugden (Lofty), 75-1
WHISPERING HOPE, Jim Reeves, 61-50
WHISPERING YOUR NAME, Alison Moyet, 94-18
WHISPERS, Elton John, 90-47
WHISTLE DOWN THE WIND, Nick Heyward, 83-13
WHISTLE DOWN THE WIND, Tina Arena, 98-24
THE WHISTLE SONG, Frankie Knuckles, 91-17
THE WHISTLE SONG, Dj Aligator Project, 00-57
THE WHISTLER, Honky, 94-41
WHITE BIRD, Vanessa-Mae, 01-66
WHITE BOY WITH A FEATHER, Jason Downs featuring Milk, 01-19
WHITE BOYS AND HEROES, Gary Numan, 82-20
WHITE CHRISTMAS:
Mantovani and his Orchestra, 52-6
Pat Boone with Mort Lindsey and his Orchestra and the Artie Malvern Singers, 57-29
Freddie Starr, 75-41
Bing Crosby, 77-5, 85-69, 98-29
Darts, 80-48
Jim Davidson, 80-52
Keith Harris and Orville, 85-40
Max Bygraves, 89-71
WHITE CLIFFS OF DOVER:
Mr. Acker Bilk and his Paramount Jazz Band, 60-30
Righteous Brothers, 66-21
Robson Green and Jerome Flynn *, 95-1
WHITE COATS [EP], New Model Army, 87-50
WHITE HORSES, Jacky, 68-10
WHITE LIE, Foreigner, 94-58
WHITE LIGHT/WHITE HEAT, David Bowie, 83-46
WHITE LIGHTNING, Fall, 90-56
WHITE LINES (DON'T DON'T DO IT):
Grand Master and Melle Mel, 83-60, 84-7, 94-59
Duran Duran featuring Mele Mel and Grandmaster Flash and the Furious Five*, 95-17
WHITE LOVE, One Dove, 93-43
(WHITE MAN) IN HAMMERSMITH PALAIS, Clash, 78-32
WHITE NO SUGAR, Clint Boon Experience!, 99-61
WHITE PUNKS ON DOPE, Tubes, 77-28
WHITE RIBBON DAY, Delirious?, 97-41
WHITE RIOT, Clash, 77-38
WHITE ROOM, Cream, 69-28
WHITE SILVER SANDS, Bill Black's Combo, 60-50
WHITE SKIES, Sunscreem, 96-25
A WHITE SPORT COAT (AND A PINK CARNATION):
King Brothers with the King Brothers and Geoff Love and his Orchestra, 57-6
Terry Dene with the Malcolm Lockyer Group *, 57-18
WHITE WEDDING, Billy Idol, 85-6
A WHITER SHADE OF PALE:
Procol Harum, 67-1, 72-13
Munich Machine introducing Chris Bennett, 78-42
Annie Lennox, 95-16
WHO?, Ed Case + Sweetie Irie, 01-29
WHO AM I?, Adam Faith, 61-5
WHO AM I (ZIM-ZIMMA), Beenie Man, 98-10
WHO ARE WE, Vera Lynn, 56-30
WHO ARE WE, Ronnie Hilton, 56-6
WHO ARE YOU, Who, 78-18
WHO CAN I RUN TO, Xscape, 96-31
WHO CAN IT BE NOW, Men At Work, 82-45
WHO CAN MAKE ME FEEL GOOD?, Bassheads, 92-38
WHO COMES TO BOOGIE, Little Benny and the Masters, 85-33
WHO COULD BE BLUER?, Jerry Lordan, 60-16
WHO DO U LOVE, Deborah Cox, 96-31
WHO DO YOU LOVE, Juicy Lucy, 70-14
WHO DO YOU LOVE, Intruders, 84-65
WHO DO YOU LOVE, Jose Padilla featuring Angela John, 98-59

Y (HOW DEEP IS YOUR LOVE), DJ Scot Project, 98-57
Y.M.C.A., Village People, 78-1, 93-12, 99-35
Y VIVA ESPANA:
Sylvia (Vrethammar), 74-4
Tony Rees and the Cottagers *, 75-46
Y VIVA SUSPENDERS, Judge Dread, 76-27
YA DON'T SEE THE SIGNS, Mark B and Blade, 01-23
YA MAMA, Fatboy Slim, 01-30
YA PLAYIN' YASELF, Jeru The Damaja, 96-67
YA YA TWIST, Petula Clark, 62-14
YAAAH, D-Shake, 90-20
YABBA DABBA DOO, Darkman, 94-49, 94-37
YAH MO B THERE, James Ingram (with Michael McDonald), 84-44, 85-12
YAKETY YAK, Coasters, 58-12
YE KE YE KE, Mory Kante, 88-29, 95-25, 96-28
YEAH?, Audioweb, 96-73
YEAH, Wannadies, 00-56
YEAH BUDDY, Royal House, 89-35
YEAH, YEAH, YEAH, YEAH, YEAH, Pogues, 88-43
YEAH YEAH YEAH YEAH YEAH, Wedding Present, 94-51
YEAR OF DECISION, Three Degrees, 74-13
YEAR OF THE CAT, Al Stewart, 77-31
YEARNING FOR YOUR LOVE, Gap Band, 81-47
YEARS FROM NOW, Dr. Hook, 80-47
YEARS GO BY, Stan Campbell, 87-65
YEARS LATER, Cactus World News, 86-59
YEARS MAY COME, YEARS MAY GO, Herman's Hermits, 70-7
YEBO!, Art Of Noise featuring Mahlathini and the Mahotella Queens, 89-63
YEH, YEH:
Georgie Fame and the Blue Flames, 64-1
Matt Bianco, 85-13
YEHA-NOHA (WISHES OF HAPPINESS AND PROSPERITY), Sacred Spirit, 95-71, 95-37
YELLOW, Coldplay, 00-4
YELLOW PEARL, Philip Lynott, 81-56, 81-14
YELLOW RIVER, Christie, 70-1
THE YELLOW ROSE OF TEXAS:
Mitch Miller with His Orchestra and Chorus, 55-2
Gary Miller with Dennis Wilson and his Orchestra and the Beryl Stott Chorus, 55-13
Ronnie Hilton, 55-15
YELLOW SUBMARINE, Beatles, 66-1, 86-63
YEP!, Duane Eddy, 59-17
YER OLD, Reef, 97-21
YES, Merry Clayton, 88-70
YES, McAlmont and Butler, 95-8
YES I DO, Shakin' Stevens, 90-60
YES I WILL, Hollies, 65-9
YES MY DARLING DAUGHTER, Eydie Gorme, 62-10
YES SIR, I CAN BOOGIE, Baccara, 77-1
YES TONIGHT, JOSEPHINE:
Johnnie Ray with Ray Conniff, 57-1
Jets, 81-25
YESTER-ME, YESTER-YOU, YESTERDAY, Stevie Wonder, 69-2
YESTERDAY:
Matt Monro, 65-8
Marianne Faithfull, 65-36
Ray Charles, 67-44
Beatles, 76-8
Wet Wet Wet, 97-4
YESTERDAY HAS GONE:
Cupids Inspiration, 68-4
P.J. Proby; Marc Almond featuring the My Life Story Orchestra, 96-58
YESTERDAY MAN, Chris Andrews, 65-3
YESTERDAY ONCE MORE:
Carpenters, 73-2
Redd Kross, 94-45
YESTERDAY TODAY, Ocean Colour Scene, 91-49
YESTERDAY WENT TOO SOON, Feeder, 99-20
YESTERDAY, WHEN I WAS MAD, Pet Shop Boys, 94-13
YESTERDAYS, Guns N' Roses, 92-8
YESTERDAY'S DREAMS, Four Tops, 68-23
YESTERDAY'S GONE, Chad Stuart and Jeremy Clyde, 63-37
YESTERDAY'S MEN, Madness, 85-18
YIM, Jez and Choopie, 98-36
THE YING TONG SONG, Goons with Maurice Ponke and his Orchestre Fromage, 56-3, 73-9
YN GYMREAG, Alarm, 89-43
YO!! SWEETNESS, M.C. Hammer, 91-16
YO YO GET FUNKY, DJ Fast Eddie, 89-54
THE YODELING SONG, Frank Ifield featuring The Backroom Boys, 91-40
YOU, Bandwagon, 69-34
YOU, George Harrison, 75-38
YOU, Randy Edelman, 77-49
YOU, Ten Sharp, 92-10
YOU, Bonnie Raitt, 94-31
YOU, Staxx featuring Carol Leeming, 95-50
YOU, Point Break, 00-14
YOU AIN'T GOING NOWHERE, Byrds, 68-45
YOU AIN'T LIVIN' TILL YOU'RE LOVIN', Marvin Gaye and Tammi Terrell, 69-21
YOU AIN'T REALLY DOWN, Status IV, 83-56
YOU AIN'T SEEN NOTHING YET:
Bachman-Turner Overdrive, 74-2
Bus Stop featuring Randy Bachman, 98-22
YOU ALL DAT, Baha Men: Guest vocal Imaani Coppolo, 01-14
YOU ALWAYS HURT THE ONE YOU LOVE:
Connie Francis, 58-13
Clarence 'Frogman' Henry, 61-6
YOU AND I, Rick James, 78-46
YOU AND I WILL NEVER SEE THINGS EYE TO EYE, Kingmaker, 95-33
YOU AND ME, Liner, 79-44
YOU AND ME, DJ Seduction, 92-26
YOU AND ME, Lisa B, 94-39
YOU + ME, Technique, 99-56
YOU + ME = LOVE:
Undisputed Truth, 77-43
Funky Worm *, 89-46
YOU & ME SONG, Wannadies, 96-18
YOU AND ME TONIGHT, Aurra, 86-12
YOU AND YOUR HEART SO BLUE, Bucks Fizz, 85-43
YOU ANGEL YOU, Manfred Mann's Earth Band, 79-54
YOU ARE, Lionel Richie, 83-43
YOU ARE ALIVE, Fragma, 01-4
YOU ARE AWFUL (BUT I LIKE YOU), Dick Emery, 73-43
YOU ARE BEAUTIFUL, Johnny Mathis with Ray Ellis and his Orchestra, 60-38
YOU ARE EVERYTHING:
Pearls, 73-41
Diana Ross and Marvin Gaye, 74-5
Melanie Williams and Joe Roberts, 95-28
YOU ARE IN MY SYSTEM, Robert Palmer, 83-53
YOU ARE MY DESTINY, Paul Anka, 58-6
YOU ARE MY FIRST LOVE, Ruby Murray with Ray Martin and his Orchestra, 56-16
YOU ARE MY HIGH, Demon vs Heartbreaker, 01-70
YOU ARE MY LADY, Freddie Jackson, 85-49
YOU ARE MY LOVE, Liverpool Express, 76-11
YOU ARE MY MELODY, Change, 84-48
YOU ARE MY WORLD, Communards/Jimmy Somerville-Richard Coles, 85-30, 87-21
YOU ARE NOT ALONE, Michael Jackson, 95-1
YOU ARE SOMEBODY, Full Intention, 98-75
YOU ARE THE ONE, A-Ha, 88-13
YOU ARE THE SUNSHINE OF MY LIFE, Stevie Wonder, 73-7
YOU ARE THE UNIVERSE, Brand New Heavies, 97-21
YOU ARE THE WAY, Primitives, 91-58
YOU ARE THE WEAKEST LINK, Echobass, 01-53
YOU BE ILLIN', Run D.M.C., 87-42
YOU BELONG IN ROCK N' ROLL, Tin Machine, 91-33
YOU BELONG TO ME, Jo Stafford with Paul Weston and his Orchestra, 52-1
YOU BELONG TO ME, Gary Glitter, 76-40
YOU BELONG TO ME, JX, 95-17
YOU BELONG TO ME, Michael Moog, 01-62
YOU BET YOUR LOVE, Herbie Hancock, 79-18
YOU BETTER, Mount Rushmore presents the Knack, 99-53
YOU BETTER YOU BET, Who, 81-9
YOU BLOW ME AWAY, Robert Palmer, 94-38
YOU BRING ME JOY:
Rhythm Factor, 95-53
Meechie, 95-74
YOU BRING ME UP, K-Ci and Jojo, 97-21
YOU BRING ON THE SUN, Londonbeat, 92-32
YOU CAME, Kim Wilde, 88-3
YOU CAME, YOU SAW, YOU CONQUERED, Pearls, 72-32
YOU CAN CALL ME AL, Paul Simon, 86-4
YOU CAN COUNT ON ME, Jaki Graham, 95-62
YOU CAN DANCE IF YOU WANT TO, Go Go Lorenzo and the Davis Pinckney Project, 86-46
YOU CAN DO IT, Al Hudson and the Partners, 79-15
YOU CAN DO MAGIC, Limmie and Family Cookin', 73-3
YOU CAN DO MAGIC, America, 82-59
YOU CAN GET IT, Maxx, 94-21
YOU CAN GET IT IF YOU REALLY WANT, Desmond Dekker, 70-2
YOU CAN GO YOUR OWN WAY, Chris Rea, 94-28
YOU CAN HAVE HIM, Dionne Warwick, 65-37
YOU CAN HAVE IT ALL, George McCrae, 74-23
YOU CAN HAVE IT ALL, Eve Gallagher, 95-43
YOU CAN HAVE IT (TAKE MY HEART), Robert Palmer, 83-66
YOU CAN LOVE ME NOW, Hothouse Flowers, 98-65
YOU CAN MAKE ME DANCE, SING OR ANYTHING (EVEN TAKE THE DOG FOR A WALK, MEND A FUSE, FOLD AWAY THE IRONING BOARD, OR ANY OTHER DOMESTIC SHORT COMINGS), Faces/Rod Stewart, 74-12
YOU CAN NEVER STOP ME LOVING YOU, Kenny Lynch, 63-10
YOU CAN TALK TO ME, Seahorses, 97-15
YOU CAN WIN IF YOU WANT, Modern Talking, 85-70
YOU CAN'T BE TRUE TO TWO, Dave King with the Roland Shaw Orchestra and the Keynotes, 56-11
YOU CAN'T BLAME LOVE, Thomas and Taylor, 86-53
YOU CAN'T CHANGE ME, Roger Sanchez featuring Armand Van Helden and N'Dea Davenport, 01-25
YOU CAN'T HIDE (YOUR LOVE FROM ME), David Joseph, 83-13
YOU CAN'T HURRY LOVE:
Supremes, 66-3
Phil Collins, 82-1
YOU CAN'T RUN FROM LOVE, Maxine Singleton, 83-57
YOU CAN'T SIT DOWN, Phil Upchurch Combo, 66-39
YOU CAN'T STOP ROCK 'N' ROLL, Twisted Sister, 83-43
YOU CAN'T STOP THE REIGN, Shaquille O'Neal, 97-40
YOU CAUGHT MY EYE, Judy Boucher, 87-18
YOU COME FROM EARTH, Lena, 93-69
YOU COULD BE MINE, Guns N' Roses, 91-3
YOU COULD BE MY EVERYTHING, Mikey Graham, 01-62
YOU COULD HAVE BEEN WITH ME, Sheena Easton, 81-54
YOU COULD'VE BEEN A LADY, Hot Chocolate, 71-22
YOU DID CUT ME, China Crisis, 85-54
YOU DISAPPEAR FROM VIEW, Teardrop Explodes, 83-41
YOU DO, McAlmont and Butler, 95-17
YOU DO SOMETHING TO ME, Paul Weller, 95-9
YOU DO SOMETHING TO ME, Dum Dums, 00-27
YOU DON'T BELIEVE ME, Stray Cats, 81-57
YOU DON'T BRING ME FLOWERS, Barbra and Neil, 78-5
YOU DON'T CARE ABOUT US, Placebo, 98-5
YOU DON'T FOOL ME – THE REMIXES, Queen, 96-17
YOU DON'T HAVE TO BE A BABY TO CRY, Caravelles, 63-6
YOU DON'T HAVE TO BE A STAR (TO BE IN MY SHOW), Marilyn McCoo and Billy Davis, Jr., 77-7
YOU DON'T HAVE TO BE IN THE ARMY TO FIGHT IN THE WAR, Mungo Jerry, 71-13
YOU DON'T HAVE TO GO, Chi – Lites, 76-3
YOU DON'T HAVE TO SAY YOU LOVE ME (IO CHE NO VIVO SENZA TE):
Dusty Springfield, 66-1
Elvis Presley, 71-9
Guys 'N' Dolls, 76-5
Mash! *, 94-37
Denise Welch, 95-23
YOU DON'T HAVE TO WORRY, Mary J. Blige, 93-36
YOU DON'T KNOW, Helen Shapiro, 61-1
YOU DON'T KNOW, Berlin, 87-39
YOU DON'T KNOW, Cyndi Lauper, 97-27
YOU DON'T KNOW, Mass Syndicate featuring Su Su Bobien, 98-71
YOU DON'T KNOW, 702, 99-36

YOU WANT THIS, Janet Jackson, 94-14
YOU WEAR IT WELL, Rod Stewart, 72-1
YOU WEAR IT WELL, El Debarge with Debarge, 85-54
(YOU WERE MADE FOR) ALL MY LOVE, Jackie Wilson, 60-33
YOU WERE MADE FOR ME, Freddie and the Dreamers, 63-3
YOU WERE MEANT FOR ME, Jewel, 97-32
YOU WERE ON MY MIND, Crispian St. Peters, 66-2
YOU WERE THERE, Heinz, 64-26
YOU WEREN'T IN LOVE WITH ME, Billy Field, 82-67
YOU WILL RISE, Sweetback featuring Amel Larrieux from Groove Theory, 97-64
YOU WIN AGAIN, Bee Gees, 87-1
YOU WOKE UP MY NEIGHBOURHOOD, Billy Bragg, 91-54
YOU WON'T BE LEAVING, Herman's Hermits, 66-20
YOU WON'T FIND ANOTHER FOOL LIKE ME, New Seekers featuring Lyn Paul, 73-1
YOU WON'T SEE ME CRY, Wilson Phillips, 92-18
YOU WOULDN'T KNOW LOVE, Cher, 90-55
YOU, YOU ROMEO, Shirley Bassey with Wally Stott and his Orchestra, 57-29
YOU YOU YOU, Alvin Stardust, 74-6
YOU'D BETTER COME HOME, Petula Clark, 65-44
YOU'LL ALWAYS BE A FRIEND, Hot Chocolate, 72-23
YOU'LL ALWAYS FIND ME IN THE KITCHEN AT PARTIES, Jona Lewie, 80-16
YOU'LL ANSWER TO ME, Cleo Laine, 61-5
YOU'LL BE IN MY HEART, Phil Collins, 99-17
YOU'LL BE MINE (PARTY TIME), Gloria Estefan, 96-18
YOU'LL BE SORRY, Steps, 01-4
YOU'LL NEVER BE SO WRONG, Hot Chocolate, 81-52
YOU'LL NEVER FIND ANOTHER LOVE LIKE MINE, Lou Rawls, 76-10
YOU'LL NEVER GET TO HEAVEN [EP], Stylistics, 76-24
YOU'LL NEVER GET TO HEAVEN (IF YOU BREAK MY HEART):
Dionne Warwick, 64-20
Stylistics (from You'll Never Get To Heaven [EP]), 76-24
YOU'LL NEVER KNOW, Shirley Bassey with the Rita Williams Singers and Geoff Love and his Orchestra, 61-6
YOU'LL NEVER KNOW, Hi-Gloss, 81-12
YOU'LL NEVER KNOW WHAT YOU'RE MISSIN' 'TIL YOU TRY, Emile Ford and the Checkmates, 60-12
YOU'LL NEVER KNOW WHAT YOU'RE MISSING, Real Thing, 77-16
YOU'LL NEVER, NEVER KNOW, Platters, 57-23
YOU'LL NEVER STOP ME LOVING YOU, Sonia, 89-1
YOU'LL NEVER WALK ALONE:
Gerry and the Pacemakers, 63-1
Elvis Presley with the Jordanaires, 68-44
Crowd, 85-1
Robson and Jerome, 96-1
Tibor Rudas presents the 3 Tenors Paris 1988: Jose Carreras, Placido Domingo, Luciano Pavarotti, 98-35
YOU'LL SEE, Madonna, 95-5
YOU'RE A BETTER MAN THAN I, Sham 69, 79-49
YOU'RE A LADY, Peter Skellern, 72-3
YOU'RE A STAR, Aquarian Dream, 79-67
YOU'RE ALL I NEED, Motley Crue, 88-23
YOU'RE ALL I NEED TO GET BY:
Marvin Gaye and Tammi Terrell, 68-19
Johnny Mathis and Deniece Williams, 78-45
YOU'RE ALL THAT MATTERS TO ME, Curtis Stigers, 92-6
YOU'RE BEEN DOING ME WRONG, Delegation, 77-49
YOU'RE BREAKING MY HEART, Keely Smith, 65-14
YOU'RE DRIVING ME CRAZY, Temperance Seven vocal refrain by Mr. Paul MacDowall, 61-1
YOU'RE EVERYTHING TO ME, Boris Gardiner, 86-11
(YOU'RE) FABULOUS BABE, Kenny Williams, 77-35
YOU'RE FREE TO GO, Jim Reeves, 72-48
YOU'RE GONNA GET NEXT TO ME, Bo Kirkland and Ruth Davis, 77-12
YOU'RE GONNA MISS ME, Turntable Orchestra, 89-52
YOU'RE GORGEOUS, Babybird, 96-3
"YOU'RE" HAVING MY BABY, Paul Anka, 74-6
YOU'RE HISTORY, Shakespear's Sister, 89-7
YOU'RE IN A BAD WAY, Saint Etienne, 93-12
YOU'RE IN LOVE, Wilson Phillips, 91-29
YOU'RE IN MY HEART, Rod Stewart, 77-3
YOU'RE IN MY HEART, David Essex, 83-59
YOU'RE INVITED (BUT YOUR FRIEND CAN'T COME), Vince Neil, 92-63
YOU'RE LOOKIN' HOT TONIGHT, Barry Manilow, 83-47
YOU'RE LYING, Linx, 80-15
YOU'RE MAKIN ME HIGH, Toni Braxton, 96-7
YOU'RE MORE THAN A NUMBER IN MY LITTLE RED BOOK, Drifters, 76-5
YOU'RE MOVING OUT TODAY, Carole Bayer Sager, 77-6
YOU'RE MY ANGEL, Mikey Graham, 00-13
YOU'RE MY BEST FRIEND, Queen, 76-7
YOU'RE MY BEST FRIEND, Don Williams, 76-35
YOU'RE MY EVERYTHING, Temptations, 67-26
YOU'RE MY EVERYTHING, Max Bygraves, 69-34
YOU'RE MY EVERYTHING:
Lee Garrett, 76-15
East Side Beat, 93-65
YOU'RE MY GIRL, Rockin' Berries, 65-40
YOU'RE MY HEART, YOU'RE MY SOUL, Modern Talking, 85-56
YOU'RE MY LAST CHANCE, 52nd Street, 86-49
YOU'RE MY LIFE, Barry Biggs, 77-36
YOU'RE MY MATE, Right Said Fred, 01-18
YOU'RE MY NUMBER ONE, S Club 7, 99-2
(YOU'RE MY ONE AND ONLY) TRUE LOVE, Ann-Marie Smith, 95-46
(YOU'RE MY) SOUL AND INSPIRATION, Righteous Brothers, 66-15
YOU'RE MY WORLD, Nick Heyward, 88-67
YOU'RE MY WORLD (IL MIO MONDO), Cilla Black, 64-1
YOU'RE NEVER TOO YOUNG, Cool Notes, 84-42
YOU'RE NO GOOD:
Swinging Blue Jeans, 64-3
Aswad, 95-35
YOU'RE NOT ALONE, Olive, 96-42, 97-1
YOU'RE NOT ALONE, Embrace, 00-14
YOU'RE NOT HERE, Tyrrel Corporation, 94-42
YOU'RE O.K., Ottawan, 80-56
YOU'RE OK, k.d. lang, 96-44
YOU'RE ONE, Imperial Teen, 96-69
(YOU'RE PUTTIN') A RUSH ON ME, Stephanie Mills, 87-62
YOU'RE READY NOW, Frankie Valli, 70-11
YOU'RE SINGING OUR LOVE SONG TO SOMEBODY ELSE, Jerry Wallace, 60-46
YOU'RE SIXTEEN:
Johnny Burnette, 61-3
Ringo Starr, 74-4
YOU'RE SO RIGHT FOR ME, Eastside Connection, 78-44
YOU'RE SO VAIN, Carly Simon, 72-3, 91-41
YOU'RE STILL THE ONE, Shania Twain, 98-10
YOU'RE SUCH A GOOD LOOKING WOMAN, Joe Dolan, 70-17
YOU'RE THE BEST THING, Style Council, 84-5
(YOU'RE THE) DEVIL IN DISGUISE, Elvis Presley with the Jordanaires, 63-1
YOU'RE THE FIRST, THE LAST, MY EVERYTHING, Barry White, 74-1
YOU'RE THE GREATEST LOVER, Jonathan King, 79-67
YOU'RE THE INSPIRATION, Chicago, 85-14
YOU'RE THE ONE, Kathy Kirby, 64-17
YOU'RE THE ONE, Petula Clark, 65-23
YOU'RE THE ONE, Bang, 89-74
YOU'RE THE ONE, SWV, 96-13
YOU'RE THE ONE FOR ME, D Train, 82-30, 85-15
YOU'RE THE ONE FOR ME – DAYBREAK – A.M., Paul Hardcastle, 84-41
YOU'RE THE ONE FOR ME, FATTY, Morrissey, 92-19
YOU'RE THE ONE I LOVE, Shola Ama, 97-3
YOU'RE THE ONE THAT I WANT:
John Travolta and Olivia Newton – John, 78-1, 98-4
Hylda Baker and Arthur Mullard, 78-22
Craig McLachlan and Debbie Gibson, 93-13
YOU'RE THE ONLY GOOD THING (THAT HAPPENED TO ME), Jim Reeves, 61-17
YOU'RE THE ONLY ONE, Val Doonican, 68-37
YOU'RE THE REASON, Wamdue Project, 00-39
YOU'RE THE REASON WHY, Rubettes, 76-28
YOU'RE THE STAR, Rod Stewart, 95-19
YOU'RE THE STORY OF MY LIFE, Judy Cheeks, 95-30
YOU'RE THE TOP-CHA, Al Saxon, 59-17
YOU'RE THE VOICE:
John Farnham, 87-6
Heart, 91-56
YOU'RE WALKING, Electribe 101, 90-50
YOU'VE BEEN GONE, Crown Heights Affair, 80-44
YOU'VE COME BACK, P.J. Proby, 66-25
(YOU'VE GOT) PERSONALITY, Lena Zavaroni, 74-33
YOU'VE GOT A FRIEND:
James Taylor, 71-4
Brand New Heavies, 97-9
YOU'VE GOT A FRIEND, Big Fun and Sonia featuring Gary Barnacle on saxophone, 90-14
YOU'VE GOT A LOT TO ANSWER FOR, Catatonia, 96-35
YOU'VE GOT ANOTHER THING COMIN', Judas Priest, 82-66
YOU'VE GOT IT, Simply Red, 89-46
YOU'VE GOT IT BAD, Ocean Colour Scene, 96-7
YOU'VE GOT LOVE, Buddy Holly and the Crickets, 64-40
YOU'VE GOT ME DANGLING ON A STRING, Chairmen Of The Board, 70-5
YOU'VE GOT ME THINKING, Beloved, 93-23
YOU'VE GOT MY NUMBER (WHY DON'T YOU USE IT!), Undertones, 79-32
YOU'VE GOT THAT SOMETHIN', Robyn, 96-54
YOU'VE GOT TO CHOOSE, Darling Buds, 89-45
YOU'VE GOT TO GIVE ME ROOM, Oleta Adams, 91-49
YOU'VE GOT TO HIDE YOUR LOVE AWAY, Silkie, 65-28
YOU'VE GOT YOUR TROUBLES, Fortunes, 65-2
YOU'VE LOST THAT LOVIN' FEELIN':
Cilla Black, 65-2
Righteous Brothers, 65-1, 69-10, 77-42, 90-3
Telly Savalas, 75-47
Daryl Hall and John Oates, 80-55
YOU'VE MADE ME SO VERY HAPPY, Blood, Sweat and Tears, 69-35
(YOU'VE) NEVER BEEN IN LOVE LIKE THIS BEFORE, Unit Four Plus Two, 65-14
YOU'VE NOT CHANGED, Sandie Shaw, 67-18
YOU'VE SAID ENOUGH, Central Line, 82-58
YOUNG AMERICANS, David Bowie, 75-18
YOUNG AMERICANS TALKING, David Van Day, 83-43
YOUNG AND FOOLISH:
Ronnie Hilton, 56-17
Edmund Hockridge with Tony Osborne and his Orchestra, 56-10
Dean Martin, 56-20
YOUNG-AT-HEART, Frank Sinatra, 54-12
YOUNG AT HEART, Bluebells, 84-8, 93-1
YOUNG BLOOD, UFO, 80-36
YOUNG BOY, Paul McCartney, 97-19
YOUNG DISCIPLES [EP], Young Disciples, 92-48
YOUNG EMOTIONS, Ricky Nelson, 60-48
YOUNG, FREE AND SINGLE, Sunfire, 83-20
YOUNG, FRESH N' NEW, Kelis, 01-32
YOUNG, GIFTED AND BLACK, Bob and Marcia, 70-5
YOUNG GIRL:
Union Gap featuring Gary Puckett, 68-1, 74-6
Joe Longthorne, 94-61
Darren Day, 94-42
YOUNG GIRLS AND HAPPY ENDINGS, Gorky's Zygotic Mynci, 97-49
YOUNG GODS, Little Angels, 91-34
YOUNG GUNS (GO FOR IT), Wham!, 82-3
YOUNG HEARTS RUN FREE:
Candi Staton, 76-2, 86-47
Kym Mazelle, 97-20
Candi Staton, 99-29

EP INDEX

ALBUM INDEX

AMNESIAC, Radiohead, 01-1
AMONG MY SWAN, Mazzy Star, 96-57
AMONG THE LIVING, Anthrax, 87-18
AMOR, Julio Iglesias, 82-14
AMORE – THE LOVE ALBUM, Luciano Pavarotti, 01-41
AMORICA, Black Crowes, 94-8
AMOUR – THE ULTIMATE LOVE COLLECTION, Various Artists: Selected Series – Ultimate, 97-3
AMPLIFIED HEART, Everything But The Girl, 94-20
AMUSED TO DEATH, Roger Waters, 92-8
THE ANALOGUE THEATRE, C.J. Bolland, 96-43
ANAM, Clannad, 90-14
ANARCHY, Chumbawamba, 94-29
ANARCHY, Busta Rhymes, 00-38
ANCIENT HEART, Tanita Tikaram, 88-3
AND, John Martyn, 96-32
AND ALL BECAUSE THE LADY LOVES . . ., Various Artists: Compilations – Dover, 89-2
AND I LOVE YOU SO, Shirley Bassey, 72-24
AND I LOVE YOU SO, Perry Como, 73-1
AND I LOVE YOU SO, Howard Keel, 84-6
. . . AND JUSTICE FOR ALL, Metallica, 88-4
AND NOW THE LEGACY BEGINS, Dream Warriors, 91-18
. . . AND OUT COME THE WOLVES, Rancid, 95-55
AND STILL I RISE, Alison Limerick, 92-53
. . . AND THE BEAT GOES ON, Various Artists: Compilations – Telstar, 88-12
. . . AND THEN THERE WERE THREE . . ., Genesis, 78-3
ANDERSON BRUFORD WAKEMAN HOWE, Anderson Bruford Wakeman Howe, 89-14
ANDREW LLOYD WEBBER – GOLD, Various Artists: Selected Series – Andrew Lloyd Webber, 01-5
ANDREW LLOYD WEBBER: REQUIEM, Placido Domingo, Sarah Brightman, Paul Miles-Kingston, Winchester Cathedral Choir and the English Chamber Orchestra conducted by Lorin Maazel, 85-4
ANDREW LLOYD WEBBER – THE PREMIERE COLLECTION, Various Artists: Compilations – Really Useful/Polydor, 88-1
ANDROMEDA HEIGHTS, Prefab Sprout, 97-7
ANDY STEWART, Andy Stewart, 62-13
ANDY WILLIAMS' GREATEST HITS, Andy Williams, 70-1
ANDY WILLIAMS SHOW, Andy Williams, 70-10
ANDY WILLIAMS' SOUND OF MUSIC, Andy Williams, 70-22
ANGEL CLARE, Art Garfunkel, 73-14
ANGEL DELIGHT, Fairport Convention, 71-8
ANGEL DUST, Faith No More, 92-2
ANGEL STATION, Manfred Mann's Earth Band, 79-30
ANGELIC UPSTARTS, Angelic Upstarts, 81-27
ANGELS & ELECTRICITY, Eddi Reader, 98-49
ANGELS WITH DIRTY FACES, Tricky, 98-23
ANIMAL BOY, Ramones, 86-38
ANIMAL MAGIC, Blow Monkeys, 86-21
ANIMAL MAGNETISM, Scorpions, 80-23
ANIMAL RIGHTS, Moby, 96-38
ANIMAL TRACKS, Animals, 65-6
ANIMALISMS, Animals, 66-4
ANIMALIZE, Kiss, 84-11
THE ANIMALS, Animals, 64-6
ANIMALS, Pink Floyd, 77-2
ANIMATION, Jon Anderson, 82-43
ANNIE, Various Artists: Films – Original Soundtracks, 82-83
ANNIVERSARY – 20 YEARS OF HITS, Tammy Wynette, 87-45
THE ANNUAL, Various Artists: Selected Series – The Annual, 95-13
THE ANNUAL II – MIXED BY PETE TONG & BOY GEORGE, Various Artists: Selected Series – The Annual, 96-1
THE ANNUAL III – PETE TONG & BOY GEORGE, Various Artists: Selected Series – The Annual, 97-1
THE ANNUAL IV – JUDGE JULES & BOY GEORGE, Various Artists: Selected Series – The Annual, 98-1
THE ANNUAL – MILLENNIUM EDITION – MIXED BY JUDGE JULES & TALL PAUL, Various Artists: Selected Series – The Annual, 99-2
THE ANNUAL – SPRING 2001, Various Artists: Selected Series – The Annual, 01-1
THE ANNUAL 2000 – MIXED BY JUDGE JULES & TALL PAUL, Various Artists: Selected Series – The Annual, 00-1
THE ANNUAL 2002 – LIMITED EDITION BOX SET, Various Artists: Selected Series – The Annual, 01-1
ANOMIE & BONHOMIE, Scritti Politti, 99-33
ANOTHER GREY AREA, Graham Parker, 82-40
ANOTHER KIND OF BLUES, U.K. Subs, 79-21
ANOTHER LEVEL, Blackstreet, 96-26
ANOTHER LEVEL, Another Level, 98-13
ANOTHER MONTY PYTHON RECORD, Monty Python's Flying Circus, 71-26
ANOTHER MUSIC IN A DIFFERENT KITCHEN, Buzzcocks, 78-15
ANOTHER NIGHT – U.S. ALBUM, Real McCoy, 95-6
ANOTHER PAGE, Christopher Cross, 83-4
ANOTHER PERFECT DAY, Motorhead, 83-20
ANOTHER PERFECT DAY, Various Artists: Compilations – Columbia, 98-13
ANOTHER PLACE AND TIME, Donna Summer, 89-17
ANOTHER SIDE OF BOB DYLAN, Bob Dylan, 64-8
ANOTHER STEP, Kim Wilde, 86-73
ANOTHER STRING OF HITS, Shadows, 80-16
ANOTHER TICKET, Eric Clapton, 81-18
ANOTHER TIME, ANOTHER PLACE, Engelbert Humperdinck, 71-48
ANOTHER TIME, ANOTHER PLACE, Bryan Ferry, 74-4
ANOTHER WORLD, Brian May, 98-23
ANOTHER YEAR, Leo Sayer, 75-8
ANSWERS TO NOTHING, Midge Ure, 88-30
ANTENNA, ZZ Top, 94-3
ANTHEM, Toyah, 81-2
ANTHEM, Black Uhuru, 84-90
THE ANTHEMS '92–'97, Various Artists: Compilations – United Dance, 97-8
THE ANTHOLOGY, Deep Purple, 85-50
ANTHOLOGY, Alien Ant Farm, 01-11
ANTHOLOGY 1, Beatles, 95-2
ANTHOLOGY 2, Beatles, 96-1
ANTHOLOGY 3, Beatles, 96-4
ANTHOLOGY – THE SOUNDS OF SCIENCE, Beastie Boys, 99-36
ANTHOLOGY – THROUGH THE YEARS, Tom Petty and the Heartbreakers, 01-14
ANTICHRIST SUPERSTAR, Marilyn Manson, 96-73
THE ANTIDOTE, Ronny Jordan, 92-52
ANTMUSIC – THE VERY BEST OF ADAM ANT, Adam Ant/Adam and the Ants, 93-6
ANUTHA ZONE, Dr. John, 98-33
THE ANVIL, Visage, 82-6
ANY LOVE, Luther Vandross, 88-3
ANYMORE FOR ANYMORE, Ronnie Lane and the band Slim Chance, 74-48
ANYTHING, Damned, 86-40
ANYTHING FOR YOU, Gloria Estefan and Miami Sound Machine, 88-1
ANYTHING IS POSSIBLE, Debbie Gibson, 91-69
ANYTIME ANYWHERE, Rita Coolidge, 77-6
ANYWAY, Family, 70-7
ANYWAYAWANNA, Beatmasters, 89-30
ANYWHERE, New Musik, 81-68
APOCADELIC, Point Break, 00-21
APOCALYPSE 91 . . . THE ENEMY STRIKES BLACK, Public Enemy, 91-8
APPETITE FOR DESTRUCTION, Guns N' Roses, 87-5
APPLE VENUS – VOLUME 1, XTC, 99-42
APPLE VENUS – VOLUME 2, XTC + Wasp Star, 00-40
APPOLONIA / FEEL THE DROP, B M Ex, 93-17
APPROVED BY THE MOTORS, Motors, 78-60
APRIL MOON, Sam Brown, 90-38
AQUALUNG, Jethro Tull, 71-4
AQUARIUM, Aqua, 97-6
AQUARIUS, Aqua, 00-24
ARBORESCENCE, Ozric Tentacles, 94-18
ARC OF A DIVER, Steve Winwood, 81-13
ARCHITECTURE & MORALITY, Orchestral Manoeuvres In The Dark, 81-3
ARCHIVE 1967-75, Genesis, 98-35
ARCHIVE ONE, Dave Clarke, 96-36
ARE YOU EXPERIENCED, Jimi Hendrix Experience, 67-2
ARE YOU GONNA GO MY WAY, Lenny Kravitz, 93-1
ARE YOU NORMAL?, Ned's Atomic Dustbin, 92-13
ARE YOU OKAY?, Was (Not Was), 90-35
ARE YOU READY?, Bucks Fizz, 82-10
ARENA, Duran Duran, 84-6
ARETHA, Aretha Franklin, 86-51
ARETHA NOW, Aretha Franklin, 68-6
ARGUS, Wishbone Ash, 72-3
ARGY BARGY, Squeeze, 80-32
THE ARGUMENT, Fugazi, 01-63
ARIA – THE OPERA ALBUM, Andrea Bocelli, 98-33
ARISE, Sepultura, 91-40
THE ARISTOCATS – REAL ALONG, Various Artists: Films – Original Soundtracks, 00-60
ARKANSAS TRAVELER, Michelle Shocked, 92-46
ARKOLOGY, Lee 'Scratch' Perry, 97-49
ARMAGEDDON, Various Artists: Films – Original Soundtracks, 98-19
ARMCHAIR MELODIES, David Gray and Tommy Tycho, 76-21
ARMCHAIR THEATRE, Jeff Lynne, 90-24
ARMED FORCES, Elvis Costello and the Attractions, 79-2
AROUND THE FUR, Deftones, 97-56
AROUND THE NEXT DREAM, BBM, 94-9
AROUND THE WORLD IN A DAY, Prince and the Revolution, 85-5
AROUND THE WORLD – LIVE IN CONCERT, Osmonds, 76-41
AROUND THE WORLD – THE JOURNEY SO FAR, East 17, 96-3
ARRIVAL, Abba, 76-1
ART AND ILLUSION, Twelfth Night, 84-83
THE ART GARFUNKEL ALBUM, Art Garfunkel, 84-12
THE ART OF CHRIS FARLOWE, Chris Farlowe, 66-37
THE ART OF FALLING APART, Soft Cell, 83-5
THE ART OF WAR, Bone Thugs-N-Harmony, 97-42
ART OFFICIAL INTELLIGENCE: MOSAIC THUMP, De La Soul, 00-22
THE ARTFUL DODGER PRESENTS RE-REWIND BACK BY PUBLIC DEMAND Various Artists: Selected Series – Artful Dodger . . . Rewind, 00-6
THE ARTFUL DODGER PRESENTS REWIND 2001 – LESSONS FROM THE UNDERGROUND, Various Artists: Selected Series – Artful Dodger . . . Rewind, 01-12
ARTIFICIAL INTELLIGENCE II, Various Artists: Compilations – Warp, 94-16
THE ARTISTS VOLUME 1, Earth Wind And Fire/Jean Carn/Rose Royce, 85-65
THE ARTISTS VOLUME 2, Luther Vandross/Teddy Pendergrass/Change/Atlantic Starr, 85-45
THE ARTISTS VOLUME III, Womack and Womack/O'Jays/Kleeer/S.O.S. Band, 85-87
AS IS, Manfred Mann, 66-22
AS IT HAPPENS, Dr. Feelgood, 79-42
AS ONE, Kool And The Gang, 82-49
AS ONE, Double Trouble, 90-73
AS RAW AS EVER, Shabba Ranks, 91-51
AS SAFE AS YESTERDAY IS, Humble Pie, 69-32
AS THE BAND TURNS, Atlantic Starr, 85-64
AS TIME GOES BY, Royal Philharmonic Orchestra conducted by Harry Rabinovitz, 84-95
AS TIME GOES BY, Various Artists: Compilations – Dino, 93-14
AS TIME GOES BY, Bryan Ferry, 99-16
AS UGLY AS THEY WANNA BE, Ugly Kid Joe, 92-9
ASIA, Asia, 82-11
ASLEEP IN THE BACK, Elbow, 01-14
ASPECTS OF LOVE, Various Artists: Stage Cast – London, 89-1
ASQUARIUS, Cud, 92-30
ASSAULT AND BATTERY, Rose Tattoo, 81-40
ASSAULT ATTACK, Michael Schenker Group, 82-19
ASSEMBLAGE, Japan, 81-26
ASTAIRE, Peter Skellern, 79-23

THE BEST OF DEL AMITRI – HATFUL OF RAIN, Del Amitri, 98-5
BEST OF DIONNE WARWICK, Dionne Warwick, 66-8
THE BEST OF DONNA SUMMER, Donna Summer, 90-24
THE BEST OF DRIVE TIME, Various Artists: Compilations – PolyGram TV, 98-12
THE BEST OF DUSTY SPRINGFIELD, Dusty Springfield, 98-19
THE BEST OF EAGLES, Eagles, 85-8
THE BEST OF EARTH WIND AND FIRE VOLUME 1, Earth, Wind And Fire, 78-6
THE BEST OF ELAINE PAIGE AND BARBARA DICKSON, Elaine Paige and Barbara Dickson, 92-22
THE BEST OF ELVIS COSTELLO – THE MAN, Elvis Costello, 85-8
BEST OF EN VOGUE, En Vogue, 98-39
THE BEST OF EVERYTHING BUT THE GIRL, Everything But The Girl, 96-23
BEST OF FRANK SINATRA, Frank Sinatra, 68-17
THE BEST OF FREE – ALL RIGHT NOW, Free, 91-9
BEST OF FRIENDS, Cleo Laine and John Williams, 78-18
BEST OF GARY NUMAN 1978 – 83, Gary Numan, 93-70
BEST OF GENE PITNEY, Gene Pitney, 69-8
THE BEST OF GLADYS KNIGHT & THE PIPS, Gladys Knight and the Pips, 76-6
THE BEST OF GLENN MILLER, Glenn Miller and his Orchestra, 69-5
THE BEST OF HANK MARVIN AND THE SHADOWS, Hank Marvin and the Shadows, 94-19
THE BEST OF HEARTBEAT, Various Artists: Selected Series – Heartbeat, 95-1
THE BEST OF HELEN REDDY, Helen Reddy, 76-6
THE BEST OF HOOKED ON CLASSICS, Royal Philharmonic Orchestra conducted by Louis Clark, 83-51
BEST OF HOUSE '88, Various Artists: Compilations – Telstar, 88-11
BEST OF HOUSE MEGAMIX, Various Artists: Compilations – Serious, 87-77
BEST OF HOUSE MEXAMIX VOLUME 2, Various Artists: Compilations – Serious, 88-73
THE BEST OF HOUSE VOLUME 1, Various Artists: Compilations – Serious, 87-55
BEST OF HOUSE VOLUME 2, Various Artists: Compilations – Serious, 87-30
BEST OF HOUSE VOLUME 3, Various Artists: Compilations – Serious, 87-61
BEST OF HOUSE VOLUME 4, Various Artists: Compilations – Serious, 88-27
THE BEST OF HOWARD JONES, Howard Jones, 93-36
THE BEST OF INCANTATION: MUSIC FROM THE ANDES, Incantation, 85-28
THE BEST OF INDIE TOP 20, Various Artists: Compilations – Beechwood Music, 91-10
THE BEST OF JAMES, James, 98-1
THE BEST OF JAMES BOND – 30TH ANNIVERSARY COLLECTION, Various Artists: Films – Related Compilations, 92-2
THE BEST OF JAMES BROWN – THE GODFATHER OF SOUL, James Brown, 87-17
THE BEST OF JASPER CARROTT, Jasper Carrott, 78-38
THE BEST OF JIM REEVES, Jim Reeves, 65-3
THE BEST OF JOHN DENVER, John Denver, 74-7
BEST OF JOHN DENVER VOLUME 2, John Denver, 77-9
THE BEST OF JOHNNY CASH, Johnny Cash, 76-48
THE BEST OF JON AND VANGELIS, Jon and Vangelis, 84-42
THE BEST OF LADYSMITH BLACK MAMBAZO – THE STAR AND THE WISEMAN, Ladysmith Black Mambazo, 98-2
THE BEST OF LENA MARTELL, Lena Martell, 77-13
THE BEST OF LOU REED AND THE VELVET UNDERGROUND, Lou Reed and the Velvet Underground, 95-56
BEST OF LUTHER VANDROSS – BEST OF LOVE, Luther Vandross, 89-14
THE BEST OF M PEOPLE, M People, 98-2
THE BEST OF MARVIN GAYE, Marvin Gaye, 76-56
THE BEST OF MASTERCUTS, Various Artists: Compilations – Virgin, 96-11
THE BEST OF MATT BIANCO, Matt Bianco, 90-49
THE BEST OF ME, Maxi Priest, 91-23
THE BEST OF ME, Bryan Adams, 99-12
THE BEST OF MICHAEL BALL, Michael Ball, 94-25
THE BEST OF MICHAEL JACKSON, Michael Jackson, 81-11
THE BEST OF MICHAEL JACKSON & THE JACKSON FIVE – THE MOTOWN YEARS, Michael Jackson and the Jackson Five, 97-5
THE BEST OF MIRAGE: JACK MIX '88, Mirage, 87-7
THE BEST OF MOTORHEAD, Motorhead, 00-52
THE BEST OF MY GOLD RECORDS, James Last, 83-42
THE BEST OF NANCI GRIFFITH, Nanci Griffith, 93-27
THE BEST OF NAT 'KING' COLE, Nat 'King' Cole, 68-5
THE BEST OF NAT 'KING' COLE VOLUME 2, Nat 'King' Cole, 70-39
THE BEST OF NEIL DIAMOND, Neil Diamond, 96-68
? (THE BEST OF NEW ORDER) /? (THE REST OF NEW ORDER), New Order, 94-4
THE BEST OF NICK CAVE AND THE BAD SEEDS, Nick Cave and the Bad Seeds, 98-11
THE BEST OF 1968-1973, Steve Miller Band, 90-34
THE BEST OF 1980-1990, U2, 98-4
THE BEST OF 1980-1990 & B-SIDES, U2, 98-1
THE BEST OF OMD, Orchestral Manoeuvres In The Dark, 88-2
THE BEST OF OL' BLUE EYES, Frank Sinatra, 75-30
THE BEST OF 100% DANCE, Various Artists: Selected Series – 100%, 95-11
BEST OF PEGGY LEE VOLUME 2, Peggy Lee, 61-18
THE BEST OF QUINCY JONES, Quincy Jones, 82-41
THE BEST OF R.E.M., R.E.M., 91-7
THE BEST OF RADIO LUXEMBOURG, Various Artists: Radio – Related Compilations , 63-14
THE BEST OF RAINBOW, Rainbow, 81-14
THE BEST OF RICHARD CLAYDERMAN, Richard Clayderman, 97-73
THE BEST OF RICKY MARTIN, Ricky Martin, 01-42
THE BEST OF ROCK 'N' ROLL LOVE SONGS, Various Artists: Compilations – Dino, 94-9
THE BEST OF ROD STEWART, Rod Stewart, 77-18
THE BEST OF ROD STEWART, Rod Stewart, 89-3
THE BEST OF ROD STEWART AND THE FACES 1971-1975, Rod Stewart and the Faces, 92-58
THE BEST OF . . . ROMANTIC CALLAS, Maria Callas (Soprano), 01-32
THE BEST OF ROXY MUSIC, Roxy Music, 01-12
THE BEST OF ROY ORBISON, Roy Orbison, 75-1
THE BEST OF SADE, Sade, 94-6
THE BEST OF SELLERS, Peter Sellers, 59-3
THE BEST OF SHIRLEY BASSEY, Shirley Bassey, 92-27
THE BEST OF SIMPLE MINDS, Simple Minds, 01-34
THE BEST OF SPANDAU BALLET, Spandau Ballet, 91-44
THE BEST OF STATUS QUO, Status Quo, 73-32
THE BEST OF – SUEDEHEAD, Morrissey, 97-26
THE BEST OF T. REX, T. Rex, 71-21
THE BEST OF TAMMY WYNETTE, Tammy Wynette, 75-4
THE BEST OF TAVARES, Tavares, 78-39
THE BEST OF 10 YEARS – 32 SUPERHITS, Boney M, 86-35
THE BEST OF THE ALAN PARSONS PROJECT, Alan Parsons Project, 83-99
THE BEST OF THE ART OF NOISE, Art Of Noise, 88-55
THE BEST OF THE B-52'S – DANCE THIS MESS AROUND, B-52's, 90-36
BEST OF THE BEACH BOYS, Beach Boys, 66-2
THE BEST OF THE BEACH BOYS, Beach Boys, 95-25
BEST OF THE BEACH BOYS VOLUME 2, Beach Boys, 67-3
BEST OF THE BEACH BOYS VOLUME 3, Beach Boys, 68-8
THE BEST OF THE BEAST, Iron Maiden, 96-16
BEST OF THE BEE GEES, Bee Gees, 69-7
THE BEST OF THE CHRISTIANS, Christians, 93-22
THE BEST OF THE CLASSICAL BITS, Various Artists: Television – Related Compilations, 93-7
THE BEST OF THE COMPOSERS: BEETHOVEN/STRAUSS/TCHAIKOWSKY/MOZART, Various Artists: Compilations – Ronco, 82-49
THE BEST OF THE CORRS, Corrs, 01-6
THE BEST OF THE DAMNED, Damned, 81-43
THE BEST OF THE DOOLEYS, Dooleys, 79-6
THE BEST OF THE DOORS, Doors, 91-17
THE BEST OF THE DOORS, Doors, 00-9
BEST OF THE DUBLINERS, Dubliners, 67-25
THE BEST OF THE FACES, Faces, 77-24
THE BEST OF THE FOUR TOPS, Four Tops, 82-13
BEST OF THE GOONS SHOWS, Goons, 59-8
BEST OF THE GOONS SHOWS VOLUME 2, Goons, 60-11
THE BEST OF THE ICICLE WORKS, Icicle Works, 92-60
THE BEST OF THE MAMAS AND PAPAS, Mamas and the Papas, 77-6
THE BEST OF THE MAVERICKS, Mavericks, 99-40
THE BEST OF THE NINETIES . . . SO FAR, Various Artists: Compilations – EMI, 96-9
THE BEST OF THE POGUES, Pogues, 91-11
THE BEST OF THE REAL THING, Real Thing, 86-24
THE BEST OF THE SEEKERS, Seekers, 68-1
THE BEST OF THE STYLISTICS, Stylistics, 75-1
BEST OF THE STYLISTICS VOLUME 2, Stylistics, 76-1
THE BEST OF THE TROGGS, Troggs, 67-24
BEST OF THE 20TH CENTURY BOY, Marc Bolan and T. Rex, 85-5
THE BEST OF THE UNDERTONES – TEENAGE KICKS, Undertones, 93-45
THE BEST OF THE VILLAGE PEOPLE, Village People, 93-72
THE BEST OF THE WATERBOYS '81-'90, Waterboys, 91-2
BEST OF THUNDER – THEIR FINEST HOUR (AND A BIT), Thunder, 95-22
BEST OF TONY CHRISTIE, Tony Christie, 76-28
THE BEST OF TUBULAR BELLS, Mike Oldfield, 01-60
THE BEST OF 2 TONE, Various Artists: Compilations – 2 Tone, 93-10
THE BEST OF UB40 – VOLUME ONE, UB40, 87-3
THE BEST OF UB40 – VOLUME TWO, UB40, 95-12
THE BEST OF VAN HALEN – VOLUME 1, Van Halen, 96-45
THE BEST OF VAN MORRISON, Van Morrison, 90-4
THE BEST OF VAN MORRISON VOLUME 2, Van Morrison, 93-31
THE BEST OF VYBIN', Various Artists: Compilations – Sony TV/Global TV, 96-12
BEST OF WEST COAST HIP HOP, Various Artists: Compilations – Street Sounds, 87-80
THE BEST OF WHAM! . . . IF YOU WERE THERE. . ., Wham!, 97-4
THE BEST OF WOMAN TO WOMAN, Various Artists: Compilations – PolyGram TV, 96-3
THE BEST OPERA ALBUM IN THE WORLD . . . EVER!, Various Artists: Selected Series – Best . . . Ever!, 96-10
THE BEST PARTY . . . EVER!, Various Artists: Selected Series – Best . . . Ever!, 95-5
THE BEST PARTY IN THE WORLD . . . EVER! 2, Various Artists: Selected Series – Best . . . Ever!, 97-7
THE BEST PARTY IN TOWN . . . EVER!, Various Artists: Selected Series – Best . . . Ever!, 01-19
THE BEST PEPSI CHART ALBUM IN THE WORLD . . . EVER!, Various Artists: Selected Series – Best . . . Ever!, 99-2

BLACK ANGEL, Mica Paris, 98-59
BLACK CELEBRATION, Depeche Mode, 86-4
BLACK COFFEE, Peggy Lee, 61-20
BLACK DIAMOND, Angie Stone, 00-62
BLACK EYED MAN, Cowboy Junkies, 92-21
BLACK IS BLACK, Los Bravos, 66-29
BLACK JOY, Various Artists: Compilations – Ronco, 77-26
BLACK LOVE, Afghan Whigs, 96-41
BLACK MAGIC, Various Artists: Compilations – Stylus, 86-26
BLACK MARKET MUSIC, Placebo, 00-6
BLACK MEANING GOOD, Rebel MC, 91-23
BLACK MOSES, Isaac Hayes, 72-38
BLACK OUT!, Method Man and Redman, 99-45
THE BLACK RIDER, Tom Waits, 93-47
BLACK ROSE (A ROCK LEGEND), Thin Lizzy, 79-2
BLACK SABBATH, Black Sabbath, 70-8
BLACK SABBATH LIVE AT LAST, Black Sabbath, 80-5
BLACK SABBATH VOLUME 4, Black Sabbath, 72-8
BLACK SEA, XTC, 80-16
BLACK SECRET TECHNOLOGY, A Guy Called Gerald, 95-64
BLACK SUNDAY, Cypress Hill, 93-13
THE BLACK SWAN, Triffids, 89-63
BLACK TIE WHITE NOISE, David Bowie, 93-1
BLACK TIGER, Y and T, 82-53
BLACK UHURU, Black Uhuru, 81-81
BLACK VELVET, Various Artists: Compilations – Warwick, 78-72
BLACKMARKET PRESENTS 2 STEP – THE BEST OF UNDERGROUND GARAGE, Various Artists: Compilations – Azuli, 00-17
BLACKOUT, Scorpions, 82-11
BLACKS' MAGIC, Salt 'N Pepa, 90-70
BLACKSTREET, Blackstreet, 94-35
BLADERUNNER [OST], Vangelis, 94-20
BLAH-BLAH-BLAH, Iggy Pop, 86-43
BLAM!!, Brothers Johnson, 78-48
BLAME IT ON THE BOOGIE, Various Artists: Compilations – PolyGram TV, 92-5
BLAME PRESENT LOGICAL PROGRESSION LEVEL 2, Various Artists: Compilations – Good Looking, 97-12
BLAST, Holly Johnson, 89-1
BLAST OFF, Stray Cats, 89-58
BLAZE OF GLORY, Joe Jackson, 89-36
BLAZE OF GLORY/YOUNG GUNS II [OST], Jon Bon Jovi, 90-2
BLAZING BULLETS, Various Artists: Compilations – Ronco, 75-17
BLEACH, Nirvana, 92-33
BLESS ITS POINTED LITTLE HEAD, Jefferson Airplane, 69-38
BLESSED BURDEN, Carleen Anderson, 98-51
BLIND, Icicle Works, 88-40
BLIND, Sundays, 92-15
BLIND BEFORE I STOP, Meat Loaf, 86-28
BLIND DOG AT ST. DUNSTAN'S, Caravan, 76-53
BLIND FAITH, Blind Faith, 69-1
THE BLIND LEADING THE NAKED, Violent Femmes, 86-81
BLIND MAN'S ZOO, 10,000 Maniacs, 89-18
BLIND MELON, Blind Melon, 94-53
THE BLISS ALBUM . . . ? (VIBRATIONS OF LOVE AND ANGER AND THE PONDERANCE OF LIFE AND EXISTENCE), PM Dawn, 93-9
BLISSED OUT, Beloved, 90-38
BLITZ, Various Artists: Stage Cast – London, 62-7
A BLITZ OF SALT-N-PEPA HITS (THE HITS REMIXED), Salt-N-Pepa, 91-70
BLOCKBUSTER! – THE SENSATIONAL 70'S, Various Artists: Compilations – Castle Communications, 92-6
BLOKE ON BLOKE, Billy Bragg, 97-72
BLONDE ON BLONDE, Bob Dylan, 66-3
BLONDES HAVE MORE FUN, Rod Stewart, 78-3
BLONDIE, Blondie, 79-75
BLOOD, This Mortal Coil, 91-28
BLOOD AND CHOCOLATE, Elvis Costello and the Attractions, 86-16
BLOOD, FIRE AND LIVE, Almighty, 90-62
BLOOD FROM STONE, Dare, 91-48
BLOOD ON THE DANCE FLOOR – HISTORY IN THE MIX, Michael Jackson, 97-1
BLOOD ON THE TRACKS, Bob Dylan, 75-4
BLOOD SUGAR SEX MAGIK, Red Hot Chili Peppers, 91-25
BLOOD SWEAT AND TEARS, Blood Sweat And Tears, 69-15
BLOOD SWEAT AND TEARS 3, Blood Sweat And Tears, 70-14
BLOODFLOWERS, Cure, 00-14
BLOODY TOURISTS, 10 C.C., 78-3
BLOW UP YOUR VIDEO, AC/DC, 88-2
BLOWBACK, Tricky, 01-34
BLUE, Joni Mitchell, 71-3
BLUE, Double, 86-69
BLUE, Mission, 96-73
BLUE, Simply Red, 98-1
BLUE BELL KNOLL, Cocteau Twins, 88-15
THE BLUE CAFE, Chris Rea, 98-10
BLUE EYED SOUL, Various Artists: Compilations – Telstar, 92-4
BLUE FOR YOU, Status Quo, 76-1
BLUE FOR YOU – THE VERY BEST OF NINA SIMONE, Nina Simone, 98-12
BLUE GENE, Gene Pitney, 64-7
BLUE HAWAII [OST], Elvis Presley with the Jordainaires, 61-1
BLUE IS THE COLOUR, Beautiful South, 96-1
BLUE JAYS, Justin Hayward and John Lodge, 75-4
BLUE LIGHT, RED LIGHT, Harry Connick Jr., 91-16
BLUE LINES, Massive, 91-13
THE BLUE MEANING, Toyah, 80-40
BLUE MOVES, Elton John, 76-3
BLUE MURDER, Blue Murder, 89-45
BLUE PRINT, Rory Gallagher, 73-12
BLUE ROSES FROM THE MOONS, Nanci Griffith, 97-64
BLUE SKIES, Frank Ifield, 64-10
BLUE SKIES, Kiri Te Kanawa with Nelson Riddle and his Orchestra, 85-40
BLUE SKY MINING, Midnight Oil, 90-28
BLUE SUEDE SHOES, Elvis Presley, 98-39
BLUE SUNSHINE, Glove, 83-35
BLUE VELVET, Bobby Vinton, 90-67
BLUE VIEWS, Paul Carrack, 96-55
THE BLUEBELLS – THE SINGLES COLLECTION, Bluebells, 93-27
BLUEBIRD, James Last, 83-57
THE BLUEPRINT, Jay-Z, 01-30
BLUES, Jimi Hendrix, 94-10
BLUES, Eric Clapton, 99-52
THE BLUES ALBUM, Various Artists: Compilations – Virgin, 95-8
BLUES ALIVE, Gary Moore, 93-8
THE BLUES ALONE, John Mayall, 67-24
BLUES ANYTIME, Various Artists: Compilations – Immediate, 68-40
BLUES BREAKERS, John Mayall with Eric Clapton, 66-6
BLUES BROTHER SOUL SISTER, Various Artists: Compilations – Dino, 93-1
BLUES BROTHER SOUL SISTER VOLUME 2, Various Artists: Compilations – Dino, 93-8
BLUES BROTHER SOUL SISTER VOLUME 3, Various Artists: Compilations – Dino, 94-5
BLUES BROTHER SOUL SISTER CLASSICS, Various Artists: Compilations – Universal Music TV, 99-8
THE BLUES BROTHERS [OST], Blues Brothers, 87-4
THE BLUES EXPERIENCE, Various Artists: Compilations – PolyGram TV, 93-7
BLUES FOR ALLAH, Grateful Dead, 75-45
BLUES FOR GREENEY, Gary Moore, 95-14
BLUES FROM LAUREL CANYON, John Mayall, 69-33
THE BLUES VOLUME 1, Various Artists: Compilations – Pye, 64-15
THE BLUES VOLUME 2, Various Artists: Compilations – Pye, 64-16
BLUR, Blur, 97-1
BLUR: THE BEST OF, Blur, 00-3
BLURRING THE EDGES, Meredith Brooks, 97-5
BO DIDDLEY, Bo Diddley, 63-11
BO DIDDLEY IS A GUNSLINGER, Bo Diddley, 63-20
BO DIDDLEY RIDES AGAIN, Bo Diddley, 63-19
BO DIDDLEY'S BEACH PARTY, Bo Diddley, 64-13
BOAT TO BOLIVIA, Martin Stephenson and the Daintees, 86-85
THE BOATMAN'S CALL, Nick Cave and the Bad Seeds, 97-22
BOB DYLAN, Bob Dylan, 65-13
BOB DYLAN AT BUDOKAN, Bob Dylan, 79-4
BOB MOULD, Bob Mould, 96-52
BOBBIE GENTRY AND GLEN CAMPBELL, Bobbie Gentry and Glen Campbell, 70-50
BOBBY, Bobby Brown, 92-11
BOBBY CRUSH, Bobby Crush, 72-15
THE BOBBY CRUSH INCREDIBLE DOUBLE DECKER PARTY 101 GREAT SONGS, Bobby Crush, 82-53
BOBBY DIGITAL IN STEREO, RZA, 98-70
BOBBY VEE MEETS THE CRICKETS, Bobby Vee and the Crickets, 62-2
A BOBBY VEE RECORDING SESSION, Bobby Vee, 63-10
THE BOBBY VEE SINGLES ALBUM, Bobby Vee, 80-5
BOBBY VEE'S GOLDEN GREATS, Bobby Vee, 63-10
BOCES, Mercury Rev, 93-43
BODIES AND SOULS, Manhattan Transfer, 84-53
BODY AND SOUL, Joe Jackson, 84-14
BODY AND SOUL – HEART AND SOUL II, Various Artists: Compilations – Heart and Soul, 90-2
THE BODY AND SOUL OF TOM JONES, Tom Jones, 73-31
BODY EXIT MIND, New Fast Automatic Daffodils, 92-57
BODY TALK, Imagination, 81-20
BODY TO BODY, Technotronic, 91-27
BODY WISHES, Rod Stewart, 83-5
THE BODYGUARD, Various Artists: Films – Original Soundtracks, 92-1
BOHEME, Deep Forest, 95-12
BOING!, Airhead, 92-29
BOLAN BOOGIE, T. Rex, 72-1
BOMBER, Motorhead, 79-12
BON JOVI, Bon Jovi, 84-71
BONA DRAG, Morrissey, 90-9
BONAFIDE, Maxi Priest, 90-11
BONE MACHINE, Tom Waits, 92-26
BONKERS 2, Various Artists: Selected Series – Bonkers, 97-10
BONKERS 3 – JOURNEY INTO MADNESS, Various Artists: Selected Series – Bonkers, 97-9
BONKERS 4 – WORLD FRENZY, Various Artists: Selected Series – Bonkers, 98-8
BONKERS 5 – ANARCHY IN THE UNIVERSE, Various Artists: Selected Series – Bonkers, 98-12
BONKERS 6 (WHEEL CRAZY), Various Artists: Selected Series – Bonkers, 99-10
BONKERS 7 – MILLENNIUM MADNESS, Various Artists: Selected Series – Bonkers, 99-18
BOOGIE BUS, Various Artists: Compilations – Polystar, 79-23
BOOGIE FEVER, Various Artists: Compilations – Ronco, 78-15
BOOGIE NIGHTS, Various Artists: Compilations – Ronco, 78-5
BOOGIE NIGHTS, Various Artists: Films – Original Soundtracks, 98-19
BOOGIE WITH CANNED HEAT, Canned Heat, 68-5
BOOK OF DAYS, Psychedelic Furs, 89-74
BOOK OF DREAMS, Steve Miller Band, 77-12
THE BOOK OF INVASIONS – A CELTIC SYMPHONY, Horslips, 77-39
BOOKBINDER'S KID, Elkie Brooks, 88-57
BOOKENDS, Simon and Garfunkel, 68-1
BOOM BOOM, John Lee Hooker, 92-15
BOOMANIA, Betty Boo, 90-4
BOOMBASTIC, Shaggy, 95-37
BOOMERANG, Various Artists: Films – Original Soundtracks, 92-17
BOOMTOWN RATS, Boomtown Rats, 77-18
BOOTH AND THE BAD ANGEL, Booth and the Bad Angel, 96-35
THE BOOTLEG SERIES VOLUMES 1 – 3, Bob Dylan, 91-32
THE BOOTLEG VERSIONS, Fugees (Refugee Camp), 96-55
BOOTS, Nancy Sinatra, 66-12
BOP TILL YOU DROP, Ry Cooder, 79-36
THE BOP WON'T STOP, Shakin' Stevens, 83-21
BORDER LINE, Ry Cooder, 80-35
BORN, China Black, 95-27
BORN, Bond, 00-16
BORN A WOMAN, Sandy Posey, 67-39
BORN AGAIN, Black Sabbath, 83-4
BORN AGAIN, Notorious B.I.G., 99-70
BORN DEAD, Body Count, 94-15

BUDDY HOLLY'S GREATEST HITS, Buddy Holly, 67-9
BUDDY'S SONG [OST], Chesney Hawkes, 91-18
BUENA VISTA SOCIAL CLUB, Ry Cooder, 97-44
BUENA VISTA SOCIAL CLUB PRESENTS . . ., Ibrahim Ferrer, 99-42
BUENAS NOCHES FROM A LONELY ROOM, Dwight Yoakam, 88-87
THE BUFFALO SKINNERS, Big Country, 93-25
BUFFY THE VAMPIRE SLAYER – THE ALBUM, Various Artists: Television – Soundtracks, 99-7
BUHLOONE MINDSTATE, De La Soul, 93-37
BUILD, Innocence, 92-66
BUILDING THE PERFECT BEAST, Don Henley, 85-14
BUILT TO DESTROY, Michael Schenker Group, 83-23
BULLET FROM A GUN, Derek B, 88-11
BULLINAMINGVASE, Roy Harper, 77-25
BULLY FOR YOU, B.A. Robertson, 81-61
BUMMED, Happy Mondays, 90-59
BUMP AHEAD, Mr. Big, 93-61
BURN, Deep Purple, 74-3
BURN MY EYES, Machine Head, 94-25
BURNED, Electrafixion, 95-38
BURNIN' SKY, Bad Company, 77-17
BURNING BLUE SOUL, The, 93-65
BURNING FROM THE INSIDE, Bauhaus, 83-13
BURNING HEARTS, Various Artists: Compilations – Telstar, 91-7
THE BURNING RED, Machine Head, 99-13
BURNT WEENY SANDWICH, Mothers Of Invention, 70-17
BURY THE HATCHET, Cranberries, 99-7
BUSINESS AS USUAL, Secret Affair, 82-84
BUSINESS AS USUAL, Men At Work, 83-1
BUSINESS AS USUAL, E.P.M.D., 91-69
BUSINESS OF PUNISHMENT, Consolidated, 94-53
BUST A NUT, Tesla, 94-51
BUSTER, Various Artists: Films – Original Soundtracks, 88-2
BUSTING AT THE SEAMS, Strawbs, 73-2
BUSY BODY, Luther Vandross, 84-42
. . . BUT SERIOUSLY, Phil Collins, 89-1
BUT SERIOUSLY FOLKS . . ., Joe Walsh, 78-16
BUTTERFLY, Mariah Carey, 97-2
BUTTON-DOWN MIND OF BOB NEWHART, Bob Newhart, 60-2
BUY NOW . . . SAVED LATER, One Minute Silence, 00-61
BUZZ, Steps, 00-4
BY ALL MEANS, By All Means, 88-80
BY ALL MEANS NECESSARY, Boogie Down Productions, 88-38
BY INVITATION ONLY, Various Artists: Compilations – Atlantic, 76-17
BY REQUEST, Salvation Army, 77-16
BY REQUEST, Lena Martell, 80-9
BY REQUEST, James Last, 87-22
BY REQUEST, Foster and Allen, 93-14
...BY REQUEST, Boyzone, 99-1
BY 7.30, Vonda Shepard, 99-39
BY THE LIGHT OF THE MOON, Los Lobos, 87-77
BY YOUR SIDE, Peters and Lee, 73-9
BY YOUR SIDE, Black Crowes, 99-34
BYE BYE BIRDIE, Various Artists: Stage Cast – London, 61-17
BYE BYE BLUES, Bert Kaempfert, 66-4
BYE BYE BLUES, Brenda Lee, 66-21
BYRDS, Byrds, 73-31
C.C.S., C.C.S., 72-23
C.M.B., Color Me Badd, 91-3
CABARET, Various Artists: Films – Original Soundtracks, 73-13
CACHARPAYA (PANPIPES OF THE ANDES), Incantation, 82-9
CADMIUM, Sky, 83-44
CAFE BLEU, Style Council, 84-2
CAFE CAROLINA, Don Williams, 84-65
CAFE DEL MAR IBIZA – VOLUMEN DOS, Various Artists: Selected Series – Cafe Del Mar, 95-17
CAFE DEL MAR IBIZA – VOLUMEN TRES, Various Artists: Selected Series – Cafe Del Mar, 96-16
CAFE DEL MAR – VOLUMEN CINCO, Various Artists: Selected Series – Cafe Del Mar, 98-16
CAFE DEL MAR – VOLUMEN CUATRO, Various Artists: Selected Series – Cafe Del Mar, 97-18
CAFE DEL MAR – VOLUMEN SEIS, Various Artists: Selected Series – Cafe Del Mar, 99-15
CAFE DEL MAR – VOLUMEN SIETE, Various Artists: Selected Series – Cafe Del Mar, 00-14
CAFE DEL MAR – VOLUMEN OCHO, Various Artists: Selected Series – Cafe Del Mar, 01-12
CAFE LATINO, Various Artists: Compilations – Telstar, 96-18
CAFE MAMBO, Various Artists: Compilations – Virgin/EMI, 97-17
CAFE MAMBO – THE REAL SOUND OF IBIZA, Various Artists: Compilations – Columbia, 00-19
THE CAGE, Tygers Of Pan Tang, 82-13
CAHOOTS, Band, 71-41
CAKE, Trash Can Sinatras, 90-74
CAL [OST], Mark Knopfler, 84-65
CALIFORNIA DREAMIN' – THE VERY BEST OF THE MAMAS AND THE PAPAS, Mamas and the Papas, 95-14
CALIFORNIA DREAMIN' – GREATEST HITS OF THE MAMAS AND THE PAPAS, Mamas and the Papas, 97-30
CALIFORNIA DREAMING, Various Artists: Compilations – K-Tel, 81-27
CALIFORNIA HOLIDAY [OST], Elvis Presley, 66-17
CALIFORNICATION, Red Hot Chili Peppers, 99-5
CALLING ALL STATIONS, Genesis, 97-2
CALLING CARD, Rory Gallagher, 76-32
CALM, Various Artists: Compilations – Decca, 00-14
CAMELOT, Various Artists: Stage Cast – Broadway, 64-10
CAMELOT, Various Artists: Stage Cast – London, 65-19
CAMELOT, Various Artists: Films – Original Soundtracks, 68-37
CAMOUFLAGE, Rod Stewart, 84-8
CAN-CAN, Various Artists: Films – Original Soundtracks, 60-2
CAN-I-BUS, Canibus, 98-43
CAN I PLAY WITH MADNESS/THE EVIL THAT MEN DO, Iron Maiden, 90-10
CAN OUR LOVE . . ., Tindersticks, 01-47
CAN U FEEL IT? – THE CHAMPION LEGEND, Various Artists: Compilations – K-Tel, 90-12
CAN YOU FEEL THE FORCE, Real Thing, 79-73
CAN YOU TELL WHAT IT IS YET?, Rolf Harris, 97-70
CAN'T BE WITH YOU TONIGHT, Judy Boucher, 87-95
CAN'T BUY A THRILL, Steely Dan, 75-38
CAN'T GET ENOUGH, Barry White, 74-4
CAN'T GET ENOUGH, Eddy Grant, 81-39
CAN'T GET USED TO LOSING YOU, Andy Williams, 65-16
CAN'T HELP FALLING IN LOVE, Andy Williams, 70-7
CAN'T SLOW DOWN, Lionel Richie, 83-1
CAN'T STAND THE REZILLOS, Rezillos, 78-16
CAN'T STOP THE CLASSICS – HOOKED ON CLASSICS 2, Louis Clark conducting the Royal Philharmonic Orchestra, 82-13
CAN'T STOP THE LOVE, Maze featuring Frankie Beverly, 85-41
CAN'T STOP THE MUSIC [OST], Village People, 80-9
CAN'T TAKE ME HOME, Pink, 00-13
CANADIAN PACIFIC, George Hamilton IV, 71-45
CANDLELAND, Ian McCulloch, 89-18
CANDLES, Heatwave, 81-29
CANDLES IN THE RAIN, Melanie, 70-5
CANDY-O, Cars, 79-30
CANDYFLOSS AND MEDICINE, Eddi Reader, 96-24
CANNED HEAT COOKBOOK, Canned Heat, 70-8
CANNED HEAT '70 CONCERT, Canned Heat, 70-15
CANTERBURY, Diamond Head, 83-32
CANTO GREGORIANO, Coro De Munjes Del Monasterio Benedictino De Santo Domingo De Silos, 94-7
CANTO NOEL, Coro De Munjes Del Monasterio Benedictino De Santo Domingo De Silos, 94-53
CAPERCAILLIE, Capercaillie, 94-61
CAPITAL GOLD LEGENDS, Various Artists: Radio – Related Compilations, 01-1
CAPITAL GOLD LEGENDS II, Various Artists: Radio – Related Compilations, 01-2
CAPITOL CLASSICS VOLUME 1, Various Artists: Compilations – Capitol, 89-16
THE CAPPUCCINO SONGS, Tanita Tikaram, 98-69
CAPTAIN BEAKY AND HIS BAND, Keith Michell and Various Artists, 80-28
CAPTAIN CORELLI'S MANDOLIN [OST], Music composed by Stephen Warbeck, 01-30
CAPTAIN FANTASTIC AND THE BROWN DIRT COWBOY, Elton John, 75-2
CAPTAIN PARALYTIC AND THE BROWN ALE COWBOY, Mike Harding, 78-60
CAPTAIN SWING, Michelle Shocked, 89-31
CAPTURED, Natasha, 82-53
CAR BOOT SOUL, Nightmares On Wax, 99-71
CAR BUTTON CLOTH, Lemonheads, 96-28
CARAVANSERAI, Santana, 72-6
CARGO, Men At Work, 83-8
CARIBBEAN GUITAR, Chet Atkins, 63-17
CARIBBEAN UNCOVERED, Various Artists: Selected Series – Uncovered, 98-10
CARIBOU, Elton John, 74-1
CARL AND THE PASSIONS/SO TOUGH, Beach Boys, 72-25
CARL COX – FACT 2, Various Artists: Compilations – Worldwide Ultimatumn, 97-13
CARL COX – NON STOP 98/01, Various Artists: Compilations – Ffrr, 98-8
CARL COX – NON STOP 2000, Various Artists: Compilations – Ffrr, 99-13
CARLOS SANTANA AND BUDDY MILES LIVE, Carlos Santana and Buddy Miles, 72-29
CARMEL 6-TRACK [EP], Carmel, 83-94
CARMEN, Orchestre National De La Radio Diffusion Francaise, conducted by Sir Thomas Beecham, 60-18
CARNIVAL, Manuel and his Music Of The Mountains, 76-3
THE CARNIVAL, Wyclef Jean and the Refugee Allstars, 97-40
CARNIVAL OF HITS, Judith Durham and the Seekers, 94-7
CARNIVAL OF LIGHT, Ride, 94-5
THE CAROLS ALBUM, Huddersfield Choral Society, 86-29
CAROUSEL, Various Artists: Films – Original Soundtracks, 58-8
CARPENTERS, Carpenters, 71-12
THE CARPENTERS COLLECTION, Richard Clayderman, 95-65
CARPENTERS GOLD – GREATEST HITS, Carpenters, 00-21
CARROTT IN NOTTS, Jasper Carrott, 76-56
CARROTT'S LIB, Jasper Carrott, 82-80
CARRY ON OI!, Various Artists: Compilations – Secret, 81-60
CARRY ON UP THE CHARTS – THE BEST OF THE BEAUTIFUL SOUTH, Beautiful South, 94-1
CARRYING A TORCH, Tom Jones, 91-44
CARS, Cars, 78-29
THE CARS GREATEST HITS, Cars, 85-27
CARVED IN SAND, Mission, 90-7
CARWASH, Various Artists: Compilations – Telstar, 98-15
CASANOVA, Divine Comedy, 96-48
CASH COWS, Various Artists: Compilations – Virgin, 80-49
CASHFLOW, Cashflow, 86-33
CASHMERE, Cashmere, 85-63
CASINO CLASSICS, Saint Etienne, 96-34
CASINO ROYALE [OST], Composed and conducted by Burt Bacharach, 67-35
CASS, JOHN, MICHELLE, DENNY, Mamas and the Papas, 67-24
THE CASSETTE OF THE ALBUM, Roland Rat Superstar, 84-67
CASSIDY LIVE, David Cassidy, 74-9
CAST YOUR FATE TO THE WIND, Sounds Orchestral, 65-17
CASUAL SEX IN THE CINEPLEX, Sultans Of Ping Fc, 93-26
THE CAT IS OUT, Judie Tzuke, 85-35
CAT SCRATCH FEVER, Ted Nugent, 77-28
CATCH AS CATCH CAN, Kim Wilde, 83-90
CATCH BULL AT FOUR, Cat Stevens, 72-2
CATCH US IF YOU CAN, Dave Clark Five, 65-8

THE COMPLETE TOM JONES, Tom Jones, 92-8
COMPLETELY HOOKED – THE BEST OF DR. HOOK, Dr. Hook, 92-3
COMPOSITIONS, Anita Baker, 90-7
COMPUTER WORLD, Kraftwerk, 81-15
THE CONCERT FOR BANGLA DESH (RECORDED LIVE), Various Artists: Concerts and Festivals, 72-1
A CONCERT FOR THE PEOPLE (BERLIN), Barclay James Harvest, 82-15
THE CONCERT IN CENTRAL PARK, Simon and Garfunkel, 82-6
CONCERT SINATRA, Frank Sinatra, 63-8
CONCERT SPECTACULAR, Mantovani, 61-16
CONCERT – THE CURE LIVE, Cure, 84-26
CONCERTO FOR GROUP AND ORCHESTRA, Deep Purple, 70-26
CONCERTS FOR THE PEOPLE OF KAMPUCHEA, Various Artists: Concerts and Festivals, 81-39
THE CONCERTS IN CHINA, Jean-Michel Jarre, 82-6
CONDITION CRITICAL, Quiet Riot, 84-71
CONEY ISLAND BABY, Lou Reed, 76-52
CONFESSIONS OF A POP GROUP, Style Council, 88-15
CONFESSIONS OF THE MIND, Hollies, 70-30
CONFRONTATION, Bob Marley and the Wailers, 83-5
CONGRATULATIONS, I'M SORRY, Gin Blossoms, 96-42
CONNECTED, Stereo MC's, 92-2
CONNECTED, Various Artists: Compilations – PolyGram TV, 98-18
CONNIE'S GREATEST HITS, Connie Francis, 61-16
CONQUEST, Uriah Heep, 80-37
CONSCIENCE, Womack and Womack, 88-4
CONSCIENCE, Beloved, 93-2
CONSEQUENCES, Kevin Godley and Lol Creme, 77-52
CONSPIRACY, Drizabone, 94-72
CONSPIRACY OF ONE, Offspring, 00-12
CONSTRICTOR, Alice Cooper, 86-41
CONSTRUCTION FOR THE MODERN IDIOT, Wonder Stuff, 93-4
CONSTRUCTION TIME AGAIN, Depeche Mode, 83-6
CONTACT, Pointer Sisters, 85-34
CONTENDERS, Easterhouse, 86-91
CONTENDERS FOR THE RECORD OF THE YEAR 2000, Various Artists: Television – Related Compilations, 00-13
CONTINENTAL ENCORES, Mantovani, 59-4
THE CONTINO SESSIONS, Death In Vegas, 99-19
CONTINUOUS PERFORMANCE, Stone The Crows, 72-33
CONTRIBUTION, Mica Paris, 90-26
CONTROL, Janet Jackson, 86-8
CONTROL – THE REMIXES, Janet Jackson, 87-20
CONVERSATION PEACE, Stevie Wonder, 95-8
CONVOY, Various Artists: Films – Original Soundtracks, 78-52
COOKIN' ON THE ROOF, Roman Holliday, 83-31
COOL FOR CATS, Squeeze, 79-45
COOL GROOVES, Various Artists: Compilations – PolyGram TV, 98-12
COOL HEAT, Various Artists: Compilations – K-Tel, 83-79
THE COOL SOUND OF THE 70S, Various Artists: Compilations – Telstar, 00-9
THE COOLEST CUTS, Shakatak, 88-73
COOLEYHIGHHARMONY, Boyz II Men, 92-7
COP YER WHACK FOR THIS, Billy Connolly, 75-10
COPPER BLUE, Sugar, 92-10
COPPERHEAD ROAD, Steve Earle, 88-42
COPPEROPOLIS, Grant Lee Buffalo, 96-34
CORE, Stone Temple Pilots, 93-27
CORNERSTONE, Styx, 79-36
CORNERSTONES – JIMI HENDRIX 1967-1970, Jimi Hendrix, 90-5
THE CORONATION STREET ALBUM, Various Artists: Television – Related Compilations, 95-20
CORRECT USE OF SOAP, Magazine, 80-28
CORRIDORS OF POWER, Gary Moore, 82-30
CORROSION, Various Artists: Compilations – Columbia, 01-17
COSA NOSTRA BECK – OLA, Jeff Beck, 69-39
COSI FAN TUTTI FRUTTI, Squeeze, 85-31
COSMIC CARROTT, Jasper Carrott, 87-66
COSMIC THING, B-52's, 89-8
COSMIC WHEELS, Donovan, 73-15
COSMO'S FACTORY, Creedence Clearwater Revival, 70-1
THE COST OF LOVING, Style Council, 87-2
COULDN'T LOVE YOU MORE, John Martyn , 92-65
COUNT THREE AND PRAY, Berlin, 87-32
COUNT YOUR BLESSINGS, Ann Williamson, 88-58
COUNTDOWN 1992-1983, Pulp, 96-10
COUNTDOWN TO EXTINCTION, Megadeth, 92-5
COUNTERFEIT [EP], Martin L. Gore, 89-51
COUNTERPARTS, Rush, 93-14
COUNTRY, Various Artists: Compilations – Sony Music TV/Universal Music TV, 99-8
COUNTRY BOY, Don Williams, 77-27
COUNTRY COMFORT, Various Artists: Compilations – K-Tel, 76-8
COUNTRY GENTLEMAN, Jim Reeves, 80-53
COUNTRY GIRL, Billie Jo Spears, 81-17
COUNTRY GIRL MEETS COUNTRY BOY, Tammy Wynette, 78-43
COUNTRY GOLD, Various Artists: Compilations – Global Television, 96-12
COUNTRY GRAMMAR, Nelly, 01-14
COUNTRY GUITAR, Various Artists: Compilations – Warwick, 80-46
COUNTRY LEGENDS, Various Artists: Compilations – Ronco, 80-9
COUNTRY LIFE, Roxy Music, 74-3
COUNTRY LIFE, Various Artists: Compilations – EMI, 79-2
COUNTRY LOVE, Various Artists: Compilations – Telstar, 93-5
COUNTRY LOVE 2, Various Artists: Compilations – Telstar, 93-11
COUNTRY MOODS, Various Artists: Compilations – PolyGram TV, 92-2
COUNTRY NUMBER ONE, Don Gibson, 80-13
COUNTRY PORTRAITS, Various Artists: Compilations – Warwick, 79-14
COUNTRY ROADS, Various Artists: Compilations – PolyGram TV, 93-3
COUNTRY ROADS, James Last, 99-18
COUNTRY ROUND UP, Various Artists: Compilations – Polystar, 80-64
COUNTRY SIDE OF JIM REEVES, Jim Reeves, 64-12
COUNTRY SUNRISE/COUNTRY SUNSET, Various Artists: Compilations – Ronco, 81-27
COUNTRY WOMEN, Various Artists: Compilations – Dino, 93-11
COUNTRY'S GREATEST HITS, Various Artists: Compilations – Telstar, 90-9
COURT AND SPARK, Joni Mitchell, 74-14
THE COVENANT, THE SWORD AND THE ARM OF THE LAW, Cabaret Voltaire, 85-57
COVER GIRL, Shawn Colvin, 94-67
COVER PLUS, Hazel O'Connor, 81-32
COVER SHOT, David Essex, 93-3
COVER TO COVER, Jeff Healey Band, 95-50
COVER UP, UB40, 01-29
COVERDALE PAGE, Coverdale Page, 93-4
COWBOY, Erasure, 97-10
COWBOY COMPILATION – THE ALBUM VOLUME 1, Various Artists: Compilations – Cowboy, 93-18
COYOTE UGLY, Various Artists: Films – Original Soundtracks, 00-16
THE CRACK, Ruts, 79-16
THE CRACKDOWN, Cabaret Voltaire, 83-31
CRACKED REAR VIEW, Hootie and the Blowfish, 95-12
"CRACKERS" – THE SLADE CHRISTMAS PARTY ALBUM, Slade, 85-34
CRAIG DOUGLAS, Craig Douglas, 60-17
CRAIG MCLACHLAN AND CHECK 1-2, Craig McLachlan and Check 1-2, 90-10
CRANK, Almighty, 94-15
CRASH, Human League, 86-7
CRASH BOOM BANG, Roxette, 94-3
CRASH COURSE, U.K. Subs, 80-8
CRASH LANDING, Jimi Hendrix, 75-35
CRAZY, Julio Iglesias, 94-6
CRAZY FROM THE HEAT, David Lee Roth, 85-91
CRAZY HORSES, Osmonds, 72-9
CRAZY LITTLE THING CALLED LOVE, Various Artists: Compilations – Warner.esp/Global TV, 99-17
CRAZY NIGHTS, Tygers Of Pan Tang, 81-51
CRAZY NIGHTS, Kiss, 87-4
CRAZY TIMES, Gene Vincent, 60-12
CRAZY WORLD, Scorpions, 90-27
THE CRAZY WORLD OF ARTHUR BROWN, Crazy World Of Arthur Brown, 68-2
CRAZYSEXYCOOL, TLC, 95-4
CRE-OLE (BEST OF KID CREOLE AND COCONUTS), Kid Creole and the Coconuts, 84-21
CREAM ANTHEMS, Various Artists: Selected Series – Cream, 95-2
CREAM ANTHEMS MIXED BY TALL PAUL AND SEB FONTAINE, Various Artists: Selected Series – Cream, 98-15
CREAM ANTHEMS '97, Various Artists: Selected Series – Cream, 97-11
CREAM ANTHEMS 2000, Various Artists: Selected Series – Cream, 99-7
CREAM ANTHEMS 2001, Various Artists: Selected Series – Cream, 00-1
CREAM ANTHEMS 2002, Various Artists: Selected Series – Cream, 01-18
CREAM IBIZA, Various Artists: Selected Series – Cream, 01-7
CREAM IBIZA – ARRIVALS, Various Artists: Selected Series – Cream, 99-2
CREAM IBIZA ARRIVALS, Various Artists: Selected Series – Cream, 00-4
CREAM IBIZA – DEPARTURES, Various Artists: Selected Series – Cream, 99-13
CREAM LIVE, Various Artists: Selected Series – Cream, 95-3
CREAM LIVE, Various Artists: Selected Series – Cream, 00-2
CREAM LIVE, Various Artists: Selected Series – Cream, 01-5
CREAM LIVE – TWO, Various Artists: Selected Series – Cream, 96-3
THE CREAM OF ERIC CLAPTON, Eric Clapton and Cream, 87-3
CREAM RESIDENT – SEB FONTAINE, Various Artists: Selected Series – Cream, 00-18
CREAM SEPARATES – THE COLLECTION, Various Artists: Selected Series – Cream, 97-16
CREAMFIELDS, Various Artists: Selected Series – Cream, 00-5
CREATING PATTERNS, 4 Hero, 01-65
CREATURES OF THE NIGHT, Kiss, 82-22
THE CREEDENCE COLLECTION, Creedence Clearwater Revival, 85-68
CREPES AND DRAPES, Showaddywaddy, 79-8
CREST OF A KNAVE, Jethro Tull, 87-19
CREW CUTS, Various Artists: Compilations – Island, 84-71
CREW CUTS – LESSON 2, Various Artists: Compilations – Island, 84-95
CRICKLEWOOD GREEN, Ten Years After, 70-4
CRIME OF THE CENTURY, Supertramp, 74-4
THE CRIMSON IDOL, W.A.S.P., 92-21
CRISES, Mike Oldfield, 83-6
CRISIS? WHAT CRISIS?, Supertramp, 75-20
THE CROCK OF GOLD, Shane MacGowan and the Popes, 97-59
CROCODILE SHOES, Jimmy Nail, 94-2
CROCODILE SHOES II, Jimmy Nail, 96-10
CROCODILES, Echo and the Bunnymen, 80-17
CROOKED RAIN CROOKED RAIN, Pavement, 94-15
CROSBY, STILLS AND NASH, Crosby, Stills and Nash, 69-25
THE CROSS OF CHANGES, Enigma 2, 94-1
CROSS PURPOSES, Black Sabbath, 94-41
CROSS ROAD – THE BEST OF BON JOVI, Bon Jovi, 94-1
CROSS THAT LINE, Howard Jones, 89-64
THE CROSSING, Big Country, 83-3
THE CROSSING, Paul Young, 93-27
CROSSING THE RED SEA WITH THE ADVERTS, Adverts, 78-38

DANGEROUS CURVES, Lita Ford, 92-51
DANGEROUS MINDS, Various Artists: Films – Original Soundtracks, 96-13
DANGEROUS MUSIC, Robin George, 85-65
THE DANIEL O'DONNELL IRISH COLLECTION, Daniel O'Donnell, 96-35
DANNY RAMPLING – LOVE GROOVE DANCE PARTY, Various Artists: Selected Series – Love Groove Dance Party, 96-10
DANNY RAMPLING – LOVE GROOVE DANCE PARTY, Various Artists: Selected Series – Love Groove Dance Party, 97-17
DANNY RAMPLING – LOVE GROOVE DANCE PARTY, Various Artists: Selected Series – Love Groove Dance Party, 01-15
DANNY RAMPLING/LOVE GROOVE PARTY 5 & 6, Various Artists: Selected Series – Love Groove Dance Party, 97-12
DANNY TENAGLIA LIVE IN ATHENS, Various Artists: Compilations – Global Underground, 99-16
DARE, Human League, 81-1
DARE TO LOVE, Jimmy Somerville, 95-38
DARING ADVENTURES, Richard Thompson, 86-92
DARK DAYS IN PARADISE, Gary Moore, 97-43
THE DARK SIDE OF THE MOON, Pink Floyd, 73-2
DARKDANCER, Les Rythmes Digitales, 99-53
DARKLANDS, Jesus And Mary Chain, 87-5
DARKNESS ON THE EDGE OF TOWN, Bruce Springsteen, 78-16
DARREN DAY, Darren Day, 98-62
DARREN EMERSON – URUGUAY, Various Artists: Compilations – Global Underground, 00-20
DART ATTACK, Darts, 79-38
DARTS, Darts, 77-9
A DATE WITH DANIEL – LIVE, Daniel O'Donnell, 93-21
A DATE WITH ELVIS, Elvis Presley, 59-4
A DATE WITH ELVIS, Cramps, 86-34
A DATE WITH THE EVERLY BROTHERS, Everly Brothers, 61-3
DAUGHTER OF TIME, Colosseum, 70-23
DAVE CLARK'S TIME THE ALBUM, Various Artists: Studio Cast, 86-21
DAVE DEE, DOZY, BEAKY, MICK AND TICH, Dave Dee, Dozy, Beaky, Mick and Tich, 66-11
DAVE PEARCE PRESENTS DANCE ANTHEMS, Various Artists: Selected Series – Dave Pearce Presents, 98-4
DAVE PEARCE PRESENTS DANCE ANTHEMS VOLUME 2, Various Artists: Selected Series – Dave Pearce Presents, 99-5
DAVE PEARCE PRESENTS 40 CLASSIC DANCE ANTHEMS, Various Artists: Selected Series – Dave Pearce Presents , 99-5
DAVE PEARCE PRESENTS 40 CLASSIC DANCE ANTHEMS 2, Various Artists: Selected Series – Dave Pearce Presents , 99-7
DAVE PEARCE PRESENTS – 40 CLASSIC DANCE ANTHEMS VOL 3, Various Artists: Selected Series – Dave Pearce Presents, 00-7
DAVE STEWART AND THE SPIRITUAL COWBOYS, Dave Stewart and the Spiritual Cowboys, 90-38
DAVID BYRNE, David Byrne, 94-44
DAVID ESSEX, David Essex, 74-2
THE DAVID ESSEX ALBUM, David Essex, 79-29
DAVID GATES AND BREAD: ESSENTIALS, David Gates and Bread, 97-9
DAVID GILMOUR, David Gilmour, 78-17
DAVID GRANT, David Grant, 83-32
DAVID LIVE, David Bowie, 74-2
DAVID MCWILLIAMS SINGS, David McWilliams, 67-38
DAVID MCWILLIAMS VOLUME 2, David McWilliams, 67-23
DAVID MCWILLIAMS VOLUME 3, David McWilliams, 68-39
DAVID SOUL, David Soul, 76-2
DAWN OF THE DICKIES, Dickies, 79-60
DAWNRAZOR, Fields Of Nephilim, 87-62
THE DAY, Babyface, 96-34
A DAY AT THE RACES, Queen, 76-1
A DAY IN THE LIFE, Eric Benet, 99-67
A DAY WITHOUT RAIN, Enya, 00-6
DAYDREAM, Lovin' Spoonful, 66-8
DAYDREAM, Mariah Carey, 95-1
DAYDREAM NATION, Sonic Youth, 88-99
DAYS IN EUROPA, Skids, 79-32
DAYS LIKE THIS, Van Morrison, 95-5
DAYS OF FUTURE PASSED, Moody Blues, 68-27
DAYS OF OPEN HAND, Suzanne Vega, 90-7
DAYS OF SPEED, Paul Weller, 01-3
DAYS OF THUNDER, Various Artists: Films – Original Soundtracks, 90-4
DAYTIME FRIENDS – THE VERY BEST OF KENNY ROGERS, Kenny Rogers, 93-16
DAZZLE SHIPS, Orchestral Manoeuvres In The Dark, 83-5
DE LA SOUL IS DEAD, De La Soul, 91-7
DE NINA A MUJER, Julio Iglesias, 81-43
DE 7, Dave Edmunds, 82-60
DEAD BEES ON A CAKE, David Sylvian, 99-31
DEAD CITIES, Future Sound Of London, 96-26
DEAD ELVIS, Death In Vegas, 97-52
DEAD LETTER OFFICE, R.E.M., 87-60
DEAD RINGER, Meat Loaf, 81-1
DEADLINE FOR MY MEMORIES, Billie Ray Martin, 96-47
DEAN MARTIN'S GREATEST HITS VOLUME 1, Dean Martin, 68-40
DEAR PERRY, Perry Como with Mitchell Ayres and his Orchestra and the Ray Charles Singers, 58-6
DEATH IS NOT THE END, Shut Up and Dance, 92-38
DEATH OF A LADIES' MAN, Leonard Cohen, 77-35
THE DEATH OF COOL, Kitchens Of Distinction, 92-72
DEATH TO THE PIXIES, Pixies, 97-28
DEATH TO THE PIXIES – DELUXE EDITION, Pixies, 97-20
DEATH WALKS BEHIND YOU, Atomic Rooster, 71-12
DEATHWISH II [OST], Jimmy Page, 82-40
DEBRAVATION, Deborah Harry, 93-24
DEBUT, Bjork, 93-3
DECADE, Neil Young, 77-46
DECADE, Duran Duran, 89-5
DECADE OF AGGRESSION – LIVE, Slayer, 91-29
DECADE OF DECADENCE '81–'91, Motley Crue, 91-20
A DECADE OF IBIZA – 1987-1997, Various Artists: Compilations – Telstar, 97-5
DECADES – THE STORY OF THE 60'S/70'S/80'S, Various Artists: Compilations – Virgin/EMI, 00-13
THE DECCA ANTHOLOGY 1965-1967, Small Faces, 96-66
DECENCY, Diesel Park West, 92-57
DECEPTION, Colourfield, 87-95
DECEPTIVE BENDS, 10 C.C., 77-3
DECKSANDRUMSANDROCKANDROLL, Propellerheads, 98-6
DECLARATION, Alarm, 84-6
DECONSTRUCTION CLASSICS – A HISTORY OF DANCE MUSIC, Various Artists: Compilations – Deconstruction, 95-17
DEDICATED TO PLEASURE, Various Artists: Compilations – EMI, 95-18
DEDICATION, Bay City Rollers, 76-4
DEDICATION, Gary 'U.S.' Bonds, 81-43
DEDICATION – THE VERY BEST OF THIN LIZZY, Thin Lizzy, 91-8
DEEP & CHILLED EUPHORIA: DIGITALLY MIXED BY RED JERRY, Various Artists: Selected Series – Euphoria, 01-5
DEEP AND MEANINGLESS, John Otway and Wild Willy Barrett, 78-44
DEEP DOWN & DIRTY, Stereo MC's., 01-17
DEEP FOREST, Deep Forest, 94-15
DEEP HEAT – 26 HOTTEST HOUSE HITS, Various Artists: Selected Series – Deep Heat, 89-1
DEEP HEAT – THE SECOND BURN, Various Artists: Selected Series – Deep Heat, 89-2
DEEP HEAT 3 – THE THIRD DEGREE, Various Artists: Selected Series – Deep Heat, 89-2
DEEP HEAT 4 – PLAY WITH FIRE, Various Artists: Selected Series – Deep Heat, 89-1
DEEP HEAT 5 – FEED THE FEVER – 32 HOTTEST CLUB HITS, Various Artists: Selected Series – Deep Heat, 90-1
DEEP HEAT 6 – THE SIXTH SENSE, Various Artists: Selected Series – Deep Heat, 90-1
DEEP HEAT 7 – SEVENTH HEAVEN, Various Artists: Selected Series – Deep Heat, 90-1
DEEP HEAT 8 – THE HAND OF FATE, Various Artists: Selected Series – Deep Heat, 90-3
DEEP HEAT 9 – NINTH LIFE – KISS THE BLISS, Various Artists: Selected Series – Deep Heat, 91-1
DEEP HEAT 10 – THE AWAKENING, Various Artists: Selected Series – Deep Heat, 91-2
DEEP HEAT 11 – SPIRIT OF ECSTASY, Various Artists: Selected Series – Deep Heat, 91-3
DEEP HEAT 1989 – FIGHT THE FLAME, Various Artists: Selected Series – Deep Heat, 89-4
DEEP HEAT 90, Various Artists: Selected Series – Deep Heat, 90-3
DEEP HEAT 93 VOLUME 1, Various Artists: Selected Series – Deep Heat, 93-2
DEEP IN THE HEART OF NOWHERE, Bob Geldof, 86-79
DEEP PURPLE, Donny and Marie Osmond, 76-48
DEEP PURPLE IN ROCK, Deep Purple, 70-4
DEEP PURPLE LIVE, Deep Purple, 76-12
DEEP PURPLE LIVE IN LONDON, Deep Purple, 82-23
DEEP SEA SKIVING, Bananarama, 83-7
DEEP WITHIN MY SOUL, Sissel, 95-58
DEEPER – EUPHORIA II: MIXED BY RED JERRY, Various Artists: Selected Series – Euphoria, 99-2
THE DEEPEST CUT – VOLUME 1, Omni Trio, 95-60
DEEPEST PURPLE, Deep Purple, 80-1
DEF DUMB AND BLONDE, Deborah Harry, 89-12
DEFECTOR, Steve Hackett, 80-9
DEFENDERS OF THE FAITH, Judas Priest, 84-19
DEFINITELY MAYBE, Oasis, 94-1
DEFINITELY MAYBE SINGLES BOX – SILVER, Oasis, 96-23
THE DEFINITIVE ALICE COOPER, Alice Cooper, 01-33
THE DEFINITIVE COLLECTION, Kinks, 93-18
THE DEFINITIVE COLLECTION, Abba, 01-17
THE DEFINITIVE FRANKIE VALLI & THE FOUR SEASONS, Frankie Valli and the Four Seasons, 01-26
THE DEFINITIVE HITS COLLECTION, Leo Sayer, 99-35
THE DEFINITIVE JIM REEVES, Jim Reeves, 92-9
THE DEFINITIVE MONKEES, Monkees, 01-15
THE DEFINITIVE PATSY CLINE 1932 – 1963, Patsy Cline, 92-11
THE DEFINITIVE RAY CHARLES, Ray Charles, 01-13
THE DEFINITIVE SIMON AND GARFUNKEL, Simon and Garfunkel, 91-8
THE DEFINITIVE SOUND OF ATLANTIC SOUL, Various Artists: Compilations – Warner.esp, 99-18
DEHUMANIZER, Black Sabbath, 92-28
DEJA VU, Crosby, Stills, Nash and Young, 70-5
DEJA VU, A.B.'S, 84-80
DELICATE SOUND OF THUNDER, Pink Floyd, 88-11
DELILAH, Tom Jones, 68-1
THE DELIQUENTS, Various Artists: Films – Original Soundtracks, 90-16
DELIVER US FROM EVIL, Budgie, 82-62
DELIVERANCE, Baby D, 96-5
DELTICS, Chris Rea, 79-54
DEMANUFACTURE, Fear Factory, 95-27
DEMOCRACY, Killing Joke, 96-71
DEMOLITION, Girlschool, 80-28
DEMONS AND WIZARDS, Uriah Heep, 72-20
DENIM AND LEATHER, Saxon, 81-9
DEREK AND CLIVE LIVE, Peter Cook and Dudley Moore, 76-12
DEREK AND THE DOMINOS IN CONCERT, Derek and the Dominos, 73-36
DERELICTS OF DIALECT, 3rd Bass, 91-46
DES O'CONNOR NOW, Des O'Connor, 84-24
DESERTER'S SONGS, Mercury Rev, 98-27
DESIGN OF A DECADE – 1986/1996, Janet Jackson, 95-2
DESIRE, Bob Dylan, 76-3
DESIRE WALKS ON, Heart, 93-32
DESIRELESS, Eagle-Eye Cherry, 98-3

DON'T LET LOVE SLIP AWAY, Freddie Jackson, 88-24
DON'T LOOK ANY FURTHER, Dennis Edwards, 84-91
DON'T LOOK BACK, Boston, 78-9
DON'T LOOK BACK, John Lee Hooker, 97-63
DON'T MIND IF I DO, Culture Club, 99-64
DON'T POINT YOUR FINGER, 9 Below Zero, 81-56
DON'T SHOOT ME I'M ONLY THE PIANO PLAYER, Elton John, 73-1
DON'T STAND ME DOWN, Dexy's Midnight Runners, 85-22
DON'T STOP, Jeffrey Osborne, 84-59
DON'T STOP DANCING, Various Artists: Compilations – Telstar, 84-11
DON'T STOP . . . DOOWOP!, Various Artists: Compilations – Telstar, 91-15
DON'T STOP ME NOW . . ., Cliff Richard, 67-23
DON'T STOP MOVIN, Livin' Joy, 96-41
DON'T STOP – THE 30TH ANNIVERSARY ALBUM, Status Quo, 96-2
DON'T STOP THE MUSIC, Various Artists: Compilations – Stylus, 89-7
DON'T SUPPOSE, Limahl, 84-63
DON'T SWEAT THE TECHNIQUE, Eric B. and Rakim, 92-73
DON'T THINK TWICE IT'S ALL RIGHT, Barbara Dickson, 92-32
DON'T TRY THIS AT HOME, Billy Bragg, 91-8
DON'T WALK – BOOGIE, Various Artists: Compilations – EMI, 78-1
DONE AND DUSTED, Dust Junkys, 98-35
DONE BY THE FORCES OF NATURE, Jungle Brothers, 90-41
DONNA SUMMER, Donna Summer, 82-13
DONNY, Donny Osmond, 75-16
DOOKIE, Green Day, 94-13
DOOLITTLE, Pixies, 89-8
DOOR TO DOOR, Cars, 87-72
THE DOORS, Doors, 91-43
THE DOORS [OST], Doors and Jim Morrison and Various Artists, 91-11
DOOWUTCHYALIKE / PACKET MAN, Digital Underground, 90-59
DOPES TO INFINITY, Monster Magnet, 95-51
DOPPELGANGER, Kid Creole and the Coconuts, 83-21
DOPPELGANGER, Curve, 92-11
DOREMI FASOL LATIDO, Hawkwind, 72-14
DOS DEDOS MIS AMIGOS, Pop Will Eat Itself, 94-11
DOTS AND LOOPS, Stereolab, 97-19
DOUBLE BARREL, Dave and Ansil Collins, 71-41
DOUBLE DEVINE, Sidney Devine, 76-14
DOUBLE DYNAMITE, Sam and Dave, 67-28
DOUBLE FANTASY, John Lennon and Yoko Ono, 80-1
DOUBLE LIVE, Garth Brooks, 98-57
DOUBLE LIVE GONZO!, Ted Nugent, 78-47
DOUBLE TROUBLE, Gillan, 81-12
DOUBLE TROUBLE [OST], Elvis Presley, 67-34
DOUBLE TROUBLE – LIVE, Molly Hatchet, 86-94
DOUBLE UP, Mase, 99-47
DOUBLE VISION, Foreigner, 78-32
DOUBLE WIDE, Uncle Kracker, 01-40
DOUBT, Jesus Jones, 91-1
DOUG LAZY GETTIN' CRAZY, Doug Lazy, 90-65
DOUGHNUT IN GRANNY'S GREENHOUSE, Bonzo Dog Doo-Dah Band, 69-40
DOWN, Jesus Lizard, 94-64
DOWN AND OUT BLUES, Sonny Boy Williamson, 64-20
DOWN DRURY LANE TO MEMORY LANE, 101 Strings, 60-1
DOWN FALL THE GOOD GUYS, Wolfsbane, 91-53
DOWN IN THE GROOVE, Bob Dylan, 88-32
DOWN MEXICO WAY, Herb Alpert and the Tijuana Brass, 70-64
DOWN ON THE FARM, Little Feat, 79-46
DOWN ON THE STREET, Shakatak, 84-17
DOWN ON THE UPSIDE, Soundgarden, 96-7
DOWN THE DUSTPIPE, Status Quo, 75-20
DOWN THE ROAD, Stephen Stills' Manassas, 73-33
DOWN TO EARTH, Rainbow, 79-6
DOWN TO EARTH, Monie Love, 90-30
DOWN TO EARTH, Ozzy Osbourne, 01-19
DOWN TWO, THEN LEFT, Boz Scaggs, 77-55
DOWN WITH THE KING, Run-D.M.C., 93-44
DOWNTOWN TONIGHT, Racing Cars, 77-39
THE DOWNWARD SPIRAL, Nine Inch Nails, 94-9
DRACONIAN TIMES, Paradise Lost, 95-16
DRAG, k.d. lang, 97-19
DRAMA, Yes, 80-2
DRAMA, Jamelia, 00-39
DRASTIC PLASTIC, Be-Bop Deluxe, 78-22
DRAWN FROM MEMORY, Embrace, 00-8
DRAWN TO THE DEEP END, Gene, 97-8
DREAM A DREAM, Charlotte Church, 00-30
THE DREAM ACADEMY, Dream Academy, 85-58
A DREAM COME TRUE, Becky Taylor, 01-67
DREAM EVIL, Dio, 87-8
A DREAM FULFILLED, Will Downing, 91-43
DREAM HARDER, Waterboys, 93-5
DREAM INTO ACTION, Howard Jones, 85-2
DREAM LOVER, Anthony Ventura Orchestra, 79-44
DREAM MELODIES, Various Artists: Compilations – Nouveau Music, 85-91
DREAM OF A LIFETIME, Marvin Gaye, 85-46
DREAM OF LIFE, Patti Smith, 88-70
DREAM OF 100 NATIONS, Transglobal Underground, 93-45
THE DREAM OF THE BLUE TURTLES, Sting, 85-3
DREAM POLICE, Cheap Trick, 79-41
DREAM WORLD, Crown Heights Affair, 78-40
DREAMBOAT ANNIE, Heart, 77-36
DREAMER, Home, 72-41
DREAMING, Various Artists: Compilations – K-Tel, 82-2
THE DREAMING, Kate Bush, 82-3
DREAMING . . ., Patsy Cline, 91-55
DREAMLAND, Black Box, 90-14
DREAMLAND, Aztec Camera, 93-21
DREAMLAND, Robert Miles, 96-7
DREAMS, Grace Slick, 80-28
DREAMS AND THEMES, Various Artists: Compilations – Ronco, 84-75
DREAMS ARE NUTHIN' MORE THAN WISHES, David Cassidy, 73-1
DREAMS CAN COME TRUE – GREATEST HITS VOL 1, Gabrielle, 01-2
DREAMS OF IRELAND, Various Artists: Compilations – Trax, 89-19
DREAMS OF REASON PRODUCE MONSTERS, Mick Karn, 87-89
DREAMSTATES, Various Artists: Compilations – Inspired, 01-18
DREAMTIME, Cult, 84-21
DREAMTIME, Stranglers, 86-16
THE DREEM TEEM IN SESSION – UK GARAGE – PAST – PRESENT AND FUTURE, Various Artists: Compilations – Telstar/4 Liberty, 01-12
DRESS FOR EXCESS, Sigue Sigue Sputnik, 89-53
DRESSED FOR THE OCCASION, Cliff Richard and the London Philharmonic Orchestra, 83-7
DRILL YOUR OWN HOLE, Gaye Bykers On Acid, 87-95
DRINK ME, Salad, 95-16
DRINKIN' AND COURTIN', Dubliners, 68-31
DRINKING GASOLINE, Cabaret Voltaire, 85-71
DRIVE ON, Mott The Hoople, 75-45
DRIVE ON, Various Artists: Compilations – Global Television, 97-10
DRIVE-THRU BOOTY, Freak Power, 95-11
DRIVE TIME – 36 OF THE GREATEST RADIO ANTHEMS . . ., Various Artists: Selected Series – Drive Time, 95-5
DRIVE TIME 2, Various Artists: Selected Series – Drive Time, 95-4
DRIVETIME 3, Various Artists: Selected Series – Drive Time, 96-4
DRIVE TIME 4, Various Artists: Selected Series – Drive Time, 96-8
DRIVE TIME USA – 22 SUMMER CRUISING GREATS, Various Artists: Compilations – K-Tel, 86-20
DRIVIN' HARD, Shakatak, 82-35
DRIVIN' ME WILD, Cliff Bennett and the Rebel Rousers, 66-25
DRIVING RAIN, Paul McCartney, 01-46
DRIVING ROCK, Various Artists: Compilations – Global Television, 95-9
DROP DEAD GORGEOUS, Various Artists: Compilations – Global Television, 98-4
DROP DEAD GORGEOUS 2, Various Artists: Compilations – Global Television, 98-10
A DROP OF THE HARD STUFF, Dubliners, 67-5
DROPPED, Mindfunk, 93-60
DROPS OF JUPITER, Train, 01-8
DRUGSTORE, Drugstore, 95-31
DRUKQS, Aphex Twin, 01-22
DRUM & BASS MIX 97, Various Artists: Compilations – PolyGram TV, 97-11
DRUM AND BASS SELECTION 2, Various Artists: Compilations – Break Down, 94-14
THE DRUM IS EVERYTHING, Carmel, 84-19
DRUMS AND WIRES, XTC, 79-34
DRUMS ARE DANGEROUS, Drum Club, 94-53
DRY, PJ Harvey, 92-11
DUB HOUSE DISCO 2000, Various Artists: Compilations – Guerilla, 93-18
DUB NO BASS WITH MY HEAD MAN, Underworld, 94-12
THE DUBLINERS 25 YEARS CELEBRATION, Dubliners, 87-43
DUCK ROCK, Malcolm McLaren, 83-18
THE DUDE, Quincy Jones, 81-19
DUETS, Frank Sinatra, 93-5
DUETS, Elton John and Various Artists, 93-5
DUETS II, Frank Sinatra, 94-29
DUETS & ARIAS, Roberto Alagna/Angela Gheorgiu, 96-42
DUKE, Genesis, 80-1
DUMB WAITERS, Korgis, 80-40
DUMBING UP, World Party, 00-64
DUMMY, Portishead, 94-2
DUOPHONIC, Charles and Eddie, 92-19
DUOTONES, Kenny G, 87-28
DURAN DURAN, Duran Duran, 81-3
DURAN DURAN (THE WEDDING ALBUM), Duran Duran, 93-4
DUSK, The, 93-2
DUSKY SAPPHO [EP], Carleen Anderson, 93-38
DUST, Screaming Trees, 96-32
DUSTY . . . DEFINITELY, Dusty Springfield, 68-30
DUSTY – THE SILVER COLLECTION, Dusty Springfield, 88-14
DUTY NOW FOR THE FUTURE, Devo, 79-49
DYLAN AND THE DEAD, Bob Dylan and the Grateful Dead, 89-38
DYNAMITE, Jermaine Jackson, 84-57
DYNASTY, Kiss, 79-50
E.C. WAS HERE, Eric Clapton, 75-14
E.1999 ETERNAL, Bone Thugs-N-Harmony, 96-39
E.S.P., Millie Jackson, 84-59
E.S.P., Bee Gees, 87-5
E.T. – THE EXTRA TERRESTRIAL STORYBOOK, Michael Jackson, 83-82
E.T. – THE EXTRATERRESTRIAL [OST], John Williams, 82-47
THE EAGLE HAS LANDED, Saxon, 82-5
EARLY DAYS – THE BEST OF LED ZEPPELIN – VOLUME ONE, Led Zeppelin, 00-40
THE EARLY TAPES JULY-AUGUST 1980, Level 42, 82-46
EARTH AND SUN AND MOON, Midnight Oil, 93-27
EARTH INFERNO, Fields Of The Nephilim, 91-39
EARTH MOVING, Mike Oldfield, 89-30
EARTH VS THE WILDHEARTS, Wildhearts, 93-46
EARTHBOUND, Conner Reeves, 97-25
EARTHLING, David Bowie, 97-6
THE EARTHQUAKE ALBUM . . . ROCK AID ARMENIA, Various Artists: Compilations – Life Aid Armenia, 90-3
EARTHQUAKE WEATHER, Joe Strummer, 89-58
EARTHRISE – THE RAINFOREST ALBUM, Various Artists: Compilations – ELF, 92-1
EAST OF THE SUN, WEST OF THE MOON, A-Ha, 90-12
EAST SIDE STORY, Squeeze, 81-19
EAST TO WEST, James Last, 78-49
THE EASTENDERS SING-ALONG ALBUM, Various Artists: Television – Related Compilations, 85-33

ENERGY RUSH DANCE HITS 94, Various Artists: Selected Series – Energy Rush, 94-3
ENERGY RUSH – EURO DANCE HITS 94, Various Artists: Selected Series – Energy Rush, 94-5
ENERGY RUSH FACTOR 5, Various Artists: Selected Series – Energy Rush, 93-3
ENERGY RUSH K9, Various Artists: Selected Series – Energy Rush, 95-3
ENERGY RUSH LEVEL 3, Various Artists: Selected Series – Energy Rush, 93-3
ENERGY RUSH PHASE 4, Various Artists: Selected Series – Energy Rush, 93-2
ENERGY RUSH PRESENTS DANCE HITS 93, Various Artists: Selected Series – Energy Rush, 93-1
ENERGY RUSH PRESENTS DANCE HITS OF THE YEAR, Various Artists: Selected Series – Energy Rush, 93-3
ENERGY RUSH – SAFE SIX, Various Artists: Selected Series – Energy Rush, 93-5
ENERGY RUSH – XTERMIN8, Various Artists: Selected Series – Energy Rush, 94-1
ENGELBERT, Engelbert Humperdinck, 69-3
ENGELBERT HUMPERDINCK, Engelbert Humperdinck, 69-5
THE ENGELBERT HUMPERDINCK COLLECTION, Engelbert Humperdinck, 87-35
ENGELBERT HUMPERDINCK – HIS GREATEST HITS, Engelbert Humperdinck, 74-1
ENGLISH SETTLEMENT, XTC, 82-5
ENJOY YOURSELF, Kylie Minogue, 89-1
ENLIGHTENMENT, Van Morrison, 90-5
ENTER THE DRU, Dru Hill, 98-42
ENTERTAINMENT, Gang Of Four, 79-45
ENTREAT, Cure, 91-10
ENVY OF ANGELS, Mutton Birds, 97-64
ENYA [OST-TV], Enya, 87-69
THE EPIC YEARS, Shaky, 92-57
EPONYMOUS, R.E.M., 88-69
THE EP'S 92-94, David Gray, 01-68
EQUALLY CURSED AND BLESSED, Catatonia, 99-1
EQUALS EXPLOSION, Equals, 68-32
EQUATOR, Uriah Heep, 85-79
EQUINOXE, Jean-Michel Jarre, 78-11
ERASURE, Erasure, 95-14
ERIC BURDON DECLARES WAR, Eric Burdon and War, 70-50
ERIC CARMEN, Eric Carmen, 76-58
ERIC CLAPTON, Eric Clapton, 70-17
EROICA, Wendy and Lisa, 90-33
EROTICA, Madonna, 92-2
ERROL FLYNN, Dogs D'Amour, 89-22
ESCAPE, Journey, 82-32
ESCAPE FROM TV, Jan Hammer, 87-34
ESCM, BT, 97-35
ESPECIALLY FOR YOU, Duane Eddy, 59-6
ESPECIALLY FOR YOU, Don Williams, 81-33
ESPECIALLY FOR YOU, Joe Longthorne, 89-22
ESPECIALLY FOR YOU, Daniel O'Donnell, 94-14
ESPECIALLY FOR YOU, Various Artists: Compilations – Columbia, 99-1
ESPRESSO LOGIC, Chris Rea, 93-8
ESSENCE, Lucinda Williams, 01-63
THE ESSENTIAL ALISON MOYET, Alison Moyet, 01-16
ESSENTIAL BALLET, Various Artists: Compilations – Decca, 92-9
THE ESSENTIAL BOB DYLAN, Bob Dylan, 01-9
THE ESSENTIAL CHILL, Various Artists: Compilations – Arcade, 92-16
ESSENTIAL CLASSICS, Various Artists: Compilations – Deutsche Grammophon, 90-6
THE ESSENTIAL COLLECTION, Elvis Presley, 94-6
THE ESSENTIAL COLLECTION, Marc Bolan and T. Rex, 95-24
THE ESSENTIAL COLLECTION, Dionne Warwick, 96-58
THE ESSENTIAL COLLECTION, Daryl Hall and John Oates, 01-26
ESSENTIAL DISCO AND DANCE, Various Artists: Compilations – Nouveau Music, 84-96
THE ESSENTIAL DOMINGO, Placido Domingo, 89-20
ESSENTIAL ELLA, Ella Fitzgerald, 94-35
THE ESSENTIAL GROOVE, Various Artists: Compilations – PolyGram TV, 95-11
ESSENTIAL HARDCORE, Various Artists: Compilations – Dino, 91-1
THE ESSENTIAL JEAN-MICHEL JARRE, Jean-Michel Jarre, 83-14
THE ESSENTIAL JOSE CARRERAS, Jose Carreras, 91-24
THE ESSENTIAL KARAJAN, Herbert Von Karajan, 88-51
THE ESSENTIAL KIRI, Kiri Te Kanawa, 92-23
ESSENTIAL MILLENNIUM – PETE TONG FATBOY SLIM PAUL OAKENFOLD, Various Artists: Selected Series – Essential Selection, 99-10
ESSENTIAL MIX – TONG COX SASHA OAKENFOLD, Various Artists: Compilations – Ffrr, 96-12
ESSENTIAL MIX 2 – TONG, MACKINTOSH . . ., Various Artists: Compilations – Ffrr, 96-6
ESSENTIAL MIX 3 – TONG, SEAMAN, JULES ETC, Various Artists: Compilations – Ffrr, 96-12
THE ESSENTIAL MOZART, Various Artists: Compilations – Decca, 91-1
ESSENTIAL OPERA, Various Artists: Compilations – Decca, 91-2
ESSENTIAL OPERA 2, Various Artists: Compilations – Decca, 93-17
THE ESSENTIAL PAVAROTTI, Luciano Pavarotti, 90-1
ESSENTIAL PAVAROTTI II, Luciano Pavarotti, 91-1
ESSENTIAL SELECTION IBIZA 2000 – THE SOUNDTRACK TO YOUR SUMMER, Various Artists: Selected Series – Essential Selection, 00-11
ESSENTIAL SELECTION '98 – PETE TONG/PAUL OAKENFOLD , Various Artists: Selected Series – Essential Selection, 98-11
ESSENTIAL SELECTION '98 – PETE TONG/PAUL OAKENFOLD, Various Artists: Selected Series – Essential Selection, 99-13
ESSENTIAL SELECTION PRESENTS THE CLUBBER'S BIBLE – YOUR SOUNDTRACK TO THE WEEKEND, Various Artists: Selected Series – Essential Selection, 00-11
ESSENTIAL SELECTION PRESENTS THE CLUBBER'S BIBLE II – THE SECOND COMING, Various Artists: Selected Series – Essential Selection, 01-6
ESSENTIAL SELECTION PRESENTS THE CLUBBER'S BIBLE WINTER 2002, Various Artists: Selected Series – Essential Selection, 01-17
ESSENTIAL SOUNDTRACKS, Various Artists: Films – Related Compilations, 99-4
ESSENTIAL SOUNDTRACKS – 40 TRACKS – THE NEW MOVIE COLLECTION, Various Artists: Films – Related Compilations, 00-8
THE ESSENTIAL TONY BENNETT, Tony Bennett, 98-49
ESSENTIAL TRACKS, Various Artists: Compilations – BMG/Telstar TV, 01-15
ESSENTIALS . . . THE VERY BEST OF GEORGE BENSON, George Benson, 98-8
ESSEX, Alison Moyet, 94-24
ESTABLISHED 1958, Cliff Richard and the Shadows, 68-30
ESTE MUNDO, Gipsy Kings, 91-19
ETERNAL FLAME – THE BEST OF THE BANGLES, Bangles, 01-15
THE ETERNAL IDOL, Black Sabbath, 87-66
ETERNAL LIGHT – MUSIC OF INNER PEACE, Priory Of The Resurrection, 01-68
ETERNAL LOVE, Various Artists: Compilations – K-Tel, 89-5
EUGENE WILDE, Eugene Wilde, 84-67
EUPHORIA, Various Artists: Selected Series – Euphoria, 99-1
EUPHORIA, Def Leppard, 99-11
EUPHORIA – LEVEL 3, Various Artists: Selected Series – Euphoria, 99-18
EUPHORIA MORNING, Chris Cornell, 99-31
EUREKA, Bible, 88-71
EUROMAN COMETH, Jean-Jacques Burnel, 79-40
EUROPOP, Eiffel 65, 00-12
EURYTHMICS LIVE 1983-1989, Eurythmics, 93-22
EV3, En Vogue, 97-9
EVANGELINE, Emmylou Harris, 81-53
EVE, Alan Parsons Project, 79-74
EVEN COW GIRLS GET THE BLUES [OST], k.d. lang, 93-36
EVEN IN THE QUIETEST MOMENTS . . ., Supertramp, 77-12
EVEN NOW, Barry Manilow, 78-12
EVEN SERPENTS SHINE, Only Ones, 79-42
EVENING FALLS, Richard Harvey and Friends, 89-72
EVENING SESSION – PRIORITY TUNES, Various Artists: Radio – Related Compilations , 96-11
AN EVENING WASTED WITH TOM LEHRER, Tom Lehrer, 60-7
AN EVENING WITH DIANA ROSS, Diana Ross, 77-52
AN EVENING WITH JOHN DENVER, John Denver, 75-31
AN EVENING WITH JOHNNERS, Brian Johnstone, 94-46
EVENTIDE, Faith Brothers, 85-66
EVERBODY WANTS TO SHAG . . . THE TEARDROP EXPLODES, Teardrop Explodes, 90-72
EVERGREEN, Mr. Acker Bilk, 78-17
EVERGREEN, Echo and the Bunnymen, 97-8
EVERLASTING, Natalie Cole, 88-62
THE EVERLY BROTHERS, Everly Brothers, 84-36
EVERLY BROTHERS REUNION CONCERT – LIVE AT THE ROYAL ALBERT HALL, Everly Brothers, 84-47
EVERY BEAT OF MY HEART, Rod Stewart, 86-5
EVERY BREATH YOU TAKE – THE SINGLES, Police, 86-1
EVERY DAY IS A NEW DAY, Diana Ross, 99-71
EVERY FACE TELLS A STORY, Cliff Richard, 77-8
EVERY GOOD BOY DESERVES FAVOUR, Moody Blues, 71-1
EVERY GOOD BOY DESERVES FUDGE, Mudhoney, 91-34
EVERY HOME SHOULD HAVE ONE, Patti Austin, 81-99
EVERY I'S A WINNER, Hot Chocolate, 78-30
EVERY PICTURE TELLS A STORY, Rod Stewart, 71-1
EVERY SONG TELLS A STORY, Various Artists: Compilations – PolyGram TV, 95-17
EVERY WOMAN, Various Artists: Compilations – RCA, 98-19
EVERYBODY, Hear'say, 01-24
EVERYBODY DANCE NOW, Various Artists: Compilations – Columbia, 91-12
EVERYBODY ELSE IS DOING IT, SO WHY CAN'T WE?, Cranberries, 93-1
EVERYBODY KNOWS, Sonia, 90-7
EVERYBODY KNOWS MILLICAN AND NESBITT, Millican and Nesbitt, 75-23
EVERYBODY LOVES A NUT, Johnny Cash, 66-28
EVERYBODY LOVES SATURDAY NIGHT, Bob Wallis and his Storyville Jazzmen, 60-20
EVERYBODY'S ANGEL, Tanita Tikaram, 91-19
EVERYBODY'S FREE, Rozalla, 92-20
EVERYBODY'S ROCKIN', Neil Young and the Shocking Pinks, 83-50
EVERYBODY'S SOMEBODY, Kele Le Roc, 99-44
EVERYONE PLAYS DARTS, Darts, 78-12
EVERYONE'S GOT ONE, Echobelly, 94-8
EVERYTHING, Climie Fisher, 88-14
EVERYTHING, Bangles, 88-5
EVERYTHING, Joe, 94-53
EVERYTHING AND NOTHING, David Sylvian, 00-57
EVERYTHING CHANGES, Take That, 93-1
EVERYTHING, EVERYTHING, Underworld Live, 00-22
EVERYTHING IS BEAUTIFUL, Ray Stevens, 70-62
EVERYTHING IS BEAUTIFUL, Dana, 80-43
EVERYTHING IS EVERYTHING, Diana Ross, 71-31
EVERYTHING IS WRONG / MIXED & REMIXED, Moby, 95-21
EVERYTHING MUST GO, Manic Street Preachers, 96-2
EVERYTHING PICTURE, Ultrasound, 99-23

FIFTY NUMBER ONES OF THE '60S, Various Artists: Compilations – Global Television, 95-8
FIFTY YEARS ON WITH JIMMY SHAND, Jimmy Shand, His Band and Guests, 83-97
52ND STREET, Billy Joel, 78-10
THE '56 SESSIONS VOLUME 1, Elvis Presley, 78-47
FIGHTING, Thin Lizzy, 75-60
FIGURE 8, Elliott Smith, 00-37
FILE UNDER EASY LISTENING, Sugar, 94-7
FILIGREE AND SHADOW, This Mortal Coil, 86-53
FILTH HOUNDS OF HADES, Tank, 82-33
FILTH PIG, Ministry, 96-43
FILTHY LUCRE LIVE, Sex Pistols, 96-26
FIN DE SIECLE, Divine Comedy, 98-9
THE FINAL, Wham!, 86-2
THE FINAL COUNTDOWN, Europe, 86-9
THE FINAL COUNTDOWN – THE VERY BEST OF SOFT METAL, Various Artists: Compilations – Telstar, 90-9
THE FINAL CUT, Pink Floyd, 83-1
THE FINAL FRONTIER, Keel, 86-83
FINALLY, Ce Ce Peniston, 92-10
FINALLY, Blackstreet, 99-27
FIND OUT, Steven Dante, 88-87
FIND YOUR WAY, Gabrielle, 93-9
FINDERS KEEPERS [OST], Cliff Richard and the Shadows, 66-6
THE FINE ART OF SURFACING, Boomtown Rats, 79-7
FINE YOUNG CANNIBALS, Fine Young Cannibals, 85-11
FINELINES, My Vitriol, 01-24
THE FINEST, Fine Young Cannibals, 96-10
FINEST HOUR, Lindisfarne, 75-55
FINGS AIN'T WOT THEY USED TO BE, Various Artists: Stage Cast – London, 60-5
FINN, Finn, 95-15
FINYL VINYL, Rainbow, 86-31
FIRE AND ICE, Yngwie Malmsteen, 92-57
FIRE & SKILL – THE SONGS OF THE JAM, Various Artists: Compilations – Ignition, 99-12
FIRE AND WATER, Free, 70-2
FIRE AND WATER, Dave Greenfield and Jean-Jacques Burnel, 83-94
FIRE DANCES, Killing Joke, 83-29
FIRE GARDEN, Steve Vai, 96-41
THE FIRE INSIDE, Bob Seger and the Silver Bullet Band, 91-54
FIRE OF UNKNOWN ORIGIN, Blue Oyster Cult, 81-29
FIREBALL, Deep Purple, 71-1
FIREWORKS, Jose Feliciano, 70-65
FIRING ON ALL SIX, Lone Star, 77-36
THE FIRM, Firm, 85-15
FIRST AND LAST AND ALWAYS, Sisters Of Mercy, 85-14
FIRST BAND ON THE MOON, Cardigans, 96-18
FIRST BLOOD . . . LAST CUTS, W.A.S.P., 93-69
FIRST CONTACT, Roger Sanchez, 01-34
THE FIRST BORN IS DEAD, Nick Cave and the Bad Seeds, 85-53
THE FIRST CHAPTER, Mission, 87-35
THE FIRST DAY, David Sylvian and Robert Fripp, 93-21
THE FIRST FAMILY, Vaughn Meader, 62-12
FIRST LADIES OF COUNTRY, Various Artists: Compilations – CBS, 80-37
THE FIRST LADY OF SOUL, Aretha Franklin, 86-89
THE FIRST LIVE RECORDINGS, Elvis Presley, 84-69
FIRST LOVE, Various Artists: Compilations – Arcade, 80-58
FIRST LOVE, Michael Ball, 96-4
THE FIRST OF A MILLION KISSES, Fairground Attraction, 88-2
THE FIRST OF TOO MANY, Senseless Things, 91-66
FIRST RAYS OF THE NEW RISING SUN, Jimi Hendrix, 97-37
FIRST STEP, Faces, 70-45
THE FIRST SUMMER OF LOVE, Various Artists: Compilations – PolyGram TV/Sony TV, 97-6
FIRST TAKE, Roberta Flack, 72-47
FIRST TEN YEARS, Joan Baez, 71-41
FIRST (THE SOUND OF MUSIC), Then Jerico, 87-35
FIRST TIME EVER I SAW YOUR FACE, Johnny Mathis, 72-40
THE FISH AND THE TREE AND THE BIRD AND THE BELL, Various Artists: Compilations – Columbia, 91-9
FISH OUT OF WATER, Chris Squire, 75-25
THE FISH PEOPLE TAPES, Alexei Sayle, 84-62
FISH RISING, Steve Hillage, 75-33
FISHERMAN'S BLUES, Waterboys, 88-13
FISHING FOR LUCKIES, Wildhearts, 96-16
5, J.J. Cale, 79-40
5, Lenny Kravitz, 98-18
FIVE, Five, 98-1
FIVE BRIDGES, Nice, 70-2
FIVE FACES OF MANFRED MANN, Manfred Mann, 64-3
FIVE GUYS NAMED MOE, Various Artists: Stage Cast – London, 91-59
FIVE MAN ACOUSTICAL JAM, Tesla, 91-59
FIVE MILES OUT, Mike Oldfield, 82-7
THE FIVE PENNIES, Various Artists: Films – Original Soundtracks, 60-2
5,000 SPIRITS OR THE LAYERS OF THE ONION, Incredible String Band, 67-25
5150, Van Halen, 86-16
FLAG, Yello, 88-56
THE FLAME, Annabel Lamb, 84-84
FLAMENCO GUITAR, Manitas De Plata, 67-40
FLAMING PIE, Paul McCartney, 97-2
FLAMING STAR AND SUMMER KISSES, Elvis Presley, 65-11
FLARED HITS AND PLATFORM SOUL, Various Artists: Compilations – Vision, 95-13
FLASH, Jeff Beck, 85-83
FLASH GORDON [OST], Queen, 80-10
FLASH LIGHT, Tom Verlaine, 87-99
FLASH TRACKS, Various Artists: Compilations – TV Records, 82-19
FLASHDANCE, Various Artists: Films – Original Soundtracks, 83-9
FLASHPOINT, Rolling Stones, 91-6
THE FLAT EARTH, Thomas Dolby, 84-14
FLAUNT IT, Sigue Sigue Sputnik, 86-10
FLAUNT THE IMPERFECTION, China Crisis, 85-9
FLEETWOOD MAC, Fleetwood Mac, 76-23
FLEETWOOD MAC LIVE, Fleetwood Mac, 80-31
FLESH AND BLOOD, Roxy Music, 80-1
FLESH AND BLOOD, Poison, 90-3
FLEX, Lene Lovich, 80-19
FLICK OF THE SWITCH, AC/DC, 83-4
FLIGHT OF ICARUS/THE TROOPER, Iron Maiden, 90-7
FLIGHT OF THE CONDOR, Various Artists: Compilations – Telstar, 92-11
THE FLIGHT OF THE CONDOR [OST-TV], Inti Illimani-Guamary, 83-62
FLIGHTS OF FANCY, Paul Leoni, 83-17
THE FLINTSTONES, Various Artists: Films – Original Soundtracks, 94-18
FLIP, Nils Lofgren, 85-36
FLOATERS, Floaters, 77-17
FLOCK, Flock, 70-59
A FLOCK OF SEAGULLS, A Flock Of Seagulls, 82-32
FLOGGING A DEAD HORSE, Sex Pistols, 80-23
FLOOD, They Might Be Giants, 90-14
FLOODLAND, Sisters Of Mercy, 87-9
FLOORED GENIUS – THE BEST OF JULIAN COPE AND THE TEARDROP EXPLODES, Julian Cope and the Teardrop Explodes, 92-22
FLORAL DANCE, Brighouse and Rastrick Brass Band, 78-10
FLOWER DRUM SONG, Various Artists: Stage Cast – Broadway, 60-2
FLOWER DRUM SONG, Various Artists: Stage Cast – London, 60-10
FLOWERS, Ace Of Base, 98-15
FLOWERS, Echo and the Bunnymen, 01-56
FLOWERS IN THE DIRT, Paul McCartney, 89-1
FLOWERS OF ROMANCE, Public Image Ltd, 81-11
FLUSH THE FASHION, Alice Cooper, 80-56
FLY, Dixie Chicks, 99-38
FLY LIKE AN EAGLE, Steve Miller Band, 76-11
FLY ON THE WALL, AC/DC, 85-7
FLYER, Nanci Griffith, 94-20
FLYING COLOURS, Chris De Burgh, 88-1
FLYING COWBOYS, Rickie Lee Jones, 89-50
FLYING LIZARDS, Flying Lizards, 80-60
FM, Various Artists: Films – Original Soundtracks, 78-37
FOCUS, Focus, 75-23
FOCUS 3, Focus, 72-6
FOCUS AT THE RAINBOW, Focus, 73-23
FOG ON THE TYNE, Lindisfarne, 71-1
FOLD YOUR HANDS CHILD, YOU WALK LIKE A PEASANT, Belle And Sebastian, 00-10
FOLK FESTIVAL OF THE BLUES (LIVE RECORDING), Various Artists: Concerts and Festivals, 64-16
FOLLOW THAT GIRL, Various Artists: Stage Cast – London, 60-5
FOLLOW THE LEADER, Eric B. and Rakim, 88-25
FOLLOW THE LEADER, Korn, 98-5
FOLLOW YOUR DREAM, Daniel O'Donnell, 92-17
F1 ROCK, Various Artists: Compilations – Telstar, 96-20
FONTANELLE, Babes In Toyland, 92-24
FONZIE'S FAVOURITES, Various Artists: Television – Related Compilations, 78-8
FOO FIGHTERS, Foo Fighters, 95-3
FOOL BRITANNIA, Anthony Newley, Peter Sellers, Joan Collins, 63-10
THE FOOL CIRCLE, Nazareth, 81-60
FOOLISH BEHAVIOUR, Rod Stewart, 80-4
FOOT LOOSE & FANCY FREE, Rod Stewart, 77-3
FOOTLOOSE, Various Artists: Films – Original Soundtracks, 84-7
FOR CERTAIN BECAUSE, Hollies, 66-23
FOR EARTH BELOW, Robin Trower, 75-26
FOR ONCE IN MY LIFE, Tony Bennett, 68-29
FOR PLEASURE, Omar, 94-50
FOR SOMEONE SPECIAL, Ken Dodd, 67-40
FOR THE BOYS [OST], Bette Midler, 92-75
FOR THE GOOD TIMES, Perry Como, 83-41
FOR THE LOVE OF STRANGE MEDICINE, Steve Perry, 94-64
FOR THE STARS, Anne Von Otter meets Elvis Costello, 01-67
FOR THOSE ABOUT TO ROCK WE SALUTE YOU, AC/DC, 81-3
FOR TO NEXT, Steve Hillage, 83-48
FOR TWISTERS ONLY, Chubby Checker, 62-17
FOR UNLAWFUL CARNAL KNOWLEDGE, Van Halen, 91-12
FOR YOU . . . 20 SONGS ESPECIALLY FOR YOU, Various Artists: Compilations – Columbia, 00-4
FOR YOUR EARS ONLY, Bentley Rhythm Ace, 00-48
FOR YOUR PLEASURE, Roxy Music, 73-4
FORBIDDEN, Black Sabbath, 95-71
THE FORCE BEHIND THE POWER, Diana Ross, 91-11
FORCE MAJEURE, Tangerine Dream, 79-26
FORCE OF VICTORY, Linton Kwesi Johnson, 79-66
FORE!, Huey Lewis and the News, 86-8
FOREIGN AFFAIR, Tina Turner, 89-1
FOREIGNER, Cat Stevens, 73-3
FOREVER, Various Artists: Compilations – EMI, 92-17
FOREVER, Cranes, 93-40
FOREVER, Damage, 97-13
FOREVER, Puff Daddy, 99-9
FOREVER, Spice Girls, 00-2
FOREVER AND EVER, Demis Roussos, 74-2
FOREVER BLUE, Chris Isaak, 95-27
FOREVER CHANGES, Love, 68-24
FOREVER ELLA, Ella Fitzgerald, 96-19
FOREVER, FOR ALWAYS, FOR LOVE, Luther Vandross, 87-23
FOREVER FOR NOW, Harry Connick Jr., 93-32
FOREVER NOW, Psychedelic Furs, 82-20
FOREVER NOW, Level 42, 94-8
FOREVER YOUR GIRL, Paula Abdul, 89-3
FORGING AHEAD, Bad Manners, 82-78
FORGIVEN, NOT FORGOTTEN, Corrs, 96-2
FORM & FUNCTION, Photek, 98-61
FORMALDEHYDE, Terrorvision, 93-75
FORMICA BLUES, Mono, 98-71
FORMULA 30, Various Artists: Compilations – Decca, 83-6

FULL HOUSE, Dooleys, 80-54
THE FULL LIFE, Jack Jones, 77-41
FULL METAL JACKET, Various Artists: Films – Original Soundtracks, 87-60
THE FULL MONTY, Various Artists: Films – Original Soundtracks, 97-1
FULL MOON, DIRTY HEARTS, Inxs, 93-3
FULL MOON FEVER, Tom Petty, 89-8
FULL ON – A YEAR IN THE LIFE OF HOUSE, Various Artists: Compilations – Deconstruction, 93-18
FULL ON DANCE, Various Artists: Compilations – Cookie Jar, 93-12
FULL ON DANCE '93, Various Artists: Compilations – Cookie Jar, 93-3
FULL ON..MASK HYSTERIA, Altern 8, 92-11
FULLY QUALIFIED SURVIVOR, Michael Chapman, 70-45
THE FUN BOY THREE, Fun Boy Three, 82-7
FUN IN ACAPULCO [OST], Elvis Presley, 63-9
FUN IN SPACE, Roger Taylor, 81-18
FUNDAMENTAL, Bonnie Raitt, 98-52
A FUNK ODYSSEY, Jamiroquai, 01-1
FUNK SOUL BROTHER – THE BEST OF DANCE SOUL & SWING, Various Artists: Compilations – Global Television, 99-19
FUNKMASTER MIX, Various Artists: Compilations – PolyGram TV, 96-16
FUNKOLOGY – ONE NATION UNDER A GROOVE, Various Artists: Compilations – WSM, 01-14
FUNKY DIVAS, En Vogue, 92-4
FUNKY DIVAS, Various Artists: Compilations – Global Television, 97-3
FUNKY DIVAS 2, Various Artists: Compilations – Global Television, 98-16
FUNKY DIVAS 3, Various Artists: Compilations – Global Television, 00-18
FUNKY DIVAS – THE VERY BEST IN SOUL DANCE AND R&B, Various Artists: Compilations – BMG/Telstar TV, 01-5
FUNKY HOUSE, Various Artists: Compilations – Telstar, 99-9
FUNKY LITTLE DEMONS, Wolfgang Press, 95-75
FUNNY GIRL, Barbra Streisand, 66-19
FUNNY GIRL [OST], Barbra Streisand, 69-11
FUR, Jane Wiedlin, 88-48
FUREYS FINEST, Fureys and Davey Arthur, 87-65
FURTHER, Geneva, 97-20
THE FURTHER ADVENTURES OF LITTLE VOICE, Jane Horrocks, 00-63
FURTHER DOWN THE ROAD, Charlie Landsborough, 97-42
FURTHEST FROM THE SUN, Family Cat, 92-55
THE FURY, Gary Numan, 85-24
FUSED, Various Artists: Compilations – PolyGram TV, 97-14
THE FUTURE, Leonard Cohen, 92-36
FUTURE BLUES, Canned Heat, 70-27
FUTURE SHOCK, Gillan, 81-2
FUTURE SHOCK, Herbie Hancock, 83-27
FUTURE SIGNS, Warm Jets, 98-40
THE FUTURE SOUND OF NEW YORK, Various Artists: Compilations – Ministry Of Sound, 95-19
FUTURESHOCK – 20 FURIOUS DANCE TUNES, Various Artists: Compilations – Dino, 93-4
FUTURISTIC DRAGON, T. Rex, 76-50
FUZZY, Grant Lee Buffalo, 93-74
FUZZY LOGIC, Super Furry Animals, 96-23
G-A-Y, Various Artists: Compilations – London, 00-18
G FORCE, Kenny G, 84-56
G.I. BLUES [OST], Elvis Presley with the Jordainaires, 60-1
G N' R THE LIES, THE SEX, THE DRUGS, THE VIOLENCE, THE SHOCKING TRUTH, Guns N' Roses, 88-22
G.O.A.T. FEATURING JAMES T. SMITH – THE GREATEST OF ALL TIME, LL Cool J, 00-29
GABRIELLE, Gabrielle, 96-11
THE GAELIC COLLECTION 1973-1995, Runrig, 98-71
GAIA (ONE WOMAN'S JOURNEY), Olivia Newton-John, 95-33
GALAXY HIT MIX, Various Artists: Compilations – Ministry Of Sound, 00-14
GALAXY MIX – BOY GEORGE, Various Artists: Compilations – Ministry Of Sound, 99-8
GALAXY WEEKEND: MIXED BY BOY GEORGE & ALLISTER WHITEHEAD, Various Artists: Compilations – Ministry Of Sound, 99-6
GALLUS, Gun, 92-14
GALORE – THE BEST OF KIRSTY MACCOLL, Kirsty MacColl, 95-6
GALORE – THE SINGLES 1987-1997, Cure, 97-37
THE GAME, Queen, 80-1
GAMES, B.B.E., 98-60
GANGSTA'S PARADISE, Coolio, 95-18
GANGSTERS OF THE GROOVE – THE 90'S MIX, Heatwave, 91-56
GAP BAND 8, Gap Band, 87-47
GARAGE ANTHEMS – MIXED BY CRAIG DAVID – THE VERY BEST OF GARAGE 2000, Various Artists: Compilations – Telstar, 00-6
GARAGE CITY, Various Artists: Compilations – Telstar, 92-8
GARAGE FLOWER, Stone Roses, 96-58
GARAGE INC., Metallica, 98-29
GARAGE NATION – LIVE MIX BY JASON KAYE, Various Artists: Compilations – Telstar, 00-10
GARAGE NATION – SUMMER 2001 – MIXED BY JASON KAYE & STICKY, Various Artists: Compilations – Incredible, 01-11
GARAGE VIBES, Various Artists: Compilations – Pure Silk, 00-20
GARBAGE, Garbage, 95-6
THE GARDEN, John Foxx, 81-24
GARDEN IN THE CITY, Melanie, 72-19
GARY GLITTER'S GREATEST HITS, Gary Glitter, 76-33
GASOLINE ALLEY, Rod Stewart, 70-62
GATECRASHER, Various Artists: Selected Series – Gatecrasher, 98-7
GATECRASHER DIGITAL, Various Artists: Selected Series – Gatecrasher, 01-6
GATECRASHER DISCO-TECH, Various Artists: Selected Series – Gatecrasher, 99-6
GATECRASHER DISCOTECH GENERATION, Various Artists: Selected Series – Gatecrasher, 01-10
GATECRASHER: GLOBAL SOUND SYSTEM, Various Artists: Selected Series – Gatecrasher, 00-3
GATECRASHER – NATIONAL ANTHEMS, Various Artists: Selected Series – Gatecrasher, 00-13
GATECRASHER RED, Various Artists: Selected Series – Gatecrasher, 99-4
GATECRASHER.WET, Various Artists: Selected Series – Gatecrasher, 99-3
GATECRASHING, Living In A Box, 89-21
GATHER ME, Melanie, 72-14
GATHERING OF FREAKS, Freak Of Nature, 94-66
GAUCHO, Steely Dan, 80-27
GAUDI, Alan Parsons Project, 87-66
GEFFERY MORGAN . . ., UB40, 84-3
GENE PITNEY'S BIG SIXTEEN, Gene Pitney, 65-12
GENE PITNEY'S BIG SIXTEEN (VOL. 3), Gene Pitney, 67-40
GENERATION TERRORISTS, Manic Street Preachers, 92-13
GENERATION X, Generation X, 78-29
GENESIS, Genesis, 83-1
GENESIS LIVE, Genesis, 73-9
THE GENIUS OF VENICE, Rondo Veneziano, 84-60
GENO, Dexy's Midnight Runners, 83-79
GENTLE ON MY MIND, Dean Martin, 69-9
GENTLE SHADES OF VAL DOONICAN, Val Doonican, 66-5
GENTLEMAN JIM, Jim Reeves, 64-3
GENTLEMEN, Afghan Whigs, 93-58
GENTLEMEN TAKE POLAROIDS, Japan, 80-45
GENTLY, Liza Minnelli, 96-58
GENUINE DUD, Dudley Moore Trio, 66-13
THE GEORGE BENSON COLLECTION, George Benson, 81-19
GEORGE BEST, Wedding Present, 87-47
GEORGE HARRISON, George Harrison, 79-39
GEORGE MCCRAE, George McCrae, 75-54
GEORGE THOROGOOD AND THE DESTROYERS, George Thorogood and the Destroyers, 78-67
GEORGIA SATELLITES, Georgia Satellites, 87-52
GERM FREE ADOLESCENTS, X-Ray Spex, 78-30
GERRY MULLIGAN MEETS BEN WEBSTER, Gerry Mulligan and Ben Webster, 60-15
GET A GRIP, Aerosmith, 93-2
GET CARTER [OST], Roy Budd, 98-68
GET CLOSE, Pretenders, 86-6
GET EVEN, Brother Beyond, 88-9
GET HAPPY!!, Elvis Costello and the Attractions, 80-2
GET HERE, Brenda Russell, 88-77
GET IN, Kenickie, 98-32
GET IN TOUCH WITH YOURSELF, Swing Out Sister, 92-27
GET INTO YOU, Dannii Minogue, 93-52
GET IT ON – GREATEST HITS OF THE 70'S, Various Artists: Compilations – The Hit Label, 93-12
GET LOOSE, Evelyn King, 82-35
GET NERVOUS, Pat Benatar, 82-73
GET ON THIS! – 30 DANCE HITS VOLUME 1, Various Artists: Compilations – Telstar, 90-2
GET ON THIS!!! 2, Various Artists: Compilations – Telstar, 90-3
GET ON UP, Various Artists: Compilations – RCA, 83-35
GET OUT AND WALK, Farmers Boys, 83-49
GET READY!, Roachford, 91-20
GET READY, 2 Unlimited, 92-37
GET READY, New Order, 01-6
GET RHYTHM, Ry Cooder, 87-75
GET RIGHT INTAE HIM, Billy Connolly, 75-6
GET STONED, Rolling Stones, 77-8
GET THAT FEELING, Jimi Hendrix and Curtis Knight, 68-39
GET THE KNACK, Knack, 79-65
GET TOGETHER WITH ANDY WILLIAMS, Andy Williams, 69-13
GET UP ON IT, Keith Sweat, 94-20
GET YER YA-YA'S OUT! – THE ROLLING STONES IN CONCERT, Rolling Stones, 70-1
GETAHEAD, Curiosity Killed The Cat, 89-29
THE GETAWAY, Chris De Burgh, 82-30
GETAWAY, Reef, 00-15
GETT OFF, Prince and the New Power Generation, 91-33
GETTIN' HIGH ON YOUR OWN SUPPLY, Apollo Four Forty, 99-20
GETTING READY, Temptations, 66-40
GETTING SENTIMENTAL, Engelbert Humperdinck, 85-35
GETTING THE HOLY GHOST ACROSS, Bill Nelson, 86-91
GETTING TO THIS, Blodwyn Pig, 70-8
GHETTO BLASTER, Crusaders, 84-46
GHETTO LOVE, Jaheim, 01-50
GHETTO MUSIC: THE BLUEPRINT OF HIP HOP, Boogie Down Productions, 89-32
GHETTO SUPASTAR, Pras, 98-44
GHOST, Various Artists: Films – Original Soundtracks, 90-15
GHOST IN THE MACHINE, Police, 81-1
GHOST OF A DOG, Edie Brickell and New Bohemians, 90-63
THE GHOST OF CAIN, New Model Army, 86-45
THE GHOST OF TOM JOAD, Bruce Springsteen, 95-16
GHOST RIDERS IN THE SKY, Slim Whitman, 79-27
GHOSTS OF PRINCES IN TOWERS, Rich Kids, 78-51
GHOSTBUSTERS, Various Artists: Films – Original Soundtracks, 84-24
GHOSTBUSTERS II, Various Artists: Films – Original Soundtracks, 89-15
GHV2: GREATEST HITS VOLUME 2 – THE BEST SONGS OF A DECADE, Madonna, 01-2
GIANT, Buddy Holly and the Crickets, 69-13
GIANT, Woodentops, 86-35
GIANT STEPS, Boo Radleys, 93-17
THE GIFT, Jam, 82-1
THE GIFT, Midge Ure, 85-2
GIFT, Sisterhood, 86-90
A GIFT FROM A FLOWER TO A GARDEN, Donovan, 68-13
THE GIFT OF GAME, Crazy Town, 01-15
A GIFT OF LOVE, Bill Tarmey, 93-15
THE GIFT OF SONG, Various Artists: Compilations – PolyGram TV, 93-7
GIFT SET, Barry Manilow, 81-62
GIGI, Various Artists: Films – Original Soundtracks, 59-2
GILBERT O'SULLIVAN HIMSELF, Gilbert O'Sullivan, 71-5

HARBOR LIGHTS, Bruce Hornsby, 93-32
HARBOUR, Jack Jones, 74-10
HARD AT PLAY, Huey Lewis and the News, 91-39
HARD DANCE ANTHEMS – MIXED BY PUBLIC DOMAIN, Various Artists: Compilations – WSM, 01-19
A HARD DAY'S NIGHT [OST], Beatles, 64-1
HARD ENERGY: MIXED BY FERGIE AND YOMANDA, Various Artists: Compilations – Ministry Of Sound, 01-10
HARD FAX, Various Artists: Compilations – Columbia, 92-3
HARD FAX 2 – TWICE THE VICE!, Various Artists: Compilations – Columbia, 92-6
HARD HOUSE EUPHORIA – MIXED BY LISA LASHES, Various Artists: Selected Series – Euphoria, 00-6
HARD HOUSE EUPHORIA – MIXED BY TIDY BOYS VS LISA PIN-UP, Various Artists: Selected Series – Euphoria, 01-12
HARD HOUSE NATION, Various Artists: Compilations – warner.esp, 00-4
HARD HOUSE NATION – 2, Various Artists: Compilations – WSM, 00-5
HARD HOUSE THREE, Various Artists: Compilations – WSM, 01-7
HARD NOSE THE HIGHWAY, Van Morrison, 73-22
HARD PROMISES, Tom Petty and the Heartbreakers, 81-32
HARD RAIN, Bob Dylan, 76-3
A HARD ROAD, John Mayall and the Bluesbreakers, 67-10
HARD TO EARN, Gang Starr, 94-29
THE HARD WAY, Steve Earle and the Dukes, 90-22
HARDCOAR DANCEFLOOR, Various Artists: Compilations – Dino, 91-2
HARDCORE DJS . . . TAKE CONTROL, Various Artists: Compilations – Perfecto, 92-15
HARDCORE ECSTASY, Various Artists: Compilations – Dino, 91-1
HARDCORE EXPLOSION '97, Various Artists: Compilations – Supreme Underground, 97-20
HARDCORE HEAVEN – VOLUME ONE, Various Artists: Compilations – Heaven Music, 97-12
HARDCORE HEAVEN – VOLUME 2, Various Artists: Compilations – Heaven Music, 97-13
HARDCORE HEAVEN – VOLUME 3, Various Artists: Compilations – Heaven Music, 98-12
HARDCORE HEAVEN – VOLUME 4, Various Artists: Compilations – Heaven Music, 98-17
HARDCORE HEAVEN – VOLUME 5, Various Artists: Compilations – Heaven Music, 99-17
HARDCORE UPROAR, Various Artists: Compilations – Dino, 91-2
HARDER . . . FASTER, April Wine, 80-34
HARDWARE, Krokus, 81-44
HAREM HOLIDAY [OST], Elvis Presley, 66-11
HARK THE HERALD ANGELS SING, Hamburg Students Choir, 60-11
HARLEM WORLD, Mase, 98-53
HARMACY, Sebadoh, 96-38
HARMONY OF CORRUPTION, Napalm Death, 90-67
HARRY POTTER AND THE PHILOSOPHER'S STONE [OST], Music Composed and Conducted by John Williams, 01-19
HARVEST, Neil Young, 72-1
HARVEST FOR THE WORLD, Isley Brothers, 76-50
HARVEST MOON, Neil Young, 92-9
HASTEN DOWN THE WIND, Linda Ronstadt, 76-32
HAT FULL OF STARS, Cyndi Lauper, 93-56
HAT TRICK, America, 73-41
HATFUL OF HOLLOW, Smiths, 84-7
HATS, Blue Nile, 89-12
HATS OFF TO DEL SHANNON, Del Shannon, 63-9
HAUNTED DANCEHALL, Sabres Of Paradise, 94-57
THE HAUNTED SCIENCE, Omni Trio, 96-43
HAUNTING MELODIES, Electric Wind Ensemble, 84-28
HAVANA MOON, Carlos Santana, 83-84
HAVE A GOOD FOREVER . . ., Cool Notes, 85-66
HAVE A LITTLE FAITH, Joe Cocker, 94-9
HAVE A NICE DAY, Roxette, 99-28
HAVE I TOLD YOU LATELY THAT I LOVE YOU, Jim Reeves, 65-12
HAVE "TWANGY" GUITAR WILL TRAVEL, Duane Eddy, 59-6
HAVE YOU EVER BEEN IN LOVE, Leo Sayer, 83-15
HAVE YOU NEVER BEEN MELLOW, Olivia Newton-John, 75-37
HAWAII, High Llamas, 96-62
HAWAIIAN PARADISE/CHRISTMAS, Wout Steenhuis, 81-28
HAWKS AND DOVES, Neil Young, 80-34
HAWKWIND, Hawkwind, 84-75
HE GOT GAME [OST], Public Enemy, 98-50
HE TOUCHED ME, Elvis Presley, 72-38
HE WALKS BESIDE ME, Elvis Presley, 78-37
HE WAS BEAUTIFUL, Iris Williams, 79-69
HE'LL HAVE TO GO, Jim Reeves, 64-16
HE'S THE DJ, I'M THE RAPPER, DJ Jazzy Jeff and Fresh Prince, 88-68
HEAD FIRST, Uriah Heep, 83-46
HEAD LIKE A ROCK, Ian McNabb, 94-29
HEAD MUSIC, Suede, 99-1
HEAD ON, Samson, 80-34
THE HEAD ON THE DOOR, Cure, 85-7
HEAD OVER HEELS, Cocteau Twins, 83-51
HEAD OVER HEELS, Various Artists: Television – Soundtracks, 93-3
HEAD OVER HEELS, Paula Abdul, 95-61
HEADED FOR THE FUTURE, Neil Diamond, 86-36
HEADHUNTERS, Krokus, 83-74
THE HEADLESS CHILDREN, W.A.S.P., 89-8
HEADLESS CROSS, Black Sabbath, 89-31
HEADLINE HITS, Various Artists: Compilations – K-Tel, 83-5
HEADLINERS: 01 – TALL PAUL LIVE AT THE GALLERY, Various Artists: Compilations – Ministry Of Sound, 00-20
HEADLINES, Midnight Star, 86-42
HEADLINES AND DEADLINES – THE HITS OF A-HA, A-Ha, 91-12
HEADQUARTERS, Monkees, 67-2
HEADRUSH, Various Artists: Compilations – Global Television, 00-10
HEADSTONE – THE BEST OF UFO, UFO, 83-39
THE HEALER, John Lee Hooker and Friends, 89-63
THE HEALING GAME, Van Morrison, 97-10
HEAR IN THE NOW FRONTIER, Queensryche, 97-46
HEAR MY CRY, Sonique, 00-6
HEAR MY SONG (THE BEST OF JOSEF LOCKE), Josef Locke, 92-7
HEAR 'N' AID, Various Artists: Compilations – Vertigo, 86-50
HEAR NOTHING, SEE NOTHING, SAY NOTHING, Discharge, 82-40
HEARSAY / ALL MIXED UP, Alexander O'Neal, 87-4
HEART, Heart, 85-19
HEART AND SOUL, Barry White, 85-34
HEART AND SOUL, Edith Piaf, 87-58
HEART & SOUL, Various Artists: Compilations – PolyGram TV, 97-17
HEART AND SOUL, Joy Division, 98-70
HEART AND SOUL – 18 CLASSIC SOUL CUTS, Various Artists: Compilations – Heart and Soul, 89-2
HEART & SOUL – NEW SONGS FROM ALLY MCBEAL [OST-TV], Vonda Shepard, 99-9
THE HEART AND SOUL OF ROCK AND ROLL, Various Artists: Compilations – Telstar, 88-60
HEART AND SOUL – THE VERY BEST OF T'PAU, T'Pau, 93-35
HEART AND SOUL III – HEART FULL OF SOUL, Various Artists: Compilations – Heart and Soul, 90-4
HEART FULL OF SOUL, Various Artists: Compilations – Dino, 93-9
HEART FULL OF SOUL, Various Artists: Compilations – Warner.esp/Global TV, 98-8
HEART FULL OF SOUL – 2, Various Artists: Compilations – Warner.esp/Global TV, 99-12
HEART IN MOTION, Amy Grant, 91-25
HEART LIKE A SKY, Spandau Ballet, 89-31
HEART 'N' SOUL, Tina Charles, 77-35
THE HEART OF A WOMAN, Johnny Mathis, 75-39
THE HEART OF CHICAGO, Chicago, 89-6
THE HEART OF CHICAGO – 1967-1997, Chicago, 99-21
A HEART OF GOLD, Various Artists: Compilations – Telstar, 93-9
THE HEART OF ROCK AND ROLL – BEST OF HUEY LEWIS AND THE NEWS, Huey Lewis and the News, 92-23
HEART OF STONE, Cher, 89-7
THE HEART OF THE 80S & 90S, Various Artists: Radio – Related Compilations , 98-9
HEART OVER MIND, Jennifer Rush, 87-48
HEART, SOUL AND VOICE, Jon Secada, 94-17
HEART STRINGS, Foster and Allen, 92-37
HEART TO HEART – 20 HOT HITS, Ray Charles, 80-29
HEART TO HEART – 24 LOVE SONG DUETS, Various Artists: Compilations – K-Tel, 86-8
HEARTBEAT, Hank Marvin, 93-17
HEARTBEAT CITY, Cars, 84-25
HEARTBEAT – FOREVER YOURS, Various Artists: Selected Series – Heartbeat, 95-1
HEARTBEAT – LOVE ME TENDER, Various Artists: Selected Series – Heartbeat, 97-6
HEARTBEAT (MUSIC FROM THE TV SERIES), Various Artists: Selected Series – Heartbeat, 92-1
HEARTBEAT – NUMBER 1 LOVE SONGS OF THE '60S, Various Artists: Selected Series – Heartbeat, 96-2
HEARTBEAT – THE OFFICIAL 10TH ANNIVERSARY, Various Artists: Selected Series – Heartbeat, 00-17
HEARTBEAT – THE 60'S GOLD COLLECTION, Various Artists: Selected Series – Heartbeat, 98-7
HEARTBEATS, Barbara Dickson, 84-21
HEARTBREAK STATION, Cinderella, 90-36
HEARTBREAKER, Free, 73-9
HEARTBREAKER, Dionne Warwick, 82-3
HEARTBREAKERS, Various Artists: Compilations – K-Tel, 77-2
HEARTBREAKERS, Matt Monro, 80-5
HEARTBREAKERS – 18 CLASSIC LOVE HITS, Various Artists: Compilations – Starblend, 86-38
HEARTLANDS, Various Artists: Compilations – Dino, 92-4
HEARTLIGHT, Neil Diamond, 82-43
HEARTS AND BONES, Paul Simon, 83-34
HEARTS AND FLOWERS, Joan Armatrading, 90-29
HEARTS OF FORTUNE, Immaculate Fools, 85-65
HEARTWORK, Carcass, 93-67
THE HEAT, Dan Reed Network, 91-15
THE HEAT, Toni Braxton , 00-3
THE HEAT IS ON!, Various Artists: Compilations – Arcade, 91-4
THE HEAT IS ON – 16 TRACKS, Various Artists: Compilations – Portrait, 86-9
HEAT OF SOUL VOLUME 1, Various Artists: Compilations – Mastersound, 87-96
HEAT TREATMENT, Graham Parker and the Rumour, 76-52
HEATHCLIFF LIVE (THE SHOW), Various Artists: Stage Cast – London, 96-41
HEAVEN AND HELL, Vangelis, 76-31
HEAVEN AND HELL, Black Sabbath, 80-9
HEAVEN AND HELL, Meat Loaf/Bonnie Tyler, 89-9
HEAVEN IS WAITING, Danse Society, 84-39
HEAVEN KNOWS, Jaki Graham, 85-48
HEAVEN ON EARTH, Belinda Carlisle, 88-4
HEAVEN OR LAS VEGAS, Cocteau Twins, 90-7
HEAVEN UP HERE, Echo and the Bunnymen, 81-10
HEAVENLY, Ladysmith Black Mambazo, 97-53
HEAVENLY HARDCORE, Various Artists: Compilations – Dino, 92-2
HEAVY, Various Artists: Compilations – K-Tel, 83-46
THE HEAVY HEAVY HITS, Madness, 98-19
HEAVY HORSES, Jethro Tull, 78-20
HEAVY NOVA, Robert Palmer, 88-17

HITS, HITS, HITS – 18 SMASH ORIGINALS, Various Artists: Compilations – Telstar, 84-6
HITS LIKE NEVER BEFORE (ESSENTIAL ELVIS VOLUME 3), Elvis Presley, 90-71
HITS 93 VOLUME 1, Various Artists: Selected Series – Hits, 93-1
HITS 93 VOLUME 2, Various Artists: Selected Series – Hits, 93-2
HITS 93 VOLUME 3, Various Artists: Selected Series – Hits, 93-2
HITS 93 VOLUME 4, Various Artists: Selected Series – Hits, 93-2
HITS 94 VOLUME 1, Various Artists: Selected Series – Hits, 94-3
HITS 96, Various Artists: Selected Series – Hits, 95-1
HITS 97, Various Artists: Selected Series – Hits, 96-2
HITS 99, Various Artists: Selected Series – Hits, 98-2
HITS OF GOLD, Mamas and the Papas, 69-7
THE HITS OF HOUSE ARE HERE, Various Artists: Compilations – K-Tel, 88-12
HITS OF THE ROCKIN' 50'S, Bobby Vee, 62-20
HITS OF THE SCREAMING 60'S, Various Artists: Compilations – Warwick, 82-24
HITS OF THE 70'S, Elvis Presley, 77-30
HITS OF THE SIXTIES, Bachelors, 66-12
HITS ON FIRE, Various Artists: Compilations – Ronco, 83-11
HITS ON OPERA, Kimera with the London Symphony Orchestra, 85-38
HITS OUT OF HELL, Meat Loaf, 85-2
HITS +, Kylie Minogue, 00-41
HITS REVIVAL, Various Artists: Compilations – K-Tel, 87-63
HITS REVIVAL, Various Artists: Compilations – K-Tel, 87-10
HITS REVIVAL 2: REPLAY, Various Artists: Compilations – K-Tel, 88-45
HITS RIGHT UP YOUR STREET, Shadows, 81-15
THE HITS/THE B-SIDES, Prince, 93-4
HITS 2000, Various Artists: Selected Series – Hits, 99-2
HITS 2001, Various Artists: Selected Series – Hits, 00-2
HITS UNLIMITED, 2 Unlimited, 95-27
HITS ZONE '97, Various Artists: Compilations – PolyGram TV, 96-11
HITS ZONE SUMMER '97, Various Artists: Compilations – PolyGram TV, 97-8
HITS ZONE – THE BEST OF '97, Various Artists: Compilations – PolyGram TV, 97-18
HITSVILLE, Various Artists: Compilations – Pye, 63-11
HITSVILLE VOLUME 2, Various Artists: Compilations – Pye, 63-20
HITZ BLITZ, Various Artists: Compilations – Global Television, 95-2
HOLD AN OLD FRIEND'S HAND, Tiffany, 88-56
HOLD ME, Bert Kaempfert, 67-36
HOLD ME, Laura Branigan, 85-64
HOLD ME IN YOUR ARMS, Rick Astley, 88-8
HOLD ME NOW, Johnny Logan, 87-83
HOLD ME, THRILL ME, KISS ME, Gloria Estefan, 94-5
HOLD ON I'M A COMIN', Sam and Dave, 67-35
HOLD OUT, Jackson Browne, 80-44
HOLD YOUR FIRE, Rush, 87-10
HOLDING BACK THE RIVER, Wet Wet Wet, 89-2
THE HOLIDAY ALBUM, Various Artists: Compilations – CBS, 87-13
HOLIDAYS IN EDEN, Marillion, 91-7
HOLLAND, Beach Boys, 73-20
HOLLIES, Hollies, 65-8
HOLLIES, Hollies, 74-38
THE HOLLIES' GREATEST, Hollies, 68-1
HOLLIES LIVE HITS, Hollies, 77-4
HOLLIES SING DYLAN, Hollies, 69-3
HOLLY IN THE HILLS, Buddy Holly and the Crickets, 65-13
HOLLYWOOD AND BROADWAY, Richard Clayderman, 86-28
HOLLYWOOD GOLDEN CLASSICS, Jose Carreras, 91-47
THE HOLLYWOOD MUSICALS, Johnny Mathis and Henry Mancini, 86-46
HOLLYWOOD VAMPIRES, L.A. Guns, 91-44
HOLST: THE PLANETS, Tomita, 77-41
HOLST: THE PLANETS, Herbert Von Karajan conducting the Berlin Philharmonic Orchestra, 91-52
THE HOLY BIBLE, Manic Street Preachers, 94-6
HOLY DIVER, Dio, 83-13
THE HOLY GROUND, Mary Black, 93-58
HOLY WOOD, Marilyn Manson, 00-23
HOME, Procol Harum, 70-49
HOME, Hothouse Flowers, 90-5
HOME, Deep Blue Something, 96-24
HOME AGAIN, New Edition, 96-22
HOME AND ABROAD, Style Council, 86-8
HOME INVASION, Ice-T, 93-15
HOME LOVIN' MAN, Andy Williams, 71-1
HOME LOVIN' MAN, Roger Whittaker, 89-20
HOME MOVIES – THE BEST OF EVERYTHING BUT THE GIRL, Everything But The Girl, 93-5
HOME ON THE RANGE, Slim Whitman, 77-2
HOME RUN, Hardfloor, 96-68
HOME THOUGHTS, Clifford T. Ward, 73-40
HOMEBASE, DJ Jazzy Jeff and the Fresh Prince, 91-69
HOMEBREW, Neneh Cherry, 92-27
HOMECOMING, America, 72-21
HOMEGROWN, Dodgy, 94-28
HOMESICK, Deaconblue, 01-59
HOMEWORK, Daft Punk, 97-8
HOMOGENIC, Bjork, 97-4
HONEY, Andy Williams, 68-4
HONEY, Robert Palmer, 94-25
HONEY HIT PARADE, Various Artists: Compilations – Pye, 62-13
HONEY LINGERS, Voice Of The Beehive, 91-17
HONEY TO THE B, Billie, 98-14
HONEY'S DEAD, Jesus And Mary Chain, 92-14
THE HONEYDRIPPERS VOLUME ONE, Honeydrippers, 84-56
HONKY CHATEAU, Elton John, 72-2
HOODOO, Alison Moyet, 91-11
HOOKED, Great White, 91-43
HOOKED ON CLASSICS, Louis Clark conducting the Royal Philharmonic Orchestra, 81-4
HOOKED ON COUNTRY, Various Artists: Compilations – K-Tel, 90-6
HOOKED ON NUMBER ONES – 100 NON-STOP GREATS, Various Artists: Compilations – K-Tel, 84-25
THE HOOPLE, Mott The Hoople, 74-11
HOORAY FOR BOOBIES, Bloodhound Gang, 00-37
HOPE AND ANCHOR FRONT ROW FESTIVAL, Various Artists: Concerts and Festivals, 78-28
HOPE AND GLORY, Tom Robinson, 84-21
HOPE IS IMPORTANT, Idlewild, 98-53
HOPES AND DREAMS, David Grant, 85-96
HORACE BROWN, Horace Brown, 96-48
HORIZON, Carpenters, 75-1
HORIZONS, Various Artists: Compilations – K-Tel, 88-13
HORIZONS – 12 DREAMHOUSE ANTHEMS, Various Artists: Compilations – PolyGram TV, 96-17
HORIZONTAL, Bee Gees, 68-16
HORMONALLY YOURS, Shakespears Sister, 92-3
THE HORNS OF JERICO, Hi-Jack, 91-54
HOST, Paradise Lost, 99-61
HOT, Melanie B, 00-28
HOT AUGUST NIGHT, Neil Diamond, 74-32
HOT AUGUST NIGHT II, Neil Diamond, 87-74
HOT CAKES, Carly Simon, 74-19
HOT CHOCOLATE, Hot Chocolate, 75-34
HOT CITY NIGHTS, Various Artists: Compilations – Vertigo, 88-1
HOT HITS 5, Various Artists: Anonymous – Music For Pleasure, 71-48
HOT HITS 6, Various Artists: Anonymous – Music For Pleasure, 71-1
HOT HITS 7, Various Artists: Anonymous – Music For Pleasure, 71-3
HOT HITS 8, Various Artists: Anonymous – Music For Pleasure, 71-2
HOT IN THE SHADE, Kiss, 89-35
HOT LOVE, David Essex, 80-75
HOT POP!, Various Artists: Compilations – Universal Music TV, 00-11
HOT RAIL, Calexico, 00-57
HOT RATS, Frank Zappa, 70-9
HOT ROCKS – THE GREATEST HITS 1964-1971, Rolling Stones, 90-3
HOT SHOT, Shaggy, 01-1
HOT SHOTS II, Beta Band, 01-13
HOT SPACE, Queen, 82-4
HOT SUMMER NIGHTS, Various Artists: Compilations – Stylus, 89-4
HOT TRACKS, Various Artists: Compilations – K-Tel, 79-31
HOT WAX, Various Artists: Compilations – K-Tel, 80-3
HOTEL CALIFORNIA, Eagles, 76-2
HOTLINE, Various Artists: Compilations – K-Tel, 83-3
HOTTER THAN JULY, Stevie Wonder, 80-2
HOTWIRED, Soup Dragons, 92-74
HOUNDS OF LOVE, Kate Bush, 85-1
THE HOUR OF BEWILDERBEAST, Badly Drawn Boy, 00-13
HOURGLASS, James Taylor, 97-46
HOURS . . ., David Bowie, 99-5
THE HOUSE COLLECTION – CLUB CLASSICS, Various Artists: Compilations – Fantazia, 96-3
THE HOUSE COLLECTION CLUB CLASSICS – 2, Various Artists: Compilations – Fantazia, 96-4
THE HOUSE COLLECTION – VOLUME 2, Various Artists: Compilations – Fantazia, 95-6
THE HOUSE COLLECTION – VOLUME 3, Various Artists: Compilations – Fantazia, 95-4
THE HOUSE COLLECTION – VOLUME 5, Various Artists: Compilations – Fantazia, 97-3
THE HOUSE COLLECTION 6 – PAUL OKENFOLD/PAUL COSFORD, Various Artists: Compilations – Fantazia, 97-10
HOUSE HALLUCINATIONS (PUMP UP LONDON VOLUME 1), Various Artists: Compilations – Breakout, 88-90
HOUSE HITS, Various Artists: Compilations – Needle, 88-25
HOUSE NATION 1, Various Artists: Compilations – React, 94-20
THE HOUSE OF BLUE LIGHT, Deep Purple, 87-10
HOUSE OF DOLLS, Gene Loves Jezebel, 87-81
THE HOUSE OF HANDBAG, Various Artists: Compilations – Ultrasound, 95-13
THE HOUSE OF HANDBAG – AUTUMN/WINTER COLLECTION, Various Artists: Compilations – Ultrasound, 95-16
HOUSE OF HANDBAG – NUOVO DISCO COLLECTION, Various Artists: Compilations – Solid State, 97-17
HOUSE OF LOVE, House Of Love, 90-8
THE HOUSE OF LOVE, House Of Love, 90-49
HOUSE OF PAIN, House Of Pain, 92-73
HOUSE OF THE BLUES, John Lee Hooker, 67-34
THE "HOUSE" SOUND OF CHICAGO, Various Artists: Compilations – Dj International, 86-52
THE "HOUSE" SOUND OF CHICAGO – VOL II, Various Artists: Compilations – Dj International, 87-38
THE HOUSE SOUND OF CHICAGO VOLUME 3, Various Artists: Compilations – Ffrr, 88-40
THE HOUSE SOUND OF LONDON VOLUME 4, Various Artists: Compilations – Ffrr, 88-70
THE HOUSE WE BUILT, Alisha's Attic, 01-55
THE HOUSEMARTINS' CHRISTMAS SINGLES BOX, Housemartins, 86-84
HOUSES OF THE HOLY, Led Zeppelin, 73-1
HOW 'BOUT US, Champaign, 81-38
HOW DARE YOU!, 10 C.C., 76-5
HOW DO I LOVE THEE, Bryn Yemm, 84-57
HOW DO YOU LIKE IT?, Gerry and the Pacemakers, 63-2
HOW DOES THAT GRAB YOU, Nancy Sinatra, 66-17
HOW GREAT THOU ART, Elvis Presley, 67-11
HOW GREAT THOU ART, Bryn Yemm, 84-67
HOW GREEN IS THE VALLEY, Men They Couldn't Hang, 86-68
HOW MEN ARE, Heaven 17, 84-12
HOW TO BE A ZILLIONAIRE, ABC, 85-28
HOW TO MAKE FRIENDS AND INFLUENCE PEOPLE, Terrorvision, 94-18
HOW TO OPERATE WITH A BLOWN MIND, Lo Fidelity Allstars, 98-15

IDEA, Bee Gees, 68-4
THE IDEAL COPY, Wire, 87-87
THE IDEAL CRASH, Deus, 99-64
THE IDIOT, Iggy Pop, 77-30
IDLEWILD, Everything But The Girl, 88-13
IDOL SONGS: 11 OF THE BEST, Billy Idol, 88-2
IF I RULED THE WORLD, Harry Secombe, 71-17
IF I SHOULD FALL FROM GRACE WITH GOD, Pogues, 88-3
IF I SHOULD LOVE AGAIN, Barry Manilow, 81-5
IF I WAS: THE VERY BEST OF MIDGE URE AND ULTRAVOX, Midge Ure/Ultravox, 93-10
IF MUSIC BE THE FOOD OF LOVE . . . PREPARE FOR INDIGESTION, Dave Dee, Dozy, Beaky, Mick and Tich, 67-27
IF ONLY I COULD REMEMBER MY NAME, David Crosby, 71-12
IF THE BEATLES HAD READ HUNTER . . . THE SINGLES, Wonder Stuff, 94-8
IF THIS IS ROCK AND ROLL, I WANT MY OLD JOB BACK, Saw Doctors, 91-69
IF WE FALL IN LOVE TONIGHT, Rod Stewart, 96-8
IF YOU CAN BELIEVE YOUR EYES AND EARS, Mamas and the Papas, 66-3
IF YOU CAN'T STAND THE HEAT, Status Quo, 78-3
IF YOU HAPPY WITH YOU NEED DO NOTHING, Alfie, 01-62
IF YOU WANT BLOOD YOU'VE GOT IT, AC/DC, 78-13
IF YOU WANT TO DEFEAT YOUR ENEMY SING HIS SONG, Icicle Works, 87-28
IF YOU'RE NEVER BEEN, Embrace, 01-9
ILL COMMUNICATION, Beastie Boys, 94-10
ILLEGAL RAVE, Various Artists: Compilations – Strictly Underground, 92-20
ILLEGAL STILLS, Stephen Stills, 76-54
ILLUMINA, Alisha's Attic, 98-15
ILLUMINATIONS, Carlos Santana and Alice Coltrane, 74-40
IMA, BT, 95-45
IMAGES, Walker Brothers, 67-6
IMAGES, Don Williams, 78-2
IMAGES, Various Artists: Compilations – K-Tel, 83-33
IMAGES, Guitar Corporation, 92-41
IMAGES – THE BEST OF JEAN MICHEL JARRE, Jean Michel Jarre, 91-14
IMAGINATION, Whispers, 81-42
IMAGINATION, Brian Wilson, 98-30
IMAGINATION – ALL THE HITS, Imagination, 89-4
IMAGINATIONS, Various Artists: Compilations – CBS, 83-15
IMAGINE, John Lennon; Plastic Ono Band (with the Flux Fiddlers), 71-1
IMAGINE: JOHN LENNON [OST], John Lennon, 88-64
THE IMMACULATE COLLECTION, Madonna, 90-1
THE IMMORTAL OTIS REDDING, Otis Redding, 68-19
IMPACT, Various Artists: Compilations – EMI, 69-15
IMPERIAL BEDROOM, Elvis Costello and the Attractions, 82-6
IMPERIAL WIZARD, David Essex, 79-12
IMPLANT, Eat Static, 94-13
THE IMPOSSIBLE DREAM, Andy Williams, 72-26
THE IMPOSSIBLE DREAM, Sensational Alex Harvey Band, 74-16
IMPRESSIONS – 15 INSTRUMENTAL IMAGES, Various Artists: Compilations – K-Tel, 87-15
IMPURITY, New Model Army, 90-23
IN BLUE, Corrs, 00-1
IN CITY DREAMS, Robin Trower, 77-58
IN CONCERT, Deep Purple, 80-30
IN CONCERT, Rolling Stones, 82-94
IN CONCERT, Carreras Domingo Pavarotti Orchestra conducted by Zubin Mehta, 90-1
IN CONCERT, Doors, 91-24
IN CONCERT – MTV PLUGGED, Bruce Springsteen, 93-4
IN CONCERT: SINATRA AT 'THE SANDS', Frank Sinatra, 66-7
IN CONCERT VOLUME 1, Peter, Paul and Mary, 65-20
IN CONCERT VOLUME 2, James Last, 74-49
IN DEEP, Argent, 73-49
IN DREAMS, Roy Orbison, 63-6
IN DREAMS, Brenda Cochrane, 91-55
IN DREAMS: THE GREATEST HITS, Roy Orbison, 87-86
IN FLIGHT, George Benson, 77-19
IN FOR THE KILL, Budgie, 74-29
IN FULL BLOOM, Rose Royce, 77-18
IN FULL EFFECT, Mantronix, 88-39
IN HARMONY, Richard Clayderman and James Last, 94-28
IN HARMONY, Ladysmith Black Mambazo, 99-15
IN HEARING OF ATOMIC ROOSTER, Atomic Rooster, 71-18
IN HIS OWN WORDS, 2 Pac, 98-65
IN IT FOR THE MONEY, Supergrass, 97-2
IN LOVE – GREATEST LOVE 5, Various Artists: Selected Series – Greatest Love, 91-5
IN MY LIFE, George Martin and Various Artists, 98-5
IN MYSTERIOUS WAYS, John Foxx, 85-85
IN NO SENSE OF NONSENSE, Art Of Noise, 87-55
IN ON THE KILLTAKER, Fugazi, 93-24
IN ORDER TO DANCE 5, Various Artists: Compilations – R&S, 94-16
IN OUR LIFETIME, Marvin Gaye, 81-48
IN PIECES, Garth Brooks, 94-2
IN RIBBONS, Pale Saints, 92-61
IN ROCK WE TRUST, Y and T, 84-33
IN SEARCH OF ANGELS, Runrig, 99-29
IN SEARCH OF SANITY, Onslaught, 89-46
IN SEARCH OF SPACE, Hawkwind, 71-18
IN SEARCH OF THE LOST CHORD, Moody Blues, 68-5
IN SIDES, Orbital, 96-5
THE IN SOUND FROM WAY OUT!, Beastie Boys, 96-45
IN SQUARE CIRCLE, Stevie Wonder, 85-5
IN STEP, Stevie Ray Vaughan and Double Trouble, 89-63
IN STEREO, Bomfunk MC's, 00-33
IN STYLE WITH THE CRICKETS, Crickets, 61-13
IN 10 CITIES, Ted Nugent, 81-75
IN THE AIR TONIGHT, Various Artists: Compilations – Virgin, 94-8
IN THE ARMY NOW, Status Quo, 86-7
IN THE BLOOD, Londonbeat, 90-34
IN THE CITY, Jam, 77-20
IN THE COURT OF THE CRIMSON KING, King Crimson, 69-5
IN THE DARK, Grateful Dead, 87-57
IN THE DYNAMITE JET SALOON, Dogs D'Amour, 88-97
IN THE EYE OF THE STORM, Roger Hodgson, 84-70
IN THE FLAT FIELD, Bauhaus, 80-72
IN THE GROOVE – THE 12 INCH DISCO PARTY, Various Artists: Compilations – Telstar, 83-20
IN THE HAND OF THE INEVITABLE, James Taylor Quartet, 95-63
IN THE HEART, Kool And The Gang, 84-18
IN THE HEAT OF THE NIGHT, Imagination, 82-7
IN THE HEAT OF THE NIGHT, Pat Benatar, 85-98
IN THE LOUNGE WITH . . . ANDY WILLIAMS, Andy Williams, 99-39
IN THE MIX IBIZA, Various Artists: Selected Series – In The Mix, 98-1
IN THE MIX – 90'S HITS, Various Artists: Selected Series – In The Mix, 96-3
IN THE MIX 96, Various Artists: Selected Series – In The Mix, 96-1
IN THE MIX 96 – 2, Various Artists: Selected Series – In The Mix, 96-2
IN THE MIX 96 – 3, Various Artists: Selected Series – In The Mix, 96-1
IN THE MIX 97, Various Artists: Selected Series – In The Mix, 97-1
IN THE MIX 97 – 2, Various Artists: Selected Series – In The Mix, 97-2
IN THE MIX 97 – 3, Various Artists: Selected Series – In The Mix, 97-2
IN THE MIX 98, Various Artists: Selected Series – In The Mix, 98-1
IN THE MIX 98, Various Artists: Selected Series – In The Mix, 98-6
IN THE MIX 2000, Various Artists: Selected Series – In The Mix, 99-3
IN THE MIX 2000 – THE ULTIMATE CLUB EXPERIENCE, Various Artists: Selected Series – In The Mix, 00-11
IN THE MODE, Roni Size Reprazent, 00-15
IN THE PINK, James Galway and Henry Mancini with the National Philharmonic Orchestra, 84-62
IN THE POCKET, Commodores, 81-69
IN THE SKIES, Peter Green, 79-32
IN THE STUDIO, Special A.K.A., 84-34
IN THE WAKE OF POSEIDON, King Crimson, 70-4
IN THE WIND, Peter, Paul and Mary, 64-11
IN THIS LIFE, Mordred, 91-70
IN THROUGH THE OUT DOOR, Led Zeppelin, 79-1
IN TOUCH, Various Artists: Compilations – Starblend, 83-89
IN TOWN, Rockin' Berries, 65-15
IN UTERO, Nirvana, 93-1
IN VISIBLE SILENCE, Art Of Noise, 86-18
IN YOUR EYES, George Benson, 83-3
IN YOUR FACE, Kingdom Come, 89-25
IN YOUR MIND, Bryan Ferry, 77-5
INARTICULATE SPEECH OF THE HEART, Van Morrison, 83-14
INCANTATIONS, Mike Oldfield, 78-14
INCESTICIDE, Nirvana, 92-14
THE INCOMPARABLE ELLA, Ella Fitzgerald, 80-40
THE INCREDIBLE PLAN, Max Boyce, 76-9
THE INCREDIBLE SHRINKING DICKIES, Dickies, 79-18
THE INCREDIBLE SOUND MACHINE, Mantronix, 91-36
INCREDIBLE SOUND OF DRUM'N'BASS: MIXED BY GOLDIE, Various Artists: Compilations – INCredible, 99-16
INCREDIBLE SOUND OF THE DREEM TEAM, Various Artists: Compilations – INCredible, 00-14
INCREDIBLE SOUND OF TREVOR NELSON, Various Artists: Compilations – INCredible, 99-14
THE INCREDIBLE STRING BAND, Incredible String Band, 68-34
INDECENT PROPOSAL, Various Artists: Films – Original Soundtracks, 93-13
INDEPENDENCE, Lulu, 93-67
INDEPENDENCE DAY [OST], David Arnold, 96-71
INDEPENDENCE DAY UK , Various Artists: Radio – Soundtracks, 96-66
INDEPENDENT WOMAN, Various Artists: Compilations – Columbia, 01-7
INDEPENDENT WORM SALOON, Butthole Surfers, 93-73
INDIAN SUMMER, Go West, 92-13
INDIE HITS, Various Artists: Compilations – Telstar, 92-13
INDIGO, Matt Bianco, 88-23
INDISCREET, Sparks, 75-18
INDISCREET, FM, 86-76
INDUSTRY, Richard and Danny Thompson, 97-69
INFECTED, The, 86-14
INFERNAL LOVE, Therapy?, 95-9
INFEST, Papa Roach, 01-9
INFIDELS, Bob Dylan, 83-9
INFINITY, Guru Josh, 90-41
INFINITY WITHIN, Deee-Lite, 92-37
INFLAMMABLE MATERIAL, Stiff Little Fingers, 79-14
INFLUENCES, Mark King, 84-77
INFORCERS 3, Various Artists: Compilations – Reinforced, 93-18
INFORMATION, Dave Edmunds, 83-92
INFOTAINMENT SCAN, Fall, 93-9
INGENUE, k.d. lang, 92-3
INITIAL SUCCESS, B.A. Robertson, 80-32
INNA DANCEHALL STYLE, Various Artists: Compilations – EMI, 93-11
INNER CHILD, Shanice, 92-21
INNER SECRETS, Santana, 78-17
INNERVISIONS, Stevie Wonder, 73-8
INNOCENCE IS NO EXCUSE, Saxon, 85-36
AN INNOCENT MAN, Billy Joel, 83-2
THE INNOCENTS, Erasure, 88-1
INNUENDO, Queen, 91-1
INSIDE INFORMATION, Foreigner, 87-64
INSIDE JOB, Don Henley, 00-25
INSIDE LIFE, Incognito, 91-44
INSIDE SHELLEY BERMAN, Shelley Berman, 60-12

JAMES GALWAY PLAYS SONGS FOR ANNIE, James Galway, flute; National Philharmonic Orchestra; Charles Gerhardt, conductor, 78-7
JAMES LAST AND HIS ORCHESTRA PLAYS ABBA, James Last and his Orchestra, 01-29
JAMES LAST GOES POP, James Last, 68-32
JAMES LAST IN CONCERT, James Last, 72-13
JAMES LAST IN RUSSIA, James Last, 73-12
JAMES LAST IN SCOTLAND, James Last, 84-68
JAMES LAST PLAYS ANDREW LLOYD WEBBER, James Last, 93-12
JAMIE OLIVER'S COOKIN' – MUSIC TO COOK BY, Various Artists: Television – Related Compilations, 00-14
JAMMIN', Various Artists: Compilations – Cookie Jar, 93-7
THE JAN AND DEAN STORY, Jan and Dean, 80-67
JANE FONDA'S WORKOUT RECORD, Jane Fonda, 83-7
JANE FONDA'S WORKOUT RECORD: NEW AND IMPROVED, Jane Fonda, 84-60
JANE MCDONALD, Jane McDonald, 98-1
JANET JACKSON'S RHYTHM NATION 1814, Janet Jackson, 89-4
JANET / JANET – REMIXED, Janet Jackson, 93-1
JANIS JOPLIN IN CONCERT, Janis Joplin, 72-30
JAPANESE WHISPERS: SINGLES NOV 82 – NOV 83, Cure, 83-26
JAR OF FLIES/SAP, Alice In Chains, 94-4
JARRE LIVE, Jean-Michel Jarre, 89-16
JARREAU, Al Jarreau, 83-39
JAWS [OST], Composed and conducted by John Williams, 76-55
JAZZ, Queen, 78-2
JAZZ CLASSICS, Louis Armstrong, 61-20
JAZZ FUNK, Incognito, 81-28
JAZZ JUICE 2, Various Artists: Compilations – Street Sounds, 86-96
JAZZ JUICE 3, Various Artists: Compilations – Street Sounds, 86-88
JAZZ JUICE 5, Various Artists: Compilations – Street Sounds, 87-97
JAZZ MOODS, Various Artists: Compilations – Telstar, 94-3
JAZZ MOODS 2, Various Artists: Compilations – Telstar, 94-18
JAZZ ON A SUMMER'S DAY, Various Artists: Compilations – Castle Communications, 92-4
JAZZ SAMBA, Stan Getz and Charlie Byrd, 63-15
JAZZ SEBASTIAN BACH, Swingle Singers, 64-13
THE JAZZ SINGER [OST], Neil Diamond, 80-3
JAZZAMATAZZ, Guru featuring Various Artists, 93-58
JAZZMATAZZ VOLUME II – THE NEW REALITY, Guru, 95-12
JEAN-MICHEL JARRE IN CONCERT LYON/HOUSTON, Jean-Michel Jarre, 87-18
JEFF BECK, TIM BOGERT & CARMINE APPICE, Jeff Beck, Tim Bogert and Carmine Appice, 73-28
JEFF WAYNE'S MUSICAL VERSION OF SPARTACUS, Jeff Wayne's Musical Version, 92-36
JEFF WAYNE'S MUSICAL VERSION OF THE WAR OF THE WORLDS, Jeff Wayne's Musical Version, 78-5
JEFF WAYNE'S MUSICAL VERSION OF THE WAR OF THE WORLDS – ULLADUBULLA THE REMIX ALBUM, Jeff Wayne's Musical Version, 00-64
JEHOVAHKILL, Julian Cope, 92-20
JENNIFER PAIGE, Jennifer Paige, 98-67
JENNIFER RUSH, Jennifer Rush, 85-7
JERKY VERSIONS OF THE DREAM, Howard Devoto, 83-57
JERRY LEE LEWIS VOLUME 2, Jerry Lee Lewis, 62-14
JESUS CHRIST SUPERSTAR, Various Artists: Studio Cast, 72-6
JESUS CHRIST SUPERSTAR, Various Artists: Films – Original Soundtracks, 73-23
THE JESUS OF COOL, Nick Lowe, 78-22
JEWEL, Marcella Detroit, 94-15
JI, Junior, 82-28
JIGSAW, Shadows, 67-8
JIM DIAMOND, Jim Diamond, 93-16
JIM REEVES AND SOME FRIENDS, Jim Reeves, 69-24
JIM REEVES' GOLDEN RECORDS, Jim Reeves, 71-9
THE JIM REEVES WAY, Jim Reeves, 65-16
JIM REEVES WRITES YOU A RECORD, Jim Reeves, 71-47
JIMI HENDRIX, Jimi Hendrix, 75-35
JIMI HENDRIX AT THE ISLE OF WIGHT, Jimi Hendrix, 71-17
THE JIMI HENDRIX CONCERTS, Jimi Hendrix, 82-16
JIMI HENDRIX – THE ULTIMATE EXPERIENCE, Jimi Hendrix, 92-25
THE JIMMY RUFFIN WAY, Jimmy Ruffin, 67-32
JINX, Rory Gallagher, 82-68
JIVE BUNNY – THE ALBUM, Jive Bunny and the Mastermixers, 89-2
JJ72, JJ72, 00-16
JOAN ARMATRADING, Joan Armatrading, 76-12
JOAN BAEZ, Joan Baez, 65-9
JOAN BAEZ IN CONCERT VOLUME 2, Joan Baez, 64-8
JOAN BAEZ NUMBER 5, Joan Baez, 65-3
JOAN BAEZ ON VANGUARD, Joan Baez, 69-15
JOB LOT, Chas and Dave, 83-59
JODY WATLEY, Jody Watley, 87-62
JOE BROWN – LIVE, Joe Brown, 63-14
JOE COCKER / WITH A LITTLE HELP FROM MY FRIENDS, Joe Cocker, 72-29
THE JOE LONGTHORNE CHRISTMAS ALBUM, Joe Longthorne, 89-44
THE JOE LONGTHORNE SONGBOOK, Joe Longthorne, 88-16
JOE SATRIANI, Joe Satriani, 95-21
JOE'S GARAGE ACT I, Frank Zappa, 79-62
JOE'S GARAGE ACTS II & III, Frank Zappa, 80-75
JOEY LAWRENCE, Joey Lawrence, 93-39
JOHN BARLEYCORN MUST DIE, Traffic, 70-11
JOHN DENVER, John Denver, 79-68
JOHN DENVER – COLLECTION, John Denver, 84-20
JOHN DIGWEED SYDNEY, Various Artists: Compilations – Global Underground, 98-16
JOHN HANSON SINGS 20 SHOWTIME GREATS, John Hanson, 77-16
JOHN LENNON/PLASTIC ONO BAND, John Lennon/Plastic Ono Band, 71-11
THE JOHN LENNON ANTHOLOGY, John Lennon, 98-62
THE JOHN LENNON COLLECTION, John Lennon, 82-1
JOHN LENNON LIVE IN NEW YORK CITY, John Lennon, 86-55
JOHN PARR, John Parr, 85-60
JOHN PAUL II – THE PILGRIM POPE, Pope John Paul II, 82-71
JOHN TAVENER: INNOCENCE, Westminster Abbey Choir/conductor: Martin Neary, 97-34
JOHN WESLEY HARDING, Bob Dylan, 68-1
JOHN WILLIAMS PLAYS THE MOVIES, John Williams, 96-54
JOHNNY CASH, Johnny Cash, 71-43
JOHNNY CASH AT FOLSOM PRISON, Johnny Cash, 68-8
JOHNNY CASH AT SAN QUENTIN, Johnny Cash, 69-2
THE JOHNNY CASH SHOW, Johnny Cash, 70-18
THE JOHNNY MATHIS COLLECTION, Johnny Mathis, 77-1
JOHNNY NASH COLLECTION, Johnny Nash, 77-18
JOHNNY THE FOX, Thin Lizzy, 76-11
JOHNNY WINTER AND . . ., Johnny Winter, 70-29
JOHNNY WINTER AND . . . LIVE, Johnny Winter, 71-20
JOIN BING AND SING ALONG, Bing Crosby, 60-7
JOIN HANDS, Siouxsie and the Banshees, 79-13
JOIN THE ARMY, Suicidal Tendencies, 87-81
JOIN TOGETHER, Who, 90-59
JOLLIFICATION, Lightning Seeds, 94-12
JON SECADA, Jon Secada, 92-20
JONATHAN BUTLER, Jonathan Butler, 87-12
JONATHAN KING'S ENTERTAINMENT FROM THE U.S.A., Various Artists: Television – Related Compilations, 86-6
JONATHAN LIVINGSTON SEAGULL [OST], Neil Diamond, 74-35
JORDAN: THE COMEBACK, Prefab Sprout, 90-7
JOSE CARRERAS COLLECTION, Jose Carreras, 88-90
JOSE CARRERAS SINGS ANDREW LLOYD WEBBER, Jose Carreras, 89-42
JOSE FELICIANO, Jose Feliciano, 69-29
JOSEPH AND THE AMAZING TECHNICOLOR DREAMCOAT, Various Artists: Stage Cast – London, 91-1
THE JOSHUA TREE, U2, 87-1
THE JOSHUA TREE SINGLES, U2, 88-100
THE JOURNEY, 911, 97-13
JOURNEY INWARDS, LTJ Bukem, 00-40
JOURNEY THROUGH THE CLASSICS – HOOKED ON CLASSICS 3, Louis Clark conducting the Royal Philharmonic Orchestra, 83-19
JOURNEY THROUGH THE SECRET LIFE OF PLANTS, Stevie Wonder, 79-8
JOURNEY TO ADDIS, Third World, 78-30
JOURNEY TO GLORY, Spandau Ballet, 81-5
JOURNEY TO THE CENTRE OF THE EARTH, Rick Wakeman with the London Symphony Orchestra and English Chamber Choir, 74-1
JOURNEY TO THE URGE WITHIN, Courtney Pine, 86-39
JOURNEYMAN, Eric Clapton, 89-2
JOURNEYS BY DJ VOLUME 4, Various Artists: Compilations – Music Unites, 94-19
JOY, Teddy Pendergrass, 88-45
JOY 1967-1990, Ultra Vivid Scene, 90-58
A JOYFUL NOISE UNTO THE CREATOR, Galliano, 92-28
JOYRIDE, Roxette, 91-2
JU JU, Siouxsie and the Banshees, 81-7
JUDGEMENT NIGHT, Various Artists: Films – Original Soundtracks, 93-16
JUDITH, Judy Collins, 75-7
JUDY AT CARNEGIE HALL, Judy Garland, 62-13
JUICY LUCY, Juicy Lucy, 70-41
JUKE BOX JIVE, Various Artists: Compilations – K-Tel, 76-3
JUKE BOX JIVE MIX – ROCK 'N' ROLL GREATS, Various Artists: Compilations – Stylus, 89-13
JULIA FORDHAM, Julia Fordham, 88-20
JULIAN COPE PRESENTS 20 MOTHERS, Julian Cope, 95-20
THE JULIET LETTERS, Elvis Costello and the Brodsky Quartet, 93-18
JULIO, Julio Iglesias, 83-5
JUMP BACK – THE BEST OF THE ROLLING STONES 1971-93, Rolling Stones, 93-16
JUMP – THE BEST OF THE POINTER SISTERS, Pointer Sisters, 89-11
JUMP UP, Elton John, 82-13
JUMPIN' JIVE, Joe Jackson's Jumpin' Jive, 81-14
JUNCTION SEVEN, Steve Winwood, 97-32
JUNGLE FEVER [OST], Stevie Wonder, 91-56
JUNGLE HITS VOLUME 1, Various Artists: Compilations – Jetstar, 94-9
JUNGLE MANIA 2, Various Artists: Compilations – Telstar, 94-5
JUNGLE MANIA 3, Various Artists: Compilations – Telstar, 95-5
JUNGLE MANIA 94, Various Artists: Compilations – Telstar, 94-7
JUNGLE TEKNO VOLUME 1, Various Artists: Compilations – Debut, 92-18
JUNIOR BOY'S OWN COLLECTION, Various Artists: Compilations – Junior Boy's Own, 94-20
JUNK CULTURE, Orchestral Manoeuvres In The Dark, 84-9
JUNK SCIENCE, Deep Dish, 98-37
JUNKYARD, Birthday Party, 82-73
JURASSIC 5, Jurassic 5, 98-70
JURASSIC PARK [OST], John Williams, 93-42
JURASSIC SHIFT, Ozric Tentacles, 93-11
JUST A BOY, Leo Sayer, 74-4
JUST A COLLECTION OF ANTIQUES AND CURIOS, Strawbs, 70-27
JUST A GIGGLE, Barron Knights, 80-45
JUST ADD LIFE, Almighty, 96-34
JUST ANOTHER WAY TO SAY I LOVE YOU, Barry White, 75-12
JUST BACKWARD OF SQUARE, Lowgold, 01-33
JUST CAN'T STOP IT, Beat, 80-3

KNOCK ON WOOD, Eddie Floyd, 67-36
KNOCKED OUT LOADED, Bob Dylan, 86-35
KNOW YOUR ENEMY, Manic Street Preachers, 01-2
KNOWING ME, KNOWING YOU 3, Alan Partridge, 95-41
KNUCKLE SANDWICH, Various Artists: Compilations – EMI, 79-19
KOHYEPT – LIVE IN LENINGRAD, Billy Joel, 87-92
KOJAK VARIETY, Elvis Costello, 95-21
KONGOS, John Kongos, 72-29
KOO KOO, Debbie Harry, 81-6
KOOL-AID, Big Audio Dynamite II, 90-55
KOOL LOVE, Kool And The Gang, 90-50
KREUZ KONTROL, Kreuz, 95-48
KT3 – KAOS THEORY 3, Various Artists: Compilations – Telstar, 92-1
KYLIE, Kylie Minogue, 88-1
KYLIE GREATEST HITS, Kylie Minogue, 92-1
KYLIE MINOGUE, Kylie Minogue, 94-4
KYLIE MINOGUE, Kylie Minogue, 98-10
L, Steve Hillage, 76-10
L, Godley and Creme, 78-47
L.A. FREEWAY, Various Artists: Compilations – Dino, 91-6
L.A. GUNS, L.A. Guns, 88-73
L.A. IS MY LADY, Frank Sinatra with the Quincy Jones Orchestra, 84-41
L.A. WOMAN, Doors, 71-28
L.A.M.F., Heartbreakers, 77-55
L IS FOR LOVER, Al Jarreau, 86-45
LA BAMBA [OST], Los Lobos/Various, 87-24
LA CARRETERA, Julio Iglesias, 95-6
LA FOLIE, Stranglers, 81-11
LA (LIGHT ALBUM), Beach Boys, 79-32
LA LUNA, Sarah Brightman, 01-37
LA PASSIONE [OST], Chris Rea, 96-43
LA VERITE, Classix Nouveaux, 82-44
THE LA'S, La's, 90-30
LABCABINCALIFORNIA, Pharcyde, 96-46
LABOUR OF LOVE, UB40, 83-1
LABOUR OF LOVE II, UB40, 89-3
LABOUR OF LOVE III, UB40, 98-8
LABOUR OF LOVE – VOLUMES I AND II [RI], UB40, 94-5
LABOUR OF LUST, Nick Lowe, 79-43
LABOURS OF LOVE – THE BEST OF HUE AND CRY, Hue And Cry, 93-27
LABYRINTH [OST], Trevor Jones, 86-38
LACE AND WHISKY, Alice Cooper, 77-33
THE LADDER, Yes, 99-36
LADIES & GENTLEMEN – THE BEST OF GEORGE MICHAEL, George Michael, 98-1
LADIES & GENTLEMEN WE ARE FLOATING IN SPACE, Spiritualized, 97-4
LADIES OF THE CANYON, Joni Mitchell, 70-8
LADY, Kenny Rogers, 81-40
LADY DAY – THE VERY BEST OF BILLIE HOLIDAY, Billie Holiday, 97-63
LADY SAMANTHA, Elton John, 80-56
THE LADY SINGS THE BLUES, Various Artists: Compilations – Pure Music, 94-9
LADY SINGS THE BLUES [OST], Diana Ross, 73-50
LADY SOUL, Aretha Franklin, 68-25
LADYKILLERS, Various Artists: Compilations – PolyGram TV, 96-3
LADYKILLERS 2, Various Artists: Compilations – PolyGram TV, 97-15
LAID, James, 93-3
THE LAMB LIES DOWN ON BROADWAY, Genesis, 74-10
LAMBADA, Various Artists: Compilations – CBS, 89-15
LAMENT, Ultravox, 84-8
LAND, Comsat Angels, 83-91
LAND OF HOPE AND GLORY, G.U.S. (Footwear) Band and the Morristown Orpheus Choir, 70-54
LAND OF MY FATHERS, Various Artists: Compilations – Universal Music TV, 99-1
LANDING ON WATER, Neil Young, 86-52
LANDMARKS, Clannad, 98-34
THE LANGUAGE OF LIFE, Everything But The Girl, 90-10
LARA CROFT TOMB RAIDER, Various Artists: Films – Original Soundtracks, 01-13
LARGER THAN LIFE, Jody Watley, 89-39
LARKS' TONGUES IN ASPIC, King Crimson, 73-20
LASER LOVE, After The Fire, 79-57
THE LAST ACTION HERO, Various Artists: Films – Original Soundtracks, 93-16
THE LAST CALL, Anti-Pasti, 81-31
THE LAST COMMAND, W.A.S.P., 85-48
THE LAST DANCE, Various Artists: Compilations – Motown, 80-1
THE LAST DOG AND PONY SHOW, Bob Mould, 98-58
LAST FOREVER, James Last, 81-88
LAST GOON SHOW OF ALL, Goons, 72-8
THE LAST IN LINE, Dio, 84-4
LAST NIGHT OF THE PROMS, Colin Davis conducting The BBC Symphony Orchestra, Singers and Chorus, 69-36
LAST OF THE INDEPENDENTS, Pretenders, 94-8
THE LAST RECORD ALBUM, Little Feat, 75-36
LAST SPLASH, Breeders, 93-5
THE LAST TEMPTATION, Alice Cooper, 94-6
THE LAST TEMPTATION OF REID, Lard, 90-69
LAST THE WHOLE NIGHT LONG, James Last, 79-2
LAST TIME I SAW HIM, Diana Ross, 74-41
THE LAST TOUR ON EARTH, Marilyn Manson, 99-61
LAST TRAIN TO LHASA, Banco De Gaia, 95-31
THE LAST WALTZ, Engelbert Humperdinck, 67-3
THE LAST WALTZ, Daniel O'Donnell, 90-46
THE LAST WALTZ [OST], Band, 78-39
LATE NIGHT GRANDE HOTEL, Nanci Griffith, 91-40
THE LATE NIGHT MIX, Various Artists: Compilations – Virgin/EMI, 00-15
LATE NIGHT SAX, After Dark, 96-18
LATERALUS, Tool, 01-16
THE LATEST AND THE GREATEST, Chuck Berry, 64-8
LATIN A LA LEE, Peggy Lee, 60-8
LATIN FEVER, Various Artists: Compilations – Sony Music TV/Universal Music TV, 00-3
LATTER DAYS – THE BEST OF LED ZEPPELIN – VOLUME 2, Led Zeppelin, 00-55
LAUGH, Terry Hall, 97-50
LAUGHING AT THE PIECES, Doctor and the Medics, 86-25
LAUGHING ON JUDGEMENT DAY, Thunder, 92-2
LAUGHING STOCK, Talk Talk, 91-26
LAUGHTER, Ian Dury and the Blockheads, 80-48
LAUGHTER AND LUST, Joe Jackson, 91-41
THE LAUGHTER AND TEARS COLLECTION, Various Artists: Compilations – Wea, 83-19
LAUGHTER AND TEARS – THE BEST OF NEIL SEDAKA TODAY, Neil Sedaka, 76-2
LAUGHTER IN THE RAIN, Neil Sedaka, 74-17
LAURENT GARNIER – LABORATOIRE MIX, Various Artists: Compilations – React, 96-16
THE LAW, Law, 91-61
LAWYERS IN LOVE, Jackson Browne, 83-37
LAZER GUIDED MELODIES, Spiritualized, 92-27
LAZY 86-88, Primitives, 89-73
LE ROI EST MORT, VIVE LE ROI!, Enigma, 96-12
THE LEAD AND HOW TO SWING IT, Tom Jones, 94-55
LEADERS OF THE PACK, Various Artists: Compilations – PolyGram TV, 93-9
LEAN INTO IT, Mr. Big, 91-28
LEARNING TO CRAWL, Pretenders, 84-11
THE LEAST WE CAN DO IS WAVE TO EACH OTHER, Van Der Graaf Generator, 70-47
LEATHER AND LACE. THE MEN AND WOMEN OF ROCK, Various Artists: Compilations – Dino, 90-3
LEATHER AND LACE – THE SECOND CHAPTER, Various Artists: Compilations – Dino, 90-14
LEATHER JACKETS, Elton John, 86-24
LEAVE HOME, Ramones, 77-45
LEAVE THE BEST TO LAST, James Last, 85-11
LED ZEPPELIN, Led Zeppelin, 69-6
LED ZEPPELIN II, Led Zeppelin, 69-1
LED ZEPPELIN 3, Led Zeppelin, 70-1
LED ZEPPELIN (BOX SET), Led Zeppelin, 90-48
LEFT ABOVE THE CLOUDS, Winx, 96-43
LEFT OF THE MIDDLE, Natalie Imbruglia, 97-5
LEFTISM, Leftfield, 95-3
LEFTOVER WINE, Melanie, 71-22
LEGAL DRUG MONEY, Lost Boyz, 96-64
LEGALIZE IT, Peter Tosh, 76-54
LEGEND (MUSIC FROM ROBIN OF SHERWOOD), Clannad, 84-15
THE LEGEND OF BILLIE HOLIDAY, Billie Holiday, 85-60
THE LEGEND OF BOBBY DARIN – HIS GREATEST HITS, Bobby Darin, 85-39
THE LEGEND OF MARIO LANZA, Mario Lanza, 81-29
LEGEND OF THE GLASS MOUNTAIN, Ron Goodwin, 70-49
LEGEND – THE BEST OF BOB MARLEY AND THE WAILERS, Bob Marley and the Wailers, 84-1
THE LEGEND – THE ESSENTIAL COLLECTION, Joe Cocker, 92-4
THE LEGENDARY BIG BANDS, Various Artists: Compilations – Ronco, 80-24
THE LEGENDARY JOE BLOGGS ALBUM 2, Various Artists: Compilations – The Hit Label, 93-15
THE LEGENDARY JOE BLOGGS DANCE ALBUM, Various Artists: Compilations – The Hit Label, 93-3
A LEGENDARY PERFORMER, Glenn Miller and his Orchestra, 76-41
A LEGENDARY PERFORMER VOLUME 2, Glenn Miller and his Orchestra, 76-53
A LEGENDARY PERFORMER VOLUME 3, Elvis Presley, 79-43
A LEGENDARY PERFORMER VOLUME 4, Elvis Presley, 83-91
THE LEGENDARY ROY ORBISON – THE GREATEST HITS, Roy Orbison, 88-1
LEGENDS AND HEROES, Various Artists: Compilations – Stylus, 89-6
LEGENDS OF SOUL – A WHOLE STACK OF SOUL, Various Artists: Compilations – Telstar, 91-15
LEISURE, Blur, 91-7
LEISURE NOISE, Gay Dad, 99-14
LEMON POPSICLE, Various Artists: Films – Original Soundtracks, 79-42
THE LENA MARTELL COLLECTION, Lena Martell, 78-12
LENA'S MUSIC ALBUM, Lena Martell, 79-5
LENNON LEGEND – THE VERY BEST OF JOHN LENNON, John Lennon, 97-4
LENNON-MCCARTNEY SONGBOOK, Keely Smith, 65-12
LENNY, Lenny Kravitz, 01-55
LENNY KRAVITZ GREATEST HITS, Lenny Kravitz, 00-12
LEO SAYER, Leo Sayer, 78-15
LEON RUSSELL AND THE SHELTER PEOPLE, Leon Russell, 71-29
LEONARD BERNSTEIN'S WEST SIDE STORY, Various Artists: Studio Cast, 93-33
LES MISERABLES, Various Artists: Stage Cast – London, 86-72
LES MISERABLES – 10TH ANNIVERSARY CONCERT, Various Artists: Stage Cast – London, 96-32
LESLEY GARRETT, Lesley Garrett, 98-34
LET IT BE, Beatles, 70-1
LET IT BEE, Voice Of The Beehive, 88-13
LET IT BLEED, Rolling Stones, 69-1
LET IT COME DOWN, Spiritualized, 01-3
LET IT RIDE, Shed Seven, 98-9
LET LOOSE, Let Loose, 94-20
LET LOVE IN, Nick Cave and the Bad Seeds, 94-12
LET LOVE RULE, Lenny Kravitz, 90-56
LET ME COME OVER, Buffalo Tom, 92-49
LET ME TRY AGAIN, Tammy Jones, 75-38
LET ME UP (I'VE HAD ENOUGH), Tom Petty and the Heartbreakers, 87-59
LET NO ONE LIVE RENT FREE IN YOUR HEAD, Nicolette, 96-36
LET THE MUSIC PLAY, Barry White, 76-22
LET THE MUSIC PLAY, Shannon, 84-52
LET THE MUSIC PLAY – 80S GROOVE, Various Artists: Compilations – Columbia, 01-18

LIVE AT THE ROYAL ALBERT HALL, Spiritualized, 98-38
LIVE AT THE ROYAL FESTIVAL HALL, Neil Sedaka, 74-48
LIVE AT THE SOCIAL – VOLUME 1, Various Artists: Compilations – Heavenly, 96-19
LIVE AT THE TALK OF THE TOWN, Seekers, 68-2
LIVE AT THE TALK OF THE TOWN, Shirley Bassey, 70-38
LIVE AT TREORCHY, Max Boyce, 75-21
'LIVE' AT WEMBLEY, Meat Loaf, 87-60
LIVE AT WEMBLEY '86, Queen, 92-2
LIVE BABY LIVE, Inxs, 91-8
LIVE BURSTING OUT, Jethro Tull, 78-17
LIVE CREAM, Cream, 70-4
LIVE CREAM VOLUME 2, Cream, 72-15
LIVE DATES II, Wishbone Ash, 80-40
LIVE – ERA '87–'93, Guns N' Roses, 99-45
LIVE EVIL, Black Sabbath, 83-13
LIVE FAST, DIE FAST, Wolfsbane, 89-48
LIVE 4 EVER, Various Artists: Compilations – Sony TV/Warner.esp, 98-11
LIVE FROM EARTH, Pat Benatar, 83-60
THE LIVE GREATEST HITS, Elvis Presley, 01-50
LIVE HERALD, Steve Hillage, 79-54
LIVE IN AUSTRALIA, Elton John and the Melbourne Symphony Orchestra, 87-43
LIVE IN BELFAST, Rowan Atkinson, 81-44
LIVE! IN EUROPE, Rory Gallagher, 72-9
LIVE IN EUROPE, Tina Turner, 88-8
LIVE IN LONDON, John Denver, 76-2
LIVE IN LOS ANGELES, Maze featuring Frankie Beverly, 86-70
LIVE IN MANCHESTER, Wonder Stuff, 95-74
LIVE IN NEW YORK CITY, Bruce Springsteen and the E Street Band, 01-12
LIVE! IN THE AIR AGE, Be-Bop Deluxe, 77-10
LIVE IN THE CITY OF LIGHT, Simple Minds, 87-1
LIVE IN THE HEART OF THE CITY, Whitesnake, 80-5
LIVE . . . IN THE RAW, W.A.S.P., 87-23
LIVE IN THE UK, Helloween, 89-26
LIVE IN YUGOSLAVIA, Anti-Nowhere League, 83-88
LIVE JAM, Jam, 93-28
LIVE KILLERS, Queen, 79-3
LIVE, LAUGH, LOVE, Daniel O'Donnell, 01-27
LIVE! LIVE! LIVE!, Bryan Adams, 94-17
LIVE MAGIC, Queen, 86-3
LIVE MCMXCIII, Velvet Underground, 93-70
LIVE/1975-1985, Bruce Springsteen and the E Street Band, 86-4
LIVE 1979, Hawkwind, 80-15
LIVE 1980-86, Joe Jackson, 88-66
LIVE 93, Orb, 93-23
LIVE ON BROADWAY, Barry Manilow, 90-19
LIVE – ON TWO LEGS, Pearl Jam, 98-68
LIVE ONE NIGHT ONLY, Bee Gees, 98-4
LIVE: RIGHT HERE, RIGHT NOW, Van Halen, 93-24
LIVE RUST, Neil Young and Crazy Horse, 79-55
LIVE SEEDS, Nick Cave and the Bad Seeds, 93-67
LIVE SHIT – BINGE AND PURGE, Metallica, 93-54
LIVE, STOLEN MOMENTS – THE LADY SINGS THE BLUES, Diana Ross, 93-45
LIVE – THE WAY WE WALK VOLUME 1: THE SHORTS, Genesis, 92-3
LIVE / THE WAY WE WALK – VOLUME TWO: THE LONGS, Genesis, 93-1
LIVE THROUGH THIS, Hole, 94-13
LIVE WOOD, Paul Weller, 94-13
LIVE (X CERT), Stranglers, 79-7
LIVE YOUR LIFE BE FREE, Belinda Carlisle, 91-7
LIVEANDIRECT, Adamski, 89-47
LIVELY UP YOURSELF, Bob Marley, 01-75
LIVERPOOL, Frankie Goes To Hollywood, 86-5
LIVES IN THE BALANCE, Jackson Browne, 86-36
LIVING ALL ALONE, Phyllis Hyman, 86-97
LIVING CLASSICS, Various Artists: Compilations – Deutsche Grammophon, 92-7
LIVING EYES, Bee Gees, 81-73
LIVING IN A BOX, Living In A Box, 87-25
LIVING IN A FANTASY, Leo Sayer, 80-15
LIVING IN OZ, Rick Springfield, 84-41
LIVING IN THE MATERIAL WORLD, George Harrison, 73-2
LIVING IN THE PAST, Jethro Tull, 72-8
LIVING IN THE PRESENT FUTURE, Eagle-Eye Cherry, 00-12
LIVING IN THE USA, Linda Ronstadt, 78-39
LIVING INSIDE YOUR LOVE, George Benson, 79-24
LIVING LEGENDS, Everly Brothers, 77-12
LIVING MY LIFE, Grace Jones, 82-15
LIVING ON THE FAULT LINE, Doobie Brothers, 77-25
LIVING ORNAMENTS 1979, Gary Numan, 81-47
LIVING ORNAMENTS 1979-1980, Gary Numan, 81-2
LIVING ORNAMENTS 1980, Gary Numan, 81-39
LIVING PROOF, Cher, 01-46
THE LIVING YEARS, Mike and the Mechanics, 88-2
LIZA WITH A 'Z', Liza Minnelli, 73-9
LIZARD, King Crimson, 71-30
LLOYD COLE, Lloyd Cole, 90-11
LLOYD WEBBER PLAYS LLOYD WEBBER, Julian Lloyd Webber with the Royal Philharmonic Orchestra, 90-15
LOAD, Metallica, 96-1
LOADED, Various Artists: Compilations – EMI/Virgin/PolyGram, 93-6
LOADED LOCK IN, Various Artists: Compilations – V2, 97-20
LOADS – THE BEST OF THE HAPPY MONDAYS, Happy Mondays, 95-41
LOCAL HERO [OST], Mark Knopfler, 83-14
LOC'ED AFTER DARK, Tone Loc, 89-22
LOCK, STOCK & TWO SMOKING BARRELS, Various Artists: Films – Original Soundtracks, 98-7
LOCK UP THE WOLVES, Dio, 90-28
LOCKED IN, Wishbone Ash, 76-36
LOCO, Fun Lovin' Criminals, 01-5
LODGER, David Bowie, 79-4
LONDON, D'Influence, 97-56
LONDON CALLING, Clash, 79-9
LONDON 0 HULL 4, Housemartins, 86-3
LONDON TOWN, Wings, 78-4
LONDON WARSAW NEW YORK, Basia, 90-68
LONE JUSTICE, Lone Justice, 85-49
THE LONE PIPER, Munros featuring David Methren, 98-46
THE LONE RANGER, Suggs, 95-14
LONE STAR, Lone Star, 76-47
LONELY AND BLUE, Roy Orbison, 63-15
LONELY IS AN EYESORE, Various Artists: Compilations – 4ad, 87-53
THE LONESOME JUBILEE, John Cougar Mellencamp, 87-31
LONG AFTER DARK, Tom Petty and the Heartbreakers, 82-45
THE LONG BLACK VEIL, Chieftains, 95-17
LONG COLD WINTER, Cinderella, 88-30
LONG DISTANCE – THE BEST OF RUNRIG, Runrig, 96-13
LONG DISTANCE VOYAGER, Moody Blues, 81-7
LONG JOHN SILVER, Jefferson Airplane, 72-30
LONG LIVE LOVE, Olivia Newton-John, 74-40
LONG LIVE ROCK 'N' ROLL, Rainbow, 78-7
LONG MAY YOU RUN, Stills-Young Band, 76-12
LONG MISTY DAYS, Robin Trower, 76-31
LONG PLAYER, Faces, 71-31
THE LONG RUN, Eagles, 79-4
LONGING IN THEIR HEARTS, Bonnie Raitt, 94-26
THE LOOK, Shalamar, 83-7
LOOK AT ME NOW, Bernie Marsden, 81-71
LOOK AT US, Sonny and Cher, 65-7
LOOK AT YOURSELF, Uriah Heep, 71-39
LOOK HEAR?, 10 C.C., 80-35
LOOK HOW LONG, Loose Ends, 90-19
LOOK INTO THE EYEBALL, David Byrne, 01-58
THE LOOK OF LOVE, Various Artists: Compilations – PolyGram TV, 96-6
THE LOOK OF LOVE, Diana Krall, 01-23
THE LOOK OF LOVE – THE BURT BACHARACH COLLECTION, Various Artists: Compilations – WSM/Universal Music TV, 01-4
LOOK OF LOVE – THE VERY BEST OF ABC, ABC, 01-69
LOOK SHARP, Joe Jackson, 79-40
LOOK SHARP!, Roxette, 89-4
LOOK TO YOUR HEART, Frank Sinatra, 59-5
LOOKIN' IN, Savoy Brown, 70-50
LOOKIN' THROUGH THE WINDOWS, Jackson 5, 72-16
LOOKIN' THRU THE EYES OF LOVE, Gene Pitney, 65-15
LOOKING BACK, John Mayall, 69-14
LOOKING EAST, Jackson Browne, 96-47
LOOKING FORWARD, Crosby, Stills, Nash and Young, 99-54
THE LOOKS OR THE LIFESTYLE, Pop Will Eat Itself, 92-15
LOONEE TUNES, Bad Manners, 80-36
LORD OF THE RINGS, Bo Hannson, 72-34
LORD UPMINSTER, Ian Dury and the Blockheads, 81-53
LORE, Clannad, 96-14
LOSS, Mull Historical Society, 01-43
LOST BOYS, Flying Pickets, 84-11
THE LOST BOYS, Various Artists: Films – Original Soundtracks, 89-1
LOST HORIZON, Various Artists: Films – Original Soundtracks, 73-36
LOST PROPERTY, Various Artists: Compilations – EMI, 96-12
THE LOST RECORDINGS, Glenn Miller and his Orchestra, 95-22
LOST SONGS 95-98, David Gray , 00-7
LOST SOULS, Doves, 00-16
LOST WITHOUT YOUR LOVE, Bread, 77-17
LOUD AND CLEAR, Sammy Hagar, 80-12
LOUD 'N' PROUD, Nazareth, 73-10
LOUDER THAN BOMBS, Smiths, 87-38
LOUDER THAN WORDS, Lionel Richie, 96-11
LOUDMOUTH – THE BEST OF THE BOOMTOWN RATS AND BOB GELDOF, Boomtown Rats and Bob Geldof, 94-10
LOVE, Cult, 85-4
LOVE, Aztec Camera, 87-10
THE LOVE ALBUM, Various Artists: Compilations – K-Tel, 80-6
THE LOVE ALBUM, Various Artists: Selected Series – Love Album, 94-1
THE LOVE ALBUM, Doris Day, 94-64
THE LOVE ALBUM II, Various Artists: Selected Series – Love Album, 95-2
THE LOVE ALBUM III, Various Artists: Selected Series – Love Album, 96-2
THE LOVE ALBUM IV, Various Artists: Selected Series – Love Album, 97-11
THE LOVE ALBUM '88, Various Artists: Compilations – Telstar, 88-51
THE LOVE ALBUM – 16 CLASSIC LOVE SONGS, Various Artists: Compilations – Telstar, 85-7
LOVE ALWAYS, K-Ci and Jojo, 97-51
LOVE AND DANCING, League Unlimited Orchestra, 82-3
LOVE AND KISSES, Dannii Minogue, 91-8
LOVE AND KISSES FROM, Brotherhood Of Man, 76-20
LOVE AND LIFE, Definition Of Sound, 91-38
LOVE & LIFE – THE VERY BEST OF DIANA ROSS, Diana Ross, 01-28
LOVE AND OTHER DEMONS, Strangelove, 96-44
LOVE AND THE RUSSIAN WINTER, Simply Red, 99-6
LOVE AND THEFT, Bob Dylan, 01-3
LOVE ANDY, Andy Williams, 68-1
LOVE AT FIRST STING, Scorpions, 84-17
LOVE AT THE GREEK – RECORDED LIVE AT THE GREEK THEATRE, LOS ANGELES, Neil Diamond, 77-3
LOVE AT THE MOVIES, Various Artists: Films – Related Compilations, 91-6
LOVE AT THE MOVIES, Jane McDonald, 01-24
LOVE AT THE MOVIES . . . THE ALBUM, Various Artists: Films – Related Compilations, 96-16
LOVE BEACH, Emerson, Lake and Palmer, 78-48
LOVE BITES, Buzzcocks, 78-13
LOVE BYRD, Donald Byrd, 81-70
LOVE CAN DO THAT, Elaine Paige, 91-36
LOVE CHILD, Diana Ross and the Supremes, 69-8
LOVE CLASSICS, Royal Philharmonic Orchestra conducted by Nick Portlock The, 83-30

MAGIC AND LOSS, Lou Reed, 92-6
MAGIC BULLETS, Mega City Four, 93-57
THE MAGIC FLUTE OF JAMES GALWAY, James Galway, 78-43
MAGIC FLY, Space, 77-11
MAGIC HOUR, Cast, 99-6
MAGIC IN THE AIR, Lindisfarne, 78-71
THE MAGIC IS YOU, Shirley Bassey, 79-40
MAGIC MOMENTS, Brendan Shine, 89-62
MAGIC, MURDER AND THE WEATHER, Magazine, 81-39
THE MAGIC OF BONEY M. – 20 GOLDEN HITS, Boney M, 80-1
THE MAGIC OF CHRISTMAS, George Mitchell Minstrels, 70-32
THE MAGIC OF DEMIS ROUSSOS, Demis Roussos, 77-29
THE MAGIC OF FOSTER AND ALLEN (THEIR GREATEST HITS), Foster and Allen, 89-29
THE MAGIC OF INSPECTOR MORSE (FROM THE ITV SERIES), Featured music by Barrington Pheloung, 00-62
THE MAGIC OF NANA MOUSKOURI, Nana Mouskouri, 88-44
MAGIC OF THE MINSTRELS, George Mitchell Minstrels, 65-9
THE MAGIC OF THE MOVIES, Doris Day, 99-63
THE MAGIC OF THE MUSICALS, Marti Webb and Mark Rattray, 92-55
THE MAGIC OF TORVILL AND DEAN, Various Artists: Compilations – Stylus, 85-35
THE MAGIC OF VAL DOONICAN, Val Doonican, 70-34
MAGIC REGGAE, Various Artists: Compilations – K-Tel, 80-9
THE MAGIC TOUCH OF ODYSSEY, Odyssey, 82-69
MAGICAL MYSTERY TOUR, Beatles, 68-31
MAGICAL RING, Clannad, 83-26
THE MAGICIAN'S BIRTHDAY, Uriah Heep, 72-28
MAGNETIC FIELDS, Jean-Michel Jarre, 81-6
MAGNIFICATION, Yes, 01-71
THE MAGNIFICENT SEVEN, Supremes and the Four Tops, 71-6
THE MAIN INGREDIENT, Pete Rock and C.L. Smooth, 94-69
MAIN OFFENDER, Keith Richards, 92-45
MAINSTREAM, Lloyd Cole and the Commotions, 87-9
MAIRE, Maire Brennan, 92-53
MAKE IT BIG, Wham!, 84-1
MAKE IT EASY ON YOURSELF, Johnny Mathis, 72-49
MAKE IT LAST FOREVER, Keith Sweat, 88-41
MAKE ME AN OFFER, Various Artists: Stage Cast – London, 60-18
MAKE THE PARTY LAST, James Last, 75-3
MAKE THE WORLD GO AWAY, Donny and Marie Osmond, 75-30
MAKE YOU SWEAT, Various Artists: Compilations – Telstar, 91-4
MAKE YOUR MOVE, Captain and Tennille, 80-33
MAKIN' MAGIC, Pat Travers, 77-40
MAKING A GOOD THING BETTER, Olivia Newton-John, 77-60
MAKING BONES, Red Snapper, 98-59
MAKING CONTACT, UFO, 83-32
MAKING HISTORY, Linton Kwesi Johnson, 84-73
MAKING LOVE AND MUSIC, Dr. Hook, 77-39
MAKING MOVIES, Dire Straits, 80-4
MAKING TRACKS, Five Penny Piece, 73-37
MAKING WAVES, Nolans, 80-11
MALADJUSTED, Morrissey, 97-8
MALPRACTICE, Dr. Feelgood, 75-17
MALPRACTICE, Redman, 01-57
MAMA SAID, Lenny Kravitz, 91-8
MAMA SAID KNOCK YOU OUT, L.L. Cool J, 90-49
MAMAS AND PAPAS DELIVER, Mamas and the Papas, 67-4
MAMMA, Luciano Pavarotti with the Henry Mancini Orchestra, 84-96
MAMMA MIA! , Various Artists: Stage Cast – London, 99-56
MAMOUNA, Bryan Ferry, 94-11
THE MAN, Barry White, 79-46
MAN, Neneh Cherry, 96-16
MAN ALIVE, 4 Of Us, 93-64
A MAN ALONE – THE WORDS AND MUSIC OF ROD MCKUEN, Frank Sinatra, 69-18
A MAN AND A WOMAN, Various Artists: Films – Original Soundtracks, 67-31
A MAN AND HIS MUSIC, Frank Sinatra, 66-9
THE MAN AND HIS MUSIC, Sam Cooke, 86-8
THE MAN FROM UTOPIA, Frank Zappa, 83-87
MAN IN BLACK, Johnny Cash, 71-18
THE MAN IN BLACK – DEFINITIVE COLLECTION, Johnny Cash, 94-15
THE MAN-MACHINE, Kraftwerk, 78-9
MAN OF COLOURS, Icehouse, 88-93
MAN ON THE LINE, Chris De Burgh, 84-11
MAN TO MAN, Hot Chocolate, 76-32
THE MAN WHO, Travis, 99-1
THE MAN WHO SOLD THE WORLD, David Bowie, 72-26
THE MAN WITH THE GOLDEN FLUTE, James Galway, 78-52
A MAN WITHOUT LOVE, Engelbert Humperdinck, 68-3
MANASSAS, Stephen Stills' Manassas, 72-30
MANE ATTRACTION, White Lion, 91-31
MANGE TOUT, Blancmange, 84-8
MANHATTAN TRANSFER, Manhattan Transfer, 77-49
MANHATTANS, Manhattans, 76-37
MANIC NIRVANA, Robert Plant, 90-15
MANIC POP THRILL, That Petrol Emotion, 86-84
MANIFESTO, Roxy Music, 79-7
MANILOW, Barry Manilow, 85-40
MANILOW MAGIC – THE BEST OF BARRY MANILOW, Barry Manilow, 79-3
MANN MADE, Manfred Mann, 65-7
MANN MADE HITS, Manfred Mann, 66-11
MANNERS AND PHYSIQUE, Adam Ant, 90-19
MANTLE PIECES, Clifford T. Ward, 74-42
MANTOVANI/HOLLYWOOD, Mantovani and his Orchestra, 67-37
MANTOVANI MAGIC, MantovanI and his Orchestra, 66-3
MANTOVANI MAGIC, Mantovani Orchestra conducted by Roland Shaw, 85-52
MANTOVANI TODAY, Mantovani and his Orchestra, 70-16
MANTOVANI'S GOLDEN HITS, Mantovani and his Orchestra, 67-10
MANUMISSION – THE MOVIE, Various Artists: Films – Original Soundtracks, 99-17
MANY HAPPY RETURNS – THE HITS, Gary Glitter, 92-35
MARA, Runrig, 95-24
MARATHON, Santana, 79-28
MARAUDER, Magnum, 80-34
MARAUDER, Blackfoot, 81-38
MARC COHN, Marc Cohn, 91-27
MARCH OR DIE, Motorhead, 92-60
MARCHIN' ALREADY, Ocean Colour Scene, 97-1
MARCY PLAYGROUND, Marcy Playground, 98-61
THE MARIA CALLAS COLLECTION, Maria Callas, 87-50
MARIA MCKEE, Maria McKee, 89-49
MARIAH CAREY, Mariah Carey, 90-6
MARIANNE FAITHFULL, Marianne Faithfull, 65-15
MARILLION.COM, Marillion, 99-53
MARIO LANZA – THE ULTIMATE COLLECTION, Mario Lanza, 94-13
MARK HOLLIS, Mark Hollis, 98-53
THE MARK, TOM AND TRAVIS SHOW (THE ENEMA STRIKES BACK), Blink-182, 00-69
THE MARK II PURPLE SINGLES, Deep Purple, 79-24
MARK RATTRAY PERFORMS THE SONGS OF THE MUSICALS, Mark Rattray, 90-46
MARK'S KEYBOARD REPAIR, Money Mark, 95-35
MAROON, Barenaked Ladies, 00-64
THE MARQUEE – 30 LEGENDARY YEARS, Various Artists: Compilations – Polydor, 89-1
MARQUEE METAL, Various Artists: Compilations – Marquee, 91-5
MARQUEE MOON, Television, 77-28
MARRYING MAIDEN, It's A Beautiful Day, 70-45
MARS AUDIAC QUINTET, Stereolab, 94-16
THE MARSHALL MATHERS LP, Eminem, 00-1
MARTIKA, Martika, 89-11
MARTIKA'S KITCHEN, Martika, 91-15
MARTIN GUERRE, Various Artists: Stage Cast – London, 96-58
MARTY ROBBINS COLLECTION, Marty Robbins, 79-5
THE MARTYR MANTRAS, Jesus Loves You, 91-60
MARVIN AT THE MOVIES, Hank Marvin, 00-17
MARVIN, WELCH AND FARRAR, Marvin, Welch and Farrar, 71-30
MARY, Mary J. Blige, 99-5
MARY JANE GIRLS, Mary Jane Girls, 83-51
MARY O'HARA AT THE ROYAL FESTIVAL HALL, Mary O'Hara, 78-37
MARY POPPINS, Various Artists: Films – Original Soundtracks, 65-2
MASK, Bauhaus, 81-30
MASK, Vangelis, 85-69
MASQUE, Mission, 92-23
MASSIVE 4, Various Artists: Compilations – London, 90-20
MASSIVE – AN ALBUM OF REGGAE HITS, Various Artists: Compilations – Virgin, 85-61
MASSIVE DANCE HITS 2000, Various Artists: Selected Series – Massive Dance, 99-11
MASSIVE DANCE MIX 96, Various Artists: Selected Series – Massive Dance, 96-9
MASSIVE DANCE: 98, Various Artists: Selected Series – Massive Dance, 97-8
MASSIVE DANCE: 98 – VOLUME 2, Various Artists: Selected Series – Massive Dance, 98-2
MASSIVE DANCE: 99, Various Artists: Selected Series – Massive Dance, 98-5
MASSIVE DANCE 99 – VOLUME 2, Various Artists: Selected Series – Massive Dance, 99-3
MASSIVE DANCE 2001, Various Artists: Selected Series – Massive Dance, 00-18
MASSIVE HITS, Various Artists: Compilations – Telstar, 91-2
MASTER OF PUPPETS, Metallica, 86-41
MASTER OF REALITY, Black Sabbath, 71-5
MASTERPIECE, Temptations, 73-28
MASTERPIECES – THE ESSENTIAL FLUTE OF JAMES GALWAY, James Galway, 93-30
MASTERPIECES – THE VERY BEST OF SKY, Sky, 84-15
THE MASTERPLAN, Oasis, 98-2
MASTERS OF METAL, Various Artists: Compilations – K-Tel, 86-38
MASTERWORKS, Jeff Jarratt and Don Reedman, 80-39
MATA LEAO, Biohazard, 96-72
MATADOR, Various Artists: Studio Cast, 87-26
MATCHBOX, Matchbox, 80-44
MATHIS MAGIC, Johnny Mathis, 79-59
THE MATRIX , Various Artists: Films – Original Soundtracks, 99-16
MATT BIANCO, Matt Bianco, 86-26
MATTERS OF THE HEART, Tracy Chapman, 92-19
MATTHEW AND SON, Cat Stevens, 67-7
MAVERICK A STRIKE, Finley Quaye, 97-3
MAX POWER – MAX BASS, Various Artists: Compilations – Break Down, 96-13
MAX Q, Max Q, 89-69
MAXI, Maxi Priest, 87-25
MAXIMUM DARKNESS, Man, 75-25
A MAXIMUM HIGH, Shed Seven, 96-8
MAXIMUM JOY, Frankie Goes To Hollywood, 00-54
MAXIMUM RAVE, Various Artists: Compilations – EMI, 92-2
MAXIMUM SECURITY, Alien Sex Fiend, 85-100
MAXIMUM SPEED, Various Artists: Compilations – Virgin/EMI, 98-3
MAXIMUM SPEED 99, Various Artists: Compilations – Virgin/EMI, 99-13
MAXINQUAYE, Tricky, 95-3
MAY EACH DAY, Andy Williams, 66-11
MAYA, Banco De Gaia, 94-34
MAYBE IT'S LIVE, Robert Palmer, 82-32
MAYBE YOU SHOULD DRIVE, Barenaked Ladies, 94-57
MAYBE YOU'VE BEEN BRAINWASHED TOO, New Radicals, 99-10
MAYFLOWER, Weather Prophets, 87-67
MCCARTNEY, Paul McCartney, 70-2
MCCARTNEY II, Paul McCartney, 80-1
THE MCCARTNEY INTERVIEW, Paul McCartney, 81-34

NOTHING LESS THAN BRILLIANT, Sandie Shaw, 94-64
. . . NOTHING LIKE THE SUN, Sting, 87-1
NOTORIOUS, Duran Duran, 86-16
THE NOTORIOUS BYRD BROTHERS, Byrds, 68-12
THE NOTORIOUS KIM, Lil' Kim, 00-67
NOTTING HILL, Various Artists: Films – Original Soundtracks, 99-4
NOW, New Seekers, 73-47
NOW!, Vic Damone, 81-28
NOW, Patrice Rushen, 84-73
NOW, Paul Rodgers, 97-30
NOW, Maxwell, 01-46
NOW AIN'T THE TIME FOR YOUR TEARS, Wendy James, 93-43
NOW & THEN, Carpenters, 73-2
NOW AND ZEN, Robert Plant, 88-10
NOW DANCE '86, Various Artists: Selected Series – Now!, 86-2
NOW DANCE 89 – THE 12" MIXES, Various Artists: Selected Series – Now!, 89-1
NOW DANCE 901 – 20 SMASH DANCE HITS – THE 12" MIXES, Various Artists: Selected Series – Now!, 90-1
NOW DANCE 902, Various Artists: Selected Series – Now!, 90-1
NOW DANCE 903 – THE 12" MIXES, Various Artists: Selected Series – Now!, 90-1
NOW DANCE 91, Various Artists: Selected Series – Now!, 91-1
NOW DANCE 92, Various Artists: Selected Series – Now!, 92-3
NOW DANCE 93, Various Artists: Selected Series – Now!, 93-1
NOW DANCE 94 VOLUME 1, Various Artists: Selected Series – Now!, 94-1
NOW! DANCE 94 VOLUME 2, Various Artists: Selected Series – Now!, 94-8
NOW DANCE 95, Various Artists: Selected Series – Now!, 95-3
NOW DANCE 97, Various Artists: Selected Series – Now!, 97-1
NOW DANCE 98, Various Artists: Selected Series – Now!, 98-3
NOW DANCE – SUMMER 94, Various Artists: Selected Series – Now!, 94-1
NOW DANCE SUMMER 95, Various Artists: Selected Series – Now!, 95-3
NOW DANCE – THE BEST OF '93, Various Artists: Selected Series – Now!, 93-1
NOW DANCE – THE BEST OF '94, Various Artists: Selected Series – Now!, 94-4
NOW DANCE – THE 12" MIXES, Various Artists: Selected Series – Now!, 85-3
NOW DANCE 2000, Various Artists: Selected Series – Now!, 99-1
NOW DANCE 2001, Various Artists: Selected Series – Now!, 00-1
NOW DANCE 2001 PART 2, Various Artists: Selected Series – Now!, 01-2
NOW DANCE 2002, Various Artists: Selected Series – Now!, 01-1
NOW I GOT WORRY, Jon Spencer Blues Explosion, 96-50
NOW I'M A COWBOY, Auteurs, 94-27
NOW IN A MINUTE, Donna Lewis, 96-52
NOW! SMASH HITS, Various Artists: Selected Series – Now!, 87-5
NOW! THAT'S WHAT I CALL LOVE, Various Artists: Selected Series – Now!, 94-6
NOW, THAT'S WHAT I CALL MUSIC, Various Artists: Selected Series – Now!, 83-1
NOW, THAT'S WHAT I CALL MUSIC II, Various Artists: Selected Series – Now!, 84-1
NOW, THAT'S WHAT I CALL MUSIC 3, Various Artists: Selected Series – Now!, 84-1
NOW, THAT'S WHAT I CALL MUSIC 4 – 32 CHART HITS, Various Artists: Selected Series – Now!, 84-2
NOW THAT'S WHAT I CALL MUSIC 5, Various Artists: Selected Series – Now!, 85-1
NOW THAT'S WHAT I CALL MUSIC 6, Various Artists: Selected Series – Now!, 85-1
NOW THAT'S WHAT I CALL MUSIC 7, Various Artists: Selected Series – Now!, 86-1
NOW THAT'S WHAT I CALL MUSIC 8, Various Artists: Selected Series – Now!, 86-1
NOW THAT'S WHAT I CALL MUSIC 9, Various Artists: Selected Series – Now!, 87-1
NOW THAT'S WHAT I CALL MUSIC 10, Various Artists: Selected Series – Now!, 87-1
NOW THAT'S WHAT I CALL MUSIC 11, Various Artists: Selected Series – Now!, 88-1
NOW THAT'S WHAT I CALL MUSIC 12, Various Artists: Selected Series – Now!, 88-1
NOW THAT'S WHAT I CALL MUSIC 13, Various Artists: Selected Series – Now!, 88-1
NOW THAT'S WHAT I CALL MUSIC 14, Various Artists: Selected Series – Now!, 89-1
NOW THAT'S WHAT I CALL MUSIC 15, Various Artists: Selected Series – Now!, 89-1
NOW THAT'S WHAT I CALL MUSIC 16, Various Artists: Selected Series – Now!, 89-1
NOW THAT'S WHAT I CALL MUSIC 17, Various Artists: Selected Series – Now!, 90-1
NOW! THAT'S WHAT I CALL MUSIC 18, Various Artists: Selected Series – Now!, 90-1
NOW! THAT'S WHAT I CALL MUSIC 19, Various Artists: Selected Series – Now!, 91-1
NOW THAT'S WHAT I CALL MUSIC! 20, Various Artists: Selected Series – Now!, 91-1
NOW THAT'S WHAT I CALL MUSIC! 21, Various Artists: Selected Series – Now!, 92-1
NOW THAT'S WHAT I CALL MUSIC! 22, Various Artists: Selected Series – Now!, 92-1
NOW THAT'S WHAT I CALL MUSIC! 23, Various Artists: Selected Series – Now!, 92-1
NOW THAT'S WHAT I CALL MUSIC! 24, Various Artists: Selected Series – Now!, 93-1
NOW THAT'S WHAT I CALL MUSIC! 25, Various Artists: Selected Series – Now!, 93-1
NOW THAT'S WHAT I CALL MUSIC! 26, Various Artists: Selected Series – Now!, 93-1
NOW THAT'S WHAT I CALL MUSIC! 27, Various Artists: Selected Series – Now!, 94-1
NOW THAT'S WHAT I CALL MUSIC! 28, Various Artists: Selected Series – Now!, 94-1
NOW THAT'S WHAT I CALL MUSIC! 29, Various Artists: Selected Series – Now!, 94-1
NOW THAT'S WHAT I CALL MUSIC! 30, Various Artists: Selected Series – Now!, 95-1
NOW THAT'S WHAT I CALL MUSIC! 31, Various Artists: Selected Series – Now!, 95-1
NOW THAT'S WHAT I CALL MUSIC! 32, Various Artists: Selected Series – Now!, 95-1
NOW THAT'S WHAT I CALL MUSIC! 33, Various Artists: Selected Series – Now!, 96-1
NOW THAT'S WHAT I CALL MUSIC! 34, Various Artists: Selected Series – Now!, 96-1
NOW THAT'S WHAT I CALL MUSIC! 35, Various Artists: Selected Series – Now!, 96-1
NOW THAT'S WHAT I CALL MUSIC! 36, Various Artists: Selected Series – Now!, 97-1
NOW THAT'S WHAT I CALL MUSIC! 37, Various Artists: Selected Series – Now!, 97-1
NOW THAT'S WHAT I CALL MUSIC! 38, Various Artists: Selected Series – Now!, 97-1
NOW THAT'S WHAT I CALL MUSIC! 39, Various Artists: Selected Series – Now!, 98-1
NOW THAT'S WHAT I CALL MUSIC! 40, Various Artists: Selected Series – Now!, 98-1
NOW THAT'S WHAT I CALL MUSIC! 41, Various Artists: Selected Series – Now!, 98-1
NOW THAT'S WHAT I CALL MUSIC! 42, Various Artists: Selected Series – Now!, 99-1
NOW THAT'S WHAT I CALL MUSIC! 43, Various Artists: Selected Series – Now!, 99-1
NOW THAT'S WHAT I CALL MUSIC! 44, Various Artists: Selected Series – Now!, 99-1
NOW THAT'S WHAT I CALL MUSIC! 45, Various Artists: Selected Series – Now!, 00-1
NOW THAT'S WHAT I CALL MUSIC! 46, Various Artists: Selected Series – Now!, 00-1
NOW THAT'S WHAT I CALL MUSIC! 47, Various Artists: Selected Series – Now!, 00-1
NOW THAT'S WHAT I CALL MUSIC! 48, Various Artists: Selected Series – Now!, 01-1
NOW THAT'S WHAT I CALL MUSIC! 49, Various Artists: Selected Series – Now!, 01-1
NOW THAT'S WHAT I CALL MUSIC! 50, Various Artists: Selected Series – Now!, 01-1
NOW, THAT'S WHAT I CALL MUSIC '86, Various Artists: Selected Series – Now!, 86-65
NOW THAT'S WHAT I CALL MUSIC! 1983, Various Artists: Selected Series – Now!, 93-10
NOW THAT'S WHAT I CALL MUSIC! 1984, Various Artists: Selected Series – Now!, 93-13
NOW THAT'S WHAT I CALL MUSIC! 1985, Various Artists: Selected Series – Now!, 93-15
NOW THAT'S WHAT I CALL MUSIC! 1986, Various Artists: Selected Series – Now!, 93-16
NOW THAT'S WHAT I CALL MUSIC! 1987, Various Artists: Selected Series – Now!, 93-17
NOW THAT'S WHAT I CALL MUSIC! 1988, Various Artists: Selected Series – Now!, 93-20
NOW THAT'S WHAT I CALL MUSIC! 1992, Various Artists: Selected Series – Now!, 93-14
NOW THAT'S WHAT I CALL MUSIC! 1993, Various Artists: Selected Series – Now!, 93-1
NOW THAT'S WHAT I CALL MUSIC! 1994, Various Artists: Selected Series – Now!, 94-1
NOW THAT'S WHAT I CALL MUSIC! 1995, Various Artists: Selected Series – Now!, 95-2
NOW THAT'S WHAT I CALL MUSIC – THE CHRISTMAS ALBUM – 18 ORGINAL CHRISTMAS HITS, Various Artists: Selected Series – Now!, 85-1
NOW THAT'S WHAT I CALL QUITE GOOD!, Housemartins, 88-8
NOW! THE CHRISTMAS ALBUM, Various Artists: Selected Series – Now!, 00-2
NOW – THE SUMMER ALBUM – 30 SUMMER HITS, Various Artists: Selected Series – Now!, 86-7
NOW THEN . . ., Stiff Little Fingers, 82-24
NOW VOYAGER, Barry Gibb, 84-85
NOW WE ARE SIX, Steeleye Span, 74-13
NOW WE MAY BEGIN, Randy Crawford, 80-10
NOW YOU SEE ME . . . NOW YOU DON'T, Cliff Richard, 82-4
NOWHERE, Ride, 90-11
***NSYNC,** *Nsync, 99-30
NU-CLEAR SOUNDS, Ash, 98-7
NUDE, Camel, 81-34
'NUFF SAID, Nina Simone, 69-11
NUISANCE, Menswear, 95-11
NUKLEUZ PRESENTZ . . . BIG ROOM DJ'S: MIXED BY MARIO PIU & NICK SENTIENCE, Various Artists: Selected Series – Nukleuz Presentz, 01-6
NUKLEUZ PRESENTS HARDHOUSE ANTHEMS, Various Artists: Selected Series – Nukleuz Presentz, 00-14
NUKLEUZ PRESENTZ . . . HARDHOUSE ANTHEMS 2 – SUMMER EDITION, Various Artists: Selected Series – Nukleuz Presentz, 00-16
NUKLEUZ PRESENTZ . . . HARDHOUSE ANTHEMS 3 – AUTUMN COLLECTION MIXED BY ED REAL, Various Artists: Selected Series – Nukleuz Presentz , 00-13
NUKLEUZ PRESENTZ . . . HARDHOUSE ANTHEMS 2001: MIXED BY BK & ED REAL, Various Artists: Selected Series – Nukleuz Presentz, 01-13
NUMA RECORDS YEAR 1, Various Artists: Compilations – Numa, 86-94
NUMBER 8, J.J. Cale, 83-47
THE NUMBER OF THE BEAST, Iron Maiden, 82-1
THE NUMBER ONE ACOUSTIC ROCK ALBUM, Various Artists: Selected Series – The Number One, 96-6
THE NUMBER ONE ALL TIME ROCK ALBUM, Various Artists: Selected Series – The Number One, 95-16
THE NUMBER ONE CHRISTMAS ALBUM, Various Artists: Selected Series – The Number One, 95-4
THE NUMBER ONE CLASSIC SOUL ALBUM, Various Artists: Selected Series – The Number One, 95-5
THE NUMBER ONE COUNTRY ALBUM, Various Artists: Selected Series – The Number One, 96-16
THE NUMBER ONE DANCE PARTY ALBUM, Various Artists: Selected Series – The Number One, 99-17
THE NUMBER ONE DRIVE ALBUM, Various Artists: Selected Series – The Number One, 97-14
THE NUMBER ONE EIGHTIES ALBUM, Various Artists: Selected Series – The Number One, 96-10
NUMBER ONE IN HEAVEN, Sparks, 79-73
THE NUMBER ONE JAZZ ALBUM, Various Artists: Selected Series – The Number One, 97-13
THE NUMBER ONE LINE DANCING ALBUM, Various

100% DANCE VOLUME 3, Various Artists: Selected Series – 100%, 93-7
100% DANCE VOLUME 4, Various Artists: Selected Series – 100%, 94-2
100% DRUM & BASS, Various Artists: Selected Series – 100%, 96-11
100% GINUWINE, Ginuwine, 99-42
100% HITS, Various Artists: Selected Series – 100%, 94-2
100% HOUSE CLASSICS – VOLUME 1, Various Artists: Selected Series – 100%, 95-16
100% PURE GROOVE, Various Artists: Selected Series – 100%, 96-4
100% PURE GROOVE 2, Various Artists: Selected Series – 100%, 96-12
100% PURE LOVE, Various Artists: Selected Series – 100%, 94-7
100% RAP, Various Artists: Selected Series – 100%, 94-3
100% REGGAE, Various Artists: Selected Series – 100%, 93-2
100% REGGAE VOLUME 2, Various Artists: Selected Series – 100%, 94-4
100% REGGAE VOLUME 3, Various Artists: Selected Series – 100%, 94-6
100% SUMMER, Various Artists: Selected Series – 100%, 94-4
100% SUMMER JAZZ, Various Artists: Selected Series – 100%, 95-11
100% SUMMER MIX 96, Various Artists: Selected Series – 100%, 96-7
100% SUMMER MIX 97, Various Artists: Selected Series – 100%, 97-8
100% SUMMER MIX 98, Various Artists: Selected Series – 100%, 98-13
100% SUMMER '95, Various Artists: Selected Series – 100%, 95-7
101, Depeche Mode, 89-5
101 DAMNATIONS, Carter – The Unstoppable Sex Machine, 91-29
101% SPEED GARAGE ANTHEMS, Various Artists: Compilations – Massive Music, 99-14
101% SPEED GARAGE VOLUME 2, Various Artists: Compilations – Massive Music, 98-16
154, Wire, 79-39
ONE IN A MILLION, Aaliyah, 96-33
ONE LOVE, Delakota, 98-58
ONE LOVE – THE VERY BEST OF BOB MARLEY & THE WAILERS, Bob Marley and the Wailers, 01-5
ONE LOVE – THE VERY BEST OF BOB MARLEY & THE WAILERS, Bob Marley and the Wailers, 01-24
ONE LOVE – THE VERY BEST OF REGGAE, Various Artists: Compilations – Arcade, 92-7
ONE MAN DOG, James Taylor, 72-27
ONE MAN SHOW, Mike Harding, 76-19
ONE MORE DREAM – THE VERY BEST OF GERRY RAFFERTY, Gerry Rafferty, 95-17
ONE MORE FOR THE ROAD, Lynyrd Skynyrd, 76-17
ONE NATION UNDER A GROOVE, Funkadelic, 78-56
ONE NIGHT AT BUDOKAN, Michael Schenker Group, 82-5
ONE NIGHT ONLY – THE GREATEST HITS, Elton John, 00-7
ONE NIGHT WITH YOU – THE BEST OF LOVE, Luther Vandross, 97-56
ONE NIL, Neil Finn, 01-14
ONE OF THE BOYS, Roger Daltrey, 77-45
ONE OF THESE NIGHTS, Eagles, 75-8
ONE ON ONE, Cheap Trick, 82-95
ONE ORIGINAL STEP BEYOND – STORY . . ., Various Artists: Compilations – Castle Communications, 93-7
ONE PIECE AT A TIME, Johnny Cash, 76-49
ONE SECOND, Yello, 87-48
ONE SECOND, Paradise Lost, 97-31
ONE STEP BEYOND..., Madness, 79-2
ONE STEP CLOSER, Doobie Brothers, 80-53
THE ONE THING, Michael Bolton, 93-4
1100 BEL AIR PLACE, Julio Iglesias, 84-14
ONE TO ONE, Howard Jones, 86-10
ONE TOUCH, Sugababes, 00-26
ONE-TRICK PONY [OST], Paul Simon, 80-17
1234, Propaganda, 90-46
ONE VICE AT A TIME, Krokus, 82-28
ONE VOICE, Barry Manilow, 79-18
ONE VOICE, Barbra Streisand, 87-27
ONE WAY OF LIFE – THE BEST OF THE LEVELLERS, Levellers, 98-15
ONE WILD NIGHT – LIVE 1985-2001, Bon Jovi, 01-2
ONE WOMAN – THE ULTIMATE COLLECTION, Diana Ross, 93-1
ONE WORLD, John Martyn, 78-54
ONE WORLD, John Denver, 86-91
ONE WORLD, Various Artists: Compilations – Global Television, 98-8
ONE WORLD ONE VOICE, One World, 90-27
ONENESS – SILVER DREAMS GOLDEN REALITY, Carlos Santana, 79-55
ONES ON 1, Various Artists: Radio – Related Compilations , 88-10
ONKA'S BIG MOKA, Toploader, 00-4
ONLY CLASSICAL ALBUM YOU'LL EVER NEED, Various Artists: Compilations – Conifer Classics, 98-17
ONLY EVERYTHING, Juliana Hatfield, 95-59
ONLY FOR THE HEADSTRONG, Various Artists: Compilations – London, 92-10
ONLY FOR THE HEADSTRONG II, Various Artists: Compilations – London, 92-18
ONLY FOREVER, Puressence, 98-36
ONLY GOD CAN JUDGE ME, Mark Morrison, 97-50
ONLY HUMAN, Dina Carroll, 96-2
THE ONLY ONES, Only Ones, 78-56
ONLY THE STRONG SURVIVE, Hurricane #1, 99-55
ONLY YAZOO – THE BEST OF YAZOO, Yazoo, 99-22
ONLY YESTERDAY – RICHARD & KAREN CARPENTER'S GREATEST HITS, Carpenters, 90-1
OOH LA LA, Faces, 73-1
OOH LAS VEGAS, Deacon Blue, 90-3
OOH WALLAH WALLAH, King Kurt, 83-99
OOH YEAH!, Daryl Hall and John Oates, 88-52
0141 632 6326, G.U.N., 97-32
OOPS! . . . I DID IT AGAIN, Britney Spears , 00-2
OOPS! SORRY WRONG PLANET, Utopia, 77-59
OPEN, Julie Driscoll and the Brian Auger Trinity, 68-12
OPEN, Steve Hillage, 79-71
OPEN ALL NIGHT, Georgia Satellites, 88-39
OPEN ROAD, Donovan, 70-30
OPEN ROAD, Gary Barlow, 97-1
OPEN TOP CARS AND GIRLS IN T'SHIRTS, Various Artists: Compilations – Telstar, 85-13
OPEN UP AND SAY . . . AAH!, Poison, 88-18
THE OPERA ALBUM 2002, Various Artists: Compilations – Virgin/EMI, 01-7
OPERA EXTRAVAGANZA, Luis Cobos, 90-72
OPERATION MINDCRIME, Queensryche, 88-58
OPERATION STACKOLA, Luniz, 96-41
OPHELIA, Natalie Merchant, 98-52
THE OPTIMIST LP, Turin Brakes, 01-27
ORANGE COLOURED SKY, Bert Kaempfert, 71-49
ORANGES AND LEMONS, XTC, 89-28
THE ORBISON WAY, Roy Orbison, 66-11
ORBISONGS, Roy Orbison, 67-40
ORBITAL, Orbital, 91-71
ORBITAL, Orbital, 93-28
THE ORB'S ADVENTURES BEYOND THE ULTRAWORLD, Orb, 91-29
ORBVS TERRARVM, Orb, 95-20
ORCHESTRA!, Sir Georg Solti and Dudley Moore, 91-38
ORCHESTRAL MANOEUVRES IN THE DARK, Orchestral Manoeuvres In The Dark, 80-27
THE ORCHESTRAL TUBULAR BELLS, Mike Oldfield with the Royal Philharmonic Orchestra, 75-17
ORDINARY MAN, Day One, 00-70
ORGAN FAN, Silverfish, 92-65
ORGANIC, Joe Cocker, 96-49
ORGANISATION, Orchestral Manoeuvres In The Dark, 80-6
ORGASMATRON, Motorhead, 86-21
ORIGIN OF SYMMETRY, Muse, 01-3
ORIGINAL FLAVA, Brand New Heavies, 94-64
ORIGINAL GREATEST HITS, Everly Brothers, 70-7
ORIGINAL MASTERS, Jethro Tull, 85-63
ORIGINAL MUSIC FROM AUF WIEDERSEHEN PET, Various Artists: Television – Soundtracks, 84-21
ORIGINAL MUSIQUARIUM 1, Stevie Wonder, 82-8
THE ORIGINAL SOUNDTRACK, 10 C.C., 75-4
ORIGINAL SOUNDTRACK, S'Express, 89-5
THE ORIGINAL SOUNDTRACK FROM TCB [OST-TV], Diana Ross and the Supremes with the Temptations, 69-11
ORIGINAL SOUNDTRACKS 1, Passengers, 95-12
THE ORIGINALS!, Various Artists: Compilations – Dino, 92-8
ORIGINALS, Various Artists: Compilations – Columbia, 93-1
ORIGINALS 2, Various Artists: Compilations – Columbia, 94-4
THE ORIGINALS: 32 ALL-TIME CLASSIC GREATS, Various Artists: Compilations – Towerbell, 86-15
OSIBISA, Osibisa, 71-11
06:21:03:11 UP EVIL, Front 242, 93-44
OSMONDS LIVE, Osmonds, 72-13
THE OTHER CHET ATKINS, Chet Atkins, 61-20
THE OTHER MAN'S GRASS IS ALWAYS GREENER, Petula Clark, 68-37
THE OTHER SIDE, Lynden David Hall, 00-36
THE OTHER SIDE OF DUDLEY MOORE, Dudley Moore, 65-11
THE OTHER SIDE OF LIFE, Moody Blues, 86-24
THE OTHER SIDE OF ME, Andy Williams, 75-60
THE OTHER SIDE OF THE MIRROR, Stevie Nicks, 89-3
OTHER VOICES, Paul Young, 90-4
OTHER VOICES/OTHER ROOMS, Nanci Griffith, 93-18
O3, Sunscreem, 93-33
OTIS BLUE: OTIS REDDING SINGS SOUL, Otis Redding, 66-6
OTIS REDDING IN EUROPE, Otis Redding, 68-14
OTO, Fluke, 95-44
OU812, Van Halen, 88-16
OUI LOVE YOU, Oui 3, 93-39
OUR BEST TO YOU, Osmonds, 74-5
OUR FAVOURITE SHOP, Style Council, 85-1
OUR FRIENDS ELECTRIC, Various Artists: Compilations – Telstar, 96-8
OUR HAPPY HARDCORE, Scooter, 96-24
OUR KID EH, Shirehorses, 01-20
OUR MEMORIES OF ELVIS, Elvis Presley, 79-72
OUR TIME IN EDEN, 10,000 Maniacs, 92-33
OUR TOWN – THE GREATEST HITS, Deacon Blue, 94-1
OUT-A-SPACE, Spotnicks, 63-20
OUT CAME THE BLUES, Various Artists: Compilations – Ace Of Hearts, 64-19
OUT HERE, Love, 70-29
OUT IN LA, Red Hot Chili Peppers, 94-61
OUT IN THE FIELDS – THE VERY BEST OF GARY MOORE, Gary Moore, 98-54
OUT IN THE SUN, Patrick Moraz, 77-44
OUT NOW! 28 HOT HITS, Various Artists: Selected Series – Out Now!, 85-2
OUT NOW!! 2 – 28 HOT HITS, Various Artists: Selected Series – Out Now!, 85-3
OUT OF AFRICA [OST], John Barry, 86-81
OUT OF HERE, Corduroy, 94-73
OUT OF ORDER, Rod Stewart, 88-11
OUT OF OUR HEADS, Rolling Stones, 65-2
OUT OF THE BLUE, Electric Light Orchestra, 77-4
OUT OF THE BLUE, Debbie Gibson, 88-26
OUT OF THE CRADLE, Lindsey Buckingham, 92-51
OUT OF THE SHADOWS, Shadows, 62-1
OUT OF THEIR SKULLS, Pirates, 77-57
OUT OF THIS WORLD, Moody Blues, 79-15
OUT OF THIS WORLD, Shakatak, 83-30
OUT OF THIS WORLD, Europe, 88-12
OUT OF THIS WORLD, Apollo 2000, 96-43
OUT OF TIME, R.E.M., 91-1
OUT ON THE STREET, David Essex, 76-31
OUT SPACED, Super Furry Animals, 98-44
OUT THERE AND BACK, Paul Van Dyk, 00-12
OUTLAND, Spear Of Destiny, 87-16
OUTLAND, Gary Numan, 91-39
OUTLANDOS D'AMOUR, Police, 79-6
OUTRIDER, Jimmy Page, 88-27
OUTROSPECTIVE, Faithless, 01-4
OUTSIDE, David Bowie, 95-8

POSITIVE REACTION, Caveman, 91-43
POSITIVE TOUCH, Undertones, 81-17
POSITIVITY, Incognito, 93-55
POSSESSED, Venom, 85-99
POST HISTORIC MONSTERS, Carter – The Unstoppable Sex Machine, 93-5
POST ORGASMIC CHILL, Skunk Anansie, 99-16
POST / TELEGRAM, Bjork, 95-2
POSTCARD, Mary Hopkin, 69-3
POSTCARDS FROM HEAVEN, Lighthouse Family, 97-2
POT LUCK, Elvis Presley, 62-1
POTATO LAND, Spirit, 81-40
POVERTY'S PARADISE, Naughty By Nature, 95-20
POWER AND PASSION, Mama's Boys, 85-55
POWER AND SOUL, Various Artists: Compilations – PolyGram TV, 94-5
POWER & SOUL, Various Artists: Compilations – PolyGram TV, 98-5
POWER AND THE GLORY, Saxon, 83-15
THE POWER AND THE GLORY, Various Artists: Compilations – Vertigo, 91-2
POWER, CORRUPTION AND LIES, New Order, 83-4
POWER CUTS – ROCK'S GREATEST HITS, Various Artists: Compilations – PolyGram TV, 92-5
POWER IN THE DARKNESS, Tom Robinson Band, 78-4
POWER OF A WOMAN, Eternal, 95-6
POWER OF A WOMAN, Various Artists: Compilations – Telstar/Warner.esp, 98-13
THE POWER OF CLASSIC ROCK, London Symphony Orchestra with the Royal Choral Society and the Roger Smith Chorale, 85-13
THE POWER OF GLORIA GAYNOR, Gloria Gaynor, 86-81
THE POWER OF LOVE, Various Artists: Compilations – West Five, 86-33
POWER OF LOVE, Luther Vandross, 91-9
THE POWER OF LOVE, Various Artists: Compilations – Quality Television, 92-4
POWER OF TEN, Chris De Burgh, 92-3
POWER RANGERS – THE ALBUM – A ROCK ADVENTURE, Mighty Morph'n Power Rangers, 94-50
THE POWER STATION, Power Station, 85-12
POWER THEMES 90, F.A.B., 90-53
POWER WINDOWS, Rush, 85-9
POWERAGE, AC/DC, 78-26
POWERLIGHT, Earth, Wind And Fire, 83-22
POWERSLAVE, Iron Maiden, 84-2
POWERTRIP, Monster Magnet, 98-65
POWERTRIPPIN', Almighty, 93-5
PRACTICE WHAT YOU PREACH, Testament, 89-40
PRAISE, Inner City, 92-52
PRAISE – 18 CHORAL MASTERPIECES, London Philharmonic Choir with the National Philharmonic Orchestra conducted by John Aldiss, 91-54
PRE-MILLENNIUM TENSION, Tricky, 96-30
THE PREACHER'S WIFE [OST], Whitney Houston, 97-35
PRECIOUS, Various Artists: Compilations – Dino, 92-11
PRECIOUS MEMORIES, Ann Williamson, 86-16
PRECIOUS METAL, Various Artists: Compilations – MCA, 80-60
PRECIOUS METAL, Various Artists: Compilations – Stylus, 89-2
PRECIOUS MOMENTS, Various Artists: Compilations – Impression, 83-77
PRECIOUS TIME, Pat Benatar, 81-30
THE PREDATOR, Ice Cube, 92-73
THE PREMIER HITS, Gary Numan/Tubeway Army, 96-21
THE PREMIERE COLLECTION – ENCORE (ANDREW LLOYD WEBBER), Various Artists: Compilations – Really Useful/Polydor, 92-2
PREMIERS SYMPTOMES, Air, 99-12
PRESENCE, Led Zeppelin, 76-1
THE PRESENT, Moody Blues, 83-15
PRESENT ARMS, UB40, 81-2
PRESENT ARMS IN DUB, UB40, 81-38
PRESENTING DIONNE WARWICK, Dionne Warwick, 64-14
THE PRESIDENTS OF THE UNITED STATES OF AMERICA, Presidents Of The United States Of America, 96-14
PRESLEY – THE ALL TIME GREATEST HITS, Elvis Presley, 87-4
PRESS TO PLAY, Paul McCartney, 86-8
PRESTO, Rush, 89-27
THE PRETENDER, Jackson Browne, 76-26
PRETENDERS, Pretenders, 80-1
PRETENDERS II, Pretenders, 81-7
PRETTY HATE MACHINE, Nine Inch Nails, 91-67
PRETTY ON THE INSIDE, Hole, 91-59
PRETTY THINGS, Pretty Things, 65-6
PRETTY WOMAN, Various Artists: Films – Original Soundtracks, 90-2
PRETZEL LOGIC, Steely Dan, 74-37
THE PRICE YOU PAY, Spear Of Destiny, 88-37
PRIDE, Robert Palmer, 83-37
PRIDE – THE VERY BEST OF SCOTLAND, Various Artists: Compilations – RCA, 95-13
PRIEST LIVE, Judas Priest, 87-47
PRIMITIVE, Neil Diamond, 84-7
PRIMITIVE, Soulfly, 00-45
PRIMITIVE COOL, Mick Jagger, 87-26
PRINCE BLIMEY, Red Snapper, 96-60
PRINCE CHARMING, Adam and the Ants, 81-2
THE PRINCE'S TRUST COLLECTION, Various Artists: Concerts and Festivals, 85-64
THE PRINCE'S TRUST CONCERT 1987, Various Artists: Concerts and Festivals, 87-44
THE PRINCE'S TRUST TENTH ANNIVERSARY BIRTHDAY PARTY, Various Artists: Concerts and Festivals, 87-76
PRINCESS, Princess, 86-15
THE PRINCIPLE OF MOMENTS, Robert Plant, 83-7
PRISONERS IN PARADISE, Europe, 91-61
PRIVATE AUDITION, Heart, 82-77
PRIVATE COLLECTION, Jon and Vangelis, 83-22
PRIVATE COLLECTION 1979 – 1988, Cliff Richard, 88-1
PRIVATE DANCER, Tina Turner, 84-2
PRIVATE EYES, Daryl Hall and John Oates, 82-8
PRIVATE PRACTICE, Dr. Feelgood, 78-41
PRIVATE REVOLUTION, World Party, 87-56
PROCOL HARUM LIVE IN CONCERT WITH THE EDMONTON SYMPHONY ORCHESTRA, Procol Harum, 72-48
PROCOL'S NINTH, Procol Harum, 75-41
PRODIGAL SISTA, Beverley Knight, 98-42
PRODIGY PRESENTS THE DIRTCHAMBER SESSIONS 1, Various Artists: Compilations – Xl Recordings, 99-3
PRODUCT 2378, Various Artists: Compilations – Telstar, 90-16
PROGNEY, Shamen, 91-23
PROGRESSION, Various Artists: Compilations – PolyGram TV, 93-9
PROGRESSION VOLUME ONE, Various Artists: Compilations – Renaissance Recordings, 01-17
PROGRESSIONS OF POWER, Triumph, 80-61
PROMISE, Sade, 85-1
THE PROMISE, T'Pau, 91-10
PROMISED LAND, Elvis Presley, 75-21
PROMISED LAND, Queensryche, 94-13
PROMISES AND LIES, UB40, 93-1
PROPAGANDA, Sparks, 74-9
PROPHESY, Nitin Sawhney, 01-40
PROPHETS, SEERS AND SAGES, THE ANGELS OF THE AGES / MY PEOPLE WERE FAIR AND HAD SKY IN THEIR HAIR BUT NOW THEY'RE CONTENT TO WEAR STARS ON THEIR BROWS [RI], Tyrannosaurus Rex, 72-1
THE PROS AND CONS OF HITCH-HIKING, Roger Waters, 84-13
PROTECT THE INNOCENT, Various Artists: Compilations – Telstar, 89-9
PROTECTION, Massive Attack, 94-4
PROTEST SONGS, Prefab Sprout, 89-18
PROTOTYPE 3 – SEB FONTAINE, Various Artists: Compilations – Prototype, 00-19
PROUD, Heather Small, 00-12
PROVISION, Scritti Politti, 88-8
PROVOCATIVE, Johnny Gill, 93-41
PROZAIC, Honeycrack, 96-34
PS I LOVE YOU, Various Artists: Compilations – Warwick, 82-68
PSALM 69, Ministry, 92-33
PSYCHE – THE ALBUM, PJ and Duncan AKA, 94-5
PSYCHEDELIC FURS, Psychedelic Furs, 80-18
PSYCHEDELIC SHACK, Temptations, 70-56
PSYCHIC KARAOKE, Transglobal Underground, 96-62
PSYCHO-CIRCUS, Kiss, 98-47
PSYCHOCANDY, Jesus And Mary Chain, 85-31
THE PSYCHOMODO, Cockney Rebel, 74-8
PSYCHOTIC SUPPER, Tesla, 91-44
PSYENCE FICTION, Unkle, 98-4
PUBLIC IMAGE, Public Image Ltd, 78-22
PULP FICTION, Various Artists: Films – Original Soundtracks, 94-5
PULSE, Pink Floyd, 95-1
PUMP, Aerosmith, 89-3
PUMP UP THE JAM, Technotronic, 90-2
PUMP UP THE VALUUM, NOFX, 00-50
PUMP UP THE VOLUME, Various Artists: Compilations – Universal Music TV, 01-11
PUNCH THE CLOCK, Elvis Costello and the Attractions, 83-3
PUNK AND DISORDERLY, Various Artists: Compilations – Abstract, 82-48
PUNK AND DISORDERLY (FURTHER CHARGES), Various Artists: Compilations – Anagram, 82-91
PUNK AND DISORDERLY – NEW WAVE 1976 – 1981, Various Artists: Compilations – Telstar, 91-18
PUNK'S NOT DEAD, Exploited, 81-20
PURE, Primitives, 89-33
PURE, Midge Ure, 91-36
PURE, 3 Colours Red, 97-16
PURE, Gary Numan, 00-58
PURE & SIMPLE, Various Artists: Compilations – Universal Music TV, 01-7
PURE ATTRACTION, Various Artists: Compilations – Columbia, 95-5
PURE CHILLOUT, Various Artists: Compilations – Virgin/EMI, 01-11
PURE CULT, Cult, 93-1
PURE DANCE '96, Various Artists: Compilations – PolyGram TV, 96-5
PURE DANCE 97, Various Artists: Compilations – PolyGram TV, 97-9
PURE EMOTIONS, Inspirations, 95-37
PURE EUPHORIA – LEVEL 4 – DIGITALLY MIXED BY MATT DAREY, Various Artists: Selected Series – Euphoria, 00-3
PURE FLAVA – MIXED BY STEVE 'SMOOTH' SUTHERLAND, Various Artists: Television – Related Compilations, 01-10
PURE GARAGE (MIXED LIVE BY EZ), Various Artists: Selected Series – Pure Garage, 00-2
PURE GARAGE II: (MIXED LIVE BY: EZ):, Various Artists: Selected Series – Pure Garage, 00-2
PURE GARAGE III: (MIXED LIVE BY EZ:), Various Artists: Selected Series – Pure Garage, 00-2
PURE GARAGE IV :(MIXED LIVE BY: EZ):, Various Artists: Selected Series – Pure Garage, 01-3
PURE GARAGE V: (MXED LIVE BY: EZ):, Various Artists: Selected Series – Pure Garage, 01-7
PURE GOLD, Various Artists: Compilations – EMI, 73-1
PURE HIP HOP – EXPLICIT BEATS – MIXED BY DJ SWERVE, Various Artists: Compilations – WSM/Universal Music TV, 01-10
PURE HIP HOP – MIXED BY SHORTEE BLITZ, Various Artists: Compilations – BMG/Telstar TV/Sony Music TV, 01-9
PURE HITS '97, Various Artists: Compilations – Telstar, 97-13
PURE JAZZ MOODS – COOL JAZZ FOR A SUMMERS DAY, Various Artists: Compilations – Dino, 96-9
PURE LIGHTNING SEEDS, Lightning Seeds, 96-27
PURE LOVERS VOLUME 1, Various Artists: Compilations – Charm, 90-14
PURE LOVERS VOLUME 2, Various Artists: Compilations – Charm, 90-12

PURE LOVERS VOLUME 3, Various Artists: Compilations – Charm, 91-16
PURE LOVERS VOLUME 4, Various Artists: Compilations – Charm, 91-19
PURE LOVERS VOLUME 5, Various Artists: Compilations – Charm, 92-13
PURE LOVERS VOLUME 6, Various Artists: Compilations – Charm, 93-17
PURE MANIA, Vibrators, 77-49
PURE MOODS, Various Artists: Compilations – Virgin, 94-1
PURE PHASE, Spiritualized Electric Mainline, 95-20
PURE PLEASURE, Shaggy, 93-67
PURE R&B – THE FINEST CUTS FOR TODAY'S R&B GENERATION, Various Artists: Selected Series – Pure R&B, 00-6
PURE R&B 2, Various Artists: Compilations – BMG Commercial/Telstar, 00-11
PURE R&B 3: REPRESENTING R&B AT ITS FINEST, Various Artists: Selected Series – Pure R&B, 01-8
PURE REGGAE, Various Artists: Compilations – Global Television, 97-12
PURE REGGAE – VOLUME 1, Various Artists: Compilations – Island, 94-10
PURE ROCK BALLADS, Various Artists: Compilations – PolyGram TV, 98-10
PURE SAX, State Of The Heart, 96-18
PURE SILK – A NEW DIMENSION, Various Artists: Compilations – Pure Music, 99-15
PURE SILK IN AYIA NAPA – THE HOME OF UK GARAGE, Various Artists: Compilations – Pure Silk, 00-8
PURE SILK IN AYIA NAPA 2, Various Artists: Compilations – Pure Silk, 01-20
PURE SILK – THE THIRD DIMENSION – MIXED BY TIMMY MAGIC, Various Artists: Compilations – Pure Silk, 00-12
PURE SOFT METAL – IT TAKES YOUR BREATH AWAY, Various Artists: Compilations – Stylus, 90-1
PURE SWING, Various Artists: Selected Series – Pure Swing, 95-2
PURE SWING TWO, Various Artists: Selected Series – Pure Swing, 95-4
PURE SWING III, Various Artists: Selected Series – Pure Swing, 95-3
PURE SWING IV, Various Artists: Selected Series – Pure Swing, 95-1
PURE SWING 5, Various Artists: Selected Series – Pure Swing, 96-6
PURE SWING 96, Various Artists: Selected Series – Pure Swing, 96-9
PURGATORY/MAIDEN JAPAN, Iron Maiden, 90-5
PURPENDICULAR, Deep Purple, 96-58
PURPLE, Stone Temple Pilots, 94-10
PURPLE RAIN [OST], Prince and the Revolution, 84-7
PURPLE RAINBOWS, Deep Purple, 91-1
THE PURSUIT OF ACCIDENTS, Level 42, 82-17
PUSH, Bros, 88-2
PUSH THE BUTTON, Money Mark, 98-17
PUTTIN' ON THE STYLE, Lonnie Donegan, 78-51
PUZZLE PEOPLE, Temptations, 70-20
PXR 5, Hawkwind, 79-59
PYE CHARTBUSTERS, Various Artists: Compilations – Pye, 71-36
PYE CHARTBUSTERS VOLUME 2, Various Artists: Compilations – Pye, 71-29
PYRAMID, Alan Parsons Project, 78-49
PYROMANIA, Def Leppard, 83-18
Q ANTHEMS, Various Artists: Magazine Related, 01-10
Q: ARE WE NOT MEN? A: NO WE ARE DEVO, Devo, 78-12
Q AWARDS: THE ALBUM, Various Artists: Magazine Related, 00-6
Q COUNTRY, Various Artists: Magazine Related, 94-20
Q RHYTHM AND BLUES, Various Artists: Magazine Related, 93-14
Q – THE ALBUM VOLUME 1, Various Artists: Magazine Related, 91-10
Q THE BLUES, Various Artists: Magazine Related, 92-6
Q-TIPS, Q-Tips, 80-50
THE QAT COLLECTION, Sasha, 94-55
QE 2, Mike Oldfield, 80-27
QUADROPHENIA, Who, 73-2
QUADROPHENIA [OST], Who, 79-23
QUALITY CONTROL, Jurassic 5, 00-23
QUALITY STREET, World Of Twist, 91-50
QUARK STRANGENESS AND CHARM, Hawkwind, 77-30
QUARTER MOON IN A TEN CENT TOWN, Emmylou Harris, 78-40
QUARTET, Ultravox, 82-6
QUEEN, Queen, 74-24
QUEEN 2, Queen, 74-5
THE QUEEN ALBUM, Elaine Paige, 88-51
QUEEN AT THE BEEB, Queen, 89-67
QUEEN GREATEST HITS, Queen, 81-1
THE QUEEN IS DEAD, Smiths, 86-2
QUEEN OF SOUL – THE VERY BEST OF ARETHA FRANKLIN, Aretha Franklin, 94-20
QUEEN ROCKS, Queen, 97-7
QUEER AS FOLK – THE WHOLE THING. SORTED, Various Artists: Television – Soundtracks, 99-2
QUEER AS FOLK 2 – SAME MEN. NEW TRACKS, Various Artists: Television – Soundtracks, 00-5
QUENCH, Beautiful South, 98-1
A QUESTION OF BALANCE, Moody Blues, 70-1
A QUICK ONE, Who, 66-4
QUICK STEP & SIDE KICK, Thompson Twins, 83-2
QUIET IS THE NEW LOUD, Kings Of Convenience, 01-72
QUICKSILVER, DJ Quicksilver, 98-26
QUIET LIFE, Japan, 80-53
THE QUIET REVOLUTION, Ronny Jordan, 93-49
QUIET REVOLUTION, Chris De Burgh, 99-23
QUINTESSENCE, Quintessence, 70-22
QUIT DREAMING AND GET ON THE BEAM, Bill Nelson, 81-7
QUO, Status Quo, 74-2
R., R. Kelly, 98-27
R, Queens Of The Stone Age, 00-54
R & S RECORDS – ORDER TO DANCE, Various Artists: Compilations – R&S, 91-18
R.I.P. PRESENTS THE REAL SOUND OF UNDERGROUND, Various Artists: Compilations – Virgin/EMI, 98-18
R. KELLY, R. Kelly, 95-18
R U STILL DOWN? (REMEMBER ME), 2Pac, 97-44
RA, Utopia, 77-27
RABBITS ON AND ON, Jasper Carrott, 75-10
RADAR, Earthling, 95-66
RADIATION, Marillion, 98-35
RADIATOR, Super Furry Animals, 97-8
RADIO, L.L. Cool J, 86-71
RADIO DREAMSCAPE – VOLUME 1, Various Artists: Compilations – Dreamscape, 95-20
RADIO K.A.O.S., Roger Waters, 87-25
RADIO M.U.S.C. MAN, Womack and Womack, 85-56
RADIO MUSICOLA, Nik Kershaw, 86-47
RADIO ONE, Jimi Hendrix, 89-30
RADIO SESSIONS, Curve, 93-72
RADIO 2 – SONGS OF THE CENTURY, Various Artists: Radio – Related Compilations, 99-9
RADIOACTIVE, Various Artists: Compilations – Ronco, 80-13
RAFI'S REVENGE, Asian Dub Foundation, 98-20
RAGE, T'Pau, 88-4
RAGE AGAINST THE MACHINE, Rage Against The Machine, 93-17
RAGE FOR ORDER, Queensryche, 86-66
RAGE IN EDEN, Ultravox, 81-4
RAGE – MAKE SOME NOISE VOLUME 1, Various Artists: Compilations – A&M, 91-12
RAGGA HEAT REGGAE BEAT, Various Artists: Compilations – Telstar, 93-4
RAGGED GLORY, Neil Young and Crazy Horse, 90-15
RAIDERS OF THE POP CHARTS, Various Artists: Compilations – Ronco, 82-1
RAIN DANCES, Camel, 77-20
RAIN DOGS, Tom Waits, 85-29
RAIN TREE CROW, Rain Tree Crow, 91-24
RAINBOW, Neil Diamond, 74-39
RAINBOW, Peters and Lee, 74-6
RAINBOW, Mariah Carey, 99-8
RAINBOW BRIDGE [OST], Jimi Hendrix, 71-16
RAINBOW CONNECTION IV, Rose Royce, 79-72
RAINBOW DOME MUSIC, Steve Hillage, 79-52
RAINBOW RISING, Ritchie Blackmore's Rainbow, 76-11
RAINBOW WARRIORS, Various Artists: Compilations – RCA, 89-2
RAINDANCE, Raindance, 96-15
RAINDANCING, Alison Moyet, 87-2
RAINDROPS KEEP FALLING ON MY HEAD, Johnny Mathis, 70-23
RAINGODS WITH ZIPPOS, Fish, 99-57
RAINTOWN, Deacon Blue, 87-14
THE RAINY SEASON, Marc Cohn, 93-24
RAISE!, Earth, Wind And Fire, 81-14
RAISE, Swervedriver, 91-44
RAISE THE PRESSURE, Electronic, 96-8
RAISE YOUR FIST AND YELL, Alice Cooper, 87-48
RAISED ON RADIO, Journey, 86-22
RAISING HELL, Fatback Band, 76-19
RAISING HELL, Run D.M.C., 86-41
RALPH TRESVANT, Ralph Tresvant, 91-37
RAM, Paul and Linda McCartney, 71-1
RAM IT DOWN, Judas Priest, 88-24
RAMPANT, Nazareth, 74-13
RAMSHACKLED, Alan White, 76-41
RANCID, Rancid, 00-68
R&B HITS, Various Artists: Compilations – Universal Music TV, 01-16
R&B MASTERS, Various Artists: Compilations – Columbia, 01-4
R&B MASTERS 2, Various Artists: Compilations – Columbia, 01-12
R&B SELECTOR, Various Artists: Compilations – Universal Music TV, 01-11
RANK, Smiths, 88-2
RANT 'N' RAVE WITH THE STRAY CATS, Stray Cats, 83-51
RAOUL AND THE KINGS OF SPAIN, Tears For Fears, 95-41
RAP ATTACK, Various Artists: Compilations – K-Tel, 89-6
RAP ATTACK, Various Artists: Compilations – Concept, 94-9
RAP FLAVAS, Various Artists: Compilations – Columbia, 96-6
RAP IT UP – RAP'S GREATEST HITS, Various Artists: Compilations – K-Tel, 86-50
RAP TO THE MAX, Various Artists: Compilations – Virgin, 94-10
RAP TRAX, Various Artists: Compilations – Stylus, 88-3
RAPPED IN REMIXES, Salt 'N' Pepa, 92-37
RAPPIN' UP THE HOUSE, Various Artists: Compilations – K-Tel, 88-19
RAPTURE, Anita Baker, 86-13
THE RAPTURE, Siouxsie and the Banshees, 95-33
RARE, David Bowie, 83-34
RARE, Various Artists: Selected Series – Rare, 87-80
RARE 2, Various Artists: Selected Series – Rare, 88-88
RARE 3, Various Artists: Selected Series – Rare, 89-15
RARE GROOVE – DYNAMIC DISCO HITS, Various Artists: Compilations – Quality Television, 92-7
RARE GROOVE MIX – 70 SMASH HITS OF THE 70'S, Various Artists: Compilations – Stylus, 88-20
RARITIES, Beatles, 79-71
RASTAMAN VIBRATION, Bob Marley and the Wailers, 76-15
RAT IN THE KITCHEN, UB40, 86-8
RATTLE AND HUM, U2, 88-1
RATTLESNAKES, Lloyd Cole and the Commotions, 84-13
RAVE, Various Artists: Compilations – Telstar, 90-10
RAVE, Various Artists: Compilations – Reachin', 91-18
RAVE 2 – STRICTLY HARDCORE!, Various Artists: Compilations – Elevate, 92-11
RAVE ALERT, Various Artists: Compilations – Telstar, 92-2
RAVE ANTHEMS, Various Artists: Compilations – Dino, 95-7
THE RAVE GENER8TOR, Various Artists: Compilations – Cookie Jar, 92-1
THE RAVE GENER8TOR 2, Various Artists: Compilations – Cookie Jar, 92-2
RAVE GENERATION, Various Artists: Compilations – Dino, 93-2
RAVE GENERATION 2, Various Artists: Compilations – Dino, 94-5
RAVE NATION, Various Artists: Compilations – Telstar, 92-2
RAVE NATION – 40 MASSIVE OLD SKOOL ANTHEMS, Various Artists: Compilations – Inspired, 01-16
RAVE 92, Various Artists: Compilations – Cookie Jar, 92-3
RAVEL'S BOLERO, London Philharmonic Orchestra, 60-15

SILVER TOWN, Men They Couldn't Hang, 89-39
THE SIMON AND GARFUNKEL COLLECTION – 17 OF THEIR ALL-TIME GREATEST RECORDINGS, Simon and Garfunkel, 81-4
SIMON AND GARFUNKEL'S GREATEST HITS, Simon and Garfunkel, 72-2
SIMON BATES – OUR TUNE, Various Artists: Radio – Related Compilations , 86-58
SIMON'S WAY, Simon May Orchestra, 86-59
SIMPLE DREAMS, Linda Ronstadt, 77-15
SIMPLE PLEASURE, Tindersticks, 99-36
SIMPLE PLEASURES, Bobby McFerrin, 88-92
SIMPLE THINGS, Zero 7, 01-28
SIMPLY. LOVE, Various Artists: Compilations – Columbia, 91-3
SIMPLY SHADOWS, Shadows, 87-11
SIMPLY THE BEST, Tina Turner, 91-2
SIMPLY THE BEST – CLASSIC SOUL, Various Artists: Selected Series – Simply The Best, 97-7
SIMPLY THE BEST CLASSICAL ANTHEMS, Various Artists: Selected Series – Simply The Best, 98-14
SIMPLY THE BEST DISCO, Various Artists: Selected Series – Simply The Best, 98-9
SIMPLY THE BEST LOVE SONGS, Various Artists: Selected Series – Simply The Best, 97-2
SIMPLY THE BEST LOVE SONGS 2, Various Artists: Selected Series – Simply The Best, 98-2
SIMPLY THE BEST RADIO HITS, Various Artists: Selected Series – Simply The Best, 98-17
SIMPLY THE BEST REGGAE ALBUM, Various Artists: Selected Series – Simply The Best, 01-12
THE SIMPSONS SING THE BLUES, Simpsons, 91-6
THE SIMPSONS – SONGS IN THE KEY OF SPRINGFIELD, Simpsons, 98-18
SIN AFTER SIN, Judas Priest, 77-23
THE SIN OF PRIDE, Undertones, 83-43
SINATRA AND COMPANY, Frank Sinatra, 71-9
SINATRA AND STRINGS, Frank Sinatra, 62-6
SINATRA – BASIE, Frank Sinatra and Count Basie, 63-2
SINATRA 80TH – ALL THE BEST, Frank Sinatra, 95-49
SINATRA PLUS, Frank Sinatra, 61-7
SINATRA SOUVENIR, Frank Sinatra, 61-18
SINATRA SWINGS, Frank Sinatra, 61-8
SINATRA – THE MAIN EVENT LIVE [OST-TV], Frank Sinatra, 75-30
SINATRA WITH SWINGING BRASS, Frank Sinatra, 62-14
SINATRA'S SINATRA, Frank Sinatra, 63-9
SINATRA'S SWINGING SESSION!!!, Frank Sinatra, 61-6
SINCE I LEFT YOU, Avalanches, 01-8
SINCE YOU'VE BEEN GONE, Damage, 01-16
SINCERE, MJ Cole, 00-14
SINCERELY, Cliff Richard, 69-24
SING A FAVOURITE SONG, Des O'Connor, 72-25
SING ALONG WITH MAX, Max Bygraves, 72-4
SING ALONG WITH MAX VOLUME 2, Max Bygraves, 72-11
SING BROTHER SING, Edgar Broughton Band, 70-18
SING IT AGAIN ROD, Rod Stewart, 73-1
SING LOFTY, Don Estelle and Windsor Davies, 76-10
SING SOMETHING SIMPLE, Cliff Adams Singers, 60-15
SING SOMETHING SIMPLE, Cliff Adams Singers, 62-15
SING SOMETHING SIMPLE, Cliff Adams Singers, 82-39
SING SOMETHING SIMPLE '76, Cliff Adams Singers, 76-23
SING THE IRVING BERLIN SONGBOOK, George Mitchell Minstrels, 68-33
SING WHEN YOU'RE WINNING, Robbie Williams, 00-1
SINGALONGAMAX VOLUME 3, Max Bygraves, 73-5
SINGALONGAMAX VOLUME 4, Max Bygraves, 73-7
SINGALONGAWARYEARS, Max Bygraves, 89-5
SINGALONGAWARYEARS VOLUME 2, Max Bygraves, 89-33
SINGALONGAXMAS, Max Bygraves, 74-21
SINGALONGPARTY SONG, Max Bygraves, 73-15
THE SINGER, Liza Minnelli, 73-45
SINGER AND THE SONG, Labi Siffre, 71-47
THE SINGER AND THE SONG, Various Artists: Compilations – Stylus, 89-5
THE SINGER AND THE SONG, Various Artists: Compilations – Virgin, 93-5
SINGING TO MY BABY, Eddie Cochran, 60-19
THE SINGLE FACTOR, Camel, 82-57
SINGLE LIFE, Cameo, 85-66
A SINGLE MAN, Elton John, 78-8
THE SINGLES, Roy Wood, 82-37
THE SINGLES, Pretenders, 87-6
SINGLES, Smiths, 95-5
SINGLES, Alison Moyet, 95-1
THE SINGLES, Inspiral Carpets, 95-17
THE SINGLES ALBUM, UB40, 82-17
THE SINGLES ALBUM, Jimi Hendrix, 83-77
THE SINGLES ALBUM, Soft Cell, 86-58
THE SINGLES ALBUM, Gladys Knight and the Pips, 89-12
THE SINGLES COLLECTION, Spandau Ballet, 85-3
THE SINGLES COLLECTION, Kool And The Gang, 88-28
THE SINGLES COLLECTION, Clash, 91-68
THE SINGLES COLLECTION, Four Tops, 92-11
THE SINGLES COLLECTION, Connie Francis, 93-12
THE SINGLES COLLECTION, David Bowie, 93-9
THE SINGLES COLLECTION 1981 – 1993, Kim Wilde, 93-11
A SINGLES COLLECTION 1982 – 1992, Marillion, 92-27
THE SINGLES COLLECTION 1984/1990, Jimmy Somerville, 90-4
THE SINGLES 81-85, Depeche Mode, 85-6
THE SINGLES 86>98, Depeche Mode, 98-5
SINGLES – 45'S AND UNDER, Squeeze, 82-3
THE SINGLES 1969 – 1973, Carpenters, 74-1
THE SINGLES 1974 – 1978, Carpenters, 78-2
SINGLES OF THE 90'S, Ace Of Base, 99-62
THE SINGLES – THE FIRST TEN YEARS, Abba, 82-1
THE SINGLES – THE UA YEARS, Stranglers, 89-57
THE SINGULAR ADVENTURES OF THE STYLE COUNCIL GREATEST HITS VOLUME 1, Style Council, 89-3
SINITTA!, Sinitta, 87-34
SIOGO, Blackfoot, 83-28
SIREN, Roxy Music, 75-4
SIREN, Heather Nova, 98-55
SIRIUS, Clannad, 87-34
SISTER ACT, Various Artists: Films – Original Soundtracks, 93-14
SISTERS, Bluebells, 84-22
SISTERS ARE DOIN' IT, Various Artists: Compilations – Towerbell, 86-27
SISTERS OF AVALON, Cyndi Lauper, 97-59
SISTERS OF SWING, Various Artists: Selected Series – Sisters Of Swing, 96-1
SISTERS OF SWING 2, Various Artists: Selected Series – Sisters Of Swing, 96-4
SISTERS OF SWING III, Various Artists: Selected Series – Sisters Of Swing, 97-7
SISTERS OF SWING 98, Various Artists: Selected Series – Sisters Of Swing, 98-5
SISTERS OF SWING 99, Various Artists: Selected Series – Sisters Of Swing, 99-9
SITTIN' ON TOP OF THE WORLD, Leann Rimes, 98-11
SITUATION:CRITICAL, Ultra Nate, 98-17
SIX, Mansun, 98-6
VI: RETURN OF THE REAL, Ice-T, 96-26
SIX WHEELS ON MY WAGON, Fluke, 93-41
THE SIX WIVES OF HENRY VIII, Rick Wakeman, 73-7
SIXPENCE NONE THE RICHER, Sixpence None The Richer, 99-27
16 DIFFERENT FLAVOURS OF HELL, Pop Will Eat Itself, 93-73
16 HITS FROM 'STARS AND GARTERS', Kathy Kirby, 64-11
16 LOVER'S LANE, Go-Betweens, 88-81
16 ORIGINAL BIG HITS – VOLUME 4, Various Artists: Compilations – Motown, 67-33
SIXTEEN STONE, Bush, 96-42
THE SIXTIES, Various Artists: Compilations – Virgin/EMI, 99-16
SIXTIES BEAT, Various Artists: Compilations – Dino, 92-1
SIXTIES MANIA, Various Artists: Compilations – Telstar, 86-19
SIXTIES MIX – 60 SEQUENCED HITS FROM THE SIXTIES, Various Artists: Compilations – Stylus, 87-3
SIXTIES MIX 2, Various Artists: Compilations – Stylus, 88-14
SIXTIES MIX 3, Various Artists: Compilations – Stylus, 90-4
SIXTIES PARTY MEGAMIX ALBUM, Various Artists: Compilations – Telstar, 87-46
60'S SOUL 90'S SOUL, Various Artists: Compilations – Parlophone, 94-6
SIXTIES SUMMER LOVE, Various Artists: Compilations – Universal Music TV, 99-16
SIXTIES SUMMER MIX, Various Artists: Compilations – Telstar, 97-5
SIXTIES SUMMER MIX 2, Various Artists: Compilations – Telstar, 98-19
60 NUMBER ONES OF THE SIXTIES, Various Artists: Compilations – Telstar, 90-7
60 NUMBER ONES OF THE SIXTIES – THE ULTIMATE SIXTIES COLECTION, Various Artists: Compilations – warner.esp, 00-13
SIZE ISN'T EVERYTHING, Bee Gees, 93-23
SKA MANIA, Various Artists: Compilations – Dino, 95-4
SKA 'N' B, Bad Manners, 80-34
SKELLERN, Peter Skellern, 78-48
SKETCHES FOR MY SWEETHEART THE DRUNK, Jeff Buckley, 98-7
SKID, Skid Row, 70-30
SKID ROW, Skid Row, 89-30
SKIDIP, Eek-A-Mouse, 82-61
THE SKIFFLE SESSIONS – LIVE IN BELFAST, Van Morrison/Lonnie Donegan/Chris Barber, 00-14
SKIN, Skin, 94-9
SKIN 'EM UP, Shakin' Pyramids, 81-48
SKIN MECHANIC, Gary Numan, 89-55
SKINBEAT – THE FIRST TOUCH, Various Artists: Compilations – Really Useful/Polydor, 90-6
SKULL & BONES, Cypress Hill, 00-6
SKUNKWORKS, Bruce Dickinson, 96-41
SKY, Sky, 79-9
SKY 2, Sky, 80-1
SKY 3, Sky, 81-3
SKY 4 – FORTHCOMING, Sky, 82-7
SKY FIVE LIVE, Sky, 83-14
SKY HIGH, Tavares, 76-22
THE SKY IS TOO HIGH, Graham Coxon, 98-31
THE SKY'S GONE OUT, Bauhaus, 82-4
SKYE BOAT SONG AND OTHER GREAT SONGS, Roger Whittaker, 86-89
SKYLARKING, XTC, 86-90
SKYNYRD'S FIRST AND LAST, Lynyrd Skynyrd, 78-50
SKYSCRAPER, David Lee Roth, 88-11
SLADE ALIVE!, Slade, 72-2
SLADE IN FLAME [OST], Slade, 74-6
SLADE ON STAGE, Slade, 82-58
SLADE SMASHES, Slade, 80-21
SLADE'S GREATZ, Slade, 84-89
SLADEST, Slade, 73-1
SLAIN BY, Urusei Yatsura, 98-64
SLAM, Dan Reed Network, 89-66
SLAMMIN', Various Artists: Compilations – A&M, 90-1
SLANG, Def Leppard, 96-5
SLANTED AND ENCHANTED, Pavement, 92-72
SLAUGHTER ON TENTH AVENUE, Mick Ronson, 74-9
SLAVE TO LOVE – THE BEST OF THE BALLADS, Bryan Ferry, 00-11
SLAVE TO THE GRIND, Skid Row, 91-5
SLAVE TO THE RHYTHM, Grace Jones, 85-12
SLAVES AND MASTERS, Deep Purple, 90-45
SLAYED?, Slade, 72-1
SLEEP NO MORE, Comsat Angels, 81-51
SLEEPING WITH THE PAST, Elton John, 89-1
SLEEPLESS IN SEATTLE, Various Artists: Films – Original Soundtracks, 93-10
SLEEPLESS NIGHTS, Lindisfarne, 82-59
SLEEPS WITH ANGELS, Neil Young and Crazy Horse, 94-2
SLEEPWALKING, Gerry Rafferty, 82-39
SLEEPWALKING, Magnum, 92-27
SLEEPWALKING, Kingmaker, 93-15

SOMETIMES WHEN WE TOUCH, Various Artists: Compilations – Ronco, 84-8
SOMETIMES YOU WIN, Dr. Hook, 79-14
SOMEWHERE IN AFRIKA, Manfred Mann's Earth Band, 83-87
SOMEWHERE IN ENGLAND, George Harrison, 81-13
SOMEWHERE IN TIME, Iron Maiden, 86-3
SOMEWHERE MY LOVE, Ray Conniff, 67-34
SOMEWHERE SOON, High, 90-59
SON OF SCHMILSSON, Nilsson, 72-41
SONG AND DANCE, Various Artists: Television – Soundtrack, 84-46
THE SONG AND DANCE MEN, Max Bygraves, 78-67
A SONG FOR ALL SEASONS, Renaissance, 78-35
A SONG FOR EUROTRASH, Various Artists: Compilations – EMI, 98-19
A SONG FOR ME, Family, 70-4
A SONG FOR YOU, Jack Jones, 72-9
A SONG FOR YOU, Carpenters, 72-13
SONG OF SEVEN, Jon Anderson, 80-38
THE SONG REMAINS THE SAME [OST], Led Zeppelin, 76-1
SONG REVIEW – A GREATEST HITS COLLECTION, Stevie Wonder, 96-19
SONG WITHOUT END, Various Artists: Films – Original Soundtracks, 61-9
SONGBIRD, Barbra Streisand, 78-50
SONGBIRD, Ruby Winters, 79-31
SONGBIRD, Eva Cassidy, 01-1
SONGS, Luther Vandross, 94-1
SONGS BY TOM LEHRER, Tom Lehrer, 58-7
SONGS FOR A TAILOR, Jack Bruce, 69-6
SONGS FOR A WINTER'S NIGHT, George Hamilton IV, 82-94
SONGS FOR BEGINNERS, Graham Nash, 71-13
SONGS FOR DRELLA, Lou Reed and John Cale, 90-22
SONGS FOR SWINGING LOVERS, Frank Sinatra, 58-8
SONGS FOR SWINGING SELLERS, Peter Sellers, 59-3
SONGS FOR THE FRONT ROW – THE BEST OF OCEAN COLOUR SCENE, Ocean Colour Scene, 01-16
SONGS FROM A ROOM, Leonard Cohen, 69-2
SONGS FROM 'ALLY MCBEAL' [OST-TV], Vonda Shepard, 98-3
SONGS FROM AN AMERICAN MOVIE – VOL. ONE: LEARNING HOW TO SMILE, Everclear, 00-51
SONGS FROM AN AMERICAN MOVIE – VOL. TWO: GOOD TIME FOR A BAD ATTITUDE, Everclear, 01-69
SONGS FROM DAWSON'S CREEK, Various Artists: Television – Soundtracks, 99-3
SONGS FROM DAWSON'S CREEK – VOLUME 2, Various Artists: Television – Soundtracks, 00-5
SONGS FROM "HEATHCLIFF", Cliff Richard, 95-15
SONGS FROM HER TV SERIES, Nana Mouskouri, 73-29
SONGS FROM MY SKETCH BOOK, Val Doonican, 90-33
SONGS FROM NORTHERN BRITAIN, Teenage Fanclub, 97-3
SONGS FROM STAGE AND SCREEN, Michael Crawford and the London Symphony Orchestra, 87-12
SONGS FROM SUN STREET, Saw Doctors, 98-24
SONGS FROM THE BIG CHAIR, Tears For Fears, 85-2
SONGS FROM THE LAST CENTURY, George Michael, 99-2
SONGS FROM THE MARDI GRAS, Feargal Sharkey, 91-27
SONGS FROM THE MIRROR, Fish, 93-46
SONGS FROM THE RAIN, Hothouse Flowers, 93-7
SONGS FROM THE WEST COAST, Elton John, 01-2
SONGS FROM THE WOOD, Jethro Tull, 77-13
SONGS FROM WHISTLE DOWN THE WIND, Various Artists: Compilations – Really Useful/Polydor, 98-3
SONGS IN A MINOR, Alicia Keys, 01-7
SONGS IN THE ATTIC, Billy Joel, 81-57
SONGS IN THE KEY OF LIFE, Stevie Wonder, 76-2
SONGS IN THE KEY OF X, Various Artists: Compilations – Warner Brothers, 96-8
THE SONGS 1975 – 1990, Barry Manilow, 90-13
SONGS OF A LIFETIME, Bing Crosby, 79-29
THE SONGS OF BOB DYLAN, Various Artists: Compilations – Start, 89-13
THE SONGS OF DISTANT EARTH, Mike Oldfield, 94-24
SONGS OF FAITH AND DEVOTION, Depeche Mode, 93-1
SONGS OF FREEDOM, Bob Marley, 92-10
SONGS OF INSPIRATION, Daniel O'Donnell, 96-11
SONGS OF JOY, Nigel Brooks Singers, 75-5
SONGS OF JOY, Pestalozzi Children's Choir, 81-65
SONGS OF LEONARD COHEN, Leonard Cohen, 68-13
SONGS OF LOVE, Richard Clayderman, 87-19
SONGS OF LOVE, Placido Domingo, 00-53
SONGS OF LOVE AND HATE, Leonard Cohen, 71-4
SONGS OF OUR HERITAGE, Duane Eddy, 60-13
SONGS OF PRAISE, Various Artists: Compilations – Warwick, 77-31
SONGS OF SANCTUARY, Adiemus, 95-35
SONGS OF THE FREE, Gang Of Four, 82-61
SONGS OF THE SEASHORE, James Galway, 79-39
SONGS OF THE VALLEYS, London Welsh Male Voice Choir, 81-61
THE SONGS THAT GOT AWAY, Sarah Brightman, 89-48
SONGS TO LEARN AND SING, Echo and the Bunnymen, 85-6
SONGS TO MAKE THE WHOLE WORLD SING, Barry Manilow, 89-20
SONGS TO REMEMBER, Scritti Politti, 82-12
SONGS TO SING IN YOUR BATH, Russ Conway, 59-8
SONGS WE LOVE TO SING, Foster and Allen, 94-41
SONGWRITER, Justin Hayward, 77-28
SONIA, Sonia, 91-33
SONIC ATTACK, Hawkwind, 81-19
SONIC FLOWER GROOVE, Primal Scream, 87-62
SONIC SYSTEM, Various Artists: Compilations – Telstar, 92-17
SONIC TEMPLE, Cult, 89-3
SONNY SIDE OF CHER, Cher, 66-11
SONS AND FASCINATIONS / SISTERS FEELINGS CALL, Simple Minds, 81-11
SONS OF SOUL, Tony! Toni! Tone!, 93-66
SOONER OR LATER, BBMak, 01-16
SOPHISTICATED BOOM BOOM, Dead Or Alive, 84-29
THE SOPHTWARE SLUMP, Grandaddy, 00-36
SOPRANO IN HOLLYWOOD, Lesley Garrett, 96-53
SOPRANO IN RED, Lesley Garrett, 95-59
A SOPRANO INSPIRED, Lesley Garrett, 97-48
THE SOPRANO'S GREATEST HITS, Lesley Garrett, 97-53
SORCERER [OST], Tangerine Dream, 77-25
SOUL, Various Artists: Compilations – PolyGram TV, 98-10
THE SOUL ALBUM, Otis Redding, 66-22
THE SOUL ALBUM, Various Artists: Compilations – Virgin, 97-1
THE SOUL ALBUM II, Various Artists: Compilations – Virgin/EMI, 98-3
SOUL ALONE, Daryl Hall, 93-55
SOUL BEAT, Various Artists: Compilations – Cookie Jar, 93-8
THE SOUL CAGES, Sting, 91-1
SOUL CITY, Various Artists: Compilations – K-Tel, 77-12
SOUL DAZE/SOUL NITES, Various Artists: Compilations – Ronco, 82-25
SOUL DECADE; THE SIXTIES, Various Artists: Compilations – Motown, 90-3
SOUL DESTRUCTION, Almighty, 91-22
SOUL DEVOTION – THE VERY BEST OF HEART & SOUL, Various Artists: Compilations – PolyGram TV, 94-1
SOUL EMOTION, Various Artists: Compilations – PolyGram TV, 92-1
SOUL INSPIRATION, Various Artists: Compilations – PolyGram TV, 93-4
SOUL KISS, Olivia Newton-John, 86-66
SOUL MATE, Various Artists: Compilations – Dino, 94-6
SOUL MEN, Sam and Dave, 68-32
SOUL MINING, The, 83-27
SOUL MOODS, Various Artists: Compilations – EMI, 93-4
SOUL MOTION, Various Artists: Compilations – K-Tel, 76-1
SOUL NIGHTS, Various Artists: Compilations – PolyGram TV, 94-3
SOUL OF MANN, Manfred Mann, 67-40
THE SOUL OF SPAIN, 101 Strings, 60-17
SOUL PROVIDER, Michael Bolton, 90-4
SOUL REFLECTION, Various Artists: Compilations – Heart and Soul, 91-2
SOUL SEARCHING, Various Artists: Compilations – Columbia, 94-6
SOUL SEARCHING TIME, Average White Band, 76-60
SOUL SURVIVORS – 40 NORTHERN SOUL ANTHEMS, Various Artists: Compilations – Telstar, 97-10
SOUL SURVIVORS 2, Various Artists: Compilations – Telstar, 98-17
SOUL'S CORE, Shawn Mullins, 99-60
SOULFLY, Soulfly, 98-16
SOULJACKER, Eels, 01-12
SOULS OF BLACK, Testament, 90-35
SOUND AFFECTS, Jam, 80-2
SOUND LOADED, Ricky Martin, 00-14
THE SOUND OF AGIA NAPA – MIXED BY ARCHITECHS, Various Artists: Compilations – Universal Music TV, 00-11
THE SOUND OF BREAD, Bread, 77-1
THE SOUND OF CLASSIC FM, Various Artists: Radio – Related Compilations, 01-16
THE SOUND OF FURY, Billy Fury, 60-18
SOUND OF GLORY, London Philharmonic Choir with the National Philharmonic Orchestra conducted by John Aldiss, 76-10
THE SOUND OF KISS 100FM, Various Artists: Selected Series – Kiss, 94-1
SOUND OF LIES, Jayhawks, 97-61
THE SOUND OF MAGIC, Various Artists: Selected Series – Magic, 99-10
THE SOUND OF MAGIC, Various Artists: Selected Series – Magic, 00-9
THE SOUND OF MAGIC LOVE Various Artists: Selected Series – Magic, 99-5
THE SOUND OF MCALMONT AND BUTLER, McAlmont and Butler, 95-33
THE SOUND OF MUSIC, Various Artists: Stage Cast – Broadway, 61-4
THE SOUND OF MUSIC, Various Artists: Stage Cast – London, 61-4
THE SOUND OF MUSIC, Various Artists: Films – Original Soundtracks, 65-1
SOUND OF MUSIC, Adicts, 82-99
SOUND OF PIBROCH, Corries, 72-39
THE SOUND OF SKA, Various Artists: Compilations – Quality Television, 92-4
THE SOUND OF SPEED, Jesus And Mary Chain, 93-15
THE SOUND OF SUPER K, Kenny, 76-56
THE SOUND OF THE CITY, Various Artists: Compilations – Columbia, 92-11
THE SOUND OF THE SHADOWS, Shadows, 65-4
THE SOUND OF THE SUBURBS, Various Artists: Compilations – Columbia, 91-1
SOUND OF WATER, Saint Etienne, 00-33
SOUND OF WHITE NOISE, Anthrax, 93-14
THE SOUND OF YOUR CRY, Elvis Presley, 82-31
SOUND ON SOUND, Bill Nelson's Red Noise, 79-33
SOUND VENTURE, Georgie Fame, 66-9
SOUND WAVES, L'Orchestre Electronique, 83-75
SOUNDCLASH, Renegade Soundwave, 90-74
SOUNDS GENTLE, Val Doonican, 69-22
SOUNDS LIKE, Herb Alpert and the Tijuana Brass, 67-21
SOUNDS LIKE THE SEARCHERS, Searchers, 65-8
SOUNDS OF SILENCE, Simon and Garfunkel, 66-13
SOUNDS OF THE SEVENTIES, Various Artists: Compilations – Global Television, 94-11
SOUNDS SENSATIONAL, Bert Kaempfert, 80-17
SOUNDTRACK RECORDINGS FROM THE FILM 'JIMI HENDRIX' [OST], Jimi Hendrix, 73-37

STEPTOE AND SON, Wilfred Brambell and Harry H. Corbett, 64-14
STEREO '57 (ESSENTIAL ELVIS VOLUME 2), Elvis Presley, 89-60
STEREO MUSICALE SHOWCASE, Various Artists: Compilations – Polydor, 66-26
THE STEVE HOWE ALBUM, Steve Howe, 79-68
STEVE MCQUEEN, Prefab Sprout, 85-21
STEVE MILLER BAND LIVE!, Steve Miller Band, 83-79
STEVE WINWOOD, Steve Winwood, 77-12
STEVE WRIGHT'S SUNDAY LOVE SONGS, Various Artists: Radio – Related Compilations, 00-6
STEVE WRIGHT'S SUNDAY LOVE SONGS – VOLUME 2, Various Artists: Radio – Related Compilations, 01-12
STEVEN HOUGHTON, Steven Houghton, 97-21
STEVEN SMITH AND FATHER AND 16 GREAT SONGS, Steven Smith and Father, 72-17
STEVIE WONDER'S GREATEST HITS, Stevie Wonder, 68-25
STICK AROUND FOR JOY, Sugarcubes, 92-16
STICK TO ME, Graham Parker and the Rumour, 77-19
STICKY FINGERS, Rolling Stones, 71-1
STIFF UPPER LIP, AC/DC, 00-12
STIFF'S LIVE STIFFS, Various Artists: Compilations – Stiff, 78-28
STIGMA, EMF, 92-19
STILETTO, Lita Ford, 90-66
STILL, Joy Division, 81-5
STILL BURNING, Mike Scott, 97-34
STILL CAN'T SAY GOODBYE, Charlie Landsborough, 99-39
STILL CLIMBING, Brownstone, 97-19
STILL CRAZY AFTER ALL THESE YEARS, Paul Simon, 75-6
STILL GOT THE BLUES, Gary Moore, 90-13
STILL I RISE, 2 Pac and the Outlawz, 00-75
STILL IN THE GAME, Keith Sweat, 98-62
STILL LIFE (AMERICAN CONCERTS 1981), Rolling Stones, 82-4
STILL NOT BLACK ENOUGH, W.A.S.P., 95-52
STILL OUT OF ORDER, Infa Riot, 82-42
STILL SEXY – THE ALBUM, Errol Brown, 01-44
STILL TOGETHER, Gladys Knight and the Pips, 77-42
STILL WATERS, Bee Gees, 97-2
STILL WATERS RUN DEEP, Four Tops, 70-29
STILLS, Stephen Stills, 75-31
THE STING, Marvin Hamlisch, 74-7
STOLEN MOMENTS, John Hiatt, 90-72
STOMPIN' AT THE SAVOY, Rufus and Chaka Khan, 84-64
STOMPIN' PARTY, Various Artists: Compilations – Dino, 92-10
STONE AGE, Rolling Stones, 71-4
STONE GON', Barry White, 74-18
STONE KILLERS, Prince Charles and the City Beat Band, 83-84
THE STONE ROSES, Stone Roses, 89-19
STONE ROSES – 10TH ANNIVERSARY EDITION, Stone Roses, 99-26
STONED AND DETHRONED, Jesus And Mary Chain, 94-13
STONED RAIDERS, Cypress Hill, 01-71
STONEDHENGE, Ten Years After, 69-6
STONES, Neil Diamond, 71-18
STONES IN THE ROAD, Mary Chapin Carpenter, 94-26
STONEY END, Barbra Streisand, 71-28
STOOSH, Skunk Anansie, 96-9
STOP!, Sam Brown, 89-4
STOP MAKING SENSE, Talking Heads, 84-24
STOP THAT TRAIN, Clint Eastwood and General Saint, 83-98
STOP THE WORLD, Black, Rock and Ron, 89-72
STOP THE WORLD – I WANT TO GET OFF, Various Artists: Stage Cast – London, 61-8
STORIES FROM THE CITY, STORIES FROM THE SEA, P J Harvey, 00-23
STORIES OF JOHNNY, Marc Almond, 85-22
STORM, Vanessa-Mae, 97-27
STORM BRINGER, Deep Purple, 74-6
STORM FRONT, Billy Joel, 89-5
A STORM IN HEAVEN, Verve, 93-27
STORM WATCH, Jethro Tull, 79-27
STORMS, Nanci Griffith, 89-38
STORMSVILLE, Johnny and the Hurricanes, 60-18
THE STORY OF A YOUNG HEART, A Flock Of Seagulls, 84-30
THE STORY OF THE CLASH – VOLUME 1, Clash, 88-7
STORY OF THE STONES, Rolling Stones, 82-24
THE STORY OF THE WHO, Who, 76-2
THE STORY SO FAR: THE VERY BEST OF ROD STEWART, Rod Stewart, 01-7
STORYVILLE, Robbie Robertson, 91-30
STRAIGHT, Dogs D'Amour, 90-32
STRAIGHT BETWEEN THE EYES, Rainbow, 82-5
STRAIGHT FROM THE HEART, Patrice Rushen, 82-24
STRAIGHT OUTTA COMPTON, N.W.A., 89-41
STRAIGHT SHOOTER, Bad Company, 75-3
STRANDED, Roxy Music, 73-1
STRANGE ANGELS, Kristin Hersh, 98-64
STRANGE BEHAVIOUR, Duran Duran, 99-70
STRANGE BOUTIQUE, Monochrome Set, 80-62
STRANGE BROTHERHOOD, New Model Army, 98-72
STRANGE CHARM, Gary Numan, 86-59
STRANGE FREE WORLD, Kitchens Of Distinction, 91-45
STRANGE FRONTIER, Roger Taylor, 84-30
STRANGE KIND OF LOVE, Love And Money, 88-71
STRANGE LITTLE GIRLS, Tori Amos, 01-16
STRANGE REFLECTIONS, Second Image, 85-100
STRANGE TIMES, Chameleons, 86-44
STRANGE WEATHER, Marianne Faithfull, 87-78
STRANGEITUDE, Ozric Tentacles, 91-70
STRANGELOVE, Strangelove, 97-67
THE STRANGER, Billy Joel, 78-25
STRANGER IN MY OWN BACK YARD, Gilbert O'Sullivan, 74-9
STRANGER IN THE CITY, John Miles, 77-37
STRANGER IN THIS TOWN, Richie Sambora, 91-20
STRANGER IN TOWN, Bob Seger and the Silver Bullet Band, 78-31
STRANGER ON THE SHORE, Mr. Acker Bilk, 62-6
STRANGERS IN THE NIGHT, Frank Sinatra, 66-4
STRANGERS IN THE NIGHT, Bert Kaempfert, 66-13
STRANGERS IN THE NIGHT, UFO, 79-8
STRANGEWAYS, HERE WE COME, Smiths, 87-2
STRANGLERS IN THE NIGHT, Stranglers, 92-33
STRANGLERS IV (RATTUS NORVEGICUS), Stranglers, 77-4
STRATOSFEAR, Tangerine Dream, 76-39
THE STRAUSS FAMILY [OST-TV], London Symphony Orchestra conducted by Cyril Ornadel, 72-2
STRAW DONKEY . . . THE SINGLES, Carter – The Unstoppable Sex Machine, 95-37
STRAWBERRIES, Damned, 82-15
STRAWBERRY SWITCHBLADE, Strawberry Switchblade, 85-25
STRAY, Aztec Camera, 90-22
STRAY CATS, Stray Cats, 81-6
STREET ANGEL, Stevie Nicks, 94-16
STREET FIGHTING YEARS, Simple Minds, 89-1
STREET JAMS, Various Artists: Compilations – Telstar TV/PolyGram TV, 98-14
STREET LEGAL, Bob Dylan, 78-2
STREET LEVEL, Various Artists: Compilations – Ronco, 80-29
STREET LIFE, Crusaders, 79-10
STREET LIFE – 20 GREAT HITS, Bryan Ferry Roxy Music, 86-1
STREET MACHINE, Sammy Hagar, 79-38
STREET MOVES, Twenty 4 Seven featuring Captain Hollywood, 91-69
STREET PARTY, Chas 'N' Dave, 95-3
STREET SOUL, Various Artists: Compilations – Virgin, 95-2
STREET SOUNDS ANTHEMS – VOLUME 1, Various Artists: Compilations – Street Sounds, 87-61
STREET SOUNDS CRUCIAL ELECTRO, Various Artists: Compilations – Street Sounds, 84-24
STREET SOUNDS CRUCIAL ELECTRO 2, Various Artists: Compilations – Street Sounds, 84-35
STREET SOUNDS CRUCIAL ELECTRO – 3, Various Artists: Compilations – Street Sounds, 87-41
STREET SOUNDS DANCE MUSIC '87, Various Artists: Compilations – Street Sounds, 87-40
STREET SOUNDS EDITION 2, Various Artists: Compilations – Street Sounds, 83-35
STREET SOUNDS EDITION 3, Various Artists: Compilations – Street Sounds, 83-21
STREET SOUNDS EDITION 4, Various Artists: Compilations – Street Sounds, 83-14
STREET SOUNDS EDITION 5, Various Artists: Compilations – Street Sounds, 83-16
STREET SOUNDS EDITION 6, Various Artists: Compilations – Street Sounds, 83-23
STREET SOUNDS EDITION 7, Various Artists: Compilations – Street Sounds, 83-48
STREET SOUNDS EDITION 8, Various Artists: Compilations – Street Sounds, 84-22
STREET SOUNDS EDITION 9, Various Artists: Compilations – Street Sounds, 84-22
STREET SOUNDS EDITION 10, Various Artists: Compilations – Street Sounds, 84-24
STREET SOUNDS EDITION 11, Various Artists: Compilations – Street Sounds, 84-48
STREET SOUNDS EDITION 12, Various Artists: Compilations – Street Sounds, 85-23
STREET SOUNDS EDITION 13, Various Artists: Compilations – Street Sounds, 85-19
STREET SOUNDS EDITION 14, Various Artists: Compilations – Street Sounds, 85-43
STREET SOUNDS EDITION 15, Various Artists: Compilations – Street Sounds, 85-58
STREET SOUNDS EDITION 16, Various Artists: Compilations – Street Sounds, 86-17
STREET SOUNDS EDITION 17, Various Artists: Compilations – Street Sounds, 86-35
STREET SOUNDS EDITION 18, Various Artists: Compilations – Street Sounds, 86-20
STREET SOUNDS EDITION 19, Various Artists: Compilations – Street Sounds, 86-61
STREET SOUNDS EDITION 20, Various Artists: Compilations – Street Sounds, 87-25
STREET SOUNDS 87 VOLUME 2, Various Artists: Compilations – Street Sounds, 87-47
STREET SOUNDS 88-1, Various Artists: Compilations – Street Sounds, 88-73
STREET SOUNDS ELECTRO 1, Various Artists: Compilations – Street Sounds, 83-18
STREET SOUNDS ELECTRO 2, Various Artists: Compilations – Street Sounds, 84-49
STREET SOUNDS ELECTRO 3, Various Artists: Compilations – Street Sounds, 84-25
STREET SOUNDS ELECTRO 4, Various Artists: Compilations – Street Sounds, 84-25
STREET SOUNDS ELECTRO 5, Various Artists: Compilations – Street Sounds, 84-17
STREET SOUNDS ELECTRO 6, Various Artists: Compilations – Street Sounds, 85-24
STREET SOUNDS ELECTRO 7, Various Artists: Compilations – Street Sounds, 85-12
STREET SOUNDS ELECTRO 8, Various Artists: Compilations – Street Sounds, 85-23
STREET SOUNDS ELECTRO 9, Various Artists: Compilations – Street Sounds, 85-18
STREET SOUNDS ELECTRO 10, Various Artists: Compilations – Street Sounds, 85-72
STREET SOUNDS HI-ENERGY NO 1, Various Artists: Compilations – Street Sounds, 84-71
STREET SOUNDS HIP-HOP 17, Various Artists: Compilations – Street Sounds, 87-38
STREET SOUNDS HIP HOP 18, Various Artists: Compilations – Street Sounds, 87-67
STREET SOUNDS HIP HOP 20, Various Artists: Compilations – Street Sounds, 88-39
STREET SOUNDS HIP HOP 21, Various Artists: Compilations – Street Sounds, 88-87
STREET SOUNDS HIP-HOP ELECTRO 11, Various Artists: Compilations – Street Sounds, 86-19
STREET SOUNDS HIP-HOP ELECTRO 12, Various Artists: Compilations – Street Sounds, 86-28
STREET SOUNDS HIP-HOP ELECTRO 13, Various Artists: Compilations – Street Sounds, 86-23

SWING STREET, Barry Manilow, 88-81
SWING WHEN YOU'RE WINNING, Robbie Williams, 01-1
SWINGIN' WITH RAYMOND, Chumbawamba, 95-70
THE SWINGING CITY, Spinners, 71-20
SWINGING SAFARI, Bert Kaempfert, 66-20
SWITCHED ON SWING, Kings Of Swing Orchestra, 82-28
SWITCHED ON – THE COOL SOUND OF TV ADVERTISING, Various Artists: Television – Related Compilations, 00-9
SWOON, Prefab Sprout, 84-22
SWORDFISHTROMBONES, Tom Waits, 83-62
SYD LAWRENCE WITH THE GLENN MILLER SOUND, Syd Lawrence Orchestra, 71-31
SYMBOL, Prince and the New Power Generation, 92-1
SYMPHONIC ROCK WITH THE VIENNA SYMPHONY ORCHESTRA, Vienna Symphony Orchestra, 87-43
SYMPHONIES FOR THE SEVENTIES, Waldo De Los Rios, 71-6
SYMPHONY OR DAMN, Terence Trent D'Arby, 93-4
SYNCHRO SYSTEM, King Sunny Ade and his African Beats, 83-93
SYNCHRONICITY, Police, 83-1
SYNKRONIZED, Jamiroquai, 99-1
THE SYNTHESIZER ALBUM, Project D, 90-13
SYNTHESIZER GOLD, Ed Starink, 93-29
SYNTHESIZER GREATEST, Ed Starink, 90-22
SYNTHESIZER 2, Project D, 90-25
T. REX, T. Rex, 71-13
T. REX IN CONCERT, T. Rex, 81-35
THE T.V. HITS ALBUM TWO – 16 ORIGINAL HIT-TV THEMES, Various Artists: Television – Related Compilations, 86-19
T.V. SKY, Young Gods, 92-54
TADPOLES, Bonzo Dog Doo-Dah Band, 69-36
TAILS, Lisa Loeb and Nine Stories, 95-39
TAJA SEVELLE, Taja Sevelle, 88-48
TAKE 2: OPERA FAVOURITES/ORCHESTRAL CLASSICS, Various Artists: Compilations – Masterworks, 92-18
TAKE A BREAK, Various Artists: Compilations – Columbia, 96-10
TAKE A LOOK, Natalie Cole, 93-16
TAKE A LOOK OVER YOUR SHOULDER (REALITY), Warren G, 97-20
TAKE A PAIR OF SPARKLING EYES, Josef Locke, 92-41
TAKE DIS, Credit To The Nation, 94-20
TAKE FAT AND PARTY, Roy 'Chubby' Brown, 95-29
TAKE GOOD CARE OF MY BABY, Bobby Vee, 62-7
TAKE GOOD CARE OF YOURSELF, Three Degrees, 75-6
TAKE IT EASY WITH THE WALKER BROTHERS, Walker Brothers, 65-3
TAKE IT HOME, B.B. King, 79-60
TAKE IT TO HEART, Michael McDonald, 90-35
TAKE ME HIGH [OST], Cliff Richard, 74-41
TAKE ME HIGHER, Diana Ross, 95-10
TAKE ME TO GOD, Jah Wobble's Invaders Of The Heart, 94-13
TAKE MY TIME, Sheena Easton, 81-17
TAKE OFF YOUR PANTS AND JACKET, Blink-182, 01-4
TAKE ONE!, Shakin' Stevens, 80-62
TAKE THAT AND PARTY, Take That, 92-2
TAKE THE HEAT OFF ME, Boney M, 77-40
TAKE TWO, Diane Solomon, 75-26
TAKE TWO, Robson and Jerome, 96-1
TAKIN' IT TO THE STREETS, Doobie Brothers, 76-42
TAKING ON THE WORLD, Gun, 89-44
TALES FROM NEW YORK – THE VERY BEST OF SIMON AND GARFUNKEL, Simon and Garfunkel, 00-8
TALES FROM THE CITY, Various Artists: Television – Related Compilations, 93-17
TALES FROM TOPOGRAPHIC OCEANS, Yes, 73-1
TALES OF MYSTERY AND IMAGINATION, Alan Parsons Project, 76-56
TALK, Yes, 94-20
TALK IS CHEAP, Keith Richards, 88-37
TALK OF THE DEVIL, Ozzy Osbourne, 82-21
TALK ON CORNERS, Corrs, 97-1
TALK TALK TALK, Psychedelic Furs, 81-30
TALKIN LOUD TWO, Various Artists: Compilations – Talkin Loud, 93-6
TALKING BACK TO THE NIGHT, Steve Winwood, 82-6
TALKING BOOK, Stevie Wonder, 73-16
TALKING HEADS '77, Talking Heads, 78-60
TALKING TIMBUKTU, Ali Farka Toure and Ry Cooder, 94-44
TALKING WITH THE TAXMAN ABOUT POETRY, Billy Bragg, 86-8
TALLULAH, Go-Betweens, 87-91
TAMING THE TIGER, Joni Mitchell, 98-57
TAMLA MOTOWN GOLD – THE SOUND OF YOUNG AMERICA, Various Artists: Compilations – Universal Music TV, 01-7
TAMLA MOTOWN HITS VOLUME 5, Various Artists: Compilations – Motown, 67-11
TAMLA MOTOWN HITS VOLUME 6, Various Artists: Compilations – Motown, 68-32
TANGO, Julio Iglesias, 96-56
TANGO IN THE NIGHT, Fleetwood Mac, 87-1
TANGRAM, Tangerine Dream, 80-36
TANX, T. Rex, 73-4
TAO, Rick Springfield, 85-68
TAP ROOT MANUSCRIPT, Neil Diamond, 71-19
TAPESTRY, Carole King, 71-4
TAPESTRY, Don McLean, 72-16
A TAPESTRY OF DREAMS, Charles Aznavour, 74-9
THE TARANTTINO COLLECTION, Various Artists: Compilations – MCA, 96-18
TARANTULA, Ride, 96-21
TARKUS, Emerson, Lake and Palmer, 71-1
TASTE – LIVE AT THE ISLE OF WIGHT, Taste, 72-41
A TASTE OF HONEY, Mr. Acker Bilk, 63-17
TATTOO, Rory Gallagher, 73-32
TATTOO YOU, Rolling Stones, 81-2
TATTOOED BEAT MESSIAH, Zodiac Mindwarp and the Love Reaction, 88-20
TATTOOED MILLIONAIRE, Bruce Dickinson, 90-14
TAXI, Bryan Ferry, 93-2
TAXI FOR THESE ANIMAL MEN, These Animal Men, 95-64
TEA FOR THE TILLERMAN, Cat Stevens, 70-20
TEACH THE WORLD TO LAUGH, Barron Knights, 79-51
TEAR DOWN THESE WALLS, Billy Ocean, 88-3
TEARDROPS, Various Artists: Compilations – Ritz, 83-37
TEARS AND LAUGHTER, Johnny Mathis, 80-1
TEARS OF HAPPINESS, Ken Dodd, 65-6
TEARS OF STONE, Chieftains, 99-36
TEARS ROLL DOWN (GREATEST HITS 1982-1992), Tears For Fears, 92-2
TEASE ME, Chaka Demus and Pliers, 93-1
TEASER AND THE FIRECAT, Cat Stevens, 71-3
TEASES AND DARES, Kim Wilde, 84-66
TECHNICAL ECSTASY, Black Sabbath, 76-13
TECHNIQUE, New Order, 89-1
TECHNO NIGHTS AMBIENT DAWN, Various Artists: Compilations – EMI, 95-16
TECHNOHEDZ – 20 FIRESTARTIN' TECHO ANTHEMS, Various Artists: Compilations – Telstar, 96-12
TECHNOSTATE – 20 SERIOUS TECHNO AND GARAGE RAVES, Various Artists: Compilations – Cookie Jar, 92-2
TED NUGENT, Ted Nugent, 76-56
TEENAGE DEPRESSION, Eddie and the Hotrods, 76-43
TEENAGE DRUG, Sultans Of Ping, 94-57
TEENAGE KICKS, Various Artists: Compilations – PolyGram TV, 95-8
TEENAGE MUTANT NINJA TURTLES, Various Artists: Films – Original Soundtracks, 90-6
TEENAGE WARNING, Angelic Upstarts, 79-29
TEENAGER OF THE YEAR, Frank Black, 94-21
TEENDREEM – THE ULTIMATE CLUB NIGHT, Various Artists: Compilations – WSM, 01-19
TELEKON, Gary Numan, 80-1
TELL GOD I'M HERE, Hurrah!, 87-71
TELL IT TO MY HEART, Taylor Dayne, 88-24
TELL ME IT'S NOT TRUE 'FROM THE MUSICAL BLOOD BROTHERS', Barbara Dickson, 83-100
TELL ME ON A SUNDAY, Marti Webb, 80-2
TELL US THE TRUTH, Sham 69, 78-25
TELLIN' STORIES, Charlatans, 97-1
TELLY, Telly Savalas, 75-12
TELLYHITS – 16 TOP TV THEMES, Various Artists: Television – Related Compilations, 85-34
TELLYHITS 2 – 16 TOP TV THEMES, Various Artists: Television – Related Compilations, 86-68
TEMPERAMENTAL, Everything But The Girl, 99-16
TEMPERANCE SEVEN 1961, Temperance Seven, 61-8
TEMPERANCE SEVEN PLUS ONE, Temperance Seven, 61-19
TEMPTATION, Various Artists: Compilations – Quality Television, 92-3
TEMPTATIONS GREATEST HITS, Temptations, 67-17
THE TEMPTATIONS LIVE!, Temptations, 67-20
TEMPTED, Various Artists: Compilations – PolyGram TV, 93-10
10, Stranglers, 90-15
TEN, Pearl Jam, 92-18
10, Wet Wet Wet, 97-2
10 C.C., 10 C.C., 73-36
TEN GOOD REASONS, Jason Donovan, 89-1
TEN NEW SONGS, Leonard Cohen, 01-26
TEN SHORT SONGS ABOUT LOVE, Gary Clark, 93-25
TEN SUMMONER'S TALES, Sting, 93-2
10 000 HZ LEGEND, Air, 01-7
10 TO 23, Jose Feliciano, 70-38
TEN YEARS NON-STOP JUBILEE, James Last, 75-5
10 YEARS OF HITS – RADIO ONE, Various Artists: Radio – Related Compilations , 77-39
TEN YEARS TOGETHER, Peter, Paul and Mary, 70-60
TENDER LOVE – 17 ROMANTIC LOVE SONGS, Various Artists: Compilations – EMI, 92-2
TENDER PREY, Nick Cave and the Bad Seeds, 88-67
TENDERLY, George Benson, 89-52
TENEMENT SYMPHONY, Marc Almond, 91-39
TENNESSEE MOON (THE NASHVILLE COLLECTION), Neil Diamond, 96-12
TENNIS, Chris Rea, 80-60
THE TENTH ANNIVERSARY ALBUM OF TOM JONES – 20 GREATEST HITS, Tom Jones, 75-1
TERENCE TRENT D'ARBY'S VIBRATOR, Terence Trent D'Arby, 95-11
TERMINATOR 2 [OST], Brad Fiedel, 91-26
TERRAPIN STATION, Grateful Dead, 77-30
TERROR TWILIGHT, Pavement, 99-19
TEST FOR ECHO, Rush, 96-25
TESTAMENT '93, Inner City, 93-33
TEXAS FEVER, Orange Juice, 84-34
THA DOGGFATHER, Snoop Doggy Dogg, 96-15
THA LAST MEAL, Snoop Dogg, 01-62
THANK CHRIST FOR THE BOMB, Groundhogs, 70-9
THANK GOD IT'S FRIDAY, Various Artists: Films – Original Soundtracks, 78-40
THANK YOU, Duran Duran, 95-12
THANK YOU AND GOODNIGHT, It Bites, 91-59
THANK YOU BABY, Stylistics, 75-5
THANK YOU FOR THE MUSIC, Abba, 83-17
THANK YOU VERY MUCH – REUNION CONCERT AT THE LONDON PALLADIUM, Cliff Richard and the Shadows, 79-5
THANKS BUT I'LL EAT IT HERE, Lowell George, 79-71
THAT ALBUM BY OCEANIC, Oceanic, 92-49
THAT LOVING FEELING, Vince Hill, 78-51
THAT LOVING FEELING, Various Artists: Selected Series – That Loving Feelng, 89-11
THAT LOVING FEELING VOLUME 2, Various Artists: Selected Series – That Loving Feelng, 90-5
THAT LOVING FEELING VOLUME 3, Various Artists: Selected Series – That Loving Feelng, 90-1

THIS YEAR'S LOVE IS FOREVER, Various Artists: Compilations – Sony TV/Global TV, 95-4
THIS YEAR'S LOVE (WILL LAST FOREVER) XXX, Various Artists: Compilations – Sony TV/Global TV, 96-12
THIS YEAR'S MODEL, Elvis Costello, 78-4
THOMPSON TWINS – THE GREATEST HITS, Thompson Twins, 90-23
THOROUGHLY MODERN MILLIE, Various Artists: Films – Original Soundtracks, 67-9
THOUGHT 'YA KNEW, Ce Ce Peniston, 94-31
THOUGHTS OF HOME, Daniel O'Donnell, 89-43
THOUGHTS OF LOVE, Shirley Bassey, 76-15
A THOUSAND LEAVES, Sonic Youth, 98-38
A THOUSAND VOLTS OF HOLT, John Holt, 75-42
THRAK, King Crimson, 95-58
III, Guy, 00-55
3 CAR GARAGE – INDIE RECORDINGS 95-96, Hanson, 98-39
THREE CHORD OPERA, Neil Diamond, 01-49
3D, Three Degrees, 79-61
THREE DEGREES, Three Degrees, 74-12
THREE DOLLAR BILL YALL$, Limp Bizkit, 00-50
THE THREE E.P.S, Beta Band, 98-35
3 FEET HIGH AND RISING, De La Soul, 89-13
THREE HEARTS IN THE HAPPY ENDING MACHINE, Daryl Hall, 86-26
THREE IMAGINARY BOYS, Cure, 79-44
THREE LIGHT YEARS, Electric Light Orchestra, 79-38
THREE MINUTE HEROES, Various Artists: Compilations – Virgin, 92-4
THREE OF A PERFECT PAIR, King Crimson, 84-30
THREE SIDES LIVE, Genesis, 82-2
III SIDES TO EVERY STORY, Extreme, 92-2
THREE SNAKES AND ONE CHARM, Black Crowes, 96-17
THREE STEPS TO HEAVEN – ROCK 'N' ROLL LEGENDS, Various Artists: Compilations – Quality Television, 92-6
THE THREE TENORS CHRISTMAS, Three Tenors, 00-57
THE 3 TENORS IN CONCERT 1994, Carreras Domingo Pavarotti with Orchestra conducted by Zubin Mehta, 94-1
THE 3 TENORS PARIS 1998, Carreras Domingo Pavarotti with James Levine, 98-14
3 YEARS, 5 MONTHS AND 2 DAYS IN THE LIFE OF ARRESTED DEVELOPMENT, Arrested Development, 92-3
3LW, 3LW, 01-75
THE THRILL OF IT ALL, Thunder, 97-14
THRILL TO THE SENSATIONAL SOUNDS OF SUPER STEREO, Various Artists: Compilations – CBS, 67-20
THRILLER, Eddie and the Hotrods, 79-50
THRILLER, Michael Jackson, 82-1
THRILLER THEMES, Chaquito Orchestra, 72-48
THROUGH A BIG COUNTRY – GREATEST HITS, Big Country, 90-2
THROUGH THE BARRICADES, Spandau Ballet, 86-7
THROUGH THE FIRE, Hagar, Schon, Aaronson, Shrieve, 84-92
THROUGH THE LOOKING GLASS, Siouxsie and the Banshees, 87-15
THROUGH THE PAST, DARKLY (BIG HITS – VOL. 2), Rolling Stones, 69-2
THROUGH THE STORM, Aretha Franklin, 89-46
THROUGH THE VEIL, Claytown Troupe, 89-72
THROUGH THE YEARS, Cilla Black, 93-41
THROWIN' DOWN, Rick James, 82-93
THROWING COPPER, Live, 95-37
THUNDER, Andy Taylor, 87-61
THUNDER AND CONSOLATION, New Model Army, 89-20
THUNDER AND LIGHTNING, Thin Lizzy, 83-4
THUNDER IN MY HEART, Leo Sayer, 77-8
TI AMO – PUCCINI'S GREATEST LOVE SONGS, Luciano Pavarotti, 93-23
TICAL 2000: JUDGEMENT DAY, Method Man, 98-49
TICKET TO RIDE, Carpenters, 72-20
TIFFANY, Tiffany, 88-5
TIGER BAY, Saint Etienne, 94-8
TIGERLILY, Natalie Merchant, 95-39
TIGERMILK, Belle And Sebastian, 99-13
TIGHT FIT, Tight Fit, 82-87
TIGHTEN UP VOLUME 1, Loose Ends, 92-40
TIGHTEN UP VOLUME 4, Various Artists: Compilations – Trojan, 71-20
TIGHTEN UP VOLUME 88, Big Audio Dynamite, 88-33
TILL DEAF US DO PART, Slade, 81-68
TILL I LOVED YOU, Barbra Streisand, 88-29
TILL WE HAVE FACES, Steve Hackett, 84-54
TILT, Cozy Powell, 81-58
TILT, Scott Walker, 95-27
TILT, Lightning Seeds, 99-46
TIME, ELO, 81-1
THE TIME, Bros, 89-4
TIME, Fleetwood Mac, 95-47
TIME, Peter Andre, 97-28
TIME, Lionel Richie, 98-31
TIME AFTER TIME, Eva Cassidy, 00-25
TIME AND A WORD, Yes, 70-45
TIME AND TIDE, Split Enz, 82-71
TIME AND TIDE, Basia, 88-61
TIME FADES AWAY, Neil Young, 73-20
TIME FOR LOVE, Bill Tarmey, 94-28
TIME FOR THE REST OF YOUR LIFE, Strangelove, 94-69
A TIME FOR US, Donny Osmond, 73-4
TIME FURTHER OUT, Dave Brubeck Quartet, 62-12
THE TIME HAS COME [EP], U.N.K.L.E., 95-73
TIME HONOURED GHOST, Barclay James Harvest, 75-32
THE TIME IS NEAR, Keef Hartley Band, 70-41
TIME, LOVE AND TENDERNESS, Michael Bolton, 91-2
TIME LOVES A HERO, Little Feat, 77-8
TIME MACHINE, Joe Satriani, 93-32
TIME OUT, Dave Brubeck Quartet, 60-11
TIME OUT OF MIND, Bob Dylan, 97-10
TIME PASSAGES, Al Stewart, 78-39
TIME PIECES – THE BEST OF ERIC CLAPTON, Eric Clapton, 82-20
TIME * SEX * LOVE *, Mary Chapin Carpenter, 01-57
TIME TELLS NO LIES, Praying Mantis, 81-60
TIME TO CELEBRATE, Russ Conway, 59-3
TIME WAS, Curtis Stigers, 95-34
TIMELESS, Goldie, 95-7
TIMELESS, Daniel O'Donnell and Mary Duff, 96-13
TIMELESS, Sarah Brightman, 97-2
TIMELESS FLIGHT, Steve Harley and Cockney Rebel, 76-18
TIMELESS – LIVE IN CONCERT, Barbra Streisand, 00-54
TIMELESS (THE CLASSICS), Michael Bolton, 92-3
TIMELESS – THE CLASSICS VOLUME 2, Michael Bolton, 99-50
TIMELESS – THE VERY BEST OF NEIL SEDAKA, Neil Sedaka, 91-10
THE TIMES THEY ARE A-CHANGIN', Bob Dylan, 64-4
TIME'S UP, Living Colour, 90-20
TIMESPACE – THE BEST OF STEVIE NICKS, Stevie Nicks, 91-15
TIN DRUM, Japan, 81-12
TIN MACHINE, Tin Machine, 89-3
TIN MACHINE II, Tin Machine, 91-23
TIN PLANET, Space, 98-3
TINDERBOX, Siouxsie and the Banshees, 86-13
TINDERSTICKS, Tindersticks, 93-56
TINSEL TOWN REBELLION, Frank Zappa, 81-55
TINY MUSIC . . . SONGS FROM THE VATICAN GIFT SHOP, Stone Temple Pilots, 96-31
TITANIC [OST], Music composed and conducted by James Horner, 98-1
TITANIC DAYS, Kirsty MacColl, 94-46
TITLE OF RECORD, Filter, 99-75
TITLES, Mick Karn, 82-74
TO BRING YOU MY LOVE, P.J. Harvey, 95-12
TO HAVE AND TO HOLD – THE WEDDING ALBUM, Various Artists: Compilations – Quality Television, 92-7
TO LOVE AGAIN, Diana Ross, 81-26
TO LOVERS EVERYWHERE, Mantovani and his Orchestra, 72-44
TO OUR CHILDREN'S CHILDREN'S CHILDREN, Moody Blues, 69-2
TO RIDE, SHOOT STRAIGHT AND SPEAK THE TRUTH, Entombed, 97-75
TO SEE THE LIGHTS, Gene, 96-11
TO THE EXTREME, Vanilla Ice, 90-4
TO THE FAITHFUL DEPARTED, Cranberries, 96-2
TO THE LIMIT, Joan Armatrading, 78-13
TO THE MAXXIMUM, Maxx, 94-66
TO THE MOON, Capercaillie, 95-41
TO THE NEXT LEVEL, MN8, 95-13
TO THE TOP, Aswad, 86-71
TO VENUS AND BACK, Tori Amos, 99-22
TO WHOM IT MAY CONCERN, Pasadenas, 88-3
TOCA, Fragma, 01-19
TOCSIN, X Mal Deutschland, 84-86
TODAY, Elvis Presley, 75-48
TOGETHER, Diana Ross and the Supremes with the Temptations, 70-28
TOGETHER, Jack Jones, 73-8
TOGETHER, New Seekers, 74-12
TOGETHER, Various Artists: Compilations – K-Tel, 79-35
TOGETHER, Various Artists: Compilations – K-Tel, 86-20
TOGETHER, Various Artists: Compilations – PolyGram TV, 95-2
TOGETHER AGAIN, Rose Marie, 88-52
TOGETHER ALONE, Crowded House, 93-4
TOGETHER AT LAST, Richard Clayderman and James Last, 91-14
TOGETHER FOR THE CHILDREN OF BOSNIA, Pavarotti and Friends, 96-11
TOGETHER FOREVER – GREATEST HITS 1983-1998, Run-DMC, 98-31
TOGETHER WITH CLIFF RICHARD, Cliff Richard, 91-10
TOM, Tom Jones, 70-4
TOM JONES AFTER DARK, Tom Jones, 89-46
TOM JONES LIVE! AT THE TALK OF THE TOWN, Tom Jones, 67-6
TOM JONES LIVE IN LAS VEGAS, Tom Jones, 69-2
TOM PETTY AND THE HEARTBREAKERS, Tom Petty and the Heartbreakers, 77-24
TOM TOM CLUB, Tom Tom Club, 81-78
TOMITA'S GREATEST HITS, Tomita, 80-66
TOMMY, Who, 69-2
TOMMY, Various Artists: Films – Original Soundtracks, 75-21
TOMMY, Wedding Present, 88-42
TOMMY [OST], Who, 75-30
TOMMY BOY GREATEST BEATS, Various Artists: Compilations – Tommy Boy/Island, 85-44
TOMORROW BELONGS TO ME, Sensational Alex Harvey Band, 75-9
TOMORROW THE GREEN GRASS, Jayhawks, 95-41
A TON OF HITS – THE BEST OF STOCK AITKEN WATERMAN, Various Artists: Compilations – Dover, 90-7
TONGUES AND TAILS, Sophie B. Hawkins, 92-46
TONI BRAXTON, Toni Braxton, 94-4
A TONIC FOR THE TROOPS, Boomtown Rats, 78-8
TONIGHT, David Bowie, 84-1
TONIGHT I'M YOURS, Rod Stewart, 81-8
TONIGHT'S THE NIGHT, Neil Young, 75-48
TONY, Anthony Newley, 61-5
TONY CHRISTIE – LIVE, Tony Christie, 75-33
TONY HADLEY, Tony Hadley, 97-45
TONY JOE, Tony Joe White, 70-63
TONY MAKES IT HAPPEN, Tony Bennett, 67-31
TONY MONOPOLY, Tony Monopoly, 76-25
TONY'S GREATEST HITS, Tony Bennett, 67-14
TOO BLIND TO SEE IT, Kym Sims, 92-39
TOO HOT TO HANDLE, Heatwave, 77-46
TOO LEGIT TO QUIT, Hammer, 91-41
TOO LONG IN EXILE, Van Morrison, 93-4
TOO LOW FOR ZERO, Elton John, 83-7
TOO MUCH PRESSURE, Selecter, 80-5
TOO OLD TO ROCK 'N' ROLL: TOO YOUNG TO DIE, Jethro Tull, 76-25

TRIVIAL PURSUIT – THE MUSIC MASTER GAME, Various Artists: Miscellaneous, 91-20
TROCADERO, Showaddywaddy, 76-41
TROGGLODYNAMITE, Troggs, 67-10
TROMPE LE MONDE, Pixies, 91-7
TROOPS OF TOMORROW, Exploited, 82-17
TROPICAL BRAINSTORM, Kirsty MacColl, 00-39
TROPICAL GANGSTERS, Kid Creole and the Coconuts, 82-3
TROPICO, Pat Benatar, 84-31
TROUBADOUR, J.J. Cale, 76-53
TROUBLE, Sailor, 76-45
TROUBLE, Whitesnake, 78-50
TROUBLE IN SHANGRI-LA, Stevie Nicks, 01-43
TROUBLE OVER HERE, TROUBLE OVER THERE, Trouble Funk, 87-54
TROUBLEGUM, Therapy?, 94-5
TROUT MASK REPLICA, Captain Beefheart and his Magic Band, 69-21
TRUE, Spandau Ballet, 83-1
TRUE BLUE, Madonna, 86-1
TRUE COLORS, Cyndi Lauper, 86-25
TRUE COLOURS, Split Enz, 80-42
TRUE COLOURS, Level 42, 84-14
TRUE CONFESSIONS, Bananarama, 86-46
TRUE EUPHORIA – MIXED BY DAVE PEARCE, Various Artists: Selected Series – Euphoria, 01-3
TRUE LOVE, Various Artists: Compilations – K-Tel, 87-38
TRUE LOVE, Pat Benatar, 91-40
TRUE LOVE WAYS, Buddy Holly, 89-8
TRUE LOVE WAYS, Various Artists: Compilations – Columbia, 94-14
TRUE SPIRIT, Carleen Anderson, 94-12
TRUE STORIES, Talking Heads, 86-7
TRUEBRIT, Various Artists: Compilations – PolyGram TV, 96-7
TRULY FOR YOU, Temptations, 84-75
TRULY – THE LOVE SONGS, Lionel Richie, 98-5
TRULY UNFORGETTABLE, Various Artists: Compilations – EMI, 90-6
TRUMPET A-GO-GO, James Last, 69-13
TRUNK FUNK – THE BEST OF THE BRAND NEW HEAVIES, Brand New Heavies, 99-13
TRUST, Elvis Costello and the Attractions, 81-9
TRUST, Brother Beyond, 89-60
TRUTH AND BEAUTY, Ian McNabb, 93-51
TRUTH AND LOVE, Hue And Cry, 92-33
TRUTH AND THE LIGHT: MUSIC FROM THE X-FILES, Mark Snow, 96-42
TRUTH BE TOLD, Shed Seven, 01-42
TRUTHDARE DOUBLEDARE, Bronski Beat, 86-18
TRY A LITTLE KINDNESS, Glen Campbell, 70-37
TRY WHISTLING THIS, Neil Finn, 98-5
TSOP – THE SOUND OF PHILADELPHIA, Various Artists: Compilations – K-Tel, 88-26
THE TUBE, Various Artists: Television – Related Compilations, 84-30
TUBEWAY ARMY, Tubeway Army, 79-14
TUBTHUMPER, Chumbawamba, 97-19
TUBULAR BELLS, Mike Oldfield, 73-1
TUBULAR BELLS II, Mike Oldfield, 92-1
TUBULAR BELLS III, Mike Oldfield, 98-4
TUESDAY NIGHT MUSIC CLUB, Sheryl Crow, 94-8
TUFF JAM PRESENTS UNDERGROUND FREQUENCIES – 1, Various Artists: Compilations – Satellite, 97-20
TUFF JAM PRESENTS UNDERGROUND FREQUENCIES – 2, Various Artists: Compilations – Satellite, 98-14
TUG OF WAR, Paul McCartney, 82-1
TUMBLEWEED CONNECTION, Elton John, 71-6
A TUNE A DAY, Supernaturals, 98-21
THE TUNNEL MIXES, Various Artists: Compilations – Limbo, 96-17
TUNNEL OF LOVE, Bruce Springsteen, 87-1
TURBO, Judas Priest, 86-33
TURBO TRAX, Various Artists: Compilations – K-Tel, 82-17
TURBULENT INDIGO, Joni Mitchell, 94-53
TURN BACK THE CLOCK, Johnny Hates Jazz, 88-1
TURN IT ON AGAIN – THE HITS, Genesis, 99-4
TURN IT UP! THE VERY BEST OF, Busta Rhymes, 01-44
TURN IT UPSIDE DOWN, Spin Doctors, 94-3
THE TURN OF A FRIENDLY CARD, Alan Parsons Project, 80-38
TURN OF THE TIDE, Barclay James Harvest, 81-55
TURN ON THE RADIO, Change, 85-39
TURN ON THE SUN, Nana Mouskouri, 71-16
TURN OUT THE LIGHTS, Bernie Torme, 82-50
TURN THE DARK OFF, Howie B, 97-58
TURN THE MUSIC UP, Players Association, 79-54
TURN, TURN, TURN, Byrds, 66-11
THE TURNING POINT, John Mayall, 69-11
TURNING STONES, Judie Tzuke, 89-57
TURNS INTO STONE, Stone Roses, 92-32
TURTLE SOUP, Mock Turtles, 91-54
TUSK, Fleetwood Mac, 79-1
TUTTI FRUTTI, Majestics, 87-64
TUTU, Miles Davis, 86-74
THE TV HITS ALBUM, Various Artists: Television – Related Compilations, 85-26
TV SPECIAL, Elvis Presley, 78-50
TV TUNES, Various Artists: Television – Related Compilations, 89-17
TV 2000, Various Artists: Television – Related Compilations, 00-16
TWANGIN', Dave Edmunds, 81-37
THE "TWANG'S" THE THANG, Duane Eddy, his "twangy" guitar and the Rebels, 60-2
TWANGY GUITAR – SILKY STRINGS, Duane Eddy, 62-13
TWELVE, Various Artists: Compilations – Warner.esp/Global TV, 96-10
THE TWELVE COMMANDMENTS OF DANCE, London Boys, 89-2
TWELVE DEADLY CYNS . . . AND THEN SOME, Cyndi Lauper, 94-2
12 GOLD BARS, Status Quo, 80-3
12 GOLD BARS VOLUME TWO – (AND ONE), Status Quo, 84-12
12 GREATEST HITS VOLUME 2, Neil Diamond, 82-32
THE 12" ALBUM, Howard Jones, 84-15
TWELVE INCHES OF PLEASURE, Various Artists: Compilations – Proto, 83-100
12 INCHES OF SNOW, Snow, 93-41
TWELVE MONTHS, ELEVEN DAYS, Gary Barlow, 99-35
TWELVE OF THOSE SONGS, Shirley Bassey, 68-38
12 PLAY, R. Kelly, 93-20
TWELVE SONGS OF CHRISTMAS, Jim Reeves, 64-3
12 X 12 MEGA MIXES, Various Artists: Compilations – Starblend, 85-77
20 ALL TIME EUROVISION FAVOURITES, Nigel Brooks Singers, 76-44
20 ALL TIME GREATEST, Petula Clark, 77-18
20 ALL TIME GREATS, Connie Francis, 77-1
20 ALL TIME GREATS, Roger Whittaker, 79-24
20 ALL TIME GREATS OF THE 50'S, Various Artists: Compilations – K-Tel, 72-1
20 CLASSIC HITS, Platters, 78-8
20 COUNTRY CLASSICS, Tammy Wynette, 77-3
TWENTY DYNAMIC HITS, Various Artists: Compilations – K-Tel, 72-1
20 FAMILY FAVOURITES, Vera Lynn, 81-25
20 FANTASTIC HITS, Various Artists: Compilations – Arcade, 72-1
20 FANTASTIC HITS VOLUME TWO, Various Artists: Compilations – Arcade, 72-2
20 FANTASTIC HITS VOLUME 3, Various Artists: Compilations – Arcade, 73-3
20 FLASH BACK GREATS OF THE SIXTIES, Various Artists: Compilations – K-Tel, 73-1
20 GIANT HITS, Nolan Sisters, 78-3
20 GOLDEN GREATS, Beach Boys, 76-1
20 GOLDEN GREATS, Buddy Holly and the Crickets, 78-1
20 GOLDEN GREATS, Nat 'King' Cole, 78-1
20 GOLDEN GREATS, Frank Sinatra, 78-4
20 GOLDEN GREATS, Hollies, 78-2
20 GOLDEN GREATS, Kinks, 78-19
20 GOLDEN GREATS, Neil Diamond, 78-2
20 GOLDEN GREATS, Doris Day, 79-12
20 GOLDEN GREATS, Mantovani and his Orchestra, 79-9
20 GOLDEN GREATS, Diana Ross, 79-2
20 GOLDEN GREATS, Dion and the Belmonts, 80-31
20 GOLDEN GREATS, Al Jolson, 81-18
20 GOLDEN GREATS, Gilbert O'Sullivan, 81-98
20 GOLDEN GREATS, Adam Faith, 81-61
20 GOLDEN GREATS OF KEN DODD, Ken Dodd, 80-8
20 GREAT ITALIAN LOVE SONGS, Various Artists: Compilations – Telstar, 83-28
20 GREATEST HITS, Real Thing, 80-56
20 GREATEST HITS, Beatles, 82-10
20 GREATEST HITS VOLUME 2, Elvis Presley, 85-98
20 GREATEST LOVE SONGS, Nat 'King' Cole, 82-7
20 HOLIDAY HITS, Various Artists: Compilations – Creole, 85-48
20 HOTTEST HITS, Hot Chocolate, 79-3
20 OF ANOTHER KIND, Various Artists: Compilations – Polydor, 79-45
20 ORIGINAL CHART HITS, Various Artists: Compilations – Philips, 73-9
20 ORIGINAL DEAN MARTIN HITS, Dean Martin, 76-7
20 ORIGINAL GREATS, Cliff Richard and the Shadows, 84-43
20 REGGAE CLASSICS, Various Artists: Compilations – Trojan, 84-89
20 SMASH DISCO HITS (THE BITCH), Various Artists: Films – Related Compilations, 79-42
20 SONGS OF JOY, Harry Secombe, 78-8
20 STAR TRACKS, Various Artists: Compilations – Ronco, 72-2
TWENTY WITH A BULLET, Various Artists: Compilations – EMI, 82-11
20 WOMBLING GREATS, Wombles, 77-29
20 YEARS OF JETHRO TULL, Jethro Tull, 88-78
20/20, Beach Boys, 69-3
20/20, George Benson, 85-9
THE 20TH ANNIVERSARY ALBUM, Various Artists: Compilations – Motown, 80-53
TWENTIETH CENTURY BLUES, Various Artists: Compilations – EMI, 98-14
21 AT 33, Elton John, 80-12
21ST CENTURY ROCK, Various Artists: Compilations – Virgin/EMI, 99-9
22 DYNAMIC HITS – VOL. II, Various Artists: Compilations – K-Tel, 72-2
22 GOLDEN GUITAR GREATS, Bert Weedon, 76-1
23AM, Robert Miles, 97-42
24 CARAT, Al Stewart, 80-55
24 CARAT PURPLE, Deep Purple, 75-14
TWENTY FOUR SEVEN, Tina Turner, 99-9
24 NIGHTS, Eric Clapton, 91-17
24 ORIGINAL HITS, Drifters, 75-2
25, Harry Connick Jr., 93-35
25 GOLDEN GREATS, Bachelors, 79-38
25 ROCKIN' & ROLLIN' GREATS, Various Artists: Compilations – K-Tel, 72-1
25 THUMPING GREAT HITS, Dave Clark Five, 78-7
25 YEARS ON, Hawklords, 78-48
25TH ANNIVERSARY, Brenda Lee, 84-65
25TH ANNIVERSARY ALBUM, Shirley Bassey, 78-3
TWICE AS KOOL – THE HITS OF KOOL & THE GANG, Kool And The Gang, 83-4
TWICE AS NICE IN AYIA NAPA – DJ SPOONY, Various Artists: Compilations – React, 99-18
TWICE AS NICE – SEXY & STYLISH – DJ SPOONY & STEVE 'SMOOTH' SUTHERLAND, Various Artists: Compilations – warner.esp, 00-5
TWICE AS NICE – SEXY & STYLISH – MIXED LIVE BY DJ SPOONY & STEVE 'SMOOTH' SUTHERLAND, Various Artists: Compilations – WSM, 01-11
TWICE AS NICE – SUMMER OF LOVE – MIXED LIVE BY DJ SPOONY & STEVE 'SMOOTH' SUNDERLAND, Various Artists: Compilations – warner.esp, 00-6
TWICE THE LOVE, George Benson, 88-16

UNFORGETTABLE: A MUSICAL TRIBUTE TO NAT KING COLE, Johnny Mathis and Natalie Cole, 83-5
THE UNFORGETTABLE FIRE, U2, 84-1
THE UNFORGETTABLE GLENN MILLER, Glenn Miller and his Orchestra, 77-4
UNFORGETTABLE NAT 'KING' COLE, Nat 'King' Cole, 65-11
THE UNFORGETTABLE NAT 'KING' COLE, Nat King Cole, 91-23
UNFORGETTABLE – WITH LOVE, Natalie Cole, 91-11
UNHALFBRICKING, Fairport Convention, 69-12
UNICORN, Tyrannosaurus Rex, 69-12
UNION, Toni Childs, 89-73
UNION, Yes, 91-7
UNION GAP, Gary Puckett and the Union Gap, 68-24
THE UNIQUE KLAUS WUNDERLICH SOUND, Klaus Wunderlich, 78-28
UNISON, Celine Dion, 95-55
UNITED DANCE PRESENTS ANTHEMS 2 – '88–'92, Various Artists: Compilations – United Dance, 97-17
UNITED DANCE – VOLUME 3, Various Artists: Compilations – Four Beat, 96-11
UNITED DANCE – VOLUME FOUR, Various Artists: Compilations – Four Beat, 96-17
UNITED DANCE – VOLUME 5, Various Artists: Compilations – Four Beat, 96-20
UNITED DANCE – VOLUME 6, Various Artists: Compilations – Four Beat, 97-10
UNITED KINGDOMS, Ultramarine, 93-49
UNIVERSAL, K-Klass, 94-73
UNIVERSAL, OMD, 96-24
UNIVERSAL MOTHER, Sinead O'Connor, 94-19
UNIVERSAL SOLDIER, Donovan, 67-5
UNIVERSE PRESENTS THE TRIBAL GATHERING, Various Artists: Compilations – Universe, 95-19
UNIVERSE – WORLD TECHNO TRIBE, Various Artists: Compilations – Universe, 93-13
UNIVERSITY, Throwing Muses, 95-10
UNKNOWN PLEASURES, Joy Division, 80-71
UNKNOWN TERRITORY, Bomb The Bass, 91-19
UNLACED, Various Artists: Compilations – EMI, 95-8
UNLEASH THE DRAGON, Sisqo, 00-15
UNLEASHED IN THE EAST, Judas Priest, 79-10
UNMASKED, Kiss, 80-48
UNPLUGGED, Eric Clapton, 92-2
UNPLUGGED, Arrested Development, 93-40
UNPLUGGED, Neil Young, 93-4
UNPLUGGED, 10,000 Maniacs, 93-40
UNPLUGGED, Bob Dylan, 95-10
UNPLUGGED, Bryan Adams, 97-19
UNPLUGGED, Corrs, 99-7
UNPLUGGED . . . AND SEATED, Rod Stewart, 93-2
UNPLUGGED IN NEW YORK, Nirvana, 94-1
UNPLUGGED – THE OFFICIAL BOOTLEG, Paul McCartney, 91-7
THE UNRECORDED JASPER CARROTT, Jasper Carrott, 79-19
UNRELEASED & REVAMPED [EP], Cypress Hill, 96-29
UNTIL THE END OF TIME, 2Pac, 01-31
UNTITLED, Byrds, 70-11
UNTITLED, Marc and the Mambas, 82-42
UNTITLED, Various Artists: Compilations – Global Television, 96-6
UNTITLED 2, Various Artists: Compilations – Global Television, 96-6
UNTITLED 3, Various Artists: Compilations – Global Television, 96-20
THE UNTOUCHABLE, Alvin Stardust, 74-4
UNUSUAL HEAT, Foreigner, 91-56
UP, ABC, 89-58
UP, Right Said Fred, 92-1
UP, R.E.M., 98-2
UP ALL NIGHT, East 17, 95-7
THE UP ESCALATOR, Graham Parker and the Rumour, 80-11
UP ON THE ROOF – SONGS FROM THE BRILL BUILDING, Neil Diamond, 93-28
UP TO DATE, Partridge Family, 72-46
UP TO OUR HIPS, Charlatans, 94-8
UPFRONT 1 – 14 DANCE TRACKS, Various Artists: Selected Series – Upfront, 86-17
UPFRONT 2 – 14 DANCE TRACKS, Various Artists: Selected Series – Upfront, 86-27
UPFRONT 3, Various Artists: Selected Series – Upfront, 86-37
UPFRONT 4, Various Artists: Selected Series – Upfront, 87-21
UPFRONT 5, Various Artists: Selected Series – Upfront, 87-21
UPFRONT 6, Various Artists: Selected Series – Upfront, 87-22
UPFRONT 7, Various Artists: Selected Series – Upfront, 87-31
UPFRONT 8, Various Artists: Selected Series – Upfront, 87-22
UPFRONT 9, Various Artists: Selected Series – Upfront, 87-92
UPFRONT 10, Various Artists: Selected Series – Upfront, 88-45
UPFRONT 89, Various Artists: Selected Series – Upfront, 89-15
UPRISING, Bob Marley and the Wailers, 80-6
THE UPS AND DOWNS, Stephen "Tin Tin" Duffy, 85-35
UPSTAIRS AT ERIC'S, Yazoo, 82-2
URBAN ACID, Various Artists: Compilations – Urban, 88-51
URBAN BEACHES, Cactus World News, 86-56
URBAN CHILL, Various Artists: Compilations – Universal Music TV, 01-15
URBAN CLASSICS, Various Artists: Compilations – Urban, 87-96
URBAN HANG SUITE, Maxwell, 96-39
URBAN HYMNS, Verve, 97-1
URBAN KISS, Various Artists: Selected Series – Kiss, 01-5
URBAN RENEWAL FEATURING THE SONGS BY PHIL COLLINS, Various Artists: Compilations – WEA, 01-16
URBAN RHYMES, Various Artists: Compilations – Global Television, 98-5
URIAH HEEP LIVE, Uriah Heep, 73-23
US, Peter Gabriel, 92-2
US AND US ONLY, Charlatans, 99-2
USE YOUR ILLUSION I, Guns N' Roses, 91-2
USE YOUR ILLUSION II, Guns N' Roses, 91-1
USE YOUR IMAGINATION, Mud, 75-33
UTAH SAINTS, Utah Saints, 93-10
UTOPIA BANISHED, Napalm Death, 92-58
UTOPIA – CHILLED CLASSICS, Various Artists: Compilations – Philips, 01-10
UTTER MADNESS, Madness, 86-29
U2 LIVE "UNDER A BLOOD RED SKY", U2, 83-2
V DEEP, Boomtown Rats, 82-64
V.U., Velvet Underground, 85-47
VACATION, Go-Go's, 82-75
VAGABOND HEART, Rod Stewart, 91-2
VAL, Val Doonican, 68-6
VAL DOONICAN ROCKS, BUT GENTLY, Val Doonican, 67-1
VALENTINE, Roy Harper, 74-27
VALENTYNE SUITE, Colosseum, 69-15
VALHALLA AVENUE, Fatima Mansions, 92-52
VALLEY OF THE DOLLS, Dionne Warwick, 68-10
VALLEY OF THE DOLLS, Generation X, 79-51
VALOTTE, Julian Lennon, 84-20
VAMP OF THE ROARING TWENTIES, Dorothy Provine, 62-9
VAN HALEN, Van Halen, 78-34
VAN HALEN II, Van Halen, 79-23
VAN HALEN 3, Van Halen, 98-43
VANESSA PARADIS, Vanessa Paradis, 92-45
VANGUARD, Finley Quaye, 00-35
VANILLA FUDGE, Vanilla Fudge, 67-31
VANISHING POINT, Primal Scream, 97-2
VARIATIONS, Andrew Lloyd Webber featuring cellist Julian Lloyd Webber, 78-2
VARIOUS POSITIONS, Leonard Cohen, 85-52
THE VAULT . . . OLD FRIENDS 4 SALE, Prince, 99-47
VAULT – THE GREATEST HITS 1980-1995, Def Leppard, 95-3
VAUXHALL AND I, Morrissey, 94-1
VEEDON FLEECE, Van Morrison, 74-41
THE VEGETARIANS OF LOVE, Bob Geldof, 90-21
THE VELVET ROPE, Janet Jackson, 97-6
VELVET WATERS, Various Artists: Compilations – Stylus, 85-54
VELVETEEN, Transvision Vamp, 89-1
VENGENCE, New Model Army, 84-73
VENICE IN PERIL, Rondo Veneziano, 83-34
VENUS AND MARS, Wings, 75-1
VERDI, Andrea Bocelli; Israel Philharmonic Orchestra; Zubin Mehta, 00-17
VERMIN IN ERMINE, Marc Almond and the Willing Sinners, 84-36
VERSION 2.0, Garbage, 98-1
VERTICAL SMILES, Blackfoot, 84-82
VERTIGO, Groove Armada, 99-23
VERY, Pet Shop Boys, 93-1
THE VERY BEST EUPHORIC CHILLOUT MIXES – BREAKDOWN, Various Artists: Selected Series – Euphoria, 01-8
THE VERY BEST OF . . ., Pogues, 01-18
THE VERY BEST OF, Chris Rea, 01-69
THE VERY BEST OF ADAM AND THE ANTS, Adam and the Ants, 99-56
THE VERY BEST OF ANDREW LLOYD WEBBER, Various Artists: Compilations – Really Useful/Polydor, 94-3
THE VERY BEST OF ANDY WILLIAMS, Andy Williams, 00-27
THE VERY BEST OF ANNE MURRAY, Anne Murray, 81-14
THE VERY BEST OF ART GARFUNKEL – ACROSS AMERICA, Art Garfunkel, 96-35
THE VERY BEST OF BANANARAMA, Bananarama, 01-43
THE VERY BEST OF BARBARA DICKSON, Barbara Dickson, 86-78
THE VERY BEST OF BEN E. KING AND THE DRIFTERS, Ben E. King and the Drifters, 90-15
THE VERY BEST OF BEN E. KING AND THE DRIFTERS, Ben E. King and the Drifters, 98-41
VERY BEST OF BLUES BROTHER SOUL SISTER, Various Artists: Compilations – Dino, 95-11
THE VERY BEST OF BRASS, Various Artists: Compilations – Dino, 97-18
THE VERY BEST OF BRENDA LEE, Brenda Lee, 85-16
THE VERY BEST OF BRENDA LEE . . . WITH LOVE, Brenda Lee, 94-20
THE VERY BEST OF BUDDY HOLLY, Buddy Holly, 96-24
THE VERY BEST OF BUDDY HOLLY AND THE CRICKETS, Buddy Holly and the Crickets, 99-25
THE VERY BEST OF CAJUN – 40 HOT CAJUN CLASSICS, Various Artists: Compilations – Dino, 96-16
THE VERY BEST OF CAT STEVENS, Cat Stevens, 90-4
THE VERY BEST OF CHARLIE LANDSBOROUGH, Charlie Landsborough, 98-41
THE VERY BEST OF CHRIS DE BURGH, Chris De Burgh, 84-6
THE VERY BEST OF CILLA BLACK, Cilla Black, 83-20
THE VERY BEST OF CLASSICAL EXPERIENCE, Various Artists: Selected Series – Classic Experience, 99-18
THE VERY BEST OF COMMODORES – 16 CLASSIC TRACKS, Commodores, 85-25
THE VERY BEST OF DANIEL O'DONNELL, Daniel O'Donnell, 91-34
THE VERY BEST OF DAVID BOWIE, David Bowie, 81-3
THE VERY BEST OF DAVID ESSEX, David Essex, 82-37
THE VERY BEST OF DEAN MARTIN – THE CAPITOL & REPRISE YEARS, Dean Martin, 99-5
THE VERY BEST OF DEAN MARTIN – VOLUME 2 – THE CAPITOL & REPRISE YEARS, Dean Martin, 00-40
THE VERY BEST OF DEXY'S MIDNIGHT RUNNERS, Dexy's Midnight Runners, 91-12
THE VERY BEST OF . . . DINA CARROLL, Dina Carroll, 01-15
THE VERY BEST OF DISNEY, Various Artists: Selected Series – Disney, 93-4
THE VERY BEST OF DISNEY 2, Various Artists: Selected Series – Disney, 94-9
THE VERY BEST OF DOLLAR, Dollar, 82-31
THE VERY BEST OF DON MCLEAN, Don McLean, 80-4
THE VERY BEST OF EARTH, WIND AND FIRE, Earth, Wind And Fire, 92-29
VERY BEST OF EDDIE COCHRAN, Eddie Cochran, 70-34
THE VERY BEST OF ELKIE BROOKS, Elkie Brooks, 86-10
THE VERY BEST OF ELKIE BROOKS, Elkie Brooks, 97-23
THE VERY BEST OF ELTON JOHN, Elton John, 80-24

VOLUME 8 – THE THREAT IS REAL!, Anthrax, 98-73
VOLUNTEERS, Jefferson Airplane, 70-34
VOODOO, D'Angelo, 00-21
VOODOO HIGHWAY, Badlands, 91-74
VOODOO LOUNGE, Rolling Stones, 94-1
VOODOO PARTY, James Last, 72-45
VOULEZ-VOUS, Abba, 79-1
VOYAGE, Voyage, 78-59
VOYAGE OF THE ACOLYTE, Steve Hackett, 75-26
VOYAGER, Mike Oldfield, 96-12
VS, Pearl Jam, 93-2
V2, Vibrators, 78-33
VULGAR DISPLAY OF POWER, Pantera, 92-64
VULTURE CULTURE, Alan Parsons Project, 85-40
VYBIN' – YOUNG SOUL REBELS, Various Artists: Compilations – Global Television, 96-9
VYBIN' 3 – NEW SOUL REBELS, Various Artists: Compilations – Global Television, 96-2
VYBIN' 4, Various Artists: Compilations – Global Television, 96-7
THE W, Wu-Tang Clan, 00-19
W.A.S.P., W.A.S.P., 84-51
W.O.W., Wendy O. Williams, 84-100
WAH WAH, James and Brian Eno, 94-11
WAIT FOR ME, Kenny Thomas, 93-10
WAITING, Fun Boy Three, 83-14
WAITING FOR BONAPARTE, Men They Couldn't Hang, 88-41
WAITING FOR COLUMBUS, Little Feat, 78-43
WAITING FOR COUSTEAU, Jean-Michel Jarre, 90-14
WAITING FOR HERB, Pogues, 93-20
WAITING FOR THE FLOODS, Armoury Show, 85-57
WAITING FOR THE PUNCHLINE, Extreme, 95-10
WAITING FOR THE SUN, Doors, 68-16
WAITING TO EXHALE, Various Artists: Films – Original Soundtracks, 96-8
THE WAKE, IQ, 85-72
WAKE ME WHEN IT'S OVER, Faster Pussycat, 89-35
WAKE UP!, Boo Radleys, 95-1
WAKE UP AND SMELL THE COFFEE, Cranberries, 01-61
WAKE UP CALL, John Mayall, 93-61
THE WAKING HOUR, Dalis Car, 84-84
WAKING HOURS, Del Amitri, 90-6
WAKING UP THE NEIGHBOURS, Bryan Adams, 91-1
WAKING UP WITH THE HOUSE ON FIRE, Culture Club, 84-2
A WALK ACROSS THE ROOFTOPS, Blue Nile, 84-80
WALK INTO LIGHT, Ian Anderson, 83-78
WALK OF LIFE, Billie Piper, 00-14
WALK ON, Boston, 94-56
WALK ON, John Hiatt, 95-74
WALK ON BY, Sybil, 90-21
WALK RIGHT BACK WITH THE EVERLYS, Everly Brothers, 75-10
WALK UNDER LADDERS, Joan Armatrading, 81-6
THE WALKER BROTHERS' STORY, Walker Brothers, 67-9
WALKING BACK HOME, Deacon Blue, 99-39
WALKING INTO CLARKSDALE, Jimmy Page and Robert Plant, 98-3
WALKING ON SUNSHINE (THE VERY BEST OF EDDY GRANT), Eddy Grant, 89-20
WALKING WITH A PANTHER, L L Cool J, 89-43
WALKING WOUNDED, Everything But The Girl, 96-4
THE WALL, Pink Floyd, 79-3
THE WALL – LIVE IN BERLIN, Roger Waters and Various Artists, 90-27
WALL OF HITS, Slade, 91-34
WALLS AND BRIDGES, John Lennon, 74-6
WALT DISNEY PRESENTS THE STORY AND SONGS OF THE JUNGLE BOOK, Various Artists: Films – Original Soundtracks, 68-5
WALTERS ROOM, Black Science Orchestra, 96-68
WALTHAMSTOW, East 17, 93-1
WALTZ DARLING, Malcolm McLaren and the Bootzilla Orchestra, 89-30
THE WANDERER, Donna Summer, 80-55
THE WANDERER, Freddie Starr, 90-33
THE WANDERERS, Various Artists: Films – Original Soundtracks, 80-48
WANDERING SPIRIT, Mick Jagger, 93-12
WANTED, Yazz, 88-3
WANTED, Cliff Richard, 01-11
WAR, U2, 83-1
WAR & PEACE – VOLUME II (THE PEACE DISC), Ice Cube, 00-56
WAR CHILD, Jethro Tull, 74-14
WAR HEROES, Jimi Hendrix, 72-23
WAREHOUSE RAVES, Various Artists: Selected Series – Warehouse Raves, 89-15
WAREHOUSE RAVES 3, Various Artists: Selected Series – Warehouse Raves, 90-12
WAREHOUSE RAVES 4, Various Artists: Selected Series – Warehouse Raves, 90-13
WAREHOUSE RAVES 5, Various Artists: Selected Series – Warehouse Raves, 91-18
WAREHOUSE RAVES 6, Various Artists: Selected Series – Warehouse Raves, 92-16
WAREHOUSE RAVES 7, Various Artists: Selected Series – Warehouse Raves, 92-20
WAREHOUSE: SONGS AND STORIES, Husker Du, 87-72
WARE'S THE HOUSE?, Various Artists: Compilations – Stylus, 89-2
WARM, Johnny Mathis, 58-6
WARM, Herb Alpert and the Tijuana Brass, 69-30
WARM LEATHERETTE, Grace Jones, 80-45
THE WARNING, Queensryche, 84-100
WARNING, Green Day, 00-4
WARNING! DANCE BOOM, Various Artists: Compilations – Telstar, 95-2
WARNING! DANCE BOOM 2, Various Artists: Compilations – Telstar, 95-7
WARRIOR ON THE EDGE OF TIME, Hawkwind, 75-13
WARRIOR ROCK – TOYAH ON TOUR, Toyah, 82-20
THE WARRIORS, Various Artists: Films – Original Soundtracks, 79-53
WARRIORS, Gary Numan, 83-12
WARRIORZ, M.O.P., 01-40
WASHING MACHINE, Sonic Youth, 95-39
WASTED IN AMERICA, Love/Hate, 92-20
WASTED YEARS/STRANGER IN A STRANGE LAND, Iron Maiden, 90-9
WASTED YOUTH, Girl, 82-92
WATCH, Manfred Mann's Earth Band, 78-33
WATCHING YOU, WATCHING ME, Bill Withers, 85-60
WATER MARK, Art Garfunkel, 78-25
WATER SIGN, Chris Rea, 83-64
WATERFRONT, Waterfront, 89-45
WATERLOO, Abba (Bjorn, Benny, Anna and Frida), 74-28
WATERMARK, Enya, 88-5
WATERTOWN, Frank Sinatra, 70-14
WATT, Ten Years After, 71-5
WATUSI, Wedding Present, 94-47
WAVE, Patti Smith Group, 79-41
WAVELENGTH, Van Morrison, 78-27
WAVES, Katrina and the Waves, 86-70
WAXWORKS – SOME SINGLES (1977-1982), XTC, 82-54
WAY BEYOND BLUE, Catatonia, 96-32
THE WAY IT IS, Bruce Hornsby and the Range, 86-16
WAY OF TODAY, Vikki Carr, 67-31
WAY OUT WEST, Way Out West, 97-42
THE WAY TO THE SKY, Neil Diamond, 81-39
THE WAY WE WERE, Andy Williams, 74-7
THE WAY WE WERE, Barbra Streisand, 74-49
WAYNE FONTANA AND THE MINDBENDERS, Wayne Fontana and the Mindbenders, 65-18
WAYNE'S WORLD, Various Artists: Films – Original Soundtracks, 92-5
WAYNE'S WORLD 2, Various Artists: Films – Original Soundtracks, 94-17
WAYSTED, Waysted, 84-73
WE ALL HAD DOCTORS' PAPERS, Max Boyce, 75-1
WE ARE FAMILY, Sister Sledge, 79-7
WE ARE IN LOVE, Harry Connick Jr., 90-7
WE ARE MOST AMUSED (THE BEST OF BRITISH COMEDY), Various Artists: Compilations – Ronco/Charisma, 81-30
WE ARE ONE, Maze featuring Frankie Beverly, 83-38
WE ARE SHAMPOO, Shampoo, 94-45
WE ARE . . . THE LEAGUE, Anti-Nowhere League, 82-24
WE ARE THE WORLD, USA For Africa, 85-31
WE CAN DO IT, Rubettes, 75-41
WE CAN MAKE IT, Peters and Lee, 73-1
WE CAN'T DANCE, Genesis, 91-1
WE CARE, Whale, 95-42
WE HAVE ALL THE TIME IN THE WORLD – THE VERY BEST OF LOUIS ARMSTRONG, Louis Armstrong, 94-10
WE LOVE LIFE, Pulp, 01-6
WE MADE IT HAPPEN, Engelbert Humperdinck, 70-17
WE MUST BELIEVE IN MAGIC, Crystal Gayle, 78-15
WE ROCK HARD, Freestylers, 98-33
WE SOLD OUR SOUL FOR ROCK 'N' ROLL, Black Sabbath, 76-35
WE THANK THEE, Jim Reeves, 64-17
WE TOO ARE ONE, Eurythmics, 89-1
WE WANT BILLY, Billy Fury, 63-14
WE WANT MOORE!, Gary Moore, 84-32
WE WILL ROCK YOU, Various Artists: Compilations – Dino, 91-3
WE WISH YOU A MERRY CHRISTMAS, Ray Conniff, 62-12
WE'D LIKE TO TEACH THE WORLD TO SING, New Seekers, 72-2
WE'LL BRING THE HOUSE DOWN, Slade, 81-25
WE'LL KEEP A WELCOME – THE WELSH ALBUM, Bryn Terfel; The Orchestra Of Welsh National Opera; Gareth Jones, 00-33
WE'LL MEET AGAIN, Vera Lynn, 89-44
WE'RE ONLY IN IT FOR THE MONEY, Mothers Of Invention, 68-32
WE'RE THE MINIPOPS, Minipops, 83-54
WE'VE GOTTA GET OUT OF THIS PLACE, Angelic Upstarts, 80-54
WEAPON IS MY LYRIC, Overlord X, 89-68
WEASELS RIPPED MY FLESH, Mothers Of Invention, 70-28
WEATHER REPORT, Weather Report, 82-88
WEATHERED, Creed, 01-48
THE WEDDING SINGER, Various Artists: Films – Original Soundtracks, 98-15
THE WEDGE, Pallas, 86-70
WEDNESDAY MORNING 3 A.M., Simon and Garfunkel, 68-24
WEEKEND IN L.A., George Benson, 78-47
WEEZER, Weezer, 95-23
WEIGHT, Rollins Band, 94-22
WEIRD SCENES INSIDE THE GOLD MINE, Doors, 72-50
WEIRD'S BAR AND GRILLS, Pop Will Eat Itself, 93-44
WELCOME, Santana, 73-8
WELCOME BACK MY FRIENDS TO THE SHOW THAT NEVER ENDS – LADIES AND GENTLEMEN: EMERSON, LAKE AND PALMER, Emerson, Lake and Palmer, 74-5
WELCOME TO MY NIGHTMARE, Alice Cooper, 75-19
WELCOME TO MY WORLD, Dean Martin, 67-39
WELCOME TO MY WORLD, Elvis Presley, 77-7
WELCOME TO THE BEAUTIFUL SOUTH, Beautiful South, 89-2
WELCOME TO THE CLUB, Ian Hunter, 80-61
WELCOME TO THE CRUISE, Judie Tzuke, 79-14
WELCOME TO THE NEIGHBOURHOOD, Meat Loaf, 95-3
WELCOME TO THE PLEASUREDOME, Frankie Goes To Hollywood, 84-1
WELCOME TO THE REAL WORLD, Mr. Mister, 86-6
WELCOME TO TOMORROW, Snap!, 94-69
WELCOME TO WHEREVER YOU ARE, Inxs, 92-1
WELD, Neil Young and Crazy Horse, 91-20
WELL KEPT SECRET, John Martyn, 82-20
WELL PLEASED, Chas and Dave, 84-27
WELL RESPECTED KINKS, Kinks, 66-5
WELL, WELL, SAID THE ROCKING CHAIR, Dean Friedman, 78-21
WELSH CONNECTION, Man, 76-40
WENDY AND LISA, Wendy and Lisa, 87-84

WIND OF CHANGE – CLASSIC ROCK, London Symphony Orchestra and the Royal Choral Society, 92-24
WIND SONG, John Denver, 75-14
WINDJAMMER II, Windjammer, 84-82
WINDOW IN THE JUNGLE, 10 C.C., 83-70
WINDSONG, Randy Crawford, 82-7
WINELIGHT, Grover Washington Jr., 81-34
WINGS AT THE SPEED OF SOUND, Wings, 76-2
WINGS GREATEST, Wings, 78-5
WINGS OF A DOVE, Anthony Way, 97-69
WINGS OF HEAVEN, Magnum, 88-5
WINGS OF JOY, Cranes, 91-52
WINGS OF LOVE, Various Artists: Compilations – A&M, 91-1
WINGS OVER AMERICA, Wings, 77-8
WINGS WILDLIFE, Wings, 71-11
WINGSPAN – HITS AND HISTORY, Paul McCartney, 01-5
WINNER IN YOU, Patti Labelle, 86-30
WINNERS, Brothers Johnson, 81-42
WINNER'S CIRCLE, Various Artists: Compilations – Expansion, 93-20
WIPEOUT – 20 INSTRUMENTAL GREATS, Various Artists: Compilations – Impression, 84-37
WIPEOUT 2097: THE SOUNDTRACK, Various Artists: Compilations – Virgin, 96-16
WIRED, Jeff Beck, 76-38
WIRED, Various Artists: Compilations – PolyGram TV, 97-2
WIRED FOR CLUBS (CLUB TRACKS VOLUME 1), Various Artists: Compilations – Mercury, 83-58
WIRED FOR SOUND, Cliff Richard, 81-4
WIRED TO THE MOON, Chris Rea, 84-35
WISEBLOOD, Corrosion Of Conformity, 96-43
WISH, Cure, 92-1
WISH YOU WERE HERE, Pink Floyd, 75-1
WISHBONE ASH, Wishbone Ash, 71-34
WISHBONE FOUR, Wishbone Ash, 73-12
WISHFUL THINKING, Propaganda, 85-82
WISHING, Martine McCutcheon, 00-25
WITH A LOT O'SOUL, Temptations, 67-19
WITH A SONG IN MY HEART, Jose Carreras, 93-73
WITH LOVE, Des O'Connor, 70-40
WITH LOVE, Brendan Shine, 84-74
WITH LOVE, Michael Crawford, 89-31
. . . WITH LOVE, Richard Clayderman, 99-62
WITH LOVING FEELING, Tony Christie, 73-19
WITH THE BEATLES, Beatles, 63-1
WITH YOU IN MIND, Charlie Landsborough, 96-49
WITHOUT A SOUND, Dinosaur Jr, 94-24
WITHOUT RESERVATIONS, Simon Dupree and the Big Sound, 67-39
WITHOUT THE AID OF A SAFETY NET (LIVE), Big Country, 94-35
WITHOUT YOU I'M NOTHING, Placebo, 98-7
WITHOUT YOUR LOVE, Dionne Warwick, 85-86
WITNESS, Halo James, 90-18
WIZZARD BREW, Wizzard, 73-29
WOLF, Hugh Cornwell, 88-98
WOMAN, Various Artists: Compilations – PolyGram TV/Sony TV, 98-5
WOMAN, Various Artists: Compilations – Sony Music TV/Universal Music TV, 00-10
WOMAN II, Various Artists: Compilations – Universal Music TV/Sony TV/Global TV, 99-4
WOMAN 2 WOMAN TWO, Various Artists: Compilations – PolyGram TV, 94-9
A WOMAN AND A MAN, Belinda Carlisle, 96-12
WOMAN IN ME, Louise, 97-5
THE WOMAN IN ME, Shania Twain, 00-7
THE WOMAN IN RED [OST], Stevie Wonder and featuring Dionne Warwick, 84-2
WOMAN TO WOMAN, Various Artists: Compilations – PolyGram TV, 93-5
WOMBLING SONGS, Wombles, 74-19
WOMEN AND CAPTAIN FIRST, Captain Sensible, 82-64
WOMEN AND CHILDREN FIRST, Van Halen, 80-15
WOMEN HOLD UP HALF THE SKY, Ruby Turner, 86-47
WOMEN IN UNIFORM/TWILIGHT ZONE, Iron Maiden, 90-10
WONDER NO.8, Honeyz, 98-33
WONDERFUL, Adam Ant, 95-24
WONDERFUL, Madness, 99-17
THE WONDERFUL AND FRIGHTENING WORLD OF . . ., Fall, 84-62
WONDERFUL LIFE, Black, 87-3
WONDERFUL LIFE [OST], Cliff Richard and the Shadows, 64-2
WONDERFUL WORLD, Various Artists: Compilations – Dino, 94-8
WONDERLAND, Erasure, 86-71
WONDERLAND, Charlatans, 01-2
THE WONDROUS WORLD OF SONNY AND CHER, Sonny and Cher, 66-15
WONDERWORLD, Uriah Heep, 74-23
WOODEN FOOT COPS ON THE HIGHWAY, Woodentops, 88-48
WOODFACE, Crowded House, 91-6
WOODSTOCK, Jimi Hendrix, 94-32
WOODSTOCK [OST], Various Artists: Concerts and Festivals, 70-35
THE WORD, Various Artists: Compilations – Zomba, 87-86
WORD GETS AROUND, Stereophonics, 97-6
WORD OF MOUTH, Toni Basil, 82-15
WORD OF MOUTH, Mike and the Mechanics, 91-11
WORD SALAD, Fischer-Z, 79-66
A WORD TO THE WISE GUY, Mighty Wah!, 84-28
WORD UP, Cameo, 86-7
THE WORD VOLUME 2, Various Artists: Compilations – Jive, 88-70
WORDS, F.R. David, 83-46
WORDS, Tony Rich Project, 96-27
WORDS AND MUSIC, Benny Hill, 71-9
WORDS AND MUSIC, Billy Connolly, 75-34
WORDS AND MUSIC, Hank Marvin, 82-66
WORDS OF LOVE, Buddy Holly and the Crickets, 93-1
WORK, LOVELIFE, MISCELLANEOUS, David Devant And His Spirit Wife, 97-70
WORK PARTY, Grandmaster Melle Mel and the Furious Five, 84-45
WORK THAT BODY, Jackie Genova, 83-74
WORKERS' PLAYTIME, Billy Bragg, 88-17
WORKIN' OVERTIME, Diana Ross, 89-23
WORKING NIGHTS, Working Week, 85-23
WORKING WITH FIRE AND STEEL – POSSIBLE POP SONGS VOLUME 2, China Crisis, 83-20
WORKINGMAN'S DEAD, Grateful Dead, 70-69
WORKS, Emerson, Lake and Palmer, 77-9
THE WORKS, Queen, 84-2
THE WORKS OF RICE AND LLOYD WEBBER, London Symphony Orchestra, 94-55
WORKS VOLUME 2, Emerson, Lake and Palmer, 77-20
WORLD, D:Ream, 95-5
THE WORLD BEATERS SING THE WORLD BEATERS, England Football World Cup Squad 1970, 70-4
WORLD CLIQUE, Deee-Lite, 90-14
WORLD COMING DOWN, Type O Negative, 99-49
WORLD DANCE – THE DRUM + BASS EXPERIENCE, Various Artists: Compilations – Firm, 97-10
WORLD DEMISE, Obituary, 94-65
WORLD GONE WRONG, Bob Dylan, 93-35
WORLD IN MOTION, Jackson Browne, 89-39
WORLD IN UNION, Union and Various Artists, 91-17
WORLD IN UNION – ANTHEMS, Various Artists: Compilations – PolyGram TV, 95-8
THE WORLD IS FULL OF MARRIED MEN, Various Artists: Films – Original Soundtracks, 79-25
WORLD MACHINE, Level 42, 85-3
WORLD MOODS, Various Artists: Compilations – Virgin/EMI, 98-17
THE WORLD NEEDS A HERO, Megadeth, 01-45
THE WORLD OF BLUES POWER, Various Artists: Selected Series – The World Of, 69-24
THE WORLD OF BRASS BANDS, Various Artists: Selected Series – The World Of, 69-13
THE WORLD OF CHARLIE KUNZ, Charlie Kunz, 69-9
THE WORLD OF CHRISTMAS, Choir Of King's College, Cambridge, 71-38
WORLD OF HIS OWN, Jools Holland, 90-71
THE WORLD OF HITS VOLUME 2, Various Artists: Selected Series – The World Of, 69-7
THE WORLD OF JOHNNY CASH, Johnny Cash, 70-5
THE WORLD OF JOSEF LOCKE TODAY, Josef Locke, 69-29
THE WORLD OF KENNETH MCKELLAR, Kenneth McKellar, 69-27
THE WORLD OF MANTOVANI, Mantovani and his Orchestra , 69-6
THE WORLD OF MANTOVANI VOL. 2, Mantovani and his Orchestra, 69-4
WORLD OF MORRISSEY, Morrissey, 95-15
A WORLD OF OUR OWN, Seekers, 65-5
WORLD OF OUR OWN, Westlife, 01-1
THE WORLD OF PHASE 4 STEREO, Various Artists: Selected Series – The World Of, 69-29
THE WORLD OF PROGRESSIVE MUSIC (WOWIE ZOWIE), Various Artists: Selected Series – The World Of, 69-17
WORLD OF THE BACHELORS, Bachelors, 69-8
WORLD OF THE BACHELORS VOLUME 2, Bachelors, 69-11
THE WORLD OF VAL DOONICAN, Val Doonican, 69-2
THE WORLD OF YOUR 100 BEST TUNES, Various Artists: Radio – Related Compilations , 71-10
THE WORLD OF YOUR 100 BEST TUNES VOLUME 2, Various Artists: Radio – Related Compilations , 71-9
THE WORLD OF YOUR 100 BEST TUNES VOLUME 10, Various Artists: Radio – Related Compilations , 75-41
WORLD OUTSIDE, Psychedelic Furs, 91-68
WORLD POWER, Snap!, 90-10
WORLD RADIO, Leo Sayer, 82-30
WORLD SERVICE, Spear Of Destiny, 85-11
WORLD SHUT YOUR MOUTH, Julian Cope, 84-40
WORLD WIDE LIVE, Scorpions, 85-18
A WORLD WITHOUT DAVE, Carter – The Unstoppable Sex Machine, 97-73
THE WORLD WITHOUT END, Mighty Lemon Drops, 88-34
THE WORLD WON'T LISTEN, Smiths, 87-2
WORLD WRESTLING FEDERATION AGGRESSION, Various Artists: Compilations – Priority, 00-13
WORLD WRESTLING FEDERATION – THE MUSIC – VOLUME 4, James A. Johnston, 99-44
WORLD WRESTLING FEDERATION – THE MUSIC – VOLUME 5, James A. Johnston, 01-11
THE WORLDS OF FOSTER AND ALLEN, Foster and Allen, 88-16
THE WORLD'S WORST RECORD SHOW, Various Artists: Compilations – K-Tel, 78-47
WORLDES BLYSSE, Mediaeval Baebes, 98-73
WORLDWIDE, Everything But The Girl, 91-29
WORLDWIDE 50 GOLD AWARD HITS VOLUME 1 – A TOUCH OF GOLD, Elvis Presley, 70-49
WORRY BOMB, Carter – The Unstoppable Sex Machine, 95-9
THE WORST ALBUM IN THE WORLD EVER . . . EVER!, Shirehorses, 97-22
WOULD YA LIKE MORE SCRATCHIN', Malcolm McLaren and the World's Famous Supreme Team Show, 84-44
WOULD YOU BELIEVE?, Hollies, 66-16
WOULDN'T YOU LIKE IT, Bay City Rollers, 75-3
WOW!, Bananarama, 87-26
WOW! – LET THE MUSIC LIFT YOU UP, Various Artists: Compilations – Arcade, 94-13
WOW WHAT A PARTY, Various Artists: Compilations – K-Tel, 87-97

CHART FACTS & FEATS

INDEX

1 MOST WEEKS ON CHART – SINGLES ARTISTS

	ARTISTS	WEEKS
1	**Elvis Presley**	1,173
2	**Cliff Richard**	1,147
3	**Madonna**	568
4	**Elton John**	567
5	**Michael Jackson**	493
6	**Rod Stewart**	462
7	**Beatles**	456
8	**David Bowie**	447
9	**Frank Sinatra**	433
10	**Queen**	420
11	**Diana Ross**	413
	Status Quo	413
13	**Stevie Wonder**	401
14	**Paul McCartney**	398
15	**Tom Jones**	390
16	**Rolling Stones**	366
17	**Shadows**	359
18	**Bee Gees**	354
19	**Everly Brothers**	345
	Roy Orbison	345
21	**UB40**	330
22	**Shirley Bassey**	326
23	**Perry Como**	323
24	**Jim Reeves**	322
25	**Lonnie Donegan**	321
26	**Hollies**	318
27	**Whitney Houston**	312
28	**Oasis**	309
29	**Pat Boone**	308
30	**Prince**	305
31	**Donna Summer**	299
32	**Four Tops**	298
33	**Hot Chocolate**	283
34	**Frankie Laine**	282
35	**Beach Boys**	281
	Billy Fury	281
37	**Slade**	279
38	**Shakin' Stevens**	277
39	**Kylie Minogue**	275
40	**Janet Jackson**	274
41	**Madness**	268
42	**Supremes**	259
43	**Electric Light Orchestra**	255
44	**U2**	254
34	**Abba**	252
	Mariah Carey	252
	Adam Faith	252
48	**George Michael**	249
49	**Petula Clark**	247
	Who	247

Others who have managed more than 250 weeks on chart:

Phil Collins 415
(228 + 187 with Genesis.)

Paul Weller 376
(62 + 205 with the Jam, 103 with the Style Council, 6 with the Council Collective.)

Robbie Williams 372
(214 + 158 with Take That.)

Annie Lennox 316
(68 + 208 with Eurythmics, 40 with the Tourists.)

Sting 299
(146 + 153 with the Police.)
Vince Clarke 297
(203 with Erasure, 55 with Yazoo, 29 with Depeche Mode, and 10 with the Assembly.)
Cher 296
(218 + 78 with Sonny.)
Midge Ure 293
(56 + 138 with Ultravox, 56 with Visage, 18 with Silk, 5 with Rich Kids, 20 as leader of Band Aid.)
David A. Stewart 281
(23 + 208 with Eurythmics, 40 with the Tourists, 10 with Vegas.)
Dusty Springfield 277
(211 + 66 with the Springfields.)
Ronan Keating 270
(57 + 213 with Boyzone.)
Tina Turner 268
(224 + 44 with Ike Turner.)

2 MOST WEEKS ON CHART – SINGLES

	SINGLES	WEEKS
1	**MY WAY** Frank Sinatra	124
2	**AMAZING GRACE** Judy Collins	67
3	**RELAX** Frankie Goes To Hollywood	59
4	**(WE'RE GONNA) ROCK AROUND THE CLOCK** Bill Haley and his Comets	57
5	**RELEASE ME** Engelbert Humperdinck	56*
6	**STRANGER ON THE SHORE** Mr. Acker Bilk with the Leon Young String Chorale	55*
7	**BLUE MONDAY** New Order	53
8	**WHATEVER** Oasis	50
9	**I LOVE YOU BECAUSE** Jim Reeves	47
10	**WHITE LINES (DON'T DON'T DO IT)** Grand Master and Melle Mel	46
11	**LET'S TWIST AGAIN** Chubby Checker	44
	ALL RIGHT NOW Free	44
	TAINTED LOVE Soft Cell	44
14	**IMAGINE** John Lennon	42
15	**DECK OF CARDS** Wink Martindale	41
16	**RIVERS OF BABLON/BROWN GIRL IN THE RING** Boney M	40*
	TIE A YELLOW RIBBON ROUND THE OLE OAK TREE Dawn featuring Tony Orlando	40
	A SCOTTISH SOLDIER (GREEN HILLS OF TYROL) Andy Stewart with the Michael Sammes Singers	40
19	**HE'LL HAVE TO GO** Jim Reeves	39
20	**SOMEWHERE MY LOVE** Mike Sammes Singers	38

*Denotes consecutive weeks on chart.

3 MOST WEEKS ON CHART – ALBUM ARTISTS

	ARTISTS	WEEKS
1	**Beatles**	1,285
2	**Queen**	1,200
3	**Elvis Presley**	1,155
4	**Dire Straits**	1,133
5	**Simon and Garfunkel**	1,107
6	**U2**	1,068
7	**Madonna**	947
8	**David Bowie**	931
9	**Elton John**	897
10	**Pink Floyd**	889
11	**Abba**	862
12	**Michael Jackson**	861
13	**Fleetwood Mac**	850
14	**Rod Stewart**	812
15	**Cliff Richard**	799
16	**Phil Collins**	796
17	**Meat Loaf**	763
18	**Rolling Stones**	761
19	**Frank Sinatra**	732
20	**Bob Dylan**	617
21	**Carpenters**	606
22	**UB40**	588
23	**Neil Diamond**	572
24	**Beach Boys**	569
25	**Simply Red**	566
26	**R.E.M.**	552
27	**Mike Oldfield**	547
28	**Diana Ross**	542
29	**Paul McCartney**	533
30	**Eric Clapton**	527
	Bob Marley and the Wailers	527
32	**Tina Turner**	521
33	**Barbra Streisand**	517
34	**Tom Jones**	493
35	**Genesis**	488
36	**Bruce Springsteen**	486
37	**Eurythmics**	476
38	**Led Zeppelin**	475
	Shadows	475
40	**Status Quo**	459
41	**Andy Williams**	452
42	**Prince**	434
43	**Oasis**	429
44	**Roxy Music**	426
45	**James Last**	421
46	**Lionel Richie**	419
47	**Madness**	412
48	**Bon Jovi**	411
49	**Electric Light Orchestra**	410
50	**Eagles**	409

Others who have managed more than 430 weeks on chart:

Sting (349 + 386 with the Police.)	735
Robbie Williams (279 + 228 with Take That.)	507
Paul Weller (201 + 182 with the Jam, 99 with the Style Council.)	490
George Michael (310 + 137 with Wham!)	447
Vince Clarke (316 with Erasure, 86 with Yazoo, 33 with Depeche Mode.)	435

4 MOST WEEKS ON CHART – ALBUMS

	ALBUMS	WEEKS
1	**RUMOURS** Fleetwood Mac	477
2	**BAT OUT OF HELL** Meat Loaf	473
3	**QUEEN GREATEST HITS** Queen (Includes 7 as a double re-issue, 5 as a triple re-issue)	462
4	**THE SOUND OF MUSIC [OST]** Various Artists	382
5	**THE DARK SIDE OF THE MOON** Pink Floyd	351
6	**GOLD – GREATEST HITS** Abba	323
7	**LEGEND – THE BEST OF BOB MARLEY AND THE WAILERS** Bob Marley and the Wailers	322
8	**BRIDGE OVER TROUBLD WATER** Simon and Garfunkel	307
9	**TUBULAR BELLS** Mike Oldfield (Includes 13 as a boxed set.)	289
10	**SOUTH PACIFIC [OST]** Various Artists	288
11	**SIMON AND GARFUNKEL'S GREATEST HITS** Simon and Garfunkel	283
12	**FACE VALUE** Phil Collins	274
13	**JEFF WAYNE'S MUSICAL VERSION OF THE WAR OF THE WORLDS** Jeff Wayne	256
14	**MAKING MOVIES** Dire Straits	251
15	**BROTHERS IN ARMS** Dire Straits	228
16	**DIRTY DANCING [OST]** Various (63 weeks in the artist chart; 153 in the compilation chart.)	216
17	**U2 LIVE: "UNDER A BLOOD RED SKY"** U2	203
18	**LOVE OVER GOLD** Dire Straits	200
19	**SGT. PEPPER'S LONELY HEARTS CLUB BAND** Beatles	197
20	**THE IMMACULATE COLLECTION** Madonna	196

5 MOST WEEKS ON CHART – EP ARTISTS

	ARTISTS	WEEKS
1	**Cliff Richard**	432
2	**Shadows**	426
3	**Beatles**	392
4	**Elvis Presley**	366
5	**Nina and Frederik**	169
6	**Seekers**	166
7	**Rolling Stones**	154
8	**Mr. Acker Bilk**	134
9	**Manfred Mann**	111
10	**Beach Boys**	108

6 MOST WEEKS ON CHART – EPS

	EPS	WEEKS
1	**NINA AND FREDERIK** Nina and Frederik	115
2	**THE SHADOWS** Shadows	86
	HIGHLIGHTS FROM "SOUTH PACIFIC" Various Artists	86
4	**THE BEACH BOY HITS** Beach Boys	82
5	**THE SHADOWS TO THE FORE** Shadows	81
6	**PETER, PAUL AND MARY** Peter, Paul and Mary	79
7	**ADAM'S HIT PARADE** Adam Faith	77
8	**HITS FROM THE SEEKERS** Seekers	73
9	**STRICTLY FOR GROWN-UPS** Paddy Roberts	66
10	**TWIST AND SHOUT** Beatles	64
	THE BUTTON-DOWN MIND OF BOB NEWHART Bob Newhart	64
	STRICTLY ELVIS Elvis Presley	64

7 MOST HITS – SINGLES

	ARTISTS	HITS
1	**Cliff Richard**	123
2	**Elvis Presley**	113
3	**Elton John**	74
4	**David Bowie**	63
5	**Rod Stewart**	58
6	**Diana Ross**	56
	Status Quo	56
8	**Madonna**	53
9	**Michael Jackson**	51
	Stevie Wonder	51

11	**Paul McCartney**	50
	Queen	50
13	**UB40**	47
14	**Prince**	46
	Rolling Stones	46
16	**Tom Jones**	39
	Donna Summer	39
18	**Bee Gees**	38
	Depeche Mode	38
20	**Shakin' Stevens**	37
21	**Janet Jackson**	36
	Tina Turner	36
23	**Elvis Costello and the Attractions**	35
	Frank Sinatra	35
	Slade	35
26	**Bryan Adams**	33
	Roy Orbison	33
	Pet Shop Boys	33
	U2	33
30	**Beatles**	32
	Gloria Estefan	32
	Whitney Houston	32
	Kylie Minogue	32

Others with more than 35 hits:

Shadows 61
(31 + 30 with Cliff Richard.)

Phil Collins 59
(30 + 29 with Genesis.)

Paul Weller 54
(18 + 18 with Jam, 17 with the Style Council, 1 with the Council Collective.)

Sting 50
(31 + 19 with Police.)

Annie Lennox 41
(10 + 26 with Eurythmics, 5 with the Tourists.)

Morrissey 41
(24 + 17 with the Smiths.)

Mike Rutherford 41
(12 with Mike & The Mechanics, 29 with Genesis.)

Cher 39
(30 + 9 with Sonny)

Bryan Ferry 38
(22 + 16 with Roxy Music.)

David A. Stewart 38
(4 + 26 with Eurythmics, 5 with the Tourists, 3 with Vegas.)

Midge Ure 38
(10 + 17 with Ultravox, 7 with Visage, 1 with Slik 1, with Rich Kids, 1 as leader of Band Aid.)

Roger Daltrey 37
(8 + 28 with the Who, 1 with High Numbers.)

George Michael 37
(27 + 10 with Wham!)

Lionel Richie 37
(24 + 13 with the Commodores.)

Suggs 36
(7 + 28 with Madness, 1 with the Fink Brothers.)

8 MOST HIT ALBUMS

	ARTISTS	HITS
1	**Elvis Presley**	102
2	**James Last**	61
3	**Cliff Richard**	55
4	**Frank Sinatra**	54
5	**Rolling Stones**	43
6	**Bob Dylan**	42
7	**Diana Ross**	41
8	**Elton John**	38
9	**David Bowie**	36
10	**Shirley Bassey**	35
11	**Neil Diamond**	34
12	**Beatles**	31
	Status Quo	31
13	**Beach Boys**	30
	Neil Young	30
15	**Shadows**	29
16	**Jim Reeves**	28
	Rod Stewart	28
18	**Jimi Hendrix**	27
	Iron Maiden	27
	Paul McCartney	27
	Andy Williams	27
22	**Jethro Tull**	26
	Tom Jones	26
24	**Eric Clapton**	25
	Van Morrison	25
	Gary Numan	25
	Who	25
28	**Deep Purple**	24
	Johnny Mathis	24
	Mike Oldfield	24
	Queen	24
	Barbra Streisand	24

Others with more than 25 hits:

Michael Jackson 34
(23 + 11 with the Jacksons.)

Paul Weller 31
(8 + 14 with Jam, 9 with the Style Council.)

Phil Collins 29
(8 + 21 with Genesis.)

Mike Rutherford 27
(2 + 6 with Mike & The Mechanics, 21 with Genesis.)

Jon Anderson 27
(3 + 19 with Yes, 4 with Vangelis, 1 with Anderson Bruford Wakeman Howe.)

9 MOST HIT EPS

	EP ARTISTS	HITS
1	Cliff Richard	22
2	Shadows	19
3	Elvis Presley	15
4	Beatles	12
5	Mr. Acker Bilk	11

10 LONGEST SPAN OF HIT SINGLES

	ARTISTS	YEARS	
1	Elvis Presley	45.53	(12 May 56 to 10 Nov 01)
2	Frank Sinatra	44.59	(10 Jul 54 to 30 Jan 99)
3	Cliff Richard	43.28	(13 Sep 58 to 15 Dec 01)
4	Shirley Bassey	42.71	(16 Feb 57 to 23 Oct 99)
5	Louis Armstrong	41.94	(20 Dec 52 to 19 Nov 94)
6	Nat 'King' Cole	41.37	(15 Nov 52 to 19 Mar 94)
7	Rolf Harris	40.25	(23 Jul 60 to 14 Oct 00)
8	Perez 'Prez' Prado & his Orchestra	39.74	(26 Mar 55 to 10 Dec 94)
9	Eartha Kitt	38.95	(2 Apr 55 to 5 Mar 94)
10	Chipmunks	37.42	(25 Jul 59 to 14 Dec 96)

Does not include re-issues of previously charted material.

11 MOST HIT SINGLES WITHOUT REACHING THE TOP 40

	ARTISTS	HITS
1	Gorky's Zygotic Mynci	8
2	That Petrol Emotion	7
3	A	6
	Deus	6
	Diesel Park West	6
	Frazier Chorus	6
	Rick James	6
	Love And Money	6
	Ragga Twins	6

12 MOST WEEKS ON CHART PER HIT – SINGLES ARTISTS

(total weeks divided by number of hits – minimum 3 hits)

	ARTISTS	WEEKS PER HIT
1	Frankie Goes To Hollywood	21.00
2	Oasis	19.31
3	Dawn	18.17
4	Spice Girls	17.90
5	Andy Stewart	16.75
6	Jackie Wilson	16.17
7	Chris Montez	15.25
8	Middle Of The Road	15.20
9	John Travolta	15.00
10	Free	15.00

13 MOST WEEKS ON CHART PER HIT – ALBUM ARTISTS

(total weeks divided by number of hits – minimum 3 hits)

	ARTISTS	WEEKS PER HIT
1	Dire Straits	103.00
2	Simon and Garfunkel	100.64
3	Phil Collins	99.50
4	U2	71.20
5	Robbie Williams	69.75
6	Meat Loaf	69.36
7	Madonna	67.64
8	Corrs	66.60
9	Jeff Wayne	65.25
10	Tina Turner	65.13
11	Wham!	64.75
12	Simply Red	62.89
13	Guns N' Roses	62.33
	Whitney Houston	62.33
15	George Michael	62.00
16	Radiohead	57.67
17	M People	55.60
18	Tracy Chapman	54.25
19	Abba	53.68
20	Oasis	53.63

14 MOST TOP 10 SINGLES

	ARTISTS	TOP 10 HITS
1	Cliff Richard	64
2	Elvis Presley	55
3	Madonna	49
4	Michael Jackson	38
5	Beatles	28
6	Elton John	27
7	Queen	26
	Rod Stewart	26
9	U2	24
10	David Bowie	23
	Paul McCartney	23
12	Status Quo	22
13	Kylie Minogue	21
	Rolling Stones	21
15	George Michael	20
	Pet Shop Boys	20

Others with more than 20 top 10 hits:

Shadows 41
(16 + 25 with Cliff Richard.)
Robbie Williams 28
(15 + 13 with Take That.)
Diana Ross 26
(18 + 8 with Supremes)

15 MOST TOP 10 ALBUMS

	ARTISTS	TOP 10 HITS
1	**Elvis Presley**	40
2	**Cliff Richard**	35
3	**Rolling Stones**	32
4	**Frank Sinatra**	30
5	**Bob Dylan**	29
6	**David Bowie**	25
7	**Beatles**	24
	Elton John	24
9	**Rod Stewart**	23
10	**Queen**	21
11	**Iron Maiden**	20
	Paul McCartney	20
12	**Status Quo**	19
13	**Genesis**	17
14	**Pink Floyd**	16
15	**Prince**	15

Others with more than 15 top 10 hits:

Shadows 27
(11 + 16 with Cliff Richard.)
Eric Clapton 20
(13 + 7 with Cream.)
Bryan Ferry 17
(8 + 9 with Roxy Music.)
Robert Plant 17
(4 + 11 with Led Zeppelin, 2 with Jimmy Page.)
Diana Ross 17
(9 + 6 with the Supremes, 1 with Marvin Gaye, 1 with the Supremes & the Temptations.)
Sting 16
(9 + 7 with the Police)

Also of note are **Depeche Mode** who have hit the Top 10 with each of their 13 releases.

16 MOST TOP 10 EPS

	ARTISTS	TOP 10 HITS
1	**Cliff Richard**	16
2	**Shadows**	13
3	**Beatles**	12
4	**Elvis Presley**	10
5	**Manfred Mann**	6

17 MOST WEEKS ON CHART WITHOUT REACHING THE TOP 10 – SINGLES

	SINGLES	WEEKS
1	**A SCOTTISH SOLDIER (GREEN HILLS OF TYROL)** Andy Stewart with the Michael Sammes Singers	40
2	**HE'LL HAVE TO GO** Jim Reeves	39
3	**SOMEWHERE MY LOVE** Mike Sammes Singers	38
4	**HI-HO SILVER LINING** Jeff Beck	29
5	**BIG SIX** Judge Dread	27
6	**MY GIRL** Otis Redding	25
7	**(YOUR LOVE KEEPS LIFTING ME) HIGHER AND HIGHER** Jackie Wilson	24
8	**BREAK 4 LOVE** Raze	23
	MY WAY Dorothy Squires	23
	SHAME Evelyn 'Champagne' King	23
	SHE SELLS SANCTUARY Cult	23

18 MOST WEEKS ON CHART WITHOUT REACHING THE TOP 10 – ALBUMS

	ALBUMS	WEEKS
1	**SOUNDS OF SILENCE** Simon And Garfunkel	105
2	**THE STONE ROSES** Stone Roses	86
3	**STOP MAKING SENSE** Talking Heads	84
4	**BLOOD SUGAR SEX MAGIK** Red Hot Chili Peppers	82
	CLOSE TO YOU Carpenters	82
	PABLO HONEY Radiohead	82
7	**HIS 12 GREATEST HITS** Neil Diamond	78
8	**CHRISTOPHER CROSS** Christopher Cross	77
9	**RAINTOWN** Deacon Blue	77
10	**BLUE LINES** Massive Attack	76
	PENTHOUSE AND PAVEMENT Heaven 17	76

19 MOST NUMBER ONES – SINGLES ARTISTS

	ARTISTS	NUMBER ONES
1	Beatles	17
	Elvis Presley	17
3	Cliff Richard	14
4	Madonna	10
5	Abba	9
	Spice Girls	9
	Westlife	9
8	Rolling Stones	8
	Take That	8
10	Michael Jackson	7
	George Michael	7
12	Blondie	6
	Boyzone	6
	Kylie Minogue	6
	Queen	6
	Slade	6
	Rod Stewart	6

Others with more than 5 number ones:

	Shadows (5 + 7 with Cliff Richard.)	12

20 MOST NUMBER ONES – SINGLES WRITERS

	SINGLES WRITERS	NUMBER ONES
1	John Lennon	28
2	Paul McCartney	27
3	Benny Anderson	11
	Melanie Chisholm (Includes 9 with the Spice Girls.)	11
	Bjorn Ulvaeus	11
6	Barry Gibb	10
	Robin Gibb	10
	Madonna	10
8	Maurice Gibb	9
	Geri Halliwell (Includes 6 with the Spice Girls.)	9
	Spice Girls	9
	Richard Stannard	9
12	Pete Waterman	8
13	Matt Aitken	7
	Burt Bacharach	7
	Gary Barlow	7
	Oscar Hammerstein II	7
	Michael Jackson	7
	Mick Jagger	7
	George Michael	7
	Keith Richards	7
	Mike Stock	7

21 MOST NUMBER ONES – SINGLES PRODUCERS

	SINGLES PRODUCERS	NUMBER ONES
1	George Martin	28
2	Norrie Paramor	27
3	Mitch Miller	17
4	Matt Aitken	16
	Mike Stock	16
	Pete Waterman	16
7	Steve Sholes	15
8	Chet Atkins	12
9	Benny Anderson	10
	Johnny Franz	10
	Madonna	10
	George Michael	10
	Bjorn Ulvaeus	10
14	Mike Chapman	9
	Richard Stannard	9

22 MOST NUMBER ONES – ALBUMS ARTISTS

	ARTISTS	NUMBER ONES
1	Beatles	15
2	Rolling Stones	10
3	Abba	9
	Queen	9
5	David Bowie	8
	Led Zeppelin	8
	U2	8
8	Michael Jackson	7
	Madonna	7
	Cliff Richard	7
	Rod Stewart	7
12	Bob Dylan	6
	Genesis	6
	Elton John	6
	Paul McCartney	6
	Elvis Presley	6

Others with more than 5 number ones:

	Shadows (4 + 4 with Cliff Richard.)	8
	Sting (2 + 5 with the Police.)	7
	Robbie Williams (4 + 3 with Take That.)	7
	Vince Clarke (5 with Erasure, 1 with Yazoo)	6
	George Michael (4 + 2 with Wham!)	6

23 MOST NUMBER ONES – EP ARTISTS

	ARTISTS	NUMBER ONES
1	**Beatles**	8
2	**Elvis Presley**	4
	Cliff Richard	4
	Shadows	4
5	**Manfred Mann**	3
	Rolling Stones	3
	Seekers	3

24 MOST WEEKS AT NUMBER ONE – SINGLES ARTISTS

	ARTISTS	WEEKS AT NUMBER ONE
1	**Elvis Presley**	73
2	**Beatles**	69
3	**Cliff Richard**	44
4	**Frankie Laine**	32
5	**Abba**	31
6	**Wet Wet Wet**	23
7	**Spice Girls**	22
8	**Madonna**	21
	Queen	21
	Take That	21

Others with more than 20 weeks at number one:

Shadows 45
(16 + 29 with Cliff Richard.)

George Michael 26
(17 + 9 with Wham!)

Mick Jagger 22
(18 with the Rolling Stones, 4 with David Bowie.)

25 MOST WEEKS AT NUMBER ONE – SINGLES

	SINGLES	WEEKS AT NUMBER ONE
1	**I BELIEVE** Frankie Laine with Paul Weston and His Orchestra	18
2	**(EVERYTHING I DO) I DO IT FOR YOU** Bryan Adams	16*
3	**LOVE IS ALL AROUND** Wet Wet Wet	15*
4	**BOHEMIAN RHAPSODY** Queen	14
5	**ROSE MARIE** Slim Whitman	11*
6	**CARA MIA** David Whitfield with Mantovani and his Orchestra and Chorus	10*
	I WILL ALWAYS LOVE YOU Whitney Houston	10*

*Denotes consecutive weeks at number one.

26 MOST WEEKS AT NUMBER ONE – ALBUMS ARTISTS

	ARTISTS	WEEKS AT NUMBER ONE
1	**Beatles**	174
2	**Abba**	55
3	**Elvis Presley**	49
4	**Simon and Garfunkel**	48
5	**Rolling Stones**	44
6	**Cliff Richard**	30
7	**Carpenters**	29
8	**Elton John**	28
9	**Rod Stewart**	27
10	**Simply Red**	26

Others with more than 25 weeks at number one:

Shadows 43
(21 + 22 with Cliff Richard)

Phil Collins 37
(25 + 12 with Genesis.)

27 MOST WEEKS AT NUMBER ONE – ALBUMS

	ALBUMS	WEEKS AT NUMBER ONE
1	**SOUTH PACIFIC (OST)** Various Artists	115
2	**THE SOUND OF MUSIC (OST)** Various Artists	70
	BRIDGE OVER TROUBLED WATER Simon and Garfunkel	41
4	**PLEASE PLEASE ME** Beatles	30*
5	**SGT. PEPPER'S LONELY HEARTS CLUB BAND** Beatles	27
6	**G.I. BLUES (OST)** Elvis Presley	22
7	**WITH THE BEATLES** Beatles	21*
	A HARD DAY'S NIGHT Beatles	21*

*Denotes consecutive weeks at number one.

28 MOST WEEKS AT NUMBER ONE – EP ARTISTS

	EP ARTISTS	WEEKS AT NUMBER ONE
1	**Beatles**	63
2	**Shadows**	59
3	**Elvis Presley**	46
4	**Rolling Stones**	37
5	**Beach Boys**	32

29 MOST WEEKS AT NUMBER ONE – EPS

	EPS	WEEKS AT NUMBER ONE
1	**THE BEACH BOY HITS** Beach Boys	32
2	**THE SHADOWS TO THE FORE** Shadows	28
3	**FOUR TOPS HITS** Four Tops	22
4	**TWIST AND SHOUT** Beatles	21
	FIVE BY FIVE Rolling Stones	21

30 FEWEST WEEKS ON CHART BY A NUMBER ONE SINGLE

	SINGLES	WEEKS
1	**BRING YOUR DAUGHTER . . . TO THE SLAUGHTER** Iron Maiden	5
2	**LET'S PARTY** Jive Bunny and the Mastermixers	6
	DO THEY KNOW IT'S CHRISTMAS? Band Aid II	6
	INNUENDO Queen	6
	THE FLY U2	6
	BLOCK ROCKIN' BEATS Chemical Brothers	6

31 FEWEST WEEKS ON CHART BY A NUMBER ONE ALBUM

	ALBUMS	WEEKS
1	**FEAR OF THE DARK** Iron Maiden	5
	JAM Little Angels	5
	VAUXHALL AND I Morrissey	5
4	**IOWA** Slipknot	7
5	**COME** Prince	8
	MUSIC FROM GRAFFITI BRIDGE Prince	8
	PURE CULT Cult	8

32 BIGGEST JUMP TO NUMBER ONE – SINGLES

	SINGLES	JUMP
1	**HEY BABY (UHH, AHH)** DJ Otzi	45-1
2	**HAPPY TALK** Captain Sensible	33-1
3	**SURRENDER (TORNA A SURRIENTO)** Elvis Presley	27-1
	PASS THE DUTCHIE Musical Youth	26-1
	GREEN DOOR Shakin' Stevens	22-1
	HEY JUDE Beatles	21-1
	(JUST LIKE) STARTING OVER John Lennon	21-1
8	**(IF PARADISE IS) HALF AS NICE** Amen Corner	19-1
	STAND BY ME Ben E. King	19-1
	LOVE ME FOR A REASON Osmonds	19-1
	ARE YOU LONESOME TONIGHT Elvis Presley	19-1

33 BIGGEST FALL FROM NUMBER ONE – SINGLES

	SINGLES	FALL
1	**MARY'S BOY CHILD** Harry Belafonte	1-12
2	**ONLY YOU** Flying Pickets	1-10
3	**BLAME IT ON THE WEATHERMAN** B*Witched	1-9
4	**BRING YOUR DAUGHTER . . . TO THE SLAUGHTER** Iron Maiden	1-9
	CHRISTMAS ALPHABET Dickie Valentine	1-9
	THESE BOOTS ARE MADE FOR WALKIN' Nancy Sinatra	1-9
	YOU'RE DRIVING ME CRAZY Temperance Seven	1-9
7	**BLOCK ROCKIN' BEATS** Chemical Brothers	1-8
	BLOOD ON THE DANCEFLOOR Michael Jackson	1-8
	FOOL AGAIN Westlife	1-8
	HELLO GOODBYE Beatles	1-8
	LONELY THIS CHRISTMAS Mud	1-8
	SAME OLD BRAND NEW YOU A1	1-8
	WHAT TOOK YOU SO LONG? Emma Bunton	1-8

34 OLDEST SOLOIST AT NUMBER ONE – SINGLES

	SINGLES ARTISTS	AGE
1	Louis Armstrong	67 years 10 months in 1968
2	Cliff Richard	59 years 2 months in 1999
3	Isaac Hayes (Chef)	56 years 5 months in 1999
4	Cher	52 years 5 months in 1998
5	Telly Savalas	51 years 1 month in 1975
6	Clive Dunn	51 years in 1971
	Elton John	50 years 6 months in 1997
	Frank Sinatra	50 years 6 months in 1966
	Charles Aznavour	50 years 1 month in 1974
	Ben E. King	48 years 5 months in 1987

35 YOUNGEST SOLOIST AT NUMBER ONE – SINGLES

	SINGLES ARTISTS	AGE
1	Little Jimmy Osmond	9 years 8 months in 1972
2	Donny Osmond	14 years 6 months in 1972
3	Helen Shapiro	14 years 10 months in 1961
4	Billie Piper	15 years 10 months in 1998
5	Paul Anka	16 years in 1957
6	Nicole	17 years in 1982
7	Britney Spears	17 years 2 months in 1999
8	Glenn Medeiros	18 years 1 month in 1988
9	Craig Douglas	18 years 1 month in 1959
10	LeAnn Rimes	18 years 2 months in 2000

36 MOST NUMBER TWO HIT SINGLES

	SINGLES ARTISTS	NUMBER TWOS
1	Cliff Richard	10
2	Kylie Minogue	9
	Elvis Presley	9
4	Madonna	8
5	Boyzone	6
	Queen	6
7	Beatles	5
	Tom Jones	5
	George Michael	5
	Sash!	5
	Steps	5
	Sweet	5

37 MOST NUMBER TWO HIT ALBUMS

	ARTISTS	NUMBER TWOS
1	Rolling Stones	7
2	Elton John	5
	Elvis Presley	5
	Cliff Richard	5
	Smiths	5
6	David Bowie	4
	Jam	4
	Madonna	4
	Paul McCartney	4
	Pet Shop Boys	4
	Queen	4
	Frank Sinatra (Includes 1 in compilation chart.)	4
	Status Quo	4
	Who	4

38 MOST POPULAR TITLE FOR A HIT SINGLE

	TITLES	NUMBER OF DIFFERENT SONGS
1	Crazy	16
2	Angel	15
	I Believe	15
4	Dreaming/Dreamin'	13
5	Stay	12
6	Heaven	11
	I Want You	11
	Tonight	11
9	Don't Stop	10
	Free	10
	Heartbeat	10
	Joy	10
	Stay With Me	10

39 LONGEST TITLE FOR A HIT SINGLE

TITLES

1 **FACES/ROD STEWART:** You can make me dance sing or anything even take the dog for a walk mend a fuse fold away the ironing board or any other domestic short coming (114 letters)

2 **CARPENTERS:** Calling occupants of interplanetary craft (the recognized anthem of world contact day (73 letters)

3 **FRESHIES:** I'm in love with the girl on a certain Manchester Virgin Megastore checkout desk (68 letters)

4 **ENNIO MORRICONE:** Chi Mai (theme from the TV series The Life and Times of David Lloyd George) (59 letters)

5 **MIKE OLDFIELD:** Mike Oldfield's single (theme from Mike Oldfield's album 'Tubular Bells') (58 letters)